Peterson's Graduate Programs in Business, Education, Health, Information Studies, Law & Social Work

2008

BOOK 6

PETERSON'S

A **nelnet** COMPANY

PETERSON'S
A nelnet COMPANY

About Peterson's, a Nelnet company

Peterson's (www.petersons.com) is a leading provider of education information and advice, with books and online resources focusing on education search, test preparation, and financial aid. Its Web site offers searchable databases and interactive tools for contacting educational institutions, online practice tests and instruction, and planning tools for securing financial aid. Peterson's serves 110 million education consumers annually.

For more information, contact Peterson's, 2000 Lenox Drive, Lawrenceville, NJ 08648; 800-338-3282; or find us on the World Wide Web at www.petersons.com/about.

© 2008 Peterson's, a Nelnet company

Previous editions © 1966, 1967, 1968, 1969, 1970, 1971, 1972, 1973, 1974, 1975, 1976, 1977, 1978, 1979, 1980, 1981, 1982, 1983, 1984, 1985, 1986, 1987, 1988, 1989, 1990, 1991, 1992, 1993, 1994, 1995, 1996, 1997, 1998, 1999, 2000, 2001, 2002, 2003, 2004, 2005, 2006, 2007

Editor: Fern A. Oram; Production Editor: Susan W. Dilts; Copy Editors: Bret Bollmann, Michael Haines, Brooke James, Sally Ross, Pam Sullivan, Valerie Bolus Vaughan; Research Project Manager: Ken Britschge; Research Associates: Cathleen Fee, James Ranish, Amy L. Weber; Programmer: Phyllis Johnson; Manufacturing Manager: Ray Golaszewski; Composition Manager: Linda M. Williams; Client Relations Representatives: Janet Garwo, Mimi Kaufman, Karen Mount, Danielle Vreeland

Peterson's makes every reasonable effort to obtain accurate, complete, and timely data from reliable sources. Nevertheless, Peterson's and the third-party data suppliers make no representation or warranty, either expressed or implied, as to the accuracy, timeliness, or completeness of the data or the results to be obtained from using the data, including, but not limited to, its quality, performance, merchantability, or fitness for a particular purpose, non-infringement or otherwise.

Neither Peterson's nor the third-party data suppliers warrant, guarantee, or make any representations that the results from using the data will be successful or will satisfy users' requirements. The entire risk to the results and performance is assumed by the user.

ISSN 1088-9442
ISBN-13: 978-0-7689-2407-7
ISBN-10: 0-7689-2407-3

Printed in the United States of America

10 9 8 7 6 5 4 3 2 1   10 09 08

Forty-second Edition

CONTENTS

CONTENTS

A Note from the Peterson's Editors

The six volumes of *Peterson's Graduate and Professional Programs*, the only annually updated reference work of its kind, provide wide-ranging information on the graduate and professional programs offered by accredited colleges and universities in the United States, U.S. territories, and Canada and by those institutions outside the United States that are accredited by U.S. accrediting bodies. More than 44,000 individual academic and professional programs at more than 2,200 institutions are listed. *Peterson's Graduate and Professional Programs* have been used for more than forty years by prospective graduate and professional students, placement counselors, faculty advisers, and all others interested in postbaccalaureate education.

Book 1: *Graduate & Professional Programs: An Overview*, contains information on institutions as a whole, while Books 2 through 6 are devoted to specific academic and professional fields.

Book 2: *Graduate Programs in the Humanities, Arts & Social Sciences*

Book 3: *Graduate Programs in the Biological Sciences*

Book 4: *Graduate Programs in the Physical Sciences, Mathematics, Agricultural Sciences, the Environment & Natural Resources*

Book 5: *Graduate Programs in Engineering & Applied Sciences*

Book 6: *Graduate Programs in Business, Education, Health, Information Studies, Law & Social Work*

The books may be used individually or as a set. For example, if you have chosen a field of study but do not know what institution you want to attend or if you have a college or university in mind but have not chosen an academic field of study, it is best to begin with Book 1.

Book 1 presents several directories to help you identify programs of study that might interest you; you can then research those programs further in Books 2 through 6. The *Directory of Graduate and Professional Programs by Field* lists the 491 fields for which there are program directories in Books 2 through 6 and gives the names of those institutions that offer graduate degree programs in each.

For geographical or financial reasons, you may be interested in attending a particular institution and will want to know what it has to offer. You should turn to the *Directory of Institutions and Their Offerings*, which lists the degree programs available at each institution, again, in the 491 academic and professional fields for which Books 2 through 6 have program directories. As in the *Directory of Graduate and Professional Programs by Field*, the level of degrees offered is also indicated.

All books in the series include advice on graduate education, including topics such as admissions tests, financial aid, and accreditation. **The Graduate Adviser** includes two essays and information about accreditation. The first essay, "The Admissions Process," discusses general admission requirements, admission tests, factors to consider when selecting a graduate school or program, when and how to apply, and how admission decisions are made. Special information for international students and tips for minority students are also included. The second essay, "Financial Support," is an overview of the broad range of support available at the graduate level. Fellowships, scholarships, and grants; assistantships and internships; federal and private loan programs, as well as Federal Work-Study; and the GI bill are detailed. This essay concludes with advice on applying for need-based financial aid. "Accreditation and Accrediting Agencies" gives information on accreditation and its purpose and lists institutional accrediting agencies first and then specialized accrediting agencies relevant to each volume's specific fields of study.

With information on more than 44,000 graduate programs in 491 disciplines, *Peterson's Graduate and Professional Programs* give you all the information you need about the programs that are of interest to you in three formats: **Profiles** (capsule summaries of basic information), **Announcements** (information that an institution or program wants to emphasize, written by administrators), and **Close-Ups** (also written by administrators, with more expansive information than the **Profiles**, emphasizing different aspects of the programs). By using these various formats of program information, coupled with **Appendixes** and **Indexes** covering directories and subject areas for all six books, you will find that these guides provide the most comprehensive, accurate, and up-to-date graduate study information available.

Peterson's publishes a full line of resources with information you need to guide you through the graduate admissions process. Peterson's publications can be found at your local bookstore or library—or visit us on the Web at www.petersons.com.

Colleges and universities will be pleased to know that Peterson's helped you in your selection. Admissions staff members are more than happy to answer questions, address specific problems, and help in any way they can. The editors at Peterson's wish you great success in your graduate program search!

THE GRADUATE ADVISER

The Admissions Process

Generalizations about graduate admissions practices are not always helpful because each institution has its own set of guidelines and procedures. Nevertheless, some broad statements can be made about the admissions process that may help you plan your strategy.

Factors Involved in Selecting a Graduate School or Program

Selecting a graduate school and a specific program of study is a complex matter. Quality of the faculty; program and course offerings; the nature, size, and location of the institution; admission requirements; cost; and the availability of financial assistance are among the many factors that affect one's choice of institution. Other considerations are job placement and achievements of the program's graduates and the institution's resources, such as libraries, laboratories, and computer facilities. If you are to make the best possible choice, you need to learn as much as you can about the schools and programs you are considering before you apply. The following steps may help you narrow your choices.

- Talk to alumni of the programs or institutions you are considering to get their impressions of how well they were prepared for work in their fields of study.
- Remember that graduate school requirements change, so be sure to get the most up-to-date information possible.
- Talk to department faculty and the graduate adviser at your undergraduate institution. They often have information about programs of study at other institutions.
- Visit the Web sites of the graduate schools in which you are interested to request a graduate catalog. Contact the department chair in your chosen field of study for additional information about the department and the field.
- Visit as many campuses as possible. Call ahead for an appointment with the graduate adviser in your field of interest and be sure to check out the facilities and talk to students.

General Requirements

Graduate schools and departments have requirements that applicants for admission must meet. Typically, these requirements include undergraduate transcripts (which provide information about undergraduate grade point average and course work applied toward a major), admission test scores, and letters of recommendation. Most graduate programs also ask for an essay or personal statement that describes your personal reasons for seeking graduate study. In some fields, such as art and music, portfolios or auditions may be required in addition to other evidence of talent. Some institutions require that the applicant have an undergraduate degree in the same subject as the intended graduate major.

Most institutions evaluate each applicant on the basis of the applicant's total record, and the weight accorded any given factor varies widely from institution to institution and from program to program.

The Application Process

You should begin the application process at least one year before you expect to begin your graduate study. Find out the application deadline for each institution (many are provided in the **Profile** section of this guide). Go to the institution Web site and find out if you can apply online. If not, request a paper application form. Fill out this form thoroughly and neatly. Assume that the school needs all the information it is requesting and that the admissions officer will be sensitive to the neatness and overall quality of what you submit. Do not supply more information than the school requires.

The institution may ask at least one question that will require a three- or four-paragraph answer. Compose your response on the assumption that the admissions officer is interested in both what you think and how you express yourself. Keep your statement brief and to the point, but, at the same time, include all pertinent information about your past experiences and your educational goals. Individual statements vary greatly in style and content, which helps admissions officers differentiate among applicants. Many graduate departments give considerable weight to this statement in making their admissions decisions, so be sure to take the time to prepare a thoughtful and concise statement.

If recommendations are a part of the admissions requirements, carefully choose the individuals you ask to write them. It is generally best to ask current or former professors to write the recommendations, provided they are able to attest to your intellectual ability and motivation for doing the work required of a graduate student. It is advisable to provide stamped, preaddressed envelopes to people being asked to submit recommendations on your behalf.

Completed applications, including references, transcripts, and admission test scores, should be received at the institution by the specified date.

Be advised that institutions do not usually make admissions decisions until all materials have been received. Enclose a self-addressed postcard with your application, requesting confirmation of receipt. Allow at least 10 days for the return of the postcard before making further inquiries.

If you plan to apply for financial support, it is imperative that you file your application early.

ADMISSION TESTS

The major testing program used in graduate admissions is the Graduate Record Examinations (GRE) testing program, sponsored by the GRE Board and administered by Educational Testing Service, Princeton, New Jersey.

The Graduate Record Examinations testing program consists of a General Test and eight Subject Tests. The General Test measures critical thinking, verbal reasoning, quantitative reasoning, and analytical writing skills. It is offered as an Internet-based test (iBT) in the United States, Canada, and many other countries.

Plans for launching an entirely new GRE General Test were dropped by ETS in early 2007 in favor of introducing new question types and improvements gradually. Some revisions to the computerized General Test are planned for November 2007. (No changes are planned for the paper-based version or the split-test administration of the GRE General Test offered in China, Korea, and Taiwan.) The fall 2007 revisions are part of the first phase of improvements endorsed by graduate school educators. When completely incorporated, the improvements will test validity, provide faculty with better information regarding applicants' performance, address security concerns, increase worldwide access to the test, and make better use of advances in technology and psychometric design. Changes planned for the verbal reasoning section may eventually include greater emphasis on higher cognitive skills and less dependence on vocabulary; more text-based materials, such as reading passages; a broader selection of reading passages; emphasis on skills related to graduate work, such as complex reasoning; and expansion of computer-enabled tasks (e.g., clicking on a sentence in a passage to highlight it). The verbal reasoning section currently consists of one 30-minute section comprised of thirty questions; beginning in November 2007, test takers may encounter a new question type in the verbal reasoning section: a text completion question that requires test takers to fill in one blank within a passage from a single multiple-choice list. Verbal scores are reported on a 200–800 score scale in 10-point increments.

Changes to the quantitative reasoning section may eventually include quantitative reasoning skills that are closer to those generally used in graduate school, an increase in the proportion of questions involving real-life scenarios and data interpretation, a decrease in the proportion of geometry questions, and better use of technology (e.g., an on-screen calculator). Currently, the quantitative reasoning section consists of one 45-minute section comprised of twenty-eight questions; beginning in November 2007, however, test takers may encounter one new question type in the quantitative reasoning section: a numeric entry question that requires test takers to type their answer as a number in a box or as a fraction in two boxes. Quantitative scores are reported on a 200–800 score scale in 10-point increments.

Changes to the analytical writing section may eventually include new, more focused prompts that reduce the possibility of reliance on memorized materials. The length of time allotted for the issue and argument tasks remains at 45 minutes and 30 minutes, respectively. Analytical writing scores are reported on a 0–6 score scale, in half-point increments.

To prepare for the new question types, be sure to check the GRE Web site at www.ets.org/gre/newquestiontypes.html.

The Subject Tests measure achievement and assume undergraduate majors or extensive background in the following eight disciplines:

- Biochemistry, Cell and Molecular Biology
- Biology
- Chemistry
- Computer Science
- Literature in English
- Mathematics
- Physics
- Psychology

The Subject Tests are available three times per year as paper-based administrations around the world. Testing time is approximately 2 hours and 50 minutes. You can obtain more information about the GRE by visiting the ETS Web site at www.ets.org or consulting the *GRE Information and Registration Bulletin*. The *Bulletin* can be obtained at many undergraduate colleges. You can also download it from the ETS Web site or obtain it by contacting Graduate Record Examinations, Educational Testing Service, PO Box 6000, Princeton, NJ 08541-6000, telephone 1-609-771-7670 or 1-866-473-4373 (toll-free for the United States, U.S. Territories, and Canada).

If you expect to apply for admission to a program that requires any of the GRE tests, you should select a test date well in advance of the application deadline. Scores on the computer-based General Test are reported within ten to fifteen days; scores on the paper-based Subject Tests are reported within six weeks.

Another testing program, the Miller Analogies Test (MAT), is administered at more than 500 Controlled Testing Centers (CTC) in the United States, Canada, and other countries. The MAT computer-based test is now available. Testing time is 60 minutes. The test consists of 120 partial analogies. There are no nationally scheduled test administrations for the MAT. Each CTC determines its own test schedule. You can obtain the *Candidate Information Booklet,* which contains a list of test centers and instructions for taking the test, from http://harcourtassessment.com/haiweb/Cultures/en-US/Harcourt/Community/PostSecondary/Products/MAT/mathome.htm, by completing a request form on the Web site, or by calling Harcourt Assessment, Inc., at 1-800-211-8378.

Always check the specific requirements of the programs to which you are applying.

How Admission Decisions Are Made

The program you apply to is directly involved in the admissions process. Although the final decision is usually made by the graduate dean (or an associate) or the faculty admissions committee, recommendations from faculty members in your intended field are important. At some institutions, an interview is incorporated into the decision process.

A Special Note for International Students

In addition to the steps already described, there are some special considerations for international students who intend to apply for gradu-

ate study in the United States. All graduate schools require an indication of competence in English. The purpose of the Test of English as a Foreign Language (TOEFL) is to evaluate the English proficiency of people who are nonnative speakers of English and want to study at colleges and universities where English is the language of instruction. The TOEFL is administered by Educational Testing Service (ETS) under the general direction of a policy board established by the College Board and the Graduate Record Examinations Board.

The TOEFL is administered as a computer-based test throughout most of the world and is available year-round by appointment only. It is not necessary to have previous computer experience to take the test. The computer-based test consists of four sections—listening, reading, structure, and writing. Total testing time is approximately 4 hours.

The TOEFL is also offered in the paper-based format in areas of the world where computer- and Internet-based testing is not available. The paper-based TOEFL consists of three sections—listening comprehension, structure and written expression, and reading comprehension. Testing time is approximately 3 hours. The Test of Written English (TWE) is also given as part of the paper-based TOEFL. TWE is a 30-minute essay that measures the examinee's ability to compose in English. Examinees receive a TWE score separate from their TOEFL score. The *Information Bulletin* contains information on local fees and registration procedures.

A new TOEFL (TOEFL iBT) that assesses the four basic language skills: listening, reading, writing, and speaking, was administered for the first time in September 2005 in the United States, Canada, France, Germany, and Puerto Rico. The second phase began in March 2006 in Africa, Europe, Eurasia, and the Middle East. (ETS will continue to introduce the iBT in selected cities and will continue to deliver the paper-based test in other locations.) The Internet-based test is administered at secure, official test centers. Testing time is approximately 4 hours. Because the TOEFL iBT includes a speaking section, the TSE will no longer be needed.

Additional information and registration materials are available from TOEFL Services, Educational Testing Service, P.O. Box 6151, Princeton, New Jersey 08541-6151. Telephone: 1-609-771-7100. E-mail: toefl@ets.org. World Wide Web: http://www.toefl.org.

International students should apply especially early because of the number of steps required to complete the admissions process. Furthermore, many United States graduate schools have a limited number of spaces for international students, and many more students apply than the schools can accommodate.

International students may find financial assistance from institutions very limited. The U.S. government requires international applicants to submit a certification of support, which is a statement attesting to the applicant's financial resources. In addition, international students *must* have health insurance coverage.

Tips for Minority Students

Indicators of a university's values in terms of diversity are found both in its recruitment programs and its resources directed to student success. Important questions: Does the institution vigorously recruit minorities for its graduate programs? Is there funding available to help with the costs associated with visiting the school? Are minorities represented in the institution's brochures or Web site or on their faculty rolls? What campus-based resources or services (including assistance in locating housing or career counseling and placement) are available? Is funding available to members of underrepresented groups?

At the program level, it is particularly important for minority students to investigate the "climate" of a program under consideration. How many minority students are enrolled and how many have graduated? What opportunities are there to work with diverse faculty and mentors whose research interests match yours? How are conflicts resolved or concerns addressed? How interested are faculty in building strong and supportive relations with students? "Climate" concerns should be addressed by posing questions to various individuals, including faculty members, current students, and alumni.

Information is also available through various organizations, such as the Hispanic Association of Colleges and Universities (HACU), and publications, such as *Diverse Issues in Higher Education* and *Hispanic Outlook* magazine. There are also books devoted to this topic, such as *The Multicultural Student's Guide to Colleges* by Robert Mitchell.

Financial Support

The range of financial support at the graduate level is very broad. The following descriptions will give you a general idea of what you might expect and what will be expected of you as a financial support recipient.

Fellowships, Scholarships, and Grants

These are usually outright awards of a few hundred to many thousands of dollars with no service to the institution required in return. Fellowships and scholarships are usually awarded on the basis of merit and are highly competitive. Grants are made on the basis of financial need or special talent in a field of study. Many fellowships, scholarships, and grants not only cover tuition, fees, and supplies but also include stipends for living expenses with allowances for dependents. However, the terms of each should be examined because some do not permit recipients to supplement their income with outside work. Fellowships, scholarships, and grants may vary in the number of years for which they are awarded.

In addition to the availability of these funds at the university or program level, many excellent fellowship programs are available at the national level and may be applied for before and during enrollment in a graduate program. A listing of many of these programs can be found at the Council of Graduate Schools' Web site: http://www.cgsnet. org. There is a wealth of information in the "Programs and Awards" section.

Assistantships and Internships

Many graduate students receive financial support through assistantships, particularly involving teaching or research duties. It is important to recognize that such appointments should not be viewed simply as employment relationships but rather should constitute an integral and important part of a student's graduate education. As such, the appointments should be accompanied by strong faculty mentoring and increasingly responsible apprenticeship experiences. The specific nature of these appointments in a given program should be considered in selecting that graduate program.

TEACHING ASSISTANTSHIPS

These usually provide a salary and full or partial tuition remission and may also provide health benefits. Unlike fellowships, scholarships, and grants, which require no service to the institution, teaching assistantships require recipients to provide the institution with a specific amount of undergraduate teaching, ideally related to the student's field of study. Some teaching assistants are limited to grading papers, compiling bibliographies, taking notes, or monitoring laboratories. At some graduate schools, teaching assistants must carry lighter course loads than regular full-time students.

RESEARCH ASSISTANTSHIPS

These are very similar to teaching assistantships in the manner in which financial assistance is provided. The difference is that recipients are given basic research assignments in their disciplines rather than teaching responsibilities. The work required is normally related to the student's field of study; in most instances, the assistantship supports the student's thesis or dissertation research.

ADMINISTRATIVE INTERNSHIPS

These are similar to assistantships in application of financial assistance funds, but the student is given an assignment on a part-time basis, usually as a special assistant with one of the university's administrative offices. The assignment may not necessarily be directly related to the recipient's discipline.

RESIDENCE HALL AND COUNSELING ASSISTANTSHIPS

These assistantships are frequently assigned to graduate students in psychology, counseling, and social work, but may be offered to students in other disciplines, especially if they have worked in this capacity during their undergraduate years. Duties can vary from being available in a dean's office for a specific number of hours for consultation with undergraduates to living in campus residences and being responsible for both counseling and administrative tasks or advising student activity groups. Residence hall assistantships often include a room and board allowance and, in some cases, tuition assistance and stipends. Contact the Housing and Student Life Office for more information.

Health Insurance

The availability and affordability of health insurance is an important issue and one that should be considered in an applicant's choice of institution and program. While often included with assistantships and fellowships, this is not always the case and, even if provided, the benefits may be limited. It is important to note that the U.S. government requires international students to have health insurance.

The GI Bill

This provides financial assistance for students who are veterans of the United States armed forces. If you are a veteran, contact your local Veterans Administration office to determine your eligibility and to get full details about benefits. There are a number of programs that offer educational benefits to current military enlistees. Some states have tuition assistance programs for members of the National Guard. Contact the VA office at the college for more information.

Federal Work-Study Program (FWS)

Employment is another way some students finance their graduate studies. The federally funded Federal Work-Study Program provides eligible students with employment opportunities, usually in public and private nonprofit organizations. Federal funds pay up to 75 percent of the wages, with the remainder paid by the employing agency. FWS is available to graduate students who demonstrate financial need. Not all schools have these funds, and some only award them to undergraduates. Each school sets its application deadline and work-study earnings limits. Wages vary and are related to the type of work done. You must file the Free Application for Federal Student Aid (FAFSA) to be eligible for this program.

Loans

Many graduate students borrow to finance their graduate programs when other sources of assistance (which do not have to be repaid) prove insufficient. You should always read and understand the terms of any loan program before submitting your application.

FEDERAL LOANS

Federal Stafford Loans. The Federal Stafford Loan Program offers government-sponsored, low-interest loans to students through a private lender such as a bank, credit union, or savings and loan association.

There are two components of the Federal Stafford Loan program. Under the *subsidized* component of the program, the federal government pays the interest on the loan while you are enrolled in graduate school on at least a half-time basis. Under the *unsubsidized* component of the program, you pay the interest on the loan from the day proceeds are issued. Eligibility for the federal subsidy is based on demonstrated financial need as determined by the financial aid office from the information you provide on the FAFSA. A cosigner is not required, since the loan is not based on creditworthiness.

Although *unsubsidized* Federal Stafford Loans may not be as desirable as *subsidized* Federal Stafford Loans from the student's perspective, they are a useful source of support for those who may not qualify for the subsidized loans or who need additional financial assistance.

Graduate students may borrow up to $20,500 per year through the Stafford Loan Program, up to a cumulative maximum of $138,500, including undergraduate borrowing. This may include up to $8500 in *subsidized* Stafford Loans annually, depending on eligibility, up to a cumulative maximum of $65,500, including undergraduate borrowing. The amount of the loan borrowed through the *unsubsidized* Stafford Program equals the total amount of the loan (as much as $20,500) minus your eligibility for a *subsidized* Stafford Loan (as much as $8500). You may borrow up to the cost of attendance at the school in which you are enrolled or will attend, minus estimated financial assistance from other federal, state, and private sources, up to a maximum of $20,500.

Stafford Loans made on or after July 1, 2006, carry a fixed interest rate of 6.8% both for in-school and in-repayment borrowers.

Two fees may be deducted from the loan proceeds upon disbursement: a Federal Default Fee of 1 percent, which is deposited in an insurance pool to ensure repayment to the lender if the borrower defaults, and a federally mandated 1.5 percent origination fee, for loans made after July 1, 2007, which is used to offset the administrative cost of the Federal Stafford Loan Program. Many lenders do offer reduced-fee or "zero fee" loans. The origination fees are scheduled to be eliminated by July 1, 2010.

Under the *subsidized* Federal Stafford Loan Program, repayment begins six months after your last date of enrollment on at least a half-time basis. Under the *unsubsidized* program, repayment of interest begins within thirty days from disbursement of the loan proceeds, and repayment of the principal begins six months after your last enrollment on at least a half-time basis. Some borrowers may choose to defer interest payments while they are in school. The accrued interest is added to the loan balance when the borrower begins repayment. There are several repayment options.

Federal Direct Loans. Some schools participate in the Department of Education's William D. Ford Direct Lending Program instead of the Federal Stafford Loan Program. The two programs are essentially the same except that with the Direct Loans, schools themselves provide the loans with funds from the federal government. Terms and interest rates are virtually the same except that there are a few additional repayment options with Federal Direct Loans.

Federal Perkins Loans. The Federal Perkins Loan is available to students demonstrating financial need and is administered directly by the school. Not all schools have these funds, and some may award them to undergraduates only. Eligibility is determined from the information you provide on the FAFSA. The school will notify you of your eligibility.

Eligible graduate students may borrow up to $6000 per year, up to a maximum of $40,000, including undergraduate borrowing (even if your previous Perkins Loans have been repaid). The interest rate for Federal Perkins Loans is 5 percent, and no interest accrues while you remain in school at least half-time. There are no guarantee, loan, or disbursement fees. Repayment begins nine months after your last date of enrollment on at least a half-time basis and may extend over a maximum of ten years with no prepayment penalty.

Federal GRADUATE PLUS Loans. Identical to the Parent Loans for Undergraduate Students, this program allows students to borrow up

to their cost of attendance, less any other aid received through this federal program. These loans have a fixed interest rate of 8.5% (7.9% for the Federal Direct PLUS), and interest begins to accrue at the time of disbursement. For more information, contact your FFELD lender or your college financial aid office.

Deferring Your Federal Loan Repayments. If you borrowed under the Federal Stafford Loan Program or the Federal Perkins Loan Program for previous undergraduate or graduate study, your repayments may be deferred when you return to graduate school, depending on when you borrowed and under which program.

There are other deferment options available if you are temporarily unable to repay your loan. Information about these deferments is provided at your entrance and exit interviews. If you believe you are eligible for a deferment of your loan repayments, you must contact your lender to complete a deferment form. The deferment must be filed prior to the time your repayment is due, and it must be refiled when it expires if you remain eligible for deferment at that time.

SUPPLEMENTAL (PRIVATE) LOANS

Many lending institutions offer supplemental loan programs and other financing plans, such as the ones described here, to students seeking additional assistance in meeting their educational expenses. Some loan programs target all types of graduate students; others are designed specifically for business, law, or medical students. In addition, you can use private loans not specifically designed for education to help finance your graduate degree.

If you are considering borrowing through a supplemental or private loan program, you should carefully consider the terms and be sure to "read the fine print." Check with the program sponsor for the most current terms that will be applicable to the amounts you intend to borrow for graduate study. Most supplemental loan programs for graduate study offer unsubsidized, credit-based loans. In general, a credit-ready borrower is one who has a satisfactory credit history or no credit history at all. A creditworthy borrower generally must pass a credit test to be eligible to borrow or act as a cosigner for the loan funds.

Many supplemental loan programs have minimum and maximum annual loan limits. Some offer amounts equal to the cost of attendance minus any other aid you will receive for graduate study. If you are planning to borrow for several years of graduate study, consider whether there is a cumulative or aggregate limit on the amount you may borrow. Often this cumulative or aggregate limit will include any amounts you borrowed and have not repaid for undergraduate or previous graduate study.

The combination of the annual interest rate, loan fees, and the repayment terms you choose will determine how much you will repay over time. Compare these features in combination before you decide which loan program to use. Some loans offer interest rates that are adjusted monthly, some quarterly, some annually. Some offer interest rates that are lower during the in-school, grace, and deferment periods, and then increase when you begin repayment. Some programs include a loan "origination" fee, which is usually deducted from the principal amount you receive when the loan is disbursed, and must be repaid along with the interest and other principal when you graduate, withdraw from school, or drop below half-time study. Sometimes the loan fees are reduced if you borrow with a qualified cosigner. Some programs allow you to defer interest and/or principal payments while you are enrolled in graduate school. Many programs allow you to capitalize your interest payments; the interest due on your loan is added to the outstanding balance of your loan, so you don't have to repay immediately, but this increases the amount you owe. Other programs allow you to pay the interest as you go, which reduces the amount you later have to repay.

Some examples of supplemental programs follow. The private loan market is very competitive and your financial aid office can help you evaluate these and other programs.

CitiAssist Loans. Offered by Citibank, these no-fee loans help graduate students fill the gap between the financial aid they receive and the money they need for school. Visit www.studentloan.com for more loan information from Citibank.

EXCEL Loan. This program, sponsored by Nellie Mae, is designed for students who are not ready to borrow on their own and wish to borrow with a creditworthy cosigner. Visit www.nelliemae.com for more information.

Key Alternative Loan. This loan can bridge the gap between education costs and traditional funding. Visit https://www.key.com/html/H-1.3.html for more information.

Graduate Access Loan. Sponsored by the Access Group, this is for graduate students enrolled at least half-time. The Web site is www.accessgroup.com.

Signature Student Loan. A loan program for students who are enrolled at least half-time, this is sponsored by Sallie Mae. Visit www.salliemae.com for more information.

Applying for Need-Based Financial Aid

Schools that award federal and institutional financial assistance based on need will require you to complete the FAFSA and, in some cases, an institutional financial aid application.

If you are applying for federal student assistance, you **must** complete the FAFSA. A service of the U.S. Department of Education, it is free to all applicants. Most applicants apply online at www.fafsa.ed.gov. Paper applications are available at the financial aid office of your local college.

After your FAFSA information has been processed, you will receive a Student Aid Report (SAR). If you provided an e-mail address on the FAFSA, this will be sent to you electronically; otherwise, it will be mailed to your home address.

Follow the instructions on the SAR if you need to correct information reported on your original application. If your situation changes after you file your FAFSA, contact your financial aid officer to discuss amending your information. You can also appeal your financial aid award if you have extenuating circumstances.

If you would like more information on federal student financial aid, visit the FAFSA Web site or download the most recent version of *The Student Guide* at http://studentaid.ed.gov/students/publications/student_guide/index.html. This guide is also available in Spanish.

The U.S. Department of Education also has a toll-free number for questions concerning federal student aid programs. The number is 1-800-4-FED AID (1-800-433-3243). If you are hearing impaired, call toll-free, 1-800-730-8913.

Summary

Remember that these are generalized statements about financial assistance at the graduate level. Because each institution allots its aid differently, you should communicate directly with the school and the specific department of interest to you. It is not unusual, for example, to find that an endowment vested within a specific department supports one or more fellowships. You may fit its requirements and specifications precisely.

Accreditation and Accrediting Agencies

Colleges and universities in the United States, and their individual academic and professional programs, are accredited by nongovernmental agencies concerned with monitoring the quality of education in this country. Agencies with both regional and national jurisdictions grant accreditation to institutions as a whole, while specialized bodies acting on a nationwide basis—often national professional associations—grant accreditation to departments and programs in specific fields.

Institutional and specialized accrediting agencies share the same basic concerns: the purpose an academic unit—whether university or program—has set for itself and how well it fulfills that purpose, the adequacy of its financial and other resources, the quality of its academic offerings, and the level of services it provides. Agencies that grant institutional accreditation take a broader view, of course, and examine university-wide or college-wide services with which a specialized agency may not concern itself.

Both types of agencies follow the same general procedures when considering an application for accreditation. The academic unit prepares a self-evaluation, focusing on the concerns mentioned above and usually including an assessment of both its strengths and weaknesses; a team of representatives of the accrediting body reviews this evaluation, visits the campus, and makes its own report; and finally, the accrediting body makes a decision on the application. Often, even when accreditation is granted, the agency makes a recommendation regarding how the institution or program can improve. All institutions and programs are also reviewed every few years to determine whether they continue to meet established standards; if they do not, they may lose their accreditation.

Accrediting agencies themselves are reviewed and evaluated periodically by the U.S. Department of Education and the Council for Higher Education Accreditation (CHEA). Recognized agencies adhere to certain standards and practices, and their authority in matters of accreditation is widely accepted in the educational community.

This does not mean, however, that accreditation is a simple matter, either for schools wishing to become accredited or for students deciding where to apply. Indeed, in certain fields the very meaning and methods of accreditation are the subject of a good deal of debate. For their part, those applying to graduate school should be aware of the safeguards provided by regional accreditation, especially in terms of degree acceptance and institutional longevity. Beyond this, applicants should understand the role that specialized accreditation plays in their field, as this varies considerably from one discipline to another. In certain professional fields, it is necessary to have graduated from a program that is accredited in order to be eligible for a license to practice, and in some fields the federal government also makes this a hiring requirement. In other disciplines, however, accreditation is not as essential, and there can be excellent programs that are not accredited. In fact, some programs choose not to seek accreditation, although most do.

Institutions and programs that present themselves for accreditation are sometimes granted the status of candidate for accreditation, or what is known as "preaccreditation." This may happen, for example, when an academic unit is too new to have met all the requirements for accreditation. Such status signifies initial recognition and indicates that the school or program in question is working to fulfill all requirements; it does not, however, guarantee that accreditation will be granted.

Institutional Accrediting Agencies—Regional

MIDDLE STATES ASSOCIATION OF COLLEGES AND SCHOOLS
Accredits institutions in Delaware, District of Columbia, Maryland, New Jersey, New York, Pennsylvania, Puerto Rico, and the Virgin Islands.
Jean Avnet Morse, President
Middle States Commission on Higher Education
3624 Market Street
Philadelphia, Pennsylvania 19104
Telephone: 267-284-5025
Fax: 215-662-5501
E-mail: info@msche.org
World Wide Web: www.msche.org

NEW ENGLAND ASSOCIATION OF SCHOOLS AND COLLEGES
Accredits institutions in Connecticut, Maine, Massachusetts, New Hampshire, Rhode Island, and Vermont.
Barbara E. Brittingham, Director
Commission on Institutions of Higher Education
209 Burlington Road
Bedford, Massachusetts 01730-1433
Telephone: 781-541-5447
Fax: 781-271-0950
E-mail: bbrittingham@neasc.org
World Wide Web: www.neasc.org

NORTH CENTRAL ASSOCIATION OF COLLEGES AND SCHOOLS
Accredits institutions in Arizona, Arkansas, Colorado, Illinois, Indiana, Iowa, Kansas, Michigan, Minnesota, Missouri, Nebraska, New Mexico, North Dakota, Ohio, Oklahoma, South Dakota, West Virginia, Wisconsin, and Wyoming.
Steven D. Crow, President
The Higher Learning Commission
30 North LaSalle Street, Suite 2400
Chicago, Illinois 60602
Telephone: 312-263-0456
Fax: 312-263-7462
E-mail: scrow@hlcommission.org
World Wide Web: www.ncahigherlearningcommission.org

NORTHWEST COMMISSION ON COLLEGES AND UNIVERSITIES
Accredits institutions in Alaska, Idaho, Montana, Nevada, Oregon, Utah, and Washington.
Sandra E. Elman, President
8060 165th Avenue, NE, Suite 100
Redmond, Washington 98052
Telephone: 425-558-4224
Fax: 425-376-0596
E-mail: selman@nwccu.org
World Wide Web: www.nwccu.org

SOUTHERN ASSOCIATION OF COLLEGES AND SCHOOLS
Accredits institutions in Alabama, Florida, Georgia, Kentucky, Louisiana, Mississippi, North Carolina, South Carolina, Tennessee, Texas, and Virginia.
Belle S. Wheelan, President
Commission on Colleges
1866 Southern Lane
Decatur, Georgia 30033
Telephone: 404-679-4512
Fax: 404-679-4558
E-mail: bwheelan@sacscoc.org
World Wide Web: www.sacscoc.org

WESTERN ASSOCIATION OF SCHOOLS AND COLLEGES
Accredits institutions in California, Guam, and Hawaii.
Ralph A. Wolff, President and Executive Director
The Senior College Commission
985 Atlantic Avenue, Suite 100
Alameda, California 94501
Telephone: 510-748-9001
Fax: 510-748-9797
E-mail: wascsr@wascsenior.org
World Wide Web: www.wascsenior.org/wasc/

Institutional Accrediting Agencies—Other

ACCREDITING COUNCIL FOR INDEPENDENT COLLEGES AND SCHOOLS
Sheryl L. Moody, Executive Director
750 First Street, NE, Suite 980
Washington, DC 20002-4242
Telephone: 202-336-6780
Fax: 202-842-2593
E-mail: smoody@acics.org
World Wide Web: www.acics.org

DISTANCE EDUCATION AND TRAINING COUNCIL
Accrediting Commission
Michael P. Lambert, Executive Director
1601 18th Street, NW
Washington, DC 20009
Telephone: 202-234-5100 Ext. 101
Fax: 202-332-1386
E-mail: detc@detc.org
World Wide Web: www.detc.org

Specialized Accrediting Agencies

[Only Book 1 of *Peterson's Graduate and Professional Programs* Series includes the complete list of specialized accrediting groups recognized by the U.S. Department of Education and the Council on Higher Education Accreditation (CHEA). The lists in Books 2, 3, 4, 5, and 6 are abridged.]

ACUPUNCTURE AND ORIENTAL MEDICINE
Dort S. Bigg, Executive Director
Accreditation Commission for Acupuncture and Oriental Medicine
Maryland Trade Center #3
7501 Greenway Center Drive, Suite 820
Greenbelt, Maryland 20770
Telephone: 301-313-0855
Fax: 301-313-0912
E-mail: dort.bigg@acaom.org
World Wide Web: www.acaom.org

BUSINESS
Jerry E. Trapnell, Executive Vice President/Chief Accreditation Officer
AACSB International--The Association to Advance Collegiate Schools of Business
777 South Harbour Island Boulevard, Suite 750
Tampa, Florida 33602
Telephone: 813-769-6500
Fax: 813-769-6559
E-mail: jerryt@aacsb.edu
World Wide Web: www.aacsb.edu

CHIROPRACTIC
Martha S. O'Connor, Executive Director
Council on Chiropractic Education
8049 North 85th Way
Scottsdale, Arizona 85258-4321
Telephone: 480-443-8877
Fax: 480-483-7333
E-mail: cce@cce-usa.org
World Wide Web: www.cce-usa.org

CLINICAL LABORATORY SCIENCES
Dianne M. Cearlock, Chief Executive Officer
National Accrediting Agency for Clinical Laboratory Sciences
8410 West Bryn Mawr Avenue, Suite 670
Chicago, Illinois 60631
Telephone: 773-714-8880
Fax: 773-714-8886
E-mail: dcearlock@naacls.org
World Wide Web: www.naacls.org

CLINICAL PASTORAL EDUCATION
Teresa E. Snorton, Executive Director
Accreditation Commission
Association for Clinical Pastoral Education, Inc.
1549 Clairmont Road, Suite 103
Decatur, Georgia 30033-4611
Telephone: 404-320-1472
Fax: 404-320-0849
E-mail: acpe@acpe.edu
World Wide Web: www.acpe.edu

DENTISTRY
Laura M. Neumann, Interim Director
Commission on Dental Accreditation
American Dental Association
211 East Chicago Avenue, 18th Floor
Chicago, Illinois 60611
Telephone: 312-440-2712
Fax: 312-440-2915
E-mail: neumannl@ada.org
World Wide Web: www.ada.org

HEALTH SERVICES ADMINISTRATION
Commission on Accreditation of Healthcare Management Education
Pamela S. Jenness
Director of Accreditation Operations
2000 14th Street North, Suite 780
Arlington, Virginia 22201
Telephone: 703-894-0960
Fax: 703-894-0941
E-mail: pjenness@cahme.org
World Wide Web: cahmeweb.org

LAW
Hulett H. Askew, Consultant on Legal Education
American Bar Association
321 North Clark Street, 21st Floor
Chicago, Illinois 60610
Telephone: 312-988-6746
Fax: 312-988-5681
E-mail: askewh@staff.abanet.org
World Wide Web: www.abanet.org/legaled/

LIBRARY
Karen O'Brien, Executive Director
Office for Accreditation
American Library Association
50 East Huron Street
Chicago, Illinois 60611
Telephone: 312-280-2434
Fax: 312-280-2433
E-mail: kobrien@ala.org
World Wide Web: www.ala.org/ala/accreditation/accreditation.htm

MEDICAL ILLUSTRATION
Commission on Accreditation of Allied Health Education Programs (CAAHEP)
Kathleen Megivern, Executive Director
1361 Park Street
Clearwater, Florida 33756
Telephone: 727-210-2350
Fax: 727-210-2354
E-mail: megivern@caahep.org
World Wide Web: www.caahep.org

MEDICINE
Liaison Committee on Medical Education (LCME)
In even-numbered years beginning each July 1, contact:

Robert H. Eaglen
Interim AAMC Secretary to the LCME
Association of American Medical Colleges
2450 N Street, NW
Washington, DC 20037

Telephone: 202-828-0596
Fax: 202-828-1125
E-mail: reaglen@aamc.org
World Wide Web: www.lcme.org
In odd-numbered years beginning each July 1,
contact:

Barbara Barzansky
Interim AMA Secretary to the LCME
American Medical Association
Council on Medical Education
515 North State Street
Chicago, Illinois 60610
Telephone: 312-464-1690
Fax: 312-464-5830
E-mail: barbara_barzansky@ama-assn.org
World Wide Web: www.ama-assn.org

NATUROPATHIC MEDICINE
Daniel Seitz, Executive Director
Council on Naturopathic Medical Education
P.O. Box 178
Great Barrington, Massachusetts 01230
Telephone: 413-528-8877
Fax: 413-528-8880
E-mail: council@cnme.org
World Wide Web: www.cnme.org

NURSE ANESTHESIA
Francis Gerbasi, Director of Accreditation and Education
Council on Accreditation of Nurse Anesthesia Educational Programs
222 South Prospect Avenue
Park Ridge, Illinois 60068
Telephone: 847-692-7050
Fax: 847-692-7137
E-mail: fgerbasi@aana.com
World Wide Web: www.aana.com

NURSE EDUCATION
Jennifer Butlin, Director
Commission on Collegiate Nursing Education (CCNE)
One Dupont Circle, NW, Suite 530
Washington, DC 20036-1120
Telephone: 202-887-6791
Fax: 202-887-8476
E-mail: jbutlin@aacn.nche.edu
World Wide Web: www.aacn.nche.edu/accreditation

NURSE MIDWIFERY
Diane Boyer, Chair
ACNM Division of Accreditation
American College of Nurse-Midwives
8403 Colesville Road, Suite 1550
Silver Spring, Maryland 20910
Telephone: 240-485-1800
Fax: 240-485-1818
E-mail: dboyer@luc.edu
World Wide Web: www.midwife.org

Mary Ann Baul, Executive Director
Midwifery Education Accreditation Council
20 East Cherry Avenue
Flagstaff, Arizona 86001-4607
Telephone: 928-214-0997
Fax: 928-773-9694
E-mail: info@meacschools.org
World Wide Web: www.meacschools.org

NURSE PRACTITIONER
Susan Wysocki, President
National Association of Nurse Practitioners in Women's Health
Council on Accreditation
505 C Street, NE
Washington, DC 20002
Telephone: 202-543-9693
Fax: 202-543-9858

E-mail: info@npwh.org
World Wide Web: www.npwh.org

NURSING
Sharon J. Tanner, Executive Director
National League for Nursing Accrediting Commission
61 Broadway, 33rd Floor
New York, New York 10006
Telephone: 800-669-1656 Ext. 451
Fax: 212-812-0364
E-mail: stanner@nlnac.org
World Wide Web: www.nlnac.org

OCCUPATIONAL THERAPY
Neil Harvison, Director of Accreditation
American Occupational Therapy Association
4720 Montgomery Lane
P.O. Box 31220
Bethesda, Maryland 20824-1220
Telephone: 301-652-2682 Ext. 2912
Fax: 301-652-7711
E-mail: nharvison@aota.org
World Wide Web: www.aota.org

OPTOMETRY
Joyce L. Urbeck, Administrative Director
Accreditation Council on Optometric Education
American Optometric Association
243 North Lindbergh Boulevard
St. Louis, Missouri 63141
Telephone: 314-991-4100 Ext. 246
Fax: 314-991-4101
E-mail: jlurbeck@aoa.org
World Wide Web: www.aoanet.org

OSTEOPATHIC MEDICINE
Konrad C. Miskowicz-Retz, Director
Commission on Osteopathic College Accreditation
American Osteopathic Association
142 East Ontario Street
Chicago, Illinois 60611
Telephone: 312-202-8048
Fax: 312-202-8202
E-mail: kretz@osteopathic.org
World Wide Web: www.osteopathic.org

PHARMACY
Peter H. Vlasses, Executive Director
Accreditation Council for Pharmacy Education
20 North Clark Street, Suite 2500
Chicago, Illinois 60602-5109
Telephone: 312-664-3575
Fax: 312-664-4652
E-mail: pvlasses@acpe-accredit.org
World Wide Web: www.acpe-accredit.org

PHYSICAL THERAPY
Mary Jane Harris, Director
Commission on Accreditation
American Physical Therapy Association
1111 North Fairfax Street
Alexandria, Virginia 22314
Telephone: 703-684-2782
Fax: 703-684-7343
E-mail: maryjaneharris@apta.org
World Wide Web: www.apta.org

PHYSICIAN ASSISTANT STUDIES
John McCarty, Executive Director
Accreditation Review Commission on Education for the Physician Assistant
12000 Findley Road, Suite 240
Duluth, Georgia 30097
Telephone: 770-476-1224
Fax: 770-476-1738

E-mail: johnmccarty@arc-pa.org
World Wide Web: www.arc-pa.org

PODIATRIC MEDICINE
Alan R. Tinkleman, Director
Council on Podiatric Medical Education
American Podiatric Medical Association
9312 Old Georgetown Road
Bethesda, Maryland 20814-1621
Telephone: 301-581-9200
Fax: 301-571-4903
E-mail: artinkleman@apma.org
World Wide Web: www.cpme.org

PUBLIC HEALTH
Laura Rasar King, Executive Director
Council on Education for Public Health
800 Eye Street, NW, Suite 202
Washington, DC 20001-3710
Telephone: 202-789-1050
Fax: 202-789-1895
E-mail: lking@ceph.org
World Wide Web: www.ceph.org

REHABILITATION EDUCATION
Marv Kuehn, Executive Director
Council on Rehabilitation Education
Commission on Standards and Accreditation
300 North Martingale Road, Suite 460
Schaumburg, Illinois 60173
Telephone: 847-944-1345
Fax: 847-944-1324
E-mail: mkuehn@emporia.edu
World Wide Web: www.core-rehab.org

SOCIAL WORK
Dean Pierce, Director
Office of Social Work Accreditation and Educational Excellence
Council on Social Work Education
1725 Duke Street, Suite 500
Alexandria, Virginia 22314
Telephone: 703-519-2044

Fax: 703-739-9048
E-mail: dpierce@cswe.org
World Wide Web: www.cswe.org

SPEECH-LANGUAGE PATHOLOGY AND AUDIOLOGY
Patrima Tice, Director of Credentialing
American Speech-Language-Hearing Association
10801 Rockville Pike
Rockville, Maryland 20852
Telephone: 301-897-5700
Fax: 301-571-0457
E-mail: ptice@asha.org
World Wide Web: www.asha.org

TEACHER EDUCATION
Arthur E. Wise, President
National Council for Accreditation of Teacher Education
2010 Massachusetts Avenue, NW, Suite 500
Washington, DC 20036
Telephone: 202-466-7496
Fax: 202-296-6620
E-mail: art@ncate.org
World Wide Web: www.ncate.org

Frank B. Murray, President
Teacher Education Accreditation Council (TEAC)
One Dupont Circle, Suite 320
Washington, DC 20036-0110
Telephone: 202-466-7236
Fax: 202-466-7238
E-mail: frank@teac.org
World Wide Web: www.teac.org

VETERINARY MEDICINE
Donald G. Simmons, Director of Education and Research Division
American Veterinary Medical Association
1931 North Meacham Road, Suite 100
Schaumburg, Illinois 60173
Telephone: 847-925-8070 Ext. 6674
Fax: 847-925-9329
E-mail: dsimmons@avma.org
World Wide Web: www.avma.org

How to Use These Guides

As you identify the particular programs and institutions that interest you, you can use both Book 1 and the specialized volumes (Books 2–6) to obtain detailed information—Book 1 for information on the institutions overall and Books 2 through 6 for details about the individual graduate units and their degree programs.

Books 2 through 6 are divided into sections that contain one or more directories devoted to programs in a particular field. If you do not find a directory devoted to your field of interest in a specific book, consult *Directories and Subject Areas in Books 2–6* (located at the end of each volume). After you have identified the correct book, consult the *Directories and Subject Areas in This Book* index, which shows (as does the more general directory) what directories cover subjects not specifically named in a directory or section title. This index in Book 2, for example, will tell you that if you are interested in sculpture, you should see the directory entitled Art/Fine Arts. The Art/Fine Arts entry will direct you to the proper page.

Books 2 through 6 have a number of general directories. These directories have entries for the largest unit at an institution granting graduate degrees in that field. For example, the general Engineering and Applied Sciences directory in Book 5 consists of **Profiles** for colleges, schools, and departments of engineering and applied sciences.

General directories are followed by other directories, or sections, that give more detailed information about programs in particular areas of the general field that has been covered. The general Engineering and Applied Sciences directory, in the previous example, is followed by nineteen sections with directories in specific areas of engineering, such as Chemical Engineering, Industrial/Management Engineering, and Mechanical Engineering.

Because of the broad nature of many fields, any system of organization is bound to involve a certain amount of overlap. Environmental studies, for example, is a field whose various aspects are studied in several types of departments and schools. Readers interested in such studies will find information on relevant programs in Book 3 under Ecology and Environmental Biology; in Book 4 under Environmental Management and Policy and Natural Resources; in Book 5 under Energy Management and Policy and Environmental Engineering; and in Book 6 under Environmental and Occupational Health. To help you find all of the programs of interest to you, the introduction to each section of Books 2 through 6 includes, if applicable, a paragraph suggesting other sections and directories with information on related areas of study.

Directory of Institutions with Programs in Business, Education, Health, Information Studies, Law & Social Work

This directory lists institutions in alphabetical order and includes beneath each name the academic fields in which each institution offers graduate programs. The degree level in each field is also indicated, provided that the institution has supplied that information in response to *Peterson's Annual Survey of Graduate and Professional Institutions.* An *M* indicates that a master's degree program is offered; a *D* indicates that a doctoral degree program is offered; a *P* indicates that the first professional degree is offered; an *O* signifies that other advanced degrees (e.g., certificates or specialist degrees) are offered; and an * (asterisk) indicates that a **Close-Up** and/or **Announcement** is located in this volume. See the index, *Close-Ups and Announcements,* for the specific page number.

Profiles of Academic and Professional Programs in Books 2–6

Each section of **Profiles** has a table of contents that lists the Program Directories, **Announcements**, and **Close-Ups.** Program Directories consist of the **Profiles** of programs in the relevant fields, with **Announcements** following if programs have chosen to include them. **Cross-Discipline Announcements**, if any programs have chosen to submit such entries, and **Close-Ups,** which are more individualized statements, again if programs have chosen to submit them, are also listed.

The **Profiles** found in the 491 directories in Books 2 through 6 provide basic data about the graduate units in capsule form for quick reference. To make these directories as useful as possible, **Profiles** are generally listed for an institution's smallest academic unit within a subject area. In other words, if an institution has a College of Liberal Arts that administers many related programs, the **Profile** for the individual program (e.g., Program in History), not the entire College, appears in the directory.

There are some programs that do not fit into any current directory and are not given individual **Profiles.** The directory structure is reviewed annually in order to keep this number to a minimum and to accommodate major trends in graduate education.

The following outline describes the **Profile** information found in the guides and explains how best to use that information. Any item that does not apply to or was not provided by a graduate unit is omitted from its listing. The format of the **Profiles** is constant, making it easy to compare one institution with another and one program with another. A description of the information in the **Profiles** in Books 2 through 6 follows; the Book 1 **Profile** description is found in that Guide's "How to Use This Guide" article.

Identifying Information. The institution's name, in boldface type, is followed by a complete listing of the administrative structure for that field of study. (For example, University of Akron, Buchtel College of Arts and Sciences, Department of Theoretical and Applied Mathematics, Program in Mathematics.) The last unit listed is the one to which all information in the **Profile** pertains. The institution's city, state, and zip code follow.

Offerings. Each field of study offered by the unit is listed with all postbaccalaureate degrees awarded. Degrees that are not preceded by a specific concentration are awarded in the general field listed in the unit name. Frequently, fields of study are broken down into subspecializations, and those appear following the degrees awarded; for example, "Offerings in secondary education (M.Ed.), including English education, mathematics education, science education." Students enrolled in the M.Ed. program would be able to specialize in any of the three fields mentioned.

Professional Accreditation. Some **Profiles** indicate whether a program is professionally accredited. Because it is possible for a program to receive or lose professional accreditation at any time, students entering fields in which accreditation is important to a career should verify the status of programs by contacting either the chairperson or the appropriate accrediting association.

Jointly Offered Degrees. Explanatory statements concerning programs that are offered in cooperation with other institutions are included in the list of degrees offered. This occurs most commonly on a regional basis (for example, two state universities offering a cooperative Ph.D. in special education) or where the specialized nature of the institutions encourages joint efforts (a J.D./M.B.A. offered by a law school at an institution with no formal business programs and an institution with a business school but lacking a law school). Only programs that are truly cooperative are listed; those involving only limited course work at another institution are not. Interested students should contact the heads of such units for further information.

Part-Time and Evening/Weekend Programs. When information regarding the availability of part-time or evening/weekend study appears in the **Profile**, it means that students are able to earn a degree exclusively through such study.

Postbaccalaureate Distance Learning Degrees. A postbaccalaureate distance learning degree program signifies that course requirements can be fulfilled with minimal or no on-campus study.

Faculty. Figures on the number of faculty members actively involved with graduate students through teaching or research are separated into full- and part-time as well as men and women whenever the information has been supplied.

Students. Figures for the number of students enrolled in graduate and professional programs pertain to the semester of highest enrollment from the 2006–07 academic year. These figures are broken down into full- and part-time and men and women whenever the data have been supplied. Information on the number of matriculated students enrolled in the unit who are members of a minority group or are international students appears here. The average age of the matriculated students is followed by the number of applicants, the percentage accepted, and the number enrolled for fall 2006.

Degrees Awarded. The number of degrees awarded in the calendar year is listed. Many doctoral programs offer a terminal master's degree if students leave the program after completing only part of the requirements for a doctoral degree; that is indicated here. All degrees are classified into one of four types: master's, doctoral, first professional, and other advanced degrees. A unit may award one or several degrees at a given level; however, the data are only collected by type and may therefore represent several different degree programs.

Median Time to Degree. If provided, information on the median amount of time required to earn the degree for full-time and part-time students is listed here. Also provided is the percentage of students who began their doctoral program in 1998 and received their degree in eight years or less.

Degree Requirements. The information in this section is also broken down by type of degree, and all information for a degree level pertains to all degrees of that type unless otherwise specified. Degree requirements are collected in a simplified form to provide some very basic information on the nature of the program and on foreign language, thesis or dissertation, comprehensive exam, and registration requirements. Many units also provide a short list of additional requirements, such as fieldwork or an internship. No information is listed on the number of courses or credits required for completion or whether a minimum or maximum number of years or semesters is needed. For complete information on graduation requirements, contact the graduate school or program directly.

Entrance Requirements. Entrance requirements are broken down into the four degree levels of master's, doctoral, first professional, and other advanced degrees. Within each level, information may be provided in two basic categories: entrance exams and other requirements. The entrance exams are identified by the standard acronyms used by the testing agencies, unless they are not well known. Other entrance requirements are quite varied, but they often contain an undergraduate or graduate grade point average (GPA). Unless otherwise stated, the GPA is calculated on a 4.0 scale and is listed as a minimum required for admission. Additional exam requirements/recommendations for international students may be listed here. Application deadlines for domestic and international students, the application fee, and whether electronic applications are accepted may be listed here. Note that the deadline should be used for reference only; these dates are subject to change, and students interested in applying should always contact the graduate unit directly about application procedures and deadlines.

Expenses. The typical cost of study for the 2006–07 academic year is given in two basic categories: tuition and fees. Cost of study may be quite complex at a graduate institution. There are often sliding scales for part-time study, a different cost for first-year students, and other variables that make it impossible to completely cover the cost of study for each graduate program. To provide the most usable information, figures are given for full-time study for a full year where available and for part-time study in terms of a per-unit rate (per credit, per semester hour, etc.). Occasionally, variances may be noted in tuition and fees for reasons such as the type of program, whether courses are taken during the day or evening, whether courses are at the master's or doctoral level, or other institution-specific reasons. Expenses are usually subject to change; for exact costs at any given time, contact your chosen schools and programs directly. Keep in mind that the tuition of Canadian institutions is usually given in Canadian dollars.

Financial Support. This section contains data on the number of awards administered by the institution and given to graduate students during the 2006–07 academic year. The first figure given represents the total number of students receiving financial support enrolled in that unit. If the unit has provided information on graduate appointments, these are broken down into three major categories: *fellowships* give money to graduate students to cover the cost of study and living expenses and are not based on a work obligation or research commitment, *research assistantships* provide stipends to graduate students for assistance in a formal research project with a faculty member, and *teaching assistantships* provide stipends to graduate students for teaching or for assisting faculty members in teaching undergraduate classes. Within each category, figures are given for the total number of awards, the average yearly amount per award, and whether full or partial tuition reimbursements are awarded. In addition to graduate appointments, the availability of several other financial aid sources is covered in this section. *Tuition waivers* are routinely part of a graduate appointment, but units sometimes waive part or all of a student's tuition even if a graduate appointment is not available. *Federal Work-Study* is made available to students who demonstrate need and meet the federal guidelines; this form of aid normally includes 10 or more hours of work per week in an office of the institution. *Institutionally sponsored loans* are low-interest loans available to graduate students to cover both educational and living expenses. *Career-related internships* or *fieldwork* offer money to students who are participating in a formal off-campus research project or practicum. Grants, scholarships, traineeships, unspecified assistantships, and other awards may also be noted. The availability of financial support to part-time students is also indicated here.

Some programs list the financial aid application deadline and the forms that need to be completed for students to be eligible for financial awards. There are two forms: FAFSA, the Free Application for Federal Student Aid, which is required for federal aid, and the CSS PROFILE®.

Faculty Research. Each unit has the opportunity to list several keyword phrases describing the current research involving faculty members and graduate students. Space limitations prevent the unit from listing complete information on all research programs. The total expenditure for funded research from the previous academic year may also be included.

Unit Head and Application Contact. The head of the graduate program for each unit is listed with academic title and telephone and fax numbers and e-mail address if available. In addition to the unit head, many graduate programs list a separate contact for application and admission information, which follows the listing for the unit head. If no unit head or application contact is given, you should contact the overall institution for information on graduate admissions.

Announcements and Close-Ups

The **Announcements** and **Close-Ups** are supplementary insertions submitted by deans, chairs, and other administrators who wish to offer an additional, more individualized statement to readers. A number of graduate school and program administrators have attached **Announcements** to the end of their **Profile** listings. In them you will find information that an institution or program wants to emphasize. The **Close-Ups** are by their very nature more expansive and flexible than the **Profiles**, and the administrators who have written them may emphasize different aspects of their programs. All of the **Close-Ups** are organized in the same way (with the exception of a few that describe research and training opportunities instead of degree programs), and in each one you will find information on the same basic topics, such as programs of study, research facilities, tuition and fees, financial aid, and application procedures. If an institution or program has submitted a **Close-Up**, a boldface cross-reference appears below its **Profile**. As with the **Announcements**, all of the **Close-Ups** in the guides have been submitted by choice; the absence of an **Announcement** or **Close-Up** does not reflect any type of editorial judgment on the part of Peterson's and their presence in the guides should not be taken as an indication of status, quality, or approval. Statements regarding a university's objectives and accomplishments are a reflection of its own beliefs and are not the opinions of the Peterson's editors.

Cross-Discipline Announcements

In addition to the regular directories that present **Profiles** of programs in each field of study, many sections in Books 2 through 6 contain special notices under the heading **Cross-Discipline Announcements**. Appearing at the end of many **Profile** sections, these **Cross-Discipline Announcements** inform you about programs that you may find of interest described in a different section. A biochemistry department, for example, may place a notice under **Cross-Discipline Announcements** in the Chemistry section (Book 4) to alert chemistry students to that course of study. **Cross-Discipline Announcements**, also written by administrators to highlight their programs, will be helpful to you not only in finding out about programs in fields related to your own but also in locating departments that are actively recruiting students with a specific undergraduate major.

Appendixes

This section contains two appendixes. The first, *Institutional Changes Since the 2007 Edition*, lists institutions that have closed, moved, merged, or changed their name or status since the last edition of the guides. The second, *Abbreviations Used in the Guides*, gives abbreviations of degree names, along with what those abbreviations stand for. These appendixes are identical in all six volumes of *Peterson's Graduate and Professional Programs*.

Indexes

There are three indexes presented here. The first index, *Close-Ups and Announcements*, gives page references for all programs that have chosen to place **Close-Ups** and **Announcements** in this volume. It is arranged alphabetically by institution; within institutions, the arrangement is alphabetical by subject area. It is not an index to all programs in the book's directories of **Profiles**; readers must refer to the directories themselves for **Profile** information on programs that have not submitted the additional, more individualized statements. The second index, *Directories and Subject Areas in Books 2–6*, gives book references for the directories in Books 2-6, for example, "Industrial Design—Book 2," and also includes cross-references for subject area names not used in the directory structure, for example, "Computing Technology (see Computer Science)." The third index, *Directories and Subject Areas in This Book*, gives page references for the directories in this volume and cross-references for subject area names not used in this volume's directory structure.

Data Collection Procedures

The information published in the directories and **Profiles** of all the books is collected through *Peterson's Annual Survey of Graduate and Professional Institutions*. The survey is sent each spring to more than 2,200 institutions offering postbaccalaureate degree programs, including accredited institutions in the United States, U.S. territories, and Canada and those institutions outside the United States that are accredited by U.S. accrediting bodies. Deans and other administrators complete these surveys, providing information on programs in the 491 academic and professional fields covered in the guides as well as overall institutional information. While every effort has been made to ensure the accuracy and completeness of the data, information is sometimes unavailable or changes occur after publication deadlines. All usable information received in time for publication has been included. The omission of any particular item from a directory or **Profile** signifies either that the item is not applicable to the institution or program or that information was not available. **Profiles** of programs scheduled to begin during the 2007–08 academic year cannot, obviously, include statistics on enrollment or, in many cases, the number of faculty members. If no usable data were submitted by an institution, its name, address, and program name appear in order to indicate the availability of graduate work.

Criteria for Inclusion in This Guide

To be included in this guide, an institution must have full accreditation or be a candidate for accreditation (preaccreditation) status by an institutional or specialized accrediting body recognized by the U.S. Department of Education or the Council for Higher Education Accreditation (CHEA). Institutional accrediting bodies, which review each institution as a whole, include the six regional associations of schools and colleges (Middle States, New England, North Central, Northwest, Southern, and Western), each of which is responsible for a specified portion of the United States and its territories. Other institutional accrediting bodies are national in scope and accredit specific kinds of institutions (e.g., Bible colleges, independent colleges, and rabbinical and Talmudic schools). Program registration by the New York State Board of Regents is considered to be the equivalent of institutional accreditation, since the board requires that all programs offered by an institution meet its standards before recognition is granted. A Canadian institution must be chartered and authorized to grant degrees by the provincial government, affiliated with a chartered institution, or accredited by a recognized U.S. accrediting body. This guide also includes institutions outside the United States that are accredited by these U.S. accrediting bodies. There are recognized specialized or professional accrediting bodies in more than fifty different fields, each of which is authorized to accredit institutions or specific programs in its particular field. For specialized institutions that offer programs in one field only, we designate this to be the equivalent of institutional accreditation. A full explanation of the accrediting process and complete information on recognized institutional (regional and national) and specialized accrediting bodies can be found online at www.chea.org or at www.ed.gov/admins/finaid/accred/index.html.

DIRECTORY OF INSTITUTIONS WITH PROGRAMS IN BUSINESS, EDUCATION, HEALTH, INFORMATION STUDIES, LAW & SOCIAL WORK

ABILENE CHRISTIAN UNIVERSITY

Accounting	M
Communication Disorders	M
Education—General	M,O
Educational Administration	M,O
Educational Measurement and Evaluation	M
Gerontological Nursing	O
Higher Education	M
Human Resources Development	M
Human Services	M,O
Nursing—General	M
Reading Education	M
Social Work	M

ACADEMY OF ART UNIVERSITY

Advertising and Public Relations	M

ACADEMY OF CHINESE CULTURE AND HEALTH SCIENCES

Acupuncture and Oriental Medicine	M

ACADEMY OF ORIENTAL MEDICINE AT AUSTIN

Acupuncture and Oriental Medicine	M

ACADIA UNIVERSITY

Counselor Education	M
Curriculum and Instruction	M
Education—General	M
Educational Administration	M
Educational Media/ Instructional Technology	M
Kinesiology and Movement Studies	M
Mathematics Education	M
Recreation and Park Management	M
Science Education	M
Social Sciences Education	M
Special Education	M

ACUPUNCTURE & INTEGRATIVE MEDICINE COLLEGE, BERKELEY

Acupuncture and Oriental Medicine	M

ACUPUNCTURE AND MASSAGE COLLEGE

Acupuncture and Oriental Medicine	M

ADAMS STATE COLLEGE

Counselor Education	M
Education—General	M
Health Education	M
Physical Education	M
Special Education	M

ADELPHI UNIVERSITY

Accounting	M
Business Administration and Management— General	M,O
Communication Disorders	M,D
Community Health	M,O
Early Childhood Education	M,O
Education—General	M,D,O*
Educational Administration	M,O
Educational Media/ Instructional Technology	M,O

Electronic Commerce	M
Elementary Education	M
English as a Second Language	M,O
Finance and Banking	M
Health Education	M,O
Human Resources Management	M,O
Management Information Systems	M
Marketing	M
Nursing—General	M,D,O*
Physical Education	M,O
Public Health—General	O
Reading Education	M
Secondary Education	M
Social Work	M,D*
Special Education	M,O

ADLER GRADUATE SCHOOL

Business Administration and Management— General	M,O
Counselor Education	M,O
Organizational Management	M,O

AGNES SCOTT COLLEGE

English Education	M*
Mathematics Education	M*
Science Education	M

AIR FORCE INSTITUTE OF TECHNOLOGY

Logistics	M,D
Management Information Systems	M

ALABAMA AGRICULTURAL AND MECHANICAL UNIVERSITY

Business Administration and Management— General	M
Communication Disorders	M
Counselor Education	M,O
Early Childhood Education	M,O
Education—General	M,O
Educational Administration	M,O
Elementary Education	M,O
Finance and Banking	M
Human Resources Management	M,O
Marketing	M
Music Education	M
Physical Education	M
Secondary Education	M,O
Social Work	M
Special Education	M,O
Vocational and Technical Education	M

ALABAMA STATE UNIVERSITY

Accounting	M
Allied Health—General	D
Business Administration and Management— General	M
Counselor Education	M,O
Early Childhood Education	M,O
Education—General	M,D,O
Educational Administration	M,D,O
Educational Media/ Instructional Technology	M,O
Educational Policy	M,D,O
Elementary Education	M,O
English Education	M,O
Health Education	M
Mathematics Education	M,O

Physical Education	M
Physical Therapy	D
Science Education	M,O
Secondary Education	M,O
Social Sciences Education	M,O
Special Education	M

ALASKA PACIFIC UNIVERSITY

Business Administration and Management— General	M
Education—General	M
Elementary Education	M
Environmental Education	M
Finance and Banking	M
Health Services Management and Hospital Administration	M
Middle School Education	M

ALBANY COLLEGE OF PHARMACY OF UNION UNIVERSITY

Pharmacy	P

ALBANY LAW SCHOOL OF UNION UNIVERSITY

Law	P,M

ALBANY MEDICAL COLLEGE

Allopathic Medicine	P
Bioethics	M,O
Nurse Anesthesia	M
Physician Assistant Studies	M

ALBANY STATE UNIVERSITY

Business Administration and Management— General	M
Business Education	M
Counselor Education	M
Early Childhood Education	M
Education—General	M,O
Educational Administration	M,O
English Education	M
Health Education	M
Health Services Management and Hospital Administration	M
Human Resources Management	M
Mathematics Education	M
Middle School Education	M
Music Education	M
Nursing—General	M
Physical Education	M
Reading Education	M
Science Education	M
Social Sciences Education	M
Special Education	M

ALBERT EINSTEIN COLLEGE OF MEDICINE

Allopathic Medicine	P

ALBERTSON COLLEGE OF IDAHO

Education—General	M

ALBERTUS MAGNUS COLLEGE

Business Administration and Management— General	M

ALBRIGHT COLLEGE

Early Childhood Education	M
Education—General	M
Elementary Education	M
English as a Second Language	M
Special Education	M

ALCORN STATE UNIVERSITY

Agricultural Education	M,O
Business Administration and Management— General	M
Counselor Education	M,O
Education—General	M,O
Elementary Education	M,O
Health Education	M,O
Nursing—General	M
Physical Education	M,O
Secondary Education	M,O
Special Education	M,O
Vocational and Technical Education	M,O

ALDERSON-BROADDUS COLLEGE

Allied Health—General	M
Emergency Medical Services	M

ALFRED UNIVERSITY

Business Administration and Management— General	M
Counselor Education	M,O
Education—General	M,O
Reading Education	M,O

ALLEN COLLEGE

Acute Care/Critical Care Nursing	M
Family Nurse Practitioner Studies	M
Health Education	M
Nursing and Healthcare Administration	M
Nursing—General	M

ALLIANCE UNIVERSITY COLLEGE

Religious Education	P,M,O

ALLIANT INTERNATIONAL UNIVERSITY–FRESNO

Education—General	M*
Educational Administration	D*
English as a Second Language	M,D,O*

ALLIANT INTERNATIONAL UNIVERSITY–IRVINE

Education—General	M,O
Educational Administration	M,D,O*
Educational Media/ Instructional Technology	M,O
Educational Psychology	M,D,O*
English as a Second Language	M,D*
Higher Education	M,D,O
Multilingual and Multicultural Education	M,O
Special Education	M,O

ALLIANT INTERNATIONAL UNIVERSITY–LOS ANGELES

Business Administration and Management— General	D*

Education—General	M*
Educational Administration	M,D,O*
Educational Psychology	M,D,O*
Higher Education	M,D,O
Student Affairs	M,D,O

ALLIANT INTERNATIONAL UNIVERSITY–MÉXICO CITY

Business Administration and Management— General	M*
Education—General	M
International Business	M

ALLIANT INTERNATIONAL UNIVERSITY–SACRAMENTO

Education—General	M*

ALLIANT INTERNATIONAL UNIVERSITY–SAN DIEGO

Business Administration and Management— General	M,D
Education—General	M,O*
Educational Administration	M,D,O*
Educational Psychology	M,D,O*
English as a Second Language	M,D,O*
Finance and Banking	M,D
Higher Education	M,D,O
International Business	M,D
Management Information Systems	M,D
Management Strategy and Policy	M,D
Marketing	M,D
Student Affairs	M,D,O

ALLIANT INTERNATIONAL UNIVERSITY–SAN FRANCISCO

Business Administration and Management— General	M
Education—General	M,O*
Educational Administration	M,D,O*
Educational Psychology	M,D,O*
Higher Education	M,D,O
Multilingual and Multicultural Education	M,O
Special Education	M,O

ALVERNIA COLLEGE

Business Administration and Management— General	M
Education—General	M
Occupational Therapy	M

ALVERNO COLLEGE

Adult Education	M
Business Administration and Management— General	M
Education—General	M
Educational Administration	M
Educational Media/ Instructional Technology	M
Nursing—General	M
Reading Education	M
Science Education	M

AMBERTON UNIVERSITY

Business Administration and Management— General	M

Human Resources Development	M
Human Resources Management	M

THE AMERICAN COLLEGE

Finance and Banking	M

AMERICAN COLLEGE OF ACUPUNCTURE AND ORIENTAL MEDICINE

Acupuncture and Oriental Medicine	M

AMERICAN COLLEGE OF COMPUTER & INFORMATION SCIENCES

Business Administration and Management— General	M

AMERICAN COLLEGE OF THESSALONIKI

Business Administration and Management— General	M,O
Entrepreneurship	M,O
Finance and Banking	M,O
Marketing	M,O

AMERICAN COLLEGE OF TRADITIONAL CHINESE MEDICINE

Acupuncture and Oriental Medicine	M,D,O

AMERICAN GRADUATE UNIVERSITY

Business Administration and Management— General	M,O
Project Management	M,O

AMERICAN INTERCONTINENTAL UNIVERSITY (CA)

Business Administration and Management— General	M
Education—General	M
Educational Media/ Instructional Technology	M
Management Information Systems	M

AMERICAN INTERCONTINENTAL UNIVERSITY (FL)

Accounting	M
Business Administration and Management— General	M
Educational Media/ Instructional Technology	M
Finance and Banking	M
Human Resources Management	M
International Business	M
Marketing	M

AMERICAN INTERCONTINENTAL UNIVERSITY BUCKHEAD CAMPUS

Accounting	M
Business Administration and Management— General	M
Finance and Banking	M

Marketing	M

AMERICAN INTERCONTINENTAL UNIVERSITY DUNWOODY CAMPUS

International Business	M
Management Information Systems	M

AMERICAN INTERCONTINENTAL UNIVERSITY-LONDON

Business Administration and Management— General	M
International Business	M
Management Information Systems	M

AMERICAN INTERCONTINENTAL UNIVERSITY ONLINE

Accounting	M
Business Administration and Management— General	M
Curriculum and Instruction	M
Education—General	M
Educational Administration	M
Educational Measurement and Evaluation	M
Educational Media/ Instructional Technology	M
Finance and Banking	M
Health Services Management and Hospital Administration	M
Human Resources Management	M
Industrial and Manufacturing Management	M
International Business	M
Marketing	M
Project Management	M

AMERICAN INTERNATIONAL COLLEGE

Business Administration and Management— General	M
Education—General	M,D,O
Educational Administration	M,D,O
Educational Psychology	M,D,O
Elementary Education	M,D,O
Human Resources Development	M
Nursing—General	M
Occupational Therapy	M
Organizational Management	M
Physical Therapy	M,D
Reading Education	M,D,O
Secondary Education	M,D,O
Special Education	M,D,O

AMERICAN JEWISH UNIVERSITY

Business Administration and Management— General	M
Education—General	M
Nonprofit Management	M
Social Work	M

AMERICAN PUBLIC UNIVERSITY SYSTEM

Business Administration and Management— General	M
Logistics	M

Public Health—General	M
Sports Management	M
Transportation Management	M

AMERICAN SENTINEL UNIVERSITY

Business Administration and Management— General	M
Health Services Management and Hospital Administration	M
Management Information Systems	M
Nursing—General	M

AMERICAN UNIVERSITY

Accounting	M
Business Administration and Management— General	M,O
Education—General	M,D,O
Educational Administration	M,D
Educational Media/ Instructional Technology	M,D
Electronic Commerce	M
Elementary Education	M,O
English as a Second Language	M,O
Entrepreneurship	M
Exercise and Sports Science	M
Finance and Banking	M,D,O
International and Comparative Education	M
International Business	M
Law	P,M,O
Legal and Justice Studies	M,D,O
Management Information Systems	M,O
Marketing	M
Organizational Management	M
Real Estate	M
Secondary Education	M,O
Special Education	M
Taxation	M

THE AMERICAN UNIVERSITY IN CAIRO

Business Administration and Management— General	M,O
English as a Second Language	M,O
Foreign Languages Education	M

THE AMERICAN UNIVERSITY IN DUBAI

Business Administration and Management— General	M
International Business	M

THE AMERICAN UNIVERSITY OF ATHENS

Business Administration and Management— General	M

AMERICAN UNIVERSITY OF BEIRUT

Allopathic Medicine	P,M
Business Administration and Management— General	M

Education—General	M
Environmental and Occupational Health	M
Epidemiology	M
Nursing—General	M
Public Health—General	M

THE AMERICAN UNIVERSITY OF PARIS

Finance and Banking	M

AMERICAN UNIVERSITY OF PUERTO RICO

Art Education	M
Education—General	M
Elementary Education	M
Physical Education	M
Science Education	M
Special Education	M

ANDERSON UNIVERSITY

Accounting	M,D
Business Administration and Management— General	M,D
Education—General	M

ANDOVER NEWTON THEOLOGICAL SCHOOL

Religious Education	P,M,D

ANDREW JACKSON UNIVERSITY

Business Administration and Management— General	M
Entrepreneurship	M
Finance and Banking	M
Health Services Management and Hospital Administration	M
Hospitality Management	M
Human Resources Management	M
International Business	M
Marketing	M

ANDREWS UNIVERSITY

Accounting	M
Allied Health—General	M
Business Administration and Management— General	M
Curriculum and Instruction	M,D,O
Education—General	M,D,O
Educational Administration	M,D,O
Educational Psychology	M,D
Elementary Education	M,D,O
English as a Second Language	M,D,O
English Education	M,D,O
Finance and Banking	M
Foreign Languages Education	M,D,O
Human Services	M
Marketing	M
Nursing—General	M
Physical Therapy	D
Reading Education	M
Religious Education	M,D,O
Science Education	M,D,O
Secondary Education	M,D,O
Social Sciences Education	M,D,O
Social Work	M
Special Education	M,D,O

ANGELO STATE UNIVERSITY

Accounting	M
Adult Nursing	M
Business Administration and Management— General	M
Counselor Education	M
Curriculum and Instruction	M
Education—General	M
Educational Administration	M
Educational Measurement and Evaluation	M
Higher Education	M
Kinesiology and Movement Studies	M
Medical/Surgical Nursing	M
Nursing Education	M
Physical Therapy	M
Reading Education	M

ANNA MARIA COLLEGE

Business Administration and Management— General	M,O
Early Childhood Education	M,O
Education—General	M,O
Elementary Education	M,O
Environmental and Occupational Health	M
Human Services	M
Reading Education	M,O

ANTIOCH UNIVERSITY LOS ANGELES

Business Administration and Management— General	M
Education—General	M
Human Resources Development	M
Organizational Management	M

ANTIOCH UNIVERSITY MCGREGOR

Business Administration and Management— General	M
Education—General	M
Educational Administration	M

ANTIOCH UNIVERSITY NEW ENGLAND

Business Administration and Management— General	M*
Education—General	M*
Educational Administration	M
Environmental Education	M
Foundations and Philosophy of Education	M
Organizational Management	O
Science Education	M

ANTIOCH UNIVERSITY SANTA BARBARA

Education—General	M
Organizational Management	M

ANTIOCH UNIVERSITY SEATTLE

Business Administration and Management— General	M
Education—General	M*

Organizational Management	M

APPALACHIAN SCHOOL OF LAW

Law	P

APPALACHIAN STATE UNIVERSITY

Accounting	M
Business Administration and Management— General	M
Communication Disorders	M
Counselor Education	M
Curriculum and Instruction	M
Education—General	M,D,O
Educational Administration	M,D,O
Educational Media/ Instructional Technology	M
Elementary Education	M
English Education	M
Exercise and Sports Science	M
Higher Education	M,O
Home Economics Education	M
Library Science	M
Mathematics Education	M
Music Education	M
Reading Education	M
Secondary Education	M
Social Sciences Education	M
Social Work	M
Special Education	M
Vocational and Technical Education	M

AQUINAS COLLEGE

Business Administration and Management— General	M
Education—General	M

AQUINAS INSTITUTE OF THEOLOGY

Health Services Management and Hospital Administration	P,M,D,O

ARCADIA UNIVERSITY

Art Education	M,D,O
Business Administration and Management— General	M
Community Health	M
Computer Education	M,D,O
Early Childhood Education	M,D,O
Education—General	M,D,O
Educational Administration	M,D,O
Educational Media/ Instructional Technology	M,D,O
Educational Psychology	M,D,O
Elementary Education	M,D,O
English Education	M,D,O
Environmental Education	M,D,O
Health Education	M
Mathematics Education	M,D,O
Music Education	M,D,O
Physical Therapy	D
Reading Education	M,D,O
Science Education	M,D,O
Secondary Education	M,D,O
Social Sciences Education	M,D,O
Special Education	M,D,O

ARGOSY UNIVERSITY, ATLANTA CAMPUS

Accounting	M,D

Business Administration and Management— General	M,D*
Counselor Education	M,D,O
Education—General	M,D,O
Educational Administration	M,D,O
Elementary Education	M,D,O
Finance and Banking	M,D
Health Services Management and Hospital Administration	M,D
Higher Education	M,D,O
International Business	M,D
Management Information Systems	M,D
Marketing	M,D
Secondary Education	M,D,O

ARGOSY UNIVERSITY, CHICAGO CAMPUS

Accounting	M,D
Business Administration and Management— General	M,D*
Community College Education	M,D,O
Counselor Education	D
Education—General	M,D,O*
Educational Administration	M,D,O
Elementary Education	M,D,O
Finance and Banking	M,D
Health Services Management and Hospital Administration	M,D
Higher Education	M,D,O
International Business	M,D
Management Information Systems	M,D
Marketing	M,D
Organizational Management	D
Secondary Education	M,D,O

ARGOSY UNIVERSITY, DALLAS CAMPUS

Business Administration and Management— General	M*
Education—General	M*
Educational Administration	M

ARGOSY UNIVERSITY, DENVER CAMPUS

Accounting	M,D
Business Administration and Management— General	M,D*
Counselor Education	M,D
Education—General	M,D*
Educational Administration	M,D
Educational Media/ Instructional Technology	M,D
Elementary Education	M,D
Finance and Banking	M,D
Health Services Management and Hospital Administration	M,D
Higher Education	M,D
International Business	M,D
Management Information Systems	M,D
Marketing	M,D
Organizational Management	M,D

ARGOSY UNIVERSITY, HAWAI'I CAMPUS

Accounting	M,D,O

Business Administration
and Management—
  General   M,D,O*
Education—General   M,D*
Educational Administration   M,D
Elementary Education   M,D
Finance and Banking   M,D,O
Health Services
Management and
  Hospital Administration   M,D,O
Higher Education   M,D
International Business   M,D,O
Management Information
  Systems   M,D,O
Marketing   M,D,O
Organizational
  Management   D
Secondary Education   M,D

ARGOSY UNIVERSITY, INLAND EMPIRE CAMPUS

Accounting   M,D
Business Administration
and Management—
  General   M,D*
Community College
  Education   M,D
Educational Administration   M,D*
Elementary Education   M,D
Finance and Banking   M,D
Health Services
Management and
  Hospital Administration   M,D
Higher Education   M,D
International Business   M,D
Management Information
  Systems   M,D
Marketing   M,D
Secondary Education   M,D

ARGOSY UNIVERSITY, NASHVILLE CAMPUS

Accounting   D
Business Administration
and Management—
  General   D*
Community College
  Education   M,D
Counselor Education   M,D
Educational Administration   M,D*
Educational Media/
  Instructional Technology   M,D
Elementary Education   M,D
Higher Education   M,D
International Business   D
Management Information
  Systems   D
Marketing   D
Secondary Education   M,D

ARGOSY UNIVERSITY, ORANGE COUNTY CAMPUS

Accounting   M,D,O
Business Administration
and Management—
  General   M,D,O*
Community College
  Education   M,D
Education—General   M,D*
Educational Administration   M,D
Educational Media/
  Instructional Technology   M,D
Elementary Education   M,D
Finance and Banking   M,D,O
Health Services
Management and
  Hospital Administration   M,D,O
Higher Education   M,D
International Business   M,D,O
Management Information
  Systems   M,D,O

Marketing   M,D,O
Organizational
  Management   M,D,O
Secondary Education   M,D

ARGOSY UNIVERSITY, PHOENIX CAMPUS

Accounting   M,D
Business Administration
and Management—
  General   M,D*
Community College
  Education   M,D,O
Education—General   M,D,O*
Educational Administration   M,D,O
Elementary Education   M,D,O
Finance and Banking   M,D
Health Services
Management and
  Hospital Administration   M,D
Higher Education   M,D,O
International Business   M,D
Management Information
  Systems   M,D
Marketing   M,D
Secondary Education   M,D,O

ARGOSY UNIVERSITY, SAN DIEGO CAMPUS

Accounting   M,D
Business Administration
and Management—
  General   M,D*
Community College
  Education   M,D
Education—General   M,D*
Educational Administration   M,D
Elementary Education   M,D
Finance and Banking   M,D
Higher Education   M,D
International Business   M,D
Management Information
  Systems   M,D
Marketing   M,D
Secondary Education   M,D

ARGOSY UNIVERSITY, SAN FRANCISCO BAY AREA CAMPUS

Accounting   M,D
Business Administration
and Management—
  General   M,D*
Community College
  Education   M,D
Education—General   M,D*
Educational Administration   M,D
Elementary Education   M,D
Finance and Banking   M,D
Health Services
Management and
  Hospital Administration   M,D
Higher Education   M,D
International Business   M,D
Management Information
  Systems   M,D
Marketing   M,D
Organizational
  Management   M,D
Secondary Education   M,D

ARGOSY UNIVERSITY, SANTA MONICA CAMPUS

Accounting   M,D
Business Administration
and Management—
  General   M,D*
Community College
  Education   M,D
Education—General   M,D*

Marketing   M,D,O
Organizational
  Management   M,D,O
Secondary Education   M,D

Educational Administration   M,D
Elementary Education   M,D
Finance and Banking   M,D
Health Services
Management and
  Hospital Administration   M,D
Higher Education   M,D
International Business   M,D
Management Information
  Systems   M,D
Marketing   M,D
Organizational
  Management   M,D
Secondary Education   M,D

ARGOSY UNIVERSITY, SARASOTA CAMPUS

Accounting   M,D,O
Business Administration
and Management—
  General   M,D,O*
Counselor Education   M,D,O
Education—General   M,D,O*
Educational Administration   M,D,O
Educational Media/
  Instructional Technology   M,D,O
Elementary Education   M,D,O
Finance and Banking   M,D,O
Health Services
Management and
  Hospital Administration   M,D,O
Higher Education   M,D,O
International Business   M,D,O
Management Information
  Systems   M,D,O
Marketing   M,D,O
Organizational
  Management   M,D,O
Secondary Education   M,D,O

ARGOSY UNIVERSITY, SCHAUMBURG CAMPUS

Accounting   M,D,O
Business Administration
and Management—
  General   M,D,O*
Community College
  Education   M,D,O
Counselor Education   M,D,O
Education—General   M,D,O*
Educational Administration   M,D,O
Elementary Education   M,D,O
Finance and Banking   M,D,O
Health Services
Management and
  Hospital Administration   M,D,O
Higher Education   M,D,O
International Business   M,D,O
Management Information
  Systems   M,D,O
Marketing   M,D,O
Organizational
  Management   M,D,O
Secondary Education   M,D,O

ARGOSY UNIVERSITY, SEATTLE CAMPUS

Accounting   M,D
Business Administration
and Management—
  General   M,D*
Community College
  Education   M,D
Education—General   M,D*
Educational Administration   M,D
Educational Media/
  Instructional Technology   M,D
Elementary Education   M,D
Finance and Banking   M,D

Educational Administration   M,D
Elementary Education   M,D
Finance and Banking   M,D
Health Services
Management and
  Hospital Administration   M,D
Higher Education   M,D
International Business   M,D
Management Information
  Systems   M,D
Marketing   M,D
Organizational
  Management   M,D
Secondary Education   M,D

ARGOSY UNIVERSITY, TAMPA CAMPUS

Accounting   M,D,O
Business Administration
and Management—
  General   M,D,O*
Community College
  Education   M,D,O
Counselor Education   M,D
Education—General   M,D,O*
Educational Administration   M,D,O
Elementary Education   M,D,O
Finance and Banking   M,D,O
Health Services
Management and
  Hospital Administration   M,D,O
Higher Education   M,D,O
International Business   M,D,O
Management Information
  Systems   M,D,O
Marketing   M,D,O
Organizational
  Management   M,D
Secondary Education   M,D,O

ARGOSY UNIVERSITY, TWIN CITIES CAMPUS

Accounting   M,D
Business Administration
and Management—
  General   M,D*
Education—General   M,D,O*
Educational Administration   M,D,O
Educational Media/
  Instructional Technology   M,D,O
Elementary Education   M,D,O
Finance and Banking   M,D
Health Services
Management and
  Hospital Administration   M,D
Higher Education   M,D,O
International Business   M,D
Management Information
  Systems   M,D
Marketing   M,D
Secondary Education   M,D,O

ARGOSY UNIVERSITY, WASHINGTON DC CAMPUS

Accounting   M,D,O
Business Administration
and Management—
  General   M,D,O*
Counselor Education   M,D
Education—General   M,D,O*
Educational Administration   M,D,O
Elementary Education   M,D,O
Finance and Banking   M,D,O
Health Services
Management and
  Hospital Administration   M,D,O
Higher Education   M,D,O
International Business   M,D,O
Management Information
  Systems   M,D,O
Marketing   M,D,O
Organizational
  Management   M,D
Secondary Education   M,D,O

ARIZONA STATE UNIVERSITY

Accounting	M,D
Business Administration and Management— General	M,D
Communication Disorders	M,D
Counselor Education	M
Curriculum and Instruction	M,D
Education—General	M,D
Educational Administration	M,D
Educational Media/ Instructional Technology	M,D
Educational Psychology	M,D
English as a Second Language	M,D
Exercise and Sports Science	D
Finance and Banking	M,D
Foundations and Philosophy of Education	M
Health Services Management and Hospital Administration	M
Health Services Research	M,D
Higher Education	M,D
Kinesiology and Movement Studies	M,D*
Law	P
Legal and Justice Studies	M,D
Management Information Systems	M,D
Marketing	M,D
Nursing—General	M
Recreation and Park Management	M
Science Education	M,D
Social Work	M,D
Special Education	M
Supply Chain Management	M,D
Transportation Management	O

ARIZONA STATE UNIVERSITY AT THE POLYTECHNIC CAMPUS

Curriculum and Instruction	M,D
Education—General	M,D
Educational Administration	M,D
Exercise and Sports Science	M,D
Management Information Systems	M
Physical Education	M,D
Transportation Management	M

ARIZONA STATE UNIVERSITY AT THE WEST CAMPUS

Accounting	O
Business Administration and Management— General	M
Education—General	M,D,O
Educational Administration	M,D,O
Elementary Education	M,D,O
Secondary Education	M,D,O
Social Work	M
Special Education	M,D,O

ARKANSAS STATE UNIVERSITY

Accounting	M
Agricultural Education	M,O
Allied Health—General	M,O
Business Administration and Management— General	M,O
Business Education	M,O
Communication Disorders	M
Community College Education	M,D,O

Counselor Education	M,O
Curriculum and Instruction	M,D,O
Early Childhood Education	M,O
Education of the Gifted	M,D,O
Education—General	M,D,O
Educational Administration	M,D,O
Educational Measurement and Evaluation	M,O
Electronic Commerce	M,O
Elementary Education	M,O
English Education	M,O
Exercise and Sports Science	M,O
Foundations and Philosophy of Education	M,D,O
Gerontological Nursing	M,O
Health Education	M,O
Management Information Systems	M,O
Music Education	M,O
Nurse Anesthesia	M,O
Nursing—General	M,O
Physical Education	M,O
Physical Therapy	M
Reading Education	M,O
Science Education	M,D,O
Social Sciences Education	M,D,O
Social Work	M
Special Education	M,D,O
Student Affairs	M,O

ARKANSAS TECH UNIVERSITY

Curriculum and Instruction	M,O
Education of the Gifted	M,O
Education—General	M,O
Educational Administration	M,O
English as a Second Language	M
English Education	M,O
Mathematics Education	M
Secondary Education	M,O
Social Sciences Education	M
Student Affairs	M,O

ARMSTRONG ATLANTIC STATE UNIVERSITY

Adult Education	M
Athletic Training and Sports Medicine	M
Business Education	M
Communication Disorders	M
Curriculum and Instruction	M
Early Childhood Education	M
Education—General	M
Elementary Education	M
English Education	M
Exercise and Sports Science	M
Health Services Management and Hospital Administration	M
Mathematics Education	M
Middle School Education	M
Nursing—General	M
Physical Therapy	M
Public Health—General	M
Science Education	M
Secondary Education	M
Social Sciences Education	M
Special Education	M

ART ACADEMY OF CINCINNATI

Art Education	M

ASBURY COLLEGE

English as a Second Language	M,O
Mathematics Education	M,O
Reading Education	M,O

Science Education	M,O
Social Sciences Education	M,O
Special Education	M,O

ASBURY THEOLOGICAL SEMINARY

Religious Education	M,O

ASHLAND UNIVERSITY

Business Administration and Management— General	M
Curriculum and Instruction	M
Early Childhood Education	M
Education of the Gifted	M
Education—General	M,D
Educational Administration	M,D
Educational Media/ Instructional Technology	M
Exercise and Sports Science	M
Foundations and Philosophy of Education	M
Middle School Education	M
Physical Education	M
Special Education	M
Sports Management	M
Student Affairs	M

ASPEN UNIVERSITY

Business Administration and Management— General	M,O
Management Information Systems	M,O
Project Management	M,O

ASSUMPTION COLLEGE

Business Administration and Management— General	M,O
Special Education	M

ATHABASCA UNIVERSITY

Adult Education	M
Allied Health—General	M,O
Business Administration and Management— General	M,O
Distance Education Development	M,O
Education—General	M,O
Family Nurse Practitioner Studies	M,O
Nursing and Healthcare Administration	M,O
Nursing—General	M,O
Organizational Management	M
Project Management	M,O

ATLANTIC INSTITUTE OF ORIENTAL MEDICINE

Acupuncture and Oriental Medicine	M

ATLANTIC UNION COLLEGE

Education—General	M

A.T. STILL UNIVERSITY OF HEALTH SCIENCES

Allied Health—General	M,D
Communication Disorders	M,D
Exercise and Sports Science	M,D

Health Education	M
Health Services Management and Hospital Administration	M
Kinesiology and Movement Studies	M,D
Occupational Therapy	M,D
Oral and Dental Sciences	P
Osteopathic Medicine	P,M
Physical Therapy	M,D
Physician Assistant Studies	M,D
Public Health—General	M

AUBURN UNIVERSITY

Accounting	M
Adult Education	M,D,O
Business Administration and Management— General	M,D
Business Education	M,D,O
Communication Disorders	M,D
Counselor Education	M,D,O
Curriculum and Instruction	M,D,O
Early Childhood Education	M,D,O
Education—General	M,D,O*
Educational Administration	M,D,O
Educational Media/ Instructional Technology	M,D,O
Educational Psychology	M,D,O
Elementary Education	M,D,O
English Education	M,D,O
Exercise and Sports Science	M,D,O
Finance and Banking	M
Foreign Languages Education	M,D,O
Health Education	M,D,O
Health Promotion	M,D,O
Higher Education	M,D,O
Human Resources Management	M,D
Management Information Systems	M,D
Mathematics Education	M,D,O
Music Education	M,D,O
Pharmaceutical Sciences	M,D
Pharmacy	P
Physical Education	M,D,O
Reading Education	M,D,O
Science Education	M,D,O
Secondary Education	M,D,O
Social Sciences Education	M,D,O
Special Education	M,D,O
Veterinary Medicine	P
Veterinary Sciences	M,D

AUBURN UNIVERSITY MONTGOMERY

Business Administration and Management— General	M
Counselor Education	M,O
Early Childhood Education	M,O
Education—General	M,O
Educational Administration	M,O
Elementary Education	M,O
Physical Education	M,O
Reading Education	M,O
Secondary Education	M,O
Special Education	M,O

AUGSBURG COLLEGE

Business Administration and Management— General	M
Community Health Nursing	M
Education—General	M
Nursing—General	M

Organizational Management	M
Physician Assistant Studies	M
Social Work	M
Transcultural Nursing	M

AUGUSTANA COLLEGE

Community Health Nursing	M
Education—General	M
Elementary Education	M
Nursing—General	M
Secondary Education	M

AUGUSTA STATE UNIVERSITY

Business Administration and Management— General	M
Counselor Education	M
Education—General	M,O
Educational Administration	M,O
Elementary Education	M,O
Health Education	M
Middle School Education	M,O
Physical Education	M
Secondary Education	M,O
Special Education	M,O

AURORA UNIVERSITY

Business Administration and Management— General	M
Curriculum and Instruction	M,D
Education—General	M,D
Educational Administration	M,D
Leisure Studies	M
Reading Education	M,D
Social Work	M

AUSTIN COLLEGE

Art Education	M
Education—General	M
Elementary Education	M
Middle School Education	M
Music Education	M
Physical Education	M
Secondary Education	M

AUSTIN PEAY STATE UNIVERSITY

Business Administration and Management— General	M
Counselor Education	M
Curriculum and Instruction	M,O
Education—General	M,O
Educational Administration	M,O
Exercise and Sports Science	M
Health Education	M
Music Education	M
Nursing—General	M
Physical Education	M
Reading Education	M,O

AVE MARIA SCHOOL OF LAW

Law	P

AVERETT UNIVERSITY

Art Education	M
Business Administration and Management— General	M
Curriculum and Instruction	M
Education—General	M
Elementary Education	M

English Education	M
Health Education	M
Mathematics Education	M
Physical Education	M
Reading Education	M
Science Education	M
Social Sciences Education	M
Special Education	M

AVILA UNIVERSITY

Accounting	M
Business Administration and Management— General	M
Education—General	M,O
English as a Second Language	M,O
Finance and Banking	M
Health Services Management and Hospital Administration	M
International Business	M
Management Information Systems	M
Marketing	M
Organizational Management	M,O*
Project Management	M,O
Reading Education	M,O

AZUSA PACIFIC UNIVERSITY

Business Administration and Management— General	M
Counselor Education	M
Curriculum and Instruction	M
Education—General	M,D
Educational Administration	M,D
Educational Media/ Instructional Technology	M
English as a Second Language	M
Higher Education	M,D
Human Resources Development	M
International Business	M
Library Science	M
Management Strategy and Policy	M
Multilingual and Multicultural Education	M
Music Education	M
Nonprofit Management	M
Nursing Education	M,D
Nursing—General	M,D
Organizational Management	M
Physical Education	M
Physical Therapy	D
Religious Education	M
Special Education	M
Student Affairs	M

BABSON COLLEGE

Business Administration and Management— General	M

BAKER COLLEGE CENTER FOR GRADUATE STUDIES

Accounting	M
Business Administration and Management— General	M
Finance and Banking	M
Health Services Management and Hospital Administration	M

Human Resources Management	M
Industrial and Manufacturing Management	M
International Business	M
Management Information Systems	M
Marketing	M
Recreation and Park Management	M

BAKER UNIVERSITY

Business Administration and Management— General	M
Education—General	M,D

BALDWIN-WALLACE COLLEGE

Accounting	M
Business Administration and Management— General	M
Education—General	M
Educational Administration	M
Educational Media/ Instructional Technology	M
Entrepreneurship	M
Health Services Management and Hospital Administration	M
Human Resources Management	M
International Business	M
Reading Education	M
Special Education	M

BALL STATE UNIVERSITY

Accounting	M
Actuarial Science	M
Adult Education	M,D
Advertising and Public Relations	M
Art Education	M
Business Administration and Management— General	M
Business Education	M
Communication Disorders	M,D
Curriculum and Instruction	M,O
Education—General	M,D,O
Educational Administration	M,D,O
Educational Psychology	M,D,O
Elementary Education	M,D
English as a Second Language	M,D
Exercise and Sports Science	D
Foundations and Philosophy of Education	D
Health Education	M
Health Promotion	M
Higher Education	M,D
Mathematics Education	M
Music Education	M,D
Nursing—General	M
Physical Education	M,D
Science Education	M,D
Secondary Education	M
Special Education	M,D,O
Vocational and Technical Education	M

BANK STREET COLLEGE OF EDUCATION

Curriculum and Instruction	M
Early Childhood Education	M
Education—General	M*
Educational Administration	M

Elementary Education	M
Foundations and Philosophy of Education	M
Maternal and Child Health	M
Mathematics Education	M
Middle School Education	M
Multilingual and Multicultural Education	M
Museum Education	M
Reading Education	M
Special Education	M

BAPTIST BIBLE COLLEGE OF PENNSYLVANIA

Counselor Education	M
Religious Education	M

BAPTIST THEOLOGICAL SEMINARY AT RICHMOND

Religious Education	P,D

BARD COLLEGE

Education—General	M*

BARNES-JEWISH COLLEGE OF NURSING AND ALLIED HEALTH

Adult Nursing	M
Allied Health—General	M,O
Family Nurse Practitioner Studies	M
Gerontological Nursing	M
Health Promotion	M,O
Health Services Management and Hospital Administration	M,O
Maternal and Child/ Neonatal Nursing	M
Nursing Education	M
Nursing—General	M
Oncology Nursing	M

BARRY UNIVERSITY

Accounting	M
Acute Care/Critical Care Nursing	M,O
Athletic Training and Sports Medicine	M
Business Administration and Management— General	M,O
Communication Disorders	M
Counselor Education	M,D,O
Curriculum and Instruction	D,O
Distance Education Development	O
Early Childhood Education	M,D,O
Education of the Gifted	M,D,O
Education—General	M,D,O
Educational Administration	M,D,O
Educational Media/ Instructional Technology	M,D,O
Elementary Education	M,D,O
English as a Second Language	M,D,O
Exercise and Sports Science	M
Family Nurse Practitioner Studies	M,O
Finance and Banking	O
Health Services Management and Hospital Administration	M,O
Higher Education	M,D
Human Resources Development	M,D
Human Resources Management	O
International Business	O

Kinesiology and
  Movement Studies | M
Law | P
Management Information
  Systems | O
Marketing | O
Nurse Anesthesia | M
Nursing and Healthcare
  Administration | M,D,O
Nursing Education | M,O
Nursing—General | M,D,O
Occupational Therapy | M
Physician Assistant
  Studies | M
Podiatric Medicine | P
Public Health—General | M
Reading Education | M,D,O
Social Work | M,D*
Special Education | M,D,O
Sports Management | M*

BASTYR UNIVERSITY

Acupuncture and Oriental
  Medicine | M,D,O*
Naturopathic Medicine | D,O*
Nurse Midwifery | D,O

BAYAMÓN CENTRAL UNIVERSITY

Accounting | M
Business Administration
  and Management—
  General | M
Counselor Education | M
Early Childhood Education | M
Education—General | M
Educational Administration | M
Elementary Education | M
Finance and Banking | M
Marketing | M
Physical Education | M
Special Education | M

BAYLOR COLLEGE OF MEDICINE

Allopathic Medicine | P
Clinical Laboratory
  Sciences/Medical
  Technology | M,D
Nurse Anesthesia | M
Physician Assistant
  Studies | M

BAYLOR UNIVERSITY

Accounting | M
Allied Health—General | M,D
Business Administration
  and Management—
  General | M
Communication Disorders | M
Curriculum and Instruction | M,D,O
Education—General | M,D,O
Educational Administration | M,O
Educational Psychology | M,D,O
Exercise and Sports
  Science | M,D
Family Nurse Practitioner
  Studies | M
Health Education | M,D
Health Services
  Management and
  Hospital Administration | M
International Business | M
Law | P
Management Information
  Systems | M
Maternal and Child/
  Neonatal Nursing | M
Music Education | M
Nursing and Healthcare
  Administration | M

Nursing—General | M
Pediatric Nursing | M
Physical Education | M,D
Physical Therapy | M,D
Social Work | M

BAY PATH COLLEGE

Entrepreneurship | M
Management Information
  Systems | M
Occupational Therapy | M

BEACON UNIVERSITY

Organizational
  Management | P,M

BELHAVEN COLLEGE (MS)

Business Administration
  and Management—
  General | M
Education—General | M
Elementary Education | M
Multilingual and
  Multicultural Education | M
Secondary Education | M

BELLARMINE UNIVERSITY

Business Administration
  and Management—
  General | M
Early Childhood Education | M
Education—General | M
Educational Administration | M
Middle School Education | M
Nursing and Healthcare
  Administration | M,D
Nursing Education | M,D
Nursing—General | M,D
Physical Therapy | M,D
Reading Education | M
Secondary Education | M
Special Education | M

BELLEVUE UNIVERSITY

Business Administration
  and Management—
  General | M
Health Services
  Management and
  Hospital Administration | M*
Human Services | M
Management Information
  Systems | M

BELMONT UNIVERSITY

Allied Health—General | M,D
Business Administration
  and Management—
  General | M
Early Childhood Education | M
Education of the Gifted | M
Education—General | M
Educational Media/
  Instructional Technology | M
Elementary Education | M
English Education | M
Mathematics Education | M
Middle School Education | M
Music Education | M
Nursing—General | M
Occupational Therapy | M,D
Physical Therapy | D
Science Education | M
Secondary Education | M
Social Sciences Education | M
Sports Management | M

BEMIDJI STATE UNIVERSITY

Education—General | M
Exercise and Sports
  Science | M
Mathematics Education | M
Science Education | M
Special Education | M
Vocational and Technical
  Education | M

BENEDICTINE COLLEGE

Business Administration
  and Management—
  General | M
Educational Administration | M

BENEDICTINE UNIVERSITY

Business Administration
  and Management—
  General | M
Curriculum and Instruction | M
Education—General | M
Educational Administration | M,D
Elementary Education | M
Exercise and Sports
  Science | M
Health Promotion | M
Higher Education | D
Management Information
  Systems | M
Organizational Behavior | M
Organizational
  Management | D
Public Health—General | M
Reading Education | M
Science Education | M
Secondary Education | M
Special Education | M

BENNINGTON COLLEGE

Allied Health—General | O
Art Education | M
Early Childhood Education | M
Education—General | M*
Elementary Education | M
English Education | M
Foreign Languages
  Education | M
Mathematics Education | M
Multilingual and
  Multicultural Education | M
Music Education | M
Science Education | M
Secondary Education | M
Social Sciences Education | M

BENTLEY COLLEGE

Accounting | M,D
Business Administration
  and Management—
  General | M,D,O*
Finance and Banking | M
Marketing | M
Real Estate | M
Taxation | M

BERNARD M. BARUCH COLLEGE OF THE CITY UNIVERSITY OF NEW YORK

Accounting | M,D
Business Administration
  and Management—
  General | M,D,O*
Educational Administration | M
Entrepreneurship | M,D
Finance and Banking | M,D

Health Services
  Management and
  Hospital Administration | M
Higher Education | M
Human Resources
  Management | M,D
International Business | M
Management Information
  Systems | M,D
Management Strategy and
  Policy | M,D
Marketing | M,D
Organizational Behavior | M,D
Organizational
  Management | M,D
Quantitative Analysis | M
Taxation | M*

BERRY COLLEGE

Business Administration
  and Management—
  General | M
Curriculum and Instruction | O
Early Childhood Education | M
Education—General | M,O
Middle School Education | M
Reading Education | M
Secondary Education | M

BETHANY UNIVERSITY

Education—General | M
Educational Administration | M

BETHEL COLLEGE (IN)

Business Administration
  and Management—
  General | M
Education—General | M
Nursing—General | M

BETHEL COLLEGE (TN)

Education—General | M
Educational Administration | M
Elementary Education | M
English Education | M
Physical Education | M
Science Education | M
Social Sciences Education | M
Special Education | M

BETHEL SEMINARY

Religious Education | P,M,D,O

BETHEL UNIVERSITY

Business Administration
  and Management—
  General | M
Education—General | M,D,O
Educational Administration | M,D,O
Higher Education | M,O
Nursing Education | M,O
Nursing—General | M,O
Organizational
  Management | M
Reading Education | M,D,O
Secondary Education | M,D,O
Special Education | M,D,O

BIOLA UNIVERSITY

Business Administration
  and Management—
  General | M
Education—General | M
English as a Second
  Language | M,D,O

Organizational
 Management — M
Religious Education — P,M,D

BIRMINGHAM-SOUTHERN COLLEGE

Business Administration
 and Management—
 General — M

BISHOP'S UNIVERSITY

Education—General — M,O
English as a Second
 Language — M,O

BLACK HILLS STATE UNIVERSITY

Business Administration
 and Management—
 General — M
Curriculum and Instruction — M
Education—General — M*

BLOOMSBURG UNIVERSITY OF PENNSYLVANIA

Adult Nursing — M
Business Administration
 and Management—
 General — M
Business Education — M
Communication Disorders — M,D
Community Health — M
Counselor Education — M
Curriculum and Instruction — M
Early Childhood Education — M
Education—General — M
Educational Media/
 Instructional Technology — M
Elementary Education — M
Exercise and Sports
 Science — M
Family Nurse Practitioner
 Studies — M
Health Physics/
 Radiological Health — M
Nursing and Healthcare
 Administration — M
Nursing—General — M
Reading Education — M
Science Education — M
Special Education — M
Student Affairs — M

BLUFFTON UNIVERSITY

Business Administration
 and Management—
 General — M
Education—General — M
Organizational
 Management — M

BOB JONES UNIVERSITY

Accounting — P,M,D,O
Business Administration
 and Management—
 General — P,M,D,O
Counselor Education — P,M,D,O
Curriculum and Instruction — P,M,D,O
Educational Administration — P,M,D,O
Elementary Education — P,M,D,O
English Education — P,M,D,O
Mathematics Education — P,M,D,O
Music Education — P,M,D,O
Secondary Education — P,M,D,O
Social Sciences Education — P,M,D,O
Special Education — P,M,D,O
Student Affairs — P,M,D,O

BOISE STATE UNIVERSITY

Accounting — M
Art Education — M
Business Administration
 and Management—
 General — M
Counselor Education — M
Curriculum and Instruction — D
Early Childhood Education — M
Education—General — M,D
Educational Administration — M,D
Educational Media/
 Instructional Technology — M
Exercise and Sports
 Science — M
Management Information
 Systems — M
Music Education — M
Public Health—General — M
Reading Education — M
Science Education — M,D
Social Work — M
Special Education — M
Sports Management — M
Taxation — M

BORICUA COLLEGE

Human Services — M

BOSTON COLLEGE

Accounting — M
Business Administration
 and Management—
 General — M
Community Health
 Nursing — M,D
Curriculum and Instruction — M,D,O
Early Childhood Education — M
Education—General — M,D,O*
Educational Administration — M,D,O
Educational Measurement
 and Evaluation — M,D
Educational Psychology — M,D
Elementary Education — M
English Education — M
Finance and Banking — M,D
Foreign Languages
 Education — M
Gerontological Nursing — M,D
Higher Education — M,D
Law — P
Maternal and Child/
 Neonatal Nursing — M,D
Mathematics Education — M
Nurse Anesthesia — M,D
Nursing—General — M,D
Organizational Behavior — D
Organizational
 Management — D
Psychiatric Nursing — M,D
Reading Education — M
Religious Education — M,D,O
Science Education — M,D
Secondary Education — M
Social Sciences Education — M
Social Work — M,D*
Special Education — M,O

THE BOSTON CONSERVATORY

Music Education — M,O

BOSTON UNIVERSITY

Accounting — M,D,O
Actuarial Science — M
Advertising and Public
 Relations — M
Allied Health—General — M,D
Allopathic Medicine — P
Art Education — M

Athletic Training and
 Sports Medicine — D
Bioethics — M
Business Administration
 and Management—
 General — M,D,O
Communication Disorders — M,D,O
Counselor Education — M,O
Curriculum and Instruction — M,D,O
Dental Hygiene — P,M,D,O
Dentistry — P,M,D,O
Early Childhood Education — M,D,O
Education—General — M,D,O*
Educational Administration — M,O
Educational Media/
 Instructional Technology — M,D,O
Electronic Commerce — M
Elementary Education — M
English as a Second
 Language — M,O
English Education — M,O
Environmental and
 Occupational Health — M,D
Epidemiology — M,D
Finance and Banking — P,M,D
Foreign Languages
 Education — M
Health Education — M,O
Health Promotion — M,D
Health Services
 Management and
 Hospital Administration — M,D,O
Human Resources
 Management — M,O
Industrial and
 Manufacturing
 Management — D
International and
 Comparative Education — M
International Business — M
International Health — M,D,O
Investment Management — M
Law — P,M
Legal and Justice Studies — M
Management Information
 Systems — D
Marketing — D
Maternal and Child Health — M,O
Mathematics Education — M,D,O
Multilingual and
 Multicultural Education — M,O
Music Education — M,D
Nonprofit Management — M,O
Nurse Midwifery — M,O
Occupational Therapy — M,D
Oral and Dental Sciences — P,M,D,O*
Organizational Behavior — D
Pharmaceutical Sciences — M,D
Physical Education — M,D,O
Physical Therapy — D
Project Management — M
Public Health—General — P,M,D,O
Reading Education — M,D,O
Rehabilitation Sciences — D
Science Education — M,D,O
Social Sciences Education — M,D,O
Social Work — M,D
Special Education — M,D,O
Taxation — P,M
Travel and Tourism — M

BOWIE STATE UNIVERSITY

Business Administration
 and Management—
 General — M
Counselor Education — M
Education—General — M
Educational Administration — M,D
Elementary Education — M
Family Nurse Practitioner
 Studies — M
Human Resources
 Development — M

Management Information
 Systems — M,O
Nursing and Healthcare
 Administration — M
Nursing Education — M
Nursing—General — M
Reading Education — M
Secondary Education — M
Special Education — M

BOWLING GREEN STATE UNIVERSITY

Accounting — M
Art Education — M
Business Administration
 and Management—
 General — M
Business Education — M
Communication Disorders — M,D
Counselor Education — M
Curriculum and Instruction — M
Early Childhood Education — M
Education of the Gifted — M
Educational Administration — M,D,O
Educational Media/
 Instructional Technology — M
Foreign Languages
 Education — M
Higher Education — D
Kinesiology and
 Movement Studies — M
Leisure Studies — M
Mathematics Education — M,D
Music Education — M,D
Organizational
 Management — M
Public Health—General — M
Reading Education — M,O
Recreation and Park
 Management — M
Science Education — M
Special Education — M
Sports Management — M
Student Affairs — M
Vocational and Technical
 Education — M

BRADLEY UNIVERSITY

Accounting — M
Business Administration
 and Management—
 General — M
Counselor Education — M
Curriculum and Instruction — M
Education—General — M,D
Educational Administration — M
Nurse Anesthesia — M
Nursing and Healthcare
 Administration — M
Nursing—General — M
Physical Therapy — D

BRANDEIS UNIVERSITY

Business Administration
 and Management—
 General — M*
Elementary Education — M
Finance and Banking — M,D
Health Services
 Management and
 Hospital Administration — M
Human Services — M
International Business — M,D
International Health — M*
Religious Education — M
Secondary Education — M

BRANDON UNIVERSITY

Counselor Education — M,O

Curriculum and Instruction	M,O
Education—General	M,O
Educational Administration	M,O
Music Education	M
Special Education	M,O

BRENAU UNIVERSITY

Accounting	M
Business Administration and Management—General	M
Early Childhood Education	M,O
Education—General	M,O
Family Nurse Practitioner Studies	M
Health Services Management and Hospital Administration	M
Management Strategy and Policy	M
Middle School Education	M,O
Nursing Education	M
Occupational Therapy	M
Organizational Management	M
Special Education	M,O

BRESCIA UNIVERSITY

Business Administration and Management—General	M
Curriculum and Instruction	M

BRIAR CLIFF UNIVERSITY

Education—General	M
Human Resources Management	M
Nursing—General	M

BRIDGEWATER STATE COLLEGE

Accounting	M
Art Education	M
Business Administration and Management—General	M
Counselor Education	M,O
Early Childhood Education	M
Education—General	M,O
Educational Administration	M,O
Educational Media/ Instructional Technology	M
Elementary Education	M
Finance and Banking	M
Health Promotion	M
Mathematics Education	M
Physical Education	M
Reading Education	M,O
Science Education	M
Secondary Education	M
Social Sciences Education	M
Social Work	M
Special Education	M

BRIERCREST SEMINARY

Business Administration and Management—General	M
Organizational Management	M

BRIGHAM YOUNG UNIVERSITY

Accounting	M
Art Education	M
Athletic Training and Sports Medicine	M,D

Business Administration and Management—General	M
Communication Disorders	M
Education—General	M,D,O
Educational Administration	M,D
Educational Media/ Instructional Technology	M,D
Educational Psychology	M,D
English as a Second Language	M,O
Exercise and Sports Science	M,D
Foreign Languages Education	M
Foundations and Philosophy of Education	M,D
Health Education	M
Health Promotion	M,D
Law	P,M
Management Information Systems	M
Mathematics Education	M
Music Education	M
Nursing—General	M*
Physical Education	M,D
Reading Education	M
Recreation and Park Management	M
Religious Education	M
Science Education	M,D
Social Work	M
Special Education	M,D,O

BROCK UNIVERSITY

Accounting	M
Allied Health—General	M
Business Administration and Management—General	M
Education—General	M,D
English as a Second Language	M
Legal and Justice Studies	M

BROOKLYN COLLEGE OF THE CITY UNIVERSITY OF NEW YORK

Accounting	M
Art Education	M,O
Communication Disorders	M,D
Community Health	M
Counselor Education	M,O
Early Childhood Education	M
Education—General	M,O
Educational Administration	O
Elementary Education	M
English Education	M,O
Environmental Education	M
Exercise and Sports Science	M
Foreign Languages Education	M,O
Health Education	M,O
Health Services Management and Hospital Administration	M
Mathematics Education	M,D,O
Middle School Education	M
Multilingual and Multicultural Education	M
Music Education	M,D,O
Physical Education	M,O
Public Health—General	M
Science Education	M,O
Secondary Education	M,O
Social Sciences Education	M,O
Special Education	M
Sports Management	M

BROOKLYN LAW SCHOOL

Law	P

BROWN UNIVERSITY

Allopathic Medicine	P
Community Health	M,D
Education—General	M
Elementary Education	M
English Education	M
Epidemiology	M,D
Health Services Research	M,D
Multilingual and Multicultural Education	M,D
Public Health—General	M
Science Education	M
Secondary Education	M
Social Sciences Education	M

BRYANT UNIVERSITY

Accounting	M,O
Business Administration and Management—General	M,O
Electronic Commerce	M,O
Finance and Banking	M,O
Industrial and Manufacturing Management	M,O
Management Information Systems	M,O
Marketing	M,O
Taxation	M,O

BRYN MAWR COLLEGE

Social Work	M,D

BUCKNELL UNIVERSITY

Counselor Education	M
Curriculum and Instruction	M
Education—General	M
Educational Administration	M
Educational Measurement and Evaluation	M
Reading Education	M

BUENA VISTA UNIVERSITY

Counselor Education	M
Education—General	M

BUFFALO STATE COLLEGE, STATE UNIVERSITY OF NEW YORK

Adult Education	M,O
Art Education	M
Business Education	M
Communication Disorders	M
Early Childhood Education	M
Educational Administration	O
Educational Media/ Instructional Technology	M
Elementary Education	M
English Education	M
Human Resources Management	M,O
Mathematics Education	M
Multilingual and Multicultural Education	M
Reading Education	M
Science Education	M
Social Sciences Education	M
Special Education	M
Student Affairs	M
Vocational and Technical Education	M

BUTLER UNIVERSITY

Business Administration and Management—General	M
Counselor Education	M
Education—General	M

Educational Administration	M
Elementary Education	M
Music Education	M
Pharmaceutical Sciences	P,M
Pharmacy	P,M
Physician Assistant Studies	P,M
Reading Education	M
Secondary Education	M
Special Education	M

CABRINI COLLEGE

Education—General	M,O
Educational Administration	M,O
Educational Media/ Instructional Technology	M,O
Organizational Management	M,O
Project Management	M,O

CALDWELL COLLEGE

Accounting	M
Business Administration and Management—General	M
Counselor Education	M
Curriculum and Instruction	M
Educational Administration	M
Special Education	M

CALIFORNIA BAPTIST UNIVERSITY

Business Administration and Management—General	M
Curriculum and Instruction	M
Education—General	M
Educational Administration	M
Educational Media/ Instructional Technology	M
Kinesiology and Movement Studies	M
Multilingual and Multicultural Education	M
Reading Education	M
Special Education	M
Vocational and Technical Education	M

CALIFORNIA COLLEGE FOR HEALTH SCIENCES

Community Health	M
Health Promotion	M
Health Services Management and Hospital Administration	M
Public Health—General	M

CALIFORNIA LUTHERAN UNIVERSITY

Business Administration and Management—General	M
Counselor Education	M
Education—General	M,O
Educational Administration	M
Entrepreneurship	M
Finance and Banking	M
Health Services Management and Hospital Administration	M
International Business	M
Management Information Systems	M
Marketing	M
Organizational Behavior	M
Reading Education	M
Special Education	M

CALIFORNIA NATIONAL UNIVERSITY FOR ADVANCED STUDIES

Business Administration and Management— General	M

CALIFORNIA POLYTECHNIC STATE UNIVERSITY, SAN LUIS OBISPO

Business Administration and Management— General	M
Education—General	M
Industrial and Manufacturing Management	M
Kinesiology and Movement Studies	M
Taxation	M

CALIFORNIA SCHOOL OF PODIATRIC MEDICINE AT SAMUEL MERRITT COLLEGE

Podiatric Medicine	P

CALIFORNIA STATE POLYTECHNIC UNIVERSITY, POMONA

Business Administration and Management— General	M
Education—General	M
Kinesiology and Movement Studies	M

CALIFORNIA STATE UNIVERSITY, BAKERSFIELD

Business Administration and Management— General	M
Counselor Education	M
Curriculum and Instruction	M
Education—General	M
Educational Administration	M
Health Services Management and Hospital Administration	M
Mathematics Education	M
Multilingual and Multicultural Education	M
Nursing—General	M
Secondary Education	M
Social Work	M
Special Education	M

CALIFORNIA STATE UNIVERSITY CHANNEL ISLANDS

Business Administration and Management— General	M
Educational Administration	M

CALIFORNIA STATE UNIVERSITY, CHICO

Business Administration and Management— General	M
Communication Disorders	M
Curriculum and Instruction	M
Education—General	M
Educational Administration	M
Educational Media/ Instructional Technology	M
Foreign Languages Education	M

Health Services Management and Hospital Administration	M
Kinesiology and Movement Studies	M
Mathematics Education	M
Multilingual and Multicultural Education	M
Nursing—General	M
Reading Education	M
Recreation and Park Management	M
Science Education	M
Social Sciences Education	M
Social Work	M
Special Education	M

CALIFORNIA STATE UNIVERSITY, DOMINGUEZ HILLS

Business Administration and Management— General	M
Computer Education	M,O
Counselor Education	M
Curriculum and Instruction	M
Education—General	M,O
Educational Administration	M
English as a Second Language	M,O
Health Education	M
International and Comparative Education	M
Mathematics Education	M
Multilingual and Multicultural Education	M
Nursing—General	M
Occupational Therapy	M
Physical Education	M
Physician Assistant Studies	M
Quality Management	M
Social Work	M
Special Education	M

CALIFORNIA STATE UNIVERSITY, EAST BAY

Accounting	M
Business Administration and Management— General	M
Communication Disorders	M
Counselor Education	M
Curriculum and Instruction	M
Education—General	M
Educational Administration	M
Educational Media/ Instructional Technology	M
Electronic Commerce	M
Entrepreneurship	M
Finance and Banking	M
Health Services Management and Hospital Administration	M
Human Resources Management	M
Industrial and Manufacturing Management	M
International Business	M
Management Information Systems	M
Management Strategy and Policy	M
Marketing	M
Physical Education	M
Quantitative Analysis	M
Social Work	M
Special Education	M
Supply Chain Management	M
Taxation	M

CALIFORNIA STATE UNIVERSITY, FRESNO

Accounting	M
Business Administration and Management— General	M
Communication Disorders	M
Counselor Education	M
Curriculum and Instruction	M
Early Childhood Education	M
Education—General	M,D
Educational Administration	M,D
English as a Second Language	M
Environmental and Occupational Health	M
Exercise and Sports Science	M
Family Nurse Practitioner Studies	M
Health Promotion	M
Health Services Management and Hospital Administration	M
Kinesiology and Movement Studies	M
Mathematics Education	M
Music Education	M
Nursing—General	M
Physical Therapy	M
Public Health—General	M
Reading Education	M
Social Work	M
Special Education	M

CALIFORNIA STATE UNIVERSITY, FULLERTON

Accounting	M
Advertising and Public Relations	M
Business Administration and Management— General	M
Communication Disorders	M
Counselor Education	M
Education—General	M
Educational Administration	M
Educational Media/ Instructional Technology	M
Elementary Education	M
English as a Second Language	M
Environmental Education	M
Finance and Banking	M
International Business	M
Management Information Systems	M
Marketing	M
Mathematics Education	M
Middle School Education	M
Multilingual and Multicultural Education	M
Music Education	M
Nursing—General	M
Physical Education	M
Public Health—General	M
Reading Education	M
Science Education	M
Secondary Education	M
Special Education	M
Taxation	M

CALIFORNIA STATE UNIVERSITY, LONG BEACH

Business Administration and Management— General	M
Communication Disorders	M
Counselor Education	M
Education—General	M,D
Health Education	M

Health Services Management and Hospital Administration	M,O
Kinesiology and Movement Studies	M
Leisure Studies	M
Mathematics Education	M
Nursing—General	M
Physical Education	M
Physical Therapy	M
Recreation and Park Management	M
Science Education	M
Social Work	M
Special Education	M
Vocational and Technical Education	M

CALIFORNIA STATE UNIVERSITY, LOS ANGELES

Accounting	M
Art Education	M
Business Administration and Management— General	M
Communication Disorders	M
Computer Education	M
Counselor Education	M
Education—General	M
Educational Media/ Instructional Technology	M
Elementary Education	M
English as a Second Language	M
Finance and Banking	M
Foundations and Philosophy of Education	M
Health Education	M
Health Services Management and Hospital Administration	M
International Business	M
Kinesiology and Movement Studies	M
Management Information Systems	M
Marketing	M
Music Education	M
Nursing—General	M
Physical Education	M
Reading Education	M
Secondary Education	M
Social Work	M
Special Education	M
Taxation	M

CALIFORNIA STATE UNIVERSITY, MONTEREY BAY

Education—General	M
Management Information Systems	M

CALIFORNIA STATE UNIVERSITY, NORTHRIDGE

Art Education	M
Business Administration and Management— General	M
Communication Disorders	M
Counselor Education	M
Early Childhood Education	M
Education—General	M
Educational Administration	M
Educational Psychology	M
Elementary Education	M
Environmental and Occupational Health	M
Health Education	M
Health Services Management and Hospital Administration	M

Industrial Hygiene	M
Kinesiology and Movement Studies	M
Mathematics Education	M
Music Education	M
Physical Therapy	M
Recreation and Park Management	M
Secondary Education	M
Social Work	M
Special Education	M

CALIFORNIA STATE UNIVERSITY, SACRAMENTO

Accounting	M
Business Administration and Management— General	M*
Communication Disorders	M
Counselor Education	M
Curriculum and Instruction	M
Early Childhood Education	M
Education—General	M
Educational Administration	M
English as a Second Language	M
Foreign Languages Education	M
Human Resources Development	M
Human Resources Management	M
Human Services	M
Management Information Systems	M
Multilingual and Multicultural Education	M
Nursing—General	M
Physical Education	M
Reading Education	M
Real Estate	M
Recreation and Park Management	M
Social Work	M
Special Education	M
Vocational and Technical Education	M

CALIFORNIA STATE UNIVERSITY, SAN BERNARDINO

Business Administration and Management— General	M
Counselor Education	M
Curriculum and Instruction	M
Education—General	M
Educational Administration	M
Educational Media/ Instructional Technology	M
Educational Psychology	M
Elementary Education	M
English as a Second Language	M
English Education	M
Environmental Education	M
Health Education	M
Health Services Management and Hospital Administration	M
Kinesiology and Movement Studies	M
Multilingual and Multicultural Education	M
Nursing—General	M
Reading Education	M
Science Education	M
Secondary Education	M
Social Sciences Education	M
Social Work	M
Special Education	M
Vocational and Technical Education	M

CALIFORNIA STATE UNIVERSITY, SAN MARCOS

Business Administration and Management— General	M
Education—General	M

CALIFORNIA STATE UNIVERSITY, STANISLAUS

Business Administration and Management— General	M
Curriculum and Instruction	M
Education—General	M
Elementary Education	M
Finance and Banking	M
Multilingual and Multicultural Education	M
Reading Education	M
Secondary Education	M
Social Work	M

CALIFORNIA UNIVERSITY OF PENNSYLVANIA

Athletic Training and Sports Medicine	M
Business Administration and Management— General	M
Communication Disorders	M
Counselor Education	M
Education—General	M
Educational Administration	M
Elementary Education	M
Exercise and Sports Science	M
Legal and Justice Studies	M
Reading Education	M
Rehabilitation Sciences	M
Secondary Education	M
Social Work	M
Special Education	M
Sports Management	M
Vocational and Technical Education	M

CALIFORNIA WESTERN SCHOOL OF LAW

Accounting	P,M
Law	P,M

CALVIN COLLEGE

Curriculum and Instruction	M
Education—General	M
Educational Administration	M
Reading Education	M
Special Education	M

CALVIN THEOLOGICAL SEMINARY

Religious Education	P,M,D

CAMBRIDGE COLLEGE

Business Administration and Management— General	M
Education—General	M,D,O
Educational Administration	M,D,O
Electronic Commerce	M

CAMERON UNIVERSITY

Business Administration and Management— General	M
Education—General	M
Educational Administration	M
Entrepreneurship	M

CAMPBELLSVILLE UNIVERSITY

Business Administration and Management— General	M
Curriculum and Instruction	M
Education—General	M
Music Education	M
Social Work	
Special Education	M

CAMPBELL UNIVERSITY

Business Administration and Management— General	M
Counselor Education	M
Education—General	M
Educational Administration	M
Elementary Education	M
English Education	M
Law	P
Mathematics Education	M
Middle School Education	M
Pharmaceutical Sciences	P,M
Pharmacy	P,M
Physical Education	M
Religious Education	P,M,D
Secondary Education	M
Social Sciences Education	M

CANADIAN COLLEGE OF NATUROPATHIC MEDICINE

Naturopathic Medicine	D*

CANADIAN MEMORIAL CHIROPRACTIC COLLEGE

Chiropractic	P,O

CANADIAN SOUTHERN BAPTIST SEMINARY

Computer Education	P,M

CANISIUS COLLEGE

Accounting	M
Business Administration and Management— General	M
Business Education	M
Communication Disorders	M
Counselor Education	M
Early Childhood Education	M
Education—General	M
Educational Administration	M
Health Promotion	M
Human Services	M
Marketing	M
Physical Education	M
Reading Education	M
Rehabilitation Sciences	M
Secondary Education	M
Special Education	M
Sports Management	M
Student Affairs	M

CAPE BRETON UNIVERSITY

Art Education	O
Business Administration and Management— General	M
Counselor Education	O
Education—General	O
Educational Media/ Instructional Technology	O

CAPELLA UNIVERSITY

Accounting	M,D,O
Adult Education	M,D,O

Business Administration and Management— General	M,D,O
Curriculum and Instruction	M,D,O
Education—General	M,D,O
Educational Administration	M,D,O
Educational Media/ Instructional Technology	M,D,O
Educational Psychology	M,D,O
Elementary Education	M,D,O
Finance and Banking	M,D,O
Health Services Management and Hospital Administration	M,D,O
Higher Education	M,D,O
Human Resources Management	M,D,O
Human Services	M,D,O
Management Information Systems	M,D,O
Marketing	M,D,O
Middle School Education	M,D,O
Multilingual and Multicultural Education	M,D,O
Nonprofit Management	M,D,O
Organizational Management	M,D,O
Project Management	M,D,O
Reading Education	M,D,O

CAPITAL UNIVERSITY

Business Administration and Management— General	M
Law	P,M
Legal and Justice Studies	M
Music Education	M
Nursing and Healthcare Administration	M
Nursing—General	M
Taxation	M

CAPITOL COLLEGE

Business Administration and Management— General	M
Management Information Systems	M

CARDEAN UNIVERSITY

Accounting	M
Business Administration and Management— General	M
Electronic Commerce	M
Finance and Banking	M
Health Services Management and Hospital Administration	M
Human Resources Management	M
International Business	M
Management Information Systems	M
Management Strategy and Policy	M
Marketing	M
Organizational Management	M
Project Management	M

CARDINAL STRITCH UNIVERSITY

Business Administration and Management— General	M*
Computer Education	M
Education—General	M,D*
Educational Administration	M,D
Finance and Banking	M

Health Services
  Management and
  Hospital Administration — M
Nursing—General — M*
Reading Education — M
Special Education — M

CARIBBEAN UNIVERSITY

Accounting — M,D
Curriculum and Instruction — M,D
Education—General — M,D
Educational Administration — M,D
Gerontological Nursing — M,D
Human Resources
  Management — M,D
Pediatric Nursing — M,D
Physical Education — M,D
Special Education — M,D

CARLETON UNIVERSITY

Business Administration
  and Management—
  General — M,D
Legal and Justice Studies — M,O
Social Work — M

CARLOS ALBIZU UNIVERSITY

Communication Disorders — M,D

CARLOS ALBIZU UNIVERSITY, MIAMI CAMPUS

Business Administration
  and Management—
  General — M,D
Education of the Gifted — M,D
English as a Second
  Language — M,D
Entrepreneurship — M,D
Nonprofit Management — M,D
Organizational
  Management — M,D
Special Education — M,D

CARLOW UNIVERSITY

Art Education — M
Early Childhood Education — M
Education—General — M
Educational Administration — M
Educational Media/
  Instructional Technology — M
Elementary Education — M
Family Nurse Practitioner
  Studies — M,O
Nonprofit Management — M
Nursing and Healthcare
  Administration — M,O
Nursing—General — M,O
Organizational
  Management — M
Secondary Education — M
Special Education — M

CARNEGIE MELLON UNIVERSITY

Accounting — D
Business Administration
  and Management—
  General — M,D*
Education—General — M,D
Electronic Commerce — M
Finance and Banking — D
Health Services
  Management and
  Hospital Administration — M*
Industrial and
  Manufacturing
  Management — M,D

Management Information
  Systems — M,D
Marketing — D
Music Education — M
Organizational Behavior — D
Organizational
  Management — D

CARROLL COLLEGE

Education—General — M
Physical Therapy — M,D

CARSON-NEWMAN COLLEGE

Counselor Education — M
Curriculum and Instruction — M
Education—General — M
Elementary Education — M
English as a Second
  Language — M
Family Nurse Practitioner
  Studies — M
Nursing—General — M
Secondary Education — M

CARTHAGE COLLEGE

Art Education — M,O
Counselor Education — M,O
Education of the Gifted — M,O
Education—General — M,O
Educational Administration — M,O
English Education — M,O
Reading Education — M,O
Science Education — M,O
Social Sciences Education — M,O

CASE WESTERN RESERVE UNIVERSITY

Accounting — M,D
Acute Care/Critical Care
  Nursing — M,D
Adult Nursing — M,D
Allopathic Medicine — P
Anesthesiologist Assistant
  Studies — M
Art Education — M
Bioethics — M,D
Business Administration
  and Management—
  General — M,D
Clinical Research — M
Communication Disorders — M,D,O
Community Health
  Nursing — M
Dentistry — P
Epidemiology — M,D
Family Nurse Practitioner
  Studies — M,D
Finance and Banking — M,D
Gerontological Nursing — M,D
Health Services
  Management and
  Hospital Administration — M,D
Human Resources
  Management — M
Industrial and
  Manufacturing
  Management — M,D
Law — P,M
Legal and Justice Studies — P,M
Logistics — M,D
Management Information
  Systems — M,D
Management Strategy and
  Policy — M
Marketing — M,D
Medical/Surgical Nursing — M,D
Music Education — M,D
Nonprofit Management — M,O*
Nurse Anesthesia — M

Nurse Midwifery — M,D
Nursing Informatics — M
Nursing—General — M,D
Oral and Dental Sciences — M,O
Organizational Behavior — M
Pediatric Nursing — M,D
Psychiatric Nursing — M,D
Public Health—General — M
Quality Management — M,D
Social Work — M,D,O*
Supply Chain
  Management — M
Women's Health Nursing — M,D

CASTLETON STATE COLLEGE

Curriculum and Instruction — M
Education—General — M,O
Educational Administration — M,O
Reading Education — M,O
Special Education — M,O

CATAWBA COLLEGE

Education—General — M
Elementary Education — M

THE CATHOLIC UNIVERSITY OF AMERICA

Adult Nursing — M,D
Business Administration
  and Management—
  General — M
Clinical Laboratory
  Sciences/Medical
  Technology — M,D
Counselor Education — M,D
Curriculum and Instruction — M,D
Education—General — M,D
Educational Administration — M,D
Educational Psychology — M,D
English as a Second
  Language — M,D
Family Nurse Practitioner
  Studies — M,D
Gerontological Nursing — M,D
Information Studies — M
Law — P
Legal and Justice Studies — D,O
Library Science — M
Music Education — M,D
Nursing and Healthcare
  Administration — M,D
Nursing Education — M,D
Nursing—General — M,D
Pediatric Nursing — M,D
Psychiatric Nursing — M,D
Social Work — M,D*

CEDAR CREST COLLEGE

Education—General — M*

CEDARVILLE UNIVERSITY

Education—General — M

CENTENARY COLLEGE

Accounting — M
Business Administration
  and Management—
  General — M
Education—General — M
Educational Administration — M
Special Education — M

CENTENARY COLLEGE OF LOUISIANA

Business Administration
  and Management—
  General — M

Curriculum and Instruction — M
Education—General — M
Educational Administration — M
Elementary Education — M
Secondary Education — M

CENTRAL CONNECTICUT STATE UNIVERSITY

Actuarial Science — M,O
Art Education — M,O
Business Administration
  and Management—
  General — M,O
Business Education — M,O
Counselor Education — M,O
Early Childhood Education — M
Education—General — M,D,O
Educational Administration — M,D,O
Educational Media/
  Instructional Technology — M
Elementary Education — M,O
English as a Second
  Language — O
Exercise and Sports
  Science — M,O
Foreign Languages
  Education — M,O
Foundations and
  Philosophy of Education — M
Information Studies — M
International Business — M
Music Education — M,O
Nurse Anesthesia — M,O
Physical Education — M,O
Reading Education — M,O
Secondary Education — M
Special Education — M
Vocational and Technical
  Education — M,O

CENTRAL EUROPEAN UNIVERSITY

Business Administration
  and Management—
  General — M
Finance and Banking — M
International Business — M,D
Law — M,D
Legal and Justice Studies — M,D
Management Information
  Systems — M
Marketing — M
Real Estate — M

CENTRAL METHODIST UNIVERSITY

Counselor Education — M
Education—General — M

CENTRAL MICHIGAN UNIVERSITY

Accounting — M
Business Administration
  and Management—
  General — M*
Business Education — M
Communication Disorders — M,D
Counselor Education — M
Early Childhood Education — M
Education—General — M,D,O
Educational Administration — M,D,O
Educational Media/
  Instructional Technology — M
Elementary Education — M
English as a Second
  Language — M
Exercise and Sports
  Science — M
Finance and Banking — M
Health Promotion — M

Health Services
Management and
Hospital Administration — M,D,O
Hospitality Management — M
Human Resources
Management — M,O
Industrial and
Manufacturing
Management — M
International Business — M
Leisure Studies — M
Management Information
Systems — M,O*
Marketing — M
Middle School Education — M
Music Education — M
Physical Education — M
Physical Therapy — M,D
Physician Assistant
Studies — M,D
Reading Education — M
Recreation and Park
Management — M
Rehabilitation Sciences — M,D
Science Education — M
Secondary Education — M
Special Education — M
Sports Management — M
Vocational and Technical
Education — M

CENTRAL STATE UNIVERSITY

Education—General — M
Educational Administration — M
Educational Media/
Instructional Technology — M
Reading Education — M

CENTRAL WASHINGTON UNIVERSITY

Accounting — M
Counselor Education — M
Education—General — M
Educational Administration — M
English as a Second
Language — M
Health Education — M
Home Economics
Education — M
Physical Education — M
Reading Education — M
Special Education — M

CHADRON STATE COLLEGE

Business Administration
and Management—
General — M
Business Education — M,O
Counselor Education — M,O
Education—General — M,O
Educational Administration — M,O
Elementary Education — M,O
English Education — M,O
Secondary Education — M,O
Social Sciences Education — M,O

CHAMINADE UNIVERSITY OF HONOLULU

Business Administration
and Management—
General — M
Education—General — M
Social Sciences Education — M

CHAPMAN UNIVERSITY

Business Administration
and Management—
General — M,O

Counselor Education — M
Curriculum and Instruction — M,D
Education—General — M,D,O
Educational Administration — M
Educational Psychology — M,O
Elementary Education — M
Human Resources
Management — M,O
Law — P,M
Physical Therapy — D
Reading Education — M
Secondary Education — M
Special Education — M
Taxation — P,M

CHARLES R. DREW UNIVERSITY OF MEDICINE AND SCIENCE

Allopathic Medicine — P

CHARLESTON SOUTHERN UNIVERSITY

Accounting — M
Business Administration
and Management—
General — M
Education—General — M
Educational Administration — M
Elementary Education — M
English Education — M
Finance and Banking — M
Health Services
Management and
Hospital Administration — M
Management Information
Systems — M
Organizational
Management — M
Science Education — M
Secondary Education — M
Social Sciences Education — M

CHATHAM UNIVERSITY

Art Education — M
Business Administration
and Management—
General — M
Early Childhood Education — M
Education—General — M
Elementary Education — M
English Education — M
Environmental Education — M
Mathematics Education — M
Nursing—General — M,D
Occupational Therapy — M,D
Organizational
Management — M
Physical Therapy — D
Physician Assistant
Studies — M
Science Education — M
Secondary Education — M
Social Sciences Education — M
Special Education — M

CHESTNUT HILL COLLEGE

Early Childhood Education — M
Education—General — M
Educational Administration — M
Educational Media/
Instructional Technology — M,O
Elementary Education — M
Human Services — M,O
Secondary Education — M

CHEYNEY UNIVERSITY OF PENNSYLVANIA

Adult Education — M
Early Childhood Education — O

Education—General — M,O
Educational Administration — M,O
Elementary Education — M
Mathematics Education — O
Special Education — M

THE CHICAGO SCHOOL OF PROFESSIONAL PSYCHOLOGY

Counselor Education — M,D,O

CHICAGO STATE UNIVERSITY

Counselor Education — M
Early Childhood Education — M
Education—General — M,D
Educational Administration — M,D
Educational Media/
Instructional Technology — M
Elementary Education — M
Foundations and
Philosophy of Education — M
Higher Education — M,D
Library Science — M
Middle School Education — M
Multilingual and
Multicultural Education — M
Physical Education — M
Reading Education — M
Secondary Education — M
Social Work — M
Special Education — M
Vocational and Technical
Education — M

CHICAGO THEOLOGICAL SEMINARY

Religious Education — P,M,D

CHRISTIAN BROTHERS UNIVERSITY

Business Administration
and Management—
General — M,O
Curriculum and Instruction — M
Education—General — M
Educational Administration — M
Finance and Banking — M,O
Project Management — M,O

CHRISTOPHER NEWPORT UNIVERSITY

Art Education — M
Computer Education — M
Education—General — M
Elementary Education — M
English Education — M
Foreign Languages
Education — M
Mathematics Education — M
Music Education — M
Science Education — M
Social Sciences Education — M

THE CITADEL, THE MILITARY COLLEGE OF SOUTH CAROLINA

Business Administration
and Management—
General — M
Counselor Education — M
Education—General — M,O
Educational Administration — M,O
Health Education — M
Physical Education — M
Reading Education — M
Secondary Education — M

CITY COLLEGE OF THE CITY UNIVERSITY OF NEW YORK

Early Childhood Education — M
Education—General — M,O
Educational Administration — M,O
Elementary Education — M
English Education — M,O
Mathematics Education — M,O
Middle School Education — M,O
Multilingual and
Multicultural Education — M
Reading Education — M
Science Education — M
Secondary Education — M,O
Social Sciences Education — M,O
Special Education — M

CITY UNIVERSITY

Accounting — M,O
Art Education — M,O
Business Administration
and Management—
General — M,O
Curriculum and Instruction — M,O
Education—General — M,O
Educational Administration — M,O
Educational Media/
Instructional Technology — M,O
Electronic Commerce — M,O
English as a Second
Language — M,O
Finance and Banking — M,O
Human Resources
Management — M,O
International Business — M,O
Management Information
Systems — M,O
Marketing — M,O
Project Management — M,O
Reading Education — M,O

CITY UNIVERSITY OF NEW YORK SCHOOL OF LAW AT QUEENS COLLEGE

Law — P

CLAFLIN UNIVERSITY

Business Administration
and Management—
General — M
Education—General — M

CLAREMONT GRADUATE UNIVERSITY

Business Administration
and Management—
General — M,D,O
Education—General — M,D,O
Educational Administration — M,D,O
Educational Measurement
and Evaluation — M,D,O
Electronic Commerce — M,D,O
Higher Education — M,D,O
Human Resources
Management — M
Information Studies — M,D,O
Management Information
Systems — M,D,O
Management Strategy and
Policy — M,D,O
Urban Education — M,D,O

CLAREMONT SCHOOL OF THEOLOGY

Religious Education — M,D

CLARION UNIVERSITY OF PENNSYLVANIA

Business Administration and Management—General	M
Communication Disorders	M
Curriculum and Instruction	M
Early Childhood Education	M
Education—General	M,O
Elementary Education	M
English Education	M
Library Science	M,O
Nursing—General	M
Reading Education	M
Rehabilitation Sciences	M
Science Education	M
Social Sciences Education	M
Special Education	M
Vocational and Technical Education	M

CLARK ATLANTA UNIVERSITY

Business Administration and Management—General	M
Counselor Education	M,D
Curriculum and Instruction	M,O
Education of the Gifted	M,O
Education—General	M,D,O
Educational Administration	M,D,O
Educational Psychology	M,D
Finance and Banking	M
International Business	M,D
Marketing	M
Quantitative Analysis	M
Science Education	M,D
Social Work	M,D

CLARKE COLLEGE

Business Administration and Management—General	M
Early Childhood Education	M
Education—General	M
Educational Administration	M
Educational Media/Instructional Technology	M
Family Nurse Practitioner Studies	M,O
Nursing and Healthcare Administration	M,O
Nursing Education	M,O
Nursing—General	M,O
Physical Therapy	M
Reading Education	M
Special Education	M

CLARKSON COLLEGE

Family Nurse Practitioner Studies	M
Nursing and Healthcare Administration	M
Nursing Education	M
Nursing—General	M

CLARKSON UNIVERSITY

Business Administration and Management—General	M
Health Services Research	M
Human Resources Management	M
Industrial and Manufacturing Management	M
Management Information Systems	M
Physical Therapy	M,D

CLARK UNIVERSITY

Accounting	M
Business Administration and Management—General	M*
Education—General	M
Finance and Banking	M
Health Services Management and Hospital Administration	M
International Business	M
Management Information Systems	M
Marketing	M

CLAYTON STATE UNIVERSITY

Business Administration and Management—General	M
Health Services Management and Hospital Administration	M
Nursing—General	M

CLEARY UNIVERSITY

Accounting	M
Business Administration and Management—General	M

CLEMSON UNIVERSITY

Accounting	M*
Agricultural Education	M*
Business Administration and Management—General	M,D*
Counselor Education	M*
Curriculum and Instruction	D*
Education—General	M,D,O
Educational Administration	M,D,O*
Electronic Commerce	M,D
Elementary Education	M*
English Education	M
Human Resources Development	M*
Industrial and Manufacturing Management	M,D
Management Strategy and Policy	M,D
Marketing	M*
Mathematics Education	M*
Middle School Education	M*
Nursing—General	M*
Reading Education	M*
Real Estate	M*
Recreation and Park Management	M,D*
Science Education	M
Secondary Education	M*
Special Education	M*
Travel and Tourism	M,D
Veterinary Sciences	M,D

CLEVELAND CHIROPRACTIC COLLEGE-KANSAS CITY CAMPUS

Chiropractic	P*

CLEVELAND CHIROPRACTIC COLLEGE-LOS ANGELES CAMPUS

Chiropractic	P*

CLEVELAND STATE UNIVERSITY

Accounting	M
Adult Education	M,O
Allied Health—General	M
Art Education	M

Bioethics	M,O
Business Administration and Management—General	M,D
Communication Disorders	M
Community Health Nursing	M
Counselor Education	M,D,O
Early Childhood Education	M
Education of the Multiply Handicapped	M
Education—General	M,D,O
Educational Administration	M,D,O
Electronic Commerce	M,D,O
English as a Second Language	M
Exercise and Sports Science	M
Finance and Banking	M,D,O
Foreign Languages Education	M
Forensic Nursing	M
Health Education	M
Health Services Management and Hospital Administration	M
Human Resources Management	M
Industrial and Manufacturing Management	D
International Business	M,D,O
Law	P,M
Management Information Systems	M,D
Marketing	M,D,O
Mathematics Education	M
Medical Physics	M
Middle School Education	M
Music Education	M
Nonprofit Management	M,O
Nursing—General	M
Occupational Therapy	M
Physical Education	M
Physical Therapy	D
Real Estate	M,O
Science Education	M
Social Work	M
Special Education	M
Sports Management	M
Student Affairs	M,O
Taxation	M
Urban Education	D

COASTAL CAROLINA UNIVERSITY

Business Administration and Management—General	M
Early Childhood Education	M
Education—General	M
Elementary Education	M
Secondary Education	M

COE COLLEGE

Education—General	M

COLGATE UNIVERSITY

Secondary Education	M

COLLEGE FOR FINANCIAL PLANNING

Finance and Banking	M

COLLEGE MISERICORDIA

Allied Health—General	M,D
Communication Disorders	M
Curriculum and Instruction	M
Education—General	M

Nursing—General	M
Occupational Therapy	M
Organizational Management	M
Physical Therapy	M,D

COLLEGE OF CHARLESTON

Accounting	M
Business Administration and Management—General	M
Early Childhood Education	M
Education—General	M,O
Elementary Education	M
English as a Second Language	O
Foreign Languages Education	M
Legal and Justice Studies	M,O
Mathematics Education	M
Science Education	M
Special Education	M

COLLEGE OF MOUNT ST. JOSEPH

Art Education	M
Early Childhood Education	M
Education—General	M
Educational Administration	M
Middle School Education	M
Multilingual and Multicultural Education	M
Music Education	M
Nursing—General	M
Organizational Management	M
Physical Therapy	M,D
Reading Education	M
Secondary Education	M

COLLEGE OF MOUNT SAINT VINCENT

Adult Nursing	M,O
Education—General	M,O
Educational Media/Instructional Technology	M,O
Family Nurse Practitioner Studies	M,O
Gerontological Nursing	M,O
Middle School Education	M,O
Multilingual and Multicultural Education	M,O
Nursing and Healthcare Administration	M,O
Nursing Education	M,O
Nursing—General	M,O
Urban Education	M,O

THE COLLEGE OF NEW JERSEY

Communication Disorders	M
Counselor Education	M
Early Childhood Education	M
Education—General	M,O
Educational Administration	M,O
Educational Media/Instructional Technology	M
Elementary Education	M
English as a Second Language	M,O
Family Nurse Practitioner Studies	M,O
Foreign Languages Education	M
Health Education	M
International and Comparative Education	M,O
Nursing—General	M,O
Physical Education	M
Reading Education	M,O
Secondary Education	M

Special Education	M,O

THE COLLEGE OF NEW ROCHELLE

Acute Care/Critical Care Nursing	M,O
Art Education	M
Communication Disorders	M
Early Childhood Education	M
Education of the Gifted	M,O
Education—General	M,O
Educational Administration	M,O
Elementary Education	M
English as a Second Language	M,O
Human Resources Development	M,O
Multilingual and Multicultural Education	M,O
Museum Education	O
Nursing and Healthcare Administration	M,O
Nursing Education	M,O
Nursing—General	M,O
Reading Education	M
Special Education	M

COLLEGE OF NOTRE DAME OF MARYLAND

Business Administration and Management— General	M
Education—General	M
Educational Administration	M,D
English as a Second Language	M
Nonprofit Management	M

COLLEGE OF ST. CATHERINE

Education—General	M
Information Studies	M
Library Science	M
Nursing—General	M
Occupational Therapy	M*
Organizational Management	M
Physical Therapy	M,D*
Public Health—General	M
Social Work	M

COLLEGE OF SAINT ELIZABETH

Business Administration and Management— General	M
Education—General	M,O
Educational Administration	M,O
Educational Media/ Instructional Technology	M,O
Health Services Management and Hospital Administration	M
Higher Education	M,O
Student Affairs	M,O

COLLEGE OF ST. JOSEPH

Business Administration and Management— General	M
Counselor Education	M
Education—General	M
Elementary Education	M
English Education	M
Mathematics Education	M
Reading Education	M
Secondary Education	M
Social Sciences Education	M
Special Education	M

THE COLLEGE OF SAINT ROSE

Accounting	M
Art Education	M,O
Business Administration and Management— General	M
Business Education	M,O
Communication Disorders	M
Counselor Education	M
Early Childhood Education	M,O
Education—General	M,O*
Educational Administration	M,O
Educational Media/ Instructional Technology	M,O
Educational Psychology	M,O
Elementary Education	M,O
Multilingual and Multicultural Education	M,O
Music Education	M,O*
Nonprofit Management	O
Reading Education	M,O
Secondary Education	M,O
Special Education	M,O
Student Affairs	M,O

THE COLLEGE OF ST. SCHOLASTICA

Business Administration and Management— General	M
Curriculum and Instruction	M
Education—General	M,O
Educational Media/ Instructional Technology	M
Exercise and Sports Science	M
Management Information Systems	M
Nursing—General	M,O
Occupational Therapy	M
Physical Therapy	D

COLLEGE OF SANTA FE

Business Administration and Management— General	M
Counselor Education	M
Curriculum and Instruction	M
Education—General	M
Educational Administration	M
Finance and Banking	M
Human Resources Management	M
Multilingual and Multicultural Education	M
Special Education	M

COLLEGE OF STATEN ISLAND OF THE CITY UNIVERSITY OF NEW YORK

Adult Nursing	M,O
Business Administration and Management— General	M
Education—General	M,O
Educational Administration	O
Elementary Education	M
Gerontological Nursing	M,O
Nursing—General	M,O
Secondary Education	M
Special Education	M

COLLEGE OF THE HUMANITIES AND SCIENCES, HARRISON MIDDLETON UNIVERSITY

Education—General	M,D
Legal and Justice Studies	M,D
Science Education	M,D

COLLEGE OF THE SOUTHWEST

Counselor Education	M
Curriculum and Instruction	M
Education—General	M
Educational Administration	M
Educational Measurement and Evaluation	M

THE COLLEGE OF WILLIAM AND MARY

Accounting	M
Business Administration and Management— General	M
Counselor Education	M,D
Curriculum and Instruction	M,D
Education of the Gifted	M
Education—General	M,D,O
Educational Administration	M,D
Educational Media/ Instructional Technology	M,D
Educational Policy	M,D
Elementary Education	M
English Education	M
Foreign Languages Education	M
Law	P,M
Mathematics Education	M
Reading Education	M
Science Education	M
Secondary Education	M
Social Sciences Education	M
Special Education	M

COLLÈGE UNIVERSITAIRE DE SAINT-BONIFACE

Education—General	M

COLORADO CHRISTIAN UNIVERSITY

Business Administration and Management— General	M
Curriculum and Instruction	M
Education—General	M

THE COLORADO COLLEGE

Art Education	M
Education—General	M
Elementary Education	M
English Education	M
Foreign Languages Education	M
Mathematics Education	M
Music Education	M
Science Education	M
Secondary Education	M
Social Sciences Education	M

COLORADO SCHOOL OF TRADITIONAL CHINESE MEDICINE

Acupuncture and Oriental Medicine	M

COLORADO STATE UNIVERSITY

Accounting	M
Advertising and Public Relations	M
Business Administration and Management— General	M
Environmental and Occupational Health	M,D
Exercise and Sports Science	M,D
Foreign Languages Education	M
Management Information Systems	M
Occupational Therapy	M
Recreation and Park Management	M,D
Social Work	M
Student Affairs	M,D
Veterinary Medicine	P
Veterinary Sciences	M,D
Vocational and Technical Education	M,D

COLORADO STATE UNIVERSITY-PUEBLO

Business Administration and Management— General	M

COLORADO TECHNICAL UNIVERSITY

Accounting	M,D
Business Administration and Management— General	M,D
Human Resources Management	M,D
Logistics	M,D
Management Information Systems	M,D
Organizational Management	M,D
Project Management	M,D

COLORADO TECHNICAL UNIVERSITY DENVER CAMPUS

Accounting	M
Business Administration and Management— General	M
Human Resources Management	M
Management Information Systems	M
Project Management	M

COLORADO TECHNICAL UNIVERSITY SIOUX FALLS CAMPUS

Business Administration and Management— General	M
Health Services Management and Hospital Administration	M
Human Resources Management	M
Management Information Systems	M
Organizational Management	M
Project Management	M

COLUMBIA COLLEGE (MO)

Business Administration and Management— General	M
Education—General	M

COLUMBIA COLLEGE (SC)

Education—General	M
Elementary Education	M
Organizational Behavior	M,O

COLUMBIA COLLEGE CHICAGO

Education—General	M
Elementary Education	M

English Education	M
Multilingual and Multicultural Education	M
Urban Education	M

COLUMBIA INTERNATIONAL UNIVERSITY

Counselor Education	M,D,O
Curriculum and Instruction	M,D,O
Early Childhood Education	M,D,O
Education—General	M,D,O
Educational Administration	M,D,O
Educational Media/ Instructional Technology	M,D,O
Elementary Education	M,D,O
English as a Second Language	M,D,O
Higher Education	M,D,O
Multilingual and Multicultural Education	M,D,O
Religious Education	P,M,D,O
Special Education	M,D,O

COLUMBIA SOUTHERN UNIVERSITY

Business Administration and Management— General	M
Electronic Commerce	M
Environmental and Occupational Health	M
Health Services Management and Hospital Administration	M
Human Resources Management	M
International Business	M
Marketing	M

COLUMBIA UNIVERSITY

Accounting	M,D
Actuarial Science	M
Adult Nursing	M,O
Allopathic Medicine	P
Business Administration and Management— General	M,D
Community Health	M,D
Dentistry	P
Entrepreneurship	M
Environmental and Occupational Health	M,D
Epidemiology	M,D
Family Nurse Practitioner Studies	M,O
Finance and Banking	M,D
Gerontological Nursing	M,O
Health Services Management and Hospital Administration	M
Human Resources Management	M
International Business	M
Kinesiology and Movement Studies	M,D
Law	P,M,D
Library Science	M
Marketing	M,D
Maternal and Child Health	M
Maternal and Child/ Neonatal Nursing	M,O
Medical Physics	M,D,O
Medical/Surgical Nursing	M,O
Nonprofit Management	M
Nurse Anesthesia	M,O
Nurse Midwifery	M
Nursing—General	M,D,O*
Occupational Therapy	M,D
Oncology Nursing	M,O
Oral and Dental Sciences	M,O
Pediatric Nursing	M,O

Physical Therapy	D
Psychiatric Nursing	M,O
Public Health—General	M,D*
Real Estate	M
Social Work	M,D*
Women's Health Nursing	O

COLUMBUS STATE UNIVERSITY

Art Education	M
Business Administration and Management— General	M
Counselor Education	M,O
Early Childhood Education	M,O
Education—General	M,O
Educational Administration	M,O
English Education	M,O
Mathematics Education	M,O
Middle School Education	M,O
Music Education	M
Physical Education	M,O
Science Education	M,O
Secondary Education	M,O
Social Sciences Education	M,O
Special Education	M,O

CONCORDIA UNIVERSITY (CA)

Business Administration and Management— General	M
Curriculum and Instruction	M
Education—General	M
Educational Administration	M
Entrepreneurship	M
Physical Education	M
Sports Management	M

CONCORDIA UNIVERSITY (CANADA)

Accounting	M,D,O
Adult Education	M,O
Art Education	M,D
Aviation Management	M,D,O
Business Administration and Management— General	M,D,O
Education—General	M,D,O
Educational Media/ Instructional Technology	M,D,O
English as a Second Language	M,O
Exercise and Sports Science	M
Health Services Management and Hospital Administration	M,D,O
Investment Management	M,D,O
Mathematics Education	M,D
Organizational Management	M
Sports Management	M,D,O
Transportation Management	M,D,O

CONCORDIA UNIVERSITY (IL)

Counselor Education	M,O
Curriculum and Instruction	M
Early Childhood Education	M,D
Education—General	M
Educational Administration	M,D,O
Exercise and Sports Science	M
Human Services	M
Reading Education	M
Religious Education	M
Urban Education	M

CONCORDIA UNIVERSITY (MI)

Educational Administration	M

Organizational Management	M

CONCORDIA UNIVERSITY (NE)

Curriculum and Instruction	M
Early Childhood Education	M
Education—General	M
Educational Administration	M
Reading Education	M
Religious Education	M

CONCORDIA UNIVERSITY (OR)

Business Administration and Management— General	M
Curriculum and Instruction	M
Education—General	M
Educational Administration	M
Elementary Education	M
Secondary Education	M

CONCORDIA UNIVERSITY AT AUSTIN

Education—General	M

CONCORDIA UNIVERSITY, ST. PAUL

Business Administration and Management— General	M
Early Childhood Education	M,O
Education—General	M,O
Human Resources Management	M
Organizational Management	M
Religious Education	M,O
Special Education	M,O

CONCORDIA UNIVERSITY WISCONSIN

Art Education	M
Business Administration and Management— General	M
Counselor Education	M
Curriculum and Instruction	M
Early Childhood Education	M
Education—General	M
Educational Administration	M
Environmental Education	M
Family Nurse Practitioner Studies	M
Finance and Banking	M
Gerontological Nursing	M
Health Services Management and Hospital Administration	M
Human Resources Management	M
Human Services	M,D
International Business	M
Management Information Systems	M
Marketing	M
Nursing Education	M
Nursing—General	M
Occupational Therapy	M
Physical Therapy	M,D
Reading Education	M
Rehabilitation Sciences	M
Special Education	M
Student Affairs	M

CONCORD LAW SCHOOL

Law	P

CONNECTICUT COLLEGE

Education—General	M
Elementary Education	M
English Education	M
Foreign Languages Education	M
Mathematics Education	M
Music Education	M
Science Education	M
Secondary Education	M

CONSERVATORIO DE MUSICA

Music Education	M

CONVERSE COLLEGE

Art Education	M,O
Curriculum and Instruction	O
Early Childhood Education	M,O
Education of the Gifted	M
Education—General	M,O
Educational Administration	M,O
Elementary Education	M
English Education	M
Mathematics Education	M
Music Education	M
Science Education	M
Secondary Education	M
Social Sciences Education	M
Special Education	M

COPPIN STATE UNIVERSITY

Adult Education	M
Curriculum and Instruction	M
Education—General	M
Family Nurse Practitioner Studies	M,O
Human Services	M
Nursing—General	M,O
Reading Education	M
Special Education	M

CORCORAN COLLEGE OF ART AND DESIGN

Art Education	M

CORNELL UNIVERSITY

Accounting	D
Adult Education	M,D
Agricultural Education	M,D
Business Administration and Management— General	M,D
Curriculum and Instruction	M,D
Education—General	M,D
Epidemiology	M,D
Facilities Management	M
Finance and Banking	D
Foreign Languages Education	M,D
Health Services Management and Hospital Administration	M,D
Hospitality Management	M,D
Human Resources Management	M,D
Information Studies	D
Law	P,M,D
Marketing	D
Mathematics Education	M,D
Organizational Behavior	M,D
Real Estate	M
Science Education	M,D
Social Work	M,D
Veterinary Medicine	P,D

CORNELL UNIVERSITY, JOAN AND SANFORD I. WEILL MEDICAL COLLEGE AND GRADUATE SCHOOL OF MEDICAL SCIENCES

Allopathic Medicine	P,M,D

Epidemiology	M
Health Services Research	M

CORNERSTONE UNIVERSITY

Religious Education	P,M

COVENANT COLLEGE

Education—General	M

CREIGHTON UNIVERSITY

Allied Health—General	P,M,D
Allopathic Medicine	P
Business Administration and Management— General	M
Counselor Education	M
Dentistry	P
Education—General	M
Educational Administration	M
Law	P,M
Management Information Systems	M
Nursing—General	M
Occupational Therapy	D
Pharmaceutical Sciences	M,D
Pharmacy	P
Physical Therapy	D
Special Education	M

CUMBERLAND UNIVERSITY

Business Administration and Management— General	M
Education—General	M
Human Resources Management	M
Organizational Management	M

CURRY COLLEGE

Adult Education	M,O
Business Administration and Management— General	M
Education—General	M,O
Educational Administration	M,O
Elementary Education	M,O
Foundations and Philosophy of Education	M,O
Reading Education	M,O
Special Education	M,O

DAEMEN COLLEGE

Business Administration and Management— General	M
Early Childhood Education	M
Education—General	M
Family Nurse Practitioner Studies	M,O
International Business	M
Medical/Surgical Nursing	M,O
Middle School Education	M
Nursing and Healthcare Administration	M,O
Nursing—General	M,O
Physical Therapy	D
Physician Assistant Studies	M
Special Education	M

DAKOTA STATE UNIVERSITY

Education—General	M
Educational Media/ Instructional Technology	M

DALHOUSIE UNIVERSITY

Allopathic Medicine	P
Business Administration and Management— General	M
Communication Disorders	M
Community Health	M
Computer Education	M
Dental Hygiene	O
Dentistry	P
Electronic Commerce	M,D
Epidemiology	M
Health Education	M
Health Services Management and Hospital Administration	M
Information Studies	M
Kinesiology and Movement Studies	M
Law	M,D
Leisure Studies	M
Library Science	M
Management Information Systems	M
Nursing—General	M
Occupational Therapy	M
Oral and Dental Sciences	P,M,O
Pharmaceutical Sciences	M,D
Social Work	M

DALLAS BAPTIST UNIVERSITY

Accounting	M
Business Administration and Management— General	M
Counselor Education	M
Curriculum and Instruction	M
Early Childhood Education	M
Education—General	M
Educational Administration	M
Electronic Commerce	M
Elementary Education	M
English as a Second Language	M
Entrepreneurship	M
Finance and Banking	M
Health Services Management and Hospital Administration	M
Higher Education	M
Human Resources Management	M
International Business	M
Management Information Systems	M
Marketing	M
Project Management	M
Reading Education	M
Religious Education	M

DALLAS THEOLOGICAL SEMINARY

Religious Education	M,D,O

DANIEL WEBSTER COLLEGE

Aviation Management	M
Business Administration and Management— General	M

DANIEL WEBSTER COLLEGE– PORTSMOUTH CAMPUS

Aviation Management	M
Business Administration and Management— General	M

DARTMOUTH COLLEGE

Business Administration and Management— General	M

Health Services Research	M,D*
Pharmaceutical Sciences	D
Public Health—General	M

DAVENPORT UNIVERSITY

Accounting	M
Business Administration and Management— General	M
Electronic Commerce	M
Finance and Banking	M
Health Services Management and Hospital Administration	M
Human Resources Management	M
International Business	M
Marketing	M

DAVENPORT UNIVERSITY

Business Administration and Management— General	M

DAVENPORT UNIVERSITY

Accounting	M
Business Administration and Management— General	M
Electronic Commerce	M
Finance and Banking	M
Health Services Management and Hospital Administration	M
Human Resources Management	M

DEFIANCE COLLEGE

Business Administration and Management— General	M
Education—General	M
Organizational Management	M

DELAWARE STATE UNIVERSITY

Business Administration and Management— General	M
Curriculum and Instruction	M
Education—General	M
Science Education	M
Social Work	M
Special Education	M

DELAWARE VALLEY COLLEGE

Educational Administration	M

DELTA STATE UNIVERSITY

Accounting	M
Aviation Management	M
Business Administration and Management— General	M
Counselor Education	M
Education—General	M,D,O
Educational Administration	M,D,O
Elementary Education	M,O
English Education	M
Marketing	M
Mathematics Education	M
Nursing—General	M
Physical Education	M
Recreation and Park Management	M
Secondary Education	M,O

Social Sciences Education	M
Special Education	M

DEPAUL UNIVERSITY

Accounting	M
Adult Education	M
Business Administration and Management— General	M
Counselor Education	M,D
Curriculum and Instruction	D
Education—General	M
Educational Administration	D
Electronic Commerce	M,D
Elementary Education	M,D
Entrepreneurship	M
Family Nurse Practitioner Studies	M
Finance and Banking	M,O
Health Services Management and Hospital Administration	M,O
Human Resources Management	M
Human Services	M,D
Industrial and Manufacturing Management	M
International Business	M
Law	P,M
Legal and Justice Studies	M,O
Management Information Systems	M,D
Management Strategy and Policy	M
Marketing	M
Mathematics Education	M,O
Multilingual and Multicultural Education	M,D
Music Education	M,O
Nonprofit Management	M,O
Nurse Anesthesia	M
Nursing—General	M
Physical Education	M,D
Reading Education	M,D
Real Estate	M
Secondary Education	M,D
Special Education	M,D
Taxation	M
Urban Education	M,D

DESALES UNIVERSITY

Business Administration and Management— General	M
Computer Education	M,O
Education—General	M,O
Educational Media/ Instructional Technology	M,O
Educational Policy	M,O
English as a Second Language	M,O
English Education	M,O
Family Nurse Practitioner Studies	M
Mathematics Education	M,O
Multilingual and Multicultural Education	M,O
Nursing Education	M
Nursing—General	M
Physician Assistant Studies	M
Science Education	M,O
Special Education	M,O

DES MOINES UNIVERSITY

Health Services Management and Hospital Administration	M
Osteopathic Medicine	P
Physical Therapy	D

Physician Assistant
  Studies — M
Podiatric Medicine — P
Public Health—General — M

DEVRY UNIVERSITY

Business Administration
and Management—
  General — M

DEVRY UNIVERSITY

Business Administration
and Management—
  General — M

DEVRY UNIVERSITY

Business Administration
and Management—
  General — M

DEVRY UNIVERSITY

Business Administration
and Management—
  General — M

DEVRY UNIVERSITY

Business Administration
and Management—
  General — M

DEVRY UNIVERSITY

Business Administration
and Management—
  General — M

DEVRY UNIVERSITY

Business Administration
and Management—
  General — M

DEVRY UNIVERSITY

Business Administration
and Management—
  General — M

DEVRY UNIVERSITY

Business Administration
and Management—
  General — M

DEVRY UNIVERSITY

Business Administration
and Management—
  General — M

DEVRY UNIVERSITY

Business Administration
and Management—
  General — M

DEVRY UNIVERSITY

Business Administration
and Management—
  General — M

DEVRY UNIVERSITY

Business Administration
and Management—
  General — M

DEVRY UNIVERSITY

Business Administration
and Management—
  General — M

DEVRY UNIVERSITY

Business Administration
and Management—
  General — M

DEVRY UNIVERSITY

Business Administration
and Management—
  General — M

DEVRY UNIVERSITY

Business Administration
and Management—
  General — M

DEVRY UNIVERSITY

Business Administration
and Management—
  General — M

DEVRY UNIVERSITY

Business Administration
and Management—
  General — M

DEVRY UNIVERSITY

Business Administration
and Management—
  General — M

DEVRY UNIVERSITY

Business Administration
and Management—
  General — M

DEVRY UNIVERSITY

Accounting — M
Business Administration
and Management—
  General — M*
Finance and Banking — M
Human Resources
  Management — M
Management Information
  Systems — M
Project Management — M

DEVRY UNIVERSITY

Business Administration
and Management—
  General — M

DEVRY UNIVERSITY

Business Administration
and Management—
  General — M

DEVRY UNIVERSITY

Business Administration
and Management—
  General — M

DEVRY UNIVERSITY (MD)

Business Administration
and Management—
  General — M,O

DEVRY UNIVERSITY

Business Administration
and Management—
  General — M

DEVRY UNIVERSITY (NV)

Business Administration
and Management—
  General — M

DEVRY UNIVERSITY

Business Administration
and Management—
  General — M

DEVRY UNIVERSITY

Business Administration
and Management—
  General — M

DEVRY UNIVERSITY

Business Administration
and Management—
  General — M

DEVRY UNIVERSITY

Business Administration
and Management—
  General — M

DEVRY UNIVERSITY (OR)

Business Administration
and Management—
  General — M

DEVRY UNIVERSITY

Business Administration
and Management—
  General — M

DEVRY UNIVERSITY

Business Administration
and Management—
  General — M

DEVRY UNIVERSITY

Business Administration
and Management—
  General — M

DEVRY UNIVERSITY

Business Administration
and Management—
  General — M

DEVRY UNIVERSITY

Business Administration
and Management—
  General — M

DEVRY UNIVERSITY

Business Administration
and Management—
  General — M

DEVRY UNIVERSITY

Business Administration
and Management—
  General — M

DOANE COLLEGE

Business Administration
and Management—
  General — M
Counselor Education — M
Curriculum and Instruction — M
Education—General — M
Educational Administration — M

DOMINICAN COLLEGE

Allied Health—General — M,D
Education—General — M
Nursing—General — M
Occupational Therapy — M
Physical Therapy — M,D

Special Education	M

DOMINICAN UNIVERSITY

Accounting	M
Business Administration and Management— General	M
Curriculum and Instruction	M
Early Childhood Education	M
Education—General	M
Educational Administration	M
Information Studies	M,O
Library Science	M,O
Management Information Systems	M
Organizational Management	M
Reading Education	M
Social Work	M
Special Education	M

DOMINICAN UNIVERSITY OF CALIFORNIA

Business Administration and Management— General	M
Curriculum and Instruction	M
Education—General	M,O
International Business	M
Management Strategy and Policy	M
Nursing Education	M
Nursing—General	M
Occupational Therapy	M
Public Health—General	M
Special Education	O

DONGGUK ROYAL UNIVERSITY

Acupuncture and Oriental Medicine	M

DORDT COLLEGE

Education—General	M

DOWLING COLLEGE

Aviation Management	M,O
Business Administration and Management— General	M,O
Education—General	M,D,O
Educational Administration	M,D,O
Educational Media/ Instructional Technology	M,D,O
Finance and Banking	M,O
Quality Management	M,O
Reading Education	M,D,O
Secondary Education	M,D,O
Special Education	M,D,O

DRAKE UNIVERSITY

Adult Education	M
Business Administration and Management— General	M
Business Education	M
Counselor Education	M
Education—General	M,D,O
Educational Administration	M,D,O
Elementary Education	M
English Education	M
Law	P*
Mathematics Education	M
Pharmacy	P
Rehabilitation Sciences	M
Science Education	M
Secondary Education	M
Social Sciences Education	M

Special Education	M

DREW UNIVERSITY

Bioethics	M,D,O

DREXEL UNIVERSITY

Accounting	M,D,O
Allied Health—General	M,D,O
Allopathic Medicine	P
Business Administration and Management— General	M,D,O
Curriculum and Instruction	M
Education—General	M,D,O*
Educational Administration	M,D
Educational Media/ Instructional Technology	D
Emergency Medical Services	M
English as a Second Language	M,D,O
Finance and Banking	M,D,O
Health Physics/ Radiological Health	M,D
Higher Education	M
Information Studies	M,D,O*
International and Comparative Education	M
Library Science	M,D,O
Management Strategy and Policy	M,D,O
Marketing	M,D,O
Medical Physics	M,D
Nurse Anesthesia	M
Nursing—General	M
Organizational Behavior	M,D,O
Physical Therapy	M,D,O
Physician Assistant Studies	M
Public Health—General	M
Quantitative Analysis	M,D,O
Taxation	M
Veterinary Sciences	M

DRURY UNIVERSITY

Business Administration and Management— General	M
Education of the Gifted	M
Education—General	M
Elementary Education	M
Human Services	M
International Business	M
Middle School Education	M
Physical Education	M
Secondary Education	M

DUKE UNIVERSITY

Acute Care/Critical Care Nursing	M,D,O
Adult Nursing	M,D,O
Allopathic Medicine	P
Business Administration and Management— General	M,D
Clinical Laboratory Sciences/Medical Technology	M
Clinical Research	M
Education—General	M
Environmental and Occupational Health	M,D,O
Family Nurse Practitioner Studies	M,D,O
Gerontological Nursing	M,D,O
Health Services Management and Hospital Administration	O
HIV/AIDS Nursing	M,D,O

Law	P,M,D
Maternal and Child/ Neonatal Nursing	M,D,O
Nurse Anesthesia	M,D,O
Nursing and Healthcare Administration	M,D,O
Nursing Education	M,D,O
Nursing Informatics	M,D,O
Nursing—General	D
Oncology Nursing	M,D,O
Pediatric Nursing	M,D,O
Physical Therapy	D
Physician Assistant Studies	M

DUQUESNE UNIVERSITY

Acute Care/Critical Care Nursing	M,O
Allied Health—General	M,D
Bioethics	M,D,O
Business Administration and Management— General	M*
Communication Disorders	M,D
Counselor Education	M,D
Curriculum and Instruction	M,D
Early Childhood Education	M
Education—General	M,D,O
Educational Administration	M,D
Educational Media/ Instructional Technology	M,D
Elementary Education	M
English as a Second Language	M,D
Family Nurse Practitioner Studies	M,O
Forensic Nursing	M,O
Foundations and Philosophy of Education	M
Health Services Management and Hospital Administration	M,D
Law	P,M
Medicinal and Pharmaceutical Chemistry	M,D
Music Education	M,O
Nursing and Healthcare Administration	M,O
Nursing Education	M,O
Nursing—General	M,D,O
Occupational Therapy	M,D
Pharmaceutical Administration	M
Pharmaceutical Sciences	M,D*
Pharmacy	P
Physical Therapy	M,D
Physician Assistant Studies	M,D
Psychiatric Nursing	M,O
Reading Education	M
Secondary Education	M
Special Education	M
Taxation	M

D'YOUVILLE COLLEGE

Chiropractic	P
Community Health Nursing	M,O
Education—General	M,O
Elementary Education	M,O
Family Nurse Practitioner Studies	M,O
Health Services Management and Hospital Administration	M,O
International Business	M
Nursing and Healthcare Administration	M,O
Nursing Education	M,O
Nursing—General	M,O*
Occupational Therapy	M

Physical Therapy	M,D,O
Physician Assistant Studies	M
Secondary Education	M,O
Special Education	M,O

EARLHAM COLLEGE

Education—General	M

EAST CAROLINA UNIVERSITY

Accounting	M
Adult Education	M,O
Allied Health—General	M,D
Allopathic Medicine	P
Business Administration and Management— General	M,D,O
Communication Disorders	M,D
Counselor Education	M,O
Curriculum and Instruction	M
Education—General	M,D,O
Educational Administration	M,D,O
Educational Media/ Instructional Technology	M,O
Elementary Education	M
English Education	M
Environmental and Occupational Health	M
Exercise and Sports Science	M,D
Health Education	M
Leisure Studies	M
Library Science	M,O
Logistics	M,D,O
Management Information Systems	M,D,O
Mathematics Education	M
Medical Physics	M,D
Middle School Education	M
Music Education	M
Nursing—General	M,D
Occupational Therapy	M
Physical Therapy	M,D
Physician Assistant Studies	M
Public Health—General	M
Reading Education	M
Recreation and Park Management	M
Rehabilitation Sciences	M
Science Education	M
Social Sciences Education	M
Social Work	M
Special Education	M
Vocational and Technical Education	M

EAST CENTRAL UNIVERSITY

Counselor Education	M
Education—General	M
Human Resources Management	M

EASTERN CONNECTICUT STATE UNIVERSITY

Early Childhood Education	M
Education—General	M
Educational Media/ Instructional Technology	M
Elementary Education	M
Organizational Management	M
Reading Education	M
Science Education	M
Secondary Education	M

EASTERN ILLINOIS UNIVERSITY

Accounting	M,O

Art Education	M
Business Administration and Management—	
General	M,O
Communication Disorders	M
Counselor Education	M
Early Childhood Education	M
Education—General	M,O
Educational Administration	M,O
Elementary Education	M
Mathematics Education	M
Middle School Education	M
Physical Education	M
Special Education	M
Student Affairs	M

EASTERN KENTUCKY UNIVERSITY

Agricultural Education	M
Allied Health—General	M
Art Education	M
Business Administration and Management—	
General	M*
Business Education	M
Communication Disorders	M
Community Health	M
Counselor Education	M
Curriculum and Instruction	M
Education—General	M
Educational Administration	M
Elementary Education	M
English Education	M
Environmental and Occupational Health	M
Family Nurse Practitioner Studies	M
Health Education	M
Health Services Management and Hospital Administration	M
Higher Education	M
Home Economics Education	M
Mathematics Education	M
Music Education	M
Nursing—General	M
Occupational Therapy	M
Physical Education	M
Reading Education	M
Recreation and Park Management	M
Science Education	M
Secondary Education	M
Social Sciences Education	M
Special Education	M
Sports Management	M
Vocational and Technical Education	M

EASTERN MENNONITE UNIVERSITY

Business Administration and Management—	
General	M
Education—General	M

EASTERN MICHIGAN UNIVERSITY

Accounting	M
Adult Nursing	M,O
Art Education	M
Athletic Training and Sports Medicine	M
Business Administration and Management—	
General	M
Clinical Research	M
Communication Disorders	M
Counselor Education	M,O
Curriculum and Instruction	M
Early Childhood Education	M
Education—General	M,D,O

Educational Administration	M,D
Educational Media/ Instructional Technology	M
Educational Psychology	M
Electronic Commerce	M
Elementary Education	M
English as a Second Language	M
Entrepreneurship	M
Exercise and Sports Science	M
Finance and Banking	M
Foundations and Philosophy of Education	M
Health Education	M
Health Promotion	M
Hospitality Management	M
Human Resources Management	M
Industrial and Manufacturing Management	M
International Business	M
Management Information Systems	M
Marketing	M
Mathematics Education	M
Middle School Education	M
Multilingual and Multicultural Education	M
Music Education	M
Nonprofit Management	M
Nursing and Healthcare Administration	M
Nursing Education	M,O
Occupational Therapy	M
Organizational Management	M
Physical Education	M
Quality Management	M
Reading Education	M
Science Education	M
Secondary Education	M
Social Work	M,O
Special Education	M
Sports Management	M
Supply Chain Management	M
Vocational and Technical Education	M

EASTERN NAZARENE COLLEGE

Early Childhood Education	M,O
Education—General	M,O
Educational Administration	M,O
Elementary Education	M,O
English as a Second Language	M,O
Middle School Education	M,O
Reading Education	M,O
Secondary Education	M,O
Special Education	M,O

EASTERN NEW MEXICO UNIVERSITY

Business Administration and Management—	
General	M
Communication Disorders	M
Counselor Education	M
Education—General	M
Human Services	M
Physical Education	M
Special Education	M

EASTERN OREGON UNIVERSITY

Education—General	M
Elementary Education	M
Secondary Education	M

EASTERN UNIVERSITY

Accounting	M
Business Administration and Management—	
General	M
Counselor Education	M
Education—General	M,O*
Educational Psychology	M
English as a Second Language	O
Finance and Banking	M
Health Education	M
Marketing	M
Multilingual and Multicultural Education	M
Nonprofit Management	M
Organizational Management	D*

EASTERN VIRGINIA MEDICAL SCHOOL

Allopathic Medicine	P
Medical/Surgical Nursing	O
Physician Assistant Studies	M
Public Health—General	M,O
Vision Sciences	O

EASTERN WASHINGTON UNIVERSITY

Adult Education	M
Business Administration and Management—	
General	M
Communication Disorders	M
Community College Education	M
Computer Education	M
Counselor Education	M
Curriculum and Instruction	M
Early Childhood Education	M
Education—General	M
Educational Administration	M
Educational Media/ Instructional Technology	M
Elementary Education	M
Foreign Languages Education	M
Foundations and Philosophy of Education	M
Higher Education	M
Mathematics Education	M
Music Education	M
Nursing Education	M
Nursing—General	M
Occupational Therapy	M
Physical Education	M
Physical Therapy	D
Reading Education	M
Science Education	M
Social Sciences Education	M
Social Work	M
Special Education	M

EAST STROUDSBURG UNIVERSITY OF PENNSYLVANIA

Communication Disorders	M
Community Health	M
Education—General	M
Educational Media/ Instructional Technology	M
Elementary Education	M
Exercise and Sports Science	M
Health Education	M
Hospitality Management	M
Physical Education	M
Public Health—General	M
Reading Education	M
Rehabilitation Sciences	M

Science Education	M
Secondary Education	M
Social Sciences Education	M
Special Education	M
Sports Management	M
Travel and Tourism	M

EAST TENNESSEE STATE UNIVERSITY

Accounting	M
Allied Health—General	M,D,O
Allopathic Medicine	P
Art Education	M
Business Administration and Management—	
General	M,O
Communication Disorders	M,D
Community Health	M,O
Counselor Education	M
Curriculum and Instruction	M
Early Childhood Education	M
Education—General	M,D,O
Educational Administration	M,D,O
Educational Media/ Instructional Technology	M
Elementary Education	M
Environmental and Occupational Health	M
Epidemiology	M,O
Exercise and Sports Science	M
Family Nurse Practitioner Studies	M,D,O
Finance and Banking	M
Health Services Management and Hospital Administration	M,D,O
Nursing—General	M,D,O
Physical Education	M
Physical Therapy	D
Public Health—General	M,O
Reading Education	M
Secondary Education	M
Social Work	M
Special Education	M,D
Sports Management	M
Vocational and Technical Education	M

EAST WEST COLLEGE OF NATURAL MEDICINE

Acupuncture and Oriental Medicine	M

EDGEWOOD COLLEGE

Business Administration and Management—	
General	M
Education—General	M,D,O
Educational Administration	M,D,O
Nursing—General	M
Special Education	M,D,O

EDINBORO UNIVERSITY OF PENNSYLVANIA

Communication Disorders	M
Counselor Education	M,O
Developmental Education	O
Early Childhood Education	M
Education—General	M,O
Educational Administration	M,O
Educational Psychology	M
Elementary Education	M
English Education	M
Family Nurse Practitioner Studies	M
Management Information Systems	M,O
Mathematics Education	M

Nursing—General	M
Reading Education	M,O
Science Education	M
Secondary Education	M
Social Work	M
Special Education	M

EDWARD VIA VIRGINIA COLLEGE OF OSTEOPATHIC MEDICINE

Osteopathic Medicine	P

ELIZABETH CITY STATE UNIVERSITY

Elementary Education	M

ELMHURST COLLEGE

Accounting	M
Business Administration and Management— General	M
Educational Administration	M
Nursing—General	M
Special Education	M
Supply Chain Management	M

ELMS COLLEGE

Communication Disorders	O
Early Childhood Education	M,O
Education—General	M,O
Elementary Education	M,O
English as a Second Language	M,O
English Education	M,O
Foreign Languages Education	M,O
Reading Education	M,O
Science Education	M,O
Secondary Education	M,O
Special Education	M,O

ELON UNIVERSITY

Business Administration and Management— General	M
Education of the Gifted	M
Education—General	M
Elementary Education	M
Law	P
Physical Therapy	D
Special Education	M

EMBRY-RIDDLE AERONAUTICAL UNIVERSITY (FL)

Aviation Management	M
Business Administration and Management— General	M

EMBRY-RIDDLE AERONAUTICAL UNIVERSITY WORLDWIDE

Aviation Management	M

EMERSON COLLEGE

Advertising and Public Relations	M
Communication Disorders	M*
Health Promotion	M
International Business	M*
Marketing	M*
Public Health—General	M*

EMMANUEL COLLEGE

Business Administration and Management— General	M
Education—General	M,O
Educational Administration	M,O
Elementary Education	M,O
Human Resources Management	M,O
Secondary Education	M,O

EMORY & HENRY COLLEGE

English Education	M
Reading Education	M

EMORY UNIVERSITY

Accounting	D
Adult Nursing	M
Allied Health—General	M,D
Allopathic Medicine	P
Anesthesiologist Assistant Studies	M
Business Administration and Management— General	M,D
Clinical Laboratory Sciences/Medical Technology	M,D
Clinical Research	M
Community Health	M,D
Education—General	M,D,O
Environmental and Occupational Health	M
Epidemiology	M,D
Family Nurse Practitioner Studies	M
Finance and Banking	D
Health Physics/ Radiological Health	D
Health Promotion	M
Health Services Management and Hospital Administration	M,D
Health Services Research	M,D
International Health	M,D
Law	P,M,O
Management Information Systems	D
Marketing	D
Medical/Surgical Nursing	M
Middle School Education	M,D,O
Nurse Anesthesia	M,D
Nurse Midwifery	M
Nursing and Healthcare Administration	M
Nursing—General	M,D*
Oncology Nursing	M
Organizational Management	D
Pediatric Nursing	M
Physical Therapy	D
Physician Assistant Studies	M
Public Health—General	M,D*
Secondary Education	M,D,O
Vision Sciences	M
Women's Health Nursing	M

EMPEROR'S COLLEGE OF TRADITIONAL ORIENTAL MEDICINE

Acupuncture and Oriental Medicine	M,D

EMPORIA STATE UNIVERSITY

Business Administration and Management— General	M
Business Education	M

Counselor Education	M
Curriculum and Instruction	M
Early Childhood Education	M
Education of the Gifted	M
Education—General	M,O
Educational Administration	M
Educational Media/ Instructional Technology	M
Elementary Education	M
English as a Second Language	M
Information Studies	M,D,O
Library Science	M,D,O
Music Education	M
Physical Education	M
Reading Education	M
Secondary Education	M
Social Sciences Education	M
Special Education	M

ENDICOTT COLLEGE

Art Education	M
Business Administration and Management— General	M
Distance Education Development	M
Elementary Education	M
Hospitality Management	M
International and Comparative Education	M
Organizational Management	M
Reading Education	M
Special Education	M
Sports Management	M

ERIKSON INSTITUTE

Early Childhood Education	M,D*
English as a Second Language	M,O

EVANGEL UNIVERSITY

Counselor Education	M
Education—General	M
Educational Administration	M
Organizational Management	M
Reading Education	M
Secondary Education	M

EVERGLADES UNIVERSITY

Business Administration and Management— General	M

EVERGLADES UNIVERSITY

Business Administration and Management— General	M

THE EVERGREEN STATE COLLEGE

Education—General	M

EXCELSIOR COLLEGE

Business Administration and Management— General	M
Nursing and Healthcare Administration	O
Nursing—General	M

FACULTAD DE DERECHO EUGENIO MARÍA DE HOSTOS

Law	P

FAIRFIELD UNIVERSITY

Accounting	M,O
Business Administration and Management— General	M,O*
Counselor Education	M,O
Education—General	M,O*
Educational Media/ Instructional Technology	M,O
Elementary Education	M,O
English as a Second Language	M,O
Family Nurse Practitioner Studies	M,O
Finance and Banking	M,O
Foreign Languages Education	M,O
Foundations and Philosophy of Education	M,O
Health Services Management and Hospital Administration	M,O
Human Resources Management	M,O
International Business	M,O
Management Information Systems	M,O
Marketing	M,O
Multilingual and Multicultural Education	M,O
Nurse Anesthesia	M,O
Nursing—General	M,O
Psychiatric Nursing	M,O
Secondary Education	M,O
Special Education	M,O
Taxation	M,O

FAIRLEIGH DICKINSON UNIVERSITY, COLLEGE AT FLORHAM

Accounting	M
Business Administration and Management— General	M,O*
Education—General	M,O
Educational Administration	M
Educational Media/ Instructional Technology	M,O
Entrepreneurship	M,O
Finance and Banking	M,O
Hospitality Management	M*
Human Resources Management	M
International Business	M,O
Marketing	M,O
Organizational Behavior	M,O
Organizational Management	M,O
Reading Education	M,O
Taxation	M,O

FAIRLEIGH DICKINSON UNIVERSITY, METROPOLITAN CAMPUS

Accounting	M,O
Business Administration and Management— General	M,O*
Clinical Laboratory Sciences/Medical Technology	M
Curriculum and Instruction	M
Education—General	M,O*
Educational Administration	M
Educational Media/ Instructional Technology	M,O

Electronic Commerce	M
Entrepreneurship	M,O
Finance and Banking	M,O
Foundations and Philosophy of Education	M
Health Services Management and Hospital Administration	M
Hospitality Management	M*
Human Resources Management	M,O
International Business	M
Management Information Systems	M,O
Marketing	M,O
Multilingual and Multicultural Education	M
Nonprofit Management	M,O
Nursing—General	M,O
Pharmaceutical Administration	M,O
Reading Education	M,O
Science Education	M
Special Education	M
Taxation	M

FASHION INSTITUTE OF TECHNOLOGY

Business Administration and Management— General	M
Marketing	M

FAULKNER UNIVERSITY

Law	P

FAYETTEVILLE STATE UNIVERSITY

Educational Administration	M,D
Elementary Education	M
Middle School Education	M
Reading Education	M
Secondary Education	M
Social Sciences Education	M
Social Work	M

FELICIAN COLLEGE

Business Administration and Management— General	M
Education—General	M*
Educational Administration	M
Elementary Education	M
Entrepreneurship	M
Family Nurse Practitioner Studies	M,O*
Health Education	M,O
Nursing—General	M,O
Religious Education	M,O
Special Education	M

FERRIS STATE UNIVERSITY

Allied Health—General	M
Business Administration and Management— General	M
Curriculum and Instruction	M
Developmental Education	M
Education—General	M
Educational Administration	M
Educational Media/ Instructional Technology	M
Electronic Commerce	M
Elementary Education	M
Human Services	M
Management Information Systems	M

Nursing and Healthcare Administration	M
Nursing Education	M
Nursing Informatics	M
Nursing—General	M
Optometry	P
Pharmacy	P
Quality Management	M
Reading Education	M
Special Education	M

FIELDING GRADUATE UNIVERSITY

Educational Administration	M,D*
Organizational Management	M,D,O*

FITCHBURG STATE COLLEGE

Accounting	M
Art Education	M,O
Business Administration and Management— General	M
Counselor Education	M,O
Early Childhood Education	M
Educational Administration	M,O
Educational Media/ Instructional Technology	M,O
Elementary Education	M
English Education	M
Forensic Nursing	M,O
Higher Education	M,O
Human Resources Management	M
Middle School Education	M
Science Education	M
Secondary Education	M
Social Sciences Education	M
Special Education	M
Vocational and Technical Education	M

FIVE BRANCHES INSTITUTE: COLLEGE OF TRADITIONAL CHINESE MEDICINE

Acupuncture and Oriental Medicine	M

FIVE TOWNS COLLEGE

Early Childhood Education	M
Music Education	M,D

FLORIDA AGRICULTURAL AND MECHANICAL UNIVERSITY

Accounting	M
Adult Education	M,D
Allied Health—General	M
Business Administration and Management— General	M
Business Education	M
Counselor Education	M,D
Early Childhood Education	M
Education—General	M,D
Educational Administration	M,D
Elementary Education	M
English Education	M
Finance and Banking	M
Health Education	M
Law	P
Management Information Systems	M
Marketing	M
Mathematics Education	M
Medicinal and Pharmaceutical Chemistry	M,D
Nursing and Healthcare Administration	M

Nursing—General	M
Pharmaceutical Administration	M,D
Pharmaceutical Sciences	M,D*
Pharmacy	P,D
Physical Education	M
Physical Therapy	M
Public Health—General	M
Recreation and Park Management	M
Science Education	M
Secondary Education	M
Social Sciences Education	M
Social Work	M
Vocational and Technical Education	M

FLORIDA ATLANTIC UNIVERSITY

Accounting	M
Adult Education	M,D,O
Art Education	M,D,O
Business Administration and Management— General	M
Communication Disorders	M
Counselor Education	M,O
Curriculum and Instruction	M,D,O
Education—General	M,D,O
Educational Administration	M,D,O
Educational Media/ Instructional Technology	M
Educational Psychology	M,D,O
Electronic Commerce	M
Elementary Education	M,D,O
Entrepreneurship	M
Exercise and Sports Science	M
Finance and Banking	M
Foreign Languages Education	M
Foundations and Philosophy of Education	M,D,O
Health Promotion	M
Health Services Management and Hospital Administration	M
Higher Education	M,D,O
International Business	M
Marketing	M
Multilingual and Multicultural Education	M,D,O
Nonprofit Management	M
Nursing and Healthcare Administration	M
Nursing—General	M,D,O
Reading Education	M,D,O
Real Estate	M
Social Work	M
Special Education	M,D
Sports Management	M
Taxation	M

FLORIDA ATLANTIC UNIVERSITY, JUPITER CAMPUS

Business Administration and Management— General	M
Education—General	M
Reading Education	M
Social Work	M
Special Education	M

FLORIDA COASTAL SCHOOL OF LAW

Law	P

FLORIDA COLLEGE OF INTEGRATIVE MEDICINE

Acupuncture and Oriental Medicine	M

FLORIDA GULF COAST UNIVERSITY

Accounting	M
Allied Health—General	M
Business Administration and Management— General	M
Counselor Education	M
Curriculum and Instruction	M
Education—General	M
Educational Administration	M
Educational Media/ Instructional Technology	M
Elementary Education	M
English Education	M
Mathematics Education	M
Nursing—General	M
Occupational Therapy	M
Physical Therapy	M
Reading Education	M
Recreation and Park Management	M
Science Education	M
Secondary Education	M
Social Sciences Education	M
Social Work	M
Special Education	M
Taxation	M

FLORIDA INSTITUTE OF TECHNOLOGY

Business Administration and Management— General	M
Computer Education	M,D,O
Electronic Commerce	M
Elementary Education	M,D,O
Environmental Education	M,D,O
Human Resources Management	M
Industrial and Manufacturing Management	M
Logistics	M
Management Information Systems	M
Mathematics Education	M,D,O
Science Education	M,D,O
Transportation Management	M

FLORIDA INTERNATIONAL UNIVERSITY

Accounting	M
Adult Education	M,D
Art Education	M,D
Athletic Training and Sports Medicine	M
Business Administration and Management— General	M,D
Communication Disorders	M
Counselor Education	M
Curriculum and Instruction	M,D,O
Early Childhood Education	M,D
Education—General	M,D,O*
Educational Administration	M,D,O
Educational Media/ Instructional Technology	M,D,O
Elementary Education	M,D
English as a Second Language	M,D,O
English Education	M,D
Exercise and Sports Science	M
Finance and Banking	M
Foreign Languages Education	M,D,O
Health Services Management and Hospital Administration	M

Higher Education	D
Hospitality Management	M
Human Resources Development	M,D
International and Comparative Education	M,D
International Business	M
Law	P
Leisure Studies	M
Management Information Systems	D
Mathematics Education	M,D
Music Education	M
Nursing—General	M,D*
Occupational Therapy	M
Physical Education	M,D,O
Physical Therapy	M
Public Health—General	M*
Reading Education	M,D
Recreation and Park Management	M
Science Education	M,D
Social Sciences Education	M,D
Social Work	M,D*
Special Education	M,D,O
Sports Management	M
Taxation	M
Urban Education	M

FLORIDA METROPOLITAN UNIVERSITY–BRANDON CAMPUS

Business Administration and Management— General	M

FLORIDA METROPOLITAN UNIVERSITY–MELBOURNE CAMPUS

Business Administration and Management— General	M

FLORIDA METROPOLITAN UNIVERSITY–NORTH ORLANDO CAMPUS

Business Administration and Management— General	M

FLORIDA METROPOLITAN UNIVERSITY–PINELLAS CAMPUS

Business Administration and Management— General	M

FLORIDA METROPOLITAN UNIVERSITY–POMPANO BEACH CAMPUS

Business Administration and Management— General	M

FLORIDA METROPOLITAN UNIVERSITY–SOUTH ORLANDO CAMPUS

Accounting	M
Business Administration and Management— General	M
Human Resources Management	M
International Business	M

FLORIDA METROPOLITAN UNIVERSITY–TAMPA CAMPUS

Accounting	M

Business Administration and Management— General	M
Human Resources Management	M
International Business	M

FLORIDA SOUTHERN COLLEGE

Accounting	M
Business Administration and Management— General	M
Education—General	M
International Business	M
Nursing—General	M

FLORIDA STATE UNIVERSITY

Accounting	M,D
Adult Education	M,D,O
Allopathic Medicine	P,D
Art Education	M,D,O
Business Administration and Management— General	M,D
Communication Disorders	M,D
Counselor Education	M,D,O
Distance Education Development	M,D,O
Early Childhood Education	M,D,O
Education—General	M,D,O
Educational Administration	M,D,O
Educational Measurement and Evaluation	M,D
Educational Media/ Instructional Technology	M,D,O
Educational Psychology	M,D
Elementary Education	M,D,O
English Education	M,D,O
Exercise and Sports Science	M,D
Family Nurse Practitioner Studies	M,O
Finance and Banking	M,D
Foundations and Philosophy of Education	M,D,O
Health Education	M,D
Health Services Research	M
Higher Education	M,D,O
Human Resources Development	M,D,O
Information Studies	M,D,O
Insurance	M,D
International and Comparative Education	M,D,O
Kinesiology and Movement Studies	M,D
Law	P
Library Science	M,D,O
Management Information Systems	M,D
Marketing	M,D
Mathematics Education	M,D,O
Multilingual and Multicultural Education	M,D,O
Music Education	M,D
Nursing Education	M,O
Nursing—General	M,O
Pediatric Nursing	M,O
Physical Education	M,D,O
Reading Education	M,D,O
Recreation and Park Management	M,D,O
Science Education	M,D,O
Social Sciences Education	M,D,O
Social Work	M,D
Special Education	M,D,O
Sports Management	M,D,O
Taxation	M,D

FONTBONNE UNIVERSITY

Accounting	M

Business Administration and Management— General	M
Communication Disorders	M
Computer Education	M
Education—General	M
Special Education	M
Taxation	M

FORDHAM UNIVERSITY

Accounting	M
Adult Education	M,D,O
Business Administration and Management— General	M
Counselor Education	M,D,O
Curriculum and Instruction	M,D,O
Early Childhood Education	M,D,O
Education—General	M,D,O*
Educational Administration	M,D,O
Educational Psychology	M,D,O
Elementary Education	M,D,O
English as a Second Language	M,D,O
Finance and Banking	M
Human Resources Management	M,D,O
Law	P,M
Management Information Systems	M
Marketing	M
Multilingual and Multicultural Education	M,D,O
Reading Education	M,D,O
Religious Education	M,D,O
Secondary Education	M,D,O
Social Work	M,D*
Special Education	M,D,O
Taxation	M

FORT HAYS STATE UNIVERSITY

Accounting	M
Business Administration and Management— General	M
Communication Disorders	M
Counselor Education	M
Education—General	M,O
Educational Administration	M,O
Educational Media/ Instructional Technology	M
Elementary Education	M
Health Education	M
Nursing—General	M
Physical Education	M
Secondary Education	M
Special Education	M

FORT VALLEY STATE UNIVERSITY

Counselor Education	M,O
Early Childhood Education	M
Environmental and Occupational Health	M
Middle School Education	M
Public Health—General	M

FRAMINGHAM STATE COLLEGE

Business Administration and Management— General	M
Curriculum and Instruction	M
Early Childhood Education	M
Educational Administration	M
Educational Media/ Instructional Technology	M
Elementary Education	M
English as a Second Language	M
English Education	M

Foreign Languages Education	M
Health Education	M
Health Services Management and Hospital Administration	M
Human Resources Management	M
Mathematics Education	M
Reading Education	M
Science Education	M
Social Sciences Education	M
Special Education	M

FRANCISCAN UNIVERSITY OF STEUBENVILLE

Business Administration and Management— General	M
Curriculum and Instruction	M
Education—General	M
Educational Administration	M
Nursing—General	M

FRANCIS MARION UNIVERSITY

Business Administration and Management— General	M
Early Childhood Education	M
Education—General	M
Elementary Education	M
Health Services Management and Hospital Administration	M
Secondary Education	M
Special Education	M

FRANKLIN PIERCE LAW CENTER

Law	P,M,O

FRANKLIN PIERCE UNIVERSITY

Business Administration and Management— General	M
Management Information Systems	M
Physical Therapy	M

FRANKLIN UNIVERSITY

Business Administration and Management— General	M
Marketing	M

FREED-HARDEMAN UNIVERSITY

Business Administration and Management— General	M
Counselor Education	M,O
Curriculum and Instruction	M,O
Education—General	M,O
Educational Administration	M,O

FRESNO PACIFIC UNIVERSITY

Business Administration and Management— General	M
Counselor Education	M
Curriculum and Instruction	M
Education of the Multiply Handicapped	M
Education—General	M
Educational Administration	M
Educational Media/ Instructional Technology	M

English as a Second
  Language — M
Kinesiology and
  Movement Studies — M
Mathematics Education — M
Multilingual and
  Multicultural Education — M
Reading Education — M
Science Education — M
Special Education — M
Student Affairs — M

FRIENDS UNIVERSITY

Business Administration
  and Management—
  General — M
Education—General — M
Educational Administration — M
Elementary Education — M
Health Services
  Management and
  Hospital Administration — M
Human Resources
  Development — M
Industrial and
  Manufacturing
  Management — M
Law — M
Management Information
  Systems — M
Secondary Education — M

FRONTIER SCHOOL OF MIDWIFERY AND FAMILY NURSING

Nurse Midwifery — M,O
Nursing—General — M,O
Women's Health Nursing — M,O

FROSTBURG STATE UNIVERSITY

Business Administration
  and Management—
  General — M
Counselor Education — M
Curriculum and Instruction — M
Education—General — M
Educational Administration — M
Educational Media/
  Instructional Technology — M
Elementary Education — M
Physical Education — M
Reading Education — M
Recreation and Park
  Management — M
Secondary Education — M
Special Education — M

FURMAN UNIVERSITY

Early Childhood Education — M
Education—General — M
Educational Administration — M
Elementary Education — M
English as a Second
  Language — M
Middle School Education — M
Reading Education — M
Special Education — M

GALLAUDET UNIVERSITY

Communication Disorders — M,D
Counselor Education — M
Early Childhood Education — M,D,O
Education of the Multiply
  Handicapped — M,D,O
Education—General — M,D,O
Educational Administration — M,D,O
Educational Measurement
  and Evaluation — O

Educational Media/
  Instructional Technology — O
Elementary Education — M,D,O
Leisure Studies — M
Secondary Education — M,D,O
Social Work — M
Special Education — M,D,O

GANNON UNIVERSITY

Accounting — O
Business Administration
  and Management—
  General — M,O
Counselor Education — M,O
Curriculum and Instruction — M
Early Childhood Education — M,O
Education—General — M,O
Educational Administration — M,O
Educational Media/
  Instructional Technology — M,O
English as a Second
  Language — O
Environmental and
  Occupational Health — M,O
Environmental Education — M
Family Nurse Practitioner
  Studies — M,O
Finance and Banking — O
Human Resources
  Management — O
Investment Management — O
Marketing — O
Medical/Surgical Nursing — M,O
Nurse Anesthesia — M,O
Nursing and Healthcare
  Administration — M,O
Nursing—General — M,O
Occupational Therapy — M,O
Organizational
  Management — O
Physical Therapy — D
Physician Assistant
  Studies — M
Reading Education — M,O
Science Education — M

GARDNER-WEBB UNIVERSITY

Business Administration
  and Management—
  General — P,M,D
Curriculum and Instruction — D
Education—General — M,D
Educational Administration — M,D
Elementary Education — M
English Education — M
Exercise and Sports
  Science — M
Middle School Education — M
Nursing—General — M,O
Physical Education — M
Religious Education — P,M,D

GARRETT-EVANGELICAL THEOLOGICAL SEMINARY

Religious Education — P,M,D

GENEVA COLLEGE

Business Administration
  and Management—
  General — M
Counselor Education — M
Education—General — M
Educational Administration — M
Higher Education — M
Organizational
  Management — M
Special Education — M

GEORGE FOX UNIVERSITY

Business Administration
  and Management—
  General — M,D
Counselor Education — M,O
Education—General — M,D,O
Educational Administration — M,D,O
Foundations and
  Philosophy of Education — M,D,O
Organizational
  Management — M

GEORGE MASON UNIVERSITY

Business Administration
  and Management—
  General — M
Community College
  Education — D,O
Counselor Education — M
Early Childhood Education — M
Education—General — M,D
Educational Administration — M
Educational Measurement
  and Evaluation — M
Educational Media/
  Instructional Technology — M
English as a Second
  Language — M
Exercise and Sports
  Science — M
Family Nurse Practitioner
  Studies — M,D,O
Foreign Languages
  Education — M
Human Resources
  Management — M
Law — P,M
Logistics — M
Medical/Surgical Nursing — M,D,O
Middle School Education — M
Multilingual and
  Multicultural Education — M
Music Education — M
Nursing and Healthcare
  Administration — M,D,O
Nursing Education — M,D,O
Nursing—General — M,D,O
Organizational
  Management — M
Reading Education — M
Secondary Education — M
Social Work — M,D,O
Special Education — M
Transportation
  Management — M

GEORGETOWN COLLEGE

Education—General — M

GEORGETOWN UNIVERSITY

Allopathic Medicine — P
Business Administration
  and Management—
  General — M
English as a Second
  Language — M,D,O
Epidemiology — M
Health Physics/
  Radiological Health — M
Health Promotion — M,D
Law — P,M,D
Multilingual and
  Multicultural Education — M,D,O
Nursing—General — M
Public Health—General — M,D
Taxation — P,M,D

THE GEORGE WASHINGTON UNIVERSITY

Accounting — M,D

Adult Nursing — M,D,O
Allopathic Medicine — P
Business Administration
  and Management—
  General — M,D
Communication Disorders — M
Community Health — M
Counselor Education — M,D,O
Curriculum and Instruction — M,D,O
Early Childhood Education — M
Education—General — M,D,O
Educational Administration — M,D,O
Educational Media/
  Instructional Technology — M
Educational Policy — M,D
Elementary Education — M
Emergency Medical
  Services — M,O
Environmental and
  Occupational Health — M,D
Epidemiology — M,D
Exercise and Sports
  Science — M
Family Nurse Practitioner
  Studies — M,D,O
Finance and Banking — M,D
Health Promotion — M,O
Health Services
  Management and
  Hospital Administration — M,D,O
Health Services Research — M,D,O
Higher Education — M,D,O
Hospitality Management — M,O
Human Resources
  Development — M,D,O
Human Resources
  Management — M,D,O
Industrial and
  Manufacturing
  Management — M
International and
  Comparative Education — M
International Business — M,D
International Health — M
Investment Management — M,D
Law — P,M,D
Logistics — M
Management Information
  Systems — M
Management Strategy and
  Policy — M,D
Marketing — M,D
Maternal and Child Health — M,O
Museum Education — M
Nonprofit Management — M
Nursing and Healthcare
  Administration — M,D,O
Oral and Dental Sciences — M
Organizational Behavior — M,D
Organizational
  Management — M,O*
Physical Therapy — D
Physician Assistant
  Studies — M
Project Management — M,D
Public Health—General — M,D,O
Real Estate — M
Secondary Education — M
Special Education — M,D,O
Sports Management — M,O
Travel and Tourism — M,O

GEORGIA CAMPUS– PHILADELPHIA COLLEGE OF OSTEOPATHIC MEDICINE

Osteopathic Medicine — P

GEORGIA COLLEGE & STATE UNIVERSITY

Accounting — M
Business Administration
  and Management—
  General — M

Early Childhood Education	M,O
Education—General	M,O
Educational Administration	M,O
Educational Media/ Instructional Technology	M,O
English Education	M,O
Health Education	M,O
Logistics	M
Management Information Systems	M
Mathematics Education	M,O
Middle School Education	M,O
Nursing—General	M
Physical Education	M,O
Science Education	M,O
Secondary Education	M,O
Social Sciences Education	M,O
Special Education	M

GEORGIA INSTITUTE OF TECHNOLOGY

Accounting	M,D,O
Business Administration and Management— General	M,D,O
Electronic Commerce	M,O
Entrepreneurship	M,O
Finance and Banking	M,D,O
Health Physics/ Radiological Health	M,D
Health Services Management and Hospital Administration	M
International Business	M,O
Management Information Systems	M,D,O
Management Strategy and Policy	M,D,O
Marketing	M,D,O
Medical Physics	M,D
Organizational Behavior	M,D,O

GEORGIAN COURT UNIVERSITY

Business Administration and Management— General	M
Education—General	M,O
Educational Administration	M,O
Educational Media/ Instructional Technology	M,O
Educational Psychology	M,O
Special Education	M,O

GEORGIA SOUTHERN UNIVERSITY

Accounting	M
Allied Health—General	M,O
Art Education	M
Business Administration and Management— General	M
Business Education	M
Community Health Nursing	M,O
Counselor Education	M,O
Curriculum and Instruction	D
Early Childhood Education	M
Education—General	M,D,O
Educational Administration	M,D,O
Educational Media/ Instructional Technology	M
English Education	M
Family Nurse Practitioner Studies	M,O
Foreign Languages Education	M
Health Education	M
Health Services Management and Hospital Administration	M
Higher Education	M

Kinesiology and Movement Studies	M
Mathematics Education	M
Middle School Education	M
Nursing—General	M,O
Physical Education	M
Public Health—General	M
Reading Education	M
Recreation and Park Management	M
Science Education	M
Social Sciences Education	M
Special Education	M
Sports Management	M
Vocational and Technical Education	M
Women's Health Nursing	M,O

GEORGIA SOUTHWESTERN STATE UNIVERSITY

Business Administration and Management— General	M
Early Childhood Education	M,O
Education—General	M,O
Health Education	M,O
Middle School Education	M,O
Physical Education	M,O
Reading Education	M,O
Secondary Education	M,O
Special Education	M,O

GEORGIA STATE UNIVERSITY

Accounting	M,D,O
Actuarial Science	M
Adult Nursing	M,D,O
Allied Health—General	M,D,O
Art Education	M,D,O
Athletic Training and Sports Medicine	M
Business Administration and Management— General	M,D
Communication Disorders	M
Counselor Education	M,D,O
Early Childhood Education	M,D,O
Education of the Multiply Handicapped	M
Education—General	M,D,O
Educational Administration	M,D,O
Educational Measurement and Evaluation	M,D
Educational Media/ Instructional Technology	M,D,O
Educational Policy	M,D,O
Educational Psychology	M,D
English as a Second Language	M,D,O
English Education	M,D,O
Entrepreneurship	M,D
Exercise and Sports Science	M,D
Family Nurse Practitioner Studies	M,D,O
Finance and Banking	M,D,O
Foundations and Philosophy of Education	M,D
Health Education	M
Health Promotion	M,D,O
Health Services Management and Hospital Administration	M
Human Resources Management	M,D
Human Services	M
Insurance	M,D
International Business	M
Law	P
Management Information Systems	M,D
Marketing	M,D
Mathematics Education	M,D,O

Middle School Education	M,O
Music Education	M,D,O
Nursing—General	M,D,O
Organizational Management	M,D
Pediatric Nursing	M,D,O
Physical Education	M
Physical Therapy	D
Psychiatric Nursing	M,D,O
Public Health—General	M,O
Reading Education	M,D,O
Real Estate	M,D,O
Science Education	M,D,O
Social Sciences Education	M,D,O
Social Work	M
Special Education	M,D
Sports Management	M
Taxation	M
Women's Health Nursing	M,D,O

GLOBAL UNIVERSITY OF THE ASSEMBLIES OF GOD

Religious Education	P,M

GODDARD COLLEGE

Business Administration and Management— General	M
Education—General	M
Health Promotion	M

GOLDEN GATE BAPTIST THEOLOGICAL SEMINARY

Early Childhood Education	P,M,D,O
Educational Administration	P,M,D,O

GOLDEN GATE UNIVERSITY

Accounting	M,D,O
Advertising and Public Relations	M,D,O
Business Administration and Management— General	M,D,O
Finance and Banking	M,D,O
Human Resources Management	M,D,O
International Business	M,D,O
Law	P,M,D
Legal and Justice Studies	P,M,D
Management Information Systems	M,D,O
Marketing	M,D,O
Taxation	P,M,D,O

GOLDEY-BEACOM COLLEGE

Business Administration and Management— General	M
Finance and Banking	M
Human Resources Management	M
Management Information Systems	M
Marketing	M

GONZAGA UNIVERSITY

Accounting	M
Business Administration and Management— General	M
Education—General	M
Educational Administration	M,D
English as a Second Language	M
Law	P
Nurse Anesthesia	M
Nursing—General	M

Organizational Management	M
Special Education	M
Sports Management	M

GOODING INSTITUTE OF NURSE ANESTHESIA

Nurse Anesthesia	M

GORDON COLLEGE

Education—General	M
Music Education	M

GORDON-CONWELL THEOLOGICAL SEMINARY

Religious Education	P,M,D

GOUCHER COLLEGE

Education—General	M

GOVERNORS STATE UNIVERSITY

Accounting	M
Business Administration and Management— General	M
Communication Disorders	M
Early Childhood Education	M
Education—General	M
Educational Administration	M
Educational Media/ Instructional Technology	M
Health Services Management and Hospital Administration	M
Legal and Justice Studies	M
Management Information Systems	M
Nursing—General	M
Occupational Therapy	M
Physical Therapy	M,D
Reading Education	M
Social Work	M
Special Education	M

GRACELAND UNIVERSITY

Education—General	M
Family Nurse Practitioner Studies	M,O
Nursing and Healthcare Administration	M,O
Nursing Education	M,O
Nursing—General	M,O

GRADUATE INSTITUTE OF APPLIED LINGUISTICS

Multilingual and Multicultural Education	M,O

GRADUATE SCHOOL AND UNIVERSITY CENTER OF THE CITY UNIVERSITY OF NEW YORK

Accounting	D
Business Administration and Management— General	D
Communication Disorders	D
Educational Psychology	D
Finance and Banking	D
Management Information Systems	D
Organizational Behavior	D
Social Work	D
Urban Education	D

GRAMBLING STATE UNIVERSITY

Curriculum and Instruction	M,D
Developmental Education	M,D
Early Childhood Education	M
Education—General	M,D
Educational Administration	M,D
Elementary Education	M
Family Nurse Practitioner Studies	M,O
Nursing Education	M,O
Nursing—General	M,O
Science Education	M,O
Social Sciences Education	M
Social Work	M
Special Education	M,D
Sports Management	M

GRAND CANYON UNIVERSITY

Business Administration and Management— General	M
Education—General	M*
Elementary Education	M
English as a Second Language	M
Reading Education	M
Secondary Education	M

GRAND RAPIDS THEOLOGICAL SEMINARY OF CORNERSTONE UNIVERSITY

Religious Education	P,M

GRAND VALLEY STATE UNIVERSITY

Accounting	M
Adult Education	M
Allied Health—General	M,D
Business Administration and Management— General	M
Early Childhood Education	M
Education of the Gifted	M
Education—General	M
Educational Administration	M
Educational Media/ Instructional Technology	M
Elementary Education	M
English as a Second Language	M
English Education	M
Family Nurse Practitioner Studies	M
Health Services Management and Hospital Administration	M
Higher Education	M
Management Information Systems	M
Middle School Education	M
Nursing and Healthcare Administration	M
Nursing Education	M
Nursing—General	M
Occupational Therapy	M
Physical Therapy	M,D
Physician Assistant Studies	M
Reading Education	M
Social Work	M
Special Education	M
Taxation	M

GRANTHAM UNIVERSITY

Business Administration and Management— General	M
Management Information Systems	M

Project Management	M

GRATZ COLLEGE

Education—General	M
Library Science	O
Religious Education	M,O
Social Work	M,O

GREEN MOUNTAIN COLLEGE

Business Administration and Management— General	M

GREENSBORO COLLEGE

Education—General	M
Elementary Education	M
English as a Second Language	M
Special Education	M

GREENVILLE COLLEGE

Education—General	M
Elementary Education	M
Secondary Education	M

GWYNEDD-MERCY COLLEGE

Adult Nursing	M
Counselor Education	M
Education—General	M
Educational Administration	M
Family Nurse Practitioner Studies	M
Gerontological Nursing	M
Nursing—General	M
Oncology Nursing	M
Pediatric Nursing	M
Reading Education	M
Special Education	M

HAMLINE UNIVERSITY

Business Administration and Management— General	M
Education—General	M,D
Law	P,M
Nonprofit Management	M

HAMPTON UNIVERSITY

Business Administration and Management— General	M
Communication Disorders	M*
Counselor Education	M
Education—General	M
Elementary Education	M
Nursing—General	M
Physical Therapy	D
Special Education	M
Student Affairs	M

HARDING UNIVERSITY

Art Education	M,O
Business Administration and Management— General	M
Counselor Education	M,O
Early Childhood Education	M,O
Education—General	M,O
Educational Administration	M,O
Elementary Education	M,O
English Education	M,O
Foreign Languages Education	M,O
Health Education	M,O

Home Economics Education	M,O
Mathematics Education	M,O
Pharmacy	P
Physician Assistant Studies	M
Reading Education	M,O
Religious Education	M,O
Science Education	M,O
Secondary Education	M,O
Social Sciences Education	M,O
Special Education	M,O

HARDIN-SIMMONS UNIVERSITY

Business Administration and Management— General	M
Counselor Education	M
Education of the Gifted	M
Education—General	M
Family Nurse Practitioner Studies	M
Maternal and Child/ Neonatal Nursing	M
Music Education	M
Nursing—General	M
Physical Education	M
Physical Therapy	D
Reading Education	M
Recreation and Park Management	M
Science Education	M,D
Sports Management	M

HARRISBURG UNIVERSITY OF SCIENCE AND TECHNOLOGY

Project Management	M

HARVARD UNIVERSITY

Allopathic Medicine	P,D
Art Education	M
Business Administration and Management— General	M,D,O
Communication Disorders	D*
Curriculum and Instruction	M
Dentistry	P,M,D,O
Education—General	M,D*
Educational Administration	M,D
Educational Measurement and Evaluation	D
Educational Media/ Instructional Technology	M,O
Educational Policy	M,D
Educational Psychology	M
Environmental and Occupational Health	M,D
Epidemiology	M,D
Foundations and Philosophy of Education	M,O
Health Promotion	M,D
Health Services Management and Hospital Administration	M,D
Higher Education	D
International and Comparative Education	M
International Health	M,D
Law	P,M,D
Management Information Systems	D
Mathematics Education	M,O
Medical Physics	D
Multilingual and Multicultural Education	M
Oral and Dental Sciences	M,D,O
Organizational Behavior	D
Public Health—General	M,D*
Reading Education	M
Science Education	M
Urban Education	D

HASTINGS COLLEGE

Education—General	M

HAWAI'I PACIFIC UNIVERSITY

Accounting	M
Business Administration and Management— General	M*
Community Health Nursing	M
Electronic Commerce	M
English as a Second Language	M*
Family Nurse Practitioner Studies	M
Finance and Banking	M
Human Resources Management	M
International Business	M
Management Information Systems	M
Marketing	M
Nursing—General	M*
Organizational Management	M
Secondary Education	M*
Social Work	M

HEBREW COLLEGE

Early Childhood Education	M,O
Education—General	M,O
Middle School Education	M,O
Music Education	M,O
Religious Education	M,O
Special Education	M,O

HEBREW UNION COLLEGE– JEWISH INSTITUTE OF RELIGION (CA)

Education—General	M,D,O
Religious Education	M,D,O
Social Work	M,O

HEBREW UNION COLLEGE– JEWISH INSTITUTE OF RELIGION (NY)

Education—General	M
Religious Education	M

HEC MONTREAL

Accounting	M,O
Business Administration and Management— General	M,D,O
Electronic Commerce	M,O
Finance and Banking	M,O
Human Resources Management	M
Industrial and Manufacturing Management	M
International Business	M
Logistics	M
Management Information Systems	M
Management Strategy and Policy	M
Marketing	M
Supply Chain Management	O
Taxation	M,O

HEIDELBERG COLLEGE

Business Administration and Management— General	M
Education—General	M

HENDERSON STATE UNIVERSITY

Business Administration and Management— General	M
Counselor Education	M
Curriculum and Instruction	M,O
Early Childhood Education	M,O
Education—General	M,O
Educational Administration	M,O
English as a Second Language	M,O
English Education	M,O
Mathematics Education	M,O
Middle School Education	M,O
Physical Education	M
Reading Education	M,O
Social Sciences Education	M,O
Special Education	M,O
Sports Management	M

HENDRIX COLLEGE

Accounting	M

HERITAGE UNIVERSITY

Counselor Education	M
Education—General	M
Educational Administration	M
English as a Second Language	M
Multilingual and Multicultural Education	M
Reading Education	M
Science Education	M
Special Education	M

HIGH POINT UNIVERSITY

Business Administration and Management— General	M
Educational Administration	M
Elementary Education	M
Exercise and Sports Science	M
Nonprofit Management	M
Special Education	M

HODGES UNIVERSITY

Business Administration and Management— General	M
Education—General	M
Law	M
Management Information Systems	M

HOFSTRA UNIVERSITY

Accounting	M
Art Education	M
Business Administration and Management— General	M,O*
Business Education	M
Communication Disorders	M,D
Counselor Education	M,O
Early Childhood Education	M,O
Education of the Gifted	M,O
Education—General	M,D,O*
Educational Administration	M,D,O
Educational Measurement and Evaluation	M
Educational Media/ Instructional Technology	M
Elementary Education	M,O
English as a Second Language	M,O
English Education	M
Finance and Banking	M

Foreign Languages Education	M
Foundations and Philosophy of Education	M,O
Health Education	M
Health Services Management and Hospital Administration	M,O
Human Resources Management	M,O
International Business	M,O
Law	P,M
Legal and Justice Studies	P,M
Management Information Systems	M
Marketing Research	M,O
Marketing	M,O
Mathematics Education	M
Middle School Education	O
Multilingual and Multicultural Education	M,O
Music Education	M
Physical Education	M
Quality Management	M,O
Quantitative Analysis	M
Reading Education	M,D,O
Science Education	M,O
Secondary Education	M,O
Social Sciences Education	M
Special Education	M,O
Taxation	M

HOLLINS UNIVERSITY

Education—General	M

HOLY FAMILY UNIVERSITY

Business Administration and Management— General	M
Education—General	M
Elementary Education	M
Human Resources Management	M
Management Information Systems	M
Nursing—General	M
Reading Education	M
Secondary Education	M

HOLY NAMES UNIVERSITY

Business Administration and Management— General	M
Community Health Nursing	M
Curriculum and Instruction	M,O
Education—General	M,O
Educational Psychology	M,O
English as a Second Language	M,O
Family Nurse Practitioner Studies	M
Music Education	M,O
Nursing—General	M
Special Education	M,O
Urban Education	M,O

HOOD COLLEGE

Business Administration and Management— General	M
Curriculum and Instruction	M,O
Early Childhood Education	M,O
Education—General	M,O
Educational Administration	M,O
Elementary Education	M,O
Foreign Languages Education	O
Mathematics Education	M,O

Reading Education	M,O
Science Education	M,O
Secondary Education	M,O
Special Education	M,O

HOPE INTERNATIONAL UNIVERSITY

Education—General	M
International Business	M
Nonprofit Management	M

HOUSTON BAPTIST UNIVERSITY

Accounting	M
Business Administration and Management— General	M
Counselor Education	M
Curriculum and Instruction	M
Education—General	M
Educational Administration	M
Educational Measurement and Evaluation	M
English as a Second Language	M
Health Services Management and Hospital Administration	M
Human Resources Management	M
Reading Education	M

HOWARD UNIVERSITY

Accounting	M
Allopathic Medicine	P,D
Business Administration and Management— General	M
Communication Disorders	M,D
Counselor Education	M,O
Dentistry	P,O
Early Childhood Education	M,O
Education—General	M,D,O
Educational Administration	M,D,O
Educational Psychology	M,D,O
Elementary Education	M
Exercise and Sports Science	M
Family Nurse Practitioner Studies	M,O
Finance and Banking	M
Health Education	M
International Business	M
Law	P,M
Leisure Studies	M
Management Information Systems	M
Marketing	M
Multilingual and Multicultural Education	M,D
Music Education	M
Nursing—General	M,O
Oral and Dental Sciences	P,O
Pharmacy	P
Physical Education	M
Reading Education	M,O
Recreation and Park Management	M
Secondary Education	M,O
Social Work	M,D
Special Education	M,O
Sports Management	M
Supply Chain Management	M

HULT INTERNATIONAL BUSINESS SCHOOL

Business Administration and Management— General	M

HUMBOLDT STATE UNIVERSITY

Athletic Training and Sports Medicine	M
Business Administration and Management— General	M
Education—General	M
Exercise and Sports Science	M .
Kinesiology and Movement Studies	M
Physical Education	M
Physical Therapy	M
Social Work	M

HUMPHREYS COLLEGE

Law	P

HUNTER COLLEGE OF THE CITY UNIVERSITY OF NEW YORK

Accounting	M
Adult Nursing	M
Communication Disorders	M
Community Health Nursing	M
Counselor Education	M
Early Childhood Education	M,O
Education of the Multiply Handicapped	M
Education—General	M,O
Educational Administration	O
Elementary Education	M
English as a Second Language	M
English Education	M
Environmental and Occupational Health	M
Family Nurse Practitioner Studies	M,O
Foreign Languages Education	M
Gerontological Nursing	M
Maternal and Child/ Neonatal Nursing	M
Mathematics Education	M
Medical/Surgical Nursing	M
Multilingual and Multicultural Education	M
Music Education	M
Nursing—General	M,O
Pediatric Nursing	M,O
Physical Therapy	M
Psychiatric Nursing	M
Public Health—General	M
Reading Education	M,O
Science Education	M,O
Secondary Education	M
Social Sciences Education	M
Social Work	M,D
Special Education	M

HURON UNIVERSITY USA IN LONDON

Advertising and Public Relations	M
Business Administration and Management— General	M
Entrepreneurship	M
Finance and Banking	M
International Business	M
Marketing	M

HUSSON COLLEGE

Business Administration and Management— General	M
Family Nurse Practitioner Studies	M

Nursing—General — M
Physical Therapy — M
Psychiatric Nursing — M

ICR GRADUATE SCHOOL
Science Education — M

IDAHO STATE UNIVERSITY
Allied Health—General — M,D,O
Business Administration and Management—
General — M,O
Communication Disorders — M,D
Community Health — O
Counselor Education — M,D,O
Curriculum and Instruction — M,O
Dental Hygiene — M,O
Dentistry — M,O
Education—General — M,D,O
Educational Administration — M,D,O
Educational Media/ Instructional Technology — M,D,O
Elementary Education — M,O
Health Education — M
Management Information Systems — M,O
Mathematics Education — M,D
Medicinal and Pharmaceutical Chemistry — M,D
Nursing—General — M,O
Occupational Therapy — M
Oral and Dental Sciences — M,O
Pharmaceutical Administration — P,M,D
Pharmaceutical Sciences — M,D
Pharmacy — P,M,D
Physical Education — M
Physical Therapy — D
Physician Assistant Studies — M
Public Health—General — M,O
Reading Education — M,O
Secondary Education — M,O
Special Education — M,D,O
Vocational and Technical Education — M

ILLINOIS COLLEGE OF OPTOMETRY
Optometry — P

ILLINOIS INSTITUTE OF TECHNOLOGY
Business Administration and Management—
General — M,D
Entrepreneurship — M
Environmental and Occupational Health — M
Finance and Banking — P,M
Health Physics/ Radiological Health — M,D
Health Services Management and Hospital Administration — M
Human Resources Development — M,D
Industrial and Manufacturing Management — M
International Business — M
Law — P,M
Management Information Systems — M,D
Management Strategy and Policy — M
Marketing — M
Mathematics Education — M,D

Nonprofit Management — M
Quality Management — M
Science Education — M,D
Taxation — P,M

ILLINOIS STATE UNIVERSITY
Accounting — M
Business Administration and Management—
General — M
Communication Disorders — M
Counselor Education — M,D
Curriculum and Instruction — M,D
Education—General — M,D
Educational Administration — M,D
Educational Policy — M,D
Educational Psychology — M,D,O
Health Education — M
Higher Education — M,D
Management Information Systems — M
Mathematics Education — D
Nurse Midwifery — M,O
Nursing—General — M,O
Physical Education — M
Reading Education — M
Social Work — M
Special Education — M,D

IMCA–INTERNATIONAL MANAGEMENT CENTRES ASSOCIATION
Business Administration and Management—
General — M,D

IMMACULATA UNIVERSITY
Counselor Education — M,D,O
Educational Administration — M,D,O
Elementary Education — M,D,O
Multilingual and Multicultural Education — M
Nursing—General — M
Organizational Management — M
Secondary Education — M,D,O
Special Education — M,D,O

INDIANA STATE UNIVERSITY
Athletic Training and Sports Medicine — M,D
Business Administration and Management—
General — M
Communication Disorders — M
Community Health — M
Counselor Education — M,D
Curriculum and Instruction — M,D
Early Childhood Education — M
Education—General — M,D,O
Educational Administration — M,D,O
Educational Media/ Instructional Technology — M,D
Educational Psychology — M,D,O
Elementary Education — M
English as a Second Language — M,O
Environmental and Occupational Health — M
Exercise and Sports Science — M
Health Education — M
Health Promotion — M
Home Economics Education — M
Human Resources Development — M
Multilingual and Multicultural Education — M,O

Nursing—General — M
Physical Education — M
Reading Education — M
Science Education — M,D
Sports Management — M
Vocational and Technical Education — M

INDIANA TECH
Accounting — M
Business Administration and Management—
General — M
Human Resources Development — M
Human Resources Management — M
Marketing — M
Science Education — M

INDIANA UNIVERSITY BLOOMINGTON
Art Education — M,D,O
Athletic Training and Sports Medicine — M,D,O
Business Administration and Management—
General — M,D
Communication Disorders — M,D
Counselor Education — M,D,O
Curriculum and Instruction — M,D,O
Education—General — M,D,O*
Educational Administration — M,D,O
Educational Media/ Instructional Technology — M,D,O
Educational Policy — M,D,O
Educational Psychology — M,D,O
Elementary Education — M,D,O
Exercise and Sports Science — M,D,O
Foreign Languages Education — M,D
Foundations and Philosophy of Education — M,D,O
Health Education — M,D
Health Promotion — M,D
Higher Education — M,D,O
Information Studies — M,D,O
International and Comparative Education — M,D,O
Kinesiology and Movement Studies — M,D,O
Law — P,M,D,O
Leisure Studies — M,D,O
Library Science — M,D,O*
Mathematics Education — M,D,O
Nonprofit Management — M,D,O
Optometry — P,M,D
Physical Education — M,D,O
Public Health—General — M,D
Reading Education — M,D,O
Recreation and Park Management — M,D,O
Science Education — M,D,O
Secondary Education — M,D,O
Social Sciences Education — M,D,O
Special Education — M,D,O
Sports Management — M,D,O

INDIANA UNIVERSITY KOKOMO
Business Administration and Management—
General — M
Education—General — M
Elementary Education — M
Secondary Education — M

INDIANA UNIVERSITY NORTHWEST
Accounting — M,O

Business Administration and Management—
General — M,O
Education—General — M
Elementary Education — M
Health Services Management and Hospital Administration — M,O
Human Services — M,O
Nonprofit Management — M,O
Secondary Education — M
Social Work — M

INDIANA UNIVERSITY OF PENNSYLVANIA
Adult Education — M
Business Administration and Management—
General — M
Communication Disorders — M
Counselor Education — M
Curriculum and Instruction — M,D
Early Childhood Education — M
Education—General — M,D,O
Educational Administration — M,D,O
Educational Media/ Instructional Technology — M
Educational Psychology — M,O
English as a Second Language — M,D
English Education — M,D
Environmental and Occupational Health — M
Exercise and Sports Science — M
Facilities Management — M
Health Education — M
Higher Education — M
Human Resources Development — M
Mathematics Education — M
Music Education — M
Nursing—General — M
Physical Education — M
Reading Education — M
Special Education — M
Sports Management — M

INDIANA UNIVERSITY–PURDUE UNIVERSITY FORT WAYNE
Business Administration and Management—
General — M
Counselor Education — M
Education—General — M
Educational Administration — M
Elementary Education — M
English as a Second Language — M,O
English Education — M,O
Nursing and Healthcare Administration — M,O
Nursing—General — M,O
Organizational Management — M
Secondary Education — M

INDIANA UNIVERSITY–PURDUE UNIVERSITY INDIANAPOLIS
Acute Care/Critical Care Nursing — M
Adult Nursing — M
Art Education — M
Bioethics — M,D,O
Business Administration and Management—
General — M
Community Health Nursing — M,D
Dentistry — P,M,D,O
Education—General — M,O

English Education	M
Family Nurse Practitioner Studies	M
Health Education	M,D
Health Services Management and Hospital Administration	M
Law	P,M,D
Library Science	M
Maternal and Child/ Neonatal Nursing	M,D
Mathematics Education	M
Nonprofit Management	M
Nursing—General	M,D
Occupational Therapy	M,D
Pediatric Nursing	M,D
Physical Education	M
Physical Therapy	M,D
Psychiatric Nursing	M,D
Public Health—General	M
Rehabilitation Sciences	M,D
Social Work	M,D,O
Travel and Tourism	M
Women's Health Nursing	M,D

INDIANA UNIVERSITY SCHOOL OF LAW-BLOOMINGTON

Law	P,M,D,O
Legal and Justice Studies	P,M,D,O

INDIANA UNIVERSITY SCHOOL OF LAW-INDIANAPOLIS

Law	P,M

INDIANA UNIVERSITY SOUTH BEND

Accounting	M
Business Administration and Management— General	M
Counselor Education	M
Education—General	M
Elementary Education	M
Health Services Management and Hospital Administration	M,O
Management Information Systems	M
Nonprofit Management	M,O
Secondary Education	M
Social Work	M
Special Education	M

INDIANA UNIVERSITY SOUTHEAST

Accounting	M,O
Business Administration and Management— General	M,O
Counselor Education	M
Education—General	M
Elementary Education	M
Finance and Banking	M,O
Industrial and Manufacturing Management	M,O
Management Information Systems	M,O
Marketing	M,O
Secondary Education	M

INDIANA WESLEYAN UNIVERSITY

Accounting	M
Business Administration and Management— General	M
Community Health Nursing	M,O
Counselor Education	M

Curriculum and Instruction	M
Education—General	M
Health Services Management and Hospital Administration	M
Nursing and Healthcare Administration	M,O
Nursing Education	M,O
Nursing—General	M,O
Organizational Management	D
Religious Education	M

INSTITUTE FOR CHRISTIAN STUDIES

Education—General	M,D

INSTITUTE FOR CLINICAL SOCIAL WORK

Social Work	D

INSTITUTE OF CLINICAL ACUPUNCTURE AND ORIENTAL MEDICINE

Acupuncture and Oriental Medicine	M

INSTITUTE OF PUBLIC ADMINISTRATION

Health Services Management and Hospital Administration	M,O

INSTITUT FRANCO-EUROPÉEN DE CHIROPRATIQUE

Chiropractic	P

INSTITUTO CENTROAMERICANO DE ADMINISTRACIÓN DE EMPRESAS

Business Administration and Management— General	M

INSTITUTO TECNOLOGICO DE SANTO DOMINGO

Allopathic Medicine	P,M
Business Administration and Management— General	M
Education—General	M
Finance and Banking	M
Human Resources Management	M
Social Sciences Education	M

INSTITUTO TECNOLÓGICO Y DE ESTUDIOS SUPERIORES DE MONTERREY, CAMPUS CENTRAL DE VERACRUZ

Business Administration and Management— General	M
Education—General	M
Educational Administration	M
Educational Media/ Instructional Technology	M
Electronic Commerce	M
Finance and Banking	M
International Business	M
Management Information Systems	M
Marketing	M

INSTITUTO TECNOLÓGICO Y DE ESTUDIOS SUPERIORES DE MONTERREY, CAMPUS CHIHUAHUA

International Business	M,O

INSTITUTO TECNOLÓGICO Y DE ESTUDIOS SUPERIORES DE MONTERREY, CAMPUS CIUDAD DE MÉXICO

Business Administration and Management— General	M,D
Education—General	M,D
Educational Media/ Instructional Technology	M,D
Finance and Banking	M,D
International Business	M,D
Law	P
Management Information Systems	M,D
Quality Management	M,D

INSTITUTO TECNOLÓGICO Y DE ESTUDIOS SUPERIORES DE MONTERREY, CAMPUS CIUDAD JUÁREZ

Business Administration and Management— General	M
Education—General	M
Finance and Banking	M
Management Information Systems	M
Quality Management	M

INSTITUTO TECNOLÓGICO Y DE ESTUDIOS SUPERIORES DE MONTERREY, CAMPUS CIUDAD OBREGÓN

Business Administration and Management— General	M
Developmental Education	M
Education—General	M
Finance and Banking	M
Management Information Systems	M
Marketing	M
Mathematics Education	M

INSTITUTO TECNOLÓGICO Y DE ESTUDIOS SUPERIORES DE MONTERREY, CAMPUS CUERNAVACA

Business Administration and Management— General	M
Finance and Banking	M
Human Resources Management	M
International Business	M
Marketing	M

INSTITUTO TECNOLÓGICO Y DE ESTUDIOS SUPERIORES DE MONTERREY, CAMPUS ESTADO DE MÉXICO

Business Administration and Management— General	M,D
Education—General	M,D
Educational Administration	M,D
Educational Media/ Instructional Technology	M,D
Electronic Commerce	M,D
Finance and Banking	M,D

Industrial and Manufacturing Management	M,D
Management Information Systems	M,D
Marketing	M,D
Quality Management	M,D

INSTITUTO TECNOLÓGICO Y DE ESTUDIOS SUPERIORES DE MONTERREY, CAMPUS GUADALAJARA

Business Administration and Management— General	M
Finance and Banking	M

INSTITUTO TECNOLÓGICO Y DE ESTUDIOS SUPERIORES DE MONTERREY, CAMPUS IRAPUATO

Business Administration and Management— General	M,D
Education—General	M,D
Educational Administration	M,D
Educational Media/ Instructional Technology	M,D
Electronic Commerce	M,D
Finance and Banking	M,D
Industrial and Manufacturing Management	M,D
International Business	M,D
Library Science	M,D
Management Information Systems	M,D
Marketing Research	M,D
Quality Management	M,D

INSTITUTO TECNOLÓGICO Y DE ESTUDIOS SUPERIORES DE MONTERREY, CAMPUS LAGUNA

Business Administration and Management— General	M
Management Information Systems	M

INSTITUTO TECNOLÓGICO Y DE ESTUDIOS SUPERIORES DE MONTERREY, CAMPUS LEÓN

Business Administration and Management— General	M

INSTITUTO TECNOLÓGICO Y DE ESTUDIOS SUPERIORES DE MONTERREY, CAMPUS MONTERREY

Business Administration and Management— General	M,D
Finance and Banking	M
International Business	M
Marketing	M
Science Education	M,D

INSTITUTO TECNOLÓGICO Y DE ESTUDIOS SUPERIORES DE MONTERREY, CAMPUS QUERÉTARO

Business Administration and Management— General	M

INSTITUTO TECNOLÓGICO Y DE ESTUDIOS SUPERIORES DE MONTERREY, CAMPUS SONORA NORTE

Business Administration and Management— General	M
Education—General	M

INSTITUTO TECNOLÓGICO Y DE ESTUDIOS SUPERIORES DE MONTERREY, CAMPUS TOLUCA

Business Administration and Management— General	M

INTER AMERICAN UNIVERSITY OF PUERTO RICO, AGUADILLA CAMPUS

Educational Administration	M
Elementary Education	M

INTER AMERICAN UNIVERSITY OF PUERTO RICO, ARECIBO CAMPUS

Community Health Nursing	M
Counselor Education	M
Education—General	M
Educational Administration	M
Nurse Anesthesia	M
Nursing—General	M

INTER AMERICAN UNIVERSITY OF PUERTO RICO, BARRANQUITAS CAMPUS

Education—General	M
Educational Administration	M
Elementary Education	M

INTER AMERICAN UNIVERSITY OF PUERTO RICO, BAYAMÓN CAMPUS

Electronic Commerce	M
Human Resources Management	M

INTER AMERICAN UNIVERSITY OF PUERTO RICO, GUAYAMA CAMPUS

Early Childhood Education	M

INTER AMERICAN UNIVERSITY OF PUERTO RICO, METROPOLITAN CAMPUS

Accounting	M
Business Administration and Management— General	M,D
Business Education	M
Clinical Laboratory Sciences/Medical Technology	M
Counselor Education	M
Education—General	M,D
Educational Administration	M
Educational Media/ Instructional Technology	M
Elementary Education	M
English as a Second Language	M
Finance and Banking	M
Health Education	M
Higher Education	M
Human Resources Development	

Human Resources Management	M
Industrial and Manufacturing Management	M
Marketing	M
Physical Education	M
Science Education	M
Social Work	M
Special Education	M
Vocational and Technical Education	M

INTER AMERICAN UNIVERSITY OF PUERTO RICO, PONCE CAMPUS

Accounting	M
Elementary Education	M
English as a Second Language	M
Finance and Banking	M
Human Resources Management	M
International Business	M
Mathematics Education	M
Science Education	M
Social Sciences Education	M

INTER AMERICAN UNIVERSITY OF PUERTO RICO, SAN GERMÁN CAMPUS

Accounting	M,D
Business Administration and Management— General	M,D
Business Education	M
Counselor Education	M
Educational Administration	M
Elementary Education	M
English as a Second Language	M
Entrepreneurship	D
Finance and Banking	M,D
Human Resources Development	M,D
Human Resources Management	M,D
International Business	M,D
Kinesiology and Movement Studies	M
Library Science	M
Management Information Systems	M,D
Marketing	M,D
Music Education	M
Physical Education	M
Science Education	M
Special Education	M

INTER AMERICAN UNIVERSITY OF PUERTO RICO SCHOOL OF LAW

Law	P

INTER AMERICAN UNIVERSITY OF PUERTO RICO SCHOOL OF OPTOMETRY

Optometry	P

INTERNATIONAL COLLEGE OF THE CAYMAN ISLANDS

Business Administration and Management— General	M
Business Education	M
Human Resources Management	M

INTERNATIONAL TECHNOLOGICAL UNIVERSITY

Business Administration and Management— General	M

INTERNATIONAL UNIVERSITY IN GENEVA

Business Administration and Management— General	M
Electronic Commerce	M
Human Resources Management	M
International Business	M
Marketing	M
Organizational Management	M

THE INTERNATIONAL UNIVERSITY OF MONACO

Business Administration and Management— General	M
Entrepreneurship	M
Finance and Banking	M
International Business	M
Marketing	M

IONA COLLEGE

Advertising and Public Relations	M
Business Administration and Management— General	M,O*
Educational Administration	M
Educational Media/ Instructional Technology	M,O
Elementary Education	M
English Education	M
Finance and Banking	M,O
Foreign Languages Education	M
Health Services Management and Hospital Administration	M,O
Human Resources Management	M,O
International Business	M,O
Marketing	M,O
Mathematics Education	M
Multilingual and Multicultural Education	M
Science Education	M
Secondary Education	M
Social Sciences Education	M

IOWA STATE UNIVERSITY OF SCIENCE AND TECHNOLOGY

Accounting	M
Agricultural Education	M,D
Art Education	M
Business Administration and Management— General	M
Counselor Education	M,D
Curriculum and Instruction	M,D
Educational Administration	M,D
Educational Measurement and Evaluation	M,D
Educational Media/ Instructional Technology	M,D
Elementary Education	M,D
Exercise and Sports Science	M,D
Foundations and Philosophy of Education	M,D
Health Education	M,D
Higher Education	M,D

Home Economics Education	M,D
Hospitality Management	M,D
Human Resources Development	M,D
Management Information Systems	M
Mathematics Education	M,D
Physical Education	M,D
Special Education	M,D
Transportation Management	M
Veterinary Medicine	P,M
Veterinary Sciences	M,D
Vocational and Technical Education	M,D

ITHACA COLLEGE

Accounting	M
Allied Health—General	M,D
Business Administration and Management— General	M
Communication Disorders	M
English Education	M
Exercise and Sports Science	M
Foreign Languages Education	M
Health Education	M
Mathematics Education	M
Music Education	M
Occupational Therapy	M
Physical Education	M
Physical Therapy	D
Science Education	M
Secondary Education	M
Social Sciences Education	M
Sports Management	M

ITT TECHNICAL INSTITUTE (IN)

Business Administration and Management— General	M

JACKSON STATE UNIVERSITY

Accounting	M
Business Administration and Management— General	M,D
Communication Disorders	M
Counselor Education	M,O
Early Childhood Education	M,D,O
Education—General	M,D,O
Educational Administration	M,D,O
Educational Media/ Instructional Technology	M,D,O
Elementary Education	M,D,O
English Education	M
Health Education	M
Mathematics Education	M
Music Education	M
Physical Education	M
Science Education	M,D
Secondary Education	M,D,O
Social Work	M,D
Special Education	M,O
Vocational and Technical Education	M

JACKSONVILLE STATE UNIVERSITY

Business Administration and Management— General	M
Counselor Education	M
Early Childhood Education	M
Education—General	M,O
Educational Administration	M,O

Educational Media/	
Instructional Technology	M
Elementary Education	M
Health Education	M
Nursing—General	M
Physical Education	M
Reading Education	M
Secondary Education	M
Special Education	M

JACKSONVILLE UNIVERSITY

Business Administration	
and Management—	
General	M
Computer Education	M
Early Childhood Education	M,O
Education—General	M,O
Educational Media/	
Instructional Technology	M
Elementary Education	M
Mathematics Education	M
Music Education	M
Nursing—General	M
Oral and Dental Sciences	O
Reading Education	M

JAMES MADISON UNIVERSITY

Accounting	M
Art Education	M
Business Administration	
and Management—	
General	M
Communication Disorders	M,D
Early Childhood Education	M
Educational Administration	M
Health Education	M
Kinesiology and	
Movement Studies	M
Middle School Education	M
Music Education	M
Nursing—General	M
Occupational Therapy	M
Physician Assistant	
Studies	M
Reading Education	M
Secondary Education	M
Special Education	M
Vocational and Technical	
Education	M

JEFFERSON COLLEGE OF HEALTH SCIENCES

Nursing and Healthcare	
Administration	M
Nursing Education	M
Nursing—General	M

THE JEWISH THEOLOGICAL SEMINARY

| Religious Education | M,D* |

JEWISH UNIVERSITY OF AMERICA

| Religious Education | M,D |

JOHN BROWN UNIVERSITY

Business Administration	
and Management—	
General	M
Counselor Education	M

JOHN CARROLL UNIVERSITY

Accounting	M
Business Administration	
and Management—	
General	M
Counselor Education	M,O

Early Childhood Education	M
Education—General	M
Educational Administration	M
Educational Psychology	M
Middle School Education	M
Nonprofit Management	M
Science Education	M
Secondary Education	M

JOHN F. KENNEDY UNIVERSITY

Business Administration	
and Management—	
General	M,O
Education—General	M
Health Education	M
Human Resources	
Development	M,O
Law	P
Organizational	
Management	M,O

JOHN JAY COLLEGE OF CRIMINAL JUSTICE OF THE CITY UNIVERSITY OF NEW YORK

| Legal and Justice Studies | M,D |
| Organizational Behavior | M,D |

JOHN MARSHALL LAW SCHOOL

International Business	P,M
Law	P,M
Legal and Justice Studies	P,M
Management Information	
Systems	P,M
Real Estate	P,M
Taxation	P,M

THE JOHNS HOPKINS UNIVERSITY

Acute Care/Critical Care	
Nursing	M,O
Adult Nursing	M,O
Allopathic Medicine	P
Business Administration	
and Management—	
General	M,O
Clinical Research	M,D
Community Health	
Nursing	M
Community Health	M,D
Counselor Education	M,O
Curriculum and Instruction	M
Education of the Gifted	M,D,O
Education—General	M,D,O
Educational Administration	M,D,O
Educational Media/	
Instructional Technology	M,D,O
Elementary Education	M
English as a Second	
Language	M
Environmental and	
Occupational Health	M,D
Epidemiology	M,D
Family Nurse Practitioner	
Studies	M,O
Finance and Banking	M,O
Health Education	M,D
Health Services	
Management and	
Hospital Administration	M,D,O
Health Services Research	M,D
Human Resources	
Development	M,O
International Health	M,D
Investment Management	M,O
Law	M,D,O
Management Information	
Systems	M,O
Marketing	M
Nursing and Healthcare	
Administration	M

Nursing—General	M,D,O
Pediatric Nursing	M,O
Public Health—General	M,D*
Reading Education	M,D,O
Real Estate	M
Science Education	M,D,O
Secondary Education	M
Special Education	M,D,O
Urban Education	M,D,O

JOHNSON & WALES UNIVERSITY

Accounting	M
Education—General	M
Educational Administration	D
Finance and Banking	M,O
Hospitality Management	M,O
Human Resources	
Development	O
International Business	M
Marketing	M
Organizational	
Management	M

JOHNSON BIBLE COLLEGE

Education—General	M
Educational Media/	
Instructional Technology	M

JOHNSON STATE COLLEGE

Counselor Education	M
Curriculum and Instruction	M
Education of the Gifted	M
Education—General	M,O
Educational Psychology	M
Reading Education	M
Science Education	M
Secondary Education	M,O
Special Education	M

JONES INTERNATIONAL UNIVERSITY

Accounting	M
Adult Education	M
Business Administration	
and Management—	
General	M
Curriculum and Instruction	M
Distance Education	
Development	M
Education—General	M
Educational Administration	M
Educational Media/	
Instructional Technology	M
Elementary Education	M
Entrepreneurship	M
Finance and Banking	M
Health Services	
Management and	
Hospital Administration	M
Higher Education	M
Organizational	
Management	M
Project Management	M
Secondary Education	M

THE JUDGE ADVOCATE GENERAL'S SCHOOL, U.S. ARMY

| Law | M |

KANSAS CITY UNIVERSITY OF MEDICINE AND BIOSCIENCES

| Bioethics | M |
| Osteopathic Medicine | P |

KANSAS STATE UNIVERSITY

| Accounting | M |

Adult Education	M,D
Business Administration	
and Management—	
General	M
Counselor Education	M,D
Curriculum and Instruction	M,D
Education—General	M,D
Educational Administration	M,D
Educational Psychology	M,D
Elementary Education	M,D
Hospitality Management	M,D
Human Services	M
Kinesiology and	
Movement Studies	M
Music Education	M
Public Health—General	M
Secondary Education	M,D
Special Education	M,D
Student Affairs	M,D
Veterinary Medicine	P
Veterinary Sciences	M

KANSAS WESLEYAN UNIVERSITY

Business Administration	
and Management—	
General	M

KEAN UNIVERSITY

Accounting	M
Adult Education	M
Art Education	M
Business Administration	
and Management—	
General	M
Communication Disorders	M
Community Health	
Nursing	M
Computer Education	M
Counselor Education	M,O
Curriculum and Instruction	M
Early Childhood Education	M
Education—General	M,O
Educational Administration	M
Educational Media/	
Instructional Technology	M
Educational Psychology	M
English as a Second	
Language	M
Exercise and Sports	
Science	M
Health Services	
Management and	
Hospital Administration	M
International Business	M
Management Information	
Systems	M
Mathematics Education	M
Multilingual and	
Multicultural Education	M
Nonprofit Management	M
Nursing and Healthcare	
Administration	M
Nursing—General	M
Occupational Therapy	M
Reading Education	M
Science Education	M
Social Work	M
Special Education	M

KEENE STATE COLLEGE

Counselor Education	M,O
Curriculum and Instruction	M
Education—General	M,O
Educational Administration	M,O
Special Education	M,O

KELLER GRADUATE SCHOOL OF MANAGEMENT

Business Administration	
and Management—	
General	M

KELLER GRADUATE SCHOOL OF MANAGEMENT

Business Administration and Management— General	M

KENNESAW STATE UNIVERSITY

Accounting	M
Business Administration and Management— General	M
Early Childhood Education	M
Education—General	M
Educational Administration	M,D,O
Family Nurse Practitioner Studies	M
Health Services Management and Hospital Administration	M
Middle School Education	M
Nursing—General	M
Social Work	M
Special Education	M

KENT STATE UNIVERSITY

Accounting	M,D
Art Education	M
Athletic Training and Sports Medicine	M
Business Administration and Management— General	M*
Communication Disorders	M,D
Counselor Education	M,D,O
Curriculum and Instruction	M,D,O
Early Childhood Education	M
Education of the Gifted	M
Education—General	M,D,O
Educational Administration	M,D,O
Educational Measurement and Evaluation	M,D
Educational Media/ Instructional Technology	M
Educational Psychology	M,D
Elementary Education	M,D,O
English as a Second Language	M,D
English Education	M,D
Exercise and Sports Science	M,D
Finance and Banking	D
Foundations and Philosophy of Education	M,D
Health Education	M,D
Higher Education	M
Human Services	M,D,O
Library Science	M
Management Information Systems	D
Marketing	D
Medical/Surgical Nursing	M,D
Middle School Education	M
Music Education	M,D
Nursing and Healthcare Administration	M,D
Nursing Education	M,D
Nursing—General	M,D
Pediatric Nursing	M,D
Physical Education	M,D
Psychiatric Nursing	M,D
Public Health—General	M
Reading Education	M
Recreation and Park Management	M
Secondary Education	M
Special Education	M,D,O
Sports Management	M
Student Affairs	M
Vocational and Technical Education	M,O

KENTUCKY STATE UNIVERSITY

Business Administration and Management— General	M
Special Education	M

KETTERING UNIVERSITY

Business Administration and Management— General	M
Industrial and Manufacturing Management	M

KEUKA COLLEGE

Business Administration and Management— General	M
Early Childhood Education	M
Occupational Therapy	M

KING COLLEGE

Business Administration and Management— General	M

KING'S COLLEGE

Business Administration and Management— General	M
Health Services Management and Hospital Administration	M
Physician Assistant Studies	M
Reading Education	M

KUTZTOWN UNIVERSITY OF PENNSYLVANIA

Art Education	M,O
Business Administration and Management— General	M
Counselor Education	M
Curriculum and Instruction	M,O
Early Childhood Education	M,O
Education—General	M,O
Educational Administration	M
Educational Media/ Instructional Technology	M,O
Elementary Education	M,O
English Education	M,O
Library Science	M,O
Mathematics Education	M,O
Music Education	O
Reading Education	M
School Nursing	O
Science Education	M,O
Secondary Education	M,O
Social Sciences Education	M,O
Social Work	M
Special Education	M,O

LAGRANGE COLLEGE

Art Education	M
Curriculum and Instruction	M
Education—General	M
Music Education	M
Secondary Education	M

LAKE ERIE COLLEGE

Business Administration and Management— General	M
Curriculum and Instruction	M
Education—General	M

Educational Administration	M
Health Services Management and Hospital Administration	M
Reading Education	M

LAKE ERIE COLLEGE OF OSTEOPATHIC MEDICINE

Health Education	P,M,O
Osteopathic Medicine	P,M,O
Pharmacy	P,M,O

LAKE FOREST GRADUATE SCHOOL OF MANAGEMENT

Business Administration and Management— General	M

LAKEHEAD UNIVERSITY

Curriculum and Instruction	M,D
Education—General	M,D
Educational Administration	M,D
Exercise and Sports Science	M
Physical Education	M
Social Work	M

LAKELAND COLLEGE

Business Administration and Management— General	M
Education—General	M

LAMAR UNIVERSITY

Accounting	M
Business Administration and Management— General	M
Communication Disorders	M,D
Counselor Education	M,D,O
Education—General	M,D,O
Educational Administration	M,D,O
Educational Media/ Instructional Technology	M,D,O
Entrepreneurship	M
Finance and Banking	M
Health Services Management and Hospital Administration	M
Kinesiology and Movement Studies	M
Management Strategy and Policy	M
Music Education	M
Nursing and Healthcare Administration	M
Nursing Education	M
Nursing—General	M
Special Education	M,D

LANCASTER BIBLE COLLEGE

Counselor Education	M
Special Education	M

LANDER UNIVERSITY

Curriculum and Instruction	M
Education—General	M
Elementary Education	M

LANGSTON UNIVERSITY

Education—General	M
Elementary Education	M
English as a Second Language	M

Multilingual and Multicultural Education	M
Physical Therapy	D
Urban Education	M

LA ROCHE COLLEGE

Family Nurse Practitioner Studies	M
Human Resources Management	M,O
Nurse Anesthesia	M
Nursing and Healthcare Administration	M
Nursing—General	M

LA SALLE UNIVERSITY

Adult Nursing	M,O
Business Administration and Management— General	M,O
Communication Disorders	M
Community Health Nursing	M,O
Education—General	M
Family Nurse Practitioner Studies	M,O
Medical/Surgical Nursing	M,O
Nursing and Healthcare Administration	M,O
Nursing Education	M,O
Nursing Informatics	M,O
Nursing—General	M,O
School Nursing	M,O

LASELL COLLEGE

Business Administration and Management— General	M*
Marketing	M

LA SIERRA UNIVERSITY

Business Administration and Management— General	M,O
Counselor Education	M,O
Curriculum and Instruction	M,D,O
Education—General	M,D,O
Educational Administration	M,D,O
Educational Psychology	M,O
Religious Education	M
Special Education	M,D,O

LAURA AND ALVIN SIEGAL COLLEGE OF JUDAIC STUDIES

Religious Education	M

LAURENTIAN UNIVERSITY

Business Administration and Management— General	M
Social Work	M

LAWRENCE TECHNOLOGICAL UNIVERSITY

Business Administration and Management— General	M,D
Educational Media/ Instructional Technology	M
Industrial and Manufacturing Management	M,D
Management Information Systems	M,D
Science Education	M

LEADERSHIP INSTITUTE OF SEATTLE

Organizational Behavior	M
Organizational Management	M

LEBANESE AMERICAN UNIVERSITY

Business Administration and Management— General	M
Pharmacy	P

LEBANON VALLEY COLLEGE

Business Administration and Management— General	M
Music Education	M
Science Education	M

LEE UNIVERSITY

Counselor Education	M
Education—General	M
Educational Administration	M
Elementary Education	M
Music Education	M
Secondary Education	M
Special Education	M

LEHIGH UNIVERSITY

Accounting	M*
Business Administration and Management— General	M,D,O*
Counselor Education	M,D,O
Education—General	M,D,O
Educational Administration	M,D,O
Educational Media/ Instructional Technology	M,D,O
Elementary Education	M,D
Finance and Banking	M
Human Services	M,D,O
Medicinal and Pharmaceutical Chemistry	M,D
Organizational Management	M,D,O
Project Management	M,D,O
Quantitative Analysis	M*
Secondary Education	M,D
Special Education	M,D,O
Supply Chain Management	M,D,O

LEHMAN COLLEGE OF THE CITY UNIVERSITY OF NEW YORK

Accounting	M
Adult Nursing	M
Business Education	M
Communication Disorders	M
Counselor Education	M
Early Childhood Education	M
Education—General	M
Elementary Education	M
English as a Second Language	M
English Education	M
Gerontological Nursing	M
Health Education	M
Health Promotion	M
Maternal and Child/ Neonatal Nursing	M
Mathematics Education	M
Multilingual and Multicultural Education	M
Music Education	M
Nursing—General	M
Pediatric Nursing	M

Reading Education	M
Recreation and Park Management	M
Science Education	M
Social Sciences Education	M
Special Education	M

LE MOYNE COLLEGE

Business Administration and Management— General	M
Education—General	M
Nursing—General	M
Physician Assistant Studies	M

LENOIR-RHYNE COLLEGE

Business Administration and Management— General	M
Counselor Education	M
Early Childhood Education	M
Education—General	M
Reading Education	M

LESLEY UNIVERSITY

Art Education	M,D,O
Computer Education	M,D,O
Curriculum and Instruction	M,D,O
Early Childhood Education	M,D,O
Education—General	M,D,O*
Elementary Education	M,D,O
Environmental Education	M,D,O
Middle School Education	M,D,O
Reading Education	M,D,O
Science Education	M,D,O
Special Education	M,D,O

LETOURNEAU UNIVERSITY

Business Administration and Management— General	M
Educational Administration	M

LEWIS & CLARK COLLEGE

Communication Disorders	M
Education—General	M,D,O
Educational Administration	M,D
Elementary Education	M
Law	P,M
Secondary Education	M
Special Education	M

LEWIS UNIVERSITY

Business Administration and Management— General	M
Counselor Education	M
Curriculum and Instruction	M
Education—General	M,O
Educational Administration	M
Nursing and Healthcare Administration	M
Nursing Education	M
Nursing—General	M
Organizational Management	M
Special Education	M
Student Affairs	M

LIBERTY UNIVERSITY

Business Administration and Management— General	M
Counselor Education	M,D,O
Curriculum and Instruction	M,D,O

Early Childhood Education	M,D,O
Education of the Gifted	M,D,O
Education—General	M,D,O
Educational Administration	M,D,O
Elementary Education	M,D,O
Law	P
Nursing—General	M,D
Reading Education	M,D,O
Secondary Education	M,D,O
Special Education	M,D,O

LIFE CHIROPRACTIC COLLEGE WEST

Chiropractic	P*

LIFE UNIVERSITY

Chiropractic	P
Exercise and Sports Science	M

LINCOLN MEMORIAL UNIVERSITY

Business Administration and Management— General	M
Counselor Education	M,O
Curriculum and Instruction	M,O
Education—General	M,O
Educational Administration	M,O
Nursing—General	M

LINCOLN UNIVERSITY (CA)

Business Administration and Management— General	M

LINCOLN UNIVERSITY (MO)

Accounting	M
Business Administration and Management— General	M
Counselor Education	M,O
Education—General	M,O
Educational Administration	M,O
Elementary Education	M,O
Entrepreneurship	M
Secondary Education	M,O
Special Education	M,O

LINCOLN UNIVERSITY (PA)

Human Services	M

LINDENWOOD UNIVERSITY

Accounting	M
Business Administration and Management— General	M
Education—General	M,D,O
Educational Administration	M,D,O
Educational Media/ Instructional Technology	M,D,O
Entrepreneurship	M
Finance and Banking	M
Health Services Management and Hospital Administration	M
Human Resources Management	M
International Business	M
Investment Management	M
Management Information Systems	M
Marketing	M
Nonprofit Management	M
Organizational Behavior	M
Organizational Management	M

Sports Management	M

LIPSCOMB UNIVERSITY

Accounting	M
Business Administration and Management— General	M
Curriculum and Instruction	M
Education—General	M
Educational Administration	M
Finance and Banking	M
Health Services Management and Hospital Administration	M
Nonprofit Management	M
Special Education	M

LOCK HAVEN UNIVERSITY OF PENNSYLVANIA

Education—General	M
Elementary Education	M
Physician Assistant Studies	M

LOGAN UNIVERSITY-COLLEGE OF CHIROPRACTIC

Chiropractic	P,M

LOMA LINDA UNIVERSITY

Allied Health—General	M,D
Allopathic Medicine	P,M,D
Bioethics	M,O
Communication Disorders	M
Counselor Education	M,D,O
Dentistry	P,M,O
Environmental and Occupational Health	M
Epidemiology	M
Gerontological Nursing	M
Health Education	M,D
Health Promotion	M,D
Health Services Management and Hospital Administration	M
International Health	M
Nursing and Healthcare Administration	M,O
Nursing—General	M,O
Oral and Dental Sciences	M,O
Pediatric Nursing	M
Physical Therapy	M,D
Physician Assistant Studies	M
Public Health—General	M,D
Social Work	M,D

LONG ISLAND UNIVERSITY, BRENTWOOD CAMPUS

Counselor Education	M
Education—General	M
Educational Administration	M
Elementary Education	M
Reading Education	M
Special Education	M

LONG ISLAND UNIVERSITY, BROOKLYN CAMPUS

Accounting	M
Adult Nursing	M,O
Athletic Training and Sports Medicine	M
Business Administration and Management— General	M
Communication Disorders	M
Community Health	M
Counselor Education	M,O

Education—General	M,O
Educational Administration	M
Educational Media/ Instructional Technology	M
Elementary Education	M
English as a Second Language	M
English Education	M
Exercise and Sports Science	M
Family Nurse Practitioner Studies	M,O
Health Education	M
Health Services Management and Hospital Administration	M
Human Resources Management	M
Mathematics Education	M
Multilingual and Multicultural Education	M
Nursing and Healthcare Administration	M
Nursing—General	M,O
Pharmaceutical Administration	M
Pharmaceutical Sciences	M,D
Physical Education	M
Physical Therapy	D
Reading Education	M
Special Education	M
Taxation	M

LONG ISLAND UNIVERSITY, C.W. POST CAMPUS

Accounting	M,O
Allied Health—General	M,O
Art Education	M
Business Administration and Management— General	M,O*
Clinical Laboratory Sciences/Medical Technology	M
Communication Disorders	M
Computer Education	M
Counselor Education	M
Early Childhood Education	M
Education—General	M,O
Educational Administration	M,O
Educational Media/ Instructional Technology	M
Elementary Education	M
English as a Second Language	M
English Education	M
Family Nurse Practitioner Studies	M,O
Finance and Banking	M,O
Foreign Languages Education	M
Health Services Management and Hospital Administration	M,O
Information Studies	M,D,O
International Business	M
Library Science	M,D,O*
Management Information Systems	M,O
Marketing	M,O
Mathematics Education	M
Medicinal and Pharmaceutical Chemistry	M
Middle School Education	M
Multilingual and Multicultural Education	M
Music Education	M
Nonprofit Management	M,O
Nursing—General	M,O
Reading Education	M
Science Education	M
Secondary Education	M

Special Education	M
Taxation	M,O

LONG ISLAND UNIVERSITY, ROCKLAND GRADUATE CAMPUS

Business Administration and Management— General	M,O
Counselor Education	M
Educational Administration	M,O
Elementary Education	M
Finance and Banking	M,O
Health Services Management and Hospital Administration	M,O
Nonprofit Management	M,O
Pharmaceutical Sciences	M
Reading Education	M
Special Education	M

LONG ISLAND UNIVERSITY, SOUTHAMPTON GRADUATE CAMPUS

Early Childhood Education	M
Education—General	M
Elementary Education	M
Reading Education	M
Special Education	M

LONG ISLAND UNIVERSITY, WESTCHESTER GRADUATE CAMPUS

Business Administration and Management— General	M
Counselor Education	M
Early Childhood Education	M
Education—General	M
Educational Psychology	M
Elementary Education	M
English as a Second Language	M
Information Studies	M
Library Science	M
Multilingual and Multicultural Education	M
Reading Education	M
Secondary Education	M
Special Education	M

LONGWOOD UNIVERSITY

Business Administration and Management— General	M
Communication Disorders	M*
Counselor Education	M
Education—General	M
Educational Administration	M
Educational Media/ Instructional Technology	M
Elementary Education	M
English Education	M
Reading Education	M
Secondary Education	M
Special Education	M

LORAS COLLEGE

Educational Administration	M
Special Education	M

LOUISIANA STATE UNIVERSITY AND AGRICULTURAL AND MECHANICAL COLLEGE

Accounting	M,D
Agricultural Education	M,D

Business Administration and Management— General	M,D
Business Education	M,D
Communication Disorders	M,D
Counselor Education	M,D,O
Education—General	M,D,O
Educational Administration	M,D,O
Educational Measurement and Evaluation	M,D,O
Educational Media/ Instructional Technology	M,D,O
Elementary Education	M,D,O
Finance and Banking	M,D
Higher Education	M,D,O
Home Economics Education	M,D
Information Studies	M,O
International and Comparative Education	M,D
Kinesiology and Movement Studies	M,D
Law	P,M
Library Science	M,O
Management Information Systems	M,D
Marketing	D
Music Education	M,D
Secondary Education	M,D,O
Social Work	M,D
Veterinary Medicine	P
Veterinary Sciences	M,D
Vocational and Technical Education	M,D

LOUISIANA STATE UNIVERSITY HEALTH SCIENCES CENTER

Adult Nursing	M,D
Allied Health—General	M
Allopathic Medicine	P,M
Communication Disorders	M
Community Health Nursing	M,D
Dentistry	P
Family Nurse Practitioner Studies	M,D
Nursing and Healthcare Administration	M,D
Nursing—General	M,D
Pediatric Nursing	M,D
Physical Therapy	M
Psychiatric Nursing	M,D
Public Health—General	M

LOUISIANA STATE UNIVERSITY HEALTH SCIENCES CENTER AT SHREVEPORT

Allopathic Medicine	P

LOUISIANA STATE UNIVERSITY IN SHREVEPORT

Business Administration and Management— General	M
Education—General	M
Health Services Management and Hospital Administration	M
Human Services	M

LOUISIANA TECH UNIVERSITY

Accounting	M,D
Business Administration and Management— General	M,D
Business Education	M,D
Communication Disorders	M
Counselor Education	M,D
Curriculum and Instruction	M,D

Education—General	M,D
Educational Administration	M,D
English Education	M,D
Exercise and Sports Science	M
Finance and Banking	M,D
Foreign Languages Education	M,D
Health Education	M,D
Marketing	M,D
Mathematics Education	M,D
Physical Education	M,D
Science Education	M,D
Secondary Education	M,D
Social Sciences Education	M,D
Special Education	M,D

LOURDES COLLEGE

Education—General	M
Educational Media/ Instructional Technology	M
Organizational Management	M

LOYOLA COLLEGE IN MARYLAND

Business Administration and Management— General	M
Communication Disorders	M,O
Counselor Education	M,O
Curriculum and Instruction	M,O
Early Childhood Education	M,O
Education—General	M
Educational Administration	M,O
Educational Media/ Instructional Technology	M
Finance and Banking	M
Marketing	M
Quantitative Analysis	M
Reading Education	M,O
Special Education	M,O

LOYOLA MARYMOUNT UNIVERSITY

Bioethics	M
Business Administration and Management— General	M
Counselor Education	M
Education—General	M,D
Educational Administration	M,D
Educational Psychology	M
Elementary Education	M
Law	P,M
Mathematics Education	M
Multilingual and Multicultural Education	M
Reading Education	M
Religious Education	M
Secondary Education	M
Special Education	M
Taxation	P,M

LOYOLA UNIVERSITY CHICAGO

Accounting	M
Acute Care/Critical Care Nursing	M
Adult Nursing	M
Allopathic Medicine	P
Business Administration and Management— General	M
Counselor Education	M,O
Curriculum and Instruction	M,D
Education—General	M,D,O
Educational Administration	M,D,O
Educational Measurement and Evaluation	M,D

Educational Media/ Instructional Technology	M
Educational Policy	M,D
Educational Psychology	M
Elementary Education	M
Environmental and Occupational Health	M
Family Nurse Practitioner Studies	M
Health Services Management and Hospital Administration	M
Higher Education	M,D
Human Resources Management	M
Law	P,M,D
Management Information Systems	M
Marketing	M
Nursing and Healthcare Administration	M
Nursing—General	M,D
Oncology Nursing	M
Reading Education	M
Religious Education	P,M,O
Science Education	M
Secondary Education	M
Social Work	M,D
Special Education	M
Women's Health Nursing	M

LOYOLA UNIVERSITY NEW ORLEANS

Business Administration and Management— General	M
Counselor Education	M
Education—General	M
Elementary Education	M
Family Nurse Practitioner Studies	M
Health Services Management and Hospital Administration	M
Law	P
Nursing—General	M
Reading Education	M
Secondary Education	M

LUTHER RICE UNIVERSITY

Religious Education	P,M,D

LYNCHBURG COLLEGE

Business Administration and Management— General	M
Counselor Education	M
Education—General	M
Educational Administration	M
Elementary Education	M
English Education	M
Science Education	M
Special Education	M

LYNDON STATE COLLEGE

Counselor Education	M
Curriculum and Instruction	M
Education—General	M
Reading Education	M
Science Education	M
Special Education	M

LYNN UNIVERSITY

Aviation Management	M,D
Business Administration and Management— General	M,D
Education of the Gifted	M,D

Educational Administration	M,D
Hospitality Management	M,D
International and Comparative Education	M,D
International Business	M,D
Investment Management	M,D
Marketing	M,D
Special Education	M,D
Sports Management	M,D

MADONNA UNIVERSITY

Adult Nursing	M
Business Administration and Management— General	M
Education—General	M
Educational Administration	M
English as a Second Language	M
Family Nurse Practitioner Studies	M
Health Services Management and Hospital Administration	M
Hospice Nursing	M
International Business	M
Nursing and Healthcare Administration	M
Nursing—General	M
Quality Management	M
Reading Education	M
Special Education	M

MAHARISHI UNIVERSITY OF MANAGEMENT

Business Administration and Management— General	M,D
Education—General	M
Elementary Education	M
Secondary Education	M

MAINE MARITIME ACADEMY

International Business	M,O
Logistics	M,O
Supply Chain Management	M,O
Transportation Management	M,O

MALASPINA UNIVERSITY-COLLEGE

Business Administration and Management— General	M

MALONE COLLEGE

Business Administration and Management— General	M
Counselor Education	M
Curriculum and Instruction	M
Education—General	M
Educational Media/ Instructional Technology	M
Family Nurse Practitioner Studies	M
Nursing—General	M
Reading Education	M
Special Education	M

MANHATTAN COLLEGE

Counselor Education	M,O
Early Childhood Education	M
Education—General	M,O
Educational Administration	M,O
Special Education	M

MANHATTANVILLE COLLEGE

Art Education	M
Early Childhood Education	M
Education—General	M*
Educational Administration	M
Elementary Education	M
English as a Second Language	M
English Education	M
Exercise and Sports Science	M
Foreign Languages Education	M
Human Resources Development	M
Human Resources Management	M
International Business	M
Management Strategy and Policy	M
Marketing	M
Mathematics Education	M
Middle School Education	M
Music Education	M
Organizational Management	M
Reading Education	M
Science Education	M
Secondary Education	M
Social Sciences Education	M
Special Education	M
Sports Management	M

MANSFIELD UNIVERSITY OF PENNSYLVANIA

Art Education	M
Education—General	M
Elementary Education	M
Information Studies	M
Library Science	M
Nursing—General	M
Secondary Education	M

MAPLE SPRINGS BAPTIST BIBLE COLLEGE AND SEMINARY

Computer Education	P,M,D,O

MARIAN COLLEGE

Education—General	M

MARIAN COLLEGE OF FOND DU LAC

Adult Nursing	M
Business Administration and Management— General	M
Education—General	M,D
Educational Administration	M,D
Nursing Education	M
Nursing—General	M
Organizational Management	M
Quality Management	M

MARIETTA COLLEGE

Education—General	M
Physician Assistant Studies	M

MARIST COLLEGE

Business Administration and Management— General	M,O*
Education—General	M,O
Educational Psychology	M,O

Industrial and Manufacturing Management	M,O
Management Information Systems	M,O

MARLBORO COLLEGE

Business Administration and Management— General	M
Computer Education	M
Education—General	M

MARQUETTE UNIVERSITY

Accounting	M
Adult Nursing	M,D,O
Advertising and Public Relations	M
Business Administration and Management— General	M
Communication Disorders	M
Dentistry	P
Education—General	M,D,O
Family Nurse Practitioner Studies	M,D,O
Foreign Languages Education	M
Gerontological Nursing	M,D,O
Human Resources Development	M
Human Resources Management	M
Law	P
Maternal and Child/ Neonatal Nursing	M,D,O
Mathematics Education	M,D
Nurse Midwifery	M,D,O
Nursing—General	M,D,O
Oral and Dental Sciences	M
Pediatric Nursing	M,D,O
Physical Therapy	D
Physician Assistant Studies	M

MARSHALL UNIVERSITY

Adult Education	M
Allopathic Medicine	P
Business Administration and Management— General	M
Communication Disorders	M
Counselor Education	M,O
Early Childhood Education	M
Education—General	M,D,O
Educational Administration	M,D,O
Elementary Education	M
Exercise and Sports Science	M
Health Education	M
Health Services Management and Hospital Administration	M
Human Resources Management	M
Nursing—General	M
Reading Education	M,O
Secondary Education	M
Special Education	M
Sports Management	M
Vocational and Technical Education	M

MARY BALDWIN COLLEGE

Education—General	M
Elementary Education	M
Middle School Education	M

MARYGROVE COLLEGE

Adult Education	M
Education—General	M
Educational Administration	M
Elementary Education	M
Human Resources Management	M
Legal and Justice Studies	M
Reading Education	M
Secondary Education	M
Urban Education	M

MARYLAND INSTITUTE COLLEGE OF ART

Art Education	M

MARYLHURST UNIVERSITY

Business Administration and Management— General	M

MARYMOUNT UNIVERSITY

Allied Health—General	M,D,O
Business Administration and Management— General	M,O
Counselor Education	M
Education—General	M,O
Educational Administration	M,O
Elementary Education	M,O
English as a Second Language	M,O
English Education	M
Family Nurse Practitioner Studies	M,O
Health Promotion	M
Health Services Management and Hospital Administration	M
Human Resources Management	M,O
Legal and Justice Studies	M,O
Management Information Systems	M,O
Nursing and Healthcare Administration	M,O
Nursing Education	M,O
Nursing—General	M,O
Physical Therapy	D
Project Management	M,O
Secondary Education	M,O
Special Education	M,O

MARYVILLE UNIVERSITY OF SAINT LOUIS

Accounting	M,O
Actuarial Science	
Allied Health—General	M,D
Art Education	M,D
Business Administration and Management— General	M,O
Business Education	M,O
Early Childhood Education	M,D
Education of the Gifted	M,D
Education—General	M,D
Educational Administration	M,D
Electronic Commerce	M,O
Elementary Education	M,D
English Education	M,D
Environmental Education	M,D
Marketing	M,O
Middle School Education	M,D
Nursing—General	M
Occupational Therapy	M
Physical Therapy	D
Reading Education	M,D
Secondary Education	M,D

MARYWOOD UNIVERSITY

Art Education	M
Business Administration and Management— General	M*
Communication Disorders	M*
Counselor Education	M,O
Early Childhood Education	M
Education—General	M
Educational Administration	M,D
Electronic Commerce	M,O
Elementary Education	M
Exercise and Sports Science	M
Finance and Banking	M
Health Education	D
Health Services Management and Hospital Administration	M
Higher Education	M,D
Investment Management	M
Library Science	M,O
Management Information Systems	M
Music Education	M
Nursing and Healthcare Administration	M
Physician Assistant Studies	M
Reading Education	M
Secondary Education	M
Social Work	M,D*
Special Education	M

MASSACHUSETTS COLLEGE OF ART

Art Education	M

MASSACHUSETTS COLLEGE OF LIBERAL ARTS

Curriculum and Instruction	M
Education—General	M
Educational Administration	M
Reading Education	M
Special Education	M

MASSACHUSETTS COLLEGE OF PHARMACY AND HEALTH SCIENCES

Health Services Management and Hospital Administration	M
Pharmaceutical Administration	M
Pharmaceutical Sciences	M,D*

MASSACHUSETTS INSTITUTE OF TECHNOLOGY

Business Administration and Management— General	M,D
Communication Disorders	D*
Logistics	M,D
Medical Physics	D
Real Estate	M

MASSACHUSETTS MARITIME ACADEMY

Facilities Management	M

MASSACHUSETTS SCHOOL OF LAW AT ANDOVER

Law	P*

MAYO MEDICAL SCHOOL

Allopathic Medicine	P

MAYO SCHOOL OF HEALTH SCIENCES

Nurse Anesthesia	M
Physical Therapy	D

MCDANIEL COLLEGE

Counselor Education	M
Curriculum and Instruction	M
Educational Administration	M
Educational Media/ Instructional Technology	M
Elementary Education	M
Human Resources Development	M
Human Services	M
Library Science	M
Physical Education	M
Reading Education	M
Secondary Education	M
Special Education	M

MCGILL UNIVERSITY

Accounting	M,D,O
Allopathic Medicine	P,M,D
Bioethics	M,D,O
Business Administration and Management— General	M,D,O
Communication Disorders	M,D
Community Health	M,D,O
Curriculum and Instruction	M,D,O
Dentistry	P,M,D,O
Education—General	M,D,O
Educational Administration	M,D,O
Educational Psychology	M,D
Entrepreneurship	M,D,O
Environmental and Occupational Health	M,D,O
Epidemiology	M,D,O
Family Nurse Practitioner Studies	M,D,O
Finance and Banking	M,D,O
Foreign Languages Education	M,D,O
Foundations and Philosophy of Education	M,D,O
Health Physics/ Radiological Health	M,D
Health Services Management and Hospital Administration	M,D,O
Industrial and Manufacturing Management	M,D,O*
Information Studies	M,D,O
International Business	M,D,O
Kinesiology and Movement Studies	M,D,O
Law	M,D,O
Library Science	M,D,O
Management Information Systems	M,D,O
Management Strategy and Policy	M,D,O
Marketing	M,D,O
Medical Physics	M,D
Music Education	M,D
Nursing—General	M,D,O
Oral and Dental Sciences	M,D
Physical Education	M,D,O
Rehabilitation Sciences	M,D
Social Work	M,D,O
Transportation Management	M,D

MCKENDREE COLLEGE

Business Administration and Management— General	M
Education—General	M

Nursing—General	M

MCMASTER UNIVERSITY

Business Administration and Management— General	M,D
Health Physics/ Radiological Health	M,D
Health Services Research	M,D
Human Resources Management	M,D
Kinesiology and Movement Studies	M,D
Management Information Systems	D
Medical Physics	M,D
Nursing—General	M,D
Occupational Therapy	M
Physical Therapy	M
Rehabilitation Sciences	M,D
Social Work	M

MCNEESE STATE UNIVERSITY

Business Administration and Management— General	M
Counselor Education	M
Curriculum and Instruction	M
Early Childhood Education	M
Education—General	M
Educational Administration	M,O
Educational Media/ Instructional Technology	M
Elementary Education	M
Exercise and Sports Science	M
Health Promotion	M
Multilingual and Multicultural Education	M
Music Education	M
Nursing—General	M
Science Education	M
Secondary Education	M
Social Sciences Education	M

MEDAILLE COLLEGE

Business Administration and Management— General	M
Curriculum and Instruction	M
Education—General	M
Elementary Education	M
Organizational Management	M
Reading Education	M
Special Education	M

MEDICAL COLLEGE OF GEORGIA

Adult Nursing	M,D
Allied Health—General	M,D
Allopathic Medicine	P
Clinical Laboratory Sciences/Medical Technology	M
Community Health Nursing	M,D
Dental Hygiene	M
Dentistry	P
Family Nurse Practitioner Studies	M,D
Health Physics/ Radiological Health	M
Maternal and Child/ Neonatal Nursing	M,D
Nurse Anesthesia	M,D
Nursing—General	M,D
Occupational Therapy	M
Oral and Dental Sciences	M,D
Physical Therapy	M,D

Physician Assistant Studies	M
Psychiatric Nursing	M,D

MEDICAL COLLEGE OF WISCONSIN

Allopathic Medicine	P
Bioethics	M
Clinical Laboratory Sciences/Medical Technology	D
Environmental and Occupational Health	M
Epidemiology	M
Public Health—General	M

MEDICAL UNIVERSITY OF SOUTH CAROLINA

Adult Nursing	M
Allied Health—General	M,D
Allopathic Medicine	P
Clinical Research	M
Communication Disorders	M
Dentistry	P
Epidemiology	M,D
Family Nurse Practitioner Studies	M
Gerontological Nursing	M
Health Services Management and Hospital Administration	M,D
Maternal and Child/ Neonatal Nursing	M
Nurse Anesthesia	M
Nurse Midwifery	M
Nursing and Healthcare Administration	M
Nursing Education	M
Nursing—General	D
Occupational Therapy	M
Pharmaceutical Sciences	P,D
Pharmacy	P,D
Physical Therapy	D
Physician Assistant Studies	M
Psychiatric Nursing	M
Rehabilitation Sciences	M,D

MEHARRY MEDICAL COLLEGE

Allopathic Medicine	P
Community Health	M
Dentistry	P
Environmental and Occupational Health	M
Health Services Management and Hospital Administration	M

MEMORIAL UNIVERSITY OF NEWFOUNDLAND

Adult Education	M,D,O
Allopathic Medicine	P
Business Administration and Management— General	M
Community Health	M,D,O
Curriculum and Instruction	M,D,O
Education—General	M,D,O
Educational Administration	M,D,O
Educational Media/ Instructional Technology	M,D,O
Educational Psychology	M,D,O
Epidemiology	M,D,O
Exercise and Sports Science	M
Kinesiology and Movement Studies	M
Nursing—General	M,O
Pharmaceutical Sciences	M,D

Physical Education	M
Social Work	M

MEMPHIS COLLEGE OF ART

Art Education	M

MERCER UNIVERSITY

Accounting	M
Allopathic Medicine	P,M
Business Administration and Management— General	M
Early Childhood Education	M,D,O
Education—General	M,D,O
Educational Administration	M,D,O
Law	P
Middle School Education	M,D,O
Nursing—General	M,O
Pharmaceutical Sciences	P,M,D
Pharmacy	P,M,D
Reading Education	M,D,O
Secondary Education	M,D,O

MERCY COLLEGE

Adult Nursing	M,O
Allied Health—General	M,O
Business Administration and Management— General	M
Communication Disorders	M
Counselor Education	M
Early Childhood Education	M
Education—General	M
Educational Administration	M
Educational Media/ Instructional Technology	M
Electronic Commerce	M
Elementary Education	M
English as a Second Language	M
Finance and Banking	M
Health Services Management and Hospital Administration	M,O
Human Resources Management	M
Marketing	M
Middle School Education	M
Multilingual and Multicultural Education	M,O
Nursing and Healthcare Administration	M
Nursing Education	M
Nursing—General	M
Occupational Therapy	M
Organizational Management	M
Physical Therapy	M
Physician Assistant Studies	M
Reading Education	M
Secondary Education	M
Special Education	M
Urban Education	M

MERCYHURST COLLEGE

Educational Administration	M,O
Multilingual and Multicultural Education	M,O
Organizational Management	M,O
Special Education	M,O

MEREDITH COLLEGE

Business Administration and Management— General	M
Education—General	M

MERRIMACK COLLEGE

Education—General	M

MESA STATE COLLEGE

Business Administration and Management— General	M

METHODIST UNIVERSITY

Business Administration and Management— General	M
Physician Assistant Studies	M

METROPOLITAN COLLEGE OF NEW YORK

Business Administration and Management— General	M
Elementary Education	M

METROPOLITAN STATE UNIVERSITY

Business Administration and Management— General	M
Finance and Banking	M
Human Resources Management	M
Information Studies	M
International Business	M
Management Information Systems	M
Marketing	M
Nonprofit Management	M
Nursing—General	M
Organizational Management	M

MGH INSTITUTE OF HEALTH PROFESSIONS

Allied Health—General	M,D,O
Clinical Research	M,O
Communication Disorders	M,O
Family Nurse Practitioner Studies	M,O
Gerontological Nursing	M,O
Medical Imaging	O
Nursing Education	M,O
Nursing—General	M,O*
Pediatric Nursing	M,O
Physical Therapy	M,D,O
Psychiatric Nursing	M,O
Reading Education	M,O
Women's Health Nursing	M,O

MIAMI UNIVERSITY

Accounting	M
Art Education	M
Business Administration and Management— General	M
Communication Disorders	M
Curriculum and Instruction	M
Early Childhood Education	M
Education—General	M,D,O
Educational Administration	M,D
Educational Psychology	M,O
Elementary Education	M
English Education	M,D
Exercise and Sports Science	M
Finance and Banking	M
Management Information Systems	M
Marketing	M

Mathematics Education	M
Music Education	M
Reading Education	M
Secondary Education	M
Social Sciences Education	M
Social Work	M
Special Education	M
Student Affairs	M

MICHIGAN SCHOOL OF PROFESSIONAL PSYCHOLOGY

Educational Psychology	M,D

MICHIGAN STATE UNIVERSITY

Accounting	M,D
Adult Education	M,D,O
Advertising and Public Relations	M,D
Allopathic Medicine	P
Bioethics	M
Business Administration and Management— General	M,D
Clinical Laboratory Sciences/Medical Technology	M
Communication Disorders	M,D
Counselor Education	M,D,O
Curriculum and Instruction	M,D,O
Education—General	M,D,O
Educational Administration	M,D,O
Educational Measurement and Evaluation	M,D,O
Educational Media/ Instructional Technology	M,D,O
Educational Policy	D
Educational Psychology	M,D,O
English as a Second Language	M,D
Epidemiology	M,D
Finance and Banking	M,D
Foreign Languages Education	D
Higher Education	M,D,O
Hospitality Management	M*
Human Resources Management	M,D
Kinesiology and Movement Studies	M,D
Management Information Systems	M,D
Marketing	M,D
Mathematics Education	M,D
Music Education	M,D
Nursing—General	M,D
Osteopathic Medicine	P
Reading Education	M
Recreation and Park Management	M,D
Science Education	M
Social Sciences Education	M,D
Social Work	M,D
Special Education	M,D,O
Supply Chain Management	M,D
Veterinary Medicine	P
Veterinary Sciences	M,D

MICHIGAN STATE UNIVERSITY COLLEGE OF LAW

Law	P,M
Legal and Justice Studies	P,M

MICHIGAN TECHNOLOGICAL UNIVERSITY

Business Administration and Management— General	M
Science Education	M

MICHIGAN THEOLOGICAL SEMINARY

Religious Education	P,M,D

MIDAMERICA NAZARENE UNIVERSITY

Business Administration and Management— General	M
Curriculum and Instruction	M
Education—General	M
Educational Media/ Instructional Technology	M
Special Education	M

MIDDLE TENNESSEE SCHOOL OF ANESTHESIA

Nurse Anesthesia	M

MIDDLE TENNESSEE STATE UNIVERSITY

Accounting	M
Business Administration and Management— General	M
Business Education	M
Counselor Education	M,O
Curriculum and Instruction	M,O
Early Childhood Education	M,O
Education—General	M,D,O
Educational Administration	M,O
Elementary Education	M,O
English as a Second Language	M,O
Exercise and Sports Science	M,D
Finance and Banking	M,D
Foreign Languages Education	M
Health Education	M,D
Health Services Management and Hospital Administration	O
Management Information Systems	M
Marketing	M
Mathematics Education	M
Middle School Education	M,O
Nursing—General	M
Physical Education	M,D
Reading Education	M
Recreation and Park Management	M,D
Science Education	M
Special Education	M,O
Vocational and Technical Education	M

MIDWEST COLLEGE OF ORIENTAL MEDICINE

Acupuncture and Oriental Medicine	M,O

MIDWESTERN BAPTIST THEOLOGICAL SEMINARY

Religious Education	P,M,D

MIDWESTERN STATE UNIVERSITY

Business Administration and Management— General	M
Counselor Education	M
Curriculum and Instruction	M
Education—General	M
Educational Administration	M
Educational Media/ Instructional Technology	M
Family Nurse Practitioner Studies	M
Health Physics/ Radiological Health	M
Health Services Management and Hospital Administration	M
Human Resources Development	M
Kinesiology and Movement Studies	M
Nursing Education	M
Nursing—General	M
Reading Education	M
Special Education	M

MIDWESTERN UNIVERSITY, DOWNERS GROVE CAMPUS

Allied Health—General	M,D
Occupational Therapy	M*
Osteopathic Medicine	P*
Pharmacy	P*
Physical Therapy	D*
Physician Assistant Studies	M*

MIDWESTERN UNIVERSITY, GLENDALE CAMPUS

Allied Health—General	P,M,O
Bioethics	M,O
Health Education	M
Nurse Anesthesia	M
Occupational Therapy	M
Osteopathic Medicine	P*
Pharmacy	P
Physician Assistant Studies	M
Podiatric Medicine	P

MIDWEST UNIVERSITY

Religious Education	P,M,D

MILLERSVILLE UNIVERSITY OF PENNSYLVANIA

Art Education	M
Business Administration and Management— General	M
Early Childhood Education	M
Education—General	M
Elementary Education	M
English Education	M
Foundations and Philosophy of Education	M
Mathematics Education	M
Nursing—General	M
Reading Education	M
Social Work	M
Special Education	M
Sports Management	M
Vocational and Technical Education	M

MILLIGAN COLLEGE

Business Administration and Management— General	M
Education—General	M
Occupational Therapy	M

MILLIKIN UNIVERSITY

Business Administration and Management— General	M

MILLSAPS COLLEGE

Accounting	M
Business Administration and Management— General	M

MILLS COLLEGE

Business Administration and Management— General	M
Curriculum and Instruction	M,D
Early Childhood Education	M,D
Education—General	M,D
Educational Administration	M,D
Elementary Education	M,D
English Education	M,D
Health Education	M,D
Mathematics Education	M,D
Science Education	M,D
Secondary Education	M,D
Social Sciences Education	M,D

MILWAUKEE SCHOOL OF ENGINEERING

Business Administration and Management— General	M
Clinical Laboratory Sciences/Medical Technology	M

MINNESOTA STATE UNIVERSITY MANKATO

Accounting	M
Allied Health—General	M,O
Art Education	M
Business Administration and Management— General	M
Communication Disorders	M
Community Health	M
Counselor Education	M,O
Curriculum and Instruction	M,O
Early Childhood Education	M
Education of the Gifted	M,O
Education—General	M,O
Educational Administration	M,O
Educational Media/ Instructional Technology	M,O
Elementary Education	M
English Education	M,O
Family Nurse Practitioner Studies	M
Finance and Banking	M
Health Education	M
Higher Education	M,O
Human Services	M
International Business	M
Marketing	M
Mathematics Education	M
Multilingual and Multicultural Education	M
Nursing and Healthcare Administration	M
Nursing Education	M
Nursing—General	M
Physical Education	M,O
Science Education	M
Social Sciences Education	M
Special Education	M,O
Student Affairs	M,O

MINNESOTA STATE UNIVERSITY MOORHEAD

Communication Disorders	M
Counselor Education	M
Curriculum and Instruction	M
Education—General	M,O
Educational Administration	M,O

Human Services	M,O
Nursing Education	M,O
Nursing—General	M,O
Reading Education	M
Special Education	M

MINOT STATE UNIVERSITY

Business Administration and Management— General	M
Communication Disorders	M
Early Childhood Education	M
Education of the Multiply Handicapped	M
Elementary Education	M
Management Information Systems	M
Mathematics Education	M
Music Education	M
Science Education	M
Special Education	M

MISSISSIPPI COLLEGE

Accounting	M,O
Advertising and Public Relations	M
Art Education	M,O
Business Administration and Management— General	M,O
Business Education	M,O
Computer Education	M,O
Counselor Education	M,O
Curriculum and Instruction	M,O
Education—General	M,O
Educational Administration	M,O
Elementary Education	M,O
English as a Second Language	M
English Education	M,O
Health Services Management and Hospital Administration	M
Higher Education	M,O
Law	P,O
Legal and Justice Studies	M,O
Mathematics Education	M,O
Music Education	M
Science Education	M,O
Secondary Education	M,O
Social Sciences Education	M,O
Special Education	M,O

MISSISSIPPI STATE UNIVERSITY

Accounting	M,D
Agricultural Education	M
Business Administration and Management— General	M,D
Counselor Education	M,D,O
Curriculum and Instruction	M,D,O
Education—General	M,D,O
Educational Administration	M,D,O
Educational Media/ Instructional Technology	M,D,O
Educational Psychology	M,D,O
Elementary Education	M,D,O
Exercise and Sports Science	M
Finance and Banking	M,D
Foreign Languages Education	M
Health Education	M
Human Resources Development	M,D,O
Kinesiology and Movement Studies	M
Management Information Systems	M
Marketing	M,D
Physical Education	M

Project Management	M,D
Secondary Education	M,D,O
Special Education	M,D,O
Sports Management	M
Taxation	M
Veterinary Medicine	P
Veterinary Sciences	M,D
Vocational and Technical Education	M,D,O

MISSISSIPPI UNIVERSITY FOR WOMEN

Communication Disorders	M
Education of the Gifted	M
Education—General	M
Educational Media/ Instructional Technology	M
Health Education	M
Nursing—General	M,O

MISSISSIPPI VALLEY STATE UNIVERSITY

Education—General	M
Elementary Education	M
Environmental and Occupational Health	M

MISSOURI STATE UNIVERSITY

Accounting	M
Agricultural Education	M
Art Education	M
Business Administration and Management— General	M*
Communication Disorders	M,D
Counselor Education	M
Curriculum and Instruction	M
Early Childhood Education	M
Education—General	M
Educational Administration	M,O
Educational Media/ Instructional Technology	M
Elementary Education	M,O
Foreign Languages Education	M
Health Promotion	M
Health Services Management and Hospital Administration	M
Management Information Systems	M
Nurse Anesthesia	M
Nursing—General	M
Physical Education	M
Physical Therapy	M
Physician Assistant Studies	M
Project Management	M
Public Health—General	M
Reading Education	M
Science Education	M
Secondary Education	M,O
Social Sciences Education	M
Social Work	M
Special Education	M,O
Sports Management	M

MOLLOY COLLEGE

Adult Nursing	M,O
Family Nurse Practitioner Studies	M,O
Nursing and Healthcare Administration	M,O
Nursing Education	M,O
Nursing Informatics	M,O
Nursing—General	M,O
Pediatric Nursing	M,O
Psychiatric Nursing	M,O

MONMOUTH UNIVERSITY

Accounting	M,O
Advertising and Public Relations	M,O
Business Administration and Management— General	M,O
Education—General	M,O
Educational Administration	M,O
Elementary Education	M,O
Family Nurse Practitioner Studies	M,O
Health Services Management and Hospital Administration	M,O
Nursing—General	M,O
Reading Education	M,O
School Nursing	M,O
Social Work	M
Special Education	M,O

MONROE COLLEGE

Business Administration and Management— General	M

MONTANA STATE UNIVERSITY

Accounting	M
Education—General	M,D,O
Family Nurse Practitioner Studies	M,O
Health Education	M
Nursing Education	M,O
Veterinary Sciences	M,D

MONTANA STATE UNIVERSITY– BILLINGS

Advertising and Public Relations	M
Athletic Training and Sports Medicine	M
Counselor Education	M
Curriculum and Instruction	M
Early Childhood Education	M
Education—General	M,O
Educational Media/ Instructional Technology	M
Health Services Management and Hospital Administration	M
Human Services	M
Physical Education	M
Reading Education	M
Secondary Education	M
Special Education	M
Sports Management	M

MONTANA STATE UNIVERSITY– NORTHERN

Counselor Education	M
Education—General	M

MONTANA TECH OF THE UNIVERSITY OF MONTANA

Industrial Hygiene	M
Project Management	M

MONTCLAIR STATE UNIVERSITY

Accounting	M
Advertising and Public Relations	M
Art Education	M,O
Business Administration and Management— General	M*
Communication Disorders	M,D
Counselor Education	M,O
Curriculum and Instruction	M,D,O*
Early Childhood Education	M,O
Education of the Multiply Handicapped	M,O
Education—General	M,O
Educational Administration	M,O
Educational Media/ Instructional Technology	M,O
Educational Psychology	M,O
Elementary Education	M,O
English as a Second Language	M,O
English Education	M,O
Environmental and Occupational Health	M,D,O
Exercise and Sports Science	M,O
Finance and Banking	M
Foundations and Philosophy of Education	M,D,O
Health Education	M,O
Home Economics Education	M,O
International Business	M
Legal and Justice Studies	M,O
Management Information Systems	M
Marketing	M
Mathematics Education	M,D,O
Middle School Education	M,O
Music Education	M,O
Physical Education	M,O
Reading Education	M,O
Science Education	M,D,O
Social Sciences Education	M
Special Education	M,O
Sports Management	M,O

MONTEREY INSTITUTE OF INTERNATIONAL STUDIES

Business Administration and Management— General	M
English as a Second Language	M*
Foreign Languages Education	M
International Business	M

MONTREAT COLLEGE

Business Administration and Management— General	M
Education—General	M
Elementary Education	M

MOODY BIBLE INSTITUTE

English as a Second Language	P,M,O

MORAVIAN COLLEGE

Business Administration and Management— General	M
Curriculum and Instruction	M
Education—General	M

MOREHEAD STATE UNIVERSITY

Adult Education	M,O
Art Education	M
Business Administration and Management— General	M
Counselor Education	M,O
Curriculum and Instruction	O
Education—General	M,O
Educational Administration	M,O
Elementary Education	M

Exercise and Sports Science	M
Health Education	M
Higher Education	M,O
International and Comparative Education	M
Management Information Systems	M
Middle School Education	M
Music Education	M
Physical Education	M
Reading Education	M
Secondary Education	M
Special Education	M
Sports Management	M
Vocational and Technical Education	M

MOREHOUSE SCHOOL OF MEDICINE

Allopathic Medicine	P
Clinical Research	M
Public Health—General	M

MORGAN STATE UNIVERSITY

Business Administration and Management— General	D
Community College Education	D
Education—General	M,D
Educational Administration	M,D
Elementary Education	M
Higher Education	D
Mathematics Education	M,D
Middle School Education	M
Public Health—General	M,D
Science Education	M,D
Secondary Education	M
Social Work	M,D
Transportation Management	M

MORNINGSIDE COLLEGE

Computer Education	M
Education—General	M
Elementary Education	M
Reading Education	M
Special Education	M

MORRISON UNIVERSITY

Business Administration and Management— General	M

MOUNTAIN STATE UNIVERSITY

Allied Health—General	M
Family Nurse Practitioner Studies	M,O
Management Strategy and Policy	M
Nurse Anesthesia	M,O
Nursing and Healthcare Administration	M,O
Nursing Education	M,O
Nursing—General	M,O*
Physician Assistant Studies	M*

MOUNT ALOYSIUS COLLEGE

Health Services Management and Hospital Administration	M

MOUNT CARMEL COLLEGE OF NURSING

Adult Nursing	M

Nursing Education	M
Nursing—General	M*

MOUNT MARTY COLLEGE

Business Administration and Management— General	M
Nurse Anesthesia	M

MOUNT MARY COLLEGE

Business Administration and Management— General	M
Counselor Education	M
Education—General	M
Health Education	M
Occupational Therapy	M

MOUNT SAINT MARY COLLEGE

Adult Nursing	M
Business Administration and Management— General	M
Early Childhood Education	M
Education—General	M
Elementary Education	M
Family Nurse Practitioner Studies	M
Finance and Banking	M
Middle School Education	M
Nursing and Healthcare Administration	M
Nursing Education	M
Nursing—General	M
Reading Education	M
Secondary Education	M
Special Education	M

MOUNT ST. MARY'S COLLEGE

Education—General	M
Educational Administration	M
Elementary Education	M
Nursing—General	M
Physical Therapy	D
Secondary Education	M
Special Education	M

MOUNT ST. MARY'S UNIVERSITY

Business Administration and Management— General	M
Education—General	M

MOUNT SAINT VINCENT UNIVERSITY

Adult Education	M
Curriculum and Instruction	M
Education—General	M
Educational Psychology	M
Elementary Education	M
English as a Second Language	M
Foundations and Philosophy of Education	M
Middle School Education	M
Reading Education	M
Special Education	M

MOUNT SINAI SCHOOL OF MEDICINE OF NEW YORK UNIVERSITY

Allopathic Medicine	P
Bioethics	M*
Community Health	M,D

MOUNT VERNON NAZARENE UNIVERSITY

Business Administration and Management— General	M
Education—General	M

MURRAY STATE UNIVERSITY

Accounting	M
Agricultural Education	M
Business Administration and Management— General	M
Communication Disorders	M
Counselor Education	M,O
Early Childhood Education	M
Education—General	M,D,O
Educational Administration	M,O
Elementary Education	M,O
English as a Second Language	M
Environmental and Occupational Health	M
Exercise and Sports Science	M
Family Nurse Practitioner Studies	M
Human Services	M
Industrial Hygiene	M
Leisure Studies	M
Middle School Education	M,O
Music Education	M
Nurse Anesthesia	M
Nursing—General	M
Physical Education	M,O
Reading Education	M,O
Secondary Education	M,O
Special Education	M
Vocational and Technical Education	M

MUSKINGUM COLLEGE

Education—General	M

MYERS UNIVERSITY

Business Administration and Management— General	M

NAROPA UNIVERSITY

Education—General	M
Recreation and Park Management	M

NATIONAL AMERICAN UNIVERSITY

Business Administration and Management— General	M

NATIONAL COLLEGE OF MIDWIFERY

Nurse Midwifery	M,D

NATIONAL COLLEGE OF NATURAL MEDICINE

Acupuncture and Oriental Medicine	M
Naturopathic Medicine	D

THE NATIONAL GRADUATE SCHOOL OF QUALITY MANAGEMENT

Business Administration and Management— General	M

Electronic Commerce	M
Quality Management	M

NATIONAL-LOUIS UNIVERSITY

Adult Education	M,D,O
Business Administration and Management— General	M
Counselor Education	M,O
Curriculum and Instruction	M,D,O
Developmental Education	M,O
Early Childhood Education	M,O
Education—General	M,D,O
Educational Administration	M,D,O
Educational Media/ Instructional Technology	M,O
Educational Psychology	M,D,O
Elementary Education	M,O
English Education	M,O
Human Resources Development	M
Human Resources Management	M
Human Services	M,O
Mathematics Education	M,O
Reading Education	M,D,O
Science Education	M,O
Secondary Education	M,O
Special Education	M,O

NATIONAL UNIVERSITY

Accounting	M
Business Administration and Management— General	M
Communication Disorders	M
Counselor Education	M
Education—General	M
Educational Administration	M
Educational Media/ Instructional Technology	M
Electronic Commerce	M
Finance and Banking	M
Health Services Management and Hospital Administration	M
Human Services	M
Management Information Systems	M
Multilingual and Multicultural Education	M
Organizational Management	M
Special Education	M
Taxation	M

NATIONAL UNIVERSITY OF HEALTH SCIENCES

Acupuncture and Oriental Medicine	P,M,D
Chiropractic	P,M,D*
Naturopathic Medicine	P,M,D

NAVAL POSTGRADUATE SCHOOL

Business Administration and Management— General	M
Human Resources Development	M
Management Information Systems	M,O

NAZARENE THEOLOGICAL SEMINARY

Religious Education	P,M,D

NAZARETH COLLEGE OF ROCHESTER

Art Education	M
Business Administration and Management— General	M
Business Education	M
Communication Disorders	M
Early Childhood Education	M
Education—General	M
Educational Media/ Instructional Technology	M
Elementary Education	M
English as a Second Language	M
Gerontological Nursing	M
Human Resources Management	M
Middle School Education	M
Music Education	M
Nursing—General	M
Physical Therapy	M,D
Reading Education	M
Social Work	M

NEBRASKA METHODIST COLLEGE

Health Promotion	M
Health Services Management and Hospital Administration	M
Nursing—General	M

NEBRASKA WESLEYAN UNIVERSITY

Nursing—General	M

NEUMANN COLLEGE

Education—General	M
Management Strategy and Policy	M
Nursing—General	M
Physical Therapy	M,D
Sports Management	M

NEW COLLEGE OF CALIFORNIA

Education—General	M
Foreign Languages Education	M
Law	P*

NEW ENGLAND COLLEGE

Business Administration and Management— General	M
Education—General	M
Educational Administration	M
Health Services Management and Hospital Administration	M
Human Services	M
Nonprofit Management	M
Organizational Management	M
Special Education	M

THE NEW ENGLAND COLLEGE OF OPTOMETRY

Optometry	P,M*
Vision Sciences	P,M

NEW ENGLAND SCHOOL OF ACUPUNCTURE

Acupuncture and Oriental Medicine	M*

NEW ENGLAND SCHOOL OF LAW

Law	P

NEW JERSEY CITY UNIVERSITY

Accounting	M
Allied Health—General	M
Art Education	M
Business Administration and Management— General	M
Community Health	M
Early Childhood Education	M
Educational Administration	M
Educational Media/ Instructional Technology	M
Educational Psychology	M,O
Elementary Education	M
English as a Second Language	M
Finance and Banking	M
Health Education	M
Health Services Management and Hospital Administration	M
Mathematics Education	M
Multilingual and Multicultural Education	M
Music Education	M
Nursing—General	M
Reading Education	M
Secondary Education	M
Special Education	M
Transcultural Nursing	M
Urban Education	M

NEW JERSEY INSTITUTE OF TECHNOLOGY

Business Administration and Management— General	M
Environmental and Occupational Health	M
Industrial Hygiene	M
Public Health—General	M
Transportation Management	M,D

NEWMAN THEOLOGICAL COLLEGE

Educational Administration	M,O
Religious Education	M,O

NEWMAN UNIVERSITY

Business Administration and Management— General	M
Curriculum and Instruction	M
Education—General	M
Educational Administration	M
English as a Second Language	M
International Business	M
Management Information Systems	M
Nurse Anesthesia	M
Organizational Management	M
Social Work	M

NEW MEXICO HIGHLANDS UNIVERSITY

Business Administration and Management— General	M
Counselor Education	M
Curriculum and Instruction	M
Education—General	M
Educational Administration	M

Exercise and Sports Science	M
Finance and Banking	M
Health Education	M
Human Resources Management	M
International Business	M
Nonprofit Management	M
Social Work	M
Special Education	M
Sports Management	M

NEW MEXICO INSTITUTE OF MINING AND TECHNOLOGY

Science Education	M

NEW MEXICO STATE UNIVERSITY

Accounting	M
Adult Nursing	M
Agricultural Education	M
Business Administration and Management— General	M,D
Communication Disorders	M,D
Community Health Nursing	M
Counselor Education	M,D,O
Curriculum and Instruction	M,D,O
Education—General	M,D,O
Educational Administration	M,D
Marketing	D
Medical/Surgical Nursing	M
Nursing—General	M
Psychiatric Nursing	M
Public Health—General	M
Reading Education	M,D,O
Social Work	M
Special Education	M,D

NEW ORLEANS BAPTIST THEOLOGICAL SEMINARY

Religious Education	P,M,D

THE NEW SCHOOL: A UNIVERSITY

English as a Second Language	M
Finance and Banking	M
Health Services Management and Hospital Administration	M,O*
Human Resources Management	M,O
International Business	M
Nonprofit Management	M*
Organizational Management	M*

NEW YORK CHIROPRACTIC COLLEGE

Acupuncture and Oriental Medicine	M
Chiropractic	P*
Health Physics/ Radiological Health	M

NEW YORK COLLEGE OF HEALTH PROFESSIONS

Acupuncture and Oriental Medicine	M

NEW YORK COLLEGE OF PODIATRIC MEDICINE

Podiatric Medicine	P

NEW YORK COLLEGE OF TRADITIONAL CHINESE MEDICINE

Acupuncture and Oriental Medicine	M

NEW YORK INSTITUTE OF TECHNOLOGY

Accounting	M,O
Business Administration and Management— General	M,O
Counselor Education	M
Distance Education Development	M,O
Education—General	M,O
Educational Administration	O
Educational Media/ Instructional Technology	M,O
Electronic Commerce	M
Elementary Education	M,O
Finance and Banking	M,O
Health Services Management and Hospital Administration	M
Human Resources Management	M,O
International Business	M,O
Management Information Systems	M,O
Management Strategy and Policy	M
Marketing	M,O
Occupational Therapy	M
Osteopathic Medicine	P
Physical Therapy	M,D
Physician Assistant Studies	M
Project Management	M

NEW YORK LAW SCHOOL

Law	P,M
Taxation	P,M

NEW YORK MEDICAL COLLEGE

Allopathic Medicine	P
Communication Disorders	M*
Community Health	M
Environmental and Occupational Health	M
Epidemiology	M,D,O*
Health Promotion	M
Health Services Management and Hospital Administration	M*
International Health	M
Maternal and Child Health	M
Physical Therapy	D*
Public Health—General	M,D,O*

NEW YORK UNIVERSITY

Accounting	M,D
Acute Care/Critical Care Nursing	M,O
Adult Nursing	M,O
Advertising and Public Relations	M
Allopathic Medicine	P
Art Education	M,D
Business Administration and Management— General	P,M,D,O
Business Education	M,O
Clinical Research	P,M,D
Communication Disorders	M,D
Counselor Education	M,D,O
Dentistry	P
Early Childhood Education	M,D,O
Education—General	M,D,O*
Educational Administration	M,D,O

Educational Measurement and Evaluation	M,D,O
Educational Media/ Instructional Technology	M,D,O
Educational Policy	M,D
Educational Psychology	M,D,O
Electronic Commerce	M,O
Elementary Education	M,D,O
English as a Second Language	M,D,O
English Education	M,D,O
Environmental and Occupational Health	M,D
Environmental Education	M
Epidemiology	M,D
Family Nurse Practitioner Studies	M,O
Finance and Banking	M,D,O
Foreign Languages Education	M,D,O
Foundations and Philosophy of Education	M,D
Gerontological Nursing	M,O
Health Education	M,D
Health Promotion	M,D,O
Health Services Management and Hospital Administration	M,O
Higher Education	M,D
Hospitality Management	M,D,O*
Human Resources Development	M,O
Human Resources Management	M,D,O*
International and Comparative Education	M,D,O
International Business	M,D
International Health	M,D
Kinesiology and Movement Studies	M,D
Law	P,M,D,O
Legal and Justice Studies	M,D
Management Information Systems	M,D,O*
Management Strategy and Policy	M,D
Marketing	M,D,O*
Mathematics Education	M
Multilingual and Multicultural Education	M,D,O
Music Education	M,D,O
Nonprofit Management	M,D,O*
Nurse Midwifery	M,O
Nursing Education	M,O
Nursing Informatics	M,O
Nursing—General	M,D,O
Occupational Therapy	M,D
Oral and Dental Sciences	M,D,O
Organizational Behavior	M,D
Organizational Management	M,D
Pediatric Nursing	M,O
Physical Therapy	M,D
Psychiatric Nursing	M,O
Quantitative Analysis	M,D,O
Reading Education	M
Real Estate	M,O*
Science Education	M
Social Sciences Education	M,D
Social Work	M,D*
Special Education	M
Sports Management	M,O
Student Affairs	M,D
Taxation	P,M,D,O
Travel and Tourism	M,O

NIAGARA UNIVERSITY

Business Administration and Management— General	M
Counselor Education	M,O
Education—General	M,O
Educational Administration	M,O

Elementary Education M
Foundations and
  Philosophy of Education M
Reading Education M
Secondary Education M
Special Education M

NICHOLLS STATE UNIVERSITY

Business Administration
  and Management—
    General M
Counselor Education M
Curriculum and Instruction M
Education—General M
Educational Administration M
Mathematics Education M

NICHOLS COLLEGE

Business Administration
  and Management—
    General M

NIPISSING UNIVERSITY

Education—General M,O

NORFOLK STATE UNIVERSITY

Early Childhood Education M
Education of the Multiply
  Handicapped M
Education—General M
Educational Administration M
Music Education M
Secondary Education M
Social Work M,D
Special Education M
Urban Education M

NORTH CAROLINA AGRICULTURAL AND TECHNICAL STATE UNIVERSITY

Adult Education M
Agricultural Education M
Art Education M
Counselor Education M
Early Childhood Education M
Education—General M
Educational Administration M
Educational Media/
  Instructional Technology M
Elementary Education M
English Education M
Health Education M
Human Resources
  Development M
Human Resources
  Management M
Mathematics Education M
Middle School Education M
Physical Education M
Reading Education M
Science Education M
Social Sciences Education M
Social Work M
Vocational and Technical
  Education M

NORTH CAROLINA CENTRAL UNIVERSITY

Business Administration
  and Management—
    General M
Communication Disorders M
Counselor Education M
Education—General M
Educational Administration M
Educational Media/
  Instructional Technology M

Elementary Education M
Information Studies M
Law P
Library Science M
Physical Education M
Recreation and Park
  Management M
Special Education M

NORTH CAROLINA STATE UNIVERSITY

Accounting M
Adult Education M,D
Agricultural Education M
Business Administration
  and Management—
    General M
Community College
  Education M,D
Counselor Education M,D
Curriculum and Instruction M,D
Developmental Education M
Education—General M,D,O
Educational Administration M,D
Educational Measurement
  and Evaluation D
Educational Media/
  Instructional Technology M,D
Epidemiology M,D
Higher Education M,D
Mathematics Education M,D
Middle School Education M
Recreation and Park
  Management M,D
Science Education M,D
Special Education M
Sports Management M,D
Supply Chain
  Management M
Travel and Tourism M,D
Veterinary Medicine P,M
Veterinary Sciences M,D

NORTH CENTRAL COLLEGE

Business Administration
  and Management—
    General M
Education—General M
Educational Administration M
Management Information
  Systems M
Nonprofit Management M

NORTH DAKOTA STATE UNIVERSITY

Agricultural Education M
Business Administration
  and Management—
    General M
Counselor Education M,D
Education—General M,D,O
Educational Administration M,O
Exercise and Sports
  Science M
Logistics M,D
Mathematics Education M,D,O
Music Education M,D,O
Nursing—General M,D
Pharmaceutical Sciences M,D
Physical Education M
Science Education M,D,O
Social Sciences Education M,D,O
Sports Management M
Transportation
  Management M,D
Veterinary Sciences M,D

NORTHEASTERN ILLINOIS UNIVERSITY

Accounting M

Business Administration
  and Management—
    General M
Counselor Education M
Education of the Gifted M
Education—General M
Educational Administration M
English Education M
Finance and Banking M
Human Resources
  Development M
Marketing M
Mathematics Education M
Multilingual and
  Multicultural Education M
Reading Education M
Special Education M
Urban Education M

NORTHEASTERN OHIO UNIVERSITIES COLLEGE OF MEDICINE

Allopathic Medicine P

NORTHEASTERN STATE UNIVERSITY

Accounting M
Business Administration
  and Management—
    General M
Communication Disorders M
Counselor Education M
Early Childhood Education M
Education—General M
Educational Administration M
Educational Media/
  Instructional Technology M
Finance and Banking M
Foundations and
  Philosophy of Education M
Health Education M
Higher Education M
Industrial and
  Manufacturing
  Management M
Mathematics Education M
Optometry P
Reading Education M
Science Education M

NORTHEASTERN UNIVERSITY

Accounting M,O
Acute Care/Critical Care
  Nursing M,O
Allied Health—General P,M,D,O
Business Administration
  and Management—
    General M,O
Communication Disorders M,D
Community Health
  Nursing M,O
Counselor Education M
Educational Psychology M
Entrepreneurship M
Exercise and Sports
  Science M
Family Nurse Practitioner
  Studies M,O
Finance and Banking M
Health Services
  Management and
  Hospital Administration M
Law P
Legal and Justice Studies M,D
Management Information
  Systems M,D
Nurse Anesthesia M
Nursing and Healthcare
  Administration M
Nursing—General M,D,O
Pediatric Nursing M,O

Pharmaceutical Sciences P,M,D
Physician Assistant
  Studies M
Psychiatric Nursing M,O
Special Education M,D,O
Student Affairs M
Taxation M,O

NORTHERN ARIZONA UNIVERSITY

Allied Health—General M,D,O
Business Administration
  and Management—
    General M
Communication Disorders M
Community College
  Education M,D
Counselor Education M
Curriculum and Instruction D
Early Childhood Education M
Education—General M,D,O
Educational Administration M,D
Educational Media/
  Instructional Technology M,O
Educational Psychology D
Elementary Education M
English as a Second
  Language M,D,O
English Education M
Exercise and Sports
  Science M
Foreign Languages
  Education M
Health Education M
Health Promotion M
Management Information
  Systems M
Mathematics Education M
Multilingual and
  Multicultural Education M,O
Music Education M
Nursing—General M,O
Physical Education M
Physical Therapy D
Public Health—General M
Science Education M,D
Secondary Education M
Special Education M
Vocational and Technical
  Education M

NORTHERN ILLINOIS UNIVERSITY

Accounting M
Adult Education M,D
Business Administration
  and Management—
    General M
Communication Disorders M,D
Counselor Education M,D
Curriculum and Instruction M,D
Early Childhood Education M,D
Education—General M,D,O
Educational Administration M,D,O
Educational Media/
  Instructional Technology M,D
Educational Psychology M,D,O
Elementary Education M,D
Foundations and
  Philosophy of Education M,D,O
Higher Education M,D
Industrial and
  Manufacturing
  Management M
Law P
Management Information
  Systems M
Nursing—General M
Physical Education M
Physical Therapy M
Public Health—General M
Reading Education M,D
Secondary Education M,D
Special Education M,D

Sports Management   M
Taxation   M

NORTHERN KENTUCKY UNIVERSITY

Accounting   M
Business Administration and Management—
   General   M
Counselor Education   M
Education—General   M,O
Educational Administration   M
Family Nurse Practitioner
   Studies   M,O
Law   P
Nonprofit Management   M,O
Nursing—General   M,O
Organizational
   Management   M
Special Education   O

NORTHERN MICHIGAN UNIVERSITY

Communication Disorders   M
Education—General   M,O
Educational Administration   M,O
Elementary Education   M
Exercise and Sports
   Science   M
Nursing—General   M
Secondary Education   M
Special Education   M

NORTHERN STATE UNIVERSITY

Counselor Education   M
Education—General   M
Educational Administration   M
Educational Media/
   Instructional Technology   M
Elementary Education   M
English Education   M
Health Education   M
Physical Education   M
Reading Education   M
Secondary Education   M
Special Education   M

NORTH GEORGIA COLLEGE & STATE UNIVERSITY

Art Education   M,O
Early Childhood Education   M,O
Education—General   M,O
Educational Administration   M,O
English Education   M,O
Family Nurse Practitioner
   Studies   M
Mathematics Education   M,O
Middle School Education   M,O
Nursing Education   M
Physical Education   M,O
Physical Therapy   D
Science Education   M,O
Secondary Education   M,O
Social Sciences Education   M,O
Special Education   M,O

NORTH GREENVILLE UNIVERSITY

Business Administration and Management—
   General   M

NORTH PARK THEOLOGICAL SEMINARY

Religious Education   M

NORTH PARK UNIVERSITY

Business Administration and Management—
   General   M
Education—General   M
Nursing—General   M

NORTHWEST CHRISTIAN COLLEGE

Business Administration and Management—
   General   M
Counselor Education   M

NORTHWESTERN HEALTH SCIENCES UNIVERSITY

Acupuncture and Oriental
   Medicine   M
Chiropractic   P
Rehabilitation Sciences   O

NORTHWESTERN OKLAHOMA STATE UNIVERSITY

Adult Education   M
Counselor Education   M
Curriculum and Instruction   M
Education—General   M
Educational Administration   M
Elementary Education   M
Reading Education   M
Secondary Education   M

NORTHWESTERN POLYTECHNIC UNIVERSITY

Business Administration and Management—
   General   M

NORTHWESTERN STATE UNIVERSITY OF LOUISIANA

Adult Education   M
Business Education   M
Counselor Education   M,O
Curriculum and Instruction   M
Early Childhood Education   M
Education—General   M,O
Educational Administration   M,O
Educational Media/
   Instructional Technology   M,O
Elementary Education   M,O
English Education   M
Health Education   M
Home Economics
   Education   M
Mathematics Education   M
Middle School Education   M
Nursing—General   M
Reading Education   M,O
Science Education   M
Secondary Education   M,O
Social Sciences Education   M
Special Education   M,O
Student Affairs   M,O

NORTHWESTERN UNIVERSITY

Accounting   D
Advertising and Public
   Relations   M
Allopathic Medicine
Business Administration and Management—
   General   M
Clinical Research   M,O
Communication Disorders   M,D*
Education—General   M,D*
Educational Media/
   Instructional Technology   M,D

Electronic Commerce   M
Elementary Education   M
Finance and Banking   D
Higher Education   M
Law   P,M,O
Management Information
   Systems   M
Management Strategy and
   Policy   D
Marketing   M,D*
Music Education   M,D
Organizational Behavior   M,D
Organizational
   Management   M,D
Physical Therapy   D
Project Management   M
Public Health—General   M
Secondary Education   M
Special Education   M,D

NORTHWEST MISSOURI STATE UNIVERSITY

Accounting   M
Agricultural Education   M
Business Administration and Management—
   General   M
Counselor Education   M
Early Childhood Education   M
Education—General   M,O
Educational Administration   M,O
Educational Media/
   Instructional Technology   M
Elementary Education   M,O
English Education   M
Health Education   M
Health Services
   Management and
   Hospital Administration   M
Management Information
   Systems   M
Mathematics Education   M
Middle School Education   M
Music Education   M
Physical Education   M
Reading Education   M
Recreation and Park
   Management   M
Science Education   M
Secondary Education   M,O
Social Sciences Education   M
Special Education   M

NORTHWEST NAZARENE UNIVERSITY

Business Administration and Management—
   General   M
Counselor Education   M
Curriculum and Instruction   M
Education—General   M
Educational Administration   M
Reading Education   M
Social Work   M
Special Education   M

NORTHWEST UNIVERSITY

Business Administration and Management—
   General   M
Education—General   M

NORTHWOOD UNIVERSITY

Business Administration and Management—
   General   M

NORWICH UNIVERSITY

Business Administration and Management—
   General   M

Education—General   M
Management Information
   Systems   M
Nursing and Healthcare
   Administration   M
Organizational
   Management   M

NOTRE DAME COLLEGE (OH)

Accounting   M,O
Business Administration and Management—
   General   M,O
Education—General   M,O
Finance and Banking   M,O
Management Information
   Systems   M,O
Reading Education   M,O
Special Education   M,O

NOTRE DAME DE NAMUR UNIVERSITY

Business Administration and Management—
   General   M
Education—General   M
Educational Administration   M,O
Educational Media/
   Instructional Technology   M,O
English as a Second
   Language   M,O
Music Education   M
Reading Education   M,O
Special Education   M,O

NOVA SOUTHEASTERN UNIVERSITY

Accounting   M
Adult Education   D
Allied Health—General   M,D
Art Education   M,O
Business Administration and Management—
   General   M,D*
Communication Disorders   M,D
Computer Education   M,D,O
Curriculum and Instruction   M,O
Dentistry   P,M
Distance Education
   Development   M,D
Early Childhood Education   M,D,O
Education of the Gifted   M,O
Education—General   M,D,O*
Educational Administration   M,D,O
Educational Media/
   Instructional Technology   M,D,O
Elementary Education   M,O
English as a Second
   Language   M,O
English Education   M,O
Health Education   D
Higher Education   D
Human Resources
   Management   M
Human Services   D
International Business   M,D
Law   P,M
Legal and Justice Studies   M
Management Information
   Systems   M,D
Mathematics Education   M,O
Multilingual and
   Multicultural Education   M,O
Nursing—General   M
Occupational Therapy   M,D
Optometry   P,M
Organizational
   Management   D
Osteopathic Medicine   P,M
Pharmacy   P
Physical Therapy   D

Physician Assistant
  Studies   M
Public Health—General   M
Reading Education   M,O
Real Estate   M
Religious Education   M,O
Science Education   M,O
Secondary Education   M,O
Social Sciences Education   M,O
Special Education   M,D,O
Sports Management   M,O
Student Affairs   M
Taxation   M
Urban Education   M,O
Vision Sciences   P,M
Vocational and Technical
  Education   D

NYACK COLLEGE

Accounting   M
Business Administration
  and Management—
    General   M
Education—General   M

OAKLAND CITY UNIVERSITY

Business Administration
  and Management—
    General   M
Education—General   M,D
Educational Administration   M,D

OAKLAND UNIVERSITY

Accounting   M,O
Adult Nursing   M
Allied Health—General   M,D,O
Business Administration
  and Management—
    General   M,O*
Early Childhood Education   M,D,O
Education—General   M,D,O
Educational Administration   M,D,O*
Educational Media/
  Instructional Technology   O
English as a Second
  Language   M,O
Entrepreneurship   M,O
Environmental and
  Occupational Health   M*
Exercise and Sports
  Science   M,O
Family Nurse Practitioner
  Studies   M,D,O
Finance and Banking   M,O
Foundations and
  Philosophy of Education   M
Gerontological Nursing   M,O
Health Promotion   O
Higher Education   M,D,O
Human Resources
  Development   M
Human Resources
  Management   M,O
Industrial and
  Manufacturing
  Management   M,O
International Business   M,O
Management Information
  Systems   M,O
Marketing   M,O
Maternal and Child Health   M,D,O
Mathematics Education   M,D,O
Medical Physics   M,D
Music Education   M,D
Nurse Anesthesia   M,O
Nursing Education   M,O
Nursing—General   M,D,O*
Physical Therapy   M,D,O
Reading Education   M,D,O
Secondary Education   M
Special Education   M,O

OCCIDENTAL COLLEGE

Education—General   M
Elementary Education   M
English Education   M
Foreign Languages
  Education   M
Mathematics Education   M
Science Education   M
Secondary Education   M
Social Sciences Education   M

OGI SCHOOL OF SCIENCE & ENGINEERING AT OREGON HEALTH & SCIENCE UNIVERSITY

Business Administration
  and Management—
    General   M,O
Environmental and
  Occupational Health   M,D
Health Services
  Management and
  Hospital Administration   M,O

OGLALA LAKOTA COLLEGE

Business Administration
  and Management—
    General   M
Educational Administration   M

OGLETHORPE UNIVERSITY

Business Administration
  and Management—
    General   M
Early Childhood Education   M
Education—General   M

OHIO COLLEGE OF PODIATRIC MEDICINE

Podiatric Medicine   P

OHIO DOMINICAN UNIVERSITY

Business Administration
  and Management—
    General   M
Education—General   M
English as a Second
  Language   M

OHIO NORTHERN UNIVERSITY

Law   P
Pharmacy   P

THE OHIO STATE UNIVERSITY

Accounting   M,D
Agricultural Education   M,D
Allied Health—General   M
Allopathic Medicine   P
Art Education   M,D
Business Administration
  and Management—
    General   M,D
Communication Disorders   M,D
Dentistry   P,M
Education—General   M,D*
Educational Administration   M,D
Educational Policy   M,D
Finance and Banking   M,D
Health Services
  Management and
  Hospital Administration   M
Higher Education   M
Home Economics
  Education   M
Hospitality Management   M,D
Human Resources
  Management   M,D

Law   P,M*
Logistics   M
Management Information
  Systems   M,D
Medicinal and
  Pharmaceutical
  Chemistry   M,D
Nursing—General   M,D
Occupational Therapy   M
Optometry   P
Oral and Dental Sciences   D
Pharmaceutical
  Administration   M,D
Pharmaceutical Sciences   M,D*
Pharmacy   P
Physical Education   M,D
Physical Therapy   M
Public Health—General   M,D
Social Work   M,D
Student Affairs   M
Veterinary Medicine   P
Veterinary Sciences   M,D
Vocational and Technical
  Education   D

THE OHIO STATE UNIVERSITY AT LIMA

Early Childhood Education   M
Education—General   M
Middle School Education   M
Social Work   M

THE OHIO STATE UNIVERSITY AT MARION

Early Childhood Education   M,D
Education—General   M,D
Middle School Education   M,D
Nursing—General   M,D
Social Work   M,D

THE OHIO STATE UNIVERSITY– MANSFIELD CAMPUS

Early Childhood Education   M
Middle School Education   M
Social Work   M

THE OHIO STATE UNIVERSITY– NEWARK CAMPUS

Early Childhood Education   M
Education—General   M
Middle School Education   M
Social Work   M

OHIO UNIVERSITY

Art Education   M
Athletic Training and
  Sports Medicine   M
Business Administration
  and Management—
    General   M
Communication Disorders   M,D
Computer Education   M,D
Counselor Education   M,D
Curriculum and Instruction   M,D
Early Childhood Education   M
Education—General   M,D
Educational Administration   M,D
Educational Measurement
  and Evaluation   M,D
Educational Media/
  Instructional Technology   M,D
English as a Second
  Language   M
Exercise and Sports
  Science   M,D
Finance and Banking   M

Health Services
  Management and
  Hospital Administration   M
Higher Education   M,D
Mathematics Education   M,D
Middle School Education   M,D
Music Education   M,O
Osteopathic Medicine   P
Physical Education   M
Physical Therapy   D
Reading Education   M
Recreation and Park
  Management   M
Science Education   M
Secondary Education   M,D
Social Sciences Education   M,D
Social Work   M
Special Education   M,D
Sports Management   M
Student Affairs   M,D

OKLAHOMA CITY UNIVERSITY

Accounting   M
Business Administration
  and Management—
    General   M
Early Childhood Education   M
Education—General   M
Educational Psychology   M
Elementary Education   M
English as a Second
  Language   M
Finance and Banking   M
Health Services
  Management and
  Hospital Administration   M
International Business   M
Law   P
Management Information
  Systems   M
Marketing   M
Nursing—General   M

OKLAHOMA STATE UNIVERSITY

Accounting   M,D
Agricultural Education   M,D
Business Administration
  and Management—
    General   M,D*
Communication Disorders   M
Counselor Education   M,D,O
Curriculum and Instruction   M,D
Education—General   M,D,O
Educational Administration   M,D
Educational Psychology   M,D,O
Emergency Medical
  Services   M
Finance and Banking   M,D
Health Education   M,D,O
Health Services
  Management and
  Hospital Administration   M
Higher Education   M,D
Hospitality Management   M,D
Industrial and
  Manufacturing
  Management   M,D
Leisure Studies   M,D,O
Management Information
  Systems   M,D
Marketing   M,D
Mathematics Education   M,D
Music Education   M
Physical Education   M,D,O
Student Affairs   M,D,O
Veterinary Medicine   P
Veterinary Sciences   M,D
Vocational and Technical
  Education   M,D

OKLAHOMA STATE UNIVERSITY CENTER FOR HEALTH SCIENCES

Osteopathic Medicine   P

OLD DOMINION UNIVERSITY

Accounting	M
Allied Health—General	M,D
Athletic Training and Sports Medicine	M
Business Administration and Management— General	M,D*
Business Education	M,D
Communication Disorders	M
Community College Education	M,D
Community Health	M
Counselor Education	M,D,O
Curriculum and Instruction	M,D
Dental Hygiene	M
Early Childhood Education	M,D
Education—General	M,D,O
Educational Administration	M,D,O
Educational Media/ Instructional Technology	M,D
Elementary Education	M
Environmental and Occupational Health	M
Exercise and Sports Science	M
Finance and Banking	D
Health Promotion	M
Health Services Management and Hospital Administration	M
Health Services Research	D
Higher Education	M,D,O
Kinesiology and Movement Studies	D
Library Science	M
Marketing	D
Middle School Education	M,D
Music Education	M
Nursing—General	M
Physical Education	M
Physical Therapy	D
Public Health—General	M
Reading Education	M,D
Recreation and Park Management	M
Science Education	M
Secondary Education	M,D
Special Education	M,D
Sports Management	M
Travel and Tourism	M
Vocational and Technical Education	M,D

OLIVET COLLEGE

Education—General	M

OLIVET NAZARENE UNIVERSITY

Business Administration and Management— General	M
Curriculum and Instruction	M
Education—General	M
Elementary Education	M
Organizational Management	M
Secondary Education	M

ORAL ROBERTS UNIVERSITY

Accounting	M
Business Administration and Management— General	M
Curriculum and Instruction	M,D
Education—General	M,D
Educational Administration	M,D
English as a Second Language	M,D
Finance and Banking	M
Higher Education	M,D

International Business	M
Marketing	M
Nonprofit Management	M
Organizational Behavior	M
Religious Education	P,M,D

OREGON COLLEGE OF ORIENTAL MEDICINE

Acupuncture and Oriental Medicine	M,D*

OREGON HEALTH & SCIENCE UNIVERSITY

Adult Nursing	M,O
Allopathic Medicine	P
Community Health Nursing	M,O
Dentistry	P
Epidemiology	M
Family Nurse Practitioner Studies	M,O
Gerontological Nursing	M,D,O
Nurse Midwifery	M,O
Nursing—General	M,D,O
Oral and Dental Sciences	M,O
Pediatric Nursing	M,O
Psychiatric Nursing	M,O
Women's Health Nursing	M,O

OREGON STATE UNIVERSITY

Adult Education	M
Agricultural Education	M
Business Administration and Management— General	M,O
Counselor Education	M,D
Education—General	M,D
Educational Administration	M
Elementary Education	M
Environmental and Occupational Health	M
Exercise and Sports Science	M,D
Health Physics/ Radiological Health	M,D
Health Promotion	M
Health Services Management and Hospital Administration	M
Kinesiology and Movement Studies	M
Mathematics Education	M,D
Music Education	M
Pharmaceutical Sciences	P,M,D
Pharmacy	P,M,D
Physical Education	M
Public Health—General	M,D
Reading Education	M
Science Education	M,D
Student Affairs	M
Veterinary Medicine	P
Veterinary Sciences	M,D

OREGON STATE UNIVERSITY– CASCADES

Education—General	M

OTTAWA UNIVERSITY

Business Administration and Management— General	M
Counselor Education	M
Curriculum and Instruction	M
Early Childhood Education	M
Education—General	M
Educational Administration	M
Educational Media/ Instructional Technology	M

Elementary Education	M
Finance and Banking	M
Human Resources Development	M
Human Resources Management	M
Marketing	M
Special Education	M

OTTERBEIN COLLEGE

Adult Nursing	M,O
Business Administration and Management— General	M
Education—General	M
Family Nurse Practitioner Studies	M,O
Nursing and Healthcare Administration	M,O
Nursing—General	M,O

OUR LADY OF HOLY CROSS COLLEGE

Counselor Education	M
Curriculum and Instruction	M
Education—General	M
Educational Administration	M

OUR LADY OF THE LAKE UNIVERSITY OF SAN ANTONIO

Business Administration and Management— General	M
Communication Disorders	M
Counselor Education	M
Curriculum and Instruction	M,D
Education—General	M,D
Educational Administration	M,D
Educational Media/ Instructional Technology	M
Finance and Banking	M
Health Services Management and Hospital Administration	M
International Business	M
Social Work	M
Special Education	M

OXFORD GRADUATE SCHOOL

Organizational Management	M,D

PACE UNIVERSITY

Accounting	M
Business Administration and Management— General	M,D,O*
Curriculum and Instruction	M,O
Education—General	M,O*
Educational Administration	M,O
Finance and Banking	M
Health Services Management and Hospital Administration	M
International Business	M
Investment Management	M
Law	P,M,D*
Legal and Justice Studies	P,M,D
Management Information Systems	M
Management Strategy and Policy	M
Marketing Research	M
Marketing	M
Nonprofit Management	M
Nursing—General	M,O*
Taxation	M

PACIFIC COLLEGE OF ORIENTAL MEDICINE

Acupuncture and Oriental Medicine	M,D

PACIFIC COLLEGE OF ORIENTAL MEDICINE-CHICAGO

Acupuncture and Oriental Medicine	M

PACIFIC COLLEGE OF ORIENTAL MEDICINE-NEW YORK

Acupuncture and Oriental Medicine	M

PACIFIC LUTHERAN UNIVERSITY

Business Administration and Management— General	M
Curriculum and Instruction	M
Education—General	M
Educational Administration	M
Family Nurse Practitioner Studies	M
Nursing and Healthcare Administration	M
Nursing—General	M

PACIFIC STATES UNIVERSITY

Accounting	M,D
Business Administration and Management— General	M,D
Finance and Banking	M,D
International Business	M,D
Management Information Systems	M,D
Real Estate	M,D

PACIFIC UNION COLLEGE

Education—General	M
Educational Administration	M

PACIFIC UNIVERSITY

Early Childhood Education	M
Education—General	M
Elementary Education	M
Middle School Education	M
Occupational Therapy	M
Pharmacy	P
Physical Therapy	D
Physician Assistant Studies	M
Secondary Education	M
Special Education	M

PALM BEACH ATLANTIC UNIVERSITY

Business Administration and Management— General	M
Counselor Education	M
Education—General	M
Elementary Education	M
Human Resources Development	M
Organizational Management	M
Pharmacy	P

PALMER COLLEGE OF CHIROPRACTIC

Chiropractic	P*
Clinical Research	M

PARKER COLLEGE OF CHIROPRACTIC

Chiropractic	P

PARK UNIVERSITY

Business Administration and Management— General	M
Education—General	M
Educational Administration	M
Entrepreneurship	M
Health Services Management and Hospital Administration	M
International Business	M
Law	M
Management Information Systems	M
Middle School Education	M
Multilingual and Multicultural Education	M
Nonprofit Management	M
Secondary Education	M
Special Education	M

PENN STATE DICKINSON SCHOOL OF LAW

Law	P,M

PENN STATE GREAT VALLEY

Business Administration and Management— General	M
Curriculum and Instruction	M
Education—General	M
Educational Media/ Instructional Technology	M
Entrepreneurship	M
Health Services Management and Hospital Administration	M
Special Education	M

PENN STATE HARRISBURG

Adult Education	M,D
Business Administration and Management— General	M*
Business Education	M,D
Curriculum and Instruction	M,D
Education—General	M,D
Health Education	M,D
Health Services Management and Hospital Administration	M,D
Management Information Systems	M

PENN STATE HERSHEY MEDICAL CENTER

Allopathic Medicine	P,M,D
Health Services Research	M
Veterinary Sciences	M

PENN STATE UNIVERSITY PARK

Accounting	M,D
Adult Education	M,D
Agricultural Education	M,D
Art Education	M,D
Communication Disorders	M,D
Counselor Education	M,D
Curriculum and Instruction	M,D
Early Childhood Education	M,D
Education—General	M,D
Educational Administration	M,D
Educational Media/ Instructional Technology	M,D
Educational Psychology	M,D
Elementary Education	M,D
Environmental and Occupational Health	M,D
Finance and Banking	M,D
Foundations and Philosophy of Education	M,D
Health Services Management and Hospital Administration	M,D*
Higher Education	M,D
Hospitality Management	M,D
Human Resources Development	M
Industrial and Manufacturing Management	M,D
Kinesiology and Movement Studies	M,D
Leisure Studies	M,D
Logistics	M,D
Management Information Systems	M,D
Marketing	M,D
Multilingual and Multicultural Education	M,D
Music Education	M,D
Nursing—General	M,D
Quality Management	M
Reading Education	M,D
Real Estate	M,D
Recreation and Park Management	M,D
Science Education	M,D
Social Sciences Education	M,D
Special Education	M,D
Student Affairs	M,D
Veterinary Sciences	D
Vocational and Technical Education	M,D

PENNSYLVANIA COLLEGE OF OPTOMETRY

Communication Disorders	M,D,O
Optometry	P
Rehabilitation Sciences	M,D,O
Special Education	M,D,O
Vision Sciences	M,D,O

PEPPERDINE UNIVERSITY

Business Administration and Management— General	M
Education—General	M,D*
Educational Administration	M,D
Educational Media/ Instructional Technology	D
Organizational Management	M

PEPPERDINE UNIVERSITY

Business Administration and Management— General	M*
International Business	M
Law	P

PERU STATE COLLEGE

Education—General	M

PFEIFFER UNIVERSITY

Business Administration and Management— General	M
Education—General	M
Elementary Education	M

Health Services Management and Hospital Administration	M
Organizational Management	M
Religious Education	M

PHILADELPHIA BIBLICAL UNIVERSITY

Curriculum and Instruction	M
Education—General	M
Educational Administration	M
Organizational Management	M

PHILADELPHIA COLLEGE OF OSTEOPATHIC MEDICINE

Osteopathic Medicine	P
Physician Assistant Studies	M*

PHILADELPHIA UNIVERSITY

Business Administration and Management— General	M
Educational Media/ Instructional Technology	M*
Finance and Banking	M
Health Services Management and Hospital Administration	M
International Business	M
Marketing	M
Nurse Midwifery	M,O
Occupational Therapy	M
Physician Assistant Studies	M
Taxation	M

PHILLIPS GRADUATE INSTITUTE

Counselor Education	M
Organizational Behavior	M

PHILLIPS THEOLOGICAL SEMINARY

Business Administration and Management— General	P,M,D
Higher Education	P,M,D
Religious Education	P,M,D
Social Work	P,M,D

PIEDMONT COLLEGE

Business Administration and Management— General	M
Curriculum and Instruction	M,O
Early Childhood Education	M,O
Education—General	M,O
Secondary Education	M,O

PIKEVILLE COLLEGE

Osteopathic Medicine	P

PITTSBURG STATE UNIVERSITY

Accounting	M
Art Education	M
Business Administration and Management— General	M
Community College Education	O
Counselor Education	M
Early Childhood Education	M
Education—General	M,O

Educational Administration	M
Educational Media/ Instructional Technology	M
Elementary Education	M
Higher Education	M,O
Human Resources Development	M,O
Music Education	M
Nursing—General	M
Physical Education	M
Reading Education	M
Secondary Education	M
Special Education	M
Vocational and Technical Education	M,O

PLYMOUTH STATE UNIVERSITY

Athletic Training and Sports Medicine	M
Business Administration and Management— General	M
Counselor Education	M
Education—General	O
Educational Administration	M
Elementary Education	M
English Education	M
Health Education	M
Mathematics Education	M
Middle School Education	M
Reading Education	M
Science Education	M
Secondary Education	M
Special Education	M,O

POINT LOMA NAZARENE UNIVERSITY

Business Administration and Management— General	M
Education—General	M,O
Nursing—General	M

POINT PARK UNIVERSITY

Business Administration and Management— General	M
Curriculum and Instruction	M
Education—General	M
Educational Administration	M
Organizational Management	M

POLYTECHNIC UNIVERSITY, BROOKLYN CAMPUS

Business Administration and Management— General	M,D*
Finance and Banking	M,O
Organizational Behavior	M
Transportation Management	M

POLYTECHNIC UNIVERSITY, LONG ISLAND GRADUATE CENTER

Business Administration and Management— General	M,O
Entrepreneurship	M,D,O

POLYTECHNIC UNIVERSITY OF PUERTO RICO

Business Administration and Management— General	M

Industrial and Manufacturing Management	M
International Business	M

POLYTECHNIC UNIVERSITY OF THE AMERICAS–MIAMI CAMPUS

Business Administration and Management—General	M

POLYTECHNIC UNIVERSITY OF THE AMERICAS–ORLANDO CAMPUS

Business Administration and Management—General	M

POLYTECHNIC UNIVERSITY, WESTCHESTER GRADUATE CENTER

Business Administration and Management—General	M
Finance and Banking	M,O
Management Information Systems	M,O

PONCE SCHOOL OF MEDICINE

Allopathic Medicine	P
Public Health—General	M

PONTIFICAL CATHOLIC UNIVERSITY OF PUERTO RICO

Accounting	M,D
Business Administration and Management—General	M,D
Clinical Laboratory Sciences/Medical Technology	O
Curriculum and Instruction	M,D
Education—General	M,D
Educational Media/Instructional Technology	M,D
English as a Second Language	M,D
Finance and Banking	M,D
Human Resources Management	M,D
Human Services	M,D
International Business	M,D
Law	P
Management Information Systems	M,D
Marketing	M,D
Medical/Surgical Nursing	M
Nursing—General	M
Psychiatric Nursing	M
Religious Education	M,D
Social Work	M,D

PONTIFICIA UNIVERSIDAD CATOLICA MADRE Y MAESTRA

Allopathic Medicine	P
Business Administration and Management—General	M
Educational Administration	M
Finance and Banking	M
Human Resources Management	M
International Business	M
Logistics	M

PORTLAND STATE UNIVERSITY

Adult Education	M,D
Business Administration and Management—General	M,D,O
Communication Disorders	M
Counselor Education	M,D
Curriculum and Instruction	M,D
Early Childhood Education	M,D
Education—General	M,D
Educational Administration	M,D
Educational Media/Instructional Technology	M,D
Educational Policy	M,D
Elementary Education	M,D
English as a Second Language	M
Finance and Banking	M
Foreign Languages Education	M
Health Education	M,O
Health Promotion	M,O
Health Services Management and Hospital Administration	M,O
Higher Education	M,D
Industrial and Manufacturing Management	M,D
International Business	M
Mathematics Education	M,D
Music Education	M
Public Health—General	M,O
Reading Education	M,D
Science Education	M,D
Secondary Education	M,D
Social Sciences Education	M
Social Work	M,D
Special Education	M,D

PRAIRIE VIEW A&M UNIVERSITY

Accounting	M
Business Administration and Management—General	M
Counselor Education	M,D
Curriculum and Instruction	M
Education—General	M,D
Educational Administration	M,D
Family Nurse Practitioner Studies	M
Health Education	M
Legal and Justice Studies	M,D
Management Information Systems	M,D
Nursing and Healthcare Administration	M
Nursing Education	M
Nursing—General	M
Physical Education	M
Special Education	M

PRATT INSTITUTE

Art Education	M
Facilities Management	M
Information Studies	M,O*
Library Science	M,O
Special Education	M

PRESCOTT COLLEGE

Education—General	M,D
English as a Second Language	M,D
Environmental Education	M
Leisure Studies	M
Multilingual and Multicultural Education	M,D

PRINCETON UNIVERSITY

Community College Education	D

Finance and Banking	M
Social Sciences Education	D

PROVIDENCE COLLEGE

Business Administration and Management—General	M*
Computer Education	M
Counselor Education	M
Education—General	M
Educational Administration	M
Mathematics Education	M
Reading Education	M
Special Education	M

PROVIDENCE COLLEGE AND THEOLOGICAL SEMINARY

English as a Second Language	P,M,D,O
Religious Education	P,M,D,O
Student Affairs	P,M,D,O

PURDUE UNIVERSITY

Accounting	M,D
Agricultural Education	M,D,O
Art Education	M,D,O
Business Administration and Management—General	M,D
Communication Disorders	M,D
Counselor Education	M,D,O
Curriculum and Instruction	M,D,O
Education of the Gifted	M,D,O
Education—General	M,D,O
Educational Administration	M,D,O
Educational Media/Instructional Technology	M,D,O
Educational Psychology	M,D,O
Elementary Education	M,D,O
English Education	M,D,O
Epidemiology	M,D
Exercise and Sports Science	M,D
Finance and Banking	M,D
Foreign Languages Education	M,D,O
Foundations and Philosophy of Education	M,D,O
Health Promotion	M,D
Higher Education	M,D,O
Home Economics Education	M,D,O
Hospitality Management	M,D
Human Resources Management	M,D
Industrial and Manufacturing Management	M,D
International Business	M
Management Information Systems	M,D
Management Strategy and Policy	M,D
Marketing	M,D
Mathematics Education	M,D,O
Medicinal and Pharmaceutical Chemistry	M,D
Organizational Behavior	M,D
Pharmaceutical Administration	M,D,O
Pharmaceutical Sciences	M,D
Pharmacy	P
Physical Education	M,D
Public Health—General	M,D
Quantitative Analysis	M,D
Reading Education	M,D,O
Science Education	M,D,O
Social Sciences Education	M,D,O
Special Education	M,D,O
Travel and Tourism	M,D

Veterinary Medicine	P
Veterinary Sciences	M,D
Vocational and Technical Education	M,D,O

PURDUE UNIVERSITY CALUMET

Accounting	M
Business Administration and Management—General	M
Counselor Education	M
Curriculum and Instruction	M
Education—General	M
Educational Administration	M
Educational Media/Instructional Technology	M
Elementary Education	M
Mathematics Education	M
Nursing—General	M
Science Education	M
Secondary Education	M

PURDUE UNIVERSITY NORTH CENTRAL

Education—General	M
Elementary Education	M

QUEENS COLLEGE OF THE CITY UNIVERSITY OF NEW YORK

Accounting	M
Art Education	M,O
Communication Disorders	M
Counselor Education	M
Early Childhood Education	M,O
Education—General	M,O
Educational Administration	O
Elementary Education	M,O
English as a Second Language	M
English Education	M,O
Exercise and Sports Science	M
Foreign Languages Education	M,O
Home Economics Education	M
Information Studies	M,O
Library Science	M,O
Mathematics Education	M,O
Multilingual and Multicultural Education	M,O
Music Education	M,O
Reading Education	M
Science Education	M,O
Secondary Education	M,O
Social Sciences Education	M,O
Special Education	M

QUEEN'S UNIVERSITY AT KINGSTON

Allopathic Medicine	P
Business Administration and Management—General	M
Education—General	M,D
Epidemiology	M
Exercise and Sports Science	M,D
Law	P,M
Nursing—General	M
Rehabilitation Sciences	M,D

QUEENS UNIVERSITY OF CHARLOTTE

Business Administration and Management—General	M
Education—General	M

Elementary Education	M
Nursing and Healthcare Administration	M
Nursing—General	M

QUINCY UNIVERSITY

Business Administration and Management— General	M
Counselor Education	M
Education—General	M

QUINNIPIAC UNIVERSITY

Accounting	M
Adult Nursing	M,O
Allied Health—General	M,D,O*
Business Administration and Management— General	M*
Clinical Laboratory Sciences/Medical Technology	M
Education—General	M*
Elementary Education	M
English Education	M
Family Nurse Practitioner Studies	M,O
Finance and Banking	M
Foreign Languages Education	M
Forensic Nursing	M,O
Health Services Management and Hospital Administration	M
International Business	M
Investment Management	M
Law	P,M
Legal and Justice Studies	M
Management Information Systems	M
Marketing	M
Mathematics Education	M
Middle School Education	M
Occupational Therapy	M
Physical Therapy	D
Physician Assistant Studies	M
Science Education	M
Secondary Education	M
Social Sciences Education	M

RADFORD UNIVERSITY

Business Administration and Management— General	M
Communication Disorders	M
Counselor Education	M
Education—General	M
Educational Administration	M
Nursing—General	M
Reading Education	M
Social Work	M
Special Education	M

REFORMED THEOLOGICAL SEMINARY–CHARLOTTE CAMPUS

Religious Education	P,M,D

REFORMED THEOLOGICAL SEMINARY–JACKSON CAMPUS

Religious Education	P,M,D,O

REGENT UNIVERSITY

Business Administration and Management— General	M,D,O
Counselor Education	M,D,O

Education—General	M,D,O
Educational Administration	M,D,O
Elementary Education	M,D,O
English as a Second Language	M,D,O
Entrepreneurship	M,D,O
Health Services Management and Hospital Administration	M
Law	P,M
Management Strategy and Policy	M,D,O
Organizational Management	M,D,O
Religious Education	M,D,O
Special Education	M,D,O

REGIONS UNIVERSITY

Organizational Behavior	P,M,D
Organizational Management	P,M,D

REGIS COLLEGE (MA)

Business Administration and Management— General	M
Education—General	M
Family Nurse Practitioner Studies	M,O
Nursing Education	M,O
Nursing—General	M,O
Organizational Management	M
Public Health—General	M

REGIS UNIVERSITY

Accounting	M,O
Adult Education	M,O
Allied Health—General	M,D
Business Administration and Management— General	M,O
Curriculum and Instruction	M,O
Early Childhood Education	M,O
Education—General	M,O
Educational Administration	M,O
Educational Media/ Instructional Technology	M,O
Electronic Commerce	M,O
Elementary Education	M,O
English as a Second Language	M,O
Finance and Banking	M,O
Foundations and Philosophy of Education	M,O
Health Services Management and Hospital Administration	M,D
Human Resources Management	M,O
Industrial and Manufacturing Management	M,O
International Business	M,O
Legal and Justice Studies	M,O
Management Information Systems	M,O
Marketing	M,O
Nonprofit Management	M,O
Nursing—General	M
Organizational Management	M,O
Physical Therapy	D
Physician Assistant Studies	M,D
Project Management	M,O
Reading Education	M,O
Science Education	M,O
Secondary Education	M,O
Special Education	M,O

RENSSELAER AT HARTFORD

Business Administration and Management— General	M

RENSSELAER POLYTECHNIC INSTITUTE

Business Administration and Management— General	M,D*
Electronic Commerce	M,D
Entrepreneurship	M,D
Finance and Banking	M,D
Industrial and Manufacturing Management	M,D
Management Information Systems	M,D
Marketing	M,D

RESEARCH COLLEGE OF NURSING

Family Nurse Practitioner Studies	M
Nursing Education	M
Nursing—General	M

RHODE ISLAND COLLEGE

Accounting	M
Art Education	M
Counselor Education	M,O
Early Childhood Education	M
Education—General	D
Educational Administration	M,O
Elementary Education	M
English as a Second Language	M,O
Finance and Banking	M
Health Education	M
Multilingual and Multicultural Education	M,O
Music Education	M
Nursing—General	M
Reading Education	M
Secondary Education	M,O
Social Work	M
Special Education	M,O

RHODE ISLAND SCHOOL OF DESIGN

Art Education	M

RHODES COLLEGE

Accounting	M

RICE UNIVERSITY

Business Administration and Management— General	M
Education—General	M

THE RICHARD STOCKTON COLLEGE OF NEW JERSEY

Business Administration and Management— General	M
Education—General	M
Educational Media/ Instructional Technology	M
Legal and Justice Studies	O
Nursing—General	M
Occupational Therapy	M
Physical Therapy	M,D

RIDER UNIVERSITY

Accounting	M
Business Administration and Management— General	M*
Business Education	M,O
Counselor Education	M,O
Curriculum and Instruction	M,O
Education—General	M,O*
Educational Administration	M,O
Elementary Education	M,O
English as a Second Language	M,O
English Education	M,O
Foreign Languages Education	M,O
Mathematics Education	M,O
Organizational Management	M
Reading Education	M,O
Science Education	M,O
Social Sciences Education	M,O
Special Education	M,O

RIVIER COLLEGE

Business Administration and Management— General	M
Counselor Education	M,O
Curriculum and Instruction	M,O
Early Childhood Education	M,O
Education—General	M,O
Educational Administration	M,O
Elementary Education	M,O
Foreign Languages Education	M
Human Resources Management	M
Management Information Systems	M
Nursing and Healthcare Administration	M
Nursing Education	M
Nursing—General	M
Organizational Management	M
Reading Education	M,O
Social Sciences Education	M
Special Education	M,O

ROBERT MORRIS UNIVERSITY

Accounting	M
Adult Education	M
Business Administration and Management— General	M
Finance and Banking	M
Human Resources Management	M
Management Information Systems	M,D
Nonprofit Management	M
Nursing—General	M
Sports Management	M
Taxation	M

ROBERTS WESLEYAN COLLEGE

Business Administration and Management— General	M,O
Counselor Education	M
Early Childhood Education	M,O
Education—General	M,O
Health Services Management and Hospital Administration	M
Human Services	M
Management Strategy and Policy	M,O
Marketing	M,O

Middle School Education M,O
Nonprofit Management M,O
Nursing and Healthcare
  Administration M
Nursing Education M
Nursing—General M
Reading Education M,O
Secondary Education M,O
Social Work M
Special Education M,O
Urban Education M,O

ROCHESTER INSTITUTE OF TECHNOLOGY

Accounting M
Art Education M
Business Administration
  and Management—
  General M
Clinical Laboratory
  Sciences/Medical
  Technology M
Educational Media/
  Instructional Technology M
Finance and Banking M
Health Services
  Management and
  Hospital Administration M,O
Hospitality Management M
Human Resources
  Development M,O
Industrial and
  Manufacturing
  Management M
International Business M
Management Information
  Systems M,O
Secondary Education M
Special Education M
Travel and Tourism M

ROCKFORD COLLEGE

Art Education M
Business Administration
  and Management—
  General M
Education—General M
Elementary Education M
English Education M
Reading Education M
Secondary Education M
Social Sciences Education M
Special Education M

ROCKHURST UNIVERSITY

Business Administration
  and Management—
  General M
Communication Disorders M
Education—General M
Occupational Therapy M
Physical Therapy D

ROGER WILLIAMS UNIVERSITY

Education—General M
Elementary Education M
Law P
Reading Education M

ROLLINS COLLEGE

Business Administration
  and Management—
  General M
Counselor Education M
Education—General M
Elementary Education M
English Education M

Human Resources
  Development M
Human Resources
  Management M
Mathematics Education M
Music Education M
Secondary Education M

ROOSEVELT UNIVERSITY

Accounting M
Actuarial Science M
Business Administration
  and Management—
  General M
Counselor Education M
Early Childhood Education M
Education—General M,D
Educational Administration M,D
Elementary Education M
Hospitality Management M
Human Resources
  Development M
Human Resources
  Management M
International Business M
Management Information
  Systems M
Music Education M,O
Organizational
  Management M,D
Reading Education M
Real Estate M,O
Secondary Education M
Special Education M

ROSALIND FRANKLIN UNIVERSITY OF MEDICINE AND SCIENCE

Allied Health—General M,D
Allopathic Medicine P
Clinical Laboratory
  Sciences/Medical
  Technology M
Health Education M
Health Services
  Management and
  Hospital Administration M
Medical Physics M,D
Physical Therapy M,D
Physician Assistant
  Studies M
Podiatric Medicine P

ROSEMONT COLLEGE

Business Administration
  and Management—
  General M
Counselor Education M
Curriculum and Instruction M
Educational Media/
  Instructional Technology M
Elementary Education M
Human Services M
Middle School Education M
Nonprofit Management M
Project Management M

ROWAN UNIVERSITY

Advertising and Public
  Relations M
Business Administration
  and Management—
  General M
Counselor Education M
Curriculum and Instruction M
Education—General M,D,O
Educational Administration M,D,O
Educational Media/
  Instructional Technology M
Higher Education M

Library Science M
Music Education M,O
Reading Education M
Secondary Education M
Special Education M

ROYAL MILITARY COLLEGE OF CANADA

Business Administration
  and Management—
  General M

ROYAL ROADS UNIVERSITY

Advertising and Public
  Relations M
Business Administration
  and Management—
  General M
Educational Administration M
Educational Media/
  Instructional Technology M
Human Resources
  Management M
Organizational
  Management M

RUSH UNIVERSITY

Acute Care/Critical Care
  Nursing M,D,O
Allopathic Medicine P
Bioethics M,O
Clinical Laboratory
  Sciences/Medical
  Technology M
Communication Disorders M,D
Community Health
  Nursing M,D,O
Family Nurse Practitioner
  Studies M,D,O
Gerontological Nursing M,D,O
Health Services
  Management and
  Hospital Administration M,D
Maternal and Child/
  Neonatal Nursing M,D,O
Medical Physics M,D
Medical/Surgical Nursing M,D,O
Nurse Anesthesia M,D,O
Nursing—General M,D,O
Occupational Therapy M
Pediatric Nursing M,D,O
Pharmaceutical Sciences M,D
Psychiatric Nursing M,D,O

RUTGERS, THE STATE UNIVERSITY OF NEW JERSEY, CAMDEN

Business Administration
  and Management—
  General M
Educational Administration M
Educational Policy M
Law P
Physical Therapy M

RUTGERS, THE STATE UNIVERSITY OF NEW JERSEY, NEWARK

Accounting M,D,O
Adult Nursing M
Business Administration
  and Management—
  General M,D,O
Community Health
  Nursing M
Family Nurse Practitioner
  Studies M
Finance and Banking M,D,O

Gerontological Nursing M
Health Services
  Management and
  Hospital Administration M,D
Human Resources
  Management M,D
International Business M,D
Law P
Management Information
  Systems M,D
Management Strategy and
  Policy M
Marketing M,D
Maternal and Child/
  Neonatal Nursing M
Nursing—General M
Organizational
  Management D
Psychiatric Nursing M
Supply Chain
  Management D
Taxation M

RUTGERS, THE STATE UNIVERSITY OF NEW JERSEY, NEW BRUNSWICK

Adult Education M
Developmental Education M
Early Childhood Education M,D
Education—General M,D
Educational Administration M,D
Educational Measurement
  and Evaluation M
Educational Policy D
Educational Psychology M,D
Elementary Education M,D
English as a Second
  Language M,D
English Education M
Finance and Banking M,D
Foreign Languages
  Education M,D
Foundations and
  Philosophy of Education M,D
Human Resources
  Management M,D*
Information Studies M,D
Legal and Justice Studies D
Library Science M
Mathematics Education M,D
Medicinal and
  Pharmaceutical
  Chemistry M,D
Music Education M,D,O
Pharmaceutical Sciences M,D
Pharmacy P
Public Health—General M,D
Quality Management M,D
Reading Education M,D
Science Education M,D
Social Sciences Education M,D
Social Work M,D
Special Education M,D

SACRED HEART UNIVERSITY

Business Administration
  and Management—
  General M
Education—General M,O
Educational Administration M,O
Educational Media/
  Instructional Technology M,O
Elementary Education M,O
Family Nurse Practitioner
  Studies M
Management Information
  Systems M,O
Nursing and Healthcare
  Administration M
Nursing—General M
Occupational Therapy M
Physical Therapy D

Reading Education — M,O
Secondary Education — M,O

SAGE GRADUATE SCHOOL

Adult Nursing — M,O
Art Education — M
Business Administration and Management—
  General — M
Community Health Nursing — M
Community Health — M
Counselor Education — M,O
Education—General — M,O
Elementary Education — M
English Education — M
Family Nurse Practitioner Studies — M,O
Finance and Banking — M
Health Education — M
Health Services Management and Hospital Administration — M
Human Resources Management — M
Human Services — M
Management Strategy and Policy — M
Marketing — M
Mathematics Education — M
Medical/Surgical Nursing — M
Nursing—General — M,O
Occupational Therapy — M
Organizational Management — M
Physical Therapy — D
Psychiatric Nursing — M
Reading Education — M
Science Education — M
Social Sciences Education — M
Special Education — M

SAGINAW VALLEY STATE UNIVERSITY

Business Administration and Management—
  General — M
Early Childhood Education — M
Education—General — M,O
Educational Administration — M,O
Educational Media/ Instructional Technology — M
Elementary Education — M
Family Nurse Practitioner Studies — M
Middle School Education — M
Nursing and Healthcare Administration — M
Nursing—General — M
Occupational Therapy — M
Physical Education — M
Reading Education — M
Science Education — M
Secondary Education — M
Special Education — M

ST. AMBROSE UNIVERSITY

Accounting — M
Business Administration and Management—
  General — M,D
Education—General — M
Educational Administration — M
Health Services Management and Hospital Administration — M,D
Human Resources Management — M,D
Nursing—General — M
Occupational Therapy — M

Organizational Management — M
Physical Therapy — D
Social Work — M
Special Education — M

ST. AUGUSTINE'S SEMINARY OF TORONTO

Religious Education — P,M,O

ST. BONAVENTURE UNIVERSITY

Accounting — M,O
Business Administration and Management—
  General — M,O
Counselor Education — M,O
Education—General — M,O
Educational Administration — M,O
Finance and Banking — M,O
Marketing — M,O
Reading Education — M

ST. CLOUD STATE UNIVERSITY

Business Administration and Management—
  General — M
Communication Disorders — M
Counselor Education — M
Curriculum and Instruction — M
Education—General — M,O
Educational Administration — M
Educational Media/ Instructional Technology — M
English as a Second Language — M
Exercise and Sports Science — M
Finance and Banking — M
Higher Education — M
Marketing — M
Music Education — M
Nonprofit Management — M
Physical Education — M
Special Education — M
Sports Management — M
Student Affairs — M

ST. EDWARD'S UNIVERSITY

Accounting — M,O
Business Administration and Management—
  General — M,O
Education—General — M
Entrepreneurship — M,O
Finance and Banking — M,O
Human Resources Management — M,O
Human Services — M,O
International Business — M,O
Management Information Systems — M,O
Marketing — M,O
Organizational Management — M
Project Management — M
Sports Management — M,O

SAINT FRANCIS MEDICAL CENTER COLLEGE OF NURSING

Family Nurse Practitioner Studies — M,O
Medical/Surgical Nursing — M,O
Nursing Education — M,O

SAINT FRANCIS UNIVERSITY

Business Administration and Management—
  General — M

Education—General — M
Educational Administration — M
Health Education — M
Human Resources Management — M
Occupational Therapy — M
Physical Therapy — D
Physician Assistant Studies — M
Reading Education — M

ST. FRANCIS XAVIER UNIVERSITY

Adult Education — M
Curriculum and Instruction — M
Education—General — M
Educational Administration — M

ST. JOHN FISHER COLLEGE

Business Administration and Management—
  General — M
Education—General — M,D,O
Educational Administration — M,D
Elementary Education — M
English Education — M
Family Nurse Practitioner Studies — M,O
Foreign Languages Education — M
Human Resources Development — M
Human Services — M
Mathematics Education — M
Middle School Education — M
Nursing Education — M,O
Pharmacy — P
Reading Education — M
Science Education — M
Social Sciences Education — M
Special Education — M,O

ST. JOHN'S UNIVERSITY (NY)

Accounting — M,O
Actuarial Science — M
Business Administration and Management—
  General — M,O
Counselor Education — M,O
Early Childhood Education — M
Education—General — M,D,O
Educational Administration — M,D,O
Elementary Education — M
English as a Second Language — M
Finance and Banking — M,O
Higher Education — O
Information Studies — M,O
Insurance — M
International Business — M,O
Law — P
Legal and Justice Studies — M
Library Science — M,O
Management Information Systems — M,O
Marketing — M,O
Multilingual and Multicultural Education — M
Pharmaceutical Administration — M
Pharmaceutical Sciences — M,D
Pharmacy — P
Quantitative Analysis — M,O
Reading Education — M,O
Secondary Education — M
Special Education — M
Taxation — M,O

SAINT JOSEPH COLLEGE

Business Administration and Management—
  General — M

Counselor Education — M,O
Early Childhood Education — M
Education—General — M
Family Nurse Practitioner Studies — M,O
Maternal and Child/ Neonatal Nursing — M,O
Nursing—General — M,O
Psychiatric Nursing — M,O
Special Education — M

ST. JOSEPH'S COLLEGE, NEW YORK

Accounting — M
Business Administration and Management—
  General — M*
Early Childhood Education — M
Education—General — M*
Nursing—General — M*
Reading Education — M
Special Education — M

SAINT JOSEPH'S COLLEGE OF MAINE

Business Administration and Management—
  General — M
Education—General — M
Health Services Management and Hospital Administration — M
Nursing and Healthcare Administration — M,O
Nursing Education — M,O
Nursing—General — M,O
Quality Management — M

ST. JOSEPH'S COLLEGE, SUFFOLK CAMPUS

Accounting — M
Business Administration and Management—
  General — M,O
Early Childhood Education — M
Health Services Management and Hospital Administration — M,O
Human Resources Management — M,O
Nursing—General — M
Organizational Management — M,O
Reading Education — M
Special Education — M

SAINT JOSEPH'S UNIVERSITY

Accounting — M
Business Administration and Management—
  General — M,O
Education—General — M,D,O
Educational Administration — M,D,O
Educational Media/ Instructional Technology — M,D,O
Electronic Commerce — M,O
Elementary Education — M,D,O
Environmental and Occupational Health — M,O
Finance and Banking — M,O*
Health Education — M
Health Services Management and Hospital Administration — M
Human Resources Management — M*
Human Services — M,O
International Business — M
Law — M,O

Management Information Systems	M
Marketing	M,O*
Nurse Anesthesia	M
Organizational Management	M,D,O
Quantitative Analysis	M
Reading Education	M,D,O
Secondary Education	M,D,O
Special Education	M,D,O

ST. LAWRENCE UNIVERSITY

Counselor Education	M,O
Education—General	M,O
Educational Administration	M,O

SAINT LEO UNIVERSITY

Accounting	M
Business Administration and Management— General	M
Curriculum and Instruction	M
Education of the Gifted	M
Education—General	M
Educational Administration	M
Human Resources Management	M
Reading Education	M
Sports Management	M

ST. LOUIS COLLEGE OF PHARMACY

Pharmaceutical Administration	M,O
Pharmacy	P

SAINT LOUIS UNIVERSITY

Accounting	M
Allied Health—General	M,D,O
Allopathic Medicine	P
Bioethics	D,O
Business Administration and Management— General	M*
Communication Disorders	M
Community Health	M
Counselor Education	M,D,O
Curriculum and Instruction	M,D
Education—General	M,D
Educational Administration	M,D,O
Finance and Banking	M
Foundations and Philosophy of Education	M,D
Health Services Management and Hospital Administration	M,D
Higher Education	M,D,O
International Business	M,D
Law	P,M
Nursing—General	M,D,O
Occupational Therapy	M
Oral and Dental Sciences	M
Organizational Management	M,D,O
Physical Therapy	M,D
Physician Assistant Studies	M
Public Health—General	M,D
Social Work	M
Special Education	M,D
Student Affairs	M,D,O

SAINT MARTIN'S UNIVERSITY

Business Administration and Management— General	M
Counselor Education	M
Education—General	M

Educational Administration	M
English as a Second Language	M
Reading Education	M
Special Education	M
Vocational and Technical Education	M

SAINT MARY-OF-THE-WOODS COLLEGE

Management Strategy and Policy	M

SAINT MARY'S COLLEGE OF CALIFORNIA

Business Administration and Management— General	M
Counselor Education	M
Curriculum and Instruction	M
Early Childhood Education	M
Education—General	M,D
Educational Administration	M,D
Kinesiology and Movement Studies	M
Reading Education	M
Special Education	M

SAINT MARY'S UNIVERSITY

Business Administration and Management— General	M,D

SAINT MARY'S UNIVERSITY OF MINNESOTA

Business Administration and Management— General	M,O
Education—General	M
Educational Administration	M,D,O
Elementary Education	M,O
Environmental and Occupational Health	M
Finance and Banking	M,O
Health Services Management and Hospital Administration	M
Human Resources Management	M
International Business	M
Nurse Anesthesia	M
Organizational Management	M
Project Management	M
Reading Education	M,O
Secondary Education	M,O

ST. MARY'S UNIVERSITY OF SAN ANTONIO

Accounting	M
Business Administration and Management— General	M
Counselor Education	D
Education—General	M,O
Educational Administration	M,O
Finance and Banking	M
Human Services	M,D,O
International Business	M
Law	P
Reading Education	M
Taxation	M

SAINT MICHAEL'S COLLEGE

Art Education	M,O

Business Administration and Management— General	M,O
Curriculum and Instruction	M,O
Education—General	M,O
Educational Administration	M,O
Educational Media/ Instructional Technology	M,O
English as a Second Language	M,O
Reading Education	M,O
Special Education	M,O

ST. NORBERT COLLEGE

Education—General	M

SAINT PETER'S COLLEGE

Accounting	M,O
Business Administration and Management— General	M
Curriculum and Instruction	M,O
Education—General	M,O
Educational Administration	M,O
Elementary Education	M,O
Finance and Banking	M
International Business	M
Management Information Systems	M
Marketing	M
Nursing—General	M
Reading Education	M
Urban Education	M

SAINTS CYRIL AND METHODIUS SEMINARY

Religious Education	P,M

ST. THOMAS AQUINAS COLLEGE

Business Administration and Management— General	M*
Education—General	M,O*
Elementary Education	M,O
Finance and Banking	M
Marketing	M
Middle School Education	M,O
Reading Education	M,O
Secondary Education	M,O
Special Education	M,O

ST. THOMAS UNIVERSITY

Accounting	M,O
Business Administration and Management— General	M,O
Counselor Education	M,O
Education—General	M,D,O
Educational Administration	M,D,O
Elementary Education	M,D,O
Health Services Management and Hospital Administration	M,O
Human Resources Management	M,O
International Business	M,O
Law	P,M
Reading Education	M,D,O
Special Education	M,D,O
Taxation	P,M

SAINT VINCENT COLLEGE

Accounting	M
Curriculum and Instruction	M
Education—General	M
Educational Administration	M

Educational Media/ Instructional Technology	M
Environmental Education	M
Special Education	M

ST. VLADIMIR'S ORTHODOX THEOLOGICAL SEMINARY

Religious Education	P,M,D

SAINT XAVIER UNIVERSITY

Adult Nursing	M,O
Business Administration and Management— General	M,O
Communication Disorders	M
Community Health Nursing	M,O
Counselor Education	M
Curriculum and Instruction	M,O
Early Childhood Education	M,O
Education—General	M,O
Educational Administration	M,O
Electronic Commerce	M,O
Elementary Education	M,O
Family Nurse Practitioner Studies	M,O
Finance and Banking	M,O
Health Services Management and Hospital Administration	M,O
Marketing	M,O
Nonprofit Management	M,O
Nursing and Healthcare Administration	M,O
Nursing—General	M,O
Psychiatric Nursing	M,O
Public Health—General	M,O
Reading Education	M,O
Secondary Education	M,O
Special Education	M,O
Travel and Tourism	M,O

SALEM COLLEGE

Early Childhood Education	M
Education—General	M
Elementary Education	M
English as a Second Language	M
Middle School Education	M
Reading Education	M
Secondary Education	M
Special Education	M

SALEM INTERNATIONAL UNIVERSITY

Business Administration and Management— General	M
Curriculum and Instruction	M
Education—General	M
Educational Administration	M
Educational Media/ Instructional Technology	M
English as a Second Language	M
Health Education	M
International Business	M
Physical Education	M

SALEM STATE COLLEGE

Art Education	M
Business Administration and Management— General	M
Counselor Education	M
Early Childhood Education	M
Education—General	M
Educational Administration	M

Educational Media/ Instructional Technology	M
Elementary Education	M
English as a Second Language	M
English Education	M
Family Nurse Practitioner Studies	M
Higher Education	M
Middle School Education	M
Multilingual and Multicultural Education	M
Nursing—General	M
Occupational Therapy	M
Physical Education	M
Reading Education	M,O
Science Education	M
Secondary Education	M
Social Work	M
Special Education	M

SALISBURY UNIVERSITY

Art Education	M
Business Administration and Management— General	M
Business Education	M
Early Childhood Education	M
Education—General	M
Educational Administration	M
Educational Media/ Instructional Technology	M
Elementary Education	M
English as a Second Language	M
English Education	M
Foreign Languages Education	M
Mathematics Education	M
Music Education	M
Nursing—General	M
Reading Education	M
Science Education	M
Secondary Education	M
Social Sciences Education	M
Social Work	M

SALVE REGINA UNIVERSITY

Business Administration and Management— General	M,O
Health Services Management and Hospital Administration	M,O
Human Resources Development	M,O
Human Resources Management	M,O
Legal and Justice Studies	M

SAMFORD UNIVERSITY

Business Administration and Management— General	M
Early Childhood Education	M,D,O
Education of the Gifted	M,D,O
Education—General	M,D,O
Educational Administration	M,D,O
Elementary Education	M,D,O
Law	P,M
Music Education	M
Nursing—General	M
Pharmacy	P

SAM HOUSTON STATE UNIVERSITY

Business Administration and Management— General	M

Counselor Education	M,D
Early Childhood Education	M
Educational Administration	M,D
Elementary Education	M
Finance and Banking	M
Kinesiology and Movement Studies	M
Library Science	M
Music Education	M
Reading Education	M
Secondary Education	M
Special Education	M
Vocational and Technical Education	M

SAMRA UNIVERSITY OF ORIENTAL MEDICINE

Acupuncture and Oriental Medicine	M,D

SAMUEL MERRITT COLLEGE

Family Nurse Practitioner Studies	M,O
Nurse Anesthesia	M,O
Nursing and Healthcare Administration	M,O
Nursing—General	M,O
Occupational Therapy	M
Physical Therapy	M
Physician Assistant Studies	M

SAN DIEGO STATE UNIVERSITY

Accounting	M
Advertising and Public Relations	M
Business Administration and Management— General	M
Communication Disorders	M,D
Counselor Education	M
Curriculum and Instruction	M
Education—General	M,D
Educational Administration	M
Educational Media/ Instructional Technology	M,D
Elementary Education	M
Emergency Medical Services	M,D
English as a Second Language	M,O
Entrepreneurship	M
Environmental and Occupational Health	M,D
Epidemiology	M,D
Exercise and Sports Science	M
Finance and Banking	M
Health Physics/ Radiological Health	M
Health Promotion	M,D
Health Services Management and Hospital Administration	M,D
Higher Education	M
Human Resources Management	M
Industrial and Manufacturing Management	M
International Business	M
Management Information Systems	M
Marketing	M
Mathematics Education	M,D
Multilingual and Multicultural Education	M,D
Music Education	M
Nursing—General	M
Pharmaceutical Administration	M

Physical Education	M
Public Health—General	M,D
Reading Education	M
Science Education	M,D
Secondary Education	M
Social Work	M
Special Education	M

SAN FRANCISCO STATE UNIVERSITY

Adult Education	M,O
Business Administration and Management— General	M
Clinical Laboratory Sciences/Medical Technology	M
Communication Disorders	M
Early Childhood Education	M
Education—General	M,D,O
Educational Administration	M,O
Educational Media/ Instructional Technology	M,O
Elementary Education	M
English as a Second Language	M
English Education	M,O
Family Nurse Practitioner Studies	M
Health Education	M
Kinesiology and Movement Studies	M
Legal and Justice Studies	M,O
Leisure Studies	M
Mathematics Education	M
Music Education	M
Nonprofit Management	M
Nursing and Healthcare Administration	M
Nursing Education	M
Nursing—General	M
Physical Therapy	M,D
Public Health—General	M
Reading Education	M,O
Recreation and Park Management	M
Secondary Education	M
Social Work	M
Special Education	M,D,O

SAN JOAQUIN COLLEGE OF LAW

Law	P

SAN JOSE STATE UNIVERSITY

Accounting	M
Business Administration and Management— General	M
Communication Disorders	M
Counselor Education	M
Education—General	M,O
Educational Administration	M,O
Educational Media/ Instructional Technology	M,O
Elementary Education	M,O
English as a Second Language	M,O
English Education	M,O
Family Nurse Practitioner Studies	M,O
Gerontological Nursing	M,O
Health Education	M,O
Higher Education	M,O
Industrial and Manufacturing Management	M
Information Studies	M
Kinesiology and Movement Studies	M
Library Science	M

Management Information Systems	M
Mathematics Education	M
Nursing and Healthcare Administration	M,O
Nursing Education	M,O
Nursing—General	M,O
Occupational Therapy	M
Public Health—General	M,O
Quality Management	M
Recreation and Park Management	M
Secondary Education	M,O
Social Work	M,O
Special Education	M,O
Student Affairs	M
Taxation	M
Transportation Management	M

SAN JUAN BAUTISTA SCHOOL OF MEDICINE

Allopathic Medicine	P

SANTA CLARA UNIVERSITY

Business Administration and Management— General	M
Counselor Education	M
Education—General	M,O
Educational Administration	M
Law	P,M,O
Management Information Systems	M
Special Education	M,O

SARAH LAWRENCE COLLEGE

Education—General	M
Public Health—General	M*

SAVANNAH COLLEGE OF ART AND DESIGN

Advertising and Public Relations	M

SAVANNAH STATE UNIVERSITY

Social Work	M

SAYBROOK GRADUATE SCHOOL AND RESEARCH CENTER

Organizational Behavior	M,D
Organizational Management	M,D

SCHILLER INTERNATIONAL UNIVERSITY (GERMANY)

Business Administration and Management— General	M
International Business	M
Management Information Systems	M

SCHILLER INTERNATIONAL UNIVERSITY

Business Administration and Management— General	M
International Business	M

SCHILLER INTERNATIONAL UNIVERSITY (SPAIN)

Business Administration and Management— General	M

International Business M

SCHILLER INTERNATIONAL UNIVERSITY

Business Administration
and Management—
General M
International Business M

SCHILLER INTERNATIONAL UNIVERSITY (UNITED KINGDOM)

Hospitality Management M
International Business M
Management Information
Systems M
Travel and Tourism M

SCHILLER INTERNATIONAL UNIVERSITY (UNITED STATES)

Business Administration
and Management—
General M
Finance and Banking M
Hospitality Management M
International Business M
Management Information
Systems M
Travel and Tourism M

SCHILLER INTERNATIONAL UNIVERSITY, AMERICAN COLLEGE OF SWITZERLAND

Business Administration
and Management—
General M
International Business M

SCHOOL FOR INTERNATIONAL TRAINING

Business Administration
and Management—
General M
Education—General M
English as a Second
Language M
Foreign Languages
Education M
International and
Comparative Education M
International Business M
Organizational
Management M

SCHOOL OF THE ART INSTITUTE OF CHICAGO

Art Education M,O

SCHOOL OF VISUAL ARTS

Art Education M

SCHREINER UNIVERSITY

Education—General M

SEATTLE INSTITUTE OF ORIENTAL MEDICINE

Acupuncture and Oriental
Medicine M

SEATTLE PACIFIC UNIVERSITY

Business Administration
and Management—
General M
Counselor Education M

Education—General M,D
Educational Administration M,D
English as a Second
Language M
Family Nurse Practitioner
Studies O
Management Information
Systems M
Nursing and Healthcare
Administration M
Nursing—General M,O
Reading Education M
Secondary Education M

SEATTLE UNIVERSITY

Accounting M
Adult Education M,O
Business Administration
and Management—
General M,O
Community Health
Nursing M
Counselor Education M,O
Curriculum and Instruction M,O
Education—General M,D,O
Educational Administration M,D,O
English as a Second
Language M,O
Family Nurse Practitioner
Studies M
Finance and Banking M,O
Law P
Nonprofit Management M
Nursing and Healthcare
Administration M
Nursing—General M
Organizational
Management M,O
Psychiatric Nursing M
Reading Education M,O
Special Education M,O
Sports Management M

SETON HALL UNIVERSITY

Accounting M
Acute Care/Critical Care
Nursing M
Adult Nursing M
Allied Health—General M,D*
Athletic Training and
Sports Medicine M*
Business Administration
and Management—
General M,O
Communication Disorders M*
Counselor Education M
Education—General M,D,O
Educational Administration M,D,O
Educational Media/
Instructional Technology M
Family Nurse Practitioner
Studies M
Finance and Banking M
Gerontological Nursing M
Health Services
Management and
Hospital Administration M*
Higher Education D
International Business M,O
Law P,M
Management Information
Systems M
Marketing M
Multilingual and
Multicultural Education O
Nonprofit Management M
Nursing and Healthcare
Administration M
Nursing Education M
Nursing—General M,D
Occupational Therapy M*
Pediatric Nursing M

Pharmaceutical
Administration M
Physical Therapy D*
Physician Assistant
Studies M*
School Nursing M
Sports Management M
Student Affairs M
Taxation M
Women's Health Nursing M

SETON HILL UNIVERSITY

Business Administration
and Management—
General M
Education—General M
Educational Media/
Instructional Technology M
Elementary Education M,O
Physician Assistant
Studies M
Special Education M,O

SHASTA BIBLE COLLEGE

Educational Administration M
Religious Education M

SHAW UNIVERSITY

Curriculum and Instruction M

SHENANDOAH UNIVERSITY

Allied Health—General M,D,O*
Athletic Training and
Sports Medicine M
Business Administration
and Management—
General M,O*
Education—General M,D,O*
Educational Administration M,D,O
Elementary Education M,D,O
English as a Second
Language M,D,O
Family Nurse Practitioner
Studies M,O
Health Services
Management and
Hospital Administration M,O
Management Information
Systems M,O
Middle School Education M,D,O
Music Education M,D,O
Nurse Midwifery M,O
Nursing—General M,O
Occupational Therapy M
Pharmacy P
Physical Therapy D
Physician Assistant
Studies M
Secondary Education M,D,O

SHEPHERD UNIVERSITY

Curriculum and Instruction M

SHERMAN COLLEGE OF STRAIGHT CHIROPRACTIC

Chiropractic P*

SHIPPENSBURG UNIVERSITY OF PENNSYLVANIA

Business Administration
and Management—
General M
Counselor Education M,O
Curriculum and Instruction M
Education—General M,O
Educational Administration M

Organizational
Management M
Reading Education M
Social Work M
Special Education M

SHORTER COLLEGE

Business Administration
and Management—
General M

SIENA HEIGHTS UNIVERSITY

Counselor Education M,O
Curriculum and Instruction M
Early Childhood Education M
Education—General M
Elementary Education M
Human Resources
Development M
Middle School Education M
Reading Education M
Secondary Education M

SIERRA NEVADA COLLEGE

Education—General M
Elementary Education M
Secondary Education M

SILVER LAKE COLLEGE

Business Administration
and Management—
General M
Education—General M
Educational Administration M
Music Education M
Organizational Behavior M
Special Education M

SIMMONS COLLEGE

Business Administration
and Management—
General M,O
Counselor Education M,D,O
Education—General M,D,O
Educational Administration M,O
Educational Media/
Instructional Technology M,D,O
Elementary Education M,O
English as a Second
Language M
Entrepreneurship M,O
Family Nurse Practitioner
Studies M,D,O
Health Education M,D,O
Health Promotion M,O
Health Services
Management and
Hospital Administration M,O
Information Studies M,D,O
Library Science M,D,O
Middle School Education M,O
Nursing—General M,D,O
Physical Therapy D
Secondary Education M,O
Social Work M,D
Special Education M,D,O
Urban Education M,O

SIMON FRASER UNIVERSITY

Business Administration
and Management—
General M
Counselor Education M
Curriculum and Instruction M,D
Education—General M,D
Educational Administration M
Educational Psychology M,D

International Business M
Kinesiology and
  Movement Studies M,D
Management Information
  Systems M
Marketing M

SIMPSON UNIVERSITY

Education—General M
Educational Administration M

SINTE GLESKA UNIVERSITY

Education—General M
Elementary Education M

SLIPPERY ROCK UNIVERSITY OF PENNSYLVANIA

Business Administration
  and Management—
  General M
Counselor Education M
Early Childhood Education M
Education—General M
Educational Administration M
Elementary Education M
Environmental Education M
Mathematics Education M
Nursing—General M
Physical Education M
Physical Therapy D
Reading Education M
Science Education M
Secondary Education M
Special Education M
Sports Management M
Student Affairs M

SMITH COLLEGE

Education—General M
Elementary Education M
English Education M
Exercise and Sports
  Science M
Foreign Languages
  Education M
Mathematics Education M
Middle School Education M
Science Education M
Secondary Education M
Social Sciences Education M
Social Work M,D*
Special Education M

SOJOURNER-DOUGLASS COLLEGE

Human Services M
Reading Education M
Urban Education M

SONOMA STATE UNIVERSITY

Business Administration
  and Management—
  General M
Counselor Education M
Curriculum and Instruction M
Education—General M
Educational Administration M
Elementary Education M
Family Nurse Practitioner
  Studies M
Kinesiology and
  Movement Studies M
Special Education M

SOUTH BAYLO UNIVERSITY

Acupuncture and Oriental
  Medicine M

SOUTH CAROLINA STATE UNIVERSITY

Allied Health—General M
Business Education M
Communication Disorders M
Counselor Education M
Early Childhood Education M
Educational Administration D,O
Elementary Education M
English Education M
Entrepreneurship M
Home Economics
  Education M
Human Services M
Mathematics Education M
Science Education M
Secondary Education M
Social Sciences Education M
Special Education M
Vocational and Technical
  Education M

SOUTH DAKOTA STATE UNIVERSITY

Counselor Education M
Curriculum and Instruction M
Education—General M
Educational Administration M
Health Education M
Hospitality Management M
Nursing—General M,D
Pharmaceutical Sciences M,D
Pharmacy P
Physical Education M
Recreation and Park
  Management M
Veterinary Sciences M,D

SOUTHEASTERN BAPTIST THEOLOGICAL SEMINARY

Religious Education P,M,D

SOUTHEASTERN LOUISIANA UNIVERSITY

Business Administration
  and Management—
  General M
Communication Disorders M
Counselor Education M
Curriculum and Instruction M
Education—General M,D
Educational Administration M,D
Elementary Education M
Health Education M
Kinesiology and
  Movement Studies M
Nursing—General M
Secondary Education M
Special Education M

SOUTHEASTERN OKLAHOMA STATE UNIVERSITY

Aviation Management M
Business Administration
  and Management—
  General M
Counselor Education M
Education—General M
Educational Administration M
Educational Media/
  Instructional Technology M
Elementary Education M
Industrial and
  Manufacturing
  Management M
Secondary Education M

SOUTHEASTERN UNIVERSITY

Accounting M

Business Administration
  and Management—
  General M
Finance and Banking M
Health Services
  Management and
  Hospital Administration M
International Business M
Management Information
  Systems M
Marketing M
Taxation M

SOUTHEAST MISSOURI STATE UNIVERSITY

Accounting M
Business Administration
  and Management—
  General M
Communication Disorders M
Counselor Education M,O
Educational Administration M,O
Elementary Education M
English as a Second
  Language M
Exercise and Sports
  Science M
Finance and Banking M
Foundations and
  Philosophy of Education M
Health Services
  Management and
  Hospital Administration M
Higher Education M,O
Industrial and
  Manufacturing
  Management M
International Business M
Leisure Studies M
Middle School Education M
Music Education M
Nursing—General M
Science Education M
Secondary Education M
Special Education M

SOUTHERN ADVENTIST UNIVERSITY

Accounting M
Adult Nursing M
Business Administration
  and Management—
  General M
Counselor Education M
Curriculum and Instruction M
Education—General M
Educational Administration M
Family Nurse Practitioner
  Studies M
Finance and Banking M
Health Services
  Management and
  Hospital Administration M
Human Resources
  Management M
Marketing M
Nursing and Healthcare
  Administration M
Nursing—General M
Reading Education M
Religious Education M

SOUTHERN ARKANSAS UNIVERSITY–MAGNOLIA

Counselor Education M
Education—General M
Educational Administration M
Elementary Education M
Kinesiology and
  Movement Studies M
Library Science M

Secondary Education M

SOUTHERN BAPTIST THEOLOGICAL SEMINARY

Religious Education P,M,D

SOUTHERN CALIFORNIA COLLEGE OF OPTOMETRY

Optometry P

SOUTHERN CALIFORNIA UNIVERSITY OF HEALTH SCIENCES

Acupuncture and Oriental
  Medicine M
Chiropractic P

SOUTHERN COLLEGE OF OPTOMETRY

Optometry P

SOUTHERN CONNECTICUT STATE UNIVERSITY

Art Education M
Business Administration
  and Management—
  General M
Communication Disorders M
Counselor Education M,O
Education—General M,D,O
Educational Administration D,O
Educational Measurement
  and Evaluation M
Educational Media/
  Instructional Technology M,O
Elementary Education M,O
English as a Second
  Language M
Environmental Education M,O
Exercise and Sports
  Science M
Foundations and
  Philosophy of Education O
Health Education M
Information Studies M,O
Leisure Studies M
Library Science M,O
Multilingual and
  Multicultural Education M
Nursing and Healthcare
  Administration M
Nursing Education M
Nursing—General M
Physical Education M
Public Health—General M
Reading Education M,O
Recreation and Park
  Management M
Science Education M,O
Social Work M
Special Education M,O

SOUTHERN EVANGELICAL SEMINARY

Religious Education P,M,O

SOUTHERN ILLINOIS UNIVERSITY CARBONDALE

Accounting M,D
Business Administration
  and Management—
  General M,D*
Communication Disorders M
Community Health M
Counselor Education M,D
Curriculum and Instruction M,D*

Education—General	M,D
Educational Administration	M,D*
Educational Measurement and Evaluation	M,D
Educational Psychology	M,D*
English as a Second Language	M
Health Education	M,D*
Higher Education	M
Law	P,M
Legal and Justice Studies	P,M
Music Education	M
Physical Education	M
Recreation and Park Management	M
Social Work	M
Special Education	M
Vocational and Technical Education	M,D*

SOUTHERN ILLINOIS UNIVERSITY EDWARDSVILLE

Accounting	M
Art Education	M
Business Administration and Management—General	M
Communication Disorders	M
Community Health Nursing	M,O
Dentistry	P
Education—General	M,D,O
Educational Administration	M,O
Educational Media/Instructional Technology	M
Elementary Education	M
English as a Second Language	M,O
English Education	M,O
Family Nurse Practitioner Studies	M,O
Finance and Banking	M
Foreign Languages Education	M
Foundations and Philosophy of Education	M
Health Education	M,O
Kinesiology and Movement Studies	M,O
Management Information Systems	M
Marketing Research	M
Mathematics Education	M
Music Education	M
Nurse Anesthesia	M,O
Nursing and Healthcare Administration	M,O
Nursing Education	M,O
Nursing—General	M,O
Pharmacy	P
Reading Education	M
Science Education	M
Secondary Education	M
Social Sciences Education	M
Social Work	M
Special Education	M

SOUTHERN METHODIST UNIVERSITY

Accounting	M
Business Administration and Management—General	M
Education—General	M
Facilities Management	M,D
Law	P,M,D
Multilingual and Multicultural Education	M,O
Music Education	M,O
Taxation	P,M,D

SOUTHERN NAZARENE UNIVERSITY

Business Administration and Management—General	M
Curriculum and Instruction	M
Education—General	M
Educational Administration	M
Nursing and Healthcare Administration	M
Nursing Education	M
Nursing—General	M

SOUTHERN NEW ENGLAND SCHOOL OF LAW

Law	P

SOUTHERN NEW HAMPSHIRE UNIVERSITY

Accounting	M,D,O
Business Administration and Management—General	M,D,O*
Business Education	M,O
Community Health	M,O
Computer Education	M,O
Curriculum and Instruction	M,O
Education—General	M,O
Educational Administration	M,O
Elementary Education	M,O
English as a Second Language	M,O
Finance and Banking	M,D,O
Hospitality Management	M,D,O
Human Resources Development	M,O
Human Resources Management	M,D,O
International Business	M,D,O
Management Information Systems	M,D,O
Marketing	M,D,O
Nonprofit Management	M,D,O
Organizational Management	M,D,O
Project Management	M,D,O
Secondary Education	M,O
Special Education	M,O
Sports Management	M,D,O
Taxation	M,D,O
Vocational and Technical Education	M,O

SOUTHERN OREGON UNIVERSITY

Business Administration and Management—General	M
Counselor Education	M
Early Childhood Education	M
Education—General	M
Educational Administration	M
Elementary Education	M
Environmental Education	M
Human Services	M
Reading Education	M
Secondary Education	M
Special Education	M

SOUTHERN POLYTECHNIC STATE UNIVERSITY

Business Administration and Management—General	M
Quality Management	M

SOUTHERN UNIVERSITY AND AGRICULTURAL AND MECHANICAL COLLEGE

Accounting	M

Business Administration and Management—General	M
Counselor Education	M
Education—General	M,D
Educational Administration	M
Educational Media/Instructional Technology	M
Elementary Education	M
Family Nurse Practitioner Studies	M,D,O
Gerontological Nursing	M,D,O
Law	P*
Mathematics Education	D
Nursing and Healthcare Administration	M,D,O
Nursing Education	M,D,O
Nursing—General	M,D,O
Recreation and Park Management	M
Science Education	D
Secondary Education	M
Special Education	M,D

SOUTHERN UNIVERSITY AT NEW ORLEANS

Social Work	M

SOUTHERN UTAH UNIVERSITY

Accounting	M
Business Administration and Management—General	M
Education—General	M

SOUTHERN WESLEYAN UNIVERSITY

Business Administration and Management—General	M
Education—General	M

SOUTH TEXAS COLLEGE OF LAW

Law	P

SOUTH UNIVERSITY (GA)

Anesthesiologist Assistant Studies	M
Pharmacy	P*
Physician Assistant Studies	M*

SOUTHWEST ACUPUNCTURE COLLEGE

Acupuncture and Oriental Medicine	M

SOUTHWEST BAPTIST UNIVERSITY

Business Administration and Management—General	M
Education—General	M,O
Educational Administration	M,O
Health Services Management and Hospital Administration	M
Physical Therapy	D

SOUTHWEST COLLEGE OF NATUROPATHIC MEDICINE AND HEALTH SCIENCES

Naturopathic Medicine	D*

SOUTHWESTERN ADVENTIST UNIVERSITY

Accounting	M
Business Administration and Management—General	M
Education—General	M
Elementary Education	M

SOUTHWESTERN ASSEMBLIES OF GOD UNIVERSITY

Curriculum and Instruction	M
Education—General	M
Educational Administration	M
Religious Education	M

SOUTHWESTERN BAPTIST THEOLOGICAL SEMINARY

Religious Education	M,D,O

SOUTHWESTERN COLLEGE (KS)

Education—General	M
Special Education	M

SOUTHWESTERN LAW SCHOOL

Law	P,M

SOUTHWESTERN OKLAHOMA STATE UNIVERSITY

Allied Health—General	M
Art Education	M
Business Administration and Management—General	M
Counselor Education	M
Early Childhood Education	M
Education—General	M
Educational Administration	M
Educational Measurement and Evaluation	M
Elementary Education	M
English Education	M
Kinesiology and Movement Studies	M
Mathematics Education	M
Music Education	M
Pharmacy	P
Recreation and Park Management	M
Science Education	M
Secondary Education	M
Social Sciences Education	M
Special Education	M

SOUTHWEST MINNESOTA STATE UNIVERSITY

Business Administration and Management—General	M
Education—General	M
Educational Administration	M
Special Education	M

SPALDING UNIVERSITY

Adult Nursing	M
Business Administration and Management—General	M
Education—General	M,D
Educational Administration	M,D
Elementary Education	M
Family Nurse Practitioner Studies	M
Middle School Education	M
Nursing and Healthcare Administration	M

Nursing—General	M
Occupational Therapy	M
Pediatric Nursing	M
Secondary Education	M
Social Work	M
Special Education	M

SPERTUS INSTITUTE OF JEWISH STUDIES

Nonprofit Management	M
Religious Education	M

SPRING ARBOR UNIVERSITY

Business Administration and Management— General	M
Education—General	M
Organizational Management	M

SPRINGFIELD COLLEGE

Counselor Education	M,O
Education—General	M
Exercise and Sports Science	M,D,O
Health Education	M,D,O
Health Services Management and Hospital Administration	M
Human Services	M
Kinesiology and Movement Studies	M,D
Occupational Therapy	M,O
Physical Education	M,D,O
Physical Therapy	M
Physician Assistant Studies	M
Recreation and Park Management	M
Secondary Education	M
Social Work	M,O*
Sports Management	M,D,O
Student Affairs	M,O

SPRING HILL COLLEGE

Business Administration and Management— General	M
Early Childhood Education	M
Education—General	M
Elementary Education	M
Nursing—General	M
Secondary Education	M

STANFORD UNIVERSITY

Allopathic Medicine	P
Art Education	M,D
Business Administration and Management— General	M,D
Computer Education	M,D
Curriculum and Instruction	M,D
Education—General	M,D
Educational Administration	M,D
Educational Measurement and Evaluation	M,D
Educational Psychology	D
English Education	M,D
Epidemiology	M,D
Foreign Languages Education	M
Foundations and Philosophy of Education	M,D
Health Services Research	M
Higher Education	M,D
International and Comparative Education	M,D
Law	P,M,D

Mathematics Education	M,D
Science Education	M,D
Social Sciences Education	M,D

STATE UNIVERSITY OF NEW YORK AT BINGHAMTON

Accounting	M,D
Business Administration and Management— General	M,D
Early Childhood Education	M
Education—General	M,D
Elementary Education	M
English Education	M
Finance and Banking	M,D
Foreign Languages Education	M
Foundations and Philosophy of Education	D
Health Services Management and Hospital Administration	M,D
Legal and Justice Studies	M,D
Mathematics Education	M
Nursing—General	M,D,O
Reading Education	M
Science Education	M
Secondary Education	M
Social Sciences Education	M
Special Education	M

STATE UNIVERSITY OF NEW YORK AT FREDONIA

Accounting	M
Business Administration and Management— General	M
Communication Disorders	M
Education—General	M,O
Educational Administration	O
Elementary Education	M
English as a Second Language	M
Music Education	M
Reading Education	M
Science Education	M
Secondary Education	M

STATE UNIVERSITY OF NEW YORK AT NEW PALTZ

Accounting	M
Adult Nursing	M,O
Art Education	M
Business Administration and Management— General	M
Communication Disorders	M
Early Childhood Education	M
Education—General	M,O
Educational Administration	M,O
Elementary Education	M
English as a Second Language	M
Gerontological Nursing	M,O
Multilingual and Multicultural Education	M
Nursing—General	M,O
Reading Education	M
Secondary Education	M
Special Education	M

STATE UNIVERSITY OF NEW YORK AT OSWEGO

Agricultural Education	M
Art Education	M
Business Administration and Management— General	M
Business Education	M

Education—General	M,O
Educational Administration	O
Elementary Education	M
Human Services	M
Reading Education	M
Secondary Education	M
Special Education	M
Vocational and Technical Education	M

STATE UNIVERSITY OF NEW YORK AT PLATTSBURGH

Communication Disorders	M
Counselor Education	M,O
Curriculum and Instruction	M
Educational Administration	O
Elementary Education	M
English Education	M
Foreign Languages Education	M
Mathematics Education	M
Reading Education	M
Science Education	M
Secondary Education	M
Social Sciences Education	M
Special Education	M

STATE UNIVERSITY OF NEW YORK COLLEGE AT BROCKPORT

Counselor Education	M,O
Curriculum and Instruction	M
Education—General	M
Educational Administration	M,O
English Education	M
Health Education	M
Leisure Studies	M
Mathematics Education	M
Middle School Education	M
Multilingual and Multicultural Education	M
Physical Education	M
Reading Education	M
Recreation and Park Management	M
Science Education	M
Social Sciences Education	M
Social Work	M

STATE UNIVERSITY OF NEW YORK COLLEGE AT CORTLAND

Early Childhood Education	M
Education—General	M,O
Educational Administration	O
English as a Second Language	M
English Education	M
Exercise and Sports Science	M*
Foreign Languages Education	M
Health Education	M
Mathematics Education	M
Physical Education	M
Reading Education	M
Recreation and Park Management	M
Science Education	M
Secondary Education	M
Social Sciences Education	M
Special Education	M
Sports Management	M*

STATE UNIVERSITY OF NEW YORK COLLEGE AT GENESEO

Communication Disorders	M
Early Childhood Education	M
Education—General	M
Elementary Education	M
Reading Education	M

Secondary Education	M

STATE UNIVERSITY OF NEW YORK COLLEGE AT OLD WESTBURY

Accounting	M*
Taxation	M

STATE UNIVERSITY OF NEW YORK COLLEGE AT ONEONTA

Counselor Education	M,O
Education—General	M,O
Educational Psychology	M,O
Elementary Education	M
Home Economics Education	M
Middle School Education	M
Reading Education	M
Secondary Education	M

STATE UNIVERSITY OF NEW YORK COLLEGE AT POTSDAM

Curriculum and Instruction	M
Educational Media/ Instructional Technology	M
Elementary Education	M
Music Education	M
Reading Education	M
Secondary Education	M
Special Education	M

STATE UNIVERSITY OF NEW YORK COLLEGE OF ENVIRONMENTAL SCIENCE AND FORESTRY

Recreation and Park Management	M,D

STATE UNIVERSITY OF NEW YORK COLLEGE OF OPTOMETRY

Optometry	P
Vision Sciences	M,D

STATE UNIVERSITY OF NEW YORK DOWNSTATE MEDICAL CENTER

Allopathic Medicine	P,M
Community Health	M
Family Nurse Practitioner Studies	M,O
Nurse Anesthesia	M
Nursing—General	M,O
Public Health—General	M*

STATE UNIVERSITY OF NEW YORK EMPIRE STATE COLLEGE

Business Administration and Management— General	M
Education—General	M

STATE UNIVERSITY OF NEW YORK INSTITUTE OF TECHNOLOGY

Accounting	M
Adult Nursing	M,O
Business Administration and Management— General	M
Family Nurse Practitioner Studies	M,O
Gerontological Nursing	M,O
Health Services Management and Hospital Administration	M
Nursing and Healthcare Administration	M,O
Nursing Education	M,O
Nursing—General	M,O

STATE UNIVERSITY OF NEW YORK MARITIME COLLEGE

Transportation Management	M*

STATE UNIVERSITY OF NEW YORK UPSTATE MEDICAL UNIVERSITY

Allopathic Medicine	P
Clinical Laboratory Sciences/Medical Technology	M
Family Nurse Practitioner Studies	M,O
Nursing—General	M,O
Physical Therapy	D

STEPHEN F. AUSTIN STATE UNIVERSITY

Accounting	M
Agricultural Education	M
Athletic Training and Sports Medicine	M
Business Administration and Management— General	M
Communication Disorders	M
Counselor Education	M
Early Childhood Education	M
Education—General	M,D
Educational Administration	M,D
Elementary Education	M
Kinesiology and Movement Studies	M
Marketing	M
Mathematics Education	M
Secondary Education	M,D
Social Work	M
Special Education	M

STEPHENS COLLEGE

Business Administration and Management— General	M
Counselor Education	M
Curriculum and Instruction	M
Health Services Management and Hospital Administration	O

STETSON UNIVERSITY

Accounting	M
Business Administration and Management— General	M
Counselor Education	M
Curriculum and Instruction	O
Education—General	M,O
Educational Administration	M,O
Law	P,M
Reading Education	M
Special Education	M

STEVENS INSTITUTE OF TECHNOLOGY

Business Administration and Management— General	M
Electronic Commerce	M,O
Entrepreneurship	M,O
Finance and Banking	M
Human Resources Management	M,O
Industrial and Manufacturing Management	M
International Business	M
Logistics	M,D,O
Management Information Systems	M,D,O
Management Strategy and Policy	M
Pharmaceutical Sciences	M,O
Project Management	M,O
Quality Management	M,O

STONEHILL COLLEGE

Accounting	M

STONY BROOK UNIVERSITY, STATE UNIVERSITY OF NEW YORK

Adult Nursing	M,O
Allopathic Medicine	P
Business Administration and Management— General	M,O*
Community Health	M,D,O
Computer Education	M*
Dentistry	P,O
Educational Administration	M,O
Educational Media/ Instructional Technology	M,O
English as a Second Language	M,D
English Education	M,O
Environmental and Occupational Health	M,O
Family Nurse Practitioner Studies	M,O
Finance and Banking	M,O
Foreign Languages Education	M,O
Gerontological Nursing	M
Health Services Management and Hospital Administration	M,D,O
Human Resources Management	M,O
Industrial and Manufacturing Management	M,O
Management Information Systems	M,D,O
Maternal and Child/ Neonatal Nursing	M,O
Mathematics Education	M,O
Medical Physics	D*
Nurse Midwifery	M,O
Nursing—General	M,O
Occupational Therapy	M,D,O
Oral and Dental Sciences	P,D,O*
Pediatric Nursing	M,O
Physical Education	M,O
Physical Therapy	M,D,O
Psychiatric Nursing	M,O
Public Health—General	M*
Science Education	M,O
Social Sciences Education	M,O
Social Work	M,D*
Women's Health Nursing	M,O

STRATFORD UNIVERSITY

Accounting	M
Business Administration and Management— General	M
Entrepreneurship	M

STRAYER UNIVERSITY

Accounting	M
Business Administration and Management— General	M
Management Information Systems	M

SUFFOLK UNIVERSITY

Accounting	M,O
Adult Education	M,O
Business Administration and Management— General	M,O
Counselor Education	M,O
Curriculum and Instruction	M,O
Education—General	M,O
Educational Administration	M,O
Finance and Banking	M,O
Foundations and Philosophy of Education	M,O
Health Services Management and Hospital Administration	M,O
Human Resources Development	M,O
Human Resources Management	M,O
International Business	M,D
Law	P,M
Nonprofit Management	M,O
Secondary Education	M
Taxation	M,O

SULLIVAN UNIVERSITY

Business Administration and Management— General	M

SUL ROSS STATE UNIVERSITY

Art Education	M
Business Administration and Management— General	M
Counselor Education	M
Education—General	M
Educational Administration	M
Educational Measurement and Evaluation	M
Elementary Education	M
International Business	M
Multilingual and Multicultural Education	M
Physical Education	M
Reading Education	M
Secondary Education	M
Vocational and Technical Education	M

SUNBRIDGE COLLEGE

Early Childhood Education	M
Education—General	M
Elementary Education	M

SWEDISH INSTITUTE, COLLEGE OF HEALTH SCIENCES

Accounting	M
Acupuncture and Oriental Medicine	M

SWEET BRIAR COLLEGE

Education—General	M

SYRACUSE UNIVERSITY

Accounting	M,D
Advertising and Public Relations	M
Art Education	M,O
Business Administration and Management— General	M,D*
Communication Disorders	M,D
Counselor Education	D
Curriculum and Instruction	M,D,O
Early Childhood Education	M
Education—General	M,D,O*
Educational Administration	M,D,O
Educational Measurement and Evaluation	M,D,O
Educational Media/ Instructional Technology	M,O
English Education	M,D
Entrepreneurship	M
Exercise and Sports Science	M
Finance and Banking	M,D
Foundations and Philosophy of Education	M,D
Health Services Management and Hospital Administration	O
Higher Education	M,D
Human Resources Development	D
Industrial and Manufacturing Management	D
Information Studies	M*
Law	P
Library Science	M,O
Management Information Systems	M,D,O
Management Strategy and Policy	D
Marketing	M,D
Mathematics Education	M,D
Music Education	M
Organizational Behavior	D
Quantitative Analysis	D
Reading Education	M,D
Science Education	M,D
Social Sciences Education	M,O
Social Work	M
Special Education	M,D
Supply Chain Management	M,D

TABOR COLLEGE

Accounting	M
Business Administration and Management— General	M

TAI SOPHIA INSTITUTE FOR THE HEALING ARTS

Acupuncture and Oriental Medicine	M

TARLETON STATE UNIVERSITY

Accounting	M
Agricultural Education	M
Business Administration and Management— General	M
Counselor Education	M
Curriculum and Instruction	M
Education—General	M,D,O
Educational Administration	M,D,O
Finance and Banking	M
Human Resources Management	M
Management Information Systems	M
Physical Education	M
Secondary Education	M,D,O
Special Education	M,D,O

TAYLOR UNIVERSITY FORT WAYNE

Business Administration and Management— General	M

TEACHERS COLLEGE COLUMBIA UNIVERSITY

Adult Education	M,D
Art Education	M,D
Communication Disorders	M,D*
Computer Education	M
Curriculum and Instruction	M,D*
Early Childhood Education	M,D
Education of the Gifted	M,D
Education—General	M,D,O
Educational Administration	M,D*
Educational Measurement and Evaluation	M,D
Educational Media/ Instructional Technology	M,D
Educational Psychology	M,D*
Elementary Education	M
English as a Second Language	M,D
English Education	M,D
Foreign Languages Education	M,D
Foundations and Philosophy of Education	M,D
Health Education	M,D
Higher Education	M,D
International and Comparative Education	M,D
Kinesiology and Movement Studies	M,D
Mathematics Education	M,D*
Multilingual and Multicultural Education	M
Music Education	M,D
Nursing and Healthcare Administration	M,D
Nursing Education	M,D
Physical Education	M,D
Reading Education	M
Religious Education	M,D
Science Education	M,D
Social Sciences Education	M,D
Special Education	M,D,O
Student Affairs	M,D

TÉLÉ-UNIVERSITÉ

Distance Education Development	M,D
Finance and Banking	M,D

TEMPLE UNIVERSITY

Accounting	M,D
Actuarial Science	M
Allied Health—General	M,D*
Allopathic Medicine	P
Art Education	M
Business Administration and Management— General	M,D
Communication Disorders	M
Community Health	M
Dentistry	P
Early Childhood Education	M,D
Education—General	M,D
Educational Administration	M,D
Educational Psychology	M,D
Electronic Commerce	M
Elementary Education	M,D
English as a Second Language	M,D
English Education	M,D
Environmental and Occupational Health	M
Epidemiology	M
Finance and Banking	M,D
Foreign Languages Education	M,D
Health Education	M
Health Services Management and Hospital Administration	M,D

Hospitality Management	M
Human Resources Management	M,D
Insurance	M,D
International Business	M,D
Kinesiology and Movement Studies	M,D
Law	P,M
Leisure Studies	M
Management Information Systems	M,D
Management Strategy and Policy	M,D
Marketing	M,D
Mathematics Education	M,D
Medicinal and Pharmaceutical Chemistry	M,D
Music Education	M,D
Nursing—General	M
Occupational Therapy	M
Oral and Dental Sciences	M,O
Pharmaceutical Sciences	M,D*
Pharmacy	P
Physical Education	M,D
Physical Therapy	D
Podiatric Medicine	P
Public Health—General	M,D
Reading Education	M,D
Recreation and Park Management	M
Science Education	M,D
Social Work	M
Special Education	M,D
Sports Management	M
Taxation	P,M
Travel and Tourism	M,D*
Urban Education	M,D
Vocational and Technical Education	M,D

TENNESSEE STATE UNIVERSITY

Allied Health—General	M,D
Business Administration and Management— General	M
Communication Disorders	M
Counselor Education	M,D
Curriculum and Instruction	M,D
Education—General	M,D,O
Educational Administration	M,D,O
Elementary Education	M,D
Exercise and Sports Science	M
Music Education	M
Nursing—General	M
Physical Education	M
Physical Therapy	M,D
Special Education	M

TENNESSEE TECHNOLOGICAL UNIVERSITY

Business Administration and Management— General	M*
Curriculum and Instruction	M,O
Early Childhood Education	M,O
Education of the Gifted	D
Education—General	M,D,O
Educational Administration	M,O
Educational Psychology	M,O
Elementary Education	M,O
Health Education	M
Kinesiology and Movement Studies	M
Library Science	M,O
Management Strategy and Policy	M
Nursing—General	M
Physical Education	M
Reading Education	M,O
Secondary Education	M,O

Special Education	M,O
Student Affairs	M,O

TENNESSEE TEMPLE UNIVERSITY

Curriculum and Instruction	M
Education—General	M
Educational Administration	M

TEXAS A&M HEALTH SCIENCE CENTER

Dental Hygiene	M
Dentistry	P
Environmental and Occupational Health	M
Epidemiology	M
Health Education	M
Health Services Management and Hospital Administration	M
Oral and Dental Sciences	P,M,D,O
Public Health—General	M

TEXAS A&M INTERNATIONAL UNIVERSITY

Accounting	M
Business Administration and Management— General	M
Counselor Education	M
Curriculum and Instruction	M,D
Early Childhood Education	M,D
Education—General	M,D
Educational Administration	M
Finance and Banking	M
Foreign Languages Education	M,D
International Business	M
Management Information Systems	M
Multilingual and Multicultural Education	M,D
Nursing—General	M
Reading Education	M,D
Special Education	M

TEXAS A&M UNIVERSITY

Accounting	M,D
Agricultural Education	M,D
Business Administration and Management— General	M,D
Counselor Education	M,D
Curriculum and Instruction	M,D
Education of the Gifted	M,D
Education—General	M,D
Educational Administration	M,D
Educational Measurement and Evaluation	M,D
Educational Media/ Instructional Technology	M,D
Educational Psychology	M,D
English Education	M,D
Epidemiology	M,D
Finance and Banking	M,D
Foundations and Philosophy of Education	M,D
Health Education	M,D
Health Physics/ Radiological Health	M,D
Human Resources Development	M,D
Human Resources Management	M,D
Industrial and Manufacturing Management	M,D
Kinesiology and Movement Studies	M,D

Management Information Systems	M,D
Marketing	M,D
Mathematics Education	M,D
Multilingual and Multicultural Education	M,D
Physical Education	M,D
Project Management	M,D
Public Health—General	M,D
Reading Education	M,D
Real Estate	M
Recreation and Park Management	M,D
Science Education	M,D
Special Education	M,D
Urban Education	M,D
Veterinary Medicine	P,M
Veterinary Sciences	M

TEXAS A&M UNIVERSITY– COMMERCE

Agricultural Education	M
Business Administration and Management— General	M
Counselor Education	M,D
Curriculum and Instruction	M,D
Early Childhood Education	M,D
Education—General	M,D
Educational Administration	M,D
Educational Media/ Instructional Technology	M,D
Educational Psychology	M,D
Elementary Education	M,D
English Education	M,D
Health Education	M,D
Higher Education	M,D
Kinesiology and Movement Studies	M,D
Music Education	M
Physical Education	M,D
Reading Education	M,D
Secondary Education	M,D
Social Sciences Education	M
Social Work	M
Special Education	M,D

TEXAS A&M UNIVERSITY–CORPUS CHRISTI

Accounting	M
Business Administration and Management— General	M
Counselor Education	M,D
Curriculum and Instruction	M,D
Early Childhood Education	M,D
Education—General	M,D
Educational Administration	M,D
Educational Media/ Instructional Technology	M,D
Elementary Education	M
Family Nurse Practitioner Studies	M
Health Services Management and Hospital Administration	M
International Business	M
Kinesiology and Movement Studies	M,D
Mathematics Education	M
Nursing and Healthcare Administration	M
Nursing—General	M
Reading Education	M,D
Secondary Education	M
Special Education	M
Vocational and Technical Education	M

TEXAS A&M UNIVERSITY– KINGSVILLE

Adult Education	M

Program	Degree
Agricultural Education	M
Business Administration and Management—General	M
Communication Disorders	M
Counselor Education	M
Early Childhood Education	M
Education—General	M,D
Educational Administration	M,D
Elementary Education	M
English as a Second Language	M
Foreign Languages Education	M
Health Education	M
Higher Education	D
Kinesiology and Movement Studies	M
Multilingual and Multicultural Education	M,D
Music Education	M
Reading Education	M
Secondary Education	M
Special Education	M

TEXAS A&M UNIVERSITY–TEXARKANA

Program	Degree
Accounting	M
Adult Education	M
Business Administration and Management—General	M
Curriculum and Instruction	M
Education—General	M
Educational Administration	M
Educational Media/Instructional Technology	M
Special Education	M

TEXAS CHIROPRACTIC COLLEGE

Program	Degree
Chiropractic	P

TEXAS CHRISTIAN UNIVERSITY

Program	Degree
Accounting	M
Adult Nursing	M
Advertising and Public Relations	M
Allied Health—General	M
Business Administration and Management—General	M,D
Communication Disorders	M
Counselor Education	M,O
Education—General	M,D,O
Educational Administration	M
Educational Measurement and Evaluation	M
Educational Psychology	M,O
Elementary Education	M,O
International Business	M
Kinesiology and Movement Studies	M
Music Education	M,O
Nurse Anesthesia	M
Nursing—General	M
Science Education	M,D
Special Education	M

TEXAS COLLEGE OF TRADITIONAL CHINESE MEDICINE

Program	Degree
Acupuncture and Oriental Medicine	M

TEXAS SOUTHERN UNIVERSITY

Program	Degree
Business Administration and Management—General	M
Counselor Education	M,D

Program	Degree
Curriculum and Instruction	M,D
Early Childhood Education	M,D
Education—General	M,D
Educational Administration	M,D
Educational Measurement and Evaluation	M,D
Elementary Education	M,D
Health Education	M
Higher Education	M,D
Human Services	M
Law	P
Multilingual and Multicultural Education	M,D
Pharmacy	P,M
Physical Education	M
Reading Education	M,D
Secondary Education	M,D
Special Education	M,D
Urban Education	M,D

TEXAS STATE UNIVERSITY-SAN MARCOS

Program	Degree
Accounting	M
Agricultural Education	M
Allied Health—General	M
Business Administration and Management—General	M
Communication Disorders	M
Counselor Education	M
Developmental Education	M,D
Early Childhood Education	M
Education—General	M,D
Educational Administration	M
Elementary Education	M
Health Education	M
Health Services Management and Hospital Administration	M
Health Services Research	M
Legal and Justice Studies	M
Leisure Studies	M
Mathematics Education	M
Multilingual and Multicultural Education	M
Music Education	M
Physical Education	M
Physical Therapy	M
Reading Education	M
Recreation and Park Management	M
Science Education	M
Secondary Education	M
Social Sciences Education	D
Social Work	M
Special Education	M
Vocational and Technical Education	M

TEXAS TECH UNIVERSITY

Program	Degree
Accounting	M,D
Agricultural Education	M,D
Art Education	M
Business Administration and Management—General	M,D
Counselor Education	M,D,O
Curriculum and Instruction	M,D
Education—General	M,D,O
Educational Administration	M,D,O
Educational Media/Instructional Technology	M,D,O
Educational Psychology	M,D,O
Elementary Education	M,D
English Education	M,D
Entrepreneurship	M
Exercise and Sports Science	M
Finance and Banking	M,D
Health Services Management and Hospital Administration	M,D

Program	Degree
Higher Education	M,D,O
Home Economics Education	M,D,O
Hospitality Management	M,D
Industrial and Manufacturing Management	M,D
International Business	M
Law	P
Management Information Systems	M,D
Marketing	M,D
Multilingual and Multicultural Education	M,D
Music Education	M,D
Quantitative Analysis	M,D
Reading Education	M,D
Secondary Education	M,D
Special Education	M,D,O

TEXAS TECH UNIVERSITY HEALTH SCIENCES CENTER

Program	Degree
Acute Care/Critical Care Nursing	M,O
Allied Health—General	M,D
Allopathic Medicine	P
Athletic Training and Sports Medicine	M
Clinical Research	M,O
Communication Disorders	M,D
Family Nurse Practitioner Studies	M,O
Gerontological Nursing	M,O
Health Services Management and Hospital Administration	M
Nursing and Healthcare Administration	M,O
Nursing Education	M,O
Nursing—General	M,O
Occupational Therapy	M
Pediatric Nursing	M,O
Pharmaceutical Sciences	M,D
Physical Therapy	M,D
Physician Assistant Studies	M

TEXAS WESLEYAN UNIVERSITY

Program	Degree
Business Administration and Management—General	M
Counselor Education	M
Education—General	M
Gerontological Nursing	M
Health Services Management and Hospital Administration	M
Law	P
Nurse Anesthesia	M
Public Health—General	M

TEXAS WOMAN'S UNIVERSITY

Program	Degree
Allied Health—General	M,D
Business Administration and Management—General	M
Communication Disorders	M
Counselor Education	M,D
Early Childhood Education	M,D
Education—General	M,D
Educational Administration	M,D
Elementary Education	M,D
Exercise and Sports Science	M
Family Nurse Practitioner Studies	M,D
Health Education	M,D
Health Services Management and Hospital Administration	M,D
Hospitality Management	M,D

Program	Degree
Kinesiology and Movement Studies	M,D
Library Science	M,D
Mathematics Education	M
Nursing Education	M,D
Nursing—General	M,D
Occupational Therapy	M,D
Physical Therapy	M,D
Reading Education	M,D
Science Education	M,D
Special Education	M,D

THOMAS COLLEGE

Program	Degree
Business Administration and Management—General	M
Business Education	M
Computer Education	M
Human Resources Management	M

THOMAS EDISON STATE COLLEGE

Program	Degree
Business Administration and Management—General	M
Educational Media/Instructional Technology	M
Human Resources Management	M
Nursing—General	M
Organizational Management	M

THOMAS JEFFERSON SCHOOL OF LAW

Program	Degree
Law	P

THOMAS JEFFERSON UNIVERSITY

Program	Degree
Allopathic Medicine	P
Clinical Laboratory Sciences/Medical Technology	M
Clinical Research	O
Health Services Research	O
Nursing—General	M*
Occupational Therapy	M
Pharmacy	P*
Physical Therapy	M,D
Public Health—General	M

THOMAS M. COOLEY LAW SCHOOL

Program	Degree
Law	P,M

THOMAS MORE COLLEGE

Program	Degree
Business Administration and Management—General	M

THOMAS UNIVERSITY

Program	Degree
Business Administration and Management—General	M
Education—General	M
Human Services	M
Nursing—General	M

THUNDERBIRD SCHOOL OF GLOBAL MANAGEMENT

Program	Degree
Business Administration and Management—General	M
International Business	M

TIFFIN UNIVERSITY

Business Administration and Management—	
General	M
Sports Management	M

TOURO COLLEGE

Health Services Management and Hospital Administration	O
Law	P,M
Occupational Therapy	M
Physical Therapy	M

TOURO UNIVERSITY COLLEGE OF OSTEOPATHIC MEDICINE

Education—General	P,M
Osteopathic Medicine	P,M
Pharmacy	P,M
Physician Assistant Studies	P,M
Public Health—General	P,M

TOURO UNIVERSITY INTERNATIONAL

Adult Education	M
Business Administration and Management—	
General	M,D
Clinical Research	M,D,O
Early Childhood Education	M
Education—General	M,D,O
Educational Administration	M,D
Educational Media/ Instructional Technology	M,D
Environmental and Occupational Health	M,D,O
Finance and Banking	M,D
Health Education	M,D,O
Health Services Management and Hospital Administration	M,D,O
Higher Education	M,D
Human Resources Management	M,D
International Business	M,D
International Health	M,D,O
Logistics	M,D
Management Information Systems	M,D,O
Nursing and Healthcare Administration	M,D,O
Public Health—General	M,D,O
Quality Management	M,D,O
Reading Education	M

TOWSON UNIVERSITY

Accounting	M
Advertising and Public Relations	O
Allied Health—General	M
Art Education	M
Business Administration and Management—	
General	M
Communication Disorders	M,D
Early Childhood Education	M,O
Education—General	M
Educational Administration	M,O
Educational Media/ Instructional Technology	M,D
Elementary Education	M
Environmental and Occupational Health	D
Health Services Management and Hospital Administration	O
Human Resources Development	M,O

Management Information Systems	M,D,O
Management Strategy and Policy	O
Mathematics Education	M
Music Education	M,O
Nursing—General	M,O
Occupational Therapy	M
Organizational Behavior	O
Physician Assistant Studies	M
Reading Education	M,O
Science Education	M
Secondary Education	M
Special Education	M

TRADITIONAL CHINESE MEDICAL COLLEGE OF HAWAII

Acupuncture and Oriental Medicine	M

TREVECCA NAZARENE UNIVERSITY

Business Administration and Management—	
General	M
Counselor Education	M
Curriculum and Instruction	M
Education—General	M,D
Educational Administration	M,D
Elementary Education	M
English as a Second Language	M
Library Science	M
Organizational Management	M
Physician Assistant Studies	M
Reading Education	M
Secondary Education	M
Vocational and Technical Education	M

TRINITY BAPTIST COLLEGE

Education—General	M
Educational Administration	M
Religious Education	M
Special Education	M

TRINITY INTERNATIONAL UNIVERSITY

Bioethics	M
Business Administration and Management—	
General	P,M,D,O
Education—General	M
Educational Administration	M
Law	P
Religious Education	P,M,D,O

TRINITY UNIVERSITY

Accounting	M
Business Administration and Management—	
General	M
Education—General	M
Educational Administration	M
Health Services Management and Hospital Administration	M*

TRINITY (WASHINGTON) UNIVERSITY

Business Administration and Management—	
General	M
Counselor Education	M

Early Childhood Education	M
Education—General	M
Educational Administration	M
Elementary Education	M
English as a Second Language	M
English Education	M
Human Resources Management	M
Mathematics Education	M
Nonprofit Management	M
Organizational Management	M
Public Health—General	M
Reading Education	M
Science Education	M
Secondary Education	M
Social Sciences Education	M
Special Education	M

TRINITY WESTERN UNIVERSITY

Educational Administration	M
English as a Second Language	M
Organizational Management	M

TRI STATE COLLEGE OF ACUPUNCTURE

Acupuncture and Oriental Medicine	M,O

TROY UNIVERSITY

Adult Education	M
Business Administration and Management—	
General	M
Counselor Education	M,O
Early Childhood Education	M,O
Education—General	M,O
Educational Administration	M,O
Elementary Education	M,O
Human Resources Management	M
Nursing—General	M
Secondary Education	M,O
Sports Management	M

TRUMAN STATE UNIVERSITY

Accounting	M
Communication Disorders	M
Education—General	M

TUFTS UNIVERSITY

Allopathic Medicine	P
Clinical Research	M,D
Dentistry	P
Early Childhood Education	M,D,O
Education—General	M,D,O
Elementary Education	M,D
Environmental and Occupational Health	M,D
Epidemiology	M,D,O
International and Comparative Education	M,D
International Business	M,D
International Health	M,D
Management Strategy and Policy	O
Middle School Education	M,D
Nonprofit Management	O
Occupational Therapy	M,D,O
Oral and Dental Sciences	M,O
Public Health—General	M
Secondary Education	M,D
Veterinary Medicine	P
Veterinary Sciences	M,D

TULANE UNIVERSITY

Allopathic Medicine	P
Business Administration and Management—	
General	M,D
Environmental and Occupational Health	M,D
Epidemiology	M,D
Health Education	M
Health Services Management and Hospital Administration	M,D
International Health	M,D
Law	P,M,D
Maternal and Child Health	M,D
Public Health—General	M,D,O
Social Work	M

TUSCULUM COLLEGE

Adult Education	M
Education—General	M
Organizational Management	M

TUSKEGEE UNIVERSITY

Veterinary Medicine	P
Veterinary Sciences	M

UNIFORMED SERVICES UNIVERSITY OF THE HEALTH SCIENCES

Allopathic Medicine	P
Environmental and Occupational Health	M,D
Family Nurse Practitioner Studies	M
International Health	M,D
Nurse Anesthesia	M
Nursing—General	M
Public Health—General	M,D

UNION COLLEGE (KY)

Education—General	M
Educational Administration	M,O
Elementary Education	M
Health Education	M
Middle School Education	M
Music Education	M
Physical Education	M
Reading Education	M
Secondary Education	M
Special Education	M

UNION COLLEGE (NE)

Physician Assistant Studies	M

UNION GRADUATE COLLEGE

Bioethics	M*
Business Administration and Management—	
General	M,O*
Education—General	M*
English Education	M
Finance and Banking	M,O
Foreign Languages Education	M
Health Services Management and Hospital Administration	M,O
Mathematics Education	M
Science Education	M
Social Sciences Education	M

UNION INSTITUTE & UNIVERSITY

Education—General	M,O

UNION THEOLOGICAL SEMINARY AND PRESBYTERIAN SCHOOL OF CHRISTIAN EDUCATION

Religious Education	M

UNION UNIVERSITY

Business Administration and Management— General	M
Education—General	M,D,O
Educational Administration	M,D,O
Higher Education	M,D,O
Nurse Anesthesia	M,O
Nursing Education	M,O
Nursing—General	M,O

UNITED STATES INTERNATIONAL UNIVERSITY

Business Administration and Management— General	M
Finance and Banking	M
Management Information Systems	M
Management Strategy and Policy	M
Marketing	M

UNITED STATES SPORTS ACADEMY

Athletic Training and Sports Medicine	M
Exercise and Sports Science	M
Physical Education	M
Sports Management	M,D*

UNIVERSIDAD ADVENTISTA DE LAS ANTILLAS

Education—General	M

UNIVERSIDAD AUTONOMA DE GUADALAJARA

Allopathic Medicine	P
Business Administration and Management— General	M,D
Education—General	M,D
International Business	M,D

UNIVERSIDAD CENTRAL DEL CARIBE

Allopathic Medicine	P,M

UNIVERSIDAD CENTRAL DEL ESTE

Accounting	M
Allopathic Medicine	P
Business Administration and Management— General	M
Human Resources Development	M
Law	P
Public Health—General	M

UNIVERSIDAD DE CIENCIAS MEDICAS

Allopathic Medicine	P,M
Health Services Management and Hospital Administration	P,M
Pharmacy	P,M

UNIVERSIDAD DE IBEROAMERICA

Allopathic Medicine	P,M
Educational Psychology	P,M
Family Nurse Practitioner Studies	P,M
Health Services Management and Hospital Administration	P,M

UNIVERSIDAD DE LAS AMERICAS, A.C.

Business Administration and Management— General	M
Education—General	M
Finance and Banking	M
Marketing Research	M
Organizational Behavior	M
Quality Management	M

UNIVERSIDAD DE LAS AMÉRICAS– PUEBLA

Business Administration and Management— General	M
Clinical Laboratory Sciences/Medical Technology	M
Education—General	M
Finance and Banking	M
Industrial and Manufacturing Management	M

UNIVERSIDAD DEL ESTE

Accounting	M
Business Administration and Management— General	M
Education—General	M
Educational Administration	M
Elementary Education	M
English as a Second Language	M
Foreign Languages Education	M
Human Resources Management	M
Social Work	M

UNIVERSIDAD DEL TURABO

Accounting	M
Business Administration and Management— General	M,D
Education—General	M
Educational Administration	M
English as a Second Language	M
Human Services	M
Logistics	M
Management Information Systems	D
Marketing	M
Multilingual and Multicultural Education	M
Special Education	M

UNIVERSIDAD IBEROAMERICANA

Allopathic Medicine	P
Dentistry	P,M
Education—General	P,M
International Business	P,M

UNIVERSIDAD METROPOLITANA

Accounting	M,O

Business Administration and Management— General	M,O
Curriculum and Instruction	M
Early Childhood Education	M
Education—General	M
Educational Administration	M
Environmental Education	M
Finance and Banking	M
Human Resources Management	M
International Business	M
Leisure Studies	M
Marketing	M
Physical Education	M
Recreation and Park Management	M
Special Education	M

UNIVERSIDAD NACIONAL PEDRO HENRIQUEZ URENA

Accounting	P,M,D
Allopathic Medicine	P
Business Administration and Management— General	P,M,D
Dentistry	P
Education—General	P,M,D
Health Services Management and Hospital Administration	P,M,D
Project Management	P,M,D
Veterinary Medicine	P,M,D

UNIVERSITÉ DE MONCTON

Business Administration and Management— General	M
Counselor Education	M
Education—General	M
Educational Administration	M
Educational Psychology	M
Law	P,M,O
Social Work	M

UNIVERSITÉ DE MONTRÉAL

Allopathic Medicine	P,O
Bioethics	M,O
Clinical Laboratory Sciences/Medical Technology	O
Communication Disorders	M,O
Community Health	M,D,O
Curriculum and Instruction	M,D,O
Dental Hygiene	M,O
Dentistry	M,O
Education—General	M,D,O
Educational Administration	M,D,O
Educational Psychology	M,D,O
Environmental and Occupational Health	M,O
Health Physics/ Radiological Health	O
Health Promotion	M,D,O
Health Services Management and Hospital Administration	M,O
Human Services	D
Information Studies	M,D,O
Kinesiology and Movement Studies	M,D,O
Law	P,M,D,O
Library Science	M,D,O
Management Information Systems	M,D,O
Maternal and Child/ Neonatal Nursing	O
Nurse Anesthesia	O
Nursing—General	M,D,O
Optometry	P
Oral and Dental Sciences	M,O

Pharmaceutical Sciences	M,D,O
Physical Education	M,D,O
Physical Therapy	O
Public Health—General	M,D,O
Social Work	O
Veterinary Medicine	P
Veterinary Sciences	M,D,O
Vision Sciences	M,O

UNIVERSITÉ DE SHERBROOKE

Accounting	M
Allopathic Medicine	P
Business Administration and Management— General	P,M,D,O
Clinical Laboratory Sciences/Medical Technology	M,D
Education—General	M,O
Educational Administration	M
Elementary Education	M,O
Finance and Banking	M
Higher Education	M,O
International Business	M
Kinesiology and Movement Studies	M,O
Law	P,M,D,O
Management Information Systems	M,O
Marketing	M
Organizational Behavior	M
Physical Education	M,O
Social Work	M
Special Education	M,O
Taxation	M,O

UNIVERSITÉ DU QUÉBEC À CHICOUTIMI

Business Administration and Management— General	M
Education—General	M,D
Project Management	M

UNIVERSITÉ DU QUÉBEC À MONTRÉAL

Accounting	M,O
Actuarial Science	O
Business Administration and Management— General	M,D,O
Education—General	M,D,O
Environmental and Occupational Health	O
Environmental Education	M,D,O
Finance and Banking	O
Kinesiology and Movement Studies	M
Law	M
Management Information Systems	M
Project Management	M,O
Social Work	M

UNIVERSITÉ DU QUÉBEC À RIMOUSKI

Business Administration and Management— General	M,O
Education—General	M,D,O
Nursing—General	M,O
Project Management	M,O

UNIVERSITÉ DU QUÉBEC À TROIS-RIVIÈRES

Accounting	O

Business Administration and Management—General	M,D
Education—General	M,O
Educational Administration	D
Educational Psychology	M
Entrepreneurship	M
Finance and Banking	O
Leisure Studies	M,O
Nursing—General	M,O
Physical Education	M
Project Management	M,O
Travel and Tourism	M,O

UNIVERSITÉ DU QUÉBEC, ÉCOLE NATIONALE D'ADMINISTRATION PUBLIQUE

International Business	M,O

UNIVERSITÉ DU QUÉBEC EN ABITIBI-TÉMISCAMINGUE

Business Administration and Management—General	M
Education—General	M,D
Project Management	M

UNIVERSITÉ DU QUÉBEC EN OUTAOUAIS

Accounting	M,O
Adult Education	O
Education—General	M,D,O
Educational Psychology	M
Finance and Banking	M,O
Nursing—General	M,O
Project Management	M,O
Social Work	M

UNIVERSITÉ LAVAL

Accounting	M,O
Advertising and Public Relations	O
Allopathic Medicine	P,O
Anesthesiologist Assistant Studies	O
Business Administration and Management—General	M,D,O
Communication Disorders	M
Community Health	M,D,O
Counselor Education	M,D
Curriculum and Instruction	M,D
Dentistry	P
Education—General	M,D,O
Educational Administration	M,D,O
Educational Measurement and Evaluation	M,D,O
Educational Media/Instructional Technology	M,D
Educational Psychology	M,D
Electronic Commerce	M,O
Emergency Medical Services	O
Entrepreneurship	M,O
Environmental and Occupational Health	O
Epidemiology	M,D
Facilities Management	M,O
Finance and Banking	M,O
Health Physics/Radiological Health	O
International Business	M,O
Kinesiology and Movement Studies	M,D
Law	M,D,O
Legal and Justice Studies	O
Management Information Systems	M,O
Marketing	M,O

Music Education	M,D
Nursing—General	M,O
Oral and Dental Sciences	M,O
Organizational Management	M,O
Pharmaceutical Sciences	M,D,O
Social Work	M,D

UNIVERSITY AT ALBANY, STATE UNIVERSITY OF NEW YORK

Accounting	M
Business Administration and Management—General	M
Counselor Education	M,D,O
Curriculum and Instruction	M,D,O
Education—General	M,D,O
Educational Administration	M,D,O
Educational Measurement and Evaluation	M,D,O
Educational Media/Instructional Technology	M,D,O
Educational Psychology	M,D,O
Environmental and Occupational Health	M,D
Epidemiology	M,D
Finance and Banking	M
Health Services Management and Hospital Administration	M
Human Resources Management	M
Library Science	M,D,O
Marketing	M
Mathematics Education	M,D
Public Health—General	M,D
Reading Education	M,D,O
Science Education	M,D
Social Work	M,D
Special Education	M
Taxation	M

UNIVERSITY AT BUFFALO, THE STATE UNIVERSITY OF NEW YORK

Accounting	M,D,O
Acute Care/Critical Care Nursing	M,D,O
Adult Nursing	M,D,O
Allied Health—General	M,D,O
Allopathic Medicine	P
Business Administration and Management—General	M,D,O
Clinical Laboratory Sciences/Medical Technology	M
Communication Disorders	M,D
Community Health	M,D
Counselor Education	M,D,O
Dentistry	P,M,D,O
Early Childhood Education	M,D,O
Education—General	M,D,O
Educational Administration	M,D,O
Educational Psychology	M,D,O
Electronic Commerce	M,D,O
Elementary Education	M,D,O
English as a Second Language	M,D,O
English Education	M,D,O
Epidemiology	M,D
Exercise and Sports Science	M,D
Finance and Banking	M,D,O
Foreign Languages Education	M,D,O
Gerontological Nursing	M,D,O
Higher Education	M,D,O
Human Resources Management	M,D,O
Information Studies	M,O
Law	P,M
Library Science	M,O

Logistics	M,D,O
Management Information Systems	M,D,O
Maternal and Child/Neonatal Nursing	M,D,O
Mathematics Education	M,D,O
Medicinal and Pharmaceutical Chemistry	M,D
Middle School Education	M,D,O
Multilingual and Multicultural Education	M,D,O
Music Education	M,D,O
Nurse Anesthesia	M,D,O
Nursing—General	M,D,O
Occupational Therapy	M
Oral and Dental Sciences	M,D,O
Pediatric Nursing	M,D,O
Pharmaceutical Sciences	M,D*
Pharmacy	P
Physical Therapy	D
Psychiatric Nursing	M,D,O
Public Health—General	M,D
Reading Education	M,D,O
Rehabilitation Sciences	M,D,O
Science Education	M,D,O
Social Sciences Education	M,D,O
Social Work	M,D
Special Education	M,D,O
Transportation Management	M,D,O
Women's Health Nursing	M,D,O

THE UNIVERSITY OF AKRON

Accounting	M
Business Administration and Management—General	M
Communication Disorders	M,D
Counselor Education	M,D
Education—General	M,D
Educational Administration	M,D
Educational Media/Instructional Technology	M
Electronic Commerce	M
Elementary Education	M,D
Entrepreneurship	M
Exercise and Sports Science	M
Finance and Banking	M
Health Services Management and Hospital Administration	M
Higher Education	M
Human Resources Management	M
International Business	M
Law	P,D
Management Information Systems	M
Marketing	M
Music Education	M
Nursing—General	M,D
Physical Education	M
Public Health—General	M,D
Secondary Education	M,D
Social Work	M
Special Education	M
Supply Chain Management	M
Taxation	M
Vocational and Technical Education	M

THE UNIVERSITY OF ALABAMA

Accounting	M,D
Advertising and Public Relations	M
Business Administration and Management—General	M,D
Communication Disorders	M

Counselor Education	M,D,O
Education of the Gifted	M,D,O
Educational Administration	M,D,O
English as a Second Language	M,D
Exercise and Sports Science	M,D
Finance and Banking	M,D
Health Education	M,D
Health Promotion	M,D
Higher Education	M,D
Hospitality Management	M
Information Studies	M,D
Kinesiology and Movement Studies	M,D
Law	P,M
Library Science	M,D
Marketing	M,D
Music Education	M,D,O
Nursing—General	M
Physical Education	M,D
Social Work	M,D
Special Education	M,D,O
Sports Management	M,D
Taxation	M,D

THE UNIVERSITY OF ALABAMA AT BIRMINGHAM

Allied Health—General	M,D,O
Allopathic Medicine	P,M,D
Art Education	M
Business Administration and Management—General	M,D
Clinical Laboratory Sciences/Medical Technology	M
Counselor Education	M
Dentistry	P
Early Childhood Education	M
Education—General	M,D,O
Educational Administration	M,D,O
Elementary Education	M
Environmental and Occupational Health	D
Epidemiology	D
Health Education	M,D
Health Promotion	D
Health Services Management and Hospital Administration	M,D
Industrial Hygiene	D
Maternal and Child Health	M
Nurse Anesthesia	M
Nursing—General	M,D
Occupational Therapy	M
Optometry	P
Oral and Dental Sciences	M
Physical Education	M
Physical Therapy	D
Physician Assistant Studies	M
Public Health—General	M,D
Rehabilitation Sciences	O
Secondary Education	M
Special Education	M
Vision Sciences	M,D

THE UNIVERSITY OF ALABAMA IN HUNTSVILLE

Accounting	M,O
Business Administration and Management—General	M,O
English as a Second Language	M,O
Human Resources Management	M,O
Management Information Systems	M,O
Maternal and Child/Neonatal Nursing	M,O

Nursing—General	M,O
Vision Sciences	M,D

UNIVERSITY OF ALASKA ANCHORAGE

Adult Education	M
Business Administration and Management— General	M
Counselor Education	M
Early Childhood Education	M,O
Education—General	M,O
Educational Administration	M,O
Family Nurse Practitioner Studies	M,O
Logistics	M,O
Nursing Education	M,O
Nursing—General	M,O
Project Management	M
Psychiatric Nursing	M,O
Public Health—General	M
Social Work	M,O
Special Education	M,O

UNIVERSITY OF ALASKA FAIRBANKS

Business Administration and Management— General	M
Counselor Education	M
Curriculum and Instruction	M
Education—General	M
English Education	M
Finance and Banking	M
Multilingual and Multicultural Education	M
Music Education	M
Reading Education	M

UNIVERSITY OF ALASKA SOUTHEAST

Business Administration and Management— General	M
Early Childhood Education	M
Education—General	M
Educational Media/ Instructional Technology	M
Elementary Education	M
Secondary Education	M

UNIVERSITY OF ALBERTA

Accounting	D
Adult Education	M,D,O
Business Administration and Management— General	M,D*
Clinical Laboratory Sciences/Medical Technology	M,D
Communication Disorders	M,D
Community Health	M,D
Counselor Education	M,D
Dental Hygiene	O
Dentistry	P
Educational Administration	M,D,O
Educational Media/ Instructional Technology	M,D
Educational Policy	M,D,O
Educational Psychology	M,D
Elementary Education	M,D
English as a Second Language	M,D
Environmental and Occupational Health	M,D
Epidemiology	M,D
Exercise and Sports Science	M,D
Finance and Banking	M,D

Health Physics/ Radiological Health	M,D
Health Promotion	M,O
Health Services Management and Hospital Administration	M,D
Health Services Research	M,D
Information Studies	M
International Business	M
International Health	M,D
Law	P,M
Library Science	M
Marketing	D
Maternal and Child/ Neonatal Nursing	P
Medical Physics	M,D
Multilingual and Multicultural Education	M
Nursing—General	M,D
Occupational Therapy	M,D
Oral and Dental Sciences	P,M,D,O
Organizational Management	D
Pharmaceutical Sciences	M,D
Pharmacy	M,D
Physical Education	M,D
Physical Therapy	M,D
Public Health—General	M,D
Recreation and Park Management	M,D
Rehabilitation Sciences	D
Secondary Education	M,D
Special Education	M,D
Sports Management	M
Vision Sciences	M,D

THE UNIVERSITY OF ARIZONA

Accounting	M
Agricultural Education	M
Allopathic Medicine	P
Art Education	M
Business Administration and Management— General	M,D
Communication Disorders	M,D
Education—General	M,D,O
Educational Administration	M,D,O
Educational Psychology	M,D
Elementary Education	M,D
English as a Second Language	M,D
English Education	M,D
Finance and Banking	M,D
Foreign Languages Education	M,D
Higher Education	M,D
Information Studies	M,D
Law	P,M
Library Science	M,D
Management Information Systems	M,D
Management Strategy and Policy	M,D
Marketing	D
Multilingual and Multicultural Education	M,D,O
Music Education	M,D
Nursing—General	M,D
Pharmaceutical Sciences	M,D
Pharmacy	P,M,D
Public Health—General	M
Reading Education	M,D,O
Secondary Education	M,D
Special Education	M,D,O

UNIVERSITY OF ARKANSAS

Accounting	M
Adult Education	M,D,O
Agricultural Education	M
Business Administration and Management— General	M,D

Communication Disorders	M
Counselor Education	M,D,O
Curriculum and Instruction	D
Early Childhood Education	M
Education—General	M,D,O
Educational Administration	M,D,O
Educational Media/ Instructional Technology	M
Elementary Education	M,O
Foundations and Philosophy of Education	M,D
Health Education	M,D
Higher Education	M,D,O
Industrial and Manufacturing Management	M
Kinesiology and Movement Studies	M,D
Law	P,M
Logistics	M
Management Information Systems	M
Mathematics Education	M
Middle School Education	M,D,O
Nursing—General	M
Physical Education	M
Recreation and Park Management	M,D
Secondary Education	M,O
Social Work	M
Special Education	M
Transportation Management	M
Vocational and Technical Education	M,D,O

UNIVERSITY OF ARKANSAS AT LITTLE ROCK

Adult Education	M
Art Education	M
Business Administration and Management— General	M
Counselor Education	M
Early Childhood Education	M
Education of the Gifted	M
Education of the Multiply Handicapped	M
Education—General	M,D,O
Educational Administration	M,D,O
Educational Media/ Instructional Technology	M
Health Services Management and Hospital Administration	M
Higher Education	D
Law	P
Management Information Systems	M
Middle School Education	M
Reading Education	M
Secondary Education	M
Social Work	M
Special Education	M

UNIVERSITY OF ARKANSAS AT MONTICELLO

Education—General	M
Educational Administration	M

UNIVERSITY OF ARKANSAS AT PINE BLUFF

Education—General	M
Elementary Education	M
English Education	M
Mathematics Education	M
Physical Education	M
Science Education	M
Secondary Education	M
Social Sciences Education	M

UNIVERSITY OF ARKANSAS FOR MEDICAL SCIENCES

Communication Disorders	M,D
Environmental and Occupational Health	M
Nursing—General	M,D
Pharmaceutical Administration	M
Pharmaceutical Sciences	M
Pharmacy	P,M

UNIVERSITY OF BALTIMORE

Accounting	M
Business Administration and Management— General	M
Finance and Banking	M
Health Services Management and Hospital Administration	M
Human Services	M
Law	P,M
Legal and Justice Studies	M
Management Information Systems	M
Marketing	M
Taxation	P,M

UNIVERSITY OF BRIDGEPORT

Acupuncture and Oriental Medicine	M
Business Administration and Management— General	M
Chiropractic	P
Computer Education	M,O
Early Childhood Education	M,O
Education—General	M,D,O
Educational Administration	D,O
Elementary Education	M,O
Human Resources Development	M
Human Services	M
International and Comparative Education	M,O
Naturopathic Medicine	D
Reading Education	M,O
Secondary Education	M,O
Student Affairs	M

THE UNIVERSITY OF BRITISH COLUMBIA

Accounting	D
Adult Education	M,D
Allopathic Medicine	P,M
Art Education	M,D
Business Administration and Management— General	M,D
Communication Disorders	M,D
Community Health	M,D
Curriculum and Instruction	M,D
Dentistry	P
Early Childhood Education	M,D
Education—General	M,D,O
Educational Administration	M,D
Educational Measurement and Evaluation	M,D,O
Educational Policy	M,D
English as a Second Language	M,D
Environmental and Occupational Health	M,D
Epidemiology	M,D
Finance and Banking	D
Foundations and Philosophy of Education	M,D
Health Services Management and Hospital Administration	M,D

Health Services Research	M,D
Higher Education	M,D
Home Economics Education	M,D
Information Studies	M
International Business	D
Kinesiology and Movement Studies	M,D
Law	M,D
Library Science	M
Management Information Systems	D
Management Strategy and Policy	D
Marketing	D
Mathematics Education	M,D
Music Education	M,D
Nursing—General	M,D
Oral and Dental Sciences	M,D,O
Organizational Behavior	D
Pharmaceutical Sciences	P,M,D
Pharmacy	P,M,D
Physical Education	M,D
Quantitative Analysis	M,D
Reading Education	M,D
Rehabilitation Sciences	M,D
Science Education	M,D
Social Sciences Education	M,D
Social Work	M,D
Special Education	M,D,O
Transportation Management	D
Vocational and Technical Education	M,D

UNIVERSITY OF CALGARY

Allopathic Medicine	P
Business Administration and Management— General	M,D
Community Health	M,D,O
Curriculum and Instruction	M,D,O
Education of the Gifted	M,D,O
Educational Administration	M,D,O
Educational Measurement and Evaluation	M,D,O
Educational Media/ Instructional Technology	M,D,O
Educational Psychology	M,D
English as a Second Language	M,D,O
Epidemiology	M,D
Exercise and Sports Science	M,D
Foreign Languages Education	M,D,O
Foundations and Philosophy of Education	M,D,O
Health Education	M,D
Higher Education	M,D,O
Kinesiology and Movement Studies	M,D
Law	P,M,O
Legal and Justice Studies	M,O
Management Strategy and Policy	M,D
Nursing—General	M,D,O
Social Work	M,D,O
Special Education	M,D
Vocational and Technical Education	M,D,O

UNIVERSITY OF CALIFORNIA, BERKELEY

Accounting	D
Allopathic Medicine	
Business Administration and Management— General	M,D
Developmental Education	
Education—General	M,D
Educational Administration	M,D

Educational Measurement and Evaluation	M,D
Environmental and Occupational Health	M,D
Epidemiology	M,D
Finance and Banking	D
Foundations and Philosophy of Education	M,D
Health Education	M
Health Services Management and Hospital Administration	M,D
Information Studies	M,D
Law	P,M,D
Legal and Justice Studies	D
Marketing	D
Maternal and Child Health	M
Mathematics Education	M,D
Multilingual and Multicultural Education	M,D
Optometry	P,O
Organizational Behavior	D
Physical Education	M,D
Public Health—General	M,D
Reading Education	M,D
Real Estate	D
Science Education	M,D
Social Work	M,D
Special Education	D
Vision Sciences	M,D

UNIVERSITY OF CALIFORNIA, DAVIS

Allopathic Medicine	P
Business Administration and Management— General	M
Clinical Research	M
Curriculum and Instruction	M,D
Education—General	M,D
Educational Psychology	M,D
Epidemiology	M,D
Exercise and Sports Science	M
Law	P,M
Maternal and Child Health	M
Transportation Management	M,D
Veterinary Medicine	P
Veterinary Sciences	M,O

UNIVERSITY OF CALIFORNIA, HASTINGS COLLEGE OF THE LAW

Law	P,M

UNIVERSITY OF CALIFORNIA, IRVINE

Allopathic Medicine	P
Business Administration and Management— General	M,D
Education—General	M,D
Educational Administration	M,D
Elementary Education	M,D
Foreign Languages Education	M,D
Secondary Education	M,D

UNIVERSITY OF CALIFORNIA, LOS ANGELES

Allopathic Medicine	P
Business Administration and Management— General	M,D*
Clinical Research	M
Community Health	M,D
Dentistry	P,O
Education—General	M,D

English as a Second Language	M
Environmental and Occupational Health	M,D
Epidemiology	M,D
Health Services Management and Hospital Administration	M,D
Information Studies	M,D,O
Law	P,M
Library Science	M,D,O
Medical Physics	M,D
Nursing—General	M,D
Oral and Dental Sciences	M,D
Public Health—General	M,D
Science Education	M,D
Social Work	M,D
Special Education	D

UNIVERSITY OF CALIFORNIA, RIVERSIDE

Business Administration and Management— General	M
Education—General	M,D

UNIVERSITY OF CALIFORNIA, SAN DIEGO

Allopathic Medicine	P
Business Administration and Management— General	M
Clinical Research	M
Communication Disorders	D
Education—General	M,D
Epidemiology	D
Health Services Management and Hospital Administration	M
Mathematics Education	D
Pharmacy	P
Public Health—General	D
Science Education	D

UNIVERSITY OF CALIFORNIA, SAN FRANCISCO

Allopathic Medicine	P
Dentistry	P
Medicinal and Pharmaceutical Chemistry	D
Nursing—General	M,D
Oral and Dental Sciences	M,D
Pharmaceutical Sciences	D
Pharmacy	P
Physical Therapy	M,D

UNIVERSITY OF CALIFORNIA, SANTA BARBARA

Education—General	M,D
Educational Administration	M,D
Educational Measurement and Evaluation	M,D
International and Comparative Education	M,D
Quantitative Analysis	M,D
Special Education	M,D

UNIVERSITY OF CALIFORNIA, SANTA CRUZ

Education—General	M,D
Social Sciences Education	M

UNIVERSITY OF CENTRAL ARKANSAS

Accounting	M

Business Administration and Management— General	M
Communication Disorders	M
Counselor Education	M
Early Childhood Education	M
Education—General	M
Educational Administration	O
Educational Media/ Instructional Technology	M
Family Nurse Practitioner Studies	M
Foreign Languages Education	M
Health Education	M
Kinesiology and Movement Studies	M
Library Science	M
Medical Physics	M
Music Education	M
Nursing—General	M
Occupational Therapy	M
Physical Therapy	D
Reading Education	M
Special Education	M
Student Affairs	M

UNIVERSITY OF CENTRAL FLORIDA

Accounting	M
Actuarial Science	M,O
Adult Nursing	D,O
Art Education	M
Business Administration and Management— General	M,D*
Communication Disorders	M,D,O
Community College Education	M,D,O
Counselor Education	M,D
Curriculum and Instruction	D
Early Childhood Education	M
Education—General	M,D,O
Educational Administration	M,D,O
Educational Media/ Instructional Technology	M,D,O
Elementary Education	M,D
English as a Second Language	M,O
English Education	M
Exercise and Sports Science	M
Foreign Languages Education	M,O
Health Promotion	M,O
Health Services Management and Hospital Administration	M,O
Hospitality Management	M
Management Information Systems	M
Mathematics Education	M,D,O
Music Education	M
Nonprofit Management	M,O
Nursing Education	D,O
Nursing—General	D,O
Pediatric Nursing	D,O
Physical Education	M
Physical Therapy	M
Reading Education	M,O
Science Education	M,O
Social Sciences Education	M
Social Work	M,O
Special Education	M,D
Sports Management	M,O
Taxation	M
Travel and Tourism	M
Vocational and Technical Education	M

UNIVERSITY OF CENTRAL MISSOURI

Accounting	M

Business Administration
and Management—
General — M
Communication Disorders — M
Counselor Education — M,O
Curriculum and Instruction — M,O
Education—General — M,D,O
Educational Administration — M,O
Educational Media/
Instructional Technology — M
Elementary Education — M,O
English as a Second
Language — M
Environmental and
Occupational Health — M,O
Exercise and Sports
Science — M
Human Services — M,O
Industrial and
Manufacturing
Management — M
Industrial Hygiene — M,O
Information Studies — M,O
Library Science — M,O
Management Information
Systems — M
Nursing—General — M
Physical Education — M
Reading Education — M,O
Secondary Education — M,O
Special Education — M,O
Student Affairs — M
Transportation
Management — M,O
Vocational and Technical
Education — M,O

UNIVERSITY OF CENTRAL OKLAHOMA

Adult Education — M
Business Administration
and Management—
General — M
Communication Disorders — M
Computer Education — M
Counselor Education — M
Early Childhood Education — M
Education—General — M
Educational Administration — M
Educational Media/
Instructional Technology — M
Elementary Education — M
English as a Second
Language — M
Health Education — M
Higher Education — M
Home Economics
Education — M
Mathematics Education — M
Music Education — M
Reading Education — M
Secondary Education — M
Special Education — M

UNIVERSITY OF CHARLESTON

Business Administration
and Management—
General — M
Pharmacy — P

UNIVERSITY OF CHICAGO

Allopathic Medicine — P
Business Administration
and Management—
General — M,D
Health Promotion — M
International Business — M
Law — P,M,D
Medical Physics — D*
Science Education — D
Social Work — M,D*

Vision Sciences — D

UNIVERSITY OF CINCINNATI

Accounting — M,D
Acute Care/Critical Care
Nursing — M,D
Adult Education — M,D,O
Adult Nursing — M,D
Allopathic Medicine — P,M
Art Education — M
Business Administration
and Management—
General — M,D
Communication Disorders — M,D,O
Community Health
Nursing — M,D
Counselor Education — M,D,O
Curriculum and Instruction — M,D
Early Childhood Education — M
Education—General — M,D,O
Educational Administration — M,D,O
Electronic Commerce — M
Elementary Education — M
English as a Second
Language — M,D,O
Environmental and
Occupational Health — M,D
Epidemiology — M,D
Family Nurse Practitioner
Studies — M,D
Finance and Banking — M,D
Foundations and
Philosophy of Education — M,D
Health Education — M,D
Health Physics/
Radiological Health — M
Industrial and
Manufacturing
Management — M,D
Industrial Hygiene — M,D
Law — P
Management Information
Systems — M
Marketing — M,D
Maternal and Child/
Neonatal Nursing — M,D
Mathematics Education — M,D
Medical Imaging — D
Medical Physics — M
Music Education — M
Nurse Anesthesia — M,D
Nurse Midwifery — M,D
Nursing and Healthcare
Administration — M,D
Nursing—General — M,D
Occupational Health
Nursing — M,D
Organizational
Management — M
Pediatric Nursing — M,D
Pharmaceutical Sciences — M,D
Pharmacy — P
Psychiatric Nursing — M,D
Quantitative Analysis — M,D
Reading Education — M,D
Rehabilitation Sciences — D
Science Education — M,D,O
Secondary Education — M
Social Sciences Education — M,D,O
Social Work — M
Special Education — M,D
Taxation — M
Women's Health Nursing — M,D

UNIVERSITY OF COLORADO AT BOULDER

Accounting — D
Business Administration
and Management—
General — M,D*
Communication Disorders — M,D
Curriculum and Instruction — M,D

Education—General — M,D
Educational Measurement
and Evaluation — D
Educational Psychology — M,D
Finance and Banking — D
Foundations and
Philosophy of Education — M,D
Kinesiology and
Movement Studies — M,D
Law — P
Marketing — D
Medical Physics — M,D
Multilingual and
Multicultural Education — M,D
Music Education — M,D

UNIVERSITY OF COLORADO AT COLORADO SPRINGS

Accounting — M
Adult Nursing — M,D
Business Administration
and Management—
General — M
Community Health
Nursing — M,D
Counselor Education — M,D
Curriculum and Instruction — M,D
Education—General — M,D
Educational Administration — M,D
Family Nurse Practitioner
Studies — M,D
Finance and Banking — M
Forensic Nursing — M,D
Gerontological Nursing — M,D
Health Services
Management and
Hospital Administration — M
Human Services — M,D
International Business — M
Management Information
Systems — M
Marketing — M
Maternal and Child/
Neonatal Nursing — M,D
Nursing and Healthcare
Administration — M,D
Nursing—General — M,D
Special Education — M,D
Women's Health Nursing — M,D

UNIVERSITY OF COLORADO AT DENVER AND HEALTH SCIENCES CENTER

Accounting — M
Advertising and Public
Relations — M,O
Allopathic Medicine — P
Business Administration
and Management—
General — M
Clinical Laboratory
Sciences/Medical
Technology — M,D
Counselor Education — M,O
Dentistry — P
Early Childhood Education — M
Education—General — M,D,O
Educational Administration — M,D,O
Educational Media/
Instructional Technology — M
Educational Psychology — M
English as a Second
Language — M,O
English Education — M,O
Epidemiology — D
Family Nurse Practitioner
Studies — M,D,O
Finance and Banking — M
Health Education — D
Health Services
Management and
Hospital Administration — M

International Business — M
Management Information
Systems — M,D
Marketing — M
Nursing—General — M,D,O
Pharmaceutical
Administration — M
Pharmaceutical Sciences — D*
Pharmacy — P,D
Physical Therapy — M,D
Physician Assistant
Studies — M
Public Health—General — M*
Social Sciences Education — M

UNIVERSITY OF CONNECTICUT

Accounting — M,D
Actuarial Science — M,D
Acute Care/Critical Care
Nursing — M,D,O
Adult Education — M,D
Adult Nursing — M,D,O
Agricultural Education — M,D
Allied Health—General — M
Business Administration
and Management—
General — M,D*
Communication Disorders — M,D
Community Health
Nursing — M,D,O
Counselor Education — M,D
Curriculum and Instruction — M,D
Education of the Gifted — M,D
Education—General — M,D
Educational Administration — D
Educational Measurement
and Evaluation — M,D
Educational Media/
Instructional Technology — M,D
Educational Psychology — M,D
Elementary Education — M,D
English Education — M,D
Environmental and
Occupational Health — M
Exercise and Sports
Science — M,D
Finance and Banking — M,D,O
Foreign Languages
Education — M,D
Foundations and
Philosophy of Education — D
Health Services
Management and
Hospital Administration — M,D
Higher Education — M
Human Resources
Development — M
Human Resources
Management — M*
Kinesiology and
Movement Studies — M,D
Law — P
Leisure Studies — M,D
Marketing — M,D
Maternal and Child/
Neonatal Nursing — M,D,O
Mathematics Education — M,D
Medicinal and
Pharmaceutical
Chemistry — M,D
Multilingual and
Multicultural Education — M,D
Music Education — M,D,O
Nonprofit Management — M,O
Nursing and Healthcare
Administration — M,D,O
Nursing—General — M,D,O
Oral and Dental Sciences — M
Pharmaceutical Sciences — M,D
Pharmacy — P
Physical Therapy — M
Psychiatric Nursing — M,D,O
Public Health—General — M

Reading Education	M,D
Science Education	M,D
Secondary Education	M,D
Social Sciences Education	M,D
Social Work	M,D
Special Education	M,D

UNIVERSITY OF CONNECTICUT HEALTH CENTER

Allopathic Medicine	P
Dentistry	P,O
Oral and Dental Sciences	M,D*
Public Health—General	M

UNIVERSITY OF DALLAS

Accounting	M
Business Administration and Management— General	M
Entrepreneurship	M
Finance and Banking	M
Health Services Management and Hospital Administration	M
Human Resources Management	M
International Business	M
Logistics	M
Management Information Systems	M
Management Strategy and Policy	M
Marketing	M
Nonprofit Management	M
Organizational Management	M
Project Management	M
Sports Management	M
Supply Chain Management	M

UNIVERSITY OF DAYTON

Art Education	M
Business Administration and Management— General	M
Counselor Education	M,O
Early Childhood Education	M
Education—General	M,D,O
Educational Administration	M,D,O
Educational Media/ Instructional Technology	M
Exercise and Sports Science	M,D
Law	P,M
Mathematics Education	M
Middle School Education	M
Music Education	M
Physical Education	M,D
Reading Education	M
Secondary Education	M
Special Education	M
Student Affairs	M,O

UNIVERSITY OF DELAWARE

Accounting	M
Adult Nursing	M,O
Business Administration and Management— General	M,D*
Business Education	M,D
Counselor Education	M,D
Curriculum and Instruction	M,D
Education—General	M,D
Educational Administration	M,D
English as a Second Language	M,D
Entrepreneurship	M,D

Exercise and Sports Science	M
Family Nurse Practitioner Studies	M,O
Foreign Languages Education	M
Gerontological Nursing	M,O
Health Promotion	M
Higher Education	M
HIV/AIDS Nursing	M,O
Hospitality Management	M
Kinesiology and Movement Studies	M,D
Management Information Systems	M*
Maternal and Child/ Neonatal Nursing	M,O
Multilingual and Multicultural Education	M,D
Music Education	M
Nonprofit Management	M,D
Nursing and Healthcare Administration	M,O
Nursing—General	M,O
Oncology Nursing	M,O
Pediatric Nursing	M,O
Physical Therapy	D
Psychiatric Nursing	M,O
Special Education	M,D
Women's Health Nursing	M,O

UNIVERSITY OF DENVER

Accounting	M
Adult Education	M,D,O
Advertising and Public Relations	M
Business Administration and Management— General	M*
Curriculum and Instruction	M,D,O
Education—General	M,D,O
Educational Administration	M,D,O
Educational Measurement and Evaluation	M,D,O
Educational Psychology	M,D,O
Electronic Commerce	M
Finance and Banking	M
Higher Education	M,D,O
Human Resources Management	M
Information Studies	M
International Business	M
Law	P,M
Legal and Justice Studies	M,O
Library Science	M,D,O
Management Information Systems	M
Marketing	M
Music Education	M,O
Organizational Management	M
Real Estate	M
Social Work	M,D,O*
Taxation	M
Transportation Management	M

UNIVERSITY OF DETROIT MERCY

Allied Health—General	M,O
Business Administration and Management— General	M,O
Counselor Education	M
Curriculum and Instruction	M
Dentistry	P
Early Childhood Education	M
Education—General	M
Educational Administration	M
Family Nurse Practitioner Studies	M,O
Health Services Management and Hospital Administration	M

Law	P
Management Information Systems	M
Mathematics Education	M
Nurse Anesthesia	M
Oral and Dental Sciences	M,O
Physician Assistant Studies	M
Special Education	M

UNIVERSITY OF DUBUQUE

Business Administration and Management— General	M

UNIVERSITY OF EVANSVILLE

Business Administration and Management— General	M
Education—General	M
Health Services Management and Hospital Administration	M
Nursing—General	M

THE UNIVERSITY OF FINDLAY

Athletic Training and Sports Medicine	M
Business Administration and Management— General	M
Early Childhood Education	M
Education—General	M
Educational Administration	M
Educational Media/ Instructional Technology	M
Elementary Education	M
English as a Second Language	M
Finance and Banking	M
Human Resources Management	M
International Business	M
Marketing	M
Multilingual and Multicultural Education	M
Occupational Therapy	M
Physical Therapy	M
Special Education	M

UNIVERSITY OF FLORIDA

Accounting	M,D
Advertising and Public Relations	M
Agricultural Education	M,D
Allied Health—General	M,D
Allopathic Medicine	P
Art Education	M,D
Athletic Training and Sports Medicine	M,D
Business Administration and Management— General	M,D,O
Clinical Research	M
Communication Disorders	M,D
Counselor Education	M,D,O
Curriculum and Instruction	M,D,O
Dentistry	P,O
Early Childhood Education	M,D,O
Education—General	M,D,O
Educational Administration	M,D,O
Educational Measurement and Evaluation	M,D,O
Educational Psychology	M,D,O
Electronic Commerce	M
Elementary Education	M,D,O
English as a Second Language	M,D,O
English Education	M,D,O

Entrepreneurship	M,D,O
Environmental and Occupational Health	M
Epidemiology	M
Exercise and Sports Science	M,D
Finance and Banking	M,D,O
Foundations and Philosophy of Education	M,D,O
Health Education	M,D,O
Health Services Management and Hospital Administration	M,D*
Health Services Research	M,D
Higher Education	M,D,O
Human Resources Management	M
Insurance	M,D,O
International Business	P,M,D
Kinesiology and Movement Studies	M,D
Law	P,M,D
Management Information Systems	M,D
Management Strategy and Policy	M
Marketing	M,D
Mathematics Education	M,D,O
Medical Imaging	M,D
Medicinal and Pharmaceutical Chemistry	P,M,D
Multilingual and Multicultural Education	M,D,O
Music Education	M,D
Nursing—General	M,D
Occupational Therapy	M
Oral and Dental Sciences	M,D,O
Pharmaceutical Administration	M,D
Pharmaceutical Sciences	D
Pharmacy	P
Physical Education	M,D
Physical Therapy	D
Physician Assistant Studies	M
Public Health—General	M
Quantitative Analysis	M
Reading Education	M,D,O
Real Estate	M,D,O
Recreation and Park Management	M,D
Rehabilitation Sciences	D
Science Education	M,D,O
Social Sciences Education	M,D,O
Special Education	M,D,O
Sports Management	M
Student Affairs	M,D,O
Supply Chain Management	M,D
Taxation	P,M,D
Veterinary Medicine	P
Veterinary Sciences	M,D,O

UNIVERSITY OF GEORGIA

Accounting	M
Adult Education	M,D,O
Agricultural Education	M
Art Education	M,D,O
Business Administration and Management— General	M,D,O
Communication Disorders	M,D,O
Counselor Education	M,D,O
Early Childhood Education	M,D,O
Education—General	M,D,O
Educational Administration	M,D,O
Educational Media/ Instructional Technology	M,D,O
Educational Policy	M,D,O
Educational Psychology	M,D,O
Elementary Education	M,D,O
Environmental and Occupational Health	M,D

Foundations and Philosophy of Education	M,D,O
Health Education	M,D,O
Health Promotion	M,D,O
Higher Education	D
Kinesiology and Movement Studies	M,D,O
Law	P,M
Marketing Research	M
Marketing	M
Mathematics Education	M,D,O
Medicinal and Pharmaceutical Chemistry	M,D
Middle School Education	M,D,O
Music Education	M,D,O
Nonprofit Management	M,D,O
Pharmaceutical Administration	M,D
Pharmaceutical Sciences	M,D
Pharmacy	P
Reading Education	M,D,O
Science Education	M,D,O
Social Sciences Education	M,D,O
Social Work	M,D,O
Special Education	M,D,O
Veterinary Medicine	P
Veterinary Sciences	M,D
Vocational and Technical Education	M,D,O

UNIVERSITY OF GREAT FALLS

Education—General	M
Human Services	M
Organizational Management	M

UNIVERSITY OF GUAM

Business Administration and Management—General	M
Counselor Education	M
Education—General	M
Educational Administration	M
English as a Second Language	M
Reading Education	M
Secondary Education	M
Special Education	M

UNIVERSITY OF GUELPH

Acute Care/Critical Care Nursing	M,D,O
Anesthesiologist Assistant Studies	M,D,O
Business Administration and Management—General	M
Epidemiology	M,D,O
Hospitality Management	M
Veterinary Medicine	M,D,O
Veterinary Sciences	M,D,O
Vision Sciences	M,D,O

UNIVERSITY OF HARTFORD

Accounting	M,O
Business Administration and Management—General	M
Community Health Nursing	M
Counselor Education	M,O
Early Childhood Education	M
Education—General	M,D,O
Educational Administration	D,O
Educational Media/ Instructional Technology	M
Elementary Education	M
Music Education	M,D,O

Nursing Education	M
Nursing—General	M
Organizational Behavior	M
Physical Therapy	M,D
Taxation	M,O

UNIVERSITY OF HAWAII AT MANOA

Accounting	M,D
Adult Nursing	M,D,O
Allopathic Medicine	P
Business Administration and Management—General	M
Communication Disorders	M
Community Health Nursing	M,D,O
Counselor Education	M
Curriculum and Instruction	M,D
Early Childhood Education	M
Education—General	M,D,O
Educational Administration	M,D
Educational Media/ Instructional Technology	M
Educational Policy	D
Educational Psychology	M,D
English as a Second Language	M,D,O
Entrepreneurship	M
Epidemiology	D
Family Nurse Practitioner Studies	M,D,O
Finance and Banking	M,D
Foreign Languages Education	M,D,O
Foundations and Philosophy of Education	M,D
Human Resources Management	M
Information Studies	M,D,O
International Business	M,D
Kinesiology and Movement Studies	M
Law	P,O
Library Science	M,D,O*
Management Information Systems	M,D,O
Marketing	M,D
Nursing and Healthcare Administration	M,D,O
Nursing—General	M,D,O
Organizational Behavior	M
Organizational Management	M,D
Public Health—General	M
Real Estate	M
Social Work	M,D
Special Education	M,D
Taxation	M
Travel and Tourism	M

UNIVERSITY OF HOUSTON

Accounting	M,D
Advertising and Public Relations	M
Art Education	M,D
Business Administration and Management—General	M,D
Communication Disorders	M
Curriculum and Instruction	M,D
Early Childhood Education	M,D
Education of the Gifted	M,D
Education—General	M,D
Educational Administration	M,D
Educational Psychology	M,D
Elementary Education	M,D
English as a Second Language	M,D
Entrepreneurship	D
Exercise and Sports Science	M,D

Finance and Banking	M
Foundations and Philosophy of Education	M,D
Health Education	M,D
Higher Education	M,D
Hospitality Management	M
Kinesiology and Movement Studies	M,D
Law	P,M
Logistics	M
Marketing	D
Mathematics Education	M,D
Multilingual and Multicultural Education	M,D
Music Education	M,D
Optometry	P
Pharmaceutical Administration	P,M,D
Pharmaceutical Sciences	P,M,D
Pharmacy	P,M,D
Physical Education	M,D
Reading Education	M,D
Science Education	M,D
Secondary Education	M,D
Social Sciences Education	M,D
Social Work	M,D
Special Education	M,D
Vision Sciences	M,D

UNIVERSITY OF HOUSTON–CLEAR LAKE

Accounting	M
Business Administration and Management—General	M
Counselor Education	M
Curriculum and Instruction	M
Early Childhood Education	M
Education—General	M,D
Educational Administration	M,D
Educational Media/ Instructional Technology	M
Exercise and Sports Science	M
Finance and Banking	M
Foundations and Philosophy of Education	M
Health Services Management and Hospital Administration	M
Human Resources Management	M
Library Science	M
Management Information Systems	M
Multilingual and Multicultural Education	M
Reading Education	M

UNIVERSITY OF HOUSTON–DOWNTOWN

Urban Education	M

UNIVERSITY OF HOUSTON–VICTORIA

Business Administration and Management—General	M*
Education—General	M

UNIVERSITY OF IDAHO

Accounting	M
Adult Education	M,D,O
Agricultural Education	M,D
Art Education	M
Business Administration and Management—General	M
Counselor Education	M,D,O

Curriculum and Instruction	M,D
Education—General	M,D,O
Educational Administration	M,D,O
English as a Second Language	M
Law	P
Physical Education	M,D
Recreation and Park Management	M
Science Education	M,D
Special Education	M,O
Veterinary Sciences	M,D
Vocational and Technical Education	M,D,O

UNIVERSITY OF ILLINOIS AT CHICAGO

Accounting	M
Allied Health—General	M,D
Allopathic Medicine	P
Business Administration and Management—General	M,D
Community Health Nursing	M
Community Health	M,D
Curriculum and Instruction	M,D
Dentistry	P
Education—General	M,D
Educational Administration	M,D
Educational Policy	M,D
Educational Psychology	M,D
Elementary Education	M,D
English as a Second Language	M
English Education	M,D
Environmental and Occupational Health	M,D
Epidemiology	M,D
Health Education	M
Health Services Management and Hospital Administration	M,D
Kinesiology and Movement Studies	M
Management Information Systems	M,D
Maternal and Child/ Neonatal Nursing	M
Mathematics Education	M
Medical/Surgical Nursing	M
Nurse Midwifery	M
Nursing and Healthcare Administration	M
Nursing—General	M,D
Occupational Therapy	M
Oral and Dental Sciences	M
Pediatric Nursing	M
Pharmaceutical Administration	M,D
Pharmaceutical Sciences	M,D
Pharmacy	P,M,D
Physical Therapy	M
Psychiatric Nursing	M
Public Health—General	M,D
Reading Education	M,D
Secondary Education	M,D
Social Work	M,D
Special Education	M,D
Urban Education	M,D

UNIVERSITY OF ILLINOIS AT SPRINGFIELD

Accounting	M
Business Administration and Management—General	M
Educational Administration	M
Human Services	M
Legal and Justice Studies	M
Management Information Systems	M

Public Health—General   M

UNIVERSITY OF ILLINOIS AT URBANA–CHAMPAIGN

Accounting	M,D
Advertising and Public Relations	M
Agricultural Education	M,D
Allopathic Medicine	
Art Education	M,D
Business Administration and Management—General	M,D
Communication Disorders	M,D
Community Health	M,D
Counselor Education	M,D,O
Curriculum and Instruction	M,D,O
Education of the Multiply Handicapped	M,D,O
Education—General	M,D,O
Educational Administration	M,D,O
Educational Policy	M,D
Educational Psychology	M,D,O
English as a Second Language	M
Finance and Banking	M,D
Foreign Languages Education	M,D,O
Health Physics/Radiological Health	M,D
Higher Education	M,D,O
Human Resources Development	M,D,O
Human Resources Management	M,D*
Information Studies	M,D,O
Kinesiology and Movement Studies	M,D
Law	P,M,D
Leisure Studies	M,D
Library Science	M,D,O*
Mathematics Education	M,D
Social Work	M,D
Special Education	M,D,O
Veterinary Medicine	P
Veterinary Sciences	M,D
Vocational and Technical Education	M,D,O

UNIVERSITY OF INDIANAPOLIS

Art Education	M
Business Administration and Management—General	M,O
Curriculum and Instruction	M
Education—General	M
Educational Administration	M
Elementary Education	M
English Education	M
Finance and Banking	M,O
Foreign Languages Education	M
Home Economics Education	M,O
Marketing	M,O
Mathematics Education	M
Nurse Midwifery	M
Nursing and Healthcare Administration	M
Nursing Education	M
Nursing—General	M
Occupational Therapy	M,D
Physical Education	M
Physical Therapy	M,D
Science Education	M
Secondary Education	M
Social Sciences Education	M
Supply Chain Management	M,O

THE UNIVERSITY OF IOWA

Accounting	M,D

Actuarial Science	M,D
Allopathic Medicine	P
Art Education	M,D
Business Administration and Management—General	M,D
Clinical Research	M,D
Communication Disorders	M,D
Community Health	M,D
Counselor Education	M,D
Curriculum and Instruction	M,D
Dentistry	P,M,D,O
Developmental Education	M,D
Early Childhood Education	M,D
Education—General	M,D,O
Educational Administration	M,D,O
Educational Measurement and Evaluation	M,D,O
Educational Policy	M,D,O
Educational Psychology	M,D,O
Elementary Education	M,D
English Education	M,D
Entrepreneurship	M
Environmental and Occupational Health	M,D,O
Epidemiology	M,D
Exercise and Sports Science	M,D
Finance and Banking	M,D
Foreign Languages Education	M,D
Foundations and Philosophy of Education	M,D,O
Health Services Management and Hospital Administration	M,D
Higher Education	M,D,O
Industrial and Manufacturing Management	M
Information Studies	M
Investment Management	M
Law	P,M
Leisure Studies	M
Library Science	M
Management Information Systems	M
Management Strategy and Policy	M
Marketing	M,D
Mathematics Education	M,D
Music Education	M,D
Nonprofit Management	M
Nursing—General	M,D
Oral and Dental Sciences	M,D,O
Pharmacy	M,D
Physical Education	M,D
Physical Therapy	D
Physician Assistant Studies	M
Public Health—General	M,D,O
Recreation and Park Management	M
Rehabilitation Sciences	D
Science Education	M,D
Secondary Education	M,D
Social Sciences Education	M,D
Social Work	M,D
Special Education	M,D
Sports Management	M
Student Affairs	M,D

UNIVERSITY OF KANSAS

Accounting	M
Allied Health—General	M,D,O
Allopathic Medicine	P
Art Education	M
Business Administration and Management—General	M,D
Communication Disorders	M,D
Curriculum and Instruction	M,D
Education—General	M,D,O

Educational Administration	M,D,O
Educational Measurement and Evaluation	M,D
Educational Policy	D
Educational Psychology	M,D
Foundations and Philosophy of Education	D
Health Services Management and Hospital Administration	M
Higher Education	M,D
Law	P
Management Information Systems	M,D
Medicinal and Pharmaceutical Chemistry	M,D
Music Education	M,D
Nurse Anesthesia	M
Nurse Midwifery	M,D,O
Nursing Education	M,D,O
Nursing—General	M,D,O
Occupational Therapy	M,D
Pharmaceutical Sciences	M
Physical Education	M,D
Physical Therapy	M,D
Psychiatric Nursing	M,D,O
Public Health—General	M
Rehabilitation Sciences	M,D
Special Education	M,D

UNIVERSITY OF KENTUCKY

Accounting	M
Allied Health—General	M,D
Allopathic Medicine	P
Art Education	M
Business Administration and Management—General	M,D
Clinical Laboratory Sciences/Medical Technology	M,D
Communication Disorders	M
Curriculum and Instruction	M,D
Dentistry	P,M
Early Childhood Education	M,D
Education—General	M,D,O
Educational Administration	M,D,O
Educational Measurement and Evaluation	M,D
Educational Media/Instructional Technology	M,D
Educational Policy	M,D
Educational Psychology	M,D,O
Exercise and Sports Science	M,D
Foreign Languages Education	M
Health Physics/Radiological Health	M
Health Promotion	M,D
Health Services Management and Hospital Administration	M
Higher Education	M,D
Hospitality Management	M
International Business	M
Kinesiology and Movement Studies	M,D
Law	P
Library Science	M
Medical Physics	M
Middle School Education	M,D
Music Education	M,D
Nursing—General	M,D
Oral and Dental Sciences	M
Pharmaceutical Sciences	M,D
Pharmacy	P
Physical Therapy	M
Physician Assistant Studies	M
Public Health—General	M
Rehabilitation Sciences	D

Social Work	M,D
Special Education	M,D
Veterinary Sciences	M,D
Vocational and Technical Education	M

UNIVERSITY OF LA VERNE

Accounting	M
Business Administration and Management—General	M,O
Counselor Education	M,O
Education—General	M,O
Educational Administration	M,D,O
Finance and Banking	M
Health Services Management and Hospital Administration	M,O
Health Services Research	M
International Business	M
Law	P
Management Information Systems	M
Marketing	M
Multilingual and Multicultural Education	O
Nonprofit Management	M,O
Organizational Management	M,D,O
Reading Education	M,O
Special Education	M
Supply Chain Management	M

UNIVERSITY OF LETHBRIDGE

Accounting	M,D
Business Administration and Management—General	M,D
Education—General	M,D
Educational Administration	M,D
Exercise and Sports Science	M,D
Finance and Banking	M,D
Human Resources Management	M,D
International Business	M,D
Kinesiology and Movement Studies	M,D
Management Information Systems	M,D
Management Strategy and Policy	M,D
Nursing—General	M,D

UNIVERSITY OF LOUISIANA AT LAFAYETTE

Business Administration and Management—General	M
Communication Disorders	M,D
Counselor Education	M
Curriculum and Instruction	M
Education of the Gifted	M
Education—General	M,D
Educational Administration	M,D
Health Services Management and Hospital Administration	M
Music Education	M
Nursing—General	M

UNIVERSITY OF LOUISIANA AT MONROE

Business Administration and Management—General	M
Communication Disorders	M
Counselor Education	M

Curriculum and Instruction	M,D
Education—General	M,D,O
Educational Administration	M,D
Elementary Education	M
Exercise and Sports Science	M
Pharmaceutical Sciences	M
Pharmacy	P,D
Reading Education	M
Secondary Education	M
Special Education	M

UNIVERSITY OF LOUISVILLE

Accounting	M
Allopathic Medicine	P
Art Education	M
Business Administration and Management—General	M
Clinical Research	M,D,O
Communication Disorders	M,D
Counselor Education	M,D
Curriculum and Instruction	D
Dentistry	P
Early Childhood Education	M
Education—General	M,D,O
Educational Administration	M,D,O
Educational Media/Instructional Technology	M
Educational Psychology	M,D
Elementary Education	M
Entrepreneurship	D
Exercise and Sports Science	M
Foreign Languages Education	M,D
Health Education	M
Higher Education	M,O
Human Resources Development	M
Law	P
Middle School Education	M
Music Education	M
Nursing—General	M,D
Oral and Dental Sciences	M
Physical Education	M
Public Health—General	M,O
Reading Education	M
Secondary Education	M
Social Work	M,D,O
Special Education	M,D
Sports Management	M
Student Affairs	M,D
Vision Sciences	D
Vocational and Technical Education	M

UNIVERSITY OF MAINE

Accounting	M
Business Administration and Management—General	M
Communication Disorders	M
Counselor Education	M,D,O
Curriculum and Instruction	M
Education—General	M,D,O*
Educational Administration	M,D,O
Educational Media/Instructional Technology	M
Elementary Education	M,O
Foreign Languages Education	M
Higher Education	M,D,O
Kinesiology and Movement Studies	M
Management Information Systems	M
Nursing—General	M,O
Physical Education	M
Reading Education	M,D,O
Science Education	M,O
Secondary Education	M,O

Social Sciences Education	M,O
Social Work	M
Special Education	M,O

UNIVERSITY OF MANAGEMENT AND TECHNOLOGY

Business Administration and Management—General	M,D,O
Management Information Systems	M,O
Project Management	M,D,O

UNIVERSITY OF MANITOBA

Adult Education	M
Business Administration and Management—General	M,D
Community Health	M,D
Counselor Education	M
Curriculum and Instruction	M
Dentistry	P
Education—General	M,D
Educational Administration	M
Educational Psychology	M
English as a Second Language	M
English Education	M
Foundations and Philosophy of Education	M
Law	M
Legal and Justice Studies	M
Nursing—General	M
Oral and Dental Sciences	M,D
Pharmaceutical Sciences	M,D
Physical Education	M
Recreation and Park Management	M
Rehabilitation Sciences	M
Social Work	M
Special Education	M

UNIVERSITY OF MARY

Business Administration and Management—General	M
Curriculum and Instruction	M
Early Childhood Education	M
Education—General	M
Educational Administration	M
Family Nurse Practitioner Studies	M
Higher Education	M
Nursing and Healthcare Administration	M
Nursing Education	M
Nursing—General	M
Occupational Therapy	M
Physical Therapy	D
Reading Education	M
Special Education	M

UNIVERSITY OF MARY HARDIN-BAYLOR

Accounting	M
Business Administration and Management—General	M
Counselor Education	M
Education—General	M,D
Educational Administration	M,D
Educational Psychology	M,D
Exercise and Sports Science	M,D
Management Information Systems	M
Reading Education	M,D
Sports Management	M

UNIVERSITY OF MARYLAND, BALTIMORE

Allopathic Medicine	P
Clinical Laboratory Sciences/Medical Technology	M
Clinical Research	M,D
Community Health Nursing	M
Dental Hygiene	M
Dentistry	P,M,O
Epidemiology	M,D
Gerontological Nursing	M
Health Services Research	M,D
Law	P
Maternal and Child/Neonatal Nursing	M
Medical/Surgical Nursing	M
Nurse Midwifery	M
Nursing and Healthcare Administration	M
Nursing Education	M
Nursing—General	M,D
Oral and Dental Sciences	P,M,D,O
Pediatric Nursing	M
Pharmaceutical Administration	M,D
Pharmaceutical Sciences	D
Pharmacy	P,M,D
Physical Therapy	D
Psychiatric Nursing	M
Rehabilitation Sciences	D
Social Work	M,D

UNIVERSITY OF MARYLAND, BALTIMORE COUNTY

Computer Education	M,O
Curriculum and Instruction	M,O
Distance Education Development	M,O
Early Childhood Education	M
Education—General	M,O
Educational Media/Instructional Technology	M,O
Elementary Education	M
Epidemiology	M
Health Education	M
Health Services Management and Hospital Administration	M
Human Services	M,D
Multilingual and Multicultural Education	M,D,O
Nonprofit Management	M,O
Secondary Education	M

UNIVERSITY OF MARYLAND, COLLEGE PARK

Advertising and Public Relations	M,D
Business Administration and Management—General	M,D
Communication Disorders	M,D
Counselor Education	M,D,O
Curriculum and Instruction	M,D,O
Early Childhood Education	M,D
Education—General	M,D,O*
Educational Administration	M,D,O
Educational Measurement and Evaluation	M,D
Educational Media/Instructional Technology	M,D,O
Educational Psychology	M,D
English as a Second Language	M,D,O
Foreign Languages Education	M,D
Foundations and Philosophy of Education	M,D,O
Health Education	M,D

Information Studies	M,D
Kinesiology and Movement Studies	M,D
Law	
Library Science*	
Music Education	M,D
Public Health—General	M,D
Reading Education	M,D,O
Secondary Education	M,D,O
Social Work	
Special Education	M,D,O
Student Affairs	M,D,O
Veterinary Medicine	P
Veterinary Sciences	M,D

UNIVERSITY OF MARYLAND EASTERN SHORE

Counselor Education	M
Education—General	M
Educational Administration	D
Organizational Management	D
Physical Therapy	D
Rehabilitation Sciences	M
Special Education	M
Vocational and Technical Education	M

UNIVERSITY OF MARYLAND UNIVERSITY COLLEGE

Accounting	M,O
Business Administration and Management—General	M,D,O
Distance Education Development	M,O
Education—General	M
Finance and Banking	M,O
Health Services Management and Hospital Administration	M,O
International Business	M,O
Management Information Systems	M,O

UNIVERSITY OF MARY WASHINGTON

Business Administration and Management—General	M
Education—General	M
Management Information Systems	M

UNIVERSITY OF MASSACHUSETTS AMHERST

Accounting	M
Business Administration and Management—General	M,D
Communication Disorders	M,D
Counselor Education	M,D,O
Curriculum and Instruction	M,D,O
Early Childhood Education	M,D,O
Education—General	M,D,O
Educational Administration	M,D,O
Educational Measurement and Evaluation	M,D,O
Educational Media/Instructional Technology	M,D,O
Elementary Education	M,D,O
Foreign Languages Education	M,D
Higher Education	M,D,O
Hospitality Management	M
International and Comparative Education	M,D,O
Kinesiology and Movement Studies	M,D

Multilingual and Multicultural Education	M,D,O
Nursing—General	M,D
Physical Education	M,D,O
Public Health—General	M,D
Reading Education	M,D,O
Secondary Education	M,D,O
Special Education	M,D,O
Sports Management	M,D
Travel and Tourism	M

UNIVERSITY OF MASSACHUSETTS BOSTON

Business Administration and Management— General	M
Counselor Education	M,O
Curriculum and Instruction	M
Education—General	M,D,O
Educational Administration	M,D,O
Elementary Education	M,D,O
English as a Second Language	M
Foreign Languages Education	M
Health Services Management and Hospital Administration	M,D,O
Higher Education	M,D,O
Human Services	M
Multilingual and Multicultural Education	M
Nursing—General	M,D
Secondary Education	M,D,O
Special Education	M
Urban Education	M,D,O

UNIVERSITY OF MASSACHUSETTS DARTMOUTH

Accounting	M,O
Art Education	M
Business Administration and Management— General	M,O
Community Health Nursing	M,D,O
Education—General	M,O
Electronic Commerce	M,O
Finance and Banking	M,O
Marketing	M,O
Organizational Management	M,O
Supply Chain Management	M,O

UNIVERSITY OF MASSACHUSETTS LOWELL

Allied Health—General	M,D
Business Administration and Management— General	M
Clinical Laboratory Sciences/Medical Technology	M
Community Health Nursing	M
Curriculum and Instruction	M,D,O
Education—General	M,D,O
Educational Administration	M,D,O
Epidemiology	M,D,O
Gerontological Nursing	M
Health Physics/ Radiological Health	M,D
Health Promotion	D
Health Services Management and Hospital Administration	M
Industrial and Manufacturing Management	M
Industrial Hygiene	M,D,O

Mathematics Education	M,D,O
Music Education	M
Nursing and Healthcare Administration	D
Nursing—General	M,D
Occupational Health Nursing	M
Physical Therapy	M
Psychiatric Nursing	M
Reading Education	M,D,O
Science Education	M,D,O

UNIVERSITY OF MASSACHUSETTS WORCESTER

Acute Care/Critical Care Nursing	M,D,O
Adult Nursing	M,D,O
Allopathic Medicine	P
Clinical Research	D
Community Health Nursing	M,D,O
Epidemiology	D
Family Nurse Practitioner Studies	M,D,O
Gerontological Nursing	M,D,O
Health Services Research	D*
Medical Physics	D
Nursing Education	M,D,O
Nursing—General	M,D,O

UNIVERSITY OF MEDICINE AND DENTISTRY OF NEW JERSEY

Adult Nursing	M,D,O
Allied Health—General	M,D,O
Allopathic Medicine	P
Clinical Laboratory Sciences/Medical Technology	M,D
Dentistry	P,M,D,O
Epidemiology	M,D,O
Family Nurse Practitioner Studies	M,O
Health Education	M,D
Health Physics/ Radiological Health	M
Health Services Management and Hospital Administration	M
Kinesiology and Movement Studies	M,D
Nurse Anesthesia	M,D,O
Nurse Midwifery	O
Nursing Education	M,O
Nursing Informatics	M
Nursing—General	M,D,O
Occupational Health Nursing	M,D,O
Oral and Dental Sciences	P,M,D,O
Osteopathic Medicine	P
Physical Therapy	M,D
Physician Assistant Studies	M
Public Health—General	M,D,O*
Transcultural Nursing	D
Women's Health Nursing	M,D,O

UNIVERSITY OF MEMPHIS

Accounting	M,D
Adult Education	M,D,O
Business Administration and Management— General	M,D
Communication Disorders	M,D
Counselor Education	M,D
Curriculum and Instruction	M,D
Early Childhood Education	M,D
Education—General	M,D,O
Educational Administration	M,D,O
Educational Measurement and Evaluation	M,D

Educational Media/ Instructional Technology	M,D
Educational Psychology	M,D
Elementary Education	M,D
Exercise and Sports Science	M
Finance and Banking	M,D
Health Promotion	M
Health Services Management and Hospital Administration	M
Higher Education	M,D,O
International Business	M
Law	P
Leisure Studies	M
Management Information Systems	M,D
Marketing	M,D
Music Education	M,D
Nonprofit Management	M
Physical Education	M
Reading Education	M,D
Real Estate	M,D
Secondary Education	M,D
Special Education	M,D
Supply Chain Management	M,D
Taxation	M

UNIVERSITY OF MIAMI

Accounting	M
Acute Care/Critical Care Nursing	M,D
Adult Nursing	M,D
Advertising and Public Relations	M,D
Allopathic Medicine	P
Athletic Training and Sports Medicine	M
Business Administration and Management— General	M*
Community Health	M,D
Counselor Education	M,O
Early Childhood Education	M,O
Education—General	M,D,O*
Educational Administration	M,O
Educational Measurement and Evaluation	M,D
Elementary Education	M
English as a Second Language	M,D
Environmental and Occupational Health	M
Epidemiology	D
Exercise and Sports Science	M,D
Family Nurse Practitioner Studies	M,D
Finance and Banking	M
Higher Education	M,O
International Business	M
Law	P,M
Management Information Systems	M
Marketing	M
Mathematics Education	M,D,O
Music Education	M,D,O
Nurse Anesthesia	M,D
Nurse Midwifery	M,D
Nursing—General	M,D
Physical Therapy	D
Psychiatric Nursing	M,D
Public Health—General	M*
Quality Management	M
Reading Education	M,D,O
Science Education	M,D,O
Special Education	M,D,O
Sports Management	M
Student Affairs	M,O
Taxation	M

UNIVERSITY OF MICHIGAN

Acute Care/Critical Care Nursing	M
Adult Nursing	M
Allopathic Medicine	P
Business Administration and Management— General	D
Clinical Research	M
Community Health Nursing	M
Computer Education	M,D
Curriculum and Instruction	M,D
Dentistry	P
Early Childhood Education	M,D
Education—General	M,D*
Educational Administration	M,D
Educational Measurement and Evaluation	M,D
Educational Media/ Instructional Technology	M,D
Elementary Education	M,D
English as a Second Language	M,D
English Education	M,D
Environmental and Occupational Health	M,D
Epidemiology	M,D
Family Nurse Practitioner Studies	M
Foreign Languages Education	M,D
Foundations and Philosophy of Education	M,D
Gerontological Nursing	M
Health Physics/ Radiological Health	M,D,O
Health Promotion	M,D
Health Services Management and Hospital Administration	M,D
Higher Education	M,D
Industrial Hygiene	M,D
Information Studies	M,D*
International Health	M,D
Kinesiology and Movement Studies	M,D
Law	P,M,D
Library Science	M,D
Mathematics Education	M,D
Medical/Surgical Nursing	M
Medicinal and Pharmaceutical Chemistry	D
Multilingual and Multicultural Education	M,D
Music Education	M,D,O
Nurse Midwifery	M
Nursing and Healthcare Administration	M
Nursing—General	M,D,O
Occupational Health Nursing	M
Oral and Dental Sciences	M,D,O
Pediatric Nursing	M
Pharmaceutical Administration	D
Pharmaceutical Sciences	D
Pharmacy	P
Psychiatric Nursing	M
Public Health—General	M,D
Reading Education	M,D
Real Estate	M,O
Science Education	M,D
Secondary Education	M,D
Social Sciences Education	M,D
Social Work	M,D*
Special Education	M,D
Sports Management	M,D
Women's Health Nursing	M,O

UNIVERSITY OF MICHIGAN–DEARBORN

Accounting	M
Business Administration and Management—General	M
Education—General	M
Educational Administration	M,O
Finance and Banking	M
Nonprofit Management	M,O
Special Education	M

UNIVERSITY OF MICHIGAN–FLINT

Business Administration and Management—General	M
Early Childhood Education	M
Education—General	M
Educational Media/Instructional Technology	M*
Elementary Education	M
Health Education	M
Multilingual and Multicultural Education	M
Nurse Anesthesia	M
Nursing—General	M
Physical Therapy	D
Reading Education	M
Special Education	M
Urban Education	M

UNIVERSITY OF MINNESOTA, DULUTH

Allopathic Medicine	P
Business Administration and Management—General	M
Communication Disorders	M
Education—General	D
Music Education	M
Social Work	M

UNIVERSITY OF MINNESOTA, TWIN CITIES CAMPUS

Accounting	M,D
Adult Education	M,D,O
Adult Nursing	M
Agricultural Education	M,D
Allopathic Medicine	P
Art Education	M,D,O
Business Administration and Management—General	M,D*
Business Education	M,D
Clinical Research	M
Communication Disorders	M,D
Community Health Nursing	M
Community Health	M
Counselor Education	M,D,O
Curriculum and Instruction	M,D,O
Dentistry	P
Early Childhood Education	M,D,O
Education of the Gifted	M,D,O
Education—General	M,D,O
Educational Administration	M,D,O
Educational Measurement and Evaluation	M,D
Educational Media/Instructional Technology	M,D,O
Educational Policy	M,D,O
Educational Psychology	M,D,O
Elementary Education	M,D,O
English as a Second Language	M
English Education	M
Entrepreneurship	M
Environmental and Occupational Health	M,D,O
Environmental Education	M,D,O
Epidemiology	M,D
Exercise and Sports Science	M,D,O
Family Nurse Practitioner Studies	M
Finance and Banking	M,D
Foreign Languages Education	M
Foundations and Philosophy of Education	M,D,O
Gerontological Nursing	M
Health Services Management and Hospital Administration	M,D*
Health Services Research	M,D
Higher Education	M,D
Human Resources Development	M,D,O
Human Resources Management	M,D*
Industrial and Manufacturing Management	M,D
Industrial Hygiene	M,D
International and Comparative Education	M,D
International Business	M
Kinesiology and Movement Studies	M,D
Law	P,M
Leisure Studies	M,D
Logistics	M,D
Management Information Systems	M,D
Management Strategy and Policy	M,D
Marketing	M,D
Maternal and Child Health	M
Mathematics Education	M
Medical Physics	M,D*
Medicinal and Pharmaceutical Chemistry	M,D
Multilingual and Multicultural Education	M
Nurse Anesthesia	M
Nurse Midwifery	M
Nursing and Healthcare Administration	M
Nursing—General	M,D
Occupational Health Nursing	M,D
Oral and Dental Sciences	M,D,O
Pediatric Nursing	M
Pharmaceutical Administration	M,D
Pharmaceutical Sciences	M,D
Pharmacy	P
Physical Education	M,D,O
Physical Therapy	D
Psychiatric Nursing	M
Public Health—General	M,D,O
Reading Education	M,D,O
Recreation and Park Management	M,D
Science Education	M
Social Sciences Education	M
Social Work	M,D
Special Education	M,D,O
Sports Management	M,D,O
Student Affairs	M,D,O
Supply Chain Management	M
Taxation	M
Veterinary Medicine	P
Veterinary Sciences	M,D
Vocational and Technical Education	M,D,O
Women's Health Nursing	M

UNIVERSITY OF MISSISSIPPI

Accounting	M,D
Art Education	M
Business Administration and Management—General	M,D
Communication Disorders	M
Counselor Education	M,D,O
Curriculum and Instruction	M,D,O
Education—General	M,D,O
Educational Administration	M,D,O
Exercise and Sports Science	M,D
Higher Education	M,D,O
Law	P
Leisure Studies	M,D
Management Information Systems	M,D
Medicinal and Pharmaceutical Chemistry	M,D
Pharmaceutical Administration	M,D
Pharmaceutical Sciences	M,D
Pharmacy	P
Recreation and Park Management	M,D
Secondary Education	M,D,O
Student Affairs	M,D,O
Taxation	M,D

UNIVERSITY OF MISSISSIPPI MEDICAL CENTER

Allied Health—General	M
Allopathic Medicine	P
Clinical Laboratory Sciences/Medical Technology	M,D
Dentistry	P,M,D
Maternal and Child Health	M
Nursing—General	M,D
Occupational Therapy	M
Oral and Dental Sciences	M,D
Physical Therapy	M

UNIVERSITY OF MISSOURI–COLUMBIA

Accounting	M,D
Adult Education	M,D,O
Agricultural Education	M,D,O
Allopathic Medicine	P
Art Education	M,D,O
Business Administration and Management—General	M,D*
Business Education	M,D,O
Communication Disorders	M
Curriculum and Instruction	M,D,O
Early Childhood Education	M,D,O
Education of the Gifted	M,D
Education—General	M,D,O
Educational Administration	M,D,O
Educational Media/Instructional Technology	M,D,O
Educational Psychology	M,D,O
Elementary Education	M,D,O
English Education	M,D,O
Exercise and Sports Science	M,D
Foreign Languages Education	M,D,O
Health Education	M,D,O
Health Physics/Radiological Health	M,D
Health Services Management and Hospital Administration	M
Higher Education	M,D,O
Hospitality Management	M,D
Information Studies	M,D,O
Law	P,M
Library Science	M,D,O
Mathematics Education	M,D,O
Medical Physics	M,D
Music Education	M,D,O
Nursing—General	M,D
Occupational Therapy	M
Physical Therapy	M
Public Health—General	M
Reading Education	M,D,O
Recreation and Park Management	M
Science Education	M,D,O
Social Sciences Education	M,D,O
Social Work	M
Special Education	M,D
Veterinary Medicine	P
Veterinary Sciences	M,D
Vocational and Technical Education	M,D,O

UNIVERSITY OF MISSOURI–KANSAS CITY

Accounting	M,D
Adult Nursing	M,D
Allopathic Medicine	P
Business Administration and Management—General	M,D
Curriculum and Instruction	M,D,O
Dental Hygiene	P,M,D,O
Dentistry	P,M,D,O
Education—General	M,D,O
Educational Administration	M,D,O
Family Nurse Practitioner Studies	M,D
Law	P,M
Maternal and Child/Neonatal Nursing	M,D
Music Education	M,D
Nursing and Healthcare Administration	M,D
Nursing Education	M,D
Nursing—General	M,D
Oral and Dental Sciences	P,M,D,O
Pediatric Nursing	M,D
Pharmaceutical Sciences	P,M,D
Pharmacy	P,M,D
Reading Education	M,D,O
Social Work	M
Special Education	M,D,O
Taxation	P,M
Women's Health Nursing	M,D

UNIVERSITY OF MISSOURI–ROLLA

Mathematics Education	M,D
Science Education	M,D

UNIVERSITY OF MISSOURI–ST. LOUIS

Accounting	M,O
Adult Education	M,D,O
Business Administration and Management—General	M,O
Counselor Education	M
Curriculum and Instruction	M,D
Education—General	M,D,O
Educational Administration	M,D,O
Educational Measurement and Evaluation	M,D,O
Educational Psychology	D,O
Elementary Education	M,D
Finance and Banking	M,O
Health Services Management and Hospital Administration	M,O
Higher Education	M,D,O
Human Resources Development	M,O
Human Resources Management	M,O
Industrial and Manufacturing Management	M,O
Logistics	M,D,O

Management Information
  Systems   M,D
Marketing   M,O
Middle School Education   M,D
Music Education   M
Nonprofit Management   M,O
Nursing—General   M,D,O
Optometry   P
Quantitative Analysis   M,O
Reading Education   M,D
Secondary Education   M,D
Social Work   M
Special Education   M,D
Supply Chain
  Management   M,D,O
Vision Sciences   M,D

UNIVERSITY OF MOBILE

Business Administration
  and Management—
    General   M
Education—General   M
Nursing—General   M

THE UNIVERSITY OF MONTANA

Accounting   M
Business Administration
  and Management—
    General   M
Counselor Education   M,D,O
Curriculum and Instruction   M,D
Education—General   M,D,O
Educational Administration   M,D,O
English Education   M
Exercise and Sports
  Science   M
Health Education   M
Health Promotion   M
Law   P
Mathematics Education   M,D
Music Education   M
Pharmaceutical Sciences   M,D
Physical Education   M
Physical Therapy   D
Public Health—General   M,O
Recreation and Park
  Management   M,D

UNIVERSITY OF MONTEVALLO

Communication Disorders   M
Counselor Education   M
Early Childhood Education   M
Education—General   M,O
Educational Administration   M,O
Elementary Education   M
Secondary Education   M

UNIVERSITY OF NEBRASKA AT KEARNEY

Art Education   M
Business Administration
  and Management—
    General   M
Communication Disorders   M
Counselor Education   M,O
Curriculum and Instruction   M
Education—General   M,O
Educational Administration   M,O
Educational Media/
  Instructional Technology   M
Exercise and Sports
  Science   M
Foreign Languages
  Education   M
Music Education   M
Physical Education   M
Reading Education   M
Science Education   M
Special Education   M

UNIVERSITY OF NEBRASKA AT OMAHA

Accounting   M
Business Administration
  and Management—
    General   M
Communication Disorders   M
Counselor Education   M
Education—General   M,D,O
Educational Administration   M,D,O
Educational Media/
  Instructional Technology   M,O
Educational Psychology   M,D,O
Elementary Education   M
English as a Second
  Language   M,O
Foreign Languages
  Education   M
Health Education   M
Management Information
  Systems   M,D
Physical Education   M
Public Health—General   M
Reading Education   M
Recreation and Park
  Management   M
Secondary Education   M
Social Work   M
Special Education   M
Urban Education   M,O

UNIVERSITY OF NEBRASKA–LINCOLN

Accounting   M,D
Actuarial Science   M
Agricultural Education   M
Business Administration
  and Management—
    General   M,D
Communication Disorders   M
Curriculum and Instruction   M,D,O
Education—General   M,D,O
Educational Administration   M,D,O
Educational Psychology   M,O
Finance and Banking   M,D
Health Education   M
Law   P,M
Legal and Justice Studies   M
Management Information
  Systems   M
Marketing   M,D
Physical Education   M
Recreation and Park
  Management   M
Special Education   M
Veterinary Sciences   M,D

UNIVERSITY OF NEBRASKA MEDICAL CENTER

Allied Health—General   M,D,O
Allopathic Medicine   P,O
Clinical Laboratory
  Sciences/Medical
  Technology   M,O
Dentistry   P,O
Nursing—General   M,D
Pharmaceutical Sciences   M,D
Pharmacy   P
Physical Therapy   D
Physician Assistant
  Studies   M
Public Health—General   M

UNIVERSITY OF NEVADA, LAS VEGAS

Accounting   M
Business Administration
  and Management—
    General   M
Counselor Education   M,D,O
Curriculum and Instruction   M,D,O
Education of the Gifted   M,D,O
Education—General   M,D,O
Educational Administration   M,D,O
Educational Media/
  Instructional Technology   M,D,O
Educational Psychology   M,D,O
Elementary Education   M,D,O
English as a Second
  Language   M,D,O
English Education   M,D,O
Exercise and Sports
  Science   M
Family Nurse Practitioner
  Studies   M,D,O
Health Physics/
  Radiological Health   M
Health Promotion   M
Hospitality Management   M,D
Kinesiology and
  Movement Studies   M
Law   P
Leisure Studies   M
Library Science   M,D,O
Management Information
  Systems   M
Mathematics Education   M,D,O
Multilingual and
  Multicultural Education   M,D,O
Music Education   M,D
Nursing Education   M,D,O
Nursing—General   M,D,O
Pediatric Nursing   M,D,O
Physical Education   M,D
Physical Therapy   M,D
Public Health—General   M
Reading Education   M,D,O
Secondary Education   M,D,O
Social Work   M
Special Education   M,D,O
Sports Management   M,D

UNIVERSITY OF NEVADA, RENO

Accounting   M
Business Administration
  and Management—
    General   M
Communication Disorders   M,D
Counselor Education   M,D,O
Curriculum and Instruction   M,D,O
Education—General   M,D,O
Educational Administration   M,D,O
Educational Psychology   M,D,O
Elementary Education   M,D,O
English as a Second
  Language   M,D,O
Environmental and
  Occupational Health   M,D
Finance and Banking   M
Foreign Languages
  Education   M
Legal and Justice Studies   M
Mathematics Education   M
Nursing—General   M
Public Health—General   M
Reading Education   M,D,O
Secondary Education   M,D,O
Social Work   M
Special Education   M,D,O

UNIVERSITY OF NEW BRUNSWICK FREDERICTON

Business Administration
  and Management—
    General   M
Education—General   M,D
Exercise and Sports
  Science   M
Family Nurse Practitioner
  Studies   M
Health Services Research   M
Law   P

Marketing   M,D
Nursing—General   M
Physical Education   M
Recreation and Park
  Management   M
Sports Management   M

UNIVERSITY OF NEW BRUNSWICK SAINT JOHN

Business Administration
  and Management—
    General   M
Electronic Commerce   M
International Business   M

UNIVERSITY OF NEW ENGLAND

Education—General   M
Educational Administration   O
Educational Measurement
  and Evaluation   M
Nurse Anesthesia   M
Occupational Therapy   M
Osteopathic Medicine   P
Physical Therapy   D
Physician Assistant
  Studies   M
Public Health—General   M,O
Reading Education   M
Social Work   M,O

UNIVERSITY OF NEW HAMPSHIRE

Accounting   M*
Business Administration
  and Management—
    General   M
Communication Disorders   M
Counselor Education   M
Early Childhood Education   M
Education—General   M,D,O
Educational Administration   M,O
Elementary Education   M
English Education   M,D
Environmental Education   M
Health Services
  Management and
  Hospital Administration   M
Higher Education   M
Kinesiology and
  Movement Studies   M
Legal and Justice Studies   M
Logistics   M,D
Mathematics Education   M,D
Music Education   M
Nursing—General   M
Occupational Therapy   M
Public Health—General   M
Reading Education   M
Recreation and Park
  Management   M
Science Education   M,D
Secondary Education   M
Social Work   M
Special Education   M

UNIVERSITY OF NEW HAMPSHIRE AT MANCHESTER

Business Administration
  and Management—
    General   M,O
Counselor Education   M,O
Education—General   M,O
Educational Administration   M,O
Public Health—General   M,O
Social Work   M,O

UNIVERSITY OF NEW HAVEN

Accounting   M

Advertising and Public Relations	M
Business Administration and Management—General	M
Education—General	M
Environmental and Occupational Health	M
Finance and Banking	M
Health Services Management and Hospital Administration	M
Hospitality Management	M
Human Resources Management	M
Industrial Hygiene	M
International Business	M
Logistics	M,O
Management Information Systems	M
Management Strategy and Policy	M
Marketing	M
Sports Management	M
Taxation	M
Travel and Tourism	M

UNIVERSITY OF NEW MEXICO

Accounting	M
Allopathic Medicine	P
Art Education	M
Business Administration and Management—General	M
Communication Disorders	M
Counselor Education	M,D
Dental Hygiene	M
Education—General	M,O
Educational Administration	M,D,O
Educational Media/ Instructional Technology	M,D,O
Educational Psychology	M,D
Elementary Education	M,O
Finance and Banking	M
Foundations and Philosophy of Education	M,D
Health Education	M
Human Resources Management	M
International Business	M
Law	P
Management Information Systems	M
Management Strategy and Policy	M
Marketing	M
Multilingual and Multicultural Education	D,O
Nursing—General	M,D
Occupational Therapy	M
Organizational Management	M
Pharmaceutical Sciences	M,D
Pharmacy	P
Physical Education	M,D,O
Physical Therapy	M
Public Health—General	M
Secondary Education	M,O
Special Education	M,D,O
Taxation	M

UNIVERSITY OF NEW ORLEANS

Accounting	M
Business Administration and Management—General	M
Counselor Education	M,D,O
Curriculum and Instruction	M,D,O
Education—General	M,D,O
Educational Administration	M,D,O
English Education	M
Finance and Banking	M,D

Foundations and Philosophy of Education	M,D,O
Health Services Management and Hospital Administration	M
Hospitality Management	M
Science Education	M
Social Sciences Education	M
Special Education	M,D,O
Taxation	M
Travel and Tourism	M

UNIVERSITY OF NORTH ALABAMA

Business Administration and Management—General	M
Counselor Education	M
Education—General	M,O
Educational Administration	M,O
Elementary Education	M,O
Nursing—General	M
Secondary Education	M
Special Education	M

THE UNIVERSITY OF NORTH CAROLINA AT CHAPEL HILL

Accounting	M,D
Allied Health—General	M,D
Allopathic Medicine	P
Athletic Training and Sports Medicine	M
Business Administration and Management—General	M,D
Communication Disorders	M,D
Community Health Nursing	M
Counselor Education	M
Curriculum and Instruction	M,D
Dentistry	P
Early Childhood Education	M,D
Education—General	M,D
Educational Administration	M,D
Educational Measurement and Evaluation	M,D
Educational Psychology	M,D
English Education	M
Environmental and Occupational Health	M,D
Epidemiology	M,D
Exercise and Sports Science	M
Finance and Banking	D
Foreign Languages Education	M
Health Education	M,D
Health Promotion	M
Health Services Management and Hospital Administration	M,D
Industrial Hygiene	M,D
Information Studies	M,D,O
Kinesiology and Movement Studies	M,D
Law	P
Leisure Studies	M
Library Science	M,D,O
Management Information Systems	D
Management Strategy and Policy	D
Marketing	D
Maternal and Child Health	M,D
Mathematics Education	M
Music Education	M
Nursing—General	M,D
Occupational Health Nursing	M
Occupational Therapy	M,D
Oral and Dental Sciences	M,D
Organizational Behavior	D
Pharmaceutical Sciences	M,D

Physical Education	M
Physical Therapy	M,D
Public Health—General	M,D
Reading Education	M,D
Recreation and Park Management	M
Science Education	M
Secondary Education	M
Social Sciences Education	M
Social Work	M,D
Sports Management	M

THE UNIVERSITY OF NORTH CAROLINA AT CHARLOTTE

Accounting	M
Adult Nursing	M
Art Education	M
Business Administration and Management—General	M,D*
Community Health Nursing	M
Counselor Education	M,D
Curriculum and Instruction	M,D,O
Education of the Gifted	M,D
Education—General	M
Educational Administration	M,D,O
Educational Media/ Instructional Technology	M,D,O
Elementary Education	M
English as a Second Language	M
English Education	M
Exercise and Sports Science	M
Family Nurse Practitioner Studies	M
Foreign Languages Education	M
Health Services Management and Hospital Administration	M
Health Services Research	D
Kinesiology and Movement Studies	M
Marketing	M
Mathematics Education	M
Middle School Education	M
Music Education	M
Nurse Anesthesia	M
Nursing—General	M
Public Health—General	M
Reading Education	M
Secondary Education	M
Social Work	M
Special Education	M,D
Sports Management	M

THE UNIVERSITY OF NORTH CAROLINA AT GREENSBORO

Accounting	M,O
Adult Education	M,D,O
Adult Nursing	M,D,O
Business Administration and Management—General	M,O
Communication Disorders	M,D
Community Health	M,D
Counselor Education	M,D,O
Curriculum and Instruction	M,D,O
Early Childhood Education	M,D,O
Education—General	M,D,O
Educational Administration	M,D,O
Educational Measurement and Evaluation	D
Educational Media/ Instructional Technology	M,D,O
Elementary Education	D
English as a Second Language	M,D,O
English Education	M,D

Exercise and Sports Science	M,D
Family Nurse Practitioner Studies	M,D,O
Finance and Banking	M,O
Foreign Languages Education	M,D,O
Gerontological Nursing	M,D,O
Higher Education	D
Information Studies	M
Library Science	M
Management Information Systems	M,D,O
Marketing	M,D
Mathematics Education	M,D,O
Middle School Education	M,D,O
Multilingual and Multicultural Education	M,D,O
Music Education	M,D
Nonprofit Management	M,O
Nurse Anesthesia	M,D,O
Nursing and Healthcare Administration	M,D,O
Nursing Education	M,D,O
Nursing—General	M,D,O
Reading Education	M,D,O
Recreation and Park Management	M
Science Education	M,D,O
Social Sciences Education	M,D,O
Social Work	M
Special Education	M,D,O
Supply Chain Management	M,D,O
Taxation	M,O

THE UNIVERSITY OF NORTH CAROLINA AT PEMBROKE

Art Education	M
Business Administration and Management—General	M
Counselor Education	M
Education—General	M
Educational Administration	M
Elementary Education	M
English Education	M
Mathematics Education	M
Middle School Education	M
Music Education	M
Physical Education	M
Reading Education	M
Science Education	M
Social Sciences Education	M

THE UNIVERSITY OF NORTH CAROLINA WILMINGTON

Accounting	M
Business Administration and Management—General	M
Curriculum and Instruction	M
Education—General	M
Educational Administration	M
Educational Media/ Instructional Technology	M
Elementary Education	M
Middle School Education	M
Nursing—General	M
Reading Education	M
Secondary Education	M
Social Work	M
Special Education	M

UNIVERSITY OF NORTH DAKOTA

Allopathic Medicine	P
Business Administration and Management—General	M

Clinical Laboratory
  Sciences/Medical
  Technology   M
Communication Disorders   M,D
Early Childhood Education   M
Education—General   M,D,O
Educational Administration   M,D,O
Educational Measurement
  and Evaluation   D
Educational Media/
  Instructional Technology   M
Elementary Education   M,D
Industrial and
  Manufacturing
  Management   M
Kinesiology and
  Movement Studies   M
Law   P
Music Education   M,D
Nursing—General   M,D
Occupational Therapy   M
Physical Therapy   M,D
Physician Assistant
  Studies   M
Reading Education   M
Secondary Education   D
Social Work   M
Special Education   M,D
Vocational and Technical
  Education   M

UNIVERSITY OF NORTHERN BRITISH COLUMBIA

Community Health   M,D,O
Education—General   M,D,O
Social Work   M,D,O

UNIVERSITY OF NORTHERN COLORADO

Communication Disorders   M,D
Community Health   M
Counselor Education   D
Early Childhood Education   M,D
Education—General   M,D,O
Educational Administration   M,D,O
Educational Measurement
  and Evaluation   M,D
Educational Media/
  Instructional Technology   M,D
Educational Psychology   M,D
Elementary Education   M,D
Exercise and Sports
  Science   M,D
Family Nurse Practitioner
  Studies   M,D
Foreign Languages
  Education   M
Mathematics Education   M,D
Music Education   M,D
Nursing Education   M,D
Nursing—General   M,D
Physical Education   M,D
Public Health—General   M
Reading Education   M
Science Education   M,D
Special Education   M,D
Sports Management   M,D

UNIVERSITY OF NORTHERN IOWA

Accounting   M
Art Education   M
Business Administration
  and Management—
  General   M
Communication Disorders   M
Community Health   M,D
Counselor Education   M,D
Curriculum and Instruction   M,D
Early Childhood Education   M
Education—General   M,D,O
Educational Administration

Educational Media/
  Instructional Technology   M
Educational Psychology   M,O
Elementary Education   M
English as a Second
  Language   M
Health Education   M,D
Higher Education   M
Leisure Studies   M,D
Mathematics Education   M
Middle School Education   M
Music Education   M
Nonprofit Management   M
Physical Education   M
Reading Education   M
Rehabilitation Sciences   M,D
Science Education   M,O
Social Work   M
Special Education   M,D
Sports Management   M,D
Student Affairs   M
Vocational and Technical
  Education   M,D

UNIVERSITY OF NORTHERN VIRGINIA

Accounting   M,D
Business Administration
  and Management—
  General   M,D
Counselor Education   M,D
Early Childhood Education   M,D
Educational Administration   M,D
Educational Media/
  Instructional Technology   M,D
English as a Second
  Language   M,D
Finance and Banking   M,D
Management Information
  Systems   M,D
Marketing   M,D
Project Management   M,D

UNIVERSITY OF NORTH FLORIDA

Accounting   M
Allied Health—General   M,O
Business Administration
  and Management—
  General   M
Community Health   M,O
Counselor Education   M
Education—General   M,D
Educational Administration   M,D
Elementary Education   M
Family Nurse Practitioner
  Studies   M,O
Health Services
  Management and
  Hospital Administration   M,O
Health Services Research   M,O
Nursing—General   M,O
Physical Therapy   M
Public Health—General   M,O
Secondary Education   M
Special Education   M

UNIVERSITY OF NORTH TEXAS

Accounting   M,D
Art Education   M,D
Business Administration
  and Management—
  General   M,D
Communication Disorders   M,D
Community Health   M
Computer Education   M,D
Counselor Education   M,D
Curriculum and Instruction   D
Early Childhood Education   M,D
Education—General   M,D,O
Educational Administration   M,D

Educational Measurement
  and Evaluation   D
Finance and Banking   M,D
Health Promotion   M
Higher Education   M,D
Hospitality Management   M
Industrial and
  Manufacturing
  Management   M,D
Information Studies   M,D
Insurance   M,D
Kinesiology and
  Movement Studies   M
Leisure Studies   M,O
Library Science   M,D
Management Information
  Systems   M,D
Management Strategy and
  Policy   M,D
Marketing   M,D
Music Education   M,D
Organizational
  Management   M,D
Quantitative Analysis   M,D
Reading Education   M,D
Real Estate   M,D
Recreation and Park
  Management   M,O
Rehabilitation Sciences   M
Secondary Education   M
Special Education   M,D
Vocational and Technical
  Education   M,D

UNIVERSITY OF NORTH TEXAS HEALTH SCIENCE CENTER AT FORT WORTH

Community Health   M,D
Environmental and
  Occupational Health   M,D
Epidemiology   M,D
Health Services
  Management and
  Hospital Administration   M,D
Osteopathic Medicine   P,M
Physician Assistant
  Studies   M
Public Health—General   M,D
Science Education   M,D

UNIVERSITY OF NOTRE DAME

Accounting   M
Business Administration
  and Management—
  General   M*
Education—General   M
Law   P,M,D
Nonprofit Management   M

UNIVERSITY OF OKLAHOMA

Accounting   M
Adult Education   M,D
Advertising and Public
  Relations   M
Business Administration
  and Management—
  General   M,D*
Counselor Education   M
Curriculum and Instruction   M,D,O
Early Childhood Education   M,D,O
Education—General   M,D
Educational Administration   M,D
Educational Psychology   M,D
Elementary Education   M,D,O
English Education   M,D,O
Environmental and
  Occupational Health   M,D
Exercise and Sports
  Science   M,D
Foundations and
  Philosophy of Education   M,D

Higher Education   M,D
Human Services   M
Information Studies   M,O
International Business   M
Law   P
Library Science   M,O
Management Information
  Systems   M
Mathematics Education   M,D,O
Multilingual and
  Multicultural Education   M,D,O
Music Education   M,D
Organizational Behavior   M
Reading Education   M,D,O
Science Education   M,D,O
Secondary Education   M,D,O
Social Sciences Education   M,D,O
Social Work   M
Special Education   M,D

UNIVERSITY OF OKLAHOMA HEALTH SCIENCES CENTER

Allied Health—General   M,D,O
Allopathic Medicine   P
Communication Disorders   M,D,O
Dentistry   P
Environmental and
  Occupational Health   M,D
Epidemiology   M,D
Health Education   D
Health Physics/
  Radiological Health   M,D
Health Promotion   M,D
Health Services
  Management and
  Hospital Administration   M,D
Medical Physics   M,D
Nursing—General   M
Occupational Therapy   M
Oral and Dental Sciences   M
Pharmaceutical Sciences   M,D
Pharmacy   P
Physical Therapy   M
Public Health—General   M,D
Rehabilitation Sciences   M
Special Education   M,D,O

UNIVERSITY OF OREGON

Accounting   M,D
Business Administration
  and Management—
  General   M,D
Education—General   M,D
Finance and Banking   D
Law   P,M
Management Information
  Systems   M
Marketing   D
Music Education   M,D
Quantitative Analysis   M

UNIVERSITY OF OTTAWA

Allopathic Medicine   P,M,D
Business Administration
  and Management—
  General   M*
Communication Disorders   M
Community Health   M,D,O
Education—General   M,D,O
Electronic Commerce   M,D,O
Epidemiology   M
Finance and Banking   D,O
Health Services
  Management and
  Hospital Administration   M
Health Services Research   D,O
Kinesiology and
  Movement Studies   M
Law   M,D
Music Education   M,O
Nursing—General   M,D,O

Project Management	M,O
Public Health—General	D
Rehabilitation Sciences	M
Social Work	M

UNIVERSITY OF PENNSYLVANIA

Accounting	M,D
Acute Care/Critical Care Nursing	M
Adult Nursing	M
Allopathic Medicine	P
Bioethics	M
Business Administration and Management—General	M,D
Dentistry	P
Early Childhood Education	M
Education—General	M,D*
Educational Administration	M,D
Educational Measurement and Evaluation	M,D
Educational Policy	M,D
Educational Psychology	M,D
Elementary Education	M
English as a Second Language	M,D
Epidemiology	M,D
Family Nurse Practitioner Studies	M,O
Finance and Banking	M,D
Health Education	M,D
Health Services Management and Hospital Administration	M,D
Insurance	M,D
International and Comparative Education	M,D
International Business	M
Law	P,M,D
Management Information Systems	M,D
Marketing	M,D
Maternal and Child/ Neonatal Nursing	M,O
Medical Physics	M,D
Multilingual and Multicultural Education	M,D
Nurse Anesthesia	M
Nurse Midwifery	M
Nursing and Healthcare Administration	M,D
Nursing—General	M,D,O
Occupational Health Nursing	M
Oncology Nursing	M
Organizational Behavior	M
Organizational Management	M
Pediatric Nursing	M
Psychiatric Nursing	M
Reading Education	M,D
Real Estate	M,D
Secondary Education	M
Social Work	M,D*
Veterinary Medicine	P
Women's Health Nursing	M

UNIVERSITY OF PHOENIX–ATLANTA CAMPUS

Business Administration and Management—General	M
Health Services Management and Hospital Administration	M
Human Resources Management	M
International Business	M
Management Information Systems	M
Nursing—General	M

UNIVERSITY OF PHOENIX–AUGUSTA CAMPUS

Accounting	M
Business Administration and Management—General	M
Health Services Management and Hospital Administration	M
Human Resources Management	M
International Business	M
Management Information Systems	M
Marketing	M
Nursing—General	M

UNIVERSITY OF PHOENIX–AUSTIN CAMPUS

Accounting	M
Business Administration and Management—General	M
Electronic Commerce	M
Health Services Management and Hospital Administration	M
Human Resources Management	M
International Business	M
Management Information Systems	M
Marketing	M

UNIVERSITY OF PHOENIX–BAY AREA CAMPUS

Accounting	M
Adult Education	M
Business Administration and Management—General	M
Curriculum and Instruction	M
Education—General	M
Electronic Commerce	M
Family Nurse Practitioner Studies	M
Health Services Management and Hospital Administration	M
Human Resources Management	M
International Business	M
Management Information Systems	M
Marketing	M

UNIVERSITY OF PHOENIX–BOSTON CAMPUS

Business Administration and Management—General	M
International Business	M
Management Information Systems	M

UNIVERSITY OF PHOENIX–CENTRAL FLORIDA CAMPUS

Accounting	M
Business Administration and Management—General	M
Curriculum and Instruction	M
Education—General	M
Educational Administration	M
Elementary Education	M
Health Services Management and Hospital Administration	M
International Business	

Management Information Systems	M
Marketing	M
Nursing—General	M
Secondary Education	M

UNIVERSITY OF PHOENIX–CENTRAL MASSACHUSETTS CAMPUS

Business Administration and Management—General	M
Education—General	M

UNIVERSITY OF PHOENIX–CENTRAL VALLEY CAMPUS

Accounting	M
Business Administration and Management—General	M
Curriculum and Instruction	M
Education—General	M
Elementary Education	M
Health Services Management and Hospital Administration	M
Human Resources Management	M
International Business	M
Marketing	M
Nursing—General	M
Secondary Education	M

UNIVERSITY OF PHOENIX–CHARLOTTE CAMPUS

Accounting	M
Allied Health—General	M
Business Administration and Management—General	M
International Business	M
Management Information Systems	M
Nursing—General	M

UNIVERSITY OF PHOENIX–CHATTANOOGA CAMPUS

Accounting	M
Business Administration and Management—General	M
Health Services Management and Hospital Administration	M
Human Resources Management	M
International Business	M
Marketing	M

UNIVERSITY OF PHOENIX–CHEYENNE CAMPUS

Business Administration and Management—General	M
Health Services Management and Hospital Administration	M
Human Resources Management	M
International Business	M
Management Information Systems	M
Marketing	M
Nursing Education	M
Nursing—General	M

UNIVERSITY OF PHOENIX–CHICAGO CAMPUS

Business Administration and Management—General	M
Electronic Commerce	M
International Business	M
Management Information Systems	M

UNIVERSITY OF PHOENIX–CINCINNATI CAMPUS

Business Administration and Management—General	M
Electronic Commerce	M
Health Services Management and Hospital Administration	M

UNIVERSITY OF PHOENIX–CLEVELAND CAMPUS

Accounting	M
Business Administration and Management—General	M
Health Services Management and Hospital Administration	M
Human Resources Management	M
International Business	M
Management Information Systems	M
Marketing	M
Nursing—General	M

UNIVERSITY OF PHOENIX–COLUMBIA CAMPUS

Business Administration and Management—General	M

UNIVERSITY OF PHOENIX–COLUMBUS GEORGIA CAMPUS

Accounting	M
Business Administration and Management—General	M
Electronic Commerce	M
Health Services Management and Hospital Administration	M
Human Resources Management	M
International Business	M
Marketing	M

UNIVERSITY OF PHOENIX–COLUMBUS OHIO CAMPUS

Business Administration and Management—General	M
Health Services Management and Hospital Administration	M
Marketing	M

UNIVERSITY OF PHOENIX–DALLAS CAMPUS

Accounting	M
Business Administration and Management—General	M
Electronic Commerce	M

Health Services
  Management and
  Hospital Administration   M
Human Resources
  Management   M
Marketing   M

UNIVERSITY OF PHOENIX–DENVER CAMPUS

Accounting   M
Business Administration
  and Management—
  General   M
Curriculum and Instruction   M
Education—General   M
Educational Administration   M
Electronic Commerce   M
Elementary Education   M
Health Services
  Management and
  Hospital Administration   M
Human Resources
  Management   M
International Business   M
Management Information
  Systems   M
Marketing   M
Nursing—General   M
Secondary Education   M

UNIVERSITY OF PHOENIX–DES MOINES CAMPUS

Accounting   M
Business Administration
  and Management—
  General   M
Health Services
  Management and
  Hospital Administration   M
Human Resources
  Management   M
International Business   M
Management Information
  Systems   M
Marketing   M

UNIVERSITY OF PHOENIX–DETROIT CAMPUS

Accounting   M
Business Administration
  and Management—
  General   M
Electronic Commerce   M
Family Nurse Practitioner
  Studies   M
Health Services
  Management and
  Hospital Administration   M
Human Resources
  Management   M
International Business   M
Management Information
  Systems   M
Marketing   M
Nursing—General   M

UNIVERSITY OF PHOENIX–EASTERN WASHINGTON CAMPUS

Business Administration
  and Management—
  General   M
Health Services
  Management and
  Hospital Administration   M

UNIVERSITY OF PHOENIX–FAIRFIELD COUNTY

Business Administration
  and Management—
  General   M

UNIVERSITY OF PHOENIX–FORT LAUDERDALE CAMPUS

Accounting   M
Business Administration
  and Management—
  General   M
Computer Education   M
Curriculum and Instruction   M
Education—General   M
Educational Administration   M
Elementary Education   M
Health Services
  Management and
  Hospital Administration   M
Human Resources
  Management   M
International Business   M
Management Information
  Systems   M
Marketing   M
Nursing Education   M
Nursing—General   M
Secondary Education   M

UNIVERSITY OF PHOENIX–HARRISBURG CAMPUS

Accounting   M
Business Administration
  and Management—
  General   M
Health Services
  Management and
  Hospital Administration   M
Human Resources
  Management   M
International Business   M
Management Information
  Systems   M
Marketing   M
Nursing Education   M
Nursing—General   M

UNIVERSITY OF PHOENIX–HAWAII CAMPUS

Accounting   M
Business Administration
  and Management—
  General   M
Curriculum and Instruction   M
Education—General   M
Educational Administration   M
Elementary Education   M
Family Nurse Practitioner
  Studies   M
Health Services
  Management and
  Hospital Administration   M
Human Resources
  Management   M
International Business   M
Management Information
  Systems   M
Marketing   M
Nursing—General   M
Secondary Education   M

UNIVERSITY OF PHOENIX–HOUSTON CAMPUS

Business Administration
  and Management—
  General   M
Electronic Commerce   M
Health Services
  Management and
  Hospital Administration   M
Human Resources
  Management   M
International Business   M

UNIVERSITY OF PHOENIX–IDAHO CAMPUS

Accounting   M

Business Administration
  and Management—
  General   M
Education—General   M
Health Services
  Management and
  Hospital Administration   M
Management Information
  Systems   M

UNIVERSITY OF PHOENIX–INDIANAPOLIS CAMPUS

Business Administration
  and Management—
  General   M
Health Services
  Management and
  Hospital Administration   M
Management Information
  Systems   M
Nursing—General   M

UNIVERSITY OF PHOENIX–JERSEY CITY CAMPUS

Accounting   M
Business Administration
  and Management—
  General   M
Health Services
  Management and
  Hospital Administration   M
Human Resources
  Management   M
International Business   M
Management Information
  Systems   M
Marketing   M

UNIVERSITY OF PHOENIX–KANSAS CITY CAMPUS

Business Administration
  and Management—
  General   M
Education—General   M
Health Services
  Management and
  Hospital Administration   M
Nursing—General   M

UNIVERSITY OF PHOENIX–LAS VEGAS CAMPUS

Allied Health—General   M
Business Administration
  and Management—
  General   M
Curriculum and Instruction   M
Education—General   M
Educational Administration   M
Elementary Education   M
Management Information
  Systems   M

UNIVERSITY OF PHOENIX–LITTLE ROCK CAMPUS

Business Administration
  and Management—
  General   M

UNIVERSITY OF PHOENIX–LOUISIANA CAMPUS

Business Administration
  and Management—
  General   M
Early Childhood Education   M
Education—General   M

UNIVERSITY OF PHOENIX–LOUISVILLE CAMPUS

Business Administration
  and Management—
  General   M
Electronic Commerce   M
Health Services
  Management and
  Hospital Administration   M

UNIVERSITY OF PHOENIX–MADISON CAMPUS

Accounting   M
Business Administration
  and Management—
  General   M
Electronic Commerce   M
Health Services
  Management and
  Hospital Administration   M
Human Resources
  Management   M
International Business   M
Management Information
  Systems   M
Marketing   M

UNIVERSITY OF PHOENIX–MARYLAND CAMPUS

Business Administration
  and Management—
  General   M
Electronic Commerce   M
Human Resources
  Management   M
Human Services   M
International Business   M
Management Information
  Systems   M
Marketing   M
Nursing Education   M
Nursing—General   M

UNIVERSITY OF PHOENIX–MEMPHIS CAMPUS

Accounting   M
Business Administration
  and Management—
  General   M
Curriculum and Instruction   M
Education—General   M
Electronic Commerce   M
Health Services
  Management and
  Hospital Administration   M
Human Resources
  Management   M
International Business   M
Management Information
  Systems   M
Marketing   M

UNIVERSITY OF PHOENIX–METRO DETROIT CAMPUS

Adult Education   M
Business Administration
  and Management—
  General   M
Curriculum and Instruction   M

Distance Education
  Development M
Education—General M
Educational Administration M
Elementary Education M
Health Services
  Management and
  Hospital Administration M
International Business M
Management Information
  Systems M
Nursing—General M
Special Education M

UNIVERSITY OF PHOENIX–MINNEAPOLIS/ST. LOUIS PARK CAMPUS

Accounting M
Business Administration
  and Management—
  General M
Family Nurse Practitioner
  Studies M
Health Services
  Management and
  Hospital Administration M
Human Resources
  Management M
International Business M
Marketing M
Nursing—General M

UNIVERSITY OF PHOENIX–NASHVILLE CAMPUS

Business Administration
  and Management—
  General M
Curriculum and Instruction M
Education—General M
Educational Administration M
Elementary Education M
Health Services
  Management and
  Hospital Administration M
Human Resources
  Management M
Management Information
  Systems M
Secondary Education M

UNIVERSITY OF PHOENIX–NEW MEXICO CAMPUS

Business Administration
  and Management—
  General M
Curriculum and Instruction M
Education—General M
Educational Administration M
Electronic Commerce M
Elementary Education M
Health Services
  Management and
  Hospital Administration M
Human Resources
  Management M
International Business M
Management Information
  Systems M
Nursing—General M
Secondary Education M

UNIVERSITY OF PHOENIX—NORTHERN NEVADA CAMPUS

Accounting M
Business Administration
  and Management—
  General M
Education—General M
Educational Administration M

Elementary Education M
Health Services
  Management and
  Hospital Administration M
Human Resources
  Management M
International Business M
Management Information
  Systems M
Marketing M
Nursing Education M
Nursing—General M

UNIVERSITY OF PHOENIX–NORTHERN VIRGINIA CAMPUS

Accounting M
Business Administration
  and Management—
  General M
Education—General M
Educational Administration M
Electronic Commerce M
Health Services
  Management and
  Hospital Administration M
Human Resources
  Management M
International Business M
Management Information
  Systems M
Marketing M
Nursing—General M

UNIVERSITY OF PHOENIX–NORTH FLORIDA CAMPUS

Accounting M
Business Administration
  and Management—
  General M
Computer Education M
Curriculum and Instruction M
Education—General M
Educational Administration M
Elementary Education M
Health Services
  Management and
  Hospital Administration M
Human Resources
  Management M
International Business M
Management Information
  Systems M
Marketing M
Nursing Education M
Nursing—General M
Secondary Education M

UNIVERSITY OF PHOENIX–NORTHWEST ARKANSAS CAMPUS

Accounting M
Business Administration
  and Management—
  General M
Health Services
  Management and
  Hospital Administration M
Human Resources
  Management M
International Business M
Management Information
  Systems M
Marketing M
Nursing Education M
Nursing—General M

UNIVERSITY OF PHOENIX–NORTHWEST INDIANA

Business Administration
  and Management—
  General M

Health Services
  Management and
  Hospital Administration M
Human Resources
  Management M
Management Information
  Systems M
Nursing Education M
Nursing—General M

UNIVERSITY OF PHOENIX–OKLAHOMA CITY CAMPUS

Business Administration
  and Management—
  General M
Electronic Commerce M
Human Resources
  Management M
Management Information
  Systems M

UNIVERSITY OF PHOENIX–OMAHA CAMPUS

Accounting M
Adult Education M
Business Administration
  and Management—
  General M
Computer Education M
Curriculum and Instruction M
Education—General M
Educational Administration M
Elementary Education M
English as a Second
  Language M
English Education M
Health Services
  Management and
  Hospital Administration M
Human Resources
  Management M
International Business M
Management Information
  Systems M
Marketing M
Mathematics Education M
Secondary Education M
Special Education M

UNIVERSITY OF PHOENIX ONLINE CAMPUS

Accounting M
Adult Education M
Business Administration
  and Management—
  General M,D
Curriculum and Instruction M
Early Childhood Education M
Education—General M,D
Educational Administration M
Educational Media/
  Instructional Technology M
Electronic Commerce M
Elementary Education M
English as a Second
  Language M
English Education M
Health Services
  Management and
  Hospital Administration M,D
Human Resources
  Management M
Management Information
  Systems M
Marketing M
Mathematics Education M
Nursing Education M
Nursing—General M
Organizational
  Management D
Secondary Education M

UNIVERSITY OF PHOENIX–OREGON CAMPUS

Accounting M
Business Administration
  and Management—
  General M
Early Childhood Education M
Education—General M
Elementary Education M
Health Services
  Management and
  Hospital Administration M
Human Resources
  Management M
International Business M
Management Information
  Systems M
Secondary Education M

UNIVERSITY OF PHOENIX–PHILADELPHIA CAMPUS

Business Administration
  and Management—
  General M
Health Services
  Management and
  Hospital Administration M
International Business M
Management Information
  Systems M

UNIVERSITY OF PHOENIX–PHOENIX CAMPUS

Business Administration
  and Management—
  General M
Curriculum and Instruction M
Education—General M
Educational Administration M
Elementary Education M
Family Nurse Practitioner
  Studies M,O
Health Services
  Management and
  Hospital Administration M,O
Nursing—General M,O
Secondary Education M

UNIVERSITY OF PHOENIX–PITTSBURGH CAMPUS

Accounting M
Business Administration
  and Management—
  General M
Electronic Commerce M
Health Services
  Management and
  Hospital Administration M
Human Resources
  Management M
International Business M
Management Information
  Systems M
Marketing M
Nursing Education M

UNIVERSITY OF PHOENIX–PUERTO RICO CAMPUS

Accounting M
Business Administration
  and Management—
  General M
Early Childhood Education M
Education—General M
Educational Administration M
Health Services
  Management and
  Hospital Administration M

Human Resources
  Management   M
International Business   M
Marketing   M

UNIVERSITY OF PHOENIX–RALEIGH CAMPUS

Accounting   M
Business Administration
  and Management—
  General   M
Electronic Commerce   M
Health Services
  Management and
  Hospital Administration   M
International Business   M
Management Information
  Systems   M

UNIVERSITY OF PHOENIX–RENTON LEARNING CENTER

Accounting   M
Business Administration
  and Management—
  General   M
Health Services
  Management and
  Hospital Administration   M
Human Resources
  Management   M
International Business   M
Management Information
  Systems   M
Marketing   M
Nursing Education   M
Nursing—General   M

UNIVERSITY OF PHOENIX–RICHMOND CAMPUS

Accounting   M
Business Administration
  and Management—
  General   M
Health Services
  Management and
  Hospital Administration   M
Human Resources
  Management   M
Human Services   M
International Business   M
Management Information
  Systems   M
Marketing   M
Nursing—General   M

UNIVERSITY OF PHOENIX–SACRAMENTO VALLEY CAMPUS

Accounting   M
Adult Education   M,O
Business Administration
  and Management—
  General   M
Curriculum and Instruction   M,O
Education—General   M,O
Elementary Education   M,O
Family Nurse Practitioner
  Studies   M
Health Services
  Management and
  Hospital Administration   M
Human Resources
  Management   M
International Business   M
Management Information
  Systems   M
Marketing   M
Nursing Education   M
Nursing—General   M
Secondary Education   M,O

UNIVERSITY OF PHOENIX–ST. LOUIS CAMPUS

Business Administration
  and Management—
  General   M
Health Services
  Management and
  Hospital Administration   M
Management Information
  Systems   M

UNIVERSITY OF PHOENIX–SAN ANTONIO CAMPUS

Accounting   M
Business Administration
  and Management—
  General   M
Electronic Commerce   M
Health Services
  Management and
  Hospital Administration   M
Human Resources
  Management   M
International Business   M
Management Information
  Systems   M
Marketing   M

UNIVERSITY OF PHOENIX–SAN DIEGO CAMPUS

Business Administration
  and Management—
  General   M
Curriculum and Instruction   M
Education—General   M
Elementary Education   M
International Business   M
Management Information
  Systems   M
Nursing—General   M
Secondary Education   M

UNIVERSITY OF PHOENIX–SAVANNAH CAMPUS

Accounting   M
Business Administration
  and Management—
  General   M
Health Services
  Management and
  Hospital Administration   M
Human Resources
  Management   M
International Business   M
Management Information
  Systems   M
Marketing   M
Nursing Education   M
Nursing—General   M

UNIVERSITY OF PHOENIX–SOUTHERN ARIZONA CAMPUS

Accounting   M
Business Administration
  and Management—
  General   M
Counselor Education   M,O
Curriculum and Instruction   M,O
Education—General   M,O
Educational Psychology   M,O
Elementary Education   M,O
Family Nurse Practitioner
  Studies   M,O
Health Services
  Management and
  Hospital Administration   M,O
International Business   M
Management Information
  Systems   M

Secondary Education   M,O
Special Education   M,O

UNIVERSITY OF PHOENIX–SOUTHERN CALIFORNIA CAMPUS

Accounting   M
Business Administration
  and Management—
  General   M
Curriculum and Instruction   M
Education—General   M
Elementary Education   M
Family Nurse Practitioner
  Studies   M,O
Health Services
  Management and
  Hospital Administration   M,O
Human Resources
  Management   M
Management Information
  Systems   M
Marketing   M
Nursing Education   M,O
Nursing—General   M,O
Secondary Education   M

UNIVERSITY OF PHOENIX–SOUTHERN COLORADO CAMPUS

Business Administration
  and Management—
  General   M
Curriculum and Instruction   M,O
Education—General   M,O
Educational Administration   M,O
Elementary Education   M,O
Health Services
  Management and
  Hospital Administration   M
Management Information
  Systems   M
Nursing—General   M
Secondary Education   M,O

UNIVERSITY OF PHOENIX–SPRINGFIELD CAMPUS

Accounting   M
Adult Education   M
Business Administration
  and Management—
  General   M
Computer Education   M
Curriculum and Instruction   M
Education—General   M
Educational Administration   M
English as a Second
  Language   M
English Education   M
Health Services
  Management and
  Hospital Administration   M
Human Resources
  Management   M
International Business   M
Management Information
  Systems   M
Marketing   M
Mathematics Education   M
Nursing and Healthcare
  Administration   M
Nursing—General   M

UNIVERSITY OF PHOENIX–TULSA CAMPUS

Business Administration
  and Management—
  General   M

UNIVERSITY OF PHOENIX–UTAH CAMPUS

Business Administration
  and Management—
  General   M

Curriculum and Instruction   M
Education—General   M
Educational Administration   M
Elementary Education   M
Management Information
  Systems   M
Nursing—General   M
Secondary Education   M

UNIVERSITY OF PHOENIX–VANCOUVER CAMPUS

Business Administration
  and Management—
  General   M
Curriculum and Instruction   M
Education—General   M
Educational Administration   M
Health Services
  Management and
  Hospital Administration   M
Management Information
  Systems   M
Nursing—General   M

UNIVERSITY OF PHOENIX–WASHINGTON CAMPUS

Business Administration
  and Management—
  General   M
Health Services
  Management and
  Hospital Administration   M

UNIVERSITY OF PHOENIX–WEST FLORIDA CAMPUS

Business Administration
  and Management—
  General   M
Curriculum and Instruction   M
Education—General   M
Educational Administration   M
Educational Media/
  Instructional Technology   M
Elementary Education   M
Health Services
  Management and
  Hospital Administration   M
Human Resources
  Management   M
International Business   M
Management Information
  Systems   M
Marketing   M
Nursing Education   M
Nursing—General   M
Secondary Education   M

UNIVERSITY OF PHOENIX–WEST MICHIGAN CAMPUS

Accounting   M
Business Administration
  and Management—
  General   M
Curriculum and Instruction   M
Education—General   M
Educational Administration   M
Electronic Commerce   M
Health Services
  Management and
  Hospital Administration   M
Human Resources
  Management   M
International Business   M
Management Information
  Systems   M
Nursing—General   M

UNIVERSITY OF PHOENIX–WICHITA CAMPUS

Business Administration
  and Management—
  General   M

UNIVERSITY OF PHOENIX–WISCONSIN CAMPUS

Business Administration and Management—General	M
Health Services Management and Hospital Administration	
Management Information Systems	M

UNIVERSITY OF PITTSBURGH

Acute Care/Critical Care Nursing	M,D
Allopathic Medicine	P
Athletic Training and Sports Medicine	M
Bioethics	M
Business Administration and Management—General	M,D
Clinical Research	M,O
Communication Disorders	M,D
Community Health	M,D,O
Dentistry	P,M,O
Early Childhood Education	M
Education—General	M,D
Educational Administration	M,D
Educational Measurement and Evaluation	M,D
Elementary Education	M
English as a Second Language	O
English Education	M,D
Environmental and Occupational Health	M
Epidemiology	M,D
Exercise and Sports Science	M,D
Family Nurse Practitioner Studies	M,D
Foreign Languages Education	M,D
Foundations and Philosophy of Education	M,D
Health Education	M,O
Health Services Management and Hospital Administration	M,D,O
Higher Education	M,D
Information Studies	M,D,O
International and Comparative Education	M,D
International Business	M
Law	P,M,O
Legal and Justice Studies	M,O
Library Science	M,D,O
Management Information Systems	M
Mathematics Education	M,D
Nonprofit Management	M
Nurse Anesthesia	M
Nursing and Healthcare Administration	M
Nursing Education	M
Nursing—General	M,D
Occupational Therapy	M
Oral and Dental Sciences	M,O
Pediatric Nursing	M,D
Pharmacy	P
Physical Therapy	M,D
Psychiatric Nursing	M,D
Public Health—General	M,D,O*
Reading Education	M,D
Rehabilitation Sciences	M,D,O
Science Education	M,D
Secondary Education	M,D
Social Sciences Education	M,D
Social Work	M,D,O
Special Education	M,D

UNIVERSITY OF PORTLAND

Business Administration and Management—General	M
Early Childhood Education	M
Education—General	M
Nursing—General	M
Secondary Education	M
Special Education	M

UNIVERSITY OF PRINCE EDWARD ISLAND

Education—General	M
Educational Administration	M
Epidemiology	M,D
Veterinary Medicine	P
Veterinary Sciences	M,D

UNIVERSITY OF PUERTO RICO, MAYAGÜEZ CAMPUS

Agricultural Education	M
Business Administration and Management—General	M
English Education	M
Finance and Banking	M
Human Resources Management	M
Industrial and Manufacturing Management	M

UNIVERSITY OF PUERTO RICO, MEDICAL SCIENCES CAMPUS

Allied Health—General	M,O
Allopathic Medicine	P
Clinical Laboratory Sciences/Medical Technology	M,O
Communication Disorders	M
Dentistry	P
Environmental and Occupational Health	M,D
Epidemiology	M
Family Nurse Practitioner Studies	M
Health Education	M,O
Health Promotion	O
Health Services Management and Hospital Administration	M
Health Services Research	M
Industrial Hygiene	M
Maternal and Child Health	M
Nurse Anesthesia	M
Nurse Midwifery	M,O
Nursing and Healthcare Administration	M
Nursing Education	M
Nursing—General	M
Oral and Dental Sciences	M,O
Pharmaceutical Sciences	P,M
Pharmacy	P,M
Physical Therapy	M
Public Health—General	M
Special Education	O

UNIVERSITY OF PUERTO RICO, RÍO PIEDRAS

Business Administration and Management—General	M,D
Counselor Education	M,D
Curriculum and Instruction	M,D
Early Childhood Education	M,D
Education—General	M,D
Educational Administration	M,D
Educational Measurement and Evaluation	M

English as a Second Language	M
English Education	M,D
Exercise and Sports Science	M
Foreign Languages Education	M,D
Information Studies	M,O
Law	P,M
Library Science	M,O
Mathematics Education	M,D
Science Education	M,D
Secondary Education	M,D
Social Sciences Education	M,D
Social Work	M,D
Special Education	M

UNIVERSITY OF PUGET SOUND

Counselor Education	M
Education—General	M
Elementary Education	M
Middle School Education	M
Occupational Therapy	M
Physical Therapy	D
Secondary Education	M

UNIVERSITY OF REDLANDS

Business Administration and Management—General	M
Communication Disorders	M
Education—General	M,D,O
Management Information Systems	M

UNIVERSITY OF REGINA

Adult Education	M
Business Administration and Management—General	M
Curriculum and Instruction	M
Education—General	M,D
Educational Administration	M
Educational Psychology	M
Human Resources Development	M
Human Resources Management	M
International Business	
Kinesiology and Movement Studies	M,D
Social Work	M,D

UNIVERSITY OF RHODE ISLAND

Accounting	M
Adult Education	M
Business Administration and Management—General	M,D
Clinical Laboratory Sciences/Medical Technology	M
Communication Disorders	M,D
Education—General	M
Elementary Education	M
Exercise and Sports Science	M,D
Family Nurse Practitioner Studies	M,D
Finance and Banking	D
Health Education	M,D
Human Resources Management	M
Industrial and Manufacturing Management	M,D
Information Studies	M
International Business	M,D
Library Science	M

Management Information Systems	D
Marketing	D
Medicinal and Pharmaceutical Chemistry	M,D
Music Education	M
Nurse Midwifery	M,D
Nursing and Healthcare Administration	M,D
Nursing Education	M,D
Nursing—General	M,D
Pharmaceutical Sciences	M,D
Pharmacy	M,D
Physical Education	M,D
Physical Therapy	D
Psychiatric Nursing	M,D
Reading Education	M
Recreation and Park Management	M,D
Secondary Education	M
Sports Management	M,D
Student Affairs	M

UNIVERSITY OF RICHMOND

Business Administration and Management—General	M
Law	P

UNIVERSITY OF RIO GRANDE

Art Education	M
Education—General	M
Mathematics Education	M
Reading Education	M
Special Education	M

UNIVERSITY OF ROCHESTER

Allopathic Medicine	P
Business Administration and Management—General	M,D
Education—General	M,D
Epidemiology	M,D
Health Services Research	D
Music Education	M,D
Nursing—General	M,D,O
Oral and Dental Sciences	M
Public Health—General	M

UNIVERSITY OF ST. AUGUSTINE FOR HEALTH SCIENCES

Occupational Therapy	M,D
Physical Therapy	M,D,O

UNIVERSITY OF ST. FRANCIS (IL)

Adult Education	M
Allied Health—General	M
Business Administration and Management—General	M
Curriculum and Instruction	M
Education—General	M
Educational Administration	M
Elementary Education	M
English Education	M
Health Services Management and Hospital Administration	M
Mathematics Education	M
Nursing—General	M
Physician Assistant Studies	M
Reading Education	M
Science Education	M
Secondary Education	M
Social Sciences Education	M
Social Work	M

Special Education — M

UNIVERSITY OF SAINT FRANCIS (IN)

Allied Health—General	M
Business Administration and Management— General	M
Counselor Education	M
Education—General	M
Nursing—General	M
Physician Assistant Studies	M
Special Education	M

UNIVERSITY OF SAINT MARY

Business Administration and Management— General	M
Curriculum and Instruction	M
Education—General	M
Special Education	M

UNIVERSITY OF ST. MICHAEL'S COLLEGE

Religious Education	P,M,D,O

UNIVERSITY OF ST. THOMAS (MN)

Accounting	M
Business Administration and Management— General	M*
Curriculum and Instruction	M,D,O
Education of the Gifted	M,D,O
Education—General	M
Educational Administration	M,D,O
Educational Media/ Instructional Technology	M,D,O
Educational Policy	M,D,O
Health Services Management and Hospital Administration	M
Industrial and Manufacturing Management	M,O
Law	P
Management Information Systems	M,O
Music Education	M
Organizational Management	M,D,O
Reading Education	M,D,O
Real Estate	M
Religious Education	M
Social Work	M
Special Education	M,O
Student Affairs	M,D,O

UNIVERSITY OF ST. THOMAS (TX)

Business Administration and Management— General	M
Education—General	M

UNIVERSITY OF SAN DIEGO

Accounting	M,O
Adult Nursing	M,D,O
Business Administration and Management— General	M,O
Counselor Education	M
Curriculum and Instruction	M,D
Education—General	M,D,O
Educational Administration	M,D,O
Family Nurse Practitioner Studies	M,D,O
Finance and Banking	M,O

Law	P,M,O
Legal and Justice Studies	P,M,O
Nonprofit Management	M,D,O
Nursing and Healthcare Administration	M,D,O
Nursing—General	M,D,O*
Pediatric Nursing	M,D,O
Supply Chain Management	M,O
Taxation	P,M,O

UNIVERSITY OF SAN FRANCISCO

Adult Nursing	M
Business Administration and Management— General	M
Counselor Education	M,D
Curriculum and Instruction	M,D
Education—General	M,D
Educational Administration	M,D
Educational Media/ Instructional Technology	M,D
Electronic Commerce	M
English as a Second Language	M,D
Entrepreneurship	M
Family Nurse Practitioner Studies	M
Finance and Banking	M
Health Services Management and Hospital Administration	M
International and Comparative Education	M,D
International Business	M
Law	P,M
Management Information Systems	M
Marketing	M
Multilingual and Multicultural Education	M,D
Nonprofit Management	M
Nursing and Healthcare Administration	M
Nursing—General	M
Organizational Management	M
Project Management	M
Religious Education	M,D
Sports Management	M

UNIVERSITY OF SASKATCHEWAN

Accounting	M
Allopathic Medicine	P
Business Administration and Management— General	M
Community Health	M,D
Curriculum and Instruction	M,D,O
Dentistry	P
Education—General	M,D,O
Educational Administration	M,D,O
Educational Psychology	M,D,O
Epidemiology	M,D
Finance and Banking	M
Foundations and Philosophy of Education	M,D,O
Health Services Management and Hospital Administration	M
International Business	M
Kinesiology and Movement Studies	M,D,O
Law	P,M
Marketing	M
Nursing—General	M
Organizational Behavior	M
Pharmaceutical Sciences	M,D
Special Education	M,D,O
Veterinary Medicine	P,M,D
Veterinary Sciences	M,D

THE UNIVERSITY OF SCRANTON

Accounting	M
Adult Nursing	M,O
Business Administration and Management— General	M
Counselor Education	M
Curriculum and Instruction	M
Early Childhood Education	M
Education—General	M
Educational Administration	M
Elementary Education	M
English as a Second Language	M
Family Nurse Practitioner Studies	M,O
Finance and Banking	M
Health Services Management and Hospital Administration	M
Human Resources Development	M
Human Resources Management	M
International Business	M
Management Information Systems	M
Marketing	M
Nurse Anesthesia	M,O
Nursing—General	M,O
Occupational Therapy	M
Organizational Management	M
Physical Therapy	M,D
Reading Education	M
Secondary Education	M
Special Education	M

UNIVERSITY OF SIOUX FALLS

Business Administration and Management— General	M
Education—General	M,O
Educational Administration	M,O
Educational Media/ Instructional Technology	M,O
Reading Education	M,O

UNIVERSITY OF SOUTH ALABAMA

Accounting	M
Adult Nursing	M,D
Allied Health—General	M,D
Allopathic Medicine	P
Business Administration and Management— General	M
Communication Disorders	M,D
Community Health Nursing	M,D
Counselor Education	M,D
Early Childhood Education	M,O
Education—General	M,D,O
Educational Administration	M,O
Educational Media/ Instructional Technology	M,D
Elementary Education	M,O
Environmental and Occupational Health	M
Exercise and Sports Science	M
Health Education	M
Leisure Studies	M
Management Information Systems	M
Maternal and Child/ Neonatal Nursing	M,D
Nursing—General	M,D
Occupational Therapy	M
Pharmacy	P
Physical Education	M
Physical Therapy	D

Physician Assistant Studies	M
Reading Education	M,O
Recreation and Park Management	M
Science Education	M,O
Secondary Education	M,O
Special Education	M,O

UNIVERSITY OF SOUTH CAROLINA

Accounting	M
Acute Care/Critical Care Nursing	M,O
Adult Nursing	M
Allopathic Medicine	P
Art Education	M,D
Business Administration and Management— General	M,D
Business Education	M,D
Communication Disorders	M,D
Community Health Nursing	M
Counselor Education	D,O
Curriculum and Instruction	M,D,O
Early Childhood Education	M,D
Education—General	M,D,O
Educational Administration	M,D,O
Educational Measurement and Evaluation	M,D
Educational Media/ Instructional Technology	M
Educational Psychology	M,D
Elementary Education	M,D
English as a Second Language	M,D,O
English Education	M,D
Environmental and Occupational Health	M,D*
Epidemiology	M,D
Exercise and Sports Science	M,D
Family Nurse Practitioner Studies	M,O
Foreign Languages Education	M,D
Foundations and Philosophy of Education	D
Health Education	M,D,O
Health Promotion	M,D,O
Health Services Management and Hospital Administration	M,D
Higher Education	M
Hospitality Management	M
Human Resources Management	M
Industrial Hygiene	M,D
Information Studies	M,O
International Business	M
Law	P
Library Science	M,O
Mathematics Education	M,D
Medical/Surgical Nursing	M
Music Education	M,D,O
Nurse Anesthesia	M
Nursing and Healthcare Administration	M
Nursing—General	M,D,O
Pediatric Nursing	M
Pharmaceutical Sciences	M,D
Pharmacy	P
Physical Education	M,D
Psychiatric Nursing	M,O
Public Health—General	M
Reading Education	M,D
Rehabilitation Sciences	M,O
Science Education	M,D
Secondary Education	M,D
Social Sciences Education	M,D,O
Social Work	M,D
Special Education	M,D

Sports Management	M
Student Affairs	M
Travel and Tourism	M
Vocational and Technical Education	M,D,O
Women's Health Nursing	M

UNIVERSITY OF SOUTH CAROLINA AIKEN

Education—General	M
Educational Media/ Instructional Technology	M
Elementary Education	M

UNIVERSITY OF SOUTH CAROLINA UPSTATE

Early Childhood Education	M
Education—General	M
Elementary Education	M
Special Education	M

THE UNIVERSITY OF SOUTH DAKOTA

Accounting	M
Allied Health—General	M,D
Allopathic Medicine	P
Business Administration and Management— General	M
Communication Disorders	M,D
Counselor Education	M,D,O
Curriculum and Instruction	M,D,O
Education—General	M,D,O
Educational Administration	M,D,O
Educational Media/ Instructional Technology	M,O
Educational Psychology	M,D,O
Elementary Education	M
Health Education	M
Law	P
Occupational Therapy	M
Physical Education	M
Physical Therapy	M,D
Physician Assistant Studies	M
Secondary Education	M
Special Education	M

UNIVERSITY OF SOUTHERN CALIFORNIA

Accounting	M
Advertising and Public Relations	M
Allopathic Medicine	P
Business Administration and Management— General	M,D
Dentistry	P,O
Education—General	M,D
Epidemiology	M,D
Finance and Banking	M
Health Promotion	M
Health Services Management and Hospital Administration	M
Health Services Research	D
International Business	M
Kinesiology and Movement Studies	M,D
Law	P,M
Management Information Systems	M
Medical Imaging	M
Music Education	M,D
Occupational Therapy	M,D
Oral and Dental Sciences	M,D
Pharmaceutical Sciences	M,D*
Pharmacy	P
Physical Therapy	M,D

Physician Assistant Studies	M
Public Health—General	M*
Real Estate	M
Social Work	M,D
Taxation	M

UNIVERSITY OF SOUTHERN INDIANA

Accounting	M
Business Administration and Management— General	M
Education—General	M
Elementary Education	M
Health Services Management and Hospital Administration	M
Industrial and Manufacturing Management	M
Nursing—General	M
Occupational Therapy	M
Secondary Education	M
Social Work	M

UNIVERSITY OF SOUTHERN MAINE

Accounting	M
Adult Education	M,O
Adult Nursing	M,O
Business Administration and Management— General	M
Counselor Education	M,O
Education—General	M,D,O
Educational Administration	M,O
English as a Second Language	M,O
Family Nurse Practitioner Studies	M,O
Health Services Management and Hospital Administration	M,O
Law	P
Medical/Surgical Nursing	M,O
Middle School Education	M,O
Nonprofit Management	M,O
Nursing—General	M,O
Occupational Therapy	M
Psychiatric Nursing	M,O
Reading Education	M,O
Social Work	M
Special Education	M
Sports Management	M,O
Vocational and Technical Education	M

UNIVERSITY OF SOUTHERN MISSISSIPPI

Accounting	M
Adult Education	M,D,O
Adult Nursing	M,D
Advertising and Public Relations	M,D
Art Education	M
Business Administration and Management— General	M
Clinical Laboratory Sciences/Medical Technology	M
Communication Disorders	M,D
Community Health Nursing	M,D
Curriculum and Instruction	M,D,O
Early Childhood Education	M,D,O
Education of the Gifted	M,D,O
Education—General	M,D,O
Educational Administration	M,D,O
Elementary Education	M,D,O

Environmental and Occupational Health	M
Epidemiology	M
Exercise and Sports Science	M,D
Family Nurse Practitioner Studies	M,D
Foreign Languages Education	M
Health Education	M
Health Services Management and Hospital Administration	M
Higher Education	M,D,O
Leisure Studies	M,D
Library Science	M,O
Management Information Systems	M
Maternal and Child/ Neonatal Nursing	M,D
Mathematics Education	M,D
Music Education	M,D
Nursing and Healthcare Administration	M,D
Nursing—General	M,D
Physical Education	M,D
Psychiatric Nursing	M,D
Public Health—General	M
Reading Education	M,D,O
Recreation and Park Management	M,D
Science Education	M,D
Secondary Education	M,D,O
Social Sciences Education	M,D,O
Social Work	M
Special Education	M,D,O
Sports Management	M,D
Vocational and Technical Education	M

UNIVERSITY OF SOUTHERN NEVADA

Pharmacy	P

UNIVERSITY OF SOUTH FLORIDA

Accounting	M
Adult Education	M,D,O
Business Administration and Management— General	M,D
Communication Disorders	D
Community College Education	M,D,O
Community Health	M,D
Counselor Education	M,D
Early Childhood Education	M,D,O
Education of the Gifted	M
Education—General	M,D,O*
Educational Administration	M,D,O
Educational Measurement and Evaluation	M,D,O
Educational Media/ Instructional Technology	M,D,O
Elementary Education	M,D,O
English Education	M,D,O
Entrepreneurship	M,O
Environmental and Occupational Health	M,D
Epidemiology	M,D
Finance and Banking	M
Foreign Languages Education	M,D,O
Health Services Management and Hospital Administration	M,D
Higher Education	M,D,O
Information Studies	M
International Health	M,D
Library Science	M
Management Information Systems	M
Mathematics Education	M,D,O

Middle School Education	M,D,O
Music Education	M
Nursing—General	M,D*
Physical Education	M
Physical Therapy	M
Public Health—General	M,D
Reading Education	M
Science Education	M,D
Secondary Education	M,D,O
Social Sciences Education	M,D,O
Social Work	M
Special Education	M
Student Affairs	M,D,O
Vocational and Technical Education	M,D,O

THE UNIVERSITY OF TAMPA

Accounting	M
Adult Nursing	M
Business Administration and Management— General	M
Education—General	M
Entrepreneurship	M
Family Nurse Practitioner Studies	M
Finance and Banking	M
International Business	M
Management Information Systems	M
Marketing	M
Mathematics Education	M
Nursing and Healthcare Administration	M
Nursing Education	M
Nursing—General	M
Reading Education	M
Science Education	M

THE UNIVERSITY OF TENNESSEE

Accounting	M,D
Adult Education	M,D
Advertising and Public Relations	M,D
Agricultural Education	M
Art Education	M,D,O
Athletic Training and Sports Medicine	M,D
Bioethics	M,D
Business Administration and Management— General	M,D
Communication Disorders	M,D,O
Community Health	M,D
Counselor Education	M,D,O
Curriculum and Instruction	M,D,O
Early Childhood Education	M,D,O
Education—General	M,D,O
Educational Administration	M,D,O
Educational Measurement and Evaluation	M,D,O
Educational Media/ Instructional Technology	M,D,O
Educational Psychology	M,D,O
Elementary Education	M,D,O
English as a Second Language	M,D,O
English Education	M,D,O
Exercise and Sports Science	M,D,O
Finance and Banking	M,D
Foreign Languages Education	M,D,O
Foundations and Philosophy of Education	M,D,O
Health Education	M
Health Promotion	M
Health Services Management and Hospital Administration	M
Hospitality Management	M

Human Resources Development	M
Industrial and Manufacturing Management	M,D
Kinesiology and Movement Studies	M,D
Law	P
Leisure Studies	M,D
Logistics	M,D
Marketing	M,D
Mathematics Education	M,D,O
Multilingual and Multicultural Education	M,D,O
Music Education	M
Nursing—General	M,D
Public Health—General	M
Reading Education	M,D,O
Recreation and Park Management	M,D
Science Education	M,D,O
Secondary Education	M,D,O
Social Sciences Education	M,D,O
Social Work	M,D
Special Education	M,D,O
Sports Management	M,D
Student Affairs	M
Transportation Management	M,D
Travel and Tourism	M
Veterinary Medicine	P

THE UNIVERSITY OF TENNESSEE AT CHATTANOOGA

Accounting	M
Adult Nursing	M
Business Administration and Management— General	M
Counselor Education	M,D,O
Education—General	M,D,O
Educational Administration	M,D,O
Educational Media/ Instructional Technology	O
Elementary Education	M,D,O
Family Nurse Practitioner Studies	M
Nurse Anesthesia	M
Nursing and Healthcare Administration	M
Nursing Education	M
Nursing—General	M
Physical Education	M
Physical Therapy	D
Secondary Education	M,D,O
Special Education	M,D,O

THE UNIVERSITY OF TENNESSEE AT MARTIN

Accounting	M
Business Administration and Management— General	M
Counselor Education	M
Education—General	M
Educational Administration	M
Elementary Education	M
Secondary Education	M

THE UNIVERSITY OF TENNESSEE HEALTH SCIENCE CENTER

Allied Health—General	M,D
Allopathic Medicine	P,M,D
Dentistry	P,M,O
Nursing—General	M,D
Oral and Dental Sciences	P,M,O
Pharmaceutical Sciences	M,D
Pharmacy	P,M,D
Physical Therapy	M,D

THE UNIVERSITY OF TEXAS AT ARLINGTON

Accounting	M,D
Business Administration and Management— General	M,D*
Curriculum and Instruction	M
Education—General	M
Educational Administration	M
English as a Second Language	M
Exercise and Sports Science	M
Family Nurse Practitioner Studies	M,D
Finance and Banking	M,D
Health Services Management and Hospital Administration	M
Human Resources Management	M
Logistics	M
Management Information Systems	M,D
Marketing Research	M
Marketing	M,D
Nursing and Healthcare Administration	M,D
Nursing Education	M,D
Nursing—General	M,D
Physical Education	M
Quantitative Analysis	M,D
Real Estate	M,D
Social Work	M,D
Taxation	M

THE UNIVERSITY OF TEXAS AT AUSTIN

Accounting	M,D
Advertising and Public Relations	M,D
Art Education	M
Business Administration and Management— General	M,D
Communication Disorders	M,D
Counselor Education	M,D
Curriculum and Instruction	M,D
Education—General	M,D
Educational Administration	M,D
Educational Psychology	M,D
Finance and Banking	D
Foreign Languages Education	M,D
Health Education	M,D
Human Resources Development	M
Information Studies	M,D
Kinesiology and Movement Studies	M,D
Law	P,M
Library Science	M,D
Management Information Systems	D
Marketing	D
Mathematics Education	M,D
Nursing—General	M,D
Pharmaceutical Sciences	M,D
Pharmacy	P
Science Education	M,D
Social Work	M,D
Special Education	M,D

THE UNIVERSITY OF TEXAS AT BROWNSVILLE

Business Administration and Management— General	M
Community Health Nursing	M
Counselor Education	M

Curriculum and Instruction	M
Early Childhood Education	M
Education—General	M
Educational Administration	M
Educational Media/ Instructional Technology	M
English as a Second Language	M
Multilingual and Multicultural Education	M
Reading Education	M
Special Education	M

THE UNIVERSITY OF TEXAS AT DALLAS

Accounting	M
Business Administration and Management— General	M,D*
Communication Disorders	M,D
Health Services Management and Hospital Administration	M
International Business	M,D
Management Information Systems	M
Mathematics Education	M
Science Education	M

THE UNIVERSITY OF TEXAS AT EL PASO

Accounting	M
Allied Health—General	M
Business Administration and Management— General	M
Communication Disorders	M
Community Health Nursing	M
Curriculum and Instruction	M
Education—General	M,D
Educational Administration	M,D
English Education	M
Exercise and Sports Science	M
Family Nurse Practitioner Studies	M
Health Education	M
Kinesiology and Movement Studies	M
Music Education	M
Nurse Midwifery	M
Nursing and Healthcare Administration	M
Nursing—General	M
Physical Education	M
Physical Therapy	M
Women's Health Nursing	M

THE UNIVERSITY OF TEXAS AT SAN ANTONIO

Accounting	M,D
Adult Education	M,D
Business Administration and Management— General	M,D
Counselor Education	M,D
Curriculum and Instruction	M
Early Childhood Education	M
Education—General	M,D
Educational Administration	M,D
Educational Media/ Instructional Technology	M
Educational Psychology	M
Elementary Education	M
English as a Second Language	M,D
Finance and Banking	M,D
Higher Education	M,D
International Business	M,D

Management Information Systems	M,D
Marketing	M
Mathematics Education	M
Multilingual and Multicultural Education	M,D
Reading Education	M
Social Work	M
Special Education	M
Taxation	M,D

THE UNIVERSITY OF TEXAS AT TYLER

Art Education	M
Business Administration and Management— General	M
Computer Education	M
Curriculum and Instruction	M
Early Childhood Education	M
Education—General	M
Educational Administration	M
English Education	M
Exercise and Sports Science	M
Family Nurse Practitioner Studies	M
Health Education	M
Health Services Management and Hospital Administration	M
Human Resources Development	M
Industrial and Manufacturing Management	M
Kinesiology and Movement Studies	M
Mathematics Education	M
Music Education	M
Nursing and Healthcare Administration	M
Nursing Education	M
Nursing—General	M
Reading Education	M
Science Education	M
Secondary Education	M
Social Sciences Education	M
Special Education	M
Vocational and Technical Education	M

THE UNIVERSITY OF TEXAS HEALTH SCIENCE CENTER AT HOUSTON

Allopathic Medicine	P
Dentistry	P,M
Medical Physics	M,D
Nursing—General	M,D
Public Health—General	M,D,O

THE UNIVERSITY OF TEXAS HEALTH SCIENCE CENTER AT SAN ANTONIO

Allopathic Medicine	P
Clinical Laboratory Sciences/Medical Technology	M
Dental Hygiene	M
Dentistry	P,M,O
Medical Physics	M,D
Nursing—General	M,D
Occupational Therapy	M
Oral and Dental Sciences	M,O
Physical Therapy	M
Physician Assistant Studies	M

THE UNIVERSITY OF TEXAS MEDICAL BRANCH

Allied Health—General	M

Allopathic Medicine	P
Community Health	M,D
Nursing—General	M,D
Occupational Therapy	M
Physical Therapy	M
Physician Assistant Studies	M
Public Health—General	M

THE UNIVERSITY OF TEXAS OF THE PERMIAN BASIN

Accounting	M
Business Administration and Management—General	M
Counselor Education	M
Early Childhood Education	M
Education—General	M
Educational Administration	M
English as a Second Language	M
Foundations and Philosophy of Education	M
Kinesiology and Movement Studies	M
Reading Education	M
Special Education	M

THE UNIVERSITY OF TEXAS–PAN AMERICAN

Adult Nursing	M
Business Administration and Management—General	M,D
Communication Disorders	M
Counselor Education	M
Early Childhood Education	M
Education of the Gifted	M
Education—General	M,D
Educational Administration	M,D
Educational Measurement and Evaluation	M
Educational Psychology	M
Elementary Education	M
English as a Second Language	M
Family Nurse Practitioner Studies	M
Kinesiology and Movement Studies	M
Management Information Systems	M,D
Multilingual and Multicultural Education	M
Music Education	M
Nursing—General	M
Occupational Therapy	M
Pediatric Nursing	M
Reading Education	M
Secondary Education	M
Social Work	M
Special Education	M

THE UNIVERSITY OF TEXAS SOUTHWESTERN MEDICAL CENTER AT DALLAS

Allopathic Medicine	P
Physical Therapy	M
Physician Assistant Studies	M

THE UNIVERSITY OF THE ARTS

Art Education	M
Museum Education	M
Music Education	M

UNIVERSITY OF THE CUMBERLANDS

Early Childhood Education	M

Education—General	M,O
Educational Administration	M,O
Elementary Education	M,O
Middle School Education	M
Reading Education	M
Secondary Education	M,O
Special Education	M

UNIVERSITY OF THE DISTRICT OF COLUMBIA

Business Administration and Management—General	M
Communication Disorders	M
Counselor Education	M
Early Childhood Education	M
Education—General	M
Law	P
Mathematics Education	M
Special Education	M

UNIVERSITY OF THE INCARNATE WORD

Adult Education	M,D,O
Business Administration and Management—General	M,O
Early Childhood Education	M,D
Education—General	M,D
Educational Media/ Instructional Technology	M,D,O
Elementary Education	M
Entrepreneurship	M,D
International Business	M,O
Kinesiology and Movement Studies	M,D
Mathematics Education	M,D
Nursing—General	M
Organizational Management	M,D,O
Pharmacy	P
Physical Education	M
Project Management	M,O
Reading Education	M,D
Science Education	M
Secondary Education	M
Special Education	M,D
Sports Management	M,O

UNIVERSITY OF THE PACIFIC

Business Administration and Management—General	M
Communication Disorders	M
Curriculum and Instruction	M,D
Dentistry	P,M,D
Education—General	M,D,O
Educational Administration	M,D
Educational Psychology	M,D,O
Exercise and Sports Science	M
Law	P,M,D
Legal and Justice Studies	P,M,D
Music Education	M
Oral and Dental Sciences	M,O
Pharmaceutical Sciences	M,D
Pharmacy	P
Physical Therapy	M,D
Special Education	M,D

UNIVERSITY OF THE SACRED HEART

Advertising and Public Relations	M
Business Administration and Management—General	M

Clinical Laboratory Sciences/Medical Technology	O
Early Childhood Education	M
Education—General	M
Educational Media/ Instructional Technology	M
Environmental and Occupational Health	M
Human Resources Management	M
Legal and Justice Studies	M
Management Information Systems	M
Marketing	M
Nonprofit Management	M
Taxation	M

UNIVERSITY OF THE SCIENCES IN PHILADELPHIA

Health Services Management and Hospital Administration	M,D
Medicinal and Pharmaceutical Chemistry	M,D
Pharmaceutical Administration	M
Pharmaceutical Sciences	M,D*
Pharmacy	P
Physical Therapy	D
Public Health—General	M

UNIVERSITY OF THE VIRGIN ISLANDS

Business Administration and Management—General	M
Education—General	M
Mathematics Education	M

UNIVERSITY OF THE WEST

Business Administration and Management—General	M
Finance and Banking	M
International Business	M
Management Information Systems	M
Nonprofit Management	M

THE UNIVERSITY OF TOLEDO

Accounting	M
Allopathic Medicine	M
Art Education	M
Business Administration and Management—General	M,D*
Business Education	M
Communication Disorders	M,D,O
Counselor Education	M,D,O
Curriculum and Instruction	M,D,O
Early Childhood Education	M,O
Education of the Gifted	O
Education—General	M,D,O
Educational Administration	M,D,O
Educational Measurement and Evaluation	M,D
Educational Media/ Instructional Technology	M,D,O
Educational Psychology	M,D
Elementary Education	D,O
English as a Second Language	M,O
English Education	M
Environmental and Occupational Health	M
Exercise and Sports Science	M,D

Family Nurse Practitioner Studies	M,O
Finance and Banking	M
Foreign Languages Education	M
Foundations and Philosophy of Education	M,D
Health Education	M,D
Health Physics/ Radiological Health	M
Health Services Management and Hospital Administration	M
Higher Education	M,D
Human Resources Management	M
Industrial and Manufacturing Management	M,D
International Business	M
Law	P,M
Leisure Studies	M
Management Information Systems	M
Marketing	M
Mathematics Education	M
Medical Physics	M
Medicinal and Pharmaceutical Chemistry	M,D
Middle School Education	M
Music Education	M
Nursing—General	M,O
Occupational Therapy	M,D
Oral and Dental Sciences	M
Pharmaceutical Administration	M
Pharmaceutical Sciences	M
Physical Education	M
Physical Therapy	M,D
Physician Assistant Studies	M
Public Health—General	M,D,O
Science Education	M
Secondary Education	M,D,O
Social Sciences Education	M,D
Social Work	M
Special Education	M,D,O
Vocational and Technical Education	M,O

UNIVERSITY OF TORONTO

Accounting	M,D
Allopathic Medicine	P,M,D
Business Administration and Management—General	M,D
Communication Disorders	M,D
Dentistry	P
Education—General	M,D
Information Studies	M,D,O
Law	P,M,D
Library Science	M,D,O
Music Education	M,D
Nursing—General	M,D,O
Oral and Dental Sciences	M,D
Pharmaceutical Sciences	M,D
Physical Education	M,D
Public Health—General	M,D,O
Rehabilitation Sciences	M
Social Work	M,D

UNIVERSITY OF TULSA

Business Administration and Management—General	M
Communication Disorders	M
Education—General	M
Finance and Banking	M*
Investment Management	M
Law	P,M,O
Mathematics Education	M

Science Education M
Taxation M

UNIVERSITY OF UTAH

Accounting	M,D
Allopathic Medicine	P
Art Education	M
Business Administration and Management—	
General	M,D
Clinical Laboratory Sciences/Medical Technology	M
Communication Disorders	M,D
Counselor Education	M,D
Education—General	M,D
Educational Administration	M,D
Educational Psychology	M,D
Elementary Education	M,D
Exercise and Sports Science	M,D
Finance and Banking	M,D
Foreign Languages Education	M,D
Foundations and Philosophy of Education	M,D
Gerontological Nursing	M,O
Health Education	M,D
Health Promotion	M,D
Law	P,M
Leisure Studies	M,D
Medicinal and Pharmaceutical Chemistry	M,D
Nursing—General	M,D
Occupational Therapy	M
Pharmacy	P,M
Physical Therapy	D,O
Physician Assistant Studies	M
Public Health—General	M,D
Recreation and Park Management	M,D
Science Education	M,D
Secondary Education	M,D
Social Work	M,D
Special Education	M,D

UNIVERSITY OF VERMONT

Allied Health—General	M,D
Allopathic Medicine	P
Business Administration and Management—	
General	M
Counselor Education	M
Curriculum and Instruction	M
Education—General	M,D
Educational Administration	M,D
Foreign Languages Education	M
Mathematics Education	M,D
Nursing—General	M
Physical Therapy	D
Reading Education	M
Science Education	M,D
Social Work	M
Special Education	M

UNIVERSITY OF VICTORIA

Art Education	M,D
Business Administration and Management—	
General	M
Counselor Education	M,D
Curriculum and Instruction	M,D
Early Childhood Education	M,D
Education—General	M,D
Educational Administration	M,D
Educational Psychology	M,D
English Education	M,D
Environmental Education	M,D

Family Nurse Practitioner Studies	M
Foreign Languages Education	M
Foundations and Philosophy of Education	M,D
Kinesiology and Movement Studies	M
Law	P,M,D
Leisure Studies	M
Mathematics Education	M,D
Medical Physics	M,D
Music Education	M,D
Nursing—General	M
Physical Education	M,D
Reading Education	M,D
Science Education	M,D
Social Sciences Education	M,D
Social Work	M
Special Education	M,D
Vocational and Technical Education	M,D

UNIVERSITY OF VIRGINIA

Accounting	M
Allopathic Medicine	P,M,D
Bioethics	M
Business Administration and Management—	
General	M,D
Clinical Research	M
Communication Disorders	M
Counselor Education	M,D,O
Curriculum and Instruction	M,D,O
Education—General	M,D,O
Educational Administration	M,D,O
Educational Measurement and Evaluation	M,D
Educational Policy	M,D
Educational Psychology	M,D,O
Health Education	M,D
Health Services Management and Hospital Administration	M
Health Services Research	M
Higher Education	D,O
Kinesiology and Movement Studies	M,D
Law	P,M,D
Management Information Systems	M
Nursing—General	M,D
Physical Education	M,D
Public Health—General	M
Science Education	M,D
Special Education	M,D,O

UNIVERSITY OF WASHINGTON

Accounting	M,D
Allopathic Medicine	P
Business Administration and Management—	
General	M,D
Business Education	M,D
Clinical Laboratory Sciences/Medical Technology	M
Communication Disorders	M,D
Counselor Education	M,D
Curriculum and Instruction	M,D
Dentistry	P
Education—General	M,D,O
Educational Administration	M,D,O
Educational Measurement and Evaluation	M,D
Educational Media/ Instructional Technology	M,D
Educational Policy	M,D
Educational Psychology	M,D
English as a Second Language	M,D
English Education	M,D

Environmental and Occupational Health	M,D*
Epidemiology	M,D
Foundations and Philosophy of Education	M,D
Health Services Management and Hospital Administration	M
Health Services Research	M,D
Higher Education	M,D
Industrial Hygiene	M,D
International Business	M,D,O
International Health	M,D
Law	P,M,D
Legal and Justice Studies	P,M,D
Library Science	M,D
Logistics	O
Maternal and Child Health	M,D
Mathematics Education	M,D
Medicinal and Pharmaceutical Chemistry	D
Multilingual and Multicultural Education	M,D
Music Education	M,D
Nursing—General	M,D
Occupational Therapy	M,D
Oral and Dental Sciences	M,D
Pharmaceutical Sciences	M,D
Pharmacy	P
Physical Therapy	M,D
Public Health—General	M,D
Reading Education	M,D
Rehabilitation Sciences	M,D
Science Education	M,D
Social Sciences Education	M,D
Social Work	M,D
Special Education	M,D
Taxation	P,M,D
Transportation Management	O
Veterinary Sciences	M

UNIVERSITY OF WASHINGTON, BOTHELL

Business Administration and Management—	
General	M
Education—General	M
Nursing—General	M

UNIVERSITY OF WATERLOO

Accounting	M,D
Actuarial Science	M,D
Business Administration and Management—	
General	M
Entrepreneurship	M
Finance and Banking	M,D
Health Education	M,D
Kinesiology and Movement Studies	M,D
Leisure Studies	M,D
Optometry	M,D
Recreation and Park Management	M,D
Taxation	M,D
Travel and Tourism	M
Vision Sciences	M,D

THE UNIVERSITY OF WEST ALABAMA

Adult Education	M
Athletic Training and Sports Medicine	M
Counselor Education	M
Early Childhood Education	M
Education—General	M
Educational Administration	M
Educational Media/ Instructional Technology	M

Elementary Education	M
English Education	M
Foundations and Philosophy of Education	M
Mathematics Education	M
Physical Education	M
Science Education	M
Secondary Education	M
Social Sciences Education	M
Special Education	M

THE UNIVERSITY OF WESTERN ONTARIO

Accounting	M,D
Allopathic Medicine	P,M
Business Administration and Management—	
General	M,D
Communication Disorders	M
Counselor Education	M
Curriculum and Instruction	M
Dentistry	P
Education—General	M
Educational Policy	M
Educational Psychology	M
Entrepreneurship	M,D
Epidemiology	M,D
Finance and Banking	M,D
Information Studies	M,D
Kinesiology and Movement Studies	M,D
Law	P,M,O
Library Science	M,D
Nursing—General	M,D
Occupational Therapy	M
Oral and Dental Sciences	M
Physical Therapy	M
Special Education	M

UNIVERSITY OF WEST FLORIDA

Accounting	M
Business Administration and Management—	
General	M
Counselor Education	M
Curriculum and Instruction	M,D,O
Early Childhood Education	M
Educational Administration	M,O
Educational Media/ Instructional Technology	M
Elementary Education	M
Exercise and Sports Science	M
Health Education	M
Leisure Studies	M
Middle School Education	M
Physical Education	M
Public Health—General	M
Reading Education	M
Science Education	M
Secondary Education	M
Special Education	M
Vocational and Technical Education	M

UNIVERSITY OF WEST GEORGIA

Accounting	M
Art Education	M
Business Administration and Management—	
General	M
Business Education	M,O
Communication Disorders	M
Counselor Education	M,O
Early Childhood Education	M,O
Education—General	M,D,O
Educational Administration	M,O
Educational Measurement and Evaluation	D
Educational Media/ Instructional Technology	M,O

English Education	M,O
Foreign Languages Education	M
Mathematics Education	M,O
Middle School Education	M,O
Music Education	M
Nursing—General	M
Physical Education	M,O
Reading Education	M
Science Education	M,O
Secondary Education	M,O
Social Sciences Education	M,O
Special Education	M,O

UNIVERSITY OF WINDSOR

Business Administration and Management— General	M
Education—General	M,D
Kinesiology and Movement Studies	M
Legal and Justice Studies	M
Nursing—General	M
Social Work	M

UNIVERSITY OF WISCONSIN–EAU CLAIRE

Business Administration and Management— General	M
Communication Disorders	M
Education—General	M
Elementary Education	M
English Education	M
Environmental and Occupational Health	M
Mathematics Education	M
Nursing—General	M
Public Health—General	M
Reading Education	M
Science Education	M
Secondary Education	M
Social Sciences Education	M
Special Education	M

UNIVERSITY OF WISCONSIN– GREEN BAY

Business Administration and Management— General	M
Education—General	M
Social Work	M

UNIVERSITY OF WISCONSIN–LA CROSSE

Athletic Training and Sports Medicine	M
Business Administration and Management— General	M
Community Health	M
Education—General	M
Elementary Education	M
Exercise and Sports Science	M
Health Education	M
Nurse Anesthesia	M
Occupational Therapy	M
Physical Education	M
Physical Therapy	M,D
Physician Assistant Studies	M
Public Health—General	M
Reading Education	M
Recreation and Park Management	M
Rehabilitation Sciences	M
Secondary Education	M
Special Education	M

Sports Management	M
Student Affairs	M

UNIVERSITY OF WISCONSIN– MADISON

Accounting	D
Actuarial Science	M
Allopathic Medicine	P
Art Education	M,D
Business Administration and Management— General	M
Communication Disorders	M,D
Community Health	M,D
Counselor Education	M
Curriculum and Instruction	M,D
Education—General	M,D,O
Educational Administration	M,D,O
Educational Policy	M,D,O
Educational Psychology	M,D
Entrepreneurship	M
Finance and Banking	M,D
Foreign Languages Education	M,D
Health Promotion	M,D
Human Resources Management	M,D
Industrial and Manufacturing Management	D
Information Studies	M,D,O
Insurance	M,D
Investment Management	D
Kinesiology and Movement Studies	M,D
Law	M,D
Legal and Justice Studies	M
Library Science	M,D,O
Management Information Systems	M,D
Management Strategy and Policy	M
Marketing Research	M
Mathematics Education	M,D
Medical Physics	M,D
Music Education	M,D
Nursing—General	M,D
Occupational Therapy	M,D
Pharmaceutical Administration	M,D
Pharmaceutical Sciences	M,D
Pharmacy	P
Real Estate	M,D
Recreation and Park Management	M
Rehabilitation Sciences	M
Science Education	M,D
Social Work	M,D
Special Education	M,D
Supply Chain Management	M
Veterinary Medicine	P
Veterinary Sciences	M,D

UNIVERSITY OF WISCONSIN– MILWAUKEE

Allied Health—General	M,D
Art Education	M
Business Administration and Management— General	M,D,O
Clinical Laboratory Sciences/Medical Technology	M
Communication Disorders	M
Curriculum and Instruction	M
Early Childhood Education	M
Education—General	M,D,O
Educational Administration	M,O
Educational Policy	M
Educational Psychology	M,O
Elementary Education	M

Foundations and Philosophy of Education	M
Human Resources Development	M,O
Information Studies	M,O
Kinesiology and Movement Studies	M
Library Science	M,O
Middle School Education	M
Nursing—General	M,D,O
Occupational Therapy	M
Reading Education	M
Secondary Education	M
Social Work	M,O
Special Education	M
Urban Education	M,D

UNIVERSITY OF WISCONSIN– OSHKOSH

Adult Nursing	M
Business Administration and Management— General	M
Counselor Education	M
Curriculum and Instruction	M
Early Childhood Education	M
Education—General	M
Educational Administration	M
Family Nurse Practitioner Studies	M
Health Services Management and Hospital Administration	M
Management Information Systems	M
Mathematics Education	M
Nursing—General	M
Reading Education	M
Social Work	M
Special Education	M

UNIVERSITY OF WISCONSIN– PARKSIDE

Business Administration and Management— General	M

UNIVERSITY OF WISCONSIN– PLATTEVILLE

Adult Education	M
Counselor Education	M
Education—General	M
Elementary Education	M
Middle School Education	M
Project Management	M
Secondary Education	M
Vocational and Technical Education	M

UNIVERSITY OF WISCONSIN– RIVER FALLS

Agricultural Education	M
Business Administration and Management— General	M
Communication Disorders	M
Counselor Education	M,O
Education—General	M
Elementary Education	M
Mathematics Education	M
Reading Education	M
Science Education	M
Social Sciences Education	M

UNIVERSITY OF WISCONSIN– STEVENS POINT

Advertising and Public Relations	M

Business Administration and Management— General	M
Communication Disorders	M,D
Counselor Education	M
Education—General	M
Educational Administration	M
Elementary Education	M
Health Promotion	M
Music Education	M
Reading Education	M
Science Education	M
Special Education	M

UNIVERSITY OF WISCONSIN– STOUT

Education—General	M,O
Human Resources Development	M
Industrial Hygiene	M
Vocational and Technical Education	M,O

UNIVERSITY OF WISCONSIN– SUPERIOR

Art Education	M
Counselor Education	M
Curriculum and Instruction	M
Education—General	M
Educational Administration	M,O
Reading Education	M
Special Education	M

UNIVERSITY OF WISCONSIN– WHITEWATER

Accounting	M
Business Administration and Management— General	M*
Business Education	M
Communication Disorders	M
Counselor Education	M
Curriculum and Instruction	M
Education—General	M
Educational Administration	M
Environmental and Occupational Health	M
Finance and Banking	M
Higher Education	M
Human Resources Management	M
International Business	M
Marketing	M
Reading Education	M
Secondary Education	M
Special Education	M
Supply Chain Management	M

UNIVERSITY OF WYOMING

Accounting	M
Adult Education	M,D,O
Business Administration and Management— General	M
Communication Disorders	M,D
Counselor Education	M,D
Curriculum and Instruction	M,D
Distance Education Development	M,D,O
Educational Administration	M,D,O
Educational Media/ Instructional Technology	M,D,O
Finance and Banking	M
Health Education	M
Law	P
Mathematics Education	M,D
Music Education	M
Nursing—General	M

Pharmacy	P
Physical Education	M
Science Education	M
Social Work	M
Special Education	M,O

UPPER IOWA UNIVERSITY

Accounting	M
Business Administration and Management— General	M
Finance and Banking	M
Human Resources Management	M
Human Services	M
International Business	M
Organizational Management	M
Quality Management	M

URBANA UNIVERSITY

Business Administration and Management— General	M
Education—General	M

URSULINE COLLEGE

Business Administration and Management— General	M
Education—General	M
Educational Administration	M
Nursing—General	M

UTAH STATE UNIVERSITY

Accounting	M
Agricultural Education	M
Business Administration and Management— General	M
Business Education	M,D
Communication Disorders	M,D,O
Counselor Education	M,D
Curriculum and Instruction	D
Education—General	M,D,O
Educational Measurement and Evaluation	M,D
Educational Media/ Instructional Technology	M,D,O
Elementary Education	M
Health Education	M
Home Economics Education	M
Human Resources Management	M
Management Information Systems	M,D
Multilingual and Multicultural Education	M
Physical Education	M
Recreation and Park Management	M,D
Secondary Education	M
Special Education	M,D,O
Veterinary Sciences	M,D
Vocational and Technical Education	M

UTICA COLLEGE

Accounting	M
Education—General	M,O
Occupational Therapy	M
Physical Therapy	D

VALDOSTA STATE UNIVERSITY

Adult Education	M,D

Business Administration and Management— General	M
Business Education	M,D
Communication Disorders	M,O
Counselor Education	M,O
Curriculum and Instruction	M,D,O
Early Childhood Education	M,O
Education—General	M,D,O
Educational Administration	M,D,O
Educational Media/ Instructional Technology	M,D,O
Health Education	M
Information Studies	M
Library Science	M
Middle School Education	M,O
Music Education	M
Nursing—General	M
Physical Education	M
Reading Education	M,O
Secondary Education	M,O
Social Work	M
Special Education	M,O
Vocational and Technical Education	M,D

VALPARAISO UNIVERSITY

Business Administration and Management— General	M,O
Education—General	M
International Business	M
Law	P,M
Nursing—General	P,M,O
Sports Management	M

VANDERBILT UNIVERSITY

Acute Care/Critical Care Nursing	M,D
Adult Nursing	M,D
Allopathic Medicine	M,D
Business Administration and Management— General	M,D
Clinical Research	M
Communication Disorders	M,D
Counselor Education	M
Curriculum and Instruction	M,D
Early Childhood Education	M,D
Education—General	M,D*
Educational Administration	M,D
Educational Measurement and Evaluation	M,D
Educational Policy	M,D
Elementary Education	M,D
English Education	M,D
Family Nurse Practitioner Studies	M,D
Finance and Banking	M,D
Foreign Languages Education	M,D
Forensic Nursing	M,D
Gerontological Nursing	M,D
Higher Education	M,D
Human Resources Development	M,D
International and Comparative Education	M,D
Law	P,M,D
Marketing	D
Maternal and Child/ Neonatal Nursing	M,D
Mathematics Education	M,D
Medical Physics	M
Medical/Surgical Nursing	M,D
Multilingual and Multicultural Education	M,D
Nurse Midwifery	M,D
Nursing and Healthcare Administration	M,D
Nursing Informatics	M,D
Nursing—General	M,D

Organizational Management	M,D
Pediatric Nursing	M,D
Psychiatric Nursing	M,D
Public Health—General	M
Reading Education	M,D
Science Education	M,D
Secondary Education	M,D
Special Education	M,D
Women's Health Nursing	M,D

VANDERCOOK COLLEGE OF MUSIC

Music Education	M

VANGUARD UNIVERSITY OF SOUTHERN CALIFORNIA

Business Administration and Management— General	M
Education—General	M

VERMONT LAW SCHOOL

Law	P
Legal and Justice Studies	M

VILLANOVA UNIVERSITY

Accounting	M
Adult Nursing	M,D,O
Business Administration and Management— General	M
Counselor Education	M*
Education—General	M*
Educational Administration	M
Elementary Education	M
Family Nurse Practitioner Studies	M,D,O
Finance and Banking	M
Gerontological Nursing	M,D,O
Health Services Management and Hospital Administration	M,D,O
Human Resources Development	M
Law	P
Nurse Anesthesia	M,D,O
Nursing and Healthcare Administration	M,D,O
Nursing Education	M,D,O
Nursing—General	M,D,O*
Pediatric Nursing	M,D,O
Secondary Education	M
Taxation	M

VIRGINIA COLLEGE AT BIRMINGHAM

Business Administration and Management— General	M

VIRGINIA COMMONWEALTH UNIVERSITY

Accounting	M,D*
Adult Education	M*
Adult Nursing	M,D,O
Advertising and Public Relations	M
Allied Health—General	D*
Allopathic Medicine	P
Art Education	M*
Athletic Training and Sports Medicine	M,D*
Business Administration and Management— General	M,D*

Clinical Laboratory Sciences/Medical Technology	M,D*
Community Health	D
Counselor Education	M*
Curriculum and Instruction	M,O*
Dentistry	P*
Early Childhood Education	M,O
Education—General	M,D,O*
Educational Administration	D*
Educational Measurement and Evaluation	D
Environmental and Occupational Health	M
Epidemiology	D*
Exercise and Sports Science	M,D*
Family Nurse Practitioner Studies	M,O
Finance and Banking	M
Health Education	M,D
Health Physics/ Radiological Health	D
Health Services Management and Hospital Administration	M,D*
Health Services Research	D*
Human Resources Development	M
Insurance	M
Management Information Systems	M,D*
Marketing	O
Medical Physics	M,D*
Middle School Education	M,O
Music Education	M*
Nonprofit Management	O*
Nurse Anesthesia	M,D*
Nursing and Healthcare Administration	M,D,O
Nursing—General	M,D,O*
Occupational Therapy	M,D*
Pediatric Nursing	M,D,O
Pharmaceutical Sciences	P,M,D*
Pharmacy	P
Physical Education	M,D
Physical Therapy	M,D*
Psychiatric Nursing	M,D,O
Public Health—General	M,D*
Quantitative Analysis	M
Reading Education	M*
Real Estate	M,O*
Recreation and Park Management	M*
Rehabilitation Sciences	M,D*
Secondary Education	M,O
Social Sciences Education	M,O
Social Work	M,D*
Special Education	M*
Taxation	M,D*
Urban Education	D
Women's Health Nursing	M,D,O

VIRGINIA POLYTECHNIC INSTITUTE AND STATE UNIVERSITY

Accounting	M,D*
Adult Education	M,D,O
Business Administration and Management— General	M,D
Counselor Education	M,D,O
Curriculum and Instruction	M,D,O
Educational Administration	D,O
Educational Measurement and Evaluation	D
Educational Media/ Instructional Technology	M
Finance and Banking	M,D
Health Education	M,D,O
Hospitality Management	M,D
Human Resources Development	M,D

Logistics	M,D
Management Information Systems	M,D
Marketing	M,D
Physical Education	M,D,O
Recreation and Park Management	M,D
Special Education	D,O
Travel and Tourism	M,D
Veterinary Medicine	P
Veterinary Sciences	M,D
Vocational and Technical Education	M,D,O

VIRGINIA STATE UNIVERSITY

Counselor Education	M
Education—General	M,O
Educational Administration	M
Mathematics Education	M
Vocational and Technical Education	M,O

VITERBO UNIVERSITY

Education—General	M
Nursing—General	M

WAGNER COLLEGE

Accounting	M
Business Administration and Management— General	M
Early Childhood Education	M
Education—General	M,O
Educational Administration	O
Elementary Education	M
Family Nurse Practitioner Studies	O
Finance and Banking	M
Health Services Management and Hospital Administration	M
International Business	M
Marketing	M
Middle School Education	M
Nursing—General	M
Physician Assistant Studies	M
Reading Education	M
Secondary Education	M

WAKE FOREST UNIVERSITY

Accounting	M
Allopathic Medicine	P
Business Administration and Management— General	M
Counselor Education	M
Education—General	M
Exercise and Sports Science	M
Health Services Research	M
Law	P,M
Secondary Education	M

WALDEN UNIVERSITY

Business Administration and Management— General	M,D,O
Education—General	M,D
Health Services Management and Hospital Administration	M,D
Human Services	M,D
Nursing—General	M,D
Public Health—General	M,D
Quantitative Analysis	M,D

WALLA WALLA COLLEGE

Curriculum and Instruction	M
Education—General	M
Educational Administration	M
Reading Education	M
Social Work	M
Special Education	M

WALSH COLLEGE OF ACCOUNTANCY AND BUSINESS ADMINISTRATION

Accounting	M
Business Administration and Management— General	M
Finance and Banking	M
Management Information Systems	M
Taxation	M

WALSH UNIVERSITY

Business Administration and Management— General	M
Counselor Education	M
Education—General	M
Physical Therapy	M

WARNER SOUTHERN COLLEGE

Business Administration and Management— General	M

WASHBURN UNIVERSITY

Business Administration and Management— General	M
Curriculum and Instruction	M
Education—General	M
Educational Administration	M
Law	P
Reading Education	M
Social Work	M
Special Education	M

WASHINGTON AND LEE UNIVERSITY

Law	P,M

WASHINGTON STATE UNIVERSITY

Accounting	M,D
Business Administration and Management— General	M,D*
Curriculum and Instruction	M,D
Education—General	M,D
Educational Administration	M,D
Educational Psychology	M,D
Elementary Education	M,D
English Education	M,D
Exercise and Sports Science	M,D
Finance and Banking	M,D
Health Services Management and Hospital Administration	M
Higher Education	M,D
Industrial and Manufacturing Management	M,D
Insurance	D
International Business	M,D,O
Management Information Systems	M,D
Marketing	M,D
Mathematics Education	M,D

Multilingual and Multicultural Education	M,D
Music Education	M
Pharmacy	P
Reading Education	M,D
Real Estate	D
Secondary Education	M,D
Sports Management	M,D
Student Affairs	M,D
Taxation	M
Veterinary Medicine	P
Veterinary Sciences	M,D

WASHINGTON STATE UNIVERSITY SPOKANE

Communication Disorders	M
Education—General	M,O
Educational Administration	M,O
Exercise and Sports Science	M,O
Health Services Management and Hospital Administration	M
Nursing—General	M
Pharmacy	P

WASHINGTON STATE UNIVERSITY TRI-CITIES

Business Administration and Management— General	M
Counselor Education	M,D
Education—General	M,D
Educational Administration	M,D
Environmental and Occupational Health	M,D
Nursing—General	M
Reading Education	M,D
Secondary Education	M,D

WASHINGTON STATE UNIVERSITY VANCOUVER

Business Administration and Management— General	M
Education—General	M,D
Nursing—General	M

WASHINGTON UNIVERSITY IN ST. LOUIS

Accounting	M
Allied Health—General	M,D,O
Allopathic Medicine	P
Business Administration and Management— General	M,D*
Clinical Research	M
Communication Disorders	M,D
Education—General	M,D*
Educational Measurement and Evaluation	D
Elementary Education	M
Finance and Banking	M
Health Services Management and Hospital Administration	M
Kinesiology and Movement Studies	D
Law	P,M,D
Mathematics Education	M,D
Occupational Therapy	M,D
Physical Therapy	D,O
Secondary Education	M
Social Work	M,D*
Special Education	M,D

WAYLAND BAPTIST UNIVERSITY

Business Administration and Management— General	M

Education—General	M
Health Services Management and Hospital Administration	M
Human Resources Management	M
International Business	M
Management Information Systems	M
Organizational Management	M

WAYNESBURG COLLEGE

Business Administration and Management— General	M

WAYNE STATE COLLEGE

Accounting	M
Business Administration and Management— General	M
Business Education	M
Counselor Education	M
Early Childhood Education	M
Education—General	M,O
Educational Administration	M,O
Elementary Education	M
English as a Second Language	M
English Education	M
Exercise and Sports Science	M
Home Economics Education	M
Mathematics Education	M
Music Education	M
Physical Education	M
Science Education	M
Social Sciences Education	M
Special Education	M
Vocational and Technical Education	M

WAYNE STATE UNIVERSITY

Accounting	M,D
Acute Care/Critical Care Nursing	M
Adult Education	M,D,O
Advertising and Public Relations	M,D
Allopathic Medicine	P
Art Education	M,D,O
Business Administration and Management— General	M,D*
Business Education	M,D,O
Clinical Laboratory Sciences/Medical Technology	M,O
Communication Disorders	M,D
Community Health Nursing	M
Community Health	M,O
Counselor Education	M,D,O
Curriculum and Instruction	M,D,O
Early Childhood Education	M,D,O
Education—General	M,D,O*
Educational Administration	M,D,O
Educational Measurement and Evaluation	M,D,O
Educational Media/ Instructional Technology	M,D,O
Educational Policy	M,D,O
Educational Psychology	M,D,O
Elementary Education	M,D,O
English Education	M,D,O
Environmental and Occupational Health	M,O
Family Nurse Practitioner Studies	M

Foreign Languages Education	M,D,O
Foundations and Philosophy of Education	M,D,O
Health Education	M,D,O
Health Physics/ Radiological Health	M,D
Higher Education	M,D,O
Human Services	O
Information Studies	M,O
Kinesiology and Movement Studies	M
Law	P,M,D
Library Science	M,O
Maternal and Child/ Neonatal Nursing	M,O
Mathematics Education	M,D,O
Medical Physics	M,D
Medical/Surgical Nursing	M
Medicinal and Pharmaceutical Chemistry	P,M,D
Multilingual and Multicultural Education	M,D,O
Music Education	M,O
Nurse Anesthesia	M,O
Nursing Education	M,O
Nursing—General	D
Occupational Therapy	M
Pediatric Nursing	M,O
Pharmaceutical Administration	P,M,D,O
Pharmaceutical Sciences	P,M,D,O
Pharmacy	P,M,D,O
Physical Education	M
Physical Therapy	M
Physician Assistant Studies	M
Psychiatric Nursing	M,O
Public Health—General	M,O
Reading Education	M,D,O
Recreation and Park Management	M
Rehabilitation Sciences	M,O
Science Education	M,D,O
Secondary Education	M,D,O
Social Sciences Education	M,D,O
Social Work	M,D,O
Special Education	M,D,O
Sports Management	M
Taxation	M,D
Vocational and Technical Education	M,D,O

WEBBER INTERNATIONAL UNIVERSITY

Accounting	M
Business Administration and Management— General	M*
Sports Management	M

WEBER STATE UNIVERSITY

Accounting	M
Business Administration and Management— General	M
Curriculum and Instruction	M
Education—General	M
Health Services Management and Hospital Administration	M
Legal and Justice Studies	M

WEBSTER UNIVERSITY

Advertising and Public Relations	M
Business Administration and Management— General	M,D
Early Childhood Education	

Education—General	M,O
Educational Administration	M,O
Educational Media/ Instructional Technology	M,O
English as a Second Language	M
Finance and Banking	M
Health Services Management and Hospital Administration	M,D
Human Resources Development	M,D
Human Resources Management	M,D
International Business	M
Legal and Justice Studies	M
Management Information Systems	M,D,O
Marketing	M,D
Mathematics Education	M,O
Music Education	M
Nurse Anesthesia	M
Nursing—General	M
Organizational Management	M
Quality Management	M,D
Social Sciences Education	M,O
Special Education	M,O

WESLEYAN COLLEGE

Business Administration and Management— General	M
Early Childhood Education	M
Education—General	M
Mathematics Education	M
Middle School Education	M
Science Education	M

WESLEY COLLEGE

Business Administration and Management— General	M
Education—General	M
Nursing—General	M

WEST CHESTER UNIVERSITY OF PENNSYLVANIA

Athletic Training and Sports Medicine	M
Business Administration and Management— General	M
Communication Disorders	M
Counselor Education	M
Education—General	M,O
Educational Measurement and Evaluation	M
Educational Media/ Instructional Technology	M,O
Electronic Commerce	M
Elementary Education	M
English as a Second Language	M
Environmental and Occupational Health	M,O
Exercise and Sports Science	M,O
Finance and Banking	M
Foreign Languages Education	M
Health Education	M,O
Health Services Management and Hospital Administration	M,O
Kinesiology and Movement Studies	M,O
Music Education	M
Nursing Education	M
Nursing—General	M
Physical Education	M,O

Public Health—General	M,O
Reading Education	M
Science Education	M
Secondary Education	M
Social Work	M
Special Education	M
Sports Management	M,O

WESTERN CAROLINA UNIVERSITY

Accounting	M
Art Education	M
Business Administration and Management— General	M
Communication Disorders	M
Community College Education	M
Counselor Education	M
Education—General	M,D,O
Educational Administration	M,D,O
Elementary Education	M
English Education	M
Entrepreneurship	M*
Health Services Management and Hospital Administration	M
Home Economics Education	M
Human Resources Development	M
Mathematics Education	M
Middle School Education	M
Music Education	M
Nursing—General	M
Physical Education	M
Physical Therapy	M
Project Management	M
Reading Education	M
Science Education	M
Secondary Education	M
Social Sciences Education	M
Special Education	M

WESTERN CONNECTICUT STATE UNIVERSITY

Accounting	M
Adult Nursing	M
Business Administration and Management— General	M
Counselor Education	M
Curriculum and Instruction	M
Education—General	M
Educational Administration	D
Educational Media/ Instructional Technology	M
English Education	M
Family Nurse Practitioner Studies	M
Health Services Management and Hospital Administration	M
Mathematics Education	M
Music Education	M
Nursing—General	M*
Reading Education	M
Special Education	M

WESTERN GOVERNORS UNIVERSITY

Business Administration and Management— General	M
Education—General	M,O
Educational Administration	M,O
Educational Measurement and Evaluation	M,O
Educational Media/ Instructional Technology	M,O
English Education	M,O
Higher Education	M,O

Management Information Systems	M
Management Strategy and Policy	M
Mathematics Education	M,O
Science Education	M,O

WESTERN ILLINOIS UNIVERSITY

Accounting	M
Business Administration and Management— General	M
Communication Disorders	M
Counselor Education	M
Distance Education Development	M,O
Education—General	M,D,O
Educational Administration	M,D,O
Educational Media/ Instructional Technology	M,O
Elementary Education	M
Foundations and Philosophy of Education	M
Health Education	M,O
Health Services Management and Hospital Administration	M,O
Kinesiology and Movement Studies	M
Nonprofit Management	M,O
Reading Education	M
Recreation and Park Management	M
Secondary Education	M
Special Education	M
Sports Management	M
Student Affairs	M
Travel and Tourism	M

WESTERN INTERNATIONAL UNIVERSITY

Business Administration and Management— General	M
Finance and Banking	M
International Business	M
Management Information Systems	M
Management Strategy and Policy	M
Marketing	M

WESTERN KENTUCKY UNIVERSITY

Art Education	M
Business Administration and Management— General	M
Business Education	M,O
Communication Disorders	M
Counselor Education	M,O
Early Childhood Education	M
Educational Administration	M,O
Educational Media/ Instructional Technology	M
Educational Psychology	M,O
Elementary Education	M,O
English as a Second Language	M
English Education	M
Health Services Management and Hospital Administration	M
Middle School Education	M,O
Music Education	M
Nursing—General	M
Physical Education	M
Public Health—General	M
Reading Education	M
Recreation and Park Management	M

Science Education	M
Secondary Education	M,O
Social Work	M
Special Education	M
Student Affairs	M,O

WESTERN MICHIGAN UNIVERSITY

Accounting	M
Athletic Training and Sports Medicine	M
Business Administration and Management— General	M
Communication Disorders	M
Counselor Education	M,D
Early Childhood Education	M
Education—General	M,D,O
Educational Administration	M,D,O
Educational Measurement and Evaluation	M,D
Elementary Education	M
English Education	M,D
Exercise and Sports Science	M
Human Resources Development	M,D,O
Mathematics Education	M,D
Middle School Education	M
Occupational Therapy	M
Physical Education	M
Physician Assistant Studies	M
Reading Education	M
Science Education	D*
Social Work	M
Special Education	M,D
Sports Management	M
Vocational and Technical Education	M

WESTERN NEW ENGLAND COLLEGE

Accounting	M
Business Administration and Management— General	M
Elementary Education	M
English Education	M
Law	P,M
Management Information Systems	M
Mathematics Education	M

WESTERN NEW MEXICO UNIVERSITY

Business Administration and Management— General	M
Counselor Education	M
Education—General	M
Educational Administration	M
Elementary Education	M
Reading Education	M
Secondary Education	M
Special Education	M

WESTERN OREGON UNIVERSITY

Early Childhood Education	M
Education of the Multiply Handicapped	M
Education—General	M
Educational Media/ Instructional Technology	M
Health Education	M
Mathematics Education	M
Multilingual and Multicultural Education	M
Science Education	M
Secondary Education	M

Social Sciences Education	M
Special Education	M

WESTERN SEMINARY

Religious Education	M,D

WESTERN STATES CHIROPRACTIC COLLEGE

Chiropractic	P

WESTERN STATE UNIVERSITY COLLEGE OF LAW

Law	P

WESTERN UNIVERSITY OF HEALTH SCIENCES

Allied Health—General	M,D
Family Nurse Practitioner Studies	M
Health Education	M
Nursing—General	M
Osteopathic Medicine	P
Pharmaceutical Sciences	M
Pharmacy	P
Physical Therapy	D
Physician Assistant Studies	M
Veterinary Medicine	P

WESTERN WASHINGTON UNIVERSITY

Adult Education	M
Business Administration and Management— General	M
Communication Disorders	M
Counselor Education	M
Education of the Gifted	M
Education—General	M
Educational Administration	M
Elementary Education	M
Environmental Education	M
Exercise and Sports Science	M
Higher Education	M
Physical Education	M
Science Education	M
Secondary Education	M

WESTFIELD STATE COLLEGE

Counselor Education	M
Early Childhood Education	M
Education—General	M,O
Educational Administration	M,O
Educational Media/ Instructional Technology	M
Elementary Education	M
Physical Education	M
Reading Education	M
Secondary Education	M
Special Education	M
Vocational and Technical Education	M,O

WESTMINSTER CHOIR COLLEGE OF RIDER UNIVERSITY

Music Education	M*

WESTMINSTER COLLEGE (PA)

Counselor Education	M,O
Education—General	M,O
Educational Administration	M,O
Reading Education	M,O

WESTMINSTER COLLEGE (UT)

Business Administration and Management— General	M,O
Education—General	M
Family Nurse Practitioner Studies	M
Nurse Anesthesia	M
Nursing Education	M
Nursing—General	M

WEST TEXAS A&M UNIVERSITY

Accounting	M
Business Administration and Management— General	M
Communication Disorders	M
Counselor Education	M
Curriculum and Instruction	M
Education—General	M
Educational Administration	M
Educational Measurement and Evaluation	M
Educational Media/ Instructional Technology	M
Exercise and Sports Science	M
Finance and Banking	M
Nursing—General	M
Reading Education	M
Special Education	M

WEST VIRGINIA SCHOOL OF OSTEOPATHIC MEDICINE

Osteopathic Medicine	P

WEST VIRGINIA UNIVERSITY

Accounting	M
Agricultural Education	M
Allopathic Medicine	P
Art Education	M
Athletic Training and Sports Medicine	M,D
Business Administration and Management— General	M
Communication Disorders	M,D
Community Health	M
Counselor Education	M
Curriculum and Instruction	M,D
Dentistry	P
Early Childhood Education	M,D
Education of the Gifted	M,D
Education of the Multiply Handicapped	M,D
Education—General	M,D
Educational Administration	M,D
Educational Psychology	M
Elementary Education	M
English as a Second Language	M
Environmental and Occupational Health	D
Environmental Education	M
Exercise and Sports Science	M,D*
Health Education	M,D
Health Promotion	M,D
Higher Education	M,D
Human Services	M
Industrial Hygiene	M
Law	P
Legal and Justice Studies	M
Marketing	M
Mathematics Education	M,D
Medicinal and Pharmaceutical Chemistry	M,D
Music Education	M,D
Nursing—General	M,D,O

Occupational Therapy	M
Oral and Dental Sciences	M
Pharmaceutical Administration	M,D
Pharmaceutical Sciences	M,D*
Pharmacy	P,M,D
Physical Education	M,D
Physical Therapy	M
Public Health—General	M
Reading Education	M
Recreation and Park Management	M
Secondary Education	M,D
Social Work	M
Special Education	M,D
Sports Management	M,D
Vocational and Technical Education	M

WEST VIRGINIA WESLEYAN COLLEGE

Business Administration and Management— General	M

WHEATON COLLEGE

Education—General	M
Elementary Education	M
English as a Second Language	M,O
Religious Education	M
Secondary Education	M

WHEELING JESUIT UNIVERSITY

Accounting	M
Business Administration and Management— General	M
Nursing—General	M
Physical Therapy	D

WHEELOCK COLLEGE

Early Childhood Education	M
Education—General	M
Educational Administration	M
Elementary Education	M
Reading Education	M
Social Work	M
Special Education	M

WHITTIER COLLEGE

Education—General	M
Educational Administration	M
Elementary Education	M
Law	P,M
Legal and Justice Studies	P,M
Secondary Education	M

WHITWORTH UNIVERSITY

Business Administration and Management— General	M
Counselor Education	M
Education of the Gifted	M
Education—General	M
Educational Administration	M
Elementary Education	M
International Business	M
Secondary Education	M
Special Education	M

WICHITA STATE UNIVERSITY

Accounting	M
Allied Health—General	M
Art Education	M

Business Administration and Management—	
General	M
Communication Disorders	M,D
Counselor Education	M,D,O
Curriculum and Instruction	M
Education—General	M,D,O
Educational Administration	M,D,O
Educational Psychology	M,D,O
Exercise and Sports Science	M
Family Nurse Practitioner Studies	M
Human Services	M
Music Education	M
Nurse Midwifery	M
Nursing and Healthcare Administration	M
Nursing—General	M
Physical Education	M
Physical Therapy	M
Public Health—General	M
Social Work	M
Special Education	M
Sports Management	M

WIDENER UNIVERSITY

Accounting	M
Adult Education	M,D
Business Administration and Management—	
General	M
Counselor Education	M,D
Early Childhood Education	M,D
Education—General	M,D
Educational Administration	M,D
Educational Media/ Instructional Technology	M,D
Educational Psychology	M,D
Elementary Education	M,D
English Education	M,D
Foundations and Philosophy of Education	M,D
Health Education	M,D
Health Services Management and Hospital Administration	M
Human Resources Management	M
Law	P,M,D*
Mathematics Education	M,D
Middle School Education	M,D
Nursing—General	M,D,O
Physical Therapy	M,D
Reading Education	M,D
Science Education	M,D
Social Sciences Education	M,D
Social Work	M*
Special Education	M,D
Taxation	M

WILFRID LAURIER UNIVERSITY

Business Administration and Management—	
General	M,D
Foundations and Philosophy of Education	M
Kinesiology and Movement Studies	M
Physical Education	M
Social Work	M,D

WILKES UNIVERSITY

Accounting	M
Business Administration and Management—	
General	M
Computer Education	M
Education—General	M
Educational Administration	M

Educational Measurement and Evaluation	M
Educational Media/ Instructional Technology	M
Elementary Education	M
English Education	M
Entrepreneurship	M
Finance and Banking	M
Human Resources Management	M
International Business	M
Marketing	M
Mathematics Education	M
Nursing—General	M
Pharmacy	P
Science Education	M
Secondary Education	M
Social Sciences Education	M
Special Education	M

WILLAMETTE UNIVERSITY

Business Administration and Management—	
General	M
Education—General	M
Law	P,M
Nonprofit Management	M

WILLIAM CAREY UNIVERSITY

Art Education	M,O
Business Administration and Management—	
General	M
Education of the Gifted	M,O
Education—General	M,O
Elementary Education	M,O
English Education	M,O
Nursing—General	M
Secondary Education	M,O
Social Sciences Education	M,O
Special Education	M,O

WILLIAM HOWARD TAFT UNIVERSITY

Education—General	M
Law	P,M
Legal and Justice Studies	P,M
Taxation	P,M

WILLIAM MITCHELL COLLEGE OF LAW

Law	P

WILLIAM PATERSON UNIVERSITY OF NEW JERSEY

Business Administration and Management—	
General	M
Communication Disorders	M
Counselor Education	M
Education—General	M
Educational Administration	M
Elementary Education	M
Nursing—General	M
Reading Education	M
Special Education	M

WILLIAM WOODS UNIVERSITY

Curriculum and Instruction	M,O
Educational Administration	M,O
Health Services Management and Hospital Administration	M,O
Human Resources Development	M,O

WILMINGTON COLLEGE (DE)

Business Administration and Management—	
General	M
Counselor Education	M
Education of the Gifted	M
Education—General	M
Educational Administration	M,D
Educational Media/ Instructional Technology	M
Elementary Education	M
Family Nurse Practitioner Studies	M
Finance and Banking	M
Health Services Management and Hospital Administration	M
Human Resources Management	M
Human Services	M
Logistics	M
Management Information Systems	M
Nursing—General	M
Organizational Management	M
Reading Education	M
Secondary Education	M
Special Education	M
Transportation Management	M
Vocational and Technical Education	M
Women's Health Nursing	M

WILMINGTON COLLEGE (OH)

Education—General	M
Reading Education	M
Special Education	M

WINGATE UNIVERSITY

Business Administration and Management—	
General	M
Education—General	M
Educational Administration	M
Elementary Education	M
Pharmacy	P
Physical Education	M
Sports Management	M

WINONA STATE UNIVERSITY

Adult Nursing	M
Counselor Education	M
Education—General	M
Educational Administration	M,O
Family Nurse Practitioner Studies	M
Nursing and Healthcare Administration	M
Nursing Education	M
Nursing—General	M
Special Education	M

WINSTON-SALEM STATE UNIVERSITY

Business Administration and Management—	
General	M
Elementary Education	M
Management Information Systems	M
Nursing—General	M
Occupational Therapy	M
Physical Therapy	M

WINTHROP UNIVERSITY

Art Education	M

Business Administration and Management—	
General	M
Counselor Education	M
Education—General	M
Educational Administration	M
Middle School Education	M
Music Education	M
Physical Education	M
Project Management	M,O
Reading Education	M
Secondary Education	M
Social Work	M
Special Education	M

WITTENBERG UNIVERSITY

Education—General	M

WOODBURY UNIVERSITY

Business Administration and Management—	
General	M
Organizational Management	M
Real Estate	M

WORCESTER POLYTECHNIC INSTITUTE

Business Administration and Management—	
General	M,O*
Management Information Systems	M,D
Marketing	M,O
Organizational Management	M
Project Management	M
Supply Chain Management	M

WORCESTER STATE COLLEGE

Accounting	M
Business Administration and Management—	
General	M
Communication Disorders	M
Community Health Nursing	M
Early Childhood Education	M
Education—General	M
Educational Administration	M
Elementary Education	M
English Education	M
Foreign Languages Education	M
Health Education	M
Health Services Management and Hospital Administration	M
Middle School Education	M
Nonprofit Management	M
Occupational Therapy	M
Organizational Management	M
Reading Education	M
Secondary Education	M
Social Sciences Education	M
Special Education	M

WORLD MEDICINE INSTITUTE: COLLEGE OF ACUPUNCTURE AND HERBAL MEDICINE

Acupuncture and Oriental Medicine	M

WRIGHT STATE UNIVERSITY

Accounting	M

Acute Care/Critical Care Nursing	M
Adult Education	O
Adult Nursing	M
Allopathic Medicine	P
Business Administration and Management— General	M
Business Education	M
Community Health Nursing	M
Computer Education	M
Counselor Education	M
Curriculum and Instruction	M,O
Early Childhood Education	M
Education of the Gifted	M
Education—General	M,O
Educational Administration	M,O
Elementary Education	M
English as a Second Language	M
Family Nurse Practitioner Studies	M
Finance and Banking	M
Health Education	M
Health Promotion	M
Health Services Management and Hospital Administration	M
Higher Education	M,O
International and Comparative Education	M
International Business	M
Library Science	M
Logistics	M
Management Information Systems	M
Marketing	M
Mathematics Education	M
Medical Physics	M
Middle School Education	M
Music Education	M
Nursing and Healthcare Administration	M
Nursing—General	M
Pediatric Nursing	M
Physical Education	M

Project Management	M
Public Health—General	M
Recreation and Park Management	M
School Nursing	M
Science Education	M
Secondary Education	M
Special Education	M
Supply Chain Management	M
Vocational and Technical Education	M

XAVIER UNIVERSITY

Business Administration and Management— General	M
Counselor Education	M
Early Childhood Education	M
Education—General	M
Educational Administration	M
Electronic Commerce	M
Elementary Education	M
Family Nurse Practitioner Studies	M
Finance and Banking	M
Health Services Management and Hospital Administration	M*
Human Resources Development	M
International Business	M
Management Information Systems	M
Marketing	M
Multilingual and Multicultural Education	M
Nursing and Healthcare Administration	M
Nursing—General	M
Occupational Therapy	M
Reading Education	M
Secondary Education	M
Special Education	M
Sports Management	M

XAVIER UNIVERSITY OF LOUISIANA

Counselor Education	M
Curriculum and Instruction	M
Education—General	M
Educational Administration	M
Pharmacy	P

YALE UNIVERSITY

Accounting	D
Allopathic Medicine	P
Business Administration and Management— General	M,D
Environmental and Occupational Health	M,D
Epidemiology	M,D
Finance and Banking	D
Health Services Management and Hospital Administration	M,D
International Health	M
Law	P,M,D
Marketing	D
Nursing—General	M,D,O
Physician Assistant Studies	M
Public Health—General	M,D*

YESHIVA UNIVERSITY

Educational Administration	M,D,O
Law	P,M
Religious Education	M,D,O
Social Work	M,D

YORK COLLEGE OF PENNSYLVANIA

Business Administration and Management— General	M
Education—General	M
Nursing—General	M

YORK UNIVERSITY

Business Administration and Management— General	M,D*
Education—General	M,D
Human Resources Management	M,D
Kinesiology and Movement Studies	M,D
Law	P,M,D
Nursing—General	M
Social Work	M,D

YO SAN UNIVERSITY OF TRADITIONAL CHINESE MEDICINE

Acupuncture and Oriental Medicine	M

YOUNGSTOWN STATE UNIVERSITY

Accounting	M
Business Administration and Management— General	M
Counselor Education	M
Early Childhood Education	M
Education of the Gifted	M
Education—General	M,D
Educational Administration	M,D
Elementary Education	M
Finance and Banking	M
Foundations and Philosophy of Education	M,D
Health Services Management and Hospital Administration	M
Human Services	M
Marketing	M
Middle School Education	M
Music Education	M
Nursing—General	M
Physical Therapy	M
Reading Education	M
Secondary Education	M
Special Education	M

ACADEMIC AND PROFESSIONAL
PROGRAMS IN BUSINESS

Section 1
Business Administration and Management

This section contains a directory of institutions offering graduate work in business administration and management, followed by in-depth entries submitted by institutions that chose to prepare detailed program descriptions. Additional information about programs listed in the directory but not augmented by an in-depth entry may be obtained by writing directly to the dean of a graduate school or chair of a department at the address given in the directory.

For programs offering related work, see also in this book Sections 2–18 and Education (Business Education), Health Services, Nursing (Nursing and Healthcare Administration), and Sports Management. In Book 2, see Art and Art History (Arts Administration), Economics, Family and Consumer Sciences (Consumer Economics), Political Science and International Affairs, Psychology (Industrial and Organizational Psychology), and Public, Regional, and Industrial Affairs (Industrial and Labor Relations). In Book 4, see Environmental Sciences and Management (Environmental Management and Policy) and Mathematical Sciences; and in Book 5, Computer Science and Information Technology, Civil and Environmental Engineering (Construction Management), Industrial Engineering, and Management of Engineering and Technology.

CONTENTS

Business Administration and Management—General

Adelphi University, School of Business, Certificate Programs in Management, Garden City, NY 11530-0701. Offers human resource management (Certificate). Part-time and evening/weekend programs available. *Entrance requirements:* For degree, GMAT or master's degree. Additional exam requirements/recommendations for international students: Required—TOEFL (minimum score 550 paper-based; 213 computer-based). *Application deadline:* For fall admission, 5/1 for international students; for spring admission, 12/1 for international students. Applications are processed on a rolling basis. Application fee: $50. Electronic applications accepted. *Financial support:* Application deadline: 3/1; *Unit head:* Brian Rothschild, Assistant Dean, 516-877-4673, Fax: 516-877-4607, E-mail: rothschild@adelphi.edu. *Application contact:* Christine Murphy, Director of Admissions, 516-877-3050, Fax: 516-877-3039, E-mail: graduateadmissions@adelphi.edu.

Adelphi University, School of Business, Department of Management, Marketing, and Decision Sciences, Garden City, NY 11530-0701. Offers management information systems (MBA); management/human resource management (MBA); marketing/e-commerce (MBA). Part-time and evening/weekend programs available. *Students:* 67 full-time (34 women), 173 part-time (85 women); includes 44 minority (24 African Americans, 11 Asian Americans or Pacific Islanders, 9 Hispanic Americans), 49 international. Average age 31. In 2006, 122 degrees awarded. *Degree requirements:* For master's, capstone course. *Entrance requirements:* For master's, GMAT, 2 letters of recommendation. Additional exam requirements/recommendations for international students: Required—TOEFL. *Application deadline:* For fall admission, 5/1 for international students; for spring admission, 12/1 for international students. Applications are processed on a rolling basis. Application fee: $50. Electronic applications accepted. *Financial support:* Research assistantships with full and partial tuition reimbursements, career-related internships or fieldwork, Federal Work-Study, institutionally sponsored loans, scholarships/grants, and unspecified assistantships available. Financial award application deadline: 3/1; financial award applicants required to submit FAFSA. *Faculty research:* Supply chain management, distribution channels, productivity benchmark analysis, data envelopment analysis, financial portfolio analysis. *Unit head:* Dr. Allan Ashley, Chairperson, 516-877-4640, E-mail: ashley@adelphi.edu. *Application contact:* Christine Murphy, Director of Admissions, 516-877-3050, Fax: 516-877-3039, E-mail: graduateadmissions@adelphi.edu.

Adler Graduate School, Program in Adlerian Studies, Richfield, MN 55423. Offers art therapy specialization (MA); clinical counseling track (MA); coaching and consulting in organizations (Certificate); management consulting and organizational leadership (MA); marriage and family track (MA); non-clinical Adlerian studies track (MA); personal and professional life coaching (Certificate); school counseling (MA). Part-time and evening/weekend programs available. *Faculty:* 4 full-time (1 woman), 36 part-time/adjunct (21 women). *Students:* Average age 37. 48 applicants, 98% accepted, 46 enrolled. In 2006, 37 degrees awarded. *Degree requirements:* For master's, thesis or alternative, 500-700 hour internship, depending on license choice. *Entrance requirements:* For master's, minimum undergraduate GPA of 3.0, 12 credits of course work in psychology or related field. *Application deadline:* For fall admission, 10/1 priority date for domestic students; for winter admission, 1/1 priority date for domestic students; for spring admission, 4/1 priority date for domestic students. Applications are processed on a rolling basis. Application fee: $50. *Financial support:* In 2006–07, 121 students received support. Career-related internships or fieldwork and tuition waivers available. Support available to part-time students. Financial award applicants required to submit FAFSA. *Unit head:* Dr. Dennis Rislove, President, 612-861-7554 Ext. 106, Fax: 612-861-7559, E-mail: rislove@alfredadler.edu. *Application contact:* Evelyn B. Haas, Director of Student Services and Admissions, 612-861-7554 Ext. 103, Fax: 612-861-7559, E-mail: ev@alfredadler.edu.

Alabama Agricultural and Mechanical University, School of Graduate Studies, School of Business, Department of Management and Marketing, Huntsville, AL 35811. Offers MBA. Part-time and evening/weekend programs available. *Faculty:* 7 full-time (0 women), 1 part-time/adjunct (0 women). *Students:* 5 full-time (4 women), 9 part-time (4 women); all minorities (all African Americans) Average age 28. In 2006, 19 degrees awarded. *Degree requirements:* For master's, thesis optional. *Entrance requirements:* For master's, GMAT, minimum undergraduate GPA of 2.5. Additional exam requirements/recommendations for international students: Required—TOEFL. *Application deadline:* For fall admission, 5/1 priority date for domestic students. Applications are processed on a rolling basis. Application fee: $25. Electronic applications accepted. *Financial support:* Research assistantships, career-related internships or fieldwork, Federal Work-Study, and institutionally sponsored loans available. Financial award application deadline: 4/1. *Faculty research:* Consumer behavior of blacks, small business marketing, economics of education, China in transition, international economics. *Unit head:* Dr. Uchenna Elike, Chair, 256-372-5088. *Application contact:* Dr. Marsha D. Griffin, Coordinator, 256-372-5494.

Alabama State University, School of Graduate Studies, College of Business Administration, Montgomery, AL 36101-0271. Offers M Acc. *Accreditation:* ACBSP. Part-time programs available. *Faculty:* 9 full-time (2 women). *Students:* 1 full-time (0 women), 9 part-time (5 women); includes 8 minority (all African Americans) 12 applicants, 83% accepted. In 2006, 6 degrees awarded. *Entrance requirements:* For master's, GMAT, graduate writing competency test. Additional exam requirements/recommendations for international students: Required—TOEFL (minimum score 500 paper-based; 173 computer-based). *Application deadline:* For fall admission, 7/15 for domestic students; for spring admission, 12/15 for domestic students. Applications are processed on a rolling basis. Application fee: $10. *Expenses:* Tuition, state resident: full-time $1,728; part-time $192 per hour. Tuition, nonresident: full-time $3,456; part-time $334 per hour. *Financial support:* In 2006–07, 2 research assistantships (averaging $9,450 per year) were awarded. *Unit head:* Dr. Percy Vaughn, Dean, 334-229-4124, Fax: 334-229-4870, E-mail: pvaughn@asunet.alasu.edu.

Alaska Pacific University, Graduate Programs, Business Administration Department, Program in Business Administration, Anchorage, AK 99508-4672. Offers business administration (MBA); global finance (MBA); health services administration (MBA). Part-time and evening/weekend programs available. *Faculty:* 6 full-time (3 women), 4 part-time/adjunct (1 woman). *Students:* 5 full-time (3 women), 46 part-time (25 women); includes 16 minority (2 African Americans, 11 American Indian/Alaska Native, 3 Asian Americans or Pacific Islanders), 1 international. Average age 37. In 2006, 11 degrees awarded. *Degree requirements:* For master's, capstone course. *Entrance requirements:* For master's, GMAT or GRE, minimum GPA of 3.0. *Application deadline:* For fall admission, 4/1 priority date for domestic students; for spring admission, 12/15 for domestic students. Applications are processed on a rolling basis. Application fee: $25. *Expenses:* Tuition: Part-time $550 per credit hour. Required fees: $100 per semester. Tuition and fees vary according to program. *Financial support:* In 2006–07, fellowships (averaging $6,300 per year), 6 research assistantships (averaging $4,112 per year) were awarded; career-related internships or fieldwork and Federal Work-Study also available. Support available to part-time students. Financial award application deadline: 4/15. *Unit head:* Dr. Tracy Stewart, Director, 907-564-8358, Fax: 907-562-4276, E-mail: tstewart@alaskapacific.edu.

Albany State University, School of Business, Albany, GA 31705-2717. Offers water policy (MBA). *Accreditation:* ACBSP. Part-time and evening/weekend programs available. Postbaccalaureate distance learning degree programs offered (no on-campus study). *Degree requirements:* For master's, comprehensive exam. *Entrance requirements:* For master's, GMAT, minimum GPA of 2.5. Electronic applications accepted. *Faculty research:* Economic impacts, employment opportunities, instructional technology.

Albertus Magnus College, Program in Leadership, New Haven, CT 06511-1189. Offers MA. *Faculty:* 3 full-time (1 woman). *Degree requirements:* For master's, thesis optional. *Entrance requirements:* For master's, interview. *Expenses:* Tuition: Full-time $10,800; part-time $1,080 per course. Tuition and fees vary according to program. *Unit head:* Dr. Howard Fero, Director of Masters in Leadership, 203-977-7100, Fax: 203-777-2112, E-mail: hfero@albertus.edu. *Application contact:* Joseph Chadwick, Director of Program Development, 203-777-0800 Ext. 114, Fax: 203-777-2112, E-mail: joe.chadwick@apollo.grp.edu.

Albertus Magnus College, Program in Management, New Haven, CT 06511-1189. Offers business administration (MBA); management (MSM). Program also offered in East Hartford, CT. Evening/weekend programs available. *Faculty:* 14 full-time (6 women), 36 part-time/adjunct (14 women). *Students:* 351 full-time, 11 part-time. Average age 35. 90 applicants, 78% accepted, 66 enrolled. In 2006, 233 degrees awarded. *Degree requirements:* For master's, thesis. *Entrance requirements:* For master's, 3 years of management or related experience, minimum GPA of 2.5. Additional exam requirements/recommendations for international students: Required—TOEFL. *Application deadline:* Applications are processed on a rolling basis. Application fee: $75. *Expenses:* Tuition: Full-time $10,800; part-time $1,080 per course. Tuition and fees vary according to program. *Financial support:* Available to part-time students. *Unit head:* Dr. John Donohue, Vice President, Academic Affairs, 203-773-8068, Fax: 203-773-8525, E-mail: jdonohue@albertus.edu. *Application contact:* Joseph Chadwick, Director of Program Development, 203-777-0800 Ext. 114, Fax: 203-777-2112, E-mail: joe.chadwick@apollo.grp.edu.

Alcorn State University, School of Graduate Studies, School of Business, Natchez, MS 39122-8399. Offers MBA. *Faculty:* 7 full-time (1 woman). *Students:* 28 full-time (14 women), 36 part-time (28 women); includes 35 minority (34 African Americans, 1 Asian American or Pacific Islander), 15 international. In 2006, 21 degrees awarded. *Application deadline:* For fall admission, 7/15 for domestic students; for spring admission, 11/25 for domestic students. *Unit head:* Dr. Steve Wells, Dean, 601-304-4300 Ext. 4309.

Alfred University, Graduate School, College of Business, Alfred, NY 14802-1205. Offers business administration (MBA). *Accreditation:* AACSB. Part-time programs available. *Students:* 6 full-time (0 women), 12 part-time (5 women). Average age 28. 33 applicants, 14 enrolled. In 2006, 11 degrees awarded. *Entrance requirements:* For master's, GMAT. Additional exam requirements/recommendations for international students: Required—TOEFL (minimum score 590 paper-based; 243 computer-based; 90 iBT), IELTS (minimum score 7). *Application deadline:* For fall admission, 6/1 priority date for international students; for spring admission, 11/1 priority date for international students. Applications are processed on a rolling basis. Application fee: $50. Electronic applications accepted. *Expenses:* Tuition: Full-time $29,600; part-time $630 per credit hour. Required fees: $850; $70 per semester. Tuition and fees vary according to program. *Financial support:* In 2006–07, 6 students received support, including research assistantships (averaging $14,225 per year); tuition waivers (partial) and unspecified assistantships also available. Financial award applicants required to submit FAFSA. *Faculty research:* Regional economic development, activity-based costing, nonprofit consumer behavior. *Unit head:* Lori Hollenbeck, Director of MBA Program, 607-871-2630, Fax: 607-871-2114, E-mail: hollenl@alfred.edu. *Application contact:* Valerie Stephens, Coordinator of Graduate Admissions, 607-871-2141, Fax: 607-871-2198, E-mail: gradinquiry@alfred.edu.

Alliant International University–Los Angeles, Marshall Goldsmith School of Management, Business Division, Alhambra, CA 91803-1360. Offers DBA.

See Close-Up on page 203.

Alliant International University–México City, Marshall Goldsmith School of Management, Mexico City, Mexico. Offers international business administration (MIBA); international relations (MA). Part-time and evening/weekend programs available. *Faculty:* 1 full-time (0 women), 11 part-time/adjunct (3 women). *Students:* 15 full-time (7 women), 11 part-time (6 women); includes 4 minority (all Hispanic Americans), 10 international. Average age 25. 17 applicants, 41% accepted. *Entrance requirements:* For master's, GMAT, minimum GPA of 3.0. Additional exam requirements/recommendations for international students: Required—TOEFL (minimum score 550 paper-based; 213 computer-based), TWE (minimum score 5). *Application deadline:* For fall admission, 8/1 priority date for domestic and international students; for spring admission, 12/1 priority date for domestic and international students. Applications are processed on a rolling basis. Application fee: $55. Electronic applications accepted. *Expenses:* Tuition: Full-time $5,640; part-time $235 per unit. Required fees: $300; $150 per semester. *Financial support:* Research assistantships, teaching assistantships, career-related internships or fieldwork, Federal Work-Study, institutionally sponsored loans, and scholarships/grants available. Support available to part-time students. Financial award application deadline: 2/15; financial award applicants required to submit FAFSA. *Faculty research:* Environmental impact and business in Mexico. *Unit head:* Dr. Jim Goodrich, Dean, 525-5264-2187, Fax: 525-5264-2188, E-mail: admissions@alliant.edu. *Application contact:* Alliant International University Central Contact Center, 866-U-ALLIANT, Fax: 858-635-4555, E-mail: admissions@alliant.edu.

See Close-Up on page 203.

Alliant International University–San Diego, Marshall Goldsmith School of Management, Business and Management Division, San Diego, CA 92131-1799. Offers business administration (MBA); information and technology management (DBA); international business (MIBA, DBA), including finance (DBA), marketing (DBA); strategic business (DBA); sustainable management (MBA). Part-time and evening/weekend programs available. *Students:* 87 full-time (22 women), 51 part-time (17 women); includes 27 minority (8 African Americans, 2 American Indian/Alaska Native, 8 Asian Americans or Pacific Islanders, 9 Hispanic Americans), 68 international. Average age 32. 104 applicants, 66% accepted, 40 enrolled. *Degree requirements:* For doctorate, thesis/dissertation. *Entrance requirements:* For master's, GMAT, minimum GPA of 3.0; for doctorate, GMAT, minimum GPA of 3.3. Additional exam requirements/recommendations for international students: Required—TOEFL (minimum score 550 paper-based; 213 computer-based), TWE (minimum score 5). *Application deadline:* For fall admission, 8/1 priority date for domestic and international students; for spring admission, 12/1 priority date for domestic and international students. Applications are processed on a rolling basis. Application fee: $55. Electronic applications accepted. *Expenses:* Tuition: Part-time $825 per unit. Tuition and fees vary according to course load, degree level and program. *Financial support:* Research assistantships, teaching assistantships, career-related internships or fieldwork, Federal Work-Study, institutionally sponsored loans, scholarships/grants, and tuition waivers (partial) available. Support available to part-time students. Financial award application deadline: 2/15; financial award applicants required to submit FAFSA. *Faculty research:* Consumer behavior, international business, strategic management, information systems. *Unit head:* Dr. Fred Phillips, Associate Dean, 866-825-5426, Fax: 855-635-4739, E-mail: admissions@alliant.edu. *Application contact:* Alliant International University Central Contact Center, 866-U-ALLIANT, Fax: 858-635-4555, E-mail: admissions@alliant.edu.

See Close-Up on page 203.

Alliant International University–San Francisco, Marshall Goldsmith School of Management, Presidio School of Management, San Francisco, CA 94133-1221. Offers sustainable management (MBA). *Students:* 75 full-time (37 women), 34 part-time (20 women). Average age 37. *Expenses:* Tuition: Part-time $825 per unit. Tuition and fees vary according to course load, degree level and program. *Unit head:* Dr. Ron Naliser, Provost.

Business Administration and Management—General

Alvernia College, Graduate and Continuing Studies, Department of Business, Reading, PA 19607-1799. Offers MBA. Part-time and evening/weekend programs available. *Degree requirements:* For master's, thesis optional. *Entrance requirements:* For master's, GMAT, GRE, or MAT. Electronic applications accepted.

Alverno College, School of Business, Milwaukee, WI 53234-3922. Offers MBA. Evening/weekend programs available. *Faculty:* 5 full-time (1 woman), 1 part-time/adjunct (0 women). *Students:* 26 full-time (25 women); includes 3 minority (all African Americans) Average age 37. 36 applicants, 72% accepted, 26 enrolled. *Entrance requirements:* For master's, 3 or more years relevant work experience. Additional exam requirements/recommendations for international students: Required—TOEFL. *Application deadline:* For fall admission, 8/1 priority date for domestic students; for spring admission, 12/15 priority date for domestic students. Applications are processed on a rolling basis. Application fee: $20. Electronic applications accepted. *Expenses: Contact institution.* Tuition and fees vary according to program. *Financial support:* Federal Work-Study available. Support available to part-time students. Financial award application deadline: 4/15; financial award applicants required to submit FAFSA. *Unit head:* William McEachern, MBA Program Director, 414-382-6238, E-mail: william.mceachern@alverno.edu. *Application contact:* Carolyn Wise, Graduate Recruiter, 800-933-3401, Fax: 414-382-6354, E-mail: carolyn.wise@alverno.edu.

Amberton University, Graduate School, Department of Business Administration, Garland, TX 75041-5595. Offers general business (MBA); management (MBA). Part-time and evening/weekend programs available. *Faculty:* 16 full-time (7 women), 45 part-time/adjunct (20 women). *Students:* 40 full-time (15 women), 250 part-time (150 women); includes 71 minority (44 African Americans, 1 American Indian/Alaska Native, 1 Asian American or Pacific Islander, 25 Hispanic Americans), 20 international. Average age 35. *Entrance requirements:* For master's, minimum GPA of 3.0. *Application deadline:* Applications are processed on a rolling basis. *Expenses:* Tuition: Full-time $4,800; part-time $600 per course. *Application contact:* Adviser, 972-279-6511 Ext. 180, Fax: 972-279-9773, E-mail: advisor@amberton.edu.

American College of Computer & Information Sciences, Department of Management Studies, Birmingham, AL 35205. Offers MBA. Part-time and evening/weekend programs available. Postbaccalaureate distance learning degree programs offered (no on-campus study). *Entrance requirements:* Additional exam requirements/recommendations for international students: Required—TOEFL (minimum score 550 paper-based; 213 computer-based). Electronic applications accepted.

American College of Thessaloniki, Department of Business Administration, Pylea, Greece. Offers banking and finance (MBA); entrepreneurship (MBA, Certificate); finance (Certificate); management (MBA, Certificate); marketing (MBA, Certificate). Part-time and evening/weekend programs available. *Faculty:* 6 full-time (1 woman), 10 part-time/adjunct (4 women). *Students:* 9 full-time (6 women), 39 part-time (24 women), 22 international. 36 applicants, 97% accepted, 26 enrolled. In 2006, 25 degrees awarded. *Degree requirements:* For master's, thesis, registration. *Application deadline:* For fall admission, 9/30 priority date for domestic students; for spring admission, 1/31 priority date for domestic students. Applications are processed on a rolling basis. Application fee: $70. Electronic applications accepted. *Expenses:* Tuition: Full-time $10,560; part-time $660 per course. Part-time tuition and fees vary according to course load. *Unit head:* Dr. Nikolaos Kourkoumelis, Chair, Business Division, E-mail: nikolaos@act.edu. *Application contact:* Vasilis Blatsas, Coordinator of Business Programs and MBA Advisor, 30-310-398206 Ext. 206.

American Graduate University, Program in Acquisition Management, Covina, CA 91724. Offers MAM, Certificate. Part-time programs available. Postbaccalaureate distance learning degree programs offered (no on-campus study). *Faculty:* 2 full-time (1 woman), 12 part-time/adjunct (2 women). In 2006, 30 master's, 3 other advanced degrees awarded. *Entrance requirements:* Additional exam requirements/recommendations for international students: Required—TOEFL. *Application deadline:* Applications are processed on a rolling basis. Application fee: $50. Electronic applications accepted. *Unit head:* Paul McDonald, President, 626-966-4576 Ext. 1006, E-mail: paulmcdonald@agu.edu. *Application contact:* Marie J. Sirney, Executive Vice President, 626-966-4576, Fax: 626-915-1709, E-mail: mariesirney@agu.edu.

American Graduate University, Program in Business Administration, Covina, CA 91724. Offers MBA. Part-time programs available. Postbaccalaureate distance learning degree programs offered (no on-campus study). *Faculty:* 2 full-time (1 woman), 12 part-time/adjunct (2 women). *Entrance requirements:* Additional exam requirements/recommendations for international students: Required—TOEFL. *Application deadline:* Applications are processed on a rolling basis. Application fee: $50. Electronic applications accepted. *Unit head:* Paul McDonald, President, 626-966-4576 Ext. 1006, E-mail: paulmcdonald@agu.edu. *Application contact:* Marie J. Sirney, Executive Vice President, 626-966-4576, Fax: 626-915-1709, E-mail: mariesirney@agu.edu.

American Graduate University, Program in Contract Management, Covina, CA 91724. Offers MCM, Certificate. Part-time programs available. Postbaccalaureate distance learning degree programs offered (no on-campus study). *Faculty:* 2 full-time (1 woman), 12 part-time/adjunct (2 women). In 2006, 9 degrees awarded. *Application deadline:* Applications are processed on a rolling basis. Application fee: $50. Electronic applications accepted. *Unit head:* Paul McDonald, President, 626-966-4576 Ext. 1006, E-mail: paulmcdonald@agu.edu. *Application contact:* Marie J. Sirney, Executive Vice President, 626-966-4576, Fax: 626-915-1709, E-mail: mariesirney@agu.edu.

American InterContinental University, Program in Business Administration, Los Angeles, CA 90066. Offers business administration (MBA); global technology management (MBA). Part-time and evening/weekend programs available. Postbaccalaureate distance learning degree programs offered. *Faculty:* 5 full-time (0 women). *Students:* 44 full-time (19 women), 4 part-time (3 women); includes 6 minority (3 African Americans, 1 Asian American or Pacific Islander, 2 Hispanic Americans), 10 international. Average age 34. In 2006, 32 degrees awarded. *Entrance requirements:* For master's, interview, proof of Baccalaureate. Additional exam requirements/recommendations for international students: Required—TOEFL (minimum score 550 paper-based; 79 iBT), IELTS (minimum score 7). *Application deadline:* Applications are processed on a rolling basis. Application fee: $50. Electronic applications accepted. *Expenses:* Tuition: Full-time $26,400. *Financial support:* Institutionally sponsored loans, scholarships/grants, and health care benefits available. Support available to part-time students. Financial award applicants required to submit FAFSA. *Faculty research:* Organizational psychology management, marketing, economics, international relations. *Unit head:* Dr. James Carroll, Dean of School of Business, 310-302-2639, E-mail: james.carroll@la.aiuniv.edu. *Application contact:* Admissions Advisor, 310-302-2000, Fax: 310-302-2410.

American InterContinental University, Program in International Business, Weston, FL 33326. Offers accounting and finance (MBA); human resource management (MBA); management (MBA); marketing (MBA). Part-time and evening/weekend programs available. Postbaccalaureate distance learning degree programs offered. *Faculty:* 3 full-time (0 women), 2 part-time/adjunct (0 women). *Students:* 87 full-time (51 women), 7 part-time (4 women); includes 62 minority (42 African Americans, 1 American Indian/Alaska Native, 1 Asian American or Pacific Islander, 18 Hispanic Americans), 5 international. Average age 34. In 2006, 51 degrees awarded. *Application deadline:* Applications are processed on a rolling basis. Application fee: $50. Electronic applications accepted. *Financial support:* Federal Work-Study and scholarships/grants available. Financial award application deadline: 1/15; financial award applicants required to submit FAFSA. *Unit head:* Dr. David Kalichavan, Acting Dean, School of Business, 954-446-6100, Fax: 954-446-6393, E-mail: dkalichavan@aiufl.edu.

American InterContinental University Buckhead Campus, Program in Business Administration, Atlanta, GA 30326-1016. Offers accounting and finance (MBA); management (MBA); marketing (MBA). Evening/weekend programs available. Postbaccalaureate distance learning degree programs offered. *Faculty:* 2 full-time (1 woman), 1 part-time/adjunct (0 women). *Students:* 19 full-time (16 women); includes 1 minority (African American) Average age 28. 10 applicants, 60% accepted, 5 enrolled. In 2006, 25 degrees awarded. *Median time to degree:* Master's–1 year full-time. *Entrance requirements:* For master's, minimum cumulative undergraduate GPA of 2.0. Additional exam requirements/recommendations for international students: Required—TOEFL (minimum score 530 paper-based; 230 computer-based). *Application deadline:* Applications are processed on a rolling basis. Application fee: $50. Electronic applications accepted. *Financial support:* In 2006–07, 14 students received support. Career-related internships or fieldwork, Federal Work-Study, institutionally sponsored loans, and scholarships/grants available. Financial award applicants required to submit FAFSA. *Faculty research:* Leadership management, international advertising. *Unit head:* Dr. Sonia Heywood, Dean of Business, 404-965-5764, Fax: 404-965-5957, E-mail: sonia.heywood@buckhead.aiuniv.edu. *Application contact:* Mike Betz, Vice President Admissions and Marketing, 404-965-5719, Fax: 404-965-5997, E-mail: mbetz@aiuniv.edu.

American InterContinental University-London, Program in Business Administration, London, United Kingdom. Offers international business (MBA). *Degree requirements:* For master's, thesis optional. *Entrance requirements:* For master's, interview, professional experience. Additional exam requirements/recommendations for international students: Required—TOEFL or IELTS recommended. Electronic applications accepted.

American InterContinental University Online, Program in Business Administration, Hoffman Estates, IL 60192. Offers accounting and finance (MBA); healthcare management (MBA); human resource management (MBA); international business (MBA); management (MBA); marketing (MBA); operations management (MBA); organizational psychology and development (MBA); project management (MBA). Evening/weekend programs available. Postbaccalaureate distance learning degree programs offered (no on-campus study). *Entrance requirements:* Additional exam requirements/recommendations for international students: Required—TOEFL (minimum score 550 paper-based; 213 computer-based). *Application deadline:* Applications are processed on a rolling basis. Application fee: $50. Electronic applications accepted. *Financial support:* Institutionally sponsored loans and scholarships/grants available. Financial award applicants required to submit FAFSA. *Unit head:* Kerri J Holloway, Vice President of Academic Affairs, 847-851-5000 Ext. 15399, Fax: 847-586-6309, E-mail: kholloway@aivonline.edu. *Application contact:* 877-701-3800, E-mail: info@aiuonline.edu.

American International College, School of Business Administration, Springfield, MA 01109-3189. Offers MBA, MSAT. Part-time and evening/weekend programs available. *Faculty:* 14 full-time (4 women), 10 part-time/adjunct (6 women). *Students:* 28 full-time (13 women), 55 part-time (34 women); includes 24 minority (14 African Americans, 6 Asian Americans or Pacific Islanders, 4 Hispanic Americans), 3 international. Average age 32. In 2006, 34 degrees awarded. *Degree requirements:* For master's, thesis (for some programs), comprehensive exam (for some programs), registration. *Entrance requirements:* Additional exam requirements/recommendations for international students: Required—TOEFL. *Application deadline:* For fall admission, 7/1 priority date for domestic and international students; for spring admission, 12/1 priority date for domestic and international students. Applications are processed on a rolling basis. Application fee: $50. *Expenses:* Tuition: Part-time $585 per semester hour. Required fees: $100 per year. Full-time tuition and fees vary according to program. *Financial support:* Career-related internships or fieldwork, Federal Work-Study, and unspecified assistantships available. Support available to part-time students. Financial award application deadline: 4/1; financial award applicants required to submit FAFSA. *Faculty research:* Leadership, strategic communication. *Unit head:* Dr. John Rogers, Dean, 413-205-3230, E-mail: john.rogers@aic.edu. *Application contact:* Keshawn Dodds, Associate Director of Graduate Admissions, 413-205-3549, Fax: 413-205-3911, E-mail: keshawn.dodds@aic.edu.

American Jewish University, Graduate School, David Lieber School of Graduate Studies, Program in Business Administration, Bel Air, CA 90077-1599. Offers general nonprofit administration (MBA); Jewish nonprofit administration (MBA). Part-time and evening/weekend programs available. *Degree requirements:* For master's, thesis, internship. *Entrance requirements:* For master's, GMAT or GRE General Test, interview, minimum undergraduate GPA of 3.0. Additional exam requirements/recommendations for international students: Required—TOEFL (minimum score 550 paper-based; 247 computer-based).

American Public University System, AMU/APU Graduate Programs, Charles Town, WV 25414. Offers business administration (MBA); criminal justice (MA); emergency and disaster management (MA); environmental policy and management (MS); history (MA); homeland security (MA); humanities (MA); intelligence (MA Strategic Intelligence); international relations and conflict resolution (MA); management (MA); military history (MA); national security studies (MA); political science (MA); public administration (MA); public health (MA); security management (MA); space studies (MS); sports management (MA); transportation and logistics management (MA). Programs offered via distance learning only. Part-time and evening/weekend programs available. Postbaccalaureate distance learning degree programs offered (no on-campus study). *Faculty:* 10 full-time (3 women), 188 part-time/adjunct (57 women). *Students:* 498 full-time (104 women), 5,272 part-time (1,209 women). Average age 34. 6,574 applicants, 100% accepted, 3508 enrolled. In 2006, 358 degrees awarded. *Degree requirements:* For master's, comprehensive exam, registration. *Entrance requirements:* For master's, bachelor's degree or equivalent, minimum GPA of 2.7 in last 60 hours of course work. *Application deadline:* For fall admission, 9/1 priority date for domestic students; for winter admission, 1/1 priority date for domestic students; for spring admission, 5/1 priority date for domestic students. Applications are processed on a rolling basis. Application fee: $0. Electronic applications accepted. *Expenses:* Tuition: Full-time $4,950; part-time $275 per credit. One-time fee: $200 full-time. *Financial support:* Applicants required to submit FAFSA. *Faculty research:* Military history, criminal justice, management performance, national security. *Unit head:* Dr. Frank McCluskey, Provost, 877-468-6268, Fax: 304-724-3780. *Application contact:* Terry Grant, Director of Enrollment Management, 877-468-6268, Fax: 304-724-3780, E-mail: info@apus.edu.

American Sentinel University, Graduate Programs, Englewood, CO 80112. Offers business administration (MBA); business intelligence (MS), computer science (MSCS); health information management (MS); healthcare (MBA); information systems (MSIS); nursing (MSN). Part-time and evening/weekend programs available. Postbaccalaureate distance learning degree programs offered (no on-campus study). *Faculty:* 40. *Students:* 400. Average age 36. In 2006, 47 degrees awarded. *Entrance requirements:* Additional exam requirements/recommendations for international students: Required—TOEFL (minimum score 600 paper-based; 215 computer-based). *Application deadline:* Applications are processed on a rolling basis. Application fee: $50. Electronic applications accepted. *Unit head:* Janette D. Marshall, Registrar, 800-729-2427 Ext. 2211, Fax: 205-326-3822, E-mail: jan.marshall@americansentinel.edu. *Application contact:* Natalie A. Nixon, Director of Admissions, 800-729-2427, Fax: 205-328-2229, E-mail: natalie.nixon@americansentinel.edu.

American University, Kogod School of Business, Washington, DC 20016-8001. Offers MBA, MS, Certificate, JD/MBA, MBA/MA. *Accreditation:* AACSB. Part-time and evening/weekend programs available. Postbaccalaureate distance learning degree programs offered. *Faculty:* 58 full-time (16 women), 21 part-time/adjunct (4 women). *Students:* 152 full-time (67 women), 261 part-time (107 women); includes 90 minority (47 African Americans, 1 American Indian/Alaska Native, 27 Asian Americans or Pacific Islanders, 15 Hispanic Americans), 69 international. Average age 31. 518 applicants, 60% accepted, 125 enrolled. In 2006, 187 degrees awarded. *Degree requirements:* For master's, residency. *Entrance requirements:* Additional exam requirements/recommendations for international students: Required—TOEFL (minimum score 550 paper-based; 213 computer-based). *Application deadline:* For fall admission, 2/1 priority date for domestic students. Applications are processed on a rolling basis. Application fee: $50. *Expenses: Contact institution.* Tuition and fees vary according to program. *Financial support:* In 2006–07, 28 students received support; fellowships, research assistantships with partial tuition reimbursements available, career-related internships or fieldwork, Federal Work-Study, institutionally sponsored loans, and tuition waivers (partial) available. Support available to part-time students. Financial award application deadline: 2/1; financial award applicants required to submit FAFSA. *Faculty research:* Management of global information technology, international business, marketing/information and technology, international accounting, international investment. *Unit head:* Dr. Richard Durand, Dean, 202-885-1900, Fax: 202-885-1955. *Application contact:* Sondra Smith, Acting Director of Graduate Programs, 202-885-1907, Fax: 202-885-1078, E-mail: sondra@american.edu.

The American University in Cairo, Graduate Studies and Research, School of Business, Economics and Communication, Department of Management, Cairo, Egypt. Offers MBA, MPA, Diploma. Part-time programs available. *Entrance requirements:* For master's, English entrance exam, GMAT. Electronic applications accepted. *Faculty research:* Privatization, public sector management, Islamic banking, information systems management, role of private sector in economic development.

The American University in Dubai, Program in International Business, Dubai, United Arab Emirates. Offers MBA. Part-time programs available. *Degree requirements:* For master's, thesis optional. *Entrance requirements:* For master's, GMAT, interview. Additional exam requirements/recommendations for international students: Required—TOEFL. Electronic applications accepted.

The American University of Athens, The School of Graduate Studies, Athens, Greece. Offers biomedical sciences (MS); business (MBA); business communication (MA); computer sciences (MS); engineering and applied sciences (MS); politics and policy making (MA); systems engineering (MS); telecommunications (MS). *Entrance requirements:* Additional exam requirements/recommendations for international students: Required—TOEFL (minimum score 550 paper-based; 213 computer-based). *Faculty research:* Nanotechnology, environmental sciences, rock mechanics, human skin studies, Monte Carlo algorithms and software.

American University of Beirut, Graduate Programs, Olayan School of Business, Beirut, Lebanon. Offers business administration (MBA); executive business administration (EMBA). Part-time and evening/weekend programs available. *Faculty:* 19 full-time (3 women), 2 part-time/adjunct (0 women). *Students:* 22 full-time (9 women), 84 part-time (43 women). Average age 27. 78 applicants, 35% accepted, 18 enrolled. In 2006, 39 degrees awarded. *Degree requirements:* For master's, one foreign language, thesis (for some programs), comprehensive exam (for some programs), registration. *Entrance requirements:* For master's, GMAT, letters of recommendation. Additional exam requirements/recommendations for international students: Required—TOEFL (minimum score 600 paper-based; 250 computer-based; 100 iBT), IELTS (minimum score 8). *Application deadline:* For fall admission, 4/30 for domestic and international students; for spring admission, 11/1 for domestic and international students. Application fee: $50. *Financial support:* In 2006–07, 9 students received support. Unspecified assistantships available. Financial award application deadline: 2/2. *Faculty research:* Capital acquisition, mergers and acquisition, corporate governance, financial reporting, international trade. Total annual research expenditures: $71,900. *Unit head:* George Najjar, Dean, 961-1340460 Ext. 3930, Fax: 961-1750214, E-mail: gnajjar@aub.edu.lb. *Application contact:* Dr. Salim Kanaan, Director of Admissions Office, 961-1-374374 Ext. 2592, Fax: 961-1-750775, E-mail: admissions@aub.edu.lb.

Anderson University, Falls School of Business, Anderson, IN 46012-3495. Offers accountancy (MA); business administration (MBA, DBA). *Accreditation:* ACBSP.

Andrew Jackson University, Brian Tracy College of Business and Entrepreneurship, Birmingham, AL 35244. Offers entrepreneurship (MBA); finance (MBA); health services management (MBA); hospitality and tourism management (MBA); human resource management (MBA); international business (MBA); management (MBA); marketing (MBA). Part-time and evening/weekend programs available. Postbaccalaureate distance learning degree programs offered (no on-campus study). *Faculty:* 13 part-time/adjunct (1 woman). *Students:* Average age 40. In 2006, 6 degrees awarded. *Entrance requirements:* For master's, course work in calculus, statistics. Additional exam requirements/recommendations for international students: Required—TOEFL (minimum score 550 paper-based; 213 computer-based). *Application deadline:* Applications are processed on a rolling basis. Application fee: $75. *Expenses:* Tuition: Part-time $705 per course. *Application contact:* Betty Howell, Director of Student Affairs, 205-871-9288 Ext. 108, Fax: 205-871-9294, E-mail: bhowell@aju.edu.

Andrews University, School of Graduate Studies, School of Business, Department of Management and Marketing, Berrien Springs, MI 49104. Offers MBA, MSA. *Entrance requirements:* For master's, GMAT. Additional exam requirements/recommendations for international students: Required—TOEFL.

Angelo State University, College of Graduate Studies, College of Business and Professional Studies, Department of Management and Marketing, San Angelo, TX 76909. Offers business administration (MBA). *Accreditation:* ACBSP. Part-time and evening/weekend programs available. *Faculty:* 18 full-time (3 women). *Students:* 8 full-time (2 women), 34 part-time (19 women); includes 6 minority (1 African American, 1 Asian American or Pacific Islander, 4 Hispanic Americans), 2 international. Average age 29. 22 applicants, 77% accepted, 13 enrolled. In 2006, 4 degrees awarded. *Entrance requirements:* For master's, GMAT. Additional exam requirements/recommendations for international students: Required—TOEFL or IELTS. *Application deadline:* For fall admission, 7/15 priority date for domestic students, 6/10 for international students; for spring admission, 12/8 for domestic students, 11/1 for international students. Applications are processed on a rolling basis. Application fee: $40 ($50 for international students). Electronic applications accepted. *Expenses:* Tuition, state resident: full-time $2,340; part-time $130 per hour. Tuition, nonresident: full-time $7,290; part-time $405 per hour. Required fees: $906; $56 per hour. *Financial support:* In 2006–07, 21 students received support. Career-related internships or fieldwork, Federal Work-Study, and scholarships/grants available. Support available to part-time students. Financial award application deadline: 3/1; financial award applicants required to submit FAFSA. *Unit head:* Dr. Tom F. Badgett, Department Head, 325-942-2383 Ext. 225, E-mail: tom.badgett@angelo.edu. *Application contact:* Dr. Dan M. Khanna, Graduate Advisor, 325-942-2383 Ext. 229, Fax: 325-942-2194, E-mail: dan.khanna@angelo.edu.

Anna Maria College, Graduate Division, Program in Business Administration, Paxton, MA 01612. Offers MBA, AC. Part-time and evening/weekend programs available. *Faculty:* 1 full-time (0 women), 6 part-time/adjunct (0 women). *Students:* 6 full-time (2 women), 34 part-time (15 women); includes 3 minority (all African Americans), 4 international. Average age 37. In 2006, 26 master's, 2 other advanced degrees awarded. *Degree requirements:* For master's, capstone project. *Entrance requirements:* For master's, minimum GPA of 2.7; for AC, MBA. *Application deadline:* For fall admission, 3/1 priority date for domestic and international students; for spring admission, 11/1 priority date for domestic and international students. Applications are processed on a rolling basis. Application fee: $40. Electronic applications accepted. *Financial support:* Applicants required to submit FAFSA. *Faculty research:* Management organization. *Unit head:* Bernard Wood, Director, 508-849-3339, Fax: 508-849-3362, E-mail: bwood@annamaria.edu. *Application contact:* Janet LaPointe, Admissions Coordinator, Graduate and Continuing Education, 508-849-3234, Fax: 508-819-3362, E-mail: jlapointe@annamaria.edu.

Antioch University Los Angeles, Graduate Programs, Program in Organizational Management, Culver City, CA 90230. Offers human resource development (MA); leadership (MA); organizational development (MA). Part-time and evening/weekend programs available. *Entrance requirements:* For master's, interview. Additional exam requirements/recommendations for international students: Required—TOEFL. *Faculty research:* Systems thinking and chaos theory, technology and organizational structure, nonprofit management, power and empowerment.

Antioch University McGregor, Graduate Programs, Individualized Liberal and Professional Studies Program, Yellow Springs, OH 45387-1609. Offers liberal and professional studies (MA), including counseling, creative writing, education, film studies, liberal studies, management, modern literature, psychology, theatre, visual arts. Part-time and evening/weekend programs available. Postbaccalaureate distance learning degree programs offered (minimal on-campus study). *Faculty:* 4 full-time (2 women), 3 part-time/adjunct (all women). *Students:* Average age 41. 31 applicants, 74% accepted, 23 enrolled. In 2006, 54 degrees awarded. *Degree requirements:* For master's, thesis or alternative, registration. *Entrance requirements:* For master's, resumé, 2 letters of reference. *Application deadline:* For fall admission, 8/25 for domestic students; for winter admission, 12/5 for domestic students; for spring admission, 3/8 for domestic students. Applications are processed on a rolling basis. Application fee: $50. Electronic applications accepted. *Expenses:* Contact institution. *Financial support:* Federal Work-Study available. Financial award applicants required to submit FAFSA. *Application contact:* Seth Gordon, Enrollment Services Officer, 937-769-1800 Ext. 1825, Fax: 937-769-1804, E-mail: sgordon@mcgregor.edu.

Antioch University McGregor, Graduate Programs, Program in Management, Yellow Springs, OH 45387-1609. Offers MA. Evening/weekend programs available. *Faculty:* 2 full-time (1 woman), 2 part-time/adjunct (1 woman). *Students:* 35 full-time (21 women), 2 part-time (both women); includes 19 minority (all African Americans) Average age 38. 23 applicants, 100% accepted, 23 enrolled. In 2006, 14 degrees awarded. *Degree requirements:* For master's, registration. *Entrance requirements:* For master's, 2 letters of reference, resumé. *Application deadline:* For fall admission, 9/1 for domestic students; for winter admission, 12/10 for domestic students; for spring admission, 3/8 for domestic students. Applications are processed on a rolling basis. Application fee: $50. Electronic applications accepted. *Expenses:* Contact institution. *Financial support:* Federal Work-Study available. Financial award applicants required to submit FAFSA. *Unit head:* Michael Robinson, Director, 937-769-1877, Fax: 937-769-1805, E-mail: rrobinson@mcgregor.edu. *Application contact:* Rob McLaughlin, Enrollment Services Manager, 937-769-1816, Fax: 937-769-1804, E-mail: rmclaughlin@mcgregor.edu.

Antioch University New England, Graduate School, Department of Organization and Management, Program in Leadership and Management, Keene, NH 03431-3552. Offers MS. *Faculty:* 3 full-time (1 woman), 5 part-time/adjunct (3 women). *Students:* 39 full-time (28 women), 7 part-time (4 women). Average age 40. 22 applicants, 100% accepted, 14 enrolled. In 2006, 23 degrees awarded. *Degree requirements:* For master's, practicum. *Entrance requirements:* For master's, previous course work and work experience in organization and management. Additional exam requirements/recommendations for international students: Required—TOEFL (minimum score 600 paper-based; 250 computer-based). *Application deadline:* For fall admission, 8/1 for domestic and international students; for spring admission, 12/1 for domestic and international students. Applications are processed on a rolling basis. Application fee: $50. Electronic applications accepted. *Expenses:* Contact institution. Tuition and fees vary according to program and student level. *Financial support:* In 2006–07, 27 students received support, including 2 fellowships; career-related internships or fieldwork and Federal Work-Study also available. Financial award applicants required to submit FAFSA. *Faculty research:* Developing a collaborative CEO performance evaluation process, search conference process as change mechanism, implementing workflow designs to increase organizational competitiveness. *Application contact:* Leatrice A. Oram, Co-Director of Admissions, 800-490-3310, Fax: 603-357-0718, E-mail: admissions@antiochne.edu.

See Close-Up on page 205.

Antioch University Seattle, Graduate Programs, Center for Creative Change, Seattle, WA 98121-1814. Offers environment and community (MA); management (MS); organizational psychology (MA); strategic communications (MA); whole system design (MA). Evening/weekend programs available. Electronic applications accepted. Expenses: Contact institution.

Appalachian State University, Cratis D. Williams Graduate School, John A. Walker College of Business, Program in Business Administration, Boone, NC 28608. Offers MBA. *Accreditation:* AACSB. *Faculty:* 48 full-time (11 women). *Students:* 14 full-time (5 women), 20 part-time (6 women), 2 international. 36 applicants, 67% accepted, 22 enrolled. In 2006, 12 degrees awarded. *Degree requirements:* For master's, comprehensive exam. *Entrance requirements:* For master's, GMAT. *Application deadline:* For fall admission, 3/1 for domestic students, 1/1 for international students; for spring admission, 6/1 for international students. Applications are processed on a rolling basis. Application fee: $50. *Expenses:* Tuition, state resident: full-time $2,600; part-time $127 per hour. Tuition, nonresident: full-time $13,200; part-time $597 per hour. Required fees: $2,000; $546 per term. *Financial support:* In 2006–07, 9 research assistantships (averaging $7,000 per year) were awarded; fellowships, teaching assistantships, career-related internships or fieldwork, Federal Work-Study, scholarships/grants, and unspecified assistantships also available. Support available to part-time students. Financial award application deadline: 7/1. *Unit head:* Dr. Phillip Witmer, Director, 828-262-2922, E-mail: witmerpr@appstate.edu.

Aquinas College, School of Management, Grand Rapids, MI 49506-1799. Offers M Mgt. Part-time and evening/weekend programs available. *Faculty:* 12 full-time (5 women), 5 part-time/adjunct (1 woman). *Students:* 11 full-time (7 women), 56 part-time (34 women); includes 2 minority (1 African American, 1 American Indian/Alaska Native), 3 international. Average age 35. 28 applicants, 79% accepted, 17 enrolled. In 2006, 26 degrees awarded. *Entrance requirements:* For master's, GMAT, minimum undergraduate GPA of 2.75, 2 years of work experience. Additional exam requirements/recommendations for international students: Required—TOEFL (minimum score 550 paper-based; 213 computer-based). *Application deadline:* Applications are processed on a rolling basis. *Expenses:* Contact institution. *Financial support:* In 2006–07, 38 students received support. Scholarships/grants available. Support available to part-time students. Financial award application deadline: 3/15; financial award applicants required to submit FAFSA. *Unit head:* Cynthia VanGelderen, Dean, 616-632-2922, Fax: 616-732-4489, E-mail: vangecyn@aquinas.edu. *Application contact:* Lynn Atkins-Rykert, Executive Assistant, School of Management, 616-632-2924, Fax: 616-732-4489, E-mail: atkinlyn@aquinas.edu.

Arcadia University, Graduate Studies, Program in Business Administration, Glenside, PA 19038-3295. Offers MBA. *Accreditation:* ACBSP. *Unit head:* Dr. Jose Marrero, Director, 215-579-2789. *Application contact:* Office of Enrollment Management, 215-572-2910, Fax: 215-572-4049, E-mail: admiss@arcadia.edu.

Argosy University, Atlanta Campus, College of Business, Atlanta, GA 30328. Offers accounting (DBA); customized professional concentration (MBA, DBA); finance (MBA); healthcare administration (MBA); information systems (DBA); information systems management (MBA); international business (MBA, DBA); management (MBA, DBA); marketing (MBA, DBA). Part-time programs available. *Students:* 53 full-time (38 women), 35 part-time (28 women); includes 73 minority (66 African Americans, 3 Asian Americans or Pacific Islanders, 4 Hispanic Americans). *Degree requirements:* For master's, comprehensive exam (for some programs), registration; for doctorate, thesis/dissertation, comprehensive exam, registration. *Entrance requirements:* For master's, minimum undergraduate GPA of 3.0; for doctorate, master's degree, minimum GPA of 3.0. Additional exam requirements/recommendations for international students: Required—TOEFL. *Application deadline:* For fall admission, 7/1 priority date for domestic students, 6/1 for international students; for spring admission, 11/1 priority date for domestic students, 10/1 for international students. Applications are processed on a rolling basis. Application fee: $50. Electronic applications accepted. *Financial support:* Applicants required to submit FAFSA. *Unit head:* Dr. Robert A. Berg, Department Chair, 770-407-1042, E-mail: rberg@argosy.edu. *Application contact:* Christa Holton, Director of Admissions, 770-671-1200 Ext. 1014, Fax: 770-671-9050, E-mail: cholton@argosy.edu.

See Close-Up on page 207.

Argosy University, Chicago Campus, College of Business, Chicago, IL 60603. Offers accounting (DBA); customized professional concentration (MBA, DBA); finance (MBA); healthcare administration (MBA); information systems (DBA); information systems management (MBA); international business (MBA, DBA); management (MBA, DBA); marketing (MBA, DBA). Part-time and evening/weekend programs available. *Faculty:* 2 full-time (both women), 4 part-time/

Business Administration and Management—General

Argosy University, Chicago Campus (continued)
adjunct (3 women). *Students:* 52 full-time (30 women), 18 part-time (7 women); includes 37 minority (24 African Americans, 7 Asian Americans or Pacific Islanders, 6 Hispanic Americans). Average age 37. 32 applicants, 81% accepted, 25 enrolled. In 2006, 9 master's, 2 doctorates awarded. *Entrance requirements:* For master's and doctorate, minimum GPA of 3.0. Additional exam requirements/recommendations for international students: Required—TOEFL (minimum score 550 paper-based; 213 computer-based). *Application deadline:* For fall admission, 2/28 for domestic and international students; for spring admission, 10/30 for domestic and international students. Applications are processed on a rolling basis. Application fee: $50. Electronic applications accepted. *Financial support:* In 2006–07, 3 students received support. Scholarships/grants available. Financial award application deadline: 4/1. *Unit head:* Dr. Cynthia Scarlett, Associate Head, 800-626-4123, Fax: 212-727-7750, E-mail: cscarlett@argosy.edu. *Application contact:* Ashley Delaney, Director of Admissions, 800-626-4123, Fax: 312-777-7750, E-mail: argosyadmissions@argosy.edu.

See Close-Up on page 209.

Argosy University, Dallas Campus, College of Business, Dallas, TX 75231. Offers management (MBA). Part-time and evening/weekend programs available. *Entrance requirements:* Additional exam requirements/recommendations for international students: Required—TOEFL. *Application deadline:* For fall admission, 5/15 priority date for domestic students, 1/15 priority date for international students; for spring admission, 10/15 priority date for domestic and international students. Applications are processed on a rolling basis. Application fee: $50. Electronic applications accepted. *Financial support:* Federal Work-Study and scholarships/grants available. *Application contact:* Kara Smith, Director of Admissions, 866-954-9900, Fax: 214-378-8555, E-mail: dallasadmissions@argosy.edu.

See Close-Up on page 211.

Argosy University, Denver Campus, College of Business, Denver, CO 80203. Offers accounting (DBA); customized professional concentraion (DBA); customized professional concentration (MBA); finance (MBA); healthcare administration (MBA); information systems (DBA); information systems management (MBA); international business (MBA, DBA); management (MBA, MSM, DBA); marketing (MBA, DBA).

See Close-Up on page 213.

Argosy University, Hawai'i Campus, College of Business, Honolulu, HI 96813. Offers accounting (DBA); customized professional concentration (MBA, DBA); finance (MBA, Certificate); healthcare administration (MBA, Certificate); information systems (DBA); information systems management (MBA, Certificate); international business (MBA, DBA, Certificate); management (MBA, DBA); marketing (MBA, DBA, Certificate). Evening/weekend programs available. *Faculty:* 12 part-time/adjunct (2 women). *Students:* 3 full-time (2 women), 1 part-time; includes 2 minority (1 Asian American or Pacific Islander, 1 Hispanic American). 6 applicants, 67% accepted, 3 enrolled. *Degree requirements:* For master's, capstone project. *Entrance requirements:* For master's, minimum GPA of 3.0 in last 60 hours. Additional exam requirements/recommendations for international students: Required—TOEFL (minimum score 550 paper-based; 213 computer-based). *Application deadline:* For fall admission, 1/15 priority date for domestic students; for spring admission, 10/15 for domestic students. Applications are processed on a rolling basis. Application fee: $50. *Financial support:* Teaching assistantships, Federal Work-Study and scholarships/grants available. Support available to part-time students. *Unit head:* Lisa Parker, Interim Chair, College of Business and Information Technology, 888-323-2777, Fax: 808-536-5505, E-mail: lparker@argosy.edu. *Application contact:* Cherie Andrade, Director of Admissions, 888-323-2777, Fax: 808-536-5505, E-mail: candrade@argosy.edu.

See Close-Up on page 215.

Argosy University, Inland Empire Campus, College of Business, San Bernardino, CA 92408. Offers accounting (DBA); customized professional concentration (MBA, DBA); finance (MBA); healthcare administration (MBA); information systems (DBA); information systems management (MBA); international business (MBA, DBA); management (DBA); mangement (MBA); marketing (MBA, DBA).

See Close-Up on page 217.

Argosy University, Nashville Campus, College of Business, Franklin, TN 37067-7226. Offers accounting (DBA); customized professional concentration (DBA); information systems (DBA); international business (DBA); management (DBA); marketing (DBA). *Degree requirements:* For doctorate, thesis/dissertation, comprehensive exam.

See Close-Up on page 219.

Argosy University, Orange County Campus, College of Business, Santa Ana, CA 92704. Offers accounting (DBA, Adv C); customized professional concentration (MBA, DBA); finance (MBA, Certificate); healthcare administration (MBA, Certificate); information systems (DBA, Adv C); information systems management (MBA); international business (MBA, DBA, Adv C, Certificate); management (MBA, MSM, DBA, EDBA); mangement (Adv C); marketing (MBA, DBA, Adv C, Certificate); organizational leadership (Ed D); public administration (MBA, Certificate). Part-time and evening/weekend programs available. *Faculty:* 4 full-time (1 woman), 20 part-time/adjunct (7 women). *Students:* 163 full-time (64 women), 41 part-time (16 women). Average age 42. 72 applicants, 51 enrolled. In 2006, 6 master's, 23 doctorates awarded. *Degree requirements:* For doctorate, thesis/dissertation, preliminary and final dissertation defense, comprehensive exam. *Entrance requirements:* For master's, minimum GPA of 3.0 in final 2 years of course work, 3 letters of recommendation, resumé; for doctorate, minimum GPA of 3.0 in graduate study, 3 letters of recommendation, resumé. Additional exam requirements/recommendations for international students: Required—TOEFL. *Application deadline:* Applications are processed on a rolling basis. Application fee: $50. Electronic applications accepted. *Financial support:* Federal Work-Study, institutionally sponsored loans, and scholarships/grants available. Support available to part-time students. Financial award applicants required to submit FAFSA. *Faculty research:* Crisis management, leadership in organizations, finance, business systems. *Unit head:* Dr. Ray London, Dean, 800-716-9598, Fax: 714-437-1284, E-mail: auocadmissions@argosy.edu. *Application contact:* Mark Betz, Director of Admissions, 800-716-9598, Fax: 714-437-1697, E-mail: mbetz@argosy.edu.

See Close-Up on page 221.

Argosy University, Phoenix Campus, College of Business, Phoenix, AZ 85021. Offers accounting (DBA); customized professional concentration (MBA, DBA); finance (MBA); healthcare administration (MBA); information systems (DBA); information systems management (MBA); international business (MBA, DBA); management (MBA, DBA); marketing (MBA, DBA). Part-time and evening/weekend programs available. *Faculty:* 1 full-time (0 women). *Students:* 7 full-time (4 women); includes 2 minority (1 African American, 1 Hispanic American). *Entrance requirements:* For doctorate, master's degree. Additional exam requirements/recommendations for international students: Required—TOEFL (minimum score 550 paper-based; 213 computer-based). Application fee: $50. *Financial support:* In 2006–07, 2 students received support. Federal Work-Study, institutionally sponsored loans, and scholarships/grants available. Support available to part-time students. Financial award applicants required to submit FAFSA. *Unit head:* Dr. Gary Berg, Program Chair, 866-216-2777, Fax: 602-216-2601. *Application contact:* Andy Hughes, Director of Admissions, 866-216-2777 Ext. 3110, Fax: 602-216-2601, E-mail: ahughes@argosyu.edu.

See Close-Up on page 223.

Argosy University, San Diego Campus, College of Business, San Diego, CA 92108. Offers accounting (DBA); customized professional concentration (MBA, DBA); finance (MBA); information systems (DBA); information systems management (MBA); international business (MBA, DBA); management (MBA, MSM, DBA); marketing (MBA, DBA); public administration (MBA).

See Close-Up on page 225.

Argosy University, San Francisco Bay Area Campus, College of Business, Point Richmond, CA 94804-3547. Offers accounting (DBA); corporate compliance (MBA); customized professional concentration (MBA, DBA); finance (MBA); healthcare administration (MBA); information systems (DBA); information systems management (MBA); international business (MBA, DBA); management (MBA, MSM, DBA); marketing (MBA, DBA). Part-time and evening/weekend programs available. *Faculty:* 2 full-time (0 women), 9 part-time/adjunct (0 women). *Students:* 29 full-time (8 women), 9 part-time (2 women); includes 30 minority (5 African Americans, 24 Asian Americans or Pacific Islanders, 1 Hispanic American). 21 applicants, 76% accepted, 13 enrolled. In 2006, 3 master's, 2 doctorates awarded. *Degree requirements:* For master's, capstone project; for doctorate, thesis/dissertation, comprehensive exam, registration. *Entrance requirements:* For master's, minimum GPA of 3.0; for doctorate, MBA or minimum GPA of 3.0. Additional exam requirements/recommendations for international students: Required—TOEFL (minimum score 550 paper-based; 213 computer-based). *Application deadline:* For fall admission, 7/1 priority date for domestic and international students; for winter admission, 11/1 priority date for domestic and international students; for spring admission, 4/1 priority date for domestic and international students. Applications are processed on a rolling basis. Application fee: $50. Electronic applications accepted. *Financial support:* Federal Work-Study and scholarships/grants available. Support available to part-time students. Financial award applicants required to submit FAFSA. *Unit head:* Dr. Anthony Martinez, Department Chair, Business and Information Technology, 866-215-0277, Fax: 510-215-0299, E-mail: amartinez@argosy.edu. *Application contact:* John Vincent Stofan, Director of Admissions, 866-215-2727 Ext. 205, Fax: 510-215-0299, E-mail: jstofan@argosyu.edu.

See Close-Up on page 227.

Argosy University, Santa Monica Campus, College of Business, Santa Monica, CA 90405. Offers accounting (DBA); customized professional concentration (MBA, DBA); finance (MBA); healthcare administration (MBA); information systems (DBA); information systems management (MBA); international business (MBA, DBA); management (MBA, MS, MSM, DBA); marketing (MBA, DBA).

See Close-Up on page 229.

Argosy University, Sarasota Campus, College of Business, Sarasota, FL 34235-8246. Offers accounting (DBA, Adv C); customized professional concentration (MBA, DBA); finance (MBA, Certificate); healtcare administration (Certificate); healthcare administration (MBA); information systems (DBA, Adv C); information systems management (MBA, Certificate); international business (MBA, DBA, Adv C, Certificate); management (MBA, MSM, DBA); mangement (Adv C); marketing (MBA, DBA, Adv C, Certificate). Part-time and evening/weekend programs available. Postbaccalaureate distance learning degree programs offered (minimal on-campus study). *Faculty:* 6 full-time (3 women), 13 part-time/adjunct (5 women). *Students:* 71 applicants, 92% accepted, 64 enrolled. In 2006, 7 master's, 30 doctorates awarded. *Degree requirements:* For doctorate, thesis/dissertation, comprehensive exam. *Entrance requirements:* For master's, minimum GPA of 3.0; for doctorate, minimum undergraduate GPA of 3.0. Additional exam requirements/recommendations for international students: Required—TOEFL. *Application deadline:* Applications are processed on a rolling basis. Application fee: $50. Electronic applications accepted. *Financial support:* Federal Work-Study and scholarships/grants available. Support available to part-time students. Financial award application deadline: 4/1; financial award applicants required to submit FAFSA. *Unit head:* Dr. Kathleen Cornett, Dean, 800-331-5995, Fax: 941-379-9464, E-mail: kcornett@argosy.edu. *Application contact:* Admissions Representative, 800-331-5995 Ext. 221, Fax: 941-379-5964.

See Close-Up on page 231.

Argosy University, Schaumburg Campus, College of Business, Schaumburg, IL 60173-5403. Offers accounting (DBA, Adv C); corporate compliance (MBA); customized professional concentration (MBA, DBA); finance (MBA, Certificate); healthcare administration (MBA, Certificate); information systems (DBA, Adv C); information systems management (MBA, Certificate); international business (MBA, DBA, Adv C, Certificate); management (MBA, DBA, Adv C, Certificate); marketing (MBA, DBA, Adv C, Certificate). Part-time and evening/weekend programs available. *Faculty:* 1 (woman) full-time, 7 part-time/adjunct (0 women). *Students:* 36 full-time, 23 part-time. 13 applicants, 69% accepted, 9 enrolled. In 2006, 5 master's, 4 doctorates awarded. *Degree requirements:* For doctorate, thesis/dissertation, comprehensive exam. *Entrance requirements:* For master's and doctorate, minimum GPA of 3.0. Additional exam requirements/recommendations for international students: Required—TOEFL. *Application deadline:* For fall admission, 3/15 priority date for domestic and international students; for spring admission, 10/15 priority date for domestic and international students. Applications are processed on a rolling basis. Application fee: $50. Electronic applications accepted. *Expenses:* Contact institution. *Financial support:* Federal Work-Study and scholarships/grants available. *Unit head:* Dr. Harriet Kandelman, Dean, 866-290-2777, Fax: 847-548-6159, E-mail: agrosyadmissions@argosy.edu. *Application contact:* Jamal Scott, Director of Admissions, 847-598-6159, Fax: 630-598-6191, E-mail: jscott@argosy.edu.

See Close-Up on page 233.

Argosy University, Seattle Campus, College of Business, Seattle, WA 98121. Offers accounting (DBA); customized professional concentration (MBA, DBA); finance (MBA); healthcare administration (MBA); information systems (DBA); information systems management (MBA); international business (MBA, DBA); management (MSM, DBA); mangement (MBA); marketing (MBA, DBA). Part-time and evening/weekend programs available. *Students:* 1 applicant, 100% accepted, 1 enrolled. In 2006, 1 degree awarded. *Degree requirements:* For master's, capstone experience; for doctorate, thesis/dissertation, comprehensive exam (for some programs). *Entrance requirements:* For master's, minimum GPA of 3.0 in last 2 years or cumulative of 2.7; for doctorate, minimum GPA of 3.0. Additional exam requirements/recommendations for international students: Required—TOEFL (minimum score 550 paper-based; 213 computer-based). *Application deadline:* For fall admission, 4/15 priority date for domestic students, 4/15 for international students; for winter admission, 10/15 priority date for domestic students. Applications are processed on a rolling basis. Application fee: $50. Electronic applications accepted. *Expenses:* Contact institution. *Financial support:* Federal Work-Study and unspecified assistantships available. Support available to part-time students. Financial award applicants required to submit FAFSA. *Unit head:* Dr. Kylene Quinn, Chair, 206-393-3543, Fax: 206-283-5777, E-mail: kquinn@argosy.edu. *Application contact:* Heather Simpson, Director of Admissions, 866-283-4500, Fax: 206-283-5777, E-mail: hsimpson@argosy.edu.

See Close-Up on page 235.

Argosy University, Tampa Campus, College of Business, Tampa, FL 33614. Offers accounting (DBA); customized professional concentration (MBA, DBA); finance (MBA, Certificate); healthcare administration (MBA, Certificate); information systems (DBA); information systems management (MBA); international business (MBA, DBA, Certificate); management (MBA, MSM, DBA); marketing (MBA, DBA, Certificate); public administration (MBA). *Entrance requirements:* For doctorate, minimum GPA of 3.0. *Unit head:* Dr. Andrew Ghillyer, Dean, 813-393-5270, E-mail: aghillyer@argosy.edu.

See Close-Up on page 237.

Argosy University, Twin Cities Campus, College of Business, Eagan, MN 55121. Offers accounting (DBA); corporate compliance (MBA); customized professional certification (DBA); customized professional concentration (MBA); finance (MBA); healthcare administration (MBA); information systems (DBA); information systems management (MBA); international business (MBA, DBA); management (MBA, MSM, DBA, EDBA); marketing (MBA, DBA). Part-time and evening/weekend programs available. *Faculty:* 1 (woman) full-time, 20 part-time/adjunct (6 women). *Students:* 47 full-time (23 women), 20 part-time (11 women); includes 21 minority (10 African Americans, 1 American Indian/Alaska Native, 9 Asian Americans or Pacific Islanders, 1 Hispanic American). Average age 39. 72 applicants, 76% accepted, 45 enrolled. In 2006, 6 degrees awarded. *Degree requirements:* For doctorate, thesis/dissertation, comprehensive exam. *Entrance requirements:* For master's, 3 letters of recommendation, bachelor's degree in a related field, minimum undergraduate GPA of 3.0, resumé; for doctorate, 3 letters of recommendation, master's degree in a related field, minimum GPA of 3.0, resumé. Additional exam requirements/recommendations for international students: Required—TOEFL (minimum score 550 paper-based; 213 computer-based). *Application deadline:* For fall admission, 5/15 priority date for domestic students, 5/15 for international students; for spring admission, 10/15 priority date for domestic students, 10/15 for international students. Applications are processed on a rolling basis. Application fee: $50. Electronic applications accepted. *Financial support:* In 2006–07, 3 fellowships with partial tuition reimbursements, 3 teaching assistantships with partial tuition reimbursements were awarded; Federal Work-Study and scholarships/grants also available. Financial award applicants required to submit FAFSA. *Unit head:* Dr. Paula King, Department Head, 651-846-3377, E-mail: pking@argosy.edu. *Application contact:* Jennifer Radke, 2nd Director of Graduate Admissions, 651-846-3300, Fax: 651-994-7954, E-mail: tcadmissions@argosy.edu.

See Close-Up on page 239.

Argosy University, Washington DC Campus, College of Business, Arlington, VA 22209. Offers accounting (DBA); customized professional concentration (MBA, DBA); finance (MBA); healthcare administration (MBA); information systems (DBA); information systems management (MBA); international business (MBA, DBA); international business marketing (Graduate Certificate); management (MBA, DBA); marketing (MBA, DBA). *Faculty:* 1 full-time (0 women), 5 part-time/adjunct (2 women). *Students:* 5 full-time (4 women), 4 part-time (1 woman); includes 4 minority (3 African Americans, 1 Asian American or Pacific Islander). 21 applicants, 86% accepted. *Degree requirements:* For master's, thesis (for some programs), comprehensive exam (for some programs); for doctorate, thesis/dissertation, comprehensive exam. *Entrance requirements:* For master's and doctorate, minimum GPA of 3.0. Additional exam requirements/recommendations for international students: Required—TOEFL (minimum score 550 paper-based; 213 computer-based). *Application deadline:* For fall admission, 6/15 priority date for domestic students; for spring admission, 10/15 priority date for domestic students. Application fee: $50. *Financial support:* Federal Work-Study and scholarships/grants available. Financial award applicants required to submit FAFSA. *Unit head:* Dr. Colleen Logan, Academic Affairs Officer, 866-703-2777, Fax: 703-521-5850, E-mail: dcadmissions@argosy.edu. *Application contact:* Emily Peck, Director of Admissions, 866-703-2777 Ext. 5851, Fax: 703-526-5850, E-mail: dcadmissions@argosy.edu.

See Close-Up on page 241.

Arizona State University, Division of Graduate Studies, W.P. Carey School of Business, Program in Business Administration, Tempe, AZ 85287. Offers accountancy (PhD); business administration (MBA); finance (PhD); health services research (PhD); information management (PhD); management (PhD); marketing (PhD); supply chain management (PhD); JD/MBA; MBA/M Arch; MBA/MHSM. MBA/MIM offered jointly with Thunderbird, The American Graduate School of International Management and Groupe Ecole Supéieure de Commerce, Toulouse, France. *Accreditation:* AACSB. *Degree requirements:* For master's, thesis optional; for doctorate, thesis/dissertation. *Entrance requirements:* For master's, GMAT.

Arizona State University at the West campus, School of Global Management and Leadership, MBA Program, Phoenix, AZ 85069-7100. Offers MBA. *Accreditation:* AACSB. Part-time and evening/weekend programs available. *Faculty:* 13 full-time (3 women), 1 part-time/adjunct (0 women). *Students:* 27 full-time (12 women), 134 part-time (48 women); includes 27 minority (4 African Americans, 8 Asian Americans or Pacific Islanders, 15 Hispanic Americans), 9 international. Average age 33. 71 applicants, 70% accepted, 43 enrolled. In 2006, 54 degrees awarded. *Median time to degree:* Master's–2.5 years full-time, 3 years part-time. *Entrance requirements:* For master's, GMAT, 2 letters of recommendation, minimum undergraduate GPA of 3.0. Additional exam requirements/recommendations for international students: Required—TOEFL (minimum score 550 paper-based; 213 computer-based; 83 iBT), IELTS (minimum score 7). *Application deadline:* For fall admission, 6/1 for domestic students, 5/1 for international students; for spring admission, 11/1 for domestic students, 10/1 for international students. Applications are processed on a rolling basis. Application fee: $50. Electronic applications accepted. *Expenses:* Tuition, state resident: full-time $5,930. Tuition, nonresident: full-time $16,516. Tuition and fees vary according to course load. *Financial support:* In 2006–07, 7 research assistantships with partial tuition reimbursements (averaging $6,400 per year) were awarded; fellowships, career-related internships or fieldwork, scholarships/grants, tuition waivers (full and partial), and unspecified assistantships also available. Financial award applicants required to submit FAFSA. *Faculty research:* Risk management, information security, cost measurement and allocation, auditing, tax compliance and policy. *Unit head:* Dr. Pierre Balthazard, Director, 602-543-6120, Fax: 602-543-6249, E-mail: pierreb@asu.edu. *Application contact:* Doris Fagin, Student Services, 602-543-6239, Fax: 602-543-6249, E-mail: dons.fagin@asu.edu.

Arkansas State University, Graduate School, College of Business, Department of Economics and Finance, Jonesboro, State University, AR 72467. Offers business administration (EMBA, MBA). *Accreditation:* AACSB. Part-time programs available. *Faculty:* 6 full-time (0 women), 1 part-time/adjunct (0 women). *Students:* 47 full-time (22 women), 104 part-time (48 women); includes 25 minority (21 African Americans, 1 American Indian/Alaska Native, 2 Asian Americans or Pacific Islanders, 1 Hispanic American), 20 international. Average age 29. 109 applicants, 68% accepted, 60 enrolled. In 2006, 60 degrees awarded. *Degree requirements:* For master's, thesis or alternative, comprehensive exam. *Entrance requirements:* For master's, GMAT, appropriate bachelor's degree, letters of reference, official transcript. Additional exam requirements/recommendations for international students: Required—TOEFL (minimum score 213 computer-based). *Application deadline:* Applications are processed on a rolling basis. Application fee: $30 ($40 for international students). Electronic applications accepted. *Expenses:* Contact institution. *Financial support:* Career-related internships or fieldwork, scholarships/grants, and unspecified assistantships available. Financial award application deadline: 7/1; financial award applicants required to submit FAFSA. *Unit head:* Dr. Jim Washam, Chair, 870-972-2280, Fax: 870-972-3863, E-mail: jwasham@astate.edu.

Arkansas State University, Graduate School, College of Business, Department of Management and Marketing, Jonesboro, State University, AR 72467. Offers business administration (SCCT); business education (SCCT). *Accreditation:* NCATE. Part-time programs available. *Faculty:* 7 full-time (2 women). *Students:* 14 applicants, 86% accepted, 0 enrolled. In 2006, 1 degree awarded. *Degree requirements:* For SCCT, comprehensive exam. *Entrance requirements:* For degree, GRE General Test or MAT, interview, master's degree, official transcript. Additional exam requirements/recommendations for international students: Required—TOEFL (minimum score 213 computer-based). *Application deadline:* Applications are processed on a rolling basis. Application fee: $30 ($40 for international students). Electronic applications accepted. *Expenses:* Contact institution. *Financial support:* Career-related internships or fieldwork, scholarships/grants, and unspecified assistantships available. Financial award application deadline: 7/1; financial award applicants required to submit FAFSA. *Unit head:* Dr. Gail Hudson, Chair, 870-972-3430, Fax: 870-972-3833, E-mail: ghud@astate.edu.

Ashland University, Dauch College of Business and Economics, Ashland, OH 44805-3702. Offers MBA. *Accreditation:* ACBSP. Part-time and evening/weekend programs available. *Faculty:* 16 full-time (4 women), 20 part-time/adjunct (6 women). *Students:* 278 full-time (129 women), 335 part-time (140 women); includes 77 minority (65 African Americans, 2 American Indian/Alaska Native, 4 Asian Americans or Pacific Islanders, 6 Hispanic Americans), 28 international. Average age 34. In 2006, 218 degrees awarded. *Degree requirements:* For master's, thesis optional. *Entrance requirements:* For master's, 2 years of full-time work experience. Additional exam requirements/recommendations for international students: Required—TOEFL. *Application deadline:* For fall admission, 8/1 priority date for domestic students; for spring admission, 12/1 priority date for domestic students. Applications are processed on a rolling basis. Application fee: $30. Electronic applications accepted. *Expenses:* Contact institution. Tuition and fees vary according to degree level and program. *Financial support:* In 2006–07, 189 students received support. Tuition waivers (partial) and unspecified assistantships available. Financial award application deadline: 4/15; financial award applicants required to submit FAFSA. *Faculty research:* Human resource management, statistical analysis, global business issues, organizational development, government and business. *Unit head:* Dr. Beverly Heimann, Chair, 419-289-5216, E-mail: bheimann@ashland.edu. *Application contact:* Stephen W. Krispinsky, Executive Director of MBA Program, 419-289-5236, Fax: 419-289-5910, E-mail: skrispin@ashland.edu.

Aspen University, Program in Business Administration, Denver, CO 80246. Offers business administration (MBA); information management (MBA); project management (MBA, Certificate). Postbaccalaureate distance learning degree programs offered (no on-campus study). Electronic applications accepted.

Assumption College, Graduate School, Department of Business Studies, Worcester, MA 01609-1296. Offers business administration (MBA, CAGS). Part-time and evening/weekend programs available. *Faculty:* 7 full-time (2 women), 8 part-time/adjunct (2 women). *Students:* 15 full-time (7 women), 137 part-time (74 women); includes 17 minority (8 African Americans, 7 Asian Americans or Pacific Islanders, 2 Hispanic Americans), 4 international. Average age 27. 86 applicants, 97% accepted. In 2006, 27 degrees awarded. *Entrance requirements:* For master's and CAGS, 3 letters of recommendation, resumé, essay. Additional exam requirements/recommendations for international students: Required—TOEFL (minimum score 540 paper-based; 200 computer-based), IELTS (minimum score 6). *Application deadline:* For fall admission, 6/1 priority date for domestic students, 5/1 priority date for international students; for spring admission, 11/1 priority date for domestic students, 10/1 priority date for international students. Applications are processed on a rolling basis. Application fee: $30. Electronic applications accepted. *Financial support:* In 2006–07, 29 students received support. Application deadline: 6/1; *Faculty research:* Workplace diversity, dynamics of team interaction, utilization of leased employees. *Unit head:* Dr. Jeffrey Hunter, Director, 508-767-7246, Fax: 508-767-7252, E-mail: jhunter@assumption.edu. *Application contact:* Adrian O. Dumas, Director of Graduate Enrollment Management and Services, 508-767-7365, Fax: 508-767-7030, E-mail: adumas@assumption.edu.

Athabasca University, Centre for Innovative Management, Athabasca, AB T9S 3A3, Canada. Offers business administration (MBA); information technology management (MBA), including policing concentration; management (GDM); project management (MBA, GDM). Part-time and evening/weekend programs available. Postbaccalaureate distance learning degree programs offered (no on-campus study). *Faculty:* 11 full-time (7 women), 63 part-time/adjunct (18 women). *Students:* Average age 39. 264 applicants, 82% accepted, 184 enrolled. In 2006, 228 degrees awarded. *Degree requirements:* For master's, thesis or alternative, applied project. *Entrance requirements:* For master's, 3 -8 years of managerial experience, 3 years with undergraduate degree, 5 years managerial experience with professional designation, 8-10 years management experience (on exception). *Application deadline:* For fall admission, 6/15 for domestic and international students; for winter admission, 10/15 for domestic and international students; for spring admission, 2/15 for domestic and international students. Applications are processed on a rolling basis. Application fee: $165. Electronic applications accepted. *Expenses:* Contact institution. *Financial support:* In 2006–07, 34 students received support. Scholarships/grants available. *Faculty research:* Human resources, project management, operations research, information technology management, corporate stewardship, energy management. *Unit head:* Dr. Lindsay Redpath, Executive Director, 780-459-1144, Fax: 780-459-2093, E-mail: lindsayr@athabascau.ca. *Application contact:* Shannon LaRose, Customer Service Representative, 800-561-4650, Fax: 800-561-4660, E-mail: cimoffice@athabascau.ca.

Auburn University, Graduate School, College of Business, Department of Management, Auburn University, AL 36849. Offers human resource management (PhD); management (MS, PhD); management information systems (MMIS, PhD). *Accreditation:* AACSB. Part-time programs available. *Faculty:* 27 full-time (4 women). *Students:* 27 full-time (6 women), 22 part-time (7 women); includes 5 minority (3 African Americans, 2 Asian Americans or Pacific Islanders), 6 international. Average age 32. 54 applicants, 35% accepted, 12 enrolled. In 2006, 17 master's, 8 doctorates awarded. *Degree requirements:* For master's, thesis (for some programs); for doctorate, thesis/dissertation. *Entrance requirements:* For master's, GMAT, GRE General Test (MS); for doctorate, GMAT, GRE General Test. Additional exam requirements/recommendations for international students: Required—TOEFL. *Application deadline:* For fall admission, 7/7 for domestic students; for spring admission, 11/24 for domestic students. Applications are processed on a rolling basis. Application fee: $25 ($50 for international students). Electronic applications accepted. *Expenses:* Tuition, state resident: full-time $5,000. Tuition, nonresident: full-time $15,000. Required fees: $416. Tuition and fees vary according to program. *Financial support:* Teaching assistantships, Federal Work-Study available. Support available to part-time students. Financial award application deadline: 3/15. *Unit head:* Dr. Sharon Oswald, Head, 334-844-4071. *Application contact:* Dr. Joe Pittman, Interim Dean of the Graduate School, 334-844-4700.

Auburn University, Graduate School, College of Business, Program in Business Administration, Auburn University, AL 36849. Offers MBA. *Accreditation:* AACSB. Part-time programs available. *Faculty:* 70 full-time (10 women). *Students:* 59 full-time (21 women), 286 part-time (72 women); includes 40 minority (16 African Americans, 1 American Indian/Alaska Native, 14 Asian Americans or Pacific Islanders, 9 Hispanic Americans), 12 international. Average age 33. 375 applicants, 56% accepted, 138 enrolled. In 2006, 149 degrees awarded. *Entrance requirements:* For master's, GMAT. *Application deadline:* For fall admission, 7/7 for domestic students; for spring admission, 11/24 for domestic students. Applications are processed on a rolling basis. Application fee: $25 ($50 for international students). Electronic applications accepted. *Expenses:* Tuition, state resident: full-time $5,000. Tuition, nonresident: full-time $15,000. Required fees: $416. Tuition and fees vary according to program. *Financial support:* Federal Work-Study available. Support available to part-time students. Financial award application deadline: 3/15. *Unit head:* Dr. Daniel M. Gropper, Director, 334-844-4060. *Application contact:* Dr. Joe Pittman, Interim Dean of the Graduate School, 334-844-4700.

Auburn University Montgomery, School of Business, Montgomery, AL 36124-4023. Offers MBA. *Accreditation:* AACSB. Part-time and evening/weekend programs available. *Faculty:* 22 full-time (3 women). *Students:* 51 full-time (28 women), 123 part-time (63 women); includes 55 minority (39 African Americans, 9 Asian Americans or Pacific Islanders, 7 Hispanic Americans). Average age 29. In 2006, 94 degrees awarded. *Degree requirements:* For master's, comprehensive exam. *Entrance requirements:* For master's, GMAT. *Application deadline:* Applications are processed on a rolling basis. Application fee: $25. Electronic applications accepted. *Financial support:* Research assistantships, career-related internships or fieldwork and scholarships/grants available. Support available to part-time students. Financial award application deadline: 3/1; financial award applicants required to submit FAFSA. *Unit head:* Dr. Jane Goodson, Dean, 334-244-3478, Fax: 334-244-3792, E-mail: jgoodson@mail.aum.edu.

Augsburg College, Program in Business Administration, Minneapolis, MN 55454-1351. Offers MBA. Evening/weekend programs available. *Faculty:* 2 full-time (1 woman), 5 part-time/adjunct (2 women). *Students:* 289 full-time (133 women), 9 part-time (2 women); includes 23 minority (11 African Americans, 1 American Indian/Alaska Native, 9 Asian Americans or Pacific Islanders, 2 Hispanic Americans), 5 international. Average age 34. 715 applicants, 13% accepted, 85 enrolled. *Application deadline:* For fall admission, 8/15 priority date for domestic students; for winter admission, 12/15 priority date for domestic students; for spring admission, 3/25 priority date for domestic students. Applications are processed on a rolling basis. Application fee: $35. Electronic applications accepted. *Expenses:* Tuition: Full-time $10,584; part-time $1,764 per course. Required fees: $300; $35 per course. Tuition and fees vary according to

Business Administration and Management—General

Augsburg College (continued)
program. *Unit head:* Dr. Robert Kramarczuk, Director, 612-330-1606, E-mail: kramarc@augsburg.edu. *Application contact:* Mike Bilden, Graduate Recruiter, 612-330-1434, E-mail: bilden@augsburg.edu.

Augusta State University, Graduate Studies, College of Business Administration, Augusta, GA 30904-2200. Offers MBA. *Accreditation:* AACSB. Part-time and evening/weekend programs available. *Faculty:* 9 full-time (6 women). *Students:* 31 full-time (16 women), 64 part-time (22 women); includes 20 minority (12 African Americans, 6 Asian Americans or Pacific Islanders, 2 Hispanic Americans). Average age 30. 44 applicants, 86% accepted, 28 enrolled. In 2006, 31 degrees awarded. *Entrance requirements:* For master's, GMAT. *Application deadline:* For fall admission, 7/15 priority date for domestic students, 7/1 for international students; for spring admission, 12/1 priority date for domestic students, 11/15 for international students. Applications are processed on a rolling basis. Application fee: $20. *Expenses:* Tuition, state resident: full-time $3,044; part-time $127 per credit hour. Tuition, nonresident: full-time $12,172; part-time $508 per credit hour. *Financial support:* Research assistantships with partial tuition reimbursements, Federal Work-Study and institutionally sponsored loans available. Support available to part-time students. Financial award application deadline: 4/15; financial award applicants required to submit FAFSA. *Unit head:* Dr. Marc D Miller, Dean, 706-737-1418, Fax: 706-667-4064, E-mail: mmiller@aug.edu. *Application contact:* Dr. Todd A Schultz, Acting Associate Dean, 706-737-1562, Fax: 706-667-4064, E-mail: tschultz@aug.edu.

Aurora University, College of Professional Studies, Dunham School of Business, Aurora, IL 60506-4892. Offers MBA. Part-time and evening/weekend programs available. *Faculty:* 6 full-time (0 women), 12 part-time/adjunct (4 women). *Students:* 27 full-time (15 women), 92 part-time (48 women); includes 23 minority (13 African Americans, 2 Asian Americans or Pacific Islanders, 8 Hispanic Americans), 1 international. Average age 36. 46 applicants, 100% accepted, 33 enrolled. In 2006, 48 degrees awarded. *Entrance requirements:* For master's, minimum GPA of 2.75, 2 years of work experience. Additional exam requirements/recommendations for international students: Required—TOEFL (minimum score 550 paper-based; 213 computer-based). *Application deadline:* For fall admission, 8/25 priority date for domestic students. Applications are processed on a rolling basis. Application fee: $25. Electronic applications accepted. *Expenses: Contact institution.* Tuition and fees vary according to campus/location and program. *Financial support:* In 2006–07, 43 students received support; fellowships, research assistantships, teaching assistantships, Federal Work-Study and scholarships/grants available. Support available to part-time students. Financial award application deadline: 4/15; financial award applicants required to submit FAFSA. *Unit head:* Dr. Shawn Green, Director, 630-844-5527, Fax: 630-844-7830, E-mail: sgreen@aurora.edu. *Application contact:* Donna DeSpain, Dean of Adult and Graduate Studies, 800-742-5281, Fax: 630-844-5535, E-mail: auadmission@aurora.edu.

Austin Peay State University, College of Graduate Studies, College of Professional Programs and Social Sciences, School of Business, Clarksville, TN 37044. Offers management (MS). Part-time and evening/weekend programs available. Postbaccalaureate distance learning degree programs offered. *Faculty:* 5 full-time (1 woman), 1 (woman) part-time/adjunct. *Students:* 17 full-time (9 women), 66 part-time (29 women); includes 25 minority (23 African Americans, 1 Asian American or Pacific Islander, 1 Hispanic American), 4 international. Average age 35. In 2006, 50 degrees awarded. *Entrance requirements:* For master's, GMAT, minimum GPA of 2.5, 3 letters of recommendation. Additional exam requirements/recommendations for international students: Required—TOEFL (minimum score 500 paper-based; 173 computer-based). *Application deadline:* For fall admission, 7/31 priority date for domestic students; for spring admission, 12/17 priority date for domestic students. Applications are processed on a rolling basis. Application fee: $25. Electronic applications accepted. *Expenses:* Tuition, state resident: full-time $5,138; part-time $272 per credit hour. Tuition, nonresident: full-time $14,832; part-time $693 per credit hour. Required fees: $1,009. *Financial support:* In 2006–07, research assistantships (averaging $10,270 per year); career-related internships or fieldwork, Federal Work-Study, institutionally sponsored loans, scholarships/grants, and unspecified assistantships also available. Support available to part-time students. Financial award application deadline: 3/1; financial award applicants required to submit FAFSA. *Unit head:* Dr. William Rayburn, Director, 931-221-7674, Fax: 931-221-7355, E-mail: rayburnw@apsu.edu.

Averett University, Program in Business Administration, Danville, VA 24541-3692. Offers MBA. Part-time and evening/weekend programs available. *Faculty:* 12 full-time (3 women), 37 part-time/adjunct (11 women). *Students:* 202 full-time (136 women), 372 part-time (225 women); includes 238 minority (207 African Americans, 4 American Indian/Alaska Native, 13 Asian Americans or Pacific Islanders, 14 Hispanic Americans). Average age 38. 41 applicants, 100% accepted, 40 enrolled. In 2006, 210 degrees awarded. *Degree requirements:* For master's, thesis or alternative, comprehensive exam, registration. *Entrance requirements:* For master's, 3 letters of recommendation, 3 years of work experience, minimum undergraduate GPA of 3.0, resumé. Additional exam requirements/recommendations for international students: Required—TOEFL (minimum score 600 paper-based; 250 computer-based). *Application deadline:* Applications are processed on a rolling basis. Application fee: $50. *Expenses: Contact institution. Financial support:* In 2006–07, 187 students received support. Federal Work-Study and scholarships/grants available. Financial award application deadline: 4/1; financial award applicants required to submit FAFSA. Total annual research expenditures: $6,000. *Unit head:* Dr. Fred Bolton, Acting Dean, 804-673-9675, Fax: 434-799-0658, E-mail: fbolton@averett.edu. *Application contact:* Katherine Pappas-Smith, Marketing and Enrollment Manager, 434-791-5844, Fax: 434-791-5850, E-mail: kapappas@averett.edu.

Avila University, School of Business, Kansas City, MO 64145-1698. Offers accounting (MBA); finance (MBA); general management (MBA); health care administration (MBA); international business (MBA); management information systems (MBA); marketing (MBA). Part-time and evening/weekend programs available. *Faculty:* 8 full-time (4 women), 17 part-time/adjunct (4 women). *Students:* 31 full-time (19 women), 165 part-time (96 women); includes 18 minority (14 African Americans, 1 American Indian/Alaska Native, 3 Hispanic Americans), 16 international. Average age 32. 77 applicants, 81% accepted, 62 enrolled. In 2006, 54 degrees awarded. *Degree requirements:* For master's, capstone course. *Entrance requirements:* For master's, GMAT, minimum GPA of 3.0. Additional exam requirements/recommendations for international students: Required—TOEFL (minimum score 550 paper-based). *Application deadline:* For fall admission, 7/30 priority date for domestic students; for winter admission, 11/30 priority date for domestic students; for spring admission, 2/28 priority date for domestic students. Applications are processed on a rolling basis. Application fee: $20. Electronic applications accepted. *Expenses:* Tuition: Full-time $7,470; part-time $415 per credit. *Financial support:* In 2006–07, 78 students received support. Career-related internships or fieldwork available. Support available to part-time students. Financial award applicants required to submit FAFSA. *Faculty research:* Leadership characteristics, financial hedging, group dynamics. *Unit head:* Dr. Richard Woodall, Dean, 816-501-3798, Fax: 816-501-2463. *Application contact:* JoAnna Giffin, MBA Admissions Director, 816-501-3601, Fax: 816-501-2463, E-mail: joanna.giffin@avila.edu.

Azusa Pacific University, School of Business and Management, Program in Business Administration, Azusa, CA 91702-7000. Offers MBA. *Students:* 22 full-time (9 women), 112 part-time (40 women); includes 43 minority (6 African Americans, 1 American Indian/Alaska Native, 10 Asian Americans or Pacific Islanders, 26 Hispanic Americans), 22 international. In 2006, 45 degrees awarded. *Expenses:* Tuition: Part-time $475 per credit.

Babson College, F. W. Olin Graduate School of Business, Wellesley, Babson Park, MA 02457-0310. Offers business administration (MBA). *Accreditation:* AACSB. Part-time and evening/weekend programs available. Postbaccalaureate distance learning degree programs offered (minimal on-campus study). *Faculty:* 137 full-time (37 women), 28 part-time/adjunct (3 women). *Students:* 414 full-time (107 women), 1,169 part-time (331 women); includes 189 minority (21 African Americans, 3 American Indian/Alaska Native, 138 Asian Americans or Pacific Islanders, 27 Hispanic Americans), 288 international. Average age 29. 580 applicants, 58% accepted, 166 enrolled. In 2006, 604 degrees awarded. *Entrance requirements:* For master's, GMAT, 2 years of work experience, resumé, letters of recommendation. Additional exam requirements/recommendations for international students: Required—TOEFL (minimum score 600 paper-based). *Application deadline:* For fall admission, 4/15 priority date for domestic students. Applications are processed on a rolling basis. Application fee: $100. Electronic applications accepted. *Expenses:* Tuition: Full-time $35,110. Required fees: $1,140. Full-time tuition and fees vary according to program. *Financial support:* In 2006–07, 54 fellowships (averaging $32,810 per year), 18 research assistantships (averaging $6,000 per year) were awarded; career-related internships or fieldwork, Federal Work-Study, scholarships/grants, tuition waivers (partial), and unspecified assistantships also available. Financial award application deadline: 4/15; financial award applicants required to submit FAFSA. *Faculty research:* Entrepreneurship, innovation and quality management, global management, e-commerce marketing, leadership and change management. *Unit head:* Mark P. Rice, Dean, 781-239-4542, Fax: 781-239-4194. *Application contact:* Martha Snelling, Admission Services Team, 781-239-4317, Fax: 781-239-4194, E-mail: mbaadmission@babson.edu.

Baker College Center for Graduate Studies, Programs in Business, Flint, MI 48507-9843. Offers accounting (MBA); computer information systems (MBA); finance (MBA); general business (MBA); health and recreation services management (MBA); health care management (MBA); human resource management (MBA); industrial management (MBA); international business (MBA); leadership (MBA); marketing (MBA). MBA in health and recreation services management enrollment limited to international students. Part-time and evening/weekend programs available. *Faculty:* 15 full-time (6 women), 425 part-time/adjunct (200 women). *Students:* 370 full-time (190 women), 1,060 part-time (560 women); includes 372 minority (205 African Americans, 27 American Indian/Alaska Native, 66 Asian Americans or Pacific Islanders, 74 Hispanic Americans), 30 international. Average age 38. 780 applicants, 85% accepted, 567 enrolled. In 2006, 202 degrees awarded. *Degree requirements:* For master's, portfolio. *Entrance requirements:* For master's, 3 years of work experience, minimum undergraduate GPA of 2.5, writing sample, letters of recommendation. Additional exam requirements/recommendations for international students: Required—TOEFL (minimum score 550 paper-based; 213 computer-based). *Application deadline:* For fall admission, 8/6 priority date for domestic students; for winter admission, 12/15 priority date for domestic students; for spring admission, 2/15 priority date for domestic students. Applications are processed on a rolling basis. Application fee: $25. Electronic applications accepted. *Expenses:* Tuition: Full-time $7,200; part-time $300 per credit hour. *Financial support:* In 2006–07, 410 students received support. Scholarships/grants available. Support available to part-time students. Financial award applicants required to submit FAFSA. *Unit head:* Dr. Michael Heberling, President, 800-469-3165, Fax: 810-766-4399, E-mail: heberling@baker.edu. *Application contact:* Chuck J. Gurden, Vice President for Graduate and Online Admissions, 800-469-3165, Fax: 810-766-2051, E-mail: chuck@baker.edu.

Baker University, School of Professional and Graduate Studies, Programs in Business, Baldwin City, KS 66006-0065. Offers MBA, MSM. *Accreditation:* ACBSP. Evening/weekend programs available. Postbaccalaureate distance learning degree programs offered (minimal on-campus study). *Students:* 727 full-time (353 women); includes 112 minority (54 African Americans, 15 American Indian/Alaska Native, 17 Asian Americans or Pacific Islanders, 26 Hispanic Americans). Average age 34. In 2006, 378 degrees awarded. *Degree requirements:* For master's, comprehensive exam, registration. *Entrance requirements:* For master's, 2 years of full-time work experience. Additional exam requirements/recommendations for international students: Required—TOEFL (minimum score 600 paper-based; 250 computer-based). *Application deadline:* Applications are processed on a rolling basis. Application fee: $45. *Financial support:* Applicants required to submit FAFSA. *Application contact:* Kelly Belk, Director of Marketing, 913-491-4432, Fax: 913-491-0470, E-mail: kbelk@bakeru.edu.

Baldwin-Wallace College, Graduate Programs, Division of Business Administration, Program in Business Administration-Systems Management, Berea, OH 44017-2088. Offers MBA. *Students:* 89 full-time (40 women), 101 part-time (53 women); includes 17 minority (13 African Americans, 1 American Indian/Alaska Native, 2 Asian Americans or Pacific Islanders, 1 Hispanic American), 2 international. Average age 32. 68 applicants, 91% accepted, 51 enrolled. In 2006, 58 degrees awarded. *Entrance requirements:* For master's, GMAT, 2 years of professional experience, minimum GPA of 3.0. *Application deadline:* For fall admission, 7/25 priority date for domestic students; for spring admission, 12/15 priority date for domestic students. Applications are processed on a rolling basis. Application fee: $25. Electronic applications accepted. *Expenses: Contact institution.* Tuition and fees vary according to program. *Unit head:* J. Peter Kelly, Director of MBA, Executive MBA and Human Resources Programs, 440-826-2391, Fax: 440-826-3868, E-mail: pkelly@bw.edu. *Application contact:* Winifred W. Gerhardt, Director of Admission for the Evening and Weekend College, 440-826-2222, Fax: 440-826-3830, E-mail: admission@bw.edu.

Baldwin-Wallace College, Graduate Programs, Division of Business Administration, Program in Executive Management, Berea, OH 44017-2088. Offers MBA. Part-time and evening/weekend programs available. *Students:* 40 full-time (14 women), 3 part-time (2 women); includes 5 minority (2 African Americans, 2 Asian Americans or Pacific Islanders, 1 Hispanic American), 1 international. Average age 40. 15 applicants, 100% accepted, 15 enrolled. In 2006, 19 degrees awarded. *Degree requirements:* For master's, project. *Entrance requirements:* For master's, interview, 10 years of work experience, current professional or managerial position. *Application deadline:* For fall admission, 7/25 priority date for domestic students; for spring admission, 12/15 for domestic students. Applications are processed on a rolling basis. Application fee: $25. Electronic applications accepted. *Expenses: Contact institution.* Tuition and fees vary according to program. *Financial support:* Applicants required to submit FAFSA. *Unit head:* J. Peter Kelly, Director of MBA, Executive MBA and Human Resources Programs, 440-826-2391, Fax: 440-826-3868, E-mail: pkelly@bw.edu. *Application contact:* Barbara McClelland, Graduate Business Coordinator, Executive and Executive Health Care MBA, 440-826-2064, Fax: 440-826-3868, E-mail: bmcclell@bw.edu.

Ball State University, Graduate School, Miller College of Business, Interdepartmental Program in Business Administration, Muncie, IN 47306-1099. Offers MBA. *Accreditation:* AACSB. *Students:* 48 full-time (12 women), 129 part-time (40 women); includes 4 minority (all African Americans), 14 international. Average age 27. 110 applicants, 62% accepted, 54 enrolled. In 2006, 83 degrees awarded. *Entrance requirements:* For master's, GMAT, resumé. *Application fee:* $25 ($35 for international students). *Financial support:* Application deadline: 3/1. *Unit head:* Inga Hill, Graduate Coordinator, 765-285-1931, Fax: 765-285-8818.

Barry University, Andreas School of Business, Graduate Certificate Programs, Miami Shores, FL 33161-6695. Offers finance (Certificate); health services administration (Certificate); international business (Certificate); management (Certificate); management information systems (Certificate); marketing (Certificate). *Application contact:* Dave Fletcher, Director of Graduate Admissions, 305-899-3113, Fax: 305-899-2971, E-mail: dfletcher@mail.barry.edu.

Barry University, Andreas School of Business, Program in Business Administration, Miami Shores, FL 33161-6695. Offers MBA, DPM/MBA, MBA/MS, MBA/MSN. *Students:* 31 full-time (15 women), 37 part-time (15 women); includes 30 minority (8 African Americans, 6 Asian Americans or Pacific Islanders, 16 Hispanic Americans), 18 international. In 2006, 36 degrees awarded. *Application contact:* Dave Fletcher, Director of Graduate Admissions, 305-899-3113, Fax: 305-899-2971, E-mail: dfletcher@mail.barry.edu.

Barry University, School of Adult and Continuing Education, Program in Administrative Studies, Miami Shores, FL 33161-6695. Offers MA. Part-time and evening/weekend programs available. *Students:* 4 full-time (0 women), 7 part-time (3 women); includes 7 minority (5 African Americans, 1 American Indian/Alaska Native, 1 Hispanic American). 17 applicants, 18% accepted, 3 enrolled. In 2006, 3 degrees awarded. *Entrance requirements:* For master's, GMAT, GRE or MAT, recommendations. *Application deadline:* Applications are processed on a rolling basis. Application fee: $30. Electronic applications accepted. *Financial support:* Applicants required to submit FAFSA. *Unit head:* Dr. Lee E. Dutter, Associate Dean for Academic Affairs,

305-899-3329, Fax: 305-899-3346, E-mail: ldutter@mail.barry.edu. *Application contact:* Dave Fletcher, Director of Graduate Admissions, 305-899-3113, Fax: 305-899-2971, E-mail: dfletcher@mail.barry.edu.

Barry University, School of Human Performance and Leisure Sciences and Andreas School of Business, Program in Sport Management and Business Administration, Miami Shores, FL 33161-6695. Offers MS/MBA. Part-time and evening/weekend programs available. *Students:* 10 full-time (4 women), 1 part-time; includes 2 minority (1 African American, 1 Hispanic American), 1 international. 19 applicants, 58% accepted, 6 enrolled. *Application deadline:* Applications are processed on a rolling basis. Application fee: $30. Electronic applications accepted. *Financial support:* Teaching assistantships with full tuition reimbursements, career-related internships or fieldwork available. Support available to part-time students. Financial award application deadline: 5/1; financial award applicants required to submit FAFSA. *Faculty research:* Economic impact of professional sports, sport marketing. *Unit head:* Dr. Annie Clement, Coordinator, 305-899-3493, Fax: 305-899-3556, E-mail: aclement@mail.barry.edu. *Application contact:* Dave Fletcher, Director of Graduate Admissions, 305-899-3113, Fax: 305-899-2971, E-mail: dfletcher@mail.barry.edu.

See Close-Up on page 2349.

Barry University, School of Nursing and Andreas School of Business, Program in Nursing Administration and Business Administration, Miami Shores, FL 33161-6695. Offers MSN/MBA. *Accreditation:* AACN. Part-time and evening/weekend programs available. *Students:* 3 applicants, 0% accepted. *Application deadline:* For fall admission, 5/1 priority date for domestic students. Applications are processed on a rolling basis. Application fee: $30. Electronic applications accepted. *Faculty research:* Power/empowerment, health delivery systems, managed care, employee health well-being. *Unit head:* Dr. Claudette Spalding, Associate Dean for Graduate Programs, 305-899-3838, Fax: 305-899-3831, E-mail: cspalding@mail.barry.edu. *Application contact:* Dave Fletcher, Director of Graduate Admissions, 305-899-3113, Fax: 305-899-2971, E-mail: dfletcher@mail.barry.edu.

Bayamón Central University, Graduate Programs, Program in Business Administration, Bayamón, PR 00960-1725. Offers accounting (MBA); finance (MBA); general business (MBA); management (MBA); management of security and protection (MBA); marketing (MBA). Part-time and evening/weekend programs available. *Degree requirements:* For master's, comprehensive exam (for some programs), registration (for some programs). *Entrance requirements:* For master's, EXADEP, bachelor's degree in business or related field.

Baylor University, Graduate School, Hankamer School of Business, Program in Business Administration, Waco, TX 76798. Offers MBA, JD/MBA, MBA/MSIS. *Accreditation:* AACSB. Part-time programs available. *Students:* 142 full-time (41 women), 3 part-time (2 women); includes 28 minority (14 African Americans, 9 Asian Americans or Pacific Islanders, 5 Hispanic Americans), 21 international. In 2006, 77 degrees awarded. *Entrance requirements:* For master's, GMAT, minimum AACSB index of 1050. *Application deadline:* For fall admission, 8/1 for domestic students; for spring admission, 12/1 for domestic students. Applications are processed on a rolling basis. Application fee: $25. *Expenses: Contact institution. Financial support:* Research assistantships, teaching assistantships, career-related internships or fieldwork, Federal Work-Study, and institutionally sponsored loans available. *Application contact:* Vicky Todd, Administrative Assistant, 254-710-3718, Fax: 254-710-1066, E-mail: mba@hsb.baylor.edu.

Belhaven College, School of Business, Jackson, MS 39202-1789. Offers business administration (MBA); business management (MSM). Evening/weekend programs available. *Entrance requirements:* For master's, GMAT, GRE General Test or MAT, minimum GPA of 2.8.

Bellarmine University, Bellarmine Center for Interdisciplinary Technology and Entrepreneurship, Louisville, KY 40205-0671. Offers MAIT. Part-time and evening/weekend programs available. *Faculty:* 1 full-time (0 women), 11 part-time/adjunct (3 women). *Students:* 12 full-time (5 women), 2 part-time (both women). Average age 33. In 2006, 9 degrees awarded. *Entrance requirements:* For master's, GRE or GMAT, minimum GPA of 2.75, letters of recommendation. Additional exam requirements/recommendations for international students: Required—TOEFL (minimum score 550 paper-based; 213 computer-based; 80 iBT). Application fee: $25. *Expenses: Contact institution.* Tuition and fees vary according to program. *Unit head:* Dr. Michael D. Mattei, Executive Director, 502-452-8441, E-mail: mmattei@bellarmine.edu.

Bellarmine University, W. Fielding Rubel School of Business, Louisville, KY 40205-0671. Offers EMBA, MBA. *Accreditation:* AACSB. Part-time and evening/weekend programs available. *Faculty:* 14 full-time (4 women), 6 part-time/adjunct (2 women). *Students:* 74 full-time (36 women), 110 part-time (44 women); includes 16 minority (8 African Americans, 5 Asian Americans or Pacific Islanders, 3 Hispanic Americans), 4 international. Average age 30. In 2006, 50 degrees awarded. *Entrance requirements:* For master's, GMAT, letters of recommendation. Additional exam requirements/recommendations for international students: Required—TOEFL (minimum score 550 paper-based; 213 computer-based; 80 iBT). *Application deadline:* Applications are processed on a rolling basis. Application fee: $25. Electronic applications accepted. *Expenses: Contact institution.* Tuition and fees vary according to program. *Financial support:* Career-related internships or fieldwork, scholarships/grants, and unspecified assistantships available. Support available to part-time students. Financial award application deadline: 7/1. *Faculty research:* Marketing, management, small business and entrepreneurship, finance, economics. *Unit head:* Daniel L. Bauer, Dean, 800-274-4723 Ext. 8026, Fax: 502-452-8013, E-mail: dbauer@bellarmine.edu. *Application contact:* Laura Richardson, Director, 800-274-4723 Ext. 8258, Fax: 502-452-8012, E-mail: lrichardson@bellarmine.edu.

Bellevue University, Graduate School, Bellevue, NE 68005-3098. Offers business (MBA); communications studies (MA, MS); computer information systems (MS); health care administration (MS); human services (MS); leadership (MA); management (MA); security management (MS). MA is delivered in an accelerated executive format. Part-time and evening/weekend programs available. Postbaccalaureate distance learning degree programs offered (no on-campus study). *Degree requirements:* For master's, thesis or project. *Entrance requirements:* For master's, minimum GPA of 2.5 in last 60 hours. Additional exam requirements/recommendations for international students: Required—TOEFL (minimum score 538 paper-based; 200 computer-based).

Belmont University, Jack C. Massey Graduate School of Business, Nashville, TN 37212-3757. Offers M Acc, MBA. *Accreditation:* AACSB. Part-time and evening/weekend programs available. *Faculty:* 22 full-time (8 women), 4 part-time/adjunct (0 women). *Students:* 21 full-time (10 women), 189 part-time (82 women); includes 32 minority (20 African Americans, 11 Asian Americans or Pacific Islanders, 1 Hispanic American), 4 international. Average age 29. 55 applicants, 80% accepted, 34 enrolled. In 2006, 81 degrees awarded. *Entrance requirements:* For master's, GMAT, 2 years of work experience (MBA). Additional exam requirements/recommendations for international students: Required—TOEFL (minimum score 550 paper-based; 213 computer-based). *Application deadline:* For fall admission, 7/1 for domestic and international students; for spring admission, 11/1 for domestic and international students. Applications are processed on a rolling basis. Application fee: $50. Electronic applications accepted. *Expenses: Contact institution. Financial support:* In 2006–07, 22 students received support. Scholarships/grants, tuition waivers (full), and unspecified assistantships available. Financial award application deadline: 7/1; financial award applicants required to submit FAFSA. *Faculty research:* Music business, strategy, ethics, finance, accounting systems. *Unit head:* Dr. Patrick Raines, Dean, 615-460-6480, Fax: 615-460-6455, E-mail: rainesp@mail.belmont.edu. *Application contact:* Tonya Hollin, Admissions Assistant, 615-460-6480, Fax: 615-460-6353, E-mail: masseyadmissions@mail.belmont.edu.

Benedictine College, Executive Master of Business Administration Program, Atchison, KS 66002-1499. Offers EMBA. Part-time and evening/weekend programs available. *Entrance requirements:* For master's, 5 years of management experience, interview. Electronic applications accepted. Expenses: Contact institution. *Faculty research:* Banking, strategic planning, ethics, leadership and entrepreneurship.

Benedictine College, Program in Business Administration, Atchison, KS 66002-1499. Offers MBA. Evening/weekend programs available. Expenses: Contact institution.

Benedictine University, Graduate Programs, Program in Business Administration, Lisle, IL 60532-0900. Offers MBA, MBA/MPH, MBA/MS. Part-time and evening/weekend programs available. Postbaccalaureate distance learning degree programs offered (minimal on-campus study). *Faculty:* 4 full-time (2 women), 24 part-time/adjunct (3 women). *Students:* 446 (196 women); includes 98 minority (41 African Americans, 1 American Indian/Alaska Native, 32 Asian Americans or Pacific Islanders, 24 Hispanic Americans) 10 international. Average age 34. 163 applicants, 91% accepted, 51 enrolled. In 2006, 134 degrees awarded. *Entrance requirements:* For master's, GMAT. Additional exam requirements/recommendations for international students: Required—TOEFL (minimum score 550 paper-based; 213 computer-based). *Application deadline:* For fall admission, 9/1 for domestic students; for winter admission, 12/1 for domestic students; for spring admission, 2/15 for domestic students. Applications are processed on a rolling basis. Application fee: $40. Electronic applications accepted. *Expenses:* Tuition: Full-time $12,150; part-time $450 per credit hour. *Financial support:* Career-related internships or fieldwork and health care benefits available. Support available to part-time students. *Faculty research:* Strategic leadership in professional organizations, sociology of professions, organizational change, social identity theory, applications to change management. *Unit head:* Dr. Sharon Borowicz, Director, 630-829-6219, E-mail: sborowicz@ben.edu. *Application contact:* Kari Gibbons, Director, Admissions, 630-829-6200, Fax: 630-829-6584, E-mail: kgibbons@ben.edu.

Benedictine University, Graduate Programs, Program in Management and Organizational Behavior, Lisle, IL 60532-0900. Offers MS, MBA/MS, MPH/MS. Part-time and evening/weekend programs available. *Faculty:* 1 full-time (0 women), 15 part-time/adjunct (7 women). *Students:* 157 (88 women); includes 22 minority (20 African Americans, 2 Hispanic Americans) 2 international. Average age 40. 56 applicants, 96% accepted, 9 enrolled. In 2006, 49 degrees awarded. *Entrance requirements:* For master's, GMAT. Additional exam requirements/recommendations for international students: Required—TOEFL (minimum score 550 paper-based; 213 computer-based). *Application deadline:* For fall admission, 9/1 for domestic students; for winter admission, 12/1 for domestic students; for spring admission, 2/15 for domestic students. Applications are processed on a rolling basis. Application fee: $40. Electronic applications accepted. *Expenses:* Tuition: Full-time $12,150; part-time $450 per credit hour. *Financial support:* Career-related internships or fieldwork and health care benefits available. Support available to part-time students. *Faculty research:* Organizational change, transformation, development, learning organizations, career transitions for academics. *Unit head:* Dr. Peter F. Sorensen, Director, 630-829-6220, Fax: 630-960-1126, E-mail: psorensen@ben.edu. *Application contact:* Kari Gibbons, Director, Admissions, 630-829-6200, Fax: 630-829-6584, E-mail: kgibbons@ben.edu.

Bentley College, The Elkin B. McCallum Graduate School of Business, Business Program, Waltham, MA 02452-4705. Offers PhD. *Faculty:* 172 full-time (56 women), 97 part-time/adjunct (25 women). *Students:* 4 full-time (1 woman), 2 part-time (both women); includes 2 minority (both Asian Americans or Pacific Islanders), 3 international. Average age 33. 28 applicants, 25% accepted, 6 enrolled. *Entrance requirements:* For doctorate, GMAT. Additional exam requirements/recommendations for international students: Required—TOEFL (minimum score 600 paper-based; 250 computer-based). *Application deadline:* For fall admission, 3/1 for domestic and international students. Application fee: $0. Electronic applications accepted. *Expenses:* Tuition: Full-time $28,440; part-time $2,844 per course. Required fees: $404; $105 per year. *Financial support:* Research assistantships, teaching assistantships available. *Unit head:* Dr. Sue Newell, PhD Program Director, 781-891-2399, Fax: 781-891-3121, E-mail: snewell@bentley.edu.

Bentley College, The Elkin B. McCallum Graduate School of Business, Day MBA Program, Waltham, MA 02452-4705. Offers MBA. *Accreditation:* AACSB. *Faculty:* 172 full-time (56 women), 97 part-time/adjunct (25 women). *Students:* 39 full-time (14 women); includes 3 minority (all Asian Americans or Pacific Islanders), 17 international. Average age 27. 122 applicants, 34% accepted, 14 enrolled. In 2006, 22 degrees awarded. *Entrance requirements:* For master's, GMAT. Additional exam requirements/recommendations for international students: Required—TOEFL (minimum score 600 paper-based; 250 computer-based). *Application deadline:* For fall admission, 6/1 priority date for domestic students, 5/1 priority date for international students; for spring admission, 11/1 priority date for domestic and international students. Applications are processed on a rolling basis. Application fee: $50. Electronic applications accepted. *Expenses:* Tuition: Full-time $28,440; part-time $2,844 per course. Required fees: $404; $105 per year. *Financial support:* In 2006–07, 24 research assistantships with partial tuition reimbursements (averaging $18,131 per year) were awarded; scholarships/grants, tuition waivers, and unspecified assistantships also available. Financial award application deadline: 4/12; financial award applicants required to submit CSS PROFILE or FAFSA. *Faculty research:* Knowledge management, information technology impact on team dynamics, innovation, new venture creation, organizational change. *Unit head:* Dr. Alan Hoffman, Director, 781-891-3433, Fax: 781-891-2464, E-mail: ahoffman@bentley.edu. *Application contact:* Sharon Hill, Director of Graduate Admissions, 781-891-2108, Fax: 781-891-2464, E-mail: shill@bentley.edu.

See Close-Up on page 243.

Bentley College, The Elkin B. McCallum Graduate School of Business, Dual Degree Program in Business, Waltham, MA 02452-4705. Offers MS/MBA. *Faculty:* 271 full-time (105 women), 202 part-time/adjunct (72 women). *Students:* 11 full-time (4 women); includes 2 minority (both Asian Americans or Pacific Islanders), 1 international. Average age 28. 31 applicants, 32% accepted, 6 enrolled. *Entrance requirements:* Additional exam requirements/recommendations for international students: Required—TOEFL. *Application deadline:* For fall admission, 6/1 priority date for domestic students, 5/1 priority date for international students; for spring admission, 11/1 priority date for domestic and international students. Applications are processed on a rolling basis. Application fee: $50. Electronic applications accepted. *Expenses:* Tuition: Full-time $28,440; part-time $2,844 per course. Required fees: $404; $105 per year. *Financial support:* Research assistantships, scholarships/grants, tuition waivers, and unspecified assistantships available. Financial award application deadline: 4/12; financial award applicants required to submit CSS PROFILE or FAFSA. *Faculty research:* Product usability; information technology ethics; business process improvement; organizational change; risk management; enterprise systems. *Unit head:* Dr. Judith B. Kamm, Director, 781-891-2867, Fax: 781-891-2464, E-mail: jkamm@bentley.edu. *Application contact:* Sharon Hill, Director of Graduate Admissions, 781-891-2108, Fax: 781-891-2464, E-mail: shill@bentley.edu.

Bentley College, The Elkin B. McCallum Graduate School of Business, Evening MBA Program, Waltham, MA 02452-4705. Offers MBA. *Accreditation:* AACSB. Part-time and evening/weekend programs available. *Faculty:* 172 full-time (56 women), 97 part-time/adjunct (25 women). *Students:* Average age 29. 267 applicants, 76% accepted, 118 enrolled. In 2006, 76 degrees awarded. *Entrance requirements:* For master's, GMAT. Additional exam requirements/recommendations for international students: Required—TOEFL (minimum score 600 paper-based; 250 computer-based). *Application deadline:* For fall admission, 6/1 priority date for domestic students, 3/1 priority date for international students; for spring admission, 11/1 priority date for domestic and international students. Applications are processed on a rolling basis. Application fee: $50. Electronic applications accepted. *Expenses:* Tuition: Full-time $28,440; part-time $2,844 per course. Required fees: $404; $105 per year. *Financial support:* Research assistantships, scholarships/grants, tuition waivers (full and partial), and unspecified assistantships available. Financial award application deadline: 4/12; financial award applicants required to submit CSS PROFILE or FAFSA. *Faculty research:* Knowledge management, information technology impact on team dynamics, innovation, new venture creation, organizational change. *Unit head:* Dr. Alan Hoffman, Director, 781-891-3433, Fax: 781-891-2464,

Business Administration and Management—General

Bentley College (continued)

E-mail: ahoffman@bentley.edu. *Application contact:* Sharon Hill, Director of Graduate Admissions, 781-891-2108, Fax: 781-891-2464, E-mail: shill@bentley.edu.

See Close-Up on page 243.

Bentley College, The Elkin B. McCallum Graduate School of Business, Graduate Business Certificate Program, Waltham, MA 02452-4705. Offers accounting (GBC); accounting information systems (GBC); business (GSS); business ethics (GBC); data analysis (GBC); financial planning (GBC); marketing analytics (GBC); taxation (GBC). Part-time and evening/weekend programs available. *Faculty:* 172 full-time (56 women), 97 part-time/adjunct (25 women). *Students:* Average age 37. 25 applicants, 92% accepted, 13 enrolled. In 2006, 6 degrees awarded. *Entrance requirements:* Additional exam requirements/recommendations for international students: Required—TOEFL (minimum score 600 paper-based; 250 computer-based). *Application deadline:* For fall admission, 6/1 priority date for domestic students, 3/1 priority date for international students; for spring admission, 11/1 priority date for domestic and international students. Applications are processed on a rolling basis. Application fee: $50. Electronic applications accepted. *Expenses:* Tuition: Full-time $28,440; part-time $2,844 per course. Required fees: $404; $105 per year. *Application contact:* Sharon Hill, Director of Graduate Admissions, 781-891-2108, Fax: 781-891-2464, E-mail: shill@bentley.edu.

Bernard M. Baruch College of the City University of New York, Zicklin School of Business, New York, NY 10010-5585. Offers MBA, MS, PhD, Certificate, JD/MBA. *Accreditation:* AACSB. Part-time and evening/weekend programs available. *Faculty:* 198 full-time (46 women), 196 part-time/adjunct (35 women). *Students:* 754 full-time (353 women), 1,499 part-time (656 women); includes 476 minority (96 African Americans, 293 Asian Americans or Pacific Islanders, 87 Hispanic Americans), 664 international. Average age 29. 1,497 applicants, 46% accepted, 482 enrolled. In 2006, 1,351 master's, 6 doctorates awarded. *Degree requirements:* For doctorate, thesis/dissertation, comprehensive exam. *Entrance requirements:* For master's, GMAT, 2 letters of recommendation, resumé, 2 years of work experience; for doctorate, GMAT. Additional exam requirements/recommendations for international students: Required—TOEFL (minimum score 590 paper-based; 243 computer-based), TWE (minimum score 5). *Application deadline:* For fall admission, 5/31 for domestic students, 4/30 for international students; for spring admission, 10/31 for domestic and international students. Applications are processed on a rolling basis. Application fee: $125. Electronic applications accepted. *Financial support:* In 2006–07, 163 students received support, including 59 fellowships (averaging $4,000 per year), 20 research assistantships (averaging $16,000 per year), 84 teaching assistantships (averaging $5,000 per year); career-related internships or fieldwork, Federal Work-Study, institutionally sponsored loans, scholarships/grants, and unspecified assistantships also available. Financial award application deadline: 4/30; financial award applicants required to submit FAFSA. *Unit head:* John Elliott, Vice President and Dean, 646-312-3030, Fax: 646-312-3031, E-mail: john_elliott@baruch.cuny.edu. *Application contact:* Frances Murphy, Office of Graduate Admissions, 646-312-1300, Fax: 646-312-1301, E-mail: zicklingradadmissions@baruch.cuny.edu.

See Close-Up on page 245.

Bernard M. Baruch College of the City University of New York, Zicklin School of Business, Zicklin Executive Programs, Executive MBA Program, New York, NY 10010-5585. Offers MBA. *Accreditation:* AACSB. *Faculty:* 19 full-time (3 women), 8 part-time/adjunct (0 women). *Students:* 71 full-time (31 women); includes 34 minority (17 African Americans, 6 Asian Americans or Pacific Islanders, 11 Hispanic Americans), 3 international. Average age 35. 62 applicants, 68% accepted, 35 enrolled. In 2006, 22 degrees awarded. *Entrance requirements:* For master's, 5 years of management-level work experience, personal interview. Additional exam requirements/recommendations for international students: Required—TOEFL. *Application deadline:* For fall admission, 5/15 priority date for domestic students, 5/15 for international students. Applications are processed on a rolling basis. Application fee: $125. *Expenses: Contact institution. Financial support:* Applicants required to submit FAFSA. *Faculty research:* Entrepreneurship, corporate governance, international finance, mergers and acquisitions. *Unit head:* Chris Koutsoutis, Director, 646-312-3100, Fax: 646-312-3101, E-mail: chris_koutsoutis@baruch.cuny.edu.

Berry College, Graduate Programs, Campbell School of Business, Mount Berry, GA 30149-0159. Offers MBA. *Accreditation:* AACSB. Part-time and evening/weekend programs available. *Faculty:* 5 part-time/adjunct (3 women). *Students:* 5 full-time (2 women), 21 part-time (7 women); includes 1 minority (Asian American or Pacific Islander), 3 international. Average age 29. In 2006, 11 degrees awarded. *Entrance requirements:* For master's, GMAT, minimum GPA of 3.0. Additional exam requirements/recommendations for international students: Required—TOEFL (minimum score 550 paper-based; 213 computer-based). *Application deadline:* For fall admission, 7/27 for domestic students; for spring admission, 12/16 for domestic students. Applications are processed on a rolling basis. Application fee: $25 ($30 for international students). *Expenses: Contact institution. Financial support:* In 2006–07, 13 students received support, including 5 research assistantships with full tuition reimbursements available (averaging $3,500 per year); scholarships/grants and unspecified assistantships also available. Support available to part-time students. Financial award application deadline: 4/1; financial award applicants required to submit FAFSA. *Faculty research:* Marketing, risk management, accounting strategies, business law, mistake proofing. Total annual research expenditures: $190,604. *Unit head:* Dr. Krishna Dhir, Dean, 706-236-2233, Fax: 706-802-6728, E-mail: kdhir@campbell.berry.edu. *Application contact:* Richard D. Paul, Dean of Admissions and Financial Aid, 706-236-2215, Fax: 706-290-2178, E-mail: dpaul@berry.edu.

Bethel College, Division of Graduate Studies, Program in Business Administration, Mishawaka, IN 46545-5591. Offers MBA. Part-time programs available. *Faculty:* 5 part-time/adjunct (2 women). *Students:* 11 full-time (4 women), 35 part-time (18 women); includes 1 minority (African American), 1 international. 43 applicants, 56% accepted, 24 enrolled. In 2006, 19 degrees awarded. *Entrance requirements:* For master's, GMAT. Additional exam requirements/recommendations for international students: Required—TOEFL (minimum score 540 paper-based; 207 computer-based). *Application deadline:* Applications are processed on a rolling basis. Application fee: $25. Electronic applications accepted. *Expenses:* Tuition: Full-time $5,940; part-time $330 per credit hour. *Faculty research:* Marketing. *Unit head:* Dr. Bradley D. Smith, Director, 574-257-3363, Fax: 574-257-7617, E-mail: smithb@bethelcollege.edu.

Bethel University, Graduate School, Department of Business, St. Paul, MN 55112-6999. Offers business administration (MBA). *Faculty:* 6 full-time (1 woman), 20 part-time/adjunct (5 women). *Students:* 105 full-time (47 women), 2 part-time (1 woman); includes 12 minority (7 African Americans, 1 American Indian/Alaska Native, 2 Asian Americans or Pacific Islanders, 2 Hispanic Americans). Average age 35. *Degree requirements:* For master's, capstone project, business plan. *Entrance requirements:* For master's, letters of reference, 1 course in managerial accounting, minimum GPA of 3.0. Additional exam requirements/recommendations for international students: Required—TOEFL. *Application deadline:* For fall admission, 5/15 priority date for domestic students. Applications are processed on a rolling basis. Application fee: $25. Electronic applications accepted. *Expenses: Contact institution.* Tuition and fees vary according to program. *Unit head:* Dr. Mary F. Whitman, Director, 651-635-8082, Fax: 651-635-8004, E-mail: m_whitman@bethel.edu. *Application contact:* Michael Price, Director of Admissions, 651-635-8000 Ext. 8017, Fax: 651-635-8004, E-mail: m_price@bethel.edu.

Biola University, Crowell School of Business, La Mirada, CA 90639-0001. Offers MBA. *Accreditation:* ACBSP. Part-time and evening/weekend programs available. *Entrance requirements:* For master's, GMAT, minimum GPA of 3.0. Additional exam requirements/recommendations for international students: Required—TOEFL (minimum score 550 paper-based; 213 computer-based). *Faculty research:* Integration of theology with business principles.

Birmingham-Southern College, Program in Public and Private Management, Birmingham, AL 35254. Offers MPPM. *Accreditation:* AACSB. Part-time and evening/weekend programs available. *Degree requirements:* For master's, thesis optional. *Entrance requirements:* For master's, GMAT, GRE, or MAT.

Black Hills State University, College of Business and Technology, Spearfish, SD 57799. Offers business services management (MS). Part-time programs available. *Degree requirements:* For master's, thesis (for some programs). *Entrance requirements:* For master's, bachelor's degree in related field. Additional exam requirements/recommendations for international students: Required—TOEFL. *Faculty research:* Tourism in western South Dakota, marketing.

Bloomsburg University of Pennsylvania, School of Graduate Studies, College of Business, Program in Business Administration, Bloomsburg, PA 17815-1301. Offers MBA. *Accreditation:* AACSB. *Faculty:* 21 full-time (2 women). *Students:* 24 full-time (9 women), 38 part-time (12 women); includes 4 minority (2 African Americans, 1 Asian American or Pacific Islander, 1 Hispanic American), 11 international. Average age 31. 22 applicants, 100% accepted, 16 enrolled. In 2006, 28 degrees awarded. *Entrance requirements:* For master's, GMAT, minimum QPA of 3.0, resumé, 3 letters of recommendation. Additional exam requirements/recommendations for international students: Required—TOEFL (minimum score 550 paper-based; 213 computer-based; 79 iBT). *Application deadline:* Applications are processed on a rolling basis. Application fee: $30. Electronic applications accepted. *Expenses:* Tuition, state resident: full-time $6,048; part-time $336 per credit. Tuition, nonresident: full-time $9,678; part-time $538 per credit. Required fees: $1,415. *Financial support:* Federal Work-Study and unspecified assistantships available. *Unit head:* Dr. A. Blair Staley, Coordinator, 570-389-4392, Fax: 570-389-3892, E-mail: astaley@bloomu.edu.

Bluffton University, Programs in Business, Bluffton, OH 45817. Offers business administration (MBA); organizational management (MA). Evening/weekend programs available. *Faculty:* 8 full-time (2 women), 4 part-time/adjunct (0 women). *Students:* 71 full-time (30 women), 10 part-time (5 women); includes 11 minority (8 African Americans, 2 Asian Americans or Pacific Islanders, 1 Hispanic American). Average age 37. 42 applicants, 100% accepted, 41 enrolled. In 2006, 43 degrees awarded. *Entrance requirements:* Additional exam requirements/recommendations for international students: Required—TOEFL. *Application deadline:* For fall admission, 7/31 priority date for domestic and international students. Applications are processed on a rolling basis. Application fee: $20. Electronic applications accepted. *Unit head:* Dr. George Lehman, Director of Graduate Programs in Business, 419-358-3302, E-mail: lehmang@bluffton.edu. *Application contact:* Betty Dills, Information Contact, 800-488-3257, Fax: 419-358-3399, E-mail: adulted@bluffton.edu.

Bob Jones University, Graduate Programs, Greenville, SC 29614. Offers accountancy (MS); Bible (MA); Bible translation (MA); Biblical studies (Certificate); broadcast management (MS); business administration (MBA); church history (MA, PhD); church ministries (MA); church music (MM); cinema and video production (MA); counseling (MS); curriculum and instruction (Ed D); divinity (M Div); dramatic production (MA); educational leadership (MS, Ed D, Ed S); elementary education (M Ed, MAT); English (M Ed, MA, MAT); fine arts (MA); graphic design (MA); history (M Ed, MA); illustration (MA); interpretative speech (MA); mathematics (M Ed, MAT); medical missions (Certificate); ministry (MM, D Min); multi-categorical special education (M Ed, MAT); music (M Ed); New Testament interpretation (PhD); Old Testament interpretation (PhD); orchestral instrument performance (MM); organ performance (MM); pastoral studies (MA); personnel services (MS, Ed S); piano pedagogy (MM); piano performance (MM); platform arts (MA); radio and television broadcasting (MS); rhetoric and public address (MA); secondary education (M Ed); studio art (MA); teaching Bible (MA); theology (MA, PhD); voice performance (MM); youth ministries (MA); M Div/MM.

Boise State University, Graduate College, College of Business and Economics, Program in Business Administration, Boise, ID 83725-0399. Offers MBA. *Accreditation:* AACSB. Part-time programs available. *Faculty:* 33 full-time (5 women), 5 part-time/adjunct (2 women). *Students:* 24 full-time (10 women), 99 part-time (36 women); includes 6 minority (4 Asian Americans or Pacific Islanders, 2 Hispanic Americans), 2 international. Average age 32. 55 applicants, 89% accepted, 23 enrolled. In 2006, 36 degrees awarded. *Entrance requirements:* For master's, GMAT, minimum GPA of 3.0. Additional exam requirements/recommendations for international students: Required—TOEFL. *Application deadline:* For fall admission, 3/1 priority date for domestic students; for spring admission, 10/1 priority date for domestic students. Applications are processed on a rolling basis. Application fee: $0. Electronic applications accepted. *Financial support:* Career-related internships or fieldwork, Federal Work-Study, institutionally sponsored loans, and unspecified assistantships available. Support available to part-time students. Financial award application deadline: 3/1. *Unit head:* Dr. Kirk Smith, Director, 208-426-3180. *Application contact:* J. Renee Anchustegui, Coordinator, 208-426-3116, Fax: 208-426-1135, E-mail: ranchust@boisestate.edu.

Boston College, The Carroll School of Management, Business Administration Program, Chestnut Hill, MA 02467-3800. Offers MBA, JD/MBA, MBA/MA, MBA/MS, MBA/MSA, MBA/MSF, MBA/MSW, MBA/PhD. *Accreditation:* AACSB. Part-time and evening/weekend programs available. *Faculty:* 42 full-time (9 women), 22 part-time/adjunct (7 women). *Students:* 169 full-time (59 women), 500 part-time (166 women); includes 67 minority (19 African Americans, 33 Asian Americans or Pacific Islanders, 15 Hispanic Americans), 70 international. Average age 27. 672 applicants, 51% accepted, 197 enrolled. In 2006, 239 degrees awarded. *Entrance requirements:* For master's, GMAT, 2 letters of recommendation, resumé. Additional exam requirements/recommendations for international students: Required—TOEFL (minimum score 600 paper-based; 250 computer-based; 100 iBT). *Application deadline:* For fall admission, 4/15 for domestic and international students; for spring admission, 10/15 for domestic students. Application fee: $100. Electronic applications accepted. *Financial support:* In 2006–07, 112 fellowships, 93 research assistantships with full and partial tuition reimbursements were awarded; career-related internships or fieldwork, Federal Work-Study, scholarships/grants, tuition waivers (full and partial), and unspecified assistantships also available. Support available to part-time students. Financial award application deadline: 3/1; financial award applicants required to submit FAFSA. *Faculty research:* Investments, e-commerce, corporate finance, management of financial services, strategic management. *Application contact:* Shelley A. Burt, Director of Graduate Enrollment, 617-552-3920, Fax: 617-552-8078, E-mail: bcmba@bc.edu.

Boston University, Metropolitan College (Continuing Education), Program in Administrative Studies, Boston, MA 02215. Offers banking and financial management (MSM); business continuity in emergency management (MSM); economics development and tourism management (MSAS); electronic commerce, systems, and technology (MSAS); financial economics (MSAS); human resource management (MSM); innovation and technology (MSAS); insurance management (MSM); international market management (MSM); multinational commerce (MSAS); project management (MSM). *Accreditation:* AACSB. Part-time and evening/weekend programs available. *Faculty:* 9 full-time (0 women), 51 part-time/adjunct (8 women). *Students:* 105 full-time (40 women), 171 part-time (65 women); includes 27 minority (5 African Americans, 18 Asian Americans or Pacific Islanders, 4 Hispanic Americans), 125 international. Average age 29. In 2006, 310 degrees awarded. *Degree requirements:* For master's, thesis optional. *Entrance requirements:* For master's, 1 year of work experience, minimum GPA of 3.0. Additional exam requirements/recommendations for international students: Required—TOEFL (minimum score 560 paper-based; 220 computer-based). *Application deadline:* Applications are processed on a rolling basis. Application fee: $65. *Expenses:* Tuition: Full-time $33,330; part-time $1,042 per credit. Required fees: $462; $40. *Financial support:* In 2006–07, 15 students received support, including research assistantships (averaging $10,000 per year); career-related internships or fieldwork and Federal Work-Study also available. *Faculty research:* International business, innovative process. *Unit head:* Dr. Kip Becker, Chairman, 617-353-3016, E-mail: adminsc@bu.edu. *Application contact:* Lucille Dicker, Administrative Sciences Department, 617-353-3016, E-mail: adminsc@bu.edu.

Boston University, School of Management, Doctorate in Business Administration Program, Boston, MA 02215. Offers accounting (DBA); information systems (DBA); management policy (DBA); marketing (DBA); operations management (DBA); organizational behavior (DBA). *Students:* 48 full-time (26 women); includes 4 minority (all Asian Americans or Pacific Islanders), 24 international. Average age 35. 120 applicants, 17% accepted, 10 enrolled. In 2006, 8 degrees awarded. *Degree requirements:* For doctorate, thesis/dissertation. *Entrance requirements:* For doctorate, GMAT or GRE General Test. *Application deadline:* For fall admission, 1/31 for domestic students. Application fee: $125. *Expenses:* Tuition: Full-time $33,330; part-time $1,042 per credit. Required fees: $462; $40. *Financial support:* Career-related internships or fieldwork, Federal Work-Study, institutionally sponsored loans, scholarships/grants, and tuition waivers available. Support available to part-time students. Financial award applicants required to submit FAFSA. *Unit head:* Dr. Sushil Vachani, Director, 617-353-4875, E-mail: dba@bu.edu. *Application contact:* Hayden Estrada, Assistant Dean, Admissions, 617-353-2670, Fax: 617-353-7368, E-mail: dba@bu.edu.

Boston University, School of Management, Executive MBA Program, Boston, MA 02215. Offers Exec MBA. *Accreditation:* AACSB. *Faculty:* 15 part-time/adjunct (2 women). *Students:* 72 full-time (21 women); includes 4 minority (3 African Americans, 1 Asian American or Pacific Islander), 4 international. Average age 39. 87 applicants, 67% accepted, 38 enrolled. In 2006, 31 degrees awarded. *Application deadline:* For winter admission, 11/1 for domestic students. Application fee: $100. *Expenses:* Tuition: Full-time $33,330; part-time $1,042 per credit. Required fees: $462; $40. *Unit head:* Kristen Sadawski, Director, 617-353-8470, Fax: 617-353-3477, E-mail: emba@bu.edu. *Application contact:* Hayden Estrada, Assistant Dean, Admissions, 617-353-2670, Fax: 617-353-7368, E-mail: emba@bu.edu.

Boston University, School of Management, Master of Business Administration Program, Boston, MA 02215. Offers advanced accounting (Certificate); general management (MBA); healthcare management (MBA); public and nonprofit management (MBA); JD/MBA; MBA/MA; MBA/MPH; MBA/MS; MBA/MSIS; MS/MBA. Part-time and evening/weekend programs available. *Faculty:* 104 full-time (21 women). *Students:* 299 full-time (114 women), 487 part-time (190 women); includes 124 minority (12 African Americans, 2 American Indian/Alaska Native, 94 Asian Americans or Pacific Islanders, 16 Hispanic Americans), 143 international. Average age 26. 1,482 applicants, 42% accepted, 300 enrolled. In 2006, 342 degrees awarded. *Entrance requirements:* For master's, GMAT. *Application deadline:* For fall admission, 5/1 for domestic students. Applications are processed on a rolling basis. Application fee: $125. Electronic applications accepted. *Expenses:* Tuition: Full-time $33,330; part-time $1,042 per credit. Required fees: $462; $40. *Financial support:* Career-related internships or fieldwork, Federal Work-Study, institutionally sponsored loans, and tuition waivers (partial) available. Support available to part-time students. Financial award applicants required to submit FAFSA. *Unit head:* Dr. John Chalykoff, Associate Dean, Academic Program, 617-353-4157, Fax: 617-353-5003, E-mail: chalykof@bu.edu. *Application contact:* Hayden Estrada, Assistant Dean, Admissions, 617-353-2670, Fax: 617-353-7368, E-mail: mba@bu.edu.

Bowie State University, Graduate Programs, Program in Administrative Management, Bowie, MD 20715-9465. Offers business administration (M Adm Mgt); public administration (M Adm Mgt). *Accreditation:* ACBSP. Part-time and evening/weekend programs available. *Degree requirements:* For master's, research paper, thesis optional. *Entrance requirements:* For master's, minimum undergraduate GPA of 2.5. *Expenses:* Tuition, state resident: full-time $7,344; part-time $306 per credit. Tuition, nonresident: full-time $14,304; part-time $396 per credit. Required fees: $1,078; $77 per credit. $539 per term. One-time fee: $40.

Bowie State University, Graduate Programs, Program in Business Administration, Bowie, MD 20715-9465. Offers MBA. Part-time and evening/weekend programs available. *Faculty:* 4 full-time (0 women), 3 part-time/adjunct (0 women). *Students:* 23 full-time (15 women), 42 part-time (22 women); includes 60 minority (59 African Americans, 1 Hispanic American), 1 international. Average age 31. 28 applicants, 96% accepted, 14 enrolled. In 2006, 23 degrees awarded. *Degree requirements:* For master's, comprehensive exam. *Entrance requirements:* For master's, GMAT, minimum undergraduate GPA of 2.5. *Application deadline:* For fall admission, 4/1 priority date for domestic and international students; for spring admission, 11/1 priority date for domestic and international students. Applications are processed on a rolling basis. Application fee: $40. Electronic applications accepted. *Expenses:* Tuition, state resident: full-time $7,344; part-time $306 per credit. Tuition, nonresident: full-time $14,304; part-time $396 per credit. Required fees: $1,078; $77 per credit. $539 per term. One-time fee: $40. *Unit head:* Dr. Falih Alsaaty, Program Coordinator, 301-860-3644, E-mail: falsaaty@bowiestate.edu. *Application contact:* Angela Issac, Information Contact.

Bowling Green State University, Graduate College, College of Business Administration, Graduate Studies in Business Program, Bowling Green, OH 43403. Offers MBA. *Accreditation:* AACSB. Part-time and evening/weekend programs available. *Faculty:* 18 full-time (5 women), 1 part-time/adjunct (0 women). *Students:* 64 full-time (26 women), 62 part-time (21 women); includes 8 minority (3 African Americans, 2 Asian Americans or Pacific Islanders, 3 Hispanic Americans), 29 international. Average age 29. 82 applicants, 45% accepted, 18 enrolled. In 2006, 83 degrees awarded. *Degree requirements:* For master's, thesis or alternative, research project. *Entrance requirements:* For master's, GMAT. Additional exam requirements/recommendations for international students: Required—TOEFL. *Application deadline:* For fall admission, 2/15 priority date for domestic students, 1/15 priority date for international students. Application fee: $30. Electronic applications accepted. *Expenses:* Tuition, state resident: part-time $535 per hour. Tuition, nonresident: part-time $884 per hour. *Financial support:* In 2006–07, 31 research assistantships with full tuition reimbursements (averaging $6,378 per year) were awarded; teaching assistantships with full tuition reimbursements, career-related internships or fieldwork, Federal Work-Study, institutionally sponsored loans, and unspecified assistantships also available. Financial award applicants required to submit FAFSA. *Faculty research:* Management of change processes, supply chain management, impacts of money on society, corporate financing strategies, macro-marketing/management of sales staff and services. *Unit head:* Dr. James McFillen, Director, 419-372-2488.

Bradley University, Graduate School, Foster College of Business Administration, Executive MBA Program, Peoria, IL 61625-0002. Offers MBA. Evening/weekend programs available. *Students:* 22 full-time (7 women); includes 2 minority (both Asian Americans or Pacific Islanders), 1 international. 22 applicants, 100% accepted, 22 enrolled. *Entrance requirements:* For master's, company sponsorship, 7 years of managerial experience, letters of recommendation. Additional exam requirements/recommendations for international students: Required—TOEFL (minimum score 550 paper-based; 213 computer-based; 79 iBT). Application fee: $40 ($50 for international students). *Expenses:* Contact institution. *Unit head:* Dr. Edward Sattler, Associate Dean, 309-677-2253. *Application contact:* Jack Russell, Director, 309-677-4425, E-mail: russellj@bradley.edu.

Bradley University, Graduate School, Foster College of Business Administration, Program in Business Administration, Peoria, IL 61625-0002. Offers MBA. *Accreditation:* AACSB. Part-time and evening/weekend programs available. *Students:* 24 full-time (10 women), 128 part-time (34 women); includes 9 minority (5 African Americans, 2 American Indian/Alaska Native, 1 Asian American or Pacific Islander, 1 Hispanic American), 24 international. 46 applicants, 65% accepted, 26 enrolled. In 2006, 37 degrees awarded. *Degree requirements:* For master's, comprehensive exam. *Entrance requirements:* For master's, GMAT, minimum undergraduate GPA of 2.75 in major, 2 letters of recommendation. Additional exam requirements/recommendations for international students: Required—TOEFL (minimum score 550 paper-based; 213 computer-based; 79 iBT). *Application deadline:* For fall admission, 5/15 priority date for domestic and international students; for spring admission, 10/15 priority date for domestic and international students. Applications are processed on a rolling basis. Application fee: $40 ($50 for international students). *Financial support:* Teaching assistantships with full and partial tuition reimbursements, career-related internships or fieldwork, institutionally sponsored loans, scholarships/grants, tuition waivers (partial), and unspecified assistantships available. Support available to part-time students. Financial award application deadline: 4/1. *Unit head:* Dr. Edward Sattler, Associate Dean, 309-677-2253. *Application contact:* Janet Davidson, Assistant Director of Graduate Programs, 309-677-2256, Fax: 309-677-3374, E-mail: jldavids@bradley.edu.

Brandeis University, The Heller School for Social Policy and Management, Program in Human Services, Waltham, MA 02454-9110. Offers child, youth, and family services (MBA); health care administration (MBA); human services (MBA); MBA/MA. Part-time and evening/weekend programs available. *Degree requirements:* For master's, team consulting project. *Entrance requirements:* For master's, GMAT. Additional exam requirements/recommendations for international students: Required—TOEFL (minimum score 600 paper-based). Electronic applications accepted. Expenses: Contact institution. *Faculty research:* Health care, child and family, elder and disabled services, general human services.

See Close-Up on page 247.

Brenau University, Graduate Programs, School of Business and Mass Communication, Gainesville, GA 30501. Offers accounting (MBA); healthcare management (MBA); leadership development (MBA); management (MBA); organizational development (MS). Part-time and evening/weekend programs available. Postbaccalaureate distance learning degree programs offered (no on-campus study). *Faculty:* 12 full-time (6 women), 16 part-time/adjunct (5 women). *Students:* 49 full-time (32 women), 148 part-time (89 women); includes 52 minority (45 African Americans, 2 Asian Americans or Pacific Islanders, 5 Hispanic Americans), 2 international. Average age 35. 222 applicants, 55% accepted, 111 enrolled. In 2006, 64 degrees awarded. *Degree requirements:* For master's, thesis (for some programs). *Entrance requirements:* For master's, GMAT, GRE General Test, or MAT, minimum undergraduate GPA of 3.0, faculty interview. Additional exam requirements/recommendations for international students: Required—TOEFL (minimum score 550 paper-based). *Application deadline:* Applications are processed on a rolling basis. Application fee: $30. Electronic applications accepted. *Expenses:* Contact institution. *Financial support:* Career-related internships or fieldwork available. Financial award application deadline: 7/15; financial award applicants required to submit FAFSA. *Faculty research:* International business, women in management entrepreneurship, simulations in business, Internet/online teaching in business, managerial leadership. *Unit head:* Dr. Bill Haney, Dean, 770-538-4707, Fax: 770-537-4701, E-mail: whaney@brenau.edu. *Application contact:* Nathan Goss, Admissions Coordinator, 770-534-6162, Fax: 770-538-4701, E-mail: ngoss@brenau.edu.

Brescia University, Program in Management, Owensboro, KY 42301-3023. Offers MSM. Part-time and evening/weekend programs available. *Entrance requirements:* For master's, GMAT, minimum GPA of 2.5.

Bridgewater State College, School of Graduate Studies, School of Business, Department of Management, Bridgewater, MA 02325-0001. Offers MSM. *Entrance requirements:* For master's, GMAT. *Application deadline:* For fall admission, 3/1 priority date for domestic students; for spring admission, 10/1 priority date for domestic students. Application fee: $50. *Financial support:* Health care benefits and unspecified assistantships available. Support available to part-time students. *Application contact:* Dr. Raymond Charles Guillette, Assistant Dean School of Graduate Studies, 508-531-2919, Fax: 508-531-6162, E-mail: rguillette@bridgew.edu.

Briercrest Seminary, Graduate Programs, Program in Leadership and Management, Caronport, SK S0H 0S0, Canada. Offers organizational leadership (MA). Part-time programs available. *Faculty:* 4 part-time/adjunct (0 women). *Students:* 1 full-time (0 women), 13 part-time (3 women). Average age 39. 10 applicants, 70% accepted, 4 enrolled. In 2006, 9 degrees awarded. *Degree requirements:* For master's, thesis optional. *Entrance requirements:* Additional exam requirements/recommendations for international students: Required—TOEFL (minimum score 550 paper-based; 213 computer-based). Application fee: $25. *Financial support:* Teaching assistantships available. *Unit head:* Dr. Dwayne Uglem, President, 306-756-3212, Fax: 306-756-5500, E-mail: duglem@briercrest.ca. *Application contact:* Kevin Weeks, Enrollment Management Officer, 306-756-3221, Fax: 306-756-5500, E-mail: kweeks@briercrest.ca.

Brigham Young University, Graduate Studies, Marriott School of Management, Executive Program in Business Administration, Provo, UT 84602-1001. Offers MBA. *Accreditation:* AACSB. Part-time and evening/weekend programs available. *Students:* Average age 33. 109 applicants, 69% accepted, 58 enrolled. In 2006, 58 degrees awarded. *Entrance requirements:* For master's, GMAT, 4 years of management experience, minimum GPA of 3.0 in last 60 undergraduate hours. Additional exam requirements/recommendations for international students: Required—TOEFL (minimum score 590 paper-based; 240 computer-based). *Application deadline:* For fall admission, 5/1 for domestic and international students. Applications are processed on a rolling basis. Application fee: $50. Electronic applications accepted. *Expenses:* Contact institution. *Unit head:* Gil Bertelson, Director, 801-422-3721, Fax: 801-422-0512, E-mail: gil@byu.edu. *Application contact:* Yvette Anderson, MBA Program Admissions Direction, 801-422-3500, Fax: 801-422-0513, E-mail: mba@byu.edu.

Brigham Young University, Graduate Studies, Marriott School of Management, Program in Business Administration, Provo, UT 84602-1001. Offers MBA, JD/MBA, MBA/MS. *Accreditation:* AACSB. *Students:* 269 full-time (44 women); includes 24 minority (2 African Americans, 1 American Indian/Alaska Native, 9 Asian Americans or Pacific Islanders, 12 Hispanic Americans), 33 international. Average age 28. 341 applicants, 57% accepted, 137 enrolled. In 2006, 124 degrees awarded. *Entrance requirements:* For master's, GMAT, minimum GPA of 3.0 in last 60 hours. Additional exam requirements/recommendations for international students: Required—TOEFL (minimum score 590 paper-based; 240 computer-based). *Application deadline:* For fall admission, 3/1 for domestic students, 1/15 for international students. Applications are processed on a rolling basis. Application fee: $50. Electronic applications accepted. *Expenses:* Contact institution. *Financial support:* In 2006–07, 196 students received support, including 25 research assistantships (averaging $2,430 per year), 25 teaching assistantships (averaging $2,430 per year); career-related internships or fieldwork, institutionally sponsored loans, scholarships/grants, and tuition waivers (full and partial) also available. Financial award application deadline: 4/15; financial award applicants required to submit FAFSA. *Faculty research:* Finance, organizational behavior/human relations, marketing, supply chain management. *Unit head:* Dr. James D. Stice, Director, 801-422-3500, Fax: 801-422-0513, E-mail: mba@byu.edu. *Application contact:* Yvette Anderson, MBA Program Admissions Direction, 801-422-3500, Fax: 801-422-0513, E-mail: mba@byu.edu.

Brock University, Faculty of Graduate Studies, Faculty of Business, Program in Business Administration, St. Catharines, ON L2S 3A1, Canada. Offers MBA. *Faculty:* 69 full-time (16 women). *Students:* 177 full-time (85 women), 32 part-time (15 women). 230 applicants, 82% accepted, 114 enrolled. In 2006, 54 degrees awarded. *Degree requirements:* For master's, thesis or alternative. *Entrance requirements:* For master's, honours degree. Additional exam requirements/recommendations for international students: Required—TOEFL (minimum score 575 paper-based; 230 computer-based; 89 iBT), IELTS (minimum score 7), TWE (minimum score 4.5). *Application deadline:* For fall admission, 5/1 for domestic students, 2/28 for international students. Application fee: $100. Electronic applications accepted. *Unit head:* Shari Sekel, Director, 905-688-5550 Ext. 3916, Fax: 905-688-4286, E-mail: shari.sekel@brocku.ca.

Brock University, Faculty of Graduate Studies, Faculty of Business, Program in Management, St. Catharines, ON L2S 3A1, Canada. Offers M Sc. Part-time programs available. *Faculty:* 69 full-time (16 women). *Degree requirements:* For master's, thesis. *Entrance requirements:* For master's, GMAT, honors degree. Additional exam requirements/recommendations for international students: Required—TOEFL (minimum score 600 paper-based; 250 computer-based; 100 iBT), IELTS (minimum score 7), TWE (minimum score 4.5). *Application deadline:* For fall admission, 5/1 for domestic students. Application fee: $75. Electronic applications accepted. *Financial support:* Fellowships, scholarships/grants, unspecified assistantships, and bursaries available. *Unit head:* Shari Sekel, Director, 905-688-5550 Ext. 3916, Fax: 905-688-4286, E-mail: shari.sekel@brocku.ca.

Bryant University, Graduate School, Graduate School of Business, Programs in Business Administration, Smithfield, RI 02917-1284. Offers accounting (MBA, CAGS); computer information systems (MBA, CAGS); e-strategy (MBA, CAGS); finance (MBA, CAGS); general business (MBA); management (MBA, CAGS); marketing (MBA, CAGS); operations manage-

Business Administration and Management—General

Bryant University (continued)
ment (MBA). *Accreditation:* AACSB. *Faculty:* 49 full-time (13 women), 2 part-time/adjunct (0 women). *Students:* 143 applicants, 41% accepted, 46 enrolled. In 2006, 106 master's, 10 other advanced degrees awarded. *Entrance requirements:* For master's, GMAT, letter of recommendation, resumé; for CAGS, GMAT, resumé. Additional exam requirements/recommendations for international students: Required—TOEFL (minimum score 580 paper-based; 237 computer-based). *Application deadline:* For fall admission, 7/15 for domestic students, 4/1 for international students; for spring admission, 11/15 for domestic and international students. Application fee: $80. *Expenses:* Tuition: Part-time $1,998 per course. *Financial support:* Research assistantships with full tuition reimbursements, unspecified assistantships available. Financial award applicants required to submit FAFSA. *Unit head:* Kristopher T. Sullivan, Assistant Dean of the Graduate School, 401-232-6230, Fax: 401-232-6494, E-mail: gradprog@bryant.edu.

Butler University, College of Business Administration, Indianapolis, IN 46208-3485. Offers MBA, MP Acc. *Accreditation:* AACSB. Part-time and evening/weekend programs available. *Faculty:* 11 full-time (3 women), 2 part-time/adjunct (0 women). *Students:* 21 full-time (10 women), 150 part-time (54 women); includes 11 minority (6 African Americans, 1 American Indian/Alaska Native, 1 Asian American or Pacific Islander, 3 Hispanic Americans), 20 international. Average age 30. 79 applicants, 57% accepted, 26 enrolled. In 2006, 62 degrees awarded. *Entrance requirements:* For master's, GMAT, minimum AACSB index of 950. *Application deadline:* For fall admission, 8/15 priority date for domestic students. Applications are processed on a rolling basis. Application fee: $35. Electronic applications accepted. *Expenses:* Tuition: Full-time $6,030; part-time $335 per credit. Tuition and fees vary according to program. *Financial support:* Career-related internships or fieldwork and institutionally sponsored loans available. Support available to part-time students. Financial award application deadline: 7/15; financial award applicants required to submit FAFSA. *Faculty research:* Real estate law, international finance, total quality management, web-based commerce, pricing policies. *Unit head:* Dr. Richard Fetter, Dean, 317-940-9221, Fax: 317-940-9455, E-mail: rfetter@butler.edu. *Application contact:* Dr. Stephanie Judge, Director—Marketing, CBA, 317-940-9886, Fax: 317-940-9455, E-mail: sjudge@butler.edu.

Caldwell College, Graduate Studies, Program in Business Administration, Caldwell, NJ 07006-6195. Offers accounting (MBA); business administration (MBA). Part-time and evening/weekend programs available. *Degree requirements:* For master's, capstone course. *Entrance requirements:* For master's, GMAT, minimum GPA of 3.0. Additional exam requirements/recommendations for international students: Required—TOEFL (minimum score 580 paper-based; 237 computer-based). Electronic applications accepted.

California Baptist University, Program in Business Administration, Riverside, CA 92504-3206. Offers MBA. *Accreditation:* ACBSP. Part-time and evening/weekend programs available. *Faculty:* 7 full-time (1 woman), 3 part-time/adjunct (1 woman). *Students:* 39 full-time (15 women), 25 part-time (10 women); includes 18 minority (7 African Americans, 1 American Indian/Alaska Native, 5 Asian Americans or Pacific Islanders, 5 Hispanic Americans), 6 international. 53 applicants, 38% accepted, 16 enrolled. In 2006, 4 degrees awarded. *Degree requirements:* For master's, thesis or alternative, comprehensive business plan. *Entrance requirements:* For master's, minimum undergraduate GPA of 2.75, course work in business. Additional exam requirements/recommendations for international students: Required—TOEFL (minimum score 575 paper-based; 230 computer-based), IELTS (minimum score 7). *Application deadline:* For fall admission, 9/1 for domestic students, 7/15 priority date for international students; for spring admission, 1/3 for domestic students, 11/1 priority date for international students. Applications are processed on a rolling basis. Application fee: $45. Electronic applications accepted. *Expenses:* Contact institution. Tuition and fees vary according to program. *Financial support:* In 2006–07, 30 students received support. Federal Work-Study available. Support available to part-time students. Financial award applicants required to submit FAFSA. *Unit head:* Dr. Andrew Herrity, Dean, School of Business, 951-343-4427, Fax: 951-343-4361, E-mail: aherrity@calbaptist.edu. *Application contact:* Gail Ronveaux, Dean of Graduate Enrollment, 951-343-5045, Fax: 951-343-5095, E-mail: graduateadmissions@calbaptist.edu.

California Lutheran University, Graduate Studies, School of Business, Thousand Oaks, CA 91360-2787. Offers finance (MBA); healthcare management (MBA); international business (MBA); management information systems (MBA); marketing (MBA); organizational behavior (MBA); small business/entrepreneurship (MBA). Evening/weekend programs available. *Entrance requirements:* For master's, GMAT, interview, minimum GPA of 3.0. Expenses: Contact institution.

California National University for Advanced Studies, College of Business Administration, Northridge, CA 91325-3576. Offers MBA, MHRM. Part-time programs available. Postbaccalaureate distance learning degree programs offered (no on-campus study). *Entrance requirements:* For master's, minimum GPA of 3.0. Additional exam requirements/recommendations for international students: Required—TOEFL (minimum score 213 computer-based). Electronic applications accepted.

California Polytechnic State University, San Luis Obispo, Orfalea College of Business, Graduate Programs in Business, San Luis Obispo, CA 93407. Offers MBA. *Faculty:* 3 full-time (1 woman), 3 part-time/adjunct (0 women). *Students:* 40 full-time (12 women), 16 part-time (8 women); includes 4 minority (3 Asian Americans or Pacific Islanders, 1 Hispanic American), 2 international. 98 applicants, 46% accepted, 40 enrolled. In 2006, 29 degrees awarded. *Degree requirements:* For master's, thesis or alternative. *Entrance requirements:* For master's, GMAT. Additional exam requirements/recommendations for international students: Required—TOEFL (minimum score 550 paper-based; 213 computer-based), TWE (minimum score 4.5). *Application deadline:* For fall admission, 7/1 for domestic students, 11/30 for international students. Applications are processed on a rolling basis. Application fee: $55. Electronic applications accepted. *Financial support:* Career-related internships or fieldwork, Federal Work-Study, institutionally sponsored loans, scholarships/grants, and unspecified assistantships available. Support available to part-time students. Financial award application deadline: 3/2; financial award applicants required to submit FAFSA. *Unit head:* Dr. Chris Carr, Associate Dean/Graduate Coordinator, 805-756-2637, Fax: 805-756-0110, E-mail: ccarr@calpoly.edu.

California State Polytechnic University, Pomona, Academic Affairs, College of Business Administration, Pomona, CA 91768-2557. Offers MBA, MSBA. *Accreditation:* AACSB. Part-time programs available. *Faculty:* 76 full-time (26 women), 57 part-time/adjunct (14 women). *Students:* 92 full-time (32 women), 68 part-time (27 women); includes 63 minority (3 African Americans, 43 Asian Americans or Pacific Islanders, 17 Hispanic Americans), 30 international. Average age 30. 132 applicants, 33% accepted, 27 enrolled. In 2006, 58 degrees awarded. *Degree requirements:* For master's, thesis, project report. *Entrance requirements:* For master's, GMAT. *Application deadline:* For fall admission, 5/1 priority date for domestic students; for winter admission, 10/15 priority date for domestic students; for spring admission, 1/2 priority date for domestic students. Applications are processed on a rolling basis. Application fee: $55. Electronic applications accepted. *Expenses:* Tuition: state resident: part-time $226 per unit. Tuition, nonresident: part-time $226 per unit. Required fees: $2,486 per year. *Financial support:* In 2006–07, 5 research assistantships, 3 teaching assistantships were awarded; career-related internships or fieldwork, Federal Work-Study, and institutionally sponsored loans also available. Support available to part-time students. Financial award application deadline: 3/2; financial award applicants required to submit FAFSA. *Faculty research:* Business strategy; investment, cash flow, and cost of capital; entrepreneurship; trade with China; creativity and innovation. *Unit head:* Dr. David Klock, Dean, 909-869-2400. *Application contact:* Dr. Eric J. McLaughlin, Director, Graduate Program, 909-869-2362, E-mail: ejmclaughlin@csupomona.edu.

California State University, Bakersfield, Division of Graduate Studies and Research, School of Business and Public Administration, Program in Administration, Bakersfield, CA 93311-1022. Offers MS. *Accreditation:* AACSB. Postbaccalaureate distance learning degree programs offered.

California State University, Bakersfield, Division of Graduate Studies and Research, School of Business and Public Administration, Program in Business Administration, Bakersfield, CA 93311-1022. Offers MBA. *Accreditation:* AACSB. *Students:* 34 full-time (12 women), 36 part-time (22 women); includes 16 minority (1 African American, 1 American Indian/Alaska Native, 7 Asian Americans or Pacific Islanders, 7 Hispanic Americans), 6 international. Average age 34. 37 applicants, 41% accepted. In 2006, 21 degrees awarded. *Entrance requirements:* For master's, GMAT. *Application deadline:* Applications are processed on a rolling basis. Application fee: $55. *Unit head:* Michael Bidell, Graduate Coordinator, 661-654-3099, Fax: 661-665-6923.

California State University Channel Islands, Extended Education, Program in Business Administration, Camarillo, CA 93012. Offers MBA. *Students:* 38. *Entrance requirements:* For master's, GMAT, 2 years work experience. Additional exam requirements/recommendations for international students: Required—TOEFL (minimum score 550 paper-based). Application fee: $55. *Unit head:* Dr. William P. Cordeiro, Director, 805-437-2748, E-mail: mba@csuci.edu. *Application contact:* Maribel Aguilera, Application Contact, 805-437-2748, Fax: 805-437-8859, E-mail: exed@csuci.edu.

California State University, Chico, Graduate School, College of Behavioral and Social Sciences, Department of Political Science, Program in Public Administration, Chico, CA 95929-0722. Offers health administration (MPA); local government management (MPA); public administration (MPA). *Accreditation:* NASPAA. *Students:* 13 full-time (7 women), 24 part-time (11 women); includes 8 minority (1 African American, 2 American Indian/Alaska Native, 1 Asian American or Pacific Islander, 4 Hispanic Americans), 1 international. Average age 32. 22 applicants, 95% accepted, 10 enrolled. In 2006, 6 degrees awarded. *Degree requirements:* For master's, thesis or alternative, oral exam. *Entrance requirements:* For master's, 2 letters of recommendation. Additional exam requirements/recommendations for international students: Required—TOEFL (minimum score 550 paper-based; 213 computer-based). *Application deadline:* For fall admission, 3/1 for domestic and international students; for spring admission, 9/15 for domestic and international students. Applications are processed on a rolling basis. Application fee: $55. Electronic applications accepted. *Financial support:* Fellowships, career-related internships or fieldwork available. *Unit head:* Dr. Donna Kemp, Graduate Coordinator, 530-898-5734.

California State University, Chico, Graduate School, College of Business, Program in Business Administration, Chico, CA 95929-0011. Offers MBA. *Accreditation:* AACSB. *Students:* 20 full-time (12 women), 12 part-time (2 women); includes 4 minority (2 Asian Americans or Pacific Islanders, 2 Hispanic Americans), 9 international. Average age 29. 31 applicants, 100% accepted, 16 enrolled. In 2006, 11 degrees awarded. *Degree requirements:* For master's, thesis or alternative. *Entrance requirements:* For master's, GMAT, 3 letters of recommendation. Additional exam requirements/recommendations for international students: Required—TOEFL (minimum score 550 paper-based; 213 computer-based). *Application deadline:* For fall admission, 3/1 for domestic and international students; for spring admission, 9/15 for domestic and international students. Applications are processed on a rolling basis. Application fee: $55. Electronic applications accepted. *Unit head:* Dr. Ray Boykin, 530-898-5895.

California State University, Dominguez Hills, College of Business Administration and Public Policy, Program in Business Administration, Carson, CA 90747-0001. Offers MBA. *Accreditation:* ACBSP. Part-time and evening/weekend programs available. Postbaccalaureate distance learning degree programs offered (no on-campus study). *Faculty:* 21 full-time (2 women), 1 part-time/adjunct (0 women). *Students:* 14 full-time (8 women), 23 part-time (16 women); includes 12 minority (7 African Americans, 3 Asian Americans or Pacific Islanders, 2 Hispanic Americans), 11 international. Average age 31. 128 applicants, 69% accepted, 7 enrolled. In 2006, 47 degrees awarded. *Entrance requirements:* For master's, GMAT, minimum GPA of 2.75. Additional exam requirements/recommendations for international students: Required—TOEFL (minimum score 570 paper-based; 230 computer-based; 88 iBT). *Application deadline:* For fall admission, 4/1 for domestic and international students; for spring admission, 11/1 for domestic students, 10/1 for international students. Application fee: $55. *Expenses:* Tuition, nonresident: part-time $339 per unit. Required fees: $1,148 per term. Tuition and fees vary according to program. *Faculty research:* Management. *Application contact:* Eileen Hall, Graduate Advisor, 310-243-3465, E-mail: ehall@csudh.edu.

California State University, East Bay, Academic Programs and Graduate Studies, College of Business and Economics, Department of Accounting and Computer Information Systems, Option in Computer Information Systems, Hayward, CA 94542-3000. Offers business administration (MBA); computer information systems (MS). Part-time and evening/weekend programs available. *Students:* 3 full-time (2 women), 11 part-time (5 women); includes 2 minority (both Asian Americans or Pacific Islanders), 5 international. Average age 32. *Degree requirements:* For master's, comprehensive exam or thesis. *Entrance requirements:* For master's, GMAT, minimum GPA of 2.75. Additional exam requirements/recommendations for international students: Required—TOEFL (minimum score 550 paper-based; 213 computer-based). *Application deadline:* For fall admission, 5/31 for domestic students, 4/30 for international students; for winter admission, 9/30 for domestic and international students; for spring admission, 12/31 for domestic students, 11/30 for international students. Application fee: $55. *Financial support:* Career-related internships or fieldwork, Federal Work-Study, and institutionally sponsored loans available. Support available to part-time students. Financial award application deadline: 3/2. *Unit head:* Doris Duncan, Director of Graduate Programs, 510-885-3364, Fax: 510-885-2176, E-mail: doris.duncan@csueastbay.edu.

California State University, East Bay, Academic Programs and Graduate Studies, College of Business and Economics, Department of Management and Finance, Option in Management Sciences, Hayward, CA 94542-3000. Offers MBA. *Accreditation:* AACSB. *Degree requirements:* For master's, comprehensive exam or thesis. *Entrance requirements:* For master's, GMAT, minimum GPA of 2.75. Additional exam requirements/recommendations for international students: Required—TOEFL (minimum score 550 paper-based; 213 computer-based). *Application deadline:* For fall admission, 5/31 for domestic students, 4/30 for international students; for winter admission, 9/30 for domestic and international students; for spring admission, 12/31 for domestic students, 11/30 for international students. Application fee: $55. *Financial support:* Application deadline: 3/2. *Unit head:* Dr. John Villareal, Coordinator, 510-885-3376, E-mail: john.villareal@csuestbay.edu. *Application contact:* Doris Duncan, Director of Graduate Programs, 510-885-3364, Fax: 510-885-2176, E-mail: doris.duncan@csueastbay.edu.

California State University, East Bay, Academic Programs and Graduate Studies, College of Business and Economics, Program in Business Administration, Hayward, CA 94542-3000. Offers MS. *Accreditation:* AACSB. *Application contact:* Doris Duncan, Director of Graduate Programs, 510-885-3364, Fax: 510-885-2176, E-mail: doris.duncan@csueastbay.edu.

California State University, Fresno, Division of Graduate Studies, Craig School of Business, Program in Business Administration, Fresno, CA 93740-8027. Offers MBA. *Accreditation:* AACSB. Part-time programs available. *Degree requirements:* For master's, thesis or alternative. *Entrance requirements:* For master's, GMAT, minimum GPA of 2.53. Additional exam requirements/recommendations for international students: Required—TOEFL. Electronic applications accepted. *Faculty research:* International trade development, entrepreneurial outreach.

California State University, Fullerton, Graduate Studies, College of Business and Economics, Department of Management, Fullerton, CA 92834-9480. Offers MBA. *Accreditation:* AACSB. Part-time and evening/weekend programs available. *Students:* 16 full-time (6 women), 28 part-time (13 women); includes 15 minority (9 Asian Americans or Pacific Islanders, 6 Hispanic Americans), 10 international. Average age 28. 74 applicants, 38% accepted, 18 enrolled. In 2006, 5 degrees awarded. *Degree requirements:* For master's, project or thesis. *Entrance requirements:* For master's, GMAT, minimum AACSB index of 950. Application fee: $55. *Expenses:* Tuition, nonresident: part-time $339 per unit. Required fees: $1,155 per semester. *Financial support:* Teaching assistantships, Federal Work-Study, institutionally sponsored loans, and scholarships/grants available. Support available to part-time students. Financial award application deadline: 3/1. *Unit head:* Dr. Ellen Dumond, Chair, 714-278-2251. *Application contact:* Robert Miyake, Assistant Dean, 714-278-2211.

California State University, Fullerton, Graduate Studies, College of Business and Economics, Program in Business Administration, Fullerton, CA 92834-9480. Offers MBA. *Accreditation:* AACSB. Part-time and evening/weekend programs available. *Students:* 42 full-time (22 women), 80 part-time (30 women); includes 46 minority (3 African Americans, 34 Asian Americans or Pacific Islanders, 9 Hispanic Americans), 26 international. Average age 30. 236 applicants, 42% accepted, 36 enrolled. In 2006, 49 degrees awarded. *Degree requirements:* For master's, project or thesis. *Entrance requirements:* For master's, GMAT. Application fee: $55. *Expenses:* Tuition, nonresident: part-time $339 per unit. Required fees: $1,155 per semester. *Financial support:* Teaching assistantships, Federal Work-Study, institutionally sponsored loans, and scholarships/grants available. Support available to part-time students. Financial award application deadline: 3/1. *Application contact:* Robert Miyake, Assistant Dean, 714-278-2211.

California State University, Long Beach, Graduate Studies, College of Business Administration, Long Beach, CA 90840. Offers MBA. *Accreditation:* AACSB. Part-time and evening/weekend programs available. *Faculty:* 8 full-time (3 women), 6 part-time/adjunct (2 women). *Students:* 100 full-time (48 women), 171 part-time (73 women); includes 73 minority (3 African Americans, 48 Asian Americans or Pacific Islanders, 22 Hispanic Americans), 42 international. Average age 32. 468 applicants, 30% accepted, 91 enrolled. In 2006, 123 degrees awarded. *Entrance requirements:* For master's, GMAT. *Application deadline:* For fall admission, 7/1 for domestic students; for spring admission, 12/1 for domestic students. Applications are processed on a rolling basis. Application fee: $55. Electronic applications accepted. *Financial support:* Career-related internships or fieldwork and scholarships/grants available. Financial award application deadline: 3/2; financial award applicants required to submit FAFSA. *Faculty research:* Attitude formation theory, consumer motivation, gift giving, derivative and synthetic securities, financial applications of artificial intelligence. *Unit head:* Dr. Mohammed B. Khan, Interim Dean, 562-985-5306, Fax: 562-985-5742, E-mail: mkhan@csulb.edu. *Application contact:* Dr. Philip Chong, Interim Associate Dean, 562-985-7696, Fax: 562-985-5742.

California State University, Los Angeles, Graduate Studies, College of Business and Economics, Department of Information Systems, Los Angeles, CA 90032-8530. Offers business information systems (MBA); management (MS); management information systems (MS); office management (MBA). Part-time and evening/weekend programs available. *Faculty:* 6 full-time (0 women). *Students:* 8 full-time (4 women), 30 part-time (7 women); includes 24 minority (1 African American, 17 Asian Americans or Pacific Islanders, 6 Hispanic Americans), 6 international. In 2006, 12 degrees awarded. *Degree requirements:* For master's, comprehensive exam (MBA), thesis (MS). *Entrance requirements:* For master's, GMAT, minimum GPA of 2.5 during previous 2 years of course work. Additional exam requirements/recommendations for international students: Required—TOEFL. *Application deadline:* For fall admission, 6/30 for domestic students; for spring admission, 11/30 for domestic students. Applications are processed on a rolling basis. Application fee: $55. *Expenses:* Tuition, nonresident: part-time $226 per unit. *Financial support:* Career-related internships or fieldwork and Federal Work-Study available. Support available to part-time students. Financial award application deadline: 3/1. *Unit head:* Dr. Adam Huarng, Chair, 323-343-2983.

California State University, Los Angeles, Graduate Studies, College of Business and Economics, Major in Business Administration, Department of Management, Los Angeles, CA 90032-8530. Offers MBA, MS. *Accreditation:* AACSB. Part-time and evening/weekend programs available. *Faculty:* 2 full-time (0 women), 1 (woman) part-time/adjunct. *Students:* 6 full-time (3 women), 26 part-time (12 women); includes 20 minority (3 African Americans, 1 American Indian/Alaska Native, 7 Asian Americans or Pacific Islanders, 9 Hispanic Americans), 3 international. *Entrance requirements:* For master's, GMAT, minimum GPA of 2.5 during previous 2 years of course work. Additional exam requirements/recommendations for international students: Required—TOEFL. *Application deadline:* For fall admission, 6/30 for domestic students; for spring admission, 11/30 for domestic students. Applications are processed on a rolling basis. Application fee: $55. *Expenses:* Tuition, nonresident: part-time $226 per unit. *Financial support:* Application deadline: 3/1. *Unit head:* Dr. Paul Washburn, Acting Chair, 323-343-2890, Fax: 323-343-6461.

California State University, Northridge, Graduate Studies, College of Business and Economics, Northridge, CA 91330. Offers MBA. *Accreditation:* AACSB. Part-time programs available. *Faculty:* 97 full-time (26 women), 61 part-time/adjunct (17 women). *Students:* 52 full-time (26 women), 181 part-time (67 women); includes 61 minority (5 African Americans, 35 Asian Americans or Pacific Islanders, 21 Hispanic Americans), 28 international. Average age 33. 198 applicants, 33% accepted, 49 enrolled. In 2006, 72 degrees awarded. *Degree requirements:* For master's, thesis or alternative. *Entrance requirements:* For master's, GMAT, minimum GPA of 3.0 in last 60 units. Additional exam requirements/recommendations for international students: Required—TOEFL. *Application deadline:* For fall admission, 11/30 for domestic students. Application fee: $55. *Expenses:* Tuition, nonresident: full-time $8,136; part-time $4,068 per year. Required fees: $3,624; $1,161 per term. *Financial support:* Teaching assistantships, Federal Work-Study available. Support available to part-time students. Financial award application deadline: 3/1. *Unit head:* Dr. William Jennings, Interim Dean, 818-677-2455. *Application contact:* Dr. Deborah Cours, Director of Graduate Programs, 818-677-2467.

California State University, Sacramento, Graduate Studies, College of Business Administration, Sacramento, CA 95819-6048. Offers MBA, MS. *Accreditation:* AACSB. Part-time and evening/weekend programs available. *Students:* 64 full-time (38 women), 150 part-time (55 women); includes 48 minority (2 African Americans, 1 American Indian/Alaska Native, 27 Asian Americans or Pacific Islanders, 18 Hispanic Americans), 19 international. Average age 30. 373 applicants, 69% accepted, 42 enrolled. *Degree requirements:* For master's, thesis or alternative, writing proficiency exam. *Entrance requirements:* For master's, GMAT. Additional exam requirements/recommendations for international students: Required—TOEFL. *Application deadline:* Applications are processed on a rolling basis. Application fee: $55. Electronic applications accepted. *Financial support:* Research assistantships, teaching assistantships, career-related internships or fieldwork and Federal Work-Study available. Support available to part-time students. Financial award application deadline: 3/1. *Unit head:* Dr. Sanjay Varshney, Dean, 916-278-6942, Fax: 916-278-5793.

See Close-Up on page 249.

California State University, San Bernardino, Graduate Studies, College of Business and Public Administration, Program in Business Administration, San Bernardino, CA 92407-2397. Offers MBA. *Accreditation:* AACSB. Part-time and evening/weekend programs available. *Faculty:* 50 full-time, 37 part-time/adjunct. *Students:* 226 full-time (89 women), 61 part-time (21 women); includes 74 minority (15 African Americans, 1 American Indian/Alaska Native, 28 Asian Americans or Pacific Islanders, 30 Hispanic Americans), 111 international. Average age 27. 310 applicants, 68% accepted, 78 enrolled. In 2006, 84 degrees awarded. *Application deadline:* For fall admission, 8/31 priority date for domestic students. Applications are processed on a rolling basis. Application fee: $55. *Financial support:* Career-related internships or fieldwork, Federal Work-Study, and institutionally sponsored loans available. Support available to part-time students. Financial award application deadline: 3/1. *Unit head:* Beth Flynn, Director, 909-537-5703, Fax: 909-537-7026, E-mail: bflynn@csusb.edu.

California State University, San Marcos, College of Business Administration, San Marcos, CA 92096-0001. Offers business management (MBA); government management (MBA). Evening/weekend programs available. *Faculty:* 26 full-time (7 women), 28 part-time/adjunct (7 women). *Students:* 65 full-time (27 women), 17 part-time (5 women); includes 17 minority (1 African American, 10 Asian Americans or Pacific Islanders, 6 Hispanic Americans), 4 international. Average age 28. 44 applicants, 30% accepted, 10 enrolled. In 2006, 47 degrees awarded. *Degree requirements:* For master's, project. *Entrance requirements:* For master's, GMAT, minimum GPA of 3.0 in last 60 units, 3 years of full-time work experience. Additional exam requirements/recommendations for international students: Required—TOEFL (minimum score 550 paper-based; 213 computer-based). *Application deadline:* For fall admission, 4/30 priority date for domestic students. Applications are processed on a rolling basis. Application fee: $55. *Expenses: Contact institution. Financial support:* In 2006–07, 35 students received support; research assistantships, teaching assistantships, Federal Work-Study available. Support available to part-time students. Financial award applicants required to submit FAFSA. *Unit head:* Dennis Guseman, Dean, 760-750-4239. *Application contact:* Keith Butler, Operations Manager, 760-750-4266, E-mail: kbutler@csusm.edu.

California State University, Stanislaus, Graduate School, College of Business Administration, Turlock, CA 95382. Offers business administration (MBA); international finance (MSBA). *Accreditation:* AACSB. Part-time and evening/weekend programs available. *Degree requirements:* For master's, thesis or alternative, comprehensive exam. *Entrance requirements:* For master's, GMAT, minimum GPA of 2.5. Additional exam requirements/recommendations for international students: Required—TOEFL (minimum score 550 paper-based; 213 computer-based).

California University of Pennsylvania, School of Graduate Studies and Research, School of Science and Technology, Program in Business Administration, California, PA 15419-1394. Offers MSBA. Part-time and evening/weekend programs available. *Faculty:* 5 full-time (0 women), 3 part-time/adjunct (0 women). *Students:* 33 full-time (15 women), 19 part-time (7 women); includes 5 minority (all African Americans) Average age 28. 32 applicants, 81% accepted, 19 enrolled. In 2006, 30 degrees awarded. *Median time to degree:* Master's–1 year full-time, 1.25 years part-time. *Degree requirements:* For master's, comprehensive exam. *Entrance requirements:* For master's, minimum QPA of 3.0. Additional exam requirements/recommendations for international students: Required—TOEFL (minimum score 550 paper-based; 213 computer-based). *Application deadline:* For fall admission, 8/1 priority date for domestic and international students; for winter admission, 12/1 priority date for domestic and international students; for spring admission, 5/1 priority date for domestic and international students. Applications are processed on a rolling basis. Application fee: $25. Electronic applications accepted. *Expenses:* Tuition, state resident: full-time $6,048; part-time $336 per credit. Tuition, nonresident: full-time $9,678; part-time $538 per credit. Required fees: $1,854; $263 per credit. Full-time tuition and fees vary according to course load, campus/location and program. *Financial support:* Career-related internships or fieldwork, scholarships/grants, traineeships, and unspecified assistantships available. Financial award applicants required to submit FAFSA. *Faculty research:* Economics, applied economics, consumer behavior, technology and business, impact of technology. *Unit head:* Dr. Arshad Chawdhry, Graduate Coordinator, 724-938-5990, Fax: 724-938-5908, E-mail: chawdhry@cup.edu.

Cambridge College, Program in Management, Cambridge, MA 02138-5304. Offers e-commerce (M Mgt); management (M Mgt). Part-time and evening/weekend programs available. *Faculty:* 4 full-time (all women), 305 part-time/adjunct (167 women). *Students:* 362 full-time (207 women), 219 part-time (135 women); includes 203 minority (131 African Americans, 2 American Indian/Alaska Native, 22 Asian Americans or Pacific Islanders, 48 Hispanic Americans), 80 international. Average age 39. 160 applicants, 96% accepted, 126 enrolled. In 2006, 165 degrees awarded. *Degree requirements:* For master's, thesis. *Application deadline:* Applications are processed on a rolling basis. Application fee: $30. *Expenses: Contact institution.* One-time fee: $130 full-time. Tuition and fees vary according to degree level and program. *Financial support:* Teaching assistantships, career-related internships or fieldwork and Federal Work-Study available. Financial award applicants required to submit FAFSA. *Unit head:* Dr. Bill Hancock, Associate Dean, 617-873-0281, Fax: 617-349-3545. *Application contact:* Michael Travaghini, Director of Graduate Admissions, 617-868-1000 Ext. 1162, Fax: 617-349-3561, E-mail: admit@cambridgecollege.edu.

Cameron University, Office of Graduate Studies, Program in Business Administration, Lawton, OK 73505-6377. Offers MBA. *Accreditation:* ACBSP. Part-time and evening/weekend programs available. Postbaccalaureate distance learning degree programs offered (no on-campus study). *Faculty:* 15 full-time (4 women), 4 part-time/adjunct (0 women). *Students:* 41 full-time (25 women), 104 part-time (59 women); includes 58 minority (29 African Americans, 14 American Indian/Alaska Native, 7 Asian Americans or Pacific Islanders, 8 Hispanic Americans). Average age 35. 121 applicants, 81% accepted. In 2006, 33 degrees awarded. *Degree requirements:* For master's, comprehensive exam, registration. *Entrance requirements:* Additional exam requirements/recommendations for international students: Required—TOEFL (minimum score 550 paper-based; 213 computer-based). *Application deadline:* Applications are processed on a rolling basis. Application fee: $15 ($35 for international students). Electronic applications accepted. *Expenses:* Tuition, state resident: full-time $2,479; part-time $138 per credit hour. Tuition, nonresident: full-time $5,976; part-time $332 per credit hour. Tuition and fees vary according to campus/location. *Financial support:* In 2006–07, 8 fellowships (averaging $2,000 per year), 4 research assistantships (averaging $7,680 per year) were awarded; teaching assistantships, career-related internships or fieldwork, Federal Work-Study, tuition waivers (partial), and unspecified assistantships also available. Support available to part-time students. Financial award application deadline: 4/15; financial award applicants required to submit FAFSA. *Faculty research:* Financial liberalization, right to work, recession, teaching evaluations, database management. *Unit head:* Bernadette Lonzanida, Graduate Advisor, 580-581-2271, Fax: 580-591-8087, E-mail: bernadel@cameron.edu. *Application contact:* Teresa Enriquez, Graduate Admissions/Enrollment Coordinator, 580-581-2987, E-mail: teresae@cameron.edu.

Campbellsville University, School of Business and Economics, Campbellsville, KY 42718-2799. Offers business administration (MBA). Part-time and evening/weekend programs available. *Faculty:* 2 full-time (0 women), 5 part-time/adjunct (1 woman). *Students:* 34 full-time (16 women), 17 part-time (10 women), 7 international. Average age 28. 40 applicants, 60% accepted, 23 enrolled. In 2006, 34 degrees awarded. *Degree requirements:* For master's, registration. *Entrance requirements:* For master's, GRE or GMAT. Additional exam requirements/recommendations for international students: Required—TOEFL (minimum score 550 paper-based; 213 computer-based). *Application deadline:* For fall admission, 9/14 priority date for domestic and international students; for winter admission, 1/18 priority date for domestic and international students; for spring admission, 4/4 priority date for domestic and international students. Applications are processed on a rolling basis. Application fee: $25. Electronic applications accepted. *Expenses: Contact institution.* Tuition and fees vary according to program. *Financial support:* In 2006–07, 11 students received support. Tuition waivers (full) and unspecified assistantships available. Financial award application deadline: 6/1; financial award applicants required to submit FAFSA. *Unit head:* Dr. Patricia H. Cowherd, Dean, 270-789-5553, Fax: 270-789-5066, E-mail: phcowherd@campbellsville.edu. *Application contact:* Karla Deaton, Assistant Director of Admissions, 270-789-5078, Fax: 270-789-5071, E-mail: krdeaton@campbellsville.edu.

Campbell University, Graduate and Professional Programs, Lundy-Fetterman School of Business, Buies Creek, NC 27506. Offers MBA, MTIM. Part-time and evening/weekend programs available. *Faculty:* 11 full-time (1 woman), 4 part-time/adjunct (0 women). *Students:* 49 full-time (18 women), 158 part-time (67 women); includes 5 minority (4 African Americans, 1 Hispanic American), 5 international. Average age 29. 90 applicants, 69% accepted, 50 enrolled. In 2006, 135 degrees awarded. *Degree requirements:* For master's, thesis or alternative, comprehensive exam, registration. *Entrance requirements:* For master's, GMAT, minimum GPA of 2.7, 3 letters of reference. Additional exam requirements/recommendations for international students: Required—TOEFL (minimum score 550 paper-based; 213 computer-based). *Application deadline:* Applications are processed on a rolling basis. Application fee: $65. *Expenses:* Tuition: Part-time $380 per semester hour. *Financial support:* In 2006–07, 3 teaching assistantships (averaging $4,000 per year) were awarded; fellowships, research assistantships, career-related internships or fieldwork, Federal Work-Study, institutionally sponsored loans, scholarships/grants, and unspecified assistantships also available. Support available to part-time students. Financial award application deadline: 3/15. *Faculty research:* Agricultural economics, investments, leadership, marketing, law and economics. *Unit head:* Dr. Ben Hawkins, Dean, 910-893-1380, Fax: 910-814-4352, E-mail: hawkinsb@campbell.edu. *Application contact:* James S. Farthing, Director of Graduate Admissions for Business and Education, 910-893-1200 Ext. 1318, Fax: 910-814-4718, E-mail: farthing@campbell.edu.

Business Administration and Management—General

Canisius College, Graduate Division, Richard J. Wehle School of Business, Department of Management and Marketing, Buffalo, NY 14208-1098. Offers business administration (MBA). *Accreditation:* AACSB. *Faculty:* 32 full-time (6 women), 8 part-time/adjunct (2 women). *Students:* 68 full-time (21 women), 167 part-time (72 women); includes 24 minority (15 African Americans, 5 Asian Americans or Pacific Islanders, 4 Hispanic Americans), 19 international. Average age 29. In 2006, 81 degrees awarded. *Entrance requirements:* For master's, GMAT. *Application deadline:* For fall admission, 7/1 priority date for domestic students; for spring admission, 11/1 priority date for domestic students. Applications are processed on a rolling basis. Application fee: $25. *Expenses: Contact institution.* Tuition and fees vary according to program. *Financial support:* Research assistantships with partial tuition reimbursements, career-related internships or fieldwork, scholarships/grants, and unspecified assistantships available. Support available to part-time students. Financial award application deadline: 6/15; financial award applicants required to submit FAFSA. *Faculty research:* Risk aversion, information security, employee relations, urban finance, student expectations. *Unit head:* Dr. George Palumbo, Director, MBA Program, 716-888-2667, Fax: 716-888-3132, E-mail: palumbo@canisius.edu. *Application contact:* Laura McEwen, Director of Graduate Programs, 716-888-2140, Fax: 716-888-8211, E-mail: gradubus@canisius.edu.

Cape Breton University, School of Business, Sydney, NS B1P 6L2, Canada. Offers community economic development (MBA). *Degree requirements:* For master's, research project, research essay. *Entrance requirements:* For master's, interview, letters of reference. Expenses: Contact institution. *Faculty research:* Community entrepreneurship, CED theory, transportation, governance, business and environmental issues in Canada.

Capella University, School of Business and Technology, Minneapolis, MN 55402. Offers accounting (MBA), including system design and programming; business (Certificate), including human resource management (MS, PhD, Certificate), information technology management (MS, PhD, Certificate), leadership (MBA, MS, PhD, Certificate); finance (MBA); general business (MBA); health care management (MBA); information technology (MS, Certificate), including general information technology (MS), information security, network architecture and design (MS), professional projects management (Certificate), project management and leadership (MS), system design and development (MS),); information technology management (MBA); marketing (MBA); organization and management (MBA, MS, PhD), including general business (PhD), general organization and management (MBA, MS), human resource management (MS, PhD, Certificate), information technology management (MS, PhD, Certificate), leadership (MBA, MS, PhD, Certificate); project management (MBA). Part-time and evening/weekend programs available. Postbaccalaureate distance learning degree programs offered (minimal on-campus study). Terminal master's awarded for partial completion of doctoral program. *Degree requirements:* For master's, integrative project, thesis optional; for doctorate, thesis/dissertation, comprehensive exam, registration. *Entrance requirements:* Additional exam requirements/recommendations for international students: Required—TOEFL (minimum score 550 paper-based; 213 computer-based), TWE (minimum score 4). Electronic applications accepted. *Faculty research:* Business policies: strategic, corporate, and financial management; interplay of technological, organizational and social change.

Capital University, Law School, Program in Business Law and Taxation, Columbus, OH 43209-2394. Offers business (LL M); business and taxation (LL M); taxation (LL M); JD/LL M. Part-time and evening/weekend programs available. *Degree requirements:* For master's, thesis or alternative. *Entrance requirements:* For master's, previous course work in accounting, business law, and taxation. Additional exam requirements/recommendations for international students: Required—TOEFL (minimum score 600 paper-based; 250 computer-based). Electronic applications accepted. *Expenses:* Tuition: Part-time $920 per credit. Part-time tuition and fees vary according to program.

Capital University, School of Management, Columbus, OH 43209-2394. Offers MBA, MBA/JD, MBA/LL M, MBA/MSN, MBA/MT. *Accreditation:* ACBSP. Part-time and evening/weekend programs available. *Faculty:* 17 full-time (7 women), 23 part-time/adjunct (1 woman). *Students:* Average age 29. *Degree requirements:* For master's, research project. *Entrance requirements:* For master's, GMAT, 2 years of work experience. Additional exam requirements/recommendations for international students: Required—TOEFL. *Application deadline:* For fall admission, 8/1 priority date for domestic students; for winter admission, 12/1 priority date for domestic students; for spring admission, 4/1 priority date for domestic students. Applications are processed on a rolling basis. Application fee: $25. Electronic applications accepted. *Expenses:* Tuition: Part-time $920 per credit. Part-time tuition and fees vary according to program. *Financial support:* In 2006–07, 2 students received support, including 2 fellowships (averaging $1,000 per year); scholarships/grants and tuition waivers (full) also available. Support available to part-time students. Financial award application deadline: 8/1; financial award applicants required to submit FAFSA. *Faculty research:* Taxation, public policy, health care, management of non-profits. *Unit head:* Dr. Keirsten Moore, Interim Dean, 614-236-6670, Fax: 614-296-6540. *Application contact:* Trudy Riesser, Director, MBA Enrollment Services, 614-236-6538, Fax: 614-236-6540, E-mail: trieser@capital.edu.

Capitol College, Graduate Programs, Laurel, MD 20708-9759. Offers business administration (MBA); computer science (MS); electrical engineering (MS); information and telecommunications systems management (MS); information architecture (MS); network security (MS). Part-time and evening/weekend programs available. Postbaccalaureate distance learning degree programs offered (no on-campus study). *Entrance requirements:* For master's, minimum GPA of 3.0. Electronic applications accepted.

Cardean University, MBA Program, Chicago, IL 60606-7204. Offers accounting and information systems (MBA); e-commerce (MBA); finance (MBA); global management (MBA); health care administration (MBA); human resources management (MBA); leadership (MBA); management of information systems (MBA); management of technology (MBA); marketing (MBA); professional accounting (MBA); project management (MBA); risk management (MBA); strategy and economics (MBA). Part-time and evening/weekend programs available. Postbaccalaureate distance learning degree programs offered (no on-campus study). *Entrance requirements:* Additional exam requirements/recommendations for international students: Required—TOEFL (minimum score 550 paper-based; 213 computer-based).

Cardinal Stritch University, College of Business and Management, Milwaukee, WI 53217-3985. Offers management for adults (MBA, MS), including business administration (MBA), financial services (MS), healthcare executives (MBA), management (MS). *Accreditation:* ACBSP. Part-time and evening/weekend programs available. *Degree requirements:* For master's, thesis (for some programs), case study, faculty recommendation. *Entrance requirements:* For master's, 3 years management or related experience, minimum GPA of 2.5. Additional exam requirements/recommendations for international students: Required—TOEFL. Expenses: Contact institution.

Announcement: The College of Business at Cardinal Stritch University designs its accelerated master's degree programs, the Master of Business Administration and the Master of Science in Management, to satisfy the needs and schedules of busy working professionals. Classes meet 1 night a week for 4 hours at one of the University's 3 regional campuses—Milwaukee or Madison, Wisconsin, or Edina, Minnesota—and at off-campus sites throughout Wisconsin and Minnesota. For more information, visit www.stritch.edu/business or call 800-347-8822, ext. 4422.

Carleton University, Faculty of Graduate Studies, Faculty of Business, Eric Sprott School of Business, Ottawa, ON K1S 5B6, Canada. Offers business administration (MBA); management (PhD). *Degree requirements:* For master's, thesis optional; for doctorate, thesis/dissertation, comprehensive exam. *Entrance requirements:* For master's, GMAT, honors degree; for doctorate, GMAT. Additional exam requirements/recommendations for international students: Required—TOEFL. *Application deadline:* Applications are processed on a rolling basis. Application fee: $75 Canadian dollars. *Financial support:* Fellowships, research assistantships, teaching assistantships, institutionally sponsored loans, scholarships/grants, and unspecified assistantships available. *Faculty research:* Business information systems, finance, international business, marketing, production and operations. *Unit head:* Roland Thomas, Director, 613-520-2600 Ext. 2388, Fax: 613-520-4427, E-mail: director_business@carleton.ca. *Application contact:* Liane Mazzuli, Graduate Secretary, 613-520-2600 Ext. 2388, Fax: 613-520-4427.

Carlos Albizu University, Miami Campus, Graduate Programs, Miami, FL 33172-2209. Offers clinical psychology (Psy D); entrepreneurship (MBA); exceptional student education (MS); industrial/organizational psychology (MS); marriage and family therapy (MS); mental health counseling (MS); nonprofit management (MBA); organizational management (MBA); psychology (MS); school counseling (MS); teaching English as a second language (MS). *Accreditation:* APA. Part-time and evening/weekend programs available. Terminal master's awarded for partial completion of doctoral program. *Degree requirements:* For master's, one foreign language, comprehensive exam, integrative project (MBA), research project (MSESE); for doctorate, one foreign language, comprehensive exam, internship, doctoral project. *Entrance requirements:* For master's, 3 letters of recommendation, interview, minimum GPA of 3.0, resumé; for doctorate, 3 letters of recommendation, minimum GPA of 3.0, resumé, interview. *Faculty research:* Psychotherapy, forensic psychology, neuropsychology, marketing strategy, entrepreneurship.

Carnegie Mellon University, H. John Heinz III School of Public Policy and Management, Program in Entertainment Industry Management, Pittsburgh, PA 15213-3891. Offers MEIM.

See Close-Up on page 251.

Carnegie Mellon University, Tepper School of Business, Pittsburgh, PA 15213-3891. Offers accounting (PhD); algorithms, combinatorics, and optimization (MS, PhD); business management and software engineering (MBMSE); civil engineering and industrial management (MS); computational finance (MSCF); economics (MS, PhD); electronic commerce (MS); environmental engineering and management (MEEM); finance (PhD); financial economics (PhD); industrial administration (MBA), including administration and public management; information systems (PhD); management of manufacturing and automation (MOM, PhD), including industrial administration (PhD), manufacturing (MOM); marketing (PhD); mathematical finance (PhD); operations research (PhD); organizational behavior and theory (PhD); political economy (PhD); production and operations management (PhD); public policy and management (MS, MSED); software engineering and business management (MS); JD/MS; JD/MSIA; M Div/MS; MOM/MSIA; MSCF/MSIA. Part-time programs available. Terminal master's awarded for partial completion of doctoral program. *Degree requirements:* For doctorate, thesis/dissertation. *Entrance requirements:* For master's, GMAT. Additional exam requirements/recommendations for international students: Required—TOEFL. Expenses: Contact institution.

Case Western Reserve University, Weatherhead School of Management, Department of Marketing and Policy Studies, Management Program for Liberal Arts Graduates, Cleveland, OH 44106. Offers MSM. *Students:* 14 full-time (7 women). Average age 22. 28 applicants, 82% accepted, 14 enrolled. *Entrance requirements:* For master's, GMAT or GRE, resumé, 2 letters of recommendation, interview. Additional exam requirements/recommendations for international students: Required—TOEFL. *Application deadline:* For fall admission, 6/15 priority date for domestic and international students. Application fee: $50. *Financial support:* Application deadline: 3/1. *Unit head:* Jon Fuller, Program Director, 216-368-0935, Fax: 216-368-5548, E-mail: jon.fuller@case.edu. *Application contact:* Cassie Solis, Admissions Counselor, 216-368-2030, Fax: 216-368-5548, E-mail: casandra.solir@case.edu.

Case Western Reserve University, Weatherhead School of Management, Department of Operations, Management Program, Cleveland, OH 44106. Offers operations research (MSM); supply chain (MSM); MBA/MSM. *Accreditation:* AACSB. Part-time and evening/weekend programs available. *Faculty:* 10 full-time (2 women). *Students:* 27 full-time (8 women), 3 part-time (1 woman); includes 2 African Americans, 23 Asian Americans or Pacific Islanders, 1 Hispanic American. Average age 28. 46 applicants, 70% accepted, 13 enrolled. In 2006, 14 degrees awarded. *Degree requirements:* For master's, registration. *Entrance requirements:* For master's, GMAT or GRE, 3 letters of recommendation, resumé. Additional exam requirements/recommendations for international students: Required—TOEFL (minimum score 600 paper-based; 250 computer-based). *Application deadline:* For fall admission, 7/1 priority date for domestic and international students; for winter admission, 5/1 priority date for domestic students, 4/1 priority date for international students; for spring admission, 12/1 priority date for domestic students, 11/1 priority date for international students. Application fee: $50. *Financial support:* Career-related internships or fieldwork, institutionally sponsored loans, scholarships/grants, tuition waivers (partial), and unspecified assistantships available. Financial award application deadline: 3/1. *Faculty research:* Supply chain management, operations management, operations/finance interface optimization, scheduling. *Application contact:* Deborah L Bibb, Admissions Coordinator, 216-368-2030, Fax: 216-368-5548, E-mail: deborah.bibb@case.edu.

Case Western Reserve University, Weatherhead School of Management, Executive Doctor of Management Program, Cleveland, OH 44106. Offers management (EDM). Part-time and evening/weekend programs available. *Faculty:* 11 full-time (0 women), 3 part-time/adjunct (2 women). *Students:* 58 full-time (18 women), 12 part-time (6 women); includes 14 minority (7 African Americans, 6 Asian Americans or Pacific Islanders, 1 Hispanic American), 10 international. Average age 46. 57 applicants, 75% accepted, 36 enrolled. In 2006, 13 degrees awarded. *Degree requirements:* For doctorate, thesis/dissertation. *Entrance requirements:* For doctorate, GMAT. *Application deadline:* For fall admission, 6/2 for domestic students. Applications are processed on a rolling basis. Application fee: $75. Electronic applications accepted. *Expenses: Contact institution. Financial support:* Fellowships with partial tuition reimbursements, institutionally sponsored loans and scholarships/grants available. Financial award application deadline: 5/1. *Faculty research:* Information technology and design, emotional intelligence and leadership, entrepreneurship, governing of NP organizations, social ethics. *Unit head:* Bo Carlsson, Program Director, 216-368-1943, E-mail: bo.carlsson@case.edu. *Application contact:* Sue Nartker, Assistant Director, 216-368-1943, Fax: 216-368-6261, E-mail: sue.nartker@case.edu.

Case Western Reserve University, Weatherhead School of Management, Executive MBA Program, Cleveland, OH 44106. Offers EMBA. *Accreditation:* AACSB. *Faculty:* 25 full-time (6 women), 3 part-time/adjunct (1 woman). *Students:* 58 full-time (13 women); includes 12 minority (7 African Americans, 2 Asian Americans or Pacific Islanders, 3 Hispanic Americans). Average age 39. 42 applicants, 95% accepted, 33 enrolled. In 2006, 21 degrees awarded. *Entrance requirements:* For master's, GMAT (required if candidate does not have an undergraduate degree from an accredited institution), work experience, interview. *Application deadline:* For fall admission, 7/1 priority date for domestic and international students. Applications are processed on a rolling basis. Application fee: $50. Electronic applications accepted. *Expenses: Contact institution. Financial support:* In 2006–07, 11 students received support. Institutionally sponsored loans available. Financial award applicants required to submit FAFSA. *Unit head:* Carleen Henderson, Director, Executive MBA, 216-368-2554, Fax: 216-368-0200, E-mail: carleen.henderson@case.edu.

Case Western Reserve University, Weatherhead School of Management, Full-time MBA program, Cleveland, OH 44106. Offers MBA, MBA/MNO, MBA/JD, MBA/M Acc, MBA/MD, MBA/MIM, MBA/MSM, MBA/MSN, MBA/MSSA. *Accreditation:* AACSB. *Students:* Average age 28. 286 applicants, 68% accepted, 75 enrolled. In 2006, 114 degrees awarded. *Entrance requirements:* For master's, GMAT, letters of recommendation, interview, work experience. Additional exam requirements/recommendations for international students: Required—TOEFL (minimum score 600 paper-based; 250 computer-based). *Application deadline:* For fall admission, 3/1 priority date for domestic and international students. Applications are processed on a rolling basis. Application fee: $50. Electronic applications accepted. *Financial support:* In 2006–07, 180 students received support. Career-related internships or fieldwork, Federal Work-Study, institutionally sponsored loans, scholarships/grants, and tuition waivers (full and partial) available. Financial award applicants required to submit FAFSA. *Unit head:* Jon Fuller, Program Director, 216-368-0935, Fax: 216-368-5548, E-mail: jon.fuller@case.edu. *Application* *contact:* Brooke Novak, Admissions Counselor, 216-368-6208, Fax: 216-368-5548, E-mail: brooke.novak@case.edu.

Case Western Reserve University, Weatherhead School of Management, Part-time MBA Program, Cleveland, OH 44106. Offers MBA, MBA/M Acc, MBA/MSM, MBA/MSSA. *Accreditation:* AACSB. Part-time and evening/weekend programs available. *Students:* Average age 29. 102 applicants, 96% accepted, 91 enrolled. In 2006, 158 degrees awarded. *Entrance requirements:* For master's, GMAT, interview, work experience. Additional exam requirements/recommendations for international students: Recommended—TOEFL (minimum score 600 paper-based; 250 computer-based). *Application deadline:* For fall admission, 7/1 priority date for domestic and international students; for winter admission, 12/1 priority date for domestic and international students; for spring admission, 5/1 priority date for domestic and international students. Applications are processed on a rolling basis. Application fee: $50. Electronic applications accepted. *Financial support:* Institutionally sponsored loans available. *Unit head:* Kevin Malecek, Program Director, 216-368-3315, Fax: 216-368-5548, E-mail: kevin.malecek@case.edu. *Application contact:* Brooke Novak, Graduate Admissions Advisor, 216-368-6208, Fax: 216-368-5548, E-mail: brooke.novak@case.edu.

The Catholic University of America, School of Arts and Sciences, Department of Business and Economics, Washington, DC 20064. Offers international political economics (MA). Part-time and evening/weekend programs available. *Faculty:* 9 full-time (3 women), 9 part-time/adjunct (4 women). *Students:* 14 full-time (10 women), 20 part-time (14 women); includes 4 minority (3 African Americans, 1 Asian American or Pacific Islander), 12 international. Average age 37. 37 applicants, 76% accepted, 21 enrolled. *Degree requirements:* For master's, comprehensive exam. *Entrance requirements:* For master's, GRE General Test, 3 letters of recommendation. Additional exam requirements/recommendations for international students: Required—TOEFL (minimum score 580 paper-based; 237 computer-based). *Application deadline:* For fall admission, 2/1 priority date for domestic students; for spring admission, 11/15 priority date for domestic students. Applications are processed on a rolling basis. Application fee: $55. Electronic applications accepted. *Expenses:* Tuition: Full-time $27,700; part-time $1,045 per credit hour. Required fees: $1,290. Part-time tuition and fees vary according to campus/location and program. *Financial support:* Teaching assistantships, career-related internships or fieldwork, Federal Work-Study, scholarships/grants, tuition waivers (full and partial), and unspecified assistantships available. Support available to part-time students. Financial award application deadline: 2/1; financial award applicants required to submit FAFSA. *Unit head:* Dr. Kevin F. Forbes, Chair, 202-319-5236, Fax: 202-319-4426, E-mail: forbes@cua.edu.

Centenary College, Program in Business Administration, Hackettstown, NJ 07840-2100. Offers MBA. Part-time and evening/weekend programs available. Postbaccalaureate distance learning degree programs offered (minimal on-campus study). *Entrance requirements:* For master's, GMAT.

Centenary College of Louisiana, Graduate Programs, Frost School of Business, Shreveport, LA 71104. Offers MBA. Part-time and evening/weekend programs available. *Degree requirements:* For master's, thesis. *Entrance requirements:* For master's, GMAT, minimum 5 years of professional/managerial experience. *Faculty research:* Leadership, organizational change strategy, market behavior, executive compensation.

Central Connecticut State University, School of Graduate Studies, School of Business, New Britain, CT 06050-4010. Offers MBA, MS, Certificate. Part-time and evening/weekend programs available. *Faculty:* 12 full-time (3 women), 8 part-time/adjunct (2 women). *Students:* 19 full-time (14 women), 53 part-time (24 women); includes 5 minority (2 African Americans, 1 Asian American or Pacific Islander, 2 Hispanic Americans), 7 international. Average age 32. 29 applicants, 28% accepted, 6 enrolled. In 2006, 29 master's, 1 other advanced degree awarded. *Degree requirements:* For master's, thesis or alternative. *Entrance requirements:* For master's, minimum GPA of 2.7. Additional exam requirements/recommendations for international students: Required—TOEFL. *Application deadline:* For fall admission, 7/1 for domestic students; for spring admission, 12/1 for domestic students. Applications are processed on a rolling basis. Application fee: $50. Electronic applications accepted. *Expenses:* Tuition, area resident: Full-time $3,970; part-time $380 per credit. Tuition, state resident: full-time $5,955; part-time $380 per credit. Tuition, nonresident: full-time $11,061; part-time $380 per credit. Required fees: $3,189. One-time fee: $62 part-time. Tuition and fees vary according to degree level and program. *Financial support:* In 2006–07, 2 students received support, including 1 research assistantship (averaging $4,800 per year); career-related internships or fieldwork, Federal Work-Study, scholarships/grants, and unspecified assistantships also available. Support available to part-time students. Financial award application deadline: 3/1; financial award applicants required to submit FAFSA. *Faculty research:* Business/marketing education, organizational management, international business. *Unit head:* Dr. Christopher Galligan, Acting Dean, 860-832-3205.

Central European University, CEU Business School, Budapest, Hungary. Offers finance (MBA); general management (MBA); information technology (M Sc); information technology management (MBA); management (EMBA); marketing (MBA); real estate management (MBA). Part-time and evening/weekend programs available. *Faculty:* 15 full-time (3 women), 30 part-time/adjunct (9 women). *Students:* 47 full-time (18 women), 158 part-time (22 women). Average age 32. 450 applicants, 43% accepted, 160 enrolled. In 2006, 77 degrees awarded. *Entrance requirements:* For master's, GMAT. Additional exam requirements/recommendations for international students: Required—TOEFL (minimum score 570 paper-based; 230 computer-based). *Application deadline:* For fall admission, 5/22 priority date for domestic students, 5/22 for international students; for winter admission, 11/13 priority date for domestic students, 11/13 for international students. Applications are processed on a rolling basis. Application fee: $0. Electronic applications accepted. *Financial support:* In 2006–07, 4 students received support, including research assistantships with partial tuition reimbursements available (averaging $3,800 per year); tuition waivers (partial) and GMAT-based tuition fee discounts also available. *Faculty research:* Social and ethical business, marketing. Total annual research expenditures: 11,000 euros. *Unit head:* Dr. Paul Garrison, Dean and Managing Director, 36-18875050, Fax: 36-18875001, E-mail: garrisonp@ceubusiness.com. *Application contact:* Tunde Hegedus, MBA Program Manager, 36-18875060, Fax: 36-18875133, E-mail: mba@ceubusiness.com.

Central Michigan University, College of Graduate Studies, College of Business Administration, Mount Pleasant, MI 48859. Offers MA, MBA, MBE, MS. *Accreditation:* AACSB. Part-time programs available. *Degree requirements:* For master's, thesis (for some programs), comprehensive exam (for some programs), registration. *Entrance requirements:* For master's, GMAT.

See Close-Up on page 255.

Central Michigan University, College of Graduate Studies, Program in Administration, Mount Pleasant, MI 48859. Offers general administration (MSA); health services administration (MSA); hospitality and tourism administration (MSA); human resource administration (MSA); information resource administration (MSA); international administration (MSA); leadership (MSA); organizational communications (MSA); public administration (MSA); recreation and park administration (MSA); software engineering (MSA); sports administration (MSA). *Accreditation:* AACSB. *Degree requirements:* For master's, thesis or alternative. *Entrance requirements:* For master's, minimum undergraduate GPA of 2.5.

See Close-Up on page 253.

Chadron State College, School of Professional and Graduate Studies, Department of Business and Economics, Chadron, NE 69337. Offers MBA. *Accreditation:* ACBSP. Part-time and evening/weekend programs available. Postbaccalaureate distance learning degree programs offered (minimal on-campus study). *Degree requirements:* For master's, thesis optional. *Entrance requirements:* For master's, GMAT, minimum GPA of 2.75 or 12 graduate hours at CSC with

minimum GPA of 3.25. Additional exam requirements/recommendations for international students: Required—TOEFL. Electronic applications accepted.

Chaminade University of Honolulu, Graduate Services, Program in Business Administration, Honolulu, HI 96816-1578. Offers MBA. Part-time and evening/weekend programs available. *Faculty:* 4 full-time (2 women), 4 part-time/adjunct (3 women). *Students:* 48 full-time (29 women), 30 part-time (24 women); includes 59 minority (2 African Americans, 51 Asian Americans or Pacific Islanders, 6 Hispanic Americans). Average age 32. 58 applicants, 86% accepted. In 2006, 41 degrees awarded. *Entrance requirements:* For master's, minimum GPA of 3.0. Additional exam requirements/recommendations for international students: Required—TOEFL. *Application deadline:* For fall admission, 9/1 priority date for domestic students; for winter admission, 12/1 for domestic students; for spring admission, 3/1 for domestic students. Applications are processed on a rolling basis. Application fee: $50. *Expenses:* Tuition: Part-time $465 per credit. *Financial support:* In 2006–07, 35 students received support. Career-related internships or fieldwork, Federal Work-Study, and institutionally sponsored loans available. Support available to part-time students. Financial award application deadline: 3/1; financial award applicants required to submit FAFSA. *Faculty research:* Environmental development, total quality management, international finance. *Unit head:* Dr. Scott J. Schroeder, Dean, 808-739-4611, Fax: 808-735-4734, E-mail: sschroed@chaminade.edu. *Application contact:* James Moses, Assistant Director, 808-739-4612, Fax: 808-735-4734, E-mail: mba@chaminade.edu.

Chapman University, Graduate Studies, The George L. Argyros School of Business and Economics, Orange, CA 92866. Offers Exec MBA, MBA, MSHRM, Certificate, JD/MBA. *Accreditation:* AACSB. Part-time and evening/weekend programs available. *Faculty:* 33 full-time (10 women), 4 part-time/adjunct (2 women). *Students:* 96 full-time (34 women), 113 part-time (54 women); includes 55 minority (3 African Americans, 38 Asian Americans or Pacific Islanders, 14 Hispanic Americans), 23 international. Average age 31. 150 applicants, 67% accepted, 64 enrolled. In 2006, 68 master's, 2 other advanced degrees awarded. *Degree requirements:* For master's, comprehensive exam (for some programs), registration. *Entrance requirements:* For master's, GMAT, minimum undergraduate GPA of 2.5. Additional exam requirements/recommendations for international students: Required—TOEFL (minimum score 550 paper-based). *Application deadline:* For fall admission, 5/1 priority date for domestic and international students; for spring admission, 12/30 priority date for domestic and international students. Application fee: $55. Electronic applications accepted. *Expenses:* Contact institution. *Financial support:* In 2006–07, 116 students received support, including 29 fellowships (averaging $5,529 per year); Federal Work-Study also available. Financial award application deadline: 6/30; financial award applicants required to submit FAFSA. *Unit head:* Dr. Arthur Kraft, Dean, 714-997-6684. *Application contact:* Debra Gonda, Associate Dean, 714-997-6894, E-mail: gonda@chapman.edu.

Charleston Southern University, Program in Business, Charleston, SC 29423-8087. Offers accounting (MBA); finance (MBA); health care administration (MBA); information systems (MBA); organizational development (MBA). Part-time and evening/weekend programs available. *Degree requirements:* For master's, thesis optional. *Entrance requirements:* For master's, GMAT. *Faculty research:* Economic forecasting.

Chatham University, Program in Business Administration, Pittsburgh, PA 15232-2826. Offers business administration (MBA); healthcare professional (MBA). Part-time and evening/weekend programs available. *Students:* 21 full-time (19 women), 18 part-time (15 women). Average age 34. 33 applicants, 73% accepted, 19 enrolled. In 2006, 31 degrees awarded. *Degree requirements:* For master's, thesis, registration. *Entrance requirements:* For master's, minimum GPA of 3.0, 2 years experience in healthcare, health MBA only, letters of recommendation, essay, official transcripts, application. Additional exam requirements/recommendations for international students: Required—TOEFL (minimum score 600 paper-based; 250 computer-based; 100 iBT); Recommended—IELTS (minimum score 7), TWE (minimum score 5). *Application deadline:* Applications are processed on a rolling basis. Application fee: $45. Electronic applications accepted. *Financial support:* Career-related internships or fieldwork available. Financial award applicants required to submit FAFSA. *Unit head:* Dr. Mary Reibe, Director, 412-365-1157, Fax: 412-365-1505, E-mail: reibe@chatham.edu. *Application contact:* 412-365-1825, Fax: 412-365-1609, E-mail: admissions@chatham.edu.

Christian Brothers University, Graduate Programs, School of Business, Memphis, TN 38104-5581. Offers business (MBA); executive leadership (MAEL); financial planning (Certificate); project management (Certificate). Part-time and evening/weekend programs available. *Faculty:* 8 full-time (3 women), 1 part-time/adjunct (0 women). *Students:* 13 full-time (1 woman), 88 part-time (38 women); includes 21 minority (18 African Americans, 2 Asian Americans or Pacific Islanders, 1 Hispanic American), 4 international. Average age 33. In 2006, 69 degrees awarded. *Entrance requirements:* For master's, GMAT. Additional exam requirements/recommendations for international students: Required—TOEFL. *Application deadline:* Applications are processed on a rolling basis. Application fee: $25. *Financial support:* Institutionally sponsored loans available. Support available to part-time students. *Faculty research:* Business ethics. *Unit head:* Dr. Mike R. Ryan, Dean, 901-321-3316. *Application contact:* Dr. Bevalee B. Pray, Director, Graduate Business Programs, 901-321-3319, Fax: 901-321-3494.

The Citadel, The Military College of South Carolina, College of Graduate and Professional Studies, School of Business Administration, Charleston, SC 29409. Offers MBA. *Accreditation:* AACSB. Part-time and evening/weekend programs available. *Students:* 24 full-time (7 women), 242 part-time (90 women); includes 32 minority (20 African Americans, 2 American Indian/Alaska Native, 8 Asian Americans or Pacific Islanders, 2 Hispanic Americans), 6 international. Average age 29. In 2006, 49 degrees awarded. *Entrance requirements:* For master's, GMAT. Additional exam requirements/recommendations for international students: Required—TOEFL (minimum score 550 paper-based; 213 computer-based). *Application deadline:* Applications are processed on a rolling basis. Application fee: $30. *Expenses:* Tuition, state resident: part-time $259 per credit hour. Tuition, nonresident: part-time $482 per credit hour. *Financial support:* Fellowships available. Financial award application deadline: 7/1; financial award applicants required to submit FAFSA. *Unit head:* Dr. Earl Walker, Head, 843-953-7466, E-mail: earl.walker@citadel.edu. *Application contact:* Dr. Raymond S. Jones, Associate Dean, College of Graduate and Professional Studies, 843-953-5089, Fax: 843-953-7630, E-mail: ray.jones@citadel.edu.

City University, Graduate Division, School of Management, Bellevue, WA 98005. Offers accounting (MBA); C++ programming (Certificate); computer systems—C++ programming (MS); computer systems—individualized study (MS); computer systems—web programming in e-commerce (MS); computer systems-web development (MS); financial management (MBA, Certificate); general management (MBA, MPA, Certificate); general management-Europe (MBA); human resource management (MPA); individualized study (MBA); information systems (MBA, Certificate); management—general management (MA); management—human resource management (MA); management—individualized study (MA); marketing (MBA, Certificate); personal financial planning (MBA, Certificate); project management (MBA, MS, Certificate); technology management (MS, Certificate); web development (Certificate); web programming in e-commerce (Certificate). Part-time and evening/weekend programs available. Postbaccalaureate distance learning degree programs offered (no on-campus study). *Entrance requirements:* Additional exam requirements/recommendations for international students: Required—TOEFL (minimum score 540 paper-based; 207 computer-based); Recommended—IELTS. Electronic applications accepted.

Claflin University, Graduate Programs, Orangeburg, SC 29115. Offers biotechnology (MS); business administration (MBA); educational studies (M Ed). *Entrance requirements:* For master's, GRE, minimum GPA of 3.0, 2 letters of recommendation. Application fee: $40 ($55 for international students).

Claremont Graduate University, Graduate Programs, Peter F. Drucker and Masatoshi Ito Graduate School of Management, Program in Executive Management, Claremont, CA 91711-

Business Administration and Management—General

Claremont Graduate University (continued)
6160. Offers advanced management (MS); executive management (EMBA); leadership (Certificate); management (MA, PhD, Certificate); strategy (Certificate). *Accreditation:* AACSB. Part-time programs available. *Students:* 46 full-time (18 women), 61 part-time (22 women); includes 35 minority (6 African Americans, 1 American Indian/Alaska Native, 12 Asian Americans or Pacific Islanders, 16 Hispanic Americans), 8 international. Average age 45. In 2006, 17 master's, 1 doctorate, 22 other advanced degrees awarded. *Entrance requirements:* For master's, GMAT or GRE General Test (EMBA). *Application deadline:* For fall admission, 2/15 priority date for domestic students. Applications are processed on a rolling basis. Electronic applications accepted. *Financial support:* Federal Work-Study and institutionally sponsored loans available. Support available to part-time students. Financial award application deadline: 2/15; financial award applicants required to submit FAFSA. *Faculty research:* Strategy and leadership, brand management, cost management and control, organizational transformation, general management. *Unit head:* Christina Wassenaar, Director, 909-607-7812, Fax: 909-607-9104, E-mail: christina.wassenaar@cgu.edu. *Application contact:* Susan Townzen, Academic Advising, 909-607-7369, Fax: 909-607-9104, E-mail: susan.n.townzen@cgu.edu.

Claremont Graduate University, Graduate Programs, Peter F. Drucker and Masatoshi Ito Graduate School of Management, Program in Management, Claremont, CA 91711-6160. Offers MBA, PhD. *Accreditation:* AACSB. Part-time programs available. *Students:* 113 full-time (39 women), 14 part-time (6 women); includes 29 minority (4 African Americans, 19 Asian Americans or Pacific Islanders, 6 Hispanic Americans), 43 international. Average age 30. In 2006, 68 master's, 1 doctorate awarded. *Entrance requirements:* For master's, GMAT. Additional exam requirements/recommendations for international students: Required—TOEFL. *Application deadline:* For fall admission, 2/15 priority date for domestic students. Applications are processed on a rolling basis. Electronic applications accepted. *Financial support:* Fellowships, research assistantships, teaching assistantships, career-related internships or fieldwork, Federal Work-Study, and institutionally sponsored loans available. Support available to part-time students. Financial award application deadline: 2/15; financial award applicants required to submit FAFSA. *Faculty research:* Strategy and leadership, brand management, cost management and control, organizational transformation, general management. *Unit head:* Kerry Boyle, Interim Director, 909-607-9060, Fax: 909-607-9104, E-mail: kerry.boyle@cgu.edu. *Application contact:* Mariaestella Cuara, Admissions and Recruiting, 909-607-7810, Fax: 909-607-9104, E-mail: mariaestella.cuara@cgu.edu.

Clarion University of Pennsylvania, Office of Research and Graduate Studies, College of Business Administration, Clarion, PA 16214. Offers MBA. *Accreditation:* AACSB. Part-time and evening/weekend programs available. *Faculty:* 23 full-time (2 women). *Students:* 27 full-time (9 women), 14 part-time (8 women); includes 3 minority (2 African Americans, 1 Hispanic American), 9 international. 53 applicants, 43% accepted. In 2006, 20 degrees awarded. *Entrance requirements:* For master's, GMAT, minimum QPA of 2.75. Additional exam requirements/recommendations for international students: Required—TOEFL (minimum score 550 paper-based; 213 computer-based). *Application deadline:* For fall admission, 8/1 priority date for domestic students, 4/15 priority date for international students; for spring admission, 12/1 priority date for domestic students, 9/15 priority date for international students. Applications are processed on a rolling basis. Application fee: $30. Electronic applications accepted. *Expenses:* Tuition, state resident: part-time $336 per credit. Tuition, nonresident: part-time $538 per credit. *Financial support:* In 2006–07, 16 research assistantships with partial tuition reimbursements (averaging $2,001 per year) were awarded; career-related internships or fieldwork also available. Support available to part-time students. Financial award application deadline: 3/1. *Unit head:* Dr. James Pesek, Interim Dean, 814-393-2600, Fax: 814-393-1910, E-mail: jpesek@clarion.edu. *Application contact:* Dr. Soga Ewedemi, MBA Director, 814-393-2605, Fax: 814-393-1910, E-mail: sewedemi@clarion.edu.

Clark Atlanta University, School of Business Administration, Atlanta, GA 30314. Offers MBA. *Accreditation:* AACSB. Part-time programs available. *Entrance requirements:* For master's, GMAT. *Faculty research:* Transportation activities, minority business management.

Clarke College, Program in Management, Dubuque, IA 52001-3198. Offers MS. Part-time and evening/weekend programs available. *Entrance requirements:* For master's, GMAT, GRE General Test or MAT, minimum GPA of 3.0 in last 60 hours, previous undergraduate course work in business. Electronic applications accepted.

Clarkson University, Graduate School, School of Business, Program in Business Administration, Potsdam, NY 13699. Offers MBA. *Accreditation:* AACSB. *Faculty:* 13 full-time (2 women). *Students:* 58 full-time (17 women), 7 part-time (4 women), 14 international. Average age 25. 160 applicants, 53% accepted, 59 enrolled. In 2006, 56 degrees awarded. *Entrance requirements:* For master's, GMAT. Additional exam requirements/recommendations for international students: Required—TOEFL. *Application deadline:* For fall admission, 5/15 priority date for domestic students; for spring admission, 10/15 priority date for domestic students. Applications are processed on a rolling basis. Application fee: $25 ($35 for international students). Electronic applications accepted. *Expenses:* Tuition: Full-time $22,776; part-time $949 per credit. Required fees: $215. *Financial support:* In 2006–07, 56 students received support. *Faculty research:* Industrial organization and regulated industries, end-user computing, systems analysis and design, technological marketing, leadership development. *Application contact:* Dr. Farzad Mahmoodi, Graduate Director, 315-268-4281 Ext. 4281, Fax: 315-268-3810, E-mail: mahmoodi@clarkson.edu.

Clark University, Graduate School, Graduate School of Management, Business Administration Program, Worcester, MA 01610-1477. Offers accounting (MBA); finance (MBA); global business (MBA); health care management (MBA); management (MBA); management of information technology (MBA); marketing (MBA). *Accreditation:* AACSB. Part-time and evening/weekend programs available. *Students:* 122 full-time (64 women), 113 part-time (42 women); includes 18 minority (3 African Americans, 9 Asian Americans or Pacific Islanders, 6 Hispanic Americans), 115 international. Average age 29. 235 applicants, 78% accepted, 80 enrolled. In 2006, 109 degrees awarded. *Degree requirements:* For master's, thesis optional. *Application deadline:* For fall admission, 6/1 priority date for domestic students; for spring admission, 12/1 priority date for domestic students. Applications are processed on a rolling basis. Application fee: $50. Electronic applications accepted. *Financial support:* In 2006–07, research assistantships with partial tuition reimbursements (averaging $6,000 per year), teaching assistantships with partial tuition reimbursements (averaging $6,000 per year) were awarded; fellowships with full and partial tuition reimbursements, career-related internships or fieldwork, Federal Work-Study, institutionally sponsored loans, and tuition waivers (partial) also available. Support available to part-time students. Financial award application deadline: 5/31. *Faculty research:* Organizational development, accounting, marketing, finance, human resource management. *Application contact:* Patricia Tollo, Admissions Director, 508-793-7406, Fax: 508-793-8822, E-mail: clarkmba@clarku.edu.

See Close-Up on page 257.

Clayton State University, School of Graduate Studies, Program in Business Administration, Morrow, GA 30260-0285. Offers MBA. *Accreditation:* AACSB.

Cleary University, Online Program in Business Administration, Ann Arbor, MI 48105-2659. Offers MBA. Part-time and evening/weekend programs available. Postbaccalaureate distance learning degree programs offered (no on-campus study). *Faculty:* 4 full-time (2 women), 16 part-time/adjunct (7 women). *Students:* 8 full-time (4 women), 57 part-time (33 women); includes 10 minority (7 African Americans, 1 American Indian/Alaska Native, 2 Asian Americans or Pacific Islanders), 1 international. Average age 34. 39 applicants, 85% accepted, 28 enrolled. In 2006, 13 degrees awarded. *Degree requirements:* For master's, thesis. *Entrance requirements:* For master's, minimum GPA of 2.5. Additional exam requirements/recommendations for international students: Required—TOEFL (minimum score 550 paper-based; 213 computer-based; 79 iBT), Michigan English Language Assessment Battery (75). *Application deadline:* For fall admission, 8/15 for domestic students, 7/15 for international students; for spring admission, 4/2 for domestic students, 1/2 for international students. Applications are processed on a rolling basis. Application fee: $50. Electronic applications accepted. *Expenses:* Tuition: Full-time $11,900; part-time $425 per credit hour. *Financial support:* In 2006–07, 14 students received support, including 14 fellowships; Federal Work-Study and scholarships/grants also available. Support available to part-time students. Financial award application deadline: 8/15; financial award applicants required to submit FAFSA. *Unit head:* Dr. Vincent Linder, Provost and Vice President Academic Affairs, 800-686-1883, Fax: 734-332-4646, E-mail: vlinder@cleary.edu. *Application contact:* Carrie Bonofiglio, Director of Student Recruiting, 800-589-1979, Fax: 517-552-7805, E-mail: cbono@cleary.edu.

Cleary University, Program in Business Administration, Ann Arbor, MI 48105-2659. Offers accounting (MBA); management (MBA). Part-time and evening/weekend programs available. Postbaccalaureate distance learning degree programs offered (minimal on-campus study). *Faculty:* 4 full-time (2 women), 16 part-time/adjunct (7 women). *Students:* 8 full-time (4 women), 57 part-time (33 women); includes 10 minority (7 African Americans, 1 American Indian/Alaska Native, 2 Asian Americans or Pacific Islanders), 1 international. Average age 34. 39 applicants, 85% accepted, 28 enrolled. In 2006, 13 degrees awarded. *Degree requirements:* For master's, comprehensive exam. *Entrance requirements:* For master's, minimum GPA of 2.5. Additional exam requirements/recommendations for international students: Required—TOEFL (minimum score 550 paper-based; 213 computer-based; 79 iBT), Michigan English Language Assessment Battery (75). *Application deadline:* For fall admission, 8/15 for domestic students, 7/15 for international students; for spring admission, 4/2 for domestic and international students. Applications are processed on a rolling basis. Application fee: $50. Electronic applications accepted. *Expenses:* Tuition: Full-time $11,900; part-time $425 per credit hour. *Financial support:* In 2006–07, 14 students received support, including 14 fellowships; Federal Work-Study and scholarships/grants also available. Support available to part-time students. Financial award application deadline: 8/15; financial award applicants required to submit FAFSA. *Faculty research:* Leadership and decision making, domestic and international corporate finance, organization structure and job satisfaction, organization culture, adoption of innovation. *Unit head:* Dr. Vincent Linder, Provost and Vice President Academic Affairs, 800-686-1883, Fax: 734-332-4646, E-mail: vlinder@cleary.edu. *Application contact:* Carrie Bonofiglio, Director of Student Recruiting, 800-589-1979 Ext. 2213, Fax: 517-552-7805, E-mail: cbono@cleary.edu.

Clemson University, Graduate School, College of Architecture, Arts, and Humanities, Department of Planning and Landscape Architecture and College of Business and Behavioral Science, Program in Real Estate Development, Clemson, SC 29634. Offers MRED. *Students:* 30 full-time (4 women), 2 part-time; includes 4 minority (3 African Americans, 1 Hispanic American). 49 applicants, 65% accepted, 19 enrolled. In 2006, 6 degrees awarded. *Entrance requirements:* For master's, GRE or GMAT, 3 letters of recommendation. Additional exam requirements/recommendations for international students: Required—TOEFL (minimum score 600 paper-based). *Application deadline:* For fall admission, 2/1 for domestic students, 4/15 for international students. Application fee: $50. *Expenses:* Tuition, state resident: full-time $8,812; part-time $450 per hour. Tuition, nonresident: full-time $18,036; part-time $760 per hour. Required fees: $474; $5 per term. *Unit head:* Dr. Terry Farris, Coordinator, 864-656-3903, Fax: 864-656-0204, E-mail: jfarris@clemson.edu. *Application contact:* Admissions, 864-656-3926, Fax: 864-656-7519.

See Close-Up on page 723.

Clemson University, Graduate School, College of Business and Behavioral Science, Department of Management, Program in Management, Clemson, SC 29634. Offers MS, PhD. *Accreditation:* AACSB. *Students:* 27 full-time (6 women), 3 part-time (1 woman); includes 2 minority (1 American Indian/Alaska Native, 1 Hispanic American), 16 international. Average age 25. 43 applicants, 28% accepted, 6 enrolled. In 2006, 23 master's, 2 doctorates awarded. *Degree requirements:* For doctorate, thesis/dissertation. *Entrance requirements:* For doctorate, GRE General Test, minimum GPA of 3.5. Additional exam requirements/recommendations for international students: Required—TOEFL. *Application deadline:* For fall admission, 2/1 for domestic students, 4/15 for international students; for spring admission, 10/1 for domestic students, 9/15 for international students. Application fee: $50. *Expenses:* Tuition, state resident: full-time $8,812; part-time $450 per hour. Tuition, nonresident: full-time $18,036; part-time $760 per hour. Required fees: $474; $5 per term. *Financial support:* In 2006–07, 11 research assistantships were awarded. Financial award applicants required to submit FAFSA. *Unit head:* Dr. Russ Purivo, Head, 864-656-3311.

See Close-Ups on pages 261 and 263.

Clemson University, Graduate School, College of Business and Behavioral Science, Program in Business Administration, Clemson, SC 29634. Offers MBA. *Accreditation:* AACSB. Part-time and evening/weekend programs available. *Students:* 57 full-time (17 women), 100 part-time (22 women); includes 9 minority (3 African Americans, 1 American Indian/Alaska Native, 2 Asian Americans or Pacific Islanders, 3 Hispanic Americans), 16 international. Average age 29. 135 applicants, 53% accepted, 43 enrolled. In 2006, 67 degrees awarded. *Entrance requirements:* For master's, GMAT. Additional exam requirements/recommendations for international students: Required—TOEFL. *Application deadline:* For fall admission, 5/1 priority date for domestic students, 4/15 for international students; for spring admission, 9/15 for international students. Applications are processed on a rolling basis. Application fee: $50. *Expenses:* Tuition, state resident: full-time $8,812; part-time $450 per hour. Tuition, nonresident: full-time $18,036; part-time $760 per hour. Required fees: $474; $5 per term. *Financial support:* In 2006–07, 26 research assistantships were awarded; fellowships, career-related internships or fieldwork and institutionally sponsored loans also available. Support available to part-time students. Financial award application deadline: 5/1; financial award applicants required to submit FAFSA. *Unit head:* Dr. Dudley W. Blair, Director, 864-656-3975, Fax: 864-656-0947, E-mail: dudley@clemson.edu. *Application contact:* Martha Duke, Associate Director, 864-656-3975, Fax: 864-656-0947, E-mail: dmartha@clemson.edu.

See Close-Up on page 259.

Cleveland State University, College of Graduate Studies, Nance College of Business Administration, Doctoral Programs in Business Administration, Cleveland, OH 44115. Offers business administration (DBA); finance (DBA); information systems (DBA); marketing (DBA); production/operations management (DBA). *Accreditation:* AACSB. In 2006, 3 degrees awarded. *Degree requirements:* For doctorate, thesis/dissertation. *Entrance requirements:* For doctorate, GMAT, MBA or equivalent. *Unit head:* Dr. Raj Shekhar G. Javalgi, Director, 216-687-3786, Fax: 216-687-9354, E-mail: r.javalgi@csuohio.edu.

Cleveland State University, College of Graduate Studies, Nance College of Business Administration, MBA Programs, Cleveland, OH 44115. Offers business statistics (MBA); finance (MBA); health care administration (MBA); marketing (MBA); operations management (MBA); JD/MBA; MSN/MBA. *Accreditation:* AACSB. Part-time and evening/weekend programs available. *Faculty:* 21 full-time (5 women), 10 part-time/adjunct (1 woman). *Students:* 276 full-time (119 women), 623 part-time (279 women); includes 120 minority (74 African Americans, 3 American Indian/Alaska Native, 32 Asian Americans or Pacific Islanders, 11 Hispanic Americans), 108 international. Average age 28. 530 applicants, 51% accepted, 146 enrolled. In 2006, 308 degrees awarded. *Entrance requirements:* For master's, GMAT or GRE. Additional exam requirements/recommendations for international students: Required—TOEFL (minimum score 525 paper-based; 197 computer-based). *Application deadline:* For fall admission, 7/15 priority date for domestic students, 5/15 for international students; for spring admission, 12/15 priority date for domestic students, 11/1 for international students. Applications are processed on a rolling basis. Application fee: $30. *Financial support:* In 2006–07, 45 research assistantships with full and partial tuition reimbursements (averaging $6,960 per year), 1 teaching assistantship with full and partial tuition reimbursement (averaging $7,800 per year) were awarded; tuition waivers (full) and unspecified assistantships also available. Financial award application deadline: 5/17; financial award applicants required to submit FAFSA. Total annual research expenditures: $63,645. *Unit head:* Bruce Gottschalk, Associate Dean, 216-687-3730, Fax: 216-687-5311, E-mail: cbacsu@csuohio.edu. *Application contact:* Patricia Hite, Director, Academic Program Support, 216-687-6925, Fax: 216-687-6888, E-mail: p.hite@csuohio.edu.

Coastal Carolina University, Wall College of Business Administration, Conway, SC 29528-6054. Offers MBA. *Accreditation:* AACSB. *Faculty:* 5 full-time (4 women). *Students:* 13 full-time (3 women), 20 part-time (12 women); includes 3 minority (1 African American, 1 Asian American or Pacific Islander, 1 Hispanic American), 2 international. Average age 29. *Entrance requirements:* For master's, GMAT, 2 letters of recommendation, resumé. *Application deadline:* For fall admission, 8/15 for domestic students. Applications are processed on a rolling basis. Application fee: $45. Electronic applications accepted. *Expenses:* Tuition, state resident: full-time $7,920; part-time $330 per credit hour. Tuition, nonresident: full-time $9,600; part-time $400 per credit hour. Required fees: $80; $40 per term. *Financial support:* Application deadline: 4/1; *Unit head:* John O. Lox, Director, 843-349-2469, E-mail: jlox@coastal.edu. *Application contact:* Dr. Judy W. Vogt, Vice President, Enrollment Services, 843-349-2037, Fax: 843-349-2127, E-mail: jvogt@coastal.edu.

College of Charleston, Graduate School, School of Business and Economics, Charleston, SC 29424-0001. Offers MS. *Accreditation:* AACSB. *Entrance requirements:* For master's, GMAT, minimum GPA of 3.0 in last 60 hours undergraduate course work, 24 hours of course work in accounting. Electronic applications accepted.

College of Notre Dame of Maryland, Graduate Studies, Program in Management, Baltimore, MD 21210-2476. Offers MA. Part-time and evening/weekend programs available. *Students:* 15 full-time (14 women), 190 part-time (160 women). *Degree requirements:* For master's, thesis optional. *Entrance requirements:* For master's, minimum GPA of 3.0. Additional exam requirements/recommendations for international students: Required—TOEFL (minimum score 500 paper-based; 173 computer-based; 61 iBT). *Application deadline:* For fall admission, 7/5 for domestic students; for winter admission, 11/5 for domestic students; for spring admission, 12/5 for domestic students. Applications are processed on a rolling basis. Application fee: $40. Electronic applications accepted. *Financial support:* Career-related internships or fieldwork and institutionally sponsored loans available. Support available to part-time students. Financial award application deadline: 6/30; financial award applicants required to submit FAFSA. *Unit head:* Dr. Ann Breihan, Head, 410-532-5554, Fax: 410-532-5333, E-mail: abreihan@ndm.edu. *Application contact:* Erica D. Jones, Graduate Admissions Coordinator, 410-532-5317, Fax: 410-532-5333, E-mail: gradadm@ndm.edu.

College of Saint Elizabeth, Department of Business Administration and Economics, Morristown, NJ 07960-6989. Offers management (MS). Part-time and evening/weekend programs available. *Faculty:* 3 full-time (1 woman), 6 part-time/adjunct (5 women). *Students:* 25 full-time (16 women), 57 part-time (50 women); includes 22 minority (12 African Americans, 2 Asian Americans or Pacific Islanders, 8 Hispanic Americans), 4 international. Average age 36. In 2006, 65 degrees awarded. *Degree requirements:* For master's, capstone seminar. *Entrance requirements:* For master's, minimum GPA of 3.0, course work in principles of management. *Application deadline:* Applications are processed on a rolling basis. Application fee: $35. Electronic applications accepted. *Financial support:* Career-related internships or fieldwork, tuition waivers (partial), and unspecified assistantships available. Support available to part-time students. Financial award application deadline: 3/15; financial award applicants required to submit FAFSA. *Faculty research:* American business history, business developments in Eastern Europe, MIS/programming languages, marketing strategy, strategic planning. *Unit head:* Dr. Kathleen Reddick, Director of the Graduate Program in Management, 973-290-4041, Fax: 973-290-4177, E-mail: kreddick@cse.edu. *Application contact:* Michael Szarek, Director of Enrollment Management, 973-290-4112, Fax: 973-290-4167, E-mail: mszarek@cse.edu.

College of St. Joseph, Graduate Program, Division of Business, Program in Business Administration, Rutland, VT 05701-3899. Offers MBA. Part-time and evening/weekend programs available. *Faculty:* 2 full-time (0 women), 4 part-time/adjunct (0 women). *Students:* 2 full-time (1 woman), 17 part-time (8 women), 1 international. Average age 38. 12 applicants, 83% accepted, 9 enrolled. In 2006, 3 degrees awarded. *Entrance requirements:* For master's, 2 letters of reference, interview. Application fee: $35. *Expenses: Contact institution.* Part-time tuition and fees vary according to program. *Financial support:* In 2006–07, 1 student received support, including teaching assistantships (averaging $3,000 per year). Financial award application deadline: 3/1. *Application contact:* Tracy Gallipo, Director of Admissions, 802-773-5900 Ext. 3262, Fax: 802-773-5900, E-mail: tracygallipo@csj.edu.

The College of Saint Rose, Graduate Studies, School of Business, Department of Business Administration, Albany, NY 12203-1419. Offers MBA, JD/MBA. *Accreditation:* ACBSP. Part-time and evening/weekend programs available. *Entrance requirements:* For master's, GMAT, graduate degree, or minimum undergraduate GPA of 3.0. Additional exam requirements/recommendations for international students: Required—TOEFL (minimum score 550 paper-based; 213 computer-based). Electronic applications accepted.

The College of St. Scholastica, Graduate Studies, Department of Management, Duluth, MN 55811-4199. Offers MA. Part-time and evening/weekend programs available. Postbaccalaureate distance learning degree programs offered (minimal on-campus study). *Faculty:* 6 full-time (1 woman), 24 part-time/adjunct (10 women). *Students:* 84 full-time (57 women), 84 part-time (49 women); includes 10 minority (4 African Americans, 3 American Indian/Alaska Native, 2 Asian Americans or Pacific Islanders, 1 Hispanic American), 1 international. Average age 36. 75 applicants, 80% accepted, 48 enrolled. In 2006, 60 degrees awarded. *Degree requirements:* For master's, thesis. *Entrance requirements:* For master's, minimum GPA of 2.8. Additional exam requirements/recommendations for international students: Required—TOEFL (minimum score 550 paper-based; 213 computer-based; 79 iBT). *Application deadline:* For fall admission, 8/1 priority date for domestic students, 8/1 for international students; for spring admission, 11/15 priority date for domestic students, 11/15 for international students. Applications are processed on a rolling basis. Application fee: $50. Electronic applications accepted. *Expenses: Contact institution. Financial support:* In 2006–07, 108 students received support. Scholarships/grants available. Support available to part-time students. Financial award applicants required to submit FAFSA. *Faculty research:* Violence in higher education and workplace, screening and selection procedures in law enforcement, Internet use in criminal justice, stress management in law enforcement. *Unit head:* Robert Hartl, Director, 218-723-6651, Fax: 218-723-6290, E-mail: rhartl@css.edu. *Application contact:* Tonya J. Roth, Graduate Recruitment Counselor, 218-723-6285, Fax: 218-733-2275, E-mail: gradstudies@css.edu.

College of Santa Fe, Department of Business Administration, Santa Fe, NM 87505-7634. Offers finance (MBA); human resources (MBA). Program also available at Albuquerque campus. Part-time and evening/weekend programs available. *Entrance requirements:* For master's, minimum GPA of 3.0 in last 60 hours (preferred).

College of Staten Island of the City University of New York, Graduate Programs, Program in Business Management, Staten Island, NY 10314-6600. Offers MS. Part-time and evening/weekend programs available. *Faculty:* 4 full-time (0 women). *Students:* 1 full-time (0 women), 34 part-time (13 women), 13 international. 32 applicants, 81% accepted, 22 enrolled. *Entrance requirements:* For master's, GMAT, minimum undergraduate GPA of 3.0. Additional exam requirements/recommendations for international students: Required—TOEFL (minimum score 550 paper-based; 213 computer-based; 79 iBT). Application fee: $125. *Expenses:* Tuition, state resident: full-time $6,400; part-time $270 per credit. Tuition, nonresident: part-time $500 per credit. Required fees: $53 per semester. *Financial support:* Fellowships, research assistantships, teaching assistantships available. *Unit head:* John Sandler, Coordinator, 718-982-2921, E-mail: sandler@mail.csi.cuny.edu. *Application contact:* Emmanuel Esperance, Deputy Director of Office of Recruitment and Admissions, 718-982-2190, Fax: 718-982-2500, E-mail: admissions@mail.csi.cuny.edu.

The College of William and Mary, Mason School of Business, Williamsburg, VA 23187-8795. Offers accounting (M Acc); business administration (MBA); JD/MBA; MBA/MPP. *Accreditation:* AACSB. Part-time and evening/weekend programs available. *Faculty:* 57 full-time (15 women), 4 part-time/adjunct (0 women). *Students:* 202 full-time (61 women), 138 part-time (25 women); includes 17 African Americans, 11 Asian Americans or Pacific Islanders, 1 Hispanic American, 58 international. Average age 32. 208 applicants, 52% accepted, 58 enrolled. In 2006, 167 degrees awarded. *Degree requirements:* For master's, field studies project. *Entrance requirements:* For master's, GMAT. Additional exam requirements/recommendations for international students: Required—TOEFL (minimum score 600 paper-based; 250 computer-based). *Application deadline:* For fall admission, 4/1 priority date for domestic students. Applications are processed on a rolling basis. Application fee: $100. Electronic applications accepted. *Expenses: Contact institution.* Tuition and fees vary according to program. *Financial support:* In 2006–07, 137 students received support, including 44 research assistantships with partial tuition reimbursements available (averaging $4,000 per year); career-related internships or fieldwork, scholarships/grants, and unspecified assistantships also available. Financial award application deadline: 3/1; financial award applicants required to submit FAFSA. *Faculty research:* Financial markets, marketing strategy, leadership and change, strategy/information, operations/inventory, supply chains. Total annual research expenditures: $305,274. *Unit head:* Dr. Lawrence Pulley, Dean, 757-221-2891, Fax: 757-221-2937, E-mail: larry.pulley@mason.wm.edu. *Application contact:* Kathy Pattison, Director of Admissions, 757-221-2898, Fax: 757-221-2958, E-mail: kpattison@business.wm.edu.

Colorado Christian University, Program in Business Administration, Lakewood, CO 80226. Offers MBA. Part-time and evening/weekend programs available. Postbaccalaureate distance learning degree programs offered (minimal on-campus study). *Degree requirements:* For master's, thesis optional. *Entrance requirements:* For master's, GMAT, 2 letters of recommendation, resumé. Additional exam requirements/recommendations for international students: Required—TOEFL. Electronic applications accepted. Expenses: Contact institution.

Colorado State University, Graduate School, College of Business, MBA Program, Fort Collins, CO 80523-0015. Offers MBA, MBA/DVM. *Accreditation:* AACSB. Part-time and evening/weekend programs available. Postbaccalaureate distance learning degree programs offered (no on-campus study). *Faculty:* 11 full-time (4 women), 1 part-time/adjunct (0 women). *Students:* 6 full-time (2 women), 443 part-time (115 women); includes 59 minority (16 African Americans, 9 American Indian/Alaska Native, 21 Asian Americans or Pacific Islanders, 13 Hispanic Americans), 25 international. Average age 36. 261 applicants, 86% accepted, 188 enrolled. In 2006, 153 degrees awarded. *Entrance requirements:* For master's, GMAT, minimum undergraduate GPA of 3.0, 4 years post-undergraduate professional work experience. Additional exam requirements/recommendations for international students: Recommended—TOEFL (minimum score 565 paper-based; 227 computer-based). *Application deadline:* For fall admission, 7/15 priority date for domestic students, 6/1 for international students; for spring admission, 11/15 priority date for domestic students, 10/1 for international students. Applications are processed on a rolling basis. Application fee: $50. Electronic applications accepted. *Expenses: Contact institution.* Tuition and fees vary according to program. *Financial support:* In 2006–07, 35 students received support, including 5 fellowships (averaging $1,500 per year), 5 teaching assistantships with full and partial tuition reimbursements available (averaging $5,000 per year); scholarships/grants and unspecified assistantships also available. Support available to part-time students. Financial award application deadline: 6/1; financial award applicants required to submit FAFSA. *Faculty research:* E-commerce, entrepreneurship. Total annual research expenditures: $105,826. *Application contact:* Rachel Stoll, Admissions Coordinator, 970-491-3704, Fax: 970-491-3481, E-mail: rachel.stoll@colostate.edu.

Colorado State University-Pueblo, Malik and Seeme Hasan School of Business, Pueblo, CO 81001-4901. Offers MBA. *Accreditation:* AACSB. Part-time and evening/weekend programs available. *Faculty:* 9 full-time (2 women), 1 part-time/adjunct (0 women). *Students:* 26 full-time (6 women), 51 part-time (25 women); includes 18 minority (2 African Americans, 1 Asian American or Pacific Islander, 15 Hispanic Americans), 22 international. Average age 28. 59 applicants, 78% accepted, 38 enrolled. In 2006, 21 degrees awarded. *Degree requirements:* For master's, thesis optional. *Entrance requirements:* For master's, GMAT, minimum GPA of 3.0. Additional exam requirements/recommendations for international students: Required—TOEFL (minimum score 550 paper-based; 217 computer-based). *Application deadline:* For fall admission, 8/18 priority date for domestic students, 7/1 for international students; for spring admission, 1/12 priority date for domestic students, 11/1 for international students. Applications are processed on a rolling basis. Application fee: $35. *Expenses:* Tuition, state resident: full-time $2,771; part-time $124 per credit hour. Tuition, nonresident: full-time $10,697; part-time $564 per credit hour. Required fees: $729; $41 per credit hour. *Financial support:* In 2006–07, 8 research assistantships (averaging $3,220 per year) were awarded; unspecified assistantships also available. Financial award applicants required to submit FAFSA. *Faculty research:* Total quality management, leadership, small business studies, case research and writing. *Unit head:* Dr. Rex D. Fuller, Dean, 719-549-2142, Fax: 719-549-2909, E-mail: rex.fuller@colostate-pueblo.edu. *Application contact:* Karen Hughes, Administrative Assistant II, 719-549-2101, Fax: 719-549-2409, E-mail: karen.hughes@colostate-pueblo.edu.

Colorado Technical University, Graduate Studies, Program in Management, Colorado Springs, CO 80907-3896. Offers business administration (MBA); business management (MSM); business technology (MSM); database management (MSM); human resources management (MSM); information technology (MSM); logistics management (MSM); management (DM); organizational leadership (MSM); project management (MSM). Part-time and evening/weekend programs available. *Degree requirements:* For master's, thesis or alternative; for doctorate, thesis/dissertation. *Entrance requirements:* For doctorate, minimum graduate GPA of 3.0, 5 years of related work experience. *Faculty research:* Sexual harassment, performance evaluation, critical thinking.

Colorado Technical University Denver Campus, Programs in Business Administration and Management, Greenwood Village, CO 80111. Offers accounting (MBA); business administration (MBA); business administration and management (EMBA); business technology (MSM); database management (MSM); human resource management (MBA); information technology (MSM); project management (MSM); technology management (MBA). Part-time and evening/weekend programs available. *Degree requirements:* For master's, thesis or alternative. *Entrance requirements:* For master's, minimum undergraduate GPA of 3.0, resumé.

Colorado Technical University Sioux Falls Campus, Programs in Business Administration and Management, Sioux Falls, SD 57108. Offers business administration (MBA); business management (MSM); health science management (MSM); human resources management (MSM); information technology (MSM); organizational leadership (MSM); project management (MBA); technology management (MBA). Evening/weekend programs available. *Degree requirements:* For master's, thesis optional. *Entrance requirements:* For master's, minimum 2 years work experience, resumé.

Columbia College, Program in Business Administration, Columbia, MO 65216-0002. Offers MBA. Part-time and evening/weekend programs available. *Faculty:* 6 full-time (1 woman), 31 part-time/adjunct (7 women). *Students:* 196 full-time (98 women); includes 47 minority (36 African Americans, 4 American Indian/Alaska Native, 3 Asian Americans or Pacific Islanders, 4 Hispanic Americans), 5 international. Average age 37. 61 applicants, 72% accepted, 35 enrolled. In 2006, 63 degrees awarded. *Degree requirements:* For master's, culminating experience, final exams, portfolio. *Entrance requirements:* For master's, minimum GPA of 3.0, bachelor's degree in business administration, 3 recommendations. Additional exam requirements/recommendations for international students: Required—TOEFL (minimum score 550 paper-based; 213 computer-based). *Application deadline:* For fall admission, 8/1 priority date for domestic and international students; for winter admission, 1/1 priority date for domestic and international students. Applications are processed on a rolling basis. Application fee: $55. *Expenses:* Tuition: Part-time $270 per credit hour. *Financial support:* Federal Work-Study and scholarships/grants available. Support available to part-time students. Financial award applica-

Business Administration and Management—General

Columbia College (continued)
tion deadline: 3/15; financial award applicants required to submit FAFSA. *Unit head:* Dr. Ken Middleton, Chair, 573-875-7535, Fax: 573-875-7209, E-mail: kamiddleton@email.ccis.edu. *Application contact:* Regina Morin, Director of Admissions, 573-875-7354, Fax: 573-875-7506, E-mail: rmmorin@ccis.edu.

Columbia Southern University, MBA Program, Orange Beach, AL 36561. Offers electronic business and technology (MBA); healthcare management (MBA); human resources management (MBA); international management (MBA); marketing (MBA); project management (MBA); public administration (MBA); sport management (MBA). Part-time and evening/weekend programs available. Postbaccalaureate distance learning degree programs offered (no on-campus study). *Entrance requirements:* Additional exam requirements/recommendations for international students: Required—TOEFL. Electronic applications accepted.

Columbia University, Graduate School of Business, Doctoral Program in Business, New York, NY 10027. Offers business (PhD), including accounting, decision, risk, and operations, finance and economics, management, marketing. *Accreditation:* AACSB. *Faculty:* 118 full-time (14 women), 106 part-time/adjunct (18 women). *Students:* 114 full-time (38 women); includes 3 Hispanic Americans, 96 international. Average age 27. 636 applicants, 6% accepted, 18 enrolled. In 2006, 15 degrees awarded. *Degree requirements:* For doctorate, thesis/dissertation, major field exam, research paper, thesis proposal, comprehensive exam, registration. *Entrance requirements:* For doctorate, GMAT, 2 letters of reference, resumé. Additional exam requirements/recommendations for international students: Required—TOEFL. *Application deadline:* For fall admission, 1/1 for domestic and international students. Application fee: $75. Electronic applications accepted. *Expenses: Contact institution. Financial support:* In 2006–07, fellowships with full tuition reimbursements (averaging $20,500 per year), research assistantships (averaging $4,000 per year) were awarded; teaching assistantships, career-related internships or fieldwork, institutionally sponsored loans, health care benefits, tuition waivers (full), and unspecified assistantships also available. *Unit head:* Elizabeth Elam Chang, Administrative Director, 212-854-2836, Fax: 212-932-2359, E-mail: phdinfo@gsb.columbia.edu.

Columbia University, Graduate School of Business, Executive MBA Global Program, New York, NY 10027. Offers EMBA. Program offered jointly with London Business School. *Faculty:* 118 full-time (14 women), 106 part-time/adjunct (18 women). *Students:* 70 full-time (17 women); includes 9 minority (7 Asian Americans or Pacific Islanders, 2 Hispanic Americans), 40 international. Average age 33. In 2006, 59 degrees awarded. *Entrance requirements:* For master's, GMAT, 2 letters of reference, interview, minimum 5 years of work experience. *Application deadline:* For spring admission, 2/1 for domestic and international students. Applications are processed on a rolling basis. Application fee: $170. Electronic applications accepted. *Expenses: Contact institution. Unit head:* Ethan R. Hanabury, Associate Dean of the Executive MBA Programs, 212-854-6019, Fax: 212-316-1473, E-mail: emba@columbia.edu. *Application contact:* Sidney Jackson, Director of Marketing and Admissions, 212-854-1183, Fax: 212-854-8998, E-mail: stj9@columbia.edu.

Columbia University, Graduate School of Business, Executive MBA Program, New York, NY 10027. Offers EMBA. Evening/weekend programs available. *Faculty:* 118 full-time (14 women), 106 part-time/adjunct (18 women). *Students:* 373 full-time (101 women); includes 62 minority (7 African Americans, 47 Asian Americans or Pacific Islanders, 8 Hispanic Americans), 111 international. Average age 33. In 2006, 238 degrees awarded. *Degree requirements:* For master's, 60 credits completed. *Entrance requirements:* For master's, GMAT, minimum 5 years of work experience, 2 letters of reference, interview. *Application deadline:* For fall admission, 6/1 for domestic and international students; for spring admission, 10/15 for domestic and international students. Applications are processed on a rolling basis. Application fee: $160. Electronic applications accepted. *Expenses: Contact institution. Financial support:* Institutionally sponsored loans available. Financial award applicants required to submit FAFSA. *Unit head:* Ethan R. Hanabury, Associate Dean of the Executive MBA Programs, 212-854-6019, Fax: 212-316-1473, E-mail: emba@columbia.edu. *Application contact:* Sidney Jackson, Director of Marketing and Admissions, 212-854-1183, Fax: 212-854-8998, E-mail: stj9@columbia.edu.

Columbia University, Graduate School of Business, Executive MBA Program, Berkeley-Columbia, New York, NY 10027. Offers EMBA. *Faculty:* 118 full-time (14 women), 106 part-time/adjunct (18 women). *Students:* 70 full-time (12 women); includes 19 minority (1 African American, 1 American Indian/Alaska Native, 14 Asian Americans or Pacific Islanders, 3 Hispanic Americans). Average age 37. In 2006, 67 degrees awarded. *Degree requirements:* For master's, 60 credits completed. *Entrance requirements:* For master's, GMAT, 2 letters of reference, interview, minimum 5 years of work experience. Additional exam requirements/recommendations for international students: Required—TOEFL. *Application deadline:* For spring admission, 2/15 for domestic and international students. Applications are processed on a rolling basis. Application fee: $165. Electronic applications accepted. *Expenses: Contact institution. Unit head:* Ethan R. Hanabury, Associate Dean of the Executive MBA Programs, 212-854-6019, Fax: 212-316-1473, E-mail: emba@columbia.edu. *Application contact:* Sidney Jackson, Director of Marketing and Admissions, 212-854-1183, Fax: 212-854-8998, E-mail: stj9@columbia.edu.

Columbia University, Graduate School of Business, MBA Program, New York, NY 10027. Offers accounting (MBA); decision, risk, and operations (MBA); entrepreneurship (MBA); finance and economics (MBA); human resource management (MBA); international business (MBA); management (MBA); marketing (MBA); media (MBA); real estate (MBA); social enterprise (MBA); DDS/MBA; JD/MBA; MBA/MIA; MBA/MPH; MBA/MS; MD/MBA. *Faculty:* 118 full-time (14 women), 106 part-time/adjunct (18 women). *Students:* 1,242 full-time (428 women); includes 291 minority (65 African Americans, 5 American Indian/Alaska Native, 189 Asian Americans or Pacific Islanders, 32 Hispanic Americans), 392 international. Average age 28. 5,372 applicants, 17% accepted, 726 enrolled. In 2006, 682 degrees awarded. *Entrance requirements:* For master's, GMAT, 2 letters of recommendation. Additional exam requirements/recommendations for international students: Required—TOEFL. *Application deadline:* For fall admission, 4/20 for domestic students, 3/1 for international students; for spring admission, 10/12 for domestic and international students. Applications are processed on a rolling basis. Application fee: $215. Electronic applications accepted. *Financial support:* Fellowships, research assistantships, teaching assistantships, career-related internships or fieldwork, Federal Work-Study, institutionally sponsored loans, scholarships/grants, and unspecified assistantships available. Financial award applicants required to submit FAFSA. *Unit head:* Prof. Amir Ziv, Vice Dean of Students and the MBA Program, 212-854-3485, Fax: 212-932-0545, E-mail: az50@columbia.edu. *Application contact:* Linda B. Meehan, Assistant Dean of Admissions, 212-854-1961, Fax: 212-662-6754, E-mail: apply@claven.gsb.columbia.edu.

Columbus State University, Graduate Studies, D. Abbott Turner College of Business, Columbus, GA 31907-5645. Offers business administration (MBA). *Accreditation:* AACSB. *Faculty:* 4 full-time (2 women). *Students:* 12 full-time (5 women), 32 part-time (17 women); includes 14 minority (7 African Americans, 5 Asian Americans or Pacific Islanders, 2 Hispanic Americans), 2 international. Average age 36. 36 applicants, 42% accepted, 14 enrolled. In 2006, 33 degrees awarded. *Entrance requirements:* For master's, GMAT. Additional exam requirements/recommendations for international students: Required—TOEFL (minimum score 550 paper-based; 213 computer-based). *Application deadline:* For fall admission, 5/1 priority date for domestic students, 5/1 for international students; for spring admission, 11/1 for domestic and international students. Applications are processed on a rolling basis. Application fee: $25. Electronic applications accepted. *Expenses:* Tuition, state resident: part-time $127 per semester hour. Tuition, nonresident: part-time $508 per semester hour. Required fees: $264 per semester. Tuition and fees vary according to course load. *Financial support:* In 2006–07, 13 students received support, including 2 research assistantships (averaging $3,000 per year). Financial award application deadline: 5/1. *Unit head:* Dr. Linda U. Hadley, Dean, 706-568-2044, Fax: 706-568-2184, E-mail: hadley_linda@colstate.edu.

Concordia University, School of Business and Professional Studies, Program in Entrepreneurial Business Administration, Irvine, CA 92612-3299. Offers MBA. *Faculty:* 3 full-time, 5 part-time/adjunct. *Students:* 58 full-time (29 women), 1 (woman) part-time; includes 9 minority (2 African Americans, 5 Asian Americans or Pacific Islanders, 2 Hispanic Americans), 10 international. Average age 32. 29 applicants, 86% accepted, 23 enrolled. In 2006, 14 degrees awarded. *Degree requirements:* For master's, thesis or alternative. *Entrance requirements:* For master's, GMAT, 2 years of work experience. Additional exam requirements/recommendations for international students: Required—TOEFL (minimum score 550 paper-based; 213 computer-based). *Application deadline:* For fall admission, 7/1 for domestic students; for spring admission, 12/1 for domestic students. Applications are processed on a rolling basis. Application fee: $25 ($300 for international students). *Financial support:* Applicants required to submit FAFSA. Total annual research expenditures: $10,000. *Application contact:* Roberto Marquez, Coordinator of Graduate Enrollment, 949-854-8002 Ext. 1133, Fax: 949-854-6894, E-mail: roberto.marquez@cui.edu.

Concordia University, School of Graduate Studies, John Molson School of Business, Montréal, QC H3G 1M8, Canada. Offers administration (M Sc, Diploma); aviation management (Certificate, Diploma); business administration (MBA, UA Undergraduate Associate, PhD), including international aviation (UA Undergraduate Associate); chartered accountancy (Diploma); community organizational development (Certificate); event management and fundraising (Certificate); executive business administration (EMBA); investment management (Diploma); investment management option (MBA); management accounting (Certificate); management of healthcare organizations (Certificate); sport administration (Diploma). *Accreditation:* AACSB. Part-time and evening/weekend programs available. *Students:* 447 full-time (174 women), 448 part-time (206 women). 925 applicants, 59% accepted, 319 enrolled. In 2006, 183 master's, 6 doctorates, 62 other advanced degrees awarded. *Degree requirements:* For master's, one foreign language, thesis (for some programs), research project; for doctorate, one foreign language, thesis/dissertation; for other advanced degree, one foreign language. *Entrance requirements:* For master's and doctorate, GMAT. Additional exam requirements/recommendations for international students: Required—TOEFL. Application fee: $50. *Expenses: Contact institution. Financial support:* Fellowships, career-related internships or fieldwork available. *Faculty research:* General business, capital markets, international business. *Unit head:* Dr. Jerry Tomberlin, Dean, 514-848-2424 Ext. 2700, Fax: 514-848-4502. *Application contact:* Dr. Michel Magnan, Associate Dean, Graduate Programs, 514-848-2424 Ext. 4145, Fax: 514-848-4208.

Concordia University, School of Management, Portland, OR 97211-6099. Offers MBA. Evening/weekend programs available. *Degree requirements:* For master's, thesis optional. *Entrance requirements:* For master's, GMAT or professional portfolio, minimum GPA of 3.0, 2 letters of recommendation, 5 years of work experience, resumé. Additional exam requirements/recommendations for international students: Required—TOEFL (minimum score 525 paper-based; 195 computer-based). *Faculty research:* Leadership characteristics in internships, marketing of MBA programs, entrepreneurship.

Concordia University, St. Paul, College of Business and Organizational Leadership, St. Paul, MN 55104-5494. Offers business and organizational leadership (MBA); criminal justice (MAHS); human resources (MAOM); organizational management (MAOM). *Accreditation:* ACBSP. Evening/weekend programs available. Postbaccalaureate distance learning degree programs offered (minimal on-campus study). *Faculty:* 11 full-time (2 women), 18 part-time/adjunct (6 women). *Students:* 186 full-time (114 women); includes 26 minority (16 African Americans, 8 Asian Americans or Pacific Islanders, 2 Hispanic Americans), 1 international. Average age 33. In 2006, 92 degrees awarded. *Entrance requirements:* Additional exam requirements/recommendations for international students: Required—TOEFL. *Application deadline:* Applications are processed on a rolling basis. Application fee: $50. Electronic applications accepted. *Financial support:* Federal Work-Study and scholarships/grants available. Financial award applicants required to submit FAFSA. *Unit head:* Dr. Robert DeGregorio, Dean, 651-641-8845, Fax: 651-641-8807, E-mail: degregorio@csp.edu. *Application contact:* Kimberly Craig, Director of Graduate and Cohort Admission, 651-603-6223, Fax: 651-603-6320, E-mail: craig@csp.edu.

Concordia University Wisconsin, Graduate Programs, School of Business and Legal Studies, MBA Program, Mequon, WI 53097-2402. Offers finance (MBA); health care administration (MBA); human resource management (MBA); international business (MBA); international business-English/Chinese (MBA); management (MBA); management information services (MBA); managerial communications (MBA); marketing (MBA); public administration (MBA); risk management (MBA). Postbaccalaureate distance learning degree programs offered (minimal on-campus study). *Students:* 504 (249 women). In 2006, 110 degrees awarded. *Degree requirements:* For master's, thesis or alternative, comprehensive exam. *Entrance requirements:* Additional exam requirements/recommendations for international students: Required—TOEFL. *Application deadline:* For fall admission, 8/1 priority date for domestic students; for spring admission, 1/15 for domestic students. Applications are processed on a rolling basis. Application fee: $50. *Expenses: Contact institution. Financial support:* Application deadline: 8/1. *Unit head:* Dr. David Borst, Director, 262-243-4298, Fax: 262-243-4428, E-mail: david.borst@cuw.edu.

Cornell University, Graduate School, Graduate Field of Management, Ithaca, NY 14853-0001. Offers accounting (PhD); behavioral decision theory (PhD); finance (PhD); marketing (PhD); organizational behavior (PhD); production and operations management (PhD). *Accreditation:* AACSB. *Faculty:* 57 full-time (11 women). *Students:* 38 full-time (14 women); includes 2 minority (both Asian Americans or Pacific Islanders), 20 international. Average age 31. 457 applicants, 5% accepted, 8 enrolled. In 2006, 4 doctorates awarded. *Degree requirements:* For doctorate, thesis/dissertation, comprehensive exam. *Entrance requirements:* For doctorate, GMAT or GRE General Test. Additional exam requirements/recommendations for international students: Required—TOEFL (minimum score 600 paper-based; 250 computer-based). *Application deadline:* For fall admission, 1/3 for domestic students. Application fee: $60. Electronic applications accepted. *Expenses: Contact institution.* Full-time tuition and fees vary according to program. *Financial support:* In 2006–07, 37 students received support, including 2 fellowships with full tuition reimbursements available, 31 research assistantships with full tuition reimbursements available, 4 teaching assistantships with full tuition reimbursements available; institutionally sponsored loans, scholarships/grants, health care benefits, tuition waivers (full and partial), and unspecified assistantships also available. Financial award applicants required to submit FAFSA. *Faculty research:* Operations and manufacturing. *Unit head:* Director of Graduate Studies, 607-255-3669. *Application contact:* Graduate Field Assistant, 607-255-9431, E-mail: js_phd@cornell.edu.

Cornell University, Johnson Graduate School of Management, Ithaca, NY 14853-0001. Offers MBA, JD/MBA, M Eng/MBA, MBA/MILR. *Accreditation:* AACSB. *Faculty:* 53 full-time (12 women), 3 part-time/adjunct (0 women). *Students:* 827 full-time (194 women); includes 147 minority (26 African Americans, 1 American Indian/Alaska Native, 98 Asian Americans or Pacific Islanders, 22 Hispanic Americans), 266 international. Average age 27. 2,043 applicants, 453 enrolled. In 2006, 346 degrees awarded. *Median time to degree:* Master's–2 years full-time. *Entrance requirements:* For master's, GMAT. Additional exam requirements/recommendations for international students: Required—TOEFL (minimum score 250 computer-based; 100 iBT); Recommended—IELTS (minimum score 7), TWE. *Application deadline:* For fall admission, 4/1 for domestic students, 1/1 for international students. Application fee: $180. *Expenses: Contact institution.* Full-time tuition and fees vary according to program. *Financial support:* Fellowships, research assistantships, career-related internships or fieldwork, Federal Work-Study, institutionally sponsored loans, and tuition waivers (full and partial) available. Financial award application deadline: 2/15; financial award applicants required to submit FAFSA. *Unit head:* Robert J. Swieringa, Dean, 607-255-6418. *Application contact:* 800-847-2082, Fax: 607-254-8886, E-mail: mba@johnson.cornell.edu.

Creighton University, Graduate School, Eugene C. Eppley College of Business Administration, Omaha, NE 68178-0001. Offers business administration (MBA); information technology

(MS); securities and portfolio management (MSAPM); JD/MBA; MBA/INR; MBA/MS-ITM; MBA/MSAPM; MS ITM/JD; Pharm D/MBA. *Accreditation:* AACSB. Part-time and evening/weekend programs available. *Faculty:* 13 full-time (3 women), 5 part-time/adjunct (3 women). *Students:* 26 full-time (9 women), 124 part-time (27 women); includes 17 minority (9 African Americans, 5 Asian Americans or Pacific Islanders, 3 Hispanic Americans), 19 international. Average age 27. 46 applicants, 100% accepted, 27 enrolled. In 2006, 65 degrees awarded. *Degree requirements:* For master's, thesis optional. *Entrance requirements:* For master's, GMAT, resumé, 2 letters of recommendation, financial statement. Additional exam requirements/recommendations for international students: Required—TOEFL (minimum score 550 paper-based; 213 computer-based; 80 iBT). *Application deadline:* For fall admission, 3/1 priority date for domestic students, 3/1 for international students; for spring admission, 10/1 priority date for domestic students, 10/1 for international students. Applications are processed on a rolling basis. Application fee: $40. Electronic applications accepted. *Expenses:* Tuition: Part-time $595 per credit hour. Required fees: $38 per semester. *Financial support:* In 2006–07, 8 research assistantships with full tuition reimbursements (averaging $8,400 per year) were awarded; career-related internships or fieldwork, tuition waivers (partial), and unspecified assistantships also available. Financial award application deadline: 3/1. *Faculty research:* Small business issues. *Unit head:* Dr. Ravi Nath, Director, 402-280-2439. *Application contact:* Gail Hafer, Coordinator, 402-280-2829, Fax: 402-280-2172, E-mail: ghafer@creighton.edu.

Cumberland University, Program in Business Administration, Lebanon, TN 37087-3408. Offers MBA. *Accreditation:* ACBSP. Part-time and evening/weekend programs available. *Faculty:* 4 full-time (1 woman). *Students:* 8 full-time (6 women), 14 part-time (6 women); includes 4 minority (2 African Americans, 1 Asian American or Pacific Islander, 1 Hispanic American), 4 international. Average age 32. 8 applicants, 100% accepted, 2 enrolled. In 2006, 5 degrees awarded. *Degree requirements:* For master's, comprehensive exam, registration. *Entrance requirements:* For master's, GMAT or GRE General Test, 3 letters of recommendation. Additional exam requirements/recommendations for international students: Required—TOEFL (minimum score 500 paper-based; 173 computer-based). *Application deadline:* Applications are processed on a rolling basis. Application fee: $50. *Expenses: Contact institution. Financial support:* Career-related internships or fieldwork, institutionally sponsored loans, and scholarships/grants available. Support available to part-time students. Financial award application deadline: 8/1; financial award applicants required to submit FAFSA. *Unit head:* Dr. Paul Stumb, Dean of the Labry School of Business, 615-444-2562 Ext. 1210, Fax: 615-444-2569, E-mail: pstumb@cumberland.edu.

Curry College, Division of Continuing Education and Graduate Studies, Program in Business Administration, Milton, MA 02186-9984. Offers MBA. Part-time and evening/weekend programs available. *Faculty:* 5 full-time (2 women), 2 part-time/adjunct (0 women). *Students:* Average age 36. 40 applicants, 88% accepted, 33 enrolled. *Degree requirements:* For master's, capstone applied project. *Entrance requirements:* For master's, resumé, recommendations, interview. Additional exam requirements/recommendations for international students: Required—TOEFL (minimum score 550 paper-based). *Application deadline:* For fall admission, 8/1 priority date for domestic students; for spring admission, 12/1 priority date for domestic students. Applications are processed on a rolling basis. Application fee: $50. *Expenses: Contact institution. Unit head:* Dr. Gail Arch, Director, 617-333-2197. *Application contact:* John Bresnahan, Director of Graduate Enrollment and Student Services, 617-333-2243, Fax: 617-333-2045, E-mail: jbresnah0104@curry.edu.

Daemen College, Program in Executive Leadership and Change, Amherst, NY 14226-3592. Offers MS. Part-time and evening/weekend programs available. *Faculty:* 1 full-time (0 women), 4 part-time/adjunct (2 women). *Students:* 7 full-time (4 women), 8 part-time (all women); includes 1 minority (African American) Average age 39. 9 applicants, 100% accepted, 5 enrolled. In 2006, 9 degrees awarded. *Degree requirements:* For master's, cohort learning sequence. *Entrance requirements:* For master's, 2 letters of recommendation, interview. Additional exam requirements/recommendations for international students: Required—TOEFL (minimum score 500 paper-based; 173 computer-based). *Application deadline:* For fall admission, 3/1 priority date for domestic and international students; for spring admission, 10/1 priority date for domestic and international students. Applications are processed on a rolling basis. Application fee: $25. Electronic applications accepted. *Expenses:* Tuition: Full-time $11,700; part-time $650 per credit hour. Required fees: $15 per credit hour. Tuition and fees vary according to course load. *Financial support:* Federal Work-Study and institutionally sponsored loans available. Financial award application deadline: 2/15; financial award applicants required to submit FAFSA. *Unit head:* Dr. John S. Frederick, Executive Director, 716-839-8342, Fax: 716-839-8261, E-mail: jfrederi@daemen.edu. *Application contact:* Karl Shallowhorn, Associate Director of Graduate Admissions, 716-839-8225, Fax: 716-839-8229, E-mail: kshallow@daemen.edu.

Dalhousie University, Faculty of Graduate Studies, Faculty of Management, School of Business Administration, Halifax, NS B3H 4R2, Canada. Offers MBA, LL B/MBA. Part-time programs available. *Entrance requirements:* For master's, GMAT. Additional exam requirements/recommendations for international students: Required—TOEFL. *Faculty research:* International business, quantitative methods, operations research, MIS, marketing, finance.

Dallas Baptist University, College of Adult Education, Professional Development Program, Dallas, TX 75211-9299. Offers accounting (MA); business (MA); church leadership (MA); corporate management (MA); counseling (MA); criminal justice (MA); English as a second language (MA); finance (MA); higher education (MA); leadership studies (MA); management (MA); management information systems (MA); marketing (MA); missions (MA). Part-time and evening/weekend programs available. *Faculty:* 49 full-time (21 women), 112 part-time/adjunct (46 women). *Students:* 31 full-time, 65 part-time. 51 applicants, 49% accepted, 15 enrolled. In 2006, 41 degrees awarded. Application fee: $25. *Expenses:* Tuition: Full-time $8,370; part-time $465 per credit hour. Required fees: $465 per credit hour. *Financial support:* Tuition waivers (full and partial) available. *Unit head:* Lynda Jackson, Director, 214-333-6830, Fax: 214-333-5558, E-mail: graduate@dbu.edu. *Application contact:* Kit P. Montgomery, Director of Graduate Programs, 214-333-5242, Fax: 214-333-5579, E-mail: graduate@dbu.edu.

Dallas Baptist University, Graduate School of Business, Business Administration Program, Dallas, TX 75211-9299. Offers accounting (MBA); business communication (MBA); conflict resolution management (MBA); e-business (MBA); entrepreneurship (MBA); finance (MBA); health care management (MBA); international business (MBA); management (MBA); management information systems (MBA); marketing (MBA); project management (MBA); technology and engineering management (MBA). *Accreditation:* ACBSP. Part-time and evening/weekend programs available. Postbaccalaureate distance learning degree programs offered (no on-campus study). *Faculty:* 49 full-time (21 women), 112 part-time/adjunct (46 women). *Students:* 103 full-time, 318 part-time. 226 applicants, 38% accepted. In 2006, 124 degrees awarded. *Entrance requirements:* For master's, GMAT, minimum GPA of 3.0. Additional exam requirements/recommendations for international students: Required—TOEFL. *Application deadline:* Applications are processed on a rolling basis. Application fee: $25. Electronic applications accepted. *Expenses:* Tuition: Full-time $8,370; part-time $465 per credit hour. Required fees: $465 per credit hour. *Financial support:* Career-related internships or fieldwork, Federal Work-Study, institutionally sponsored loans, scholarships/grants, and tuition waivers (full and partial) available. Support available to part-time students. *Faculty research:* Sports management, services marketing, retailing, strategic management, financial planning/investments. *Unit head:* Dr. Sandra S. Reid, Director, 214-333-5244, Fax: 214-333-5293, E-mail: graduate@dbu.edu. *Application contact:* Kit P. Montgomery, Director of Graduate Programs, 214-333-5242, Fax: 214-333-5579, E-mail: graduate@dbu.edu.

Dallas Baptist University, Graduate School of Business, Management Program, Dallas, TX 75211-9299. Offers business communication (MA); conflict resolution management (MA); general management (MA); health care management (MA); human resource management (MA). Part-time and evening/weekend programs available. Postbaccalaureate distance learning degree programs offered (no on-campus study). *Faculty:* 49 full-time (21 women), 112 part-time/adjunct (46 women). *Students:* 46 full-time, 194 part-time. 96 applicants. In 2006, 77 degrees awarded. *Entrance requirements:* For master's, minimum GPA of 3.0. Additional exam requirements/recommendations for international students: Required—TOEFL. *Application deadline:* Applications are processed on a rolling basis. Application fee: $25. Electronic applications accepted. *Expenses:* Tuition: Full-time $8,370; part-time $465 per credit hour. Required fees: $465 per credit hour. *Financial support:* Federal Work-Study, institutionally sponsored loans, scholarships/grants, and tuition waivers (full and partial) available. Support available to part-time students. *Faculty research:* Organizational behavior, conflict personalities. *Unit head:* Connie F. Throne, Director of Organizational Management Program, 214-333-5244, Fax: 214-333-5579, E-mail: graduate@dbu.edu. *Application contact:* Kit P. Montgomery, Director of Graduate Programs, 214-333-5242, Fax: 214-333-5579, E-mail: graduate@dbu.edu.

Dallas Baptist University, School of Leadership and Christian Education, Program in Christian Education, Dallas, TX 75211-9299. Offers adult ministry (MA); Baptist student ministry (MA); business ministry (MA); children's ministry (MA); collegiate ministry (MA); counseling ministry (MA); education ministry (MA); general ministry (MA); ministry with students (MA); missions ministry (MA); worship ministry (MA); youth ministry (MA). Part-time and evening/weekend programs available. *Faculty:* 49 full-time (21 women), 112 part-time/adjunct (46 women). *Students:* 40 full-time, 45 part-time. 50 applicants, 32% accepted, 15 enrolled. In 2006, 19 degrees awarded. *Entrance requirements:* For master's, GRE, ACT or SAT, minimum GPA of 2.8. Additional exam requirements/recommendations for international students: Required—TOEFL. *Application deadline:* Applications are processed on a rolling basis. Application fee: $25. Electronic applications accepted. *Expenses:* Tuition: Full-time $8,370; part-time $465 per credit hour. Required fees: $465 per credit hour. *Financial support:* Federal Work-Study, institutionally sponsored loans, scholarships/grants, and tuition waivers (full and partial) available. Support available to part-time students. *Unit head:* Dr. Judy Morris, Director, 214-333-5246, Fax: 214-333-5115, E-mail: graduate@dbu.edu. *Application contact:* Kit P. Montgomery, Director of Graduate Programs, 214-333-5242, Fax: 214-333-5579, E-mail: graduate@dbu.edu.

Daniel Webster College, MBA Program, Nashua, NH 03063-1300. Offers applied management (MBA). Postbaccalaureate distance learning degree programs offered.

Daniel Webster College–Portsmouth Campus, MBA Program, Portsmouth, NH 03801. Offers applied management (MBA).

Dartmouth College, Tuck School of Business at Dartmouth, Hanover, NH 03755. Offers MBA, MBA/MA, MBA/MALD, MBA/MEM, MBA/MPA, MBA/MPH, MBA/MSEL, MD/MBA. *Accreditation:* AACSB. *Faculty:* 45 full-time (12 women), 15 part-time/adjunct (5 women). *Students:* 490 full-time (156 women); includes 71 minority (15 African Americans, 2 American Indian/Alaska Native, 38 Asian Americans or Pacific Islanders, 16 Hispanic Americans), 154 international. Average age 28. 2,276 applicants, 20% accepted, 248 enrolled. In 2006, 258 degrees awarded. *Degree requirements:* For master's, the Tuck First Year project. *Entrance requirements:* For master's, GMAT, letters of recommendation, transcript, essays. Additional exam requirements/recommendations for international students: Required—TOEFL. *Application deadline:* For fall admission, 10/12 for domestic and international students; for winter admission, 1/11 for domestic and international students; for spring admission, 4/5 for domestic and international students. Application fee: $220. Electronic applications accepted. *Expenses: Contact institution. Financial support:* In 2006–07, 395 students received support. Career-related internships or fieldwork, institutionally sponsored loans, scholarships/grants, and health care benefits available. Financial award application deadline: 4/17; financial award applicants required to submit FAFSA. *Faculty research:* Corporate governance, corporate citizenship, international business, digital strategies, private equity and entrepreneurship. *Unit head:* Paul Danos, Dean, 603-646-2460, Fax: 603-646-1308, E-mail: tuck.public.relations@dartmouth.edu. *Application contact:* Dawna Clarke, Director of Admissions, 603-646-3162, Fax: 603-646-1441, E-mail: tuck.admissions@dartmouth.edu.

Davenport University, Sneden Graduate School, Grand Rapids, MI 49503. Offers MBA. Evening/weekend programs available. *Entrance requirements:* For master's, GMAT, minimum undergraduate GPA of 2.75. Additional exam requirements/recommendations for international students: Required—TOEFL. Electronic applications accepted. *Faculty research:* Leadership, management, marketing, organizational culture.

Davenport University, Sneden Graduate School, Warren, MI 48092-5209. Offers accounting (MBA); commerce (MBA); finance (MBA); health care management (MBA); human resources management (MBA); management (MBA). *Entrance requirements:* For master's, minimum undergraduate GPA of 2.7.

Davenport University, Sneden Graduate School, Dearborn, MI 48126-3799. Offers accounting (MBA); e-business (MBA); finance (MBA); global business (MBA); health care management (MBA); human resources management (MBA); management (MBA); marketing (MBA). Part-time and evening/weekend programs available. Postbaccalaureate distance learning degree programs offered (no on-campus study). *Entrance requirements:* For master's, minimum GPA of 2.7, previous course work in accounting and statistics. *Faculty research:* Accounting, international accounting, social and environmental accounting, finance.

Defiance College, Program in Business and Organizational Leadership, Defiance, OH 43512-1610. Offers MBOL. Part-time and evening/weekend programs available. *Degree requirements:* For master's, thesis. *Entrance requirements:* For master's, minimum GPA of 2.5.

Delaware State University, Graduate Programs, Department of Economics and Business Administration, Program in Business Administration, Dover, DE 19901-2277. Offers MBA. *Accreditation:* AACSB. Part-time and evening/weekend programs available. *Entrance requirements:* For master's, GMAT, minimum GPA of 3.0 in major, 2.75 overall. Electronic applications accepted. *Faculty research:* Managerial economics, strategic management, qualitative effort, finance.

Delta State University, Graduate Programs, College of Business, Cleveland, MS 38733-0001. Offers MBA, MCA, MPA. *Accreditation:* ACBSP. Part-time and evening/weekend programs available. Postbaccalaureate distance learning degree programs offered (minimal on-campus study). *Faculty:* 9 full-time (1 woman), 8 part-time/adjunct (3 women). *Students:* 37 full-time (20 women), 47 part-time (20 women); includes 31 minority (27 African Americans, 1 American Indian/Alaska Native, 3 Asian Americans or Pacific Islanders). Average age 28. In 2006, 42 degrees awarded. *Entrance requirements:* For master's, GMAT. *Application deadline:* For fall admission, 8/1 priority date for domestic students; for spring admission, 12/1 priority date for domestic students. Applications are processed on a rolling basis. Application fee: $0. *Financial support:* Research assistantships, career-related internships or fieldwork, Federal Work-Study, and institutionally sponsored loans available. Support available to part-time students. Financial award application deadline: 6/1. *Unit head:* Dr. Billy Moore, Dean, 662-846-4200, Fax: 662-846-4215, E-mail: bcmoore@deltastate.edu. *Application contact:* Carla Johnson, Coordinator, College of Business Graduate Programs, 662-846-4234, Fax: 662-846-4215, E-mail: cjohnson@deltastate.edu.

DePaul University, Charles H. Kellstadt Graduate School of Business, Chicago, IL 60604-2287. Offers M Acc, MA, MBA, MS, MSA, MSF, MSHR, MSMA, MST, JD/MBA. *Accreditation:* AACSB. Part-time and evening/weekend programs available. *Faculty:* 134 full-time (32 women), 158 part-time/adjunct (36 women). *Students:* 969 full-time (356 women), 837 part-time (335 women); includes 247 minority (53 African Americans, 4 American Indian/Alaska Native, 136 Asian Americans or Pacific Islanders, 54 Hispanic Americans), 153 international. Average age 28. 750 applicants, 84% accepted, 367 enrolled. In 2006, 624 degrees awarded. *Entrance requirements:* For master's, GMAT, 2 letters of recommendation, resumé. Additional exam requirements/recommendations for international students: Required—TOEFL (minimum score 550 paper-based; 213 computer-based; 80 iBT). *Application deadline:* For fall admission, 7/1 for domestic students, 6/1 for international students; for winter admission, 10/1 for domestic students, 9/1 for international students; for spring admission, 2/1 for domestic students, 1/1 for international students. Applications are processed on a rolling basis. Application fee: $60.

Business Administration and Management—General

DePaul University (continued)
Electronic applications accepted. *Expenses:* Contact institution. *Financial support:* In 2006–07, 701 students received support. Career-related internships or fieldwork, Federal Work-Study, institutionally sponsored loans, scholarships/grants, tuition waivers (full and partial), and unspecified assistantships available. Support available to part-time students. Financial award application deadline: 4/1. *Unit head:* Robert T. Ryan, Assistant Dean and Director, 312-362-8810, Fax: 312-362-6677, E-mail: rryan1@depaul.edu. *Application contact:* Christopher E. Kinsella, Director of Cohort MBA Programs, 312-362-8810, Fax: 312-362-6677, E-mail: kgsb@depaul.edu.

DeSales University, Graduate Division, Department of Business, Center Valley, PA 18034-9568. Offers business administration (MBA). *Accreditation:* ACBSP. Part-time and evening/weekend programs available. Postbaccalaureate distance learning degree programs offered (no on-campus study). *Students:* 394. In 2006, 99 degrees awarded. *Entrance requirements:* For master's, minimum GPA of 3.0, 2 years of work experience. Additional exam requirements/recommendations for international students: Required—TOEFL. *Application deadline:* Applications are processed on a rolling basis. Application fee: $50. Electronic applications accepted. *Expenses:* Contact institution. *Financial support:* Career-related internships or fieldwork available. *Faculty research:* Quality improvement, executive development, productivity, cross-cultural managerial differences, leadership. *Unit head:* Dr. Mohamed Latib, Director, 610-282-1100 Ext. 1450, Fax: 610-282-2254, E-mail: mohamed.latib@desales.edu. *Application contact:* Maryann Falk, Associate Director and Program Coordinator, 610-282-1100 Ext. 1448, Fax: 610-282-2869, E-mail: maryann.falk@desales.edu.

DeVry University, Keller Graduate School of Management, Phoenix, AZ 85021-2995. Offers MAFM, MBA, MHRM, MISM, MNCM, MPA, MPM.

DeVry University, Keller Graduate School of Management, Fremont, CA 94555. Offers MAFM, MBA, MHRM, MISM, MNCM, MPA, MPM.

DeVry University, Keller Graduate School of Management, Long Beach, CA 90806. Offers MAFM, MBA, MHRM, MISM, MNCM, MPA, MPM.

DeVry University, Keller Graduate School of Management, Pomona, CA 91768-2642. Offers MAFM, MBA, MHRM, MISM, MNCM, MPA, MPM.

DeVry University, Keller Graduate School of Management, West Hills, CA 91304. Offers MAFM, MBA, MHRM, MISM, MNCM, MPA, MPM.

DeVry University, Keller Graduate School of Management, Colorado Springs, CO 80910. Offers MAFM, MBA, MHRM, MISM, MNCM, MPA, MPM.

DeVry University, Keller Graduate School of Management, Miramar, FL 33027-4150. Offers MAFM, MBA, MHRM, MISM, MNCM, MPA, MPM.

DeVry University, Keller Graduate School of Management, Orlando, FL 32839. Offers MAFM, MBA, MHRM, MISM, MNCM, MPA, MPM.

DeVry University, Keller Graduate School of Management, Alpharetta, GA 30004. Offers MAFM, MBA, MHRM, MISM, MNCM, MPA, MPM.

DeVry University, Keller Graduate School of Management, Decatur, GA 30030-2198. Offers MAFM, MBA, MHRM, MISM, MNCM, MPA, MPM.

DeVry University, Keller Graduate School of Management, Tinley Park, IL 60477. Offers MAFM, MBA, MHRM, MISM, MNCM, MPA, MPM.

DeVry University, Keller Graduate School of Management, Columbus, OH 43209-2705. Offers MAFM, MBA, MHRM, MISM, MNCM, MPA, MPM.

DeVry University, Keller Graduate School of Management, Fort Washington, PA 19034. Offers MAFM, MBA, MHRM, MISM, MNCM, MPA, MPM.

DeVry University, Keller Graduate School of Management, Irving, TX 75063-2439. Offers MAFM, MBA, MHRM, MISM, MNCM, MPA, MPM.

DeVry University, Keller Graduate School of Management, Arlington, VA 22202. Offers MAFM, MBA, MHRM, MISM, MNCM, MPA, MPM.

DeVry University, Keller Graduate School of Management, Federal Way, WA 98001. Offers MAFM, MBA, MHRM, MISM, MNCM, MPA, MPM.

DeVry University, Keller Graduate School of Management, Mesa, AZ 85210-2011. Offers MAFM, MBA, MHRM, MISM, MNCM, MPA, MPM.

DeVry University, Keller Graduate School of Management, Scottsdale, AZ 85258-5140. Offers MAFM, MBA, MHRM, MISM, MNCM, MPA, MPM.

DeVry University, Keller Graduate School of Management, Irvine, CA 92612-1682. Offers MAFM, MBA, MHRM, MISM, MNCM, MPA, MPM.

DeVry University, Keller Graduate School of Management, Elk Grove, CA 95758. Offers MAFM, MBA, MHRM, MISM, MNCM, MPA, MPM.

DeVry University, Keller Graduate School of Management, San Diego, CA 92108-1633. Offers MAFM, MBA, MHRM, MISM, MNCM, MPA, MPM.

DeVry University, Keller Graduate School of Management, San Francisco, CA 94105-2472. Offers MAFM, MBA, MHRM, MISM, MNCM, MPA, MPM.

DeVry University, Keller Graduate School of Management, Miami, FL 33131-5351. Offers MAFM, MBA, MHRM, MISM, MNCM, MPA, MPM.

DeVry University, Keller Graduate School of Management, Tampa, FL 33607-5901. Offers MAFM, MBA, MHRM, MISM, MNCM, MPA, MPM.

DeVry University, Keller Graduate School of Management, Atlanta, GA 30305-1543. Offers MAFM, MBA, MHRM, MISM, MNCM, MPA, MPM.

DeVry University, Keller Graduate School of Management, Duluth, GA 30096-7671. Offers MAFM, MBA, MHRM, MISM, MNCM, MPA, MPM.

DeVry University, Keller Graduate School of Management, Elgin, IL 60123-9341. Offers MAFM, MBA, MHRM, MISM, MNCM, MPA, MPM.

DeVry University, Keller Graduate School of Management, Lincolnshire, IL 60069-4460. Offers MAFM, MBA, MHRM, MISM, MNCM, MPA, MPM.

DeVry University, Keller Graduate School of Management, Schaumburg, IL 60173-5009. Offers MAFM, MBA, MHRM, MISM, MNCM, MPA, MPM.

DeVry University, Keller Graduate School of Management, Gurnee, IL 60031-9126. Offers MAFM, MBA, MHRM, MISM, MNCM, MPA, MPM.

DeVry University, Keller Graduate School of Management, Indianapolis, IN 46240-2158. Offers MAFM, MBA, MHRM, MISM, MNCM, MPA, MPM.

DeVry University, Keller Graduate School of Management, Merrillville, IN 46410-5673. Offers MAFM, MBA, MHRM, MISM, MNCM, MPA, MPM.

DeVry University, Keller Graduate School of Management, Bethesda, MD 20814-3304. Offers MAFM, MBA, MHRM, MISM, MNCM, MPA, MPM, Graduate Certificate.

DeVry University, Keller Graduate School of Management, Kansas City, MO 64105-2112. Offers MAFM, MBA, MHRM, MISM, MNCM, MPA, MPM.

DeVry University, Keller Graduate School of Management, St. Louis, MO 63146-4020. Offers MAFM, MBA, MHRM, MISM, MNCM, MPA, MPM.

DeVry University, Keller Graduate School of Management, Charlotte, NC 28211-3627. Offers MAFM, MBA, MHRM, MISM, MNCM, MPA, MPM.

DeVry University, Keller Graduate School of Management, Henderson, NV 89074-7120. Offers MAFM, MBA, MHRM, MISM, MNCM, MPA, MPM.

DeVry University, Keller Graduate School of Management, Cleveland, OH 44114-2301. Offers MAFM, MBA, MHRM, MISM, MNCM, MPA, MPM.

DeVry University, Keller Graduate School of Management, Seven Hills, OH 44131-6907. Offers MAFM, MBA, MHRM, MISM, MNCM, MPA, MPM.

DeVry University, Keller Graduate School of Management, Portland, OR 97225-6651. Offers MAFM, MBA, MHRM, MISM, MNCM, MPA, MPM.

DeVry University, Keller Graduate School of Management, Pittsburgh, PA 15222-9123. Offers MAFM, MBA, MHRM, MISM, MNCM, MPA, MPM.

DeVry University, Keller Graduate School of Management, Chesterbrook, PA 19087-5612. Offers MAFM, MBA, MHRM, MISM, MNCM, MPA, MPM.

DeVry University, Keller Graduate School of Management, Plano, TX 75075-8435. Offers MAFM, MBA, MHRM, MISM, MNCM, MPA, MPM.

DeVry University, Keller Graduate School of Management, Houston, TX 77041. Offers MBA, MISM, MPA, MPM.

DeVry University, Keller Graduate School of Management, McLean, VA 22102-3832. Offers MAFM, MBA, MHRM, MISM, MNCM, MPA, MPM.

DeVry University, Keller Graduate School of Management, Bellevue, WA 98004-5519. Offers MAFM, MBA, MHRM, MISM, MNCM, MPA, MPM.

DeVry University, Keller Graduate School of Management, Milwaukee, WI 53202-4107. Offers MAFM, MBA, MHRM, MISM, MNCM, MPA, MPM.

DeVry University, Keller Graduate School of Management, Waukesha, WI 53186-4047. Offers MAFM, MBA, MHRM, MISM, MNCM, MPA, MPM.

DeVry University, Keller Graduate School of Management, Naperville, IL 60563-2361. Offers MAFM, MBA, MHRM, MISM, MNCM, MPA, MPM.

DeVry University, Keller Graduate School of Management, Oakbrook Terrace, IL 60181. Offers accounting and financial management (MAFM); business administration (MBA); human resources management (MHRM); information systems management (MISM); network and communications management (MNCM); project management (MPM); public administration (MPA); telecommunications management (MTM). Part-time and evening/weekend programs available. Postbaccalaureate distance learning degree programs offered (no on-campus study). *Degree requirements:* For master's, business plan (MBA), capstone project (MHRM, MPM, MTM, MAFM). *Entrance requirements:* For master's, GMAT, GRE General Test, or institutional assessment, interview. Additional exam requirements/recommendations for international students: Required—TOEFL (minimum score 500 paper-based; 173 computer-based). Electronic applications accepted.

See Close-Up on page 265.

Doane College, Program in Management, Crete, NE 68333-2430. Offers MA. *Accreditation:* ACBSP. Part-time and evening/weekend programs available. *Degree requirements:* For master's, thesis. *Entrance requirements:* For master's, minimum GPA of 3.0. Expenses: Contact institution.

Dominican University, Edward A. and Lois L. Brennan School of Business, River Forest, IL 60305-1099. Offers accounting (MSA); business administration (MBA); computer information systems (MSCIS); management information systems (MSMIS); organization management (MSOM); JD/MBA; MBA/MLIS. *Accreditation:* ACBSP. Part-time and evening/weekend programs available. *Faculty:* 12 full-time (4 women), 32 part-time/adjunct (9 women). *Students:* 171 full-time (46 women), 193 part-time (84 women); includes 26 minority (11 African Americans, 3 Asian Americans or Pacific Islanders, 12 Hispanic Americans), 173 international. Average age 30. 133 applicants, 98% accepted, 106 enrolled. In 2006, 118 degrees awarded. *Entrance requirements:* For master's, GMAT. Additional exam requirements/recommendations for international students: Required—TOEFL (minimum score 550 paper-based; 213 computer-based); Recommended—IELTS (minimum score 6). *Application deadline:* Applications are processed on a rolling basis. Application fee: $25. Electronic applications accepted. *Expenses:* Contact institution. Tuition and fees vary according to campus/location and program. *Financial support:* Career-related internships or fieldwork, tuition waivers (partial), and unspecified assistantships available. Support available to part-time students. Financial award applicants required to submit FAFSA. *Faculty research:* Entrepreneurship, small business finance, business ethics, marketing strategy. *Unit head:* Dr. Molly Burke, Dean, 708-524-6810, Fax: 708-524-6939, E-mail: burkemq@dom.edu. *Application contact:* Linda Puvogel, Assistant Dean for Graduate Business Programs, 708-524-6507, Fax: 708-524-6939, E-mail: lpuvogel@dom.edu.

Dominican University of California, Graduate Programs, School of Business, Education and Leadership, Division of Business and International Studies, Program in Management, San Rafael, CA 94901-2298. Offers MAM. Program offered through strategic alliance with the California Management Institute (CMI).

Dowling College, School of Business, Oakdale, NY 11769-1999. Offers aviation management (MBA, Certificate); banking and finance (MBA, Certificate); general management (MBA); public management (MBA, Certificate); total quality management (MBA, Certificate). Part-time and evening/weekend programs available. *Students:* 239 full-time (105 women), 566 part-time (273 women); includes 132 African Americans, 55 Asian Americans or Pacific Islanders, 48 Hispanic Americans, 3 international. Average age 31. 414 applicants, 82% accepted, 166 enrolled. In 2006, 471 master's, 1 other advanced degree awarded. *Degree requirements:* For master's, thesis optional. *Entrance requirements:* For master's, minimum GPA of 2.8, 2 letters of recommendation, courses in accounting and finance or seminar in accounting/finance, resumé. Additional exam requirements/recommendations for international students: Required—TOEFL (minimum score 550 paper-based). *Application deadline:* For fall admission, 9/1 priority date for domestic students; for winter admission, 1/1 priority date for domestic students; for spring admission, 2/1 priority date for domestic students. Applications are processed on a rolling basis. Application fee: $25. Electronic applications accepted. *Expenses:* Tuition: Full-time $16,008; part-time $667 per credit. Tuition and fees vary according to course load. *Financial support:* In 2006–07, 126 students received support, including 30 research assistantships (averaging $3,150 per year); career-related internships or fieldwork, Federal Work-Study, scholarships/grants, and unspecified assistantships also available. Support available to part-time students. Financial award application deadline: 6/30; financial award applicants required to submit FAFSA. *Faculty research:* International finance, computer applications, labor relations, executive development. *Unit head:* Dr. Elana Zolfo, Dean of the School of Business, 631-244-3190, Fax: 631-244-1018, E-mail: zdfoe@dowling.edu. *Application contact:* Franks S. Pizzardi, Director of Admissions Operations, 631-244-3227, Fax: 631-244-1059, E-mail: pizzardf@dowling.edu.

Drake University, College of Business and Public Administration, Des Moines, IA 50311-4516. Offers M Acc, MBA, MFM, MPA, JD/MBA, JD/MPA, Pharm D/MBA, Pharm D/MPA. *Accreditation:* AACSB. Part-time and evening/weekend programs available. *Faculty:* 3 full-time (0 women), 7 part-time/adjunct (1 woman). *Students:* 9 full-time (5 women), 451 part-time (242 women); includes 32 minority (11 African Americans, 1 American Indian/Alaska Native, 13 Asian Americans or Pacific Islanders, 7 Hispanic Americans), 36 international. Average age 24. 297 applicants, 68% accepted, 112 enrolled. In 2006, 201 degrees awarded. *Degree requirements:* For master's, thesis (for some programs), internships, comprehensive exam (for some programs), registration. *Entrance requirements:* For master's, GMAT, letters of recommendation, resumé. Additional exam requirements/recommendations for international students: Required—TOEFL (minimum score 550 paper-based; 213 computer-based). *Application deadline:* For fall admission, 8/15 priority date for domestic students; for winter admission, 12/20 priority date for domestic students; for spring admission, 12/1 priority date for domestic students. Applications are processed on a rolling basis. Application fee: $25. Electronic applications accepted. *Expenses: Contact institution. Financial support:* Fellowships with tuition reimbursements, teaching assistantships, career-related internships or fieldwork and institutionally sponsored loans available. Support available to part-time students. Financial award application deadline: 3/1; financial award applicants required to submit FAFSA. *Unit head:* Dr. Charles Edwards, Dean, 515-271-2871, Fax: 515-271-4518, E-mail: charles.edwards@drake.edu. *Application contact:* Danette Kenne, Director of Graduate Programs, 515-271-2188, Fax: 515-271-4518, E-mail: cbpa.gradprograms@drake.edu.

Drexel University, LeBow College of Business, Program in Business Administration, Philadelphia, PA 19104-2875. Offers business administration (MBA, PhD, APC), including accounting (MBA, PhD), decision sciences (PhD), economics (MBA, PhD), finance (MBA, PhD), legal studies (MBA), management (MBA), marketing (MBA, PhD), organizational sciences (PhD), quantitative methods (MBA), strategic management (PhD). *Accreditation:* AACSB. Part-time and evening/weekend programs available. Postbaccalaureate distance learning degree programs offered (minimal on-campus study). Terminal master's awarded for partial completion of doctoral program. *Entrance requirements:* For master's, GMAT, minimum GPA of 2.75; for doctorate, GMAT. Additional exam requirements/recommendations for international students: Required—TOEFL. Electronic applications accepted. *Faculty research:* Decision support systems, individual and group behavior, operations research, techniques and strategy.

Drury University, Breech School of Business Administration, Springfield, MO 65802. Offers MBA, MBA/MIM. *Accreditation:* ACBSP. Part-time and evening/weekend programs available. *Entrance requirements:* For master's, GMAT. Additional exam requirements/recommendations for international students: Required—TOEFL. Electronic applications accepted. Expenses: Contact institution. *Faculty research:* Health care management, cross cultural management, philosophical orientation and decision making.

Duke University, Fuqua School of Business, Cross Continent Executive MBA Program, Durham, NC 27708-0586. Offers EMBA. *Faculty:* 110 full-time (23 women), 31 part-time/adjunct (3 women). *Students:* 239 full-time (57 women); includes 85 minority (3 African Americans, 70 Asian Americans or Pacific Islanders, 12 Hispanic Americans). Average age 30. In 2006, 119 degrees awarded. *Degree requirements:* For master's, one foreign language. *Entrance requirements:* For master's, GMAT. *Application deadline:* Applications are processed on a rolling basis. Application fee: $185. Electronic applications accepted. *Financial support:* Fellowships with tuition reimbursements available. *Unit head:* John Gallagher, Associate Dean for Executive MBA Programs, 919-660-7641, E-mail: johng@duke.edu. *Application contact:* Dan McCleary, Director of EMBA Admissions, 919-60-8002, Fax: 919-681-8026, E-mail: admissions-info@fuqua.duke.edu.

Duke University, Fuqua School of Business, Duke-Goethe Executive MBA Program, Durham, NC 27708-0586. Offers EMBA. *Faculty:* 110 full-time (23 women), 31 part-time/adjunct (3 women). *Students:* 68 full-time (11 women). Average age 34. *Financial support:* Fellowships available. *Unit head:* John Gallagher, Associate Dean for Executive MBA Programs, 919-660-7641, E-mail: johng@duke.edu. *Application contact:* Eric McCloe, Admissions and CRM Manager, Goethe Business School, 49 69 905 50 3755, E-mail: admissions@gbs.uni-frankford.de.

Duke University, Fuqua School of Business, Global Executive MBA Program, Durham, NC 27708-0586. Offers GEMBA. *Faculty:* 110 full-time (23 women), 31 part-time/adjunct (3 women). *Students:* 170 full-time (27 women); includes 60 minority (7 African Americans, 3 American Indian/Alaska Native, 41 Asian Americans or Pacific Islanders, 9 Hispanic Americans). Average age 38. In 2006, 67 degrees awarded. *Application deadline:* Applications are processed on a rolling basis. Application fee: $185. Electronic applications accepted. *Financial support:* Fellowships with tuition reimbursements available. *Unit head:* John Gallagher, Associate Dean for Executive MBA Programs, 919-660-7641, E-mail: johng@duke.edu. *Application contact:* Dan McCleary, Director of EMBA Admissions, 919-60-8002, Fax: 919-681-8026, E-mail: admissions-info@fuqua.duke.edu.

Duke University, Fuqua School of Business, Weekend Executive MBA Program, Durham, NC 27708-0586. Offers WEMBA. Evening/weekend programs available. *Faculty:* 110 full-time (23 women), 31 part-time/adjunct (3 women). *Students:* 214 full-time (34 women); includes 74 minority (5 African Americans, 64 Asian Americans or Pacific Islanders, 5 Hispanic Americans). Average age 34. In 2006, 103 degrees awarded. *Degree requirements:* For master's, one foreign language. *Entrance requirements:* For master's, GMAT. *Application deadline:* Applications are processed on a rolling basis. Application fee: $185. Electronic applications accepted. *Financial support:* Fellowships with tuition reimbursements available. *Unit head:* John Gallagher, Associate Dean for Executive MBA Programs, 919-660-7641, E-mail: johng@duke.edu. *Application contact:* Dan McCleary, Director of EMBA Admissions, 919-60-8002, Fax: 919-681-8026, E-mail: admissions-info@fuqua.duke.edu.

Duke University, Graduate School, Department of Business Administration, Durham, NC 27708. Offers PhD. *Faculty:* 95 full-time. *Students:* 79 full-time (28 women); includes 12 minority (1 African American, 9 Asian Americans or Pacific Islanders, 2 Hispanic Americans), 42 international. 458 applicants, 7% accepted, 14 enrolled. In 2006, 6 doctorates awarded. *Degree requirements:* For doctorate, thesis/dissertation. *Entrance requirements:* For doctorate, GMAT or GRE General Test. Additional exam requirements/recommendations for international students: Required—TOEFL (minimum score 550 paper-based; 213 computer-based; 83 iBT), IELTS (minimum score 7). *Application deadline:* For fall admission, 12/15 for domestic and international students. Application fee: $75. Electronic applications accepted. *Financial support:* Fellowships with full tuition reimbursements, research assistantships, career-related internships or fieldwork, Federal Work-Study, and institutionally sponsored loans available. Financial award application deadline: 12/31; financial award applicants required to submit FAFSA. *Unit head:* James Bettman, Director of Graduate Studies, 919-660-7851, Fax: 919-681-6245, E-mail: bobbiec@mail.duke.edu.

Duquesne University, John F. Donahue Graduate School of Business, Pittsburgh, PA 15282-0001. Offers business administration (MBA); taxation (MS); JD/MBA; MBA/MA; MBA/MES; MBA/MHMS; MBA/MLLS; MBA/MS; MBA/MSN. *Accreditation:* AACSB. Part-time and evening/weekend programs available. *Faculty:* 50 full-time (5 women), 20 part-time/adjunct (5 women). *Students:* 110 full-time (49 women), 233 part-time (86 women); includes 26 minority (15 African Americans, 1 American Indian/Alaska Native, 1 Asian American or Pacific Islander, 9 Hispanic Americans), 31 international. Average age 31. 174 applicants, 69% accepted, 75 enrolled. In 2006, 146 degrees awarded. *Entrance requirements:* For master's, GMAT, letter of recommendation. Additional exam requirements/recommendations for international students: Required—TOEFL (minimum score 550 paper-based; 213 computer-based); Recommended—TWE. *Application deadline:* For fall admission, 6/1 priority date for domestic students, 6/1 for international students; for spring admission, 11/1 for domestic and international students. Applications are processed on a rolling basis. Application fee: $50. Electronic applications accepted. *Expenses:* Tuition: Part-time $723 per credit. Required fees: $71 per credit. Tuition and fees vary according to degree level and program. *Financial support:* In 2006–07, 31 students received support, including 27 research assistantships with partial tuition reimbursements available; career-related internships or fieldwork and unspecified assistantships also available. Support available to part-time students. Financial award application deadline: 7/1; financial award applicants required to submit FAFSA. *Faculty research:* International business, investment management, business ethics, technology management, supply chain management, business strategy, finance. *Unit head:* Alan R. Miciak, Dean, 412-396-5848, Fax: 412-396-5304, E-mail: miciak@duq.edu. *Application contact:* Dr. Patricia Moore, Assistant Director, 412-396-6276, Fax: 412-396-1726, E-mail: moorep@duq.edu.

See Close-Up on page 267.

East Carolina University, Graduate School, College of Business, Department of Management, Greenville, NC 27858-4353. Offers MBA. *Students:* 204 full-time (87 women), 299 part-time (137 women); includes 82 minority (59 African Americans, 6 American Indian/Alaska Native, 11 Asian Americans or Pacific Islanders, 6 Hispanic Americans), 11 international. Average age 29. In 2006, 141 degrees awarded. *Unit head:* Dr. Joseph M. Tomkiewicz, Director, 252-328-6883, E-mail: tomkiewiczj@ecu.edu.

East Carolina University, Graduate School, College of Technology and Computer Science, Department of Technology Systems, Greenville, NC 27858-4353. Offers computer network professional (Certificate); industrial technology (MS), including computer networking management, digital communications, industrial distribution and logistics, information security, manufacturing, performance improvement, planning; information assurance (Certificate); occupational safety (MS); technology management (PhD); Website developer (Certificate). *Students:* 27 full-time (8 women), 114 part-time (28 women); includes 34 minority (25 African Americans, 1 American Indian/Alaska Native, 3 Asian Americans or Pacific Islanders, 5 Hispanic Americans), 4 international. Average age 34. 53 applicants, 28% accepted, 13 enrolled. In 2006, 65 degrees awarded. *Entrance requirements:* For master's and Certificate, GRE General Test or MAT, minimum GPA of 2.5; for doctorate, GRE General Test, related work experience. *Application deadline:* For fall admission, 6/1 priority date for domestic students. Applications are processed on a rolling basis. Application fee: $50. *Financial support:* Application deadline: 6/1. *Unit head:* Dr. Andrew Jackson, Chair, 252-737-1468, Fax: 252-328-1618, E-mail: jacksona@ecu.edu. *Application contact:* Jenny Simpkins, Information Contact, 252-328-9653, Fax: 252-328-1618, E-mail: best@ecu.edu.

Eastern Illinois University, Graduate School, Lumpkin College of Business and Applied Sciences, Program in Business Administration, Charleston, IL 61920-3099. Offers accountancy (Certificate); general management (MBA). *Accreditation:* AACSB. Part-time programs available. *Faculty:* 35 full-time (8 women). In 2006, 58 degrees awarded. *Entrance requirements:* For master's, GMAT. *Application deadline:* For fall admission, 7/31 priority date for domestic students. Applications are processed on a rolling basis. Application fee: $30. *Expenses:* Tuition, state resident: part-time $169 per semester hour. Tuition, nonresident: part-time $508 per semester hour. Required fees: $60 per semester hour. *Financial support:* In 2006–07, 4 research assistantships with tuition reimbursements (averaging $7,200 per year), 8 teaching assistantships with tuition reimbursements (averaging $7,200 per year) were awarded. *Unit head:* Dr. James Jordan-Wagner, Department Chair, 217-581-3028, E-mail: jjordanwagner@eiu.edu. *Application contact:* Dr. Cheryl Noll, Coordinator, 217-581-3028, Fax: 217-581-6029, E-mail: clnoll@eiu.edu.

Eastern Kentucky University, The Graduate School, College of Business and Technology, Program in Business Administration, Richmond, KY 40475-3102. Offers MBA. *Accreditation:* AACSB. *Faculty:* 9 full-time (4 women). *Students:* 12 full-time (6 women), 53 part-time (24 women); includes 3 minority (2 African Americans, 1 Asian American or Pacific Islander), 11 international. Average age 29. 97 applicants, 32% accepted, 15 enrolled. In 2006, 18 degrees awarded. Application fee: $35. *Expenses:* Tuition, state resident: full-time $5,610. Tuition, nonresident: full-time $15,910. *Financial support:* In 2006–07, research assistantships (averaging $6,500 per year), teaching assistantships (averaging $6,500 per year) were awarded. *Unit head:* Judith W. Spain, JD, Director, MBA Program, 859-622-1775, Fax: 859-622-1413, E-mail: judy.spain@eku.edu.

See Close-Up on page 269.

Eastern Mennonite University, Program in Business Administration, Harrisonburg, VA 22802-2462. Offers MBA. Part-time and evening/weekend programs available. *Faculty:* 4 full-time (0 women), 6 part-time/adjunct (2 women). *Students:* Average age 34. 13 applicants, 100% accepted, 13 enrolled. In 2006, 6 degrees awarded. *Degree requirements:* For master's, final capstone course. *Entrance requirements:* For master's, GMAT, minimum GPA of 2.5, 2 years of work experience, 2 letters of reference. Additional exam requirements/recommendations for international students: Required—TOEFL (minimum score 500 paper-based). *Application deadline:* Applications are processed on a rolling basis. Application fee: $25. *Expenses: Contact institution. Financial support:* Application deadline: 6/30; *Faculty research:* Information security, Anabaptist/Mennonite experiences and perspectives, limits of multi-cultural education, international development performance criteria. Total annual research expenditures:$4,000. *Unit head:* Allon H. Lefever, Director MBA Program, 540-432-4545, Fax: 540-432-4071, E-mail: allon.lefever@emu.edu. *Application contact:* Patricia S. Eckard, Office Coordinator, Business and Economics, 540-432-4150, Fax: 540-432-4071, E-mail: eckardp@emu.edu.

Eastern Michigan University, Graduate School, College of Business, Department of Management, Ypsilanti, MI 48197. Offers human resources management and organizational development (MSHROD); management of human resources (MBA); management organizational development (MBA); production and operations management (MBA); strategic quality management (MBA). Part-time and evening/weekend programs available. Postbaccalaureate distance learning degree programs offered (minimal on-campus study). *Students:* Average age 29. *Degree requirements:* For master's, thesis optional. *Entrance requirements:* For master's, GMAT. Additional exam requirements/recommendations for international students: Required—TOEFL. *Application deadline:* For fall admission, 5/15 priority date for domestic and international students; for winter admission, 10/15 priority date for domestic and international students; for spring admission, 3/15 priority date for domestic and international students. Applications are processed on a rolling basis. Application fee: $35. *Expenses:* Tuition, state resident: part-time $341 per credit hour. Tuition, nonresident: full-time $16,104; part-time $671 per credit hour. Required fees: $816; $34 per credit hour. $40 per term. One-time fee: $82 full-time. Tuition and fees vary according to course level, course load, degree level and reciprocity agreements. *Financial support:* Fellowships, research assistantships with full tuition reimbursements, teaching assistantships with full tuition reimbursements, career-related internships or fieldwork, Federal Work-Study, institutionally sponsored loans, scholarships/grants, tuition waivers (partial), and unspecified assistantships available. Support available to part-time students. Financial award applicants required to submit FAFSA. *Unit head:* Dr. Fraya Wagner-Marsh, Head, 734-487-3240, Fax: 734-487-4100, E-mail: fraya.wagner@emich.edu.

Eastern Michigan University, Graduate School, College of Business, Program in Business Administration, Ypsilanti, MI 48197. Offers business administration (MBA); e-business (MBA); enterprise business intelligence (MBA); entrepreneurship (MBA); finance (MBA); human resources (MBA); information systems (MBA); internal auditing (MBA); international business (MBA); nonprofit management (MBA); supply chain management (MBA). *Accreditation:* AACSB. Part-time and evening/weekend programs available. Postbaccalaureate distance learning degree programs offered (minimal on-campus study). *Students:* 98 full-time (36 women), 192 part-time (86 women); includes 50 minority (26 African Americans, 19 Asian Americans or Pacific Islanders, 5 Hispanic Americans), 76 international. Average age 29. In 2006, 109 degrees awarded. *Entrance requirements:* For master's, GMAT. Additional exam requirements/recommendations for international students: Required—TOEFL. *Application deadline:* For fall admission, 5/15 priority date for domestic students, 5/1 priority date for international students; for winter admission, 10/15 priority date for domestic students, 10/1 priority date for international students; for spring admission, 3/15 priority date for domestic students, 3/1 priority date for international students. Applications are processed on a rolling basis. Application fee: $35. *Expenses:*

Business Administration and Management—General

Eastern Michigan University (continued)
Tuition, state resident: part-time $341 per credit hour. Tuition, nonresident: full-time $16,104; part-time $671 per credit hour. Required fees: $816; $34 per credit hour. $40 per term. One-time fee: $82 full-time. Tuition and fees vary according to course level, course load, degree level and reciprocity agreements. *Financial support:* Fellowships, research assistantships with full tuition reimbursements, teaching assistantships with full tuition reimbursements, career-related internships or fieldwork, Federal Work-Study, institutionally sponsored loans, scholarships/grants, tuition waivers (partial), and unspecified assistantships available. Support available to part-time students. Financial award applicants required to submit FAFSA. *Unit head:* Dawn Gaymer, Assistant Dean, Graduate Business Programs, 734-487-4444, Fax: 734-483-1316, E-mail: dawn.malone@emich.edu. *Application contact:* K. Michelle Henry, Coordinator, 734-487-4444, Fax: 734-483-1316, E-mail: michelle.henry@emich.edu.

Eastern New Mexico University, Graduate School, College of Business, Portales, NM 88130. Offers MBA. *Accreditation:* ACBSP. Part-time and evening/weekend programs available. Postbaccalaureate distance learning degree programs offered (minimal on-campus study). *Faculty:* 8 full-time (1 woman). *Students:* 6 full-time (3 women), 45 part-time (26 women); includes 16 minority (3 African Americans, 4 Asian Americans or Pacific Islanders, 9 Hispanic Americans), 1 international. Average age 34. 45 applicants, 76% accepted. In 2006, 9 degrees awarded. *Degree requirements:* For master's, comprehensive exam. *Entrance requirements:* For master's, GMAT, minimum GPA of 2.5. *Application deadline:* For fall admission, 8/20 priority date for domestic students. Applications are processed on a rolling basis. Application fee: $0. Electronic applications accepted. *Expenses:* Tuition, state resident: full-time $2,478; part-time $103 per credit hour. Tuition, nonresident: full-time $8,034; part-time $335 per credit hour. Required fees: $35 per credit hour. *Financial support:* In 2006–07, 7 research assistantships (averaging $8,200 per year), teaching assistantships (averaging $8,200 per year) were awarded; fellowships, Federal Work-Study also available. Support available to part-time students. Financial award application deadline: 3/1. *Unit head:* Dr. John Groesbeck, Dean, 505-562-2343, E-mail: john.groesbeck@enmu.edu. *Application contact:* Dr. John Stockmeyer, Graduate Coordinator, 505-562-2352, E-mail: john.stockmeyer@enmu.edu.

Eastern University, Graduate Business Programs, St. Davids, PA 19087-3696. Offers business administration (MBA), including accounting, economics, finance, management, marketing; economic development (MBA, MS); nonprofit management (MBA, MS); M Div/MBA; M Div/MS. Part-time and evening/weekend programs available. *Degree requirements:* For master's, thesis (for some programs). *Entrance requirements:* For master's, GMAT (MBA), minimum GPA of 2.5. *Expenses:* Contact institution. *Faculty research:* Micro-level economic development, China welfare and economic development, macroethics, micro- and macro-level economic development in transitional economics, organizational effectiveness.

Eastern Washington University, Graduate Studies, College of Business and Public Administration, Business Administration Program, Cheney, WA 99004-2431. Offers MBA, MBA/MPA. *Accreditation:* AACSB. *Degree requirements:* For master's, thesis optional. *Entrance requirements:* For master's, GMAT, minimum GPA of 3.0.

East Tennessee State University, School of Graduate Studies, College of Business and Technology, Johnson City, TN 37614. Offers M Acc, MBA, MCM, MPM, MS, Certificate. *Accreditation:* AACSB. Part-time and evening/weekend programs available. *Degree requirements:* For master's, comprehensive exam. *Entrance requirements:* For master's, GMAT, minimum GPA of 2.5. Additional exam requirements/recommendations for international students: Required—TOEFL (minimum score 550 paper-based; 213 computer-based). *Faculty research:* Artificial intelligence and accounting, profit vs. non-profit hospital comparisons, environmental compliance issues in manufacturing, international finance, case law on Americans with disabilities.

Edgewood College, Program in Business, Madison, WI 53711-1997. Offers MBA. *Accreditation:* ACBSP. Part-time and evening/weekend programs available. *Students:* 19 full-time (9 women), 156 part-time (78 women); includes 12 minority (3 African Americans, 5 Asian Americans or Pacific Islanders, 4 Hispanic Americans), 4 international. Average age 33. In 2006, 72 degrees awarded. *Entrance requirements:* For master's, GMAT, minimum GPA of 2.75, 2 letters of recommendation. Additional exam requirements/recommendations for international students: Required—TOEFL. *Application deadline:* For fall admission, 8/24 for domestic students, 8/1 for international students; for spring admission, 1/10 for domestic students, 10/1 for international students. Applications are processed on a rolling basis. Application fee: $25. Electronic applications accepted. *Financial support:* Career-related internships or fieldwork available. *Unit head:* Dr. Gary Schroeder, Chair, 608-663-3374, Fax: 608-663-3291, E-mail: gschroeder@edgewood.edu. *Application contact:* Paula O'Malley, Graduate Student Admissions Counselor, 608-663-2282, Fax: 608-663-3291, E-mail: gradprograms@edgewood.edu.

Elmhurst College, Graduate Programs, Program in Business Administration, Elmhurst, IL 60126-3296. Offers MBA. Part-time and evening/weekend programs available. *Faculty:* 6 full-time (0 women), 11 part-time/adjunct (1 woman). *Students:* Average age 31. 70 applicants, 89% accepted, 46 enrolled. In 2006, 35 degrees awarded. *Median time to degree:* Master's–2 years part-time. *Entrance requirements:* For master's, 3 recommendations. Additional exam requirements/recommendations for international students: Required—TOEFL (minimum score 550 paper-based; 213 computer-based). *Application deadline:* Applications are processed on a rolling basis. Application fee: $25. Electronic applications accepted. *Expenses:* Tuition: Part-time $781 per hour. Required fees: $75 per hour. Part-time tuition and fees vary according to course load and student level. *Financial support:* In 2006–07, 3 students received support. Federal Work-Study and scholarships/grants available. Support available to part-time students. Financial award application deadline: 6/1; financial award applicants required to submit FAFSA. *Application contact:* Elizabeth D. Kuebler, Director of Adult and Graduate Admission, 630-617-3069, Fax: 630-617-5501, E-mail: betsyk@elmhurst.edu.

Elon University, Program in Business Administration, Elon, NC 27244-2010. Offers MBA. *Accreditation:* AACSB. Part-time and evening/weekend programs available. *Faculty:* 26 full-time (6 women), 3 part-time/adjunct (1 woman). *Students:* 3 full-time (1 woman), 101 part-time (32 women); includes 13 minority (all African Americans), 2 international. Average age 31. 90 applicants, 74% accepted, 55 enrolled. In 2006, 25 degrees awarded. *Entrance requirements:* For master's, GMAT. Additional exam requirements/recommendations for international students: Required—TOEFL (minimum score 550 paper-based; 213 computer-based; 79 iBT). *Application deadline:* For fall admission, 8/1 priority date for domestic students; for spring admission, 2/1 priority date for domestic students. Applications are processed on a rolling basis. Application fee: $50. Electronic applications accepted. *Financial support:* In 2006–07, 5 students received support, including 2 fellowships (averaging $8,112 per year); Federal Work-Study and scholarships/grants also available. Support available to part-time students. Financial award application deadline: 3/15; financial award applicants required to submit FAFSA. *Faculty research:* Business ethics; international business and global economics; sales force management; sustainable business practices; consumer behavior. *Unit head:* Dr. Scott Buechler, Director, 336-278-6000, Fax: 336-278-5952. *Application contact:* Art Fadde, Director of Graduate Admissions, 800-334-8448 Ext. 3, Fax: 336-278-7699, E-mail: afadde@elon.edu.

Embry-Riddle Aeronautical University, Daytona Beach Campus Graduate Program, Department of Business Administration, Daytona Beach, FL 32114-3900. Offers business administration in aviation (MBAA). *Accreditation:* ACBSP. Part-time and evening/weekend programs available. *Students:* 74 full-time (17 women), 59 part-time (11 women); includes 16 minority (5 African Americans, 1 American Indian/Alaska Native, 5 Asian Americans or Pacific Islanders, 5 Hispanic Americans), 31 international. Average age 30. 46 applicants, 67% accepted, 22 enrolled. In 2006, 56 degrees awarded. *Degree requirements:* For master's, thesis or alternative. *Entrance requirements:* For master's, minimum GPA of 2.5. Additional exam requirements/recommendations for international students: Required—TOEFL. *Application deadline:* For fall admission, 8/1 priority date for domestic students; for spring admission, 12/1 priority date for domestic students. Applications are processed on a rolling basis. *Expenses:* Tuition: Full-time

$12,240; part-time $1,020 per credit. *Financial support:* In 2006–07, 53 students received support, including 18 research assistantships with partial tuition reimbursements available (averaging $2,872 per year); fellowships with partial tuition reimbursements available, career-related internships or fieldwork, Federal Work-Study, and unspecified assistantships also available. Support available to part-time students. Financial award application deadline: 4/15; financial award applicants required to submit FAFSA. *Faculty research:* Aircraft safety operations analysis; energy consumption analysis; statistical analysis of general aviation accidents; airport funding strategies; industry assessment and marketing analysis for ENAER aerospace. Total annual research expenditures: $120,079. *Unit head:* Dr. Blaise Waguespack, Program Coordinator, 386-226-7235, Fax: 386-226-6696, E-mail: waguespb@erau.edu. *Application contact:* Tom Shea, Director, International and Graduate Admissions, 800-388-3728, Fax: 386-226-7070, E-mail: graduate.admissions@erau.edu.

Emmanuel College, Graduate Programs, Program in Management, Boston, MA 02115. Offers MSM. Part-time and evening/weekend programs available. *Faculty:* 22 part-time/adjunct (5 women). *Students:* Average age 36. 41 applicants, 44% accepted, 17 enrolled. In 2006, 30 degrees awarded. *Degree requirements:* For master's, thesis or alternative. *Entrance requirements:* For master's, interview, leadership statement, resumé, 2 letters of recommendation, critical analysis essay. Additional exam requirements/recommendations for international students: Required—TOEFL (minimum score 600 paper-based; 250 computer-based). *Application deadline:* For fall admission, 8/15 priority date for domestic students; for spring admission, 12/8 priority date for domestic students. Applications are processed on a rolling basis. Application fee: $50. Electronic applications accepted. *Expenses:* Tuition: Full-time $5,256. *Unit head:* Brian Minchello, Associate Director, Graduate and Professional Programs, 617-735-9928, Fax: 617-735-9708, E-mail: gpp@emmanuel.edu. *Application contact:* Kristin Balutis, Graduate Management Programs, 617-735-9859, Fax: 617-735-9708, E-mail: balutkr@emmanuel.edu.

Emory University, Roberto C. Goizueta Business School, Atlanta, GA 30322-1100. Offers business (EMBA, MBA, WEMBA, PhD), including accounting (PhD), finance (PhD), information systems (PhD), marketing (PhD), organization and management (PhD); JD/MBA; M Div/MBA; MBA/MPH. *Accreditation:* AACSB. Part-time and evening/weekend programs available. Postbaccalaureate distance learning degree programs offered (minimal on-campus study). *Faculty:* 84 full-time (23 women), 10 part-time/adjunct (1 woman). *Students:* 504 full-time (139 women), 230 part-time (69 women); includes 141 minority (56 African Americans, 65 Asian Americans or Pacific Islanders, 20 Hispanic Americans), 188 international. Average age 30. 989 applicants, 34% accepted, 149 enrolled. In 2006, 361 master's, 1 doctorate awarded. *Median time to degree:* Master's–2 years full-time, 3 years part-time; doctorate–4 years full-time. *Degree requirements:* For doctorate, thesis/dissertation, comprehensive exam. *Entrance requirements:* For master's, GMAT, previous course work in calculus or statistics, at least one year of work experience, 2-3 essays, 2 recommendations. Additional exam requirements/recommendations for international students: Required—TOEFL (minimum score 600 paper-based; 250 computer-based). *Application deadline:* For fall admission, 3/15 priority date for domestic students, 2/1 priority date for international students; for winter admission, 10/1 priority date for domestic students; for spring admission, 3/1 priority date for domestic students. Applications are processed on a rolling basis. Application fee: $140. Electronic applications accepted. *Expenses:* Contact institution. *Financial support:* In 2006–07, 462 students received support, including 50 research assistantships (averaging $8,840 per year), 50 teaching assistantships (averaging $8,840 per year); fellowships with full tuition reimbursements available, career-related internships or fieldwork, Federal Work-Study, institutionally sponsored loans, and scholarships/grants also available. Support available to part-time students. Financial award application deadline: 4/1; financial award applicants required to submit FAFSA. *Faculty research:* Financial markets and banking, corporate disclosure and investor relations, marketing strategy, organizational innovation, electronic markets. *Unit head:* Lawrence Benveniste, Dean, 404-727-6377, Fax: 404-727-0868, E-mail: larry_benveniste@bus.emory.edu. *Application contact:* Julie Barefoot, Associate Dean, 404-727-6311, Fax: 404-727-4612, E-mail: admissions@bus.emory.edu.

Emporia State University, School of Graduate Studies, School of Business, Department of Business Administration and Education, Emporia, KS 66801-5087. Offers business administration (MBA); business education (MSBE). *Accreditation:* NCATE (one or more programs are accredited). *Faculty:* 16 full-time (3 women). *Students:* 64 full-time (24 women), 28 part-time (18 women); includes 3 minority (2 African Americans, 1 Asian American or Pacific Islander), 33 international. 29 applicants, 100% accepted, 24 enrolled. In 2006, 36 degrees awarded. *Entrance requirements:* For master's, GMAT (MBA), appropriate bachelor's degree. Additional exam requirements/recommendations for international students: Required—TOEFL (minimum score 550 paper-based). *Application deadline:* For fall admission, 8/15 priority date for domestic students. Applications are processed on a rolling basis. Application fee: $30 ($75 for international students). Electronic applications accepted. *Expenses:* Tuition, state resident: full-time $3,438; part-time $143 per credit hour. Tuition, nonresident: full-time $10,398; part-time $433 per credit hour. Required fees: $724; $44 per credit hour. *Financial support:* In 2006–07, 6 research assistantships with full tuition reimbursements (averaging $6,752 per year), teaching assistantships with full tuition reimbursements (averaging $6,752 per year) were awarded; fellowships, career-related internships or fieldwork, Federal Work-Study, institutionally sponsored loans, health care benefits, and unspecified assistantships also available. Financial award application deadline: 3/15; financial award applicants required to submit FAFSA. *Unit head:* Dr. William Smith, Chair, 620-341-5345, Fax: 620-341-6345, E-mail: wsmith@emporia.edu. *Application contact:* Dr. Donald Miller, Director, MBA Program, 620-341-5456, Fax: 620-341-6523, E-mail: dmiller1@emporia.edu.

Endicott College, Van Loan School of Graduate and Professional Studies, Program in Business Administration, Beverly, MA 01915-2096. Offers MBA. Part-time and evening/weekend programs available. *Faculty:* 2 full-time (0 women), 18 part-time/adjunct (8 women). *Students:* 42 full-time (23 women), 83 part-time (40 women); includes 5 minority (2 African Americans, 2 Asian Americans or Pacific Islanders, 1 Hispanic American), 25 international. Average age 32. 90 applicants, 89% accepted, 75 enrolled. In 2006, 50 degrees awarded. *Degree requirements:* For master's, thesis, masters project. *Entrance requirements:* For master's, GMAT, letters of recommendation, resumé. Additional exam requirements/recommendations for international students: Required—TOEFL. *Application deadline:* Applications are processed on a rolling basis. Application fee: $50. *Expenses:* Tuition: Part-time $279 per credit. Tuition and fees vary according to program. *Financial support:* Tuition waivers (full) available. *Faculty research:* Adult learning and development, supply chain management, marketing, ethics. *Unit head:* Dr. Jayanti Bandyopadhyay, Associate Dean of Graduate School, 978-232-2744, Fax: 978-232-3000, E-mail: jbandyop@endicott.edu.

Everglades University, Graduate Programs, Orlando, FL 32807. Offers aviation science (MSA); business administration (MBA).

Everglades University, Graduate Programs, Program in Business Administration, Boca Raton, FL 33431. Offers MBA. *Entrance requirements:* Additional exam requirements/recommendations for international students: Recommended—TOEFL (minimum score 500 paper-based; 173 computer-based). Electronic applications accepted.

Excelsior College, School of Business and Technology, Albany, NY 12203-5159. Offers MBA. Part-time and evening/weekend programs available. Postbaccalaureate distance learning degree programs offered (no on-campus study). *Faculty:* 10 part-time/adjunct (5 women). *Students:* Average age 45. *Application deadline:* Applications are processed on a rolling basis. Application fee: $100. *Expenses:* Tuition: Part-time $365 per credit hour. *Unit head:* Dr. Harpal S. Dhillon, Dean, 518-464-8500, Fax: 518-464-8777, E-mail: hdhillon@excelsior.edu. *Application contact:* Admissions, 888-647-2388 Ext. 133, Fax: 518-464-8777, E-mail: admissions@excelsior.edu.

Fairfield University, Charles F. Dolan School of Business, Fairfield, CT 06824-5195. Offers accounting (MBA, MS, CAS); finance (MBA, MS, CAS); general management (MBA); human resource management (MBA, CAS); information systems and operations (MBA); information systems and operations management (CAS); international business (MBA, CAS); marketing (MBA, CAS); taxation (MBA, MS, CAS). *Accreditation:* AACSB. Part-time and evening/weekend programs available. *Faculty:* 43 full-time (17 women), 2 part-time/adjunct (1 woman). *Students:* 65 full-time (31 women), 125 part-time (54 women); includes 4 Asian Americans or Pacific Islanders, 4 Hispanic Americans, 22 international. Average age 27. 99 applicants, 45% accepted, 38 enrolled. In 2006, 78 degrees awarded. *Degree requirements:* For master's, registration. *Entrance requirements:* For master's, GMAT, 2 letters of reference, resumé. Additional exam requirements/recommendations for international students: Required—TOEFL (minimum score 550 paper-based; 213 computer-based; 79 iBT). *Application deadline:* For fall admission, 8/15 priority date for domestic students, 5/15 priority date for international students; for spring admission, 11/15 priority date for domestic students, 10/15 priority date for international students. Applications are processed on a rolling basis. Application fee: $55. Electronic applications accepted. *Expenses:* Contact institution. *Financial support:* Unspecified assistantships available. *Faculty research:* Optimal investment strategies, organization structure, international finance, strategic management, customer behavior. *Unit head:* Dr. Norman A. Solomon, Dean, 203-254-4000 Ext. 4070, Fax: 203-254-4105, E-mail: nsolomon@mail.fairfield.edu. *Application contact:* Marianne Gumpper, Director of Graduate and Continuing Studies Admissions, 203-254-4184, Fax: 203-254-4073, E-mail: gradadmis@mail.fairfield.edu.

See Close-Up on page 271.

Fairleigh Dickinson University, College at Florham, Anthony J. Petrocelli College of Continuing Studies, School of Administrative Science, Program in Administrative Science, Madison, NJ 07940-1099. Offers MAS. *Students:* Average age 25. 1 applicant, 100% accepted, 1 enrolled. In 2006, 1 degree awarded. Application fee: $40.

Fairleigh Dickinson University, College at Florham, Silberman College of Business, Madison, NJ 07940-1099. Offers MBA, MS, Certificate, MA/MBA, MBA/MA. *Accreditation:* AACSB. Part-time and evening/weekend programs available. *Students:* 117 full-time (48 women), 313 part-time (139 women), 23 international. Average age 31. 201 applicants, 70% accepted, 106 enrolled. In 2006, 144 degrees awarded. *Application deadline:* Applications are processed on a rolling basis. Application fee: $40. *Unit head:* Dr. David Steele, Dean, 201-692-7200, Fax: 201-692-7199, E-mail: steele@fdu.edu.

See Close-Up on page 273.

Fairleigh Dickinson University, College at Florham, Silberman College of Business, Departments of Management, Marketing, and Entrepreneurial Studies, Program in Management, Madison, NJ 07940-1099. Offers evolving technology (Certificate); management (MBA); MBA/MA. *Students:* 13 full-time (8 women), 37 part-time (14 women), 1 international. Average age 31. 26 applicants, 54% accepted, 11 enrolled. In 2006, 17 degrees awarded. *Application deadline:* Applications are processed on a rolling basis. Application fee: $40.

Fairleigh Dickinson University, Metropolitan Campus, Anthony J. Petrocelli College of Continuing Studies, School of Administrative Science, Program in Administrative Science, Teaneck, NJ 07666-1914. Offers MAS, Certificate. *Students:* 64 full-time (31 women), 565 part-time (239 women), 30 international. Average age 39. 234 applicants, 94% accepted, 143 enrolled. In 2006, 220 degrees awarded. *Application deadline:* Applications are processed on a rolling basis. *Unit head:* Ronald Calissi, Director/Executive Associate Dean, School of Administrative Science, 201-692-2000.

Fairleigh Dickinson University, Metropolitan Campus, Silberman College of Business, Teaneck, NJ 07666-1914. Offers MBA, MS, Certificate, MBA/MA. *Accreditation:* AACSB. *Students:* 217 full-time (95 women), 152 part-time (74 women), 143 international. Average age 31. 360 applicants, 61% accepted, 109 enrolled. In 2006, 209 degrees awarded. *Entrance requirements:* For master's, GMAT. *Application deadline:* Applications are processed on a rolling basis. Application fee: $40. *Unit head:* Dr. Robert Greenfield, Dean, 201-692-2000.

See Close-Up on page 273.

Fairleigh Dickinson University, Metropolitan Campus, Silberman College of Business, Center for Healthcare Management Studies, Program in Management for Health System Executives, Teaneck, NJ 07666-1914. Offers MBA. *Students:* 10 full-time (6 women), 2 part-time (1 woman). Average age 38. 2 applicants, 50% accepted, 0 enrolled. In 2006, 7 degrees awarded. *Application deadline:* Applications are processed on a rolling basis. *Unit head:* Dr. Peter Caliguari, Director, Center for Healthcare Management Studies, 201-692-2000.

Fairleigh Dickinson University, Metropolitan Campus, Silberman College of Business, Departments of Management, Marketing, and Entrepreneurial Studies, Program in Management, Teaneck, NJ 07666-1914. Offers management (MBA); management information systems (Certificate). *Accreditation:* AACSB. *Students:* 31 full-time (17 women), 20 part-time (8 women), 26 international. Average age 29. 101 applicants, 47% accepted, 20 enrolled. In 2006, 38 degrees awarded. *Application deadline:* Applications are processed on a rolling basis. Application fee: $40. *Unit head:* Dr. Robert Greenfield, Dean, Silberman College of Business, 201-692-2000.

Fashion Institute of Technology, School of Graduate Studies, Program in Global Fashion Management, New York, NY 10001-5992. Offers MPS. *Expenses:* Tuition, state resident: full-time $6,900; part-time $288 per credit. Tuition, nonresident: full-time $10,920; part-time $455 per credit. Required fees: $420; $30 per term. *Unit head:* Pamela Ellsworth, Acting Associate Chair, 212-217-5714.

Felician College, Program in Business, Lodi, NJ 07644-2117. Offers innovation and entrepreneurship (MBA). Part-time and evening/weekend programs available. *Students:* 47. 28 applicants, 89% accepted, 24 enrolled. *Entrance requirements:* For master's, GMAT. *Application deadline:* Applications are processed on a rolling basis. Application fee: $40. *Expenses:* Tuition: Part-time $675 per credit. Tuition and fees vary according to program. *Unit head:* Dr. William Morgan, Dean, Division of Business and Management Services, 201-559-6140, E-mail: morganw@felician.edu. *Application contact:* Dominic DiGioacching, Associate Director of Adult and Graduate Admission, 201-559-6097, Fax: 201-559-6138, E-mail: digioacchinod@felician.edu.

Ferris State University, College of Business, Big Rapids, MI 49307. Offers application development (MSISM); database administration (MSISM); e-business (MSISM); information systems (MBA); networking (MSISM); quality management (MBA); security (MSISM). Part-time and evening/weekend programs available. *Faculty:* 5 full-time (2 women), 2 part-time/adjunct (both women). *Students:* 35 full-time (12 women), 60 part-time (24 women); includes 5 minority (3 African Americans, 1 American Indian/Alaska Native, 1 Asian American or Pacific Islander), 13 international. Average age 34. 90 applicants, 72% accepted, 29 enrolled. In 2006, 40 degrees awarded. *Degree requirements:* For master's, thesis. *Entrance requirements:* For master's, GRE or GMAT, minimum GPA of 3.0 in CIS and business core, 2.75 overall; writing sample; 3 letters of reference; resumé. Additional exam requirements/recommendations for international students: Required—TOEFL (minimum score 500 paper-based; 173 computer-based). *Application deadline:* For fall admission, 7/1 priority date for domestic students, 6/15 for international students; for winter admission, 11/1 priority date for domestic students, 10/15 for international students; for spring admission, 3/1 priority date for domestic students, 2/15 for international students. Applications are processed on a rolling basis. Electronic applications accepted. *Expenses:* Tuition, state resident: part-time $355 per credit hour. Tuition, nonresident: part-time $687 per credit hour. *Financial support:* In 2006–07, 40 research assistantships, 10 teaching assistantships were awarded; career-related internships or fieldwork, Federal Work-Study, and unspecified assistantships also available. Support available to part-time students. Financial award applicants required to submit FAFSA. *Faculty research:* Quality improvement, client/server end-user computing, information management and policy, learning space/Lotus Notes, security. *Unit head:* Dr. Bill Boras, Department Chair, 231-591-2168, Fax: 231-591-2973, E-mail: cbgp@ferris.edu. *Application contact:* Shannon Yost, Department Secretary, 231-591-2168, Fax: 231-591-2973, E-mail: yosts@ferris.edu.

Fitchburg State College, Division of Graduate and Continuing Education, Program in Business Administration, Fitchburg, MA 01420-2697. Offers accounting (MBA); human resource management (MBA); management (MBA). Part-time and evening/weekend programs available. *Students:* 42 full-time (8 women), 36 part-time (19 women); includes 13 minority (6 African Americans, 3 Asian Americans or Pacific Islanders, 4 Hispanic Americans), 25 international. Average age 31. 51 applicants, 98% accepted, 41 enrolled. In 2006, 47 degrees awarded. *Entrance requirements:* For master's, GMAT, minimum GPA of 2.8, letters of recommendation, resumé. Additional exam requirements/recommendations for international students: Required—TOEFL (minimum score 550 paper-based; 213 computer-based; 79 iBT). *Application deadline:* Applications are processed on a rolling basis. Application fee: $25 ($50 for international students). *Expenses:* Tuition, state resident: part-time $150 per credit. Tuition, nonresident: part-time $150 per credit. Required fees: $90 per credit. *Financial support:* In 2006–07, research assistantships with partial tuition reimbursements (averaging $5,500 per year); Federal Work-Study, scholarships/grants, and unspecified assistantships also available. Support available to part-time students. Financial award application deadline: 3/1; financial award applicants required to submit FAFSA. *Unit head:* Joseph McAloon, Chair, 978-665-3745, Fax: 978-665-3658, E-mail: gce@fsc.edu. *Application contact:* Director of Admissions, 978-665-3144, Fax: 978-665-4540, E-mail: admissions@fsc.edu.

Florida Agricultural and Mechanical University, Division of Graduate Studies, Research, and Continuing Education, School of Business and Industry, Tallahassee, FL 32307-3200. Offers accounting (MBA); finance (MBA); management information systems (MBA); marketing (MBA). *Degree requirements:* For master's, residency. *Entrance requirements:* For master's, GMAT, minimum GPA of 3.0.

Florida Atlantic University, College of Business, Department of Management, International Business and Entrepreneurship, Boca Raton, FL 33431-0991. Offers business administration (Exec MBA, MBA), including accounting (MBA), electronic commerce (MBA), finance (MBA), financial planning (MBA), global entrepreneurship (MBA), health administration (MBA), international business (MBA), marketing (MBA), operations management (MBA), real estate (MBA), sport management (MBA). *Faculty:* 64 full-time (17 women), 15 part-time/adjunct (3 women). *Students:* 215 full-time (89 women), 365 part-time (189 women); includes 150 minority (49 African Americans, 2 American Indian/Alaska Native, 36 Asian Americans or Pacific Islanders, 63 Hispanic Americans), 54 international. Average age 32. 414 applicants, 55% accepted, 167 enrolled. In 2006, 196 master's awarded. *Degree requirements:* For master's, thesis optional. *Entrance requirements:* For master's, GMAT, minimum GPA of 3.0. Additional exam requirements/recommendations for international students: Required—TOEFL (minimum score 600 paper-based; 250 computer-based). *Application deadline:* For fall admission, 7/1 priority date for domestic students, 2/15 priority date for international students; for winter admission, 11/1 priority date for domestic students, 8/15 priority date for international students; for spring admission, 4/1 priority date for domestic students, 1/15 priority date for international students. Applications are processed on a rolling basis. Application fee: $30. Electronic applications accepted. *Expenses:* Tuition, area resident: Full-time $4,394. Tuition, nonresident: full-time $16,441. *Financial support:* Research assistantships, teaching assistantships, career-related internships or fieldwork, Federal Work-Study, institutionally sponsored loans, tuition waivers (partial), and unspecified assistantships available. Support available to part-time students. Financial award application deadline: 3/1; financial award applicants required to submit FAFSA. *Unit head:* Dr. Brenda Richey, Head, 561-297-3194, E-mail: brichey@fau.edu. *Application contact:* Fredrick G. Taylor, Graduate Adviser, 561-297-2768, Fax: 561-297-1315, E-mail: mba@fau.edu.

Florida Atlantic University, Jupiter Campus, College of Business, Jupiter, FL 33458. Offers MBA.

Florida Gulf Coast University, College of Business, Master of Business Administration Program, Fort Myers, FL 33965-6565. Offers MBA. *Accreditation:* AACSB. Part-time and evening/weekend programs available. *Faculty:* 51 full-time (14 women), 18 part-time/adjunct (0 women). *Students:* 91 full-time (40 women), 44 part-time (25 women); includes 21 minority (6 African Americans, 1 Asian American or Pacific Islander, 14 Hispanic Americans), 8 international. Average age 31. 78 applicants, 86% accepted, 51 enrolled. In 2006, 42 degrees awarded. *Entrance requirements:* For master's, GMAT, minimum GPA of 3.0. Additional exam requirements/recommendations for international students: Required—TOEFL (minimum score 550 paper-based; 213 computer-based). *Application deadline:* For fall admission, 7/1 priority date for domestic students; for spring admission, 11/1 for domestic students. Applications are processed on a rolling basis. Application fee: $30. Electronic applications accepted. *Expenses:* Tuition, state resident: full-time $4,326. Tuition, nonresident: full-time $18,523. Required fees: $1,211. One-time fee: $5 full-time. *Faculty research:* Fraud in audits, production planning in cell manufacturing systems, collaborative learning in distance courses, characteristics of minority- and women-owned businesses. *Unit head:* Dr. Gerald Schoenfeld, Chair, 239-590-7300, Fax: 239-590-7330. *Application contact:* Carol Burnette, Associate Dean, 239-590-7350, Fax: 239-590-7330, E-mail: burnette@fgcu.edu.

Florida Institute of Technology, Graduate Programs, College of Business, Melbourne, FL 32901-6975. Offers EMBA, MBA. Part-time and evening/weekend programs available. *Faculty:* 12 full-time (6 women), 2 part-time/adjunct (0 women). *Students:* 19 full-time (7 women), 64 part-time (21 women); includes 7 minority (3 African Americans, 1 American Indian/Alaska Native, 2 Asian Americans or Pacific Islanders, 1 Hispanic American), 10 international. Average age 30. 58 applicants, 64% accepted, 15 enrolled. In 2006, 16 degrees awarded. *Degree requirements:* For master's, thesis optional. *Entrance requirements:* For master's, GMAT, minimum GPA of 3.0, 2 letters of recommendation, resumé. Additional exam requirements/recommendations for international students: Required—TOEFL (minimum score 550 paper-based; 213 computer-based). *Application deadline:* Applications are processed on a rolling basis. Application fee: $50. Electronic applications accepted. *Expenses:* Tuition: Part-time $900 per credit. *Financial support:* Institutionally sponsored loans, unspecified assistantships, and tuition remissions available. Financial award application deadline: 3/1; financial award applicants required to submit FAFSA. *Faculty research:* Investment analysis, marketing research, strategy analysis, ethics, small business. Total annual research expenditures: $1.2 million. *Unit head:* Dr. Robert H. Fronk, Interim Dean, 321-674-7327, Fax: 321-674-8896, E-mail: fronk@fit.edu. *Application contact:* Carolyn P. Farrior, Director of Graduate Admissions, 321-674-7118, Fax: 321-723-9468, E-mail: cfarrior@fit.edu.

Florida Institute of Technology, Graduate Programs, University College, Melbourne, FL 32901-6975. Offers acquisition and contract management (MS, PMBA); aerospace engineering (MS); business administration (PMBA); computer information systems (MS); computer science (MS); e-business (PMBA); electrical engineering (MS); engineering management (MS); human resource management (PMBA); human resources management (MS); information systems (PMBA); logistics management (MS); management (MS), including acquisition and contract management, e-business, human resource management, information systems, logistics management, transportation management; materiel acquisition management (MS); mechanical engineering (MS); operations research (MS); project management (MS), including information systems, operations research; public administration (MPA); software engineering (MS); space systems (MS); space systems management (MS); systems management (MS), including information systems, operations research. Part-time and evening/weekend programs available. Postbaccalaureate distance learning degree programs offered (no on-campus study). *Faculty:* 11 full-time (4 women), 129 part-time/adjunct (17 women). *Students:* 78 full-time (34 women), 1,258 part-time (507 women); includes 384 minority (252 African Americans, 9 American Indian/Alaska Native, 58 Asian Americans or Pacific Islanders, 65 Hispanic Americans), 28 international. Average age 36. 629 applicants, 65% accepted, 320 enrolled. In 2006, 505 degrees awarded. *Degree requirements:* For master's, registration. *Entrance requirements:* For master's, minimum GPA of 3.0. Additional exam requirements/recommendations for inter-

Business Administration and Management—General

Florida Institute of Technology (continued)

national students: Required—TOEFL (minimum score 550 paper-based; 213 computer-based). *Application deadline:* Applications are processed on a rolling basis. Application fee: $50. Electronic applications accepted. *Expenses:* Tuition: Part-time $900 per credit. *Financial support:* Institutionally sponsored loans available. Financial award application deadline: 3/1; financial award applicants required to submit FAFSA. *Unit head:* Dr. Clifford Bragdon, Dean, 321-674-8821, Fax: 321-951-7694, E-mail: cbragdon@fit.edu. *Application contact:* Carolyn P. Farrior, Director of Graduate Admissions, 321-674-7118, Fax: 321-723-9468, E-mail: cfarrior@fit.edu.

Florida International University, Alvah H. Chapman, Jr. Graduate School of Business, Program in Business Administration, Miami, FL 33199. Offers MBA, MS, PhD. *Accreditation:* AACSB. Part-time and evening/weekend programs available. *Students:* 307 full-time (145 women), 181 part-time (65 women); includes 283 minority (32 African Americans, 34 Asian Americans or Pacific Islanders, 217 Hispanic Americans), 120 international. Average age 37. 533 applicants, 37% accepted, 124 enrolled. In 2006, 204 master's, 4 doctorates awarded. *Entrance requirements:* For master's, GMAT, minimum AACSB index of 1000, minimum GPA of 3.0. Additional exam requirements/recommendations for international students: Required—TOEFL. *Application deadline:* For fall admission, 4/1 priority date for domestic students; for spring admission, 10/1 for domestic students. Applications are processed on a rolling basis. Application fee: $25. *Expenses:* Tuition, state resident: part-time $249 per credit hour. Tuition, nonresident: part-time $753 per credit hour. Tuition and fees vary according to program. *Financial support:* Research assistantships, teaching assistantships available. *Faculty research:* Whole brain learning approach, management style. *Unit head:* Dr. Joyce J. Elam, Executive Dean, Alvah H. Chapman, Jr. Graduate School of Business, 305-348-2751, Fax: 305-348-3278, E-mail: elamj@fiu.edu.

Florida Metropolitan University–Brandon Campus, Program in Business Administration, Tampa, FL 33619. Offers MBA. Part-time and evening/weekend programs available. Postbaccalaureate distance learning degree programs offered (minimal on-campus study). *Faculty:* 1 (woman) full-time, 4 part-time/adjunct (2 women). *Students:* 6 full-time (4 women), 32 part-time (18 women); includes 14 minority (7 African Americans, 7 Hispanic Americans). Average age 34. In 2006, 28 degrees awarded. *Entrance requirements:* Additional exam requirements/recommendations for international students: Required—TOEFL (minimum score 550 paper-based; 213 computer-based). *Application deadline:* Applications are processed on a rolling basis. Application fee: $25. *Expenses:* Tuition: Full-time $14,016; part-time $438 per credit. Required fees: $60 per quarter. *Financial support:* Federal Work-Study, institutionally sponsored loans, and scholarships/grants available. *Unit head:* James Jehs, Chair, 813-621-0041 Ext. 140, Fax: 813-623-5769. *Application contact:* Shandretta Pointer, Admissions Office, 813-621-0041 Ext. 106, Fax: 813-628-0919, E-mail: spointer@cci.edu.

Florida Metropolitan University–Melbourne Campus, Program in Business Administration, Melbourne, FL 32935-6657. Offers MBA.

Florida Metropolitan University–North Orlando Campus, Division of Business Administration, Orlando, FL 32810-5674. Offers MBA. Part-time and evening/weekend programs available. *Degree requirements:* For master's, thesis or alternative.

Florida Metropolitan University–Pinellas Campus, Graduate School of Business, Clearwater, FL 33759. Offers MBA. *Faculty research:* Management fads, learning styles, effective use of technology.

Florida Metropolitan University–Pompano Beach Campus, School of Business, Pompano Beach, FL 33062. Offers MBA. Part-time and evening/weekend programs available. *Entrance requirements:* For master's, minimum GPA of 3.0. *Faculty research:* E-learning.

Florida Metropolitan University–South Orlando Campus, Program in Business Administration, Orlando, FL 32819. Offers accounting (MBA); general management (MBA); human resources (MBA); international management (MBA).

Florida Metropolitan University–Tampa Campus, Department of Business Administration, Tampa, FL 33614-5899. Offers accounting (MBA); human resources (MBA); international business (MBA). Part-time and evening/weekend programs available. *Degree requirements:* For master's, thesis optional. *Entrance requirements:* For master's, GMAT or GRE, minimum GPA of 3.0.

Florida Southern College, Program in Business Administration, Lakeland, FL 33801-5698. Offers accounting (MBA); business administration (MBA); international business (MBA). Part-time and evening/weekend programs available. *Faculty:* 12 full-time (2 women). *Students:* Average age 31. 15 applicants, 80% accepted, 8 enrolled. In 2006, 9 degrees awarded. *Entrance requirements:* For master's, GMAT or GRE General Test, minimum GPA of 2.75. Additional exam requirements/recommendations for international students: Required—TOEFL (minimum score 550 paper-based). *Application deadline:* For fall admission, 8/1 for domestic students; for spring admission, 12/1 for domestic students. Applications are processed on a rolling basis. Application fee: $30. *Expenses:* Tuition: Part-time $250 per credit hour. Required fees: $10 per term. Tuition and fees vary according to program. *Financial support:* In 2006–07, 9 students received support. Scholarships/grants available. Support available to part-time students. Financial award applicants required to submit FAFSA. *Unit head:* Dr. Larry Ross, Program Coordinator, 863-680-4285, Fax: 863-680-4355, E-mail: lross@flsouthern.edu. *Application contact:* Craig Story, Evening Program Director, 863-680-6276, Fax: 863-680-4205, E-mail: cstory@flsouthern.edu.

Florida State University, Graduate Studies, College of Business, Tallahassee, FL 32306. Offers accounting (M Acc), including accounting information systems, assurance services, corporate accounting, taxation; business administration (MBA, PhD), including accounting (PhD), finance (PhD), information and management science (PhD), management (PhD), marketing (PhD), risk and insurance (PhD); insurance (MSM); management information systems (MS); JD/MBA. *Accreditation:* AACSB. Part-time and evening/weekend programs available. Postbaccalaureate distance learning degree programs offered (no on-campus study). *Faculty:* 107 full-time (26 women), 21 part-time/adjunct (2 women). *Students:* 145 full-time (62 women), 444 part-time (143 women); includes 147 minority (58 African Americans, 3 American Indian/Alaska Native, 45 Asian Americans or Pacific Islanders, 41 Hispanic Americans). Average age 29. 789 applicants, 50% accepted, 321 enrolled. In 2006, 263 master's, 19 doctorates awarded. Terminal master's awarded for partial completion of doctoral program. *Degree requirements:* For master's, registration; for doctorate, thesis/dissertation, comprehensive exam, registration. *Entrance requirements:* For master's, GMAT, substantial work experience (MBA, MS), minimum GPA of 3.0, letters of recommendation; for doctorate, GMAT, minimum graduate GPA of 3.5, letters of recommendation. Additional exam requirements/recommendations for international students: Required—TOEFL (minimum score 600 paper-based; 250 computer-based). *Application deadline:* For fall admission, 5/1 for domestic and international students; for spring admission, 10/1 for domestic students, 9/1 for international students. Applications are processed on a rolling basis. Application fee: $30. Electronic applications accepted. *Expenses:* Tuition, state resident: full-time $5,822; part-time $243 per credit hour. Tuition, nonresident: full-time $20,976; part-time $874 per credit hour. Tuition and fees vary according to program. *Financial support:* In 2006–07, 126 students received support, including 40 fellowships with partial tuition reimbursements available (averaging $4,600 per year), 37 research assistantships with partial tuition reimbursements available (averaging $4,600 per year), 49 teaching assistantships with partial tuition reimbursements available (averaging $10,500 per year); unspecified assistantships also available. Financial award application deadline: 1/1. Total annual research expenditures: $1.5 million. *Unit head:* Dr. Caryn Beck-Dudley, Dean, 850-644-3090, Fax: 850-644-0915. *Application contact:* Lisa Beverly, Coordinator, Graduate Programs Admissions, 850-644-6458, Fax: 850-644-0588, E-mail: lbeverly@cob.fsu.edu.

Fontbonne University, Graduate Programs, Department of Business Administration, Options Program in Business Administration, St. Louis, MO 63105-3098. Offers MBA. Evening/weekend programs available. *Faculty:* 40 part-time/adjunct (8 women). *Students:* 172 full-time (109 women), 47 part-time (29 women); includes 115 minority (111 African Americans, 2 Asian Americans or Pacific Islanders, 2 Hispanic Americans), 1 international. Average age 35. 104 applicants, 91% accepted, 94 enrolled. *Degree requirements:* For master's, applied management project. *Entrance requirements:* For master's, minimum GPA of 2.5. *Application deadline:* For fall admission, 8/1 priority date for domestic students. Applications are processed on a rolling basis. Application fee: $25. *Expenses:* Contact institution. Full-time tuition and fees vary according to course load and program. *Financial support:* Application deadline: 4/1; *Unit head:* Carol Drury, Executive Director, 314-889-4588, Fax: 314-889-1451, E-mail: cdrury@fontbonne.edu. *Application contact:* Cindy Bluestone, Director of Marketing and Enrollment, 314-889-4576, Fax: 314-863-0917, E-mail: cbbushue@apollogrp.edu.

Fontbonne University, Graduate Programs, Department of Business Administration, Options Program in Management, St. Louis, MO 63105-3098. Offers MM. *Faculty:* 21 part-time/adjunct (8 women). *Students:* 95 full-time (66 women), 6 part-time (5 women); includes 70 minority (67 African Americans, 2 American Indian/Alaska Native, 1 Asian American or Pacific Islander). Average age 37. 45 applicants, 93% accepted, 40 enrolled. In 2006, 37 degrees awarded. *Application deadline:* For fall admission, 8/1 priority date for domestic students. Applications are processed on a rolling basis. Application fee: $25. *Expenses:* Contact institution. Full-time tuition and fees vary according to course load and program. *Financial support:* Application deadline: 4/1; *Unit head:* Carol Drury, Executive Director, 314-889-4588, Fax: 314-889-1451, E-mail: cdrury@fontbonne.edu. *Application contact:* Cindy Bluestone, Director of Marketing and Enrollment, 314-889-4576, Fax: 314-863-0917, E-mail: cbbushue@apollogrp.edu.

Fontbonne University, Graduate Programs, Department of Business Administration, Program in Business Administration, St. Louis, MO 63105-3098. Offers MBA. Part-time and evening/weekend programs available. *Faculty:* 4 full-time (0 women), 19 part-time/adjunct (6 women). *Students:* 41 full-time (21 women), 36 part-time (18 women); includes 12 minority (10 African Americans, 2 Asian Americans or Pacific Islanders), 36 international. Average age 31. 23 applicants, 87% accepted, 17 enrolled. *Entrance requirements:* For master's, minimum GPA of 2.5. *Application deadline:* For fall admission, 8/1 priority date for domestic students. Applications are processed on a rolling basis. Application fee: $25. *Expenses:* Tuition: Full-time $4,890; part-time $489 per credit. Required fees: $160; $76 per credit. Full-time tuition and fees vary according to course load and program. *Financial support:* Application deadline: 4/1; *Unit head:* Dr. Linda Maurer, Dean of Business, 314-889-1423, Fax: 314-889-1451, E-mail: lmaurer@fontbonne.edu. *Application contact:* William D. Foster, Administrative Director, Business and Administration, 314-889-1418, Fax: 314-889-1451, E-mail: bfoster@fontbonne.edu.

Fordham University, Graduate School of Business, New York, NY 10023. Offers accounting (MBA); communications and media management (MBA); finance (MBA, MS); information systems (MBA, MS); management systems (MBA); marketing (MBA); media management (MS); taxation (MS); JD/MBA; MBA/MIM; MS/MBA. *Accreditation:* AACSB. Part-time and evening/weekend programs available. *Faculty:* 87 full-time, 41 part-time/adjunct. *Students:* 345 full-time (132 women), 1,183 part-time (448 women); includes 238 minority (59 African Americans, 1 American Indian/Alaska Native, 116 Asian Americans or Pacific Islanders, 62 Hispanic Americans), 77 international. 1,081 applicants, 65% accepted, 422 enrolled. In 2006, 454 degrees awarded. *Entrance requirements:* For master's, GMAT. Additional exam requirements/recommendations for international students: Required—TOEFL (minimum score 600 paper-based; 250 computer-based). *Application deadline:* For fall admission, 6/1 priority date for domestic students, 5/1 priority date for international students; for winter admission, 11/1 priority date for domestic students, 10/1 priority date for international students; for spring admission, 3/1 priority date for domestic students, 2/1 priority date for international students. Applications are processed on a rolling basis. Application fee: $65. Electronic applications accepted. *Expenses:* Contact institution. *Financial support:* In 2006–07, 7 fellowships (averaging $27,000 per year), 128 research assistantships were awarded; career-related internships or fieldwork, institutionally sponsored loans, scholarships/grants, and unspecified assistantships also available. Support available to part-time students. Financial award application deadline: 5/1; financial award applicants required to submit FAFSA. *Unit head:* Dr. Howard Tuckman, Dean, 212-636-6165, Fax: 212-307-1779, E-mail: tuckman@fordham.edu. *Application contact:* Frank Fletcher, Director of Admissions and Financial Aid, 212-636-6200, Fax: 212-636-7076, E-mail: admissionsgb@fordham.edu.

Fort Hays State University, Graduate School, College of Business and Leadership, Department of Management and Marketing, Hays, KS 67601-4099. Offers accounting (MBA); management (MBA). *Faculty:* 19 full-time (1 woman). *Students:* 14 full-time (6 women), 8 part-time (3 women); includes 10 minority (all Asian Americans or Pacific Islanders) Average age 31. 39 applicants, 59% accepted. In 2006, 18 degrees awarded. *Degree requirements:* For master's, thesis optional. *Entrance requirements:* For master's, GMAT. Additional exam requirements/recommendations for international students: Required—TOEFL (minimum score 550 paper-based; 213 computer-based). *Application deadline:* For fall admission, 7/1 priority date for domestic students. Applications are processed on a rolling basis. Application fee: $35. Electronic applications accepted. *Financial support:* In 2006–07, 5 teaching assistantships (averaging $5,000 per year) were awarded; research assistantships, institutionally sponsored loans and tuition waivers (full) also available. Support available to part-time students. *Faculty research:* Organizational behavior and performance appraisal, data processing, international marketing. *Unit head:* Dr. Micol Maughan, Chair, 785-628-5877.

Framingham State College, Division of Graduate and Continuing Education, Program in Business Administration, Framingham, MA 01701-9101. Offers MA. Part-time and evening/weekend programs available. *Faculty:* 4 full-time, 4 part-time/adjunct. *Students:* 101. In 2006, 22 degrees awarded. *Entrance requirements:* For master's, GMAT, GRE, or MAT. *Unit head:* Dr. Andrew Hall, Director, 508-626-4892, Fax: 508-626-4030, E-mail: ahall2@frc.mass.edu. *Application contact:* 508-626-4550, Fax: 508-626-4030, E-mail: dgce@frc.mass.edu.

Franciscan University of Steubenville, Graduate Programs, Department of Business, Steubenville, OH 43952-1763. Offers MBA. Part-time and evening/weekend programs available. *Degree requirements:* For master's, research paper. *Entrance requirements:* For master's, GMAT, minimum undergraduate GPA of 2.5. Expenses: Contact institution.

Francis Marion University, Graduate Programs, School of Business, Florence, SC 29501-0547. Offers business (MBA); health management (MBA). *Accreditation:* AACSB. Part-time and evening/weekend programs available. *Faculty:* 16 full-time (2 women). *Students:* 7 full-time (5 women), 49 part-time (24 women); includes 11 minority (8 African Americans, 1 Asian American or Pacific Islander, 2 Hispanic Americans), 1 international. Average age 31. 32 applicants, 100% accepted, 13 enrolled. In 2006, 18 degrees awarded. *Degree requirements:* For master's, comprehensive exam. *Entrance requirements:* For master's, GMAT. *Application deadline:* For fall admission, 4/15 priority date for domestic students; for spring admission, 10/15 priority date for domestic students. Applications are processed on a rolling basis. Application fee: $30. *Expenses:* Tuition, state resident: full-time $6,527; part-time $326 per credit hour. Tuition, nonresident: full-time $13,054; part-time $653 per credit hour. Required fees: $185; $5 per credit hour. $45 per term. *Financial support:* In 2006–07, 2 research assistantships (averaging $3,000 per year) were awarded; unspecified assistantships also available. Support available to part-time students. Financial award application deadline: 3/1; financial award applicants required to submit FAFSA. *Faculty research:* Ethics, directions of MBA, international business, regional economics, environmental issues. *Unit head:* Dr. M. Barry O'Brien, Dean, 843-661-1419, Fax: 843-661-1432, E-mail: mbobrien@fmarion.edu.

Franklin Pierce University, Graduate Studies, Rindge, NH 03461-0060. Offers information technology management (MS); leadership (MBA); physical therapy (MS). *Accreditation:* APTA. Part-time and evening/weekend programs available. *Entrance requirements:* For master's, minimum GPA of 2.5. Additional exam requirements/recommendations for international students: Required—TOEFL (minimum score 550 paper-based; 195 computer-based). Electronic applications accepted.

Franklin University, Graduate School of Business, Columbus, OH 43215-5399. Offers MBA. Part-time and evening/weekend programs available. Postbaccalaureate distance learning degree programs offered (minimal on-campus study). *Faculty:* 3 full-time (0 women), 33 part-time/adjunct (12 women). *Students:* 483 full-time (242 women), 91 part-time (47 women); includes 176 minority (119 African Americans, 44 Asian Americans or Pacific Islanders, 13 Hispanic Americans), 30 international. Average age 35. In 2006, 125 degrees awarded. *Degree requirements:* For master's, registration. *Entrance requirements:* For master's, minimum undergraduate GPA of 2.75. Additional exam requirements/recommendations for international students: Required—TOEFL (minimum score 550 paper-based; 213 computer-based). *Application deadline:* For fall admission, 8/1 priority date for domestic students; for winter admission, 1/2 priority date for domestic students; for spring admission, 4/4 priority date for domestic students. Applications are processed on a rolling basis. Application fee: $30. Electronic applications accepted. *Expenses:* Tuition: Full-time $7,110; part-time $395 per credit hour. Tuition and fees vary according to campus/location and program. *Financial support:* In 2006–07, 267 students received support. Institutionally sponsored loans available. Financial award application deadline: 6/30; financial award applicants required to submit FAFSA. *Unit head:* Dr. Terry Boyd, Program Chair, 614-947-6140, Fax: 614-224-4025. *Application contact:* Graduate Services Office, 614-797-4700, Fax: 614-221-7723, E-mail: gradschl@franklin.edu.

Freed-Hardeman University, Program in Business Administration, Henderson, TN 38340-2399. Offers MBA. *Accreditation:* ACBSP. *Students:* 10 full-time (2 women), 8 part-time (3 women). Average age 30. *Entrance requirements:* Additional exam requirements/recommendations for international students: Required—TOEFL (minimum score 500 paper-based; 173 computer-based). Application fee: $32. *Expenses:* Tuition: Part-time $334 per credit hour. Required fees: $10 per credit hour. *Unit head:* Dr. Tom Deberry, Director of Graduate Studies, School of Business, 731-989-6659, E-mail: tdelberry@fhu.edu.

Fresno Pacific University, Graduate Programs, Program in Leadership and Organizational Studies, Fresno, CA 93702-4709. Offers MA. Part-time and evening/weekend programs available. *Faculty:* 2 full-time (1 woman), 2 part-time/adjunct (0 women). *Students:* 23 full-time (17 women), 44 part-time (26 women); includes 22 minority (6 African Americans, 1 American Indian/Alaska Native, 3 Asian Americans or Pacific Islanders, 12 Hispanic Americans), 3 international. Average age 40. 16 applicants, 94% accepted, 0 enrolled. In 2006, 14 degrees awarded. *Degree requirements:* For master's, thesis, registration. *Entrance requirements:* For master's, MAT, GRE or GMAT, interview, 2 writing samples. Additional exam requirements/recommendations for international students: Required—TOEFL (minimum score 550 paper-based; 213 computer-based). *Application deadline:* For fall admission, 7/15 for domestic and international students; for spring admission, 11/15 for domestic and international students. Applications are processed on a rolling basis. Application fee: $90. Electronic applications accepted. *Expenses:* Contact institution. *Financial support:* In 2006–07, 33 students received support. Scholarships/grants and tuition waivers (full and partial) available. Support available to part-time students. Financial award applicants required to submit FAFSA. *Faculty research:* Ethics, servant leadership, communication, creative problem solving. *Unit head:* Duane Ruth-Heffelbower, Director, 559-253-7202, Fax: 559-252-4800, E-mail: duane.ruth-heffelbower@fresno.edu.

Friends University, Graduate School, Division of Business, Technology, and Leadership, Program in Business Administration, Wichita, KS 67213. Offers MBA. Program also offered at Kansas City and Topeka campuses. Evening/weekend programs available. *Students:* 136 full-time. *Entrance requirements:* Additional exam requirements/recommendations for international students: Required—TOEFL (minimum score 560 paper-based; 220 computer-based). *Application deadline:* For fall admission, 6/1 priority date for domestic students, 5/1 priority date for international students; for spring admission, 11/1 priority date for domestic students, 10/1 priority date for international students. Application fee: $45 ($65 for international students). Electronic applications accepted. *Application contact:* Craig Davis, Director of Graduate Admissions, 800-794-6945 Ext. 5573, Fax: 316-295-5050, E-mail: cdavis@friends.edu.

Friends University, Graduate School, Division of Business, Technology, and Leadership, Program in Executive Business Administration, Wichita, KS 67213. Offers EMBA. Evening/weekend programs available. *Faculty:* 1 full-time (0 women), 2 part-time/adjunct (1 woman). In 2006, 21 degrees awarded. *Entrance requirements:* Additional exam requirements/recommendations for international students: Required—TOEFL (minimum score 560 paper-based; 220 computer-based). *Application deadline:* For fall admission, 8/15 priority date for domestic students, 7/15 priority date for international students; for spring admission, 12/15 for domestic students, 11/15 priority date for international students. Applications are processed on a rolling basis. Application fee: $45 ($65 for international students). Electronic applications accepted. *Application contact:* Craig Davis, Director of Graduate Admissions, 800-794-6945 Ext. 5573, Fax: 316-295-5050, E-mail: cdavis@friends.edu.

Friends University, Graduate School, Division of Business, Technology, and Leadership, Program in Management, Wichita, KS 67213. Offers MSM. Evening/weekend programs available. *Faculty:* 3 full-time (1 woman), 4 part-time/adjunct (1 woman). *Students:* 41 full-time. In 2006, 43 degrees awarded. *Entrance requirements:* Additional exam requirements/recommendations for international students: Required—TOEFL (minimum score 560 paper-based; 220 computer-based). *Application deadline:* For fall admission, 8/15 priority date for domestic students, 7/15 priority date for international students; for spring admission, 12/15 priority date for domestic students, 11/15 priority date for international students. Applications are processed on a rolling basis. Application fee: $45 ($65 for international students). Electronic applications accepted. *Unit head:* Director, 316-295-5621 Ext. 5661, Fax: 316-295-5040. *Application contact:* Craig Davis, Director of Graduate Admissions, 800-794-6945 Ext. 5573, Fax: 316-295-5050, E-mail: cdavis@friends.edu.

Friends University, Graduate School, Division of Business, Technology, and Leadership, Program of Studies in Business Law, Wichita, KS 67213. Offers MBL. Evening/weekend programs available. *Faculty:* 1 (woman) full-time, 3 part-time/adjunct (1 woman). *Students:* 33 full-time. In 2006, 19 degrees awarded. *Entrance requirements:* Additional exam requirements/recommendations for international students: Required—TOEFL (minimum score 560 paper-based; 220 computer-based). *Application deadline:* For fall admission, 6/1 priority date for domestic and international students. Applications are processed on a rolling basis. Application fee: $45 ($65 for international students). Electronic applications accepted. *Unit head:* Dr. Dixie Madden, Director, 800-794-6945 Ext. 5906. *Application contact:* Craig Davis, Director of Graduate Admissions, 800-794-6945 Ext. 5573, Fax: 316-295-5050, E-mail: cdavis@friends.edu.

Frostburg State University, Graduate School, College of Business, Frostburg, MD 21532-1099. Offers MBA. *Accreditation:* AACSB. Part-time and evening/weekend programs available. *Entrance requirements:* For master's, GMAT. Electronic applications accepted. *Faculty research:* Cooperative teaching methods, strategic change processes, political marketing.

Gannon University, School of Graduate Studies, College of Humanities, Business, and Education, School of Business, Program in Business Administration, Erie, PA 16541-0001. Offers MBA. *Accreditation:* ACBSP. Part-time and evening/weekend programs available. Postbaccalaureate distance learning degree programs offered (no on-campus study). *Students:* 33 full-time (11 women), 56 part-time (31 women); includes 4 minority (2 African Americans, 2 Asian Americans or Pacific Islanders), 17 international. Average age 29. 82 applicants, 65% accepted, 25 enrolled. In 2006, 30 degrees awarded. *Degree requirements:* For master's, computer workshop, research project. *Entrance requirements:* For master's, GMAT. Additional exam requirements/recommendations for international students: Required—TOEFL (minimum score 500 paper-based; 173 computer-based). *Application deadline:* Applications are processed on a rolling basis. Application fee: $25. *Expenses:* Tuition: Full-time $12,240; part-time $680 per credit. Required fees: $496; $16 per credit. Tuition and fees vary according to course load, degree level, campus/location and program. *Financial support:* Career-related internships or fieldwork, scholarships/grants, and administrative assistantships available. Support available to part-time students. Financial award application deadline: 7/1; financial award applicants required to submit FAFSA. *Application contact:* Debra Meszaros, Director of Graduate Recruitment, 814-871-5819, Fax: 814-871-5827, E-mail: cfal@gannon.edu.

Gannon University, School of Graduate Studies, College of Humanities, Business, and Education, School of Business, Program in Risk Management, Erie, PA 16541-0001. Offers Certificate. Part-time and evening/weekend programs available. *Entrance requirements:* For degree, GMAT. Additional exam requirements/recommendations for international students: Required—TOEFL (minimum score 500 paper-based; 173 computer-based). *Application deadline:* Applications are processed on a rolling basis. Application fee: $25. *Expenses:* Tuition: Full-time $12,240; part-time $680 per credit. Required fees: $496; $16 per credit. Tuition and fees vary according to course load, degree level, campus/location and program. *Financial support:* Application deadline: 7/1; *Application contact:* Debra Meszaros, Director of Graduate Recruitment, 814-871-5819, Fax: 814-871-5827, E-mail: cfal@gannon.edu.

Gardner-Webb University, Graduate School of Business, Boiling Springs, NC 28017. Offers IMBA, M Acc, MBA. *Accreditation:* ACBSP. Part-time and evening/weekend programs available. Postbaccalaureate distance learning degree programs offered (no on-campus study). *Faculty:* 12 full-time (1 woman), 6 part-time/adjunct (1 woman). *Students:* 55 full-time (29 women), 362 part-time (193 women); includes 103 minority (86 African Americans, 6 Asian Americans or Pacific Islanders, 11 Hispanic Americans), 1 international. Average age 33. 147 applicants, 80% accepted, 117 enrolled. In 2006, 138 degrees awarded. *Entrance requirements:* For master's, GMAT, 2 semesters of course work in each economics and statistics, 2 semesters course work in accounting. *Application deadline:* For fall admission, 8/29 for domestic students; for spring admission, 1/13 for domestic students. Applications are processed on a rolling basis. Application fee: $25. Electronic applications accepted. *Expenses:* Contact institution. *Financial support:* In 2006–07, 23 students received support. Unspecified assistantships available. Support available to part-time students. Financial award applicants required to submit FAFSA. *Unit head:* Dr. Anthony Negbenebor, Director, 704-406-4622, Fax: 704-406-3895, E-mail: anegbenebor@gardner-webb.edu. *Application contact:* Kristen J. Setzer, Director of Admissions, 800-457-4622, Fax: 704-434-3895, E-mail: ksetzer@gardner-webb.edu.

Gardner-Webb University, M. Christopher White School of Divinity, Boiling Springs, NC 28017. Offers business administration (MA); Christian education (M Div); English (MA); ministry (D Min); missiology (M Div); pastoral care and counseling (M Div); pastoral ministry (M Div). *Accreditation:* ACIPE; ATS. Part-time programs available. *Faculty:* 9 full-time (2 women), 7 part-time/adjunct (1 woman). *Students:* 106 full-time (29 women), 58 part-time (12 women); includes 29 minority (27 African Americans, 2 Hispanic Americans). Average age 34. 69 applicants, 97% accepted, 59 enrolled. In 2006, 33 master's, 5 doctorates awarded. *Degree requirements:* For first-professional, 2 foreign languages. *Entrance requirements:* For M Div, minimum GPA of 2.0; for master's, minimum GPA of 2.5; for doctorate, minimum GPA of 2.75. *Application deadline:* For fall admission, 8/1 priority date for domestic students; for spring admission, 12/15 priority date for domestic students. Applications are processed on a rolling basis. Application fee: $25. *Expenses:* Contact institution. *Financial support:* Fellowships, institutionally sponsored loans and unspecified assistantships available. Support available to part-time students. Financial award application deadline: 5/15. *Faculty research:* Jewish Christian dialogue, Islam. *Unit head:* Dr. Robert W. Canoy, Dean, 704-406-4400, Fax: 704-406-3935, E-mail: rcanoy@gardner-webb.edu. *Application contact:* Dr. Toby Ziglar, Director of Admissions, 704-406-3205, Fax: 704-406-3935, E-mail: tziglar@gardner-webb.edu.

Geneva College, Program in Business Administration, Beaver Falls, PA 15010-3599. Offers MBA. *Accreditation:* ACBSP. Part-time and evening/weekend programs available. *Entrance requirements:* For master's, 2 letters of recommendation. Electronic applications accepted.

George Fox University, School of Management, Newberg, OR 97132-2697. Offers MBA, DM. Part-time and evening/weekend programs available. *Faculty:* 11 full-time (4 women), 7 part-time/adjunct (1 woman). *Students:* 1 full-time (0 women), 239 part-time (79 women); includes 24 minority (4 African Americans, 2 American Indian/Alaska Native, 11 Asian Americans or Pacific Islanders, 7 Hispanic Americans), 1 international. Average age 36. 79 applicants, 76% accepted, 49 enrolled. In 2006, 99 degrees awarded. *Degree requirements:* For master's, project. *Entrance requirements:* For master's, minimum undergraduate GPA of 3.0 during previous 2 years, 2 years of professional or managerial work experience. *Application deadline:* For fall admission, 7/1 for domestic students; for spring admission, 10/15 for domestic students. Applications are processed on a rolling basis. Application fee: $40. Electronic applications accepted. *Expenses:* Contact institution. *Financial support:* Applicants required to submit FAFSA. *Unit head:* Dr. Dirk Barran, Acting Dean, 800-631-0921, E-mail: dbarram@georgefox.edu. *Application contact:* Amber Russell, Admissions Counselor, 800-631-0921, Fax: 503-554-3856, E-mail: arussell@georgefox.edu.

George Mason University, School of Management, Program in Business Administration, Fairfax, VA 22030. Offers EMBA, MBA. *Accreditation:* AACSB. Part-time and evening/weekend programs available. *Faculty:* 74 full-time (25 women), 37 part-time/adjunct (12 women). *Students:* 93 full-time (35 women), 218 part-time (79 women); includes 61 minority (12 African Americans, 2 American Indian/Alaska Native, 39 Asian Americans or Pacific Islanders, 8 Hispanic Americans), 39 international. Average age 35. 336 applicants, 47% accepted, 114 enrolled. In 2006, 154 degrees awarded. *Entrance requirements:* For master's, GMAT, 2 years of work experience. Additional exam requirements/recommendations for international students: Required—TOEFL. *Application deadline:* For fall admission, 5/1 for domestic students; for spring admission, 11/1 for domestic students. Applications are processed on a rolling basis. Application fee: $60 ($75 for international students). Electronic applications accepted. *Expenses:* Tuition, state resident: full-time $5,724; part-time $238 per credit. Tuition, nonresident: full-time $16,896; part-time $704 per credit. Required fees: $1,656; $69 per credit. *Financial support:* Fellowships, research assistantships, teaching assistantships, career-related internships or fieldwork and Federal Work-Study available. Support available to part-time students. Financial award application deadline: 3/1; financial award applicants required to submit FAFSA. *Faculty research:* Electronic commerce, marketing information systems, group decision making, corporate governance, risk management. *Unit head:* Angel Burgos, Director, 703-993-2136, Fax: 703-993-1778.

Georgetown University, Graduate School of Arts and Sciences, McDonough School of Business, Washington, DC 20057. Offers business administration (MBA); JD/MBA; MBA/MPP; MBA/MS; MD/MBA. *Accreditation:* AACSB. *Entrance requirements:* For master's, GMAT. Additional exam requirements/recommendations for international students: Required—TOEFL. Expenses: Contact institution.

The George Washington University, School of Business, Department of Management Science, Washington, DC 20052. Offers human resources management (MBA); information systems management (MBA); logistics, operations, and materials management (MBA); management and organization (PhD); management decision making (MBA, PhD); management information systems (MSIST); management of science, technology, and innovation (MBA); organizational behavior and development (MBA); project management (MS). *Accreditation:* AACSB. Part-time and evening/weekend programs available. *Degree requirements:* For doctorate, thesis/dissertation. *Entrance requirements:* For master's, GMAT; for doctorate, GMAT or GRE. Additional exam requirements/recommendations for international students: Required—TOEFL. *Faculty research:* Artificial intelligence, technological entrepreneurship, expert systems, strategic planning/management.

Georgia College & State University, Graduate School, The J. Whitney Bunting School of Business, Milledgeville, GA 31061. Offers accountancy (MACCT); business (MBA); informa-

Business Administration and Management—General

Georgia College & State University (continued)
tion systems (MIS). *Accreditation:* AACSB. Part-time and evening/weekend programs available. Postbaccalaureate distance learning degree programs offered (no on-campus study). *Faculty:* 43 full-time (18 women). *Students:* 44 full-time (19 women), 139 part-time (71 women); includes 28 minority (19 African Americans, 6 Asian Americans or Pacific Islanders, 3 Hispanic Americans), 17 international. Average age 30. 135 applicants, 56% accepted, 42 enrolled. In 2006, 76 degrees awarded. *Entrance requirements:* For master's, GMAT. Additional exam requirements/recommendations for international students: Required—TOEFL (minimum score 500 paper-based; 173 computer-based). *Application deadline:* For fall admission, 7/1 priority date for domestic students; for spring admission, 11/15 priority date for domestic students. Applications are processed on a rolling basis. Application fee: $25. Electronic applications accepted. *Expenses:* Tuition, state resident: full-time $3,222; part-time $179 per credit hour. Tuition, nonresident: full-time $12,870; part-time $715 per credit hour. Required fees: $391 per semester. Tuition and fees vary according to course load. *Financial support:* In 2006–07, 24 research assistantships with tuition reimbursements were awarded; career-related internships or fieldwork, Federal Work-Study, and unspecified assistantships also available. Support available to part-time students. Financial award application deadline: 3/1; financial award applicants required to submit FAFSA. *Faculty research:* Artificial intelligence, international trade, business ethics, curriculum issues. *Unit head:* Dr. Faye Gilbert, Dean, 478-445-5497, E-mail: faye.gilbert@gcsu.edu. *Application contact:* Lynn Hanson, Director of Graduate Programs in Business, 478-445-5115, E-mail: lynn.hanson@gcsu.edu.

Georgia Institute of Technology, Graduate Studies and Research, College of Management, Program in Business Administration, Atlanta, GA 30332-0001. Offers accounting (MBA); e-commerce (Certificate); engineering entrepreneurship (MBA); entrepreneurship (Certificate); finance (MBA); information technology management (MBA); international business (MBA, Certificate); management of technology (Certificate); marketing (MBA); operations management (MBA); organizational behavior (MBA); strategic management (MBA). *Accreditation:* AACSB.

Georgia Institute of Technology, Graduate Studies and Research, College of Management, Program in Management, Atlanta, GA 30332-0001. Offers accounting (PhD); finance (PhD); information technology management (PhD); marketing (PhD); operations management (PhD); organizational behavior (PhD); quantitative and computational finance (MS); strategic management (PhD). *Accreditation:* AACSB. *Degree requirements:* For doctorate, thesis/dissertation, oral exams, comprehensive exam. *Entrance requirements:* For master's and doctorate, GMAT. Additional exam requirements/recommendations for international students: Required—TOEFL. *Faculty research:* MIS, management of technology, international business, entrepreneurship, operations management.

Georgian Court University, School of Business, Lakewood, NJ 08701-2697. Offers MBA. *Accreditation:* ACBSP. Part-time and evening/weekend programs available. *Faculty:* 8 full-time (4 women), 8 part-time/adjunct (3 women). *Students:* 36 full-time (29 women), 130 part-time (93 women); includes 27 minority (9 African Americans, 7 Asian Americans or Pacific Islanders, 11 Hispanic Americans), 5 international. Average age 34. 55 applicants, 95% accepted, 40 enrolled. In 2006, 61 degrees awarded. *Entrance requirements:* For master's, GMAT or CPA exam, 3 letters of recommendation. Additional exam requirements/recommendations for international students: Required—TOEFL (minimum score 550 paper-based; 213 computer-based). *Application deadline:* For fall admission, 8/1 priority date for domestic students, 4/1 for international students; for spring admission, 1/1 priority date for domestic students, 7/1 for international students. Applications are processed on a rolling basis. Application fee: $40. Electronic applications accepted. *Financial support:* Scholarships/grants, health care benefits, and unspecified assistantships available. Financial award application deadline: 4/15; financial award applicants required to submit FAFSA. *Unit head:* Dr. Siamack Shoisi, Dean, 732-987-2724. *Application contact:* Eugene Soltys, Director of Graduate Admissions, 732-987-2760 Ext. 2760, Fax: 732-987-2000, E-mail: admissions@georgian.edu.

Georgia Southern University, Jack N. Averitt College of Graduate Studies, College of Business Administration, Program in Business Administration, Statesboro, GA 30460. Offers MBA. *Accreditation:* AACSB. Part-time and evening/weekend programs available. *Students:* 81 full-time (33 women), 106 part-time (43 women); includes 42 minority (34 African Americans, 2 American Indian/Alaska Native, 5 Asian Americans or Pacific Islanders, 1 Hispanic American), 21 international. Average age 28. 95 applicants, 77% accepted, 58 enrolled. In 2006, 85 degrees awarded. *Entrance requirements:* For master's, GMAT. Additional exam requirements/recommendations for international students: Required—TOEFL (minimum score 550 paper-based; 213 computer-based). *Application deadline:* For fall admission, 3/1 priority date for domestic students, 6/1 for international students; for spring admission, 10/1 priority date for domestic students, 10/1 for international students. Applications are processed on a rolling basis. Application fee: $50. Electronic applications accepted. *Financial support:* In 2006–07, 99 students received support, including research assistantships with partial tuition reimbursements available (averaging $5,500 per year), teaching assistantships with partial tuition reimbursements available (averaging $5,500 per year); career-related internships or fieldwork, Federal Work-Study, scholarships/grants, tuition waivers (partial), and unspecified assistantships also available. Support available to part-time students. Financial award application deadline: 4/15; financial award applicants required to submit FAFSA. *Faculty research:* Organizational theory and development, management science, production/operations research, business ethics, labor relations. *Unit head:* Dr. James Michael McDonald, Director, 912-681-5483, Fax: 912-681-0710, E-mail: mmcdonal@georgiasouthern.edu. *Application contact:* 912-681-5384, Fax: 912-681-0740, E-mail: gradadmissions@georgiasouthern.edu.

Georgia Southwestern State University, Graduate Studies, School of Business Administration, Americus, GA 31709-4693. Offers MBA. *Accreditation:* ACBSP. *Entrance requirements:* For master's, GMAT or GRE General Test, minimum GPA of 2.5. Electronic applications accepted.

Georgia State University, J. Mack Robinson College of Business, Department of Managerial Sciences, Atlanta, GA 30303-3083. Offers business analysis (MBA, MS); entrepreneurship (MBA); human resources management (MBA, MS); management (MBA, PhD); operations management (MBA, MS, PhD); organization change (MS). Part-time and evening/weekend programs available. *Faculty:* 34 full-time (14 women). *Students:* 53 full-time (18 women), 177 part-time (61 women); includes 37 minority (21 African Americans, 11 Asian Americans or Pacific Islanders, 5 Hispanic Americans), 19 international. Average age 32. 68 applicants, 35% accepted, 20 enrolled. In 2006, 98 master's, 4 doctorates awarded. *Degree requirements:* For doctorate, thesis/dissertation. *Entrance requirements:* For master's and doctorate, GMAT. Additional exam requirements/recommendations for international students: Required—TOEFL (minimum score 610 paper-based; 255 computer-based; 101 iBT). *Application deadline:* For fall admission, 5/1 for domestic students, 2/1 for international students; for spring admission, 10/15 for domestic students, 5/1 for international students. Applications are processed on a rolling basis. Application fee: $50. Electronic applications accepted. *Unit head:* Dr. Todd J. Maurer, Chair, 404-651-3400, E-mail: tmaurer@gsu.edu.

Georgia State University, J. Mack Robinson College of Business, Program in General Business Administration, Atlanta, GA 30303-3083. Offers accounting/information systems (MBA); enterprise risk management (MBA); general business (MBA); general business administration (EMBA, PMBA); information systems consulting (MBA); information systems risk management (MBA); international business and information technology (MBA); international entrepreneurship (MBA); MBA/JD. *Accreditation:* AACSB. Part-time and evening/weekend programs available. *Faculty:* 1 (woman) full-time. *Students:* 183 full-time (83 women), 212 part-time (57 women); includes 118 minority (73 African Americans, 36 Asian Americans or Pacific Islanders, 9 Hispanic Americans), 42 international. 294 applicants, 74% accepted, 182 enrolled. In 2006, 98 degrees awarded. *Entrance requirements:* For master's, GMAT. Additional exam requirements/recommendations for international students: Required—TOEFL (minimum score 610 paper-based; 255 computer-based; 101 iBT). *Application deadline:* For fall admission, 5/1 for domestic students, 2/1 for international students; for spring admission, 10/15 for domestic students, 5/1 for international students. Applications are processed on a rolling basis. Application fee: $50. Electronic applications accepted. *Financial support:* Research assistantships, tuition waivers (partial) available. Support available to part-time students. Financial award application deadline: 5/1; financial award applicants required to submit FAFSA. *Application contact:* Graduate Student and Alumni Services, 404-463-4568, Fax: 404-651-2721, E-mail: mastersadmissions@gsu.edu.

Goddard College, Graduate Program, Program in Socially Responsible Business and Sustainable Communities, Plainfield, VT 05667-9432. Offers MA. *Students:* 11 full-time. 9 applicants, 100% accepted. *Degree requirements:* For master's, thesis, registration. *Entrance requirements:* For master's, 3 letters of recommendation, preliminary study plan and bib.. Application fee: $40. *Expenses:* Tuition: Full-time $12,506; part-time $10,392 per year. Required fees: $998; $499 per term. *Financial support:* In 2006–07, 11 students received support. *Unit head:* Ann Driscoll, Director, 802-454-8311, E-mail: ann.driscoll@goddard.edu. *Application contact:* Lara Duston, Admissions Counselor, 800-906-8312 Ext. 205, Fax: 802-454-1029, E-mail: lara.duston@goddard.edu.

Golden Gate University, Ageno School of Business, San Francisco, CA 94105-2968. Offers accounting (M Ac, MBA); business administration (EMBA, MBA, DBA); finance (MBA, MS, Certificate); financial planning (MS, Certificate); human resource management (MBA, MS); human resources management (Certificate); information technology (MBA); information technology management (MS, Certificate); integrated marketing and communications (MS, Certificate); international business (MBA); management (MBA); marketing (MBA, MS, Certificate); operations management (Certificate); psychology (MA, Certificate); public relations (MS, Certificate); JD/MBA. Part-time and evening/weekend programs available. *Students:* 355 full-time (192 women), 977 part-time (465 women); includes 447 minority (85 African Americans, 5 American Indian/Alaska Native, 274 Asian Americans or Pacific Islanders, 83 Hispanic Americans), 226 international. Average age 34. 548 applicants, 74% accepted, 201 enrolled. In 2006, 545 master's, 21 doctorates awarded. *Degree requirements:* For doctorate, thesis/dissertation. *Entrance requirements:* For master's, GMAT (MBA), minimum GPA of 2.5 (MS). Additional exam requirements/recommendations for international students: Required—TOEFL. *Application deadline:* Applications are processed on a rolling basis. Application fee: $55 ($90 for international students). *Financial support:* Career-related internships or fieldwork, Federal Work-Study, and institutionally sponsored loans available. Support available to part-time students. Financial award applicants required to submit FAFSA. *Unit head:* Terry Connelly, Dean, 415-442-6519, Fax: 415-442-5369. *Application contact:* Enrollment Services, 415-442-7800, Fax: 415-442-7807, E-mail: info@ggu.edu.

Goldey-Beacom College, Graduate Program, Wilmington, DE 19808-1999. Offers business administration (MBA); financial management (MBA); human resource management (MBA); information technology (MBA); management (MM); marketing management (MBA). *Accreditation:* ACBSP. Part-time and evening/weekend programs available. *Entrance requirements:* For master's, GMAT, minimum GPA of 3.0. Additional exam requirements/recommendations for international students: Required—TOEFL (minimum score 525 paper-based; 195 computer-based). Electronic applications accepted.

Gonzaga University, School of Business Administration, Spokane, WA 99258. Offers M Acc, MBA, JD/M Acc, JD/MBA. *Accreditation:* AACSB. Part-time and evening/weekend programs available. *Faculty:* 24 full-time (1 woman). *Students:* 67 full-time (25 women), 134 part-time (51 women); includes 25 minority (1 African American, 14 American Indian/Alaska Native, 5 Asian Americans or Pacific Islanders, 5 Hispanic Americans), 10 international. Average age 31. In 2006, 88 degrees awarded. *Entrance requirements:* For master's, GMAT. Additional exam requirements/recommendations for international students: Required—TOEFL. *Application deadline:* For fall admission, 7/20 priority date for domestic students; for spring admission, 11/1 for domestic students. Applications are processed on a rolling basis. Application fee: $40. *Expenses:* Tuition: Full-time $10,620; part-time $590 per credit. *Financial support:* Teaching assistantships, Federal Work-Study available. Support available to part-time students. Financial award application deadline: 3/1. *Unit head:* Dr. Clarence H. Barnes, Dean, 509-328-4220 Ext. 5502.

Governors State University, College of Business and Public Administration, Program in Business Administration, University Park, IL 60466-0975. Offers MBA. *Accreditation:* ACBSP. Evening/weekend programs available. *Students:* 25 full-time, 102 part-time. Average age 34. *Degree requirements:* For master's, competency exams in elementary and intermediate algebra, thesis optional. *Entrance requirements:* For master's, GMAT. *Application deadline:* For fall admission, 7/15 priority date for domestic students; for spring admission, 11/10 for domestic students. Applications are processed on a rolling basis. Application fee: $25. *Expenses:* Tuition, state resident: full-time $4,104; part-time $171 per hour. Tuition, nonresident: part-time $513 per hour. *Financial support:* Research assistantships, Federal Work-Study, institutionally sponsored loans, scholarships/grants, and tuition waivers (full and partial) available. Support available to part-time students. Financial award application deadline: 5/1. *Unit head:* Dr. Akkanad Isaac, Head, 708-534-4951, E-mail: a-isaac@goust.edu.

Graduate School and University Center of the City University of New York, Graduate Studies, Program in Business, New York, NY 10016-4039. Offers accounting (PhD); behavioral science (PhD); finance (PhD); management planning systems (PhD). *Faculty:* 66 full-time (5 women). *Students:* 55 full-time (27 women); includes 7 minority (2 African Americans, 1 American Indian/Alaska Native, 2 Asian Americans or Pacific Islanders, 2 Hispanic Americans), 26 international. Average age 33. 74 applicants, 32% accepted, 11 enrolled. In 2006, 9 degrees awarded. *Degree requirements:* For doctorate, thesis/dissertation. *Entrance requirements:* For doctorate, GMAT, writing sample (15 pages). Additional exam requirements/recommendations for international students: Required—TOEFL. *Application deadline:* For fall admission, 1/15 for domestic students. Application fee: $125. Electronic applications accepted. *Financial support:* In 2006–07, 40 fellowships, 5 teaching assistantships were awarded; research assistantships, career-related internships or fieldwork, Federal Work-Study, institutionally sponsored loans, and tuition waivers (full and partial) also available. Financial award application deadline: 2/1; financial award applicants required to submit FAFSA. *Unit head:* Dr. Joseph Weintrop, Executive Officer, 646-312-3092, Fax: 646-312-3031.

Grand Canyon University, College of Business, Phoenix, AZ 85017-1097. Offers MBA. *Accreditation:* ACBSP. Part-time and evening/weekend programs available. *Entrance requirements:* For master's, GMAT. Additional exam requirements/recommendations for international students: Required—TOEFL.

Grand Valley State University, Seidman College of Business, Program in Business Administration, Allendale, MI 49401-9403. Offers MBA, MSN/MBA. *Accreditation:* AACSB. Part-time and evening/weekend programs available. *Faculty:* 18 full-time (3 women), 10 part-time/adjunct (1 woman). *Students:* 31 full-time (11 women), 238 part-time (68 women); includes 12 minority (5 African Americans, 1 American Indian/Alaska Native, 5 Asian Americans or Pacific Islanders, 1 Hispanic American), 14 international. Average age 30. 79 applicants, 80% accepted, 49 enrolled. In 2006, 65 degrees awarded. *Entrance requirements:* For master's, GMAT. Additional exam requirements/recommendations for international students: Required—TOEFL. *Application deadline:* For fall admission, 8/1 priority date for domestic students, 5/1 priority date for international students; for winter admission, 12/1 priority date for domestic students, 11/1 priority date for international students; for spring admission, 4/1 priority date for domestic students, 3/1 priority date for international students. Applications are processed on a rolling basis. Application fee: $30. Electronic applications accepted. *Expenses:* Tuition, state resident: full-time $5,850; part-time $325 per credit. Tuition, nonresident: full-time $10,800; part-time $600 per credit. Tuition and fees vary according to course load. *Financial support:* In 2006–07, 70 students received support, including 13 research assistantships with full tuition reimbursements available (averaging $8,000 per year); institutionally sponsored loans and unspecified assistantships also available. Support available to part-time students. Financial award application deadline: 2/15. *Faculty research:* E-commerce, continuous improvement, currency futures, manufacturing flexibility. *Unit head:* Dr. Jaideep Motwani, Director, 616-331-7490, Fax: 616-331-7389, E-mail: bajemac@gvsu.edu. *Application contact:* Claudia J. Bajema, Director, Graduate Business Programs, 616-331-7387, Fax: 616-331-7389, E-mail: bajemac@gvsu.edu.

Grantham University, Mark Skousen School of Business, Kansas City, MO 64153. Offers information management (MBA); project management (MBA). Part-time and evening/weekend programs available. Postbaccalaureate distance learning degree programs offered (no on-campus study). *Faculty:* 30. *Students:* 372 full-time. Average age 36. *Degree requirements:* For master's, thesis, registration. *Entrance requirements:* Additional exam requirements/recommendations for international students: Required—TOEFL (minimum score 500 paper-based). *Application deadline:* Applications are processed on a rolling basis. Application fee: $0. Electronic applications accepted. *Financial support:* Institutionally sponsored loans and scholarships/grants available. *Application contact:* DeAnn Wandler, Director of Admissions, 800-955-2527, Fax: 816-595-5757, E-mail: admissions@grantham.edu.

Green Mountain College, Program in Business Administration, Poultney, VT 05764-1199. Offers MBA. Distance learning only. Postbaccalaureate distance learning degree programs offered (no on-campus study). *Faculty:* 8 full-time (1 woman), 3 part-time/adjunct (1 woman). *Students:* 13 full-time (10 women). Average age 35. 20 applicants, 70% accepted, 13 enrolled. *Entrance requirements:* For master's, GMAT or Quantitative Skills Assessment, 3 recommendations. *Application deadline:* Applications are processed on a rolling basis. Application fee: $30. Electronic applications accepted. *Expenses:* Tuition: Part-time $550 per credit. Tuition and fees vary according to program. *Financial support:* In 2006–07, 3 students received support. *Faculty research:* Migrant farm workers and world systems theory ecosystem assessments. *Unit head:* Dr. William H. Prado, Director of MBA, 802-287-8241, E-mail: pradow@greenmtn.edu. *Application contact:* Susan Whiting, Administrative Assistant, 802-287-8319, E-mail: mba@greenmtn.edu.

Hamline University, Graduate School of Management, St. Paul, MN 55104-1284. Offers management (MAM); nonprofit management (MANM); public administration (MAPA); JD/MAM; JD/MANM; JD/MAPA. Part-time and evening/weekend programs available. *Faculty:* 10 full-time (5 women), 29 part-time/adjunct (13 women). *Students:* 184 full-time (101 women), 145 part-time (87 women); includes 29 minority (14 African Americans, 2 American Indian/Alaska Native, 9 Asian Americans or Pacific Islanders, 4 Hispanic Americans), 65 international. Average age 33. 145 applicants, 72% accepted, 86 enrolled. In 2006, 92 master's awarded. *Degree requirements:* For master's, thesis/dissertation. *Entrance requirements:* For master's, personal statement, c.v., official transcripts, letters of recommendation, writing sample. Additional exam requirements/recommendations for international students: Required—TOEFL (minimum score 550 paper-based; 213 computer-based). *Application deadline:* For fall admission, 3/30 priority date for domestic students. Applications are processed on a rolling basis. Application fee: $30. Electronic applications accepted. *Expenses:* Tuition: Full-time $5,104; part-time $319 per credit. One-time fee: $175. Tuition and fees vary according to course load, degree level and program. *Financial support:* Federal Work-Study available. Financial award applicants required to submit FAFSA. *Unit head:* Julian Schuster, Dean, 651-523-2335, Fax: 651-523-3098, E-mail: jschuster01@hamline.edu. *Application contact:* Rae A. Lenway, Director Graduate Recruitment and Admission, 651-523-2592, Fax: 458, E-mail: rlenway01@hamline.edu.

Hampton University, Graduate College, Program in Business, Hampton, VA 23668. Offers MBA. Part-time and evening/weekend programs available. *Entrance requirements:* For master's, GRE General Test.

Harding University, College of Business Administration, Searcy, AR 72149-0001. Offers MBA. *Accreditation:* ACBSP. Part-time and evening/weekend programs available. Postbaccalaureate distance learning degree programs offered (no on-campus study). *Faculty:* 27 part-time/adjunct (3 women). *Students:* 88 full-time (50 women), 72 part-time (28 women); includes 14 minority (10 African Americans, 2 American Indian/Alaska Native, 2 Hispanic Americans), 44 international. Average age 28. 70 applicants, 100% accepted, 55 enrolled. In 2006, 39 degrees awarded. *Degree requirements:* For master's, registration. *Entrance requirements:* For master's, minimum GPA of 3.0, 2 letters of recommendation, resumé. Additional exam requirements/recommendations for international students: Required—TOEFL (minimum score 550 paper-based; 213 computer-based; 80 iBT). *Application deadline:* For fall admission, 8/1 priority date for domestic and international students; for spring admission, 12/1 priority date for domestic and international students. Application fee: $35. Electronic applications accepted. *Expenses:* Tuition: Part-time $455 per semester hour. Required fees: $20 per semester hour. Tuition and fees vary according to course load. *Financial support:* Unspecified assistantships available. Financial award application deadline: 7/30; financial award applicants required to submit FAFSA. *Unit head:* Allen Figley, Director of Graduate Studies, 501-279-5790, Fax: 501-279-4805, E-mail: afigley@harding.edu. *Application contact:* Suzanne Guymon, Marketing Manager, 501-279-5726, Fax: 501-279-4805, E-mail: sguymon1@harding.edu.

Hardin-Simmons University, The Acton MBA in Entrepreneurship, Austin, TX 78701. Offers MBA. *Entrance requirements:* For master's, GMAT, letters of recommendation. Additional exam requirements/recommendations for international students: Required—TOEFL. *Application deadline:* For fall admission, 3/15 priority date for domestic students. Application fee: $50. *Expenses:* Tuition: Full-time $9,090; part-time $505 per hour. Required fees: $490; $66 per semester. One-time fee: $50. Tuition and fees vary according to course load and degree level. *Application contact:* Jessica Blanchard, Director of Recruiting, 512-703-1231, E-mail: jblanchard@actonmba.org.

Hardin-Simmons University, Graduate School, Kelley College of Business, Abilene, TX 79698-0001. Offers MBA. *Accreditation:* ACBSP. Part-time and evening/weekend programs available. *Faculty:* 7 full-time (1 woman), 1 part-time/adjunct (0 women). *Students:* 4 full-time (1 woman), 18 part-time (8 women); includes 1 minority (American Indian/Alaska Native). Average age 34. 13 applicants, 85% accepted, 8 enrolled. In 2006, 5 degrees awarded. *Degree requirements:* For master's, thesis or alternative. *Entrance requirements:* For master's, GMAT, minimum GPA of 3.0 in upper level course work, resumé, interview. Additional exam requirements/recommendations for international students: Required—TOEFL (minimum score 600 paper-based; 232 computer-based). *Application deadline:* For fall admission, 8/15 priority date for domestic students; for spring admission, 1/5 priority date for domestic students. Applications are processed on a rolling basis. Application fee: $50 ($100 for international students). *Expenses:* Tuition: Full-time $9,090; part-time $505 per hour. Required fees: $490; $66 per semester. One-time fee: $50. Tuition and fees vary according to course load and degree level. *Financial support:* In 2006–07, 22 students received support; fellowships, scholarships/grants available. Support available to part-time students. Financial award application deadline: 6/30; financial award applicants required to submit FAFSA. *Unit head:* Dr. Charles Walts, Director, 325-670-1293, Fax: 325-670-1523, E-mail: cwalts@hsutx.edu. *Application contact:* Dr. Gary Stanlake, Dean of Graduate Studies, 325-670-1298, Fax: 325-670-1564, E-mail: gradoff@hsutx.edu.

Harvard University, Business School, Doctoral Programs in Management, Boston, MA 02163. Offers business administration (DBA); business economics (PhD); health policy management (PhD); information and technology management (PhD); organizational behavior (PhD). *Degree requirements:* For doctorate, thesis/dissertation, comprehensive exam (for some programs). *Entrance requirements:* For doctorate, GRE General Test or GMAT. Additional exam requirements/recommendations for international students: Required—TOEFL. *Expenses:* Tuition: Full-time $30,275. Full-time tuition and fees vary according to program and student level.

Harvard University, Business School, Master's Program in Business Administration, Boston, MA 02163. Offers MBA, JD/MBA. *Entrance requirements:* For master's, GMAT. Additional exam requirements/recommendations for international students: Required—TOEFL. *Expenses:* Tuition: Full-time $30,275. Full-time tuition and fees vary according to program and student level.

Harvard University, Extension School, Cambridge, MA 02138-3722. Offers applied sciences (CAS); biotechnology (ALM); educational technologies (ALM); educational technology (CET);

English for graduate and professional studies (DGP); environmental management (ALM); CEM); information technology (ALM); journalism (ALM); liberal arts (ALM); management (ALM, CM); mathematics for teaching (ALM); museum studies (ALM); premedical studies (Diploma); publication and communication (CPC). Part-time and evening/weekend programs available. *Faculty:* 236 part-time/adjunct. *Students:* 101 full-time (56 women), 564 part-time (278 women); includes 167 minority (35 African Americans, 1 American Indian/Alaska Native, 84 Asian Americans or Pacific Islanders, 47 Hispanic Americans). Average age 36. In 2006, 112 master's, 184 Diplomas awarded. *Degree requirements:* For master's, thesis. *Entrance requirements:* For master's, 3 completed graduate courses with grade of B or higher. Additional exam requirements/recommendations for international students: Required—TOEFL (minimum score 600 paper-based; 250 computer-based), TWE (minimum score 5). *Application deadline:* Applications are processed on a rolling basis. Application fee: $75. *Expenses:* Contact institution. Full-time tuition and fees vary according to program and student level. *Financial support:* In 2006–07, 268 students received support. Scholarships/grants available. Support available to part-time students. Financial award application deadline: 8/6; financial award applicants required to submit FAFSA. *Unit head:* Michael Shinagel, Dean. *Application contact:* Program Director, 617-495-4024, Fax: 617-495-9176.

Hawai'i Pacific University, College of Business Administration, Honolulu, HI 96813. Offers accounting/CPA (MBA); communication (MBA); e-business (MBA); economics (MBA); finance (MBA); human resource management (MBA); information systems (MBA); international business (MBA); management (MBA); marketing (MBA); organizational change (MBA); travel industry management (MBA). Part-time and evening/weekend programs available. *Faculty:* 40 full-time (16 women), 30 part-time/adjunct (10 women). *Students:* 320 full-time (150 women), 205 part-time (95 women); includes 168 minority (17 African Americans, 7 American Indian/Alaska Native, 137 Asian Americans or Pacific Islanders, 7 Hispanic Americans), 232 international. Average age 31. 279 applicants, 67% accepted, 166 enrolled. In 2006, 172 degrees awarded. *Degree requirements:* For master's, thesis. *Entrance requirements:* For master's, GMAT. Additional exam requirements/recommendations for international students: Recommended—TOEFL (minimum score 550 paper-based; 213 computer-based), TWE (minimum score 5). *Application deadline:* For fall admission, 2/15 priority date for domestic students; for spring admission, 10/15 priority date for domestic students. Applications are processed on a rolling basis. Application fee: $50. Electronic applications accepted. *Expenses:* Tuition: Full-time $10,080; part-time $560 per credit. *Financial support:* In 2006–07, 118 students received support; research assistantships, career-related internships or fieldwork, Federal Work-Study, scholarships/grants, and unspecified assistantships available. Support available to part-time students. Financial award application deadline: 3/1; financial award applicants required to submit FAFSA. *Faculty research:* Statistical control process as used by management, studies in comparative cross-cultural management styles, not-for-profit management. *Unit head:* Dr. Charles Steilen, Dean, 808-544-9301, Fax: 808-544-0283, E-mail: csteilen@hpu.edu. *Application contact:* Danny Lam, Assistant Director of Graduate Admissions, 808-544-1135, Fax: 808-544-0280, E-mail: graduate@hpu.edu.

See Close-Up on page 275.

HEC Montreal, School of Business Administration, Diploma Programs in Administration, Program in Management, Montréal, QC H3T 2A7, Canada. Offers Diploma. All courses are given in French. *Accreditation:* AACSB. Part-time programs available. *Students:* 83 full-time (33 women), 405 part-time (202 women). In 2006, 101 degrees awarded. *Degree requirements:* For Diploma, one foreign language. *Application deadline:* For fall admission, 4/15 for domestic and international students; for winter admission, 10/1 for domestic and international students; for spring admission, 2/15 for domestic and international students. Application fee: $60 Canadian dollars. Electronic applications accepted. Tuition and fees charges are reported in Canadian dollars. *Expenses:* Tuition, nonresident: part-time $56 Canadian dollars per credit. Required fees: $30 Canadian dollars per semester. *Financial support:* Scholarships/grants available. *Application contact:* Francine Blais, Administrative Director, 514-340-6112, Fax: 514-340-6411, E-mail: francine.blais@hec.ca.

HEC Montreal, School of Business Administration, Diploma Programs in Administration, Program in Management and Sustainable Development, Montréal, QC H3T 2A7, Canada. Offers Diploma. Part-time programs available. *Students:* 9 full-time (4 women), 20 part-time (9 women). *Application deadline:* For fall admission, 5/15 for domestic students. Application fee: $60. Tuition and fees charges are reported in Canadian dollars. *Expenses:* Tuition, nonresident: part-time $56 Canadian dollars per credit. Required fees: $30 Canadian dollars per semester. *Application contact:* Francine Blais, Administrative Director, 514-340-6112, Fax: 514-340-6411, E-mail: francine.blais@hec.ca.

HEC Montreal, School of Business Administration, Doctoral Program in Administration, Montréal, QC H3T 2A7, Canada. Offers PhD. *Accreditation:* AACSB. *Students:* 165 full-time (64 women). 68 applicants, 43% accepted, 19 enrolled. In 2006, 9 degrees awarded. *Degree requirements:* For doctorate, one foreign language, thesis/dissertation. *Entrance requirements:* For doctorate, GMAT, GRE, master's degree in administration or related field. *Application deadline:* For fall admission, 2/1 for domestic and international students; for winter admission, 9/15 for domestic and international students. Application fee: $60. Electronic applications accepted. Tuition and fees charges are reported in Canadian dollars. *Expenses:* Tuition, nonresident: part-time $56 Canadian dollars per credit. Required fees: $30 Canadian dollars per semester. *Unit head:* Dr. Francois Bellavance, Director, 514-340-6485, Fax: 514-340-5690, E-mail: francois.bellavance@hec.ca. *Application contact:* Francine Blais, Administrative Director, 514-340-6112, Fax: 514-340-6411, E-mail: francine.blais@hec.ca.

HEC Montreal, School of Business Administration, Master of Science Programs in Administration, Montréal, QC H3T 2A7, Canada. Offers applied economics (M Sc); applied financial economics (M Sc); business intelligence (M Sc); controllership (M Sc); finance (M Sc); financial engineering (M Sc); human resources management (M Sc); information systems (M Sc); international business (M Sc); international management (M Sc); logistics (M Sc); management (M Sc); marketing (M Sc); production and operations management (M Sc). *Accreditation:* AACSB. Part-time programs available. *Students:* 622 full-time (308 women), 11 part-time (7 women). 523 applicants, 41% accepted, 127 enrolled. In 2006, 225 degrees awarded. *Degree requirements:* For master's, one foreign language, thesis. *Entrance requirements:* For master's, bachelor's degree in business administration or equivalent. Additional exam requirements/recommendations for international students: Required—GMAT or TAGE-MAGE and TFI. *Application deadline:* For fall admission, 3/15 for domestic and international students; for winter admission, 9/15 for domestic and international students. Application fee: $60 Canadian dollars. Electronic applications accepted. Tuition and fees charges are reported in Canadian dollars. *Expenses:* Tuition, nonresident: part-time $56 Canadian dollars per credit. Required fees: $30 Canadian dollars per semester. *Financial support:* Research assistantships, teaching assistantships, scholarships/grants available. *Unit head:* Dr. Francois Bellavance, Director, 514-340-6485, Fax: 514-340-5690, E-mail: francois.bellavance@hec.ca. *Application contact:* Francine Blais, Administrative Director, 514-340-6112, Fax: 514-340-6411, E-mail: francine.blais@hec.ca.

HEC Montreal, School of Business Administration, Master's Program in Business Administration and Management, Montréal, QC H3T 2A7, Canada. Offers MBA. Courses are given in French or English. *Accreditation:* AACSB. Part-time programs available. *Students:* 190 full-time (65 women), 253 part-time (77 women). 525 applicants, 41% accepted, 210 enrolled. In 2006, 203 degrees awarded. *Degree requirements:* For master's, one foreign language. *Entrance requirements:* For master's, GMAT, 3 years of related work experience. Additional exam requirements/recommendations for international students: Required—TOEFL (minimum score 550 paper-based; 213 computer-based). *Application deadline:* For fall admission, 3/15 for domestic and international students; for winter admission, 10/1 for domestic students. Application fee: $60 Canadian dollars. Electronic applications accepted. Tuition and fees charges are reported in Canadian dollars. *Expenses:* Tuition, nonresident: part-time $56 Canadian dollars per credit. Required fees: $30 Canadian dollars per semester. *Financial*

Business Administration and Management—General

HEC Montreal (continued)
support: Scholarships/grants available. *Unit head:* Dr. Jean Talbot, Director, 514-340-6293, Fax: 514-340-6880, E-mail: jean.talbot@hec.ca. *Application contact:* Diane St-Pierre, Administrative Director, 514-340-6136, Fax: 514-340-5640, E-mail: diane.st-pierre@hec.ca.

Heidelberg College, Program in Business, Tiffin, OH 44883-2462. Offers MBA. Part-time and evening/weekend programs available. *Faculty:* 1 full-time (0 women), 2 part-time/adjunct (1 woman). *Students:* 26 full-time (12 women), 36 part-time (24 women); includes 5 minority (4 African Americans, 1 Asian American or Pacific Islander), 1 international. 23 applicants, 100% accepted, 17 enrolled. In 2006, 5 degrees awarded. *Degree requirements:* For master's, thesis or alternative, internship, practicum. *Entrance requirements:* For master's, previous undergraduate course work in business, minimum GPA of 2.7. Additional exam requirements/recommendations for international students: Required—TOEFL. *Application deadline:* Applications are processed on a rolling basis. Application fee: $25. *Expenses: Contact institution.* Tuition and fees vary according to program. *Financial support:* In 2006–07, 17 students received support. Federal Work-Study available. Support available to part-time students. Financial award applicants required to submit FAFSA. *Unit head:* Dr. Henry G. Rennie, Director of Graduate Studies in Business, 419-448-2221, Fax: 419-448-2072, E-mail: hrennie@nike.heidelberg.edu. *Application contact:* Dr. G. Michael Pratt, Graduate Studies Office, 419-448-2288, Fax: 419-448-2072, E-mail: mpratt@heidelberg.edu.

Henderson State University, Graduate Studies, School of Business Administration, Arkadelphia, AR 71999-0001. Offers MBA. *Accreditation:* AACSB. Part-time programs available. *Faculty:* 10 full-time (1 woman). *Students:* 28 full-time (11 women), 13 part-time (10 women); includes 11 minority (10 African Americans, 1 American Indian/Alaska Native), 4 international. Average age 27. In 2006, 20 degrees awarded. *Entrance requirements:* For master's, GMAT, minimum AACSB index of 1000, minimum GPA of 2.5. *Application deadline:* For fall admission, 5/1 priority date for domestic students, 5/1 for international students; for winter admission, 10/1 for international students; for spring admission, 12/1 priority date for domestic students, 4/1 for international students. Applications are processed on a rolling basis. Application fee: $0 ($30 for international students). *Expenses:* Tuition, state resident: full-time $3,294; part-time $183 per credit hour. Tuition, nonresident: full-time $6,588; part-time $366 per credit hour. Required fees: $176 per term. *Financial support:* In 2006–07, 7 teaching assistantships with tuition reimbursements (averaging $4,000 per year) were awarded; research assistantships, Federal Work-Study and institutionally sponsored loans also available. Support available to part-time students. Financial award application deadline: 7/31. *Unit head:* Dr. Paul Huo, Dean, 870-230-5310, Fax: 870-230-5286, E-mail: huoy@hsu.edu. *Application contact:* Dr. Marck L. Beggs, Graduate Dean, 870-230-5126, Fax: 870-230-5479, E-mail: beggsm@hsu.edu.

High Point University, Norcross Graduate School, High Point, NC 27262-3598. Offers business administration (MBA); educational leadership (M Ed); elementary education (M Ed); history (MA); nonprofit organizations (MPA); special education (M Ed); sport studies (MS). *Accreditation:* ACBSP; NCATE. Part-time and evening/weekend programs available. *Faculty:* 31 full-time (11 women), 1 part-time/adjunct (0 women). *Students:* 49 full-time (29 women), 202 part-time (130 women); includes 72 minority (66 African Americans, 1 American Indian/Alaska Native, 2 Asian Americans or Pacific Islanders, 3 Hispanic Americans), 11 international. Average age 33. 171 applicants, 71% accepted, 94 enrolled. In 2006, 95 degrees awarded. *Degree requirements:* For master's, thesis (for some programs), comprehensive exam (for some programs), registration. *Entrance requirements:* For master's, GMAT (MBA), GRE, MAT, minimum GPA of 3.0. Additional exam requirements/recommendations for international students: Required—TOEFL (minimum score 550 paper-based). *Application deadline:* For fall admission, 4/15 priority date for domestic and international students; for spring admission, 10/15 priority date for domestic and international students. Applications are processed on a rolling basis. Application fee: $50. Electronic applications accepted. *Expenses:* Tuition: Full-time $9,270; part-time $1,545 per course. *Financial support:* In 2006–07, 190 students received support. Federal Work-Study, scholarships/grants, and unspecified assistantships available. Support available to part-time students. Financial award application deadline: 3/1; financial award applicants required to submit FAFSA. *Application contact:* Dr. Alberta Haynes Herron, Dean of Norcross Graduate School, 336-841-9198, Fax: 336-888-6378, E-mail: aherron@highpoint.edu.

Hodges University, Graduate Programs, Naples, FL 34119. Offers business administration (MBA); computer information technology (MS); criminal justice (MCJ); education (MPS); information systems management (MIS); interdisciplinary (MPS); law (MPS); management (MSM); professional studies (MPS); psychology (MPS); public administration (MPA). Part-time and evening/weekend programs available. Postbaccalaureate distance learning degree programs offered (no on-campus study). *Faculty:* 17 full-time (4 women). *Students:* 35 full-time (22 women), 156 part-time (100 women); includes 52 minority (24 African Americans, 1 American Indian/Alaska Native, 4 Asian Americans or Pacific Islanders, 23 Hispanic Americans). Average age 32. In 2006, 101 degrees awarded. *Median time to degree:* Master's–1.5 years full-time, 2.5 years part-time. *Degree requirements:* For master's, comprehensive exam (for some programs), registration. *Entrance requirements:* For master's, in-house entrance exam. Application fee: $50. Electronic applications accepted. *Financial support:* Federal Work-Study and scholarships/grants available. Financial award applicants required to submit FAFSA. *Unit head:* Terry McMahan, President, 239-513-1122, Fax: 239-598-6253, E-mail: tmcmahan@internationalcollege.edu. *Application contact:* Rita Lampus, Vice President of Student Enrollment Management, 239-513-1122, Fax: 239-598-6253, E-mail: rlampus@internationalcollege.edu.

Hofstra University, Frank G. Zarb School of Business, Hempstead, NY 11549. Offers EMBA, MBA, MS, Advanced Certificate. *Accreditation:* AACSB. Part-time and evening/weekend programs available. *Faculty:* 42 full-time (8 women), 8 part-time/adjunct (1 woman). *Students:* 194 full-time (72 women), 451 part-time (198 women); includes 126 minority (43 African Americans, 58 Asian Americans or Pacific Islanders, 25 Hispanic Americans), 54 international. Average age 31. 429 applicants, 85% accepted, 217 enrolled. In 2006, 176 master's, 3 other advanced degrees awarded. *Degree requirements:* For master's, capstone. *Entrance requirements:* For master's, GMAT, 2 letters of recommendation, resumé, minimum 7 years of management experience (EMBA), essay, interview. Additional exam requirements/recommendations for international students: Required—TOEFL (minimum score 550 paper-based; 213 computer-based). *Application deadline:* Applications are processed on a rolling basis. Application fee: $60. Electronic applications accepted. *Expenses:* Tuition: Full-time $13,320; part-time $740 per credit. Required fees: $930; $155 per term. *Financial support:* In 2006–07, 110 students received support, including 79 fellowships with tuition reimbursements available (averaging $6,259 per year), 11 research assistantships with full and partial tuition reimbursements available (averaging $4,866 per year); career-related internships or fieldwork, Federal Work-Study, scholarships/grants, health care benefits, tuition waivers (full and partial), and unspecified assistantships also available. Support available to part-time students. Financial award applicants required to submit FAFSA. *Faculty research:* Impact of Sarbanes-Oxley, enterprise planning- SAP, business strategy, corporate finance/derivative markets, business/personal ethics, cross cultural consumer behavior. Total annual research expenditures:$24,000. *Unit head:* Salvatore F. Sodano, Dean, 516-463-5685, Fax: 516-463-5268, E-mail: bizsfs@hofstra.edu. *Application contact:* Carol Drummer, Dean of Graduate Admissions, 516-463-4876, Fax: 516-463-4664, E-mail: gradstudent@hofstra.edu.

See Close-Up on page 277.

Holy Family University, Graduate School, School of Business, Philadelphia, PA 19114-2094. Offers human resources management (MS); information systems management (MS). Part-time and evening/weekend programs available. *Degree requirements:* For master's, thesis optional. *Entrance requirements:* For master's, GMAT, GRE, or MAT, minimum GPA of 3.0.

Holy Names University, Graduate Division, Department of Business, Oakland, CA 94619-1699. Offers management (MBA). Part-time and evening/weekend programs available. *Faculty:* 2 full-time (1 woman), 3 part-time/adjunct (0 women). *Students:* 34 full-time (23 women), 17 part-time (13 women); includes 35 minority (28 African Americans, 7 Asian Americans or Pacific Islanders), 9 international. Average age 34. 34 applicants, 74% accepted, 21 enrolled. In 2006, 2 degrees awarded. *Entrance requirements:* For master's, minimum undergraduate GPA of 2.6 overall, 3.0 in major. Additional exam requirements/recommendations for international students: Required—TOEFL (minimum score 550 paper-based). *Application deadline:* For fall admission, 8/1 priority date for domestic students; for spring admission, 12/1 priority date for domestic students. Applications are processed on a rolling basis. Application fee: $50. *Expenses:* Tuition: Full-time $10,800; part-time $600 per unit. Required fees: $240; $120 per term. *Financial support:* In 2006–07, 22 students received support. Available to part-time students. Application deadline: 3/2; *Faculty research:* Business ethics, sustainable economics, accounting models, cross cultural management, diversity in organizations. *Unit head:* Dr. Marcia Frideger, Program Director, 510-436-1205, E-mail: frideger@hnu.edu. *Application contact:* 800-430-1351, Fax: 510-436-1325, E-mail: admissions@hnu.edu.

Hood College, Graduate School, Department of Economics and Management, Frederick, MD 21701-8575. Offers administration and management (MBA). Part-time and evening/weekend programs available. *Faculty:* 4 full-time (1 woman), 9 part-time/adjunct (1 woman). *Students:* 25 full-time (11 women), 147 part-time (91 women); includes 19 minority (10 African Americans, 6 Asian Americans or Pacific Islanders, 3 Hispanic Americans), 18 international. Average age 32. 69 applicants, 97% accepted, 37 enrolled. In 2006, 32 degrees awarded. *Entrance requirements:* For master's, minimum GPA of 2.5, resumé, letters of recommendation. *Application deadline:* Applications are processed on a rolling basis. *Expenses:* Tuition: Part-time $350 per credit. Required fees: $20 per semester. *Financial support:* Applicants required to submit FAFSA. *Faculty research:* Corporate strategy and sustainable competitive advantages, business ethics, entrepreneurship, investments management, economic development. *Unit head:* Dr. Anita Jose, Program Director, 301-696-3691, Fax: 301-696-3597, E-mail: ajose@hood.edu. *Application contact:* Dr. Kathleen C. Bands, Associate Dean of Graduate School, 301-696-3811, Fax: 301-696-3597, E-mail: gofurther@hood.edu.

Houston Baptist University, College of Business and Economics, Program in Business Administration, Houston, TX 77074-3298. Offers MBA, MSM. Part-time and evening/weekend programs available. *Degree requirements:* For master's, registration. *Entrance requirements:* For master's, GMAT, minimum GPA of 2.5. Additional exam requirements/recommendations for international students: Required—TOEFL (minimum score 550 paper-based; 213 computer-based). Expenses: Contact institution.

Howard University, School of Business, Graduate Programs in Business, Washington, DC 20059-0002. Offers accounting (MBA); entrepreneurship (MBA); finance (MBA); information systems (MBA); international business (MBA); marketing (MBA); supply chain management (MBA); JD/MBA. *Accreditation:* AACSB. Part-time and evening/weekend programs available. Postbaccalaureate distance learning degree programs offered (no on-campus study). *Entrance requirements:* For master's, GMAT, minimum 1 year post undergraduate work experience, resumé, 3 letters of recommendation, advanced college algebra. Additional exam requirements/recommendations for international students: Required—TOEFL. *Faculty research:* Marketing research in multi-ethnic populations, U.S. trade policies and international relations, risk management (finance).

Hult International Business School, Graduate Program, Cambridge, MA 02141. Offers MBA. *Faculty:* 4 full-time (2 women), 28 part-time/adjunct (4 women). *Students:* 129 full-time (37 women); includes 51 minority (3 African Americans, 30 Asian Americans or Pacific Islanders, 18 Hispanic Americans), 59 international. Average age 30. 532 applicants, 46% accepted, 129 enrolled. In 2006, 107 degrees awarded. *Entrance requirements:* For master's, GMAT, 3 years of management experience. Additional exam requirements/recommendations for international students: Required—TOEFL (minimum score 240 computer-based). *Application deadline:* For fall admission, 6/1 priority date for domestic and international students; for winter admission, 11/1 priority date for domestic and international students; for spring admission, 12/1 priority date for domestic and international students. Applications are processed on a rolling basis. Application fee: $150. Electronic applications accepted. *Expenses:* Tuition: Full-time $39,250. *Financial support:* In 2006–07, 125 students received support, including 8 fellowships with tuition reimbursements available (averaging $4,000 per year); institutionally sponsored loans, scholarships/grants, and tuition waivers (partial) also available. Financial award application deadline: 6/1; financial award applicants required to submit FAFSA. *Faculty research:* Management for international development. *Application contact:* Ashley M. Ludovicy, Recruiting Coordinator, 617-746-1990, Fax: 617-746-1991, E-mail: admissions@hult.edu.

Humboldt State University, Graduate Studies, College of Professional Studies, School of Business, Arcata, CA 95521-8299. Offers MBA. Part-time and evening/weekend programs available. *Students:* 23 full-time (18 women), 2 part-time (both women); includes 3 minority (1 African American, 1 Asian American or Pacific Islander, 1 Hispanic American), 4 international. Average age 31. 33 applicants, 73% accepted, 17 enrolled. In 2006, 14 degrees awarded. *Degree requirements:* For master's, thesis or alternative. *Entrance requirements:* For master's, GMAT, minimum GPA of 2.5. Additional exam requirements/recommendations for international students: Required—TOEFL (minimum score 500 paper-based; 173 computer-based). *Application deadline:* For fall admission, 6/30 for domestic and international students; for spring admission, 12/15 for domestic and international students. Applications are processed on a rolling basis. Application fee: $55. *Financial support:* Fellowships, Federal Work-Study available. Support available to part-time students. Financial award application deadline: 3/1; financial award applicants required to submit FAFSA. *Faculty research:* International business development, small town entrepreneurship, international trade: Pacific Rim. *Unit head:* Dr. Saeed Mortazavi, Chair, 707-826-3846, Fax: 707-826-6666, E-mail: sm5@humboldt.edu. *Application contact:* Dr. Michael Thomas, MBA Graduate Coordinator, 707-826-6022, Fax: 707-826-6666, E-mail: mft5@humboldt.edu.

Huron University USA in London, Graduate Programs, Program in Business Administration, London, United Kingdom. Offers entrepreneurship (MBA); international business (MBA); international finance (MBA); marketing (MBA). Part-time programs available. *Degree requirements:* For master's, thesis, internship, comprehensive exam. *Entrance requirements:* Additional exam requirements/recommendations for international students: Required—TOEFL (minimum score 580 paper-based; 237 computer-based), TWE (minimum score 5). Electronic applications accepted.

Husson College, Graduate Studies Division, Program in Business, Bangor, ME 04401-2999. Offers MSB. Part-time and evening/weekend programs available. *Degree requirements:* For master's, thesis optional. *Entrance requirements:* For master's, GMAT, minimum GPA of 2.5.

Idaho State University, Office of Graduate Studies, College of Business, Pocatello, ID 83209. Offers business administration (MBA, Postbaccalaureate Certificate); computer information systems (MS, Postbaccalaureate Certificate). *Accreditation:* AACSB. Part-time and evening/weekend programs available. Postbaccalaureate distance learning degree programs offered (minimal on-campus study). *Faculty:* 26 full-time (4 women). *Students:* 55 full-time (11 women), 73 part-time (16 women); includes 3 minority (1 African American, 1 Asian American or Pacific Islander, 1 Hispanic American), 14 international. Average age 31. In 2006, 45 degrees awarded. *Degree requirements:* For master's, thesis (for some programs), comprehensive exam, registration; for Postbaccalaureate Certificate, thesis (for some programs), 6 hours of clerkship, comprehensive exam, registration. *Entrance requirements:* For master's, GMAT, GRE General Test, minimum GPA of 3.0, resumé outlining work experience, 2 letters of reference; for Postbaccalaureate Certificate, GMAT, GRE General Test, minimum upper level GPA of 3.0. Additional exam requirements/recommendations for international students: Required—TOEFL (minimum score 550 paper-based; 213 computer-based; 80 iBT). *Application deadline:* For fall admission, 7/1 for domestic students, 6/1 for international students; for spring admission, 12/1 for domestic students, 11/1 for international students. Applications are processed on a rolling basis. Application fee: $55. *Expenses:* Tuition, state resident: part-time $251 per credit. Tuition, nonresident: part-time $366 per credit. Tuition and fees vary according to degree level, program and reciprocity agreements. *Financial support:* In 2006–07, 9 teaching assistantships with full and partial tuition reimbursements (averaging $8,694 per year) were awarded; career-related internships or fieldwork, Federal Work-Study, traineeships, tuition waivers (full and partial), and unspecified assistantships also available. Support available to part-time students. Financial award application deadline: 1/1. *Faculty research:* Information assurance, computer information technology, finance management, marketing. Total annual research expenditures: $236,510. *Unit head:* Dr. William Stratton, Dean, 208-282-3585, Fax: 208-282-4367.

Illinois Institute of Technology, Stuart School of Business, Program in Business Administration, Chicago, IL 60616-3793. Offers entrepreneurship (MBA); financial management (MBA); financial markets (MBA); healthcare management (MBA); information technology management (MBA); international business (MBA); management science (MBA); marketing (MBA); operations, quality, and technology management (MBA); strategic management of organizations (MBA); sustainable enterprise (MBA); JD/MBA; MBA/MS. *Accreditation:* AACSB. Part-time and evening/weekend programs available. *Faculty:* 13 full-time (1 woman), 9 part-time/adjunct (0 women). *Students:* 74 full-time (29 women), 42 part-time (16 women); includes 17 minority (5 African Americans, 11 Asian Americans or Pacific Islanders, 1 Hispanic American), 74 international. Average age 29. 247 applicants, 70% accepted, 51 enrolled. In 2006, 45 degrees awarded. *Entrance requirements:* For master's, GMAT. Additional exam requirements/recommendations for international students: Required—TOEFL (minimum score 600 paper-based; 250 computer-based). *Application deadline:* For fall admission, 8/15 priority date for domestic students, 7/1 for international students; for winter admission, 11/1 priority date for domestic students, 10/1 for international students; for spring admission, 1/1 priority date for domestic students, 1/1 for international students. Applications are processed on a rolling basis. Application fee: $75. Electronic applications accepted. *Expenses: Contact institution.* Tuition and fees vary according to class time, course level, course load, program and student level. *Financial support:* Career-related internships or fieldwork, Federal Work-Study, institutionally sponsored loans, scholarships/grants, traineeships, health care benefits, tuition waivers, and unspecified assistantships available. Support available to part-time students. Financial award applicants required to submit FAFSA. *Faculty research:* Knowledge management, healthcare management, sustainability in supply chain. *Unit head:* Dr. George P. Nassos, Interim Director, 312-906-6543, Fax: 312-906-6549, E-mail: george.nassos@iit.edu. *Application contact:* Brian Jansen, Director of Graduate Admissions, 312-906-6521, Fax: 312-906-6549, E-mail: admission@stuart.iit.edu.

Illinois Institute of Technology, Stuart School of Business, Program in Management Science, Chicago, IL 60616-3793. Offers PhD. *Accreditation:* AACSB. Part-time programs available. *Faculty:* 1 full-time (0 women), 1 part-time/adjunct (0 women). *Students:* 17 full-time (5 women), 16 part-time (4 women); includes 3 minority (2 Asian Americans or Pacific Islanders, 1 Hispanic American), 17 international. Average age 36. 27 applicants, 89% accepted, 20 enrolled. In 2006, 2 degrees awarded. *Degree requirements:* For doctorate, thesis/dissertation, qualifying exam, comprehensive exam. *Entrance requirements:* For doctorate, GMAT. Additional exam requirements/recommendations for international students: Required—TOEFL (minimum score 600 paper-based; 250 computer-based). *Application deadline:* For fall admission, 8/15 priority date for domestic students, 7/1 for international students; for winter admission, 11/1 priority date for domestic students, 10/1 for international students; for spring admission, 1/1 priority date for domestic students, 1/1 for international students. Applications are processed on a rolling basis. Application fee: $75. Electronic applications accepted. *Expenses: Contact institution.* Tuition and fees vary according to class time, course level, course load, program and student level. *Financial support:* Career-related internships or fieldwork, Federal Work-Study, institutionally sponsored loans, scholarships/grants, traineeships, health care benefits, tuition waivers (full and partial), and unspecified assistantships available. Support available to part-time students. Financial award applicants required to submit FAFSA. *Faculty research:* Scheduling systems, queuing systems, optimization, quality systems. *Unit head:* Dr. Zia Hassan, Dean Emeritus, 312-906-6500, E-mail: hassan@stuart.iit.edu. *Application contact:* Brian Jansen, Director of Graduate Admissions, 312-906-6521, Fax: 312-906-6549, E-mail: admission@stuart.iit.edu.

Illinois State University, Graduate School, College of Business, Program in Business Administration, Normal, IL 61790-2200. Offers MBA. *Accreditation:* AACSB. Part-time programs available. *Faculty:* 23 full-time (5 women), 1 part-time/adjunct (0 women). *Students:* 61 full-time (18 women), 107 part-time (40 women); includes 15 minority (2 African Americans, 11 Asian Americans or Pacific Islanders, 2 Hispanic Americans), 31 international. 56 applicants, 75% accepted. In 2006, 55 degrees awarded. *Degree requirements:* For master's, thesis optional. *Entrance requirements:* For master's, GMAT, minimum GPA of 2.75 during previous 2 years of course work. Additional exam requirements/recommendations for international students: Required—TOEFL. *Application deadline:* Applications are processed on a rolling basis. Application fee: $40. *Expenses:* Tuition, state resident: full-time $3,330; part-time $185 per credit hour. Tuition, nonresident: full-time $6,948; part-time $438 per credit hour. Required fees: $1,259; $52 per credit hour. *Financial support:* In 2006–07, 46 research assistantships (averaging $6,475 per year), 4 teaching assistantships (averaging $6,750 per year) were awarded; tuition waivers (full) also available. Financial award application deadline: 4/1. *Faculty research:* McLean County small business development center. *Unit head:* Dr. Lee Graff, Director of Graduate Programs and Research, 309-438-8386.

IMCA–International Management Centres Association, Programs in Business Administration, Buckingham, United Kingdom. Offers M Phil, MBA, D Phil, DBA. Postbaccalaureate distance learning degree programs offered (no on-campus study).

Indiana State University, School of Graduate Studies, College of Business, Terre Haute, IN 47809-1401. Offers MBA. *Accreditation:* AACSB. Part-time and evening/weekend programs available. *Faculty:* 18 full-time (7 women), 6 part-time/adjunct (0 women). *Students:* 32 full-time (13 women), 19 part-time (9 women); includes 5 minority (2 African Americans, 3 Asian Americans or Pacific Islanders), 17 international. Average age 27. 92 applicants, 74% accepted, 15 enrolled. In 2006, 36 degrees awarded. *Degree requirements:* For master's, thesis optional. *Entrance requirements:* For master's, GMAT. *Application deadline:* For fall admission, 7/1 priority date for domestic students; for spring admission, 11/1 priority date for domestic students. Applications are processed on a rolling basis. Application fee: $35. Electronic applications accepted. *Expenses:* Tuition, state resident: part-time $278 per credit. Tuition, nonresident: part-time $552 per credit. *Financial support:* In 2006–07, 14 research assistantships with partial tuition reimbursements (averaging $6,300 per year) were awarded; career-related internships or fieldwork and tuition waivers (partial) also available. Financial award application deadline: 3/1; financial award applicants required to submit FAFSA. *Faculty research:* Small business and entrepreneurial sciences, production and operations management. *Unit head:* Dr. Ronald Green, Dean, 812-237-2000.

Indiana Tech, Program in Business Administration, Fort Wayne, IN 46803-1297. Offers accounting (MBA); human resources (MBA); management (MBA); marketing (MBA). Part-time and evening/weekend programs available. *Entrance requirements:* For master's, minimum undergraduate GPA of 2.5, GMAT or 2 years of work experience. Additional exam requirements/recommendations for international students: Required—TOEFL (minimum score 550 paper-based). Electronic applications accepted.

Indiana Tech, Program in Management, Fort Wayne, IN 46803-1297. Offers MSM. Part-time and evening/weekend programs available. *Entrance requirements:* For master's, minimum undergraduate GPA of 2.5, GMAT or 2 years work experience. Additional exam requirements/recommendations for international students: Required—TOEFL (minimum score 550 paper-based). Electronic applications accepted.

Indiana University Bloomington, Kelley School of Business, Bloomington, IN 47405-7000. Offers MBA, MPA, MS, DBA, PhD, DBA/MIS, JD/MBA, JD/MPA, MBA/MA, PhD/MIS. PhD offered through the University Graduate School. *Faculty:* 87 full-time (15 women). *Students:* 634 full-time (173 women), 35 part-time (13 women); includes 88 minority (20 African Americans, 55 Asian Americans or Pacific Islanders, 13 Hispanic Americans), 256 international. Average age 27. In 2006, 350 master's, 18 doctorates awarded. *Degree requirements:* For doctorate, thesis/dissertation. *Entrance requirements:* For master's, GMAT; for doctorate, GMAT, GRE General Test. Additional exam requirements/recommendations for international students: Required—TOEFL. *Application deadline:* For fall admission, 1/15 priority date for domestic students, 12/1 priority date for international students; for winter admission, 3/1 priority date for domestic students; for spring admission, 4/15 for domestic students, 9/1 for international students. Application fee: $50 ($60 for international students). Electronic applications accepted. *Expenses: Contact institution. Financial support:* Fellowships with full and partial tuition reimbursements, research assistantships, teaching assistantships, career-related internships or fieldwork, Federal Work-Study, institutionally sponsored loans, tuition waivers (full and partial), and unspecified assistantships available. Support available to part-time students. Financial award application deadline: 3/1; financial award applicants required to submit FAFSA. Total annual research expenditures: $1.1 million. *Unit head:* Daniel Smith, Dean, 812-855-8100, Fax: 812-855-8679, E-mail: business@indiana.edu. *Application contact:* Director of Admissions and Financial Aid, 812-855-8006, Fax: 812-855-9039.

Indiana University Kokomo, School of Business, Kokomo, IN 46904-9003. Offers business administration (MBA). *Accreditation:* AACSB. Part-time and evening/weekend programs available. *Faculty:* 14 full-time (6 women). *Students:* 7 full-time (1 woman), 38 part-time (18 women); includes 4 minority (2 African Americans, 1 Asian American or Pacific Islander, 1 Hispanic American), 4 international. Average age 34. 27 applicants, 81% accepted, 22 enrolled. In 2006, 19 degrees awarded. *Degree requirements:* For master's, research project, thesis optional. *Entrance requirements:* For master's, GMAT. Additional exam requirements/recommendations for international students: Required—TOEFL (minimum score 550 paper-based; 213 computer-based). *Application deadline:* For fall admission, 8/1 priority date for domestic and international students; for spring admission, 12/15 priority date for domestic and international students. Applications are processed on a rolling basis. Application fee: $40 ($60 for international students). *Expenses: Contact institution. Financial support:* In 2006–07, 2 students received support; fellowships, research assistantships, teaching assistantships, career-related internships or fieldwork and tuition waivers (partial) available. *Faculty research:* Investments, outsourcing, technology, adoption. *Unit head:* Dr. Niranjan Pati, Dean, 756-455-9275, Fax: 756-455-9348, E-mail: npati@iuk.edu. *Application contact:* Dr. Linda Ficht, Director of MBA Program, 765-455-9275, Fax: 765-455-9348, E-mail: lficht@iuk.edu.

Indiana University Northwest, School of Business and Economics, Gary, IN 46408-1197. Offers accountancy (M Acc); accounting (Certificate); business administration (MBA). *Accreditation:* AACSB. Part-time and evening/weekend programs available. *Faculty:* 5 full-time (0 women). *Students:* 11 full-time (7 women), 72 part-time (38 women); includes 19 minority (10 African Americans, 1 Asian American or Pacific Islander, 8 Hispanic Americans). Average age 32. In 2006, 39 degrees awarded. *Degree requirements:* For master's, registration. *Entrance requirements:* For master's, GMAT, letter of recommendation. *Application deadline:* For fall admission, 7/15 priority date for domestic students; for spring admission, 11/15 for domestic students. Applications are processed on a rolling basis. Application fee: $25. *Expenses: Contact institution.* Tuition and fees vary according to course load, campus/location and program. *Financial support:* In 2006–07, 9 students received support. Federal Work-Study, institutionally sponsored loans, and unspecified assistantships available. Support available to part-time students. Financial award application deadline: 7/15. *Faculty research:* International finance, wellness in the workplace, handicapped employment, MIS, regional economic forecasting. *Unit head:* Anna Rominger, Dean, 219-980-6636, Fax: 219-980-6916, E-mail: iunbiz@iun.edu. *Application contact:* John Gibson, Director of Graduate Program, 219-980-6500, Fax: 219-980-6916, E-mail: jagibson@iun.edu.

Indiana University of Pennsylvania, School of Graduate Studies and Research, Eberly College of Business and Information Technology, Program in Business Administration, Indiana, PA 15705-1087. Offers MBA. *Accreditation:* AACSB. Part-time programs available. *Faculty:* 26 full-time (4 women), 1 part-time/adjunct (0 women). *Students:* 115 full-time (45 women), 123 part-time (35 women); includes 10 minority (1 African American, 6 Asian Americans or Pacific Islanders, 3 Hispanic Americans), 164 international. Average age 26. 274 applicants, 69% accepted. In 2006, 81 degrees awarded. *Degree requirements:* For master's, thesis optional. *Entrance requirements:* For master's, GMAT, 2 letters of recommendation. Additional exam requirements/recommendations for international students: Required—TOEFL. *Application deadline:* For fall admission, 7/1 priority date for domestic students; for spring admission, 11/1 for domestic students. Applications are processed on a rolling basis. Application fee: $30. *Expenses:* Tuition, state resident: full-time $6,048; part-time $336 per credit. Tuition, nonresident: full-time $9,678; part-time $538 per credit. Required fees: $1,069; $148 per year. *Financial support:* In 2006–07, 1 fellowship (averaging $250 per year), 60 research assistantships with full and partial tuition reimbursements (averaging $1,372 per year) were awarded; career-related internships or fieldwork and Federal Work-Study also available. Support available to part-time students. Financial award application deadline: 3/15; financial award applicants required to submit FAFSA. *Unit head:* Dr. Krish Krishnan, Graduate Coordinator, 724-357-2522, E-mail: krishnan@iup.edu.

Indiana University–Purdue University Fort Wayne, School of Business and Management Sciences, Fort Wayne, IN 46805-1499. Offers business administration (MBA). *Accreditation:* AACSB. Part-time programs available. *Faculty:* 31 full-time (8 women). *Students:* 32 full-time (13 women), 114 part-time (39 women); includes 8 minority (2 African Americans, 5 Asian Americans or Pacific Islanders, 1 Hispanic American), 14 international. Average age 30. 64 applicants, 78% accepted, 49 enrolled. In 2006, 39 degrees awarded. *Entrance requirements:* For master's, GMAT, minimum GPA of 3.0, letters of recommendation. Additional exam requirements/recommendations for international students: Required—TOEFL (minimum score 600 paper-based; 260 computer-based). *Application deadline:* For fall admission, 7/1 for domestic students, 5/1 for international students; for spring admission, 11/1 for domestic students, 10/1 for international students. Applications are processed on a rolling basis. Application fee: $30. *Expenses:* Tuition, state resident: full-time $4,039; part-time $224 per credit. Tuition, nonresident: full-time $9,220; part-time $512 per credit. Required fees: $429; $24 per credit. Tuition and fees vary according to course load. *Financial support:* In 2006–07, 11 teaching assistantships with partial tuition reimbursements (averaging $11,950 per year) were awarded; scholarships/grants and unspecified assistantships also available. Support available to part-time students. Financial award application deadline: 3/1; financial award applicants required to submit FAFSA. *Faculty research:* Intellectual property asset management, arbitration and lexicology, organizational citizenship behaviors at work. Total annual research expenditures: $4,600. *Unit head:* Dr. John L. Wellington, Dean, 260-481-6461, Fax: 260-481-6879, E-mail: wellingj@ipfw.edu. *Application contact:* Dr. Zoher Shipchandler, Interim Director Graduate Programs, 260-481-6474, Fax: 260-481-6879, E-mail: shipchan@ipfw.edu.

Indiana University–Purdue University Indianapolis, Kelley School of Business, Indianapolis, IN 46202-2896. Offers MBA, MPA. *Accreditation:* AACSB. Part-time and evening/weekend programs available. Postbaccalaureate distance learning degree programs offered (minimal on-campus study). *Faculty:* 20 full-time (4 women), 1 part-time/adjunct (0 women). *Students:* 116 full-time (47 women), 932 part-time (226 women); includes 140 minority (42 African Americans, 3 American Indian/Alaska Native, 81 Asian Americans or Pacific Islanders, 14 Hispanic Americans), 135 international. Average age 32. In 2006, 400 degrees awarded. *Entrance requirements:* For master's, GMAT, previous course work in accounting, statistics. *Application deadline:* For fall admission, 4/15 priority date for domestic and international students; for spring admission, 11/1 priority date for domestic and international students. Application fee: $50 ($55 for international students). Electronic applications accepted. *Expenses: Contact institution.* Tuition and fees vary according to course load, campus/location and program. *Financial support:* Fellowships, Federal Work-Study, institutionally sponsored loans, and scholarships/grants available. Support available to part-time students. Financial award application deadline: 3/1; financial award applicants required to submit FAFSA. *Unit head:* Roger W. Schmenner, Associate Dean, Indianapolis Programs, 317-274-2481, Fax: 317-274-2483, E-mail: busugrad@iupui.edu. *Application contact:* Julie L. Moore, Recorder/Admission Coordinator, 317-274-4895, Fax: 317-274-2483, E-mail: mbaindy@iupui.edu.

Business Administration and Management—General

Indiana University South Bend, School of Business and Economics, South Bend, IN 46634-7111. Offers accounting (MSA); business administration (MBA); management of information technologies (MS). Part-time and evening/weekend programs available. *Faculty:* 17 full-time (2 women), 3 part-time/adjunct (1 woman). *Students:* 69 full-time (39 women), 118 part-time (43 women); includes 13 minority (5 African Americans, 4 Asian Americans or Pacific Islanders, 4 Hispanic Americans), 55 international. Average age 31. 49 applicants, 100% accepted, 47 enrolled. In 2006, 51 degrees awarded. *Entrance requirements:* For master's, GMAT. Additional exam requirements/recommendations for international students: Required—TOEFL (minimum score 550 paper-based; 213 computer-based). *Application deadline:* For fall admission, 7/1 priority date for domestic and international students; for spring admission, 11/1 priority date for domestic and international students. Applications are processed on a rolling basis. Application fee: $45 ($55 for international students). *Expenses: Contact institution. Financial support:* Federal Work-Study and institutionally sponsored loans available. Support available to part-time students. Financial award applicants required to submit FAFSA. *Faculty research:* Financial accounting, consumer research, capital budgeting research, business strategy research. *Unit head:* Dr. P. N. Saksena, Assistant Dean, Director of Graduate Studies, 574-520-4456, Fax: 574-520-4866, E-mail: psakena@iusb.edu. *Application contact:* Sharon Peterson, Secretary—Graduate Business, 574-520-4138, Fax: 574-520-4866, E-mail: spetersо@iusb.edu.

Indiana University Southeast, School of Business, New Albany, IN 47150-6405. Offers accounting (Certificate); business administration (MBA); economics (Certificate); finance (Certificate); general business (Certificate); information and operations management (Certificate); management and marketing (Certificate); strategic finance (MS). *Accreditation:* AACSB. *Faculty:* 11 full-time (2 women). *Students:* 10 full-time (4 women), 201 part-time (65 women); includes 12 minority (2 African Americans, 8 Asian Americans or Pacific Islanders, 2 Hispanic Americans), 5 international. Average age 31. In 2006, 60 degrees awarded. *Degree requirements:* For master's, community service. *Entrance requirements:* For master's, GMAT, work experience. Additional exam requirements/recommendations for international students: Required—TOEFL. Application fee: $35. *Expenses: Contact institution.* Tuition and fees vary according to course load, campus/location and program. *Unit head:* Chris Bjornson, Dean, 812-941-2362, Fax: 812-941-2672. *Application contact:* Dr. Jay White, Director of Graduate Business Programs, 812-941-2364, Fax: 812-941-2581, E-mail: jwhite04@ius.edu.

Indiana Wesleyan University, College of Adult and Professional Studies, Program in Business Administration, Marion, IN 46953-4974. Offers accounting (MBA); applied management (MBA); health care management (MBA). Evening/weekend programs available. Postbaccalaureate distance learning degree programs offered (no on-campus study). *Faculty:* 13 full-time (1 woman), 162 part-time/adjunct (31 women). *Students:* 1,163 full-time. Average age 34. In 2006, 792 degrees awarded. *Degree requirements:* For master's, applied management project. *Entrance requirements:* For master's, minimum GPA of 2.5, related 3 years full time work experience, math/statistics (3 hours or proficiency exam). Additional exam requirements/recommendations for international students: Required—TOEFL (minimum score 550 paper-based; 213 computer-based). *Application deadline:* Applications are processed on a rolling basis. Application fee: $25. Electronic applications accepted. *Expenses:* Tuition: Full-time $16,000; part-time $400 per credit. Required fees: $3,000. Tuition and fees vary according to degree level, campus/location and program. *Financial support:* Applicants required to submit FAFSA. *Unit head:* Dr. Jim Kraai, Director, 765-677-2882, Fax: 765-677-2023, E-mail: jim.kraai@indwes.edu. *Application contact:* Kris Douglas, Marketing Manager, 800-234-5327, Fax: 765-674-8028, E-mail: kris.douglas@apollogrp.org.

Indiana Wesleyan University, College of Adult and Professional Studies, Program in Management, Marion, IN 46953-4974. Offers MS. Evening/weekend programs available. *Faculty:* 13 full-time (1 woman), 162 part-time/adjunct (31 women). *Students:* 467 full-time. Average age 38. 216 applicants, 99% accepted. In 2006, 145 degrees awarded. *Entrance requirements:* For master's, minimum GPA of 2.5, related experience. Additional exam requirements/recommendations for international students: Required—TOEFL (minimum score 550 paper-based; 213 computer-based). *Application deadline:* Applications are processed on a rolling basis. Application fee: $25. *Expenses:* Tuition: Full-time $16,000; part-time $400 per credit. Required fees: $3,000. Tuition and fees vary according to degree level, campus/location and program. *Financial support:* Available to part-time students. Applicants required to submit FAFSA. *Unit head:* Dr. Jim Kraai, Director, 765-677-2882, Fax: 765-677-2023, E-mail: jim.kraai@indwes.edu. *Application contact:* Kris Douglas, Marketing Manager, 800-234-5327, Fax: 765-674-8028, E-mail: kris.douglas@apollogrp.org.

Instituto Centroamericano de Administración de Empresas, Graduate Programs, La Garita, Costa Rica. Offers agribusiness (MIAM); business administration (EMBA); entrepreneurial economics (MBA); industry and technology (MBA); sustainable development (MBA). *Degree requirements:* For master's, essay. *Entrance requirements:* For master's, GMAT or GRE, fluency in Spanish, interview, letters of recommendation, minimum 1 year of work experience. Electronic applications accepted. *Faculty research:* Competitiveness, production.

Instituto Tecnologico de Santo Domingo, Graduate School, Santo Domingo, Dominican Republic. Offers corporate finance (M Mgmt); education (M Ed); engineering (M Eng), including data telecommunications, industrial engineering, sanitary and environmental engineering, structural engineering; environmental science (M En S); human resources administration (M Mgmt); management (M Mgmt); psychology (MA); social science (M Ed). *Entrance requirements:* For master's, birth certificate, minimum GPA of 2.0.

Instituto Tecnológico y de Estudios Superiores de Monterrey, Campus Central de Veracruz, Graduate Programs, Córdoba, Mexico. Offers administration (MA); administration of information technologies (MTI); computer sciences (MCC); education (MEE); educational institution administration (MAD); educational technology (MTE); electronic commerce (MCE); finance (MAF); humanistic studies (MEH); international business for Latin America (MNL); marketing (MMT); science (MCP); technology management (MTT). Part-time and evening/weekend programs available. Postbaccalaureate distance learning degree programs offered (minimal on-campus study). *Degree requirements:* For master's, thesis (for some programs). *Entrance requirements:* For master's, PAEP College Board. Electronic applications accepted.

Instituto Tecnológico y de Estudios Superiores de Monterrey, Campus Ciudad de México, Division of Business, Ciudad de Mexico, Mexico. Offers business administration (EMBA, MBA, PhD); economy (MBA); finance (MBA). Part-time and evening/weekend programs available. Postbaccalaureate distance learning degree programs offered (minimal on-campus study). *Entrance requirements:* For master's and doctorate, Instituto entrance exam. Additional exam requirements/recommendations for international students: Required—TOEFL.

Instituto Tecnológico y de Estudios Superiores de Monterrey, Campus Ciudad Juárez, Program in Business Administration, Ciudad Juárez, Mexico. Offers MBA.

Instituto Tecnológico y de Estudios Superiores de Monterrey, Campus Ciudad Obregón, Program in Administration, Ciudad Obregón, Mexico. Offers MA.

Instituto Tecnológico y de Estudios Superiores de Monterrey, Campus Cuernavaca, Programs in Business Administration, Temixco, Mexico. Offers finance (MA); human resources management (MA); international business (MA); marketing (MA).

Instituto Tecnológico y de Estudios Superiores de Monterrey, Campus Estado de México, Professional and Graduate Division, Estado de Mexico, Mexico. Offers administration of information technologies (MITA); architecture (M Arch); business administration (GMBA, MBA); computer sciences (MCS, PhD); education (M Ed); educational institution administration (MAD); educational technology and innovation (PhD); electronic commerce (MEC); environmental systems (MS); finance (MAF); humanistic studies (MHS); information sciences and knowledge management (MISKM); information systems (MS); manufacturing systems (MS); marketing (MEM); quality systems and productivity (MS); science and materials engineering (PhD); telecommunications management (MTM). Part-time programs available. Postbaccalaureate distance learning degree programs offered (minimal on-campus study). *Degree requirements:* For master's, one foreign language, thesis (for some programs), registration; for doctorate, one foreign language, thesis/dissertation, registration (for some programs). *Entrance requirements:* For master's, E-PAEP 500, interview; for doctorate, E-PAEP 500, research proposal. Additional exam requirements/recommendations for international students: Required—TOEFL (minimum score 550 paper-based). *Faculty research:* Surface treatments by plasmas, mechanical properties, robotics, graphical computing, mechatronics security protocols.

Instituto Tecnológico y de Estudios Superiores de Monterrey, Campus Guadalajara, Program in Business Administration, Zapopan, Mexico. Offers MBA. Part-time and evening/weekend programs available. Postbaccalaureate distance learning degree programs offered. *Degree requirements:* For master's, one foreign language. *Entrance requirements:* For master's, ITESM admission test. *Faculty research:* Strategic alliances in small business, family business practice in Mexico, competitiveness under NAFTA for Mexican firms.

Instituto Tecnológico y de Estudios Superiores de Monterrey, Campus Irapuato, Graduate Programs, Irapuato, Mexico. Offers administration (MBA); administration of information technology (MAIT); administration of telecommunications (MAT); architecture (M Arch); computer science (MCS); education (M Ed); educational administration (MEA); educational innovation and technology (DEIT); educational technology (MET); electronic commerce (MBA); environmental administration and planning (MEAP); environmental systems (MES); finances (MBA); humanistic studies (MHS); international management for Latin American executives (MIMLAE); library and information science (MLIS); manufacturing quality management (MMQM); marketing research (MBA).

Instituto Tecnológico y de Estudios Superiores de Monterrey, Campus Laguna, Graduate School, Torreón, Mexico. Offers business administration (MBA); industrial engineering (MIE); management information systems (MS). Part-time programs available. *Entrance requirements:* For master's, GMAT. *Faculty research:* Computer communications from home to the University.

Instituto Tecnológico y de Estudios Superiores de Monterrey, Campus León, Program in Business Administration, León, Mexico. Offers MBA. Part-time programs available.

Instituto Tecnológico y de Estudios Superiores de Monterrey, Campus Monterrey, Graduate School of Business Administration and Leadership, Program in Business Administration, Monterrey, Mexico. Offers business administration (MA, MBA); finance (M Sc); international business (M Sc); marketing (M Sc). Part-time programs available. *Degree requirements:* For master's, one foreign language, thesis. *Entrance requirements:* For master's, GMAT. Additional exam requirements/recommendations for international students: Required—TOEFL. *Faculty research:* Technology management, quality management, organizational theory and behavior.

Instituto Tecnológico y de Estudios Superiores de Monterrey, Campus Monterrey, Graduate School of Business Administration and Leadership, Program in Management, Monterrey, Mexico. Offers PhD. Part-time programs available. *Degree requirements:* For doctorate, one foreign language, thesis/dissertation. *Entrance requirements:* For doctorate, GMAT. Additional exam requirements/recommendations for international students: Required—TOEFL. *Faculty research:* Quality management, manufacturing and technology management, information systems, managerial economics, business policy.

Instituto Tecnológico y de Estudios Superiores de Monterrey, Campus Querétaro, School of Business, Santiago de Querétaro, Mexico. Offers MBA. *Entrance requirements:* For master's, GRE General Test. *Faculty research:* Organizational analysis, industrial marketing, international trade.

Instituto Tecnológico y de Estudios Superiores de Monterrey, Campus Sonora Norte, Program in Business, Hermosillo, Mexico. Offers MA. *Entrance requirements:* For master's, GMAT.

Instituto Tecnológico y de Estudios Superiores de Monterrey, Campus Toluca, Graduate Programs, Toluca, Mexico. Offers MBA. Part-time and evening/weekend programs available. *Degree requirements:* For master's, one foreign language. *Entrance requirements:* For master's, master's admission test. *Faculty research:* Management in the industrial valley of Toluca.

Inter American University of Puerto Rico, Metropolitan Campus, Graduate Programs, Faculty of Economics and Administrative Sciences, San Juan, PR 00919-1293. Offers accounting (MBA); business and management development (PhD); business education (MA); finance (MBA); human resources (MBA); industrial management (MBA); labor relations (MA); marketing (MBA). Part-time and evening/weekend programs available. *Degree requirements:* For master's, comprehensive exam. *Entrance requirements:* For master's, GRE or PAEG, interview. Electronic applications accepted. *Faculty research:* Economic development, production and operations, lean manufacturing, productivity, applied business economics.

Inter American University of Puerto Rico, San Germán Campus, Graduate Studies Center, Graduate Program in Business Administration, San Germán, PR 00683-5008. Offers accounting (MBA); finance (MBA); human resources (MBA, PhD); industrial relations (MBA); international business (PhD); labor relations (PhD); management information systems (MBA); marketing (MBA); quality organizational design (MBA). Part-time and evening/weekend programs available. *Faculty:* 12 full-time, 4 part-time/adjunct. *Students:* 265. Average age 27. In 2006, 67 master's, 1 doctorate awarded. *Degree requirements:* For master's, comprehensive exam. *Entrance requirements:* For master's, GRE General Test or EXADEP, minimum GPA of 3.0. *Application deadline:* For fall admission, 4/30 priority date for domestic students; for spring admission, 11/15 for domestic students. Applications are processed on a rolling basis. Application fee: $31. *Expenses:* Tuition: Part-time $175 per credit. Required fees: $238 per semester. Tuition and fees vary according to degree level. *Financial support:* Teaching assistantships, Federal Work-Study and unspecified assistantships available. *Application contact:* Prof. Duay Rivera, Graduate Coordinator, 787-264-1912 Ext. 7218, Fax: 787-892-7510, E-mail: durivera@sg.inter.edu.

Inter American University of Puerto Rico, San Germán Campus, Graduate Studies Center, Graduate Program in Entrepreneurial and Managerial Development, San Germán, PR 00683-5008. Offers human resources (PhD); interregional and international business (PhD); labor relations (PhD). Part-time and evening/weekend programs available. *Faculty:* 12 full-time, 4 part-time/adjunct. *Students:* 52. Average age 41. In 2006, 1 degree awarded. *Degree requirements:* For doctorate, thesis/dissertation, comprehensive exam. *Entrance requirements:* For doctorate, EXADEP or GMAT, minimum graduate GPA of 3.25. *Application deadline:* For fall admission, 4/30 priority date for domestic students; for spring admission, 11/15 for domestic students. Applications are processed on a rolling basis. Application fee: $75. *Expenses:* Tuition: Part-time $175 per credit. Required fees: $238 per semester. Tuition and fees vary according to degree level. *Financial support:* Teaching assistantships available. *Application contact:* Dr. Carlos E. Irizarry, Director of Graduate Studies Center, 787-264-1912 Ext. 7357, Fax: 787-892-6350, E-mail: carlos.irizarry@sg.inter.edu.

International College of the Cayman Islands, Graduate Program in Management, Newlands, Cayman Islands. Offers business administration (MBA); management (MS), including education, human resources. Part-time and evening/weekend programs available. *Degree requirements:* For master's, comprehensive exam. *Faculty research:* International human resources administration.

International Technological University, MBA Program, Santa Clara, CA 95050. Offers MBA. Part-time and evening/weekend programs available. *Degree requirements:* For master's, thesis or alternative. *Entrance requirements:* For master's, 1 semester of calculus, minimum GPA of 2.5. Additional exam requirements/recommendations for international students: Required—TOEFL. *Faculty research:* High tech management, business management, international marketing.

International University in Geneva, MBA Program, Geneva, Switzerland. Offers e-commerce (MBA); human relations (MBA); international business (Exec MBA, MBA); marketing (MBA);

organizational development (MBA); telecommunications (MBA). Part-time and evening/weekend programs available. *Degree requirements:* For master's, comprehensive exam, registration. *Entrance requirements:* For master's, GMAT. Additional exam requirements/recommendations for international students: Required—TOEFL. Electronic applications accepted.

The International University of Monaco, Graduate Programs, Monte Carlo, Monaco. Offers entrepreneurship (EMBA, MBA); financial engineering (M Sc); international marketing (EMBA, MBA); luxury goods and services (EMBA, M Sc, MBA); wealth and asset management (EMBA, MBA). Part-time programs available. *Degree requirements:* For master's, applied research project. *Entrance requirements:* Additional exam requirements/recommendations for international students: Required—TOEFL (minimum score 550 paper-based; 213 computer-based), IELTS. Electronic applications accepted. *Faculty research:* Gaming, leadership, disintermediation.

Iona College, Hagan School of Business, New Rochelle, NY 10801-1890. Offers MBA, PMC. *Accreditation:* AACSB. Part-time and evening/weekend programs available. *Faculty:* 27 full-time (5 women), 12 part-time/adjunct (2 women). *Students:* 34 full-time (18 women), 232 part-time (110 women); includes 27 minority (15 African Americans, 7 Asian Americans or Pacific Islanders, 5 Hispanic Americans), 10 international. Average age 31. 96 applicants, 84% accepted, 68 enrolled. In 2006, 118 master's, 40 other advanced degrees awarded. *Entrance requirements:* For master's, GMAT, 2 letters of recommendation. Additional exam requirements/recommendations for international students: Required—TOEFL (minimum score 550 paper-based; 213 computer-based). *Application deadline:* For fall admission, 8/15 priority date for domestic students, 8/1 for international students; for winter admission, 11/15 priority date for domestic students, 11/1 for international students; for spring admission, 2/15 priority date for domestic students, 2/1 for international students. Applications are processed on a rolling basis. Application fee: $50. Electronic applications accepted. *Expenses: Contact institution. Financial support:* In 2006–07, 2 fellowships with tuition reimbursements (averaging $7,000 per year) were awarded; Federal Work-Study, scholarships/grants, tuition waivers (partial), and unspecified assistantships also available. Support available to part-time students. *Faculty research:* Artificial intelligence, financial services, value-based management, public policy, business ethics. *Unit head:* Dr. Vincent Calluzo, Dean, 914-633-2256, E-mail: vcalluzo@iona.edu. *Application contact:* Veronica Jarek-Prinz, Graduate Admissions, 914-633-2289, Fax: 914-633-2012, E-mail: vjarekprinz@iona.edu.

See Close-Up on page 279.

Iowa State University of Science and Technology, Graduate College, College of Business, Ames, IA 50011. Offers M Acc, MBA, MS, M Arch/MBA, MBA/MCRP, MBA/MS. *Accreditation:* AACSB. *Faculty:* 64 full-time, 2 part-time/adjunct. *Students:* 156 full-time (73 women), 121 part-time (51 women); includes 13 minority (1 African American, 7 Asian Americans or Pacific Islanders, 5 Hispanic Americans), 51 international. 247 applicants, 57% accepted, 104 enrolled. In 2006, 130 degrees awarded. *Entrance requirements:* For master's, GMAT. Additional exam requirements/recommendations for international students: Required—TOEFL. Application fee: $30 ($70 for international students). Electronic applications accepted. *Expenses: Contact institution. Financial support:* In 2006–07, 54 research assistantships with full and partial tuition reimbursements (averaging $17,059 per year), 5 teaching assistantships with full and partial tuition reimbursements (averaging $17,232 per year) were awarded; fellowships, scholarships/grants, health care benefits, and unspecified assistantships also available. *Unit head:* Dr. Labh S Hira, Dean, 515-294-2422, E-mail: busgrad@iastate.edu.

Ithaca College, Graduate Studies, School of Business, Program in Business Administration, Ithaca, NY 14850-7020. Offers MBA. *Accreditation:* AACSB. Part-time programs available. *Faculty:* 19 full-time (4 women). *Students:* 11 full-time (5 women), 7 part-time (2 women). Average age 27. 25 applicants, 64% accepted, 12 enrolled. In 2006, 10 master's awarded. *Degree requirements:* For master's, registration. *Entrance requirements:* For master's, GMAT, minimum GPA of 3.0. Additional exam requirements/recommendations for international students: Required—TOEFL (minimum score 550 paper-based; 213 computer-based). *Application deadline:* For fall admission, 8/1 for domestic students; for spring admission, 12/1 for domestic students. Applications are processed on a rolling basis. Application fee: $40. *Financial support:* In 2006–07, 13 students received support, including 8 fellowships (averaging $3,867 per year); Federal Work-Study, institutionally sponsored loans, and scholarships/grants also available. Support available to part-time students. Financial award application deadline: 4/15; financial award applicants required to submit FAFSA. *Unit head:* Dr. Donald Eckrich, Chairperson, 607-274-3936.

ITT Technical Institute, Online MBA Program, Indianapolis, IN 46268-1119. Offers MBA.

Jackson State University, Graduate School, School of Business, Department of Business Administration, Jackson, MS 39217. Offers PhD. *Accreditation:* AACSB. Part-time and evening/weekend programs available. *Faculty:* 11 full-time (3 women). *Students:* 9 full-time (5 women); includes 4 minority (all African Americans), 3 international. *Degree requirements:* For doctorate, thesis/dissertation, comprehensive exam. *Entrance requirements:* For doctorate, MAT, GMAT. *Application deadline:* For fall admission, 3/1 priority date for domestic students. Applications are processed on a rolling basis. Application fee: $20. *Financial support:* Career-related internships or fieldwork and Federal Work-Study available. Financial award application deadline: 3/1; financial award applicants required to submit FAFSA. *Unit head:* Dr. Jean Claude Assad, Director, 601-979-4326, Fax: 601-979-1205, E-mail: jean-claude.assad@jsums.edu. *Application contact:* Curtis Gore, Director of Graduate Admissions, 601-979-2455, Fax: 601-974-4325, E-mail: cgore@ccaix.jsums.edu.

Jackson State University, Graduate School, School of Business, Department of Economics, Finance and General Business, Jackson, MS 39217. Offers business administration (MBA). Part-time and evening/weekend programs available. *Faculty:* 11 full-time (3 women). *Students:* 40 full-time (22 women), 40 part-time (27 women); includes 64 minority (62 African Americans, 2 Asian Americans or Pacific Islanders), 8 international. In 2006, 57 degrees awarded. *Degree requirements:* For master's, thesis, comprehensive exam. *Entrance requirements:* For master's, GRE General Test, GMAT. Additional exam requirements/recommendations for international students: Required—TOEFL. *Application deadline:* For fall admission, 3/1 priority date for domestic students; for spring admission, 10/1 for domestic students. Applications are processed on a rolling basis. Application fee: $20. *Financial support:* Federal Work-Study, scholarships/grants, tuition waivers (full and partial), and unspecified assistantships available. Support available to part-time students. Financial award application deadline: 3/1. *Unit head:* Dr. Jean Claude Assad, Director, 601-979-4326, Fax: 601-979-1205, E-mail: jean-claude.assad@jsums.edu. *Application contact:* Curtis Gore, Director of Graduate Admissions, 601-979-2455, Fax: 601-974-4325, E-mail: cgore@ccaix.jsums.edu.

Jacksonville State University, College of Graduate Studies and Continuing Education, College of Commerce and Business Administration, Jacksonville, AL 36265-1602. Offers MBA. *Accreditation:* AACSB. Part-time and evening/weekend programs available. *Faculty:* 11 full-time (4 women). *Students:* 10 full-time (7 women), 55 part-time (25 women); includes 15 minority (7 African Americans, 1 American Indian/Alaska Native, 5 Asian Americans or Pacific Islanders, 2 Hispanic Americans), 3 international. In 2006, 20 degrees awarded. *Entrance requirements:* For master's, GMAT. *Application deadline:* Applications are processed on a rolling basis. Application fee: $20. *Expenses:* Tuition, state resident: full-time $5,400; part-time $225 per credit hour. Tuition, nonresident: full-time $10,800; part-time $450 per credit hour. One-time fee: $20 full-time. *Financial support:* In 2006–07, 4 research assistantships were awarded. Support available to part-time students. Financial award application deadline: 4/1. *Unit head:* Dr. William Fielding, Dean, 256-782-5508. *Application contact:* 256-782-5329.

Jacksonville University, Davis College of Business, Executive Master's in Business Administration Program, Jacksonville, FL 32211-3394. Offers Exec MBA. Part-time and evening/weekend programs available. *Entrance requirements:* For master's, 5 years of managerial or professional experience. Additional exam requirements/recommendations for international students: Required—TOEFL. *Faculty research:* Economic impact, vicarious learning, psychology and advertising.

Jacksonville University, Davis College of Business, Master's in Business Administration Program, Jacksonville, FL 32211-3394. Offers MBA. Part-time and evening/weekend programs available. *Entrance requirements:* For master's, GMAT. Additional exam requirements/recommendations for international students: Required—TOEFL.

James Madison University, College of Graduate and Outreach Programs, College of Business, Program in Business Administration, Harrisonburg, VA 22807. Offers MBA. *Accreditation:* AACSB. Part-time and evening/weekend programs available. Postbaccalaureate distance learning degree programs offered (no on-campus study). *Students:* 16 full-time (5 women), 87 part-time (28 women); includes 13 minority (4 African Americans, 1 American Indian/Alaska Native, 8 Asian Americans or Pacific Islanders), 3 international. Average age 27. In 2006, 46 degrees awarded. *Entrance requirements:* For master's, GMAT, resumé, 2 letters of recommendation. Additional exam requirements/recommendations for international students: Required—TOEFL. *Application deadline:* For fall admission, 5/1 priority date for domestic students. Applications are processed on a rolling basis. Application fee: $55. Electronic applications accepted. *Expenses:* Tuition, state resident: full-time $6,336; part-time $264 per credit hour. Tuition, nonresident: full-time $17,832; part-time $743 per credit hour. *Financial support:* In 2006–07, 6 students received support. Federal Work-Study and unspecified assistantships available. Financial award application deadline: 3/1; financial award applicants required to submit FAFSA. *Unit head:* Dr. Kenneth D. Bahn, Director, 540-568-3009.

John Brown University, Department of Business Administration, Siloam Springs, AR 72761-2121. Offers business administration (MBA); leadership and ethics (MS). Part-time and evening/weekend programs available. *Degree requirements:* For master's, supervised fieldwork. *Entrance requirements:* For master's, GRE General Test, MAT, or GMAT, minimum GPA of 3.0. Additional exam requirements/recommendations for international students: Required—TOEFL (minimum score 550 paper-based; 173 computer-based). Electronic applications accepted.

John Carroll University, Graduate School, John M. and Mary Jo Boler School of Business, University Heights, OH 44118-4581. Offers accountancy (MS); business (MBA). *Accreditation:* AACSB. Part-time and evening/weekend programs available. *Faculty:* 33 full-time (6 women), 2 part-time/adjunct (0 women). *Students:* 31 full-time (13 women), 171 part-time (72 women); includes 14 minority (12 African Americans, 1 Asian American or Pacific Islander, 1 Hispanic American). Average age 29. 62 applicants, 81% accepted, 36 enrolled. In 2006, 91 degrees awarded. *Entrance requirements:* For master's, GMAT. Additional exam requirements/recommendations for international students: Required—TOEFL (minimum score 550 paper-based; 213 computer-based). *Application deadline:* Applications are processed on a rolling basis. Application fee: $25 ($35 for international students). *Expenses: Contact institution.* Tuition and fees vary according to program. *Financial support:* In 2006–07, 6 research assistantships with full tuition reimbursements (averaging $8,000 per year) were awarded; scholarships/grants and unspecified assistantships also available. Financial award application deadline: 3/15; financial award applicants required to submit FAFSA. *Faculty research:* Accounting, economics and finance, management, marketing and logistics. *Unit head:* Dr. Karen Schuele, Associate Dean, 216-397-4606, Fax: 216-397-1728, E-mail: kschuele@jcu.edu. *Application contact:* Gayle T. Bruno-Gannon, Assistant to the Dean, 216-397-1970, Fax: 216-397-1728, E-mail: ggannon@jcu.edu.

John F. Kennedy University, School of Management, Program in Business Administration, Pleasant Hill, CA 94523-4817. Offers business administration (MBA); organizational leadership (Certificate). Part-time and evening/weekend programs available. *Degree requirements:* For master's, thesis or alternative. *Entrance requirements:* For master's, interview. Additional exam requirements/recommendations for international students: Required—TOEFL.

The Johns Hopkins University, Carey Business School, Department of Management, Baltimore, MD 21218-2699. Offers leadership development (Certificate); organization development and strategic human resources (MS); skilled facilitator (Certificate). Part-time and evening/weekend programs available. *Students:* 44 full-time (30 women), 127 part-time (93 women); includes 52 minority (44 African Americans, 2 Asian Americans or Pacific Islanders, 6 Hispanic Americans), 3 international. Average age 33. 147 applicants, 82% accepted, 104 enrolled. In 2006, 33 master's, 44 other advanced degrees awarded. *Degree requirements:* For master's, project. *Entrance requirements:* For master's and Certificate, minimum GPA of 3.0, resumé, work experience, two letters of recommendation. Additional exam requirements/recommendations for international students: Required—TOEFL (minimum score 600 paper-based; 250 computer-based; 100 iBT). *Application deadline:* For fall admission, 5/1 for international students; for spring admission, 10/15 for international students. Applications are processed on a rolling basis. Application fee: $60. *Expenses:* Tuition: Full-time $32,976. Tuition and fees vary according to degree level and program. *Financial support:* Scholarships/grants available. Support available to part-time students. Financial award application deadline: 6/1; financial award applicants required to submit FAFSA. *Unit head:* Dr. Toni Ungaretti, Chair, 410-516-7190, Fax: 410-230-4257, E-mail: toni@jhu.edu. *Application contact:* Robin Reed, Senior Academic Coordinator, 800-gotojhu, Fax: 410-872-1251, E-mail: onestop.admissions@jhu.edu.

The Johns Hopkins University, Carey Business School, MBA Department, Baltimore, MD 21218-2699. Offers MBA, MBA/MA, MBA/MSITS. Part-time and evening/weekend programs available. Postbaccalaureate distance learning degree programs offered (minimal on-campus study). *Students:* 149 full-time (67 women), 525 part-time (204 women); includes 121 minority (55 African Americans, 2 American Indian/Alaska Native, 48 Asian Americans or Pacific Islanders, 16 Hispanic Americans), 6 international. Average age 33. 528 applicants, 67% accepted, 302 enrolled. In 2006, 301 degrees awarded. *Degree requirements:* For master's, project. *Entrance requirements:* For master's, GMAT or GRE, minimum GPA of 3.0, resumé, work experience, two letters of recommendation. Additional exam requirements/recommendations for international students: Required—TOEFL (minimum score 600 paper-based; 250 computer-based; 100 iBT). *Application deadline:* For fall admission, 5/1 for international students; for spring admission, 10/15 for international students. Applications are processed on a rolling basis. Application fee: $60. *Expenses:* Tuition: Full-time $32,976. Tuition and fees vary according to degree level and program. *Financial support:* Scholarships/grants available. Support available to part-time students. Financial award application deadline: 6/1; financial award applicants required to submit FAFSA. *Unit head:* Dr. Rick Milter, Interim Chair, 410-516-0249, Fax: 410-516-2033, E-mail: milter@jhu.edu. *Application contact:* Robin Reed, Senior Academic Coordinator, 800-gotojhu, Fax: 410-872-1251, E-mail: onestop.admissions@jhu.edu.

The Johns Hopkins University, School of Professional Studies in Business and Education, School of Education, Division of Public Safety Leadership, Baltimore, MD 21218-2699. Offers management (MS). Part-time and evening/weekend programs available. *Students:* 139 full-time (27 women); includes 29 minority (26 African Americans, 2 American Indian/Alaska Native, 1 Asian American or Pacific Islander), 2 international. Average age 40. 99 applicants, 95% accepted, 89 enrolled. In 2006, 55 degrees awarded. *Degree requirements:* For master's, registration. *Entrance requirements:* For master's, minimum GPA of 3.0, interview, resumé, letters of recommendation. Additional exam requirements/recommendations for international students: Required—TOEFL (minimum score 600 paper-based; 250 computer-based; 100 iBT). *Application deadline:* For fall admission, 5/1 for international students; for spring admission, 10/15 for international students. Applications are processed on a rolling basis. Application fee: $60. *Expenses:* Tuition: Full-time $32,976. Tuition and fees vary according to degree level and program. *Financial support:* Scholarships/grants available. Support available to part-time students. Financial award application deadline: 6/1; financial award applicants required to submit FAFSA. *Faculty research:* Ethics and integrity, counter terrorism, school safety, Homeland Security, identity theft. *Unit head:* Dr. Sheldon Greenberg, Associate Dean, 410-

Business Administration and Management—General

The Johns Hopkins University (continued)

312-4401, Fax: 410-290-1061, E-mail: greenberg@jhu.edu. *Application contact:* Kelly Williams, Academic Administrator, 410-312-4409, Fax: 410-290-1061, E-mail: kelly.williams@jhu.edu.

Jones International University, Graduate School of Business Administration, Centennial, CO 80112. Offers accounting (MBA); business communication (MABC); entrepreneurship (MABC, MBA); finance (MBA); global enterprise management (MBA); health care management (MBA); information security management (MBA); information technology management (MBA); leadership and influence (MABC); leading the customer-driven organization (MABC); negotiation and conflict management (MBA); project management (MABC, MBA). Program only offered online. Part-time and evening/weekend programs available. Postbaccalaureate distance learning degree programs offered (no on-campus study). *Degree requirements:* For master's, capstone project. *Entrance requirements:* For master's, minimum cumulative GPA of 2.5. Additional exam requirements/recommendations for international students: Recommended—TOEFL (minimum score 550 paper-based; 213 computer-based). Electronic applications accepted.

Kansas State University, Graduate School, College of Business Administration, Program in Business Administration, Manhattan, KS 66506. Offers MBA. *Accreditation:* AACSB. Part-time programs available. *Faculty:* 24 full-time (2 women). *Students:* 101 full-time (31 women), 17 part-time (11 women); includes 5 minority (1 African American, 4 Asian Americans or Pacific Islanders), 15 international. Average age 28. 45 applicants, 91% accepted, 35 enrolled. In 2006, 33 degrees awarded. *Degree requirements:* For master's, comprehensive exam. *Entrance requirements:* For master's, GMAT, minimum undergraduate GPA of 3.0. Additional exam requirements/recommendations for international students: Required—TOEFL (minimum score 550 paper-based; 213 computer-based). *Application deadline:* For fall admission, 7/1 for domestic students, 2/1 for international students; for spring admission, 12/1 for domestic students, 8/1 for international students. Applications are processed on a rolling basis. Application fee: $50 ($60 for international students). *Expenses:* Tuition, state resident: full-time $6,352; part-time $240 per credit hour. Tuition, nonresident: full-time $14,296; part-time $571 per credit hour. Required fees: $585. *Financial support:* Research assistantships with partial tuition reimbursements, teaching assistantships with partial tuition reimbursements, institutionally sponsored loans and scholarships/grants available. Support available to part-time students. Financial award application deadline: 3/1; financial award applicants required to submit FAFSA. *Faculty research:* Organizational citizenship behavior, service marketing, impression management, human resources management, lean manufacturing and supply chain management, financial market behavior and investment management. *Unit head:* Jeff Katz, Director, 785-532-7451, E-mail: jkatz@ksu.edu.

Kansas Wesleyan University, Program in Business Administration, Salina, KS 67401-6196. Offers MBA. Part-time and evening/weekend programs available. *Entrance requirements:* For master's, GMAT, minimum graduate GPA of 3.0 or undergraduate GPA of 3.25.

Kean University, College of Education, Program in Educational Administration, Union, NJ 07083. Offers principals and supervisors (MA); school business administration (MA); supervisors (MA). *Accreditation:* NCATE. Part-time and evening/weekend programs available. *Faculty:* 5 full-time (1 woman). *Students:* 13 full-time (9 women), 247 part-time (153 women); includes 68 minority (34 African Americans, 5 Asian Americans or Pacific Islanders, 29 Hispanic Americans), 1 international. Average age 34. 111 applicants, 95% accepted, 86 enrolled. In 2006, 107 degrees awarded. *Degree requirements:* For master's, portfolio, field experience, research component. *Entrance requirements:* For master's, GRE General Test or MAT, interview, 2 letters of recommendation, 1 year of teaching experience, teaching certificate. *Application deadline:* For fall admission, 5/1 for domestic students; for spring admission, 11/1 for domestic students. Application fee: $60 ($150 for international students). Electronic applications accepted. *Expenses:* Tuition, state resident: full-time $8,856; part-time $369 per credit. Tuition, nonresident: full-time $11,256; part-time $469 per credit. *Financial support:* Research assistantships with full tuition reimbursements, unspecified assistantships available. *Unit head:* Dr. Leonard Elovitz, Program Coordinator, 908-737-4276, E-mail: lelovitz@kean.edu. *Application contact:* Joanne Morris, Director of Graduate Admissions, 908-737-3355, Fax: 908-737-3354, E-mail: grad-adm@kean.edu.

Keller Graduate School of Management, Keller Graduate School of Management, Long Island City, NY 11101-3051. Offers MBA, MISM.

Keller Graduate School of Management, Keller Graduate School of Management, New York, NY 10036-4041. Offers MBA, MISM.

Kennesaw State University, Michael J. Coles College of Business, Program in Business Administration, Kennesaw, GA 30144-5591. Offers MBA. Part-time and evening/weekend programs available. Postbaccalaureate distance learning degree programs offered (no on-campus study). *Students:* 143 full-time (47 women), 462 part-time (168 women); includes 128 minority (71 African Americans, 4 American Indian/Alaska Native, 37 Asian Americans or Pacific Islanders, 16 Hispanic Americans), 53 international. Average age 34. 308 applicants, 81% accepted, 217 enrolled. In 2006, 195 degrees awarded. *Entrance requirements:* For master's, GMAT, 2.80 GPA, 1 year work experience. Additional exam requirements/recommendations for international students: Required—TOEFL (minimum score 550 paper-based; 213 computer-based; 80 iBT), IELTS (minimum score 6). *Application deadline:* For fall admission, 6/15 for domestic students; for winter admission, 11/15 for domestic students; for spring admission, 4/15 for domestic students. Application fee: $50. Electronic applications accepted. *Expenses:* Tuition, state resident: full-time $3,044; part-time $127 per semester hour. Tuition, nonresident: full-time $12,172; part-time $508 per semester hour. Required fees: $353 per semester. Full-time tuition and fees vary according to campus/location and program. *Financial support:* Unspecified assistantships available. *Unit head:* Dr. Sher True, Director, 770-423-6087, E-mail: strue@kennesaw.edu. *Application contact:* Vilma Marquez, Admissions Counselor, 770-420-4377, Fax: 770-423-6885, E-mail: ksugrad@kennesaw.edu.

Kent State University, Graduate School of Management, Master's Program in Business Administration, Kent, OH 44242-0001. Offers MBA. *Accreditation:* AACSB. Part-time and evening/weekend programs available. *Faculty:* 58 full-time (12 women). *Students:* 142 full-time (60 women), 141 part-time (71 women); includes 20 minority (5 African Americans, 1 American Indian/Alaska Native, 13 Asian Americans or Pacific Islanders, 1 Hispanic American), 20 international. Average age 29. 192 applicants, 84% accepted, 121 enrolled. In 2006, 109 degrees awarded. *Entrance requirements:* For master's, GMAT, minimum GPA of 2.75, interview. Additional exam requirements/recommendations for international students: Required—TOEFL (minimum score 550 paper-based; 213 computer-based). *Application deadline:* For fall admission, 7/1 for domestic students, 4/1 for international students; for spring admission, 12/15 for domestic students. Applications are processed on a rolling basis. Application fee: $30. Electronic applications accepted. *Financial support:* In 2006–07, 33 students received support, including 33 research assistantships with full tuition reimbursements available (averaging $6,500 per year); fellowships, career-related internships or fieldwork, Federal Work-Study, and institutionally sponsored loans also available. Financial award application deadline: 4/1; financial award applicants required to submit FAFSA. *Unit head:* Director, 330-672-2282, Fax: 330-672-7303. *Application contact:* Felecia A. Urbanek, Coordinator, Graduate Programs, 330-672-2282, Fax: 330-672-7303, E-mail: gradbus@bsa3.kent.edu.

Announcement: The Graduate School of Management at Kent State University is AACSB-accredited and offers an innovative curriculum, high-caliber faculty, and leading-edge technology. Programs include the MBA, MA in financial engineering, MS in accounting, MA in economics, and PhD in business administration. Graduate assistantships are available for all programs.

Kentucky State University, College of Professional Studies, Frankfort, KY 40601. Offers business (MBA); public administration (MPA); special education (MA). Part-time and evening/weekend programs available. *Faculty:* 11 full-time (2 women). *Students:* 44 full-time (26 women), 69 part-time (40 women); includes 67 minority (64 African Americans, 1 Asian American or Pacific Islander, 2 Hispanic Americans), 1 international. Average age 32. 70 applicants, 74% accepted, 41 enrolled. In 2006, 26 degrees awarded. *Degree requirements:* For master's, thesis optional. *Entrance requirements:* For master's, GMAT. Additional exam requirements/recommendations for international students: Required—TOEFL. *Application deadline:* For fall admission, 7/1 priority date for domestic students, 4/1 priority date for international students; for spring admission, 11/15 priority date for domestic students, 8/15 priority date for international students. Applications are processed on a rolling basis. Application fee: $30 ($100 for international students). Electronic applications accepted. *Expenses:* Tuition, state resident: part-time $285 per credit. Tuition, nonresident: part-time $685 per credit. Required fees: $35 per credit. *Financial support:* In 2006–07, 4 research assistantships (averaging $613 per year) were awarded. Financial award application deadline: 4/15; financial award applicants required to submit FAFSA. *Unit head:* Dr. Gashaw Lake, Dean, E-mail: gashaw.lake@kysu.edu. *Application contact:* James Burrell, Director of Admission, 502-597-6322, Fax: 502-597-5814, E-mail: james.burrell@kysu.edu.

Kettering University, Graduate School, Department of Business, Flint, MI 48504-4898. Offers business administration (MBA); engineering management (MSEM); information technology (MSIT); manufacturing management (MSMM); manufacturing operations (MSMO); operations management (MSOM). *Accreditation:* ACBSP. *Faculty:* 13 full-time (5 women), 8 part-time/adjunct (1 woman). *Students:* 10 full-time (4 women), 455 part-time (122 women); includes 108 minority (53 African Americans, 1 American Indian/Alaska Native, 11 Asian Americans or Pacific Islanders, 43 Hispanic Americans), 2 international. Average age 33. 142 applicants, 91% accepted, 90 enrolled. In 2006, 158 degrees awarded. *Entrance requirements:* Additional exam requirements/recommendations for international students: Required—TOEFL (minimum score 550 paper-based; 213 computer-based). *Application deadline:* For fall admission, 8/15 for domestic students, 4/1 for international students; for winter admission, 11/15 for domestic students; for spring admission, 2/15 for domestic students. Applications are processed on a rolling basis. Electronic applications accepted. *Expenses:* Tuition: Part-time $629 per credit. *Application contact:* Allison Fleming, Graduate Admissions Assistant, 810-762-7953, Fax: 810-762-9935, E-mail: afleming@kettering.edu.

Keuka College, Program in Management, Keuka Park, NY 14478-0098. Offers MS. Evening/weekend programs available. *Faculty:* 3 full-time (1 woman), 16 part-time/adjunct (3 women). *Students:* 46 full-time (29 women), 56 part-time (33 women); includes 9 minority (4 African Americans, 1 American Indian/Alaska Native, 2 Asian Americans or Pacific Islanders, 2 Hispanic Americans). 47 applicants, 100% accepted, 47 enrolled. In 2006, 41 degrees awarded. *Degree requirements:* For master's, thesis, registration. *Entrance requirements:* For master's, 2 letters of reference, minimum GPA of 3.0. Additional exam requirements/recommendations for international students: Required—TOEFL (minimum score 550 paper-based; 213 computer-based). *Application deadline:* For fall admission, 8/15 priority date for domestic students; for winter admission, 12/15 priority date for domestic students; for spring admission, 4/15 priority date for domestic students. Applications are processed on a rolling basis. Application fee: $30. *Expenses:* Contact institution. *Faculty research:* Leadership, adult education, decision making, strategic planning, business ethics. *Unit head:* Gary M. Smith, Chair, Division of Business and Management, 315-279-5352, E-mail: gsmith@mail.keuka.edu.

King College, School of Business and Economics, Bristol, TN 37620-2699. Offers MBA. Part-time and evening/weekend programs available. Postbaccalaureate distance learning degree programs offered (no on-campus study). *Degree requirements:* For master's, thesis optional. *Entrance requirements:* For master's, GMAT, 2 years of work experience. Additional exam requirements/recommendations for international students: Required—TOEFL (minimum score 550 paper-based). Electronic applications accepted. *Faculty research:* Leadership, international monetary policy.

King's College, William G. McGowan School of Business, Wilkes-Barre, PA 18711-0801. Offers health care administration (MS). *Accreditation:* AACSB; CAHME. Part-time and evening/weekend programs available. *Faculty:* 4 full-time (1 woman), 1 part-time/adjunct (0 women). *Students:* Average age 35. In 2006, 6 degrees awarded. *Entrance requirements:* Additional exam requirements/recommendations for international students: Required—TOEFL (minimum score 600 paper-based; 250 computer-based). *Application deadline:* For fall admission, 7/31 priority date for domestic students; for spring admission, 12/1 priority date for domestic students. Applications are processed on a rolling basis. Application fee: $35. *Expenses:* Tuition: Full-time $26,598; part-time $625 per credit. Required fees: $900. *Unit head:* Dr. John J. Ryan, Director, 570-208-5932, Fax: 570-826-5989, E-mail: jjryan@kings.edu. *Application contact:* Dr. Elizabeth S. Lott, Director of Graduate Programs, 570-208-5991, Fax: 570-825-9049, E-mail: eslott@kings.edu.

Kutztown University of Pennsylvania, College of Graduate Studies and Extended Learning, College of Business, Program in Business Administration, Kutztown, PA 19530-0730. Offers MBA. Part-time and evening/weekend programs available. *Faculty:* 12 full-time (2 women). *Students:* 22 full-time (10 women), 73 part-time (24 women); includes 9 minority (4 African Americans, 3 Asian Americans or Pacific Islanders, 2 Hispanic Americans), 7 international. Average age 32. 48 applicants, 27% accepted, 11 enrolled. In 2006, 32 degrees awarded. *Degree requirements:* For master's, thesis (for some programs), comprehensive exam. *Entrance requirements:* For master's, GMAT. Additional exam requirements/recommendations for international students: Required—TOEFL. *Application deadline:* For fall admission, 3/1 for domestic students; for spring admission, 8/1 for domestic students. Applications are processed on a rolling basis. Application fee: $35. *Expenses:* Tuition, state resident: full-time $6,048; part-time $336 per credit. Tuition, nonresident: full-time $9,678; part-time $538 per credit. *Financial support:* In 2006–07, research assistantships with full tuition reimbursements (averaging $5,000 per year); career-related internships or fieldwork, Federal Work-Study, tuition waivers (partial), and unspecified assistantships also available. Financial award application deadline: 3/15; financial award applicants required to submit FAFSA. *Unit head:* Dr. Fidelis M. Ikem, Interim Dean, 610-683-4575, Fax: 610-683-4573, E-mail: ikem@kutztown.edu.

Lake Erie College, Division of Management Studies, Painesville, OH 44077-3389. Offers general management (MBA); management healthcare administration (MBA). Part-time and evening/weekend programs available. *Faculty:* 6 full-time (2 women), 4 part-time/adjunct (1 woman). *Students:* Average age 33. 40 applicants, 98% accepted, 29 enrolled. In 2006, 22 degrees awarded. *Entrance requirements:* For master's, GMAT, resumé, references. Additional exam requirements/recommendations for international students: Required—TOEFL (minimum score 590 paper-based). *Application deadline:* For fall admission, 8/1 priority date for domestic students, 6/1 for international students; for spring admission, 12/15 for domestic students, 10/1 for international students. Applications are processed on a rolling basis. Application fee: $25 ($50 for international students). Electronic applications accepted. *Expenses:* Tuition: Part-time $595 per credit hour. Required fees: $45 per credit hour. *Financial support:* Career-related internships or fieldwork available. Financial award applicants required to submit FAFSA. *Faculty research:* Organizational effectiveness. *Unit head:* Prof. Robert Trebar, Associate Dean, 440-375-7115, Fax: 440-375-7005, E-mail: rtrebar@lec.edu. *Application contact:* Admissions Office, 440-375-7050, Fax: 440-375-7005, E-mail: admissions@lec.edu.

Lake Forest Graduate School of Management, MBA Program, Program at Chicago, Lake Forest, IL 60045. Offers MBA. Part-time and evening/weekend programs available. *Faculty:* 160 part-time/adjunct (26 women). *Students:* Average age 37. 55 applicants, 96% accepted, 51 enrolled. In 2006, 29 master's awarded. *Entrance requirements:* For master's, GMAT, 4 years business experience, interview, 2 letters of recommendation. *Application deadline:* For fall admission, 8/13 priority date for domestic students; for spring admission, 1/15 priority date for domestic students. Applications are processed on a rolling basis. Application fee: $0. Electronic applications accepted. *Expenses:* Tuition: Part-time $2,475 per course. *Financial support:* In 2006–07, 43 students received support. Scholarships/grants available. Support available to part-time students. Financial award applicants required to submit FAFSA. *Unit* *head:* Sue Lawler, Associate Dean, 312-884-7962, E-mail: slawler@lfgsm.edu. *Application contact:* Joanna Ficorilli, Senior Admissions Manager, 800-737-4MBA, Fax: 312-435-5333, E-mail: admiss@lfgsm.edu.

Lake Forest Graduate School of Management, MBA Program, Program at Lake Forest, Lake Forest, IL 60045. Offers MBA. Part-time and evening/weekend programs available. *Faculty:* 160 part-time/adjunct (26 women). *Students:* Average age 37. 105 applicants, 97% accepted, 88 enrolled. In 2006, 175 degrees awarded. *Entrance requirements:* For master's, GMAT, 4 years of work experience, interview, 2 letters of recommendation. *Application deadline:* For fall admission, 8/13 priority date for domestic students; for spring admission, 1/15 priority date for domestic students. Applications are processed on a rolling basis. Application fee: $0. Electronic applications accepted. *Expenses:* Tuition: Part-time $2,475 per course. *Financial support:* In 2006–07, 122 students received support. Scholarships/grants available. Support available to part-time students. Financial award applicants required to submit FAFSA. *Unit head:* Frank Brletich, Associate Dean, 847-574-5182, E-mail: fbrletich@lfgsm.edu. *Application contact:* Angel Baldassano, Senior Admissions Manager, 800-737-4MBA, Fax: 847-295-3656, E-mail: admiss@lfgsm.edu.

Lake Forest Graduate School of Management, MBA Program, Program at Schaumburg, Lake Forest, IL 60045. Offers MBA. Part-time and evening/weekend programs available. *Faculty:* 160 part-time/adjunct (26 women). *Students:* Average age 37. 43 applicants, 35 enrolled. In 2006, 58 degrees awarded. *Entrance requirements:* For master's, GMAT, 4 years of work experience, interview, 2 letters of recommendation. *Application deadline:* For fall admission, 8/15 priority date for domestic students; for spring admission, 1/15 priority date for domestic students. Applications are processed on a rolling basis. Electronic applications accepted. *Expenses:* Tuition: Part-time $2,475 per course. *Financial support:* In 2006–07, 37 students received support. Scholarships/grants available. Support available to part-time students. Financial award applicants required to submit FAFSA. *Unit head:* Arlene Mayzel, Vice President and Academic Dean, 847-574-5198, Fax: 847-574-5199, E-mail: amayzel@lfgsm.edu. *Application contact:* Marty Parker, Admissions Manager, 800-737-4MBA, Fax: 847-576-1213, E-mail: admiss@lfgsm.edu.

Lakeland College, Graduate Studies Division, Program in Business Administration, Sheboygan, WI 53082-0359. Offers MBA. *Entrance requirements:* For master's, GMAT. Expenses: Contact institution.

Lamar University, College of Graduate Studies, College of Business, Beaumont, TX 77710. Offers accounting (MBA); experiential business and Entrepreneurship (MBA); financial management (MBA); healthcare administration (MBA); information systems (MBA); management (MBA). *Accreditation:* AACSB. Part-time and evening/weekend programs available. *Faculty:* 20 full-time (8 women), 2 part-time/adjunct (1 woman). *Students:* 55 full-time (27 women), 45 part-time (20 women); includes 17 minority (9 African Americans, 4 Asian Americans or Pacific Islanders, 4 Hispanic Americans), 14 international. Average age 29. 131 applicants, 34% accepted, 29 enrolled. In 2006, 29 degrees awarded. *Degree requirements:* For master's, thesis optional. *Entrance requirements:* For master's, GMAT. Additional exam requirements/recommendations for international students: Required—TOEFL (minimum score 525 paper-based; 197 computer-based). *Application deadline:* For fall admission, 3/15 priority date for domestic students; for spring admission, 10/1 priority date for domestic students. Applications are processed on a rolling basis. Application fee: $25 ($50 for international students). *Expenses:* Tuition, nonresident: part-time $33 per hour. Required fees: $43 per hour. $110 per semester. *Financial support:* In 2006–07, 12 students received support, including 4 research assistantships with partial tuition reimbursements available; fellowships with tuition reimbursements available, career-related internships or fieldwork, Federal Work-Study, institutionally sponsored loans, scholarships/grants, and tuition waivers (partial) also available. Support available to part-time students. Financial award application deadline: 4/1; financial award applicants required to submit FAFSA. *Faculty research:* Marketing, finance, quantitative methods, MIS, legal, environmental. Total annual research expenditures: $26,000. *Unit head:* Dr. Enrique R. Venta, Dean, 409-880-8604, Fax: 409-880-8088, E-mail: henry.venta@lamar.edu. *Application contact:* Dr. Brad Mayer, Professor and Associate Dean, 409-880-2383, Fax: 409-880-8605, E-mail: bradley.mayer@lamar.edu.

La Salle University, School of Business, Philadelphia, PA 19141-1199. Offers MBA, MS, Certificate, MSN/MBA. *Accreditation:* AACSB. Part-time and evening/weekend programs available. *Entrance requirements:* For master's, GMAT; for Certificate, MBA. Additional exam requirements/recommendations for international students: Required—TOEFL. Electronic applications accepted. Expenses: Contact institution. *Faculty research:* Small business development, unemployment insurance costs, nonprofit business, transfer pricing, forecasting.

Lasell College, Program in Management, Newton, MA 02466-2709. Offers elder care administration (MS); elder care marketing (MS); management (MS); marketing (MS). Part-time and evening/weekend programs available. *Entrance requirements:* Additional exam requirements/recommendations for international students: Required—TOEFL (minimum score 500 paper-based). Electronic applications accepted.

See Close-Up on page 281.

La Sierra University, School of Business and Management, Riverside, CA 92515. Offers business administration and management (MBA); executive business administration (EMBA); leadership, values, and ethics for business and management (Certificate). *Degree requirements:* For master's, research project. *Entrance requirements:* For master's, GMAT, minimum GPA of 3.0. Additional exam requirements/recommendations for international students: Required—TOEFL. *Faculty research:* Financial econometrics, institutional assessment and strategic planning, legal issues in management, behavioral finance, content of financial reports.

Laurentian University, School of Graduate Studies and Research, School of Commerce and Administration, Sudbury, ON P3E 2C6, Canada. Offers MBA. Part-time and evening/weekend programs available. *Entrance requirements:* For master's, GMAT, 2 years of work experience. *Faculty research:* Small business and entrepreneurship development, mutual fund performance, donorship behavior, stress and organizations, quality programs.

Lawrence Technological University, College of Management, Southfield, MI 48075-1058. Offers business administration (MBA, DBA); information systems (MS); information technology (DM); operations management (MS). *Accreditation:* ACBSP. Part-time and evening/weekend programs available. *Faculty:* 11 full-time (4 women), 61 part-time/adjunct (13 women). *Students:* 47 full-time (20 women), 702 part-time (235 women); includes 285 minority (98 African Americans, 178 Asian Americans or Pacific Islanders, 9 Hispanic Americans), 15 international. Average age 34. 337 applicants, 90% accepted, 192 enrolled. In 2006, 281 degrees awarded. *Entrance requirements:* For master's, GMAT. Additional exam requirements/recommendations for international students: Required—TOEFL (minimum score 550 paper-based; 213 computer-based). *Application deadline:* For fall admission, 8/1 priority date for domestic students; for winter admission, 12/1 priority date for domestic students; for spring admission, 5/1 for domestic students. Applications are processed on a rolling basis. Application fee: $50. Electronic applications accepted. *Financial support:* Institutionally sponsored loans available. Support available to part-time students. Financial award application deadline: 3/1; financial award applicants required to submit FAFSA. *Unit head:* Dr. Lou DeGennaro, Dean, 248-204-3050, E-mail: degennaro@ltu.edu. *Application contact:* Jane Rohrback, Director of Admissions, 248-204-3160, Fax: 248-204-3188, E-mail: admissions@ltu.edu.

Lebanese American University, School of Business, Beirut, Lebanon. Offers MBA.

Lebanon Valley College, Graduate Studies and Continuing Education, Program in Business Administration, Annville, PA 17003-1400. Offers MBA. Part-time and evening/weekend programs available. *Faculty:* 6 part-time/adjunct (1 woman). *Students:* Average age 34. In 2006, 22 degrees awarded. *Entrance requirements:* For master's, GMAT. *Application deadline:* Applications are processed on a rolling basis. Application fee: $30. Electronic applications accepted. *Expenses:* Tuition: Full-time $28,280; part-time $390 per credit. Required fees: $575. *Financial support:* Application deadline: 5/1; *Unit head:* Dr. Barney T Raffield, Coordinator MBA, Professor of Business Administration, 717-867-6335.

Lehigh University, College of Business and Economics, Bethlehem, PA 18015-3094. Offers accounting (MS), including accounting and information analysis; business administration (MBA); economics (MS, PhD), including economics, health and bio-pharmaceutical economics (MS); entrepreneurship (Certificate); finance (MS), including analytical finance, finance; organizational leadership (Certificate); project management (Certificate); supply chain management (Certificate); MBA/E; MBA/M Ed. *Accreditation:* AACSB. Part-time and evening/weekend programs available. Postbaccalaureate distance learning degree programs offered (minimal on-campus study). *Faculty:* 64 full-time (14 women), 12 part-time/adjunct (0 women). *Students:* 87 full-time (25 women), 219 part-time (60 women); includes 34 minority (9 African Americans, 22 Asian Americans or Pacific Islanders, 3 Hispanic Americans), 56 international. 371 applicants, 69% accepted, 151 enrolled. In 2006, 103 master's, 2 doctorates awarded. Terminal master's awarded for partial completion of doctoral program. *Degree requirements:* For master's, thesis optional; for doctorate, thesis/dissertation, proposal defense, comprehensive exam. *Entrance requirements:* For master's, GMAT, GRE General Test; for doctorate, GMAT or GRE General Test. Additional exam requirements/recommendations for international students: Required—TOEFL (minimum score 600 paper-based; 250 computer-based). *Application deadline:* For fall admission, 7/15 for domestic students, 5/1 for international students; for spring admission, 12/1 for domestic and international students. Applications are processed on a rolling basis. Application fee: $60. Electronic applications accepted. *Expenses: Contact institution. Financial support:* In 2006–07, 2 fellowships with full tuition reimbursements (averaging $13,200 per year), 8 research assistantships with full and partial tuition reimbursements (averaging $1,000 per year), 13 teaching assistantships with full tuition reimbursements (averaging $13,200 per year) were awarded; career-related internships or fieldwork, scholarships/grants, health care benefits, tuition waivers (full and partial), and unspecified assistantships also available. Support available to part-time students. Financial award application deadline: 1/15. *Faculty research:* Public finance, energy, investments, activity-based costing, management information systems. *Unit head:* Michael G. Kolchin, Graduate Business Programs, 610-758-4450, Fax: 610-758-5283, E-mail: mgk1@lehigh.edu. *Application contact:* Mary- Theresa Taglang, Director of Graduate Programs, 610-758-5285, Fax: 610-758-5283, E-mail: mtt4@lehigh.edu.

See Close-Ups on pages 283, 285, and 1807.

Le Moyne College, Division of Management, Syracuse, NY 13214. Offers MBA. Part-time and evening/weekend programs available. *Faculty:* 18 full-time (3 women), 1 part-time/adjunct (0 women). *Students:* 3 full-time (2 women), 98 part-time (45 women); includes 7 minority (4 African Americans, 1 American Indian/Alaska Native, 2 Asian Americans or Pacific Islanders). Average age 33. 80 applicants, 85% accepted, 68 enrolled. In 2006, 38 degrees awarded. *Entrance requirements:* For master's, GMAT, interview, Bachelors, 3.0 GPA, resumè, 2 letters of recommendation, application. Additional exam requirements/recommendations for international students: Required—TOEFL (minimum score 550 paper-based; 213 computer-based). *Application deadline:* Applications are processed on a rolling basis. Application fee: $0. *Expenses:* Tuition: Full-time $9,846; part-time $547 per credit hour. Tuition and fees vary according to program. *Financial support:* In 2006–07, 27 students received support. Scholarships/grants and unspecified assistantships available. Support available to part-time students. Financial award applicants required to submit FAFSA. *Faculty research:* Performance evaluation outcomes assessment, technology outsourcing, international business, systems for web-based information seeking. *Unit head:* Dr. George Kulick, Director of MBA Program, 315-445-4786, Fax: 315-445-4787, E-mail: kulick@lemoyne.edu. *Application contact:* Kristen P. Trapasso, Director of Graduate Admission, 315-445-4265, Fax: 315-445-6027, E-mail: trapaskp@lemoyne.edu.

Lenoir-Rhyne College, Graduate Programs, Charles M. Snipes School of Business, Hickory, NC 28603. Offers MBA. *Accreditation:* ACBSP. Part-time and evening/weekend programs available. *Degree requirements:* For master's, capstone course. *Entrance requirements:* For master's, GMAT, minimum undergraduate GPA of 2.7, graduate 3.0. Additional exam requirements/recommendations for international students: Required—TOEFL (minimum score 600 paper-based). Electronic applications accepted. Expenses: Contact institution.

LeTourneau University, Graduate and Professional Studies, Longview, TX 75607-7001. Offers business administration (MBA); educational leadership (MBA). Part-time and evening/weekend programs available. Postbaccalaureate distance learning degree programs offered (no on-campus study). *Faculty:* 7 full-time (0 women), 29 part-time/adjunct (7 women). *Students:* 217 full-time (135 women), 123 part-time (71 women); includes 165 minority (124 African Americans, 8 American Indian/Alaska Native, 7 Asian Americans or Pacific Islanders, 26 Hispanic Americans), 2 international. Average age 37. 394 applicants, 90% accepted, 337 enrolled. In 2006, 182 degrees awarded. *Entrance requirements:* For master's, minimum GPA of 2.8, 3 years of full-time work experience. Additional exam requirements/recommendations for international students: Required—TOEFL. *Application deadline:* Applications are processed on a rolling basis. Application fee: $50. Electronic applications accepted. *Expenses:* Tuition: Full-time $10,043; part-time $510 per credit hour. Required fees: $975; $50 per credit hour. One-time fee: $75 full-time. *Financial support:* Applicants required to submit FAFSA. *Unit head:* Dr. Scott Ray, Associate Vice President for the school of Graduate and Professional Studies, 903-233-3250, Fax: 903-233-3227, E-mail: scottray@letu.edu. *Application contact:* Chris Fontaine, Assistant VP for Enrollment Management and Market Research, 903-233-3250, Fax: 903-233-3227, E-mail: chrisfontaine@letu.edu.

Lewis University, College of Business, Graduate School of Management, Romeoville, IL 60446. Offers accounting (MBA); e-business (MBA); finance (MBA); healthcare management (MBA); human resources management (MBA); international business (MBA); management information systems (MBA); marketing (MBA); technology and operations management (MBA). Part-time programs available. *Entrance requirements:* For master's, interview.

Liberty University, School of Business, Lynchburg, VA 24502. Offers MBA. Part-time programs available. Postbaccalaureate distance learning degree programs offered (minimal on-campus study). *Faculty:* 9 full-time (0 women), 6 part-time/adjunct (3 women). *Students:* 206 full-time (88 women), 644 part-time (202 women); includes 197 minority (154 African Americans, 4 American Indian/Alaska Native, 18 Asian Americans or Pacific Islanders, 21 Hispanic Americans), 22 international. Average age 34. 712 applicants, 92% accepted, 334 enrolled. In 2006, 265 degrees awarded. *Entrance requirements:* For master's, minimum undergraduate GPA of 3.0. Additional exam requirements/recommendations for international students: Required—TOEFL (minimum score 600 paper-based; 250 computer-based). *Application deadline:* For fall admission, 6/1 for domestic students; for spring admission, 11/1 for domestic students. Applications are processed on a rolling basis. Application fee: $35. Electronic applications accepted. *Expenses: Contact institution. Financial support:* In 2006–07, 625 students received support. *Faculty research:* International business, export management strategy, knowledge management, global industries and operations, tourism. *Unit head:* Dr. Bruce K. Bell, Dean, 434-592-3863, Fax: 434-582-2366, E-mail: bkbell@liberty.edu. *Application contact:* Kyle A Falce, Director of Graduate Admissions, 800-424-9596, Fax: 800-628-7977, E-mail: gradadmissions@liberty.edu.

Lincoln Memorial University, School of Business, Harrogate, TN 37752-1901. Offers MBA. Part-time and evening/weekend programs available. *Faculty:* 4 full-time (0 women). *Students:* 18 full-time (8 women), 37 part-time (18 women); includes 2 minority (both African Americans), 6 international. 72 applicants, 88% accepted. In 2006, 22 degrees awarded. *Degree requirements:* For master's, thesis optional. *Entrance requirements:* For master's, GMAT, minimum GPA of 2.5 in business, 3.0 overall; interview; writing sample. *Application deadline:* For fall admission, 8/10 priority date for domestic students. Applications are processed on a rolling basis. Application fee: $25. *Financial support:* Career-related internships or fieldwork and unspecified assistantships available. Support available to part-time students. Financial award application deadline: 4/1; financial award applicants required to submit FAFSA. *Unit head:* Dr. Bill Hamby, Dean, 423-869-7085, Fax: 423-869-6269, E-mail: bill.hamby@lmunet.

Business Administration and Management—General

Lincoln Memorial University *(continued)*
edu. *Application contact:* Robin Lamb, Office Assistant, Graduate Studies, 423-869-6254, Fax: 423-869-6269, E-mail: robin.lamb@lmunet.edu.

Lincoln University, Business Administration Program, Oakland, CA 94612. Offers MBA. *Degree requirements:* For master's, thesis. *Entrance requirements:* For master's, minimum GPA of 2.7. Electronic applications accepted.

Lincoln University, School of Graduate Studies and Continuing Education, College of Business and Professional Studies, Department of Business and Economics, Jefferson City, MO 65102. Offers business administration (MBA), including accounting, entrepreneurship, management, public administration and policy. *Accreditation:* ACBSP. Part-time and evening/weekend programs available. *Faculty:* 7 part-time/adjunct (2 women). *Students:* 39 full-time (26 women), 23 part-time (14 women); includes 18 minority (17 African Americans, 1 American Indian/Alaska Native), 24 international. Average age 31. 28 applicants, 96% accepted, 14 enrolled. In 2006, 31 degrees awarded. *Degree requirements:* For master's, portfolio, thesis optional. *Entrance requirements:* For master's, GMAT. Additional exam requirements/recommendations for international students: Required—TOEFL (minimum score 500 paper-based; 173 computer-based; 61 iBT). *Application deadline:* For fall admission, 7/1 priority date for domestic and international students; for spring admission, 12/1 priority date for domestic and international students. Applications are processed on a rolling basis. Application fee: $17. *Expenses:* Tuition, state resident: part-time $189 per credit hour. Tuition, nonresident: part-time $351 per credit hour. Required fees: $15 per credit hour. $20 per semester. *Financial support:* Federal Work-Study and scholarships/grants available. Financial award application deadline: 4/1; financial award applicants required to submit FAFSA. *Unit head:* Dr. Ogugua Anunoby, Department Head, 573-681-5487, Fax: 573-681-6085, E-mail: anunobyo@lincolnu.edu.

Lindenwood University, Graduate Programs, Division of Management, St. Charles, MO 63301-1695. Offers accounting (MBA, MS); business administration (MBA); entrepreneurial studies (MBA); finance (MBA, MS); human resource management (MBA); human resources (MS); international business (MBA, MS); management (MBA, MS); management information systems (MBA, MS); managing business to business (MA); managing human resources (MA); managing international business (MA); managing investment management (MA); managing leadership (MA); managing marketing (MA); managing organizational behavior (MA); managing sales (MA); managing, training and development (MA); marketing (MBA, MS); nonprofit administration (MA); public management (MBA, MS); sport management (MA). Part-time and evening/weekend programs available. *Faculty:* 38 full-time (15 women), 20 part-time/adjunct (5 women). *Students:* 177 full-time (78 women), 138 part-time (67 women); includes 43 minority (27 African Americans, 4 American Indian/Alaska Native, 6 Asian Americans or Pacific Islanders, 6 Hispanic Americans), 73 international. Average age 30. In 2006, 159 degrees awarded. *Degree requirements:* For master's, thesis (for some programs). *Entrance requirements:* For master's, interview, minimum GPA of 3.0. Additional exam requirements/recommendations for international students: Required—TOEFL (minimum score 550 paper-based; 173 computer-based). *Application deadline:* For fall admission, 7/30 priority date for domestic students, 9/30 priority date for international students; for winter admission, 12/30 priority date for domestic and international students; for spring admission, 3/30 priority date for domestic and international students. Applications are processed on a rolling basis. Application fee: $30 ($100 for international students). Electronic applications accepted. *Expenses:* Tuition: Part-time $340 per credit hour. Tuition and fees vary according to course level, course load, degree level and program. *Financial support:* Career-related internships or fieldwork, Federal Work-Study, institutionally sponsored loans, and tuition waivers (partial) available. Financial award application deadline: 6/30; financial award applicants required to submit FAFSA. *Unit head:* Ed Morris, Dean, 636-949-4832, Fax: 636-949-4910, E-mail: emorris@lindenwood.edu. *Application contact:* Brett Barger, Dean Adult, Corporate and Graduate Admissions, 636-949-4366, Fax: 636-949-4109, E-mail: bbarger@lindenwood.edu.

Lindenwood University, Graduate Programs, Programs in Individualized Education, St. Charles, MO 63301-1695. Offers administration (MSA); business administration (MBA); communications (MA); criminal justice and administration (MS); gerontology (MA); health management (MS); human resource management (MS); management (MSA); marketing (MSA); writing (MFA). Part-time and evening/weekend programs available. *Faculty:* 18 full-time (9 women), 50 part-time/adjunct (25 women). *Students:* 595 full-time (348 women), 55 part-time (37 women); includes 176 minority (163 African Americans, 1 American Indian/Alaska Native, 5 Asian Americans or Pacific Islanders, 7 Hispanic Americans), 10 international. Average age 34. In 2006, 303 degrees awarded. *Degree requirements:* For master's, thesis. *Entrance requirements:* For master's, interview, minimum GPA of 3.0. Additional exam requirements/recommendations for international students: Required—TOEFL. *Application deadline:* For fall admission, 9/30 priority date for domestic and international students; for winter admission, 12/30 priority date for domestic and international students; for spring admission, 3/30 priority date for domestic and international students. Applications are processed on a rolling basis. Application fee: $30 ($100 for international students). *Expenses:* Tuition; Part-time $340 per credit hour. Tuition and fees vary according to course level, course load, degree level and program. *Financial support:* Career-related internships or fieldwork, institutionally sponsored loans, tuition waivers (partial), and unspecified assistantships available. Financial award application deadline: 6/30; financial award applicants required to submit FAFSA. *Unit head:* Dan Kemper, Dean of LCIE, 636-916-9125, E-mail: dkemper@lindenwood.edu. *Application contact:* Brett Barger, Dean, Adult, Corporate and Graduate Admissions, 636-949-4934, Fax: 636-949-4109, E-mail: adultadmissions@lindenwood.edu.

Lipscomb University, MBA Program, Nashville, TN 37204-3951. Offers accounting (MBA); business administration (general) (MBA); conflict management (MBA); financial services (MBA); healthcare management (MBA); leadership (MBA); nonprofit management (MBA). *Accreditation:* ACBSP. Part-time and evening/weekend programs available. *Faculty:* 11 full-time (3 women), 6 part-time/adjunct (0 women). *Students:* 18 full-time (6 women), 50 part-time (23 women); includes 5 minority (4 African Americans, 1 American Indian/Alaska Native), 2 international. Average age 30. 48 applicants, 73% accepted, 27 enrolled. In 2006, 30 degrees awarded. *Median time to degree:* Master's–1 year full-time, 2.3 years part-time. *Entrance requirements:* For master's, GMAT, interview, 2 references, resumé. Additional exam requirements/recommendations for international students: Required—TOEFL (minimum score 570 paper-based; 230 computer-based). *Application deadline:* For fall admission, 7/1 for domestic students, 2/1 for international students; for winter admission, 12/1 for domestic students, 6/1 for international students. Applications are processed on a rolling basis. Application fee: $50 ($75 for international students). Electronic applications accepted. *Expenses:* Contact institution. *Financial support:* In 2006–07, 25 students received support. Career-related internships or fieldwork, Federal Work-Study, scholarships/grants, tuition waivers (partial), and unspecified assistantships available. Support available to part-time students. Financial award application deadline: 7/1; financial award applicants required to submit FAFSA. *Faculty research:* Impact of spirituality on organization commitment; leadership; psychological empowerment; training. *Unit head:* Dr. Steven K. Yoho, Associate Dean of Graduate Business Studies, 615-966-1833, Fax: 615-966-1818, E-mail: steven.yoho@lipscomb.edu. *Application contact:* Jackie Cash, MBA Assistant, 615-966-1833, Fax: 615-966-1818, E-mail: jackie.cash@lipscomb.edu.

Long Island University, Brooklyn Campus, School of Business, Public Administration and Information Sciences, Program in Business Administration, Brooklyn, NY 11201-8423. Offers MBA. Part-time and evening/weekend programs available. *Entrance requirements:* For master's, GMAT or GRE General Test, 2 letters of recommendation. Additional exam requirements/recommendations for international students: Required—TOEFL (minimum score 500 paper-based; 173 computer-based). Electronic applications accepted.

Long Island University, C.W. Post Campus, College of Management, School of Business, Brookville, NY 11548-1300. Offers accounting and taxation (Certificate); business administration (Certificate); finance (MBA, Certificate); general business administration (MBA); international business (MBA, Certificate); management (MBA, Certificate); management information systems (MBA, Certificate); marketing (MBA, Certificate). *Accreditation:* AACSB. Part-time and evening/weekend programs available. *Entrance requirements:* For master's, GMAT, resumé, minimum GPA of 3.0, 2 letters of recommendation. Additional exam requirements/recommendations for international students: Required—TOEFL (minimum score 527 paper-based; 197 computer-based). Electronic applications accepted. *Faculty research:* Financial markets, consumer behavior.

Announcement: The College of Management at the C. W. Post Campus of Long Island University offers full- and part-time programs. Degrees, accredited by AACSB–International, are awarded in business administration. The MBA curriculum has been wholly redesigned and now requires between 36 and 48 credits to complete. Courses are offered on weekdays and Saturdays on this campus and on the Brentwood campus. A highly regarded Corporate Program presents classes on-site at various corporate locations. NASPAA-accredited MPA degrees are awarded in public administration and health-care administration. Dual JD/MPA and JD/MBA degrees are offered with Touro Law School. MS degrees are awarded in taxation and accountancy, which offer concentrations in information systems, taxation, and professional accountancy. Accelerated BS/MS and BS/MBA in accountancy are also available for qualified students who wish to combine a BS in accountancy with an MS in accounting or an MBA. Advanced certificates are offered in business, business administration, criminal justice, nonprofit management, and gerontology. Contact 516-299-2100 (telephone), campusmba@cwpost.liu.edu (e-mail), or http://www.liu.edu/com.htm

---

Long Island University, Rockland Graduate Campus, Graduate School, Program in Business Administration, Orangeburg, NY 10962. Offers MBA, Post Master's Certificate. *Entrance requirements:* For master's, GMAT.

Long Island University, Westchester Graduate Campus, Program in Business Administration, Purchase, NY 10577. Offers MBA. Part-time and evening/weekend programs available. *Faculty:* 1 full-time (0 women), 7 part-time/adjunct (3 women). *Students:* 13 applicants, 77% accepted, 7 enrolled. In 2006, 18 degrees awarded. *Entrance requirements:* For master's, GMAT. Additional exam requirements/recommendations for international students: Required—TOEFL (minimum score 500 paper-based; 173 computer-based). *Application deadline:* Applications are processed on a rolling basis. Application fee: $30. *Expenses:* Tuition: Part-time $790 per credit. *Financial support:* In 2006–07, 4 students received support. Scholarships/grants, tuition waivers (partial), and unspecified assistantships available. Financial award applicants required to submit FAFSA. *Unit head:* Dr. Lynn Johnson, Program Director, 914-831-2711, Fax: 914-251-5959, E-mail: lynn.johnson@liu.edu. *Application contact:* Ellen Brief, Coordinator of Admissions, Marketing, Student Services and Public Relations, 914-831-2701, Fax: 914-251-5959, E-mail: ellen.brief@liu.edu.

Longwood University, Office of Graduate Studies, College of Business and Economics, Farmville, VA 23909. Offers retail management (MBA). *Accreditation:* AACSB. *Degree requirements:* For master's, internship. *Entrance requirements:* For master's, GMAT.

Louisiana State University and Agricultural and Mechanical College, Graduate School, E. J. Ourso College of Business, Department of Finance, Baton Rouge, LA 70803. Offers business administration (PhD), including finance; finance (MS). *Faculty:* 13 full-time (3 women), 2 part-time/adjunct (0 women). *Students:* 21 full-time (3 women), 4 part-time (1 woman); includes 1 African American, 11 international. Average age 30. 43 applicants, 37% accepted, 3 enrolled. In 2006, 11 master's, 2 doctorates awarded. *Degree requirements:* For master's, thesis or alternative; for doctorate, thesis/dissertation. *Entrance requirements:* For master's and doctorate, GMAT. Additional exam requirements/recommendations for international students: Required—TOEFL (minimum score 550 paper-based; 213 computer-based; 79 iBT). *Application deadline:* For fall admission, 1/25 priority date for domestic students, 5/15 for international students; for spring admission, 10/15 for international students. Applications are processed on a rolling basis. Application fee: $25. *Financial support:* In 2006–07, 12 students received support, including 5 research assistantships with full and partial tuition reimbursements available (averaging $12,400 per year), 5 teaching assistantships with full and partial tuition reimbursements available (averaging $12,000 per year); fellowships, career-related internships or fieldwork, Federal Work-Study, scholarships/grants, and unspecified assistantships also available. Support available to part-time students. Financial award application deadline: 4/1; financial award applicants required to submit FAFSA. *Faculty research:* Derivatives and risk management, capital structure, asset pricing, spatial statistics, financial institutions and underwriting. Total annual research expenditures: $16,562. *Unit head:* Dr. William R. Lane, Chair, 225-578-6367, Fax: 225-578-6366, E-mail: filane@lsu.edu.

Louisiana State University and Agricultural and Mechanical College, Graduate School, E. J. Ourso College of Business, Department of Management, Baton Rouge, LA 70803. Offers business administration (PhD), including management. *Accreditation:* AACSB. *Faculty:* 12 full-time (1 woman). *Students:* 9 full-time (3 women), 5 international. Average age 33. 12 applicants, 8% accepted, 1 enrolled. In 2006, 3 degrees awarded. *Degree requirements:* For doctorate, thesis/dissertation. *Entrance requirements:* For doctorate, GMAT. Additional exam requirements/recommendations for international students: Required—TOEFL (minimum score 550 paper-based; 213 computer-based; 79 iBT). *Application deadline:* For fall admission, 1/25 priority date for domestic students, 5/15 for international students; for spring admission, 10/15 for international students. Applications are processed on a rolling basis. Application fee: $25. Electronic applications accepted. *Financial support:* In 2006–07, 8 students received support, including 2 research assistantships with full and partial tuition reimbursements available (averaging $16,000 per year), 6 teaching assistantships with full and partial tuition reimbursements available (averaging $13,792 per year); fellowships, Federal Work-Study, institutionally sponsored loans, scholarships/grants, and unspecified assistantships also available. Support available to part-time students. Financial award applicants required to submit FAFSA. *Faculty research:* Human resource management, organizational behavior, strategy. Total annual research expenditures: $4,970. *Unit head:* Dr. Robert Justis, Chair, 225-578-6402, Fax: 225-578-6983, E-mail: rjustis@lsu.edu. *Application contact:* Jean McGuire, Graduate Adviser, 225-578-5187, Fax: 225-578-6140, E-mail: mcguire@lsu.edu.

Louisiana State University and Agricultural and Mechanical College, Graduate School, E. J. Ourso College of Business, Department of Marketing, Baton Rouge, LA 70803. Offers business administration (PhD), including marketing. Part-time programs available. *Faculty:* 9 full-time (2 women). *Students:* 10 full-time (6 women), 3 part-time (1 woman), 8 international. Average age 33. 16 applicants, 38% accepted, 4 enrolled. In 2006, 3 degrees awarded. *Degree requirements:* For doctorate, thesis/dissertation. *Entrance requirements:* Additional exam requirements/recommendations for international students: Required—TOEFL (minimum score 550 paper-based; 213 computer-based; 79 iBT). *Application deadline:* For fall admission, 1/25 priority date for domestic students, 5/15 for international students; for spring admission, 10/15 for international students. Applications are processed on a rolling basis. Application fee: $25. Electronic applications accepted. *Financial support:* In 2006–07, 10 students received support, including 9 teaching assistantships with full and partial tuition reimbursements available (averaging $16,533 per year); fellowships, research assistantships with partial tuition reimbursements available, career-related internships or fieldwork, Federal Work-Study, institutionally sponsored loans, scholarships/grants, and unspecified assistantships also available. Support available to part-time students. Financial award applicants required to submit FAFSA. *Faculty research:* Consumer behavior, marketing strategy, global marketing, e-commerce, branding/brand equity. *Unit head:* Dr. Alvin C. Burns, Chair, 225-578-8786, Fax: 225-578-8616, E-mail: alburns@lsu.edu. *Application contact:* Dr. William C. Black, Graduate Adviser, 225-578-8403, Fax: 225-578-8616, E-mail: wcblack@lsu.edu.

Louisiana State University and Agricultural and Mechanical College, Graduate School, E. J. Ourso College of Business, Flores MBA Program, Baton Rouge, LA 70803. Offers EMBA, MBA, PMBA. *Accreditation:* AACSB. *Students:* 191 full-time (57 women), 107 part-time (38 women); includes 34 minority (23 African Americans, 1 American Indian/Alaska Native, 4 Asian Americans or Pacific Islanders, 6 Hispanic Americans), 18 international.

Average age 29. 257 applicants, 64% accepted, 42 enrolled. In 2006, 138 degrees awarded. *Entrance requirements:* Additional exam requirements/recommendations for international students: Required—TOEFL (minimum score 550 paper-based; 213 computer-based; 79 iBT). *Application deadline:* For fall admission, 1/25 priority date for domestic students, 5/15 for international students; for spring admission, 10/15 for international students. Application fee: $25. Electronic applications accepted. *Financial support:* In 2006–07, 83 students received support, including 3 fellowships (averaging $17,823 per year), 52 research assistantships with partial tuition reimbursements available (averaging $9,316 per year), 8 teaching assistantships with full and partial tuition reimbursements available (averaging $10,301 per year); Federal Work-Study, institutionally sponsored loans, scholarships/grants, and unspecified assistantships also available. Support available to part-time students. Financial award applicants required to submit FAFSA. *Unit head:* Dr. David Crary, Director, 225-578-8867, Fax: 225-578-2421, E-mail: dcrary2@lsu.edu. *Application contact:* Kathleen L. Bosworth, Assistant to the Director and Counselor, 225-578-8867, Fax: 225-578-2421, E-mail: babosw@lsu.edu.

Louisiana State University in Shreveport, College of Business Administration, Shreveport, LA 71115-2399. Offers healthcare (MBA). *Accreditation:* AACSB. Part-time and evening/weekend programs available. *Entrance requirements:* For master's, GMAT. Additional exam requirements/recommendations for international students: Required—TOEFL (minimum score 550 paper-based; 213 computer-based). *Faculty research:* Real estate, organizational behavior, finance, operations research, information systems technology.

Louisiana Tech University, Graduate School, College of Administration and Business, Ruston, LA 71272. Offers MBA, MPA, DBA. *Accreditation:* AACSB. Part-time programs available. *Degree requirements:* For doctorate, thesis/dissertation. *Entrance requirements:* For master's and doctorate, GMAT.

Loyola College in Maryland, Graduate Programs, Sellinger School of Business and Management, Program in Business Administration, Baltimore, MD 21210-2699. Offers decision sciences (MBA); economics (MBA); finance (MBA); marketing/management (MBA). *Accreditation:* AACSB. Part-time and evening/weekend programs available. *Students:* 47 full-time (17 women), 733 part-time (315 women); includes 111 minority (59 African Americans, 1 American Indian/Alaska Native, 37 Asian Americans or Pacific Islanders, 14 Hispanic Americans), 19 international. Average age 31. In 2006, 215 degrees awarded. *Entrance requirements:* For master's, GMAT. Additional exam requirements/recommendations for international students: Required—TOEFL (minimum score 550 paper-based; 213 computer-based). *Application deadline:* For fall admission, 8/15 priority date for domestic students; for spring admission, 11/20 priority date for domestic students. Applications are processed on a rolling basis. Application fee: $50. *Financial support:* Applicants required to submit FAFSA. *Unit head:* Ann Attanasio, Director, 410-617-2308, E-mail: aattanasio@loyola.edu.

Loyola College in Maryland, Graduate Programs, Sellinger School of Business and Management, Program in Executive Business Administration, Baltimore, MD 21210-2699. Offers MBA, XMBA. *Accreditation:* AACSB. Part-time and evening/weekend programs available. *Students:* 145 full-time (51 women); includes 5 minority (4 African Americans, 1 Asian American or Pacific Islander). Average age 38. In 2006, 53 degrees awarded. *Entrance requirements:* For master's, GMAT. Additional exam requirements/recommendations for international students: Required—TOEFL (minimum score 550 paper-based; 213 computer-based). *Application deadline:* For fall admission, 8/15 priority date for domestic students; for spring admission, 11/20 priority date for domestic students. Applications are processed on a rolling basis. Application fee: $50. *Financial support:* Applicants required to submit FAFSA. *Unit head:* Manette Gates, Director, 410-617-2836, E-mail: mgates@loyola.edu.

Loyola Marymount University, Graduate Division, College of Business Administration, Los Angeles, CA 90045-2659. Offers MBA, JD/MBA. *Accreditation:* AACSB. Part-time and evening/weekend programs available. *Faculty:* 54 full-time (10 women), 25 part-time/adjunct (2 women). *Students:* 284 full-time (103 women), 48 part-time (24 women); includes 119 minority (24 African Americans, 1 American Indian/Alaska Native, 54 Asian Americans or Pacific Islanders, 40 Hispanic Americans), 29 international. Average age 25. 291 applicants, 69% accepted, 129 enrolled. In 2006, 162 degrees awarded. *Degree requirements:* For master's, thesis (for some programs). *Entrance requirements:* For master's, GMAT, minimum AACSB index of 1125. Additional exam requirements/recommendations for international students: Required—TOEFL (minimum score 600 paper-based; 250 computer-based). *Application deadline:* Applications are processed on a rolling basis. Application fee: $50. Electronic applications accepted. *Expenses:* Contact institution. *Financial support:* In 2006–07, 122 students received support, including 9 research assistantships (averaging $12,370 per year); Federal Work-Study and scholarships/grants also available. Support available to part-time students. Financial award application deadline: 6/1; financial award applicants required to submit FAFSA. *Faculty research:* International management, business ethics, strategy implementation. *Unit head:* Dr. John T. Wholihan, Dean, 310-338-7504, Fax: 310-338-2899. *Application contact:* Dr. Rachelle Katz, Associate Dean and Director of MBA Program, 310-338-2848, E-mail: rkatz@lmu.edu.

Loyola University Chicago, Graduate School of Business, Chicago, IL 60611-2196. Offers accountancy (MS, MSA); business administration (MBA); healthcare management (MBA); human resources and employee relations (MS, MSHR); information systems and operations management (MS), including information systems management; marketing (MS, MSIMC), including integrated marketing communications (MS), marketing (MSIMC); strategic financial services (MBA); JD/MBA; MBA/MSA; MSIMC/MBA; MSISM/MBA; MSN/MBA. *Accreditation:* AACSB. Part-time and evening/weekend programs available. *Faculty:* 64 full-time (14 women). *Students:* 180 full-time (94 women), 546 part-time (262 women); includes 153 minority (44 African Americans, 73 Asian Americans or Pacific Islanders, 36 Hispanic Americans). Average age 27. 717 applicants, 72% accepted, 314 enrolled. In 2006, 329 degrees awarded. *Entrance requirements:* For master's, GMAT, letters of recommendation, personal statement. Additional exam requirements/recommendations for international students: Required—TOEFL (minimum score 550 paper-based; 213 computer-based; 80 iBT). *Application deadline:* For fall admission, 7/1 for domestic and international students; for winter admission, 9/1 for domestic and international students; for spring admission, 1/3 for domestic and international students. Applications are processed on a rolling basis. Application fee: $50. Electronic applications accepted. *Expenses:* Contact institution. *Financial support:* In 2006–07, 25 students received support, including 14 research assistantships with partial tuition reimbursements available (averaging $5,000 per year); career-related internships or fieldwork, Federal Work-Study, and institutionally sponsored loans also available. Support available to part-time students. Financial award application deadline: 3/10; financial award applicants required to submit FAFSA. *Faculty research:* Financial markets, marketing research, futures and options, e-commerce strategy, business ethics. *Unit head:* Dr. Mary Ann McGrath, Associate Dean, 312-915-7107, Fax: 312-915-6136, E-mail: mmcgrat@luc.edu. *Application contact:* Olivia Heath, Enrollment Advisor, 312-915-8908, Fax: 312-915-7207, E-mail: oheath@luc.edu.

Loyola University New Orleans, Joseph A. Butt, S.J., College of Business Administration, Program in Business Administration, New Orleans, LA 70118-6195. Offers MBA, JD/MBA. *Accreditation:* AACSB. Part-time and evening/weekend programs available. Postbaccalaureate distance learning degree programs offered (minimal on-campus study). *Degree requirements:* For master's, capstone course. *Entrance requirements:* For master's, GMAT, minimum GPA of 3.0, resumé, 2 letters of recommendation, work experience in field. Additional exam requirements/recommendations for international students: Required—TOEFL (minimum score 550 paper-based; 213 computer-based). Electronic applications accepted. *Faculty research:* Ethics, international business, entrepreneurship, quality management, risk management.

Lynchburg College, Graduate Studies, School of Business and Economics, Lynchburg, VA 24501-3199. Offers business (MBA). Part-time and evening/weekend programs available. *Faculty:* 6 full-time (1 woman), 1 part-time/adjunct (0 women). *Students:* 14 full-time (6 women), 34 part-time (18 women); includes 5 minority (2 African Americans, 1 American Indian/Alaska Native, 2 Hispanic Americans). Average age 34. 22 applicants, 55% accepted, 11 enrolled. In 2006, 9 degrees awarded. *Median time to degree:* Master's–2 years full-time, 4 years part-time. *Entrance requirements:* For master's, GMAT, GRE Subject Test. Additional exam requirements/recommendations for international students: Required—TOEFL. *Application deadline:* For fall admission, 7/31 for domestic students, 6/1 for international students; for spring admission, 11/30 for domestic students, 10/1 for international students. Application fee: $30. *Expenses:* Tuition: Full-time $6,300; part-time $350 per credit. Required fees: $100. *Financial support:* Fellowships, teaching assistantships, Federal Work-Study, institutionally sponsored loans, and scholarships/grants available. Financial award applicants required to submit FAFSA. *Unit head:* Dr. Dan Messerschmidt, Dean, 434-522-8417. *Application contact:* Dr. Sally Selden, MBA Program Director, 434-544-8266.

Lynn University, College of Business and Management, Boca Raton, FL 33431-5598. Offers aviation management (MBA); financial valuation and investment management (MBA); global leadership (PhD); hospitality management (MBA); international business (MBA); marketing (MBA); mass communication and media management (MBA); sports and athletics administration (MBA). Part-time and evening/weekend programs available. Postbaccalaureate distance learning degree programs offered. *Faculty:* 13 full-time (5 women), 7 part-time/adjunct (3 women). *Students:* 71 full-time (37 women), 113 part-time (47 women); includes 35 minority (13 African Americans, 6 Asian Americans or Pacific Islanders, 16 Hispanic Americans), 55 international. Average age 32. 114 applicants, 88% accepted, 71 enrolled. In 2006, 83 master's, 9 doctorates awarded. *Degree requirements:* For master's, project; for doctorate, thesis/dissertation, qualifying paper. *Entrance requirements:* For master's, GMAT or GRE, minimum undergraduate GPA of 3.0, resumé, 2 letters of recommendation; for doctorate, GRE or GMAT, minimum graduate GPA of 3.25, resumé, 2 letters of recommendation. Additional exam requirements/recommendations for international students: Required—TOEFL (minimum score 550 paper-based; 213 computer-based). *Application deadline:* Applications are processed on a rolling basis. Application fee: $50. Electronic applications accepted. *Expenses:* Tuition: Full-time $26,200. Required fees: $1,500. Tuition and fees vary according to class time, course load and degree level. *Financial support:* In 2006–07, 160 students received support. Career-related internships or fieldwork, Federal Work-Study, institutionally sponsored loans, scholarships/grants, tuition waivers (full and partial), and unspecified assistantships available. Support available to part-time students. Financial award application deadline: 8/1; financial award applicants required to submit FAFSA. *Faculty research:* Labor relations, dynamic balance in leisure-time skills, ethics in athletics, hotel development. *Unit head:* Dr. Russell Boisjoly, Dean, 561-237-7458, Fax: 561-237-7014, E-mail: rboisjoly@lynn.edu. *Application contact:* Dr. Larissa Baia, Assistant Director of Graduate Admissions, 561-237-7916, Fax: 561-237-7100, E-mail: admissionpm@lynn.edu.

Madonna University, School of Business, Livonia, MI 48150-1173. Offers business administration (MBA); international business (MSBA); leadership studies (MSBA); leadership studies in criminal justice (MSBA); quality and operations management (MSBA). Part-time and evening/weekend programs available. Postbaccalaureate distance learning degree programs offered (minimal on-campus study). *Faculty:* 12 full-time (3 women), 14 part-time/adjunct (3 women). *Students:* 34 full-time (21 women), 214 part-time (107 women); includes 26 minority (7 African Americans, 7 American Indian/Alaska Native, 4 Asian Americans or Pacific Islanders, 8 Hispanic Americans), 88 international. Average age 36. 60 applicants, 60% accepted. In 2006, 41 degrees awarded. *Degree requirements:* For master's, thesis (for some programs), foreign language proficiency (international business). *Entrance requirements:* For master's, GMAT, GRE General Test, minimum GPA of 3.0. *Application deadline:* For fall admission, 8/1 priority date for domestic students; for winter admission, 12/1 priority date for domestic students; for spring admission, 4/1 priority date for domestic students. Applications are processed on a rolling basis. Application fee: $25 ($200 for international students). Electronic applications accepted. *Financial support:* Career-related internships or fieldwork, institutionally sponsored loans, and scholarships/grants available. Support available to part-time students. *Faculty research:* Management, women in management, future studies. *Unit head:* Dr. Stuart Arends, Dean, 734-432-5366, Fax: 734-432-5364, E-mail: sarends@madonna.edu. *Application contact:* Sandra Kellums, Coordinator of Graduate Admissions and Records, 734-432-5667, Fax: 734-432-5862, E-mail: skellum@madonna.edu.

Maharishi University of Management, Graduate Studies, Program in Business Administration, Fairfield, IA 52557. Offers MBA, PhD. Evening/weekend programs available. Postbaccalaureate distance learning degree programs offered (minimal on-campus study). *Degree requirements:* For doctorate, thesis/dissertation. *Entrance requirements:* For master's, GMAT, minimum GPA of 3.0; for doctorate, minimum GPA of 3.0. Additional exam requirements/recommendations for international students: Required—TOEFL. *Faculty research:* Leadership, effects of the group dynamics of consciousness on the economy, innovation, employee development, cooperative strategy.

Malaspina University-College, Program in Business Administration, Nanaimo, BC V9R 5S5, Canada. Offers EMBA, IMBA, MBA. Program offered jointly with University of Hertfordshire. Part-time and evening/weekend programs available. *Degree requirements:* For master's, thesis. *Entrance requirements:* Additional exam requirements/recommendations for international students: Required—TOEFL (minimum score 550 paper-based; 213 computer-based). Electronic applications accepted. *Faculty research:* Tourism development, entrepreneurship, organizational development, strategic planning, international business strategy.

Malone College, School of Business, Graduate Program in Business, Canton, OH 44709-3897. Offers MBA. Part-time and evening/weekend programs available. *Faculty:* 8 full-time (3 women), 8 part-time/adjunct (3 women). *Students:* 1 full-time (0 women), 43 part-time (18 women); includes 5 minority (2 African Americans, 2 American Indian/Alaska Native, 1 Asian American or Pacific Islander), 1 international. Average age 34. In 2006, 14 degrees awarded. *Entrance requirements:* For master's, GMAT, minimum GPA of 3.0. *Application deadline:* Applications are processed on a rolling basis. Application fee: $25. *Expenses:* Contact institution. *Financial support:* Tuition waivers (partial) available. Support available to part-time students. Financial award application deadline: 6/30. *Faculty research:* Leadership, business ethics, mathematical modeling, globalization, non-profit financial management. *Unit head:* Dr. John P. Harris, Director, 330-471-8247, Fax: 330-471-8563, E-mail: jharris@malone.edu. *Application contact:* Dr. David Kleffman, Recruiter, 330-471-8447, Fax: 330-471-8343, E-mail: dkleffman@malone.edu.

Marian College of Fond du Lac, Business Division, Fond du Lac, WI 54935-4699. Offers organizational leadership and quality (MS). Part-time and evening/weekend programs available. *Faculty:* 6 part-time/adjunct (0 women). *Students:* 1 full-time (0 women), 95 part-time (55 women); includes 7 minority (5 African Americans, 1 American Indian/Alaska Native, 1 Hispanic American). Average age 38. 44 applicants, 100% accepted, 44 enrolled. In 2006, 33 degrees awarded. *Degree requirements:* For master's, comprehensive group project. *Entrance requirements:* For master's, 3 years of managerial experience, minimum GPA of 2.75, letters of professional reference. *Application deadline:* Applications are processed on a rolling basis. Application fee: $25. Electronic applications accepted. *Expenses:* Contact institution. Tuition and fees vary according to degree level and program. *Financial support:* In 2006–07, 23 students received support. Institutionally sponsored loans available. Support available to part-time students. Financial award application deadline: 3/1; financial award applicants required to submit FAFSA. *Faculty research:* Organizational values, statistical decision making, learning organization, quality planning, customer research. *Unit head:* David McPhail, Dean of Lifelong Learning, 920-923-8760, Fax: 920-923-7167, E-mail: dmcphail@mariancollege.edu. *Application contact:* Tracy Qualman, Director of Marketing and Admission, 920-923-7159, Fax: 920-923-7167, E-mail: tqualmann@mariancollege.edu.

Marist College, Graduate Programs, School of Management, Business Administration Program, Poughkeepsie, NY 12601-1387. Offers business administration (MBA); executive leadership (Adv C). *Accreditation:* AACSB. Part-time and evening/weekend programs available. Postbaccalaureate distance learning degree programs offered (no on-campus study). *Faculty:* 13 full-time (7 women), 4 part-time/adjunct (2 women). *Students:* 9 full-time (4 women), 201 part-time (72 women); includes 22 minority (3 African Americans, 14 Asian Americans or

Business Administration and Management—General

Marist College *(continued)*
Pacific Islanders, 5 Hispanic Americans), 9 international. Average age 33. 80 applicants, 89% accepted, 51 enrolled. In 2006, 43 master's, 2 other advanced degrees awarded. *Entrance requirements:* For master's, GMAT, resumé, 2 letters of recommendation, official transcripts, response to essay question. Additional exam requirements/recommendations for international students: Required—TOEFL (minimum score 550 paper-based; 213 computer-based; 80 iBT); Recommended—IELTS (minimum score 6). *Application deadline:* For fall admission, 7/1 for domestic students, 6/1 for international students; for spring admission, 12/15 for domestic students, 10/15 for international students. Applications are processed on a rolling basis. Application fee: $50. Electronic applications accepted. *Expenses:* Tuition: Full-time $11,340; part-time $630 per credit. Required fees: $60; $30 per semester. *Financial support:* In 2006–07, 46 students received support. Scholarships/grants available. Support available to part-time students. Financial award application deadline: 8/15; financial award applicants required to submit FAFSA. *Faculty research:* International trade law, process management, AIDS and the medical provider, mid-Hudson region economics, time quality management and organizational behavior. *Unit head:* Dr. Katherine Jackson, Director, 845-575-3225, E-mail: katherine.jackson@marist.edu. *Application contact:* Anu R. Ailawadhi, Director of Graduate Admissions, 845-575-3800, Fax: 845-575-3166, E-mail: graduate@marist.edu.

See Close-Up on page 287.

Marlboro College, Graduate Center, Program in Business Administration, Marlboro, VT 05344. Offers managing for sustainability (MBA). *Degree requirements:* For master's, capstone project. *Entrance requirements:* For master's, GMAT. *Application deadline:* For fall admission, 6/1 priority date for domestic students. Electronic applications accepted. *Expenses:* Tuition: Full-time $18,900; part-time $630 per credit. Tuition and fees vary according to program. *Unit head:* Ralph Meima, Program Director, 802-251-7690, Fax: 802-258-9201, E-mail: rmeima@marlboro.edu. *Application contact:* Bethany Catron, Director of Admissions, 802-258-9209, Fax: 802-258-9201, E-mail: bcatron@gradcenter.marlboro.edu.

Marlboro College, Graduate Center, Program in Management, Marlboro, VT 05344. Offers MS. Evening/weekend programs available. Postbaccalaureate distance learning degree programs offered (minimal on-campus study). *Faculty:* 9 part-time/adjunct (4 women). *Students:* 1 (woman) full-time, 4 part-time (3 women); includes 1 minority (Asian American or Pacific Islander) Average age 40. In 2006, 1 degree awarded. *Degree requirements:* For master's, capstone project. *Application deadline:* For fall admission, 3/1 priority date for domestic students. Applications are processed on a rolling basis. Application fee: $0. Electronic applications accepted. *Expenses:* Tuition: Full-time $18,900; part-time $630 per credit. Tuition and fees vary according to program. *Financial support:* Applicants required to submit FAFSA. *Unit head:* Kevin Bell, Academic Director, 802-258-9203, Fax: 802-258-9201, E-mail: kbell@gradcenter.marlboro.edu. *Application contact:* Bethany Catron, Director of Admissions, 802-258-9209, Fax: 802-258-9201, E-mail: bcatron@gradcenter.marlboro.edu.

Marquette University, Graduate School, College of Business Administration, Executive MBA Program, Milwaukee, WI 53201-1881. Offers MBA. *Accreditation:* AACSB. *Faculty:* 3 full-time (1 woman), 2 part-time/adjunct (0 women). *Students:* 44 full-time (15 women), 2 part-time; includes 12 minority (1 African American, 4 American Indian/Alaska Native, 7 Asian Americans or Pacific Islanders), 1 international. Average age 37. 31 applicants, 84% accepted, 25 enrolled. In 2006, 25 degrees awarded. *Entrance requirements:* For master's, GMAT. *Application deadline:* Applications are processed on a rolling basis. Electronic applications accepted. *Unit head:* Dr. Jeanne Simmons, Graduate Director, 414-288-7145, Fax: 414-288-1660, E-mail: jeanne.simmons@marquette.edu.

Marquette University, Graduate School, College of Business Administration, Program in Business Administration, Milwaukee, WI 53201-1881. Offers MBA, JD/MBA. *Accreditation:* AACSB. Part-time and evening/weekend programs available. *Faculty:* 36 full-time (7 women), 19 part-time/adjunct (5 women). *Students:* 37 full-time (15 women), 403 part-time (126 women); includes 33 minority (4 African Americans, 24 Asian Americans or Pacific Islanders, 5 Hispanic Americans), 35 international. Average age 31. 306 applicants, 73% accepted, 184 enrolled. In 2006, 159 degrees awarded. *Entrance requirements:* For master's, GMAT. Additional exam requirements/recommendations for international students: Required—TOEFL. Application fee: $40. *Financial support:* In 2006–07, 4 research assistantships, 13 teaching assistantships were awarded; Federal Work-Study, institutionally sponsored loans, scholarships/grants, and tuition waivers (full and partial) also available. Support available to part-time students. Financial award application deadline: 2/15. *Faculty research:* Ethics in the professions, services marketing, technology impact on decision making, mentoring. Total annual research expenditures: $99,528. *Unit head:* Dr. Jeanne Simmons, Graduate Director, 414-288-7145, Fax: 414-288-1660, E-mail: jeanne.simmons@marquette.edu.

Marshall University, Academic Affairs Division, Lewis College of Business, Graduate School of Management, Huntington, WV 25755. Offers MBA, MS. *Accreditation:* AACSB. Part-time and evening/weekend programs available. *Faculty:* 17 full-time (5 women), 2 part-time/adjunct (0 women). *Students:* 155 full-time (93 women), 70 part-time (35 women); includes 10 minority (5 African Americans, 2 American Indian/Alaska Native, 2 Asian Americans or Pacific Islanders, 1 Hispanic American), 35 international. Average age 29. In 2006, 108 degrees awarded. *Degree requirements:* For master's, comprehensive assessment. *Application deadline:* Applications are processed on a rolling basis. Application fee: $40. *Expenses:* Contact institution. *Financial support:* Career-related internships or fieldwork and tuition waivers (full) available. Support available to part-time students. Financial award applicants required to submit FAFSA. *Unit head:* Dr. Andrew Sikula, Associate Dean, 304-746-1956, E-mail: sikula@marshall.edu. *Application contact:* Information Contact, 304-746-1900, Fax: 304-746-1902, E-mail: services@marshall.edu.

Marylhurst University, Department of Business Administration, Marylhurst, OR 97036-0261. Offers MBA. Part-time and evening/weekend programs available. Postbaccalaureate distance learning degree programs offered (no on-campus study). *Faculty:* 2 full-time (0 women), 18 part-time/adjunct (6 women). *Students:* 14 full-time (8 women), 215 part-time (107 women); includes 13 minority (3 African Americans, 1 American Indian/Alaska Native, 7 Asian Americans or Pacific Islanders, 2 Hispanic Americans), 11 international. Average age 37. In 2006, 69 degrees awarded. *Degree requirements:* For master's, capstone course. *Entrance requirements:* For master's, interview, GMAT if GPA less than 3.0 and fewer than 5 years of work experience, resumé, 2 letters of recommendation. Additional exam requirements/recommendations for international students: Recommended—TOEFL (minimum score 550 paper-based). *Application deadline:* Applications are processed on a rolling basis. Application fee: $40 ($50 for international students). Electronic applications accepted. *Expenses:* Tuition: Part-time $395 per credit. Required fees: $8 per credit. *Financial support:* Federal Work-Study and scholarships/grants available. Support available to part-time students. Financial award applicants required to submit FAFSA. *Unit head:* Bob Hanks, Director of Business Programming, 503-675-3961, Fax: 503-697-5597, E-mail: mba@marylhurst.edu. *Application contact:* Kathleen Schneff, Admissions Specialist, 800-634-9982 Ext. 3322, Fax: 503-635-6585, E-mail: admissions@marylhurst.edu.

Marymount University, Corporate Outreach Program, Arlington, VA 22207-4299. Offers management studies (Certificate). Part-time and evening/weekend programs available. *Faculty:* 1 (woman) part-time/adjunct. *Students:* Average age 38. 16 applicants, 100% accepted, 13 enrolled. In 2006, 14 degrees awarded. *Entrance requirements:* For degree, resumé. Additional exam requirements/recommendations for international students: Required—TOEFL (minimum score 600 paper-based; 250 computer-based). *Application deadline:* Applications are processed on a rolling basis. Application fee: $40. Electronic applications accepted. *Expenses:* Tuition: Full-time $11,160; part-time $620 per credit. Required fees: $113; $630 per credit. *Unit head:* Dr. Stuart Werner, Director, 703-284-5962, E-mail: stuart.werner@marymount.edu.

Marymount University, School of Business Administration, Program in Business Administration, Arlington, VA 22207-4299. Offers MBA. *Accreditation:* ACBSP. Part-time and evening/

weekend programs available. *Students:* 37 full-time (19 women), 148 part-time (69 women); includes 65 minority (28 African Americans, 2 American Indian/Alaska Native, 15 Asian Americans or Pacific Islanders, 20 Hispanic Americans), 21 international. Average age 31. 57 applicants, 91% accepted, 33 enrolled. In 2006, 69 degrees awarded. *Entrance requirements:* For master's, GMAT, resumé. Additional exam requirements/recommendations for international students: Required—TOEFL (minimum score 600 paper-based; 250 computer-based). *Application deadline:* Applications are processed on a rolling basis. Application fee: $40. Electronic applications accepted. *Expenses:* Tuition: Full-time $11,160; part-time $620 per credit. Required fees: $113; $630 per credit. *Financial support:* Research assistantships with full tuition reimbursements, career-related internships or fieldwork, scholarships/grants, and unspecified assistantships available. Support available to part-time students. Financial award applicants required to submit FAFSA. *Unit head:* Dr. Terri Long, Director, 703-284-5918, E-mail: terri.long@marymount.edu.

Marymount University, School of Business Administration, Program in Management, Arlington, VA 22207-4299. Offers advanced leadership (Certificate); leading and managing change (Certificate); management (MS); management studies (Certificate); project management (Certificate). Part-time and evening/weekend programs available. *Students:* 2 full-time (1 woman), 20 part-time (13 women); includes 5 minority (4 African Americans, 1 Hispanic American), 1 international. Average age 38. 13 applicants, 100% accepted, 9 enrolled. In 2006, 5 master's, 4 other advanced degrees awarded. *Entrance requirements:* For master's, GRE or GMAT, resumé; for Certificate, resumé. Additional exam requirements/recommendations for international students: Required—TOEFL (minimum score 600 paper-based; 250 computer-based). *Application deadline:* Applications are processed on a rolling basis. Electronic applications accepted. *Expenses:* Tuition: Full-time $11,160; part-time $620 per credit. Required fees: $113; $630 per credit. *Financial support:* Research assistantships with full tuition reimbursements, career-related internships or fieldwork, scholarships/grants, and unspecified assistantships available. Support available to part-time students. Financial award applicants required to submit FAFSA. *Unit head:* Dr. Lorri Cooper, Director, 703-284-5950, Fax: 703-527-3830, E-mail: lorri.cooper@marymount.edu.

Maryville University of Saint Louis, The John E. Simon School of Business, St. Louis, MO 63141-7299. Offers accounting (MBA, PGC); business studies (PGC); e-business (MBA, PGC); management (MBA, PGC); marketing (MBA, PGC). *Accreditation:* ACBSP. Part-time and evening/weekend programs available. *Students:* 34 full-time (23 women), 162 part-time (101 women); includes 9 African Americans, 8 Asian Americans or Pacific Islanders, 2 international. Average age 31. 56 applicants, 96% accepted, 38 enrolled. In 2006, 89 degrees awarded. *Entrance requirements:* For master's, GMAT (unless applicant possesses a graduate degree or an undergraduate degree in business with a minimum GPA of 3.0), minimum AACSB index of 950. Additional exam requirements/recommendations for international students: Required—TOEFL (minimum score 550 paper-based). *Application deadline:* Applications are processed on a rolling basis. Application fee: $35 ($50 for international students). Electronic applications accepted. *Expenses:* Tuition: Full-time $17,800; part-time $555 per credit. Required fees: $55 per semester. Tuition and fees vary according to degree level and program. *Financial support:* Career-related internships or fieldwork, Federal Work-Study, tuition waivers (partial), and campus employment available. Financial award application deadline: 7/31; financial award applicants required to submit FAFSA. *Faculty research:* International business, e-business, strategic planning, interpersonal management skills, financial analysis. *Unit head:* Dr. Pamela Horwitz, Dean, 314-529-9418, Fax: 314-529-9975, E-mail: horwitz@maryville.edu. *Application contact:* Kathy Dougherty, Director of MBA Admissions and Enrollment, 314-529-9382, Fax: 314-529-9975, E-mail: business@marville.edu.

Marywood University, Academic Affairs, Insalaco College of Creative Arts and Management, Department of Business and Managerial Science, Scranton, PA 18509-1598. Offers finance and investments (MBA); general management (MBA); management information systems (MBA, MS). Part-time and evening/weekend programs available. *Students:* 7 full-time (5 women), 44 part-time (26 women); includes 3 minority (2 African Americans, 1 Hispanic American), 2 international. Average age 35. In 2006, 21 degrees awarded. *Degree requirements:* For master's, comprehensive exam. *Entrance requirements:* For master's, GMAT. Additional exam requirements/recommendations for international students: Required—TOEFL (minimum score 550 paper-based; 213 computer-based). *Application deadline:* For fall admission, 4/15 priority date for domestic and international students; for spring admission, 11/15 priority date for domestic and international students. Applications are processed on a rolling basis. Application fee: $30. Electronic applications accepted. *Expenses:* Tuition: Part-time $672 per credit. Tuition and fees vary according to degree level, campus/location and program. *Financial support:* Research assistantships with tuition reimbursements, career-related internships or fieldwork, scholarships/grants, tuition waivers (partial), and unspecified assistantships available. Support available to part-time students. Financial award application deadline: 2/15; financial award applicants required to submit FAFSA. *Faculty research:* Problem formulation in ill-structured situations, corporate tax structures. *Unit head:* Dr. Art Comstock, Head, 570-348-6211 Ext. 2449, E-mail: comstock@es.marywood.edu. *Application contact:* Dr. Deborah M. Flynn, Coordinator of Graduate Advising (Enrollment Management), 570-348-6211, E-mail: flynn@ac.marywood.edu.

See Close-Up on page 289.

Massachusetts Institute of Technology, Sloan School of Management, Cambridge, MA 02139-4307. Offers MBA, MS, SM, PhD, SM/MBA, SM/SM. *Accreditation:* AACSB. Postbaccalaureate distance learning degree programs offered. *Faculty:* 106 full-time (17 women). *Students:* 781 full-time (242 women); includes 170 minority (15 African Americans, 4 American Indian/Alaska Native, 130 Asian Americans or Pacific Islanders, 21 Hispanic Americans), 234 international. Average age 28. 2,944 applicants, 20% accepted. *Degree requirements:* For master's, thesis (for some programs); for doctorate, thesis/dissertation, exams. *Entrance requirements:* For master's, GMAT, previous course work in calculus and economics; for doctorate, GMAT, GRE, previous course work in calculus and economics. Additional exam requirements/recommendations for international students: Required—TOEFL. *Application deadline:* For fall admission, 1/10 for domestic and international students. Application fee: $230. Electronic applications accepted. *Expenses:* Contact institution. Part-time tuition and fees vary according to course load. *Financial support:* Fellowships with tuition reimbursements, research assistantships with tuition reimbursements, teaching assistantships with tuition reimbursements, institutionally sponsored loans available. *Faculty research:* Financial engineering, entrepreneurship, e-business, work and employment, leaders for manufacturing. *Unit head:* Richard L. Schmalensee, Dean, 617-253-2957, Fax: 617-258-6617, E-mail: rschmal@mit.edu. *Application contact:* Rod Garcia, Director of Admissions, MBA Program, 617-253-5434, Fax: 617-253-6405, E-mail: mbaadmissions@sloan.mit.edu.

McGill University, Faculty of Graduate and Postdoctoral Studies, Desautels Faculty of Management, Montréal, QC H3A 2T5, Canada. Offers administration (PhD); entrepreneurial studies (MBA); finance (MBA); general management (Post Master's Certificate); information systems (MBA); international business (exchange program) (MBA); international Master's program in practicing management (MM); management (MBA); management for development (MBA); manufacturing management (MMM); marketing (MBA); operations management (MBA); public accountancy (Diploma); strategic management (MBA); MBA/LL B; MD/MBA. Part-time programs available. *Entrance requirements:* For master's, GMAT, minimum undergraduate GPA of 3.0, 2 years work experience; for doctorate, GMAT or GRE General Test, 2 letters of recommendation, preferably by professors in chosen field of specialization; for other advanced degree, 2 years of work experience, MBA, minimum GPA of 3.0 (Post-MBA Certificate). Additional exam requirements/recommendations for international students: Required—TOEFL (minimum score 600 paper-based; 250 computer-based), IELTS (minimum score 7). Electronic applications accepted. Expenses: Contact institution. *Faculty research:* Social innovation, leadership, strategy.

McKendree College, Graduate Programs, Lebanon, IL 62254-1299. Offers business administration (MBA); counseling (MA); education (M Ed); nursing (MSN).

McMaster University, School of Graduate Studies, Faculty of Business, Hamilton, ON L8S 4M2, Canada. Offers MBA, PhD. *Accreditation:* AACSB. Part-time programs available. *Faculty:* 51 full-time. *Students:* 218 full-time, 101 part-time. *Degree requirements:* For doctorate, thesis/dissertation, comprehensive exam. *Entrance requirements:* For master's, GMAT; for doctorate, GMAT or GRE, master's degree. Additional exam requirements/recommendations for international students: Required—TOEFL (minimum score 580 paper-based; 237 computer-based). *Application deadline:* For fall admission, 6/1 for domestic students. Application fee: $90. *Financial support:* In 2006–07, teaching assistantships (averaging $8,440 per year); fellowships, research assistantships, career-related internships or fieldwork, Federal Work-Study, and scholarships/grants also available. *Faculty research:* Mergers, acquisitions, and restructuring; business investment; capital structure and dividend policy; employee pay/reward systems; pay and employment equity. *Unit head:* Paul Bates, Dean, 905-525-9140 Ext. 24431, Fax: 905-526-0852, E-mail: deanbus@mcmaster.ca. *Application contact:* Denise Anderson, Manager, Recruitment and Admissions, 905-525-9140 Ext. 23940, Fax: 905-521-8995, E-mail: anderd@mcmaster.ca.

McNeese State University, Graduate School, College of Business, Department of Business Administration, Lake Charles, LA 70609. Offers MBA. *Accreditation:* AACSB. Evening/weekend programs available. *Faculty:* 11 full-time (0 women). *Students:* 38 full-time (14 women), 36 part-time (20 women); includes 7 minority (3 African Americans, 2 Asian Americans or Pacific Islanders, 2 Hispanic Americans), 21 international. In 2006, 18 degrees awarded. *Degree requirements:* For master's, written exam. *Entrance requirements:* For master's, GMAT. *Application deadline:* For fall admission, 5/15 priority date for domestic students. Applications are processed on a rolling basis. Application fee: $20 ($30 for international students). *Expenses:* Tuition, area resident: Full-time $2,226; part-time $193 per hour. Required fees: $919; $106 per hour. *Financial support:* Research assistantships, teaching assistantships, Federal Work-Study available. Support available to part-time students. Financial award application deadline: 5/1. *Faculty research:* Management development, integrating technology into the work force, union/management relations, economic development. *Unit head:* Dr. Bruce Swindle, Director, 337-475-5576, Fax: 337-475-5986, E-mail: mbaprog@mcneese.edu.

Medaille College, Program in Business Administration—Amherst, Buffalo, NY 14214-2695. Offers business administration (MBA); organizational leadership (MA). Evening/weekend programs available. *Faculty:* 4 full-time (1 woman), 30 part-time/adjunct (15 women). *Students:* 228 full-time (136 women); includes 64 minority (49 African Americans, 2 American Indian/Alaska Native, 2 Asian Americans or Pacific Islanders, 11 Hispanic Americans). Average age 36. 135 applicants, 96% accepted, 127 enrolled. In 2006, 86 degrees awarded. *Degree requirements:* For master's, thesis or alternative. *Entrance requirements:* For master's, GMAT, minimum undergraduate GPA of 2.7, 3 years of work experience. Additional exam requirements/recommendations for international students: Required—TOEFL (minimum score 550 paper-based; 213 computer-based). *Application deadline:* Applications are processed on a rolling basis. Application fee: $100. *Expenses: Contact institution.* Full-time tuition and fees vary according to program. *Financial support:* In 2006–07, 150 students received support. Federal Work-Study available. Financial award applicants required to submit FAFSA. *Unit head:* Jennifer Bavifard, Associate Dean for Special Programs, 716-631-1061 Ext. 150, Fax: 716-631-1380, E-mail: jbavifar@medaille.edu. *Application contact:* Susan Greenwald, Executive Director of Admissions, 716-635-5033 Ext. 2011, Fax: 716-631-1380, E-mail: sgreenwald@medaille.edu.

Medaille College, Program in Business Administration—Rochester, Buffalo, NY 14214-2695. Offers business administration (MBA); organizational leadership (MA). Evening/weekend programs available. *Faculty:* 3 full-time (2 women), 53 part-time/adjunct (27 women). *Students:* 46 full-time (32 women); includes 14 minority (9 African Americans, 5 Hispanic Americans). Average age 36. 31 applicants, 87% accepted, 25 enrolled. In 2006, 18 degrees awarded. *Degree requirements:* For master's, thesis or alternative. *Entrance requirements:* For master's, GMAT, 3 years of work experience, minimum undergraduate GPA of 2.7. Additional exam requirements/recommendations for international students: Required—TOEFL (minimum score 550 paper-based; 213 computer-based). *Application deadline:* Applications are processed on a rolling basis. Application fee: $100. *Expenses: Contact institution.* Full-time tuition and fees vary according to program. *Financial support:* In 2006–07, 34 students received support. Federal Work-Study available. Financial award applicants required to submit FAFSA. *Unit head:* Lorraine Beach-Horner, Branch Campus Director, 585-272-0030 Ext. 102, Fax: 585-273-0057, E-mail: lbeach-horner@medaille.edu. *Application contact:* Jane Rowlands, Marketing Support, 585-272-0030, Fax: 585-272-0057, E-mail: jrowlands@medaille.edu.

Memorial University of Newfoundland, School of Graduate Studies, Faculty of Business Administration, St. John's, NL A1C 5S7, Canada. Offers EMBA, MBA. *Accreditation:* AACSB. Part-time programs available. *Degree requirements:* For master's, thesis (for some programs). *Entrance requirements:* For master's, GMAT. Additional exam requirements/recommendations for international students: Required—TOEFL (minimum score 580 paper-based; 237 computer-based), TWE (minimum score 4). Electronic applications accepted. *Faculty research:* International business, marketing, organizational theory and behavior, management science and information systems, small business.

Mercer University, Graduate Studies, Cecil B. Day Campus, Eugene W. Stetson School of Business and Economics, Atlanta, GA 30341. Offers business administration (MBA, XMBA); Pharm D/MBA. *Accreditation:* AACSB. Part-time and evening/weekend programs available. *Faculty:* 19 full-time (5 women), 6 part-time/adjunct (0 women). *Students:* 195 full-time (81 women), 147 part-time (70 women); includes 111 minority (90 African Americans, 2 American Indian/Alaska Native, 14 Asian Americans or Pacific Islanders, 5 Hispanic Americans), 37 international. Average age 32. In 2006, 158 degrees awarded. *Entrance requirements:* For master's, GMAT. Additional exam requirements/recommendations for international students: Required—TOEFL (minimum score 550 paper-based; 213 computer-based; 80 iBT). *Application deadline:* For fall admission, 7/1 priority date for domestic students; for spring admission, 11/1 priority date for domestic students. Applications are processed on a rolling basis. Application fee: $50 ($100 for international students). Electronic applications accepted. *Financial support:* Federal Work-Study available. *Faculty research:* Entrepreneurship, market studies, international business strategy, financial analysis. *Unit head:* Karen G. Herlitz, Assistant Vice President of Admissions, 678-547-6206, Fax: 678-547-6367, E-mail: herlitz.kg@mercer.edu.

Mercer University, Graduate Studies, Macon Campus, Eugene W. Stetson School of Business and Economics, Macon, GA 31207-0003. Offers MBA. *Accreditation:* AACSB. Part-time and evening/weekend programs available. *Faculty:* 9 full-time (3 women). *Students:* 9 full-time (5 women), 39 part-time (21 women); includes 8 minority (6 African Americans, 2 Asian Americans or Pacific Islanders), 6 international. Average age 27. 16 applicants, 94% accepted, 15 enrolled. In 2006, 18 degrees awarded. *Entrance requirements:* For master's, GMAT. Additional exam requirements/recommendations for international students: Required—TOEFL (minimum score 550 paper-based; 213 computer-based). *Application deadline:* For fall admission, 8/1 for domestic students; for spring admission, 12/1 for domestic students. Applications are processed on a rolling basis. Application fee: $50 ($100 for international students). *Faculty research:* Federal Reserve System, management of nurses, sales promotion, systems for common stock selection, interest rate premiums. *Unit head:* Dr. William S. Mounts, Dean, 478-301-2837, Fax: 478-301-2635, E-mail: mounts_ws@mercer.edu. *Application contact:* Robert Holland, Director, Academic Administrator, 478-301-2835, Fax: 478-301-2635, E-mail: holland_r@mercer.edu.

Mercy College, Division of Business and Accounting, Program in Business Administration, Dobbs Ferry, NY 10522-1189. Offers MBA. *Students:* 5 full-time (3 women), 96 part-time (54 women); includes 41 minority (27 African Americans, 4 Asian Americans or Pacific Islanders, 10 Hispanic Americans), 18 international. Average age 31. In 2006, 21 degrees awarded. *Entrance requirements:* For master's, GMAT, interview. *Application deadline:* Applications are processed on a rolling basis. Application fee: $37. Electronic applications accepted. *Expenses:* Tuition: Part-time $595 per credit. Required fees: $9 per credit. Tuition and fees vary according to program.

Meredith College, John E. Weems Graduate School, School of Business, Raleigh, NC 27607-5298. Offers business administration (MBA). Part-time and evening/weekend programs available. *Faculty:* 4 full-time (all women), 2 part-time/adjunct (0 women). *Students:* 2 full-time (both women), 58 part-time (46 women); includes 15 minority (8 African Americans, 5 Asian Americans or Pacific Islanders, 2 Hispanic Americans). Average age 32. 39 applicants, 59% accepted, 18 enrolled. In 2006, 27 degrees awarded. *Degree requirements:* For master's, thesis optional. *Entrance requirements:* For master's, GMAT, interview, minimum GPA of 2.5, letters of recommendation. Additional exam requirements/recommendations for international students: Required—TOEFL. *Application deadline:* For fall admission, 7/1 priority date for domestic and international students; for spring admission, 11/1 priority date for domestic and international students. Applications are processed on a rolling basis. Application fee: $50. Electronic applications accepted. *Financial support:* Career-related internships or fieldwork, institutionally sponsored loans, scholarships/grants, and tuition waivers (partial) available. Support available to part-time students. Financial award application deadline: 2/15; financial award applicants required to submit FAFSA. *Unit head:* Dr. Denise Rotundo, Dean, 919-760-8471, Fax: 919-760-8470. *Application contact:* Page Midyette, Coordinator, 919-760-2281, Fax: 919-760-2898, E-mail: midyette@meredith.edu.

Mesa State College, School of Business and Professional Studies, Grand Junction, CO 81501-3122. Offers MBA. Part-time and evening/weekend programs available. *Degree requirements:* For master's, internship or thesis. *Entrance requirements:* For master's, GMAT, MAT, or GRE. Electronic applications accepted.

Methodist University, School of Graduate Studies, Fayetteville, NC 28311-1498. Offers business administration (MBA); justice administration (MJA); physician assistant studies (MPA).

Metropolitan College of New York, Program in General Management, New York, NY 10013-1919. Offers MBA. Evening/weekend programs available. *Faculty:* 2 full-time (1 woman), 13 part-time/adjunct (6 women). *Students:* 42 full-time (20 women); includes 24 African Americans, 4 Hispanic Americans, 3 international. Average age 36. 42 applicants, 71% accepted, 26 enrolled. In 2006, 29 degrees awarded. *Median time to degree:* Master's–1 year full-time, 1.5 years part-time. *Degree requirements:* For master's, thesis, 10 day study abroad. *Entrance requirements:* For master's, GMAT. Additional exam requirements/recommendations for international students: Required—TOEFL (minimum score 600 paper-based; 220 computer-based). *Application deadline:* For fall admission, 7/15 priority date for domestic students; for winter admission, 11/15 priority date for domestic students; for spring admission, 3/30 priority date for domestic students. Applications are processed on a rolling basis. Application fee: $45. Electronic applications accepted. *Expenses: Contact institution. Financial support:* In 2006–07, 39 students received support. Scholarships/grants available. Financial award application deadline: 8/15; financial award applicants required to submit FAFSA. *Unit head:* Dr. Robert Gilmore, Dean, Graduate School for Business, 212-343-1234 Ext. 2209. *Application contact:* Emery Ailes, MBA Recruiter, 212-343-1234, Fax: 212-343-8470.

Metropolitan State University, College of Management, St. Paul, MN 55106-5000. Offers finance (MBA); human resource management (MBA); information management (MMIS); international business (MBA); law enforcement (MPNA); management information systems (MBA); marketing (MBA); nonprofit management (MPNA); organizational studies (MBA); public administration (MPNA); purchasing management (MBA); systems management (MMIS). Part-time and evening/weekend programs available. *Degree requirements:* For master's, computer language (MMIS), thesis optional. *Entrance requirements:* For master's, GMAT (MBA), resumé. Additional exam requirements/recommendations for international students: Required—TOEFL (minimum score 550 paper-based; 213 computer-based). *Faculty research:* Yugoslav economic system, workers' cooperatives, participative management and job enrichment, global business systems.

Miami University, Graduate School, Richard T. Farmer School of Business Administration, Oxford, OH 45056. Offers accountancy (M Acc); business administration (MBA); economics (MA); finance (MBA); general management (MBA); management information systems (MBA); marketing (MBA); quality and process improvement (MBA). *Accreditation:* AACSB. Part-time programs available. *Entrance requirements:* For master's, GMAT, minimum undergraduate GPA of 3.0 during previous 2 years or 2.75 overall. Additional exam requirements/recommendations for international students: Required—TOEFL (minimum score 550 paper-based; 213 computer-based), TWE (minimum score 4).

Michigan State University, The Graduate School, Eli Broad Graduate School of Management, Department of Management, East Lansing, MI 48824. Offers business administration (PhD). *Faculty:* 15 full-time (3 women). *Students:* 14 full-time (4 women), 1 part-time; includes 3 minority (1 African American, 1 American Indian/Alaska Native, 1 Hispanic American), 2 international. Average age 32. 45 applicants, 7% accepted. In 2006, 1 doctorate awarded. *Entrance requirements:* Additional exam requirements/recommendations for international students: Required—TOEFL (minimum score 550 paper-based; 213 computer-based). Electronic applications accepted. *Expenses:* Tuition, state resident: part-time $346 per credit hour. Tuition, nonresident: part-time $730 per credit hour. Tuition and fees vary according to program. *Financial support:* In 2006–07, 7 fellowships with tuition reimbursements, 9 research assistantships with tuition reimbursements (averaging $14,092 per year), 2 teaching assistantships with tuition reimbursements (averaging $14,921 per year) were awarded. Total annual research expenditures: $97,679. *Unit head:* Dr. Donald E. Conlon, Chairperson, 517-353-1878, Fax: 517-432-1111, E-mail: conlon@bus.msu.edu. *Application contact:* Application Contact, 517-535-1878, E-mail: mgt@msu.edu.

Michigan State University, The Graduate School, Eli Broad Graduate School of Management, Department of Marketing and Supply Chain Management, East Lansing, MI 48824. Offers business administration (PhD); manufacturing and engineering management (MS); supply chain management (MS). Part-time programs available. *Faculty:* 32 full-time (3 women). *Students:* 34 full-time (10 women), 35 part-time (10 women); includes 8 minority (5 African Americans, 1 American Indian/Alaska Native, 1 Asian American or Pacific Islander, 1 Hispanic American), 16 international. Average age 33. 65 applicants, 14% accepted. In 2006, 22 master's, 7 doctorates awarded. *Degree requirements:* For master's, field study, research project; for doctorate, thesis/dissertation, oral defense of dissertation proposal and dissertation, comprehensive exam. *Entrance requirements:* For master's, GMAT, bachelor's degree in related field, letters of recommendation, 2-3 years of work experience, minimum GPA of 3.0 in last 2 years of undergraduate course work; for doctorate, GMAT or GRE, letters of recommendation. Additional exam requirements/recommendations for international students: Required—TOEFL. Electronic applications accepted. *Expenses: Contact institution.* Tuition and fees vary according to program. *Financial support:* In 2006–07, 5 fellowships with tuition reimbursements, 23 research assistantships with tuition reimbursements (averaging $14,743 per year), 4 teaching assistantships with tuition reimbursements (averaging $12,000 per year) were awarded. Total annual research expenditures: $485,815. *Unit head:* Dr. Robert W. Nason, Chairperson, 517-355-2240, Fax: 517-432-1112, E-mail: nason@msu.edu. *Application contact:* Program Information, 517-353-6381, E-mail: mslogs@bus.msu.edu.

Michigan State University, The Graduate School, Eli Broad Graduate School of Management, Program in Business Administration, East Lansing, MI 48824. Offers business administration (MBA, PhD); corporate business administration (MBA); integrative management (MBA). Evening/weekend programs available. *Faculty:* 4 full-time (2 women). *Students:* 488 full-time (128 women), 1 part-time; includes 90 minority (31 African Americans, 1 American Indian/Alaska Native, 46 Asian Americans or Pacific Islanders, 12 Hispanic Americans), 102 international. Average age 32. 638 applicants, 33% accepted. In 2006, 192 degrees awarded. *Degree requirements:* For master's, enrichment experience. *Entrance requirements:* For master's, GMAT. Additional exam requirements/recommendations for international students: Required—TOEFL. *Application deadline:* Applications are processed on a rolling basis. Application fee: $50. Electronic applications accepted. *Expenses: Contact institution.* Tuition and fees vary according to program. *Financial support:* In 2006–07, 115 fellowships with tuition reimbursements, 58 research assistantships with tuition reimbursements (averaging $11,757 per year),

Business Administration and Management—General

Michigan State University (continued)
21 teaching assistantships with tuition reimbursements (averaging $12,151 per year) were awarded. Total annual research expenditures: $634. *Unit head:* Dr. Cheri T. Speier, Acting Associate Dean for MBA and MS Programs, 517-432-5100, Fax: 517-353-6395, E-mail: cspeier@bus.msu.edu. *Application contact:* Program Information, 517-432-5100, E-mail: mba@msu.edu.

Michigan Technological University, Graduate School, School of Business and Economics, Houghton, MI 49931-1295. Offers MS. *Accreditation:* AACSB. Part-time programs available. *Degree requirements:* For master's, thesis or alternative, registration. *Entrance requirements:* For master's, GMAT, minimum GPA of 2.9. Additional exam requirements/recommendations for international students: Required—TOEFL (minimum score 590 paper-based; 240 computer-based). Electronic applications accepted. *Faculty research:* High tech ventures, supply chain management, management of 15 workforce, corporate finance, environmental management systems and standards (15014000).

MidAmerica Nazarene University, Graduate Studies in Management, Olathe, KS 66062-1899. Offers MAOA, MBA. Evening/weekend programs available. *Entrance requirements:* For master's, minimum undergraduate GPA of 3.0, mathematical assessment, letters of recommendation. Additional exam requirements/recommendations for international students: Required—TOEFL. Electronic applications accepted. *Faculty research:* Economic development, international finance, business development, employee evaluation.

Middle Tennessee State University, College of Graduate Studies, College of Business, Department of Management and Marketing, Murfreesboro, TN 37132. Offers MBA. *Accreditation:* AACSB. Part-time and evening/weekend programs available. Postbaccalaureate distance learning degree programs offered. *Faculty:* 18 full-time (4 women). *Students:* 67 full-time (22 women), 235 part-time (108 women); includes 68 minority (37 African Americans, 24 Asian Americans or Pacific Islanders, 7 Hispanic Americans). Average age 28. 103 applicants, 100% accepted. In 2006, 113 degrees awarded. *Degree requirements:* For master's, comprehensive exam. *Entrance requirements:* For master's, GMAT. Additional exam requirements/recommendations for international students: Required—TOEFL (minimum score 525 paper-based; 195 computer-based). *Application deadline:* For fall admission, 8/1 priority date for domestic students. Applications are processed on a rolling basis. Application fee: $25. Electronic applications accepted. *Financial support:* In 2006–07, 6 students received support. Institutionally sponsored loans available. Support available to part-time students. Financial award application deadline: 5/1; financial award applicants required to submit FAFSA. *Faculty research:* International business, business strategy, organizational culture/leadership, consumer behavior, services marketing. *Unit head:* Dr. Jill Austin, Chair, 615-898-2736, Fax: 615-898-5308, E-mail: jaustin@mtsu.edu.

Midwestern State University, Graduate Studies, College of Business Administration, Wichita Falls, TX 76308. Offers business administration (MBA); health services administration (MBA). *Accreditation:* ACBSP. Part-time and evening/weekend programs available. *Faculty:* 13 full-time (1 woman). *Students:* 21 full-time (12 women), 35 part-time (12 women); includes 6 minority (2 African Americans, 4 Hispanic Americans), 19 international. Average age 30. 19 applicants, 68% accepted, 12 enrolled. In 2006, 15 degrees awarded. *Degree requirements:* For master's, thesis optional. *Entrance requirements:* For master's, GMAT. Additional exam requirements/recommendations for international students: Required—TOEFL (minimum score 550 paper-based; 213 computer-based). *Application deadline:* For fall admission, 7/1 for domestic students, 4/1 for international students; for spring admission, 11/1 for domestic students, 8/1 for international students. Applications are processed on a rolling basis. Application fee: $35 ($50 for international students). Electronic applications accepted. *Financial support:* In 2006–07, 34 students received support, including 2 teaching assistantships with partial tuition reimbursements available (averaging $7,766 per year); career-related internships or fieldwork, Federal Work-Study, institutionally sponsored loans, tuition waivers (partial), and unspecified assistantships also available. Support available to part-time students. Financial award application deadline: 5/1; financial award applicants required to submit FAFSA. *Faculty research:* Small business management, health care personnel administration, Pacific Rim trade, AIDS in the workplace, technology transfer. *Unit head:* Anthony Chelte, Dean, 940-397-4088, Fax: 940-397-4280, E-mail: anthony.chelte@mwsu.edu. *Application contact:* Dr. David Wierschem, Graduate Coordinator, 940-397-6260, Fax: 940-397-4280, E-mail: david.wierschem@mwsu.edu.

Millersville University of Pennsylvania, Graduate School, School of Humanities and Social Sciences, Department of Business Administration, Millersville, PA 17551-0302. Offers MBA. *Accreditation:* ACBSP. Part-time and evening/weekend programs available. *Faculty:* 16 full-time (3 women), 7 part-time/adjunct (2 women). *Students:* 14 full-time (8 women), 26 part-time (8 women); includes 4 minority (2 African Americans, 1 Asian American or Pacific Islander, 1 Hispanic American), 4 international. Average age 29. 12 applicants, 92% accepted, 8 enrolled. In 2006, 18 degrees awarded. *Entrance requirements:* For master's, GMAT, resumé. Additional exam requirements/recommendations for international students: Required—TOEFL (minimum score 500 paper-based; 183 computer-based). *Application deadline:* For fall admission, 3/1 priority date for domestic students; for spring admission, 10/1 priority date for domestic students. Applications are processed on a rolling basis. Application fee: $35. *Expenses:* Tuition, state resident: full-time $6,048; part-time $336 per credit. Tuition, nonresident: full-time $9,678; part-time $538 per credit. Required fees: $1,244. Tuition and fees vary according to course load. *Financial support:* In 2006–07, 12 students received support, including 12 research assistantships with full and partial tuition reimbursements available (averaging $4,250 per year); unspecified assistantships also available. Financial award application deadline: 3/1; financial award applicants required to submit FAFSA. *Faculty research:* Tax legislation, fraud controls, ethical behavior in the workplace, comparative business and legal systems. *Unit head:* Dr. Howard C. Ellis, Chair, 717-872-3881, Fax: 717-871-5434, E-mail: howard.ellis@millersville.edu. *Application contact:* Dr. Victor S. DeSantis, Dean of Graduate Studies, 717-872-3099, Fax: 717-871-2022, E-mail: victor.desantis@millersville.edu.

Milligan College, Program in Business Administration, Milligan College, TN 37682. Offers MBA. *Entrance requirements:* For master's, writing sample; GMAT if undergraduate GPA is below 3.0; 2 professional recommendations; 3 years related work experience. *Expenses:* Tuition: Part-time $305 per hour. Tuition and fees vary according to course load and program. *Unit head:* John Keyt, Director, 423-461-8482, Fax: 423-461-8789, E-mail: jckeyt@milligan.edu. *Application contact:* Courtney Kieslich, Admissions Specialist, 423-461-8482, Fax: 423-461-8789, E-mail: ckieslich@milligan.edu.

Millikin University, Tabor School of Business, Decatur, IL 62522-2084. Offers MBA. *Accreditation:* ACBSP. *Faculty research:* E-commerce, international marketing, pedagogy, total quality management, auditing.

Millsaps College, Else School of Management, Jackson, MS 39210-0001. Offers accounting (M Acc); business administration (MBA). *Accreditation:* AACSB. Part-time programs available. *Faculty:* 16 full-time (6 women), 1 part-time/adjunct (0 women). *Students:* 40 full-time (21 women), 41 part-time (21 women); includes 8 minority (6 African Americans, 1 Asian American or Pacific Islander, 1 Hispanic American), 5 international. Average age 26. 109 applicants, 76% accepted, 45 enrolled. In 2006, 31 degrees awarded. *Entrance requirements:* For master's, GMAT. Additional exam requirements/recommendations for international students: Required—TOEFL. *Application deadline:* For fall admission, 7/1 priority date for domestic students; for spring admission, 11/15 priority date for domestic students. Applications are processed on a rolling basis. Application fee: $25. Electronic applications accepted. *Expenses:* Tuition: Part-time $816 per hour. *Financial support:* In 2006–07, research assistantships (averaging $2,500 per year); career-related internships or fieldwork, Federal Work-Study, institutionally sponsored loans, scholarships/grants, and tuition waivers (partial) also available. Support available to part-time students. Financial award application deadline: 7/1; financial award applicants required to submit FAFSA. *Faculty research:* Ethics, audit independence, satisfaction with assurance services, political business cycles. *Unit head:* Howard L McMillan, Dean, 601-974-1250, Fax: 601-974-1260. *Application contact:* Dr. Bill Brisler, Associate Director of Graduate Business Admissions, 601-974-1277, Fax: 601-974-1260, E-mail: mbamacc@millsaps.edu.

Mills College, Graduate Studies, Program in Management, Oakland, CA 94613-1000. Offers MBA. *Faculty:* 5 full-time (2 women), 8 part-time/adjunct (7 women). *Students:* 52 full-time (49 women); includes 33 minority (13 African Americans, 2 American Indian/Alaska Native, 13 Asian Americans or Pacific Islanders, 5 Hispanic Americans), 2 international. Average age 32. 47 applicants, 87% accepted, 31 enrolled. In 2006, 15 degrees awarded. *Application deadline:* For fall admission, 2/1 for domestic and international students. *Financial support:* In 2006–07, 11 fellowships with partial tuition reimbursements (averaging $3,500 per year) were awarded. *Faculty research:* Information systems, corporate and financial planning, interest-based marketing, organizational behavior, international trade and finance. *Unit head:* Nancy Thornborrow, Director, 510-430-2344, Fax: 510-430-3314, E-mail: nancy@mills.edu. *Application contact:* Randy McGlauthing, Director of Graduate Admissions, 510-430-2355, Fax: 510-430-2159, E-mail: rmcglaut@mills.edu.

Milwaukee School of Engineering, Rader School of Business, Milwaukee, WI 53202-3109. Offers engineering management (MS); medical informatics (MS). Part-time and evening/weekend programs available. *Faculty:* 5 full-time (0 women), 8 part-time/adjunct (2 women). *Students:* 14 full-time (6 women), 149 part-time (31 women); includes 11 minority (7 African Americans, 1 Asian American or Pacific Islander, 3 Hispanic Americans), 5 international. Average age 25. 64 applicants, 61% accepted, 25 enrolled. In 2006, 41 degrees awarded. *Median time to degree:* Master's–1 year full-time, 4 years part-time. *Degree requirements:* For master's, thesis defense or capstone project. *Entrance requirements:* For master's, GMAT, GRE General Test, or MCAT, BS in engineering, science, business or related fields; 2 letters of recommendation. Additional exam requirements/recommendations for international students: Required—TOEFL (minimum score 550 paper-based; 213 computer-based). *Application deadline:* Applications are processed on a rolling basis. Application fee: $30. Electronic applications accepted. *Expenses:* Tuition: Part-time $526 per credit. *Financial support:* In 2006–07, 57 students received support. Career-related internships or fieldwork available. Support available to part-time students. Financial award applicants required to submit FAFSA. *Unit head:* Dr. Steven Bialer, Chairman, Rader School of Business, 414-277-7364, Fax: 414-277-7479, E-mail: bialer@msoe.edu. *Application contact:* Julie A. Schuster, Graduate Admissions, 800-332-6763, Fax: 414-277-7475, E-mail: schuster@msoe.edu.

Minnesota State University Mankato, College of Graduate Studies, College of Business, Mankato, MN 56001. Offers accounting and business law (MBA); finance (MBA); management (MBA); marketing and international business (MBA). *Accreditation:* AACSB. *Students:* 8 full-time (3 women), 32 part-time (13 women). *Entrance requirements:* For master's, GMAT, 2 letters of reference. Additional exam requirements/recommendations for international students: Required—TOEFL. *Application deadline:* For fall admission, 6/1 for domestic students; for spring admission, 10/1 for domestic students. Electronic applications accepted. *Unit head:* Scott Johnson, Dean, 507-389-5420.

Minot State University, Graduate School, Program in Management, Minot, ND 58707-0002. Offers MS. *Students:* 19. 39 applicants, 82% accepted. In 2006, 36 degrees awarded. *Degree requirements:* For master's, thesis (for some programs), comprehensive exam (for some programs). *Entrance requirements:* For master's, minimum GPA of 2.75. Additional exam requirements/recommendations for international students: Required—TOEFL. *Application deadline:* Applications are processed on a rolling basis. Application fee: $35. *Financial support:* In 2006–07, 2 students received support, including 2 teaching assistantships with partial tuition reimbursements available (averaging $1,000 per year); research assistantships with partial tuition reimbursements available, career-related internships or fieldwork, institutionally sponsored loans, scholarships/grants, traineeships, tuition waivers (partial), and unspecified assistantships also available. Support available to part-time students. *Faculty research:* Distance education. *Unit head:* Dr. Gary Ross, Chairperson, 701-858-3110, Fax: 701-858-3111, E-mail: ross@minotstateu.edu. *Application contact:* Brenda Anderson, Administrative Assistant, 701-858-3250, Fax: 701-858-4286, E-mail: brenda.anderson@minotstateu.edu.

Mississippi College, Graduate School, School of Business, Clinton, MS 39058. Offers accounting (Certificate); business administration (MBA), including accounting; business education (M Ed); JD/MBA. *Accreditation:* ACBSP. Part-time and evening/weekend programs available. *Faculty:* 12 full-time (2 women), 1 part-time/adjunct (0 women). *Students:* 55 full-time (28 women), 111 part-time (58 women); includes 41 minority (35 African Americans, 6 Asian Americans or Pacific Islanders), 32 international. Average age 29. In 2006, 45 master's, 5 other advanced degrees awarded. *Degree requirements:* For master's, thesis optional. *Entrance requirements:* For master's, GMAT, minimum GPA of 2.5, 24 hours of undergraduate course work in business. Additional exam requirements/recommendations for international students: Recommended—IELTS. *Application deadline:* For fall admission, 8/15 priority date for domestic students. Applications are processed on a rolling basis. Application fee: $25. Electronic applications accepted. *Expenses:* Tuition: Full-time $7,290; part-time $405 per hour. Required fees: $150 per term. Tuition and fees vary according to campus/location and program. *Financial support:* Federal Work-Study and unspecified assistantships available. Support available to part-time students. Financial award application deadline: 4/1; financial award applicants required to submit FAFSA. *Unit head:* Dr. Marcelo Eduardo, Dean, 601-925-3420, E-mail: eduardo@mc.edu.

Mississippi State University, College of Business and Industry, Graduate Studies in Business, Mississippi State, MS 39762. Offers business administration (MBA, PhD), including accounting (PhD), business information systems (PhD), finance (PhD), management (PhD), marketing (PhD); project management (MBA). *Accreditation:* AACSB. Part-time and evening/weekend programs available. Postbaccalaureate distance learning degree programs offered. *Faculty:* 66 full-time (18 women), 18 part-time/adjunct (9 women). *Students:* 143 full-time (52 women), 159 part-time (52 women); includes 30 minority (24 African Americans, 1 American Indian/Alaska Native, 2 Asian Americans or Pacific Islanders, 3 Hispanic Americans), 35 international. Average age 30. 605 applicants, 34% accepted, 142 enrolled. In 2006, 107 master's, 10 doctorates awarded. Terminal master's awarded for partial completion of doctoral program. *Degree requirements:* For doctorate, thesis/dissertation. *Entrance requirements:* For master's, GMAT, minimum GPA of 3.0 in last 60 hours of course work; for doctorate, GMAT, minimum GPA of 2.75 in last 60 undergraduate hours, 3.25 in last 60 graduate hours. Additional exam requirements/recommendations for international students: Required—TOEFL. *Application deadline:* For fall admission, 7/1 for domestic students; for spring admission, 11/1 for domestic students. Applications are processed on a rolling basis. Application fee: $30. Electronic applications accepted. *Expenses:* Tuition, state resident: full-time $4,550; part-time $253 per hour. Tuition, nonresident: full-time $10,552; part-time $584 per hour. International tuition: $10,882 full-time. Tuition and fees vary according to course load. *Financial support:* In 2006–07, 29 teaching assistantships with full tuition reimbursements (averaging $10,778 per year) were awarded; research assistantships with full tuition reimbursements, Federal Work-Study, institutionally sponsored loans, and unspecified assistantships also available. Financial award applicants required to submit FAFSA. *Unit head:* Dr. Barbara Spencer, Director, 662-325-1891, Fax: 662-325-8161, E-mail: gsb@cobilan.msstate.edu. *Application contact:* Dr. Phil Bonfanti, Director of Admissions, 662-325-4104, Fax: 662-325-8872, E-mail: admit@msstate.edu.

Missouri State University, Graduate College, College of Business Administration, Department of Computer Information Systems, Springfield, MO 65804-0094. Offers computer information systems (MS); secondary education (MS Ed), including business. Part-time and evening/weekend programs available. *Faculty:* 13 full-time (4 women). *Students:* 30 full-time (8 women), 9 part-time (7 women); includes 2 minority (1 African American, 1 Hispanic American), 2 international. Average age 35. 30 applicants, 40% accepted, 12 enrolled. In 2006, 11 degrees awarded. *Degree requirements:* For master's, thesis optional. *Entrance requirements:* For master's, GMAT, 3 years of work experience in computer information systems, minimum

GPA of 2.75 (MS), 9-12 teaching certification (MS Ed). Additional exam requirements/recommendations for international students: Required—TOEFL (minimum score 550 paper-based; 213 computer-based; 79 iBT), IELTS (minimum score 6). *Application deadline:* For fall admission, 7/20 priority date for domestic students; for spring admission, 12/20 priority date for domestic students. Applications are processed on a rolling basis. Application fee: $35. *Expenses:* Contact institution. Full-time tuition and fees vary according to course level, course load, program and reciprocity agreements. *Financial support:* Teaching assistantships with full tuition reimbursements, career-related internships or fieldwork, institutionally sponsored loans, scholarships/grants, tuition waivers (partial), and unspecified assistantships available. Support available to part-time students. Financial award application deadline: 3/31; financial award applicants required to submit FAFSA. *Unit head:* Dr. Jerry Chin, Head, 417-836-4131, Fax: 417-836-6907, E-mail: jerrychin@missouristate.edu.

Missouri State University, Graduate College, College of Business Administration, Program in Business Administration, Springfield, MO 65804-0094. Offers MBA. *Accreditation:* AACSB. Part-time and evening/weekend programs available. Postbaccalaureate distance learning degree programs offered (no on-campus study). *Faculty:* 29 full-time (6 women). *Students:* 202 full-time (89 women), 165 part-time (56 women); includes 18 minority (11 African Americans, 2 American Indian/Alaska Native, 4 Asian Americans or Pacific Islanders, 1 Hispanic American), 99 international. Average age 27. 141 applicants, 65% accepted, 85 enrolled. In 2006, 149 degrees awarded. *Degree requirements:* For master's, thesis optional. *Entrance requirements:* For master's, GMAT, minimum GPA of 2.75. Additional exam requirements/recommendations for international students: Required—TOEFL (minimum score 550 paper-based; 213 computer-based; 79 iBT). *Application deadline:* For fall admission, 7/20 priority date for domestic students; for spring admission, 12/20 priority date for domestic students. Applications are processed on a rolling basis. Application fee: $35. Electronic applications accepted. *Expenses:* Tuition, state resident: full-time $3,582; part-time $199 per credit hour. Tuition, nonresident: full-time $6,984; part-time $199 per credit hour. Required fees: $548. Full-time tuition and fees vary according to course level, course load, program and reciprocity agreements. *Financial support:* In 2006–07, 2 research assistantships with full tuition reimbursements (averaging $9,000 per year), 5 teaching assistantships with full tuition reimbursements (averaging $6,780 per year) were awarded; career-related internships or fieldwork, institutionally sponsored loans, scholarships/grants, tuition waivers (partial), and unspecified assistantships also available. Support available to part-time students. Financial award application deadline: 3/31; financial award applicants required to submit FAFSA. *Unit head:* James Simmerman, Director, 417-836-5646, Fax: 417-836-4407, E-mail: jamessimmerman@missouristate.edu.

See Close-Up on page 291.

Monmouth University, Graduate School, School of Business Administration, West Long Branch, NJ 07764-1898. Offers accounting (MBA); business administration (MBA); health care management (MBA, Certificate). *Accreditation:* AACSB. Part-time and evening/weekend programs available. *Faculty:* 30 full-time (11 women), 3 part-time/adjunct (1 woman). *Students:* 36 full-time (18 women), 198 part-time (88 women); includes 22 minority (9 African Americans, 1 American Indian/Alaska Native, 6 Asian Americans or Pacific Islanders, 6 Hispanic Americans), 12 international. Average age 30. 123 applicants, 89% accepted, 54 enrolled. In 2006, 74 degrees awarded. *Degree requirements:* For master's, capstone course. *Entrance requirements:* For master's, GMAT, minimum GPA of 3.0 in major, 2.75 overall. Additional exam requirements/recommendations for international students: Required—TOEFL (minimum score 550 paper-based; 213 computer-based; 79 iBT), IELTS (minimum score 5), MELAB 77, Cambridge A, B, C. *Application deadline:* For fall admission, 7/15 priority date for domestic students, 6/1 for international students; for spring admission, 11/15 priority date for domestic students, 11/1 for international students. Applications are processed on a rolling basis. Application fee: $50. Electronic applications accepted. *Expenses:* Tuition: Full-time $12,780; part-time $710 per credit. Required fees: $628; $314 per term. *Financial support:* In 2006–07, 126 fellowships (averaging $1,459 per year), 12 research assistantships (averaging $8,362 per year) were awarded; career-related internships or fieldwork, scholarships/grants, tuition waivers (partial), and unspecified assistantships also available. Support available to part-time students. Financial award application deadline: 3/1; financial award applicants required to submit FAFSA. *Faculty research:* Information technology and marketing, behavioral research in accounting, human resources, management of technology. *Unit head:* Donald Smith, Program Director, 732-571-7536, Fax: 732-263-5517, E-mail: dsmith@monmouth.edu. *Application contact:* Kevin Roane, Director, Office of Graduate Admission, 732-571-3452, Fax: 732-263-5123, E-mail: gradadm@monmouth.edu.

Monroe College, King School of Business, Bronx, NY 10468-5407. Offers business management (MBA). Program also offered in New Rochelle, NY. Postbaccalaureate distance learning degree programs offered.

Montclair State University, The Graduate School, School of Business, Montclair, NJ 07043-1624. Offers MA, MBA. *Accreditation:* AACSB. Part-time and evening/weekend programs available. *Faculty:* 73 full-time (19 women), 34 part-time/adjunct (13 women). *Students:* 56 full-time (31 women), 254 part-time (111 women); includes 49 minority (8 African Americans, 1 American Indian/Alaska Native, 24 Asian Americans or Pacific Islanders, 16 Hispanic Americans), 32 international. 238 applicants, 40% accepted, 62 enrolled. In 2006, 137 degrees awarded. *Degree requirements:* For master's, comprehensive exam. *Entrance requirements:* For master's, GMAT (MBA), GRE (MA), 2 letters of recommendation, resumé. Additional exam requirements/recommendations for international students: Required—TOEFL (minimum score 83 computer-based). *Application deadline:* For fall admission, 6/1 for international students; for spring admission, 10/1 for international students. Applications are processed on a rolling basis. Application fee: $60. Electronic applications accepted. *Expenses:* Tuition, state resident: part-time $450 per credit. Tuition, nonresident: part-time $682 per credit. Tuition and fees vary according to degree level and program. *Financial support:* In 2006–07, 28 students received support, including 17 research assistantships with full tuition reimbursements available (averaging $7,000 per year); Federal Work-Study, scholarships/grants, and unspecified assistantships also available. Support available to part-time students. Financial award application deadline: 3/1; financial award applicants required to submit FAFSA. *Unit head:* Dr. Alan Oppenheim, Dean, 973-655-4303, E-mail: oppenheima@mail.montclair.edu. *Application contact:* Dr. Carla M. Narrett, Dean of the Graduate School, 973-655-5147, Fax: 973-655-7869, E-mail: graduate.school@montclair.edu.

See Close-Up on page 293.

Monterey Institute of International Studies, Fisher Graduate School of International Business, Monterey, CA 93940-2691. Offers MBA. *Accreditation:* AACSB. *Faculty:* 7 full-time (1 woman), 3 part-time/adjunct (0 women). *Students:* 68 full-time (31 women), 1 part-time; includes 12 minority (1 African American, 6 Asian Americans or Pacific Islanders, 5 Hispanic Americans), 19 international. Average age 28. 86 applicants, 94% accepted, 41 enrolled. In 2006, 43 degrees awarded. *Degree requirements:* For master's, one foreign language, thesis. *Entrance requirements:* For master's, GMAT, minimum GPA of 3.0, proficiency in a foreign language. Additional exam requirements/recommendations for international students: Required—TOEFL (minimum score 550 paper-based; 213 computer-based; 80 iBT). *Application deadline:* For fall admission, 3/15 priority date for domestic students; for spring admission, 10/1 priority date for domestic students. Applications are processed on a rolling basis. Application fee: $50. Electronic applications accepted. *Expenses:* Tuition: Full-time $26,500; part-time $1,200 per credit. Required fees: $200. *Financial support:* In 2006–07, 59 students received support, including 2 research assistantships with partial tuition reimbursements available (averaging $4,000 per year); career-related internships or fieldwork, Federal Work-Study, institutionally sponsored loans, scholarships/grants, tuition waivers (partial), and unspecified assistantships also available. Support available to part-time students. Financial award application deadline: 3/15; financial award applicants required to submit FAFSA. *Faculty research:* Cross-cultural consumer behavior, foreign direct investment, marketing and entrepreneurial orientation, political risk analysis and area studies, managing international human resources. *Unit head:* Dr. Ernest J. Scalberg, Dean, 831-647-4140, Fax: 831-647-6506, E-mail: fgsib@miis.edu. *Application contact:* 831-647-4123, Fax: 831-647-6405, E-mail: admit@miis.edu.

Montreat College, School of Professional and Adult Studies, Montreat, NC 28757-1267. Offers business administration (MBA); K-6 education (MA Ed). Evening/weekend programs available. Postbaccalaureate distance learning degree programs offered. *Entrance requirements:* Additional exam requirements/recommendations for international students: Required—TOEFL (minimum score 500 paper-based; 190 computer-based).

Moravian College, The Comenius Center for Continuing, Professional, and Graduate Studies, Business and Management Programs, Bethlehem, PA 18018-6650. Offers MBA. Part-time and evening/weekend programs available. *Faculty:* 5 full-time (1 woman), 3 part-time/adjunct (0 women). *Students:* 105. Average age 33. 15 applicants, 100% accepted, 15 enrolled. In 2006, 11 degrees awarded. *Entrance requirements:* For master's, GMAT. Additional exam requirements/recommendations for international students: Required—TOEFL. *Application deadline:* Applications are processed on a rolling basis. Application fee: $40. *Expenses:* Contact institution. *Financial support:* In 2006–07, 1 fellowship with full tuition reimbursement was awarded. *Faculty research:* Marketing, interest rate, labor relations, personnel and public administration, strategic planning. *Unit head:* Dr. William A. Kleintop, Associate Dean for Business and Management Programs, 610-507-1400, Fax: 610-861-1466, E-mail: comenius@moravian.edu. *Application contact:* Linda J. Doyle, Information Contact, 610-807-4444, Fax: 610-861-1466, E-mail: mba@moravian.edu.

Morehead State University, Graduate Programs, College of Business, Morehead, KY 40351. Offers MBA, MSIS. *Accreditation:* AACSB. Part-time and evening/weekend programs available. Postbaccalaureate distance learning degree programs offered (minimal on-campus study). *Faculty:* 13 full-time (2 women), 10 part-time/adjunct (3 women). *Students:* 33 full-time (16 women), 149 part-time (84 women); includes 13 minority (8 African Americans, 3 Asian Americans or Pacific Islanders, 2 Hispanic Americans), 3 international. Average age 32. In 2006, 57 degrees awarded. *Degree requirements:* For master's, comprehensive exam. *Entrance requirements:* For master's, GMAT, GRE General Test, minimum GPA of 2.5. Additional exam requirements/recommendations for international students: Required—TOEFL (minimum score 525 paper-based; 197 computer-based). *Application deadline:* For fall admission, 8/1 for domestic and international students; for spring admission, 12/1 for domestic and international students. Applications are processed on a rolling basis. Application fee: $0 ($55 for international students). Electronic applications accepted. *Financial support:* In 2006–07, 13 teaching assistantships (averaging $6,000 per year) were awarded; career-related internships or fieldwork, Federal Work-Study, and unspecified assistantships also available. Financial award application deadline: 4/1; financial award applicants required to submit FAFSA. *Faculty research:* Regional economic development, accounting systems, banking market structures, macroeconomics, distance learning. *Unit head:* Dr. Robert L. Albert, Dean, 606-783-2174, Fax: 606-783-5025, E-mail: r.albert@moreheadstate.edu. *Application contact:* Michelle Barber, Graduate Admissions Counselor, 606-783-2039, Fax: 606-783-5061, E-mail: m.barber@moreheadstate.edu.

Morgan State University, School of Graduate Studies, Earl G. Graves School of Business and Management, PhD Program in Business Administration, Baltimore, MD 21251. Offers PhD. *Students:* 14 (3 women); includes 10 minority (all African Americans) 4 international. In 2006, 1 degree awarded. *Degree requirements:* For doctorate, thesis/dissertation. *Entrance requirements:* For doctorate, GMAT. Additional exam requirements/recommendations for international students: Required—TOEFL (minimum score 550 paper-based; 213 computer-based). *Application deadline:* For fall admission, 2/1 priority date for domestic students; for spring admission, 10/1 priority date for domestic students. Applications are processed on a rolling basis. Application fee: $0. *Expenses:* Tuition, state resident: part-time $272 per credit. Tuition, nonresident: part-time $478 per credit. Required fees: $38 per credit. *Financial support:* Fellowships, research assistantships, teaching assistantships available. Financial award application deadline: 2/1. *Unit head:* Dr. Franklyn Manu, Graduate Coordinator, 443-885-3357. *Application contact:* Dr. Maurice C. Taylor, Dean, 443-885-3185, Fax: 443-885-8226, E-mail: mctaylor@moac.morgan.edu.

Morrison University, Graduate School, Reno, NV 89521. Offers business administration (MBA). Part-time and evening/weekend programs available. *Degree requirements:* For master's, thesis. *Entrance requirements:* For master's, GMAT, minimum 3 years minimum work experience, interview, minimum GPA of 3.0. Electronic applications accepted.

Mount Marty College, Graduate Studies Division, Yankton, SD 57078-3724. Offers business administration (MBA); nurse anesthesia (MS); pastoral ministries (MPM). *Accreditation:* AANA/CANAEP (one or more programs are accredited). *Faculty:* 4 full-time (3 women), 1 part-time/adjunct (0 women). *Students:* 70 full-time (42 women); includes 4 minority (2 African Americans, 1 Asian American or Pacific Islander, 1 Hispanic American). 140 applicants, 28% accepted, 39 enrolled. In 2006, 37 degrees awarded. *Degree requirements:* For master's, thesis or alternative. *Entrance requirements:* For master's, GRE General Test, minimum GPA of 3.0. *Application deadline:* For fall admission, 12/1 priority date for domestic students. Applications are processed on a rolling basis. Application fee: $35. Electronic applications accepted. *Financial support:* In 2006–07, 70 students received support. Scholarships/grants available. Financial award application deadline: 8/1; financial award applicants required to submit FAFSA. *Faculty research:* Clinical anesthesia, professional characteristics, motivations of applicants. *Unit head:* Brandi Tschumper, Vice President of Enrollment, 800-658-4552, Fax: 605-688-1508, E-mail: mmcadmit@mtmc.edu.

Mount Mary College, Graduate Programs, Program in Business Administration, Milwaukee, WI 53222-4597. Offers MBA. *Degree requirements:* For master's, terminal project. *Entrance requirements:* For master's, GPA of 2.75. Additional exam requirements/recommendations for international students: Required—TOEFL (minimum score 500 paper-based; 173 computer-based). *Application deadline:* For fall admission, 8/1 priority date for domestic and international students; for spring admission, 12/1 priority date for domestic and international students. Application fee: $35 ($75 for international students). *Expenses:* Tuition: Part-time $490 per credit. Required fees: $48 per term. Tuition and fees vary according to course load and program. *Unit head:* Robert Crombie, Director, 414-258-4810 Ext. 478, E-mail: crombier@mtmary.edu.

Mount Saint Mary College, Division of Business, Newburgh, NY 12550-3494. Offers business (MBA); financial planning (MBA). Part-time and evening/weekend programs available. *Faculty:* 6 full-time (2 women), 4 part-time/adjunct (1 woman). *Students:* 20 full-time (13 women), 43 part-time (24 women); includes 20 minority (12 African Americans, 3 Asian Americans or Pacific Islanders, 5 Hispanic Americans). Average age 33. 23 applicants, 100% accepted, 22 enrolled. In 2006, 24 degrees awarded. *Degree requirements:* For master's, thesis. *Entrance requirements:* For master's, GMAT. *Application deadline:* Applications are processed on a rolling basis. Application fee: $35. *Expenses:* Tuition: Full-time $11,880; part-time $660 per credit. *Financial support:* In 2006–07, 8 students received support. Unspecified assistantships available. Financial award application deadline: 3/15. *Faculty research:* Financial reform, entrepreneurship and small business development, global business relations, technology's impact on business decision-making, college-assisted business education. *Unit head:* David R. Rant, Coordinator, 845-569-3124, Fax: 845-562-6762, E-mail: rant@msmc.edu. *Application contact:* Janice Banker, Secretary, 845-569-3582, Fax: 845-569-3885, E-mail: banker@msmc.edu.

Mount St. Mary's University, Program in Business Administration, Emmitsburg, MD 21727-7799. Offers MBA. Part-time and evening/weekend programs available. *Faculty:* 10 full-time (1 woman), 9 part-time/adjunct (1 woman). *Students:* 32 full-time (18 women), 197 part-time (99 women); includes 13 minority (6 African Americans, 3 Asian Americans or Pacific Islanders, 4 Hispanic Americans), 6 international. Average age 32. 96 applicants, 99% accepted, 52 enrolled. In 2006, 92 degrees awarded. *Median time to degree:* Master's–3 years part-time. *Degree requirements:* For master's, thesis. *Entrance requirements:* For master's, GMAT, minimum GPA of 2.75. Additional exam requirements/recommendations for international students: Required—TOEFL (minimum score 550 paper-based; 213 computer-based). *Application*

Business Administration and Management—General

Mount St. Mary's University (continued)

deadline: For fall admission, 8/21 priority date for domestic students; for winter admission, 10/14 priority date for domestic students; for spring admission, 2/24 priority date for domestic students. Applications are processed on a rolling basis. Application fee: $35. *Expenses: Contact institution.* Tuition and fees vary according to program. *Financial support:* In 2006–07, 68 students received support. Career-related internships or fieldwork and unspecified assistantships available. Financial award applicants required to submit FAFSA. *Faculty research:* Corporate social responsibility, aviation law, managerial economics, the monetary transmission mechanism, data mining. *Application contact:* Sandy Kauffman, Administrative Assistant, 301-447-5326, Fax: 301-447-5335, E-mail: kauffman@msmary.edu.

Mount Vernon Nazarene University, Program in Management, Mount Vernon, OH 43050-9500. Offers MSM. Part-time and evening/weekend programs available.

Murray State University, College of Business and Public Affairs, MBA Program, Murray, KY 42071. Offers MBA. *Accreditation:* AACSB. Part-time and evening/weekend programs available. *Faculty:* 16 full-time (3 women). *Students:* 91 full-time (37 women), 101 part-time (49 women); includes 2 minority (both Asian Americans or Pacific Islanders), 66 international. Average age 28. 159 applicants, 81% accepted, 61 enrolled. In 2006, 55 degrees awarded. *Entrance requirements:* For master's, GMAT. Additional exam requirements/recommendations for international students: Required—TOEFL. *Application deadline:* Applications are processed on a rolling basis. Application fee: $25. *Financial support:* In 2006–07, research assistantships with partial tuition reimbursements (averaging $48,000 per year); teaching assistantships, Federal Work-Study also available. Financial award application deadline: 4/1. *Unit head:* Dr. Gerry Muuka, Coordinator, 270-809-4190, Fax: 270-809-3482, E-mail: gerry.muuka@murraystate.edu.

Myers University, Charles R. McDonald School of Business, Cleveland, OH 44114-4624. Offers MBA, MFP, MMG. Part-time and evening/weekend programs available. Postbaccalaureate distance learning degree programs offered (no on-campus study). *Degree requirements:* For master's, registration. *Entrance requirements:* For master's, references, interview.

National American University, Graduate Programs, Rapid City, SD 57701. Offers MBA, MM. Programs also offered in Wichita, KS; Albuquerque, NM; Bloomington, MN; Brooklyn Center, MN; Colorado Springs, CO; Denver, CO; Independence, MO; Overland Park, KS; Rio Rancho, NM; Roseville, MN; Zona Rosa, MO. Part-time and evening/weekend programs available. Postbaccalaureate distance learning degree programs offered. *Entrance requirements:* For master's, minimum undergraduate GPA of 2.75. Additional exam requirements/recommendations for international students: Required—TOEFL, TWE. Electronic applications accepted. *Faculty research:* Tourism, finance, marketing.

The National Graduate School of Quality Management, Program in Quality Systems Management, Falmouth, MA 02541. Offers e-commerce (MS); management (MS); six sigma (MS).

National-Louis University, College of Management and Business, Program in Business Administration, Chicago, IL 60603. Offers MBA. *Students:* 102 full-time (69 women), 9 part-time (5 women); includes 52 minority (32 African Americans, 8 Asian Americans or Pacific Islanders, 12 Hispanic Americans), 1 international. Average age 34. *Entrance requirements:* For master's, college-administered critical thinking and writing skills test, minimum GPA of 3.0, resumé. *Application deadline:* Applications are processed on a rolling basis. Application fee: $25. *Expenses:* Tuition: Full-time $17,685. One-time fee: $40 full-time. *Financial support:* Federal Work-Study, institutionally sponsored loans, and scholarships/grants available. Support available to part-time students. *Unit head:* Paul O'Neil, Associate Professor, 630-874-4411, E-mail: poneill@nl.edu. *Application contact:* David McCulloch, Vice President for University Services, 800-443-5522 Ext. 5127, Fax: 847-465-0593, E-mail: dmcc@wheeling1.nl.edu.

National-Louis University, College of Management and Business, Program in Management, Chicago, IL 60603. Offers MS. Evening/weekend programs available. *Students:* 53 full-time (25 women), 2 part-time; includes 19 minority (15 African Americans, 1 American Indian/Alaska Native, 1 Asian American or Pacific Islander, 2 Hispanic Americans). Average age 41. 48 applicants, 98% accepted. *Entrance requirements:* For master's, college-administered critical thinking and writing skills test, minimum GPA of 3.0, resumé. *Application deadline:* Applications are processed on a rolling basis. Application fee: $25. *Expenses:* Tuition: Full-time $17,685. One-time fee: $40 full-time. *Financial support:* Federal Work-Study, institutionally sponsored loans, and scholarships/grants available. Support available to part-time students. Financial award applicants required to submit FAFSA. *Unit head:* Robert Skenes, Associate Professor, 703-394-6932, E-mail: rskenes@nl.edu. *Application contact:* David McCulloch, Vice President for University Services, 800-443-5522 Ext. 5127, Fax: 847-465-0593, E-mail: dmcc@wheeling1.nl.edu.

National University, Academic Affairs, School of Business and Management, La Jolla, CA 92037-1011. Offers EMBA, MA, MBA, MFS, MS. Part-time and evening/weekend programs available. Postbaccalaureate distance learning degree programs offered (no on-campus study). *Faculty:* 38 full-time (8 women), 528 part-time/adjunct (133 women). *Students:* 808 full-time (422 women), 1,458 part-time (753 women); includes 817 minority (251 African Americans, 12 American Indian/Alaska Native, 262 Asian Americans or Pacific Islanders, 292 Hispanic Americans), 173 international. Average age 35. 1,413 applicants, 1220 enrolled. In 2006, 550 degrees awarded. *Degree requirements:* For master's, thesis. *Entrance requirements:* For master's, interview, minimum GPA of 2.5. Additional exam requirements/recommendations for international students: Required—TOEFL (minimum score 550 paper-based; 213 computer-based; 80 iBT), IELTS (minimum score 6). *Application deadline:* Applications are processed on a rolling basis. Application fee: $60 ($65 for international students). Electronic applications accepted. *Expenses:* Tuition: Full-time $7,722; part-time $286 per unit. One-time fee: $60. *Financial support:* Career-related internships or fieldwork, scholarships/grants, and tuition waivers (partial) available. Support available to part-time students. Financial award application deadline: 6/30; financial award applicants required to submit FAFSA. *Unit head:* Dr. Wali Mondal, Dean, 858-642-8439, Fax: 858-642-8406, E-mail: wmondal@nu.edu. *Application contact:* Dominick Giovanniello, Associate Regional Dean—San Diego, 800-NAT-UNIV, Fax: 858-642-8709, E-mail: dgiovann@nu.edu.

Naval Postgraduate School, Graduate Programs, School of Business and Public Policy, Monterey, CA 93943. Offers contract management (MS); defense-focused business administration (MBA); executive business administration (MBA); leadership and human resource development (MS); management (MS); program management (MS); systems engineering management (MS). Program only open to commissioned officers of the United States and friendly nations and selected United States federal civilian employees. *Accreditation:* AACSB; NASPAA. Part-time programs available. Postbaccalaureate distance learning degree programs offered (minimal on-campus study). *Degree requirements:* For master's, thesis.

Nazareth College of Rochester, Graduate Studies, Department of Business, Program in Management, Rochester, NY 14618-3790. Offers MS. Part-time and evening/weekend programs available. *Faculty:* 3 full-time (0 women), 3 part-time/adjunct (0 women). *Students:* 19 applicants, 95% accepted, 12 enrolled. In 2006, 18 degrees awarded. *Entrance requirements:* For master's, minimum GPA of 3.0. *Application deadline:* For fall admission, 8/1 for domestic students; for spring admission, 11/1 for domestic students. Application fee: $40. *Financial support:* Research assistantships with partial tuition reimbursements available. Financial award application deadline: 3/1; financial award applicants required to submit FAFSA. *Application contact:* Judith G. Baker, Director, Graduate Admissions, 585-389-2050, Fax: 585-389-2817, E-mail: gradstudies@naz.edu.

New England College, Program in Management, Henniker, NH 03242-3293. Offers healthcare administration (MS); nonprofit leadership (MS); organizational leadership (MS). Part-time and evening/weekend programs available. *Degree requirements:* For master's, independent research project. Electronic applications accepted.

New Jersey City University, Graduate and Continuing Education, College of Professional Studies, Department of Business Administration, Jersey City, NJ 07305-1597. Offers accounting (MS); finance (MS). *Accreditation:* ACBSP. Evening/weekend programs available. *Faculty:* 9. *Students:* 2 full-time (1 woman), 33 part-time (10 women); includes 10 minority (3 African Americans, 4 Asian Americans or Pacific Islanders, 3 Hispanic Americans), 2 international. Average age 35. In 2006, 6 degrees awarded. *Application deadline:* For fall admission, 8/1 priority date for domestic students; for spring admission, 12/1 for domestic students. Applications are processed on a rolling basis. Application fee: $0. *Expenses:* Tuition, state resident: full-time $7,038; part-time $391 per credit. Tuition, nonresident: full-time $12,510; part-time $695 per credit. Required fees: $65 per credit. *Financial support:* Career-related internships or fieldwork and unspecified assistantships available. *Unit head:* Dr. Marilyn Ettinger, Head, 201-200-3353, E-mail: mettinger@njcu.edu.

New Jersey Institute of Technology, Office of Graduate Studies, School of Management, Program in Management of Business Administration, Newark, NJ 07102. Offers MBA. *Accreditation:* AACSB. Part-time and evening/weekend programs available. *Students:* 113 full-time (31 women), 84 part-time (25 women); includes 79 minority (18 African Americans, 1 American Indian/Alaska Native, 46 Asian Americans or Pacific Islanders, 14 Hispanic Americans), 48 international. Average age 34. 250 applicants, 61% accepted, 75 enrolled. In 2006, 73 degrees awarded. *Entrance requirements:* Additional exam requirements/recommendations for international students: Required—TOEFL (minimum score 550 paper-based; 213 computer-based). *Application deadline:* For fall admission, 6/5 priority date for domestic students; for spring admission, 10/15 for domestic students. Applications are processed on a rolling basis. Application fee: $60. Electronic applications accepted. *Expenses:* Tuition, state resident: full-time $11,896; part-time $648 per credit. Tuition, nonresident: full-time $16,900; part-time $892 per credit. Required fees: $336; $66 per credit. $168 per term. Tuition and fees vary according to course load. *Financial support:* Fellowships with full and partial tuition reimbursements, research assistantships with full and partial tuition reimbursements, teaching assistantships with full and partial tuition reimbursements, career-related internships or fieldwork, Federal Work-Study, institutionally sponsored loans, and unspecified assistantships available. Financial award application deadline: 3/15. *Application contact:* Kathryn Kelly, Director of Admissions, 973-596-3300, Fax: 973-596-3461, E-mail: admissions@njit.edu.

Newman University, School of Business, Wichita, KS 67213-2097. Offers international business (MBA); leadership (MBA); management (MBA); technology (MBA). Part-time programs available. *Faculty:* 6 full-time (2 women), 3 part-time/adjunct (1 woman). *Students:* 34 full-time (14 women), 76 part-time (30 women); includes 14 minority (6 African Americans, 1 American Indian/Alaska Native, 3 Asian Americans or Pacific Islanders, 4 Hispanic Americans), 31 international. Average age 31. 74 applicants, 80% accepted, 46 enrolled. In 2006, 76 degrees awarded. *Degree requirements:* For master's, thesis optional. *Entrance requirements:* For master's, interview; minimum GPA of 3.0; 3 letters of recommendation; course work in algebra, statistics, macroeconomics. Additional exam requirements/recommendations for international students: Required—TOEFL (minimum score 600 paper-based; 250 computer-based; 100 iBT). *Application deadline:* For fall admission, 8/1 priority date for domestic students; for winter admission, 1/1 priority date for domestic students; for spring admission, 1/1 priority date for domestic students. Applications are processed on a rolling basis. Application fee: $25 ($40 for international students). Electronic applications accepted. *Expenses: Contact institution.* *Financial support:* In 2006–07, 3 students received support. Federal Work-Study and tuition waivers available. Financial award application deadline: 8/15; financial award applicants required to submit FAFSA. *Unit head:* Dr. Joe Goetz, Dean, 316-942-4291 Ext. 2111, Fax: 316-942-4486, E-mail: goetzj@newmanu.edu. *Application contact:* Linda Kay Sabala, Director of Graduate Admissions, 316-942-4291 Ext. 2230, Fax: 316-942-4483, E-mail: sabalal@newmanu.edu.

New Mexico Highlands University, Graduate Studies, School of Business, Las Vegas, NM 87701. Offers business administration (MBA), including human resource management, international business, non-profit financial management. *Accreditation:* ACBSP. *Faculty:* 12 full-time (4 women), 1 part-time/adjunct (0 women). *Students:* 57 full-time (39 women), 103 part-time (69 women); includes 97 minority (1 African American, 26 American Indian/Alaska Native, 4 Asian Americans or Pacific Islanders, 66 Hispanic Americans), 17 international. Average age 35. 69 applicants, 84% accepted, 42 enrolled. In 2006, 29 degrees awarded. *Degree requirements:* For master's, thesis or alternative, comprehensive exam, registration. *Entrance requirements:* For master's, minimum undergraduate GPA of 3.0. Additional exam requirements/recommendations for international students: Required—TOEFL (minimum score 540 paper-based; 190 computer-based). *Application deadline:* For fall admission, 8/1 priority date for domestic students. Applications are processed on a rolling basis. Application fee: $15. *Expenses:* Tuition, state resident: part-time $101 per credit hour. Tuition, nonresident: part-time $101 per credit hour. *Financial support:* In 2006–07, 67 students received support, including 8 teaching assistantships with full and partial tuition reimbursements available (averaging $6,500 per year); career-related internships or fieldwork, Federal Work-Study, institutionally sponsored loans, scholarships/grants, tuition waivers (full and partial), and unspecified assistantships also available. Support available to part-time students. Financial award application deadline: 3/1; financial award applicants required to submit FAFSA. *Unit head:* Dr. William Taylor, Dean, 505-454-3344, Fax: 505-454-3354. *Application contact:* Diane Trujillo, Administrative Assistant Graduate Studies, 505-454-3266, Fax: 505-454-3558, E-mail: dtrujillo@nmhu.edu.

New Mexico State University, Graduate School, College of Business, Department of Management, Las Cruces, NM 88003-8001. Offers business administration (PhD), including management. *Faculty:* 12 full-time (4 women), 1 (woman) part-time/adjunct. *Students:* 14 full-time (5 women), 2 part-time (1 woman); includes 1 minority (American Indian/Alaska Native), 8 international. Average age 35. 17 applicants, 29% accepted. *Degree requirements:* For doctorate, thesis/dissertation, comprehensive exam. *Entrance requirements:* For doctorate, GMAT or GRE, references, writing sample, statement of purpose. Additional exam requirements/recommendations for international students: Required—TOEFL (minimum score 530 paper-based; 197 computer-based). *Application deadline:* For fall admission, 2/15 priority date for domestic and international students. Application fee: $30 ($50 for international students). Electronic applications accepted. *Financial support:* In 2006–07, 10 students received support, including 10 teaching assistantships; health care benefits also available. *Unit head:* Dr. Bonnie F. Daily, Head, 505-646-1201, Fax: 505-646-1372, E-mail: bdaily@nmsu.edu. *Application contact:* Dr. Philip G. Benson, Professor, 505-646-5695, Fax: 505-646-1372, E-mail: phddirector@business.nmsu.edu.

New Mexico State University, Graduate School, College of Business, Program in Business Administration, Las Cruces, NM 88003-8001. Offers MBA, PhD. *Accreditation:* AACSB. Part-time and evening/weekend programs available. *Students:* 56 full-time (28 women), 129 part-time (55 women); includes 83 minority (1 African American, 1 American Indian/Alaska Native, 3 Asian Americans or Pacific Islanders, 78 Hispanic Americans), 11 international. Average age 34. 116 applicants, 83% accepted. In 2006, 46 master's, 4 doctorates awarded. *Degree requirements:* For master's, thesis optional; for doctorate, thesis/dissertation, comprehensive exam, registration. *Entrance requirements:* For master's, GMAT; for doctorate, GMAT or GRE, MBA, writing samples, letters of reference. Additional exam requirements/recommendations for international students: Required—TOEFL (minimum score 530 paper-based; 197 computer-based). *Application deadline:* For fall admission, 7/1 priority date for domestic students, 3/1 priority date for international students; for spring admission, 11/1 priority date for domestic students, 10/1 priority date for international students. Applications are processed on a rolling basis. Application fee: $30 ($50 for international students). Electronic applications accepted. *Financial support:* In 2006–07, 4 fellowships with partial tuition reimbursements, 2 research assistantships with partial tuition reimbursements, 32 teaching assistantships with partial tuition reimbursements were awarded; Federal Work-Study, institutionally sponsored loans, scholarships/grants, health care benefits, and unspecified assistantships also available. Financial award application deadline: 3/1. *Faculty research:* Small business/entrepreneurship, international business/global marketing, e-business, total quality management, supply chain management. *Unit head:* Dr. Bobbie Green, Director, 505-646-8003, Fax: 505-646-7977, E-mail: mba@nmsu.edu.

New York Institute of Technology, Ellis College, Old Westbury, NY 11568. Offers accounting and information systems (MBA); e-commerce (MBA); finance (MBA); global management (MBA); healthcare administration (MBA); human resources management (MBA); leadership (MBA); management of information systems (MBA); management of technology (MBA); marketing (MBA); professional accounting (MBA); project management (MBA); risk management (MBA); strategy and economics (MBA). Ellis College is a collaboration between New York Institute of Technology and UNext online learning company. Part-time and evening/weekend programs available. Postbaccalaureate distance learning degree programs offered (no on-campus study). *Entrance requirements:* For master's, interview. Additional exam requirements/recommendations for international students: Required—TOEFL (minimum score 550 paper-based; 213 computer-based). Electronic applications accepted. *Expenses:* Tuition: Full-time $16,800; part-time $700 per credit.

New York Institute of Technology, Graduate Division, School of Management, Program in Business Administration, Old Westbury, NY 11568-8000. Offers accounting (Advanced Certificate); business administration (MBA); finance (Advanced Certificate); international business (Advanced Certificate); management of information systems (Advanced Certificate); marketing (Advanced Certificate). Part-time and evening/weekend programs available. *Students:* 481 full-time (120 women), 1,300 part-time (670 women); includes 297 minority (153 African Americans, 6 American Indian/Alaska Native, 81 Asian Americans or Pacific Islanders, 57 Hispanic Americans), 215 international. Average age 29. 1,049 applicants, 87% accepted, 137 enrolled. In 2006, 917 degrees awarded. *Degree requirements:* For master's, thesis (for some programs). *Entrance requirements:* For master's, minimum QPA of 2.85. Additional exam requirements/recommendations for international students: Required—TOEFL (minimum score 550 paper-based; 213 computer-based). *Application deadline:* For fall admission, 7/1 priority date for domestic students; for spring admission, 12/1 priority date for domestic students. Applications are processed on a rolling basis. Application fee: $50. Electronic applications accepted. *Expenses:* Tuition: Full-time $16,800; part-time $700 per credit. *Financial support:* Fellowships, research assistantships with partial tuition reimbursements, institutionally sponsored loans, tuition waivers (full and partial), and unspecified assistantships available. Support available to part-time students. Financial award applicants required to submit FAFSA. *Faculty research:* Instructor performance appraisal; relationship between TOEFL, GMAT, GRE, and performance in foreign students. *Unit head:* Dr. Gurumurthy Kalyanuram, Director, 516-686-7972, E-mail: gkalyana@nyit.edu. *Application contact:* Jacquelyn Nealon, Dean of Admissions and Financial Aid, 516-686-7925, Fax: 516-686-7613, E-mail: jnealon@nyit.edu.

New York University, Leonard N. Stern School of Business, Department of Marketing, New York, NY 10012-1019. Offers entertainment, media and technology (MBA); general marketing (MBA); marketing (PhD); product management (MBA). *Expenses:* Tuition: Part-time $1,080 per unit. Required fees: $56 per unit. $329 per term. Tuition and fees vary according to program.

New York University, Robert F. Wagner Graduate School of Public Service, Program in Management, New York, NY 10012-1019. Offers international public service organizations management (MS); management (MS); MA/MS; MSW/MS. *Accreditation:* AACSB. Part-time and evening/weekend programs available. *Faculty:* 29 full-time (15 women), 58 part-time/adjunct (31 women). *Students:* 5 full-time (4 women), 18 part-time (14 women); includes 4 minority (2 African Americans, 2 Asian Americans or Pacific Islanders), 3 international. Average age 39. 68 applicants, 22% accepted, 7 enrolled. In 2006, 21 degrees awarded. *Entrance requirements:* For master's, minimum undergraduate GPA of 3.0. Additional exam requirements/recommendations for international students: Required—TOEFL (minimum score 600 paper-based; 250 computer-based), TWE (minimum score 4). *Application deadline:* For fall admission, 6/1 for domestic students, 1/15 for international students; for spring admission, 11/15 for domestic students, 10/1 for international students. Applications are processed on a rolling basis. Application fee: $70. Electronic applications accepted. *Expenses: Contact institution.* Tuition and fees vary according to program. *Financial support:* In 2006–07, 4 students received support, including 1 fellowship (averaging $3,176 per year); research assistantships with full and partial tuition reimbursements available, institutionally sponsored loans, scholarships/grants, health care benefits, and unspecified assistantships also available. Support available to part-time students. Financial award application deadline: 1/15; financial award applicants required to submit FAFSA. *Unit head:* Debra Gabrera, Administrator, 212-998-7400, Fax: 212-995-4164, E-mail: debra.gabrera@nyu.edu. *Application contact:* Bethany Godsoe, Assistant Dean, Enrollment and Student Services, 212-998-7414, Fax: 212-995-4164, E-mail: wagner.admissions@nyu.edu.

New York University, School of Law, New York, NY 10012-1019. Offers law (JD, LL M, JSD); law and business (Advanced Certificate); tax (Advanced Certificate); JD/LL M; JD/MA; JD/MBA; JD/MPA; JD/MSW; JD/PhD. *Accreditation:* ABA. Part-time programs available. *Faculty:* 117 full-time (35 women), 64 part-time/adjunct (18 women). *Students:* 1,442 full-time (667 women); includes 345 minority (124 African Americans, 153 Asian Americans or Pacific Islanders, 68 Hispanic Americans), 53 international. 7,571 applicants, 448 enrolled. In 2006, 465 JDs, 472 master's, 6 doctorates awarded. *Entrance requirements:* LSAT. *Application deadline:* For fall admission, 2/1 for domestic students. Application fee: $85. Electronic applications accepted. *Expenses: Contact institution.* Tuition and fees vary according to program. *Financial support:* Fellowships, research assistantships, teaching assistantships, career-related internships or fieldwork, Federal Work-Study, institutionally sponsored loans, scholarships/grants, tuition waivers (partial), and loan repayment assistance available. Financial award application deadline: 4/15; financial award applicants required to submit FAFSA. *Faculty research:* Constitutional law, environmental law, corporate law, globalization of law, philosophy of law. *Unit head:* Richard L. Revesz, Dean, 212-998-6000, Fax: 212-995-3150. *Application contact:* Kenneth J. Kleinrock, Assistant Dean for Admissions, 212-998-6060, Fax: 212-995-4527.

Niagara University, Graduate Division of Business Administration, Niagara Falls, Niagara University, NY 14109. Offers business (MBA); commerce (MBA). *Accreditation:* AACSB. Part-time and evening/weekend programs available. *Faculty:* 7 full-time (2 women). *Students:* 89 full-time (42 women), 37 part-time (12 women); includes 8 minority (4 African Americans, 1 American Indian/Alaska Native, 2 Asian Americans or Pacific Islanders, 1 Hispanic American), 29 international. Average age 30. 89 applicants, 73% accepted. In 2006, 41 degrees awarded. *Entrance requirements:* For master's, GMAT. Additional exam requirements/recommendations for international students: Required—TOEFL. *Application deadline:* For fall admission, 8/1 for domestic students; for spring admission, 11/1 for domestic students. Applications are processed on a rolling basis. Application fee: $30. *Financial support:* In 2006–07, 3 fellowships, 2 research assistantships were awarded; career-related internships or fieldwork and Federal Work-Study also available. Support available to part-time students. Financial award application deadline: 8/1; financial award applicants required to submit FAFSA. *Faculty research:* Capital flows, Federal Reserve policy, human resource management, public policy, issues in marketing. *Unit head:* Wick Hannan, Director, 716-286-8178, Fax: 716-286-8206, E-mail: wkh@niagara.edu.

Nicholls State University, Graduate Studies, College of Business Administration, Thibodaux, LA 70310. Offers MBA. *Accreditation:* AACSB. Part-time and evening/weekend programs available. *Faculty:* 27 full-time (5 women). *Students:* 40 full-time (20 women), 62 part-time (34 women); includes 8 minority (7 African Americans, 1 Asian American or Pacific Islander), 15 international. Average age 27. 56 applicants, 98% accepted, 36 enrolled. In 2006, 26 degrees awarded. *Degree requirements:* For master's, thesis optional. *Entrance requirements:* For master's, GMAT. Additional exam requirements/recommendations for international students: Required—TOEFL (minimum score 550 paper-based; 213 computer-based). *Application deadline:* For fall admission, 8/1 priority date for domestic students, 7/1 priority date for international students; for spring admission, 12/1 priority date for domestic students, 11/1 priority date for international students. Applications are processed on a rolling basis. Application fee: $20 ($30 for international students). Electronic applications accepted. *Expenses:* Tuition, state resident: part-time $450 per hour. Tuition, nonresident: part-time $450 per hour. *Financial support:* In 2006–07, 16 students received support, including 16 research assistantships with full tuition reimbursements available (averaging $4,000 per year); unspecified assistantships also available. Financial award application deadline: 6/1. *Unit head:* Dr. Shawn Mauldin, Dean, 985-448-4172, Fax: 985-448-4922.

Nichols College, Graduate Program in Business Administration, Dudley, MA 01571-5000. Offers MBA. Part-time and evening/weekend programs available. Postbaccalaureate distance learning degree programs offered (no on-campus study). *Faculty:* 5 full-time (2 women), 20 part-time/adjunct (6 women). *Students:* 33 full-time (16 women), 218 part-time (107 women); includes 17 minority (12 African Americans, 1 American Indian/Alaska Native, 1 Asian American or Pacific Islander, 3 Hispanic Americans), 3 international. Average age 34. In 2006, 77 degrees awarded. *Entrance requirements:* Additional exam requirements/recommendations for international students: Required—TOEFL. *Application deadline:* Applications are processed on a rolling basis. Application fee: $25. Electronic applications accepted. *Expenses:* Tuition: Part-time $495 per credit. *Financial support:* Career-related internships or fieldwork available. *Unit head:* Laurie Albert, Dean, Graduate and Professional Studies, 508-213-2440, Fax: 508-213-2490. *Application contact:* Rayanne Drouin, Director of Enrollment Services, 508-213-2150, Fax: 508-213-2490, E-mail: rayanne.drouin@nichols.edu.

North Carolina Central University, Division of Academic Affairs, School of Business, Durham, NC 27707-3129. Offers MBA, JD/MBA. *Accreditation:* AACSB; ACBSP. Part-time and evening/weekend programs available. *Degree requirements:* For master's, thesis. *Entrance requirements:* For master's, GMAT. Additional exam requirements/recommendations for international students: Required—TOEFL. *Faculty research:* Small business issues, research of pedagogy, African business environment.

North Carolina State University, Graduate School, College of Management, Program in Business Administration, Raleigh, NC 27695. Offers financial management (MBA); information technology management (MBA); marketing management (MBA); product innovation management (MBA); supply chain management (MBA); technology commercialization (MBA). *Accreditation:* AACSB. Part-time programs available. *Degree requirements:* For master's, thesis optional. *Entrance requirements:* For master's, GMAT. Additional exam requirements/recommendations for international students: Required—TOEFL. Electronic applications accepted. *Faculty research:* Manufacturing strategy, information systems, technology commercialization, managing research and development, historical stock returns.

North Central College, Graduate Programs, Department of Business, Program in Business Administration, Naperville, IL 60566-7063. Offers MBA. *Degree requirements:* For master's, project. *Entrance requirements:* For master's, interview.

North Central College, Graduate Programs, Department of Leadership Studies, Naperville, IL 60566-7063. Offers MLD. Part-time and evening/weekend programs available. *Degree requirements:* For master's, project. *Entrance requirements:* For master's, interview.

North Dakota State University, The Graduate School, College of Business Administration, Fargo, ND 58105. Offers MBA. *Accreditation:* AACSB. Part-time and evening/weekend programs available. *Faculty:* 25 full-time (5 women). *Students:* 21 full-time (9 women), 75 part-time (35 women); includes 4 minority (2 African Americans, 2 Hispanic Americans). Average age 29. 55 applicants, 76% accepted, 38 enrolled. In 2006, 32 degrees awarded. *Entrance requirements:* For master's, GMAT. Additional exam requirements/recommendations for international students: Required—TOEFL. *Application deadline:* For fall admission, 7/15 priority date for domestic students; for spring admission, 11/15 for domestic students. Applications are processed on a rolling basis. Application fee: $45 ($60 for international students). *Financial support:* In 2006–07, 14 students received support, including 13 research assistantships, 1 teaching assistantship; institutionally sponsored loans and tuition waivers (partial) also available. Support available to part-time students. Financial award application deadline: 5/15; financial award applicants required to submit FAFSA. *Faculty research:* Labor management, operations, international finance, agency, internet marketing. *Unit head:* Dr. Ron Johnson, Dean, 701-231-8805. *Application contact:* Paul R. Brown, Director, 701-231-7681, Fax: 701-231-7508, E-mail: paul.brown@ndsu.edu.

Northeastern Illinois University, Graduate College, College of Business and Management, Chicago, IL 60625-4699. Offers accounting (MBA); finance (MBA); management (MBA); marketing (MBA). Part-time and evening/weekend programs available. *Faculty:* 24 full-time (3 women), 13 part-time/adjunct (4 women). *Students:* 24 full-time (12 women), 40 part-time (16 women); includes 15 minority (4 African Americans, 8 Asian Americans or Pacific Islanders, 3 Hispanic Americans), 21 international. Average age 31. 23 applicants, 91% accepted. In 2006, 13 degrees awarded. *Degree requirements:* For master's, thesis optional. *Entrance requirements:* For master's, GMAT, minimum GPA of 2.75. Additional exam requirements/recommendations for international students: Required—TOEFL. *Application deadline:* For fall admission, 4/1 priority date for domestic students; for spring admission, 8/15 for domestic students. Applications are processed on a rolling basis. Application fee: $25. *Financial support:* In 2006–07, 20 students received support, including 8 research assistantships with full tuition reimbursements available (averaging $6,600 per year); career-related internships or fieldwork, Federal Work-Study, institutionally sponsored loans, and tuition waivers (full and partial) also available. Support available to part-time students. *Faculty research:* Perception of accountants and non-accountants toward future of the accounting industry, asynchronous learning outcomes, cost and efficiency of financial markets, impact of deregulation on airline industry, analysis of derivational instruments.

Northeastern State University, Graduate College, College of Business and Technology, Program in Business Administration, Tahlequah, OK 74464-2399. Offers MBA. *Accreditation:* ACBSP. Part-time and evening/weekend programs available. *Faculty:* 9 full-time (2 women). *Students:* 18 full-time (8 women), 43 part-time (15 women); includes 24 minority (4 African Americans, 19 American Indian/Alaska Native, 1 Asian American or Pacific Islander), 2 international. In 2006, 16 degrees awarded. *Degree requirements:* For master's, thesis, business plan, oral exam, comprehensive exam. *Entrance requirements:* For master's, GMAT, minimum GPA of 2.5. Additional exam requirements/recommendations for international students: Required—TOEFL (minimum score 213 computer-based). *Application deadline:* For fall admission, 6/1 priority date for domestic students. Applications are processed on a rolling basis. Application fee: $0 ($25 for international students). Electronic applications accepted. *Financial support:* Teaching assistantships, Federal Work-Study available. Financial award application deadline: 3/1. *Unit head:* Dr. Sandra Edwards, Chair, 918-683-0400 Ext. 5219.

Northeastern University, Graduate School of Business Administration, Boston, MA 02115-5096. Offers EMBA, MBA, MSF, MST, CAGS, JD/MBA, JD/MS/MBA, MBA/MSN, MS/MBA. *Accreditation:* AACSB. Part-time and evening/weekend programs available. *Faculty:* 102 full-time (20 women), 34 part-time/adjunct. *Students:* 224 full-time (88 women), 552 part-time (215 women). Average age 30. 529 applicants, 41% accepted. In 2006, 365 degrees awarded. *Entrance requirements:* For master's, GMAT. *Application deadline:* Applications are processed on a rolling basis. Application fee: $50. Electronic applications accepted. *Expenses: Contact institution.* *Financial support:* In 2006–07, 49 teaching assistantships (averaging $12,298 per year) were awarded; fellowships, research assistantships, career-related internships or fieldwork, Federal Work-Study, institutionally sponsored loans, and unspecified assistantships also available. Support available to part-time students. Financial award application deadline: 3/1; financial award applicants required to submit FAFSA. *Faculty research:* Investing in bankruptcy, planning for technology-based companies, organizational leadership, characteristics of small business managers. *Unit head:* Kate Klepper, Director of Graduate Programs, 617-373-5417, Fax: 617-373-8564, E-mail: gsba@cba.neu.edu. *Application contact:* Admissions Coordinator, 617-373-4951.

Business Administration and Management—General

Northern Arizona University, Graduate College, College of Business Administration, Flagstaff, AZ 86011. Offers general management (MBA); management information systems (MBA). *Accreditation:* AACSB. Part-time programs available. *Entrance requirements:* For master's, GMAT. Expenses: Contact institution. *Faculty research:* Data processing applications to business situations and problems, accounting fraud, effects of sales tactics, self-efficacy and performance.

Northern Illinois University, Graduate School, College of Business, MBA Program, De Kalb, IL 60115-2854. Offers MBA. *Accreditation:* AACSB. Part-time and evening/weekend programs available. *Faculty:* 53 full-time (17 women), 3 part-time/adjunct (0 women). *Students:* 100 full-time (26 women), 465 part-time (157 women); includes 113 minority (14 African Americans, 2 American Indian/Alaska Native, 77 Asian Americans or Pacific Islanders, 20 Hispanic Americans), 5 international. Average age 32. 245 applicants, 56% accepted, 99 enrolled. In 2006, 224 degrees awarded. *Degree requirements:* For master's, seminar, thesis optional. *Entrance requirements:* For master's, GMAT, minimum GPA of 2.75. Additional exam requirements/recommendations for international students: Required—TOEFL (minimum score 550 paper-based; 213 computer-based). *Application deadline:* For fall admission, 6/1 for domestic students, 5/1 for international students; for spring admission, 11/1 for domestic students, 10/1 for international students. Applications are processed on a rolling basis. Application fee: $30. Electronic applications accepted. *Financial support:* In 2006–07, 6 research assistantships with full tuition reimbursements, 2 teaching assistantships with full tuition reimbursements were awarded; fellowships with full tuition reimbursements, career-related internships or fieldwork, Federal Work-Study, scholarships/grants, tuition waivers (full), and unspecified assistantships also available. Support available to part-time students. Financial award applicants required to submit FAFSA. *Unit head:* Harold Wright, Director, 815-753-6277, E-mail: hwright@niu.edu.

Northern Kentucky University, Office of Graduate Programs, College of Business, Program in Business Administration, Highland Heights, KY 41099. Offers MBA, JD/MBA. *Accreditation:* AACSB. Part-time and evening/weekend programs available. *Faculty:* 15 full-time (8 women), 10 part-time/adjunct (1 woman). *Students:* 29 full-time (15 women), 193 part-time (78 women); includes 19 minority (12 African Americans, 7 Asian Americans or Pacific Islanders), 8 international. Average age 30. 100 applicants, 53% accepted, 40 enrolled. In 2006, 66 degrees awarded. *Entrance requirements:* For master's, GMAT, minimum undergraduate GPA of 2.5. Additional exam requirements/recommendations for international students: Required—TOEFL (minimum score 550 paper-based; 213 computer-based; 79 iBT), Michigan (must be taken at NKU). *Application deadline:* For fall admission, 8/1 priority date for domestic students, 6/1 priority date for international students; for spring admission, 12/1 priority date for domestic students, 10/1 priority date for international students. Applications are processed on a rolling basis. Application fee: $30. Electronic applications accepted. *Financial support:* In 2006–07, 85 students received support. Unspecified assistantships available. *Unit head:* Dr. Gregory Farfsing, Director of MBA Programs, 859-572-6357, Fax: 859-572-6177, E-mail: farfsingg@nku.edu. *Application contact:* Dr. Peg Griffin, Director of Graduate Programs, 859-572-1555, Fax: 859-572-6670, E-mail: gradprog@nku.edu.

Northern Kentucky University, Office of Graduate Programs, College of Business, Program in Executive Leadership and Organizational Change, Highland Heights, KY 41099. Offers MA. Part-time and evening/weekend programs available. *Faculty:* 5 full-time (2 women), 2 part-time/adjunct (both women). *Students:* 44 applicants, 66% accepted, 26 enrolled. *Entrance requirements:* For master's, minimum GPA of 2.5. Additional exam requirements/recommendations for international students: Required—TOEFL (minimum score 600 paper-based), Michigan (must be taken at NKU). *Application deadline:* For fall admission, 8/1 priority date for domestic students, 6/1 for international students; for spring admission, 12/1 priority date for domestic students, 10/1 for international students. Applications are processed on a rolling basis. Application fee: $30. Electronic applications accepted. *Financial support:* In 2006–07, 11 students received support. Unspecified assistantships available. *Faculty research:* Emotional and social intelligence, organizational changes, leadership, team work/ life issues. *Unit head:* Dr. Kenneth Rhee, Program Director, 859-572-6310, Fax: 859-572-5150, E-mail: rhee@nku.edu. *Application contact:* Dr. Peg Griffin, Director of Graduate Programs, 859-572-1555, Fax: 859-572-6670, E-mail: gradprog@nku.edu.

North Greenville University, T. Walter Brashier Graduate School, Tigerville, SC 29688-1892. Offers business administration (MBA); Christian ministry (MCM). Part-time and evening/weekend programs available. *Students:* 47 full-time (17 women), 35 part-time (10 women); includes 9 minority (7 African Americans, 2 Hispanic Americans), 6 international. Average age 32. 120 applicants, 79% accepted, 32 enrolled. In 2006, 1 degree awarded. *Median time to degree:* Master's–1.5 years full-time, 3 years part-time. *Degree requirements:* For master's, thesis or alternative, comprehensive exam (for some programs), registration. *Entrance requirements:* For master's, GMAT, GRE, minimum GPA of 2.25 overall, 2.5 in major. Additional exam requirements/recommendations for international students: Required—TOEFL (minimum score 550 paper-based). *Application deadline:* Applications are processed on a rolling basis. Application fee: $30. Electronic applications accepted. *Financial support:* In 2006–07, 35 students received support. Federal Work-Study, institutionally sponsored loans, scholarships/grants, and tuition waivers (partial) available. Support available to part-time students. *Faculty research:* Organizational behavior, church growth, homiletics. *Unit head:* Dr. J. Samuel Isgett, Vice President and Dean for Graduate Studies, 864-877-3052, Fax: 864-877-1653, E-mail: sisgett@ngu.edu. *Application contact:* Tawana Scott, Director of Graduate Enrollment, 864-877-1598, Fax: 864-877-1653, E-mail: tscott@ngu.edu.

North Park University, Center for Management Education, Chicago, IL 60625-4895. Offers MBA, MM, MBA/MS. Part-time and evening/weekend programs available. *Entrance requirements:* For master's, GMAT. Expenses: Contact institution.

Northwest Christian College, School of Business and Management, Eugene, OR 97401-3745. Offers MBA. Part-time and evening/weekend programs available. *Degree requirements:* For master's, thesis. *Entrance requirements:* For master's, GMAT, GRE, MAT, interview, minimum GPA of 3.0 (undergraduate). *Faculty research:* Ethics in business, spirituality in the workplace.

Northwestern Polytechnic University, School of Business and Information Technology, Fremont, CA 94539-7482. Offers MBA. Part-time and evening/weekend programs available. *Degree requirements:* For master's, thesis optional. *Entrance requirements:* For master's, GMAT, minimum GPA of 3.0. Additional exam requirements/recommendations for international students: Required—TOEFL (minimum score 550 paper-based; 213 computer-based). Expenses: Contact institution. *Faculty research:* Entrepreneurship, accounting, information technology.

Northwestern University, The Graduate School, Kellogg School of Management, MBA Programs, Evanston, IL 60208. Offers business administration (MBA); JD/MBA; MBA/MEM; MD/MBA. *Accreditation:* CAHME (one or more programs are accredited). Part-time and evening/weekend programs available. *Faculty:* 176 full-time, 101 part-time/adjunct. *Students:* 1,089 full-time (337 women), 1,279 part-time (371 women). Average age 28. 4,072 applicants, 24% accepted, 556 enrolled. In 2006, 1300 degrees awarded. *Entrance requirements:* For master's, GMAT, interview. Additional exam requirements/recommendations for international students: Required—TOEFL. *Application deadline:* For fall admission, 10/20 for domestic students; for winter admission, 1/5 for domestic students; for spring admission, 3/9 for domestic students. Application fee: $225. Electronic applications accepted. *Financial support:* Fellowships, career-related internships or fieldwork, institutionally sponsored loans, and scholarships/grants available. Support available to part-time students. Financial award application deadline: 5/15; financial award applicants required to submit FAFSA. *Application contact:* Beth Flye, Director of Admissions and Financial Aid, 847-491-3308, Fax: 847-491-4960, E-mail: mbaadmissions@kellogg.northwestern.edu.

Northwest Missouri State University, Graduate School, Melvin and Valorie Booth College of Business and Professional Studies, Program in Business Administration, Maryville, MO 64468-6001. Offers MBA. *Accreditation:* ACBSP. *Faculty:* 15 full-time (2 women). *Students:* 40 full-time (14 women), 11 part-time (9 women); includes 2 minority (1 Asian American or Pacific Islander, 1 Hispanic American), 13 international. 53 applicants, 70% accepted, 15 enrolled. In 2006, 31 degrees awarded. *Degree requirements:* For master's, comprehensive exam. *Entrance requirements:* For master's, GMAT, minimum GPA of 2.5. Additional exam requirements/recommendations for international students: Required—TOEFL (minimum score 550 paper-based; 213 computer-based). *Application deadline:* For fall admission, 7/1 for domestic and international students; for spring admission, 12/1 for domestic students, 11/15 for international students. Applications are processed on a rolling basis. Application fee: $0 ($50 for international students). Electronic applications accepted. *Financial support:* In 2006–07, 3 research assistantships with full tuition reimbursements (averaging $6,000 per year) were awarded; teaching assistantships, unspecified assistantships also available. Financial award application deadline: 3/1; financial award applicants required to submit FAFSA. *Unit head:* Dr. Mark Jelavich, Head, 660-562-1763. *Application contact:* Dr. Frances Shipley, Dean of Graduate School, 660-562-1145, Fax: 660-562-1096, E-mail: gradsch@nwmissouri.edu.

Northwest Nazarene University, Graduate Studies, Program in Business Administration, Nampa, ID 83686-5897. Offers MBA. *Accreditation:* ACBSP. Part-time and evening/weekend programs available. *Faculty:* 11 full-time (2 women), 10 part-time/adjunct (3 women). *Students:* 73 full-time (27 women), 12 part-time (3 women); includes 1 minority (Asian American or Pacific Islander), 2 international. Average age 35. In 2006, 22 degrees awarded. *Entrance requirements:* For master's, GMAT, minimum GPA of 3.0. *Application deadline:* Applications are processed on a rolling basis. Application fee: $40. Electronic applications accepted. *Expenses: Contact institution. Unit head:* Dr. William Russell, Director, 208-467-8415, Fax: 208-467-8440, E-mail: mba@nnu.edu.

Northwest University, School of Business, Kirkland, WA 98033. Offers MBA. Evening/weekend programs available. *Faculty:* 1 full-time (0 women), 6 part-time/adjunct (2 women). *Students:* 43 full-time (9 women); includes 3 minority (1 African American, 2 Asian Americans or Pacific Islanders). Average age 34. In 2006, 18 degrees awarded. *Median time to degree:* Master's–1.5 years full-time. *Degree requirements:* For master's, formalized graduate research. *Entrance requirements:* For master's, GMAT, 4 foundation courses. Additional exam requirements/recommendations for international students: Required—TOEFL (minimum score 550 paper-based). *Application deadline:* Applications are processed on a rolling basis. Electronic applications accepted. *Expenses:* Tuition: Full-time $12,938; part-time $691 per credit. Required fees: $85 per term. Tuition and fees vary according to course load and program. *Financial support:* Federal Work-Study, scholarships/grants, health care benefits, and tuition waivers (full) available. Financial award applicants required to submit FAFSA. *Unit head:* Dr. E. Arthur Self, Dean, School of Business, 425-889-5754, E-mail: woody.self@northwestu.edu. *Application contact:* Darrell Hughes, Director of Graduate and Professional Studies Enrollment, 425-889-7787, Fax: 425-803-3059, E-mail: gpse@northwestu.edu.

Northwood University, Richard DeVos Graduate School of Management, Midland, MI 48640-2398. Offers EMBA, MBA, MMBA. Part-time and evening/weekend programs available. *Degree requirements:* For master's, capstone project. *Entrance requirements:* For master's, GMAT, interview, letters of recommendation, resumé. Additional exam requirements/recommendations for international students: Required—TOEFL (minimum score 550 paper-based; 213 computer-based). Electronic applications accepted.

Norwich University, School of Graduate Studies, Program in Business Administration, Northfield, VT 05663. Offers MBA. *Accreditation:* ACBSP. Postbaccalaureate distance learning degree programs offered (no on-campus study). *Students:* 145 full-time (50 women). Average age 35. *Degree requirements:* For master's, comprehensive exam (for some programs). *Entrance requirements:* For master's, minimum undergraduate GPA of 2.75. Additional exam requirements/recommendations for international students: Required—TOEFL (minimum score 550 paper-based). *Application deadline:* For fall admission, 7/1 for domestic and international students; for winter admission, 11/1 for domestic and international students; for spring admission, 3/1 for domestic and international students. Application fee: $50. Electronic applications accepted. *Financial support:* Scholarships/grants available. Financial award application deadline: 6/1. *Unit head:* Dr. Bill Jolley, Program Director, 802-485-2730, Fax: 802-485-2533, E-mail: jolley@norwich.edu. *Application contact:* Janet Mara, Administrative Director, 802-485-2567, Fax: 802-485-2533, E-mail: jmara@norwich.edu.

Notre Dame College, Graduate Studies, South Euclid, OH 44121-4293. Offers accounting (Certificate); creative critical thinking (M Ed); financial services management (Certificate); information systems (Certificate); learning disabilities (M Ed); management (Certificate); paralegal (Certificate); pastoral ministry (Certificate); reading (M Ed); teacher education (Certificate). Part-time and evening/weekend programs available. *Degree requirements:* For master's, thesis. *Entrance requirements:* For master's, GRE General Test, MAT, minimum GPA of 2.75, valid teaching certificate. *Faculty research:* Cognitive psychology, teaching critical thinking in the classroom.

Notre Dame de Namur University, Division of Academic Affairs, School of Business and Management, Department of Business Administration, Belmont, CA 94002-1908. Offers MBA. Part-time and evening/weekend programs available. *Faculty:* 7 full-time (1 woman), 6 part-time/adjunct (0 women). *Students:* 21 full-time (11 women), 80 part-time (55 women); includes 37 minority (2 African Americans, 2 American Indian/Alaska Native, 15 Asian Americans or Pacific Islanders, 18 Hispanic Americans), 9 international. Average age 31. 53 applicants, 98% accepted, 40 enrolled. In 2006, 38 degrees awarded. *Entrance requirements:* For master's, GMAT (if GPA less than 3.5), minimum GPA of 2.5. Additional exam requirements/recommendations for international students: Required—TOEFL. *Application deadline:* For fall admission, 8/1 priority date for domestic students; for spring admission, 12/1 priority date for domestic students. Applications are processed on a rolling basis. Application fee: $50. Electronic applications accepted. *Expenses:* Tuition: Part-time $655 per credit. *Financial support:* Career-related internships or fieldwork available. Support available to part-time students. Financial award applicants required to submit FAFSA. *Unit head:* Dr. James Fogal, Director, 650-508-3721, E-mail: jfogal@ndnu.edu. *Application contact:* Helen Valine, Director of Graduate Admissions, 650-508-3534, Fax: 650-508-3426, E-mail: grad.admit@ndnu.edu.

Notre Dame de Namur University, Division of Academic Affairs, School of Business and Management, Department of Management, Belmont, CA 94002-1908. Offers MSM. Part-time and evening/weekend programs available. *Faculty:* 3 full-time (1 woman), 1 part-time/adjunct (0 women). *Students:* 4 full-time (2 women), 24 part-time (13 women); includes 11 minority (7 Asian Americans or Pacific Islanders, 4 Hispanic Americans), 1 international. Average age 34. 14 applicants, 100% accepted, 13 enrolled. In 2006, 7 degrees awarded. *Entrance requirements:* For master's, minimum GPA of 2.5. Additional exam requirements/recommendations for international students: Required—TOEFL. *Application deadline:* For fall admission, 8/1 priority date for domestic students; for spring admission, 12/1 priority date for domestic students. Applications are processed on a rolling basis. Application fee: $50. Electronic applications accepted. *Expenses:* Tuition: Part-time $655 per credit. *Financial support:* Applicants required to submit FAFSA. *Unit head:* Dr. James Fogal, Director, 650-508-3721, E-mail: jfogal@ndnu.edu. *Application contact:* Helen Valine, Director of Graduate Admissions, 650-508-3534, Fax: 650-508-3426, E-mail: grad.admit@ndnu.edu.

Nova Southeastern University, H. Wayne Huizenga School of Business and Entrepreneurship, Doctoral Program in Business Administration, Fort Lauderdale, FL 33314-7796. Offers DBA. Part-time and evening/weekend programs available. *Students:* 13 full-time (3 women), 225 part-time (74 women); includes 74 minority (44 African Americans, 1 American Indian/Alaska Native, 13 Asian Americans or Pacific Islanders, 16 Hispanic Americans), 10 international. Average age 45. In 2006, 67 degrees awarded. *Degree requirements:* For doctorate, thesis/dissertation. *Entrance requirements:* For doctorate, GMAT. *Application deadline:* Applications are processed on a rolling basis. Application fee: $50. *Financial support:* Available to part-time students. *Unit head:* Kristie Tetrault, Director, 954-262-5158, Fax: 954-262-3849, E-mail:

kristie@nova.edu. *Application contact:* Dennis Dannacher, Director, Recruitment and Admissions, 954-262-5033, Fax: 954-262-3822, E-mail: dannachr@huizenga.nova.edu.

See Close-Up on page 295.

Nova Southeastern University, H. Wayne Huizenga School of Business and Entrepreneurship, Master's Program in Business Administration, Fort Lauderdale, FL 33314-7796. Offers MBA, JD/MBA, MBA/MHSA. Evening/weekend programs available. *Students:* 278 full-time (153 women), 1,413 part-time (818 women); includes 955 minority (477 African Americans, 4 American Indian/Alaska Native, 71 Asian Americans or Pacific Islanders, 403 Hispanic Americans), 159 international. In 2006, 601 degrees awarded. *Degree requirements:* For master's, thesis optional. *Entrance requirements:* For master's, GMAT. *Application deadline:* For fall admission, 8/15 for domestic students; for spring admission, 2/10 for domestic students. Applications are processed on a rolling basis. Application fee: $50. *Financial support:* Career-related internships or fieldwork, Federal Work-Study, and scholarships/grants available. Support available to part-time students. *Unit head:* Steve Harvey, Assistant Dean, 954-262-5047, Fax: 954-262-3829, E-mail: harvey@nsu.nova.edu. *Application contact:* Karen Goldberg, Assistant Director, 954-262-5039, Fax: 954-262-3822, E-mail: karen@nova.edu.

See Close-Up on page 295.

Nova Southeastern University, H. Wayne Huizenga School of Business and Entrepreneurship, Program in Leadership, Fort Lauderdale, FL 33314-7796. Offers MS. Evening/weekend programs available. *Students:* 8 full-time (1 woman), 140 part-time (92 women); includes 88 minority (56 African Americans, 1 American Indian/Alaska Native, 6 Asian Americans or Pacific Islanders, 25 Hispanic Americans), 6 international. In 2006, 25 degrees awarded. *Unit head:* Steve Harvey, Assistant Dean, 954-262-5047, Fax: 954-262-3829, E-mail: harvey@nsu.nova.edu. *Application contact:* Karen Goldberg, Assistant Director, 954-262-5039, Fax: 954-262-3822, E-mail: karen@nova.edu.

See Close-Up on page 295.

Nyack College, Graduate and Professional Programs, School of Business, Nyack, NY 10960-3698. Offers accounting (MBA); business administration (MBA). Evening/weekend programs available. *Degree requirements:* For master's, thesis. *Entrance requirements:* For master's, GMAT (may be waived based on business experience), minimum GPA of 3.0. Expenses: Contact institution.

Oakland City University, School of Adult and Extended Learning, Oakland City, IN 47660-1099. Offers MS Mgt. Part-time and evening/weekend programs available. *Degree requirements:* For master's, thesis or alternative. *Entrance requirements:* For master's, GMAT, GRE, or MAT, appropriate bachelor's degree, computer literacy. Additional exam requirements/recommendations for international students: Required—TOEFL. *Faculty research:* Leadership and management styles, international business, new technologies.

Oakland University, Graduate Study and Lifelong Learning, School of Business Administration, Rochester, MI 48309-4401. Offers M Acc, MBA, MS, Certificate. *Accreditation:* AACSB. Part-time and evening/weekend programs available. *Faculty:* 30 full-time (5 women), 9 part-time/adjunct (2 women). *Students:* 84 full-time (31 women), 478 part-time (156 women); includes 83 minority (17 African Americans, 1 American Indian/Alaska Native, 53 Asian Americans or Pacific Islanders, 12 Hispanic Americans), 60 international. Average age 31. 147 applicants, 90% accepted, 85 enrolled. In 2006, 194 master's, 1 other advanced degree awarded. *Entrance requirements:* For master's, GMAT, minimum GPA of 3.0 for unconditional admission. Additional exam requirements/recommendations for international students: Required—TOEFL (minimum score 550 paper-based; 213 computer-based). *Application deadline:* For fall admission, 8/15 priority date for domestic students, 5/1 priority date for international students; for winter admission, 12/1 priority date for domestic students, 9/1 priority date for international students; for spring admission, 4/15 priority date for domestic students. Applications are processed on a rolling basis. Application fee: $35. Electronic applications accepted. *Expenses: Contact institution. Financial support:* Career-related internships or fieldwork, Federal Work-Study, institutionally sponsored loans, and tuition waivers (full) available. Financial award application deadline: 3/1; financial award applicants required to submit FAFSA. *Faculty research:* Rotor manufacturing induced anomaly database, Globalization Challenges project. *Unit head:* Dr. Jonathan Silberman, Dean, 248-370-3286, Fax: 248-370-4974. *Application contact:* Donna Free, Coordinator, 248-370-3281.

See Close-Up on page 297.

OGI School of Science & Engineering at Oregon Health & Science University, Graduate Studies, Department of Management in Science and Technology, Beaverton, OR 97006-8921. Offers health care management (Certificate); management in science and technology (MS, Certificate). Part-time and evening/weekend programs available. *Faculty:* 3 full-time (1 woman), 39 part-time/adjunct (15 women). *Students:* Average age 38. 8 applicants, 38% accepted, 2 enrolled. In 2006, 26 master's, 10 other advanced degrees awarded. *Degree requirements:* For master's, thesis, registration. *Entrance requirements:* For master's, 2 years of work experience. Additional exam requirements/recommendations for international students: Recommended—TOEFL (minimum score 625 paper-based; 263 computer-based). *Application deadline:* Applications are processed on a rolling basis. Application fee: $65. Electronic applications accepted. *Expenses:* Tuition, nonresident: full-time $22,760; part-time $625 per credit. Required fees: $65 per term. *Financial support:* Tuition waivers (partial) available. *Unit head:* Jim Huntzicker, Head, 503-748-3075. *Application contact:* Shelly Charles, Enrollment Manager, 503-748-1335, Fax: 503-748-1285, E-mail: charles@ohsu.edu.

Oglala Lakota College, Graduate Studies, Program in Lakota Leadership and Management, Kyle, SD 57752-0490. Offers MA. Part-time and evening/weekend programs available. *Degree requirements:* For master's, thesis. *Entrance requirements:* For master's, minimum GPA of 2.5. *Faculty research:* Curriculum, values, retention of administrators, behavior, graduate follow-up.

Oglethorpe University, Division of Business Administration, Atlanta, GA 30319-2797. Offers MBA. *Degree requirements:* For master's, thesis. *Entrance requirements:* For master's, GMAT, GRE General Test. Expenses: Contact institution.

Ohio Dominican University, Graduate Programs, Division of Business, Columbus, OH 43219-2099. Offers MBA. Program also offered in Dayton, OH. Part-time and evening/weekend programs available. *Students:* 249 full-time (110 women), 33 part-time (14 women); includes 80 minority (71 African Americans, 1 American Indian/Alaska Native, 5 Asian Americans or Pacific Islanders, 3 Hispanic Americans), 10 international. Average age 32. In 2006, 132 degrees awarded. *Degree requirements:* For master's, thesis or alternative, registration. *Entrance requirements:* For master's, minimum GPA of 3.0, 3 letters of recommendation. Additional exam requirements/recommendations for international students: Required—TOEFL (minimum score 550 paper-based; 213 computer-based). *Application deadline:* For fall admission, 8/15 priority date for domestic and international students; for spring admission, 1/13 priority date for domestic and international students. Applications are processed on a rolling basis. Application fee: $25. *Expenses:* Tuition: Part-time $450 per credit. Required fees: $10 per semester. *Financial support:* Applicants required to submit FAFSA. *Unit head:* Antonio Emanuel, Director of Graduate Business Programs, 614-251-4559, E-mail: emanuela@ohiodominican.edu. *Application contact:* Jill M. Westerfeld, Graduate Admissions Recruiter, 614-251-4725, Fax: 614-251-4634, E-mail: westerfj@ohiodominican.edu.

The Ohio State University, Graduate School, Max M. Fisher College of Business, Program in Business Administration, Columbus, OH 43210. Offers MA, MBA, PhD. *Accreditation:* AACSB. *Faculty:* 75. *Students:* 397 full-time (115 women), 225 part-time (66 women); includes 102 minority (15 African Americans, 72 Asian Americans or Pacific Islanders, 15 Hispanic Americans), 146 international. Average age 30. 608 applicants, 50% accepted, 136 enrolled. In 2006, 296 master's, 6 doctorates awarded. *Degree requirements:* For doctorate, thesis/dissertation. *Entrance requirements:* For master's and doctorate, GMAT. Additional exam requirements/recommendations for international students: Required—TOEFL (minimum score 600 paper-based; 250 computer-based). *Application deadline:* For fall admission, 8/15 priority date for domestic students, 7/1 priority date for international students; for winter admission, 12/1 priority date for domestic students, 11/1 priority date for international students; for spring admission, 3/1 priority date for domestic students, 2/1 priority date for international students. Applications are processed on a rolling basis. Application fee: $40 ($50 for international students). Electronic applications accepted. *Expenses:* Tuition, state resident: full-time $9,438. Tuition, nonresident: full-time $22,791. Tuition and fees vary according to course load, campus/location and program. *Financial support:* Fellowships, research assistantships, teaching assistantships, Federal Work-Study, institutionally sponsored loans, and unspecified assistantships available. Support available to part-time students. *Unit head:* Ingrid Werner, Head, 614-292-6040, Fax: 614-292-9006, E-mail: werner.47@osu.edu. *Application contact:* 614-292-9444, Fax: 614-292-3895, E-mail: domestic.grad@osu.edu.

The Ohio State University, Graduate School, Max M. Fisher College of Business, Program in Business Logistics and Engineering, Columbus, OH 43210. Offers MBLE. *Students:* 17 full-time (8 women), 3 part-time (1 woman); includes 1 minority (Hispanic American), 17 international. Average age 27. 32 applicants, 66% accepted, 14 enrolled. In 2006, 2 degrees awarded. *Entrance requirements:* For master's, GRE or GMAT. Additional exam requirements/recommendations for international students: Required—TOEFL. *Application deadline:* Applications are processed on a rolling basis. Electronic applications accepted. *Expenses:* Tuition, state resident: full-time $9,438. Tuition, nonresident: full-time $22,791. Tuition and fees vary according to course load, campus/location and program. *Unit head:* Walter Zinn, Graduate Studies Committee Chair, 416-292-0797, Fax: 416-292-9006, E-mail: zinn.13@osu.edu. *Application contact:* Graduate Admissions, 614-292-9444, Fax: 614-292-3895, E-mail: domestic.grad@osu.edu.

Ohio University, Graduate Studies, College of Business, Executive Business Administration Program, Athens, OH 45701-2979. Offers EMBA. *Accreditation:* AACSB. Part-time and evening/weekend programs available. *Faculty:* 44 full-time (15 women), 16 part-time/adjunct (7 women). *Students:* 56 full-time (11 women); includes 8 minority (4 African Americans, 4 Asian Americans or Pacific Islanders). Average age 34. 48 applicants, 79% accepted. In 2006, 28 degrees awarded. *Entrance requirements:* For master's, work experience in management (7–10 years). *Application deadline:* For fall admission, 6/1 priority date for domestic students. Applications are processed on a rolling basis. Application fee: $45. *Expenses: Contact institution. Faculty research:* Business, strategy, issues. *Application contact:* Virginia Finsterwald, Assistant Director, 740-593-2028, Fax: 740-593-0319, E-mail: finsterw@ohio.edu.

Ohio University, Graduate Studies, College of Business, Program in Business Administration, Athens, OH 45701-2979. Offers MBA. *Accreditation:* AACSB. Part-time and evening/weekend programs available. *Faculty:* 44 full-time (15 women), 16 part-time/adjunct (7 women). *Students:* 60 full-time (27 women), 8 part-time (2 women); includes 6 minority (5 African Americans, 1 Hispanic American), 23 international. In 2006, 182 degrees awarded. *Entrance requirements:* For master's, GMAT, minimum GPA of 3.0. Additional exam requirements/recommendations for international students: Required—TOEFL (minimum score 600 paper-based; 250 computer-based). *Application deadline:* For fall admission, 2/1 priority date for domestic students, 1/15 priority date for international students. Applications are processed on a rolling basis. Application fee: $45. Electronic applications accepted. *Expenses: Contact institution. Financial support:* In 2006–07, 20 research assistantships with full and partial tuition reimbursements (averaging $8,000 per year) were awarded; career-related internships or fieldwork and institutionally sponsored loans also available. Financial award application deadline: 2/1. *Application contact:* Jan Ross, Assistant Dean, 740-593-2007, Fax: 740-593-1388, E-mail: rossj@ohio.edu.

Oklahoma City University, Meinders School of Business, Program in Business Administration, Oklahoma City, OK 73106-1402. Offers finance (MBA); health administration (MBA); information technology (MBA); integrated marketing communications (MBA); international business (MBA); marketing (MBA); JD/MBA. *Accreditation:* ACBSP. Part-time and evening/weekend programs available. *Faculty:* 30 full-time (7 women), 24 part-time/adjunct (5 women). *Students:* 291 full-time (112 women), 186 part-time (68 women); includes 57 minority (27 African Americans, 9 American Indian/Alaska Native, 12 Asian Americans or Pacific Islanders, 9 Hispanic Americans), 218 international. Average age 27. In 2006, 341 degrees awarded. *Degree requirements:* For master's, comprehensive exam. *Entrance requirements:* For master's, minimum GPA of 2.5. Additional exam requirements/recommendations for international students: Required—TOEFL (minimum score 510 paper-based). *Application deadline:* For fall admission, 8/22 for domestic students; for spring admission, 1/15 for domestic students. Applications are processed on a rolling basis. Application fee: $30 ($70 for international students). *Financial support:* Fellowships with partial tuition reimbursements, career-related internships or fieldwork, Federal Work-Study, institutionally sponsored loans, and tuition waivers (partial) available. Support available to part-time students. Financial award application deadline: 8/1. *Faculty research:* Management information systems, international business strategies. *Unit head:* Dr. Mahmood Shandiz, Head, 405-208-5130, Fax: 405-208-5098, E-mail: mshandiz@okcu.edu. *Application contact:* Leslie McKenzie, Director, Graduate Admissions, 800-633-7242, Fax: 405-208-5356, E-mail: gadmissions@okcu.edu.

Oklahoma City University, Petree College of Arts and Sciences, Program in Liberal Arts, Oklahoma City, OK 73106-1402. Offers art (MLA); general studies (MLA); leadership/management (MLA); literature (MLA); mass communications (MLA); philosophy (MLA); writing (MLA). Part-time and evening/weekend programs available. *Faculty:* 18 full-time (7 women), 14 part-time/adjunct (4 women). *Students:* 33 full-time (21 women), 21 part-time (13 women); includes 12 minority (6 African Americans, 3 American Indian/Alaska Native, 2 Asian Americans or Pacific Islanders, 1 Hispanic American), 20 international. Average age 30. 20 applicants, 95% accepted. In 2006, 19 degrees awarded. *Degree requirements:* For master's, thesis optional. *Entrance requirements:* Additional exam requirements/recommendations for international students: Required—TOEFL. *Application deadline:* For fall admission, 8/22 for domestic students; for spring admission, 1/15 for domestic students. Applications are processed on a rolling basis. Application fee: $30 ($70 for international students). *Expenses:* Tuition: Full-time $12,780; part-time $710 per hour. Required fees: $89 per hour. *Financial support:* Fellowships with partial tuition reimbursements, career-related internships or fieldwork, Federal Work-Study, institutionally sponsored loans, and tuition waivers (partial) available. Support available to part-time students. Financial award application deadline: 8/1; financial award applicants required to submit FAFSA. *Unit head:* Dr. Regina Benuett, Director, 405-208-5178, Fax: 405-208-5451, E-mail: rebeunett@okcu.edu. *Application contact:* Leslie McKenzie, Director, Graduate Admissions, 800-633-7242, Fax: 405-208-5356, E-mail: gadmissions@okcu.edu.

Oklahoma State University, William S. Spears School of Business, Department of Management, MBA Program, Stillwater, OK 74078. Offers MBA. *Accreditation:* AACSB. *Faculty:* 2 full-time (1 woman). *Students:* 132 full-time (46 women), 232 part-time (95 women); includes 45 minority (12 African Americans, 19 American Indian/Alaska Native, 5 Asian Americans or Pacific Islanders, 9 Hispanic Americans), 29 international. Average age 29. 411 applicants, 39% accepted, 124 enrolled. In 2006, 105 master's awarded. *Entrance requirements:* For master's, GMAT. *Application deadline:* For fall admission, 3/1 priority date for international students; for spring admission, 8/1 priority date for international students. Application fee: $40 ($75 for international students). *Expenses:* Tuition, state resident: part-time $146 per credit hour. Tuition, nonresident: part-time $516 per credit hour. Required fees: $44 per credit hour. Tuition and fees vary according to program. *Financial support:* In 2006–07, 11 research assistantships (averaging $4,017 per year), 61 teaching assistantships (averaging $4,553 per year) were awarded; Federal Work-Study, scholarships/grants, health care benefits, and unspecified assistantships also available. Support available to part-time students. *Unit head:* Dr. David Carter, MBA Director, 405-744-2951.

Announcement: Oklahoma State University's MBA program is fully accredited by AACSB and is designed to meet the needs of students with business and nonbusiness undergraduate degrees. There are 3 program options. The 52-hour full-time program is designed for the

Business Administration and Management—General

Oklahoma State University *(continued)*
individual seeking a traditional cohort structured program that, in addition to business-course offerings, emphasizes student professional development through exposure to high-level executives, networking, and career-related activities. In addition, a 48-hour part-time program and a 36-hour professional program are both designed for students seeking more flexibility in course offerings and scheduling. The part-time and professional programs are offered at OSU-Tulsa and through distance learning.

Oklahoma State University, William S. Spears School of Business, Department of Management Science and Information Systems, Stillwater, OK 74078. Offers management information systems (PhD); management information systems/accounting information systems (MS); management science (PhD); operations management (PhD); telecommunications management (MS, PhD). *Faculty:* 17 full-time (3 women), 1 part-time/adjunct (0 women). *Students:* 64 full-time (15 women), 66 part-time (15 women); includes 6 minority (2 American Indian/Alaska Native, 3 Asian Americans or Pacific Islanders, 1 Hispanic American), 77 international. Average age 31. 144 applicants, 55% accepted, 35 enrolled. In 2006, 62 master's, 1 doctorate awarded. *Degree requirements:* For doctorate, thesis/dissertation. *Entrance requirements:* For master's and doctorate, GMAT. *Application deadline:* For fall admission, 3/1 priority date for international students; for spring admission, 8/1 priority date for international students. Applications are processed on a rolling basis. Application fee: $40 ($75 for international students). Electronic applications accepted. *Expenses:* Tuition, state resident: part-time $146 per credit hour. Tuition, nonresident: part-time $516 per credit hour. Required fees: $44 per credit hour. Tuition and fees vary according to program. *Financial support:* In 2006–07, 2 research assistantships (averaging $4,620 per year), 19 teaching assistantships (averaging $7,334 per year) were awarded; career-related internships or fieldwork, Federal Work-Study, scholarships/grants, health care benefits, and unspecified assistantships also available. Support available to part-time students. *Unit head:* Dr. Rick Wilson, Head, 405-744-5084.

Old Dominion University, College of Business and Public Administration, Doctoral Program in Business Administration, Norfolk, VA 23529. Offers finance (PhD); management (PhD); marketing (PhD). *Accreditation:* AACSB. *Faculty:* 20 full-time (2 women). *Students:* 21 full-time (7 women), 20 part-time (7 women); includes 4 minority (1 African American, 3 Asian Americans or Pacific Islanders), 28 international. Average age 35. 29 applicants, 59% accepted, 10 enrolled. In 2006, 5 degrees awarded. *Degree requirements:* For doctorate, thesis/dissertation, comprehensive exam. *Entrance requirements:* For doctorate, GMAT. Additional exam requirements/recommendations for international students: Required—TOEFL. *Application deadline:* For fall admission, 4/1 priority date for domestic and international students. Applications are processed on a rolling basis. Application fee: $40. Electronic applications accepted. *Expenses:* Tuition, area resident: Part-time $285 per credit hour. Tuition, nonresident: part-time $715 per credit hour. Required fees: $94 per semester. *Financial support:* In 2006–07, 11 research assistantships with full tuition reimbursements (averaging $11,500 per year), 9 teaching assistantships with full tuition reimbursements (averaging $11,500 per year) were awarded; fellowships, career-related internships or fieldwork and scholarships/grants also available. Financial award application deadline: 3/15; financial award applicants required to submit FAFSA. *Faculty research:* International business, buyer behavior, financial markets, strategy, operations research. *Unit head:* Dr. Sylvia C. Hudgins, Graduate Program Director, 757-683-3551, Fax: 757-683-4076, E-mail: shudgins@odu.edu.

See Close-Up on page 299.

Old Dominion University, College of Business and Public Administration, Master's Program in Business Administration, Norfolk, VA 23529. Offers MBA. *Accreditation:* AACSB. Part-time and evening/weekend programs available. *Faculty:* 66 full-time (15 women), 6 part-time/adjunct (1 woman). *Students:* 76 full-time (33 women), 196 part-time (77 women); includes 48 minority (28 African Americans, 16 Asian Americans or Pacific Islanders, 4 Hispanic Americans), 29 international. Average age 31. 235 applicants, 74% accepted, 134 enrolled. In 2006, 87 degrees awarded. *Degree requirements:* For master's, registration. *Entrance requirements:* For master's, GMAT, letters of reference, resumé, essay, transcripts, calculus. Additional exam requirements/recommendations for international students: Required—TOEFL (minimum score 550 paper-based; 213 computer-based; 80 iBT). *Application deadline:* For fall admission, 6/1 priority date for domestic students, 4/15 priority date for international students; for spring admission, 11/1 priority date for domestic students, 10/1 priority date for international students. Applications are processed on a rolling basis. Application fee: $40. Electronic applications accepted. *Expenses:* Tuition, area resident: Part-time $285 per credit hour. Tuition, nonresident: part-time $715 per credit hour. Required fees: $94 per semester. *Financial support:* In 2006–07, 30 students received support, including 27 research assistantships with partial tuition reimbursements available (averaging $6,300 per year), 3 teaching assistantships with partial tuition reimbursements available (averaging $5,800 per year); career-related internships or fieldwork, scholarships/grants, and unspecified assistantships also available. Support available to part-time students. Financial award application deadline: 2/15; financial award applicants required to submit FAFSA. *Faculty research:* International business, buyer behavior, financial markets, strategy, operations research. *Unit head:* Dr. Bruce Rubin, Graduate Program Director, 757-683-3585 Ext. 3585, Fax: 757-683-5750, E-mail: mbainfo@odu.edu. *Application contact:* Rhyanne Henley, Associate Director, 757-683-3585, Fax: 757-683-5750, E-mail: mbainfo@odu.edu.

See Close-Up on page 299.

Olivet Nazarene University, Graduate School, Department of Business, Bourbonnais, IL 60914-2271. Offers business administration (MBA). Evening/weekend programs available. *Degree requirements:* For master's, thesis or alternative. Expenses: Contact institution.

Oral Roberts University, School of Business, Tulsa, OK 74171-0001. Offers accounting (MBA); finance (MBA); international business (MBA); management (MBA); marketing (MBA); non-profit management (M Man, MBA); organizational dynamics (M Man); sales marketing (M Man). *Accreditation:* ACBSP. Part-time programs available. Postbaccalaureate distance learning degree programs offered (minimal on-campus study). *Faculty:* 9 full-time (2 women), 4 part-time/adjunct (2 women). *Students:* 33 full-time (18 women), 67 part-time (28 women); includes 28 minority (17 African Americans, 3 American Indian/Alaska Native, 6 Asian Americans or Pacific Islanders, 2 Hispanic Americans), 15 international. Average age 29. 69 applicants, 84% accepted, 33 enrolled. In 2006, 21 degrees awarded. *Degree requirements:* For master's, thesis optional. *Entrance requirements:* For master's, minimum GPA of 3.0. Additional exam requirements/recommendations for international students: Required—TOEFL (minimum score 550 paper-based; 213 computer-based). *Application deadline:* For fall admission, 7/1 priority date for domestic students, 5/1 priority date for international students; for spring admission, 12/1 priority date for domestic students, 10/1 priority date for international students. Applications are processed on a rolling basis. Application fee: $35. *Expenses:* Contact institution. *Financial support:* In 2006–07, 9 research assistantships (averaging $3,600 per year) were awarded; scholarships/grants and unspecified assistantships also available. Financial award application deadline: 6/1; financial award applicants required to submit FAFSA. *Faculty research:* Non-profit, international business and marketing. *Unit head:* Dr. Mark Lewandowski, Dean, 918-495-7040, Fax: 918-495-7876, E-mail: mlewandowski@oru.edu. *Application contact:* 918-495-6989, Fax: 918-495-7965, E-mail: alsc@oru.edu.

Oregon State University, Graduate School, College of Business, Corvallis, OR 97331. Offers MAIS, MBA, Certificate. *Accreditation:* AACSB. Part-time programs available. *Faculty:* 37 full-time (7 women), 12 part-time/adjunct (2 women). *Students:* 53 full-time (21 women), 22 part-time (13 women); includes 5 minority (1 American Indian/Alaska Native, 2 Asian Americans or Pacific Islanders, 2 Hispanic Americans), 24 international. Average age 30. In 2006, 39 degrees awarded. *Degree requirements:* For master's, portfolio. *Entrance requirements:* For master's, GMAT, minimum GPA of 3.0 in last 90 hours. Additional exam requirements/recommendations for international students: Required—TOEFL. *Application deadline:* For fall admission, 3/15 for domestic students. Applications are processed on a rolling basis. Applica-

tion fee: $50. *Financial support:* Fellowships, teaching assistantships, career-related internships or fieldwork, Federal Work-Study, and institutionally sponsored loans available. Financial award application deadline: 2/1. *Faculty research:* Financial and account services, market analysis and planning, innovation, family business, tourism. *Unit head:* Dr. Ilene K. Kleinsorge, Dean, 541-737-6024, Fax: 541-737-3033. *Application contact:* Clara Horne, Head Adviser, 541-737-3716, Fax: 541-737-4890, E-mail: horne@bus.orst.edu.

Ottawa University, Graduate Studies-Arizona, Programs in Business, Ottawa, KS 66067-3399. Offers business administration (MBA); finance (MBA); human resources (MA, MBA); leadership (MBA); marketing (MBA). Programs offered in Mesa, Phoenix, Tempe and West Valley, AZ. Part-time and evening/weekend programs available. Postbaccalaureate distance learning degree programs offered. *Faculty:* 3 full-time (1 woman), 11 part-time/adjunct (3 women). *Students:* 5 full-time (1 woman), 125 part-time (73 women); includes 21 minority (7 African Americans, 1 American Indian/Alaska Native, 2 Asian Americans or Pacific Islanders, 11 Hispanic Americans), 5 international. Average age 39. In 2006, 42 degrees awarded. *Degree requirements:* For master's, thesis or alternative, registration. *Entrance requirements:* For master's, minimum undergraduate GPA of 3.0. Additional exam requirements/recommendations for international students: Required—TOEFL (minimum score 550 paper-based; 213 computer-based). *Application deadline:* For fall admission, 7/1 priority date for domestic students; for winter admission, 11/1 priority date for domestic students; for spring admission, 2/1 priority date for domestic students. Applications are processed on a rolling basis. Application fee: $50. Electronic applications accepted. *Unit head:* Dr. Tony Muscia, Director of Business Graduate Studies, 602-371-1188, E-mail: tony.muscia@ottawa.edu. *Application contact:* Sharon Lind, Advisement Assistant, 602-371-1188, Fax: 602-371-0035, E-mail: sharon.lind@ottawa.edu.

Ottawa University, Graduate Studies-International, Ottawa, KS 66067-3399. Offers business administration (MBA). Postbaccalaureate distance learning degree programs offered (minimal on-campus study). *Faculty:* 1 full-time (0 women), 2 part-time/adjunct (1 woman). *Students:* 3 full-time (2 women), 22 part-time (11 women), (all international). Average age 35. In 2006, 21 degrees awarded. *Degree requirements:* For master's, thesis or alternative, registration. *Entrance requirements:* For master's, minimum undergraduate GPA of 3.0. Additional exam requirements/recommendations for international students: Required—TOEFL (minimum score 550 paper-based; 213 computer-based). *Application deadline:* Applications are processed on a rolling basis. Application fee: $50. Electronic applications accepted. *Expenses: Contact institution.* *Unit head:* Buddy Jo Tanck, Program Coordinator, 785-242-5200, E-mail: tanckb@ottawa.edu. *Application contact:* Misti Thuro, Admissions Coordinator, 785-242-5200, Fax: 785-229-1007, E-mail: misti.thuro@ottawa.edu.

Ottawa University, Graduate Studies-Kansas City, Overland Park, KS 66211. Offers business administration (MBA); human resources (MA). Part-time and evening/weekend programs available. Postbaccalaureate distance learning degree programs offered (minimal on-campus study). *Faculty:* 4 full-time (1 woman), 8 part-time/adjunct (4 women). *Students:* 4 full-time (all women), 63 part-time (42 women); includes 10 minority (7 African Americans, 2 Asian Americans or Pacific Islanders, 1 Hispanic American). Average age 37. In 2006, 30 degrees awarded. *Degree requirements:* For master's, thesis or alternative, registration. *Entrance requirements:* For master's, resumé, 3 letters of recommendation. Additional exam requirements/recommendations for international students: Required—TOEFL (minimum score 550 paper-based; 213 computer-based). *Application deadline:* Applications are processed on a rolling basis. Application fee: $65. Electronic applications accepted. *Expenses: Contact institution.* *Unit head:* Dr. W. A. Breytspraak, Director of Graduate Studies, 913-451-1431, Fax: 913-451-0806, E-mail: breytspraak@ottawa.edu. *Application contact:* Alisa Jones, Enrollment Coordinator, 913-451-1431, Fax: 913-451-0806, E-mail: alisa.jones@ottawa.edu.

Ottawa University, Graduate Studies-Wisconsin, Brookfield, WI 53005. Offers business administration (MBA). Part-time and evening/weekend programs available. Postbaccalaureate distance learning degree programs offered. *Faculty:* 1 (woman) full-time, 5 part-time/adjunct (4 women). *Students:* Average age 39. In 2006, 2 degrees awarded. *Degree requirements:* For master's, thesis or alternative, registration. *Entrance requirements:* For master's, resumé, 3 letters of recommendation. Additional exam requirements/recommendations for international students: Required—TOEFL (minimum score 550 paper-based; 213 computer-based). *Application deadline:* Applications are processed on a rolling basis. Application fee: $50. Electronic applications accepted. *Unit head:* Elaine George, Instructor in Business Administration, 262-879-0200, Fax: 262-879-0096, E-mail: elaine.george@ottawa.edu. *Application contact:* Trisha Frederick, Enrollment Manager, 262-879-0200, Fax: 262-879-0096, E-mail: trisha.frederick@ottawa.edu.

Otterbein College, Department of Business, Accounting and Economics, Westerville, OH 43081. Offers MBA. Part-time and evening/weekend programs available. *Students:* 53 full-time, 50 part-time; includes 13 minority (7 African Americans, 5 Asian Americans or Pacific Islanders, 1 Hispanic American). Average age 33. 23 applicants, 83% accepted, 14 enrolled. In 2006, 55 degrees awarded. *Degree requirements:* For master's, consulting project team. *Entrance requirements:* For master's, GMAT, all official transcripts, 2 reference forms, personal statement, resumé. Additional exam requirements/recommendations for international students: Required—TOEFL (minimum score 550 paper-based; 213 computer-based; 79 iBT). *Application deadline:* For fall admission, 8/10 priority date for domestic students, 7/10 priority date for international students; for winter admission, 12/7 priority date for domestic students, 11/7 priority date for international students; for spring admission, 2/28 priority date for domestic students, 1/31 priority date for international students. Applications are processed on a rolling basis. Application fee: $35. *Expenses: Contact institution.* Tuition and fees vary according to program. *Financial support:* Available to part-time students. Applicants required to submit FAFSA. *Faculty research:* Organizational design, dispute resolution international trade, developing economies, marketing consumer goods, human resources development. *Unit head:* Dr. Don Eskew, Chair, 614-823-1212, Fax: 614-823-1014, E-mail: deskew@otterbein.edu. *Application contact:* Deb Williams, Administrative Assistant, Office of Graduate Programs, 614-823-3210, Fax: 614-823-3208, E-mail: grad@otterbein.edu.

Our Lady of the Lake University of San Antonio, School of Business, San Antonio, TX 78207-4689. Offers general (MBA), including finance, international business, management; health care management (MBA). *Accreditation:* ACBSP. Part-time and evening/weekend programs available. *Degree requirements:* For master's, thesis optional. *Entrance requirements:* For master's, GMAT, GRE General Test, or MAT. Electronic applications accepted. *Faculty research:* International marketing, employee benefits, decision process.

Pace University, Lubin School of Business, New York, NY 10038. Offers MBA, MS, DPS, APC, JD/MBA. *Accreditation:* AACSB. Part-time and evening/weekend programs available. Postbaccalaureate distance learning degree programs offered (minimal on-campus study). *Faculty:* 128 full-time, 62 part-time/adjunct. *Students:* 159 full-time (84 women), 844 part-time (349 women); includes 236 minority (46 African Americans, 134 Asian Americans or Pacific Islanders, 56 Hispanic Americans), 250 international. Average age 30. 995 applicants, 58% accepted, 233 enrolled. In 2006, 483 master's, 7 doctorates, 4 other advanced degrees awarded. *Degree requirements:* For doctorate, thesis/dissertation, oral and written exams. *Entrance requirements:* For master's, GMAT; for doctorate, GMAT, interview. *Application deadline:* For fall admission, 7/31 priority date for domestic students; for spring admission, 11/30 for domestic students. Applications are processed on a rolling basis. Application fee: $65. Electronic applications accepted. *Expenses: Contact institution. Financial support:* Research assistantships, career-related internships or fieldwork, Federal Work-Study, and tuition waivers (full and partial) available. Support available to part-time students. Financial award applicants required to submit FAFSA. *Unit head:* Dr. Arthur Centonze, Dean, 212-346-1963. *Application contact:* Joanna Broda, Director of Admissions, 212-346-1652, Fax: 212-346-1585, E-mail: gradnyc@pace.edu.

See Close-Up on page 301.

Pacific Lutheran University, Division of Graduate Studies, School of Business, Tacoma, WA 98447. Offers business administration (MBA), including technology and innovation management. *Accreditation:* AACSB. Part-time and evening/weekend programs available. *Faculty:* 8 full-time (4 women), 2 part-time/adjunct (0 women). *Students:* 49 full-time (15 women), 24 part-time (11 women); includes 9 minority (3 African Americans, 4 Asian Americans or Pacific Islanders, 2 Hispanic Americans), 15 international. Average age 31. 46 applicants, 100% accepted, 30 enrolled. In 2006, 27 degrees awarded. *Degree requirements:* For master's, registration. *Entrance requirements:* For master's, GMAT. Additional exam requirements/recommendations for international students: Required—TOEFL (minimum score 550 paper-based; 213 computer-based). *Application deadline:* Applications are processed on a rolling basis. Application fee: $40. *Expenses:* Tuition: Full-time $17,544. Part-time tuition and fees vary according to program. *Financial support:* In 2006–07, 10 students received support, including 7 fellowships (averaging $20,066 per year); career-related internships or fieldwork, Federal Work-Study, scholarships/grants, and unspecified assistantships also available. Financial award application deadline: 3/1. *Unit head:* Dr. Andrew Turner, Dean, 253-535-7445, Fax: 253-535-8723. *Application contact:* Abby Wigstrom, Director, MBA Program, Fax: 253-535-8723, E-mail: wigstraj@plu.edu.

Pacific States University, College of Business, Los Angeles, CA 90006. Offers accounting (MBA); business administration (DBA); finance (MBA); international business (MBA); management of information technology (MBA); real estate management (MBA). Part-time and evening/weekend programs available. Postbaccalaureate distance learning degree programs offered (no on-campus study). *Faculty:* 3 full-time (0 women), 11 part-time/adjunct (0 women). *Students:* 106 full-time (47 women); includes 10 minority (all Asian Americans or Pacific Islanders), 96 international. Average age 32. 36 applicants, 81% accepted, 26 enrolled. In 2006, 68 degrees awarded. *Entrance requirements:* For master's, minimum undergraduate GPA of 2.5 during last 90 hours of course work. Additional exam requirements/recommendations for international students: Required—TOEFL (minimum score 133 computer-based). *Application deadline:* For fall admission, 8/15 priority date for domestic students; for winter admission, 10/15 priority date for domestic students; for spring admission, 1/15 priority date for domestic students. Applications are processed on a rolling basis. Application fee: $100. *Expenses:* Tuition: Full-time $6,360. Required fees: $1,080. Full-time tuition and fees vary according to course load and degree level. *Financial support:* Fellowships, research assistantships, teaching assistantships, scholarships/grants available. Financial award applicants required to submit FAFSA. *Unit head:* Dr. Kamol Somvichian, Director, 888-200-0383, Fax: 323-731-2383, E-mail: admission@psuca.edu. *Application contact:* Marina Miller, Assistant Director of Admissions, 323-731-2383 Ext. 11, Fax: 323-731-7276, E-mail: admissions@psuca.edu.

Palm Beach Atlantic University, Rinker School of Business, West Palm Beach, FL 33416-4708. Offers MBA. Part-time and evening/weekend programs available. *Faculty:* 6 full-time (2 women), 5 part-time/adjunct (0 women). *Students:* 27 full-time (16 women), 86 part-time (42 women); includes 31 minority (15 African Americans, 1 American Indian/Alaska Native, 5 Asian Americans or Pacific Islanders, 10 Hispanic Americans), 11 international. Average age 33. 36 applicants, 94% accepted, 31 enrolled. In 2006, 46 degrees awarded. *Entrance requirements:* For master's, GMAT, minimum GPA of 3.0. Additional exam requirements/recommendations for international students: Required—TOEFL (minimum score 550 paper-based; 213 computer-based). *Application deadline:* For fall admission, 7/15 priority date for domestic students; for spring admission, 11/15 priority date for domestic students. Applications are processed on a rolling basis. Application fee: $35. Electronic applications accepted. *Expenses:* Tuition: Full-time $10,665; part-time $395 per credit. Required fees: $90 per semester. *Financial support:* Career-related internships or fieldwork and unspecified assistantships available. Support available to part-time students. Financial award applicants required to submit FAFSA. *Unit head:* Dr. Edgar Langlois, Interim Dean, 561-803-2462, E-mail: edgar_langlois@pba.edu. *Application contact:* Laura A. Leinweber, Director of Graduate and Evening Admissions, 888-468-6722, Fax: 561-803-2115, E-mail: grad@pba.edu.

Park University, College of Graduate and Professional Studies, Kansas City, MO 54105. Offers adult education (M Ed); at-risk students (M Ed); disaster and emergency management (MPA); educational administration (M Ed); entrepreneurship (MBA); general business (MBA); general education (M Ed); government/business relations (MPA); healthcare/services management (MBA, MPA); international business (MBA); K-12 certification (MAT); management information systems (MBA); management of information systems (MPA); middle school certification (MAT); multi-cultural education (M Ed); nonprofit management (MPA); public management (MPA); school law (M Ed); secondary school certification (MAT); special education (M Ed). Part-time and evening/weekend programs available. Postbaccalaureate distance learning degree programs offered (no on-campus study). *Degree requirements:* For master's, thesis (for some programs), comprehensive exam, registration. *Entrance requirements:* For master's, GRE, GMAT, teacher certification (M Ed). Additional exam requirements/recommendations for international students: Required—TOEFL (minimum score 550 paper-based). Electronic applications accepted. *Faculty research:* Literacy, leadership, brain based research, multicultural education, diversity.

Penn State Great Valley, Graduate Studies, Management Division, Malvern, PA 19355-1488. Offers biotechnology and health industry management (MBA); business administration (MBA); finance (M Fin); leadership development (MLD); new venture and entrepreneurial studies (MBA);).

Penn State Harrisburg, Graduate School, School of Business Administration, Program in Business Administration, Middletown, PA 17057-4898. Offers MBA, MBA/JD, MBA/PhD. *Accreditation:* AACSB. *Entrance requirements:* For master's, GMAT. *Expenses:* Tuition, state resident: full-time $13,224; part-time $551 per credit. Tuition, nonresident: full-time $18,652; part-time $777 per credit. Required fees: $84 per semester.

See Close-Up on page 303.

Pepperdine University, The Graziadio School of Business and Management, Los Angeles, CA 90045. Offers business (MBA), including business administration; executive business administration (MBAA); organizational development (MSOD); technology management (MSTM). *Accreditation:* AACSB. Part-time and evening/weekend programs available. *Faculty:* 83 full-time (15 women), 47 part-time/adjunct (11 women). *Students:* 606 full-time (229 women), 766 part-time (301 women); includes 433 minority (43 African Americans, 6 American Indian/Alaska Native, 250 Asian Americans or Pacific Islanders, 134 Hispanic Americans), 54 international. 764 applicants, 71% accepted, 415 enrolled. In 2006, 681 degrees awarded. *Entrance requirements:* For master's, GMAT or MAT. Additional exam requirements/recommendations for international students: Required—TOEFL (minimum score 550 paper-based). *Application deadline:* For fall admission, 6/28 for domestic students. Applications are processed on a rolling basis. Application fee: $45. *Expenses: Contact institution. Financial support:* Career-related internships or fieldwork, institutionally sponsored loans, scholarships/grants, and unspecified assistantships available. Support available to part-time students. Financial award applicants required to submit FAFSA. *Unit head:* Dr. Linda A. Livingstone, Dean, 310-568-5689, Fax: 310-568-5766, E-mail: linda.livingstone@pepperdine.edu. *Application contact:* Darrell Eriksen, Director of Admission and Student Accounts, 310-568-5525, E-mail: darrell.eriksen@pepperdine.edu.

Pepperdine University, Malibu Graduate Business Programs, Malibu, CA 90263. Offers business administration (MBA); international business (MIB); JD/MBA. *Accreditation:* AACSB. *Faculty:* 10 full-time (4 women). *Students:* 241 full-time (111 women), 3 part-time; includes 34 minority (1 African American, 1 American Indian/Alaska Native, 24 Asian Americans or Pacific Islanders, 8 Hispanic Americans), 94 international. 627 applicants, 62% accepted, 164 enrolled. In 2006, 86 degrees awarded. *Degree requirements:* For master's, foreign language (MIB). *Entrance requirements:* For master's, GMAT, MAT, 2 letters of recommendation, resumé. Additional exam requirements/recommendations for international students: Required—TOEFL (minimum score 550 paper-based; 220 computer-based). *Application deadline:* For fall admission, 5/1 for domestic and international students. Applications are processed on a rolling basis. Application fee: $45. Electronic applications accepted. *Expenses: Contact institution.* Full-time tuition and fees vary according to program. *Financial support:* Career-related internships or fieldwork, institutionally sponsored loans, scholarships/grants, and unspecified assistantships available. Financial award application deadline: 6/1; financial award applicants required to submit FAFSA. *Unit head:* Dr. Mark Mallinger, Director, Full-Time Programs, 310-506-6962, Fax: 310-506-4126, E-mail: mark.mallinger@pepperdine.edu. *Application contact:* Paul E. Pinckley, Executive Director, Recruitment and Student Recruitment, 310-506-4858, Fax: 310-506-4126, E-mail: paul.pinckley@pepperdine.edu.

See Close-Up on page 305.

Pfeiffer University, Program in Business Administration, Misenheimer, NC 28109-0960. Offers business administration (MBA); organizational management (MS); MBA/MHA; MBA/MS. Part-time and evening/weekend programs available. Postbaccalaureate distance learning degree programs offered (minimal on-campus study). *Faculty:* 13 full-time (3 women), 15 part-time/adjunct (2 women). *Students:* 108 full-time (46 women), 395 part-time (248 women); includes 202 minority (182 African Americans, 9 Asian Americans or Pacific Islanders, 11 Hispanic Americans), 43 international. Average age 36. In 2006, 223 degrees awarded. *Entrance requirements:* For master's, GMAT, minimum GPA of 3.0. *Application deadline:* For fall admission, 8/21 for domestic students. Applications are processed on a rolling basis. Application fee: $75. *Expenses:* Tuition: Part-time $380 per semester hour. Tuition and fees vary according to campus/location. *Financial support:* Unspecified assistantships available. Support available to part-time students. Financial award applicants required to submit FAFSA. *Unit head:* Dr. Robert K. Spear, Director of the MBA Program, 704-521-9116 Ext. 244, Fax: 704-521-8617, E-mail: rks@pfeiffer.edu.

Philadelphia University, School of Business Administration, Program in Business Administration, Philadelphia, PA 19144-5497. Offers business administration (MBA); finance (MBA); health care management (MBA); international business (MBA); marketing (MBA); MBA/MS. Part-time and evening/weekend programs available. Postbaccalaureate distance learning degree programs offered (no on-campus study). *Faculty:* 10 full-time (2 women), 8 part-time/adjunct (0 women). *Students:* 43 full-time (24 women), 87 part-time (45 women); includes 3 Asian Americans or Pacific Islanders. 154 applicants, 56% accepted, 37 enrolled. In 2006, 85 degrees awarded. *Entrance requirements:* For master's, GMAT. Additional exam requirements/recommendations for international students: Required—TOEFL (minimum score 550 paper-based; 213 computer-based; 79 iBT). *Application deadline:* Applications are processed on a rolling basis. Application fee: $35. *Financial support:* In 2006–07, research assistantships with full tuition reimbursements (averaging $2,500 per year); career-related internships or fieldwork, Federal Work-Study, scholarships/grants, and unspecified assistantships also available. Support available to part-time students. Financial award applicants required to submit FAFSA. *Unit head:* MarySheila McDonald, Assistant Dean for Graduate Programs, 215-951-2950, Fax: 215-951-2653, E-mail: mcdonaldm@philau.edu. *Application contact:* Jack A. Klett, Director of Graduate Admissions, 215-951-2943, Fax: 215-951-2907, E-mail: gradadm@philau.edu.

Phillips Theological Seminary, Programs in Theology, Tulsa, OK 74116. Offers administration of church agencies (M Div); campus ministry (M Div); church-related social work (M Div); college and seminary teaching (M Div); global mission work (M Div); institutional chaplaincy (M Div); ministerial vocations in Christian education (M Div); ministry (D Min), including parish ministry, pastoral counseling, practices of ministry; ministry and culture (MAMC), including Christian education, congregational leadership, history and practice of Christian spirituality, theology, ethics, and culture; ministry of music (M Div); pastoral care and counseling (M Div); pastoral ministry (M Div); theological studies (MTS). *Accreditation:* ATS. Part-time programs available. Postbaccalaureate distance learning degree programs offered (minimal on-campus study). *Degree requirements:* For master's, thesis (for some programs); for doctorate, thesis/dissertation. *Entrance requirements:* For master's, minimum GPA of 2.5; for doctorate, M Div, minimum GPA of 3.0. *Faculty research:* Biblical studies, historical studies, theology and culture, practical theology, theology and film.

Piedmont College, School of Business, Demorest, GA 30535-0010. Offers MBA. *Faculty:* 3 full-time (1 woman), 10 part-time/adjunct (4 women). *Students:* 77 full-time (32 women), 36 part-time (15 women); includes 17 minority (all African Americans) 37 applicants, 89% accepted, 27 enrolled. In 2006, 29 degrees awarded. *Entrance requirements:* For master's, GMAT, GRE or MAT, minimum GPA of 2.5. Additional exam requirements/recommendations for international students: Required—TOEFL (minimum score 550 paper-based; 213 computer-based). *Application deadline:* For fall admission, 7/15 for domestic students; for spring admission, 12/1 for domestic students. Application fee: $30. *Expenses:* Tuition: Part-time $310 per credit hour. *Financial support:* Unspecified assistantships available. Financial award applicants required to submit FAFSA. *Unit head:* Dr. William Piper, Dean, 706-778-3000 Ext. 1349, Fax: 706-778-0701, E-mail: bpiper@piedmont.edu. *Application contact:* Carol E. Kokesh, Director of Graduate Studies, 706-778-8500 Ext. 1181, Fax: 706-776-6635, E-mail: ckokesh@piedmont.edu.

Pittsburg State University, Graduate School, Kelce College of Business, Department of Management and Marketing, Pittsburg, KS 66762. Offers general administration (MBA). *Accreditation:* AACSB. *Students:* 68. *Degree requirements:* For master's, thesis or alternative. *Entrance requirements:* For master's, GMAT. Application fee: $35 ($60 for international students). *Expenses:* Tuition, state resident: full-time $2,144; part-time $181 per credit hour. Tuition, nonresident: full-time $5,273; part-time $442 per credit hour. Tuition and fees vary according to course load and campus/location. *Financial support:* In 2006–07, teaching assistantships (averaging $5,000 per year); research assistantships, career-related internships or fieldwork, Federal Work-Study, and unspecified assistantships also available. Financial award application deadline: 3/1. *Faculty research:* Consumer behavior, productions management, forecasting interest rate swaps, strategy management. *Unit head:* Dr. Richard Dearth, Chairperson, 620-235-4588. *Application contact:* Marvene Darraugh, Administrative Officer, 620-235-4220, Fax: 620-235-4219, E-mail: mdarraug@pittstate.edu.

Plymouth State University, College of Graduate Studies, Department of Graduate Studies in Business, Plymouth, NH 03264-1595. Offers MBA. *Accreditation:* ACBSP. Part-time and evening/weekend programs available. *Faculty:* 21 full-time (4 women), 4 part-time/adjunct (1 woman). *Students:* 8 full-time (3 women), 211 part-time (84 women); includes 14 minority (4 African Americans, 1 American Indian/Alaska Native, 3 Asian Americans or Pacific Islanders, 6 Hispanic Americans). Average age 36. 63 applicants, 100% accepted, 63 enrolled. In 2006, 44 degrees awarded. *Degree requirements:* For master's, registration. *Entrance requirements:* For master's, minimum GPA of 2.5. Additional exam requirements/recommendations for international students: Required—TOEFL (minimum score 550 paper-based). *Application deadline:* For fall admission, 5/15 for international students; for winter admission, 5/15 for international students; for spring admission, 10/15 for international students. Applications are processed on a rolling basis. Application fee: $75. *Expenses: Contact institution.* Tuition and fees vary according to course level. *Financial support:* In 2006–07, 5 teaching assistantships with full tuition reimbursements (averaging $4,000 per year) were awarded; career-related internships or fieldwork, institutionally sponsored loans, scholarships/grants, and unspecified assistantships also available. Support available to part-time students. Financial award application deadline: 4/15; financial award applicants required to submit FAFSA. *Unit head:* Craig Zamzow, MBA Coordinator, 603-535-3020, Fax: 603-535-2572, E-mail: czamzow@plymouth.edu. *Application contact:* Cheryl B. Baker, Director of Recruitment and Outreach, 603-535-2737, Fax: 603-535-2572, E-mail: cbaker@plymouth.edu.

Point Loma Nazarene University, Graduate Studies, Program in Business Administration, San Diego, CA 92106-2899. Offers MBA. *Accreditation:* ACBSP. Part-time and evening/weekend programs available. Postbaccalaureate distance learning degree programs offered (minimal on-campus study). *Faculty:* 14 full-time (3 women). *Students:* 22 full-time (5 women), 5 part-time (3 women); includes 11 minority (1 African American, 6 Asian Americans or Pacific Islanders, 4 Hispanic Americans), 1 international. Average age 32. *Entrance requirements:* For

Business Administration and Management—General

Point Loma Nazarene University (continued)
master's, GMAT, letters of recommendation. *Application deadline:* For fall admission, 5/1 for domestic students. Application fee: $30. *Unit head:* Dr. Bruce Schooling, Dean.

Point Park University, School of Business, Pittsburgh, PA 15222-1984. Offers business (MBA); organizational leadership (MA). Part-time and evening/weekend programs available. *Faculty:* 13 full-time, 21 part-time/adjunct. *Students:* 133 full-time (72 women), 138 part-time (85 women); includes 60 minority (55 African Americans, 1 American Indian/Alaska Native, 2 Asian Americans or Pacific Islanders, 2 Hispanic Americans), 24 international. Average age 31. 269 applicants, 74% accepted, 140 enrolled. In 2006, 132 degrees awarded. *Entrance requirements:* For master's, minimum QPA of 2.75. Additional exam requirements/recommendations for international students: Required—TOEFL. *Application deadline:* Applications are processed on a rolling basis. Application fee: $30. Electronic applications accepted. *Expenses:* Tuition: Full-time $9,828; part-time $546 per credit. Required fees: $360; $20 per credit. *Financial support:* In 2006–07, 29 students received support, including 3 research assistantships with full tuition reimbursements available (averaging $5,400 per year); career-related internships or fieldwork and scholarships/grants also available. Support available to part-time students. Financial award application deadline: 5/1; financial award applicants required to submit FAFSA. *Faculty research:* Technology issues, foreign direct investment, multinational corporate issues, cross-cultural international organizations/administrations, regional integration issues. *Unit head:* Margaret Gilfillan, Interim Dean, 412-392-3942, Fax: 412-765-2570, E-mail: mgilfillan@pointpark.edu. *Application contact:* Kathryn B. Ballas, Director, Adult Enrollment, 412-392-3808, Fax: 412-392-6164, E-mail: kballas@pointpark.edu.

Polytechnic University, Brooklyn Campus, Department of Management, Brooklyn, NY 11201-2990. Offers management (MS); management of technology (MS); organizational behavior (MS); technology management (PhD); telecommunications and information management (MS). Part-time and evening/weekend programs available. *Faculty:* 8 full-time (1 woman), 33 part-time/adjunct (4 women). *Students:* 234 full-time (75 women), 113 part-time (41 women); includes 57 minority (23 African Americans, 30 Asian Americans or Pacific Islanders, 4 Hispanic Americans), 115 international. Average age 32. 398 applicants, 89% accepted, 177 enrolled. In 2006, 125 degrees awarded. *Degree requirements:* For master's, thesis (for some programs), comprehensive exam (for some programs), registration; for doctorate, thesis/dissertation, comprehensive exam, registration. *Entrance requirements:* For master's, GMAT, minimum B average in undergraduate course work. Additional exam requirements/recommendations for international students: Required—TOEFL (minimum score 550 paper-based; 213 computer-based); Recommended—IELTS (minimum score 7). *Application deadline:* For fall admission, 7/15 priority date for domestic students, 4/1 priority date for international students; for spring admission, 12/15 priority date for domestic students, 10/1 priority date for international students. Applications are processed on a rolling basis. Application fee: $55. Electronic applications accepted. *Expenses:* Tuition: Full-time $17,784; part-time $988 per credit. *Financial support:* Fellowships, research assistantships, teaching assistantships available. Total annual research expenditures: $80,000. *Unit head:* Dr. Barry Blecherman, Associate Dean, 718-260-3760, Fax: 718-260-3874, E-mail: blecherm@poly.edu. *Application contact:* Anthea Jeffrey, Graduate Admissions, 718-260-3200, Fax: 718-260-3624, E-mail: gradinfo@poly.edu.

See Close-Up on page 307.

Polytechnic University, Long Island Graduate Center, Graduate Programs, Department of Management, Melville, NY 11747. Offers financial engineering (MS, AC); management (MS). Part-time and evening/weekend programs available. *Faculty:* 8 full-time (1 woman), 33 part-time/adjunct (4 women). *Students:* 1 full-time (0 women), 17 part-time (4 women); includes 3 minority (all Asian Americans or Pacific Islanders), 1 international. Average age 32. 10 applicants, 80% accepted, 1 enrolled. In 2006, 3 degrees awarded. *Degree requirements:* For master's, thesis (for some programs), comprehensive exam (for some programs), registration. *Entrance requirements:* Additional exam requirements/recommendations for international students: Required—TOEFL (minimum score 550 paper-based; 213 computer-based); Recommended—IELTS (minimum score 7). *Application deadline:* For fall admission, 7/15 priority date for domestic students, 4/1 priority date for international students; for spring admission, 12/15 priority date for domestic students, 10/1 priority date for international students. Applications are processed on a rolling basis. Application fee: $55. Electronic applications accepted. *Expenses:* Tuition: Full-time $17,184. *Financial support:* Fellowships, research assistantships, teaching assistantships, institutionally sponsored loans available. Support available to part-time students. Financial award applicants required to submit FAFSA. *Unit head:* Dr. Barry Blecherman, Associate Dean, 718-260-3760, Fax: 718-260-3874, E-mail: blecherm@poly.edu. *Application contact:* Prof. Sunil Kumar, Graduate Admissions, 718-260-3482, Fax: 718-260-3624, E-mail: gradinfo@poly.edu.

Polytechnic University of Puerto Rico, Graduate School, Hato Rey, PR 00919. Offers business administration (MBA), including general studies, management of information systems, management of international enterprises; civil engineering (ME, MS); competitiveness manufacturing (MCM, MMC, MS); computer engineering (ME, MS); electrical engineering (ME, MS); engineering management (MEM); environmental management (MEPM); manufacturing engineering (ME, MS). Part-time and evening/weekend programs available. *Entrance requirements:* For master's, 3 letters of recommendation.

Polytechnic University of the Americas–Miami Campus, Graduate School, Miami, FL 33166. Offers business administration (MBA); engineering management (MEM). Part-time and evening/weekend programs available. Postbaccalaureate distance learning degree programs offered (no on-campus study). *Faculty:* 8 part-time/adjunct (1 woman). *Students:* 29 full-time (15 women); includes 28 minority (2 African Americans, 26 Hispanic Americans). Average age 35. In 2006, 4 degrees awarded. *Entrance requirements:* For master's, minimum GPA of 3.0. *Application deadline:* Applications are processed on a rolling basis. Application fee: $30 ($250 for international students). Electronic applications accepted. *Expenses:* Tuition: Full-time $7,110; part-time $395 per credit. Required fees: $620. One-time fee: $30 full-time. *Financial support:* In 2006–07, 13 students received support. Applicants required to submit FAFSA. *Unit head:* Gustavo B. Marin, Campus Director, 305-418-4220 Ext. 205, Fax: 305-418-4325, E-mail: gmarin@pupr.edu. *Application contact:* Ernesto Castro, Academic and Enrollment Director, 305-418-4220 Ext. 206, Fax: 305-418-4325, E-mail: ecastro@pupr.edu.

Polytechnic University of the Americas–Orlando Campus, Graduate School, Orlando, FL 32792. Offers business administration (MBA); engineering management (MEM). Part-time and evening/weekend programs available. Postbaccalaureate distance learning degree programs offered (no on-campus study). *Faculty:* 5 part-time/adjunct (1 woman). *Students:* 12 full-time (6 women); all minorities (all Hispanic Americans) Average age 30. 5 applicants, 100% accepted, 5 enrolled. In 2006, 5 degrees awarded. *Degree requirements:* For master's, registration. *Entrance requirements:* For master's, minimum GPA of 3.0. *Application deadline:* For fall admission, 8/6 priority date for domestic students, 7/6 priority date for international students; for winter admission, 11/6 priority date for domestic students, 10/6 priority date for international students; for spring admission, 3/7 priority date for domestic students, 2/7 priority date for international students. Applications are processed on a rolling basis. Application fee: $30. Electronic applications accepted. *Financial support:* Applicants required to submit FAFSA. *Unit head:* Carlos Perez, Campus Director, 407-677-5661 Ext. 301, Fax: 407-677-5082, E-mail: cperez@pupr.edu. *Application contact:* Luis Mercado, Admissions Director, 407-677-5661, Fax: 407-677-5082, E-mail: lmercado@pupr.edu.

Polytechnic University, Westchester Graduate Center, Graduate Programs, Department of Management, Major in Management, Hawthorne, NY 10532-1507. Offers MS. Part-time and evening/weekend programs available. *Students:* Average age 32. In 2006, 1 degree awarded. *Degree requirements:* For master's, thesis (for some programs), comprehensive exam (for some programs), registration. *Entrance requirements:* Additional exam requirements/recommendations for international students: Required—TOEFL (minimum score 550 paper-based; 213 computer-based); Recommended—IELTS (minimum score 7). *Application deadline:*

For fall admission, 7/15 priority date for domestic students, 4/1 priority date for international students; for spring admission, 12/15 priority date for domestic students, 10/1 priority date for international students. Applications are processed on a rolling basis. Application fee: $55. Electronic applications accepted. *Expenses:* Tuition: Full-time $17,184; part-time $988 per credit.

Pontifical Catholic University of Puerto Rico, College of Business Administration, Ponce, PR 00717-0777. Offers accounting (MBA); business administration (PhD); finance (MBA); general business (MBA); human resources (MBA); international business (MBA); management (MBA); management information systems (MBA); marketing (MBA); office administration (MBA). Part-time and evening/weekend programs available. *Degree requirements:* For master's, thesis/dissertation; for doctorate, thesis/dissertation, comprehensive exam. *Entrance requirements:* For master's, GRE, interview, minimum GPA of 2.75; for doctorate, 2 letters of recommendation, 2 years experience in a related field, interview.

Pontificia Universidad Catolica Madre y Maestra, Graduate School, Santiago, Dominican Republic. Offers administration (M Adm, M Ed); architecture of interiors (M Arch); architecture of tourist lodgings (M Arch); construction administration (ME); convergent networks (ME); earthquake-resistant engineering (ME); environmental engineering (MEE); financial (M Mgmt); human resources (EMBA); international (M Mgmt); labor law and Social Security (M Mgmt); logistics management (ME); urban planning (M Urb). *Entrance requirements:* For master's, curriculum vitae, interview.

Portland State University, Graduate Studies, School of Business Administration, Portland, OR 97207-0751. Offers MBA, MIM, MSFA, PhD. *Accreditation:* AACSB. Part-time and evening/weekend programs available. *Faculty:* 60 full-time (24 women), 44 part-time/adjunct (7 women). *Students:* 205 full-time (85 women), 233 part-time (91 women); includes 67 minority (8 African Americans, 2 American Indian/Alaska Native, 45 Asian Americans or Pacific Islanders, 12 Hispanic Americans), 54 international. Average age 31. 328 applicants, 84% accepted, 199 enrolled. In 2006, 156 degrees awarded. *Degree requirements:* For doctorate, thesis/dissertation. *Entrance requirements:* For master's, GMAT. Additional exam requirements/recommendations for international students: Required—TOEFL (minimum score 550 paper-based; 213 computer-based). *Application deadline:* For fall admission, 4/1 for domestic students, 3/1 for international students. Applications are processed on a rolling basis. Application fee: $50. *Expenses:* Tuition, state resident: full-time $6,426; part-time $238 per credit. Tuition, nonresident: full-time $11,016; part-time $408 per credit. Tuition and fees vary according to course load. *Financial support:* Research assistantships with full tuition reimbursements, teaching assistantships with full tuition reimbursements, career-related internships or fieldwork, Federal Work-Study, scholarships/grants, tuition waivers (partial), and unspecified assistantships available. Support available to part-time students. Financial award application deadline: 3/1; financial award applicants required to submit FAFSA. Total annual research expenditures: $246,428. *Unit head:* Dr. Scott Dawson, Dean, 503-725-3721, Fax: 503-725-5850, E-mail: scottd@sba.pdx.edu. *Application contact:* Pam Mitchell, Administrator, 503-725-3730, Fax: 503-725-5850, E-mail: pamm@sba.pdx.edu.

Portland State University, Graduate Studies, Systems Science Program, Portland, OR 97207-0751. Offers computational intelligence (Certificate); computer modeling and simulation (Certificate); systems science (MS); systems science/anthropology (PhD); systems science/business administration (PhD); systems science/civil engineering (PhD); systems science/economics (PhD); systems science/engineering management (PhD); systems science/general (PhD); systems science/mathematical sciences (PhD); systems science/mechanical engineering (PhD); systems science/psychology (PhD); systems science/sociology (PhD). *Faculty:* 3 full-time (0 women). *Students:* 11 full-time (3 women), 10 part-time (1 woman); includes 1 minority (Asian American or Pacific Islander), 3 international. Average age 38. 2 applicants, 100% accepted, 0 enrolled. In 2006, 1 master's, 2 doctorates awarded. *Degree requirements:* For doctorate, variable foreign language requirement, thesis/dissertation. *Entrance requirements:* For doctorate, GMAT, GRE General Test, minimum undergraduate GPA of 3.0. Additional exam requirements/recommendations for international students: Required—TOEFL. *Application deadline:* For fall admission, 2/1 for domestic students; for spring admission, 11/1 for domestic students. Application fee: $50. *Expenses:* Tuition, state resident: full-time $6,426; part-time $238 per credit. Tuition, nonresident: full-time $11,016; part-time $408 per credit. Required fees: $1,226; $23 per credit. $59 per term. Tuition and fees vary according to course load. *Financial support:* In 2006–07, 1 research assistantship with full tuition reimbursement (averaging $5,940 per year) was awarded; teaching assistantships with full tuition reimbursements, career-related internships or fieldwork, Federal Work-Study, scholarships/grants, and unspecified assistantships also available. Support available to part-time students. Financial award application deadline: 3/1; financial award applicants required to submit FAFSA. *Faculty research:* Systems theory and methodology, artificial intelligence neural networks, information theory, nonlinear dynamics/chaos, modeling and simulation. Total annual research expenditures: $103,759. *Unit head:* George Lendaris, Acting Director, 503-725-4960. *Application contact:* Dawn Sharafi, Administrative Assistant, 503-725-4960, E-mail: dawn@sysc.pdx.edu.

Prairie View A&M University, Graduate School, College of Business, Prairie View, TX 77446-0519. Offers accounting (MS); general business administration (MBA). *Accreditation:* AACSB. Evening/weekend programs available. *Faculty:* 30 full-time (7 women), 7 part-time/adjunct (2 women). *Students:* 10 full-time (6 women), 124 part-time (72 women); includes 118 minority (107 African Americans, 1 American Indian/Alaska Native, 8 Asian Americans or Pacific Islanders, 2 Hispanic Americans), 6 international. Average age 30. 76 applicants, 29% accepted. In 2006, 36 degrees awarded. *Degree requirements:* For master's, registration. *Entrance requirements:* For master's, GMAT, minimum GPA of 2.45. Additional exam requirements/recommendations for international students: Required—TOEFL. *Application deadline:* For fall admission, 7/1 priority date for domestic students, 6/1 priority date for international students; for spring admission, 11/1 priority date for domestic students, 10/1 priority date for international students. Applications are processed on a rolling basis. Application fee: $50. *Financial support:* In 2006–07, 4 research assistantships (averaging $1,500 per year) were awarded; career-related internships or fieldwork, Federal Work-Study, institutionally sponsored loans, and tuition waivers (partial) also available. Support available to part-time students. Financial award application deadline: 4/1; financial award applicants required to submit FAFSA. *Faculty research:* Operations management, international finance, marketing strategy, accounting theory, human resource management. Total annual research expenditures: $25,000. *Unit head:* John W. Dyck, Dean, 936-261-9217, Fax: 936-261-9232, E-mail: john_dyck@pvamo.edu. *Application contact:* Crystal Allen, Assistant to the Dean, 936-261-9237, Fax: 936-261-9241, E-mail: cjallen@pvamu.edu.

Providence College, Graduate Studies, Department of Business Administration, Providence, RI 02918. Offers MBA. Part-time and evening/weekend programs available. *Faculty:* 9 full-time (2 women), 8 part-time/adjunct (0 women). *Students:* 26 full-time (14 women), 60 part-time (23 women); includes 6 minority (4 African Americans, 2 Hispanic Americans), 4 international. Average age 30. 30 applicants, 97% accepted. In 2006, 44 degrees awarded. *Degree requirements:* For master's, thesis optional. *Entrance requirements:* For master's, GMAT. Additional exam requirements/recommendations for international students: Required—TOEFL (minimum score 550 paper-based; 213 computer-based). *Application deadline:* For fall admission, 8/1 priority date for domestic students; for spring admission, 12/1 for domestic students. Applications are processed on a rolling basis. Application fee: $55. *Expenses:* Contact institution. *Financial support:* In 2006–07, 22 research assistantships with full tuition reimbursements (averaging $8,400 per year) were awarded; institutionally sponsored loans and unspecified assistantships also available. Support available to part-time students. Financial award application deadline: 8/1; financial award applicants required to submit FAFSA. *Unit head:* Dr. John Shaw, Director, 401-865-2333, E-mail: jshaw@providence.edu.

See Close-Up on page 309.

Purdue University, Graduate School, Krannert School of Management, Department of Management, West Lafayette, IN 47907. Offers accounting (PhD); business administration (MBA); finance (PhD); management information systems (PhD); marketing (PhD); operations management (PhD); quantitative methods (PhD); strategic management (PhD). *Students:* 56 full-time (21 women); includes 5 minority (3 Asian Americans or Pacific Islanders, 2 Hispanic Americans), 41 international. Average age 30. 421 applicants, 7% accepted, 19 enrolled. In 2006, 11 degrees awarded. *Median time to degree:* Doctorate–5 years full-time. Of those who began their doctoral program in fall 1998, 98% received their degree in 8 years or less. *Degree requirements:* For doctorate, thesis/dissertation, comprehensive exam, registration. *Entrance requirements:* For master's and doctorate, GMAT. Additional exam requirements/recommendations for international students: Required—TOEFL (minimum score 575 paper-based; 233 computer-based; 77 iBT), IELTS (minimum score 7). *Application deadline:* For fall admission, 2/15 for domestic and international students. Application fee: $55. Electronic applications accepted. *Financial support:* In 2006–07, 7 fellowships with partial tuition reimbursements (averaging $16,800 per year), 79 research assistantships with partial tuition reimbursements (averaging $16,800 per year), 8 teaching assistantships with partial tuition reimbursements (averaging $16,800 per year) were awarded; scholarships/grants and unspecified assistantships also available. Financial award application deadline: 2/15; financial award applicants required to submit FAFSA. *Faculty research:* Corporate finance, international business, enterprise integration. *Unit head:* Dr. John M. Barron, Head, 765-494-4451, Fax: 765-494-1526. *Application contact:* Kelly Felty, Assistant Director of Administration for Doctoral Programs, 765-494-4375, Fax: 765-494-1526, E-mail: phd@krannert.purdue.edu.

Purdue University Calumet, Graduate School, School of Management, Hammond, IN 46323-2094. Offers accountancy (M Acc); business administration (MBA). Part-time and evening/weekend programs available. *Entrance requirements:* For master's, GMAT. Additional exam requirements/recommendations for international students: Required—TOEFL. Electronic applications accepted.

Queen's University at Kingston, Queens School of Business, Program in Business Administration, Kingston, ON K7L 3N6, Canada. Offers MBA. *Accreditation:* AACSB. *Degree requirements:* For master's, research project, thesis optional. *Entrance requirements:* For master's, GMAT, minimum B+ average. Additional exam requirements/recommendations for international students: Required—TOEFL. Electronic applications accepted. *Faculty research:* Management fundamentals, strategic thinking, global business, innovation and change, leadership.

Queen's University at Kingston, Queens School of Business, Program in Business Administration for Science and Technology, Kingston, ON K7L 3N6, Canada. Offers MBA. *Accreditation:* AACSB. *Degree requirements:* For master's, thesis optional. *Entrance requirements:* For master's, GMAT, bachelor's degree in engineering or science, 2 years of work experience in field, minimum B+ average, 3 letters of reference. Additional exam requirements/recommendations for international students: Required—TOEFL. Electronic applications accepted. *Faculty research:* Management information systems, organizational behavior, finance, marketing, management science, strategic management.

Queens University of Charlotte, McColl Graduate School of Business, Charlotte, NC 28274-0002. Offers EMBA, MBA. *Accreditation:* AACSB; ACBSP. Part-time and evening/weekend programs available. *Faculty:* 11 full-time (2 women), 3 part-time/adjunct (1 woman). *Students:* 52 full-time (12 women), 127 part-time (58 women); includes 25 minority (14 African Americans, 6 Asian Americans or Pacific Islanders, 5 Hispanic Americans), 3 international. Average age 31. 62 applicants, 85% accepted, 37 enrolled. In 2006, 55 degrees awarded. *Degree requirements:* For master's, capstone course. *Entrance requirements:* For master's, GMAT, minimum GPA of 2.5. Additional exam requirements/recommendations for international students: Required—TOEFL. *Application deadline:* Applications are processed on a rolling basis. Application fee: $50. Electronic applications accepted. *Expenses: Contact institution. Financial support:* In 2006–07, 40 fellowships were awarded; institutionally sponsored loans also available. Support available to part-time students. *Unit head:* Terry Broderick, Chair, 704-337-2234. *Application contact:* Robert Mobley, Director of MBA Admissions, 704-337-2224, Fax: 704-337-2594.

Quincy University, Division of Business, Quincy, IL 62301-2699. Offers MBA. Part-time and evening/weekend programs available. *Faculty:* 6 full-time (3 women). *Students:* 10 full-time (4 women), 34 part-time (18 women); includes 1 minority (Hispanic American), 2 international. Average age 29. In 2006, 14 degrees awarded. *Entrance requirements:* For master's, GMAT, previous course work in accounting, economics, finance, management, marketing, and statistics. *Application deadline:* Applications are processed on a rolling basis. Application fee: $25. *Financial support:* In 2006–07, 26 students received support. Available to part-time students. Applicants required to submit FAFSA. *Faculty research:* Macroeconomic forecasting, business ethics/social responsibility. *Unit head:* Dr. John Palmer, Director, MBA Program, 217-228-5387, E-mail: palmejo@quincy.edu. *Application contact:* Kevin Brown, Director of Admissions, 217-228-5210, Fax: 217-228-5648, E-mail: admissions@quincy.edu.

Quinnipiac University, School of Business, Program in Business Administration, Hamden, CT 06518-1940. Offers accounting (MBA); economics (MBA); finance (MBA); healthcare management (MBA); information systems management (MBA); international business (MBA); management (MBA); marketing (MBA); JD/MBA. *Accreditation:* AACSB. Part-time and evening/weekend programs available. *Faculty:* 16 full-time (2 women), 2 part-time/adjunct (1 woman). *Students:* 53 full-time (21 women), 112 part-time (48 women); includes 13 minority (2 African Americans, 1 American Indian/Alaska Native, 4 Asian Americans or Pacific Islanders, 6 Hispanic Americans), 7 international. Average age 26. 80 applicants, 65% accepted, 34 enrolled. In 2006, 73 degrees awarded. *Median time to degree:* Master's–1.5 years full-time, 2.5 years part-time. *Entrance requirements:* For master's, GMAT, minimum GPA of 3.0. Additional exam requirements/recommendations for international students: Required—TOEFL (minimum score 575 paper-based; 233 computer-based; 90 iBT), IELTS (minimum score 7). *Application deadline:* For fall admission, 7/30 priority date for domestic students, 5/30 priority date for international students; for spring admission, 12/15 priority date for domestic students, 10/15 priority date for international students. Applications are processed on a rolling basis. Application fee: $45. Electronic applications accepted. *Expenses:* Tuition: Part-time $675 per credit. Required fees: $30 per credit. *Financial support:* Tuition waivers (partial) and unspecified assistantships available. Support available to part-time students. Financial award application deadline: 4/15; financial award applicants required to submit FAFSA. *Faculty research:* Equity compensation, marketing relationships and public policy, corporate governance, international business. *Unit head:* Kevin B. Taylor, Director, 203-582-3676, Fax: 203-582-8664, E-mail: mba@quinnipiac.edu. *Application contact:* 800-462-1944, Fax: 203-582-3443, E-mail: graduate@quinnipiac.edu.

See Close-Up on page 311.

Radford University, Graduate College, College of Business and Economics, Program in Business Administration, Radford, VA 24142. Offers MBA. *Accreditation:* AACSB. Part-time and evening/weekend programs available. Postbaccalaureate distance learning degree programs offered (minimal on-campus study). *Faculty:* 7 full-time (1 woman). *Students:* 33 full-time (11 women), 30 part-time (13 women); includes 13 minority (all African Americans) Average age 30. 43 applicants, 91% accepted, 28 enrolled. In 2006, 27 degrees awarded. *Degree requirements:* For master's, comprehensive exam. *Entrance requirements:* For master's, GMAT. Additional exam requirements/recommendations for international students: Required—TOEFL. *Application deadline:* For fall admission, 3/1 priority date for domestic students, 4/1 for international students; for spring admission, 10/1 for domestic students, 8/1 for international students. Applications are processed on a rolling basis. Application fee: $40. Electronic applications accepted. *Expenses:* Tuition, state resident: full-time $4,680; part-time $260 per credit hour. Tuition, nonresident: full-time $8,604; part-time $478 per credit hour. *Financial support:* In 2006–07, 23 students received support, including 21 research assistantships with partial tuition reimbursements available (averaging $8,000 per year), teaching assistantships with partial tuition reimbursements available (averaging $8,700 per year); career-related internships or fieldwork, Federal Work-Study, institutionally sponsored loans, scholarships/grants, and unspecified assistantships also available. Financial award application deadline: 3/1; financial award applicants required to submit FAFSA. *Unit head:* Dr. Clarence C. Rose, Director of MBA and Academic Outreach, 540-831-5185, Fax: 540-831-6103, E-mail: rumba@radford.edu.

Regent University, Graduate School, School of Global Leadership and Entrepreneurship, Virginia Beach, VA 23464-9800. Offers business administration (MBA); management (MA); organizational leadership (MA, PhD, Certificate); strategic foresight (MA); strategic leadership (DSL). Part-time programs available. Postbaccalaureate distance learning degree programs offered (minimal on-campus study). *Faculty:* 20 full-time (3 women), 36 part-time/adjunct (6 women). *Students:* 68 full-time (40 women), 482 part-time (170 women); includes 144 minority (110 African Americans, 6 American Indian/Alaska Native, 9 Asian Americans or Pacific Islanders, 19 Hispanic Americans), 37 international. Average age 40. 395 applicants, 37% accepted, 64 enrolled. In 2006, 100 master's, 69 doctorates awarded. *Degree requirements:* For master's, thesis or alternative, 3 credit hour culminating experience; for doctorate, thesis/dissertation. *Entrance requirements:* For master's, GRE, GMAT or MAT, minimum undergraduate GPA of 2.75, computer literacy survey, 2 recommendations, resumé; for doctorate, GRE, GMAT or MAT, sample of writing, minimum of 3 years of relevant experience, computer literacy survey, 2 recommendations, resumé; for Certificate, GRE, GMAT or MAT, writing sample. Additional exam requirements/recommendations for international students: Required—TOEFL (minimum score 577 paper-based; 233 computer-based). *Application deadline:* For fall admission, 5/1 priority date for domestic students; for spring admission, 10/1 priority date for domestic students. Applications are processed on a rolling basis. Application fee: $50. Electronic applications accepted. *Expenses: Contact institution. Financial support:* In 2006–07, 321 students received support. Scholarships/grants and tuition waivers (full and partial) available. Support available to part-time students. Financial award application deadline: 9/1. *Faculty research:* Servant leadership, ethics and values, telecommuting and family values, organizational communications, distance education. *Unit head:* Dr. Bruce Winston, Dean, 757-226-4306, Fax: 757-226-4634, E-mail: brucwin@regent.edu. *Application contact:* Althea Bishard, Registrar and Executive Director of Enrollment and Academic Services, 800-373-5504, Fax: 757-226-4381, E-mail: admissions@regent.edu.

Regis College, Department of Management and Leadership, Weston, MA 02493. Offers leadership and organizational change (MS). Part-time and evening/weekend programs available. *Faculty:* 1 full-time (0 women), 1 part-time/adjunct (0 women). *Students:* 1 (woman) full-time, 17 part-time (15 women); includes 3 minority (1 Asian American or Pacific Islander, 2 Hispanic Americans). Average age 36. 5 applicants, 100% accepted, 5 enrolled. In 2006, 9 degrees awarded. *Degree requirements:* For master's, thesis. *Entrance requirements:* For master's, GRE General Test. *Application deadline:* Applications are processed on a rolling basis. Application fee: $50. *Expenses:* Tuition: Full-time $23,680; part-time $665 per credit hour. *Financial support:* Applicants required to submit FAFSA. *Faculty research:* Leadership, service and learning, building high commitment organizations. *Unit head:* Dr. Phillip Jutras, Director, 781-768-7436, Fax: 781-768-7159, E-mail: phillip.jutras@regiscollege.edu.

Regis University, School for Professional Studies, Program in Business, Denver, CO 80221-1099. Offers accounting (MS); business administration (MBA); finance (MBA); finance and accounting (MBA); international business (MBA); marketing (MBA); operations management (MBA); organization leadership (MS); project management (Certificate); technical management (Certificate). Offered at Colorado Springs Campus, Northwest Denver Campus, Southeast Denver Campus, Fort Collins Campus, Broomfield Campus, Henderson (Nevada) Campus, and Summerlin (Nevada) Campus. Part-time and evening/weekend programs available. Postbaccalaureate distance learning degree programs offered (no on-campus study). *Faculty:* 16 full-time (4 women), 82 part-time/adjunct (22 women). *Students:* 1,770 (834 women). Average age 36. In 2006, 560 degrees awarded. *Degree requirements:* For master's, capstone project, thesis optional. *Entrance requirements:* For master's, GMAT, interview, 2 years of full-time business work experience; for Certificate, GMAT. Additional exam requirements/recommendations for international students: Required—TOEFL or university-based test. *Application deadline:* For fall admission, 8/22 for domestic and international students; for winter admission, 1/2 for domestic and international students; for spring admission, 4/30 for domestic and international students. Applications are processed on a rolling basis. Application fee: $75. Electronic applications accepted. *Financial support:* Federal Work-Study available. Support available to part-time students. Financial award applicants required to submit FAFSA. *Unit head:* Dr. Michael Goess, Chair, 303-458-4302, Fax: 303-964-5538. *Application contact:* 800-677-9270 Ext. 4080, Fax: 303-964-5538, E-mail: masters@regis.edu.

Regis University, School for Professional Studies, Program in Organization Leadership, Denver, CO 80221-1099. Offers computer information technology (MSOL); executive international management (Certificate); executive leadership (Certificate); human resource management (MSOL); organizational leadership (MSOL); project leadership and management (MSOL, Certificate); strategic business (Certificate); strategic human resource (Certificate). Offered at Boulder Campus, Fort Collins Campus, Northwest Denver Campus, Southeast Denver Campus, Colorado Springs Campus, and Broomfield Campus. Part-time and evening/weekend programs available. Postbaccalaureate distance learning degree programs offered. *Faculty:* 55. *Students:* Average age 35. In 2006, 61 degrees awarded. *Median time to degree:* Master's–3 years full-time. *Degree requirements:* For master's, capstone course; for Certificate, final research project. *Entrance requirements:* For master's, 3 years of management-related experience, resumé. Additional exam requirements/recommendations for international students: Required—TOEFL, TWE (minimum score 5), TOEFL or university-based test. *Application deadline:* For fall admission, 8/13 priority date for domestic students, 7/13 for international students; for winter admission, 10/8 priority date for domestic students, 9/8 for international students; for spring admission, 12/17 priority date for domestic students, 11/11 for international students. Applications are processed on a rolling basis. Application fee: $75. Electronic applications accepted. *Expenses: Contact institution. Financial support:* Federal Work-Study available. Support available to part-time students. Financial award applicants required to submit FAFSA. *Faculty research:* Organizational behavior, leadership, change, quality control, global economics. *Unit head:* Dr. Donna VanDusen, Chair, 303-458-4302, Fax: 303-964-5538. *Application contact:* 800-677-9270, Fax: 303-964-5538, E-mail: masters@regis.edu.

Rensselaer at Hartford, Lally School of Management and Technology, Hartford, CT 06120-2991. Offers MBA, MS. Part-time and evening/weekend programs available. Postbaccalaureate distance learning degree programs offered (no on-campus study). *Degree requirements:* For master's, capstone course. *Entrance requirements:* For master's, GMAT (MBA). Additional exam requirements/recommendations for international students: Required—TOEFL (minimum score 600 paper-based; 250 computer-based). Electronic applications accepted.

Rensselaer Polytechnic Institute, Graduate School, Lally School of Management and Technology, Troy, NY 12180-3590. Offers MBA, MS, PhD. *Accreditation:* AACSB. Part-time and evening/weekend programs available. Postbaccalaureate distance learning degree programs offered (no on-campus study). *Faculty:* 50 full-time (9 women), 1 part-time/adjunct (0 women). *Students:* 121 full-time (62 women), 525 part-time (184 women); includes 137 minority (43 African Americans, 60 Asian Americans or Pacific Islanders, 34 Hispanic Americans), 71 international. Average age 28. 416 applicants, 70% accepted, 240 enrolled. In 2006, 215 master's, 6 doctorates awarded. *Median time to degree:* Of those who began their doctoral program in fall 1998, 25% received their degree in 8 years or less. *Degree requirements:* For doctorate, thesis/dissertation. *Entrance requirements:* For master's, GMAT, 2 letters of recommendation, resumé; for doctorate, GMAT or GRE General Test, 2 letters of recommendation. Additional exam requirements/recommendations for international students: Required—TOEFL (minimum score 600 paper-based; 250 computer-based; 100 iBT); Recommended—IELTS (minimum score 7). *Application deadline:* For fall admission, 3/15 priority date for domestic and international students. Applications are processed on a rolling basis. Application fee: $75. Electronic applications accepted. *Expenses:* Tuition: Full-time $32,600; part-time $1,358 per credit. Required fees: $1,629. *Financial support:* In 2006–07, 48 students received support; fellowships with partial tuition reimbursements available, research assistantships with partial

Business Administration and Management—General

Rensselaer Polytechnic Institute (continued)
tuition reimbursements available, teaching assistantships with partial tuition reimbursements available, career-related internships or fieldwork, institutionally sponsored loans, and scholarships/grants available. Financial award application deadline: 3/15; financial award applicants required to submit FAFSA. *Faculty research:* Technological entrepreneurship operations mgmt, new product development and mgmt marketing finance, information systems. Total annual research expenditures: $24,747. *Unit head:* Dr. David A. Gautschi, Dean, 518-276-6586, Fax: 518-276-2665, E-mail: lallymba@rpi.edu. *Application contact:* Michele M. Martens, Manager of Graduate Programs, 518-276-6586, Fax: 518-276-2665, E-mail: martem@rpi.edu.

See Close-Up on page 313.

Rice University, Graduate Programs, Jesse H. Jones Graduate School of Management, Houston, TX 77251-1892. Offers business administration (EMBA, MBA, PMBA); MBA/M Eng; MD/MBA. *Accreditation:* AACSB. Evening/weekend programs available. *Faculty:* 58 full-time (16 women), 46 part-time/adjunct (8 women). *Students:* 459 full-time (125 women); includes 125 minority (28 African Americans, 1 American Indian/Alaska Native, 55 Asian Americans or Pacific Islanders, 41 Hispanic Americans), 91 international. 437 applicants, 48% accepted, 105 enrolled. In 2006, 160 degrees awarded. *Entrance requirements:* For master's, GMAT. Additional exam requirements/recommendations for international students: Required—TOEFL (minimum score 600 paper-based; 250 computer-based). *Application deadline:* For fall admission, 11/13 priority date for domestic and international students; for winter admission, 1/22 priority date for domestic and international students; for spring admission, 3/26 priority date for domestic and international students. Applications are processed on a rolling basis. Application fee: $100. Electronic applications accepted. *Expenses: Contact institution. Financial support:* Fellowships, career-related internships or fieldwork, Federal Work-Study, institutionally sponsored loans, scholarships/grants, and tuition waivers (full and partial) available. Financial award application deadline: 5/15; financial award applicants required to submit FAFSA. *Faculty research:* Marketing strategy, technology transfer initiatives, management accounting, leadership and change management, financial management. *Unit head:* Dr. William H. Glick, Dean, 713-348-4838, Fax: 713-348-5110, E-mail: bill.glick@rice.edu. *Application contact:* Lisa W. Anderson, Director of Admissions, 713-348-4918, Fax: 713-348-6147, E-mail: ricemba@rice.edu.

The Richard Stockton College of New Jersey, Graduate Programs, Program in Business Studies, Pomona, NJ 08240-0195. Offers MBA. *Faculty:* 22 full-time (12 women), 1 (woman) part-time/adjunct. *Students:* 10 full-time (2 women), 45 part-time (27 women); includes 13 minority (4 African Americans, 5 Asian Americans or Pacific Islanders, 4 Hispanic Americans). Average age 35. 30 applicants, 77% accepted. In 2006, 14 degrees awarded. *Degree requirements:* For master's, project. *Entrance requirements:* For master's, GMAT. *Application deadline:* For fall admission, 4/1 for domestic students. Applications are processed on a rolling basis. Application fee: $50. *Expenses:* Tuition, state resident: full-time $9,746. Tuition, nonresident: full-time $14,462. Required fees: $2,340. *Financial support:* In 2006–07, 9 students received support. Career-related internships or fieldwork and Federal Work-Study available. Support available to part-time students. Financial award application deadline: 3/1; financial award applicants required to submit FAFSA. *Faculty research:* Business ethics, marketing channels development, event studies, total quality management. *Unit head:* Dr. Gurprit Chhatwal, Director, 609-652-4615, E-mail: mba@stockton.edu. *Application contact:* Alison Henry, Associate Director of Admissions, 609-652-4261, Fax: 609-626-5541, E-mail: admissions@stockston.edu.

Rider University, College of Business Administration, Lawrenceville, NJ 08648-3001. Offers M Acc, MBA. *Accreditation:* AACSB. Part-time and evening/weekend programs available. *Faculty:* 23 full-time (6 women), 12 part-time/adjunct (0 women). *Students:* 68 full-time (27 women), 270 part-time (124 women); includes 69 minority (19 African Americans, 1 American Indian/Alaska Native, 39 Asian Americans or Pacific Islanders, 10 Hispanic Americans), 18 international. Average age 29. 129 applicants, 71% accepted, 62 enrolled. In 2006, 112 degrees awarded. *Entrance requirements:* For master's, GMAT, minimum AACSB index of 1050, resumé. Additional exam requirements/recommendations for international students: Required—TOEFL (minimum score 550 paper-based; 213 computer-based). *Application deadline:* For fall admission, 8/1 priority date for domestic students, 6/1 priority date for international students; for spring admission, 12/1 priority date for domestic students, 11/1 priority date for international students. Applications are processed on a rolling basis. Application fee: $50. Electronic applications accepted. *Expenses: Contact institution. Financial support:* In 2006–07, 90 students received support. Career-related internships or fieldwork, Federal Work-Study, institutionally sponsored loans, unspecified assistantships, and institutional work-study available. Support available to part-time students. Financial award applicants required to submit FAFSA. *Unit head:* Dr. John Farrell, MBA Program Director, 609-895-5776, Fax: 609-896-5304. *Application contact:* Jamie L Mitchell, Director of Graduate Admissions, 609-896-5036, Fax: 609-895-5680, E-mail: jmitchell@rider.edu.

See Close-Up on page 315.

Rivier College, School of Graduate Studies, Department of Business Administration, Nashua, NH 03060-5086. Offers business administration (MBA); health care administration (MBA); human resources management (MS); organizational leadership (EMBA). Part-time and evening/weekend programs available. *Faculty:* 4 full-time (2 women), 21 part-time/adjunct (6 women). *Students:* 12 full-time (10 women), 60 part-time (35 women); includes 7 minority (2 African Americans, 2 Asian Americans or Pacific Islanders, 3 Hispanic Americans), 6 international. Average age 36. In 2006, 37 degrees awarded. *Degree requirements:* For master's, registration. *Application deadline:* Applications are processed on a rolling basis. Application fee: $25. *Financial support:* Available to part-time students. Application deadline: 2/1; *Unit head:* Maria Matarazzo, Division Chair, 603-897-8532, Fax: 603-897-8885, E-mail: mmatarazzo@rivier.edu. *Application contact:* Diane Monahan, Director of Graduate Admissions, 603-897-8129, Fax: 603-897-8810, E-mail: gradadm@rivier.edu.

Robert Morris University, Graduate Studies, School of Business, Moon Township, PA 15108-1189. Offers accounting (MS); business administration and management (MBA); finance (MS); human resource management (MS); nonprofit management (MS); sport management (MS); taxation (MS). Part-time and evening/weekend programs available. *Faculty:* 27 full-time (12 women), 6 part-time/adjunct (1 woman). *Students:* Average age 31. 253 applicants, 59% accepted, 103 enrolled. In 2006, 139 degrees awarded. *Entrance requirements:* For master's, GMAT, letters of recommendation. Additional exam requirements/recommendations for international students: Required—TOEFL (minimum score 550 paper-based; 213 computer-based). *Application deadline:* For fall admission, 7/1 priority date for domestic and international students; for spring admission, 11/1 priority date for domestic and international students. Applications are processed on a rolling basis. Application fee: $35. Electronic applications accepted. *Expenses:* Tuition: Part-time $580 per credit. Part-time tuition and fees vary according to degree level and program. *Financial support:* Research assistantships with partial tuition reimbursements, Federal Work-Study, institutionally sponsored loans, and unspecified assistantships available. Support available to part-time students. Financial award application deadline: 5/1; financial award applicants required to submit FAFSA. *Unit head:* Dr. Derya A. Jacobs, Dean, 412-262-8451, Fax: 412-262-8494, E-mail: jacobs@rmu.edu. *Application contact:* Kellie L. Laurenzi, Dean of Enrollment, 412-262-8235, Fax: 412-299-2425, E-mail: laurenzi@rmu.edu.

Roberts Wesleyan College, Division of Business, Rochester, NY 14624-1997. Offers nonprofit leadership (Certificate); strategic leadership (MS); strategic marketing (MS). Evening/weekend programs available. *Faculty:* 3 full-time (0 women), 13 part-time/adjunct (3 women). *Students:* 57 full-time (28 women). Average age 34. 45 applicants, 89% accepted. In 2006, 26 degrees awarded. *Degree requirements:* For master's, thesis or alternative. *Entrance requirements:* For master's, GMAT, minimum GPA of 2.75, verifiable work experience. *Application deadline:* Applications are processed on a rolling basis. Application fee: $35. *Expenses: Contact institution. Financial support:* In 2006–07, 15 students received support. Applicants required to submit FAFSA. *Unit head:* Dr. Steven Bovee, Chair, 716-594-6571, Fax: 716-594-6316, E-mail: bovees@roberts.edu.

Rochester Institute of Technology, Graduate Enrollment Services, E. Philip Saunders College of Business, Department of Business Administration, Executive MBA Program, Rochester, NY 14623-5603. Offers Exec MBA. *Accreditation:* AACSB. *Students:* 57 full-time (22 women); includes 6 minority (3 African Americans, 2 Asian Americans or Pacific Islanders, 1 Hispanic American). 28 applicants, 100% accepted, 27 enrolled. In 2006, 9 degrees awarded. *Entrance requirements:* For master's, GMAT, minimum GPA of 2.5. Additional exam requirements/recommendations for international students: Required—TOEFL (minimum score 580 paper-based; 237 computer-based; 92 iBT). *Application deadline:* For fall admission, 3/1 priority date for domestic students. Applications are processed on a rolling basis. Application fee: $50. *Expenses: Contact institution.*

Rochester Institute of Technology, Graduate Enrollment Services, E. Philip Saunders College of Business, Department of Business Administration, Program in Business Administration, Rochester, NY 14623-5603. Offers MBA. *Accreditation:* AACSB. *Students:* 167 full-time (60 women), 135 part-time (55 women); includes 27 minority (7 African Americans, 11 Asian Americans or Pacific Islanders, 9 Hispanic Americans), 74 international. 271 applicants, 67% accepted, 98 enrolled. In 2006, 179 degrees awarded. *Entrance requirements:* For master's, GMAT, minimum GPA of 2.5. Additional exam requirements/recommendations for international students: Required—TOEFL (minimum score 580 paper-based; 237 computer-based; 92 iBT). *Application deadline:* For fall admission, 3/1 priority date for domestic students. Applications are processed on a rolling basis. Application fee: $50. *Expenses:* Tuition: Full-time $28,491; part-time $800 per credit. Required fees: $201. *Financial support:* Research assistantships, career-related internships or fieldwork available. *Application contact:* Brian O'Neil, Associate Dean, 585-475-7784, E-mail: boneil@cob.rit.edu.

Rockford College, Graduate Studies, Program in Business Administration, Rockford, IL 61108-2393. Offers MBA. Part-time and evening/weekend programs available. *Entrance requirements:* For master's, GMAT.

Rockhurst University, Helzberg School of Management, Kansas City, MO 64110-2561. Offers MBA. *Accreditation:* AACSB. Part-time and evening/weekend programs available. Postbaccalaureate distance learning degree programs offered (minimal on-campus study). *Faculty:* 29 full-time (6 women), 14 part-time/adjunct (3 women). *Students:* 112 full-time (33 women), 341 part-time (135 women); includes 58 minority (23 African Americans, 1 American Indian/Alaska Native, 24 Asian Americans or Pacific Islanders, 10 Hispanic Americans), 4 international. Average age 30. 184 applicants, 47% accepted, 74 enrolled. In 2006, 179 degrees awarded. *Entrance requirements:* For master's, GMAT. Additional exam requirements/recommendations for international students: Required—TOEFL. *Application deadline:* For fall admission, 7/25 priority date for domestic students; for spring admission, 12/15 for domestic students. Applications are processed on a rolling basis. Application fee: $0. Electronic applications accepted. *Expenses:* Tuition: Full-time $9,810; part-time $6,540 per year. Required fees: $400 per term. *Financial support:* Career-related internships or fieldwork available. Support available to part-time students. Financial award application deadline: 4/1; financial award applicants required to submit FAFSA. *Faculty research:* Offshoring/outsourcing, systems analysis/synthesis, work teams, multilateral trade, path dependencies/creation. *Unit head:* Dr. James Daley, Dean, 816-501-4201, Fax: 816-501-4650, E-mail: james.daley@rockhurst.edu. *Application contact:* Ron Filipowicz, Director of Graduate Admission, 816-501-4731, Fax: 816-501-4241, E-mail: ron.filipowicz@rockhurst.edu.

Rollins College, Crummer Graduate School of Business, Winter Park, FL 32789-4499. Offers MBA. *Accreditation:* AACSB. Part-time and evening/weekend programs available. *Faculty:* 23 full-time (3 women). *Students:* 261 full-time (105 women), 171 part-time (65 women); includes 83 minority (24 African Americans, 2 American Indian/Alaska Native, 21 Asian Americans or Pacific Islanders, 36 Hispanic Americans), 17 international. Average age 30. In 2006, 175 degrees awarded. *Degree requirements:* For master's, thesis optional. *Entrance requirements:* For master's, GMAT. *Application deadline:* For fall admission, 4/1 priority date for domestic students; for spring admission, 12/1 for domestic students. Applications are processed on a rolling basis. Application fee: $50. Electronic applications accepted. *Expenses: Contact institution. Financial support:* Fellowships, research assistantships, career-related internships or fieldwork, Federal Work-Study, scholarships/grants, and tuition waivers (full) available. *Unit head:* Dr. Craig M. McAllaster, Dean, 407-646-2249, Fax: 407-646-1550, E-mail: cmcallaster@rollins.edu. *Application contact:* Student Admissions Office, 407-646-2405, Fax: 407-646-1550.

Roosevelt University, Graduate Division, Walter E. Heller College of Business Administration, Program in Business Administration, Chicago, IL 60605-1394. Offers MBA. *Accreditation:* ACBSP. Part-time and evening/weekend programs available. *Students:* 85 full-time (43 women), 486 part-time (278 women); includes 201 minority (130 African Americans, 4 American Indian/Alaska Native, 36 Asian Americans or Pacific Islanders, 31 Hispanic Americans), 25 international. Average age 33. 317 applicants, 64% accepted, 193 enrolled. In 2006, 186 degrees awarded. *Entrance requirements:* For master's, GMAT. *Application deadline:* For fall admission, 6/1 priority date for domestic students. Applications are processed on a rolling basis. Application fee: $25 ($35 for international students). *Financial support:* Application deadline: 2/15. *Unit head:* Marilyn Nance, Assistant Dean and Director, 312-281-3280, Fax: 312-341-3827. *Application contact:* Joanne Canyon-Heller, Coordinator of Graduate Admission, 877-APPLY RU, Fax: 312-281-3356, E-mail: applyru@roosevelt.edu.

Rosemont College, Graduate School, Accelerated Program in Management, Rosemont, PA 19010-1699. Offers arts/culture/project management (MSM); criminal justice (MSM); not for profit (MSM); training and leadership (MSM). Part-time and evening/weekend programs available. *Degree requirements:* For master's, thesis or alternative. *Entrance requirements:* For master's, GRE or MAT. Expenses: Contact institution.

Rosemont College, Graduate School, Program in Business Administration, Rosemont, PA 19010-1699. Offers MBA. Part-time and evening/weekend programs available. *Degree requirements:* For master's, thesis optional.

Rowan University, Graduate School, William G. Rohrer College of Business, Program in Business Administration, Glassboro, NJ 08028-1701. Offers MBA. *Accreditation:* AACSB. Part-time and evening/weekend programs available. *Students:* 13 full-time (5 women), 57 part-time (25 women); includes 7 minority (3 African Americans, 3 Asian Americans or Pacific Islanders, 1 Hispanic American). Average age 30. 13 applicants, 54% accepted, 7 enrolled. In 2006, 29 degrees awarded. *Degree requirements:* For master's, thesis. *Entrance requirements:* For master's, GMAT, minimum GPA of 2.8. Additional exam requirements/recommendations for international students: Required—TOEFL. *Application deadline:* Applications are processed on a rolling basis. Application fee: $50. Electronic applications accepted. *Expenses:* Tuition, state resident: full-time $9,882; part-time $549 per credit. Tuition, nonresident: full-time $9,882; part-time $549 per credit. Tuition and fees vary according to degree level. *Financial support:* Federal Work-Study and unspecified assistantships available. Support available to part-time students. *Unit head:* Dr. Daniel McFarland, Director, MBA Program, 856-256-5426, E-mail: mcfarland@rowan.edu.

Royal Military College of Canada, Division of Graduate Studies and Research, Continuing Studies, Department of Business Administration, Kingston, ON K7K 7B4, Canada. Offers MBA. *Degree requirements:* For master's, thesis, registration. *Entrance requirements:* For master's, GMAT. Electronic applications accepted.

Royal Roads University, Graduate Studies, School of Business, Victoria, BC V9B 5Y2, Canada. Offers digital technologies management (MBA); executive management (MBA), including global aviation management, knowledge management, leadership; human resources management (MBA); public relations and communications management (MBA). Postbaccalaureate distance learning degree programs offered (minimal on-campus study). *Degree requirements:* For master's, thesis. *Entrance requirements:* For master's, 5-7 years of related work experience. Additional exam requirements/recommendations for international students: Required—TOEFL (paper-based 570; computer-based 233) or IELTS (paper-based 7) (recommended). Electronic applications accepted. Expenses: Contact institution. *Faculty research:* Global venture analysis standards; computer assisted venture opportunity screening; teaching philosophies, instructions and methods.

Rutgers, The State University of New Jersey, Camden, School of Business, Camden, NJ 08102-1401. Offers MBA. *Accreditation:* AACSB. Part-time and evening/weekend programs available. *Faculty:* 33 full-time (9 women), 7 part-time/adjunct (2 women). *Students:* 40 full-time, 226 part-time; includes 61 minority (16 African Americans, 41 Asian Americans or Pacific Islanders, 4 Hispanic Americans). Average age 28. 186 applicants, 74% accepted, 76 enrolled. In 2006, 94 degrees awarded. *Entrance requirements:* For master's, GMAT, minimum GPA of 2.5. Additional exam requirements/recommendations for international students: Required—TOEFL (minimum score 230 computer-based; 89 iBT). *Application deadline:* For fall admission, 7/1 priority date for domestic students, 2/1 for international students; for spring admission, 11/1 priority date for domestic students, 9/1 for international students. Applications are processed on a rolling basis. Application fee: $50. Electronic applications accepted. *Expenses: Contact institution. Financial support:* In 2006–07, 5 students received support. Career-related internships or fieldwork and scholarships/grants available. Financial award applicants required to submit FAFSA. *Faculty research:* Efficiency in utility industry, management information systems development, management/labor relations. Total annual research expenditures: $60,000. *Unit head:* Mitchell P. Koza, Dean, 856-225-6217, Fax: 856-225-6231, E-mail: mitchell.koza@camden.rutgers.edu. *Application contact:* Barbara Bickart, MBA Director, 856-225-6593, Fax: 856-225-6231, E-mail: bickart@camden.rutgers.edu.

Rutgers, The State University of New Jersey, Newark, Graduate School, Program in Management, Newark, NJ 07102. Offers accounting (PhD); accounting information systems (PhD); computer information systems (PhD); finance (PhD); information technology (PhD); international business (PhD); management science (PhD); marketing (PhD); organization management (PhD). *Accreditation:* AACSB. *Faculty:* 101 full-time (16 women), 3 part-time/adjunct (1 woman). *Students:* 60 full-time (29 women), 32 part-time (17 women); includes 57 minority (6 African Americans, 49 Asian Americans or Pacific Islanders, 2 Hispanic Americans). 279 applicants, 13% accepted, 32 enrolled. In 2006, 10 degrees awarded. *Degree requirements:* For doctorate, thesis/dissertation, cumulative exams. *Entrance requirements:* For doctorate, GMAT or GRE, minimum undergraduate B average. Additional exam requirements/recommendations for international students: Required—TOEFL. *Application deadline:* For fall admission, 4/1 for domestic students; for spring admission, 11/1 for domestic students. Applications are processed on a rolling basis. Application fee: $50. Electronic applications accepted. *Financial support:* In 2006–07, 8 fellowships with full and partial tuition reimbursements (averaging $18,000 per year), 7 research assistantships with full tuition reimbursements (averaging $18,347 per year), teaching assistantships with full tuition reimbursements (averaging $18,347 per year) were awarded; institutionally sponsored loans and tuition waivers (full and partial) also available. Support available to part-time students. Financial award application deadline: 2/15. *Faculty research:* Technology management, leadership and teams, consumer behavior, financial and markets, logistics. *Unit head:* Dr. Glenn Shafer, Director, 973-353-1604, Fax: 973-353-5691, E-mail: gshafer@rbs.rutgers.edu. *Application contact:* Goncalo Filipe, Senior Academic Coordinator, 973-353-1002, Fax: 973-353-5691, E-mail: gfilipe@rbsmail.rutgers.edu.

Rutgers, The State University of New Jersey, Newark, Rutgers Business School: Graduate Programs-Newark/New Brunswick, Newark, NJ 07102. Offers M Accy, MBA, MQF, PhD, Certificate, JD/MBA, MBA/MS, MD/MBA, MPH/MBA, MS/MBA. *Accreditation:* AACSB. Part-time and evening/weekend programs available. Terminal master's awarded for partial completion of doctoral program. *Degree requirements:* For doctorate, thesis/dissertation. *Entrance requirements:* For doctorate, GMAT. Additional exam requirements/recommendations for international students: Required—TOEFL. Electronic applications accepted. Expenses: Contact institution. *Faculty research:* Finance/economics, accounting, international business, operations research, marketing, organizational behavior.

Sacred Heart University, Graduate Studies, The John F. Welch College of Business, Fairfield, CT 06825-1000. Offers MBA, MSN/MBA. *Accreditation:* AACSB. Part-time and evening/weekend programs available. *Faculty:* 35 full-time, 27 part-time/adjunct. *Students:* 26 full-time (10 women), 138 part-time (72 women); includes 30 minority (13 African Americans, 8 Asian Americans or Pacific Islanders, 9 Hispanic Americans), 7 international. Average age 32. 58 applicants, 90% accepted, 47 enrolled. In 2006, 88 degrees awarded. *Degree requirements:* For master's, thesis or alternative. *Entrance requirements:* For master's, GMAT. Additional exam requirements/recommendations for international students: Required—TOEFL (minimum score 550 paper-based; 213 computer-based). *Application deadline:* Applications are processed on a rolling basis. Application fee: $50 ($100 for international students). Electronic applications accepted. *Expenses: Contact institution.* Full-time tuition and fees vary according to degree level and program. *Financial support:* Career-related internships or fieldwork, institutionally sponsored loans, and unspecified assistantships available. Support available to part-time students. Financial award applicants required to submit FAFSA. *Faculty research:* Management of organizations, international business management of technology. *Unit head:* Dr. Stephen Brown, Dean, 203-396-8084. *Application contact:* Meredith Woerz, Director of Graduate Admissions, 203-365-2619, Fax: 203-365-4732, E-mail: gradstudies@sacredheart.edu.

Sage Graduate School, Graduate School, Division of Management, Communications and Legal Studies, Program in Business Administration, Troy, NY 12180-4115. Offers business strategy (MBA); finance (MBA); human resources (MBA); marketing (MBA); JD/MBA; MBA/MS. Part-time and evening/weekend programs available. *Faculty:* 3 full-time (1 woman), 4 part-time/adjunct (2 women). *Students:* 9 full-time (5 women), 60 part-time (35 women); includes 10 minority (7 African Americans, 3 Hispanic Americans), 2 international. Average age 31. 58 applicants, 67% accepted, 27 enrolled. In 2006, 12 degrees awarded. *Entrance requirements:* For master's, minimum GPA of 2.75. Additional exam requirements/recommendations for international students: Required—TOEFL (minimum score 550 paper-based; 213 computer-based). *Application deadline:* Applications are processed on a rolling basis. Application fee: $40. *Expenses:* Tuition: Full-time $9,270; part-time $515 per credit hour. *Financial support:* Career-related internships or fieldwork, scholarships/grants, and unspecified assistantships available. Support available to part-time students. Financial award application deadline: 3/1; financial award applicants required to submit FAFSA. *Unit head:* Dr. David Kiner, Director, 518-292-1761, E-mail: kinerd@sage.edu. *Application contact:* Shannon K. Easton, Director of Graduate and Adult Admission, 518-244-2443, Fax: 518-244-6880, E-mail: sgsadm@sage.edu.

Saginaw Valley State University, College of Business and Management, Program in Business Administration, University Center, MI 48710. Offers MBA. *Accreditation:* AACSB. Part-time and evening/weekend programs available. *Faculty:* 10 full-time (3 women), 1 part-time/adjunct (0 women). *Students:* 22 full-time (7 women), 44 part-time (15 women); includes 4 minority (2 African Americans, 2 Asian Americans or Pacific Islanders), 17 international. Average age 30. 50 applicants, 88% accepted, 19 enrolled. In 2006, 23 degrees awarded. *Application deadline:* Applications are processed on a rolling basis. Application fee: $25. Electronic applications accepted. *Expenses:* Tuition, state resident: full-time $7,225; part-time $301 per credit hour. Tuition, nonresident: full-time $13,888; part-time $579 per credit hour. Required fees: $330; $14 per credit hour. Tuition and fees vary according to course load. *Financial support:* Federal Work-Study available. Support available to part-time students. Financial award application deadline: 4/15; financial award applicants required to submit FAFSA.

St. Ambrose University, College of Business, Program in Business Administration, Davenport, IA 52803-2898. Offers business administration (DBA); health care (MBA); human resources (MBA). *Accreditation:* ACBSP. Part-time and evening/weekend programs available. *Faculty:* 29 full-time (4 women), 24 part-time/adjunct (5 women). *Students:* 99 full-time (47 women), 352 part-time (164 women); includes 48 minority (28 African Americans, 6 Asian Americans or Pacific Islanders, 14 Hispanic Americans), 16 international. Average age 35. 201 applicants, 84% accepted, 112 enrolled. In 2006, 119 master's, 5 doctorates awarded. *Degree requirements:* For master's, thesis or alternative, capstone seminar, comprehensive exam (for some programs), registration; for doctorate, thesis/dissertation, oral and written exams, comprehensive exam, registration. *Entrance requirements:* For master's, GMAT; for doctorate, GMAT, master's degree. Additional exam requirements/recommendations for international students: Required—TOEFL. *Application deadline:* For fall admission, 8/15 priority date for domestic students; for winter admission, 12/15 for domestic students; for spring admission, 1/1 for domestic students. Applications are processed on a rolling basis. Application fee: $25. Electronic applications accepted. *Expenses: Contact institution. Financial support:* In 2006–07, 338 students received support, including 8 research assistantships with partial tuition reimbursements available; career-related internships or fieldwork, scholarships/grants, tuition waivers (partial), and unspecified assistantships also available. Support available to part-time students. Financial award application deadline: 3/15; financial award applicants required to submit FAFSA. *Unit head:* Allison S. Ambrose, Director of MBA Academic Services, 563-333-6155, Fax: 563-333-6243, E-mail: ambroseallisons@sau.edu. *Application contact:* Elizabeth Berridge, Director of Graduate Student Recruitment, 563-333-6271, Fax: 563-333-6268, E-mail: berridgeelizabethb@sau.edu.

St. Bonaventure University, School of Graduate Studies, School of Business, St. Bonaventure, NY 14778-2284. Offers accounting (Adv C); accounting and finance (MBA); finance (Adv C); management (Adv C); management and marketing (MBA); marketing (Adv C); professional leadership (Adv C). *Accreditation:* AACSB. Part-time and evening/weekend programs available. *Entrance requirements:* For master's, GMAT. Additional exam requirements/recommendations for international students: Required—TOEFL. *Faculty research:* Stock options, small business, market relationships, auditing, taxes.

St. Cloud State University, School of Graduate Studies, G.R. Herberger College of Business, St. Cloud, MN 56301-4498. Offers management and finance (MBA), including finance; marketing and general business (MBA), including marketing. *Accreditation:* AACSB. Part-time and evening/weekend programs available. *Faculty:* 62 full-time (17 women), 4 part-time/adjunct (1 woman). *Students:* 35 full-time (11 women), 98 part-time (39 women); includes 9 minority (5 African Americans, 1 American Indian/Alaska Native, 3 Asian Americans or Pacific Islanders), 21 international. 67 applicants, 84% accepted. In 2006, 87 degrees awarded. *Degree requirements:* For master's, thesis or alternative. *Entrance requirements:* For master's, GMAT, minimum GPA of 2.75. Additional exam requirements/recommendations for international students: Required—MELAB; Recommended—TOEFL (minimum score 550 paper-based; 213 computer-based), IELTS (minimum score 7). *Application deadline:* For fall admission, 6/1 priority date for domestic students, 4/1 for international students; for spring admission, 10/1 priority date for domestic students, 8/1 for international students. Applications are processed on a rolling basis. Application fee: $35. Electronic applications accepted. *Expenses: Contact institution. Financial support:* Federal Work-Study, scholarships/grants, and unspecified assistantships available. Financial award application deadline: 3/1. *Unit head:* Dr. P.N. Subba, Graduate Director, 320-308-3212. *Application contact:* Linda Lou Krueger, School of Graduate Studies, 320-308-2113, Fax: 320-308-5371, E-mail: lekrueger@stcloudstate.edu.

St. Edward's University, School of Management and Business, Austin, TX 78704. Offers MA, MBA, MS, Certificate. Part-time and evening/weekend programs available. *Faculty:* 21 full-time (9 women), 33 part-time/adjunct (8 women). *Students:* 69 full-time (40 women), 569 part-time (281 women); includes 179 minority (40 African Americans, 3 American Indian/Alaska Native, 36 Asian Americans or Pacific Islanders, 100 Hispanic Americans), 27 international. Average age 34. 254 applicants, 76% accepted, 160 enrolled. In 2006, 218 degrees awarded. *Degree requirements:* For master's, minimum 24 hours in residence. *Entrance requirements:* For master's, GMAT or GRE General Test, minimum GPA of 2.75 in last 60 hours of course work. Additional exam requirements/recommendations for international students: Required—TOEFL (minimum score 550 paper-based; 213 computer-based; 79 iBT). *Application deadline:* For fall admission, 8/1 for domestic students, 7/1 for international students; for spring admission, 12/1 for domestic students, 11/1 for international students. Applications are processed on a rolling basis. Application fee: $45 ($50 for international students). Electronic applications accepted. *Expenses:* Tuition: Full-time $11,682; part-time $649 per credit hour. Full-time tuition and fees vary according to course load and program. *Financial support:* In 2006–07, 9 students received support. Scholarships/grants available. Financial award applicants required to submit FAFSA. *Faculty research:* Business ethics, organizational management, minority entrepreneurship, globalization, system design. *Unit head:* Marsha Kelliher, Dean, 512-448-8588, Fax: 512-448-8492, E-mail: marshak@stedwards.edu. *Application contact:* Bridget Sowinski, Director, Center for Academic Progress, 512-428-1061, Fax: 512-428-1032, E-mail: bridgets@stedwards.edu.

Saint Francis University, Graduate School of Business and Human Resource Management, Business Administration Program, Loretto, PA 15940-0600. Offers MBA. Part-time and evening/weekend programs available. *Faculty:* 7 full-time (1 woman), 4 part-time/adjunct (1 woman). *Students:* 8 full-time (3 women), 131 part-time (37 women); includes 2 minority (both African Americans) Average age 32. 35 applicants, 97% accepted, 30 enrolled. In 2006, 32 degrees awarded. *Entrance requirements:* For master's, GMAT, 2 letters of recommendation, minimum GPA of 2.75. Additional exam requirements/recommendations for international students: Required—TOEFL (minimum score 550 paper-based; 213 computer-based; 57 iBT). *Application deadline:* For fall admission, 8/1 priority date for domestic and international students; for spring admission, 12/1 for domestic and international students. Applications are processed on a rolling basis. Application fee: $30. *Expenses: Contact institution. Financial support:* Unspecified assistantships available. *Application contact:* Roxane Hogue, Coordinator, Graduate Business Programs, 814-472-3026, Fax: 814-472-3369, E-mail: rhogue@franics.edu.

St. John Fisher College, Office of the Provost, Ronald L. Bittner School of Business, MBA Program, Rochester, NY 14618-3597. Offers MBA. *Accreditation:* AACSB. Part-time and evening/weekend programs available. *Faculty:* 11 full-time (2 women), 1 part-time/adjunct (0 women). *Students:* 34 full-time (21 women), 54 part-time (20 women); includes 4 African Americans, 3 Asian Americans or Pacific Islanders, 1 Hispanic American. Average age 33. 74 applicants, 61% accepted, 35 enrolled. In 2006, 41 degrees awarded. *Degree requirements:* For master's, capstone project. *Entrance requirements:* For master's, GMAT, minimum GPA of 3.0, 2 letters of recommendation. Additional exam requirements/recommendations for international students: Required—TOEFL (minimum score 575 paper-based; 233 computer-based; 80 iBT). *Application deadline:* For fall admission, 7/1 for domestic students; for spring admission, 10/30 for domestic students. Applications are processed on a rolling basis. Application fee: $30. *Expenses: Contact institution.* Tuition and fees vary according to program. *Financial support:* Federal Work-Study and scholarships/grants available. Financial award application deadline: 2/15; financial award applicants required to submit FAFSA. *Faculty research:* Business strategy, consumer behavior, cross-cultural management practices, international finance, organizational trust. *Application contact:* Dina Natale, MBA Admissions Coordinator, 585-385-8357, Fax: 585-385-8344, E-mail: dnatale@sjfc.edu.

St. John's University, The Peter J. Tobin College of Business, Queens, NY 11439. Offers MBA, MS, Adv C, JD/MBA. *Accreditation:* AACSB. Part-time and evening/weekend programs available. *Faculty:* 98 full-time (20 women), 65 part-time/adjunct (13 women). *Students:* 239 full-time (125 women), 434 part-time (192 women); includes 162 minority (52 African Americans, 66 Asian Americans or Pacific Islanders, 44 Hispanic Americans), 202 international. Average age 27. 716 applicants, 66% accepted, 225 enrolled. In 2006, 300 degrees awarded. *Degree requirements:* For master's, thesis optional. *Entrance requirements:* For master's, GMAT, minimum GPA of 3.0, 2 letters of recommendation, resumé. Additional exam requirements/recommendations for international students: Required—TOEFL (minimum score 500 paper-based; 173 computer-based). *Application deadline:* For fall admission, 5/1 priority date for domestic and international students; for spring admission, 11/1 priority date for domestic and

Business Administration and Management—General

St. John's University (continued)
international students. Applications are processed on a rolling basis. Application fee: $40. Electronic applications accepted. *Expenses: Contact institution.* Tuition and fees vary according to program. *Financial support:* In 2006–07, 364 students received support, including 47 research assistantships with full and partial tuition reimbursements available (averaging $15,894 per year); scholarships/grants also available. Support available to part-time students. Financial award application deadline: 3/1; financial award applicants required to submit FAFSA. Total annual research expenditures: $10,107. *Unit head:* Dr. Steven Papamarcos, Dean, 718-990-6477, Fax: 718-990-5966, E-mail: papamars@stjohns.edu. *Application contact:* Nicole T. Bryan, Assistant Dean, 718-990-2599, Fax: 718-990-5242, E-mail: mbaadmissions@stjohns.edu.

Saint Joseph College, Graduate Division, Department of Management Science, West Hartford, CT 06117-2700. Offers MS. *Entrance requirements:* For master's, letters of recommendation, minimum GPA of 2.67. Electronic applications accepted.

St. Joseph's College, New York, Graduate Programs, Program in Business, Field of Executive Business Administration, Brooklyn, NY 11205-3688. Offers EMBA.

See Close-Up on page 317.

Saint Joseph's College of Maine, Program in Business Administration, Standish, ME 04084-5263. Offers quality leadership (MBA). Part-time programs available. *Faculty:* 15 part-time/adjunct (5 women). *Students:* Average age 40. 71 applicants, 93% accepted, 61 enrolled. *Entrance requirements:* For master's, 2 years work experience. *Expenses:* Tuition: Part-time $350 per credit. *Unit head:* Dr. Gregory Gull, Director, 207-893-7988, Fax: 207-892-7423, E-mail: ggull@sjcme.edu. *Application contact:* 800-752-4723, Fax: 207-892-7480, E-mail: info@sjcme.edu.

St. Joseph's College, Suffolk Campus, Executive MBA Program, Patchogue, NY 11772-2399. Offers EMBA.

St. Joseph's College, Suffolk Campus, Program in Management, Patchogue, NY 11772-2399. Offers health care (AC); health care management (MS); human resource management (AC); human resources management (MS); organizational management (MS).

Saint Joseph's University, Erivan K. Haub School of Business, Philadelphia, PA 19131-1395. Offers MBA, MS, Certificate, Post Master's Certificate, DO/MBA. *Accreditation:* AACSB. Part-time and evening/weekend programs available. Postbaccalaureate distance learning degree programs offered (minimal on-campus study). *Faculty:* 39 full-time (9 women), 27 part-time/adjunct (5 women). *Students:* 186 full-time (66 women), 674 part-time (315 women); includes 117 minority (60 African Americans, 1 American Indian/Alaska Native, 35 Asian Americans or Pacific Islanders, 21 Hispanic Americans), 61 international. Average age 32. In 2006, 326 degrees awarded. *Entrance requirements:* For master's, GMAT, MAT, GRE, letters of recommendation, resumé. Additional exam requirements/recommendations for international students: Required—TOEFL (minimum score 550 paper-based; 213 computer-based). *Application deadline:* For fall admission, 7/15 priority date for domestic students, 4/15 for international students; for winter admission, 1/15 for international students; for spring admission, 11/15 priority date for domestic students, 10/15 for international students. Applications are processed on a rolling basis. Application fee: $35. Electronic applications accepted. *Financial support:* In 2006–07, 29 students received support, including research assistantships with full and partial tuition reimbursements available (averaging $4,000 per year), teaching assistantships with full and partial tuition reimbursements available (averaging $4,000 per year); scholarships/grants and unspecified assistantships also available. Financial award application deadline: 2/1; financial award applicants required to submit FAFSA. *Faculty research:* Food marketing, agriculture, finance and accounting systems, consumer acceptance. Total annual research expenditures: $3.4 million. *Unit head:* Dr. Joseph A. DiAngelo, Dean, 610-660-1645, Fax: 610-660-1649, E-mail: jodiange@sju.edu. *Application contact:* Sena Owereko-Andah, Assistant Director of Graduate Admissions, 610-660-1108, Fax: 610-660-1224, E-mail: sowereko@sju.edu.

Saint Joseph's University, Erivan K. Haub School of Business, Professional MBA Program, Program in Management, Philadelphia, PA 19131-1395. Offers MBA. *Accreditation:* AACSB. Part-time and evening/weekend programs available. *Faculty:* 12 full-time (1 woman), 6 part-time/adjunct (1 woman). *Students:* 5 full-time (0 women), 66 part-time (28 women); includes 5 minority (4 African Americans, 1 Asian American or Pacific Islander), 3 international. Average age 30. In 2006, 25 degrees awarded. *Entrance requirements:* For master's, GMAT, 2 letters of recommendation, resumé. Additional exam requirements/recommendations for international students: Required—TOEFL. *Application deadline:* For fall admission, 7/15 for domestic students, 4/15 for international students; for spring admission, 11/15 for domestic students, 10/15 for international students. Applications are processed on a rolling basis. Application fee: $35. *Financial support:* In 2006–07, 2 research assistantships with partial tuition reimbursements (averaging $2,000 per year) were awarded; unspecified assistantships also available. Financial award application deadline: 5/1. *Unit head:* Dr. Elizabeth Doherty, Chair, 610-660-1987, E-mail: doherty@sju.edu.

Saint Leo University, Graduate Business Studies, Saint Leo, FL 33574-6665. Offers accounting (MBA); business (MBA); criminal justice (MBA); human resource administration (MBA); information security management (MBA); sport business (MBA). Part-time and evening/weekend programs available. Postbaccalaureate distance learning degree programs offered (no on-campus study). *Faculty:* 17 full-time (5 women), 24 part-time/adjunct (6 women). *Students:* 298 full-time (187 women), 368 part-time (215 women); includes 195 minority (132 African Americans, 3 American Indian/Alaska Native, 23 Asian Americans or Pacific Islanders, 37 Hispanic Americans), 6 international. Average age 36. 863 applicants, 59% accepted, 282 enrolled. In 2006, 156 degrees awarded. *Degree requirements:* For master's, thesis. *Entrance requirements:* For master's, GMAT, 5 years of professional work experience, resumé, 2 letters of recommendation. Additional exam requirements/recommendations for international students: Required—TOEFL (minimum score 550 paper-based; 213 computer-based). *Application deadline:* For fall admission, 7/1 priority date for domestic students; for spring admission, 11/12 priority date for domestic students. Applications are processed on a rolling basis. Application fee: $45. Electronic applications accepted. *Expenses: Contact institution. Financial support:* In 2006–07, 39 students received support. Career-related internships or fieldwork, Federal Work-Study, and scholarships/grants available. Support available to part-time students. Financial award application deadline: 3/1; financial award applicants required to submit FAFSA. *Unit head:* Dr. Robert Robertson, Director, 352-588-8758, Fax: 352-588-8912, E-mail: mba@saintleo.edu. *Application contact:* Scott Cathcart, Vice President of Enrollment, 800-707-8846, Fax: 352-588-7873, E-mail: grad.admission@saintleo.edu.

Saint Louis University, Graduate School, John Cook School of Business, Program in Business Administration, St. Louis, MO 63103-2097. Offers MBA. *Accreditation:* AACSB. Part-time and evening/weekend programs available. *Faculty:* 37 full-time (9 women), 15 part-time/adjunct (4 women). *Students:* 50 full-time (16 women), 244 part-time (85 women); includes 31 minority (12 African Americans, 1 American Indian/Alaska Native, 11 Asian Americans or Pacific Islanders, 7 Hispanic Americans), 8 international. Average age 29. 256 applicants, 55% accepted, 109 enrolled. In 2006, 87 degrees awarded. *Entrance requirements:* For master's, GMAT, letter of recommendation, resumé. Additional exam requirements/recommendations for international students: Required—TOEFL (minimum score 525 paper-based; 194 computer-based). *Application deadline:* For fall admission, 4/15 priority date for domestic and international students. Applications are processed on a rolling basis. Application fee: $90. Electronic applications accepted. *Expenses: Contact institution. Financial support:* In 2006–07, 63 students received support. Federal Work-Study, scholarships/grants, traineeships, health care benefits, and unspecified assistantships available. Support available to part-time students. Financial award application deadline: 6/1; financial award applicants required to submit FAFSA. *Unit head:* Kathy Day, Director, 314-977-2201, Fax: 314-977-3897, E-mail: dayka@slu.edu. *Application contact:* 314-977-2013, Fax: 314-977-1416, E-mail: mba@slu.edu.

See Close-Up on page 319.

Saint Martin's University, Graduate Programs, Division of Economics and Business Administration, Lacey, WA 98503-1297. Offers MBA. Part-time and evening/weekend programs available. *Entrance requirements:* For master's, GMAT. Additional exam requirements/recommendations for international students: Required—TOEFL.

Saint Mary's College of California, Graduate Business Programs, Evening MBA Program, Moraga, CA 94575. Offers MBA. Part-time and evening/weekend programs available. *Faculty:* 3 full-time (2 women), 6 part-time/adjunct (0 women). *Students:* Average age 28. 29 applicants, 86% accepted, 17 enrolled. In 2006, 18 degrees awarded. *Degree requirements:* For master's, 4 half-day management practica. *Entrance requirements:* For master's, GMAT. Additional exam requirements/recommendations for international students: Required—TOEFL. *Application deadline:* Applications are processed on a rolling basis. Application fee: $50. *Expenses: Contact institution. Financial support:* Available to part-time students. Application deadline: 3/2; *Application contact:* Bob Peterson, Director of Admissions, 925-631-4505, Fax: 925-376-6521, E-mail: smcmba@stmarys-ca.edu.

Saint Mary's College of California, Graduate Business Programs, Executive MBA Program, Moraga, CA 94575. Offers MBA. Part-time and evening/weekend programs available. *Faculty:* 12 full-time (2 women), 10 part-time/adjunct (0 women). *Students:* 158 full-time (54 women); includes 49 minority (8 African Americans, 22 Asian Americans or Pacific Islanders, 19 Hispanic Americans). Average age 38. 96 applicants, 86% accepted, 73 enrolled. In 2006, 102 degrees awarded. *Entrance requirements:* For master's, 5 years of business experience, managerial position. Additional exam requirements/recommendations for international students: Required—TOEFL. *Application deadline:* Applications are processed on a rolling basis. Application fee: $50. *Expenses: Contact institution. Financial support:* Available to part-time students. Application deadline: 3/2; *Application contact:* Bob Peterson, Director of Admissions, 925-631-4504, Fax: 925-376-6521, E-mail: smcmba@stmarys-ca.edu.

Saint Mary's College of California, School of Liberal Arts, Program in Leadership, Moraga, CA 94575. Offers MA. Part-time and evening/weekend programs available. Postbaccalaureate distance learning degree programs offered (minimal on-campus study). *Faculty:* 14 part-time/adjunct (8 women). *Students:* Average age 42. 14 applicants, 93% accepted. In 2006, 43 degrees awarded. *Degree requirements:* For master's, research project. *Entrance requirements:* For master's, letters of recommendation, interview. *Application deadline:* For fall admission, 9/1 priority date for domestic students; for winter admission, 12/1 priority date for domestic students; for spring admission, 3/31 priority date for domestic students. Applications are processed on a rolling basis. Application fee: $50. *Expenses: Contact institution. Financial support:* In 2006–07, 2 students received support. Available to part-time students. Applicants required to submit FAFSA. *Faculty research:* Futures, leadership, organizational change, values, adult learning, transformative learning. *Unit head:* Kenneth Otter, Director of Admissions, 925-631-8692, Fax: 925-631-9412, E-mail: kotter@stmarys-ca.edu. *Application contact:* Kenneth Otter, Director of Admissions, 925-631-8692, Fax: 925-631-9412, E-mail: kotter@stmarys-ca.edu.

Saint Mary's University, Faculty of Commerce, Halifax, NS B3H 3C3, Canada. Offers business administration (MBA); management (PhD). *Accreditation:* AACSB. Part-time and evening/weekend programs available. *Degree requirements:* For master's, research project; for doctorate, thesis/dissertation. *Entrance requirements:* For master's, GMAT, minimum B average; for doctorate, GMAT or GRE, MBA or other masters level degree, minimum B+ average. Expenses: Contact institution.

Saint Mary's University of Minnesota, School of Graduate and Professional Programs, Program in Business Administration, Winona, MN 55987-1399. Offers business administration (MBA); executive business leadership (Certificate); finance manager (Certificate). *Unit head:* Dr. Karen Gulliver, Director, 612-728-5147, Fax: 612-728-5121, E-mail: kgulliver@smumn.edu.

Saint Mary's University of Minnesota, School of Graduate and Professional Programs, Program in Management, Minneapolis, MN 55404. Offers MA. *Unit head:* Dushan G. Knezevich, Director, 612-728-5156, Fax: 612-728-5121, E-mail: dknezevi@smumn.edu.

St. Mary's University of San Antonio, Graduate School, Bill Greehey School of Business, San Antonio, TX 78228-8507. Offers accounting (M Acc), including taxation; business administration (MBA), including finance, international business, management; JD/M Acc; JD/MBA. *Accreditation:* AACSB. Part-time and evening/weekend programs available. Postbaccalaureate distance learning degree programs offered (minimal on-campus study). *Faculty:* 17 full-time (6 women), 1 part-time/adjunct (0 women). *Students:* 20 full-time (9 women), 88 part-time (42 women); includes 45 minority (2 African Americans, 2 Asian Americans or Pacific Islanders, 41 Hispanic Americans), 4 international. Average age 30. In 2006, 37 degrees awarded. *Degree requirements:* For master's, thesis, comprehensive exam, registration. *Entrance requirements:* For master's, GMAT. Additional exam requirements/recommendations for international students: Required—TOEFL (minimum score 550 paper-based; 213 computer-based). *Application deadline:* Applications are processed on a rolling basis. Application fee: $30. Electronic applications accepted. *Expenses:* Tuition: Full-time $10,890; part-time $605 per hour. Required fees: $500. Tuition and fees vary according to degree level. *Financial support:* Research assistantships, career-related internships or fieldwork, Federal Work-Study, institutionally sponsored loans, scholarships/grants, health care benefits, and unspecified assistantships available. Financial award application deadline: 3/31. *Faculty research:* International operations, job satisfaction, total quality management, taxation, stress management. *Unit head:* Dr. Keith A Russell, Dean.

Saint Michael's College, Graduate Programs, Program in Administration and Management, Colchester, VT 05439. Offers MSA, CAMS. Part-time and evening/weekend programs available. *Faculty:* 8 full-time (2 women), 10 part-time/adjunct (2 women). *Students:* 7 full-time (3 women), 51 part-time (32 women); includes 1 minority (Asian American or Pacific Islander), 4 international. Average age 37. 11 applicants, 64% accepted, 7 enrolled. In 2006, 27 degrees awarded. *Degree requirements:* For master's, portfolio. *Entrance requirements:* For master's, 3 years of work experience or GMAT or GRE, minimum undergraduate GPA of 2.8. Additional exam requirements/recommendations for international students: Required—TOEFL (minimum score 550 paper-based; 213 computer-based). *Application deadline:* Applications are processed on a rolling basis. Application fee: $35. Electronic applications accepted. *Financial support:* Teaching assistantships with full tuition reimbursements, Federal Work-Study, scholarships/grants, and unspecified assistantships available. Financial award application deadline: 4/15; financial award applicants required to submit FAFSA. *Faculty research:* Learnership/leadership, international banking, top-quality management and organizational changes, national health care, management and ethics. *Unit head:* Dr. Robert Letovsky, Director, 802-654-2477. *Application contact:* Dr. Paul Olsen, Assistant Director, 802-654-2369, Fax: 802-654-2664, E-mail: polsen@smcvt.edu.

Saint Peter's College, MBA Programs, Jersey City, NJ 07306-5997. Offers finance (MBA); international business (MBA); management (MBA); management information systems (MBA); marketing (MBA); MBA/MS. Part-time and evening/weekend programs available. *Degree requirements:* For master's, exit presentation. *Entrance requirements:* For master's, GMAT or MAT. *Faculty research:* International finance, operations research, expert systems, networking, decision support systems.

St. Thomas Aquinas College, Division of Business Administration, Sparkill, NY 10976. Offers business administration (MBA); finance (MBA); management (MBA); marketing (MBA). Part-time and evening/weekend programs available. *Entrance requirements:* For master's, GMAT. Additional exam requirements/recommendations for international students: Required—TOEFL. Electronic applications accepted.

Announcement: The Master of Business Administration is for individuals seeking to obtain an MBA in finance, management, marketing, or general business studies. This program is held on weekends. Friday, Saturday, or Sunday classes run for 9 weeks each. For information, call 845-398-4109.

St. Thomas University, School of Graduate Studies, Department of Business Administration, Miami Gardens, FL 33054-6459. Offers M Acc, MBA, Certificate. Part-time and evening/weekend programs available. *Degree requirements:* For master's, comprehensive exam. *Entrance requirements:* Additional exam requirements/recommendations for international students: Required—TOEFL. Electronic applications accepted.

St. Thomas University, School of Graduate Studies, Department of Management, Miami Gardens, FL 33054-6459. Offers accounting (MBA); general management (MSM, Certificate); health management (MBA, MSM, Certificate); human resource management (MBA, MSM, Certificate); international business (MBA, MIB, MSM, Certificate); justice administration (MSM, Certificate); management accounting (MSM, Certificate); public management (MSM, Certificate). Part-time and evening/weekend programs available. *Degree requirements:* For master's, comprehensive exam. *Entrance requirements:* For master's, interview, minimum GPA of 3.0 or GMAT. Additional exam requirements/recommendations for international students: Required—TOEFL. Electronic applications accepted.

Saint Xavier University, Graduate Studies, Graham School of Management, Chicago, IL 60655-3105. Offers e-commerce (MBA); employee health benefits (Certificate); finance (MBA, MS); financial analysis and investments (MBA); financial planning (MBA, Certificate); financial trading and practice (MBA, Certificate); generalist/administration (MBA); health administration (MBA, MS); managed care (Certificate); management (MBA, MS); marketing (MBA); public and non-profit management (MBA); public health (MPH); service management (MBA); training and performance management (MBA); MBA/MS. *Accreditation:* ACBSP. Part-time and evening/weekend programs available. *Faculty:* 27. *Students:* 67 full-time (32 women), 291 part-time (152 women). Average age 35. In 2006, 61 degrees awarded. *Entrance requirements:* For master's, GMAT, minimum GPA of 3.0, 2 years of work experience. *Application deadline:* For fall admission, 8/15 for domestic students. Applications are processed on a rolling basis. Application fee: $35. Electronic applications accepted. *Expenses: Contact institution. Financial support:* Career-related internships or fieldwork available. Support available to part-time students. Financial award applicants required to submit FAFSA. *Unit head:* Dr. John Eber, Dean, 773-298-3601, Fax: 773-298-3601, E-mail: eber@sxu.edu. *Application contact:* Beth Gierach, Managing Director of Admission, 773-298-3053, Fax: 773-298-3076, E-mail: gierach@sxu.edu.

Salem International University, School of Business, Salem, WV 26426-0500. Offers information security (eMBA); international business (MBA). Part-time programs available. Postbaccalaureate distance learning degree programs offered (no on-campus study). *Faculty:* 8 full-time (2 women), 13 part-time/adjunct (4 women). *Students:* 50 full-time (22 women), 88 part-time (31 women); includes 1 minority (African American), 87 international. 9 applicants, 56% accepted, 5 enrolled. In 2006, 1 degree awarded. *Degree requirements:* For master's, registration. *Entrance requirements:* For master's, GRE or GMAT, minimum undergraduate GPA of 2.5, course work in business, resumé. Additional exam requirements/recommendations for international students: Required—TOEFL (minimum score 550 paper-based). *Application deadline:* For fall admission, 8/15 priority date for domestic and international students; for winter admission, 12/15 priority date for domestic and international students; for spring admission, 4/15 priority date for domestic and international students. Applications are processed on a rolling basis. Application fee: $25. Electronic applications accepted. *Expenses: Contact institution.* One-time fee: $25 part-time. Tuition and fees vary according to program. *Financial support:* In 2006–07, 1 student received support. Career-related internships or fieldwork, institutionally sponsored loans, and tuition waivers (partial) available. *Faculty research:* Organizational behavior strategy, marketing services. *Unit head:* Dean, 304-326-1609, Fax: 304-326-1246. *Application contact:* Thomas White, Director of Admissions, 304-326-1549, Fax: 304-326-1246, E-mail: admission@salemiu.edu.

Salem State College, Graduate School, Program in Business Administration, Salem, MA 01970-5353. Offers MBA. Part-time and evening/weekend programs available. *Faculty:* 12 part-time/adjunct (1 woman). *Students:* 28 full-time (15 women), 48 part-time (23 women); includes 4 minority (1 African American, 3 Asian Americans or Pacific Islanders), 22 international. Average age 32. In 2006, 20 degrees awarded. *Entrance requirements:* For master's, GMAT. *Application deadline:* Applications are processed on a rolling basis. Application fee: $35. *Unit head:* Raminder Luther, Coordinator, 978-542-7006, E-mail: rluther@salemstate.edu.

Salisbury University, Graduate Division, Department of Business Administration, Salisbury, MD 21801-6837. Offers MBA. *Accreditation:* AACSB. Part-time and evening/weekend programs available. *Faculty:* 10 full-time (0 women), 1 (woman) part-time/adjunct. *Students:* 41 full-time (22 women), 45 part-time (27 women); includes 5 minority (1 African American, 2 Asian Americans or Pacific Islanders, 2 Hispanic Americans), 15 international. Average age 28. 51 applicants, 100% accepted, 41 enrolled. In 2006, 39 degrees awarded. *Entrance requirements:* For master's, GMAT, resumé. Additional exam requirements/recommendations for international students: Required—TOEFL (minimum score 550 paper-based; 213 computer-based). *Application deadline:* For fall admission, 8/1 for domestic students; for spring admission, 1/1 for domestic students. Applications are processed on a rolling basis. Application fee: $45. Electronic applications accepted. *Expenses:* Tuition, state resident: part-time $260 per credit hour. Tuition, nonresident: part-time $546 per credit hour. Required fees: $52 per credit hour. *Financial support:* In 2006–07, 2 research assistantships with full tuition reimbursements were awarded; institutionally sponsored loans and scholarships/grants also available. Support available to part-time students. Financial award applicants required to submit FAFSA. *Unit head:* Janine M. Vienna, Director, 410-548-3983, Fax: 410-546-6208, E-mail: jmvienna@ssu.edu.

Salve Regina University, Graduate Studies, Program in Business Administration, Newport, RI 02840-4192. Offers business administration (MBA); business studies (Certificate); human resources management (Certificate); management (Certificate); organizational development (Certificate). Part-time and evening/weekend programs available. Postbaccalaureate distance learning degree programs offered (minimal on-campus study). *Faculty:* 1 (woman) full-time, 9 part-time/adjunct (2 women). *Students:* 21 full-time (6 women), 70 part-time (30 women); includes 1 minority (African American) Average age 35. 90 applicants, 70% accepted, 54 enrolled. In 2006, 42 degrees awarded. *Entrance requirements:* For master's, GMAT, GRE General Test, or MAT, 6 undergraduate credits each in accounting, economics, and quantitative analysts. Additional exam requirements/recommendations for international students: Required—TOEFL or IELTS. *Application deadline:* For fall admission, 3/15 priority date for domestic and international students; for spring admission, 9/15 priority date for domestic and international students. Applications are processed on a rolling basis. Application fee: $50. Electronic applications accepted. *Financial support:* Career-related internships or fieldwork and Federal Work-Study available. Support available to part-time students. Financial award application deadline: 3/1. *Unit head:* Dr. Myra Edelstein, Director, 401-341-2153, E-mail: edelstem@salve.edu. *Application contact:* Karen E. Johnson, Graduate Admissions Counselor, 401-341-2153, Fax: 401-341-2973, E-mail: johnsonke@salve.edu.

Salve Regina University, Graduate Studies, Program in Management, Newport, RI 02840-4192. Offers MS, Certificate. Postbaccalaureate distance learning degree programs offered. *Unit head:* Dr. Myra Edelstein, Director, 401-341-2153, E-mail: edelstem@salve.edu.

Samford University, School of Business, Birmingham, AL 35229-0002. Offers M Acc, MBA, JD/M Acc, JD/MBA, M Div/MBA, MBA/M Acc, MBA/MSN. *Accreditation:* AACSB. Part-time and evening/weekend programs available. *Faculty:* 11 full-time (1 woman). *Students:* 20 full-time (13 women), 69 part-time (44 women); includes 15 minority (14 African Americans, 1 Hispanic American), 3 international. Average age 29. 67 applicants, 79% accepted, 18 enrolled. In 2006, 39 degrees awarded. *Entrance requirements:* For master's, GMAT. Additional exam requirements/recommendations for international students: Required—TOEFL (minimum score 550 paper-based; 213 computer-based). *Application deadline:* For fall admission, 7/15 priority date for domestic students; for spring admission, 12/15 for domestic students. Applications are processed on a rolling basis. Application fee: $25. *Expenses:* Tuition: Part-time $500 per credit. One-time fee: $25 part-time. Full-time tuition and fees vary according to program and student level. *Financial support:* In 2006–07, 6 students received support. Career-related internships or fieldwork and institutionally sponsored loans available. Support available to part-time students. Financial award applicants required to submit FAFSA. *Faculty research:* Health care, organizational behavior, leadership, supply chain, management information system. *Unit head:* Dr. Beck Taylor, Dean, 205-726-2364, Fax: 205-726-2464, E-mail: btaylor@samford.edu. *Application contact:* Doug Smith, Director of Graduate Programs, 205-726-2931, Fax: 205-726-2540, E-mail: dusmith@samford.edu.

Sam Houston State University, College of Business Administration, Huntsville, TX 77341. Offers business administration (MBA); general business and finance (MS), including finance. *Accreditation:* AACSB. Part-time and evening/weekend programs available. *Faculty:* 31 full-time (7 women). *Students:* 95 full-time (40 women), 118 part-time (56 women); includes 37 minority (12 African Americans, 1 American Indian/Alaska Native, 6 Asian Americans or Pacific Islanders, 18 Hispanic Americans), 15 international. Average age 30. In 2006, 81 degrees awarded. *Entrance requirements:* For master's, GMAT. *Application deadline:* For fall admission, 8/1 for domestic students; for spring admission, 12/1 for domestic students. Applications are processed on a rolling basis. Application fee: $20. *Expenses:* Tuition, state resident: full-time $5,904; part-time $164 per semester hour. Tuition, nonresident: full-time $15,804; part-time $439 per semester hour. Required fees: $1,374; $462 per semester. *Financial support:* Research assistantships, Federal Work-Study, institutionally sponsored loans, and unspecified assistantships available. Financial award application deadline: 5/31; financial award applicants required to submit FAFSA. *Unit head:* Dr. R. Dean Lewis, Dean, 936-294-1254, Fax: 936-294-3612, E-mail: bed_rdl@shsu.edu. *Application contact:* Dr. Leroy Ashorn, Advisor, 936-294-4040, E-mail: busgrad@shsu.edu.

San Diego State University, Graduate and Research Affairs, College of Business Administration, Department of Management, San Diego, CA 92182. Offers entrepreneurship (MS); human resources management (MS); management science (MS). Part-time and evening/weekend programs available. *Students:* 16 full-time (6 women), 23 part-time (13 women); includes 5 minority (4 Asian Americans or Pacific Islanders, 1 Hispanic American), 9 international. Average age 30. 24 applicants, 75% accepted, 6 enrolled. In 2006, 21 degrees awarded. *Degree requirements:* For master's, thesis or alternative. *Entrance requirements:* For master's, GMAT, resumé, letters of reference. Additional exam requirements/recommendations for international students: Required—TOEFL. *Application deadline:* For fall admission, 4/15 for domestic and international students; for spring admission, 11/1 for domestic students, 10/1 for international students. Applications are processed on a rolling basis. Application fee: $55. Electronic applications accepted. *Financial support:* In 2006–07, 14 teaching assistantships were awarded; fellowships, research assistantships, career-related internships or fieldwork also available. Financial award applicants required to submit FAFSA. Total annual research expenditures: $11,500. *Unit head:* Gangaram Singh, Chair, 619-594-5306, Fax: 619-594-3272. *Application contact:* Information Contact, E-mail: sdsumba@mail.sdsu.edu.

San Diego State University, Graduate and Research Affairs, College of Business Administration, Program in Business Administration, San Diego, CA 92182. Offers MBA. *Accreditation:* AACSB. Part-time programs available. *Students:* 131 full-time (52 women), 136 part-time (39 women); includes 53 minority (1 African American, 2 American Indian/Alaska Native, 37 Asian Americans or Pacific Islanders, 13 Hispanic Americans), 47 international. 516 applicants, 42% accepted, 59 enrolled. In 2006, 103 degrees awarded. *Degree requirements:* For master's, thesis or alternative. *Entrance requirements:* For master's, GMAT, resumé, letters of reference. Additional exam requirements/recommendations for international students: Required—TOEFL. *Application deadline:* For fall admission, 5/1 for domestic and international students; for spring admission, 11/1 for domestic students, 10/1 for international students. Applications are processed on a rolling basis. Electronic applications accepted. *Financial support:* In 2006–07, 1 teaching assistantship was awarded. Financial award applicants required to submit FAFSA. *Unit head:* Dr. Ken Marino, Associate Dean, 619-594-5217. *Application contact:* Information Contact, E-mail: sdsumba@mail.sdsu.edu.

San Francisco State University, Division of Graduate Studies, College of Business, Program in Business Administration, San Francisco, CA 94132-1722. Offers MBA. *Accreditation:* AACSB. Part-time and evening/weekend programs available. *Faculty:* 100. *Students:* 850 (408 women). 839 applicants, 56% accepted, 241 enrolled. In 2006, 220 degrees awarded. *Degree requirements:* For master's, thesis, essay test. *Entrance requirements:* For master's, GMAT, minimum GPA of 2.7 in last 60 units. Additional exam requirements/recommendations for international students: Required—TOEFL (minimum score 550 paper-based; 213 computer-based). *Application deadline:* For fall admission, 5/1 priority date for domestic students, 4/1 for international students; for spring admission, 11/1 for domestic students, 10/15 for international students. Applications are processed on a rolling basis. Application fee: $55. *Financial support:* Application deadline: 3/1. *Application contact:* Armaan Moattori, Graduate Admission Coordinator, 415-338-1395, Fax: 415-405-0495, E-mail: amoatt@sfsu.edu.

San Jose State University, Graduate Studies and Research, Lucas Graduate School of Business, Programs in Business Administration, San Jose, CA 95192-0001. Offers MBA. *Accreditation:* AACSB. *Students:* 39 full-time (11 women), 172 part-time (75 women); includes 92 minority (1 African American, 83 Asian Americans or Pacific Islanders, 8 Hispanic Americans), 38 international. Average age 32. 332 applicants, 34% accepted, 32 enrolled. In 2006, 159 degrees awarded. *Degree requirements:* For master's, thesis or alternative, comprehensive exam. *Entrance requirements:* For master's, GMAT, minimum GPA of 3.0. *Application deadline:* For fall admission, 6/29 for domestic students; for spring admission, 11/30 for domestic students. Applications are processed on a rolling basis. Application fee: $59. Electronic applications accepted. *Financial support:* Applicants required to submit FAFSA.

Santa Clara University, Leavey School of Business, Executive Business Administration Program, Santa Clara, CA 95053. Offers EMBA. *Accreditation:* AACSB. *Students:* 57 full-time (9 women); includes 18 minority (2 African Americans, 15 Asian Americans or Pacific Islanders, 1 Hispanic American), 4 international. Average age 40. 47 applicants, 74% accepted, 29 enrolled. In 2006, 30 degrees awarded. *Entrance requirements:* Additional exam requirements/recommendations for international students: Required—TOEFL. *Application deadline:* For fall admission, 6/1 for domestic students. Applications are processed on a rolling basis. Application fee: $75. Electronic applications accepted. *Expenses:* Tuition: Part-time $627 per unit. Tuition and fees vary according to program. *Financial support:* Application deadline: 3/1; *Unit head:* Elizabeth Ford, Assistant Dean of Admissions, 408-554-2752, Fax: 408-554-4571.

Santa Clara University, Leavey School of Business, Program in Business Administration, Santa Clara, CA 95053. Offers MBA, JD/MBA. *Accreditation:* AACSB. Part-time programs available. *Students:* 160 full-time (68 women), 828 part-time (246 women); includes 353 minority (9 African Americans, 1 American Indian/Alaska Native, 325 Asian Americans or Pacific Islanders, 18 Hispanic Americans), 215 international. Average age 33. 381 applicants, 65% accepted, 179 enrolled. In 2006, 279 degrees awarded. *Entrance requirements:* For master's, GMAT. Additional exam requirements/recommendations for international students: Required—TOEFL. *Application deadline:* For fall admission, 6/1 for domestic students; for winter admission, 9/1 for domestic students; for spring admission, 12/1 for domestic students. Applications are processed on a rolling basis. Application fee: $75 ($100 for international students). Electronic applications accepted. *Expenses:* Tuition: Part-time $627 per unit. Tuition and fees vary according to program. *Financial support:* Fellowships, research assistantships, career-related internships or fieldwork, Federal Work-Study, institutionally sponsored loans, and scholarships/grants available. Support available to part-time students. Financial award application deadline: 3/1; financial award applicants required to submit FAFSA. *Unit head:* Dr. David F. Caldwell, Senior Associate Dean, 408-554-4114. *Application contact:* Elizabeth Ford, Assistant Dean of Admissions, 408-554-2752, Fax: 408-554-4571.

Schiller International University, MBA Program, Madrid, Spain, Madrid, Spain. Offers international business (MBA). Part-time programs available. *Faculty:* 6 full-time, 4 part-time/adjunct. *Students:* 7 full-time, 3 part-time. Average age 28. *Degree requirements:* For master's, thesis optional. *Entrance requirements:* Additional exam requirements/recommendations for

Business Administration and Management—General

Schiller International University (continued)
international students: Required—TOEFL (minimum score 550 paper-based; 213 computer-based). *Application deadline:* For fall admission, 8/1 priority date for domestic and international students; for spring admission, 12/1 priority date for domestic and international students. Applications are processed on a rolling basis. Application fee: $60. *Expenses:* Tuition: Full-time $20,958; part-time $1,652 per course. Tuition and fees vary according to degree level. *Financial support:* In 2006–07, 8 students received support. Career-related internships or fieldwork, scholarships/grants, tuition waivers (partial), and unspecified assistantships available. Support available to part-time students. Financial award application deadline: 3/30; financial award applicants required to submit FAFSA. *Unit head:* Lynn Bergunde, Adviser, 34-91-448-2488, Fax: 34-91-445-2110, E-mail: admissions@schillermadrid.edu. *Application contact:* Susan Russeff, Associate Director of Admissions, 727-736-5082, Fax: 727-734-0359, E-mail: admissions@schiller.edu.

Schiller International University, MBA Program Paris, France, Paris, France. Offers international business (MBA). Bilingual French/English MBA available for native French speakers. Part-time and evening/weekend programs available. *Faculty:* 5 full-time (1 woman), 10 part-time/adjunct (5 women). *Students:* 50. In 2006, 12 degrees awarded. *Degree requirements:* For master's, thesis or alternative, comprehensive exam, registration. *Entrance requirements:* Additional exam requirements/recommendations for international students: Required—TOEFL (minimum score 550 paper-based; 213 computer-based). *Application deadline:* For fall admission, 8/1 priority date for domestic and international students; for spring admission, 12/1 priority date for domestic and international students. Applications are processed on a rolling basis. Application fee: $60. Tuition charges are reported in euros. *Expenses:* Tuition: Full-time 21,812 euros; part-time 1,724 euros per course. Tuition and fees vary according to degree level. *Financial support:* In 2006–07, 14 students received support; teaching assistantships, scholarships/grants, tuition waivers (partial), and unspecified assistantships available. Support available to part-time students. Financial award application deadline: 3/30; financial award applicants required to submit FAFSA. *Unit head:* Hassan Mansoor, Adviser, 1-4538-5601, Fax: 1-4538-5430, E-mail: info-schiller@schillerparis.com. *Application contact:* Kamala Dontamsetti, Associate Director of Admissions, 813-736-5082 Ext. 240, Fax: 813-734-0359, E-mail: admissions@schiller.edu.

Schiller International University, MBA Programs, Florida, Largo, FL 33770. Offers financial planning (MBA); information technology (MBA); international business (MBA); international hotel and tourism management (MBA). Part-time and evening/weekend programs available. Postbaccalaureate distance learning degree programs offered (no on-campus study). *Faculty:* 5 full-time (0 women), 10 part-time/adjunct (1 woman). *Students:* 146. Average age 25. In 2006, 39 degrees awarded. *Degree requirements:* For master's, thesis optional. *Entrance requirements:* Additional exam requirements/recommendations for international students: Required—TOEFL (minimum score 550 paper-based; 213 computer-based). *Application deadline:* For fall admission, 8/1 priority date for domestic and international students; for spring admission, 12/1 priority date for domestic and international students. Applications are processed on a rolling basis. Application fee: $60. *Expenses:* Tuition: Full-time $17,920; part-time $1,420 per course. *Financial support:* Federal Work-Study, scholarships/grants, tuition waivers (partial), and unspecified assistantships available. Support available to part-time students. Financial award application deadline: 3/30; financial award applicants required to submit FAFSA. *Unit head:* Dr. Cathy Eberhart, Head, 727-736-5082, Fax: 727-734-0359. *Application contact:* Susan Russeff, Associate Director of Admissions, 727-736-5082, Fax: 727-734-0359, E-mail: admissions@schiller.edu.

Schiller International University, MBA Programs, Heidelberg, Germany, Heidelberg, Germany. Offers international business (MBA, MIM); management of information technology (MBA). Part-time and evening/weekend programs available. *Faculty:* 7 full-time (3 women), 14 part-time/adjunct (4 women). *Students:* 28 full-time, 4 part-time. Average age 28. In 2006, 15 degrees awarded. *Degree requirements:* For master's, thesis optional. *Entrance requirements:* Additional exam requirements/recommendations for international students: Required—TOEFL (minimum score 550 paper-based; 213 computer-based). *Application deadline:* For fall admission, 8/1 priority date for domestic and international students; for spring admission, 12/1 priority date for domestic and international students. Applications are processed on a rolling basis. Application fee: $60. Tuition charges are reported in euros. *Expenses:* Tuition: Full-time 20,938 euros; part-time 1,651 euros per course. *Financial support:* In 2006–07, 32 students received support. Scholarships/grants, tuition waivers (partial), and unspecified assistantships available. Support available to part-time students. Financial award application deadline: 3/30; financial award applicants required to submit FAFSA. *Faculty research:* Leadership, international economy, foreign direct investment. *Unit head:* Dr. Nicolle Macho, Director, 49-6221-458135, Fax: 49-6221-402703, E-mail: campus@siu-heidelberg.de. *Application contact:* Susan Russeff, Assistant Director of Admissions, 727-736-5082, Fax: 727-734-0359, E-mail: admissions@schiller.edu.

Schiller International University, MBA Program, Strasbourg, France Campus, Strasbourg, France. Offers international business (MBA). Part-time and evening/weekend programs available. Postbaccalaureate distance learning degree programs offered (no on-campus study). *Faculty:* 8. *Students:* Average age 28. In 2006, 13 degrees awarded. *Degree requirements:* For master's, GMAT before graduation, oral comprehensive exam or thesis. *Entrance requirements:* For master's, BBA. Additional exam requirements/recommendations for international students: Recommended—TOEFL (minimum score 550 paper-based; 213 computer-based). *Application deadline:* For fall admission, 8/1 priority date for domestic and international students; for spring admission, 12/1 priority date for domestic and international students. Applications are processed on a rolling basis. Application fee: $60. *Expenses:* Tuition: Part-time $1,282 per course. *Financial support:* Teaching assistantships, tuition waivers (partial) and unspecified assistantships available. Support available to part-time students. Financial award application deadline: 3/30; financial award applicants required to submit FAFSA. *Unit head:* Anne Zedler, Director, 33-3884-58464, Fax: 33-3884-58460, E-mail: siustrmba@aol.com. *Application contact:* Kamala Dontamsetti, Associate Director of Admissions, 727-736-5082 Ext. 240, Fax: 727-734-0359, E-mail: admissions@schiller.edu.

Schiller International University, American College of Switzerland, MBA Program, Leysin, Switzerland. Offers international business (MBA). Part-time programs available. Postbaccalaureate distance learning degree programs offered (no on-campus study). *Faculty:* 6. *Students:* 8 full-time. Average age 23. *Degree requirements:* For master's, thesis or alternative, comprehensive exam, registration. *Entrance requirements:* For master's, bachelor's degree in business or BA with specific core courses. Additional exam requirements/recommendations for international students: Recommended—TOEFL (minimum score 550 paper-based; 213 computer-based). *Application deadline:* For fall admission, 8/1 priority date for domestic and international students; for spring admission, 12/1 priority date for domestic and international students. Applications are processed on a rolling basis. Application fee: $60. *Expenses:* Tuition: Full-time $22,622; part-time $1,178 per course. *Financial support:* In 2006–07, 3 students received support, including teaching assistantships (averaging $6,895 per year); career-related internships or fieldwork, scholarships/grants, tuition waivers (partial), and unspecified assistantships also available. Support available to part-time students. Financial award application deadline: 4/1; financial award applicants required to submit FAFSA. *Unit head:* Nancy Carroll, Provost, 41-244930303, Fax: 41-244930300, E-mail: acs_provost@bluewin.ch. *Application contact:* Bethani Ann Delong Vehapi, Director of Admissions, 41-244930309, Fax: 41-244930300, E-mail: siuadmissions@bluewin.ch.

School for International Training, Graduate Programs, Master's Programs in Intercultural Service, Leadership, and Management, Brattleboro, VT 05302-0676. Offers conflict transformation (MA); intercultural service, leadership, and management (MA); international education (MA); management (MS); social justice in intercultural relations (MA); sustainable development (MA). Postbaccalaureate distance learning degree programs offered (minimal on-campus study). *Students:* 182 full-time (116 women), 298 part-time (215 women); includes 60 minority (27 African Americans, 1 American Indian/Alaska Native, 14 Asian Americans or Pacific Islanders, 18 Hispanic Americans), 96 international. Average age 30. 634 applicants, 73% accepted, 157 enrolled. In 2006, 84 master's awarded. *Degree requirements:* For master's, one foreign language, thesis. *Entrance requirements:* For master's, 3 letters of reference. Additional exam requirements/recommendations for international students: Required—TOEFL. *Application deadline:* Applications are processed on a rolling basis. Application fee: $50. *Expenses:* Tuition: Full-time $27,355; part-time $638 per credit hour. Required fees: $1,092. *Financial support:* Career-related internships or fieldwork, Federal Work-Study, institutionally sponsored loans, and scholarships/grants available. Financial award application deadline: 3/1; financial award applicants required to submit FAFSA. *Faculty research:* Intercultural communication, conflict resolution, advising and training, world issues, international business. *Unit head:* Marla Solomon, Graduate Dean, 802-258-3325, Fax: 802-258-3241, E-mail: marla.solomon@sit.edu. *Application contact:* Information Contact, 800-336-1616, Fax: 802-258-3500, E-mail: admissions@sit.edu.

Seattle Pacific University, Graduate School, School of Business and Economics, Program in Business Administration, Seattle, WA 98119-1997. Offers MBA. *Accreditation:* AACSB. *Students:* 18 full-time (7 women), 73 part-time (34 women); includes 19 minority (6 African Americans, 11 Asian Americans or Pacific Islanders, 2 Hispanic Americans), 7 international. 47 applicants, 81% accepted, 21 enrolled. In 2006, 37 degrees awarded. *Application contact:* Debbie Wysomierski, Assistant Graduate Director, 206-281-2753, Fax: 206-281-2733, E-mail: mba@spu.edu.

Seattle University, Albers School of Business and Economics, Program in Business Administration, Seattle, WA 98122-1090. Offers MBA, MIB, Certificate, JD/MBA, JD/MIB. *Accreditation:* AACSB. Part-time and evening/weekend programs available. *Faculty:* 20 full-time (5 women), 13 part-time/adjunct (5 women). *Students:* 120 full-time (50 women), 528 part-time (215 women); includes 128 minority (12 African Americans, 2 American Indian/Alaska Native, 100 Asian Americans or Pacific Islanders, 14 Hispanic Americans), 73 international. Average age 30. 304 applicants, 52% accepted, 124 enrolled. In 2006, 167 master's, 7 other advanced degrees awarded. *Entrance requirements:* For master's, GMAT, minimum GPA of 3.0, 1 year of related work experience. Additional exam requirements/recommendations for international students: Required—TOEFL. *Application deadline:* For fall admission, 8/20 priority date for domestic students; for winter admission, 11/20 for domestic students; for spring admission, 2/20 for domestic students. Applications are processed on a rolling basis. Application fee: $55. *Financial support:* Career-related internships or fieldwork and Federal Work-Study available. Support available to part-time students. Financial award applicants required to submit FAFSA. *Unit head:* Dr. Bill Weis, Director, 206-296-5701, Fax: 206-296-5795. *Application contact:* Janet Shandley, Associate Dean of Graduate Admissions, 206-296-5900, Fax: 206-298-5656, E-mail: grad_admissions@seattleu.edu.

Seton Hall University, Stillman School of Business, South Orange, NJ 07079-2692. Offers MBA, MS, Certificate, MADIR/MSIB, MBA/MSIB. *Accreditation:* AACSB. Part-time and evening/weekend programs available. *Faculty:* 57 full-time (13 women), 30 part-time/adjunct (3 women). *Students:* 70 full-time (19 women), 404 part-time (165 women); includes 52 minority (20 African Americans, 19 Asian Americans or Pacific Islanders, 13 Hispanic Americans). Average age 27. 271 applicants, 49% accepted, 77 enrolled. In 2006, 195 degrees awarded. *Median time to degree:* Master's–1.5 years full-time, 2.5 years part-time. *Degree requirements:* For master's, registration. *Entrance requirements:* For master's, GMAT (or 10 years of managerial experience), minimum GPA of 2.75; for Certificate, master's degree. Additional exam requirements/recommendations for international students: Required—TOEFL (minimum score 550 paper-based; 213 computer-based). *Application deadline:* For fall admission, 6/1 priority date for domestic students, 5/1 for international students; for spring admission, 11/1 priority date for domestic students, 10/1 for international students. Applications are processed on a rolling basis. Application fee: $75 ($100 for international students). Electronic applications accepted. *Expenses:* Contact institution. *Financial support:* In 2006–07, 60 students received support, including research assistantships with full and partial tuition reimbursements available (averaging $5,400 per year); career-related internships or fieldwork, Federal Work-Study, scholarships/grants, health care benefits, and unspecified assistantships also available. Support available to part-time students. Financial award application deadline: 6/1; financial award applicants required to submit FAFSA. *Faculty research:* Financial, hedge funds, international business, legal issues, disclosure and branding. Total annual research expenditures: $500,000. *Unit head:* Dr. Karen E. Boroff, Dean, 973-761-9013, Fax: 973-275-2465, E-mail: boroffka@shu.edu. *Application contact:* Catherine Bianchi, Director of Graduate Admissions, 973-761-9220, Fax: 973-761-9208, E-mail: biancha@shu.edu.

Seton Hill University, Program in Business Administration, Greensburg, PA 15601. Offers MBA. Part-time and evening/weekend programs available. *Faculty:* 4 full-time (2 women), 8 part-time/adjunct (2 women). *Students:* 34 full-time (24 women), 64 part-time (41 women); includes 8 minority (5 African Americans, 2 Asian Americans or Pacific Islanders, 1 Hispanic American), 5 international. Average age 33. 49 applicants, 84% accepted, 34 enrolled. In 2006, 52 master's awarded. *Entrance requirements:* For master's, resumé, minimum GPA of 3.0. Additional exam requirements/recommendations for international students: Required—TOEFL (minimum score 600 paper-based; 250 computer-based). *Application deadline:* For fall admission, 8/15 priority date for domestic students; for spring admission, 12/15 for domestic students. Applications are processed on a rolling basis. Application fee: $35. Electronic applications accepted. *Expenses:* Tuition: Part-time $620 per credit. Required fees: $100 per semester. *Financial support:* In 2006–07, 84 students received support. Scholarships/grants, tuition waivers (partial), and unspecified assistantships available. Support available to part-time students. Financial award application deadline: 8/15; financial award applicants required to submit FAFSA. *Faculty research:* Women in business, entrepreneurship. *Unit head:* Paul Mahady, Interim Director, 724-830-1012, Fax: 724-830-1294, E-mail: mahady@setonhill.edu. *Application contact:* Michelle Kelly, Advisor, 724-830-4634, Fax: 724-830-1891, E-mail: mkelly@setonhill.edu.

Shenandoah University, Byrd School of Business, Winchester, VA 22601-5195. Offers business administration (MBA); health care management (Certificate); information systems and computer technology (Certificate). *Accreditation:* AACSB. Part-time and evening/weekend programs available. *Faculty:* 11 full-time (2 women), 1 part-time/adjunct (0 women). *Students:* 23 full-time (9 women), 10 part-time (3 women); includes 1 minority (Asian American or Pacific Islander), 7 international. Average age 29. 27 applicants, 59% accepted, 12 enrolled. In 2006, 23 degrees awarded. *Entrance requirements:* For master's, GMAT or GRE, 2 letters of recommendation, resumé. Additional exam requirements/recommendations for international students: Required—TOEFL (minimum score 527 paper-based; 197 computer-based; 71 iBT). *Application deadline:* Applications are processed on a rolling basis. Application fee: $30. Electronic applications accepted. *Expenses:* Tuition: Full-time $12,200; part-time $610 per credit. Required fees: $150. Full-time tuition and fees vary according to course load and program. *Financial support:* In 2006–07, 28 students received support, including 4 fellowships with partial tuition reimbursements available (averaging $1,518 per year), 8 teaching assistantships with partial tuition reimbursements available (averaging $4,278 per year); career-related internships or fieldwork, institutionally sponsored loans, and unspecified assistantships also available. Support available to part-time students. Financial award application deadline: 3/15; financial award applicants required to submit FAFSA. *Faculty research:* Business and economics, marketing. *Unit head:* Dr. Randy Boxx, Dean, 540-665-4572, Fax: 540-665-5437, E-mail: rboxx@su.edu. *Application contact:* David Anthony, Dean of Admissions, 540-665-4581, Fax: 540-665-4627, E-mail: admit@su.edu.

See Close-Up on page 321.

Shippensburg University of Pennsylvania, School of Graduate Studies, John L. Grove College of Business, Shippensburg, PA 17257-2299. Offers business administration (MBA). *Accreditation:* AACSB. Part-time and evening/weekend programs available. Postbaccalaureate distance learning degree programs offered (minimal on-campus study). *Faculty:* 21 full-time (7 women), 3 part-time/adjunct (0 women). *Students:* 13 full-time (5 women), 96 part-time (38 women); includes 8 minority (3 African Americans, 3 Asian Americans or Pacific Islanders, 2 Hispanic Americans), 1 international. Average age 30. 76 applicants, 66% accepted, 34 enrolled. In 2006, 21 degrees awarded. *Entrance requirements:* For master's, GMAT (if GPA less than 3.0), resumé, relevant work/classroom experience. Additional exam requirements/recommendations for international students: Required—TOEFL (minimum score 560 paper-based; 220 computer-based). *Application deadline:* For fall admission, 3/1 for international students; for spring admission, 7/1 for international students. Applications are processed on a rolling basis. Application fee: $30. Electronic applications accepted. *Expenses:* Tuition, state resident: part-time $336 per credit. Tuition, nonresident: part-time $538 per credit. *Financial support:* In 2006–07, 4 research assistantships with full tuition reimbursements (averaging $3,125 per year) were awarded; career-related internships or fieldwork, scholarships/grants, and unspecified assistantships also available. Support available to part-time students. Financial award application deadline: 3/1; financial award applicants required to submit FAFSA. *Unit head:* Dr. Robert Rollins, Director, 717-477-1483, Fax: 717-477-4015, E-mail: rdroll@ship.edu. *Application contact:* Renee Payne, Associate Dean of Graduate Admissions, 717-477-1231, Fax: 717-477-4016, E-mail: rmpayn@ship.edu.

Shorter College, School of Business, Rome, GA 30165. Offers business administration (MBA); business leadership (MA). Evening/weekend programs available. *Degree requirements:* For master's, project. *Entrance requirements:* For master's, GMAT, MAT (optional), minimum undergraduate GPA of 2.75 in last 60 hours, 3 years of work experience. Additional exam requirements/recommendations for international students: Required—TOEFL (minimum score 551 paper-based; 213 computer-based). *Faculty research:* Systems design, leadership, pedagogy using technology.

Silver Lake College, Division of Graduate Studies, Program in Management and Organizational Behavior, Manitowoc, WI 54220-9319. Offers MS. Part-time and evening/weekend programs available. Postbaccalaureate distance learning degree programs offered (minimal on-campus study). *Faculty:* 19 part-time/adjunct (8 women). *Students:* 15 full-time (13 women), 54 part-time (35 women). Average age 35. 30 applicants, 67% accepted, 15 enrolled. In 2006, 39 degrees awarded. *Degree requirements:* For master's, thesis optional. *Entrance requirements:* For master's, interview, minimum undergraduate GPA of 3.0, writing sample, two letters of recommendation. Additional exam requirements/recommendations for international students: Required—TOEFL. *Application deadline:* For fall admission, 8/1 priority date for domestic students; for spring admission, 12/1 priority date for domestic students. Applications are processed on a rolling basis. Application fee: $35. Electronic applications accepted. *Expenses:* Tuition: Full-time $6,120; part-time $340 per credit. *Financial support:* Career-related internships or fieldwork, Federal Work-Study, and scholarships/grants available. Support available to part-time students. Financial award applicants required to submit FAFSA. *Unit head:* Suzanne Lawrence, Director- MOB Program, 920-686-6198, Fax: 920-684-9734, E-mail: law@silver.sl.edu. *Application contact:* Jamie Grant, Associate Director- Admissions, 800-236-4752 Ext. 186, Fax: 920-684-7082, E-mail: jgrant@silver.sl.edu.

Simmons College, Simmons School of Management, Boston, MA 02115. Offers entrepreneurship (Certificate); management (MBA). Part-time and evening/weekend programs available. *Faculty:* 25 full-time (21 women), 8 part-time/adjunct (4 women). *Students:* 32 full-time (all women), 117 part-time (all women); includes 23 minority (14 African Americans, 7 Asian Americans or Pacific Islanders, 2 Hispanic Americans), 2 international. Average age 31. 98 applicants, 82% accepted, 53 enrolled. In 2006, 99 master's, 5 other advanced degrees awarded. *Entrance requirements:* For master's, GMAT, 3 letters of recommendation, minimum 2 years experience, resumé. Additional exam requirements/recommendations for international students: Required—TOEFL. *Application deadline:* For fall admission, 6/30 priority date for domestic and international students; for spring admission, 12/1 priority date for domestic students, 11/15 priority date for international students. Applications are processed on a rolling basis. Application fee: $75. Electronic applications accepted. *Expenses: Contact institution. Financial support:* Institutionally sponsored loans, scholarships/grants, and unspecified assistantships available. Support available to part-time students. Financial award application deadline: 3/1; financial award applicants required to submit FAFSA. *Faculty research:* Women, leadership, gender equity, organizational effectiveness, general management negotiations, entrepreneurship. *Unit head:* Dr. Deborah Merrill-Sands, Dean, 617-521-3827, Fax: 617-521-3881. *Application contact:* Denise Haile, Director of Admissions, 617-521-3840, Fax: 617-521-3880, E-mail: somadm@simmons.edu.

Simon Fraser University, Graduate Studies, Faculty of Business Administration, Burnaby, BC V5A 1S6, Canada. Offers business administration (EMBA); decision support systems (MBA); international business (MBA); management, organization studies (MBA); marketing (MBA); MBA/MRM. *Accreditation:* AACSB. Postbaccalaureate distance learning degree programs offered. *Degree requirements:* For master's, thesis or written project. *Entrance requirements:* For master's, minimum GPA of 3.0. Additional exam requirements/recommendations for international students: Required—TOEFL. Expenses: Contact institution. *Faculty research:* Leadership, marketing and technology, wealth management.

Slippery Rock University of Pennsylvania, Graduate Studies (Recruitment), College of Business, Information, and Social Sciences, Slippery Rock, PA 16057-1383. Offers MS. *Accreditation:* ACBSP. Part-time programs available. *Entrance requirements:* For master's, GMAT (preferred), GRE General Test, or MAT, CPA certificate, minimum GPA of 2.75, professional experience. Additional exam requirements/recommendations for international students: Required—TOEFL (minimum score 550 paper-based; 213 computer-based). *Application deadline:* For fall admission, 7/1 priority date for domestic and international students; for spring admission, 11/1 priority date for domestic and international students. Applications are processed on a rolling basis. Application fee: $25. Electronic applications accepted. *Expenses:* Tuition, state resident: part-time $336 per credit. Tuition, nonresident: part-time $538 per credit. Required fees: $84 per credit. $37 per semester. *Financial support:* Career-related internships or fieldwork, Federal Work-Study, scholarships/grants, and unspecified assistantships available. Support available to part-time students. Financial award application deadline: 5/1; financial award applicants required to submit FAFSA. *Unit head:* Dr. Bruce Russell, Dean, 724-738-2607, Fax: 724-738-4767, E-mail: bruce.russell@sru.edu. *Application contact:* April Longwell, Interim Director of Graduate Studies, 724-738-2051 Ext. 2116, Fax: 724-738-2146, E-mail: graduate.studies@sru.edu.

Sonoma State University, School of Business and Economics, Department of Business Administration, Rohnert Park, CA 94928-3609. Offers MBA. *Accreditation:* AACSB. Part-time and evening/weekend programs available. *Faculty:* 5 full-time (1 woman), 1 part-time/adjunct (0 women). *Students:* 4 full-time (1 woman), 37 part-time (13 women); includes 1 minority (African American) Average age 31. 24 applicants, 63% accepted, 7 enrolled. In 2006, 21 degrees awarded. *Degree requirements:* For master's, thesis or alternative. *Entrance requirements:* For master's, GMAT. *Application deadline:* For fall admission, 1/31 for domestic students; for spring admission, 8/31 for domestic students. Applications are processed on a rolling basis. Application fee: $55. *Expenses:* Tuition, nonresident: part-time $339 per unit. Required fees: $1,464 per term. *Financial support:* Fellowships, career-related internships or fieldwork, Federal Work-Study, and institutionally sponsored loans available. Support available to part-time students. Financial award application deadline: 3/2. *Unit head:* Dr. T. K. Clarke, Chair, 707-664-3115, E-mail: tk.clarke@sonoma.edu.

Southeastern Louisiana University, College of Business, Hammond, LA 70402. Offers business administration (MBA). *Accreditation:* AACSB. Part-time and evening/weekend programs available. *Faculty:* 25 full-time (4 women). *Students:* 111 full-time (51 women), 61 part-time (26 women); includes 19 minority (9 African Americans, 1 American Indian/Alaska Native, 4 Asian Americans or Pacific Islanders, 5 Hispanic Americans), 27 international. Average age 27. 65 applicants, 78% accepted, 38 enrolled. In 2006, 85 degrees awarded. *Entrance requirements:* For master's, GMAT, minimum AACSB index of 950, bachelor's degree with minimum GPA of 2.5. Additional exam requirements/recommendations for international students: Required—TOEFL (minimum score 525 paper-based; 195 computer-based). *Application deadline:* For fall admission, 7/15 priority date for domestic students, 6/1 priority date for international students; for spring admission, 12/1 priority date for domestic students, 10/1 priority date for international students. Applications are processed on a rolling basis. Application fee: $20 ($30 for international students). Electronic applications accepted. *Expenses:* Tuition, state resident: full-time $2,216; part-time $123 per credit. Tuition, nonresident: full-time $6,212; part-time $345 per credit. Required fees: $986; $55 per credit. Part-time tuition and fees vary according to course load. *Financial support:* Career-related internships or fieldwork, Federal Work-Study, institutionally sponsored loans, scholarships/grants, unspecified assistantships, and administrative assistantships available. Support available to part-time students. Financial award application deadline: 5/1; financial award applicants required to submit FAFSA. *Faculty research:* Radio frequency identification, corporate and portfolio diversification, effect of inexperienced workers on organizational performance, improving information technology project management, pay-for-performance methods. *Unit head:* Dr. Randy Settoon, Dean, 985-549-2258, Fax: 985-549-5038, E-mail: rsettoon@selu.edu. *Application contact:* Sandra Meyers, Graduate Admissions Analyst, 985-549-2066, Fax: 985-549-5632, E-mail: admissions@selu.edu.

Southeastern Oklahoma State University, Graduate School, School of Business, Durant, OK 74701-0609. Offers MBA, MS. *Accreditation:* ACBSP. Part-time and evening/weekend programs available. *Degree requirements:* For master's, thesis optional. *Entrance requirements:* For master's, GMAT, minimum GPA of 3.0 in last 60 hours or 2.75 overall. Additional exam requirements/recommendations for international students: Required—TOEFL (minimum score 550 paper-based; 213 computer-based). Electronic applications accepted.

Southeastern University, College of Graduate Studies, Program in Business Management, Washington, DC 20024-2788. Offers international management (MBA); management (MBA). Part-time and evening/weekend programs available. *Degree requirements:* For master's, thesis optional. *Entrance requirements:* Additional exam requirements/recommendations for international students: Required—TOEFL.

Southeast Missouri State University, School of Graduate Studies, Harrison College of Business, Cape Girardeau, MO 63701-4799. Offers accounting (MBA); environmental management (MBA); finance (MBA); general management (MBA); health administration (MBA); industrial management (MBA); international business (MBA). *Accreditation:* AACSB. Part-time and evening/weekend programs available. Postbaccalaureate distance learning degree programs offered (no on-campus study). *Faculty:* 33 full-time (10 women). *Students:* 35 full-time (18 women), 40 part-time (24 women); includes 5 minority (2 African Americans, 3 Asian Americans or Pacific Islanders), 9 international. Average age 27. 35 applicants, 86% accepted. In 2006, 23 degrees awarded. *Degree requirements:* For master's, applied research project. *Entrance requirements:* For master's, GMAT, minimum undergraduate GPA of 2.5. Additional exam requirements/recommendations for international students: Required—TOEFL (minimum score 550 paper-based; 213 computer-based). *Application deadline:* For fall admission, 8/1 for domestic students, 4/1 for international students; for spring admission, 11/21 for domestic students, 10/1 for international students. Applications are processed on a rolling basis. Application fee: $20 ($100 for international students). *Financial support:* In 2006–07, 54 students received support, including 31 research assistantships with full tuition reimbursements available (averaging $7,100 per year); career-related internships or fieldwork and unspecified assistantships also available. Financial award applicants required to submit FAFSA. *Unit head:* Dr. Kenneth Heischmidt, Director MBA Program, 573-651-2912, Fax: 573-651-5032, E-mail: kheischmidt@semo.edu. *Application contact:* Marsha L. Arant, Senior Administrative Assistant, Office of Graduate Studies, 573-651-2192, Fax: 573-651-2001, E-mail: marant@semo.edu.

Southern Adventist University, School of Business and Management, Collegedale, TN 37315-0370. Offers accounting (MBA); administration (MS); financial services (MFS); health care administration (MBA); human resource management (MBA); management (MBA); marketing (MBA). Part-time and evening/weekend programs available. Postbaccalaureate distance learning degree programs offered (no on-campus study). *Faculty:* 7 full-time (0 women), 2 part-time/adjunct (1 woman). *Students:* 18 full-time (8 women), 66 part-time (37 women); includes 15 minority (6 African Americans, 7 Asian Americans or Pacific Islanders, 2 Hispanic Americans). Average age 35. 32 applicants, 84% accepted, 24 enrolled. In 2006, 11 degrees awarded. *Entrance requirements:* For master's, GMAT. Additional exam requirements/recommendations for international students: Required—TOEFL. *Application deadline:* For fall admission, 8/1 priority date for domestic students, 7/1 for international students; for winter admission, 12/1 priority date for domestic students, 11/1 for international students; for spring admission, 4/1 priority date for domestic students, 3/1 for international students. Applications are processed on a rolling basis. Application fee: $25. Electronic applications accepted. *Financial support:* In 2006–07, 32 students received support. Scholarships/grants available. Financial award application deadline: 9/1; financial award applicants required to submit FAFSA. *Unit head:* Dr. Don Van Ornam, Dean, 423-236-2750, Fax: 423-236-1527, E-mail: dvanorna@southern.edu. *Application contact:* Linda Wilhelm, Admissions Coordinator, 423-236-2751, Fax: 423-236-1527, E-mail: sbm@southern.edu.

Southern Connecticut State University, School of Graduate Studies, School of Business, Department of Business Administration, New Haven, CT 06515-1355. Offers MBA. Part-time and evening/weekend programs available. *Faculty:* 7 full-time, 2 part-time/adjunct. *Students:* 64 full-time (30 women), 109 part-time (46 women); includes 67 minority (34 African Americans, 20 Asian Americans or Pacific Islanders, 13 Hispanic Americans). 107 applicants, 59% accepted, 46 enrolled. In 2006, 62 degrees awarded. *Entrance requirements:* For master's, GMAT, interview. *Application deadline:* For fall admission, 7/1 priority date for domestic students. Applications are processed on a rolling basis. Application fee: $50. Electronic applications accepted. *Financial support:* Application deadline: 4/15; *Unit head:* Dr. Omid Nodoushani, Director, 203-392-7030, Fax: 203-392-5988, E-mail: nodoushanio1@southernct.edu.

Southern Illinois University Carbondale, Graduate School, College of Business and Administration, Department of Business Administration, Carbondale, IL 62901-4701. Offers MBA, PhD, JD/MBA, MBA/MA, MBA/MS. *Accreditation:* AACSB. *Faculty:* 32 full-time (3 women). *Students:* 98 full-time (42 women), 69 part-time (26 women); includes 12 minority (3 African Americans, 1 American Indian/Alaska Native, 5 Asian Americans or Pacific Islanders, 3 Hispanic Americans), 82 international. Average age 26. 232 applicants, 34% accepted, 21 enrolled. In 2006, 92 master's, 14 doctorates awarded. *Degree requirements:* For doctorate, thesis/dissertation. *Entrance requirements:* For master's, GMAT, minimum GPA of 2.7; for doctorate, GMAT, minimum graduate GPA of 3.25. Additional exam requirements/recommendations for international students: Required—TOEFL. *Application deadline:* For fall admission, 6/15 priority date for domestic students. Applications are processed on a rolling basis. Application fee: $20. *Financial support:* In 2006–07, 108 students received support, including 2 fellowships with full tuition reimbursements available, 42 research assistantships with full tuition reimbursements available, 49 teaching assistantships with full tuition reimbursements available; Federal Work-Study, institutionally sponsored loans, and tuition waivers (full) also available. Support available to part-time students. *Faculty research:* Marketing, corporate finance, organizational behavior, accounting, MIS, international business. Total annual research expenditures: $200,000. *Application contact:* Julie Virgo, Administrative Aide, 618-453-3030, Fax: 618-453-7961, E-mail: jvirgo@siu.edu.

Announcement: The PhD in business administration degree program at SIUC is designed to prepare highly qualified individuals for teaching and research at academic institutions and for high-level administrative positions in business and government. Candidates must demonstrate in-depth knowledge of business administration and a high potential to undertake significant research in their selected area of specialization.

See Close-Up on page 323.

Southern Illinois University Edwardsville, Graduate Studies and Research, School of Business, Program in Business Administration, Edwardsville, IL 62026-0001. Offers business administration (MBA); management information systems (MBA). *Accreditation:* AACSB. Part-

Business Administration and Management—General

Southern Illinois University Edwardsville (continued)
time and evening/weekend programs available. *Students:* 33 full-time (18 women), 123 part-time (54 women); includes 8 minority (6 African Americans, 2 Asian Americans or Pacific Islanders), 7 international. Average age 33. 89 applicants, 58% accepted. In 2006, 66 degrees awarded. *Degree requirements:* For master's, thesis or alternative, final exam. *Entrance requirements:* For master's, GMAT. Additional exam requirements/recommendations for international students: Required—TOEFL. *Application deadline:* For fall admission, 7/20 for domestic students, 6/1 for international students; for spring admission, 12/14 for domestic students, 10/1 for international students. Application fee: $30. Electronic applications accepted. *Financial support:* Fellowships with full tuition reimbursements, research assistantships with full tuition reimbursements, teaching assistantships with full tuition reimbursements, career-related internships or fieldwork, Federal Work-Study, institutionally sponsored loans, traineeships, and unspecified assistantships available. Support available to part-time students. Financial award application deadline: 3/1; financial award applicants required to submit FAFSA. *Unit head:* Dr. Janice Joplin, Director, 618-650-2485.

Southern Methodist University, Cox School of Business, Dallas, TX 75275. Offers accounting (MSA); business (Exec MBA, MBA); management (MSM); JD/MBA; MBA/MA. *Accreditation:* AACSB. Part-time and evening/weekend programs available. *Faculty:* 68 full-time (16 women), 31 part-time/adjunct (8 women). *Students:* 472 full-time (130 women), 455 part-time (126 women); includes 231 minority (43 African Americans, 4 American Indian/Alaska Native, 112 Asian Americans or Pacific Islanders, 72 Hispanic Americans), 104 international. Average age 30. 318 applicants, 57% accepted, 76 enrolled. In 2006, 391 degrees awarded. *Degree requirements:* For master's, community service project, oral and written proficiency exams. *Entrance requirements:* For master's, GMAT. Additional exam requirements/recommendations for international students: Required—TOEFL. *Application deadline:* For fall admission, 4/30 priority date for domestic students; for spring admission, 12/30 priority date for domestic students. Applications are processed on a rolling basis. Application fee: $75. Electronic applications accepted. *Expenses: Contact institution. Financial support:* In 2006–07, 165 fellowships (averaging $20,000 per year), 10 research assistantships (averaging $2,800 per year) were awarded; career-related internships or fieldwork, scholarships/grants, and unspecified assistantships also available. Support available to part-time students. Financial award application deadline: 3/1; financial award applicants required to submit FAFSA. *Faculty research:* Corporate liquidity, strategy and network formation, outsourcing practices, advertising responses. *Unit head:* Dr. Albert W. Niemi, Dean, 214-768-3012, Fax: 214-768-3713, E-mail: aniemi@mail.cox.smu.edu. *Application contact:* Path Cudney, Director of MBA Admissions, 214-768-3001, Fax: 214-768-3956, E-mail: pcudney@mail.cox.smu.edu.

Southern Nazarene University, Graduate College, School of Business, Bethany, OK 73008. Offers MBA, MS Mgt. Part-time and evening/weekend programs available. *Students:* 152. Average age 27. In 2006, 151 degrees awarded. *Degree requirements:* For master's, thesis optional. *Entrance requirements:* For master's, GMAT, English proficiency exam, minimum GPA of 3.0 in last 60 hours/major, 2.7 overall. *Application deadline:* For fall admission, 8/1 priority date for domestic students. Applications are processed on a rolling basis. Application fee: $25 ($35 for international students). Electronic applications accepted. *Expenses:* Tuition: Part-time $507 per credit. *Unit head:* Jeff Seyfert, Interim Chair, 405-491-6358, E-mail: jseyfert@snu.edu.

Southern New Hampshire University, School of Business, Manchester, NH 03106-1045. Offers accounting (MS); business administration (MBA, Certificate), including accounting (Certificate), business administration (MBA), finance (Certificate), forensic accounting (Certificate), human resources management (Certificate), international business (Certificate), international sport management (Certificate), leadership of not for profit organizations (Certificate), marketing (Certificate), operations management (Certificate), sport management (Certificate), taxation (Certificate); finance (MS); hospitality and tourism leadership (Certificate); information technology (MS, Certificate); information technology/international business (Certificate); integrated marketing communications (Certificate); international business (MS, DBA); marketing (MS); operations and project management (MS); organizational leadership (MS); project management (Certificate); sport management (MS); MBA/Certificate. *Accreditation:* ACBSP. Part-time and evening/weekend programs available. Postbaccalaureate distance learning degree programs offered (no on-campus study). *Faculty:* 45 full-time, 75 part-time/adjunct. *Students:* 427 full-time (184 women), 774 part-time (428 women). Average age 32. In 2006, 682 master's, 1 doctorate awarded. Terminal master's awarded for partial completion of doctoral program. *Degree requirements:* For master's, one foreign language, thesis or alternative, comprehensive exam (for some programs); for doctorate, one foreign language, thesis/dissertation, comprehensive exam. *Entrance requirements:* For master's, minimum GPA of 2.5; for doctorate, GMAT. Additional exam requirements/recommendations for international students: Required—TOEFL (minimum score 500 paper-based). *Application deadline:* Applications are processed on a rolling basis. Application fee: $25. Electronic applications accepted. *Financial support:* Career-related internships or fieldwork, Federal Work-Study, institutionally sponsored loans, tuition waivers (partial), and unspecified assistantships available. Support available to part-time students. Financial award applicants required to submit FAFSA. *Unit head:* Dr. Martin Bradley, Dean, 603-644-3102, Fax: 603-644-3144, E-mail: m.bradley@snhu.edu. *Application contact:* Scott Durand, Director of Graduate Enrollment Services, 603-644-3102 Ext. 3338, Fax: 603-644-3144, E-mail: s.durand@snhu.edu.

See Close-Up on page 325.

Southern Oregon University, Graduate Studies, School of Business, Ashland, OR 97520. Offers MA Ed, MIM, MS Ed. *Degree requirements:* For master's, comprehensive exam. *Entrance requirements:* For master's, GMAT. Electronic applications accepted.

Southern Polytechnic State University, School of Engineering Technology and Management, Department of Business Administration, Marietta, GA 30060-2896. Offers MBA. *Accreditation:* ACBSP. Part-time and evening/weekend programs available. *Faculty:* 7 full-time (3 women), 2 part-time/adjunct (0 women). *Students:* 36 full-time (12 women), 54 part-time (22 women); includes 40 minority (32 African Americans, 8 Asian Americans or Pacific Islanders), 26 international. Average age 32. 75 applicants, 56% accepted, 30 enrolled. In 2006, 31 degrees awarded. *Degree requirements:* For master's, thesis optional. *Entrance requirements:* For master's, GMAT. Additional exam requirements/recommendations for international students: Required—TOEFL (minimum score 550 paper-based; 213 computer-based). *Application deadline:* For fall admission, 7/1 priority date for domestic students, 5/1 priority date for international students; for spring admission, 11/1 priority date for domestic students, 9/1 priority date for international students. Applications are processed on a rolling basis. Application fee: $20. Electronic applications accepted. *Expenses:* Tuition, state resident: part-time $422 per credit hour. Tuition, nonresident: part-time $835 per credit hour. *Financial support:* In 2006–07, 89 students received support, including 11 research assistantships with tuition reimbursements available (averaging $1,500 per year); career-related internships or fieldwork, scholarships/grants, and unspecified assistantships also available. Support available to part-time students. Financial award application deadline: 5/1; financial award applicants required to submit FAFSA. *Faculty research:* Management of technology, quality management, capacity planning, human-computer interaction/interface, enterprise integration planning, economic impact of educational institutions. *Unit head:* Dr. Ronny Richardson, Chair, 678-915-7440, Fax: 678-915-4967, E-mail: rrichard@spsu.edu. *Application contact:* Virginia A. Head, Director of Admissions, 678-915-4188, Fax: 678-915-7292, E-mail: vhead@spsu.edu.

Southern University and Agricultural and Mechanical College, Graduate School, College of Business, Baton Rouge, LA 70813. Offers MPA. *Accreditation:* AACSB. *Degree requirements:* For master's, comprehensive exam. *Entrance requirements:* For master's, GMAT. Additional exam requirements/recommendations for international students: Required—TOEFL. *Faculty research:* Accounting theory, auditing, governmental and non-profit accounting.

Southern Utah University, School of Business, Program in Business Administration, Cedar City, UT 84720-2498. Offers MBA. *Accreditation:* AACSB; ACBSP. Part-time programs available. *Faculty:* 7 full-time (1 woman). *Students:* 8 full-time (1 woman), 20 part-time (8 women); includes 1 minority (African American) Average age 30. 69 applicants, 87% accepted. In 2006, 29 degrees awarded. *Degree requirements:* For master's, thesis or alternative. *Application deadline:* For fall admission, 8/1 priority date for domestic students. Applications are processed on a rolling basis. Application fee: $50. *Expenses: Contact institution.* Tuition and fees vary according to program. *Financial support:* In 2006–07, 5 research assistantships with full tuition reimbursements (averaging $4,916 per year) were awarded; career-related internships or fieldwork, institutionally sponsored loans, tuition waivers (full and partial), and unspecified assistantships also available. *Application contact:* Paula Alger, Curriculum Coordinator and Adviser, 435-865-8157, Fax: 435-586-5493, E-mail: alger@suu.edu.

Southern Wesleyan University, Program in Business Administration, Central, SC 29630-1020. Offers MBA. Evening/weekend programs available. *Degree requirements:* For master's, comprehensive exam. *Entrance requirements:* For master's, GMAT, GRE, or MAT.

Southern Wesleyan University, Program in Management, Central, SC 29630-1020. Offers MSM. Evening/weekend programs available. *Degree requirements:* For master's, comprehensive exam. *Entrance requirements:* For master's, GMAT, GRE, or MAT. Expenses: Contact institution.

Southwest Baptist University, Graduate Studies, Program in Business, Bolivar, MO 65613-2597. Offers business administration (MBA); health administration (MBA). *Accreditation:* ACBSP. Part-time and evening/weekend programs available. *Degree requirements:* For master's, comprehensive exam. *Entrance requirements:* For master's, interviews, minimum GPA of 2.75. Additional exam requirements/recommendations for international students: Required—TOEFL (minimum score 550 paper-based; 213 computer-based).

Southwestern Adventist University, Business Department, Graduate Program, Keene, TX 76059. Offers accounting (MBA). Part-time and evening/weekend programs available. *Degree requirements:* For master's, capstone course. *Entrance requirements:* For master's, GMAT, GRE General Test.

Southwestern Oklahoma State University, College of Professional and Graduate Studies, School of Business and Technology, Weatherford, OK 73096-3098. Offers MBA. MBA distance learning degree program offered to Oklahoma residents only. Part-time and evening/weekend programs available. Postbaccalaureate distance learning degree programs offered (minimal on-campus study). *Degree requirements:* For master's, comprehensive exam. *Entrance requirements:* For master's, GMAT, minimum GPA of 2.5. Additional exam requirements/recommendations for international students: Required—TOEFL.

Southwest Minnesota State University, Department of Business Administration, Marshall, MN 56258. Offers business administration (MBA); management (MS). *Faculty:* 13 full-time (3 women). *Students:* 12 full-time (4 women), 60 part-time (28 women); includes 6 minority (3 African Americans, 3 Asian Americans or Pacific Islanders), 10 international. 18 applicants. In 2006, 46 degrees awarded. *Degree requirements:* For master's, thesis. *Application deadline:* Applications are processed on a rolling basis. Application fee: $20. Electronic applications accepted. *Expenses:* Tuition, area resident: Full-time $4,835. Tuition, state resident: full-time $4,835; part-time $269 per credit. Tuition, nonresident: part-time $269 per credit. Required fees: $589; $33 per credit. Tuition and fees vary according to course load and reciprocity agreements. *Unit head:* Dr. Mark Goodenow, Department Chair, 507-537-6260. *Application contact:* Rich Shearer, Director of Enrollment Management, 507-537-6286, E-mail: shearerr@southwestmsu.edu.

Spalding University, Graduate Studies, College of Business and Communication, Louisville, KY 40203-2188. Offers business communication (MS). Part-time and evening/weekend programs available. *Degree requirements:* For master's, project. *Entrance requirements:* For master's, GRE or GMAT, writing sample, interview, letters of recommendation. Additional exam requirements/recommendations for international students: Required—TOEFL (minimum score 535 paper-based). Electronic applications accepted. *Faculty research:* Curriculum development, consumer behavior, interdisciplinary pedagogy.

Spring Arbor University, School of Business and Management, Spring Arbor, MI 49283-9799. Offers MBA. Part-time and evening/weekend programs available. *Faculty:* 9 full-time (3 women), 9 part-time/adjunct (5 women). *Students:* 40 full-time (21 women), 55 part-time (28 women); includes 10 minority (6 African Americans, 1 Asian American or Pacific Islander, 3 Hispanic Americans), 4 international. Average age 37. 28 applicants, 71% accepted, 18 enrolled. In 2006, 41 degrees awarded. *Entrance requirements:* Additional exam requirements/recommendations for international students: Required—TOEFL (minimum score 550 paper-based; 220 computer-based). *Application deadline:* Applications are processed on a rolling basis. Application fee: $30. *Expenses:* Tuition: Full-time $4,200; part-time $350 per credit. Required fees: $140; $48 per term. Tuition and fees vary according to course load and program. *Financial support:* Career-related internships or fieldwork, scholarships/grants, and tuition waivers (partial) available. Support available to part-time students. Financial award application deadline: 8/25; financial award applicants required to submit FAFSA. *Unit head:* Dr. Caleb K. Chan, Director, MBA Program, 517-750-6538, Fax: 517-750-6624, E-mail: cchan@arbor.edu. *Application contact:* Michelle Coats, Secretary, School of Business and Management, 517-750-6315, Fax: 517-750-6624, E-mail: mcoats@arbor.edu.

Spring Hill College, Graduate Programs, Program in Business Administration, Mobile, AL 36608-1791. Offers MBA. *Accreditation:* ACBSP. Part-time and evening/weekend programs available. *Faculty:* 3 full-time (1 woman), 1 (woman) part-time/adjunct. *Students:* 1 (woman) full-time, 26 part-time (10 women); includes 3 minority (2 African Americans, 1 American Indian/Alaska Native), 1 international. Average age 32. In 2006, 12 degrees awarded. *Degree requirements:* For master's, capstone course. *Entrance requirements:* For master's, GMAT. Additional exam requirements/recommendations for international students: Required—TOEFL (minimum score 550 paper-based; 213 computer-based). *Application deadline:* For fall admission, 8/1 priority date for domestic students, 6/1 priority date for international students; for spring admission, 12/1 priority date for domestic students, 11/1 priority date for international students. Applications are processed on a rolling basis. Application fee: $25 ($35 for international students). Electronic applications accepted. *Expenses: Contact institution. Financial support:* In 2006–07, 16 students received support. Career-related internships or fieldwork and scholarships/grants available. Support available to part-time students. Financial award applicants required to submit FAFSA. *Unit head:* Dr. Robert M. Bracken, Director, Graduate Business Program, 251-380-4119, Fax: 251-460-2178, E-mail: rbracken@shc.edu. *Application contact:* Joyce Genz, Dean of Life Long Learning and Director of Graduate Programs, 251-380-3094, Fax: 251-460-2190, E-mail: grad@shc.edu.

Stanford University, Graduate School of Business, Stanford, CA 94305-9991. Offers MBA, PhD, JD/MBA, MBA/MS. *Accreditation:* AACSB. Terminal master's awarded for partial completion of doctoral program. *Degree requirements:* For doctorate, thesis/dissertation. *Entrance requirements:* For master's, GMAT; for doctorate, GMAT, GRE. Electronic applications accepted. Expenses: Contact institution.

State University of New York at Binghamton, Graduate School, School of Management, Program in Business Administration, Binghamton, NY 13902-6000. Offers business administration (MBA, PhD); health care professional executive (MBA). *Accreditation:* AACSB. *Students:* 234 full-time (89 women), 30 part-time (11 women); includes 14 minority (3 African Americans, 11 Asian Americans or Pacific Islanders), 123 international. Average age 29. 449 applicants, 51% accepted. In 2006, 101 master's, 2 doctorates awarded. *Degree requirements:* For doctorate, thesis/dissertation. *Entrance requirements:* For master's and doctorate, GMAT. Additional exam requirements/recommendations for international students: Required—TOEFL. *Application deadline:* For fall admission, 4/15 priority date for domestic students, 1/15 priority date for international students; for spring admission, 11/1 for domestic students, 10/1 priority date for international students. Applications are processed on a rolling basis. Application fee: $60. Electronic applications accepted. *Financial support:* In 2006–07, 39 students received support, including 1 fellowship with full tuition reimbursement available (averaging $8,700 per year), 34 teaching assistantships with full tuition reimbursements available (averaging $7,302 per year); research assistantships, career-related internships or fieldwork, Federal Work-Study, institutionally sponsored loans, tuition waivers (full and partial), and unspecified assistantships also available. Support available to part-time students. Financial award application deadline: 2/15. *Unit head:* George Bobinski, Associate Dean, 607-777-2315, E-mail: gbobins@binghamton.edu.

State University of New York at Fredonia, Graduate Studies, Department of Business Administration, Fredonia, NY 14063-1136. Offers accounting (MS). *Faculty:* 2 full-time (0 women). In 2006, 1 degree awarded. *Application deadline:* For fall admission, 8/5 for domestic students; for spring admission, 12/1 for domestic students. Application fee: $50. *Expenses:* Tuition, state resident: full-time $6,900; part-time $288 per credit hour. Tuition, nonresident: full-time $10,920; part-time $455 per credit hour. Required fees: $1,132; $47 per credit hour. *Financial support:* In 2006–07, 1 teaching assistantship (averaging $6,500 per year) was awarded; research assistantships, career-related internships or fieldwork and tuition waivers (full and partial) also available. Support available to part-time students. *Unit head:* Dr. Mojtaba Seyedian, Chair, 716-673-4603, E-mail: mojtaba.seyedian@fredonia.edu.

State University of New York at New Paltz, Graduate School, School of Business, New Paltz, NY 12561. Offers business administration (MBA); public accountancy (MBA). Part-time and evening/weekend programs available. *Faculty:* 25 full-time (6 women), 4 part-time/adjunct (1 woman). *Students:* 58 full-time (29 women), 48 part-time (24 women); includes 17 minority (3 African Americans, 11 Asian Americans or Pacific Islanders, 3 Hispanic Americans), 31 international. Average age 30. In 2006, 51 degrees awarded. *Entrance requirements:* For master's, GMAT, minimum GPA of 3.0. Additional exam requirements/recommendations for international students: Required—TOEFL (minimum score 550 paper-based; 213 computer-based; 80 iBT). *Application deadline:* For fall admission, 5/15 priority date for domestic students, 5/15 for international students; for spring admission, 11/15 for domestic and international students. Applications are processed on a rolling basis. Application fee: $50. Electronic applications accepted. *Expenses: Contact institution. Financial support:* In 2006–07, 14 students received support, including 8 research assistantships with partial tuition reimbursements available (averaging $5,000 per year), 1 teaching assistantship with partial tuition reimbursement available (averaging $5,000 per year). *Unit head:* Dr. Hadi Salavitabar, Dean, 845-257-3720, E-mail: mba@newpaltz.edu. *Application contact:* Rania Al-Haddad, Coordinator, 845-257-2968, E-mail: mba@newpaltz.edu.

State University of New York at Oswego, Graduate Studies, School of Business, Program in Business Administration, Oswego, NY 13126. Offers MBA. *Accreditation:* AACSB. Part-time and evening/weekend programs available. *Faculty:* 6 full-time, 12 part-time/adjunct. *Students:* 46 full-time (14 women), 30 part-time (12 women); includes 5 minority (3 African Americans, 2 Asian Americans or Pacific Islanders), 18 international. Average age 32. 87 applicants, 90% accepted. In 2006, 30 degrees awarded. *Entrance requirements:* For master's, GMAT, minimum GPA of 2.6. Additional exam requirements/recommendations for international students: Required—TOEFL (minimum score 560 paper-based; 220 computer-based). *Application deadline:* For fall admission, 4/15 for domestic students; for spring admission, 11/1 for domestic students. Applications are processed on a rolling basis. Application fee: $50. *Expenses:* Tuition, state resident: part-time $288 per credit. Tuition, nonresident: part-time $455 per credit. Tuition and fees vary according to program. *Financial support:* In 2006–07, 7 students received support, including 1 fellowship; teaching assistantships with partial tuition reimbursements available, career-related internships or fieldwork, Federal Work-Study, institutionally sponsored loans, scholarships/grants, health care benefits, tuition waivers (partial), and unspecified assistantships also available. Support available to part-time students. Financial award application deadline: 4/1; financial award applicants required to submit FAFSA. *Faculty research:* Marketing, industrial finance, technology. *Unit head:* Dr. Ding Zhang, Director, 315-312-2911, E-mail: zhang@oswego.edu.

State University of New York Empire State College, Graduate Studies, Program in Business Administration, Saratoga Springs, NY 12866-4391. Offers MBA. Part-time programs available. Postbaccalaureate distance learning degree programs offered (minimal on-campus study). *Degree requirements:* For master's, thesis or alternative. *Entrance requirements:* For master's, previous course work in statistics, macroeconomics, microeconomics, and accounting. Additional exam requirements/recommendations for international students: Required—TOEFL (minimum score 600 paper-based; 250 computer-based). Electronic applications accepted. Expenses: Contact institution. *Faculty research:* Corporate strategy, managerial competencies, decision analysis, economics in transition, organizational communication.

State University of New York Empire State College, Graduate Studies, Program in Business and Policy Studies, Saratoga Springs, NY 12866-4391. Offers MA. Part-time and evening/weekend programs available. Postbaccalaureate distance learning degree programs offered (minimal on-campus study). *Degree requirements:* For master's, thesis, exam. *Entrance requirements:* For master's, proficiency in statistics. Additional exam requirements/recommendations for international students: Required—TOEFL (minimum score 600 paper-based; 280 computer-based). Electronic applications accepted. *Faculty research:* Business history, applied business statistics, labor/management relations, American social problems and business, effect of government economic policies on business.

State University of New York Institute of Technology, School of Business, Utica, NY 13504-3050. Offers accountancy (MS); business administration in technology management (MBA), including technology management; health services administration (MS). Part-time and evening/weekend programs available. Postbaccalaureate distance learning degree programs offered (no on-campus study). *Faculty:* 15 full-time (4 women), 3 part-time/adjunct (0 women). *Students:* 62 full-time (27 women), 154 part-time (77 women); includes 25 minority (11 African Americans, 11 Asian Americans or Pacific Islanders, 3 Hispanic Americans), 12 international. *Entrance requirements:* For master's, GMAT, minimum GPA of 3.0. Additional exam requirements/recommendations for international students: Required—TOEFL (minimum score 550 paper-based; 213 computer-based). *Application deadline:* For fall admission, 6/15 priority date for domestic students. Applications are processed on a rolling basis. Application fee: $50. *Expenses:* Tuition, state resident: full-time $3,452; part-time $288 per credit hour. Tuition, nonresident: full-time $10,920; part-time $455 per credit hour. Required fees: $927; $38 per credit hour. *Financial support:* In 2006–07, 1 fellowship (averaging $7,500 per year), 8 research assistantships (averaging $7,500 per year) were awarded; career-related internships or fieldwork, Federal Work-Study, scholarships/grants, health care benefits, and unspecified assistantships also available. Financial award application deadline: 6/1; financial award applicants required to submit FAFSA. *Faculty research:* Bond performance, paying for college tuition, mergers with utilities companies. *Unit head:* Dr. Stephen Havlovic, Dean, 315-792-7429, Fax: 315-792-7138. *Application contact:* Marybeth Lyons, Director of Admissions, 315-792-7500, Fax: 315-792-7837, E-mail: smbl@sunyit.edu.

Stephen F. Austin State University, Graduate School, College of Business, Program in Business Administration, Nacogdoches, TX 75962. Offers business (MBA); management and marketing (MBA). *Accreditation:* AACSB. Part-time and evening/weekend programs available. *Degree requirements:* For master's, comprehensive exam. *Entrance requirements:* For master's, GMAT, minimum AACSB index of 1000. Additional exam requirements/recommendations for international students: Required—TOEFL (minimum score 550 paper-based; 213 computer-based). *Faculty research:* Strategic implications, information search, multinational firms, philosophical guidance.

Stephens College, Division of Graduate and Continuing Studies, Program in Business Administration, Columbia, MO 65215-0002. Offers MBA. Part-time programs available. Postbaccalaureate distance learning degree programs offered (minimal on-campus study). *Faculty:* 5 part-time/adjunct. *Students:* 20 applicants, 75% accepted, 15 enrolled. *Entrance requirements:* For master's, minimum GPA of 3.0 in last 60 hours. Additional exam requirements/recommendations for international students: Required—TOEFL (minimum score 213 computer-based). *Application deadline:* Applications are processed on a rolling basis. Application fee: $25. Electronic applications accepted. *Unit head:* Susan Bartel, Program Chair, 800-388-7579. *Application contact:* Mellodie Wilson, Associate Director, 800-388-7579, E-mail: online@stephens.edu.

Stetson University, School of Business Administration, Program in Business Administration, DeLand, FL 32723. Offers MBA, JD/MBA. *Accreditation:* AACSB. Part-time and evening/weekend programs available. *Students:* 74 full-time (24 women), 128 part-time (51 women); includes 23 minority (6 African Americans, 5 Asian Americans or Pacific Islanders, 12 Hispanic Americans), 14 international. Average age 29. In 2006, 119 degrees awarded. *Entrance requirements:* For master's, GMAT. *Application deadline:* For fall admission, 7/1 for domestic students. Application fee: $25. *Financial support:* Application deadline: 3/15. *Unit head:* Dr. Frank DeZoort, Director, 386-822-7410. *Application contact:* Jeanne Bosco, Administrative Assistant, 386-822-7410, Fax: 386-822-7413, E-mail: jbosco@stetson.edu.

Stevens Institute of Technology, Graduate School, Wesley J. Howe School of Technology Management, Program in Business Administration, Hoboken, NJ 07030. Offers engineering management (MBA); financial management (MBA); global technology management (MBA); information management (MBA); information technology in financial services (MBA); information technology in the pharmaceutical industry (MBA); information technology outsourcing (MBA); pharmaceutical technology management (MBA); project management (MBA); telecommunications management (MBA).

Stevens Institute of Technology, Graduate School, Wesley J. Howe School of Technology Management, Program in Management, Hoboken, NJ 07030. Offers general management (MS); global innovation management (MS); human resource management (MS); information management (MS); project management (MS); technology commercialization (MS); technology management (MS). Part-time programs available. *Degree requirements:* For master's, thesis optional. *Entrance requirements:* For master's, GMAT, GRE General Test. Additional exam requirements/recommendations for international students: Required—TOEFL. Electronic applications accepted. *Faculty research:* Industrial economics.

Stony Brook University, State University of New York, Graduate School, College of Business, Program in Business Administration, Stony Brook, NY 11794. Offers business administration (MBA); finance (Certificate). *Students:* 150 full-time (70 women), 58 part-time (23 women); includes 43 minority (7 African Americans, 24 Asian Americans or Pacific Islanders, 12 Hispanic Americans), 54 international. In 2006, 48 master's, 22 other advanced degrees awarded. Application fee: $60. *Expenses:* Tuition, state resident: full-time $6,900; part-time $288 per credit. Tuition, nonresident: full-time $10,920; part-time $455 per credit. *Application contact:* Dr. Jeff Casey, Director, Graduate Program, 631-632-7171, E-mail: jcasey@notes.cc.sunysb.edu.

See Close-Up on page 327.

Stony Brook University, State University of New York, Graduate School, College of Business, W. Averell Harriman School for Management and Policy, Stony Brook, NY 11794. Offers business administration (MBA); industrial management (Certificate); management policy (MS); technology management (MS). Part-time and evening/weekend programs available. *Degree requirements:* For master's, internship. *Expenses:* Tuition, state resident: full-time $6,900; part-time $288 per credit. Tuition, nonresident: full-time $10,920; part-time $455 per credit. *Financial support:* Fellowships, research assistantships, teaching assistantships, career-related internships or fieldwork available.

Announcement: The MBA program in the College of Business recognizes two critical features of the modern business world. First, business is truly global and, second, business changes rapidly. Students are educated to realize that the big picture includes business, government, and nonprofit organizations interacting around the world. That theory is put into play in alliances with over 130 firms that work with and have hired Stony Brook's MBA graduates, who are ready to contribute to today's challenging business environment.

Stratford University, Graduate Programs, Falls Church, VA 22043. Offers business administration (MBA); enterprise business management (MS); entrepreneurial business (MS); information systems (MS); software engineering (MS). Part-time and evening/weekend programs available. Postbaccalaureate distance learning degree programs offered (minimal on-campus study). *Entrance requirements:* Additional exam requirements/recommendations for international students: Required—TOEFL (minimum score 500 paper-based). Electronic applications accepted.

Strayer University, Graduate Studies, Washington, DC 20005-2603. Offers accounting (MS); business administration (MBA); communications technology (MS); information systems (MS); management information systems (MS). Part-time and evening/weekend programs available. Postbaccalaureate distance learning degree programs offered (minimal on-campus study). *Degree requirements:* For master's, thesis. *Entrance requirements:* For master's, GMAT, GRE General Test, bachelor's degree from an accredited college or university, minimum undergraduate GPA of 2.75. Electronic applications accepted.

Suffolk University, Sawyer Business School, Management Graduate Programs, Boston, MA 02108-2770. Offers business administration (MBA, APC); executive business administration (EMBA); global business administration (GMBA); JD/MBA. *Accreditation:* AACSB. Part-time and evening/weekend programs available. Postbaccalaureate distance learning degree programs offered (no on-campus study). *Faculty:* 85 full-time (22 women), 64 part-time/adjunct (19 women). *Students:* 163 full-time (62 women), 410 part-time (191 women); includes 46 minority (16 African Americans, 27 Asian Americans or Pacific Islanders, 3 Hispanic Americans), 88 international. Average age 29. 462 applicants, 73% accepted, 158 enrolled. In 2006, 308 degrees awarded. *Entrance requirements:* For master's, GMAT, minimum undergraduate GPA of 2.75 (MBA), 5 years of managerial experience (EMBA). Additional exam requirements/recommendations for international students: Required—TOEFL (minimum score 550 paper-based; 213 computer-based). *Application deadline:* For fall admission, 6/15 priority date for domestic students, 6/15 for international students; for spring admission, 11/1 priority date for domestic students, 11/1 for international students. Applications are processed on a rolling basis. Application fee: $50. Electronic applications accepted. *Financial support:* In 2006–07, 109 fellowships with full and partial tuition reimbursements (averaging $8,555 per year) were awarded; career-related internships or fieldwork, Federal Work-Study, and institutionally sponsored loans also available. Support available to part-time students. Financial award application deadline: 4/1; financial award applicants required to submit FAFSA. *Faculty research:* Foreign investments; career strategies and boundaryless careers; corporate ethics codes; interest rates, inflation, and growth options; innovation and product development performance. *Unit head:* Lillian Hallberg, Assistant Dean of Graduate Programs, Director of MBA Programs, 617-573-6306, E-mail: lhallberg@suffolk.edu. *Application contact:* Judith Reynolds, Director of Graduate Admissions, 617-573-8302, Fax: 617-523-0116, E-mail: grad.admission@suffolk.edu.

Sullivan University, School of Business, Louisville, KY 40205. Offers business (EMBA, MBA); dispute resolution (MSDR); management of information technology (MSMIT). *Entrance requirements:* Additional exam requirements/recommendations for international students: Required—TOEFL.

Sul Ross State University, Rio Grande College of Sul Ross State University, Alpine, TX 79832. Offers business administration (MBA); teacher education (M Ed), including bilingual education, counseling, educational diagnostics, elementary education, general education, reading, school administration, secondary education. Part-time and evening/weekend programs available. *Degree requirements:* For master's, thesis optional. *Entrance requirements:* For master's, GMAT or GRE General Test, minimum GPA of 2.5 in last 60 hours of undergraduate work. *Faculty research:* Drug and substance abuse counseling, U.S.-Mexico border economic development.

Business Administration and Management—General

Sul Ross State University, School of Professional Studies, Department of Business Administration, Alpine, TX 79832. Offers international trade (MBA); management (MBA). Part-time and evening/weekend programs available. *Degree requirements:* For master's, thesis optional. *Entrance requirements:* For master's, GMAT or GRE General Test, minimum GPA of 2.5 in last 60 hours of undergraduate work. *Faculty research:* Cross-cultural comparisons, U.S.-Mexico management relations.

Syracuse University, Martin J. Whitman School of Management, Syracuse, NY 13244. Offers MBA, MS Acct, MSF, PhD, JD/MBA, JD/MS Acct, JD/MSF. *Accreditation:* AACSB. Part-time programs available. Postbaccalaureate distance learning degree programs offered (minimal on-campus study). *Faculty:* 71 full-time (16 women), 2 part-time/adjunct (1 woman). *Students:* 115 full-time (36 women), 285 part-time (85 women); includes 84 minority (45 African Americans, 33 Asian Americans or Pacific Islanders, 6 Hispanic Americans), 66 international. 458 applicants, 22% accepted, 39 enrolled. In 2006, 146 master's, 8 doctorates awarded. *Degree requirements:* For master's, registration; for doctorate, thesis/dissertation, summer research paper, comprehensive exam, registration. *Entrance requirements:* For master's, GMAT, 2 letters of recommendation; for doctorate, GMAT, 3 letters of recommendation. Additional exam requirements/recommendations for international students: Required—TOEFL (minimum score 600 paper-based; 250 computer-based; 100 iBT). *Application deadline:* For fall admission, 1/30 priority date for domestic and international students. Applications are processed on a rolling basis. Application fee: $75. Electronic applications accepted. *Expenses: Contact institution. Financial support:* In 2006–07, 45 students received support; fellowships with full tuition reimbursements available, research assistantships with partial tuition reimbursements available, teaching assistantships with partial tuition reimbursements available, career-related internships or fieldwork, scholarships/grants, tuition waivers (partial), unspecified assistantships, and paid hourly positions available. Financial award application deadline: 1/30; financial award applicants required to submit FAFSA. *Unit head:* Dr. Melvin T. Stiten, Dean, 315-443-3751. *Application contact:* Carol J. Swanberg, Director of Graduate Admissions and Financial Aid, 315-443-9214, Fax: 315-443-9517, E-mail: mbainfo@syr.edu.

See Close-Up on page 329.

Tabor College, Graduate Program, Hillsboro, KS 67063. Offers accounting (MBA). Program offered at the Wichita campus only.

Tarleton State University, College of Graduate Studies, College of Business Administration, Stephenville, TX 76402. Offers MBA, MS. *Accreditation:* ACBSP. Part-time and evening/weekend programs available. Postbaccalaureate distance learning degree programs offered (minimal on-campus study). *Faculty:* 31 full-time (5 women), 3 part-time/adjunct (1 woman). *Students:* 99 full-time (53 women), 290 part-time (164 women); includes 101 minority (62 African Americans, 4 American Indian/Alaska Native, 11 Asian Americans or Pacific Islanders, 24 Hispanic Americans), 31 international. Average age 36. In 2006, 117 degrees awarded. *Degree requirements:* For master's, thesis optional. *Entrance requirements:* For master's, GMAT or GRE General Test, minimum GPA of 3.0. Additional exam requirements/recommendations for international students: Required—TOEFL (minimum score 550 paper-based; 220 computer-based). *Application deadline:* For fall admission, 8/5 priority date for domestic students; for spring admission, 12/1 for domestic students. Applications are processed on a rolling basis. Application fee: $25 ($75 for international students). *Financial support:* In 2006–07, 4 teaching assistantships (averaging $12,000 per year) were awarded; research assistantships, career-related internships or fieldwork, Federal Work-Study, and institutionally sponsored loans also available. Support available to part-time students. Financial award application deadline: 5/1; financial award applicants required to submit FAFSA. *Unit head:* Dr. Ruby Barker, Dean, 254-968-9350.

Taylor University Fort Wayne, Master of Business Administration Program, Fort Wayne, IN 46807-2197. Offers MBA. Electronic applications accepted.

Temple University, Graduate School, Fox School of Business and Management, Doctoral Programs in Business, Philadelphia, PA 19122-6096. Offers accounting (PhD); economics (PhD); finance (PhD); general and strategic management (PhD); healthcare management (PhD); human resource administration (PhD); international business administration (PhD); management information systems (PhD); management science/operations research (PhD); marketing (PhD); risk, insurance, and health-care management (PhD); statistics (PhD); tourism (PhD). *Accreditation:* AACSB. *Entrance requirements:* For doctorate, GRE General Test, minimum GPA of 3.0, master's degree. Additional exam requirements/recommendations for international students: Required—TOEFL. *Expenses:* Tuition, state resident: full-time $12,264; part-time $511 per credit. Tuition, nonresident: full-time $17,904; part-time $746 per credit. Required fees: $84 per course. Tuition and fees vary according to program.

Temple University, Graduate School, Fox School of Business and Management, Masters Programs in Business, MBA/MS Programs, Philadelphia, PA 19122-6096. Offers IMBA/MS, MBA/MS. *Entrance requirements:* Additional exam requirements/recommendations for international students: Required—TOEFL. *Expenses:* Tuition, state resident: full-time $12,264; part-time $511 per credit. Tuition, nonresident: full-time $17,904; part-time $746 per credit. Required fees: $84 per course. Tuition and fees vary according to program.

Temple University, Graduate School, Fox School of Business and Management, Masters Programs in Business, MBA Programs, Philadelphia, PA 19122-6096. Offers accounting (MBA); business administration (EMBA, MBA); e-business (MBA); economics (MBA); finance (MBA); general and strategic management (MBA); healthcare management (MBA); human resource administration (MBA); international business (IMBA); management information systems (MBA); management science/operations management (MBA); marketing (MBA); risk management and insurance (MBA); statistics (MBA). EMBA offered in Philadelphia, PA and Tokyo, Japan. *Accreditation:* AACSB. *Entrance requirements:* For master's, GMAT, minimum undergraduate GPA of 3.0. Additional exam requirements/recommendations for international students: Required—TOEFL. *Expenses:* Tuition, state resident: full-time $12,264; part-time $511 per credit. Tuition, nonresident: full-time $17,904; part-time $746 per credit. Required fees: $84 per course. Tuition and fees vary according to program.

Temple University, Graduate School, Fox School of Business and Management, Masters Programs in Business, MS Programs, Philadelphia, PA 19122-6096. Offers accounting and financial management (MS); actuarial science (MS); e-business (MS); finance (MS); healthcare financial management (MS); human resource administration (MS); management information systems (MS); management science/operations management (MS); marketing (MS); statistics (MS). *Accreditation:* AACSB. *Entrance requirements:* For master's, GRE General Test, minimum undergraduate GPA of 3.0. Additional exam requirements/recommendations for international students: Required—TOEFL. *Expenses:* Tuition, state resident: full-time $12,264; part-time $511 per credit. Tuition, nonresident: full-time $17,904; part-time $746 per credit. Required fees: $84 per course. Tuition and fees vary according to program.

Tennessee State University, The School of Graduate Studies and Research, College of Business, Nashville, TN 37209-1561. Offers MBA. *Accreditation:* AACSB. Part-time and evening/weekend programs available. Postbaccalaureate distance learning degree programs offered. *Faculty:* 13 full-time (3 women), 1 part-time/adjunct (0 women). *Students:* 31 full-time (19 women), 60 part-time (34 women); includes 56 minority (46 African Americans, 9 Asian Americans or Pacific Islanders, 1 Hispanic American), 11 international. Average age 30. 129 applicants, 36% accepted, 37 enrolled. In 2006, 30 degrees awarded. *Entrance requirements:* For master's, GMAT. Application fee: $25. *Financial support:* In 2006–07, 6 research assistantships (averaging $3,198 per year), teaching assistantships (averaging $3,198 per year) were awarded. *Faculty research:* Supply chain management, health economics, accounting, e-commerce, international business. *Unit head:* Dr. Tilden J. Curry, Dean, 615-963-7121, Fax: 615-963-7139, E-mail: tcurry@tnstate.edu. *Application contact:* Dr. Raovl Russell, Director, 615-963-7170, Fax: 615-963-7139, E-mail: rrussell3@tnstate.edu.

Tennessee Technological University, Graduate School, College of Business Administration, Cookeville, TN 38505. Offers MBA. *Accreditation:* AACSB. Part-time and evening/weekend programs available. *Faculty:* 28 full-time (5 women). *Students:* 42 full-time (21 women), 145 part-time (69 women); includes 19 minority (7 African Americans, 1 American Indian/Alaska Native, 7 Asian Americans or Pacific Islanders, 4 Hispanic Americans). Average age 25. 175 applicants, 59% accepted, 70 enrolled. In 2006, 64 degrees awarded. *Entrance requirements:* For master's, GMAT, interview. Additional exam requirements/recommendations for international students: Required—TOEFL. *Application deadline:* For fall admission, 3/1 priority date for domestic students; for spring admission, 8/1 for domestic students. Application fee: $25 ($30 for international students). *Expenses:* Tuition, state resident: full-time $8,748; part-time $319 per hour. Tuition, nonresident: full-time $23,524; part-time $740 per hour. *Financial support:* In 2006–07, 5 fellowships (averaging $10,000 per year), 18 research assistantships (averaging $4,000 per year), teaching assistantships (averaging $4,000 per year) were awarded. Support available to part-time students. Financial award application deadline: 4/1. *Unit head:* Dr. Bob G. Wood, Director, 931-372-3600, Fax: 931-372-6249. *Application contact:* Dr. Francis O. Otuonye, Associate Vice President for Research and Graduate Studies, 931-372-3233, Fax: 931-372-3497, E-mail: fotuonye@tntech.edu.

See Close-Up on page 331.

Texas A&M International University, Office of Graduate Studies and Research, College of Business Administration, Laredo, TX 78041-1900. Offers MBA, MP Acc, MSIS. *Accreditation:* AACSB. Part-time and evening/weekend programs available. *Faculty:* 22 full-time (2 women), 8 part-time/adjunct (0 women). *Students:* 114 full-time (42 women), 155 part-time (53 women); includes 140 minority (1 African American, 2 Asian Americans or Pacific Islanders, 137 Hispanic Americans), 120 international. Average age 28. 272 applicants, 57% accepted, 117 enrolled. In 2006, 107 degrees awarded. *Degree requirements:* For master's, thesis (for some programs). *Entrance requirements:* For master's, GMAT or GRE General Test. Additional exam requirements/recommendations for international students: Required—TOEFL (minimum score 550 paper-based; 213 computer-based). *Application deadline:* For fall admission, 7/15 priority date for domestic students; for spring admission, 11/12 for domestic students. Applications are processed on a rolling basis. Application fee: $25. *Expenses:* Tuition, state resident: full-time $1,580. Tuition, nonresident: full-time $5,432. Required fees: $3,808. *Financial support:* In 2006–07, 105 students received support, including 40 fellowships; Federal Work-Study and institutionally sponsored loans also available. Support available to part-time students. Financial award application deadline: 11/1; financial award applicants required to submit FAFSA. *Unit head:* Dr. Jacky So, Dean, 956-328-2480. *Application contact:* Imelda Lopez, Graduate Admissions Counselor, 956-326-2485, Fax: 956-326-2459, E-mail: lopez@tamiu.edu.

Texas A&M University, Mays Business School, Department of Management, College Station, TX 77843. Offers human resource management (MS); management (PhD). *Faculty:* 32 full-time (10 women), 9 part-time/adjunct (2 women). *Students:* 60 full-time (37 women). Average age 31. 76 applicants, 28% accepted. In 2006, 19 master's, 3 doctorates awarded. Terminal master's awarded for partial completion of doctoral program. *Degree requirements:* For master's, comprehensive exam; for doctorate, thesis/dissertation. *Entrance requirements:* For master's, GMAT or GRE; for doctorate, GMAT or GRE General Test. Additional exam requirements/recommendations for international students: Required—TOEFL. *Application deadline:* For fall admission, 3/1 priority date for domestic students; for spring admission, 8/1 for domestic students. Applications are processed on a rolling basis. Application fee: $50 ($75 for international students). *Expenses:* Tuition, state resident: full-time $4,697. Tuition, nonresident: full-time $11,297. Required fees: $2,272. *Financial support:* In 2006–07, 25 students received support; fellowships, research assistantships, teaching assistantships, career-related internships or fieldwork and institutionally sponsored loans available. Financial award application deadline: 2/1. *Faculty research:* Strategic and human resource management, business and public policy, organizational behavior, organizational theory. *Unit head:* Dr. Duane Ireland, Head, 979-845-4851, Fax: 979-845-9641. *Application contact:* Kristi Mora, Information Contact, 979-845-4045.

Texas A&M University, Mays Business School, Executive MBA Program, College Station, TX 77843. Offers EMBA. *Accreditation:* AACSB. *Faculty:* 28 full-time (4 women). *Students:* 90 full-time (20 women). In 2006, 46 degrees awarded. *Entrance requirements:* For master's, GMAT or GRE. Additional exam requirements/recommendations for international students: Required—TOEFL. *Application deadline:* For fall admission, 3/1 priority date for domestic students. Applications are processed on a rolling basis. Application fee: $50 ($75 for international students). Electronic applications accepted. *Expenses: Contact institution. Financial support:* Application deadline: 2/1. *Unit head:* Julie Orzabal, Director, 979-845-0361, Fax: 979-862-6296, E-mail: emba@tamu.edu.

Texas A&M University, Mays Business School, MBA Program, College Station, TX 77843. Offers MBA. *Accreditation:* AACSB. *Students:* 145 full-time (30 women). Average age 27. 372 applicants, 35% accepted, 76 enrolled. In 2006, 76 degrees awarded. *Entrance requirements:* For master's, GMAT. Additional exam requirements/recommendations for international students: Required—TOEFL (minimum score 600 paper-based; 250 computer-based; 100 iBT), IELTS (minimum score 7). *Application deadline:* For fall admission, 1/1 for domestic students, 11/1 for international students; for winter admission, 1/4 for domestic and international students; for spring admission, 2/28 for domestic and international students. Application fee: $50 ($75 for international students). Electronic applications accepted. *Expenses: Contact institution. Financial support:* Fellowships, research assistantships, career-related internships or fieldwork, Federal Work-Study, institutionally sponsored loans, scholarships/grants, health care benefits, and unspecified assistantships available. Financial award application deadline: 1/15. *Unit head:* Kelli Kilpatrick, Director, MBA Program, 979-845-4714, Fax: 979-862-2393, E-mail: kkilpatrick@mays.tamu.edu. *Application contact:* Wendy Flynn, Director of MBA Admissions, 979-845-4714, Fax: 979-862-2393, E-mail: wflynn@mays.tamu.edu.

Texas A&M University–Commerce, Graduate School, College of Business and Technology, Department of General Business and Systems Management, Commerce, TX 75429-3011. Offers business administration (MBA). *Accreditation:* AACSB. Part-time programs available. *Degree requirements:* For master's, thesis (for some programs), comprehensive exam. *Entrance requirements:* For master's, GMAT.

Texas A&M University–Corpus Christi, Graduate Studies and Research, College of Business, Corpus Christi, TX 78412-5503. Offers accounting (M Acc); health care administration (MBA); international business (MBA). *Accreditation:* AACSB. Part-time and evening/weekend programs available. *Degree requirements:* For master's, thesis (for some programs), comprehensive exam, registration. *Entrance requirements:* For master's, GMAT. Additional exam requirements/recommendations for international students: Required—TOEFL. Electronic applications accepted.

Texas A&M University–Kingsville, College of Graduate Studies, College of Business Administration, Kingsville, TX 78363. Offers MBA, MS. *Accreditation:* ACBSP. Part-time and evening/weekend programs available. *Degree requirements:* For master's, thesis or alternative, comprehensive exam. *Entrance requirements:* For master's, GMAT, minimum GPA of 2.5. Additional exam requirements/recommendations for international students: Required—TOEFL. *Faculty research:* Capital budgeting, international trade.

Texas A&M University–Texarkana, Graduate Studies and Research, College of Business, Texarkana, TX 75505-5518. Offers accounting (MSA); business administration (MBA, MS). Part-time and evening/weekend programs available. *Students:* 178. Average age 32. 81 applicants, 91% accepted. In 2006, 87 degrees awarded. *Degree requirements:* For master's, thesis or alternative. *Entrance requirements:* For master's, minimum GPA of 2.5 in last 60 hours of bachelor's degree. Additional exam requirements/recommendations for international students: Required—TOEFL. *Application deadline:* For fall admission, 7/15 priority date for domestic students; for spring admission, 12/1 priority date for domestic students. Applications are processed on a rolling basis. Application fee: $0 ($25 for international students). Electronic applications accepted. *Expenses:* Tuition, state resident: part-time $112 per credit hour. Tuition, nonresident: part-time $387 per credit hour. Required fees: $8 per credit hour. $8 per term. *Financial support:* Career-related internships or fieldwork and scholarships/grants available. Financial award application deadline: 3/1; financial award applicants required to submit FAFSA. *Unit head:* Dr. Edward Bashaw, Dean, 903-223-3106, E-mail: edward.bashaw@tamut.edu. *Application contact:* Patricia E. Black, Director of Admissions and Registrar, 903-223-3068, Fax: 903-223-3140, E-mail: pat.black@tamut.edu.

Texas Christian University, College of Science and Engineering, Department of Physics and Astronomy, Fort Worth, TX 76129-0002. Offers physics (MA, MS, PhD), including astrophysics (PhD), business (PhD), physics (PhD). Part-time and evening/weekend programs available. *Degree requirements:* For doctorate, thesis/dissertation, qualifying exams. *Entrance requirements:* For doctorate, GRE General Test. Additional exam requirements/recommendations for international students: Required—TOEFL. *Application deadline:* For fall admission, 3/1 for domestic students; for spring admission, 12/1 for domestic students. Applications are processed on a rolling basis. Application fee: $0. *Expenses:* Tuition: Part-time $800 per credit hour. *Financial support:* Fellowships, teaching assistantships available. Financial award application deadline: 3/1. *Unit head:* Dr. T. W. Zerda, Chairperson, 817-257-7375. *Application contact:* Dr. Bonnie Melhart, Associate Dean, College of Science and Engineering, E-mail: b.melhart@tcu.edu.

Texas Christian University, M. J. Neeley School of Business, Program in Business Administration, Fort Worth, TX 76129-0002. Offers MBA. *Accreditation:* AACSB. Part-time and evening/weekend programs available. *Entrance requirements:* For master's, GMAT, 6 hours of course work in economics, 3 hours of course work in college algebra. Additional exam requirements/recommendations for international students: Required—TOEFL. *Application deadline:* For fall admission, 4/30 priority date for domestic students. Applications are processed on a rolling basis. Application fee: $50. Electronic applications accepted. *Expenses:* Tuition: Part-time $800 per credit hour. *Financial support:* Career-related internships or fieldwork, Federal Work-Study, institutionally sponsored loans, and unspecified assistantships available. Support available to part-time students. Financial award application deadline: 5/1; financial award applicants required to submit FAFSA. *Faculty research:* Emerging financial markets, derivative trading activity, salesforce deployment, examining sales activity, litigation against tax practitioners. Total annual research expenditures: $2.5 million. *Unit head:* Dr. Bill Cron, Associate Dean, Graduate Programs, 817-257-7531. *Application contact:* Peggy Conway, Director, MBA Admissions, 817-257-7531, Fax: 817-257-6431, E-mail: mbainfo@tcu.edu.

Texas Southern University, Graduate School, Jesse H. Jones School of Business, Program in Business Administration, Houston, TX 77004-4584. Offers MBA. *Accreditation:* AACSB. Part-time and evening/weekend programs available. *Faculty:* 11 full-time (2 women), 5 part-time/adjunct (2 women). *Students:* 57 full-time (33 women), 34 part-time (21 women); includes 82 minority (78 African Americans, 3 Asian Americans or Pacific Islanders, 1 Hispanic American), 9 international. Average age 30. 55 applicants, 82% accepted, 34 enrolled. In 2006, 36 degrees awarded. *Degree requirements:* For master's, comprehensive exam. *Entrance requirements:* For master's, GMAT, minimum GPA of 2.5. *Application deadline:* For fall admission, 7/15 priority date for domestic students; for spring admission, 11/15 for domestic students. Applications are processed on a rolling basis. Application fee: $50 ($75 for international students). *Financial support:* In 2006–07, 2 students received support, including 2 research assistantships (averaging $8,623 per year); career-related internships or fieldwork and unspecified assistantships also available. Financial award application deadline: 5/1. *Unit head:* Dr. K. V. Ramaswamy, Chairperson, 713-313-7309, Fax: 713-313-7705, E-mail: ramaswamy@aol.com. *Application contact:* Bobbie J. Richardson, Executive Secretary, 713-313-7309, Fax: 713-313-7705, E-mail: richardson_bj@tsu.edu.

Texas State University-San Marcos, Graduate School, Emmett & Miriam McCoy College of Business Administration, Program in Business Administration, San Marcos, TX 78666. Offers MBA. *Accreditation:* AACSB. Part-time programs available. *Faculty:* 19 full-time (3 women). *Students:* 74 full-time (37 women), 145 part-time (51 women); includes 52 minority (10 African Americans, 3 American Indian/Alaska Native, 17 Asian Americans or Pacific Islanders, 22 Hispanic Americans), 13 international. Average age 28. 78 applicants, 79% accepted, 46 enrolled. In 2006, 106 degrees awarded. *Degree requirements:* For master's, thesis optional. *Entrance requirements:* For master's, GMAT, minimum GPA of 2.0 in last 60 hours of undergraduate work. *Application deadline:* For fall admission, 6/1 for domestic and international students; for spring admission, 10/1 for domestic and international students. Applications are processed on a rolling basis. Application fee: $40 ($90 for international students). *Financial support:* In 2006–07, 102 students received support, including 2 research assistantships (averaging $4,991 per year), 8 teaching assistantships (averaging $7,488 per year); Federal Work-Study and institutionally sponsored loans also available. Support available to part-time students. Financial award application deadline: 4/1; financial award applicants required to submit FAFSA. *Faculty research:* Organizational change and communication, artificial intelligence systems. *Unit head:* Dr. Robert Davis, Associate Dean, 512-245-3692, Fax: 512-245-7973, E-mail: rd23@txstate.edu.

Texas Tech University, Jerry S. Rawls College of Business Administration, Area of Management, Lubbock, TX 79409. Offers PhD. *Accreditation:* AACSB. Part-time programs available. *Faculty:* 17 full-time (3 women), 1 part-time/adjunct (0 women). *Students:* 10 full-time (5 women), 2 international. Average age 32. 9 applicants, 33% accepted, 3 enrolled. In 2006, 1 doctorate awarded. *Degree requirements:* For doctorate, thesis/dissertation, qualifying exams, comprehensive exam, registration. *Entrance requirements:* For doctorate, GMAT, holistic profile of academic credentials. Additional exam requirements/recommendations for international students: Required—TOEFL (minimum score 550 paper-based; 213 computer-based; 79 iBT). *Application deadline:* For fall admission, 7/1 priority date for domestic students, 3/1 priority date for international students; for spring admission, 11/1 priority date for domestic students, 9/1 priority date for international students. Applications are processed on a rolling basis. Application fee: $50 ($60 for international students). Electronic applications accepted. *Expenses:* Tuition, state resident: full-time $4,440. Tuition, nonresident: full-time $11,040. Required fees: $2,136. *Financial support:* In 2006–07, 5 research assistantships (averaging $8,000 per year), 4 teaching assistantships (averaging $16,930 per year) were awarded; career-related internships or fieldwork, Federal Work-Study, and scholarships/grants also available. Financial award applicants required to submit FAFSA. *Faculty research:* Entrepreneurship, Leadership, Health Care, Organization Theory. *Unit head:* Dr. William Gardner, Area Coordinator, 806-742-1055, Fax: 806-742-2308, E-mail: william.gardner@ttu.edu. *Application contact:* Cynthia D. Barnes, Director, Graduate Services Center, 806-742-3184, Fax: 806-742-3958, E-mail: ba_grad@ttu.edu.

Texas Tech University, Jerry S. Rawls College of Business Administration, Programs in Business Administration, Lubbock, TX 79409. Offers agricultural business (MBA); entrepreneurship (MBA); finance (MBA); general business (MBA); health organization management (MBA); international business (MBA); management and leadership skills (MBA); management information systems (MBA); marketing (MBA); statistics (MBA); JD/MBA; MBA/M Arch; MBA/MA; MBA/MD; MBA/MS. Part-time and evening/weekend programs available. *Students:* 65 full-time (16 women), 347 part-time (121 women); includes 74 minority (5 African Americans, 5 American Indian/Alaska Native, 24 Asian Americans or Pacific Islanders, 40 Hispanic Americans), 24 international. Average age 25. 382 applicants, 82% accepted, 244 enrolled. In 2006, 150 degrees awarded. *Degree requirements:* For master's, capstone course. *Entrance requirements:* For master's, GMAT, holistic review of academic credentials. Additional exam requirements/recommendations for international students: Required—TOEFL (minimum score 550 paper-based; 213 computer-based; 79 iBT). *Application deadline:* For fall admission, 7/1 priority date for domestic students, 3/1 priority date for international students; for spring admission, 11/1 priority date for domestic students, 9/1 priority date for international students. Applications are processed on a rolling basis. Application fee: $50 ($60 for international students). Electronic applications accepted. *Expenses:* Tuition, state resident: full-time $4,440. Tuition, nonresident: full-time $11,040. Required fees: $2,136. *Financial support:* In 2006–07, 36 research assistantships (averaging $8,000 per year) were awarded; teaching assistantships, career-related internships or fieldwork, Federal Work-Study, scholarships/grants, health care benefits, and unspecified assistantships also available. Support available to part-time students. Financial award applicants required to submit FAFSA. *Unit head:* Dr. W. Jay Conover, Director, 806-742-1546, Fax: 806-742-3958, E-mail: jay.conover@ttu.edu. *Application contact:* Cynthia D. Barnes, Director, Graduate Services Center, 806-742-3184, Fax: 806-742-3958, E-mail: ba_grad@ttu.edu.

Texas Wesleyan University, Graduate Programs, Programs in Business Administration, Fort Worth, TX 76105-1536. Offers business administration (MBA); geriatrics (MSHA); health administration (MSHA); public health (MSHA). *Accreditation:* ACBSP. Part-time and evening/weekend programs available. *Faculty:* 13 full-time (3 women), 4 part-time/adjunct (1 woman). *Students:* 15 full-time (7 women), 42 part-time (30 women); includes 27 minority (14 African Americans, 1 American Indian/Alaska Native, 4 Asian Americans or Pacific Islanders, 8 Hispanic Americans). Average age 31. In 2006, 18 degrees awarded. *Degree requirements:* For master's, capstone course. *Entrance requirements:* For master's, GMAT, minimum GPA of 3.0 in final 60 hours of undergraduate course work, 2.75 overall. *Application deadline:* Applications are processed on a rolling basis. Application fee: $30 ($50 for international students). Electronic applications accepted. *Expenses:* Contact institution. Tuition and fees vary according to program. *Financial support:* Federal Work-Study, scholarships/grants, and tuition waivers (full and partial) available. Support available to part-time students. Financial award application deadline: 3/15; financial award applicants required to submit FAFSA. *Unit head:* Dr. Charles Little, Director, 817-531-6500, Fax: 817-531-6585.

Texas Woman's University, Graduate School, College of Arts and Sciences, School of Management, Denton, TX 76201. Offers MBA, MHSM. Part-time programs available. *Students:* 388 full-time (313 women), 190 part-time (152 women); includes 299 minority (198 African Americans, 3 American Indian/Alaska Native, 38 Asian Americans or Pacific Islanders, 60 Hispanic Americans), 37 international. Average age 36. In 2006, 238 degrees awarded. *Degree requirements:* For master's, thesis optional. *Entrance requirements:* For master's, GMAT, 3 letters of reference, resumé, minimum GPA of 3.0, 5 years relevant experience may be required. Additional exam requirements/recommendations for international students: Required—TOEFL (minimum score 550 paper-based; 213 computer-based; 79 iBT). *Application deadline:* For fall admission, 4/1 for international students; for spring admission, 8/1 for international students. Applications are processed on a rolling basis. Application fee: $30 ($50 for international students). Electronic applications accepted. *Expenses:* Tuition, area resident: Part-time $168 per unit. Tuition, state resident: full-time $4,369. Tuition, nonresident: full-time $9,373; part-time $443 per unit. Required fees: $20 per unit. $177 per term. *Financial support:* In 2006–07, 9 research assistantships (averaging $9,468 per year), 2 teaching assistantships (averaging $9,468 per year) were awarded; career-related internships or fieldwork, Federal Work-Study, institutionally sponsored loans, scholarships/grants, traineeships, health care benefits, and unspecified assistantships also available. Support available to part-time students. Financial award application deadline: 3/1; financial award applicants required to submit FAFSA. *Faculty research:* Leadership, tax, women in management, sales, job satisfaction. *Unit head:* Dr. P. Ann Hughes, Director, 940-898-2111, Fax: 940-898-2120, E-mail: pahughes@twu.edu. *Application contact:* Samuel Wheeler, Coordinator of Graduate Admissions, 940-898-3188, Fax: 940-898-3081, E-mail: wheelersr@twu.edu.

Thomas College, Graduate School, Programs in Business, Waterville, ME 04901-5097. Offers business (MBA); computer technology education (MS); education (MS); human resource management (MBA). Part-time and evening/weekend programs available. *Entrance requirements:* For master's, GMAT or minimum GPA of 3.3 in first 3 graduate-level courses, GRE or minimum GPA of 3.3 in first 3 graduate-level courses, MAT or minimum GPA of 3.3 in first 3 graduate-level courses.

Thomas Edison State College, School of Business and Management, Program in Management, Trenton, NJ 08608-1176. Offers human resource management (MSM); online learning and teaching (MSM); organizational leadership (MSM); public sector auditing (MSM); public service leadership (MSM). Part-time programs available. Postbaccalaureate distance learning degree programs offered (minimal on-campus study). *Students:* Average age 42. 77 applicants, 60 enrolled. In 2006, 55 degrees awarded. *Degree requirements:* For master's, capstone/thesis, applied project. *Entrance requirements:* For master's, 3-5 years of work experience. Additional exam requirements/recommendations for international students: Required—TOEFL (minimum score 550 paper-based; 213 computer-based). *Application deadline:* For fall admission, 8/15 priority date for domestic and international students; for winter admission, 11/15 priority date for domestic and international students; for spring admission, 2/15 priority date for domestic and international students. Applications are processed on a rolling basis. Application fee: $75. Electronic applications accepted. *Expenses:* Tuition, nonresident: part-time $422 per credit. Part-time tuition and fees vary according to program. *Financial support:* Applicants required to submit FAFSA. *Application contact:* Renee San Giacomo, Director of Admissions, 888-442-8372, Fax: 609-984-8447, E-mail: admissions@tesc.edu.

Thomas More College, Program in Business Administration, Crestview Hills, KY 41017-3495. Offers MBA. Evening/weekend programs available. *Faculty:* 11 full-time (3 women). *Students:* 75 full-time (36 women); includes 4 minority (1 African American, 2 Asian Americans or Pacific Islanders, 1 Hispanic American). Average age 32. 47 applicants, 68% accepted, 28 enrolled. In 2006, 69 degrees awarded. *Degree requirements:* For master's, final project. *Entrance requirements:* For master's, GMAT, minimum GPA of 2.7. Additional exam requirements/recommendations for international students: Required—TOEFL (minimum score 600 paper-based; 250 computer-based). *Application deadline:* Applications are processed on a rolling basis. Application fee: $25. Electronic applications accepted. *Expenses:* Tuition: Full-time $10,330. One-time fee: $125 full-time. *Financial support:* In 2006–07, 60 students received support. Institutionally sponsored loans available. Financial award application deadline: 3/15; financial award applicants required to submit FAFSA. *Faculty research:* Comparison level and consumer satisfaction, history of U.S. business development, share price reaction, quality and competition, personnel development. *Unit head:* Nathan Hartman, Director of Lifelong Learning, 859-344-3602, Fax: 859-344-3686, E-mail: nathan.hartman@thomasmore.edu.

Thomas University, Department of Business Administration, Thomasville, GA 31792-7499. Offers MBA. Part-time programs available. *Faculty:* 4 full-time (3 women). *Students:* 3 full-time (2 women), 7 part-time (6 women); includes 5 minority (all African Americans) Average age 27. In 2006, 10 degrees awarded. *Entrance requirements:* For master's, resumé, 3 professional or academic references. Additional exam requirements/recommendations for international students: Required—TOEFL (minimum score 600 paper-based; 250 computer-based). *Application deadline:* For fall admission, 8/1 priority date for domestic students, 6/1 for international students; for spring admission, 12/1 priority date for domestic students, 10/1 for international students. Applications are processed on a rolling basis. Application fee: $50 ($125 for international students). Electronic applications accepted. *Expenses:* Tuition: Part-time $376 per credit. Required fees: $130 per semester. *Financial support:* Applicants required to submit FAFSA. *Unit head:* Dr. Jenny Swearingen, Assistant Professor, Chair of Business, 229-226-1621 Ext. 133, Fax: 229-226-1653, E-mail: jswearingen@thomasu.edu. *Application contact:* Adrienne Diggs, Assistant Director of Admissions, 229-226-1621 Ext. 127, Fax: 229-227-6919, E-mail: adiggs@thomasu.edu.

Thunderbird School of Global Management, Graduate Programs, Master's Programs in Global Management, Glendale, AZ 85306-6000. Offers global affairs and management (MA); global management (MS). *Accreditation:* AACSB. *Faculty:* 40 full-time (10 women), 3 part-time/adjunct (1 woman). *Degree requirements:* For master's, one foreign language. *Entrance requirements:* For master's, GMAT/GRE. Additional exam requirements/recommendations for international students: Required—TOEFL (minimum score 567 paper-based). Application fee: $125. *Expenses:* Tuition: Full-time $36,630. Required fees: $1,220. One-time fee: $625 full-time. Part-time tuition and fees vary according to course load and program. *Financial support:*

Business Administration and Management—General

Thunderbird School of Global Management (continued)
Career-related internships or fieldwork, Federal Work-Study, scholarships/grants, and unspecified assistantships available. *Unit head:* Dr. Glenn Fong, Unit Head, 602-978-7000.

Tiffin University, Program in Business Administration, Tiffin, OH 44883-2161. Offers general management (MBA); leadership (MBA); safety and security (MBA); sports management (MBA). *Accreditation:* ACBSP. Part-time and evening/weekend programs available. Postbaccalaureate distance learning degree programs offered (no on-campus study). *Faculty:* 29 full-time (8 women), 28 part-time/adjunct (9 women). *Students:* 89 full-time (54 women), 159 part-time (87 women); includes 31 minority (28 African Americans, 3 Hispanic Americans), 8 international. Average age 31. 182 applicants, 68% accepted, 88 enrolled. In 2006, 145 degrees awarded. *Entrance requirements:* For master's, minimum undergraduate GPA of 2.5, work experience. Additional exam requirements/recommendations for international students: Required—TOEFL (minimum score 550 paper-based; 213 computer-based). *Application deadline:* For fall admission, 9/3 for domestic students, 8/1 for international students; for spring admission, 1/9 for domestic students, 12/1 for international students. Applications are processed on a rolling basis. Application fee: $50. Electronic applications accepted. *Expenses:* Tuition: Part-time $700 per credit hour. *Financial support:* In 2006–07, 94 students received support. Available to part-time students. Application deadline: 7/31; *Faculty research:* Small business, executive development operations, research and statistical analysis, market research, management information systems. *Unit head:* Dr. Shawn P. Daly, Dean of the School of Business, 419-448-3404, Fax: 419-443-5002, E-mail: sdaly@tiffin.edu. *Application contact:* Kristi Krintzline, Director of Graduate Admissions, 800-968-6446 Ext. 3445, Fax: 419-443-5002, E-mail: krintzlineka@tiffin.edu.

Touro University International, College of Business Administration, Program in Business Administration, Cypress, CA 90630. Offers business administration (PhD); conflict and negotiation management (MBA); criminal justice administration (MBA); entrepreneurship (MBA); finance (MBA); general management (MBA); human resource management (MBA); information technology management (MBA); international business (MBA); logistics management (MBA); public management (MBA); strategic leadership (MBA). Part-time and evening/weekend programs available. Postbaccalaureate distance learning degree programs offered (no on-campus study). In 2006, 631 master's, 30 doctorates awarded. *Degree requirements:* For doctorate, thesis/dissertation, defense of dissertation, comprehensive exam. *Entrance requirements:* For master's, minimum GPA of 3.0; for doctorate, minimum GPA of 3.4, curriculum vitae, course work in research methods or statistics. Additional exam requirements/recommendations for international students: Required—TOEFL (minimum score 550 paper-based). *Application deadline:* Applications are processed on a rolling basis. Application fee: $75. Electronic applications accepted. *Expenses:* Tuition: Part-time $300 per credit hour. Tuition and fees vary according to course level and program.

Towson University, Joint University of Baltimore/Towson University (UB/Towson) MBA Program, Baltimore, MD 21201. Offers accounting and business advisory services (MS); business administration (MBA); MBA/JD; MBA/MSN; MBA/PhD; MBA/Pharm D. *Students:* 21 full-time (3 women). *Entrance requirements:* For master's, GMAT, 2 letters of recommendation, minimum GPA of 3.0, resumé. *Application deadline:* Applications are processed on a rolling basis. Application fee: $50. Electronic applications accepted. *Expenses:* Tuition, state resident: part-time $275 per unit. Tuition, nonresident: part-time $577 per unit. Required fees: $72 per unit. *Unit head:* Ron Desi, Graduate Program Director, 410-704-3562, E-mail: rdesi@towson.edu. *Application contact:* Graduate School, 410-837-4777, E-mail: grads@towson.edu.

Trevecca Nazarene University, Graduate Division, School of Business and Management, Major in Business Administration, Nashville, TN 37210-2877. Offers MBA. Evening/weekend programs available. In 2006, 28 degrees awarded. *Entrance requirements:* For master's, GMAT, proficiency exam (quantitative skills), minimum GPA of 2.5, resumé, employer letter of recommendation, 2 letters of recommendation, written business analysis. Additional exam requirements/recommendations for international students: Required—TOEFL (minimum score 500 paper-based; 173 computer-based). *Application deadline:* Applications are processed on a rolling basis. Application fee: $25. *Expenses: Contact institution.* Tuition and fees vary according to degree level and program. *Financial support:* Applicants required to submit FAFSA. *Unit head:* Dr. Ken Burger, Director, 615-248-1529, E-mail: management@trevecca.edu. *Application contact:* Marcus Lackey, Admissions Counselor, 615-248-1529, Fax: 615-248-1700, E-mail: management@trevecca.edu.

Trinity International University, Trinity Evangelical Divinity School, Deerfield, IL 60015-1284. Offers Biblical and Near Eastern archaeology and languages (MA); Christian studies (MA, Certificate); Christian thought (MA); church history (MA, Th M); congregational ministry: pastor-teacher (M Div); congregational ministry: team ministry (M Div); counseling ministries (MA); counseling psychology (MA); cross-cultural ministry (M Div); educational studies (PhD); evangelism (MA); general studies (MAR); history of Christianity in America (MA); intercultural studies (MA, PhD); leadership and ministry management (D Min); military chaplaincy (D Min); ministry (MA); mission and evangelism (Th M); missions and evangelism (D Min); New Testament (MA, Th M); Old Testament (Th M); Old Testament and Semitic languages (MA); pastoral care (M Div); pastoral care and counseling (D Min); pastoral counseling and psychology (Th M); pastoral theology (Th M); philosophy of religion (MA); preaching (D Min); research ministry (M Div); systematic theology (Th M); theological studies (PhD); urban ministry (MA, MAR). *Accreditation:* ATS (one or more programs are accredited). Part-time programs available. Postbaccalaureate distance learning degree programs offered (minimal on-campus study). *Faculty:* 39 full-time (3 women), 68 part-time/adjunct (10 women). *Students:* 515 full-time (105 women), 716 part-time (180 women); includes 163 minority (32 African Americans, 1 American Indian/Alaska Native, 119 Asian Americans or Pacific Islanders, 11 Hispanic Americans), 135 international. 489 applicants, 88% accepted, 212 enrolled. In 2006, 76 first professional degrees, 136 master's, 47 doctorates, 31 other advanced degrees awarded. *Degree requirements:* For M Div, 2 foreign languages; for master's, thesis, fieldwork, comprehensive exam; for doctorate, thesis/dissertation, comprehensive exam (for some programs); for Certificate, integrative papers. *Entrance requirements:* For M Div, GRE, MAT; for master's, GRE, MAT, minimum cumulative undergraduate GPA of 3.0; for doctorate, GRE, minimum cumulative graduate GPA of 3.2; for Certificate, GRE, MAT, minimum undergraduate GPA of 2.5. Additional exam requirements/recommendations for international students: Required—TOEFL (minimum score 580 paper-based; 237 computer-based), TWE (minimum score 4). *Application deadline:* For fall admission, 7/15 priority date for domestic and international students. Applications are processed on a rolling basis. Application fee: $25. Electronic applications accepted. *Expenses: Contact institution. Financial support:* In 2006–07, 929 students received support, including 6 fellowships with partial tuition reimbursements available, 12 teaching assistantships with partial tuition reimbursements available; career-related internships or fieldwork, Federal Work-Study, scholarships/grants, and tuition waivers (partial) also available. Financial award application deadline: 4/1; financial award applicants required to submit FAFSA. *Unit head:* Dr. Tite Tiénou, Academic Dean, 847-317-8086, Fax: 847-317-8014, E-mail: ttienou@teds.edu. *Application contact:* Ron Campbell, Director of Admissions, 800-345-8337, Fax: 847-317-8097, E-mail: rcampbel@tiu.edu.

Trinity University, Department of Business Administration, San Antonio, TX 78212-7200. Offers accounting (MS). *Accreditation:* AACSB. Part-time programs available. *Faculty:* 4 full-time (2 women). *Students:* 21 full-time (13 women), 2 part-time (1 woman); includes 4 minority (all Hispanic Americans), 1 international. Average age 23. In 2006, 27 degrees awarded. *Entrance requirements:* For master's, GMAT, minimum GPA of 3.0, course work in accounting and business law. *Application deadline:* For fall admission, 2/1 priority date for domestic students. Application fee: $40. *Financial support:* In 2006–07, 12 research assistantships were awarded. Financial award application deadline: 4/1. *Unit head:* Dr. Petrea K. Sandlin, Director of the Accounting Program, 210-999-7296, Fax: 210-999-8134, E-mail: psandlin@trinity.edu.

Trinity (Washington) University, School of Professional Studies, Washington, DC 20017-1094. Offers business administration (MBA); communication (MA); information security management (MS); organizational management (MSA), including federal program management, human resource management, nonprofit management, organizational development, public and community health. Part-time and evening/weekend programs available. *Degree requirements:* For master's, thesis (for some programs), capstone project (MSA). *Entrance requirements:* For master's, minimum GPA of 2.5. Additional exam requirements/recommendations for international students: Required—TOEFL (minimum score 550 paper-based; 213 computer-based).

Troy University, Graduate School, College of Business, Troy, AL 36082. Offers business administration (EMBA, MBA); human resource management (MS); management (MS, MSM). *Accreditation:* ACBSP. Part-time and evening/weekend programs available. Postbaccalaureate distance learning degree programs offered. *Students:* 1,274 full-time (604 women), 1,592 part-time (818 women); includes 1,615 minority (1,410 African Americans, 13 American Indian/Alaska Native, 97 Asian Americans or Pacific Islanders, 95 Hispanic Americans). Average age 33. In 2006, 1148 degrees awarded. *Degree requirements:* For master's, thesis or alternative, registration. *Entrance requirements:* For master's, GMAT, GRE General Test, minimum GPA of 2.5. Additional exam requirements/recommendations for international students: Required—TOEFL (minimum score 523 paper-based; 200 computer-based). *Application deadline:* Applications are processed on a rolling basis. Application fee: $50. Electronic applications accepted. *Expenses:* Tuition, state resident: full-time $4,368; part-time $182 per hour. Tuition, nonresident: full-time $8,736; part-time $364 per hour. Required fees: $50 per term. *Financial support:* In 2006–07, 5 research assistantships were awarded; career-related internships or fieldwork also available. Support available to part-time students. Financial award applicants required to submit FAFSA. *Faculty research:* Public accounting, investment, employee relations, networking, supply chain management. *Unit head:* Dr. Don Hines, Dean, 334-670-3143, Fax: 334-670-3708, E-mail: dhines@troy.edu. *Application contact:* Brenda K. Campbell, Director of Graduate Admissions, 334-670-3178, Fax: 334-670-3733, E-mail: bcamp@troy.edu.

Troy University, Graduate School, Program in Business Administration, Troy, AL 36082. Offers EMBA, MBA. Part-time and evening/weekend programs available. *Students:* 400 full-time (212 women), 629 part-time (332 women); includes 484 minority (417 African Americans, 4 American Indian/Alaska Native, 43 Asian Americans or Pacific Islanders, 20 Hispanic Americans). Average age 29. In 2006, 49 degrees awarded. *Degree requirements:* For master's, thesis or alternative, registration. *Entrance requirements:* Additional exam requirements/recommendations for international students: Required—TOEFL (minimum score 523 paper-based; 200 computer-based). *Application deadline:* Applications are processed on a rolling basis. Application fee: $50. *Expenses:* Tuition, state resident: full-time $4,368; part-time $182 per hour. Tuition, nonresident: full-time $8,736; part-time $364 per hour. Required fees: $50 per term. *Unit head:* Dr. Henry M. Findley, Interim Chair, Professor, 334-670-3271, Fax: 334-670-3599, E-mail: hfindley@troy.edu. *Application contact:* Brenda K. Campbell, Director of Graduate Admissions, 334-670-3178, Fax: 334-670-3733, E-mail: bcamp@troy.edu.

Troy University, Graduate School, Program in Management, Troy, AL 36082. Offers MS, MSM. Evening/weekend programs available. *Students:* 698 full-time (262 women), 501 part-time (151 women); includes 693 minority (585 African Americans, 8 American Indian/Alaska Native, 42 Asian Americans or Pacific Islanders, 58 Hispanic Americans), 1 international. Average age 35. In 2006, 881 degrees awarded. *Degree requirements:* For master's, thesis or alternative, registration. *Entrance requirements:* Additional exam requirements/recommendations for international students: Required—TOEFL (minimum score 523 paper-based; 200 computer-based). *Application deadline:* Applications are processed on a rolling basis. Application fee: $50. Electronic applications accepted. *Expenses: Contact institution. Unit head:* Dr. Henry M. Findley, Interim Chair, Professor, 334-670-3271, Fax: 334-670-3599, E-mail: hfindley@troy.edu. *Application contact:* Brenda K. Campbell, Director of Graduate Admissions, 334-670-3178, Fax: 334-670-3733, E-mail: bcamp@troy.edu.

Tulane University, A. B. Freeman School of Business, New Orleans, LA 70118-5669. Offers EMBA, M Acct, M Fin, MBA, PMBA, PhD, JD/M Acct, JD/MBA, MBA/M Acc, MBA/MA, MBA/MD, MBA/ME, MBA/MPH. *Accreditation:* AACSB. Part-time and evening/weekend programs available. *Faculty:* 65 full-time (15 women), 64 part-time/adjunct (21 women). *Students:* 337 full-time, 222 part-time; includes 58 minority (30 African Americans, 3 American Indian/Alaska Native, 11 Asian Americans or Pacific Islanders, 14 Hispanic Americans), 177 international. Average age 27. 495 applicants, 72% accepted, 173 enrolled. In 2006, 325 master's, 16 doctorates awarded. Terminal master's awarded for partial completion of doctoral program. *Entrance requirements:* For master's, GMAT, interview. Additional exam requirements/recommendations for international students: Required—TOEFL. *Application deadline:* For fall admission, 5/1 priority date for domestic students; for spring admission, 12/1 priority date for domestic students. Application fee: $40 ($50 for international students). Electronic applications accepted. *Expenses: Contact institution. Financial support:* In 2006–07, 68 students received support, including 50 fellowships with full and partial tuition reimbursements available; research assistantships, teaching assistantships, career-related internships or fieldwork, Federal Work-Study, tuition waivers (full and partial), and unspecified assistantships also available. Support available to part-time students. Financial award application deadline: 4/15; financial award applicants required to submit FAFSA. *Unit head:* Angelo S. DeNisi, Dean, 504-865-5407, Fax: 504-865-5491. *Application contact:* Bill D. Sandefer, Director, Graduate Admissions and Financial Aid, 504-865-5410, Fax: 504-865-6770, E-mail: freeman.admissions@tulane.edu.

Union Graduate College, School of Management, Program in Business Administration, Schenectady, NY 12308-3107. Offers MBA, Certificate. *Accreditation:* AACSB. Part-time and evening/weekend programs available. *Students:* 77 full-time (37 women), 189 part-time (70 women); includes 8 African Americans, 10 Asian Americans or Pacific Islanders, 6 Hispanic Americans, 20 international. Average age 27. 101 applicants, 70% accepted, 57 enrolled. In 2006, 58 master's, 2 other advanced degrees awarded. *Degree requirements:* For master's, internship, capstone course. *Entrance requirements:* For master's, GMAT, minimum GPA of 3.0. Additional exam requirements/recommendations for international students: Required—TOEFL (minimum score 550 paper-based; 213 computer-based). *Application deadline:* Applications are processed on a rolling basis. Application fee: $60. *Financial support:* Research assistantships, career-related internships or fieldwork, Federal Work-Study, scholarships/grants, health care benefits, and tuition waivers (partial) available. Support available to part-time students. Financial award applicants required to submit FAFSA. *Application contact:* Rhonda Sheehan, Director of Graduate Admissions Registrar, 518-388-6238, Fax: 518-388-6686, E-mail: sheehanr@union.edu.

See Close-Up on page 333.

Union University, McAfee School of Business Administration, Jackson, TN 38305-3697. Offers MBA. Also available at Germantown campus. Evening/weekend programs available. *Entrance requirements:* For master's, GMAT, minimum GPA of 2.5. Electronic applications accepted. Expenses: Contact institution. *Faculty research:* Personal financial management, strategy, accounting, marketing, economics.

United States International University, School of Business Administration, Nairobi, Kenya. Offers finance (MBA); information technology management (MBA); integrated studies (MBA); management and organizational development (MS); marketing (MBA); strategic management (MBA). Part-time and evening/weekend programs available. *Degree requirements:* For master's, thesis, registration. *Entrance requirements:* For master's, GMAT, 2 letters of reference, resumé. Additional exam requirements/recommendations for international students: Required—TOEFL (minimum score 550 paper-based; 213 computer-based). *Faculty research:* Marketing in small business enterprises, total quality management in Kenya.

Universidad Autonoma de Guadalajara, Graduate Programs, Guadalajara, Mexico. Offers architecture (M Arch); computational science (MCC); education (Ed M, Ed D); international business (MIB); manufacturing systems (MMS); quality systems (MQS);).

Universidad Central del Este, Graduate School, San Pedro de Macoris, Dominican Republic. Offers accounting (M Ad); administration (M Ad); architecture (M Arch); civil engineering (ME); electromechanical engineering (ME); human resources (M Ad); industrial engineering (ME); public health (MPH). *Entrance requirements:* For master's, letters of recommendation.

Universidad de las Americas, A.C., Program in Business Administration, Mexico City, Mexico. Offers finance (MBA); marketing research (MBA); production and quality (MBA).

Universidad de las Américas–Puebla, Division of Graduate Studies, School of Business Administration, Puebla, Mexico. Offers business administration (MBA); finance (M Adm). Part-time and evening/weekend programs available. *Degree requirements:* For master's, one foreign language, thesis. *Entrance requirements:* Additional exam requirements/ recommendations for international students: Required—TOEFL. *Faculty research:* System dynamics, information technology, marketing, international business, strategic planning, quality.

Universidad del Este, Graduate School, Carolina, PR 00983. Offers accounting (MBA); administration (M Ed); criminal justice and criminology (MA); education (M Ed); elementary education (M Ed); human resources (MBA); management (MBA); social work (MA); teaching English (M Ed); teaching Spanish (M Ed).

Universidad del Turabo, Graduate Programs, School in Business Administration, Program in Management, Gurabo, PR 00778-3030. Offers MBA, DBA. Part-time and evening/weekend programs available. *Entrance requirements:* For master's, GRE, EXADEP, interview.

Universidad Metropolitana, School of Business Administration, San Juan, PR 00928-1150. Offers accounting (MBA); finance (MBA); human resources management (MBA); international business (MBA); management (MBA); marketing (MBA); public accounting (Certificate). Part-time and evening/weekend programs available. *Degree requirements:* For master's, thesis or alternative. Electronic applications accepted. *Faculty research:* Latin American trade, international investments, central city business development, Hispanic consumer research, Caribbean and Asian trade cooperation.

Universidad Nacional Pedro Henriquez Urena, Graduate School, Santo Domingo, Dominican Republic. Offers accounting and auditing (M Acct); animal production (M Agr); business administration (MBA, PhD); Caribbean tropical architecture (M Arch); conservation of monuments and cultural goods (M Arch); economics (M Econ); education (PhD); environmental engineering (MEE); horticulture (M Agr); hospital administration (PhD); humanities (PhD); international relations (MPS); management of natural resources (MNRM); project management (M Man, MPM); public administration (MPS); sanitary engineering (ME); social science (PhD); veterinary medicine (DVM).

Université de Moncton, Faculty of Administration, Moncton, NB E1A 3E9, Canada. Offers MBA, LL B/MBA. Part-time and evening/weekend programs available. Postbaccalaureate distance learning degree programs offered (no on-campus study). *Faculty:* 11 full-time (3 women), 2 part-time/adjunct (0 women). *Students:* 42 full-time (5 women), 88 part-time (45 women), 34 international. Average age 28. 100 applicants, 45% accepted, 25 enrolled. In 2006, 36 degrees awarded. *Degree requirements:* For master's, one foreign language. *Entrance requirements:* For master's, minimum undergraduate GPA of 3.0. *Application deadline:* For fall admission, 6/1 for domestic students, 2/1 for international students; for winter admission, 11/15 for domestic students, 9/1 for international students; for spring admission, 3/31 for domestic students, 1/1 for international students. Applications are processed on a rolling basis. Application fee: $39. *Financial support:* In 2006–07, 7 fellowships (averaging $2,500 per year) were awarded; teaching assistantships, institutionally sponsored loans also available. Support available to part-time students. Financial award application deadline: 5/30. *Faculty research:* Services management, corporate reputation, financial management, accounting, supply chain. Total annual research expenditures: $150,000. *Unit head:* Dr. Tania Morris, Director, 506-858-4218, Fax: 506-858-4093, E-mail: tania.morris@umoncton.ca. *Application contact:* Natalie LeBlanc, Admission Counselor, 506-858-4273, Fax: 506-858-4093, E-mail: natalie.r.leblanc@umoncton.ca.

Université de Sherbrooke, Faculty of Administration, Doctoral Program in Business Administration, Sherbrooke, QC J1K 2R1, Canada. Offers DBA.

Université de Sherbrooke, Faculty of Administration, Program in Business Administration, Sherbrooke, QC J1K 2R1, Canada. Offers EMBA, MBA, Diploma.

Université de Sherbrooke, Faculty of Law, Sherbrooke, QC J1K 2R1, Canada. Offers alternative dispute resolution (LL M, Diploma); biotechnology (LL B); business administration (LL B); business law (Diploma); health law (LL M, Diploma); law (LL B, LL D); legal management (Diploma); notarial law (DDN); transnational law (Diploma). Part-time and evening/weekend programs available. *Degree requirements:* For master's, thesis; for other advanced degree, one foreign language. *Entrance requirements:* For master's and other advanced degree, LL B. Electronic applications accepted.

Université du Québec à Chicoutimi, Graduate Programs, Program in Small and Medium-Sized Organization Management, Chicoutimi, QC G7H 2B1, Canada. Offers M Sc. Part-time programs available. *Degree requirements:* For master's, thesis. *Entrance requirements:* For master's, appropriate bachelor's degree, proficiency in French.

Université du Québec à Montréal, Graduate Programs, PhD Program in Business Administration, Montréal, QC H3C 3P8, Canada. Offers PhD. Part-time programs available. *Degree requirements:* For doctorate, thesis/dissertation. *Entrance requirements:* For doctorate, appropriate master's degree or equivalent, proficiency in French.

Université du Québec à Montréal, Graduate Programs, Program in Business Administration (Professional), Montréal, QC H3C 3P8, Canada. Offers business administration (MBA); management consultant (Diploma). Part-time programs available. *Entrance requirements:* For master's and Diploma, appropriate bachelor's degree or equivalent, proficiency in French.

Université du Québec à Montréal, Graduate Programs, Program in Business Administration (Research), Montréal, QC H3C 3P8, Canada. Offers MBA. Part-time programs available. *Entrance requirements:* For master's, appropriate bachelor's degree or equivalent and proficiency in French.

Université du Québec à Rimouski, Graduate Programs, Program in Business Administration, Rimouski, QC G5L 3A1, Canada. Offers MBA. *Students:* 47 full-time (17 women), 5 part-time (2 women). *Unit head:* Jules Bouchard, Director, 418-833-8800 Ext. 3227, Fax: 418-833-1113, E-mail: jules_bouchard@uqar.ca. *Application contact:* Marc Berube, Office of Admission, 418-724-1433, Fax: 418-724-1525, E-mail: marc_berube@uqar.ca.

Université du Québec à Rimouski, Graduate Programs, Program in Management of People in Working Situation, Rimouski, QC G5L 3A1, Canada. Offers M Sc, Diploma. *Students:* 11 full-time, 28 part-time. Application fee: $50. *Unit head:* Jean-Pierre Roger, Director, 418-724-1546, Fax: 418-724-1525, E-mail: jean-pierreroger@uqar.ca. *Application contact:* Marc Berube, Office of Admission, 418-724-1433, Fax: 418-724-1525, E-mail: marcberube@uqar.ca.

Université du Québec à Trois-Rivières, Graduate Programs, Program in Business Administration, Trois-Rivières, QC G9A 5H7, Canada. Offers DBA. *Degree requirements:* For doctorate, thesis/dissertation.

Université du Québec à Trois-Rivières, Graduate Programs, Program in Management of Small and Medium-Sized Enterprises and Their Environment, Trois-Rivières, QC G9A 5H7, Canada. Offers M Sc. Part-time programs available. *Degree requirements:* For master's, research report. *Entrance requirements:* For master's, appropriate bachelor's degree, proficiency in French.

Université du Québec en Abitibi-Témiscamingue, Graduate Programs, Program in Business Administration, Rouyn-Noranda, QC J9X 5E4, Canada. Offers MBA.

Université du Québec en Abitibi-Témiscamingue, Graduate Programs, Program in Organization Management, Rouyn-Noranda, QC J9X 5E4, Canada. Offers M Sc. Part-time programs available. *Degree requirements:* For master's, thesis. *Entrance requirements:* For master's, appropriate bachelor's degree, proficiency in French.

Université Laval, Faculty of Administrative Sciences, Program in Organizations Management and Development, Québec, QC G1K 7P4, Canada. Offers Diploma. Part-time programs available. *Entrance requirements:* For degree, knowledge of French. Electronic applications accepted.

Université Laval, Faculty of Administrative Sciences, Programs in Administrative Studies, Québec, QC G1K 7P4, Canada. Offers administrative studies (M Sc, PhD); financial engineering (M Sc). *Accreditation:* AACSB. Terminal master's awarded for partial completion of doctoral program. *Degree requirements:* For master's, thesis (for some programs); for doctorate, thesis/dissertation, comprehensive exam. *Entrance requirements:* For master's and doctorate, knowledge of French and English. Electronic applications accepted.

Université Laval, Faculty of Administrative Sciences, Programs in Business Administration, Québec, QC G1K 7P4, Canada. Offers accounting (MBA); agri-food management (MBA); electronic business (MBA, Diploma); factory management and logistics (MBA); finance (MBA); firm management (MBA); information technology management (MBA); international management (MBA); management (MBA); management accounting (MBA, Diploma); marketing (MBA); modelization and organizational decision (MBA); occupational health and safety management (MBA); pharmacy management (MBA); technological entrepreneurship (Diploma). *Accreditation:* AACSB. Part-time and evening/weekend programs available. Postbaccalaureate distance learning degree programs offered (no on-campus study). *Entrance requirements:* For master's and Diploma, knowledge of French and English. Electronic applications accepted.

University at Albany, State University of New York, School of Business, Albany, NY 12222-0001. Offers MBA, MS. *Accreditation:* AACSB. Part-time and evening/weekend programs available. *Students:* 199 full-time (93 women), 189 part-time (74 women); includes 44 minority (11 African Americans, 2 American Indian/Alaska Native, 26 Asian Americans or Pacific Islanders, 5 Hispanic Americans), 53 international. Average age 31. In 2006, 216 master's awarded. Terminal master's awarded for partial completion of doctoral program. *Degree requirements:* For master's, project. *Entrance requirements:* For master's, GMAT. Additional exam requirements/ recommendations for international students: Required—TOEFL (minimum score 550 paper-based; 213 computer-based). *Application deadline:* For fall admission, 3/1 for domestic students, 5/1 for international students. Applications are processed on a rolling basis. Application fee: $75. Electronic applications accepted. *Expenses:* Tuition, state resident: full-time $6,900; part-time $288 per credit. Tuition, nonresident: full-time $10,920; part-time $455 per credit. Required fees: $1,139. *Financial support:* Fellowships, research assistantships, career-related internships or fieldwork and Federal Work-Study available. *Unit head:* Paul Leonard, Dean, 518-442-4910. *Application contact:* Michael DeRensis, Director, Graduate Admissions, 518-442-3980, Fax: 518-442-3922, E-mail: graduate@uamail.albany.edu.

University at Buffalo, the State University of New York, Graduate School, School of Management, Buffalo, NY 14260. Offers accounting (MS); business administration (MBA); finance (MS); information assurance (Certificate); management (PhD); management information systems (MS); supply chains and operations management (MS); Au D/MBA; JD/MBA; M Arch/MBA; MA/MBA; MD/MBA; MPH/MBA; MSW/MBA; Pharm D/MBA. *Accreditation:* AACSB. Part-time and evening/weekend programs available. *Faculty:* 65 full-time (18 women), 30 part-time/adjunct (3 women). *Students:* 493 full-time (192 women), 212 part-time (55 women); includes 53 minority (11 African Americans, 3 American Indian/Alaska Native, 31 Asian Americans or Pacific Islanders, 8 Hispanic Americans), 283 international. Average age 27. 1,058 applicants, 55% accepted, 369 enrolled. In 2006, 260 master's, 5 doctorates, 3 other advanced degrees awarded. *Degree requirements:* For doctorate, thesis/dissertation, comprehensive exam. *Entrance requirements:* For master's, GMAT, GRE General Test (all master's degrees except accounting); for doctorate, GMAT or GRE. Additional exam requirements/recommendations for international students: Required—TOEFL (minimum score 230 computer-based). *Application deadline:* For fall admission, 6/1 priority date for domestic students, 3/1 priority date for international students. Applications are processed on a rolling basis. Application fee: $50. Electronic applications accepted. *Expenses:* Contact institution. *Financial support:* In 2006–07, 91 students received support, including 17 fellowships with full and partial tuition reimbursements available (averaging $3,917 per year), 38 research assistantships with full and partial tuition reimbursements available (averaging $11,907 per year), 26 teaching assistantships with full and partial tuition reimbursements available (averaging $7,571 per year); career-related internships or fieldwork, Federal Work-Study, institutionally sponsored loans, scholarships/ grants, health care benefits, and unspecified assistantships also available. Financial award application deadline: 2/15; financial award applicants required to submit FAFSA. *Faculty research:* Information assurance, relationship marketing, global processes, credit analysis in banking, disaster mitigation and response. Total annual research expenditures: $330,551. *Unit head:* John M. Thomas, Dean, 716-645-3221, Fax: 716-645-5926, E-mail: jmthomas@buffalo.edu. *Application contact:* David W. Frasier, Administrative Director of Graduate Programs and Assistant Dean, 716-645-3204, Fax: 716-645-2341, E-mail: davidf@buffalo.edu.

The University of Akron, Graduate School, College of Business Administration, Department of Management, Akron, OH 44325. Offers electronic business (MBA); entrepreneurship (MBA); management (MBA); management of technology (MBA); management-health services administration (MSM); management-human resources (MSM); management-information systems (MSM); management-supply chain management (MSM); JD/MBA; JD/MSM. *Accreditation:* AACSB. Part-time and evening/weekend programs available. *Faculty:* 19 full-time (3 women), 6 part-time/adjunct (1 woman). *Students:* 70 full-time (29 women), 72 part-time (24 women); includes 4 minority (2 African Americans, 1 Asian American or Pacific Islander, 1 Hispanic American), 40 international. Average age 29. 91 applicants, 70% accepted, 29 enrolled. In 2006, 31 degrees awarded. *Entrance requirements:* For master's, GMAT, minimum GPA of 2.75. Additional exam requirements/recommendations for international students: Required—TOEFL (minimum score 550 paper-based; 213 computer-based; 79 iBT). *Application deadline:* For fall admission, 8/15 for domestic students. Applications are processed on a rolling basis. Application fee: $30 ($40 for international students). Electronic applications accepted. *Expenses:* Tuition, state resident: full-time $6,164; part-time $342 per credit. Tuition, nonresident: full-time $10,575; part-time $588 per credit. Required fees: $806; $43 per credit. $12 per term. Tuition and fees vary according to course load, degree level and program. *Financial support:* In 2006–07, 26 research assistantships with full tuition reimbursements, 1 teaching assistantship with full tuition reimbursement were awarded; career-related internships or fieldwork, Federal Work-Study, and tuition waivers (partial) also available. *Faculty research:* Information systems management, supply chain management, health care management, organizational development and leadership, strategy and globalization. *Unit head:* Dr. Ravi Krovi, Chair, 330-972-8108, Fax: 330-972-6588, E-mail: krovi@uakron.edu. *Application contact:* Dr. James Divoky, Director of Graduate Business Programs, 330-972-7043, Fax: 330-972-6588, E-mail: jdivoky@uakron.edu.

The University of Alabama, Graduate School, Manderson Graduate School of Business, Department of Information Systems, Statistics, and Management Science, Program of Information Systems, Statistics, and Management Science—Operations Management, Tuscaloosa, AL 35487. Offers operations management (MS, PhD). Part-time programs available. Postbaccalaureate distance learning degree programs offered (no on-campus study). *Students:* 9 full-time (1 woman), 6 part-time (3 women); includes 1 minority (African American), 2 international. In 2006, 17 master's, 6 doctorates awarded. Terminal master's awarded for partial completion of doctoral program. *Median time to degree:* Of those who began their doctoral program in fall 1998, 75% received their degree in 8 years or less. *Degree requirements:* For master's, business calculus; for doctorate, thesis/dissertation, comprehensive exam. *Entrance requirements:* For master's, GMAT or GRE, TOEFL or IELTS; for doctorate, GRE or GMAT. Additional exam

Business Administration and Management—General

The University of Alabama (continued)
requirements/recommendations for international students: Required—TOEFL (minimum score 550 paper-based; 213 computer-based), IELTS (minimum score 7). *Application deadline:* For spring admission, 3/1 priority date for domestic and international students. Application fee: $25. *Financial support:* In 2006–07, 7 teaching assistantships with full tuition reimbursements (averaging $13,500 per year) were awarded; scholarships/grants and health care benefits also available. Financial award application deadline: 3/1. *Application contact:* Dana Merchant, Administrative Secretary, 205-348-8904, E-mail: dmerchan@cba.ua.edu.

The University of Alabama, Graduate School, Manderson Graduate School of Business, Department of Management and Marketing, Program in Management, Tuscaloosa, AL 35487. Offers accounting (MA, PhD); applied statistics (PhD); economics (MA, PhD); finance (MS, PhD); management (MA, PhD); operations management (MS, PhD); statistics (MS); tax accounting (MA). *Faculty:* 27 full-time (8 women), 2 part-time/adjunct (0 women). *Students:* Average age 29. 112 applicants, 36% accepted. In 2006, 20 master's, 1 doctorate awarded. Terminal master's awarded for partial completion of doctoral program. *Median time to degree:* Master's–2.4 years part-time; doctorate–4 years full-time, 2 years part-time. Of those who began their doctoral program in fall 1998, 100% received their degree in 8 years or less. *Degree requirements:* For master's, thesis (for some programs), formal project paper, comprehensive exam (for some programs); registration; for doctorate, thesis/dissertation, comprehensive exam, registration. *Entrance requirements:* For master's and doctorate, GMAT or GRE, minimum GPA of 3.0. Additional exam requirements/recommendations for international students: Required—TOEFL. *Application deadline:* For fall admission, 6/30 priority date for domestic students, 1/31 for international students. Applications are processed on a rolling basis. Application fee: $25. *Financial support:* In 2006–07, 5 fellowships (averaging $2,000 per year), 2 research assistantships (averaging $2,000 per year), 2 teaching assistantships (averaging $2,000 per year) were awarded. *Faculty research:* Relationship marketing, team building, e-commerce strategy, entrepreneurship, health care management, service marketing.

The University of Alabama, Graduate School, Manderson Graduate School of Business, Program in General Commerce and Business, Tuscaloosa, AL 35487. Offers MBA. Part-time programs available. *Students:* 126 full-time (38 women), 2 part-time; includes 6 African Americans, 1 American Indian/Alaska Native, 3 Asian Americans or Pacific Islanders, 17 international. In 2006, 77 degrees awarded. *Financial support:* In 2006–07, 22 research assistantships (averaging $5,400 per year), 4 teaching assistantships were awarded. *Application contact:* Pam Vickers, Manager of Admissions and Student Services, 205-348-9122, Fax: 205-348-4504, E-mail: pvickers@cba.ua.edu.

The University of Alabama at Birmingham, School of Business, Birmingham, AL 35294. Offers M Acct, MBA, PhD. *Accreditation:* AACSB. *Students:* 149 full-time (65 women), 244 part-time (89 women); includes 68 minority (37 African Americans, 2 American Indian/Alaska Native, 23 Asian Americans or Pacific Islanders, 6 Hispanic Americans), 40 international. Average age 28. 176 applicants, 79% accepted. In 2006, 166 degrees awarded. *Entrance requirements:* For master's, GMAT. *Application deadline:* Applications are processed on a rolling basis. Application fee: $35 ($60 for international students). Electronic applications accepted. *Expenses:* Tuition, state resident: part-time $170 per credit hour. Tuition, nonresident: part-time $425 per credit hour. Required fees: $15 per credit hour. $122 per term. Tuition and fees vary according to program. *Financial support:* Fellowships, career-related internships or fieldwork available. *Unit head:* Dr. Robert E. Holmes, Dean, 205-934-8800, Fax: 205-934-8886, E-mail: holmesr@uab.edu. *Application contact:* Director, 205-934-8817.

The University of Alabama in Huntsville, School of Graduate Studies, College of Administrative Science, Department of Management, Huntsville, AL 35899. Offers human resource management (Certificate); management (MS, MSM). *Accreditation:* AACSB. Part-time and evening/weekend programs available. *Faculty:* 7 full-time (2 women), 6 part-time/adjunct (5 women). *Students:* 9 full-time (5 women), 63 part-time (29 women); includes 11 minority (3 African Americans, 2 American Indian/Alaska Native, 4 Asian Americans or Pacific Islanders, 2 Hispanic Americans), 4 international. Average age 32. 36 applicants, 83% accepted, 23 enrolled. In 2006, 36 master's, 2 other advanced degrees awarded. *Degree requirements:* For master's, thesis or alternative, comprehensive exam, registration. *Entrance requirements:* For master's, GMAT, minimum AACSB index of 1000. Additional exam requirements/recommendations for international students: Required—TOEFL (minimum score 550 paper-based; 213 computer-based). *Application deadline:* For fall admission, 8/10 for domestic students; for spring admission, 12/10 for domestic students. Application fee: $40. *Expenses:* Tuition, state resident: full-time $6,072; part-time $253 per credit hour. Tuition, nonresident: full-time $12,476; part-time $519 per credit hour. *Financial support:* Research assistantships, teaching assistantships with full and partial tuition reimbursements, career-related internships or fieldwork, Federal Work-Study, institutionally sponsored loans, scholarships/grants, health care benefits, and unspecified assistantships available. Support available to part-time students. Financial award application deadline: 4/1; financial award applicants required to submit FAFSA. *Unit head:* Dr. James Simpson, Chair, 256-824-6408, Fax: 256-824-7571, E-mail: msmprog@email.uah.edu.

University of Alaska Anchorage, College of Business and Public Policy, Program in Business Administration, Anchorage, AK 99508-8060. Offers MBA. *Accreditation:* AACSB. Part-time programs available. *Students:* 20 full-time (16 women), 52 part-time (39 women); includes 17 minority (4 African Americans, 8 American Indian/Alaska Native, 3 Asian Americans or Pacific Islanders, 2 Hispanic Americans), 2 international. 53 applicants, 75% accepted. In 2006, 25 degrees awarded. *Degree requirements:* For master's, thesis (for some programs), capstone projects, comprehensive exam, registration. *Entrance requirements:* Additional exam requirements/recommendations for international students: Required—TOEFL (minimum score 550 paper-based; 213 computer-based). *Application deadline:* For fall admission, 7/1 priority date for domestic students, 7/1 for international students; for spring admission, 11/1 for domestic and international students. Applications are processed on a rolling basis. Application fee: $45. *Expenses:* Tuition, state resident: part-time $268 per credit. Tuition, nonresident: part-time $547 per credit. Required fees: $124 per semester. Tuition and fees vary according to reciprocity agreements and student level. *Financial support:* Research assistantships with full tuition reimbursements, Federal Work-Study, scholarships/grants, health care benefits, and unspecified assistantships available. Support available to part-time students. Financial award application deadline: 4/1; financial award applicants required to submit FAFSA. *Faculty research:* Complex global environments. *Unit head:* Dr. Edward Forrest, Chair, 907-786-4161, Fax: 907-786-4119. *Application contact:* Pat Lee, CBPP Graduate Programs Assistant, 907-786-4101, Fax: 907-786-4119, E-mail: pat.lee@uaa.alaska.edu.

University of Alaska Fairbanks, School of Management, Department of Business Administration, Fairbanks, AK 99775-7520. Offers capital markets (MBA); general management (MBA). *Accreditation:* AACSB. Part-time programs available. *Faculty:* 9 full-time (2 women), 2 part-time/adjunct (1 woman). *Students:* 16 full-time (5 women), 8 part-time (7 women); includes 1 minority (Asian American or Pacific Islander), 6 international. Average age 33. 16 applicants, 56% accepted, 5 enrolled. In 2006, 7 degrees awarded. *Degree requirements:* For master's, thesis or alternative, comprehensive exam, registration. *Entrance requirements:* For master's, GMAT. Additional exam requirements/recommendations for international students: Required—TOEFL (minimum score 550 paper-based; 213 computer-based). *Application deadline:* For fall admission, 6/1 priority date for domestic students, 2/1 for international students; for spring admission, 10/15 priority date for domestic students, 9/1 for international students. Applications are processed on a rolling basis. Application fee: $50. Electronic applications accepted. *Financial support:* In 2006–07, 1 research assistantship with tuition reimbursement (averaging $4,800 per year), 5 teaching assistantships with tuition reimbursements (averaging $10,773 per year) were awarded; fellowships with tuition reimbursements, career-related internships or fieldwork, Federal Work-Study, and scholarships/grants also available. Financial award applicants required to submit FAFSA. *Faculty research:* Consumer behavior, portfolio theory, marketing,

international finance and business, asset pricing. *Unit head:* Dr. Laura Milner, Director, MBA Program, 907-474-5294, Fax: 907-474-5219, E-mail: fflmm@uaf.edu.

University of Alaska Southeast, Graduate Programs, Program in Business Administration, Juneau, AK 99801. Offers MBA. Part-time and evening/weekend programs available. Post-baccalaureate distance learning degree programs offered (minimal on-campus study). *Faculty:* 9 full-time (3 women). *Students:* 6 full-time (all women), 38 part-time (24 women); includes 11 minority (1 African American, 8 American Indian/Alaska Native, 2 Asian Americans or Pacific Islanders), 1 international. Average age 37. In 2006, 5 degrees awarded. *Degree requirements:* For master's, residential seminar. *Entrance requirements:* For master's, curriculum vitae, letters of reference, minimum GPA of 3.0. *Application deadline:* For fall admission, 5/1 priority date for domestic students. Application fee: $50. Electronic applications accepted. *Financial support:* Institutionally sponsored loans and tuition waivers (partial) available. *Faculty research:* Services marketing; marketing and technology issues: social capital and entrepreneurship; motivation and managerial tactics. *Unit head:* Dr. Karen Schmitt, Dean, 907-796-6357, Fax: 907-796-6383. *Application contact:* Valentina Jimmerson, Administrative Assistant, 800-478-9069, Fax: 877-465-6549, E-mail: valentina.jimmerson@vas.alaska.edu.

University of Alberta, Faculty of Graduate Studies and Research, Doctoral Program in Business, Edmonton, AB T6G 2E1, Canada. Offers accounting (PhD); finance (PhD); human resources/industrial relations (PhD); management science (PhD); marketing (PhD); organizational analysis (PhD); MBA/PhD. *Accreditation:* AACSB. Part-time programs available. *Faculty:* 41 full-time (7 women), 1 part-time/adjunct (0 women). *Students:* 46 full-time (27 women), 5 part-time (3 women). Average age 34. 307 applicants, 7% accepted, 11 enrolled. In 2006, 2 degrees awarded. *Median time to degree:* Of those who began their doctoral program in fall 1998, 60% received their degree in 8 years or less. *Degree requirements:* For doctorate, thesis/dissertation, comprehensive exam. *Entrance requirements:* For doctorate, GMAT. Additional exam requirements/recommendations for international students: Required—TOEFL (minimum score 550 paper-based; 213 computer-based). *Application deadline:* For fall admission, 6/1 priority date for domestic students; for winter admission, 5/1 for domestic students. Application fee: $0. Electronic applications accepted. *Financial support:* In 2006–07, 29 students received support, including 11 fellowships with full tuition reimbursements available (averaging $17,000 per year); scholarships/grants and tuition waivers (partial) also available. *Faculty research:* Accounting, capital markets and corporate finance, organizational change and human resource management, marketing, strategic management. Total annual research expenditures: $7.7 million. *Unit head:* Dr. Mike Percy, Director, 780-492-2361, Fax: 780-492-3325, E-mail: busphd@ualberta.ca. *Application contact:* Jeanette Gosine, Program Coordinator, 780-492-2361, Fax: 780-492-3325, E-mail: busphd@ualberta.ca.

See Close-Up on page 335.

University of Alberta, Faculty of Graduate Studies and Research, Executive MBA Program, Edmonton, AB T6G 2E1, Canada. Offers business administration (Exec MBA). *Accreditation:* AACSB. *Students:* 14 full-time (5 women). 18 applicants, 83% accepted. In 2006, 7 degrees awarded. *Entrance requirements:* For master's, GMAT. Additional exam requirements/recommendations for international students: Required—TOEFL. *Application deadline:* For fall admission, 5/15 priority date for domestic students. Applications are processed on a rolling basis. Application fee: $0. Electronic applications accepted. *Expenses:* Contact institution. *Unit head:* Dr. Vern Jones, Director, 780-465-3946, Fax: 403-465-8760. *Application contact:* Marjorie McCullen, Information Contact, 780-492-4213, Fax: 780-492-7825, E-mail: mba@ualberta.ca.

University of Alberta, Faculty of Graduate Studies and Research, Program in Business Administration, Edmonton, AB T6G 2E1, Canada. Offers international business (MBA); leisure and sport management (MBA); natural resources and energy (MBA); technology commercialization (MBA); MBA/LL B; MBA/M Ag; MBA/M Eng; MBA/MF; MBA/PhD. *Accreditation:* AACSB. Part-time and evening/weekend programs available. *Faculty:* 77 full-time, 20 part-time/adjunct. *Students:* 131 full-time (56 women), 109 part-time (51 women). Average age 29. 525 applicants, 30% accepted, 90 enrolled. In 2006, 114 degrees awarded. *Degree requirements:* For master's, thesis or alternative. *Entrance requirements:* For master's, GMAT. Additional exam requirements/recommendations for international students: Required—TOEFL (minimum score 600 paper-based; 250 computer-based). *Application deadline:* For fall admission, 4/30 priority date for domestic students, 4/30 for international students. Applications are processed on a rolling basis. Application fee: $0. Electronic applications accepted. *Financial support:* Fellowships, research assistantships, teaching assistantships, career-related internships or fieldwork, scholarships/grants, health care benefits, and unspecified assistantships available. *Faculty research:* Natural resources and energy/management and policy/family enterprise/international business/healthcare research management. Total annual research expenditures: $1 million. *Unit head:* Dr. Douglas Olsen, Associate Dean, 780-492-5412, Fax: 780-492-7825. *Application contact:* Joan A. White, Secretary, 780-492-3679, Fax: 780-492-2024, E-mail: mba@ualberta.ca.

The University of Arizona, Graduate College, College of Business and Public Administration, Eller Graduate School of Management, Tucson, AZ 85721. Offers accounting (M Ac); business administration (MBA); economics (MA, PhD); finance (MS, PhD); management (PhD), including accounting, finance, management (MS, PhD), management information systems (MS, PhD), marketing; management and organizations (MS, PhD), including management; management information systems (MS), including management information systems (MS, PhD); marketing (MS, PhD); JD/MA; JD/MBA; JD/PhD. *Accreditation:* AACSB. Evening/weekend programs available. *Faculty:* 116. *Students:* 251 full-time (70 women); includes 44 minority (7 African Americans, 4 American Indian/Alaska Native, 12 Asian Americans or Pacific Islanders, 21 Hispanic Americans), 54 international. Average age 30. 402 applicants, 58% accepted, 147 enrolled. In 2006, 136 degrees awarded. *Degree requirements:* For doctorate, thesis/dissertation. *Entrance requirements:* For master's, GMAT, minimum GPA of 3.0, interview, 3 letters of recommendation; for doctorate, GRE General Test, GRE Subject Test, minimum GPA of 3.0. Additional exam requirements/recommendations for international students: Required—TOEFL (minimum score 600 paper-based; 250 computer-based; 100 iBT). *Application deadline:* For fall admission, 4/15 for domestic students, 2/15 for international students. Applications are processed on a rolling basis. Application fee: $50. Electronic applications accepted. *Expenses:* Contact institution. *Financial support:* In 2006–07, 81 students received support, including 46 teaching assistantships (averaging $8,000 per year); career-related internships or fieldwork, Federal Work-Study, scholarships/grants, health care benefits, tuition waivers (partial), and unspecified assistantships also available. Financial award application deadline: 3/15. *Unit head:* Dr. E. LaBrent Chrite, Associate Dean and MBA Director, 520-626-3372, Fax: 520-621-2606. *Application contact:* Marissa B. Cox, Director of Admissions, 520-621-6227, Fax: 520-621-2606, E-mail: mbaadmissions@eller.arizona.edu.

University of Arkansas, Graduate School, Sam M. Walton College of Business Administration, Program in Business Administration, Fayetteville, AR 72701-1201. Offers MBA, PhD. *Accreditation:* AACSB. Part-time and evening/weekend programs available. Postbaccalaureate distance learning degree programs offered (minimal on-campus study). *Students:* 17 full-time (6 women), 108 part-time (29 women); includes 16 minority (4 African Americans, 10 Asian Americans or Pacific Islanders, 2 Hispanic Americans), 14 international. 29 applicants, 31% accepted. In 2006, 96 master's, 4 doctorates awarded. *Degree requirements:* For doctorate, thesis/dissertation. *Entrance requirements:* For master's and doctorate, GMAT. Application fee: $40 ($50 for international students). *Financial support:* In 2006–07, 19 fellowships with tuition reimbursements, 12 research assistantships, 13 teaching assistantships were awarded; career-related internships or fieldwork and Federal Work-Study also available. Support available to part-time students. Financial award application deadline: 4/1; financial award applicants required to submit FAFSA. *Unit head:* Dr. William Curington, Associate Dean, 479-575-2851. *Application contact:* Jennifer Williams, Assistant Director of Marketing and Recruiting, 479-575-6123, E-mail: gsb@walton.uark.edu.

University of Arkansas at Little Rock, Graduate School, College of Business Administration, Little Rock, AR 72204-1099. Offers business administration (MBA); management information system (MIS); JD/MBA. *Accreditation:* AACSB. Part-time and evening/weekend programs available. *Entrance requirements:* For master's, GMAT, minimum undergraduate GPA of 2.7. Additional exam requirements/recommendations for international students: Required—TOEFL (minimum score 525 paper-based; 195 computer-based).

University of Baltimore, Graduate School, Merrick School of Business, Baltimore, MD 21201-5779. Offers MBA, MS, JD/MBA, MBA/MSN, MBA/Pharm D. Part-time and evening/weekend programs available. Postbaccalaureate distance learning degree programs offered (no on-campus study). *Faculty:* 54 full-time (11 women), 36 part-time/adjunct (6 women). *Students:* 133 full-time (66 women), 419 part-time (195 women); includes 134 minority (83 African Americans, 2 American Indian/Alaska Native, 35 Asian Americans or Pacific Islanders, 14 Hispanic Americans), 74 international. Average age 31. 543 applicants, 66% accepted, 253 enrolled. In 2006, 199 degrees awarded. *Entrance requirements:* For master's, GMAT. Additional exam requirements/recommendations for international students: Required—TOEFL (minimum score 550 paper-based; 213 computer-based). *Application deadline:* For fall admission, 8/1 priority date for domestic students, 6/1 for international students; for spring admission, 12/1 for domestic students, 11/1 for international students. Applications are processed on a rolling basis. Application fee: $45. Electronic applications accepted. *Expenses:* Tuition, state resident: full-time $5,322; part-time $591 per credit. Tuition, nonresident: full-time $7,527; part-time $830 per credit. *Financial support:* Fellowships, research assistantships, career-related internships or fieldwork and Federal Work-Study available. Support available to part-time students. Financial award application deadline: 4/1; financial award applicants required to submit FAFSA. *Faculty research:* Finance, economics, accounting, health care, MIS. Total annual research expenditures: $1.2 million. *Unit head:* Dr. Susan Zacur, Dean, 410-837-4955. *Application contact:* Dean Dreibelbis, Assistant Director, Office of Graduate Admissions, 410-837-6565, Fax: 410-837-4793, E-mail: gradadmissions@ubalt.edu.

University of Baltimore, Joint University of Baltimore/Towson University (UB/Towson) MBA Program, Baltimore, MD 21201-5779. Offers MBA, JD/MBA, MBA/MSN, MBA/Pharm D. *Accreditation:* AACSB. Part-time and evening/weekend programs available. Postbaccalaureate distance learning degree programs offered (no on-campus study). *Faculty:* 44 full-time (12 women), 36 part-time/adjunct (6 women). *Students:* 103 full-time (48 women), 331 part-time (147 women); includes 113 minority (72 African Americans, 2 American Indian/Alaska Native, 27 Asian Americans or Pacific Islanders, 12 Hispanic Americans), 47 international. Average age 30. 367 applicants, 63% accepted, 151 enrolled. In 2006, 151 degrees awarded. *Entrance requirements:* For master's, GMAT. Additional exam requirements/recommendations for international students: Required—TOEFL (minimum score 550 paper-based; 213 computer-based). *Application deadline:* For fall admission, 8/1 priority date for domestic students, 6/1 for international students; for spring admission, 12/1 for domestic students, 11/1 for international students. Applications are processed on a rolling basis. Application fee: $45. *Expenses:* Tuition, state resident: full-time $5,322; part-time $591 per credit. Tuition, nonresident: full-time $7,527; part-time $830 per credit. *Financial support:* In 2006–07, 16 research assistantships were awarded; fellowships, career-related internships or fieldwork and Federal Work-Study also available. Support available to part-time students. Financial award application deadline: 4/1; financial award applicants required to submit FAFSA. Total annual research expenditures: $184,507. *Unit head:* Ray Frederick, Graduate Advisor, 410-837-4944, E-mail: rfrederick@ubalt.edu. *Application contact:* Dean Dreibelbis, Assistant Director, Office of Graduate Admissions, 410-837-6565, Fax: 410-837-4793, E-mail: gradadmissions@ubalt.edu.

University of Bridgeport, School of Business, Program in Business Administration, Bridgeport, CT 06604. Offers MBA. *Accreditation:* ACBSP. Postbaccalaureate distance learning degree programs offered (minimal on-campus study). *Faculty:* 11 full-time (2 women), 12 part-time/adjunct (5 women). *Students:* 227 full-time (100 women), 131 part-time (54 women); includes 46 minority (21 African Americans, 15 Asian Americans or Pacific Islanders, 10 Hispanic Americans), 272 international. Average age 29. 503 applicants, 76% accepted, 141 enrolled. In 2006, 70 degrees awarded. *Degree requirements:* For master's, thesis optional. *Entrance requirements:* For master's, GMAT. Additional exam requirements/recommendations for international students: Required—TOEFL. *Application deadline:* For fall admission, 8/1 priority date for domestic students; for spring admission, 12/1 priority date for domestic students. Applications are processed on a rolling basis. Application fee: $25 ($35 for international students). Electronic applications accepted. *Financial support:* In 2006–07, 69 students received support; research assistantships, career-related internships or fieldwork available. Financial award application deadline: 6/1; financial award applicants required to submit FAFSA. *Unit head:* Dr. Ward Thrasher, MBA Director, 203-576-4368, Fax: 203-576-4388, E-mail: mba@bridgeport.edu.

The University of British Columbia, Sauder School of Business, Doctoral Program in Commerce and Business Administration, Vancouver, BC V6T 1Z1, Canada. Offers accounting (PhD); finance (PhD); international business (PhD); management information systems (PhD); management science (PhD); marketing (PhD); organizational behavior (PhD); policy analysis and strategy (PhD); transportation and logistics (PhD); urban land economics (PhD). *Degree requirements:* For doctorate, thesis/dissertation, comprehensive exam. *Entrance requirements:* For doctorate, GMAT or GRE. Additional exam requirements/recommendations for international students: Required—TOEFL. Electronic applications accepted.

The University of British Columbia, Sauder School of Business, MBA Program, Vancouver, BC V6T 1Z1, Canada. Offers IMBA, MBA. *Accreditation:* AACSB. Part-time and evening/weekend programs available. Postbaccalaureate distance learning degree programs offered (minimal on-campus study). *Entrance requirements:* For master's, GMAT, minimum B average in undergraduate course work. Additional exam requirements/recommendations for international students: Required—TOEFL, IELTS or Michigan English Language Assessment Battery. Electronic applications accepted. Expenses: Contact institution. *Faculty research:* Financial economics and reporting, human resources, information systems, management science, marketing.

University of Calgary, Faculty of Graduate Studies, Haskayne School of Business, Alberta/Haskayne Executive MBA Program, Calgary, AB T2N 1N4, Canada. Offers EMBA. Program offered with School of Business at The University of Alberta. *Accreditation:* AACSB. Part-time programs available. *Faculty:* 27 full-time (5 women). *Students:* 82 full-time (18 women). Average age 35. 60 applicants, 85% accepted, 51 enrolled. In 2006, 39 degrees awarded. *Entrance requirements:* For master's, GMAT, minimum GPA of 3.0, minimum 7 years of work experience, 3 letters of reference. Additional exam requirements/recommendations for international students: Required—TOEFL (minimum score 600 paper-based; 250 computer-based). *Application deadline:* For fall admission, 5/15 priority date for domestic and international students. Applications are processed on a rolling basis. Application fee: $100. *Expenses: Contact institution. Financial support:* Employer funding support available. *Faculty research:* Accounting, data analysis and modeling, strategy, entrepreneurship, negotiations. *Unit head:* Dr. Jack Kulchitsky, Academic Director, 403-220-3358, Fax: 403-282-0095, E-mail: jack.kulchitsky@haskayne.ucalgary.ca. *Application contact:* Karen Amonson, Program Coordinator, 403-220-8828, Fax: 403-282-0095, E-mail: karen.amonson@haskayne-emba.com.

University of Calgary, Faculty of Graduate Studies, Haskayne School of Business, Program in Business Administration, Calgary, AB T2N 1N4, Canada. Offers MBA, MBA/LL B, MBA/MBT, MBA/MD, MBA/MSW. *Accreditation:* AACSB. Part-time and evening/weekend programs available. *Faculty:* 52 full-time (15 women), 15 part-time/adjunct (3 women). *Students:* 146 full-time (53 women), 140 part-time (52 women). Average age 30. 200 applicants, 61% accepted, 64 enrolled. In 2006, 131 degrees awarded. *Degree requirements:* For master's, thesis optional. *Entrance requirements:* For master's, GMAT, minimum GPA of 3.0, resumé, 3 years of work experience, 3 letters of reference, 4 year bachelor degree. Additional exam requirements/recommendations for international students: Required—TOEFL (minimum score 600 paper-based; 250 computer-based). *Application deadline:* For fall admission, 5/1 for domestic students, 3/1 for international students. Applications are processed on a rolling basis. Application fee: $100 ($130 for international students). Electronic applications accepted. *Expenses: Contact institution. Financial support:* In 2006–07, 45 students received support. Career-related internships or fieldwork, scholarships/grants, health care benefits, unspecified assistantships, and $10000 international student grant available. Support available to part-time students. Financial award application deadline: 5/1. *Faculty research:* Sustainability, accounting, entrepreneurship, ethics, strategy. *Unit head:* Dr. Laurie Milton, Associate Dean, Graduate Programs, 403-220-8523, Fax: 403-282-0095, E-mail: laurie.milton@haskayne.ucalgary.ca. *Application contact:* Barbara Lunn, Administrative Coordinator, 403-220-3808, Fax: 403-282-0095, E-mail: barbara.lunn@haskayne.ucalgary.ca.

University of Calgary, Faculty of Graduate Studies, Haskayne School of Business, Program in Management, Calgary, AB T2N 1N4, Canada. Offers MBA, PhD. *Accreditation:* AACSB. *Faculty:* 38 full-time (12 women). *Students:* 37 full-time (10 women). Average age 37. 38 applicants, 18% accepted, 6 enrolled. In 2006, 1 master's, 11 doctorates awarded. Terminal master's awarded for partial completion of doctoral program. *Median time to degree:* Of those who began their doctoral program in fall 1998, 50% received their degree in 8 years or less. *Degree requirements:* For master's, one foreign language, thesis, comprehensive exam, registration; for doctorate, one foreign language, thesis/dissertation, written and oral exams, comprehensive exam, registration. *Entrance requirements:* For master's, GMAT, GRE, minimum GPA of 3.3 in last 2 years of course work, 3 letters of ref.; for doctorate, GMAT, GRE, minimum GPA of 3.5 in last 2 years of course work, 3 letters of reference. Additional exam requirements/recommendations for international students: Required—TOEFL (minimum score 600 paper-based; 250 computer-based), IELTS (minimum score 7). *Application deadline:* For fall admission, 1/15 for domestic and international students; for winter admission, 10/15 for domestic students. Application fee: $100 ($130 for international students). Electronic applications accepted. *Financial support:* In 2006–07, 47 fellowships (averaging $3,569 per year), 14 research assistantships with tuition reimbursements (averaging $6,915 per year), 26 teaching assistantships (averaging $4,410 per year) were awarded; scholarships/grants, health care benefits, and unspecified assistantships also available. Financial award application deadline: 2/1. *Faculty research:* Operations management, entrepreneurship and international business, environmental management, management information systems, accounting. *Unit head:* Dr. Tom Rohleder, Associate Dean, 403-220-7147, Fax: 403-282-0095, E-mail: tom.rohleder@haskayne.ucalgary.ca. *Application contact:* Louise Chapman, Graduate Program Administrator, 403-220-3803, Fax: 403-282-0095, E-mail: louise.chapman@haskayne.ucalgary.ca.

University of California, Berkeley, Graduate Division, Haas School of Business, Berkeley-Columbia Executive MBA Program, Berkeley, CA 94720-1500. Offers MBA. *Accreditation:* AACSB. Part-time programs available. *Students:* Average age 38. In 2006, 67 degrees awarded. *Entrance requirements:* For master's, GMAT. Additional exam requirements/recommendations for international students: Required—TOEFL (minimum score 570 paper-based; 230 computer-based). *Application deadline:* For winter admission, 2/2 priority date for domestic students, 2/21 priority date for international students. Application fee: $175. Electronic applications accepted. *Expenses: Contact institution. Financial support:* Unspecified assistantships available. Financial award application deadline: 3/2; financial award applicants required to submit FAFSA. *Unit head:* Robert Gleeson, Executive Director, 510-643-2188, Fax: 510-642-0631, E-mail: gleeson@haas.berkeley.edu. *Application contact:* Marjorie Degraca, Berkeley-Columbia Executive MBA Admissions Office, 510-643-1046, Fax: 510-642-5902, E-mail: emba@haas.berkeley.edu.

University of California, Berkeley, Graduate Division, Haas School of Business and School of Law, Concurrent JD/MBA Program, Berkeley, CA 94720-1500. Offers JD/MBA. *Accreditation:* AACSB; ABA. *Students:* 2 full-time (both women); includes 1 minority (Asian American or Pacific Islander) Average age 28. *Entrance requirements:* Additional exam requirements/recommendations for international students: Required—TOEFL. *Application deadline:* For fall admission, 3/10 for domestic and international students. Application fee: $175. Electronic applications accepted. *Financial support:* Fellowships, career-related internships or fieldwork, scholarships/grants, and unspecified assistantships available. Financial award application deadline: 3/2; financial award applicants required to submit FAFSA. *Unit head:* Julia Hwang, Director, MBA Program, 510-642-1405, Fax: 510-643-6659, E-mail: julia_hwang@haas.berkeley.edu. *Application contact:* Office of Admissions, 510-642-1405, Fax: 510-643-6659, E-mail: admissions@boalt.berkeley.edu.

University of California, Berkeley, Graduate Division, Haas School of Business and Group in International and Area Studies, Concurrent MBA/MIAS Program in International and Area Studies, Berkeley, CA 94720-1500. Offers MBA/MIAS. *Accreditation:* AACSB. *Entrance requirements:* Additional exam requirements/recommendations for international students: Required—TOEFL. *Application deadline:* For fall admission, 3/10 for domestic and international students. Application fee: $175. *Financial support:* Fellowships with full tuition reimbursements, research assistantships, teaching assistantships with partial tuition reimbursements, career-related internships or fieldwork, scholarships/grants, and unspecified assistantships available. Support available to part-time students. Financial award application deadline: 3/2; financial award applicants required to submit FAFSA. *Unit head:* Julia Hwang, Director, MBA Program, 510-642-1405, Fax: 510-643-6659, E-mail: julia_hwang@haas.berkeley.edu. *Application contact:* 510-642-1405, Fax: 510-643-6659.

University of California, Berkeley, Graduate Division, Haas School of Business and School of Public Health, Concurrent MBA/MPH Program, Berkeley, CA 94720-1500. Offers MBA/MPH. *Accreditation:* AACSB; CAHME; CEPH. *Students:* 34 full-time (22 women); includes 12 minority (1 African American, 10 Asian Americans or Pacific Islanders, 1 Hispanic American), 5 international. Average age 28. *Entrance requirements:* Additional exam requirements/recommendations for international students: Required—TOEFL. *Application deadline:* For fall admission, 3/10 for domestic and international students. Application fee: $175. Electronic applications accepted. *Financial support:* Fellowships with tuition reimbursements, teaching assistantships with tuition reimbursements, career-related internships or fieldwork, scholarships/grants, and unspecified assistantships available. Financial award application deadline: 3/2; financial award applicants required to submit FAFSA. *Unit head:* Prof. Kristi Raube, Director, Health Services Management Program, 510-642-5023, Fax: 510-643-6659, E-mail: raube@haas.berkeley.edu. *Application contact:* Lee Forgue, Student Affairs Officer, 510-642-5023, Fax: 510-643-6659, E-mail: eilis@haas.berkeley.edu.

University of California, Berkeley, Graduate Division, Haas School of Business, Evening and Weekend MBA Program, Berkeley, CA 94720-1500. Offers MBA. *Accreditation:* AACSB. Part-time and evening/weekend programs available. *Students:* Average age 32. 697 applicants, 42% accepted, 243 enrolled. In 2006, 188 degrees awarded. *Degree requirements:* For master's, academic retreat. *Entrance requirements:* For master's, GMAT. Additional exam requirements/recommendations for international students: Required—TOEFL (minimum score 570 paper-based; 230 computer-based). *Application deadline:* For fall admission, 3/1 for domestic and international students. Application fee: $175. Electronic applications accepted. *Expenses: Contact institution. Financial support:* Scholarships/grants and unspecified assistantships available. Support available to part-time students. Financial award application deadline: 3/2; financial award applicants required to submit FAFSA. *Unit head:* Jennifer Chizuk, Director, 510-642-1406, Fax: 510-643-5902, E-mail: ewmbaadm@haas.berkeley.edu. *Application contact:* Evening and Weekend MBA Admissions Officer, 510-642-0292, Fax: 510-643-5902, E-mail: ewmbaadm@haas.berkeley.edu.

University of California, Berkeley, Graduate Division, Haas School of Business, Full-Time MBA Program, Berkeley, CA 94720-1500. Offers MBA. *Accreditation:* AACSB. *Faculty:* 72 full-time, 142 part-time/adjunct. *Students:* 505 full-time (174 women); includes 119 minority (7 African Americans, 100 Asian Americans or Pacific Islanders, 12 Hispanic Americans), 146 international. Average age 28. 2,727 applicants, 17% accepted, 240 enrolled. In 2006, 229 degrees awarded. *Entrance requirements:* For master's, GMAT. Additional exam requirements/recommendations for international students: Required—TOEFL (minimum score 570 paper-based; 230 computer-based), IELTS. *Application deadline:* For fall admission, 3/10 for domestic and international students. Application fee: $175. Electronic applications accepted. *Expenses:*

Business Administration and Management—General

University of California, Berkeley (continued)
Contact institution. *Financial support:* Fellowships with full tuition reimbursements, research assistantships with tuition reimbursements, teaching assistantships with partial tuition reimbursements, career-related internships or fieldwork, scholarships/grants, and unspecified assistantships available. Support available to part-time students. Financial award application deadline: 3/2; financial award applicants required to submit FAFSA. *Unit head:* Julia Hwang, Director, MBA Program, 510-642-1405, Fax: 510-643-6659, E-mail: julia_hwang@haas.berkeley.edu. *Application contact:* Pete Johnson, Co-Director, 510-642-1405, Fax: 510-643-6659.

University of California, Berkeley, Graduate Division, Haas School of Business, Program in Business, Berkeley, CA 94720-1500. Offers accounting (PhD); business and public policy (PhD); finance (PhD); marketing (PhD); organizational behavior and industrial relations (PhD); real estate (PhD). *Accreditation:* AACSB. *Students:* 83 full-time (28 women); includes 17 minority (14 Asian Americans or Pacific Islanders, 3 Hispanic Americans), 33 international. Average age 30. 347 applicants, 16 enrolled. In 2006, 17 degrees awarded. *Median time to degree:* Of those who began their doctoral program in fall 1998, 88% received their degree in 8 years or less. *Degree requirements:* For doctorate, thesis/dissertation, oral exam, written preliminary exams, comprehensive exam. *Entrance requirements:* For doctorate, GMAT or GRE, minimum GPA of 3.0. Additional exam requirements/recommendations for international students: Required—TOEFL (minimum score 570 paper-based; 230 computer-based), IELTS (minimum score 7). *Application deadline:* For fall admission, 12/15 for domestic and international students. Application fee: $60 ($80 for international students). Electronic applications accepted. *Financial support:* Fellowships with full and partial tuition reimbursements, research assistantships with full and partial tuition reimbursements, teaching assistantships with full and partial tuition reimbursements, career-related internships or fieldwork, Federal Work-Study, scholarships/grants, health care benefits, tuition waivers (full), and unspecified assistantships available. Financial award application deadline: 12/15; financial award applicants required to submit FAFSA. *Unit head:* Miguel Villas-Boas, Director, 510-642-1409, Fax: 510-643-4255, E-mail: kimg@haas.berkeley.edu. *Application contact:* Kim Guilfoyle, Administrative Director, 510-642-3944, Fax: 510-643-4255, E-mail: kimg@haas.berkeley.edu.

University of California, Davis, Graduate School of Management, Daytime MBA Program, Davis, CA 95616. Offers MBA, JD/MBA, M Engr/MBA, MBA/MS, MD/MBA. *Faculty:* 27 full-time (7 women), 19 part-time/adjunct (3 women). *Students:* 116 full-time (45 women); includes 22 minority (2 American Indian/Alaska Native, 16 Asian Americans or Pacific Islanders, 4 Hispanic Americans), 22 international. Average age 30. 316 applicants, 28% accepted, 55 enrolled. *Degree requirements:* For master's, registration. *Entrance requirements:* For master's, letters of recommendation, resumé. Additional exam requirements/recommendations for international students: Required—TOEFL (minimum score 600 paper-based; 250 computer-based; 100 iBT). *Application deadline:* For fall admission, 3/14 priority date for domestic and international students. Applications are processed on a rolling basis. Application fee: $100. Electronic applications accepted. *Financial support:* In 2006–07, 80 students received support; research assistantships with partial tuition reimbursements available, teaching assistantships with partial tuition reimbursements available, career-related internships or fieldwork, Federal Work-Study, institutionally sponsored loans, scholarships/grants, tuition waivers (partial), and unspecified assistantships available. Financial award application deadline: 3/1; financial award applicants required to submit FAFSA. *Faculty research:* Technology management, finance, marketing, corporate governance and investor welfare, organizational behavior. *Application contact:* Kathy Gleed, Director, Admissions and Student Services, 530-754-5476, Fax: 530-754-9355, E-mail: krgleed@ucdavis.edu.

University of California, Davis, Graduate School of Management, Working Professional MBA Program, Davis, CA 95616. Offers MBA. Part-time and evening/weekend programs available. *Faculty:* 27 full-time (7 women), 19 part-time/adjunct (3 women). *Students:* Average age 31. 196 applicants, 79% accepted, 114 enrolled. *Degree requirements:* For master's, registration. *Entrance requirements:* For master's, GMAT, letters of recommendation, resumé. Additional exam requirements/recommendations for international students: Required—TOEFL (minimum score 600 paper-based; 250 computer-based; 100 iBT). *Application deadline:* For fall admission, 4/4 priority date for domestic and international students. Applications are processed on a rolling basis. Application fee: $100. Electronic applications accepted. *Expenses:* Contact institution. *Financial support:* Scholarships/grants available. Financial award applicants required to submit FAFSA. *Faculty research:* Technology management, finance, marketing, corporate governance and investor welfare, organizational behavior. *Unit head:* Nicole W. Biggart, Dean, 530-752-7366, Fax: 530-752-2924, E-mail: nwbiggart@ucdavis.edu. *Application contact:* Kathy Gleed, Director, Admissions and Student Services, 530-754-5476, Fax: 530-754-9355, E-mail: krgleed@ucdavis.edu.

University of California, Irvine, Office of Graduate Studies, The Paul Merage School of Business, Irvine, CA 92697. Offers business administration (MBA); management (PhD). *Accreditation:* AACSB. Part-time and evening/weekend programs available. *Students:* 784 full-time (258 women), 7 part-time (4 women); includes 176 minority (9 African Americans, 2 American Indian/Alaska Native, 143 Asian Americans or Pacific Islanders, 22 Hispanic Americans), 122 international. Average age 32. In 2006, 363 master's, 2 doctorates awarded. Terminal master's awarded for partial completion of doctoral program. *Degree requirements:* For doctorate, thesis/dissertation. *Entrance requirements:* For master's, GMAT, minimum GPA of 3.0; for doctorate, GMAT or GRE, minimum GPA of 3.0. Additional exam requirements/recommendations for international students: Required—TOEFL (minimum score 570 paper-based; 230 computer-based). *Application deadline:* For fall admission, 12/1 priority date for domestic students; for spring admission, 5/1 for domestic students. Applications are processed on a rolling basis. Application fee: $75. Electronic applications accepted. *Expenses:* Contact institution. *Financial support:* Career-related internships or fieldwork, Federal Work-Study, institutionally sponsored loans, scholarships/grants, traineeships, health care benefits, and unspecified assistantships available. Support available to part-time students. Financial award application deadline: 3/1; financial award applicants required to submit FAFSA. *Faculty research:* Organizational behavior, finance, informational technology, marketing, accounting. *Unit head:* Jone Pearce, Dean, 949-824-6505, Fax: 949-824-8469, E-mail: jlpearce@uci.edu. *Application contact:* Wendy Gillett, Admissions Coordinator, 949-824-8318, Fax: 949-824-2944, E-mail: wgillett@uci.edu.

University of California, Los Angeles, Graduate Division, UCLA Anderson School of Management, Los Angeles, CA 90095. Offers MBA, MS, PhD, JD/MBA, MBA/MA, MBA/MLIS, MBA/MPH, MBA/MS, MBA/MSN, MD/MBA, MD/PhD. *Accreditation:* AACSB. Part-time programs available. *Students:* 686 full-time (208 women), 646 part-time (181 women); includes 355 minority (17 African Americans, 302 Asian Americans or Pacific Islanders, 36 Hispanic Americans), 108 international. Average age 28. 3,227 applicants, 32% accepted, 608 enrolled. In 2006, 607 degrees awarded. *Degree requirements:* For master's, thesis (MS); for doctorate, thesis/dissertation, oral and written qualifying exams. *Entrance requirements:* For master's, GMAT (MBA); GMAT or GRE General Test (MS), minimum GPA of 3.0; for doctorate, GMAT or GRE General Test, minimum undergraduate GPA of 3.0. *Application deadline:* Applications are processed on a rolling basis. Application fee: $175. *Expenses:* Contact institution. *Financial support:* In 2006–07, 120 fellowships, 23 research assistantships, 25 teaching assistantships were awarded; career-related internships or fieldwork, Federal Work-Study, institutionally sponsored loans, scholarships/grants, and tuition waivers (full and partial) also available. Financial award application deadline: 3/1. *Unit head:* Judy D. Olian, Dean, 310-825-7982, Fax: 310-206-2073. *Application contact:* Linda Baldwin, Director of Admissions, 310-825-6944, E-mail: mba.admissions@anderson.ucla.edu.

See Close-Up on page 337.

University of California, Riverside, Graduate Division, A. Gary Anderson Graduate School of Management, Riverside, CA 92521-0102. Offers MBA. *Accreditation:* AACSB. Part-time and evening/weekend programs available. *Faculty:* 21 full-time (4 women). *Students:* 104 full-time (51 women), 11 part-time (5 women); includes 22 minority (18 Asian Americans or Pacific Islanders, 4 Hispanic Americans), 67 international. Average age 26. In 2006, 39 degrees awarded. *Degree requirements:* For master's, thesis optional. *Entrance requirements:* For master's, GMAT, minimum GPA of 3.2. Additional exam requirements/recommendations for international students: Required—TOEFL (minimum score 550 paper-based; 213 computer-based; 80 iBT). *Application deadline:* For fall admission, 5/1 for domestic students, 2/1 for international students; for winter admission, 9/1 for domestic students, 7/1 for international students; for spring admission, 12/1 for domestic students, 10/1 for international students. Applications are processed on a rolling basis. Application fee: $60 ($75 for international students). *Expenses:* Contact institution. *Financial support:* In 2006–07, teaching assistantships (averaging $15,610 per year); fellowships, research assistantships, career-related internships or fieldwork, Federal Work-Study, institutionally sponsored loans, scholarships/grants, and tuition waivers (full) also available. Financial award application deadline: 2/1; financial award applicants required to submit FAFSA. *Faculty research:* Option pricing, consumer attribution, feminization of management styles, artificial intelligence, new technologies in cost accounting. *Unit head:* Dr. Anil Deolalikar, Interim Dean, 951-827-1575, Fax: 951-827-5685, E-mail: econgrad@ucr.edu. *Application contact:* Charlotte Weber, Assistant Dean, 951-827-4551, Fax: 951-827-3970, E-mail: mba@agsmmail.ucr.edu.

University of California, San Diego, Office of Graduate Studies, Rady School of Management, La Jolla, CA 92093. Offers MBA.

University of Central Arkansas, Graduate School, College of Business Administration, Program in Business Administration, Conway, AR 72035-0001. Offers MBA. *Accreditation:* AACSB. Part-time and evening/weekend programs available. *Faculty:* 11 full-time (2 women). *Students:* 33 full-time (13 women), 40 part-time (16 women); includes 5 minority (2 African Americans, 2 Asian Americans or Pacific Islanders, 1 Hispanic American), 12 international. 34 applicants, 97% accepted, 33 enrolled. In 2006, 39 degrees awarded. *Entrance requirements:* For master's, GMAT, minimum GPA of 2.7. Additional exam requirements/recommendations for international students: Required—TOEFL (minimum score 550 paper-based; 213 computer-based). *Application deadline:* For fall admission, 3/1 priority date for domestic and international students; for spring admission, 10/1 priority date for domestic and international students. Applications are processed on a rolling basis. Application fee: $25 ($40 for international students). *Expenses:* Tuition, state resident: full-time $4,194; part-time $233 per semester. Tuition, nonresident: full-time $5,963; part-time $429 per semester. International tuition: $6,162 full-time. Required fees: $65; $23 per semester. One-time fee: $65 part-time. *Financial support:* In 2006–07, 4 research assistantships with partial tuition reimbursements (averaging $5,000 per year) were awarded; career-related internships or fieldwork, Federal Work-Study, scholarships/grants, tuition waivers (partial), and unspecified assistantships also available. Support available to part-time students. Financial award application deadline: 2/15. *Unit head:* Dr. David Kim, MBA Director, 501-450-5316, Fax: 501-450-5302, E-mail: davidk@uca.edu. *Application contact:* Brenda Herring, Admissions Assistant, 501-450-5065, Fax: 501-450-5678, E-mail: bherring@uca.edu.

University of Central Florida, College of Business Administration, Department of Management, Orlando, FL 32816. Offers MSM. *Accreditation:* AACSB. *Faculty:* 32 full-time (10 women), 1 part-time/adjunct (0 women). *Students:* 7 full-time (5 women), 18 part-time (16 women); includes 9 minority (4 African Americans, 2 Asian Americans or Pacific Islanders, 3 Hispanic Americans), 1 international. In 2006, 20 degrees awarded. *Entrance requirements:* For master's, GMAT, minimum GPA of 3.0 in last 60 hours. *Application deadline:* For fall admission, 2/1 priority date for domestic students; for spring admission, 11/1 priority date for domestic students. Application fee: $30. Electronic applications accepted. *Expenses:* Tuition, state resident: full-time $6,167; part-time $257 per credit hour. Tuition, nonresident: full-time $22,790; part-time $950 per credit hour. *Financial support:* In 2006–07, 2 research assistantships (averaging $6,000 per year) were awarded; fellowships, teaching assistantships also available. *Unit head:* Dr. Foard Jones, Chair, 407-823-2925, Fax: 407-823-3725.

University of Central Florida, College of Business Administration, Program in Business Administration, Orlando, FL 32816. Offers MBA, PhD. *Accreditation:* AACSB. Part-time and evening/weekend programs available. *Students:* 285 full-time (124 women), 264 part-time (102 women); includes 107 minority (31 African Americans, 3 American Indian/Alaska Native, 33 Asian Americans or Pacific Islanders, 40 Hispanic Americans), 76 international. In 2006, 232 master's, 10 doctorates awarded. *Degree requirements:* For master's, exam; for doctorate, thesis/dissertation, departmental candidacy exam. *Entrance requirements:* For master's and doctorate, GMAT, minimum GPA of 3.0 in last 60 hours. Additional exam requirements/recommendations for international students: Required—TOEFL. *Application deadline:* For fall admission, 2/1 priority date for domestic students; for spring admission, 11/1 priority date for domestic students. Application fee: $30. Electronic applications accepted. *Expenses:* Tuition, state resident: full-time $6,167; part-time $257 per credit hour. Tuition, nonresident: full-time $22,790; part-time $950 per credit hour. *Financial support:* In 2006–07, 12 fellowships with partial tuition reimbursements (averaging $4,000 per year), 44 research assistantships with partial tuition reimbursements (averaging $5,400 per year), 36 teaching assistantships with partial tuition reimbursements (averaging $13,700 per year) were awarded; career-related internships or fieldwork, Federal Work-Study, institutionally sponsored loans, tuition waivers (partial), and unspecified assistantships also available. Financial award application deadline: 3/1; financial award applicants required to submit FAFSA. *Application contact:* Judy Ryder, Director, Graduate Admissions, 407-823-2364, Fax: 407-823-0219, E-mail: judy.ryder@bus.ucf.edu.

See Close-Up on page 339.

University of Central Missouri, The Graduate School, Harmon College of Business Administration, Department of Management and Business Communication, Warrensburg, MO 64093. Offers business administration (MBA). *Accreditation:* AACSB. Part-time programs available. *Faculty:* 10 full-time (5 women). *Students:* 15 full-time (2 women), 18 part-time (6 women); includes 6 minority (1 African American, 4 Asian Americans or Pacific Islanders, 1 Hispanic American), 15 international. Average age 28. 24 applicants. In 2006, 24 degrees awarded. *Entrance requirements:* For master's, GMAT, minimum GPA of 2.5. Additional exam requirements/recommendations for international students: Required—TOEFL (minimum score 500 paper-based; 173 computer-based). *Application deadline:* For fall admission, 6/1 priority date for domestic students, 5/1 priority date for international students; for spring admission, 10/1 priority date for domestic students, 10/1 for international students. Applications are processed on a rolling basis. Application fee: $30 ($50 for international students). *Expenses:* Tuition, state resident: full-time $5,448; part-time $227 per credit hour. Tuition, nonresident: full-time $10,896; part-time $454 per credit hour. Required fees: $336; $14 per credit hour. *Financial support:* In 2006–07, 5 students received support; teaching assistantships with full and partial tuition reimbursements available, career-related internships or fieldwork, Federal Work-Study, scholarships/grants, unspecified assistantships, and administrative and laboratory assistantships available. Support available to part-time students. Financial award application deadline: 3/1; financial award applicants required to submit FAFSA. *Faculty research:* Business communication, supply chain management, pedagogy in management education, team based learning. *Unit head:* Dr. Christine Wright, Chair, 660-543-4247, E-mail: wright@ucmo.edu.

University of Central Oklahoma, College of Graduate Studies and Research, College of Business Administration, Program in Business Administration, Edmond, OK 73034-5209. Offers MBA. *Accreditation:* ACBSP. *Degree requirements:* For master's, thesis optional. *Entrance requirements:* For master's, GMAT. Additional exam requirements/recommendations for international students: Required—TOEFL (minimum score 550 paper-based; 213 computer-based). Electronic applications accepted.

University of Charleston, Accelerated Business Administration Program, Charleston, WV 25304-1099. Offers MBA. *Faculty:* 3 full-time (0 women), 2 part-time/adjunct (1 woman). *Students:* 13 full-time (6 women), 3 part-time (2 women); includes 4 minority (3 African Americans, 1 Asian American or Pacific Islander), 2 international. Average age 23. 13 applicants, 92% accepted, 8 enrolled. In 2006, 7 degrees awarded. *Entrance requirements:* For master's,

GMAT, minimum 5 years of professional work experience. Application fee: $40. *Financial support:* In 2006–07, 10 students received support. Application deadline: 3/1; *Unit head:* Dr. Robert B. Bliss, Director, 304-357-4865, Fax: 304-357-4872, E-mail: robertbliss@ucwr.edu.

University of Charleston, Executive Business Administration Program, Charleston, WV 25304-1099. Offers EMBA. Part-time and evening/weekend programs available. *Faculty:* 5 full-time (1 woman). *Students:* 33 full-time (10 women). Average age 36. 28 applicants, 96% accepted, 22 enrolled. In 2006, 11 degrees awarded. *Degree requirements:* For master's, registration. *Entrance requirements:* For master's, GMAT, minimum 5 years of professional work experience or approval of director. Additional exam requirements/recommendations for international students: Required—TOEFL. *Application deadline:* Applications are processed on a rolling basis. Application fee: $40. Electronic applications accepted. *Financial support:* In 2006–07, 18 students received support. Available to part-time students. Application deadline: 3/1; *Unit head:* Dr. Robert B. Bliss, Director, 304-357-4865, Fax: 304-357-4872, E-mail: robertbliss@ucwr.edu. *Application contact:* Dr. Robert B. Bliss, Director, 304-357-4865, Fax: 304-357-4872, E-mail: robertbliss@ucwr.edu.

University of Chicago, Graduate School of Business, Doctoral Program in Business, Chicago, IL 60637-1513. Offers PhD. *Accreditation:* AACSB. *Students:* 110 full-time (36 women). Average age 28. In 2006, 23 degrees awarded. *Degree requirements:* For doctorate, thesis/dissertation, workshops, curriculum paper. *Entrance requirements:* For doctorate, GMAT or GRE, resumé, transcripts, letters of referral, essay. Additional exam requirements/recommendations for international students: Required—TOEFL, IELTS. *Application deadline:* For fall admission, 1/1 for domestic and international students. Application fee: $65. Electronic applications accepted. *Expenses:* Tuition: Full-time $34,920. Required fees: $612. One-time fee: $35 full-time. Full-time tuition and fees vary according to course load, degree level and program. *Financial support:* In 2006–07, 100 students received support; fellowships with tuition reimbursements available, research assistantships with tuition reimbursements available, teaching assistantships with tuition reimbursements available, tuition waivers (full) available. *Faculty research:* Accounting, finance, marketing economics, econometrics and statistics. *Unit head:* Pradeep Chintagunta, Director, 773-702-7298, Fax: 773-702-5257. *Application contact:* Malaina Brown, Associate Director, 773-702-7298, Fax: 773-702-5257, E-mail: mbrown@chicagogsb.edu.

University of Chicago, Graduate School of Business, Part-Time MBA Program-Evening, Chicago, IL 60637-1513. Offers MBA. *Accreditation:* AACSB. Part-time and evening/weekend programs available. *Faculty:* 127 full-time, 43 part-time/adjunct. *Students:* Average age 29. In 2006, 383 degrees awarded. *Entrance requirements:* For master's, GMAT, 2 letters of recommendation, interview, essays, transcripts. Additional exam requirements/recommendations for international students: Required—TOEFL (minimum score 600 paper-based; 250 computer-based), IELTS. *Application deadline:* For fall admission, 7/13 for domestic and international students; for winter admission, 10/19 for domestic and international students; for spring admission, 1/19 for domestic and international students. Applications are processed on a rolling basis. Application fee: $175. Electronic applications accepted. *Expenses: Contact institution.* One-time fee: $35 full-time. Full-time tuition and fees vary according to course load, degree level and program. *Financial support:* Applicants required to submit FAFSA. *Faculty research:* Finance, entrepreneurialship, strategy, marketing, international business. *Unit head:* Kristine Mackey, Associate Dean, 312-464-8660, Fax: 312-464-8778, E-mail: kmackey@chicagogsb.edu. *Application contact:* Information Contact, 312-464-8700, Fax: 312-464-8778, E-mail: eveningweekend-admissions@chicagogsb.edu.

University of Chicago, Graduate School of Business, Part-Time MBA Program-Weekend, Chicago, IL 60637-1513. Offers MBA. *Accreditation:* AACSB. Part-time and evening/weekend programs available. *Faculty:* 127 full-time, 43 part-time/adjunct. *Students:* Average age 30. In 2006, 112 degrees awarded. *Entrance requirements:* For master's, GMAT, 2 letters of recommendation, interview, resumé. Additional exam requirements/recommendations for international students: Required—TOEFL or IELTS. *Application deadline:* For fall admission, 6/9 for domestic and international students. Application fee: $175. *Expenses:* Tuition: Full-time $34,920. Required fees: $612. One-time fee: $35 full-time. Full-time tuition and fees vary according to course load, degree level and program. *Faculty research:* Finance, marketing, international business, strategy, entrepreneurialship. *Unit head:* Kristine Mackey, Associate Dean, 312-464-8660, Fax: 312-464-8778, E-mail: kmackey@chicagogsb.edu. *Application contact:* Information Contact, 312-464-8700, E-mail: eveningweekend-admission@chicagogsb.edu.

University of Cincinnati, Division of Research and Advanced Studies, College of Business, Cincinnati, OH 45221-0020. Offers MBA, MS, PhD, JD/MBA, MBA/MA, MBA/MD, MBA/MS, MBA/MSN. *Accreditation:* AACSB. Part-time and evening/weekend programs available. *Faculty:* 85 full-time (24 women), 23 part-time/adjunct (8 women). *Students:* 243 full-time (97 women), 432 part-time (153 women); includes 56 minority (30 African Americans, 15 Asian Americans or Pacific Islanders, 11 Hispanic Americans), 177 international. Average age 31. 586 applicants, 67% accepted, 233 enrolled. In 2006, 236 master's, 8 doctorates awarded. *Median time to degree:* Of those who began their doctoral program in fall 1998, 90% received their degree in 8 years or less. *Degree requirements:* For master's, thesis (for some programs), capstone project (MBA); for doctorate, thesis/dissertation, comprehensive exam. *Entrance requirements:* For master's, resumé, letters of recommendation; for doctorate, GMAT, GRE. Additional exam requirements/recommendations for international students: Required—TOEFL (minimum score 600 paper-based; 250 computer-based; 100 iBT). *Application deadline:* For fall admission, 6/1 priority date for domestic students, 2/15 priority date for international students. Applications are processed on a rolling basis. Application fee: $40. Electronic applications accepted. *Financial support:* In 2006–07, 105 students received support, including 27 research assistantships (averaging $9,800 per year), 20 teaching assistantships (averaging $16,000 per year); scholarships/grants, tuition waivers (full and partial), and unspecified assistantships also available. Financial award application deadline: 2/15; financial award applicants required to submit FAFSA. Total annual research expenditures: $50,000. *Unit head:* Dr. Willard McIntosh, Dean, 513-556-7001, Fax: 513-556-4891, E-mail: will.mcintosh@uc.edu. *Application contact:* Valerie Robinson, Associate Director, MBA Admissions, 513-556-7024, Fax: 513-558-7006, E-mail: valerie.robinson@uc.edu.

University of Colorado at Boulder, Leeds School of Business, Boulder, CO 80309. Offers accounting (MS); business (PhD), including accounting, finance, management, marketing; business administration (MBA, PhD); JD/MBA; MBA/MA; MBA/MS. *Accreditation:* AACSB. Part-time and evening/weekend programs available. *Faculty:* 48 full-time (11 women). *Students:* 167 full-time (58 women), 113 part-time (20 women); includes 25 minority (16 Asian Americans or Pacific Islanders, 9 Hispanic Americans), 35 international. Average age 30. 135 applicants, 96% accepted. In 2006, 121 master's, 8 doctorates awarded. *Degree requirements:* For doctorate, thesis/dissertation, research internship. *Entrance requirements:* For master's, GMAT, minimum undergraduate GPA of 2.75; for doctorate, GMAT. *Application deadline:* For fall admission, 3/1 priority date for domestic students, 3/1 for international students. Applications are processed on a rolling basis. Application fee: $50 ($60 for international students). Electronic applications accepted. *Expenses: Contact institution. Financial support:* In 2006–07, 7 fellowships (averaging $4,254 per year), 26 research assistantships (averaging $14,883 per year), 20 teaching assistantships (averaging $11,984 per year) were awarded; career-related internships or fieldwork, Federal Work-Study, scholarships/grants, and unspecified assistantships also available. Financial award application deadline: 3/1. Total annual research expenditures: $2.4 million. *Unit head:* Dennis Ahlburg, Dean, 303-492-1809, Fax: 303-492-7676, E-mail: dennis.ahlburg@colorado.edu. *Application contact:* Information Contact, 303-492-1809, Fax: 303-492-1727, E-mail: busgrad@spot.colorado.edu.

See Close-Up on page 341.

University of Colorado at Colorado Springs, Graduate School, Graduate School of Business Administration, Colorado Springs, CO 80933-7150. Offers accounting (MBA); finance (MBA); general health care administration (MBA); information systems (MBA); international business management (MBA); marketing (MBA); service management/technology management (MBA). *Accreditation:* AACSB. Part-time and evening/weekend programs available. *Faculty:* 15 full-time (4 women), 4 part-time/adjunct (0 women). *Students:* 158 full-time (70 women), 290 part-time (87 women); includes 48 minority (11 African Americans, 1 American Indian/Alaska Native, 20 Asian Americans or Pacific Islanders, 16 Hispanic Americans), 7 international. Average age 33. 158 applicants, 75% accepted, 51 enrolled. In 2006, 119 degrees awarded. *Entrance requirements:* For master's, GMAT. *Application deadline:* For fall admission, 6/1 for domestic students; for spring admission, 11/1 for domestic students. Application fee: $60 ($75 for international students). *Expenses: Contact institution.* Tuition and fees vary according to course load, campus/location and program. *Financial support:* Career-related internships or fieldwork, Federal Work-Study, and institutionally sponsored loans available. Support available to part-time students. Financial award applicants required to submit FAFSA. *Faculty research:* Quality financial reporting, investments and corporate governance, group support systems, environmental and project management, customer relationship management. Total annual research expenditures: $99,250. *Unit head:* Dr. Venkateshwar Reddy, Dean, 719-262-3113, Fax: 719-262-3494, E-mail: vreddy@uccs.edu. *Application contact:* Amy DeLourenco, MBA Program Director, 719-262-3408, Fax: 719-262-3100, E-mail: busadvsr@uccs.edu.

University of Colorado at Denver and Health Sciences Center, Business School, Executive MBA Program, Denver, CO 80248-0006. Offers Exec MBA. *Accreditation:* AACSB. Evening/weekend programs available. *Entrance requirements:* For master's, GMAT, 10 years of work experience, including 5 years of management experience. Electronic applications accepted. Expenses: Contact institution.

University of Colorado at Denver and Health Sciences Center, Business School, Master of Business Administration Program, Denver, CO 80217-3364. Offers MBA. *Accreditation:* AACSB. Part-time and evening/weekend programs available. *Students:* 128 full-time (55 women), 440 part-time (165 women); includes 82 minority (5 African Americans, 5 American Indian/Alaska Native, 39 Asian Americans or Pacific Islanders, 33 Hispanic Americans), 36 international. Average age 31. 323 applicants, 77% accepted, 102 enrolled. In 2006, 384 degrees awarded. *Entrance requirements:* For master's, GMAT. Additional exam requirements/recommendations for international students: Required—TOEFL (minimum score 525 paper-based; 197 computer-based). *Application deadline:* For fall admission, 6/1 for domestic students, 3/15 for international students; for spring admission, 11/1 for domestic students, 10/1 for international students. Applications are processed on a rolling basis. Application fee: $50 ($75 for international students). *Financial support:* Federal Work-Study, institutionally sponsored loans, and scholarships/grants available. Support available to part-time students. Financial award application deadline: 4/1; financial award applicants required to submit FAFSA. *Unit head:* Elizabeth Cooperman, Director, 303-556-5948, Fax: 303-556-5899. *Application contact:* Shelly Townley, Admissions Coordinator, 303-556-5956, Fax: 303-556-5904, E-mail: shelly.townley@cudenver.edu.

University of Colorado at Denver and Health Sciences Center, Business School, Program in Management and Organization, Denver, CO 80217-3364. Offers MS. *Accreditation:* AACSB. Part-time and evening/weekend programs available. *Students:* 5 full-time (3 women), 17 part-time (10 women); includes 4 minority (1 American Indian/Alaska Native, 2 Asian Americans or Pacific Islanders, 1 Hispanic American), 2 international. Average age 30. 10 applicants, 50% accepted, 4 enrolled. In 2006, 13 degrees awarded. *Entrance requirements:* For master's, GMAT. Additional exam requirements/recommendations for international students: Required—TOEFL (minimum score 525 paper-based; 197 computer-based). *Application deadline:* For fall admission, 6/1 for domestic students, 3/15 for international students; for spring admission, 11/1 for domestic students, 10/1 for international students. Applications are processed on a rolling basis. Application fee: $50 ($75 for international students). Electronic applications accepted. *Financial support:* Federal Work-Study, institutionally sponsored loans, and scholarships/grants available. Support available to part-time students. Financial award application deadline: 4/1; financial award applicants required to submit FAFSA. *Faculty research:* Human resource management, management of catastrophe, turnaround strategies. *Unit head:* Blair Gifford, Program Director, 303-556-5866, Fax: 303-556-6619, E-mail: blair.gifford@cudenver.edu. *Application contact:* Shelly Townley, Admissions Coordinator, 303-556-5956, Fax: 303-556-5904, E-mail: shelly.townley@cudenver.edu.

University of Connecticut, Graduate School, School of Business, Storrs, CT 06269. Offers accounting (MS, PhD); business administration (Exec MBA, MBA, PhD); finance (PhD); health care management and insurance studies (MBA); management (PhD); management consulting (MBA); marketing (PhD); marketing intelligence (MBA); MA/MBA; MBA/MSW. *Accreditation:* AACSB. *Faculty:* 70 full-time (14 women). *Students:* 378 full-time (126 women), 852 part-time (322 women); includes 154 minority (43 African Americans, 5 American Indian/Alaska Native, 71 Asian Americans or Pacific Islanders, 35 Hispanic Americans), 171 international. Average age 30. 632 applicants, 72% accepted, 452 enrolled. In 2006, 413 master's, 9 doctorates awarded. *Degree requirements:* For master's, comprehensive exam; for doctorate, thesis/dissertation. *Entrance requirements:* For master's and doctorate, GMAT. Additional exam requirements/recommendations for international students: Required—TOEFL (minimum score 550 paper-based; 213 computer-based). *Application deadline:* For fall admission, 2/1 priority date for domestic and international students; for spring admission, 11/1 for domestic students, 10/1 for international students. Applications are processed on a rolling basis. Electronic applications accepted. *Financial support:* In 2006–07, 107 research assistantships with full tuition reimbursements, 4 teaching assistantships with full tuition reimbursements were awarded; fellowships, career-related internships or fieldwork, Federal Work-Study, scholarships/grants, health care benefits, and unspecified assistantships also available. Financial award application deadline: 2/1; financial award applicants required to submit FAFSA. *Unit head:* William Curt Hunter, Dean, 860-486-2317, Fax: 860-846-0889, E-mail: william.hunter@uconn.edu. *Application contact:* Richard Dino, Admissions Chairperson, 860-486-4483, E-mail: rich.dino@uconn.edu.

See Close-Up on page 343.

University of Dallas, Graduate School of Management, Irving, TX 75062-4736. Offers accounting (MBA, MS); business management (MBA); corporate finance (MBA, MM); engineering management (MBA, MM); entrepreneurship (MBA, MM); financial services (MBA, MM); global business (MBA, MM); health services management (MBA, MM); human resource management (MBA, MM, MS); information assurance (MBA, MM, MS); information technology (MBA, MM, MS); information technology service management (MBA); IT service management (MS); marketing (MM); marketing management (MBA); not-for-profit management (MBA); organization development (MBA); project management (MBA, MM); sports and entertainment management (MBA, MM); strategic leadership (MBA); supply chain management (MBA); supply chain management and market logistics (MM); telecommunications management (MBA, MM). *Accreditation:* ACBSP. Part-time and evening/weekend programs available. Postbaccalaureate distance learning degree programs offered (no on-campus study). *Faculty:* 26 full-time (5 women), 85 part-time/adjunct (18 women). *Students:* 227 full-time (98 women), 1,160 part-time (446 women); includes 473 minority (209 African Americans, 3 American Indian/Alaska Native, 143 Asian Americans or Pacific Islanders, 118 Hispanic Americans), 224 international. Average age 34. 556 applicants, 86% accepted, 291 enrolled. In 2006, 476 degrees awarded. *Entrance requirements:* Additional exam requirements/recommendations for international students: Required—TOEFL. *Application deadline:* Applications are processed on a rolling basis. Application fee: $50. Electronic applications accepted. *Expenses: Contact institution. Financial support:* In 2006–07, 468 students received support. Scholarships/grants and unspecified assistantships available. Financial award application deadline: 2/15; financial award applicants required to submit FAFSA. *Unit head:* Dr. J. Lee Whittington, Dean, 972-721-5230. *Application contact:* Sarah Stivison, Director of Graduate Admissions, 972-721-5198, Fax: 972-721-4009, E-mail: admiss@gsm.udallas.edu.

University of Dayton, Graduate School, School of Business Administration, Dayton, OH 45469-1300. Offers MBA, JD/MBA. *Accreditation:* AACSB. Part-time and evening/weekend programs avail-

Business Administration and Management—General

University of Dayton (continued)
able. *Faculty:* 80. *Students:* 115 full-time (43 women), 115 part-time (37 women); includes 25 minority (11 African Americans, 5 Asian Americans or Pacific Islanders, 9 Hispanic Americans), 17 international. Average age 29. 205 applicants, 65% accepted, 77 enrolled. In 2006, 128 degrees awarded. *Entrance requirements:* For master's, GMAT. Additional exam requirements/recommendations for international students: Required—TOEFL (minimum score 550 paper-based; 213 computer-based). *Application deadline:* For fall admission, 3/1 priority date for international students. Applications are processed on a rolling basis. Application fee: $0. Electronic applications accepted. *Expenses: Contact institution.* Tuition and fees vary according to degree level and program. *Financial support:* In 2006–07, 5 fellowships with partial tuition reimbursements, 9 research assistantships with full and partial tuition reimbursements were awarded; career-related internships or fieldwork, institutionally sponsored loans, scholarships/grants, health care benefits, and unspecified assistantships also available. Support available to part-time students. Financial award application deadline: 2/15; financial award applicants required to submit FAFSA. *Faculty research:* Management information systems, economics, finance, production operations management, marketing. *Unit head:* Janice M. Glynn, Director, 937-229-3733, Fax: 937-229-3882, E-mail: mba@udayton.edu. *Application contact:* Erika Eavers, Graduate Admission Processor, 937-229-3065, Fax: 937-229-4729, E-mail: erika.eavers@notes.udayton.edu.

University of Delaware, Alfred Lerner College of Business and Economics, Program in Business Administration, Newark, DE 19716. Offers MBA, MA/MBA, MBA/MIB, MBA/MS. *Accreditation:* AACSB. Part-time and evening/weekend programs available. *Entrance requirements:* For master's, GMAT, 2 letters of recommendation, resumé. Additional exam requirements/recommendations for international students: Required—TOEFL (minimum score 600 paper-based; 260 computer-based). Electronic applications accepted. Expenses: Contact institution. *Faculty research:* Finance, corporate governance, information systems, leadership, marketing.

See Close-Up on page 345.

University of Delaware, College of Agriculture and Natural Resources, Department of Entomology and Wildlife Ecology, Newark, DE 19716. Offers entomology and applied ecology (MS, PhD), including avian ecology, evolution and taxonomy, insect biological control, insect ecology and behavior (MS), insect genetics, pest management, plant-insect interactions, wildlife ecology and management. Part-time programs available. *Degree requirements:* For master's, thesis, oral exam, seminar, comprehensive exam; for doctorate, thesis/dissertation, qualifying exam, seminar, comprehensive exam. *Entrance requirements:* For master's, GRE General Test, minimum GPA of 3.0 in field, 2.8 overall; for doctorate, GRE General Test, GRE Subject Test (biology), minimum GPA of 3.0 in field, 2.8 overall. Additional exam requirements/recommendations for international students: Required—TOEFL. Electronic applications accepted. *Faculty research:* Genetics and resistance, biological control, chemically mediated behavioral ecology, ecology and evolution of plant-insect interactions, ecology of wildlife conservation and management.

University of Denver, Daniels College of Business, Denver, CO 80208. Offers IMBA, M Acc, MBA, MS. *Accreditation:* AACSB. Part-time and evening/weekend programs available. *Faculty:* 83 full-time (17 women). *Students:* 425 full-time (149 women), 479 part-time (146 women); includes 79 minority (12 African Americans, 3 American Indian/Alaska Native, 41 Asian Americans or Pacific Islanders, 23 Hispanic Americans), 173 international. Average age 30. 1,070 applicants, 73% accepted. In 2006, 468 degrees awarded. *Entrance requirements:* For master's, GMAT. *Application deadline:* For fall admission, 1/15 priority date for domestic students. Applications are processed on a rolling basis. Application fee: $50. Electronic applications accepted. *Expenses:* Tuition: Full-time $29,628; part-time $823 per credit. *Financial support:* In 2006–07, 63 teaching assistantships with full and partial tuition reimbursements (averaging $2,027 per year) were awarded; career-related internships or fieldwork, Federal Work-Study, institutionally sponsored loans, and scholarships/grants also available. Support available to part-time students. Financial award application deadline: 2/15; financial award applicants required to submit FAFSA. *Unit head:* Dr. Karen Newman, Dean, 303-871-3416. *Application contact:* Admissions, 303-871-3416, Fax: 303-571-4466, E-mail: daniels@du.edu.

See Close-Up on page 347.

University of Denver, University College, Denver, CO 80208. Offers applied communication (MAS, MPS); computer information systems (MAS); environmental policy and management (MAS); geographic information systems (MAS); human resource administration (MPS); knowledge and information technologies (MAS); liberal studies (MLS); modern languages (MLS); organizational leadership (MPS); technology management (MAS); telecommunications (MAS). Part-time and evening/weekend programs available. Postbaccalaureate distance learning degree programs offered (no on-campus study). *Students:* 57 full-time (28 women), 453 part-time (253 women); includes 84 minority (37 African Americans, 1 American Indian/Alaska Native, 21 Asian Americans or Pacific Islanders, 25 Hispanic Americans), 39 international. Average age 26. 159 applicants, 84% accepted. In 2006, 171 master's awarded. *Entrance requirements:* Additional exam requirements/recommendations for international students: Required—TOEFL (minimum score 550 paper-based; 213 computer-based). *Application deadline:* Applications are processed on a rolling basis. Application fee: $75. Electronic applications accepted. *Expenses: Contact institution. Financial support:* Applicants required to submit FAFSA. *Unit head:* Dr. James Davis, Dean, 303-871-2291, Fax: 303-871-4047, E-mail: jdavis@du.edu. *Application contact:* Information Contact, 303-871-3069.

University of Detroit Mercy, College of Business Administration, Program in Business Administration, Detroit, MI 48221. Offers MBA, JD/MBA. *Accreditation:* AACSB. Part-time and evening/weekend programs available. *Faculty:* 17 full-time (2 women). *Students:* 22 full-time (5 women), 86 part-time (38 women); includes 13 minority (10 African Americans, 2 American Indian/Alaska Native, 1 Hispanic American), 46 international. Average age 31. In 2006, 62 degrees awarded. *Degree requirements:* For master's, thesis or alternative. *Entrance requirements:* For master's, GMAT, minimum GPA of 2.75. *Application deadline:* For fall admission, 8/1 priority date for domestic students. Applications are processed on a rolling basis. Application fee: $30 ($50 for international students). *Expenses:* Tuition: Full-time $15,750; part-time $875 per credit hour. Required fees: $570. *Financial support:* Research assistantships, career-related internships or fieldwork and Federal Work-Study available. Support available to part-time students. Financial award application deadline: 8/1. *Application contact:* Dr. Bonnie Naski, Coordinator for Graduate Programs, 313-993-1202, Fax: 313-993-1052, E-mail: gradbusiness@udmercy.edu.

University of Detroit Mercy, College of Business Administration, Program in Business Turnaround Management, Detroit, MI 48221. Offers MS, Certificate. *Faculty:* 17 full-time (2 women). *Students:* 1 full-time (0 women), 11 part-time (5 women); includes 4 minority (3 African Americans, 1 Asian American or Pacific Islander), 1 international. *Expenses:* Tuition: Full-time $15,750; part-time $875 per credit hour. Required fees: $570. *Application contact:* Dr. Bonnie Naski, Coordinator for Graduate Programs, 313-993-1202, Fax: 313-993-1052, E-mail: gradbusiness@udmercy.edu.

University of Detroit Mercy, College of Business Administration, Program in Executive MBA, Detroit, MI 48221. Offers EMBA. *Faculty:* 17 full-time (2 women). *Students:* 22 full-time (8 women), 13 part-time (2 women); includes 13 minority (11 African Americans, 2 Asian Americans or Pacific Islanders). *Expenses:* Tuition: Full-time $15,750; part-time $875 per credit hour. Required fees: $570. *Application contact:* Dr. Bonnie Naski, Coordinator for Graduate Programs, 313-993-1202, Fax: 313-993-1052, E-mail: gradbusiness@udmercy.edu.

University of Dubuque, Program in Business Administration, Dubuque, IA 52001-5099. Offers MBA. Part-time and evening/weekend programs available. *Faculty:* 5 full-time (1 woman), 4 part-time/adjunct (3 women). *Students:* 18 full-time (10 women), 42 part-time (17 women); includes 13 minority (1 African American, 1 American Indian/Alaska Native, 11 Asian Americans or Pacific Islanders), 1 international. Average age 33. In 2006, 42 degrees awarded. *Entrance requirements:* For master's, GMAT. Additional exam requirements/recommendations for international students: Required—TOEFL. *Application deadline:* For fall admission, 8/15 priority date for domestic students, 7/15 priority date for international students. Applications are processed on a rolling basis. Application fee: $25. Electronic applications accepted. *Financial support:* In 2006–07, 4 teaching assistantships with full tuition reimbursements were awarded; Federal Work-Study also available. Support available to part-time students. Financial award application deadline: 4/1; financial award applicants required to submit FAFSA. *Unit head:* Richard Birkenbeuel, Director of Domestic and International MBA Programs, 319-589-3417, Fax: 319-589-3184, E-mail: rbirkenb@dbq.edu. *Application contact:* Carol A. Knockle, Graduate Program Coordinator, 563-589-3300, Fax: 563-589-3184, E-mail: mba@dbq.edu.

University of Evansville, School of Business Administration, Evansville, IN 47722. Offers executive business administration (MBA). *Accreditation:* AACSB. Part-time and evening/weekend programs available. *Entrance requirements:* For master's, GMAT or GRE, minimum 5 years professional experience, 2 letters of recommendation. Additional exam requirements/recommendations for international students: Required—TOEFL (minimum score 500 paper-based; 61 iBT). *Application deadline:* Applications are processed on a rolling basis. Application fee: $75. *Expenses: Contact institution. Financial support:* Available to part-time students. Application deadline: 6/1; *Unit head:* Dr. Robert Clark, Dean, 812-488-2851, Fax: 812-488-2872, E-mail: rc60@evansville.edu. *Application contact:* Anna Newton, Executive MBA Program Coordinator, 812-488-2455, Fax: 812-488-2872, E-mail: emba@evansville.edu.

The University of Findlay, Graduate and Professional Studies, MBA Program, Findlay, OH 45840-3653. Offers financial management (MBA); human resource management (MBA); international management (MBA); management (MBA); marketing (MBA); public management (MBA). Part-time and evening/weekend programs available. Postbaccalaureate distance learning degree programs offered (no on-campus study). *Faculty:* 16 full-time, 1 part-time/adjunct. *Students:* 80 full-time (26 women), 456 part-time (168 women); includes 20 minority (13 African Americans, 1 American Indian/Alaska Native, 4 Asian Americans or Pacific Islanders, 2 Hispanic Americans), 289 international. Average age 35. 208 applicants, 88% accepted, 181 enrolled. In 2006, 210 degrees awarded. *Degree requirements:* For master's, thesis, cumulative project. *Entrance requirements:* For master's, GMAT, minimum undergraduate GPA of 3.0 in last 60 hours of course work. Additional exam requirements/recommendations for international students: Required—TOEFL (minimum score 550 paper-based). *Application deadline:* Applications are processed on a rolling basis. Application fee: $25. Electronic applications accepted. *Expenses: Contact institution. Financial support:* In 2006–07, 1 student received support, including 1 teaching assistantship with full tuition reimbursement available (averaging $6,000 per year); unspecified assistantships also available. Financial award application deadline: 4/1; financial award applicants required to submit FAFSA. *Faculty research:* Health care management, operations and logistics management. *Unit head:* Dr. Paul Sears, Dean, 419-434-4704, Fax: 419-434-4822. *Application contact:* Heather Riffle, Director, Graduate and Special Programs, 419-434-4640, Fax: 419-434-5517, E-mail: riffle@findlay.edu.

University of Florida, Graduate School, Warrington College of Business Administration, Department of Finance, Insurance and Real Estate, Gainesville, FL 32611. Offers business administration (MS), including entrepreneurship, insurance, real estate and urban analysis, retailing; finance (PhD); financial services (Certificate); insurance (PhD); real estate and urban analysis (PhD); JD/MS. *Faculty:* 15 full-time (1 woman). *Students:* 69 (17 women); includes 14 minority (2 African Americans, 5 Asian Americans or Pacific Islanders, 7 Hispanic Americans) 12 international. In 2006, 54 master's, 1 doctorate awarded. Terminal master's awarded for partial completion of doctoral program. *Degree requirements:* For doctorate, thesis/dissertation. *Entrance requirements:* For master's, GMAT or GRE General Test, minimum GPA of 3.0 for last 60 hours of undergraduate degree, work experience (preferred); for doctorate, GMAT or GRE General Test, minimum GPA of 3.0. Additional exam requirements/recommendations for international students: Required—TOEFL (minimum score 550 paper-based; 213 computer-based). *Application deadline:* For fall admission, 5/1 priority date for domestic students. Applications are processed on a rolling basis. Application fee: $30. Electronic applications accepted. *Expenses:* Tuition, state resident: full-time $6,827. Tuition, nonresident: full-time $21,951. Required fees: $999. *Financial support:* In 2006–07, 10 research assistantships (averaging $23,562 per year), 1 teaching assistantship (averaging $40,989 per year) were awarded; fellowships, career-related internships or fieldwork, scholarships/grants, and unspecified assistantships also available. *Faculty research:* Financial management, financial markets and institutions, investments, risk and insurance, real estate development. *Unit head:* Dr. Michael D. Ryngaert, Chair, 352-392-9765, Fax: 352-392-0301, E-mail: michael.ryngaert@cba.ufl.edu. *Application contact:* Pamela De Michele, Director of Admissions and Student Services, 352-273-0310, Fax: 352-392-0301, E-mail: pam.demichele@cba.ufl.edu.

University of Florida, Graduate School, Warrington College of Business Administration, Department of Management, Gainesville, FL 32611. Offers international business (MAIB); management (MS, PhD). *Accreditation:* AACSB. *Faculty:* 13 full-time (2 women). *Students:* 108 (55 women); includes 20 minority (3 African Americans, 7 Asian Americans or Pacific Islanders, 10 Hispanic Americans) 11 international. In 2006, 92 master's, 4 doctorates awarded. Terminal master's awarded for partial completion of doctoral program. *Degree requirements:* For master's and doctorate, thesis/dissertation. *Entrance requirements:* For master's and doctorate, GMAT or GRE General Test, minimum GPA of 3.0. Additional exam requirements/recommendations for international students: Required—TOEFL (minimum score 550 paper-based; 213 computer-based). *Application deadline:* For fall admission, 2/16 for domestic students. Applications are processed on a rolling basis. Application fee: $30. Electronic applications accepted. *Expenses:* Tuition, state resident: full-time $6,827. Tuition, nonresident: full-time $21,951. Required fees: $999. *Financial support:* In 2006–07, 6 research assistantships (averaging $19,959 per year), 4 teaching assistantships (averaging $21,479 per year) were awarded; fellowships, unspecified assistantships also available. *Faculty research:* Organizational behavior, organizational theory, strategy and business policy. *Unit head:* Dr. Larry A. DiMatteo, Chair, 352-392-0163, Fax: 352-392-6020, E-mail: larry.dimatteo@cba.ufl.edu. *Application contact:* Mary Cano, Coordinator of Student Affairs, 352-273-0341, Fax: 352-392-6020, E-mail: mary.cano@cba.ufl.edu.

University of Florida, Graduate School, Warrington College of Business Administration, Programs in Business Administration, Gainesville, FL 32611. Offers accounting (MBA); arts administration (MBA); business strategy and public policy (MBA); competitive strategy (MBA); decision and information sciences (MBA); electronic commerce (MBA); finance (MBA); general business (MBA); global management (MBA); Graham-Buffett security analysis (MBA); health administration (MBA); human resources management (MBA); international studies (MBA); Latin American business (MBA); management (MBA); marketing (MBA); sports administration (MBA); JD/MBA; MBA/MS; MBA/PhD; MBA/Pharm D; MD/MBA. *Accreditation:* AACSB. Part-time and evening/weekend programs available. Postbaccalaureate distance learning degree programs offered. *Faculty:* 14. *Students:* 950 (282 women); includes 189 minority (31 African Americans, 2 American Indian/Alaska Native, 66 Asian Americans or Pacific Islanders, 90 Hispanic Americans) 56 international. In 2006, 481 degrees awarded. *Entrance requirements:* For master's, GMAT, minimum GPA of 3.0, interview. Additional exam requirements/recommendations for international students: Required—TOEFL (minimum score 550 paper-based; 213 computer-based). *Application deadline:* For fall admission, 4/15 for domestic students; for winter admission, 10/15 priority date for domestic students; for spring admission, 2/15 for domestic students. Applications are processed on a rolling basis. Application fee: $30. Electronic applications accepted. *Expenses:* Tuition, state resident: full-time $6,827. Tuition, nonresident: full-time $21,951. Required fees: $999. *Financial support:* Fellowships, research assistantships, teaching assistantships, career-related internships or fieldwork, scholarships/grants, and unspecified assistantships available. Support available to part-time students. Financial award application deadline: 2/15; financial award applicants required to submit FAFSA. *Faculty research:* Accounting, finance, insurance, management, real estate and urban analysis marketing. *Unit head:* Alex Sevilla, Director, 352-392-7992 Ext. 1206. *Application* *contact:* Patrick Foran, Associate Director of Admissions, 352-392-7992 Ext. 282, Fax: 352-392-8791, E-mail: patrick.foran@cba.ufl.edu.

University of Georgia, Graduate School, College of Education, Department of Workforce Education, Leadership and Social Foundations, Athens, GA 30602. Offers M Ed, MA, MAT, Ed D, PhD, Ed S. *Accreditation:* NCATE. *Faculty:* 19 full-time (10 women). *Students:* 45 full-time (27 women), 181 part-time (109 women); includes 37 minority (34 African Americans, 1 American Indian/Alaska Native, 1 Asian American or Pacific Islander, 1 Hispanic American), 5 international. 139 applicants, 72% accepted, 62 enrolled. In 2006, 52 master's, 18 doctorates, 7 other advanced degrees awarded. *Entrance requirements:* For master's, GRE General Test, MAT; for doctorate, GRE General Test; for Ed S, GRE General Test or MAT. *Application deadline:* For fall admission, 7/1 priority date for domestic students; for spring admission, 11/15 for domestic students. Application fee: $50. Electronic applications accepted. *Financial support:* Fellowships, research assistantships, teaching assistantships, unspecified assistantships available. *Unit head:* Dr. Roger B. Hill, Head, 706-542-4100, Fax: 706-542-4054, E-mail: rbhill@uga.edu. *Application contact:* Dr. Mura N. Womble, Graduate Coordinator, 706-542-4503, Fax: 706-542-4054, E-mail: mwomble@uga.edu.

University of Georgia, Graduate School, Terry College of Business, Program in Business Administration, Athens, GA 30602. Offers MA, MBA, PhD, JD/MBA. *Accreditation:* AACSB. *Faculty:* 79 full-time (18 women). *Students:* 370 full-time (114 women), 214 part-time (68 women); includes 105 minority (58 African Americans, 1 American Indian/Alaska Native, 32 Asian Americans or Pacific Islanders, 14 Hispanic Americans), 62 international. 625 applicants, 43% accepted, 222 enrolled. In 2006, 201 master's, 13 doctorates awarded. *Degree requirements:* For master's, thesis (MA); for doctorate, thesis/dissertation. *Entrance requirements:* For master's, GMAT (MBA), GRE General Test (MA); for doctorate, GMAT or GRE General Test. *Application deadline:* For fall admission, 7/1 priority date for domestic students; for spring admission, 11/15 for domestic students. Application fee: $50. Electronic applications accepted. *Financial support:* Fellowships, research assistantships, teaching assistantships, unspecified assistantships available. *Unit head:* Dr. Melvin R. Crask, Interim Associate Dean, 706-542-8068, Fax: 706-542-5351, E-mail: mcrask@terry.uga.edu.

University of Guam, Graduate School and Research, College of Business and Public Administration, Master of Business Administration Program, Mangilao, GU 96923. Offers MBA. *Entrance requirements:* For master's, GMAT. Additional exam requirements/recommendations for international students: Required—TOEFL.

University of Guelph, Graduate Program Services, College of Management and Economics, Faculty of Management, Guelph, ON N1G 2W1, Canada. Offers business administration (MBA), including agribusiness management, hospitality and tourism management; leadership (MA). Part-time and evening/weekend programs available. Postbaccalaureate distance learning degree programs offered. *Entrance requirements:* For master's, minimum B average, minimum 3 years managerial experience. Additional exam requirements/recommendations for international students: Required—TOEFL (minimum score 550 paper-based; 213 computer-based). Electronic applications accepted. *Faculty research:* Marketing, operations management, business policy, financial management, organizational behavior.

University of Hartford, Barney School of Business, Program in Business Administration, West Hartford, CT 06117-1599. Offers EMBA, MBA, MBA/M Eng. *Accreditation:* AACSB. Part-time and evening/weekend programs available. *Faculty:* 16 full-time (5 women), 10 part-time/adjunct (3 women). *Students:* 98 full-time (39 women), 348 part-time (135 women); includes 76 minority (28 African Americans, 1 American Indian/Alaska Native, 28 Asian Americans or Pacific Islanders, 19 Hispanic Americans), 40 international. Average age 32. 181 applicants, 73% accepted, 100 enrolled. In 2006, 131 degrees awarded. *Entrance requirements:* For master's, GMAT, 2 letters of recommendation, resumé. Additional exam requirements/recommendations for international students: Required—TOEFL (minimum score 550 paper-based; 213 computer-based). *Application deadline:* For fall admission, 7/1 priority date for domestic students; for spring admission, 12/1 for domestic students. Applications are processed on a rolling basis. Application fee: $40 ($55 for international students). Electronic applications accepted. *Expenses:* Tuition: Part-time $515 per credit. Required fees: $200 per term. *Financial support:* In 2006–07, 1 fellowship with full tuition reimbursement (averaging $12,000 per year), 37 research assistantships (averaging $3,400 per year) were awarded; career-related internships or fieldwork also available. Support available to part-time students. Financial award application deadline: 5/1.

University of Hartford, College of Education, Nursing, and Health Professions, Program in Nursing, West Hartford, CT 06117-1599. Offers community/public health nursing (MSN); nursing education (MSN); nursing management (MSN). *Accreditation:* AACN. Part-time and evening/weekend programs available. *Faculty:* 6 full-time (all women), 2 part-time/adjunct (both women). *Students:* 1 (woman) full-time, 170 part-time (163 women); includes 12 minority (5 African Americans, 1 American Indian/Alaska Native, 6 Hispanic Americans). Average age 43. 60 applicants, 97% accepted, 54 enrolled. In 2006, 46 degrees awarded. *Degree requirements:* For master's, research project. *Entrance requirements:* For master's, BSN, Connecticut RN license. Additional exam requirements/recommendations for international students: Required—TOEFL (minimum score 550 paper-based; 213 computer-based). *Application deadline:* For fall admission, 4/15 priority date for domestic students; for spring admission, 12/1 for domestic students. Application fee: $40 ($55 for international students). Electronic applications accepted. *Expenses:* Contact institution. *Financial support:* Teaching assistantships, Federal Work-Study available. Support available to part-time students. Financial award application deadline: 6/1; financial award applicants required to submit FAFSA. *Faculty research:* Child development, women in doctoral study, applying feminist theory in teaching methods, near death experience, grandmothers as primary care providers. *Unit head:* Mary Beth Mathews, Chair, 860-768-4217, Fax: 860-768-5346, E-mail: mbmathews@hartford.edu. *Application contact:* Marlene Hall, Assistant Dean, 860-768-5116, E-mail: mhall@hartford.edu.

University of Hawaii at Manoa, Graduate Division, Shidler College of Business, Program in Business Administration, Honolulu, HI 96822. Offers Asian business studies (MBA); Chinese business studies (MBA); decision sciences (MBA); entrepreneurship (MBA); finance (MBA); finance and banking (MBA); human resources management (MBA); information management (MBA); information technology (MBA); international business (MBA); Japanese business studies (MBA); marketing (MBA); organizational behavior (MBA); organizational management (MBA); real estate (MBA); student-designed track (MBA). *Accreditation:* AACSB. Part-time programs available. *Faculty:* 48 full-time (9 women). *Students:* 207 full-time (77 women), 158 part-time (60 women); includes 93 minority (2 African Americans, 1 American Indian/Alaska Native, 88 Asian Americans or Pacific Islanders, 2 Hispanic Americans), 58 international. Average age 33. 235 applicants, 55% accepted, 68 enrolled. In 2006, 147 degrees awarded. *Degree requirements:* For master's, thesis optional. *Entrance requirements:* For master's, GMAT, minimum GPA of 3.0. Additional exam requirements/recommendations for international students: Required—TOEFL (minimum score 500 paper-based; 173 computer-based; 61 iBT). *Application deadline:* For fall admission, 5/1 for domestic and international students; for spring admission, 9/1 for domestic and international students. Application fee: $50. *Financial support:* In 2006–07, 7 research assistantships (averaging $17,409 per year), 3 teaching assistantships (averaging $14,028 per year) were awarded. *Application contact:* Ting Bui, Information Contact, 808-956-5565, Fax: 808-956-6889.

University of Hawaii at Manoa, Graduate Division, Shidler College of Business, Program in Executive Education, Honolulu, HI 96822. Offers executive business administration (EMBA); Vietnam focused business administration (EMBA). Part-time programs available. *Entrance requirements:* For master's, GMAT, minimum GPA of 3.0. *Application deadline:* For fall admission, 5/1 for domestic and international students; for spring admission, 11/1 for domestic and international students. Application fee: $50. *Application contact:* Program Office, 808-956-3260, Fax: 808-956-3251.

University of Houston, Bauer College of Business, Houston, TX 77204. Offers M Acy, MBA, MS, PhD. *Accreditation:* AACSB. Part-time and evening/weekend programs available. *Faculty:* 52 full-time (12 women), 35 part-time/adjunct (7 women). *Students:* 461 full-time (195 women), 498 part-time (161 women); includes 317 minority (48 African Americans, 3 American Indian/Alaska Native, 200 Asian Americans or Pacific Islanders, 66 Hispanic Americans), 166 international. Average age 30. 628 applicants, 62% accepted, 294 enrolled. In 2006, 377 master's, 4 doctorates awarded. *Degree requirements:* For doctorate, thesis/dissertation, comprehensive exam. *Entrance requirements:* For master's, GMAT; for doctorate, GMAT or GRE. Additional exam requirements/recommendations for international students: Required—TOEFL. *Application deadline:* For fall admission, 5/1 for domestic students; for spring admission, 10/1 for domestic students. Applications are processed on a rolling basis. Application fee: $75 ($150 for international students). *Expenses:* Tuition, state resident: full-time $5,429; part-time $226 per credit. Tuition, nonresident: full-time $12,029; part-time $501 per credit. Required fees: $2,454. *Financial support:* In 2006–07, 8 fellowships with full tuition reimbursements (averaging $10,150 per year), 97 teaching assistantships with full tuition reimbursements (averaging $7,000 per year) were awarded; research assistantships with full tuition reimbursements, career-related internships or fieldwork, Federal Work-Study, institutionally sponsored loans, scholarships/grants, health care benefits, and unspecified assistantships also available. Support available to part-time students. Financial award application deadline: 3/10; financial award applicants required to submit FAFSA. *Faculty research:* Accountancy and taxation, finance, international business, management. Total annual research expenditures: $1.9 million. *Unit head:* Dr. Arthur Warga, Dean, 713-743-4604, Fax: 713-743-4622, E-mail: warga@uh.edu. *Application contact:* Andrew Wayne Edwards, Office of Student Services, 713-743-4852, Fax: 713-743-4942, E-mail: aedwards@uh.edu.

University of Houston–Clear Lake, School of Business, Program in Business Administration, Houston, TX 77058-1098. Offers MBA. *Accreditation:* AACSB. Part-time and evening/weekend programs available. *Students:* 140 full-time, 261 part-time; includes 107 minority (30 African Americans, 1 American Indian/Alaska Native, 35 Asian Americans or Pacific Islanders, 41 Hispanic Americans), 76 international. 236 applicants, 53% accepted, 85 enrolled. In 2006, 148 degrees awarded. *Degree requirements:* For master's, thesis optional. *Entrance requirements:* For master's, GMAT. Additional exam requirements/recommendations for international students: Required—TOEFL (minimum score 550 paper-based; 213 computer-based). *Application deadline:* For fall admission, 8/1 for domestic students, 6/1 for international students; for spring admission, 12/1 for domestic students, 10/1 for international students. Applications are processed on a rolling basis. Application fee: $35 ($75 for international students). Electronic applications accepted. *Financial support:* Career-related internships or fieldwork, Federal Work-Study, and institutionally sponsored loans available. Support available to part-time students. Financial award application deadline: 5/1; financial award applicants required to submit FAFSA. *Unit head:* Dr. R. McGlashan, Head, 281-283-3124, E-mail: mcglashan@uhcl.edu. *Application contact:* Janis S. Bigelow, Assistant Director of Admissions, Recruitment and Communications, 281-283-2540, Fax: 281-283-2530, E-mail: bigelow@uhcl.edu.

University of Houston–Victoria, School of Business Administration, Victoria, TX 77901-4450. Offers MBA. *Accreditation:* AACSB. Part-time and evening/weekend programs available. Postbaccalaureate distance learning degree programs offered (no on-campus study). *Faculty:* 25 full-time (5 women). *Students:* 144 full-time (75 women), 504 part-time (251 women); includes 356 minority (133 African Americans, 4 American Indian/Alaska Native, 144 Asian Americans or Pacific Islanders, 75 Hispanic Americans), 26 international. Average age 34. In 2006, 158 degrees awarded. *Entrance requirements:* For master's, GMAT. Additional exam requirements/recommendations for international students: Required—TOEFL (minimum score 550 paper-based; 213 computer-based). *Application deadline:* For fall admission, 6/1 for international students; for spring admission, 10/1 for international students. Applications are processed on a rolling basis. Application fee: $0. Electronic applications accepted. *Expenses:* Tuition, state resident: full-time $3,168; part-time $176 per semester hour. Tuition, nonresident: full-time $7,218; part-time $401 per semester hour. Required fees: $756; $42 per semester hour. Tuition and fees vary according to course load. *Financial support:* In 2006–07, research assistantships with partial tuition reimbursements (averaging $2,000 per year), teaching assistantships with partial tuition reimbursements (averaging $2,000 per year) were awarded; career-related internships or fieldwork, Federal Work-Study, scholarships/grants, and unspecified assistantships also available. Support available to part-time students. Financial award application deadline: 4/15; financial award applicants required to submit FAFSA. *Faculty research:* Economic development, marketing, finance. *Unit head:* Charles Bullock, Dean, 361-570-4230, Fax: 361-570-4229, E-mail: bullockc@uhv.edu. *Application contact:* Rosie McCusker, Recruitment Coordinator, 832-842-2858, E-mail: mccuskerr@uhv.edu.

See Close-Up on page 349.

University of Idaho, College of Graduate Studies, College of Business and Economics, Moscow, ID 83844-2282. Offers M Acct. *Accreditation:* AACSB. *Students:* 15. In 2006, 16 degrees awarded. *Degree requirements:* For master's, comprehensive exam. *Application deadline:* For fall admission, 8/1 for domestic students; for spring admission, 12/15 for domestic students. Application fee: $55 ($60 for international students). *Expenses:* Tuition, nonresident: full-time $9,600; part-time $140 per credit. Required fees: $4,740; $227 per credit. *Financial support:* Research assistantships, teaching assistantships, Federal Work-Study and scholarships/grants available. Support available to part-time students. Financial award application deadline: 2/15. *Unit head:* Dr. John Morris, Dean, 208-885-6478.

University of Illinois at Chicago, Graduate College, Liautaud Graduate School of Business, Program in Business Administration, Chicago, IL 60607-7128. Offers MBA, PhD, MBA/MA, MBA/MPH, MBA/MS. *Accreditation:* AACSB. Part-time programs available. *Entrance requirements:* For master's, GMAT, minimum GPA of 2.75; for doctorate, GMAT. Additional exam requirements/recommendations for international students: Required—TOEFL. Electronic applications accepted.

University of Illinois at Springfield, Graduate Programs, College of Business and Management, Program in Business Administration, Springfield, IL 62703-5407. Offers MBA. *Accreditation:* AACSB. Part-time and evening/weekend programs available. *Faculty:* 11 full-time (2 women). *Students:* 58 full-time (21 women), 58 part-time (28 women); includes 8 minority (2 African Americans, 4 Asian Americans or Pacific Islanders, 2 Hispanic Americans), 5 international. Average age 29. 85 applicants, 78% accepted, 39 enrolled. In 2006, 44 degrees awarded. *Degree requirements:* For master's, closure course. *Entrance requirements:* For master's, GMAT, 3 letters of reference. Additional exam requirements/recommendations for international students: Required—TOEFL (minimum score 550 paper-based; 213 computer-based). *Application deadline:* Applications are processed on a rolling basis. Application fee: $50 ($60 for international students). Electronic applications accepted. *Expenses:* Tuition, state resident: full-time $4,722; part-time $197 per credit hour. Tuition, nonresident: full-time $12,558; part-time $523 per credit hour. Required fees: $1,614; $8 per credit hour. $597 per term. *Financial support:* In 2006–07, research assistantships with full tuition reimbursements (averaging $7,425 per year), teaching assistantships with full tuition reimbursements (averaging $7,425 per year) were awarded; career-related internships or fieldwork, Federal Work-Study, scholarships/grants, health care benefits, and unspecified assistantships also available. Support available to part-time students. Financial award application deadline: 11/15; financial award applicants required to submit FAFSA. *Unit head:* Dr. Michael Small, Program Administrator, 217-206-7927, Fax: 217-206-7543, E-mail: small.michael@uis.edu.

University of Illinois at Urbana–Champaign, Graduate College, College of Business, Department of Business Administration, Champaign, IL 61820. Offers business administration (PhD); technology management (MSTM). *Accreditation:* AACSB. *Faculty:* 45 full-time (16 women), 5 part-time/adjunct (0 women). *Students:* 98 full-time (33 women), 10 part-time (2 women); includes 5 minority (1 African American, 4 Asian Americans or Pacific Islanders), 78 international. 316 applicants, 26% accepted, 60 enrolled. In 2006, 25 master's, 7 doctorates awarded. *Degree requirements:* For doctorate, thesis/dissertation. *Entrance requirements:* For master's and doctorate, GMAT, minimum GPA of 3.0. *Application deadline:* Applications are processed

Business Administration and Management—General

University of Illinois at Urbana–Champaign (continued)
on a rolling basis. Application fee: $50 ($60 for international students). Electronic applications accepted. *Expenses: Contact institution. Financial support:* In 2006–07, 38 fellowships, 39 research assistantships, 24 teaching assistantships were awarded; tuition waivers (full and partial) also available. Financial award application deadline: 2/15. *Unit head:* Huseyin Leblebici, Head, 217-333-4240, Fax: 217-244-7969, E-mail: hleblebi@uiuc.edu. *Application contact:* J.E. Miller, Coordinator of Graduate Programs, 217-244-8002, Fax: 217-244-7969, E-mail: j-miller@uiuc.edu.

University of Illinois at Urbana–Champaign, Graduate College, College of Business, Program in Business Administration, Champaign, IL 61820. Offers MBA, Ed M/MBA, JD/MBA, M Arch/MBA, MCS/MBA, MS/MBA. *Accreditation:* AACSB. *Students:* 98 full-time (33 women), 10 part-time (2 women); includes 5 minority (1 African American, 4 Asian Americans or Pacific Islanders), 78 international. 316 applicants, 26% accepted, 60 enrolled. In 2006, 25 master's awarded. Application fee: $50 ($60 for international students). *Financial support:* In 2006–07, 41 fellowships, 39 research assistantships, 24 teaching assistantships were awarded. *Unit head:* Mary Miller, Dean, 217-244-8019, Fax: 217-333-1156, E-mail: mmillero@uiuc.edu. *Application contact:* Annetta Culver, Director, MBA Student Affairs, 217-244-6424, Fax: 217-333-1156, E-mail: arculver@uiuc.edu.

University of Indianapolis, Graduate Programs, School of Business, Graduate Business Programs, Indianapolis, IN 46227-3697. Offers business (EMBA); business administration (MBA); finance (Graduate Certificate); global supply chains management (Graduate Certificate); marketing (Graduate Certificate); organizational leadership (Graduate Certificate); technology management (Graduate Certificate). *Accreditation:* ACBSP. Part-time and evening/weekend programs available. *Faculty:* 6 full-time (2 women), 6 part-time/adjunct (1 woman). *Students:* 50 full-time (16 women), 92 part-time (32 women); includes 12 minority (4 African Americans, 7 Asian Americans or Pacific Islanders, 1 Hispanic American), 10 international. Average age 32. In 2006, 57 degrees awarded. *Entrance requirements:* For master's, GMAT, interview, minimum GPA of 2.8, 2 letters of recommendation, resumé. Additional exam requirements/recommendations for international students: Required—TOEFL (minimum score 550 paper-based; 213 computer-based). *Application deadline:* Applications are processed on a rolling basis. Application fee: $50. *Expenses: Contact institution. Financial support:* Federal Work-Study and unspecified assistantships available. Financial award application deadline: 5/1; financial award applicants required to submit FAFSA. *Faculty research:* Integration of microcomputers into decision making, communication skills, application of synthesized theories. *Unit head:* Dr. Matthew Will, Associate Dean, 317-788-3370, E-mail: mwill@uindy.edu.

The University of Iowa, Henry B. Tippie College of Business, Department of Accounting, Iowa City, IA 52242-1316. Offers accountancy (M Ac); business administration (PhD); JD/M Ac. *Accreditation:* AACSB. Part-time programs available. *Faculty:* 13 full-time (4 women). *Students:* 50 full-time (22 women); includes 2 minority (both Asian Americans or Pacific Islanders) Average age 25. 103 applicants, 49% accepted, 31 enrolled. In 2006, 40 degrees awarded. *Degree requirements:* For doctorate, thesis/dissertation, thesis defense, comprehensive exam, registration. *Entrance requirements:* For master's and doctorate, GMAT. Additional exam requirements/recommendations for international students: Required—TOEFL (minimum score 600 paper-based; 250 computer-based; 100 iBT). *Application deadline:* For fall admission, 7/15 for domestic students, 4/15 for international students; for spring admission, 12/1 for domestic students, 10/1 for international students. Application fee: $60 ($85 for international students). Electronic applications accepted. *Financial support:* In 2006–07, 44 students received support, including fellowships with full tuition reimbursements available (averaging $18,000 per year), research assistantships with partial tuition reimbursements available (averaging $15,736 per year), teaching assistantships with partial tuition reimbursements available (averaging $15,985 per year); career-related internships or fieldwork, Federal Work-Study, institutionally sponsored loans, scholarships/grants, and unspecified assistantships also available. Financial award applicants required to submit FAFSA. *Faculty research:* Auditing judgment and decision making; corporate financial reporting and capital markets; cost structure: analysis, estimation, and management; experimental and prediction economics; income taxes and interaction of financial and tax reporting systems. *Unit head:* Prof. W Bruce Johnson, Department Executive Officer, 319-335-0910, Fax: 319-335-1956. *Application contact:* Prof. Lynn M. Pringle, Director, Master of Accountancy Program, 319-335-0894, Fax: 319-335-1956, E-mail: lynn-pringle@uiowa.edu.

The University of Iowa, Henry B. Tippie College of Business, Department of Management and Organizations, Iowa City, IA 52242-1316. Offers business administration (PhD). *Accreditation:* AACSB. *Faculty:* 12 full-time (5 women), 44 part-time/adjunct (17 women). *Students:* 13 full-time (4 women), 4 international. Average age 30. 47 applicants, 9% accepted, 2 enrolled. In 2006, 2 degrees awarded. *Degree requirements:* For doctorate, thesis/dissertation, thesis defense, comprehensive exam, registration. *Entrance requirements:* For doctorate, GMAT or GRE. Additional exam requirements/recommendations for international students: Required—TOEFL (minimum score 600 paper-based; 250 computer-based). *Application deadline:* For fall admission, 2/1 for domestic and international students. Applications are processed on a rolling basis. Application fee: $60 ($85 for international students). Electronic applications accepted. *Financial support:* In 2006–07, 13 students received support, including 1 fellowship with full tuition reimbursement available (averaging $18,000 per year), 2 research assistantships with full tuition reimbursements available (averaging $15,985 per year), 10 teaching assistantships with full tuition reimbursements available (averaging $15,985 per year); institutionally sponsored loans, scholarships/grants, health care benefits, unspecified assistantships, and Department of Management and Operations pays full tuition also available. Financial award application deadline: 2/1; financial award applicants required to submit FAFSA. *Faculty research:* Decision making, human resources, personal selection, organizational behavior, training. Total annual research expenditures: $340,497. *Unit head:* Prof. Frank L. Schmidt, Department Executive Officer, 319-335-0927, Fax: 319-335-1956, E-mail: frank-schmidt@uiowa.edu. *Application contact:* Renea L. Jay, PhD Program Coordinator, 319-335-0830, Fax: 319-335-1956, E-mail: renea-jay@uiowa.edu.

The University of Iowa, Henry B. Tippie College of Business, Department of Management Sciences, Iowa City, IA 52242-1316. Offers business administration (PhD). *Accreditation:* AACSB. *Faculty:* 15 full-time (2 women), 2 part-time/adjunct (0 women). *Students:* 12 full-time (3 women), 9 international. Average age 30. 38 applicants, 8% accepted, 0 enrolled. In 2006, 1 degree awarded. *Degree requirements:* For doctorate, thesis/dissertation, thesis defense, comprehensive exam, registration. *Entrance requirements:* For doctorate, GRE General Test or GMAT, minimum GPA of 3.0. Additional exam requirements/recommendations for international students: Required—TOEFL (minimum score 600 paper-based; 250 computer-based). *Application deadline:* For fall admission, 2/15 for domestic and international students. Application fee: $60 ($85 for international students). Electronic applications accepted. *Financial support:* In 2006–07, 12 students received support, including research assistantships with full tuition reimbursements available (averaging $15,985 per year), teaching assistantships with full tuition reimbursements available (averaging $15,985 per year); institutionally sponsored loans, scholarships/grants, health care benefits, unspecified assistantships, and Department of Management Sciences pays full tuition also available. Financial award application deadline: 2/15. *Faculty research:* Optimization, supply chain management, data mining, logistics, knowledge management. Total annual research expenditures: $82,724. *Unit head:* Prof. Kurt Anstreicher, Department Executive Officer, 319-335-0858, Fax: 319-335-1956, E-mail: kurt-anstreicher@uiowa.edu. *Application contact:* Renea L. Jay, PhD Program Coordinator, 319-335-0830, Fax: 319-335-1956, E-mail: renea-jay@uiowa.edu.

The University of Iowa, Henry B. Tippie College of Business, Henry B. Tippie School of Management, Iowa City, IA 52242-1316. Offers accounting (MBA); corporate finance (MBA); entrepreneurship (MBA); finance (MBA); individually designed concentration (MBA); investment management (MBA); management information systems (MBA); marketing (MBA); nonprofit management (MBA); operations management (MBA); strategic management and consulting (MBA); JD/MBA; MBA/MA; MBA/MD; MBA/MHA; MBA/MSN. *Accreditation:* AACSB. Part-time and evening/weekend programs available. *Faculty:* 94 full-time (23 women), 65 part-time/adjunct (21 women). *Students:* 230 full-time (67 women), 712 part-time (234 women); includes 62 minority (6 African Americans, 1 American Indian/Alaska Native, 43 Asian Americans or Pacific Islanders, 12 Hispanic Americans), 127 international. Average age 30. 431 applicants, 61% accepted, 217 enrolled. In 2006, 363 degrees awarded. *Median time to degree:* Master's–2 years full-time, 3.5 years part-time. *Degree requirements:* For master's, registration. *Entrance requirements:* For master's, GMAT, work experience. Additional exam requirements/recommendations for international students: Required—TOEFL (minimum score 600 paper-based; 250 computer-based; 100 iBT). *Application deadline:* For fall admission, 7/15 for domestic students, 4/15 for international students; for spring admission, 12/15 priority date for domestic students, 11/1 priority date for international students. Applications are processed on a rolling basis. Application fee: $60 ($85 for international students). Electronic applications accepted. *Expenses: Contact institution. Financial support:* In 2006–07, 72 fellowships (averaging $3,892 per year), 55 research assistantships with partial tuition reimbursements (averaging $10,260 per year) were awarded; career-related internships or fieldwork, Federal Work-Study, institutionally sponsored loans, scholarships/grants, health care benefits, and unspecified assistantships also available. Support available to part-time students. Financial award application deadline: 4/15; financial award applicants required to submit FAFSA. *Faculty research:* Capital markets, econometrics, optimization, investments and empirical corporate finance, Iowa electronic markets. *Unit head:* Prof. Gary J. Gaeth, Associate Dean, MBA Programs, 800-622-4692, Fax: 319-335-3604, E-mail: gary-gaeth@uiowa.edu. *Application contact:* Jodi Schafer, Director of Student Recruitment and Marketing, 319-335-0864, Fax: 319-335-3604, E-mail: jodi-schafer@uiowa.edu.

The University of Iowa, Henry B. Tippie College of Business, Program in Accounting, Iowa City, IA 52242-1316. Offers business administration (PhD). *Faculty:* 13 full-time (4 women). *Students:* 13 full-time (2 women); includes 2 minority (both Asian Americans or Pacific Islanders), 3 international. Average age 31. 44 applicants, 7% accepted, 0 enrolled. In 2006, 1 degree awarded. *Degree requirements:* For doctorate, thesis/dissertation, thesis defense, comprehensive exam, registration. *Entrance requirements:* For doctorate, GMAT. Additional exam requirements/recommendations for international students: Required—TOEFL (minimum score 600 paper-based; 250 computer-based). *Application deadline:* For fall admission, 1/31 for domestic and international students. Applications are processed on a rolling basis. Application fee: $60 ($85 for international students). Electronic applications accepted. *Financial support:* In 2006–07, 1 fellowship with full tuition reimbursement (averaging $18,000 per year), 1 research assistantship with full tuition reimbursement (averaging $15,985 per year), 13 teaching assistantships with full tuition reimbursements (averaging $15,985 per year) were awarded; scholarships/grants, health care benefits, unspecified assistantships, and Program in Accounting pays full tuition also available. Financial award application deadline: 1/31. *Unit head:* Prof. W. Bruce Johnson, Department Executive Officer, 319-355-0910, Fax: 319-335-1956, E-mail: bruce-johnson@uiowa.edu. *Application contact:* Renea L. Jay, PhD Program Coordinator, 319-335-0830, Fax: 319-335-1956, E-mail: renea-jay@uiowa.edu.

University of Kansas, Graduate Studies, School of Business, Program in Business, Lawrence, KS 66045. Offers MS, PhD. *Accreditation:* AACSB. *Faculty:* 47 full-time (10 women). *Students:* 27 full-time (14 women), 8 part-time (3 women); includes 2 minority (1 African American, 1 Asian American or Pacific Islander), 23 international. Average age 32. 72 applicants, 21% accepted. In 2006, 7 master's, 4 doctorates awarded. *Degree requirements:* For doctorate, thesis/dissertation, departmental qualifying exam, comprehensive exam. *Entrance requirements:* For master's, GMAT; for doctorate, GMAT or GRE. Additional exam requirements/recommendations for international students: Required—TOEFL (minimum score 570 paper-based; 230 computer-based; 88 iBT). *Application deadline:* For fall admission, 1/15 for domestic and international students. Applications are processed on a rolling basis. Application fee: $65. Electronic applications accepted. *Expenses:* Tuition, area resident: Part-time $227 per credit. Tuition, state resident: part-time $543 per credit. Tuition and fees vary according to course load, campus/location, program and reciprocity agreements. *Financial support:* Fellowships with full tuition reimbursements, research assistantships with full tuition reimbursements, teaching assistantships with tuition reimbursements, scholarships/grants, tuition waivers (full), and unspecified assistantships available. *Faculty research:* Tax, mergers and acquisitions, risk analysis personality and work outcomes, services, marketing, business ethics, corporate turnarounds. *Unit head:* Surendra Singh, Director, 785-864-7531. *Application contact:* Charly Edmonds, Associate Director, 785-864-3841, E-mail: bschoolphd@ku.edu.

University of Kansas, Graduate Studies, School of Business, Program in Business Administration, Lawrence, KS 66045. Offers MBA, JD/MBA, MBA/MA, MBA/MHSA. *Accreditation:* AACSB. Part-time and evening/weekend programs available. *Faculty:* 60 full-time (15 women), 28 part-time/adjunct (8 women). *Students:* 124 full-time (27 women), 194 part-time (51 women); includes 38 minority (6 African Americans, 2 American Indian/Alaska Native, 24 Asian Americans or Pacific Islanders, 6 Hispanic Americans), 30 international. Average age 30. 168 applicants, 61% accepted. In 2006, 135 degrees awarded. *Degree requirements:* For master's, 52 credit hours. *Entrance requirements:* For master's, GMAT, 2 years of professional work experience for MBA. Additional exam requirements/recommendations for international students: Required—TOEFL. *Application deadline:* For fall admission, 1/15 priority date for domestic and international students; for spring admission, 11/1 priority date for domestic students, 10/1 for international students. Applications are processed on a rolling basis. Application fee: $65. Electronic applications accepted. *Expenses:* Tuition, area resident: Part-time $227 per credit. Tuition, state resident: part-time $543 per credit. Tuition and fees vary according to course load, campus/location, program and reciprocity agreements. *Financial support:* Career-related internships or fieldwork, Federal Work-Study, institutionally sponsored loans, scholarships/grants, and unspecified assistantships available. Financial award application deadline: 6/1; financial award applicants required to submit FAFSA. *Faculty research:* Advanced audit technologies, real options and asset pricing, corporate governance, foreign direct investment, CEO characteristics and organizational innovation. *Unit head:* Dr. Charles Krider, Director of MBA Programs, 785-864-7543, E-mail: ckrider@ku.edu. *Application contact:* Dee Steinle, Administative Director of Masters Programs, 785-864-7596, Fax: 785-864-5376, E-mail: dsteinle@ku.edu.

University of Kentucky, Graduate School, Gatton College of Business and Economics, Program in Business Administration, Lexington, KY 40506-0032. Offers MBA, PhD. *Accreditation:* AACSB. *Faculty:* 36 full-time (5 women), 1 part-time/adjunct (0 women). *Students:* 195 full-time (66 women), 126 part-time (49 women); includes 10 minority (4 African Americans, 2 Asian Americans or Pacific Islanders, 4 Hispanic Americans), 132 international. Average age 29. 145 applicants, 31% accepted, 13 enrolled. In 2006, 116 master's, 9 doctorates awarded. *Median time to degree:* Of those who began their doctoral program in fall 1998, 77% received their degree in 8 years or less. *Degree requirements:* For master's, comprehensive exam; for doctorate, thesis/dissertation, comprehensive exam. *Entrance requirements:* For master's, GMAT, minimum undergraduate GPA of 2.75; for doctorate, GMAT, minimum undergraduate GPA of 3.0. Additional exam requirements/recommendations for international students: Required—TOEFL (minimum score 550 paper-based; 213 computer-based). *Application deadline:* For fall admission, 7/17 priority date for domestic students, 2/1 priority date for international students; for spring admission, 12/13 priority date for domestic students, 6/15 priority date for international students. Application fee: $40 ($55 for international students). Electronic applications accepted. *Expenses:* Tuition, state resident: full-time $7,670; part-time $401 per credit hour. Tuition, nonresident: full-time $16,158; part-time $873 per credit hour. *Financial support:* In 2006–07, 11 fellowships with full tuition reimbursements (averaging $2,960 per year), 37 teaching assistantships with full tuition reimbursements (averaging $12,450 per year) were awarded; research assistantships with full tuition reimbursements, Federal Work-Study, institutionally sponsored loans, scholarships/grants, traineeships, health care benefits, tuition waivers (partial), and unspecified assistantships also available. Support available to part-time students. Financial award application deadline: 3/15. *Faculty research:* Expert systems in manufacturing, knowledge acquisition and management, financial institutions, market in service organizations, strategic planning. *Unit head:* Dr. Paul Jarley, Associate

Dean for Academic Affairs, 859-257-7692, Fax: 859-257-4822, E-mail: pjarl@uky.edu. *Application contact:* Dr. Brian Jackson, Senior Associate Dean, 859-257-4667, Fax: 859-257-4676, E-mail: brian.jackson@uky.edu.

University of La Verne, College of Business and Public Management, Graduate Programs in Business Administration, La Verne, CA 91750-4443. Offers accounting (MBA); business (MBIT); executive management (MBA-EP); finance (MBA, MBA-EP); health services management (MBA); information technology (MBA, MBA-EP); international business (MBA, MBA-EP); leadership (MBA-EP); managed care (MBA); management (MBA, MBA-EP); marketing (MBA, MBA-EP). Part-time and evening/weekend programs available. *Faculty:* 15 full-time (7 women), 13 part-time/adjunct (7 women). *Students:* 277 full-time (133 women), 112 part-time (64 women); includes 144 minority (32 African Americans, 3 American Indian/Alaska Native, 70 Asian Americans or Pacific Islanders, 39 Hispanic Americans), 160 international. Average age 30. In 2006, 142 degrees awarded. *Entrance requirements:* For master's, minimum undergraduate GPA of 3.0, 2 letters of recommendation, resumé. Additional exam requirements/recommendations for international students: Required—TOEFL (minimum score 550 paper-based; 213 computer-based). *Application deadline:* Applications are processed on a rolling basis. Application fee: $50. *Expenses:* Contact institution. *Financial support:* Career-related internships or fieldwork, institutionally sponsored loans, and scholarships/grants available. Financial award application deadline: 3/2; financial award applicants required to submit FAFSA. *Unit head:* Dr. Ibrahim Helou, Chairperson, 909-593-3511 Ext. 4211, Fax: 909-392-2704, E-mail: heloua@ulv.edu. *Application contact:* Dr. Julius Walecki, Marketing Director, 909-593-3511 Ext. 4192, Fax: 909-392-2704, E-mail: cbpm@ulv.edu.

University of La Verne, College of Business and Public Management, Program in Gerontology, La Verne, CA 91750-4443. Offers business administration (MS); counseling (MS); gerontology (Certificate); gerontology administration (MS); health services management (MS); public administration (MS). Part-time programs available. *Faculty:* 7 full-time (2 women), 8 part-time/adjunct (4 women). *Students:* 7 full-time (all women), 21 part-time (20 women); includes 16 minority (7 African Americans, 1 American Indian/Alaska Native, 2 Asian Americans or Pacific Islanders, 6 Hispanic Americans). Average age 45. In 2006, 12 degrees awarded. *Entrance requirements:* For master's, minimum GPA of 2.5. Additional exam requirements/recommendations for international students: Required—TOEFL (minimum score 550 paper-based; 213 computer-based). *Application deadline:* Applications are processed on a rolling basis. Application fee: $50. *Expenses:* Contact institution. *Financial support:* Institutionally sponsored loans available. Financial award application deadline: 3/2; financial award applicants required to submit FAFSA. *Unit head:* Joan Branin, Chairperson, 909-593-3511 Ext. 4247, E-mail: braninj@ulv.edu. *Application contact:* Jo Nell Baker, Director, Graduate Admissions and Academic Services, 909-593-3511 Ext. 4244, Fax: 909-392-2761, E-mail: gradadmt@ulv.edu.

University of La Verne, College of Business and Public Management, Program in Organizational Management and Leadership, La Verne, CA 91750-4443. Offers leadership and management (MS); nonprofit management (Certificate); organizational leadership (Certificate). Part-time programs available. *Faculty:* 15 full-time (7 women), 13 part-time/adjunct (7 women). *Students:* 20 full-time (13 women), 40 part-time (25 women); includes 37 minority (5 African Americans, 5 American Indian/Alaska Native, 3 Asian Americans or Pacific Islanders, 24 Hispanic Americans), 2 international. Average age 35. In 2006, 21 degrees awarded. *Degree requirements:* For master's, thesis or research project. *Entrance requirements:* For master's, minimum undergraduate GPA of 2.75, 2 letters of recommendation, interview, resumé. Additional exam requirements/recommendations for international students: Required—TOEFL (minimum score 550 paper-based; 213 computer-based). *Application deadline:* Applications are processed on a rolling basis. Application fee: $50. *Expenses:* Contact institution. *Financial support:* Institutionally sponsored loans available. Financial award application deadline: 3/2; financial award applicants required to submit FAFSA. *Unit head:* Dr. Bernice Ledbetter, Chairperson, 909-593-3511 Ext. 4345, E-mail: bledbetter@ulv.edu. *Application contact:* Jo Nell Baker, Director, Graduate Admissions and Academic Services, 909-593-3511 Ext. 4244, Fax: 909-392-2761, E-mail: gradadmt@ulv.edu.

University of La Verne, Regional Campus Administration, Graduate Programs, Central Coast/Vandenberg Air Force Base Campuses, La Verne, CA 91750-4443. Offers business (MBA-EP), including health services management, information technology; health administration (MHA); leadership and management (MS). *Faculty:* 6 part-time/adjunct (0 women). *Students:* 14 full-time (5 women), 20 part-time (8 women); includes 7 minority (1 African American, 1 American Indian/Alaska Native, 5 Hispanic Americans). Average age 38. In 2006, 11 degrees awarded. *Entrance requirements:* For master's, 2 letters of recommendation, resumé. *Application deadline:* Applications are processed on a rolling basis. Application fee: $50. *Expenses:* Contact institution. *Financial support:* Institutionally sponsored loans available. Financial award application deadline: 3/2; financial award applicants required to submit FAFSA. *Unit head:* Kitt Vincent, Director, Central Coast Campus, 805-542-9690 Ext. 321, Fax: 805-542-9735, E-mail: vincentk@ulv.edu.

University of La Verne, Regional Campus Administration, Graduate Programs, High Desert Campus, Victorville, CA 91750-4443. Offers business (MBA-EP); health administration (MHA); leadership and management (MS). *Faculty:* 2 part-time/adjunct (0 women). *Students:* 1 full-time (0 women), 13 part-time (7 women); includes 8 minority (5 African Americans, 1 American Indian/Alaska Native, 2 Hispanic Americans). Average age 41. In 2006, 1 degree awarded. *Entrance requirements:* For master's, 2 letters of recommendation, resumé. *Application deadline:* Applications are processed on a rolling basis. Application fee: $50. *Expenses:* Contact institution. *Financial support:* Application deadline: 3/2; *Unit head:* Teresa Anderson, Director, 760-843-0086, Fax: 760-843-9505, E-mail: tanderson7@ulv.edu.

University of La Verne, Regional Campus Administration, Graduate Programs, Inland Empire Campus, Ranche Cucamonga, CA 91750-4443. Offers business (MBA-EP), including health services management, information technology, management, marketing; health administration (MHA); leadership and management (MS). *Faculty:* 2 full-time (1 woman), 8 part-time/adjunct (2 women). *Students:* 21 full-time (16 women), 32 part-time (18 women); includes 29 minority (13 African Americans, 1 American Indian/Alaska Native, 4 Asian Americans or Pacific Islanders, 11 Hispanic Americans). Average age 37. In 2006, 17 degrees awarded. *Entrance requirements:* For master's, 2 letters of recommendation, resumé. *Application deadline:* Applications are processed on a rolling basis. Application fee: $50. *Expenses:* Contact institution. *Financial support:* Institutionally sponsored loans available. Financial award application deadline: 3/2; financial award applicants required to submit FAFSA. *Unit head:* Jerry Ford, Director, 909-484-3858 Ext. 228, Fax: 909-484-9469, E-mail: fordj@ulv.edu.

University of La Verne, Regional Campus Administration, Graduate Programs, Kern County Campus, Bakersfield, CA 93301. Offers business (MBA-EP), including information technology, management, marketing; health administration (MHA); leadership and management (MS). *Faculty:* 4 part-time/adjunct (2 women). *Students:* 2 full-time (1 woman), 7 part-time (4 women); includes 2 minority (1 African American, 1 Hispanic American). Average age 37. In 2006, 4 degrees awarded. *Entrance requirements:* For master's, 2 letters of recommendation, resumé. *Application deadline:* Applications are processed on a rolling basis. Application fee: $50. *Expenses:* Contact institution. *Financial support:* Institutionally sponsored loans available. Financial award application deadline: 3/2; financial award applicants required to submit FAFSA. *Unit head:* Val Garcia, 661-328-1430, E-mail: vgarcia6@ulv.edu.

University of La Verne, Regional Campus Administration, Graduate Programs, Orange County Campus, Garden Grove, CA 92840. Offers business (MBA-EP), including health services management, information technology, management, marketing, supply chain management; health administration (MHA); leadership and management (MS); public administration (MPA). *Faculty:* 4 full-time (1 woman), 3 part-time/adjunct (1 woman). *Students:* 19 full-time (8 women), 64 part-time (29 women); includes 37 minority (4 African Americans, 2 American Indian/Alaska Native, 15 Asian Americans or Pacific Islanders, 16 Hispanic Americans). Average age 41. In 2006, 18 degrees awarded. *Entrance requirements:* For master's, 2 letters of recommendation, resumé. *Application deadline:* Applications are processed on a rolling basis. Application fee: $50. *Expenses:* Contact institution. *Financial support:* Institutionally sponsored loans available. Financial award application deadline: 3/2; financial award applicants required to submit FAFSA. *Unit head:* Pamela Bergovoy, Director, 714-534-4860, Fax: 714-534-4865, E-mail: bergovoy@ulv.edu.

University of La Verne, Regional Campus Administration, Graduate Programs, San Fernando Valley Campus, Burbank, CA 91505. Offers business (MBA-EP), including health services management, information technology, management, marketing; health administration (MHA); leadership and management (MS). *Faculty:* 3 full-time (2 women), 6 part-time/adjunct (2 women). *Students:* 24 full-time (12 women), 57 part-time (31 women); includes 42 minority (12 African Americans, 1 American Indian/Alaska Native, 9 Asian Americans or Pacific Islanders, 20 Hispanic Americans), 1 international. Average age 39. In 2006, 45 degrees awarded. *Entrance requirements:* For master's, 2 letters of recommendation, resumé. *Application deadline:* Applications are processed on a rolling basis. Application fee: $50. *Expenses:* Contact institution. *Financial support:* Institutionally sponsored loans available. Financial award application deadline: 3/2; financial award applicants required to submit FAFSA. *Unit head:* Nelly Kazman, Director, 818-846-4008 Ext. 26, Fax: 818-566-1047, E-mail: kazmann@ulv.edu.

University of La Verne, Regional Campus Administration, Graduate Programs, Ventura County/Point Mugu Naval Air Station Campuses, La Verne, CA 91750-4443. Offers business (MBA-EP), including health services management, information technology, management, marketing; business organizational management (MS); health administration (MHA); leadership and management (MS). *Faculty:* 2 full-time (0 women), 8 part-time/adjunct (1 woman). *Students:* 22 full-time (7 women), 29 part-time (16 women); includes 19 minority (4 African Americans, 7 Asian Americans or Pacific Islanders, 8 Hispanic Americans). Average age 40. In 2006, 26 degrees awarded. *Entrance requirements:* For master's, 2 letters of recommendation, resumé. Application fee: $50. *Expenses:* Contact institution. *Financial support:* Institutionally sponsored loans available. Financial award application deadline: 3/2; financial award applicants required to submit FAFSA. *Unit head:* Janet Meyer, Director, Ventura Campus, 805-981-8030 Ext. 225, Fax: 805-981-8033, E-mail: jmeyer2@ulv.edu.

University of La Verne, Regional Campus Administration, Graduate Program, ULV Online, La Verne, CA 91750-4443. Offers business administration (MBA). *Faculty:* 7 full-time (4 women), 2 part-time/adjunct (1 woman). *Students:* 25 full-time (15 women), 41 part-time (22 women); includes 23 minority (11 African Americans, 2 American Indian/Alaska Native, 4 Asian Americans or Pacific Islanders, 6 Hispanic Americans). Average age 35. In 2006, 11 degrees awarded. *Entrance requirements:* For master's, resumé, 2 letters of recommendation. *Application deadline:* Applications are processed on a rolling basis. Application fee: $50. *Financial support:* Application deadline: 3/2; *Unit head:* Unit Head, 800-695-4858 Ext. 5322.

University of Lethbridge, School of Graduate Studies, Lethbridge, AB T1K 3M4, Canada. Offers accounting (MScM); addictions counseling (M Sc); agricultural biotechnology (M Sc); agricultural studies (M Sc, MA); anthropology (MA); archaeology (MA); art (MA); biochemistry (M Sc); biological sciences (M Sc); biomolecular science (PhD); biosystems and biodiversity (PhD); Canadian studies (MA); chemistry (M Sc); computer science (M Sc); computer science and geographical information science (M Sc); counseling psychology (M Ed); dramatic arts (MA); earth, space, and physical science (PhD); economics (MA); educational leadership (M Ed); English (MA); environmental science (M Sc); evolution and behavior (PhD); exercise science (M Sc); finance (MScM); French (MA); French/German (MA); French/Spanish (MA); general education (M Ed); general management (MScM); geography (M Sc, MA); German (MA); health sciences (M Sc, MA); history (MA); human resource management and labour relations (MScM); individualized multidisciplinary (M Sc, MA); information systems (MScM); international management (MScM); kinesiology (M Sc, MA); management (M Sc, MA); marketing (MScM); mathematics (M Sc); music (MA); Native American studies (MA); neuroscience (M Sc, PhD); new media (MA); nursing (M Sc); philosophy (MA); physics (M Sc); policy and strategy (MScM); political science (MA); psychology (M Sc, MA); religious studies (MA); sociology (MA); theoretical and computational science (PhD); urban and regional studies (MA). Part-time and evening/weekend programs available. *Students:* 200 full-time, 90 part-time. In 2006, 105 master's, 3 doctorates awarded. *Degree requirements:* For doctorate, thesis/dissertation, comprehensive exam. *Entrance requirements:* For master's, GMAT (M Sc management), bachelor's degree in related field, minimum GPA of 3.0 during previous 20 graded semester courses, 2 years teaching or related experience (M Ed); for doctorate, master's degree, minimum graduate GPA of 3.5. Additional exam requirements/recommendations for international students: Required—TOEFL. Application fee: $60 Canadian dollars. *Financial support:* Fellowships, research assistantships, teaching assistantships, scholarships/grants, health care benefits, and unspecified assistantships available. *Faculty research:* Movement and brain plasticity, gibberellin physiology, photosynthesis, carbon cycling, molecular properties of main-group ring components. *Unit head:* Dr. Jo-Anne Fiske, Interim Dean, 403-329-2121, Fax: 403-329-2097. *Application contact:* Kathy Schrage, Administrative Assistant, Office of the Academic Vice President, 403-329-2121, Fax: 403-329-2097, E-mail: inquiries@uleth.ca.

University of Louisiana at Lafayette, Graduate School, College of Business Administration, Lafayette, LA 70504. Offers business administration (MBA); health care administration (MBA); health care certification (MBA). *Accreditation:* AACSB. Part-time programs available. *Faculty:* 34 full-time (11 women). *Students:* 68 full-time (28 women), 106 part-time (55 women); includes 18 minority (8 African Americans, 3 American Indian/Alaska Native, 3 Asian Americans or Pacific Islanders, 4 Hispanic Americans), 17 international. Average age 28. 122 applicants, 43% accepted, 38 enrolled. In 2006, 63 degrees awarded. *Entrance requirements:* For master's, GMAT, minimum GPA of 2.75. *Application deadline:* For fall admission, 5/15 for domestic and international students; for spring admission, 10/1 for domestic and international students. Application fee: $25 ($30 for international students). *Expenses:* Tuition, state resident: full-time $3,247; part-time $93 per credit hour. Tuition, nonresident: full-time $9,427; part-time $350 per credit hour. *Financial support:* In 2006–07, 15 research assistantships with full tuition reimbursements (averaging $5,500 per year) were awarded; Federal Work-Study, tuition waivers (full), and unspecified assistantships also available. Support available to part-time students. Financial award application deadline: 5/1. *Unit head:* Ellen Cook, Acting Dean, 337-482-6491, Fax: 337-482-5883, E-mail: edcook@louisiana.edu. *Application contact:* Dr. P. Robert Viguerie, Director, MBA, 337-482-6119, Fax: 337-482-5883, E-mail: mbadirector@louisiana.edu.

University of Louisiana at Monroe, Graduate Studies and Research, College of Business Administration, Monroe, LA 71209-0001. Offers MBA. *Accreditation:* AACSB. Part-time and evening/weekend programs available. *Faculty:* 14 full-time (4 women). *Students:* 27 full-time (19 women), 44 part-time (32 women); includes 12 African Americans, 3 Asian Americans or Pacific Islanders, 8 international. Average age 29. In 2006, 40 degrees awarded. *Entrance requirements:* For master's, GMAT, minimum GPA of 2.5, minimum AACSB index of 950. Additional exam requirements/recommendations for international students: Required—TOEFL. *Application deadline:* For fall admission, 6/1 for domestic students; for spring admission, 11/1 for domestic students. Application fee: $20 ($30 for international students). *Expenses:* Tuition, state resident: part-time $124 per credit hour. Tuition, nonresident: part-time $124 per credit hour. *Financial support:* Research assistantships, teaching assistantships, Federal Work-Study available. Financial award application deadline: 7/1. *Unit head:* Dr. Ron Berry, Dean, 318-342-1100, E-mail: rberry@ulm.edu. *Application contact:* Dr. Donna Luse, Program Chair, 318-342-1106, E-mail: luse@ulm.edu.

University of Louisville, Graduate School, College of Business, MBA Programs, Louisville, KY 40292-0001. Offers MBA. *Accreditation:* AACSB. *Students:* 118 full-time (50 women), 229 part-time (89 women); includes 30 minority (9 African Americans, 16 Asian Americans or Pacific Islanders, 5 Hispanic Americans), 79 international. Average age 31. In 2006, 216 degrees awarded. *Entrance requirements:* For master's, GMAT, 2 letters of reference, personal interview, resum[00e9]. *Unit head:* Dr. Robert D. Nixon, Associate Dean for Masters Programs, 502-852-4847, Fax: 502-852-7557, E-mail: robert.nixon@louisville.edu. *Application contact:*

Business Administration and Management—General

University of Louisville (continued)
Kevin J. Kane, Director of Masters Programs, 502-852-2169, Fax: 502-852-7557, E-mail: kevin.kane@louisville.edu.

University of Maine, Graduate School, College of Business, Public Policy and Health, The Maine Business School, Orono, ME 04469. Offers accounting (MS); business administration (MBA). *Accreditation:* AACSB. Part-time and evening/weekend programs available. *Faculty:* 20. *Students:* 56 full-time (19 women), 25 part-time (15 women); includes 1 minority (Asian American or Pacific Islander), 15 international. Average age 29. 48 applicants, 56% accepted, 19 enrolled. In 2006, 38 degrees awarded. *Entrance requirements:* For master's, GMAT. Additional exam requirements/recommendations for international students: Required—TOEFL (minimum score 550 paper-based; 213 computer-based). *Application deadline:* For fall admission, 6/1 priority date for domestic and international students; for spring admission, 11/1 priority date for domestic and international students. Applications are processed on a rolling basis. Application fee: $50. Electronic applications accepted. *Expenses:* Contact institution. *Financial support:* In 2006–07, 16 students received support, including 4 research assistantships with tuition reimbursements available (averaging $11,000 per year); career-related internships or fieldwork, Federal Work-Study, institutionally sponsored loans, scholarships/grants, tuition waivers (full and partial), and unspecified assistantships also available. Financial award application deadline: 3/1. *Faculty research:* Entrepreneurship, investment management, international markets, decision support systems, strategic planning. *Unit head:* Richard A. Grant, Director of Graduate Programs, 207-581-1971, Fax: 207-581-1930, E-mail: mba@maine.edu. *Application contact:* Scott G. Delcourt, Associate Dean of the Graduate School, 207-581-3219, Fax: 207-581-3232, E-mail: graduate@maine.edu.

University of Management and Technology, Program in Business Administration, Arlington, VA 22209. Offers acquisition management (DBA); general management (MBA, DBA); project management (MBA, DBA). Part-time and evening/weekend programs available. Postbaccalaureate distance learning degree programs offered (no on-campus study). *Degree requirements:* For master's, comprehensive exam. *Entrance requirements:* For master's, 3 recommendations, current resumé. Additional exam requirements/recommendations for international students: Required—TOEFL (minimum score 550 paper-based; 213 computer-based). *Application deadline:* Applications are processed on a rolling basis. Application fee: $30. Electronic applications accepted. *Unit head:* Dr. J. Davidson Frame, Academic Dean, 703-516-0035 Ext. 25.

University of Management and Technology, Program in Management, Arlington, VA 22209. Offers acquisition management (MS, AC); management (MS); project management (MS, AC); public administration (MPA, MS, AC); public management (MS); telecommunications management (MS). Part-time and evening/weekend programs available. Postbaccalaureate distance learning degree programs offered (no on-campus study). *Entrance requirements:* For master's, 3 recommendations, current resumé. Additional exam requirements/recommendations for international students: Required—TOEFL (minimum score 550 paper-based; 213 computer-based). *Application deadline:* Applications are processed on a rolling basis. Application fee: $30. Electronic applications accepted. *Unit head:* Dr. J. Davidson Frame, Academic Dean, 703-516-0035 Ext. 25.

University of Manitoba, Faculty of Graduate Studies, Faculty of Management, Winnipeg, MB R3T 2N2, Canada. Offers MBA, PhD. *Accreditation:* AACSB. *Degree requirements:* For master's, thesis or alternative.

University of Mary, Program in Business Administration, Bismarck, ND 58504-9652. Offers MBA. Part-time and evening/weekend programs available. *Faculty:* 200 full-time (64 women). *Students:* 291 full-time (140 women), 33 part-time (20 women); includes 54 minority (15 African Americans, 30 American Indian/Alaska Native, 6 Asian Americans or Pacific Islanders, 3 Hispanic Americans), 17 international. Average age 34. 177 applicants, 100% accepted, 167 enrolled. In 2006, 193 degrees awarded. *Degree requirements:* For master's, strategic planning seminar. *Entrance requirements:* For master's, minimum GPA of 2.5. *Application deadline:* Applications are processed on a rolling basis. Application fee: $40. *Financial support:* Career-related internships or fieldwork available. Support available to part-time students. Financial award applicants required to submit FAFSA. *Unit head:* Brenda Kaspari, Director of the School of Accelerated and Distance Education, 701-255-7500. *Application contact:* Wayne G. Maruska, Graduate Program Advisor, 701-355-8134, Fax: 701-255-7687, E-mail: wmaruska@umary.edu.

University of Mary, Program in Management, Bismarck, ND 58504-9652. Offers M Mgmt. Part-time and evening/weekend programs available. Postbaccalaureate distance learning degree programs offered (no on-campus study). *Faculty:* 207 part-time/adjunct (72 women). *Students:* 108 full-time (63 women), 38 part-time (23 women); includes 31 minority (2 African Americans, 24 American Indian/Alaska Native, 5 Hispanic Americans), 3 international. 99 applicants, 100% accepted, 92 enrolled. In 2006, 146 degrees awarded. *Degree requirements:* For master's, strategic planning seminar. *Entrance requirements:* For master's, minimum GPA of 2.5. *Application deadline:* Applications are processed on a rolling basis. Application fee: $40. *Financial support:* Career-related internships or fieldwork available. Support available to part-time students. Financial award application deadline: 8/1; financial award applicants required to submit FAFSA. *Unit head:* Brenda Kaspari, Director of the School of Accelerated and Distance Education, 701-255-7500. *Application contact:* Wayne G. Maruska, Graduate Program Advisor, 701-355-8134, Fax: 701-255-7687, E-mail: wmaruska@umary.edu.

University of Mary Hardin-Baylor, College of Business, Graduate Studies in Business Administration, Belton, TX 76513. Offers accounting (MBA); management (MBA); sport management (MBA). Part-time and evening/weekend programs available. *Faculty:* 10 full-time (3 women), 3 part-time/adjunct (1 woman). *Students:* 4 full-time (2 women), 19 part-time (10 women); includes 3 minority (all Hispanic Americans) Average age 24. In 2006, 9 degrees awarded. *Degree requirements:* For master's, practicum. *Entrance requirements:* For master's, GMAT, minimum GPA of 3.0, work experience, interview. *Application deadline:* For fall admission, 6/1 priority date for domestic students; for spring admission, 11/1 for domestic students. Applications are processed on a rolling basis. Application fee: $35 ($135 for international students). Electronic applications accepted. *Expenses:* Tuition: Full-time $8,910; part-time $495 per hour. Required fees: $906; $47 per hour. $30 per term. Tuition and fees vary according to course load. *Financial support:* Federal Work-Study and scholarships (for some active duty military personnel only) available. Financial award applicants required to submit FAFSA. *Unit head:* Dr. Chrisann Merriman, Director, 254-295-4647, E-mail: chrisann.merriman@umhb.edu.

University of Maryland, College Park, Graduate Studies, Interdepartmental Programs, Joint Program in Business and Management/Public Policy, College Park, MD 20742. Offers MBA/MPM. *Accreditation:* AACSB. *Students:* 3 full-time (1 woman), 1 (woman) part-time; includes 1 minority (African American) 10 applicants, 40% accepted, 2 enrolled. *Application deadline:* For fall admission, 2/1 for domestic and international students. Applications are processed on a rolling basis. Application fee: $60. Electronic applications accepted. *Financial support:* In 2006–07, 1 fellowship (averaging $990 per year) was awarded; research assistantships, teaching assistantships. Financial award applicants required to submit FAFSA. *Application contact:* Dean of Graduate School, 301-405-0358, Fax: 301-314-9305.

University of Maryland, College Park, Graduate Studies, Robert H. Smith School of Business, Combined MSW/MBA Program, College Park, MD 20742. Offers MSW/MBA. *Accreditation:* AACSB. *Students:* 2 applicants, 0% accepted. *Entrance requirements:* Additional exam requirements/recommendations for international students: Required—TOEFL. *Application deadline:* For fall admission, 2/1 for domestic and international students. Application fee: $60. *Financial support:* In 2006–07, 1 fellowship (averaging $25,961 per year) was awarded. *Application contact:* Dean of Graduate School, 301-405-0358, Fax: 301-314-9305.

University of Maryland, College Park, Graduate Studies, Robert H. Smith School of Business, Executive MBA Program, College Park, MD 20742. Offers EMBA. *Students:* 113 full-time (32 women); includes 34 minority (9 African Americans, 17 Asian Americans or Pacific Islanders, 8 Hispanic Americans), 5 international. In 2006, 42 master's awarded. *Entrance requirements:* For master's, minimum GPA of 3.0, 7-12 years professional experience. Additional exam requirements/recommendations for international students: Required—TOEFL. *Application deadline:* For fall admission, 2/1 for domestic and international students. Application fee: $60. *Financial support:* In 2006–07, 16 fellowships (averaging $14,001 per year) were awarded. *Application contact:* Dean of Graduate School, 301-405-0358, Fax: 301-314-9305.

University of Maryland, College Park, Graduate Studies, Robert H. Smith School of Business, Joint Program in Business and Management, College Park, MD 20742. Offers MBA/MS. *Students:* 14 full-time (3 women), 14 part-time (2 women); includes 4 minority (all Asian Americans or Pacific Islanders), 4 international. 29 applicants, 7% accepted, 1 enrolled. *Entrance requirements:* Additional exam requirements/recommendations for international students: Required—TOEFL. *Application deadline:* For fall admission, 2/1 for domestic and international students. Applications are processed on a rolling basis. Application fee: $60. Electronic applications accepted. *Financial support:* In 2006–07, 20 fellowships (averaging $17,006 per year), 7 teaching assistantships (averaging $13,493 per year) were awarded. *Application contact:* Dean of Graduate School, 301-405-0358, Fax: 301-314-9305.

University of Maryland, College Park, Graduate Studies, Robert H. Smith School of Business, Program in Business Administration, College Park, MD 20742. Offers MBA. *Accreditation:* AACSB. Part-time and evening/weekend programs available. Postbaccalaureate distance learning degree programs offered. *Students:* 565 full-time (171 women), 587 part-time (159 women); includes 318 minority (81 African Americans, 3 American Indian/Alaska Native, 192 Asian Americans or Pacific Islanders, 42 Hispanic Americans), 172 international. 1,277 applicants, 51% accepted, 426 enrolled. In 2006, 473 degrees awarded. *Entrance requirements:* For master's, GMAT, minimum GPA of 3.0, resumé, 3 letters of recommendation. Additional exam requirements/recommendations for international students: Required—TOEFL. *Application deadline:* For fall admission, 2/1 for domestic and international students. Applications are processed on a rolling basis. Application fee: $60. Electronic applications accepted. *Financial support:* In 2006–07, 75 fellowships (averaging $8,580 per year) were awarded. Financial award applicants required to submit FAFSA. *Faculty research:* Accounting, entrepreneurship, finance management and organization, management server and statistical information systems. *Unit head:* Dr. Vernard S. Koerwer, Associate Dean, 301-405-5266, Fax: 301-314-9862, E-mail: skoerwer@rhsmith.umd.edu. *Application contact:* Dean of Graduate School, 301-405-0358.

University of Maryland, College Park, Graduate Studies, Robert H. Smith School of Business, Program in Business and Management, College Park, MD 20742. Offers MS, PhD. *Accreditation:* AACSB. Part-time programs available. *Students:* 98 full-time (49 women), 1 part-time; includes 11 minority (3 African Americans, 8 Asian Americans or Pacific Islanders), 60 international. 554 applicants, 5% accepted, 19 enrolled. In 2006, 19 master's, 20 doctorates awarded. *Median time to degree:* Of those who began their doctoral program in fall 1998, 67% received their degree in 8 years or less. *Degree requirements:* For master's, thesis optional; for doctorate, thesis/dissertation, comprehensive exam. *Entrance requirements:* For master's, GMAT, minimum GPA of 3.0, resumé, 2 letters of recommendation; for doctorate, GMAT or GRE, minimum GPA of 3.0, resumé, 2 letters of recommendation. Additional exam requirements/recommendations for international students: Required—TOEFL. *Application deadline:* For fall admission, 2/1 for domestic and international students. Applications are processed on a rolling basis. Application fee: $60. Electronic applications accepted. *Financial support:* In 2006–07, 20 fellowships with full tuition reimbursements (averaging $17,006 per year), 98 teaching assistantships with tuition reimbursements (averaging $13,464 per year) were awarded; research assistantships with tuition reimbursements. Financial award applicants required to submit FAFSA. *Unit head:* Dr. Vernard S. Koerwer, Associate Dean, 301-405-5266, Fax: 301-314-9862, E-mail: skoerwer@rhsmith.umd.edu. *Application contact:* Director of MBA/MS Admissions, 301-405-0358.

University of Maryland, College Park, Graduate Studies, Robert H. Smith School of Business, Program in Business Management/Law, College Park, MD 20742. Offers JD/MBA. *Accreditation:* AACSB. *Students:* 5 full-time (0 women); includes 3 minority (1 African American, 1 Asian American or Pacific Islander, 1 Hispanic American). 11 applicants, 55% accepted, 4 enrolled. *Entrance requirements:* Additional exam requirements/recommendations for international students: Required—TOEFL. *Application deadline:* For fall admission, 2/1 for domestic and international students. Applications are processed on a rolling basis. Application fee: $60. *Financial support:* In 2006–07, 1 fellowship (averaging $23,814 per year), 1 teaching assistantship (averaging $13,224 per year) were awarded. Financial award applicants required to submit FAFSA. *Application contact:* Dean of Graduate School, 301-405-0358, Fax: 301-314-9305.

University of Maryland University College, Graduate School of Management and Technology, Doctoral Program in Management, Adelphi, MD 20783. Offers management (DM). Part-time programs available. *Students:* 1 full-time (0 women), 136 part-time (44 women); includes 25 minority (18 African Americans, 4 Asian Americans or Pacific Islanders, 3 Hispanic Americans), 23 international. Average age 46. 126 applicants, 87% accepted, 17 enrolled. *Degree requirements:* For doctorate, thesis/dissertation, comprehensive exam. *Application deadline:* Applications are processed on a rolling basis. Application fee: $100. Electronic applications accepted. *Financial support:* Federal Work-Study and scholarships/grants available. Support available to part-time students. Financial award application deadline: 6/1; financial award applicants required to submit FAFSA. *Unit head:* Dr. Bryan Booth, 301-985-7200, Fax: 301-985-4611, E-mail: bbooth@umuc.edu. *Application contact:* Coordinator, Graduate Admissions- DM Admissions, 301-985-6428, E-mail: gradinfo@umuc.edu.

University of Maryland University College, Graduate School of Management and Technology, Program in Business Administration, Adelphi, MD 20783. Offers Exec MBA, MBA. Part-time and evening/weekend programs available. Postbaccalaureate distance learning degree programs offered (no on-campus study). *Students:* 12 full-time (7 women), 2,021 part-time (1,097 women); includes 966 minority (712 African Americans, 8 American Indian/Alaska Native, 174 Asian Americans or Pacific Islanders, 72 Hispanic Americans), 46 international. Average age 34. 662 applicants, 100% accepted, 488 enrolled. In 2006, 467 degrees awarded. *Degree requirements:* For master's, thesis or alternative. *Application deadline:* Applications are processed on a rolling basis. Application fee: $50. Electronic applications accepted. *Expenses:* Contact institution. *Financial support:* Federal Work-Study and scholarships/grants available. Support available to part-time students. Financial award application deadline: 6/1; financial award applicants required to submit FAFSA. *Unit head:* Dr. Michael Evanchik, 301-985-7200, Fax: 301-985-7175, E-mail: mevanchik@umuc.edu. *Application contact:* Coordinator, Graduate Admissions, 301-985-7155, Fax: 301-985-7175, E-mail: gradinfo@umuc.edu.

University of Maryland University College, Graduate School of Management and Technology, Program in Management, Adelphi, MD 20783. Offers management (MS, Certificate). Offered evenings and weekends only. Part-time and evening/weekend programs available. Postbaccalaureate distance learning degree programs offered (no on-campus study). *Students:* 91 full-time (59 women), 2,337 part-time (1,575 women); includes 1,288 minority (1,041 African Americans, 10 American Indian/Alaska Native, 124 Asian Americans or Pacific Islanders, 113 Hispanic Americans), 24 international. Average age 35. 628 applicants, 100% accepted, 475 enrolled. In 2006, 452 master's, 70 other advanced degrees awarded. *Degree requirements:* For master's, thesis or alternative. *Application deadline:* Applications are processed on a rolling basis. Application fee: $50. Electronic applications accepted. *Financial support:* Federal Work-Study and scholarships/grants available. Support available to part-time students. Financial award application deadline: 6/1; financial award applicants required to submit FAFSA. *Unit head:* Dr. Theresa Marron-Grodsky, 301-985-7200, Fax: 301-985-4611, E-mail: tmarron-grodsky@umuc.edu. *Application contact:* Coordinator, Graduate Admissions, 301-985-7155, Fax: 301-985-7175, E-mail: gradinfo@umuc.edu.

University of Mary Washington, College of Graduate and Professional Studies, Fredericksburg, VA 22406-7239. Offers business administration (MBA); education (M Ed); management information systems (MSMIS). Part-time and evening/weekend programs available. *Faculty:* 25 full-time (17 women), 20 part-time/adjunct (10 women). *Students:* 121 full-time (92 women), 507 part-time (367 women); includes 95 minority (59 African Americans, 1 American Indian/Alaska Native, 10 Asian Americans or Pacific Islanders, 25 Hispanic Americans), 4 international. Average age 35. In 2006, 14 degrees awarded. *Entrance requirements:* For master's, GMAT (MBA), PRAXIS I (M Ed), minimum GPA of 3.0. Additional exam requirements/recommendations for international students: Required—TOEFL (minimum score 600 paper-based; 250 computer-based; 100 iBT). *Application deadline:* For fall admission, 6/1 priority date for domestic students, 6/1 for international students; for spring admission, 10/1 for domestic and international students. Application fee: $45. *Expenses:* Tuition, area resident: Part-time $275 per credit hour. Tuition, state resident: part-time $626 per credit. Required fees: $25 per term. One-time fee: $45 part-time. *Financial support:* In 2006–07, 46 students received support. Scholarships/grants available. Support available to part-time students. Financial award application deadline: 3/15; financial award applicants required to submit FAFSA. *Unit head:* Dr. Meta R. Braymer, Vice President for Graduate and Professional Studies and Dean of the Faculty, 540-286-8000, Fax: 540-286-8005, E-mail: mbraymer@umw.edu. *Application contact:* Matthew E. Mejia, Assistant Dean for Graduate and Professional Studies and Dean of the Faculty, 540-286-8017, Fax: 540-286-8085, E-mail: mmejia@umw.edu.

University of Massachusetts Amherst, Graduate School, Isenberg School of Management, Professional Master's of Business Administration Program, Amherst, MA 01003. Offers PMBA. *Accreditation:* AACSB. *Students:* 30 full-time (9 women), 611 part-time (181 women); includes 70 minority (9 African Americans, 2 American Indian/Alaska Native, 41 Asian Americans or Pacific Islanders, 18 Hispanic Americans), 34 international. Average age 36. 249 applicants, 90% accepted, 191 enrolled. *Entrance requirements:* For master's, GMAT, minimum GPA of 3.0. Additional exam requirements/recommendations for international students: Required—TOEFL (minimum score 530 paper-based; 197 computer-based). *Application deadline:* For fall admission, 2/1 priority date for domestic and international students; for spring admission, 7/1 for domestic and international students. Applications are processed on a rolling basis. Application fee: $40 ($65 for international students). Electronic applications accepted. *Expenses:* Tuition, state resident: full-time $2,640; part-time $110 per credit. Tuition, nonresident: full-time $9,936; part-time $414 per credit. Required fees: $8,969; $3,129 per term. One-time fee: $257 full-time. Tuition and fees vary according to class time, course load, campus/location and reciprocity agreements. *Financial support:* Fellowships with full tuition reimbursements, research assistantships with full tuition reimbursements, teaching assistantships with full tuition reimbursements, career-related internships or fieldwork, Federal Work-Study, scholarships/grants, traineeships, and unspecified assistantships available. Support available to part-time students. Financial award application deadline: 2/1. *Unit head:* Dr. Eric Berkowitz, Director, 413-545-5663, Fax: 413-545-3858, E-mail: enb@mktg.umass.edu.

University of Massachusetts Amherst, Graduate School, Isenberg School of Management, Program in Management, Amherst, MA 01003. Offers MBA, MS, PhD. *Accreditation:* AACSB. *Faculty:* 55 full-time (13 women). *Students:* 86 full-time (42 women), 23 part-time (10 women); includes 13 minority (4 African Americans, 1 American Indian/Alaska Native, 3 Asian Americans or Pacific Islanders, 5 Hispanic Americans), 43 international. Average age 31. 321 applicants, 21% accepted, 37 enrolled. In 2006, 217 master's, 12 doctorates awarded. *Degree requirements:* For doctorate, thesis/dissertation, oral and written exams. *Entrance requirements:* For master's and doctorate, GMAT, minimum GPA of 3.0. Additional exam requirements/recommendations for international students: Required—TOEFL (minimum score 530 paper-based; 197 computer-based). *Application deadline:* For fall admission, 2/1 priority date for domestic and international students; for spring admission, 7/1 for domestic and international students. Applications are processed on a rolling basis. Application fee: $40 ($65 for international students). Electronic applications accepted. *Expenses:* Tuition, state resident: full-time $2,640; part-time $110 per credit. Tuition, nonresident: full-time $9,936; part-time $414 per credit. Required fees: $8,969; $3,129 per term. One-time fee: $257 full-time. Tuition and fees vary according to class time, course load, campus/location and reciprocity agreements. *Financial support:* In 2006–07, 9 fellowships with full tuition reimbursements (averaging $7,590 per year), 102 research assistantships with full tuition reimbursements (averaging $9,825 per year), 25 teaching assistantships with full tuition reimbursements (averaging $8,787 per year) were awarded; career-related internships or fieldwork, Federal Work-Study, scholarships/grants, traineeships, and unspecified assistantships also available. Support available to part-time students. Financial award application deadline: 2/1. *Unit head:* Dr. D. Anthony Butterfield, Director, 413-545-5678, Fax: 413-545-3858, E-mail: dabutter@som.umass.edu.

University of Massachusetts Boston, Office of Graduate Studies, College of Management, Program in Business Administration, Boston, MA 02125-3393. Offers MBA, MS/MBA. *Accreditation:* AACSB. Part-time and evening/weekend programs available. *Students:* 87 full-time (43 women), 220 part-time (102 women); includes 64 minority (19 African Americans, 35 Asian Americans or Pacific Islanders, 10 Hispanic Americans). Average age 30. 297 applicants, 38% accepted, 45 enrolled. In 2006, 68 degrees awarded. *Median time to degree:* Master's–3 years full-time. *Degree requirements:* For master's, capstone project. *Entrance requirements:* For master's, GMAT, minimum GPA of 3.0. *Application deadline:* For fall admission, 3/1 priority date for domestic students; for spring admission, 11/1 for domestic students. Application fee: $25 ($40 for international students). *Expenses:* Tuition, state resident: full-time $2,590; part-time $301 per credit. Tuition, nonresident: full-time $9,758; part-time $427 per credit. One-time fee: $495 full-time. *Financial support:* In 2006–07, 13 research assistantships with full tuition reimbursements (averaging $13,000 per year), teaching assistantships with full tuition reimbursements (averaging $13,000 per year) were awarded; career-related internships or fieldwork, Federal Work-Study, and unspecified assistantships also available. Support available to part-time students. Financial award application deadline: 3/1; financial award applicants required to submit FAFSA. *Faculty research:* International finance, human resource management, management information systems, investment and corporate finance, international marketing. *Unit head:* Dr. William Koehler, Director, 617-287-7855, E-mail: william.koehler@umb.edu.

University of Massachusetts Dartmouth, Graduate School, Charlton College of Business, Program in Business Administration, North Dartmouth, MA 02747-2300. Offers accounting (Postbaccalaureate Certificate); business administration (MBA); e-commerce (PMC); finance (PMC); general management (PMC); leadership (PMC); management (Postbaccalaureate Certificate); marketing (PMC); supply chain management (PMC). *Accreditation:* AACSB. Part-time programs available. *Faculty:* 41 full-time (11 women), 22 part-time/adjunct (8 women). *Students:* 66 full-time (20 women), 111 part-time (54 women); includes 16 minority (5 African Americans, 6 Asian Americans or Pacific Islanders, 5 Hispanic Americans), 46 international. Average age 30. 167 applicants, 83% accepted, 83 enrolled. In 2006, 73 master's, 20 other advanced degrees awarded. *Entrance requirements:* For master's, GMAT, resumé, letters of recommendation. Additional exam requirements/recommendations for international students: Required—TOEFL (minimum score 500 paper-based). *Application deadline:* For fall admission, 6/1 for domestic students, 4/1 for international students; for spring admission, 10/1 for domestic students, 8/1 for international students. Application fee: $40 ($60 for international students). Electronic applications accepted. *Expenses:* Tuition, state resident: full-time $2,071; part-time $86 per credit. Tuition, nonresident: full-time $8,099; part-time $337 per credit. *Financial support:* In 2006–07, 2 research assistantships with full tuition reimbursements (averaging $11,985 per year), 6 teaching assistantships with full tuition reimbursements (averaging $7,200 per year) were awarded; Federal Work-Study and unspecified assistantships also available. Support available to part-time students. Financial award application deadline: 3/1; financial award applicants required to submit FAFSA. *Faculty research:* Organizational identity dynamics in strategic alliances and partnerships, market analysis in cranberry industry, consumer choice modeling. Total annual research expenditures: $508,000. *Unit head:* Matthew Roy, Assistant Dean, 508-999-8409, Fax: 508-999-8776, E-mail: mroy@umassd.edu. *Application contact:* Carol Novo, Graduate Admissions Officer, 508-999-8604, Fax: 508-999-8183, E-mail: graduate@umassd.edu.

University of Massachusetts Lowell, Graduate School, College of Management, Program in Business Administration, Lowell, MA 01854-2881. Offers MBA. *Accreditation:* AACSB. Part-time and evening/weekend programs available. *Entrance requirements:* For master's, GMAT.

University of Memphis, Graduate School, Fogelman College of Business and Economics, Program in Business Administration, Memphis, TN 38152. Offers accounting (MBA, PhD); economics (MBA, PhD); executive business administration (MBA); finance (PhD); finance, insurance, and real estate (MBA, MS); international business administration (MBA); management (MBA, MS, PhD); management information systems (MBA, MS, PhD); management science (MBA); marketing (MBA, MS); marketing and supply chain management (PhD); real estate development (MS); JD/MBA. *Accreditation:* AACSB. *Faculty:* 84 full-time (14 women), 3 part-time/adjunct (0 women). *Students:* 222 full-time (92 women), 163 part-time (52 women); includes 62 minority (43 African Americans, 14 Asian Americans or Pacific Islanders, 5 Hispanic Americans), 119 international. Average age 29. In 2006, 196 master's, 12 doctorates awarded. *Degree requirements:* For master's, comprehensive exam; for doctorate, thesis/dissertation, comprehensive exam. *Entrance requirements:* For master's, GMAT, resumé; for doctorate, GMAT, interview, minimum GPA of 3.4, resumé, letter of recommendation. Additional exam requirements/recommendations for international students: Required—TOEFL (minimum score 550 paper-based; 220 computer-based). *Application deadline:* For fall admission, 8/1 for domestic students; for spring admission, 12/1 for domestic students. Application fee: $25 ($50 for international students). *Financial support:* Research assistantships with full tuition reimbursements, teaching assistantships, career-related internships or fieldwork, scholarships/grants, and unspecified assistantships available. Financial award application deadline: 3/1. *Faculty research:* Competitive business strategy, finance microstructures, supply chain management innovations, health care economics, litigation risks and corporate audits. Total annual research expenditures: $2.7 million. *Application contact:* Dr. Carol V. Danehower, Associate Dean for Programs, 901-678-5402, Fax: 901-678-3579, E-mail: fcbegp@memphis.edu.

University of Miami, Graduate School, School of Business Administration, Department of Management Science, Coral Gables, FL 33124. Offers management science (MS), including applied statistics, operations research, quality management. Part-time and evening/weekend programs available. Postbaccalaureate distance learning degree programs offered. *Faculty:* 9 full-time (1 woman). *Students:* 3 full-time (1 woman), 3 part-time (1 woman); includes 2 minority (both Asian Americans or Pacific Islanders), 1 international. Average age 36. 7 applicants, 71% accepted, 3 enrolled. In 2006, 1 degree awarded. *Degree requirements:* For master's, thesis optional. *Entrance requirements:* For master's, GRE General Test. Additional exam requirements/recommendations for international students: Required—TOEFL. *Application deadline:* For fall admission, 6/30 priority date for domestic students; for spring admission, 10/31 for domestic students. Applications are processed on a rolling basis. Application fee: $50. *Financial support:* Career-related internships or fieldwork and Federal Work-Study available. Financial award application deadline: 3/1. *Faculty research:* Mathematical programming, applied probability, logistics, statistical process control. Total annual research expenditures: $20,000. *Unit head:* Dr. Anuj Mehrotra, Chairman, 305-284-6595, Fax: 305-284-2321, E-mail: anuj@miami.edu. *Application contact:* Dr. Howard Gitlow, Director, 305-284-4296, Fax: 305-284-2321, E-mail: hgitlow@miami.edu.

University of Miami, Graduate School, School of Business Administration, Program in Business Administration, Coral Gables, FL 33124. Offers accounting (MBA); computer information systems (MBA); executive and professional (MBA), including international business, management; finance (MBA); international business (MBA); management (MBA); management science (MBA); marketing (MBA); professional management (MSPM); JD/MBA; MBA/MSIE. *Accreditation:* AACSB. Evening/weekend programs available. *Faculty:* 105 full-time (25 women). *Students:* 734 full-time (269 women), 19 part-time (4 women); includes 194 minority (24 African Americans, 1 American Indian/Alaska Native, 23 Asian Americans or Pacific Islanders, 146 Hispanic Americans), 115 international. Average age 31. 453 applicants, 71% accepted, 152 enrolled. In 2006, 394 degrees awarded. *Degree requirements:* For master's, comprehensive exam, registration. *Entrance requirements:* For master's, GMAT. Additional exam requirements/recommendations for international students: Required—TOEFL (minimum score 550 paper-based; 213 computer-based; 59 iBT). *Application deadline:* For fall admission, 7/30 priority date for domestic students, 6/30 priority date for international students; for spring admission, 12/31 priority date for domestic students, 10/31 priority date for international students. Applications are processed on a rolling basis. Application fee: $50. Electronic applications accepted. *Financial support:* In 2006–07, 418 students received support, including 19 fellowships with partial tuition reimbursements available; unspecified assistantships also available. Financial award application deadline: 3/1; financial award applicants required to submit FAFSA. *Faculty research:* Leadership, e-commerce, supply chain management. *Unit head:* Daniela Mu±iz, Associate Director, Graduate Business Programs, 305-284-4626, Fax: 305-284-1878, E-mail: dmuniz@miami.edu. *Application contact:* David S. Green, Director of Graduate Business Recruiting and Admissions, 305-284-4607, Fax: 305-284-1878, E-mail: mba@miami.edu.

Announcement: The University of Miami School of Business Administration is located in Coral Gables, Florida. The School offers an MBA program with various concentrations, including management, computer information systems, accounting, international business, finance, and marketing; a JD/MBA program; and various MS degrees. Tuition is $1350 per credit hour. Contact 305-284-4607, fax: 305-284-1878, e-mail: mba@miami.edu, Web site: http://www.bus.miami.edu/grad.

University of Michigan, Ross School of Business at the University of Michigan, Doctoral Program in Business Administration, Ann Arbor, MI 48109. Offers PhD. Offered through the Horace H. Rackham School of Graduate Studies. *Accreditation:* AACSB. *Degree requirements:* For doctorate, oral defense of dissertation, preliminary exam. *Entrance requirements:* For doctorate, GMAT or GRE. Additional exam requirements/recommendations for international students: Required—TOEFL (minimum score 600 paper-based; 250 computer-based), IELTS, TOEFL or IELTS. Electronic applications accepted. *Faculty research:* Finance, accounting, marketing, operations and management science, corporate strategy.

University of Michigan–Dearborn, School of Management, Dearborn, MI 48128-1491. Offers accounting (MS); finance (MS); management (MBA); MBA/MHSA; MBA/MSE; MBA/MSF. *Accreditation:* AACSB. Part-time and evening/weekend programs available. Postbaccalaureate distance learning degree programs offered (no on-campus study). *Degree requirements:* For master's, registration. *Entrance requirements:* For master's, GMAT, 2 years of work experience (MBA); course work in computer applications, statistics, and pre-calculus or finite mathematics. Additional exam requirements/recommendations for international students: Required—TOEFL (minimum score 560 paper-based; 220 computer-based). Expenses: Contact institution. *Faculty research:* Cultural diversity, buyer-supplier relations, error detection in data, economic evolution.

University of Michigan–Flint, School of Management, Flint, MI 48502-1950. Offers MBA. *Accreditation:* AACSB. Part-time programs available. Postbaccalaureate distance learning degree programs offered (minimal on-campus study). *Faculty:* 12 full-time (2 women), 2 part-time/adjunct (0 women). *Students:* 12 full-time (6 women), 174 part-time (64 women); includes 21 minority (12 African Americans, 1 American Indian/Alaska Native, 7 Asian Americans or Pacific Islanders, 1 Hispanic American), 15 international. Average age 32. 92 applicants, 77% accepted, 62 enrolled. In 2006, 77 degrees awarded. *Degree requirements:* For master's, thesis or alternative. *Entrance requirements:* For master's, GMAT, 2 years of work experience, minimum GPA of 3.0, 1 year college course work in mathematics. Additional exam requirements/recommendations for international students: Required—TOEFL (minimum score 560 paper-based; 220 computer-based), IELTS (minimum score 7). *Application deadline:* For fall admission, 8/1 priority date for domestic and international students; for winter admission, 12/1 priority date for domestic and international students; for spring admission, 2/15 priority date for domestic and international students. Applications are processed on a rolling basis. Application fee: $55. Electronic applications accepted. *Expenses:* Tuition, state resident: full-time $6,790; part-time $377 per credit. Tuition, nonresident: full-time $10,186; part-time $566 per credit. Required

Business Administration and Management—General

University of Michigan–Flint (continued)
fees: $258 per term. Full-time tuition and fees vary according to degree level and program. Part-time tuition and fees vary according to course load and degree level. *Financial support:* Federal Work-Study and scholarships/grants available. Support available to part-time students. Financial award applicants required to submit FAFSA. *Faculty research:* Business performance evaluations, consumer satisfaction, M&A success. *Unit head:* Dr. Douglas Moon, Dean, 810-762-3160, Fax: 810-762-3287. *Application contact:* D. Nicol Taylor, MBA Program Coordinator, 810-237-6591, Fax: 810-237-6685, E-mail: dntaylor@umflint.edu.

University of Minnesota, Duluth, Graduate School, Labovitz School of Business and Economics, Program in Business Administration, Duluth, MN 55812-2496. Offers MBA. *Accreditation:* AACSB. Part-time and evening/weekend programs available. *Faculty:* 36 full-time (7 women). *Students:* Average age 34. 19 applicants, 89% accepted, 16 enrolled. In 2006, 24 degrees awarded. *Degree requirements:* For master's, registration. *Entrance requirements:* For master's, GMAT, minimum GPA of 3.0; course work in accounting, business administration, and economics. Additional exam requirements/recommendations for international students: Required—TOEFL (minimum score 550 paper-based; 213 computer-based). *Application deadline:* For fall admission, 7/15 for domestic and international students; for spring admission, 11/1 for domestic and international students. Applications are processed on a rolling basis. Application fee: $55 ($75 for international students). *Expenses: Contact institution. Financial support:* In 2006–07, 6 students received support, including 6 research assistantships with full and partial tuition reimbursements available (averaging $12,000 per year); institutionally sponsored loans also available. Financial award application deadline: 5/1; financial award applicants required to submit FAFSA. *Faculty research:* Regional economic analysis, marketing, management, human resources, organizational behavior. *Unit head:* Dr. Rajiv Vaidyanathan, Director of Graduate Studies, 218-726-6817, Fax: 218-726-7578, E-mail: rvaidyan@d.umn.edu. *Application contact:* Candy Furo, Associate Administrator, 218-726-8986, Fax: 218-726-6789, E-mail: cfuro@d.umn.edu.

University of Minnesota, Twin Cities Campus, Carlson School of Management, Minneapolis, MN 55455-0213. Offers EMBA, M Acc, MA, MBA, MBT, MS, MSMOT, PhD, JD/MBA, MD/MBA, MHA/MBA. *Accreditation:* AACSB. Part-time and evening/weekend programs available. *Faculty:* 126 full-time (28 women), 120 part-time/adjunct. *Students:* 2,517 (767 women). Average age 29. In 2006, 581 master's, 20 doctorates awarded. Terminal master's awarded for partial completion of doctoral program. *Degree requirements:* For doctorate, thesis/dissertation. Electronic applications accepted. *Expenses: Contact institution.* Full-time tuition and fees vary according to class time, course load, program, reciprocity agreements and student level. *Financial support:* In 2006–07, 247 fellowships with full and partial tuition reimbursements, 85 research assistantships with full tuition reimbursements, 84 teaching assistantships with full and partial tuition reimbursements were awarded; career-related internships or fieldwork, Federal Work-Study, institutionally sponsored loans, scholarships/grants, health care benefits, tuition waivers (full and partial), and unspecified assistantships also available. Support available to part-time students. Financial award application deadline: 4/1; financial award applicants required to submit FAFSA. *Faculty research:* Management information systems, operations management, decision sciences, marketing. Total annual research expenditures: $3.7 million. *Unit head:* Dr. Allison Davis-Blake, Dean, 612-624-7876, Fax: 612-624-6374, E-mail: adavis-blake@csom.umn.edu.

Announcement: Admission is based on potential for research and teaching and commitment to a career based on the PhD degree. Students in the doctoral program represent a wide range of undergraduate and graduate disciplines. A combination of fellowships and teaching and research assistantships provide a minimum of 5 years of funding to all matriculants. Applications should be submitted by December 31.

University of Mississippi, Graduate School, School of Business Administration, Oxford, University, MS 38677. Offers business administration (MBA, PhD); systems management (MS); JD/MBA. *Accreditation:* AACSB. *Faculty:* 44 full-time (13 women), 18 part-time/adjunct (5 women). *Students:* 62 full-time (19 women), 26 part-time (7 women); includes 2 Asian Americans or Pacific Islanders, 17 international. 203 applicants, 39% accepted, 55 enrolled. In 2006, 36 master's, 11 doctorates awarded. *Degree requirements:* For doctorate, thesis/dissertation. *Entrance requirements:* For master's, GMAT, minimum GPA of 3.0; for doctorate, GMAT. Additional exam requirements/recommendations for international students: Required—TOEFL. *Application deadline:* For fall admission, 2/1 for domestic students; for spring admission, 10/1 for domestic students. Applications are processed on a rolling basis. Application fee: $25. Electronic applications accepted. *Expenses:* Tuition, state resident: full-time $4,602; part-time $256 per credit hour. Tuition, nonresident: full-time $10,566; part-time $587 per credit hour. *Financial support:* Fellowships, career-related internships or fieldwork, scholarships/grants, tuition waivers (full), and unspecified assistantships available. Financial award application deadline: 3/1; financial award applicants required to submit FAFSA. *Unit head:* Dr. Brian Reithel, Dean, 662-915-5820, Fax: 662-915-5821, E-mail: breithel@bus.olemiss.edu.

University of Missouri–Columbia, Graduate School, College of Business, School of Business, Columbia, MO 65211. Offers MBA, PhD. *Accreditation:* AACSB. *Faculty:* 45 full-time (9 women). *Students:* 195 full-time (80 women), 9 part-time (3 women); includes 7 minority (5 Asian Americans or Pacific Islanders, 2 Hispanic Americans), 76 international. In 2006, 88 master's, 12 doctorates awarded. *Degree requirements:* For doctorate, thesis/dissertation. *Entrance requirements:* For master's and doctorate, GMAT, minimum GPA of 3.0. *Application deadline:* For fall admission, 2/1 priority date for domestic students. Applications are processed on a rolling basis. Application fee: $45 ($60 for international students). *Financial support:* Research assistantships, teaching assistantships, institutionally sponsored loans available. *Unit head:* Dr. Allen C. Bluedorn, Director of Graduate Studies, 573-882-3089, E-mail: bluedorna@missouri.edu.

See Close-Up on page 351.

University of Missouri–Kansas City, Henry W. Bloch School of Business and Public Administration, Kansas City, MO 64110-2499. Offers accounting (MS); business administration (MBA); public affairs (MPA, PhD); JD/MBA; LL M/MPA. *Accreditation:* AACSB; NASPAA. Part-time and evening/weekend programs available. *Faculty:* 42 full-time (11 women), 16 part-time/adjunct (7 women). *Students:* 201 full-time (104 women), 395 part-time (177 women); includes 80 minority (41 African Americans, 5 American Indian/Alaska Native, 21 Asian Americans or Pacific Islanders, 13 Hispanic Americans), 41 international. Average age 30. 464 applicants, 63% accepted, 226 enrolled. In 2006, 186 degrees awarded. Terminal master's awarded for partial completion of doctoral program. *Entrance requirements:* For master's, GMAT, GRE, 2 writing essays, 2 references and support of employer; for doctorate, GRE, minimum GPA of 3.0. Additional exam requirements/recommendations for international students: Required—TOEFL. *Application deadline:* For fall admission, 5/1 priority date for domestic students, 4/1 priority date for international students; for winter admission, 10/1 priority date for domestic students, 9/1 priority date for international students. Applications are processed on a rolling basis. Application fee: $35 ($50 for international students). Electronic applications accepted. *Expenses:* Tuition, state resident: full-time $4,975; part-time $276 per credit. Tuition, nonresident: full-time $12,847; part-time $713 per credit. Required fees: $595; $595 per year. *Financial support:* In 2006–07, 407 students received support, including 26 research assistantships with partial tuition reimbursements available (averaging $10,483 per year), 3 teaching assistantships with partial tuition reimbursements available (averaging $11,080 per year); fellowships, career-related internships or fieldwork, Federal Work-Study, institutionally sponsored loans, scholarships/grants, tuition waivers (full and partial), and unspecified assistantships also available. Support available to part-time students. Financial award application deadline: 3/1; financial award applicants required to submit FAFSA. *Faculty research:* Entrepreneurship, finance, non-profit, risk management. Total annual research expenditures: $803,340. *Unit head:* Dr. O. Homer Erekson, Dean, 816-235-2204, Fax: 816-235-2206, E-mail: ereksonh@umkc.edu. *Application contact:* 816-235-1111, E-mail: admit@umkc.edu.

University of Missouri–St. Louis, College of Business Administration, Program in Business Administration, St. Louis, MO 63121. Offers accounting (MBA); business administration (Certificate); finance (MBA); human resource management (Certificate); logistics and supply chain management (MBA, Certificate); management (MBA); marketing (MBA); marketing management (Certificate); operations (MBA); quantitative management science (MBA); telecommunications management (Certificate). *Accreditation:* AACSB. Part-time and evening/weekend programs available. *Faculty:* 26 full-time (6 women), 2 part-time/adjunct (0 women). *Students:* 242 full-time (156 women), 186 part-time (123 women); includes 48 minority (17 African Americans, 1 American Indian/Alaska Native, 27 Asian Americans or Pacific Islanders, 3 Hispanic Americans), 96 international. Average age 33. In 2006, 138 degrees awarded. *Entrance requirements:* For master's, GMAT, 2 letters of recommendation. Additional exam requirements/recommendations for international students: Required—TOEFL (minimum score 550 paper-based; 213 computer-based). *Application deadline:* For fall admission, 7/1 for domestic students; for spring admission, 11/1 for domestic students. Applications are processed on a rolling basis. Application fee: $35 ($40 for international students). Electronic applications accepted. *Expenses:* Tuition, state resident: part-time $332 per credit hour. Tuition, nonresident: part-time $770 per credit hour. *Financial support:* Research assistantships with full and partial tuition reimbursements, teaching assistantships with full and partial tuition reimbursements, career-related internships or fieldwork, Federal Work-Study, and institutionally sponsored loans available. Support available to part-time students. Financial award application deadline: 4/1; financial award applicants required to submit FAFSA. *Faculty research:* Human resources, strategic management, marketing strategy, consumer behavior product development, advertising. *Application contact:* 314-516-5458, Fax: 314-516-6996, E-mail: gradadm@umsl.edu.

University of Missouri–St. Louis, Graduate School, Program in Public Policy Administration, St. Louis, MO 63121. Offers health policy (MPPA); local government management (MPPA); managing human resources and organization (MPPA); nonprofit organization management (MPPA); nonprofit organization management and leadership (Certificate); policy research and analysis (MPPA); public sector human resources management (MPPA). *Accreditation:* NASPAA. Part-time and evening/weekend programs available. *Faculty:* 8 full-time (5 women), 5 part-time/adjunct (1 woman). *Students:* 21 full-time (13 women), 61 part-time (35 women); includes 22 minority (18 African Americans, 1 American Indian/Alaska Native, 2 Asian Americans or Pacific Islanders, 1 Hispanic American), 4 international. Average age 34. In 2006, 22 degrees awarded. *Entrance requirements:* For master's, 3 letters of recommendation. Additional exam requirements/recommendations for international students: Required—TOEFL (minimum score 550 paper-based; 213 computer-based). *Application deadline:* For fall admission, 7/15 priority date for domestic students; for spring admission, 12/15 priority date for domestic students. Applications are processed on a rolling basis. Application fee: $35 ($40 for international students). Electronic applications accepted. *Expenses:* Tuition, state resident: part-time $332 per credit hour. Tuition, nonresident: part-time $770 per credit hour. *Financial support:* In 2006–07, 2 research assistantships with full tuition reimbursements (averaging $14,100 per year) were awarded; teaching assistantships with partial tuition reimbursements, career-related internships or fieldwork also available. *Faculty research:* Urban policy, public finance, evaluation. *Unit head:* Brady Baybeck, Director, 314-516-5145, Fax: 314-516-5210, E-mail: baybeck@umsl.edu. *Application contact:* 314-516-5458, Fax: 314-516-6996, E-mail: gradadm@umsl.edu.

University of Mobile, Graduate Programs, Program in Business Administration, Mobile, AL 36613. Offers MBA. *Accreditation:* ACBSP. Part-time and evening/weekend programs available. *Faculty:* 9 full-time (5 women), 3 part-time/adjunct (0 women). *Students:* 3 full-time, 31 part-time; includes 20 minority (all African Americans), 1 international. Average age 32. In 2006, 14 degrees awarded. *Degree requirements:* For master's, comprehensive exam. *Entrance requirements:* For master's, GMAT. Additional exam requirements/recommendations for international students: Required—TOEFL. *Application deadline:* For fall admission, 8/3 priority date for domestic students; for spring admission, 12/23 for domestic students. Applications are processed on a rolling basis. Application fee: $40 ($50 for international students). *Expenses:* Tuition: Part-time $340 per hour. Required fees: $121 per term. Tuition and fees vary according to course load. *Financial support:* Research assistantships, Federal Work-Study available. Support available to part-time students. Financial award application deadline: 8/1. *Faculty research:* Management, personnel management, small business, diversity. *Unit head:* Dr. Anne B. Lowery, Dean, School of Business, 251-442-2219, Fax: 251-442-2523, E-mail: alowery@mail.umobile.edu. *Application contact:* Dr. Kaye F. Brown, Associate Vice President for Academic Affairs, 251-442-2289, Fax: 251-442-2523, E-mail: kayeb@mail.umobile.edu.

The University of Montana, Graduate School, School of Business Administration, MBA Professional Program, Missoula, MT 59812-0002. Offers MBA, JD/MBA, MBA/Pharm D. *Accreditation:* AACSB. Part-time and evening/weekend programs available. Postbaccalaureate distance learning degree programs offered (minimal on-campus study). *Degree requirements:* For master's, thesis optional. *Entrance requirements:* For master's, GMAT. Additional exam requirements/recommendations for international students: Required—TOEFL. *Faculty research:* Information systems, research methods, international business, human resource management, marketing.

University of Nebraska at Kearney, College of Graduate Study, College of Business and Technology, Department of Business, Kearney, NE 68849-0001. Offers business administration (MBA). *Accreditation:* AACSB. Part-time and evening/weekend programs available. *Faculty:* 19 full-time (9 women). *Students:* 17 full-time (10 women), 21 part-time (9 women), 5 international. 12 applicants, 75% accepted. In 2006, 13 degrees awarded. *Degree requirements:* For master's, thesis optional. *Entrance requirements:* For master's, GMAT. Additional exam requirements/recommendations for international students: Required—TOEFL (minimum score 550 paper-based; 213 computer-based). *Application deadline:* For fall admission, 5/1 for domestic and international students; for spring admission, 8/15 for domestic students, 8/1 for international students. Application fee: $45. Electronic applications accepted. *Expenses:* Tuition, state resident: part-time $161 per hour. Tuition, nonresident: part-time $332 per hour. Required fees: $57 per hour. *Financial support:* In 2006–07, 9 research assistantships with full tuition reimbursements (averaging $8,200 per year) were awarded; career-related internships or fieldwork, scholarships/grants, and unspecified assistantships also available. Support available to part-time students. Financial award application deadline: 3/1; financial award applicants required to submit FAFSA. *Faculty research:* Small business financial management, employment law, expert systems, international trade and marketing, environmental economics. *Unit head:* Dr. Dave Palmer, Director, 308-865-8346, Fax: 308-865-8114. *Application contact:* Lori Skarka, Information Contact, 308-865-8346, Fax: 308-865-8114, E-mail: skarkala@unk.edu.

University of Nebraska at Omaha, Graduate Studies and Research, College of Business Administration, Program in Business Administration, Omaha, NE 68182. Offers EMBA, MBA. *Accreditation:* AACSB. Part-time and evening/weekend programs available. *Faculty:* 25 full-time (7 women). *Students:* 57 full-time (18 women), 210 part-time (78 women); includes 14 minority (3 African Americans, 8 Asian Americans or Pacific Islanders, 3 Hispanic Americans), 16 international. Average age 33. 153 applicants, 48% accepted, 52 enrolled. In 2006, 86 degrees awarded. *Degree requirements:* For master's, thesis (for some programs), capstone course. *Entrance requirements:* For master's, GMAT, minimum AACSB index of 1040, minimum GPA of 3.0, resumé. Additional exam requirements/recommendations for international students: Required—TOEFL (minimum score 550 paper-based; 213 computer-based; 80 iBT). *Application deadline:* For fall admission, 7/1 for domestic students; for spring admission, 11/15 for domestic students. Applications are processed on a rolling basis. Application fee: $45. Electronic applications accepted. *Financial support:* In 2006–07, 83 students received support; research assistantships with tuition reimbursements available, Federal Work-Study, institutionally sponsored loans, scholarships/grants, tuition waivers (partial), and unspecified assistantships available. Support available to part-time students. Financial award application deadline: 3/1; financial award applicants required to submit FAFSA. *Unit head:* Dr. Lynn Harland, Associate Dean, 402-554-2303. *Application contact:* Lex Kaczmarek, Director, 402-554-2303.

University of Nebraska–Lincoln, Graduate College, College of Business Administration, Interdepartmental Area of Business, Lincoln, NE 68588. Offers accountancy (PhD); business (MBA); finance (MA, PhD), including business; management (MA, PhD), including business; marketing (MA, PhD), including business; JD/MA; JD/MBA; M Arch/MBA. *Accreditation:* AACSB. Part-time programs available. Postbaccalaureate distance learning degree programs offered. *Degree requirements:* For doctorate, thesis/dissertation, comprehensive exam. *Entrance requirements:* For master's and doctorate, GMAT. Additional exam requirements/recommendations for international students: Required—TOEFL (minimum score 550 paper-based; 213 computer-based). Electronic applications accepted.

University of Nevada, Las Vegas, Graduate College, College of Business, Program in Business Administration, Las Vegas, NV 89154-9900. Offers MBA. *Accreditation:* AACSB. Part-time and evening/weekend programs available. *Faculty:* 47 full-time (6 women). *Students:* 156 full-time (56 women), 86 part-time (37 women); includes 40 minority (8 African Americans, 1 American Indian/Alaska Native, 19 Asian Americans or Pacific Islanders, 12 Hispanic Americans), 25 international. 248 applicants, 38% accepted, 79 enrolled. In 2006, 81 degrees awarded. *Entrance requirements:* For master's, GMAT, minimum GPA of 3.0. Additional exam requirements/recommendations for international students: Required—TOEFL (minimum score 550 paper-based; 213 computer-based; 80 iBT). *Application deadline:* For fall admission, 6/1 for domestic students, 5/1 for international students; for spring admission, 11/15 for domestic students, 10/1 for international students. Application fee: $60 ($75 for international students). Electronic applications accepted. *Financial support:* In 2006–07, 18 research assistantships with partial tuition reimbursements (averaging $10,000 per year) were awarded; career-related internships or fieldwork, Federal Work-Study, institutionally sponsored loans, scholarships/grants, health care benefits, and unspecified assistantships also available. Support available to part-time students. Financial award application deadline: 3/1. *Unit head:* Prof. Robert Chatfield, Director, 702-895-3655. *Application contact:* Graduate College Admissions Evaluator, 702-895-3320, Fax: 702-895-4180, E-mail: gradcollege@unlv.edu.

University of Nevada, Reno, Graduate School, College of Business Administration, Department of Business Administration, Reno, NV 89557. Offers MBA. *Accreditation:* AACSB. Part-time and evening/weekend programs available. *Faculty:* 20. *Students:* 61 full-time (28 women), 158 part-time (65 women); includes 32 minority (1 American Indian/Alaska Native, 23 Asian Americans or Pacific Islanders, 8 Hispanic Americans), 8 international. Average age 32. 72 applicants, 86% accepted, 46 enrolled. In 2006, 45 degrees awarded. *Degree requirements:* For master's, thesis optional. *Entrance requirements:* For master's, GMAT, minimum GPA of 2.75. Additional exam requirements/recommendations for international students: Required—TOEFL. *Application deadline:* For fall admission, 2/1 priority date for domestic students; for spring admission, 11/1 for domestic students. Applications are processed on a rolling basis. Application fee: $60 ($95 for international students). *Financial support:* Research assistantships, teaching assistantships, Federal Work-Study and institutionally sponsored loans available. Financial award application deadline: 3/1. *Unit head:* Dr. Kambiz Raffiee, Graduate Program Director, 775-682-9142.

University of New Brunswick Fredericton, School of Graduate Studies, Faculty of Business Administration, Fredericton, NB E3B 5A3, Canada. Offers MBA, MBA/LL B. Part-time programs available. *Faculty:* 34 full-time (9 women). *Students:* 57 full-time (30 women), 46 part-time (21 women). In 2006, 29 degrees awarded. *Entrance requirements:* For master's, GMAT, resumé. Additional exam requirements/recommendations for international students: Required—TOEFL, TWE. *Application deadline:* For fall admission, 3/1 priority date for domestic students. Applications are processed on a rolling basis. Application fee: $50 Canadian dollars. *Financial support:* In 2006–07, 19 teaching assistantships were awarded. *Unit head:* Daniel Coleman, Dean, 506-543-4869, Fax: 506-453-3561, E-mail: dan@unb.ca. *Application contact:* Karen Hansen, Graduate Secretary, 506-453-4766, Fax: 506-453-3561, E-mail: karen@unb.ca.

University of New Brunswick Saint John, Faculty of Business, Saint John, NB E2L 4L5, Canada. Offers administration (MBA); electronic commerce (MBA); international business (MBA); natural resource management (MBA). Part-time programs available. *Degree requirements:* For master's, thesis optional. *Entrance requirements:* For master's, GMAT. Additional exam requirements/recommendations for international students: Required—TOEFL (minimum score 550 paper-based). Expenses: Contact institution.

University of New Hampshire, Graduate School, Whittemore School of Business and Economics, Department of Business Administration, Durham, NH 03824. Offers business administration (MBA); executive business administration (MBA); health management (MBA); management of technology (MS). *Accreditation:* AACSB. Part-time and evening/weekend programs available. *Faculty:* 30 full-time. *Students:* 166 full-time (53 women), 125 part-time (38 women); includes 20 minority (4 African Americans, 15 Asian Americans or Pacific Islanders, 1 Hispanic American), 24 international. Average age 33. 171 applicants, 85% accepted, 115 enrolled. In 2006, 92 degrees awarded. *Entrance requirements:* For master's, GMAT. Additional exam requirements/recommendations for international students: Required—TOEFL (minimum score 550 paper-based; 213 computer-based). *Application deadline:* For fall admission, 7/1 priority date for domestic students, 4/1 for international students. Applications are processed on a rolling basis. Application fee: $60. *Expenses: Contact institution.* Tuition and fees vary according to course load, program and reciprocity agreements. *Financial support:* In 2006–07, 7 fellowships, 2 research assistantships were awarded; teaching assistantships, career-related internships or fieldwork, Federal Work-Study, scholarships/grants, and tuition waivers (full and partial) also available. Financial award application deadline: 2/15. *Unit head:* George Abraham, Chairperson, 603-862-1367. *Application contact:* Jason Brodeur, Administrative Assistant, 603-862-3326, E-mail: wsbe.grad@unh.edu.

University of New Hampshire at Manchester, Center for Graduate and Professional Studies, Manchester, NH 03101-1113. Offers business administration (MBA); counseling (M Ed); education (M Ed, MAT); educational administration and supervision (M Ed, CAGS); industrial statistics (Certificate); public administration (MPA); public health (MPH, Certificate); social work (MSW).

University of New Haven, Graduate School, School of Business, Executive Program in Business Administration, West Haven, CT 06516-1916. Offers EMBA. Expenses: Contact institution.

University of New Haven, Graduate School, School of Business, Program in Business Administration, West Haven, CT 06516-1916. Offers accounting (MBA); business policy and strategy (MBA); finance (MBA); health care management (MBA); human resources management (MBA); international business (MBA); marketing (MBA); public relations (MBA); sports management (MBA); technology management (MBA); MBA/MPA; MBA/MSIE. Part-time and evening/weekend programs available. *Degree requirements:* For master's, thesis or alternative. *Entrance requirements:* For master's, GMAT.

University of New Mexico, Robert O. Anderson Graduate School of Management, Albuquerque, NM 87131-2039. Offers accounting (M Acc, MBA), including accounting, tax accounting (MBA); financial, international and technology management (MBA), including financial management, international management, international management in Latin America, management of technology; marketing, information and decision sciences (MBA), including management information systems, marketing management, operations management; organizational studies (MBA), including human resources management, policy and planning; JD/MBA; MBA/MA; MBA/MEME. *Accreditation:* AACSB. Part-time and evening/weekend programs available. *Entrance requirements:* For master's, GMAT. Additional exam requirements/recommendations for international students: Required—TOEFL (minimum score 550 paper-based; 213 computer-based). *Faculty research:* Organizational and social aspects of accounting, entrepreneurial learning, information requirements analysis, product disposition and replacement.

University of New Orleans, Graduate School, College of Business Administration, Program in Business Administration, New Orleans, LA 70148. Offers MBA. *Accreditation:* AACSB. *Students:* 429 (225 women). Average age 31. In 2006, 283 degrees awarded. *Degree requirements:* For master's, thesis optional. *Entrance requirements:* For master's, GMAT. Additional exam requirements/recommendations for international students: Required—TOEFL (minimum score 550 paper-based; 213 computer-based). *Application deadline:* For fall admission, 7/1 priority date for domestic students, 6/1 for international students; for spring admission, 11/15 priority date for domestic students, 10/1 for international students. Applications are processed on a rolling basis. Application fee: $40. Electronic applications accepted. *Financial support:* Fellowships, research assistantships, teaching assistantships, Federal Work-Study available. Financial award application deadline: 3/15; financial award applicants required to submit FAFSA. *Unit head:* Dr. Paul Hensel, Associate Dean, 504-280-6954, Fax: 504-280-6693, E-mail: phensel@uno.edu. *Application contact:* Barbara Moran, Assistant to Associate Dean, 504-280-6279, Fax: 504-280-6693, E-mail: mba@uno.edu.

University of North Alabama, College of Business, Florence, AL 35632-0001. Offers MBA. *Accreditation:* ACBSP. Part-time and evening/weekend programs available. *Faculty:* 1 full-time (0 women), 18 part-time/adjunct (3 women). *Students:* 214 full-time (87 women), 410 part-time (195 women); includes 183 minority (49 African Americans, 5 American Indian/Alaska Native, 125 Asian Americans or Pacific Islanders, 4 Hispanic Americans), 92 international. Average age 31. In 2006, 190 degrees awarded. *Entrance requirements:* For master's, GMAT, minimum GPA of 2.75 in last 60 hours, 2.5 overall on a 3.0 scale; 27 hours of course work in business and economics. *Application deadline:* For fall admission, 7/1 priority date for domestic students; for spring admission, 12/1 for domestic students. Applications are processed on a rolling basis. Application fee: $25. Electronic applications accepted. *Expenses:* Tuition, state resident: full-time $4,080. Tuition, nonresident: full-time $8,160. Required fees: $764. *Financial support:* Federal Work-Study available. Support available to part-time students. Financial award application deadline: 4/1. *Unit head:* Dr. Kerry Gatlin, Dean, 256-765-4261, Fax: 256-765-4170, E-mail: kpgatlin@una.edu. *Application contact:* Dr. Sue Wilson, Dean of Enrollment Management, 256-765-4316, Fax: 256-765-4349, E-mail: sjwilson@una.edu.

The University of North Carolina at Chapel Hill, Kenan-Flagler Business School, Doctoral Program in Business Administration, Chapel Hill, NC 27599. Offers accounting (PhD); finance (PhD); marketing (PhD); operations management (PhD); organizational behavior (PhD); strategy (PhD). *Accreditation:* AACSB. *Degree requirements:* For doctorate, thesis/dissertation. *Entrance requirements:* For doctorate, GMAT or GRE General Test. Electronic applications accepted. Expenses: Contact institution.

The University of North Carolina at Chapel Hill, Kenan-Flagler Business School, Executive MBA Programs, Chapel Hill, NC 27599. Offers MBA. *Accreditation:* AACSB. Evening/weekend programs available. Postbaccalaureate distance learning degree programs offered (minimal on-campus study). *Degree requirements:* For master's, exams, project. *Entrance requirements:* For master's, GMAT, 5 years of full-time work experience, interview. Electronic applications accepted. Expenses: Contact institution.

The University of North Carolina at Chapel Hill, Kenan-Flagler Business School, MBA Program, Chapel Hill, NC 27599. Offers MBA, MBA/JD, MBA/MHA, MBA/MRP, MBA/MSIS. *Accreditation:* AACSB. *Degree requirements:* For master's, exams, practicum. *Entrance requirements:* For master's, GMAT, interview, minimum 2 years of work experience. Additional exam requirements/recommendations for international students: Required—TOEFL. Electronic applications accepted.

The University of North Carolina at Charlotte, Graduate School, Belk College of Business Administration, Program in Business Administration, Charlotte, NC 28223-0001. Offers MBA, PhD. *Accreditation:* AACSB. Part-time and evening/weekend programs available. *Faculty:* 37 full-time (11 women), 3 part-time/adjunct (0 women). *Students:* 80 full-time (35 women), 269 part-time (67 women); includes 34 minority (16 African Americans, 2 American Indian/Alaska Native, 14 Asian Americans or Pacific Islanders, 2 Hispanic Americans), 87 international. Average age 30. 261 applicants, 70% accepted, 134 enrolled. In 2006, 94 degrees awarded. *Entrance requirements:* For master's, GMAT, minimum GPA of 3.0 in undergraduate major, 2.8 overall. Additional exam requirements/recommendations for international students: Required—TOEFL (minimum score 557 paper-based; 220 computer-based). *Application deadline:* For fall admission, 7/15 for domestic students, 5/1 for international students; for spring admission, 11/15 for domestic students, 10/1 for international students. Applications are processed on a rolling basis. Application fee: $55. Electronic applications accepted. *Expenses:* Tuition, state resident: full-time $2,719; part-time $170 per credit. Tuition, nonresident: full-time $12,926; part-time $808 per credit. Required fees: $1,555. *Financial support:* In 2006–07, 1 research assistantship (averaging $10,000 per year), 42 teaching assistantships (averaging $7,891 per year) were awarded; fellowships, career-related internships or fieldwork, Federal Work-Study, institutionally sponsored loans, scholarships/grants, and unspecified assistantships also available. Support available to part-time students. Financial award application deadline: 4/1; financial award applicants required to submit FAFSA. *Unit head:* Ronald A Veith, Director, MBA Program, 704-687-6058, Fax: 704-687-4014, E-mail: raveith@email.uncc.edu. *Application contact:* Kathy B. Giddings, Director of Graduate Admissions, 704-687-3366, Fax: 704-687-3279, E-mail: gradadm@email.uncc.edu.

See Close-Up on page 353.

The University of North Carolina at Greensboro, Graduate School, Bryan School of Business and Economics, Department of Business Administration, Greensboro, NC 27412-5001. Offers MBA, PMC, Postbaccalaureate Certificate, MS/MBA, MSN/MBA. *Accreditation:* AACSB. *Faculty:* 15 full-time (3 women), 13 part-time/adjunct (4 women). *Students:* 154 full-time (56 women), 75 part-time (30 women); includes 64 minority (16 African Americans, 37 Asian Americans or Pacific Islanders, 11 Hispanic Americans). 209 applicants, 35% accepted. *Entrance requirements:* For master's, GMAT, GRE General Test, managerial experience. Additional exam requirements/recommendations for international students: Required—TOEFL. *Application deadline:* For fall admission, 7/1 priority date for domestic students; for spring admission, 11/1 for domestic students. Applications are processed on a rolling basis. Application fee: $45. Electronic applications accepted. *Expenses:* Tuition, state resident: full-time $2,692. Tuition, nonresident: full-time $13,742. *Financial support:* In 2006–07, 29 students received support; fellowships with full tuition reimbursements available, research assistantships with full tuition reimbursements available, teaching assistantships with full tuition reimbursements available, career-related internships or fieldwork, Federal Work-Study, scholarships/grants, and traineeships available. Support available to part-time students. *Unit head:* Dr. Stephen R. Lucas, Head, 336-334-4524, Fax: 336-334-4141. *Application contact:* Michelle Harkleroad, Director of Graduate Admissions, 336-334-4884, Fax: 336-334-4424, E-mail: mbharkle@uncg.edu.

The University of North Carolina at Pembroke, Graduate Studies, School of Business, Program in Business Administration, Pembroke, NC 28372-1510. Offers MBA. Part-time and evening/weekend programs available. *Faculty:* 6 full-time (0 women). *Students:* 13 full-time (7 women), 23 part-time (4 women); includes 6 minority (2 African Americans, 2 American Indian/Alaska Native, 2 Asian Americans or Pacific Islanders). Average age 34. 36 applicants, 100% accepted, 36 enrolled. In 2006, 5 degrees awarded. *Degree requirements:* For master's, thesis optional. *Entrance requirements:* For master's, GMAT, minimum GPA of 3.0 in major or 2.5 overall. Additional exam requirements/recommendations for international students: Required—TOEFL. *Application deadline:* For fall admission, 7/15 priority date for domestic and international students; for spring admission, 12/1 priority date for domestic and international students. Applications are processed on a rolling basis. Application fee: $40. *Expenses:* Tuition, state resident: full-time $3,516; part-time $1,091 per semester. Tuition, nonresident: full-time $12,924; part-time $4,619 per semester. Tuition and fees vary according to class time, course load, degree level and campus/location. *Financial support:* In 2006–07, 1 research assistantship with full tuition reimbursement (averaging $6,000 per year) was awarded; unspecified assistantships also available. Support available to part-time students. Financial award application deadline: 4/15; financial award applicants required to submit FAFSA. *Unit head:* Dr.

Business Administration and Management—General

The University of North Carolina at Pembroke (continued)
Carmen F. Calabrese, Director, 910-521-5712, Fax: 910-521-6564, E-mail: carmen.calabrese@uncp.edu. *Application contact:* Dr. Kathleen C. Hilton, Dean of Graduate Studies, 910-521-6271, Fax: 910-521-6751, E-mail: grad@uncp.edu.

The University of North Carolina Wilmington, School of Business, Program in Business Administration, Wilmington, NC 28403-3297. Offers MBA. *Accreditation:* AACSB. Part-time and evening/weekend programs available. *Students:* Average age 31. 46 applicants, 93% accepted, 40 enrolled. In 2006, 43 degrees awarded. *Degree requirements:* For master's, final project. *Entrance requirements:* For master's, GMAT, 1 year of appropriate work experience. *Application deadline:* For fall admission, 2/1 for domestic students. Applications are processed on a rolling basis. Application fee: $45. *Financial support:* In 2006–07, 1 teaching assistantship was awarded; career-related internships or fieldwork and Federal Work-Study also available. Support available to part-time students. Financial award application deadline: 3/15. *Unit head:* Dr. Vince Howe, Coordinator, 910-962-3882, E-mail: howe@uncw.edu. *Application contact:* Dr. Robert D. Roer, Dean, Graduate School, 910-962-4117, Fax: 910-962-3787, E-mail: roer@uncw.edu.

University of North Dakota, Graduate School, College of Business and Public Administration, Business Administration Program, Grand Forks, ND 58202. Offers MBA. *Accreditation:* AACSB. Part-time and evening/weekend programs available. Postbaccalaureate distance learning degree programs offered (minimal on-campus study). *Faculty:* 32 full-time (10 women). *Students:* 11 full-time (4 women), 95 part-time (33 women); includes 5 minority (1 African American, 2 American Indian/Alaska Native, 1 Asian American or Pacific Islander, 1 Hispanic American), 15 international. 41 applicants, 68% accepted, 27 enrolled. In 2006, 28 degrees awarded. *Degree requirements:* For master's, thesis or alternative, project, comprehensive exam. *Entrance requirements:* For master's, GMAT, minimum GPA of 3.25. Additional exam requirements/recommendations for international students: Required—TOEFL (minimum score 550 paper-based; 213 computer-based; 79 iBT), IELTS (minimum score 6). *Application deadline:* For fall admission, 2/15 priority date for domestic and international students; for spring admission, 10/15 priority date for domestic and international students. Applications are processed on a rolling basis. Application fee: $35. Electronic applications accepted. *Expenses:* Tuition, state resident: full-time $5,650; part-time $214 per credit. Tuition, nonresident: full-time $14,248; part-time $572 per credit. Required fees: $1,008; $42 per credit. Tuition and fees vary according to reciprocity agreements. *Financial support:* In 2006–07, 27 students received support, including 13 research assistantships with full tuition reimbursements available, 8 teaching assistantships with full tuition reimbursements available (averaging $6,312 per year); fellowships, Federal Work-Study, institutionally sponsored loans, scholarships/grants, tuition waivers (full and partial), and unspecified assistantships also available. Support available to part-time students. Financial award application deadline: 3/15; financial award applicants required to submit FAFSA. *Unit head:* Dr. Timothy P. O'Keefe, Graduate Director, 701-777-2135, Fax: 701-777-2019, E-mail: mba@mail.business.und.edu. *Application contact:* Brenda Halle, Admissions Specialist, 701-777-2947, Fax: 701-777-3619, E-mail: brendahalle@mail.und.edu.

University of Northern Iowa, Graduate College, College of Business Administration, Program in Business Administration, Cedar Falls, IA 50614. Offers MBA. *Accreditation:* AACSB. Part-time and evening/weekend programs available. *Faculty:* 33 full-time (9 women), 1 part-time/adjunct (0 women). *Students:* 37 full-time (16 women), 36 part-time (12 women); includes 1 minority (Asian American or Pacific Islander), 45 international. 35 applicants, 66% accepted, 19 enrolled. In 2006, 62 degrees awarded. *Entrance requirements:* For master's, GMAT. Additional exam requirements/recommendations for international students: Required—TOEFL (minimum score 500 paper-based; 180 computer-based; 61 iBT). *Application deadline:* For fall admission, 8/1 priority date for domestic students. Applications are processed on a rolling basis. Application fee: $30 ($50 for international students). Electronic applications accepted. *Expenses:* Tuition, state resident: full-time $5,936. Tuition, nonresident: full-time $14,074. *Financial support:* Career-related internships or fieldwork, Federal Work-Study, scholarships/grants, and tuition waivers (full and partial) available. Support available to part-time students. Financial award application deadline: 2/1. *Unit head:* Leslie K. Wilson, Acting Associate Dean, 319-273-6240, Fax: 319-273-2922, E-mail: leslie.wilson@uni.edu.

University of Northern Virginia, Graduate Programs, Manassas, VA 20109. Offers accountancy (MS); accounting (MBA); business administration (DBA); computer science (MS); counseling education (M Ed); early childhood education (M Ed); educational communication and instructional technology (M Ed); educational leadership (M Ed); finance (MBA); information systems technology (MS); management (MBA); marketing (MBA); project management (MBA); public administration (MPA); teaching English to speakers of other languages (M Ed). Part-time and evening/weekend programs available. Postbaccalaureate distance learning degree programs offered (no on-campus study). *Degree requirements:* For doctorate, thesis/dissertation, comprehensive exam, registration. *Entrance requirements:* Additional exam requirements/recommendations for international students: Required—TOEFL (minimum score 550 paper-based; 230 computer-based), IELTS (minimum score 6). Electronic applications accepted.

University of North Florida, Coggin College of Business, Department of Management, Marketing, and Logistics, Jacksonville, FL 32224-2645. Offers business administration (MBA). *Accreditation:* AACSB. Part-time and evening/weekend programs available. *Faculty:* 24 full-time (5 women). *Students:* 119 full-time (59 women), 298 part-time (126 women); includes 63 minority (24 African Americans, 27 Asian Americans or Pacific Islanders, 12 Hispanic Americans), 28 international. Average age 29. 267 applicants, 52% accepted, 109 enrolled. In 2006, 179 degrees awarded. *Entrance requirements:* For master's, GMAT, minimum GPA of 3.0 in last 60 hours. Additional exam requirements/recommendations for international students: Required—TOEFL (minimum score 550 paper-based; 213 computer-based). *Application deadline:* For fall admission, 7/6 priority date for domestic students, 5/1 for international students; for spring admission, 11/1 priority date for domestic students, 10/1 for international students. Applications are processed on a rolling basis. Application fee: $30. *Expenses:* Tuition, state resident: full-time $4,948; part-time $206 per semester hour. Tuition, nonresident: full-time $19,140; part-time $408 per semester hour. *Financial support:* In 2006–07, 99 students received support, including 1 teaching assistantship (averaging $3,356 per year); research assistantships, Federal Work-Study and tuition waivers (partial) also available. Support available to part-time students. Financial award application deadline: 4/1; financial award applicants required to submit FAFSA. *Faculty research:* Performance measures, costing, and inventory issues in logistics and supply chain management; inter-organizational systems; international management and marketing practices; e-Commerce; organizational learning and socialization processes. *Unit head:* Dr. H. Eugene Baker, Chair, 904-620-2780, E-mail: gbaker@unf.edu. *Application contact:* Denise Guerra, Graduate Adviser, 904-620-1453, Fax: 904-620-2832, E-mail: dguerra@unf.edu.

University of North Texas, Robert B. Toulouse School of Graduate Studies, College of Business Administration, Denton, TX 76203. Offers EMBA, MBA, MS, PhD. *Accreditation:* AACSB. Part-time and evening/weekend programs available. *Faculty:* 108 full-time (24 women). *Students:* 224 full-time (103 women), 337 part-time (139 women); includes 121 minority (52 African Americans, 3 American Indian/Alaska Native, 32 Asian Americans or Pacific Islanders, 34 Hispanic Americans), 109 international. Average age 28. 562 applicants, 81% accepted, 104 enrolled. In 2006, 181 master's, 9 doctorates awarded. *Degree requirements:* For master's, thesis or alternative; for doctorate, thesis/dissertation. *Entrance requirements:* For master's and doctorate, GMAT or GRE General Test. Additional exam requirements/recommendations for international students: Required—TOEFL (minimum score 550 paper-based; 213 computer-based). *Application deadline:* For fall admission, 7/15 for domestic students. Applications are processed on a rolling basis. Application fee: $50 ($75 for international students). *Expenses:* Tuition, state resident: full-time $3,573; part-time $198 per credit. Tuition, nonresident: full-time $8,577; part-time $476 per credit. Required fees: $1,258; $126 per credit. One-time fee: $150 full-time. Tuition and fees vary according to course load. *Financial support:* Fellowships, research assistantships, teaching assistantships, career-related internships or fieldwork, Federal Work-Study, and institutionally sponsored loans available. *Faculty research:* Oil and gas accounting, expert systems, stock returns, occupational safety, service marketing. *Unit head:* Dr. Kathleen Cooper, Dean, 940-565-3037, Fax: 940-565-4930, E-mail: cooperk@unt.edu. *Application contact:* Denise Galubenski, Graduate Advisor, 940-565-3027, Fax: 940-369-8978, E-mail: galubens@cobaf.unt.edu.

University of Notre Dame, Mendoza College of Business, Executive Master of Business Administration Program, Notre Dame, IN 46556. Offers MBA. Evening/weekend programs available. Postbaccalaureate distance learning degree programs offered (minimal on-campus study). *Faculty:* 33 full-time (3 women), 4 part-time/adjunct (2 women). *Students:* 244 full-time (52 women); includes 32 minority (9 African Americans, 11 Asian Americans or Pacific Islanders, 12 Hispanic Americans), 10 international. Average age 37. 310 applicants, 50% accepted, 127 enrolled. In 2006, 120 degrees awarded. *Entrance requirements:* For master's, 5 years of work experience in management. *Application deadline:* For fall admission, 6/1 for domestic students; for winter admission, 11/2 for domestic students. Applications are processed on a rolling basis. Application fee: $100. Electronic applications accepted. *Expenses:* Contact institution. *Financial support:* In 2006–07, 120 students received support. Institutionally sponsored loans available. Financial award application deadline: 4/1; financial award applicants required to submit FAFSA. *Faculty research:* Exchange rates, compensation, market microstructure or volatility in foreign currency, ethical negotiation/decision making. *Unit head:* Leo F. Burke, Associate Dean and Director, 574-631-3622, Fax: 574-631-6783, E-mail: leo.burke.77@nd.edu. *Application contact:* Dr. Barry J. VanDyck, Director of Degree Programs, Executive Education, 574-631-3622, Fax: 574-631-6783, E-mail: barry.vandyck.1@nd.edu.

See Close-Up on page 355.

University of Notre Dame, Mendoza College of Business, Master of Business Administration Program, Notre Dame, IN 46556. Offers MBA, MBA/JD. *Accreditation:* AACSB. *Faculty:* 99 full-time (33 women), 39 part-time/adjunct (6 women). *Students:* 321 full-time (73 women); includes 45 minority (7 African Americans, 3 American Indian/Alaska Native, 16 Asian Americans or Pacific Islanders, 19 Hispanic Americans), 78 international. Average age 27. 582 applicants, 47% accepted, 138 enrolled. In 2006, 185 degrees awarded. *Entrance requirements:* For master's, GMAT, work experience. Additional exam requirements/recommendations for international students: Required—TOEFL (minimum score 600 paper-based; 250 computer-based). *Application deadline:* For fall admission, 11/15 priority date for domestic and international students; for winter admission, 1/15 priority date for domestic and international students; for spring admission, 4/15 for domestic and international students. Applications are processed on a rolling basis. Application fee: $100. Electronic applications accepted. *Financial support:* In 2006–07, 212 fellowships with full and partial tuition reimbursements (averaging $17,049 per year), 99 teaching assistantships (averaging $3,000 per year) were awarded; career-related internships or fieldwork, Federal Work-Study, institutionally sponsored loans, scholarships/grants, and unspecified assistantships also available. Financial award application deadline: 3/15; financial award applicants required to submit FAFSA. *Faculty research:* Market microstructure, marketing and public policy, corporate finance and accounting, corporate governance and ethical behavior, high performing organizations. *Unit head:* Dr. Edward J. Conlon, Associate Dean, Graduate Programs, 574-631-9295, Fax: 574-631-4825, E-mail: econlon@nd.edu. *Application contact:* Brian T. Lohr, Director of MBA Admissions, 574-631-8488, Fax: 574-631-8800, E-mail: blohr@nd.edu.

See Close-Up on page 355.

University of Oklahoma, Graduate College, College of Arts and Sciences, School of International and Area Studies, Norman, OK 73019-0390. Offers international studies (MA), including global affairs, global management. Part-time programs available. *Faculty:* 1 (woman) full-time. *Students:* 5 full-time (2 women), 8 part-time (4 women); includes 2 minority (1 Asian American or Pacific Islander, 1 Hispanic American), 2 international. 12 applicants, 75% accepted, 4 enrolled. In 2006, 3 degrees awarded. *Degree requirements:* For master's, one foreign language, thesis optional. *Entrance requirements:* For master's, GMAT or GRE. Additional exam requirements/recommendations for international students: Required—TOEFL (minimum score 550 paper-based; 213 computer-based). *Application deadline:* For fall admission, 2/15 for domestic students, 4/1 for international students; for spring admission, 10/15 for domestic students, 9/1 for international students. Applications are processed on a rolling basis. Application fee: $40 ($90 for international students). *Expenses:* Tuition, state resident: full-time $3,180; part-time $133 per credit hour. Tuition, nonresident: full-time $11,347; part-time $473 per credit hour. Required fees: $1,729; $62 per credit hour. $117 per semester. Tuition and fees vary according to course load and program. *Financial support:* In 2006–07, 5 students received support, including 3 research assistantships (averaging $13,500 per year), teaching assistantships with partial tuition reimbursements available (averaging $13,500 per year); career-related internships or fieldwork, scholarships/grants, and unspecified assistantships also available. Financial award applicants required to submit FAFSA. *Faculty research:* International relations, comparative politics, international economics, global environmental affairs, contemporary history. Total annual research expenditures: $1,000. *Unit head:* Dr. Robert Cox, Director, 405-325-1584, Fax: 405-325-7738, E-mail: rhcox@ou.edu. *Application contact:* Mitchell P. Amirh, Associate Professor and Director of Graduate Studies, 405-325-8893, Fax: 405-325-0718, E-mail: mps@ou.edu.

University of Oklahoma, Graduate College, Michael F. Price College of Business, Division of Management Information Systems, Norman, OK 73019-0390. Offers management (MS). Part-time and evening/weekend programs available. *Faculty:* 12 full-time (4 women). *Students:* 2 full-time (0 women), (both international). 8 applicants, 13% accepted, 1 enrolled. In 2006, 7 degrees awarded. *Entrance requirements:* Additional exam requirements/recommendations for international students: Required—TOEFL (minimum score 550 paper-based; 213 computer-based). *Application deadline:* For fall admission, 2/1 for domestic and international students; for spring admission, 11/1 for domestic students, 9/1 for international students. Applications are processed on a rolling basis. Application fee: $40 ($90 for international students). *Expenses:* Tuition, state resident: full-time $3,180; part-time $133 per credit hour. Tuition, nonresident: full-time $11,347; part-time $473 per credit hour. Required fees: $1,729; $62 per credit hour. $117 per semester. Tuition and fees vary according to course load and program. *Financial support:* In 2006–07, 6 research assistantships with full tuition reimbursements (averaging $12,450 per year), 4 teaching assistantships with full tuition reimbursements (averaging $16,272 per year) were awarded; Federal Work-Study, scholarships/grants, health care benefits, and unspecified assistantships also available. Financial award applicants required to submit FAFSA. *Faculty research:* Outsourcing and governance, virtual teams, systems analysis, data warehousing, project management. Total annual research expenditures: $26,022. *Unit head:* Lakshamanan Chidambaram, Director, 405-325-1957, Fax: 405-325-1957, E-mail: laku@ou.edu. *Application contact:* Jim Smith, Academic Counselor, 405-325-3744, Fax: 405-325-7753, E-mail: jlsmith@ou.edu.

University of Oklahoma, Graduate College, Michael F. Price College of Business, Program in Business Administration, Norman, OK 73019-0390. Offers MBA, PhD, JD/MBA, MBA/MA, MBA/MPH, MBA/MS. *Accreditation:* AACSB. Part-time and evening/weekend programs available. *Students:* 131 full-time (46 women), 129 part-time (34 women); includes 33 minority (4 African Americans, 9 American Indian/Alaska Native, 14 Asian Americans or Pacific Islanders, 6 Hispanic Americans), 46 international. 154 applicants, 57% accepted, 69 enrolled. In 2006, 71 master's, 5 doctorates awarded. Terminal master's awarded for partial completion of doctoral program. *Degree requirements:* For master's, comprehensive exam (for some programs); for doctorate, thesis/dissertation. *Entrance requirements:* For master's, GMAT, minimum GPA of 3.2; for doctorate, GMAT. Additional exam requirements/recommendations for international students: Required—TOEFL (minimum score 550 paper-based; 213 computer-based). *Application deadline:* For fall admission, 6/1 for domestic students, 4/1 for international students; for spring admission, 11/1 for domestic students, 9/1 for international students. Applications are processed on a rolling basis. Application fee: $40 ($90 for international students). *Expenses:* Tuition, state resident: full-time $3,180; part-time $133 per credit hour. Tuition, nonresident: full-time $11,347; part-time $473 per credit hour. Required fees: $1,729; $62 per credit hour. $117 per semester. Tuition and fees vary according to course load and program. *Financial support:* In 2006–07, 51 students received support, including 13 fellowships with full tuition reimbursements available (averaging $1,196 per year); career-related internships or fieldwork, Federal Work-Study, scholarships/grants, health care benefits, and unspecified assistantships also available. Financial award applicants required to submit FAFSA. *Faculty research:* Corporate finance entrepreneurship, supply chain, management, investment management. *Application contact:* Jillian Duty, Academic Counselor, 405-325-5815, Fax: 405-325-7753, E-mail: jduty@ou.edu.

See Close-Up on page 357.

University of Oregon, Graduate School, Charles H. Lundquist College of Business, Department of Management, Eugene, OR 97403. Offers PhD. *Accreditation:* AACSB. Part-time programs available. *Students:* 5 full-time (3 women). 3 applicants, 100% accepted. In 2006, 3 degrees awarded. Terminal master's awarded for partial completion of doctoral program. *Degree requirements:* For doctorate, thesis/dissertation, 2 comprehensive exams. *Entrance requirements:* For doctorate, GMAT. Additional exam requirements/recommendations for international students: Required—TOEFL. *Application deadline:* For fall admission, 2/1 for domestic students. Application fee: $50. *Financial support:* Teaching assistantships, career-related internships or fieldwork and Federal Work-Study available. *Unit head:* Michael Russo, Head, 541-346-5182. *Application contact:* Perri McGee, Admissions Contact, 541-346-1462, E-mail: pcrone@uoregon.edu.

University of Oregon, Graduate School, Charles H. Lundquist College of Business, Department of Management: General Business, Eugene, OR 97403. Offers MBA. *Accreditation:* AACSB. *Students:* 108 full-time (40 women), 43 part-time (16 women); includes 11 minority (2 African Americans, 9 Asian Americans or Pacific Islanders), 19 international. Average age 27. 156 applicants, 53% accepted. In 2006, 125 degrees awarded. *Entrance requirements:* For master's, GMAT. Additional exam requirements/recommendations for international students: Required—TOEFL. Application fee: $50. *Financial support:* In 2006–07, 33 teaching assistantships were awarded; fellowships, research assistantships, career-related internships or fieldwork and Federal Work-Study also available. *Unit head:* Andrew Verner, Director, 541-346-3306. *Application contact:* Perri McGee, Admissions Contact, 541-346-1462, E-mail: pcrone@uoregon.edu.

University of Ottawa, Faculty of Graduate and Postdoctoral Studies, School of Management, Business Administration Program, Ottawa, ON K1N 6N5, Canada. Offers MBA. *Accreditation:* AACSB. Part-time and evening/weekend programs available. *Degree requirements:* For master's, thesis optional. *Entrance requirements:* For master's, GMAT, bachelor's degree or equivalent, minimum B average, minimum 2 years of work experience. Additional exam requirements/recommendations for international students: Recommended—TOEFL (minimum score 237 computer-based). Electronic applications accepted.

See Close-Up on page 359.

University of Ottawa, Faculty of Graduate and Postdoctoral Studies, School of Management, Executive Business Administration Program, Ottawa, ON K1N 6N5, Canada. Offers EMBA. *Accreditation:* AACSB. Evening/weekend programs available. *Entrance requirements:* For master's, bachelor's degree or equivalent, minimum B average, business experience. Additional exam requirements/recommendations for international students: Recommended—TOEFL (minimum score 237 computer-based). Electronic applications accepted. Expenses: Contact institution.

University of Pennsylvania, Wharton School, Management Department, Philadelphia, PA 19104. Offers MBA, PhD. *Accreditation:* AACSB. *Entrance requirements:* For master's, GMAT; for doctorate, GMAT or GRE. *Faculty research:* Cross-cultural leadership, international technology transfers, human resource management, financial services.

University of Pennsylvania, Wharton School, Wharton Doctoral Programs Division, Philadelphia, PA 19104. Offers accounting (PhD); business and public policy (PhD); finance (PhD); health care systems (PhD); insurance and risk management (PhD); management (PhD); marketing (PhD); operations and information management operations research (PhD); real estate (PhD); statistics (PhD). *Accreditation:* AACSB. *Degree requirements:* For doctorate, thesis/dissertation. *Entrance requirements:* For doctorate, GMAT or GRE. Additional exam requirements/recommendations for international students: Required—TOEFL, TWE. Electronic applications accepted.

University of Pennsylvania, Wharton School, Wharton Executive MBA Division, Program in Executive MBA—East, Philadelphia, PA 19104. Offers MBA. *Accreditation:* AACSB. Evening/weekend programs available. *Entrance requirements:* For master's, GMAT.

University of Pennsylvania, Wharton School, Wharton Executive MBA Division, Program in Executive MBA—West, Philadelphia, PA 19104. Offers MBA. *Accreditation:* AACSB. Evening/weekend programs available. *Entrance requirements:* For master's, GMAT.

University of Pennsylvania, Wharton School, Wharton MBA Division, Philadelphia, PA 19104. Offers MBA, DMD/MBA, JD/MBA, MBA/DSW, MBA/MA, MBA/MS, MBA/MSN, MBA/MSW, MBA/PhD, MD/MBA, VMD/MBA. *Accreditation:* AACSB. *Entrance requirements:* For master's, GMAT. Additional exam requirements/recommendations for international students: Required—TOEFL. Electronic applications accepted. *Faculty research:* Entrepreneurial studies, finance, management of technology.

University of Phoenix–Atlanta Campus, John Sperling School of Business, College of Graduate Business and Management, Sandy Springs, GA 30350-4153. Offers business administration (MBA); global management (MBA); human resources management (MBA); management (MM). Evening/weekend programs available. *Faculty:* 25 full-time (15 women), 151 part-time/adjunct (31 women). *Students:* 605 full-time (375 women); includes 323 minority (303 African Americans, 1 American Indian/Alaska Native, 10 Asian Americans or Pacific Islanders, 9 Hispanic Americans), 22 international. Average age 36. In 2006, 156 degrees awarded. *Degree requirements:* For master's, thesis (for some programs), registration. *Entrance requirements:* For master's, minimum undergraduate GPA of 3.0, 3 years of work experience. Additional exam requirements/recommendations for international students: Required—TOEFL (minimum score 550 paper-based; 213 computer-based; 79 iBT). *Application deadline:* Applications are processed on a rolling basis. *Expenses:* Tuition: Full-time $10,560. Required fees: $760. *Financial support:* Institutionally sponsored loans and scholarships/grants available. Financial award applicants required to submit FAFSA. *Unit head:* Dr. Brian Lindquist, Associate Vice President and Dean/Executive Director, 480-557-1221, E-mail: brian.lindquist@phoenix.edu. *Application contact:* Chair, 678-731-0555, Fax: 678-731-9666.

University of Phoenix–Augusta Campus, College of Graduate Business and Management, Augusta, GA 30909-4583. Offers accounting (MBA); business and management (MBA, MM); global management (MBA); human resources management (MBA, MM); marketing (MBA); public administration (MBA, MM).

University of Phoenix–Austin Campus, College of Graduate Business and Management, Austin, TX 78759. Offers accounting (MBA); business and management (MBA); e-business (MBA); global management (MBA); human resources management (MBA, MM); management (MM); marketing (MBA); public administration (MBA).

University of Phoenix–Bay Area Campus, John Sperling School of Business, College of Graduate Business and Management, Pleasanton, CA 94588-3677. Offers accounting (MBA); business administration (MBA); global management (MBA); human resource management (MBA); marketing (MBA); public administration (MBA). Evening/weekend programs available. *Faculty:* 30 full-time (3 women), 390 part-time/adjunct (106 women). *Students:* 523 full-time (279 women); includes 185 minority (40 African Americans, 2 American Indian/Alaska Native, 110 Asian Americans or Pacific Islanders, 33 Hispanic Americans), 84 international. Average age 37. In 2006, 205 degrees awarded. *Degree requirements:* For master's, thesis (for some programs), registration. *Entrance requirements:* For master's, minimum undergraduate GPA of 3.0, 3 years of work experience. Additional exam requirements/recommendations for international students: Required—TOEFL (minimum score 550 paper-based; 213 computer-based; 79 iBT). *Application deadline:* Applications are processed on a rolling basis. Application fee: $45. Electronic applications accepted. *Expenses:* Tuition: Full-time $12,648. Required fees: $760. *Financial support:* Institutionally sponsored loans and scholarships/grants available. Financial award applicants required to submit FAFSA. *Unit head:* Dr. Brian Lindquist, Associate Vice President and Dean/Executive Director, 480-557-1221, E-mail: brian.lindquist@phoenix.edu. *Application contact:* Chair, 408-435-8500, Fax: 408-435-8250.

University of Phoenix–Boston Campus, John Sperling School of Business, College of Graduate Business and Management, Braintree, MA 02184-4949. Offers administration (MBA); global management (MBA). Evening/weekend programs available. *Faculty:* 34 full-time (30 women), 126 part-time/adjunct (0 women). *Students:* 136 full-time (76 women). Average age 36. In 2006, 55 degrees awarded. *Degree requirements:* For master's, thesis (for some programs), registration. *Entrance requirements:* For master's, 3 years of work experience, minimum undergraduate GPA of 3.0. Additional exam requirements/recommendations for international students: Required—TOEFL (minimum score 550 paper-based; 213 computer-based; 79 iBT). *Application deadline:* Applications are processed on a rolling basis. Application fee: $45. *Expenses:* Tuition: Full-time $13,848. Required fees: $760. *Financial support:* Institutionally sponsored loans and scholarships/grants available. Financial award applicants required to submit FAFSA. *Unit head:* Dr. Brian Lindquist, Associate Vice President and Dean/Executive Director, 480-557-1221, E-mail: brian.lindquist@phoenix.edu. *Application contact:* Chair, 781-843-0844, Fax: 781-843-8646.

University of Phoenix–Central Florida Campus, John Sperling School of Business, College of Graduate Business and Management, Maitland, FL 32751-7057. Offers accounting (MBA); business administration (MBA); business and management (MM); global management (MBA); management (MM); marketing (MBA). Evening/weekend programs available. *Faculty:* 50 full-time (11 women), 136 part-time/adjunct (32 women). *Students:* 440 full-time (265 women); includes 175 minority (102 African Americans, 4 American Indian/Alaska Native, 16 Asian Americans or Pacific Islanders, 53 Hispanic Americans), 38 international. Average age 36. In 2006, 149 degrees awarded. *Degree requirements:* For master's, thesis (for some programs), registration. *Entrance requirements:* For master's, minimum undergraduate GPA of 3.0, 3 years work experience. Additional exam requirements/recommendations for international students: Required—TOEFL (minimum score 550 paper-based; 213 computer-based; 79 iBT). *Application deadline:* Applications are processed on a rolling basis. Application fee: $45. Electronic applications accepted. *Expenses:* Tuition: Full-time $9,450. Required fees: $760. *Financial support:* Institutionally sponsored loans and scholarships/grants available. Financial award applicants required to submit FAFSA. *Unit head:* Dr. Brian Lindquist, Associate Vice President and Dean/Executive Director, 480-557-1221, E-mail: brian.lindquist@phoenix.edu. *Application contact:* Chair, 407-667-0555, Fax: 407-667-0560.

University of Phoenix–Central Florida Campus, John Sperling School of Business, College of Information Systems and Technology, Maitland, FL 32751-7057. Offers management (MIS); technology management (MBA). Evening/weekend programs available. *Faculty:* 25 full-time (1 woman), 62 part-time/adjunct (9 women). *Students:* 1 full-time (0 women); minority (Asian American or Pacific Islander) Average age 39. In 2006, 24 degrees awarded. *Degree requirements:* For master's, thesis (for some programs), registration. *Entrance requirements:* For master's, minimum undergraduate GPA of 3.0, 3 years work experience. Additional exam requirements/recommendations for international students: Required—TOEFL (minimum score 550 paper-based; 213 computer-based; 79 iBT). *Application deadline:* Applications are processed on a rolling basis. Application fee: $45. Electronic applications accepted. *Expenses:* Tuition: Full-time $9,450. Required fees: $760. *Financial support:* Institutionally sponsored loans and scholarships/grants available. Financial award applicants required to submit FAFSA. *Application contact:* Chair, 407-667-0555, Fax: 407-667-0560.

University of Phoenix–Central Massachusetts Campus, John Sperling School of Business, College of Graduate Business and Management, Westborough, MA 01581-3906. Offers business administration (MBA); global management (MBA). Evening/weekend programs available. *Faculty:* 11 full-time (5 women), 84 part-time/adjunct (14 women). *Students:* 58 full-time (27 women); includes 9 minority (5 African Americans, 4 Hispanic Americans), 1 international. Average age 39. In 2006, 18 degrees awarded. *Degree requirements:* For master's, thesis (for some programs), registration. *Entrance requirements:* For master's, minimum undergraduate GPA of 3.0, 3 years of work experience. Additional exam requirements/recommendations for international students: Required—TOEFL (minimum score 550 paper-based; 213 computer-based; 79 iBT). *Application deadline:* Applications are processed on a rolling basis. Application fee: $45. Electronic applications accepted. *Expenses:* Tuition: Full-time $13,848. Required fees: $760. *Financial support:* Institutionally sponsored loans available. Financial award applicants required to submit FAFSA. *Unit head:* Dr. Brian Lindquist, Associate Vice President and Dean/Executive Director, 480-557-1221, E-mail: brian.lindquist@phoenix.edu. *Application contact:* Campus College Chair, 508-614-4100.

University of Phoenix–Central Valley Campus, College of Graduate Business and Management, Fresno, CA 93720. Offers accounting (MBA); business administration (MBA); global management (MBA); human resources management (MBA); management (MM); marketing (MBA); public administration (MBA).

University of Phoenix–Charlotte Campus, John Sperling School of Business, College of Graduate Business and Management, Charlotte, NC 28273-3409. Offers accounting (MBA); administration (MBA); global management (MBA). Evening/weekend programs available. *Faculty:* 18 full-time (2 women), 111 part-time/adjunct (33 women). *Students:* 423 full-time (272 women); includes 221 minority (211 African Americans, 6 Asian Americans or Pacific Islanders, 4 Hispanic Americans), 21 international. Average age 36. In 2006, 78 degrees awarded. *Degree requirements:* For master's, thesis (for some programs), registration. *Entrance requirements:* For master's, minimum undergraduate GPA of 3.0, 3 years work experience. Additional exam requirements/recommendations for international students: Required—TOEFL (minimum score 550 paper-based; 213 computer-based; 79 iBT). *Application deadline:* Applications are processed on a rolling basis. Application fee: $45. Electronic applications accepted. *Expenses:* Tuition: Full-time $10,320. Required fees: $760. *Financial support:* Institutionally sponsored loans and scholarships/grants available. Financial award applicants required to submit FAFSA. *Unit head:* Dr. Brian Lindquist, Associate Vice President and Dean/Executive Director, 480-557-1221, E-mail: brian.lindquist@phoenix.edu. *Application contact:* College Chair, 704-504-5409, Fax: 704-504-5360.

University of Phoenix–Chattanooga Campus, College of Graduate Business and Management, Chattanooga, TN 37421-3707. Offers accounting (MBA); business and management (MBA); global management (MBA); human resources management (MBA, MM); management (MM); marketing (MBA); public administration (MBA, MM).

University of Phoenix–Cheyenne Campus, College of Graduate Business and Management, Cheyenne, WY 82009. Offers business and management (MM); global management (MBA); human resources management (MBA, MM); marketing (MBA); public administration (MBA, MM).

University of Phoenix–Chicago Campus, John Sperling School of Business, College of Graduate Business and Management, Schaumburg, IL 60173-4399. Offers administration (MBA); global management (MBA); information systems (MIS); management (MM). Evening/weekend programs available. *Faculty:* 39 full-time (12 women), 109 part-time/adjunct (28 women). *Students:* 259 full-time (156 women); includes 99 minority (69 African Americans, 1 American Indian/Alaska Native, 17 Asian Americans or Pacific Islanders, 12 Hispanic Americans), 21 international. Average age 37. In 2006, 91 degrees awarded. *Degree requirements:* For

Business Administration and Management—General

University of Phoenix–Chicago Campus (continued)
master's, thesis (for some programs), registration. *Entrance requirements:* For master's, minimum undergraduate GPA of 3.0, 3 years of work experience. Additional exam requirements/recommendations for international students: Required—TOEFL (minimum score 550 paper-based; 213 computer-based; 79 iBT). *Application deadline:* Applications are processed on a rolling basis. Application fee: $45. Electronic applications accepted. *Expenses:* Tuition: Full-time $12,120. Required fees: $760. *Financial support:* Institutionally sponsored loans and scholarships/grants available. Financial award applicants required to submit FAFSA. *Unit head:* Dr. Brian Lindquist, Associate Vice President and Dean/Executive Director, 480-557-1221, E-mail: brian.lindquist@phoenix.edu. *Application contact:* Campus College Chair—Graduate Business, 847-413-1922, Fax: 847-413-8706.

University of Phoenix–Cincinnati Campus, John Sperling School of Business, College of Graduate Business and Management, West Chester, OH 45069-4875. Offers business and management (MBA). Evening/weekend programs available. *Faculty:* 26 full-time (7 women), 53 part-time/adjunct (15 women). *Students:* 183 full-time (134 women); includes 54 minority (49 African Americans, 3 Asian Americans or Pacific Islanders, 2 Hispanic Americans), 6 international. Average age 38. In 2006, 85 degrees awarded. *Degree requirements:* For master's, thesis (for some programs), registration. *Entrance requirements:* For master's, minimum undergraduate GPA of 3.0, 3 years of work experience. Additional exam requirements/recommendations for international students: Required—TOEFL (minimum score 550 paper-based; 213 computer-based; 79 iBT). *Application deadline:* Applications are processed on a rolling basis. Application fee: $45. Electronic applications accepted. *Expenses:* Tuition: Full-time $11,832. Required fees: $760. *Financial support:* Institutionally sponsored loans and scholarships/grants available. Financial award applicants required to submit FAFSA. *Unit head:* Dr. Brian Lindquist, Associate Vice President and Dean/Executive Director, 480-557-1221. *Application contact:* College Chair, 573-772-9600.

University of Phoenix–Cleveland Campus, John Sperling School of Business, College of Graduate Business and Management, Independence, OH 44131-2194. Offers accounting (MBA); business administration (MBA); global management (MBA); human resources management (MM); management (MM); marketing (MBA); public administration (MBA, MM). Evening/weekend programs available. *Faculty:* 10 full-time (1 woman), 68 part-time/adjunct (16 women). *Students:* 178 full-time (107 women); includes 115 minority (66 African Americans, 1 American Indian/Alaska Native, 5 Asian Americans or Pacific Islanders, 43 Hispanic Americans), 9 international. Average age 37. In 2006, 25 degrees awarded. *Degree requirements:* For master's, thesis (for some programs), registration. *Entrance requirements:* For master's, minimum undergraduate GPA of 3.0, 3 years of work experience. Additional exam requirements/recommendations for international students: Required—TOEFL (minimum score 550 paper-based; 213 computer-based; 79 iBT). *Application deadline:* Applications are processed on a rolling basis. Application fee: $45. Electronic applications accepted. *Expenses:* Tuition: Full-time $11,608. Required fees: $760. *Financial support:* Institutionally sponsored loans and scholarships/grants available. Financial award applicants required to submit FAFSA. *Unit head:* Dr. Brian Lindquist, Associate Vice President and Dean/Executive Director, 480-557-1221, E-mail: brian.linquist@phoenix.edu. *Application contact:* Chair, 216-447-8807, Fax: 216-447-9144.

University of Phoenix–Columbia Campus, College of Graduate Business and Management, Columbia, SC, SC 29223. Offers business and management (MBA).

University of Phoenix–Columbus Georgia Campus, John Sperling School of Business, College of Graduate Business and Management, Columbus, GA 31904-6321. Offers accounting (MBA); administration (MBA); global management (MBA); human resource management (MBA); marketing (MBA); public administration (MBA). Evening/weekend programs available. *Faculty:* 11 full-time (1 woman), 53 part-time/adjunct (15 women). *Students:* 52 full-time (35 women); includes 27 minority (22 African Americans, 1 Asian American or Pacific Islander, 4 Hispanic Americans). Average age 37. In 2006, 10 degrees awarded. *Degree requirements:* For master's, thesis (for some programs), registration. *Entrance requirements:* For master's, minimum undergraduate GPA of 3.0, 3 years of work experience. Additional exam requirements/recommendations for international students: Required—TOEFL (minimum score 550 paper-based; 213 computer-based; 79 iBT). *Application deadline:* Applications are processed on a rolling basis. Application fee: $45. Electronic applications accepted. *Expenses:* Tuition: Full-time $10,200. Required fees: $760. *Financial support:* Institutionally sponsored loans and scholarships/grants available. Financial award applicants required to submit FAFSA. *Unit head:* Dr. Brian Lindquist, Associate Vice President/Dean/Executive Director, 480-557-1221, E-mail: brian.lindquist@phoenix.edu. *Application contact:* College Chair, 706-320-1262.

University of Phoenix–Columbus Ohio Campus, John Sperling School of Business, College of Graduate Business and Management, Columbus, OH 43240-4032. Offers administration (MBA); marketing (MBA). Evening/weekend programs available. *Faculty:* 12 full-time (5 women), 27 part-time/adjunct (3 women). *Students:* 145 full-time (88 women); includes 40 minority (36 African Americans, 3 Asian Americans or Pacific Islanders, 1 Hispanic American), 6 international. Average age 37. In 2006, 40 degrees awarded. *Degree requirements:* For master's, thesis (for some programs), registration. *Entrance requirements:* For master's, minimum undergraduate GPA of 3.0, 3 years of work experience. Additional exam requirements/recommendations for international students: Required—TOEFL (minimum score 550 paper-based; 213 computer-based; 79 iBT). *Application deadline:* Applications are processed on a rolling basis. Application fee: $45. Electronic applications accepted. *Expenses:* Tuition: Full-time $11,832. Required fees: $760. *Financial support:* Institutionally sponsored loans and scholarships/grants available. Financial award applicants required to submit FAFSA. *Unit head:* Dr. Brian Lindquist, Associate Vice President and Dean/Executive Director, 480-557-1221, E-mail: brian.lindquist@phoenix.edu.

University of Phoenix–Dallas Campus, John Sperling School of Business, College of Graduate Business and Management, Dallas, TX 75251-2009. Offers accounting (MBA); administration (MBA); human resources management (MBA, MM); management (MM); marketing (MBA); public administration (MBA, MM). Evening/weekend programs available. *Faculty:* 27 full-time (5 women), 130 part-time/adjunct (34 women). *Students:* 517 full-time (320 women); includes 217 minority (166 African Americans, 7 American Indian/Alaska Native, 11 Asian Americans or Pacific Islanders, 33 Hispanic Americans), 68 international. Average age 37. In 2006, 127 degrees awarded. *Degree requirements:* For master's, thesis (for some programs), registration. *Entrance requirements:* For master's, 3 years of work experience, minimum undergraduate GPA of 3.0. Additional exam requirements/recommendations for international students: Required—TOEFL (minimum score 550 paper-based; 213 computer-based; 79 iBT). *Application deadline:* Applications are processed on a rolling basis. Application fee: $45. Electronic applications accepted. *Expenses:* Tuition: Full-time $11,832. Required fees: $760. *Financial support:* Institutionally sponsored loans and scholarships/grants available. Financial award applicants required to submit FAFSA. *Unit head:* Dr. Brian Lindquist, Associate Vice President and Dean/Executive Director, 480-557-1221, E-mail: brian.lindquist@phoenix.edu. *Application contact:* Chair, 972-385-1055, Fax: 972-385-1700.

University of Phoenix–Denver Campus, John Sperling School of Business, College of Graduate Business and Management, Lone Tree, CO 80124-5453. Offers accounting (MBA); business administration (MBA); e-business (MBA); global management (MBA); human resources management (MBA, MM); management (MM); marketing (MBA); public administration (MBA, MM). Evening/weekend programs available. *Faculty:* 63 full-time (22 women), 254 part-time/adjunct (56 women). *Students:* 289 full-time (139 women); includes 59 minority (25 African Americans, 1 American Indian/Alaska Native, 9 Asian Americans or Pacific Islanders, 24 Hispanic Americans), 20 international. Average age 37. In 2006, 93 degrees awarded. *Degree requirements:* For master's, thesis (for some programs), registration. *Entrance requirements:* For master's, minimum undergraduate GPA of 3.0, 3 years work experience. Additional exam requirements/recommendations for international students: Required—TOEFL (minimum score 550 paper-based; 213 computer-based; 79 iBT). *Application deadline:* Applications are processed on a rolling basis. Application fee: $45. Electronic applications accepted. *Expenses:* Tuition: Full-time $10,032. Required fees: $760. *Financial support:* Institutionally sponsored loans and scholarships/grants available. Financial award applicants required to submit FAFSA. *Unit head:* Dr. Brian Lindquist, Associate Vice President and Dean/Executive Director, 480-557-1221, E-mail: brian.lindquist@phoenix.edu. *Application contact:* Chair, 303-694-9093, Fax: 303-662-0911.

University of Phoenix–Denver Campus, John Sperling School of Business, College of Information Systems and Technology, Lone Tree, CO 80124-5453. Offers e-business (MBA); management (MIS); technology management (MBA). Evening/weekend programs available. *Faculty:* 26 full-time (9 women), 118 part-time/adjunct (25 women). *Students:* 7 full-time (2 women); includes 1 minority (Hispanic American) Average age 38. In 2006, 11 master's awarded. *Degree requirements:* For master's, thesis (for some programs), registration. *Entrance requirements:* For master's, minimum undergraduate GPA of 3.0, 3 years of work experience. Additional exam requirements/recommendations for international students: Required—TOEFL (minimum score 550 paper-based; 213 computer-based; 79 iBT). *Application deadline:* Applications are processed on a rolling basis. Application fee: $45. Electronic applications accepted. *Expenses:* Tuition: Full-time $10,032. Required fees: $760. *Financial support:* Institutionally sponsored loans and scholarships/grants available. Financial award applicants required to submit FAFSA. *Unit head:* Dr. Adam Honea, Dean/Executive Director, 480-557-1659, E-mail: adam.honea@phoenix.edu. *Application contact:* Chair, 303-694-9093, Fax: 303-662-0911.

University of Phoenix–Des Moines Campus, College of Graduate Business and Management, Des Moines, IA 50266. Offers accounting (MBA); business administration (MBA); global management (MBA); human resources management (MBA, MM); management (MM); marketing (MBA); public administration (MBA, MM).

University of Phoenix–Detroit Campus, College of Graduate Business and Management, Southfield, MI 48076. Offers accounting (MBA); business administration (MBA); e-business (MBA); global management (MBA); human resources management (MBA, MM); management (MM); marketing (MBA); public administration (MBA).

University of Phoenix–Eastern Washington Campus, John Sperling School of Business, College of Graduate Business and Management, Spokane Valley, WA 99212-2531. Offers MBA. Evening/weekend programs available. *Faculty:* 14 full-time (0 women), 62 part-time/adjunct (15 women). *Students:* 38 full-time (19 women); includes 1 minority (American Indian/Alaska Native), 10 international. Average age 34. In 2006, 11 degrees awarded. *Degree requirements:* For master's, thesis (for some programs), registration. *Entrance requirements:* For master's, minimum undergraduate GPA of 3.0, 3 years of work experience. Additional exam requirements/recommendations for international students: Required—TOEFL (minimum score 550 paper-based; 213 computer-based; 79 iBT). *Application deadline:* Applications are processed on a rolling basis. Application fee: $45. Electronic applications accepted. *Expenses:* Tuition: Full-time $9,120. Required fees: $760. *Financial support:* Institutionally sponsored loans and scholarships/grants available. Financial award applicants required to submit FAFSA. *Unit head:* Dr. Brian Lindquist, Associate Vice President and Dean/Executive Director, 480-557-1221, E-mail: brian.lindquist@phoenix.edu.

University of Phoenix–Fairfield County, College of Graduate Business and Management, Norwalk, CT 06854-1799. Offers MBA.

University of Phoenix–Fort Lauderdale Campus, John Sperling School of Business, College of Graduate Business and Management, Fort Lauderdale, FL 33309. Offers accounting (MBA); business administration (MBA); global management (MBA); human resource management (MBA); human resources management (MM); management (MM); marketing (MBA); public administration (MBA). Evening/weekend programs available. *Faculty:* 31 full-time (13 women), 117 part-time/adjunct (33 women). *Students:* 433 full-time (273 women); includes 196 minority (113 African Americans, 3 American Indian/Alaska Native, 8 Asian Americans or Pacific Islanders, 72 Hispanic Americans), 64 international. Average age 38. In 2006, 112 degrees awarded. *Degree requirements:* For master's, thesis (for some programs), registration. *Entrance requirements:* For master's, minimum undergraduate GPA of 3.0, 3 years work experience. Additional exam requirements/recommendations for international students: Required—TOEFL (minimum score 550 paper-based; 213 computer-based; 79 iBT). *Application deadline:* Applications are processed on a rolling basis. Application fee: $45. Electronic applications accepted. *Expenses:* Tuition: Full-time $9,450. Required fees: $760. *Financial support:* Institutionally sponsored loans and scholarships/grants available. Financial award applicants required to submit FAFSA. *Unit head:* Dr. Brian Linquist, Associate V.P. & Dean/Executive Director, 480-557-1221, E-mail: brian.linquist@phoenix.edu. *Application contact:* Chair, 954-382-5303, Fax: 954-382-5304.

University of Phoenix–Fort Lauderdale Campus, John Sperling School of Business, College of Information Systems and Technology, Fort Lauderdale, FL 33309. Offers management (MIS); technology management (MBA). Evening/weekend programs available. *Faculty:* 11 full-time (3 women), 53 part-time/adjunct (4 women). *Students:* 16 full-time (8 women); includes 9 minority (5 African Americans, 4 Hispanic Americans), 2 international. Average age 40. In 2006, 10 degrees awarded. *Degree requirements:* For master's, thesis (for some programs), registration. *Entrance requirements:* For master's, minimum undergraduate GPA of 3.0, 3 years of work experience. Additional exam requirements/recommendations for international students: Required—TOEFL (minimum score 550 paper-based; 213 computer-based; 79 iBT). *Application deadline:* Applications are processed on a rolling basis. Application fee: $45. Electronic applications accepted. *Expenses:* Tuition: Full-time $9,450. Required fees: $760. *Financial support:* Institutionally sponsored loans and scholarships/grants available. Financial award applicants required to submit FAFSA. *Application contact:* Chair, 954-382-5303, Fax: 954-382-5304.

University of Phoenix–Harrisburg Campus, College of Graduate Business and Management, Harrisburg, PA 17112. Offers accounting (MBA); business and management (MBA); glboal management (MBA); human resources management (MBA, MM); management (MM); marketing (MBA); public administration (MBA, MM).

University of Phoenix–Hawaii Campus, John Sperling School of Business, College of Graduate Business and Management, Honolulu, HI 96813-4317. Offers accounting (MBA); business administration (MBA); global management (MBA); human resources management (MBA, MM); management (MM); marketing (MBA); public administration (MBA, MM). Evening/weekend programs available. *Faculty:* 17 full-time (4 women), 92 part-time/adjunct (23 women). *Students:* 72 full-time (39 women); includes 18 minority (3 African Americans, 13 Asian Americans or Pacific Islanders, 2 Hispanic Americans), 30 international. Average age 37. In 2006, 20 master's awarded. *Degree requirements:* For master's, thesis (for some programs), registration. *Entrance requirements:* For master's, minimum undergraduate GPA of 3.0, 3 years of work experience. Additional exam requirements/recommendations for international students: Required—TOEFL (minimum score 550 paper-based; 213 computer-based; 79 iBT). *Application deadline:* Applications are processed on a rolling basis. Application fee: $45. Electronic applications accepted. *Expenses:* Tuition: Full-time $11,520. Required fees: $760. *Financial support:* Institutionally sponsored loans and scholarships/grants available. Financial award applicants required to submit FAFSA. *Unit head:* Dr. Brian Lindquist, Associate Vice President and Dean/Executive Director, 480-557-1221, E-mail: brian.lindquist@phoenix.edu. *Application contact:* Chair, 808-536-2686, Fax: 808-536-3848.

University of Phoenix–Hawaii Campus, John Sperling School of Business, College of Information Systems and Technology, Honolulu, HI 96813-4317. Offers management (MIS); technology management (MBA). Evening/weekend programs available. *Faculty:* 7 full-time (1 woman), 57 part-time/adjunct (7 women). *Students:* 16 full-time (3 women); includes 5 minority (2 African Americans, 3 Asian Americans or Pacific Islanders), 6 international. Average age 37. In 2006, 11 degrees awarded. *Degree requirements:* For master's, thesis (for some programs), registration. *Entrance requirements:* For master's, minimum undergraduate GPA of 3.0, 3 years of work experience. Additional exam requirements/recommendations for international students: Required—TOEFL (minimum score 550 paper-based; 213 computer-based; 79 iBT). *Application deadline:* Applications are processed on a rolling basis. Application fee: $45. Electronic applications accepted. *Expenses:* Tuition: Full-time $11,520. Required fees: $760. *Financial support:* Institutionally sponsored loans and scholarships/grants available. Financial award applicants required to submit FAFSA. *Unit head:* Dr. Adam Honea, Dean/Executive Director, 480-557-1659, E-mail: adam.honea@phoenix.edu. *Application contact:* Chair, 808-536-2686, Fax: 808-536-3848.

University of Phoenix–Houston Campus, John Sperling School of Business, College of Graduate Business and Management, Houston, TX 77079-2004. Offers business administration (MBA); global management (MBA); human resources management (MBA); public administration (MBA). Evening/weekend programs available. *Faculty:* 28 full-time (9 women), 149 part-time/adjunct (43 women). *Students:* 666 full-time (417 women); includes 350 minority (274 African Americans, 1 American Indian/Alaska Native, 34 Asian Americans or Pacific Islanders, 41 Hispanic Americans), 45 international. Average age 37. In 2006, 244 degrees awarded. *Degree requirements:* For master's, thesis (for some programs), registration. *Entrance requirements:* For master's, 3 years of work experience, minimum undergraduate GPA of 3.0. Additional exam requirements/recommendations for international students: Required—TOEFL (minimum score 550 paper-based; 213 computer-based; 79 iBT). *Application deadline:* Applications are processed on a rolling basis. Application fee: $45. Electronic applications accepted. *Expenses:* Tuition: Full-time $11,832. Required fees: $760. *Financial support:* Institutionally sponsored loans available. Financial award applicants required to submit FAFSA. *Unit head:* Dr. Brian Lindquist, Associate Vice President and Dean/Executive Director, 480-557-1221, E-mail: brian.lindquist@phoenix.edu. *Application contact:* 713-465-9966, Fax: 713-465-2686.

University of Phoenix–Idaho Campus, John Sperling School of Business, College of Graduate Business and Management, Meridian, ID 83642-3014. Offers accounting (MBA); administration (MBA); management (MM). Evening/weekend programs available. *Faculty:* 7 full-time (0 women), 52 part-time/adjunct (12 women). *Students:* 104 full-time (34 women); includes 6 minority (1 African American, 2 Asian Americans or Pacific Islanders, 3 Hispanic Americans), 11 international. Average age 35. In 2006, 22 degrees awarded. *Degree requirements:* For master's, thesis (for some programs), registration. *Entrance requirements:* For master's, 3 years of work experience, minimum undergraduate GPA of 3.0. Additional exam requirements/recommendations for international students: Required—TOEFL (minimum score 550 paper-based; 213 computer-based). *Application deadline:* Applications are processed on a rolling basis. Application fee: $45. Electronic applications accepted. *Expenses:* Tuition: Full-time $9,104. *Financial support:* Institutionally sponsored loans and scholarships/grants available. Financial award applicants required to submit FAFSA. *Unit head:* Dr. Brian Lindquist, Dean, 480-557-1221, E-mail: brian.lindquist@phoenix.edu. *Application contact:* Chair, 208-888-1505, Fax: 208-888-4775.

University of Phoenix–Indianapolis Campus, John Sperling School of Business, College of Graduate Business and Management, Indianapolis, IN 46250-932. Offers business and management (MBA); management (MM). Evening/weekend programs available. *Faculty:* 13 full-time (6 women), 77 part-time/adjunct (22 women). *Students:* 102 full-time (52 women); includes 28 minority (24 African Americans, 3 Asian Americans or Pacific Islanders, 1 Hispanic American), 10 international. Average age 36. In 2006, 35 degrees awarded. *Degree requirements:* For master's, thesis (for some programs), registration. *Entrance requirements:* For master's, minimum undergraduate GPA of 3.0, 3 years of work experience. Additional exam requirements/recommendations for international students: Required—TOEFL (minimum score 550 paper-based; 213 computer-based). *Application deadline:* Applications are processed on a rolling basis. Application fee: $45. Electronic applications accepted. *Expenses:* Tuition: Full-time $10,320. Required fees: $760. *Financial support:* Institutionally sponsored loans and scholarships/grants available. Financial award applicants required to submit FAFSA. *Unit head:* Dr. Brian Lindquist, Provost, 480-557-1221, E-mail: brian.lindquist@phoenix.edu. *Application contact:* Chair, 317-585-8616.

University of Phoenix–Jersey City Campus, College of Graduate Business and Management, Jersey City, NJ 07310. Offers accounting (MBA); business and management (MBA); global management (MBA); human resources management (MBA, MM); management (MM); marketing (MBA); public administration (MBA, MM).

University of Phoenix–Kansas City Campus, John Sperling School of Business, College of Graduate Business and Management, Kansas City, MO 64131-4517. Offers business administration (MBA); management (MM). Evening/weekend programs available. *Faculty:* 22 full-time (3 women), 143 part-time/adjunct (34 women). *Students:* 226 full-time (105 women); includes 44 minority (36 African Americans, 1 American Indian/Alaska Native, 7 Hispanic Americans), 32 international. Average age 34. In 2006, 78 degrees awarded. *Degree requirements:* For master's, thesis (for some programs), registration. *Entrance requirements:* For master's, minimum undergraduate GPA of 3.0, 3 years of work experience. Additional exam requirements/recommendations for international students: Required—TOEFL (minimum score 550 paper-based; 213 computer-based). *Application deadline:* Applications are processed on a rolling basis. Application fee: $45. Electronic applications accepted. *Expenses:* Tuition: Full-time $11,064. Required fees: $760. *Financial support:* Institutionally sponsored loans and scholarships/grants available. Financial award applicants required to submit FAFSA. *Unit head:* Dr. Brian Lindquist, Associate Vice President/Dean/Executive Director, 480-557-1142. *Application contact:* Chair, 816-943-9600, Fax: 816-943-6675.

University of Phoenix–Las Vegas Campus, John Sperling School of Business, College of Graduate Business and Management, Las Vegas, NV 89128. Offers business administration (MBA); management (MM). Evening/weekend programs available. *Faculty:* 28 full-time (6 women), 144 part-time/adjunct (30 women). *Students:* 467 full-time (261 women); includes 152 minority (97 African Americans, 5 American Indian/Alaska Native, 17 Asian Americans or Pacific Islanders, 33 Hispanic Americans), 19 international. Average age 37. In 2006, 155 degrees awarded. *Degree requirements:* For master's, thesis (for some programs), registration. *Entrance requirements:* For master's, minimum undergraduate GPA of 3.0, 3 years of work experience. Additional exam requirements/recommendations for international students: Required—TOEFL (minimum score 550 paper-based; 213 computer-based; 79 iBT). *Application deadline:* Applications are processed on a rolling basis. Application fee: $45. Electronic applications accepted. *Expenses:* Tuition: Full-time $9,576. Required fees: $760. *Financial support:* Institutionally sponsored loans and scholarships/grants available. Financial award applicants required to submit FAFSA. *Unit head:* Dr. Brian Lindquist, Associate Vice President and Dean/Executive Director, 480-557-1221, E-mail: brian.lindquist@phoenix.edu. *Application contact:* Chair, 702-638-7249, Fax: 702-638-8035.

University of Phoenix–Little Rock Campus, John Sperling School of Business, College of Graduate Business and Management, Little Rock, AR 72211-3500. Offers MBA, MM. Evening/weekend programs available. *Faculty:* 6 full-time (3 women), 85 part-time/adjunct (23 women). *Students:* 170 full-time (113 women); includes 89 minority (88 African Americans, 1 Asian American or Pacific Islander). Average age 33. In 2006, 32 degrees awarded. *Degree requirements:* For master's, thesis (for some programs), registration. *Entrance requirements:* For master's, minimum undergraduate GPA of 3.0, 3 years of work experience. Additional exam requirements/recommendations for international students: Required—TOEFL (minimum score 550 paper-based; 213 computer-based). *Application deadline:* Applications are processed on a rolling basis. Application fee: $45. Electronic applications accepted. *Expenses:* Tuition: Full-time $9,576. Required fees: $760. *Financial support:* Institutionally sponsored loans and scholarships/grants available. Financial award applicants required to submit FAFSA. *Unit head:* Dr. Brian Lindquist, Associate Vice President/Dean/Executive Director, 480-557-1221, E-mail: brian.lindquist@phoenix.edu. *Application contact:* Campus College Chair, 501-225-9337.

University of Phoenix–Louisiana Campus, John Sperling School of Business, College of Graduate Business and Management, Metairie, LA 70001-2082. Offers business administration (MBA); human resource management (MBA, MM); public administration (MBA). Evening/weekend programs available. *Faculty:* 14 full-time (6 women), 123 part-time/adjunct (40 women). *Students:* 445 full-time (325 women); includes 225 minority (218 African Americans, 6 Asian Americans or Pacific Islanders, 1 Hispanic American), 38 international. Average age 35. In 2006, 126 degrees awarded. *Degree requirements:* For master's, thesis (for some programs), registration. *Entrance requirements:* For master's, minimum undergraduate GPA of 3.0, 3 years work experience. Additional exam requirements/recommendations for international students: Required—TOEFL (minimum score 550 paper-based; 213 computer-based; 79 iBT). *Application deadline:* Applications are processed on a rolling basis. Application fee: $45. Electronic applications accepted. *Expenses:* Tuition: Full-time $11,832. Required fees: $760. *Financial support:* Institutionally sponsored loans and scholarships/grants available. Financial award applicants required to submit FAFSA. *Unit head:* Dr. Brian Lindquist, Associate Vice President and Dean/Executive Director, 480-557-1221, E-mail: brian.linguist@phoenix.edu. *Application contact:* Chair, 504-461-8852, Fax: 504-464-6373.

University of Phoenix–Louisville Campus, College of Graduate Business and Management, Louisville, KY 40223-3839. Offers business and management (MBA, MM); e-business (MBA).

University of Phoenix–Madison Campus, College of Graduate Business and Management, Madison, WI 53718-2416. Offers accounting (MBA); business and management (MBA, MM); e-business (MBA); global management (MBA); human resources management (MBA, MM); marketing (MBA); public administration (MBA).

University of Phoenix–Maryland Campus, John Sperling School of Business, College of Graduate Business and Management, Columbia, MD 21045-5424. Offers business administration (MBA); e-business (MBA); global management (MBA); human resources management (MBA, MM); marketing (MBA); public administration (MBA, MM). Evening/weekend programs available. *Faculty:* 22 full-time (6 women), 136 part-time/adjunct (35 women). *Students:* 357 full-time (223 women); includes 148 minority (128 African Americans, 2 American Indian/Alaska Native, 9 Asian Americans or Pacific Islanders, 9 Hispanic Americans), 38 international. Average age 37. In 2006, 111 master's awarded. *Degree requirements:* For master's, thesis (for some programs), registration. *Entrance requirements:* For master's, minimum undergraduate GPA of 3.0, 3 years of work experience. Additional exam requirements/recommendations for international students: Required—TOEFL (minimum score 550 paper-based; 213 computer-based; 79 iBT). *Application deadline:* Applications are processed on a rolling basis. Application fee: $45. Electronic applications accepted. *Expenses:* Tuition: Full-time $13,200. Required fees: $760. *Financial support:* Institutionally sponsored loans and scholarships/grants available. Financial award applicants required to submit FAFSA. *Unit head:* Dr. Brian Lindquist, Associate Vice President and Dean/Executive Director, 480-557-1221, E-mail: brian.lindquist@phoenix.edu. *Application contact:* Chair, 410-872-9001, Fax: 410-536-5727.

University of Phoenix–Memphis Campus, College of Graduate Business and Management, Cordova, TN 38018. Offers acounting (MBA); business and management (MBA); e-business (MBA); global management (MBA); human resources management (MBA, MM); marketing (MBA); public administration (MBA, MM).

University of Phoenix–Metro Detroit Campus, John Sperling School of Business, College of Graduate Business and Management, Troy, MI 48098-2623. Offers business administration (MBA); global management (MBA). Evening/weekend programs available. *Faculty:* 32 full-time (9 women), 223 part-time/adjunct (61 women). *Students:* 607 full-time (394 women); includes 267 minority (254 African Americans, 3 American Indian/Alaska Native, 7 Asian Americans or Pacific Islanders, 3 Hispanic Americans), 19 international. Average age 39. In 2006, 216 master's awarded. *Degree requirements:* For master's, thesis (for some programs), registration. *Entrance requirements:* For master's, minimum undergraduate GPA of 3.0, 3 years work experience. Additional exam requirements/recommendations for international students: Required—TOEFL (minimum score 550 paper-based; 213 computer-based; 79 iBT). *Application deadline:* Applications are processed on a rolling basis. Application fee: $45. Electronic applications accepted. *Expenses:* Tuition: Full-time $12,168. Required fees: $760. *Financial support:* Institutionally sponsored loans and scholarships/grants available. Financial award applicants required to submit FAFSA. *Unit head:* Dr. Brian Lindquist, Associate Vice President and Dean/Executive Director, 480-557-1221, E-mail: brian.lindquist@phoenix.edu. *Application contact:* Chair, 800-834-2438, Fax: 248-267-0147.

University of Phoenix–Metro Detroit Campus, John Sperling School of Business, College of Information Systems and Technology, Troy, MI 48098-2623. Offers management (MIS); technology management (MBA). Evening/weekend programs available. *Faculty:* 20 full-time (5 women), 98 part-time/adjunct (18 women). *Students:* 49 full-time (20 women); includes 19 minority (17 African Americans, 2 Asian Americans or Pacific Islanders), 7 international. Average age 38. In 2006, 32 degrees awarded. *Degree requirements:* For master's, thesis (for some programs), registration. *Entrance requirements:* For master's, minimum undergraduate GPA of 3.0, 3 years work experience. Additional exam requirements/recommendations for international students: Required—TOEFL (minimum score 550 paper-based; 213 computer-based; 79 iBT). *Application deadline:* Applications are processed on a rolling basis. Application fee: $45. Electronic applications accepted. *Expenses:* Tuition: Full-time $12,168. Required fees: $760. *Financial support:* Institutionally sponsored loans and scholarships/grants available. Financial award applicants required to submit FAFSA. *Unit head:* Dr. Adam Honea, Dean/Executive Director, 480-557-1659, E-mail: adam.honea@phoenix.edu. *Application contact:* Chair, 800-834-2438, Fax: 248-267-0147.

University of Phoenix–Minneapolis/St. Louis Park Campus, College of Graduate Business and Management, St. Louis Park, MN 55426. Offers accounting (MBA); business administration (MBA); global management (MBA); human resources management (MBA); marketing (MBA).

University of Phoenix–Nashville Campus, John Sperling School of Business, College of Graduate Business and Management, Nashville, TN 37214-5048. Offers business administration (MBA); human resource management (MBA); management (MM). Evening/weekend programs available. *Faculty:* 29 full-time (2 women), 66 part-time/adjunct (20 women). *Students:* 246 full-time (145 women); includes 95 minority (90 African Americans, 1 American Indian/Alaska Native, 1 Asian American or Pacific Islander, 3 Hispanic Americans), 7 international. Average age 36. In 2006, 61 degrees awarded. *Degree requirements:* For master's, thesis (for some programs), registration. *Entrance requirements:* For master's, minimum undergraduate GPA of 3.0, 3 years of work experience. Additional exam requirements/recommendations for international students: Required—TOEFL (minimum score 550 paper-based; 213 computer-based; 79 iBT). *Application deadline:* Applications are processed on a rolling basis. Application fee: $45. Electronic applications accepted. *Expenses:* Tuition: Full-time $10,104. Required fees: $760. *Financial support:* Institutionally sponsored loans and scholarships/grants available. Financial award applicants required to submit FAFSA. *Unit head:* Dr. Brian Lindquist, Associate Vice President and Dean/Executive Director, 480-557-1221. *Application contact:* Chair, 615-872-0188.

University of Phoenix–New Mexico Campus, John Sperling School of Business, College of Graduate Business and Management, Albuquerque, NM 87109-4645. Offers business administration (MBA); global management (MBA); human resource management (MBA). Evening/weekend programs available. *Faculty:* 25 full-time (6 women), 305 part-time/adjunct (77 women). *Students:* 507 full-time (273 women); includes 235 minority (12 African Americans, 9 American Indian/Alaska Native, 7 Asian Americans or Pacific Islanders, 207 Hispanic Americans), 21 international. Average age 37. In 2006, 129 degrees awarded. *Degree requirements:* For master's, thesis (for some programs), registration. *Entrance requirements:* For master's, 3 years of work experience, minimum undergraduate GPA of 3.0. Additional exam requirements/recommendations for international students: Required—TOEFL (minimum score 550 paper-based; 213 computer-based; 79 iBT). *Application deadline:* Applications are processed on a rolling basis. Application fee: $45. Electronic applications accepted. *Expenses:* Tuition: Full-

Business Administration and Management—General

University of Phoenix–New Mexico Campus (continued)
time $9,005. Required fees: $760. *Financial support:* Institutionally sponsored loans and scholarships/grants available. Financial award applicants required to submit FAFSA. *Unit head:* Dr. Brian Lindquist, Associate Vice President and Dean/Executive Director, 480-557-1221, E-mail: brian.lindquist@phoenix.edu. *Application contact:* Graduate Business Chair, 505-821-4800, Fax: 505-821-5551.

University of Phoenix–Northern Nevada Campus, College of Graduate Business and Management, Reno, NV 89511. Offers accounting (MBA); business and management (MBA); global management (MBA); human resources management (MBA, MM); management (MM); marketing (MBA); public administration (MBA, MM).

University of Phoenix–Northern Virginia Campus, College of Graduate Business and Management, Reston, VA 20190. Offers accounting (MBA); business administration (MBA); e-business (MBA); global management (MBA); human resources management (MBA, MM); management (MM); marketing (MBA); public administration (MBA).

University of Phoenix–Northern Virginia Campus, College of Information Systems and Technology, Reston, VA 20190. Offers information systems and technology (MIS); management (MIS); technology management (MBA).

University of Phoenix–North Florida Campus, John Sperling School of Business, College of Graduate Business and Management, Jacksonville, FL 32216-0959. Offers accounting (MBA); business administration (MBA); global management (MBA); human resources management (MBA, MM); management (MM); marketing (MBA); public administration (MBA). Evening/weekend programs available. *Faculty:* 40 full-time (15 women), 105 part-time/adjunct (25 women). *Students:* 392 full-time (237 women); includes 135 minority (117 African Americans, 1 American Indian/Alaska Native, 12 Asian Americans or Pacific Islanders, 5 Hispanic Americans), 20 international. Average age 31. In 2006, 134 degrees awarded. *Degree requirements:* For master's, thesis (for some programs), registration. *Entrance requirements:* For master's, minimum undergraduate GPA of 3.0, 3 years work experience. Additional exam requirements/recommendations for international students: Required—TOEFL (minimum score 550 paper-based; 213 computer-based; 79 iBT). *Application deadline:* Applications are processed on a rolling basis. Application fee: $45. Electronic applications accepted. *Financial support:* Institutionally sponsored loans available. Financial award applicants required to submit FAFSA. *Unit head:* Dr. Brian Lindquist, Associate Vice President and Dean/Executive Director, 480-557-1221, E-mail: brian.lindquist@phoenix.edu. *Application contact:* Chair, 904-636-6645, Fax: 904-636-0998.

University of Phoenix–North Florida Campus, John Sperling School of Business, College of Information Systems and Technology, Jacksonville, FL 32216-0959. Offers information systems (MIS); management (MIS). Evening/weekend programs available. *Faculty:* 20 full-time (5 women), 50 part-time/adjunct (6 women). *Students:* 20 full-time (3 women); includes 4 minority (3 African Americans, 1 Asian American or Pacific Islander), 3 international. Average age 36. In 2006, 4 master's awarded. *Degree requirements:* For master's, thesis (for some programs), registration. *Entrance requirements:* For master's, minimum undergraduate GPA of 3.0, 3 years work experience. Additional exam requirements/recommendations for international students: Required—TOEFL (minimum score 550 paper-based; 213 computer-based; 79 iBT). *Application deadline:* Applications are processed on a rolling basis. Application fee: $45. Electronic applications accepted. *Financial support:* Institutionally sponsored loans and scholarships/grants available. Financial award applicants required to submit FAFSA. *Unit head:* Dr. Adam Honea, Dean, 480-557-1659, E-mail: adam.honea@phoenix.edu. *Application contact:* Chair, 904-636-6645, Fax: 904-636-0998.

University of Phoenix–Northwest Arkansas Campus, College of Graduate Business and Management, Rogers, AR 72756-9615. Offers accounting (MBA); business and management (MBA); global management (MBA); human resources management (MBA, MM); management (MM); marketing (MBA); public administration (MBA, MM).

University of Phoenix–Northwest Indiana, College of Graduate Business and Management, Merrillville, IN 46410. Offers business and management (MBA, MM); human resources management (MM); public administration (MBA, MM).

University of Phoenix–Oklahoma City Campus, John Sperling School of Business, College of Graduate Business and Management, Oklahoma City, OK 73116-8244. Offers business administration (MBA); business and management (MM); human resource management (MBA). Evening/weekend programs available. *Faculty:* 10 full-time (0 women), 135 part-time/adjunct (33 women). *Students:* 150 full-time (92 women); includes 45 minority (32 African Americans, 3 American Indian/Alaska Native, 4 Asian Americans or Pacific Islanders, 6 Hispanic Americans), 12 international. Average age 37. In 2006, 41 degrees awarded. *Degree requirements:* For master's, thesis (for some programs), registration. *Entrance requirements:* For master's, minimum undergraduate GPA of 3.0, 3 years of work experience. Additional exam requirements/recommendations for international students: Required—TOEFL (minimum score 550 paper-based; 213 computer-based; 79 iBT). *Application deadline:* Applications are processed on a rolling basis. Application fee: $45. Electronic applications accepted. *Expenses:* Tuition: Full-time $10,608. Required fees: $760. *Financial support:* Institutionally sponsored loans and scholarships/grants available. Financial award applicants required to submit FAFSA. *Unit head:* Dr. Brian Lindquist, Associate Vice President and Dean/Executive Director, 480-557-1221, E-mail: brian.lindquist@phoenix.edu. *Application contact:* Chair, 405-842-8007, Fax: 405-841-3386.

University of Phoenix–Omaha Campus, College of Graduate Business and Management, Omaha, NE 68154-5240. Offers accounting (MBA); business and management (MBA); global management (MBA); human resources management (MM); human resources managemetn (MBA); management (MM); marketing (MBA); public administration (MM); public adminstration (MBA).

University of Phoenix Online Campus, John Sperling School of Business, College of Graduate Business and Management, Phoenix, AZ 85034-7209. Offers accounting (MBA); administration (MBA); global management (MBA); human resources management (MBA); management (MM); marketing (MBA); public administration (MBA, MM). Evening/weekend programs available. *Faculty:* 25 full-time (15 women), 4,861 part-time/adjunct (1,504 women). *Students:* 17,914 full-time (10,655 women); includes 4,983 minority (3,259 African Americans, 113 American Indian/Alaska Native, 651 Asian Americans or Pacific Islanders, 960 Hispanic Americans), 1,805 international. Average age 36. In 2006, 1,740 master's awarded. *Degree requirements:* For master's, thesis (for some programs), registration. *Entrance requirements:* For master's, 3 years of work experience, minimum undergraduate GPA of 3.0. Additional exam requirements/recommendations for international students: Required—TOEFL (minimum score 550 paper-based; 213 computer-based; 79 iBT). *Application deadline:* Applications are processed on a rolling basis. Application fee: $45. Electronic applications accepted. *Expenses:* Tuition: Full-time $12,664. Required fees: $760. *Financial support:* Institutionally sponsored loans and scholarships/grants available. Financial award applicants required to submit FAFSA. *Unit head:* Brian Lindquist, Dean/Executive Director and Associate Vice President, 480-557-1221, E-mail: brian.lindquist@phoenix.edu. *Application contact:* Brian Lindquist, Dean/Executive Director and Associate Vice President, 480-557-1221, E-mail: brian.lindquist@phoenix.edu.

University of Phoenix Online Campus, John Sperling School of Business, College of Information Systems and Technology, Phoenix, AZ 85034-7209. Offers e-business (MBA); management (MIS); technology management (MBA). Evening/weekend programs available. *Faculty:* 7 full-time (3 women), 2,317 part-time/adjunct (528 women). *Students:* 4,315 full-time (1,423 women); includes 967 minority (552 African Americans, 19 American Indian/Alaska Native, 222 Asian Americans or Pacific Islanders, 174 Hispanic Americans), 581 international. Average age 38. In 2006, 7359 degrees awarded. *Degree requirements:* For master's, thesis (for some programs), registration. *Entrance requirements:* For master's, 3 years of work experience, minimum undergraduate GPA of 3.0. Additional exam requirements/recommendations for international students: Required—TOEFL (minimum score 550 paper-based; 213 computer-based; 79 iBT). *Application deadline:* Applications are processed on a rolling basis. Application fee: $45. Electronic applications accepted. *Expenses:* Tuition: Full-time $12,664. Required fees: $760. *Financial support:* Institutionally sponsored loans and scholarships/grants available. Financial award applicants required to submit FAFSA. *Unit head:* Dr. Adam Honea, Dean/Executive Director, 480-557-1659, E-mail: adam.honea@phoenix.edu. *Application contact:* Dr. Adam Honea, Dean/Executive Director, 480-557-1659, E-mail: adam.honea@phoenix.edu.

University of Phoenix Online Campus, School of Advanced Studies, Phoenix, AZ 85034-7209. Offers business administration (DBA); education (Ed D); health administration (DHA); organizational management (DM). Evening/weekend programs available. *Faculty:* 36 full-time (13 women), 551 part-time/adjunct (224 women). *Students:* 4,544 full-time (2,756 women); includes 1,550 minority (1,136 African Americans, 32 American Indian/Alaska Native, 152 Asian Americans or Pacific Islanders, 230 Hispanic Americans), 378 international. Average age 44. In 2006, 210 degrees awarded. *Degree requirements:* For doctorate, thesis/dissertation. *Entrance requirements:* For doctorate, 3 letters of recommendation, minimum master's GPA of 3.0, 3 years professional work experience. Additional exam requirements/recommendations for international students: Required—TOEFL (minimum score 550 paper-based; 213 computer-based; 79 iBT). *Application deadline:* Applications are processed on a rolling basis. Application fee: $45. Electronic applications accepted. *Expenses:* Tuition: Full-time $12,664. Required fees: $760. *Financial support:* Institutionally sponsored loans and scholarships/grants available. Financial award applicants required to submit FAFSA. *Unit head:* Dr. Dawn Iwamoto, Dean/Executive Director, 480-557-3228, E-mail: dawn.iwamoto@phoenix.edu. *Application contact:* Information Contact, 800-697-8223.

University of Phoenix–Oregon Campus, The John Sperling School of Business, College of Graduate Business and Management, Tigard, OR 97223. Offers accounting (MBA); business administration (MBA); global management (MBA); human resource management (MM); human resources management (MBA); management (MM). Evening/weekend programs available. *Faculty:* 28 full-time (4 women), 104 part-time/adjunct (24 women). *Students:* 241 full-time (103 women); includes 31 minority (7 African Americans, 4 American Indian/Alaska Native, 14 Asian Americans or Pacific Islanders, 6 Hispanic Americans), 21 international. Average age 39. In 2006, 66 degrees awarded. *Degree requirements:* For master's, thesis (for some programs), registration. *Entrance requirements:* For master's, minimum undergraduate GPA of 3.0, 3 years of work experience. Additional exam requirements/recommendations for international students: Required—TOEFL (minimum score 550 paper-based; 213 computer-based; 79 iBT). *Application deadline:* Applications are processed on a rolling basis. Application fee: $45. Electronic applications accepted. *Expenses:* Tuition: Full-time $10,200. Required fees: $760. *Financial support:* Institutionally sponsored loans and scholarships/grants available. Financial award applicants required to submit FAFSA. *Unit head:* Dr. Brian Lindquist, Associate Vice President and Dean/Executive Director, 480-557-1221, E-mail: brian.lindquist@phoenix.edu. *Application contact:* Chair, 503-403-2900, Fax: 503-670-0614.

University of Phoenix–Philadelphia Campus, The John Sperling School of Business, College of Graduate Business and Management, Wayne, PA 19087-2121. Offers business administration (MBA); global management (MBA); management (MM). Evening/weekend programs available. *Faculty:* 21 full-time (4 women), 85 part-time/adjunct (19 women). *Students:* 271 full-time (160 women); includes 96 minority (86 African Americans, 3 American Indian/Alaska Native, 5 Asian Americans or Pacific Islanders, 2 Hispanic Americans), 18 international. Average age 36. In 2006, 102 degrees awarded. *Degree requirements:* For master's, thesis (for some programs), registration. *Entrance requirements:* For master's, minimum undergraduate GPA of 3.0, 3 years work experience. Additional exam requirements/recommendations for international students: Required—TOEFL (minimum score 550 paper-based; 213 computer-based; 79 iBT). *Application deadline:* Applications are processed on a rolling basis. Application fee: $45. Electronic applications accepted. *Expenses:* Tuition: Full-time $13,560. Required fees: $760. *Financial support:* Institutionally sponsored loans and scholarships/grants available. Financial award applicants required to submit FAFSA. *Unit head:* Dr. Brian Lindquist, Associate Vice President and Dean/Executive Director, 480-557-1221, E-mail: brian.lindquist@phoenix.edu. *Application contact:* Campus College Chair, 610-984-0880, Fax: 610-989-0881.

University of Phoenix–Phoenix Campus, The John Sperling School of Business, College of Graduate Business and Management, Phoenix, AZ 85040-1958. Offers business administration (MBA); management (MM). Evening/weekend programs available. *Faculty:* 63 full-time (14 women), 833 part-time/adjunct (228 women). *Students:* 1,291 full-time (615 women); includes 265 minority (73 African Americans, 12 American Indian/Alaska Native, 55 Asian Americans or Pacific Islanders, 125 Hispanic Americans), 86 international. Average age 35. In 2006, 496 degrees awarded. *Degree requirements:* For master's, thesis (for some programs), registration. *Entrance requirements:* For master's, 3 years of work experience, minimum undergraduate GPA of 3.0. Additional exam requirements/recommendations for international students: Required—TOEFL (minimum score 550 paper-based; 213 computer-based; 79 iBT). *Application deadline:* Applications are processed on a rolling basis. Application fee: $45. Electronic applications accepted. *Financial support:* Institutionally sponsored loans and scholarships/grants available. Financial award applicants required to submit FAFSA. *Unit head:* Dr. Brian Lindquist, Dean/Executive Director, 480-557-1221, E-mail: brian.lindquist@phoenix.edu. *Application contact:* Campus College Chair, 480-804-7400, Fax: 480-557-2320.

University of Phoenix–Phoenix Campus, The John Sperling School of Business, College of Information Systems and Technology, Phoenix, AZ 85040-1958. Offers management (MIS). Evening/weekend programs available. *Faculty:* 24 full-time (3 women), 393 part-time/adjunct (63 women). *Students:* 30 full-time (9 women); includes 6 minority (4 African Americans, 1 American Indian/Alaska Native, 1 Hispanic American), 3 international. Average age 40. In 2006, 65 degrees awarded. *Degree requirements:* For master's, thesis (for some programs), registration. *Entrance requirements:* For master's, 3 years of work experience, minimum undergraduate GPA of 3.0. Additional exam requirements/recommendations for international students: Required—TOEFL (minimum score 550 paper-based; 213 computer-based; 79 iBT). *Application deadline:* Applications are processed on a rolling basis. Application fee: $45. Electronic applications accepted. *Financial support:* Institutionally sponsored loans and scholarships/grants available. Financial award applicants required to submit FAFSA. *Unit head:* Dr. Adam Honea, Provost, 480-557-1659, E-mail: adam.honea@phoenix.edu. *Application contact:* Campus College Chair, 480-804-7400, Fax: 480-557-2320.

University of Phoenix–Pittsburgh Campus, John Sperling School of Business, College of Graduate Business and Management, Pittsburgh, PA 15276. Offers accounting (MBA); business administration (MBA); global management (MBA); human resource management (MBA); human resources management (MM); management (MM); marketing (MBA); public administration (MBA, MM). Evening/weekend programs available. *Faculty:* 19 full-time (6 women), 49 part-time/adjunct (13 women). *Students:* 84 full-time (43 women); includes 16 minority (13 African Americans, 2 Asian Americans or Pacific Islanders, 1 Hispanic American), 4 international. Average age 37. In 2006, 35 degrees awarded. *Degree requirements:* For master's, thesis (for some programs), registration. *Entrance requirements:* For master's, minimum undergraduate GPA of 3.0, 3 years work experience. Additional exam requirements/recommendations for international students: Required—TOEFL (minimum score 550 paper-based; 213 computer-based; 79 iBT). *Application deadline:* Applications are processed on a rolling basis. Application fee: $45. Electronic applications accepted. *Expenses:* Tuition: Full-time $13,560. Required fees: $760. *Financial support:* Institutionally sponsored loans and scholarships/grants available. Financial award applicants required to submit FAFSA. *Unit head:* Dr. Brian Lindquist, Associate Vice President and Dean/Executive Director, 480-551-1221, E-mail: brian.lindquist@phoenix.edu. *Application contact:* College Chair, 412-747-9000, Fax: 412-747-0676.

University of Phoenix–Puerto Rico Campus, John Sperling School of Business, College of Graduate Business and Management, Guaynabo, PR 00968. Offers accounting (MBA); business administration (MBA); global management (MBA); human resource management (MBA); marketing (MBA). Evening/weekend programs available. *Faculty:* 19 full-time (8 women), 73 part-time/adjunct (25 women). *Students:* 1,122 full-time (671 women); includes 636 minority (2 African Americans, 3 American Indian/Alaska Native, 3 Asian Americans or Pacific Islanders, 628 Hispanic Americans), 31 international. Average age 34. In 2006, 281 degrees awarded. *Degree requirements:* For master's, thesis (for some programs), registration. *Entrance requirements:* For master's, minimum undergraduate GPA of 3.0, 3 years work experience. Additional exam requirements/recommendations for international students: Required—TOEFL (minimum score 550 paper-based; 213 computer-based; 79 iBT). *Application deadline:* Applications are processed on a rolling basis. Application fee: $45. Electronic applications accepted. *Expenses:* Tuition: Full-time $5,816. Required fees: $760. *Financial support:* Institutionally sponsored loans and scholarships/grants available. Financial award applicants required to submit FAFSA. *Unit head:* Dr. Brian Lindquist, Associate Vice President and Dean/Executive Director, 480-557-1221, E-mail: brian.lindquist@phoenix.edu. *Application contact:* Chair, 787-931-5400, Fax: 787-931-1510.

University of Phoenix–Raleigh Campus, College of Graduate Business and Management, Raleigh, NC 27606. Offers accounting (MBA); business administration (MBA); e-business (MBA); global management (MBA).

University of Phoenix–Raleigh Campus, College of Information Systems and Technology, Raleigh, NC 27606. Offers information systems and technology (MIS); management (MIS); technology management (MBA).

University of Phoenix–Renton Learning Center, College of Graduate Business and Management, Renton, WA 98005. Offers accounting (MBA); business and management (MBA, MM); global management (MBA); human resources management (MBA, MM); marketing (MBA); public administration (MBA, MM).

University of Phoenix–Richmond Campus, John Sperling School of Business, College of Graduate Business and Management, Richmond, VA 23230. Offers accounting (MBA); business administration (MBA); global management (MBA); human resources management (MBA, MM); management (MM); marketing (MBA); public administration (MBA, MM). Evening/weekend programs available. *Faculty:* 6 full-time (4 women), 60 part-time/adjunct (7 women). *Students:* 103 full-time (73 women); includes 42 minority (38 African Americans, 1 American Indian/Alaska Native, 2 Asian Americans or Pacific Islanders, 1 Hispanic American), 10 international. Average age 36. In 2006, 1 degree awarded. *Degree requirements:* For master's, thesis (for some programs), registration. *Entrance requirements:* For master's, minimum undergraduate GPA 3.0, 3 years work experience. Additional exam requirements/recommendations for international students: Required—TOEFL (minimum score 550 paper-based; 213 computer-based; 79 iBT). *Application deadline:* Applications are processed on a rolling basis. Application fee: $45. Electronic applications accepted. *Financial support:* Institutionally sponsored loans and scholarships/grants available. Financial award applicants required to submit FAFSA. *Unit head:* Dr. Brian Lindquist, Associate Vice President/Dean, 480-557-1221, E-mail: brian.lindquist@phoenix.edu. *Application contact:* Chair, 804-288-3390.

University of Phoenix–Sacramento Valley Campus, John Sperling School of Business, College of Graduate Business and Management, Sacramento, CA 95833-3632. Offers accounting (MBA); business administration (MBA); global management (MBA); human resources management (MBA); marketing (MBA); public administration (MBA). Evening/weekend programs available. *Faculty:* 36 full-time (19 women), 291 part-time/adjunct (83 women). *Students:* 395 full-time (197 women); includes 120 minority (62 African Americans, 2 American Indian/Alaska Native, 32 Asian Americans or Pacific Islanders, 24 Hispanic Americans), 34 international. Average age 37. In 2006, 138 master's awarded. *Degree requirements:* For master's, thesis (for some programs), registration. *Entrance requirements:* For master's, minimum undergraduate GPA of 3.0, 3 years work experience. Additional exam requirements/recommendations for international students: Required—TOEFL (minimum score 550 paper-based; 213 computer-based; 79 iBT). *Application deadline:* Applications are processed on a rolling basis. Application fee: $45. Electronic applications accepted. *Expenses:* Tuition: Full-time $12,024. Required fees: $760. *Financial support:* Institutionally sponsored loans and scholarships/grants available. Financial award applicants required to submit FAFSA. *Unit head:* Dr. Brian Lindquist, Associate Vice President and Dean/Executive Director, 480-557-1221, E-mail: brian.lindquist@phoenix.edu. *Application contact:* Campus College Chair, 916-923-2107, Fax: 916-923-3914.

University of Phoenix–Sacramento Valley Campus, John Sperling School of Business, College of Information Systems and Technology, Sacramento, CA 95833-3632. Offers management (MIS); technology management (MBA). Evening/weekend programs available. *Faculty:* 15 full-time (4 women), 144 part-time/adjunct (25 women). *Students:* 19 full-time (2 women); includes 8 minority (4 African Americans, 3 Asian Americans or Pacific Islanders, 1 Hispanic American), 2 international. Average age 41. In 2006, 22 degrees awarded. *Degree requirements:* For master's, thesis (for some programs), registration. *Entrance requirements:* For master's, minimum undergraduate GPA of 3.0, 3 years work experience. Additional exam requirements/recommendations for international students: Required—TOEFL (minimum score 550 paper-based; 213 computer-based; 79 iBT). *Application deadline:* Applications are processed on a rolling basis. Application fee: $45. Electronic applications accepted. *Expenses:* Tuition: Full-time $12,024. Required fees: $760. *Financial support:* Institutionally sponsored loans and scholarships/grants available. Financial award applicants required to submit FAFSA. *Unit head:* Dr. Adam Honea, Provost/Dean, Vice President Academic Research and Development, 480-557-1659, E-mail: adam.honea@phoenix.edu. *Application contact:* Campus College Chair, 916-923-2107, Fax: 916-923-3914.

University of Phoenix–St. Louis Campus, John Sperling School of Business, College of Graduate Business and Management, St. Louis, MO 63043-4828. Offers business administration (MBA). Evening/weekend programs available. *Faculty:* 14 full-time (8 women), 64 part-time/adjunct (14 women). *Students:* 129 full-time (88 women); includes 34 minority (26 African Americans, 1 American Indian/Alaska Native, 5 Asian Americans or Pacific Islanders, 2 Hispanic Americans), 4 international. Average age 36. In 2006, 57 master's awarded. *Degree requirements:* For master's, thesis (for some programs), registration. *Entrance requirements:* For master's, 3 years of work experience, minimum undergraduate GPA of 3.0. Additional exam requirements/recommendations for international students: Required—TOEFL (minimum score 550 paper-based; 213 computer-based; 79 iBT). *Application deadline:* Applications are processed on a rolling basis. Application fee: $45. Electronic applications accepted. *Expenses:* Tuition: Full-time $11,832. Required fees: $762. *Financial support:* Institutionally sponsored loans available. Financial award applicants required to submit FAFSA. *Unit head:* Dr. Brian Lindquist, Associate Vice President and Dean/Executive Director, 480-557-1221, E-mail: brain.lindquist@phoenix.edu. *Application contact:* Campus College Chair—Graduate Business, 314-298-9755, Fax: 314-291-2901.

University of Phoenix–San Antonio Campus, College of Graduate Business and Management, San Antonio, TX 78230. Offers accounting (MBA); business and management (MBA); e-business (MBA); global management (MBA); human resources management (MBA, MM); management (MM); marketing (MBA); public administration (MBA, MM).

University of Phoenix–San Diego Campus, John Sperling School of Business, College of Graduate Business and Management, San Diego, CA 92123. Offers business administration (MBA); global management (MBA); management (MM). Evening/weekend programs available. *Faculty:* 39 full-time (4 women), 217 part-time/adjunct (39 women). *Students:* 437 full-time (211 women); includes 139 minority (32 African Americans, 2 American Indian/Alaska Native, 48 Asian Americans or Pacific Islanders, 57 Hispanic Americans), 24 international. Average age 36. In 2006, 127 degrees awarded. *Degree requirements:* For master's, thesis (for some programs), registration. *Entrance requirements:* For master's, 3 years of work experience, minimum undergraduate GPA of 3.0. Additional exam requirements/recommendations for international students: Required—TOEFL (minimum score 550 paper-based; 213 computer-based; 79 iBT). *Application deadline:* Applications are processed on a rolling basis. Application fee: $45. Electronic applications accepted. *Expenses:* Tuition: Full-time $11,419. Required fees: $760. *Financial support:* Institutionally sponsored loans and scholarships/grants available. Financial award applicants required to submit FAFSA. *Unit head:* Dr. Brian Lindquist, Associate Vice President and Dean/Executive Director, 480-557-1221, E-mail: brian.lindquist@phoenix.edu. *Application contact:* Campus Information Center, 888-UOP-INFO, Fax: 858-509-4399.

University of Phoenix–San Diego Campus, John Sperling School of Business, College of Information Systems and Technology, San Diego, CA 92123. Offers management (MIS); technology management (MBA). Evening/weekend programs available. *Faculty:* 13 full-time (0 women), 133 part-time/adjunct (13 women). *Students:* 23 full-time (4 women); includes 3 minority (1 African American, 2 Hispanic Americans), 1 international. Average age 40. In 2006, 39 degrees awarded. *Degree requirements:* For master's, thesis (for some programs), registration. *Entrance requirements:* For master's, minimum undergraduate GPA of 3.0, 3 years work experience. Additional exam requirements/recommendations for international students: Required—TOEFL (minimum score 550 paper-based; 213 computer-based; 79 iBT). *Application deadline:* Applications are processed on a rolling basis. Application fee: $45. Electronic applications accepted. *Expenses:* Tuition: Full-time $11,419. Required fees: $760. *Financial support:* Institutionally sponsored loans and scholarships/grants available. Financial award applicants required to submit FAFSA. *Unit head:* Dr. Adam Honea, Provost/Dean, Vice President Academic Research and Development, 480-557-1659, E-mail: adam.honea@phoenix.edu. *Application contact:* Campus College Chair, 888-UOP-INFO, Fax: 858-509-4399.

University of Phoenix–Savannah Campus, College of Graduate Business and Management, Savannah, GA 31405-7400. Offers accounting (MBA); business administration (MBA); business and management (MM); global management (MBA); human resources management (MBA, MM); marketing (MBA); public administration (MBA, MM).

University of Phoenix–Southern Arizona Campus, John Sperling School of Business, College of Graduate Business and Management, Tucson, AZ 85712-2732. Offers accounting (MBA); business administration (MBA); global management (MBA); management (MM). Evening/weekend programs available. *Faculty:* 29 full-time (13 women), 207 part-time/adjunct (40 women). *Students:* 412 full-time (205 women); includes 107 minority (23 African Americans, 7 American Indian/Alaska Native, 10 Asian Americans or Pacific Islanders, 67 Hispanic Americans), 24 international. Average age 36. In 2006, 141 degrees awarded. *Degree requirements:* For master's, thesis (for some programs), registration. *Entrance requirements:* For master's, minimum undergraduate GPA of 3.0, 3 years of work experience. Additional exam requirements/recommendations for international students: Required—TOEFL (minimum score 550 paper-based; 213 computer-based; 79 iBT). *Application deadline:* Applications are processed on a rolling basis. Application fee: $45. Electronic applications accepted. *Expenses:* Tuition: Full-time $8,669. Required fees: $760. *Financial support:* Institutionally sponsored loans and scholarships/grants available. Financial award applicants required to submit FAFSA. *Unit head:* Dr. Brian Lindquist, Associate Vice President and Dean/Executive Director, 480-557-1221, E-mail: brian.lindquist@phoenix.edu. *Application contact:* Campus College Chair, 520-881-6512, Fax: 520-795-6177.

University of Phoenix–Southern California Campus, John Sperling School of Business, College of Graduate Business and Management, Costa Mesa, CA 92626. Offers accounting (MBA); business administration (MBA); business and management (MM); human resource management (MBA); marketing (MBA). Evening/weekend programs available. *Faculty:* 47 full-time (13 women), 513 part-time/adjunct (138 women). *Students:* 1,491 full-time (852 women); includes 558 minority (233 African Americans, 7 American Indian/Alaska Native, 124 Asian Americans or Pacific Islanders, 194 Hispanic Americans), 116 international. Average age 38. In 2006, 401 degrees awarded. *Degree requirements:* For master's, thesis (for some programs), registration. *Entrance requirements:* For master's, minimum undergraduate GPA of 3.0, 3 years work experience. Additional exam requirements/recommendations for international students: Required—TOEFL (minimum score 550 paper-based; 213 computer-based; 79 iBT). *Application deadline:* Applications are processed on a rolling basis. Application fee: $45. Electronic applications accepted. *Expenses:* Tuition: Full-time $13,512. Required fees: $760. *Financial support:* Institutionally sponsored loans and scholarships/grants available. Financial award applicants required to submit FAFSA. *Unit head:* Dr. Brian Lindquist, Associate Vice President and Dean/Executive Director, 480-557-1221, E-mail: brian.lindquist@phoenix.edu. *Application contact:* Campus College Chair, 714-378-1878, Fax: 714-378-5875.

University of Phoenix–Southern Colorado Campus, John Sperling School of Business, College of Graduate Business and Management, Colorado Springs, CO 80919-2335. Offers business administration (MBA). Evening/weekend programs available. *Faculty:* 209 part-time/adjunct (51 women). *Students:* 107 full-time (53 women); includes 21 minority (8 African Americans, 1 American Indian/Alaska Native, 5 Asian Americans or Pacific Islanders, 7 Hispanic Americans), 4 international. Average age 38. In 2006, 47 master's awarded. *Degree requirements:* For master's, thesis (for some programs), registration. *Entrance requirements:* For master's, minimum undergraduate GPA of 3.0, 3 years of work experience. Additional exam requirements/recommendations for international students: Required—TOEFL (minimum score 550 paper-based; 213 computer-based; 79 iBT). *Application deadline:* Applications are processed on a rolling basis. Application fee: $45. Electronic applications accepted. *Expenses:* Tuition: Full-time $10,291. Required fees: $760. *Financial support:* Institutionally sponsored loans and scholarships/grants available. Financial award applicants required to submit FAFSA. *Unit head:* Dr. Brian Lindquist, Associate Vice President and Dean/Executive Director, 480-557-1221, E-mail: brian.lindquist@phoenix.edu. *Application contact:* Chair, 719-599-5282, Fax: 719-599-7973.

University of Phoenix–Springfield Campus, College of Graduate Business and Management, Springfield, MO 65804-7211. Offers accounting (MBA); business and management (MBA); global management (MBA); human resources management (MBA, MM); management (MM); marketing (MBA); public administration (MBA, MM).

University of Phoenix–Tulsa Campus, John Sperling School of Business, College of Graduate Business and Management, Tulsa, OK 74146-3801. Offers business administration (MBA); business and management (MM). Evening/weekend programs available. *Faculty:* 16 full-time (7 women), 160 part-time/adjunct (50 women). *Students:* 142 full-time (71 women); includes 30 minority (20 African Americans, 3 American Indian/Alaska Native, 2 Asian Americans or Pacific Islanders, 5 Hispanic Americans), 17 international. Average age 38. In 2006, 50 degrees awarded. *Degree requirements:* For master's, thesis (for some programs), registration. *Entrance requirements:* For master's, minimum undergraduate GPA of 3.0, 3 years work experience. Additional exam requirements/recommendations for international students: Required—TOEFL (minimum score 550 paper-based; 213 computer-based; 79 iBT). *Application deadline:* Applications are processed on a rolling basis. Application fee: $45. *Expenses:* Tuition: Full-time $10,608. Required fees: $760. *Financial support:* Institutionally sponsored loans and scholarships/grants available. Financial award applicants required to submit FAFSA. *Unit head:* Dr. Brian Lindquist, Associate Vice President and Dean/Executive Director, 480-557-1221, E-mail: brian.lindquist@phoenix.edu. *Application contact:* Campus College Chair, 918-622-4877, Fax: 918-622-4981.

University of Phoenix–Utah Campus, The Artemis School, College of Health and Human Services, Salt Lake City, UT 84123-4617. Offers business administration healthcare (MSN); mental health counseling (MSC); nursing (MSN). Evening/weekend programs available. *Faculty:* 25 full-time (8 women), 105 part-time/adjunct (46 women). *Students:* 381 full-time (264 women); includes 20 minority (2 African Americans, 1 American Indian/Alaska Native, 8 Asian Americans or Pacific Islanders, 9 Hispanic Americans), 9 international. Average age 38. In 2006, 59 degrees awarded. *Degree requirements:* For master's, thesis (for some programs), registration. *Entrance requirements:* For master's, minimum undergraduate GPA of 2.5, 3 years work experience, RN license. Additional exam requirements/recommendations for international

Business Administration and Management—General

University of Phoenix–Utah Campus *(continued)*
students: Required—TOEFL (minimum score 550 paper-based; 213 computer-based; 79 iBT). *Application deadline:* Applications are processed on a rolling basis. Application fee: $45. Electronic applications accepted. *Expenses:* Tuition: Full-time $9,104. Required fees: $760. *Financial support:* Institutionally sponsored loans and scholarships/grants available. Financial award applicants required to submit FAFSA. *Unit head:* Dr. Gil Linne, Dean/Executive Director, 480-557-1751, E-mail: gil.linne@phoenix.edu. *Application contact:* Chair, 801-263-1444, Fax: 801-269-9766.

University of Phoenix–Utah Campus, John Sperling School of Business, College of Graduate Business and Management, Salt Lake City, UT 84123-4617. Offers business administration (MBA). Evening/weekend programs available. *Faculty:* 58 full-time (7 women), 155 part-time/adjunct (14 women). *Students:* 618 full-time (158 women); includes 32 minority (4 African Americans, 3 American Indian/Alaska Native, 14 Asian Americans or Pacific Islanders, 11 Hispanic Americans), 21 international. Average age 36. In 2006, 251 degrees awarded. *Degree requirements:* For master's, thesis (for some programs), registration. *Entrance requirements:* For master's, minimum undergraduate GPA of 3.0, 3 years of work experience. Additional exam requirements/recommendations for international students: Required—TOEFL (minimum score 550 paper-based; 213 computer-based; 79 iBT). *Application deadline:* Applications are processed on a rolling basis. Application fee: $45. Electronic applications accepted. *Expenses:* Tuition: Full-time $9,104. Required fees: $760. *Financial support:* Institutionally sponsored loans and scholarships/grants available. Financial award applicants required to submit FAFSA. *Unit head:* Dr. Brian Lindquist, Associate Vice President and Dean/Executive Director, 480-557-1221, E-mail: brian.lindquist@phoenix.edu. *Application contact:* Chair, 801-263-1444, Fax: 801-269-9766.

University of Phoenix–Vancouver Campus, John Sperling School of Business, College of Graduate Business and Management, Burnaby, BC V5C 6G9, Canada. Offers business administration (MBA). Evening/weekend programs available. *Faculty:* 39. *Students:* 101 full-time (38 women); includes 45 minority (2 African Americans, 1 American Indian/Alaska Native, 40 Asian Americans or Pacific Islanders, 2 Hispanic Americans). Average age 36. In 2006, 38 degrees awarded. *Degree requirements:* For master's, thesis (for some programs), registration. *Entrance requirements:* For master's, minimum undergraduate GPA of 3.0, 3 years of work experience. Additional exam requirements/recommendations for international students: Required—TOEFL (minimum score 550 paper-based; 213 computer-based; 79 iBT). *Application deadline:* Applications are processed on a rolling basis. Application fee: $45. Electronic applications accepted. *Expenses:* Tuition: Full-time $12,840. Required fees: $760. *Financial support:* Institutionally sponsored loans and scholarships/grants available. *Unit head:* Dr. Brian Lindquist, Associate Vice President and Dean/Executive Director, 480-557-1221, E-mail: brian.lindquist@phoenix.edu. *Application contact:* Chair, 604-205-6999.

University of Phoenix–Washington Campus, John Sperling School of Business, College of Graduate Business and Management, Seattle, WA 98188-7500. Offers business administration (MBA). Evening/weekend programs available. *Faculty:* 30 full-time (11 women), 117 part-time/adjunct (27 women). *Students:* 262 full-time (125 women); includes 57 minority (15 African Americans, 1 American Indian/Alaska Native, 27 Asian Americans or Pacific Islanders, 14 Hispanic Americans), 7 international. Average age 37. In 2006, 109 degrees awarded. *Degree requirements:* For master's, thesis (for some programs), registration. *Entrance requirements:* For master's, minimum undergraduate GPA of 3.0, 3 years of work experience. Additional exam requirements/recommendations for international students: Required—TOEFL (minimum score 550 paper-based; 213 computer-based; 79 iBT). *Application deadline:* Applications are processed on a rolling basis. Application fee: $45. Electronic applications accepted. *Expenses:* Tuition: Full-time $10,200. Required fees: $760. *Financial support:* Institutionally sponsored loans and scholarships/grants available. Financial award applicants required to submit FAFSA. *Unit head:* Dr. Brian Lindquist, Associate Vice President and Dean/Executive Director, 480-557-1221, E-mail: brian.lindquist@phoenix.edu. *Application contact:* Chair, 206-268-5800, Fax: 206-241-8848.

University of Phoenix–West Florida Campus, The John Sperling School of Business, College of Graduate Business and Management, Temple Terrace, FL 33637. Offers business administration (MBA); global management (MBA); human resource management (MBA); human resources management (MM); management (MM); marketing (MBA); public administration (MBA). Evening/weekend programs available. *Faculty:* 39 full-time (19 women), 145 part-time/adjunct (45 women). *Students:* 475 full-time (272 women); includes 150 minority (98 African Americans, 4 American Indian/Alaska Native, 9 Asian Americans or Pacific Islanders, 39 Hispanic Americans), 43 international. Average age 36. In 2006, 165 degrees awarded. *Degree requirements:* For master's, thesis (for some programs), registration. *Entrance requirements:* For master's, 3 years of work experience, minimum undergraduate GPA of 3.0. Additional exam requirements/recommendations for international students: Required—TOEFL (minimum score 550 paper-based; 213 computer-based; 79 iBT). *Application deadline:* Applications are processed on a rolling basis. Application fee: $45. Electronic applications accepted. *Expenses:* Tuition: Full-time $9,450. Required fees: $760. *Financial support:* Institutionally sponsored loans and scholarships/grants available. Financial award applicants required to submit FAFSA. *Unit head:* Dr. Brian Lindquist, Associate Vice President and Dean/Executive Director, 480-557-1221, E-mail: brian.lindquist@phoenix.edu. *Application contact:* Chair, 813-626-7911, Fax: 813-977-1449.

University of Phoenix–West Michigan Campus, The John Sperling School of Business, College of Graduate Business and Management, Walker, MI 49544. Offers accounting (MBA); business administration (MBA); global management (MBA); human resource management (MBA). Evening/weekend programs available. *Faculty:* 26 full-time (0 women), 95 part-time/adjunct (42 women). *Students:* 124 full-time (62 women); includes 16 minority (15 African Americans, 1 Hispanic American), 4 international. Average age 37. In 2006, 50 degrees awarded. *Degree requirements:* For master's, thesis (for some programs), registration. *Entrance requirements:* For master's, minimum undergraduate GPA of 3.0, 3 years work experience. Additional exam requirements/recommendations for international students: Required—TOEFL (minimum score 550 paper-based; 213 computer-based; 79 iBT). *Application deadline:* Applications are processed on a rolling basis. Application fee: $45. Electronic applications accepted. *Expenses:* Tuition: Full-time $12,043. Required fees: $760. *Financial support:* Institutionally sponsored loans and scholarships/grants available. Financial award applicants required to submit FAFSA. *Unit head:* Dr. Brian Lindquist, Associate Vice President and Dean/Executive Director, 480-557-1221, E-mail: brian.lindquist@phoenix.edu. *Application contact:* Chair, 888-345-9699, Fax: 616-784-5300.

University of Phoenix–Wichita Campus, John Sperling School of Business, College of Graduate Business and Management, Wichita, KS 67226-4011. Offers MBA. Evening/weekend programs available. *Faculty:* 8 full-time (1 woman), 55 part-time/adjunct (12 women). *Students:* 59 full-time (38 women); includes 11 minority (4 African Americans, 1 American Indian/Alaska Native, 5 Asian Americans or Pacific Islanders, 1 Hispanic American), 12 international. Average age 37. In 2006, 15 degrees awarded. *Degree requirements:* For master's, thesis (for some programs), registration. *Entrance requirements:* For master's, minimum undergraduate GPA of 3.0, 3 years of work experience. Additional exam requirements/recommendations for international students: Required—TOEFL (minimum score 550 paper-based; 213 computer-based; 79 iBT). *Application deadline:* Applications are processed on a rolling basis. Application fee: $45. Electronic applications accepted. *Expenses:* Tuition: Full-time $10,560. Required fees: $760. *Financial support:* Institutionally sponsored loans and scholarships/grants available. Financial award applicants required to submit FAFSA. *Unit head:* Dr. Brian Lindquist, Associate Vice President and Dean/Executive Director, 480-557-1221, E-mail: brian.lindquist@phoenix.edu. *Application contact:* Campus College Chair, 316-630-8121.

University of Phoenix–Wisconsin Campus, John Sperling School of Business, College of Graduate Business and Management, Brookfield, WI 53045-6608. Offers administration (MBA).

Evening/weekend programs available. *Faculty:* 15 full-time (10 women), 135 part-time/adjunct (48 women). *Students:* 245 full-time (137 women); includes 51 minority (37 African Americans, 5 American Indian/Alaska Native, 5 Asian Americans or Pacific Islanders, 4 Hispanic Americans), 9 international. Average age 35. In 2006, 64 degrees awarded. *Degree requirements:* For master's, thesis (for some programs), registration. *Entrance requirements:* For master's, 3 years of work experience, minimum undergraduate GPA of 3.0. Additional exam requirements/recommendations for international students: Required—TOEFL (minimum score 550 paper-based; 213 computer-based; 79 iBT). *Application deadline:* Applications are processed on a rolling basis. Application fee: $45. Electronic applications accepted. *Expenses:* Tuition: Full-time $10,944. Required fees: $760. *Financial support:* Institutionally sponsored loans and scholarships/grants available. Financial award applicants required to submit FAFSA. *Unit head:* Dr. Brian Lindquist, Associate Vice President/Dean, 480-557-1221, E-mail: brian.lindquist@phoenix.edu. *Application contact:* Chair, 262-785-0608, Fax: 262-785-0977.

University of Pittsburgh, Graduate School of Public and International Affairs, Executive Programs in Public Policy and Management, Pittsburgh, PA 15260. Offers development planning (MPPM); international development (MPPM); international political economy (MPPM); international security studies (MPPM); management of non profit organizations (MPPM); metropolitan management and regional development (MPPM); policy analysis and evaluation (MPPM). Part-time programs available. *Faculty:* 35 full-time (11 women), 16 part-time/adjunct (9 women). *Students:* 15 full-time (4 women), 32 part-time (14 women); includes 5 minority (3 African Americans, 1 Asian American or Pacific Islander, 1 Hispanic American), 4 international. Average age 38. 25 applicants, 76% accepted, 16 enrolled. In 2006, 26 degrees awarded. *Degree requirements:* For master's, capstone seminar, thesis optional. *Entrance requirements:* For master's, 2 letters of recommendation, resumé. Additional exam requirements/recommendations for international students: Required—TOEFL (minimum score 600 paper-based; 250 computer-based), TWE (minimum score 4); Recommended—IELTS (minimum score 7). *Application deadline:* For fall admission, 5/1 priority date for domestic students, 2/1 for international students; for spring admission, 10/1 priority date for domestic students, 8/1 for international students. Applications are processed on a rolling basis. Application fee: $50. Electronic applications accepted. *Financial support:* In 2006–07, 4 students received support, including 4 fellowships (averaging $5,308 per year), institutionally sponsored loans and scholarships/grants also available. Support available to part-time students. Financial award application deadline: 2/1. *Faculty research:* Executive training and technical assistance for U.S. and international clients. Total annual research expenditures: $1.1 million. *Unit head:* Michele Garrity, Director, Executive Education, 412-648-7610, Fax: 412-648-2605, E-mail: garrity@birch.gspia.pitt.edu. *Application contact:* Maureen O'Malley, Admissions Counselor, 412-648-7640, Fax: 412-648-7641, E-mail: pronobis@birch.gspia.pitt.edu.

University of Pittsburgh, Joseph M. Katz Graduate School of Business, Doctoral Program in Business Administration, Pittsburgh, PA 15260. Offers PhD. *Accreditation:* AACSB. *Faculty:* 56 full-time (12 women). *Students:* 59 full-time (22 women); includes 30 minority (1 African American, 4 Asian Americans or Pacific Islanders, 25 Hispanic Americans), 28 international. Average age 34. 221 applicants, 8% accepted, 9 enrolled. In 2006, 13 degrees awarded. *Degree requirements:* For doctorate, thesis/dissertation, comprehensive exam. *Entrance requirements:* For doctorate, GMAT, GRE. Additional exam requirements/recommendations for international students: Required—TOEFL. *Application deadline:* For fall admission, 2/1 priority date for domestic students. Applications are processed on a rolling basis. Application fee: $50. Electronic applications accepted. *Financial support:* In 2006–07, 26 research assistantships with tuition reimbursements (averaging $17,145 per year), 9 teaching assistantships with tuition reimbursements (averaging $20,992 per year) were awarded; Federal Work-Study, health care benefits, and unspecified assistantships also available. Financial award application deadline: 2/1. *Faculty research:* Accounting, marketing, finance, strategy, information systems. *Unit head:* Dr. John E. Prescott, Director, 412-648-1523, Fax: 412-624-3633, E-mail: prescott@katz.pitt.edu.

University of Pittsburgh, Joseph M. Katz Graduate School of Business, Executive MBA Program, Pittsburgh, PA 15260. Offers EMBA. *Accreditation:* AACSB. Evening/weekend programs available. *Faculty:* 41 full-time (5 women), 1 (woman) part-time/adjunct. *Students:* 72 full-time (13 women); includes 4 minority (all Asian Americans or Pacific Islanders), 48 international. Average age 37. 31 applicants, 97% accepted, 26 enrolled. In 2006, 63 degrees awarded. *Degree requirements:* For master's, participation in 3 Global Forums. *Entrance requirements:* For master's, GMAT, 3 credits of course work in college-level calculus, minimum 5 years management experience, corporate sponsorship. Additional exam requirements/recommendations for international students: Required—TOEFL (minimum score 600 paper-based; 250 computer-based). *Application deadline:* For fall admission, 9/20 for domestic students; for spring admission, 3/1 priority date for international students. Applications are processed on a rolling basis. *Expenses:* Contact institution. *Faculty research:* Strategic planning and management control; market mode labor relations; human resource management; process improvement initiatives; entrepreneurship; transitional economies. *Unit head:* Anne M. Nemer, Executive Director for EMBA Worldwide, 412-648-1694, Fax: 412-648-1787, E-mail: annemer@katz.pitt.edu.

University of Pittsburgh, Joseph M. Katz Graduate School of Business, Master's Program in Business Administration, Pittsburgh, PA 15260. Offers MBA, MS, JD/MBA, MBA/MA, MBA/MIB, MBA/MPIA, MBA/MS, MBA/MSIE. *Accreditation:* AACSB. Part-time and evening/weekend programs available. *Faculty:* 70 full-time (13 women), 27 part-time/adjunct (10 women). *Students:* 198 full-time (61 women), 451 part-time (154 women); includes 51 minority (13 African Americans, 1 American Indian/Alaska Native, 31 Asian Americans or Pacific Islanders, 6 Hispanic Americans), 102 international. Average age 28. 795 applicants, 62% accepted, 329 enrolled. In 2006, 234 master's awarded. *Entrance requirements:* For master's, GMAT. Additional exam requirements/recommendations for international students: Required—TOEFL (minimum score 600 paper-based; 250 computer-based). *Application deadline:* For fall admission, 3/1 for domestic and international students. Application fee: $50. Electronic applications accepted. *Financial support:* Fellowships with tuition reimbursements, career-related internships or fieldwork, institutionally sponsored loans, scholarships/grants, and tuition waivers (full and partial) available. Financial award application deadline: 3/15; financial award applicants required to submit FAFSA. *Faculty research:* Finance, marketing, strategy, MIS, accounting. Total annual research expenditures: $2.1 million. *Application contact:* Kelly R. Wilson, Assistant Dean and Director, MBA Admissions Office, 412-648-1700, Fax: 412-648-1659, E-mail: mba@katz.pitt.edu.

University of Portland, Graduate School, Dr. Robert B. Pamplin, Jr. School of Business, Portland, OR 97203-5798. Offers MBA. *Accreditation:* AACSB. Part-time and evening/weekend programs available. *Faculty:* 24 full-time (5 women). *Students:* 68 full-time, 77 part-time. *Entrance requirements:* For master's, GMAT, minimum GPA of 3.0, resumé, 2 letters of recommendation. Additional exam requirements/recommendations for international students: Required—TOEFL (minimum score 570 paper-based; 89 iBT). *Application deadline:* For fall admission, 8/1 priority date for domestic students; for spring admission, 12/1 for domestic students. Applications are processed on a rolling basis. Application fee: $50. *Expenses:* Contact institution. Tuition and fees vary according to program. *Financial support:* Federal Work-Study, scholarships/grants, and tuition waivers (partial) available. Support available to part-time students. Financial award application deadline: 3/1; financial award applicants required to submit FAFSA. *Unit head:* Dr. Robin Anderson, Dean, 503-943-7224, E-mail: anderson@up.edu. *Application contact:* Melissa McCarthy, Academic Specialist, 503-943-7225, E-mail: mccarthy@up.edu.

University of Puerto Rico, Mayagüez Campus, Graduate Studies, College of Business Administration, Mayagüez, PR 00681-9000. Offers business administration (MBA); finance (MBA); human resources (MBA); industrial management (MBA). Part-time and evening/weekend programs available. *Faculty:* 52 full-time (30 women). *Students:* 32 full-time (15 women), 52 part-time (37 women); includes 73 minority (all Hispanic Americans), 11 international. 47 applicants, 70% accepted, 24 enrolled. In 2006, 13 degrees awarded. *Degree requirements:*

For master's, comprehensive exam. *Entrance requirements:* For master's, GMAT or EXADEP, bachelor's degree with courses in calculus, microeconomics, accounting and statistics. Additional exam requirements/recommendations for international students: Required—TOEFL (minimum score 500 paper-based; 173 computer-based). *Application deadline:* For fall admission, 2/15 for domestic and international students; for spring admission, 9/15 for domestic and international students. Applications are processed on a rolling basis. Application fee: $25. *Expenses:* Tuition, nonresident: full-time $4,655. Required fees: $210. One-time fee: $77 full-time. Part-time tuition and fees vary according to course load and reciprocity agreements. *Financial support:* In 2006–07, 10 students received support, including fellowships (averaging $12,000 per year), 7 research assistantships (averaging $15,000 per year), 3 teaching assistantships (averaging $8,500 per year); Federal Work-Study and institutionally sponsored loans also available. *Faculty research:* Organizational studies, management, accounting. Total annual research expenditures: $264,836. *Unit head:* Prof. Eva Quinnnones, Dean, 787-265-3800, Fax: 787-832-5320, E-mail: quinones-e@rigel.uprm.edu. *Application contact:* Dr. Yolanda Ruiz, Director, 787-265-3887, Fax: 787-832-5320, E-mail: yruiz@caribe.net.

University of Puerto Rico, Río Piedras, College of Business Administration, San Juan, PR 00931-3300. Offers MBA, PhD. Part-time programs available. *Students:* 125 full-time (81 women), 199 part-time (135 women); all minorities (all Hispanic Americans) In 2006, 50 master's, 3 doctorates awarded. *Degree requirements:* For master's, thesis or alternative, research project, comprehensive exam. *Entrance requirements:* For master's, GMAT or PAEG, minimum GPA of 3.0, letter of recommendation; for doctorate, GMAT, PAEG, minimum GPA of 3.0, master degree. *Application deadline:* For fall admission, 2/1 for domestic and international students. Application fee: $17. *Expenses:* Tuition, state resident: part-time $100 per credit. Tuition, nonresident: part-time $291 per credit. Required fees: $72 per semester. *Financial support:* Fellowships, research assistantships, teaching assistantships, Federal Work-Study, institutionally sponsored loans, and tuition waivers (partial) available. Financial award application deadline: 5/31. *Faculty research:* Accounting, international affairs, production management, finance. *Unit head:* Dr. Emilio Pontojas, Coordinator of Master Programs, 787-764-0000, Fax: 787-763-6944. *Application contact:* Information Contact, 787-764-0000 Ext. 4142, Fax: 787-763-6944.

University of Redlands, School of Business, Redlands, CA 92373-0999. Offers business (MBA); information technology (MS); management (MA). Evening/weekend programs available. *Faculty:* 22 full-time, 138 part-time/adjunct. *Students:* 576 full-time (257 women); includes 247 minority (60 African Americans, 8 American Indian/Alaska Native, 54 Asian Americans or Pacific Islanders, 125 Hispanic Americans), 22 international. Average age 36. In 2006, 275 degrees awarded. *Entrance requirements:* For master's, minimum GPA of 3.0, 2 letters of recommendation. *Application deadline:* For fall admission, 9/1 priority date for domestic students; for spring admission, 2/1 priority date for domestic students. Applications are processed on a rolling basis. Application fee: $0. *Expenses:* Tuition: Part-time $584 per credit. Required fees: $20 per course. Full-time tuition and fees vary according to program. *Financial support:* Applicants required to submit FAFSA. *Faculty research:* Human resources management, educational leadership, humanities, teacher education. *Unit head:* Dr. Stuart Noble-Goodman, Interim Dean, 909-793-2121, Fax: 909-335-3400. *Application contact:* Kimmi Grulke, Campus Director, 885-999-9844, Fax: 909-335-5325, E-mail: schoolofbusiness@redlands.edu.

University of Regina, Faculty of Graduate Studies and Research, Kenneth Levene Graduate School of Business, Regina, SK S4S 0A2, Canada. Offers MBA, MHRM, Master's Certificate. Part-time and evening/weekend programs available. *Faculty:* 24 full-time (5 women), 3 part-time/adjunct (0 women). *Students:* 66 full-time (27 women), 45 part-time (21 women). 104 applicants, 88% accepted. In 2006, 17 degrees awarded. *Entrance requirements:* Additional exam requirements/recommendations for international students: Required—TOEFL (minimum score 580 paper-based; 287 computer-based; 88 iBT). *Application deadline:* Applications are processed on a rolling basis. Application fee: $60 ($100 for international students). Electronic applications accepted. *Expenses:* Contact institution. *Financial support:* In 2006–07, 4 fellowships (averaging $14,886 per year), 1 research assistantship (averaging $12,750 per year), 3 teaching assistantships (averaging $13,501 per year) were awarded; scholarships/grants also available. Financial award application deadline: 6/15. *Faculty research:* Management of public and private sector organizations. *Unit head:* Dr. Anne Lavack, Director, 306-585-4716, Fax: 306-585-4805, E-mail: anne.lavack@uregina.ca. *Application contact:* Heidi Eger, 306-585-4735, E-mail: heidi.eger@uregina.ca.

University of Rhode Island, Graduate School, College of Business Administration, Kingston, RI 02881. Offers accounting (MS); business administration (PhD), including finance, management, management science and information systems, marketing; finance (MBA); international business (MBA); international sports management (MBA); management (MBA); management science (MBA), including management information systems, manufacturing; marketing (MBA). *Accreditation:* AACSB. In 2006, 86 master's, 1 doctorate awarded. *Entrance requirements:* For master's and doctorate, GMAT. Additional exam requirements/recommendations for international students: Required—TOEFL. *Application deadline:* For fall admission, 4/15 priority date for domestic students. Applications are processed on a rolling basis. Application fee: $35. *Expenses:* Tuition, state resident: full-time $6,032; part-time $335 per credit. Tuition, nonresident: full-time $17,288; part-time $960 per credit. Required fees: $65 per credit. $30 per semester. One-time fee: $80 part-time. *Financial support:* Unspecified assistantships available. *Unit head:* Mark Higgins, Dean, 401-874-2337. *Application contact:* Dr. Laura Beauvais, Director of Graduate Programs, 401-874-4341.

University of Richmond, Robins School of Business, Richmond, University of Richmond, VA 23173. Offers MBA, JD/MBA. *Accreditation:* AACSB. Part-time and evening/weekend programs available. *Faculty:* 48 full-time (10 women), 13 part-time/adjunct (4 women). *Students:* Average age 29. 78 applicants, 77% accepted, 43 enrolled. In 2006, 38 degrees awarded. *Median time to degree:* Master's–2 years full-time, 3 years part-time. *Degree requirements:* For master's, capstone project. *Entrance requirements:* For master's, GMAT, 2 years of work experience. Additional exam requirements/recommendations for international students: Required—TOEFL (minimum score 600 paper-based; 250 computer-based; 100 iBT). *Application deadline:* For fall admission, 5/1 for domestic and international students. Applications are processed on a rolling basis. Application fee: $50. *Expenses:* Contact institution. *Financial support:* In 2006–07, 59 students received support, including 8 research assistantships with tuition reimbursements available; unspecified assistantships also available. Support available to part-time students. Financial award applicants required to submit FAFSA. *Faculty research:* Entrepreneurship, investments, auditing, consumer behavior, strategic management. *Unit head:* Dr. Jorge Haddock, Dean, 804-289-8550, Fax: 804-287-6544, E-mail: jhaddock@richmond.edu. *Application contact:* Dr. Richard S. Coughlan, Associate Dean for Graduate and Executive Programs, 804-289-8553, Fax: 804-287-1228, E-mail: rcoughla@richmond.edu.

University of Rochester, William E. Simon Graduate School of Business Administration, Doctoral Program in Business Administration, Rochester, NY 14627-0250. Offers PhD. *Accreditation:* AACSB. *Degree requirements:* For doctorate, thesis/dissertation, qualifying exam, comprehensive exam. *Entrance requirements:* For doctorate, GMAT or GRE, previous course work in calculus. Additional exam requirements/recommendations for international students: Required—TOEFL. Expenses: Contact institution.

University of Rochester, William E. Simon Graduate School of Business Administration, Master's Program in Business Administration, Rochester, NY 14627-0250. Offers MBA, MS. *Accreditation:* AACSB. Part-time and evening/weekend programs available. *Entrance requirements:* For master's, GMAT, previous course work in calculus. Additional exam requirements/recommendations for international students: Required—TOEFL.

University of St. Francis, College of Business, Joliet, IL 60435-6169. Offers business (MBA); management (MS). Part-time and evening/weekend programs available. Postbaccalaureate distance learning degree programs offered (no on-campus study). *Faculty:* 4 full-time (0 women), 12 part-time/adjunct (4 women). *Students:* 29 full-time (19 women), 115 part-time (71 women); includes 22 minority (15 African Americans, 2 Asian Americans or Pacific Islanders, 5 Hispanic Americans). Average age 38. 89 applicants, 76% accepted, 47 enrolled. In 2006, 64 degrees awarded. *Degree requirements:* For master's, registration. *Entrance requirements:* For master's, GMAT or 2 years of work experience, minimum undergraduate GPA of 2.75, computer competency, 2 letters of recommendation. Additional exam requirements/recommendations for international students: Required—TOEFL (minimum score 550 paper-based; 213 computer-based). *Application deadline:* Applications are processed on a rolling basis. Application fee: $30. Electronic applications accepted. *Expenses:* Contact institution. Part-time tuition and fees vary according to campus/location and program. *Financial support:* In 2006–07, 65 students received support. Tuition waivers (partial) available. Support available to part-time students. Financial award applicants required to submit FAFSA. *Unit head:* Dr. Michael LaRocco, Dean, 815-740-3452, Fax: 815-774-2920, E-mail: mlarocco@stfrancis.edu. *Application contact:* Sandra Sloka, Director of Admissions for Graduate and Degree Completion Programs, 800-735-7500, Fax: 815-740-5032, E-mail: ssloka@stfrancis.edu.

University of Saint Francis, Graduate School, Department of Business Administration, Fort Wayne, IN 46808-3994. Offers MBA, MS. Part-time and evening/weekend programs available. *Faculty:* 8 full-time (5 women), 2 part-time/adjunct (0 women). *Students:* 9 full-time (6 women), 44 part-time (23 women); includes 5 minority (4 African Americans, 1 Asian American or Pacific Islander). Average age 37. 25 applicants, 92% accepted. In 2006, 21 degrees awarded. *Entrance requirements:* For master's, GMAT, minimum AACSB index of 900, minimum GPA of 2.5. *Application deadline:* For fall admission, 7/1 priority date for domestic students; for spring admission, 11/1 priority date for domestic students. Applications are processed on a rolling basis. Application fee: $20. *Financial support:* In 2006–07, 4 students received support. Federal Work-Study and unspecified assistantships available. Financial award applicants required to submit FAFSA. *Unit head:* Dr. Lillian Schumacher, Director of Graduate Programs, 260-399-7700 Ext. 8305, Fax: 260-399-8174, E-mail: lschumacher@st.edu. *Application contact:* James Lashdollar, Admissions Counselor, 260-434-3279, E-mail: jcashdollar@sf.edu.

University of Saint Mary, Graduate Programs, Program in Business Administration, Leavenworth, KS 66048-5082. Offers MBA. Part-time and evening/weekend programs available. *Degree requirements:* For master's, thesis. *Entrance requirements:* For master's, minimum undergraduate GPA of 2.75.

University of Saint Mary, Graduate Programs, Program in Management, Leavenworth, KS 66048-5082. Offers MS. Part-time and evening/weekend programs available. *Degree requirements:* For master's, thesis, oral or written exam. *Entrance requirements:* For master's, minimum undergraduate GPA of 2.75.

University of St. Thomas, Cameron School of Business, Houston, TX 77006-4696. Offers MBA, MIB, MSA, MSIS. *Accreditation:* ACBSP. Part-time and evening/weekend programs available. *Faculty:* 22 full-time (9 women), 17 part-time/adjunct (5 women). *Students:* 194 full-time (101 women), 359 part-time (172 women); includes 224 minority (64 African Americans, 4 American Indian/Alaska Native, 46 Asian Americans or Pacific Islanders, 110 Hispanic Americans), 103 international. Average age 31. 154 applicants, 97% accepted, 119 enrolled. In 2006, 237 degrees awarded. *Entrance requirements:* For master's, GMAT, minimum GPA of 2.5. Additional exam requirements/recommendations for international students: Required—TOEFL (minimum score 550 paper-based; 213 computer-based). *Application deadline:* For fall admission, 6/30 for domestic and international students; for spring admission, 10/31 for domestic and international students. Applications are processed on a rolling basis. Application fee: $35. *Expenses:* Tuition: Full-time $11,880; part-time $660 per credit. Required fees: $52; $21 per semester. *Financial support:* In 2006–07, 280 students received support. Federal Work-Study, scholarships/grants, and unspecified assistantships available. Support available to part-time students. Financial award application deadline: 3/1; financial award applicants required to submit FAFSA. *Faculty research:* Trade theory, development theory, financial institutions, monetary and accounting theory. *Unit head:* Dr. Bahman Mirshab, Dean, 713-525-2100, Fax: 713-525-2110, E-mail: mirshab@stthom.edu. *Application contact:* Sandra Flanagan, Enrollment Coordinator, 713-525-2115, Fax: 713-525-2110, E-mail: flanags@stthom.edu.

University of St. Thomas, Graduate Studies, Opus College of Business, Evening MBA Program, St. Paul, MN 55105-1096. Offers MBA. Part-time and evening/weekend programs available. *Faculty:* 33 full-time (14 women), 52 part-time/adjunct (11 women). *Students:* Average age 33. 312 applicants, 69% accepted, 177 enrolled. In 2006, 448 degrees awarded. *Entrance requirements:* For master's, GMAT. Additional exam requirements/recommendations for international students: Required—TOEFL. *Application deadline:* For fall admission, 6/1 priority date for domestic and international students; for spring admission, 12/1 priority date for domestic and international students. Applications are processed on a rolling basis. Application fee: $60 ($90 for international students). Electronic applications accepted. *Financial support:* In 2006–07, 5 students received support. Scholarships/grants available. Financial award application deadline: 7/1; financial award applicants required to submit FAFSA. *Unit head:* Dr. David P. Brennan, Assistant Dean, 651-962-4071, Fax: 651-962-4208, E-mail: dpbrennan@stthomas.edu. *Application contact:* Rachelle D. Holm, Director of Admissions, 651-962-4889, Fax: 651-962-4129, E-mail: rdholm@stthomas.edu.

University of St. Thomas, Graduate Studies, Opus College of Business, Executive UST MBA Program, St. Paul, MN 55105-1096. Offers MBA. Part-time and evening/weekend programs available. *Faculty:* 2 full-time (0 women), 11 part-time/adjunct (3 women). *Students:* Average age 40. 66 applicants, 50% accepted, 32 enrolled. In 2006, 43 degrees awarded. *Entrance requirements:* For master's, MAT, 5 years of management experience. Additional exam requirements/recommendations for international students: Required—TOEFL. *Application deadline:* For fall admission, 6/30 priority date for domestic students; for winter admission, 9/30 priority date for domestic students; for spring admission, 1/31 priority date for domestic students. Applications are processed on a rolling basis. Application fee: $100. Electronic applications accepted. *Expenses:* Contact institution. *Financial support:* Scholarships/grants available. Support available to part-time students. Financial award application deadline: 12/1. *Unit head:* Nick Lauer, Director, 651-962-4230, Fax: 651-962-4235, E-mail: execmba@stthomas.edu. *Application contact:* Katherine R. Johnson, Program Services Manager, 651-962-4238, Fax: 651-962-4235, E-mail: krjohnson@stthomas.edu.

See Close-Up on page 361.

University of St. Thomas, Graduate Studies, Opus College of Business, Full-time UST MBA Program, St. Paul, MN 55105-1096. Offers MBA. *Faculty:* 22 full-time (6 women), 11 part-time/adjunct (3 women). *Students:* 80 full-time (31 women); includes 7 minority (3 African Americans, 3 Asian Americans or Pacific Islanders, 1 Hispanic American), 14 international. Average age 28. 104 applicants, 64% accepted, 41 enrolled. In 2006, 30 degrees awarded. *Median time to degree:* Master's–1 year full-time. *Degree requirements:* For master's, registration. *Entrance requirements:* For master's, GMAT. Additional exam requirements/recommendations for international students: Required—TOEFL. *Application deadline:* For fall admission, 4/1 priority date for domestic students. Application fee: $60 ($90 for international students). *Financial support:* In 2006–07, 66 students received support; fellowships, research assistantships available. Support available to part-time students. Financial award application deadline: 7/1. *Application contact:* Rachelle D. Holm, Director of Admissions, 651-962-4889, Fax: 651-962-4129, E-mail: rdholm@stthomas.edu.

See Close-Up on page 361.

University of San Diego, School of Business Administration, San Diego, CA 92110-2492. Offers accounting and financial management (MS); business administration (MBA); executive leadership (MSEL); global leadership (MSGL); international business administration (IMBA); real estate (MSRE); supply chain management (MS, Certificate); taxation (MS); JD/IMBA; JD/MBA; MBA/MSIT; MBA/MSN; MBA/MSRE. *Accreditation:* AACSB. Part-time and evening/weekend programs available. *Faculty:* 35 full-time (10 women), 18 part-time/adjunct (4 women). *Students:* 187 full-time (76 women), 265 part-time (89 women); includes 55 minority (5 African Americans, 1 American Indian/Alaska Native, 32 Asian Americans or Pacific Islanders, 17 Hispanic Americans), 45 international. Average age 32. 517 applicants, 66% accepted, 187

Business Administration and Management—General

University of San Diego *(continued)*
enrolled. In 2006, 256 degrees awarded. *Entrance requirements:* For master's, GMAT, minimum GPA of 3.0, minimum 2 years of full-time work experience. Additional exam requirements/recommendations for international students: Required—TOEFL (minimum score 580 paper-based; 237 computer-based), TWE. *Application deadline:* For fall admission, 5/1 priority date for domestic students; for spring admission, 11/15 priority date for domestic students. Applications are processed on a rolling basis. Application fee: $45. Electronic applications accepted. *Financial support:* Career-related internships or fieldwork, Federal Work-Study, institutionally sponsored loans, scholarships/grants, tuition waivers (partial), and unspecified assistantships available. Support available to part-time students. Financial award application deadline: 5/1; financial award applicants required to submit FAFSA. *Faculty research:* Business management, production, purchasing, quantitative methods, accounting. *Unit head:* Dr. Andy Allen, Interim Dean, 619-260-4886, E-mail: sbadean@sandiego.edu. *Application contact:* Stephen Pultz, Director of Admissions, 619-260-4524, Fax: 619-260-4158, E-mail: grads@sandiego.edu.

University of San Francisco, Masagung Graduate School of Management, Professional MBA for Executives Program, San Francisco, CA 94117-1080. Offers MBA. *Accreditation:* AACSB. *Faculty:* 5 full-time (1 woman). *Students:* 42 full-time (12 women); includes 11 minority (8 Asian Americans or Pacific Islanders, 3 Hispanic Americans). Average age 40. 25 applicants, 96% accepted, 19 enrolled. In 2006, 22 degrees awarded. Application fee: $50. *Expenses:* Contact institution. Tuition and fees vary according to degree level, campus/location and program. *Financial support:* In 2006–07, 19 students received support. Applicants required to submit FAFSA. *Unit head:* Dr. Karl Boedecker, Director, 415-422-2511, Fax: 415-422-6315. *Application contact:* Kelly Tarry, Secretary, Executive Programs, 415-422-2525.

University of San Francisco, Masagung Graduate School of Management, Program in Business Administration, San Francisco, CA 94117-1080. Offers business economics (MBA); e-business (MBA); entrepreneurship (MBA); finance and banking (MBA); international business (MBA); management (MBA); marketing (MBA); telecommunications management and policy (MBA); JD/MBA; MSN/MBA. *Accreditation:* AACSB. *Faculty:* 27 full-time (4 women), 21 part-time/adjunct (7 women). *Students:* 191 full-time (73 women), 71 part-time (33 women); includes 51 minority (4 African Americans, 1 American Indian/Alaska Native, 35 Asian Americans or Pacific Islanders, 11 Hispanic Americans), 102 international. Average age 28. 373 applicants, 70% accepted, 106 enrolled. In 2006, 163 degrees awarded. *Entrance requirements:* For master's, GMAT, minimum undergraduate GPA of 3.2. Additional exam requirements/recommendations for international students: Required—TOEFL. *Application deadline:* For fall admission, 7/1 priority date for domestic students; for spring admission, 11/30 for domestic students. Applications are processed on a rolling basis. Application fee: $55 ($65 for international students). *Expenses:* Tuition: Full-time $17,370; part-time $965 per unit. Tuition and fees vary according to degree level, campus/location and program. *Financial support:* In 2006–07, 104 students received support; fellowships available. Financial award application deadline: 3/2; financial award applicants required to submit FAFSA. *Faculty research:* International financial markets, technology transfer licensing, international marketing, strategic planning. Total annual research expenditures: $50,000. *Unit head:* Carol Langlois, Director, 415-422-6314, Fax: 415-422-2502.

University of Saskatchewan, College of Graduate Studies and Research, College of Commerce, Saskatoon, SK S7N 5A2, Canada. Offers M Sc, MBA, MPAcc. Part-time programs available. *Degree requirements:* For master's, thesis (for some programs), registration. *Entrance requirements:* For master's, GMAT. Additional exam requirements/recommendations for international students: Required—TOEFL.

The University of Scranton, Graduate School, Program in Business Administration, Scranton, PA 18510. Offers accounting (MBA); enterprise management technology (MBA); finance (MBA); general business administration (MBA); international business (MBA); management information systems (MBA); marketing (MBA); operations management (MBA). *Accreditation:* AACSB. Part-time and evening/weekend programs available. *Faculty:* 34 full-time (8 women). *Students:* 39 full-time (11 women), 54 part-time (15 women); includes 3 minority (1 American Indian/Alaska Native, 2 Hispanic Americans), 31 international. Average age 28. 58 applicants, 83% accepted. In 2006, 52 degrees awarded. *Degree requirements:* For master's, capstone experience. *Entrance requirements:* For master's, GMAT, minimum GPA of 2.75. Additional exam requirements/recommendations for international students: Required—TOEFL (minimum score 500 paper-based; 173 computer-based), IELTS (minimum score 6). *Application deadline:* Applications are processed on a rolling basis. Application fee: $50. *Expenses:* Tuition: Part-time $684 per credit. Required fees: $25 per term. *Financial support:* In 2006–07, 11 teaching assistantships with full tuition reimbursements (averaging $5,600 per year) were awarded; fellowships, career-related internships or fieldwork, Federal Work-Study, and unspecified assistantships also available. Support available to part-time students. Financial award application deadline: 3/1. *Faculty research:* Financial markets, strategic impact of total quality management, internal accounting controls, consumer preference, information systems and the Internet. *Unit head:* Dr. Murli Rajan, Director, 570-941-4043, Fax: 570-941-4342.

University of Sioux Falls, Program in Business Administration, Sioux Falls, SD 57105-1699. Offers MBA. Part-time and evening/weekend programs available. *Faculty:* 8 full-time (3 women), 7 part-time/adjunct (2 women). In 2006, 15 degrees awarded. *Degree requirements:* For master's, project. *Entrance requirements:* For master's, minimum GPA of 3.0. Additional exam requirements/recommendations for international students: Required—TOEFL. Application fee: $25. *Expenses:* Contact institution. Part-time tuition and fees vary according to program. *Financial support:* In 2006–07, 47 students received support. Institutionally sponsored loans and scholarships/grants available. Financial award applicants required to submit FAFSA. *Unit head:* Rebecca T. Murdock, Director, 605-575-2068, E-mail: mba@usiouxfalls.edu.

University of South Alabama, Graduate School, Mitchell College of Business, Program in Business Management, Mobile, AL 36688-0002. Offers general management (MBA). *Accreditation:* AACSB. Part-time and evening/weekend programs available. *Faculty:* 8 full-time (4 women). *Students:* 71 full-time (23 women), 23 part-time (8 women); includes 11 minority (6 African Americans, 2 American Indian/Alaska Native, 1 Asian American or Pacific Islander, 2 Hispanic Americans), 18 international. 114 applicants, 68% accepted, 58 enrolled. In 2006, 36 degrees awarded. *Degree requirements:* For master's, comprehensive exam. *Entrance requirements:* For master's, GMAT, minimum undergraduate GPA of 3.0. *Application deadline:* For fall admission, 9/1 priority date for domestic students. Applications are processed on a rolling basis. Application fee: $25. *Financial support:* Research assistantships available. Support available to part-time students. Financial award application deadline: 4/1. *Unit head:* Dr. John Gamble, Chair, 251-460-6418.

University of South Carolina, The Graduate School, The Darla Moore School of Business, Columbia, SC 29208. Offers accountancy (M Acc), including business measurement and assurance; business administration (PMBA, PhD); economics (MA, PhD); human resources (MHR); international business administration (IMBA); JD/IMBA; JD/M Acc; JD/MA; JD/MHR. *Accreditation:* AACSB. Part-time and evening/weekend programs available. Postbaccalaureate distance learning degree programs offered (minimal on-campus study). *Degree requirements:* For doctorate, one foreign language, thesis/dissertation. *Entrance requirements:* For master's, GMAT, GRE, minimum GPA of 3.0; for doctorate, GMAT or GRE. Additional exam requirements/recommendations for international students: Required—TOEFL (minimum score 600 paper-based; 250 computer-based). Electronic applications accepted. Expenses: Contact institution. *Faculty research:* Finance, marketing, strategic management, international management, operations.

The University of South Dakota, Graduate School, Program in Administrative Studies, Vermillion, SD 57069-2390. Offers MS. Part-time and evening/weekend programs available. Postbaccalaureate distance learning degree programs offered (no on-campus study). *Students:* 121 (77 women). In 2006, 15 degrees awarded. *Degree requirements:* For master's, thesis or

alternative. *Entrance requirements:* For master's, 3 years of work or experience, minimum GPA of 2.7. Additional exam requirements/recommendations for international students: Required—TOEFL (minimum score 550 paper-based; 213 computer-based; 79 iBT). *Application deadline:* Applications are processed on a rolling basis. Application fee: $35. Electronic applications accepted. *Expenses:* Tuition, state resident: part-time $120 per credit hour. Tuition, nonresident: part-time $355 per credit hour. Required fees: $90 per credit hour. *Financial support:* In 2006–07, teaching assistantships with partial tuition reimbursements (averaging $4,626 per year). *Unit head:* Dr. Anthony Molina, Head, 605-677-6405, Fax: 605-677-5202, E-mail: msas@usd.edu. *Application contact:* Holli Novak, Program Assistant, 605-677-6405, Fax: 605-677-5202, E-mail: msas@usd.edu.

The University of South Dakota, Graduate School, School of Business, Department of Business Administration, Vermillion, SD 57069-2390. Offers MBA, JD/MBA. *Accreditation:* AACSB. Part-time and evening/weekend programs available. Postbaccalaureate distance learning degree programs offered (no on-campus study). *Faculty:* 26 full-time (5 women). *Students:* 130 (57 women). In 2006, 74 degrees awarded. *Degree requirements:* For master's, thesis or alternative. *Entrance requirements:* For master's, GMAT, minimum GPA of 2.7. Additional exam requirements/recommendations for international students: Required—TOEFL (minimum score 550 paper-based; 213 computer-based; 79 iBT). *Application deadline:* For fall admission, 6/1 priority date for domestic students, 5/1 priority date for international students; for spring admission, 10/1 priority date for domestic students, 9/1 priority date for international students. Applications are processed on a rolling basis. Application fee: $35. Electronic applications accepted. *Expenses:* Contact institution. *Financial support:* Research assistantships with partial tuition reimbursements, teaching assistantships with partial tuition reimbursements, career-related internships or fieldwork, Federal Work-Study, and unspecified assistantships available. Financial award applicants required to submit FAFSA. *Unit head:* Dr. Angeline Lavin, MBA and Executive Education Dean, 605-677-5232, Fax: 605-677-5058, E-mail: mba@usd.edu.

University of Southern California, Graduate School, Marshall School of Business, Los Angeles, CA 90089. Offers M Acc, MBA, MBT, MS, PhD, DDS/MBA, JD/MBA, JD/MBT, MBA/M Pl, MBA/MA, MBA/MRED, MBA/MS, Pharm D/MBA. *Accreditation:* AACSB. *Students:* 1,385 full-time (432 women), 432 part-time (132 women); includes 708 minority (33 African Americans, 3 American Indian/Alaska Native, 579 Asian Americans or Pacific Islanders, 93 Hispanic Americans), 297 international. In 2006, 698 master's, 8 doctorates awarded. *Degree requirements:* For doctorate, thesis/dissertation. *Entrance requirements:* For master's, GMAT; for doctorate, GMAT or GRE General Test. *Application deadline:* For fall admission, 12/1 priority date for domestic students. Application fee: $85. *Expenses:* Tuition: Full-time $33,314; part-time $1,121 per credit. Required fees: $522. Full-time tuition and fees vary according to program. *Financial support:* In 2006–07, research assistantships (averaging $18,500 per year), teaching assistantships (averaging $18,500 per year) were awarded; fellowships, Federal Work-Study, institutionally sponsored loans, and scholarships/grants also available. Support available to part-time students. Financial award application deadline: 2/15; financial award applicants required to submit FAFSA. *Unit head:* James Ellis, Dean, 213-740-6422, E-mail: dean@marshall.usc.edu.

University of Southern Indiana, Graduate Studies, College of Business, Program in Business Administration, Evansville, IN 47712-3590. Offers MBA. *Accreditation:* AACSB. Part-time and evening/weekend programs available. *Faculty:* 9 full-time (3 women). *Students:* 4 full-time (0 women), 87 part-time (35 women); includes 3 minority (all Hispanic Americans), 2 international. Average age 31. 26 applicants, 85% accepted, 16 enrolled. In 2006, 26 degrees awarded. *Entrance requirements:* For master's, GMAT, minimum GPA of 2.5, resumé. Additional exam requirements/recommendations for international students: Required—TOEFL (minimum score 550 paper-based; 213 computer-based). *Application deadline:* For fall admission, 8/15 for domestic students, 3/1 priority date for international students. Applications are processed on a rolling basis. Application fee: $25. *Expenses:* Tuition, state resident: full-time $3,888; part-time $216 per credit hour. Tuition, nonresident: full-time $7,688; part-time $426 per credit hour. Required fees: $220; $23 per term. Tuition and fees vary according to course load and reciprocity agreements. *Financial support:* In 2006–07, 22 students received support. Federal Work-Study, scholarships/grants, tuition waivers (full and partial), and unspecified assistantships available. Financial award application deadline: 3/1; financial award applicants required to submit FAFSA. *Unit head:* Dr. Gregory Murphy, 812-464-5348, E-mail: gbmurphy@usi.edu.

University of Southern Maine, Lewiston-Auburn College, Program in Leadership Studies, Portland, ME 04104-9300. Offers MLS. *Expenses:* Tuition, state resident: full-time $4,860; part-time $270 per credit hour. Tuition, nonresident: full-time $13,572; part-time $754 per credit hour. Required fees: $222 per semester. Tuition and fees vary according to course load. *Unit head:* Marvin Druker, Head, 207-780-4141.

University of Southern Maine, School of Business, Portland, ME 04104-9300. Offers accounting (MSA); business administration (MBA); JD/MBA; MBA/MSA; MBA/MSN; MS/MBA. *Accreditation:* AACSB. Part-time and evening/weekend programs available. *Faculty:* 20 full-time (4 women). *Students:* 43 full-time (26 women), 117 part-time (45 women); includes 8 minority (1 American Indian/Alaska Native, 7 Asian Americans or Pacific Islanders), 2 international. Average age 32. 77 applicants, 82% accepted, 54 enrolled. In 2006, 32 degrees awarded. *Degree requirements:* For master's, registration. *Entrance requirements:* For master's, GMAT, minimum AACSB index of 1100. Additional exam requirements/recommendations for international students: Required—TOEFL (minimum score 550 paper-based; 213 computer-based; 79 iBT). *Application deadline:* For fall admission, 8/1 priority date for domestic students, 5/1 priority date for international students; for spring admission, 12/1 priority date for domestic students, 9/1 priority date for international students. Applications are processed on a rolling basis. Application fee: $50. Electronic applications accepted. *Expenses:* Tuition, state resident: full-time $4,860; part-time $270 per credit hour. Tuition, nonresident: full-time $13,572; part-time $754 per credit hour. Required fees: $222 per semester. Tuition and fees vary according to course load. *Financial support:* In 2006–07, 108 students received support, including 3 research assistantships with partial tuition reimbursements available (averaging $9,000 per year), 3 teaching assistantships with partial tuition reimbursements available (averaging $9,000 per year); career-related internships or fieldwork, Federal Work-Study, scholarships/grants, tuition waivers (full and partial), and unspecified assistantships also available. Support available to part-time students. Financial award application deadline: 2/15; financial award applicants required to submit FAFSA. *Faculty research:* Economic development, MIS, real options, system dynamics, simulation. *Unit head:* James B. Shaffer, Dean, 207-780-4020, Fax: 207-780-4662, E-mail: jshaffer@usm.maine.edu. *Application contact:* Alice B. Cash, Graduate Programs Director, 207-780-4184, Fax: 207-780-4662, E-mail: acash@usm.maine.edu.

University of Southern Mississippi, Graduate School, College of Business, Department of Management and Marketing, Hattiesburg, MS 39406-0001. Offers business administration (MBA). *Accreditation:* AACSB. Part-time and evening/weekend programs available. *Faculty:* 37 full-time (6 women). *Students:* 26 full-time (7 women), 41 part-time (18 women); includes 9 minority (6 African Americans, 1 Asian American or Pacific Islander, 2 Hispanic Americans). Average age 31. 100 applicants, 42% accepted, 31 enrolled. In 2006, 49 degrees awarded. *Degree requirements:* For master's, comprehensive exam, registration. *Entrance requirements:* For master's, GMAT. Additional exam requirements/recommendations for international students: Required—TOEFL. *Application deadline:* For fall admission, 7/15 priority date for domestic students, 7/15 for international students; for spring admission, 11/15 priority date for domestic students, 11/15 for international students. Application fee: $25 ($30 for international students). Electronic applications accepted. *Financial support:* In 2006–07, 11 research assistantships with full and partial tuition reimbursements (averaging $5,406 per year) were awarded; Federal Work-Study and institutionally sponsored loans also available. Support available to part-time students. Financial award application deadline: 3/15. *Faculty research:* Inflation accounting, self-esteem training, international trade policy, health care marketing, ethics in strategic planning. *Unit head:* Dr. Barry Babin, Chair, 601-266-4627. *Application contact:* Dr. Francis Daniel, Graduate Coordinator, 601-266-4664, Fax: 601-266-5814.

University of South Florida, Graduate School, College of Business Administration, Department of Business Administration, Tampa, FL 33620-9951. Offers MBA, PhD. *Accreditation:* AACSB. Part-time and evening/weekend programs available. *Faculty:* 22 full-time (6 women), 3 part-time/adjunct (0 women). *Students:* 240 full-time (88 women), 289 part-time (107 women); includes 106 minority (17 African Americans, 2 American Indian/Alaska Native, 45 Asian Americans or Pacific Islanders, 42 Hispanic Americans), 78 international. Average age 28. 426 applicants, 66% accepted, 188 enrolled. In 2006, 203 master's, 6 doctorates awarded. *Entrance requirements:* For master's, GMAT, minimum GPA of 3.0 in last 60 hours of course work. Additional exam requirements/recommendations for international students: Required—TOEFL (minimum score 550 paper-based; 213 computer-based). *Application deadline:* For fall admission, 12/1 for domestic students. Application fee: $30. *Financial support:* Health care benefits and unspecified assistantships available. Financial award applicants required to submit FAFSA. Total annual research expenditures: $49,968. *Unit head:* Wendy Baker, Assistant Director of Graduate Studies, 813-974-3335, Fax: 813-974-4518, E-mail: wbaker@coba.usf.edu. *Application contact:* Cathy Slagle, Admissions/Registrar's Office, 813-974-3335, Fax: 813-974-4518, E-mail: cslagle@coba.usf.edu.

University of South Florida, Graduate School, College of Business Administration, Executive Program in Business Administration, Tampa, FL 33620-9951. Offers Exec MBA. *Accreditation:* AACSB. Evening/weekend programs available. *Students:* 69 full-time (19 women), 1 (woman) part-time; includes 19 minority (9 Asian Americans or Pacific Islanders, 10 Hispanic Americans), 2 international. Average age 34. 51 applicants, 92% accepted, 39 enrolled. In 2006, 38 degrees awarded. *Entrance requirements:* For master's, GMAT, minimum 5 years of work experience. *Application deadline:* For fall admission, 6/1 for domestic students. Applications are processed on a rolling basis. Application fee: $30. *Application contact:* Katie Knoth, Coordinator, Executive Programs, 813-974-4876, Fax: 813-975-6604, E-mail: emba@coba.usf.edu.

University of South Florida, Graduate School, College of Business Administration, School of Management, Tampa, FL 33620-9951. Offers MSM. *Faculty:* 12 full-time (4 women), 3 part-time/adjunct (1 woman). *Students:* 1 (woman) full-time, 28 part-time (14 women); includes 5 minority (2 African Americans, 3 Hispanic Americans). 27 applicants, 67% accepted, 16 enrolled. In 2006, 11 degrees awarded. *Entrance requirements:* For master's, GMAT. Application fee: $30. *Application contact:* MBA Program Staff, 813-974-3335, Fax: 813-974-4518, E-mail: mba@coba.usf.edu.

The University of Tampa, John H. Sykes College of Business, Tampa, FL 33606-1490. Offers accounting (MBA, MS); economics (MBA); entrepreneurship (MBA); finance (MBA, MS); information systems management (MBA); innovation management (MS); international business (MBA); management (MBA); marketing (MBA, MS). *Accreditation:* AACSB. Part-time and evening/weekend programs available. *Faculty:* 39 full-time (9 women), 1 part-time/adjunct (0 women). *Students:* 143 full-time (52 women), 381 part-time (158 women); includes 78 minority (18 African Americans, 3 American Indian/Alaska Native, 19 Asian Americans or Pacific Islanders, 38 Hispanic Americans), 89 international. Average age 31. 486 applicants, 59% accepted, 231 enrolled. In 2006, 127 degrees awarded. *Median time to degree:* Master's–1.8 years full-time, 2.8 years part-time. *Entrance requirements:* For master's, GMAT. Additional exam requirements/recommendations for international students: Required—TOEFL (minimum score 577 paper-based; 230 computer-based; 90 iBT). *Application deadline:* For fall admission, 2/15 priority date for domestic students, 6/15 for international students; for spring admission, 12/15 for domestic students, 11/15 for international students. Applications are processed on a rolling basis. Application fee: $40. Electronic applications accepted. *Expenses:* Tuition: Part-time $426 per credit hour. Required fees: $35 per year. *Financial support:* In 2006–07, 57 students received support, including 57 research assistantships with tuition reimbursements available (averaging $3,000 per year); career-related internships or fieldwork and unspecified assistantships also available. Support available to part-time students. Financial award applicants required to submit FAFSA. *Faculty research:* Industrial organization and antitrust, artificial intelligence, corporate quality, leadership, ethics, quality. *Unit head:* Dr. William L. Rhey, Dean Graduate Studies, 813-253-6211, Fax: 813-259-5403, E-mail: wrhey@ut.edu. *Application contact:* Fernals Nolasco, Director of Graduate Studies, 813-253-6211, Fax: 813-259-5403, E-mail: fnolasco@ut.edu.

The University of Tennessee, Graduate School, College of Business Administration, Program in Business Administration, Knoxville, TN 37996. Offers accounting (PhD); finance (MBA, PhD); logistics and transportation (MBA, PhD); management (PhD); marketing (MBA, PhD); operations management (MBA); professional business administration (MBA); statistics (PhD); JD/MBA; MS/MBA. *Accreditation:* AACSB. Postbaccalaureate distance learning degree programs offered. *Students:* 344 (105 women); includes 42 minority (20 African Americans, 4 American Indian/Alaska Native, 9 Asian Americans or Pacific Islanders, 9 Hispanic Americans) 49 international. In 2006, 169 master's, 9 doctorates awarded. *Degree requirements:* For master's, thesis or alternative; for doctorate, thesis/dissertation. *Entrance requirements:* For master's and doctorate, GMAT, minimum GPA of 2.7. Additional exam requirements/recommendations for international students: Required—TOEFL. *Application deadline:* For fall admission, 2/1 priority date for domestic students. Application fee: $35. Electronic applications accepted. *Expenses:* Tuition, state resident: full-time $5,574. Tuition, nonresident: full-time $16,840. Required fees: $792. *Financial support:* In 2006–07, 6 fellowships, 3 research assistantships, 35 teaching assistantships were awarded; career-related internships or fieldwork, Federal Work-Study, institutionally sponsored loans, and unspecified assistantships also available. Financial award application deadline: 2/1; financial award applicants required to submit FAFSA. *Unit head:* Dr. Sarah Gardial, Assistant Dean, 865-974-5033, Fax: 865-974-3826, E-mail: sgardial@utk.edu. *Application contact:* Donna Potts, Graduate Representative, 865-974-5033, Fax: 865-974-3826, E-mail: dpotts@utk.edu.

The University of Tennessee, Graduate School, College of Business Administration, Program in Management Science, Knoxville, TN 37996. Offers MS, PhD. *Accreditation:* AACSB. *Students:* 18 (9 women); includes 1 African American 10 international. In 2006, 5 master's, 1 doctorate awarded. *Degree requirements:* For master's, thesis or alternative; for doctorate, thesis/dissertation. *Entrance requirements:* For master's and doctorate, GMAT or GRE General Test, minimum GPA of 2.7. Additional exam requirements/recommendations for international students: Required—TOEFL. *Application deadline:* For fall admission, 2/1 priority date for domestic students. Applications are processed on a rolling basis. Application fee: $35. Electronic applications accepted. *Expenses:* Tuition, state resident: full-time $5,574. Tuition, nonresident: full-time $16,840. Required fees: $792. *Financial support:* Fellowships, career-related internships or fieldwork, Federal Work-Study, and institutionally sponsored loans available. Financial award application deadline: 2/1; financial award applicants required to submit FAFSA. *Unit head:* Dr. Oscar Fowler, Head, 865-974-4116, Fax: 865-974-3163, E-mail: ofowler@utk.edu. *Application contact:* Dr. Charles Noon, Graduate Representative, 865-974-4116, E-mail: cnoon@utk.edu.

The University of Tennessee at Chattanooga, Graduate School, College of Business Administration, Program in Business Administration, Chattanooga, TN 37403-2598. Offers general business administration (MBA). *Accreditation:* AACSB. Part-time and evening/weekend programs available. *Faculty:* 12 full-time (3 women). *Students:* 70 full-time (33 women), 191 part-time (70 women); includes 33 minority (22 African Americans, 1 American Indian/Alaska Native, 5 Asian Americans or Pacific Islanders, 5 Hispanic Americans), 4 international. Average age 33. 95 applicants, 85% accepted, 50 enrolled. In 2006, 84 degrees awarded. *Entrance requirements:* For master's, GMAT. *Application deadline:* For fall admission, 8/1 priority date for domestic students; for spring admission, 12/1 priority date for domestic students. Applications are processed on a rolling basis. Application fee: $30. *Expenses:* Tuition, state resident: full-time $5,434; part-time $339 per hour. Tuition, nonresident: full-time $14,830; part-time $861 per hour. Required fees: $940; $178 per hour. *Financial support:* Fellowships, research assistantships, Federal Work-Study and institutionally sponsored loans available. Support available to part-time students. Financial award application deadline: 4/1; financial award applicants required to submit FAFSA. *Faculty research:* Diversity; operations/production management; entrepreneurial processes; customer satisfaction and retention; branding. Total annual research expenditures: $7,000. *Unit head:* Kimberly Gee, Executive Director, 423-425-4210, Fax: 423-425-5255, E-mail: kimberly-gee@utc.edu. *Application contact:* Dr. Deborah E. Arfken, Dean of Graduate Studies, 423-425-4666, Fax: 423-425-5223, E-mail: deborah-arfken@utc.edu.

The University of Tennessee at Martin, Graduate Programs, College of Business and Public Affairs, Program in Business, Martin, TN 38238-1000. Offers MBA. *Accreditation:* AACSB. Part-time programs available. Postbaccalaureate distance learning degree programs offered (no on-campus study). *Students:* 107 (46 women); includes 8 African Americans. 60 applicants, 72% accepted, 35 enrolled. In 2006, 53 degrees awarded. *Degree requirements:* For master's, comprehensive exam. *Entrance requirements:* For master's, GMAT, minimum GPA of 2.5, resumé. Additional exam requirements/recommendations for international students: Required—TOEFL (minimum score 525 paper-based; 197 computer-based). *Application deadline:* For fall admission, 8/1 priority date for domestic students, 8/1 for international students; for spring admission, 1/1 priority date for domestic students, 1/1 for international students. Applications are processed on a rolling basis. Application fee: $30 ($50 for international students). Electronic applications accepted. *Expenses:* Tuition, state resident: part-time $303 per credit hour. Tuition, nonresident: part-time $829 per credit hour. *Financial support:* In 2006–07, 9 students received support. Career-related internships or fieldwork, scholarships/grants, tuition waivers (partial), and unspecified assistantships available. Support available to part-time students. Financial award application deadline: 3/1. *Unit head:* Dr. Kevin Hammond, Coordinator, 731-881-7236, Fax: 731-881-7241, E-mail: bagrad@utm.edu.

The University of Texas at Arlington, Graduate School, College of Business Administration, Program in Business Administration, Arlington, TX 76019. Offers accounting (PhD); business administration (PhD); business statistics (PhD); finance (MBA); information systems (MBA, PhD); management (MBA); management sciences (MBA); marketing (MBA, PhD); real estate (MBA). *Accreditation:* AACSB. Part-time and evening/weekend programs available. Postbaccalaureate distance learning degree programs offered (no on-campus study). *Faculty:* 1 full-time (0 women). *Students:* 156 full-time (60 women), 319 part-time (110 women); includes 123 minority (38 African Americans, 4 American Indian/Alaska Native, 52 Asian Americans or Pacific Islanders, 29 Hispanic Americans), 88 international. 502 applicants, 85% accepted, 199 enrolled. In 2006, 417 master's, 11 doctorates awarded. Terminal master's awarded for partial completion of doctoral program. *Degree requirements:* For master's, thesis optional; for doctorate, thesis/dissertation. *Entrance requirements:* For master's, GMAT; for doctorate, GMAT, minimum GPA of 3.0 (undergraduate), 3.4 (graduate); 30 hours of graduate course work. Additional exam requirements/recommendations for international students: Required—TOEFL (minimum score 550 paper-based; 213 computer-based). *Application deadline:* For fall admission, 6/15 for domestic students, 4/1 for international students; for spring admission, 10/15 for domestic students, 9/1 for international students. Applications are processed on a rolling basis. Application fee: $35 ($50 for international students). Electronic applications accepted. *Expenses:* Tuition, state resident: full-time $5,528. Tuition, nonresident: full-time $10,478. International tuition: $10,608 full-time. *Financial support:* In 2006–07, 1 fellowship (averaging $1,000 per year), 14 research assistantships (averaging $6,432 per year) were awarded; teaching assistantships, career-related internships or fieldwork, scholarships/grants, and unspecified assistantships also available. Financial award application deadline: 6/1; financial award applicants required to submit FAFSA. *Application contact:* Dr. Mike West, Assistant Dean, 817-272-1287, Fax: 817-272-5799, E-mail: mpwest@uta.edu.

See Close-Up on page 363.

The University of Texas at Austin, Graduate School, McCombs School of Business, Department of Management, Austin, TX 78712-1111. Offers PhD. *Accreditation:* AACSB. *Degree requirements:* For doctorate, thesis/dissertation. *Entrance requirements:* For doctorate, GMAT or GRE. Electronic applications accepted.

The University of Texas at Austin, Graduate School, McCombs School of Business, Executive MBA Program in Mexico City, Austin, TX 78712-1111. Offers MBA. *Accreditation:* AACSB. *Entrance requirements:* For master's, GMAT, 5 years of work experience. Additional exam requirements/recommendations for international students: Required—TOEFL.

The University of Texas at Austin, Graduate School, McCombs School of Business, Programs in MBA, Austin, TX 78712-1111. Offers MBA, JD/MBA, MBA/M Eng, MBA/MA, MBA/MP Aff, MBA/MSE, MBA/MSN. *Accreditation:* AACSB. Part-time programs available. *Entrance requirements:* For master's, GMAT, minimum 2 years of full-time work experience. Additional exam requirements/recommendations for international students: Required—TOEFL. Electronic applications accepted.

The University of Texas at Brownsville, Graduate Studies, School of Business, Brownsville, TX 78520-4991. Offers MBA. Part-time and evening/weekend programs available. Postbaccalaureate distance learning degree programs offered (minimal on-campus study). *Degree requirements:* For master's, capstone courses. *Entrance requirements:* For master's, GRE General Test. Additional exam requirements/recommendations for international students: Required—TOEFL. *Faculty research:* Binational and international business.

The University of Texas at Dallas, School of Management, Program in Business Administration, Richardson, TX 75083-0688. Offers EMBA, MBA. *Accreditation:* AACSB. Part-time and evening/weekend programs available. Postbaccalaureate distance learning degree programs offered. *Faculty:* 70 full-time (12 women), 6 part-time/adjunct (2 women). *Students:* 325 full-time (112 women), 771 part-time (274 women); includes 299 minority (44 African Americans, 188 Asian Americans or Pacific Islanders, 67 Hispanic Americans), 269 international. Average age 30. 857 applicants, 68% accepted, 359 enrolled. In 2006, 438 degrees awarded. *Degree requirements:* For master's, thesis optional. *Entrance requirements:* For master's, GMAT, 10 years of business experience (EMBA), minimum GPA of 3.0. Additional exam requirements/recommendations for international students: Required—TOEFL (minimum score 550 paper-based; 213 computer-based). Application fee: $50 ($100 for international students). Electronic applications accepted. *Expenses: Contact institution. Financial support:* In 2006–07, 6 research assistantships with tuition reimbursements (averaging $9,509 per year), 20 teaching assistantships with tuition reimbursements (averaging $9,465 per year) were awarded; fellowships, Federal Work-Study also available. Support available to part-time students. Financial award application deadline: 4/30; financial award applicants required to submit FAFSA. *Faculty research:* Production scheduling, trade and finance, organizational decision making, life/work planning. *Unit head:* Dr. Steve Perkins, MBA Coordinator, 972-883-6789, E-mail: perkins@utdallas.edu. *Application contact:* David B. Ritchey, Director of Advising, 972-883-2701, Fax: 972-883-6425, E-mail: davidr@utdallas.edu.

See Close-Up on page 365.

The University of Texas at Dallas, School of Management, Program in Management and Administrative Sciences, Richardson, TX 75083-0688. Offers information technology and management (MS); management and administrative science (MS); medical management (MS). *Accreditation:* AACSB. Part-time and evening/weekend programs available. *Faculty:* 53 full-time (8 women), 4 part-time/adjunct (1 woman). *Students:* 67 full-time (25 women), 127 part-time (53 women); includes 46 minority (12 African Americans, 1 American Indian/Alaska Native, 27 Asian Americans or Pacific Islanders, 6 Hispanic Americans), 86 international. Average age 31. 140 applicants, 89% accepted, 74 enrolled. In 2006, 73 degrees awarded. *Degree requirements:* For master's, thesis optional. *Entrance requirements:* For master's, GMAT. Additional exam requirements/recommendations for international students: Required—TOEFL (minimum score 550 paper-based; 213 computer-based). *Application deadline:* Applications are processed on a rolling basis. Application fee: $50 ($100 for international students). Electronic applications accepted. *Financial support:* In 2006–07, 1 research assistantship with tuition reimbursement (averaging $9,000 per year), 22 teaching assistantships with tuition

Business Administration and Management—General

The University of Texas at Dallas (continued)
reimbursements (averaging $13,457 per year) were awarded; fellowships, career-related internships or fieldwork, Federal Work-Study, institutionally sponsored loans, and scholarships/grants also available. Support available to part-time students. Financial award application deadline: 4/30; financial award applicants required to submit FAFSA. *Faculty research:* Integrated and detailed knowledge of functional areas of management, as well as analytical tools for effective appraisal and decision making. *Unit head:* Dr. Diane McNulty, Associate Dean and College Master, 972-883-2705, Fax: 972-883-2799, E-mail: dmcnulty@utdallas.edu. *Application contact:* David B. Ritchey, Director of Advising, 972-883-2701, Fax: 972-883-6425, E-mail: davidr@utdallas.edu.

See Close-Up on page 365.

The University of Texas at Dallas, School of Management, Programs in Management Science, Richardson, TX 75083-0688. Offers PhD. *Accreditation:* AACSB. Part-time and evening/weekend programs available. *Faculty:* 26 full-time (1 woman), 3 part-time/adjunct (1 woman). *Students:* 51 full-time (24 women), 4 part-time (2 women); includes 1 minority (Asian American or Pacific Islander), 46 international. Average age 31. 113 applicants, 34% accepted, 20 enrolled. In 2006, 19 degrees awarded. *Degree requirements:* For doctorate, thesis/dissertation. *Entrance requirements:* For doctorate, GMAT, minimum GPA of 3.0. Additional exam requirements/recommendations for international students: Required—TOEFL (minimum score 550 paper-based; 213 computer-based). *Application deadline:* Applications are processed on a rolling basis. Application fee: $50 ($100 for international students). Electronic applications accepted. *Financial support:* In 2006–07, 50 teaching assistantships with tuition reimbursements (averaging $14,514 per year) were awarded; fellowships, research assistantships, career-related internships or fieldwork, Federal Work-Study, institutionally sponsored loans, and scholarships/grants also available. Support available to part-time students. Financial award application deadline: 4/30. *Faculty research:* Empirical generalizations in marketing, diffusion of generations of technology, stochastic brand-choice theory, acceptance of trade deals by supermarkets, nonparametric estimations of market share response. *Unit head:* Program Director, 972-883-2744, E-mail: som-phd@utdallas.edu. *Application contact:* David B. Ritchey, Director of Advising, 972-883-2701, Fax: 972-883-6425, E-mail: davidr@utdallas.edu.

See Close-Up on page 365.

The University of Texas at El Paso, Graduate School, College of Business Administration, Department of Business Administration, El Paso, TX 79968-0001. Offers MBA. *Accreditation:* AACSB. Part-time and evening/weekend programs available. Postbaccalaureate distance learning degree programs offered (no on-campus study). *Entrance requirements:* For master's, GMAT, minimum GPA of 2.7. Additional exam requirements/recommendations for international students: Required—TOEFL. Electronic applications accepted.

The University of Texas at San Antonio, College of Business, Department of Management, San Antonio, TX 78249-0617. Offers international business (MBA); management (PhD); management science (MBA). *Accreditation:* AACSB. Part-time and evening/weekend programs available. *Faculty:* 12 full-time (4 women), 7 part-time/adjunct (2 women). *Students:* 11 full-time (3 women), 15 part-time (3 women); includes 10 minority (1 African American, 5 Asian Americans or Pacific Islanders, 4 Hispanic Americans), 6 international. Average age 29. 17 applicants, 53% accepted, 8 enrolled. In 2006, 11 degrees awarded. *Degree requirements:* For master's, thesis optional. *Entrance requirements:* For master's, GMAT, minimum GPA of 3.0. Additional exam requirements/recommendations for international students: Required—TOEFL (minimum score 500 paper-based; 173 computer-based). *Application deadline:* For fall admission, 7/1 for domestic students, 4/1 for international students; for spring admission, 11/1 for domestic students, 9/1 for international students. Applications are processed on a rolling basis. Application fee: $45 ($80 for international students). Electronic applications accepted. *Expenses:* Tuition, state resident: full-time $1,730; part-time $192 per credit hour. Tuition, nonresident: full-time $6,680; part-time $742 per credit hour. Required fees: $733; $308,359 per credit hour. *Financial support:* In 2006–07, 3 research assistantships (averaging $20,800 per year), 5 teaching assistantships (averaging $15,600 per year) were awarded; career-related internships or fieldwork, Federal Work-Study, scholarships/grants, and unspecified assistantships also available. Support available to part-time students. *Unit head:* Dr. Robert L. Cardy, Chair, 210-458-7480, Fax: 210-458-6335, E-mail: robert.cardy@utsa.edu.

The University of Texas at San Antonio, College of Business, Department of Management Science and Statistics, San Antonio, TX 78249-0617. Offers applied statistics (PhD); management science (MBA); statistics (MS). *Accreditation:* AACSB. Part-time and evening/weekend programs available. *Faculty:* 11 full-time (3 women), 1 part-time/adjunct (0 women). *Students:* 14 full-time (7 women), 29 part-time (13 women); includes 20 minority (1 African American, 6 Asian Americans or Pacific Islanders, 13 Hispanic Americans), 6 international. Average age 35. 28 applicants, 71% accepted, 19 enrolled. In 2006, 14 degrees awarded. *Degree requirements:* For master's, thesis optional. *Entrance requirements:* For master's, GMAT, minimum GPA of 3.0. Additional exam requirements/recommendations for international students: Required—TOEFL (minimum score 500 paper-based; 173 computer-based). *Application deadline:* For fall admission, 7/1 for domestic students, 4/1 for international students; for spring admission, 11/1 for domestic students, 9/1 for international students. Applications are processed on a rolling basis. Application fee: $45 ($80 for international students). Electronic applications accepted. *Expenses:* Tuition, state resident: full-time $1,730; part-time $192 per credit hour. Tuition, nonresident: full-time $6,680; part-time $742 per credit hour. Required fees: $733; $308,359 per credit hour. *Financial support:* In 2006–07, 1 research assistantship (averaging $21,944 per year), 9 teaching assistantships (averaging $15,975 per year) were awarded. Total annual research expenditures: $17,468. *Unit head:* Dr. Nandini Kannan, 210-458-5691, Fax: 210-458-6350, E-mail: nkannan@utsa.edu.

The University of Texas at Tyler, Graduate Studies, College of Business and Technology, Tyler, TX 75799-0001. Offers business administration (MBA); general management (MBA); health care track (MBA); human resource development and technology (MS), including human resource development, industrial distribution, industrial safety, industrial technology, instructional technology, technology systems; MSN/MBA. *Accreditation:* AACSB. Part-time and evening/weekend programs available. Postbaccalaureate distance learning degree programs offered (no on-campus study). *Entrance requirements:* Additional exam requirements/recommendations for international students: Required—TOEFL (minimum score 215 computer-based). Electronic applications accepted. *Expenses:* Tuition, state resident: part-time $50 per credit hour. Tuition, nonresident: part-time $328 per credit hour. Required fees: $107 per credit hour. $426 per term. *Faculty research:* Business ethics, financial policy, policy and strategy, economic multipliers, tax policy.

The University of Texas of the Permian Basin, Office of Graduate Studies, School of Business, Program in Management, Odessa, TX 79762-0001. Offers MBA. *Accreditation:* AACSB. *Degree requirements:* For master's, registration. *Entrance requirements:* For master's, GMAT. Additional exam requirements/recommendations for international students: Required—TOEFL (minimum score 550 paper-based; 213 computer-based).

The University of Texas–Pan American, College of Business Administration, Edinburg, TX 78539. Offers MBA, MS, PhD. *Accreditation:* AACSB. Part-time and evening/weekend programs available. *Degree requirements:* For master's, thesis optional; for doctorate, one foreign language, thesis/dissertation, internship. *Entrance requirements:* For master's, GMAT, minimum AACSB index of 1000 (based on last 60 semester hours); for doctorate, GMAT. Additional exam requirements/recommendations for international students: Required—TOEFL. *Expenses:* Tuition, state resident: full-time $2,577; part-time $143 per credit hour. Tuition, nonresident: full-time $7,527; part-time $418 per credit hour. Required fees: $561.

University of the District of Columbia, School of Business and Public Administration, Department of Management, Marketing, and Information Systems, Program in Business Administration, Washington, DC 20008-1175. Offers MBA. *Accreditation:* ACBSP. *Students:* 11 full-time (6 women), 14 part-time (6 women); 23 African Americans, 2 Asian Americans or Pacific Islanders. Average age 34. 50 applicants, 60% accepted. In 2006, 10 degrees awarded. *Degree requirements:* For master's, thesis optional. *Entrance requirements:* For master's, GMAT, writing proficiency exam. *Application deadline:* For fall admission, 6/15 priority date for domestic students; for spring admission, 11/1 for domestic students. Applications are processed on a rolling basis. Application fee: $20. *Financial support:* Career-related internships or fieldwork and Federal Work-Study available. *Application contact:* LaVerne Hill Flannigan, Director of Admission, 202-274-6069.

University of the Incarnate Word, School of Graduate Studies and Research, H-E-B School of Business and Administration, Programs in Administration, San Antonio, TX 78209-6397. Offers adult education (MAA); applied administration (MAA); communication arts (MAA); English (MAA); instructional technology (MAA); international business (Certificate); multidisciplinary sciences (MAA); nutrition (MAA); organizational development (MAA, Certificate); project management (Certificate); sports management (MAA); urban administration (MAA). *Students:* 1 (woman) full-time, 161 part-time (102 women); includes 17 African Americans, 1 American Indian/Alaska Native, 82 Hispanic Americans, 18 international. Average age 34. In 2006, 78 degrees awarded. *Entrance requirements:* For master's, GMAT, GRE, MAT. Additional exam requirements/recommendations for international students: Required—TOEFL. *Application deadline:* For fall admission, 8/15 priority date for domestic students; for spring admission, 12/31 for domestic students. Applications are processed on a rolling basis. Application fee: $20. *Expenses:* Tuition: Part-time $570 per credit hour. Required fees: $54 per credit hour. One-time fee: $195 part-time. Tuition and fees vary according to degree level. *Financial support:* Federal Work-Study and scholarships/grants available. *Unit head:* Dr. Dan Dominguez, MAA Director, 210-829-3180, Fax: 210-805-3564, E-mail: domingue@uiwtx.edu. *Application contact:* Andrea Cyterski-Acosta, Dean of Enrollment, 210-829-6005, Fax: 210-829-3921, E-mail: cyterski@uiwtx.edu.

University of the Incarnate Word, School of Graduate Studies and Research, H-E-B School of Business and Administration, Programs in Business Administration, San Antonio, TX 78209-6397. Offers international business (MBA); sports management (MBA); MBA/MSN. *Accreditation:* ACBSP. Part-time and evening/weekend programs available. *Students:* 19 full-time (13 women), 219 part-time (120 women); includes 123 minority (13 African Americans, 3 American Indian/Alaska Native, 4 Asian Americans or Pacific Islanders, 103 Hispanic Americans), 35 international. Average age 31. In 2006, 99 degrees awarded. *Entrance requirements:* For master's, GMAT. Additional exam requirements/recommendations for international students: Required—TOEFL. *Application deadline:* For fall admission, 8/15 priority date for domestic students; for spring admission, 12/31 for domestic students. Applications are processed on a rolling basis. Application fee: $20. *Expenses:* Tuition: Part-time $570 per credit hour. Required fees: $54 per credit hour. One-time fee: $195 part-time. Tuition and fees vary according to degree level. *Financial support:* Federal Work-Study, scholarships/grants, and tuition waivers (partial) available. Financial award application deadline: 5/31. *Faculty research:* Small business, Mexico/U.S. business, organizational development. *Unit head:* Dr. Connie Green, MBA Director, 210-829-3182, Fax: 210-805-3564, E-mail: greenc@uiwtx.edu. *Application contact:* Andrea Cyterski-Acosta, Dean of Enrollment, 210-829-6005, Fax: 210-829-3921, E-mail: cyterski@uiwtx.edu.

University of the Pacific, Eberhardt School of Business, Stockton, CA 95211-0197. Offers MBA, JD/MBA. *Accreditation:* AACSB. Part-time programs available. *Faculty:* 25 full-time (8 women), 1 part-time/adjunct (0 women). *Students:* 35 full-time (19 women), 11 part-time (4 women); includes 12 minority (1 African American, 8 Asian Americans or Pacific Islanders, 3 Hispanic Americans), 5 international. Average age 27. 85 applicants, 53% accepted, 20 enrolled. In 2006, 23 degrees awarded. *Entrance requirements:* For master's, GMAT. Additional exam requirements/recommendations for international students: Required—TOEFL (minimum score 475 paper-based; 150 computer-based). *Application deadline:* For fall admission, 7/31 priority date for domestic students; for spring admission, 11/30 for domestic students. Applications are processed on a rolling basis. Application fee: $75. *Expenses:* Tuition: Full-time $26,920. Required fees: $430. Tuition and fees vary according to course load. *Financial support:* Fellowships, research assistantships, Federal Work-Study and institutionally sponsored loans available. Support available to part-time students. Financial award application deadline: 3/1; financial award applicants required to submit FAFSA. *Unit head:* Dr. Charles Williams, Dean, 209-946-2466, Fax: 209-946-2586. *Application contact:* Dr. Chris Lozano, MBA Recruiting Director, 209-946-2597, Fax: 209-946-2586, E-mail: clozano@pacific.edu.

University of the Sacred Heart, Graduate Programs, Department of Business Administration, San Juan, PR 00914-0383. Offers human resource management (MBA); management information systems (MBA); marketing (MBA); taxation (MBA). Part-time and evening/weekend programs available. *Degree requirements:* For master's, thesis. *Entrance requirements:* For master's, EXADEP, minimum undergraduate GPA of 2.75, interview.

University of the Virgin Islands, Graduate Programs, Division of Business Administration, Saint Thomas, VI 00802-9990. Offers MBA. Part-time and evening/weekend programs available. *Faculty:* 6 full-time (0 women). *Students:* 3 full-time (2 women), 21 part-time (17 women); includes 22 minority (21 African Americans, 1 American Indian/Alaska Native), 1 international. Average age 34. 22 applicants, 73% accepted, 16 enrolled. In 2006, 14 degrees awarded. *Degree requirements:* For master's, comprehensive exam or thesis. *Entrance requirements:* For master's, GMAT, minimum GPA of 2.5. *Application deadline:* For fall admission, 4/30 for domestic and international students; for spring admission, 10/30 for domestic and international students. Application fee: $25. *Expenses:* Tuition, area resident: Full-time $4,950; part-time $275 per credit. Tuition, nonresident: full-time $9,900; part-time $550 per credit. Required fees: $130 per term. Tuition and fees vary according to course load and degree level. *Financial support:* Application deadline: 4/15. *Faculty research:* Management information systems. *Unit head:* Dr. Paul G. Simmonds, Chairperson, 340-692-4151, Fax: 340-692-4009, E-mail: psimmon@uvi.edu. *Application contact:* Carolyn Cook-Roberts, Director of Admissions, 340-693-1224, Fax: 340-693-1155, E-mail: ccook@uvi.edu.

University of the West, Department of Business Administration, Rosemead, CA 91770. Offers business administration (EMBA); finance (MBA); information technology and management (MBA); international business (MBA); nonprofit organization management (MBA). Part-time and evening/weekend programs available. *Entrance requirements:* Additional exam requirements/recommendations for international students: Required—TOEFL.

The University of Toledo, College of Graduate Studies, College of Business Administration, Toledo, OH 43606-3390. Offers EMBA, MBA, MS Acct, MSA, DME. *Accreditation:* AACSB. Part-time and evening/weekend programs available. *Faculty:* 28 full-time (3 women), 18 part-time/adjunct (1 woman). *Students:* 192 full-time (75 women), 175 part-time (55 women); includes 21 minority (14 African Americans, 2 Asian Americans or Pacific Islanders, 5 Hispanic Americans), 90 international. Average age 29. 260 applicants, 65% accepted, 105 enrolled. In 2006, 150 master's, 7 doctorates awarded. *Degree requirements:* For doctorate, thesis/dissertation. *Entrance requirements:* For master's and doctorate, GMAT. Additional exam requirements/recommendations for international students: Required—TOEFL. *Application deadline:* For fall admission, 8/1 priority date for domestic students. Applications are processed on a rolling basis. Application fee: $45. Electronic applications accepted. *Financial support:* In 2006–07, 59 research assistantships with tuition reimbursements (averaging $7,500 per year), 1 teaching assistantship with tuition reimbursement (averaging $5,500 per year) were awarded; fellowships, career-related internships or fieldwork, Federal Work-Study, institutionally sponsored loans, scholarships/grants, tuition waivers (full), and administrative assistantships also available. Support available to part-time students. Financial award application deadline: 4/1; financial award applicants required to submit FAFSA. *Unit head:* Dr. Thomas G. Gutteridge, Dean, 419-530-4060, Fax: 419-530-7260, E-mail: mba@uoft01.utoledo.edu.

See Close-Up on page 367.

The University of Toledo, College of Graduate Studies, College of Business Administration, Department of Management, Program in Management, Toledo, OH 43606-3390. Offers MBA. *Students:* 16 full-time (5 women), 18 part-time (8 women); includes 2 minority (1 African American, 1 Hispanic American), 3 international. Average age 29. 21 applicants, 57% accepted, 7 enrolled. In 2006, 16 degrees awarded. *Entrance requirements:* For master's, GMAT. *Financial support:* Research assistantships with tuition reimbursements available. *Application contact:* Graduate School Office, 419-530-4723, Fax: 419-530-4724, E-mail: gradsch@utnet.utoledo.edu.

University of Toronto, School of Graduate Studies, Social Sciences Division, Faculty of Management, Toronto, ON M5S 1A1, Canada. Offers EMBA, MBA, MMPA, PhD, JD/MBA, MBA/MA, MBA/MN. *Accreditation:* AACSB. Part-time and evening/weekend programs available. *Degree requirements:* For doctorate, thesis/dissertation. *Entrance requirements:* For master's, GMAT (MBA, MMPA; for EMBA: only applicants without an undergraduate degree), minimum mid-B average in final undergraduate year (MMPA, MBA), 2 years of full-time work experiences (MBA), 8 years work experience preferred (EMBA), 2-3 letters of reference; for doctorate, GMAT, minimum B+ average, master's degree in business administration, 2-3 letters of reference. Expenses: Contact institution. *Faculty research:* Natural resources, organizational behavior, finance.

University of Tulsa, Graduate School, College of Business Administration, Online Program in Business Administration, Tulsa, OK 74104-3189. Offers MBA. *Accreditation:* AACSB. Part-time and evening/weekend programs available. Postbaccalaureate distance learning degree programs offered (minimal on-campus study). *Faculty:* 12 full-time (4 women). *Students:* Average age 34. 4 applicants, 100% accepted, 3 enrolled. In 2006, 10 degrees awarded. *Median time to degree:* Master's–2.5 years full-time. *Degree requirements:* For master's, final team project. *Entrance requirements:* For master's, GMAT. Additional exam requirements/recommendations for international students: Required—TOEFL (minimum score 575 paper-based; 231 computer-based), IELTS (minimum score 7). *Application deadline:* Applications are processed on a rolling basis. Application fee: $40. Electronic applications accepted. *Expenses: Contact institution. Financial support:* Tuition waivers (full and partial) available. Financial award application deadline: 2/1; financial award applicants required to submit FAFSA. *Unit head:* Markham Collins, Associate Dean, 918-631-2783, Fax: 918-631-2142, E-mail: markham-collins@utulsa.edu.

University of Tulsa, Graduate School, College of Business Administration, Program in Business Administration, Tulsa, OK 74104-3189. Offers MBA, JD/MBA. *Accreditation:* AACSB. Part-time and evening/weekend programs available. *Faculty:* 12 full-time (4 women). *Students:* 57 full-time (24 women), 50 part-time (16 women); includes 11 minority (2 African Americans, 5 American Indian/Alaska Native, 2 Asian Americans or Pacific Islanders, 2 Hispanic Americans), 20 international. Average age 27. 51 applicants, 88% accepted, 40 enrolled. In 2006, 45 degrees awarded. *Median time to degree:* Master's–2 years full-time. *Entrance requirements:* For master's, GMAT. Additional exam requirements/recommendations for international students: Required—TOEFL (minimum score 575 paper-based; 231 computer-based), IELTS (minimum score 7). *Application deadline:* Applications are processed on a rolling basis. Application fee: $40. Electronic applications accepted. *Expenses:* Tuition: Full-time $13,338; part-time $741 per credit hour. *Financial support:* In 2006–07, 42 students received support, including 3 research assistantships with full and partial tuition reimbursements available (averaging $7,520 per year), 38 teaching assistantships with full and partial tuition reimbursements available (averaging $10,125 per year); fellowships with full and partial tuition reimbursements available, career-related internships or fieldwork, Federal Work-Study, institutionally sponsored loans, scholarships/grants, tuition waivers (full and partial), and unspecified assistantships also available. Support available to part-time students. Financial award application deadline: 2/1; financial award applicants required to submit FAFSA. *Faculty research:* International trade and development, expert systems, leadership, creativity, entrepreneurship. *Unit head:* Markham Collins, Associate Dean, 918-631-2783, Fax: 918-631-2142, E-mail: markham-collins@utulsa.edu.

University of Utah, The Graduate School, David Eccles School of Business, Salt Lake City, UT 84112-1107. Offers M Pr A, M Stat, MBA, MS, PhD, JD/MBA, MBA/M Acc. *Accreditation:* AACSB. Part-time and evening/weekend programs available. *Faculty:* 63 full-time (18 women), 7 part-time/adjunct (1 woman). *Students:* 610 full-time (137 women), 74 part-time (22 women); includes 66 minority (2 African Americans, 4 American Indian/Alaska Native, 36 Asian Americans or Pacific Islanders, 24 Hispanic Americans), 51 international. Average age 31. 867 applicants, 63% accepted, 418 enrolled. In 2006, 296 master's, 9 doctorates awarded. *Median time to degree:* Of those who began their doctoral program in fall 1998, 100% received their degree in 8 years or less. *Degree requirements:* For doctorate, thesis/dissertation, oral qualifying exams, written qualifying exams, comprehensive exam. *Entrance requirements:* For master's, GMAT, minimum undergraduate GPA of 3.0; for doctorate, GMAT, GRE. Additional exam requirements/recommendations for international students: Required—TOEFL (minimum score 600 paper-based; 256 computer-based). *Application deadline:* For fall admission, 4/1 for domestic and international students; for spring admission, 11/1 for domestic and international students. Application fee: $45 ($65 for international students). Electronic applications accepted. *Expenses: Contact institution.* Tuition and fees vary according to class time and program. *Financial support:* In 2006–07, 1 fellowship (averaging $12,000 per year), 41 research assistantships (averaging $750 per year), 39 teaching assistantships with partial tuition reimbursements (averaging $7,635 per year) were awarded; career-related internships or fieldwork, health care benefits, and unspecified assistantships also available. Financial award application deadline: 2/1; financial award applicants required to submit FAFSA. *Faculty research:* Information systems, investment, financial accounting, international strategy. Total annual research expenditures: $1.6 million. *Unit head:* Dr. Jack Brittain, Dean, 801-587-3860, Fax: 801-587-3380, E-mail: jack.brittain@business.utah.edu. *Application contact:* Lori Frandsden, Academic Coordinator, 801-581-8625, Fax: 801-587-3380, E-mail: lori.frandsen@business.utah.edu.

University of Vermont, Graduate College, School of Business Administration, Burlington, VT 05405. Offers MBA. *Accreditation:* AACSB. Part-time programs available. *Faculty:* 25. *Students:* 56 (24 women); includes 4 minority (all Asian Americans or Pacific Islanders) 6 international. 42 applicants, 71% accepted, 21 enrolled. In 2006, 15 degrees awarded. *Entrance requirements:* For master's, GMAT. Additional exam requirements/recommendations for international students: Required—TOEFL (minimum score 550 paper-based; 213 computer-based). *Application deadline:* For fall admission, 4/1 priority date for domestic students. Applications are processed on a rolling basis. Application fee: $40. *Expenses:* Tuition, state resident: part-time $434 per credit. Tuition, nonresident: part-time $1,096 per credit. *Financial support:* Fellowships, teaching assistantships, Federal Work-Study available. Financial award application deadline: 3/1. *Unit head:* Dr. R. DeWitt, Dean, 802-656-3177. *Application contact:* Dr. W. Averyt, Coordinator, 802-656-3177.

University of Victoria, Faculty of Graduate Studies, Faculty of Business, Victoria, BC V8W 2Y2, Canada. Offers MBA, MBA/LL B. Part-time programs available. *Entrance requirements:* For master's, GMAT, minimum B average. Additional exam requirements/recommendations for international students: Required—TOEFL (minimum score 575 paper-based; 233 computer-based), IELTS (minimum score 7). Electronic applications accepted. Expenses: Contact institution. *Faculty research:* Organizational design and analysis, negotiation and conflict management, human resources management, entrepreneurship, international marketing and tourism.

University of Virginia, Darden Graduate School of Business Administration, Charlottesville, VA 22903. Offers MBA, PhD, MBA/JD, MBA/MA, MBA/ME, MBA/MSN. *Accreditation:* AACSB. *Faculty:* 62 full-time (13 women), 2 part-time/adjunct (1 woman). *Students:* 693 full-time (147 women), 1 part-time; includes 92 minority (25 African Americans, 1 American Indian/Alaska Native, 47 Asian Americans or Pacific Islanders, 19 Hispanic Americans), 165 international. Average age 29. 1,780 applicants, 32% accepted, 329 enrolled. In 2006, 300 master's, 3 doctorates awarded. *Degree requirements:* For doctorate, thesis/dissertation. *Entrance requirements:* For master's and doctorate, GMAT. Additional exam requirements/recommendations for international students: Required—TOEFL. *Application deadline:* Applications are processed on a rolling basis. Application fee: $140. Electronic applications accepted. *Expenses: Contact institution. Financial support:* Fellowships, research assistantships, career-related internships or fieldwork available. Financial award applicants required to submit FAFSA. *Unit head:* Robert F. Bruner, Dean, 434-924-7481, E-mail: brunerr@virginia.edu. *Application contact:* Dawna Clarke, Director of Admissions, 434-924-4809, E-mail: darden@virginia.edu.

University of Virginia, McIntire School of Commerce, Charlottesville, VA 22903. Offers accounting (MS); management of information technology (MS). *Accreditation:* AACSB. *Faculty:* 58 full-time (14 women), 4 part-time/adjunct (3 women). *Students:* 125 full-time (42 women), 55 part-time (24 women); includes 8 minority (3 African Americans, 2 Asian Americans or Pacific Islanders, 3 Hispanic Americans), 25 international. Average age 27. In 2006, 172 degrees awarded. *Entrance requirements:* For master's, GMAT. Additional exam requirements/recommendations for international students: Required—TOEFL. *Application deadline:* For fall admission, 2/15 for domestic students, 1/15 priority date for international students. Applications are processed on a rolling basis. Application fee: $60. Electronic applications accepted. *Expenses: Contact institution. Financial support:* Fellowships, research assistantships, teaching assistantships, career-related internships or fieldwork and Federal Work-Study available. Financial award application deadline: 3/15; financial award applicants required to submit FAFSA. *Unit head:* Carl P. Zeithaml, Dean, 434-924-3110. *Application contact:* Cyndy Huddleston, Assistant Dean, Graduate Marketing and Admissions, 434-924-3110, E-mail: mcintiregrad@virginia.edu.

University of Washington, Graduate School, Business School, Seattle, WA 98195-3200. Offers auditing and assurance (MP Acc); business (PhD); evening part-time (MBA); executive (MBA); full time (MBA); global executive (MBA); taxation (MP Acc); technology management (MBA); JD/MBA; MBA/MAIS; MBA/MHA. *Accreditation:* AACSB. Part-time and evening/weekend programs available. *Degree requirements:* For master's, registration; for doctorate, thesis/dissertation, comprehensive exam, registration. *Entrance requirements:* For master's, GMAT; for doctorate, GMAT, GRE. Additional exam requirements/recommendations for international students: Required—TOEFL (minimum score 600 paper-based; 250 computer-based). Electronic applications accepted. Expenses: Contact institution.

University of Washington, Bothell, Program in Business Administration, Bothell, WA 98011-8246. Offers MA. *Faculty:* 10 full-time (1 woman). *Students:* 77 full-time (26 women), 5 part-time (1 woman); includes 2 African Americans, 14 Asian Americans or Pacific Islanders. Average age 34. 89 applicants, 46% accepted, 38 enrolled. In 2006, 35 degrees awarded. *Degree requirements:* For master's, thesis. *Entrance requirements:* For master's, GRE General Test. Additional exam requirements/recommendations for international students: Required—TOEFL. *Application deadline:* For fall admission, 2/5 priority date for domestic students. Applications are processed on a rolling basis. Application fee: $45. Electronic applications accepted. *Financial support:* Federal Work-Study available. *Faculty research:* Innovation and technology, management, finance, leadership, ethics. *Unit head:* Prof. Steven Holland, Director of Business Program, 425-352-5232, Fax: 425-352-5277, E-mail: sholland@uwb.edu. *Application contact:* Don Whitney, MBA Manager, 425-352-5434, Fax: 425-352-5277.

University of Waterloo, Graduate Studies, Centre for Business, Entrepreneurship and Technology, Waterloo, ON N2L 3G1, Canada. Offers MBET. *Faculty:* 15 full-time. *Students:* 33 full-time (11 women). 57 applicants, 63% accepted, 23 enrolled. In 2006, 31 degrees awarded. *Degree requirements:* For master's, registration. *Entrance requirements:* For master's, honors degree. Additional exam requirements/recommendations for international students: Required—TOEFL (minimum score 550 paper-based; 213 computer-based), TWE. *Application deadline:* Applications are processed on a rolling basis. Application fee: $75. Electronic applications accepted. *Unit head:* Dr. Howard Armitage, Director, 519-888-4567 Ext. 35776, Fax: 519-888-7562, E-mail: howard@uwaterloo.ca. *Application contact:* Emily Stafford, Administrative Liaison and Support, 519-888-4567 Ext. 31167, Fax: 519-888-7562, E-mail: estaffor@uwaterloo.ca.

The University of Western Ontario, Richard Ivey School of Business, London, ON N6A 3K7, Canada. Offers biotechnology stream (MBA); business (EMBA, PhD); certified management accountant (MBA); China business stream (MBA); entrepreneurship (MBA); finance stream (MBA); LL B/MBA. Part-time and evening/weekend programs available. *Degree requirements:* For master's, thesis (for some programs); for doctorate, thesis/dissertation. *Entrance requirements:* For master's, GMAT, 3 years of full-time work experience, interview; for doctorate, GMAT. Additional exam requirements/recommendations for international students: Required—TOEFL. Electronic applications accepted. *Faculty research:* Strategy, organizational behavior, international business, finance, operations management.

University of West Florida, College of Business, Program in Business Administration, Pensacola, FL 32514-5750. Offers MBA. *Accreditation:* AACSB. Part-time and evening/weekend programs available. *Faculty:* 20 full-time (6 women), 10 part-time/adjunct (5 women). *Students:* 20 full-time (9 women), 108 part-time (48 women); includes 11 minority (6 African Americans, 3 Asian Americans or Pacific Islanders, 2 Hispanic Americans), 17 international. Average age 31. 75 applicants, 64% accepted, 41 enrolled. In 2006, 76 degrees awarded. *Degree requirements:* For master's, thesis optional. *Entrance requirements:* For master's, GMAT. Additional exam requirements/recommendations for international students: Required—TOEFL (minimum score 550 paper-based; 213 computer-based). *Application deadline:* For fall admission, 6/30 for domestic students, 5/15 for international students; for spring admission, 11/1 for domestic students, 10/1 for international students. Applications are processed on a rolling basis. Application fee: $30. *Expenses:* Tuition, state resident: full-time $5,871; part-time $245 per credit hour. Tuition, nonresident: full-time $21,241; part-time $885 per credit hour. *Financial support:* In 2006–07, 61 fellowships (averaging $500 per year), 26 research assistantships with partial tuition reimbursements (averaging $7,000 per year) were awarded; scholarships/grants and unspecified assistantships also available. Support available to part-time students. Financial award application deadline: 4/15; financial award applicants required to submit FAFSA. *Faculty research:* Robotics, corporate behavior, international trade, franchising, counterfeiting. *Unit head:* Dr. Arup Mukerjee, Chairperson, 850-474-2313. *Application contact:* Cheryl Y. Powell, Academic Advisor, 850-474-2662.

University of West Georgia, Graduate School, Richards College of Business, Program of Business Administration, Carrollton, GA 30118. Offers MBA. *Accreditation:* AACSB. Part-time and evening/weekend programs available. Postbaccalaureate distance learning degree programs offered (no on-campus study). *Faculty:* 11 full-time (2 women), 1 part-time/adjunct (0 women). *Students:* 9 full-time (3 women), 20 part-time (6 women); includes 1 minority (African American), 5 international. Average age 21. In 2006, 30 degrees awarded. *Degree requirements:* For master's, comprehensive exam. *Entrance requirements:* For master's, GMAT, minimum GPA of 2.5. Additional exam requirements/recommendations for international students: Required—TOEFL. *Application deadline:* For fall admission, 7/25 for domestic students, 6/5 for international students; for spring admission, 12/8 for domestic students, 10/2 for international students. Applications are processed on a rolling basis. Application fee: $20. Electronic applications accepted. *Expenses:* Tuition, state resident: full-time $2,286; part-time $127 per credit. Tuition, nonresident: full-time $9,144; part-time $508 per credit. Required fees: $494; $27 per credit. $121 per semester. *Financial support:* In 2006–07, 8 research assistantships with full tuition reimbursements (averaging $8,000 per year) were awarded; career-related internships or fieldwork, tuition waivers (partial), and unspecified assistantships also available. Support available to part-time students. Financial award application deadline: 7/1; financial award applicants required to submit FAFSA. *Faculty research:* Distance learning, small business development, e-commerce, computer self-efficancy. *Unit head:* Dr. John Anderson, Associate Dean/MBA Director, 678-839-6467, Fax: 678-839-5039, E-mail: janderson@westga.edu. *Application contact:* Dr. Charles W. Clark, Chair, 678-839-6508, E-mail: cclark@westga.edu.

University of Windsor, Faculty of Graduate Studies and Research, Odette School of Business, Windsor, ON N9B 3P4, Canada. Offers MBA, MM, MBA/LL B. Evening/weekend programs available. *Degree requirements:* For master's, thesis or alternative. *Entrance*

Business Administration and Management—General

University of Windsor (continued)
requirements: For master's, GMAT, minimum B average. Additional exam requirements/recommendations for international students: Required—TOEFL (minimum score 600 paper-based; 250 computer-based). Electronic applications accepted. *Faculty research:* Accounting, administrative studies, finance, marketing, business policy and strategy.

University of Wisconsin–Eau Claire, College of Business, Program in Business Administration, Eau Claire, WI 54702-4004. Offers MBA. *Accreditation:* AACSB. Part-time programs available. *Faculty:* 32 full-time (8 women), 2 part-time/adjunct (0 women). *Students:* 7 full-time (2 women), 170 part-time (77 women); includes 18 minority (4 African Americans, 3 American Indian/Alaska Native, 7 Asian Americans or Pacific Islanders, 4 Hispanic Americans), 6 international. Average age 32. 108 applicants, 66% accepted, 71 enrolled. In 2006, 26 degrees awarded. *Degree requirements:* For master's, applied field project. *Entrance requirements:* For master's, GMAT, minimum GPA of 2.75 overall or 2.9 in final 10 credit hours. *Application deadline:* For fall admission, 7/1 for domestic students; for spring admission, 12/1 for domestic students. Applications are processed on a rolling basis. Application fee: $45. *Expenses:* Tuition, state resident: full-time $6,533; part-time $363 per credit. Tuition, nonresident: full-time $17,143; part-time $952 per credit. Tuition and fees vary according to program and reciprocity agreements. *Financial support:* In 2006–07, 23 students received support, including 3 fellowships, 3 teaching assistantships (averaging $3,800 per year); Federal Work-Study also available. Support available to part-time students. Financial award applicants required to submit FAFSA. *Unit head:* Dr. Robert Erffmeyer, Director, 715-836-6019, Fax: 715-836-3923, E-mail: erffmerc@uwec.edu.

University of Wisconsin–Green Bay, Graduate Studies, Program in Management, Green Bay, WI 54311-7001. Offers MS. Part-time programs available. *Faculty:* 5 full-time (1 woman). *Students:* 2 full-time (1 woman), 36 part-time (26 women); includes 5 minority (1 African American, 2 American Indian/Alaska Native, 1 Asian American or Pacific Islander, 1 Hispanic American), 1 international. Average age 32. 29 applicants, 72% accepted, 14 enrolled. In 2006, 11 degrees awarded. *Degree requirements:* For master's, thesis or alternative. *Entrance requirements:* For master's, GMAT or GRE General Test, minimum GPA of 3.0. *Application deadline:* For fall admission, 8/1 for domestic students; for spring admission, 11/1 for domestic students. Applications are processed on a rolling basis. Application fee: $45. Electronic applications accepted. *Expenses:* Tuition, state resident: full-time $5,910; part-time $246 per credit. Tuition, nonresident: full-time $16,520; part-time $688 per credit. Required fees: $1,148; $48 per credit. *Financial support:* Career-related internships or fieldwork, Federal Work-Study, and institutionally sponsored loans available. Financial award application deadline: 7/15; financial award applicants required to submit FAFSA. *Faculty research:* Planning methods, budgeting, decision making, organizational behavior and theory, management. *Unit head:* Dr. Karl Zehms, Chair, 920-465-2553. *Application contact:* Don McCartney, Management Program Advisor, 920-465-2520, E-mail: mccartnd@uwgb.edu.

University of Wisconsin–La Crosse, Office of University Graduate Studies, College of Business Administration, La Crosse, WI 54601-3742. Offers MBA. *Accreditation:* AACSB. Part-time and evening/weekend programs available. *Faculty:* 26 full-time (5 women), 2 part-time/adjunct (1 woman). *Students:* 12 full-time (3 women), 32 part-time (13 women); includes 2 minority (1 Asian American or Pacific Islander, 1 Hispanic American), 8 international. Average age 31. 30 applicants, 77% accepted, 14 enrolled. In 2006, 17 degrees awarded. *Degree requirements:* For master's, thesis optional. *Entrance requirements:* For master's, GMAT. Additional exam requirements/recommendations for international students: Required—TOEFL (minimum score 550 paper-based; 213 computer-based). *Application deadline:* For fall admission, 5/1 priority date for domestic students; for spring admission, 10/1 priority date for domestic students. Applications are processed on a rolling basis. Application fee: $45. *Expenses: Contact institution. Financial support:* In 2006–07, 6 research assistantships with partial tuition reimbursements (averaging $5,914 per year) were awarded; Federal Work-Study, health care benefits, tuition waivers (partial), and unspecified assistantships also available. Support available to part-time students. Financial award application deadline: 3/15; financial award applicants required to submit FAFSA. *Faculty research:* Tax Circular 230, supply chain solutions, economics of sports, internet privacy and regulation, stock predictions. *Unit head:* Dr. Bruce May, Dean, 608-785-8095, Fax: 608-785-6700, E-mail: may.bruce@uwlax.edu. *Application contact:* Amelia Dittman, Assistant to the Dean, 608-785-8092, Fax: 608-785-6700, E-mail: dittman.amel@uwlax.edu.

University of Wisconsin–Madison, Graduate School, School of Business, Wisconsin Full-Time MBA Programs, Madison, WI 53706-1380. Offers applied corporate finance (MBA); applied security analysis (MBA); arts administration (MBA); brand and product management (MBA); entrepreneurial management (MBA); information systems (MBA); marketing research (MBA); operations and technology management (MBA); real estate (MBA); risk management and insurance (MBA); strategic human resource management (MBA); strategic management in the life and engineering sciences (MBA); supply chain management (MBA). *Faculty:* 84. *Students:* 231 full-time (74 women); includes 21 minority (10 African Americans, 5 Asian Americans or Pacific Islanders, 6 Hispanic Americans), 59 international. Average age 28. 405 applicants, 43% accepted, 121 enrolled. In 2006, 110 degrees awarded. *Entrance requirements:* For master's, GMAT, bachelors or equivalent degree, 2 years of work experience. Additional exam requirements/recommendations for international students: Required—TOEFL (minimum score 600 paper-based; 250 computer-based; 90 iBT). *Application deadline:* For fall admission, 11/1 for domestic and international students; for winter admission, 1/23 for domestic and international students; for spring admission, 3/26 for domestic and international students. Applications are processed on a rolling basis. Application fee: $45. Electronic applications accepted. *Financial support:* In 2006–07, 177 students received support, including 20 fellowships with full and partial tuition reimbursements available (averaging $16,566 per year), 105 research assistantships with full tuition reimbursements available (averaging $8,098 per year), 33 teaching assistantships with full tuition reimbursements available (averaging $10,112 per year); scholarships/grants, health care benefits, and unspecified assistantships also available. *Unit head:* Gary Lessuise, Assistant Dean, Masters Programs, 608-265-5102, Fax: 608-265-4192, E-mail: glessuise@bus.wisc.edu. *Application contact:* Betsy Kacizak, Director of Admissions and Financial Aid—Full Time MBA, 608-262-4000, Fax: 608-265-4192, E-mail: mba@bus.wisc.edu.

University of Wisconsin–Milwaukee, Graduate School, Sheldon B. Lubar School of Business, Milwaukee, WI 53201-0413. Offers MBA, MS, PhD, Certificate. *Accreditation:* AACSB. Part-time and evening/weekend programs available. *Faculty:* 64 full-time (17 women). *Students:* 247 full-time (96 women), 366 part-time (147 women); includes 57 minority (16 African Americans, 4 American Indian/Alaska Native, 29 Asian Americans or Pacific Islanders, 8 Hispanic Americans), 86 international. Average age 32. 457 applicants, 46% accepted, 172 enrolled. In 2006, 291 master's, 11 doctorates awarded. *Degree requirements:* For doctorate, thesis/dissertation, comprehensive exam. *Entrance requirements:* For master's and doctorate, GMAT or GRE General Test. *Application deadline:* For fall admission, 1/1 priority date for domestic students; for spring admission, 9/1 for domestic students. Applications are processed on a rolling basis. Application fee: $45 ($75 for international students). *Expenses: Contact institution.* Tuition and fees vary according to program. *Financial support:* In 2006–07, 5 fellowships, 35 teaching assistantships were awarded; research assistantships, career-related internships or fieldwork, Federal Work-Study, and unspecified assistantships also available. Support available to part-time students. Financial award application deadline: 4/15. *Faculty research:* Applied management research in finance, MIS, marketing, operations research, organizational sciences. *Unit head:* Sarah Sandin, Representative, 414-229-5403, Fax: 414-229-2372, E-mail: ssandin@uwm.edu. *Application contact:* Velagapudi K. Prasad, Associate Dean, 414-229-4235.

University of Wisconsin–Oshkosh, The School of Graduate Studies, College of Business Administration, Program in Business Administration, Oshkosh, WI 54901. Offers MBA. *Accreditation:* AACSB. Part-time programs available. *Degree requirements:* For master's, registration. *Entrance requirements:* For master's, GMAT, GRE, minimum undergraduate GPA of 2.75. Additional exam requirements/recommendations for international students: Required—TOEFL (minimum score 550 paper-based; 213 computer-based). Electronic applications accepted.

University of Wisconsin–Parkside, School of Business and Technology, Kenosha, WI 53141-2000. Offers MBA, MSCIS. *Accreditation:* AACSB. Part-time and evening/weekend programs available. *Faculty:* 24 full-time (7 women). *Students:* 15 full-time (5 women), 82 part-time (34 women); includes 23 minority (8 African Americans, 11 Asian Americans or Pacific Islanders, 4 Hispanic Americans). Average age 30. 28 applicants, 96% accepted, 24 enrolled. In 2006, 23 degrees awarded. *Entrance requirements:* For master's, GMAT. Additional exam requirements/recommendations for international students: Required—TOEFL (minimum score 550 paper-based; 216 computer-based; 79 iBT). *Application deadline:* For fall admission, 8/1 for domestic students, 6/1 for international students; for spring admission, 12/15 for domestic students, 10/1 for international students. Applications are processed on a rolling basis. Application fee: $45. Electronic applications accepted. *Expenses: Contact institution. Financial support:* Available to part-time students. Application deadline: 7/1. *Faculty research:* Business strategy, ethics in accounting and finance, mutual funds, decision analysis and neural networks, management skills. *Unit head:* Dr. Fred Ebeid, Dean, 262-595-2243, Fax: 262-595-2680, E-mail: ebeid@uwp.edu. *Application contact:* Bradley Piazza, Assistant Dean, 262-595-2046, Fax: 262-595-2680, E-mail: piazza@uwp.edu.

University of Wisconsin–River Falls, Outreach and Graduate Studies, College of Business and Economics, River Falls, WI 54022-5001. Offers MM. *Accreditation:* AACSB. *Degree requirements:* For master's, thesis or alternative, registration. Electronic applications accepted.

University of Wisconsin–Stevens Point, College of Letters and Science, Division of Business and Economics, Stevens Point, WI 54481-3897. Offers MBA. *Application deadline:* Applications are processed on a rolling basis. Application fee: $45. *Expenses:* Tuition, state resident: full-time $5,910; part-time $328 per credit. Tuition, nonresident: full-time $16,520; part-time $918 per credit. Required fees: $756; $73 per credit. *Financial support:* Application deadline: 5/1; *Unit head:* Dr. Gary Mullins, Chair, 715-346-2728.

University of Wisconsin–Whitewater, School of Graduate Studies, College of Business and Economics, Program in Business Administration, Whitewater, WI 53190-1790. Offers finance (MBA); human resource management (MBA); information technology management (MBA); international business (MBA); management (MBA); marketing (MBA); operations and supply chain management (MBA); technology and training (MBA). *Accreditation:* AACSB. Part-time and evening/weekend programs available. Postbaccalaureate distance learning degree programs offered (no on-campus study). *Students:* 67 full-time (26 women), 331 part-time (136 women); includes 71 minority (20 African Americans, 40 Asian Americans or Pacific Islanders, 11 Hispanic Americans). Average age 28. 167 applicants, 62% accepted, 75 enrolled. In 2006, 141 degrees awarded. *Degree requirements:* For master's, thesis or alternative. *Entrance requirements:* For master's, GMAT, minimum AACSB index of 1000, minimum GPA of 2.75. Additional exam requirements/recommendations for international students: Required—TOEFL (minimum score 550 paper-based; 213 computer-based). *Application deadline:* For fall admission, 7/15 for domestic students, 7/15 priority date for international students; for spring admission, 12/1 for domestic and international students. Applications are processed on a rolling basis. Application fee: $45. Electronic applications accepted. *Expenses:* Tuition, state resident: full-time $3,311. Tuition, nonresident: full-time $8,616. Required fees: $368 per credit. *Financial support:* In 2006–07, 11 research assistantships (averaging $7,385 per year) were awarded; Federal Work-Study, unspecified assistantships, and out of state fee waiver also available. Support available to part-time students. Financial award application deadline: 3/15; financial award applicants required to submit FAFSA. *Faculty research:* Interface between social institutions and individual behavior, technology and innovation management, occupational mental health, workplace deviance and workplace romance. *Unit head:* Dr. Donald Zahn, Associate Dean, 262-472-1945, Fax: 262-472-4863, E-mail: zahnd@uww.edu.

Announcement: Whitewater's Master of Business Administration (MBA) program provides advanced academic work in the functional aspects of public and private organizations. This professional degree program provides students with general competencies for overall management and allows a degree of specialization in the areas of finance, human resource management, international business, IT management, management, marketing, operations and supply chain management, and technology and training. Internationalization and globalization are important ingredients in courses. A variety of teaching methods are used. Problem-solving and communication skills are emphasized through projects, case studies, and formal and informal presentations. There is diversity among students and faculty members. Many students are employed full-time. There are a significant number of international students. MBA courses are available over the Internet. Also offered are a Master of Professional Accountancy (MPA) degree, which prepares students for the CPA exam, and a certificate program in human resource management.

University of Wyoming, Graduate School, College of Business, Program in Business Administration, Laramie, WY 82070. Offers MBA. *Accreditation:* AACSB. Part-time and evening/weekend programs available. Postbaccalaureate distance learning degree programs offered (minimal on-campus study). *Faculty:* 13. *Students:* 26 full-time (8 women), 56 part-time (15 women); includes 4 minority (1 African American, 1 American Indian/Alaska Native, 1 Asian American or Pacific Islander, 1 Hispanic American), 1 international. Average age 32. 83 applicants, 71% accepted. In 2006, 38 degrees awarded. *Degree requirements:* For master's, thesis or alternative. *Entrance requirements:* For master's, GMAT, GRE General Test, minimum GPA of 3.0. Additional exam requirements/recommendations for international students: Required—TOEFL (minimum score 525 paper-based; 197 computer-based). *Application deadline:* For fall admission, 3/1 priority date for domestic students. Applications are processed on a rolling basis. Application fee: $50. Electronic applications accepted. *Financial support:* In 2006–07, 16 research assistantships with partial tuition reimbursements (averaging $5,031 per year) were awarded; fellowships, teaching assistantships, career-related internships or fieldwork, Federal Work-Study, institutionally sponsored loans, and unspecified assistantships also available. Financial award application deadline: 2/1; financial award applicants required to submit FAFSA. *Faculty research:* Natural resource marketing and product development, work place violence. *Unit head:* Dr. Lanny Stevens, Director, 307-766-3154, Fax: 307-766-4028, E-mail: mba@uwyo.edu. *Application contact:* 307-766-2449, Fax: 307-766-4028, E-mail: mba@uwyo.edu.

Upper Iowa University, Online Master's Programs, Fayette, IA 52142-1857. Offers accounting (MBA); corporate financial management (MBA); global business (MBA); health and human services (MPA); homeland security (MPA); human resources management (MBA); justice administration (MPA); organizational development (MPA); public personnel management (MPA); quality management (MBA). MBA also available at Madison, Wisconsin campus. Part-time and evening/weekend programs available. Postbaccalaureate distance learning degree programs offered (no on-campus study). *Degree requirements:* For master's, research project. *Entrance requirements:* For master's, GMAT, GRE, or minimum GPA of 2.7 during last 60 hours. Additional exam requirements/recommendations for international students: Required—TOEFL (minimum score 570 paper-based; 230 computer-based). Electronic applications accepted. *Faculty research:* Total quality management, CQI, teams, organization culture and climate, management.

Urbana University, Division of Business Administration, Urbana, OH 43078-2091. Offers MBA. Part-time and evening/weekend programs available. *Degree requirements:* For master's, thesis or alternative, comprehensive exam. *Entrance requirements:* For master's, GMAT, minimum GPA of 2.7, BS in business, 3 letters of recommendation, work experience. Additional exam requirements/recommendations for international students: Required—TOEFL (minimum score 550 paper-based; 213 computer-based). *Faculty research:* Organizational behavior, taxation, segmentation, information systems, retail gravitation.

Ursuline College, School of Graduate Studies, Program in Management, Pepper Pike, OH 44124-4398. Offers MM. Part-time programs available. *Faculty:* 1 (woman) full-time, 3 part-time/adjunct (2 women). *Students:* 14 full-time (13 women); includes 8 minority (all African Americans) Average age 41. 4 applicants, 100% accepted, 4 enrolled. In 2006, 10 degrees awarded. *Degree requirements:* For master's, project. *Entrance requirements:* For master's, minimum undergraduate GPA of 3.0. Additional exam requirements/recommendations for international students: Required—TOEFL (minimum score 500 paper-based; 173 computer-based). *Application deadline:* For fall admission, 8/1 priority date for domestic students. Applications are processed on a rolling basis. Application fee: $25. *Expenses:* Tuition: Full-time $12,078; part-time $671 per credit hour. Required fees: $60 per semester. *Financial support:* In 2006–07, 12 students received support. Federal Work-Study available. Financial award application deadline: 3/1; financial award applicants required to submit FAFSA. *Unit head:* Director, 440-646-8332, Fax: 440-684-6088, E-mail: bbraun@ursuline.edu. *Application contact:* Jo Mann, Secretary, 440-646-8119, Fax: 440-684-6088, E-mail: gradsch@ursuline.edu.

Utah State University, School of Graduate Studies, College of Business, Program in Business Administration, Logan, UT 84322. Offers MBA. *Accreditation:* AACSB. Part-time and evening/weekend programs available. Postbaccalaureate distance learning degree programs offered (minimal on-campus study). *Faculty:* 40 full-time (5 women). *Students:* 363 full-time (76 women), 277 part-time (43 women); includes 5 minority (all Hispanic Americans), 109 international. Average age 29. 396 applicants, 78% accepted, 243 enrolled. In 2006, 58 degrees awarded. *Degree requirements:* For master's, comprehensive exam, registration. *Entrance requirements:* For master's, GMAT or GRE, minimum GPA of 3.0. Additional exam requirements/recommendations for international students: Required—TOEFL. *Application deadline:* For fall admission, 2/15 priority date for domestic and international students; for spring admission, 10/15 priority date for domestic students. Applications are processed on a rolling basis. Application fee: $50 ($60 for international students). Electronic applications accepted. *Financial support:* In 2006–07, 4 fellowships with partial tuition reimbursements (averaging $3,000 per year), 14 research assistantships with partial tuition reimbursements (averaging $2,500 per year), 1 teaching assistantship with partial tuition reimbursement (averaging $2,500 per year) were awarded; career-related internships or fieldwork, Federal Work-Study, institutionally sponsored loans, and tuition waivers (full and partial) also available. Financial award application deadline: 4/1. *Faculty research:* Marketing strategy, technology and innovation, public utility finance, international competitiveness. *Unit head:* Mary Jo Blahna, Director, 435-797-2360, Fax: 435-797-2634, E-mail: maryjo.blahna@usu.edu. *Application contact:* Teri Guy, Staff Assistant, 435-797-2360, Fax: 435-797-2634, E-mail: teri.guy@usu.edu.

Valdosta State University, Graduate School, Langdale College of Business Administration, Program in Business Administration, Valdosta, GA 31698. Offers MBA. *Accreditation:* AACSB. Part-time programs available. *Degree requirements:* For master's, comprehensive written and/or oral exams. *Entrance requirements:* For master's, GMAT, minimum GPA of 2.75. Additional exam requirements/recommendations for international students: Required—TOEFL (minimum score 523 paper-based; 193 computer-based). Electronic applications accepted.

Valparaiso University, Graduate Division, College of Business Administration, Valparaiso, IN 46383. Offers business administration (MBA); engineering management (MEM); management (Certificate); JD/MBA; MBA/MSN. *Accreditation:* AACSB. Part-time and evening/weekend programs available. *Faculty:* 13 part-time/adjunct (4 women). *Students:* 32 full-time (13 women), 34 part-time (14 women); includes 4 minority (3 African Americans, 1 Hispanic American), 1 international. Average age 26. In 2006, 25 degrees awarded. *Entrance requirements:* For master's, GMAT, minimum GPA of 3.0. Additional exam requirements/recommendations for international students: Required—TOEFL (minimum score 550 paper-based; 213 computer-based). *Application deadline:* Applications are processed on a rolling basis. Application fee: $30 ($50 for international students). Electronic applications accepted. *Expenses: Contact institution.* Tuition and fees vary according to program. *Financial support:* Available to part-time students. Applicants required to submit FAFSA. *Unit head:* Dr. Dean Schroeder, Director, 219-464-5177, Fax: 219-464-5789, E-mail: dean.schroeder@valpo.edu. *Application contact:* Erin Brown, Assistant MBA Director, 219-465-7952, Fax: 219-464-5789, E-mail: erin.brown@valpo.edu.

Vanderbilt University, Owen Graduate School of Management, Business Administration Program, Nashville, TN 37240-1001. Offers MBA, JD/MBA, MBA/M Div, MBA/MA, MBA/MD, MBA/MSN. Students in the 5-year MBA program enter as undergraduates. *Accreditation:* AACSB. *Faculty:* 46 full-time (8 women), 25 part-time/adjunct (4 women). *Students:* 358 full-time (91 women); includes 28 minority (15 African Americans, 2 American Indian/Alaska Native, 10 Asian Americans or Pacific Islanders, 1 Hispanic American), 108 international. Average age 28. 779 applicants, 45% accepted, 161 enrolled. In 2006, 176 degrees awarded. *Median time to degree:* Master's–2 years full-time. *Entrance requirements:* For master's, GMAT, minimum 2 years of work experience (strongly recommended). Additional exam requirements/recommendations for international students: Required—TOEFL; Recommended—TWE. *Application deadline:* For fall admission, 11/15 priority date for domestic students, 11/30 priority date for international students; for winter admission, 1/15 priority date for domestic and international students; for spring admission, 3/1 priority date for domestic students, 3/15 priority date for international students. Applications are processed on a rolling basis. Application fee: $100. Electronic applications accepted. *Expenses:* Tuition: Full-time $24,462. Required fees: $2,515. One-time fee: $30 full-time. Full-time tuition and fees vary according to course load, degree level and program. *Financial support:* In 2006–07, 184 students received support. Scholarships/grants and tuition waivers (full and partial) available. Financial award application deadline: 5/1; financial award applicants required to submit FAFSA. *Faculty research:* Financial markets, services marketing, operations, organization studies, health care. Total annual research expenditures: $201,000. *Unit head:* John Roeder, Director of Admissions, 615-322-6469, Fax: 615-343-1175, E-mail: admissions@owen.vanderbilt.edu. *Application contact:* Sue Miller, Operations Manager, 615-322-4269, Fax: 615-343-1175, E-mail: admissions@owen.vanderbilt.edu.

Vanderbilt University, Owen Graduate School of Management, Executive Business Administration Program, Nashville, TN 37240-1001. Offers MBA. Evening/weekend programs available. *Faculty:* 46 full-time (8 women), 25 part-time/adjunct (4 women). *Students:* 81 full-time (13 women); includes 11 minority (5 African Americans, 3 Asian Americans or Pacific Islanders, 3 Hispanic Americans). Average age 35. 97 applicants, 60% accepted, 46 enrolled. In 2006, 38 degrees awarded. *Median time to degree:* Master's–2 years full-time. *Entrance requirements:* For master's, GMAT, minimum of 5 years of work experience. Additional exam requirements/recommendations for international students: Required—TOEFL. *Application deadline:* For fall admission, 6/1 for domestic students. Applications are processed on a rolling basis. Application fee: $100. Electronic applications accepted. *Expenses: Contact institution.* One-time fee: $30 full-time. Full-time tuition and fees vary according to course load, degree level and program. *Financial support:* In 2006–07, 1 student received support. Scholarships/grants available. *Faculty research:* Management, business policy, finance, marketing, operations management, health care. *Unit head:* Tami Fassinger, Associate Dean of Executive Education, Fax: 615-343-2293. *Application contact:* Juli Bennett, Coordinator, 615-322-9865, Fax: 615-343-2293, E-mail: juli.bennett@owen.vanderbilt.edu.

Vanderbilt University, Owen Graduate School of Management and Graduate School, Program in Management, Nashville, TN 37240-1001. Offers finance (PhD); marketing (PhD); operations management (PhD); organization studies (PhD). PhD offered through the Graduate School. *Accreditation:* AACSB. *Faculty:* 46 full-time (8 women). *Students:* 19 full-time (6 women); includes 12 minority (all Asian Americans or Pacific Islanders) Average age 28. 169 applicants, 5% accepted, 5 enrolled. In 2006, 3 degrees awarded. *Median time to degree:* Doctorate–5 years full-time. Of those who began their doctoral program in fall 1998, 100% received their degree in 8 years or less. *Degree requirements:* For doctorate, thesis/dissertation, registration. *Entrance requirements:* For doctorate, GMAT or GRE. Additional exam requirements/recommendations for international students: Required—TOEFL. *Application deadline:* For fall admission, 1/15 priority date for domestic students; for spring admission, 3/15 for domestic students. Application fee: $0. Electronic applications accepted. *Expenses: Contact institution.* One-time fee: $30 full-time. Full-time tuition and fees vary according to course load, degree level and program. *Financial support:* In 2006–07, 19 students received support, including 4 fellowships with full tuition reimbursements available (averaging $20,500 per year); scholarships/grants, health care benefits, and tuition waivers (full and partial) also available. Financial award application deadline: 5/1. *Faculty research:* Financial marketing, operations, human resources. *Unit head:* Dr. Clifford Ball, Director, 615-322-2909, E-mail: cliff.ball@owen.vanderbilt.edu. *Application contact:* Janet Sisco, Information Contact, 615-322-5652, E-mail: janet.sisco@owen.vanderbilt.edu.

Vanguard University of Southern California, School of Business and Management, Costa Mesa, CA 92626-9601. Offers MBA. Part-time and evening/weekend programs available. *Faculty:* 2 full-time (0 women), 4 part-time/adjunct (1 woman). *Students:* 17 full-time (6 women), 2 part-time (1 woman); includes 9 minority (2 African Americans, 4 Asian Americans or Pacific Islanders, 3 Hispanic Americans), 1 international. Average age 35. 17 applicants, 53% accepted, 8 enrolled. In 2006, 12 degrees awarded. *Entrance requirements:* For master's, MAT or GMAT, minimum GPA of 3.0. Additional exam requirements/recommendations for international students: Required—TOEFL (minimum score 550 paper-based; 213 computer-based; 79 iBT). *Application deadline:* For fall admission, 4/1 priority date for domestic and international students; for spring admission, 10/1 priority date for domestic and international students. Applications are processed on a rolling basis. Application fee: $45. Electronic applications accepted. *Expenses: Contact institution. Financial support:* Applicants required to submit FAFSA. *Unit head:* Dr. David Alford, Dean, 714-556-3610 Ext. 3701, Fax: 714-662-5228, E-mail: dalford@vanguard.edu. *Application contact:* Jill Zeiger, Graduate Coordinator, 714-556-3610 Ext. 3704, Fax: 714-662-5228, E-mail: jzeiger@vanguard.edu.

Villanova University, Villanova School of Business, Executive MBA Program, Villanova, PA 19085-1699. Offers EMBA. *Accreditation:* AACSB. Evening/weekend programs available. *Faculty:* 9 full-time (0 women), 10 part-time/adjunct (1 woman). *Students:* 62 full-time (14 women); includes 7 minority (3 African Americans, 2 Asian Americans or Pacific Islanders, 2 Hispanic Americans). Average age 37. In 2006, 27 degrees awarded. *Application deadline:* For fall admission, 4/6 priority date for domestic and international students. Applications are processed on a rolling basis. Application fee: $75. Electronic applications accepted. *Expenses: Contact institution. Financial support:* In 2006–07, 7 students received support. Application deadline: 3/15; *Faculty research:* Leadership, management, corporate valuation, systems thinking, strategy. *Unit head:* Doug Dickel, Director, 610-523-1739, Fax: 610-523-1798, E-mail: douglas.dickel@villanova.edu.

Villanova University, Villanova School of Business, Full-Time Equivalent MBA Program, Villanova, PA 19085-1699. Offers MBA. *Accreditation:* AACSB. Part-time and evening/weekend programs available. *Faculty:* 9 full-time, 3 part-time/adjunct. *Students:* Average age 29. 46 applicants, 57% accepted, 19 enrolled. In 2006, 39 degrees awarded. *Entrance requirements:* For master's, GMAT, 2-3 years of professional work experience. Additional exam requirements/recommendations for international students: Required—TOEFL (minimum score 600 paper-based; 250 computer-based; 100 iBT). *Application deadline:* For fall admission, 7/15 for domestic and international students. Applications are processed on a rolling basis. Application fee: $50. Electronic applications accepted. *Expenses:* Tuition: Part-time $565 per credit. *Financial support:* Application deadline: 3/31; *Unit head:* Simone L. Pollard, Director of Graduate Business, 610-519-4336, Fax: 610-519-6273, E-mail: simone.pollard@villanova.edu. *Application contact:* Elizabeth A. Eshleman, Associate Director/Corporate Liaison, 610-519-5939, Fax: 610-519-6273, E-mail: elizabeth.eshleman@villanova.edu.

Villanova University, Villanova School of Business, Master of Business Administration Program, Villanova, PA 19085-1699. Offers MBA, JD/MBA. *Accreditation:* AACSB. Part-time and evening/weekend programs available. Postbaccalaureate distance learning degree programs offered (minimal on-campus study). *Faculty:* 95 full-time, 61 part-time/adjunct. *Students:* 487 (155 women); includes 50 minority (10 African Americans, 1 American Indian/Alaska Native, 36 Asian Americans or Pacific Islanders, 3 Hispanic Americans). Average age 28. 300 applicants, 91% accepted, 156 enrolled. *Entrance requirements:* For master's, GMAT. Additional exam requirements/recommendations for international students: Required—TOEFL (minimum score 600 paper-based; 250 computer-based; 100 iBT). *Application deadline:* For fall admission, 7/15 for domestic and international students; for spring admission, 11/15 for domestic and international students. Applications are processed on a rolling basis. Application fee: $50. Electronic applications accepted. *Expenses:* Tuition: Part-time $565 per credit. *Financial support:* In 2006–07, 19 research assistantships with full tuition reimbursements (averaging $12,165 per year) were awarded. Support available to part-time students. Financial award application deadline: 3/31. *Faculty research:* Technology management, marketing of services, tax accounting, asset liability management. *Unit head:* Simone L. Pollard, Director of Graduate Business, 610-519-4336, Fax: 610-519-6273, E-mail: simone.pollard@villanova.edu. *Application contact:* Elizabeth A. Eshleman, Associate Director/Corporate Liaison, 610-519-5939, Fax: 610-519-6273, E-mail: elizabeth.eshleman@villanova.edu.

Virginia College at Birmingham, Program in Business Administration, Birmingham, AL 35209. Offers MBA. Part-time and evening/weekend programs available. Postbaccalaureate distance learning degree programs offered (no on-campus study). *Financial support:* Career-related internships or fieldwork, Federal Work-Study, institutionally sponsored loans, and scholarships/grants available. Support available to part-time students. *Unit head:* Mike Largent, Unit Head, 877-812-8428, E-mail: admissions@vc.edu. *Application contact:* Joe Rogalski, Vice President of Admissions, 205-802-1200, E-mail: admissions@vc.edu.

Virginia College at Birmingham, Virginia College Online, Birmingham, AL 35209. Offers business administration (MBA); criminal justice (MCJ); cybersecurity (MC). Part-time and evening/weekend programs available. Postbaccalaureate distance learning degree programs offered (no on-campus study). *Unit head:* Stan Banks, President, Virginia College Online, 888-827-7770, E-mail: vcadm@vc.edu. *Application contact:* Darrel Hanbury, Director of Admissions, 888-827-7770, E-mail: vcoadm@vc.edu.

Virginia Commonwealth University, Graduate School, School of Business, Program in Business Administration, Richmond, VA 23284-9005. Offers MBA, PhD. *Faculty:* 26 full-time (2 women). *Students:* 103 full-time (38 women), 212 part-time (72 women); includes 59 minority (29 African Americans, 23 Asian Americans or Pacific Islanders, 7 Hispanic Americans), 28 international. 226 applicants, 77% accepted. In 2006, 103 master's, 1 doctorate awarded. *Degree requirements:* For doctorate, thesis/dissertation. *Entrance requirements:* For master's and doctorate, GMAT. *Application deadline:* For fall admission, 4/1 priority date for domestic students; for spring admission, 11/1 for domestic students. Applications are processed on a rolling basis. Application fee: $50. *Financial support:* Fellowships, research assistantships, teaching assistantships, Federal Work-Study, institutionally sponsored loans, and tuition waivers (full and partial) available. Financial award application deadline: 3/15. *Unit head:* Dr. Glenn H. Gilbreath, Chair, 804-828-6468, Fax: 804-828-8884, E-mail: ghgilbre@vcu.edu. *Application contact:* Tracy Green, Graduate Program Director, 804-828-1741, Fax: 804-828-7174, E-mail: tsgreen@vcu.edu.

See Close-Up on page 369.

Virginia Polytechnic Institute and State University, Graduate School, Pamplin College of Business, Department of Business Information Technology, Blacksburg, VA 24061. Offers business administration (PhD); business information technology (MS, PhD). *Faculty:* 23 full-time (7 women), 2 part-time/adjunct (0 women). *Students:* 3 full-time (1 woman), 2 part-time; includes 1 minority (African American), 2 international. Average age 30. 7 applicants. In 2006, 1 degree awarded. *Entrance requirements:* For master's and doctorate, GMAT. Additional exam requirements/recommendations for international students: Required—TOEFL (minimum score 600 paper-based; 250 computer-based). *Application deadline:* For fall admission, 5/15 for international students; for spring admission, 10/15 for international students. Applications

Business Administration and Management—General

Virginia Polytechnic Institute and State University (continued)
are processed on a rolling basis. Application fee: $45. Electronic applications accepted. *Expenses:* Tuition, state resident: full-time $7,017; part-time $390 per credit hour. Tuition, nonresident: full-time $12,414; part-time $690 per credit hour. International tuition: $11,296 full-time. Required fees: $1,523; $256 per term. *Financial support:* In 2006–07, 4 teaching assistantships with full tuition reimbursements (averaging $15,538 per year) were awarded; career-related internships or fieldwork, Federal Work-Study, scholarships/grants, and unspecified assistantships also available. Financial award application deadline: 4/1. *Faculty research:* Mathematical programming, computer simulation, decision support systems, production/operations research, information technology. *Unit head:* Dr. Bernard W. Taylor, Head, 540-231-6596, Fax: 540-231-7916, E-mail: betaylo3@vt.edu. *Application contact:* Cliff Ragsdale, Information Contact, 540-231-4697, Fax: 540-231-7916, E-mail: cragsdal@vt.edu.

Virginia Polytechnic Institute and State University, Graduate School, Pamplin College of Business, Department of Management, Blacksburg, VA 24061. Offers business administration/management (MS, PhD). *Accreditation:* AACSB. *Faculty:* 18 full-time (4 women), 1 (woman) part-time/adjunct. *Students:* 9 full-time (4 women), 2 part-time (1 woman); includes 1 minority (Asian American or Pacific Islander), 7 international. Average age 35. 21 applicants, 24% accepted, 3 enrolled. In 2006, 1 degree awarded. *Entrance requirements:* For master's and doctorate, GMAT. Additional exam requirements/recommendations for international students: Required—TOEFL (minimum score 600 paper-based; 250 computer-based). *Application deadline:* For fall admission, 5/15 for international students; for spring admission, 10/15 for international students. Applications are processed on a rolling basis. Application fee: $45. Electronic applications accepted. *Expenses:* Tuition, state resident: full-time $7,017; part-time $390 per credit hour. Tuition, nonresident: full-time $12,414; part-time $690 per credit hour. International tuition: $11,296 full-time. Required fees: $1,523; $256 per term. *Financial support:* In 2006–07, 8 teaching assistantships with full tuition reimbursements (averaging $11,305 per year) were awarded; career-related internships or fieldwork, Federal Work-Study, scholarships/grants, and unspecified assistantships also available. Financial award application deadline: 1/31. *Faculty research:* Compensation, organization effectiveness, selection, strategic planning, labor/management relations. *Unit head:* Dr. Richard E. Wokutch, Head, 540-231-6353, Fax: 540-231-4487, E-mail: wokutch@vt.edu. *Application contact:* Karen Poe, Information Contact, 540-231-5250, Fax: 540-231-4487, E-mail: kpoe@vt.edu.

Virginia Polytechnic Institute and State University, Graduate School, Pamplin College of Business, Program in Business Administration, Blacksburg, VA 24061. Offers MBA. *Accreditation:* AACSB. *Faculty:* 110 full-time (30 women), 5 part-time/adjunct (1 woman). *Students:* 173 full-time (51 women), 173 part-time (45 women); includes 54 minority (15 African Americans, 5 American Indian/Alaska Native, 26 Asian Americans or Pacific Islanders, 8 Hispanic Americans), 70 international. Average age 31. 261 applicants, 61% accepted, 110 enrolled. In 2006, 127 degrees awarded. *Entrance requirements:* For master's, GMAT. Additional exam requirements/recommendations for international students: Required—TOEFL (minimum score 550 paper-based; 213 computer-based). *Application deadline:* For fall admission, 5/15 for international students; for spring admission, 10/15 for international students. Applications are processed on a rolling basis. Application fee: $45. Electronic applications accepted. *Expenses:* Tuition, state resident: full-time $7,017; part-time $390 per credit hour. Tuition, nonresident: full-time $12,414; part-time $690 per credit hour. International tuition: $11,296 full-time. Required fees: $1,523; $256 per term. *Financial support:* In 2006–07, 5 teaching assistantships (averaging $10,015 per year) were awarded; career-related internships or fieldwork, Federal Work-Study, scholarships/grants, and unspecified assistantships also available. Financial award application deadline: 4/1. *Unit head:* Dr. Stephen Skripak, Head, 540-231-6152, Fax: 540-231-4487, E-mail: sskripak@vt.edu. *Application contact:* Susan V. Vest, Enrollment Services Coordinator, 540-231-6152, Fax: 540-231-4487, E-mail: susanv@vt.edu.

Wagner College, Division of Graduate Studies, Department of Business Administration, Staten Island, NY 10301-4495. Offers accelerated MBA (MBA); accounting (MS); finance (MBA); health care administration (MBA); international business (MBA); management (Exec MBA, MBA); marketing (MBA). *Accreditation:* ACBSP. Part-time and evening/weekend programs available. *Faculty:* 9 full-time (3 women), 15 part-time/adjunct (5 women). *Students:* 109 full-time (51 women), 28 part-time (15 women); includes 20 minority (7 African Americans, 1 American Indian/Alaska Native, 8 Asian Americans or Pacific Islanders, 4 Hispanic Americans), 1 international. 91 applicants, 95% accepted, 81 enrolled. In 2006, 83 degrees awarded. *Degree requirements:* For master's, thesis optional. *Entrance requirements:* For master's, GMAT, minimum GPA of 2.75, proficiency in computers and math. Additional exam requirements/recommendations for international students: Required—TOEFL (minimum score 550 paper-based; 217 computer-based). *Application deadline:* For fall admission, 8/1 priority date for domestic students, 6/30 priority date for international students; for spring admission, 12/10 for domestic students, 11/15 for international students. Applications are processed on a rolling basis. Application fee: $50 ($85 for international students). *Expenses:* Tuition: Full-time $15,120; part-time $840 per credit. *Financial support:* Fellowships, tuition waivers (partial) and unspecified assistantships available. Financial award applicants required to submit FAFSA. *Unit head:* Prof. Donald Crooks, Director, 718-390-3429, E-mail: dcrooks@wagner.edu. *Application contact:* Susan Rosenberg, Office of Graduate Studies, 718-390-3106, Fax: 718-390-3456, E-mail: graduate@wagner.edu.

Wake Forest University, Babcock Graduate School of Management, Evening MBA Program–Charlotte, Winston-Salem, NC 27109. Offers MBA. *Accreditation:* AACSB. Evening/weekend programs available. *Faculty:* 36 full-time (5 women), 6 part-time/adjunct (1 woman). *Students:* 83 full-time (21 women); includes 12 minority (3 African Americans, 6 Asian Americans or Pacific Islanders, 3 Hispanic Americans), 2 international. Average age 31. In 2006, 49 degrees awarded. *Degree requirements:* For master's, registration. *Entrance requirements:* For master's, GMAT, interview, letters of recommendation. *Application deadline:* Applications are processed on a rolling basis. Application fee: $75. Electronic applications accepted. *Expenses:* Contact institution. *Financial support:* In 2006–07, 5 students received support. Scholarships/grants available. Financial award applicants required to submit FAFSA. *Faculty research:* Impact of operations strategy on competitiveness, information technology management, change management, impact of strategic decisions by corporations and financial intermediaries, consumer behavior and product management. *Unit head:* Leslye Gervasi, Director, 704-365-1717, Fax: 704-365-3511, E-mail: clt.mba@mba.wfu.edu. *Application contact:* Judith Wright, Administrative Assistant, 704-365-1717, Fax: 704-365-3511, E-mail: clt.mba@mba.wfu.edu.

Wake Forest University, Babcock Graduate School of Management, Evening MBA Program–Winston-Salem, Winston-Salem, NC 27109. Offers MBA, PhD/MBA. *Accreditation:* AACSB. Evening/weekend programs available. *Faculty:* 36 full-time (5 women), 6 part-time/adjunct (1 woman). *Students:* 97 full-time (26 women); includes 23 minority (13 African Americans, 8 Asian Americans or Pacific Islanders, 2 Hispanic Americans). Average age 30. In 2006, 55 degrees awarded. *Degree requirements:* For master's, registration. *Entrance requirements:* For master's, GMAT, interview, letters of recommendation. *Application deadline:* Applications are processed on a rolling basis. Application fee: $75. Electronic applications accepted. *Expenses:* Contact institution. *Financial support:* In 2006–07, 10 students received support. Scholarships/grants available. Financial award applicants required to submit FAFSA. *Faculty research:* Impact of operations strategy on competitiveness, information technology management, change management, impact of strategic decisions by corporations and financial intermediaries, consumer behavior and product management. *Unit head:* Jamie Barnes, Director, 336-758-4584, Fax: 336-758-5830, E-mail: evening.exec@mba.wfu.edu. *Application contact:* Pat Peacock, Associate Director, 336-758-4584, Fax: 336-758-5830, E-mail: evening.exec@mba.wfu.edu.

Wake Forest University, Babcock Graduate School of Management, Fast-Track Executive MBA Program, Winston-Salem, NC 27109. Offers MBA. *Accreditation:* AACSB. Evening/weekend programs available. *Faculty:* 36 full-time (5 women), 6 part-time/adjunct (1 woman). *Students:* 82 full-time (21 women); includes 15 minority (11 African Americans, 2 Asian Americans or Pacific Islanders, 2 Hispanic Americans), 1 international. Average age 38. In 2006, 42 degrees awarded. *Degree requirements:* For master's, registration. *Entrance requirements:* For master's, GMAT, interview, letter of recommendation. *Application deadline:* Applications are processed on a rolling basis. Application fee: $75. Electronic applications accepted. *Expenses:* Contact institution. *Financial support:* In 2006–07, 15 students received support. Scholarships/grants available. Financial award applicants required to submit FAFSA. *Faculty research:* Impact of operations on competitiveness, information technology management, change management, impact of strategic decisions by corporations and financial intermediaries, consumer behavior and product management. *Unit head:* Jamie Barnes, Director, 336-758-4584, Fax: 336-758-5830, E-mail: evening.exec@mba.wfu.edu. *Application contact:* Pat Peacock, Associate Director, 336-758-4584, Fax: 336-758-5830, E-mail: evening.exec@mba.wfu.edu.

Wake Forest University, Babcock Graduate School of Management, Full-time MBA Program, Winston-Salem, NC 27109. Offers MA, MBA, JD/MBA, MBA/MSA, MD/MBA. *Accreditation:* AACSB. Evening/weekend programs available. *Faculty:* 36 full-time (5 women), 6 part-time/adjunct (1 woman). *Students:* 189 full-time (55 women); includes 17 minority (8 African Americans, 6 Asian Americans or Pacific Islanders, 3 Hispanic Americans), 52 international. Average age 28. In 2006, 106 degrees awarded. *Degree requirements:* For master's, registration. *Entrance requirements:* For master's, GMAT, interview, letter of recommendation. Additional exam requirements/recommendations for international students: Required—TOEFL (minimum score 600 paper-based; 250 computer-based; 100 iBT). *Application deadline:* For fall admission, 4/1 priority date for domestic and international students. Applications are processed on a rolling basis. Application fee: $75. Electronic applications accepted. *Expenses:* Contact institution. *Financial support:* In 2006–07, 110 students received support. Career-related internships or fieldwork, scholarships/grants, and unspecified assistantships available. Financial award application deadline: 2/1; financial award applicants required to submit FAFSA. *Faculty research:* Impact of operations strategy of competitiveness, information technology management, change management, impact of strategic decisions by corporations and financial intermediaries, consumer behavior and product management. *Unit head:* Stacy Owen, Director, Fulltime Admissions, 336-758-5422, Fax: 336-758-5830, E-mail: admissions@mba.wfu.edu. *Application contact:* Ginny Kerlin, Administrative Assistant, 336-758-5422, Fax: 336-758-5830, E-mail: admissions@mba.wfu.edu.

Wake Forest University, Babcock Graduate School of Management, Saturday MBA Program–Charlotte, Winston-Salem, NC 27109. Offers MBA. *Accreditation:* AACSB. Evening/weekend programs available. *Faculty:* 36 full-time (5 women), 6 part-time/adjunct (1 woman). *Students:* 70 full-time (22 women); includes 13 minority (3 African Americans, 9 Asian Americans or Pacific Islanders, 1 Hispanic American), 1 international. Average age 31. In 2006, 36 degrees awarded. *Degree requirements:* For master's, registration. *Entrance requirements:* For master's, GMAT, interview, letters of recommendation. *Application deadline:* Applications are processed on a rolling basis. Application fee: $75. Electronic applications accepted. *Expenses:* Contact institution. *Financial support:* In 2006–07, 7 students received support. Scholarships/grants available. Financial award applicants required to submit FAFSA. *Faculty research:* Impact of operations strategy on competitiveness, information technology management, change management, impact of strategic decisions by corporations and financial intermediaries, and consumer behavior and product management. *Unit head:* Leslye Gervasi, Director, 704-365-1717, Fax: 704-365-3511, E-mail: clt.mba@mba.wfu.edu. *Application contact:* Judith Wright, Administrative Assistant, 704-365-1717, Fax: 704-365-3511, E-mail: clt.mba@mba.wfu.edu.

Walden University, Graduate Programs, NTU School of Engineering and Applied Science, Minneapolis, MN 55401. Offers computer engineering (MBA); computer science (MBA); electrical engineering (MBA); engineering (MS); engineering and technology management (Certificate); engineering management (MBA); high-tech business administration (MBA); software engineering (MBA); systems engineering (MBA). Part-time and evening/weekend programs available. Postbaccalaureate distance learning degree programs offered (minimal on-campus study). *Faculty:* 44. *Students:* 69 full-time (13 women), 336 part-time (50 women); includes 71 minority (29 African Americans, 2 American Indian/Alaska Native, 24 Asian Americans or Pacific Islanders, 16 Hispanic Americans), 14 international. Average age 33. 220 applicants, 58% accepted, 82 enrolled. In 2006, 13 degrees awarded. *Degree requirements:* For master's, thesis optional. *Entrance requirements:* For master's, minimum GPA of 3.0. Additional exam requirements/recommendations for international students: Required—TOEFL (minimum score 550 paper-based; 213 computer-based), IELTS (minimum score 7). *Application deadline:* For fall admission, 8/15 priority date for domestic and international students; for winter admission, 11/15 priority date for domestic and international students; for spring admission, 12/15 priority date for domestic and international students. Applications are processed on a rolling basis. Application fee: $50. Electronic applications accepted. *Unit head:* Dr. Ahmed Naumaan, Chair, 800-925-3368.

Walden University, Graduate Programs, School of Management, Minneapolis, MN 55401. Offers applied management and decision sciences (PhD). Part-time and evening/weekend programs available. Postbaccalaureate distance learning degree programs offered (minimal on-campus study). *Faculty:* 264. *Students:* 2,212 full-time (1,216 women), 752 part-time (390 women); includes 756 minority (626 African Americans, 11 American Indian/Alaska Native, 49 Asian Americans or Pacific Islanders, 70 Hispanic Americans), 22 international. Average age 40. 967 applicants, 83% accepted, 600 enrolled. In 2006, 267 master's, 55 doctorates awarded. *Degree requirements:* For doctorate, thesis/dissertation, brief dispersed residency sessions. *Entrance requirements:* For master's, minimum GPA of 3.0; for doctorate, 3 years of professional experience, master's degree. Additional exam requirements/recommendations for international students: Required—TOEFL (minimum score 550 paper-based; 213 computer-based), IELTS (minimum score 7). *Application deadline:* For fall admission, 8/15 priority date for domestic and international students; for winter admission, 11/15 priority date for domestic and international students; for spring admission, 12/15 priority date for domestic and international students. Applications are processed on a rolling basis. Application fee: $50. Electronic applications accepted. *Financial support:* In 2006–07, 1 fellowship with partial tuition reimbursement (averaging $750 per year) was awarded; scholarships/grants and tuition waivers (partial) also available. Support available to part-time students. Financial award application deadline: 6/1; financial award applicants required to submit FAFSA. *Faculty research:* International business, organizational behavior, entrepreneurship, economics, HR management. *Unit head:* Dr. Kathleen Simmons, Chair, 800-925-3368, Fax: 612-338-5092. *Application contact:* 866-4-WALDEN, Fax: 410-843-8780, E-mail: request@waldenu.edu.

Walsh College of Accountancy and Business Administration, Graduate Programs, Program in Business Administration, Troy, MI 48007-7006. Offers MBA. *Faculty:* 2 full-time (0 women), 22 part-time/adjunct (6 women). *Students:* 39 full-time (16 women), 858 part-time (427 women). Average age 32. 258 applicants, 88% accepted, 227 enrolled. In 2006, 268 degrees awarded. *Entrance requirements:* For master's, GMAT, minimum GPA of 2.75, previous course work in business. Additional exam requirements/recommendations for international students: Required—TOEFL. *Application deadline:* For fall admission, 8/24 priority date for domestic students; for winter admission, 1/1 priority date for domestic students; for spring admission, 4/1 priority date for domestic students. Applications are processed on a rolling basis. Application fee: $25. Electronic applications accepted. *Expenses:* Tuition: Part-time $435 per hour. Required fees: $119 per semester. One-time fee: $50. *Financial support:* Application deadline: 6/30. *Unit head:* Dr. David Odett, Chair, Management and Marketing Department, 248-823-1261, Fax: 248-689-9066, E-mail: dodett@walshcollege.edu. *Application contact:* Karen Mahaffy, Director of Admissions and Academic Advising, 248-823-1610, Fax: 248-689-0938, E-mail: kmahaffy@walshcollege.edu.

Walsh College of Accountancy and Business Administration, Graduate Programs, Program in Management, Troy, MI 48007-7006. Offers MSM. Part-time and evening/weekend programs available. *Faculty:* 2 full-time (1 woman), 22 part-time/adjunct (6 women). *Students:*

10 full-time (5 women), 271 part-time (160 women). Average age 34. 85 applicants, 93% accepted, 79 enrolled. *Entrance requirements:* For master's, minimum GPA of 2.75, previous course work in business. Additional exam requirements/recommendations for international students: Required—TOEFL. *Application deadline:* For fall admission, 8/24 priority date for domestic students; for winter admission, 1/1 priority date for domestic students; for spring admission, 4/1 priority date for domestic students. Applications are processed on a rolling basis. Application fee: $25. Electronic applications accepted. *Expenses:* Tuition: Part-time $435 per hour. Required fees: $119 per semester. One-time fee: $50. *Financial support:* Available to part-time students. Application deadline: 6/30. *Unit head:* Dr. David Odett, Director, 248-823-1261, Fax: 248-689-0920, E-mail: dodett@walshcollege.edu. *Application contact:* Karen Mahaffy, Director of Admissions and Academic Advising, 248-823-1610, Fax: 248-689-0938, E-mail: kmahaffy@walshcollege.edu.

Walsh University, Graduate Programs, Program in Business Administration, North Canton, OH 44720-3396. Offers MBA. Part-time and evening/weekend programs available. *Faculty:* 9 full-time (3 women), 5 part-time/adjunct (2 women). *Students:* 7 full-time (5 women), 73 part-time (34 women); includes 5 minority (2 African Americans, 1 Asian American or Pacific Islander, 2 Hispanic Americans), 2 international. Average age 36. 53 applicants, 75% accepted, 39 enrolled. In 2006, 21 degrees awarded. *Entrance requirements:* For master's, GMAT, minimum GPA of 3.0. Additional exam requirements/recommendations for international students: Required—TOEFL (minimum score 500 paper-based; 173 computer-based). *Application deadline:* For fall admission, 7/15 priority date for domestic students. Applications are processed on a rolling basis. Application fee: $25. Electronic applications accepted. *Expenses:* Tuition: Full-time $8,910; part-time $495 per credit. *Financial support:* In 2006–07, 21 students received support, including 17 research assistantships with partial tuition reimbursements available (averaging $3,310 per year); tuition waivers (partial), unspecified assistantships, and tuition discounts also available. Financial award application deadline: 12/31. *Faculty research:* Academic integrity and business ethics, assessing outcomes of experiential learning project. *Unit head:* Dr. Therese Maskulka, Coordinator, 330-490-4690, Fax: 330-490-7165. *Application contact:* Brett D. Freshour, Vice President of Enrollment Management, 330-490-7286, Fax: 330-490-7165, E-mail: bfreshour@walsh.edu.

Warner Southern College, School of Business, Lake Wales, FL 33859. Offers MBA. *Degree requirements:* For master's, comprehensive exam. *Entrance requirements:* For master's, GMAT, minimum GPA of 3.0, letters of recommendation (2). Additional exam requirements/recommendations for international students: Required—TOEFL.

Washburn University, School of Business, Topeka, KS 66621. Offers MBA. *Accreditation:* AACSB. Part-time and evening/weekend programs available. *Faculty:* 16 full-time (5 women), 3 part-time/adjunct (1 woman). *Students:* 19 full-time (13 women), 138 part-time (67 women); includes 13 minority (3 African Americans, 6 Asian Americans or Pacific Islanders, 4 Hispanic Americans). Average age 29. 40 applicants, 53% accepted, 21 enrolled. In 2006, 36 degrees awarded. *Entrance requirements:* For master's, GMAT, minimum GPA of 3.0. Additional exam requirements/recommendations for international students: Required—TOEFL (minimum score 550 paper-based; 213 computer-based). *Application deadline:* For fall admission, 7/1 priority date for domestic and international students; for spring admission, 11/15 priority date for domestic and international students. Applications are processed on a rolling basis. Application fee: $40 ($60 for international students). Electronic applications accepted. *Expenses:* Tuition, state resident: full-time $4,338; part-time $241 per credit hour. Tuition, nonresident: full-time $8,820; part-time $490 per credit hour. Required fees: $62; $31 per semester. *Financial support:* In 2006–07, 21 students received support. Available to part-time students. Application deadline: 2/15; *Faculty research:* Ethics in information technology, forecasting for shareholder value creation, model for measuring expected losses from litigation contingencies, business vs. family commitment in family businesses, calculated intangible value and brand recognition. Total annual research expenditures: $40,000. *Unit head:* Dr. David L. Sollars, Dean, 785-670-1308, Fax: 785-670-1063, E-mail: david.sollars@washburn.edu. *Application contact:* Dr. Robert J. Boncella, MBA Program Director, 785-670-2047, Fax: 785-670-1063, E-mail: mba.advisor@washburn.edu.

Washington State University, Graduate School, College of Business, Graduate Programs in Business, Pullman, WA 99164. Offers accounting and business law (M Acc); business administration (MBA, PhD), including accounting (PhD), finance (PhD), management and operations (PhD), management information systems (PhD), marketing (PhD); JD/MBA. *Accreditation:* AACSB. *Faculty:* 38. *Students:* 105 full-time (39 women), 14 part-time (5 women); includes 3 minority (1 American Indian/Alaska Native, 2 Asian Americans or Pacific Islanders), 62 international. Average age 30. 328 applicants, 32% accepted, 43 enrolled. In 2006, 56 master's, 8 doctorates awarded. *Degree requirements:* For master's, thesis (for some programs), final presentation, comprehensive exam (for some programs); for doctorate, thesis/dissertation, oral and written exams, comprehensive exam. *Entrance requirements:* For master's and doctorate, GMAT, minimum GPA of 3.0, 3 letters of recommendation. Additional exam requirements/recommendations for international students: Required—TOEFL. *Application deadline:* For fall admission, 3/1 priority date for domestic students, 3/1 for international students; for spring admission, 6/1 priority date for domestic students, 6/1 for international students. Applications are processed on a rolling basis. Application fee: $50. Electronic applications accepted. *Expenses:* Tuition, state resident: full-time $7,066. Tuition, nonresident: full-time $17,204. *Financial support:* In 2006–07, 102 students received support, including 9 fellowships (averaging $6,000 per year), 8 research assistantships with full and partial tuition reimbursements available (averaging $13,917 per year), 75 teaching assistantships with full and partial tuition reimbursements available (averaging $13,056 per year); career-related internships or fieldwork, Federal Work-Study, institutionally sponsored loans, health care benefits, tuition waivers (partial), unspecified assistantships, and teaching associateships also available. Financial award application deadline: 4/1. *Unit head:* Dr. Charles Munson, Associate Dean, 509-335-1193, E-mail: mba@wsu.edu. *Application contact:* Graduate School Admissions, 800-GRADWSU, Fax: 509-335-1949, E-mail: gradsch@wsu.edu.

Announcement: The MBA and M Acc programs are nationally recognized and accredited by AACSB International. The MBA program focuses on the delivery of innovation, positive societal impact, and globally competitive leadership. The PhD program is highly research oriented and leads to high-level academic competence in all business areas. Web site: http://www.cb.wsu.edu/graduate. Telephone: 509-335-7617.

Washington State University Tri-Cities, Graduate Programs, College of Business, Richland, WA 99352-1671. Offers business management (MBA); technology management (MTM). Part-time and evening/weekend programs available. *Faculty:* 6 full-time (1 woman), 3 part-time/adjunct (2 women). *Students:* 6 full-time (2 women), 30 part-time (13 women); includes 4 minority (all Hispanic Americans) Average age 35. 27 applicants, 22% accepted, 4 enrolled. *Degree requirements:* For master's, thesis (for some programs), oral presentation exam. *Entrance requirements:* For master's, GMAT, minimum GPA of 3.0, 3 letters of recommendation. Additional exam requirements/recommendations for international students: Required—TOEFL (minimum score 550 paper-based; 213 computer-based). *Application deadline:* For fall admission, 2/1 priority date for domestic students, 3/1 for international students; for spring admission, 9/1 priority date for domestic students, 7/1 for international students. Application fee: $50. *Expenses:* Tuition, state resident: full-time $7,066. Tuition, nonresident: full-time $17,204. *Financial support:* In 2006–07, 17 students received support. *Faculty research:* Strategy, organizational transformation, technology and instructional effectiveness, market research effects of type (fonts), optimization of price structure, accounting ethic. *Unit head:* Dr. John Thornton, Graduate Program Director, 509-372-7000, Fax: 509-372-7354. *Application contact:* Graduate School Admissions, 800-GRADWSU, Fax: 509-335-1949, E-mail: gradsch@wsu.edu.

Washington State University Vancouver, Graduate Programs, Program in Business Administration, Vancouver, WA 98686. Offers MBA. *Faculty:* 12. *Students:* 2 full-time (0 women), 41 part-time (13 women); includes 2 minority (1 Asian American or Pacific Islander, 1 Hispanic American). Average age 35. 29 applicants, 41% accepted, 11 enrolled. *Degree requirements:* For master's, thesis (for some programs), final presentation, portfolio, comprehensive exam (for some programs), registration. *Entrance requirements:* For master's, GMAT, minimum GPA of 3.0, 3 letters of recommendation, resumé. Additional exam requirements/recommendations for international students: Required—TOEFL. *Application deadline:* For fall admission, 3/1 for domestic and international students; for spring admission, 10/1 for domestic students, 7/1 for international students. Application fee: $50. *Expenses:* Tuition, state resident: full-time $7,066. Tuition, nonresident: full-time $17,204. *Financial support:* In 2006–07, 14 students received support, including 1 teaching assistantship with full tuition reimbursement available (averaging $13,056 per year). *Faculty research:* Liquidity, cost of capital and firm value, business ethics, corporate governance, finance and nonfinancial performance measurement, negotiations, project management. *Unit head:* Dr. Jane Cote, Academic Director, 360-546-9756, E-mail: cotej@vancouver.wsu.edu. *Application contact:* Graduate School Admissions, 800-GRADWSU, Fax: 509-335-1949, E-mail: gradsch@wsu.edu.

Washington University in St. Louis, John M. Olin School of Business, St. Louis, MO 63130-4899. Offers EMBA, M Acc, MBA, MS, PhD, JD/MBA, M Arch/MBA, M Eng/MBA, MBA/MA, MBA/MSW. *Accreditation:* AACSB. Electronic applications accepted.

See Close-Up on page 371.

Wayland Baptist University, Graduate Programs, Programs in Business Administration/Management, Plainview, TX 79072-6998. Offers general business (MBA); health care administration (MBA); human resource management (MBA); international management (MBA); management (MA, MBA), including human resource management (MA), organization management (MA); management information systems (MBA). Part-time and evening/weekend programs available. Postbaccalaureate distance learning degree programs offered (no on-campus study). *Faculty:* 3 full-time (0 women). *Students:* 1 full-time (0 women), 7 part-time (2 women); includes 1 minority (Hispanic American) Average age 28. 1 applicant, 100% accepted, 1 enrolled. In 2006, 2 degrees awarded. *Degree requirements:* For master's, capstone course. *Entrance requirements:* For master's, GMAT, GRE or MAT. Additional exam requirements/recommendations for international students: Required—TOEFL (minimum score 500 paper-based; 173 computer-based). *Application deadline:* Applications are processed on a rolling basis. Application fee: $35. *Expenses:* Tuition: Full-time $6,120; part-time $340 per credit hour. Required fees: $50 per term. *Financial support:* Federal Work-Study, institutionally sponsored loans, and scholarships/grants available. Support available to part-time students. Financial award application deadline: 5/1; financial award applicants required to submit FAFSA. *Unit head:* Dr. Otto Schacht, Chairman, 806-291-1020, Fax: 806-291-1957.

Waynesburg College, Graduate and Professional Studies, Waynesburg, PA 15370-1222. Offers M Ed, MBA, MSN, MSN/MBA. *Accreditation:* AACN. Part-time and evening/weekend programs available. Electronic applications accepted.

Wayne State College, School of Business and Technology, Wayne, NE 68787. Offers MBA. Part-time and evening/weekend programs available. Postbaccalaureate distance learning degree programs offered (minimal on-campus study). *Faculty:* 8 part-time/adjunct (4 women). *Students:* 3 full-time (2 women), 52 part-time (25 women); includes 1 Hispanic American. Average age 34. In 2006, 16 degrees awarded. *Entrance requirements:* For master's, GMAT, minimum overall GPA of 3.0. Additional exam requirements/recommendations for international students: Required—TOEFL (minimum score 550 paper-based; 213 computer-based). *Application deadline:* Applications are processed on a rolling basis. Application fee: $30. *Expenses:* Tuition, state resident: full-time $3,114; part-time $130 per credit hour. Tuition, nonresident: full-time $6,228; part-time $260 per credit hour. Required fees: $894; $37 per credit hour. Tuition and fees vary according to course load. *Financial support:* In 2006–07, 2 teaching assistantships with full tuition reimbursements (averaging $4,000 per year) were awarded; unspecified assistantships also available. Financial award applicants required to submit FAFSA. *Unit head:* Dr. Vaughn Benson, Dean, 402-375-7245, E-mail: vabenso1@wsc.edu.

Wayne State University, School of Business Administration, Detroit, MI 48202. Offers accounting (MS); business administration (MBA, PhD); interdisciplinary studies (PhD); taxation (MS); JD/MBA. *Accreditation:* AACSB. Part-time and evening/weekend programs available. *Faculty:* 64 full-time (11 women), 5 part-time/adjunct (1 woman). *Students:* 218 full-time (92 women), 1,021 part-time (446 women); includes 313 minority (179 African Americans, 2 American Indian/Alaska Native, 111 Asian Americans or Pacific Islanders, 21 Hispanic Americans), 153 international. Average age 30. 526 applicants, 73% accepted, 276 enrolled. In 2006, 386 degrees awarded. *Degree requirements:* For master's, thesis optional. *Entrance requirements:* For master's, GMAT. Additional exam requirements/recommendations for international students: Required—TOEFL (minimum score 550 paper-based; 213 computer-based); Recommended—TWE (minimum score 6). *Application deadline:* For fall admission, 8/1 for domestic students, 6/1 for international students; for winter admission, 10/1 for international students; for spring admission, 4/1 for domestic students, 2/1 for international students. Applications are processed on a rolling basis. Application fee: $30 ($50 for international students). Electronic applications accepted. *Financial support:* In 2006–07, 10 research assistantships (averaging $13,222 per year) were awarded; career-related internships or fieldwork, Federal Work-Study, and scholarships/grants also available. Support available to part-time students. Financial award applicants required to submit FAFSA. *Faculty research:* Corporate financial valuation, strategic advertising, information technology effectiveness, financial accounting and taxation, organizational performance and effectiveness. Total annual research expenditures: $188,100. *Unit head:* Dr. Richard Gabrys, Dean, 313-577-4501, Fax: 313-577-4557, E-mail: az4994@wayne.edu. *Application contact:* Linda Zaddach, Assistant Dean, 313-577-4510, E-mail: l.s.zaddach@wayne.edu.

See Close-Up on page 373.

Webber International University, Graduate School of Business, Babson Park, FL 33827-0096. Offers accounting (MBA); management (MBA); sports management (MBA). Part-time and evening/weekend programs available. *Degree requirements:* For master's, thesis or alternative. *Entrance requirements:* For master's, previous course work in financial and managerial accounting. Additional exam requirements/recommendations for international students: Required—TOEFL. *Faculty research:* Finance strategy, market research, investments, intranet.

See Close-Up on page 375.

Weber State University, John B. Goddard School of Business and Economics, Program in Business Administration, Ogden, UT 84408-1001. Offers MBA. *Accreditation:* AACSB. Part-time and evening/weekend programs available. *Faculty:* 6 full-time (0 women), 4 part-time/adjunct (1 woman). *Students:* 74 full-time (10 women), 93 part-time (18 women); includes 6 minority (1 African American, 2 Asian Americans or Pacific Islanders, 3 Hispanic Americans), 2 international. Average age 31. 135 applicants, 79% accepted, 98 enrolled. In 2006, 37 degrees awarded. *Entrance requirements:* For master's, GMAT, resumé, letters of recommendation. *Application deadline:* For fall admission, 2/15 priority date for domestic students; for spring admission, 10/4 for domestic students. Applications are processed on a rolling basis. Application fee: $60 ($75 for international students). Electronic applications accepted. *Expenses:* Tuition, state resident: full-time $3,950; part-time $203 per semester. Tuition, nonresident: full-time $10,371; part-time $518 per semester. Required fees: $544; $24 per semester. Tuition and fees vary according to course load and program. *Financial support:* In 2006–07, 8 students received support. Institutionally sponsored loans, scholarships/grants, and tuition waivers (partial) available. Support available to part-time students. *Unit head:* Dr. Brian Davis, Director, 801-626-7307, Fax: 801-626-7423, E-mail: bdavis@weber.edu. *Application contact:* Dr. Mark A. Stevenson, MBA Enrollment Director, 801-395-3528, Fax: 801-626-7423, E-mail: mba@weber.edu.

Webster University, School of Business and Technology, Department of Business, St. Louis, MO 63119-3194. Offers business (MA); business and organizational security management

Business Administration and Management—General

Webster University (continued)
(MBA); computer resources and information management (MBA); environmental management (MBA); finance (MA, MBA); health services management (MBA); human resources development (MBA); human resources management (MBA); international business (MA, MBA); management and leadership (MBA); marketing (MBA); procurement and acquisitions management (MBA); telecommunications management (MBA). Part-time and evening/weekend programs available. Postbaccalaureate distance learning degree programs offered (no on-campus study). *Students:* 1,205 full-time (629 women), 4,197 part-time (2,153 women); includes 2,005 minority (1,467 African Americans, 29 American Indian/Alaska Native, 212 Asian Americans or Pacific Islanders, 297 Hispanic Americans), 485 international. Average age 33. *Application deadline:* Applications are processed on a rolling basis. Application fee: $25 ($50 for international students). *Expenses:* Tuition: Full-time $8,820; part-time $490 per credit. Tuition and fees vary according to degree level, campus/location and program. *Financial support:* Federal Work-Study available. Support available to part-time students. Financial award application deadline: 4/1; financial award applicants required to submit FAFSA. *Unit head:* Bradford Scott, Chair, 314-961-2260 Ext. 7574, Fax: 314-968-7077, E-mail: buschair@webster.edu. *Application contact:* Director of Graduate and Evening Student Admissions, Fax: 314-968-7116, E-mail: gadmit@webster.edu.

Webster University, School of Business and Technology, Department of Management, St. Louis, MO 63119-3194. Offers business and organizational security management (MA); computer resources and information management (MA); environmental management (MS); health care management (MA); health services management (MA); human resources development (MA); human resources management (MA); management (DM); management and leadership (MA); marketing (MA); procurement and acquisitions management (MA); public administration (MA); quality management (MA); space systems operations management (MS); telecommunications management (MA). Part-time and evening/weekend programs available. Postbaccalaureate distance learning degree programs offered (no on-campus study). *Students:* 1,396 full-time (746 women), 4,727 part-time (2,579 women); includes 3,065 minority (2,374 African Americans, 45 American Indian/Alaska Native, 158 Asian Americans or Pacific Islanders, 488 Hispanic Americans), 128 international. Average age 37. In 2006, 9 degrees awarded. *Degree requirements:* For doctorate, thesis/dissertation, written exam. *Entrance requirements:* For doctorate, GMAT, 3 years of work experience, MBA. *Application deadline:* Applications are processed on a rolling basis. Application fee: $25 ($50 for international students). *Expenses:* Tuition: Full-time $8,820; part-time $490 per credit. Tuition and fees vary according to degree level, campus/location and program. *Financial support:* Federal Work-Study available. Support available to part-time students. Financial award application deadline: 4/1; financial award applicants required to submit FAFSA. *Unit head:* Jeffrey Haldeman, Chair, 314-961-2660 Ext. 7552, Fax: 314-968-7077, E-mail: mgtchair@webster.edu. *Application contact:* Director of Graduate and Evening Student Admissions, Fax: 314-968-7116, E-mail: gadmit@webster.edu.

Wesleyan College, Department of Business and Economics, EMBA Program, Macon, GA 31210-4462. Offers EMBA. Evening/weekend programs available. *Faculty:* 5 full-time (4 women), 4 part-time/adjunct (2 women). *Students:* 47 full-time (38 women); includes 37 minority (35 African Americans, 2 Hispanic Americans), 1 international. Average age 37. 41 applicants, 61% accepted, 22 enrolled. In 2006, 33 degrees awarded. *Entrance requirements:* For master's, GMAT, LSAT, GRE or MAT, 5 years of work experience, 5 years of management experience. Additional exam requirements/recommendations for international students: Required—TOEFL (minimum score 550 paper-based). *Application deadline:* For fall admission, 7/1 priority date for domestic students, 5/1 for international students; for spring admission, 12/1 priority date for domestic students, 8/1 for international students. Applications are processed on a rolling basis. Application fee: $60. Electronic applications accepted. *Expenses:* Tuition: Full-time $14,500. Tuition and fees vary according to program. *Unit head:* Dr. Philip Davis Taylor, Director of Graduate Business Programs, 478-757-5184, Fax: 478-757-5183, E-mail: ptaylor@wesleyancollege.edu. *Application contact:* Danielle Lodge, Director of Recruiting, 478-757-5180, Fax: 478-757-3780, E-mail: dlodge@wesleyancollege.edu.

Wesley College, Business Program, Dover, DE 19901-3875. Offers MBA. Part-time and evening/weekend programs available. *Faculty:* 3 full-time (2 women), 7 part-time/adjunct (4 women). *Students:* 45 full-time (27 women), 32 part-time (19 women); includes 27 minority (21 African Americans, 4 Asian Americans or Pacific Islanders, 2 Hispanic Americans). Average age 30. 45 applicants, 93% accepted, 32 enrolled. In 2006, 26 degrees awarded. *Entrance requirements:* For master's, GMAT or GRE, minimum undergraduate GPA of 2.75. *Application deadline:* Applications are processed on a rolling basis. Application fee: $25. *Expenses:* Tuition: Full-time $6,120; part-time $340 per credit. Required fees: $60; $60 per year. *Financial support:* Unspecified assistantships available. *Unit head:* G. R. Myers, Director of Graduate Admissions, 302-736-2343, E-mail: myersgr@wesley.edu. *Application contact:* William H. Firman, Dean of Enrollment Management, 302-736-2400, Fax: 302-736-2301, E-mail: firmanwh@wesley.edu.

West Chester University of Pennsylvania, Graduate Studies, School of Business and Public Affairs, Program in Business Administration, West Chester, PA 19383. Offers economics/finance (MBA); executive business administration (MBA); general business (MBA); management (MBA); technology and electronic commerce (MBA). *Accreditation:* AACSB. Part-time and evening/weekend programs available. *Students:* 2 full-time (1 woman), 68 part-time (19 women); includes 3 African Americans, 8 Asian Americans or Pacific Islanders, 2 Hispanic Americans, 5 international. Average age 34. 39 applicants, 77% accepted, 27 enrolled. In 2006, 41 degrees awarded. *Degree requirements:* For master's, thesis optional. *Entrance requirements:* For master's, GMAT, interview, minimum GPA of 3.0. *Application deadline:* For fall admission, 4/15 priority date for domestic students; for spring admission, 10/15 for domestic students. Applications are processed on a rolling basis. Application fee: $35. *Financial support:* In 2006–07, 4 research assistantships with full tuition reimbursements (averaging $5,000 per year) were awarded; unspecified assistantships also available. Support available to part-time students. Financial award application deadline: 2/15; financial award applicants required to submit FAFSA. *Unit head:* Dr. Pual Christ, Director, 610-436-2608, E-mail: pchrist@wcupa.edu. *Application contact:* Dr. Pual Christ, Graduate Coordinator, 610-436-2608, E-mail: mba@wcupa.edu.

Western Carolina University, Graduate School, College of Business, Program in Business Administration, Cullowhee, NC 28723. Offers MBA. *Accreditation:* AACSB. Part-time and evening/weekend programs available. *Degree requirements:* For master's, comprehensive exam. *Entrance requirements:* For master's, GMAT. Additional exam requirements/recommendations for international students: Required—TOEFL (minimum score 550 paper-based; 213 computer-based).

Western Connecticut State University, Division of Graduate Studies, Ancell School of Business, Program in Business Administration, Danbury, CT 06810-6885. Offers accounting (MBA); business administration (MBA). Part-time and evening/weekend programs available. *Faculty:* 12 full-time (3 women), 1 part-time/adjunct (0 women). *Students:* 2 full-time (1 woman), 57 part-time (23 women); includes 7 minority (1 African American, 5 Asian Americans or Pacific Islanders, 1 Hispanic American), 1 international. Average age 32. In 2006, 23 degrees awarded. *Entrance requirements:* For master's, GMAT. *Application deadline:* For fall admission, 8/1 priority date for domestic students. Applications are processed on a rolling basis. Application fee: $40. *Financial support:* Fellowships, career-related internships or fieldwork available. Support available to part-time students. Financial award application deadline: 5/1; financial award applicants required to submit FAFSA. *Unit head:* Dr. Fred Tesch, Professor, 203-837-8654. *Application contact:* Chris Shankle, Associate Director of Graduate Admissions, 203-837-8244, Fax: 203-837-8338, E-mail: shanklec@wcsu.edu.

Western Governors University, Programs in Business, Salt Lake City, UT 84107. Offers information technology management (MBA); management and strategy (MBA); strategic leadership (MBA). Electronic applications accepted.

Western Illinois University, School of Graduate Studies, College of Business and Technology, Program in Business Administration, Macomb, IL 61455-1390. Offers MBA. *Accreditation:* AACSB. Part-time programs available. *Students:* 63 full-time (24 women), 67 part-time (32 women); includes 8 minority (4 African Americans, 1 Asian American or Pacific Islander, 3 Hispanic Americans), 11 international. Average age 30. 64 applicants, 70% accepted. In 2006, 46 degrees awarded. *Degree requirements:* For master's, thesis or alternative. *Entrance requirements:* For master's, GMAT. Additional exam requirements/recommendations for international students: Required—TOEFL (minimum score 550 paper-based; 213 computer-based; 80 iBT). *Application deadline:* Applications are processed on a rolling basis. Application fee: $30. Electronic applications accepted. *Expenses:* Tuition, state resident: part-time $200 per credit hour. Tuition, nonresident: part-time $400 per credit hour. *Financial support:* In 2006–07, 25 students received support, including 25 research assistantships with full tuition reimbursements available (averaging $6,568 per year). Financial award applicants required to submit FAFSA. *Unit head:* Dr. Larry Wall, Director, 309-298-2442. *Application contact:* Dr. Barbara Baily, Director of Graduate Studies/Associate Provost, 309-298-1806, Fax: 309-298-2345, E-mail: grad-office@wiu.edu.

Western International University, Graduate Programs in Business, Phoenix, AZ 85021-2718. Offers MA, MBA, MPA, MS. Evening/weekend programs available. Postbaccalaureate distance learning degree programs offered (no on-campus study). *Faculty:* 149 part-time/adjunct (49 women). *Students:* 576 full-time (281 women); includes 136 minority (38 African Americans, 7 American Indian/Alaska Native, 32 Asian Americans or Pacific Islanders, 59 Hispanic Americans), 89 international. Average age 35. In 2006, 140 degrees awarded. *Degree requirements:* For master's, thesis. *Entrance requirements:* For master's, minimum GPA of 2.75. Additional exam requirements/recommendations for international students: Required—TOEFL (minimum score 550 paper-based; 213 computer-based), IELTS (minimum score 7), TWE (minimum score 5). *Application deadline:* Applications are processed on a rolling basis. Application fee: $85 ($100 for international students). *Expenses:* Tuition: Full-time $9,600; part-time $400 per credit. One-time fee: $85 full-time. *Financial support:* In 2006–07, 103 students received support. Career-related internships or fieldwork and scholarships/grants available. Support available to part-time students. Financial award applicants required to submit FAFSA. *Unit head:* Dr. Deborah DeSimone, Chief Academic Officer, 602-943-2311 Ext. 1135, Fax: 602-749-0752, E-mail: deborah.desimone@apollogrp.edu. *Application contact:* Karen Janitell, Director of Enrollment, 602-943-2311 Ext. 1063, Fax: 602-371-8637, E-mail: karen_janitell@apollogrp.edu.

Western Kentucky University, Graduate Studies, Gordon Ford College of Business, College of Business Administration, Bowling Green, KY 42101. Offers MBA. *Accreditation:* AACSB. Part-time and evening/weekend programs available. *Faculty:* 9 full-time (1 woman), 1 part-time/adjunct (0 women). *Students:* 36 full-time (22 women), 88 part-time (44 women); includes 10 minority (6 African Americans, 3 Asian Americans or Pacific Islanders, 1 Hispanic American), 41 international. Average age 30. 56 applicants, 41% accepted, 13 enrolled. In 2006, 25 master's awarded. *Degree requirements:* For master's, thesis optional. *Entrance requirements:* For master's, GMAT, minimum GPA of 2.5. Additional exam requirements/recommendations for international students: Required—TOEFL (minimum score 555 paper-based; 213 computer-based; 79 iBT). *Application deadline:* For fall admission, 2/1 priority date for domestic students, 12/1 for international students; for spring admission, 7/1 priority date for domestic students, 6/1 for international students. Application fee: $35. *Expenses:* Tuition, state resident: full-time $6,520; part-time $226 per hour. Tuition, nonresident: full-time $7,140; part-time $357 per hour. International tuition: $15,820 full-time. *Financial support:* In 2006–07, 12 students received support, including 4 research assistantships with partial tuition reimbursements available (averaging $9,500 per year); Federal Work-Study, institutionally sponsored loans, tuition waivers (partial), and service awards also available. Support available to part-time students. Financial award application deadline: 4/1; financial award applicants required to submit FAFSA. *Faculty research:* Business and international education, web page development, management training, international studies, globalization. *Unit head:* Dr. Bob Hatfield, MBA Program Director, 270-745-5458, Fax: 270-745-3893, E-mail: bob.hatfield@wku.edu.

Western Michigan University, Graduate College, Haworth College of Business, Program in Business Administration, Kalamazoo, MI 49008-5202. Offers MBA. *Accreditation:* AACSB. *Entrance requirements:* For master's, GMAT.

Western New England College, School of Business, Program in Business Administration (General), Springfield, MA 01119. Offers MBA. *Accreditation:* AACSB. Part-time and evening/weekend programs available. *Entrance requirements:* For master's, GMAT, 2 letters of reference.

Western New Mexico University, Graduate Division, Department of Business Administration and Criminal Justice, Silver City, NM 88062-0680. Offers business management (MBA). *Accreditation:* ACBSP. Part-time and evening/weekend programs available. *Entrance requirements:* For master's, GMAT. Additional exam requirements/recommendations for international students: Required—TOEFL (minimum score 550 paper-based; 213 computer-based). Electronic applications accepted. *Expenses:* Tuition, state resident: full-time $1,329. Tuition, nonresident: full-time $4,779.

Western Washington University, Graduate School, College of Business and Economics, Bellingham, WA 98225-5996. Offers MBA. *Accreditation:* AACSB. Part-time and evening/weekend programs available. *Faculty:* 51. *Students:* 50 full-time (23 women), 6 part-time (3 women); includes 9 minority (2 African Americans, 6 Asian Americans or Pacific Islanders, 1 Hispanic American), 3 international. 26 applicants, 69% accepted, 13 enrolled. In 2006, 31 degrees awarded. *Degree requirements:* For master's, comprehensive exam. *Entrance requirements:* For master's, GMAT, minimum GPA of 3.0 in last 60 semester hours or last 90 quarter hours. Additional exam requirements/recommendations for international students: Required—TOEFL (minimum score 567 paper-based; 227 computer-based). *Application deadline:* For fall admission, 5/1 for domestic students. Applications are processed on a rolling basis. Application fee: $50. *Expenses:* Tuition, state resident: full-time $6,609; part-time $199 per credit. Tuition, nonresident: full-time $16,845; part-time $540 per credit. *Financial support:* In 2006–07, 10 teaching assistantships with partial tuition reimbursements (averaging $9,339 per year) were awarded; Federal Work-Study, institutionally sponsored loans, scholarships/grants, tuition waivers (partial), and unspecified assistantships also available. Support available to part-time students. Financial award application deadline: 2/15; financial award applicants required to submit FAFSA. *Unit head:* Dennis Murphy, Dean, 360-650-3896, Fax: 360-650-4844, E-mail: dennis.murphy@wwu.edu. *Application contact:* Carrie Thurman, Graduate Program Coordinator, 360-650-3898, Fax: 360-650-4844, E-mail: carrie.thurman@wwu.edu.

Westminster College, The Bill and Vieve Gore School of Business, Salt Lake City, UT 84105-3697. Offers business administration (MBA, Certificate); technology management (MBATM). *Accreditation:* ACBSP. Part-time and evening/weekend programs available. Postbaccalaureate distance learning degree programs offered (no on-campus study). *Faculty:* 23 full-time (7 women), 7 part-time/adjunct (5 women). *Students:* 165 full-time (49 women), 189 part-time (56 women); includes 38 minority (3 African Americans, 1 American Indian/Alaska Native, 22 Asian Americans or Pacific Islanders, 12 Hispanic Americans), 12 international. Average age 32. 221 applicants, 71% accepted, 124 enrolled. In 2006, 168 master's, 38 other advanced degrees awarded. *Entrance requirements:* For master's, GMAT, 2 professional recommendations, employer letter of support, personal resumé. Additional exam requirements/recommendations for international students: Required—TOEFL (minimum score 550 paper-based; 213 computer-based). *Application deadline:* For fall admission, 8/1 priority date for domestic students. Applications are processed on a rolling basis. Application fee: $40. Electronic applications accepted. *Expenses:* Contact institution. *Financial support:* In 2006–07, 167 students received support. Career-related internships or fieldwork and tuition remissions available. Support available to part-time students. Financial award applicants required to submit FAFSA. *Faculty research:* China-America business studies, entrepreneurial excellence, civic engagement. *Unit head:* James Clark, Dean, 801-832-2600, Fax: 801-832-3106, E-mail:

jclark@westminstercollege.edu. *Application contact:* Joel Bauman, Vice President of Enrollment Services, 801-832-2200, Fax: 801-832-3101, E-mail: admission@westminstercollege.edu.

West Texas A&M University, College of Business, Department of Management, Marketing, and General Business, Canyon, TX 79016-0001. Offers business administration (MBA). *Accreditation:* ACBSP. Part-time and evening/weekend programs available. Postbaccalaureate distance learning degree programs offered (minimal on-campus study). *Degree requirements:* For master's, registration. *Entrance requirements:* For master's, GMAT. Additional exam requirements/recommendations for international students: Required—TOEFL (minimum score 550 paper-based). Electronic applications accepted. *Faculty research:* Human resources, international business, southern Asian markets, global strategies, international trade composition.

West Virginia University, College of Business and Economics, Program in Business Administration, Morgantown, WV 26506. Offers MBA, JD/MBA. *Accreditation:* AACSB. Part-time and evening/weekend programs available. *Students:* 50 full-time (13 women), 164 part-time (72 women); includes 8 minority (6 African Americans, 1 American Indian/Alaska Native, 1 Asian American or Pacific Islander), 18 international. Average age 32. 248 applicants, 51% accepted, 85 enrolled. In 2006, 114 degrees awarded. *Entrance requirements:* For master's, GMAT. Additional exam requirements/recommendations for international students: Required—TOEFL. *Application deadline:* For fall admission, 10/15 priority date for domestic and international students; for spring admission, 3/1 priority date for domestic and international students. Application fee: $50. Electronic applications accepted. *Expenses:* Tuition, state resident: full-time $4,926; part-time $276 per credit hour. Tuition, nonresident: full-time $14,278; part-time $796 per credit hour. Tuition and fees vary according to program. *Financial support:* Research assistantships, teaching assistantships, career-related internships or fieldwork, Federal Work-Study, institutionally sponsored loans, scholarships/grants, unspecified assistantships, and graduate administrative assistantships available. Financial award application deadline: 2/1; financial award applicants required to submit FAFSA. *Faculty research:* Financial management, managerial accounting, marketing, planning, corporate finance. *Unit head:* Dr. Cyril Logar, Associate Dean, Interim Director for Graduate Programs, 304-293-7956, Fax: 304-293-5652, E-mail: cyril.logar@mail.wvu.edu. *Application contact:* Bonnie Anderson, Associate Director, 304-293-7812, Fax: 304-293-2385, E-mail: bonnie.anderson@mail.wvu.edu.

West Virginia Wesleyan College, Department of Business and Economics, Buckhannon, WV 26201. Offers MBA. Part-time and evening/weekend programs available. *Degree requirements:* For master's, exit evaluation. *Entrance requirements:* For master's, GMAT. Additional exam requirements/recommendations for international students: Required—TOEFL.

Wheeling Jesuit University, Department of Business, Wheeling, WV 26003-6295. Offers accounting (MS); business administration (MBA). Part-time and evening/weekend programs available. *Faculty:* 6 full-time (0 women). *Students:* 19 full-time (5 women), 28 part-time (15 women), 2 international. Average age 31. 31 applicants, 97% accepted, 23 enrolled. In 2006, 18 degrees awarded. *Entrance requirements:* For master's, GMAT, minimum undergraduate GPA of 2.8. Additional exam requirements/recommendations for international students: Required—TOEFL (minimum score 600 paper-based; 250 computer-based; 80 iBT). *Application deadline:* For fall admission, 8/1 priority date for domestic students, 8/1 for international students; for spring admission, 12/15 priority date for domestic students, 12/15 for international students. Applications are processed on a rolling basis. Application fee: $25. Electronic applications accepted. *Expenses:* Tuition: Full-time $8,910; part-time $405 per credit hour. Required fees: $105 per semester. One-time fee: $380 full-time. Full-time tuition and fees vary according to course load, degree level and program. *Financial support:* In 2006–07, 38 students received support. Career-related internships or fieldwork, Federal Work-Study, and unspecified assistantships available. Financial award application deadline: 8/1; financial award applicants required to submit FAFSA. *Faculty research:* Forensic economics, philosophic economics, consumer behavior, international business, economic development. *Unit head:* Dr. Edward W Younkins, Director, 304-243-2255, Fax: 304-243-8703, E-mail: younkins@wju.edu. *Application contact:* Becky Forney, Associate Dean of Adult Education, 304-243-2250, Fax: 304-243-4441, E-mail: bforney@wju.edu.

Whitworth University, School of Global Commerce and Management, Program in Business Administration, Spokane, WA 99251-0001. Offers business administration (MBA); international management (MBA). Part-time and evening/weekend programs available. *Faculty:* 4 full-time (3 women), 14 part-time/adjunct (11 women). *Students:* 13 full-time (8 women), 4 part-time (3 women); includes 1 Hispanic American, 2 international. 17 applicants, 65% accepted, 11 enrolled. *Entrance requirements:* For master's, GMAT, minimum GPA of 3.0, 2 letters of recommendation, resumé, completion of prerequisite courses in micro-economics, macro-economics, accounting, marketing, finance and statistics. Additional exam requirements/recommendations for international students: Required—TOEFL (minimum score 213 computer-based). *Application deadline:* For fall admission, 8/20 priority date for domestic students; for spring admission, 1/8 priority date for domestic students. Applications are processed on a rolling basis. Application fee: $35. *Financial support:* In 2006–07, 2 students received support; fellowships with tuition reimbursements available, career-related internships or fieldwork, Federal Work-Study, institutionally sponsored loans, and scholarships/grants available. Support available to part-time students. Financial award applicants required to submit FAFSA. *Faculty research:* International business (European, Central America and Asian topics), micro-finance, entrepreneurship. *Unit head:* 509-777-4606, Fax: 509-777-3723. *Application contact:* Bonnie Wakefield, Assistant Director, Graduate Studies in Business, 509-777-4606, Fax: 509-777-3723, E-mail: bwakefield@whitworth.edu.

Wichita State University, Graduate School, W. Frank Barton School of Business, Department of Business, Wichita, KS 67260. Offers EMBA, MBA, MS, MSN/MBA. *Accreditation:* AACSB. Part-time and evening/weekend programs available. *Degree requirements:* For master's, thesis optional. *Entrance requirements:* For master's, GMAT, minimum GPA of 2.75. Additional exam requirements/recommendations for international students: Required—TOEFL. Electronic applications accepted.

Widener University, School of Business Administration, Chester, PA 19013-5792. Offers MBA, MHA, MHR, MS, JD/MBA, MD/MBA, MD/MHA, ME/MBA, Psy D/MBA, Psy D/MHA, Psy D/MHR. *Accreditation:* AACSB. Part-time and evening/weekend programs available. *Entrance requirements:* For master's, minimum GPA of 2.5. Electronic applications accepted. Expenses: Contact institution. *Faculty research:* Cost containment in health care, human resource management, productivity, globalization.

Wilfrid Laurier University, Faculty of Graduate Studies, School of Business and Economics, Department of Business, Program in Business, Waterloo, ON N2L 3C5, Canada. Offers MBA. *Accreditation:* AACSB. Part-time and evening/weekend programs available. *Faculty:* 74 full-time, 4 part-time/adjunct. *Students:* 83 full-time, 401 part-time. 345 applicants, 57% accepted, 139 enrolled. In 2006, 183 degrees awarded. *Entrance requirements:* For master's, GMAT, minimum 2 years of business experience, minimum B average in a 4 yr. BA program. Additional exam requirements/recommendations for international students: Required—TOEFL (minimum score 230 computer-based; 89 iBT). *Application deadline:* For fall admission, 5/1 for domestic students. Application fee: $100. Electronic applications accepted. *Financial support:* Fellowships, research assistantships, teaching assistantships available. *Faculty research:* MBA, MBA with CMA option, MBA with CFA option, MBA with FCIP option, MBA co-op option. *Unit head:* Dr. Peter Carayannopoulos, Director, 519-884-0710 Ext. 3613. *Application contact:* SBE Marketing Office, 519-884-0710 Ext. 6220, E-mail: wlumba@wlu.ca.

Wilfrid Laurier University, Faculty of Graduate Studies, School of Business and Economics, Department of Business, Program in Management, Waterloo, ON N2L 3C5, Canada. Offers PhD. *Faculty:* 100 full-time. *Students:* 9 full-time. 31 applicants, 29% accepted, 5 enrolled. *Degree requirements:* For doctorate, thesis/dissertation. *Entrance requirements:* For doctorate, master's degree, minimum B+ average, GMAT required. Additional exam requirements/recommendations for international students: Required—TOEFL (minimum score 230 computer-based; 89 iBT). *Application deadline:* For fall admission, 2/1 priority date for domestic students. Application fee: $100. Electronic applications accepted. *Financial support:* Fellowships, research assistantships, teaching assistantships available. *Faculty research:* Financial economics, management and organizational behavior, operations and supply chain management. *Unit head:* Dr. Hamid Noori, Director, 519-884-0710 Ext. 2571. *Application contact:* Dianne Duffy, Student Contact, 519-884-0710 Ext. 3127, Fax: 519-884-1020, E-mail: gradstudies@wlu.ca.

Wilkes University, Graduate Studies and Continued Learning, Jay S. Sidhu School of Business and Leadership, Wilkes-Barre, PA 18766-0002. Offers accounting (MBA); entrepreneurship (MBA); finance (MBA); human resource management (MBA); international business (MBA); management (MBA); marketing (MBA). *Accreditation:* ACBSP. Part-time and evening/weekend programs available. *Students:* 30 full-time (16 women), 149 part-time (73 women); includes 5 minority (1 African American, 2 Asian Americans or Pacific Islanders, 2 Hispanic Americans), 4 international. Average age 30. In 2006, 48 degrees awarded. *Entrance requirements:* For master's, GMAT. Additional exam requirements/recommendations for international students: Required—TOEFL (minimum score 500 paper-based; 173 computer-based). *Application deadline:* Applications are processed on a rolling basis. Application fee: $40. *Expenses:* Contact institution. *Financial support:* Federal Work-Study and unspecified assistantships available. Financial award application deadline: 3/1; financial award applicants required to submit FAFSA. *Unit head:* Dr. Paul Browne, Dean, 570-408-4701, Fax: 570-408-4700, E-mail: paul.browne@wilkes.edu. *Application contact:* Kathleen Houlihan, Director of Graduate Studies, 570-408-3235, Fax: 570-408-7846, E-mail: kathleen.houlihan@wilkes.edu.

Willamette University, George H. Atkinson Graduate School of Management, Salem, OR 97301-3931. Offers business (MBA); government (MBA); not-for-profit management (MBA); JD/MBA. *Accreditation:* AACSB; NASPAA. Part-time programs available. *Faculty:* 15 full-time (3 women), 9 part-time/adjunct (2 women). *Students:* 116 full-time (38 women), 7 part-time (2 women); includes 15 minority (1 African American, 2 American Indian/Alaska Native, 8 Asian Americans or Pacific Islanders, 4 Hispanic Americans), 28 international. Average age 25. 101 applicants, 95% accepted, 50 enrolled. In 2006, 56 degrees awarded. *Median time to degree:* Master's–2 years full-time. *Entrance requirements:* For master's, GMAT or GRE. Additional exam requirements/recommendations for international students: Required—TOEFL (minimum score 570 paper-based; 230 computer-based; 88 iBT), Require TOEFL or IELTS. *Application deadline:* For fall admission, 1/9 priority date for domestic and international students; for winter admission, 3/1 priority date for domestic and international students; for spring admission, 5/1 priority date for domestic and international students. Applications are processed on a rolling basis. Application fee: $50. Electronic applications accepted. *Expenses:* Contact institution. *Financial support:* In 2006–07, 115 students received support, including 12 research assistantships (averaging $1,500 per year); teaching assistantships, career-related internships or fieldwork, Federal Work-Study, scholarships/grants, and unspecified assistantships also available. Financial award application deadline: 5/1; financial award applicants required to submit FAFSA. *Faculty research:* General management, finance, marketing, public management, human resources. *Unit head:* Debra J. Ringold, Interim Dean, 503-370-6440, Fax: 503-370-3011, E-mail: dringold@willamette.edu. *Application contact:* Judy O'Neill, Director of Admission, 503-370-6167, Fax: 503-370-3011, E-mail: joneill@willamette.edu.

William Carey University, Graduate Studies, School of Business, Hattiesburg, MS 39401-5499. Offers MBA. Part-time programs available. *Faculty:* 9 full-time (4 women), 1 part-time/adjunct (0 women). *Students:* 87 full-time (46 women), 35 part-time (23 women); includes 48 minority (42 African Americans, 1 Asian American or Pacific Islander, 5 Hispanic Americans). 45 applicants, 32 enrolled. In 2006, 88 degrees awarded. *Entrance requirements:* For master's, GMAT. Additional exam requirements/recommendations for international students: Required—TOEFL (minimum score 500 paper-based; 213 computer-based). *Application deadline:* For fall admission, 8/7 for domestic and international students; for winter admission, 10/30 for domestic and international students; for spring admission, 2/12 for domestic and international students. Application fee: $25. *Expenses:* Tuition: Full-time $5,040; part-time $240 per credit hour. Tuition and fees vary according to course load. *Financial support:* In 2006–07, 60 students received support. Federal Work-Study and scholarships/grants available. Support available to part-time students. Financial award applicants required to submit FAFSA. *Unit head:* Dr. Cheryl D. Dale, Dean, 601-318-6199, Fax: 601-318-6281, E-mail: cheryl.dale@wmcarey.edu. *Application contact:* Jason Douglas, Clerical Assistant, Graduate Admissions, 601-318-6774, Fax: 601-318-6765, E-mail: jason.douglas@wmcarey.edu.

William Paterson University of New Jersey, College of Business, Wayne, NJ 07470-8420. Offers MBA. *Accreditation:* AACSB. Part-time and evening/weekend programs available. *Students:* 14 full-time (8 women), 32 part-time (12 women); includes 11 minority (5 African Americans, 3 Asian Americans or Pacific Islanders, 3 Hispanic Americans). In 2006, 23 degrees awarded. *Entrance requirements:* For master's, GMAT, minimum AACSB index of 1000. *Application deadline:* Applications are processed on a rolling basis. Application fee: $50. Electronic applications accepted. *Financial support:* Research assistantships with full tuition reimbursements, unspecified assistantships available. Support available to part-time students. Financial award application deadline: 4/1; financial award applicants required to submit FAFSA. *Faculty research:* Appropriate marketing variables for international food retail chains, racial attitudes among corporate managers in northern New Jersey. *Unit head:* Sam Basu, Dean, 973-720-2964. *Application contact:* Danielle Liautaud, Director, 973-720-3579, Fax: 973-720-2035, E-mail: liautaudd@wpunj.edu.

Wilmington College, Division of Business, New Castle, DE 19720-6491. Offers business administration (MBA); finance (MBA); health care administration (MBA, MS); human resource management (MS); management (MS); management information systems (MBA); organizational leadership (MS); public administration (MS); transportation and logistics (MBA, MS). Part-time and evening/weekend programs available. *Faculty:* 3 full-time (0 women). *Students:* 230 full-time (138 women), 432 part-time (274 women); includes 109 minority (98 African Americans, 1 American Indian/Alaska Native, 3 Asian Americans or Pacific Islanders, 7 Hispanic Americans). Average age 34. 229 applicants, 100% accepted, 156 enrolled. In 2006, 273 degrees awarded. *Entrance requirements:* Additional exam requirements/recommendations for international students: Required—TOEFL (minimum score 500 paper-based; 173 computer-based). *Application deadline:* Applications are processed on a rolling basis. Application fee: $25. *Financial support:* Applicants required to submit FAFSA. *Unit head:* Dr. Robert Edelson, Chair, 302-295-1147, Fax: 302-328-7021, E-mail: robert.e.edelson@wilmcoll.edu. *Application contact:* Chris Ferguson, Director of Admissions and Financial Aid, 302-328-9407 Ext. 256, Fax: 302-328-5164, E-mail: inquire@wilmcoll.edu.

Wingate University, Program in Business Administration, Wingate, NC 28174-0159. Offers MBA. *Accreditation:* ACBSP. Part-time and evening/weekend programs available. *Faculty:* 3 full-time (0 women), 2 part-time/adjunct (0 women). *Students:* Average age 29. 15 applicants, 93% accepted, 14 enrolled. In 2006, 12 degrees awarded. *Entrance requirements:* For master's, GMAT, work experience, 2 letters of recommendation. *Application deadline:* For fall admission, 8/15 priority date for domestic students; for spring admission, 12/15 priority date for domestic students. Applications are processed on a rolling basis. Application fee: $50. Electronic applications accepted. *Expenses:* Contact institution. *Financial support:* In 2006–07, 9 students received support. Federal Work-Study and scholarships/grants available. Support available to part-time students. Financial award application deadline: 8/1; financial award applicants required to submit FAFSA. *Faculty research:* Stochastic processes, business ethics, regional economic development, municipal finance, consumer behavior. *Unit head:* Joseph M. Graham, Dean, 704-233-8148, Fax: 704-233-8146, E-mail: graham@wingate.edu. *Application contact:* Mary May, MBA Coordinator, 704-233-8148, Fax: 704-233-8146.

Winston-Salem State University, Program in Business Administration, Winston-Salem, NC 27110-0003. Offers MBA. *Accreditation:* AACSB. Part-time and evening/weekend programs available. Postbaccalaureate distance learning degree programs offered (minimal on-campus study). *Faculty:* 17 full-time (5 women). *Students:* 5 full-time (4 women), 37

Business Administration and Management—General

Winston-Salem State University (continued)
part-time (14 women); includes 24 minority (21 African Americans, 1 Asian American or Pacific Islander, 2 Hispanic Americans). Average age 40. 33 applicants, 30% accepted, 10 enrolled. In 2006, 13 degrees awarded. *Degree requirements:* For master's, registration. *Entrance requirements:* For master's, GMAT, resumé, 3 letters of recommendation. *Application deadline:* For fall admission, 7/15 for domestic and international students; for spring admission, 11/15 for domestic and international students. Applications are processed on a rolling basis. Application fee: $40. Electronic applications accepted. *Expenses:* Tuition, state resident: full-time $2,010. Tuition, nonresident: full-time $10,502. Tuition and fees vary according to course load. *Financial support:* In 2006–07, 10 students received support, including 4 research assistantships (averaging $5,000 per year), 4 teaching assistantships (averaging $5,000 per year); career-related internships or fieldwork, institutionally sponsored loans, and tuition waivers (partial) also available. *Faculty research:* Innovative entrepreneurship and customer service, econometrics and operations research. *Unit head:* Dr. Suresh Gopalan, Unit Head, 336-750-2344, Fax: 336-750-2335, E-mail: gopalans@wssu.edu. *Application contact:* Graduate Studies and Research, 336-750-2102, Fax: 336-750-3042, E-mail: graduate@wssu.edu.

Winthrop University, College of Business Administration, Program in Business Administration, Rock Hill, SC 29733. Offers MBA. *Accreditation:* AACSB. *Faculty:* 14 full-time (7 women), 3 part-time/adjunct (2 women). *Students:* 99 full-time (35 women), 93 part-time (51 women); includes 49 minority (36 African Americans, 1 American Indian/Alaska Native, 11 Asian Americans or Pacific Islanders, 1 Hispanic American), 23 international. Average age 28. In 2006, 87 master's awarded. *Expenses:* Tuition, state resident: full-time $9,148; part-time $383 per hour. Tuition, nonresident: full-time $16,864; part-time $704 per hour. *Unit head:* Peggy Hager, Director of Graduate Studies, 803-323-2408, E-mail: hagerp@winthrop.edu. *Application contact:* 800-411-7041, Fax: 803-323-2292, E-mail: graduatestu@winthrop.edu.

Woodbury University, School of Business and Management, Burbank, CA 91504-1099. Offers business administration (MBA); organizational leadership (MA). *Accreditation:* ACBSP. Part-time and evening/weekend programs available. *Faculty:* 16 part-time/adjunct (4 women). *Students:* 120 full-time (75 women), 25 part-time (11 women); includes 41 minority (9 African Americans, 1 American Indian/Alaska Native, 10 Asian Americans or Pacific Islanders, 21 Hispanic Americans), 25 international. Average age 29. 80 applicants, 60% accepted, 37 enrolled. In 2006, 54 degrees awarded. *Entrance requirements:* Additional exam requirements/recommendations for international students: Required—TOEFL (minimum score 550 paper-based; 213 computer-based; 80 iBT), IELTS (minimum score 6). *Application deadline:* For fall admission, 8/1 priority date for domestic students; for spring admission, 12/1 for domestic and international students. Applications are processed on a rolling basis. Application fee: $35 ($50 for international students). *Expenses:* Tuition: Full-time $8,052; part-time $671 per unit. Tuition and fees vary according to course load and campus/location. *Financial support:* In 2006–07, 2 fellowships with tuition reimbursements (averaging $12,000 per year) were awarded. Financial award application deadline: 7/15; financial award applicants required to submit FAFSA. *Faculty research:* Total quality management, leadership. *Unit head:* Dr. Andre Van Niekerk, Dean, 818-767-0888 Ext. 264, Fax: 818-767-0032. *Application contact:* Frank Frias, MBA Recruitment, 818-767-0888 Ext. 224, Fax: 818-767-7520, E-mail: frank.frias@woodbury.edu.

Worcester Polytechnic Institute, Graduate Studies and Enrollment, Department of Management, Worcester, MA 01609-2280. Offers customized management (Certificate); information security management (Certificate); information technology (MS, Certificate), including information security management (MS), information technology and applications development (MS), information technology and entrepreneurship (MS), information technology project management (MS), manufacturing and service information technology applications (MS), marketing information technology applications (MS); management of technology (Certificate); marketing and technological innovation (MS); operations design and leadership (MS), including process design, supply chain management; technology (MBA); technology marketing (Certificate). *Accreditation:* AACSB. Part-time and evening/weekend programs available. Postbaccalaureate distance learning degree programs offered (no on-campus study). *Faculty:* 21 full-time (9 women), 5 part-time/adjunct (2 women). *Students:* 23 full-time (8 women), 178 part-time (48 women); includes 21 minority (2 African Americans, 2 American Indian/Alaska Native, 14 Asian Americans or Pacific Islanders, 3 Hispanic Americans), 30 international. Average age 32. 85 applicants, 76% accepted, 34 enrolled. In 2006, 31 degrees awarded. *Median time to degree:* Master's–2 years full-time, 4 years part-time. *Degree requirements:* For master's, thesis optional. *Entrance requirements:* For master's, GMAT (MBA), GMAT or GRE General Test (MS), 3 letters of recommendation, statement of purpose. Additional exam requirements/recommendations for international students: Required—TOEFL (minimum score 550 paper-based; 213 computer-based; 79 iBT), IELTS (minimum score 7). *Application deadline:* For fall admission, 6/1 priority date for domestic and international students; for spring admission, 10/15 priority date for domestic students, 10/1 priority date for international students. Applications are processed on a rolling basis. Application fee: $70. Electronic applications accepted. *Expenses:* Tuition: Part-time $1,042 per credit hour. Required fees: $1,009 per year. *Financial support:* In 2006–07, 10 students received support, including 1 research assistantship with full tuition reimbursement available; fellowships with full tuition reimbursements available, career-related internships or fieldwork, institutionally sponsored loans, scholarships/grants, and unspecified assistantships also available. Financial award application deadline: 6/1. *Faculty research:* Organizational aesthetics, resistance in organizations, dynamics of product innovation, economic approaches to productivity, corporate earnings forecasts and value relevance. Total annual research expenditures: $125,538. *Unit head:* Dr. McRae C. Banks, Head, 508-831-5218, Fax: 508-831-5720, E-mail: macb@wpi.edu. *Application contact:* Norm D. Wilkinson, Director, Graduate Management Programs, 508-831-5957, Fax: 508-831-5720, E-mail: nwilkins@wpi.edu.

See Close-Up on page 377.

Worcester State College, Graduate Studies, Program in Management, Worcester, MA 01602-2597. Offers accounting (MS); organizational leadership (MS). *Students:* 1 (woman) full-time, 14 part-time (8 women), 4 international. Average age 28. 20 applicants, 80% accepted, 12 enrolled. *Expenses:* Tuition, state resident: full-time $4,518; part-time $251 per credit hour. Tuition, nonresident: full-time $4,518; part-time $251 per credit hour. *Unit head:* Dr. Lauri Dahlin, Coordinator, 508-929-8094.

Wright State University, School of Graduate Studies, Raj Soin College of Business, Program in Business Administration, Dayton, OH 45435. Offers MBA. *Unit head:* Michael Evans, Director of MBA Programs, 937-775-2437, Fax: 937-775-3545, E-mail: michael.evans@wright.edu.

Xavier University, Williams College of Business, Master of Business Administration Program, Cincinnati, OH 45207. Offers business administration (Exec MBA, MBA); e-commerce (MBA); finance (MBA); international business (MBA); management information systems (MBA); marketing (MBA);); MBA/MHSA; MSN/MBA. *Accreditation:* AACSB. Part-time and evening/weekend programs available. *Faculty:* 59 full-time (22 women), 29 part-time/adjunct (8 women). *Students:* 227 full-time (66 women), 708 part-time (252 women); includes 99 minority (41 African Americans, 1 American Indian/Alaska Native, 43 Asian Americans or Pacific Islanders, 14 Hispanic Americans), 43 international. Average age 31. 486 applicants, 63% accepted, 229 enrolled. In 2006, 294 degrees awarded. *Entrance requirements:* For master's, GMAT, resumé. Additional exam requirements/recommendations for international students: Required—TOEFL (minimum score 550 paper-based; 213 computer-based; 79 iBT). *Application deadline:* For fall admission, 8/1 priority date for domestic students, 6/1 for international students; for winter admission, 12/1 priority date for domestic students; for spring admission, 4/1 priority date for domestic students, 10/1 for international students. Applications are processed on a rolling basis. Application fee: $35. Electronic applications accepted. *Expenses: Contact institution.* Part-time tuition and fees vary according to degree level, campus/location and program. *Financial support:* In 2006–07, 175 students received support, including 11 research assistantships with full and partial tuition reimbursements available; career-related internships or fieldwork, scholarships/grants, and tuition waivers (partial) also available. Support available to part-time students. Financial award application deadline: 4/30; financial award applicants required to submit FAFSA. *Faculty research:* Supply chain management, category management, data mining, off-shoring. *Unit head:* Dr. Raghu Tadepalli, Associate Dean, 513-745-3525, Fax: 513-745-2929, E-mail: tadepalli@xavier.edu. *Application contact:* Jennifer Bush, Executive Director, MBA Programs, 513-745-3525, Fax: 513-745-2929, E-mail: xumba@xavier.edu.

Yale University, Yale School of Management and Graduate School of Arts and Sciences, Doctoral Program in Management, New Haven, CT 06520. Offers accounting (PhD); financial economics (PhD); marketing (PhD). *Accreditation:* AACSB. *Faculty:* 55 full-time (7 women). *Students:* 25 full-time (6 women); includes 2 minority (both Asian Americans or Pacific Islanders), 20 international. Average age 28. 300 applicants, 4% accepted. In 2006, 6 doctorates awarded. *Degree requirements:* For doctorate, thesis/dissertation, comprehensive exam. *Entrance requirements:* For doctorate, GMAT or GRE General Test. Additional exam requirements/recommendations for international students: Required—TOEFL, IELTS. *Application deadline:* For fall admission, 1/2 for domestic and international students. Application fee: $85. Electronic applications accepted. *Expenses: Contact institution. Financial support:* Fellowships with full tuition reimbursements, research assistantships with full tuition reimbursements, teaching assistantships with full tuition reimbursements, institutionally sponsored loans, scholarships/grants, and health care benefits available. Financial award application deadline: 1/2. *Faculty research:* Pricing of options and futures, term structure of interest rates, use of accounting numbers in debt contracts, product differentiation, e-commerce and marketing, behavioral finance. *Unit head:* Mary Ellen Nichols, Registrar, 203-432-3955, Fax: 203-432-0342, E-mail: maryellen.nichols@yale.edu.

Yale University, Yale School of Management, Program in Business Administration, New Haven, CT 06520. Offers MBA, PhD, JD/MBA, M Arch/MBA, M Div/MBA, MBA/MA, MBA/MF, MBA/MFA, MBA/MPH, MD/MBA. *Accreditation:* AACSB. *Faculty:* 56 full-time (8 women), 22 part-time/adjunct (6 women). *Students:* 425 full-time (154 women); includes 103 minority (18 African Americans, 69 Asian Americans or Pacific Islanders, 16 Hispanic Americans), 88 international. Average age 28. 2,220 applicants, 22% accepted, 208 enrolled. In 2006, 215 master's, 2 doctorates awarded. *Degree requirements:* For doctorate, thesis/dissertation, comprehensive exam. *Entrance requirements:* For master's, GMAT; for doctorate, GMAT or GRE General Test (preferred). Additional exam requirements/recommendations for international students: Required—TOEFL (minimum score 600 paper-based; 250 computer-based). *Application deadline:* For fall admission, 10/26 priority date for domestic students, 10/20 priority date for international students; for winter admission, 1/11 priority date for domestic and international students; for spring admission, 3/15 priority date for domestic and international students. Application fee: $180. Electronic applications accepted. *Expenses: Contact institution. Financial support:* In 2006–07, 332 students received support. Career-related internships or fieldwork, Federal Work-Study, institutionally sponsored loans, and scholarships/grants available. Financial award application deadline: 3/1; financial award applicants required to submit FAFSA. *Faculty research:* Finance, strategy, marketing, leadership, operations. *Application contact:* Bruce DelMonico, Director of Admissions, 203-432-5635, Fax: 203-432-7004, E-mail: mba.admissions@yale.edu.

York College of Pennsylvania, Department of Business Administration, York, PA 17405-7199. Offers MBA. *Accreditation:* ACBSP. Part-time and evening/weekend programs available. *Entrance requirements:* For master's, GMAT. Additional exam requirements/recommendations for international students: Required—TOEFL.

York University, Faculty of Graduate Studies, Schulich School of Business, Toronto, ON M3J 1P3, Canada. Offers EMBA, IMBA, MBA, MPA, PhD, MBA/LL B, MBA/MA, MBA/MFA, MPA/LL B. Part-time and evening/weekend programs available. *Degree requirements:* For doctorate, thesis/dissertation, comprehensive exam. *Entrance requirements:* For master's, GMAT, minimum GPA of 3.0; for doctorate, GMAT, minimum GPA of 3.3. Electronic applications accepted.

See Close-Up on page 379.

Youngstown State University, Graduate School, Warren P. Williamson Jr. College of Business Administration, Youngstown, OH 44555-0001. Offers EMBA, MBA. *Accreditation:* AACSB. Part-time and evening/weekend programs available. *Degree requirements:* For master's, thesis optional. *Entrance requirements:* For master's, GMAT, minimum GPA of 2.7. Additional exam requirements/recommendations for international students: Required—TOEFL. *Faculty research:* Taxation and compliance, business ethics, operations management, organizational behavior, gender issues.

ALLIANT INTERNATIONAL UNIVERSITY

Marshall Goldsmith School of Management
Division of Business and Management

Programs of Study	The Marshall Goldsmith School of Management (MGSM) at Alliant International University prepares students to be managers and change agents in the world of business. The School recognizes the great need for forward-looking leadership and reliable management, and all its degrees are guided by an educational philosophy that puts the learner at the center. Students can pursue the Master in Business Administration (San Diego), the Master in International Business Administration (San Diego and Mexico City), or the Doctor of Business Administration (San Diego and Los Angeles). Programs offered in conjunction with the Division of Organizational Psychology, all on the San Diego campus, are the dual M.B.A. and M.A. in industrial/organizational (IO) psychology and the joint M.B.A. and Ph.D. in consulting psychology or in IO psychology. Classes are held in the evenings and weekends to accommodate the needs of working professionals. The Master in Business Administration (M.B.A.) and the Master in International Business Administration (M.I.B.A.) each require 39 semester units; however, the M.I.B.A. heavily emphasizes the international aspects of the world of business and management. Concentrations are available in finance, information and technology management, marketing, or strategic management. The Doctor of Business Administration (D.B.A.) program (60 semester units) emphasizes the discovery of new knowledge that can be applied to enhance successful management of business firms, government organizations, and not-for-profit organizations. Graduates hold senior positions in business, consulting, teaching, and research in universities, corporations, government agencies, and nongovernment organizations in the United States and around the world. Students select an area of emphasis in international business–finance, international business–marketing, or strategic management. In the dual- and joint-degree programs, M.B.A. courses provide students with advanced skills in the context of the overall dynamics of business firms. M.A. course work prepares graduates for careers in such fields as human resources or organizational development, with classes that apply psychology to the workplace. Doctoral work helps students become skilled in enhancing human performance, developing highly competent managers, and improving organizational productivity. The total number of credits for the M.A./M.B.A., the M.B.A./Ph.D. in consulting psychology, and the M.B.A./Ph.D. in IO psychology are 92, 152, and 153, respectively. Students have the opportunity to gain hands-on experience by having an internship in the industry, thereby keeping up-to-date with the latest developments. International students have the option to apply for a one-year practical experience in the United States after graduation. This valuable opportunity allows international students to gain work experience in the United States before returning to their home country. Students also have the option—and are strongly encouraged—to spend a semester at Alliant International University in Mexico City.
Research Facilities	Alliant International offers excellent research facilities throughout the system. Its libraries maintain a diverse collection of more than 160,000 books, 1,150 current print journal subscriptions, twelve electronic database subscriptions, approximately 995 psychological test titles, and more than 3,000 audiotapes and videotapes. Each campus library is a resource for a variety of research topics and works in cooperation with several other four-year institutions in the immediate area. Each academic school or college has research clusters, labs, and/or other resources to support original scholarly and applied research.
Financial Aid	Financial aid is available to graduate students in the form of long-term, low-interest loans (Federal Perkins Loans and Federal Subsidized and Unsubsidized Stafford Loans) and part-time employment (Federal Work-Study Program). Most international and domestic applicants are eligible for Alliant merit scholarships. The amount of a scholarship depends on the student's academic performance in the bachelor's degree (for master's applicants) and M.B.A. degree (for doctoral applicants). In other words, the merit scholarship is based on the incoming GPA. More information is available from the graduate program director.
Cost of Study	Tuition for the M.B.A. and M.I.B.A. programs is $800 per semester unit; for all other degree programs, the cost is $865 per semester unit.
Living and Housing Costs	In San Diego, the estimated cost of living for a graduate student (including housing and food, transportation, and personal expenses) for the nine-month academic year is $17,300. The estimated cost for books and supplies is $1500 per year. The San Diego campus offers student housing; the cost for a double room is $8000. There is no on-campus housing in Mexico City or Los Angeles. Most students live in communities adjacent to campus.
Student Group	Alliant's diverse student population in San Diego reflects the area itself—the campus welcomes about one third of its students from countries other than the United States. On the Mexico City campus, there are 3 full-time and 3 part-time graduate business students. The average age on all campuses is 32.
Student Outcomes	Alliant International alumni have successful careers internationally and domestically with financial institutions, government agencies, multinational corporations, export companies, not-for-profit groups, educational institutions, and professional psychology, practice, and entrepreneurial enterprises.
Location	Often called "America's Finest City," San Diego is a dynamic, vibrant, multicultural location with a laid-back, small-town feel. The area is filled with an incredible selection of activities and attractions that make San Diego one of the most popular spots in the United States. The Mexico City campus is situated downtown, in the city's main shopping and cultural area, near the historic center and within walking distance of the primary financial district. The campus is housed in an attractive historic building, surrounded by restaurants, bookstores, museums, and cultural centers. The Los Angeles–area campus is located in Alhambra, conveniently situated 6 miles east of downtown Los Angeles and easily accessible from the San Bernardino and Long Beach freeways. The Alhambra complex features 24-hour gated security and plenty of parking space for students and faculty and staff members.
The School and The Division	The Marshall Goldsmith School of Management is widely recognized for its adherence to the scholar-practitioner model of education, its demonstrated commitment to international education and multicultural competence, and the excellence of its alumni. What distinguishes MGSM is its emphasis on people—its superb faculty members, bright and able students from many different backgrounds, helpful staff members, and a star-studded cast of alumni. Graduates learn as much about people—how to understand them, work with them, and motivate them—as they do about other aspects of business and organizational studies. The Division of Business and Management at MGSM provides students with a range of knowledge, skills, and problem-solving abilities, enabling them to respond to the need for successful management of business firms, government organizations, and other not-for-profit organizations in a changing transnational environment. The Division's degree programs incorporate traditional face-to-face teaching methods, online distance-learning technology, and work on projects that require collaborative efforts and that help students integrate what they learn with the real world of business.
Applying	In general, students should have an overall GPA of at least 3.0 in all undergraduate and, if applicable, graduate work. Applicants should submit the completed application, the application fee ($55 for master's programs and $70 for the doctoral program), all official transcripts, a two-page personal essay, official GMAT scores for doctoral applicants only (GMAT scores are not required for master's degree programs), and letters of recommendation (two for master's students, three for doctoral). International students must also submit TOEFL scores.
Correspondence and Information	Central Contact Center Alliant International University 10455 Pomerado Road San Diego, California 92131 Phone: 866-U-ALLIANT (toll-free) Fax: 858-635-4555 E-mail: admissions@alliant.edu Web site: http://marshallgoldsmith.alliant.edu

Alliant International University

THE FACULTY AND THEIR RESEARCH

Los Angeles and San Diego Campuses

David Bainbridge, Associate Professor; M.S., California, Davis, 1973. Sustainable management, environmental accounting, industrial ecology, environmental restoration, alternative building materials, ecotourism. Nitrogen pollution. In *Teaching Green: The High School Years*. Gabriola Island, BC: New Society Press, 2007.

Jay Finkelman, Professor; Ph.D., NYU, 1970. Forensic industrial-organizational psychology; gender, race, age, disability, and other sources of employment discrimination; sexual harassment; contingent workforce staffing practices and productivity; attitudes and organizational citizenship; human resource management policies and practices; information processing and human factors engineering.

Ute Jamrozy, Assistant Professor; Ph.D., Clemson, 1996. Consumer psychology, sustainable and international marketing and sustainable tourism.

Louise Kelly, Professor; Ph.D., Concordia, 1996. Strategic management, international entrepreneurship. Founder centrality and strategy in the family-owned firm. *Entrepreneurship Theory Pract.* January 2001 (with Athanassiou and Crittenden).

Mohamed Ali Khalil, Professor; Ph.D., UCLA, 1967. International business and finance.

Meenakshi S. Krishnamoorthy, Professor; Ph.D., Manchester, 1960. Production/operations management, management science, technology management, project management, tourism economics, quantitative methods and total quality management,.

Rachna Kumar, Professor; Ph.D., NYU, 1994. Information systems, software process and productivity metrics, transfer of technology skills to developing cultures, technology synchronization and organizational performance, technology-mediated learning and knowledge retention, technology intervention and emotional maturity.

Alfred Lewis, Professor; D.B.A., US International, 1989. International trade and finance, political economy, strategic management. Analysis of the political-economy of Turkey and the European Union evaluation of foreign exchange regimes in the context of the global economy. *Eur. Business Rev.* 2005.

René M. Naert, Associate Professor; Ph.D., Walden, 1996. Information and technology management systems, computer-mediated distance education, video and audio compression algorithms, network engineering and administration, information sciences.

Fred Phillips, Professor and Associate Dean and Associate Provost for Research; Ph.D., Texas, 1978. Technology management, high-tech regional economic development, management education. Technology and the management imagination. *Pragmatics Cognition* 13:3:533–65, 2005.

Hamid Rahman, Professor; Ph.D., Syracuse, 1987. Corporate finance, investments, international finance, managerial accounting.

James V. Sullivan, Associate Professor; Ph.D., US International, 1993. Cross-cultural management, economics, leadership and management.

Akunna Winston, Principal Lecturer; D.B.A., US International, 2002. Consumer behavior, international business and marketing, hospitality management.

Mexico City Campus

Ilya Adler, Professor and Program Director, International Studies; Ph.D., Wisconsin–Madison, 1988. Communications and organizational development, cross-cultural issues.

Arturo Cherbowski, Professor; Ph.D., Yale, 2000. Public policy and development, Latin American affairs.

Clarisa Desouches, Professor; Ph.D., Universidad Nacional Autónoma de México, 2000; Ph.D.; Université de Dijon. Conflict-resolution issues in Latin America and Africa.

David Felsen, Assistant Professor; D.Phil., Oxford, 2001. International relations, comparative politics, public policy.

Mohamed Yakan, Professor; Ph.D., Michigan, 1965. International relations, political science, international law, organization, economics, political theory.

ANTIOCH UNIVERSITY NEW ENGLAND

Department of Organization & Management

Programs of Study

Antioch University New England's (ANE) organization and management programs help students discover their potential as leaders and continue their forward momentum. The Department attracts students whose jobs may have hit a plateau and who need to recharge their professional energy. The programs focus on training and educating creative thinkers to position themselves at the forefront of managing the inevitable changes that accompany progress. These low-residency programs provide high-impact growth, blending thoughtful instruction with practical experience. Professors are also practitioners in their fields, and the real world is an integral part of the curriculum.

Antioch New England's cohort model establishes a group of learners who begin their education together and move through the curriculum as a team. This approach creates a community of enthusiastic students whose similarities and differences spark lively interactions, creativity, and synergy—important ingredients for a powerful, insightful experience. Students come from nonprofit organizations; small or midsize businesses; and technical, product-based, health-care, or service industries and are connected by a common thread—the desire to develop organizations with work environments in which employees can grow and realize their full potential. This is the multiple bottom line, where success is measured as the sum of a company's financial health, high standards, sustainable growth, quality of work life, and social responsibility.

A working professional who seeks to advance along a career path should not have to abandon that path while pursuing a graduate education. ANE's programs are designed to accommodate busy lives, meeting approximately one weekend a month. Some programs have one-week summer intensives, and others meet for the regular weekend sessions.

Degrees offered are the Master of Science (M.S.) in management, the Master of Education (M.Ed.) in administration and supervision, and the Master of Business Administration (M.B.A.) in organizational and environmental sustainability. The University also offers the Organization Development Certificate.

Research Facilities

The Edward J. Tomey Center for Organization Development supports the development of vibrant, successful, sustainable organizations in nonprofit, public, and for-profit sectors. The center's aim is to support organizations so they can consistently fulfill their mission and vision, provide outstanding service to customers or consumers, achieve sustainable growth with respectable financial return, maintain a work culture in which employees thrive, and act as responsible community citizens. The Tomey Center is a vital educational link for Organization & Management graduate students who want supervised experience applying theory to practice through center projects and internships.

The Institute for Nonprofit Management, developed by the Department of Organization & Management at Antioch New England Graduate School, is a comprehensive curriculum of seminars for nonprofit executives. The program provides information in areas such as human resources, fund-raising, board development, marketing, business planning, and team-building. It is offered annually at various locations around the state of New Hampshire.

The librarians at Antioch New England offer professional and personalized reference service for graduate research. Extensive class and research support is available via the library Web site. Access to the library catalog is available through Horace, the library's automated catalog system. Also available are specialized online reference pages for classes and key topics, access to many online bibliographic databases, reserve reading, and links to scholarly Internet resources with full Internet access. In addition, detailed reference instruction, specific research information, an electronic book collection, and specific class-support resources are also available on the library Web site. All library services, such as book requests, renewals, reference help, and interlibrary loan requests, are available online.

The focused library collection includes print and electronic books and journals, dissertations and theses, audiovisual materials, and government documents. This collection is enhanced by the large collection of more than 300,000 books and 13,000 journal titles at Antioch College, the Graduate School's partner in the larger Antioch University Library system. Recent additions include OhioLINK, which offers more than 100 electronic-research databases, including a variety of full-text resources and RefWORKS, a bibliographic management program. The Antioch New England Library also participates in local, regional, and national interlibrary loan services.

Financial Aid

Approximately 70 percent of students receive some type of aid, usually in the form of federal loans and work-study. The Jonathan Daniels Scholarship, established in 2003, strives to increase the diversity of the student body in its racial, ethnic, cultural, international, and socioeconomic makeup and to encourage service to underserved groups. All full-time Antioch New England students are eligible, although funding is limited. The completed scholarship form, along with relevant information from the Office of Financial Aid, is forwarded to each academic department for decisions. Awards range from $500 to 50 percent of tuition for a given year.

Cost of Study

In 2007–08, tuition per semester is $5625 for those enrolled in the M.S. and M.Ed. programs as fall starters and $6750 for spring starters, $6500 for those enrolled in the Green M.B.A. program, and $5200 for the Organization Development Certificate program. Each student must pay a $250 comprehensive fee each semester.

Living and Housing Costs

ANE's location enables a large portion of students to commute to classes from their established homes in various parts of New England. Other students move close to Antioch New England, where they have a varied selection of settings—urban, rural, semirural, coast, mountains, or valley—in which to live. The Office of Admissions provides information resources for those relocating to the Monadnock region, the greater Brattleboro area, or northern Massachusetts.

Student Group

Approximately 1,200 students attend Antioch New England. The average age ranges between 25 and 55; women make up 69 percent of the population. Students have an average of three to six years of professional experience upon entering their program, and most continue employment while pursuing their studies.

Location

Located in Keene, New Hampshire, Antioch New England is in the heart of the Monadnock region, a picturesque area that has been described as the Currier & Ives corner of New Hampshire. The School is geographically situated so that students also have easy access to several popular metropolitan areas, including Boston and Montreal. With a population of nearly 23,000, Keene has been named by the National Trust for Historic Preservation as one of America's Dozen Distinctive Destinations.

The University and The Department

Antioch New England offers a rich array of master's and doctoral-level academic programming and institutional activities. The values-driven mission and focus on experiential learning, peer interaction, and reflective practice make the Antioch experience unique for each individual who is part of this learning community.

The Department of Organization & Management develops leaders and managers who can articulate their purpose, goals, and values and have the knowledge and skills to put them into action. Students and graduates are vital contributors to their organizations and communities, positioned for dynamic careers.

Applying

Students must submit the completed application form, including a resume and an essay; a nonrefundable application fee of $50; an official transcript from each accredited college or university attended, indicating courses taken and degree(s) earned; and three letters of recommendation (four letters for Alternative Admissions Process applicants), preferably from persons who are, or have been, in a position to evaluate the applicant's work. An interview with a Department faculty member is required. Antioch New England does not require master's-level applicants to take the Graduate Record Examinations (GRE) or similar written examinations.

Application deadlines are August 1 for fall admission and December 1 for a spring start.

Correspondence and Information

Antioch University New England
40 Avon Street
Keene, New Hampshire 03431-3516
Phone: 800-490-3310 (toll-free)
Fax: 603-357-0718
E-mail: petersons@antiochne.edu
Web site: http://www.antiochne.edu

Antioch University New England

THE FACULTY AND THEIR RESEARCH

Sunny Bradford, Associate Core Faculty; Ph.D., California, Santa Barbara. Organizational behavior, managing diversity, designing and conducting a workshop, coaching for excellence.

John Carr, Adjunct Faculty; Ed.D., Montana. Organizational theory and leadership in schools and school districts, planning, school law, rural leadership, middle school, staff development.

Wendy M. Elliott, Adjunct Faculty; M.Ed., Antioch New England. Team development, meeting facilitation, strategic planning, workshop design.

William T. Griffith, Interdisciplinary Core Faculty; Ph.D., Massachusetts Amherst; Ph.D., Boston College. Information technology and systems, postmodernism and social criticism, models of communication, technology and culture, and applications of narrative.

Steven P. Guerriero, Chair; Ph.D., Fielding Institute. Organizational behavior, research design, group dynamics, leadership and conflict resolution.

Robbie Hertneky, Associate Chair; M.Ed., Antioch New England. Group dynamics and leadership, team and leadership development.

Donna L. Mellen, Core Faculty; Ed.D., Massachusetts Amherst. Organization development, group dynamics and leadership, human resource development, self-knowledge for leadership.

Peter M. Smith, Core Faculty; M.B.A., Youngstown State. Leadership development, building of effective management teams, redesign of organizations and work processes to improve results.

Edward J. Tomey, Faculty Emeritus; M.Ed., Harvard. Organizational analysis and problem solving, strategic planning, marketing, team building, management development, supervisor-employee relations, performance appraisal, organizational and interpersonal communications, training.

ARGOSY UNIVERSITY

ARGOSY UNIVERSITY, ATLANTA CAMPUS

College of Business

Programs of Study

Argosy University, Atlanta Campus, offers the Master of Business Administration (M.B.A.) and the Doctor of Business Administration (D.B.A.) degrees. The business programs are designed to serve the needs of talented students, regardless of their undergraduate degrees. The College of Business welcomes and encourages students from diverse academic backgrounds.

The Master of Business Administration program offers a solutions-based, action-oriented approach to organizational change and human dynamics. It is designed to develop a new breed of leader—one who can identify challenges and opportunities, draw on the latest technology and information, use advanced analytical and planning approaches, and execute plans for positive change. Core courses include a broad array of foundation subjects, all relevant to meeting challenges and problems encountered in modern organizations. Students are required to choose from a variety of concentrations: customized professional concentration, finance, health-care administration, information systems management, international business, management, or marketing. This program can enhance future career potential and prepare students for postgraduate work in business.

The Doctor of Business Administration program provides industry and academic professionals the opportunity to build upon core skills and knowledge gained through the master's program. Students develop advanced comprehension of theoretical and applied literature in a chosen discipline and a higher level of competence in conducting action research. The program is designed to develop critical knowledge and skills for success in service to the profession and the community and in attaining credentials essential to leading, consulting, and teaching. Students must choose a concentration in accounting, customized professional concentration, information systems, international business, management, or marketing.

Research Facilities

Argosy University libraries provide curriculum support and educational resources, including current text materials, diagnostic training documents, reference materials and databases, journals and dissertations, and major and current titles in program areas. They provide an online public-access catalog of library resources throughout the Argosy University system. Students enjoy full remote access to their campus library database, enabling them to study and conduct research at home. Academic databases offer dissertation abstracts, academic journals, and professional periodicals. All library computers are Internet accessible. Software applications include Word, Excel, PowerPoint, SPSS, and various test-scoring programs.

Financial Aid

A wide range of financial aid options is available to students who qualify. Argosy University's Atlanta Campus offers access to federal and state aid programs, merit-based awards, grants, loans, and a work-study program. As a first step, students should complete the Free Application for Federal Student Aid (FAFSA). Prospective students can apply electronically at http://www.fafsa.ed.gov or at the campus. To receive consideration for the maximum amount of aid and ensure timely receipt of funds, it is best to submit an application promptly.

Cost of Study

Tuition varies by program. Students should contact Argosy University's Atlanta Campus for tuition information.

Living and Housing Costs

Students typically live in apartments in the metropolitan Atlanta area. Living expenses vary according to each student's preferred standard of living, housing, and transportation. The University does not offer or operate student housing. Most students are full-time working professionals who live within driving distance of the campus. Several nearby hotels offer special rates for those who commute from long distances. The Admissions Department also maintains a list of housing options, including contact information, for University students who wish to share housing. For more information, students should contact the Admissions Department.

Student Group

Admission to Argosy University's Atlanta Campus is selective to ensure a highly qualified student body. It encourages diversity in academic and employment backgrounds and promotes integration of the student body into professional life through established connections with local and national professional associations. Argosy University offers a professionally oriented education with rich opportunities to gain practical experience in class, field placements, and internships. Full-time students and working professionals gain the extensive knowledge and range of skills necessary for effective performance in their chosen fields.

Student Outcomes

Students can register with the University's online career-services system and use select services from a distance, such as degree-specific career e-mail lists, national job posts, and virtual job fairs. Students should contact the University for more information.

Location

Argosy University's Atlanta Campus is housed in a modern building in Sandy Springs, a northern suburb of Atlanta. The campus features a café and an outdoor lakeside terrace. Beyond the University, students find a wide selection of affordable housing options. This major metropolitan area offers many social and recreational opportunities, from clubs and concerts to galleries and museums, from a growing restaurant scene to Braves baseball games and in-line skating in Piedmont Park.

Many businesses in the area provide excellent, varied opportunities for student training. Atlanta's thriving business environment includes high-technology companies such as EarthLink and Macquarium as well as corporate giants such as the Coca-Cola Company, CNN, Delta Air Lines, AT&T, and Georgia Pacific.

The University

Argosy University is a private institution with eighteen locations across the nation. Argosy University's Atlanta Campus provides students with a career resources office, an academic resources center, and extensive information access for research. It offers the resources of a large university, plus the friendliness and personal attention of a small campus.

The innovative programs feature dynamic, relevant, and practical curricula delivered in flexible class formats. Students enjoy scheduling options that make it easier to fit school into their busy lives, choosing from day and evening courses, on campus or online. Many students find a combination of class formats to be an ideal way of continuing their education while meeting family and professional demands.

Argosy University is accredited by the Higher Learning Commission and is a member of the North Central Association (NCA, 30 North LaSalle Street, Suite 2400, Chicago, Illinois 60602; 800-621-7440 (toll-free); http://www.ncahlc.org).

Applying

Argosy University, Atlanta Campus, accepts students year-round on a rolling admissions basis, depending on availability of required courses. Applications for admission are available online or by contacting the campus.

Correspondence and Information

Argosy University, Atlanta Campus
980 Hammond Drive, Suite 100
Atlanta, Georgia 30328
Phone: 770-671-1200
        888-671-4777 (toll-free)
Fax: 770-671-0476
E-mail: auadmissions@argosy.edu
Web site: http://www.argosy.edu/atlanta

Argosy University, Atlanta Campus

THE FACULTY

The Argosy University faculty comprises working professionals who are eager to help students succeed. Members bring real-world experience and the latest practice innovations to the academic setting. The diverse faculty members of the College of Business are widely recognized for contributions to the field. Many are published scholars, and most hold doctoral degrees. They provide a substantive education that combines comprehensive knowledge with critical skills and practical workplace relevance. Above all, faculty members are committed to their students' personal and professional growth.

ARGOSY UNIVERSITY

ARGOSY UNIVERSITY, CHICAGO CAMPUS

College of Business

Programs of Study

Argosy University, Chicago Campus offers the Master of Business Administration (M.B.A.) and the Doctor of Business Administration (D.B.A.) degrees. The business programs are designed to serve the needs of talented students, regardless of their undergraduate degrees. The College of Business welcomes and encourages students from diverse academic backgrounds.

The Master of Business Administration program offers a solutions-based, action-oriented approach to organizational change and human dynamics. It is designed to develop a new breed of leader—one who can identify challenges and opportunities, draw on the latest technology and information, use advanced analytical and planning approaches, and execute plans for positive change. Core courses include a broad array of foundation subjects, all relevant to meeting challenges and problems encountered in modern organizations. Students are required to choose from a variety of concentrations: customized professional concentration, finance, health-care administration, information systems management, international business, management, or marketing. This program can enhance future career potential and prepare students for postgraduate work in business.

The Doctor of Business Administration program provides industry and academic professionals the opportunity to build upon core skills and knowledge gained through the master's program. Students develop advanced comprehension of theoretical and applied literature in a chosen discipline and a higher level of competence in conducting action research. The program is designed to develop critical knowledge and skills for success in service to the profession and the community, and in attaining credentials essential to leading, consulting, and teaching. Students must choose a concentration in accounting, customized professional concentration, information systems, international business, management, or marketing.

Research Facilities

Argosy University libraries provide curriculum support and educational resources, including current text materials, diagnostic training documents, reference materials and databases, journals and dissertations, and major and current titles in program areas. They provide an online public-access catalog of library resources throughout the Argosy University system. Students enjoy full remote access to their campus library database, enabling them to study and conduct research at home. Academic databases offer dissertation abstracts, academic journals, and professional periodicals. All library computers are Internet accessible. Software applications include Word, Excel, PowerPoint, SPSS, and various test-scoring programs.

Financial Aid

A wide range of financial aid options is available to students who qualify. Argosy University's Chicago Campus offers access to federal and state aid programs, merit-based awards, grants, loans, and a work-study program. As a first step, students should complete the Free Application for Federal Student Aid (FAFSA). Prospective students can apply electronically at http://www.fafsa.ed.gov or at the campus. To receive consideration for the maximum amount of aid and ensure timely receipt of funds, it is best to submit an application promptly.

Cost of Study

Tuition varies by program. Students should contact Argosy University's Chicago Campus for tuition information.

Living and Housing Costs

Students typically live in apartments in the metropolitan Chicago area. Living expenses vary according to each student's preferred standard of living, housing, and transportation. The University does not offer or operate student housing. Most of the students are full-time working professionals who live within driving distance of the campus. Several nearby hotels offer special rates for those who commute from long distances. The Admissions Department also maintains a list of housing options, including contact information for university students who wish to share housing. For more information, students should contact the Admissions Department.

Student Group

Admission to Argosy University's Chicago Campus is selective to ensure a highly qualified student body. It encourages diversity in academic and employment backgrounds and promotes integration of the student body into professional life through established connections with local and national professional associations. Argosy University offers a professionally oriented education with rich opportunities to gain practical experience in class, field placements, and internships. Full-time students and working professionals gain the extensive knowledge and range of skills necessary for effective performance in their chosen fields.

Student Outcomes

Students can register with the University's online career-services system and use select services from a distance, such as degree-specific career e-mail lists, national job posts, and virtual job fairs. Students should contact the University for more information.

Location

Chicago is a city of world-class status and beauty, drawing visitors from around the globe. Argosy University's Chicago Campus sits in the heart of The Loop, the city's business and entertainment center. Located on the shores of Lake Michigan, Chicago is home to world-champion sports teams, an internationally acclaimed symphony orchestra, renowned architecture, and a variety of history and art museums. Recreational opportunities include hiking and cycling on miles of lakefront trails, golfing, and shopping. Many businesses in the area provide excellent opportunities for student training. Chicago's thriving business environment includes a broad array of companies including Boeing and Pepsi America. The commercial banking headquarters of JP Morgan Chase is also located in Chicago.

The University

Argosy University is a private institution with eighteen locations across the nation. Argosy University's Chicago Campus provides students with an academic resources center and extensive information access for research. It offers the resources of a large university plus the friendliness and personal attention of a small campus. Argosy University's Chicago Campus is closely associated with the University's Schaumburg Campus located 45 minutes from downtown Chicago.

The innovative programs feature dynamic, relevant, and practical curricula delivered in flexible class formats. Students enjoy scheduling options that make it easier to fit school into their busy lives, choosing from day and evening courses, on campus or online. Many students find a combination of class formats to be an ideal way of continuing their education while meeting family and professional demands.

Argosy University is accredited by the Higher Learning Commission and is a member of the North Central Association (NCA, 30 North LaSalle Street, Suite 2400, Chicago, Illinois 60602; 800-621-7440 (toll-free); http://www.ncahlc.org).

Applying

Argosy University, Chicago Campus accepts students year-round on a rolling admissions basis, depending on availability of required courses. Applications for admission are available online or by contacting the campus.

Correspondence and Information

Argosy University, Chicago Campus
350 North Orleans Street
Chicago, Illinois 60654
Phone: 312-777-7600
       800-626-4123 (toll-free)
Fax: 312-777-7748
E-mail: auadmissions@argosy.edu
Web site: http://www.argosy.edu/chicago

Argosy University, Chicago Campus

THE FACULTY

The Argosy University faculty comprises working professionals who are eager to help students succeed. Members bring real-world experience and the latest practice innovations to the academic setting. The diverse faculty members of the College of Business are widely recognized for contributions to their fields. Many are published scholars, and most hold doctoral degrees. They provide a substantive education that combines comprehensive knowledge with critical skills and practical workplace relevance. Above all, faculty members are committed to their students' personal and professional development.

ARGOSY UNIVERSITY.

ARGOSY UNIVERSITY, DALLAS CAMPUS

College of Business

Programs of Study
Argosy University, Dallas Campus, offers the Master of Business Administration (M.B.A.) degree. The program is designed to serve the needs of talented students, regardless of their undergraduate degrees. The College of Business welcomes and encourages students from diverse academic backgrounds.

The Master of Business Administration program offers a solutions-based, action-oriented approach to organizational change and human dynamics. It is designed to develop a new breed of leader—one who can identify challenges and opportunities, draw on the latest technology and information, use advanced analytical and planning approaches, and execute plans for positive change. Core courses include a broad array of foundation subjects, all relevant to meeting challenges and problems encountered in modern organizations. The program includes a concentration in management. This course of study can enhance future career potential and prepare students for postgraduate work in business.

Research Facilities
Argosy University libraries provide curriculum support and educational resources, including current text materials, diagnostic training documents, reference materials and databases, journals and dissertations, and major and current titles in program areas. They provide an online public-access catalog of library resources throughout the Argosy University system. Students enjoy full remote access to their campus library database, enabling them to study and conduct research at home. Academic databases offer dissertation abstracts, academic journals, and professional periodicals. All library computers are Internet accessible. Software applications include Word, Excel, PowerPoint, SPSS, and various test-scoring programs.

Financial Aid
A wide range of financial aid options is available to students who qualify. Argosy University's Dallas Campus offers access to federal and state aid programs, merit-based awards, grants, loans, and a work-study program. As a first step, students should complete the Free Application for Federal Student Aid (FAFSA). Prospective students can apply electronically at http://www.fafsa.ed.gov or at the campus. To receive consideration for the maximum amount of aid and ensure timely receipt of funds, it is best to submit an application promptly.

Cost of Study
Tuition varies by program. Students should contact Argosy University's Dallas Campus for tuition information.

Living and Housing Costs
Students typically live in apartments in the metropolitan Dallas area. Living expenses vary according to each student's preferred standard of living, housing, and transportation. The University does not offer or operate student housing. Most of the students are full-time working professionals who live within driving distance of the campus. Several nearby hotels offer special rates for those who commute from long distances. The Admissions Department also maintains a list of housing options, including contact information, for University students who wish to share housing. For more information, students should contact the Admissions Department.

Student Group
Admission to Argosy University's Dallas Campus is selective to ensure a highly qualified student body. It encourages diversity in academic and employment backgrounds and promotes integration of the student body into professional life through established connections with local and national professional associations. Argosy University offers a professionally oriented education with rich opportunities to gain practical experience in class, field placements, and internships. Full-time students and working professionals gain the extensive knowledge and range of skills necessary for effective performance in their chosen fields.

Student Outcomes
Students can register with the University's online career-services system and use select services from a distance, such as degree-specific career e-mail lists, national job posts, and virtual job fairs. Students should contact the University for more information.

Location
Argosy University's Dallas Campus offers a north-central location in Dallas, with easy access to freeways, neighboring colleges and universities, libraries, shops, restaurants, theaters, art museums, and other tourist attractions. Many businesses in the metropolitan area offer excellent training facilities for students. The city is home to a broad array of companies, including Lockheed Martin Corporation, Baylor University Medical System, and Southwest Airlines.

The University
Argosy University is a private institution with eighteen locations across the nation. Argosy University's Dallas Campus provides students with a career resources office, an academic resources center, and extensive information access for research. It offers the resources of a large university, plus the friendliness and personal attention of a small campus.

Argosy University's Dallas Campus offers the unique opportunity to take one class at a time, with each class lasting for one month. Students are never required to study for multiple exams at the same time. New classes start each month. This flexible format lets students begin working on a graduate degree without waiting for the traditional semester to start.

Argosy University is accredited by the Higher Learning Commission and is a member of the North Central Association (NCA, 30 North LaSalle Street, Suite 2400, Chicago, Illinois 60602; 800-621-7440 (toll-free); http://www.ncahlc.org).

Applying
Argosy University, Dallas Campus, accepts students year-round on a rolling admissions basis, depending on availability of required courses. Applications for admission are available online or by contacting the campus.

Correspondence and Information
Argosy University, Dallas Campus
8080 Park Lane, Suite 500
Dallas, Texas 75231
Phone: 214-890-9900
　　　 866-954-9900 (toll-free)
Fax: 214-696-3900
E-mail: auadmissions@argosy.edu
Web site: http://www.argosy.edu/dallas

Argosy University, Dallas Campus

THE FACULTY

The Argosy University faculty comprises working professionals who are eager to help students succeed. Members bring real-world experience and the latest practice innovations to the academic setting. The diverse faculty members of the College of Business are widely recognized for contributions to the field. Many are published scholars, and most hold doctoral degrees. They provide a substantive education that combines comprehensive knowledge with critical skills and practical workplace relevance. Above all, faculty members are committed to their students' personal and professional development.

ARGOSY UNIVERSITY.

ARGOSY UNIVERSITY, DENVER CAMPUS

College of Business

Programs of Study

Argosy University, Denver Campus, offers the Master of Business Administration (M.B.A.), the Master of Science (M.S.) in management, and the Doctor of Business Administration (D.B.A.) degrees. The business programs are designed to serve the needs of talented students, regardless of their undergraduate degrees. The College of Business welcomes and encourages students from diverse academic backgrounds.

The Master of Business Administration program offers a solutions-based, action-oriented approach to organizational change and human dynamics. It is designed to develop a new breed of leader—one who can identify challenges and opportunities, draw on the latest technology and information, use advanced analytical and planning approaches, and execute plans for positive change. Core courses include a broad array of foundation subjects, all relevant to meeting challenges and problems encountered in modern organizations. Students are required to choose from a variety of concentrations: customized professional concentration, finance, health-care administration, information systems management, international business, management, or marketing. This program can enhance future career potential and prepare students for postgraduate work in business.

The Master of Science in Management program was designed to develop leadership and operational skills in those who wish to hold managerial or supervisory positions in public, private, and not-for-profit industries. Students learn the multifaceted process of business administration. The program enables students to diagnose multiple organizational circumstances, determine and evaluate options, and then implement and evaluate a plan of action.

The Doctor of Business Administration program provides industry and academic professionals the opportunity to build upon core skills and knowledge gained through the master's program. Students develop advanced comprehension of theoretical and applied literature in a chosen discipline and a higher level of competence in conducting action research. The program is designed to develop critical knowledge and skills for success in service to the profession and the community and in attaining credentials essential to leading, consulting, and teaching. Students must choose a concentration in accounting, customized professional concentration, information systems, international business, management, or marketing.

Research Facilities

Argosy University libraries provide curriculum support and educational resources, including current text materials, diagnostic training documents, reference materials and databases, journals and dissertations, and major and current titles in program areas. They provide an online public-access catalog of library resources throughout the Argosy University system. Students enjoy full remote access to their campus library database, enabling them to study and conduct research at home. Academic databases offer dissertation abstracts, academic journals, and professional periodicals. All library computers are Internet accessible. Software applications include Word, Excel, PowerPoint, SPSS, and various test-scoring programs.

Financial Aid

A wide range of financial aid options is available to students who qualify. Argosy University's Denver Campus offers access to federal and state aid programs, merit-based awards, grants, loans, and a work-study program. As a first step, students should complete the Free Application for Federal Student Aid (FAFSA). Prospective students can apply electronically at http://www.fafsa.ed.gov or at the campus. To receive consideration for the maximum amount of aid and ensure timely receipt of funds, it is best to submit an application promptly.

Cost of Study

Tuition varies by program. Students should contact Argosy University's Denver Campus for tuition information.

Living and Housing Costs

Students typically live in apartments in the metropolitan Denver area. Living expenses vary according to each student's preferred standard of living, housing, and transportation. The University does not offer or operate student housing. Most of the students are full-time working professionals who live within driving distance of the campus. Several nearby hotels offer special rates for those who commute from long distances. The Admissions Department also maintains a list of housing options, including contact information for University students who wish to share housing. For more information, students should contact the Admissions Department.

Student Group

Admission to Argosy University's Denver Campus is selective to ensure a highly qualified student body. It encourages diversity in academic and employment backgrounds and promotes integration of the student body into professional life through established connections with local and national professional associations. Argosy University offers a professionally oriented education with rich opportunities to gain practical experience in class, field placements, and internships. Full-time students and working professionals gain the extensive knowledge and range of skills necessary for effective performance in their chosen fields.

Student Outcomes

Students can register with the University's online career-services system and use select services from a distance, such as degree-specific career e-mail lists, national job posts, and virtual job fairs. Students should contact the University for more information.

Location

Argosy University, Denver Campus, is located at 1200 Lincoln Street in Denver, Colorado. The ten-story downtown facility includes classrooms, computer labs, a resource center with Internet access, a student lounge, staff and faculty offices, and other amenities. The campus is close to a variety of local libraries, shops, restaurants, theaters, and art museums. Denver's thriving professional organizations, major corporations, high-tech companies, hospitals, schools, clinics, and social service agencies can also provide outstanding training opportunities for students.

The University

Argosy University is a private institution with eighteen locations across the nation. Argosy University's Denver Campus provides students with a career resources office, an academic resources center, and extensive information access for research. It offers the resources of a large university, plus the friendliness and personal attention of a small campus.

The innovative programs feature dynamic, relevant, and practical curricula delivered in flexible class formats. Students enjoy scheduling options that make it easier to fit school into their busy lives, choosing from day and evening courses, on campus or online. Many students find a combination of class formats to be an ideal way of continuing their education while meeting family and professional demands.

Argosy University is accredited by the Higher Learning Commission and is a member of the North Central Association (NCA, 30 North LaSalle Street, Suite 2400, Chicago, Illinois 60602; 800-621-7440 (toll-free); http://www.ncahlc.org).

Applying

Argosy University, Denver Campus, accepts students year-round on a rolling admissions basis, depending on availability of required courses. Applications for admission are available online or by contacting the campus.

Correspondence and Information

Argosy University, Denver Campus
1200 Lincoln Street
Denver, Colorado 80203

Phone: 303-248-2700
        866-431-5981 (toll-free)
Fax: 303-248-2800
E-mail: auadmissions@argosy.edu
Web site: http://www.argosy.edu/denver

Argosy University, Denver Campus

THE FACULTY

The Argosy University faculty comprises working professionals who are eager to help students succeed. Members bring real-world experience and the latest practice innovations to the academic setting. The diverse faculty members of the College of Business are widely recognized for contributions to the field. Many are published scholars, and most hold doctoral degrees. They provide a substantive education that combines comprehensive knowledge with critical skills and practical workplace relevance. Above all, faculty members are committed to their students' personal and professional development.

ARGOSY UNIVERSITY

ARGOSY UNIVERSITY, HAWAI'I CAMPUS

College of Business

Programs of Study	Argosy University, Hawai'i Campus, offers the Master of Business Administration (M.B.A.) and the Doctor of Business Administration (D.B.A.) degrees. The business programs are designed to serve the needs of talented students, regardless of their undergraduate degrees. The College of Business welcomes and encourages students from diverse academic backgrounds. The Master of Business Administration program offers a solutions-based, action-oriented approach to organizational change and human dynamics. It is designed to develop a new breed of leader—one who can identify challenges and opportunities, draw on the latest technology and information, use advanced analytical and planning approaches, and execute plans for positive change. Core courses include a broad array of foundation subjects, all relevant to meeting challenges and problems encountered in modern organizations. Students are required to choose from a variety of concentrations: customized professional concentration, finance, health-care administration, information systems management, international business, management, or marketing. This program can enhance future career potential and prepare students for postgraduate work in business. The Doctor of Business Administration program provides industry and academic professionals the opportunity to build upon core skills and knowledge gained through the master's program. Students develop advanced comprehension of theoretical and applied literature in a chosen discipline and a higher level of competence in conducting action research. The program is designed to develop critical knowledge and skills for success in service to the profession and the community and in attaining credentials essential to leading, consulting, and teaching. Students must choose a concentration in accounting, customized professional concentration, information systems, international business, management, or marketing.
Research Facilities	Argosy University libraries provide curriculum support and educational resources, including current text materials, diagnostic training documents, reference materials and databases, journals and dissertations, and major and current titles in program areas. They provide an online public-access catalog of library resources throughout the Argosy University system. Students enjoy full remote access to their campus library database, enabling them to study and conduct research at home. Academic databases offer dissertation abstracts, academic journals, and professional periodicals. All library computers are Internet accessible. Software applications include Word, Excel, PowerPoint, SPSS, and various test-scoring programs.
Financial Aid	A wide range of financial aid options is available to students who qualify. Argosy University's Hawai'i Campus offers access to federal and state aid programs, merit-based awards, grants, loans, and a work-study program. As a first step, students should complete the Free Application for Federal Student Aid (FAFSA). Prospective students can apply electronically at http://www.fafsa.ed.gov or at the campus. To receive consideration for the maximum amount of aid and ensure timely receipt of funds, it is best to submit an application promptly.
Cost of Study	Tuition varies by program. Students should contact Argosy University's Hawai'i Campus for tuition information.
Living and Housing Costs	Students typically live in apartments in the metropolitan Honolulu area. Living expenses vary according to each student's preferred standard of living, housing, and transportation. The University does not offer or operate student housing. Most of the students are full-time working professionals who live within driving distance of the campus. Several nearby hotels offer special rates for those who commute from long distances. The Admissions Department also maintains a list of housing options, including contact information for University students who wish to share housing. For more information, students should contact the Admissions Department.
Student Group	Admission to Argosy University's Hawai'i Campus is selective to ensure a highly qualified student body. The University encourages diversity in academic and employment backgrounds and promotes integration of the student body into professional life through established connections with local and national professional associations. Argosy University offers a professionally oriented education with rich opportunities to gain practical experience in class, field placements, and internships. Full-time students and working professionals gain the extensive knowledge and range of skills necessary for effective performance in their chosen fields.
Student Outcomes	Students can register with the University's online career-services system and use select services from a distance, such as degree-specific career e-mail lists, national job posts, and virtual job fairs. Students should contact the University for more information.
Location	Argosy University's Hawai'i Campus is located in downtown Honolulu on O'ahu. Additional satellite locations on Maui and in Hilo on the Island of Hawai'i offer programs to communities on the neighboring islands. These locations connect the campus to Hawai'i and to the local and native communities of the Pacific Islands and the Pacific Rim. Students enjoy the cultural and recreational opportunities that these locations provide. University faculty and staff members often work in cooperation with the Hawai'i community to create an educational focus on social issues, human diversity, and programs that make a difference to underserved populations. Honolulu's thriving business environment includes a broad array of companies. The area's largest employers include Bank of Hawaii, Queens Medical Center, and the U.S. government. Many businesses in the metropolitan area provide excellent, varied opportunities for student training.
The University	Argosy University is a private institution with eighteen locations across the nation. Argosy University's Hawai'i Campus provides students with a career resources office, an academic resources center, and extensive information access for research. It offers the resources of a large university, plus the friendliness and personal attention of a small campus. The innovative programs feature dynamic, relevant, and practical curricula delivered in flexible class formats. Students enjoy scheduling options that make it easier to fit school into their busy lives, choosing from day and evening courses, on campus or online. Many students find a combination of class formats to be an ideal way of continuing their education while meeting family and professional demands. Argosy University is accredited by the Higher Learning Commission and is a member of the North Central Association (NCA, 30 North LaSalle Street, Suite 2400, Chicago, Illinois 60602; 800-621-7440 (toll-free); http://www.ncahlc.org).
Applying	Argosy University, Hawai'i Campus, accepts students year-round on a rolling admissions basis, depending on availability of required courses. Applications for admission are available online or by contacting the campus.
Correspondence and Information	Argosy University, Hawai'i Campus 400 ASB Tower 1001 Bishop Street Honolulu, Hawaii 96813 Phone: 808-536-5555 888-323-2777 (toll-free) Fax: 808-536-5505 E-mail: auadmissions@argosy.edu Web site: http://www.argosy.edu/honolulu

Argosy University, Hawai'i Campus

THE FACULTY

The Argosy University faculty comprises working professionals who are eager to help students succeed. Members bring real-world experience and the latest practice innovations to the academic setting. The diverse faculty members of the College of Business are widely recognized for contributions to the field. Many are published scholars, and most hold doctoral degrees. They provide a substantive education that combines comprehensive knowledge with critical skills and practical workplace relevance. Above all, faculty members are committed to their students' personal and professional development.

ARGOSY UNIVERSITY, INLAND EMPIRE CAMPUS

ARGOSY UNIVERSITY

College of Business

Programs of Study

Argosy University, Inland Empire Campus, offers the Master of Business Administration (M.B.A.) and the Doctor of Business Administration (D.B.A.) degrees. The business programs are designed to serve the needs of talented students, regardless of their undergraduate degrees. The College of Business welcomes and encourages students from diverse academic backgrounds.

The Master of Business Administration program offers a solutions-based, action-oriented approach to organizational change and human dynamics. It is designed to develop a new breed of leader—one who can identify challenges and opportunities, draw on the latest technology and information, use advanced analytical and planning approaches, and execute plans for positive change. Core courses include a broad array of foundation subjects, all relevant to meeting challenges and problems encountered in modern organizations. Students are required to choose from a variety of concentrations: customized professional concentration, finance, health-care administration, information systems management, international business, management, or marketing. This program can enhance future career potential and prepare students for postgraduate work in business.

The Doctor of Business Administration program provides industry and academic professionals the opportunity to build upon core skills and knowledge gained through the master's program. Students develop advanced comprehension of theoretical and applied literature in a chosen discipline and a higher level of competence in conducting action research. The program is designed to develop critical knowledge and skills for success in service to the profession and the community and in attaining credentials essential to leading, consulting, and teaching. Students must choose a concentration in accounting, customized professional concentration, information systems, international business, management, or marketing.

Research Facilities

Argosy University libraries provide curriculum support and educational resources, including current text materials, diagnostic training documents, reference materials and databases, journals and dissertations, and major and current titles in program areas. They provide an online public-access catalog of library resources throughout the Argosy University system. Students enjoy full remote access to their campus library database, enabling them to study and conduct research at home. Academic databases offer dissertation abstracts, academic journals, and professional periodicals. All library computers are Internet accessible. Software applications include Word, Excel, PowerPoint, SPSS, and various test-scoring programs.

Financial Aid

A wide range of financial aid options is available to students who qualify. Argosy University's Inland Empire Campus offers access to federal and state aid programs, merit-based awards, grants, loans, and a work-study program. As a first step, students should complete the Free Application for Federal Student Aid (FAFSA). Prospective students can apply electronically at http://www.fafsa.ed.gov or at the campus. To receive consideration for the maximum amount of aid and ensure timely receipt of funds, it is best to submit an application promptly.

Cost of Study

Tuition varies by program. Students should contact Argosy University's Inland Empire Campus for tuition information.

Living and Housing Costs

Students typically live in apartments in the metropolitan San Bernardino area. Living expenses vary according to each student's preferred standard of living, housing, and transportation. The University does not offer or operate student housing. Most of the students are full-time working professionals who live within driving distance of the campus. Several nearby hotels offer special rates for those who commute from long distances. The Admissions Department also maintains a list of housing options, including contact information for university students who wish to share housing. For more information, students should contact the Admissions Department.

Student Group

Admission to Argosy University's Inland Empire Campus is selective to ensure a highly qualified student body. The University encourages diversity in academic and employment backgrounds and promotes integration of the student body into professional life through established connections with local and national professional associations. Argosy University offers a professionally oriented education with rich opportunities to gain practical experience in class, field placements, and internships. Full-time students and working professionals gain the extensive knowledge and range of skills necessary for effective performance in their chosen fields.

Student Outcomes

Students can register with the University's online career-services system and use select services from a distance, such as degree-specific career e-mail lists, national job posts, and virtual job fairs. Students should contact the University for more information.

Location

Argosy University's Inland Empire Campus is conveniently located in the Hospitality Lane section of San Bernardino, California. The facility features classrooms, computer labs, a resource center with Internet access, student lounge, staff and faculty offices, and proximity to the region's many cultural and recreational attractions. The University provides a supportive educational environment with convenient class options that enable students to earn a degree while fulfilling other life responsibilities. All of the programs are thoroughly oriented to the real working world with a focus on developing technical proficiency in each student's field as well as an overall professional career approach. Many businesses in the area provide excellent, varied opportunities for student training.

The University

Argosy University is a private institution with eighteen locations across the nation. Argosy University's Inland Empire Campus provides students with a career resources office, an academic resources center, and extensive information access for research. It offers the resources of a large university plus the friendliness and personal attention of a small campus.

The innovative programs feature dynamic, relevant, and practical curricula delivered in flexible class formats. Students enjoy scheduling options that make it easier to fit school into their busy lives, choosing from day and evening courses, on campus or online. Many students find a combination of class formats to be an ideal way of continuing their education while meeting family and professional demands.

Argosy University is accredited by the Higher Learning Commission and is a member of the North Central Association (NCA, 30 North LaSalle Street, Suite 2400, Chicago, Illinois 60602; 800-621-7440 (toll-free); http://www.ncahlc.org).

Applying

Argosy University, Inland Empire Campus, accepts students year-round on a rolling admissions basis, depending on availability of required courses. Applications for admission are available online or by contacting the campus.

Correspondence and Information

Argosy University, Inland Empire Campus
636 East Brier Drive, Suite 235
San Bernardino, California 92408
Phone: 909-915-3800
        866-217-9075 (toll-free)
Fax: 909-915-3810
E-mail: auadmissions@argosy.edu
Web site: http://www.argosy.edu/inlandempire

Argosy University, Inland Empire Campus

THE FACULTY

The Argosy University faculty comprises working professionals who are eager to help students succeed. Members bring real-world experience and the latest practice innovations to the academic setting. The diverse faculty members of the College of Business are widely recognized for contributions to the field. Many are published scholars, and most hold doctoral degrees. They provide a substantive education that combines comprehensive knowledge with critical skills and practical workplace relevance. Above all, faculty members are committed to their students' personal and professional development.

ARGOSY UNIVERSITY

ARGOSY UNIVERSITY, NASHVILLE CAMPUS

College of Business

Program of Study

Argosy University, Nashville Campus, offers the Doctor of Business Administration (D.B.A.) degree. The business programs are designed to serve the needs of talented students, regardless of their undergraduate degrees. The College of Business welcomes and encourages students from diverse academic backgrounds.

The Doctor of Business Administration program provides industry and academic professionals the opportunity to build upon core skills and knowledge gained through the master's program. Students develop advanced comprehension of theoretical and applied literature in a chosen discipline and a higher level of competence in conducting action research. The program is designed to develop critical knowledge and skills for success in service to the profession and the community and in attaining credentials essential to leading, consulting, and teaching. Students must choose a concentration in accounting, customized professional concentration, information systems, international business, management, or marketing.

Research Facilities

Argosy University libraries provide curriculum support and educational resources, including current text materials, diagnostic training documents, reference materials and databases, journals and dissertations, and major and current titles in program areas. They provide an online public-access catalog of library resources throughout the Argosy University system. Students enjoy full remote access to their campus library database, enabling them to study and conduct research at home. Academic databases offer dissertation abstracts, academic journals, and professional periodicals. All library computers are Internet accessible. Software applications include Word, Excel, PowerPoint, SPSS, and various test-scoring programs.

Financial Aid

A wide range of financial aid options is available to students who qualify. Argosy University's Nashville Campus offers access to federal and state aid programs, merit-based awards, grants, loans, and a work-study program. As a first step, students should complete the Free Application for Federal Student Aid (FAFSA). Prospective students can apply electronically at http://www.fafsa.ed.gov or at the campus. To receive consideration for the maximum amount of aid and ensure timely receipt of funds, it is best to submit an application promptly.

Cost of Study

Tuition varies by program. Students should contact Argosy University's Nashville Campus for tuition information.

Living and Housing Costs

Students typically live in apartments in the metropolitan Nashville area. Living expenses vary according to each student's preferred standard of living, housing, and transportation. The University does not offer or operate student housing. Most of the students are full-time working professionals who live within driving distance of the campus. Several nearby hotels offer special rates for those who commute from long distances. The Admissions Department also maintains a list of housing options, including contact information, for University students who wish to share housing. For more information, students should contact the Admissions Department.

Student Group

Admission to Argosy University's Nashville Campus is selective to ensure a highly qualified student body. It encourages diversity in academic and employment backgrounds and promotes integration of the student body into professional life through established connections with local and national professional associations. Argosy University offers a professionally oriented education with rich opportunities to gain practical experience in class, field placements, and internships. Full-time students and working professionals gain the extensive knowledge and range of skills necessary for effective performance in their chosen fields.

Student Outcomes

Students can register with the University's online career-services system and use select services from a distance, such as degree-specific career e-mail lists, national job posts, and virtual job fairs. Students should contact the University for more information.

Location

Argosy University's Nashville Campus is located at 100 Centerview Drive in Nashville, Tennessee. This growing city offers a variety of recreational activities, including the ballet and symphony, the newly established Frist Museum of Art, and professional sports. Nashville is known as Music City, USA, and is home to the Country Music Hall of Fame. The thriving business environment includes companies such as Moses Cone Health Systems, Inc., and Novant Health, Inc.

The University

Argosy University is a private institution with eighteen locations across the nation. Argosy University's Nashville Campus provides students with a career resources office, an academic resources center, and extensive information access for research. It offers the resources of a large university, plus the friendliness and personal attention of a small campus.

The innovative programs feature dynamic, relevant, and practical curricula delivered in flexible class formats. Students enjoy scheduling options that make it easier to fit school into their busy lives, choosing from day and evening courses, on campus or online. Many students find a combination of class formats to be an ideal way of continuing their education while meeting family and professional demands.

Argosy University is accredited by the Higher Learning Commission and is a member of the North Central Association (NCA, 30 North LaSalle Street, Suite 2400, Chicago, Illinois 60602; 800-621-7440 (toll-free); http://www.ncahlc.org).

Applying

Argosy University, Nashville Campus, accepts students year-round on a rolling admissions basis, depending on availability of required courses. Applications for admission are available online or by contacting the campus.

Correspondence and Information

Argosy University, Nashville Campus
100 Centerview Drive, Suite 225
Nashville, Tennessee 37214
Phone: 615-525-2800
   866-833-6598 (toll-free)
Fax: 615-525-2900
E-mail: auadmissions@argosy.edu
Web site: http://www.argosy.edu/nashville

Argosy University, Nashville Campus

THE FACULTY

The Argosy University faculty comprises working professionals who are eager to help students succeed. Members bring real-world experience and the latest practice innovations to the academic setting. The diverse faculty members of the College of Business are widely recognized for contributions to the field. Most hold doctoral degrees. They provide a substantive education that combines comprehensive knowledge with critical skills and practical workplace relevance. Above all, faculty members are committed to their students' personal and professional development.

ARGOSY UNIVERSITY, ORANGE COUNTY CAMPUS

ARGOSY UNIVERSITY

College of Business

Programs of Study	Argosy University, Orange County Campus, offers the Master of Business Administration (M.B.A.), the Master of Science (M.S.) in management, and the Doctor of Business Administration (D.B.A.) degrees. The business programs are designed to serve the needs of talented students, regardless of their undergraduate degrees. The College of Business welcomes and encourages students from diverse academic backgrounds.

The Master of Business Administration program offers a solutions-based, action-oriented approach to organizational change and human dynamics. It is designed to develop a new breed of leader—one who can identify challenges and opportunities, draw on the latest technology and information, use advanced analytical and planning approaches, and execute plans for positive change. Core courses include a broad array of foundation subjects, all relevant to meeting challenges and problems encountered in modern organizations. Students are required to choose from a variety of concentrations: customized professional concentration, finance, health-care administration, information systems management, international business, management, or marketing. This program can enhance future career potential and prepare students for postgraduate work in business.

The Master of Science in Management program was designed to develop leadership and operational skills in those who wish to hold managerial or supervisory positions in public, private, and not-for-profit industries. Students learn the multifaceted process of business administration. The program enables students to diagnose multiple organizational circumstances, determine and evaluate options, and then implement and evaluate a plan of action.

The Doctor of Business Administration program provides industry and academic professionals the opportunity to build upon core skills and knowledge gained through the master's program. Students develop advanced comprehension of theoretical and applied literature in a chosen discipline and a higher level of competence in conducting action research. The program is designed to develop critical knowledge and skills for success in service to the profession and the community and in attaining credentials essential to leading, consulting, and teaching. Students must choose a concentration in accounting, customized professional concentration, information systems, international business, management, or marketing. |
Research Facilities	Argosy University libraries provide curriculum support and educational resources, including current text materials, diagnostic training documents, reference materials and databases, journals and dissertations, and major and current titles in program areas. They provide an online public-access catalog of library resources throughout the Argosy University system. Students enjoy full remote access to their campus library database, enabling them to study and conduct research at home. Academic databases offer dissertation abstracts, academic journals, and professional periodicals. All library computers are Internet accessible. Software applications include Word, Excel, PowerPoint, SPSS, and various test-scoring programs.
Financial Aid	A wide range of financial aid options is available to students who qualify. Argosy University's Orange County Campus offers access to federal and state aid programs, merit-based awards, grants, loans, and a work-study program. As a first step, students should complete the Free Application for Federal Student Aid (FAFSA). Prospective students can apply electronically at http://www.fafsa.ed.gov or at the campus. To receive consideration for the maximum amount of aid and ensure timely receipt of funds, students should submit an application promptly.
Cost of Study	Tuition varies by program. Students should contact Argosy University's Orange County Campus for tuition information.
Living and Housing Costs	Students typically live in apartments in the Santa Ana metropolitan area. Living expenses vary according to each student's preferred standard of living, housing, and transportation. The University does not offer or operate student housing. Most of the students are full-time working professionals who live within driving distance of the campus. Several nearby hotels offer special rates for those who commute from long distances. The Admissions Department also maintains a list of housing options, including contact information, for University students who wish to share housing. For more information, students should contact the Admissions Department.
Student Group	Admission to Argosy University's Orange County Campus is selective to ensure a highly qualified student body. It encourages diversity in academic and employment backgrounds and promotes integration of the student body into professional life through established connections with local and national professional associations. Argosy University offers a professionally oriented education with rich opportunities to gain practical experience in class, field placements, and internships. Full-time students and working professionals gain the extensive knowledge and range of skills necessary for effective performance in their chosen fields.
Student Outcomes	Students can register with the University's online career-services system and use select services from a distance, such as degree-specific career e-mail lists, national job posts, and virtual job fairs. Students should contact the University for more information.
Location	Argosy University's Orange County Campus attracts students from Southern California as well as around the country and the world. Orange County features a temperate climate, sunny beaches, and a host of cultural and entertainment options. The campus is located approximately 30 miles south of downtown Los Angeles, 90 miles north of San Diego, and just minutes from one of the many freeways that connect the Southern California basin. Regional parks and preserved lands provide opportunities for hiking, biking, riding, and other recreational activities. Whether it is ultrachic Newport Beach, artsy Laguna Beach, or unspoiled Catalina Island, Orange County's oceanside personalities are as varied as the people who visit the area.

Many businesses in the area provide excellent opportunities for student training. Orange County's thriving business environment includes a broad array of companies. The area's largest employers include Ingram Micro Inc., the *Orange County Register,* ITT Industries, and OneSource. |
| **The University** | Argosy University is a private institution with eighteen locations across the nation. Argosy University's Orange County Campus provides students with a career resources office, an academic resources center, and extensive information access for research. It offers the resources of a large university plus the friendliness and personal attention of a small campus.

The innovative programs feature dynamic, relevant, and practical curricula delivered in flexible class formats. Students enjoy scheduling options that make it easier to fit school into their busy lives, choosing from day and evening courses, on campus or online. Many students find a combination of class formats to be an ideal way of continuing their education while meeting family and professional demands.

Argosy University is accredited by the Higher Learning Commission and is a member of the North Central Association (NCA, 30 North LaSalle Street, Suite 2400, Chicago, Illinois 60602; 800-621-7440 (toll-free); http://www.ncahlc.org). |
| **Applying** | Argosy University, Orange County Campus, accepts students year-round on a rolling admissions basis, depending on availability of required courses. Applications for admission are available online or by contacting the campus. |
| **Correspondence and Information** | Argosy University, Orange County Campus
3501 West Sunflower Avenue, Suite 110
Santa Ana, California 92704
Phone: 714-338-6200
    800-716-9598 (toll-free)
Fax: 714-437-1697
E-mail: auadmissions@argosy.edu
Web site: http://www.argosy.edu/orangecounty |

Argosy University, Orange County Campus

THE FACULTY

The Argosy University faculty comprises working professionals who are eager to help students succeed. Members bring real-world experience and the latest practice innovations to the academic setting. The diverse faculty members of the College of Business are widely recognized for contributions to the field. Many are published scholars, and most hold doctoral degrees. They provide a substantive education that combines comprehensive knowledge with critical skills and practical workplace relevance. Above all, faculty members are committed to their students' personal and professional development.

ARGOSY UNIVERSITY.

ARGOSY UNIVERSITY, PHOENIX CAMPUS

College of Business

Programs of Study

Argosy University, Phoenix Campus, offers the Master of Business Administration (M.B.A.) and the Doctor of Business Administration (D.B.A.) degrees. The business programs are designed to serve the needs of talented students, regardless of their undergraduate degrees. The College of Business welcomes and encourages students from diverse academic backgrounds.

The Master of Business Administration program offers a solutions-based, action-oriented approach to organizational change and human dynamics. It is designed to develop a new breed of leader—one who can identify challenges and opportunities, draw on the latest technology and information, use advanced analytical and planning approaches, and execute plans for positive change. Core courses include a broad array of foundation subjects, all relevant to meeting challenges and problems encountered in modern organizations. Students are required to choose from a variety of concentrations: customized professional concentration, finance, health-care administration, information systems management, international business, management, or marketing. This program can enhance future career potential and prepare students for postgraduate work in business.

The Doctor of Business Administration program provides industry and academic professionals the opportunity to build upon core skills and knowledge gained through the master's program. Students develop advanced comprehension of theoretical and applied literature in a chosen discipline and a higher level of competence in conducting action research. The program is designed to develop critical knowledge and skills for success in service to the profession and the community and in attaining credentials essential to leading, consulting, and teaching. Students must choose a concentration in accounting, customized professional concentration, information systems, international business, management, or marketing.

Research Facilities

Argosy University libraries provide curriculum support and educational resources, including current text materials, diagnostic training documents, reference materials and databases, journals and dissertations, and major and current titles in program areas. They provide an online public-access catalog of library resources throughout the Argosy University system. Students enjoy full remote access to their campus library database, enabling them to study and conduct research at home. Academic databases offer dissertation abstracts, academic journals, and professional periodicals. All library computers are Internet accessible. Software applications include Word, Excel, PowerPoint, SPSS, and various test-scoring programs.

Financial Aid

A wide range of financial aid options is available to students who qualify. Argosy University's Phoenix Campus offers access to federal and state aid programs, merit-based awards, grants, loans, and a work-study program. As a first step, students should complete the Free Application for Federal Student Aid (FAFSA). Prospective students can apply electronically at http://www.fafsa.ed.gov or at the campus. To receive consideration for the maximum amount of aid and ensure timely receipt of funds, it is best to submit an application promptly.

Cost of Study

Tuition varies by program. Students should contact Argosy University's Phoenix Campus for tuition information.

Living and Housing Costs

Students typically live in apartments in the metropolitan Phoenix area. Living expenses vary according to each student's preferred standard of living, housing, and transportation. The University does not offer or operate student housing. Most of the students are full-time working professionals who live within driving distance of the campus. Several nearby hotels offer special rates for those who commute from long distances. The Admissions Department also maintains a list of housing options, including contact information for University students who wish to share housing. For more information, students should contact the Admissions Department.

Student Group

Admission to Argosy University's Phoenix Campus is selective to ensure a highly qualified student body. It encourages diversity in academic and employment backgrounds and promotes integration of the student body into professional life through established connections with local and national professional associations. Argosy University offers a professionally oriented education with rich opportunities to gain practical experience in class, field placements, and internships. Full-time students and working professionals gain the extensive knowledge and range of skills necessary for effective performance in their chosen fields.

Student Outcomes

Students can register with the University's online career-services system and use select services from a distance, such as degree-specific career e-mail lists, national job posts, and virtual job fairs. Students should contact the University for more information.

Location

Argosy University's Phoenix Campus offers a high-quality education in an intimate, small-group setting. The campus is conveniently located near I-17, close to shops, restaurants, and recreational areas. Phoenix is home to several major league sports teams, and the city offers an array of cultural activities ranging from opera and theater to science museums. The multicultural environment of Arizona, coupled with Argosy University's professional training affiliations throughout the state, creates an exciting opportunity for students to work with urban, rural, and culturally diverse populations.

Many businesses in the area provide excellent, varied opportunities for student training. The thriving business environment in Phoenix includes a wide variety of companies such as Intel and Go Daddy Group, an Internet company. Wells Fargo, Home Depot, Lowe's, and Wal-Mart also represent some of the area's largest employers.

The University

Argosy University is a private institution with eighteen locations across the nation. Argosy University's Phoenix Campus provides students with a career resources office, an academic resources center, and extensive information access for research. It offers the resources of a large university, plus the friendliness and personal attention of a small campus. The innovative programs feature dynamic, relevant, and practical curricula delivered in flexible class formats. Students enjoy scheduling options that make it easier to fit school into their busy lives, choosing from day and evening courses, on campus or online. Many students find a combination of class formats to be an ideal way of continuing their education while meeting family and professional demands.

Argosy University is accredited by the Higher Learning Commission and is a member of the North Central Association (NCA, 30 North LaSalle Street, Suite 2400, Chicago, Illinois 60602; 800-621-7440 (toll-free); http://www.ncahlc.org).

Applying

Argosy University, Phoenix Campus, accepts students year-round on a rolling admissions basis, depending on availability of required courses. Applications for admission are available online or by contacting the campus.

Correspondence and Information

Argosy University, Phoenix Campus
2233 West Dunlap Avenue
Phoenix, Arizona 85021
Phone: 602-216-2600
　　　　866-216-2777 (toll-free)
Fax: 602-216-2601
E-mail: auadmissions@argosy.edu
Web site: http://www.argosy.edu/phoenix

Argosy University, Phoenix Campus

THE FACULTY

The Argosy University faculty comprises working professionals who are eager to help students succeed. Members bring real-world experience and the latest practice innovations to the academic setting. The diverse faculty members of the College of Business are widely recognized for contributions to the field. Many are published scholars, and most hold doctoral degrees. They provide a substantive education that combines comprehensive knowledge with critical skills and practical workplace relevance. Above all, faculty members are committed to their students' personal and professional development.

ARGOSY UNIVERSITY, SAN DIEGO CAMPUS

College of Business

ARGOSY UNIVERSITY

Programs of Study
Argosy University, San Diego Campus, offers the Master of Business Administration (M.B.A.), the Master of Science (M.S.) in management, and the Doctor of Business Administration (D.B.A.) degrees. The business programs are designed to serve the needs of talented students, regardless of their undergraduate degrees. The College of Business welcomes and encourages students from diverse academic backgrounds.

The Master of Business Administration program offers a solutions-based, action-oriented approach to organizational change and human dynamics. It is designed to develop a new breed of leader—one who can identify challenges and opportunities, draw on the latest technology and information, use advanced analytical and planning approaches, and execute plans for positive change. Core courses include a broad array of foundation subjects, all relevant to meeting challenges and problems encountered in modern organizations. Students are required to choose from a variety of concentrations: customized professional concentration, finance, information systems management, international business, management, or marketing. This program can enhance future career potential and prepare students for postgraduate work in business.

The Master of Science in Management program was designed to develop leadership and operational skills in those who wish to hold managerial or supervisory positions in public, private, and not-for-profit industries. Students learn the multifaceted process of business administration. The program enables students to diagnose multiple organizational circumstances, determine and evaluate options, and then implement and evaluate a plan of action.

The Doctor of Business Administration program provides industry and academic professionals the opportunity to build upon core skills and knowledge gained through the master's program. Students develop advanced comprehension of theoretical and applied literature in a chosen discipline and a higher level of competence in conducting action research. The program is designed to develop critical knowledge and skills for success in service to the profession and the community and in attaining credentials that are essential to leading, consulting, and teaching. Students must choose a concentration in accounting, customized professional concentration, information systems, international business, management, or marketing.

Research Facilities
Argosy University libraries provide curriculum support and educational resources, including current text materials, diagnostic training documents, reference materials and databases, journals and dissertations, and major and current titles in program areas. They provide an online public-access catalog of library resources throughout the Argosy University system. Students enjoy full remote access to their campus library database, enabling them to study and conduct research at home. Academic databases offer dissertation abstracts, academic journals, and professional periodicals. All library computers are Internet accessible. Software applications include Word, Excel, PowerPoint, SPSS, and various test-scoring programs.

Financial Aid
A wide range of financial aid options is available to students who qualify. Argosy University's San Diego Campus offers access to federal and state aid programs, merit-based awards, grants, loans, and a work-study program. As a first step, students should complete the Free Application for Federal Student Aid (FAFSA). Prospective students can apply electronically at http://www.fafsa.ed.gov or at the campus. To receive consideration for the maximum amount of aid and ensure timely receipt of funds, it is best to submit an application promptly.

Cost of Study
Tuition varies by program. Students should contact Argosy University's San Diego Campus for tuition information.

Living and Housing Costs
Students typically live in apartments in the metropolitan San Diego area. Living expenses vary according to each student's preferred standard of living, housing, and transportation. The University does not offer or operate student housing. Most of the students are full-time working professionals who live within driving distance of the campus. Several nearby hotels offer special rates for those who commute from long distances. The Admissions Department also maintains a list of housing options, including contact information, for University students who wish to share housing. For more information, students should contact the Admissions Department.

Student Group
Admission to Argosy University's San Diego Campus is selective to ensure a highly qualified student body. It encourages diversity in academic and employment backgrounds and promotes integration of the student body into professional life through established connections with local and national professional associations. Argosy University offers a professionally oriented education with rich opportunities to gain practical experience in class, field placements, and internships. Full-time students and working professionals gain the extensive knowledge and range of skills necessary for effective performance in their chosen fields.

Student Outcomes
Students can register with the University's online career-services system and use select services from a distance, such as degree-specific career e-mail lists, national job posts, and virtual job fairs. Students should contact the University for more information.

Location
San Diego, southern California's second-largest city, offers an ideal climate year-round, 70 miles of beautiful beaches, colorful neighborhoods, and a dynamic downtown district. Argosy University's San Diego Campus offers classrooms, a library resource center, a student lounge, staff and faculty offices, and other amenities. The area offers numerous attractions, including the famous San Diego Zoo and Wild Animal Park and Sea World.

Many businesses in the area provide excellent, varied opportunities for student training. San Diego's thriving business environment includes several Fortune 500 companies such as QUALCOMM and Pfizer, Inc., and a concentration of high-tech companies.

The University
Argosy University is a private institution with eighteen locations across the nation. Argosy University's San Diego Campus provides students with a career resources office, an academic resources center, and extensive information access for research. It offers the resources of a large university, plus the friendliness and personal attention of a small campus.

The innovative programs feature dynamic, relevant, and practical curricula delivered in flexible class formats. Students enjoy scheduling options that make it easier to fit school into their busy lives, choosing from day and evening courses, on campus or online. Many students find a combination of class formats to be an ideal way of continuing their education while meeting family and professional demands.

Argosy University is accredited by the Higher Learning Commission and is a member of the North Central Association (NCA, 30 North LaSalle Street, Suite 2400, Chicago, Illinois 60602; 800-621-7440 (toll-free); http://www.ncahlc.org).

Applying
Argosy University, San Diego Campus, accepts students year-round on a rolling admissions basis, depending on availability of required courses. Applications for admission are available online or by contacting the campus.

Correspondence and Information
Argosy University, San Diego Campus
7650 Mission Valley Road
San Diego, California 92108
Phone: 858-598-1900
        866-505-0333 (toll-free)
Fax: 619-292-0553
E-mail: auadmissions@argosy.edu
Web site: http://www.argosy.edu/sandiego

Argosy University, San Diego Campus

THE FACULTY

The Argosy University faculty comprises working professionals who are eager to help students succeed. Members bring real-world experience and the latest practice innovations to the academic setting. The diverse faculty members of the College of Business are widely recognized for contributions to the field. Many are published scholars, and most hold doctoral degrees. They provide a substantive education that combines comprehensive knowledge with critical skills and practical workplace relevance. Above all, faculty members are committed to their students' personal and professional development.

ARGOSY UNIVERSITY.

ARGOSY UNIVERSITY, SAN FRANCISCO BAY AREA CAMPUS
College of Business

Programs of Study

Argosy University, San Francisco Bay Area Campus, offers the Master of Business Administration (M.B.A.), the Master of Science (M.S.) in management, and the Doctor of Business Administration (D.B.A.) degrees. The business programs are designed to serve the needs of talented students, regardless of their undergraduate degrees. The College of Business welcomes and encourages students from diverse academic backgrounds.

The Master of Business Administration program offers a solutions-based, action-oriented approach to organizational change and human dynamics. It is designed to develop a new breed of leader—one who can identify challenges and opportunities, draw on the latest technology and information, use advanced analytical and planning approaches, and execute plans for positive change. Core courses include a broad array of foundation subjects, all relevant to meeting challenges and problems encountered in modern organizations. Students are required to choose from a variety of concentrations: corporate compliance, customized professional concentration, finance, health-care administration, information systems management, international business, management, or marketing. This program can enhance future career potential and prepare students for postgraduate work in business.

The Master of Science in Management program was designed to develop leadership and operational skills in those who wish to hold managerial or supervisory positions in public, private, and not-for-profit industries. Students learn the multifaceted process of business administration. The program enables students to diagnose multiple organizational circumstances, determine and evaluate options, and then implement and evaluate a plan of action.

The Doctor of Business Administration program provides industry and academic professionals the opportunity to build upon core skills and knowledge gained through the master's program. Students develop advanced comprehension of theoretical and applied literature in a chosen discipline and a higher level of competence in conducting action research. The program is designed to develop critical knowledge and skills for success in service to the profession and the community and in attaining credentials essential to leading, consulting, and teaching. Students must choose a concentration in accounting, customized professional concentration, information systems, international business, management, or marketing.

Research Facilities

Argosy University libraries provide curriculum support and educational resources, including current text materials, diagnostic training documents, reference materials and databases, journals and dissertations, and major and current titles in program areas. They provide an online public-access catalog of library resources throughout the Argosy University system. Students enjoy full remote access to their campus library database, enabling them to study and conduct research at home. Academic databases offer dissertation abstracts, academic journals, and professional periodicals. All library computers are Internet accessible. Software applications include Word, Excel, PowerPoint, SPSS, and various test-scoring programs.

Financial Aid

A wide range of financial aid options is available to students who qualify. Argosy University's San Francisco Bay Area Campus offers access to federal and state aid programs, merit-based awards, grants, loans, and a work-study program. As a first step, students should complete the Free Application for Federal Student Aid (FAFSA). Prospective students can apply electronically at http://www.fafsa.ed.gov or at the campus. To receive consideration for the maximum amount of aid and ensure timely receipt of funds, it is best to submit an application promptly.

Cost of Study

Tuition varies by program. Students should contact Argosy University's San Francisco Bay Area Campus for tuition information.

Living and Housing Costs

Students typically live in apartments in the metropolitan San Francisco area. Living expenses vary according to each student's preferred standard of living, housing, and transportation. The University does not offer or operate student housing. Most of the students are full-time working professionals who live within driving distance of the campus. Several nearby hotels offer special rates for those who commute from long distances. The Admissions Department also maintains a list of housing options, including contact information for university students who wish to share housing. For more information, students should contact the Admissions Department.

Student Group

Admission to Argosy University's San Francisco Bay Area Campus is selective to ensure a highly qualified student body. The University encourages diversity in academic and employment backgrounds and promotes integration of the student body into professional life through established connections with local and national professional associations. Argosy University offers a professionally oriented education with rich opportunities to gain practical experience in class, field placements, and internships. Full-time students and working professionals gain the extensive knowledge and range of skills necessary for effective performance in their chosen fields.

Student Outcomes

Students can register with the University's online career-services system and use select services from a distance, such as degree-specific career e-mail lists, national job posts, and virtual job fairs. Students should contact the University for more information.

Location

Located in northern California, Argosy University's San Francisco Bay Area Campus attracts students from the immediate area as well as from around the country and the world. In July 2007, the San Francisco Bay Area Campus moved to its new location at 1005 Atlantic Avenue in Alameda. The energy in San Francisco is contagious. Numerous surveys rank San Francisco as the most wired city in the world, thanks to its high concentration of computer-savvy citizens and businesses.

Many businesses in the area provide excellent, varied opportunities for student training. The Bay Area and nearby Silicon Valley are home to leading new media companies such as Pixar, ILM, and Sega. A who's who of technology companies call the Bay Area home, including Apple, Cisco, Hewlett-Packard, Intel, Oracle, and Sun Microsystems. San Francisco also is the home of traditional companies such as BankAmerica, Chevron, Levi-Strauss, Safeway, and Wells Fargo.

The University

Argosy University is a private institution with eighteen locations across the nation. Argosy University's San Francisco Bay Area Campus provides students with a career resources office, an academic resources center, and extensive information access for research. It offers the resources of a large university plus the friendliness and personal attention of a small campus.

The innovative programs feature dynamic, relevant, and practical curricula delivered in flexible class formats. Students enjoy scheduling options that make it easier to fit school into their busy lives, choosing from day and evening courses, on campus or online. Many students find a combination of class formats to be an ideal way of continuing their education while meeting family and professional demands.

Argosy University is accredited by the Higher Learning Commission and is a member of the North Central Association (NCA, 30 North LaSalle Street, Suite 2400, Chicago, Illinois 60602; 800-621-7440 (toll-free); http://www.ncahlc.org).

Applying

Argosy University, San Francisco Bay Area Campus, accepts students year-round on a rolling admissions basis, depending on availability of required courses. Applications for admission are available online or by contacting the campus.

Correspondence and Information

Argosy University, San Francisco Bay Area Campus
1005 Atlantic Avenue
Alameda, California 94501
Phone: 510-215-0277
          866-215-2777 (toll-free)
Fax: 510-215-0299
E-mail: auadmissions@argosy.edu
Web site: http://www.argosy.edu/sanfrancisco

Argosy University, San Francisco Bay Area Campus

THE FACULTY

The Argosy University faculty comprises working professionals who are eager to help students succeed. Members bring real-world experience and the latest practice innovations to the academic setting. The diverse faculty members of the College of Business are widely recognized for contributions to the field. Many are published scholars, and most hold doctoral degrees. They provide a substantive education that combines comprehensive knowledge with critical skills and practical workplace relevance. Above all, faculty members are committed to their students' personal and professional development.

ARGOSY UNIVERSITY.

ARGOSY UNIVERSITY, SANTA MONICA CAMPUS

College of Business

Programs of Study

Argosy University, Santa Monica Campus, offers the Master of Business Administration (M.B.A.), the Master of Science (M.S.) in management, and the Doctor of Business Administration (D.B.A.) degrees. The business programs are designed to serve the needs of talented students, regardless of their undergraduate degrees. The College of Business welcomes and encourages students from diverse academic backgrounds.

The Master of Business Administration program offers a solutions-based, action-oriented approach to organizational change and human dynamics. It is designed to develop a new breed of leader—one who can identify challenges and opportunities, draw on the latest technology and information, use advanced analytical and planning approaches, and execute plans for positive change. Core courses include a broad array of foundation subjects, all relevant to meeting challenges and problems encountered in modern organizations. Students are required to choose from a variety of concentrations: customized professional concentration, finance, health-care administration, information systems management, international business, management, or marketing. This program can enhance future career potential and prepare students for postgraduate work in business.

The Master of Science in Management program was designed to develop leadership and operational skills in those who wish to hold managerial or supervisory positions in public, private, and not-for-profit industries. Students learn the multifaceted process of business administration. The program enables students to diagnose multiple organizational circumstances, determine and evaluate options, and then implement and evaluate a plan of action.

The Doctor of Business Administration program provides industry and academic professionals the opportunity to build upon core skills and knowledge gained through the master's program. Students develop advanced comprehension of theoretical and applied literature in a chosen discipline and a higher level of competence in conducting action research. The program is designed to develop critical knowledge and skills for success in service to the profession and the community and in attaining credentials essential to leading, consulting, and teaching. Students must choose a concentration in accounting, customized professional concentration, information systems, international business, management, or marketing.

Research Facilities

Argosy University libraries provide curriculum support and educational resources, including current text materials, diagnostic training documents, reference materials and databases, journals and dissertations, and major and current titles in program areas. They provide an online public-access catalog of library resources throughout the Argosy University system. Students enjoy full remote access to their campus library database, enabling them to study and conduct research at home. Academic databases offer dissertation abstracts, academic journals, and professional periodicals. All library computers are Internet accessible. Software applications include Word, Excel, PowerPoint, SPSS, and various test-scoring programs.

Financial Aid

A wide range of financial aid options is available to students who qualify. Argosy University's Santa Monica Campus offers access to federal and state aid programs, merit-based awards, grants, loans, and a work-study program. As a first step, students should complete the Free Application for Federal Student Aid (FAFSA). Prospective students can apply electronically at http://www.fafsa.ed.gov or at the campus. To receive consideration for the maximum amount of aid and ensure timely receipt of funds, it is best to submit an application promptly.

Cost of Study

Tuition varies by program. Students should contact Argosy University's Santa Monica Campus for tuition information.

Living and Housing Costs

Students typically live in apartments in the metropolitan Santa Monica area. Living expenses vary according to each student's preferred standard of living, housing, and transportation. The University does not offer or operate student housing. Most of the students are full-time working professionals who live within driving distance of the campus. Several nearby hotels offer special rates for those who commute from long distances. The Admissions Department also maintains a list of housing options, including contact information for university students who wish to share housing. For more information, students should contact the Admissions Department.

Student Group

Admission to Argosy University's Santa Monica Campus is selective to ensure a highly qualified student body. The University encourages diversity in academic and employment backgrounds and promotes integration of the student body into professional life through established connections with local and national professional associations. Argosy University offers a professionally oriented education with rich opportunities to gain practical experience in class, field placements, and internships. Full-time students and working professionals gain the extensive knowledge and range of skills necessary for effective performance in their chosen fields.

Student Outcomes

Students can register with the University's online career-services system and use select services from a distance, such as degree-specific career e-mail lists, national job posts, and virtual job fairs. Students should contact the University for more information.

Location

Argosy University's Santa Monica Campus is located in the beach community of Santa Monica, California. Coupled with the charm of the famous Santa Monica Pier, beautiful beaches, and Farmer's Markets is an undeniable sophisticated urban environment. On campus, the main facility covers approximately 107,000 square feet and houses classrooms, laboratories, offices, a student lounge, and a library. Many businesses in the area provide excellent, varied opportunities for student training. The thriving business environment in Santa Monica includes a broad array of companies, including a proliferation of entertainment, high tech, and software firms. Principal employers in the area include Yahoo, MTV Networks, RAND Corporation, and Symantec Corporation.

The University

Argosy University is a private institution with eighteen locations across the nation. Argosy University's Santa Monica Campus provides students with a career resources office, an academic resources center, and extensive information access for research. It offers the resources of a large university plus the friendliness and personal attention of a small campus.

The innovative programs feature dynamic, relevant, and practical curricula delivered in flexible class formats. Students enjoy scheduling options that make it easier to fit school into their busy lives, choosing from day and evening courses, on campus or online. Many students find a combination of class formats to be an ideal way of continuing their education while meeting family and professional demands.

Argosy University is accredited by the Higher Learning Commission and is a member of the North Central Association (NCA, 30 North LaSalle Street, Suite 2400, Chicago, Illinois 60602; 800-621-7440 (toll-free); http://www.ncahlc.org).

Applying

Argosy University, Santa Monica Campus, accepts students year-round on a rolling admissions basis, depending on availability of required courses. Applications for admission are available online or by contacting the campus.

Correspondence and Information

Argosy University, Santa Monica Campus
2950 31st Street
Santa Monica, California 90405
Phone: 310-866-4000
866-505-0332 (toll-free)
Fax: 310-399-1804
E-mail: auadmissions@argosy.edu
Web site: http://www.argosy.edu/santamonica

Argosy University, Santa Monica Campus

THE FACULTY

The Argosy University faculty comprises working professionals who are eager to help students succeed. Members bring real-world experience and the latest practice innovations to the academic setting. The diverse faculty members of the College of Business are widely recognized for contributions to the field. Many are published scholars, and most hold doctoral degrees. They provide a substantive education that combines comprehensive knowledge with critical skills and practical workplace relevance. Above all, faculty members are committed to their students' personal and professional development.

ARGOSY UNIVERSITY, SARASOTA CAMPUS

ARGOSY UNIVERSITY.

College of Business

Programs of Study

Argosy University, Sarasota Campus, offers the Master of Business Administration (M.B.A.), the Master of Science (M.S.) in management, and the Doctor of Business Administration (D.B.A.) degrees. The business programs are designed to serve the needs of talented students, regardless of their undergraduate degrees. The College of Business welcomes and encourages students from diverse academic backgrounds.

The Master of Business Administration Program offers a solutions-based, action-oriented approach to organizational change and human dynamics. It is designed to develop a new breed of leader—one who can identify challenges and opportunities, draw on the latest technology and information, use advanced analytical and planning approaches, and execute plans for positive change. Core courses include a broad array of foundation subjects, all relevant to meeting challenges and problems encountered in modern organizations. Students are required to choose from a variety of concentrations: customized professional concentration, finance, health-care administration, information systems management, international business, management, or marketing. This program can enhance future career potential and prepare students for postgraduate work in business.

The Master of Science in Management Program was designed to develop leadership and operational skills in those who wish to hold managerial or supervisory positions in public, private, and not-for-profit industries. Students learn the multifaceted process of business administration. The program enables students to diagnose multiple organizational circumstances, determine and evaluate options, and then implement and evaluate a plan of action.

The Doctor of Business Administration Program provides industry and academic professionals the opportunity to build upon core skills and knowledge gained through the master's program. Students develop advanced comprehension of theoretical and applied literature in a chosen discipline and a higher level of competence in conducting action research. The program is designed to develop critical knowledge and skills for success in service to the profession and the community and in attaining credentials essential to leading, consulting, and teaching. Students must choose a concentration in accounting, customized professional concentration, information systems, international business, management, or marketing.

Research Facilities

Argosy University libraries provide curriculum support and educational resources, including current text materials, diagnostic training documents, reference materials and databases, journals and dissertations, and major and current titles in program areas. They provide an online public-access catalog of library resources throughout the Argosy University system. Students enjoy full remote access to their campus library database, enabling them to study and conduct research at home. Academic databases offer dissertation abstracts, academic journals, and professional periodicals. All library computers are Internet accessible. Software applications include Word, Excel, PowerPoint, SPSS, and various test-scoring programs.

Financial Aid

A wide range of financial aid options is available to students who qualify. Argosy University's Sarasota Campus offers access to federal and state aid programs, merit-based awards, grants, loans, and a work-study program. As a first step, students should complete the Free Application for Federal Student Aid (FAFSA). Prospective students can apply electronically at http://www.fafsa.ed.gov or at the campus. To receive consideration for the maximum amount of aid and ensure timely receipt of funds, students should submit an application promptly.

Cost of Study

Tuition varies by program. Students should contact Argosy University's Sarasota Campus for tuition information.

Living and Housing Costs

Students typically live in apartments in the metropolitan Sarasota area. Living expenses vary according to each student's preferred standard of living, housing, and transportation. The University does not offer or operate student housing. Most of the students are full-time working professionals who live within driving distance of the campus. Several nearby hotels offer special rates for those who commute from long distances. The Admissions Department also maintains a list of housing options, including contact information for University students who wish to share housing. For more information, students should contact the Admissions Department.

Student Group

Admission to Argosy University's Sarasota Campus is selective to ensure a highly qualified student body. It encourages diversity in academic and employment backgrounds and promotes integration of the student body into professional life through established connections with local and national professional associations. Argosy University offers a professionally oriented education with rich opportunities to gain practical experience in class, field placements, and internships. Full-time students and working professionals gain the extensive knowledge and range of skills necessary for effective performance in their chosen fields.

Student Outcomes

Students can register with the University's online career-services system and use select services from a distance, such as degree-specific career e-mail lists, national job posts, and virtual job fairs. Students should contact the University for more information.

Location

Located in northeast Sarasota, the campus is specifically designed for postsecondary and graduate-level instruction through a unique combination of in-residence course work, tutorials, and online study courses. Several of the programs are off-site tutorials and intensive one-week classroom sessions. Students may also complete up to 49 percent of the work of some degree programs via online courses that allow interaction with faculty members and classmates from any Internet connection.

Sarasota is recognized as Florida's cultural center and is home to a professional symphony, ballet, and opera as well as dozens of theaters and art galleries. Well-known vacation attractions such as Disney World, Busch Gardens-Tampa, and the city of Miami are within a few hours' drive. The area enjoys mild winters and endless summer beauty.

The growing business sector in the Gulf Coast community helps make it one of the top 20 places to live and work. ASO Corporation, Nelson Publishing, and Select Technology Group are among the numerous companies headquartered in Sarasota County. The area's top employers include Sarasota Memorial Hospital and Publix Supermarkets. Many businesses in the area provide excellent, varied opportunities for student training.

The University

Argosy University is a private institution with eighteen locations across the nation. Argosy University's Sarasota Campus provides students with a career resources office, an academic resources center, and extensive information access for research. It offers the resources of a large university plus the friendliness and personal attention of a small campus. The innovative programs feature dynamic, relevant, and practical curricula delivered in flexible class formats.

Students enjoy scheduling options that make it easier to fit school into their busy lives, choosing from day and evening courses, on campus or online. Many students find a combination of class formats to be an ideal way of continuing their education while meeting family and professional demands.

Argosy University is accredited by the Higher Learning Commission and is a member of the North Central Association (NCA, 30 North LaSalle Street, Suite 2400, Chicago, Illinois 60602; 800-621-7440 (toll-free); http://www.ncahlc.org).

Applying

Argosy University, Sarasota Campus, accepts students year-round on a rolling admissions basis, depending on availability of required courses. Applications for admission are available online or by contacting the campus.

Correspondence and Information

Argosy University, Sarasota Campus
5250 17th Street
Sarasota, Florida 34235
Phone: 941-379-0404
　　　 800-331-5995 (toll-free)
Fax: 941-371-8910
E-mail: auadmissions@argosy.edu
Web site: http://www.argosy.edu/sarasota

Argosy University, Sarasota Campus

THE FACULTY

The Argosy University faculty comprises working professionals who are eager to help students succeed. Members bring real-world experience and the latest practice innovations to the academic setting. The diverse faculty members of the College of Business are widely recognized for contributions to the field. Many are published scholars, and most hold doctoral degrees. They provide a substantive education that combines comprehensive knowledge with critical skills and practical workplace relevance. Above all, faculty members are committed to their students' personal and professional development.

ARGOSY UNIVERSITY

ARGOSY UNIVERSITY, SCHAUMBURG CAMPUS

College of Business

Programs of Study
Argosy University, Schaumburg Campus, offers the Master of Business Administration (M.B.A.) and the Doctor of Business Administration (D.B.A.) degrees. The business programs are designed to serve the needs of talented students, regardless of their undergraduate degrees. The College of Business welcomes and encourages students from diverse academic backgrounds.

The Master of Business Administration program offers a solutions-based, action-oriented approach to organizational change and human dynamics. It is designed to develop a new breed of leader—one who can identify challenges and opportunities, draw on the latest technology and information, use advanced analytical and planning approaches, and execute plans for positive change. Core courses include a broad array of foundation subjects, all relevant to meeting challenges and problems encountered in modern organizations. Students are required to choose from a variety of concentrations: corporate compliance, customized professional concentration, finance, health-care administration, information systems management, international business, management, or marketing. This program can enhance future career potential and prepare students for postgraduate work in business.

The Doctor of Business Administration program provides industry and academic professionals the opportunity to build upon core skills and knowledge gained through the master's program. Students develop advanced comprehension of theoretical and applied literature in a chosen discipline and a higher level of competence in conducting action research. The program is designed to develop critical knowledge and skills for success in service to the profession and the community and in attaining credentials essential to leading, consulting, and teaching. Students must choose a concentration in accounting, customized professional concentration, information systems, international business, management, or marketing.

Research Facilities
Argosy University libraries provide curriculum support and educational resources, including current text materials, diagnostic training documents, reference materials and databases, journals and dissertations, and major and current titles in program areas. They provide an online public-access catalog of library resources throughout the Argosy University system. Students enjoy full remote access to their campus library database, enabling them to study and conduct research at home. Academic databases offer dissertation abstracts, academic journals, and professional periodicals. All library computers are Internet accessible. Software applications include Word, Excel, PowerPoint, SPSS, and various test-scoring programs.

Financial Aid
A wide range of financial aid options is available to students who qualify. Argosy University's Schaumburg Campus offers access to federal and state aid programs, merit-based awards, grants, loans, and a work-study program. As a first step, students should complete the Free Application for Federal Student Aid (FAFSA). Prospective students can apply electronically at http://www.fafsa.ed.gov or at the campus. To receive consideration for the maximum amount of aid and ensure timely receipt of funds, it is best to submit an application promptly.

Cost of Study
Tuition varies by program. Students should contact Argosy University's Schaumburg Campus for tuition information.

Living and Housing Costs
Students typically live in apartments in the metropolitan Schaumburg area. Living expenses vary according to each student's preferred standard of living, housing, and transportation. The University does not offer or operate student housing. Most of the students are full-time working professionals who live within driving distance of the campus. Several nearby hotels offer special rates for those who commute from long distances. The Admissions Department also maintains a list of housing options, including contact information for university students who wish to share housing. For more information, students should contact the Admissions Department.

Student Group
Admission to Argosy University's Schaumburg Campus is selective to ensure a highly qualified student body. The University encourages diversity in academic and employment backgrounds and promotes integration of the student body into professional life through established connections with local and national professional associations. Argosy University offers a professionally oriented education with rich opportunities to gain practical experience in class, field placements, and internships. Full-time students and working professionals gain the extensive knowledge and range of skills necessary for effective performance in their chosen fields.

Student Outcomes
Students can register with the University's online career-services system and use select services from a distance, such as degree-specific career e-mail lists, national job posts, and virtual job fairs. Students should contact the University for more information.

Location
Argosy University's Schaumburg Campus is located in the northwest suburban area, approximately 45 minutes from downtown Chicago. The campus's small size allows it to offer a highly personal atmosphere and flexible programs tailored to students' needs. Visitors to Chicago experience a range of attractions to stimulate both intellectual and recreational pursuits. Located on the shores of Lake Michigan in the Midwest, Chicago is home to world-champion sports teams, an internationally acclaimed symphony orchestra, renowned architecture, and nearly three million residents. Among the variety of history and art museums in the city, the Chicago Cultural Center offers more than 600 art programs and exhibits each year. Recreational opportunities include hiking and cycling on miles of lakefront trails, golfing, and shopping.

Many businesses in the area provide excellent, varied opportunities for student training. Schaumburg's thriving business environment includes 5,000 businesses that employ 80,000 people. The area's largest employers are Motorola, Experian, Cingular, and IBM.

The University
Argosy University is a private institution with eighteen locations across the nation. Argosy University's Schaumburg Campus provides students with a career resources office, an academic resources center, and extensive information access for research. It offers the resources of a large university plus the friendliness and personal attention of a small campus. Argosy University's Schaumburg Campus is an approved degree site that is closely associated with the University's Chicago Campus.

The innovative programs feature dynamic, relevant, and practical curricula delivered in flexible class formats. Students enjoy scheduling options that make it easier to fit school into their busy lives, choosing from day and evening courses, on campus or online. Many students find a combination of class formats to be an ideal way of continuing their education while meeting family and professional demands.

Argosy University is accredited by the Higher Learning Commission and is a member of the North Central Association (NCA, 30 North LaSalle Street, Suite 2400, Chicago, Illinois 60602; 800-621-7440 (toll-free); http://www.ncahlc.org).

Applying
Argosy University, Schaumburg Campus, accepts students year-round on a rolling admissions basis, depending on availability of required courses. Applications for admission are available online or by contacting the campus.

Correspondence and Information
Argosy University, Schaumburg Campus
An approved degree site
999 N. Plaza Drive, Suite 111
Schaumburg, Illinois 60173-5403
Phone: 847-969-4900
866-290-2777 (toll-free)
Fax: 847-969-4998
E-mail: auadmissions@argosy.edu
Web site: http://www.argosy.edu/schaumburg

Argosy University, Schaumburg Campus

THE FACULTY

The Argosy University faculty comprises working professionals who are eager to help students succeed. Members bring real-world experience and the latest practice innovations to the academic setting. The diverse faculty members of the College of Business are widely recognized for contributions to their fields. Many are published scholars, and most hold doctoral degrees. They provide a substantive education that combines comprehensive knowledge with critical skills and practical workplace relevance. Above all, faculty members are committed to their students' personal and professional development.

ARGOSY UNIVERSITY.

ARGOSY UNIVERSITY, SEATTLE CAMPUS

College of Business

Programs of Study

Argosy University, Seattle Campus offers the Master of Business Administration (M.B.A.), the Master of Science (M.S.) in management, and the Doctor of Business Administration (D.B.A.) degrees. The business programs are designed to serve the needs of talented students, regardless of their undergraduate degrees. The College of Business welcomes and encourages students from diverse academic backgrounds.

The Master of Business Administration program offers a solutions-based, action-oriented approach to organizational change and human dynamics. It is designed to develop a new breed of leader—one who can identify challenges and opportunities, draw on the latest technology and information, use advanced analytical and planning approaches, and execute plans for positive change. Core courses include a broad array of foundation subjects, all relevant to meeting challenges and problems encountered in modern organizations. Students are required to choose from a variety of concentrations: customized professional concentration, finance, healthcare administration, information systems management, international business, management, or marketing. This program can enhance future career potential and prepare students for postgraduate work in business.

The Master of Science in management program was designed to develop leadership and operational skills in those who wish to hold managerial or supervisory positions in public, private, and not-for-profit industries. Students learn the multifaceted process of business administration. The program enables students to diagnose multiple organizational circumstances, determine and evaluate options, and then implement and evaluate a plan of action.

The Doctor of Business Administration program provides industry and academic professionals the opportunity to build upon core skills and knowledge gained through the master's program. Students develop advanced comprehension of theoretical and applied literature in a chosen discipline and a higher level of competence in conducting action research. The program is designed to develop critical knowledge and skills for success in service to the profession and the community and in attaining credentials essential to leading, consulting, and teaching. Students must choose a concentration in accounting, customized professional concentration, information systems, international business, management, or marketing.

Research Facilities

Argosy University libraries provide curriculum support and educational resources, including current text materials, diagnostic training documents, reference materials and databases, journals and dissertations, and major and current titles in program areas. They provide an online public-access catalog of library resources throughout the Argosy University system. Students enjoy full remote access to their campus library database, enabling them to study and conduct research at home. Academic databases offer dissertation abstracts, academic journals, and professional periodicals. All library computers are Internet accessible. Software applications include Word, Excel, PowerPoint, SPSS, and various test-scoring programs.

Financial Aid

A wide range of financial aid options is available to students who qualify. Argosy University's Seattle Campus offers access to federal and state aid programs, merit-based awards, grants, loans, and a work-study program. As a first step, students should complete the Free Application for Federal Student Aid (FAFSA). Prospective students can apply electronically at http://www.fafsa.ed.gov or at the campus. To receive consideration for the maximum amount of aid and ensure timely receipt of funds, it is best to submit an application promptly.

Cost of Study

Tuition varies by program. Students should contact Argosy University's Seattle Campus for tuition information.

Living and Housing Costs

Students typically live in apartments in the metropolitan Seattle area. Living expenses vary according to each student's preferred standard of living, housing, and transportation. The University does not offer or operate student housing. Most of the students are full-time working professionals who live within driving distance of the campus. Several nearby hotels offer special rates for those who commute from long distances. The Admissions Department also maintains a list of housing options, including contact information for university students who wish to share housing. For more information, students should contact the Admissions Department.

Student Group

Admission to Argosy University's Seattle Campus is selective to ensure a highly qualified student body. It encourages diversity in academic and employment backgrounds and promotes integration of the student body into professional life through established connections with local and national professional associations. Argosy University offers a professionally oriented education with rich opportunities to gain practical experience in class, field placements, and internships. Full-time students and working professionals gain the extensive knowledge and range of skills necessary for effective performance in their chosen fields.

Student Outcomes

Students can register with the University's online career-services system and use select services from a distance, such as degree-specific career e-mail lists, national job posts, and virtual job fairs. Students should contact the University for more information.

Location

The faculty and staff members at Argosy University's Seattle Campus aspire to provide a supportive, collaborative, engaging, yet challenging learning environment. Easily reached through the King County Public Transportation System, the campus offers convenient access to local libraries, shops, and restaurants. Seattle offers numerous historical and multicultural museums, a symphony, ballet, and many theater companies. Seattle is home to several major league sports teams, and offers a myriad of outdoor recreational opportunities, such as camping, hiking, fishing, skiing, and rock-climbing.

Many businesses in the area provide excellent, varied opportunities for student training. Seattle's thriving business environment encompasses a wide range of industries and features such giants as Microsoft, Boeing, and Alaska Air Group. The Port of Seattle and University of Washington are also among the area's largest employers.

The University

Argosy University is a private institution with eighteen locations across the nation. Argosy University's Seattle Campus provides students with a career resources office, an academic resources center, and extensive information access for research. It offers the resources of a large university plus the friendliness and personal attention of a small campus.

The innovative programs feature dynamic, relevant, and practical curricula delivered in flexible class formats. Students enjoy scheduling options that make it easier to fit school into their busy lives, choosing from day and evening courses, on campus or online. Many students find a combination of class formats to be an ideal way of continuing their education while meeting family and professional demands.

Argosy University is accredited by the Higher Learning Commission and is a member of the North Central Association (NCA, 30 North LaSalle Street, Suite 2400, Chicago, Illinois 60602; 800-621-7440 (toll-free); http://www.ncahlc.org).

Applying

Argosy University, Seattle Campus accepts students year-round on a rolling admissions basis, depending on availability of required courses. Applications for admission are available online or by contacting the campus.

Correspondence and Information

Argosy University, Seattle Campus
2601-A Elliott Avenue
Seattle, Washington 98121
Phone: 206-283-4500
      866-283-2777 (toll-free)
Fax: 206-283-5777
E-mail: auadmissions@argosy.edu
Web site: http://www.argosy.edu/seattle

Argosy University, Seattle Campus

THE FACULTY

The Argosy University faculty comprises working professionals who are eager to help students succeed. Members bring real-world experience and the latest practice innovations to the academic setting. The diverse faculty members of the College of Business are widely recognized for contributions to their field. Many are published scholars, and most hold doctoral degrees. They provide a substantive education that combines comprehensive knowledge with critical skills and practical workplace relevance. Above all, faculty members are committed to their students' personal and professional development.

ARGOSY UNIVERSITY

ARGOSY UNIVERSITY, TAMPA CAMPUS

College of Business

Programs of Study

Argosy University, Tampa Campus, offers the Master of Business Administration (M.B.A.), the Master of Science (M.S.) in management, and the Doctor of Business Administration (D.B.A.) degrees. The business programs are designed to serve the needs of talented students, regardless of their undergraduate degrees. The College of Business welcomes and encourages students from diverse academic backgrounds.

The Master of Business Administration program offers a solutions-based, action-oriented approach to organizational change and human dynamics. It is designed to develop a new breed of leader—one who can identify challenges and opportunities, draw on the latest technology and information, use advanced analytical and planning approaches, and execute plans for positive change. Core courses include a broad array of foundation subjects, all relevant to meeting challenges and problems encountered in modern organizations. Students are required to choose from a variety of concentrations: customized professional concentration, finance, health-care administration, information systems management, international business, management, or marketing. This program can enhance future career potential and prepare students for postgraduate work in business.

The Master of Science in Management program was designed to develop leadership and operational skills in those who wish to hold managerial or supervisory positions in public, private, and not-for-profit industries. Students learn the multifaceted process of business administration. The program enables students to diagnose multiple organizational circumstances, determine and evaluate options, and then implement and evaluate a plan of action.

The Doctor of Business Administration program provides industry and academic professionals the opportunity to build upon core skills and knowledge gained through the master's program. Students develop advanced comprehension of theoretical and applied literature in a chosen discipline and a higher level of competence in conducting action research. The program is designed to develop critical knowledge and skills for success in service to the profession and the community and in attaining credentials essential to leading, consulting, and teaching. Students must choose a concentration in accounting, customized professional concentration, information systems, international business, management, or marketing.

Research Facilities

Argosy University libraries provide curriculum support and educational resources, including current text materials, diagnostic training documents, reference materials and databases, journals and dissertations, and major and current titles in program areas. They provide an online public-access catalog of library resources throughout the Argosy University system. Students enjoy full remote access to their campus library database, enabling them to study and conduct research at home. Academic databases offer dissertation abstracts, academic journals, and professional periodicals. All library computers are Internet accessible. Software applications include Word, Excel, PowerPoint, SPSS, and various test-scoring programs.

Financial Aid

A wide range of financial aid options is available to students who qualify. Argosy University's Tampa Campus offers access to federal and state aid programs, merit-based awards, grants, loans, and a work-study program. As a first step, students should complete the Free Application for Federal Student Aid (FAFSA). Prospective students can apply electronically at http://www.fafsa.ed.gov or on the campus. To receive consideration for the maximum amount of aid and ensure timely receipt of funds, students should submit an application promptly.

Cost of Study

Tuition varies by program. Students should contact Argosy University's Tampa Campus for tuition information.

Living and Housing Costs

Students typically live in apartments in the metropolitan Tampa area. Living expenses vary according to each student's preferred standard of living, housing, and transportation. The University does not offer or operate student housing. Most of the students are full-time working professionals who live within driving distance of the campus. Several nearby hotels offer special rates for those who commute from long distances. The Admissions Department also maintains a list of housing options, including contact information for University students who wish to share housing. For more information, students should contact the Admissions Department.

Student Group

Admission to Argosy University's Tampa Campus is selective to ensure a highly qualified student body. It encourages diversity in academic and employment backgrounds and promotes integration of the student body into professional life through established connections with local and national professional associations. Argosy University offers a professionally oriented education with rich opportunities to gain practical experience in class, field placements, and internships. Full-time students and working professionals gain the extensive knowledge and range of skills necessary for effective performance in their chosen fields.

Student Outcomes

Students can register with the University's online career-services system and use select services from a distance, such as degree-specific career e-mail lists, national job posts, and virtual job fairs. Students should contact the University for more information.

Location

Located in sunny Florida, Argosy University's Tampa Campus attracts a diverse student population from throughout the United States, the Caribbean, Europe, Africa, and Asia. Tampa's central location affords students the opportunity to work for major corporations and hear speakers of international acclaim. The school offers rigorous programs of study in a supportive, collaborative environment. The campus sits within an hour's drive of some of the most popular tourist destinations in the world, including the Disney theme parks, Busch Gardens, and the Florida Gulf Coast beaches. Major-league sporting events, concerts, theaters, world-renowned restaurants, recreational facilities, and a cosmopolitan social scene are all within easy reach. The University's location provides easy access to I-4 and I-75. Tampa combines the opportunities of a large city with the friendliness of a small town with a strong sense of community.

The Tampa-St. Petersburg-Clearwater metropolitan area offers a diversified economic base fueled by a broad array of companies, including Verizon Communications and JP Morgan Chase. In addition, Tampa serves as headquarters for three Fortune 100 companies—OSI Restaurant Partners; TECO, an energy provider; and Raymond Jones Financial. Many businesses in the area provide excellent, varied opportunities for student training.

The University

Argosy University is a private institution with eighteen locations across the nation. Argosy University's Tampa Campus provides students with a career resources office, an academic resources center, and extensive information access for research. It offers the resources of a large university plus the friendliness and personal attention of a small campus.

The innovative programs feature dynamic, relevant, and practical curricula delivered in flexible class formats. Students enjoy scheduling options that make it easier to fit school into their busy lives, choosing from day and evening courses, on campus or online. Many students find a combination to be an ideal way of continuing their education while meeting family and professional demands.

Argosy University is accredited by the Higher Learning Commission and is a member of the North Central Association (NCA, 30 North LaSalle Street, Suite 2400, Chicago, Illinois 60602; 800-621-7440 (toll-free); http://www.ncahlc.org).

Applying

Argosy University, Tampa Campus, accepts students on a rolling admissions basis year-round, depending on availability of required courses. Applications for admission are available online or by contacting the campus.

Correspondence and Information

Argosy University, Tampa Campus
Parkside at Tampa Bay Park
4401 North Himes Avenue, Suite 150
Tampa, Florida 33614
Phone: 813-393-5290
           800-850-6488 (toll-free)
Fax: 813-874-1989
E-mail: auadmissions@argosy.edu
Web site: http://www.argosy.edu/tampa

Argosy University, Tampa Campus

THE FACULTY

The Argosy University faculty comprises working professionals who are eager to help students succeed. Members bring real-world experience and the latest practice innovations to the academic setting. The diverse faculty members of the College of Business are widely recognized for contributions to the field. Many are published scholars, and most hold doctoral degrees. They provide a substantive education that combines comprehensive knowledge with critical skills and practical workplace relevance. Above all, faculty members are committed to their students' personal and professional development.

ARGOSY UNIVERSITY.

ARGOSY UNIVERSITY, TWIN CITIES CAMPUS

College of Business

Programs of Study

Argosy University, Twin Cities Campus, offers the Master of Business Administration (M.B.A.), the Master of Science (M.S.) in management, and the Doctor of Business Administration (D.B.A.) degrees. The business programs are designed to serve the needs of talented students, regardless of their undergraduate degrees. The College of Business welcomes and encourages students from diverse academic backgrounds.

The Master of Business Administration program offers a solutions-based, action-oriented approach to organizational change and human dynamics. It is designed to develop a new breed of leader—one who can identify challenges and opportunities, draw on the latest technology and information, use advanced analytical and planning approaches, and execute plans for positive change. Core courses include a broad array of foundation subjects, all relevant to meeting challenges and problems encountered in modern organizations. Students are required to choose from a variety of concentrations: corporate compliance, customized professional concentration, finance, health-care administration, information systems management, international business, management, or marketing. This program can enhance future career potential and prepare students for postgraduate work in business.

The Master of Science in Management program was designed to develop leadership and operational skills in those who wish to hold managerial or supervisory positions in public, private, and not-for-profit industries. Students learn the multifaceted process of business administration. The program enables students to diagnose multiple organizational circumstances, determine and evaluate options, and then implement and evaluate a plan of action.

The Doctor of Business Administration program provides industry and academic professionals the opportunity to build upon core skills and knowledge gained through the master's program. Students develop advanced comprehension of theoretical and applied literature in a chosen discipline and a higher level of competence in conducting action research. The program is designed to develop critical knowledge and skills for success in service to the profession and the community and in attaining credentials essential to leading, consulting, and teaching. Students must choose a concentration in accounting, customized professional concentration, information systems, international business, management, or marketing.

Research Facilities

Argosy University libraries provide curriculum support and educational resources, including current text materials, diagnostic training documents, reference materials and databases, journals and dissertations, and major and current titles in program areas. They provide an online public-access catalog of library resources throughout the Argosy University system. Students enjoy full remote access to their campus library database, enabling them to study and conduct research at home. Academic databases offer dissertation abstracts, academic journals, and professional periodicals. All library computers are Internet accessible. Software applications include Word, Excel, PowerPoint, SPSS, and various test-scoring programs.

Financial Aid

A wide range of financial aid options is available to students who qualify. Argosy University's Twin Cities Campus offers access to federal and state aid programs, merit-based awards, grants, loans, and a work-study program. As a first step, students should complete the Free Application for Federal Student Aid (FAFSA). Prospective students can apply electronically at http://www.fafsa.ed.gov or at the campus. To receive consideration for the maximum amount of aid and ensure timely receipt of funds, it is best to submit an application promptly.

Cost of Study

Tuition varies by program. Students should contact Argosy University's Twin Cities Campus for tuition information.

Living and Housing Costs

Students typically live in apartments in the metropolitan Eagan area. Living expenses vary according to each student's preferred standard of living, housing, and transportation. The University does not offer or operate student housing. Most of the students are full-time working professionals who live within driving distance of the campus. Several nearby hotels offer special rates for those who commute from long distances. The Admissions Department also maintains a list of housing options, including contact information for university students who wish to share housing. For more information, students should contact the Admissions Department.

Student Group

Admission to Argosy University's Twin Cities Campus is selective to ensure a highly qualified student body. The University encourages diversity in academic and employment backgrounds and promotes integration of the student body into professional life through established connections with local and national professional associations. Argosy University offers a professionally oriented education with rich opportunities to gain practical experience in class, field placements, and internships. Full-time students and working professionals gain the extensive knowledge and range of skills necessary for effective performance in their chosen fields.

Student Outcomes

Students can register with the University's online career-services system and use select services from a distance, such as degree-specific career e-mail lists, national job posts, and virtual job fairs. Students should contact the University for more information.

Location

Argosy University's Twin Cities Campus offers rigorous academics in a supportive environment. The campus is nestled in a parklike suburban setting within 10 miles of the airport and the Mall of America. Students enjoy the convenience of nearby shops, restaurants, and housing and easy freeway access. The neighboring Eagan Community Center offers many amenities, including walking paths, a fitness center, meeting rooms, and an outdoor amphitheater. The Twin Cities of Minneapolis and St. Paul have been rated by popular magazines as one of the most livable metropolitan areas in the country. With a population of 2.5 million, the area offers an abundance of recreational activities. Year-round outdoor activities, nationally acclaimed venues for theater art and music, and professional sports teams attract residents and visitors alike.

Many businesses in the area provide excellent, varied opportunities for student training. The Minneapolis-St. Paul metropolitan area offers a diversified economic base fueled by a broad array of companies. Among the numerous publicly traded companies headquartered in the area are Target, UnitedHealth Group, 3M, General Mills, and U.S. Bancorp.

The University

Argosy University is a private institution with eighteen locations across the nation. Argosy University's Twin Cities Campus provides students with a career resources office, an academic resources center, and extensive information access for research. It offers the resources of a large university plus the friendliness and personal attention of a small campus.

The innovative programs feature dynamic, relevant, and practical curricula delivered in flexible class formats. Students enjoy scheduling options that make it easier to fit school into their busy lives, choosing from day and evening courses, on campus or online. Many students find a combination of class formats to be an ideal way of continuing their education while meeting family and professional demands.

Argosy University is accredited by the Higher Learning Commission and is a member of the North Central Association (NCA, 30 North LaSalle Street, Suite 2400, Chicago, Illinois 60602; 800-621-7440 (toll-free); http://www.ncahlc.org).

Applying

Argosy University, Twin Cities Campus, accepts students year-round on a rolling admissions basis, depending on availability of required courses. Applications for admission are available online or by contacting the campus.

Correspondence and Information

Argosy University, Twin Cities Campus
1515 Central Parkway
Eagan, Minnesota 55121
Phone: 651-846-2882
　　　　888-844-2004 (toll-free)
Fax: 651-994-7956
E-mail: auadmissions@argosy.edu
Web site: http://www.argosy.edu/twincities

Argosy University, Twin Cities Campus

THE FACULTY

The Argosy University faculty comprises working professionals who are eager to help students succeed. Members bring real-world experience and the latest practice innovations to the academic setting. The diverse faculty members of the College of Business are widely recognized for contributions to the field. Many are published scholars, and most hold doctoral degrees. They provide a substantive education that combines comprehensive knowledge with critical skills and practical workplace relevance. Above all, faculty members are committed to their students' personal and professional development.

ARGOSY UNIVERSITY, WASHINGTON DC CAMPUS

ARGOSY UNIVERSITY

College of Business

Programs of Study	Argosy University, Washington DC Campus, offers the Master of Business Administration (M.B.A.) and the Doctor of Business Administration (D.B.A.) degrees. The business programs are designed to serve the needs of talented students, regardless of their undergraduate degrees. The College of Business welcomes and encourages students from diverse academic backgrounds.
	The Master of Business Administration program offers a solutions-based, action-oriented approach to organizational change and human dynamics. It is designed to develop a new breed of leader—one who can identify challenges and opportunities, draw on the latest technology and information, use advanced analytical and planning approaches, and execute plans for positive change. Core courses include a broad array of foundation subjects, all relevant to meeting challenges and problems encountered in modern organizations. Students are required to choose from a variety of concentrations: customized professional concentration, finance, health-care administration, information systems management, international business, management, or marketing. This program can enhance future career potential and prepare students for postgraduate work in business.
	The Doctor of Business Administration program provides industry and academic professionals the opportunity to build upon core skills and knowledge gained through the master's program. Students develop advanced comprehension of theoretical and applied literature in a chosen discipline and a higher level of competence in conducting action research. The program is designed to develop critical knowledge and skills for success in service to the profession and the community and in attaining credentials essential to leading, consulting, and teaching. Students must choose a concentration in accounting, customized professional concentration, information systems, international business, management, or marketing.
Research Facilities	Argosy University libraries provide curriculum support and educational resources, including current text materials, diagnostic training documents, reference materials and databases, journals and dissertations, and major and current titles in program areas. They provide an online public-access catalog of library resources throughout the Argosy University system. Students enjoy full remote access to their campus library database, enabling them to study and conduct research at home. Academic databases offer dissertation abstracts, academic journals, and professional periodicals. All library computers are Internet accessible. Software applications include Word, Excel, PowerPoint, SPSS, and various test-scoring programs.
Financial Aid	A wide range of financial aid options is available to students who qualify. Argosy University's Washington DC Campus offers access to federal and state aid programs, merit-based awards, grants, loans, and a work-study program. As a first step, students should complete the Free Application for Federal Student Aid (FAFSA). Prospective students can apply electronically at http://www.fafsa.ed.gov or at the campus. To receive consideration for the maximum amount of aid and ensure timely receipt of funds, it is best to submit an application promptly.
Cost of Study	Tuition varies by program. Students should contact Argosy University's Washington DC Campus for tuition information.
Living and Housing Costs	Students typically live in apartments in the metropolitan Arlington, Virginia, area. Living expenses vary according to each student's preferred standard of living, housing, and transportation. The University does not offer or operate student housing. Most of the students are full-time working professionals who live within driving distance of the campus. Several nearby hotels offer special rates for those who commute from long distances. The Admissions Department also maintains a list of housing options, including contact information for University students who wish to share housing. For more information, students should contact the Admissions Department.
Student Group	Admission to Argosy University's Washington DC Campus is selective to ensure a highly qualified student body. It encourages diversity in academic and employment backgrounds and promotes integration of the student body into professional life through established connections with local and national professional associations. Argosy University offers a professionally oriented education with rich opportunities to gain practical experience in class, field placements, and internships. Full-time students and working professionals gain the extensive knowledge and range of skills necessary for effective performance in their chosen fields.
Student Outcomes	Students can register with the University's online career-services system and use select services from a distance, such as degree-specific career e-mail lists, national job posts, and virtual job fairs. Students should contact the University for more information.
Location	Argosy University's Washington DC Campus is located in suburban Arlington, Virginia. The University is conveniently situated to provide access to most major highways in the area and is easily accessible by public transportation. In proximity to Georgetown, students enjoy access to the many diverse attractions of the D.C. area. Additional campus space is located at The Art Institute of Washington Building (1820 Fort Myer Drive). The University houses administrative offices and seven classrooms at this location. Perhaps best known as the home of the Pentagon and Arlington National Cemetery, Arlington, Virginia, is one of the most highly educated areas in the nation. It is also one of the most diverse.
	Many businesses in the area provide excellent, varied opportunities for student training. Major employers in the region include MCI Telecommunications Corporation; Bell Atlantic Network Services, Inc.; and Gannett/USA Today Company, Inc.
	Argosy University, Washington DC Campus, is certified to operate by the State Council of Higher Education for Virginia (James Monroe Building, 101 North 14th Street, Richmond, Virginia 23219; 804-225-2600).
The University	Argosy University is a private institution with eighteen locations across the nation. Argosy University's Washington DC Campus provides students with a career resources office, an academic resources center, and extensive information access for research. It offers the resources of a large university, plus the friendliness and personal attention of a small campus. The innovative programs feature dynamic, relevant, and practical curricula delivered in flexible class formats. Students enjoy scheduling options that make it easier to fit school into their busy lives, choosing from day and evening courses, on campus or online. Many students find a combination of class formats to be an ideal way of continuing their education while meeting family and professional demands.
	Argosy University is accredited by the Higher Learning Commission and is a member of the North Central Association (NCA, 30 North LaSalle Street, Suite 2400, Chicago, Illinois 60602; 800-621-7440 (toll-free); http://www.ncahlc.org).
Applying	Argosy University, Washington DC Campus, accepts students year-round on a rolling admissions basis, depending on availability of required courses. Applications for admission are available online or by contacting the campus.
Correspondence and Information	Argosy University, Washington DC Campus 1550 Wilson Boulevard, Suite 600 Arlington, Virginia 22209 Phone: 703-526-5800 866-703-2777 (toll-free) Fax: 703-243-8973 E-mail: auadmissions@argosy.edu Web site: http://www.argosy.edu/washingtondc

Argosy University, Washington DC Campus

THE FACULTY

The Argosy University faculty comprises working professionals who are eager to help students succeed. Members bring real-world experience and the latest practice innovations to the academic setting. The diverse faculty members of the College of Business are widely recognized for contributions to the field. Many are published scholars, and most hold doctoral degrees. They provide a substantive education that combines comprehensive knowledge with critical skills and practical workplace relevance. Above all, faculty members are committed to their students' personal and professional development.

BENTLEY
www.bentley.edu

BENTLEY COLLEGE

McCallum Graduate School of Business

Programs of Study

Bentley has been transformed into a premier business school over the past decade, and at the center of that transformation is the McCallum School. The McCallum Graduate School of Business presents the Bentley Portfolio 360, which offers students comprehensive graduate business programs that are flexible to fit student schedules, streamlined to build on their personal backgrounds, and easily customized to meet the demands of their careers. In other words, its a graduate business degree just the way they want it. Bentley's M.B.A. and eight Master of Science (M.S.) programs integrate business, technology, ethics, and global understanding, focused through experiential learning, so students will be fluent in the principles and practices that drive corporate decision-making today.

The M.B.A. prepares students by integrating strategic business processes and information technology applications that are critical to effective management and business operations. Developed with teams from more than a dozen major companies, the two-year, daytime cohort program (Day M.B.A.) option is designed to prepare graduates for leadership in the information-rich, technology-driven global arena. The flexible Evening M.B.A. program option emphasizes choice to meet the needs of working professionals. The program's well-rounded curriculum, field-based learning, and international, ethical, and strategic perspectives offer students the tools to be successful in today's marketplace.

The Bentley Master of Accountancy program (M.S.A.) provides students with the opportunity to build and sharpen professional skills in one of the few graduate programs to earn a separate accreditation in accountancy from AACSB International–The Association to Advance Collegiate Schools of Business. The distinction means that the M.S.A. program fulfills the academic requirement for graduates to become licensed CPAs in Massachusetts and many other states.

The M.S.I.T. program prepares professionals for careers that require the integration of information systems knowledge with a strong understanding of the global business environment. The program imparts current technical knowledge of the IS field as it is being shaped by IT-enabled business processes, Web technologies, distributed architectures, new infrastructure standards, and advances in mobile computing.

The M.S.F. program provides specialized skills in financial analysis and decision making for individuals with a professional interest in finance. The program develops students' analytical and critical-thinking skills through the use of state-of-the-art information assessment and analysis software, and other resources available in Bentley's Financial Trading Room. Students gain an additional competitive advantage in the marketplace through a rigorous curriculum that integrates mathematics, economics, accounting, and associated disciplines with the theories and application of finance.

The M.S.M.A. program meets the changing needs of today's global and information-driven marketing environment. Students gain the critical expertise in qualitative and quantitative analysis that is in high demand among leading companies across a range of industries. With the M.S.M.A. program, marketing classes make extensive use of the Center for Marketing Technology.

The M.S.H.F.I.D. program addresses the advanced degree needs of technical communicators, information designers, and instructional design specialists. It combines an in-depth examination of human factors principles with a solid foundation in managing projects in the fast-paced technology field.

The M.S.F.P. is designed for the financial planner of the next century and provides students with a strong background in the practical areas of financial planning, including estate planning, investment advising, retirement counseling, insurance practice, and tax consulting. The M.S.T. is designed to meet the needs of people with taxation, accounting, or legal experience who want to specialize as tax advisers, consultants, or tax executives. Many practicing tax professionals enroll to enhance their careers.

The M.S.R.E.M. is the only graduate program in New England focused on the management—as opposed to the development—of commercial and residential property. Students acquire a solid understanding of business processes for planning, organizing, and controlling real estate holdings and acquisitions, along with the leadership and interpersonal skills needed to pursue a meaningful real estate career in a global environment.

Research Facilities

The Center for Marketing Technology is a dynamic facility with the latest technologies and software that are changing the global marketplace. Bentley's on-site Financial Trading Room offers access to real-time data from Reuters, Bloomberg, and Bridge and cutting-edge software applications such as MultexNet, DataStream and FirstCall. The Design and Usability Testing Center is one of the most sophisticated usability testing facilities in the country for making software and Web interfaces easier to navigate and use. The library houses more than 200,000 volumes, receives more than 1,700 periodicals, and has 155,000 microform titles. The Accounting Center for Electronic Learning and Business Measurement allows students to gain firsthand experience with the same sophisticated technologies used in the accounting profession today. Study rooms and computer terminals are available for students' use, as are the various databases (e.g., LexisNexis, NAARS, Dow Jones, and InfoTrac) and the up-to-date Media Services Department, which provides television facilities, films, conferencing telephones, videoconferencing, and recordings for both instruction and group-work support.

Financial Aid

Bentley awards scholarships to highly qualified full- and part-time graduate students. Awards are based primarily on academic, professional, and personal merit, with consideration given to the contributions that each individual can make to the diversity of the graduate student population—usually without regard to financial need. Some scholarships may have a work requirement in the form of a graduate or research assistantship. Need-based financial aid programs at Bentley assist students whose resources are insufficient to meet the costs of attendance. These programs consist of grants and loans. All awards are based on financial need as determined by the Free Application for Federal Student Aid (FAFSA) and the Bentley Graduate Aid application. In addition, the Bentley Financial Aid Office assists students in identifying potential alternative loan resources.

Cost of Study

Tuition for the 2007–08 academic year is $2958 per 3-credit course. Payment for tuition is due by the start of classes each semester and may be paid by check, MasterCard, VISA, or Discover. For convenience, Bentley offers two payment plan options. For more information, students should contact the Student Accounts Office at 781-891-2171.

Living and Housing Costs

Bentley offers limited off-campus housing for graduate students. Interested students should visit Bentley's Web site at http://www.bentley.edu for more information.

Student Group

The Graduate School enrolls approximately 1,300 students representing more than fifty countries: 350 full-time, 950 part-time. Students average four to seven years' work experience.

Location

Bentley is ideally located in Waltham, Massachusetts, at the heart of a high-technology region. The 163-acre campus is minutes from Boston's business, financial, and cultural resources and Cambridge's culturally diverse Harvard Square; 30 minutes from Logan International Airport; and a 3-hour drive from New York City.

The College

Founded in 1917 by Harry C. Bentley, a pioneer in American business education, Bentley is an independent, coeducational institution recognized internationally for its excellence in professional business education. In addition to the students at the Graduate School, Bentley also enrolls nearly 4,200 undergraduates in nine business majors. Bentley is accredited nationally by AACSB International–The Association to Advance Collegiate Schools of Business and regionally by the New England Association of Schools and Colleges (NEASC).

Applying

Applications for the Evening M.B.A. program option and the M.S. programs are accepted for the fall and spring semesters. Applications for the Day M.B.A. program option are accepted only for the fall term. All applicants must submit an application form, official transcripts of all academic work beyond high school, scores on the Graduate Management Admission Test (GMAT), two letters of recommendation, and a resume (an interview is also required for the Day M.B.A. program). M.S.A., M.S.F.P., and M.S.T. applicants may submit evidence of successful completion of the CPA or bar examination or receipt of an appropriate master's or doctoral degree in lieu of GMAT scores. International students must submit their scores on the TOEFL and must complete an International Student Data Form (ISDF) upon acceptance. There is a $50 nonrefundable application fee.

Correspondence and Information

Office of Graduate Admissions
McCallum Graduate School of Business
Bentley College
175 Forest Street
Waltham, Massachusetts 02452-4705
Phone: 781-891-2108
          800-442-4723 (toll-free)
Fax: 781-891-2464
Web site: http://www.bentley.edu/graduate

Bentley College

THE FACULTY

Bentley is a practitioner-oriented institution where excellence in research and teaching is valued and rewarded. All classes are taught by faculty members; none are taught by teaching assistants. Faculty members maintain professional working relationships with executives in the business world to stay abreast of current developments. The majority of the faculty members publish articles in leading business publications, make professional presentations, and conduct applied research. Their commitment to scholarly pursuits and professional involvement supports classroom excellence.

As one of the largest nationally accredited graduate business schools in the United States, Bentley's Graduate School courses are taught primarily by full-time faculty members drawn from a pool of more than 200. They are supplemented by working professionals who serve as adjunct professors when appropriate. For a complete listing of the faculty members currently teaching in the Graduate School, students should request a copy of the McCallum Graduate School of Business catalog.

Bentley's dynamic facilities have the latest and most sophisticated software and technology available.

Bentley's on-site Financial Trading Center offers access to real-time data.

BERNARD M. BARUCH COLLEGE
OF THE CITY UNIVERSITY OF NEW YORK
Zicklin School of Business

Programs of Study

The Zicklin School's graduate business programs, including the Master of Business Administration (M.B.A.), the Master of Science (M.S.) in business, and the Executive M.B.A. and M.S. programs, provide exceptional opportunities to prepare for greater career responsibility, advance present skills, acquire new expertise, and gain a better understanding of the effective functioning of a complex and competitive society. Zicklin's premier program is the Full-Time Honors M.B.A., a selective, cohort-based program featuring a collaborative learning environment emphasizing teamwork and leadership. Admission to the program is highly competitive. Applications are accepted for the fall semester only. The traditional M.B.A. and M.S. programs, which are now called the Flex-Time Programs, are available for study at either a full- or part-time pace and allow students to switch back and forth as their work and study needs dictate. With courses offered primarily in the evening, this program is particularly well suited for those who wish to remain employed while they earn their degree. Students in the Flex-Time Programs may begin in the fall or spring semester. The Accelerated Part-Time M.B.A., a special twenty-eight-month program, offers an alternative for those who wish to study part-time while working full-time. In addition, students enjoy the benefits of a cohort-based core curriculum. Applications are accepted for the fall semester only. The Zicklin M.B.A. programs are cohort in style. Students follow a prescribed sequence of introductory courses before selecting a major from one of the following areas: accounting, computer information systems, decision sciences, economics, finance, general business, health-care administration (a joint program with the Mt. Sinai School of Medicine), industrial/organizational psychology, international business, management/entrepreneurship and small-business management, management/operations management, management/organizational behavior/human resource management, marketing, real estate, statistics, and taxation. A J.D./M.B.A. program is offered in conjunction with Brooklyn Law School or New York Law School. Master of Science programs in accounting, business computer information systems, marketing, quantitative methods and modeling, statistics, and taxation are available for students who seek in-depth study in a subject area. Baruch's Executive M.B.A. program is designed for high-achieving individuals who need an alternative to the traditional M.B.A. program. Classes are held on Fridays and Saturdays, allowing students to finish the program in two years. Executive M.S. programs in finance and industrial and labor relations are available. The City University of New York (CUNY) offers a Ph.D.; the program is located at Baruch College and comprises specializations in accounting, finance, information systems, marketing, and organizational behavior.

Research Facilities

The William and Anita Newman Library is one of the most technologically advanced facilities in New York. In addition to books and periodicals, the library maintains local area networks that provide access to information resources in CD-ROM format and to several hundred online databases through the Dow Jones News/Retrieval, LexisNexis, and Dialog services. Baruch College students and faculty and staff members also have access to the 4.5 million volumes in the CUNY library system and to the collections of the world-famous New York Public Library. The Baruch Computing and Technology Center provides more than 500 computer workstations with Web access and multimedia capability. Baruch's Subotnick Financial Services Center is a unique educational facility for students and the financial community that features a fully equipped simulated trading environment with continuous live data feed by Reuters, integrating financial services practice into the M.B.A. curriculum. Baruch's 800,000-square-foot Vertical Campus building features 102 classrooms, fourteen research labs, and thirty-six computer labs that are all fully equipped with state-of-the-art instructional technology.

Financial Aid

Merit-based graduate assistantships are awarded to qualified full-time master's students. The assistantships carry an annual stipend of $5000 and are renewable for one year; they do not include a tuition waiver. The Mitsui USA Foundation awards $5000 scholarships in the fall to 2 newly admitted full-time students pursuing an M.B.A. degree in international business. Applicants must be U.S. citizens or permanent residents. Twenty to twenty-five Full-Time Honors M.B.A. Scholarships of $2000 to $5000 are awarded each year to new students in the Full-Time Honors M.B.A. program. The Carl Spielvogel '56 Scholarship in International Marketing provides annual support of $5000 to 1 or more graduate students who intend to study international marketing and pursue a career in that field. It is renewable for one year. Financial aid also is available through a variety of state, federal, and College programs. International students are eligible to apply for graduate assistantships and College work-study. Prospective doctoral students should contact the Admissions Office at the City University Graduate Center for financial aid information.

Cost of Study

M.S. tuition for state residents in fall 2007 was $3200 per semester for full-time and $270 per credit for part-time study. For out-of-state residents and international students, tuition was $500 per credit. M.B.A. tuition for state residents in fall 2007 was $4400 per term for full-time and $400 per credit for part-time study. For out-of-state residents and international students, tuition was $600 per credit. Doctoral students may contact the Admissions Office at the City University Graduate Center for tuition information.

Living and Housing Costs

Baruch College does not offer student housing at this time; students must provide for their own room and board. A single student should anticipate spending approximately $16,900 per year for housing, food, utilities, books, transportation, entertainment, and incidental expenses.

Student Group

With an earned reputation for excellence that extends to all parts of the world, Baruch College attracts students from New York, neighboring states, and abroad. In the traditional M.B.A. and M.S. programs, the Zicklin School enrolls approximately 600 full-time students, about half of whom are international students representing thirty-seven countries worldwide.

Student Outcomes

Graduates of Baruch's programs are hired to work in a variety of industries and professional functions. Top employers of recent Baruch College graduates include Citigroup, Colgate Palmolive, Ernst & Young, KPMG, Lehman Brothers, and PricewaterhouseCoopers.

Location

Baruch College occupies five buildings in the Gramercy Park area of Manhattan, the heart of one of the world's most dynamic cultural and financial centers.

The College

Baruch College has evolved from the innovative School of Business and Civic Administration, which was established in 1919 by the trustees of the City College of New York. The first master's degree program in business administration was offered by the School in 1920. In 1953, the name of the School was changed to the Bernard M. Baruch School of Business and Public Administration, in honor of the distinguished financier and statesman who was an alumnus and a trustee of the City College. In 1968, the School became an independent senior college of the City University of New York. In 1998, in response to an $18-million gift from alumnus Lawrence Zicklin, the business school became the Zicklin School of Business. Baruch College is accredited by AACSB International–The Association to Advance Collegiate Schools of Business and by the Middle States Association of Colleges and Schools.

Applying

For master's programs, students must have a baccalaureate degree from a regionally accredited college or its equivalent. Applicants must submit GMAT scores. Applicants for the Ph.D. in business must have earned an acceptable bachelor's and/or master's degree from an accredited institution whose requirements for the particular degree are substantially equivalent to those of the City University of New York. The GMAT is required.

Correspondence and Information

For M.B.A. and M.S. programs:
Graduate Admissions
Zicklin School of Business
Baruch College of the City University of New York
One Bernard Baruch Way
Box H-0820
New York, New York 10010-5518
Phone: 646-312-1300
Fax: 646-312-1301
E-mail: ZicklinGradAdmissions@baruch.cuny.edu
Web site: http://www.zicklin.baruch.cuny.edu

For the Executive M.B.A. program:
Executive M.B.A. Program
Baruch College of the City University of New York
One Bernard Baruch Way
Box B13-282
New York, New York 10010-5518
Phone: 646-312-3100
Fax: 646-312-3101
E-mail: exprog_bus@baruch.cuny.edu
Web site: http://www.zicklin.baruch.cuny.edu

For doctoral degree programs:
Admissions Office
The Graduate Center
City University of New York
365 Fifth Avenue
New York, New York 10016-4309
Phone: 646-312-3090 (business)
E-mail: phd@baruch.cuny.edu
Web site: http://www.gc.cuny.edu

Bernard M. Baruch College of the City University of New York

FACULTY HEADS AND AREAS OF RESEARCH

John A. Elliott, Vice President and Dean of the Zicklin School of Business; Ph.D., Cornell.
Joseph Weintrop, Executive Officer of the Doctoral Program in Business; Ph.D., Oregon.

The Zicklin School of Business faculty members in every department continue to develop major research contributions over a wide range of topics. During the academic year, faculty members published more than thirty text and reference books, contributed scholarly pieces that appeared in more than forty additional books, and published nearly 200 articles in many of the leading professional journals. During this period, faculty members also held major editorial positions with more than fifty business journals and research publications.

Department of Accountancy

Masako N. Darrough, Ph.D., Chair. Major areas of research include financial accounting, managerial accounting, auditing, and taxation. Both theoretical and applied research is conducted, with most of the faculty members emphasizing basic research. The department stresses high-quality research targeted to the most selective publications. Recent research interests include auditing standards, derivative and hedge accounting, auditing professionalism, disclosure of earnings estimates, accounting information, estate and gift taxation, leasing and the cost of capital, CEO compensation, mandated accounting changes and managerial discretion, insider trading and analysts' earnings forecasts, accounting ethics, statement analysis, pension accounting and corporate takeovers, and the poetry and politics of accounting.

Department of Economics and Finance

Kishore Tandon, Ph.D., Chair. The department's faculty members conduct both applied and theoretical research, broadly covering many areas of economics and finance. The department has particular research strength in derivative markets, financial institutions, and investment theory. Examples of recent work include operational efficiency in banking, treasury yield curve, stock market reaction to dividend changes, valuation of interest rate–sensitive securities, buy-write securities, investment analysis software, asset pricing implications, equity derivatives, options and valuation of inventory, foreign acquisitions in the United States, foreign ownership restrictions and premiums for international investments, economies of scale and cost complementaries in commercial banking, future markets efficiency, and import and hedging uncertainty in international trade.

Department of Law

Elliot Axelrod, J.D., Chair. Major areas of research include practically all areas of business law, including heavy emphasis on contract law, corporations, partnerships, computer law, real estate law, international trade law, health-care law, the Uniform Commercial Code, antitrust law, and employment law, as well as some areas of constitutional, intellectual property, environmental, consumer, and criminal law.

Department of Management

Harry Rosen, Ph.D., Chair. Major areas of research include strategic management, temporal issues in strategy, competitive dynamics and industry structure, social issues in management, business ethics, operations management, international and comparative management, organizational behavior, work and family, economic justification of advanced manufacturing systems, technology and strategy, flexible manufacturing systems, inspection policy design, critical thinking, managing strategic flexibility, linking strategies with work redesign, ethical preferences and future orientations of business executives, optimal maintenance policies, the ceiling effect on work motivation, effects of failure on group performance, repeat purchase behavior as a criterion of teaching effectiveness, human dilemmas in work organizations, research and development in biotechnology firms, black economic empowerment in post-apartheid South Africa, and vehicle routing systems.

Department of Marketing

Kapil Bawa, Ph.D., Chair. Major areas of research include advertising and marketing communications, consumer behavior, marketing research, international marketing, marketing management, retailing and sales, direct marketing, and all areas of international business. Recent research interests have included the conceptual domain of international business, the consequences of whistle-blowing, casual inferences in consumer safety judgments, how consumers assess the value of advertising, gender effects in consumer research, marketing strategies of Japanese auto manufacturers, social and governmental environment of business, comparative institutional analysis of marketing systems, globalization and quality-of-life considerations, entrepreneurship education for minorities, environmental standards and European consumer-goods marketing, consumer marketing relationship programs, managing imitative strategies, geographical market diffusion, analysis of price and exposure of network prime-time advertising, and managing cultural differences.

Department of Real Estate

Ko Wang, Ph.D., Chair and Newman Chair in Real Estate Finance. Situated in a historical landmark and sponsored by a pioneer in the real estate field, the Department of Real Estate at the Zicklin School of Business seeks to become a center of excellence in producing and disseminating cutting-edge real estate knowledge. As the anchor of the William Newman Programs in Real Estate, the department currently offers an M.B.A. with a concentration in real estate, a Ph.D. program in real estate, and electives for other programs. It is the department's goal to offer executive training programs in the near future. Baruch College aims to establish a department that is renowned for its breadth and depth. All aspects of real estate are covered, and the curriculum includes substantial opportunities for internships. The Scholar in Residence program, job fairs, career panels, and real estate clubs offer excellent opportunities for students to be in close contact with and to network with industry leaders.

Department of Statistics and Computer Information Systems

Albert Croker, Ph.D., Chair. Major areas of research include database systems; information retrieval; telecommunications and networks; privacy; multimedia systems; organizational diffusion of information technologies; information systems in the human service and nonprofit sectors; information system ethics; control and audit of information systems; electronic commerce; financial information systems; system development methodologies; computer simulation; Bayesian analysis; business application of linear and integer programming; generalized assignment problem; health-care systems; nonparametric data analysis; categorical data analysis; expert systems; mathematical programming applied to information technology; combinatorics; polyhedral theory; cryptology; group decision support systems; Meta Analysis; statistics in sports; statistics in auditing; sampling theory; medical statistics; incomplete, censored, and truncated data; total quality management; bootstrap and Gibbs sampling; legal statistics; time-series analysis; robust methods; and experimental design.

BRANDEIS UNIVERSITY

The Heller School for Social Policy and Management
Human Services M.B.A.

Programs of Study

The Heller M.B.A. program offers the technical foundation found in traditional business programs within the context of social policy and mission-driven management. It provides not only rigorous skills, such as financial management and strategic planning, but also tools to address the unique management issues facing nonprofit, public, and for-profit entities that attend to the needs of underserved and vulnerable populations. The M.B.A. program is designed to train the next generation of leaders and decision makers to be able to find resources, use them effectively, and deliver on a social good. Graduates of the program are able to bring solid management tools, honed analytical skills, and personal commitment to bear on answering some of today's most pressing social problems. Heller M.B.A. students become innovative forces working within, and almost despite, the systems in which they find health and human services as well as other mission-driven organizations.

The management curriculum is distinct in that it is taught as a context-specific discipline. It integrates major contextual forces, including social policies and programs as well as market forces that affect the role of managers in mission-driven organizations. The full-time core curriculum is planned as an intensive academic program to minimize time in school and time away from the job market, covering the usual two years of work found in traditional business, public administration, social work, public health, or other comparable programs in four consecutive semesters (fifteen months). The seventeen-course curriculum combines key management courses such as organizational behavior, strategic management, and accounting with social policy courses in areas of specific interest to the student. Policy courses provide broader perspectives needed to truly manage mission-oriented programs in not just the most efficient, but the most effective way. Students may choose policy concentrations in the areas of child, youth, and family policy and management; health care; health care policy and management; social policy and management; or sustainable development. Students may opt for the Heller/Hornstein Dual-Degree Program with Brandeis University's Master of Arts in Jewish Communal Service.

The Heller M.B.A. culminates in the Team Consulting Project: a real-world, practical experience where students have the opportunity to apply the analytical and problem-solving skills they have developed at Heller to an actual mission-driven organization. Working under the supervision of a faculty adviser, students work in teams of 3 to 5 and provide management consulting services to a variety of community-based organizations and agencies during a four-month period. By working on a real world problem—with its human resource, technical, financial, strategic, or other management challenges—students are better prepared to function as professionals after graduation.

Research Facilities

Students benefit from course offerings by and association with an expert research staff in six nationally recognized policy centers.

Financial Aid

The Heller School attempts to assist as many students as possible in securing financial aid. Candidates for admission are expected to explore a variety of outside funding sources such as private scholarships, G.I. bill benefits, and government loan programs. The School also offers partial scholarships and fellowships. Forms may be obtained from the Office of Admissions. Aid decisions are made on the combined basis of financial need and academic merit. Part-time students can apply for student loans by filing the FAFSA form.

Cost of Study

For 2006–07, the cost of study was $65,902 for the full-time, sixteen-month (four consecutive semesters) program. Part-time study was $2945 per course.

Living and Housing Costs

In 2006–07, the cost of living for a single student was about $1300 a month. University housing at Brandeis University is limited; most students rent nearby apartments.

Student Group

The M.B.A. Program enrolls 40 to 50 students per year. Full-time students complete the program in sixteen months (August through December of the following year), which is a considerable advantage in cost and time over equivalent two-year programs. Part-time students finish in two to five years.

Student Outcomes

The educational goal of the M.B.A. Program is to develop outstanding leaders who are well prepared for managerial roles in health and human services organizations and responsible citizenship in the community. Heller's management program develops in graduates the capacity to frame, analyze, and solve managerial problems; make and execute effective decisions; and lead health and human services organizations through a complex and changing environment. Alumni have gone on to hold a variety of challenging positions in the not-for-profit, public, and for-profit sectors. From a recent survey, 74 percent are in management/administration and 26 percent are in research/policy analysis, direct care, and consulting.

Location

Minutes from Boston, The Heller School is on Brandeis' picturesque 235-acre suburban campus in Waltham. Shuttle buses and the commuter train link the campus to the state capital, which is rich in history and offers many attractions and cultural resources and easy access to beaches and mountains.

The University

Founded in 1948, Brandeis has become one of the leading small private research universities in the United States, having earned recognition by Phi Beta Kappa only thirteen years after its founding—the youngest institution to be so honored in more than 100 years. In a national review, Brandeis was named the top rising research institution in the United States. The University has a student population of 5,189, of whom 1,922 are graduate students. Brandeis offers students a broad diversity of cultural events and opportunities. Student groups and clubs exist for a wide variety of academic and leisure activity. The Gosman Sports Center is a facility with an indoor track, multipurpose courts, a swimming pool, and weight/fitness rooms.

Applying

Application forms and financial aid information can be obtained from the Office of Admissions. Students must submit a completed application, transcripts, recommendations, writing samples, and GMAT test scores. Students must have an undergraduate degree and two or more years of work experience, although some applicants who have excellent academic records and evidence of leadership potential are accepted directly out of undergraduate programs. The application fee is $55. Completed applications are reviewed as they are received throughout the year. Review of applications begins in November; early application is encouraged. Prospective applicants are invited to attend information sessions which are held monthly between September and February.

Correspondence and Information

Office of Admissions
The Heller School for Social Policy and Management/MS 035
Brandeis University
Waltham, Massachusetts 02454-9110
Phone: 781-736-3820
Fax: 781-736-2774
E-mail: helleradmissions@brandeis.edu
Web site: http://heller.brandeis.edu

Brandeis University

THE FACULTY AND THEIR RESEARCH

Faculty

Stuart H. Altman, Sol C. Chaiken Professor of National Health Policy and Dean; Ph.D., UCLA.
Brenda Anderson, Adjunct Lecturer; Ph.D., Massachusetts Amherst.
Jeffrey Ashe, Adjunct Professor; M.A., Boston University.
Lawrence Neil Bailis, Associate Professor; Ph.D., Harvard.
Sarita Bhalotra, Assistant Professor; Ph.D., Brandeis.
Christine E. Bishop, Professor and Director, Ph.D. Program; Ph.D., Harvard.
David Boyer, Adjunct Lecturer; M.S., Antioch New England.
Jon A. Chilingerian, Associate Professor; Ph.D., MIT.
Susan P. Curnan, Associate Professor; M.F.S., Yale.
Michael T. Doonan, Assistant Professor; Ph.D., Brandeis.
Stephen Fournier, Lecturer; Ph.D., MIT.
Barry L. Friedman, Professor; Ph.D., MIT.
Deborah Garnick, Professor; Sc.D., Johns Hopkins.
David G. Gil, Professor of Social Policy; D.S.W., Pennsylvania.
Jody H. Gittell, Professor; Ph.D., MIT.
Ricardo A. Godoy, Professor; Ph.D., Columbia.
Maria Green, Assistant Professor; J.D., Harvard.
Jose Suaya Grezzi, Lecturer; Ph.D., Brandeis.
Andrew B. Hahn, Professor; Ph.D., Brandeis.
Anita Hill, Professor of Social Policy, Law, and Women's Studies; J.D., Yale.
Dominic Hodgkin, Assistant Professor; Ph.D., Boston University.
Susan Holcombe, Professor of the Practice; Ph.D., NYU.
Constance M. Horgan, Professor; Sc.D., Johns Hopkins.
Milton Obote Joshua, Adjunct Lecturer; M.A., Nairobi.
Sajed Kamal, Adjunct Lecturer; Ph.D., Boston University.
Attila O. Klein, Adjunct Lecturer; Ph.D., Indiana.
Lorraine Klerman, Professor; Dr.P.H., Harvard.
Marty Wyngaarden Krauss, Professor and Provost; Ph.D., Brandeis.
Ravi Lakshmikanthan, Lecturer; M.A., Brandeis.
Walter N. Leutz, Associate Professor; Ph.D., Brandeis.
Thomas McLaughlin, Adjunct Lecturer; M.B.A., Boston University
Ellen Messer, Adjunct Lecturer; Ph.D., Michigan.
Phyllis H. Mutschler, Associate Professor; Ph.D., Brandeis.
A. K. Nandakumar, Professor; Ph.D., Boston University.
Huong H. Nguyen, Assistant Professor; Ph.D., Michigan State.
Eric Olson, Adjunct Lecturer; Ph.D., Pennsylvania.
Jeffrey Prottas, Professor; Ph.D., MIT.
Jehan Raheem, Adjunct Professor; M.B.A., CUNY, Baruch.
Carol A. (Kelley) Ready, Adjunct Lecturer; Ph.D., CUNY Graduate Center.
Laura Roper, Adjunct Lecturer; Ph.D., Pennsylvania.
Leonard Saxe, Professor; Ph.D., Pittsburgh.
Ann Seidman, Adjunct Lecturer; Ph.D., Wisconsin–Madison.
Robert Seidman, Adjunct Professor; L.L.M., Columbia.
Thomas Shapiro, Pokross Professor of Law and Social Policy; Ph.D., Washington (St. Louis).

Donald Shephard, Professor; Ph.D., Harvard.
Joseph Short, Adjunct Professor; Ph.D., Columbia.
Laurence Simon, Professor; Ph.D., Clark.
Christopher Tompkins, Associate Professor; Ph.D., Brandeis.
Stanley S. Wallack, Professor; Ph.D., Washington (St. Louis).
David Whalen, Adjunct Lecturer; M.B.A., Brandeis.

Professors Emeriti

Jim Callahan, Ph.D., Brandeis.
Janet Giele, Ph.D., Harvard.
Ken Jones, Ed.D., Harvard.
Norman R. Kurtz, Ph.D., Colorado.
Robert Perlman, Ph.D., Brandeis.
James H. Schulz, Ph.D., Yale.
Roland Warren, Ph.D., Heidelberg.
Constance Williams, Ph.D., Brandeis.

Research Staff

Janet Boguslaw, Senior Research Associate; Ph.D., Boston College.
Mary Brolin, Senior Research Associate; Ph.D., Brandeis.
Cathy Burak, Senior Research Associate; Ed.D., Harvard.
Garen Corbett, Senior Research Associate; M.S., Massachusetts Boston.
Marilyn Daley, Senior Research Associate; Ph.D., Brandeis.
Joseph Frees, Senior Research Associate; Ph.D., Minnesota.
Deborah Gurewich, Senior Research Associate; Ph.D., Brandeis.
Della Hughes, Senior Research Associate; M.S.S.W., Tennessee; M.Div., Vanderbilt.
John Kaufman, Senior Scientist; Sc.D., Harvard.
Christopher Kingsley, Senior Program Associate; B.S., Clarkson.
Peter Kreiner, Scientist, Ph.D., USC.
Brad Krevor, Senior Research Associate; Ph.D., Boston University.
Susan Lanspery, Senior Research Associate; Ph.D., Brandeis.
A. James Lee, Senior Scientist; Ph.D., Wisconsin–Madison.
Margaret T. Lee, Scientist; Ph.D., Berkeley.
Tim Martin, Senior Research Associate; Ph.D., Brandeis.
Alan Melchior, Senior Research Associate; B.A., Brandeis.
Elizabeth Merrick, Scientist; Ph.D., Brandeis.
Sharon Reif, Scientist; Ph.D., Brandeis.
Grant Ritter, Senior Scientist and Lecturer; Ph.D., Cornell.
Amy Smalarz, Senior Research Associate; Ph.D., Brandeis.
William Stason, Senior Scientist; M.D., Harvard.
Cindy Thomas, Senior Scientist; Ph.D., Brandeis.
Elizabeth Tighe, Senior Research Associate; Ph.D., Brandeis.
Sandy Venner, Senior Program Associate; M.S.S.W., Wisconsin.
Marjorie Erickson Warfield, Scientist; Ph.D., Brandeis.

CALIFORNIA STATE UNIVERSITY, SACRAMENTO

College of Business Administration

Programs of Study

The College of Business Administration at California State University, Sacramento, strives to be an exemplary regional educational institution graduating community-minded students with a strong foundation in business knowledge, skills, and values for the new information age. The College offers a high-quality business education that is responsive to the changing regional, global, and technology-driven environment and fulfills its mission through the pursuit of excellence in teaching and learning, scholarship, and service to the community as well through collaborative efforts among the faculty and staff members, students, the administration, and community members.

Guided by dynamic faculty members who are dedicated to preparing competent, community-minded graduates, the College's goals are supported by its partnerships with such institutes as the Center for Small Businesses and the Government Accounting Institute and through such programs as the Business Ventures Lecture Series, which brings together students, alumni, and industry professionals.

The College offers a Master of Business Administration (M.B.A.) degree, an Executive Master of Business Administration (E.M.B.A.) degree, a Master of Science degree in accountancy (M.S./ACCY), a Master of Science degree in urban land development (M.S./ULD), and a Master of Science in Business Administration with concentrations in management information systems (M.S.B.A./MIS) and taxation (M.S.B.A./TAX). The M.S./ACCY and the M.S.B.A./TAX programs are interactive, synchronous online programs. A Certificate in Advanced Business Studies (CABS) is also available through the College. The graduate programs require 30 to 54 semester units beyond the baccalaureate degree, including required courses, electives, and a master's project or other culminating experience. Students who do not have an undergraduate business degree may be required to take foundation courses to gain proficiency in key business areas.

The College of Business Administration is fully accredited by AACSB International–The Association to Advance Collegiate Schools of Business.

Research Facilities

The University Library holds more than 1 million volumes; thousands of maps, slides, and pamphlets; and several million pieces of microforms and nonprint media as well as subscriptions to some 4,000 magazines, technical and scholarly journals, and newspapers. Thousands of additional journals are available electronically. The library is a depository for California State publications and for selected United States government materials, and it provides access to EUREKA and other databases. University Computing and Communications Services (UCCS) is responsible for all University-wide computing and data communications equipment, software, and networking. There are more than 4,000 workstations located throughout the campus for use by students and faculty members.

Financial Aid

More than forty College of Business Administration departmental scholarships are available to business majors in all concentrations and are awarded to these students each academic year on a semester or annual basis. The University also awards three Graduate Diversity Grants of $1500 ($3000 for doctoral candidates) every year to students who have experienced economic and educational disadvantages. The Solano Association of Realtors Scholarship Foundation awards scholarships of $1000 to students from southern Solano County who intend to study real estate or a related field, such as business or finance. California residents who demonstrate financial need are also eligible for CalGrants.

Cost of Study

In 2007–08, tuition for California residents is $1372 per semester for up to 6 units and $2088 per semester for 7 units or more. Nonresidents pay the resident fees plus $339 per unit. Other fees such as parking and health insurance may also be applicable. Some programs are provided through the College of Continuing Education, and the fee structure is set for each program.

Living and Housing Costs

In 2007–08, the rate for a double room on campus is $4772 per academic year, plus an additional $3088 for ten meals per week or $2720 for fifteen meals per week. A single room costs an additional $200 per semester. Off-campus housing is available and costs $600 to $900 per month for a one-bedroom apartment or $900 to $1300 per month for a two-bedroom unit.

Student Group

Every year, approximately 350 students enroll in the graduate programs. Approximately 40 percent are full-time, and approximately 40 percent are women. The majority range in age from 24 to 34.

Student Outcomes

Graduates of the College find jobs in a number of industries, including finance, accounting, information technology, banking, and real estate. They work as CEOs, CFOs, COOs, MIS specialists, CPAs, developers, treasurers, and financial planners and in other executive roles.

Location

The campus is located in Sacramento, whose mild climate, rivers, and nearby recreation areas make it popular with outdoor enthusiasts. The city also offers art galleries, museums, theater, and shopping. Sacramento hosts the world's largest traditional jazz festival each Memorial Day weekend, and it is a short drive from San Francisco, the Napa and Sonoma Valleys, and the ski slopes of Lake Tahoe.

The University

Founded in 1947, California State University, Sacramento is dedicated to offering students an education that balances liberal arts with an in-depth knowledge in a discipline, providing an excellent opportunity for those who aspire to prepare themselves for meaningful lives, careers, and service to their community. The University offers sixty undergraduate degrees and forty graduate degrees to 28,000 students who take advantage of the University's access to extensive research and internship opportunities in one of the fastest-growing regions in the nation.

Applying

Admission to the business graduate programs requires an application for admission, two transcripts from all universities previously attended that show a GPA of 2.5 or higher from the last 60 credits earned, a minimum GMAT score of 500 and placement in the thirtieth percentile, letters of recommendation, a current resume or CV, and a $55 application fee. Prospective students should visit the Web site at http://www.cba.csus.edu/mba for the admission criteria and requirements for submission of application materials for each program.

Correspondence and Information

Office of Graduate Programs
Tahoe Hall, Room 1035
California State University, Sacramento
Sacramento, California 95819-6088

Phone: 916-278-6772
Fax: 916-278-4233
E-mail: cbagrad@csis.edu
Web site: http://cbaweb.cba.csus.edu/

California State University, Sacramento

THE FACULTY AND THEIR RESEARCH

Hamid A. Ahmadi, Professor of Finance; Ph.D., Claremont.

Jaime R. Alvayay, Professor of Real Estate and Land Use Affairs; Ph.D., Georgia. Housing and urban land markets, mortgage markets and financial institutions, corporate finance, valuation of real assets.

Seung Bai Bach, Assistant Professor of Management; Ph.D., Tennessee, Knoxville. Entrepreneurial rent creation, venture survival, social network.

Thomas J. Beirne Jr., Professor of Accountancy; Ph.D., Oklahoma. Financial accounting.

Herbert Blake Jr., Professor of Operations/Strategic Management and Chair, Department of Management; Ph.D., Santa Clara. Operations management.

H. David Brecht, Professor of Accountancy; Ph.D., Texas. Accounting, pedagogy, and IT in teaching accounting; financial accounting, managerial accounting.

Claudia Bridges, Assistant Professor of Management; Ph.D., Arizona State. Environmental sustainability, salesmanship, distance education, online shopping habits.

Donald Carper, Professor of Business Law; J.D., University of the Pacific. Adaptation of a North American mediation model in Russia and Africa, conflict management in business and public administration, alternative dispute resolution, business arbitrations.

Patricia Cheshier, Professor of Finance and Insurance; Ph.D., Nebraska–Lincoln. Risk management and insurance, finance, business policy.

Kenichiro Chinen, Assistant Professor of Operations Management; Ph.D., New Mexico State. International business and marketing (country of origin).

Russell K. H. Ching, Professor of Management Information Systems and Chair, Management Information Science. Ph.D., Arkansas. Effects of information load on use of inferences in decision making.

Beom-Jin Choi, Assistant Professor; Ph.D., Arizona State. Information technology standards, virtual communities of practice, knowledge management.

John Clark, Professor of Marketing; Ph.D., Texas Tech. Retailing, general marketing.

Margaret A. Cleek, Professor and Chair of Department of Organizational Behavior and Environment; Ph.D., Wayne State. Personality disorders in the work environment, application of natural models to organizational behavior, assessment, development of work sample assessment exercises.

John Corless, Professor of Accountancy; Ph.D., Minnesota; CPA. Accounting.

Stephen Crow, Professor of Accountancy; Ph.D., USC; CPA. Taxation, with focus on international taxation, tax treaties and cross-border tax issues, and fiscal and cultural impact of cross-border taxation.

Charles Davis, Professor of Accountancy; Ph.D., Illinois. Issues within financial accounting, including standard setting, improvements in financial reporting, international accounting standards, accounting aspects of information systems.

Jerry Estenson, Professor of Organizational Behavior; D.P.A., USC. Communication systems used in facilitating organizational change and leadership in rapidly changing environments.

Reginald Goodfellow, Professor of Organizational Behavior and Human Resources Management; Ph.D., Bowling Green State. Employee recruitment, selection and evaluation, attitudes, legal aspects of HRM/organizational behavior.

Jordan Halgas, Assistant Professor of Business and Employment Law; Ph.D., Ohio State. Employment law, labor law, business law, constitutional law.

Yongliang Han, Assistant Professor of Operations Management; Ph.D., USC. Strategic alliances in hi-tech industries, strategy and structure of firms in emerging markets, innovation management, venture capital.

Lindle Hatton, Professor of Strategic Management; D.B.A., Kentucky. Business strategy, entrepreneurship, corporate governance, business ethics and social responsibility.

Arthur Jensen, Professor of Marketing; Ph.D., Arizona State. Sacramento Forecast Project.

Necmi Karagozoglu, Professor of Operations/Strategic Management; Ph.D., Oregon. Entrepreneurial opportunity recognition, e-commerce and SMES, creative strategic management.

Serge Karalli, Professor; Ph.D., Case Western Reserve. Multiple-family economic lot-scheduling problems with safety stocks, logistics: warehouse location, physical distribution, revenue management.

Craig Kelley, Professor of Marketing; Ph.D., Arizona State. Marketing research, marketing management.

Jong Kim, Professor of Accountancy; Ph.D., Missouri. Financial accounting issues, small business issues.

James Kuhle, Professor of Finance; Ph.D., Texas at Austin. Investment in real estate assets.

Monica Lam, Professor; Ph.D., Wisconsin–Madison. Object-oriented databases and data warehouse, neural network models for machine learning, business values of information systems, knowledge models for strategic management accounting.

John LaRocco, Professor of Law; J.D., San Diego; LL.M., Georgetown. Arbitration, mediation, labor law, negotiation, industrial relations, employment law.

Leonardo Legorreta, Assistant Professor of Management Information Systems; Ph.D., Oregon. E-business metrics, impact of IT on organizational development, e-business architecture, alignment of IT and business strategy.

Min Li, Assistant Professor of Decision Sciences; Ph.D., Cincinnati. Bayesian statistics, empirical finance, marketing research.

Caixing Liu, Assistant Professor of Accountancy; Ph.D., Hawaii. Earnings management, corporate governance.

James Mackey, Professor of Accountancy; Ph.D., Illinois; CMA, CPA. Cost managerial accounting.

Richard Marens, Assistant Professor of Organizational Behavior and Environment; Ph.D., Washington (Seattle). Corporate governance and stakeholder interests, practicality of stakeholder theory, political economy of globalization, history of business organization.

Kent Meyer, Professor of Accountancy; Ph.D., Texas at Austin; J.D., University of the Pacific.

Amy E. Mickel, Assistant Professor of Human Resources Management; Ph.D., Washington (Seattle). Quality of life, money-related individual differences, interactive teaching practices.

Suzanne Ogilby, Professor of Accountancy; Ph.D., Wisconsin. Financial accounting, governmental and nonprofit accounting, pedagogical research.

Thian-Huat Ong, Assistant Professor of Management Information Systems; Ph.D., Arizona. Knowledge management, data mining, multilingual systems.

Hakan Ozcelik, Assistant Professor; Ph.D., British Columbia. Organizational communications, organizational behavior.

Walter Perlick, Professor of Finance; Ph.D., Penn State. Banking, entrepreneurship, general management.

Hugh Pforsich, Assistant Professor; Ph.D., Washington State. Decisions made under risk, information systems and new technologies that influence those decisions.

Ralph Pope, Professor of Finance; D.B.A., Mississippi State. Financial management, international business.

Joseph Richards, Assistant Professor of Finance; Ph.D., Syracuse. Marketing, business strategy.

Laura T. Riolli, Associate Professor of Organizational Behavior and Environment; Ph.D., Nebraska–Lincoln. Impact of individual and group factors on employees' stress, turnover, and performance; organizational culture and cross-cultural issues; human resources management; consumer behavior and the Internet.

Chris Sablynski, Assistant Professor of Human Resources Management; Ph.D., Washington (Seattle). General areas of employee retention, job embeddedness and workplace aggression.

Thomas Sandman, Professor of Management Information Systems; Ph.D., Arizona State. Computer information systems.

David Scanlan, Professor of Management Information Systems; Ed.D., Northern Illinois.

Peter Sharp, Professor of Finance; Ph.D., Claremont. Financial markets, currency markets.

Craig Stanley, Professor of Real Estate and Land Use Affairs; Ph.D., Claremont. Course assessment in real estate, hybrid Web/on-campus course design, using e-mail to teach writing skills and foster learning in real estate.

Laurence Takeuchi, Professor of Marketing; Ph.D., Claremont. Statistical methods, consumer behavior models, cognitive models, neural networks, expert systems, empirical studies that link cognitive states/variables with behavioral outcomes, technology diffusion and innovation, academic planning and assessment.

Stanley Taylor, Professor of Decision Sciences; Ph.D., Oregon. Statistics.

Gail Tom, Professor of Marketing; Ph.D., California, Davis. Marketing, advertising, retailing, psychology and education, consumer behavior.

Dennis Tootelian, Professor of Marketing and Director, Center for Small Business; Ph.D., Arizona State. Health-care marketing, gaming, leisure-time marketing, environmental protection, governmental marketing impact of business on marketplace economics, small business management.

Nancy Tsai, Professor of Management Information Systems; Ph.D., Texas at Austin. Database, networking, information system security, system analysis and design, infrastructure of strategic planning and management for information technology.

Chiang Wang, Professor of Operations/Strategic Management; Ph.D., Iowa. Operations management, quality management, productivity management.

Ruth Wang, Professor of Operations/Strategic Management; Ph.D., Iowa. International operating strategies, international business ethics, international marketing, East Asian markets.

Martha Wilson, Assistant Professor of Management; Ph.D., Washington (Seattle). Supply-chain dynamics, system-dynamics simulation, transportation.

Haroldene Wunder, Professor of Accountancy; Ph.D., South Carolina. Taxation, international accounting.

Yan Xiong, Assistant Professor of Accountancy; Ph.D., Washington State. Capital markets research with an emphasis in earnings management in IPO firms, auditor litigation, and firm valuation; accounting educational research; accounting information systems research.

Carnegie Mellon

CARNEGIE MELLON UNIVERSITY

H. John Heinz III School of Public Policy and Management
Master of Entertainment Industry Management

Program of Study	The Master of Entertainment Industry Management (M.E.I.M.) program complements the creative and aesthetic skills honed in undergraduate school with a set of management skills that prepares students for a leadership career in the entertainment industry. What distinguishes this degree program is its unique blend of Carnegie Mellon's renowned rigorous, high-quality academic training with on-site, hands-on training within the film and television industry in Los Angeles. Students spend the first year of study in Pittsburgh, taking core management course work to build the skills and ways of thinking that they need to succeed. During the second year, the students are in Los Angeles, expanding and enriching their management skills, theories, and techniques through specialized course work taught by some of the entertainment industry's leading professionals. In addition, M.E.I.M. students work side-by-side with industry professionals throughout the year as full-time apprentices in a studio or production company. The curriculum blends the theoretical and the practical, offering classroom experiences that provide the theoretical foundations and key management skills and techniques. Core courses cover management, technology, financial, quantitative, and communication skills within the context of creative enterprises in both the nonprofit and for-profit sectors. Case studies—based on issues confronted by actual organizations—serve as the basis for analysis and discussion in many of the courses. Seminars and special presentations are scheduled throughout the first academic year and feature key national and international figures in the arts, entertainment, and related policy areas. The capstone project tests students' acquired skills through the development of a business plan for a creative project, which could be a student's first venture in the industry.
Research Facilities	Carnegie Mellon's University Libraries house more than 890,000 volumes, 3,800 periodicals, and extensive electronic databases. Reciprocal borrowing agreements with nearby universities and colleges, including the University of Pittsburgh, provide students with virtually unlimited library resources. The main branch of the Carnegie Library of Pittsburgh is a few minutes' walk from campus. More than 400 UNIX, Macintosh, and Windows computers are available in public clusters.
Financial Aid	The Heinz School offers merit-based scholarships to eligible students entering the M.E.I.M. program and a limited number of Regional Leaders Scholarships to incoming full-time students who have demonstrated a commitment to the Pittsburgh community. A variety of other scholarships are available. First-year students undertake a production management assignment in the School of Drama for a maximum of 200 hours of work with a salary of $10 per hour.
Cost of Study	In the 2007–08 academic year, full-time tuition is $17,300. Other expenses include $1000 annually for health insurance and $200 per semester in miscellaneous fees. Students can also expect to spend approximately $460 per semester on books and supplies.
Living and Housing Costs	A wide range of affordable housing options are available close to the Carnegie Mellon campus. Housing costs in Pittsburgh are typically lower than those in other urban settings. Room and board for a single graduate student average around $5600 per semester. Carnegie Mellon does not provide housing for graduate students.
Student Group	Students have a passion for telling a story—and they do it very well. Many students enter the program immediately after completing their undergraduate degree, while others have worked in the entertainment field for a time.
Location	Carnegie Mellon is located in Oakland, a cultural center of Pittsburgh, Pennsylvania, on a 90-acre campus adjacent to Schenley Park, the city's largest park. The campus is conveniently located for easy access to many cultural and sporting events and is only 4 miles from the downtown business and cultural district. Pittsburgh is the thirteenth-largest metropolitan area in the United States. The city has good public transportation, diverse cultural attractions, and three professional sports teams. New York City, Philadelphia, Toronto, and Washington, D.C., are all within driving distance. Many recreational facilities, including ski areas and state parks, are located nearby.
The University and The School	Carnegie Mellon was first established in 1900 as the Carnegie Technical School through a gift from Andrew Carnegie. In 1912, the name of the school was changed to Carnegie Institute of Technology. Mellon Institute, founded in 1913 by A. W. and R. B. Mellon, merged with Carnegie Institute of Technology in 1967 to become Carnegie Mellon University. The University has an enrollment of about 10,000, approximately 4,000 of whom are engaged in graduate study. Rated one of the country's top public policy schools by *U.S. News & World Report*, the Heinz School advances public interest through research and education. By strategically integrating expertise in policy, management, and information technology, the faculty focuses on critical public issues, including arts management, crime and violence, health care, information systems and technology, and public policy.
Applying	Candidates must have an undergraduate degree from an accredited university in the United States or its equivalent abroad, and they should have taken at least one college-level course in statistics. Students must submit the online application form (including essay and resume), official transcripts from all colleges and universities attended, three letters of recommendation, and scores from the GRE or GMAT. Nonnative English speakers are required to submit TOEFL or IELTS results as part of their application for admission. The early decision deadline is December 1; applicants are notified by January 15 and must respond to the offer of admission no later than January 31. February 1 is the final application deadline, but if the class is not full, the program continues to accept applications until all spaces are filled.
Correspondence and Information	Dan Martin, Associate Dean and M.E.I.M. Program Director H. John Heinz III School of Public Policy and Management Carnegie Mellon University 5000 Forbes Avenue Pittsburgh, Pennsylvania 15213-3890 Phone: 412-268-2164 E-mail: hnzadmit@andrew.cmu.edu Web site: http://www.heinz.cmu.edu/meim/

Carnegie Mellon University

THE FACULTY

Faculty members in the H. John Heinz III School of Public Policy and Management include:

Alessandro Acquisti, Assistant Professor of Information Technology and Public Policy.
Samuel Alfano, Adjunct Faculty.
Ashish Arora, Professor of Economics and Public Policy.
Linda C. Babcock, James M. Walton Professor of Economics.
Joseph Balestreire, Adjunct Associate Professor in Health Systems.
Edward Barr, Associate Teaching Professor.
Alfred Blumstein, Erik S. Jonsson University Professor of Urban Systems and Operations Research.
Silvia Borzutzky, Teaching Professor.
Dawn Cappelli, Adjunct Faculty.
Maurizio Carbone, Adjunct Faculty.
Kathleen Carley, Professor of Organizational Sociology.
Jonathan P. Caulkins, Professor of Operations Research and Public Policy.
Karen B. Clay, Visiting Assistant Professor of History and Public Policy.
Marilyn Coleman, Adjunct Faculty.
Jerry A. Coltin, Adjunct Faculty.
Marnie Conley, Adjunct Faculty.
George T. Duncan, Professor of Statistics.
Dennis Epple, Thomas Lord Professor of Economics.
David J. Farber, Distinguished Career Professor of Computer Science and Public Policy, School of Computer Science.
Scott Farrow, Principal Research Engineer and Director of the Center for the Study and Improvement of Regulation.
Penny S. Ferreira, Distinguished Service Professor of Environmental and Policy Law.
Martin S. Gaynor, E. J. Barone Professor of Economics and Health Policy.
Wilpen L. Gorr, Professor of Public Policy and Information Systems.
Jason L. Hansen, Adjunct Faculty.
John Huber, Adjunct Faculty.
Anne Humphreys, Adjunct Faculty.
Jeffrey Hunker, Professor of Technology and Public Policy.
Laks Iyengar, Adjunct Associate Professor of Management.
Michael P. Johnson, Associate Professor of Management Science and Urban Affairs.
Steven Klepper, Professor of Economics and Social Science.
David M. Krackhardt, Professor of Organizations and Public Policy.
Ramayya Krishnan, William W. and Ruth F. Cooper Professor of Management Science and Information Systems.
Lester B. Lave, James Higgins Professor of Economics and Finance, Professor of Urban and Public Affairs, Professor of Engineering and Public Policy.
Gordon H. Lewis, Associate Professor of Sociology.
Pamela Lewis, Teaching Professor.
Martin Lindner, Adjunct Faculty.
Peter Madsen, Senior Lecturer in Ethics and Public Policy.
Rahmi Marasli, Adjunct Faculty.
Donald Marinelli, Professor of Drama and Arts Management.
Dan Martin, Associate Professor of Drama, College of Fine Arts.
Sharon McCarthy, Adjunct Faculty.
Theodore McConnell, Adjunct Faculty.
Kevin McMahon, Adjunct Faculty.
M. Granger Morgan, Professor of Engineering and Public Policy, Electrical and Computer Engineering.
Dennis Moul, Adjunct Faculty.
Thomas Murray, Adjunct Faculty.
Daniel Nagin, Teresa and H. John Heinz III Professor of Public Policy.
Celeste Nalwasky, Adjunct Faculty.
George Novacky, Adjunct Faculty.
Rema Padman, Professor of Operations Research and Information Management.
Jeanne Pearlman, Adjunct Faculty.
Toni Pellegrini, Adjunct Instructor in Law.
Dana Phillips, Adjunct Instructor of Management.
Ron D. Porter, Adjunct Instructor of Management.
Jonathan Rosenoer, Adjunct Faculty.
Denise M. Rousseau, H. J. Heinz II Professor of Organizational Behavior.
Velma Saire, Adjunct Professor of Educational Management.
Kathryn Shaw, Professor of Economics.
Kathleen Smith, Associate Teaching Professor.
Melvin Stephens, Assistant Professor of Economics.
Marc Sternberger, Adjunct Faculty.
Shelby Stewman, Professor of Sociology and Demography.
Robert P. Strauss, Professor of Economics and Public Policy.
Joel Tarr, Richard S. Caliguiri Professor of Urban and Environmental History and Policy.
Lowell J. Taylor, Professor of Economics and Public Policy.
Rahul Telang, Assistant Professor of Information Systems.
Brian To, Adjunct Professor of Management.
Karyl Troup-Leasure, Adjunct Faculty.
Randall Trzeciak, Adjunct Faculty.
William B. Vogt, Assistant Professor of Economics.

CENTRAL MICHIGAN UNIVERSITY

Program in Administration

Program of Study
The Master of Science in Administration (M.S.A.) degree program at Central Michigan University (CMU) is an interdisciplinary program that was developed in the early 1970s to meet the educational needs and interests of administrators in the public and nonprofit sectors. Its faculty includes members from many CMU departments, such as physical education and sport, accounting, political science, management, finance, and communication and health sciences. The central purpose of the M.S.A. degree is to prepare managers, administrators, and supervisors in both private- and public-sector environments to function effectively within all types of organizations and at all levels of administration. The degree is highly sensitive to the constituencies and the demographics and cultural environments it serves and has the unique ability to adapt the necessary academic processes and course work to an organization's rapidly changing informational and technological needs.

All M.S.A. students are required to take three courses: Administrative Research and Report Methods, Managerial Accounting or Financial Management, and Quantitative Applications in Administrative Decision Making. Other core courses must be selected in consultation with an academic adviser. A total of 15 to 21 hours must be taken in the administrative core, plus a 3-credit Integrative Analysis of Administration course, which is designed to combine practical experience, integrate knowledge from the academic program, and demonstrate ability to design and execute a research project.

Students must also choose from the following concentrations: acquisitions administration, general administration, health services administration, human resources administration, information resource management, international administration, leadership, organizational communication, public administration, recreation and park administration, sport administration, and vehicle-design administration. All concentrations are not offered at all locations.

The M.S.A. program is also offered through CMU's Off-Campus Programs in more than sixty locations in the United States, Canada, and Mexico. Additional information and program locations are available online at http://www.cmuoffcampus.com or by contacting Off-Campus Programs at 800-950-1144 (toll-free).

Research Facilities
The University's library system includes off-campus library services, the Clarke Historical Library, and the main library, with numerous books and publications, electronic and paper journals, and access to several databases. There are three large public computer labs on campus that contain 400 PC and Mac workstations, and the Library offers more than 300 public workstations, which are distributed throughout the facility. A large selection of general software is available, including Adobe Photoshop, Microsoft Office, SPSS, SAS, and Minitab.

Financial Aid
The M.S.A. program offers graduate assistantships, and assistantships may be available through other University departments. On-campus students whose research is accepted for publication or presentation are eligible for Publication and Presentation Grants worth up to $300. Research grants of up to $700 are awarded on the basis of proposals received by the Research Grants Committee. Nonresidents may pay resident tuition if they have minimum undergraduate GPAs of 3.0 and minimum GMAT scores of 600 or a minimum GRE score of 560/600. In addition, students with an acceptable grade point average from Illinois, Indiana, Ohio, and Ontario, Canada, pay resident tuition. Additional financial aid information is available online at http://financialaid.cmich.edu.

Cost of Study
For the 2007–08 academic year, tuition is $388 per credit for Michigan residents and $719 per credit for out-of-state students.

Living and Housing Costs
Single-student and one- to three-bedroom family apartments are available in apartment complexes on campus. Rent includes electricity, gas, water, heat, telephone, cable TV, and other such services as the University deems appropriate. Off-campus housing is available from $250 per month, depending on the neighborhood, number of roommates, and size of the apartment.

Student Group
The program is designed for administrators in the public and nonprofit sectors. The on-campus program has approximately 100 students, both full- and part-time, and an additional 5,000 students are enrolled in CMU's Off-Campus Programs. Many of the full-time students are international and come from a variety of countries, including Thailand, Taiwan, Venezuela, Chile, Turkey, Japan, Ghana, India, and Nigeria.

Student Outcomes
Graduates of the program are prepared to serve as managers, administrators, and supervisors who function effectively within all types of organizations and at all levels of administration in both private- and public-sector environments.

Location
Mt. Pleasant is located in Michigan's lower peninsula. The downtown district features specialty stores and boutiques of all types within walking distance of the campus. Thirteen golf courses are located within a 30-minute drive, while surrounding state preserves are frequented by local hunters. Eleven parks covering 300 acres—plus another 900 acres in Isabella County—offer venues for swimming, canoeing, hiking, camping, and cross-country skiing.

The University
Central Michigan University opened its doors in 1892 to formally train teachers in the state. Bachelor's degrees were first awarded in 1918, and graduate courses were first offered in 1938. Today, the University enrolls more than 27,000 students in more than 200 programs, leading to twenty-seven degrees at the bachelor's, master's, specialist's, and doctoral levels. The University's $50-million New Vision of Excellence Campaign is a broadly focused initiative to raise academic standards, strengthen discovery and creative activity, and enhance learning-environment facilities and technology.

Applying
Those who hold a bachelor's degree with a GPA of 2.7 or, optimally, 3.0 in the final 60 semester hours of graded course work, may be considered for admission, which also requires a completed application form, one official copy of undergraduate or graduate transcripts, a statement of personal and professional goals and how the program will help achieve those goals, and a $35 application fee ($45 for international applicants). GRE and GMAT scores are not required. International students must also submit a minimum TOEFL score of 213 (computer-based), 79 (Internet-based), or 550 (paper-based) to be considered for regular admission.

Correspondence and Information
Master of Science in Administration Program Director
College of Graduate Studies
Ronan Hall 309
Central Michigan University
Mount Pleasant, Michigan 48859
Phone: 989-774-6525
Fax: 989-774-2575
E-mail: msa@cmich.edu
Web site: http://www.grad.cmich.edu/msa

Central Michigan University

THE FACULTY

As an interdisciplinary degree, the Master of Science in Administration (M.S.A.) degree program utilizes faculty members from many Central Michigan University departments and experienced administrators with successful professional backgrounds.

CENTRAL MICHIGAN UNIVERSITY

College of Business Administration

Program of Study

The Master of Business Administration (M.B.A.) program at Central Michigan University (CMU) is designed to prepare graduate business students for leadership positions in today's global economy. The program features an active student-learning environment with a curriculum that meets the needs of both part-time and full-time students from all over the world. Emphasis is placed on developing oral and written communication skills as well as the interpersonal, analytical, and integrative abilities that are needed in order to function well in dynamic organizations.

Classes are available both on the CMU campus and in Midland, Michigan. Two-credit-hour courses have been created for the core courses. This structure permits classes to meet once a week over eight weeks instead of the traditional sixteen weeks, increasing flexibility in scheduling and allowing for more breadth in the core.

Foundation requirements are satisfied with course work earned either before or after admission to the program. Students must show sufficient course work in accounting, business communications, quantitative methods and statistics, economics, legal and social environment of business, management, production/operations management, marketing, and finance. In addition, students must demonstrate a working knowledge of advanced applications in spreadsheet, database, and presentation graphics.

The M.B.A. program requires a minimum of 31 credit hours. Students must complete nine core courses, as well as a minimum of 8 hours in one of the following concentrations: consulting, finance, general business, international business, and management information systems. During the capstone experience, students apply their skills and competencies to actual business problems, developing integrated business solutions with the guidance of a faculty supervisor.

The program is accredited by the AACSB International–The Association to Advance Collegiate Schools of Business.

Research Facilities

The LaBelle Entrepreneurial Center (LEC) is a focal point for new business development and educational activities related to entrepreneurship and small business management. Currently, an advisory board of 13 entrepreneurs helps to direct the LEC, with guidance from a committee of faculty members from the College of Business Administration. The University's library system includes off-campus library services, the Clarke Historical Library, and the main library, with numerous books and publications, electronic and paper journals, and access to several databases. There are three large public labs on campus, which contain 400 PC and Mac workstations. The library also offers more than 300 public workstations distributed throughout the facility. A large selection of general software is available, including Adobe Photoshop, Microsoft Office, SPSS, SAS, and Minitab.

Financial Aid

Graduate assistantships are available for full-time students with a cumulative GPA of at least 3.0 in all graduate work. In 2006–07, graduate assistants received a stipend of $4850 per semester and a certain number of hours of tuition-free enrollment. Research grants of up to $700 are awarded on the basis of proposals received by the Research Grants Committee. Nonresidents may pay resident tuition if they have a minimum undergraduate GPA of 3.0 and a GMAT score of at least 600 or GRE score of at least 560/600. Martin Luther King Jr./César Chávez/Rosa Parks Future Faculty Program awards of up to $20,000, plus a tuition waiver for all graduate classes, are given to minority students in an effort to increase the number of teachers in Michigan.

Cost of Study

In the 2007–08 academic year, tuition is $388 per credit for Michigan residents and $719 per credit for out-of-state students.

Living and Housing Costs

Single-student or one- to three-bedroom family apartments are available in apartment complexes on campus. Rent includes electricity, gas, water, heat, telephone, cable TV, and other such services as the University deems appropriate. Off-campus housing is available from $250 per month, depending on the neighborhood, number of roommates, and size of the apartment.

Student Group

The program is designed to meet the needs of individuals who seek to develop a more general management perspective in anticipation of further advancement, students seeking a general business education that allows them to move into management positions, and persons with limited work experience who plan to use the M.B.A. as a foundation from which to begin their careers.

Student Outcomes

Graduates of the program develop as leaders and team players and develop integrity, social responsibility, and a high degree of professionalism. They develop oral- and written-communication skills as well as the interpersonal, analytical, and integrative abilities necessary to function in dynamic organizations.

Location

Mt. Pleasant is located in Michigan's lower peninsula. The downtown district features specialty stores and boutiques of all types within walking distance of campus. Thirteen golf courses are located within a 30-minute drive, while surrounding state preserves are frequented by local hunters. Eleven parks covering 300 acres—plus another 900 acres in Isabella County—offer venues for picnicking, swimming, canoeing, hiking, camping, and cross-country skiing.

The University

Central Michigan University opened its doors in 1892 to formally train teachers in the state. Bachelor's degrees were first awarded in 1918; graduate courses were first offered in 1938. Today, the University enrolls more than 28,000 students in more than 200 programs that lead to twenty-seven degrees at the bachelor's, master's, specialist's, and doctoral levels. The University's $50-million New Vision of Excellence Campaign is a broadly focused initiative to raise academic standards, strengthen discovery and creative activity, and enhance learning-environment facilities and technology.

Applying

Admission to the program requires an acceptable undergraduate GPA and a GMAT score of at least 450. Prospective students must submit an application form; official copies of undergraduate and graduate transcripts; official copies of GMAT scores; a statement of purpose and general plans for graduate study, including career plans after graduation; and a $35 application fee. Applications must be sent to the appropriate address below.

Correspondence and Information

Applications must be sent to:
Graduate Admissions
College of Graduate Studies
Foust 100
Central Michigan University
Mount Pleasant, Michigan 48859

For other correspondence and inquiries:
College of Business Administration
Central Michigan University
150 E. Bellows
Mount Pleasant, Michigan 48859
Phone: 989-774-3150
Fax: 989-774-1320
E-mail: mba@cmich.edu
Web site: http://www.cba.cmich.edu/mba/

Central Michigan University

THE FACULTY AND THEIR RESEARCH

Bruce Benet, Professor; Ph.D., North Carolina at Chapel Hill, 1989. Finance.

Debasish Chakraborty, Professor; Ph.D., Pittsburgh, 1987. Empirical tests of the random walk on the Cyprus stock exchange; macroeconomic conditions; opening up Argentina, Chili, and India.

Michael Garver, Professor; Ph.D., Tennessee, 1998. Best practices in identifying improvement opportunities, customer satisfaction audits, subscription supply chains, data mining applications in customer satisfaction research.

Deborah Gray, Professor; Ph.D., London, 2003. Marketing.

Randall Hayes, Professor; Ph.D., Michigan, 1980. Using real-option concepts to guide the nature and measured benefit of consulting interventions involving investment analysis, accounting for stock options, enterprise resource planning and SAP R/3.

Monica Holmes, Professor and Associate Dean; Ph.D., North Texas, 1995. Decision-support systems in information technology assimilation, issues in information systems, cross-cultural differences and information systems developer values.

Hyungu Kang, Professor; Ph.D., Rensselaer, 2002. Technology management in services, strategic technology planning for competitive advantage.

Anil Kumar, Professor; Ph.D., Memphis, 1997. IS planning in nonprofit organizations, understanding the role of information technology in global organizations.

Lawrence Lepisto, Professor; Ph.D., Penn State, 1974. Applying the concept of a knowledge-intensive firm to a management-consulting graduate program, applying work-role attachment theory to retirement decisions.

John Mitchell, Professor; D.B.A., Kent State, 1979. Web-based student evaluation of professors, a stochastic model of citation, citation patterns in finance literature.

Shanthakumar Palaniswami, Professor; Ph.D., IIT, 1985. Impact of information technology and e-commerce on supply chain management, evaluation and comparisons of cellular systems vs. traditional systems using simulation.

Michael Pisani, Professor; Ph.D., Pan American, 2000. Sectoral selection and informality, microcredit and micro- and small-enterprise development in Belize, penetration of the Mexican peso into United States retail operations.

Daniel Vetter, Professor and Senior Associate Dean; Ph.D., Nebraska–Lincoln. Finance and law.

J. Holton Wilson, Professor; D.B.A., Kent State, 1973. Business economics, forecasting, teaching pedagogy.

CLARK UNIVERSITY

Graduate School of Management

Programs of Study

Clark University offers high-quality education to those interested in deepening their understanding of the corporate world and sharpening their expertise to become highly effective managers of people and resources.

To prepare leaders to meet the demands of the twenty-first century, Clark's Graduate School of Management encourages a global perspective. Both curriculum and faculty develop students to be insightful managers who understand the economic, technological, and political changes that are shaping the world's business communities. The program prepares managers not only to balance the complex and often conflicting demands of a changing work force but also to respond to a new mix of national and international competitors.

The Graduate School of Management offers an environment that features small classes, easy access to faculty members, and the stimulation that comes from exposure to a wide range of students from many different professional settings and levels of management experience.

The Graduate School of Management offers a Master of Business Administration (M.B.A.) degree program with a variety of concentrations and a Master of Science in Finance (M.S.F.). Clark University's management programs are internationally accredited by AACSB International–The Association to Advance Collegiate Schools of Business, the premier accrediting agency for business schools.

To accommodate students' schedules, classes and seminars are held during the morning, afternoon, and evening. Evening classes are held in two locations: Worcester and Framingham, Massachusetts.

Research Facilities

Personal computers, available exclusively for use by management students, are located in the MIS Laboratory in the Graduate School of Management. The Robert Hutchings Goddard Library houses 600,000 volumes as well as the Morton and Vivien Sigel Machine Readable Management Database in CD-ROM format. Extensive research facilities are also available through ten other local colleges and universities that compose the Worcester Consortium.

Financial Aid

Graduate assistantships and/or scholarships are awarded to more than 40 percent of the entering full-time class. Graduate assistantships require research, teaching, or administrative duties in exchange for tuition remission. Both scholarship and assistantship awards are based on merit.

Cost of Study

For the 2007–08 academic year, graduate tuition is $3020 per course unit. Other charges include a $50 application fee, a one-time student services fee of $1250, and an annual $80 student activities fee.

Living and Housing Costs

A limited number of University-owned apartments are available to graduate students through the Office of Housing and Residential Programs. Off-campus apartments are available in the immediate area at a cost of approximately $400 per person per month.

Student Group

The University has approximately 2,000 undergraduate and 900 graduate students. There are about 170 full-time and 140 part-time students enrolled at the Graduate School of Management.

Student Outcomes

The class of 2006 found employment in the following functional areas: advertising, marketing, and sales; finance and accounting; human resources; and other areas, including technology and operations. Employers of program graduates include American Express Financial Services, Deutsche Bank, Merrill Lynch, Saint-Gobain Bonded Abrasives, Smith Barney Citigroup, Fidelity Investments, World Bank, Genzyme, and Evergreen America Corporation.

Location

Worcester is one of the largest cities in New England. It is located in central Massachusetts, New England's high-technology area, within an hour's drive of Boston and near the region's numerous recreational attractions. The city has diversified industry and is distinguished as an educational center. The ten institutions of higher education in the Worcester area, which have more than 15,000 students enrolled, have formed the Worcester Consortium for Higher Education. Clark students have many opportunities to meet with area chief executive officers and senior executives through a variety of special programs.

The University

Clark University is an urban, independent university that was founded in 1887 as a graduate institution. By design, the University has remained small in order to offer its students the educational experience of close personal relationships among the faculty members and students.

Applying

The priority admission deadline for full-time M.B.A. applicants who wish to receive full consideration for scholarships and assistantships is April 1. The regular admission deadlines for the full-time M.B.A. program are June 1 for the fall semester and December 1 for the spring semester. After those dates, students are accepted on a space-available basis. The deadline for part-time M.B.A. applicants who wish to receive full consideration for scholarships and assistantships is July 1. The regular admission deadlines for the part-time M.B.A. program are August 1 for the fall semester and December 15 for the spring semester. After those dates, students are accepted on a space-available basis.

Fixed deadlines are in effect for applications to the M.S.F. program. Deadlines for full-time M.S.F. applicants are February 1 for the fall semester and November 1 for the spring semester. Part-time M.S.F. applicants must apply by July 1 for fall admission and December 15 for spring admission. All applicants who meet these deadlines are considered for scholarships and assistantships.

Admission to the M.B.A. and M.S.F. programs is based on prior academic performance (transcripts are required), GMAT/GRE scores, professional and extracurricular experiences, a personal statement, and letters of recommendation. All undergraduate majors are given equal weight in the admission decision.

Many part-time M.B.A. applicants take advantage of the opportunity to enroll through the Alternative Admissions Track. The Alternative Admissions Track allows applicants to apply for provisional admission before taking the GMAT/GRE, based on their prior academic record and professional experience. Part-time M.B.A. students who are admitted provisionally may take up to 4 units of course work before submitting GMAT or GRE scores. If the student achieves at least a 3.5 GPA on completion of 4 units of course work, the GMAT/GRE entrance requirement is waived. On request, further information is available from the Office of Admissions.

Students interested in the M.B.A. of M.S.F. programs should request program information through the General Admissions e-mail address. Those who wish to apply should complete the application form and submit the required supporting documents. When all supporting documents have been received, the application is reviewed by the Admissions Committee, which meets throughout the year.

Correspondence and Information

Lynn Davis
Director of Enrollment and Marketing
Graduate School of Management
Clark University
950 Main Street
Worcester, Massachusetts 01610-1477
Phone: 508-793-7406
Fax: 508-421-3825
E-mail: clarkmba@clarku.edu (General Admissions)
Web site: http://www.clarku.edu/mba

Clark University

THE FACULTY

Edward J. Ottensmeyer, Associate Professor of Management and Dean, Graduate School of Management; Ph.D., Indiana, 1983.
Margarete Arndt, Professor of Health Administration; D.B.A., Boston University, 1991.
Sarita Bhalotra, Affiliate Assistant Professor; Ph.D., Brandeis, 1997.
Barbara Bigelow, Professor of Management; Ph.D., MIT, 1987.
Mary Ellen Boyle, Associate Professor of Management; Ph.D., Boston College, 1997.
Robert C. Bradbury, Professor Emeritus of Health Administration; Ph.D., Ohio State, 1975.
Gary N. Chaison, Professor of Industrial Relations; Ph.D., SUNY at Buffalo, 1972.
Robin Chase, Lecturer; Ph.D., USC, 1992.
Pilsik Choi, Assistant Professor of Marketing; Ph.D., Illinois at Urbana-Champaign, 2005.
Keith S. Coulter, Associate Professor of Marketing; Ph.D., Connecticut, 1995.
John L. Crawley, Lecturer; J.D., New England Law, 1989.
Joan Cole Densberger, Affiliate Assistant Professor; J.D., Boston College, 1986.
Dileep G. Dhavale, Professor of Accounting; Ph.D., Penn State, 1975; CPA, CPIM.
Priscilla Elsass, Associate Professor of Management and Associate Dean, Graduate School of Management; Ph.D., Connecticut, 1992.
Donna M. Gallo, Visiting Instructor of Global Business; Ph.D. candidate, Massachusetts Amherst.
Jane N. Gilligan, Lecturer; M.A., Boston College, 1967.
Laura M. Graves, Associate Professor of Management; Ph.D., Connecticut, 1982.
Michael A. Holbrook, Lecturer; M.B.A., Anna Maria, 1990.
Gerald D. McCarthy, Lecturer; Ph.D., Pennsylvania, 1976.
Saeed Mohaghegh, Lecturer; M.A., Clark, 1986.
William F. Mosher, Visiting Instructor of Mathematics and Economics; M.A., Clark.
John Rainey, Lecturer; M.B.A., Babson, 1976.
Ruth E. Rowan, Lecturer; S.M., MIT, 1977.
Joseph Sarkis, Associate Professor of Operations Management; Ph.D., SUNY at Buffalo, 1992.
Inshik Seol, Assistant Professor of Accounting; Ph.D., Connecticut, 1996.
Richard B. Spurgin, Associate Professor of Finance; Ph.D., Massachusetts Amherst, 1995.
Joel S. Sternberg, Assistant Professor of Finance; Ph.D., Berkeley, 1986.
Maurry Tamarkin, Professor of Finance; Ph.D., Washington (St. Louis), 1979.
Kristie L. Thompson, Lecturer; M.Ed., Massachusetts Amherst.
Dennis Wadsworth, Lecturer; M.B.A., Notre Dame.
Russell D. Wass, Lecturer; M.S.M., MIT, 1989.
Jing Zhang, Assistant Professor of Management; Ph.D., SUNY at Albany, 2003.

Professor Mary-Ellen Boyle provides advice to M.B.A. students on their group project in Goddard Library.

Professor Maurry Tamarkin guides a Master of Science in Finance student on her finance project.

The front view of Jonas Clark Hall, the University's flagship building.

CLEMSON UNIVERSITY

Master of Business Administration

Programs of Study

The Clemson Master of Business Administration (M.B.A.) programs, both day and evening, provide advanced business education to prepare graduates for successful careers in a global market. M.B.A. students come from a wide variety of business and nonbusiness backgrounds.

The two-year day M.B.A. program (62 to 64 hours) is held on the Clemson campus. This intensive program starts in the fall only and allows students the flexibility to tailor their degree to meet specific career goals through four formal specializations—entrepreneurship and innovation, supply chain and information management, real estate finance, and marketing research—or by designing their own specialization. Such self-designed specializations have included accounting, architecture, bioengineering, construction management, consulting, engineering, finance, international trade, marketing, operations management, and tourism. Self-designed tracks also allow the pursuit of a second, dual master's degree (such as an M.B.A./M.S. in engineering or architecture), which can typically be earned in as little as one extra semester. The first year (34 hours) provides a strong foundation in advanced business topics. M.B.A. seminars include top industry speakers, company tours, career-enhancing workshops, and etiquette sessions. In the second year (28 to 30 hours), students take four specialization courses specific to their professional career objectives, three tools courses to strengthen analytical and managerial decision-making skills, two electives, and strategic management. During the summer, students typically do internships or study abroad.

The evening M.B.A. (33 to 44 hours) is offered in a live classroom setting in Greenville, South Carolina, at the University Center. Each class meets one night per week. Five foundation courses (11 hours) provide basic business knowledge and may be waived with prior, acceptable academic work. The eleven advanced-level classes (33 hours) include three electives and eight required courses in accounting, economics, finance, marketing, operations, organizational behavior, statistics, and strategic management. It typically takes two to three years to complete this program. Evening students may also pursue a dual master's degree.

Research Facilities

M.B.A. students engage in applied research projects through the Clemson University Center for International Trade, which enhances the ability of organizations and policy makers to respond effectively to a changing international economy; the Center for the Advancement of Marketing and Social Sciences, which connects students, faculty members, and organizations in solving customer-defined, market-related problems; and the Spiro Center for Entrepreneurial Leadership, which promotes entrepreneurial activity and economic development.

Financial Aid

Approximately 80 percent of the on-campus day students have graduate assistantships. Qualified applicants with at least two years of work experience and a nonbusiness undergraduate major have an excellent chance of obtaining an assistantship. In addition to reduced tuition rates of around 80 percent, graduate assistants receive an annual stipend of $6000. All domestic students may apply for Stafford loans, and those desiring part-time work find opportunities both on and off campus.

Cost of Study

Tuition for the on-campus day program in 2007–08 is estimated at $3641 per semester for in-state students and $7285 per semester for nonresidents. Graduate assistants pay a flat fee of $950 per semester and approximately $250 per course during the summer. Tuition for the evening program at the University Center is currently $535 per credit hour for in-state students and $918 per credit hour for nonresidents.

Living and Housing Costs

On-campus housing is available; for information, students should visit http://www.housing.clemson.edu. The cost of living in Clemson is quite low compared to the national average; students who choose to live off campus typically spend $300–$400 per month for rent, depending on location, amenities, roommates, and other factors.

Student Group

The ideal candidate for the day program has a nonbusiness undergraduate degree with a GPA of around 3.0, a solid GMAT score, and a couple of years of work experience. In the evening program, two years of work experience is required and no specific undergraduate major is needed. The combined programs have approximately 180 students. Twenty-nine percent are women, 65 percent attend the evening program, and 15 percent are international students.

Student Outcomes

M.B.A. students are hired by a wide variety of businesses and organizations located primarily in the southeastern part of the United States. Recent employers have included financial institutions, manufacturers, market researchers, real estate companies, consulting firms, pharmaceuticals, health-related companies, accounting firms, food services, construction companies, advertising firms, high-technology agencies, and the public sector. About 10 percent of the graduates continue their education by entering Ph.D. or J.D. programs.

Location

Clemson is a small, beautiful college town near the Blue Ridge Mountains and Lake Hartwell in Upstate South Carolina. The Upstate is one of the country's fastest-growing areas and is an important part of the I-85 corridor, a multistate area along Interstate 85 that runs from metro Atlanta to Richmond, Virginia, and encompasses Charlotte, North Carolina, and North Carolina's Research Triangle. Atlanta and Charlotte are each a 2-hour drive away. Many financial institutions and other industries have a major presence in the Upstate, including Wachovia, Bank of America, BMW, Bon Secours St. Francis Health System, Bosch North America, Bowater, Charter Communications, Ernst & Young, Fluor Corporation, IBM, Microsoft, Michelin of North America, and many others.

The University

Clemson is classified by the Carnegie Foundation as a Research University (high research activity), a category comprising just 10 percent of all graduate degree–granting universities in America. The University's mission is to fulfill the covenant between its founder and the people of South Carolina to establish a "high seminary of learning" through its responsibilities of teaching, research, and extended public service. The University has identified eight areas of academic emphasis that create collaborations that, in turn, help fulfill the University's mission.

Applying

Applicants may apply on the Web at http://www.grad.clemson.edu/p_apply.html. The application fee is $50. Complete application packages should be received by the appropriate M.B.A. office no later than four weeks prior to registration for the evening program and for the day program, by June 15 for domestic applicants and April 15 for international applicants.

Correspondence and Information

Day, on-campus M.B.A.:
The Clemson M.B.A. Program
124 Sirrine Hall
Clemson University
Clemson, South Carolina 29634-1315
Phone: 864-656-3975
Fax: 864-656-0947
E-mail: MBA@clemson.edu
Web site: http://business.clemson.edu/MBA/Info/Fulltime.htm

Evening, off-campus M.B.A.:
The Clemson Evening M.B.A. Program
University Center
P.O. Box 5616
225 South Pleasantburg Drive
Greenville, South Carolina 29606
Phone: 864-250-8888
Fax: 864-250-8889
E-mail: EMBA@clemson.edu
Web site: http://business.clemson.edu/MBA/Info/Parttime.htm

Clemson University

THE FACULTY AND THEIR RESEARCH

John C. Alexander Jr., Breazeale Professor of Financial Planning; Ph.D., Florida State. Financial planning.

Nagraj Balakrishnan, Professor; Ph.D., Purdue. Management.

Daniel K. Benjamin, Professor; Ph.D., UCLA. Economics.

Dudley W. Blair, Professor; Ph.D., Texas A&M. Economics.

Daniel J. Bradley, Assistant Professor; Ph.D., Kentucky. Economics.

E. Earl Burch Jr., Professor; Ph.D., Clemson. Mathematical science.

R. Stephen Cantrell, Professor; Ph.D., North Carolina State. Economics and statistics.

Les Carlson, Professor; Ph.D., Nebraska. Marketing.

L. Stephen Cash, Professor; J.D., Tennessee; LL.M., Washington (Seattle); CPA. Accounting.

Michael D. Crino, Professor; Ph.D., Florida. Management.

John Stephen Davis, Professor; Ph.D., Georgia Tech. Information and computer science.

Thomas L. Dickens, Professor; Ph.D., Texas A&M; CPA, CMA. Accounting.

Michael J. Dorsch, Associate Professor; Ph.D., Arkansas. Marketing.

William R. Dougan, Professor; Ph.D., Chicago. Economics.

Charles R. Duke, Professor; Ph.D., Texas at Arlington. Marketing.

Frances L. Edwards, Associate Professor; J.D., Kansas. Legal studies.

Lawrence D. Fredendall, Associate Professor; Ph.D., Michigan State. Operations management.

William B. Gartner, Arthur M. Spiro Professor of Entrepreneurial Leadership; Ph.D., Washington (Seattle). Business policy.

Roger Gomes, Associate Professor; Ph.D., Virginia Tech. Marketing.

David W. Grigsby, Professor and Associate Dean; Ph.D., North Carolina at Chapel Hill. Management.

Stephen J. Grove, Professor; Ph.D., Oklahoma State. Marketing.

John M. Harris Jr., Associate Professor; Ph.D., South Carolina. Finance.

Christopher D. Hopkins, Assistant Professor; Ph.D., Mississippi State. Marketing.

William E. Kilbourne, Professor; Ph.D., Houston. Marketing.

R. Lawrence Laforge, Alumni Professor; Ph.D., Georgia. Operations management.

Terry L. Leap, Professor and Department Chair; Ph.D., Iowa. Industrial relations.

Robert E. McCormick, Professor; Ph.D., Texas A&M. Economics.

Robert B. McElreath, Professor and Department Chair; Ph.D., Georgia State. Finance.

Mark A. McKnew, Professor and Associate Dean; Ph.D., MIT. Industrial engineering.

Jeffrey J. McMillan, Professor; Ph.D., South Carolina. Accounting.

Janis L. Miller, Associate Professor; Ph.D., Missouri–Columbia. Management.

John Mittelstaedt, Associate Professor; Ph.D., Iowa. Marketing.

Jesse N. Moore, Associate Professor; Ph.D., South Florida. Marketing.

Gregory M. Pickett, Professor and Department Chair; Ph.D., Oklahoma State. Marketing.

Dennis L. Placone, Professor; Ph.D., Pittsburgh. Economics.

Tina L. Robbins, Associate Professor; Ph.D., South Carolina. Management.

Curtis J. Simon, Associate Professor; Ph.D., SUNY at Binghamton. Economics.

Michael F. Spivey, Professor; Ph.D., Tennessee. Finance.

V. Sridharan, Professor; Ph.D., Iowa. Management.

Caron St. John, Professor; Ph.D., Georgia State. Management.

Wayne H. Stewart Jr., Associate Professor; Ph.D., North Texas. Management.

Fred S. Switzer, Professor; Ph.D., Illinois at Urbana-Champaign. Psychology.

Mary Anne Taylor, Professor; Ph.D., Akron. Industrial and organizational psychology.

Neil G. Waller, Professor; Ph.D., Texas. Finance.

Ralph E. Welton Jr., Professor and Department Director; Ph.D., LSU. Accounting.

Alan J. Winters, Professor; Ph.D., Texas Tech. Accounting.

CLEMSON UNIVERSITY

Master of Science in Management

Program of Study

The Department of Management at Clemson University awards the Master of Science in Management (M.S.M.) degree. The M.S.M. program, which currently offers a concentration only in operations management, is designed to provide a comprehensive education to current and future managers of manufacturing and service operations as well as to students who are interested in further study in operations management at the doctoral level. The program focuses on the capabilities and resources of operations and the role of operations in the formulation and implementation of organization strategies for both manufacturing and service industries. The program requires 30 semester hours of courses beyond the program's co-requisites as well as a final examination. Full-time students may complete the M.S.M. program in as little as one calendar year, depending on the co-requisite courses that may be needed.

Research Facilities

Students have access to an extensive computer network on campus. All users have access to the Internet, e-mail, and word processing and spreadsheet applications as well as a course management system that supports extensive file sharing, team communications, and project activities. Standard statistical packages and simulation software are also available.

The Clemson University libraries have a collection of more than 7,000 serial titles and 1,500,000 volumes that were developed to support the undergraduate and graduate curricula and research. Several commercial bibliographic databases and locally created full-text databases may be searched online from local and remote computers. The library is linked electronically through OCLC, Inc., to more than 11,000 other libraries worldwide for cataloging and interlibrary loan services.

The Department of Management also has a dedicated Manufacturing Management Lab, which provides access to manufacturing resource planning software.

Financial Aid

The Department of Management currently does not offer financial aid to students in the M.S.M. program.

Cost of Study

Tuition for 2007–08 is $3641 per semester for in-state students and $7285 per semester for nonresidents. Off-campus rates are $330 per hour for in-state students and $660 per hour for nonresidents. Graduate assistants pay a flat fee of $950 per semester and $315 per summer session. Graduate fellows pay South Carolina resident fees.

Living and Housing Costs

On-campus housing is available. For information, students should visit http://www.housing.clemson.edu. The cost of living in Clemson is quite low compared to the national average. Students who choose to live off the campus typically spend $300–$400 per month for rent, depending on location, amenities, roommates, etc.

Student Group

The M.S.M. program seeks students who are highly motivated to follow a business career path that focuses on operations management. Approximately 20 percent of the students in the program are women, virtually all students attend on a full-time basis, and more than 50 percent are international students.

Student Outcomes

M.S.M. graduates are employed as operations analysts, managers, and consultants in a variety of organizations, including Michelin, Milliken, ABB, Price Waterhouse Coopers, GE, Siemens, Schlumberger, FedEx, Ford, Sonoco, Accenture, Ahold, and Oracle. Several graduates have gone on to pursue a Ph.D. degree either at Clemson or another university.

Location

Clemson is a small, beautiful college town near the Blue Ridge Mountains and Lake Hartwell in upstate South Carolina. The Upstate is one of the country's fastest-growing areas and is the midpoint of the Charlotte-to-Atlanta I-85 corridor, a multistate area along Interstate 85 that runs from metro Atlanta to Richmond, Virginia, and encompasses Charlotte, North Carolina, and North Carolina's Research Triangle. Atlanta and Charlotte are each a 2-hour drive away. Many financial institutions and other industries have national headquarters for a major presence in the Upstate, including Wachovia, Bank of America, BMW, Bon Secours St. Francis Health System, Bosch North America, Bowater, Charter Communications, Ernst & Young, Fluor Corporation, IBM, Microsoft, Michelin of North America, and many others.

The University

Clemson is classified by the Carnegie Foundation as an RU/H: Research University (high research activity), a category comprising just 10 percent of all graduate degree–granting universities in America. The University's mission is to fulfill the covenant between its founder and the people of South Carolina to establish a "high seminary of learning" through its responsibilities of teaching, research, and extended public service. The University has identified eight areas of academic emphasis that create collaborations that, in turn, help fulfill the University's mission.

Applying

Applicants may apply on the Web at http://www.grad.clemson.edu/p_apply.html. Applications with a $50 nonrefundable fee should be received no later than five weeks prior to registration. Every required item in support of the application must be on file by that date. Students are advised to contact the department for the deadlines of the program of proposed study.

Correspondence and Information

Dr. Russell Purvis
Graduate Coordinator
Department of Management
106 Sirrine Hall
Clemson University
Clemson, South Carolina 29634-1305

Phone: 864-656-3770
Fax: 864-656-2015
E-mail: rlpurvi@clemson.edu
Web site: http://business.clemson.edu/managemt/Acad_Overview/L1_msmgt.html

Clemson University

THE FACULTY AND THEIR RESEARCH

Nagraj (Raju) Balakrishnan, Professor and Department Chair; Ph.D., Purdue. Operations and supply chain management, decision modeling, scheduling, transportation planning.

R. Stephen Cantrell, Professor; Ph.D., North Carolina State. Managerial economics, business statistics, statistical and research methods.

John S. Davis, Professor; Ph.D., Georgia Tech. Information systems, computer science, information systems in supply chain management, electronic commerce.

Scott C. Ellis, Assistant Professor; Ph.D., SUNY at Buffalo. Operations and supply chain management, logistics, transportation planning.

Lawrence D. Fredendall, Associate Professor; Ph.D., Michigan State. Operations and supply chain management, quality management, lean production.

William B. Gartner, Arthur M. Spiro Professor; Ph.D., Washington (Seattle). Entrepreneurship, leadership, entrepreneurial behavior, the use of narrative in the process of organizing.

Peter T. Gianiodis, Assistant Professor; Ph.D., Georgia. Strategic management, entrepreneurship, innovation management, commercialization, technology-based entrepreneurship, resource-based rivalry.

Kimberly M. Green, Assistant Professor; Ph.D., Indiana. Strategic management, entrepreneurship, corporate entrepreneurship, corporate venturing, strategic management of innovation firms.

David W. Grigsby, Professor; Ph.D., North Carolina at Chapel Hill. Organizational behavior, human resource management, bargaining/negotiation behavior, international strategic management.

Varun Grover, William S. Lee Distinguished Professor; Ph.D., Pittsburgh. Management information systems; strategic, process, organizational, and interorganizational impacts of IT.

Raymond M. Henry, Assistant Professor; Ph.D., Pittsburgh. Management information systems, IT governance, systems development, human–computer interaction.

Richard E. Klein Jr., Assistant Professor; Ph.D., Georgia State. Management information systems, electronic intermediation, digitally-enabled supply chain management initiatives.

Robert L. LaForge, Alumni Distinguished Professor; Ph.D., Georgia. Operations and supply chain management, operations planning, control systems, enterprise resource planning systems.

Terry L. Leap, Professor; Ph.D., Iowa. Organizational behavior and human resource management, white-collar crime, organizational deviance, counterproductive behaviors in organizations.

Mark A. McKnew, Professor; Ph.D., MIT. Management science, operations research, production/supply chain modeling, international programs.

Janis L. Miller, Associate Professor; Ph.D., Missouri. Decision modeling, international business, service recovery, international management.

J. Wayne Patterson, Professor; Ph.D., Arkansas. Business statistics, operations and supply chain management, theory of constraints, improvement management.

Russell L. Purvis, Associate Professor and Graduate Coordinator; Ph.D., Florida State. Management information systems, project management, IT implementation, the diffusion of innovations.

Tina L. Robbins, Associate Professor; Ph.D., South Carolina. Organizational behavior and human resource management, organizational justice, business ethics, innovations in distance learning.

Aleda V. Roth, Burlington Industries Professor; Ph.D., Ohio State. Operations and supply chain management, global operations, technology strategy, service innovation.

Philip L. Roth, Professor; Ph.D., Houston. Organizational behavior and human resource management, personnel selection, performance and research methods.

Kristin D. Scott, Assistant Professor; Ph.D., Kentucky. Organizational behavior and human resource management, organizational reward systems, dysfunctional organizational behavior, group dynamics.

V. Sridharan, Professor; Ph.D., Iowa. Operations and supply chain management, supply chain strategy, revenue management, interorganization information sharing.

Caron H. St. John, Professor; Ph.D., Georgia State. Operations strategy; competitive, technology, and operations strategies of new and established firms; management of innovation; regional clusters and innovation.

Wayne H. Stewart Jr., Associate Professor; Ph.D., North Texas. Strategic management, individual and team issues in venture creation and performance, strategic change and firm development, the organization-environment interface.

Jason B. Thatcher, Assistant Professor; Ph.D., Florida State. Management information systems, innovation and diffusion of information technology, individual characteristics and beliefs of the use of information technology, management of the IT workforce.

Thomas Zagenczyk, Assistant Professor; Ph.D., Pittsburgh. Organizational behavior, human resource management, employer-employee relationship, social influence in organizations, developmental relationships.

Yanfeng Zheng, Assistant Professor; Ph.D., Wisconsin–Madison. Strategic management, entrepreneurship, organizational learning, capability development.

CLEMSON UNIVERSITY

Ph.D. in Management

Programs of Study

The Department of Management at Clemson University awards a doctoral degree in management, with specializations in two tracks: operations management (OM) and information systems (IS).

The Ph.D. program is designed to produce scholars who are capable of contributing to the body of knowledge through research and teaching at leading U.S. and international universities. The OM track is concerned with the systems, processes, and activities that produce the goods and services of an organization. The IS track deals with the effective deployment, use, and impact of information technologies on individuals, groups, and organizations. The program requires 57 semester hours of course work, including 18 hours of dissertation credit, a comprehensive examination, and successful completion of the doctoral dissertation. Full-time students may complete the program in four calendar years. Faculty members are actively involved in guiding student research, which covers a wide spectrum of OM and IS issues. All Ph.D. students are required to obtain classroom teaching experience before graduation.

Research Facilities

Students have access to an extensive computer network on campus. All users have access to the Internet, e-mail, and word processing and spreadsheet applications as well as a course management system that supports extensive file sharing, team communications, and project activities. All Ph.D. student cubicles have dedicated high-speed Internet access. Standard statistical packages and simulation software are also available.

The Clemson University libraries have a collection of more than 7,000 serial titles and 1,500,000 volumes that were developed to support the undergraduate and graduate curricula and research. Several commercial bibliographic databases and locally created full-text databases may be searched online from local and remote computers. The library is linked electronically through OCLC, Inc., to more than 11,000 other libraries worldwide for cataloging and interlibrary loan services.

The Department of Management also has a dedicated Manufacturing Management Lab, which provides access to manufacturing resource planning software.

Financial Aid

The Department offers financial aid packages that are comparable to peer Ph.D. programs. Assistantships typically pay an annual stipend of $16,050 for 20 hours of duties per week and include significant tuition reduction. The stipend is slightly higher in semesters when the Ph.D. student teaches a class. Ph.D. assistantships are renewable for up to four years, pending satisfactory performance and degree progress. In addition to these assistantships, Graduate school fellowships ranging from $5000 to $15,000 may be awarded to outstanding Ph.D. students.

Cost of Study

Tuition for 2007–08 is $3641 per semester for in-state students and $7285 per semester for nonresidents. Off-campus rates are $330 per hour for in-state students and $660 per hour for nonresidents. Graduate assistants pay a flat fee of $950 per semester and $315 per summer session. Graduate fellows pay South Carolina resident fees.

Living and Housing Costs

On-campus housing is available. For information, students should visit http://www.housing.clemson.edu. The cost of living in Clemson is quite low compared to the national average. Students who choose to live off the campus typically spend $300–$400 per month for rent, depending on location, amenities, roommates, etc.

Student Group

The program has approximately 22 students, all of whom attend on a full-time basis. A significant percentage of students are women, and more than 50 percent are international students.

Student Outcomes

Recent Ph.D. graduates serve on the business school faculties of prominent national and international universities, including Auburn, Colorado, University of North Carolina at Charlotte, University of Texas at Arlington, Wichita State, and Kasetsart University (Thailand).

Location

Clemson is a small, beautiful college town near the Blue Ridge Mountains and Lake Hartwell in upstate South Carolina. The Upstate is one of the country's fastest-growing areas and is the midpoint of the Charlotte-to-Atlanta I-85 corridor, a multistate area along Interstate 85 that runs from metro Atlanta to Richmond, Virginia, and encompasses Charlotte, North Carolina, and North Carolina's Research Triangle. Atlanta and Charlotte are each a 2-hour drive away. Many financial institutions and other industries have national headquarters for a major presence in the Upstate, including Wachovia, Bank of America, BMW, Bon Secours St. Francis Health System, Bosch North America, Bowater, Charter Communications, Ernst & Young, Fluor Corporation, IBM, Microsoft, Michelin of North America, and many others.

The University

Clemson is classified by the Carnegie Foundation as an RU/H: Research University (high research activity), a category comprising just 10 percent of all graduate degree–granting universities in America. The University's mission is to fulfill the covenant between its founder and the people of South Carolina to establish a "high seminary of learning" through its responsibilities of teaching, research, and extended public service. The University has identified eight areas of academic emphasis that create collaborations that, in turn, help fulfill the University's mission.

Applying

The emphasis is on exceptionally talented students who exhibit the capabilities, desire, and motivation to succeed as an academic at a top-tier research institution. Applicants may apply on the Web at http://www.grad.clemson.edu/p_apply.html. Applications with a $50 nonrefundable fee should be received no later than five weeks prior to registration. Every required item in support of the application must be on file by that date. Students are advised to contact the department for the deadlines of the program of proposed study.

Correspondence and Information

Dr. Russell Purvis
Graduate Coordinator
106 Sirrine Hall
Department of Management
Clemson University
Clemson, South Carolina 29634-1305
Phone: 864-656-3770
Fax: 864-656-2015
E-mail: rlpurvi@clemson.edu
Web site: http://business.clemson.edu/managemt/Management_PhD/index.html

Clemson University

THE FACULTY AND THEIR RESEARCH

Nagraj (Raju) Balakrishnan, Professor and Department Chair; Ph.D., Purdue. Operations and supply chain management, decision modeling, scheduling, transportation planning.

R. Stephen Cantrell, Professor; Ph.D., North Carolina State. Managerial economics, business statistics, statistical and research methods.

John S. Davis, Professor; Ph.D., Georgia Tech. Information systems, computer science, information systems in supply chain management, electronic commerce.

Scott C. Ellis, Assistant Professor; Ph.D., SUNY at Buffalo. Operations and supply chain management, logistics, transportation planning.

Lawrence D. Fredendall, Associate Professor; Ph.D., Michigan State. Operations and supply chain management, quality management, lean production.

William B. Gartner, Arthur M. Spiro Professor; Ph.D., Washington (Seattle). Entrepreneurship, leadership, entrepreneurial behavior, the use of narrative in the process of organizing.

Peter T. Gianiodis, Assistant Professor; Ph.D., Georgia. Strategic management, entrepreneurship, innovation management, commercialization, technology-based entrepreneurship, resource-based rivalry.

Kimberly M. Green, Assistant Professor; Ph.D., Indiana. Strategic management, entrepreneurship, corporate entrepreneurship, corporate venturing, strategic management of innovation firms.

David W. Grigsby, Professor; Ph.D., North Carolina at Chapel Hill. Organizational behavior and human resource management, bargaining/negotiation behavior, international strategic management.

Varun Grover, William S. Lee Distinguished Professor; Ph.D., Pittsburgh. Management information systems; strategic, process, organizational, and interorganizational impacts of IT.

Raymond M. Henry, Assistant Professor; Ph.D., Pittsburgh. Management information systems, IT governance, systems development, human–computer interaction.

Richard E. Klein Jr., Assistant Professor; Ph.D., Georgia State. Management information systems, electronic intermediation, digitally-enabled supply chain management initiatives.

Robert L. LaForge, Alumni Distinguished Professor; Ph.D., Georgia. Operations and supply chain management, operations planning, control systems, enterprise resource planning systems.

Terry L. Leap, Professor; Ph.D., Iowa. Organizational behavior and human resource management, white-collar crime, organizational deviance, counterproductive behaviors in organizations.

Mark A. McKnew, Professor; Ph.D., MIT. Management science, operations research, production/supply chain modeling, international programs.

Janis L. Miller, Associate Professor; Ph.D., Missouri. Decision modeling, international business, service recovery, international management.

J. Wayne Patterson, Professor; Ph.D., Arkansas. Business statistics, operations and supply chain management, theory of constraints, improvement management.

Russell L. Purvis, Associate Professor and Graduate Coordinator; Ph.D., Florida State. Management information systems, project management, IT implementation, the diffusion of innovations.

Tina L. Robbins, Associate Professor; Ph.D., South Carolina. Organizational behavior and human resource management, organizational justice, business ethics, innovations in distance learning.

Aleda V. Roth, Burlington Industries Professor; Ph.D., Ohio State. Operations and supply chain management, global operations, technology strategy, service innovation.

Philip L. Roth, Professor; Ph.D., Houston. Organizational behavior and human resource management, personnel selection, performance and research methods.

Kristin D. Scott, Assistant Professor; Ph.D., Kentucky. Organizational behavior and human resource management, organizational reward systems, dysfunctional organizational behavior, group dynamics.

V. Sridharan, Professor; Ph.D., Iowa. Operations and supply chain management, supply chain strategy, revenue management, interorganization information sharing.

Caron H. St. John, Professor; Ph.D., Georgia State. Operations strategy; competitive, technology, and operations strategies of new and established firms; management of innovation; regional clusters and innovation.

Wayne H. Stewart Jr., Associate Professor; Ph.D., North Texas. Strategic management, individual and team issues in venture creation and performance, strategic change and firm development, the organization-environment interface.

Jason B. Thatcher, Assistant Professor; Ph.D., Florida State. Management information systems, innovation and diffusion of information technology, individual characteristics and beliefs of the use of information technology, management of the IT workforce.

Thomas Zagenczyk, Assistant Professor; Ph.D., Pittsburgh. Organizational behavior, human resource management, employer-employee relationship, social influence in organizations, developmental relationships.

Yanfeng Zheng, Assistant Professor; Ph.D., Wisconsin–Madison. Strategic management, entrepreneurship, organizational learning, capability development.

DEVRY UNIVERSITY

Keller Graduate School of Management
Master of Business Administration Program

Programs of Study

In today's rapidly changing business environment, managers' responsibilities are increasingly complex. Technological advances, increasing demographic diversity, and global competition have prompted an ever-growing need for highly skilled and adaptive managers in all fields. As one of the nation's largest M.B.A. programs, DeVry University's Keller Graduate School of Management's curriculum provides a unique blend of management theories and concepts and helps students apply these ideas to the realities of everyday business. Keller's faculty consists of practicing business professionals—leaders in the corporate community as well as in the classroom. These professionals bring business contacts as well as hands-on knowledge and experience to graduate students.

The M.B.A. program at DeVry University's Keller Graduate School of Management requires successful completion of sixteen courses (3 semester credit hours each). These include four management core courses, one quantitative course, and five program-specific courses, one of which is an integrative capstone course. Also required are six electives, which may be chosen in accounting, e-commerce, educational management, finance, general management, health services, human resources, information security, information systems, international business, marketing, project management, public administration, and telecommunications. The curriculum provides a solid business management foundation in critical areas such as information technology, leadership, new product development, and project and change management.

Keller's students are working adults who have multiple real-world demands. Class hours are designed to accommodate work and family responsibilities. Classes are offered in eight-week sessions during each of the three semesters per year. Courses are delivered in "blended" or "all-online" formats. In the blended format, students and faculty members meet face-to-face on-site for 3½ hours per week, either on weekday evenings or Saturdays, and also participate in an average of 2 hours of instructor-guided online activities. The all-online format integrates today's high-tech capabilities with proven methodology through DeVry University's Online Center. Whether individual courses are taken or entire degrees are earned online (http://online.keller.edu), students receive a solid education enhanced by the latest in interactive information technology (computer-mediated e-mail and threaded conversations, videotapes, and the Internet). Students can send feedback to and receive feedback from instructors as well as participate in various group and team activities with fellow online students. Distance learning courses demand the same dedicated student efforts as traditional classroom-based courses. Online students read course materials, write papers, conduct applied research, and take exams. Students have access to the same full range of support services they would receive if they were attending a traditional location.

For students who wish to complete their M.B.A. in less than 1½ years without disrupting their work week, the M.B.A. program is offered in an accelerated format on Saturdays. For students who wish to specialize in business administration without completing the entire M.B.A. degree program, a certificate option is available.

Research Facilities

A variety of accommodations are offered at all of the program's locations, and all provide comfortable areas in which to study, relax, and learn. Most centers include spacious classrooms, student lounges, and convenient hours for computer labs and information centers. The information centers, many of which are open 24 hours a day, seven days a week, offer Internet access to 300 databases, alternative texts, student study guides, career service materials, and periodicals.

Financial Aid

Keller M.B.A. students may apply for both subsidized and unsubsidized Federal Stafford Student Loans.

Cost of Study

At current rates, tuition per course (3 semester credit hours) differs by state, ranging from $1715 to $2050. After acceptance, new students pay a $100 deposit, which is credited toward the first term's tuition. Tuition is payable in full at registration or in installments of two or three payments (with small handling fees for the latter two choices). Books and materials average $175 per course.

Student Group

Students attending Keller Graduate School are working adults who bring their diverse experiences to the classroom. Nearly 7,000 professionals nationwide have turned to DeVry University's Keller Graduate School for their advanced business education. A bachelor's degree in business is not required to enter the program; more than half of all Keller students hold undergraduate degrees in nonbusiness fields.

Location

DeVry University offers graduate programs at more than seventy locations nationwide as well as online, enabling adult students to continue their education while continuing to meet their other responsibilities. In addition, having so many locations and options to choose from enables students to continue their programs of study even after job transfers, temporary assignments, or other relocations with the least possible disruption to their academic schedules.

Centers are located near major metropolitan areas with accessible transportation routes, keeping commuting time to a minimum. There are one or more centers in each of the following states: Arizona, California, Colorado, Florida, Georgia, Illinois, Indiana, Maryland, Minnesota, Missouri, Nevada, New York, North Carolina, Ohio, Oklahoma, Oregon, Pennsylvania, Tennessee, Texas, Utah, Virginia, Washington, and Wisconsin.

The School

The Keller Graduate School of Management was founded in 1973 on the idea that the most important components of management education are effective teaching and student mastery of practical management skills. In addition, the School has a long tradition of, and commitment to, serving working adults that is reflected in the flexibility and tenor of its programs.

Applying

For regular admission, applicants must hold a baccalaureate degree (in any field) from a U.S. institution that is accredited by, or in candidacy status with, a regional accrediting agency recognized by the U.S. Department of Education (international applicants must hold a degree equivalent to a U.S. baccalaureate degree); pass the Graduate Management Admission Test (GMAT) or the Graduate Record Examinations (GRE) or Keller's alternative admission test; complete a personal interview with an admissions representative; and complete a written application. Applicants with postbaccalaureate degrees from accredited graduate schools must complete an application and an interview as well as document their degree. An admissions test is not required for these applicants.

Students may begin their program in either of the two 8-week sessions offered each semester. There are three full semesters each year, beginning in July, November, and March. There is no application fee.

Correspondence and Information

Keller Graduate School of Management
DeVry University
One Tower Lane, 9th Floor
Oakbrook Terrace, Illinois 60181
Phone: 630-571-1960
Web site: http://www.keller.edu

DeVry University

THE FACULTY

Keller faculty members are working professionals who are effective communicators, coaches, and mentors as well as practitioners with extensive management experience. They deal with cutting-edge business and management issues and bring their expertise to the classroom, emphasizing theories, practices, and issues that most benefit students in the working world.

The faculty includes both part- and full-time instructors. Those who teach full-time commit most of their working hours to teaching and curricula development while remaining actively involved in business as consultants and participants in professional organizations. Part-time instructors are full-time managers whose teaching provides adult students with vital professional enrichment and perspectives. All faculty members have developed contacts and relationships with a variety of academic and professional fields and geographic locations. The relationships students develop with these instructors often lead to mentoring arrangements, professional contacts, and even job offers.

DUQUESNE UNIVERSITY

John F. Donahue Graduate School of Business
Master of Business Administration

Programs of Study

Fully accredited by AACSB International, the Donahue M.B.A. program prepares students to meet today's management challenges. The M.B.A. curriculum developed by the School's diverse faculty emphasizes learning that is current and managerially relevant, with a high potential for immediate application and impact. Participants deal with the pressing workplace and marketplace challenges confronting today's managers and executives. Both students who are working managers and full-time students participating in internships and collaborative work projects with the region's leading employers have the opportunity to immediately apply these lessons in professional activities.

The M.B.A. curriculum stresses the relationships among business disciplines to enable students to evaluate business activity as a series of value-added processes that contribute to a firm's competitiveness and profitability. Important contemporary business issues such as the ethical dimensions of decision making, the globalization of business, the impact of technology, the value chain, managing diversity, and leading change are emphasized. By being one of the few M.B.A. programs to require the Understanding the Value Chain course, the Donahue School is distinguished in its field. Provided with an overview of business as a process early in their course of study, students learn how business disciplines work together as a process to create value for customers, employees, and shareholders. Understanding the value chain lays the foundation for cross-disciplinary integration in the core M.B.A. curriculum. The focus on business as a process is reinforced again in Strategy Formulation and Implementation, a capstone experience that includes formal presentations to panels of business professionals.

The M.B.A. program is available on both a full-time and a part-time basis. Concentrations are offered in business ethics, environmental management, finance, health-care management, human resource management, information systems management, international business, marketing, management, supply chain management, and taxation.

Duquesne University's John F. Donahue Graduate School of Business also provides students with the opportunity to earn the M.B.A. degree by attending classes on a part-time basis on Saturdays. The program may be completed in eleven 12-week terms (less than three calendar years). In addition, the M.B.A. program can be completed at off-campus sites in Cranberry, Monroeville, and Latrobe, Pennsylvania.

The Donahue School offers students a unique opportunity to earn the joint M.B.A./M.S.I.S.M. degree. This combination of business and information systems studies provides participants with a competitive advantage as contemporary organizations aggressively seek business school graduates who have a depth of understanding of the link between key business functions and information technology. Students in the program need to complete 24 credits beyond the M.B.A. to earn the joint degree. This program is available to full- and part-time students.

The Donahue Graduate School of Business has developed important partnerships with other schools on the campus to offer dual-degree programs. The M.B.A. degree and degrees in corporate communication, environmental science and management, health-management systems, industrial pharmacy, leadership, liberal studies, law, nursing, and public policy are offered. In addition and upon prior approval, students may also take up to 6 elective credits in other graduate programs on campus.

There are also study-abroad opportunities for M.B.A. students. These for-credit experiences range from three weeks to an entire year.

Research Facilities

The School operates several independent centers designed to provide students and faculty members with an opportunity for professional development as well as provide services to the University and the community at large. Among the most active of the Business School's centers are the Investment Center, the Beard Center for Leadership in Ethics, the Chrysler Corporation Small Business Development Center, the Center for Corporate and Executive Education, the Center for Competitive Workforce Development, and the Center for International Regulatory Assistance.

Duquesne University's Investment Center offers students instant access to information and sophisticated analytical techniques in a classroom setting that mimics worldwide trading operations. The center provides data feeds that supply real-time news and market data on stocks, bonds, international markets, futures, and options and other securities. Also, a state-of-the-art technology center features three technology-rich classroom learning centers that provide access to enterprise resource planning (ERP) software applications, a networking laboratory, and a general computer laboratory available for use by students and faculty members in courses throughout the graduate curriculum.

Through its Distinguished Ethics Speaker Series, ethics courses, and student organizations, the Beard Center provides an invaluable focus and public forum for students to study the tangled ethical questions as they prepare for their careers in business. Promoting moral integrity and behavior through ethics education and training, the Donahue School's Eugene Beard Center for Leadership in Ethics prepares students to encounter moral challenges in the corporate world.

The Institute for Economic Transformation provides another way through which the Donahue School contributes to the economic development of the Western Pennsylvania economy. Much of the institute's work is funded by major Pittsburgh-based foundations and includes projects ranging from workforce development to studies that focus on the region's manufacturing base. The Institute's Center for Corporate Development and Center for Executive Education offer a wide range of noncredit seminars and workshops, some of which are available to students in the Donahue School.

The mission of the Small Business Development Center is to further the economic development of the region. M.B.A. students are provided with an opportunity to work on the center's projects through various practicums.

The University's Gumberg Library houses nearly 500,000 volumes, more than 3,700 journal titles, and an extensive microprint and audiovisual center. Other library facilities include an online card catalog and a CD-ROM center that gives students access to hundreds of additional periodicals not physically housed in the library.

Financial Aid

A limited number of graduate assistantships, which provide up to 9 credits of tuition remission each semester and a monthly cash stipend, are available to full-time students.

Cost of Study

Tuition for the 2005–06 academic year was $660 per credit. There was also a $69 University fee charged for each credit.

Living and Housing Costs

Room and board were $3741 per semester, based on double occupancy. Housing is also available off campus. The University's Office of Residence Life can assist students in locating off-campus housing.

Student Group

The student body of approximately 350 students is diverse. Full-time students, who make up approximately 25 percent of the enrollment, get an enriching experience by sharing classes with full-time business professionals who are working toward their degrees on a part-time basis. Part-time students bring an average of five years of professional work experience to the classroom, providing a rich source of real-world issues that add value to the educational experience. The student body also represents countries from around the world, including those in Africa, Asia, Europe, and Latin America, who bring an important international dimension to the program.

Location

Long noted as one of the world's great business centers, Pittsburgh combines the features of big-city living with many of the charms and personal characteristics of a much smaller town. Pittsburgh has one of the largest concentrations of corporate headquarters in the United States and has developed a strong civic identity and sense of pride in its rebirth as a modern urban community. Students from Duquesne and other colleges and universities in the city can choose from a wide variety of cultural, social, and sporting events and programs.

The University

Nestled in a private 43-acre campus in the heart of Pittsburgh, Duquesne University provides a unique world-renowned education that continues to be grounded in the values of the Holy Spirit Fathers who founded it in 1878. Faculty members are recognized time and again both nationally and internationally for their instruction and research, and their support and encouragement provide an energetic and productive environment in which students thrive.

Applying

Candidates who have earned an undergraduate degree from an accredited four-year college or university (or its equivalent in another country) are eligible for admission. Admissions criteria include the undergraduate grade point average; the quality of undergraduate course work completed; scores on the Graduate Management Admissions Test; at least two letters of recommendation from those who can make reasonable judgments on the candidate's potential for graduate study, including professors and/or business associates; and a personal essay. International students are required to provide proof of adequate financial support and, if their native language is not English, take the Test of English as a Foreign Language (TOEFL). The application fee is $50 (waived for online applicants).

Correspondence and Information

John F. Donahue Graduate School of Business
704 Rockwell Hall
Duquesne University
600 Forbes Avenue
Pittsburgh, Pennsylvania 15282

Phone: 412-396-6276
E-mail: grad-bus@duq.edu
Web site: http://www.bus.duq.edu/grad

Duquesne University

THE FACULTY AND THEIR RESEARCH

The faculty members of the Donahue Graduate School of Business are committed to teaching excellence, scholarship that focuses on real business problems, and developing creative academic-business partnerships. The academic and professional experiences of the faculty members are complemented by the executive adjunct faculty members who teach classes in their areas of expertise, directly relating their daily experiences to the material covered in the courses. Graduate students benefit from exposure to a roster of executives who share their knowledge and experience.

Priscilla Austin, Assistant Professor of Accounting; M.B.A., Duquesne; CPA. Financial accounting, auditing.

Philip L. Baird III, Associate Professor of Finance and Chair, Finance and Investment Management; M.B.A., Ph.D., Tennessee. Economic analysis of U.S. Treasury security transactions data, developing software for fixed income trading applications, mergers and acquisitions and derivatives.

Vashishta Bhaskar, Assistant Professor of Finance and Director, Investment Center of Finance; M.B.A., Penn State. Investments, commodity and futures markets, asset allocation, rule-based security selection.

George Bodnar, Associate Professor of Accounting; M.B.A., Ph.D., Pennsylvania (Wharton). Auditing information services, educational software development.

James Burnham, Professor of Finance; Ph.D., Washington (St. Louis). Domestic and international financial markets and institutions, international trade policy with special attention on the steel industry, local government finance.

Petros Christofi, Associate Professor of Management Science; Ph.D., Penn State. Productivity and TQM analysis.

Antony Davies, Associate Professor of Economics; Ph.D., SUNY at Albany. Forecasting and rational expectations, consumer behavior, public policy.

Ronald J. Dick, Assistant Professor of Marketing; M.B.A., Saint Joseph's (Pennsylvania); Ed.D., Temple. Sports marketing.

Matthew Drake, Assistant Professor of Supply Chain Management; M.S.I.E., Ph.D., Georgia Tech. Supply chain coordination and collaboration, revenue management for nontravel industries, ethics of supply chain management, behavioral decision-making analysis in supply chain management, pedagogical tools for teaching operations and supply chain management.

Mordechai Gal-Or, Assistant Professor of Information Systems Management; Ph.D., Pittsburgh. Addressable advertising, multiple classifier systems, data mining, knowledge discovery in databases, data driven application development.

Mark Giallonardo, Adjunct Instructor of Taxation; J.D., Duquesne; L.L.M., Villanova. Business taxation, with a special emphasis on flow-through entities and Pennsylvania state taxation.

Sharon Green, Associate Professor of Accounting; M.B.A., Indiana of Pennsylvania; Ph.D., Pittsburgh. Innovative teaching methods.

Audrey Guskey, Associate Professor of Marketing; M.B.A., Ph.D., Pittsburgh. Consumer trends, service encounters, customer satisfaction.

David Hanson, Associate Professor of International Business; Ph.D., Florida; J.D., Michigan. European market and related quality standards.

Kathleen S. Hartzel, Associate Professor of Information Systems Management and Chair, Information Systems, Supply Chain, and Operations Management; M.B.A., Penn State; Ph.D., Pittsburgh. Management of attitudes and behaviors during system development and use, effects of computer-mediated support on decision making and attitudes, impact of interorganizational information systems on interorganizational cooperation and competition.

Trevor H. Jones, Associate Professor of Information Systems Management; Ph.D., Drexel; CIMA. Information systems disaster recovery planning, information security.

Maryellen Kelly, Assistant Professor of Marketing; M.B.A., Ohio State; Ph.D., Union (Ohio). Product management, innovation and entrepreneurship, Pennsylvania small-cap companies, qualitative research, innovative pedagogy.

Lance Kurke, Associate Professor of Leadership and Change Management and Director, M.B.A. Program; M.B.A., M.A., Ph.D., Cornell. Business strategy and leadership.

Conway Lackman, Associate Professor of Marketing; Ph.D., Cincinnati. New product development, marketing intelligence, market forecasting.

Ohn M. Lanasa, Associate Professor of Marketing and Chair, Marketing and Entrepreneurship; M.B.A., Duquesne; Ph.D., Pittsburgh. New product development, marketing education.

S. Jay Liebowitz, Associate Professor of Organizational Behavior of Leadership and Change Management; Ph.D., Tennessee. Effects of organizational behavior on the success of global, virtual, new product development teams; managing high-potential employees; transformational leadership; managing resistance to change; teaching online; self-managing work teams; terminating employees appropriately.

Gustav Lundberg, Professor of Quantitative Sciences; Ph.D., SUNY at Albany. Decision support and expert systems, modeling and simulation.

Matthew Marlin, Professor of Economics and Chair, Economics and Quantitative Science; Ph.D., Florida State. Forensic economics, municipal bonds, global economic perspectives.

J. Kenneth Matejka, Professor of Leadership and Change Management; M.B.A., Missouri–Kansas City; Ph.D., Arkansas. Visionary leadership, motivation practices, leading organizational change.

John Mawhinney, Executive Associate Professor in Residence of Supply Chain Management; M.B.A., Pittsburgh. Developing metrics to evaluate the impact of supply chain management strategies on corporate performance, supply chain management outcomes assessment in higher education.

Thomas McCue, Associate Professor of Finance; M.B.A., Virginia Tech; Ph.D., North Carolina at Chapel Hill. Institutional investment in real estate valuation, corporate applications of derivatives, relationship between the macroeconomy and investment returns.

Elaine McGivern, Assistant Professor of Quantitative Sciences; Ph.D., Pittsburgh. Design of new methodologies for the study of moral reasoning processes, e-business adoption strategies of midsize manufacturers.

Thomas J. Murrin, Distinguished Service Professor of Leadership and Change Management; D.M.S., Duquesne; L.H.D., Fordham. Contemporary global issues and the business environment.

Brian Nagle, Associate Professor of Accounting; Ph.D., Saint Louis. Auditor cognition, going concern decisions, impacts of Sarbanes-Oxley.

David Pentico, Professor of Management Science of Operations Management; Ph.D., Carnegie Mellon. Development and testing of heuristics in scheduling and production and inventory planning control systems.

Thomas A. Pollack, Associate Dean, Academic Support and Accreditation, and Associate Professor of Information Systems Management; M.Ed., Duquesne; Ph.D., Pittsburgh. Information ethics and security and information technology curricula.

William D. Presutti Jr., Associate Professor of Supply Chain Management; Ph.D., Carnegie Mellon. E-procurement strategy, impact of reverse auctions on buyer-supplier relationships, making a business case for e-procurement.

Stephen Rau, Associate Professor of Accounting; M.B.A., Ph.D., Pittsburgh. Auditors' cognitive processes, ethics, Sarbanes-Oxley, risks and controls associated with technology implementation.

Jeffrey Alan Roberts, Assistant Professor of Information Systems Management; M.B.A., Texas; M.S., Ph.D., Carnegie Mellon. Information systems.

Kenneth Saban, Associate Professor of Marketing; M.S.J., Northwestern; Ph.D., Pittsburgh. Internet security.

Jan N. Saykiewicz, Professor of Marketing and International Marketing; Ph.D., D.Sc., Central School of Planning and Statistics (Warsaw). Comparative marketing systems and issues in international marketing.

Seleshi Sisaye, Professor of Accounting; M.B.A., Ph.D., Pittsburgh; Ph.D., Cornell. The behavioral issues relating to the practice of managerial accounting.

Nagaraj Sivasubramaniam, Chair, Leadership and Change Management, Ethics and Global Business, and Associate Professor of Leadership and Change Management; Ph.D., Florida International. The effects of leadership at multiple levels on performance, evolution of capabilities in start-ups, and consequences of managerial actions on firm survival.

William E. Spangler, Associate Dean, Academic Affairs and Research, and Associate Professor of Information Systems Management; M.B.A., Hawaii; Ph.D., Pittsburgh. Computational modeling for decision support in complex systems, machine learning and data mining.

Gerald Tatar, Associate Professor of Information Systems Management; M.Ed., California of Pennsylvania; Ph.D., Pittsburgh. Computer crime and security; network operating systems, including Windows server 2003 and Redhat Linux Fedora Core 5.

James Weber, Professor of Business Ethics and Director, Beard Center for Leadership in Ethics of Leadership and Change Management; M.B.A., St. Louis; Ph.D., Pittsburgh. Ethical issues in business and managers' moral reasoning.

Valerie Trott Williams, Assistant Professor of Accounting and Director, Accounting Honors Institute of Accounting; M.B.A., Pittsburgh; CPA, CIA, CHFP. The integration of enterprise resource planning systems into business school curricula, accounting information systems, forensic auditing.

EASTERN KENTUCKY UNIVERSITY

Program in Business Administration

Program of Study	Eastern Kentucky University's (EKU) M.B.A. program is committed to providing students with the tools and experiences they need to broaden their professionalism and add value to their companies and the communities where they live. Classes are scheduled on nights and weekends and are taught by full-time professors who integrate technology into the curriculum and assign projects based on real-world issues. Students may attend on a full-time or part-time basis. The program is accredited by AACSB International–The Association to Advance Collegiate Schools of Business.
	Students must complete 30 credit hours of course work to earn the degree. These include 24 hours in core courses, covering business communications, accounting, information systems, financial management, and other relevant business topics, plus 6 hours in electives such as finance, auditing, global management, and taxation. The program culminates in a capstone course and either a comprehensive examination or a master's thesis. Students are required to have taken prerequisite courses in accounting, management, marketing, finance, economics, and computer information systems.
	Beginning in fall 2007, M.B.A. students may select concentrations in accounting or integrated communications. Students choosing the accounting option experience a unique blend of M.B.A. courses designed to complement those who have an accounting background. The additional courses offered in the accounting option help students prepare for the professional certification exams. Students choosing the integrated communications option experience a unique integration of public relations, marketing, and corporate communications courses. This option delivers a set of integrated communication methodologies and experiences to address strategic communication initiatives in a corporate setting.
Research Facilities	The John Grant Crabbe Library and Thomas and Hazel Little addition contains 760,000 volumes and seats more than 2,100 students. The building houses several large reading rooms as well as smaller areas for individual and group study. Other libraries house special collections and University archives. The libraries provide many Web-based databases, including e.Quest, the online catalog. Most can be accessed from any campus or off-campus center and from home or remote locations.
Financial Aid	Graduate assistants perform such duties as teaching, laboratory supervision, research- or service-related tasks, and residence hall work. The usual stipend is $5000 per semester, but some awards may be higher. The Jack Kent Cooke Foundation Scholarship Program provides fellowships of up to $50,000 per year. The Federal Perkins Loan is awarded to exceptionally needy students at a 5 percent interest rate. The Federal Stafford Student Loan is available to students who are enrolled at least half-time; the maximum is $8500 in subsidized loans or $18,500 in unsubsidized loans. The Student Aid Society Emergency Loan Program provides emergency short-term loans.
Cost of Study	In 2006–07, tuition was $311 per credit hour for Kentucky residents and $883 for nonresidents. Fees were $341 per credit for residents and $935 for nonresidents.
Living and Housing Costs	Single students may live in an apartment on campus for $260 per month. Housing is also available for married students and their families. Meal plans range from $300 to $500 per semester. Students living off campus can expect to spend $375 to $500 per month in rent, depending on apartment size and location. Other expenses, including books and incidentals, typically cost $1000 to $1200 per semester.
Student Group	The program is designed for working professionals in central Kentucky. Many students hold undergraduate degrees in business, and many others hold nonbusiness degrees, including engineering, health sciences, and social sciences. Most of the students in the program are already involved in their business careers and want to use the M.B.A. as a vehicle for advancement into upper management. There are approximately 140 students currently active in the program.
Location	Situated near the heart of the Bluegrass, Richmond is one of Kentucky's fastest-growing cities, offering a regional shopping mall, theaters, live entertainment, fine dining, and cultural events and activities. Many areas of historic interest are nearby, including Fort Boonesborough State Park, the birthplace of Kentucky. Richmond is within driving distance of Lexington, Cincinnati, and Louisville and is easily accessible from major highways.
The University	Eastern Kentucky University was founded in 1906 as a comprehensive public university dedicated to high-quality instruction, scholarship, and service. Today, it offers 168 liberal arts, preprofessional, and applied and technical degree programs on six campuses and serves more than 16,000 students per year. Since its inception, EKU has been driven by its core values, including civic responsibility, dignity and integrity, excellence and innovation, and opportunity and access, and it employs these values in its efforts to serve the community.
Applying	Prospective students must submit a completed application, official undergraduate transcripts showing a GPA of 2.5 or higher, official GMAT scores of 410 or higher, a current resume, a statement of personal and professional objectives, three letters of recommendation, and a $35 application fee. The deadline to apply is July 9 for fall admission, November 20 for spring admission, and April 5 for summer admission.
Correspondence and Information	Master of Business Administration Program Business and Technology Center, Room 252 Eastern Kentucky University 521 Lancaster Avenue Richmond, Kentucky 40475 Phone: 859-622-1775 E-mail: mba@eku.edu Web site: http://www.mba.eku.edu

Eastern Kentucky University

THE FACULTY AND THEIR RESEARCH

Faridah Awang, Assistant Professor of Corporate Communications and Technology; Ph.D., Southern Illinois Carbondale, 2002. Intercultural communication, ethical communication, workplace skills, communication technology.

Steve Brown, Professor of Management and Marketing and of Administrative Communication; Ph.D., Southern Illinois, 1974. Strategy, entrepreneurship, operations, quality management, supply chain.

Lana Carnes, Associate Professor of Corporate Communications and Technology; Ed.D., Kentucky, 1996. International business communication, communication in the workplace.

Mark Case, Assistant Professor of Marketing; Ph.D., Old Dominion, 2004. Multicultural comparative research methods, political advertising, marketing strategy.

Richard Chen, Professor of Accounting, Finance, and Information Systems; Ph.D., Texas, 1980. Managerial accounting.

Bjoern Claassen, Assistant Professor of Accounting, Finance, and Information Systems; Ph.D., Mississippi, 2005. Efficient markets, stock price performance related to analyst recommendations.

Jan Colbert, Professor of Accounting, Finance, and Information Systems; Ph.D., Georgia, 1984. Internal control audits and Section 404, ethics awareness.

Norb Elbert, Professor and Chair; D.B.A., Kentucky, 1976. International human resource management.

Allen Engle, Professor of Management; D.B.A., Kentucky, 1990. Ethics, international management, human resource management.

Zekeriya Eser, Assistant Professor of Finance; Ph.D., Kentucky, 2007. Agency problems in mutual fund management, Japanese banking system, Japanese stock market, numerical methods in derivative pricing, performance measurement in actively managed mutual funds.

Ed Fenton, Professor of Accounting, Finance, and Information Systems; D.B.A., Kentucky, 1986. Forensic accounting, litigation support, natural resource taxation.

S. J. Garner, Professor of Marketing; D.B.A., Mississippi State, 1983. Advertising, consumer behavior topics, ethics in marketing, marketing education, promotion techniques, services marketing.

Tim Kiessling, Assistant Professor of Management; Ph.D., Oklahoma, 2005. International human resources, mergers and acquisitions, strategy, top management team.

Chang-Yang Lin, Professor of Accounting, Finance, and Information Systems; Ph.D., Arkansas, 1983. Project management, database migration, hypermedia.

Teresa McGlone, Professor of Marketing; D.B.A., Kentucky. Marketing research design, quantitative methods, integration of marketing and management science tools to solve defined marketing problems.

Mike Roberson, Professor of Management; Ph.D., Tennessee, 1985. Applied statistics and psychometrics, competency/skills assessment centers, global business management, HR metrics, human capital strategy and systems, managing people for competitive advantage.

Marcel Robles, Associate Professor of Corporate Communications and Technology; Ph.D., North Dakota, 1996. Assessment, business communication, educational technology.

Judy Spain, Professor and Program Director; J.D., Capital, 1981. Employment and labor law, ethics, security law.

FAIRFIELD UNIVERSITY

Charles F. Dolan School of Business

Programs of Study

The Charles F. Dolan School of Business at Fairfield University offers the following graduate programs: Master of Business Administration (M.B.A.), Master of Science in Accounting, Master of Science in Finance, Master of Science in Taxation, and Certificate Programs for Advanced Study. The School is accredited by AACSB International–The Association to Advance Collegiate Schools of Business.

The M.B.A. program has three components: core courses, breadth courses, and specialization or concentration courses. The core curriculum (18 credits) includes financial reporting, analysis and markets, domestic and global economic environments of organizations, creation and distribution of goods and services, and human behavior in organizations. Most students are able to waive selected core courses on the basis of previous course work or relevant work experience. Students must also take 18 credits of breadth courses as well as four concentration courses (12 credits) in accounting, finance, general management, human resource management, information systems and operations management, international business, marketing, or taxation. The elective (a designated research course in the student's area of concentration) is usually taken following the completion of the core and breadth courses. The M.B.A. curriculum includes practical applications of critical business skills, including negotiation and dispute resolution and market valuation and analysis. Many courses emphasize the role of technology in the competitive position of the firm in a global economy.

The Master of Science in Accounting (M.S.A.) program is designed to prepare students for careers in the field of accounting. Students learn to use professional and other resources to critically consider and resolve complex issues associated with accounting and financial reporting. Students also learn to analyze accounting issues from an ethical perspective. The program consists of ten 3-credit courses (seven required and three electives), and it is designed to address the educational requirements for certification in Connecticut and most other states.

The Master of Science in Finance program provides unique opportunities for individuals who want to enhance their career opportunities in the areas of investments, corporate finance, or banking. The program consists of ten 3-credit courses (seven required and three electives) and is especially useful for those who want to pursue advanced certification, such as the CFA, CFM, and CFP.

The Master of Science in Taxation program is designed to prepare students for careers in the field of taxation. Students learn to use a variety of tax authorities (i.e., statutory, judicial, and administrative) and other resources to critically consider and resolve complex tax issues. The program consists of ten 3-credit courses (seven required and three electives), and it is especially useful for industry managers and executives, financial services and public accounting professionals, and others seeking a specialized education in taxation.

The Certificate Programs for Advanced Study in accounting, finance, human resource management, information systems and operations management, international business, marketing, and taxation provide opportunities for qualified professionals to enhance their competency and update their skills in an area of specialization. The 15-credit program is designed to provide a complete integration to the theory and practice of contemporary business. Students must complete all requirements within three years of the start of their course work.

All students are expected to demonstrate and/or attain proficiency in the use of microcomputers and the mainframe computer during their program of study. Computer use is integrated throughout the curriculum. The School provides fully equipped microcomputer labs for student use, and each student may obtain a computer account for access to the University's mainframe systems.

Research Facilities

The Nyselius Library contains approximately 300,000 volumes, the equivalent of 92,000 volumes in microform, and 1,800 journals and newspapers, with extensive business collections, including World Wide Web subscription databases such as Disclosure Global Access, IAC's Business & Company ASAP, RIA Checkpoint, Westlaw, LexisNexis, and Encyclopedia Britannica Online. ABI-Inform on CD-ROM is also available. Access to library facilities throughout the area is available as well. The library recently completed a major expansion and renovation project, doubling its size and including a 24-hour computer lab and increased group study space. The computer center includes a DEC Alpha 2100, with terminals throughout the campus; buildings on the campus are equipped with fiber optics, and a campuswide network of microcomputers is in place.

Financial Aid

Scholarship aid is limited. Most students are employed and receive substantial financial support from their employers. Students may apply for financial assistance after having been accepted into a program. Assistance is usually limited to U.S. citizens.

Cost of Study

In 2006–07, tuition was $600 per credit hour. The registration fee was $25 per semester.

Living and Housing Costs

The large majority of graduate students live off campus in the surrounding communities. Housing costs in the area vary widely.

Student Group

Students in Fairfield's M.B.A. program have a wide variety of academic and work experience. Although some students in the program are recent college graduates, the average age of students is 27, with four years of full-time work experience. The student body represents many nations, with connections to many major international corporations.

Location

Fairfield University is situated in a suburban area on the Connecticut shore of Long Island Sound about 1 hour from New York City and 3 hours from Boston. The University is in America's academic corridor, along with many cultural, recreational, and intellectual activities.

The University and The School

Fairfield University is a coeducational institution of higher learning founded by the Society of Jesus in 1942 and proudly aspires to the Jesuit tradition of developing the whole intellectual potential of its students and creating the true sense of ethical and social responsibility within them. Fairfield partners with Jesuit universities throughout the U.S. to facilitate the transfer of courses and degree completion should graduate students be required to relocate to another geographic area. The 200-acre campus is among the most beautiful in the country.

The Charles F. Dolan School of Business includes modern classrooms, team workrooms, and state-of-the-art technology that make it a model teaching and learning environment. The School has been the recipient of several major corporate grants for support of curriculum and faculty development. A close relationship exists with dozens of major corporations in Fairfield County, which is the third-largest center of corporate headquarters in the nation. The School also has an outstanding Advisory Council of business leaders from the nation's largest corporations. Corporate executives participate extensively as guests and lecturers in many courses every semester.

Applying

The criteria for admission to the M.B.A. and the M.S. programs are a strong undergraduate grade point average and an appropriate score on the Graduate Management Admission Test (GMAT). A formula score of at least 1100, derived by multiplying the grade point average by 200 and adding the GMAT score, is usually required for admission. The $55 application fee, complete official transcripts of all undergraduate and graduate work, two letters of recommendation, and a letter of self-evaluation or an enumeration of work experience must also be submitted.

Applicants to the Certificate Program for Advanced Study must submit a completed Application for Admission for the Certificate Program form, a $55 application fee, a recent resume, and official transcripts of previous undergraduate and graduate work. Students applying to the certificate program are not required to submit GMAT scores.

The International Programs and Student Services Offices offer special services for international students. International students must attend on a full-time basis and fulfill visa eligibility requirements, including evidence of full financial support. A score of 550 or higher on the Test of English as a Foreign Language (TOEFL) is also required.

Applications are accepted on a revolving basis and should be completed by August 15 for the fall semester, December 15 for the spring semester, and May 15 for the summer semester. International students should apply by June 15 for fall admission and November 15 for spring admission.

Correspondence and Information

Committee on Graduate Admissions
Charles F. Dolan School of Business
Fairfield University
1073 North Benson Road
Fairfield, Connecticut 06824
Phone: 203-254-4180
Fax: 203-254-4029
E-mail: gradadmis@mail.fairfield.edu
Web site: http://www.fairfield.edu/x757.html

Fairfield University

THE FACULTY

Students in the Charles F. Dolan School of Business are engaged with a faculty that is distinguished by scholarly achievements and business experience. Faculty members have published books and articles, presented their research at national and international conferences, and earned international awards for research and teaching.

Christy Ashley, Assistant Professor of Marketing; M.B.A., Miami (Florida); Ph.D., Rhode Island.
Bharat B. Bhalla, Professor of Finance; M.B.A., Delhi (India); Ph.D., Cornell.
Mousumi Bhattacharya, Associate Professor of Management; M.B.A., Jadavpur (India); Ph.D., Syracuse.
Bruce Bradford, Associate Professor of Accounting; M.S., Ph.D., Virginia Tech; M.B.A., Arkansas State; D.B.A., Memphis; CPA.
Gerard M. Campbell, Associate Professor of Information Systems and Operations Management; M.B.A., Connecticut; M.S., Rensselaer; Ph.D., Indiana.
Paul Caster, Associate Professor of Accounting; M.B.A., Chicago; Ph.D., North Texas; CPA.
Gerald O. Cavallo, Associate Professor of Marketing; M.B.A., Columbia; M.B.A., Ph.D., CUNY.
J. Michael Cavanaugh, Associate Professor of Management; M.S., Georgetown; M.B.A., Rensselaer; Ph.D., Massachusetts.
Arjun Chaudhuri, Rev. Thomas R. Fitzgerald, S.J., Professor of Marketing; M.A., Calcutta; M.A., Ph.D., Connecticut.
Thomas E. Conine Jr., Professor of Finance; M.B.A., Ph.D., NYU.
JoAnn Drusbowsky, Visiting Professor of Accounting; M.S., New Haven.
Catherine Giapponi, Assistant Professor of Management; M.B.A., Connecticut; Sc.D., New Haven.
Donald E. Gibson, Associate Professor of Management; M.A., San Francisco State; M.B.A., Ph.D., UCLA.
Xin (James) He, Professor of Information Systems and Operations Management; M.B.A., Shanghai; Ph.D., Penn State.
Walter F. Hlawitschka, Associate Professor of Finance; M.B.A., Cornell; M.A., Ph.D., Virginia.
Christopher L. Huntley, Associate Professor of Information Systems and Operations Management and Chair, Information Systems and Operations Management Department; Ph.D., Virginia.
Lucy V. Katz, Robert C. Wright Professor of Business Law, Ethics, and Dispute Resolution; J.D., NYU.
Gregory D. Koutmos, Gerald M. Levin Professor of Finance and Chair, Finance Department; Ph.D., CUNY Graduate Center.
Robert W. Kravet, Assistant Professor of Accounting; M.S., Massachusetts; CPA.
Nikiforos Laopodis, Associate Professor of Finance; Ph.D., Catholic University.
Patrick S. Lee, Associate Professor of Operations Management and Information Technology; Ph.D., Carnegie Mellon.
Sooyeon Nikki Lee-Wingate, Assistant Professor of Marketing; M.B.A., Seoul National University; M.Phil., Ph.D., NYU.
Mark Ligas, Associate Professor of Marketing and Chair, Marketing Department; Ph.D., Connecticut.
Lisa A. Mainiero, Professor of Management; Ph.D., Yale.
Valeria Martinez, Assistant Professor of Finance; M.S., Warwick (England).
Dawn W. Massey, Associate Professor of Accounting and Chair, Accounting Department; M.B.A., Fordham; Ph.D., Connecticut; CPA.
John McDermott, Associate Professor of Finance; M.B.A., Columbia; Ph.D., Connecticut.
Roselie McDevitt, Assistant Professor of Accounting; M.B.A., Pace; Sc.D., New Haven; CPA.
Sharlene A. McEvoy, Professor of Business Law; J.D., Connecticut; Ph.D., UCLA.
Camelia C. Micu, Assistant Professor of Marketing; Ph.D., Connecticut.
Yasin Ozcelik, Assistant Professor of Information Systems and Operations Management; Ph.D., Purdue.
Milo W. Peck Jr., Assistant Professor of Accounting; J.D., Suffolk; LL.M., Boston University; CPA.
Patricia M. Poli, Associate Professor of Accounting; Ph.D., NYU; CPA.
Rajasree K. Rajamma, Assistant Professor of Marketing; M.B.A., Cochin (India); M.B.A., Indiana; Ph.D., North Texas.
Katsiaryna Salavei, Assistant Professor of Finance; B.S., Belarussian State University of Informatics and Radioelectronics (Belarus); B.A., Hartwick.
Carl A. Scheraga, Professor of Business Strategy and Technology Management; Ph.D., Connecticut.
David P. Schmidt, Associate Professor of Ethics and Chair, Management Department; Ph.D., Chicago.
Norman A. Solomon, Professor of Management and Dean, Dolan School of Business; Ph.D., Wisconsin.
Debra Strauss, Assistant Professor of Business Law; J.D., Yale.
Winston Tellis, Camille and Stephen Schramm Professor of Information Systems and Operations Management; Ph.D., Nova Southeastern.
Cheryl L. Tromley, Professor of Management; Ph.D., Yale.
Michael T. Tucker, Professor of Finance; D.B.A., Boston University.
Joan L. Van Hise, Associate Professor of Accounting; M.B.A., Fordham; Ph.D., NYU; CPA.
Vishnu Vinekar, Assistant Professor of Information Systems and Operations Management; M.S., Texas A&M.
Kathleen Weiden, Assistant Professor of Accounting; Ph.D., CUNY, Baruch; CPA.

Faculty Emeriti
Henry E. Allinger, Assistant Professor of Accounting.
Robert L. DeMichiell, Professor of Information Systems.
Suzanne D. Lyngaas, Assistant Professor of Accounting.
R. Keith Martin, Professor of Information Systems and Operations Management.
Krishna Mohan, Associate Professor of Marketing.
Richard F. Tyler, Assistant Professor of Management.

THE LEADER IN GLOBAL EDUCATION

FAIRLEIGH DICKINSON UNIVERSITY

FAIRLEIGH DICKINSON UNIVERSITY

Silberman College of Business

Programs of Study

The Silberman College of Business at Fairleigh Dickinson University (FDU) offers programs that lead to the degrees of Master of Business Administration (M.B.A.) (including an Executive M.B.A. and Executive M.B.A. in health care and life sciences), Master of Science in Taxation (M.S.T.), Master of Science in Accounting (M.S.A.), and a one-year, full-time M.B.A. in global business management. Courses for most M.B.A., M.S.T., and M.S.A. degrees are scheduled during the evenings and on Saturdays. Programs may be pursued either full-time or part-time. Students are required to finish their studies within in six calendar years, with two 1-semester leaves of absence.

The M.B.A. programs are cross-functional in nature and emphasize managerial skills, global-thinking strategy, and entrepreneurship. The traditional M.B.A. is offered in entrepreneurial studies, finance, human resource management, international business, management, management (with concentrations in information systems and corporate communication), marketing, and pharmaceutical management. All traditional M.B.A. programs require 48 credits. The total number of credits may be decreased to a minimum of 30 through petition to waive core courses. Both the Executive M.B.A. in management and Executive M.B.A. in health care and life sciences require completion of 48 credits and are offered in a Saturday format. The Executive M.B.A. programs include a two-week international immersion experience, which is held at a variety of international locations. Recent seminars have been held in such countries as Brazil, Central/Eastern Europe, and China. The M.S.T. is designed for those who currently practice in the field. The M.S.A. offers two tracks, both of which qualify students to sit for New Jersey's CPA exam. Both the M.S.T. and M.S.A. programs require completion of 30 credits. The College also offers a 12-credit post-M.B.A. certificate in eleven different subject areas for individuals who already hold their M.B.A. but are interested in updating their business skills or in developing expertise in a particular area of study.

Research Facilities

The University maintains extensive library facilities at all locations, including multidisciplinary databases. A business research library is located on the Metropolitan Campus. The library offers interlibrary capability to enable students to acquire material that is not available locally. The University also maintains computer laboratories at all locations, including the latest in personal computer technology and software as well as Compaq Alpha, Sun E450, Sun E250, and Cisco Power Network computers.

Financial Aid

Students can obtain loans through several national programs. The College of Business also offers a number of graduate fellowships on both campuses.

Cost of Study

Tuition for most programs is $893 per credit hour in 2007–08. The annual technology fee is $608 for full-time study and $288 for part-time study. There are special program fees for the M.B.A. in global management and both Executive M.B.A. programs, which include all books and materials; travel, room, and board for an international immersion seminar; and all University fees.

Living and Housing Costs

Fairleigh Dickinson University makes available a limited amount of graduate housing. Housing in the community is readily available to students.

Student Group

The graduate enrollment at Fairleigh Dickinson University includes 2,593 full- and part-time graduate students at the Metropolitan Campus, including 361 enrolled in graduate business programs. At the College at Florham, there are 934 full- and part-time graduate students, including 439 graduate business students. The M.B.A. in global management is offered only at the Metropolitan Campus. All Executive M.B.A. classes are offered at the Hamilton Park Conference Center, a world-class conference center located adjacent to the University's College at Florham location in Madison, New Jersey.

Location

Fairleigh Dickinson University has two campuses in northern New Jersey, both of which are located in attractive residential suburbs within easy reach of the cultural and social advantages of New York City. The University also owns and operates Wroxton College, its overseas campus in England.

The University

Founded in 1942, Fairleigh Dickinson University today is the largest private university in New Jersey, enrolling 12,112 students. The Metropolitan Campus was opened in 1954, and the College at Florham became operational in 1958. Wroxton College, a center for graduate and undergraduate study, was opened in 1965 at historic Wroxton Abbey in England. In fall 2007, the University began offering undergraduate business at its newest international location in Vancouver, British Columbia, Canada.

Applying

Applications should be filed during the semester preceding the one for which enrollment is sought. Applications for domestic students are processed on a rolling basis, and early application is encouraged. Applications for international students for the fall semester are due by July 1 and for the spring semester are due by December 1. Applicants must hold a baccalaureate degree from a regionally accredited institution and must file the appropriate graduate studies application. The application and fee, official transcripts of all education beyond high school, and scores from the Graduate Management Admission Test (GMAT) should be forwarded to the admissions office.

Correspondence and Information

Silberman College of Business
Fairleigh Dickinson University
1000 River Road, T-KB1-01
Teaneck, New Jersey 07666
Web site: http://www.fdu.edu
    http://www.fdu/edu/business (Business Web site)

Office of Graduate Admissions (Domestic Students)
Phone: 201-692-2554
E-mail: grad@fdu.edu

Office of International Admissions (International Students)
Phone: 201-692-2205
E-mail: global@fdu.edu

Fairleigh Dickinson University

THE FACULTY

Administration

James Almeida, Associate Professor of Entrepreneurial Studies and Associate Dean; Ph.D., South Carolina.
James Barrood, Executive Director, Rothman Institute of Entrepreneurial Studies; M.B.A., Texas A&M.
Scott Behson, Chair of Management; Ph.D., SUNY at Albany.
Peter Caliguari, Director, Center for Executive Leadership and Director of Executive M.B.A. Program; M.B.A., Fairleigh Dickinson.
Robert DeFilippis, Chair of Accounting, Taxation and Law; M.B.A., Rutgers.
Evangelos S. Djimopoulos, Chair of Economics, Finance and International Business; Ph.D., Columbia.
Gerard Farias, Executive Director, Center for Human Resource Management Studies and the Institute for Sustainable Enterprise; Ph.D., Texas Tech.
Robert Greenfield, Professor of Economics and Finance and Interim Dean; Ph.D., Rutgers.
Karin Hamilton, Director of Graduate and Global Programs; M.B.A., Fairleigh Dickinson.
Roger Koppl, Executive Director, Institute for Forensic Science Administration; Ph.D., Auburn.
Ethné Swartz, Chair of Marketing and Entrepreneurship; Ph.D., Manchester (England).
Ron West, Director, Tax Program; LL.M., NYU.
K. Paul Yoon, Chair of Information Systems and Decision Sciences; Ph.D., Kansas State.

Department of Accounting, Taxation, and Law.

Frank Brunetti, Professor of Law and Taxation; LL.M., NYU. Matthew Calderisi, Associate Professor of Accounting; Ph.D., Columbia; CPA. J. Richard Chaplin, Professor of Accounting; M.B.A., St. John's (New York); CPA. Theodore M. David, Associate Professor of Taxation; LL.M., NYU. Henry Fuentes, Associate Professor of Accounting; M.B.A., Seton Hall; CPA. Kenneth R. Gillies, Associate Professor of Accounting; M.B.A., Rutgers; CPA. Jonathan Schiff, Professor of Accounting; J.D., Fordham. John H. Skarbnik, Professor of Taxation; LL.M., NYU; CPA. Frederic M. Stiner Jr., Professor of Accounting; Ph.D., Nebraska. Rosemarie Twomey, Professor of Business Law; J.D., West Virginia.

Department of Economics, Finance, and International Business

Petros Anastasopoulus, Associate Professor of Economics; Ph.D., New School. Kenneth Betz, Lecturer in Economics; M.B.A., Fairleigh Dickinson. Karen Denning, Associate Professor of Finance; Ph.D., Pittsburgh. Frederick Englander, Professor of Economics; Ph.D., Rutgers. Christine Farias, Lecturer of Economics; Ph.D., Texas Tech. Patrick Gaughan, Professor of Economics and Finance; Ph.D., CUNY. Claude Jonnard, Associate Professor of Economics and Finance; M.A., NYU. Adam Kessler, Associate Professor of Economics; Ph.D., NYU. Joseph J. Kiernan, Associate Professor of Economics and Finance; Ph.D., Fordham. Richard W. Kjetsaa, Associate Professor of Economics and Finance; Ph.D., Fordham. Roger Koppl, Professor of Economics and Finance; Ph.D., Auburn. Chee K. Ng, Associate Professor of Finance; Ph.D., Arizona State. Van Nguen, Assistant Professor of Finance; Ph.D., Arizona State. Braimoh Oseghale, Associate Professor of Economics and Finance; Ph.D., Temple. Sorin Tuluca, Associate Professor of Finance; D.B.A., Cleveland State. Burton Zwick, Lecturer of Finance; Ph.D., Carnegie Mellon.

Department of Information Systems and Decision Sciences

Gary J. Bronson, Professor of Information Systems; Ph.D., Stevens. Hee-Kyung Cho, Assistant Professor of Management Information Systems; Ph.D., NJIT. Jeffrey Hsu, Assistant Professor of Management Information Systems; Ph.D., Rutgers. Maureen Kieff, Assistant Professor of Quantitative Analysis; M.A., Fordham. Yongbeom Kim, Associate Professor of Information Systems; Ph.D., NYU. Govindasami Naadimuthu, Professor of Information Systems and Sciences; Ph.D., Kansas; PE. Richard Panicucci, Professor of Quantitative Analysis; M.B.A., Fairleigh Dickinson. Mohammod Sedaghat, Lecturer in Operations Management; Ph.D., Polytechnic. Mel Stern, Lecturer of Management Information Systems; M.S., NYU. Zhaobo Wang, Assistant Professor of Production and Operations Management; Ph.D., Rutgers. Mahmoud Watad, Associate Professor of Information Sciences; Ph.D., NYU.

Department of Management

Scott Behson, Associate Professor of Management; Ph.D., SUNY at Albany. Gerard W. Cleaves, Assistant Professor of Management; M.B.A., Harvard. Kent Fairfield, Assistant Professor of Management; Ph.D., Columbia. Joel I. Harmon, Professor of Management; Ph.D., SUNY at Albany. Gwen Jones, Associate Professor of Management; Ph.D., SUNY at Albany. Osita Nwachukwu, Associate Professor of Management; Ph.D., Mississippi. Dennis Scotti, Professor of Health Systems and Management; Ph.D., Temple. Joan Slepian, Lecturer of Management; Ph.D., Yale. Gordon Sollars, Assistant Professor of Management; Ph.D., Virginia. Daniel F. Twomey, Professor of Management; D.B.A., Kent State. J. Daniel Wischnevsky, Associate Professor of Management; Ph.D., Rutgers.

Department of Marketing and Entrepreneurship

Richard Archambault, Lecturer in Entrepreneurial Studies; M.B.A., Fairleigh Dickinson. Rajesh Chandrashekaran, Professor of Marketing; Ph.D., Rutgers. Arthur Dolinsky, Associate Professor of Marketing; Ph.D., Pennsylvania. Ronald Heim, Associate Professor of Marketing; Ph.D., Cornell. Eleanor Ann Huser, Lecturer of Marketing; M.S., MIT. James Hutton, Associate Professor of Marketing; Ph.D., Texas at Austin. Caroline K. L. Munoz, Assistant Professor of Marketing; Ph.D., Auburn. Shahana Sen, Assistant Professor of Marketing; Ph.D., NYU.

Department of Statistics

Alan Fask, Associate Professor of Statistics; Ph.D., NYU. Gaston Mendoza, Associate Professor of Statistics; Ph.D., Temple.

HAWAI'I PACIFIC UNIVERSITY

College of Business Administration

Programs of Study

Hawai'i Pacific University, an established institution with leading programs in business administration, information systems, and management, offers a comprehensive Master of Business Administration (M.B.A.) degree program. This program is noted for several distinctive features. First, it is pragmatic, emphasizing real-world applications, case studies, and specific skills and competencies needed in contemporary business. Second, most courses include both an entrepreneurial and an international perspective. Third, computer applications are integrated into many of the M.B.A. courses. Fourth, interpersonal and communication skills are stressed throughout the curriculum. Fifth, as a major partner in the downtown business community, Hawai'i Pacific University coordinates a large internship program that provides part-time and full-time managerial, technical, and professional positions in leading business firms. Through this internship program, M.B.A. candidates have the opportunity to supplement their income while earning academic credit.

The M.B.A. program at Hawai'i Pacific University requires 42 semester hours of graduate work. Prerequisite courses in business subjects may be required. The curriculum is organized into nine core courses (27 semester hours), three elective courses tailored to the student's individual needs (9 semester hours), and a capstone sequence, including a policy and strategy formulation course and a professional paper (6 semester hours). Students may concentrate in any one of several business areas, including accounting, corporate communication, e-business, economics, finance, human resource management, information systems, international business, management, marketing, organizational change, and travel industry management.

The University also offers an M.A. in global leadership and sustainable development, which is designed for the exceptional student whose background, education, and worldview have inspired an interest in assuming leadership positions in the global community. In addition, the M.A. in organizational change examines the models and strategies for leading change, continuous improvement, and performance management. Courses include organizational change and development, national and community change and development, culture and human organization, and organizational behavior.

Research Facilities

To support graduate studies, University libraries, with a collection exceeding 153,000 volumes, add an average of 2,500 volumes annually, 15 percent of which are on business topics. A significant number of business reference books are available, including national and international business directories, investment and financial services, accounting and tax information sources, and a collection of annual reports. Periodical titles number more than 1,700, and 205,000 pieces of microfiche and 5,300 rolls of microfilm are maintained. Dial-up access to local area databases of public and state university library catalogs, legislative information, and business-oriented statistical data is available in the library. Other in-house, business-related, and commercially vendored databases support specialized information needs. The University's accessible on-campus computer center houses more than 100 IBM-compatible microcomputers with stand-alone and networked configurations that support the graduate program's integrated computer applications approach.

Financial Aid

The University participates in all federal financial aid programs designated for graduate students. These programs provide aid in the form of subsidized (need-based) and unsubsidized (non-need-based) Federal Stafford Student Loans. Through these loans, funds may be available to cover the student's entire cost of education. To apply for aid, students must submit the Free Application for Federal Student Aid (FAFSA) after January 1. Mailing of student award letters usually begins by the end of March.

Cost of Study

For the 2007–08 academic year, graduate tuition is $560 per credit, and books cost approximately $1500 for the entire program.

Living and Housing Costs

The University has both on-campus residence halls and an apartment referral service. Including tuition, books, housing, food, health insurance, and miscellaneous expenses, the cost of living for a typical single student for two semesters (nine months) is approximately $25,840.

Student Group

University enrollment currently stands at nearly 9,000, including more than 1,200 graduate students. All fifty states and more than 100 countries are represented.

Location

The University has three campuses linked by shuttle. Hawai'i Pacific combines the excitement of an urban, downtown campus with the serenity of the windward side of the island. The main campus is located in downtown Honolulu, the business and financial center of the Pacific. The Hawai'i Loa campus is 8 miles away situated on 135 acres in Kaneohe at the base of the Ko'olau Mountains; it is the site of the School of Nursing, the marine science program, and a variety of other course offerings. The third campus, Oceanic Institute, is an applied aquaculture research facility located on a 56-acre site at Makapu'u Point on the windward coast.

The University

Hawai'i Pacific University is the largest private postsecondary institution in the state of Hawai'i. The University is coeducational, with a faculty of more than 300 members, a student-faculty ratio of 18:1, and an average class size of 20. A wide range of counseling and other student support services are available. There are more than ninety student organizations on campus, including the Graduate Student Organization.

Applying

Hawai'i Pacific University seeks students with academic promise, outstanding career potential, and high motivation. Applicants should complete and forward a graduate admissions application form, have official transcripts sent from all colleges or universities previously attended, have two letters of recommendation forwarded, and submit GMAT results (M.B.A. applicants). International applicants should submit results of the TOEFL. Admissions decisions are made on a rolling basis, and applicants are notified between one and two weeks after all documents have been submitted. Applicants to Hawai'i Pacific University's graduate program are encouraged to submit applications online at http://www.hpu.edu/mba.

Correspondence and Information

Graduate Admissions
Hawai'i Pacific University
1164 Bishop Street, #911
Honolulu, Hawai'i 96813
Phone: 808-544-1135
        866-GRAD-HPU (toll-free)
Fax: 808-544-0280
E-mail: graduate@hpu.edu
Web site: http://www.hpu.edu/grad

Hawai'i Pacific University

THE FACULTY AND THEIR RESEARCH

Jerome Agrusa, Ph.D., Texas A&M. Travel industry management.
Leinaala Ahu-Isa, Ed.D., Hawai'i at Manoa. Management.
Michelle Alarcon-Catt, M.B.A., Pepperdine; J.D., Loyola Marymount. Management.
Justin Cho, Ph.D., MIT. Management.
Yooncheong Cho, Ph.D., Rutgers. Marketing.
Ron Cranfill, M.S., Chapman. Management.
Eric Drabkin, Ph.D., UCLA. Economics.
Antonina Espiritu, Ph.D., Nebraska–Lincoln. Economics.
Daniel Flood, Ph.D., Union (Ohio). Management.
Susan Fox-Wolfgramm, M.P.A., Ph.D., Texas Tech. Management.
Ken Guyette, M.S., North Dakota; M.B.A., Texas Tech. Accounting.
Joseph Ha, Ph.D., Rutgers. Marketing.
Ted Haggblom, Ph.D., Michigan State. Marketing.
Thomas Kam, M.B.A., Hawai'i at Manoa; CPA. Accounting.
John Karbens, M.B.A., Ed.D., Hawai'i at Manoa; CPA. Accounting.
Lauren Kelly, Ph.D., Alabama. Accounting.
Mary Kelly, Ph.D., Greenwich. Economics.
Wendy Lam, M.B.A., Hawai'i at Manoa. Travel industry management.
Mark A. Lane, Ph.D., Missouri–Columbia. Finance.
Leroy Laney, Ph.D., Colorado at Boulder. Finance and economics.
Binsheng Li, Ph.D., Hawai'i at Manoa. Economics.
Ernesto Lucas, Ph.D., Hawai'i at Manoa. Agricultural economics.
Gunter Meissner, Ph.D., Kiel (Germany). Finance, derivatives.
U. Aytun Ozturk, Ph.D., Pittsburgh. Quantitative methods.
Joseph D. Patoskie, Ph.D., Texas Tech. Travel industry management.
Stephen Phillips, M.B.A., Central Michigan. Management.
Brett Saraniti, Ph.D., Northwestern. Economics.
Ken Schoolland, M.S.F.S., Georgetown. Economics.
Michael Seiler, D.B.A., Cleveland State. Finance.
Joseph Smith, Ed.D., USC. Management.
Niti Villinger, Ph.D., Cambridge. Management.
James Waddington, M.B.A., Hawai'i Manoa; CPA. Accounting.
Gary Waters, M.S.A., Central Michigan. Management.
Warren Wee, Ph.D., Washington (Seattle); M.B.A., Hawai'i at Manoa; CPA. Accounting.

HOFSTRA UNIVERSITY

Frank G. Zarb School of Business

Programs of Study

Hofstra University offers 155 graduate degree programs—each designed to give students the edge they need to succeed.

The Frank G. Zarb School of Business offers a wide range of graduate programs leading to the following degrees: Master of Business Administration (M.B.A.), Executive M.B.A. (EMBA), and Master of Science (M.S.). A combined program leading to the Juris Doctor/ M.B.A. (J.D./M.B.A.) (offered with the Hofstra School of Law) is also available.

The Zarb School's programs in accounting and general business are accredited by AACSB International–The Association to Advance Collegiate Schools of Business, making it one of the few schools nationally with dual accreditation.

The School's challenging M.B.A. program gives students broad exposure to the functional areas of business, opportunities to gain hands-on experience in a specific field, and specialized instruction in the leadership aspects of business. Students choose from a wide selection of concentrations, including accounting, finance, and marketing. To keep pace with changes in business, the School recently added new concentrations in health services management, quality management, and sports and entertainment management. The M.B.A. internship program takes advantage of the proximity of New York City, allowing students to gain on-the-job experience in their field of specialization.

The EMBA program features a schedule designed to allow working professionals to complete their degrees.

The M.S. program allows students to gain expertise in a specific field of business. Starting in the fall of 2007, the School plans to offer a new concentration in quantitative finance.

The J.D./M.B.A. program offers students integrated study of law and business.

Both day and evening classes are offered.

Research Facilities

Hofstra's graduate programs are supported by extensive academic resources and state-of-the-art facilities.

The Hofstra libraries contain 1.4 million print volumes and provide 24/7 electronic access to more than 50,000 journals and electronic books. Additionally, students have access to about 30 business databases. C.V. Starr Hall, home to the Zarb School of Business, features the Martin B. Greenberg Trading Room, a state-of-the-art academic trading room complete with Bloomberg terminals and Internet access at every student seat.

The Merrill Lynch Center for the Study of International Financial Services and Markets at the Zarb School promotes and facilitates faculty and student research and innovation in the field of international financial services and markets. Research areas include the globalization process for financial institutions, the development of financial services in global markets, and the development of emerging financial markets.

Financial Aid

Financial aid is available in the form of fellowships, scholarships, grants, loans, and graduate assistantship positions. All students applying for financial aid must file the Free Application for Federal Student Aid (FAFSA). Information about graduate financial aid may be obtained from the Office of Financial Aid or the graduate academic departments.

Cost of Study

Graduate tuition is $820 per credit hour in 2007–08. Hofstra is a private institution, so tuition is the same for residents and nonresidents of New York State. University fees range from $78 to $300 per semester, depending on the number of credits taken.

Living and Housing Costs

The cost of housing in University residence halls for 2007–08 ranges from $2775 to $6000 per semester, depending on the type of accommodation. Board prices range from $495 to $1700 per semester, depending on the plan chosen. The Office of Residential Life maintains listings of available off-campus accommodations.

Student Group

Students enrolled in the graduate programs at the Zarb School form a dynamic, achievement-oriented community. These students represent ten states and twenty-three countries. About 25 percent are members of minority groups, 24 percent are international students, and 37 percent are women. Many students in these graduate programs have previous work experience.

Location

Hofstra's distinctive 240-acre campus, a registered arboretum, is located in suburban Long Island, just 25 miles from New York City.

With New York City just a short ride away, students take advantage of the museums, concerts, and professional sports as well as internships the city offers. Students can also explore Long Island, which offers spectacular beaches, museums, and internship opportunities.

The University

Hofstra University is a dynamic private institution where students find their edge to succeed in 140 undergraduate and 155 graduate programs in the liberal arts and sciences, business, communication, education and allied human services, and law.

With an outstanding faculty, advanced technological resources, and state-of-the-art facilities, Hofstra has a growing national reputation. Yet the average graduate class size is just 13, ensuring that students receive the personal attention they deserve.

Applying

Candidates generally are required to complete the graduate application and all supporting forms and to submit two letters of recommendation, a resume, a statement of professional objectives, official transcripts from every college or university attended, and scores obtained on the Graduate Management Admission Test (GMAT). International students are also required to submit scores obtained on the TOEFL. Application requirements vary depending on the program. For further information, candidates should contact the Office of Graduate Admissions or individual departments.

Correspondence and Information

Office of Graduate Admissions
126 Hofstra University
105 Memorial Hall
Hofstra University
Hempstead, New York 11549-1260
Phone: 516-463-4723
      800-HOFSTRA Ext. 624 (toll-free)
Fax: 516-463-4664
E-mail: graddean@hofstra.edu
Web site: http://www.hofstra.edu/graduate

Hofstra University

DEPARTMENT CHAIRPERSONS

Accounting, Taxation, and Legal Studies in Business
Nathan S. Slavin, Associate Professor and Chairperson; Ph.D., CUNY, Baruch, 1980.

Business Computer Information Systems and Quantitative Methods
John F. Affisco, Professor and Chairperson; Ph.D., CUNY Graduate Center, 1981.

Finance
Nancy A. White, Associate Professor and Chairperson; Ph.D., CUNY, 1992.

Management, Entrepreneurship, and General Business
Mamdouh I. Farid, Associate Professor and Chairperson; Ph.D., CUNY, 1988.

Marketing and International Business
Benny Z. Barak, Professor and Chairperson; Ph.D., CUNY Graduate Center, 1979.

IONA COLLEGE

Hagan School of Business

Programs of Study

The Hagan School of Business offers classes leading to the Master of Business Administration (M.B.A.) degree and to the Post-Master's Certificate (PMC) in business administration.

The programs are designed to meet the needs of both full-time and part-time students and are organized on a trimester basis during the academic year, September to May. Two summer sessions are also available in June and July.

The goal of the M.B.A. program is to prepare students for management careers in business and other organizations. Effective managers must know themselves, work in teams, lead organizational change, and understand the macro factors affecting the future. They must also appreciate the role of information technology, ethically and socially responsible decision making, and the globalization of business. The School's concentrations in financial management, human resource management, information and decision technology management, management, and marketing provide solid knowledge in a specific functional area of business. Required course work consists of 27 credits in the core curriculum and 30 credits in the major and related fields. Waivers are possible out of the core curriculum if certain criteria are met. Students must complete at least 33 credits of graduate work at Iona. The M.B.A. program is offered at the main campus at New Rochelle and at a branch campus in Pearl River, New York. The program also offers certificate options in international business and e-commerce, which can be completed concurrently with the M.B.A. curriculum.

The Post-Master's Certificate in business administration is designed to meet specific individual professional needs at the post-M.B.A. level through a program of advanced courses in one of the major fields or in business continuity and risk management, e-commerce, or international business. A minimum of 15 credits is required to earn the New York State–approved certificate.

Research Facilities

The Hagan School is fully supported by Iona's state-of-the-art computing capabilities and facilities. There are more than 550 workstations available for student use on campus. In 2001 Iona became the first New York metropolitan area to boast a completely wireless local area network (LAN), and students continue to benefit from the 24-hour access to the College's computer network, library databases, and the Internet.

Financial Aid

Tuition scholarships based on exceptional GMAT scores are available. Loans are provided through the Federal Stafford Student Loan program. Employment opportunities are also available on campus and at local corporate businesses.

Cost of Study

Tuition for 2007–08 was $712 per credit. The initial application fee is $50. A $15 registration fee is charged for the summer sessions. Other charges depend upon the course of study.

Living and Housing Costs

Rooms and apartments are available in the local community and the nearby metropolitan area for students attending Iona College.

Student Group

There are approximately 350 students enrolled in the M.B.A. program; 85 percent are part-time students.

Location

The main campus is located in New Rochelle, a suburban community in Westchester County, 15 miles north of Manhattan. All degree programs are offered on this site. A branch campus is located in Rockland County. Major highways and public transportation connect both campuses with the cultural and business centers of the Greater New York metropolitan area.

The College

Founded in 1940, Iona is a private coeducational institution with a total enrollment of 3,100 students, of whom 884 study at the graduate level. The Hagan School of Business was instituted in 1965.

Applying

Candidates may enter the graduate program in the fall (September), winter (November), or spring (March) trimester and summer sessions. The completed application, with fee, must be supported by official transcripts from each institution of higher education attended, two letters of recommendation, and Graduate Management Admission Test (GMAT) scores. All required documents should be received no later than two weeks prior to the start of the trimester or summer session for which the candidate is applying.

Correspondence and Information

Director of Admissions
Hagan School of Business
Iona College
New Rochelle, New York 10801
Phone: 914-633-2288
Fax: 914-633-2012
Web site: http://www.iona.edu/hagan

Iona College

DEPARTMENT AND PROGRAM HEADS

Accounting: Robert Strittmatter, Associate Professor and Chair; M.B.A., NYU; CPA.
Finance, Business Economics and Legal Studies: Anand Shetty, Professor and Chair; Ph.D., Pittsburgh.
IDTM: Robert Richardson, Associate Professor and Chair; Ph.D., Pittsburgh.
Management/Business Administration: Ursula Wittig-Berman, Associate Professor and Chair; Ph.D., CUNY, Baruch.
Marketing/International Business: Fredrica Rudell, Associate Professor and Chair; Ph.D., Columbia.

LASELL COLLEGE

Master of Science in Management

Programs of Study	The Master of Science in Management (M.S.M.) degree at Lasell College is designed to deliver an academically substantial yet career-focused management education. The M.S.M. program offers concentrations in elder-care administration, elder-care marketing, human resources management, management, marketing, nonprofit management, and project management. The program is appropriate for both the experienced working professional and the new career entrant. Working with faculty members who are scholars and practitioners in their fields, students enhance their management skills while developing greater perspective in their chosen area of concentration.

The Master of Science in Management program is a 36-credit curriculum rooted in a core of seven courses that provide a solid and competitive foundation in management and business operations. Among other courses, the core includes Fundamentals of Executive Management, Management Information Systems, Financial Management, and a capstone Internship/Research Project. Students with appropriate academic achievement and relevant course work may waive up to 6 credits of the core. In addition to the core, students complete 15 credits in their area of concentration, which provides them with a foundation mastering the theory and skills that are essential to their career field. All courses are tied to central themes of professional communications, ethics and social responsibility, teamwork, dynamic change, a global perspective, and hands-on learning.

Students may choose to complete a graduate certificate in any of the above-mentioned concentrations. A graduate certificate is composed of five 3-credit courses that can be completed in six months and may be used either as a stand-alone for the working professional seeking a career change or as a foundation that can be built upon toward earning Lasell's M.S.M. degree.

Graduate courses are offered in a variety of formats. Traditional-format courses meet one evening per week. Hybrid courses are offered in six- or thirteen-week sessions alternating on-campus time with online study. The Master of Science in Management degree program and all graduate certificates are also offered 100 percent online.

Research Facilities Students in elder care have direct access to two distinguished on-campus resources. Lasell Village is both a nationally ranked continuing-care retirement community and a groundbreaking experiment in lifelong education and intergenerational exchange. The Fuss Center for Research on Aging and Intergenerational Studies is dedicated to enhancing the quality of life for older adults through research, teaching, intergenerational programs, and community partnerships. Located at Lasell Village, the center seeks to convene conferences, workshops, and lectures to facilitate research studies initiated by the members of the Lasell community and support scholars and research groups from inside and outside the College community who wish to conduct studies on aging and intergenerational learning.

The Jessie S. Brennan Library maintains a working collection of books and periodicals. As a member of the Minuteman Library Network, a consortium of more than forty libraries, Brennan Library provides students with easy access to more than 5 million books and materials through the online computer catalog.

Financial Aid In order to qualify for loan resources, students must complete the online Free Application for Federal Student Aid (FAFSA) at http://www.fafsa.ed.gov and the Lasell College Graduate School Financial Aid Application, which is available at http://www.lasell.edu. Lasell's FAFSA code is 002158.

Cost of Study The 2007–08 tuition cost is $475 per credit, with a $50 comprehensive fee per semester. The comprehensive fee includes technology, parking, and a College ID.

Living and Housing Costs Lasell College offers limited housing for international graduate students on its campus. However, the local area has an abundance of opportunities for temporary housing. For further information, interested students should contact the Office of Graduate Admission.

Student Group There are 73 full- and part-time students enrolled in the Master of Science in Management program. Many of the graduate students are working professionals.

Location Lasell College is located in Newton, Massachusetts, just 8 miles west of Boston near the intersection of Route 128 and I-90 (Massachusetts Turnpike). The College is within walking distance of the T's Riverside Green Line and a short walk from the Auburndale commuter rail. An express T bus stops at the corner of the campus. There is ample parking available for graduate students.

The University and The School Founded in 1851, Lasell College is a coeducational, independent institution of higher education that is accredited by the New England Association of Schools and Colleges. Lasell offers career-oriented master's and bachelor's degree programs. Central to the Lasell plan of education is Connected Learning, a teaching philosophy stating that students acquire and retain knowledge most effectively when classroom theory is reinforced by practical application through internships, projects, and case studies.

Applying Students are admitted on a rolling admission basis for sessions beginning in September, October, January, March, May, and July. To apply to the program, applicants must submit the following information: a completed application for graduate admission with a $40 application fee, official transcripts of all academic work beyond high school, and two letters of recommendation. Candidates do not need to take the GRE or GMAT. International students applying to the program must also submit a TOEFL score, a certified copy of a financial declaration, and a copy of their passport.

Correspondence and Information
Office of Graduate Admission
Lasell College
1844 Commonwealth Avenue
Newton, Massachusetts 02466
Phone: 617-243-2400
Fax: 617-243-2450
E-mail: gradinfo@lasell.edu
Web site: http://www.lasell.edu

Lasell College

THE FACULTY

Janice Barrett, Associate Professor; Ed.D., Harvard.
Jeffrey Corcoran, Assistant Professor; M.S., Boston University; M.B.A., Nichols.
Richard T. Fredericks, Assistant Professor; M.S., Bentley.
Emily Meyer, Instructor; Ph.D., Brandeis.
Paula Deangelis Panchuck, Associate Professor; Ph.D., Lesley.
Gerald Pineault, Lecturer; M.B.A., Northeastern.
Mark Sciegaj, Dean of Graduate and Professional Studies; Ph.D., Brandeis.
Derrek Shulman, Instructor; M.A., Massachusetts.
Nancy R. Waldron, Assistant Professor; M.B.A., Plymouth State; Ph.D., Capella.
Martin Walsh, Assistant Professor; M.B.A., Anna Maria; Ph.D., Northeastern.

LEHIGH UNIVERSITY

College of Business and Economics

Program of Study

The College of Business and Economics offers an M.B.A; an online M.B.A.; Master of Science (M.S.) programs in accounting and information analysis, analytical finance, economics, and health and biopharmaceutical economics; and the degree of Ph.D. in business and economics. The 36-credit program can be completed on a part-time or full-time basis and is specifically designed to mirror business challenges and decision-making situations in a dynamic and rapidly changing corporate environment.

The M.S. in economics program requires 30 credit hours of course work and can be completed in one calendar year, with no requirement for prior work experience. The M.S. in accounting and information analysis program is a flexible, 30-hour program offering either a general degree emphasizing assurance services or concentrations in consulting and business risk management, financial services, and strategic cost management. The M.S. in analytical finance, for students with a highly quantitative background in engineering, physics, or mathematics, prepares its graduates for positions in the financial field. The M.S. program in health and biopharmaceutical economics focuses on outcomes assessments in health care and related fields. Both the M.S. in analytical finance and in health and bio-pharmaceutical economics are one-year degree programs and can be pursued directly after completing the undergraduate degree.

The Ph.D. program provides its graduates with extensive knowledge complemented by a demonstrated ability to conduct independent research and requires a minimum of 72 credit hours of work beyond the bachelor's degree or 48 credit hours beyond the master's degree. Students must pass comprehensive examinations in microeconomic and macroeconomic theory and two areas of specialization. A dissertation is also required.

Faced with dramatic changes in the way of conducting business in the twenty-first century, which produce unprecedented challenges in the preparation of future business leaders, Lehigh's graduate students are exposed to the thought leaders of today, faculty members whose research is published in top academic journals and whose expertise is called on by national and international media. Students have the resources to learn, adapt, and influence the corporate environment in today's complex business world.

Research Facilities

The Rauch Business Center, a $17.8-million headquarters for the graduate programs in the College of Business and Economics, is a modern, dynamic, professional environment for learning and teaching. There are forty well-equipped classrooms, computer labs, auditoriums, and conference rooms. A wireless, state-of-the-art Financial Services Laboratory offers students access to real-time financial information and a window on the world of financial markets. The Clayton Conference Center wing has excellent facilities for executive education programs, conferences, seminars, and other special programs, with plenty of comfortable places to gather and study. Lehigh's distance learning facilities on the Mountaintop Campus provide a state-of-the-art environment for students to interact with students at corporate sites throughout the United States. Along with books and journals, Lehigh's library system includes electronic databases and microfilm, computer software, and media collections. Via the campuswide integrated voice and data communication network, users can access the Internet, the libraries' online catalog, and hundreds of national and international electronic databases and can submit reference inquires, place orders, and request media services and the delivery of documents electronically. The campus network provides access to mainframe computers, the Integrated Library System, and other computers on campus.

Financial Aid

Aside from that offered to graduate students by Lehigh as a whole, the College of Business and Economics offers several types of financial aid. There are twenty-two teaching assistantships, which provide up to 9 credit hours of tuition each semester and an annual stipend of $11,000 to $13,500. Teaching assistants provide classroom support, teach recitation sections, and work 20 hours per week. Graduate assistants, hired to assist departments and faculty members with research and/or administrative duties, work up to 15 hours a week and may receive tuition waivers and hourly pay. Business analysts assist small and growing businesses in the Lehigh Valley area through the Small Business Development Center. They work 20 hours a week, receive an hourly wage, and receive tuition waivers for up to 10 credit hours of tuition each semester. These positions offer tremendous opportunity for experiential learning and are available to M.B.A. students only. Scholarships are available for both full-time and part-time students. Ph.D. students are eligible to apply for fellowships that cover up to 10 credits of tuition and an annual stipend.

Cost of Study

In 2007–08, tuition is $630 per credit hour. Full-time students are assessed a $150 technology fee each semester. Online courses also require a $100 technology fee.

Living and Housing Costs

Information on graduate student housing is available through the Department of Residential Services at 610-758-3500. On-campus housing costs range from $470 to $625 per month. Off-campus listings are also available through Residential Services. Students should budget approximately $28,000 per year in tuition and living expenses.

Student Group

About 387 graduate students are enrolled in the College of Business and Economics, of whom about 32 percent are women. Of the 258 M.B.A. students, about 60 percent come from an engineering, technical, or scientific background. Eleven students are currently enrolled in the M.S. in economics, 24 in the M.S. in accounting and information analysis, 8 in the health and biopharmaceutical economics program, 10 in the M.S. in analytical finance, and 16 in the Ph.D. program. Sixty students are non-degree-seeking students. Ninety-three students attend full-time.

Student Outcomes

Graduates of the M.B.A. and M.S. programs have taken positions in a variety of industries, including consulting, health care, marketing, operations, and financial institutions. Ph.D. graduates have accepted teaching positions in academia and research positions in financial institutions, business, and government.

Location

Lehigh University consists of three distinctive, continuous areas, totaling more than 1,600 acres. Located 90 miles southwest of New York City and 50 miles north of Philadelphia, the Lehigh Valley is Pennsylvania's fourth-largest metropolitan area. Bethlehem, one of three principal cities of the Lehigh Valley, is a center of industry, high technology, culture, and education.

The University and The College

Lehigh University, founded in 1865, was one of the first American institutions to offer a technical education. Its first five schools included a school of general literature and four scientific schools. The innovative concept of offering both technical and nontechnical courses of study has continued to be a successful formula at Lehigh. Today, Lehigh has a graduate school of education and three colleges: Engineering and Applied Science, Arts and Sciences, and Business and Economics. Thirty-five percent of the students are enrolled in the College of Engineering and Applied Science. Women have always been admitted to Lehigh at the graduate level, and in 1971, the University began admitting women at the undergraduate level. In 1987, the campus expanded to 1,600 acres, with the addition of the former Homer Labs of the Bethlehem Steel Corporation. The Mountaintop Campus houses several engineering departments and centers.

Applying

Candidates must have completed an undergraduate program at an accredited U.S. college or university. International students must have sixteen years of formal education, including four years at the university level. A TOEFL score is required of all applicants for whom English is not the native language. The credentials evaluated by the faculty admission committee include the candidate's undergraduate background, GMAT scores, personal essay, and letters of recommendation.

Lehigh evaluates applications on a rolling basis and usually notifies applicants of admissions decisions within three weeks of receiving a completed application. Deadlines for regular students are May 1 for the fall semester, December 1 for the spring semester, April 30 for summer session I, and May 30 for summer session II. The deadline for financial aid is January 15 for the upcoming academic year.

Correspondence and Information

Corinn McBride
Director of Recruitment and Admissions
College of Business and Economics
Graduate Programs Office
Lehigh University
621 Taylor Street
Bethlehem, Pennsylvania 18015
Phone: 610-758-5280
Fax: 610-758-5283
E-mail: business@lehigh.edu
Web site: http://www.lehigh.edu/mba

Lehigh University

THE FACULTY AND THEIR RESEARCH

Mark R. Adams, Professor of Practice, Business Minor Program; M.B.A., Pittsburgh; J.D., Baltimore; CFA, CPA. Accounting, corporate reporting, finance, capital evaluations and investments.

Anne-Marie Anderson, Assistant Professor of Finance; M.B.A., Tulsa, 1998; Ph.D., Arizona, 2003. Corporate restructuring, mergers and acquisitions, valuation.

J. Richard Aronson, William L. Clayton Professor of Business and Economics and Director, Martindale Center for the Study of Private Enterprise; Ph.D., Clark, 1964. Tax and expenditure analysis, pension funds, municipal bond analysis, fiscal federalism.

Richard W. Barsness, Professor Emeritus; Ph.D., Minnesota, 1963. International business, corporate strategy in the airline industry.

John W. Bonge, Professor Emeritus; Ph.D., Northwestern, 1968. Business strategy and entrepreneurship.

Paul R. Brown, Professor of Accounting and Dean, College of Business and Economics; Ph.D., Texas at Austin. Financial statement analysis, FASB/SEC policy analysis, international reporting and analysis, earnings measurement and management, managing earnings expectations.

Stephen G. Buell, Professor; Ph.D., Lehigh, 1977. High-yield bonds, corporate bankruptcy.

Franklin J. Carter, Assistant Professor of Marketing; Ph.D., Carnegie Mellon, 1997. Business-to-business marketing, sales force management, diffusion of innovation.

Ravi Chitturi, Assistant Professor of Marketing; M.B.A., 1996, Ph.D., 2003, Texas at Austin. Technology and innovation, design and consumer emotions, brand value and marketing strategy.

Shin-Yi Chou, Assistant Professor of Economics; Ph.D., Duke, 1999. Health economics.

Karen M. Collins, Associate Professor; Ph.D., Virginia Tech, 1988. Behavioral dimensions of public accounting practice (including stress, turnover, and upward mobility of women), ethnic diversity.

James A. Dearden, Professor; Ph.D., Penn State, 1987. Game theory, marketing science, institution design, microeconomics.

Mary E. Deily, Associate Professor; Ph.D., Harvard, 1985. Industrial organization, exit behavior, industries in transition.

Dale F. Falcinelli, Swartley Professor of Finance, Professor of Practice in Marketing and Management, and Chairman, vSeries Corporate Entrepreneurship; M.A., Lehigh, 1972. Contemporary marketing, business management policies, entrepreneurship, strategic business analysis.

Robert C. Giambatista, Assistant Professor of Management; Ph.D., Wisconsin–Madison, 1999. Leadership, groups, decision making, diversity.

Paul Gordon, Professor of Practice; M.B.A., Wisconsin–Madison; CPA. Financial accounting.

James A. Greenleaf, Associate Professor; Ph.D., NYU, 1973. Portfolio management, derivative instruments, international investments, quantitative applications to investments.

Frank Gunter, Associate Professor; Ph.D., Johns Hopkins, 1985. Economies of Colombia, Iraq, China, and Latvia; capital flight; customs; unions.

Parveen P. Gupta, Frank L. McGee Professor of Accounting; Ph.D., Penn State, 1987. Process redesign through reengineering and benchmarking within manufacturing and service organizations; assessment of business risks and controls within the value chain; business valuation; financial analysis, corporate governance, and internal auditing.

Reetika Gupta, Assistant Professor of Marketing: Ph.D., CUNY, Baruch. Complexity in interactive consumption environments, consumer learning of new products.

James A. Hall, Associate Professor; Ph.D., Oklahoma State, 1979. Systems design, internal control of systems, computer systems auditing.

Thomas J. Hyclak, Professor; Ph.D., Notre Dame, 1976. Labor market developments in transition economies, urban economic development.

Arthur E. King, Professor; Ph.D., Ohio State, 1976. Applied econometrics, comparative economics, economics of Central Europe.

Richard J. Kish, Professor; Ph.D., Florida, 1988. Fixed-income securities, efficient markets, international mergers.

Michael G. Kolchin, Professor; D.B.A., Indiana, 1980. Comparative buying processes, purchasing education and training, purchasing effectiveness, supply chain management optimization.

Nevena T. Koukova, Assistant Professor of Marketing; Ph.D., Maryland, 2005. Pricing of digital products, bundling and unbundling of electronic content, and behavioral aspects of bundling; marketing strategy; consumer analysis; marketing research; principles of marketing; services marketing.

Robert Kuchta, Professor of Practice; M.S., NJIT, 1982. Marketing as a business.

James A. Largay, Professor; Ph.D., Cornell, 1971. Cash flow reporting, intercorporate investments, derivative financial investments.

James M. Maskulka, Associate Professor; D.B.A., Kent State, 1984. Marketing communications, branding, media.

Teresa McCarthy, Assistant Professor of Supply Chain Management; Ph.D., Tennessee, 2003. Role of marketing in demand management, demand planning and demand forecasting, market orientation and supply chain orientation, collaboration forecasting and sales force forecasting management, e-commerce demand management.

Judith A. McDonald, Associate Professor; Ph.D., Princeton, 1986. United States–Canada economic relations, external debt and tropical deforestation issues, pay equity, gender differences in starting salaries.

Matthew A. Melone, Associate Professor; J.D., Pennsylvania, 1993. Taxation, law and accounting, real estate law, partnership and LLC taxation.

Erin Moore, Assistant Professor of Accounting; Ph.D., Massachusetts, 2006; CPA. Earnings restatements, firm valuation.

Vincent G. Munley, Professor; Ph.D., SUNY at Binghamton, 1979. Political economy of state and local government finances.

David H. Myers, Professor of Practice; Ph.D., Washington (Seattle), 2001. Conditional performance measurement of mutual funds; pension funds, portfolio strategies, Japanese equity markets, international investing, stochastic programming applications for asset/liability management.

George A. Nation III, Professor; J.D., Villanova, 1983. Commercial lending law topics, environmental liability for lenders, promissory notes, guaranty and surety law, product liability.

Nandkumar Nayar, Professor and Hans Baer Chair in Finance; Ph.D., Iowa, 1988. Investment banking and financing methods, derivative securities, working capital management, tax issues, game theory modeling.

Anthony P. O'Brien, Professor; Ph.D., Berkeley, 1986. Business history, economic history, microeconomics.

John W. Paul, Professor; Ph.D., Lehigh, 1978. Audits of small businesses, audits of information systems, statistical sampling in auditing, cost allocation, activity-based costing.

Catherine M. Ridings, Assistant Professor; Ph.D., Drexel, 2000. Virtual communities, trust, e-commerce, management of technical personnel.

Heibatollah Sami, Eugene and Sue Mercy Professor of Accounting; Ph.D., Louisiana State, 1984. Impact of accounting information on capital markets, international accounting, auditing.

Michael D. Santoro, Associate Professor; Ph.D., Rutgers, 1998. Organizational strategy, entrepreneurship and intrapreneurship, sources of technological innovation, role of industry-university collaboration in advancing new technologies.

Theodore W. Schlie, Associate Professor; Ph.D., Northwestern, 1973. Advanced manufacturing and competitive strategy, globalization of industrial research and development, international competitiveness.

Susan A. Sherer, Kenan Professor of Information Technology Management, Business Information Systems Program Director, and Co-director for the Center for Value Chain Research; Ph.D., Pennsylvania, 1988. Software failure risk, management of software development, manufacturing networks, interorganizational information systems, strategic information systems, IT investment management.

Kenneth P. Sinclair, Professor and Accounting Department Chairman; Ph.D., Massachusetts, 1972. Performance evaluation, human resource accounting, case studies in managerial accounting.

K. Sivakumar, Arthur Tauck Professor of International Marketing and Logistics and Professor and Chairperson of Marketing; Ph.D., Syracuse, 1992. Pricing, international marketing, innovation management.

Quingjiu (Tom) Tao, Assistant Professor of Management; Ph.D., Pittsburgh, 2004. Strategic alliance in emerging market environments, institutions and firm behavior, first mover advantage in international market entry.

Larry W. Taylor, Professor; Ph.D., North Carolina, 1984. Specification testing for economic models, finite-sample issues in econometrics, econometric methodology, macroeconomic modeling, qualitative dependent variables.

Stephen F. Thode, Associate Professor and Director, Goodman Center for Real Estate Studies; D.B.A., Indiana, 1980. New mortgage products, mortgage pricing, affordable housing financing, taxation of real estate investments, real option pricing.

Robert J. Thornton, Charles W. MacFarlane Professor of Economics and Program Director; Ph.D., Illinois, 1970. Unionism and collective bargaining, public employment, labor market discrimination, forensic economics.

Robert J. Trent, Associate Professor and Program Director, Supply Chain Management Program; Ph.D., Michigan State, 1993. Cross-functional teams in purchasing.

Geraldo M. Vasconcellos, Allen DuBois Professor of Finance and Economics and Director, Business Minor Program; Ph.D., Illinois at Urbana-Champaign, 1986. Cross-border mergers and acquisitions foreign direct investment, international financial markets, privatizations, financial structure and development.

Todd A. Watkins, Associate Professor; Ph.D., Harvard, 1986. Technology and industrial policy, economics and management of innovation, defense and optoelectronics industries.

Samuel C. Weaver, Swartley Professor of Finance; Ph.D., Lehigh, 1985. Value-based management, performance metrics, capital evaluation, cost of capital, mergers and acquisitions.

Wenlong Weng, Assistant Professor; Ph.D., Stanford, 2001. Managerial economics, planning and decision making under uncertainty, real options, financial risk measurement and management.

Yuliang (Oliver) Yao, Assistant Professor of Business Information Systems; M.B.A., Rensselaer, 1997; Ph.D., Maryland, 2002. Supply chain management, electronic commerce, technology issues in supply chains, logistics modeling/simulation.

LEHIGH UNIVERSITY

College of Business and Economics
P. C. Rossin College of Engineering and Applied Science

Program of Study

In a world where crossing boundaries can mean the difference between success and mediocrity, the Lehigh Master of Business Administration and Engineering (M.B.A.&E.) forges the path to excellence.

Decisions in business and industry rarely involve only one area of the company. Technical professionals must work successfully on teams requiring advanced skills in both management and technology.

Anticipating the needs of today's challenging technical environment, Lehigh has developed an interdisciplinary degree—the M.B.A.&E.—designed to provide those skills that are necessary for individuals and companies to achieve a competitive edge. Building on Lehigh's commitment to developing leaders in business and industry, the M.B.A.&E. brings together two premier programs in one powerful joint degree, offering a solid foundation in both business and engineering. In this 45-credit-hour program, students may choose a concentration in business or in engineering, enabling them to develop strategic career goals. A concentration in business may include information systems management, corporate entrepreneurship, management, marketing, and supply chain management. Engineering concentrations include chemical, civil, computer, computer science, electrical, industrial, manufacturing systems, mechanical, materials science, and polymer science.

Elective courses, jointly developed by the highly respected P. C. Rossin College of Engineering and Applied Science and the College of Business and Economics, integrate technical and business concepts designed to prepare graduates for real-world applications. An integrative team project, sponsored by a corporate partner, provides the opportunity to apply knowledge in an industry setting. Students may pursue this degree on a full-time or part-time basis. Graduates of the program offer to their employers specialized skills in leadership, communication, technology, integrative problem solving, and managing information.

Research Facilities

The Rauch Business Center is a modern, professional environment for learning and teaching, including forty well-equipped classrooms, computer labs, auditoriums, and conference rooms. Along with books and journals, Lehigh's library system includes electronic databases and microfilm, computer software, and media collections. Via the campuswide integrated voice and data communication network, users can access the Internet, the libraries' online catalog, and hundreds of national and international electronic databases and can submit reference inquires, place orders, request media services, and request delivery of documents electronically. The campus network provides access to mainframe computers, the Integrated Library System, and other computers on campus. The Computing Center houses several mainframes and maintains hundreds of microcomputers in sites across the campus.

Financial Aid

Financial aid for graduate students is based on academic performance and, in the case of M.B.A.&E. students, work experience. Students interested in financial aid must file a complete application and be admitted to both the College of Business and Economics and the College of Engineering by January 15 for the following academic year.

Financial aid is dispersed through teaching assistantships (which cover tuition and pay a stipend of $11,000 to $13,500 for the academic year), graduate assistantships, fellowships, and positions in the Small Business Development Center. Domestic students receive priority for financial aid.

The primary loan source for graduate students is the Federal Stafford Student Loan. Students must file the Free Application for Federal Student Aid (FAFSA), an institutional application, and their most recent 1040. Students may complete the FAFSA at http://www.fafsa.ed.gov.

Cost of Study

Tuition for the M.B.A.&E. program is $760 per credit hour. Full-time students are assessed a $150 technology fee each semester. Online courses also require a $100 technology fee.

Living and Housing Costs

Information on graduate student housing is available through the Department of Residential Services at 610-758-3500. On-campus housing costs range from $470 per month to $625 per month. Off-campus listings are also available through residential services. Students should budget approximately $30,000 per year.

Student Group

There are currently 17 students in the M.B.A.&E. program.

Student Outcomes

Students graduating with the M.B.A.&E. degree have secured positions in industry as engineering managers, company principals, and consultants.

Location

Lehigh University, founded in 1865, consists of three distinctive, continuous areas, totaling more than 1,600 acres. Located 90 miles southwest of New York City and 50 miles north of Philadelphia, the Lehigh Valley is Pennsylvania's fourth-largest metropolitan area. Bethlehem, one of three principal cities of the Lehigh Valley, is a center of industry, high technology, culture, and education.

The University

Lehigh University, founded in 1865, was one of the first American institutions to offer a technical education. Its first five schools included a school of general literature and four scientific schools. The innovative concept of offering both technical and nontechnical courses of study has continued to be a successful formula at Lehigh. Today, Lehigh has a graduate school of education and three colleges: Engineering and Applied Science, Arts and Sciences, and Business and Economics. Thirty-five percent of the students are enrolled in the College of Engineering and Applied Science. Women have always been admitted to Lehigh at the graduate level, and, in 1971, the University began admitting women at the undergraduate level. In 1987, the campus expanded to 1,600 acres, with the addition of the former Homer Labs of the Bethlehem Steel Corporation. The Mountaintop Campus houses several engineering departments and centers.

Applying

Lehigh evaluates applications on a rolling basis and usually notifies applicants of admissions decisions within three weeks of receiving a completed application. Prospective students must have achieved a bachelor's degree in engineering or applied science. A TOEFL score is required of all candidates for whom English is not their native language. Either a GMAT or a GRE score is required, depending on the engineering discipline to be pursued. Applications to the M.B.A.&E. degree program must be accepted by both colleges. Deadlines for regular full-time students are May 1 for fall semester (July 15 for part-time students), December 1 for spring semester, April 30 for summer session I, and May 30 for summer session II. Associate students (those who have conditional status) may apply up to two weeks before classes begin in any semester or summer session. The deadline for financial aid is January 15 for the upcoming academic year.

Correspondence and Information

Corinn McBride
Director of Recruitment and Admissions
Graduate Programs Office
College of Business and Economics
Lehigh University
621 Taylor Street
Bethlehem, Pennsylvania 18015
Phone: 610-758-5280
Fax: 610-758-5283
E-mail: mbaadmissions@lehigh.edu
Web site: http://www.lehigh.edu/mba

Dr. John Coulter
Associate Dean of Graduate Studies
P. C. Rossin College of Engineering
  and Applied Science
Packard Laboratory
Lehigh University
Bethlehem, Pennsylvania 18015
Phone: 610-758-6310
E-mail: jc0i@lehigh.edu
Web site: http://www.lehigh.edu/~ineas

Lehigh University

THE FACULTY AND THEIR RESEARCH

Mark R. Adams, Professor of Practice, Business Minor Program; M.B.A., Pittsburgh; J.D., Baltimore; CFA, CPA. Accounting, corporate reporting, finance, capita evaluations and investments.

Anne-Marie Anderson, Assistant Professor of Finance; M.B.A., Tulsa, 1998; Ph.D., Arizona, 2003. Corporate restructuring, mergers and acquisitions, valuation.

J. Richard Aronson, William L. Clayton Professor of Business and Economics and Director, Martindale Center for the Study of Private Enterprise; Ph.D., Clark, 1964. Tax and expenditure analysis, pension funds, municipal bond analysis, fiscal federalism.

Richard W. Barsness, Professor Emeritus; Ph.D., Minnesota, 1963. International business, corporate strategy in the airline industry.

John W. Bonge, Professor Emeritus; Ph.D., Northwestern, 1968. Business strategy and entrepreneurship.

Paul R. Brown, Professor of Accounting and Dean, College of Business and Economics; Ph.D., Texas at Austin. Financial statement analysis, FASB/SEC policy analysis, international reporting and analysis, earnings measurement and management, managing earnings expectations.

Stephen G. Buell, Professor; Ph.D., Lehigh, 1977. High-yield bonds, corporate bankruptcy.

Franklin J. Carter, Assistant Professor of Marketing; Ph.D., Carnegie Mellon, 1997. Business-to-business marketing, sales force management, diffusion of innovation.

Ravi Chitturi, Assistant Professor of Marketing; M.B.A., 1996, Ph.D., 2003, Texas at Austin. Technology and innovation, design and consumer emotions, brand value and marketing strategy.

Shin-Yi Chou, Assistant Professor of Economics; Ph.D., Duke, 1999. Health economics.

Karen M. Collins, Associate Professor; Ph.D., Virginia Tech, 1988. Behavioral dimensions of public accounting practice (including stress, turnover, and upward mobility of women), ethnic diversity.

James A. Dearden, Professor; Ph.D., Penn State, 1987. Game theory, marketing science, institution design, microeconomics.

Mary E. Deily, Associate Professor; Ph.D., Harvard, 1985. Industrial organization, exit behavior, industries in transition.

Dale F. Falcinelli, Swartley Professor of Finance, Professor of Practice in Marketing and Management, and Chairman, vSeries Corporate Entrepreneurship; M.A., Lehigh, 1972. Contemporary marketing, business management policies, entrepreneurship, strategic business analysis.

Robert C. Giambatista, Assistant Professor of Management; Ph.D., Wisconsin–Madison, 1999. Leadership, groups, decision making, diversity.

Paul Gordon, Professor of Practice; M.B.A., Wisconsin–Madison; CPA. Financial accounting.

James A. Greenleaf, Associate Professor; Ph.D., NYU, 1973. Portfolio management, derivative instruments, international investments, quantitative applications to investments.

Frank Gunter, Associate Professor; Ph.D., Johns Hopkins, 1985. Economies of Colombia, Iraq, China, and Latvia; capital flight; customs; unions.

Parveen P. Gupta, Frank L. McGee Professor of Accounting; Ph.D., Penn State, 1987. Process redesign through reengineering and benchmarking within manufacturing and service organizations; assessment of business risks and controls within the value chain; business valuation; financial analysis, corporate governance, and internal auditing.

Reetika Gupta, Assistant Professor of Marketing: Ph.D., CUNY, Baruch. Complexity in interactive consumption environments, consumer learning of new products.

James A. Hall, Associate Professor; Ph.D., Oklahoma State, 1979. Systems design, internal control of systems, computer systems auditing.

Thomas J. Hyclak, Professor; Ph.D., Notre Dame, 1976. Labor market developments in transition economies, urban economic development.

Arthur E. King, Professor; Ph.D., Ohio State, 1976. Applied econometrics, comparative economics, economics of Central Europe.

Richard J. Kish, Professor; Ph.D., Florida, 1988. Fixed-income securities, efficient markets, international mergers.

Michael G. Kolchin, Professor; D.B.A., Indiana, 1980. Comparative buying processes, purchasing education and training, purchasing effectiveness, supply chain management optimization.

Nevena T. Koukova, Assistant Professor of Marketing; Ph.D., Maryland, 2005. Pricing of digital products, bundling and unbundling of electronic content, and behavioral aspects of bundling; marketing strategy; consumer analysis; marketing research; principles of marketing; services marketing.

Robert Kuchta, Professor of Practice; M.S., NJIT, 1982. Marketing as a business.

James A. Largay, Professor; Ph.D., Cornell, 1971. Cash flow reporting, intercorporate investments, derivative financial investments.

James M. Maskulka, Associate Professor; D.B.A., Kent State, 1984. Marketing communications, branding, media.

Teresa McCarthy, Assistant Professor of Supply Chain Management; Ph.D., Tennessee, 2003. Role of marketing in demand management, demand planning and demand forecasting, market orientation and supply chain orientation, collaboration forecasting and sales force forecasting management, e-commerce demand management.

Judith A. McDonald, Associate Professor; Ph.D., Princeton, 1986. United States–Canada economic relations, external debt and tropical deforestation issues, pay equity, gender differences in starting salaries.

Matthew A. Melone, Associate Professor; J.D., Pennsylvania, 1993. Taxation, law and accounting, real estate law, partnership and LLC taxation.

Erin Moore, Assistant Professor of Accounting; Ph.D., Massachusetts, 2006; CPA. Earnings restatements, firm valuation.

Vincent G. Munley, Professor; Ph.D., SUNY at Binghamton, 1979. Political economy of state and local government finances.

David H. Myers, Professor of Practice; Ph.D., Washington (Seattle), 2001. Conditional performance measurement of mutual funds; pension funds, portfolio strategies, Japanese equity markets, international investing, stochastic programming applications for asset/liability management.

George A. Nation III, Professor; J.D., Villanova, 1983. Commercial lending law topics, environmental liability for lenders, promissory notes, guaranty and surety law, product liability.

Nandkumar Nayar, Professor and Hans Baer Chair in Finance; Ph.D., Iowa, 1988. Investment banking and financing methods, derivative securities, working capital management, tax issues, game theory modeling.

Anthony P. O'Brien, Professor; Ph.D., Berkeley, 1986. Business history, economic history, microeconomics.

John W. Paul, Professor; Ph.D., Lehigh, 1978. Audits of small businesses, audits of information systems, statistical sampling in auditing, cost allocation, activity-based costing.

Catherine M. Ridings, Assistant Professor; Ph.D., Drexel, 2000. Virtual communities, trust, e-commerce, management of technical personnel.

Heibatollah Sami, Eugene and Sue Mercy Professor of Accounting; Ph.D., Louisiana State, 1984. Impact of accounting information on capital markets, international accounting, auditing.

Michael D. Santoro, Associate Professor; Ph.D., Rutgers, 1998. Organizational strategy, entrepreneurship and intrapreneurship, sources of technological innovation, role of industry-university collaboration in advancing new technologies.

Theodore W. Schlie, Associate Professor; Ph.D., Northwestern, 1973. Advanced manufacturing and competitive strategy, globalization of industrial research and development, international competitiveness.

Susan A. Sherer, Kenan Professor of Information Technology Management, Business Information Systems Program Director, and Co-director for the Center for Value Chain Research; Ph.D., Pennsylvania, 1988. Software failure risk, management of software development, manufacturing networks, interorganizational information systems, strategic information systems, IT investment management.

Kenneth P. Sinclair, Professor and Accounting Department Chairman; Ph.D., Massachusetts, 1972. Performance evaluation, human resource accounting, case studies in managerial accounting.

K. Sivakumar, Arthur Tauck Professor of International Marketing and Logistics and Professor and Chairperson of Marketing; Ph.D., Syracuse, 1992. Pricing, international marketing, innovation management.

Quingjiu (Tom) Tao, Assistant Professor of Management; Ph.D., Pittsburgh, 2004. Strategic alliance in emerging market environments, institutions and firm behavior, first mover advantage in international market entry.

Larry W. Taylor, Professor; Ph.D., North Carolina, 1984. Specification testing for economic models, finite-sample issues in econometrics, econometric methodology, macroeconomic modeling, qualitative dependent variables.

Stephen F. Thode, Associate Professor and Director, Goodman Center for Real Estate Studies; D.B.A., Indiana, 1980. New mortgage products, mortgage pricing, affordable housing financing, taxation of real estate investments, real option pricing.

Robert J. Thornton, Charles W. MacFarlane Professor of Economics and Program Director; Ph.D., Illinois, 1970. Unionism and collective bargaining, public employment, labor market discrimination, forensic economics.

Robert J. Trent, Associate Professor and Program Director, Supply Chain Management Program; Ph.D., Michigan State, 1993. Cross-functional teams in purchasing.

Geraldo M. Vasconcellos, Allen DuBois Professor of Finance and Economics and Director, Business Minor Program; Ph.D., Illinois at Urbana-Champaign, 1986. Cross-border mergers and acquisitions foreign direct investment, international financial markets, privatizations, financial structure and development.

Todd A. Watkins, Associate Professor; Ph.D., Harvard, 1986. Technology and industrial policy, economics and management of innovation, defense and optoelectronics industries.

Samuel C. Weaver, Swartley Professor of Finance; Ph.D., Lehigh, 1985. Value-based management, performance metrics, capital evaluation, cost of capital, mergers and acquisitions.

Wenlong Weng, Assistant Professor; Ph.D., Stanford, 2001. Managerial economics, planning and decision making under uncertainty, real options, financial risk measurement and management.

Yuliang (Oliver) Yao, Assistant Professor of Business Information Systems; M.B.A., Rensselaer, 1997; Ph.D., Maryland, 2002. Supply chain management, electronic commerce, technology issues in supply chains, logistics modeling/simulation.

The faculty members of the P. C. Rossin College of Engineering participate in the M.B.A.&E. Graduate Program at Lehigh University. The faculty members with whom a student has contact are determined by the area of concentration or department that is chosen upon entrance into the program. Faculty members can be viewed on the pages listed by the following departments: chemical engineering, civil and environmental engineering, computer science and engineering, electrical and computer science, industrial and systems engineering, materials science and engineering, and mechanical engineering and mechanics.

MARIST COLLEGE

School of Management

Programs of Study

The School of Management at Marist College offers master's degrees in business administration, public administration, and technology management designed to meet the unique needs of working adults. Structured for part-time study and offered in both traditional campus-based classrooms and online formats, the graduate management degree programs at Marist provide a high-quality, broad-based business management education that emphasizes the application of management theory to practice and the use of technology to enhance student learning.

The 30-credit Master of Business Administration (M.B.A.) program is accredited by AACSB International–The Association to Advance Collegiate Schools of Business, the premier accrediting body for business programs worldwide. The curriculum is designed to cultivate managers who are effective decision makers and to provide the tools they need to advance their career with their current employers, prepare themselves to take a position of influence within a new organization, or pursue an entirely new career path. The program emphasizes the management process and the behavioral influences that significantly affect the success of modern organizations. M.B.A. graduates possess the strategic perspective necessary to identify opportunities and risks when there are competing demands and finite resources available. M.B.A. course requirements consist of a combination of foundation, core, and elective courses designed to develop the professional analytical, communication, and leadership skills needed to keep pace with the competitive demands of a global economy.

The School of Management created the 39-credit Master of Public Administration (M.P.A.) program to provide students with the knowledge and skills they need to be effective public-sector and not-for-profit program administrators. The curriculum stresses the ethical, legal, and social context of administration. Graduates of Marist College's M.P.A. program understand how to develop and sustain positive organizational behavior. They know how to effectively utilize a full range of management and administrative techniques to analyze critical issues, solve complex problems, and lead important programs.

The Master of Science in Technology Management (M.S.T.M.) is an interdisciplinary program offered jointly by the School of Management and the School of Computer Science and Mathematics. The M.S.T.M. focuses on educating technology professionals in bridging the gap between technology-driven and managerial thought processes. Marist's M.S.T.M. is fully online, allowing students to set up time management according to their personal schedule. The Marist M.S.T.M. additionally includes three residencies that allow students to interact and network: an orientation residency at the beginning and a capping residency at the end of the program as well as a ten-day international residency that allows students to encounter technology management in the global context. A class recently traveled to Beijing, China, for their ten-day residency.

Research Facilities

Marist's state-of-the-art James A. Cannavino Library opened in 1999. The 83,000-square-foot structure houses the library's circulating collection, print periodicals, and archives that include special collections of distinctive resources. The library collection includes more than 170,000 book and periodical volumes. Current periodical subscriptions exceed 6,000 titles in several formats. More than 4,500 videocassettes and videodisks on a variety of topics are available in the library as components of assigned course work.

The James A. Cannavino Library is an innovator in developing and implementing computerized information resources and information literacy programs as well as a variety of services especially for distance education and nonresident students. The MERIT electronic reserve room, developed in conjunction with IBM, provides students with online access to reserve material in any format—print, radio, and video—from several locations on campus. The library also provides online access to full-text periodical articles and has continued to expand and upgrade access to journal literature through its Web page and remote database access.

Financial Aid

Financial aid for graduate students is available primarily in the form of student loans and federal grants. Employer tuition reimbursement programs are also honored.

Cost of Study

Graduate tuition for the 2007–08 academic year is $665 per credit Fees include a one-time matriculation fee of $30. In addition, a $30 registration fee is charged per semester. Costs for books and supplies are estimated to be $125 per course.

Living and Housing Costs

The College does not offer housing to graduate students, but off-campus housing is available.

Location

Marist College is located on the east bank of the majestic Hudson River, midway between New York City and Albany, in Poughkeepsie, New York. The scenic 130-acre campus is situated just minutes from several important historic sites, including the Vanderbilt mansion; the Franklin Delano Roosevelt home and museum; Eleanor Roosevelt's retreat house, Val-Kill; and the Culinary Institute of America.

The College

Marist College has been recognized for excellence by *U.S. News & World Report*, *Barron's Best Buys in College Education*, and is listed among the Princeton Review's "Best 351 Colleges" and "Best 257 Best Business Schools" nationwide. Founded by the Marist Brothers in 1929, the College is one of the leading liberal arts institutions in the Northeast. In 2006, the *Princeton Review* and *Forbes* named Marist College one of the "25 Most Connected Campuses" in America.

Applying

Applicants to the M.B.A., M.P.A., or M.S.T.M. program must submit a completed Marist Graduate Admission Application (available online); a nonrefundable $50 application fee, made payable to Marist College; official transcripts from all prior undergraduate and graduate institutions attended; a current resume; completed recommendation forms from two references; response to essay question; and official GRE or GMAT scores as required by the program. The Graduate Admissions Office accepts applications on a rolling basis. Admission is made according to published deadlines.

Correspondence and Information

The Office of Graduate Enrollment
Marist College
3399 North Road
Poughkeepsie, New York 12601
Phone: 845-575-3800
        888-877-7900 (toll-free)
E-mail: graduate@marist.edu
Web site: http://www.marist.edu/graduate

Marist College

THE FACULTY

For information about faculty members and their current research, students should visit the Marist Web site at http://www.marist.edu/graduate.

MARYWOOD UNIVERSITY

Program in Business Administration

Programs of Study	The Master of Business Administration (M.B.A.) degree at Marywood University provides students with a common body of knowledge in business administration via the required core courses and undergraduate prerequisites for the degree. With the selection of a concentration area in finance and investments, general management, or management information systems (MIS), students gain the experience and skills to be considered specialists within their respective fields. While enhancing a student's broad business knowledge—and to successfully complete the program—36 semester hours of graduate-level courses are taken within the core, 12 of which make up the concentration.
	The Master of Science in Management Information Systems is a more specialized program that offers students the opportunity to elect three courses that complement the management information systems concentration (the electives must be approved by the program chairperson or the student's adviser). A total of 36 semester hours, which includes 15 in core courses plus the required prerequisites, must be completed.
Research Facilities	The Business and Managerial Science Programs benefit from Marywood University's commitment to provide all students with state-of-the-art technology. Computer facilities, with the latest financial and statistical software, are available in the McGowan Center and throughout the campus. The library, located in the Learning Resources Center, has holdings of more than 216,190 volumes, 338,190 microforms, 43,530 media items, and 965 current periodicals. The library also participates in a national and international interlibrary loan network.
Financial Aid	Assistantships, scholarships, and loans are available to graduate students. Students enrolled for at least 6 credits per semester can borrow under the Federal Stafford Student Loan. Information is available from the financial aid office.
Cost of Study	Tuition is $695 per credit. The per-semester general fee is $140 for students enrolled in 4–11 credits and $425 for those enrolled in 12 or more credits.
Living and Housing Costs	Students can pursue off-campus housing. Marywood is located in a residential area, and rental apartments are available for graduate students.
Student Group	Of the 13 full-time and 65 part-time students, 34 are women and 6 are members of minority groups.
Location	Marywood University is situated in a suburban area known as the Green Ridge section of Scranton, a city of about 75,000. Located a little more than 100 miles west of New York City and 100 miles north of Philadelphia, Scranton is served by the Scranton–Wilkes-Barre International Airport and is accessible by a network of superhighways. The Pocono Mountains resort areas and several beautiful lakes can be reached within 45 minutes or less. The Montage Mountain recreation area is only 15 minutes away.
The University and The Program	Marywood University, which was established 1915, is an independent, comprehensive Catholic university that is owned and sponsored by the Congregation of Sisters, Servants of the Immaculate Heart of Mary. Graduate studies were inaugurated in 1921. The Business and Managerial Science Programs enable students to acquire and further develop their managerial and leadership competencies to successfully meet the dynamic challenges of a knowledge-based society and to nurture values that are conducive to ethical and socially responsible behavior. The Business Programs are accredited by the Association of Collegiate Business Schools and Programs (ACBSP).
Applying	Most applicants with undergraduate backgrounds in business will likely have completed the necessary courses in accounting concepts, business economics, computer technologies for management, financial tools, managerial concepts, marketing and sales concepts, the legal environment of business, and review of business statistics. For students with undergraduate backgrounds outside of business, 1-credit modules are offered to meet the prerequisites. For students pursuing the M.B.A. degree with a concentration in management information systems (MIS), prerequisites also include two programming languages, such as C++, COBOL, RPG, Visual Basic, or Java.
	Students should submit the completed application, the $30 application fee, and scores from the GMAT. International students should also submit TOEFL scores. The preferred application deadline is April 15 for the fall semester and November 15 for the spring semester, but applications are processed on a rolling basis.
Correspondence and Information	Dr. Arthur Comstock Business and Managerial Science Programs Marywood University 2300 Adams Avenue Scranton, Pennsylvania 18509 Phone: 866-279-9663 Ext. 6274 (toll-free) Fax: 570-961-4762 E-mail: comstock@marywood.edu Web site: http://www.marywood.edu/departments/business/graduate/gradindex.html

Marywood University

THE FACULTY AND THEIR RESEARCH

Marywood's business faculty members have the practical business experience to add credence to the academic knowledge they impart. Possessing graduate degrees from a wide range of geographical areas, instructors present various business philosophies of both the United States and the international sector, as applied by multinational enterprises. The congenial atmosphere on campus is felt not only among the students but also by the faculty members, whose dedication is immediately apparent.

Arthur B. Comstock, Associate Professor of Business and Managerial Science; Ph.D., Lehigh. Investments and corporate finance.

Samir P. Dagher, Professor of Business and Managerial Science; Ph.D., Ohio State; CMFC. Strategic planning and management.

Uldarico Rex Dumdum Jr., Associate Professor of Business and Managerial Science; Ph.D., SUNY at Binghamton. Information systems.

Dennis Grimes, Adjunct Professor of Business and Managerial Science; M.B.A., Marywood. Information technology and programming.

Chris Haran, Adjunct Professor of Business and Managerial Science; M.S., SUNY at Binghamton. Management of technology.

Gale A. Jaeger, Associate Professor of Business and Managerial Science; Ed.D., Temple. Marketing and human resource management.

Brian Kelly, Assistant Professor of Business and Managerial Science; M.B.A., Wilkes. Information technology and database systems.

Charles J. Lipinski, Assistant Professor of Business and Managerial Science; D.B.A., Nova Southeastern. Hospitality management.

George Marcinek, Assistant Professor of Business and Managerial Science; M.B.A., Scranton; CPA. Accounting rules and federal taxation.

Brian Petula, Assistant Professor of Business and Managerial Science; J.D., M.B.A., Wake Forest. Legal responsibilities of corporate executives.

Tim Rosser, Director of the Aviation Management Program; M.B.A., Marywood. Aviation management.

Chris Speicher, Assistant Professor of Business and Managerial Science; Ph.D., Temple. Organizational behavior.

MISSOURI STATE UNIVERSITY

College of Business Administration

Programs of Study

The College of Business Administration (COBA) offers four graduate study programs: the Master of Accountancy (M.Acc.), the Master of Business Administration (M.B.A.), the Master of Science (M.S.) in computer information systems, and the Master of Health Administration (M.H.A.). Both day and evening classes are available to accommodate a variety of schedules.

The M.Acc. degree fulfills the education needs of professional accountants, enhancing both their business and specialized accounting knowledge. The program meets the 150-hour education requirement for membership in the American Institute of Certified Public Accountants and the statutory education requirements for certification as a public accountant.

Along with integrating a variety of courses offered by the five departments in COBA, the M.B.A. program gives students the opportunity to tailor their degree to meet their career needs. Students take 21 hours of required courses and may choose an area of concentration.

Developed exclusively for IT professionals with three or more years of IT work experience, the M.S. program enables students to earn an accredited degree in just twenty-three months—without interrupting their careers. The program gained national recognition for being one of the first accredited graduate programs designed exclusively for IT professionals that combined classroom and distance learning.

The 48-credit M.H.A. degree program is designed for students who wish to further their careers in the administration of health organizations, including integrated systems, hospitals, group practices, long-term-care facilities, clinics, and managed-care and other types of health organizations. Degree requirements and specific program information can be found in the graduate catalog, which is available online at http://graduate.missouristate.edu/.

Research Facilities

The Center for Business and Economic Development is home to both the Small Business Development Center and the Management Development Institute. The Small Business Development Center, a nonprofit entity, provides consultation and seminar training for potential and existing small businesses in nineteen southwest Missouri counties. The Management Development Institute offers a wide range of seminars in order to assist managers and supervisors with developing tools, techniques, and strategies that motivate people, solve problems, and keep worker performance and work quality at high levels.

Missouri State University libraries have comprehensive electronic resources, including an online catalog, electronic indexes and full-text resources, and Internet accessibility. The University is a member of the Center for Research Libraries and is both a U.S. and United Nations document depository.

Financial Aid

A limited number of graduate assistantships are available and are awarded on a competitive basis. An assistantship provides a minimum stipend of $7050 for the nine-month academic year and a tuition scholarship for up to 12 credit hours of course work for both the fall and spring semesters. In addition, students who have served as assistants for both the fall and spring semesters are eligible to receive a scholarship for up to 6 hours of graduate course work for the following summer semester. Graduate students are also eligible for federal financial assistance through the Federal Perkins Loan, the Federal Subsidized Stafford Student Loan, and the Federal Unsubsidized Stafford Student Loan.

Cost of Study

In 2006–07, graduate-level course fees were $199 per credit hour for in-state residents and $388 per credit hour for nonresidents. An additional student services fee ($274 for full-time students) is assessed per semester, based on enrolled credit hours.

Living and Housing Costs

The average cost per year for room and board in residence halls was $5445 in 2006–07. Exact rates depend on room style and meal plan. Furnished apartments are available for graduate, married, and nontraditional students for $422 to $562 per month. University and privately owned apartments are within a reasonable distance of the campus.

Student Group

In fall 2006, COBA had about 500 graduate students, 75 of whom were enrolled in the M.Acc. program; 370 were M.B.A. students. The remainder was evenly split between the M.S. and M.H.A. programs.

Location

Missouri State University is located in Springfield, the third-largest city in Missouri, with a metropolitan service region of 330,000. Located in the heart of the Ozarks recreational area, the University is within easy driving distance of numerous lakes, streams, and parks. The community of Springfield is supported by an industrial/manufacturing base and an expanding service industry in tourism, with people drawn by the natural beauty and recreation of the Ozarks and the musical attractions in nearby Branson. Springfield has an extensive health and medical economy serving southwest Missouri, northwest Arkansas, southeast Kansas, and northeast Oklahoma.

The University and The College

Missouri State University, founded in 1905, is a multicampus metropolitan university system with a statewide mission in public affairs. The University offers more than 150 undergraduate majors and forty-three graduate programs, many of which are the strongest of their kind in the state. The students experience college life at its best, with NCAA Division I athletics and more than 250 student organizations.

The College of Business Administration comprises two divisions: the Business Unit and the Department of Industrial Management. The Business Unit, which consists of the School of Accountancy, the Department of Computer Information Systems, the Department of Finance and General Business, the Department of Management, and the Department of Marketing, is accredited by AACSB International–The Association to Advance Collegiate Schools of Business. The Department of Industrial Management is accredited by the National Association of Industrial Technology.

Applying

Admission requirements vary by program but can be obtained by contacting the College. In general, students should have a bachelor's degree from an accredited institution and a minimum GPA of 2.75 for the last 60 hours of academic work. Students should submit the completed application form, the $35 application fee, GMAT or GRE scores, official transcripts from all institutions attended, and two letters of recommendation. International applicants whose native language is not English are required to submit TOEFL scores (minimum of 550 on the paper-based test or 213 on the computer-based test). The early action deadline is December 1.

Correspondence and Information

College of Business Administration
Glass Hall 400
Missouri State University
901 South National Avenue
Springfield, Missouri 65897

Phone: 417-836-5646
Fax: 417-836-4407
E-mail: coba@missouristate.edu
Web site: http://www.coba.missouristate.edu

Missouri State University

THE FACULTY

Accountancy
Ronald R. Bottin, Professor and Dean; Ph.D., Missouri, 1974.
Anita V. Brand, Lecturer; M.B.A., Missouri State, 2005.
Radie G. Bunn, Professor; J.D., William Mitchell Law, 1977; M.S. (taxation), Hartford.
David B. Byrd, Professor and Director, M.Acc. Program; Ph.D., Arkansas, 1979; CPA.
Sandra D. Byrd, Professor; Ph.D., Arkansas, 1979; CPA.
Margaret V. Cerullo, Professor; Ph.D., LSU, 1990; CPA, CFE.
Michael J. Cerullo, Professor; Ph.D., LSU, 1971; CPA, CFE, CDE.
Kurt E. Chaloupecky, Associate Professor; Ph.D., Missouri–Columbia, 1977; CPA.
Sidney R. Ewer, Professor; Ph.D., Mississippi, 1989; CPA, CMA, CIA.
Olen L. Greer, Professor; Ph.D., Colorado, 1986; CMA.
Michael Hammond, Lecturer; M.Acc., Missouri State, 2002; CPA.
Phillip D. Harsha, Associate Professor; Ph.D., Georgia State, 1983; CMA, CIA.
A. Craig Keller, Assistant Professor; Ph.D., Texas A&M, 2000.
Geanie W. Margavio, Associate Professor; Ph.D., Alabama, 1990; CPA.
Robert S. McDuffie, Professor; D.B.A., Louisiana Tech, 1990; CPA.
Debra H. Oden, Associate Professor; J.D., LL.M. (tax), Missouri–Kansas City, 1981; CPA.
Stevan K. Olson, Professor; Ph.D., Wisconsin–Madison, 1974; CPA.
George D. Schmelzle, Associate Professor; Ph.D., Mississippi, 1992; CPA.
Donald G. Smillie, Lecturer; M.Acc., Missouri State, 1999; CPA.
John R. Williams, Associate Professor and Director, School of Accountancy; Ph.D., Mississippi, 1992; CPA, CMA.

Computer Information Systems
Tonya B. Barrier, Professor; Ph.D., Texas at Arlington, 1990.
Sheryl Brahnam, Assistant Professor; Ph.D., CUNY Graduate Center, 2002.
Richard Burton, Lecturer; M.B.A., Duke, 1986.
Jerry M. Chin, Professor and Department Head; D.B.A., Memphis, 1989.
David A. Crockett, Instructor; M.B.A., Drury, 1984.
Ronald S. Dattero, Professor; Ph.D., Purdue, 1982.
Karen Eagles, Lecturer; M.A., Missouri State, 1993.
Michael A. Hignite, Professor and Director, M.B.A. Program; Ph.D., Missouri–Columbia, 1990.
Michelle Hulett, Lecturer; M.B.A., Missouri State, 1998.
Richard Johnson, Associate Professor; Ph.D., Arkansas, 1997.
Rajeev Kaula, Professor; Ph.D., SUNY at Binghamton, 1990.
Chung S. Kim, Professor; Ph.D., Texas Tech, 1987.
Thomas Margavio, Professor; Ph.D., Alabama, 1990.
Shannon McMurtrey, Lecturer; M.B.A., Missouri State, 1997.
David B. Meinert, Professor and Director, M.S.C.I.S. Program; Ph.D., Mississippi, 1990.
Juan Meraz, Lecturer; M.B.A., Missouri State, 1997.
Duane Moses, Associate Professor; Ph.D., Missouri–Columbia, 1990.
Heidi R. Perreault, Professor; Ed.D., Oklahoma State, 1983.
John Satzinger, Professor; Ph.D., Claremont, 1991.
Randall Sexton, Associate Professor; Ph.D., Mississippi, 1996.
Glenna Vanderhoof, Lecturer; Ph.D., Missouri–Columbia, 1994.
Cathy VanLanduyt, Lecturer; M.B.A., Missouri State, 1995.
Hong Zhang, Assistant Professor; M.S., SUNY at Buffalo, 2003.

Finance and General Business
Stanley R. Adamson, Associate Professor; Ph.D., Pennsylvania (Wharton), 1991.
Wayne L. Anderson, Professor; J.D., California Western Law, 1980; M.B.A., Drury, 1988.
John S. Bowdidge, Professor; Ph.D., Missouri–Kansas City, 1967.
C. Edward Chang, Professor; Ph.D., Illinois at Urbana-Champaign, 1989.
Susan J. Crain, Associate Professor; Ph.D., Oklahoma, 1997.
Kee S. Kim, Professor; Ph.D., Texas at Austin, 1978.
Stan Leasure, Assistant Professor; J.D., Tulsa, 1980.
Carol J. Miller, Professor; J.D., 1978, M.B.A., 1984, Missouri–Columbia.
Walt A. Nelson, Associate Professor; Ph.D., Georgia State, 1992.
Robert W. Owens, Professor; Ph.D., Washington (Seattle), 1978.
James Pettijohn, Professor; Ph.D., Nebraska–Lincoln, 1980.
James Philpot, Assistant Professor; Ph.D., Arkansas, 1994.

Kent Ragan, Associate Professor; Ph.D., Missouri–Columbia, 2000; CFA.
James R. Scott, Assistant Professor; Ph.D., Georgia, 1991.
George S. Swales, Professor and Department Head; Ph.D., Arkansas, 1984.

Industrial Management
Richard Neal Callahan, Associate Professor; Ph.D., Missouri–Rolla, 1999.
William H. Drake, Associate Professor; Ph.D., Texas A&M, 1983.
Rita S. Hawkins, Assistant Professor; Ph.D., Arkansas, 2005.
Clifford L. House, Professor; Ph.D., Tulsa, 1977.
Steven W. McCrary, Associate Professor; Ph.D., Missouri–Rolla, 1991.
John H. Reposa, Assistant Professor; Ph.D., Florida Tech, 1996.
Rathel R. Smith, Assistant Professor; M.S., Central Missouri State, 1983; CPIM, CIRM.
Shawn D. Strong, Associate Professor and Department Head; Ph.D., Iowa State, 1999.

Management
Yohannan T. Abraham, Professor; Ph.D., Oklahoma, 1976.
Karen Brown, Associate Professor; D.B.A., Louisiana Tech, 1994.
Mary K. Coulter, Associate Professor; Ph.D., Arkansas, 1984.
Michal Dale, Lecturer; M.A., Missouri State, 1999.
D. Keith Denton, Professor; Ph.D., Southern Illinois, 1982.
Patricia Feltes, Associate Professor; Ph.D., Nebraska, 1988.
Vinay Garg, Assistant Professor; Ph.D., Texas at Arlington, 2000.
Ben Goss, Assistant Professor; Ed.D., Southern Mississippi, 1999.
Corinne Karuppan, Professor; Ph.D., Nebraska, 1991.
Tami Knotts, Associate Professor; D.B.A., Louisiana Tech, 2000.
Patricia Ann Lambert, Lecturer; M.B.A., Missouri State, 1995.
Melody LaPreze, Assistant Professor; Ph.D., Missouri–Columbia, 1997.
Robert Lunn, Professor and Director of Master of Health Administration Program; M.H.A., Duke, 1973; Ph.D., North Carolina at Chapel Hill, 1981.
Peter Richardson, Professor and Director of Assessment; Ph.D., Houston, 1979.
Philip C. Rothschild, Assistant Professor and Entertainment Management Program Director; Ph.D., Florida State, 1996.
Elizabeth Rozell, Professor; Ph.D., Mississippi, 1992.
Wesley A. Scroggins, Assistant Professor; Ph.D., New Mexico State, 2003.
Lawrence Summers, Assistant Professor; Ph.D. candidate, Missouri–Columbia.
Steven Thomas, Professor; Ph.D., Kansas, 1989.
Joyce E. Traylor, Lecturer; M.S., Missouri State, 1993.
Barry L. Wisdom, Professor and Department Head; Ph.D., Arkansas, 1981.
Karen Lee Woodall, Assistant Professor; Ed.D., Tennessee, 1982.

Marketing
T. Sam Brown, Professor; Ph.D., Texas Christian, 1970.
Melissa S. Burnett, Associate Professor; Ph.D., Oklahoma State, 1988.
Mary Chin, Lecturer; M.B.A., Missouri State, 1994.
Sherry Cook, Lecturer; M.B.A., Missouri State, 1981.
Ronald L. Coulter, Professor; Ph.D., Arkansas, 1985.
Christopher Ellis, Lecturer; M.S., Georgia Tech, 1989.
Peggy S. Gilbert, Assistant Professor; M.B.A., Northeast Louisiana, 1970.
Diana Haytko, Associate Professor; Ph.D., Wisconsin–Madison, 1997.
Charles Hermans, Assistant Professor; Ph.D., New Mexico State, 2003.
Nancy K. Keith, Professor; Ph.D., Purdue, 1978.
John Kent, Associate Professor; Ph.D., Tennessee, 1997.
Robert H. Luke, Professor and Department Head; Ph.D., Missouri–Columbia, 1974.
R. Stephen Parker, Professor; D.B.A., Louisiana Tech, 1984.
Janice E. Parmley, Assistant Professor; M.A., Central Missouri State, 1967.
Dane K. Peterson, Professor; Ph.D., Southern Illinois, 1982.
Charles E. Pettijohn, Professor; D.B.A., Louisiana Tech, 1986.
Linda S. Pettijohn, Professor; D.B.A., Louisiana Tech, 1987.
Allen D. Schaefer, Professor; Ph.D., Oklahoma State, 1992.
Lois M. Shufeldt, Professor; Ph.D., New Mexico State, 1977.
Carlo D. Smith, Assistant Professor; Ph.D., Tennessee, 2000.
Sara M. Smith, Assistant Professor; Ph.D., Georgia, 2005.
Gerald G. Udell, Professor and Director, Center for Business and Economic Development; Ph.D., Wisconsin–Madison, 1972.

MONTCLAIR STATE UNIVERSITY

School of Business
Programs in Business Administration

Programs of Study

The goal of the Montclair State University (MSU) M.B.A. program is to combine conceptual approaches to business with practical application in order to give students the skills to be competitive and effective managers in today's global economy. This blend of theory and practice builds a strong foundation for immediate practical application as well as postgraduate professional growth. M.B.A. courses have a maximum enrollment of 25 students, and students and alumni cite the seminar-style classes and friendly, informal atmosphere as major strengths of the program, facilitating both learning and networking. Each individual has the opportunity to shape the M.B.A. experience.

Concentrations are available in accounting, finance, international business, management, management information systems, and marketing. The curriculum consists of 48 credits, but this may be reduced by up to 15 credits in the business core through prior academic course work, challenge exams, and/or graduate transfer credits. All advanced courses must be completed at MSU. Courses are held on weeknights or Saturdays, meeting once a week; this M.B.A. is designed to accommodate busy professionals who work full-time. There is also a Saturday-only accelerated cohort program, which allows completion of the M.B.A. in just two years; classes are held at Brookdale Community College in Lincroft, New Jersey. Structured in a similar manner to an executive M.B.A. program, the Montclair State M.B.A. at Brookdale is for those who prefer a weekend course schedule and can manage the rapid pace of instruction.

Post-M.B.A. certificate programs in accounting, international business, and management are also available, and additional certificates are planned in finance, marketing, and MIS.

Research Facilities

The Harry A. Sprague Library owns more than 1.5 million items, including 410,000 books, 2,600 periodical subscriptions, 65,000 government documents, and more than a million nonprint media. The library provides wireless access to the MSU computer network, business and other research databases, and the Internet; M.B.A. students have access to a study room for graduate student and faculty use only. The School of Business provides access to additional business databases and resources, and all instructional spaces are wireless enabled.

Financial Aid

Several kinds of financial aid sources are available to graduate students who meet all admission requirements, including graduate assistantships and graduate scholarships. Graduate assistants receive remission of tuition and University-wide fees for up to 24 graduate credits per academic year and a stipend for the full ten-month appointment. Montclair offers a number of scholarship opportunities to full-time and part-time students; most notably, the Saul and Adelaide Goldfarb Graduate Scholarship ranges from $1500 to $7000 per year.

Cost of Study

Tuition is $470 per credit for New Jersey residents and $629 per credit for out-of-state residents on the main campus; for the Saturday-only Brookdale M.B.A., tuition is $520 per credit for New Jersey residents and $679 per credit for out-of-state residents. Required fees are $56 per credit. The cost of books and supplies varies by course load.

Living and Housing Costs

Campus housing for graduate students is available for approximately $8250 for a nine-month period. Optional summer housing is available for about $2000 for three months. Housing is also readily available off campus in the Montclair area.

Student Group

There are more than 325 M.B.A. students; 40 percent are women, and approximately 75 percent attend classes on a part-time basis while working full-time. Most full-time students are international (about 20 percent of the total enrollment), and 15 percent of students entering the program already hold another graduate degree. Montclair State M.B.A. students have diverse professional backgrounds in a wide range of industries across the region, especially in financial services, consumer products and services, health care, pharmaceutical manufacturing, and biotechnology. Upon graduation, many students report salary increases, promotions, and/or other significant career changes.

Location

The University is conveniently located on a beautiful 200-acre hilltop campus in Montclair, New Jersey. This suburban town is surrounded by a rich diversity of cultural and recreational opportunities in northern New Jersey and in New York City, which is located 14 miles from campus. New York City can be reached by train and bus from the campus.

The University and The School

Montclair State is New Jersey's second-largest university, offering the advantages of a large, comprehensive research and teaching institution with a broad undergraduate curriculum, a global focus, a wide variety of superior graduate programs, a diverse faculty and student body, and small class sizes. The School of Business offers outstanding undergraduate and graduate programs that prepare students for successful careers in business, nonprofit institutions, and public service. The School is an accredited member of AACSB International–The Association to Advance Collegiate Schools of Business.

Applying

The M.B.A. program accepts all undergraduate majors; the only prerequisite is an undergraduate course in calculus. Candidates without calculus on their transcripts may apply and be accepted to the Montclair State M.B.A. on a conditional basis, completing the calculus course prior to enrolling in the core Statistical Methods course. Admission requirements include a completed written or online application to the Graduate School, one official academic transcript from each college or university (to document an earned undergraduate degree), official GMAT scores, a personal statement of professional objectives, two letters of recommendation, and a nonrefundable application fee of $60. Applications are processed on a rolling basis and may be submitted at any time.

Correspondence and Information

Karen Dennis, Assistant Dean and M.B.A. Director
M.B.A. Office, PA 210
Montclair State University
1 Normal Avenue
Upper Montclair, New Jersey 07043
Phone: 973-655-4306
Fax: 973-655-3449
E-mail: mba@mail.montclair.edu
Web site: http://www.montclair.edu/mba

Montclair State University

THE FACULTY

Accounting, Law, and Taxation

Frank Aquilino, Chair; M.B.A., St. John's (New York); CPA.
Chiaho Chang, Associate Professor; Ph.D., NYU.
James DiGabrielle, Assistant Professor; D.P.S., Pace.
Irene Douma, Professor; Ph.D., CUNY, Baruch; CPA.
Michele Evans, Assistant Professor; J.D., Pace.
Nashwa George, Professor; Ph.D., CUNY, Baruch.
Peggy Ann Hughes, Associate Professor; Ph.D., Rutgers.
Agatha Jeffers, Assistant Professor; Ph.D., Rutgers; CPA.
Lili-Anne Kihn, Associate Professor; D.Sc., Turku (Finland).
Leonard Lauricella, Assistant Professor; J.D., Georgetown; CPA.
Betsy Lin, Assistant Professor; Ph.D., Rutgers.
Joseph LiPari, Assistant Professor; M.B.A., Fairleigh Dickinson.
Santanu Mitra, Associate Professor; Ph.D., LSU.
Ramesh Narasimhan, Associate Professor; Ph.D., Virginia Tech; CPA,
    CIA, CMA.
JoAnn Pinto, Associate Professor; Ph.D., Rutgers; CPA.
Wing Poon, Associate Professor; Ph.D., LSU; CPA.
James Yang, Professor; M.Ph., M.B.A., NYU; CPA.

Economics and Finance

Sang-Hoon Kim, Chair; Ph.D., Wisconsin–Madison.
Ahmet Baytas, Professor; Ph.D., CUNY Graduate Center.
Harold Flint, Professor; Ph.D., Southern Illinois.
Phillip LeBel, Professor; Ph.D., Boston University.
Serpil Leveen, Professor; Ph.D., NYU.
Richard Lord, Professor; Ph.D., Georgia.
A. Seddik Meziani, Professor; Ph.D., Rensselaer.
Deniz Ozenbas, Professor; Ph.D., CUNY, Baruch.
Kamrouz Pirouz, Professor; Ph.D., Hawaii.
Glenville Rawlins, Professor; Ph.D., NYU.
Farahmand Rezvani, Professor; Ph.D., CUNY Graduate Center.
Cecilia Ricci, Professor; Ph.D., University of International Business
    and Economics (China).
Hermann Sintim, Professor; Ph.D., New Orleans.
Ira Sohn, Professor; Ph.D., NYU.
Susana Yu, Associate Professor; Ph.D., CUNY, Baruch.
Zaman Zamanian, Professor; Ph.D., Indiana.

International Business

Chandana Chakraborty, Chair; Ph.D., Rensselaer.
Suresh Desai, Professor; Ph.D., UCLA.
Ikechi Ekeledo, Associate Professor; Ph.D., Illinois.
Nadeem Firoz, Professor; Ph.D., North Texas State.
C. Jayachandran, Professor; Ph.D., Madras.

Dong-Kyoong Kim, Assistant Professor; Ph.D., South Carolina.
Luis San Vicente Portes, Assistant Professor; Ph.D., Georgetown.
Carl Rodrigues, Professor; D.P.A., Nova Southeastern.
Nilufer Usmen, Professor; Ph.D., CUNY, Baruch.
Jun Xia, Assistant Professor; Ph.D., Texas Tech.

Management Information Systems

Richard Peterson, Chair; Ph.D., Penn State.
Mark R. Allyn, Assistant Professor; Ph.D., Stanford.
Mark Berenson, Professor; Ph.D., CUNY, Baruch.
Edward Bewayo, Professor; D.P.A., SUNY at Albany.
Harvey Blumberg, Professor; Ph.D., CUNY, Baruch.
Qiyang Chen, Professor; Ph.D., Maryland.
Eleanor Flanigan, Professor; Ed.D., Temple.
Eileen Kaplan, Professor; Ph.D., Rutgers.
Kimberly Killmer Hollister, Professor; Ph.D., Pennsylvania.
Soo Kim, Assistant Professor; Ph.D., Penn State.
Nicole Koppel, Professor; Ph.D., Rutgers.
Charles Lee, Associate Professor; Ph.D., Clemson.
Zu-Hsu Lee, Professor; Ph.D., Berkeley.
Li-Chun Lin, Assistant Professor; Ph.D., Kansas State.
Ross Malaga, Associate Professor; Ph.D., George Mason.
Byung Min, Professor; Ph.D., Penn State.
Ram Misra, Professor; Ph.D., Texas A&M.
Jeffrey Monacelli, Assistant Professor/Executive in Residence; M.B.A.,
    Fairleigh Dickinson.
David J. Radosevich, Assistant Professor; Ph.D., SUNY at Albany.
Ram Subramanian, Professor; Ph.D., North Texas.
John Wang, Professor; Ph.D., Temple.
Ruben Xing, Professor; Ed.D., Columbia Teachers College.
James Yao, Professor; Ph.D., Mississippi State.
Michael Zey, Professor; Ph.D., Rutgers.

Marketing

John McGinnis, Chair; Ed.D., NYU.
Patrali Chatterjee, Associate Professor; Ph.D., Bombay.
Ralph DiPietro, Professor; Ph.D., NYU.
Mark E. Hill, Associate Professor; D.B.A., Southern Illinois.
Mark S. Johnson, Associate Professor; Ph.D., Colorado.
Mark J. Kay, Associate Professor; Ph.D., CUNY, Baruch.
Avinandan Mukherjee, Professor; Ph.D., Indian Institute of Management
    (Ahmedabad).
Jack Samuels, Professor; Ph.D., Temple.
Yawei Wang, Assistant Professor; Ph.D., Clemson.
Susan Weston, Associate Professor; Ed.D. Rutgers.

NOVA SOUTHEASTERN UNIVERSITY

H. Wayne Huizenga School of Business and Entrepreneurship

Programs of Study

The H. Wayne Huizenga School of Business and Entrepreneurship at Nova Southeastern University (NSU) offers the Master of Business Administration (M.B.A.) in entrepreneurship, finance, and real estate development. Other master's degree programs include the Master of Accounting, the Master of Science in Human Resource Management, the Master of International Business Administration, the Master of Public Administration, the Master of Taxation, and the Master of Science in Leadership. The School also offers concurrent or postdegree specializations and certificates in entrepreneurship, finance, human resource development, human resource management, information security, international business, international economics, international logistics, international management, international strategy, leadership, management information systems, marketing, and real estate development.

The doctoral programs are designed to enable students to assume increased responsibility, enhance problem-solving skills, and design, implement, and evaluate research. These programs include the Doctor of Business Administration (D.B.A.) in accounting, finance, human resource management, international business, management, marketing, or operations management and the Doctor of Public Administration. Flexible formats (including weeklong and weekend classes) help students to more easily meet their educational goals.

Research Facilities

Information services are offered via traditional and technology-driven approaches in the libraries, which are stocked with carefully selected print materials and are readily available to various electronic resources. The NSU libraries are nationally known for their excellent services to distance education students. With its 325,000-square-foot structure, the Alvin Sherman Library, Research, and Information Technology Center is the largest library building in Florida. It is a joint-use facility between the Broward County Board of County Commissioners and NSU, and it is ultramodern in its application of both wireline and wireless technology. The facility has individual study rooms, large conference rooms, exhibit areas, electronic classrooms, a café, and the Rose and Alfred Miniaci 500-seat Performing Arts Center.

Financial Aid

NSU offers various loans, student employment, and scholarships to graduate students. Although administered by the colleges, many of the scholarships are funded by private individuals and institutions. Financial aid awards are based on the completion of the Free Application for Federal Student Aid (FAFSA), accuracy and timeliness of information, receipt of appropriate documentation, and the availability of funds. More information is available for prospective students at http://www.nova.edu/cwis/finaid/.

Cost of Study

Graduate tuition for 2007–08 varies by program. The tuition ranges from $556 to $615 per credit hour for master's courses and is $726 per credit hour for doctoral courses.

Living and Housing Costs

The Office of Residential Life helps students with their housing needs and concerns. Graduate housing is available in the Cultural Living Center (CLC) and The Commons, located on the main campus. The CLC, built in 1984, houses approximately 125 graduate students during the academic year and costs between $2840 and $4140. The Commons, the newest residence hall, opened in August 2007. The Commons houses 120 graduate students during the academic year and costs between $7536 and $10,280. All rates include unlimited laundry, NSU-secured wireless Internet, furnishings, utilities, air conditioning, cable TV, and local telephone service. More information about student housing is available for prospective students at http://www.nova.edu/reslife/.

Student Group

The typical weekend graduate student enrolled in the master's degree programs is 30–35 years old; 35–40 years old in the doctoral programs. Most work full-time—in the middle to upper levels of management—and are engaged in study for the purpose of professional development and advancement. The average age of full-time students is 23.

Student Outcomes

Graduates of the Huizenga School work for such companies as Alamo; American Broadcast Company (ABC); American Express; American University; AT&T; AutoNation USA; Bank of America; Baptist Hospital; Beckman Coulter Electronics; BellSouth; BellSouth Mobility; Blockbuster Entertainment; Boeing Aircraft; Burger King; Busch Gardens; CALA; Chrysler Credit; Citicorp; City of Fort Lauderdale; City of Houston; Coca-Cola; Computer Sciences Corporation; CSX; Department of Energy; DHL; Digital Equipment Corporation; Disney World; EG&G; Exxon-Mobil; Federal Express; First Data; Florida Power; Ford Motor Company; FPL; General Electric; General Mills; General Motors; GlaxoSmithKlein; Hewlett-Packard; Hughes Aerospace; Humana Health Care Plus; Hyundai Electronics; IBM; Jackson Memorial Hospital; John Alden Financial; Johnson & Johnson; Johnson & Johnson Cordis; Kaiser Engineering; Knight-Ridder; Lenox; Lucent Technologies; Martin Marietta; McDonald's; Microsoft; Modcomp; Motorola; NASA; Northern Telecom; Parke-Davis; Pepsico; Perrier; Petro Canada; PricewaterhouseCoopers; Quaker Oats; Raymond James and Associates; Rexall Sundown; Rockwell Collins; Royal Caribbean Cruise Lines; Rubbermaid; Ryder; Sears, Roebuck and Co.; Sensormatic; Siemens; TVA Tropicana; Unisys; United Parcel Service; United States Military (Air Force, Army, Coast Guard, Marines, National Guard, Navy); United Technologies; Verizon; Westinghouse Savannah River Company, Inc.; Xerox; and ZPMC, Co., Ltd.

Location

Founded in 1964, Nova Southeastern University is the largest not-for-profit institution in Florida. NSU maintains four campuses in the Miami–Fort Lauderdale area of southern Florida, all within 20 miles of the main campus in Davie. The main campus consists of 300 acres with general-purpose athletic fields and NCAA-qualifying soccer and baseball fields. The residence halls on the main campus serve undergraduate, graduate, health professions, and law students.

Davie, a city of more than 80,000, maintains a sense of small-town intimacy while its location between major highways is near both an international airport and a seaport, which offers access to the state's metropolitan centers. The area is famous for its wide expanses of sandy beach and its tropical climate. Nearby Fort Lauderdale is home to numerous museums, art galleries, and a performing arts center.

The University and The School

NSU offers a wide range of undergraduate, graduate, and professional degree programs to more than 25,000 students every year. It is the sixth-largest independent institution in the nation. The University Center, which opened in August of 2006, is a 300,000-square-foot facility that is home to a 5,500-seat sports arena, recreation and wellness center, student union, and a performing arts theater. In early 2004, the Carl DeSantis Building, home to the H. Wayne Huizenga School of Business and Entrepreneurship, opened its doors. Its design includes general-purpose classrooms, compressed video/teleconferencing classrooms, a lecture theater, computer labs, multipurpose facilities, conference facilities, business services/copy center, and a full service café as well as administrative and student offices with support facilities.

Applying

Master's applicants must submit a graduate admission application form with a nonrefundable application fee; provide official transcripts in English, showing the degree conferred and all undergraduate course work from all colleges and universities attended; and have unrestricted access to a PC. Those with an undergraduate degree from a regionally accredited institution should have a GPA of 2.5 or greater overall (or in the last 60 hours) on a 4.0 scale. Applicants whose undergraduate GPA is greater than or equal to 2.25 but less than 2.5 must submit a GMAT score of 450 or greater (or GRE score of 1000 or greater). International students must have a TOEFL score of 550 or greater on the written test, 79 or greater on the Internet-based test, or the equivalent of 213 or greater on the computer-based test. Applicants may also be considered for admission through corporate sponsorship. A letter on company letterhead verifying corporate sponsorship, signed by the corporate tuition benefits officer or appropriate human resources official, must accompany the application.

Doctoral candidates must submit a completed doctoral application form with a nonrefundable application fee; an earned master's degree (preferably in business or public administration as appropriate); specific prerequisite courses with a B or better at the master's level; a career essay that describes professional development goals and the reasons for entering the doctoral program; a resume or curriculum vitae with detailed explanation of previous and present employment responsibilities that demonstrates at least seven years' professional-level experience in business, industry, government, military service, education, or consulting; official transcripts in English from all undergraduate and graduate institutions attended, received directly from each institution; and official GMAT or GRE scores taken within the past five years. Those with a master's degree from a regionally accredited institution should have a graduate GPA of 3.25 or greater on a 4.0 scale and a GMAT score of 500 or greater (or GRE score of 1,110 or better). International students should have a minimum TOEFL score of 600 (paper-based), 100 (Internet-based), or 250 (computer-based) and a GMAT score of 500 or greater (or GRE score of 1,110 or better). Applicants must own or have unrestricted access to a personal computer and modem that can be used to complete course work.

Students are admitted on a year-round basis and may begin classes in any of four terms in the master's programs (January, April, July, and October) or any of three terms in the doctoral programs (January, May, and September).

Correspondence and Information

H. Wayne Huizenga School of Business and Entrepreneurship
Carl DeSantis Building
Nova Southeastern University
3301 College Avenue
Fort Lauderdale, Florida 33314
Phone: 954-262-5168
       800-672-7223 Ext. 5168 (toll-free)
E-mail: info@huizenga.nova.edu
Web site: http://www.huizenga.nova.edu

Nova Southeastern University

THE FACULTY AND THEIR RESEARCH

Rebecca Abraham, Professor of Business Administration; D.B.A., US International, 1989. Investments and industrial/organizational psychology.

Russell Abratt, Professor of Marketing; D.B.A. Marketing and sales management.

Young Baek, Co-Chair and Assistant Professor of Finance; Ph.D., South Carolina, 1999. International corporate finance, agency theory, management compensation, foreign exchange and foreign direct investment.

Barry Barnes, Professor; Ph.D., Kansas, 1996. Innovative business practices of the legendary rock band, the Grateful Dead.

James Barry, Associate Professor of Marketing; D.B.A., Nova Southeastern. Marketing communications, salesmanship, Internet marketing, international marketing.

Michael Bendixen, Professor of Research Methods; Ph.D. Research methodology, statistics, business forecasting, organizational culture.

Charlie Blackwell, Associate Professor of Management; D.P.A., Nova. Management history, communications, customer service, leadership and total quality management.

Nicholas Castaldo, Lecturer; M.B.A., Harvard. Management, marketing.

Frank Cavico, Professor of Business Law and Ethics; J.D., St. Mary's. Trade secret law and the law of intentional interference with contract, comparative legal and ethical analysis of whistleblowing in the private sector, tort of intentional infliction of emotional distress in the private employment sector.

Ramdas Chandra, Professor of International Business; Ph.D., NYU.

Ruth Clarke, Associate Professor and Chair of International Business; Ph.D., Massachusetts Amherst, 1989. Strategy, new venture creation, international business.

Charles Collver, Assistant Professor of Finance; Ph.D. Economic thinking, applying managerial finance, futures and options.

Barbara Dastoor, Associate Professor of Management Science; Ph.D., Texas at Dallas. Organizational behavior and human resource management.

Peter Di Paolo, Professor; D.B.A., Nova Southeastern. Research and development, management development, employee recruitment and development, strategic and fiscal planning.

J. Wayne Falbey, Assistant Professor of Management and Real Estate; D.B.A., Nova Southeastern.

J. Robert Field, Assistant Professor of Statistics and Research Methods; Ph.D.

Peter Finley, Assistant Professor of Sport Management; Ph.D., Northern Colorado, 1998. Sport marketing, sport law, sociology of sports.

Jeffrey Fountain, Assistant Professor of Sports Management; Ph.D., Northern Colorado. Sport and wellness management; sport and wellness in institutions; sports, wellness, and diversity; sport and wellness administration; sport marketing; sport finance.

Jane Gibson, Professor of Management; D.B.A., Nova Southeastern. Leadership and online education.

George Hanbury, Executive Vice President for Administration; Ph.D., Florida Atlantic. Leadership, organizational development, organizational theory, public-policy analysis, public administration, budgeting and finance, comparative government and economics.

Charlie Harrington, Professor of Economics; Ph.D., Northeastern, 1975. Economics.

William Harrington, Associate Professor of Management; Ph.D., Nova Southeastern. Human resource management, organizational behavior, values integration, organizational health and reward systems, values-based leadership.

Judith Harris, Professor; D.B.A., Boston University, 1988. Cost and managerial accounting.

Michael Hoffman, Professor of Taxation; D.B.A., Indiana. Financial, retirement, and estate planning; corporate income taxation.

Merriam "Micki" Johnson, Professor of Business Administration; M.B.A., New Hampshire, 1985. Organizational development and change, management and marketing.

J. Preston Jones, Associate Dean; D.B.A., Nova Southeastern. Business administration, accounting.

Joung Kim, Associate Professor of Accounting; Ph.D., South Carolina.

Barbara Landau, Assistant Professor of Accounting; J.D., New York. Corporate and partnership taxation, estate and gift tax and fiduciary income taxation, taxation of pension and profit-sharing plans and tax-exempt organizations, taxation of LLCs and Subchapter S corporations, real estate taxation.

Terrell Manyak, Professor of Public Administration; Ph.D., UCLA. Public policy and economic development.

Tim McCartney, Professor, Clinical Psychologist, and Organizational Development Consultant; Ph.D., Strasbourg. Psychology and mental health in the Americas.

Karen McKenzie, Professor of Accounting; Ph.D., LSU. Governmental and financial accounting.

Walter Moore, Director and Faculty Chair of Accounting and Taxation; Ph.D., Nova, 1996. Private and public accounting.

Bahaudin Mujtaba, Director of Institutional Relations, Planning, and Accreditation; Ph.D., Nova Southeastern. Learning outcome assessment, customer value/service and diversity management.

Ron Needleman, Associate Professor of Economics and Chair of the Institutional Review Board; Ph.D., CUNY Graduate Center. State and local finance, energy and urban problems such as poverty, welfare, health services, and manpower.

Ordean Olson, Associate Professor; D.B.A., US International. Financial management and international finance.

Pedro F. Pellet, Professor; Ph.D., Miami (Florida). Applied economics.

Jack Pinkowski, Executive Director of the NSU Institute of Government and Public Policy; Ph.D., Florida Atlantic. Public finance, economic development, globalization, international economic and organizational impacts of the Internet, evolution of e-commerce and its impacts on state and local government finance.

Randy Pohlman, Dean; Ph.D., Oklahoma State. Finance and organizational behavior.

Robert Preziosi, Professor of Management Education and Chair of the Master of Science in Human Resource Management; D.P.A. Leadership, values, and adult learning.

Randall Rentfro, Assistant Professor of Accounting; Ph.D., Florida Atlantic, 2000. Behaviors of financial statement preparers and the factors that influence those behaviors.

Robert Sellani, Assistant Professor; D.B.A., Nova Southeastern. Cost management and business systems development.

John Sennetti, Professor of Accounting, Auditing, and Information Systems; Ph.D., Virginia Tech. Auditing and ethics.

Belay Seyoum, Associate Professor of International Business; Ph.D., McGill. High-technology trade and global e-commerce.

Randi Sims, Associate Professor; D.B.A., Florida Atlantic. The relationship between employee ethical decision making and national culture.

Leslie Tworoger, Assistant Professor; M.B.A., Nova Southeastern. Leadership, uses of power in organizations and privatization.

Tom Tworoger, Assistant Professor of Entrepreneurship; D.B.A., Nova Southeastern. Entrepreneurship.

Art Weinstein, Professor; Ph.D., Florida International. Market definition and segmentation.

Albert Williams, Assistant Professor of Economics; Ph.D., Georgia. Managerial economics, statistics, monetary policy, corporate finance.

Pan Yatrakis, Professor of Finance and Economics; Ph.D., NYU. Efficient markets and behavioral finance.

OAKLAND UNIVERSITY

Master of Business Administration

Program of Study

A program leading to the Master of Business Administration (M.B.A.) with special emphasis in information technology or international business is offered by the School of Business Administration (SBA) at Oakland University (OU). The program is designed to educate students for managerial roles in private, public, or not-for-profit sectors of the economy. Courses are offered weekday evenings at the Rochester campus and at OU Centers in Birmingham and in Macomb County. Saturday morning classes are also offered at the Rochester campus.

The M.B.A. program is designed for undergraduate majors from any discipline, including business or management. It is preferred that students with an undergraduate degree in business or one of the functional areas of management have two years of work experience before entering the M.B.A. program. A typical entering class consists of students with undergraduate majors from engineering, the natural and social sciences, computer science, mathematics, business, health care, education, and the humanities.

The program is based on the belief that an education in management should prepare students for careers involving problem identification, problem solving, decision making, and leadership in any type of organization. To accomplish this, the program seeks to emphasize the determination of goals and the effective utilization of scarce resources; help students understand and deal with the emerging workplace issues of globalization and diversity; assist students in understanding the effects of—and successfully deal with—the changing social, legal, ethical, and technological environments of organizations; and stress the importance of the management of information and information resources in the successful operation of an organization. Because much of management relates to people—understanding them, communicating with them, working with them, and leading them—the program also stresses an understanding of human behavior and the organizational setting.

The Oakland M.B.A. is distinguished by its curricular emphasis on international business and information. More information is available on the M.B.A. Web site at http://www.sba.oakland.edu/grad/programs/mba/.

Research Facilities

The Office of Grants, Contracts and Sponsored Research supports research and scholarship at Oakland University. In particular, the office acts as the coordinating office between Oakland University and the federal and state agencies, foundations, and public and private corporations that provide funds for research, education, training and service programs.

Located in the center of campus, the Kresge Library houses collections of books, journals, reference works, government documents, musical scores, and recordings, as well as a wireless network and computer workstations to access an array of digital resources. The Kresge Library's collections include over 727,000 books, approximately 1,400 print journal subscriptions and electronic access to more than 15,000 titles, over 240,000 federal and state documents, and more than 1.1 million microforms. The Library's homepage and online catalog serve as gateways to dozens of specialized and general research databases, hundreds of full-text electronic journals, and e-books covering a wide range of disciplines and research areas.

Financial Aid

In order to assist eligible graduate students in financing their education, Oakland University participates in the Federal College Work-Study Program and the William Ford Federal Direct Loan Program.

Cost of Study

Graduate tuition in the 2007–08 academic year is $472.50 per credit hour for Michigan residents and $814.50 per credit hour for non-residents. For current tuition rates, students should visit http://www.oakland.edu/tuitionandfees.

Living and Housing Costs

The 2006–07 rate for room and board was $6385 for the academic year. Facilities with a selected number of single rooms are available to graduate students. For students with families, a limited number of two-bedroom town houses and two- to four-bedroom student apartments are available.

Student Group

Total enrollment at OU for fall 2006 was 17,737. Twenty-three percent of the total enrollment is graduate students. Within the graduate enrollment, 66 percent are women and 11.4 percent are members of ethnic minority groups. The diverse student body includes international students representing many different countries.

Location

Oakland University is located in Oakland County, the third-most-affluent county in the United States and the fastest growing county in Michigan. Rochester, Michigan, OU's hometown, was named thirty-ninth in a list of top 100 cities in which to live and was the highest-ranking Michigan city in a survey by *Money* magazine and *CNN Money* in 2005. Rochester and the surrounding area were ranked based on population, number of educational facilities, safety, environment, housing affordability, taxes, weather, commute times, and job market.

In addition, the area's rolling hills, wetlands, and woodlands provide beautiful neighborhoods and plenty of year-round recreation. The surrounding community also offers an abundance of entertainment, cultural, and social opportunities. Together, all this makes Oakland County and Rochester a great place to live, work, and go to school.

The University

Oakland University, founded in 1957, is a comprehensive state-supported institution of higher education. The University is organized into the College of Arts and Sciences and the Schools of Business Administration, Education and Human Services, Engineering and Computer Science, Health Sciences, and Nursing.

Applying

Students applying to the M.B.A. program need to submit the Application for Admission to Graduate Study, the application processing fee, GMAT scores, and supporting documents to Graduate Admissions. Both a paper and online application process are available. Information about application requirements and deadlines is available online at http://www.oakland.edu/grad/apply. Information specific to the M.B.A. is found at http://www.sba.oakland.edu/grad/admissions.

Correspondence and Information

Graduate Admissions
160 North Foundation Hall
Oakland University
2200 North Squirrel Road
Rochester, Michigan 48309
Phone: 248-370-3167
E-mail: gradmail@oakland.edu
Web site: http://www.oakland.edu/gograd

Oakland University

THE FACULTY

Henry Aigbedo, Associate Professor of Production Operations Management.
Lizabeth A. Barclay, Professor of Management.
Mohammad Sadi Bazaz, Professor of Accounting.
Mukesh Bhargava, Associate Professor of Marketing.
Joseph H. Callaghan, Professor of Accounting.
Vivienne Chen, Assistant Professor of Marketing.
Addington Coppin, Professor of Economics and Chair, Department of Economics.
Mohammad Dadashzadeh, Professor of Management Information Systems and Director, Applied Technology in Business (ATiB).
Xiaodong Deng, Associate Professor of Management Information Systems.
Gadis J. Dillon, Professor of Accounting.
David P. Doane, Professor of Quantitative Methods.
Edward J. Farragher, Professor of Finance.
Eugene B. Fliedner, Associate Professor of Production Operations Management.
Sherman T. Folland, Professor of Economics.
Donna Free, Special Instructor of Accounting.
Fuad Hasanov, Assistant Professor of Economics.
John W. Henke Jr., Associate Professor of Marketing.
Frederick G. Hoffman, Special Instructor of Management.
Mark Isken, Associate Professor of Management Information Systems.
Oded Izraeli, Professor of Economics.
Joy Jiang, Assistant Professor of Management, International Business.
John Kim, Associate Professor of Marketing.
Thomas W. Lauer, Professor of Management Information Systems and Chair, Department of Decision and Information Sciences.
Paul Licker, Professor of Management Information Systems and Faculty M.B.A. Program Director.
Carol Liu, Assistant Professor of Accounting.
Karl Majeske, Assistant Professor of Quantitative Methods.
Karen Markel, Assistant Professor of Management.
Kieran Mathieson, Associate Professor of Management Information Systems.
Don Mayer, Professor of Management.
Robin McCutcheon, Visiting Instructor of Economics.
Cynthia E. Miree, Associate Professor of Management.
Nivedita Mukherji, Associate Professor of Economics.
J. Austin Murphy, Professor of Finance.
Kevin J. Murphy, Professor of Economics.
Robert Nehmer, Assistant Professor of Accounting.
Ram Orzach, Assistant Professor of Economics.
Ravi Parameswaran, Professor of Marketing and Chair, Department of Management and Marketing.
Mohinder Parkash, Associate Professor of Accounting and Chair, Department of Accounting and Finance.
Sandra Pelfrey, Associate Professor of Accounting.
Louis W. Petro, Assistant Professor of Accounting.
Ram Mohan Pisharodi, Associate Professor of Marketing.
Hong Qian, Assistant Professor of Finance.
Balaji Rajagopalan, Associate Professor of Management Information Systems.
Anandi P. Sahu, Professor of Economics.
Joseph Schiele, Assistant Professor of Production Operations Management.
Howard S. Schwartz, Professor of Management.
James S. Serocki, Assistant Professor of Accounting.
Srinarayan Sharma, Associate Professor of Management Information Systems.
David D. Sidaway, Special Instructor of Accounting.
Jonathan Silberman, Professor of Economics.
Mark Simon, Associate Professor of Management.
Rajeev Singhal, Assistant Professor of Finance.
Miron Stano, Professor of Economics.
Vijayan Sugumaran, Professor of Management Information Systems.
Mohan Tanniru, Dean.
Kasaundra Tomlin, Assistant Professor of Economics.
Janell Townsend, Assistant Professor of Marketing.
Ronald L. Tracy, Associate Professor of Economics, Associate Dean.
Catherine Tyler, Assistant Professor of Management.
T. J. Wharton, Associate Professor of Production Operations Management.
Floyd G. Willoughby, Associate Professor of Management.
Kenneth M. York, Professor of Management.
Ellen Yun Zhu, Assistant Professor of Finance.
Xie Zhu, Assistant Professor of Economics.

OLD DOMINION UNIVERSITY

College of Business and Public Administration
Graduate Programs in Business and Public Administration

Programs of Study

The College of Business and Public Administration offers eight degree programs and three certificate programs. All are designed to promote professional competency in the student's selected area of study. The programs are fully accredited by the appropriate organization: AACSB International–The Association to Advance Collegiate Schools of Business or the National Association of Schools of Public Affairs and Administration (NASPAA).

Graduate programs of study lead to the degrees of Master of Arts in Economics, Master of Business Administration, Master of Public Administration, Master of Science in Accounting, Master of Science in computer information science, Master of Urban Studies, Doctor of Philosophy in business administration, and Doctor of Philosophy in public administration and urban policy.

Graduate students come from a variety of backgrounds and from different colleges and universities. The master's programs are open to any qualified holder of a bachelor's degree regardless of the undergraduate field of study. Graduates in education, engineering, liberal arts and sciences, and business administration are encouraged to apply. Many students are midcareer professionals who are returning for their professional degree or those who have reached managerial levels in their careers.

Graduate courses are taught during the day and in the evening, facilitating flexible combinations of formal learning and full- or part-time employment. In addition to courses offered at the Old Dominion University campus, off-campus centers at Virginia Beach and the peninsula have been established to serve the needs of students who seek a graduate education. The College offers M.B.A. and M.P.A. courses at the centers.

The Doctor of Philosophy program in business administration is a scholarly research–based and internationally focused program with a professional orientation. The objective of the program is to prepare individuals of superior promise and potential for careers in higher education, teaching, and research and for administrative and research careers in the private and public sectors. In addition to a strong international business orientation the program is based on established business disciplines.

The Doctor of Philosophy in public administration and urban policy is a research-based program. The objective of the program is to develop graduates with a substantive knowledge of a body of work in public administration and urban policy, as well as to acquire analytic and research skills that enable them to become educators, leaders, and researchers in their chosen specialty areas. The Ph.D. program in public administration and urban policy, therefore, focuses on developing effective public, nonprofit sector, and urban policy leaders throughout Hampton Roads, the Commonwealth of Virginia, and the nation who have both content knowledge and research skills; educating individuals who intend to pursue teaching as a vocation in colleges and universities in Virginia, as well as nationally and internationally; building collaborative research and demonstration initiatives with community and state agencies that link research to public management, urban policy improvement, and economic development; and providing the linkages among content knowledge, research, and field experiences for all doctoral students.

Research Facilities

The University Library provides a full complement of services and materials, with approximately 1.5 million items, including monographs, government publications, periodicals and serials, microforms, scores, and recordings for student and faculty use. Computer-assisted searches of more than 200 indexing and abstracting services, in addition to instruction in the use of the library and its services and resources, are available in the reference department. The Office of Computing and Communications Services offers services ranging from software development to professional consulting to training programming and analysis support, all of which are provided for users as diverse as faculty members, students, and administrators.

Financial Aid

Financial aid is available for graduate students in the form of University fellowships, doctoral fellowships, tuition grants, teaching or research assistantships, and doctoral teaching fellowships. In addition, graduate students in the College of Business and Public Administration may apply for the Theodore F. and Constance C. Constant and Simon Fellowships. Graduate students may also qualify for various University scholarships, such as the Alumni Association Outstanding Scholar Fellowship, the Meredith Construction Company Scholarship, the Herman E. Valentine Scholarship, and Special Part-Time Minority Tuition Grants.

Cost of Study

Tuition and fees in 2006–07 were $285 per credit hour for Virginia residents and $715 per credit hour for nonresidents.

Living and Housing Costs

A wide variety of housing is available for rent on campus and in the immediate community within walking, biking, or easy commuting distance.

Student Group

Currently, Old Dominion University has more than 13,500 undergraduate students and 6,500 graduate students.

Location

Old Dominion University is located in Norfolk, Virginia, which is the center of a metropolitan area with a population of approximately 1.5 million. Norfolk is the hub of the world's largest natural harbor and is regarded as one of the nation's leading cities in business and industry. The area is a major recreational area that is known for its beach and historical landmarks. Norfolk also benefits from its heavy military concentration and its proximity to Washington, D.C., and the Outer Banks of North Carolina.

The University and The College

Old Dominion University interacts closely with a vigorous community at the heart of the seven-city Hampton Roads region. The University had its formal beginning in 1930 as a branch of the College of William and Mary, and, by 1969, Old Dominion University was an independent institution with university status. At present, it has more than 22,000 students.

The College of Business and Public Administration is one of approximately 400 schools in the world to have achieved accreditation on the graduate and undergraduate levels by AACSB International. The College's highly productive faculty is dedicated to the intellectual development of students through a variety of course offerings that are enhanced by an impressive spectrum of research and service activities. The Master of Public Administration is accredited by the NASPAA.

Applying

The College of Business and Public Administration welcomes applications from men and women who have earned a bachelor's degree from an accredited institution. Admission to the program is competitive and is granted only to those who show high ability and likely success in graduate study. To apply, students must submit application forms for graduate study, official transcripts of all previous college work, one letter of recommendation, scores on the Graduate Management Admission Test or Graduate Record Examinations, and a goals and interest statement. Applicants whose native language is not English are also required to achieve an acceptable score on the Test of English as a Foreign Language (TOEFL).

Correspondence and Information

For program information:

Graduate Programs
College of Business and Public
    Administration
Old Dominion University
Norfolk, Virginia 23529
Phone: 757-683-3520
Fax: 757-683-4076
Web site: http://www.odu.edu

For application forms:

Graduate Admissions
Old Dominion University
Norfolk, Virginia 23529
Phone: 757-683-3637
    800-348-7926 (toll-free)
Web site: http://www.odu.edu

For application for M.B.A. program:

M.B.A. Program Director
College of Business and Public
    Administration
Old Dominion University
1026 Constant Hall
Norfolk, Virginia 23529
Phone: 757-683-3585
Fax: 757-683-5750
E-mail: mbainfo@odu.edu
Web site: http://www.odu-mba.org

Old Dominion University

THE FACULTY

Department of Accounting

Walter W. Berry, Senior Lecturer; M.B.A., Old Dominion. Patricia M. Doherty, Senior Lecturer; M.B.A., Golden Gate. Laurie J. Henry, Associate Professor; Ph.D., Mississippi. Chansong (Francis) Kim, Associate Professor; Ph.D., Baruch College of City University. Terry Kubichan, Senior Lecturer; M.S., Old Dominion. Otto B. Martinson, Professor; Ph.D., George Washington. Timothy McKee, Associate Professor; J.D., Indiana. Robert E. Pinsker, Assistant Professor; Ph.D., South Florida. Randall Spurrier, Instructor; M.B.A., Hawaii. Michael Stein, Associate Professor; Ph.D., British Columbia. Yin Xu, Assistant Professor; Ph.D., South Carolina. Douglas E. Ziegenfuss, Associate Professor; Ph.D., Virginia Commonwealth.

Department of Business Administration

Barbara R. Bartkus, Associate Professor; Ph.D., Texas A&M. Paul J. Champagne, Professor; Ph.D., Massachusetts. Ateba Crocker, Instructor; M.A., Portland State. Jon R. Crunkleton, Associate Professor; Ph.D., South Carolina. Roy R. Cunningham, Senior Lecturer; M.S., Nebraska. Diana L. Deadrick, Associate Professor; Ph.D., Virginia Tech. John A. Doukas, Professor; Ph.D., NYU. John B. Ford, Professor; Ph.D., Georgia. Myron Glassman, Professor; Ph.D., Illinois. Mahesh Gopinath, Assistant Professor; Ph.D., Michigan. John M. Griffith, Associate Professor; Ph.D., Alabama. Sylvia C. Hudgins, Professor; Ph.D., Virginia Tech. William Q. Judge, Professor; Ph.D., North Carolina. John G. Keeling, Senior Lecturer; M.B.A., Virginia Tech. James S. Key, Lecturer; M.B.A., Virginia. Kiran Kirande, Associate Professor; Ph.D., Houston. Soo-Hoon Lee, Assistant Professor; Ph.D., Washington (Seattle). Shaomin Li, Professor; Ph.D., Princeton. Yuping Liu, Assistant Professor; Ph.D., Rutgers. Steve Maurer, Professor; Ph.D., Oregon. R. Bruce McAfee, Professor; Ph.D., Wayne State. D. Brian McNatt, Assistant Professor; Ph.D., Iowa. Sara A. Morris, Associate Professor; Ph.D., Texas at Austin. Anil Nair, Associate Professor; Ph.D., NYU. Mohammad S. Najand, Professor; Ph.D., Syracuse. Bruce L. Rubin, Associate Professor; Ph.D., Case Western Reserve. Bruce M. Seifert, Professor; Ph.D., Michigan. Deepak Sethi, Assistant Professor; Ph.D., Texas. J. Taylor Sims, Professor; Ph.D., Illinois. Anusorn Singhapakdi, Professor; Ph.D., Mississippi. Maurine Stiner, Instructor; M.B.A., Pittsburgh. Licheng Sun, Assistant Professor; Ph.D., Georgia State. Leona Tam, Assistant Professor; Ph.D., Texas A&M. Kenneth K. Yung, Professor; Ph.D., Georgia. Michael T. Zugelder, Associate Professor; J.D., Toledo.

Department of Economics

Vinod Agarwal, Professor; Ph.D., California, Santa Barbara. Eric E. Anderson, Associate Professor; Ph.D., Washington (Seattle). Melanie Carter, Instructor; M.A., Old Dominion. Christopher B. Colburn, Associate Professor; Ph.D., Texas A&M. Berna Demiralp, Assistant Professor; Ph.D., John Hopkins. Larry Filer, Assistant Professor; Ph.D., Kentucky. Martha Hofler, Senior Lecturer; M.A., Old Dominion. James V. Koch, Professor; Ph.D., Northwestern. David D. Selover, Assistant Professor; Ph.D., California, San Diego. Wayne K. Talley, Professor; Ph.D., Kentucky. Charlie G. Turner, Associate Professor; Ph.D., Harvard. Gilbert R. Yochum, Professor; Ph.D., West Virginia. Haiwen Zhou, Assistant Professor; Ph.D., Maryland.

Department of Information Systems and Technology and Decision Sciences

Alireza Ardalan, Professor and Associate Dean; Ph.D., Arizona. Roya Ardalan, Lecturer; Ph.D., Old Dominion. Lan Cao, Assistant Professor; Ph.D., Georgia State. Jimmie Carraway, Senior Lecturer; M.B.A., Old Dominion. David P. Cook, Associate Professor; Ph.D., Kentucky. Denise Copeland, Instructor; M.S., Naval Postgraduate School. Samuel F. Coppage, Associate Professor; Ph.D., NYU. Russell Haines, Assistant Professor; Ph.D., Houston. Vijay Kalburgi, Senior Lecturer; Ph.D., Old Dominion. Ling Li, Associate Professor; Ph.D., Ohio State. Joan Mann, Associate Professor; Ph.D., Georgia. Carol A. Markowski, Professor; Ph.D., Penn State. Edward P. Markowski, Professor; Ph.D., Penn State. G. Steven Rhiel, Associate Professor; Ph.D., Northern Colorado. Kathryn E. Strozak, Instructor; M.S., Adelphi. John Watson, Instructor; M.P.A., Virginia Commonwealth. Renee A. Weather, Lecturer; M.S., Polytechnic. Marek Wermus, Associate Professor; Ph.D., Wroclaw Technical (Poland). Darryl Wilson, Associate Professor; Ph.D., Ohio State. Harris Wu, Assistant Professor; Ph.D., Michigan. Li D. Xu, Professor; Ph.D., Portland State. Harry Zhou, Assistant Professor; Ph.D., MIT.

Graduate Center for Urban Studies and Public Administration

Pamela A. Gibson, Assistant Professor; Ph.D., Virginia Commonwealth. William Leavitt, Associate Professor; Ph.D., Colorado. John Lombard, Assistant Professor; Ph.D., Buffalo. Berhanu Mengistu, Professor; Ph.D., Delaware. John C. Morris, Associate Professor; Ph.D., Mississippi State. Leonard L. Ruchelman, Professor; Ph.D., Columbia.

Students on the campus of Old Dominion University.

The College of Business and Public Administration.

PACE UNIVERSITY

Lubin School of Business
Graduate Programs

Programs of Study

The Lubin School of Business offers innovative full-time and part-time graduate programs leading to the Master of Business Administration (M.B.A.), Master of Science (M.S.), and Doctor of Professional Studies (D.P.S.) degrees. Also available are the J.D./M.B.A. and B.B.A./M.B.A. programs. Lubin continues to receive national recognition. *U.S. News & World Report* ranks Lubin's part-time M.B.A. program in the top 20 nationwide in its "Best Graduate Schools 2007" survey. The M.B.A. program prepares students for broad management responsibilities with a team-oriented, cross-disciplinary approach. The practice-oriented curriculum has been streamlined to 52 credits with a strong emphasis on globalization and technology. Concentrations include accounting, financial management, information systems, international business, international economics, management, management science, marketing management, and taxation.

Now in its seventh year, the e.MBA@PACE is a fully accredited, two-year, Web-assisted executive M.B.A. program that combines online learning with brief residencies and is team taught by dedicated faculty members in a module-based format. In a recent survey of the best online graduate programs, *U.S. News & World Report* lists Lubin's e.MBA@PACE program among the top online programs nationwide. The M.S. program provides fundamental principles and advanced technical knowledge and is designed for students who seek intensive study in a specialized area. Concentrations are offered in accounting, accounting information systems, financial management, human resources management, investment management, personal financial planning, and taxation. Students need at least 30–36 credit hours to earn an M.S. degree.

The doctoral program (D.P.S.) delivers advanced education that enables successful executives and business professionals to enhance or transition their careers as senior line managers, staff members, experts, business consultants, and faculty members. This executive doctorate is a delicate balance of breadth and depth, a deliberate blend of theory and application, and a distinctive combination of research and insight. Graduates earn a respected credential while expanding and enriching their knowledge, conceptualizing and generalizing their experience, and extending and sharpening their skills. Convenient schedules, with limited visits to the campus, allow candidates to continue full-time employment while completing degree requirements in just four years.

Certificate programs are also offered for professionals with advanced degrees to stay current with developments in their industries, acquire new responsibilities, or qualify for licensing or certification. The Lubin School of Business is accredited by AACSB International–The Association to Advance Collegiate Schools of Business.

Research Facilities

The Pace University Library is a comprehensive teaching library and student-learning center, a virtual library that combines strong core collections with ubiquitous access to global Internet resources to support broad and diversified curricula. Reciprocal borrowing and access accords, traditional interlibrary loan services, and commercial document delivery options supplement the aggregate library. Pace offers Instructional Services Librarians, a state-of-the-art electronic classroom, digital reference services, and multimedia applications. Pace's computer resource centers are linked to high-speed data networks and feature sophisticated hardware and software to facilitate active learning. Recognized as one of America's most wired universities, Pace supports high-speed Internet and Internet2 access on every campus; resident facilities are wired, and most public areas are enabled for wireless connectivity. Full-motion videoconference facilities enable remote delivery of instruction between campus sites for synchronous learning applications. Many courses are Web-assisted with state-of-the-art software, and some courses and programs are completely Web-based.

Financial Aid

Pace's comprehensive student financial assistance program includes scholarships, graduate assistantships, student loans, and tuition payment plans. Scholarships are awarded to students in recognition of academic achievement and are available for full- and part-time study. Highly qualified students may be eligible for assistantships awarded by departments, which paid stipends of up to $5100 and tuition remission up to 24 credits during the 2006–07 academic year. Pace participates in all major federal and state financial aid programs, such as federal loans, the New York State Tuition Assistance Program (TAP), Perkins Loans, and the Federal Work-Study Program. All students are encouraged to apply for these programs by filing the Free Application for Federal Student Aid (FAFSA).

Cost of Study

Tuition for graduate courses is $857 per credit in 2007–08.

Living and Housing Costs

Residence facilities are available on campus in both New York City and Westchester. Double-occupancy rooms range from approximately $8500 to $12,000 in 2007–08. University-operated off-campus housing is available in proximity of the New York City campus.

Student Group

Pace students represent diversified personal, cultural, and educational backgrounds. Many students are employed and pursue graduate study for personal growth and career advancement. Sixty-two percent are enrolled part-time in evening classes. Current enrollment in graduate business programs is approximately 1,400 students.

Location

Pace University is a multicampus institution with campuses in both New York City and Westchester County, New York. All locations are within reach of cultural, business, and social resources and opportunities. The downtown Manhattan campus is adjacent to Wall Street and City Hall. Pace's Midtown Center is a short distance from Times Square, theaters, and Grand Central Station. The Pleasantville/Briarcliff campus is a suburban setting, surrounded by towns offering various forms of recreation. The Graduate Center and the School of Law are located in White Plains, among major retail districts and many corporate headquarters. All locations are accessible by public transportation. Graduate business programs are available at both the New York City and Westchester campuses.

The University

Founded in 1906, Pace University is a private, nonsectarian, coeducational institution. Originally founded as a school of accounting, Pace Institute was designated Pace College in 1948. Through growth and various successes, it was renamed Pace University, as approved by the New York State Board of Regents, in 1973. Today, Pace offers comprehensive undergraduate, graduate, doctoral, and professional programs at several campus locations through six schools and colleges.

Applying

Admission to Pace University requires successful completion of a U.S. baccalaureate degree or its equivalent from an accredited institution. Students must submit a completed application, the application fee, official transcripts from all postsecondary institutions, a personal statement, a resume, and two letters of recommendation. International students must submit official TOEFL scores and official transcripts in the native language with a professional English translation. Applicants must demonstrate satisfactory performance on the Graduate Management Admission Test (GMAT). Applications should be submitted by August 1 for the fall semester, December 1 for the spring semester, and May 1 for summer sessions. Applications for the D.P.S. program should be submitted by July 1 for the fall semester and November 1 for the spring semester. Applications for the e.MBA program should be submitted by July 15 for the fall semester. International applications should be submitted one month prior to these dates.

Correspondence and Information

Office of Graduate Admission
Pace University
1 Pace Plaza
New York, New York 10038

Phone: 212-346-1531
Fax: 212-346-1585
E-mail: gradnyc@pace.edu
Web site: http://www.pace.edu

Office of Graduate Admission
Pace University
1 Martine Avenue
White Plains, New York 10606

Phone: 914-422-4283
Fax: 914-422-4287
E-mail: gradwp@pace.edu
Web site: http://www.pace.edu

Pace University

THE FACULTY

Lewis Altfest, Associate Professor of Finance; Ph.D., CUNY Graduate Center.

Andrew A. Anabila, Assistant Professor of Accounting; Ph.D., Columbia.

Uzo Anakwe, Associate Professor of Management; Ph.D., Drexel.

Walter Antognini, Associate Professor of Taxation; LL.M., NYU.

Bruce Bachenheimer, Clinical Professor of Management; M.B.A., Australian Graduate School of Management.

Vincent Barrella, Associate Professor of Taxation; LL.M., NYU.

Dan Baugher, Professor of Management; Ph.D., Rutgers.

Karen A. Berger, Associate Professor of Marketing; Ph.D., NYU.

Narendra C. Bhandari, Professor of Management; Ph.D., Georgia.

Vasanthakumar Bhat, Associate Professor of Management Science; Ph.D., Yale.

Stephen Blank, Professor of Management; Ph.D., Harvard.

Lawrence Bridwell, Associate Professor of Management; Ph.D., CUNY, Baruch.

Steven A. Brownstein, Lecturer of Marketing; Ph.D. candidate, Arizona State.

Branko Bucar, Assistant Professor of Management; Ph.D., Case Western Reserve.

John C. Byrne, Assistant Professor of Management; Ph.D., Stevens.

Roberta Cable, Professor of Accounting; Ph.D., Columbia.

John Carter, Professor of Management Science; Ph.D., Columbia.

Arthur L. Centonze, Associate Professor of Economics and Dean; Ph.D., NYU.

Kam C. Chan, Professor of Accounting; Ph.D., South Carolina.

Larry Chiagouris, Associate Professor of Marketing; Ph.D., CUNY, Baruch.

Kwang-Hyun Chung, Professor of Accounting; Ph.D., CUNY, Baruch.

Robert Dennehy, Professor of Management; Ph.D., NYU.

Joseph C. DiBenedetto, Professor of Accounting; J.D., Brooklyn Law.

Bairj Donabedian, Associate Professor of Accounting; Ph.D., Columbia.

John Dory, Associate Professor of Management; D.B.A., Harvard.

Alan B. Eisner, Associate Professor of Management; Ph.D., NYU.

Samir El-Gazzar, KPMG Professor of Accounting; Ph.D., CUNY, Baruch.

Ronald W. Filante, Associate Professor of Finance; Ph.D., Purdue.

Phillip Finn, Associate Professor of Accounting; M.S., Columbia.

Natalia Gershun, Assistant Professor of Finance; Ph.D., Columbia.

David Gertner, Assistant Professor of Marketing; Ph.D., Northwestern.

Rosane K. Gertner, Visiting Assistant Professor of Marketing; D.Sc., Coppe, Federal University of Rio de Janeiro.

Rosario J. Girasa, Professor of Legal Studies; Ph.D., Fordham.

Barry Gold, Associate Professor of Management; Ph.D., Columbia.

Elena Goldman, Assistant Professor of Finance; Ph.D., Rutgers.

Pradeep Gopalakrishna, Professor of Marketing; Ph.D., North Texas.

Aron A. Gottesman, Assistant Professor of Finance; Ph.D., York.

James Gould, Professor of Marketing; Ph.D., Cornell.

Claudia G. Green, Associate Professor of Management; Ph.D., Virginia Tech.

James Hall, Professor of Management and Associate Dean for Planning and Assessment; Ph.D., Chicago.

Patricia Healy, Associate Professor of Accounting; M.B.A., Rutgers.

Peter Hoefer, Professor of Management Science and Associate Dean and Director of Graduate Programs; Ph.D., CUNY Graduate Center.

Alvin Hwang, Associate Professor of Management; Ph.D., UCLA.

Robert Isaak, Professor of Management; Ph.D., NYU.

Rudolph Jacob, Professor of Accounting; Ph.D., NYU.

Sertan Kabadayi, Visiting Lecturer of Marketing; Ph.D. candidate, CUNY, Baruch.

Padma Kadiyala, Associate Professor of Finance; Ph.D., Ohio State.

Albert Kalter, Professor of Taxation; LL.M., NYU.

Surendra K. Kaushik, Professor of Finance; Ph.D., Boston University.

Warren Keegan, Distinguished Professor of Marketing; D.B.A., Harvard.

Eric Kessler, Associate Professor of Management; Ph.D., Rutgers.

Chu-hua Kuei, Associate Professor of Management Science; Ph.D., CUNY, Baruch.

John Lee, Schaeberle Professor of Accounting; Ph.D., LSU.

Picheng Lee, Assistant Professor of Accounting; Ph.D., Rutgers.

Chunyan Li, Assistant Professor of Accounting; Ph.D., Rutgers.

Mary Long, Associate Professor of Marketing; Ph.D., CUNY, Baruch.

Raymond H. Lopez, Professor of Finance; Ph.D., NYU.

Qi Lu, Visiting Assistant Professor of Finance; Ph.D., Northwestern.

Christian Madu, Professor/Research Scholar of Management Science; Ph.D., CUNY, Baruch.

Carl I. Malinowski, Associate Professor of Marketing; Ph.D., CUNY Graduate Center.

Edmund Mantell, Professor of Finance; Ph.D., Pennsylvania.

Matthew R. Morey, Associate Professor of Finance; Ph.D., California, Irvine.

Ira Morrow, Associate Professor of Management; Ph.D., NYU.

Jouahn Nam, Associate Professor of Finance; Ph.D., Georgia State.

Bernard Newman, Professor of Accounting; Ph.D., NYU.

Lawrence Newman, Professor of Taxation; S.J.D., New York Law.

Susanne O'Callaghan, Associate Professor of Accounting; Ph.D., Cincinnati.

Richard E. Ottoo, Assistant Professor of Finance; Ph.D., CUNY, Baruch.

Merav Ozair, Visiting Assistant Professor of Accounting; Ph.D., NYU.

Robert H. Parks, Professor of Finance; Ph.D., Pennsylvania.

Joseph M. Pastore, Emeritus Professor of Management; Ph.D., Saint Louis.

J. Marion Posey, Professor of Accounting; Ph.D., Arkansas.

Corinne A. Post, Assistant Professor of Management; Ph.D., Rutgers.

Randi L. Priluck, Associate Professor of Marketing; Ph.D., Drexel.

Noushi Rahman, Assistant Professor of Management; Ph.D. candidate, CUNY, Baruch.

James Russell, Associate Professor of Management and Associate Dean and Director of Undergraduate Programs; Ph.D., NYU.

Joseph A. Russo, Professor of Accounting; Ph.D., Rutgers.

Joseph Salerno, Professor of Economics; Ph.D., Rutgers.

Linda Sama, Associate Professor of Management; Ph.D., CUNY, Baruch.

Dennis Sandler, Associate Professor of Marketing; Ph.D., NYU.

Lewis Schier, Professor of Accounting; Ph.D., NYU.

Kaustav Sen, Associate Professor of Accounting; Ph.D., Rutgers.

Fred Silverman, Professor of Management Science; Ph.D., Columbia.

Michael Szenberg, Distinguished Professor of Economics; Ph.D., CUNY Graduate Center.

Charles Tang, Associate Professor of Accounting; Ph.D., CUNY, Baruch.

Ibraiz Tarique, Assistant Professor of Management; Ph.D. candidate, Rutgers.

John L. Teall, Professor of Finance; Ph.D., NYU.

Pelis Thottathil, Professor of Finance; Ph.D., Columbia.

Daniel Tinkelman, Associate Professor of Accounting; Ph.D., NYU.

Martin Topol, Professor of Marketing; Ph.D., CUNY Graduate Center.

Alan Tucker, Associate Professor of Finance; Ph.D., Florida State.

Michael Ulinski, Assistant Professor of Accounting; Ph.D., NYU.

Robert Vambery, Professor of Marketing; Ph.D., Columbia.

Andrew Varanelli, Professor of Management; Ph.D., Rutgers.

P. V. Viswanath, Professor of Finance; Ph.D., Chicago.

Thomas Webster, Professor of Economics; Ph.D., CUNY Graduate Center.

Ellen S. Weisbord, Associate Professor of Management; Ph.D., CUNY Graduate Center.

Berry K. Wilson, Associate Professor of Finance; Ph.D., NYU.

Janice Winch, Associate Professor of Management Science; Ph.D., Rutgers.

Kathryn Winsted, Associate Professor of Marketing; Ph.D., Colorado State.

Kevin Wynne, Associate Professor of Finance; Ph.D., Fordham.

Jack Yurkiewicz, Professor of Management Science; Ph.D., Yale.

Martin Zern, Professor of Taxation; LL.M., NYU.

PENN STATE HARRISBURG

School of Business Administration

Programs of Study

At the graduate-program level, the School of Business Administration at Penn State Harrisburg offers the Master of Business Administration (M.B.A.), the Master of Science in Information Systems (M.S.I.S.), and several joint degrees, including the M.B.A./J.D., the M.S.I.S./J.D., and the M.B.A./Ph.D. in pharmacology. The minimum credit completion requirement for the M.B.A. and M.S.I.S. degree programs is 30 credits, unless students have not met all prerequisites. Students are expected to complete degree requirements within six years of starting the program.

Fully accredited by AACSB International–The Association to Advance Collegiate Schools of Business, the M.B.A. and M.S.I.S. degree programs not only satisfy current needs for professional growth, but also foster lifelong learning. High priority is placed on teaching and currency of curriculum. In order to accommodate both full- and part-time students, courses are primarily offered in the evening.

As an outcome of the M.B.A. degree program, students develop skills in problem solving, collaborative learning, and critical thinking as well as gain technical expertise and knowledge of business ethics and corporate governance. Oral and written communication, research techniques, and the integration of concepts across functional areas are emphasized. The twofold nature of the M.S.I.S. degree program requires a manager to have competence both in information technology and in management theory; therefore, the curriculum combines the highly technical content of information science with the managerial emphasis of information systems.

Research Facilities

In 2000, Penn State Harrisburg welcomed the opening of its $17.3-million library. This 115,000-square-foot building contains shelving space for 400,000 volumes and seats more than 730 people, of whom 90 percent have access to data ports for use of online electronic resources. The library also has eleven group-study rooms, thirty-six locker carrels for graduate students and faculty members, a snack bar with data access, two technology-enhanced classrooms, two seminar rooms, a state-of-the-art library instruction lab, and a gallery/reception hall.

Technology resources include high-speed communications connected to state-of-the-art technology resources that are located throughout the University system. Access to a myriad of software ranges from compilers to sophisticated application packages as well as a multitude of databases. In addition, the University is linked to Internet services that provide access to communications worldwide.

Financial Aid

There are a limited number of scholarships, fellowships, and research grants available, as well as several graduate assistantships. For more information on these, students should contact the School of Business Administration. To find other options available, students should contact one of the following offices: Financial Aid Office at 717-948-6307 or Office of Research and Graduate Studies at 717-948-6303.

Cost of Study

Graduate business tuition for the 2006–07 academic year was $620 per credit for Pennsylvania residents. Additional fees included a $45 application fee, a per-semester computer fee based on the number of credits taken ($69 to $202), and a per-semester student activity fee based on the number of credits taken ($15 to $49), course materials/books, and living expenses.

Living and Housing Costs

On- and off-campus housing in apartments is available. Due to the number of options and price ranges, it is best for students to contact Penn State Harrisburg's Food and Housing Services at 717-948-6244 for further information.

Student Group

Penn State Harrisburg has an enrollment of more than 3,800 students, many of whom are nontraditional. The School offers several graduate honor societies for students.

Location

The College is located 8 miles east of the state capitol in Harrisburg. It is easily accessible via interstate routes from Philadelphia, Baltimore, New York, and Washington, D.C. The surrounding area offers many historical and entertainment activities, including Hershey Park, Gettysburg Battle Fields, the Amish country of Lancaster, and the James Buchanan Homestead.

The University and The School

Penn State Harrisburg was established in 1966. As a graduate center, it offers twenty master's degree programs and two doctoral degrees.

The School of Business Administration offers the M.B.A. degree to approximately 200 candidates and the M.S.I.S. degree to about 70 candidates. Nearly all of the School's 36 full-time faculty members hold doctorates. The School is fully accredited by AACSB International and the Middle States Association of Colleges and Schools.

Applying

Applicants must hold a baccalaureate degree from a regionally accredited college or university. Admission decisions are based primarily on undergraduate junior/senior grade point average and the GMAT score. Postbaccalaureate course work, professional experience, and statements provided in the application are also taken into account. The Test of English as a Foreign Language (TOEFL) must be taken by applicants for whom English is not their first language. Applications can be made online at http://www.hbg.psu.edu/admissions/endtour.html.

Correspondence and Information

School of Business Administration
Graduate Programs E-355 Olmsted
Penn State Harrisburg
777 West Harrisburg Pike
Middletown, Pennsylvania 17057-4898
Phone: 717-948-6140
Fax: 717-948-6456
E-mail: mbahbg@psu.edu
          msishbg@psu.edu
Web site: http:// www.hbg.psu.edu/hbg/academicunits.html

Penn State Harrisburg

THE FACULTY

School Director: Stephen Schappe, Associate Professor of Management; Ph.D., Ohio State, 1993.

Associate Directors
John Trussel, Associate Professor of Accounting and Director, Undergraduate Studies; Ph.D., George Washington, 1993.
Gayle Yaverbaum, Professor of Information Systems and Director, Information Technology Programs; Ph.D., Temple, 1983.
Richard R. Young, Professor of Supply Chain Management and Director, M.B.A. Program; Ph.D., Penn State, 1993.

Program Coordinators
Finance and Economics: Oranee Tawatnuntachai, Associate Professor of Finance; Ph.D., New Orleans, 1999.
Information Systems: Girish Subramanian, Professor of Information Systems; Ph.D., Temple, 1991.
Management: Refik Culpan, Professor of Management and International Business; Ph.D., NYU, 1973.
Marketing: Ugur Yucelt, Associate Professor of Marketing; Ph.D., NYU, 1980.
Professional Accountancy: Thomas Buttross, Associate Professor of Accounting; Ph.D., Mississippi, 1991.

Faculty Members
Thomas Amlie, Assistant Professor of Accounting; Ph.D., Maryland, 1996.
Nihal Bayraktar, Assistant Professor of Economics; Ph.D., Maryland, 2002.
Melvin Blumberg, Professor of Management; Ph.D., Penn State, 1977.
Stephan Brady, Assistant Professor of Operations and Supply Chain Management; Ph.D., Penn State, 1999.
Terence A. Brown, Associate Professor of Transportation and Marketing; D.B.A., Maryland, 1971.
Keunsuk Chung, Assistant Professor of Economics; Ph.D., Washington (Seattle), 2005.
Patrick Cusatis, Assistant Professor of Finance; Ph.D., Penn State, 1992.
Jacob De Rooy, Associate Professor of Managerial Economics and Statistics; Ph.D., Rutgers, 1969.
Douglas Friedman, Assistant Professor of Marketing; Ph.D., Michigan, 2005.
Jean Harris, Associate Professor of Professional Accountancy; Ph.D., Virginia Tech, 1990.
Rhoda Joseph, Assistant Professor of Information Systems; Ph.D., CUNY Graduate Center, 2005.
Erdener Kaynak, Professor of Marketing; Ph.D., Cranfield Institute of Management (England), 1975.
David Morand, Professor of Management; Ph.D., Cornell, 1991.
Kurt Parkum, Emeritus Professor of Management; Ph.D., Wisconsin, 1969.
Parag Pendharkar, Associate Professor of Information Systems; Ph.D., Southern Illinois at Carbondale, 1997.
Robert Russell, Assistant Professor of Management; Ph.D., Pittsburgh, 1986.
Peter Swan, Assistant Professor of Logistics and Operation Management; Ph.D., Michigan, 1997.
Premal Vora, Associate Professor of Finance; Ph.D., Penn State, 1991.

PEPPERDINE UNIVERSITY

The Graziadio School of Business and Management
Malibu Graduate Business Programs

Programs of Study

The Graziadio School of Business and Management offers full-time programs leading to the degrees of Master of Business Administration (M.B.A.) and International Master of Business Administration (I.M.B.A.). Joint programs culminating in both the M.B.A./Juris Doctor (J.D.) and the M.B.A./Master of Public Policy (M.P.P.) are also offered. Combined, these programs constitute the Full-time Graduate Business Programs.

The M.B.A. is designed to provide students with a working knowledge of business administration and management. The one-year, 48-unit accelerated program is geared toward students who have completed the necessary business prerequisites and have a minimum of three years of professional work experience. The fifteen-month fast-track M.B.A. program (60 units) is for students with at least three years of experience who study through the summer to graduate early. The two-year, 66-unit program includes an opportunity for a summer internship and the option to study abroad for a week or a trimester. The twenty-month M.B.A. programs offer concentrations in marketing, entrepreneurship, finance, leadership and managing organizational change, and dispute resolution.

For students who pursue business from a multinational perspective, Pepperdine's International M.B.A. (I.M.B.A.) program offers comprehensive real-world learning both in the classroom and on location overseas in countries across Europe, Latin America, and Asia. The I.M.B.A. program offers the foundational courses found in the Pepperdine M.B.A., with a concentration of international business electives and a trimester abroad (studying in English or the host country's language) to provide students with the global experience essential to succeed in today's multinational organizations. In addition, students gain practical experience through an internship or consulting project with an international or multinational company.

Research Facilities

In addition to the Center for Learning and Technology at the Drescher Graduate Complex, students have access to a variety of library sources, including Payson Library and the School of Law Library at Malibu, Pepperdine University Library in West Los Angeles, and reference centers throughout southern California. Several online databases are available in the centers for researching journal articles and reference information. Library materials are listed in the online catalog.

Financial Aid

Financial aid is available to qualified students enrolled in a program at the School. The Graziadio School offers financial aid through merit-based scholarships and graduate assistantships. Applicants are reviewed on the basis of academic and professional experience. The University participates in state and federal financial aid programs administered through the Financial Aid Office. In addition, limited loan funds are available through the School. Candidates are selected for these resources on the basis of academic achievement and financial need.

Cost of Study

Tuition was $16,372 per trimester for the 2006–07 academic year. The one-year M.B.A. program consists of a total of three consecutive trimesters; the fifteen-month M.B.A., a total of four consecutive trimesters; and the two-year M.B.A. and I.M.B.A., a total of four trimesters, with a summer internship after the first year.

Living and Housing Costs

On-campus housing costs are approximately $5200 per trimester for the 2007–08 academic year. Most students choose to live off campus in the surrounding areas, spending an average of $1200 per person per month for rent. Additional costs include food, books, supplies, and insurance. I.M.B.A. and study-abroad students are also responsible for transportation costs to and from the host country.

Student Group

Each year, the full-time Graduate Business Program enrolls approximately 150 new students with diverse backgrounds from all regions of the world. About 110 students enroll in the two-year program, 25 in the one-year program, and 15 in the I.M.B.A. program. The average class size is 26 students.

Location

Nestled in the Santa Monica mountains and overlooking the Pacific Ocean in Malibu, Pepperdine's campus is located just 35 miles northwest of downtown Los Angeles. The economy of southern California is as varied as its population, thriving in the areas of banking, agribusiness, technology, and entertainment. A primary focus of the School revolves around providing students with the chance to take advantage of the rich opportunities afforded by the area through practicum, internship, and mentorship experiences.

The University and The School

Founded in 1937, Pepperdine University presents a unique combination of academic excellence and a strong emphasis on values. It is an independent institution that enrolls 8,000 students in five schools. The business school was established in 1969, developing its hallmark by its practical approach of teaching students ethical business concepts that are applicable in the real world. Including all programs, the School is the fifth-largest accredited business school in the country. It was endowed as the Graziadio School of Business and Management in 1996.

Applying

The application deadline is May 1 for all full-time M.B.A. programs (April 1 for international students). After the deadline, applications are reviewed on a space-available basis. A completed application is composed of an application form, a $100 fee ($50 online), four essays, two recommendations, a resume, a GMAT score, and all college transcripts. A minimum TOEFL score of 600 (250 on the computer-based test; 80 on the Internet-based test) is required for students whose first language is not English. Interviews are strongly recommended but not required.

Correspondence and Information

Admission Office
The Graziadio School
Pepperdine University
24255 Pacific Coast Highway
Malibu, California 90263-4858

Phone: 310-506-4858
      800-726-9283 (toll-free within the U.S.)
E-mail: gsbmadm@pepperdine.edu
Web site: http://bschool.pepperdine.edu

Pepperdine University

THE FACULTY

Michael Davis, Associate Professor of Accounting; Ph.D., Massachusetts.
Terri Egan, Assistant Professor of Organization Behavior; Ph.D., California, Irvine.
Steven R. Ferraro, Assistant Professor of Finance; Ph.D., LSU.
Bruce J. Hanson, Assistant Professor of Management; Ph.D., Case Western Reserve.
Rick Hesse, Professor of Quantitative Methods; Ph.D., Washington (St. Louis).
Michael Magasin, Associate Professor of Business Law; J.D., UCLA.
Mark Mallinger, Professor of Organization Behavior; Ph.D., USC.
James T. Martinoff, Professor of Finance; Ph.D., USC; Ph.D., Claremont; M.D., Bulgaria.
Linnea Bernard McCord, Associate Professor of Business Law; J.D./M.B.A., Houston.
Robert McQuaid, Assistant Professor of Quantitative Methods; Ph.D., North Texas.
Charles Morrissey, Associate Professor of Information Systems; Ph.D., Claremont.
Bob Namvar, Assistant Professor of Economics; Ph.D., California, Riverside.
Fred A. Petro, Professor of Accounting; Ph.D., Arkansas; CMA.
Margaret E. Phillips, Assistant Professor of Organization and Management; Ph.D., UCLA.
John E. Richardson, Associate Professor of Management; D.Min., Fuller Theological Seminary.
David M. Smith, Assistant Professor of Economics; Ph.D., Michigan State.
William Smith, Associate Professor of Marketing; Ph.D., North Carolina at Chapel Hill.
Darrol Stanley, Professor of Finance and Accounting; D.B.A., USC.
Wayne L. Strom, Professor of Behavioral Science; Ph.D., UCLA.
Nikolai Wasilewski, Associate Professor of Strategy; Ph.D., NYU.
W. Bradley Zehner, Assistant Professor of Business Strategy; Ph.D., Claremont.

The Graziadio School of Business and Management, with a mountain landscape overlooking the Pacific Ocean, is located on the main campus of Pepperdine University in the coastal community of Malibu, California.

POLYTECHNIC UNIVERSITY, BROOKLYN CAMPUS
Department of Management

Programs of Study

The Department of Management at Polytechnic University is committed to meeting its objective of providing the highest-quality learning, research, and development in the discipline of management. Its customized educational programs are continually revised to meet today's changing, technology-driven environment. These courses are pragmatic in nature and progressive in scope and provide a superior learning experience for dealing with the junction at which telecommunication, networking, information technologies, and management meet.

The Master of Science in Management (M.S.M.), with classes scheduled in the evenings, allows candidates to build managerial skills by focusing on one of eight concentrations: construction management, electronic business, entrepreneurship, human resource management, information management, operations management, technology management, and telecommunications management. For busy professionals, the evening format Master of Science (M.S.) degree program in organizational behavior is scheduled after business hours. The Department also offers Executive Format Master of Science Degree Programs in management of technology (MOT) and in technology and information management (TIM), with tracks in biopharmaceuticals, e-business decision making, financial services, and retailing. Designed for the modern manager, the program offers small, weekend classes; a contemporary work environment; and close collaboration with industry participants. Students can earn a Master of Science degree in twenty-eight weekends over fifteen months. Advanced certificates are offered with concentrations in construction management, electronic business management, entrepreneurship, financial engineering, financial technology management, human resource management, information management, operations management, organizational behavior, risk management, technology management, and telecommunications management. An extension course is available within the Department of Management in Rehovot, Israel, home of the Weizmann Institute of Science. The program is equal to the M.S.M. evening curriculum in New York, focusing on and working with professionals and managers in Israeli business and industry.

Polytechnic's Ph.D. in technology management program focuses on an interdisciplinary business understanding of how technology can affect an organization's behavior and structure and the effective use and control of information and computer systems by management. The program stresses both the technical aspects and the organizational impact of information management. This doctoral program is geared toward preparing high-level researchers, educators, and practitioners.

Research Facilities

The current areas of research handled by the Department are electronic retailing, new media management, high-tech entrepreneurship, technology in finance services, pervasive computing, and electronic publishing. The diverse research and development work of the Department includes books, articles in well-regarded industry journals, and current case studies on Web-based digital formats. This material forms a portion of the Department's educational programs, thus keeping the curriculum current and unique. The Department is also committed to integrating technology into all of its educational programs, and the Bern Dibner Library of Science and Technology, the center of Polytechnic's information resources, is available to all students. The library and its vast databases are accessible online from any location, 24 hours a day, seven days a week. The University maintains large computer facilities, including a total wired and wireless LAN-equipped infrastructure.

Financial Aid

Polytechnic University offers a variety of financial assistance options to its students, including merit-based graduate fellowships, research fellowships, need-based tuition awards, federal and private loans, the New York State Tuition Assistance Program (TAP), tuition reduction programs, on-campus employment, and a range of flexible payment plans. The University also participates in a unique Educational Investment Program that is based on a student's expected future earnings. More information may be obtained through Polytechnic's Graduate Admissions Office.

Cost of Study

Graduate tuition is $988 per credit, and each 3-credit course costs $2964. There is an additional University fee that may apply. The all-inclusive costs of the executive degree programs vary.

Living and Housing Costs

Campus housing is available for matriculated, full-time graduate students. On-campus housing is approximately $10,000 per academic year and includes a meal plan. Students interested in off-campus housing may obtain information through postings on bulletin boards.

Student Group

Nearly all of the Department of Management students are employed part-time. Industries represented include financial services, information technology, electronic business, telecommunications, chemicals, pharmaceuticals, energy, utilities, media entertainment, defense, aerospace, retailing, health, government, transportation, and construction. The University provides career placement specialists for those students interested in job opportunities.

Location

The M.S.M. program is offered at Polytechnic's main campus at MetroTech Center in Brooklyn. The executive programs (MOT, TIM) are held at 55 Broad Street in downtown Manhattan and at the University's two graduate centers in Melville, Long Island, and at Hawthorne, New York, in Westchester County.

The University

Polytechnic University was founded in 1854 in Brooklyn, New York, and is the nation's second-oldest private engineering university. It has grown to be one of the New York metropolitan area's finest educational institutions in science, technology, and research. Private and coeducational, Polytechnic has a distinguished history of excellence in electrical engineering, polymer chemistry, aerospace and microwave engineering, and technology management, and it is known for its outstanding research centers, including the Institute for Technology and Enterprise.

Applying

Applicants must have a bachelor's degree with at least a B average from an accredited college or university. Satisfactory scores on the GMAT or an acceptable equivalent test may be required for admission. Polytechnic operates on a rolling admissions schedule. Scholarship applications for spring semester should be submitted before October 1, and before April 1 for fall semester. Applications for the spring/regular admission must be submitted by November 1. Applications for the executive degree programs are accepted for the fall only. TOEFL scores are required for all students whose native language is not English. The application fee is $55.

Correspondence and Information

Graduate Center
Polytechnic University
Six MetroTech Center
Brooklyn, New York 11201
Phone: 718-260-3182
Fax: 718-260-3624
E-mail: gradinfo@poly.edu

Dibner/CATT Building, Room 401
Polytechnic University
Six MetroTech Center
Brooklyn, New York 11201-3840
Phone: 718-260-3760
Fax: 718-260-3874
E-mail: msm@poly.edu
Web site: http://www.poly.edu/management

Manhattan Location:
Polytechnic University
55 Broad Street, Suite 13B
New York, New York 10004
Phone: 212-547-7030 Ext. 207
Fax: 212-547-7029
E-mail: msm@poly.edu
Web site: http://www.poly.edu/management

Polytechnic University, Brooklyn Campus

THE FACULTY

Mel Horwitch, Professor of Management and Department Head; Director, Othmer Institute for Interdisciplinary Studies, Institute for Technology and Enterprise; and Co-director, Executive Management Master's Programs; D.B.A., Harvard.

Nina D. Ziv, Industry Associate Professor of Management; Academic Director, Institute for Technology and Enterprise; and Co-director, Executive Management Master's Programs; Ph.D., NYU.

Harold G. Kaufman, Professor of Management; Academic Director, Organizational Behavior Program; and Academic Director, M.S.M. Extension in Israel; Ph.D., NYU.

Yair Berson, Assistant Professor of Management; Ph.D., SUNY at Binghamton.

Anne-Laure Fayard, Assistant Professor; Ph.D., École des Hautes Études en Sciences Sociales (Paris).

Oded Nov, Assistant Professor of Management; Ph.D., Cambridge.

Bharat P. Rao, Associate Professor of Management; Ph.D., Georgia.

A. George Schillinger, Professor Emeritus and Research Professor; Eng.Sc.D., Columbia.

PROVIDENCE COLLEGE

Graduate Business Program

Program of Study

The Graduate Business Program offers a program of graduate study leading to the degree of Master of Business Administration (M.B.A.) that consists of practical courses that are useful in the workplace. Every course is planned so that it will be a meaningful learning experience that is beneficial to the individual in his or her career. Many of the courses have a quantitative emphasis with computer applications. Courses are offered in the late afternoon and evening from Monday through Thursday. Two to four electives are offered on Saturday mornings. While M.B.A. programs are often criticized for producing graduates who master technique but lack substance, the Providence College program gives due consideration to the social purpose and responsibilities as well as to the technical aspects of business. In short, Providence College recognizes the critically important challenge of "humanizing" business administration programs.

The Providence College M.B.A. Program fosters an interdisciplinary approach to the problems facing Rhode Island and American businesses. The faculty includes professors not only from the business department but also from the political science, sociology, psychology, and economics departments. In addition, about a third of the courses are taught by adjunct faculty members who bring to their classes a wealth of current, practical business experience.

The M.B.A. Program requires a total of twelve to nineteen courses, depending upon the student's undergraduate background. Theses, while not required, are encouraged; they may be purely academic, but practical, applied topics are also welcomed. The M.B.A. Program has links with local businesses and with the state government for the promotion of research projects and internships.

Research Facilities

M.B.A. students have access to seven public computer laboratories. The labs are open from 8 a.m. until midnight, Sunday through Thursday; until 8 p.m. on Friday evenings; and from 9 a.m. to 5 p.m. on Saturdays. The labs are equipped with state-of-the-art Pentium III computers running the Windows XP professional edition. All computers have access to the Internet via a T3 pipeline. All seven computer labs are part of the campus network, and printing is available at each location. Providence College has a Helpdesk available in Accinno Hall, room 102, which is open during the computer laboratory hours and is staffed by student assistants who can provide help with the supported software packages installed on the lab computers.

The Phillips Memorial Library holds 300,000 volumes in open stacks and has seating accommodations for 1,000 students. The library is a member of the Consortium of Rhode Island Academic and Research Libraries (which includes the libraries of Brown University, the University of Rhode Island, and the Naval War College), making the resources of most of the libraries of the state available to Providence College students. The library is also a member of the New England Library Network (NELINET) and the Online Computer Library Center (OCLC), which has 3,800 member libraries and a database containing more than 10.6 million records. Through interlibrary loan, most of the resources of these libraries are available to Providence College students.

Financial Aid

Nearly all M.B.A. students have full-time employment, and about half receive financial aid in the form of tuition reimbursement from their employer. There are a limited number of graduate assistantships available for full-time graduate students.

Cost of Study

For the 2007–08 academic year, tuition is $1140 per 3-credit course. The total tuition cost for the M.B.A. program ranges from $13,680 (for twelve courses) to $19,750 (for twenty courses). The cost of books averages $150 per course. The graduation fee is $150.

Living and Housing Costs

No College housing is available for M.B.A. students, but there is an adequate supply of rental accommodations in the Providence College area. While prices vary widely depending upon quality, a two-bedroom apartment in the area rents for approximately $500 to $700 per month.

Student Group

Ninety percent of the 250 M.B.A. students work full-time. The 2007 graduating class of 37 students averaged 28 years of age and consisted of 17 men and 20 women. More than 90 percent of the entering students score above 1100 points on the AACSB International–The Association to Advance Collegiate Schools of Business criteria (200 times the undergraduate GPA plus the GMAT score). More than 90 percent of the students are from Rhode Island and nearby Massachusetts and Connecticut, but more and more students are being attracted from other regions of the United States and from other nations; in the past few years, students have been accepted from Africa, Argentina, Brazil, Canada, Ecuador, England, Germany, India, Indonesia, Ireland, Japan, Pakistan, the Panama Canal Zone, the People's Republic of China, Philippines, Poland, Russia, Spain, Sri Lanka, Switzerland, Thailand, and Turkey.

Location

Providence College's beautiful 105-acre campus is located about a mile from the state capitol and 3 miles from the center of Providence, Rhode Island. The College enjoys the advantages of an atmosphere that is far removed from the traffic and commerce of the metropolitan area, yet it provides easy access to the many cultural attractions of a city that is not only the capital of one of the original thirteen states but also the location of a variety of institutions of higher learning.

The College

Providence College is primarily a four-year college of the liberal arts and sciences, with an undergraduate enrollment of approximately 3,600 men and women. It is conducted under the auspices of the Order of Preachers of the Province of St. Joseph, commonly known as the Dominicans. Founded in 1917 under an Act of Incorporation approved by the General Assembly of the State of Rhode Island, the College states in its charter: "No person shall be denied any of the privileges, honors or degrees of said college on account of the religious opinions he may entertain." Providence College is a coeducational, equal opportunity institution and is duly accredited by the New England Association of Schools and Colleges. It is also a member of AACSB International and, wherever feasible, adheres to its principles.

Applying

Application materials may be obtained from the M.B.A. Program director. Applications are considered throughout the year, and students may enter the program in any semester. Full semesters start in September and January, and two 5-week semesters start in May and July, along with a three-week semester during the Christmas holidays. Detailed application instructions are contained in the Graduate School catalog. Students must submit the completed application form, the application fee ($55), two letters of reference (preferably one academic and one professional), and an official undergraduate transcript from a regionally accredited U.S. college or university (or, if an international institution, one recognized by the American Council on Education). Applicants are required to take the GMAT prior to admission to the M.B.A. Program. Applicants whose native language is not English are required to take the TOEFL.

Correspondence and Information

M.B.A. Office
Koffler Hall, Room 116
Providence College
Providence, Rhode Island 02918-0001
Phone: 401-865-2333
Fax: 401-865-2978

Providence College

THE FACULTY AND THEIR RESEARCH

Deirdre Bird, Assistant Professor; Ph.D., Purdue. International marketing.

Paul A. Brule, Adjunct Instructor; J.D., Suffolk. Legal environment for business.

Helen M. Caldwell, Assistant Professor; Ph.D., Connecticut. Advertising, international marketing, promotion strategy.

Ronald P. Cerwonka, Professor Emeritus; Ph.D., Missouri. Financial analysis, theory of finance.

Clement DeMayo, Professor; Ph.D., Clark. Statistical concepts.

Norman Desmarais, Associate Professor; M.B.A., Providence. Computer systems.

Cemal A. Ekin, Associate Professor; Ph.D., Academy of Economics and Commercial Sciences (Turkey). Marketing theory, management information systems.

Richard B. Goldstein, Professor; Ph.D., Brown. Statistics, management information systems.

Peter S. Goodrich, Associate Professor; Ph.D., Manchester; CMA. International accounting, the politics of information.

Carol A. Hartley, Assistant Professor; M.B.A., Rhode Island; CPA. EDP audit.

Linda F. Jamieson, Associate Professor; Ph.D., Texas. Research methodology.

John R. King, Associate Professor; M.A., Boston College. Statistics, management information systems.

MaryJane Lenon, Associate Professor; Ph.D., Connecticut. Urban economics, managerial economics.

Chunlin Liu, Adjunct Instructor; Ph.D., Rhode Island. Financial institutions, stock and bond markets, portfolio management.

James W. Martin, Adjunct Instructor; M.S., Northeastern. Production management, operations research, industrial organization, economic forecasting.

Stephen G. Misovich, Professor; Ph.D., Connecticut. Human resource management, personnel psychology.

Ian G. Morris, Adjunct Instructor; D.B.A., Oxford (England). Business planning and development, industrial organization, international marketing, marketing research.

Francine Newth, Assistant Professor; D.B.A., Nova Southeastern. Business policy, global strategic alliances, international business.

Francis T. O'Brien, Associate Professor; M.A., Boston College. Collective bargaining, labor relations.

Vivian Okere, Assistant Professor; Ph.D., Rhode Island. Econometrics, financial modeling, international finance, investments.

Theodore J. Przybyla, Adjunct Instructor; M.B.A., Bryant. Money and capital markets, international finance, derivatives, investment theory.

John J. Shaw, Professor; D.B.A., Oklahoma. Consumer behavior, international marketing, marketing management.

Pamela Sherer, Associate Professor; Ph.D., Massachusetts. Human resource management, diversity in the workplace, organizational behavior.

Qing Shui, Adjunct Instructor; M.B.A., Providence. Computer software packages for business computer systems.

Vincent C. Trofi, Assistant Professor; Ph.D., Detroit. Business communication.

William J. Waters, Adjunct Instructor; Ph.D., Ohio State. Managed health-care systems, strategic planning in health care, seminar in health care.

David A. Zalewski, Assistant Professor; Ph.D., Clark. Managerial economics, international finance.

Thomas Flaherty, Ph.D., Dean of the Graduate School.

Harkins Hall, built in 1917, is the main administration building.

QUINNIPIAC
UNIVERSITY

QUINNIPIAC UNIVERSITY

School of Business
Master of Business Administration Program

Programs of Study

The Master of Business Administration (M.B.A.) program at Quinnipiac University is carefully designed to help individuals develop both today's required technical skills and the knowledge and conceptual base needed to meet career challenges of the new millennium. The program teaches people how to think, not what to think, and develops leaders who can capitalize on opportunities, take risks, and participate actively in teams. Apart from providing training for business careers, the Quinnipiac M.B.A. can furnish opportunities to enter or advance in professional positions in government, education, health care, and a wide variety of social services.

The program is built on a broad-based foundation of business knowledge and includes the opportunity to gain expertise in a chosen area. Knowledge is relayed to students through distinct experiences inside and outside the classroom. The traditional one-sided lecture is replaced by discussion, Internet-based learning, and provocative case studies. The integrated approach to learning includes faculty members and students working in teams to solve problems and develop strategies in areas such as marketing, international business, finance, computer information systems, health services administration, and management. To keep in step with the business environment, the curriculum is continually reviewed by the Business Advisory Council, which is composed of CEOs and other company executives. Many of these council members are guest speakers in classes and act as mentors to students. The M.B.A. program also features a lecture series, which brings in prominent corporate executives who shape today's business issues. Every curriculum area addresses the problems and challenges of doing business globally, and Quinnipiac M.B.A. students also have the opportunity to analyze global concerns through an optional three-week summer session that has taken students to Europe, Latin America, and Asia. This intensive experience includes seminars, comprehensive studies, and meetings with corporate executives and government officials.

The M.B.A. program is a total of 46 credits: a 34 credit core and 12 credits of electives. Electives are available in accounting/taxation, computer information systems, finance, health-care management, international business, management, and marketing. Students can choose to take electives within one discipline for greater depth of knowledge in that area or spread their electives across various disciplines for a broad-based view.

Part-time students can complete the M.B.A. program in as little as three years, depending on the number of classes taken each semester. Full-time students can complete the program in under two years.

The M.B.A. program can be completed by following the general M.B.A. curriculum, or applicants can elect to join the M.B.A.-CFA® Track program (Chartered Financial Analyst), M.B.A./HCM (health-care management) program, or the M.B.A./J.D. joint-degree program. A Health Care Compliance Certificate program is also offered.

Research Facilities

The School of Business is designed to accommodate the particular needs of graduate students. Recently ranked as a top 10 "most wired school," the classrooms include the most up-to-date technology. Computer rooms have monitors and keyboards at each desk with line-of-sight contact with the discussion leader. Case rooms allow groups to work on business problems in lecture-discussions. Team-study rooms provide a technologically advanced, learning-conducive environment in which to develop problem-solving strategies with classmates. Technology is effectively integrated into learning modules, and many classes use Internet-based curricula to bring global resources and databases into the classroom. In addition, television monitors throughout the center display breaking financial news from such sources as CNN and CNBC. A partnership between the School of Business and the *Wall Street Journal* gives students access to free copies of the *Wall Street Journal*. Of the 1,700 business schools nationwide, only a few have an academic partnership with the *Journal*.

The newly renovated and expanded Arnold Bernhard Library is one of the most technologically advanced centers for electronic information and learning resources anywhere in the country. In this 47,000-square-foot facility, nearly 100 Internet-accessible workstations open the door to online business resources and digital archives, and there are computer ports throughout the facility for laptop computers. The Research Library provides M.B.A. students with access to such databases as ABI/INFORM, LexisNexis, and the Business Periodicals Index on CD-ROM. In addition, there is a large library of the latest versions of software used by business and industry for student use. Online access to the Dialog database is also available, as is a comprehensive collection of business holdings in hard copy. Off-campus e-mail users have full access to the University's computer network.

The Terry W. Goodwin '67 Financial Technology Center is Quinnipiac's version of Wall Street. The 1,500-square-foot center is where students become mini-stockbrokers and learn how the financial market ticks. Software installed in the center's computer workstations allows students to access real-time financial data, practice analytical finance methods, conduct trading simulations, analyze economic databases, and develop financial models.

Financial Aid

The Financial Aid Office offers all students assistance in obtaining publicly and privately funded loans. Graduate assistantships are available on a limited basis to both full- and part-time students.

Cost of Study

Tuition in 2006–07 was $625 per credit hour. In addition, student fees were $275 per semester for full-time students and $30 per credit for part-time students.

Living and Housing Costs

Privately owned housing is available near the campus. For more information concerning off-campus housing, students should contact the Office of Residential Life or visit the University's Web site.

Student Group

There are approximately 220 students enrolled in the program; 47 percent are women. The students represent a rich mix of backgrounds and experiences, ranging from mid- and top-level managers, beginning and veteran entrepreneurs, and family and small-business owners to recent baccalaureate recipients preparing to enter the business world. As today's managers must organize, motivate, and work with specialists from various disciplines, all of the students in the program benefit from the wide variety of backgrounds and experiences of the participants.

Student Outcomes

Quinnipiac M.B.A. graduates hold top positions in such companies as United Technologies, Bayer Corporation, Aetna, and General Electric. On-campus recruiters include all the "big four" accounting firms, a division of NBC in New York, Pratt & Whitney, regional manufacturing firms, insurance companies, banks, pharmaceutical, health-care organizations, and government agencies. Over 200 companies attend Quinnipiac University's annual job fair. Most graduates find positions in their fields within three months of graduation.

Location

The University is nestled on a beautiful campus located across the street from Sleeping Giant State Park in Hamden, Connecticut, a suburb of New Haven. It is approximately 30 minutes from Hartford, 90 minutes from New York City, and 2 hours from Boston.

The University and The School

Quinnipiac University is nationally recognized as one of the leading centers for higher learning in the Northeast and is consistently ranked among the best master's-level universities in the North in *U.S. News & World Report*'s "Guide to America's Best Colleges." All programs have integrated computer technology into academic and campus life, and Quinnipiac has been recognized in *Yahoo! Internet Life* for its achievements in technology. In 2006, Quinnipiac was ranked ninth in *PC Magazine*'s 2007 Top Wired Colleges.

The School of Business has been one of the traditional strengths of the University for more than sixty years and has strong relationships with local and national businesses. The School has studied new markets in Japan for Connecticut companies and the economic impact of a regional airport and consulted on health management programs in Central America and the Caribbean.

Applying

Admission is competitive, as Quinnipiac University is one of the few AACSB International–accredited schools in the state. A complete application consists of an application form accompanied by the application fee, GMAT scores, two letters of recommendation, a letter of intent (personal letter), a current resume, and college transcripts.

Correspondence and Information

Office of Graduate Admissions
Quinnipiac University
275 Mount Carmel Avenue
Hamden, Connecticut 06518
Phone: 203-582-8672
      800-462-1944 (toll-free)
Fax: 203-582-3443
E-mail: graduate@quinnipiac.edu
Web site: http://www.quinnipiac.edu

M.B.A. Program Office
Quinnipiac University
275 Mount Carmel Avenue
Hamden, Connecticut 06518
Phone: 203-582-8793
E-mail: mbainfo@quinnipiac.edu
Web site: http://www.quinnipiac.edu/mba

Quinnipiac University

THE FACULTY AND THEIR RESEARCH

Guiding Quinnipiac's M.B.A. program are faculty members with exceptional academic credentials and proven business experience. Although their first commitment is to teaching, Quinnipiac's faculty members are also active professionals, knowledgeable about the latest developments in their fields through consulting, leading executive seminars, research, publication, and attendance at conferences and workshops. Among their many areas of expertise are information systems, entrepreneurship, organizational development, fiscal policy, marketing, and competitive strategy.

Henry Adobor, Associate Professor of Management; Ph.D., Concordia (Montreal). International marketing.
Janice Ammons, Professor of Accounting; Ph.D., Michigan. Cost management practices, design of cost systems at universities, accounting education.
Christopher Ball, Assistant Professor of Economics; Ph.D., Texas A&M. Trade deficits, exchange rates, effects of an economic collapse on a country.
Blaine Branchik, Assistant Professor of Marketing; Ph.D., Florida Atlantic.
Charles M. Brooks, Associate Dean and Professor of Marketing; Ph.D., Georgia State. Geographic information systems, retail site selection modeling, sales force management.
Juanita Brooks, Assistant Professor of Information Systems Management; Ph.D., Arkansas.
Eric Brunner, Associate Professor of Economics; Ph.D., California, San Diego.
David T. Cadden, Professor of Management; Ph.D., CUNY, Baruch. Expert systems, neural networks, quality controls.
Wendy Ceccucci, Associate Professor of Information Systems Management; Ph.D., Virginia Tech. Management science.
Tilottama Chowdhury, Assistant Professor of Marketing; Ph.D., Connecticut.
Thomas Coe, Associate Professor of Finance; Ph.D., New Orleans. International financial markets, small-business financial management.
Mohammad Elahee, Associate Professor in International Business; Ph.D., Texas–Pan American. Cross-cultural negotiation, foreign-direct investment, business ethics.
Robert L. Engle, Associate Professor of International Business; D.B.A., Nova Southeastern. Global marketing, occupational stress and work-life outcomes, job satisfaction among sales representatives.
Mark P. Gius, Professor of Economics; Ph.D., Penn State. Baseball economics, wage discrimination in professional basketball.
Martin L. Gosman, Professor of Accounting; Ph.D., Wisconsin–Madison. Effects of lease accounting on firms' reported debt levels, economic effects and adequacy of financial-reporting disclosures, bankers' use of cash flow statements.
Xiaohong He, Professor and Chair of International Business; Ph.D., Texas at Dallas. Foreign direct investment.
Dale W. Jasinski, Associate Professor and Chair of Management; Ph.D., Colorado. Strategic management and entrepreneurship.
Donn M. Johnson, Professor of Economics and Chair of Accounting and Economics; Ph.D., Colorado State. Sports economics, environmental economics.
Brian Jones, Professor of Marketing and Advertising; Ph.D., Queens.
Osman Kilic, Professor of Finance; Ph.D., New Orleans. Financial markets and institutions, international finance.
Norris L. Larrymore, Assistant Professor of Finance; Ph.D., Arkansas. Finance.
Angela Mattie, Assistant Professor of Management; M.P.H., Yale; J.D., Connecticut. Health care, heart attack survival, medical and financial outcomes of motor vehicle crashes.
Richard V. McCarthy, Professor of Information Systems Management; D.B.A., Nova Southeastern. Information systems management.
Mary Meixell, Associate Professor of Management; Ph.D., Lehigh.
Chadwick C. Nehrt, Professor of International Business; Ph.D., Michigan. International diversification, dual diversification, environmental strategies.
Patricia Norberg, Assistant Professor of Marketing and Advertising; Ph.D., Rhode Island.
Mario Norbis, Professor of Management; Ph.D., Massachusetts Amherst. Production scheduling, decision support systems, optimization methods.
Matthew O'Connor, Professor and Chair of Finance; Ph.D., Syracuse. Mutual funds, options.
Rowena Ortiz-Walters, Assistant Professor of Management; Ph.D., Connecticut.
Robert Porter, Assistant Professor of Finance; Ph.D., Rutgers.
Matthew C. Rafferty, Associate Professor of Economics; Ph.D., California, Davis. Business cycles and long-run growth, monetary policy and financial markets, demand fluctuation.
Abhik Roy, Professor of Advertising and Chair of Marketing; Ph.D., UCLA. Competitive pricing strategy, bargaining, retailing.
Farid Sadrieh, Associate Professor in International Business; Ph.D., Temple. International marketing.
Aamer Sheikh, Assistant Professor of Accounting; Ph.D., Georgia; CPA.
Ramesh Subramanian, Professor of Information Systems Management; Ph.D., Rutgers. Computers and information systems.
Mark Thompson, Dean of School of Business; Ph.D., Georgia State. Impact of intellectual property protection on economic growth, economic consequences of discrimination, issues related to regional economic development.
Michael J. Tucker, Professor of Accounting; Ph.D., Houston; LL.M., Georgetown; CPA. Taxes, entrepreneurship in the former Soviet Union.
Bruce A. White, Professor and Chair of Information Systems Management; Ph.D., Nebraska–Lincoln. Electronic commerce undergraduate programs, industry/academic relations success factors.

RENSSELAER POLYTECHNIC INSTITUTE

Lally School of Management and Technology

Programs of Study

The Lally School of Management and Technology graduates technologically sophisticated business leaders who are prepared to guide their organizations in the integration of technology for new products, businesses, and systems. An M.B.A., an executive M.B.A., a Master of Science, specialized certificate programs, and a Ph.D. research program are offered. An international exchange program is also available. The Lally School is accredited by AACSB International–The Association to Advance Collegiate Schools of Business. The Lally M.B.A. program prepares business leaders with the skills and thinking that are essential for meeting the day-to-day, real-world challenges of running a business within the evolving dynamics of the global economy. Through experiential hands-on instruction, students acquire an overall understanding of the new sources of value creation brought about by the convergence of globalization and the information technology (IT) revolution.

The curriculum is built on five course streams of knowledge, enabling students to gain critical expertise in launching, running, and growing a successful business: creating and managing an enterprise; value creation, managing networks, and driving innovation; developing innovative products and services; formulating and executing competitive business strategies; and managing the business implications of emerging technologies. These five streams of knowledge focus on critical business issues in today's global marketplace and integrate all discrete business functions, from finance and operations to global marketing and supply chain management, within the dynamics of each course experience.

To ensure that each M.B.A. student graduates with the necessary in-depth business skills, key modules complement the five streams of knowledge. Modules include global business, decision models, social responsibility and business ethics, and succeeding in knowledge-intensive organizations. Students also have the opportunity to specialize in one of five areas: strategy and entrepreneurship, management of information systems, finance, new product development and marketing, and production and operations management.

The three-year Pathfinders M.B.A. program at the Lally School of Management and Technology is designed for the recent graduating senior of an engineering, science, or math program. Students in the Pathfinders M.B.A. program attend M.B.A. classes on the Rensselaer campus for the first year of the program; get paid experience during the second year through participation in a One-Year Co-op in the U.S. or abroad; and, in the third year, return to campus to complete the M.B.A. program. Classes and the co-op program reflect the tenets of a Lally School education: Experience in global innovation and technological entrepreneurship.

The Master of Science in management is a focused degree for students with professional experience. Students may also pursue an M.S. in management with a special focus in technology commercialization and entrepreneurship or financial technology.

The Ph.D. program is designed for students with superior abilities, a technological orientation, and interest in a career as an educator, researcher, or professional specialist. Interdisciplinary graduate programs include those leading to the Ph.D. degree in decision sciences and engineering systems and to M.S. degrees in operations research and statistics, manufacturing systems engineering, industrial and management engineering, and environmental management and policy.

Research Facilities

The Lally School of Management and Technology houses the Paul J. '69 and Kathleen M. Severino Center for Technological Entrepreneurship. The Severino Center was created to assist entrepreneurs in setting the stage for the technological breakthroughs necessary for long-term sustainability for corporations and start-ups alike. The Center for the Study of Financial Technology examines financial engineering, financial modeling, the impact of information technology on financial markets, and entrepreneurial finance. The Lighting Research Center pursues a wide range of lighting research and is a source of patented technology ready for commercialization in conjunction with Lally School technological entrepreneurship initiatives. The Center for the Study of Science, Technology, and Innovation in Greater China is an initiative that provides joint research and training opportunities in the identification and analysis of technological developments in the greater China region and their implications for business policy and research and development strategy.

The Pittsburgh Building is a state-of-the-art facility in a historic building that serves as the home of the Lally School. Fully networked, it contains computer-interactive, videoconferencing, and distance education classrooms. The Rensselaer Research Libraries provide the university community with information resources and services in support of both teaching and research missions. Researchers can access more than 400,000 print volumes, 40,000 electronic and print journals, and 32,000 electronic books and view several extensive image databases. When researchers need material that is not held by one of the Research Libraries, they can initiate online interlibrary loan requests or use the Connect NY service to borrow books directly—and receive rapid delivery—from a statewide consortium holding more than 5 million items.

Financial Aid

Financial aid is available in the form of teaching and research assistantships, which include tuition scholarships and stipends. Rensselaer assistantships and university, corporate, or national fellowships fund many of Rensselaer's full-time graduate students. Outstanding students may qualify for university-sponsored Rensselaer Graduate Fellowship Awards, which carry a minimum stipend of $20,000 and a full-tuition-and-fees scholarship. All fellowship awards are calendar-year awards for full-time graduate students. Summer support is also available in many departments. Low-interest, deferred-repayment graduate loans are also available to U.S. citizens with demonstrated need.

Cost of Study

Full-time graduate tuition for the 2007–08 academic year is $34,900. Other costs (estimated living expenses, insurance, etc.) are projected to be about $12,605. Therefore, the cost of attendance for full-time graduate study is approximately $47,505. Part-time study and cohort programs are priced differently. Students should contact Rensselaer for specific cost information related to the program they wish to study.

Living and Housing Costs

Graduate students at Rensselaer may choose from a variety of housing options. On campus, students can select one of the many residence halls and immerse themselves in campus life or choose from a select number of apartments designed for graduate students only. There are abundant, affordable options off campus as well, many within easy walking distance.

Student Group

Of the 1,228 graduate students, 30 percent are women, 92 percent are full-time, and 72 percent study at the doctoral level.

Student Outcomes

Rensselaer's graduate students are hired in a variety of industries and sectors of the economy and by private and public organizations, the government, and institutions of higher education. Their starting salaries average $72,231 for master's degree recipients and $74,238 for Ph.D. recipients.

Location

Located just 10 miles northeast of Albany, New York State's capital city, Rensselaer's historic 275-acre campus sits on a hill overlooking the city of Troy, New York, and the Hudson River. The area offers a relaxed lifestyle with many cultural and recreational opportunities, with easy access to both the high-energy metropolitan centers of the Northeast—such as Boston, New York City, and Montreal, Canada—and the quiet beauty of the neighboring Adirondack Mountains.

The Institute

Recognized as a leader in interactive learning and interdisciplinary research, Rensselaer continues a tradition of excellence and technological innovation dating back to 1824. Rensselaer has five schools—Architecture, Engineering, Management, Science, and Humanities and Social Sciences—that offer more than 100 graduate programs in more than fifty disciplines, attracting top students, researchers, and professors. The discovery of new scientific concepts and technologies, especially in emerging interdisciplinary fields, is the lifeblood of Rensselaer's culture and a core goal for the faculty and staff members and students. Fueled by significant support from government, industry, and private donors, Rensselaer provides a world-class education in an environment tailored to the individual.

Applying

Applications and all supporting credentials should be submitted well in advance of the preferred semester of entry to allow sufficient time for departmental review and processing. Since the first departmental awards are made in early February for the next academic year, applicants are encouraged to submit all required credentials by January 1 to ensure full consideration for admission and assistance. Late applications are considered only with departmental approval, though M.B.A. applications are generally accepted beyond the January deadline.

Correspondence and Information

For written information about graduate work:

Graduate Admissions
Lally School of Management and Technology
Rensselaer Polytechnic Institute
110 8th Street
Troy, New York 12180-3590
Phone: 518-276-6565
Web site: http://lallyschool.rpi.edu/

For applications and admissions information:

Rensselaer Admissions
Rensselaer Polytechnic Institute
110 8th Street
Troy, New York 12180-3590
Phone: 518-276-6216
Web site: gradadmissions.rpi.edu

Rensselaer Polytechnic Institute

THE FACULTY AND THEIR RESEARCH

Professors
Robert A. Baron, Dean R. Wellington '83 Professorship in Management; Ph.D., Iowa. Organizational behavior, entrepreneurship.
Daniel Berg, Ph.D., Yale. Information systems and operations management.
David A. Gautschi, Ph.D., Berkeley. Marketing, economics.
Iftekar Hasan, Acting Dean; Ph.D., Houston. Finance.
Albert S. Paulson, Frank and Lillian Gilbreth Professor in the Technologies of Management; Ph.D., Virginia Tech. Operations research and statistics, risk management and investment analysis.

Clinical Professors
Pier A. Abetti, Ph.D., IIT; PE. Management of technology, international business development and strategic planning, entrepreneurship.
Greg Hughes, Ph.D., Princeton. Strategy, entrepreneurship, information technology.

Associate Professors
Jeffrey Durgee, Ph.D., Pittsburgh. Marketing research and advertising.
Bill Francis, Ph.D., Toronto. Corporate finance, international finance and economics.
David H. Goldenberg, Ph.D., Florida. Investments, derivatives markets, mathematical and computational finance.
Chris McDermott, Ph.D., North Carolina at Chapel Hill. Manufacturing strategy, operations management.
Satish Nambisan, Ph.D., Syracuse. Information systems.
Gina O'Connor, Ph.D., NYU. Marketing, product management.
Lois S. Peters, Ph.D., NYU. Science and technology policy, innovation and R&D management, entrepreneurship, organization theory, international business.
Phil Phan, Warren H. Bruggeman '46 and Pauline Urban Bruggeman Distinguished Associate Professor; Ph.D., Washington (Seattle). Strategic management, entrepreneurship.
Thiagarajan Ravichandran, Ph.D., Southern Illinois at Carbondale. Management information systems.
Susan S. Sanderson, Ph.D., Pittsburgh. International business, manufacturing policy, new product development.
Robert Veryzer, Ph.D., Florida. Marketing and consumer behavior.

Clinical Associate Professors
L. B. Dickenson-Peters, Ph.D., Rensselaer. Management information systems.
R. Miccio, J.D., Albany Law. Law, ethics.
W. C. St. John, Ph.D., Rensselaer. Accounting, finance.
T. Triscari, Ph.D., Rensselaer. Information systems.

Assistant Professors
L. Chi, Ph.D., Kentucky. Telecommunications and computer networks.
A. Choo, Ph.D., Minnesota, Twin Cities. Operations management, knowledge management, operations strategy.
A. Corbett, Ph.D., Colorado at Boulder. Entrepreneurship.
A. Cui, Ph.D., Michigan State. Marketing strategy and innovation.
T. Golden, Ph.D., Connecticut. Organizational behavior, human resource management.
J. Kuruzovich, Ph.D., Maryland. Information systems.
S. Jayanthi, Ph.D., Minnesota, Twin Cities. Manufacturing operations, operations management.
Y. Jiao, Ph.D., Boston College. Corporate and entrepreneurial finance.
J. C. Park, Ph.D., Carnegie Mellon. Corporate finance, financial accounting and reporting.
Y.-C. Shin, Ph.D., MIT. Financial accounting.

Clinical Assistant Professors
G. Karaatli, Ph.D., Rensselaer. Marketing.
S. Mehta, Ph.D., Texas Southwestern Medical Center at Dallas. Biotechnology management and entrepreneurship.
R. Sands, M.S., M.B.A., SUNY at Albany. Organizational behavior and human resource management.

Adjunct Faculty
R. Alben, Ph.D., Harvard. Physics, operations management.
H. Johnson, A.B., Dartmouth. Financial markets and analysis.
W. Nealon, M.B.A., Rensselaer. Accounting.
P. Nugent, Ph.D., SUNY at Albany. Organization theory.
S. Russell, Ph.D., Fielding Institute. Human organizational systems.
F. Wright, M.S.E.E., Naval Postgraduate School. General management, manufacturing operations, international business.

For a list of faculty members from Rensselaer at Hartford, students should contact the Admissions Office.

RIDER UNIVERSITY

College of Business Administration
Business Administration and Accountancy Programs

Programs of Study

The graduate business programs at Rider University are accredited by AACSB International–The Association to Advance Collegiate Schools of Business. The Master of Business Administration (M.B.A.) Program provides advanced preparation for successful participation as managers and leaders in today's rapidly changing business environment. The M.B.A. program provides an effective and distinctive learning environment that emphasizes advanced business theory, interpersonal communication, management skills, and an integration of theory and application. Program flexibility is encouraged; students may pursue a general M.B.A. program; an M.B.A. with a concentration in the functional disciplines of computer information systems, finance, management and human resources, or marketing; or an M.B.A. with an interdisciplinary concentration in global business, health-care administration, or entrepreneurship. The Executive M.B.A. program enables managers to become leaders by mastering the latest financial techniques and managerial approaches to make decisions at the executive level.

The Master of Accountancy (M.Acc.) Program prepares individuals for careers in the rapidly changing field of accounting. Students pursuing a career in public accounting develop required technical competencies and meet evolving credit-hour requirements for licensure. Career paths in areas outside of public accounting, including corporate, financial, or governmental entities, are facilitated through the use of elective course offerings. Required courses emphasize an integration and synthesis of accounting subject matter. Course work assumes a basic understanding of accounting. Students holding a baccalaureate degree in an area other than accounting must complete preliminary course requirements in addition to the required M.Acc. course work. Students may choose an M.Acc. Program with a concentration in computer information systems, management and human resources, marketing, finance, global business, health-care administration, or entrepreneurship.

The programs are organized for students with full-time career track positions and/or similar work experience. Most courses are offered in the evenings, Monday through Thursday. Selected M.Acc. courses are offered during the day. Executive M.B.A. course work is offered each Saturday with five Friday sessions throughout the twenty-one-month program. While most students attend part-time, full-time enrollment is possible in up to four courses per semester.

Research Facilities

The College of Business Administration is centrally housed in an award-winning facility that includes computer labs, terminals, and networking capabilities. A central library contains extensive hard copy, database, and media collections to support research. The Ernst and Young Resource Center provides M.Acc. students with networking and computing capabilities in a small practice office setting.

Financial Aid

Financial aid is available to qualified graduate students under several state and federal loan programs, including the Federal Stafford Student Loan program. A limited number of graduate assistantship positions are also available.

Cost of Study

M.B.A. and M.Acc. tuition for 2007–08 is $735 per credit hour, plus any applicable fees. Executive M.B.A. tuition is $55,000 and covers the full cost of the entire twenty-one–month program, payable in installments.

Living and Housing Costs

On-campus graduate student housing is available. Students must be enrolled in two or more graduate courses each semester. The cost is approximately $3640 per semester. The optional University meal plan is approximately $2070 per semester. A community kitchen facility is also available.

Student Group

Fifty-six percent of the students are men. Eighty percent are pursuing their program of study on a part-time basis. The majority of M.B.A. students are employed in professional or managerial positions and bring a wealth of business experience to the classroom to share with their peers. Most M.Acc. students are employed by public accounting firms, corporations, and financial institutions.

Student Outcomes

Graduates of the M.B.A. and M.Acc. programs have accepted employment in area Fortune 500 corporations, public accounting firms, and in corporate/financial and governmental entities.

Location

Rider University maintains campuses in Lawrenceville and Princeton, New Jersey—locations rich in tradition, culture, and beauty. The College of Business Administration is housed on the Lawrenceville campus in Sweigart Hall. The campus location is in the heart of the New York and Philadelphia corridor, a major center of corporate, financial, and cultural vitality.

The University and The College

Rider University has historically been recognized for its ability to educate business professionals. Department faculty members view themselves as teachers-scholars, dedicated to effective teaching and to adding value to a student's academic pursuits.

The College of Business Administration at Rider University was accredited by AACSB International in 1993 and was reaffirmed in 2007. The accounting program was further recognized for excellence with AACSB International accounting accreditation in 2000.

Applying

Applicants must submit a completed graduate application, a $50 application fee, professional resume, personal statement, official GMAT scores, and official transcripts from each college/university attended. For applicants whose native language is not English, satisfactory results on the TOEFL are required. International applicants must provide transcripts evaluated by a recognized credential evaluation service. The application for admission should be submitted by August 1 for the fall semester, December 1 for the spring semester, and May 1 for the summer session. Students applying for the Executive M.B.A. program require a personal interview.

Correspondence and Information

Office of Graduate Admission
Rider University
2083 Lawrenceville Road
Lawrenceville, New Jersey 08648
Phone: 609-896-5036
Fax: 609-895-5680
E-mail: gradadm@rider.edu
Web site: http://www.rider.edu

Rider University

THE GRADUATE BUSINESS FACULTY

Mohammad Ahsanullah, Professor of Management Sciences; M.S.C., Calcutta; Ph.D., North Carolina State.
William J. Amadio, Associate Professor of Computer Information Systems; Ph.D., Polytechnic of New York.
Paul Benchener, Lecturer of Marketing; B.S., California State, Long Beach; M.Div., Southwestern Baptist Theological Seminary.
Jerome T. Bentley, Associate Professor of Economics; Ph.D., Pittsburgh.
Edward H. Bonfield, Professor of Marketing; Ph.D., Illinois at Urbana-Champaign.
Anne M. Carroll, Associate Professor of Finance; Ph.D., Pennsylvania.
Radha Chaganti, Professor of Business Policy and Environment; M.B.A., Indian Institute of Mangi; Ph.D., SUNY at Buffalo.
Judy F. Cohen, Associate Professor of Marketing; M.B.A., Chicago; Ph.D., Syracuse.
Ronald G. Cook, Professor of Management of Human Resources; M.B.A., Ph.D., Syracuse.
Lewis Coopersmith, Associate Professor of Management Science; M.S., Ph.D., NYU.
Hope Corman, Professor of Economics; Ph.D., CUNY.
James W. Dailey, Associate Professor of Computer Information Systems; Ph.D., Case Western Reserve.
Jean C. Darian, Associate Professor of Marketing; M.C.D., Liverpool; Ph.D., Pennsylvania.
Susan Denbo, Associate Professor of Business Policy and Environment; J.D., Villanova.
Jie Joyce Ding, Associate Professor of Management Sciences; Ph.D., Texas at Austin.
John J. Donovan, Associate Professor of Management and Human Resources; Ph.D., SUNY at Albany.
Kathleen Dunne, Associate Professor of Accounting; Ph.D., Temple.
Lauren Eder, Associate Professor of Computer Information Systems; M.B.A., Ph.D., Drexel.
Benjamin H. Eichhorn, Associate Professor of Management Sciences; Ph.D., Berkeley.
Ralph Gallay, Associate Professor of Marketing; M.B.A., Ph.D., NYU.
Zhihong Gao, Assistant Professor of Marketing; M.A., Wake Forest; Ph.D., Illinois at Urbana-Champaign.
Herbert E. Gishlick, Professor of Economics; Ph.D., Pennsylvania.
Ilene V. Goldberg, Associate Professor of Business Policy and Environment; J.D., Temple.
Linguo Gong, Associate Professor of Management Sciences; Ph.D., Texas.
Cengiz Haksever, Professor of Management Sciences; M.B.A., Texas A&M; Ph.D., Texas at Austin.
Mary Elizabeth Haywood-Sullivan, Assistant Professor of Accounting; Ph.D., Georgia.
Sigfredo Hernandez, Associate Professor of Marketing; Ph.D., Temple.
Joe H. Kim, Associate Professor of Marketing; M.B.A., Yon-sei (Korea); Ph.D., Saint Louis.
Sion Kim, Assistant Professor of Business Policy and Environment; J.D., Columbia.
Gerald D. Klein, Associate Professor of Organizational Behavior and Management; M.B.A., Harvard; Ph.D., Case Western Reserve.
Steven Klein, Associate Professor of Management Sciences; M.B.A., NYU; Ph.D., Rutgers.
Christine Lentz, Associate Professor of Management and Human Resources; Ph.D., Northwestern.
Sherry Li, Assistant Professor of Business Economics; D.B.A., Massachusetts.
Feng-Ying Liu, Professor of Finance; M.B.A., Ph.D., Drexel.
Charmen Loh, Associate Professor of Finance; M.B.A., Ph.D., Arkansas.
Steven J. Lorenzet, Associate Professor of Management and Human Resources and Associate Dean of the College of Business; Ph.D., SUNY at Albany.
Biju Mathew, Associate Professor of Computer Information Systems; Ph.D., Pittsburgh.
Charles W. McCall, Associate Professor of Economics; Ph.D., Temple.
Evelyn McDowell, Assistant Professor of Accounting; M.Acc., Ph.D., Case Western Reserve.
Dorothy McMullen, Associate Professor of Accounting; M.B.A., Ph.D., Drexel; CPA.
Ilhan Meric, Professor of Finance; Ph.D., Lehigh.
John Moussourakis, Professor of Management Sciences; M.B.A., Iona; Ph.D., NYU.
Cynthia Newman, Assistant Professor of Marketing; Ph.D., Pennsylvania.
Larry Newman, Dean of the College of Business Administration; M.B.A., Drexel; Ph.D., Penn State.
Kelly Noonan, Associate Professor of Economics; Ph.D., SUNY at Stony Brook.
Lan Ma Nygren, Assistant Professor of Management Sciences; M.A., Ohio State; Ph.D., NYU.
Margaret O'Reilly-Allen, Chairperson of Accounting; M.B.A., Ph.D., Drexel; CPA.
Obeua S. Persons, Associate Professor of Accounting; M.P.A., Ph.D., Texas; CPA.
Larry M. Prober, Associate Professor of Accounting; M.B.A., Massachusetts; Ph.D., Temple; CPA.
Drew Procaccino, Associate Professor of Computer Information Systems; M.B.A., Rider.
Maury R. Randall, Professor and Chairperson of Finance; Ph.D., NYU.
Mitchell Ratner, Associate Professor of Finance; M.B.A., Ph.D., Drexel.
Thomas L. Ruble, Associate Professor and Chairperson of Management and Human Resources; M.B.A., Ph.D., UCLA.
Maria Sanchez, Assistant Professor of Accounting; M.B.A., Ph.D., Drexel.
Mark E. Sandberg, Professor Emeritus and Associate Professor of Management and Human Resources; M.B.A., Drexel; Ph.D., Cornell.
Joy A. Schneer, Professor of Management and Organizational Behavior; M.B.A., Ph.D., CUNY, Baruch.
Harold Schneider, Associate Professor of Management Sciences; M.S., Ph.D., Chicago.
Wayne J. Smeltz, Associate Professor of Business Policy and Environment; M.B.A., Ph.D., Houston.
Ira B. Sprotzer, Associate Professor and Chairperson of Business Policy and Environment; J.D., Boston College; M.B.A., Miami (Ohio).
David Suk, Associate Professor of Finance; Ph.D., Ohio State.
Alan R. Sumutka, Associate Professor of Accounting; M.B.A., Seton Hall; CPA.
Leonore S. Taga, Associate Professor of Economics; Ph.D., Berkeley.
Arthur Taylor, Lecturer of Computer Information Systems; M.I.S., George Mason.
Carol D. Watson, Professor of Management and Human Resources; Ph.D., Columbia.
Alan R. Wiman, Associate Professor of Marketing; M.B.A., D.B.A., Tennessee.
Donald E. Wygal, Associate Professor of Accounting; M.B.A., Ph.D., Pittsburgh.
Zaher Z. Zantout, Associate Professor of Finance; M.B.A., American University of Beirut; Ph.D., Drexel.

ST. JOSEPH'S COLLEGE

Programs in Business

Programs of Study

The Graduate Management Programs at St. Joseph's College (SJC) were designed around two interrelated concepts—developing specific abilities needed for success in the workplace and relating theoretical knowledge to the real world. Consonant with the values espoused in the mission and goals of the College, the programs support ethical behavior and social responsibility as a foundation of managerial practice. The curricula encourage a proactive perspective relative to the challenges and opportunities inherent in promoting diversity in the workplace.

Designed for working adults holding leadership positions in the public-service, private, and nonprofit sectors, the M.B.A. in Accounting, the M.S. in Management, and the Executive M.B.A. programs promote managerial effectiveness and the enhancement of human performance in organizations. Each program is solidly rooted in groundbreaking research—that is, innovative scholarly investigation into the key distinctions between superior leaders and average performers in the workplace. Based on this research, the programs help students strengthen a variety of abilities, including goal and action management, people management, and analytic reasoning. Students create an individualized plan to target those abilities they wish to develop.

The Self-Directed Managerial Applications Component of each course addresses an appropriate issue, problem, or task within an actual organizational environment. Students learn to apply classroom knowledge and develop one or more managerial-effectiveness abilities. Students are also required to complete a minimum of two projects as participants in management teams. Certificates in health-care management and human resources management are also offered. These 15-credit programs are designed to provide practitioners with advanced study of current health-care or human resources trends and practices and the latest leadership and management tools necessary to advance their careers.

Research Facilities

The Callahan Library at the Long Island Campus is a modern, 25,000-square-foot, freestanding facility with seating for more than 300 readers. A curriculum library, seminar rooms, administrative offices, and two classrooms are housed in this building. Holdings include more than 105,000 volumes and 307 periodical titles, and they are supplemented by videos and other instructional aids. Patrons have access to the Internet and to several online academic databases. A fully automated library system, Endeavor, ensures the efficient retrieval and management of all library resources. Other resources include the library at St. Joseph's Brooklyn Campus, with more than 109,000 volumes, and membership in the Long Island Library Resources Council, which facilitates cooperative associations with the academic and special libraries on Long Island. Internet access, subscriptions to several online full-text databases, and membership in the international bibliographic utility, OCLC, allow almost limitless access to available information.

McEntegart Hall is a fully air-conditioned five-level structure. Three spacious reading areas with a capacity for 300 readers, including individual study carrels and shelf space for 200,000 volumes, provide an excellent environment for research. In addition, McEntegart Hall houses the college archives, a curriculum library, three computer laboratories, a nursing education laboratory, and a videoconference room. There are eight classrooms, a chapel, cafeteria, and faculty and student lounges.

A high-speed fiber-optic intracampus network connects all offices, instructional facilities, computer laboratories, and libraries on both the Brooklyn and Patchogue campuses. The network provides Internet access to all students and faculty and staff members. An integrated online library system enables students to search for and check out books at either campus. Online databases and other electronic resources are available to students from either campus or from their home computers. Two wireless laptop classrooms with "smart classroom" features provide flexible instruction spaces with the latest technologies. Videoconferencing facilities connect the two campuses, allowing for real-time distance learning in a small-group setting.

Financial Aid

Financial aid is available in the form of federal and private loans, scholarships, and work-study programs. Students should contact the Financial Aid Office for more information (Brooklyn Campus, telephone: 718-636-6808; Long Island Campus, telephone: 631-447-3214).

Cost of Study

In 2006–07, tuition was $530 per credit. Per semester, the college and technology fees for 12 or more credits totaled $200.

Living and Housing Costs

On-campus housing is not available. The St. George Hotel, New York's number-one resource for student housing, and St. Joseph's College have partnered to offer off-campus housing. In 2006–07, the cost was $5450 per semester, or $10,900 for the year. Accommodations include a double room, cable TV, high-speed access, a completely furnished bedroom, a full bath, a closet, a kitchen on each floor, and 24-hour security. Housing applications are available online.

Student Group

The total enrollment for all graduate programs on both campuses is 508.

Location

St. Joseph's College has two campuses—the main campus in the residential Clinton Hill section of Brooklyn and the campus in Patchogue, Long Island. The main campus offers easy access to all transit lines; to the Long Island Expressway; to all bridges in Brooklyn, Manhattan, and Queens; and to the Verrazano-Narrows Bridge to Staten Island. Within the space of half an hour, students leaving St. Joseph's College may find themselves in the Metropolitan Museum of Art, the 42nd Street Library, Carnegie Hall and Lincoln Center, the Broadway theater district, Madison Square Garden, or Shea Stadium. The College itself stands in the center of one of the nation's most diversified academic communities, consisting of six colleges and universities within a 2-mile radius of each other. The 27-acre Long Island campus, adjacent to Great Patchogue Lake, is an ideal setting for studying, socializing, and partaking in extracurricular activities. Just off Sunrise Highway, the College is easily accessible from all parts of Long Island.

The University

St. Joseph's College is a fully accredited institution that has been dedicated to providing a diverse population of students in the New York metropolitan area with an affordable education rooted in the liberal arts tradition since 1916. Independent and coeducational, the College provides a strong academic and value-oriented education at the undergraduate and graduate levels. For the fifth year in a row, the 2007 ranking of America's Best Colleges by *U.S. News & World Report* named St. Joseph's College to the top tier of the Northern Comprehensive Colleges–Bachelor's category.

Applying

All applicants must have a baccalaureate degree from an accredited institution of higher education with an undergraduate grade point average of at least 3.0. In addition, applicants typically are required to be employed in a full-time position and to have substantial work experience involving supervision, program development, specialized training, considerable responsibility, and/or independent judgment. When an applicant's experiential qualifications fall short of the aforementioned criteria, the GMAT is required. Students must submit the completed application; the application fee; official transcripts; a current chronological resume; a completed verification of employment form, with a verification letter outlining designated duties from the current (or previous) employer; and two letters of recommendation. An interview is required.

Correspondence and Information

Brooklyn Campus
St. Joseph's College
245 Clinton Avenue
Brooklyn, New York 11205
Phone: 718-399-0068
E-mail: msmbab@sjcny.edu
Web site: http://www.sjcny.edu/page.php/prmID/185

Long Island Campus
St. Joseph's College
155 West Roe Boulevard
Patchogue, New York 11772
Phone: 631-447-3250
E-mail: msmbab@sjcny.edu

St. Joseph's College

THE FACULTY

FULL-TIME FACULTY
James J. Barkocy, Assistant Professor of Business; M.B.A., NYU.
Mary Chance, Assistant Professor of Business and Director of Graduate Management Studies; M.S.T., Long Island; CPA.
Stanley Chu, Accounting; M.B.A., St. John's (New York).
Stanley F. Fox, Associate Professor of Business; Ph.D., Walden.
Eileen White Jahn, Associate Professor of Business; Ph.D., CUNY, Baruch.
William Cotesworth Keller, Associate Professor of Business; Ph.D., Walden.
Robert A. Marose, Associate Professor of Business; Ph.D., Polytechnic.
Robert J. Nobile, Assistant Professor of Business; J.D., St. John's (New York).
Charles J. Pendola, Assistant Professor of Business; J.D., Touro; CPA.
Lauren Grace Pete, Associate Professor of Health Administration; J.D., Yeshiva; Ph.D., CUNY Graduate Center.
Diane Pfadenhauer, Assistant Professor of Business; J.D., St. John's (New York).
John Sardelis, Assistant Professor of Health Administration; Dr.P.H., Columbia.
Robert Seperson, Assistant Professor of Business; M.B.A., Dowling.
John J. Skinnon, Assistant Professor of Accounting; M.S.T., Long Island; CPA.
Richard Torz, Associate Professor of Economics; Ph.D., CUNY Graduate Center.

PRECEPTORS
Sharon Didier, Business; Ph.D., Capella.
Charles Dyon, Business; M.B.A., NYU.
Thomas Horan, Business; M.S., Long Island; CPA.
Marie Losquadro, Associate Dean of the Suffolk Campus, Business; M.S., NYIT.
Jay Zuckerman, Health Administration; M.P.A., SUNY at Albany; M.S., SUNY at Stony Brook.

LECTURERS
Ivo Antoniazzi, Business; Ed.D., Columbia.
Hsien-hung Chiu, Economics; M.A., Fu-Jen Catholic; M.A., SUNY at Stony Brook.
John Furnari, Business; M.A., CUNY, Queens.
Brenda Gill, Business; J.D., Fordham.
Heidi Hayden, Business; M.S., St. Joseph's (New York).
Steven Jarmon, Business; M.A., Denver.
Linda Lombardi, Health Administration; Ph.D., CUNY Graduate Center.
Verina Mathis-Crawford, Business; M.B.A., Pace.
Arthur Rescigno, Business; M.S., Columbia.
M. Par Rostom, Business; M.A, Temple.
Alan Vitters, Business; Ph.D., Utah.
Gail Whelan, Business; M.S., NYIT.

SAINT LOUIS
UNIVERSITY

SAINT LOUIS UNIVERSITY

John Cook School of Business

Programs of Study

The John Cook School of Business opens doors of opportunity for future business and community leaders. As the oldest business school west of the Mississippi, the School is well respected in the business community, and its programs prepare business professionals, leaders, and educators to perform effectively and ethically in today's fast-changing global environment.

The part-time M.B.A. program requires 45 credit hours, including 12 hours in foundation courses, 15 hours in breadth courses, 6 hours in required courses, and 12 elective hours. Students can expect to complete the degree in two years. The one-year, full-time M.B.A. immerses students in their studies and provides an integrated curriculum that encourages thinking across disciplines. Students typically enroll for three semesters, with a two-week study-abroad program to Hong Kong in January. The Ph.D. program consists of 54 credit hours, including 12 hours in research techniques, 21 hours in an area of concentration, 9 hours in research topics, and 12 hours in dissertation research, and a comprehensive examination that includes a written and an oral component. Students are expected to enroll full-time and complete the degree in five years or less.

Specialized master's degree programs are geared toward students who want to gain expertise in a specific area. These include the Master of Accounting for students who want to take the CPA exam, the Master of Finance for students who are interested in how markets function, and the Executive Master of International Business for professionals who wish to gain global business expertise. The School also offers three dual degrees: the J.D./M.B.A. for legal advisers, the M.H.A./M.B.A. for health-care managers and policy advisers, and the M.D./M.B.A. for clinician-managers pursuing careers that balance delivery of patient care.

Research Facilities

The Cook School has three computer labs, including one dedicated lab with twenty-eight workstations, one classroom/lab with thirty-seven workstations, and one dedicated classroom with thirty-six workstations. All labs are linked by a Novell local area network and are equipped with leading-edge technology. The combined holdings of the libraries total more than 1.6 million volumes, 12,800 serial subscriptions, 2 million microfilms, more than 400,000 government documents, and numerous electronic resources. The libraries of the University provide on-site and remote access to library holdings of Saint Louis University and the four campuses of the University of Missouri.

Financial Aid

All admitted students are considered for merit-based scholarships, which typically range from $1000 to $14,000 per semester, depending on the program of study. The 97.1 FM TALK Scholarship program awards one $25,000 scholarship to a qualified full-time M.B.A. student. Other scholarships of varying amounts may be available from other organizations. A limited number of graduate assistantships are available, offering a stipend of up to $1800 per semester in exchange for 10 hours of work per week. The USX Loan Fund provides short-term emergency loans for graduate students. Students may borrow up to $1200, with no interest if repaid within ninety days.

Cost of Study

In 2007–08, tuition for full-time day M.B.A. students is $47,785. This includes the cost of a two-week study-abroad trip. Part-time evening students pay $840 per credit hour.

Living and Housing Costs

Students who live in an apartment on campus can expect to spend anywhere from $2395 per semester to share a room in a two-bedroom apartment to $3585 per semester for a studio apartment. Meal plans range from $200 to $1855 per semester, depending on number of meals eaten in campus dining facilities. Students living off campus typically pay $750 to $1300 per month for a two-bedroom apartment.

Student Group

The School's programs are designed for current business professionals who are seeking expertise in a particular business area or for future professionals who already hold an undergraduate degree in business or a related field and would like to strengthen their skills in business and management. Students come from throughout the United States and around the world and present a diverse demographic profile.

Student Outcomes

Graduates are provided the tools to pursue careers in the business and legal professions, including investment and commercial banking, management consulting, government regulation, health care, and business policy analysis.

Location

The campus is located near downtown St. Louis, a center of business activity for the Midwest and the site of the famous Gateway Arch. To the north is the city's revitalized arts and entertainment district, and to the west is Forest Park, one of the largest urban parks in the nation. The nearby Ozarks offer hiking, mountain biking, and camping opportunities, and vineyards dot the landscape.

The University and The School

Founded in 1818, Saint Louis University is the oldest university west of the Mississippi and the second-oldest Jesuit university in the United States. It also ranks among the top research institutions in the nation; in 2005, its health sciences researchers received a record $72.7 million in grants and contracts. The John Cook School of Business was founded in 1910, making it the fifteenth-oldest business school in the nation. It is accredited by AACSB International–The Association to Advance Collegiate Schools of Business. The part-time M.B.A. program was ranked number 26 in the nation by *U.S. News & World Report*, while the Princeton Review ranks the school among the "Best of the Midwest."

Applying

Prospective students must submit a completed application, official transcripts of previous university work, official GMAT scores, a current resume, two letters of recommendation, a personal statement of 500 words or less describing academic and professional goals, and a nonrefundable $90 application fee. Qualified candidates are contacted for an interview by the Admissions Committee. The deadline to apply is April 15; applications received after that date are reviewed on a space-available basis.

Correspondence and Information

John Cook School of Business
Saint Louis University
3674 Lindell Boulevard
St. Louis, Missouri 63108
Phone: 314-977-3800
Fax: 314-977-3897
Web site: http://gradbiz.slu.edu

Saint Louis University

THE FACULTY AND THEIR RESEARCH

Michael J. Alderson, Professor of Finance; Ph.D., Illinois at Urbana-Champaign. Corporate finance, capital structure, financial distress.

Hadi Alhorr, Assistant Professor of International Business; Ph.D., Texas Tech. Global strategy, geopolitics, implications of economic integrations on business strategies, international cooperative strategies, cross-border mergers and acquisitions, international joint ventures and cross-cultural negotiations.

Lyn S. Amine, Professor of Marketing and International Business; Ph.D., Bradford. Global marketing, consumer behavior, green marketing, principles of marketing, international marketing, cross-cultural consumer marketing, big emerging markets, export marketing.

Mark Arnold, Associate Professor of Marketing; Ph.D., Saint Louis. International marketing strategy, global e-commerce, consumer behavior, retail management.

Heather Bednarek, Assistant Professor of Economics; Ph.D., Michigan State, 1999. Public economics, health economics, labor economics, economic impact of disease.

Brian Betker, Professor of Finance and Department Chair; Ph.D., UCLA, 1991. Investments, corporate finance.

Jennifer Blaskovich, Assistant Professor of Accounting; Ph.D., Nebraska, 2005. Information systems, auditing, managerial accounting.

Laurel Boone, Assistant Professor of Management; J.D., Indiana, 1980. Legal environment of business, intellectual property, cyberlaw, ethics in business.

Paul D. Boughton, Associate Professor of Marketing; Ph.D., Saint Louis, 1980. Marketing research and marketing strategy, customer satisfaction and market research, use of online surveys.

Brett Boyle, Associate Professor of Marketing; Ph.D., Cincinnati, 1991. Sports marketing, sales and sales management, interfirm exchange issues, ethical issues in marketing.

Bidisha Chakrabarty, Assistant Professor of Finance; Ph.D., SUNY at Buffalo, 2004. Behavior of market participants, design of markets, functioning of markets, investment strategies, database- and data-related issues, mergers and acquisitions, corporate governance and control.

Mark E. Ferris, Associate Professor of Decision Sciences/MIS; Ph.D., Illinois at Urbana-Champaign, 1982. Statistics, transportation, quantitative business analysis.

James E. Fisher, Associate Professor of Marketing; Ph.D., Illinois at Urbana-Champaign, 1988. Marketing management and business ethics, case research, business ethics, marketing and public policy, consumer complaining behavior.

Denise Guithues-Amrhein, Associate Professor of Accounting; Ph.D., Saint Louis. Managerial accounting, electronic business applications, cash flows, bankruptcy prediction.

Donald E. Hardaway, Associate Professor of Decision Sciences/MIS; Ph.D., Houston, 1988. Multimedia technology, emerging education technologies, strategic planning for technology.

Ellen F. Harshman, Associate Professor of Management and Dean; Ph.D., Saint Louis. Legal environment of business, women in management, organizational communications, employment law, ethics in business grant preparation and administration.

Xiaouri Hu, Associate Professor of Decision Sciences/MIS; Ph.D., Texas at Austin, 2000. Electronic commerce and e-market, industrial organization, risk management, financial modeling and optimization, database management, data communication.

Muhammad Q. Islam, Associate Professor of Economics and Department Chair; Ph.D., Indiana, 1989. Public-sector economics, principles of economics, microeconomic theory econometrics.

James P. Jennings, Professor of Accounting; Ph.D., Missouri. Corporate financial reporting, managerial accounting.

Lawrence Jones, Assistant Professor of Decision Sciences/MIS; Ph.D., Saint Louis. Mathematical programming, simulation modeling, critical path techniques, artificial intelligence, expert systems.

David Kaplan, Assistant Professor of Management; Ph.D., Illinois at Urbana-Champaign, 2000. Human resources management; planning and staffing; employment law; perceptions of organizational culture interacting with motivation, attitude, and efficacy.

Jerome A. Katz, Professor of Entrepreneurship; Ph.D., Michigan, 1981. Business planning, entrepreneurship, strategic management, e-business, Web-based education and training, entrepreneurial careers, virtual marketplaces, endowed positions.

John P. Keithley, Professor of Accounting; Ph.D., Missouri–Columbia, 1972. Financial reporting, strategic applications of management accounting, social applications of accounting, business ethics.

Seung H. Kim, Professor of International Business and Department Chair; Ph.D., NYU. International finance, foreign direct investment, global joint ventures, international corruption.

John N. Kissinger, Associate Professor of Accounting; Ph.D., Michigan State, 1974. Financial accounting, accounting for income taxes.

NoKyoon Kwak, Professor of Decision Sciences/MIS; Ph.D., USC, 1964. Management science/operations research, mathematical programming, production and operations management, global logistics and operations management data envelopment analysis modeling.

Ik-Whan Kwon, Professor of Decision Sciences/MIS; Ph.D., Georgia, 1968. Business statistics, multivariate analysis in business and health-care economics, supply chain management design and strategies.

Cynthia LeRouge, Assistant Professor of Decision Sciences/MIS; Ph.D., South Florida, 2003. Health information systems, systems analysis and design, project management, IT auditing, technology-mediated learning, IT training and education.

Reuven R. Levary, Professor of Decision Sciences/MIS; Ph.D., Case Western Reserve. Global manufacturing, integration and optimization of supply chains, computer simulation, artificial intelligence and expert systems for management sciences.

Carl Maertz, Assistant Professor of Management; Ph.D., Purdue, 1998. Human resource management and international/cross-cultural human resource management, employee turnover and attachment, expatriate adjustment and withdrawal, work-family conflicts.

Doug Marcouiller, Associate Professor of Economics; Ph.D., Texas at Austin, 1994. International trade, economic development, friction in international trade.

John R. McGowan, Professor of Accounting; Ph.D., Southern Illinois at Carbondale, 1988. Tax policy.

Stephen W. Miller, Professor of Marketing and Associate Dean; D.B.A., Kent State, 1973. Marketing management, strategic assessment and planning, international/global marketing, international banking and financial services.

Thomas Miller, Professor of Finance and Associate Dean; Ph.D., Washington (Seattle), 1992. Teaching interests: introductory corporate finance, investments, and derivatives. Research interests: market volatility, short-dated option pricing, and portfolio performance from asset allocation.

Alireza Nasseh, Professor of Finance; Ph.D., Michigan State, 1982. Corporate finance and financial economics, banking and financial markets.

Fred Niederman, Professor of Decision Sciences/MIS; Ph.D., Minnesota, 1990. Systems analysis and design, global information management, human-computer interface, MIS personnel, group decision-support systems, MIS project management, health information systems.

Arun Pereira, Associate Professor of Marketing; Ph.D., Houston, 1991. New product management, marketing research, marketing decision models, branding, market entry, international marketing.

Hailong Qian, Associate Professor of Economics; Ph.D., Michigan State. Applied and theoretical econometrics.

David Rapach, Associate Professor of Economics; Ph.D., American, 1994. Macroeconomics, money and banking, international economics, applied time series, monetary economics, international finance.

Scott R. Safranski, Associate Professor of Management and Associate Dean; Ph.D., Indiana, 1983. Organization structures and environments, comparative leadership and management, organizational assessment.

Thomas Scheiding, Assistant Professor of Economics; Ph.D., Notre Dame, 2006. Microeconomics, labor economics, public finance, economics of science, history of economic thought.

Ananth Seetharaman, Professor of Accounting and Department Chair; Ph.D., Georgia State, 1991. Tax and management accounting.

Neil E. Seitz, Professor of Finance; Ph.D., Ohio State, 1973. Financial management and strategy, capital investments and engineering economics.

Micheal C. Shaner, Professor of Management; Ph.D., South Carolina. Strategic management, employee motivation, leadership, situational leadership, team building, change management.

Philipp Stoeberl, Professor of Management and Department Chair; Ph.D., Saint Louis. Business policy/strategy, business decision making and policy formulation, strategic management, current issues in management and management theory.

Jack K. Strauss, Professor of Economics; Ph.D., Duke, 1989. International macroeconomics/exchange rates, macroeconomics, international economics, applied econometrics, economic growth.

Brian D. Till, Associate Professor of Marketing and Department Chair; Ph.D., South Carolina, 1993.

Weiman Wang, Assistant Professor of Accounting; Ph.D., Washington (St. Louis). Capital markets, corporate governance, intangible assets.

Patrick J. Welch, Professor of Economics; Ph.D., Pittsburgh, 1973. Industrial organization, principles of economics, history of economic thought, antitrust economics.

Bonnie Wilson, Assistant Professor of Economics; Ph.D., Illinois at Urbana-Champaign, 1999. Macroeconomics, international economics, financial economics.

Frederick C. Yeager, Professor of Finance; Ph.D., West Virginia. Financial management, financial institutions and markets, international financial markets, ethics and technology.

Hongxin Zhao, Professor of International Business; Ph.D., George Washington, 1992. Asian business, business strategy FDI, knowledge transfer, e-commerce.

SHENANDOAH UNIVERSITY

Harry F. Byrd, Jr. School of Business

Programs of Study

The Harry F. Byrd, Jr. School of Business is committed to providing high-quality educational programs that assist individuals in their preparation to become leaders within an international business environment. The main goal of the M.B.A. degree program is to provide students with skills and competencies critical in today's organizations—a global perspective, communication proficiency, functional knowledge across business disciplines, leadership and teamwork skills, strategic thinking, and informed, ethical decision making. The program is premised on the notion that education is value added for both the individuals who are pursuing the degree and for the organizations that support them in their quest for higher education. The program is applicable for managers and leaders working in entrepreneurial enterprises, corporations, and governmental agencies regardless of their undergraduate studies. Classroom discussions, seminars, and integrated, case-study situations prove especially valuable to managers whose formal undergraduate education was highly specialized. The entire M.B.A. program consists of sixteen courses. For students with the appropriate undergraduate preparation, the first four prerequisite courses may be waived, but the remaining twelve are required. All M.B.A. students are required to have laptop computers.

Two certificate programs are offered. Upon the successful completion of the required 12 credit hours, M.B.A. students can enroll in the Certificate of Health Care Management. The four-course certificate consists of two courses included in the core requirement of the M.B.A. program and two electives in health-care management courses. When M.B.A. students complete the required 15 credit hours, they can earn the Certificate in Information Systems and Computer Technology. The five-course certificate consists of two courses included in the core requirement of the M.B.A. program and three electives in information systems and computer technology. Both certificates can be completed simultaneously with the M.B.A. degree or as stand-alone programs.

Research Facilities

The library collections of Shenandoah University are housed in two facilities. The Alson H. Smith Jr. Library, located in the center of the Winchester campus, is the main library facility for the University. The branch Health Sciences Library is located in the Health Professions Building on the grounds of the Winchester Medical Center. Current total holdings number more than 275,000 items, including 123,000 books and bound journals, 13,000 recordings, 16,000 scores, 1,500 videotapes, and 115,000 ERIC documents. The University subscribes to more than 1,100 print periodicals and has access to more than 10,000 electronic journals. More than 60 Internet-accessible databases are available through the library's Web site. Subject disciplines represented in the Smith Library are biology, business, chemistry, computer science, education, history, literature, mathematics, music, philosophy, physics, psychology, religion, and sociology. Most materials in occupational therapy and physical therapy are located in the Smith Library. The Smith Library also houses the media center, the Macintosh computer lab, and the Children's Literature Center.

Financial Aid

A limited number of assistantships, which cover up to 9 credits and provide a stipend, and scholarships may be available for full-time students. Fellowships are available to meritorious part-time M.B.A. students and may cover up to 2 credits per academic trimester. Loans through commercial and governmental sources are available. Information regarding financial aid may be obtained from the Office of Financial Aid.

Cost of Study

Students can expect to spend about $3660 in tuition per semester, plus additional fees.

Living and Housing Costs

Room and board costs range from $2656 to $3795 per term, depending on the meal plan chosen. Off-campus housing is also available.

Student Group

The University attracts students from throughout the region and around the globe. Total enrollment is approximately 3,000 students. Of these, 57 percent are from Virginia; the remaining students represent forty-five states and forty-one countries. Forty percent of the students are men. There are 18 full-time and 10 part-time M.B.A. students; 8 are women, and 10 are international students.

Location

The Shenandoah campus is located 72 miles west of Washington, D.C., in the historic Shenandoah Valley of Virginia. The University is on the southeast edge of the city of Winchester, Virginia. Winchester–Frederick County, rich in history, is a vigorous community of approximately 70,000 people. Shenandoah's students have the distinct advantage of being on a small campus near large metropolitan cultural centers.

The University and The School

Shenandoah University, established in 1875, is a comprehensive Level V private university. The University offers more than sixty programs of study at the undergraduate, master's, doctoral, and professional levels at the main campus in Winchester, the Health Professions Building on the campus of the Winchester Medical Center, and the Northern Virginia Campus in Leesburg.

The Harry F. Byrd, Jr. School of Business prepares students with the knowledge, skills, and competencies to function effectively in the global environment. The School does not believe in using graduate assistants for teaching purposes, so experienced faculty members who deeply care for students teach all courses. Proximity to Washington, D.C., significantly expands the on-campus learning environment. Internships and field experiences are available for acquiring the real-world aspects of a business education. Outside business executives share their experiences and provide real and current examples of business principles and practices that are discussed and learned from. The pursuit of accreditation by AACSB International–The Association to Advance Collegiate Schools of Business shows a real commitment to building a high-quality academic program through continuous improvement.

Applying

Applicants must have a bachelor's degree in any field of study from a regionally or, in the case of international students, nationally accredited institution. Students must submit a completed application, the $30 application fee, official transcripts from all institutions of higher education previously attended, GMAT or GRE scores, two letters of recommendation, and a brief narrative (two to three pages) of their career, professional development, and professional goals as they relate to the M.B.A. program. In addition, international students must send in their TOEFL scores. As soon as all required documents have been received, an interview with the program director is arranged.

Correspondence and Information

Office of Admissions
Shenandoah University
Winchester, Virginia 22601
Phone: 540-665-4581
Fax: 540-665-4627
E-mail: admit@su.edu
Web site: http://www.su.edu/bsb/prospectives.asp

Shenandoah University

THE FACULTY AND THEIR RESEARCH

Robert Bonometti, Professor of Information Systems and Computer Technology; Ph.D., MIT. Business development for advanced high-payoff rapid-time-to-market products, technology benchmarking and competitive analyses, executive decision support systems, computing and communications networking and interoperability, advanced telecommunications and radio technologies, space systems.

W. Randy Boxx, Professor of Management and Dean; Ph.D., Arkansas. Organizational behavior and general management.

Yvonne Chen, Associate Professor of Finance/Economics; Ph.D., Wisconsin. Ecological economics, international macroeconomics, dynamic optimization.

Nabie Y. Conteh, Assistant Professor of Information Systems and Computer Technology; Ph.D., Maryland. Decision support systems, systems modeling and simulation, artificial intelligence/expert systems, systems analysis and design, knowledge management, organizational learning.

Miles K. Davis, Assistant Professor of Management; Ph.D., George Washington. Planned change in organizations, with particular interest in how technology impacts organizational structure, processes, and culture.

Harry B. Folk, Visiting Associate Professor of Business; M.I.M., American Graduate School of International Management.

Bruce K. Gouldey, Associate Professor of Economics and Finance; Ph.D., Pittsburgh. Corporate finance, investment and portfolio theory, commercial bank management.

Giles A. Jackson, Associate Professor of Marketing; Ph.D., Virginia Tech. Industrial marketing, with special interest in advanced composites sector; sustainable business; innovation and entrepreneurship.

Young K. "Sally" Kim, Assistant Professor of Marketing and International Business; Ph.D., George Washington. Services marketing, customer satisfaction, loyalty, consumer penalty.

Sonia Manzoor, Visiting Assistant Professor of Economics; Ph.D., Texas A&M. Public finance and econometrics.

Daniel A. Pavsek, Durell Professor of Money and Banking; Ph.D., Case Western Reserve. International economics, money and banking, basic MIS.

Gary M. Pecquet, Visiting Assistant Professor of Economics and Accounting; Ph.D., Virginia Tech.

Charles J. Pineno, Professor of Accounting and Lillian Cook Braun Chair in Accounting; Ph.D., Penn State. Accounting, with emphasis on management accounting, with recent emphasis on the balanced scorecard.

John D. Proe, Professor of Management and Health Care Administration; Ph.D., Iowa. Organizational studies and leadership.

Travis L. Sample, Professor of Public Administration; D.P.A., USC. Organizational behavior and change and public administration/policies.

William D. Schulte Jr., Associate Professor of Organizational Behavior; Ph.D., George Washington. Knowledge management, cross-cultural aspects of international management, innovation and entrepreneurship.

Clifford F. Thies, Professor of Money, Banking, and Finance; Ph.D., Boston College. Economics and finance.

Mark Tyree, Professor of Accounting and Yount, Hyde, and Barbour Chair in Accounting; Ed.D., William and Mary. Financial accounting, taxation.

John I. Winn, Associate Professor of Business Law; J.D., Campbell.

Jim Wong, Professor of Marketing and Management; Ph.D., Ohio State. Marketing and management, consumer behavior, organizational behavior, business policy, labor relations, marketing management.

SOUTHERN ILLINOIS UNIVERSITY CARBONDALE

College of Business and Administration
Ph.D. Program

Programs of Study

The Doctor of Philosophy in business administration degree program is designed to prepare individuals for faculty research and teaching positions in academic institutions and for high-level administrative or staff positions in business, government, or other organizations. Ph.D. candidates in business administration must demonstrate in-depth knowledge of business and administration and a high potential to undertake significant research. Students in the college-wide degree program choose a major area in accountancy, finance, management (including management information systems, production/operations management, and organizational studies), and marketing.

Research Facilities

The University's Morris Library contains more than 3.4 million volumes and 4.6 million microform units and subscribes to more than 44,000 current serials. Supplementing the resources of Morris Library is the Center for Research Libraries (Chicago), in which the University holds membership. Students also have access to I-Share, the statewide automated catalog, circulation, and interlibrary loan system, and to a comprehensive array of databases and other electronic data files. Information Technology operates a general-purpose computing facility that provides a wide range of technology services and support to the University academic and research community. In addition, the College of Business and Administration houses state-of-the-art classrooms, networked offices, and a modern computer laboratory and offers wireless Internet access and laptops for checkout by students.

Financial Aid

Financial assistance is available to qualified students in several forms. Graduate Fellowships are awarded by the Graduate School and include a monthly stipend and tuition waiver. Graduate teaching and research assistantships are available within the College of Business and Administration and are awarded on the basis of student potential or academic performance in the program. Graduate assistants receive a monthly stipend and tuition scholarship. Other sources of financial assistance in the form of fellowships and loans are available through the Financial Aid Office.

Cost of Study

In-state graduate tuition is $275 per credit hour in 2007–08. Out-of-state tuition is 2½ times the in-state tuition rate ($687.50 per credit hour). Graduate students with at least a 25 percent appointment as a graduate assistant receive a tuition waiver. Fees vary from $490.11 (1 credit hour) to $1272.45 (12 credit hours).

Living and Housing Costs

For married couples, students with families, and single graduate students, the University has 589 efficiency and one-, two-, and three-bedroom apartments that rent for $460 to $532 per month in 2007–08. Residence halls for single graduate students are also available, as are accessible residence hall rooms and apartments for students with disabilities.

Student Group

Enrollment in the Ph.D. program for fall 2006 was 66 students. Nearly 50 percent were international students representing eighteen different countries.

Location

Carbondale, with a population of 20,700, is located approximately 100 miles southeast of St. Louis, Missouri. Immediately south of Carbondale are the Illinois Ozarks, some of the most beautiful and rugged terrain in the state. Within 10 miles of the campus are two state parks, four recreational lakes, and the 240,000-acre Shawnee National Forest. Camping, caving, rock climbing, boating, hunting, and fishing are just a few of the diversions that are easily accessible.

The University and The College

Southern Illinois University Carbondale became a four-year, degree-granting institution in 1907. Graduate work was instituted in 1943, with the first doctoral degrees granted in 1959. Fall 2006 total enrollment was 16,294 undergraduates and 4,709 graduate students. SIUC has more than 1,150 international students currently enrolled, representing more than 100 nations.

The College of Business and Administration was established in 1956 and was accredited six years later. Offices for the College are located in Rehn Hall. Independently affiliated with the College is the Pontikes Center for Management of Information. Placement services are provided by University Career Services and by the College's H. Scott Hines Placement Center.

Applying

Applicants to the Ph.D. program are required to submit a Graduate School application, a College of Business and Administration application, official transcripts, three letters of recommendation, GMAT scores, brief essay responses, a description of previous work experience, and a nonrefundable $45 application fee. All international applicants are required to submit a copy of their passport page that lists their name and date of birth. International applicants whose native language is not English are also required to submit TOEFL scores, with a minimum score of 550 on the paper-based test or 220 on the computer-based test. Applications are considered on a case-by-case basis. Decisions are made based upon the entire application. Students typically enter the program in August, but January or June entry is also possible.

Correspondence and Information

Director of Doctoral Studies
Graduate Programs
College of Business and Administration
133 Rehn Hall
Mail Code 4625
Southern Illinois University Carbondale
Carbondale, Illinois 62901-4625
Phone: 618-453-3030
Fax: 618-453-7961
Web site: http://www.cba.siu.edu/

Southern Illinois University Carbondale

THE FACULTY AND THEIR RESEARCH

School of Accountancy

Allan Karnes, Professor; M.A., J.D., Southern Illinois Carbondale, 1986; CPA. Taxation and auditing.

Michael M. Masoner, Associate Professor; Ph.D., Minnesota, 1975; CPA. Accounting systems, cost accounting.

Marcus Dean Odom, Associate Professor and Director; Ph.D., Oklahoma State, 1993; CPA. Accounting information systems.

Richard Rivers, Professor; D.B.A., Kent State, 1976; CPA. Quantitative decisions models, information systems, managerial accounting.

Ania M. Rose, Assistant Professor; Ph.D., Texas A&M, 1998. Audit judgment, markets for audit services, internal control evaluation, fraud, accounting education.

Jacob M. Rose, Associate Professor; Ph.D., Texas A&M, 1998. Judgment, decision making and learning, effects of IT on knowledge structure development and decision making.

Julie Sobery, Associate Professor; Ph.D., Saint Louis, 1982; CPA. Financial accounting, accounting theory.

Raymond Wacker, Associate Professor; Ph.D., Houston, 1989; CPA. Taxation.

Robert B. Welker, Professor; Ph.D., Arizona State, 1977. Managerial accounting, accounting theory.

Department of Finance

Marcia M. Cornett, Rehn Professor of Business; Ph.D., Indiana, 1983. Corporate finance, financial institutions and markets.

Wallace N. Davidson III, Rehn Professor of Finance; Ph.D., Ohio State, 1982. Corporate finance, corporate control and governance.

Vincent Intintoli, Assistant Professor; Ph.D., Arizona, 2007. Corporate finance, corporate governance.

Ike Mathur, Rehn Professor of Finance; Ph.D., Cincinnati, 1974. Financial management, international finance.

James Musumeci, Associate Professor and Chair; Ph.D., Texas, 1987. Investments and corporate finance.

Mark A. Peterson, Associate Professor; Ph.D., Penn State, 1996. Investments, corporate finance, market microstructure.

David A. Rakowski, Assistant Professor; Ph.D., Georgia State, 2003. Investments, international finance.

Basak Tanyeri, Assistant Professor; Ph.D., Boston College, 2006. Corporate finance, financial institutions and markets, mergers and acquisitions.

Xiaoxin Wang, Assistant Professor; Ph.D., Penn State, 2003. Market microstructures, investments.

Department of Management

Steven J. Karau, Associate Professor; Ph.D., Purdue, 1993. Organizational behavior, human resource management.

Charles R. Litecky, Professor; Ph.D., Minnesota, 1974. Management information systems.

William A. McKinley, Rehn Professor of Management; Ph.D., Columbia, 1983. Organization theory, organizational behavior, strategic management.

Arlyn J. Melcher, Professor; Ph.D., Chicago, 1964. Organization theory, strategic management, research methodology.

Michael Michalisin, Associate Professor; Ph.D., Kent State, 1996. Strategic management, organization theory, international business.

Peter P. Mykytyn Jr., Professor; Ph.D., Arizona State, 1985. Computer information systems.

Jim Nelson, Assistant Professor; Ph.D., Colorado, 1999. Data and process models, cognitive processes in object-oriented technology, business value of IT.

Kay Nelson, Professor; Ph.D., Texas, 1995. IS and organizational flexibility, change, and knowledge; software maintenance, architecture, and metrics; IS personnel issues; business value of IT.

Reed Nelson, Professor; Ph.D., Cornell, 1983. Organizational behavior and theory.

John M. Pearson, Associate Professor; D.B.A., Mississippi State, 1991. Management systems, information systems.

Charles Stubbart, Associate Professor; Ph.D., Pittsburgh, 1983. Strategic management, international business, entrepreneurship.

Suresh K. Tadisina, Associate Professor; Ph.D., Cincinnati, 1987. Operations management and management sciences.

Gregory P. White, Professor and Chair; Ph.D., Cincinnati, 1976. Production management and management sciences.

Department of Marketing

Mavis T. Adjei, Assistant Professor; Ph.D., Mississippi, 2006. Marketing relationships, customer retention in services.

Siva K. Balasubramanian, Rehn Professor of Marketing; Ph.D., SUNY at Buffalo, 1986. Advertising/promotional management, consumer behavior, new product diffusion models, measurement issues in marketing.

Gordon C. Bruner II, Professor; Ph.D., North Texas, 1983. Consumer behavior, promotion management, scale compilation.

David A. Campbell, Assistant Professor; Ph.D., Mississippi, 2007. Marketing strategy: competitive dynamics and use of competitor information.

Terry Clark, Professor and Chair; Ph.D., Texas A&M, 1987. Marketing strategy, global marketing, global business strategy, relationship marketing.

Dennis Cradit, Professor and Dean; Ph.D., Iowa, 1984. Marketing segmentation, quantitative methods, business-to-business marketing.

John P. Fraedrich, Professor; Ph.D., Texas A&M, 1988. Ethics, international marketing, industrial sales.

Maryon F. King, Associate Professor; Ph.D., Indiana, 1989. Marketing management, consumer behavior, promotion management.

Lynette Knowles, Associate Professor; Ph.D., Ohio State, 1990. International business and marketing, marketing channels, physical distribution.

Suzanne Altobello Nasco, Assistant Professor; Ph.D., Notre Dame, 1999. Counter-factual analysis, statistics, consumer behavior.

John H. Summey, Associate Professor; Ph.D., Arizona State, 1974. Marketing management, product strategy and marketing research.

SOUTHERN NEW HAMPSHIRE UNIVERSITY

School of Business

Programs of Study

At Southern New Hampshire University, there are no limits to what students can achieve. With a culture that inspires every person, every day, to do more, learn more, try harder, and exceed expectations, the University is dedicated to helping students realize their potential. Southern New Hampshire University is a premier university with a small-college feel. Students find caring, credentialed faculty members; high-quality academic programs; small classes; state-of-the-art facilities; and an exciting campus culture.

The School of Business at Southern New Hampshire University offers a variety of graduate programs, including the Global Master of Business Administration (M.B.A.) degree and Master of Science degree programs in accounting, finance, information technology, international business, marketing, operations and project management, organizational leadership, and sport management. The Global M.B.A. and M.S. programs can be pursued in conjunction with graduate certificate programs in many fields. It is also possible to earn a graduate certificate independent of a degree. The graduate program also offers the Doctor of Business Administration (D.B.A.) in international business. All degree programs and certificates offered within the School of Business are offered during the day at the main campus in Manchester, New Hampshire. The Global M.B.A., the M.S. in organizational leadership, and select graduate certificates are also offered evenings and weekends at other locations, including Laconia, Manchester, Nashua, Portsmouth, and Salem, New Hampshire, and Brunswick, Maine. The M.B.A. and the M.S. programs in international business and organizational leadership are also offered online.

Research Facilities

Library collections are developed to support the University's business, community economic development, liberal arts, education, and hospitality and tourism curricula at all levels. There are extensive core holdings in management, administration, finance, nonprofit management, international business, and economic development. The collections contain more than 96,000 paper and electronic books, 20,700 paper and online periodical subscriptions, and 12,000 company financial and annual reports. The microfiche collection includes more than 345,000 items. There is networked access to more than 50 proprietary databases. A strong, dynamic bibliographic instruction program provides orientation and reinforced research instruction for all students. Southern New Hampshire University's computing resource center supports a variety of business programming languages. Statistical and analytical packages such as SPSS and simulation and commonly used software, including Microsoft Office, Microsoft Project, Microsoft Visio, SPSS, SAS, Crystal Ball, Eviews, MatLab, Quickbooks Peachtree, ProSeries, Creative Solutions, Great Plains, Maptitude, and 3DS Max, are available.

Financial Aid

Graduate students are eligible for Federal Stafford Student Loans and other assistance. Students should contact the University's financial aid office at finaid@snhu.edu or 603-645-9645 for more information.

Cost of Study

Graduate tuition for the 2006–07 academic year ranged from $99 to $1434 per course. Full-time day graduate students also paid up to $650 in fees. There is an additional charge for any student who takes specified prerequisite courses at the University. Tuition for online courses was $1497 per course.

Living and Housing Costs

Limited on-campus housing for single students is available and cost $14,060 for twelve months in 2006–07. A variety of off-campus options are available in the Manchester area.

Student Group

The evening/weekend graduate programs comprise a total of more than 2,000 students, predominantly individuals who are employed full-time in the private and public sectors and who have work experience. The day graduate programs have a total enrollment of approximately 425 students. The day student body includes students from various parts of the United States and from dozens of countries around the world.

Student Outcomes

Last year's graduates were hired for career positions in leading regional, national, and international business environments. Examples include consultant, KPMG Peat Marwick LLP; manager, product development, L. L. Bean, Inc.; retail sales engineer, Esso Columbiana Ltd.; supervisor, audit and analysis, Lockheed Martin Commercial Electronics; senior portfolio manager, Ram Trust Services; senior financial analyst, UNUM Corp.; client relations representative, The Boston Company; analyst programmer, MIT; and director of international sales, Eastern Air Devices.

Location

The University is located on the Merrimack River in Manchester, New Hampshire, northern New England's largest city and the "most livable" city in the East, according to *Money* magazine. Downtown Manchester, just minutes away, is home to a number of fine and casual and ethnically diverse restaurants as well as clubs, cultural attractions, sports venues, and the Verizon Wireless Arena. It is an hour's drive from Boston and the state's seacoast, lakes, and mountain recreational areas.

The University

Southern New Hampshire University is a private, nonprofit, coeducational institution that has been graduating successful leaders for more than seventy years. The undergraduate and graduate academic programs are designed with the real world in mind. The University offers associate, bachelor's, master's, and doctoral degree programs in business, the culinary and hospitality fields, community economic development, education, and the liberal arts. The programs and students are career-focused, yet the University provides a well-rounded education that incorporates the liberal arts, so graduates are truly prepared for the real world. Students may attend on a full- or part-time basis and take classes on campus, on location at the University's centers in New Hampshire and Maine, or online. Faculty members in all schools and programs combine real-world experience with their academic credentials to add a practical dimension to classroom instruction.

The University is accredited by the New England Association of Schools and Colleges, the Association of Collegiate Business Schools and Programs (ACBSP), the New Hampshire State Department for Teacher Certification, the American Culinary Federation's Educational Institute, and the North American Society for Sport Management.

Applying

Students may enter the full-time or part-time master's programs in September, December, March, or June. Applications are accepted on a rolling basis. Admission to several programs within the School of Business requires a foundation of undergraduate preparation in business. Students lacking some or all of the foundation prerequisites may be admitted on a conditional basis, pending completion of the required course work as part of their program of studies. The application deadline for doctoral programs is April 1; the application fee is $25.

Correspondence and Information

Graduate Admission and Enrollment Services
Southern New Hampshire University
2500 North River Road
Manchester, New Hampshire 03106-1045
Phone: 603-644-3102
Web site: http://www.snhu.edu

Southern New Hampshire University

THE FACULTY

Administration

Martin J. Bradley, Dean of the School of Business; Ed.D., Vanderbilt.
C. Richard Erskine, Associate Dean; Ed.D., Vanderbilt.
Patricia Gerard, Assistant Dean; M.B.A., Southern New Hampshire.
Ron Biron, Assistant Dean; M.B.A., Southern New Hampshire.
Ashley Liadis, Assistant to the Dean; M.S., Southern New Hampshire.

Faculty

Micheline Anstey, Lecturer in Marketing; M.B.A., New Hampshire College.
C. Bulent Aybar, Professor of International Business; Ph.D., Ohio State.
Doug Blais, Associate Professor of Sport Management; Ph.D., Connecticut.
Kimberly L. Bogle, Assistant Professor of Sport Management; Ph.D., Florida State.
Steven O. Booth, Assistant Professor of Business Law; J.D., Ohio Northern.
Martin J. Bradley, Professor of Organizational Leadership; Ph.D., Vanderbilt.
Charlotte Broaden, Associate Professor of International Business and Organizational Leadership; D.B.A., Southern New Hampshire.
Karin L. Caruso, Associate Professor of Accountancy and Taxation and Organizational Leadership; M.B.A., Southern New Hampshire.
Tom S. Chan, Associate Professor of Information Technology; D.Ed., Texas Tech.
J. Stephanie Collins, Professor of Information Technology; Ph.D., Wisconsin–Milwaukee.
Tej S. Dhakar, Professor of Quantitative Studies and Operations Management; Ph.D., Alabama.
David L. Doyon, Assistant Professor of Accountancy and Taxation; M.B.A., Southern New Hampshire; CPA.
Euclid A. Dupuis, Professor of Accountancy and Taxation; M.S., Bentley; CPA.
C. Richard Erskine, Assistant Professor of Organizational Leadership; Ed.D., Vanderbilt.
John K. Evans, Professor of Organizational Leadership; Ed.D., Boston University.
David W. Fehr, Associate Professor of Finance and Economics; M.B.A., Rochester.
Philip Vos Fellman, Professor of International Business; Ph.D., Cornell.
Aysun Ficici, Assistant Professor of International Business; D.B.A., Southern New Hampshire.
James Freiburger, Professor of Organizational Leadership; Ph.D., Connecticut.
Philip H. Funk Jr., Associate Professor of Information Technology; S.M., MIT.
Yvonne C. Hall, Professor of Finance and Economics; Ph.D., Colorado State.
Shaikh A. Hamid, Associate Professor of Finance and Economics; D.B.A., Boston University.
Richard O. Hanson, Professor of Accountancy and Taxation; D.B.A., Nova Southeastern; CPA, CMA, CFM.
Gerald I. Harel, Professor of Quantitative Studies and Operations Management; Ph.D., Temple.
Mahboubul Hassan, Professor of Finance and Economics; D.B.A., Nova Southeastern.
Mark G. Hecox, Associate Professor of Sport Management; D.B.A., Southern New Hampshire.
James Isaak, Assistant Professor of Information Technology; M.S.E.E., Stanford.
Gerald E. Karush, Professor of Information Technology; Ph.D., Pennsylvania.
Beth Jowdy, Assistant Professor of Sport Management; Ph.D., Massachusetts Amherst.
Diane M. Lander, Associate Professor of Finance and Economics; Ph.D., Kansas.
Louis B. Lanzillotti, Associate Professor of Accounting; M.B.A., Northeastern; CPA.
Jane M. Legacy, Associate Professor of Business Education; Ed.D., Houston.
Lundy Lewis, Associate Professor of Information Technology; Ph.D., Georgia.
Susan Losapio, Lecturer of Organizational Leadership; M.S., Antioch.
Robert C. Losik, Professor of Organizational Leadership; Ed.D., Vanderbilt.
Andy Lynch, Assistant Professor of Marketing; Ph.D., Southern Illinois.
Kimberly Monk, Associate Professor of Hospitality Management; Ed.D., Argosy.
Shahriar Movafaghi, Associate Professor of Information Technology; Ph.D., Northwestern.
Nicholas Nugent, Professor of International Business; Ph.D., Florida State.
Maria E. Manus Painchaud, Instructor of Organizational Leadership; Ed.D., Argosy.
Steven R. Painchaud, Associate Professor of Organizational Leadership; D.Ed., Boston College.
Ravi Pandit, Associate Professor of Hospitality Management; Ph.D., Penn State.
Laurence J. Pelletier Jr., Professor of Accountancy and Taxation; Ed.D., Nova Southeastern.
Kishore K. Pochampally, Assistant Professor of Quantitative Studies and Operations Management; Ph.D., Northeastern.
Greg Randolph, Assistant Professor of Economics; Ph.D., West Virginia.
Marc A. Rubin, Associate Professor of Marketing; M.B.A., Northeastern.
Massood V. Samii, Professor of International Business; Ph.D., SUNY.
Paul Schneiderman, Professor of Finance and Economics; Ph.D., Clark.
Susan Schragle-Law, Professor of Organizational Leadership; Ed.D., Massachusetts Amherst.
Robert Seidman, Professor of Information Technology; Ph.D., Syracuse.
Denis Shea, Lecturer in Accounting and Taxation; M.S., New Hampshire College.
Patricia Spirou, Associate Professor of Marketing; D.B.A., Nova Southeastern.
Karen Curry Stone, Professor of Marketing; Ph.D., Boston College.
Michael Tasto, Assistant Professor of Economics; Ph.D., Georgia State.
Jeannemarie Thorpe, Assistant Professor of Marketing; M.B.A., Southern New Hampshire; M.Ed., Rivier.
Susan Torrey, Associate Professor of Hospitality Management; M.S., Lesley.
Gary P. Tripp, Associate Professor of Finance and Economics; Ph.D., Clark.
John C. VanSantvoord, Professor of Accountancy and Taxation; M.B.A., New Hampshire.
Charles V. A. White, Professor of Finance and Economics; Ph.D., Ohio State.
Steven L. Widener, Associate Professor of Finance and Economics; Ph.D., New Hampshire.

STATE UNIVERSITY OF NEW YORK
STONY BROOK
THE GRADUATE SCHOOL

STONY BROOK UNIVERSITY, STATE UNIVERSITY OF NEW YORK

College of Business
M.B.A. Program

Programs of Study

The College of Business offers an M.B.A. degree with concentrations in finance, health care management, human resources, information systems management, management, and marketing. The regular M.B.A. consists of a 60 credit program plus an internship. Students with more than five years of business experience or an advanced degree beyond the bachelor's may qualify for the accelerated program, which consists of a 48 credit program. Courses for the M.B.A. program are held during the day, in the evening, and on Saturdays. Most courses are offered on the Stony Brook campus, but a few courses are offered in Manhattan on weekday evenings for the convenience of students who work or live in New York City.

The College also offers its Stony Brook Fast Track M.B.A. Program, which consists of a combined undergraduate degree and M.B.A. degree, typically taken over a five year period. Students in this program complete an undergraduate major outside of the College of Business and take the regular M.B.A. program with courses beginning in the summer before the senior year.

The College has an Executive M.B.A. program for employees of businesses that contract with Stony Brook. Students in these programs must have at least five years of business experience. Courses for these programs are often held on the employer's premises, with tuition paid for by the employer. One such Executive M.B.A. is exclusively offered for law firm managers, with most courses offered at Stony Brook's Manhattan facility.

In addition, advanced graduate certificate programs in finance, health care management, human resource management, information systems management, are open to M.B.A. students or other graduate students at Stony Brook. Students who meet the M.B.A. degree admissions requirements of the College may also apply the certificate credits toward the M.B.A. degree. These programs are also open to non-matriculated students who wish to earn an advanced graduate certificate without completing an M.B.A. degree. Students should note that, although it is a valuable academic credential, an advanced graduate certificate is not a degree.

Research Facilities

Research support is provided by the Frank Melville Jr. Memorial Library, the Health Sciences Library, and six branch science libraries, holding more than 2 million volumes and 3 million publications in microformat. The Business Learning Center is also a major asset for the department's students. Sun, IBM, and DEC computers in the Division of Information Technology and in other academic departments are available for general research use. There are more than 800 publicly available, state-of-the-art computers for student use. E-mail and Internet accounts are provided to all full-time students. Other research facilities include the Institute for Theoretical Physics, the Humanities Institute, and the Marine Science Research Center.

Financial Aid

Because Stony Brook is committed to attracting high-quality students, the Graduate School provides two competitive fellowships for U.S. citizens and permanent residents. Graduate Council fellowships are for outstanding doctoral candidates studying in any discipline, and the W. Burghardt Turner Fellowships target outstanding African-American, Hispanic-American, and Native American students entering either a doctoral or master's degree program. For doctoral students, both fellowships provide a minimum annual stipend of $15,975 for up to five years, as well as a full tuition scholarship. For master's students, the Turner Fellowship provides an annual stipend of $10,000 for up to two years, along with a full tuition scholarship. Health insurance subsidies are also provided within a scale, depending on the size of the fellow's dependent family. Departments and degree programs award approximately 900 teaching and graduate assistantships and approximately 600 research assistantships on an annual basis. Full assistantships carry a stipend amount that usually ranges from $11,947 to $18,000, depending on the department.

Cost of Study

In 2006–07, full-time tuition at 12 credits for entering in-state residents was $3450 per semester, while out-of-state residents and international students paid $5460. Additional fees for each semester, including (but not limited to) the infirmary, activity, technology, and transportation fee, amount to about $430. International students also pay a service fee of $35 per semester and an orientation fee of $50. Fees for the mandatory Student Health Insurance Plan vary depending on citizenship and employment status.

Living and Housing Costs

For 2006–07, Stony Brook calculated the cost of education excluding tuition, fees, and insurance at $13,520 per year. On-campus apartments range in cost from approximately $316 per month to approximately $1456 per month, depending on the size of the unit and the number of students sharing the space. Off-campus housing options include rooms, houses, and apartments that can be rented from $350 to $2500 per month. Costs including books, food, and transportation may vary depending on academic program and/or personal circumstances.

Student Outcomes

Alumni find careers in all areas of business, nonprofit management, and public-sector management and policymaking.

Location

Stony Brook's campus is approximately 50 miles east of Manhattan on the north shore of Long Island. The cultural offerings of New York City and Suffolk County's countryside and seashore are conveniently located nearby. Cold Spring Harbor Laboratory and Brookhaven National Laboratory are easily accessible from, and have close relationships with, the University.

The University

Established in 1957, the University achieved national stature within a generation. Founded in Oyster Bay, Long Island, the school moved to its present location in 1962. Stony Brook has grown to encompass more than 110 buildings on 1,100 acres. There are over 1,568 faculty members, and the annual budget is more than $805 million. The Graduate Student Organization oversees the spending of the student activity fee for graduate student campus events. International students find that the additional four-week Summer Institute in American Living is very helpful. The Intensive English Center offers classes in English as a second language. The Career Development Office assists with career planning and has information on permanent full-time employment. Disabled Student Services has a Resource Center that offers placement testing, tutoring, vocational assessment, and psychological counseling. The Counseling Center provides individual, group, family, and marital counseling and psychotherapy. Day-care services are provided in four on-campus facilities. The Writing Center offers tutoring in all phases of writing.

Applying

The College of Business is designed for ambitious and able students who are capable of applying what they learn toward the solution of organizational problems. Each student is asked to forward with the application a statement of career objectives and the way in which he or she expects to realize these objectives through the program. Students must satisfy the following admissions requirements in addition to the minimum requirements of the Graduate School: a bachelor's degree, with a minimum grade point average of 3.0 (in exceptional cases, students not meeting this requirement may be admitted on a conditional basis); an aptitude for quantitative analysis, demonstrated through previous course work, standardized tests, or practical experience; successful completion of an introductory calculus course (MAT 123 or equivalent) with a grade of C or higher; submission of (GMAT) scores (preferred), or GRE General Test scores; three letters of recommendation (one, if possible, from a professional working in a private company or public agency who is capable of evaluating the applicant's motivation and potential, and at least one from a college faculty member, counselor, or administrator); acceptance by both the College of Business and the Graduate School; and the $60 application fee. Although not required, examples of an applicant's creative work will be considered. These might include project reports or published articles. Admission is available for both the fall and spring semesters. Applications for fall should be submitted by April 15 and for spring by October 1. Earlier submissions are encouraged, especially for candidates for University-wide fellowships. Applications are reviewed on a rolling basis and, if seats are available, are considered after the application deadlines. Application forms may be obtained on the College of Business M.B.A. Web site (http://www.stonybrook.edu/sbbusiness/mba.shtml) or by contacting the Office of Student Services, Harriman Hall, Room 102, College of Business, University at Stony Brook, Stony Brook, New York 11794-3775; 631-632-7171; oss@notes.cc.sunysb.edu.

Correspondence and Information

T. Owen Carroll
Graduate Studies Director
College of Business
Stony Brook University, State University of New York
Stony Brook, New York 11794-3775

Phone: 631-632-7476
Fax: 631-632-7243
E-mail: Owen.Carroll@stonybrook.edu
Web site: http://www.stonybrook.edu/sbbusiness/mba.shtml

Stony Brook University, State University of New York

THE FACULTY AND THEIR RESEARCH

William H. Turner, Dean; M.B.A., NYU. Marketing, leadership, business strategy.

Manuel London, Associate Dean; Ph.D., Ohio State. Industrial and organizational psychology, human resource management, organizational development, organizational behavior.

Joseph W. McDonnell., Associate Dean; Ph.D., USC. Management, corporate communications, crisis management, entrepreneurship.

Carl Allocca, Director, Undergraduate Studies; M.S.T., LIU, C.W. Post; CPA. Public and private accounting, auditing, taxation, internal systems development and review.

T. Owen Carroll, Director, Graduate Studies; Ph.D., Cornell. Engineering physics, management information systems, finance.

Jeff T. Casey; Ph.D., Wisconsin–Madison. Psychology and organizational behavior, human resource management, negotiation and conflict resolution, business strategy.

Robert Clark, M.S., SUNY at Stony Brook. Operations management, management science, entrepreneurship.

Robert Ettl, M.B.A., Iona; M.C.A., NYIT; M.B.A., Penn State. Global and domestic operations in both services and product marketing management.

Dmytro Holod, Ph.D., Kentucky. Economics, banking and financial intermediation, financial markets and institutions, monetary policy, economic growth.

Herbert Lewis, Ph.D., SUNY at Stony Brook. Applied mathematics and statistics, operations research, management science.

Michael Nugent, M.B.A., Dowling. Financial engineering, derivatives, international finance, capital markets and institutions, foreign exchange markets, investment analysis, corporate finance, business strategy.

Mark R. Palermo, M.B.A., Adelphi; J.D., Hofstra. Banking, finance, law, general management.

Timothy M. Quey, M.S., Stanford. Management, marketing/product development, marketing of high technology, new product development, product design market research, entrepreneurship.

Thomas R. Sexton, Ph.D., SUNY at Stony Brook. Applied mathematics and statistics, health-care management, productivity analysis.

Jadranka Skorin-Kapov, Ph.D., British Columbia. Management science, management information systems, systems analysis and design, operations research.

Harry Weiner, S.M., MIT. Business-government relations, managerial ethics.

Gerrit Wolf, Ph.D., Cornell. Social psychology, business strategy, organizational behavior, entrepreneurship, communications.

SYRACUSE UNIVERSITY

Martin J. Whitman School of Management

Programs of Study

The M.B.A. curriculum is designed to produce manager-leaders for business. The heart of the curriculum is its highly integrated group of professional core courses required of every student. Elective courses are also integral to the program, offering students the opportunity to tailor the program to their own professional and career interests. Concentrations are offered in the following areas: accounting; entrepreneurship, innovation, and global leadership; finance; general management; innovation management; management of technology; marketing management; and supply chain management. Elective courses may also be selected from other graduate programs in the University. Summer internship programs are available with companies in the United States and in the cities of London, Madrid, Shanghai, Singapore, and Cape Town. Other international internship locations are also available. Part-time M.B.A. study is accomplished through the School's Independent Study M.B.A. (iMBA) program.

Additional graduate degree programs include the Master of Science (M.S.) in accounting, the M.S. in finance, and the M.S. in media management offered jointly with the S. I. Newhouse School of Public Communications. Joint-degree programs include the Juris Doctor (J.D./M.B.A. and J.D./M.S. in accounting) in cooperation with the College of Law and the Master of Public Administration (M.P.A./M.B.A.) with the Maxwell School of Citizenship and Public Affairs, as well as with other graduate programs throughout Syracuse University.

The Ph.D. program requires students to complete a prescribed series of advanced courses, write a summer research paper, demonstrate their knowledge through a comprehensive written examination, and develop and orally defend a written dissertation. The doctoral program is strictly a full-time program requiring year-round residency. All students have exposure to teaching-related activities.

Research Facilities

The University libraries serve the informational and research needs of the entire Syracuse University community. The library system is one of the largest in the country and ranks in the top 2 percent of university libraries nationally. It contains more than 10 million books, periodicals, and pieces of microform information, housed in the main Ernest Stevenson Bird Library and five branch libraries. Research centers within the Whitman School offer graduate students the opportunity to work with faculty members on projects of mutual interest. For specific areas of faculty research, students can visit the School's Web site. The academic computing systems at Syracuse are interconnected by a data network to about 4,000 public workstations located on the main campus, and the entire campus has wireless access throughout. Also available are sixteen microcomputer clusters, which are located at several campus locations, including two in the Whitman School—one specifically dedicated to graduate students. The new state-of-the-art Whitman facility incorporates the newest technology available, including videoconferencing, multimedia classrooms, high-tech team meeting rooms, and wireless access throughout.

Financial Aid

Approximately 60 percent of the M.B.A. students receive merit-based assistance in the form of scholarships. The majority of Ph.D. students are funded with graduate or teaching assistantships or fellowships that provide competitive stipends. Financial need-based programs include federal loan programs. Applicants for those programs must submit the Free Application for Federal Student Aid.

Cost of Study

Tuition in 2006–07 was $940 per credit hour. Books and other course materials were estimated at $1325 per academic year.

Living and Housing Costs

For 2006–07, living expenses were estimated at $12,490 for a single graduate student for nine months. A limited amount of University housing is available for single and married graduate students. Off-campus housing is plentiful.

Student Group

There are approximately 150 full-time and 200 part-time M.B.A. students. Of the full-time students, 31 percent are women, 55 percent are international students, and the majority of students have full-time work experience prior to enrollment. There are about 30 full-time Ph.D. students.

Location

Syracuse lies in the geographic center of New York State, 250 miles northwest of New York City. Nearby are Lake Ontario, the Finger Lakes, the Thousand Islands, and the Adirondack Mountains. New York City, Boston, Cleveland, Philadelphia, Pittsburgh, Toronto, Montreal, and Washington, D.C., are all less than half a day's drive away. With a metropolitan population of 500,000, Syracuse is an important educational, commercial, medical, and cultural center.

The University

Founded in 1870, Syracuse University is a private, nonsectarian, liberal arts institution and is one of the largest and most comprehensive independent universities in the nation. The Whitman School of Management, in existence since 1919, has offered graduate programs since 1947.

Applying

Applications for admission to the full-time M.B.A. program should be submitted no later than May 1 for fall admission. The deadline for Ph.D. applicants is February 15 for first consideration. Applicants must submit transcripts of all previous college work, a GMAT score, a completed application for admission, and two letters of recommendation (three for Ph.D. applicants), together with a $60 application fee. Prior work experience is strongly preferred, and personal interviews are encouraged. Applicants may apply for any of the University's programs online.

Correspondence and Information

For the master's programs:
Carol J. Swanberg
Director of Admissions and Financial Aid
M.B.A. and M.S. Programs
Martin J. Whitman School of Management
Syracuse University
721 University Avenue, Suite 315
Syracuse, New York 13244-2450
Phone: 315-443-9214
Fax: 315-443-9517
E-mail: MBAinfo@syr.edu
Web site: http://whitman.syr.edu/mba

For the Ph.D. program:
Ravi Dharwadkar
Director, Ph.D. Program
Martin J. Whitman School of Management
Syracuse University
721 University Avenue
Syracuse, New York 13244-2450
Phone: 315-443-1001
Fax: 315-443-9517
E-mail: phd@som.syr.edu
Web site: http://whitman.syr.edu/phd

Syracuse University

THE FACULTY AND THEIR RESEARCH

Todd Alessandri, Ph.D., North Carolina. Managing external and internal uncertainty related to capital investment opportunities.

Sumitro Banerjee, Ph.D., INSEAD. Timing of introduction, sequencing research, and development of new products

Amiya K. Basu, Ph.D., Stanford. Quantitative research in marketing, agency theory.

Michel Benaroch, Ph.D., NYU. Knowledge modeling, ontology-centered knowledge representations, intelligent reasoning architectures, methodologies for building knowledge systems, investments in information technology, intelligent decision support.

Pam Brandes, Ph.D., Cincinnati. Organizational cynicism, social exchange theory, contemporary workplace behaviors, privatization in emerging economies.

William Brown, Ph.D., Massachusetts Amherst. How decision makers use financial information in investment decisions.

George Burman, Ph.D., Chicago. Economics of regulation, energy, economics, entrepreneurship, corporate leadership.

Kristin Byron, Ph.D., Georgia State. Emotion in the workplace, nonverbal and electronic communication, employee responses to mistreatment, intersection of employers' work and nonwork lives.

Elletta Sangrey Callahan, J.D., Syracuse. Whistle-blowing, at-will employment, environmental policy, academic integrity.

Donald Cardarelli, M.B.A., Syracuse. Dynamics of leadership in stressed business environments.

Hsihui Chang, Ph.D., Minnesota. Financial accounting, managerial accounting, information technology, public policy, data envelopment analysis.

Chung Chen, Ph.D., Wisconsin. Time-series modeling, forecasting methods, statistical quality control, neural network methods, comparative studies of reforms in Central/Eastern Europe and China.

Anna Chernobai, Ph.D., California, Santa Barbara. Financial mathematics and applied statistics/probability applied to the management and modeling of financial risks in banking institutions.

Patrick Cihon, LL.M., Yale. Employment law, employment discrimination law, labor relations and dispute resolution.

Linda Cushman, Ph.D., Tennessee. Needs of retail-industry employers.

Ravi Dharwadkar, Ph.D., Cincinnati. International management issues in emerging markets, strategic human-resource management, changes in employee attitudes within organizations.

Fernando Diz, Ph.D., Cornell. Trading, energy trading, market volatility, derivative securities, use of managed derivatives in investment portfolios.

Fred Easton, Ph.D., Washington (Seattle). Capacity management issues in service and manufacturing organizations.

Randal Elder, Ph.D., Michigan State. Audit quality, governmental auditing, auditor decision making.

Mitch Franklin, M.S., Syracuse. Financial planning.

Yitzhak Fried, Ph.D., Illinois at Urbana-Champaign. Work stress, job and office design, motivation, performance appraisal, diversity.

Dennis J. Gillen, Ph.D., Maryland. Transformational leadership, organizational learning, teamwork, executive education, strategic management.

Leon Hanouille, Ph.D., Syracuse. Educational development, case writing.

David G. Harris, Ph.D., Michigan. Effects of taxation on business decisions and in the interaction between firms' financial disclosures and markets' value evaluations.

Maurice Harris, Ph.D., Syracuse. Market microstructure, asset volatility, corporate finance.

Donald Harter, Ph.D., Carnegie Mellon. Project management and software process improvement.

J. Michael Haynie, Ph.D., Colorado. Entrepreneurship and emerging enterprises.

Sandra Hurd, J.D., Syracuse. Employment testing, international liability and safety.

Badr Ismail, Ph.D., Illinois. Strategic cost management issues, role of cash flows in capital markets.

Moon Kim, Ph.D., Illinois at Urbana-Champaign. Inflation's impact on financial management and investors; capital assets pricing; relationship among accounting, income statements, and securities prices.

Lisa Knych, J.D., Syracuse. Commercial transactions.

Peter Koveos, Ph.D., Penn State. International financial market behavior, especially as it pertains to economic systems in transition; theory and practice of financial system reform.

Gary LaPoint, M.B.A., Syracuse. Aspects of supply chain management.

E. Scott Lathrop, Ph.D., Cornell. Adaptive decision-making process, decision making in complex choice tasks, behavioral consequences of brand equity.

Eunkyu Lee, Ph.D., Duke. Analytical and empirical investigations, channel management, price competition, differentiation strategy, consumer survey response errors.

Susan B. Long, Ph.D., Washington (Seattle). Measurement and evaluation methods, information technology, data visualization, government regulatory policy.

Yogesh Malhotra, Ph.D., Pittsburgh. IT acceptance, utilization, and management for effective business performance; knowledge management for e-business model innovation and new organization forms and e-services; IT infrastructures for electronic commerce, e-business, and knowledge management.

Catherine Maritan, Ph.D., Purdue. Strategy process and how firms build and use capabilities.

Stephen Matyas, M.B.A., Syracuse. Business education.

Tridib Mazumdar, Ph.D., Virginia Tech. Behavioral and psychological approaches to studying consumer reactions to price.

Michael Morris, Chris Witting Chair of Entrepreneurship; Ph.D., Virginia Tech. Entrepreneurship and emerging enterprises.

Amanda Nicholson, M.S., Syracuse. Role of communications in the retention of retail employees.

Martin Nunlee, Ph.D., Illinois at Urbana-Champaign. Empirical and analytical modeling techniques in the analysis of strategic and institutional issues as they relate to channels of distribution.

Kofi Okyere, Ph.D., Wisconsin–Madison. Corporate governance and financial reporting, managerial incentives and earnings management, financial disclosure.

Mohamed Onsi, Ph.D., Illinois. Strategic management control systems, design of strategic cost systems for competitive advantage.

Patrick Penfield, M.B.A., LeMoyne. Helping practitioners bring their supply chain management activities into the twenty-first century.

Milena Petrova, Ph.D., Florida. Real estate capital markets, REITs, commercial real estate, corporate finance and corporate governance.

Sandra Phillips, Ph.D., Saint Louis. Mortgage and housing discrimination, predatory lending, impact of financial policy on consumers.

Kira Reed, Ph.D., Connecticut. Development and management of intellectual capital in organizations, as well as issues in strategic human-resource management.

Byong Duk Rhee, Ph.D., Michigan. E-commerce and its conflict with conventional channel intermediaries, wireless phone number portability in the telecommunications industry, impact of customer satisfaction on repurchase decisions.

Minet Schindehutte, Ph.D., South Africa. Interface between entrepreneurship, innovation, and strategy; entrepreneurship under conditions of adversity; factors affecting performance and the role of values in entrepreneurial companies.

Ravi Shukla, Ph.D., SUNY at Buffalo. Investments, asset pricing, methodological issues.

Melvin T. Stith, Dean; Ph.D., Syracuse. Impact of value systems on consumer purchase behavior.

Clint B. Tankersley, Ph.D., Cincinnati. Marketing strategy implementation issues, corporate venturing.

Alex Thevaranjan, Ph.D., Minnesota. Agency theory and organizational control.

Frances Gaither Tucker, Ph.D., Ohio State. Logistics contributions to corporate and marketing strategy and profits.

Raja Velu, Ph.D., Wisconsin. Multivariate methods, longitudinal and time-series modeling, exploratory data analysis.

Padmal Vitharana, Ph.D., Wisconsin–Milwaukee. Software quality and process improvement, the Internet and e-commerce, group support systems.

William Walsh, M.B.A., Syracuse. Taxes for closely held businesses.

Boyce Watkins, Ph.D., Ohio State. International and domestic asset pricing, investments, and capital markets.

Craig Watters, Ph.D., Syracuse. Growth of ventures of small-business owners and minority entrepreneurs.

Scott Webster, Ph.D., Indiana. Improving competitiveness through logistics, including scheduling, policies for managing a supply chain, and the design of distribution networks.

David Wilemon, Ph.D., Michigan State. Managing innovative marketing and technology teams and organizations.

Ray Wimer, M.A., M.S., Syracuse. Personality type in selling, strategic history of retail organizations, human-resource communications.

Chunchi Wu, Ph.D., Illinois at Urbana-Champaign. Investments, securities markets, corporate financial policies.

Yildiray Yildirim, Ph.D., Cornell. Applied probability, stochastic processes, statistical estimation of model parameters, time-series analysis, asset pricing theory, credit risks.

Allan Young, Ph.D., Columbia. Privatization, capital and financial infrastructure development, emerging and developing security and other capital markets, transition economies and entrepreneurship.

Pierre Yourougou, Ph.D., NYU. Emerging markets, corporate finance, financial markets and institutions.

Paul Zinszer, Ph.D., Ohio State. Logistics, supply chain segmentation of services in markets.

Frances Zollers, J.D., Syracuse. Business-government relations, product liability, product safety.

TENNESSEE TECHNOLOGICAL UNIVERSITY

College of Business
Division of M.B.A. Studies

Program of Study

The College of Business offers a program of study leading to the Master of Business Administration (M.B.A.) degree. The M.B.A. program is accredited by AACSB International–The Association to Advance Collegiate Schools of Business. Tennessee Tech is one of approximately 130 U.S. schools that have the additional accounting accreditation. The program is offered both in the traditional campus-based setting and in a technology-based distance setting. The entirely doctorally qualified faculty, the curriculum, and the courses are the same for the distance-based and the campus-based M.B.A. Both methods of delivery offer professional preparation for high-level careers in business. Course materials provide students with the opportunity to develop managerial competence through extensive use of a variety of pedagogical methods to move quickly beyond the basics to applying business concepts to real-world situations. The distance-based course of study is designed to fit the businessperson's lifestyle. It features faculty lectures on CD-ROM and other technology-based delivery systems combined with Internet communication between students and faculty members. Case discussions, virtual project teams, and other active-learning approaches connect academic subjects and the issues facing managers in today's global and highly technological business environment.

The program is designed for students with business or nonbusiness undergraduate majors as well as for experienced managers. Students with an undergraduate degree in business from an AACSB-accredited university must complete common courses and electives for a total of 30 semester hours. The full-time program may be completed in one calendar year (three semesters). Students with other undergraduate degrees are required to complete either a series of CD-ROM-based noncredit modules and pass a competency-based validation exam or complete additional foundation courses. The pre-M.B.A. CD-ROM-based modules are flexible, portable, and affordable.

Research Facilities

The College has excellent research facilities and is recognized for its leadership in information technology applications. Two computer centers, a business multimedia center, a distance-learning and telecommunications center, and an external relations division are located in the College. Housed in the College are the Chairs of Excellence in Management Information Systems, Quality, and Portfolio Management. The M.B.A. division also participates in the Center for Manufacturing Research at Tennessee Tech University.

Financial Aid

Sources of aid for the on-campus program include scholarships, assistantships, and out-of-state tuition waivers. A number of whole and half-time assistantships are awarded to superior applicants. Graduate assistants receive a full tuition waiver and a monthly stipend; in-state tuition and monthly stipends are reduced by one half for the half-time assistants. Scholarships are available through the College of Business Board of Trustees; applications are accepted with admission applications.

Cost of Study

Information about tuition and fees for in-state and out-of-state residents may be found on the Web at http://www.tntech.edu/bursar/fees.htm. In 2006–07, maintenance fees for on-campus students were $319 per hour (up to $2916 per semester), and tuition, paid only by out-of-state students, was $421 per hour (up to $4847 per semester). Fees for the distance M.B.A. in 2006–07 were $392 per hour for in-state students and $813 per hour for out-of-state students.

Living and Housing Costs

University housing includes both dormitories and apartments. Costs in 2006–07 were $1472 to $1822 per semester in residence halls and $280 to $330 per month in student apartments. Housing is also available in the community.

Student Group

The M.B.A. class in fall 2006 was composed of 187 students, of whom 48.1 percent were women. The mean GPA was 3.3, and the mean GMAT score was 525. Students enter the program with a variety of undergraduate degrees. About 62 percent have full-time work experience. A total of 106 distance M.B.A. students enrolled during the 2006–07 school year.

Location

Tennessee Tech is located in Cookeville, Tennessee, on Interstate 40 approximately 80 miles east of Nashville. Several state parks, golf courses, rivers, and beautiful lakes are within a few minutes' drive of the city. Cookeville, often listed by *USA Today* as one of "America's Most Affordable Cities," is the trade center of the 280,000 people who live in the Upper Cumberland region of middle Tennessee.

The University and The College

The University, founded in 1916, is a state-supported coeducational institution. The 2006 *U.S. News & World Report* ranking of universities listed Tennessee Tech as one of the top ten public schools in the South and included it in its top tier of Best Universities–Master's category in the South. In addition, the University was recently named as one of the "Best in the Southeast" by the *Princeton Review.*

The College is composed of the Department of Accounting and Business Law; the Department of Economics, Finance, and Marketing; the Department of Decision Sciences and Management; and the Division of M.B.A. Studies. Nonacademic units include the Business Media Training Center, the Business Technology Incubator, the Distance Learning Center, the Small Business Development Center, two computer centers, and the Division of External Relations. The University enrolls about 9,700 students per semester; the College enrolls about 1,500 undergraduates and 187 graduate students, including a number who attend part-time while pursuing full-time careers.

Applying

Admission is open to qualified students with a bachelor's degree from an accredited institution. Previous business courses are not required. Qualification is determined by undergraduate grade point average and scores on the GMAT. Students must have a score of 1000 points (200 x grade point average + GMAT score), a minimum 2.5 GPA, and a minimum 450 GMAT score. Employment experience is also considered. International students must submit (directly from the testing agency) a minimum score of 550 (213 computer-based, 79–80 Internet-based) on the TOEFL. Applications for admission should be received at least one month before the semester in which the student plans to enroll (six months for international students). Although students can begin the program in any semester in the year, it is recommended that students begin the program in the fall to facilitate program completion. Distance M.B.A. students can begin the program in any semester in the year. Applications for assistantships and scholarships for the on-campus program should be submitted by April 1 to be considered for fall semester support. Although assistantships may be available during the year, most appointments are made in the spring for the following academic year.

Correspondence and Information

College of Business
Tennessee Tech University
P.O. Box 5023
Cookeville, Tennessee 38505
Phone: 931-372-3600
Fax: 931-372-6544
E-mail: mbastudies@tntech.edu
Web site: http://www.tntech.edu/mba

Tennessee Technological University

THE FACULTY AND THEIR RESEARCH

Ismet Anitsal, Ph.D., Tennessee, 2005. Marketing.
Curtis P. Armstrong, Ph.D., Florida State, 1995. Information and management science.
Bonita Barger, Ed.D., Vanderbilt, 1996. Human resources development.
Robert R. Bell, Ph.D., Florida, 1972. Human resources management, organizational behavior.
Jon A. Booker, Ph.D., North Texas State, 1971. Accounting standards and financial reporting, microcomputer applications in accounting.
Charles W. Caldwell, D.B.A., Florida State, 1979. Accounting.
Rodney L. Carlson, Ph.D., LSU, 1976. Quantitative modeling.
Robert C. Elmore, Ph.D., Mississippi, 1986. Managerial and cost accounting, tax.
Robert D. Fesler, D.B.A., Mississippi State, 1986. Managerial accounting.
Tor Guimaraes, Ph.D., Minnesota, 1981. Information systems.
Brian Huguenard, Ph.D., Carnegie Mellon, 1993. Information systems.
Seisel N. Jonakin, Ph.D., Tennessee, 1992. Economics.
Brian Jones, Ph.D., Pittsburgh, 2003. Information systems.
Linda D. Lerner, Ph.D., Tennessee, 1990. Strategic management.
Lawrence D. Maples, D.B.A., Mississippi State, 1976. Taxation, accounting standards, financial reporting.
Deryl W. Martin, Ph.D., Texas A&M, 1984. Investments and portfolio management.
Christine Miller, Ph.D., Houston, 1994. Management.
Virginia M. Moore, J.D., Tennessee, 1966. Business law.
Ramachandran Natarajan, Ph.D., Kansas, 1984. Operations management, productivity management.
Robert E. Niebuhr, Ph.D., Ohio State, 1977. Management.
Mary M. Pashley, D.B.A., Tennessee, 1986. Mergers and acquisitions, corporate divestitures.
Julie Moore Pharr, D.B.A., Mississippi State, 1987. Retailing, marketing management, international marketing.
Gary C. Pickett, D.B.A., Mississippi State, 1978. Computer resources management, information systems implementation.
Rodley Pineda, Ph.D., Texas Tech, 1994. Management.
Richard Rand, Ph.D., South Carolina, 1989. Accounting and international business.
Magdalena I. Rappl, Ph.D., South Carolina, 1985. Economics.
Mark Stephens, Ph.D., Tennessee, 1985. International trade and finance, development strategies for Third World economies.
G. A. Swanson, Ph.D., Georgia State, 1982. General systems theory, accounting history.
Tom A. Timmerman, Ph.D., Tulane, 1996. Organizational behavior.
J. Donald Weinrauch, Ph.D., Arkansas, 1973. Small business/entrepreneurship, industrial marketing, marketing management.
F. Stuart Wells, D.B.A., Louisiana Tech, 1988. Management information systems, systems analysis.
Bob G. Wood, Ph.D., LSU, 1994. Corporate and international finance.

UNION GRADUATE COLLEGE

M.B.A. Programs

Programs of Study

The Union Graduate College M.B.A. program is attuned to the needs of students and employers alike. Employers recognize graduates for their high degree of professionalism, strong analytical skills and ability to work on a broad range of problems and issues, and their strong interpersonal and communication skills and ability to work well with many different kinds of people. Employers consider the Union M.B.A. an immediate return on investment; individuals able to "hit the ground running" and able to tackle complex business issues from the start. This is what employers value; this is exactly what management education at Union Graduate College offers.

Union Graduate College offers two graduate management degree programs: Master of Business Administration (M.B.A.) and Master of Business Administration in Healthcare Management. The M.B.A. program allows students to pick an area of concentration. The core curriculum provides a foundation in the essentials of management with a heavy emphasis on effective problem solving within complex systems. Beyond the core, students select an area of focus from the fields of finance, management, marketing, human resource management, operations/management science, and international business. The Master of Business Administration in Healthcare Management program prepares graduates with the skills needed to succeed in the health-care business environment. The core courses overlap with the general management program. The advanced courses are specific to health care.

The M.B.A. programs take approximately two years of full-time study. Students with appropriate backgrounds may waive up to eight courses. Both M.B.A. programs are accredited by AACSB International–The Association to Advance Collegiate Schools of Business. The M.B.A. in Healthcare Management is one of a select few that is also accredited by the Commission on Accreditation of Healthcare Management (CAHME). The College also offers several unique joint degrees, including an M.B.A./J.D. with Albany Law School and an M.B.A./ Pharm.D. with Albany College of Pharmacy. Students must apply separately to each institution.

A 400-hour required internship is a critical component of both M.B.A. programs. There is a Career Services professional who is dedicated to helping students secure resume-building internship positions. The internship prepares graduates to meet the high expectations of demanding employers.

Research Facilities

Graduate College students have complete access to the Schaffer Library, positioned at the hub of Union College's grounds. The library houses more than 500,000 volumes and 1,600 current periodical subscriptions, a periodicals reading room, group-study spaces, and more than 500 individual study spaces. It operates on the open-stack plan and offers bibliographic instruction, interlibrary loan, online bibliographic retrieval services, electronic document delivery, and Internet workstations for access to indexes, abstracts, and full-text journals online. Automated circulation of books and other library materials as well as the online catalog are in place. The library has been a depository for federal documents since 1901. Professional reference service is offered during nearly all hours that the library is open. The Writing Center, located in the Schaffer Library, is open afternoons and evenings. The Olin Center is a state-of-the-art high-technology building. The building contains laboratories and classrooms equipped for computer-intensive instruction, as well as a multimedia auditorium and collaborative computer classrooms.

Financial Aid

The M.B.A. programs award merit-based scholarships consisting of tuition waivers. These awards are made based on undergraduate GPA and GMAT scores as well as other considerations, such as work experience and need. Low-interest, deferred-repayment graduate loans are also available to U.S. citizens with demonstrated need.

Cost of Study

Tuition was $2200 per course in 2006–07 (full-time load is generally nine courses per academic year). The cost of books and supplies is approximately $600 per year. Full-time students pay a resource and facility fee of $250 per academic year. Health insurance is available for full-time students.

Living and Housing Costs

Private off-campus room and apartment rents range from $300 to $600 per month. Off-campus housing is located within walking distance of the College.

Student Group

Current enrollment is approximately 250 full-time and part-time students in the M.B.A. program. The Graduate Student Activities Committee is the most active student group on campus. They organize multiple social and educational events designed to enrich the student experience. The Investment Club is another popular student group. Students work closely with a faculty adviser and conduct simulated portfolio investment and research.

Location

The Graduate College is located on the Union College campus in Schenectady, New York. The area belongs to the New York Tech Valley, which was recently ranked as a "Best Place for Business" by *Forbes* magazine. In addition to economic and business opportunities, there are many opportunities for recreational activities, such as skiing, hiking, and water sports, in New York's Adirondack Forest Preserve and in nearby Vermont. New York City, Boston, and Montreal are all within a 3-hour drive. Tanglewood, Massachusetts (the summer home of the Boston Symphony), and Saratoga, New York, are close by.

The College

In July 2003, all of the graduate programs at Union College, including its M.B.A. programs, were reorganized into a separate independent college called Union Graduate College. All programmatic accreditations carried over to the new Graduate College. This new college, chartered by the Board of Regents of the State of New York, continues to be housed on the campus of Union College. It is part of a consortium of colleges known as Union University. Other consortium colleges included Union College, Albany Law School, Albany Medical College, and the Albany College of Pharmacy.

Applying

The College operates on a trimester schedule and holds two summer sessions. The application fee is $60. Selection is based on undergraduate GPA, GMAT scores, and leadership potential. International students must also submit their scores on the Test of English as a Foreign Language (TOEFL). Students must submit an essay, all official college transcripts, GMAT scores, and three letters of recommendation.

Correspondence and Information

Rhonda Sheehan
Director of Graduate Admissions and Registrar
Union Graduate College
807 Union Street
Schenectady, New York 12308
Phone: 518-388-6238
Fax: 518-388-6686
E-mail: sheehanr@union.edu
Web site: http://www.uniongraduatecollege.edu

Union Graduate College

THE FACULTY AND THEIR RESEARCH

Susan Lehrman, President; Ph.D., Berkeley. Strategic planning, organization theory.
Donald Arnold, Professor; Ph.D., SUNY at Buffalo. Accounting.
Robert Baker, Professor; Ph.D., Minnesota. Philosophy, ethics.
Alan Bowman, Professor; Ph.D., Cornell. Operations research.
Jay Carlson, Assistant Professor; Ph.D., South Carolina. Marketing.
Zhilan Feng, Assistant Professor; Ph.D., Connecticut. Finance.
James Lambrinos, Professor; Ph.D., Rutgers. Managerial and health economics.
Presha Neidermeyer, Associate Professor; Ph.D., Virginia Commonwealth. Accounting.
Rudy Nydegger, Professor; Ph.D., Washington (St. Louis). Organizational behavior.
Josef Schmee, Professor; Ph.D., Union (New York). Statistics.
Martin A. Strosberg, Professor; Ph.D., Syracuse. Health policy.

Adjunct Faculty
Alan T. Belasen, Ph.D., SUNY at Albany. Organizational theory.
Jane Openlander, Ph.D., Union (New York). Statistics.

UNIVERSITY OF ALBERTA

School of Business
Business Ph.D. Program

Program of Study

The University of Alberta Ph.D. in business is a research-focused program that emphasizes high-quality research, develops teaching skills, and takes four to five years to complete. The program builds on the research strength of the School of Business (ranked in the top three in Canada and in the top fifty worldwide). Students are prepared for academic careers and may specialize in any of the following areas: accounting, finance, human resources management/industrial relations, management science, marketing, and organizational analysis. Students conduct research in the functional fields of business and related disciplines.

There are two distinct stages: (1) completion of course work and comprehensive examinations and (2) candidacy, for thesis completion. Students complete course work in one major and two complementary minor fields of study and write comprehensive examinations. To enter the candidacy stage, students prepare a dissertation proposal and take an oral examination intended to determine their ability to conduct advanced research on their dissertation topic. During the candidacy period, students research and write a dissertation grounded in the major study area, which is then examined.

Ph.D. students work throughout the year furthering their research training, completing prerequisite and major/minor support courses, preparing for comprehensive and candidacy examinations, conducting research, or satisfying the program's teaching requirement. In addition, students complete a teaching component and take part in research workshops and seminars. They can expect to work closely with faculty members in their area of interest throughout their program. The minimum period of residence is two academic years for full-time students and one academic year for part-time students. Part-time students are admitted on an exceptional basis.

Research Facilities

The campus library system, with more than 5 million volumes, over 41,000 serial subscriptions, and a substantial microform collection, can be accessed at http://www.library.ualberta.ca. The Winspear Library in the School of Business, part of the University's library system, contains course materials for the Ph.D. program, including a wide selection of business periodicals. The School prides itself in having very extensive and well-supported bibliographic, financial, and corporate databases.

The Business Building is equipped with the latest computer and audiovisual resources. Full-time students are provided with a University-owned laptop computer up until their fourth year in the program. Students beyond the fourth year have access to desktop computer support. The Stollery Centre is a fully equipped executive training facility in the building. Computer labs, including a designated lab for Ph.D. students, are regularly updated with an extensive array of software. There are also a number of specialized centers and institutes designed to promote research activity and student interaction with business and government communities.

Financial Aid

All students are competitively funded, typically for four years. Some teaching and research duties are normally required. In addition, students may work with faculty members on their funded research projects. Students can also apply for University and government-supported research grants and awards. Students in the candidacy stage may apply for temporary teaching positions in their respective departments. These positions are subject to the availability of departmental funds and cannot be guaranteed. Spouses of international students are eligible to work on or off campus.

Cost of Study

Students are responsible for textbooks and related study costs for the duration of their program. Textbook expenses are approximately Can$1000 per year. Information on tuition and fees can be found under Registration and Fees at http://www.ualberta.ca/gradstudies/.

Living and Housing Costs

Edmonton is a low-cost and safe Canadian city. Accommodation is available on campus and at privately owned rental properties at varying costs. Detailed information on estimated living expenses for students can be found at http://www.international.ualberta.ca.

Student Group

With about 69 candidates enrolled at any given time, the program is relatively small and can accommodate the individual needs of students. The percentages of men, women, and international students enrolled vary from year to year, but there are currently about 44 percent women and 23 percent international students. The program seeks candidates whose intellectual and research interests form a good match with the expertise that exists within the School.

Student Outcomes

Most graduates have built successful academic careers at leading universities in Canada, the United States, and other locations that include Australia, China, India, New Zealand, and the United Kingdom. Recent graduates have accepted positions at the Australian Graduate School of Management, York University, City University of Hong Kong, St. Mary's University, and the University of Wollongong.

Location

Edmonton, with a population of about 1 million people, is a bustling community with many cultural and recreational opportunities and is located a few hours' drive from the majestic Rocky Mountains. It is the site of most provincial government offices and is the production center for the province's petroleum and petrochemical industries. The University campus is located just south of the city center.

The University and The School

The University of Alberta, with an enrollment of more than 36,000, has programs spanning twenty faculties. The School of Business, with an excellent reputation in research and teaching, has been accredited since 1968 by AACSB International. The Business Ph.D. Program began in 1984, had its first graduate in 1989, and now has more than 80 graduates.

Applying

Applicants are required to provide a statement of purpose, information on degrees obtained (with grade point averages), and GMAT score (recommended score: approximately in the 90th percentile). Where English language proficiency is required, scores from the TOEFL (minimum 550, paper-based test, or 213, computer-based) or IELTS (minimum 6.5, with a band of 5 in each area) are required. Applications are accepted throughout the year; however, application decisions are normally made between January and March. A financial offer is normally made when an offer of admission is recommended.

Correspondence and Information

Business Ph.D. Program
School of Business
University of Alberta
Edmonton, Alberta T6G 2R6
Canada
Phone: 780-492-2361
Fax: 780-492-3325
E-mail: busphd@ualberta.ca
Web site: http://www.bus.ualberta.ca/PhD/

University of Alberta

THE FACULTY

Michael Percy, Professor, Dean, and Stanley A. Milner Professor; Ph.D., Queen's at Kingston.

Accounting

Amy Choy, Assistant Professor; Ph.D., Washington (St. Louis).

David Cooper, Professor, Director of Business Ph.D. Program, and CGA Professor of Accounting; Ph.D., Manchester (England).

James Gaa, Professor; Ph.D., Illinois at Urbana-Champaign.

Yanmin Gao, Assistant Professor; Ph.D., British Columbia.

Mike Gibbins, Professor and Winspear Professor of Professional Accounting; Ph.D., Cornell.

Andrew Hilton, Assistant Professor; Ph.D., Waterloo.

Karim Jamal, Professor and Chartered Accountants Distinguished Chair in Accounting; Ph.D., Minnesota.

Jennifer Kao, Professor and Alex Hamilton Professor of Business; Ph.D., British Columbia.

Jason Lee, Associate Professor; Ph.D., Alberta.

Thomas Matthews, Assistant Professor; Ph.D., Waterloo.

Florin Sabac, Assistant Professor; Ph.D., South Carolina, Ph.D., British Columbia.

Tom Scott, Professor and Vice Dean (Administration); Ph.D., Queen's at Kingston.

Jie Tian, Assistant Professor; Ph.D., Florida.

Peter Tiessen, Professor and Department Chair (Accounting and Management Information Systems); Ph.D., Minnesota.

Heather Wier, Associate Professor; Ph.D., Cornell.

Business Economics and Law

Dick Beason, Professor; Ph.D., Michigan.

Tania Bubela, Assistant Professor; Ph.D., Sydney (Australia); LL.B., Alberta.

Joseph Doucet, Associate Professor and H.& R. Drilling Professor of Regulatory Economics; Ph.D., Berkeley.

Rasmus Fatum, Associate Professor; Ph.D., California, Santa Cruz.

Elaine Geddes, Assistant Dean (Undergraduate Programs); LL.M., Alberta.

Andrew Leach, Assistant Professor; Ph.D., Queens at Kingston.

Runjuan Liu, Assistant Professor; Ph.D. candidate, Toronto.

Nadia Massoud, Assistant Professor and Life Underwriters Fellow (also with Finance); Ph.D., Queens at Kingston.

Barry Scholnick, Associate Professor; Ph.D., Cambridge.

Entrepreneurship

Karen Hughes, Associate Professor (also with Sociology); Ph.D., Cambridge.

Jennifer Jennings, Assistant Professor; Ph.D., British Columbia.

Michael Percy, Professor, Stanley A. Milner Professor, and Dean; Ph.D., Queen's at Kingston.

Patricia Reay, Assistant Professor; Ph.D., Alberta.

Lloyd Steier, Professor, Endowed Chair, and Academic Director, Centre for Entrepreneurship and Family Enterprise; Ph.D., Alberta.

Finance

Felipe Aguerrevere, Assistant Professor and Alberta Stock Exchange Fellow; Ph.D., UCLA.

Mark Huson, Associate Professor, Peter H. Pocklington Professor in Free Enterprise, and Jarislowsky Fellow; Ph.D., Rochester.

Aditya Kaul, Associate Professor, Jarislowsky Fellow, Life Underwriters Fellow, and Alberta Stock Exchange Fellow; Ph.D., Rochester.

Jung-Wook Kim, Assistant Professor; Ph.D., Harvard.

Nadia Massoud, Assistant Professor and Life Underwriters Fellow; Ph.D., Queen's at Kingston.

David McLean, Assistant Professor; Ph.D., Boston College.

Vikas Mehrotra, Associate Professor, Collins Professor of Finance, and Jarislowsky Fellow; Ph.D., Oregon.

Randall Morck, Professor, University Professor, and Jarislowsky Distinguished Professor of Finance; Ph.D., Harvard.

Akiko Watanabe, Assistant Professor; Ph.D., Yale.

Human Resources/Industrial Relations

Jed Fisher, Professor; Ph.D., British Columbia.

Andrew Luchak, Associate Professor; Ph.D., Toronto.

Yonatan Reshef, Professor and Department Chair (Strategic Management and Organization); Ph.D., Illinois.

Management Information Systems

Ofer Arazy, Assistant Professor; Ph.D., British Columbia.

Kursad Asdemir, Assistant Professor; Ph.D., Texas at Dallas.

Yonghua Ji, Assistant Professor; Ph.D., Texas at Dallas.

Ray Patterson, Associate Professor and Canadian Research Chair in Management Information Systems; Ph.D., Ohio State.

Management Science

Terry Daniel, Professor; Ph.D., Stanford.

Erhan Erkut, Professor and Vargo Distinguished Teaching Chair; Ph.D., Florida. (On leave)

Armann Ingolfsson, Associate Professor; Ph.D., MIT.

Bora Kolfal, Assistant Professor; Ph.D. candidate, Northwestern.

Alice Nakamura, Professor; Ph.D., Johns Hopkins.

Ken Schultz, Associate Professor; Ph.D., Cornell.

Prem Talwar, Professor, Life Underwriters Fellow, and Acting Department Chair (Finance and Management Science); Ph.D., Carnegie Mellon.

Dawit Zerom, Assistant Professor; Ph.D., Amsterdam.

Marketing

Jennifer Argo, Assistant Professor; Ph.D., Manitoba.

Terry Elrod, Professor and Francis Winspear Professor of Business; Ph.D., Columbia.

Adam Finn, Professor and Banister Professor in Marketing; Ph.D., Illinois at Urbana-Champaign.

Robert Fisher, Professor; Ph.D., Colorado.

Gerald Häubl, Associate Professor and Banister Professor of Electronic Commerce; Ph.D., Vienna.

Ric Johnson, Associate Professor and Department Chair (Marketing, Business Economics, and Law); Ph.D., Iowa.

Yu Ma, Assistant Professor; Ph.D., Washington (St. Louis).

Paul Messinger, Associate Professor and Academic Director of the Canadian Institute of Retailing and Services; Ph.D., Berkeley.

Douglas Olsen, Associate Professor and Associate Dean (M.B.A. Programs); Ph.D., Alberta.

Peter Popkowski Leszczyc, Associate Professor; Ph.D., Texas at Dallas.

John Pracejus, Assistant Professor; Ph.D., Florida.

Organizational Behavior

Richard Field, Professor; Ph.D., Toronto.

Ian Gellatly, Associate Professor; Ph.D., Western Ontario.

Ray Rasmussen, Professor Emeritus and TransAlta Professor of Environmental Policy; Ph.D., Berkeley.

Michelle Innes, Assistant Professor; Ph.D., Queen's at Kingston.

Organization Theory/Strategic Management

David Deephouse, Associate Professor; Ph.D., Minnesota.

Bob Gephart, Professor; Ph.D., British Columbia.

Royston Greenwood, Professor, TELUS Professor of Strategic Management, Director of the Centre for Professional Service Firms Management, and Associate Dean (Research); Ph.D., Birmingham.

Bob Hinings, Professor Emeritus and Senior Research Fellow; B.A., Leeds.

Devereaux Jennings, Professor; Ph.D., Stanford.

Michael Lounsbury, Associate Professor (joint appointment with NRC National Institute for Nanotechnology); Ph.D., Northwestern.

Roy Suddaby, Assistant Professor; Ph.D., Alberta.

UNIVERSITY OF CALIFORNIA, LOS ANGELES

UCLA Anderson School of Management
Master of Business Administration Program

Programs of Study

Professional management education at the UCLA Anderson School of Management requires rigorous study, creativity and imagination, analytical thinking, problem diagnosis and solution, and teamwork. The UCLA Anderson School M.B.A. program is designed for highly motivated, exceptional students and is structured to ensure that each graduate leaves with a leadership-level knowledge of all key management disciplines, as well as the conceptual and analytical frameworks underlying those disciplines. Consisting of three components—the management core, advanced electives, and the applied management research project (formerly management field study)—the curriculum is regularly updated to address the evolving challenges today's business managers must meet.

The management core is a set of ten courses that provides the fundamental knowledge of the major functional fields of management and builds a foundation for advanced study in a variety of areas. The integrated and sequential nature of the management core courses ensures that each successive course builds upon the knowledge gained in prior courses.

Chosen from course offerings in ten curriculum areas and several interdisciplinary areas, advanced electives compose about half of the M.B.A. curriculum. The large number of advanced electives lends great flexibility and diversity to each student's program of study. Because of the program's general management focus, M.B.A. students are not required to declare a major or concentration. Traditional areas of study offered at the UCLA Anderson School are discipline-based. Students may tailor an individual M.B.A. program that reflects several interdisciplinary areas of study. These include entrepreneurial studies, international business and comparative management, and real estate.

The applied management research project is the capstone requirement of the M.B.A. program and is conducted during the second year of the program. In this project, students integrate and apply their knowledge and skills in a professional setting outside the classroom.

Research Facilities

The UCLA Library System is ranked in the top five among the nation's college and university libraries. While the resources of all UCLA libraries are available to UCLA Anderson School students, the collections, online systems, and services available in the School's Rosenfeld Library are of particular value. Holdings include 147,000 volumes; subscriptions to nearly 3,000 journals, periodicals, and newspapers; 445,000 items on microfilm and microfiche; and 85,000 pamphlets including annual reports and working papers from other schools. Research programs and study centers associated with the School and its faculty include the Harold Price Center for Entrepreneurial Studies, the Center for International Business Education and Research, the Richard S. Ziman Center for Real Estate, the UCLA Anderson Forecast, the Center for Management in the Information Economy, and the Entertainment & Media Management Institute.

Financial Aid

All applicants to UCLA Anderson School interested in obtaining financial assistance must complete a Free Application for Federal Student Aid (FAFSA) by March 2, regardless of when they are admitted. The FAFSA may be accessed on the Web at http://www.ed.gov/. All admitted full-time students who are U.S. citizens or permanent residents may apply for need-based financial aid. A limited number of research and teaching assistantship positions are also available. Merit-based fellowships for entering students attending the UCLA Anderson School are awarded by the Anderson Admissions Office based on academic performance and leadership activities as seen in the application for admission. Private student loans are available for all students, including international students.

Cost of Study

For 2007–08, tuition and fees per academic year total $26,932 for California residents and $36,082 for nonresidents. These costs are subject to change.

Living and Housing Costs

Room and board for the 2006–07 academic year were $12,927. Books and supplies were $5900 (including a $3500 laptop computer). Transportation, entertainment, and miscellaneous costs were $6180. These costs are for students living off campus in shared housing. Additional costs may include support of dependents and medical expenses. Married students should expect to budget about $4000 in additional costs from personal resources as financial aid only covers the student's costs.

Student Group

UCLA Anderson has a vibrant student body whose extraordinary intellectual, cultural, social, and athletic energies spill out of the classroom into a plethora of nonacademic activities. The average student is 28 years old, with more than four years of full-time work experience. Women compose 32 percent of the student population, members of minority groups make up 21 percent, and international students make up 28 percent.

Location

Strolling to classes through the serene gardens on UCLA's campus, it is easy to forget that UCLA Anderson is located in the middle of the second-largest city in the U.S. and one of the most vital economic and cultural areas in the world. For Anderson students, Los Angeles offers the best of many worlds. Beach, mountain, and desert recreation areas are plentiful and easily accessible by car. Los Angeles museums house some of the finest art collections in the country, and theaters and the splendid Music Center offer some of the world's most acclaimed entertainment. Westwood Village, which adjoins the UCLA campus to the south, offers shopping, dining, and a wide range of services.

The School

UCLA Anderson's management education complex is a testament to the School's vision of the growing importance of superior management education. Continuing the School's reputation as a national leader in the use of computing in M.B.A. instruction, the eleven specially designed case study rooms have data ports at each seating station to integrate the instructional program of each faculty member with the School's central computing facility in the Rosenfeld Library.

Applying

Applicants may apply for fall 2007 admission from September 1, 2006, through April 25, 2007. The Admissions Committee begins considering applications in November of each year.

Correspondence and Information

Ms. Lydia Heyman
Director of M.B.A. Admissions
UCLA Anderson School of Management
110 Westwood Plaza, Suite B201
Box 951481
Los Angeles, California 90095-1481
Phone: 310-825-6944
Fax: 310-825-8582
E-mail: mba.admissions@anderson.ucla.edu
Web site: http://www.anderson.ucla.edu/programs/mba/

University of California, Los Angeles

THE FACULTY

Judy D. Olian, Dean and John E. Anderson Chair in Management, UCLA Anderson School of Management; Ph.D. (industrial relations), Wisconsin–Madison.

Accounting
David Aboody, Professor; Ph.D., Berkeley. Shlomo Benartzi, Professor; Ph.D., Cornell. Gonzalo Freixes, Lecturer; J.D., Loyola Marymount. Carla Hayn, Associate Professor; Ph.D., Michigan. John S. Hughes, Professor and Ernst and Young Chair in Accounting; Ph.D., Purdue. Gordon Klein, J.D., Lecturer. Danny Litt, Lecturer; M.B.A., UCLA. Jing Liu, Associate Professor; Ph.D., Columbia. Bruce L. Miller, Professor; Ph.D., Stanford. Eric Sussman, Lecturer; M.B.A., Stanford. Brett Trueman, Professor and Area Chair; Ph.D., Columbia. Li Zhang, Associate Professor; Ph.D., Carnegie Mellon.

Decisions, Operations, and Technology Management
Reza Ahmadi, Professor; Ph.D., Texas at Austin. Sushil Bikhchandani, Professor and Associate Dean; Ph.D., Stanford. Scott Carr, Assistant Professor; Ph.D., Michigan. Charles Corbett, Associate Professor and Associate Dean; Ph.D., INSEAD. Donald Erlenkotter, Professor Emeritus; Ph.D., Stanford. Robert Foster, Adjunct Associate Professor; M.B.A., UCLA. Ariella Herman, Senior Lecturer; Ph.D., Paris. Uday S. Karmarkar, Professor and Times Mirror Chair in Management Strategy and Policy; Ph.D., MIT. Kevin McCardle, Professor; Ph.D., UCLA. Donald Morrison, William E. Leonhard Professor of Management; Ph.D., Stanford. William P. Pierskalla, Professor Emeritus and Former Dean; Ph.D., Stanford. Kumar Rajaram, Associate Professor; Ph.D., Pennsylvania. Rakesh K. Sarin, Professor, Paine Chair in Management, and Faculty Chair; Ph.D., UCLA. Richard Stern, Lecturer; Ph.D., Chicago. Christopher S. Tang, Professor and Edward W. Carter Chair in Business Administration; Ph.D., Yale.

Finance
Antonio E. Bernardo, Professor; Ph.D., Stanford. Michael J. Brennan, Professor Emeritus; Ph.D., MIT. Bhagwan Chowdhry, Professor; Ph.D., Chicago. William Cockrum, Adjunct Professor; M.B.A., Harvard. Bradford Cornell, Professor; Ph.D., Stanford. Mark Garmaise, Assistant Professor; Ph.D., Stanford. Robert L. Geske, Associate Professor; Ph.D., Berkeley. Mark S. Grinblatt, Professor; Ph.D., Yale. Francis Longstaff, Professor and Allstate Chair of Insurance and Finance; Ph.D., Chicago. Richard W. Roll, Professor and Japan Alumni Chair in International Finance; Ph.D., Chicago. Pedro Santa-Clara, Associate Professor; Ph.D., INSEAD. Eduardo S. Schwartz, Professor and California Chair in Real Estate and Land Economics; Ph.D., British Columbia. Avanidhar Subrahmanyam, Professor; Ph.D., UCLA. Walt Torous, Professor; Ph.D., Pennsylvania.

Global Economics and Management
Antonio Bernardo, Professor; Ph.D., Stanford. Matías Braun, Assistant Professor; Ph.D., Harvard. Bhagwan Chowdhry, Professor; Ph.D., Chicago. Jose de la Torre, Professor Emeritus; Ph.D., Harvard. Sebastian Edwards, Professor and Henry Ford II Chair in International Management; Ph.D., Chicago. Mark Garmaise, Assistant Professor; Ph.D., Stanford. Larry J. Kimbell, Professor Emeritus; Ph.D., Texas at Austin. Clay LaForce, Dean Emeritus; Ph.D., UCLA. Edward E. Leamer, Professor and Chauncey J. Medberry Chair in Management; Ph.D., Michigan. Alfred E. Osborne Jr., Associate Professor and Senior Associate Dean; Ph.D., Stanford. Richard W. Roll, Professor and Japan Alumni Chair in International Finance; Ph.D., Chicago. Hans Schollhammer, Professor; D.B.A., Indiana. Victor Tabbush, Adjunct Professor; Ph.D., UCLA.

Human Resources and Organizational Behavior
Corinne Bendersky, Assistant Professor; Ph.D., MIT. Samuel A. Culbert, Professor; Ph.D., UCLA. Christopher L. Erickson, Professor; Ph.D., MIT. Eric G. Flamholtz, Professor; Ph.D., Michigan. Sanford M. Jacoby, Professor and Howard Noble Chair in Management; Ph.D., Berkeley. Barbara S. Lawrence, Professor; Ph.D., MIT. David Lewin, Professor, Neil Jacoby Chair in Management, and Senior Associate Dean; Ph.D., UCLA. Fred Massarik, Professor Emeritus; Ph.D., UCLA. Daniel J. B. Mitchell, Professor and Ho-Su Wu Chair in Management; Ph.D., MIT. Judy D. Olian, Dean and John E. Anderson Chair in Management; Ph.D., Wisconsin–Madison. William G. Ouchi, Professor and Sanford and Betty Sigoloff Chair in Corporate Renewal; M.B.A., Stanford; Ph.D., Chicago.

Information Systems
Jason Frand, Adjunct Assistant Professor, Assistant Dean, and Director; Ph.D., UCLA. George Geis, Adjunct Professor; Ph.D., USC. Martin Greenberger, Professor and IBM Chair in Computers and Information Systems; Ph.D., Harvard. Bennet P. Lientz, Professor; Ph.D., Washington (Seattle). R. Clay Sprowls, Professor Emeritus; Ph.D. Chicago. E. Burton Swanson, Professor; Ph.D., Berkeley.

Marketing
Andrew Ainslie, Associate Professor; Ph.D., Chicago. Anand Bodapati, Associate Professor; Ph.D., Stanford. Bart Bronnenberg, Professor; Ph.D., INSEAD. Randolph E. Bucklin, Professor; Ph.D., Stanford. Lee G. Cooper, Professor Emeritus; Ph.D., Illinois. Ely Dahan, Assistant Professor; Ph.D., Stanford. Aimee Drolet, Associate Professor; Ph.D., Stanford. Dominique M. Hanssens, Professor and Bud Knapp Chair in Management; Ph.D., Purdue. Harold Kassarjian, Professor Emeritus; Ph.D., UCLA. Donald G. Morrison, Professor and William E. Leonhard Chair in Management; Ph.D., Stanford. Carol A. Scott, Professor; Ph.D., Northwestern. Sanjay Sood, Associate Professor; Ph.D., Stanford. Shi Zhang, Associate Professor; Ph.D., Columbia and Arizona.

Policy
Sushil Bikhchandani, Professor and Area Chair; Ph.D., Stanford. Michael R. Darby, Professor and Warren C. Cordner Chair in Money and Financial Markets; Ph.D., Chicago. Craig Fox, Associate Professor; Ph.D., Stanford. Marvin B. Lieberman, Professor; Ph.D., Harvard. Steven A. Lippman, Professor and George W. Robbins Chair in Management; Ph.D., Stanford. John Mamer, Professor; Ph.D., Berkeley. Kevin McCardle, Professor; Ph.D., UCLA. Richard P. Rumelt, Professor and Harry and Elsa Kunin Chair in Business & Society; D.B.A., Harvard. Mariko Sakakibara, Associate Professor; Ph.D., Harvard. Olav Sorenson, Associate Professor; Ph.D., Stanford.

Strategy and Organization
Bill McKelvey, Professor; Ph.D., MIT. William G. Ouchi, Professor and Sanford and Betty Sigoloff Chair in Corporate Renewal; M.B.A., Stanford; Ph.D., Chicago. Hans Schollhammer, Professor; D.B.A., Indiana. Sanford Sigoloff, Adjunct Professor; B.S., UCLA. Bruce G. Willison, Professor, Dean, and John E. Anderson Chair in Management; M.B.A., USC. James Q. Wilson, Professor Emeritus and James A. Collins Chair Emeritus in Management; Ph.D., Chicago.

A view of the campus at UCLA.

UNIVERSITY OF CENTRAL FLORIDA

College of Business Administration

Programs of Study

The College of Business Administration at the University of Central Florida (UCF) offers nine professional degree programs: the Master of Business Administration (M.B.A.), Executive M.B.A. (E.M.B.A.), Professional M.B.A. (P.M.B.A.), Master of Science in Accounting (M.S.A.), Master of Science in Management Information Systems (M.S.M.I.S.), Master of Science in Taxation (M.S.T.), Master of Science in Economics (M.S.Eco.), Master of Sport Business Management (M.S.B.M.), the Ph.D. in business administration, and the Ph.D. in economics. UCF's graduate and undergraduate programs in business are accredited by AACSB International–The Association to Advance Collegiate Schools of Business.

The M.B.A. program is designed to develop students' analytical, decision-making, and problem-solving capabilities to meet the challenges of leadership in professional management positions at present and in the changing world of the future. The program has a broad-based administrative emphasis that permits a limited degree of specialization in a particular field of business. A thesis is not required. The program involves between 39 and 51 semester hours of course work, depending on the student's prior academic preparation. The M.B.A. program is open to students with baccalaureate degrees in nonbusiness or business fields and can be pursued on a part-time basis.

The E.M.B.A. program is designed to prepare executives and managers for the challenges they face as they develop and refine their full career potential during this program. The program is made up of 39 hours and an international residency. Classes meet all day Friday and Saturday every other weekend for twenty-one months. Students should have a minimum of five years of full-time, progressive managerial experience and hold a bachelor's degree or its equivalent from an accredited university or institution. The P.M.B.A. program is tailored to professionals on regional campuses in the greater Orlando area and meets two evenings a week in a lockstep-type program. A one-year, full-time M.B.A. program is also available. This program is offered as a cohort group and begins every fall. The M.S.A. degree program stresses the development of advanced accounting skills to provide resources for decision making and problem solving in public, private, and government accounting. Course work is practice-oriented, emphasizing quantitative techniques and computer skills. There is considerable flexibility with regard to advanced accounting areas of concentration. The length of the program depends on the student's background in accounting and other business disciplines.

The M.S.M.I.S. program is designed to educate students in the technical and managerial topics that are essential for a successful career in the information technology (IT) field. Individuals are needed who can design and manage large and complex information systems and who can communicate effectively with both customers and management. Forward-looking companies must invest wisely in IT and the human expertise necessary to make them competitive and successful in the future. The program core consists of 30 to 52 hours. A technical and basic management background is required. The M.S.T. degree program stresses the development of advanced knowledge of taxation for use in decision making and problem solving in public, private, and government accounting positions. Course work is practice-oriented, emphasizing quantitative techniques and the development of research skills. The length of the program depends on the student's background in accounting and other disciplines. For a student with an accounting background, the program involves 15 semester hours of required tax courses and 15 hours of restricted electives. The M.S.Eco. degree program, which requires 30 semester hours, provides specialization in economics for students who are embarking on careers as economists in the academic, government, business, and financial communities. The M.S.B.M. program is designed to serve professionals who work in the sport industry and undergraduates interested in sport business management. This program prepares students to work in professional and collegiate sport organizations with the necessary tools to lead and manage the business of sport.

The Ph.D. in business administration is designed to prepare students for academic careers in higher education and management careers in profit and nonprofit organizations. Success in the program is judged by the student's understanding of the issues and methodologies essential to the advancement of knowledge. Doctoral work is based on the achievement of academic and research competencies rather than a specific number of courses. Students must have an M.B.A. or an equivalent degree to enter the program. This is a full-time Ph.D. program. The objective of the Ph.D. in economics is to prepare students for careers in academe, business, and government. The program focuses on environmental and natural resource (ENR) economics and equips students with theoretical, conceptual, and quantitative skills to research a broad range of ENR problems.

Research Facilities

Extensive computer facilities for batch and interactive modes are available both in the College of Business Administration and in the many University computer centers. Graduate business students have access to equipment that ranges from large mainframe computers to minicomputers and microcomputers. The University Library has more than 4.3 million holdings and other research materials necessary to support high-caliber graduate programs. The library also participates in online information searching through a variety of services.

Financial Aid

Financial aid is available in the form of graduate assistantships, tuition waivers, fellowships and scholarships, and student loan programs. Assistantship stipends were $6400 plus a partial tuition fee waiver for the 2006–07 academic year and required 20 hours of service per week to the College of Business Administration.

Cost of Study

Tuition, which is subject to change, was $257 per semester hour for Florida residents and $950 per semester hour for out-of-state residents in 2006–07.

Living and Housing Costs

Off-campus living accommodations for graduate students are available throughout the Orlando area; some are within walking distance of the University.

Student Group

Enrollment on campus is more than 46,700, with 9,000 students in the College of Business Administration. Approximately 1,100 graduate students are pursuing degrees in the College; approximately half of these students have undergraduate degrees in nonbusiness fields. Diverse geographical backgrounds and areas of professional experience are represented.

Location

Metropolitan Orlando is a growing, dynamic area of more than 2.5 million people. Cultural and recreational activities and facilities are abundant. Although best known for its various tourist attractions, Orlando also has an extremely broad technical and industrial base. Central Florida has an ideal climate, with an average temperature of 72°F, which makes it possible to enjoy outdoor activities during the whole year. The Atlantic Ocean is an hour's drive east of campus.

The University

The University of Central Florida, formerly known as Florida Technological University, was founded in 1963. A youthful, dynamic institution, UCF is part of the State University System of Florida. The picturesque campus, located 13 miles east of downtown Orlando, consists of 1,227 acres. Baccalaureate, master's, and doctoral degrees are offered in a wide variety of fields.

Applying

Students may enter the M.S.A., M.S.M.I.S., and M.S.T. degree programs in the fall, spring, or summer semester. The M.B.A., M.S.Eco., and M.S.B.M. programs begin in the fall semester. The M.B.A. thirty-three-month lockstep evening program is a part-time program, and the one-year full-time M.B.A., M.S.B.M., and M.S.Eco. are full-time programs. Applications should be made at least four months prior to the desired enrollment date. Admission is open to students showing a high promise of success. A bachelor's degree from a regionally accredited college or university, submission of satisfactory scores on the Graduate Management Admission Test (GMAT), an essay, a resume, and three recommendations are required for admission consideration. Ph.D. in business administration applicants are accepted every other year (in odd-numbered years) in the fall semester. Ph.D. in economics applicants are admitted each fall semester.

Correspondence and Information

Director of Graduate Programs
College of Business Administration, Suite 240
University of Central Florida
Orlando, Florida 32816-1400

Phone: 407-823-4723
E-mail: cbagrad@bus.ucf.edu
Web site: http://www.bus.ucf.edu

University of Central Florida

THE FACULTY

Richard Ajayi, Associate Professor of Finance; Ph.D., Temple, 1983.
Jeffery W. Allen, Associate Professor of Marketing; D.B.A., Kentucky, 1988.
Maureen K. Ambrose, Professor of Management; Ph.D., Illinois, 1986.
Amber Anand, Assistant Professor of Finance; Ph.D., CUNY, Baruch, 2001.
Wilma Anton, Assistant Professor of Economics; Ph.D., Illinois at Urbana-Champaign, 2001.
Vicky Arnold, Professor of Accounting; Ph.D., Arkansas, 1989.
Bruce Barringer, Associate Professor of Management; Ph.D., Missouri–Columbia, 1995.
Tanya Benford, Assistant Professor of Accounting; Ph.D., South Florida, 1994.
Donna Bobeck, Associate Professor of Accounting; Ph.D., Florida, 1997.
Walter A. Bogumil, Associate Professor of Management; Ph.D., Georgia, 1972.
Stephen F. Borde, Associate Professor of Finance; Ph.D., Florida Atlantic, 1993.
Bradley M. Braun, Associate Professor of Economics and Associate Dean; Ph.D., Tulane, 1986.
Anthony K. Byrd, Associate Professor of Finance; Ph.D., South Carolina, 1992.
Michael Caputo, Professor of Economics; Ph.D., Washington (Seattle), 1986.
Honghui Chen, Associate Professor of Finance; Ph.D., Virginia Tech, 1999.
John M. Cheney, Associate Professor of Finance; D.B.A., Tennessee, 1977.
Paul Cheney, Professor of Management Information Systems; Ph.D., Minnesota.
Yoon Choi, Associate Professor of Finance; Ph.D., Michigan, 1990.
James Courtney, Professor of Management Information Systems; Ph.D., Texas at Austin, 1974.
Duane L. Davis, Professor of Marketing; D.B.A., Kentucky, 1978.
Ramarao Desiraju, Associate Professor of Marketing; Ph.D., Florida, 1999.
Mark Dickie, Professor of Economics; Ph.D., Wyoming, 1987.
Peggy D. Dwyer, Associate Professor of Accounting; Ph.D., Missouri, 1988.
Rajagopal R. Echambadi, Associate Professor of Marketing; Ph.D., Houston, 1998.
E. Taylor Ellis, Associate Professor of Hospitality Management and Associate Dean; Ph.D., Texas A&M, 1976.
Robert Folger, Professor of Management; Ph.D., North Carolina at Chapel Hill, 1975.
Cameron Ford, Associate Professor of Management; Ph.D., Penn State, 1997.
Robert C. Ford, Professor of Management; Ph.D., Arizona State, 1972.
Melissa Frye, Associate Professor of Finance; Ph.D., Georgia Tech, 1999.
Jaishankar Ganesh, Associate Professor of Marketing and Associate Dean; Ph.D., Houston, 1995.
Shelby Gerking, Professor of Economics; Ph.D., Indiana, 1975.
W. Ernest Gibbs, Associate Professor of Economics; Ph.D., Rutgers, 1987.
James Gilkeson, Associate Professor of Finance; Ph.D., Duke, 1993.
Paul Goldwater, Associate Professor of Accounting; Ph.D., LSU, 1989.
Stephen H. Goodman, Associate Professor of Management Information Systems; Ph.D., Penn State, 1972.
Glenn Harrison, Professor of Economics; Ph.D., UCLA, 1982.
Xin He, Assistant Professor of Marketing; Ph.D., Arizona State.
Ross Hightower, Associate Professor of Management Information Systems; Ph.D., Georgia State, 1999.
Richard A. Hofler, Professor of Economics; Ph.D., North Carolina at Chapel Hill, 1982.
Djehane Hosni, Associate Professor of Economics; Ph.D., Arkansas, 1978.
Richard S. Huseman, Professor of Management; Ph.D., Illinois, 1965.
Kyung-So Im, Associate Professor of Economics; Ph.D., Michigan State.
James J. Jiang, Professor of Management Information Systems; Ph.D., Cincinatti.
Walter L. Johnson, Associate Professor of Accounting; Ph.D., Texas at Austin, 1974; CPA.
Foard F. Jones, Associate Professor of Management; Ph.D., Georgia, 1991.
Amit Joshi, Assistant Professor of Marketing; Ph.D., UCLA, 2005.
Andrew Judd, Associate Professor of Accounting; Ph.D., Florida, 1985.
Charles Kelliher, Associate Professor of Accounting; Ph.D., Texas A&M, 1990.
Thomas L. Keon, Professor of Management and Dean; Ph.D., Michigan State, 1979.
Junyong Kim, Assistant Professor of Marketing; Ph.D., Illinois at Urbana-Champaign.
Anand Krishnamoorthy, Assistant Professor of Marketing; Ph.D., Texas at Dallas.
Jo Lacy, Assistant Professor of Accounting; Ph.D., George Washington, 1994.
Richard Lapchick, Professor of Sport Business Management; Ph.D., Denver, 1993.
William E. Leigh, Professor of Management; Ph.D., Cincinnati, 1984.
Thomas L. Martin, Associate Professor of Economics; Ph.D., Rice, 1981.
Carolyn Massiah, Assistant Professor of Marketing; Ph.D., Arizona State, 2007.
David Mayer, Assistant Professor of Management; Ph.D., Maryland, 2004.
Michael McDonald, Assistant Professor of Management; Ph.D., Texas at Austin.
Warren W. McHone, Professor of Economics; Ph.D., Pennsylvania, 1980.
Ron Michaels, Professor of Marketing and Chair; Ph.D., Indiana, 1983.
O. Mikhail, Assistant Professor of Economics; Ph.D., McGill, 2001.
J. Walter Milon, Professor of Economics; Ph.D., Florida State, 1979.
Naval K. Modani, Associate Professor of Finance; Ph.D., South Carolina, 1980.
Mihir Parikh, Assistant Professor of Management Information Systems; Ph.D., Georgia State.
Hoon Park, Associate Professor of Finance; Ph.D., Georgia State, 1988.
Robert L. Pennington, Associate Professor of Economics; Ph.D., Texas A&M, 1977.
Ronald Piccolo, Assistant Professor of Management; Ph.D., Florida.
Roberto Ragozzino, Assistant Professor of Finance; Ph.D., Ohio State, 2004.
Pradipkumar Ramanlal, Associate Professor of Finance; Ph.D., Michigan, 1991.
Robin W. Roberts, Professor of Accounting and Chair; Ph.D., Arkansas, 1987.
Pamela B. Roush, Associate Professor of Accounting; Ph.D., Georgia State, 1989.
Ronald S. Rubin, Professor of Marketing; Ph.D., Massachusetts, 1973.
E. Elisabet Rutström, Professor of Economics; Ph.D., Stockholm School of Economics, 1990.
Mitrabarum Sarkar, Associate Professor of Management; Ph.D., Michigan State, 1999.
Carol Saunders, Professor of Management Information Systems; Ph.D., Houston, 1979.
Marshall J. Schminke, Professor of Management; Ph.D., Carnegie Mellon, 1986.
Charles Schnitzlein, Associate Professor of Finance; Ph.D., Washington (St. Louis), 1994.
David Scrogin, Assistant Professor of Economics; Ph.D., New Mexico, 1999.
Stanley D. Smith, Professor of Finance and Sun Trust Chair of Banking; Ph.D., Arizona State, 1971.
Mark D. Soskin, Associate Professor of Economics; Ph.D., Penn State, 1979.
Axel Stock, Assistant Professor of Marketing; Ph.D., Purdue, 2003.
Steve Sutton, Professor of Accounting; Ph.D., Missouri–Columbia, 1987.
William Sutton, Professor of Sport Business Management; Ed.D., Oklahoma State.
Wouter Vanhouche, Assistant Professor of Marketing; Ph.D., Florida, 2005.
Craig Van Slyke, Assistant Professor of Management Information Systems; Ph.D., South Florida, 1998.
William C. Weaver, Associate Professor of Finance; Ph.D., Georgia State, 1983.
Judith K. Welch, Associate Professor of Accounting; Ph.D., Florida State, 1985.
Lawrence West, Associate Professor of Management Information Systems; Ph.D., Texas A&M, 1996.
Kenneth R. White, Associate Professor of Economics; Ph.D., Oklahoma, 1971.
Ann Marie Whyte, Associate Professor of Finance; Ph.D., Florida Atlantic, 1991.
Kanghyun Yoon, Assistant Professor of Marketing; Ph.D., Wisconsin–Milwaukee.

UNIVERSITY OF COLORADO AT BOULDER

Master of Business Administration Program

College of Business & Administration

Developing The Leaders of Tomorrow

Program of Study

Students at the University of Colorado's (CU) Leeds School of Business can do more than get a degree—they can blaze a trail! Students are encouraged to take advantage of all the opportunities the school's M.B.A. experience offers. The time students spend in the Leeds M.B.A. program can be one of the most significant and rewarding experiences of their lives. This personal program immerses students in the Leeds School, the University, and the surrounding community. The curriculum helps students build their skills and challenges them to grow in new directions. Opportunities for personal interaction with faculty members, business professionals, successful entrepreneurs, mentors, and alumni allow students to expand their horizons and apply their new skills. In addition, their classmates in this cooperative and team-based culture challenge them to do their best and expect the same in return. The journey students make together at Leeds helps to shape their lives.

The flexibility of the curriculum structure allows students to design an M.B.A. that supports their personal and professional goals. The M.B.A. curriculum provides a comprehensive general management education through the core courses while adding a breadth and depth of knowledge through electives. The M.B.A. requires 55 credits with a minimum GPA of 3.0 for graduation. The required core courses create a strong foundation in business theory and application (28 credits). Electives allow students to develop breadth and depth in a functional area of expertise (finance, marketing, systems, or management) balanced with options in the program's niche areas of specialization—entrepreneurship, real estate, and the newest focus—sustainability.

Dual-degree agreements with other graduate schools and departments on campus offer students a variety of opportunities to earn two master's degrees in less time in combination than if taken sequentially. Leeds' dual-degree options include the J.D./M.B.A. with the School of Law; M.B.A./M.S. degrees in conjunction with computer science, environmental studies, or telecommunications; and M.B.A./M.A. degrees in conjunction with anthropology, fine arts, theater and dance, or Germanic languages.

Research Facilities

The William M. White Business Library includes research materials for management and administration as well as corporate annual shareholder reports, SEC 10-K reports for Colorado and Fortune 500 companies, and proxy statements for all companies on primary U.S. exchanges. The Douglas H. Buck Electronic Media Center provides access to more than 50 online databases. The Business Research Division conducts research that assists companies, educational institutions, and governmental agencies in making sound business and policy decisions. Its primary competencies are in the areas of manufacturing issues and trends, the impact of government policy, and the impact of technology. The Richard M. Burridge Center for Securities Analysis and Valuation supports the creation and dissemination of new knowledge about the world financial markets, with an emphasis on the U.S. financial markets. The Center for Sustainable Tourism provides a forum for the assessment of economic, social, cultural, and environmental implications of the tourism industry as well as for the designing and planning for sustainable tourism development.

Financial Aid

University of Colorado Foundation fellowships are awarded to incoming M.B.A. students each year. The Robert H. and Beverly A. Deming Center for Entrepreneurship offers fellowships to students who plan to pursue the study of entrepreneurship. The CU Real Estate Center offers fellowships to students who plan to pursue the study of real estate. The Barney Ford Fellowship creates additional support for people of diverse backgrounds. Students may apply for Federal Work-Study or federal grants or loans. Second-year students who have established high levels of achievement in core courses may qualify for paid teaching assistantships or work in research positions.

Cost of Study

Full-time tuition per year (9 or more credits) for 2006–07 was $8982 for residents and $24,156 for nonresidents. Students also pay approximately $1200 in required fees each year.

Living and Housing Costs

Students living on campus can expect to pay $4654 to $5224 per year for room and board, including fifteen to nineteen meals per week, or $4509 to $5079 for room and board, including ten meals per week. Apartment- and family-style housing costs $685–$800 per month for one bedroom and $790–$1000 per month for two bedrooms. Off-campus housing typically costs $500–$1200 per month.

Student Group

In 2006–07, 53 students (out of 225 applicants) enrolled in the program. Of these, 34 percent were women, 9 percent were members of minority groups, and 17 percent came from other countries. They entered the program with an average GMAT score of 630 and an average undergraduate GPA of 3.2. On average, they were 28 years old with five years of work experience in industries ranging from consulting and engineering to tourism, marketing, and technology.

Student Outcomes

Graduates of the program have found employment in some of the world's largest companies across a wide range of industries; examples include 3M, Ernst & Young, LLP, IBM, Hitachi Consulting, Horizon Organic Dairy, Celestial Seasonings, Coors Brewing Company, Level 3 Communications, Merrill Lynch, the National Park Service, and Wild Oats Markets. Many work in their company's finance department, but others work in IT, marketing, engineering, and consulting.

Location

Boulder is regarded as one of the most desirable places to live in the country, with a mild, dry climate and 300 days of sunshine per year. Rocky Mountain National Park is located only 45 miles from Boulder, and Eldora Mountain is approximately 20 miles away. Other popular attractions include the Colorado Shakespeare Festival and Chautauqua Park Historic District.

The University

Founded in 1876 at the base of the Rocky Mountains, the University of Colorado at Boulder is now one of the most prestigious universities in the nation. More than 28,500 students are enrolled in 165 degree programs and participate in research at ninety research centers, institutes, and laboratories. *U.S. News & World Report* ranked the M.B.A. program twenty-sixth in the country, and the school is one of thirty-four U.S. public research universities invited to join the prestigious Association of American Universities.

Applying

Prospective students should submit an online application for admission, official college transcripts, answers to specific essay questions, official GMAT scores, three letters of recommendation, and a $70 application fee. Deadlines for applying to the M.B.A. program are December 1 (for candidates requesting an early decision), February 1 (encouraged for international candidates and applicants requesting fellowship consideration), and April 1 (final application deadline).

Correspondence and Information

Leeds School of Business
UCB 419
University of Colorado at Boulder
Boulder, Colorado 80302
Phone: 303-492-8397
Fax: 303-492-1727
E-mail: LeedsMBA@Colorado.edu
Web site: http://leeds.colorado.edu/mba/

University of Colorado at Boulder

THE FACULTY AND THEIR RESEARCH

David Balkin, Professor of Strategy and Organization Management and Chair, Management Division; Ph.D., Minnesota, 1981. Relationship between pay policies and firm strategy, strategic human resource management, corporate governance.

John Ballantine Jr., Senior Instructor of Business Law; J.D., Colorado, 1990. Tax, corporate law, alternative dispute resolution, business law, financial and managerial accounting.

Sanjai Bhagat, Professor of Finance; Ph.D., Washington (Seattle), 1982. Corporate lawsuits, business valuation, corporate finance, corporate governance, entrepreneurial finance.

R. Wayne Boss, Professor of Strategy and Organizational Management; D.P.A., Georgia, 1973. Organization effectiveness, organization development, consultation skills, organization behavior.

Thomas Buchman, Associate Professor of Accounting; Ph.D., Illinois at Urbana-Champaign, 1976. Financial reporting, financial accounting.

Cathleen Burns, Senior Instructor of Accounting; Ph.D., New Mexico State, 1995. Effects of accounting information and accounting personnel on organizational behavior, new developments in cost management, project management, self-managed work groups.

Margaret C. Campbell, Assistant Professor of Marketing; Ph.D., Stanford, 1992. Consumer understanding of persuasion, perceptions of unfairness in prices and marketing, branding, advertising effects.

Dipankar Chakravarti, Professor of Marketing; Ph.D., Carnegie-Mellon, 1979. Consumer and managerial decisions, consumer and market measurement methods, marketing in developing economies.

Thomas Dean, Anderson Professor of Entrepreneurial Development; Ph.D., Colorado at Boulder, 1992. Influence of organizational contexts on new venture creation, strategy, performance, market failure and entrepreneurial opportunity.

Calvin Duncan, Associate Professor of Marketing and Chair, Marketing Division; D.B.A., Indiana, 1977. Effects of message structure and content on advertising effectiveness, influence of consumer heuristics on information search and brand/store choice behaviors.

Garland Durham, Assistant Professor of Finance; Ph.D., North Carolina at Chapel Hill, 2001. Finance, econometrics, statistics.

Maw der Foo, Assistant Professor of Management; Ph.D., MIT, 1999. Emotion management in organizations, entrepreneurship, opportunity recognition.

David Frederick, Associate Professor of Accounting; Ph.D., Michigan, 1986. The nature of expertise, consideration of fraud in financial statement audits, gender equity in intercollegiate athletics, analysis of sports enterprise.

John Garnand, Senior Instructor of Business Economics, Management, and Operations; Ph.D., Colorado at Boulder, 1976. Policy implications of business management and operations, business ethics and employment law applications.

Fred Glover, Professor of Operations Management and Operations Research; Ph.D., Carnegie Tech, 1965. Real-world applications of optimization and computer decision-support systems.

Kenneth Gordon, Senior Instructor of Operations Management and International Business; Ph.D., Northwestern, 1973. International management and international operations.

Susan Jung Grant, Assistant Professor of Marketing; Ph.D., Northwestern, 2002. Effects of contextual factors on consumer information processing, persuasion, judgment and decision making, temporal framing, goal states and motivation, psychology of financial decision making, advertising effects.

Mathew L. A. Hayward, Assistant Professor of Management; Ph.D., Columbia, 1998. Confidence in decision making, media accounts of and effects on organizations, power and learning in organizations.

Chuan He, Assistant Professor of Marketing; Ph.D., Washington (St. Louis), 2002. Promotion, pricing strategies, channel contracts, Internet marketing, experimental economics.

Paul Herr, Professor of Marketing and Director, Marketing Doctoral Program; Ph.D., Indiana, 1983. Consumer memory and judgment, affect, attitude theory, decision making, brand management.

Eric Hughson, Associate Professor of Finance; Ph.D., Carnegie Mellon, 1990. Timing of offers and existence of equilibrium in market microstructure, splitting orders, discrete pricing and the design of dealership markets, investment and insider trading.

Betty Jackson, Professor of Accounting; Ph.D., Texas at Austin, 1982. Behavioral/cognitive analysis of judgments by tax professionals and taxpayers, identification and measurement of intangible assets.

John Jacob, Associate Professor of Accounting; Ph.D., Northwestern, 1995. Firms' diversification decisions, analysts' earnings forecasts and recommendations, market anomalies, electric utility industry.

Kenneth Kozar, Professor of Information Systems; Ph.D., Minnesota, 1972. Human and organizational impacts of information systems technology, information systems usefulness and usability, aligning information technology with organization strategy, developing Web sites accessible to persons with disabilities.

Manuel Laguna, Professor of Operations Management Systems and Chair, Systems Doctoral Programs; Ph.D., Texas at Austin, 1990. Developing models and solution methods for combinatorial optimization problems, interface between operations research and artificial intelligence as applied to heuristic search, model formulation and solution methods for decision problems under uncertainty.

Kai Larsen, Assistant Professor of Information Systems; Ph.D., SUNY at Albany, 2000. Implementation of information systems, organizational impacts of emerging technologies.

Stephen Lawrence, Associate Professor of Operations Management; Ph.D., Carnegie Mellon, 1988. Technology management, technology adoption, operations scheduling, operations strategy, entrepreneurship.

J. Chris Leach, Associate Professor of Finance; Ph.D., Cornell, 1988. Corporate and venture financing, mergers and acquisitions, structure of securities markets, real options, information economics and game theory.

Jintae Lee, Associate Professor of Information Systems; Ph.D., MIT, 1991. Knowledge management, knowledge sharing, organizational memory.

Donald R. Lichtenstein, Professor of Marketing; Ph.D., South Carolina, 1984. Consumer perceptions of reference price advertising, consumer price-quality perceptions, consumer perception of sales promotion techniques, consumer marketplace attribution.

Patrick Long, Professor of Tourism Management; Ed.D., Western Michigan, 1977. Tourism planning and development; tourism impacts on the social, economic, and environmental aspects of community life; sustainable tourism practices; social and economic effects of second homes; rural destinations and tourism; gambling tourism.

Stanley Martin, Senior Instructor of Finance; Ph.D., Kansas, 1976. Corporate finance, financial markets, security analysis.

Sharon Matusik, Assistant Professor of Management; Ph.D., Washington (Seattle), 1998. Strategic management, firm knowledge and innovation, entrepreneurship innovation, entrepreneurship.

A. Peter McGraw, Assistant Professor of Marketing; Ph.D., Ohio State, 2002. Judgment and decision making, emotions, social relational theory, consumer behavior.

Ronald Melicher, Professor of Finance and Chair, Finance Division; D.B.A., Washington (St. Louis), 1968. Corporate mergers, bankruptcy, and other restructuring; asymmetric information and financial signaling topics; entrepreneurial finance issues.

Ramiro Montealegre, Associate Professor of Information Systems and Chair, Systems Division; D.B.A., Harvard, 1994. Assimilation of information technology, organizational transformation through implementation of information technology, transfer of technology to less developed countries.

Page Moreau, Assistant Professor of Marketing; Ph.D., Columbia, 1998. Consumer learning and knowledge transfer, new-product development and acceptance, creativity, product design.

Elaine Mosakowski, Professor of Management and Director, Organizational Management Doctoral Program; Ph.D., Berkeley, 1988. Entrepreneurial role in firm strategy, sources of profit generation, strategy making under causal ambiguity, global organizations, evolution of entrepreneurial firms, corporate governance, innovation.

Nathalie Moyen, Assistant Professor of Finance; Ph.D., British Columbia, 1999. Corporate finance, derivative securities.

Michael Palmer, Professor of Finance; Ph.D., Washington (Seattle), 1967. International debt and sovereign debt rescheduling, management and assessment of country risk, international finance and foreign exchange markets, economic trading blocs.

Steven Rock, Assistant Professor of Accounting; Ph.D., Penn State, 1996. Earnings management, financial analyst forecasting and behavior, relations between prices and earnings, earnings-based bonus plans, initial public offerings.

Joseph Rosse, Professor of Management; Ph.D., Illinois at Urbana-Champaign, 1983. Employee recruitment and retention, counterproductive employee behavior, employee satisfaction and stress, workplace safety.

Frank Selto, Professor of Accounting and Chair, Accounting Division; Ph.D., Washington (Seattle), 1977. Effects of accounting information and performance measurement on managerial decision making and organizational performance.

Lori Seward, Senior Instructor of Information Systems; Ph.D., Virginia Tech, 1998. Probability theory, maintenance planning, stochastic processes.

Philip Shane, Associate Professor of Accounting; Ph.D., Oregon, 1982. Valuation implications of financial accounting information, stock market efficiency with respect to financial accounting information and the intermediary role of financial analysts, financial reporting quality, corporate social responsibility.

Atanu Sinha, Assistant Professor of Marketing; Ph.D., NYU, 1992. Pricing, auctions, and bundling; loyalty rewards; theoretical and empirical marketing strategy.

Naomi Soderstrom, Associate Professor of Accounting; Ph.D., Northwestern, 1990. Empirical managerial accounting, accounting for environmental costs and health care.

Michael Stutzer, Professor of Finance; Ph.D., Minnesota, 1981. Continuing development of a unified approach to investment, securities valuation, valuation model parameter estimation based on the statistical theory of large deviations.

Thomas Thibodeau, Professor of Finance; Ph.D., SUNY at Stony Brook, 1980. Measuring and modeling spatial and temporal variation in real estate prices, identifying real estate submarket boundaries, real estate investment.

Thomas Vossen, Assistant Professor of Operations Management and Information Systems; Ph.D., Maryland, 2002. Modeling and analysis of real-time transportation and logistics operations, collaborative decision making in air traffic flow management, hybrid artificial intelligence/integer programming techniques applied to planning and scheduling.

Richard Wobbekind, Associate Professor of Business Economics and Director, Business Research Division. Ph.D., Colorado at Boulder, 1984. Public policy, macroeconomic forecasting, regional economic development, economics of salary arbitration.

Chris Yung, Assistant Professor of Finance; Ph.D., Washington (St. Louis), 2002. Security issuance, initial public offerings, asymmetric information.

Jaime Zender, Associate Professor of Finance; Ph.D., Yale, 1988. Corporate control, corporate finance, financial contracting, auction theory.

UNIVERSITY OF CONNECTICUT

School of Business
M.B.A. Program

Program of Study

The University of Connecticut's (UConn) M.B.A. program integrates experiential learning across all functional business areas. The M.B.A. curriculum requires a total of nineteen courses (57 credits) to earn the degree, which takes two academic years. UConn's experiential learning opportunities are what distinguish it from other top-quality M.B.A. programs. These dynamic multipartner initiatives create a multidimensional environment that significantly leverages the learning process, allowing students to acquire a business education like no other. One of UConn's earliest experiential learning opportunities is the "integration project" component. Assigned to groups from day one, students work together throughout their first years as members of cross-functional teams. The spring semester culminates in a live, real-company integration project that draws upon formal course instruction as well as preprogram work experience. Presentations are made to faculty members and business leaders, and students are given structured feedback to hone their technical, analytical, and interpersonal skills. Partnering companies have included Aetna, GE, Pitney Bowes, Pratt & Whitney, and Xerox. A second experiential opportunity is UConn's $2-million student-managed investment fund (SMF). Reporting to the University's investment oversight board, the SMF gives M.B.A. students majoring in finance the opportunity to serve as actual portfolio managers—investing $2 million of the University's endowment funds. UConn was one of the first schools in the country to provide real money for student investing experience.

UConn's SS&C Technologies Financial Accelerator is a robust multipartner environment in which students, faculty members, and business executives utilize the latest financial technologies and real-time databases to develop solutions to real insurance and financial challenges. The Innovation Accelerator, UConn's latest learning accelerator, provides a set of services geared toward capturing opportunities in new, developing, and existing markets for both established and start-up businesses that populate the numerous supply chains in the strategically important industry clusters of Connecticut. These services include identifying market opportunities, building the road maps to capture those opportunities, evaluating emerging technologies, assessing competitive threats, and improving business processes.

During the second year, students focus their studies in any two of the five M.B.A. concentrations: operations and information management, finance, health-care management and insurance studies, management consulting, and marketing intelligence. At this time, students also participate actively in externally directed programs of the School, such as business consulting projects, and work with the School's career services to pursue placement opportunities. The University, together with the School of Business, also offers the following dual-degree programs: M.B.A./J.D., M.B.A./M.A. in international studies, M.B.A./M.S.W., M.B.A./M.S. in nursing, M.B.A./M.A. of international management (MIM), and M.B.A./M.D. Evening M.B.A. and Executive M.B.A. programs are also available.

Research Facilities

An experiential learning initiative offered by UConn is a nationally recognized $2.5-million, 10,000-square-foot e-lab, *edgelab*, funded by General Electric, which offers a superb research facility providing an exceptional learning and applied research experience for M.B.A. students. The *edgelab* serves as an advanced e-business center where M.B.A. students, faculty members, and GE managers jointly explore new IT technologies and develop IT strategies that yield real business value.

The School of Business, the Placement Office, the Small Business Institute, and the Centers for Real Estate and Urban Economic Studies, Health Care and Insurance Studies, and Research in Financial Services provide specialized resources for students at the University of Connecticut. The University Library, directly across the street from the School of Business, contains 2.6 million volumes, 6,000 currently received print periodicals, 41,000 electronic journals, 2.8 million units of microform, 35,000 reference sources, 200,000 maps, sound and video recordings, musical scores, and a growing array of electronic resources, including e-books, e-sound recordings, and image databases.

Financial Aid

Although the cost of a UConn M.B.A. is reasonable, candidates often need financial assistance. Most financial aid is awarded on the basis of established need, primarily determined through an analysis of an applicant's Free Application for Federal Student Aid (FAFSA). For further information, students may also contact the University of Connecticut's Financial Aid Office at 860-486-2819 or at their Web site at http://www.financialaid.uconn.edu. In order to receive financial aid on a timely basis, it is imperative that students file the application for financial aid as soon after January 1 as possible. Candidates without sufficient financial resources may be able to attend the program by applying for and obtaining the necessary financial aid. Out-of-state candidates who have demonstrated a high likelihood of success can also benefit from the Tuition Assistance Program. In this program, out-of-state students receive the benefit of paying in-state tuition fees. There are a limited number of these awards, so work experience and GMAT scores are important determinants. Graduate assistantships are another opportunity for financial assistance. Students with a graduate assistantship work for 150 hours over the course of the semester, typically 10 hours a week for fifteen weeks. In exchange, students receive a tuition waiver (University fees must still be paid), health and dental insurance, and a stipend of approximately $4000 per semester. In 2004, more than 38 percent of all students were awarded graduate assistantships. Early applicants receive preference for graduate assistantships if they apply before April 15.

Cost of Study

Tuition and fees for the 2006–07 academic year (two semesters) for the Full-Time M.B.A. program at UConn were $9510 for Connecticut residents and $22,290 for nonresidents. Additional costs, including required health insurance, textbooks, mobile computer, laundry, and incidentals, can add up to an estimated $7000. Fees are subject to change without notice.

Living and Housing Costs

For a nine-month academic year, the approximate cost of living, in addition to tuition and fees, is estimated to be $9300. Many unmarried students reside in the Graduate Residence in single dormitory rooms. Specific information is available by contacting the Graduate Dormitory Assignments Office, Department of Residential Life, University of Connecticut, 233 Glenbrook Road, Unit 4022, Storrs, Connecticut 06269. A wide variety of off-campus housing is available to students. A visit to the area is recommended for all students interested in finding off-campus housing.

Student Group

M.B.A. students come to the School of Business from a wide variety of undergraduate institutions, both domestic and international. Their undergraduate degrees represent majors in many diverse areas—from engineering to English, from natural sciences to fine arts, and, of course, from business to economics. In a typical class of students, 34 percent are women, the average age is 28, and approximately 35 percent are international students. Friendliness and informality characterize student life at the main campus. Social and professional organizations offer a variety of activities to satisfy the needs of students.

Student Outcomes

In 2006, eighty-nine percent of UConn's M.B.A. graduates were employed three months after graduation. The median salary was $70,000 and went as high as $95,000 plus bonus. Employers who hire the most University of Connecticut M.B.A. graduates include General Electric, "Big 4" accounting firms, CIGNA, Aetna, IBM, United Technologies Corp., Wachovia, Hartford Financial Services, PricewaterhouseCoopers, Gerber Technologies, ESPN, and UBS Warburg.

Location

The University of Connecticut is located on 3,100 acres in the Storrs section of the town of Mansfield in northeastern Connecticut. It is approximately 30 minutes from Hartford, the state capital and prominent insurance center. Boston is a 90-minute drive, while New York City is 3 hours away.

The University and The School

Fifteen schools and colleges constitute the University, which has a student population of approximately 28,000. There are 140 students in the full-time program in Storrs; 900 in the part-time program in Stamford, Hartford, and Waterbury; and 100 in the Executive M.B.A. program. The M.B.A. program is nationally accredited by AACSB International–The Association to Advance Collegiate Schools of Business. The School of Business is a member of the Graduate Management Admissions Council (GMAC) and the European Foundation for Management Development (EFMD).

Applying

Individuals with degrees from accredited institutions are encouraged to apply. The admissions committee evaluates an individual on academic and professional accomplishments, potential for success, recommendations, information provided in the online application, and scores on the Graduate Management Admission Test. Students may enter the M.B.A. program at the Storrs campus only in the fall. The application and all accompanying materials should be received as early as possible.

Correspondence and Information

For the master's program:
Full-Time M.B.A. Director, Storrs
School of Business
University of Connecticut
2100 Hillside Road, Unit 1041
Storrs, Connecticut 06269-1041

Phone: 860-486-2872
Fax: 860-486-5222
E-mail: uconnmba@business.uconn.edu
Web site: http://www.business.uconn.edu

For the Ph.D. program:
Ph.D. Director
School of Business
University of Connecticut
2100 Hillside Road, Unit 1041
Storrs, Connecticut 06269-1041

Phone: 860-486-5822
Fax: 860-486-0270
E-mail: phdmail@business.uconn.edu
Web site: http://www.business.uconn.edu

University of Connecticut

THE FACULTY

Accounting
Stanley F. Biggs, Ph.D., Minnesota.
Amy Dunbar, Ph.D., Texas at Austin.
Lawrence J. Gramling, Ph.D., Maryland.
Robert E. Hoskin, Ph.D., Cornell.
Richard Hurley, Ph.D., Connecticut.
Mohamed E. Hussein, Ph.D., Pittsburgh.
Alfred Zhu Liu, Ph.D., California, Irvine.
Cliff Nelson, D.B.A., Illinois.
Jose Oaks, M.B.A., NYU.
John Phillips, Ph.D., Iowa.
George Plesco, Ph.D., Wisconsin–Madison.
Michael Redemske, M.S., DePaul.
Andrew J. Rosman, Ph.D., North Carolina at Chapel Hill.
Gim S. Seow, Ph.D., Oregon.
David P. Weber, Ph.D., Colorado at Boulder.
Michael Willenborg, Ph.D., Penn State.

Finance
John M. Clapp, Ph.D., Columbia.
Walter Dolde, Ph.D., Yale.
Assaf Eisdorfer, Ph.D., Rochester.
Chinmoy Ghosh, Ph.D., Penn State.
Carmelo Giaccotto, Ph.D., Kentucky.
Joseph Golec, Ph.D., Washington (St. Louis).
John P. Harding, Ph.D., Berkeley.
Shantaram P. Hegde, Ph.D., Massachusetts.
Ray Kehrhahn, M.B.A., Connecticut.
Linda S. Klein, Ph.D., Florida State.
John Knopf, Ph.D., NYU.
Jeffrey Kramer, Ph.D., Connecticut.
Norman H. Moore, Ph.D., Florida State.
Kenneth P. Nunn, Ph.D., Massachusetts.
Thomas J. O'Brien, Ph.D., Florida.
Katherine Pancak, J.D., Boston College.
Rexford Santerre, Ph.D., Connecticut.
James Sfiridis, Ph.D., Connecticut.
C. F. Sirmans, Ph.D., Georgia.
John Vernon, Ph.D., Pennsylvania.

Management
Lane Barrow, M.A., Harvard.
Qing Cao, Ph.D., Maryland.
Kathleen Dechant, Ed.D., Columbia.
Richard N. Dino, Associate Dean; Ph.D., SUNY at Buffalo.
Eric Gedajlovic, Ph.D., Concordia.
Lucy L. Gilson, Ph.D., Georgia Tech.
Jodi Goodman, Ph.D., Georgia Tech.
Michael H. Lubatkin, Ph.D., Tennessee.
Nora Madjar, Ph.D., Illinois.
John E. Mathieu, Ph.D., Old Dominion.
Gary N. Powell, Ph.D., Massachusetts.

Eugene M. Salorio, D.B.A., Harvard.
Zeki Simsek, Ph.D. candidate, Connecticut.
John F. Veiga, D.B.A., Kent State.

Marketing and Business Law
Robert J. Bird, J.D., Boston University.
Vincent A. Carrafiello, J.D., Connecticut.
Robin A. Coulter, Ph.D., Pittsburgh.
Mark DeAngelis, J.D., Suffolk.
Karla H. Fox, J.D., Duke.
Wynd Harris, Ph.D., Oklahoma.
Subhash C. Jain, Ph.D., Oregon.
V. Kumar, Ph.D., Texas at Austin.
Joseph Pancras, Ph.D., NYU.
Charles Peterson, M.B.A., NYU.
Girish N. Punj, Ph.D., Carnegie Mellon.
Samuel Schrager, J.D., Miami.
Murphy A. Sewall, Ph.D., Washington (St. Louis).
Susan Spiggle, Ph.D., Connecticut.
Mark Spurling, J.D., Western New England.
Narasimhan Srinivasan, Ph.D., SUNY at Buffalo.
Srinivasaraghavan Sriram, Ph.D., Purdue.

Operations and Information Management
Sulin Ba, Ph.D., Texas at Austin.
Ravi Bapna, Ph.D., Connecticut.
Sudip Bhattacharjee, Ph.D., SUNY at Buffalo.
Fidan Boylu, Ph.D., Florida.
Jose Cruz, Ph.D., Massachusetts Amherst.
Robert Day, Ph.D., Maryland, College Park.
Moustapha V. Diaby, Ph.D., SUNY at Buffalo.
Timothy J. Dowding, Ph.D., Connecticut.
Robert S. Garfinkel, Ph.D., Johns Hopkins.
Paulo B. Goes, Ph.D., Rochester.
Ram Gopal, Ph.D., SUNY at Buffalo.
Wei-Kuang Huang, Ph.D., Rutgers.
Robert E. Johnson, Ph.D., Rochester.
Cuihong Li, Ph.D., Carnegie Mellon.
Xinxin Li, Ph.D., Pennsylvania.
James R. Marsden, Ph.D., Purdue.
Suresh K. Nair, Ph.D., Northwestern.
Manuel A. Nunez, Ph.D., MIT.
Jeffrey Rummel, Ph.D., Rochester.
Ramesh Sankaranarayanan, Ph.D., NYU.
George M. Scott, Ph.D., Washington (Seattle).
Jan Stallaert, Ph.D., UCLA.
Lakshman S. Thakur, Eng.Sc.D., Columbia.
Yung-Chin Tung, Ph.D., Kentucky.
Michael Vertefeuille, B.A., Central Connecticut.
Fang Yin, Ph.D., Texas.
Zhongju (John) Zhang, Ph.D., Washington (Seattle).

UConn provides state-of-the-art experiential learning opportunities through such collaborative initiatives as the SS&C Technologies Financial Accelerator.

The University of Connecticut's $27-million School of Business facility opened its doors in fall 2001.

UNIVERSITY OF DELAWARE

Alfred Lerner College of Business and Economics
Master of Business Administration Programs

Programs of Study

The Alfred Lerner College of Business and Economics offers rigorous programs for superior students leading to the M.B.A. and the M.A./M.B.A. degrees. The combination of academically accomplished faculty members, highly qualified students, and ideal location—a small university town in the midst of a large eastern megalopolis—provides the necessary environment for an outstanding experience in graduate business education.

The Delaware M.B.A. program's curriculum includes courses that focus on capable leadership, effective team building, group decision making, strategic use of technology, power negotiating, creative problem-solving techniques, international concerns, coordinating an effective Total Quality Management process, and ethical considerations. The College of Business and Economics offers M.B.A. programs that are designed to serve different groups of students. The Professional M.B.A. program is highly flexible and offers students the option to pursue full- or part-time study. Students who attend full-time are exposed to a combination of course work and opportunities to apply their skills in business settings, work with faculty members on research, attend presentations by business leaders, and become involved in volunteer projects to develop the skills required for successful placement after graduation. Full-time students complete the program in twenty-one months. The part-time study option is designed for the adult who is working full-time and needs the flexibility to complete the M.B.A. in three years through a series of courses offered in the evening. All Professional M.B.A. students have the opportunity to select concentrations from a diverse set of alternatives and to participate in special programs, such as a condensed study-abroad experience or a dual-degree program. Dual-degree options include M.B.A./M.S. Information Systems Technology Management, M.B.A./M.S. Organizational Effectiveness Development and Change, and M.B.A./M.A. Economics.

The Executive M.B.A. program, designed for senior-level managers with extensive work experience, is offered in lock-step format on Friday evenings and all day Saturdays for nineteen months. All programs are accredited by AACSB International–The Association to Advance Collegiate Schools of Business. The University of Delaware is also a long-standing member of the Graduate Management Admissions Council.

The Lerner M.B.A. programs are highly selective and comparatively small, allowing for a high level of student involvement. The combination of small classroom size, classroom theory, and students' practical experiences creates a stimulating environment for the analysis of today's business world.

Research Facilities

The University library, a modern research facility with more than 2.5 million volumes and 3.3 million microforms, is a member of the Association of Research Libraries and is a depository for U.S. government documents and patents.

All computing at the University is conducted over a high-speed, fiber-optic network connecting all buildings, laboratories, offices, and student housing on campus. Also connected to the network are an array of computing resources, ranging from NT servers to supercomputing clusters. The College offers a high-speed network, computing labs, computer classrooms, a variety of NT servers, an SAP environment, multimedia conferencing, and a behavioral research facility.

Financial Aid

Various financial aid packages are available to superior full-time Professional M.B.A. students. These include corporate assistantships, fellowships, graduate assistantships, and tuition grants, which are awarded on a competitive basis. Awards to first-year students are based on prior academic performance, work experience, and test scores. Awards to second-year students are based on academic performance in the program.

A typical aid package may include a stipend of $7000 per year and/or a 50 percent waiver of tuition. A corporate assistant position provides full tuition remission and a $14,000 stipend per academic year. This requires that the student interns with the corporate partner. Members of minority groups may qualify for an additional fellowship program that includes a stipend and full tuition.

Cost of Study

The 2006–07 yearly tuition for full-time M.B.A. students was $8552 for Delaware residents and $17,690 for nonresidents. Part-time study was $476 per credit hour for Delaware residents and $983 per credit hour for nonresident students. Tuition for the Executive M.B.A. program was $51,500.

Living and Housing Costs

Rental costs for shared occupancy in a graduate student complex were $450 per month in 2006–07. University and privately owned apartments, furnished and unfurnished, were available at costs ranging from $500 to $1200 per month.

Student Group

While a minimum GMAT score is not strictly enforced, a score of 550 or above is preferred, and most entering classes typically average 600. The College also prefers to admit students who hold undergraduate GPAs of not less than 2.7. Entering classes for the past several years have an average minimum GPA of 3.0.

Location

The University of Delaware is located in Newark, a suburban community of approximately 30,000. Newark is situated in the northwest corner of Delaware within 3 miles of the Pennsylvania and Maryland borders. It is located within easy driving distance of Philadelphia (45 miles), Baltimore (50 miles), Washington, D.C. (100 miles), and New York City (130 miles). Nearby Wilmington is a major center for credit banking and the chemical industry. More than 50 percent of all Fortune 500 companies are incorporated in Delaware. The College maintains strong ties with the corporate sector. The Wilmington campus is ideal for part-time M.B.A. students whose jobs are located nearby. The Executive M.B.A. program is offered exclusively on the Wilmington campus.

The University and The College

The University of Delaware, founded in 1743 as a small liberal arts school, was moved to Newark, where it became both a land-grant and a sea-grant college. It now ranks among the finest of the nation's medium-sized universities, with approximately 16,000 undergraduate and 3,000 graduate students. Included in the College of Business and Economics are the four Departments: Accounting, Business Administration, Economics, and Finance. All accounting and business programs are accredited by AACSB International–The Association to Advance Collegiate Schools of Business.

Applying

Students must have two years of full-time professional work experience prior to entering the program and need to submit a resume, official copies of all undergraduate and graduate transcripts, GMAT scores, answers to essay questions, and two letters of recommendation. A personal interview is also required for qualified applicants. All students whose native language is not English must have a minimum score of 600 on the TOEFL. Although there are no prerequisite courses, applicants are expected to possess basic skills in written and oral communication, mathematics, and computer usage.

Correspondence and Information

M.B.A. Program Admissions
Alfred Lerner College of Business and Economics
103 Alfred Lerner Hall
University of Delaware
Newark, Delaware 19716
Phone: 302-831-2221
Fax: 302-831-3329
E-mail: mbaprogram@udel.edu
Web site: http://www.mba.udel.edu

University of Delaware

THE FACULTY AND ADMINISTRATION

ADMINISTRATION

Conrado (Bobby) Gempesaw, Dean, Alfred Lerner College of Business and Economics; Ph.D., Penn State.
Gloria Diodato, Assistant Dean, Graduate and Executive Programs; M.B.A., Delaware.
Amy Estey, Manager, M.B.A. Programs; B.S., Ohio State.
Robert B. Barker, Director, M.B.A. Career Services and Corporate Relations; M.B.A./M.Ed., Delaware.
Denise Waters, Director, Recruitment and Admissions; M.S.Ed., Johns Hopkins.
Paul Rollison, Program Manager, Executive Programs; M.Ed., New Hampshire.

FACULTY

Burton A. Abrams, Professor of Economics; Ph.D., Ohio State.
Richard J. Agnello, Associate Professor of Economics; Ph.D., Johns Hopkins.
John H. Antil, Associate Professor of Marketing; Ph.D., Penn State.
Karl F. Aquino, Assistant Professor of Management; Ph.D., Northwestern.
Michael A. Arnold, Associate Professor of Economics; Ph.D., UCLA.
Stacie Beck, Associate Professor of Economics; Ph.D., Pennsylvania.
Thomas E. Becker, Associate Professor of Management; Ph.D., Ohio State.
Kenneth R. Biederman, Professor of Finance; Ph.D., Purdue.
David E. Black, Associate Professor of Economics; Ph.D., MIT.
Helen M. Bowers, Associate Professor of Finance; Ph.D., South Carolina.
Dale A. Buckmaster, Professor of Accounting; Ph.D., Penn State; CPA.
James L. Butkiewicz, Professor of Economics; Ph.D., Virginia.
Terry L. Campbell, Assistant Professor of Finance; Ph.D., Penn State.
Jay F. Coughenour, Assistant Professor of Finance; Ph.D., Pittsburgh.
Eleanor D. Craig, Associate Professor of Economics and Associate Chair; M.A., Pennsylvania.
Joseph I. Daniel, Associate Professor of Economics; Ph.D., Minnesota.
Darwin J. Davis, Assistant Professor of Operations Management; Ph.D., Indiana.
Araya Debessay, Professor of Accounting; Ph.D., Penn State; CPA.
Lawrence P. Donnelley, Associate Professor of Economics; Ph.D., Brown.
Charles Elson, Edgar S. Woolard Jr. Professor of Corporate Governance, Professor of Finance, and Director of the Center for Corporate Governance; J.D., Virginia.
Evangelos Falaris, Associate Professor of Economics; Ph.D., Minnesota.
Diane L. Ferry, Associate Professor of Management; Ph.D., Pennsylvania.
M. Andrew Fields, Associate Professor of Finance and Chair of Finance; Ph.D., Virginia Tech.
Daniel Freeman, Assistant Professor; Ph.D., Arizona.
Meryl P. Gardner, Associate Professor of Marketing; Ph.D., Carnegie Mellon.
Howard Garland, Chaplin Tyler Professor of Business; Ph.D., Cornell.
Guido L. Geerts, Assistant Professor; Ph.D., Free University of Brussels.
William V. Gehrlein, Professor of Operations Management; Ph.D., Penn State.
Jackson E. Gillespie, Associate Professor of Accounting; Ph.D., Virginia Tech; CMA.
Jennifer Gregan-Paxton, Assistant Professor of Marketing; Ph.D., Minnesota.
Farley Grubb, Professor of Economics; Ph.D., Chicago.
Jeffrey Harris, Assistant Professor of Finance; Ph.D., Ohio State.
William Harris, Associate Professor of Economics; Ph.D., Virginia Tech.
Saul D. Hoffman, Professor of Economics and Chair of Economics; Ph.D., Michigan.
Gregory D. Kane, Associate Professor of Accounting; Ph.D., Virginia Tech; CPA.
Robert J. Kent, Associate Professor of Marketing and Head of Marketing; Ph.D., Cincinnati.
Mary C. Kernan, Associate Professor of Management; Ph.D., Akron.
Phyllis Y. Keys, Assistant Professor of Finance; Ph.D., Florida State.
Hemant V. Kher, Assistant Professor of Operations Management; Ph.D., South Carolina.
John L. Kmetz, Associate Professor of Management; D.B.A., Maryland.
Yasemin Y. Kor, Assistant Professor; Ph.D., Illinois.
Christine T. Kydd, Associate Professor of Operations Management; Ph.D., Pennsylvania.
William R. Latham III, Associate Professor of Economics and Associate Professor of Urban Affairs; Ph.D., Illinois.
Kenneth A. Lewis, Chaplin Tyler Professor of Business and Associate Chair of Economics; Ph.D., Princeton.
Charles R. Link, Professor of Economics; Ph.D., Wisconsin.
Ajay K. Manrai, Professor of Marketing and Faculty Director of M.B.A. Programs; Ph.D., Northwestern.
Lalita A. Manrai, Professor of Marketing; Ph.D., Northwestern.
Jeffrey B. Miller, Professor of Economics; Ph.D., Pennsylvania.
James G. Mulligan, Professor of Economics; Ph.D., Minnesota.
James B. O'Neill, Professor of Economics; Ph.D., Purdue.
Robert L. Paretta, Associate Professor of Accounting; Ph.D., Syracuse; CPA.
Neal Phillips, Assistant Professor of Accounting and M.I.S.; J.D., Villanova.
Sheldon D. Pollack, Associate Professor of Business Law; J.D., Ph.D., Cornell.
John F. Preble, Associate Professor of Management; Ph.D., Massachusetts.
Janis R. Reeder, Associate Professor of Accounting; Ph.D., South Carolina; CPA.
Breck L. Robinson, Assistant Professor of Finance; Ph.D., Tennessee.
Erwin M. Saniga, Professor of Operations Management and Head of Operations Management Faculty; Ph.D., Penn State.
John E. Sawyer, Associate Professor of Management and Interim Chair of Business Administration; Ph.D., Illinois.
Robert L. Schweitzer, Professor of Finance; Ph.D., Duke.
Winifred Scott, Assistant Professor of Accounting; Ph.D., Florida State; CPA.
Laurence S. Seidman, Professor of Economics and Chaplin Tyler Professor of Business; Ph.D., Berkeley.
Mark Serva, Assistant Professor of Accounting; Ph.D., Texas at Austin.
Stewart A. Shapiro, Assistant Professor of Marketing; Ph.D., Arizona.
E. Kent St. Pierre, Professor of Accounting, Chair of Accounting, and Director of M.S. Program; Ph.D., Washington (St. Louis); CPA.
David R. Stockman, Assistant Professor of Economics; Ph.D., Chicago.
Daniel P. Sullivan, Associate Professor of Management; Ph.D., South Carolina.
Raj S. Varma, Associate Professor of Finance; Ph.D., Penn State.
Uma Velury, Assistant Professor of Accounting; Ph.D., South Carolina.
Siyan Wang, Assistant Professor of Economics; Ph.D., USC.
Sharon Watson, Assistant Professor of Management; Ph.D., South Carolina.
Gary R. Weaver, Associate Professor of Management; Ph.D., Iowa; Ph.D., Penn State.
Richard M. Weiss, Associate Professor of Management; Ph.D., Cornell.
Clinton E. White, Associate Professor of Accounting and Head of M.I.S. Faculty; D.B.A., Indiana.
John H. Wragge, Associate Professor of Accounting and Faculty Director of Executive Education; Ph.D., Houston; CPA.
Ravindra Yatawara, Assistant Professor of Economics; Ph.D., Columbia.
John S. Ying, Associate Professor of Economics; Ph.D., Berkeley.

UNIVERSITY OF DENVER

Daniels College of Business

Programs of Study

Daniels College of Business at the University of Denver takes an innovative approach to preparing students for the rapidly changing world of business. Recognizing that ethics and values-based leadership, along with technical business knowledge, are prerequisites for success in business today, Daniels requires graduate students to take the Daniels Compass, an unprecedented "curriculum within a curriculum" that integrates values, global perspective, and leadership with foundational business knowledge.

Relevancy, innovation, and a commitment to value creation set the Daniels curriculum apart from other universities. Daniels faculty members are seasoned practitioners, not theorists. They put to use deep methods of applied learning, including case studies, actual work-environment studies, and experiential learning that teaches collaboration and leadership skills. As a result, students develop a comprehensive view of business and acquire leadership and analytical skills that will guide them throughout their careers.

The College's dedication to values was recently recognized by the *Wall Street Journal*. Daniels is ranked (among other prominent academic distinctions) number three in the world for producing students with high ethical standards. This is the fourth year in a row that the *Journal* has recognized Daniels as among the world's best.

Daniels offers full- and part-time M.B.A. programs with several concentrations, including a customized option. Daniels also offers an International M.B.A.; Master of Science degrees in finance, marketing, business intelligence, and real estate and construction management; a Master of Accountancy; and a Master of Taxation. The Daniels dual-degree program allows students to complete a combination of two graduate degrees. The oldest (thirty years and counting) in the nation, the Daniels Executive M.B.A. for experienced professionals is one of the most rigorous programs of its kind. A variety of certificate programs are also offered for working professionals.

Research Facilities

In September 1999, the $25-million Daniels College of Business building opened. Designed for collaboration, it has team breakout rooms, more than 3,000 data ports for instant access to the Daniels network and Internet, and wireless access throughout the facility. It houses the Advanced Technology Center, a state-of-the-art laboratory with the latest software and hardware, and the Marsico Investment Center. Computer facilities include labs with networked PCs that support word processing, spreadsheet and visual presentation software, print and multimedia design and authoring software, UNIX mainframes that provide statistical packages, and Internet and information research database access.

Financial Aid

Merit-based scholarships and assistantships are available, are awarded at the time of decision, and do not require a separate application. Daniels also offers guidance for student loan applications. Tuition and fee structures for the Executive M.B.A. are different. Students should visit http://daniels.du.edu/gradadmission for complete details.

Cost of Study

Tuition in 2007–08 for all graduate students is $873 per credit hour (tuition varies for executive and professional programs). Daniels assesses experiential learning and technology and other fees.

Living and Housing Costs

On-campus room and board for graduate students are available. For more information, students should contact the Department of Residence at 303-871-2246. Many students prefer to live off campus, as one-bedroom apartments near the University are available for as little as $600 per month.

Student Group

Daniels students are a mirror of the Rocky Mountain West community: collaborative and innovative, supportive and engaging, ethically sound, and principles-driven. Students have a wide range of academic and professional backgrounds and represent more than thirty countries around the world. With an average of seven years' professional experience, students provide diverse perspectives that add to dynamic classroom environments and group projects.

Location

Daniels is located in the middle of Colorado business and at the foot of the spectacular Rocky Mountains. The College was ranked in the top 10 in the 2004 *Princeton Review* for Best Campus Environment, which factors in safety, location, and attractiveness. The University of Denver is undergoing extraordinary transformation, investing approximately $378 million to add many new buildings to its campus—buildings with such lasting, timeless architecture that they are quickly becoming Denver landmarks. Located minutes from Colorado's two main business hubs—Downtown Denver and the Denver Tech Center—students enjoy easy access to the cosmopolitan population, cultural activities, and lifestyle of Denver. Daniels is close to some of the best outdoor activities in the world.

The College

Founded in 1908, the University of Denver Daniels College of Business is the eighth-oldest school of business in the United States and has been accredited by AACSB International–The Association to Advance Collegiate Schools of Business since 1923. The $25-million Daniels College of Business building opened in 1999 and adds leading-edge educational technology and facilities to the learning environment. The Daniels College of Business's 80 full-time faculty members combine a love of teaching with a commitment to teamwork and communications to create an engaging, balanced learning environment. They are also business consultants and practitioners, ensuring relevant and current course work. The Daniels College of Business enrolls nearly 3,000 students; the University of Denver enrolls approximately 10,850 students.

Applying

Candidates who demonstrate a commitment to advanced learning, display leadership potential, are committed to high ethical standards, and show promise in their chosen careers are encouraged to apply. Admission to the Daniels College of Business is selective, and decisions are based on a qualitative evaluation of a candidate's potential professional, intellectual, and interpersonal contributions to the Daniels learning environment.

More information about the Daniels application process, including scholarship opportunities, deadlines, and test score requirements for both domestic and international students, can be found on the Web at http://daniels.du.edu/gradadmission.

Correspondence and Information

Daniels College of Business
Rifkin Center for Student Services
University of Denver
2101 South University Boulevard, #255
Denver, Colorado 80208-3416
Phone: 303-871-3416
      800-622-4723 (toll-free)
Fax: 303-871-4466
E-mail: daniels@du.edu
Web site: http://daniels.du.edu

University of Denver

FACULTY HEADS

Karen L. Newman, Dean; Ph.D., Chicago.
Glyn Hanbery, Senior Associate Dean; Ph.D., Arizona State.
William Silver, Chief Operating Officer and Senior Associate Dean; Ph.D., Washington (Seattle).

Schools and Departments

School of Accountancy: A. Ronald Kucic, Director; Ph.D., NYU.
Franklin L. Burns School of Real Estate and Construction Management: Mark L. Levine, Director; LL.M., NYU; Ph.D., Century.
Reiman School of Finance: Louis D'Antonio, Co-Director; Ph.D., Colorado at Denver. Ron Rizzuto, Co-Director; Ph.D., NYU.
Department of Business Ethics and Legal Studies: Buie Seawell, Chair; J.D., Denver.
Department of Information Technology and Electronic Commerce: Richard Scudder, Chair; Ph.D., Colorado.
Department of Management: Dennis Wittmer, Chair; Ph.D., Syracuse.
Department of Marketing: Steven Hartley, Chair; Ph.D., Minnesota.
Department of Statistics and Operations Technology: Tony Hayter, Chair; Ph.D., Cornell.

Program Areas

Master of Business Administration: David Cox, Director of Graduate Programs; Ph.D., Texas Tech.
Executive M.B.A.: Barbara Kreisman, Director; Ph.D., Texas at Austin.
International M.B.A.: Douglas Allen, Director; Ph.D., Michigan.
Master of Science in Finance: Maclyn Clouse, Director; Ph.D., Washington (Seattle).
Master of Accountancy: A. Ronald Kucic, Director; Ph.D., NYU.
Master of Real Estate and Construction Management: Mark L. Levine, Director; LL.M., NYU; Ph.D., Century.
Master of Science in Information Technology: Richard Scudder, Director; Ph.D., Colorado.
Graduate Tax Program: Mark Vogel, Director; LL.M., Denver.

The Daniels College of Business building opened in 1999.

The picturesque Rocky Mountains near Denver.

UNIVERSITY OF HOUSTON–VICTORIA

School of Business Administration

Program of Study

The School of Business Administration (SoBA) at the University of Houston–Victoria (UH–Victoria) is accredited by AACSB International–The Association to Advance Collegiate Schools of Business, the hallmark of excellence in management education. It is committed to providing high-quality academic programs at all levels and ensuring that graduates possess the knowledge and skills necessary for successful careers in business and society. An integrated curriculum blends theoretical concepts with practical applications to ensure that students receive the knowledge and skills to successfully manage organizations in a dynamic environment. SoBA primarily serves nontraditional, working professional students.

UH–Victoria is a leader in online course delivery and offers all course work for the Master of Business Administration (M.B.A.) and the Global M.B.A. (G-M.B.A.) program entirely online. UH–Victoria offers the M.B.A. evening programs at two locations in the Houston metropolitan area—Sugar Land and Katy.

UH–Victoria's Fourth Year Bridge Program offers international students whose baccalaureate degrees were completed in three years (the equivalent of fewer than 120 credit hours) the opportunity to join either the M.B.A or G-M.B.A. program.

The M.B.A. curriculum is management-based, relevant, and highly integrated, using the strategic-planning process. The Global M.B.A. provides students with the knowledge and skills needed to function as managers in the global marketplace. Required courses use cases and projects to give students a real-world context for the program. Specifically, the program seeks to develop a student's capacity to understand and adapt to the changing business, political, and social environments; evaluate and respond to emerging threats and opportunities; interact with and effectively lead diverse groups; analyze and evaluate business operations and processes; and synthesize and apply cross-functional approaches to organizational issues. The program concludes with an M.B.A. conference that is held each fall and spring at a conference center in the Houston, Texas area, at which students participate in a team-case competition as part of the Seminar in Strategic Management course. The one-day M.B.A. conference is the only element of the program that cannot be completed online.

Students of the strategic M.B.A. must take 36 hours of core business courses, which include such courses as Economics for Managers, Management and Organizational Behavior, Business and Society, Financial Reporting and Analysis, and Management Information Systems. Students must also take 12 hours of elective courses to form a concentration in either accounting, finance, general business, international business, management, or marketing, for a total of 48 hours. The Global M.B.A. consists of up to 24 hours of foundation courses, 18 hours of core courses, and 12 hours of concentration courses in either finance or management. Students who have completed a B.B.A. degree in the last five years may qualify for up to 24 hours of foundation course waivers.

Research Facilities

The Victoria College/University of Houston–Victoria (VC/UHV) Library occupies an attractive three-story building with a seating capacity of more than 300. Professional librarians are available to assist in locating information and using the library's resources. Interlibrary loan, a full program of bibliographic instruction, electronic reserves, and an online catalog that is shared with the Victoria Public Library are available to all students and faculty members. The VC/UHV Library is committed to serving distance learners at the Sugar Land and Katy campuses and online.

The library's main collection contains more than 200,000 print volumes, more than 10,500 subscriptions to print and electronic journals, and more than 500,000 items on microforms. The library's audiovisual collection is located in the Media Library, which is on the third floor of UH–Victoria's University Center building. This facility houses approximately 7,500 audiovisual items, including compact discs, audiotapes, and videotapes. The Media Library houses the VC/UHV Library's collection of state-adopted textbooks and curriculum materials.

Financial Aid

Students may apply for financial aid, scholarships, and loans. Students are notified of any award or missing documents through "Awards by Web," which sends notices to the student's University e-mail address. There are limited opportunities for graduate assistantship positions within SoBA.

Cost of Study

The 2006–07 graduate tuition for Texas residents was $176 per semester credit hour, while nonresidents paid $401 per semester credit hour. In addition to tuition, all M.B.A. students must pay $97 per semester credit hour in additional fees. Fees for 2007–08 are not yet available.

Living and Housing Costs

UH–Victoria has no on-campus student housing. An apartment guide and maps of Victoria, Sugar Land, and Katy are available to prospective students.

Student Group

More than 600 students from the Coastal Bend region of Texas, around the country, and throughout the world are enrolled in UH–Victoria's M.B.A. programs each semester through live or online courses. The enrollment is characterized by diversity—geographically, ethnically, academically, and professionally. In fall 2006, of the 137 full-time students, 68 were women. The total enrollment included 377 students who were members of minority groups (124 African Americans, 149 Asian Americans or Pacific Islanders, 71 Hispanic Americans, and 33 international students).

Student Outcomes

SoBA graduates have found professional success in a variety of fields—not only in traditional business careers, such as public accounting and sales management, but also in careers that combine business education with a previous degree or experience in such fields as engineering, medicine, law, or education. Each graduate of the M.B.A. program emerges with a unique set of qualifications on which to build a successful career.

Location

Faculty members teach all of the M.B.A. courses in the evenings at three South Texas locations. Classes meet from 7 to 9:45 p.m. Monday through Thursday at Victoria and UH System Centers in Sugar Land and Cinco Ranch (Katy), which are approximately 30 miles west of downtown Houston. Students may blend online with face-to-face courses. Victoria, the center of the South Texas Crossroads in the heart of the Golden Gulf Coast, is an expanding historic city on the banks of the Guadalupe River. More than 150 years old, Victoria is one of the first three towns chartered by the new Republic when Texas won its independence from Mexico in 1836. Pioneer charm and high-tech industry mingle in the city of 62,000 near the Gulf of Mexico, on a popular coastal route between Houston and Mexico. The campus is approximately 90 miles from Houston, San Antonio, Austin, and Corpus Christi. Victoria is the home of many petrochemical companies, such as DuPont, Alcoa, and Dow. Surrounded by vast expanses of ranch lands owned by descendants of early Texas settlers, Victoria offers economic as well as cultural diversity.

The University

The University of Houston–Victoria is an upper-level institution that offers more than thirty undergraduate and graduate degree programs and concentrations to citizens in the Coastal Bend region. For three decades, UH–Victoria has proudly served the higher-education needs of the region through the School of Arts and Sciences, the School of Business Administration, and the School of Education. UH–Victoria and the UH System Centers in Sugar Land and Cinco Ranch (Katy) are home to an outstanding faculty and staff, whose members serve to enhance students' studies and University experience. The University emphasizes student learning, related research, responsiveness to student needs, and collaboration in the development and delivery of academic programs.

Applying

Applicants to the M.B.A. and G-M.B.A. program must have at least a four-year bachelor's degree in any field, with a minimum GPA of 2.5 (cumulative or last 60 hours, whichever is higher), and a GMAT score of at least 450 (verbal and quantitative scores combined). Students who do not meet the GMAT requirement may be eligible for temporary or conditional admission and take up to 12 hours of courses. Under certain circumstances, conditional admission may be granted without the GMAT to applicants who have an undergraduate GPA of 3.0 or higher and at least two years of relevant professional and/or management/supervisory experience. Conditional admission is subject to earning a B or better in QMS 6351 and MGT 6351. International students must also have a minimum TOEFL score of 550 (213 on the computer-based test) and are not eligible for conditional admission.

Applications, official transcripts, and official scores should be submitted to the Office of Admissions, University of Houston–Victoria, 3007 North Ben Wilson Street, Victoria, Texas 77901. International students should submit all application materials by June 1 for the fall semester, October 1 for the spring semester, and March 1 for the summer semester.

Correspondence and Information

Charles A. Bullock, Dean
School of Business Administration
University of Houston–Victoria
3007 North Ben Wilson Street
Victoria, Texas 77901
Phone: 800-687-4293 (toll free)
Fax: 361-570-4229
E-mail: busadvisor@uhv.edu
Web site: http://www.uhv.edu/bus/

University of Houston–Victoria

THE FACULTY

Accounting

Charles Bullock, Associate Professor and Dean; LL.M. (taxation), Denver, 1984; J.D., Texas Tech, 1982.
Jonathan Du, Assistant Professor; Ph.D. (international business and accounting), St. Louis, 2002.
Yong Lee, Assistant Professor; Ph.D. (accounting), Georgia State, 1993.
David Satava, Associate Professor; Ph.D. (accounting), Mississippi State, 1994.

Economics and Quantitative Management Science

Vera Adamchik, Assistant Professor; Ph.D. (business and economics), Lehigh, 1999.
Chien-Ping Chen, Assistant Professor; Ph.D. (economics), Houston, 1999.
Yong Glasure, Associate Professor; Ph.D. (economics), California, Santa Barbara, 1987.
Louie Ren, Associate Professor; Ph.D. (information system and quantitative science), Texas Tech, 1986.

Finance

Xavier Garza-Gomez, Assistant Professor; Ph.D. (economics), Nagoya City (Japan), 2001.
Massoud Metghalchi, Professor and Chair; Ph.D. (economics), Oklahoma State, 1981.
Yixi Ning, Assistant Professor; Ph.D., Southern Illinois Carbondale, 2004.

Management

Peggy Cloninger, Assistant Professor; Ph.D. (business administration), Georgia State, 2000.
Nigel Cohen, Adjunct Instructor; M.B.A. (management), Texas–Pan American, 2004.
Jun-Yeon Lee, Assistant Professor; M.S., Korean Advanced Institute of Science and Technology, 1993.
June Lu, Assistant Professor; Ph.D. (education), Georgia, 1995.
Nagarajan Ramamoorthy, Assistant Professor and Interim Chair; Ph.D. (business and management), Maryland, 1996.
Ronald J. Salazar, Visiting Assistant Professor; Ph.D., Texas at Austin, 1990.
Ron Sardessai, Professor; Ph.D. (management), North Texas, 1977.
T. T. (Rajan) Selvarajan, Assistant Professor; Ph.D., Arizona State, 2000.
David Summers, Assistant Professor; Ph.D. (organization theory and strategy), North Texas, 1998.
Jifu Wang, Assistant Professor; Ph.D. (management), Auburn, 2001.
Chun-Sheng Yu, Assistant Professor; Ph.D., Mississippi State, 1998.

Marketing

Joseph Ben-Ur, Associate Professor; Ph.D. (marketing), Illinois at Urbana–Champaign, 1997.
Linda Hayes, Assistant Professor; Ph.D. (marketing), Berkeley, 1991.
Ziad Swaidan, Assistant Professor; Ph.D., Mississippi, 1999.
James Walton, Assistant Professor; Ph.D., Texas Tech, 2001.

UNIVERSITY OF MISSOURI–COLUMBIA

College of Business

Programs of Study

The College of Business at the University of Missouri–Columbia (MU) offers fully accredited programs of study leading to the degrees of Doctor of Philosophy (Ph.D.) in business administration or accountancy, Master of Business Administration (M.B.A.), and Master of Accountancy (M.Acc.).

The Ph.D. programs in business administration and accountancy prepare graduates for careers as effective university researchers and teachers or for senior research positions in business or government. Business administration students may concentrate study in finance, management, or marketing. The Ph.D. programs are residential and full-time only, normally requiring four years beyond the master's degree.

The Gordon E. Crosby, Jr., M.B.A. program is flexible and individualized, designed to prepare superior graduate students for managerial careers in corporations or public organizations or as entrepreneurs. Course work may vary from 32 to 59 semester hours, depending on previous college work. Up to 6 hours of course work outside the College may be included, and students may develop individualized specialties. Dual-degree programs exist with health administration, industrial engineering, and law.

The M.Acc. program is a flexible program for superior graduate students interested in becoming high-level accounting professionals. It is a broadly based program that allows students to develop specialized expertise in financial accounting, auditing, information systems, and taxation. Most students in the M.Acc. program matriculate as part of the integrated 150-hour program in accountancy. Admission is limited and highly competitive.

Research Facilities

The collection of the University libraries includes 3.2 million volumes and 6.8 million microforms. Friendly, professional staff members are available to answer questions, help solve research problems, and support online and CD-ROM databases. Cornell Hall, a new state-of-the-art building, houses the College of Business. It features a building-wide wireless network, several three-station e-mail kiosks, a distance learning classroom with two-way video capabilities, and computer classrooms. Computer labs contain the latest versions of business software. Online databases available to graduates students include the Wharton Data Management System, including CRSP (Daily Stocks, Monthly Stocks, Mutual Funds, Monthly Bonds), Compustat (Annual Quarterly Industrial, Business and Geographic, Canadian Industrial Annual and Quarterly Executive Compensation, Global), I/B/ES, NYSE TAQ, ISSM, Thomson Financial, Eventus, Audit Analytics, IRRC, and First Call along with a number of other databases. The College also subscribes to AICPA, ARN, FARS, FEN, ERN, Government Account Research System, LIPPER, SDC Platinum, and Stock Trak.

Financial Aid

A large number of assistantships are available to qualified students. Master's assistantships involve 10 hours of work per week at a rate of $4667 per year and typically include a waiver of educational fees. Scholarships that may waive out-of-state tuition charges are also available. Scholarships, grants, and loans are available through the University of Missouri–Columbia Financial Aid Office. International students may qualify for financial support, and once enrolled at MU can apply for a Curator's Grant-in-Aid. Assistantships for Ph.D. students involve approximately 20 hours of work per week. Doctoral funding, including assistantships and scholarships, totals $17,833 annually, waives the educational fees, and continues for up to four years.

Cost of Study

For the academic year 2006–07, graduate students paid in-state or out-of-state educational fees of $276.40 or $734.09 per credit hour, respectively. Other miscellaneous fees of approximately $300 per semester and a supplemental College of Business fee of $32 per credit hour are also assessed.

Living and Housing Costs

MU has a number of excellent residence halls. Off-campus housing is also readily available. Housing costs are so reasonable that some MU students own their own homes. Estimated living expenses per year include $9000 for room and board and $3500 for books, supplies, and miscellaneous items.

Student Group

Of MU's more than 28,250 students, more than 5,000 are graduate students. During 2006–07, the College of Business enrolled approximately 300 master's candidates and 42 Ph.D. candidates. Students admitted to the College's graduate programs are committed to and capable of academic and professional success. Programs are kept small; the average class size is 25. College of Business graduate students represent colleges and universities in many U.S. states and a host of international countries.

Student Outcomes

Employment opportunities have been excellent for recent College of Business graduates. M.Acc. and M.B.A. graduates typically accept employment with Big 4 accounting and consulting firms, with medium-size and large firms based in the Midwest, or in entrepreneurial ventures. In the last ten years, most Ph.D. graduates in business and accountancy have entered teaching/research positions at a variety of national and regional universities.

Location

Columbia, located midway between St. Louis and Kansas City, is a warm, friendly, cosmopolitan, and safe college community with a population of more than 84,000. The city's growing economy and low unemployment rate offer job opportunities for student family members. Sidewalk restaurants, pubs and coffeehouses, and the quaint downtown shopping district are within three blocks of the campus and help make the community a pleasant place to live.

The University and The College

The University of Missouri–Columbia is the oldest state university west of the Mississippi River. MU is one of the most comprehensive and diverse universities in the nation, with 267 degree programs. It is classified as a Research Extensive Institution by the Carnegie Foundation for the Advancement of Teaching. MU is a premier provider of graduate and professional education. The College of Business was among the first in the nation to have accredited business programs. The College has more than 29,000 alumni, who can be found contributing their expertise to organizations in every state and in a multitude of international countries.

Applying

Applicants for graduate degree programs in accountancy or business administration are required to submit a score from the Graduate Management Admission Test (GMAT). Application deadlines and requirements vary by degree program.

Correspondence and Information

Director of the 150-Hour Accountancy Program (M.Acc.) or
    Director of Ph.D. in Accountancy
College of Business
303 Cornell Hall
University of Missouri–Columbia
Columbia, Missouri 65211

Phone: 573-882-4463
E-mail: accountancy@missouri.edu

Graduate Studies in Business
College of Business
213 Cornell Hall
University of Missouri–Columbia
Columbia, Missouri 65211

Phone: 573-882-2750
E-mail: grad@missouri.edu

University of Missouri–Columbia

THE FACULTY

Vairam Arunachalam, Professor of Accountancy and PricewaterhouseCoopers/Joseph A. Silvoso Distinguished Professor; Ph.D., Illinois, 1991.

Peter H. Bloch, Professor of Marketing; Ph.D., Texas at Austin, 1981.

Allen C. Bluedorn, Professor and Chair of Management and Emma S. Hibbs Distinguished Professor; Ph.D., Iowa, 1976.

Paul Brockman, Associate Professor of Finance and State Farm Risk Management Fellow; Ph.D., Louisiana State, 1994.

Todd H. Chiles, Assistant Professor of Management; Ph.D., Oregon, 1996.

Suraj Commuri, Assistant Professor of Marketing; Ph.D., Nebraska, 2001.

Thomas W. Dougherty, Professor of Management and Emma S. Hibbs/Harry Gunnison Brown Chair of Business and Economics; Ph.D., Houston, 1981.

Kenneth R. Evans, Professor of Marketing, Pinkney C. Walker Professor of Teaching Excellence, Associate Dean, and Director of Graduate Studies in Business; Ph.D., Colorado, 1980.

David Farber, Assistant Professor of Accountancy; Ph.D., Cornell, 2002.

Stephen P. Ferris, Professor of Finance; James Harvey Rogers Chair of Money, Credit, and Banking; and Director of the Financial Research Institute; Ph.D., Pittsburgh, 1984.

Jere R. Francis, Curators' Professor and KPMG Distinguished Research Professor; Ph.D., University of New England (Australia), 1982.

Charles R. Franz, Associate Professor of Management; Ph.D., Nebraska, 1979.

Lori S. Franz, Professor of Management; Ph.D., Nebraska, 1980.

Dan W. French, Professor and Chair of Finance; Ph.D., Louisiana Tech, 1979.

Srinath Gopalakrishna, Associate Professor of Marketing; Ph.D., Purdue, 1988.

Daniel W. Greening, Associate Professor of Management; Ph.D., Penn State, 1991.

Qing Hao, Assistant Professor of Finance; Ph.D., Florida, 2005.

Mark B. Houston, Associate Professor of Marketing and David and Judy O'Neal MBA Professor; Ph.D., Arizona State, 1995.

Thomas P. Howard, Joseph A. Silvoso Director of the School of Accountancy; Ph.D., Arizona State, 1978.

John S. Howe, Missouri Bankers Chair Professor of Finance and Chartered Financial Analyst; Ph.D., Purdue, 1981.

Arthur G. Jago, Professor of Management and Frances Ridge Gay MBA Professor; Ph.D., Yale, 1977.

Richard A. Johnson, Professor of Management and Emma S. Hibbs/Frederick C. Middlebush Chair in Entrepreneurship; Ph.D., Texas A&M, 1992.

Inder K. Khurana, Professor of Accountancy and Deloitte Professor; Ph.D., Arizona State, 1989.

Murali K. Mantrala, Sam M. Walton Professor of Marketing; Ph.D., Northwestern, 1987.

Elaine G. Mauldin, Associate Professor of Accountancy and BKD Professor; Ph.D., Nebraska, 1997.

Douglas D. Moesel, Associate Professor of Management; Ph.D., Texas A&M, 1996.

Sandra Mortal, Assistant Professor of Finance; Ph.D., Georgia, 2003.

William J. Moser, Assistant Professor of Accountancy; Ph.D., Arizona, 2005.

Loren A. Nikolai, Ernst & Young Distinguished Professor of Accountancy and Director of the Masters of Accountancy Program; Ph.D., Minnesota, 1973.

Raynolde Pereira, Assistant Professor of Accountancy; Ph.D., Arizona, 2001.

Jenice J. Prather-Kinsey, Associate Professor of Accountancy; Ph.D., Alabama, 1985.

Walter A. Puckett, Assistant Professor of Finance; Ph.D., Georgia, 2004.

S. Ratneshwar, Bailey K. Howard World Book Chair of Marketing and Department Chair; Ph.D., Vanderbilt, 1987.

Marsha L. Richins, Professor of Marketing and Myron Watkins Distinguished Professor; Ph.D., Texas at Austin, 1979.

Christopher Robert, Assistant Professor of Management; Ph.D., Illinois, 1998.

Lisa K. Scheer, Associate Professor of Marketing and Emma S. Hibbs Distinguished Professor; Ph.D., Northwestern, 1990.

Karen A. Schnatterly, Assistant Professor of Management; Ph.D., Michigan, 2000.

Kenneth W. Shaw, Associate Professor of Accountancy; Ph.D., Wisconsin, 1995.

Antonie Stam, Professor of Management and Legget and Platt Distinguished Professor of Information Systems; Ph.D., Kansas, 1986.

Christopher S. Tuggle, Assistant Professor of Management; Ph.D., Texas A&M, 2005.

Daniel B. Turban, Professor of Management and Stephen Furbacher Professor in Organizational Change; Ph.D., Houston, 1989.

Bruce J. Walker, Lansford Professor of Leadership and Dean of College of Business; Ph.D., Colorado, 1971.

James A. Wall Jr., Curator's Professor of Management; Ph.D., North Carolina, 1972.

David A. West, Professor of Finance and CTMT Scholar; Ph.D., Arkansas, 1961.

Patrick R. Wheeler, Assistant Professor of Accountancy; Ph.D., Georgia State, 1999.

Xuemin Yan, Assistant Professor of Finance; Ph.D., Iowa, 2001.

May H. Zhang, Assistant Professor of Accountancy; Ph.D., Texas at Austin, 2005.

Shaoming Zou, Associate Professor of Marketing; Ph.D., Michigan State, 1994.

THE BELK COLLEGE of BUSINESS
UNC CHARLOTTE

UNIVERSITY OF NORTH CAROLINA AT CHARLOTTE

The Belk College of Business
Doctoral Program in Business Administration
Master's Programs in Accountancy, Business Administration, Economics, and Mathematical Finance

Programs of Study

The Belk College of Business is accredited by AACSB International–The Association to Advance Collegiate Schools of Business and is one of only three schools in North Carolina to award business degrees at the bachelor's, master's, and doctoral levels. The Belk College offers four graduate degrees: Master of Accountancy (M.Acc.), Master of Business Administration (M.B.A.), M.B.A. in sports marketing and management, Master of Science (M.S.) in economics, and M.S. in mathematical finance. In addition, in fall 2006, the Belk College is scheduled to enroll its first cohort of students for the Ph.D. program in business administration with a major in finance.

The Master of Accountancy (M.Acc.) degree is a 30 credit-hour program designed to respond to the significant changes impacting the accounting profession. The program strengthens the technical competency of students in specialized accounting fields, including tax and financial accounting/auditing, and develops students' analytical and communication skills so they may advance in modern organizations. The M.Acc. program offers four curriculum tracks: Professional Accounting, for students with a non-accounting undergraduate degree who wish to become professional accountants and prepare for the CPA exam; Financial Accounting/Auditing, for accounting majors who wish to become CPAs; Tax, for CPAs and non-CPAs who wish to specialize in taxation; and Individualized, for students who wish to design a concentration based on a personal or professional interest. Graduates of this program are qualified for careers and advancement in taxation, public accounting, managerial accounting, and corporate financial accounting.

The M.B.A. program offers a comprehensive, 37-credit-hour curriculum for aspiring managers and leaders. With flexible course loads, a distinguished resident faculty, and academic concentrations, the UNC Charlotte M.B.A. program offers a top-quality program at an outstanding economic value. The M.B.A. is an evening program, with classes offered both on the main campus and at UNC Charlotte Uptown. With the flexible scheduling, students may take from one to four courses each semester. Students on the "fast track" can complete their M.B.A. in about eighteen months (taking three courses each semester and one course each summer session). Students on the "flexible track" can finish their degree at their own pace, taking anywhere from 2½ years or longer, if desired. The M.B.A. program admits students year-round, so students can begin during any of the four available terms.

The M.B.A. in sports marketing and management is designed to address the growing need for highly skilled business professionals in sports-related organizations. The program is delivered in a full-time two-year cohort-based format combining the strength and rigor of the M.B.A. with the application of this knowledge, though geared directly to the sports industry. A full-time six-month internship is required during the second year of the M.B.A. program, providing students with valuable hands-on experience from seasoned professionals.

In addition to the Charlotte-based programs, the Belk College offers a number of international M.B.A. programs, including a joint M.B.A. with EGADE in Monterrey, Mexico, and an Executive M.B.A. in Taiwan and Hong Kong.

The M.S. in Economics Program features a curriculum that is flexible yet thorough in its approach to theoretical training and applied course work. This 30-semester-hour program offers concentrations in economics and in finance. Students completing this program are prepared for analytical and management positions that require the integration of economic analysis and advanced quantitative methods. Employment opportunities for economists with a master's degree exist in both the public and private sectors. In addition, students with a master's degree may choose to pursue additional graduate education leading to a doctoral degree in economics or finance.

The M.S. in Mathematical Finance Program is designed to prepare students to pursue careers in finance. The 30-credit-hour program consists of 9 hours in mathematics, 9 hours in finance, 6 hours in economics courses, and 6 elective hours. The M.S. in Mathematical Finance Program is a joint program with the Departments of Economics and Finance in the Belk College of Business and the Department of Mathematics. Students take courses from all three departments in an integrated curriculum and may use electives to tailor the program to their specific interests.

The new Ph.D. in business administration with a major in finance offers a research-oriented curriculum and is designed to prepare graduates for academic teaching and research careers. The program includes core courses covering all business disciplines, combined with in-depth study in both the theoretical and empirical aspects of finance. Students minor in economics and complete a research-methods sequence in mathematics. They also teach undergraduate courses to receive training in pedagogy. Graduates will be qualified for tenure-track professor positions at both national and international teaching universities and other educational institutions.

Research Facilities

The Belk College makes its home in the Friday Building on the main campus of UNC Charlotte. Constructed in 1982 and expanded in 1995, the building holds lecture halls, classrooms, an interactive student trading room, faculty and administrative offices, computer labs, and a dedicated study and lounge area for graduate students.

Other facilities at UNC Charlotte include the J. Murray Atkins Library, the largest research library in the southeast Piedmont region. The library contains more than 1 million volumes and over 1 million microforms and subscribes to 14,000 periodicals, two thirds of which are accessible electronically. The library provides state-of-the-art information technologies, including wireless networking and 250 public computer stations for research. Atkins Library is a member of the Association of Southeastern Research Libraries (ASERL). UNC Charlotte also has a satellite campus in the center of the city, which is heavily utilized by Belk College graduate programs.

Financial Aid

The College offers a variety of need- and merit-based financial assistance opportunities for students, including scholarships, graduate assistantships, and tuition-remission awards. Additional information is available on the Belk College Web site.

Cost of Study

The 2006–07 tuition and fees for the M.Acc. and M.S. programs were $2137 per semester for full-time North Carolina resident graduate students and $7215 per semester for full-time nonresident students. M.B.A. program tuition and fees were $4637 per semester for full-time North Carolina residents and $9741 per semester for full-time nonresident students. These costs do not include books or supplies.

Living and Housing Costs

On-campus housing costs, including a campus meal plan, ranged from approximately $3000 to $4000 per semester for the 2006–07 academic year. Private apartments are also available near the University. Housing, food, and miscellaneous living expenses in the Charlotte area compare favorably with national averages.

Student Group

Graduate enrollment in the Belk College for fall 2006 was 561 students, which included 47 students enrolled in the international M.B.A. programs. In the Charlotte-based programs, 33 percent of students were women, approximately 7 percent were international, and 72 percent attended on a part-time basis. The Belk College graduate student body is diverse in age, race, gender, national origin, educational background, and work experience. Students bring a unique perspective and a wide range of professional backgrounds to the program, with alumni representing more than 200 different employers. Students range in age from 20 to 57 years, with an average age of 29.

Location

Known as the "Queen City," Charlotte is the twenty-sixth-largest city in the U.S. and the heart of the nation's fifth-largest urban region. *Fortune* magazine has ranked Charlotte as having the nation's best pro-business attitude. As the nation's second-largest banking center, Charlotte is a business location for more than 300 Fortune 500 companies, including nine corporate headquarters. The fifteen-county Charlotte region is home to 617 internationally owned firms, representing nearly 70 percent of those firms in North Carolina. More than 600,000 people reside within the city of Charlotte, and approximately 2 million people call the region around the city home.

Charlotte hosts a number of professional sports teams, including the NBA's Charlotte Bobcats and the NFL's Carolina Panthers. Automobile racing is an important local industry. Charlotte was recently selected to be the site of the NASCAR Hall of Fame, and Lowe's Motor Speedway is located just north of the UNC Charlotte campus. Residents of the Charlotte region enjoy a variety of arts and cultural resources, including the Mint Museums, the North Carolina Blumenthal Performing Arts Center, and Discovery Place. Charlotte-Mecklenburg's Arts and Science Council is the second-largest arts oversight group in the country.

Charlotte is located in the Piedmont of North Carolina, with a climate that is mild and sunny. The beautiful Blue Ridge Mountains are a 2-hour car ride away, and the beaches of North and South Carolina are about 3½ hours away. Some of the world's best golf courses are within in a few hours' drive of Charlotte.

The University and The College

A research-intensive university, UNC Charlotte is the fourth largest of the sixteen institutions within the University of North Carolina system and the largest institution in the Charlotte region. The University comprises seven professional colleges and currently offers sixteen doctoral programs, fifty-nine master's degree programs, and eighty-three programs leading to bachelor's degrees. There are more than 800 full-time faculty members, and the 2005 fall enrollment exceeded more than 20,700 students. UNC Charlotte has more than 75,000 living alumni and adds 4,000 to 4,500 new alumni each year.

UNC Charlotte has been educating future business leaders since the 1960s. Today, with more than 2,500 undergraduate students, 550 graduate students, 84 full-time faculty members, and more than 17,000 alumni, the Belk College of Business is one of the Carolinas' largest business programs. The Belk College provides a broad range of excellent undergraduate and graduate educational programs that are relevant to business practice and ethics and foster economic development. The College strongly supports the University's research mission by encouraging the creation of new knowledge and its dissemination through publication, teaching, and outreach activities. The College offers international programs that enhance educational opportunities for students and faculty members.

Applying

Applications are reviewed on an ongoing basis. The suggested deadlines for domestic students are May 1 for fall admission, October 1 for spring admission, and April 1 for summer admission. International students must apply by May 1 for fall admission and October 1 for spring. The GMAT is required for admission to the M.B.A., M.Acc., and Ph.D. programs. The GRE is required for admission to the economics program. The GRE or the GMAT is required for admission to the mathematical finance program. For additional information, students should contact the appropriate admissions office or visit the Belk College Web site.

Correspondence and Information

Belk College of Business
University of North Carolina at Charlotte
9201 University City Boulevard
Charlotte, North Carolina 28223

Phone: 704-687-2569
Fax: 704-687-2809
Web site: http://www.belkcollege.uncc.edu

Graduate Admissions
Phone: 704-687-3366
E-mail: gradadm@email.uncc.edu
Web site: http://www.uncc.edu/gradmiss

International Admissions
Phone: 704-687-2694
E-mail: intnladm@email.uncc.edu

University of North Carolina at Charlotte

THE FACULTY AND THEIR RESEARCH

Claude C. Lilly, Dean of the Belk College of Business (Finance); Ph.D., Georgia State. Insurance company operations, reinsurance, rate making, self-insurance.

Christie H. Amato (Marketing); Ph.D., Alabama. Marketing research and strategy.
Ted Amato (Economics); Ph.D., South Carolina. Antitrust, industrial relations, retailing.
Frank C. Barnes (BISOM); Ph.D., Georgia State. Synchronous manufacturing processes, computer-integrated manufacturing.
Joyce M. Beggs (Management); Ph.D., Tennessee, Knoxville. Business ethics, case writing, strategic management.
Surasakdi Bhamornsiri (Accounting); D.B.A., Tennessee, Knoxville. Financial accounting, managerial accounting.
Alan Blankley (Accounting); Ph.D., Texas A&M. Financial analysis, computer distribution channel financial performance issues, accounting information systems.
Cynthia Blanthorne (Accounting); Ph.D., Arizona State. Taxation.
Lloyd Blenman (Finance); Ph.D., Virginia Tech. International finance, financial markets, investments and asset pricing theory.
Charles D. Bodkin (Marketing); Ph.D., Virginia Tech. Retail strategy, salesperson behavior and performance.
Rosemary Booth (Management); Ph.D., Kentucky. Gender and management communication and media relations.
Hughlene A. Burton (Accounting); Ph.D., San Jose State. Corporate integration, tax policy, corporate and international tax issues.
Richard Buttimer (Finance); Ph.D., Georgia. Real estate finance/development, financial derivatives.
Fred H. Campbell (Marketing); Ph.D., North Carolina at Greensboro. Advertising, marketing strategy, health-care marketing, consumer marketing.
Claudio Carpano (Management); Ph.D., South Carolina. International strategy and competition.
Jack M. Cathey (Accounting); Ph.D., Virginia Tech; CPA. Microcomputers, EDI, internal control.
Steven P. Clark (Finance); Ph.D., Clemson. Mathematical finance, corporate finance, statistical modeling.
Richard M. Conboy (Management); Ph.D., Virginia Tech. Organizational structure and control, school finance, strategic planning.
John E. Connaughton (Economics); Ph.D., Northeastern. Forecasting.
W. Douglas Cooper (BISOM); Ph.D., North Carolina State. Decision support systems, synchronous manufacturing systems.
W. Young Davis (Economics); Ph.D., Georgia. Labor relations.
Nabil Elias (Accounting); Ph.D., Minnesota. Managing costing and reporting for sustainability, conflict resolution, intellectual capital.
Sunil Erevelles (Marketing); Ph.D., Ohio State. Marketing strategy, consumer behavior, brand management.
Frances H. Fabian (Management); Ph.D., Texas. Managerial cognition, information and knowledge.
John M. Gandar (Economics); Ph.D., Missouri. Applied macroeconomics; health, labor, and sports economics.
L. Howard Godfrey (Accounting); Ph.D., Alabama; CPA. Tax research, tax planning, evaluation of closely held companies.
Christine Henle (Management); Ph.D., Colorado State. Workplace deviance, organizational justice, employment law.
I. Edward Jernigan III (Management); D.B.A., Memphis State. Employment training.
David S. Kerr (Accounting); Ph.D., Michigan State. Accounting.
Moutaz J. Khouja (BISOM); Ph.D., Kent State. Materials management, computer-integrated manufacturing.
Gary F. Kohut (Management); Ph.D., Southern Illinois. Strategic and corporate communication.
Ram L. Kumar (BISOM); Ph.D., Maryland, College Park. Management of information systems.
Hwan-Chyang Lin (Economics); Ph.D., Illinois at Urbana-Champaign. Computational economics, international economics.
Gaines H. Liner (Economics); Ph.D., Clemson. Employment and age discrimination, econometric analysis.
Ronald A. Madsen (Economics); D.B.A., Arizona State. Regional development and labor force demographics.
Edward G. Malmgren (Accounting); Ph.D., Iowa. Financial accounting.
Michele Matherly (Accounting); Ph.D., Alabama. Accounting information systems auditing, managerial accounting.
Rob Roy McGregor (Economics); Ph.D., South Carolina. Monetary policy.
J. Jerome Miller (Finance and Business Law); J.D., Samford. Business law, corporate taxation, real property, regulatory environment.
Hermann A. Ndofor (Management); Ph.D., Wisconsin–Milwaukee. Competitive dynamics, entrepreneurship, strategic management.
Faith R. Neale (Finance); Ph.D., Florida State. Insurance industry regulation, insurer solvency, medical malpractice.
James F. Nebus (Management); Ph.D., South Carolina. International business, management of innovation, political economy.
Bennie H. Nunnally Jr. (Finance); D.B.A., Virginia. Small-business finance and valuation.
Steven Ott (Finance and Business Law); Ph.D., Wisconsin–Madison. Option pricing techniques.
Gordon H. Otto (BISOM); Ph.D., North Carolina State. Biostatistics, quality engineering.
Sungjune Park (BISOM); Ph.D., SUNY at Buffalo. Supply chain management, neural network applications.
Marcelo Pinheiro (Finance); Ph.D., Princeton. Applied theory, asset-pricing models, corporate finance.
Anthony Plath (Finance); D.B.A., Kent State. Banking, corporate finance, lending.
S. Douglas Pugh (Management); Ph.D., Tulane. Organizational climate and culture, customer service, layoffs, race and diversity issues.
Stanislav Radchenko (Economics); Ph.D., Rutgers. Time-series econometrics, Bayesian econometrics, industrial organization.
Stephanie S. Robbins (BISOM); Ph.D., Alabama/LSU. MIS for marketing.
Beth A. Rubin (Management); Ph.D., Indiana Bloomington. Workplace and economic restructuring, labor and market structures.
Judson Russell (Finance and Business Law); Ph.D., Alabama. Investments, capital markets, derivative securities.
Benjamin Russo (Economics); Ph.D., Iowa. Fiscal policy, federal tax policy, interest rates and saving.
Cem A. Saydam (BISOM); Ph.D., Clemson. Decision support systems and project management.
Richard G. Schroeder (Accounting); Ph.D., Arizona. Financial accounting, impact on behavior.
Peter M. Schwarz (Economics); Ph.D., Ohio State. Airline pricing/issues and privatization.
Calvin W. Sealey (Finance); Ph.D., Montreal. Banking and financial services industry.
Suzanne K. Sevin (Accounting); Ph.D., Georgia. Financial accounting, managerial accounting, capital markets.
Ellen M. Sewell (Economics); Ph.D., Florida. Applied microeconomics, industrial organization.
Alan T. Shao (Marketing); Ph.D., Alabama. International marketing and advertising.
Thomas H. Stevenson (Marketing); Ph.D., Case Western Reserve. Sales management issues.
Antonis C. Stylianou (BISOM); Ph.D., Kent State. Expert systems.
Chandrasekar Subramaniam (BISOM); Ph.D., Illinois at Urbana-Champaign. E-commerce, enterprise business processes, value and impact of IT.
Linda E. Swayne (Marketing); Ph.D., North Texas State. Strategic marketing and promotional strategies.
Louis A. Trosch (Finance and Business Law); J.D., West Virginia. Age and gender discrimination, business law, employment and discrimination law.
Jennifer Troyer (Economics); Ph.D., Florida State. Health economics, industrial organization, labor economics.
Irvin B. Tucker (Economics); Ph.D., South Carolina. Sports economics.
Hui-Kuan "Alice" Tseng (Economics); Ph.D., Illinois at Urbana-Champaign. Economic impact studies, international finance.
Casper Wiggins (Accounting); Ph.D., Tennessee, Knoxville. Accounting information systems.
Kelly L. Zellars (Management); Ph.D., Florida State. Job stress, personality and individual differences in organizations, equity in workplace.
Richard A. Zuber (Economics); Ph.D., Kentucky. Economics of sports and crime.

UNIVERSITY OF NOTRE DAME

Mendoza College of Business
Master of Business Administration Program

Programs of Study

The University of Notre Dame's M.B.A. program is solidly based on the vision of its founders—to help develop the student's fullest potential and send him or her forth to make a difference in the world. This is accomplished by developing in the student the following portfolio of skills: critical thinking, teamwork, effective communication, a global business perspective, and the manager's ability to make practical and ethical business decisions. With more than 100 elective courses, seven concentration tracks, and two formats, the Notre Dame M.B.A. program provides students with a challenging and flexible educational experience.

The Two-Year Program is appropriate for students with little or no academic background in business. In the first year of the program, students study the core business disciplines. The curriculum is integrated so that students learn to analyze situations from the vantage point of each of the functional areas. The second year allows students to select the concentration track that furthers their interests and future prospects. Students are required to complete 63 credit hours of work over four semesters.

The One-Year Program is designed for students who have an undergraduate degree in business. This program enables students to begin study in May and graduate the following May. Beginning with a ten-week summer semester, students attend intensive sessions in the core disciplines that are normally explored during the first year of the Two-Year Program. After the summer semester, students move directly into the second year of the Two-Year Program. They take courses in problem solving, business ethics, and strategic decision making while customizing the remainder of their elective courses by choosing courses from the seven concentration tracks. Students must complete 46 credit hours of work over eleven months.

The M.B.A. program utilizes two seven-week modules plus a one-week interterm module that provides students greater schedule flexibility and course selection. A signature course, Problem Solving, is required for all students. Working in teams, students diagnose organizational problems, disaggregate the critical issues, structure and execute the problem-solving effort, and then test the implementability of their proposed recommendation against a range of obstacles.

Every year, Notre Dame attracts corporate executives who speak on campus through a variety of lecture series and classroom visits. Some of the most interesting networking discussions take place in small classroom settings where students work directly with corporate executives on classroom projects. For example, in Organizational Consulting and through a number of Live Case interterm courses, students have the opportunity to test-drive their new problem-solving skills by tackling actual business problems for organizations such as GE, HP, and OfficeMax, developing the solutions and pitching ideas directly to the organization for feedback. Students in entrepreneurship work directly with start-ups from coast to coast to develop a business plan for their product or service ideas.

M.B.A. students can learn global perspectives firsthand by participating in one of several study-abroad programs in locations such as Europe, Asia, and South and Central America. Leading up to the study-abroad experience is an international business course. Students may also choose to spend a module in Santiago, Chile. Students who choose to study in Santiago begin with a two-week orientation, during which they are immersed in the Spanish language and the cultural norms and traditions of South America. Courses are conducted in English at the Universidad Alberto Hurtado by eminent Chilean business faculty members. Chile serves as an ideal laboratory for learning about developing economies. Included in the program are visits to the Ministry of Finance and the stock exchange as well as tours of nearby copper mines and vineyards. M.B.A. students can also participate in a summer internship in South Africa that combines service with valuable business experience. Through this outreach, students spend eight weeks in the townships of South Africa where they help small-business owners and entrepreneurs develop marketing and business plans.

Three joint-degree programs are available to M.B.A. students. Students may pursue a joint Master of Business Administration/Juris Doctor (M.B.A./J.D.) degree program that is offered jointly by the Mendoza College of Business and the Notre Dame Law School. Students can complete both degrees in a total of four years. Students must apply to each school separately and be accepted to both programs. A joint Five-Year M.B.A./Science Program and a joint Five-Year M.B.A./Engineering Program are also available.

Research Facilities

Notre Dame's state-of-the-art Mendoza College of Business complex, opened in 1995, features a multimedia amphitheater, a computer lab, a two-level M.B.A. lounge, team rooms equipped with networked computers, and Media-on-Call classrooms with computer controls and a fiber-optic network that provides faculty members with access to satellite feeds from major international networks. The Doermer Family M.B.A. Career Development Center opened in 1999 and is equipped with the latest videoconferencing technology. In August 2003, Mendoza opened the Giovanini Commons, an 8,500-square-foot facility. To facilitate communication, creative thinking, and group problem solving, the design allows for complete flexibility and customization.

Notre Dame is a campus without boundaries. Every student is linked to the University's advanced computer network and has instant desktop access to the latest versions of leading business application software. The Thomas J. Mahaffey Jr. Business Information Center (BIC) provides students with easy online access to complete electronic business resources, such as Dow Jones News Retrieval Service, LexisNexis, General BusinessFile ASAP, and Bridge real-time investment information. The Mendoza College of Business's Management Information Systems (MIS) Laboratory enables students to develop software applications, test innovative hardware and software configurations, and explore entrepreneurial opportunities that are based on information technology applications. In most classrooms, every seat is equipped with an Ethernet port for student access.

Financial Aid

Fellowships are awarded primarily on merit and are open to all domestic and international applicants. All applicants are considered for fellowship awards if they mark the appropriate box on the application. Loans and campus employment opportunities are available to qualified students through the University's Financial Aid Office.

Cost of Study

Tuition for the 2007–08 academic year is $35,490. Tuition for the 2007 ten-week summer semester was $14,200. Books and supplies average about $1500 per year.

Living and Housing Costs

Living expenses, including room, board, and personal expenses, total approximately $10,200 per academic year for an average single student living on or off campus. Married students should expect to increase their living expenses by about $400 a month.

Student Group

Notre Dame attracts high-caliber students from more than 200 undergraduate institutions, forty-eight states, and twenty-five countries. Approximately 26 percent of the student body are international students, 28 percent are from the Midwest, 19 percent are from the West, 10 percent are from the Northeast, 6 percent are from the South, 6 percent are from the Mid-Atlantic, and 5 percent are from the Southwest. The Two-Year students at Notre Dame represent a varied mix of undergraduate majors, including business, engineering, economics, math, science, and humanities. Notre Dame M.B.A. students range in age from 21 to 41 years, and they enter the program with an average of more than four years of meaningful work experience. More than 23 percent of the students are women, and roughly 18 percent of domestic students are members of minority groups.

Location

The University's 1,250-acre campus is situated immediately north of the city of South Bend, Indiana. The campus's twin lakes and many wooded areas provide a setting of natural beauty for more than 160 University buildings. With a population of approximately 265,000, South Bend has a familiar hometown feel yet is large and diverse enough to provide students with myriad cultural, shopping, and entertainment opportunities. The area is served by numerous city parks, golf courses, and county facilities that offer a variety of outdoor recreational activities. Medical and religious needs are adequately met by three hospitals and more than 300 churches and synagogues of all major denominations.

The University and The College

Notre Dame was founded in 1842 by Rev. Edward Frederick Sorin and 6 brothers of the French religious community known as the Congregation of Holy Cross. The total University enrollment is about 10,800 students, of whom approximately 8,038 are enrolled at the undergraduate level. The Law School, the graduate division of the Mendoza College of Business, and the Graduate School enroll a combined 2,762 students.

At Notre Dame, graduate business education is composed of three elements: thought leadership, action leadership, and values leadership. Through these three elements, students are mentored to become leaders who make the future better by the privilege of the positions they will hold, the decisions that they will make, the resources they will develop and use, and the people whose lives they will touch. This is the vision embedded in the founding of the University of Notre Dame by Father Edward Sorin, C.S.C., in 1842, and a dream that today continues to call forth the collective passion and energy of the faculty and staff members of the Mendoza College of Business.

Applying

The M.B.A. program seeks highly qualified and well-rounded applicants. Typically, there are three characteristics of incoming students that have proven to be reliable gauges of success in the Notre Dame M.B.A. program: a demonstrated history and aptitude for academic success, meaningful work experience, and leadership qualities that prove the student will be an active participant in the M.B.A. community. Because Notre Dame seeks well-rounded candidates, students are encouraged to apply even if their profile is atypical. The Graduate Management Admission Test (GMAT) is required for all applicants to the M.B.A. program. Average GMAT scores and GPA were 667 and 3.21, respectively, for the class of 2008. The Test of English as a Foreign Language (TOEFL) is required for all applicants who have not earned a bachelor's degree from an institution in the U.S., U.K., or Canada. Admission decisions are made on a rolling basis. Applicants must submit all application materials on or before May 1, with a decision mailed within thirty days after the application is received.

Correspondence and Information

M.B.A. Admission
276 Mendoza College of Business
University of Notre Dame
Notre Dame, Indiana 46556
Phone: 574-631-8488
        800-631-8488 (toll-free)
Fax: 574-631-8800
E-mail: mba.1@nd.edu
Web site: http://www.nd.edu/~mba/

University of Notre Dame

THE FACULTY AND THEIR RESEARCH

DEPARTMENT OF ACCOUNTANCY

Thomas J. Frecka, Vincent and Rose Lizzadro Professor of Accountancy; Ph.D., Syracuse. Financial reporting, financial statements analysis, accounting fraud investigation.

Jeff McGowan, Adjunct Instructor; M.B.A., Notre Dame.

H. Fred Mittelstaedt, Professor and PricewaterhouseCoopers Faculty Fellow; Ph.D., Illinois. Financial accounting, pension and retiree health benefits.

James O'Brien, Associate Professional Specialist; J.D., Notre Dame. Business law, federal and state taxation, nonprofit law/legal environment.

Margot O'Brien, Professional Specialist; J.D., Notre Dame. Business law.

Ramachandran Ramanan, Professor; Ph.D., Northwestern. Insider trading, management compensation, accounting choices.

Juan M. Rivera, Associate Professor; Ph.D., Illinois. International accounting, foreign exchange transactions, foreign reporting and disclosures, agribusiness and development, NAFTA.

Thomas Stober, Associate Professor and Assistant Chair; Ph.D., Chicago. Financial statements analysis, accounting-based valuation models, financial accounting and reporting, capital markets and accounting.

DEPARTMENT OF FINANCE

Robert Battalio, Associate Professor; Ph.D., Indiana. Trading costs in security markets, market design.

Jeffrey Bergstrand, Professor; Ph.D., Wisconsin. International trade and regional economic integration, foreign direct investment and multinational enterprises, macroeconomics, U.S. economy.

Shane A. Corwin, Viola D. Hank Associate Professor of Finance; Ph.D., Ohio State. Investments, market microstructure, investment banking.

John A. Halloran, Associate Professor; Ph.D., Washington (Seattle). Management of financial institutions, corporate finance, working capital management.

Michael L. Hemler, Associate Professor; Ph.D., Chicago; Ph.D., Washington (St. Louis). Financial derivatives, market timing.

Roger D. Huang, Kenneth R. Meyer Professor and Department Chair; Ph.D., Pennsylvania. International financial management, financial market microstructure.

Barry P. Keating, Jesse H. Jones Professor; Ph.D., Notre Dame. Business forecasting, experimental economics, economic regulation and government policy, not-for-profit organizations.

Jerry Langley, Professional Specialist; M.B.A., Northwestern. Banking, investment management, international finance, corporate finance.

Timothy Loughran, C. R. Smith Professor of Finance; Ph.D., Illinois at Urbana-Champaign. Behavioral finance, market microstructure.

Bill D. McDonald, Professor; Ph.D., Arizona State. Econometrics, capital markets.

Richard R. Mendenhall, Professor; Ph.D., Indiana. Stock market anomalies, stock market response to information, characteristics of analysts' forecasts.

Paul Schultz, John W. and Maude Clark Professor of Finance; M.B.A., Ph.D., Chicago. Corporate finance, market microstructure.

Frank K. Reilly, Bernard J. Hank Professor of Finance; Ph.D., Chicago. Security analysis, capital markets, credit analysis, security market indexes.

Joseph Rizzi, Adjunct Professor.

Paul Schultz, John W. and Maude Clark Professor of Finance; Ph.D., Chicago. Corporate finance, market microstructure.

Ann Sherman, Assistant Professor; Ph.D., Minnesota. Initial public offerings, shelf registration.

Katherine Spiess, Associate Professor; Ph.D., Missouri. Mergers and acquisitions, corporate financing decisions, initial public offerings.

Lee Tavis, C.R. Smith Emeritus Professor; D.B.A., Indiana. International financial management, international ethics.

DEPARTMENT OF MANAGEMENT

Robert Audi, David E. Gallo Professor of Business Ethics; Ph.D., Michigan. Ethics, theory, and applications, especially in business; theory of knowledge and justification; philosophy of action; philosophy of religion.

Viva Bartkus, Associate Professor; D.Phil., Oxford.

J. Michaels Bea, Adjunct Instructor; M.A., Minnesota.

Matt Bloom, Associate Professor; Ph.D., Cornell. Innovation and creativity, employee motivation, intrinsic motivation and employee engagement.

Robert Bretz, Joe and Jane Giovanini Professor of Management and Department Chair; Ph.D., Kansas. Job applicant decision processes, human resource management.

Kevin Butterbaugh, Adjunct Instructor; M.S., Indiana.

Sondra Byrnes, Associate Professional Specialist; J.D., Detroit.

Jay Caponigro, Concurrent Instructor and Director, Robinson Learning Center.

Sandra Collins, Associate Professional Specialist/Concurrent Assistant Professor; Ph.D., Notre Dame.

Edward J. Conlon, Edward Frederick Sorin Society Professor of Management and Associate Dean; Ph.D., Carnegie-Mellon. Organizational design, organizational behavior, decision making, conflict management.

J. Michael Crant, Professor; Ph.D., North Carolina at Chapel Hill. Proactive personality and behavior, organizational behavior, intrinsic and extrinsic motivation, personality and technology use.

Carolyn Crystal, Adjunct Professor.

John D'Arcy, Adjunct Professor.

James H. Davis, Associate Professor and Director of the Gigot Center for Entrepreneurial Studies; Ph.D., Iowa. Family business, entrepreneurship, corporate governance, strategic planning, trust, organizational social capital.

Sarv Devaraj, Viola D. Hank Associate Professor of Management; Ph.D., Minnesota. Management of technology, quality and productivity management, manufacturing strategy, electronic commerce, information technology payoff.

Samuel Gaglio, Concurrent Instructor and Assistant Dean; M.S., USC. Systems management.

David B. Hartvigsen, Professor; Ph.D., Carnegie-Mellon. Algorithms, operations research.

H. David Hayes, William Alexander Nolan Director in Family Business Enterprise; M.B.A., Notre Dame. Change/transition/organizational culture, human resources management, executive development, strategic planning, family business planning.

Rajesh Kothari, Adjunct Instructor.

Lee Krajewski, William and Cassie Daley Professor of Manufacturing Strategy; Ph.D., Wisconsin. Manufacturing strategy, supply chain management, operations management.

Khalil F. Matta, Professor and Director of Management Information Systems Programs; Ph.D., Notre Dame. Total quality management, strategic use of information systems, inventory management.

Mark Noeldner, Adjunct Instructor; M.A., Marquette.

James O'Rourke IV, Professional Specialist and Concurrent Professor and Arthur F. and Mary J. O'Neil Director, Eugene D. Fanning Center for Business Communication; Ph.D., Syracuse. Corporate communication, reputation management, public speaking, business writing.

Gerard Pannekoek, Adjunct Instructor.

Theresa Sedlack, Program Manager, Gigot Center for Entrepreneurial Studies.

Ann Tenbrunsel, Professor and Arthur F. and Mary J. O'Neil Co-Director of the Institute for Ethical Business Worldwide; Ph.D., Northwestern. Decision making, negotiations, ethics.

Jerry Cheyung Wei, Associate Professor; Ph.D., Texas A&M. Supply chain integration, manufacturing planning and control, international operations, lean process design and analysis.

Kevin White, Associate Professor and Athletic Director; Ph.D., Southern Illinois. Sports business.

Charles Wood, Assistant Professor; Ph.D. Java, C++, ASP, and XML programming; seller behavior in electronic commerce; electronic commerce and Internet dynamics.

Xuying Zhao, Assistant Professor; Ph.D., Texas at Dallas. Interface between operations and marketing, supply chain optimization, computational economics (including mechanism design and game theory).

DEPARTMENT OF MARKETING

W. S. Dee, Adjunct Professor.

Sandra DuCoffe, Adjunct Instructor.

Georges Enderle, Professor of International Business Ethics and John T. Ryan, Jr., Chair in Business Ethics; Dr. habil., St. Gallen; Dr. rer. pol., Fribourg. Corporate ethics, business ethics, managerial ethical leadership, international issues.

Yusaku Furuhashi, Ray W. and Kenneth G. Herrick Professor Emeritus of Business Administration; M.B.A., Washington (Seattle); Ph.D., Illinois. Comparative business and management; international trade, business, and marketing.

Timothy Gilbride, Assistant Professor; Ph.D., Ohio State. Discrete choice models, Bayesian applications in marketing, noncompensatory decision models.

Yoshiko Green, Adjunct Professor.

Joseph P. Guiltinan, Professor; D.B.A., Indiana. Pricing, marketing strategy, new-product marketing.

Elizabeth S. Moore, Notre Dame Associate Professor of Marketing; Ph.D., Florida. Marketing and society, marketing to children, intergenerational studies.

Patrick E. Murphy, Professor and C. R. Smith Co-Director of the Institute for Ethical Business Worldwide; Ph.D., Houston. Business and marketing ethics, public policy issues in marketing.

Carol Phillips, Adjunct Instructor; M.A., Michigan State. Brand strategy and research, brand ROI, online qualitative and quantitative research.

Joan M. Phillips, Assistant Professor; Ph.D., Illinois at Urbana-Champaign. Interorganizational relationships, marketing and society, survey research methodology.

Constance Porter, Assistant Professor; Ph.D., Georgia State. Trust and relationship marketing, virtual communities and interactive marketing, and technology adoption, acceptance, and use.

John F. Sherry Jr., Raymond W. and Kenneth G. Herrick Professor of Marketing and Department Chair; Ph.D., Illinois at Urbana-Champaign. Consumer experience, symbolic communication, ethnographic methods, cultural analysis, servicescapes.

Joel Urbany, Professor; Ph.D., Ohio State. Buyer information search and price perception, information economics, price competition, competitive conjecture and decision making.

John A. Weber, Associate Professor; Ph.D., Wisconsin. Value-based marketing, business-to-business marketing, integrity in selling, marketing and selling complex solutions.

William L. Wilkie, Aloysius and Eleanor Nathe Professor of Marketing; Ph.D., Stanford. Consumer behavior, marketing and society, public policy issues, advertising.

EXECUTIVE EDUCATION

Joseph Holt, Concurrent Assistant Professor.

RESEARCH CENTERS

The **Center for Accounting Research and Education** supports domestic and international faculty members in the creation and dissemination of accounting knowledge in order to strengthen the bridges between accounting research, accounting education, and accounting practice. (http://www.nd.edu/~carecob/)

The **Center for Ethics and Religious Values** seeks to strengthen ethical foundations in business and public policy decisions by fostering dialogue among academic and corporate leaders, as well as through research and publications. The center's ethics curriculum is integrated throughout Notre Dame's business course work. (http://www.nd.edu/~ethics)

The **Fanning Center for Business Communication** provides course work in all facets of human communication, from writing and speaking to listening and group interaction. In addition to classroom success, Fanning center faculty members have also earned an international reputation for their research and publications. (http://www.nd.edu/~fanning/)

The **Gigot Center for Entrepreneurial Studies** fosters innovation among current and aspiring entrepreneurs. Through a unique curriculum, business plan competitions, and mentoring opportunities with Notre Dame alumni, students gain vital experience and the skills necessary to build successful businesses. (http://www.nd.edu/~entrep/)

The **Institute for Ethical Business Worldwide** seeks to promote positive illustrations of ethical and socially responsible business conduct throughout the world. The importance of ethical leadership as a cornerstone to building a stronger sense of integrity and values into all business firms is stressed. (http://www.ethicalbusiness.nd.edu/)

UNIVERSITY OF OKLAHOMA

The Michael F. Price College of Business

Programs of Study

The Michael F. Price College of Business at the University of Oklahoma (OU) offers the following graduate programs: the Master of Business Administration (M.B.A.), the Master of Accountancy (M.Acc.), the Master of Science in Management Information Systems (M.S. in MIS), and the Doctor of Philosophy (Ph.D.). Dual-degree programs offered are M.B.A./M.S. in MIS, M.B.A./J.D., M.B.A./M.S. in mathematics, M.B.A./M.A. in language (French, German, Spanish), M.B.A./M.S. in pharmacy administration, M.B.A./Master of Library and Information Studies, M.B.A./M.S. in construction administration, M.B.A./Master of Public Health, and M.B.A./M.S. in public health administration. For the dual-degree programs, applicants must apply and be admitted to each program separately. Programs in the Michael F. Price College of Business are fully accredited by AACSB International–The Association to Advance Collegiate Schools of Business.

The full-time M.B.A. is a 42-credit-hour, twenty-one-month program, with all courses taken at the graduate level. The Professional M.B.A. requires 42 to 54 credit hours, depending on the student's undergraduate background. All courses are at the graduate level and are offered in the evening. Both programs require that the student become familiar with the functional areas of business, the necessary tools for management decision making, and the environment in which business firms operate. Knowledge prerequisites include an introduction to calculus, matrix algebra, and linear programming; computer familiarity; and communication skills. Students from all undergraduate majors are encouraged to apply.

The M.Acc. is a 33-hour program for students with an undergraduate degree in accounting from a program accredited by AACSB International. Other students may enter this program, but they must take a minimum of 24 hours of undergraduate accounting courses as well as other core business courses. The core business courses are all graduate courses. The Master of Accountancy is a terminal professional degree.

The M.S. in MIS is a 33-hour program designed for people with an undergraduate degree in a discipline other than MIS who wish to embark on a career as information system analysts or designers. The program combines a solid base of business and organizational knowledge with an in-depth exposure to information systems technologies. The curriculum contains 12 to 15 hours of graduate business courses and 18 to 21 hours of graduate MIS courses. In addition, candidates must demonstrate competency in two programming languages. The M.S. in MIS program admits a small number of highly qualified students.

The full-time Ph.D. program is small and research oriented. The program requires a minimum of 90 graduate hours past a bachelor's degree. Eighteen hours of course work are stipulated; most degree requirements and major and supporting fields are determined on an individual basis. Close association with faculty members, as well as early research involvement, is standard. Doctoral students normally receive financial aid. Doctoral majors are available in accounting, finance, management, management information systems, and marketing/supply chain management. A master's degree is not required to enter the doctoral program.

Research Facilities

Research facilities that are available to graduate students include an extensive University library, the Amoco Business Resource Information Center, a graduate computer lab, the Bass Business History Collection, the Oklahoma University Research Institute, the Center for Economic and Management Research, and extensive computer facilities.

Financial Aid

Graduate assistantships of up to $15,300 a year, special instructorships, fellowships and scholarships, and tuition-waiver scholarships are available for qualified graduate students. Graduate assistantships may include a partial waiver of resident and nonresident tuition.

Cost of Study

Tuition in 2006–07 for full-time state residents was $215 per credit hour; nonresident students paid $555 per credit hour. Books and supplies are estimated at $1250 per academic year; other fees vary by program.

Living and Housing Costs

Many graduate students live on campus in one of the University's three apartment complexes or in the residence halls. Prices for apartments vary from $475 to $1000 per month. Room and board rates for the residence halls are approximately $3100 for one semester. For more information, students should call 405-325-2511 or visit the Web site at http://www.housing.ou.edu.

Student Group

Typically, 33 percent of an M.B.A. class consists of business majors, 29 percent engineering majors, and the remainder science and humanities majors. More than 60 percent have two years or more of work experience. The average age is 27, and approximately 30 percent are women. There are generally 300 to 350 graduate students in the College.

Location

Although part of the Oklahoma City metropolitan area, Norman began and continues as an independent community with a permanent population of nearly 105,000. It has extensive parks and recreation programs, a 10,000-acre lake and park area, a community theater, an art center and art league, and other amenities of a university town. Norman is minutes from downtown Oklahoma City and 3 hours from Dallas. Summers are hot with high humidity, and winters are mild to cold.

The University

The University of Oklahoma, which was founded in 1890, is a doctoral-degree-granting research university. The Norman campus serves as home to all of the University's academic programs, except health-related fields. Both the Norman and Health Sciences Center Colleges offer programs at the Schusterman Center, the site of OU-Tulsa. OU enrolls more than 31,000 students, has more than 2,000 full-time faculty members, and has twenty colleges offering 153 majors at the baccalaureate level, 133 majors at the master's level, seventy-five majors at the doctoral level, twenty majors at the first-professional level, and eighteen graduate certificates.

Applying

There is a nonrefundable application processing fee of $40 for U.S. citizens and permanent residents and $90 for international applicants. Admission is open to qualified individuals holding a bachelor's degree from an accredited college or university who show high promise of success in graduate study. Applicants need not have undergraduate backgrounds in business. All applicants must submit satisfactory scores on the Graduate Management Admission Test (GMAT). International applicants must submit satisfactory scores on the Test of English as a Foreign Language (TOEFL) or the Cambridge IELTS. In addition, the Test of Spoken English (TSE) is required of international applicants to the Ph.D. program. Letters of recommendation are required for all applicants.

Students may enter the fall semester beginning in late August, the spring semester beginning in early January, or the eight-week summer session beginning in early June. Students may only enter the full-time M.B.A. program, M.S. in MIS program, and doctoral programs in the fall semester.

Correspondence and Information

Graduate Programs Office
Michael F. Price College of Business
1003 Asp Avenue, Suite 1040
University of Oklahoma
Norman, Oklahoma 73019-4302

Phone: 405-325-4107
Fax: 405-325-7753
E-mail: ougpo@ou.edu
Web site: http://price.ou.edu/mba/

University of Oklahoma

THE FACULTY AND THEIR RESEARCH

Frances L. Ayres, John W. Jr. and Barbara J. Branch Professor of Accounting and Director, School of Accounting; Ph.D., Iowa. Financial accounting, tax policy.

Samir Barman, Ph.D., Clemson. Production/operations, job scheduling, inventory modeling.

Mark Bolino, Ph.D., South Carolina. Organizational behavior, international business.

Michael R. Buckley, Tom G. Clark Presidential Professor and Director, Division of Management; Ph.D., Auburn. Human resource management, performance appraisal, interviewing.

Lowell A. Busenitz, McCasland Foundation Professor of American Free Enterprise; Ph.D., Texas A&M. Strategic management, entrepreneurship.

Traci A. Carte, Ph.D., Georgia. Systems implementation.

Laku Chidambaram, Wood Professor of Management Information Systems; Ph.D., Indiana. W. P. Application of information technology.

Terry L. Crain, Dale Looper Chair in Accounting; Ph.D., Texas Tech. Taxpayer compliance and policy, estate taxation and international taxation.

Andrew D. Cuccia, Ph.D., Florida. Judgment and decision making.

Robert C. Dauffenbach, Director, Center for Economic and Management Research and Associate Dean for Graduate Programs and Research; Ph.D., Illinois at Urbana-Champaign. Regional economics and business.

Patricia J. Daugherty, Director, Division of Marketing and Supply Chain Management, and Robin Siegfried Centennial Chair of Marketing and Supply Chain Management; Ph.D., Michigan State. Logistical trends, supply chain management.

Parthiban David, Rath Chair in Strategic Management; Ph.D., Texas A&M. Corporate governance, strategy and firm performance.

Louis H. Ederington, Michael F. Price Chair in Finance; Ph.D., Washington (St. Louis). Fixed-income securities, futures and options, financial markets and institutions, interest rate structure.

Gary W. Emery, Michael F. Price College of Business Professor in Finance and Senior Associate Dean; Ph.D., Kansas. Corporate finance and investments.

Chitru S. Fernando, Ph.D., Pennsylvania. Corporate and international finance, energy markets and regulation, financial markets and risk management.

Dipankar Ghosh, Ph.D., Penn State. Managerial accounting, accounting information for judgment and decision making, transfer pricing and negotiation.

Evgenia Golubeva, Ph.D., Utah. Asset pricing and market microstructure.

H. Ann Hamilton, Accounting Coordinator of Student Relations; M.B.A., Oklahoma.

John A. Hobbs, Coordinator of Applied Business Programs; M.L.A., Oklahoma City.

Kevan L. Jensen, Ph.D., Florida. Market for audit services both as a control mechanism and as a provider of assurance.

Richard A. Johnson, Ph.D., Texas A&M. Corporate restructuring and governance, international business, strategic management and corporate social performance.

Jack J. Kasulis, Associate Dean for Undergraduate Programs; Ph.D., Northwestern. Consumer behavior, channels of distribution and retailing strategy.

Carol A. Knapp, Ph.D., Oklahoma. Judgment and decision making in the context of auditing and fraud detection by auditors.

M. Chris Knapp, McLaughlin Chair in Business Ethics; Ph.D., Oklahoma. Policy issues related to the professional practice of public accounting and behavioral issues concerning the author-client dyad.

Timothy D. Landry, Ph.D., Missouri. Electronic business, including customer relationships and Internet communities, interpersonal dynamics in sales and service encounters, and technology's impact on boundary-spanning employees.

Scott Linn, Hindman Professor of Finance; Ph.D., Purdue. Corporate finance; corporate governance; corporate control; capital markets and security pricing and behavior; risk management, including investment and portfolio management; behavior of intermediaries in real markets.

Marlys Gascho Lipe, Rath Chair in Accounting; Ph.D., Chicago. Judgment and decision making.

Robert C. Lipe, KPMG Centennial Professor in Accounting; Ph.D., Chicago. Corporate financial reports.

Anne M. Magro, Ph.D., Illinois at Urbana-Champaign. Characteristics and development of expertise and the effects of institutional and task characteristics on information processing.

William L. Megginson, Rainbolt Chair in Finance; Ph.D., Florida State. International finance and corporate finance issues.

Soonhong Min, Ph.D., Tennessee. The marketing concept and a market orientation in a channel setting, supply chain management, marketing and logistics strategic interface and buyer-seller relationships.

Shaila Miranda, Ph.D., Georgia. Outsourcing, electronic collaboration, knowledge management and sociological and organizational theory.

John Robert Mitchell, Ph.D., Indiana. Entrepreneurial cognition, focusing specifically on how thinking shapes and is affected by entrepreneurial behaviors and outcomes.

Ning Nan, Ph.D., Michigan. Behavioral and economic factors in management information systems.

Daniel T. Ostas, James G. Harlow Jr. Chair in Business Ethics and Community Service; Ph.D., J.D., Indiana. Economic analysis of marketplace ethics, institutional economic analysis of law and corporate social responsibility.

R. Leon Price, D.B.A., Oklahoma. Management information systems, systems analysis and design and computer auditing.

David A. Ralston, Price Chair in International Business; D.B.A., Florida State. Cross-cultural management.

Manonita M. Ratwatte, M.S., Georgia. IT issues in developing nations, e-commerce opportunities for poor nations, and overcoming technology barriers.

Nim Razook Jr., J.D., Oklahoma. The legal environment, ethics, commercial law.

Anthony S. Roath, Ph.D., Michigan State. Efficiency of global logistics systems and relationship management of cross-border alliances.

Craig J. Russell, Ph.D., Iowa. Advancing theory and practice in the selection and development of organizational leaders.

Fran McKee Ryan, Ph.D., Arizona State. Unemployment and helping employees through difficult transitions, such as the job-loss experience.

Jeffrey B. Schmidt, Ph.D., Michigan. Managerial decision making during new product development, new product performance, adaptation of products for international markets, and marketing strategy.

A. B. Schwarzkopf, Ph.D., Virginia. Database and end-user computing applications.

Teresa Shaft, Ph.D., Penn State. Cognitive processes used by IS professionals during systems development and maintenance and the role of IS in environmental management.

Mark Sharfman, Ph.D., Arizona. How the business environment affects the firm, how the firm affects the natural environment, and how firms manage the social issues they face in the business environment.

Rajeev Sharma, Ph.D., New South Wales (Australia). Implementation of IS innovations, management of IS projects, strategic management of IS.

Ford Smith, M.B.A., Texas.

Bryan E. Stanhouse, Director, Division of Finance; Ph.D., Illinois at Urbana-Champaign. Impact of learning on risky asset prices and information economics.

Duane R. Stock, Michael F. Price Student Managed Investment Fund Professor; Ph.D., Illinois at Urbana-Champaign. Corporate bonds, municipal bonds, options, interest rate risk and banking.

Wayne Thomas, John W. Mertes, Jr. Presidential Professor; Ph.D., Oklahoma State. Market-based accounting research, earnings management, time-series properties of earnings and earnings components, segment disclosures, financial statement analysis and international accounting issues.

Vahap Bulent Uysal, Ph.D., Texas. Corporate finance, capital structure, mergers and acquisitions.

Jeffrey P. Wallman, Ph.D., Wisconsin–Madison. Marketing strategies and strategy on performance.

G. Lee Willinger, John F. Stambaugh Centennial Professor of Accounting; D.B.A., Florida State. Financial accounting, empirical research in accounting and accounting theory.

Pradeep K. Yadav, W. Ross Johnston Chair in Finance; Ph.D., Texas. Market microstructure; derivatives, including risk management, index futures pricing, early exercise premiums, and implied distributions; ownership structure and corporate governance; mergers and acquisitions; performance of managed funds.

Han Yi, Ph.D., Michigan State. Financial reporting—causes and consequences of accounting choices, earnings management and benchmarks, and financial reporting regulations.

Robert W. Zmud, Michael F. Price Chair in Management Information Systems and Director, Division of Management Information Systems; Ph.D., Arizona. Impact of IT in facilitating organizational behaviors and organizational efforts involved with planning, managing, and diffusing information technology.

UNIVERSITY OF OTTAWA

Telfer School of Management
Master of Business Administration

Programs of Study

The Telfer School of Management M.B.A. program is an intensive and challenging program that prepares talented professionals to become accomplished managers and business leaders. Ideally located in Canada's capital, at the crossroads of business, trade, policy, and government, the Telfer M.B.A. links modern management theory and practice by offering exciting and unique opportunities to complete a major consulting project with an industry or public-sector partner. The M.B.A. experience in Ottawa is rooted in the application of technology and the integration of management skills, strategic thinking, leadership, and teamwork in a multicultural global framework. The program provides a strong foundation in all management disciplines, develops management and people skills, and refines the students' abilities to review and analyze issues, opportunities, and situations from a strategic perspective, allowing them to become responsible agents of change. Emphasis is placed on relevant, contemporary management models and philosophies with an integrated approach to problem solving. Program delivery is unique in its flexibility. It offers full- and part-time study, allowing students to complete the degree requirements in as little as twelve months or to spread out their studies as long as sixty months. The program is offered in English or in French, and students may complete elective courses in either language. It offers courses in a variety of formats, from the 36-hour, full-course delivery over twelve weeks with day or evening classes, to the 18-hour half course delivered intensively over a weekend. There are also opportunities to undertake directed readings or a thesis.

Using the extensive network within the local business community and the public sector, students must complete a major project under the supervision of a faculty member and the mentorship of a Certified Management Consultant from the Canadian Association of Management (CAMC) and an executive from the host organization as they apply their newly acquired knowledge and skills, balance theory and practice, and gain valuable management experience. Recent projects have been completed for Adobe, Fasken Martineau DuMoulin LLP, Foreign Affairs Canada, International Trade Canada, Live Work Learn Play LLP, Lumenera Corporation, March Networks, Nature Canada, National Research Council (NRC), PAI Medical Group, Volvo Cars of Canada, Yellow Pages/Pages Jaunes.

Work groups composed of students with different academic and professional profiles are carefully created by the program. As they progress through the core modules of the program within their work group, students are exposed to all the basic management disciplines and develop the skills to think strategically.

The Telfer M.B.A. draws students from around the world, from a variety of educational backgrounds and professional experiences. It is designed to build on the diversity and wealth of its students' profiles. A cohort environment allows students to work and learn together, benefiting from each other's strengths, capabilities, and experiences. Students participate in national and international case competitions annually. The strong performance of the School's M.B.A. teams over the years is a reflection of the excellence of its students and of the high quality of the Telfer M.B.A.

Other graduate management programs include the Executive M.B.A. (EMBA), a twenty-one-month program with classes one day a week; the Master of Health Administration (M.H.A.), a sixteen-month program that includes a four-month administrative residency; the Master of Science in management (M.Sc.); the Master of Science in Health Systems (M.Sc.); and e-commerce and e-business graduate certificates.

Research Facilities

The Telfer School has recently moved in the new Desmarais Building. This twelve-storey structure offers management students an unparalleled learning environment.

The Telfer School fosters the development of the students' high-tech skills by providing them with state-of-the-art computing and teaching facilities. From private rooms to multimedia labs and teaching rooms, students can prepare their assignments using common and specialized software, advanced financial and accounting databases, the Internet, electronic mail, and the computerized libraries of the University.

A dedicated Management Library ensure that students can access—directly and easily—indispensable learning materials, such as all the latest academic journals and trade publications and the increasing number of online databases and electronic resources applied to management

The Telfer School of Management has a state-of-the-art Career Centre dedicated exclusively to management students. The purpose of the Career Centre is to partner with students, alumni, and employers in order to create employment opportunities, enhance student value, and facilitate the employers' recruitment process. The center organizes and assists with career fairs, company information sessions, workshops, and networking events. Employers post jobs on the Career Centre's Web site in order to offer employment opportunities for full-time, part-time, and summer job positions. Interested students can visit the Web site at http://www.telfer.uOttawa.ca/careercentre/.

The University also offers a variety of services and resources that contribute to the student's professional development and success in achieving career goals.

Financial Aid

The Telfer School of Management's goal is to attract top quality candidates to its M.B.A. program. Numerous scholarships are awarded, which reflects the Telfer School's ongoing commitment to reward exceptional students for their academic successes and achievements. To learn more about scholarships and awards, students should visit the Web site at http://www.telfer.uOttawa.ca.

Canadian citizens and permanent residents in need of financial aid can apply for government assistance. The Telfer School of Management provides funds for teaching assistants and research assistants. The University also offers various awards primarily for Canadian citizens or permanent residents who intend to pursue or are pursuing full-time graduate studies.

Cost of Study

Tuition for a full-time M.B.A. program (three semesters) is Can$15,145 for Canadian students and Can$24,960 for international students. For part-time students, tuition is Can$281 per credit, with 54 credits needed.

Living and Housing Costs

Other estimated costs for the academic year include housing (off campus), Can$6000; food, Can$4800; books, Can$1500; and for non-Canadians, health insurance, Can$750.

Location

In the heart of the nation's capital in Silicon Valley North, Canada's highest concentration of high-tech and telecommunications firms, the Telfer School of Management at the University of Ottawa is at the center of an extensive group of government and private organizations that drive most of Canada's business and trade nationally and internationally. The main campus covers an area of 1 kilometer by ½ kilometer, bordering the Rideau Canal, near the downtown core. The campus is within walking distance of shopping malls, restaurants, cinemas, and museums.

The University and The School

The University of Ottawa is a cosmopolitan campus where nearly 31,500 students from a variety of cultural heritages live and learn in an atmosphere of tolerance and understanding. International students benefit from the University's long tradition of excellence in teaching and research while learning about the multicultural Canadian social mosaic. The Telfer School of Management provides a rich educational experience, both inside and outside the classroom, that prepares students to be leaders in the new global, knowledge-based economy. The School's graduates are in demand by high-technology companies, leading consulting firms, financial institutions, and public-sector organizations in Canada and abroad. The Telfer School of Management at the University of Ottawa received accreditation from AACSB International in 2003 and from AMBA in 2005. It is the only Ottawa-based business school to be recognized by these prestigious international organizations.

Applying

Admission to the Ottawa M.B.A. program is competitive and granted to candidates who clearly demonstrate high promise of success. The admission requirements are: a baccalaureate degree with at least a B or a 70 percent overall standing, at least two years of full-time work experience, and at least a 50th percentile score on the GMAT. Application deadlines are January 1 for international students and April 1 for students from the United States and Canada. Students should allow four to six weeks for notification. Preference is given to candidates who have greater work experience, particularly where there is evidence of career progression.

Correspondence and Information

Master of Business Administration (M.B.A.)
University of Ottawa Telfer School of Management
55 Laurier Avenue East
Ottawa, Ontario K1N 6N5
Canada
Phone: 613-562-5884
         800-965-5512 (toll-free)
Fax: 613-562-5912
E-mail: mba@telfer.uottawa.ca
Web site: http://www.mba.uOttawa.ca

University of Ottawa

THE FACULTY

Many of the School's faculty members serve as consultants to major corporations and government organizations around the world. Holders of numerous teaching and research awards, the professors combine excellence in teaching with outstanding scholarship.

Administration

Dean: Micheál J. Kelly, Professor; Ph.D., Carleton.
Associate Dean (Programs) and Vice-Dean: François Julien, Associate Professor; Ph.D., Waterloo.
Associate Dean (Academic) and Secretary: Joanne Leck, Associate Professor; M.B.A., Ph.D., McGill.
Associate Dean (Strategy, Planning and Management Systems): Michel Nedzela, Associate Professor; M.S., Stanford.
Director of the Master of Business Administration (M.B.A.) Program: Philip McIlkenny, Associate Professor; Ph.D., Essex.
Director of the Executive M.B.A. (EMBA) Program: Terrence Kulka, Ph.D., McGill.
Acting Director of the Master of Health Administration (M.H.A.) Program: François Julien, Associate Professor; Ph.D., Waterloo.
Director, Undergraduate Program and Assistant Dean, Student Services: Peter Koppel; M.B.A., York; CLU.

Section Coordinators

Merridee Bujaki, Associate Professor; Ph.D., Queen's at Kingston; CA.
Swee Goh, Professor; M.B.A., Ph.D., Toronto.
Patrick Woodcock, Assistant Professor; M.B.A., Ph.D., Western Ontario.

Professors

Fodil Adjaoud, Professor; M.B.A., Ph.D., Laval.
Douglas Angus, Professor; M.A., Ottawa.
Jacques Barrette, Associate Professor; Ph.D., Montréal.
Julie Beauchamp, Assistant Professor; Ph.D., McGill.
Sarah Ben Amor, Assistant Professor; Ph.D., Laval.
Morad Benyoucef, Assistant Professor; Ph.D., Montréal.
Silvia Bonaccio, Assistant Professor; Ph.D., Purdue.
Ameur Boujenoui, Assistant Professor; Lic. en sc. econ., Rabat; Ph.D., HEC-Montréal.
Richard Bozec, Associate Professor; Ph.D., Montréal.
Kevin Brand, Assistant Professor; S.M., Sc.D., Harvard.
Tom Brzustowski, Visiting Professor; Ph.D., Princeton.
Jonathan Calof, Associate Professor; M.B.A., Ph.D., Western Ontario.
A. Louis Calvet, Professor; M.B.A., Queen's at Kingston; Ph.D., MIT.
Denis H. J. Caro, Professor; M.B.A., Ph.D., Minnesota.
Jules Carrière, Associate Professor; Ph.D., Montréal.
Tyler Chamberlin, Assistant Professor; Ph.D., Manchester.
Imed Eddine Chkir, Associate Professor; Ph.D., HEC-Montréal.
Samia Chreim, Associate Professor; Ph.D., HEC-Montréal.
Robert Collier, Teaching Associate; B.A., Carleton; CMA.
Brian Conheady, Teaching Associate, M.B.A., McGill; CMA.
Jean Couillard, Associate Professor; M.B.A., Ph.D., Laval.
Margaret Dalziel, Assistant Professor; M.B.A., McGill; Ph.D., Montréal.
Anna Dodonova, Assistant Professor; Ph.D., Michigan.
David Doloreux, Associate Professor; Ph.D., Waterloo.
Sylvain Durocher, Associate Professor; Ph.D., Quebec (Montréal).
Ronald Eden, Associate Professor; M.B.A., Dalhousie; Ph.D., NYU; CA.
Prescott Ensign, Assistant Professor; M.B.A., Clemson; Ph.D., HEC-Montréal.
Leila Hamzaoui Essoussi, Assistant Professor; D.E.A., Doctorat en Gestion, Aix en Provence.
Dominique J. Ferrand, Associate Professor; D.E.S.C., Paris; M.S.G., Paris IX; Ph.D., Laval.
Bruce M. Firestone, Entrepreneur-in-Residence; Ph.D., Australian National.
Mark Freel, Associate Professor; Ph.D., Aberdeen.
Chen Guo, Associate Professor; M.B.A., Ph.D., Queen's at Kingston.
Michael Guolla, Teaching Associate; Ph.D., Michigan.

Pavlo Kalyta, Assistant Professor; Ph.D., Concordia.
Yuri Khoroshilov, Assistant Professor; Ph.D., Michigan.
Gurprit S. Kindra, Professor; M.B.A., Northwest Missouri State; Ph.D., Iowa.
Kaouthar Lajili-Kobeissi, Associate Professor; Ph.D., Illinois.
Natalie Lam, Associate Professor; Ph.D., Berkeley.
Daniel E. Lane, Professor; Ph.D., British Columbia.
Laurent Lapierre, Associate Professor; Ph.D., McMaster.
David Large, Assistant Professor; M.B.A., Ph.D., Western Ontario.
Sharon Leiba-O'Sullivan, Associate Professor; M.B.A., McGill; Ph.D., Toronto.
Brigitte Levy, Associate Professor; D.E.A., Doct.S.Écon., Paris X.
Jonathan Linton, Associate Professor; Ph.D., York.
Pranlal Manga, Professor; Ph.D., Toronto.
Wojtek Michalowski, Professor; M.Econ., Ph.D., Warsaw.
Muriel Mignerat, Assistant Professor; Ph.D., HEC-Montréal.
Michael Miles, Assistant Professor; Ph.D., Fielding Institute.
Michael Mulvey, Assistant Professor; Ph.D., Penn State.
John Nash, Professor; D.Phil., Oxford.
Christian Navarre, Professor; M.Sc., Agrégé de l'Université, D.Ét., Lille.
Barbara Orser, Associate Professor; Ph.D., Bradford.
Alan O'Sullivan, Assistant Professor; M.B.A., Dublin; Ph.D., McGill.
Kathryn Pedwell, Assistant Professor; M.B.A., Ph.D., Calgary.
Ajax Persaud, Associate Professor; M.Ms., Ph.D., Carleton.
Rhonda Pyper, Lecturer; M.B.A. Laurentian.
Tony Quon, Associate Professor; Ph.D., Princeton.
Bijan Raajemi, Assistant Professor; Ph.D., Waterloo.
Abdul Rahman, Associate Professor; Ph.D., Concordia.
William Rentz, Associate Professor; Ph.D., Rochester.
Greg Richards, Visiting Professor; Cognos Professorship, Carleton.
Allan Riding, Professor; Ph.D., McGill.
Jean-Louis Schaan, Associate Professor; Ph.D., Western.
Martine Spence, Associate Professor; M.B.A., Concordia; Ph.D., Middlesex.
Geneviève Tellier, Associate Professor; Ph.D., Laval.
David J. Wright, Professor; Ph.D., Cambridge.
Daniel Zeghal, Professor; M.B.A., Ph.D., Laval; CGA.
David Zussman, Jarislowsky Chair; Ph.D., McGill.

UNIVERSITY OF ST. THOMAS

College of Business

UNIVERSITY
of ST.THOMAS
MINNESOTA

Programs of Study

The College of Business at the University of St. Thomas (UST) offers a Full-time UST M.B.A. (twenty-one-months), an Evening UST M.B.A. for working professionals, a weekend Executive UST M.B.A., a Health Care UST M.B.A. for physicians and health-care professionals, a Master of Business Communication, an M.S. in accountancy for CPA seekers, and an M.S. in real estate. The goal of the College of Business is to be recognized nationally and internationally for its overall excellence in educating highly principled global business leaders. Faculty members are leading scholars in their fields who also understand the value of practical experience. This recognized combination of theory and practice gives students the relevance necessary for rapid advancement in their careers.

The Full-time UST M.B.A. offers a traditional business core curriculum augmented by unique learning laboratories that prepare students with advanced analytical, communications, and problem-solving skills. Special attention is given to understanding the process of ethical decision making in today's complicated global environment. Elective options cover a variety of career tracks, and students have access to extensive career counseling and a network of successful alumni.

The Evening UST M.B.A. offers flexible class schedules to accommodate working professionals. Classes meet one night per week, with selected courses available on Saturdays. A similar variety of elective tracks enables students to tailor the program to support their career interests. The typical time to complete the degree is approximately 4½ years. Industrious part-time students can finish in under four years.

The weekend Executive UST M.B.A. is designed for leaders and managers who have the flexibility to attend class on a Friday and Saturday one weekend per month. The program is an accelerated M.B.A. with a curriculum that emphasizes strategic and conceptual managerial competencies across industries, organizations, and functions.

The Health Care UST M.B.A. offers course delivery through a combination of distance technology and intensive residencies to accommodate working health-care professionals from throughout the continental United States and Canada.

The Master of Business Communication is a part-time evening program designed for communicators who want to expand their communication expertise while building core business knowledge. The program includes specialties such as public relations, advertising, and marketing communication.

The Master of Science in Accountancy program is designed for students with an undergraduate accounting major and prepares them for a fast track in the accounting profession while meeting the 150-hour education requirement.

The Master of Science in Real Estate program provides the opportunity for real estate professionals to enhance their business and real estate acumen to advance in the field of commercial real estate.

All programs feature smaller class sizes designed to enable each student to have regular interactions with members of the highly talented faculty. The Full-time UST M.B.A., the Executive UST M.B.A., and the Health Care UST M.B.A. are all cohort-based programs. Cocurricular activities include an investment management course in which students actively manage $2 million and a venture capital fund that invests in technology-based start-up businesses. Other activities include clubs and organizations, such as the Accounting and Finance Club; Marketing, Consulting, and New Venture Clubs; and the UST MBA Student Association.

Research Facilities

The majority of graduate programs at the UST College of Business take place at its downtown Minneapolis campus. This state-of-the-art facility offers comprehensive services and a dynamic educational environment. An 86,000-square-foot technology-laden School of Entrepreneurship opened in fall 2005. The College of Business also conducts classes and programs in St. Paul on the beautiful, 78-acre original campus. In addition, graduate courses also take place in the surrounding Minnesota communities of Anoka, Chaska, Eagan, Owatonna, Woodbury, Rochester, and Bloomington. Students have access to state-of-the-art computing facilities and leading-edge software. Comprehensive library resources, with more than 300,000 volumes, are located on both the Minneapolis and St. Paul campuses. All students in the Full-time UST M.B.A. participate in an applied business research course designed to give them extensive practical experience in collecting relevant information for business decisions.

Financial Aid

Financial aid is available through a variety of private, institutional, and federal programs on both a need and merit basis. For information on these programs, students should contact Student Financial Services at 651-962-6550. In addition, many employers pay or subsidize their employees' tuition expenses.

Cost of Study

Tuition for 2006–07 was between $669 and $1150 per credit hour, depending on the program. Expenses for course materials vary by program and course. Nondegree professional development courses are also available for both companies and individuals through the UST Center for Business Excellence.

Living and Housing Costs

Most graduate students live off campus. Both Minneapolis and St. Paul offer a variety of reasonably priced housing options. Students who elect to live in St. Paul can take advantage of a free shuttle service that runs throughout the day between the campuses. A number of services and publications in the Twin Cities area provide off-campus residential listings. The Student Life Office in the Full-time UST M.B.A. program maintains a roommate referral listing service.

Student Group

Students in the part-time graduate business programs include a variety of working professionals, and students in the Full-time UST M.B.A. include individuals who have left the workforce to pursue full-time study. The student body has broad ethnic diversity and maintains close connections with the National Black MBA Association (NBMBAA) and the National Society for Hispanic MBAs (NSHMBA).

Location

The Twin Cities of Minneapolis and St. Paul are among the country's most vibrant cultural centers. The business community features a number of Fortune 500 corporations. The Twin Cities are also home to two world-class symphonies and internationally acclaimed theaters and art museums. In addition, Minneapolis features many professional sports teams and provides a wide range of opportunities for recreational athletes. The Mall of America in Bloomington is within minutes of the St. Paul and Minneapolis campuses.

The University

The University of St. Thomas is a comprehensive, coeducational, Catholic university. Founded in 1885, St. Thomas is now the largest private university in Minnesota. It is dedicated to providing career-oriented, value-centered education in a dynamic, stimulating environment. St. Thomas does not discriminate on the basis of race, color, creed, religion, national origin, sex, age, marital status, sexual orientation, or disability in its programs and activities.

Applying

Admission requirements vary by degree program, especially with regard to previous work or managerial experience; however, most programs require official scores from the GMAT, transcripts from all undergraduate institutions attended, and TOEFL scores for those students whose native language is not English and who did not graduate from a North American undergraduate institution. Personal interviews are required for certain programs.

Students can apply online at the Web site (http://www.stthomas.edu/cob/graduate) or through the traditional application forms available on the Internet or from the program office. Applications are considered on a rolling basis for most programs. The Full-time UST M.B.A. offers fall admission only, but applications are considered in five rounds, beginning in November. The other programs offer fall and spring admission. For specific information and application materials, students should contact the College of Business.

Correspondence and Information

College of Business
TMH 100
University of St. Thomas
1000 LaSalle Avenue
Minneapolis, Minnesota 55403-2025
Phone: 651-962-4200
　　　　800-328-6819 Ext. 2-4200 (toll-free)
E-mail: cob@stthomas.edu
Web site: http://www.stthomas.edu/cob/graduate

University of St. Thomas

THE FACULTY

The St. Thomas full-time and adjunct faculty members, many of whom are leaders in their industries, bring a wealth of business and academic experience to the classroom. This unique mixture of expertise results in leading-edge curricula and the real-world applied approach that makes a University of St. Thomas degree so valued in the business community. Students benefit from this expertise through the accessibility that results from small class sizes and the advisory or mentoring roles assumed by many faculty members.

Deans and Directors of the Master's Programs

Christopher P. Puto, Dean.
William Raffield, Senior Associate Dean.
David P. Brennan, Assistant Dean.

Rachelle Holm, Director of UST M.B.A. Admissions.
Nick Lauer, Director of the Executive UST M.B.A.
Nona Mason, Director of the Master of Business Communication.
John Militello, Director of the Health Care UST M.B.A.
Tom Musil, Director of the M.S. in Real Estate.
Janice Raffield, Director of the M.S. in Accountancy.

THE UNIVERSITY OF TEXAS AT ARLINGTON

College of Business Administration

Programs of Study

The College of Business Administration at The University of Texas at Arlington (UT Arlington), accredited by AACSB International–The Association to Advance Collegiate Schools of Business, offers four versions of the M.B.A. and ten specialized master's degrees. Students may begin their studies in any semester and complete those studies on either a part-time or full-time basis. Programs may require up to 30 hours of foundation work for students with nonbusiness backgrounds.

The Master of Professional Accounting (42 semester hours in accounting) is appropriate for students without prior study in business or accounting. The M.S. in accounting (36 semester hours) allows specialization in accounting information systems, auditing, financial accounting, and managerial accounting. The M.S. in taxation (36 semester hours) is open to students with undergraduate degrees in accounting and includes course work in the following areas of taxation: corporations, partnerships, estates, gifts, trusts, state and local, practice and procedure, international, and research. The M.S. in information systems (30 to 33 semester hours) offers management and technology courses to prepare students for careers in software and systems development, security and CSI, and systems management. The M.S. in marketing research (37 semester hours) prepares students for careers in marketing research, product/service management, and marketing planning. The M.S. in human resource management (36 semester hours) has courses in compensation administration, employee relations law, diversity, planning and policy, industrial and labor relations, staffing, and performance management. The M.S. in real estate (36 semester hours) is a specialized degree in real estate decision making and focuses on appraisal, architecture, investment analysis, land utilization, mortgage-backed securities, primary and secondary mortgage markets, real asset management, real property law, and urban and regional planning. The M.A. in economics (30 to 36 semester hours) prepares students for jobs in government, business, research, and teaching. The program can be tailored to fit the student's interests, with special emphasis in forecasting, international business, and quantitative analysis. The M.S. in health-care administration (36 semester hours) is a twenty-four-month, cohort-based program that integrates business topics with the delivery of health-care services to prepare students for various positions in the health-care industry. The M.B.A. program includes a 36-hour advanced program with areas of study in accounting, economics, finance, information systems, management, operations management, marketing, or real estate. The Professional Cohort M.B.A. program (48 semester hours) allows working professionals with no business background to complete their degrees in twenty-eight months. The Monday evening and Saturday morning schedule enables students to focus on one course at a time. The online M.B.A. program is a general management (36–48 semester hours) degree offered exclusively online. The new executive M.B.A. targets mid-level executives/managers with at least seven to eight years of work experience. The program, offered in Fort Worth, features sixty-two class meetings, a four-day orientation, and a thirteen-day China International Residency experience. Classes are held alternating Friday and Saturday weekends. The Ph.D. in business administration (67 semester hours) is a research-oriented program. Major fields of study are accounting, economics, finance, management, information systems, operations management, and marketing.

Research Facilities

Teaching and research activities take place in a newly renovated building with 149,000 square feet of space. The building has six computer lab facilities with more than 211 desktop systems, one specialty lab with ten desktop systems, and one mobile "lab" with twenty-four laptops. In addition, there are twenty-four classrooms, each with a multimedia teaching station that is connected to the campus network and the Internet, and a distance learning classroom operated by UT Arlington's Distance Education. The Goolsby Leadership Academy, the Center for Research on Organizational and Managerial Excellence, the Center for Research in Information Technology Management, the Center for Marketing Research, and the Ryan-Reilly Center for Urban Land Utilization provide research assistance to faculty members and graduate students.

Financial Aid

Approximately eighty-five assistantships are available to students on a competitive basis. For 2006–07, master's and doctoral stipends were $5994 and approximately $12,000 to $14,000, respectively, for a nine-month period. Individuals desiring part-time work off campus are served by one of the nation's best student employment service centers. Students with excellent academic credentials may apply for scholarships and fellowships.

Cost of Study

In 2006–07, tuition and fees for Texas residents were $4047 for 12 semester hours, while nonresidents paid $7347 for the same course work. Students with assistantships, fellowships, or scholarships may qualify for resident tuition rates.

Living and Housing Costs

Information about University and off-campus housing can be obtained by contacting the housing office at 817-272-2827. An ample supply of moderately priced apartments is available for both single and married students.

Student Group

The College enrolls approximately 1,000 master's students and 80 doctoral students. These students come from a variety of academic backgrounds in more than 200 universities in the United States and seventy-two other countries. Nearly 80 percent of the students have significant professional and technical work experience.

Location

Arlington, with a population of more than 362,970, is one of the fastest-growing cities in north Texas. It is located in the center of the vast Dallas–Fort Worth metroplex, which is a regional market and distribution center, a major convention site, a growing financial and cultural center, the tenth-largest market in the United States, and the home of the largest industrial district in the Southwest.

The University

The University of Texas at Arlington was founded in 1895 as a private liberal arts college called Arlington College. In recent years, it has grown significantly and is one of the largest institutions in the University of Texas System (19,205 undergraduate and 5,620 graduate students). The University is composed of nine academic units, of which the College of Business Administration is one of the largest (approximately 5,000 students).

Applying

Application may be made for fall, spring, or summer semesters. U.S. students are encouraged to submit their applications and all related material prior to May 15 for the fall semester, September 15 for the spring semester, and February 15 for the summer semester. International students are encouraged to submit their applications by April 1, September 1, and January 1, respectively. Applications, official transcripts, scores on the GMAT, and three letters of recommendation are required. International students are required to provide a TOEFL score (and a TSE-A score if seeking graduate assistantships), financial statements, and statements of educational background.

Correspondence and Information

Director for Graduate Business Services
College of Business Administration
UTA Box 19376
University of Texas at Arlington
Arlington, Texas 76019
Phone: 817-272-3005
E-mail: admit@uta.edu
Web site: http://www.uta.edu/gradbiz

University of Texas at Arlington

THE FACULTY AND THEIR RESEARCH

Ryan C. Amacher, Ph.D., Virginia, 1971. International economics, microeconomics, public finance.
Vincent Apilado, Ph.D., Michigan, 1970. Financial institutions and markets.
R. C. Baker, Ph.D., Texas A&M, 1971. Production, quality, and operations management.
Myrtle Bell, Ph.D., Texas at Arlington, 1996. Human resource management and diversity.
George Benson, Ph.D., USC, 2002. Human resource management.
Elten Briggs, Ph.D., Oklahoma, 2006. Services marketing.
Alan Cannon, Ph.D., Clemson, 1999. Operations management.
Wendy J. Casper, Ph.D., George Mason, 2000. Industrial/organizational psychology.
C. Y. Choy, Ph.D., Ohio State, 2000. International macroeconomics and finance, time-series econometrics, money and macroeconomics.
William J. Crowder, Ph.D., Arizona State, 1992. International money and finance.
Deepak Datta, Ph.D., Pittsburgh, 1986. Strategic planning and policy, industrial economics.
Craig A. Depken II, Ph.D., Georgia, 1996. Industrial organization.
Roger Dickinson, Ph.D., Columbia, 1967. Marketing, retail management.
J. David Diltz, Ph.D., Illinois, 1980. Corporate finance, capital budgeting.
Mark Eakin, Ph.D., Texas A&M, 1980. Management science, statistics.
Gregory Frazier, Ph.D., Texas A&M, 1989. Operations management.
John Gallo, Ph.D., Texas at Arlington, 1992. Finance.
David Gray, Ph.D., Massachusetts, 1974. Management, industrial relations.
Douglas Grisaffe, Ph.D., Vanderbilt, 1989. Consumer research, decision making.
Bethane Jo Pierce Hall, Ph.D., North Texas State, 1987. Accounting, taxation.
Thomas W. Hall, Ph.D., Oklahoma State, 1980. Financial accounting, auditing.
Andrew Hansz, Ph.D., Georgia State, 1999. Real estate finance.
Darren K. Hayunga, Ph.D., LSU, 2006. Real estate investments.
Daniel Himarios, Ph.D., Virginia Tech, 1984. Macroeconomics.
Li Chin Ho, Ph.D., Texas at Austin, 1990. Managerial and financial accounting.
Jorge Fernando Jaramillo, Ph.D., South Florida, 2004. Sales-force performance and marketing strategy.
Cagatay Koc, Ph.D., Texas at Austin, 2000. Applied econometrics, health economics, industrial organization, applied microeconomics.
Courtney LaFountain, Ph.D., Washington (St. Louis), 2003. Urban and regional economics, microeconomics.
James Lavelle, Ph.D., Utah, 1999. Organizational behavior.
Xueming Luo, D.B.A., Louisiana Tech, 2003. Strategic marketing, modeling, international business/marketing.
Radha Mahapatra, Ph.D., Texas A&M, 1994. Information systems.
Richard Mark, LL.M., Denver, 1977. Accounting, taxation.
Donald McConnell, Ph.D., North Texas State, 1981. Financial accounting and auditing.
Carl McDaniel, Ph.D., Arizona State, 1970. Marketing, global research.
Jeff McGee, Ph.D., Georgia, 1992. Venture development, small business management.
Gary McMahan, Ph.D., Texas A&M, 1993. Human resource management.
Roger Meiners, Ph.D., Virginia Tech, 1978. Law and economics.
Sridhar Nerur, Ph.D., Texas at Arlington, 1994. Information systems.
Liliana Nordtvedt, Ph.D., Memphis, 2005. Strategic and international management.
Don Panton, Ph.D., Arizona, 1972. Corporate finance, investments.
Shushanik Papanyan, Ph.D., Houston, 2006. Time-series econometrics, applied macroeconomics, international economics.
Edmund Prater, Ph.D., Georgia Tech, 1999. Operations management, supply chain management.
Kenneth Price, Ph.D., Michigan State, 1973. Organizational behavior, management.
James C. Quick, Ph.D., Houston, 1977. Management, organizational behavior.
M. K. Raja, Ph.D., Texas Tech, 1971. Management information systems.
Abdul Rasheed, Ph.D., Pittsburgh, 1988. Management, business policy.
Sanjiv Sabherwal, Ph.D., Georgia Tech, 2000. International finance and investments.
Salil K. Sarkar, Ph.D., LSU, 1991. Corporate finance and investments.
Riyaz Sikora, Ph.D., Illinois, 1994. Information systems.
Craig Slinkman, Ph.D., Minnesota, 1982. Statistics, information systems.
Aaron D. Smallwood, Ph.D., Florida State, 2001. Time-series econometrics, international finance and international trade.
Robert Sonora, Ph.D., Ohio State, 1998. International macroeconomics.
Chandra Subramaniam, Ph.D., Minnesota, 1993. Corporate governance and executive compensation.
Patricia Swafford, Ph.D., Georgia Tech, 2003. Supply chain management.
Peggy Swanson, Ph.D., SMU, 1978. Corporate and international finance.
Martin E. Taylor, Ph.D., Texas at Austin, 1974. Auditing.
James T. C. Teng, Ph.D., Minnesota, 1980. E-commerce, information management.
Jeffrey Tsay, Ph.D., Missouri, 1973. Managerial accounting, information systems.
Larry Walther, Ph.D., Oklahoma State, 1980. Financial accounting, auditing.
Michael Ward, Ph.D., Chicago, 1993. Applied price theory, industrial organization.
Kenneth Wheeler, Ph.D., Minnesota, 1978. Personnel and human resource management.
Mary Whiteside, Ph.D., Texas Tech, 1974. Statistics, management science.
Dennis Wilson, Ph.D., Kentucky, 1999. Applied microeconomic theory, public economics, sport economics.
Li Yong, Ph.D., Texas at Austin, 2005. Investments and corporate finance.

THE UNIVERSITY OF TEXAS AT DALLAS

School of Management

Programs of Study

The University of Texas at Dallas (UTD) School of Management (SOM) offers the Master of Business Administration (M.B.A.), the Master of Arts (M.A.) in international management studies, the Master of Science (M.S.) in accounting and information management, the M.S. in management and administrative sciences with various concentration areas, and the M.S. in information technology management.

The 53-credit-hour part-time Professional M.B.A. is the largest program in the School. SOM's Professional M.B.A. is offered in evening and online classes and caters primarily to students who work full-time. The School also offers a lockstep, full-time, day-format Cohort M.B.A. program that students complete in sixteen months. *U.S. News & World Report* ranks the Cohort M.B.A. program among the top fifty-four full-time M.B.A. programs in the nation and among the top twenty-five at public colleges and universities.

Both the M.A. and M.S. programs require 36 hours of study, with classes offered on both a part-time and full-time basis. Classes, primarily at night, allow the student to specialize in accounting, international management, finance, marketing, organizational strategies, information technology and management, innovation and entrepreneurship, and supply chain management.

The Global Leadership Executive M.B.A. program, cited by *Forbes* magazine as one of the best on the Web, is an online executive program designed for experienced managers and senior professionals. The curriculum, typically completed in thirty-two months, is 53 credit hours and is delivered using an online learning model that incorporates Web-based interactive technologies, teleconferencing, and on-campus sessions offered at a series of weekend retreats. Students participate in a ten-day international study tour. Admissions are in November, April, and July.

A specialized Executive M.B.A. (E.M.B.A.) focuses on management for change, with a curriculum that stresses skills and perspectives needed for leadership in the twenty-first century. *Financial Times* ranks the UTD E.M.B.A. forty-sixth in the world and twenty-fourth in the U.S. Participants are assigned an individual coach to mentor/assist in career strategic planning. The E.M.B.A. is a lockstep, twenty-one-month program for executives with at least ten years of managerial experience. Classes meet on one Friday and two Saturdays a month.

In addition, the School offers an executive education program in project management. This module leads to Project Management Institute (PMI) certification and can become a master's degree track with 18 additional hours or an M.B.A. with 35 additional hours. The UTD School of Management's Project Management Program is one of only five such programs in the world to have earned accreditation from the Project Management Institute. *PM Network* magazine has listed the program as one of the "Best Bets" worldwide for project managers seeking graduate and continuing education. The School's executive education division also offers M.S. and M.B.A. degrees in medical management for practicing physicians.

For students who prefer the flexibility of online learning, the School extends delivery, via the Internet, of M.B.A. program resources through the Global M.B.A. Online, which charges standard tuition rates.

The School's Doctor of Philosophy (Ph.D.) program is distinguished by its emphasis on interdisciplinary research. It provides rigorous training in theoretical and empirical skills that are applied to problems faced by managers. Students work closely with internationally renowned faculty members to address questions at the leading edge of their field. Research supervision is available in areas of accounting, economics, finance, information systems, international management, marketing, operations research, organizations, and strategy. Students entering the Ph.D. program are provided financial aid in the form of teaching or research assistantships. The School offers Ph.D. degrees in international management studies and management science.

Research Facilities

Academic Computer Services provides central computing facilities, workstations, microcomputer equipment, and network services for student and faculty and staff member use in instruction and research.

Complementing existing campus labs, two new School of Management computer labs, based on Windows-NT, are open to management students. The Microcomputer Center, located in the McDermott Library building, provides a modern, fully networked personal computing environment with both IBM-compatible and Macintosh computers. The Computing Lab, located in the Jonsson Building, is the focal point for student access to the University's extensive UNIX environment, which is based primarily on SUN servers accessed via X-Windows terminals. Dedicated servers support such functions as campus information services, programming instruction, applications instruction, research-related instruction, and computationally intense applications.

Financial Aid

The UTD School of Management Scholarship Committee awards a variety of scholarships each fall. Applications are available from the Office of Financial Aid. UTD participates in most federal and state aid programs. Short-term loans are also available. In addition, students can apply for Dean's Excellence Scholarship funds given on a semester basis. The School offers scholarships to master's students with strong academic potential. For more information, students should visit the UTD School of Management's Web site at http://som.utdallas.edu.

Cost of Study

Tuition and most student fees are billed per semester hour, depending on course load. A full-time Texas resident student carrying 9 hours pays $3000 per semester; a non-Texas resident student pays $5475 per semester. A minimum tuition of $675 per hour is charged for all Texas resident students and $950 per hour for all non-Texas resident students. Fees include advising, career-planning placement, and intern/co-op services.

Living and Housing Costs

UTD has many affordable housing options near its campus in the Dallas suburbs of Richardson and Plano. The Waterview Park Apartments, run by a private company, are available on campus and are approved student residences.

Student Group

Many participants in the graduate programs work full-time and have a minimum of five years of managerial experience. About 57 percent are pursuing their degrees part-time. About 42 percent of master's students are women, 27 percent are members of minority groups, and 29 percent are from other countries. Students range in age from 20 to over 70; the average age is 30.

Location

The University of Texas at Dallas is located just north of Dallas in a growing suburban area of more than 400,000 people.

The University

Now known for its innovative teaching practices, UTD was created in 1969 by the Texas legislature after existing for eight years as a privately sponsored graduate-level teaching and research institution, the Southwest Center for Advanced Studies. The University first admitted undergraduates in 1975. The UTD School of Management was established in 1972 as an upper-level graduate institution. It is fully accredited by AACSB International–The Association to Advance Collegiate Schools of Business.

Applying

All applicants must have obtained a bachelor's degree, not necessarily in business, from an accredited institution. Prerequisites vary according to program and may include completion of an undergraduate calculus class, personal computer proficiency, and spreadsheet proficiency. Also required are GMAT scores and three letters of reference. A TOEFL score is required for applicants whose native language is not English. Applicants are evaluated based on their personal qualities and academic backgrounds following the admission formula guidelines as set forth by the International Association for Management Education. Personal interviews are not required. The application deadline for fall admission is July 1, spring admission is November 1, and summer admission is April 1.

Correspondence and Information

Dr. Steve Perkins
Associate Dean for Graduate Studies
The School of Management
The University of Texas at Dallas
P.O. Box 830688, SM40
Richardson, Texas 75083-0688
Phone: 972-883-6789
Fax: 972-883-4095
E-mail: grad-admission@utdallas.edu
Web site: http://som.utdallas.edu

Dee Ellington
Office of Recruitment and Orientation
School of Management
The University of Texas at Dallas
P.O. Box 830688, SM40
Richardson, Texas 75083-0688
Phone: 972-883-2750
Fax: 972-883-6425
E-mail: delling@utdallas.edu
PMBA@utdallas.edu

The University of Texas at Dallas

THE FACULTY AND THEIR RESEARCH

Hans-Joachim Adler, Senior Lecturer of ISOM; Ph.D., Lyon (France).

Arthur Agulnek, Senior Lecturer of Accounting/Information Management; B.S., Brooklyn State.

Ashiq Ali, Professor of Accounting/Information Management; Ph.D., Columbia.

Mark Anderson, Associate Professor of Accounting/Information Management; Ph.D., Florida.

Jasper Arnold, Senior Lecturer and Executive Director of Executive M.B.A. Program; Ph.D., Harvard.

Jai Asundi, Assistant Professor of ISOM; Ph.D., Carnegie Mellon.

Nina Baranchuk, Assistant Professor of Finance; Ph.D., Washington (St. Louis).

Indranil Bardhan, Assistant Professor of Accounting/Information Management; Ph.D., Texas at Austin.

George Barnes, Senior Lecturer of OSIM/International Business Management; M.A., Tufts.

Frank Bass, Eugene McDermott Professor of Marketing; Ph.D., Illinois.

Alain Bensoussan, Distinguished Research Professor of Risk Management, Operations Management; Ph.D., Paris.

Abhijit Biswas, Senior Lecturer of Marketing; Ph.D., Purdue.

Ron Blair, Senior Lecturer of Accounting/Information Management; M.B.A., Oklahoma.

Tiffany Bortz, Senior Lecturer of Accounting/Information Management; M.S., Texas A&M.

Norris Bruce, Assistant Professor of Marketing; Ph.D., Duke.

Alexander Butler, Assistant Professor of Finance; Ph.D., Indiana.

Metin Cakanyildirim, Assistant Professor of ISOM; Ph.D., Cornell.

Octavian Carare, Assistant Professor of Finance and Managerial Economics; Ph.D., Rutgers.

Mary Chaffin, Senior Lecturer of Finance; Ph.D., Texas at Dallas.

William Cready, Professor of Accounting/Information Management; Ph.D., Ohio State.

Zhonglan (Di) Dai, Assistant Professor of Accounting/Information Management; Ph.D., North Carolina at Chapel Hill.

Tevfik Dalgic, Clinical Professor of OSIM; Ph.D., Gazi (Turkey).

Milind Dawande, Associate Professor of ISOM; Ph.D., Carnegie Mellon.

Ted Day, Professor of Finance; Ph.D., Stanford.

David Deeds, Associate Professor of OSIM; Ph.D., Washington (Seattle).

Greg Dess, Andrew R. Cecil Endowed Chair in Applied Ethics; Ph.D., Washington (Seattle).

Kutsal Dogan, Assistant Professor of ISOM; Ph.D., Florida.

Adolf Enthoven, Professor of Accounting/Information Management; Ph.D., Rotterdam.

Anne Ferrante, Senior Lecturer of MISM; Ph.D., Fielding Institute.

Richard Fisher, Senior Lecturer of ISOM; M.S., Texas at Dallas.

David Ford, Professor of OSIM; Ph.D., Wisconsin–Madison.

Laurel Frazen, Assistant Professor of Accounting/Information Management; Ph.D., Washington (Seattle).

Mary Beth Goodrich, Senior Lecturer of Accounting/Information Management; M.B.A., LSU.

Umit Gurun, Assistant Professor of Accounting/Information Management; Ph.D., Michigan State.

Richard Harrison, Associate Professor of International Management Studies; Ph.D., Stanford.

Ernan Haruvy, Assistant Professor of Marketing; Ph.D., Texas at Austin.

David Heroy, Senior Lecturer of ISOM; Ph.D., Texas Christian.

Jonathon Hochberg, Senior Lecturer of Information Management Studies; Ed.D., Nova Southeastern.

Varghese Jacob, Professor of ISOM and Senior Associate Dean; Ph.D., Purdue.

Surya Janakiraman, Assistant Professor of Accounting/Information Management; Ph.D., Pennsylvania.

Marilyn Kaplan, Senior Lecturer of OSIM; Ph.D., Texas at Dallas.

Robert Kieschnick, Assistant Professor of Finance; Ph.D., Texas at Austin.

Constantine Konstans, Professor of Accounting/Information Management; Ph.D., Michigan State.

Nanda Kumar, Assistant Professor of Marketing; Ph.D., Chicago.

Mark Laplante, Assistant Professor of Finance; Ph.D., Washington (Seattle).

Seung-Hyun Lee, Assistant Professor of OSIM; Ph.D., Ohio State.

Peter Lewin, Senior Lecturer of Finance and Managerial Economics; Ph.D., Chicago.

Xu Li, Assistant Professor of Accounting/Information Management; Ph.D., MIT.

Stan Liebowitz, Professor of Managerial Economics; Ph.D., UCLA.

Zhiang Lin, Associate Professor of OSIM; Ph.D., Carnegie Mellon.

Xiaohui (Gloria) Liu, Assistant Professor of Accounting/Information Management; Ph.D., Northwestern.

Holly Lutze, Assistant Professor of ISOM; Ph.D., Stanford.

Sumit Majumdar, Professor of ISOM; Ph.D., Minnesota.

Livia Markoczy, Associate Professor of OSIM; Ph.D., Cambridge.

John McCracken, Senior Lecturer of Medical Management; Ph.D., Pennsylvania (Wharton).

Diane McNulty, Associate Dean for External Affairs and Senior Lecturer of Business Policy; Ph.D., Texas at Dallas.

Nirup Menon, Assistant Professor of ISOM; Ph.D., Arizona.

Syam Menon, Assistant Professor of ISOM; Ph.D., Chicago.

Larry Merville, Professor of Finance; Ph.D., Texas at Austin.

Radha Mookerjee, Senior Lecturer of ISOM; Ph.D., Purdue.

Vijay Mookerjee, Professor of ISOM; Ph.D., Purdue.

B. P. S. Murthi, Associate Professor of Marketing; Ph.D., Carnegie Mellon.

Volkan Muslu, Assistant Professor of Accounting/Information Management; Ph.D., MIT.

Kumar Nair, Senior Lecturer of Strategy, Organizational Performance, and Leadership; Ph.D., Twente (Netherlands).

Ramachandran Natarajan, Associate Professor of Accounting/Information Management; Ph.D., Pennsylvania (Wharton).

Shun-Chen Niu, Professor of ISOM; Ph.D., Berkeley.

Michael Oliff, Clinical Professor of Corporate Strategy; Ph.D., Clemson.

Mike Peng, Provost's Distinguished Professor of Global Strategy, Organizations, Strategy, and International Management; Ph.D., Washington (Seattle).

Steve Perkins, Associate Dean of Masters Program; Ph.D., Texas at Dallas.

Joseph Picken, Senior Lecturer of ISOM; Ph.D., Texas at Arlington.

Hasan Pirkul, Dean and Caruth Chair Professor of Decision Sciences; Ph.D., Rochester.

Ashutosh Prasad, Assistant Professor of Marketing; Ph.D., Texas at Austin.

Suresh Radhakrishnan, Professor of Accounting/Information Management; Ph.D., NYU.

Srinivasan Raghunathan, Associate Professor of ISOM; Ph.D., Pittsburgh.

Ram Rao, Founders Professor of Marketing; Ph.D., Carnegie Mellon.

Suk Rhee, Assistant Professor of ISOM; Ph.D., Ohio State.

Orlando Richard, Assistant Professor of OSIM; Ph.D., Kentucky.

Robert Robb, Senior Lecturer of OSIM; M.S., Utah.

Young Ryu, Associate Professor of ISOM; Ph.D., Texas at Dallas.

Mark Salamasick, Senior Lecturer of Accounting/Information Management; M.B.A., Central Michigan.

Jane Salk, Associate Professor of OSIM; Ph.D., MIT.

Sumit Sarkar, Professor of ISOM; Ph.D., Rochester.

Michael Savoie, Director of Center for Information Technology and Management and Senior Lecturer of ISOM; Ph.D., North Texas.

Suresh Sethi, Ashbell Smith Professor of Operations Management and Fellow of the Royal Society of Canada and the New York Academy; Ph.D., Carnegie Mellon.

Charles Solcher, Senior Lecturer of Accounting/Information Management; J.D., South Texas Law.

David Springate, Associate Dean for Executive Education and Associate Professor of Finance; D.B.A., Harvard.

Chelliah Sriskandarajah, Professor of ISOM; Ph.D., National Polytechnique (France).

Kathryn Stecke, Professor of ISOM; Ph.D., Purdue.

Andrei Strinjnev, Assistant Professor of Marketing; Ph.D., Washington (St. Louis).

Rafal Szwejkowski, Assistant Professor of Accounting/Information Management Programs; Ph.D., Arizona.

Lou Thompson, Senior Lecturer of ISOM; M.S., DePaul.

Amy Troutman, Assistant Director of Accounting/Information Management Programs and Senior Lecturer; M.P.A., Texas at Austin.

Mark Vargus, Assistant Professor of Accounting/Information Management; Ph.D., Pennsylvania (Wharton).

Davina Vora, Assistant Professor of OSIM; Ph.D., South Carolina.

John Wiorkowski, Professor of Mathematical Statistics; Ph.D., Chicago.

Habte Woldu, Senior Lecturer of OSIM/International Business Management; Ph.D., Poznan (Poland).

Yexiao Xu, Associate Professor of Finance and Managerial Economics; Ph.D., Princeton.

Wei Yue, Assistant Professor of ISOM; Ph.D., Purdue.

Alejandro Zentner, Assistant Professor of Finance and Managerial Economics; Ph.D., Chicago.

Harold Zhang, Professor of Finance and Managerial Economics; Ph.D., Duke.

Qin Zhang, Assistant Professor of Marketing; Ph.D., Washington (St. Louis).

Laurie Ziegler, Senior Lecturer of OSIM; Ph.D., Texas at Arlington.

THE UNIVERSITY OF TOLEDO

College of Business Administration

Programs of Study

The College of Business Administration at The University of Toledo (UT) offers a master's degree in accounting (M.S.A.), the Master of Business Administration (M.B.A.) degree in a traditional and executive format (Executive M.B.A.), and a doctoral degree (Ph.D. in manufacturing management) to serve a diverse population in a global and entrepreneurial environment. The College also has a joint-degree program with the College of Law in which students with undergraduate degrees in business can earn an M.B.A. and a J.D. in 3½ years. The joint-degree program is open to all students regardless of background. The M.B.A. is a comprehensive program with specializations available in administration, customer relationship management and marketing intelligence, finance, human resource management, information systems, international business, marketing, operations management, and professional sales. The Master of Science in Accountancy (M.S.A.) is a 30-semester-hour program that prepares students for a professional career in accounting and fulfills the requirements to sit for the uniform CPA exam in the state of Ohio. The Executive M.B.A. Program is designed to provide a learning experience for executives in order to effectively manage the change and growth component in today's competitive global environment. The curriculum includes fifteen courses built around three major integrative themes. The program takes five quarters—fifteen months—to complete and allows for normal holidays and a summer break. Classes meet Friday evenings and Saturday in a two-weekends-on, one-weekend-off format. An international or domestic study trip of seven to ten days is planned for the final term. Responding proactively to a national need in the area of manufacturing management, the College of Business Administration, in cooperation with the College of Engineering, started the Ph.D. program in manufacturing management in 1989. The University of Toledo is one of the few universities in the United States offering this degree. The program educates scholars in meeting traditional and emerging standards of excellence in and contributing to the field through research, teaching, and seminal publications in academic and professional journals and monographs. Graduates of the Ph.D. program pursue careers in university teaching, industry, consulting, or research.

Research Facilities

The University of Toledo offers an outstanding setting for its College of Business Administration. Housed in Stranahan Hall, an attractive and modern facility in the heart of the campus, faculty members and students have access to multimedia classrooms and state-of-the-art computer labs. The College of Business will soon be breaking ground on the Savage and Associates Complex for Business Learning and Engagement, a $13-million expansion that will place the College of Business among the national leaders in classroom technology. The Savage and Associates Complex is scheduled for completion in the fall of 2009. The College currently houses several 24-hour computer labs, including a virtual lab where students can check out laptops and tablet PCs to use in and out of the classroom. All classrooms are equipped with the latest wireless technology. The College is also home to the award-winning Center for Family Business, the Executive Center for Global Competitiveness, the Edward Schmidt School of Professional Sales, the Small Business and Entrepreneurship Institute, and the International Business Institute. These centers work closely with all academic departments to provide advanced study and research within the College.

Financial Aid

Most full-time graduate students receive some financial support. College fellowships, teaching assistantships, and research assistantships, which include a stipend and a tuition waiver, are available for qualified students on a competitive basis. The out-of-state tuition surcharge normally charged to out-of-state and international students is waived for students whose permanent address is within one of the following Michigan counties: Hillsdale, Lenawee, Macomb, Oakland, Washtenaw, and Wayne. In addition, The University of Toledo offers an out-of-state tuition surcharge waiver to cities and regions that are a part of the Sister Cities Agreement. These regions include Toledo, Spain; Londrina, Brazil; Qinhuangdao, China; Csongrad County, Hungary; Delmenhorst, Germany; Toyohashi, Japan; Tanga, Tanzania; Bekaa Valley, Lebanon; and Poznan, Poland. The University of Toledo Graduate School offers a variety of memorial and minority scholarship awards, including the Ronald E. McNair Postbaccalaureate Achievement Scholarship, the Graduate Minority Assistantship Award, and several full University fellowships.

Cost of Study

The graduate tuition rate for the 2007–08 academic year is $448.15 per semester credit hour for in-state students. For nonresidents, the out-of-state surcharge is $367.15 per semester credit hour. Additional fees are required and include the general fee, technology fee, and mandatory health-care insurance.

Living and Housing Costs

The University of Toledo has a diverse offering of student housing options, including suite-style and traditional residential halls. Housing is offered to graduate students through Residence Life or contracted individually by the student. Affordable, high-quality off-campus apartment-style housing within walking distance of campus is abundant.

Student Group

There are approximately 20,000 students at the University of Toledo. About 3,300 are graduate and professional students. The University has a rich diversity of student organizations. Students join groups that are organized around common cultural, religious, athletic, and educational interests.

Location

The University of Toledo has several campus sites in the city of Toledo. M.B.A. students take classes on UT's main campus, which is located on Bancroft Street in suburban western Toledo. With a population of 300,000, Toledo is the sixtieth-largest city in the United States. It is located on the western shores of Lake Erie, 2 hours west of Cleveland and 1 hour south of Detroit.

Toledo boasts several outstanding attractions in the area, lending itself to be an attractive location to study and live. The Toledo Zoo and the Toledo Public Library have both been ranked in the top 10 in their respective categories by national publications. The Toledo Museum of Art and Center for the Visual Arts have been featured in *The New York Times* for the outstanding Glass Pavilion. The Toledo Mud Hens have won consecutive Governor's Cup Championships in International League AAA baseball play while playing at Fifth Third Field, a five-year-old park that *Newsweek* called the "best park in the minors." COSI, the Toledo Speedway, Toledo Botanical Gardens, and a new downtown sporting arena round out just a sampling of all there is to do in Toledo.

The University and The College

The University of Toledo was founded by Jessup W. Scott in 1872 as a municipal institution and became part of the state of Ohio's system of higher education in 1967. On July 1, 2006, The University of Toledo merged with the Medical University of Ohio becoming one of only seventeen American universities to offer professional and graduate academic programs in medicine, law, pharmacy, nursing, health sciences, engineering, and business.

Established in 1930, the College of Business Administration is fully accredited by AACSB International–The Association to Advance Collegiate Schools of Business, which is the premier accrediting agency for business schools. Only 15 percent of business schools worldwide are currently accredited by AACSB. The Princeton Review has also selected the College of Business Administration's graduate programs for inclusion in the 2008 edition of *Best 290 Business Schools*.

Applying

Students applying to the M.B.A. and M.S.A. programs must have an undergraduate or professional degree earned from an accredited college or university, a 2.7 or better GPA, and three letters of recommendation. All applicants must also take the Graduate Management Admissions Test (GMAT). Specific admission guidelines can be found online. For the J.D./M.B.A. dual-degree program, students must submit separate applications and be admitted to both programs. The Law School Admission Test (LSAT) is accepted by the College of Business in lieu of GMAT scores.

To enroll in the Executive M.B.A. Program, students must submit the application, the employer nomination, and the optional employer sponsorship forms along with the $45 application fee. Applicants must send official transcripts from each educational institution attended and two letters of recommendation from individuals familiar with the applicant's managerial experience to the Executive M.B.A. Office, which then arranges an interview with the candidate. Applications for both the M.B.A. and Executive M.B.A. Programs are considered on a rolling, space-available basis.

Ph.D. applicants must send a completed application, three sets of transcripts for each institution attended (at least one set of transcripts must be official), three letters of recommendation, GMAT scores, and the $45 application fee. Students are admitted to the Ph.D. program on the basis of past academic performance and their potential for sustained study at the graduate level. Letters of recommendation for the applicant and a statement of career objectives are considered in the admissions process.

All international applicants from non-English-speaking countries must submit TOEFL scores and a completed financial statement.

Correspondence and Information

M.B.A. Office, Stranahan Hall, Room 1033
College of Business Administration
University of Toledo
2801 West Bancroft Street
Toledo, Ohio 43606-3390
Phone: 419-530-2775
Fax: 419-530-7260
E-mail: mba@utoledo.edu
Web site: http://www.utoledo.edu/business

The University of Toledo

THE FACULTY

Accounting

Diana Franz, Professor and Department Chair; Ph.D., Texas Tech; CPA (Ohio).
Philip Fink, Professor; J.D., Ohio Northern; CPA (Ohio).
Hassan Hassab-Elnaby, Assistant Professor; Ph.D., Cairo.
Brian Laverty, Professor; Ph.D., Michigan State; CPA (Michigan).
Bhanu Ragu-Nathan, Professor; Ph.D., Pittsburgh.
Donald Saftner, Professor; Ph.D., Penn State.
Amal Said, Assistant Professor; Ph.D., Virginia Commonwealth.
Nicholas Schroeder, Professor; D.B.A., Colorado; CPA (Ohio).
Nancy Snow, Lecturer; M.S.A., Toledo; CPA (Ohio).
Glenn Wolfe, Associate Professor; Ph.D., Virginia Tech.

Finance and Business Economics

Andrew Solocha, Associate Professor and Department Chair; Ph.D., Michigan State.
Richard Boden, Associate Professor; Ph.D., Maryland.
Linda Bowyer, Associate Professor; Ph.D., Iowa State.
Maureen Conroy, Professor; M.B.A., Bowling Green State.
Mine Ertugrul, Professor; Ph.D., Connecticut.
Gary Moore, Associate Professor; J.D., Iowa; Ph.D., Arizona State.
Ozcan Sezer, Assistant Professor; Ph.D., Connecticut.
Michael Sherman, Associate Professor; Ph.D., Purdue.
Herbert Weinraub, Professor; Ph.D., Michigan State.

Information Operations and Technology Management

T. S. Ragu-Nathan, Professor and Department Chair; Ph.D., Pittsburgh.
Mesbah Ahmed, Professor; Ph.D., Texas Tech.
Xiao Fang, Assistant Professor; Ph.D. Arizona.
Bassam Hasan, Assistant Professor; Ph.D., Mississippi.
Paul Hong, Associate Professor; Ph.D., Toledo.
Jerzy Kamburowski, Professor; Ph.D., Wroclaw Technical (Poland).
Anand Kunnathur, Professor and Associate Dean; Ph.D., Tennessee.
Kee Lim, Lecturer; Ph.D., Toledo.
Udayan Nandkeolyar, Associate Professor; Ph.D., Penn State.
James Pope, Professor; Ph.D., North Carolina at Chapel Hill.
Ram Rachamadugu, Professor; Ph.D., Carnegie Mellon.
S. Subba Rao, Professor; Ph.D., Delhi.
Arthur Smith, Professor; Ph.D., Oklahoma.
P. S. Sundaraghavan, Professor; Ph.D., Tennessee.
Monideepa Tarafdar, Assistant Professor; Ph.D., Indian Institute of Management (Calcutta).
Mark Vonderembse, Professor; Ph.D., Michigan.

Management

Dale Dwyer, Professor and Department Chair; Ph.D., Nebraska–Lincoln.
Sonny Ariss, Associate Professor; Ph.D., Ohio State.

Dale Eesley, Assistant Professor; Ph.D., Wisconsin–Madison.
Larry Fink, Associate Professor; Ph.D., Purdue.
Margaret Hopkins, Assistant Professor; Ph.D., Case Western Reserve.
Clinton Longenecker, Stranahan Professor of Leadership and Organizational Excellence; Ph.D., Penn State.
Nick Nykodym, Professor; Ph.D., Nebraska.
Frederick Post, Associate Professor; J.D., Toledo.
Tim Schramko, Assistant Professor; E.D.M., Case Western Reserve.
Robert Schwartz, Associate Professor; Ph.D., Michigan.
Nancy Waldeck, Assistant Professor; Ph.D., Ohio State.
Donald Wedding, Associate Professor; J.D., American.
Robert Yonker, Assistant Professor; Ph.D., Missouri.

Marketing and International Business

Anthony Koh, Associate Professor and Department Chair; Ph.D., Alabama.
Ainsworth Bailey, Professor; Ph.D., Iowa.
Don Beeman, Professor; D.B.A., Indiana.
Richard Buehrer, Professor; Ph.D., Toledo.
William Darley, Professor; Ph.D., Indiana.
Bashar Gammoh, Assistant Professor; Ph.D., Oklahoma State.
Robin Hadwick.
Ken Kim, Professor; D.B.A., Indiana, 1985.
Thuong Le, Professor; Ph.D., Michigan State.
Jeen Lim, Professor; Ph.D., Indiana.
Sylvia Long-Tolbert, Professor; Ph.D., Ohio State.
Michael Mallin, Assistant Professor; Ph.D., Kent State.
Sam Okoroafo, Professor; Ph.D., Michigan State.
Ellen Pullins, Associate Professor; Ph.D., Ohio State.
Thomas Sharkey, Associate Professor; Ph.D., Indiana.
Ron Zallocco, Professor; Ph.D., Kent State.

Visiting Faculty

Jackie Flom, M.B.A., Toledo. (Management)
Laura Frisbie, M.B.A., Toledo. (Management)
Deirdre Jones, M.B.A., Toledo. (Marketing and International Business)
Amy Latimer, B.S., Southern New Hampshire. (Accounting)
Kimberly Lehman, M.B.A., Toledo. (Marketing and International Business)
Amy O'Donnell, M.S., Miami (Ohio). (Management)
Susan Shultz, M.B.A., Toledo. (Management)
Norman Spohler, J.D., Toledo. (Management)
Laura Williams, M.B.A., Toledo. (Management)

VIRGINIA COMMONWEALTH UNIVERSITY

School of Business

Programs of Study

The School of Business at Virginia Commonwealth University (VCU) offers degree programs leading to the Master of Arts in economics, the Master of Accountancy, the Master of Business Administration, the Master of Business Administration/Master of Science in Information Systems, the Master of Science in business, the Master of Science in information systems, the Master of Taxation, the Ph.D. in business, and the Pharm.D./M.B.A.

The M.A. in economics enhances students' abilities to use economic modeling to conduct applied analytical and econometric research. Students are expected to demonstrate competence over a rigorous and current core curriculum in microeconomic and macroeconomic theory and in econometrics.

The purpose of the Master of Accountancy program is to provide the skills and knowledge necessary to be future leaders in the professional business community and the public sector for students who wish to specialize in the areas of accounting/information systems, auditing financial reporting, accounting, or other fields of business.

The M.B.A. provides a balance of business theory and practical applications. Through a variety of instructional methods, including case studies, students acquire the skills and knowledge needed to lead complex business organizations, and they become well-prepared for the responsibilities and rigors of management. Students may choose a general course of study or specialize in one or more concentrations, such as decision sciences, economics, finance, human resource management and industrial relations, information systems, marketing, or real estate and urban land development.

The M.S. in information systems program is focused on the rapidly emerging area known as enterprise information systems (EIS). Graduates can take significant roles in planning, organizing, managing, designing, configuring, and implementing EIS systems using state-of-the-art technologies within organizations. Students in the fast-track M.B.A. program have the option to continue with the fast-track executive M.S. in information systems with an information technology management concentration, after having completed the requirements for the fast-track M.B.A., to earn both degrees.

The M.S. in business program provides in-depth knowledge of one business discipline and allows students to develop and build technical skills in their specific area of interest. Concentrations are available in decision sciences, finance, global marketing management, and real estate valuation.

The Ph.D. in business is designed specifically for individuals intending to fill positions at institutions that require a balance of scholarly training, teaching, and practical application of the appropriate field of study. Three areas of study are offered—accounting, information systems, and management.

The Master of Taxation gives existing tax professionals an opportunity to update and expand existing tax knowledge; the program also prepares students for entry-level positions in the field of taxation. The curriculum includes a comprehensive study of tax laws and regulations, administrative practice and procedure, and tax research fundamentals.

The Pharm.D./M.B.A. program seeks to prepare pharmacists for careers that encompass pharmacy and business theories and principles. The program is designed to take advantage of efficiencies and electives in both the Pharm.D. and M.B.A. programs. Students in the combined program can earn both degrees and save as much as one year or more over the time required for enrolling in the programs separately.

Research Facilities

VCU libraries provide a combined capacity of more than 1.7 million volumes and 10,200 periodical titles and an online bibliographic search service accessing hundreds of databases. In addition, the Virginia State and Richmond Public Libraries are within walking distance of both VCU campuses. Academic Computing provides a variety of microcomputer, minicomputer, and mainframe computing services to support the research and instructional endeavors of the faculty and students, including consultation, instruction, and computer acquisition.

Financial Aid

The School of Business offers a limited number of graduate assistantship positions to full-time students. Scholarship opportunities exist for graduate students after they have completed at least one semester of study. Students may apply for need-based assistance with the University's Financial Aid Office. Current information on financial aid programs, policies, and procedures is available at http://www.vcu.edu/enroll/finaid.

Cost of Study

For full-time study (9–15 credits) in 2007–08, Virginia residents pay tuition and fees of $4452 per semester; nonresidents, $8876 per semester. For part-time study, Virginia residents pay tuition and fees of $465 per hour; nonresidents, $954 per hour. Some programs require additional fees. On the Medical College of Virginia (MCV) campus, tuition, fees, and other expenses vary in the medicine, pharmacy, nurse anesthesia, dentistry, and School of Allied Health programs.

Living and Housing Costs

Graduate student housing is available on both the MCV campus and the academic campus of Virginia Commonwealth University. Many graduate students live in off-campus housing, which is reasonably priced and readily available in a variety of styles and settings in nearby residential areas or within easy commuting distance. On- and off-campus housing information is available on the Web at http://www.housing.vcu.edu/.

Student Group

VCU enrolls 30,452 students, 7,611 of whom are graduate students. More than 200 clubs and organizations reflect the diverse social, recreational, educational, political, and religious interests of the student body.

Location

Richmond is Virginia's capital and a major East Coast financial and manufacturing center that offers students a wide range of cultural, educational, and recreational activities. Richmond is located in central Virginia at the intersection of Interstates 95 and 64, 2 hours south of Washington, D.C., and nestled between the Blue Ridge Mountains and the Atlantic coast. The Richmond region is easily accessible by plane, car, and train. With nearly 1 million residents, the historic city of Richmond combines big-city offerings with small-town hospitality. Applicants are encouraged to explore http://www.visit.richmond.com/ for more information on the city.

The University

VCU is a state-supported coeducational university with a graduate school, a major teaching hospital, and twelve academic and professional units that offer fifty-two undergraduate, twenty-two postbaccalaureate certificate, sixty-five master's, six post-master's certificate, and twenty-nine Ph.D. programs. VCU also offers M.D., D.D.S., D.P.T., and Pharm.D. programs as well as cooperative degree programs with other major Virginia colleges and universities. VCU has one of the largest evening colleges in the United States. The academic campus is located in Richmond's historic Fan District. The health sciences campus and hospital are located 2 miles east in the downtown business district. A University bus service provides free intercampus transportation for faculty members and students.

With more than $211 million in annual research funding, Virginia Commonwealth University is classified as one of the nation's top research universities by the Carnegie Foundation for the Advancement of Teaching. More than 29,000 undergraduate, certificate, graduate, post-master's, professional, and doctoral students are enrolled in 162 academic programs, forty of which are unique in the commonwealth of Virginia. The faculty members represent the finest American and international graduate institutions and enhance the University's position among the important institutions of higher learning in the United States and the world via their work in the classroom, laboratory, studio, and clinic and in their scholarly publications.

Applying

Admission procedures and program requirements are detailed in the *Graduate Bulletin*. Application deadlines and materials, including the application and the *Graduate Bulletin*, are available online at the Graduate School Web site at http://www.graduate.vcu.edu. Virginia Commonwealth University is an equal opportunity/affirmative action institution providing access to education and employment without regard to age, race, color, national origin, gender, religion, sexual orientation, veteran's status, political affiliation, or disability.

Correspondence and Information

Jana P. McQuaid, Graduate Program Director
School of Business
Virginia Commonwealth University
1015 Floyd Avenue
Richmond, Virginia 23284-4000
Phone: 804-828-1595
E-mail: jpmcquaid@vcu.edu
Web site: http://www.gsib.bus.vcu.edu/index.html

Virginia Commonwealth University

THE FACULTY AND THEIR RESEARCH

ACCOUNTING

Edward N. Coffman, Professor; D.B.A., George Washington. Financial accounting, accounting history.

Wayne Edmunds, Associate Professor; M.L.T., J.D., William and Mary; CPA.

Ruth W. Epps, Professor and Chair; Ph.D., Virginia Commonwealth; CPA. Governmental/not-for-profit accounting, corporate governance.

John O. Everett, Professor; Ph.D., Oklahoma State; CPA. Taxation, computer solutions to tax planning problems, tax policy issues.

Carolyn Norman, Assistant Professor; Ph.D., Texas A&M.

Philip R. Olds, Associate Professor; Ph.D., Georgia State; CPA. Accounting education.

Myung Park, Assistant Professor; Ph.D., Purdue. Capital market research, earnings management, fair-value accounting, and other topics in financial, managerial accounting, and accounting information systems.

Edward C. Spede, Associate Professor; Ph.D., Virginia Tech. Financial accounting, accounting education.

Roxanne Spindle, Associate Professor; Ph.D., Colorado; CPA. Public policy and the tax structure, individual tax planning.

Rasoul H. Tondkar, Professor; Ph.D., North Texas. International accounting.

Jayaraman Vijayakumar, Associate Professor; Ph.D., Pittsburgh. State and local government finances and accounting, capital markets, financial reporting, insider trading.

Benson Wier, Professor; Ph.D., Texas Tech; CPA. Behavioral facets of managerial accounting.

ECONOMICS

Douglas D. Davis, Professor; Ph.D., Indiana. Tools used by antitrust authorities for detecting collusion and for identifying problematic mergers.

David Harless, Professor; Ph.D., Indiana. Applied econometrics, health economics, behavior under risk and uncertainty.

George E. Hoffer, Professor; Ph.D., Virginia. Pricing and consumer topics related to the automobile industry.

Oleg Korenok, Assistant Professor; Ph.D., Rutgers. Prices and inflation: price/information stickiness (macroeconomics), price discovery (financial economics), price formation mechanisms (experimental economics).

Carol Scotese Lehr, Associate Professor; Ph.D., Penn State. Institutional aspects of economic development.

Edward L. Millner, Professor and Chair; Ph.D., North Carolina at Chapel Hill. Experimental economics, decision making in the face of uncertainty, economic analysis of business strategies and tactics.

Shannon K. Mitchell, Associate Professor; Ph.D., Virginia. Health care in developing countries, particularly AIDS in sub-Saharan Africa; development economics; and international trade theory.

Dennis M. O'Toole, Associate Professor; Ph.D., Ohio. Factors that lead college students to alter their enrollment behavior—switching between full-time, part-time, and stop-out status.

Steven P. Peterson, Director of Research, Virginia Retirement System; Ph.D., Indiana. Econometrics of financial markets, risk and distress models, neural networks, covariance misspecification in asset allocation.

Michael D. Pratt, Professor; Ph.D., Kansas. Experimental economics directed to public choice theory, controls for and analysis of risk aversion, industrial organization.

Laura Razzolini, Associate Professor; Ph.D., Southern Methodist. Mechanism design and experimental economics.

Robert J. Reilly, Professor; Ph.D., Tennessee. Experimental economics, individual behavior under uncertainty, biodiversity and ecological economics, applied microeconomics.

Leslie S. Stratton, Associate Professor; Ph.D., MIT. Interaction between market and nonmarket activities, particularly as they influence market outcomes; undergraduate enrollment patterns.

James N. Wetzel, Professor; Ph.D., North Carolina. Environmental, urban, and managerial economics and public finance.

FINANCE, INSURANCE, AND REAL ESTATE

Etti Baranoff, Associate Professor; Ph.D., Texas. Insurance law and regulation, all coverages (personal and commercial lines), insurers' financial stability, alternative risk financing, risk management information systems (RMIS).

Kenneth N. Daniels, Professor; Ph.D., Connecticut. Municipal bonds, corporate finance, financial institutions, small-business development, financial economics of minorities.

David Downs, Professor and Alfred L. Blake Chair; Ph.D., North Carolina at Chapel Hill. Real estate finance and investment, issues relevant to institutional real estate investors, the implications of real estate regulation.

John Guthmann, Assistant Professor; Ph.D., New Mexico.

R. Michael McDonald, Associate Professor; Ed.D., Virginia Tech. Impediments to organizational change and the application of concept-mapping techniques to holistic problem analysis and strategic planning.

E. G. Miller, Senior Associate Dean; Ph.D., Alabama. Statistical applications in the insurance industry and insurance regulation.

Oghenovo Obrimah, Assistant Professor; Ph.D., Maryland.

Richard A. Phillips, Associate Professor; Ph.D., North Carolina at Chapel Hill. Real estate finance and economics, housing economics, and economics of transportation and public policy.

Daniel P. Salandro, Associate Professor; Ph.D., Pittsburgh.

Tai S. Shin, Professor; Ph.D., Illinois. Corporate finance, investment, banking, and international finance.

David E. Upton, Professor and Chair; Ph.D., North Carolina. Security analysis, portfolio management, investments.

INFORMATION SYSTEMS

Peter Aiken, Associate Professor; Ph.D., George Mason.

Amita Chin, Associate Professor; Ph.D., Maryland. Collaborative and WWW technologies, database systems, women in technology, information technology curricula.

Richard J. Coppins, Associate Professor; Ph.D., North Carolina State. Computer/network security and application of operations research techniques to problems related to computer systems.

Gupreet Dhillon, Professor; Ph.D., London. Information security, its right use, and the range of related ethical and philosophical issues.

George Kasper, Professor; Ph.D., SUNY at Buffalo. Computer-human interaction, decision-support systems.

Allen S. Lee, Professor; Ph.D., MIT. Qualitative, interpretive, and case research on information technology and organizations; communications; research methodologies in information systems research and the social sciences; action research.

Kweku-Muata (Noel) Osei-Bryson, Professor; Ph.D., Maryland, College Park. Data mining, database systems, expert systems, decision-support systems, group-support systems, multicriteria decision analysis, cluster analysis, integer programming, and parametric programming.

Richard T. Redmond, Associate Professor; D.B.A., Kent State. Software productivity, expert systems, applications of AI to business, database/imagebase design theory and compression theory.

John Sutherland, Professor; Ph.D., UCLA.

Heinz R. Weistroffer, Associate Professor; Ph.D., Free University of Berlin. Software engineering, decision support systems, conceptual modeling, portfolio decision making, economics of information technology.

James Wynne, Associate Professor; Ph.D., Nebraska–Lincoln. Software project management, software training and curriculum development, group-decision support systems, systems analysis and design.

MANAGEMENT

R. Jon Ackley, Associate Professor; Ed.D., Utah State. Applied statistics and quantitative methods.

Robert L. Andrews, Associate Professor; Ph.D., Virginia Tech. Applied statistics, decision analysis, quantitative methods.

Randolph T. Barker, Professor; Ph.D., Florida State. Multidimensional aspects of organizational communication including team leadership, listening, and strategy.

Charles M. Byles, Associate Professor; D.B.A., Kent State. Relationship between strategy and human resource management practices, differences in cognitive styles among managers in several countries.

George C. Canavos, Professor; Ph.D., Virginia Tech.

José Dulá, Associate Professor; Ph.D., Michigan.

Glenn H. Gilbreath, Professor and Chair; Ph.D., Alabama. Statistics and quality management.

George R. Gray, Ph.D., Alabama.

Ronald Humphrey, Associate Professor; Ph.D., Michigan. Cognitive and emotional processes in organizations, especially with regard to performance appraisals, personnel selection, assessment centers, group dynamics, and decision-making.

Iris W. Johnson, Ed.D., Virginia Tech.

Jeffrey Krug, Associate Professor; Ph.D., Indiana. Corporate strategy, mergers and acquisitions, corporate governance, top management teams, global strategy.

Ibrahim Kurtulus, Associate Professor; Ph.D., North Carolina at Chapel Hill. Purchasing, logistics, MRP, JIT, and resource-constrained scheduling.

Michael A. McDaniel, Professor; Ph.D., George Washington. Situational judgment tests, race and sex differences in work-related variables, effects of applicant faking on employment decisions and issues concerning older workers, applications of meta-analysis in the evaluation of personnel selection methods.

Marianne Miller, Associate Professor; Ph.D., Oregon. Employee recruitment, selection, and socialization; management of a diverse work force, particularly issues related to inclusion and accommodation of people with disabilities.

Elliott D. Minor III, Associate Professor; Ph.D., South Carolina.

Subhash C. Narula, Professor; Ph.D., Iowa.

Michael W. Pitts, Associate Professor; D.B.A., Tennessee. Strategic management process in former Soviet-type economic systems and competitive intelligence activities.

Anson Seers, Professor; Ph.D., Cincinnati. Work roles and relationships, including leadership, the development of effective teamwork, and employee motivation.

Randall G. Sleeth, Associate Professor; Ph.D., Massachusetts. Leadership processes, computer-mediated instruction.

Robert R. Trumble, Professor; Ph.D., Minnesota. Human resources, labor relations and strategic planning.

Larry Williams, Professor; Ph.D., Indiana. Application of structural equation methods to various substantive and methodological concerns in the field of organizational behavior.

Margaret Williams, Associate Professor; Ph.D., Indiana. Employee compensation programs, particularly employee reactions to benefits; work-life issues, with a particular emphasis on part-time or reduced load work at the managerial and professional levels and work-life issues in small organizations; leadership and motivation issues within organizations.

D. Robley Wood Jr., Professor; D.B.A., Tennessee. Characteristics of successful formal planning for the operations function of commercial banks.

MARKETING AND BUSINESS LAW

Deborah L. Cowles, Associate Professor; Ph.D., Arizona State. Relationship marketing (including database marketing), e-commerce (including retail and business-to-business), services marketing (including service quality, customer service, and customer satisfaction).

Frank J. Franzak, Associate Professor and Chair; Ph.D., Maryland. New product development, global marketing strategy, marketing of technology products, public policy issues, evaluation research methods.

Haeran Jae, Assistant Professor; Ph.D., Kentucky. Low-literate consumers, linguistically isolated consumers.

Michael W. Little, Associate Professor; Ph.D., Michigan State. Electronic retail/marketing on the World Wide Web.

Dennis R. McDermott, Associate Professor; Ph.D., Ohio State. Strategic marketing, marketing management, marketing education.

David J. Urban, Professor; Ph.D., Michigan. Customer satisfaction research, retailing, and distribution channel management.

Heiko de B. Wijnholds, Associate Professor; D.Com., South Africa. International marketing, marketing management, forensic marketing, forecasting.

Van R. Wood, Professor and Phillip Morris Chair in International Business; Ph.D., Oregon. International marketing/globalization (risk assessment, market development and management in international markets), marketing management (strategic planning and assessment).

WASHINGTON UNIVERSITY IN ST. LOUIS

John M. Olin School of Business

Programs of Study

The John M. Olin School of Business offers several options for graduate study. The Master of Science in finance is a ten- to twelve-month program that prepares students for advanced entry-level career opportunities in financial services and corporate financial management. The Master of Accounting is a one- to two-year graduate program that prepares students for careers that require extensive accounting knowledge in both public and corporate accounting settings. A two-year program, the full-time M.B.A. offers an intensely personalized curriculum that allows students to target areas of interest, develop career-specific skills, and capitalize on hands-on learning opportunities. The professional M.B.A. (PMBA) program, designed for working professionals, features a class cohort system where students attend classes with the same individuals for their first four semesters. Students take classes in the evening and usually complete the degree in three years. The St. Louis– and Shanghai-based eighteen-month weekend executive M.B.A. (EMBA) programs emphasize strategy, leadership, and effective organization in their effort to transform high-caliber executives into innovative, critical thinkers capable of dealing effectively with complex, unstructured problems. The School also offers a Ph.D. program that provides an intellectually challenging core curriculum that emphasizes microeconomics, statistics, and quantitative methods; features one-on-one mentoring relationships with highly respected faculty members; and prepares students for careers in scholarship and teaching.

Research Facilities

The Boeing Center for Technology, Information, and Manufacturing was set up jointly by Washington University's John M. Olin School of Business, the Boeing Company, and other corporate partners in order to foster a more meaningful, mutually beneficial interaction between industry and academia. The center focuses on issues relating to technology in general, and information technology (IT) in particular, and their impact on the firm in general and, more specifically, on the management of its operations and those of its supply chain partners.

The Center for Research in Economics and Strategy (CRES) advances the understanding of firms and markets by supporting scientific research on these subjects, especially research that employs state-of-the-art analytical and/or empirical methods to address substantive questions and that is intended to be published in top-tier academic journals.

The Reuben C. Taylor Experimental Laboratory is a state-of-the-art facility for conducting experimental research on decision making, bargaining, and markets. The backbone of the laboratory is a network of computers that enables participants to make decisions and communicate with others.

The Kopolow Business Library keeps students and faculty members up-to-the-minute with online resources, including Dow Jones Interactive, LexisNexis, InfoTrac, and ABI, as well as databases provided by Moody's, Standard & Poor's, Hoover's, and Disclosure. The library also receives comprehensive real-time information on stocks and other markets through Bloomberg and Bridge Information Systems. The library maintains a book collection of about 30,000 volumes and subscriptions to more than 400 major business journals, magazines, and newspapers.

Financial Aid

The full-time M.B.A. program has full- and partial-tuition scholarships and assistantships available. Many EMBA students receive full or partial financial support from their organizations, and a limited number of scholarships for up to 50 percent of tuition are offered to individuals working for nonprofit organizations. PMBA students may apply for loans to pay for education-related expenses, including tuition, books, course materials, and computer hardware and software. All Ph.D. students who make satisfactory progress are guaranteed financial aid for five years, including full-tuition remission plus a stipend for living expenses distributed over twelve months. The minimum annual stipend is $17,000. There are no scholarships or special financial aid packages for the Master of Science or the Master of Accounting programs. Student loans are available for students who do not receive full financial support.

Cost of Study

Tuition is $1085 per credit hour. The full-time M.B.A. costs $17,975 per semester. The total program cost for the executive M.B.A. program, including lodging at the Knight Center for the opening residency, meals, textbooks, study materials, and on-campus parking, is $79,900.

Living and Housing Costs

Most graduate students live off campus in large and affordable apartments that range from $600 to $900 per month. The University's estimate of living expenses for the nine-month academic year, including room and board, books and supplies, clothing, recreation, incidentals, and medical insurance, is $18,260.

Student Group

There are 507 full-time and 349 part-time students, 224 of whom are women and 142, international.

Location

St. Louis, the "Gateway to the West," offers a multitude of appealing destinations, unique neighborhoods, and a rich history. St. Louis is the home of premier educational institutions, varied cultural attractions, Fortune 500 companies that dominate their industries, and research facilities that are making breakthroughs in agriculture, medicine, and technology. With its innovative, entrepreneurial environment, St. Louis is poised for a bright and vibrant future.

The University and The School

An independent institution founded in 1853, Washington University in St. Louis seeks excellence in everything it does. With 13,000 students and 3,000 faculty members, the University is counted among the world's leaders in teaching and research and draws students from all fifty states and approximately 130 other nations. Parts of the 1904 World's Fair and Olympics were held on the 169-acre campus, which is bordered on the east by St. Louis's famed Forest Park and on the north, west, and south by well-established suburbs. Twenty-three Nobel Prize winners have been associated with the University.

The John M. Olin School of Business was founded in 1917. Its longstanding reputation for outstanding management education comes from the School's unique combination of highly accomplished researchers, professors, and students; tailored curriculum; and strong sense of community.

Applying

In general, students should submit the completed application form, the application fee ($75–$100, depending on the program), official transcripts of all prior undergraduate and graduate work, and two to three letters of recommendation. Some programs require GMAT or GRE scores and a resume. International applicants should send in TOEFL scores. Deadlines vary by program. Students should check online for more information.

Correspondence and Information

John M. Olin School of Business
Campus Box 1133
Washington University in St. Louis
1 Brookings Drive
St. Louis, Missouri 63130-4899

Phone: 314-935-7301
Fax: 314-935-6309
E-mail: mba@olin.wustl.edu (Full-Time and Professional M.B.A.)
      embainfo@olin.wustl.edu (Executive M.B.A.)
      phdinfo@olin.wustl.edu (Ph.D.)
      hochberg@wustl.edu (M.S. in Finance)
      maccinfo@wustl.edu (M.S. in Accounting)
Web site: http://www.olin.wustl.edu

Washington University in St. Louis

THE FACULTY AND THEIR RESEARCH

Yossi Aviv, Associate Professor of Operations and Manufacturing Management; Ph.D., Columbia, 1998. Production and operations management, logistics and distribution systems, supply chain management, decision analysis, stochastic processes.

Markus Baer, Assistant Professor of Organizational Behavior; Ph.D., Illinois at Urbana-Champaign, 2006. Creativity and innovation at the individual, team, and organizational levels of analysis; cross-cultural effects of organizational climate/culture (e.g., error management culture) on organizational performance; social network theory.

William P. Bottom, Joyce and Howard Wood Distinguished Professor of Organizational Behavior; Ph.D., Illinois at Urbana-Champaign, 1989. Organizational behavior, behavioral decision theory, negotiation.

J. Stuart Bunderson, Associate Professor of Organizational Behavior; Ph.D., Minnesota, 1998. Knowledge management and the coordination of specialized expertise.

Tat Y. Chan, Assistant Professor of Marketing; Ph.D., Yale, 2001. Industrial organization, applied econometrics, applied microeconomics, marketing.

Anchanda Charoenrook, Visiting Assistant Professor of Finance; M.S./Ph.D. (electrical engineering), Washington (Seattle), 1995; Ph.D., Michigan, 2000. Theoretical and empirical asset pricing, derivative securities, risk management, corporate finance theory as related to security pricing, problems in economic modeling.

Sergio Chayet, Assistant Professor of Operations and Manufacturing Management; Ph.D., Northwestern, 1999. Strategic planning for production and service organizations, using queuing and game-theoretic models; control and management of manufacturing systems; stochastic models for production systems; customer-supplier relationships.

Amar Cheema, Assistant Professor of Marketing; Ph.D., Colorado, 2003. Consumer behavior in auctions, consumer spending with credit, behavioral decision theory, measuring consumer valuation of products, customer purchase patterns in grocery stores, psychophysiology.

Siddhartha Chib, Harry C. Hartkopf Professor of Econometrics and Statistics; Ph.D., California, Santa Barbara, 1986. Bayesian statistics and econometrics, Markov chain Monte Carlo methods.

Samuel Chun, Lecturer; Ph.D., Washington (St. Louis), 1995. Marketing.

Martin Cripps, John K. Wallace, Jr. and Ellen A. Wallace Distinguished Professor of Managerial Economics; Ph.D., London School of Economics, 1986. Economics, bargaining, debt, reputation, the strategic foundations of competitive markets.

Charles Cuny, Visiting Assistant Professor of Finance; Ph.D., Stanford, 1990. Capital structure, financial innovation, venture capital, employee stock options, stock index changes, corporate payout policy.

Shawn Davis, Visiting Assistant Professor of Accounting; Ph.D., Washington (St. Louis). Audit judgment and decision making; experimental and capital markets research, specifically economic theories and psychology theories of market reactions.

Kurt T. Dirks, Associate Professor of Organizational Behavior; Ph.D., Minnesota, 1997. Organizational behavior, trust in work relationships, feelings of ownership in the workplace, teams.

Lingxiu Dong, Associate Professor of Operations and Manufacturing Management; Ph.D., Stanford, 1999. Operations management, production and distribution systems, supply chain management, information in supply chains.

Philip H. Dybvig, Boatmen's Bancshares Professor of Banking and Finance; Ph.D., Yale, 1979. Banking, corporate finance, financial markets, fixed income securities, industrial organization, portfolio management.

Daniel Elfenbein, Assistant Professor of Organization and Strategy; Ph.D., Harvard, 2004. Governance of complex transactions, markets for intellectual property, innovation and technological change, university-industry technology transfer, incentives in organizations.

Michael W. Faulkender, 2006–07 Marcile and James Reid Professor and Assistant Professor of Finance; Ph.D., Northwestern, 2002. Empirical corporate finance: capital structure, derivatives usage, debt characteristics.

Thomas D. Fields, Lecturer in Accounting; Ph.D., Northwestern, 2004. Accounting, specifically financial reporting.

Richard Frankel, Associate Professor of Accounting; Ph.D., Stanford, 1993. Accounting-based valuation, voluntary disclosure.

Amanda Friedenberg, Assistant Professor of Economics; Ph.D., Harvard, 2003. Game theory, microeconomic theory, political economy.

Armando Gomes, Associate Professor of Finance; Ph.D., Harvard, 1997. Corporate finance, mergers and acquisitions, corporate governance, economic theory.

Radhakrishnan Gopalan, Assistant Professor of Finance; Ph.D., Michigan, 2006. Corporate finance, specifically corporate governance, emerging market financial systems, mergers and acquisitions, corporate restructuring, and entrepreneurial finance.

Michael R. Gordinier, Senior Lecturer in Management; Ph.D., Wisconsin, 1980. Statistics, management science, financial planning, investments, insurance.

Todd Gormley, Assistant Professor of Finance; Ph.D., MIT, 2006. Corporate finance, banking and financial institutions, economic development.

Gautam Gowrisankaran, Assistant Professor of Economics; Ph.D., Yale, 1995. Industrial organization, health economics, applied econometrics.

Stuart I. Greenbaum, Bank of America Professor of Managerial Leadership; Ph.D., Johns Hopkins, 1964. Banking and financial intermediation.

Mahendra R. Gupta, Geraldine J. and Robert L. Virgil Professor of Accounting and Management and Dean; Ph.D., Stanford, 1990. Managerial accounting, strategic cost management and control.

Dirk Hackbarth, Assistant Professor of Finance; Ph.D., Berkeley, 2003. Corporate finance: banking, bankruptcy, capital structure; behavioral finance: managerial aspects.

Barton H. Hamilton, Robert Brookings Smith Distinguished Professor of Entrepreneurship; Ph.D., Stanford, 1993. Entrepreneurship, health economics, labor economics, econometrics.

Zeynep K. Hansen, Assistant Professor of Organization and Strategy; Ph.D., Arizona, 2002. Technology licensing and management, strategic R&D collaborations, R&D and innovation, organizational strategy, pharmaceutical and biotechnology industries, property rights and economic policy.

Kenneth Harrington, Senior Lecturer in Entrepreneurship and Managing Director, Skandalaris Center for Entrepreneurial Studies; M.B.A., Pennsylvania, 1987.

Nicole Thorne Jenkins, Assistant Professor of Accounting; Ph.D., Iowa, 2002. Financial accounting and corporate governance.

Ohad Kadan, Assistant Professor of Finance and 2006–07 Marcile and James Reid Professor; Ph.D., Hebrew (Jerusalem), 2002. Corporate finance, market microstructure, economics of information, game theory.

Ronald R. King, Myron Northrop Professor of Accounting; Ph.D., Arizona, 1986. Business, law, and economics; auditing; experimental economics.

Anne Marie Knott, Assistant Professor of Strategy; Ph.D., UCLA, 1996. Innovation, R&D, entrepreneurship, managerial value, sustainable advantage.

Panos Kouvelis, Emerson Distinguished Professor of Operations and Manufacturing Management and Director, Boeing Center for Technology, Information, and Manufacturing; Ph.D., Stanford, 1988. International operations, supply chain management, e-business and e-fulfillment strategies, marketing/manufacturing interfaces, manufacturing strategy, lean manufacturing, project management, cyclic scheduling, manufacturing system design, discrete optimization.

Dmitri Kuksov, Assistant Professor of Marketing; Ph.D., Berkeley, 2003. Competitive strategy, consumer information processing, customer satisfaction, brand image, Internet marketing.

Claus Langfred, Associate Professor of Organizational Behavior; Ph.D., Northwestern, 1998. Self-management, autonomy (at multiple levels), trust, conflict, and interdependence in organizations.

Lubomir Litov, Assistant Professor of Finance; Ph.D., NYU, 2005. Corporate finance, corporate governance, international corporate finance, behavioral corporate finance.

James T. Little, Professor of Finance and Economics; Ph.D., Minnesota, 1977. Microeconomics, international economics, corporate strategy, insurance regulation.

Hong Liu, Associate Professor of Finance; Ph.D., Pennsylvania, 1998. Optimal consumption and investment with frictions, asset pricing, market microstructure.

Chris P. Long, Assistant Professor of Organizational Behavior; Ph.D., Duke, 2002. Organizational fairness, trust, and control within both traditional organizations and new organizational forms.

Glenn MacDonald, Senior Associate Dean and John M. Olin Distinguished Professor of Economics and Strategy; Ph.D., Rochester, 1979. Industry evolution, strategy and value appropriation, microeconomics/industrial organization, investor protection, compensation.

Vladimir N. Mares, Assistant Professor of Economics; Ph.D., Rutgers, 2001. Industrial organization, microeconomic theory, game theory, auction and bargaining theory, antitrust economics, finance, economies in transition.

Raj Mashruwala, Assistant Professor of Accounting; Ph.D., Texas at Dallas, 2002. Managerial accounting, especially the role of nonfinancial measures in performance measurement and business value models; role of nonfinancial measures in executive labor and capital markets; impact of information technology on performance.

Brian P. McManus, Assistant Professor of Economics; Ph.D., Virginia, 2002. Industrial organization, empirical microeconomics, theoretical microeconomics.

Todd Milbourn, Associate Professor of Finance; Ph.D., Indiana, 1995. Corporate finance, managerial career concerns, management compensation, economics of asymmetric information.

Chakravarthi Narasimhan, Philip L. Siteman Professor of Marketing and Director, Ph.D. Program; Ph.D., Rochester, 1982. Supply chain strategies, especially under uncertainty; competitive strategies in information-intensive environments (e-strategies); modeling customer profitability; choice modeling.

Jackson A. Nickerson, Professor of Organization and Strategy; Ph.D., Berkeley, 1997. Business strategy and public policy, organizational economics, new institutional economics, intellectual capital management, technology licensing, organizational theory.

Tava Lennon Olsen, Associate Professor of Operations and Manufacturing Management; Ph.D., Stanford, 1994. Supply chain management, e-commerce, manufacturing systems analysis and control, control of wireless communication networks, queuing theory.

Judi McLean Parks, Reuben C. and Anne Carpenter Taylor Professor of Organizational Behavior; Ph.D., Iowa, 1990. Organizational behavior, conflict management and dispute resolution, psychological contracts and workplace justice, diversity and sociocultural/cross-cultural management factors, revenge in the workplace, organizational identity.

Robert A. Pollak, Hernreich Distinguished Professor of Economics; Ph.D., MIT, 1964. Environmental economics and policy; consumer demand analysis and consumer behavior; demography, labor economics, and economics of the family.

Ambar G. Rao, Fossett Distinguished Professor of Marketing; Ph.D., Pennsylvania, 1967. Product strategy, marketing management, advertising, new-product management.

Mark E. Soczek, Lecturer in Accounting; Director, Center for Experiential Learning; and Director, M.S.B.A. Program in Accounting; Ph.D. candidate, Northwestern. Corporate disclosure policy, financial reporting.

Raymond T. Sparrowe, Associate Professor of Organizational Behavior; Ph.D., Illinois at Chicago, 1998. Leadership, informal relationships in organizations, group processes and outcomes.

Jeroen M. Swinkels, August A. Busch Jr., Distinguished Professor of Managerial Economics and Strategy; Ph.D., Princeton, 1990. Economics, competitive strategy, game theory, auctions and bidding, design of incentive schemes.

Anjan Thakor, John E. Simon Professor of Finance and Senior Associate Dean; Ph.D., Northwestern, 1979. Corporate finance, financial intermediation, economics of asymmetric information.

Ozge Turut, Assistant Professor of Marketing; D.B.A., Harvard, 2006. Innovation strategies under market uncertainty, marketing–R&D interface, asymmetric information models, impact of the Internet on retail channel competition.

Annette Veech, Senior Lecturer of Business Communications; Ph.D., Illinois at Urbana-Champaign, 1988. Communications and training and development.

Ying Xie, Visiting Assistant Professor of Marketing; Ph.D., Northwestern, 2004. Advertising, consumer behavior in financial decision making, marketing response modeling, pharmaceutical marketing, sales-force management, social contagion.

Tzachi Zach, Assistant Professor of Accounting; Ph.D., Rochester, 2003. Financial accounting, capital markets research, earnings management.

Todd R. Zenger, Robert and Barbara Frick Professor of Business Strategy; Ph.D., UCLA, 1989. Corporate strategy, economic theories of the firm, compensation, organizational design, business strategy, managing technology.

Guofu Zhou, Associate Professor of Finance; Ph.D., Duke, 1990. Asset pricing tests, futures and options markets, structure of interest rates.

WAYNE STATE UNIVERSITY

School of Business Administration

Programs of Study

The accelerated Master of Business Administration (M.B.A.) program at Wayne State University (WSU) is designed to incorporate the fluid nature of the twenty-first century's business and industry. By emphasizing functional conceptual knowledge, the comprehensive, high-impact M.B.A. program prepares individuals for successful careers in business, government, and other types of organizations. A wide range of elective courses in accounting, business economics, entrepreneurship, finance, human resources management, industrial relations, information systems and manufacturing, international business, management and organizational behavior, marketing, quality management, and taxation are offered. Fulfillment of foundation requirements in accounting, computing, economics, finance, management, marketing, production management, and business writing is essential. Applicants who do not fulfill the foundation requirements must enroll in accelerated foundation courses. The M.B.A. program is accredited by AACSB International–The Association to Advance Collegiate Schools of Business, the organization with the highest standard of achievement for business schools worldwide. Member institutions confirm their commitment to quality and continuous improvement through a rigorous and comprehensive peer review.

The Master of Science in Taxation (M.S.T.) is designed to prepare students for entry into professional tax practice in both the public and private sectors. Through the interdisciplinary nature of the program, students learn the accounting, legal, and public policy aspects of taxation. Students with a bachelor's degree in accounting usually meet all of the program's foundation requirements. Applicants with a baccalaureate degree in a field other than accounting may have to complete foundation courses in the areas of accounting, business law, management information systems, and statistics. Concentration areas consist of accounting and taxation, public finance, and public administration.

The Master of Science in Accounting program (M.S.A.) prepares individuals for professional careers in public accounting. The primary objective of the program is to prepare students for public accounting careers rather than entry-level jobs, while meeting the 150-hour education requirement for licensure as a certified public accountant in the state of Michigan. Secondary objectives are to better prepare students for professional examinations, especially the CPA exam. Student with undergraduate degrees in accounting who are pursuing careers in private industry, financial institutions, and government and nonprofit organizations benefit from the expanded study in accounting and business.

The academic year has two 15-week semesters (fall and winter). The spring-summer semester is divided into two terms. A full schedule of graduate courses is offered each term. Students can complete their entire program of study either on the main campus in Detroit, at the Oakland Center in Farmington Hills, through the Online MBA Program, or a combination of these options. All M.B.A. requirements can be completed on Saturdays at the Oakland Center in Farmington Hills.

The Wayne State University School of Business Administration launched a Ph. D. program commencing September 2007. The principal objective of the Ph. D. program is to prepare students to become faculty members at major research universities. The program focuses on quantitative skills—enabling students to engage in research projects with faculty members—and will place a heavy emphasis on a global perspective. Assistantships, scholarships, and fellowships will be available to doctoral students on a competitive basis.

Research Facilities

The Wayne State University School of Business Administration (SBA) has a dedicated computer laboratory exclusively for SBA students. It is equipped with the latest PC workstations and cutting-edge business software. In addition, the SBA has two dedicated distance-learning classrooms linking WSU's main campus in Detroit with the Oakland Center campus in Farmington Hills. SBA students have access to a wide range of computing resources: wireless Internet is accessible throughout the School and in and around all libraries and many classroom buildings on campus; most M.B.A. courses are available online; classrooms have high-speed Internet access with network printing; and computers also have access to multiple financial datasets and file storage on an Oracle Server for instructional and student use. If necessary, students can securely access WSU's Internet from a remote location.

Wayne State University has a high-speed, fiber-optic Gigabit Ethernet network interconnecting buildings on its main and medical campuses. With high-performance connections to the commercial Internet, Internet2, and the Michigan LambdaRail (MiLR) research network, WSU's network infrastructure supports the reach of University research and collaboration to academic institutions around the country and abroad, including national laboratories and supercomputing centers.

Wayne State also operates a centrally managed Grid-enabled computing system, which houses research-related projects involving high-speed computation, data management, statistical analysis, and other computationally intensive applications. The WSU Grid infrastructure is designed to allow students access to many different programs and data-storage options, depending on the research being performed. More information about the WSU Grid is available online at https://www.grid.wayne.edu.

The University Library System provides access to many business resources, including electronic indexes with abstracts and full text and subject guides that focus on specific areas of research. Many of these resources can be accessed directly online at http://www.lib.wayne.edu. The library system provides open-access computing labs for the entire campus community, including more than 800 computers with a variety of applications in support of student learning. The 24-hour Extended Study Center is open during the fall and winter semesters.

Financial Aid

The Office of Scholarships and Financial Aid provides students with information regarding sources of funds. The University offers graduate and professional scholarships to both full- and part-time graduate students. The SBA offers graduate teaching and research assistantships through its Departments of Accounting and Business (finance, information systems and manufacturing, management, and marketing areas). Stipends for 2007–08 average $13,672, plus tuition and benefits, for nine-month appointments.

Cost of Study

Tuition per semester in 2007–08 for Michigan residents is $415 per credit hour. The cost for non-Michigan residents is $847 per credit hour.

Living and Housing Costs

WSU Housing offers a number of options for students from modern apartment buildings with views of the city to historic apartments on campus. In addition, the University's new residence halls, located in the heart of the campus, are just steps from the 24-hour Undergraduate Library, the Recreation and Fitness Center, the Student Center, and classes. The Towers Residential Suites provides housing for sophomores, juniors, seniors, graduate, and professional students. Depending on one's enrollment status at WSU, prices for the 2007–08 academic year (fall and winter semesters) range from $392 per month for an efficiency apartment to $1205 per month for a room in a three-bedroom apartment. Residence halls (including a meal plan) range from $6702 to $8982 for the academic year. For more information, students should visit http://www.housing.wayne.edu.

Student Group

The School of Business Administration enrolls approximately 250 full-time and 1,000 part-time graduate students. Classes average 35 students. The average age of M.B.A. students is 27. Of the students enrolled, 43 percent are women and nearly 5 percent are international students. On average, the M.B.A. students have five years of work experience, and approximately 93 percent are employed either full- or part-time, with more than half holding supervisory positions.

Student Outcomes

Most students pursuing a master's degree in business administration, taxation, or accounting have already made impressive starts to their careers. An advanced degree can be a vehicle to broaden one's expertise, enhance one's opportunities for advancement, and increase one's earning potential. While more than 30 percent of the graduate students work for the major automotive companies, the majority work in nonautomotive settings that include health care, accounting, government, banking, and finance and a host of other industries. Several students have initiated successful businesses of their own.

Location

WSU is located in the heart of Detroit's University Cultural Center, the home of renowned museums, galleries, and theaters—most within walking distance. The University's main campus encompasses 203 acres of beautifully landscaped walkways and gathering spots, linking 100 education and research buildings. The five extension centers in the metropolitan area provide convenient access to a wide selection of courses.

The University

Wayne State University is Michigan's only urban research university, filling a unique niche by providing access to a world-class education at a great value. Wayne State's eleven schools and colleges offer more than 350 major subject areas to its 33,000 graduate and undergraduate students. Since its founding in 1868, Wayne State has continued growing to meet educational needs. In 1994, Wayne State became one of only eighty-eight Carnegie Research I Universities out of a total of 3,600 accredited universities in the U.S. WSU offers a broad range of baccalaureate programs while demonstrating a commitment to graduate education and a significant capacity for research.

Applying

The M.B.A., M.S.T., and M.S.A. programs are open to students who hold bachelor's degrees from regionally accredited institutions and who demonstrate considerable promise of success in pursuing graduate study. A completed application for graduate admission, the $50 application fee, official transcripts from all collegiate institutions attended, and GMAT results are required. Admission is granted each semester. The application and other required documents are due by July 1 for fall semester admission, November 1 for winter semester admission, and March 15 for spring-summer semester admission. International students must provide required materials four months prior to the beginning of the term. Semesters begin in September, January, and May.

Applicants to the Ph. D. programs may be admitted with a bachelor's or a master's degree and are expected to have competence in math, computing, and statistics sufficient to satisfy prerequisites for the quantitative courses in the Ph. D. curriculum. Students who have not completed macroeconomics and microeconomics as well as calculus prerequisites prior to admission must enroll in these courses during the first year of the doctoral program. Minimum requirements include 3.0 undergraduate GPA (or 3.0 upper-division GPA), 3.5 graduate GPA, and a minimum 600 GMAT score. International applicants must meet the University requirements for TOEFL scores. Three letters of recommendation and an essay on career objectives must be included with applications for admission.

Correspondence and Information

Office of Student Services
School of Business Administration
Wayne State University
Detroit, Michigan 48202
Phone: 313-577-4510
        800-910-EARN (toll-free)
Fax: 313-577-5299
Web site: http://www.busadm.wayne.edu

Wayne State University

THE FACULTY

Angela Andrews, Assistant Professor of Accounting; Ph.D., Michigan State.

Clinton Andrews, Lecturer in Finance; M.S., Chicago.

Neveen Faraq Awad, Assistant Professor of Information Systems and Manufacturing; Ph.D., Michigan.

Mark E. Bayless, Associate Professor of Finance; Ph.D., Washington (St. Louis).

John D. Beard, Associate Professor of Business Communication; D.A., Michigan.

Richard F. Beltramini, Professor of Marketing and Academic Associate Dean; Ph.D., Texas at Austin.

B. Anthony Billings, Professor of Tax; Ph.D., Texas A&M.

Abhijit Biswas, Professor of Marketing and Kmart Endowed Chair; Ph.D., Houston.

William Burrell, Lecturer in Information Systems and Manufacturing; M.B.A., Wayne State.

Timothy W. Butler, Associate Professor of Information Systems and Manufacturing; Ph.D., South Carolina.

Hugh M. Cannon, Adcraft/Simons-Michelson Professor of Advertising; Ph.D., NYU.

Clyde Chaffee, Lecturer in Finance; M.B.A., Michigan State.

Sudip Datta, Professor of Finance and T. Norris Hitchman Chair; Ph.D., SUNY.

Ranjan D'Mello, Associate Professor of Finance; Ph.D., Ohio State.

Sujay Dutta, Assistant Professor of Marketing; Ph.D., LSU.

Richard M. Gabrys, Lecturer in Accounting and Dean; B.S., King's.

Ali Hammoud, Lecturer in Finance; M.B.A., Henderson State.

Jia Hao, Assistant Professor of Finance; Ph.D., Utah.

Mai Iskandar-Datta, Professor of Finance; Ph.D., Missouri–Columbia.

Deborah Jones, Senior Lecturer of Accounting and Taxation; Ph.D., Kent State.

Catherine Kirchmeyer, Associate Professor of Management; Ph.D., York.

K. S. Krishnan, Associate Professor of Information Systems and Manufacturing; Ph.D., Pennsylvania.

Frank LaMarra, Lecturer in Accounting; M.B.A., Wayne State; CPA.

Jaegul Lee, Assistant Professor of Management; Ph.D., Carnegie Mellon.

Ariel Levi, Senior Lecturer in Management; Ph.D., Yale.

James T. Low, Associate Professor of Marketing; Ph.D., Michigan.

David Lucas, Senior Lecturer in Management; Ph.D., Wayne State.

James E. Martin, Professor of Management and Industrial Relations; Ph.D., Washington (St. Louis).

Cathleen Miller, Associate Professor of Accounting; Ph.D., Kentucky.

Santanu Mitra, Associate Professor of Accounting; Ph.D., LSU.

Mbodja Mougoué, Associate Professor of Finance; Ph.D., New Orleans.

Thomas J. Naughton, Associate Professor of Management and Associate Chair of the Business Department; Ph.D., SUNY at Buffalo.

Richard N. Osborn, Distinguished University Professor of Management; D.B.A., Kent State.

Randolph Paschke, Chair of the Accounting Department; B.B.A., Michigan; CPA.

Joan Penner-Hahn, Assistant Professor of Management; Ph.D., Michigan.

Barbara Price, Associate Professor of Information Systems and Manufacturing and Associate Provost for Academic Personnel; Ph.D., Utah.

Kelly R. Price, Associate Professor of Finance; Ph.D., Michigan.

William Pritchard, Lecturer in Information Systems and Manufacturing; M.B.A., Wayne State.

Arik Ragowsky, Associate Professor of Information Systems and Manufacturing and Director, Center for Information Systems and Manufacturing; Ph.D., Tel Aviv.

Paul Reagan, Senior Lecturer in Management; Ph.D., Michigan State.

Irvin D. Reid, Professor of Management and University President; Ph.D., Pennsylvania.

Alan Reinstein, George Husband Endowed Professor of Accounting; D.B.A., Kentucky; CPA.

Edward A. Riordan, Professor of Marketing; D.B.A., Kentucky.

Celia Livermore Romm, Professor of Information Systems and Manufacturing; Ph.D., Toronto.

Gary Shields, Lecturer of Management; M.B.A., Wayne State.

Margaret Smoller, Associate Professor of Finance; Ph.D., Florida.

Toni M. Somers, Professor of Information Systems and Manufacturing; Ph.D., Toledo.

Albert D. Spalding Jr., Associate Professor of Business Law and Taxation; J.D., M.B.A., George Washington; CPA.

William Spaulding, Lecturer in Management; M.B.A., Wayne State.

Myles S. Stern, Associate Professor of Accounting; Ph.D., Michigan State; CMA.

Jeffrey J. Stoltman, Associate Professor of Marketing; Ph.D., Syracuse.

Joseph Tan, Professor of Information Systems and Manufacturing; Ph.D., British Columbia.

Amanuel G. Tekleab, Assistant Professor of Management; Ph.D., Maryland.

Frank Vandervegt, Senior Lecturer in Information Systems and Manufacturing; Ph.D., Michigan.

Harish L. Verma, Associate Professor of Information Systems and Manufacturing and Chair of the Business Department; Ph.D., Michigan State.

William H. Volz, Professor of Business Law; J.D., Wayne State; M.B.A., Harvard.

John D. Wagster, Associate Professor of Finance; Ph.D., Texas A&M.

Daniel Weimer, Lecturer in Accounting; Ph.D. candidate, Michigan; CPA.

Mary Ann Welden, Lecturer in Accounting; M.B.A., Notre Dame; CPA.

David L. Williams, Associate Professor of Marketing; Ph.D., Wayne State.

Sandra Williams, Senior Lecturer in Management; Ph.D., Wayne State.

Attila Yaprak, Professor of Marketing; Ph.D., Georgia State.

WEBBER INTERNATIONAL UNIVERSITY

Graduate School of Business

Program of Study

The Webber International University Graduate School of Business offers a unique nineteen-month, full-time program leading to a Master of Business Administration (M.B.A.), with options in accounting, management, or sport management. The degree consists of 36 credit hours, with courses offered one night a week over six 10-week periods. The University is accredited by the Southern Association of Colleges and Schools and the International Assembly for Collegiate Business Education.

The Webber M.B.A. aims to assist students in enhancing managerial skills through the delivery of techniques and best practices that integrate academic theory with contemporary applications. The program places a premium level of concentration on developing students' critical-thinking skills, so that they may more easily adapt to paradigm shifts within business.

The Webber International University Graduate School of Business offers an M.B.A. program that focuses on the interdisciplinary nature of business practices. The program capitalizes on the faculty's ability to focus on proven traditional methods of teaching that integrate the various facets of effective business administration, while utilizing information technology to enhance problem-solving skills.

Through the practicum course(s), students undertake group-based consulting projects. Through these projects, students have the opportunity to test theoretical concepts in an applied setting.

Research Facilities

The Roger Babson Learning Center, located in the central part of the campus, is a modern and comprehensive library facility that contains extensive collections of reference, research, and reserve materials keyed to business research. The center also offers access to several external data sources, such as EbscoHost, LexisNexis Academic Universe, LIRN-Library, and several others.

The computer resource center is a data processing center and teaching facility whose microcomputers offer the latest modern technology for developing student excellence in business, communication, and creativity.

Financial Aid

Financial aid is available in the form of student loans for eligible students. For more information, prospective students should contact the Financial Aid Office (telephone: 863-638-2929). In addition, many employers provide for or subsidize their employees' tuition expenses.

Cost of Study

Tuition for the 2007–08 academic year is $485 per credit hour. Book expenses vary by course.

Living and Housing Costs

On-campus housing is available to graduate students. Housing costs range from $1000 to $1230 per ten-week term. A meal plan is available for $685 per ten-week term. Additional fees include a cable and microfridge fee per term.

Student Group

The Graduate School of Business is small in size, with approximately 60 graduate students. With small class sizes, there is ample opportunity for students to exchange ideas with other students and interact closely with the faculty.

The students are distinguished by the diversity of their professional and ethnic backgrounds. The average age of the students in the M.B.A. program is 30, and approximately 55 percent of the class has had one year or more of professional, full-time employment experience. Students come from several states as well as several different countries. Approximately half are women and approximately 60 percent are employed full- or part-time.

Student Outcomes

Approximately 68 percent of Webber graduates live and work in Florida. Thirty-two percent are located throughout the United States and the world. A sample of position titles of recent graduates includes partner, manager, human resource manager, and assistant controller.

Location

Webber International University is located on a beautiful 110-acre campus along the shoreline of Lake Caloosa, approximately 45 minutes south of Orlando. The town of Babson Park, a small rural residential community, is located in the heart of Florida's citrus country near a chain of freshwater lakes. Babson Park is conveniently located near many major recreational facilities and national tourist attractions in central Florida.

The University and The School

Webber International University was founded in 1927 by Grace Knight and Roger W. Babson as a women's college, with the exclusive purpose of teaching women about business. It was the first school chartered under the educational and charitable laws of the state of Florida as a nonprofit organization. In September 1971, the college began admitting men.

Webber is a small university with a total student body of approximately 650.

The Graduate School of Business was established in September 1997. The Graduate School of Business granted its first degrees in February 1999.

Applying

Men and women with baccalaureate degrees from regionally accredited colleges or universities or the international equivalent are eligible for consideration for admission. Admission to the Graduate School is based on both quantitative and qualitative criteria. In addition to the application, the applicant must submit a resume, an essay, and three letters of recommendation, and some may need to submit results from the GMAT. Academic qualifications are determined by evaluation of student performance at previous higher education institutions. In addition, international applicants are required to submit results from the TOEFL unless they have obtained a degree from a college or university where English is the language of instruction.

The standard academic year for the full-time M.B.A. program begins in late August and ends in mid July. Applications are accepted on a first-come, first-served basis. Applications may be submitted online, downloaded from the University's Web site, or requested and sent through conventional mail.

Correspondence and Information

Director of Admissions
Graduate School of Business
Webber International University
1201 North Scenic Highway
P.O. Box 96
Babson Park, Florida 33827-0096

Phone: 863-638-2927
Fax: 863-638-1591
E-mail: mba@webber.edu
Web site: http://www.webber.edu

Webber International University

THE FACULTY

The Webber International University Graduate School of Business faculty members bring both professional and academic expertise to the classroom. The faculty members are distinguished in their fields and are dedicated to teaching. The Webber International University Graduate School of Business emphasizes strong faculty-student interaction, as indicated by the small class size and the nature of the course work.

The Conference Center.

The campus of Webber International University.

WORCESTER POLYTECHNIC INSTITUTE

Department of Management

Programs of Study

While traditional business schools scramble to keep pace with technological changes, the Department of Management at Worcester Polytechnic Institute (WPI) has a better approach. As part of one of the nation's leading technological universities, the Department offers leading-edge, hands-on management programs aimed at the intersection of business and technology. The result is WPI's students enjoy a distinct advantage in today's technology-driven business environment. WPI's education, research, and outreach focus on leading and managing technology-based organizations, integrating technology into the workplace, and creating new processes, products, services, and organizations based on technology. All programs are accredited by AACSB International–The Association to Advance Collegiate Schools of Business.

The Department offers an M.B.A. and three Master of Science (M.S.) programs: information technology, marketing and technological innovation, and operations design and leadership. WPI also offers several graduate management certificate programs.

The M.B.A. requires the completion of 49 credits. Students acquire a managerial toolset and an executive-level perspective, both with an application toward technology-driven environments. Specialization areas are formed within the 12-credit elective block. The program concludes with a company-sponsored capstone project. The result is WPI graduates hit the ground running; WPI's placement record and alumni success rival any school in the U.S.

The M.S. in information technology requires the completion of 35 hours, including one of the following 12-credit concentrations: applications development, entrepreneurship, information security management, manufacturing and service IT applications, marketing IT applications, or project management.

The M.S. in marketing and technological innovation (MSMTI) is a 32-credit program aimed at preparing leaders in the marketing and innovation areas. The program includes 18 elective credits within which students customize their programs.

The M.S. in operations design and leadership requires 35 credits and offers students the choice of a supply chain management or process design track; or students may customize their elective track.

Graduate certificates require 14 to 16 credit hours of course work; certificate credits may be applied to a degree program at a later time. Certificate programs are available in information security management, information technology, management of technology, and technology marketing as well as customized certificate programs.

Research Facilities

The Collaborative for Entrepreneurship and Innovation capitalizes upon the synergy between WPI's many different entrepreneurship and innovation initiatives. It offers programs that nurture entrepreneurship and innovation and accelerate knowledge and action in the transfer of technology, working frequently with entrepreneurs, investors, researchers, incubators, small-business organizations, service providers, private foundations, and government organizations.

The Information Technology Research Centers consist of a number of component centers or research projects that work together on information technology–related topics. Its mission is to foster cooperative industry-university efforts to improve the effectiveness and efficiency of organizations through improved information technology practices.

The Center for Research in Electronic Commerce Technology is an industry-university consortium that works to improve the delivery of information through the Internet and investigates how to best utilize emerging software and hardware technologies in support of electronic commerce.

The George C. Gordon Library contains 36,000 electronic journals and more than 900 hard-copy journals, 39,000 electronic books and 272,000 print books, and over 150 databases.

Financial Aid

The Robert H. Goddard Graduate Research Fellowships are awarded on a competitive basis across all fields of study; these fellowships provide recipients with a twelve-month stipend and tuition support. The Department has a limited number of graduate management assistantships, which are available for entering full-time students and provide compensation of up to $4800 per academic year in exchange for working with a faculty member in a research or administrative capacity. Financial assistance is also available in the form of student loans; students must be enrolled in 2 or more courses per semester to qualify. Many part-time graduate students may also receive tuition benefits from their employers.

Cost of Study

In the 2007–08 academic year, tuition is $1042 per credit hour. Full-time students are expected to enroll in 9 credit hours each semester (fall and spring).

Living and Housing Costs

On-campus graduate student housing is limited to a space-available basis. There is no on-campus housing for married students. Apartments and rooms in private homes near the campus are available at varying costs. For further information and apartment listings, students should visit the Residential Services Office online at http://www.wpi.edu/Admin/RSO/Offcampus/.

Student Group

Students in the M.B.A. or M.S. programs have the analytic aptitude necessary to complete a technology-focused business program. The majority of WPI graduate management students come from engineering or science backgrounds, though that is not a prerequisite for admission. There are approximately 250 graduate students in the Department of Management. Twenty-eight percent of the students are women and 19 percent are international students.

Location

The university is located on an 80-acre campus in a residential section of Worcester. The city, the third-largest in New England, has many colleges and an unusual variety of cultural opportunities. Located three blocks from the campus, the nationally famous Worcester Art Museum contains one of the finest permanent collections in the country. From the renown Worcester Music Festival to Foothills Theatre, the community provides outstanding programs in music and theater. The DCU Center offers rock concerts and hosts the American Hockey League's Worcester Sharks. The Tornadoes, of baseball's Can Am League, play at nearby Fitton Field. Easily reached for recreation are Boston and Cape Cod to the east and the Berkshires to the west; good skiing is nearby to the north. Complete athletic and recreational facilities and a program of concerts and special events are available on campus to graduate students.

The Institute

Founded in 1865, Worcester Polytechnic Institute is one of the nation's earliest and most prestigious technological universities. Its eighteen academic departments offer more than fifty degree programs to over 3,800 students. WPI's reputation for research is strong, with professors working on cutting-edge research and more than twenty project centers around the world. WPI is consistently ranked among the nation's top 65 doctoral universities by *U.S. News & World Report*. WPI was also ranked ninth for "best career prospects" and eighth for "greatest opportunities for women" for M.B.A. graduates by the *Princeton Review*.

Applying

Admission to the program is competitive. Candidates should have a high likelihood of success in a challenging, technology-focused management program, based on their academic and professional records. Applicants should have the analytic aptitude and academic preparation necessary to complete a technology-oriented management program, including a minimum of three semesters of college-level math or two semesters of college-level calculus.

Applications are available online at http://mgt.wpi.edu/Graduate/admission.html. Prospective students must submit an application form, official transcripts from all previously attended colleges/universities, three letters of recommendation, official GMAT scores (GRE may be substituted for M.S. applicants), and a $70 application fee. Students whose native language is not English and who have not received a degree from an institution where the language of instruction is English are required to submit official TOEFL scores.

Applications are evaluated on a rolling basis, but it is recommended that applicants submit them before July 1 for fall admission (June 1 for international students) and November 1 for spring admission (October 1 for international students).

Correspondence and Information

Department of Management
Worcester Polytechnic Institute
100 Institute Road
Worcester, Massachusetts 01609-2280

Phone: 508-831-5218
Fax: 508-831-5720
E-mail: mgt@wpi.edu
Web site: http://www.mgt.wpi.edu

Worcester Polytechnic Institute

THE FACULTY AND THEIR RESEARCH

McRae C. Banks, Professor, Department Head, and Director, Collaborative for Entrepreneurship and Innovation; Ph.D., Virginia Tech. Entrepreneurial teams, rural entrepreneurship, economic development and entrepreneurship, strategic planning in small and entrepreneurial companies, entrepreneurship in technological organizations, re-engineering business education.

Erwin Danneels, Associate Professor; Ph.D., Penn State. Growth and renewal of corporations through product innovation, nature and consequences of product innovativeness, characteristics of corporations with innovative new-product programs, performance effects of innovative new-product programs.

Soussan Djamasbi, Assistant Professor; Ph.D., Hawaii at Manoa. Decision making, decision support systems, information overload, decision making under crisis. affect and decision making.

Michael B. Elmes, Professor; Ph.D., Syracuse. Workplace resistance and ideological control, critical perspectives on spirituality in the workplace, implementation of IT in organizations, organizations in the natural environment, narrative and aesthetic perspectives on organizational phenomena, psychodynamics of group and intergroup behavior.

Arthur Gerstenfeld, Professor; Ph.D., MIT. Industrial engineering, innovation.

Huong Ngo Higgins, Associate Professor; Ph.D., Georgia State. Financial accounting, focusing on earnings expectation and international accounting.

Sharon A. Johnson, Associate Professor and Director of Industrial Engineering Program; Ph.D., Cornell. Lean process design, enterprise engineering, process analysis and modeling, reverse logistics.

Chickery J. Kasouf, Associate Professor; Ph.D., Syracuse. Product management, marketing strategy in fragmented industries, innovation management, marketing information use, strategic alliances.

Eleanor Loiacono, Associate Professor; Ph.D., Georgia. Web site quality, information systems accessibility, e-commerce, affect in information systems.

Fabienne Miller, Assistant Professor; Ph.D., Michigan State. Managerial accounting and contracting in inter- and intra-firm relationships.

Kankana Mukherjee, Assistant Professor; Ph.D., Connecticut. Efficiency and productivity analysis applied to manufacturing, banking, and other sectors.

Frank Noonan, Associate Professor; Ph.D., Massachusetts Amherst. Operations management, decision/risk analysis, environmental management.

John T. O'Connor, Professor; Ph.D., Notre Dame. Economics, finance, accounting, medical-care financial and delivery systems.

Jerome J. Schaufeld, Visiting Instructor of Entrepreneurship; M.B.A., Northeastern. Entrepreneurship, technology commercialization, business acquisition and development.

Diane M. Strong, Associate Professor; Ph.D., Carnegie Mellon. Advanced information technologies, such as enterprise systems, and their use in organizations; MIS quality issues, with primary focus on data and information quality.

Steven S. Taylor, Assistant Professor; Ph.D., Boston College. Aesthetics of organizational action.

Bengisu Tulu, Assistant Professor; Ph.D., Claremont. Medical informatics, Voice over Internet Protocol (VoIP), information security, telecommunications and networking, system analysis and design.

Helen G. Vassallo, Professor; Ph.D., Clark. Organizational behavior, project management, management of planned change, management of biotechnology, medical product liability.

Amy Z. Zeng, Associate Professor; Ph.D., Penn State. Modeling and analysis of decisions in supply and/or distribution networks, applications of operations research and operations management techniques to supply chain process design and improvement, global supply chain management and international business.

Willie Zhao, Assistant Professor; Ph.D., Temple. Corporate governanace, international finance/business, financial markets/institutions.

Joe Zhu, Associate Professor; Ph.D., Massachusetts Amherst. Information technology and productivity, e-business, performance evaluation and benchmarking.

redefine **THE POSSIBLE.**

Programs of Study	Established in 1966, the Schulich School of Business at York University is Canada's Global Business School™. Schulich programs emphasize relevance to real-world contexts, an applied focus, the application of multiple perspectives to decision making, globalization, and critical skills such as group, negotiation, and presentation skills. In addition to becoming strong generalists, students have exceptional opportunities for multiple specializations. Areas of study and specialization include industry sectors (arts and media, financial engineering, financial services, health industry management, nonprofit management and leadership, public sector management, and real property), management functions (accounting, applied economics, finance, human resource management, information systems, marketing, operations management, and strategic management), and special areas (business and sustainability, arts and media management, business consulting, business ethics, entrepreneurial studies and family business, and international business).

Schulich has become a global business school, with worldwide strategic alliances, including academic exchange agreements with close to eighty leading international management schools.

At the master's level, Schulich offers the following degrees: the regular M.B.A., the Kellogg-Schulich Executive M.B.A (E.M.B.A.), the International M.B.A. (I.M.B.A.), and the Master of Public Administration (M.P.A.). M.B.A. and M.P.A. students can study on a full-time and/or a part-time basis three semesters a year. Admission is in September or January. Schulich also offers a joint M.B.A./LL.B. degree with Osgoode Hall Law School at York and a joint M.B.A./M.F.A. degree with the Faculty of Fine Arts at York.

The Kellogg-Schulich Executive M.B.A., with Northwestern University, is an eighteen-month program that emphasizes U.S., Canadian, and international perspectives on global leadership and strategic management. The program includes three residence weeks, alternating weekends, and International Study Seminars abroad.

The I.M.B.A. is a twenty-month (five-semester) full-time program that admits 40–50 students each September. In addition to taking foundations of management and international business courses, students develop specialized region and country expertise, master a foreign language, complete a twelve- to sixteen-week Work Term abroad, and have the option of studying abroad for a semester.

The Ph.D. in administration program exposes students to quantitative and qualitative research methods and techniques through core and elective courses. Students may tailor specializations to individual needs in either management functions or thematic issues such as international business and change management.

Research Facilities	York University houses five libraries with considerable resources, including a book collection of more than 2 million volumes and more than 20,000 serials (periodicals, magazines, reports and digests, collections of microfiche, maps, videos, films, sound recordings, compact discs, and databases in CD-ROM and diskette to which the students have access). In addition, the University has one of the best business reference collections in metropolitan Toronto.
Financial Aid	Entrance scholarships are offered to a limited number of students each fall. Students may also apply for graduate assistantships and teaching assistantships throughout their stay at York University.
Cost of Study	For M.B.A. programs, based on an academic year of 30 semester credits, the 2007–08 tuition for Canadian students is approximately Can$17,500 and for international students, approximately Can$25,000. Tuition for the two-year Executive M.B.A. is Can$100,000 for both Canadian and international students.
Living and Housing Costs	On-campus housing is available at reasonable rates. Travel and personal expenses vary with each student; a single student should anticipate a budget between Can$6000 and Can$8000 per semester.
Student Group	Students admitted to the School are expected to be of the highest caliber, with demonstrated leadership qualities and experience to build on. At any one time, there are approximately 600 full-time and 600–700 part-time master's students enrolled in the School.
Location	Toronto is Canada's industrial, commercial, and financial heartland and the capital of Ontario. Canada offers all business students the advantage of its traditional role as a major international trading nation with a balanced perspective on global issues. Transportation to the main campus from the downtown area takes approximately 50 minutes by public transit or 30 minutes by car, depending on traffic. The majority of the School's students commute.
The University	Founded in 1959, York University soon achieved an international reputation for excellence in teaching, research, and scholarship in both undergraduate and graduate studies. Today, York is the third-largest university in Canada and is similar to other large urban North American commuter universities.
Applying	Decisions on admission are made after a thorough review of the applicant's file. In addition to previous academic performance and the GMAT score (not required for the E.M.B.A.), the applicant's work experience, demonstrated leadership qualities, and communication skills, as well as apparent creativity and innovation, are taken into consideration. Further, previous managerial experience, volunteer and extracurricular activity (particularly in a leadership capacity), and evidence of writing ability and interpersonal skills are examined. Work experience may be a significant factor for candidates whose applications are not consistently strong in all areas. Admission may be offered to some applicants without an undergraduate degree under the nonbaccalaureate category. Applicants in this group must present several years of management-level working experience and acceptable GMAT results.

The regular M.B.A. admits students in September and January. The E.M.B.A. offers January admission only. The I.M.B.A. offers September admission only.

Correspondence and Information	Division of Student Services and International Relations Schulich School of Business York University 4700 Keele Street Toronto, Ontario M3J 1P3 Canada Phone: 416-736-5059 Fax: 416-650-8174 E-mail: intladmissions@schulich.yorku.ca Web site: http://www.schulich.yorku.ca

York University

THE FACULTY

Dezsö J. Horváth, Professor of Policy, Dean, and Tanna H. Schulich Chair in Strategic Management; Ph.D., Umeå (Sweden).

Accounting

Marcia Annisete, Associate Professor; Ph.D., Manchester (England). Thomas H. Beechy, Professor Emeritus; D.B.A., Washington (St. Louis); CPA, Illinois. Kathryn Bewley, Associate Professor; Ph.D., Waterloo; CA, Ontario. Janne Chung, Associate Professor; Ph.D., Edith Cowan (Australia). Cameron Graham, Assistant Professor; Ph.D., Calgary. Sylvia Hsingwen Hsu, Assistant Professor; Ph.D., Wisconsin–Madison. Amin Mawani, Associate Professor; Ph.D., Waterloo. Sandy Qian Qu, Assistant Professor; Ph.D., Alberta. Alan J. Richardson, Professor; Ph.D., Queen's at Kingston; CGA, FCGA. Linda Thorne, Associate Professor; Ph.D., McGill; CA, Ontario. Viswanath Umashanker Trivedi, Associate Professor; Ph.D., Arizona.

Economics

Irene Henriques, Associate Professor; Ph.D., Queen's at Kingston. Fred Lazar, Associate Professor; Ph.D., Harvard. Perry A. Sadorsky, Associate Professor; Ph.D., Queen's at Kingston. John N. Smithin, Professor; Ph.D., McMaster. A. Bhanich Supapol, Associate Professor; Ph.D., Carleton (Ottawa). Bernard M. Wolf, Professor; Ph.D., Yale.

Finance

Melanie Cao, Associate Professor; Ph.D., Toronto. Douglas Cumming, Associate Professor; Ph.D., Toronto. Ming Dong, Associate Professor; Ph.D., Ohio. Fred Gorbet, CIT Chair in Financial Services; Ph.D., Duke. Mark Kamstra, Associate Professor; Ph.D., California, San Diego. Nadia Massoud, Associate Professor; Ph.D., Queen's at Kingston. Elizabeth M. Maynes, Associate Professor; Ph.D., Queen's at Kingston. Moshe Arye Milevsky, Associate Professor; Ph.D., York. Debarshi Nandy, Assistant Professor; Ph.D., Boston College. Eliezer Prisman, Professor and Nigel Martin Chair in Finance; D.Sc., Technion (Israel). Gordon Roberts, Professor and CIBC Professor of Financial Services; Ph.D., Boston College. Pauline Shum, Associate Professor; Ph.D., Toronto. Yisong Sam Tian, Associate Professor; Ph.D., York.

Marketing

Russell Belk, Professor and Kraft Foods Canada Chair in Marketing; Ph.D., Minnesota. Samuel K. Bonsu, Assistant Professor; Ph.D., Rhode Island. Alexandra Campbell, Associate Professor; Ph.D., Toronto. Peter Darke, Associate Professor; Ph.D., Toronto. Eileen Fischer, Professor and Anne and Max Tanenbaum Chair in Entrepreneurship and Family Enterprise; Ph.D., Queen's at Kingston. Brenda Gainer, Associate Professor and Royal Bank Professor of Nonprofit Management; Ph.D., York. Markus Giesler, Assistant Professor; Ph.D., Witten/Herdecke (Germany). Roger M. Heeler, Professor Emeritus; Ph.D., Stanford. Ashwin Joshi, Associate Professor; Ph.D., Queen's at Kingston. Robert Kozinets, Associate Professor; Ph.D., Queen's at Kingston. Alan Middleton, Assistant Professor; Ph.D., York. Yigang Pan, Professor; Ph.D., Columbia. Marshall D. Rice, Associate Professor; Ph.D., Illinois. Ajay K. Sirsi, Associate Professor; Ph.D., Arizona. Donald N. Thompson, Professor Emeritus; Ph.D., Berkeley. Detlev Zwick, Associate Professor; Ph.D., Rhode Island.

Operations Management and Information Systems

Markus Biehl, Associate Professor; Ph.D., Georgia Tech. John Buzacott, Professor Emeritus; Ph.D., Birmingham (England). Wade D. Cook, Professor and Gordon Charlton Shaw Professor of Management Science; Ph.D., Dalhousie. Richard H. Irving, Associate Professor; Ph.D., Waterloo. David Johnston, Associate Professor; Ph.D., Western Ontario. Henry Kim, Associate Professor; Ph.D., Toronto. Mehmet Murat Kristal, Assistant Professor; Ph.D., North Carolina. Ronald J. McClean, Assistant Professor; Ph.D., Waterloo. Dorit Nevo, Assistant Professor; Ph.D., British Columbia. Mark Pagell, Associate Professor; Ph.D., Michigan. Daniele Thomassin-Singh, Assistant Professor; Ph.D., Case Western Reserve. Michael Wade, Associate Professor; Ph.D., Western Ontario. J. Scott Yeomans, Associate Professor; Ph.D., McMaster.

Organizational Behavior and Industrial Relations

Chris Bell, Assistant Professor; Ph.D., Duke. Patricia Bradshaw, Associate Professor; Ph.D., York. Ronald J. Burke, Professor Emeritus; Ph.D., Michigan. André deCarufel, Associate Professor; Ph.D., North Carolina. David E. Dimick, Associate Professor; Ph.D., Minnesota. Ingo Holzinger, Assistant Professor; Ph.D., Wisconsin–Madison. Rekha Karambayya, Associate Professor; Ph.D., Northwestern. Robert G. Lucas, Associate Professor; Ph.D., Cornell. Gareth Morgan, Distinguished Research Professor; Ph.D., Lancaster (England). Christine Oliver, Professor and Henry J. Knowles Chair in Organizational Strategy; Ph.D., Toronto. Hazel Rosin, Associate Professor; Ph.D., Yale. Eleanor Westney, Professor and Scotiabank Chair in International Business; Ph.D., Princeton. Lorna Wright, Associate Professor; Ph.D., Western Ontario.

Policy/Strategic Management

Jean Adams, Assistant Professor; Ph.D., York. Preet Aulakh, Associate Professor and Pierre Lassonde Chair in International Business; Ph.D., Texas at Austin. Ellen Auster, Professor; Ph.D., Cornell. Cyril Bouquet, Assistant Professor; Ph.D., Western Ontario. Wesley Cragg, Professor Emeritus; D.Phil., Oxford. Andrew Crane, Professor; Ph.D., Nottingham (England). James L. Darroch, Associate Professor; Ph.D., York. Jerry D. Dermer, Professor; Ph.D., Illinois. Yuval Deutsch, Associate Professor; Ph.D., British Columbia. Burkard Eberlein, Assistant Professor; Ph.D., Konstanz (Germany). Moshe Farjoun, Associate Professor; Ph.D., Northwestern. James M. Gillies, Professor Emeritus; Ph.D., Indiana. Dezsö J. Horváth, Dean and Tanna H. Schulich Chair in Strategic Management; Ph.D., Umeå (Sweden). Thomas Keil, Assistant Professor; D.Sc., Helsinki Tech. Matthias Kipping, Professor and Chair in Business History; D.Phil., München (Germany). Stan Li, Associate Professor; Ph.D., Toronto. H. Ian Macdonald, Professor Emeritus and President Emeritus; B.Phil., Oxford. Anoop Madhok, Professor; Ph.D., McGill. Dirk Matten, Professor; Dr.rer.pol., Dr.habil., Düsseldorf (Germany). James McKellar, Professor; M.C.P./M.Arch., Pennsylvania. Charles J. McMillan, Professor; Ph.D., Bradford (England). Theodore Peridis, Associate Professor; Ph.D., NYU. Rein Peterson, Professor Emeritus; Ph.D., Cornell. Willow Sheremata, Associate Professor; Ph.D., NYU. Justin Tan, Professor and Newmont Mining Chair in Business Strategy; Ph.D., Virginia Tech. Stephen Weiss, Associate Professor; Ph.D., Pennsylvania. Tom Wesson, Associate Professor; Ph.D., Harvard. Joyce Zemans, University Professor; D.F.A. Hon., Nova Scotia College of Art & Design. Brenda Zimmerman, Associate Professor; Ph.D., York; CA, Ontario.

The Schulich School of Business and Executive Learning Centre.

Section 2
Accounting and Finance

This section contains a directory of institutions offering graduate work in accounting and finance, followed by in-depth entries submitted by institutions that chose to prepare detailed program descriptions. Additional information about programs listed in the directory but not augmented by an in-depth entry may be obtained by writing directly to the dean of a graduate school or chair of a department at the address given in the directory.

For programs offering related work, see also in this book Business Administration and Management, International Business, and Nonprofit Management. In Book 2, see Economics and Family and Consumer Sciences (Consumer Economics). In Book 4, see Mathematical Sciences; and in Book 5, Computer Science and Information Technology.

CONTENTS

Program Directories

Close-Ups

Accounting

Abilene Christian University, Graduate School, College of Business Administration, Abilene, TX 79699-9100. Offers M Acc. *Accreditation:* AACSB. Part-time programs available. *Faculty:* 6 part-time/adjunct (0 women). *Students:* 22 full-time (7 women), 4 part-time (1 woman); includes 1 minority (African American), 3 international. 23 applicants, 83% accepted, 16 enrolled. In 2006, 26 degrees awarded. *Degree requirements:* For master's, comprehensive exam. *Entrance requirements:* For master's, GMAT or GRE General Test. Additional exam requirements/recommendations for international students: Required—TOEFL (minimum score 525 paper-based; 197 computer-based). *Application deadline:* For fall admission, 4/1 priority date for domestic students; for spring admission, 11/1 for domestic students. Applications are processed on a rolling basis. Application fee: $40 ($45 for international students). Electronic applications accepted. *Expenses:* Tuition: Full-time $12,504; part-time $521 per hour. Required fees: $700; $34 per hour. *Financial support:* Teaching assistantships, Federal Work-Study available. Support available to part-time students. Financial award application deadline: 4/1. *Faculty research:* Organizational structure, financial management, cost accounting, unit analysis management. *Unit head:* Bill Fowler, Department Chair, 325-674-2080, Fax: 325-674-2564, E-mail: bill.fowler@coba.acu.edu. *Application contact:* William Horn, Graduate Admissions Counselor, 325-674-2656, Fax: 325-674-6717, E-mail: gradinfo@acu.edu.

Adelphi University, School of Business, Department of Accounting, Finance and Economics, Garden City, NY 11530-0701. Offers accounting (MBA); finance (MBA, MS). Part-time and evening/weekend programs available. *Students:* 1 (woman) full-time, 8 part-time (4 women); includes 3 minority (1 African American, 1 American Indian/Alaska Native, 1 Asian American or Pacific Islander), 4 international. Average age 39. In 2006, 9 degrees awarded. *Entrance requirements:* For master's, GMAT, 2 letters of recommendation. Additional exam requirements/recommendations for international students: Required—TOEFL (minimum score 550 paper-based; 213 computer-based). *Application deadline:* For fall admission, 5/1 for international students; for spring admission, 12/1 for international students. Applications are processed on a rolling basis. Application fee: $50. Electronic applications accepted. *Financial support:* Research assistantships with full and partial tuition reimbursements, career-related internships or fieldwork, Federal Work-Study, institutionally sponsored loans, scholarships/grants, and unspecified assistantships available. Financial award application deadline: 3/1; financial award applicants required to submit FAFSA. *Faculty research:* Capital market, executive compensation, business ethics, classical value theory, labor economics. *Unit head:* Dr. Bruce Swensen, Chairperson, 516-877-4655, E-mail: swensen@adelphi.edu. *Application contact:* Christine Murphy, Director of Admissions, 516-877-3050, Fax: 516-877-3039, E-mail: graduateadmissions@adelphi.edu.

Alabama State University, School of Graduate Studies, College of Business Administration, Department of Accounting and Finance, Montgomery, AL 36101-0271. Offers accountancy (M Acc). *Faculty:* 3 full-time (1 woman). *Students:* 1 full-time (0 women), 9 part-time (5 women); includes 8 minority (all African Americans) 12 applicants, 83% accepted. In 2006, 6 degrees awarded. *Entrance requirements:* For master's, GMAT, graduate writing competency test. Additional exam requirements/recommendations for international students: Required—TOEFL (minimum score 500 paper-based; 173 computer-based). *Application deadline:* For fall admission, 7/15 for domestic students; for spring admission, 12/15 for domestic students. Applications are processed on a rolling basis. Application fee: $10. *Expenses:* Tuition, state resident: full-time $1,728; part-time $192 per hour. Tuition, nonresident: full-time $3,456; part-time $334 per hour. *Financial support:* In 2006–07, 2 research assistantships (averaging $9,450 per year) were awarded. *Unit head:* Dr. Jean Crawford, Chair, 334-229-4134, Fax: 334-229-4870, E-mail: jcrawford@asunet.alasu.edu.

American InterContinental University, Program in International Business, Weston, FL 33326. Offers accounting and finance (MBA); human resource management (MBA); management (MBA); marketing (MBA). Part-time and evening/weekend programs available. Postbaccalaureate distance learning degree programs offered. *Faculty:* 3 full-time (0 women), 2 part-time/adjunct (0 women). *Students:* 87 full-time (51 women), 7 part-time (4 women); includes 62 minority (42 African Americans, 1 American Indian/Alaska Native, 1 Asian American or Pacific Islander, 18 Hispanic Americans), 5 international. Average age 34. In 2006, 51 degrees awarded. *Application deadline:* Applications are processed on a rolling basis. Application fee: $50. Electronic applications accepted. *Financial support:* Federal Work-Study and scholarships/grants available. Financial award application deadline: 1/15; financial award applicants required to submit FAFSA. *Unit head:* Dr. David Kalichavan, Acting Dean, School of Business, 954-446-6100, Fax: 954-446-6393, E-mail: dkalichavan@aiufl.edu.

American InterContinental University Buckhead Campus, Program in Business Administration, Atlanta, GA 30326-1016. Offers accounting and finance (MBA); management (MBA); marketing (MBA). Evening/weekend programs available. Postbaccalaureate distance learning degree programs offered. *Faculty:* 2 full-time (1 woman), 1 part-time/adjunct (0 women). *Students:* 19 full-time (16 women); includes 1 minority (African American) Average age 28. 10 applicants, 60% accepted, 5 enrolled. In 2006, 25 degrees awarded. *Median time to degree:* Master's–1 year full-time. *Entrance requirements:* For master's, minimum cumulative undergraduate GPA of 2.0. Additional exam requirements/recommendations for international students: Required—TOEFL (minimum score 530 paper-based; 230 computer-based). *Application deadline:* Applications are processed on a rolling basis. Application fee: $50. Electronic applications accepted. *Financial support:* In 2006–07, 14 students received support. Career-related internships or fieldwork, Federal Work-Study, institutionally sponsored loans, and scholarships/grants available. Financial award applicants required to submit FAFSA. *Faculty research:* Leadership management, international advertising. *Unit head:* Dr. Sonia Heywood, Dean of Business, 404-965-5764, Fax: 404-965-5957, E-mail: sonia.heywood@buckhead.aiuniv.edu. *Application contact:* Mike Betz, Vice President Admissions and Marketing, 404-965-5719, Fax: 404-965-5997, E-mail: mbetz@aiuniv.edu.

American InterContinental University Online, Program in Business Administration, Hoffman Estates, IL 60192. Offers accounting and finance (MBA); healthcare management (MBA); human resource management (MBA); international business (MBA); management (MBA); marketing (MBA); operations management (MBA); organizational psychology and development (MBA); project management (MBA). Evening/weekend programs available. Postbaccalaureate distance learning degree programs offered (no on-campus study). *Entrance requirements:* Additional exam requirements/recommendations for international students: Required—TOEFL (minimum score 550 paper-based; 213 computer-based). *Application deadline:* Applications are processed on a rolling basis. Application fee: $50. Electronic applications accepted. *Financial support:* Institutionally sponsored loans and scholarships/grants available. Financial award applicants required to submit FAFSA. *Unit head:* Kerri J Holloway, Vice President of Academic Affairs, 847-851-5000 Ext. 15399, Fax: 847-586-6309, E-mail: kholloway@aivonline.edu. *Application contact:* 877-701-3800, E-mail: info@aiuonline.edu.

American University, Kogod School of Business, Department of Accounting, Program in Accounting, Washington, DC 20016-8001. Offers MBA. Part-time and evening/weekend programs available. *Students:* 19 full-time (10 women), 8 part-time (4 women); includes 2 minority (1 African American, 1 Hispanic American), 7 international. Average age 29. In 2006, 9 degrees awarded. *Entrance requirements:* For master's, GMAT. Additional exam requirements/recommendations for international students: Required—TOEFL. *Application deadline:* For fall admission, 2/1 priority date for domestic students; for spring admission, 10/1 priority date for domestic students. Applications are processed on a rolling basis. Application fee: $50. *Expenses:* Tuition: Full-time $18,864; part-time $1,048 per credit. Required fees: $380. Tuition and fees vary according to program. *Financial support:* Fellowships, research assistantships, career-related internships or fieldwork, Federal Work-Study, and institutionally sponsored loans available. Support available to part-time students. Financial award application deadline: 2/1.

Anderson University, Falls School of Business, Anderson, IN 46012-3495. Offers accountancy (MA); business administration (MBA, DBA). *Accreditation:* ACBSP.

Andrews University, School of Graduate Studies, School of Business, Department of Accounting, Economics and Finance, Berrien Springs, MI 49104. Offers MBA, MSA.

Angelo State University, College of Graduate Studies, College of Business and Professional Studies, Department of Accounting, Economics, and Finance, San Angelo, TX 76909. Offers accounting (MBA); professional accountancy (MPAC). Part-time and evening/weekend programs available. *Faculty:* 18 full-time (3 women). *Students:* 13 full-time (10 women), 4 part-time (1 woman); includes 3 minority (all Hispanic Americans), 1 international. Average age 28. 7 applicants, 57% accepted, 3 enrolled. In 2006, 12 degrees awarded. *Entrance requirements:* For master's, GMAT. Additional exam requirements/recommendations for international students: Required—TOEFL or IELTS. *Application deadline:* For fall admission, 7/15 priority date for domestic students, 6/10 for international students; for spring admission, 12/1 for domestic students, 11/1 for international students. Applications are processed on a rolling basis. Application fee: $40 ($50 for international students). Electronic applications accepted. *Expenses:* Tuition, state resident: full-time $2,340; part-time $130 per hour. Tuition, nonresident: full-time $7,290; part-time $405 per hour. Required fees: $906; $56 per hour. *Financial support:* In 2006–07, 15 students received support. Career-related internships or fieldwork, Federal Work-Study, and scholarships/grants available. Support available to part-time students. Financial award application deadline: 3/1; financial award applicants required to submit FAFSA. *Unit head:* Dr. Thomas A. Bankston, Department Head, 325-942-2046 Ext. 248, E-mail: thomas.bankston@angelo.edu. *Application contact:* Dr. Norman A. Sunderman, Graduate Advisor, 325-942-2046 Ext. 245, E-mail: norman.sunderman@angelo.edu.

Appalachian State University, Cratis D. Williams Graduate School, John A. Walker College of Business, Department of Accounting, Boone, NC 28608. Offers MS. Part-time programs available. *Faculty:* 12 full-time (3 women). *Students:* 37 full-time (16 women), 5 part-time (2 women); includes 1 minority (Asian American or Pacific Islander) Average age 23. 44 applicants, 91% accepted, 32 enrolled. In 2006, 36 degrees awarded. *Degree requirements:* For master's, thesis or alternative, comprehensive exam. *Entrance requirements:* For master's, GMAT. Additional exam requirements/recommendations for international students: Required—TOEFL (minimum score 550 paper-based; 230 computer-based). *Application deadline:* For fall admission, 7/1 for domestic students, 1/1 for international students; for spring admission, 11/1 for domestic students, 6/1 for international students. Applications are processed on a rolling basis. Application fee: $50. *Expenses:* Tuition, state resident: full-time $2,600; part-time $127 per hour. Tuition, nonresident: full-time $13,200; part-time $597 per hour. Required fees: $2,000; $546 per term. *Financial support:* In 2006–07, 9 research assistantships (averaging $7,000 per year) were awarded; fellowships, teaching assistantships, Federal Work-Study, scholarships/grants, and unspecified assistantships also available. Financial award application deadline: 7/1; financial award applicants required to submit FAFSA. *Faculty research:* Audit assurance risk, state taxation, financial accounting inconsistencies, management information systems, charitable contribution taxation. *Unit head:* Dr. Timothy Forsyth, Chairman, 828-262-2036, Fax: 828-262-6640. *Application contact:* Dr. William Pollard, Director, 828-262-6232, Fax: 828-262-6640, E-mail: pollardwb@appstate.edu.

Argosy University, Atlanta Campus, College of Business, Atlanta, GA 30328. Offers accounting (DBA); customized professional concentration (MBA, DBA); finance (MBA); healthcare administration (MBA); information systems (DBA); information systems management (MBA); international business (MBA, DBA); management (MBA, DBA); marketing (MBA, DBA). Part-time programs available. *Students:* 53 full-time (38 women), 35 part-time (28 women); includes 73 minority (66 African Americans, 3 Asian Americans or Pacific Islanders, 4 Hispanic Americans). *Degree requirements:* For master's, comprehensive exam (for some programs), registration; for doctorate, thesis/dissertation, comprehensive exam, registration. *Entrance requirements:* For master's, minimum undergraduate GPA of 3.0; for doctorate, master's degree, minimum GPA of 3.0. Additional exam requirements/recommendations for international students: Required—TOEFL. *Application deadline:* For fall admission, 7/1 priority date for domestic students, 6/1 for international students; for spring admission, 11/1 priority date for domestic students, 10/1 for international students. Applications are processed on a rolling basis. Application fee: $50. Electronic applications accepted. *Financial support:* Applicants required to submit FAFSA. *Unit head:* Dr. Robert A. Berg, Department Chair, 770-407-1042, E-mail: rberg@argosy.edu. *Application contact:* Christa Holton, Director of Admissions, 770-671-1200 Ext. 1014, Fax: 770-671-9050, E-mail: cholton@argosy.edu.

See Close-Up on page 207.

Argosy University, Chicago Campus, College of Business, Chicago, IL 60603. Offers accounting (DBA); customized professional concentration (MBA, DBA); finance (MBA); healthcare administration (MBA); information systems (DBA); information systems management (MBA); international business (MBA, DBA); management (MBA, DBA); marketing (MBA, DBA). Part-time and evening/weekend programs available. *Faculty:* 2 full-time (both women), 4 part-time/adjunct (3 women). *Students:* 52 full-time (30 women), 18 part-time (7 women); includes 37 minority (24 African Americans, 7 Asian Americans or Pacific Islanders, 6 Hispanic Americans). Average age 37. 32 applicants, 81% accepted, 25 enrolled. In 2006, 9 master's, 2 doctorates awarded. *Entrance requirements:* For master's and doctorate, minimum GPA of 3.0. Additional exam requirements/recommendations for international students: Required—TOEFL (minimum score 550 paper-based; 213 computer-based). *Application deadline:* For fall admission, 2/28 for domestic and international students; for spring admission, 10/30 for domestic and international students. Applications are processed on a rolling basis. Application fee: $50. Electronic applications accepted. *Financial support:* In 2006–07, 3 students received support. Scholarships/grants available. Financial award application deadline: 4/1. *Unit head:* Dr. Cynthia Scarlett, Associate Head, 800-626-4123, Fax: 212-727-7750, E-mail: cscarlett@argosy.edu. *Application contact:* Ashley Delaney, Director of Admissions, 800-626-4123, Fax: 312-777-7750, E-mail: argosyadmissions@argosy.edu.

See Close-Up on page 209.

Argosy University, Denver Campus, College of Business, Denver, CO 80203. Offers accounting (DBA); customized professional concentraion (DBA); customized professional concentration (MBA); finance (MBA); healthcare administration (MBA); information systems (DBA); information systems management (MBA); international business (MBA, DBA); management (MBA, MSM, DBA); marketing (MBA, DBA).

See Close-Up on page 213.

Argosy University, Hawai'i Campus, College of Business, Honolulu, HI 96813. Offers accounting (DBA); customized professional concentration (MBA, DBA); finance (MBA, Certificate); healthcare administration (MBA, Certificate); information systems (DBA); information systems management (MBA, Certificate); international business (MBA, DBA, Certificate); management (MBA, DBA); marketing (MBA, DBA, Certificate). Evening/weekend programs available. *Faculty:* 12 part-time/adjunct (2 women). *Students:* 3 full-time (2 women), 1 part-time; includes 2 minority (1 Asian American or Pacific Islander, 1 Hispanic American). 6 applicants, 67% accepted, 3 enrolled. *Degree requirements:* For master's, capstone project. *Entrance requirements:* For master's, minimum GPA of 3.0 in last 60 hours. Additional exam requirements/recommendations for international students: Required—TOEFL (minimum score 550 paper-based; 213 computer-based). *Application deadline:* For fall admission, 1/15 priority date for domestic students; for spring admission, 10/15 for domestic students. Applications are processed on a rolling basis. Application fee: $50. *Financial support:* Teaching assistantships, Federal Work-Study and scholarships/grants available. Support available to part-time students. *Unit head:* Lisa Parker, Interim Chair, College of Business and Information Technology, 888-323-

2777, Fax: 808-536-5505, E-mail: lparker@argosy.edu. *Application contact:* Cherie Andrade, Director of Admissions, 888-323-2777, Fax: 808-536-5505, E-mail: candrade@argosy.edu.

See Close-Up on page 215.

Argosy University, Inland Empire Campus, College of Business, San Bernardino, CA 92408. Offers accounting (DBA); customized professional concentration (MBA, DBA); finance (MBA); healthcare administration (MBA); information systems (DBA); information systems management (MBA); international business (MBA, DBA); management (DBA); mangement (MBA); marketing (MBA, DBA).

See Close-Up on page 217.

Argosy University, Nashville Campus, College of Business, Franklin, TN 37067-7226. Offers accounting (DBA); customized professional concentration (DBA); information systems (DBA); international business (DBA); management (DBA); marketing (DBA). *Degree requirements:* For doctorate, thesis/dissertation, comprehensive exam.

See Close-Up on page 219.

Argosy University, Orange County Campus, College of Business, Santa Ana, CA 92704. Offers accounting (DBA, Adv C); customized professional concentration (MBA, DBA); finance (MBA, Certificate); healthcare administration (MBA, Certificate); information systems (DBA, Adv C); information systems management (MBA); international business (MBA, DBA, Adv C, Certificate); management (MBA, MSM, DBA, EDBA); mangement (Adv C); marketing (MBA, DBA, Adv C, Certificate); organizational leadership (Ed D); public administration (MBA, Certificate). Part-time and evening/weekend programs available. *Faculty:* 4 full-time (1 woman), 20 part-time/adjunct (7 women). *Students:* 163 full-time (64 women), 41 part-time (16 women). Average age 42. 72 applicants, 51 enrolled. In 2006, 6 master's, 23 doctorates awarded. *Degree requirements:* For doctorate, thesis/dissertation, preliminary and final dissertation defense, comprehensive exam. *Entrance requirements:* For master's, minimum GPA of 3.0 in final 2 years of course work, 3 letters of recommendation, resumé; for doctorate, minimum GPA of 3.0 in graduate study, 3 letters of recommendation, resumé. Additional exam requirements/recommendations for international students: Required—TOEFL. *Application deadline:* Applications are processed on a rolling basis. Application fee: $50. Electronic applications accepted. *Financial support:* Federal Work-Study, institutionally sponsored loans, and scholarships/grants available. Support available to part-time students. Financial award applicants required to submit FAFSA. *Faculty research:* Crisis management, leadership in organizations, finance, business systems. *Unit head:* Dr. Ray London, Dean, 800-716-9598, Fax: 714-437-1284, E-mail: auocadmissions@argosy.edu. *Application contact:* Mark Betz, Director of Admissions, 800-716-9598, Fax: 714-437-1697, E-mail: mbetz@argosy.edu.

See Close-Up on page 221.

Argosy University, Phoenix Campus, College of Business, Phoenix, AZ 85021. Offers accounting (DBA); customized professional concentration (MBA, DBA); finance (MBA); healthcare administration (MBA); information systems (DBA); information systems management (MBA); international business (MBA, DBA); management (MBA, DBA); marketing (MBA, DBA). Part-time and evening/weekend programs available. *Faculty:* 1 full-time (0 women). *Students:* 7 full-time (4 women); includes 2 minority (1 African American, 1 Hispanic American). *Entrance requirements:* For doctorate, master's degree. Additional exam requirements/recommendations for international students: Required—TOEFL (minimum score 550 paper-based; 213 computer-based). Application fee: $50. *Financial support:* In 2006–07, 2 students received support. Federal Work-Study, institutionally sponsored loans, and scholarships/grants available. Support available to part-time students. Financial award applicants required to submit FAFSA. *Unit head:* Dr. Gary Berg, Program Chair, 866-216-2777, Fax: 602-216-2601. *Application contact:* Andy Hughes, Director of Admissions, 866-216-2777 Ext. 3110, Fax: 602-216-2601, E-mail: ahughes@argosyu.edu.

See Close-Up on page 223.

Argosy University, San Diego Campus, College of Business, San Diego, CA 92108. Offers accounting (DBA); customized professional concentration (MBA, DBA); finance (MBA); information systems (DBA); information systems management (MBA); international business (MBA, DBA); management (MBA, MSM, DBA); marketing (MBA, DBA); public administration (MBA).

See Close-Up on page 225.

Argosy University, San Francisco Bay Area Campus, College of Business, Point Richmond, CA 94804-3547. Offers accounting (DBA); corporate compliance (MBA); customized professional concentration (MBA, DBA); finance (MBA); healthcare administration (MBA); information systems (DBA); information systems management (MBA); international business (MBA, DBA); management (MBA, MSM, DBA); marketing (MBA, DBA). Part-time and evening/weekend programs available. *Faculty:* 2 full-time (0 women), 9 part-time/adjunct (0 women). *Students:* 29 full-time (8 women), 9 part-time (2 women); includes 30 minority (5 African Americans, 24 Asian Americans or Pacific Islanders, 1 Hispanic American). 21 applicants, 76% accepted, 13 enrolled. In 2006, 3 master's, 2 doctorates awarded. *Degree requirements:* For master's, capstone project; for doctorate, thesis/dissertation, comprehensive exam, registration. *Entrance requirements:* For master's, minimum GPA of 3.0; for doctorate, MBA or minimum GPA of 3.0. Additional exam requirements/recommendations for international students: Required—TOEFL (minimum score 550 paper-based; 213 computer-based). *Application deadline:* For fall admission, 7/1 priority date for domestic and international students; for winter admission, 11/1 priority date for domestic and international students; for spring admission, 4/1 priority date for domestic and international students. Applications are processed on a rolling basis. Application fee: $50. Electronic applications accepted. *Financial support:* Federal Work-Study and scholarships/grants available. Support available to part-time students. Financial award applicants required to submit FAFSA. *Unit head:* Dr. Anthony Martinez, Department Chair, Business and Information Technology, 866-215-0277, Fax: 510-215-0299, E-mail: amartinez@argosy.edu. *Application contact:* John Vincent Stofan, Director of Admissions, 866-215-2727 Ext. 205, Fax: 510-215-0299, E-mail: jstofan@argosyu.edu.

See Close-Up on page 227.

Argosy University, Santa Monica Campus, College of Business, Santa Monica, CA 90405. Offers accounting (DBA); customized professional concentration (MBA, DBA); finance (MBA); healthcare administration (MBA); information systems (DBA); information systems management (MBA); international business (MBA, DBA); management (MBA, MS, MSM, DBA); marketing (MBA, DBA).

See Close-Up on page 229.

Argosy University, Sarasota Campus, College of Business, Sarasota, FL 34235-8246. Offers accounting (DBA, Adv C); customized professional concentration (MBA, DBA); finance (MBA, Certificate); healtcare administration (Certificate); healthcare administration (MBA); information systems (DBA, Adv C); information systems management (MBA, Certificate); international business (MBA, DBA, Adv C, Certificate); management (MBA, MSM, DBA); mangement (Adv C); marketing (MBA, DBA, Adv C, Certificate). Part-time and evening/weekend programs available. Postbaccalaureate distance learning degree programs offered (minimal on-campus study). *Faculty:* 6 full-time (3 women), 13 part-time/adjunct (5 women). *Students:* 71 applicants, 92% accepted, 64 enrolled. In 2006, 7 master's, 30 doctorates awarded. *Degree requirements:* For doctorate, thesis/dissertation, comprehensive exam. *Entrance requirements:* For master's, minimum GPA of 3.0; for doctorate, minimum undergraduate GPA of 3.0. Additional exam requirements/recommendations for international students: Required—TOEFL. *Application deadline:* Applications are processed on a rolling basis. Application fee: $50. Electronic applications accepted. *Financial support:* Federal Work-Study and scholarships/grants available. Support available to part-time students. Financial award application deadline: 4/1; financial award applicants required to submit FAFSA. *Unit head:* Dr. Kathleen Cornett, Dean, 800-331-5995, Fax: 941-379-9464, E-mail: kcornett@argosy.edu. *Application contact:* Admissions Representative, 800-331-5995 Ext. 221, Fax: 941-379-5964.

See Close-Up on page 231.

Argosy University, Schaumburg Campus, College of Business, Schaumburg, IL 60173-5403. Offers accounting (DBA, Adv C); corporate compliance (MBA); customized professional concentration (MBA, DBA); finance (MBA, Certificate); healthcare administration (MBA, Certificate); information systems (DBA, Adv C); information systems management (MBA, Certificate); international business (MBA, DBA, Adv C, Certificate); management (MBA, DBA, Adv C, Certificate); marketing (MBA, DBA, Adv C, Certificate). Part-time and evening/weekend programs available. *Faculty:* 1 (woman) full-time, 7 part-time/adjunct (0 women). *Students:* 36 full-time, 23 part-time. 13 applicants, 69% accepted, 9 enrolled. In 2006, 5 master's, 4 doctorates awarded. *Degree requirements:* For doctorate, thesis/dissertation, comprehensive exam. *Entrance requirements:* For master's and doctorate, minimum GPA of 3.0. Additional exam requirements/recommendations for international students: Required—TOEFL. *Application deadline:* For fall admission, 3/15 priority date for domestic and international students; for spring admission, 10/15 priority date for domestic and international students. Applications are processed on a rolling basis. Application fee: $50. Electronic applications accepted. *Expenses: Contact institution. Financial support:* Federal Work-Study and scholarships/grants available. *Unit head:* Dr. Harriet Kandelman, Dean, 866-290-2777, Fax: 847-548-6159, E-mail: agrosyadmissions@argosy.edu. *Application contact:* Jamal Scott, Director of Admissions, 847-598-6159, Fax: 630-598-6191, E-mail: jscott@argosy.edu.

See Close-Up on page 233.

Argosy University, Seattle Campus, College of Business, Seattle, WA 98121. Offers accounting (DBA); customized professional concentration (MBA, DBA); finance (MBA); healthcare administration (MBA); information systems (DBA); information systems management (MBA); international business (MBA, DBA); management (MSM, DBA); mangement (MBA); marketing (MBA, DBA). Part-time and evening/weekend programs available. *Students:* 1 applicant, 100% accepted, 1 enrolled. In 2006, 1 degree awarded. *Degree requirements:* For master's, capstone experience; for doctorate, thesis/dissertation, comprehensive exam (for some programs). *Entrance requirements:* For master's, minimum GPA of 3.0 in last 2 years or cumulative of 2.7; for doctorate, minimum GPA of 3.0. Additional exam requirements/recommendations for international students: Required—TOEFL (minimum score 550 paper-based; 213 computer-based). *Application deadline:* For fall admission, 4/15 priority date for domestic students, 4/15 for international students; for winter admission, 10/15 priority date for domestic students. Applications are processed on a rolling basis. Application fee: $50. Electronic applications accepted. *Expenses: Contact institution. Financial support:* Federal Work-Study and unspecified assistantships available. Support available to part-time students. Financial award applicants required to submit FAFSA. *Unit head:* Dr. Kylene Quinn, Chair, 206-393-3543, Fax: 206-283-5777, E-mail: kquinn@argosy.edu. *Application contact:* Heather Simpson, Director of Admissions, 866-283-4500, Fax: 206-283-5777, E-mail: hsimpson@argosy.edu.

See Close-Up on page 235.

Argosy University, Tampa Campus, College of Business, Tampa, FL 33614. Offers accounting (DBA); customized professional concentration (MBA, DBA); finance (MBA, Certificate); healthcare administration (MBA, Certificate); information systems (DBA); information systems management (MBA); international business (MBA, DBA, Certificate); management (MBA, MSM, DBA); marketing (MBA, DBA, Certificate); public administration (MBA). *Entrance requirements:* For doctorate, minimum GPA of 3.0. *Unit head:* Dr. Andrew Ghillyer, Dean, 813-393-5270, E-mail: aghillyer@argosy.edu.

See Close-Up on page 237.

Argosy University, Twin Cities Campus, College of Business, Eagan, MN 55121. Offers accounting (DBA); corporate compliance (MBA); customized professional certification (DBA); customized professional concentration (MBA); finance (MBA); healthcare administration (MBA); information systems (DBA); information systems management (MBA); international business (MBA, DBA); management (MBA, MSM, DBA, EDBA); marketing (MBA, DBA). Part-time and evening/weekend programs available. *Faculty:* 1 (woman) full-time, 20 part-time/adjunct (6 women). *Students:* 47 full-time (23 women), 20 part-time (11 women); includes 21 minority (10 African Americans, 1 American Indian/Alaska Native, 9 Asian Americans or Pacific Islanders, 1 Hispanic American). Average age 39. 72 applicants, 76% accepted, 45 enrolled. In 2006, 6 degrees awarded. *Degree requirements:* For doctorate, thesis/dissertation, comprehensive exam. *Entrance requirements:* For master's, 3 letters of recommendation, bachelor's degree in a related field, minimum undergraduate GPA of 3.0, resumé; for doctorate, 3 letters of recommendation, master's degree in a related field, minimum GPA of 3.0, resumé. Additional exam requirements/recommendations for international students: Required—TOEFL (minimum score 550 paper-based; 213 computer-based). *Application deadline:* For fall admission, 5/15 priority date for domestic students, 5/15 for international students; for spring admission, 10/15 priority date for domestic students, 10/15 for international students. Applications are processed on a rolling basis. Application fee: $50. Electronic applications accepted. *Financial support:* In 2006–07, 3 fellowships with partial tuition reimbursements, 3 teaching assistantships with partial tuition reimbursements were awarded; Federal Work-Study and scholarships/grants also available. Financial award applicants required to submit FAFSA. *Unit head:* Dr. Paula King, Department Head, 651-846-3377, E-mail: pking@argosy.edu. *Application contact:* Jennifer Radke, 2nd Director of Graduate Admissions, 651-846-3300, Fax: 651-994-7954, E-mail: tcadmissions@argosy.edu.

See Close-Up on page 239.

Argosy University, Washington DC Campus, College of Business, Arlington, VA 22209. Offers accounting (DBA); customized professional concentration (MBA, DBA); finance (MBA); healthcare administration (MBA); information systems (DBA); information systems management (MBA); international business (MBA, DBA); international business marketing (Graduate Certificate); management (MBA, DBA); marketing (MBA, DBA). *Faculty:* 1 full-time (0 women), 5 part-time/adjunct (2 women). *Students:* 5 full-time (4 women), 4 part-time (1 woman); includes 4 minority (3 African Americans, 1 Asian American or Pacific Islander). 21 applicants, 86% accepted. *Degree requirements:* For master's, thesis (for some programs), comprehensive exam (for some programs); for doctorate, thesis/dissertation, comprehensive exam. *Entrance requirements:* For master's and doctorate, minimum GPA of 3.0. Additional exam requirements/recommendations for international students: Required—TOEFL (minimum score 550 paper-based; 213 computer-based). *Application deadline:* For fall admission, 6/15 priority date for domestic students; for spring admission, 10/15 priority date for domestic students. Application fee: $50. *Financial support:* Federal Work-Study and scholarships/grants available. Financial award applicants required to submit FAFSA. *Unit head:* Dr. Colleen Logan, Academic Affairs Officer, 866-703-2777, Fax: 703-521-5850, E-mail: dcadmissions@argosy.edu. *Application contact:* Emily Peck, Director of Admissions, 866-703-2777 Ext. 5851, Fax: 703-526-5850, E-mail: dcadmissions@argosy.edu.

See Close-Up on page 241.

Arizona State University, Division of Graduate Studies, W.P. Carey School of Business, Program in Business Administration, Tempe, AZ 85287. Offers accountancy (PhD); business administration (MBA); finance (PhD); health services research (PhD); information management (PhD); management (PhD); marketing (PhD); supply chain management (PhD); JD/MBA; MBA/M Arch; MBA/MHSM. MBA/MIM offered jointly with Thunderbird, The American Graduate School of International Management and Groupe Ecole Supéieure de Commerce, Toulouse, France. *Accreditation:* AACSB. *Degree requirements:* For master's, thesis optional; for doctorate, thesis/dissertation. *Entrance requirements:* For master's, GMAT.

Arizona State University, Division of Graduate Studies, W.P. Carey School of Business, School of Accountancy and Information Management, Tempe, AZ 85287. Offers M Tax, MAIS,

Accounting

Arizona State University (continued)
MBA/M Tax, MBA/MAIS. *Accreditation:* AACSB. *Degree requirements:* For master's, thesis optional. *Entrance requirements:* For master's, GMAT.

Arizona State University at the West campus, School of Global Management and Leadership, Program in Accounting, Phoenix, AZ 85069-7100. Offers professional accountancy (Certificate). *Accreditation:* AACSB. *Faculty:* 6 full-time (3 women), 1 part-time/adjunct (0 women). *Students:* 28 full-time (15 women), 161 part-time (80 women); includes 33 minority (4 African Americans, 2 American Indian/Alaska Native, 11 Asian Americans or Pacific Islanders, 16 Hispanic Americans). Average age 32. 106 applicants, 98% accepted, 84 enrolled. *Entrance requirements:* Additional exam requirements/recommendations for international students: Required—TOEFL (minimum score 550 paper-based; 213 computer-based; 83 iBT), IELTS (minimum score 7). *Application deadline:* For fall admission, 8/1 for domestic students; for spring admission, 1/1 for domestic students. Applications are processed on a rolling basis. Application fee: $50. Electronic applications accepted. *Expenses:* Tuition, state resident: full-time $5,930. Tuition, nonresident: full-time $16,516. Tuition and fees vary according to course load. *Unit head:* Dr. Bruce Baldwin, Interim Chair, 602-543-1622, Fax: 602-543-6303, E-mail: bruce.baldwin@asu.edu. *Application contact:* Michael Del Valle, Student Support Coordinator, 602-543-6278, Fax: 602-543-6303, E-mail: michael.delvalle@asu.edu.

Arkansas State University, Graduate School, College of Business, Department of Accounting and Law, Jonesboro, State University, AR 72467. Offers accountancy (M Acc). Part-time programs available. *Faculty:* 5 full-time (2 women), 2 part-time/adjunct (1 woman). *Students:* 14 full-time (10 women), 5 part-time (3 women); includes 1 minority (African American) Average age 26. 15 applicants, 93% accepted, 13 enrolled. In 2006, 8 degrees awarded. *Degree requirements:* For master's, thesis or alternative, comprehensive exam. *Entrance requirements:* For master's, GMAT, appropriate bachelor's degree, letters of reference, official transcript. *Application deadline:* Applications are processed on a rolling basis. Application fee: $30 ($40 for international students). Electronic applications accepted. *Expenses: Contact institution. Financial support:* Career-related internships or fieldwork, scholarships/grants, and unspecified assistantships available. Financial award application deadline: 7/1; financial award applicants required to submit FAFSA. *Unit head:* Dr. Tina Quinn, Chair, 870-972-3038, Fax: 870-972-3868, E-mail: tquinn@astate.edu.

Auburn University, Graduate School, College of Business, School of Accountancy, Auburn University, AL 36849. Offers M Acc. *Accreditation:* AACSB. Part-time programs available. *Faculty:* 15 full-time (5 women). *Students:* 45 full-time (24 women), 28 part-time (17 women); includes 1 minority (African American) Average age 26. 139 applicants, 55% accepted, 55 enrolled. In 2006, 55 degrees awarded. *Entrance requirements:* For master's, GMAT, GRE General Test. Additional exam requirements/recommendations for international students: Required—TOEFL. *Application deadline:* For fall admission, 7/7 for domestic students; for spring admission, 11/24 for domestic students. Applications are processed on a rolling basis. Application fee: $25 ($50 for international students). Electronic applications accepted. *Expenses:* Tuition, state resident: full-time $5,000. Tuition, nonresident: full-time $15,000. Required fees: $416. Tuition and fees vary according to program. *Financial support:* Teaching assistantships, Federal Work-Study available. Support available to part-time students. Financial award application deadline: 3/15. *Unit head:* Norman H. Godwin, Director, 334-844-5340. *Application contact:* Dr. Joe Pittman, Interim Dean of the Graduate School, 334-844-4700.

Avila University, School of Business, Kansas City, MO 64145-1698. Offers accounting (MBA); finance (MBA); general management (MBA); health care administration (MBA); international business (MBA); management information systems (MBA); marketing (MBA). Part-time and evening/weekend programs available. *Faculty:* 8 full-time (4 women), 17 part-time/adjunct (4 women). *Students:* 31 full-time (19 women), 165 part-time (96 women); includes 18 minority (14 African Americans, 1 American Indian/Alaska Native, 3 Hispanic Americans), 16 international. Average age 32. 77 applicants, 81% accepted, 62 enrolled. In 2006, 54 degrees awarded. *Degree requirements:* For master's, capstone course. *Entrance requirements:* For master's, GMAT, minimum GPA of 3.0. Additional exam requirements/recommendations for international students: Required—TOEFL (minimum score 550 paper-based). *Application deadline:* For fall admission, 7/30 priority date for domestic students; for winter admission, 11/30 priority date for domestic students; for spring admission, 2/28 priority date for domestic students. Applications are processed on a rolling basis. Application fee: $20. Electronic applications accepted. *Expenses:* Tuition: Full-time $7,470; part-time $415 per credit. *Financial support:* In 2006–07, 78 students received support. Career-related internships or fieldwork available. Support available to part-time students. Financial award applicants required to submit FAFSA. *Faculty research:* Leadership characteristics, financial hedging, group dynamics. *Unit head:* Dr. Richard Woodall, Dean, 816-501-3798, Fax: 816-501-2463. *Application contact:* JoAnna Giffin, MBA Admissions Director, 816-501-3601, Fax: 816-501-2463, E-mail: joanna.giffin@avila.edu.

Baker College Center for Graduate Studies, Programs in Business, Flint, MI 48507-9843. Offers accounting (MBA); computer information systems (MBA); finance (MBA); general business (MBA); health and recreation services management (MBA); health care management (MBA); human resource management (MBA); industrial management (MBA); international business (MBA); leadership (MBA); marketing (MBA). MBA in health and recreation services management enrollment limited to international students. Part-time and evening/weekend programs available. *Faculty:* 15 full-time (6 women), 425 part-time/adjunct (200 women). *Students:* 370 full-time (190 women), 1,060 part-time (560 women); includes 372 minority (205 African Americans, 27 American Indian/Alaska Native, 66 Asian Americans or Pacific Islanders, 74 Hispanic Americans), 30 international. Average age 38. 780 applicants, 85% accepted, 567 enrolled. In 2006, 202 degrees awarded. *Degree requirements:* For master's, portfolio. *Entrance requirements:* For master's, 3 years of work experience, minimum undergraduate GPA of 2.5, writing sample, letters of recommendation. Additional exam requirements/recommendations for international students: Required—TOEFL (minimum score 550 paper-based; 213 computer-based). *Application deadline:* For fall admission, 8/6 priority date for domestic students; for winter admission, 12/15 priority date for domestic students; for spring admission, 2/15 priority date for domestic students. Applications are processed on a rolling basis. Application fee: $25. Electronic applications accepted. *Expenses:* Tuition: Full-time $7,200; part-time $300 per credit hour. *Financial support:* In 2006–07, 410 students received support. Scholarships/grants available. Support available to part-time students. Financial award applicants required to submit FAFSA. *Unit head:* Dr. Michael Heberling, President, 800-469-3165, Fax: 810-766-4399, E-mail: heberling@baker.edu. *Application contact:* Chuck J. Gurden, Vice President for Graduate and Online Admissions, 800-469-3165, Fax: 810-766-2051, E-mail: chuck@baker.edu.

Baldwin-Wallace College, Graduate Programs, Division of Business Administration, Program in Accounting, Berea, OH 44017-2088. Offers MBA. Part-time and evening/weekend programs available. *Students:* 27 full-time (13 women), 10 part-time (8 women); includes 7 minority (3 African Americans, 4 Asian Americans or Pacific Islanders), 2 international. Average age 31. 19 applicants, 84% accepted, 13 enrolled. In 2006, 36 degrees awarded. *Entrance requirements:* For master's, GMAT, minimum GPA of 3.0, work experience. *Application deadline:* For fall admission, 7/25 priority date for domestic students; for spring admission, 12/15 priority date for domestic students. Applications are processed on a rolling basis. Application fee: $25. Electronic applications accepted. *Expenses: Contact institution.* Tuition and fees vary according to program. *Unit head:* Roger A. Grugle, Director of Accounting MBA, 440-826-2363, Fax: 440-826-3868, E-mail: rgrugle@bw.edu. *Application contact:* Winifred W. Gerhardt, Director of Admission for the Evening and Weekend College, 440-826-2222, Fax: 440-826-3830, E-mail: admission@bw.edu.

Ball State University, Graduate School, Miller College of Business, Department of Accounting, Muncie, IN 47306-1099. Offers MS. *Accreditation:* AACSB. *Faculty:* 11. *Students:* 29 full-time (14 women), 4 part-time (2 women); includes 5 minority (1 African American, 1 American Indian/Alaska Native, 3 Hispanic Americans), 1 international. Average age 25. 37 applicants, 86% accepted, 25 enrolled. In 2006, 17 degrees awarded. Application fee: $25 ($35 for international students). *Financial support:* In 2006–07, 5 teaching assistantships with full tuition reimbursements (averaging $8,356 per year) were awarded; research assistantships with full tuition reimbursements. Financial award application deadline: 3/1. *Unit head:* Dr. Lucinda Van Alst, Head, 765-285-5100, E-mail: lvanalst@bsu.edu. *Application contact:* Dr. Mark Myring, Information Contact, 765-285-5100, Fax: 765-285-8024.

Barry University, Andreas School of Business, Program in Accounting, Miami Shores, FL 33161-6695. Offers MSA. *Students:* 4 full-time (3 women), 3 part-time (1 woman); includes 2 minority (both Hispanic Americans), 2 international. In 2006, 6 degrees awarded. *Application contact:* Dave Fletcher, Director of Graduate Admissions, 305-899-3113, Fax: 305-899-2971, E-mail: dfletcher@mail.barry.edu.

Bayamón Central University, Graduate Programs, Program in Business Administration, Bayamón, PR 00960-1725. Offers accounting (MBA); finance (MBA); general business (MBA); management (MBA); management of security and protection (MBA); marketing (MBA). Part-time and evening/weekend programs available. *Degree requirements:* For master's, comprehensive exam (for some programs), registration (for some programs). *Entrance requirements:* For master's, EXADEP, bachelor's degree in business or related field.

Baylor University, Graduate School, Hankamer School of Business, Department of Accounting and Business Law, Waco, TX 76798. Offers M Acc, MT, JD/M Acc, JD/MT. *Accreditation:* AACSB. Part-time programs available. *Faculty:* 11 full-time (2 women). *Students:* 3 full-time (1 woman). In 2006, 41 degrees awarded. *Entrance requirements:* For master's, GMAT. *Application deadline:* For fall admission, 8/1 for domestic students; for spring admission, 12/1 for domestic students. Applications are processed on a rolling basis. Application fee: $25. *Financial support:* Research assistantships, career-related internships or fieldwork, Federal Work-Study, and institutionally sponsored loans available. *Faculty research:* Continuing professional education (CPE), accounting education, retirement plans. *Unit head:* Dr. Jane Baldwin, Adviser, 254-710-3536, Fax: 254-710-2421, E-mail: jane_baldwin@baylor.edu. *Application contact:* Vicky Todd, Administrative Assistant, 254-710-3718, Fax: 254-710-1066, E-mail: mba@hsb.baylor.edu.

Bentley College, The Elkin B. McCallum Graduate School of Business, Accountancy Program, Waltham, MA 02452-4705. Offers PhD. *Faculty:* 27 full-time (10 women), 17 part-time/adjunct (6 women). *Students:* 4 full-time (all women), 1 part-time; includes 1 minority (African American) Average age 38. 7 applicants, 71% accepted, 5 enrolled. *Entrance requirements:* For doctorate, GMAT. Additional exam requirements/recommendations for international students: Required—TOEFL (minimum score 600 paper-based; 250 computer-based). *Application deadline:* For fall admission, 3/1 for domestic and international students. Application fee: $0. Electronic applications accepted. *Expenses:* Tuition: Full-time $28,440; part-time $2,844 per course. Required fees: $404; $105 per year. *Financial support:* Research assistantships, teaching assistantships available. *Unit head:* Dr. Sue Newell, PhD Program Director, 781-891-2399, Fax: 781-891-3121, E-mail: snewell@bentley.edu.

Bentley College, The Elkin B. McCallum Graduate School of Business, Master's Program in Accounting, Waltham, MA 02452-4705. Offers MSA. *Accreditation:* AACSB. Part-time and evening/weekend programs available. *Faculty:* 27 full-time (10 women), 17 part-time/adjunct (6 women). *Students:* 68 full-time (45 women), 91 part-time (54 women); includes 24 minority (6 African Americans, 14 Asian Americans or Pacific Islanders, 4 Hispanic Americans), 25 international. Average age 27. 204 applicants, 82% accepted, 102 enrolled. In 2006, 25 degrees awarded. *Entrance requirements:* For master's, GMAT. Additional exam requirements/recommendations for international students: Required—TOEFL (minimum score 600 paper-based; 250 computer-based). *Application deadline:* For fall admission, 6/1 priority date for domestic students, 3/1 priority date for international students; for spring admission, 11/1 priority date for domestic and international students. Applications are processed on a rolling basis. Application fee: $50. Electronic applications accepted. *Expenses:* Tuition: Full-time $28,440; part-time $2,844 per course. Required fees: $404; $105 per year. *Financial support:* Research assistantships, scholarships/grants, tuition waivers, and unspecified assistantships available. Financial award application deadline: 4/12; financial award applicants required to submit CSS PROFILE or FAFSA. *Faculty research:* Audit risk assessment, ethics in accounting, corporate governance, accounting information systems and management control. *Unit head:* Martha Howe, Director, 781-891-2573. *Application contact:* Sharon Hill, Director of Graduate Admissions, 781-891-2108, Fax: 781-891-2464, E-mail: shill@bentley.edu.

Bernard M. Baruch College of the City University of New York, Zicklin School of Business, Department of Accounting, Program in Accounting, New York, NY 10010-5585. Offers MBA, MS, PhD. *Accreditation:* AACSB. Part-time and evening/weekend programs available. *Faculty:* 33 full-time (9 women), 33 part-time/adjunct (6 women). *Students:* 130 full-time (73 women), 219 part-time (115 women); includes 141 minority (14 African Americans, 108 Asian Americans or Pacific Islanders, 19 Hispanic Americans). In 2006, 97 master's, 1 doctorate awarded. *Degree requirements:* For doctorate, thesis/dissertation, comprehensive exam. *Entrance requirements:* For master's, GMAT, 2 letters of recommendation, resumé, 2 years of work experience; for doctorate, GMAT. Additional exam requirements/recommendations for international students: Required—TOEFL (minimum score 590 paper-based; 243 computer-based), TWE (minimum score 5). *Application deadline:* For fall admission, 5/31 for domestic students, 4/30 for international students; for spring admission, 10/31 for domestic and international students. Application fee: $125. *Financial support:* Fellowships, research assistantships, teaching assistantships, career-related internships or fieldwork, Federal Work-Study, scholarships/grants, and unspecified assistantships available. Financial award application deadline: 4/30; financial award applicants required to submit FAFSA. *Application contact:* Frances Murphy, Office of Graduate Admissions, 646-312-1300, Fax: 646-312-1301, E-mail: zicklingradadmissions@baruch.cuny.edu.

Bob Jones University, Graduate Programs, Greenville, SC 29614. Offers accountancy (MS); Bible (MA); Bible translation (MA); Biblical studies (Certificate); broadcast management (MS); business administration (MBA); church history (MA, PhD); church ministries (MA); church music (MM); cinema and video production (MA); counseling (MS); curriculum and instruction (Ed D); divinity (M Div); dramatic production (MA); educational leadership (MS, Ed D, Ed S); elementary education (M Ed, MAT); English (M Ed, MA, MAT); fine arts (MA); graphic design (MA); history (M Ed, MA); illustration (MA); interpretative speech (MA); mathematics (M Ed, MAT); medical missions (Certificate); ministry (MM, D Min); multi-categorical special education (M Ed, MAT); music (M Ed); New Testament interpretation (PhD); Old Testament interpretation (PhD); orchestral instrument performance (MM); organ performance (MM); pastoral studies (MA); personnel services (MS, Ed S); piano pedagogy (MM); piano performance (MM); platform arts (MA); radio and television broadcasting (MS); rhetoric and public address (MA); secondary education (M Ed); studio art (MA); teaching Bible (MA); theology (MA, PhD); voice performance (MM); youth ministries (MA); M Div/MM.

Boise State University, Graduate College, College of Business and Economics, Program in Accountancy, Boise, ID 83725-0399. Offers accountancy (MSA); taxation (MSA). *Accreditation:* AACSB. Part-time programs available. *Faculty:* 8 full-time (0 women), 3 part-time/adjunct (1 woman). *Students:* 19 full-time (6 women), 33 part-time (22 women); includes 1 minority (Hispanic American), 2 international. Average age 35. 21 applicants, 86% accepted, 9 enrolled. In 2006, 20 degrees awarded. *Entrance requirements:* For master's, GMAT, minimum GPA of 3.0. Additional exam requirements/recommendations for international students: Required—TOEFL. *Application deadline:* For fall admission, 3/1 priority date for domestic students; for spring admission, 10/1 priority date for domestic students. Applications are processed on a rolling basis. Application fee: $0. Electronic applications accepted. *Financial support:* Career-related internships or fieldwork, Federal Work-Study, institutionally sponsored loans, and unspecified assistantships available. Support available to part-time students. Financial award application deadline: 3/1. *Unit head:* Dr. Kirk Smith, Director, 208-426-3180. *Application contact:* J. Renee Anchustegui, Coordinator, 208-426-3116, Fax: 208-426-1135, E-mail: ranchust@boisestate.edu.

Boston College, The Carroll School of Management, Programs in Accounting, Chestnut Hill, MA 02467-3800. Offers MSA. *Faculty:* 4 full-time (0 women), 1 part-time/adjunct (0 women). *Students:* 86 full-time (38 women); includes 18 minority (1 American Indian/Alaska Native, 17 Asian Americans or Pacific Islanders), 20 international. Average age 24. 64 applicants, 91% accepted, 45 enrolled. In 2006, 90 degrees awarded. *Entrance requirements:* For master's, GMAT, recommendations, resumé. Additional exam requirements/recommendations for international students: Required—TOEFL (minimum score 600 paper-based; 250 computer-based; 100 iBT). *Application deadline:* For fall admission, 3/15 for domestic and international students; for spring admission, 2/15 for domestic and international students. Application fee: $100. Electronic applications accepted. *Financial support:* Tuition waivers (partial) available. *Faculty research:* Financial reporting, auditing, tax planning, financial statement analysis. *Application contact:* Shelley A. Burt, Director of Graduate Enrollment, 617-552-3920, Fax: 617-552-8078, E-mail: bcmba@bc.edu.

Boston University, School of Management, Doctorate in Business Administration Program, Boston, MA 02215. Offers accounting (DBA); information systems (DBA); management policy (DBA); marketing (DBA); operations management (DBA); organizational behavior (DBA). *Students:* 48 full-time (26 women); includes 4 minority (all Asian Americans or Pacific Islanders), 24 international. Average age 35. 120 applicants, 17% accepted, 10 enrolled. In 2006, 8 degrees awarded. *Degree requirements:* For doctorate, thesis/dissertation. *Entrance requirements:* For doctorate, GMAT or GRE General Test. *Application deadline:* For fall admission, 1/31 for domestic students. Application fee: $125. *Expenses:* Tuition: Full-time $33,330; part-time $1,042 per credit. Required fees: $462; $40. *Financial support:* Career-related internships or fieldwork, Federal Work-Study, institutionally sponsored loans, scholarships/grants, and tuition waivers available. Support available to part-time students. Financial award applicants required to submit FAFSA. *Unit head:* Dr. Sushil Vachani, Director, 617-353-4875, E-mail: dba@bu.edu. *Application contact:* Hayden Estrada, Assistant Dean, Admissions, 617-353-2670, Fax: 617-353-7368, E-mail: dba@bu.edu.

Boston University, School of Management, Master of Business Administration Program, Boston, MA 02215. Offers advanced accounting (Certificate); general management (MBA); healthcare management (MBA); public and nonprofit management (MBA); JD/MBA; MBA/MA; MBA/MPH; MBA/MS; MBA/MSIS; MS/MBA. Part-time and evening/weekend programs available. *Faculty:* 104 full-time (21 women). *Students:* 299 full-time (114 women), 487 part-time (190 women); includes 124 minority (12 African Americans, 2 American Indian/Alaska Native, 94 Asian Americans or Pacific Islanders, 16 Hispanic Americans), 143 international. Average age 26. 1,482 applicants, 42% accepted, 300 enrolled. In 2006, 342 degrees awarded. *Entrance requirements:* For master's, GMAT. *Application deadline:* For fall admission, 5/1 for domestic students. Applications are processed on a rolling basis. Application fee: $125. Electronic applications accepted. *Expenses:* Tuition: Full-time $33,330; part-time $1,042 per credit. Required fees: $462; $40. *Financial support:* Career-related internships or fieldwork, Federal Work-Study, institutionally sponsored loans, and tuition waivers (partial) available. Support available to part-time students. Financial award applicants required to submit FAFSA. *Unit head:* Dr. John Chalykoff, Associate Dean, Academic Program, 617-353-4157, Fax: 617-353-5003, E-mail: chalykof@bu.edu. *Application contact:* Hayden Estrada, Assistant Dean, Admissions, 617-353-2670, Fax: 617-353-7368, E-mail: mba@bu.edu.

Bowling Green State University, Graduate College, College of Business Administration, Program in Accountancy, Bowling Green, OH 43403. Offers M Acc. *Accreditation:* AACSB. Part-time programs available. *Faculty:* 12 full-time (1 woman). *Students:* 51 full-time (25 women), 1 (woman) part-time; includes 10 minority (2 African Americans, 2 Asian Americans or Pacific Islanders, 6 Hispanic Americans), 17 international. Average age 25. 80 applicants, 70% accepted, 49 enrolled. In 2006, 45 degrees awarded. *Degree requirements:* For master's, thesis or alternative. *Entrance requirements:* For master's, GMAT. Additional exam requirements/recommendations for international students: Required—TOEFL. *Application deadline:* For fall admission, 2/15 priority date for domestic students. Application fee: $30. Electronic applications accepted. *Expenses:* Tuition, state resident: part-time $535 per hour. Tuition, nonresident: part-time $884 per hour. *Financial support:* In 2006–07, 44 research assistantships with full tuition reimbursements (averaging $4,820 per year), 1 teaching assistantship with full tuition reimbursement (averaging $4,060 per year) were awarded; Federal Work-Study and unspecified assistantships also available. Financial award applicants required to submit FAFSA. *Faculty research:* Financial reporting and auditing, accounting information systems, taxation. *Unit head:* Dr. Larry Kowalski, Chair, 419-372-8160. *Application contact:* Alan Lord, Director, 419-372-8045.

Bradley University, Graduate School, Foster College of Business Administration, Program in Accounting, Peoria, IL 61625-0002. Offers MSA. *Accreditation:* AACSB. Part-time and evening/weekend programs available. *Students:* 2 full-time (1 woman), 2 part-time (1 woman), 1 international. 8 applicants, 50% accepted, 1 enrolled. In 2006, 18 degrees awarded. *Degree requirements:* For master's, comprehensive exam. *Entrance requirements:* For master's, GMAT, minimum undergraduate GPA of 2.75 in major, 2 letters of recommendation. Additional exam requirements/recommendations for international students: Required—TOEFL (minimum score 550 paper-based; 213 computer-based; 79 iBT). *Application deadline:* For fall admission, 5/15 priority date for domestic and international students; for spring admission, 10/15 priority date for domestic and international students. Applications are processed on a rolling basis. Application fee: $40 ($50 for international students). *Financial support:* Research assistantships with full and partial tuition reimbursements, career-related internships or fieldwork, institutionally sponsored loans, scholarships/grants, tuition waivers (partial), and unspecified assistantships available. Support available to part-time students. Financial award application deadline: 4/1. *Unit head:* Dr. Edward Sattler, Associate Dean, 309-677-2253. *Application contact:* Janet Davidson, Assistant Director of Graduate Programs, 309-677-2256, Fax: 309-677-3374, E-mail: jdavids@bradley.edu.

Brenau University, Graduate Programs, School of Business and Mass Communication, Gainesville, GA 30501. Offers accounting (MBA); healthcare management (MBA); leadership development (MBA); management (MBA); organizational development (MS). Part-time and evening/weekend programs available. Postbaccalaureate distance learning degree programs offered (no on-campus study). *Faculty:* 12 full-time (6 women), 16 part-time/adjunct (5 women). *Students:* 49 full-time (32 women), 148 part-time (89 women); includes 52 minority (45 African Americans, 2 Asian Americans or Pacific Islanders, 5 Hispanic Americans), 2 international. Average age 35. 222 applicants, 55% accepted, 111 enrolled. In 2006, 64 degrees awarded. *Degree requirements:* For master's, thesis (for some programs). *Entrance requirements:* For master's, GMAT, GRE General Test, or MAT, minimum undergraduate GPA of 3.0, faculty interview. Additional exam requirements/recommendations for international students: Required—TOEFL (minimum score 550 paper-based). *Application deadline:* Applications are processed on a rolling basis. Application fee: $30. Electronic applications accepted. *Expenses: Contact institution. Financial support:* Career-related internships or fieldwork available. Financial award application deadline: 7/15; financial award applicants required to submit FAFSA. *Faculty research:* International business, women in management entrepreneurship, simulations in business, Internet/online teaching in business, managerial leadership. *Unit head:* Dr. Bill Haney, Dean, 770-538-4707, Fax: 770-537-4701, E-mail: whaney@brenau.edu. *Application contact:* Nathan Goss, Admissions Coordinator, 770-534-6162, Fax: 770-538-4701, E-mail: ngoss@brenau.edu.

Bridgewater State College, School of Graduate Studies, School of Business, Department of Accounting and Finance, Bridgewater, MA 02325-0001. Offers MSM. Part-time and evening/weekend programs available. *Entrance requirements:* For master's, GMAT. *Application deadline:* For fall admission, 3/1 priority date for domestic students; for spring admission, 10/1 priority date for domestic students. Application fee: $50. *Financial support:* Health care benefits and unspecified assistantships available. Support available to part-time students. *Application contact:* Dr. Raymond Charles Guillette, Assistant Dean School of Graduate Studies, 508-531-2919, Fax: 508-531-6162, E-mail: rguillette@bridgew.edu.

Brigham Young University, Graduate Studies, Marriott School of Management, School of Accountancy, Provo, UT 84602-1001. Offers M Acc, JD/M Acc. *Accreditation:* AACSB. *Students:* 142 full-time (36 women); includes 7 minority (4 Asian Americans or Pacific Islanders, 3 Hispanic Americans), 7 international. Average age 25. 266 applicants, 65% accepted. In 2006, 133 degrees awarded. *Entrance requirements:* For master's, GMAT, minimum GPA of 3.0 in last 60 hours. Additional exam requirements/recommendations for international students: Required—TOEFL (minimum score 580 paper-based; 230 computer-based). *Application deadline:* For fall admission, 3/1 for domestic and international students. Application fee: $50. Electronic applications accepted. *Expenses: Contact institution. Financial support:* In 2006–07, 142 students received support, including 39 research assistantships with full and partial tuition reimbursements available (averaging $4,200 per year); career-related internships or fieldwork, institutionally sponsored loans, scholarships/grants, and tuition waivers (full and partial) also available. Financial award application deadline: 4/15; financial award applicants required to submit FAFSA. *Faculty research:* Judgment and decision making, international accounting, fraud and corrupt corporate taxation, auditing. *Unit head:* Dr. Kevin D. Stocks, Director, 801-422-4613, Fax: 801-422-0621, E-mail: kevin_stocks@byu.edu. *Application contact:* Julie Averett, Academic Advisor, 801-422-3951, Fax: 801-422-0621, E-mail: soa@byu.edu.

Brock University, Faculty of Graduate Studies, Faculty of Business, Program in Accountancy, St. Catharines, ON L2S 3A1, Canada. Offers M Acc. *Faculty:* 69 full-time (16 women). *Students:* 49 full-time (28 women). 85 applicants, 66% accepted, 42 enrolled. In 2006, 43 degrees awarded. *Degree requirements:* For master's, thesis or alternative. *Entrance requirements:* For master's, honours degree. Additional exam requirements/recommendations for international students: Required—TOEFL (minimum score 550 paper-based; 213 computer-based; 80 iBT), IELTS (minimum score 7), TWE (minimum score 4.5). *Application deadline:* For fall admission, 2/28 for international students. Application fee: $100. Electronic applications accepted. *Unit head:* Shari Sekel, Director, 905-688-5550 Ext. 3916, Fax: 905-688-4286, E-mail: shari.sekel@brocku.ca.

Brooklyn College of the City University of New York, Division of Graduate Studies, Department of Economics, Brooklyn, NY 11210-2889. Offers accounting (MA, MS); economics (MA); economics and computer and information science (MPS); economics/accounting (MA). Part-time and evening/weekend programs available. *Students:* 5 full-time (3 women), 119 part-time (68 women); includes 51 minority (35 African Americans, 11 Asian Americans or Pacific Islanders, 5 Hispanic Americans), 38 international. 92 applicants, 63% accepted, 29 enrolled. In 2006, 41 degrees awarded. *Degree requirements:* For master's, thesis or alternative. *Entrance requirements:* For master's, 2 letters of recommendation. Additional exam requirements/recommendations for international students: Required—TOEFL. *Application deadline:* For fall admission, 3/1 priority date for domestic students, 2/1 priority date for international students; for spring admission, 11/1 priority date for domestic students, 10/1 priority date for international students. Applications are processed on a rolling basis. Application fee: $125. Electronic applications accepted. *Expenses:* Tuition, state resident: full-time $6,400; part-time $270 per credit. Tuition, nonresident: full-time $12,000; part-time $500 per credit. Required fees: $118 per semester. *Financial support:* Career-related internships or fieldwork, Federal Work-Study, institutionally sponsored loans, and scholarships/grants available. Support available to part-time students. Financial award application deadline: 5/1; financial award applicants required to submit FAFSA. *Faculty research:* Econometrics, environmental economics, microeconomics, macroeconomics, taxation. *Unit head:* Dr. Robert Bell, Chairperson, 718-951-5317, E-mail: robertibell@compuserve.com. *Application contact:* Karen Alleyne-Pierre, Director of Admissions Services and Enrollment Communications, 718-951-5902, Fax: 718-951-4506, E-mail: grads@brooklyn.cuny.edu.

Bryant University, Graduate School, Graduate School of Business, Program in Professional Accounting, Smithfield, RI 02917-1284. Offers MPAC. *Faculty:* 8 full-time (2 women), 1 (woman) part-time/adjunct. *Expenses:* Tuition: Part-time $1,998 per course. *Unit head:* Dr. Denis M. Bline, Professor, 401-232-6402, E-mail: dbline@bryant.edu.

Bryant University, Graduate School, Graduate School of Business, Programs in Business Administration, Smithfield, RI 02917-1284. Offers accounting (MBA, CAGS); computer information systems (MBA, CAGS); e-strategy (MBA, CAGS); finance (MBA, CAGS); general business (MBA); management (MBA, CAGS); marketing (MBA, CAGS); operations management (MBA). *Accreditation:* AACSB. *Faculty:* 49 full-time (13 women), 2 part-time/adjunct (0 women). *Students:* 143 applicants, 41% accepted, 46 enrolled. In 2006, 106 master's, 10 other advanced degrees awarded. *Entrance requirements:* For master's, GMAT, letter of recommendation, resumé; for CAGS, GMAT, resumé. Additional exam requirements/recommendations for international students: Required—TOEFL (minimum score 580 paper-based; 237 computer-based). *Application deadline:* For fall admission, 7/15 for domestic students, 4/1 for international students; for spring admission, 11/15 for domestic and international students. Application fee: $80. *Expenses:* Tuition: Part-time $1,998 per course. *Financial support:* Research assistantships with full tuition reimbursements, unspecified assistantships available. Financial award applicants required to submit FAFSA. *Unit head:* Kristopher T. Sullivan, Assistant Dean of the Graduate School, 401-232-6230, Fax: 401-232-6494, E-mail: gradprog@bryant.edu.

Caldwell College, Graduate Studies, Program in Business Administration, Caldwell, NJ 07006-6195. Offers accounting (MBA); business administration (MBA). Part-time and evening/weekend programs available. *Degree requirements:* For master's, capstone course. *Entrance requirements:* For master's, GMAT, minimum GPA of 3.0. Additional exam requirements/recommendations for international students: Required—TOEFL (minimum score 580 paper-based; 237 computer-based). Electronic applications accepted.

California State University, East Bay, Academic Programs and Graduate Studies, College of Business and Economics, Department of Accounting and Computer Information Systems, Option in Accounting, Hayward, CA 94542-3000. Offers MBA. *Degree requirements:* For master's, comprehensive exam or thesis. *Entrance requirements:* For master's, GMAT, minimum GPA of 2.75. Additional exam requirements/recommendations for international students: Required—TOEFL (minimum score 550 paper-based; 213 computer-based). *Application deadline:* For fall admission, 5/31 for domestic students, 2/29 for international students; for winter admission, 9/30 for domestic students, 8/31 for international students; for spring admission, 12/31 for domestic students, 11/30 for international students. Application fee: $55. *Financial support:* Career-related internships or fieldwork, Federal Work-Study, and institutionally sponsored loans available. Support available to part-time students. Financial award application deadline: 3/2. *Unit head:* Diane Satin, Graduate Adviser, 510-885-3141, E-mail: diane.satin@csueastbay.edu. *Application contact:* Doris Duncan, Director of Graduate Programs, 510-885-3364, Fax: 510-885-2176, E-mail: doris.duncan@csueastbay.edu.

California State University, Fresno, Division of Graduate Studies, Craig School of Business, Department of Accountancy, Fresno, CA 93740-8027. Offers MS. Part-time programs available. *Degree requirements:* For master's, comprehensive exam. *Entrance requirements:* For master's, GMAT, minimum GPA of 2.75. Additional exam requirements/recommendations for international students: Required—TOEFL. Electronic applications accepted.

California State University, Fullerton, Graduate Studies, College of Business and Economics, Department of Accounting, Fullerton, CA 92834-9480. Offers accounting (MBA, MS); taxation (MS). *Accreditation:* AACSB. Part-time and evening/weekend programs available. *Students:* 85 full-time (54 women), 81 part-time (54 women); includes 76 minority (1 African American, 63 Asian Americans or Pacific Islanders, 12 Hispanic Americans), 41 international. Average age 30. 170 applicants, 61% accepted, 62 enrolled. In 2006, 27 degrees awarded. *Degree requirements:* For master's, thesis or alternative, project. *Entrance requirements:* For master's, GMAT, minimum AACSB index of 950. Application fee: $55. *Expenses:* Tuition, nonresident: part-time $339 per unit. Required fees: $1,155 per semester. *Financial support:* Teaching assistantships, Federal Work-Study, institutionally sponsored loans, and scholarships/grants available. Support available to part-time students. Financial award application deadline: 3/1. *Unit head:* Dr. Betty Chavis, Chair, 714-278-2225.

Accounting

California State University, Los Angeles, Graduate Studies, College of Business and Economics, Department of Accounting, Los Angeles, CA 90032-8530. Offers accountancy (MS), including business taxation, financial accounting, information systems, management accounting; accounting (MBA). Part-time and evening/weekend programs available. *Faculty:* 6 full-time (0 women), 2 part-time/adjunct (0 women). *Students:* 45 full-time (36 women), 44 part-time (29 women); includes 40 minority (39 Asian Americans or Pacific Islanders, 1 Hispanic American), 37 international. In 2006, 25 degrees awarded. *Degree requirements:* For master's, comprehensive exam (MBA), thesis (MS). *Entrance requirements:* For master's, GMAT, minimum GPA of 2.5 during previous 2 years of course work. Additional exam requirements/recommendations for international students: Required—TOEFL. *Application deadline:* For fall admission, 6/30 for domestic students; for spring admission, 11/30 for domestic students. Applications are processed on a rolling basis. Application fee: $55. *Expenses:* Tuition, nonresident: part-time $226 per unit. *Financial support:* Career-related internships or fieldwork and Federal Work-Study available. Support available to part-time students. Financial award application deadline: 3/1. *Unit head:* Dr. Greg Kunkel, Chair, 323-343-2830, Fax: 323-343-6439.

California State University, Sacramento, Graduate Studies, College of Business Administration, Department of Accountancy, Sacramento, CA 95819-6048. Offers MS. Part-time and evening/weekend programs available. *Students:* Average age 30. 46 applicants, 96% accepted, 2 enrolled. *Degree requirements:* For master's, thesis or alternative, writing proficiency exam. *Entrance requirements:* For master's, GMAT. Additional exam requirements/recommendations for international students: Required—TOEFL. *Application deadline:* Applications are processed on a rolling basis. Application fee: $55. Electronic applications accepted. *Financial support:* Research assistantships, teaching assistantships, career-related internships or fieldwork and Federal Work-Study available. Support available to part-time students. Financial award application deadline: 3/1.

California Western School of Law, Graduate and Professional Programs, San Diego, CA 92101-3090. Offers law (JD, LL M); JD/MBA; JD/MSW; JD/PhD; MCL/LL M. *Accreditation:* ABA. Part-time programs available. *Entrance requirements:* LSAT. Additional exam requirements/recommendations for international students: Required—TOEFL. Electronic applications accepted. *Faculty research:* Biotechnology, child and family law, international law, labor and employment law, sports law.

Canisius College, Graduate Division, Richard J. Wehle School of Business, Department of Accounting, Buffalo, NY 14208-1098. Offers accounting (MBA); professional accounting (MBAPA). Part-time and evening/weekend programs available. *Faculty:* 6 full-time (0 women), 5 part-time/adjunct (2 women). *Students:* 24 full-time (7 women), 23 part-time (15 women); includes 7 minority (2 African Americans, 4 Asian Americans or Pacific Islanders, 1 Hispanic American), 4 international. Average age 29. In 2006, 18 degrees awarded. *Entrance requirements:* For master's, GMAT. *Application deadline:* For fall admission, 7/1 priority date for domestic students; for spring admission, 11/1 priority date for domestic students. Applications are processed on a rolling basis. Application fee: $25. *Expenses:* Tuition: Part-time $645 per credit hour. Required fees: $19 per credit hour. Tuition and fees vary according to program. *Financial support:* Research assistantships, career-related internships or fieldwork, scholarships/grants, health care benefits, tuition waivers (partial), and unspecified assistantships available. Support available to part-time students. Financial award application deadline: 6/15; financial award applicants required to submit FAFSA. *Unit head:* Dr. Ian J. Redpath, Chair, 716-888-2868. *Application contact:* Laura McEwen, Director, 716-888-2140, Fax: 716-888-3211, E-mail: gradubus@canisius.edu.

Capella University, School of Business and Technology, Minneapolis, MN 55402. Offers accounting (MBA), including system design and programming; business (Certificate), including human resource management (MS, PhD, Certificate), information technology management (MS, PhD, Certificate), leadership (MBA, MS, PhD, Certificate), finance (MBA); general business (MBA); health care management (MBA); information technology (MS, Certificate), including general information technology (MS), information security, network architecture and design (MS), professional projects management (Certificate), project management and leadership (MS), system design and development (MS),); information technology management (MBA); marketing (MBA); organization and management (MBA, MS, PhD), including general business (PhD), general organization and management (MBA, MS), human resource management (MS, PhD, Certificate), information technology management (MS, PhD, Certificate), leadership (MBA, MS, PhD, Certificate); project management (MBA). Part-time and evening/weekend programs available. Postbaccalaureate distance learning degree programs offered (minimal on-campus study). Terminal master's awarded for partial completion of doctoral program. *Degree requirements:* For master's, integrative project, thesis optional; for doctorate, thesis/dissertation, comprehensive exam, registration. *Entrance requirements:* Additional exam requirements/recommendations for international students: Required—TOEFL (minimum score 550 paper-based; 213 computer-based), TWE (minimum score 4). Electronic applications accepted. *Faculty research:* Business policies: strategic, corporate, and financial management; interplay of technological, organizational and social change.

Cardean University, MBA Program, Chicago, IL 60606-7204. Offers accounting and information systems (MBA); e-commerce (MBA); finance (MBA); global management (MBA); health care administration (MBA); human resources management (MBA); leadership (MBA); management of information systems (MBA); management of technology (MBA); marketing (MBA); professional accounting (MBA); project management (MBA); risk management (MBA); strategy and economics (MBA). Part-time and evening/weekend programs available. Postbaccalaureate distance learning degree programs offered (no on-campus study). *Entrance requirements:* Additional exam requirements/recommendations for international students: Required—TOEFL (minimum score 550 paper-based; 213 computer-based).

Caribbean University, Graduate School, Bayamón, PR 00960-0493. Offers accounting (MBA); administration and supervision (MA Ed); criminal justice (MA); curriculum and instruction (MA Ed); education (PhD); gerontology (MSN); human resources (MBA); museology, archiving and art history (MA Ed); neonatal pediatrics (MSN); physical education (MA Ed); special education (MA Ed). *Entrance requirements:* For master's, interview, minimum GPA of 2.5.

Carnegie Mellon University, Tepper School of Business, Program in Accounting, Pittsburgh, PA 15213-3891. Offers PhD. *Degree requirements:* For doctorate, thesis/dissertation. *Entrance requirements:* For doctorate, GRE.

Case Western Reserve University, Weatherhead School of Management, Department of Accountancy, Cleveland, OH 44106. Offers M Acc, PhD, MBA/M Acc. *Accreditation:* AACSB. Evening/weekend programs available. *Faculty:* 8 full-time (1 woman), 3 part-time/adjunct (0 women). *Students:* 42 full-time (20 women), 4 part-time (2 women); includes 15 minority (1 African American, 13 Asian Americans or Pacific Islanders, 1 Hispanic American), 8 international. Average age 25. In 2006, 25 degrees awarded. *Degree requirements:* For doctorate, thesis/dissertation. *Entrance requirements:* For master's and doctorate, GMAT. *Application deadline:* For fall admission, 4/15 priority date for domestic students. Applications are processed on a rolling basis. Application fee: $50. *Financial support:* Career-related internships or fieldwork, Federal Work-Study, institutionally sponsored loans, scholarships/grants, and tuition waivers (full and partial) available. Support available to part-time students. Financial award application deadline: 5/1; financial award applicants required to submit FAFSA. *Faculty research:* Auditing, regulation, financial reporting, public interest, efficient markets. *Unit head:* Larry Parker, Chairman, 216-368-2065, E-mail: larry.parker@case.edu. *Application contact:* Tiffany Welch, Director of Marketing and Admissions, 216-368-2058, Fax: 216-368-4776, E-mail: clg3@po.cwru.edu.

Centenary College, Program in Professional Accounting, Hackettstown, NJ 07840-2100. Offers MS. Part-time and evening/weekend programs available. Postbaccalaureate distance learning degree programs offered (minimal on-campus study).

Central Michigan University, College of Graduate Studies, College of Business Administration, Department of Accounting, Mount Pleasant, MI 48859. Offers MBA. *Accreditation:* AACSB. *Degree requirements:* For master's, thesis (for some programs), comprehensive exam (for some programs), registration. *Entrance requirements:* For master's, GMAT. *Faculty research:* Accounting and financial reporting for local government, tax accounting for partnerships and small corporations, accounting for employee stock ownership plans.

Central Washington University, Graduate Studies, Research and Continuing Education, College of Business, Department of Accounting, Ellensburg, WA 98926. Offers MPA. Part-time programs available. *Faculty:* 8 full-time (3 women). *Students:* 20 full-time (11 women), 5 part-time (3 women); includes 4 minority (all Asian Americans or Pacific Islanders) 25 applicants, 72% accepted, 16 enrolled. In 2006, 16 degrees awarded. *Degree requirements:* For master's, thesis or alternative. *Entrance requirements:* For master's, GMAT, minimum GPA of 3.0. Additional exam requirements/recommendations for international students: Required—TOEFL (minimum score 550 paper-based; 213 computer-based; 79 iBT). *Application deadline:* For fall admission, 4/1 priority date for domestic students; for winter admission, 10/1 for domestic students; for spring admission, 1/1 for domestic students. Applications are processed on a rolling basis. Application fee: $50. Electronic applications accepted. *Expenses:* Tuition, state resident: full-time $6,312. Tuition, nonresident: full-time $14,112. Tuition and fees vary according to course load and degree level. *Financial support:* In 2006–07, 2 research assistantships with partial tuition reimbursements (averaging $8,100 per year) were awarded; Federal Work-Study, health care benefits, and unspecified assistantships also available. *Unit head:* Dr. Ronald Tidd, Chair, 509-963-3340, Fax: 509-963-2875, E-mail: tiddr@cwu.edu. *Application contact:* Justine Eason, Admissions Program Coordinator, 509-963-3103, Fax: 509-963-1799, E-mail: masters@cwu.edu.

Charleston Southern University, Program in Business, Charleston, SC 29423-8087. Offers accounting (MBA); finance (MBA); health care administration (MBA); information systems (MBA); organizational development (MBA). Part-time and evening/weekend programs available. *Degree requirements:* For master's, thesis optional. *Entrance requirements:* For master's, GMAT. *Faculty research:* Economic forecasting.

City University, Graduate Division, School of Management, Bellevue, WA 98005. Offers accounting (MBA); C++ programming (Certificate); computer systems—C++ programming (MS); computer systems—individualized study (MS); computer systems—web programming in e-commerce (MS); computer systems-web development (MS); financial management (MBA, Certificate); general management (MBA, MPA, Certificate); general management-Europe (MBA); human resource management (MPA); individualized study (MBA); information systems (MBA, Certificate); management—general management (MA); management—human resource management (MA); management—individualized study (MA); marketing (MBA, Certificate); personal financial planning (MBA, Certificate); project management (MBA, MS, Certificate); technology management (MS, Certificate); web development (Certificate); web programming in e-commerce (Certificate). Part-time and evening/weekend programs available. Postbaccalaureate distance learning degree programs offered (no on-campus study). *Entrance requirements:* Additional exam requirements/recommendations for international students: Required—TOEFL (minimum score 540 paper-based; 207 computer-based); Recommended—IELTS. Electronic applications accepted.

Clark University, Graduate School, Graduate School of Management, Business Administration Program, Worcester, MA 01610-1477. Offers accounting (MBA); finance (MBA); global business (MBA); health care management (MBA); management (MBA); management of information technology (MBA); marketing (MBA). *Accreditation:* AACSB. Part-time and evening/weekend programs available. *Students:* 122 full-time (64 women), 113 part-time (42 women); includes 18 minority (3 African Americans, 9 Asian Americans or Pacific Islanders, 6 Hispanic Americans), 115 international. Average age 29. 235 applicants, 78% accepted, 80 enrolled. In 2006, 109 degrees awarded. *Degree requirements:* For master's, thesis optional. *Application deadline:* For fall admission, 6/1 priority date for domestic students; for spring admission, 12/1 priority date for domestic students. Applications are processed on a rolling basis. Application fee: $50. Electronic applications accepted. *Financial support:* In 2006–07, research assistantships with partial tuition reimbursements (averaging $6,000 per year), teaching assistantships with partial tuition reimbursements (averaging $6,000 per year) were awarded; fellowships with full and partial tuition reimbursements, career-related internships or fieldwork, Federal Work-Study, institutionally sponsored loans, and tuition waivers (partial) also available. Support available to part-time students. Financial award application deadline: 5/31. *Faculty research:* Organizational development, accounting, marketing, finance, human resource management. *Application contact:* Patricia Tollo, Admissions Director, 508-793-7406, Fax: 508-793-8822, E-mail: clarkmba@clarku.edu.

See Close-Up on page 257.

Cleary University, Program in Business Administration, Ann Arbor, MI 48105-2659. Offers accounting (MBA); management (MBA). Part-time and evening/weekend programs available. Postbaccalaureate distance learning degree programs offered (minimal on-campus study). *Faculty:* 4 full-time (2 women), 16 part-time/adjunct (7 women). *Students:* 8 full-time (4 women), 57 part-time (33 women); includes 10 minority (7 African Americans, 1 American Indian/Alaska Native, 2 Asian Americans or Pacific Islanders), 1 international. Average age 34. 39 applicants, 85% accepted, 28 enrolled. In 2006, 13 degrees awarded. *Degree requirements:* For master's, comprehensive exam. *Entrance requirements:* For master's, minimum GPA of 2.5. Additional exam requirements/recommendations for international students: Required—TOEFL (minimum score 550 paper-based; 213 computer-based; 79 iBT), Michigan English Language Assessment Battery (75). *Application deadline:* For fall admission, 8/15 for domestic students, 7/15 for international students; for spring admission, 4/2 for domestic and international students. Applications are processed on a rolling basis. Application fee: $50. Electronic applications accepted. *Expenses:* Tuition: Full-time $11,900; part-time $425 per credit hour. *Financial support:* In 2006–07, 14 students received support, including 14 fellowships; Federal Work-Study and scholarships/grants also available. Support available to part-time students. Financial award application deadline: 8/15; financial award applicants required to submit FAFSA. *Faculty research:* Leadership and decision making, domestic and international corporate finance, organization structure and job satisfaction, organization culture, adoption of innovation. *Unit head:* Dr. Vincent Linder, Provost and Vice President Academic Affairs, 800-686-1883, Fax: 734-332-4646, E-mail: vlinder@cleary.edu. *Application contact:* Carrie Bonofiglio, Director of Student Recruiting, 800-589-1979 Ext. 2213, Fax: 517-552-7805, E-mail: cbono@cleary.edu.

Clemson University, Graduate School, College of Business and Behavioral Science, School of Accountancy and Legal Studies, Clemson, SC 29634. Offers MP Acc. *Accreditation:* AACSB. Part-time programs available. *Faculty:* 17 full-time (6 women). *Students:* 26 full-time (20 women), 7 part-time (6 women); includes 2 minority (1 African American, 1 Asian American or Pacific Islander), 1 international. Average age 30. 56 applicants, 52% accepted, 20 enrolled. In 2006, 22 degrees awarded. *Degree requirements:* For master's, oral final exam. *Entrance requirements:* For master's, GMAT, BS in accounting or equivalent, minimum GPA of 3.0. Additional exam requirements/recommendations for international students: Required—TOEFL. *Application deadline:* For fall admission, 5/1 priority date for domestic students, 4/15 for international students; for spring admission, 10/1 for domestic students, 9/15 for international students. Applications are processed on a rolling basis. Application fee: $50. *Expenses:* Tuition, state resident: full-time $8,812; part-time $450 per hour. Tuition, nonresident: full-time $18,036; part-time $760 per hour. Required fees: $474; $5 per term. *Financial support:* In 2006–07, 1 research assistantship was awarded. Financial award applicants required to submit FAFSA. *Unit head:* Dr. Ralph E. Welton, Director, 864-656-4881, Fax: 864-656-4892. *Application contact:* Dr. Thomas L. Dickens, Program Coordinator, 864-656-4890, Fax: 864-656-4892, E-mail: dickent@clemson.edu.

See Close-Up on page 451.

Cleveland State University, College of Graduate Studies, Nance College of Business Administration, Department of Accounting, Cleveland, OH 44115. Offers financial accounting/audit (MAC); taxation (MAC). *Accreditation:* AACSB. Part-time and evening/weekend programs available. *Faculty:* 15 full-time (3 women), 3 part-time/adjunct (1 woman). *Students:* 23 full-time (13 women), 47 part-time (23 women); includes 14 minority (8 African Americans, 5 Asian Americans or Pacific Islanders, 1 Hispanic American), 17 international. Average age 31. 82 applicants, 56% accepted, 24 enrolled. In 2006, 30 degrees awarded. *Entrance requirements:* For master's, GMAT, minimum GPA of 2.75. Additional exam requirements/recommendations for international students: Required—TOEFL (minimum score 525 paper-based; 197 computer-based). *Application deadline:* For fall admission, 7/15 priority date for domestic students; for spring admission, 12/15 priority date for domestic students. Applications are processed on a rolling basis. Application fee: $30. *Financial support:* In 2006–07, 3 research assistantships with full and partial tuition reimbursements (averaging $6,960 per year) were awarded; career-related internships or fieldwork, Federal Work-Study, scholarships/grants, and unspecified assistantships also available. *Faculty research:* Internal auditing, computer auditing, accounting education, managerial accounting. *Unit head:* Dr. Dennis J. Gaffney, Chair, 216-687-4720, Fax: 216-687-9212, E-mail: dennis.gaffney@csuohio.edu. *Application contact:* Bruce Gottschalk, Associate Dean, 216-687-3730, Fax: 216-687-5311, E-mail: cbacsu@csuohio.edu.

College of Charleston, Graduate School, School of Business and Economics, Program in Accountancy, Charleston, SC 29424-0001. Offers MS. *Accreditation:* AACSB. *Entrance requirements:* For master's, GMAT, minimum GPA of 3.0 in last 60 hours of undergraduate course work, 24 hours of course work in accounting. Electronic applications accepted.

The College of Saint Rose, Graduate Studies, School of Business, Department of Accounting, Albany, NY 12203-1419. Offers MS. Part-time and evening/weekend programs available. *Entrance requirements:* For master's, GMAT, graduate degree, or minimum undergraduate GPA of 3.0. Additional exam requirements/recommendations for international students: Required—TOEFL (minimum score 550 paper-based; 213 computer-based). Electronic applications accepted.

The College of William and Mary, Mason School of Business, Williamsburg, VA 23187-8795. Offers accounting (M Acc); business administration (MBA); JD/MBA; MBA/MPP. *Accreditation:* AACSB. Part-time and evening/weekend programs available. *Faculty:* 57 full-time (15 women), 4 part-time/adjunct (0 women). *Students:* 202 full-time (61 women), 138 part-time (25 women); includes 17 African Americans, 11 Asian Americans or Pacific Islanders, 1 Hispanic American, 58 international. Average age 32. 208 applicants, 52% accepted, 58 enrolled. In 2006, 167 degrees awarded. *Degree requirements:* For master's, field studies project. *Entrance requirements:* For master's, GMAT. Additional exam requirements/recommendations for international students: Required—TOEFL (minimum score 600 paper-based; 250 computer-based). *Application deadline:* For fall admission, 4/1 priority date for domestic students. Applications are processed on a rolling basis. Application fee: $100. Electronic applications accepted. *Expenses: Contact institution.* Tuition and fees vary according to program. *Financial support:* In 2006–07, 137 students received support, including 44 research assistantships with partial tuition reimbursements available (averaging $4,000 per year); career-related internships or fieldwork, scholarships/grants, and unspecified assistantships also available. Financial award application deadline: 3/1; financial award applicants required to submit FAFSA. *Faculty research:* Financial markets, marketing strategy, leadership and change, strategy/information, operations/inventory, supply chains. Total annual research expenditures: $305,274. *Unit head:* Dr. Lawrence Pulley, Dean, 757-221-2891, Fax: 757-221-2937, E-mail: larry.pulley@mason.wm.edu. *Application contact:* Kathy Pattison, Director of Admissions, 757-221-2898, Fax: 757-221-2958, E-mail: kpattison@business.wm.edu.

Colorado State University, Graduate School, College of Business, Department of Accounting, Fort Collins, CO 80523-0015. Offers M Acc. Part-time programs available. *Faculty:* 8 full-time (1 woman). *Students:* Average age 29. *Degree requirements:* For master's, thesis or alternative. *Entrance requirements:* For master's, GMAT, minimum GPA of 3.0; BA/BS. Additional exam requirements/recommendations for international students: Required—TOEFL (minimum score 565 paper-based; 227 computer-based; 86 iBT). *Application deadline:* For fall admission, 7/15 for domestic students, 4/1 for international students; for spring admission, 11/15 for domestic students, 10/1 for international students. Applications are processed on a rolling basis. Application fee: $50. Electronic applications accepted. *Expenses:* Tuition, state resident: full-time $4,248; part-time $236 per credit. Tuition, nonresident: full-time $15,642; part-time $869 per credit. Required fees: $66 per credit. Tuition and fees vary according to program. *Financial support:* In 2006–07, 10 fellowships (averaging $1,500 per year) were awarded; research assistantships, teaching assistantships with full and partial tuition reimbursements, career-related internships or fieldwork, Federal Work-Study, and traineeships also available. Financial award application deadline: 3/1. *Unit head:* Dr. Barry L. Lewis, Chair, 970-491-2977, Fax: 970-491-2676, E-mail: barry.lewis@business.colostate.edu. *Application contact:* Laura L. McGrath, Administrative Assistant III, 970-491-5102, Fax: 970-491-2676, E-mail: lmcgrath@lamar.colostate.edu.

Colorado Technical University, Graduate Studies, Program in Management, Colorado Springs, CO 80907-3896. Offers business administration (MBA); business management (MSM); business technology (MSM); database management (MSM); human resources management (MSM); information technology (MSM); logistics management (MSM); management (DM); organizational leadership (MSM); project management (MSM). Part-time and evening/weekend programs available. *Degree requirements:* For master's, thesis or alternative; for doctorate, thesis/dissertation. *Entrance requirements:* For doctorate, minimum graduate GPA of 3.0, 5 years of related work experience. *Faculty research:* Sexual harassment, performance evaluation, critical thinking.

Colorado Technical University Denver Campus, Programs in Business Administration and Management, Greenwood Village, CO 80111. Offers accounting (MBA); business administration (MBA); business administration and management (EMBA); business technology (MSM); database management (MSM); human resource management (MBA); information technology (MSM); project management (MSM); technology management (MBA). Part-time and evening/weekend programs available. *Degree requirements:* For master's, thesis or alternative. *Entrance requirements:* For master's, minimum undergraduate GPA of 3.0, resumé.

Columbia University, Graduate School of Business, Doctoral Program in Business, New York, NY 10027. Offers business (PhD), including accounting, decision, risk, and operations, finance and economics, management, marketing. *Accreditation:* AACSB. *Faculty:* 118 full-time (14 women), 106 part-time/adjunct (18 women). *Students:* 114 full-time (38 women); includes 3 Hispanic Americans, 96 international. Average age 27. 636 applicants, 6% accepted, 18 enrolled. In 2006, 15 degrees awarded. *Degree requirements:* For doctorate, thesis/dissertation, major field exam, research paper, thesis proposal, comprehensive exam, registration. *Entrance requirements:* For doctorate, GMAT, 2 letters of reference, resumé. Additional exam requirements/recommendations for international students: Required—TOEFL. *Application deadline:* For fall admission, 1/1 for domestic and international students. Application fee: $75. Electronic applications accepted. *Expenses: Contact institution. Financial support:* In 2006–07, fellowships with full tuition reimbursements (averaging $20,500 per year), research assistantships (averaging $4,000 per year) were awarded; teaching assistantships, career-related internships or fieldwork, institutionally sponsored loans, health care benefits, tuition waivers (full), and unspecified assistantships also available. *Unit head:* Elizabeth Elam Chang, Administrative Director, 212-854-2836, Fax: 212-932-2359, E-mail: phdinfo@gsb.columbia.edu.

Columbia University, Graduate School of Business, MBA Program, New York, NY 10027. Offers accounting (MBA); decision, risk, and operations (MBA); entrepreneurship (MBA); finance and economics (MBA); human resource management (MBA); international business (MBA); management (MBA); marketing (MBA); media (MBA); real estate (MBA); social enterprise (MBA); DDS/MBA; JD/MBA; MBA/MIA; MBA/MPH; MBA/MS; MD/MBA. *Faculty:* 118 full-time (14 women), 106 part-time/adjunct (18 women). *Students:* 1,242 full-time (428 women); includes 291 minority (65 African Americans, 5 American Indian/Alaska Native, 189 Asian Americans or Pacific Islanders, 32 Hispanic Americans), 392 international. Average age 28. 5,372 applicants, 17% accepted, 726 enrolled. In 2006, 682 degrees awarded. *Entrance requirements:* For master's, GMAT, 2 letters of recommendation. Additional exam requirements/recommendations for international students: Required—TOEFL. *Application deadline:* For fall admission, 4/20 for domestic students, 3/1 for international students; for spring admission, 10/12 for domestic and international students. Applications are processed on a rolling basis. Application fee: $215. Electronic applications accepted. *Financial support:* Fellowships, research assistantships, teaching assistantships, career-related internships or fieldwork, Federal Work-Study, institutionally sponsored loans, scholarships/grants, and unspecified assistantships available. Financial award applicants required to submit FAFSA. *Unit head:* Prof. Amir Ziv, Vice Dean of Students and the MBA Program, 212-854-3485, Fax: 212-932-0545, E-mail: az50@columbia.edu. *Application contact:* Linda B. Meehan, Assistant Dean of Admissions, 212-854-1961, Fax: 212-662-6754, E-mail: apply@claven.gsb.columbia.edu.

Concordia University, School of Graduate Studies, John Molson School of Business, Montréal, QC H3G 1M8, Canada. Offers administration (M Sc, Diploma); aviation management (Certificate, Diploma); business administration (MBA, UA Undergraduate Associate, PhD), including international aviation (UA Undergraduate Associate); chartered accountancy (Diploma); community organizational development (Certificate); event management and fundraising (Certificate); executive business administration (EMBA); investment management (Diploma); investment management option (MBA); management accounting (Certificate); management of healthcare organizations (Certificate); sport administration (Diploma). *Accreditation:* AACSB. Part-time and evening/weekend programs available. *Students:* 447 full-time (174 women), 448 part-time (206 women). 925 applicants, 59% accepted, 319 enrolled. In 2006, 183 master's, 6 doctorates, 62 other advanced degrees awarded. *Degree requirements:* For master's, one foreign language, thesis (for some programs), research project; for doctorate, one foreign language, thesis/dissertation; for other advanced degree, one foreign language. *Entrance requirements:* For master's and doctorate, GMAT. Additional exam requirements/recommendations for international students: Required—TOEFL. Application fee: $50. *Expenses: Contact institution. Financial support:* Fellowships, career-related internships or fieldwork available. *Faculty research:* General business, capital markets, international business. *Unit head:* Dr. Jerry Tomberlin, Dean, 514-848-2424 Ext. 2700, Fax: 514-848-4502. *Application contact:* Dr. Michel Magnan, Associate Dean, Graduate Programs, 514-848-2424 Ext. 4145, Fax: 514-848-4208.

Cornell University, Graduate School, Graduate Field of Management, Ithaca, NY 14853-0001. Offers accounting (PhD); behavioral decision theory (PhD); finance (PhD); marketing (PhD); organizational behavior (PhD); production and operations management (PhD). *Accreditation:* AACSB. *Faculty:* 57 full-time (11 women). *Students:* 38 full-time (14 women); includes 2 minority (both Asian Americans or Pacific Islanders), 20 international. Average age 31. 457 applicants, 5% accepted, 8 enrolled. In 2006, 4 doctorates awarded. *Degree requirements:* For doctorate, thesis/dissertation, comprehensive exam. *Entrance requirements:* For doctorate, GMAT or GRE General Test. Additional exam requirements/recommendations for international students: Required—TOEFL (minimum score 600 paper-based; 250 computer-based). *Application deadline:* For fall admission, 1/3 for domestic students. Application fee: $60. Electronic applications accepted. *Expenses: Contact institution.* Full-time tuition and fees vary according to program. *Financial support:* In 2006–07, 37 students received support, including 2 fellowships with full tuition reimbursements available, 31 research assistantships with full tuition reimbursements available, 4 teaching assistantships with full tuition reimbursements available; institutionally sponsored loans, scholarships/grants, health care benefits, tuition waivers (full and partial), and unspecified assistantships also available. Financial award applicants required to submit FAFSA. *Faculty research:* Operations and manufacturing. *Unit head:* Director of Graduate Studies, 607-255-3669. *Application contact:* Graduate Field Assistant, 607-255-9431, E-mail: js_phd@cornell.edu.

Dallas Baptist University, College of Adult Education, Professional Development Program, Dallas, TX 75211-9299. Offers accounting (MA); business (MA); church leadership (MA); corporate management (MA); counseling (MA); criminal justice (MA); English as a second language (MA); finance (MA); higher education (MA); leadership studies (MA); management (MA); management information systems (MA); marketing (MA); missions (MA). Part-time and evening/weekend programs available. *Faculty:* 49 full-time (21 women), 112 part-time/adjunct (46 women). *Students:* 31 full-time, 65 part-time. 51 applicants, 49% accepted, 15 enrolled. In 2006, 41 degrees awarded. Application fee: $25. *Expenses:* Tuition: Full-time $8,370; part-time $465 per credit hour. Required fees: $465 per credit hour. *Financial support:* Tuition waivers (full and partial) available. *Unit head:* Lynda Jackson, Director, 214-333-6830, Fax: 214-333-5558, E-mail: graduate@dbu.edu. *Application contact:* Kit P. Montgomery, Director of Graduate Programs, 214-333-5242, Fax: 214-333-5579, E-mail: graduate@dbu.edu.

Dallas Baptist University, Graduate School of Business, Business Administration Program, Dallas, TX 75211-9299. Offers accounting (MBA); business communication (MBA); conflict resolution management (MBA); e-business (MBA); entrepreneurship (MBA); finance (MBA); health care management (MBA); international business (MBA); management (MBA); management information systems (MBA); marketing (MBA); project management (MBA); technology and engineering management (MBA). *Accreditation:* ACBSP. Part-time and evening/weekend programs available. Postbaccalaureate distance learning degree programs offered (no on-campus study). *Faculty:* 49 full-time (21 women), 112 part-time/adjunct (46 women). *Students:* 103 full-time, 318 part-time. 226 applicants, 38% accepted. In 2006, 124 degrees awarded. *Entrance requirements:* For master's, GMAT, minimum GPA of 3.0. Additional exam requirements/recommendations for international students: Required—TOEFL. *Application deadline:* Applications are processed on a rolling basis. Application fee: $25. Electronic applications accepted. *Expenses:* Tuition: Full-time $8,370; part-time $465 per credit hour. Required fees: $465 per credit hour. *Financial support:* Career-related internships or fieldwork, Federal Work-Study, institutionally sponsored loans, scholarships/grants, and tuition waivers (full and partial) available. Support available to part-time students. *Faculty research:* Sports management, services marketing, retailing, strategic management, financial planning/investments. *Unit head:* Dr. Sandra S. Reid, Director, 214-333-5244, Fax: 214-333-5293, E-mail: graduate@dbu.edu. *Application contact:* Kit P. Montgomery, Director of Graduate Programs, 214-333-5242, Fax: 214-333-5579, E-mail: graduate@dbu.edu.

Davenport University, Sneden Graduate School, Warren, MI 48092-5209. Offers accounting (MBA); commerce (MBA); finance (MBA); health care management (MBA); human resources management (MBA); management (MBA). *Entrance requirements:* For master's, minimum undergraduate GPA of 2.7.

Davenport University, Sneden Graduate School, Dearborn, MI 48126-3799. Offers accounting (MBA); e-business (MBA); finance (MBA); global business (MBA); health care management (MBA); human resources management (MBA); management (MBA); marketing (MBA). Part-time and evening/weekend programs available. Postbaccalaureate distance learning degree programs offered (no on-campus study). *Entrance requirements:* For master's, minimum GPA of 2.7, previous course work in accounting and statistics. *Faculty research:* Accounting, international accounting, social and environmental accounting, finance.

Delta State University, Graduate Programs, College of Business, Division of Accounting, Computer Information Systems, and Finance, Cleveland, MS 38733-0001. Offers accountancy (MPA). *Application contact:* Carla Johnson, Coordinator, College of Business Graduate Programs, 662-846-4234, Fax: 662-846-4215, E-mail: cjohnson@deltastate.edu.

DePaul University, Charles H. Kellstadt Graduate School of Business, School of Accountancy and Management Information Systems, Chicago, IL 60604-2287. Offers accountancy (M Acc, MSA); business information technology (MS); e-business (MBA, MS); financial management and control (MBA); management accounting (MBA); management information systems (MBA); taxation (MST). Part-time and evening/weekend programs available. *Faculty:* 30 full-time (9 women), 54 part-time/adjunct (7 women). *Students:* 127 full-time (53 women), 209 part-time

Accounting

DePaul University *(continued)*
(101 women); includes 53 minority (13 African Americans, 3 American Indian/Alaska Native, 28 Asian Americans or Pacific Islanders, 9 Hispanic Americans), 56 international. Average age 30. In 2006, 141 degrees awarded. *Entrance requirements:* For master's, GMAT, 2 letters of recommendation, resumé. Additional exam requirements/recommendations for international students: Required—TOEFL (minimum score 550 paper-based; 213 computer-based). *Application deadline:* For fall admission, 7/1 for domestic students; for winter admission, 10/1 for domestic students; for spring admission, 2/1 for domestic students. Applications are processed on a rolling basis. Application fee: $60. *Financial support:* In 2006–07, 7 research assistantships with full tuition reimbursements (averaging $4,100 per year) were awarded; institutionally sponsored loans also available. Financial award application deadline: 4/2. *Faculty research:* Tax policy, property transactions, stock options as compensation, standards setting, activity-based costing in health care. *Application contact:* Christopher E. Kinsella, Director of Cohort MBA Programs, 312-362-8810, Fax: 312-362-6677, E-mail: kgsb@depaul.edu.

DeVry University, Keller Graduate School of Management, Oakbrook Terrace, IL 60181. Offers accounting and financial management (MAFM); business administration (MBA); human resources management (MHRM); information systems management (MISM); network and communications management (MNCM); project management (MPM); public administration (MPA); telecommunications management (MTM). Part-time and evening/weekend programs available. Postbaccalaureate distance learning degree programs offered (no on-campus study). *Degree requirements:* For master's, business plan (MBA), capstone project (MHRM, MPM, MTM, MAFM). *Entrance requirements:* For master's, GMAT, GRE General Test, or institutional assessment, interview. Additional exam requirements/recommendations for international students: Required—TOEFL (minimum score 500 paper-based; 173 computer-based). Electronic applications accepted.

See Close-Up on page 265.

Dominican University, Edward A. and Lois L. Brennan School of Business, River Forest, IL 60305-1099. Offers accounting (MSA); business administration (MBA); computer information systems (MSCIS); management information systems (MSMIS); organization management (MSOM); JD/MBA; MBA/MLIS. *Accreditation:* ACBSP. Part-time and evening/weekend programs available. *Faculty:* 12 full-time (4 women), 32 part-time/adjunct (9 women). *Students:* 171 full-time (46 women), 193 part-time (84 women); includes 26 minority (11 African Americans, 3 Asian Americans or Pacific Islanders, 12 Hispanic Americans), 173 international. Average age 30. 133 applicants, 98% accepted, 106 enrolled. In 2006, 118 degrees awarded. *Entrance requirements:* For master's, GMAT. Additional exam requirements/recommendations for international students: Required—TOEFL (minimum score 550 paper-based; 213 computer-based); Recommended—IELTS (minimum score 6). *Application deadline:* Applications are processed on a rolling basis. Application fee: $25. Electronic applications accepted. *Expenses: Contact institution.* Tuition and fees vary according to campus/location and program. *Financial support:* Career-related internships or fieldwork, tuition waivers (partial), and unspecified assistantships available. Support available to part-time students. Financial award applicants required to submit FAFSA. *Faculty research:* Entrepreneurship, small business finance, business ethics, marketing strategy. *Unit head:* Dr. Molly Burke, Dean, 708-524-6810, Fax: 708-524-6939, E-mail: burkemq@dom.edu. *Application contact:* Linda Puvogel, Assistant Dean for Graduate Business Programs, 708-524-6507, Fax: 708-524-6939, E-mail: lpuvogel@dom.edu.

Drexel University, LeBow College of Business, Department of Accounting, Program in Accounting, Philadelphia, PA 19104-2875. Offers MS. *Entrance requirements:* For master's, GMAT, minimum GPA of 2.75. Additional exam requirements/recommendations for international students: Required—TOEFL. Electronic applications accepted.

Drexel University, LeBow College of Business, Program in Business Administration, Philadelphia, PA 19104-2875. Offers business administration (MBA, PhD, APC), including accounting (MBA, PhD), decision sciences (PhD), economics (MBA, PhD), finance (MBA, PhD), legal studies (MBA), management (MBA), marketing (MBA, PhD), organizational sciences (PhD), quantitative methods (MBA), strategic management (PhD). *Accreditation:* AACSB. Part-time and evening/weekend programs available. Postbaccalaureate distance learning degree programs offered (minimal on-campus study). Terminal master's awarded for partial completion of doctoral program. *Entrance requirements:* For master's, GMAT, minimum GPA of 2.75; for doctorate, GMAT. Additional exam requirements/recommendations for international students: Required—TOEFL. Electronic applications accepted. *Faculty research:* Decision support systems, individual and group behavior, operations research, techniques and strategy.

East Carolina University, Graduate School, College of Business, Department of Accounting, Greenville, NC 27858-4353. Offers MS. *Students:* 61 full-time (30 women), 13 part-time (6 women); includes 5 minority (4 African Americans, 1 Asian American or Pacific Islander), 7 international. Average age 25. In 2006, 44 degrees awarded. *Unit head:* Dr. Dan Schisler, Chair, 252-328-6055, E-mail: schislerd@ecu.edu.

Eastern Illinois University, Graduate School, Lumpkin College of Business and Applied Sciences, Program in Business Administration, Charleston, IL 61920-3099. Offers accountancy (Certificate); general management (MBA). *Accreditation:* AACSB. Part-time programs available. *Faculty:* 35 full-time (8 women). In 2006, 58 degrees awarded. *Entrance requirements:* For master's, GMAT. *Application deadline:* For fall admission, 7/31 priority date for domestic students. Applications are processed on a rolling basis. Application fee: $30. *Expenses:* Tuition, state resident: part-time $169 per semester hour. Tuition, nonresident: part-time $508 per semester hour. Required fees: $60 per semester hour. *Financial support:* In 2006–07, 4 research assistantships with tuition reimbursements (averaging $7,200 per year), 8 teaching assistantships with tuition reimbursements (averaging $7,200 per year) were awarded. *Unit head:* Dr. James Jordan-Wagner, Department Chair, 217-581-3028, E-mail: jjordanwagner@eiu.edu. *Application contact:* Dr. Cheryl Noll, Coordinator, 217-581-3028, Fax: 217-581-6029, E-mail: clnoll@eiu.edu.

Eastern Michigan University, Graduate School, College of Business, Department of Accounting and Finance, Ypsilanti, MI 48197. Offers accounting (MSA); accounting and taxation (MBA); accounting, financial, and operational control (MBA). Part-time and evening/weekend programs available. Postbaccalaureate distance learning degree programs offered (minimal on-campus study). *Faculty:* 24 full-time (7 women). *Students:* 69 full-time (50 women), 39 part-time (28 women); includes 19 minority (4 African Americans, 14 Asian Americans or Pacific Islanders, 1 Hispanic American), 29 international. Average age 29. In 2006, 61 degrees awarded. *Entrance requirements:* For master's, GMAT. Additional exam requirements/recommendations for international students: Required—TOEFL. *Application deadline:* For fall admission, 5/15 priority date for domestic students, 5/1 priority date for international students; for winter admission, 10/15 priority date for domestic students, 10/1 priority date for international students; for spring admission, 3/15 priority date for domestic students, 3/1 priority date for international students. Applications are processed on a rolling basis. Application fee: $35. *Expenses:* Tuition, state resident: part-time $341 per credit hour. Tuition, nonresident: full-time $16,104; part-time $671 per credit hour. Required fees: $816; $34 per credit hour. $40 per term. One-time fee: $82 full-time. Tuition and fees vary according to course level, course load, degree level and reciprocity agreements. *Financial support:* Fellowships, research assistantships with full tuition reimbursements, teaching assistantships with full tuition reimbursements, career-related internships or fieldwork, Federal Work-Study, institutionally sponsored loans, scholarships/grants, tuition waivers (partial), and unspecified assistantships available. Support available to part-time students. Financial award applicants required to submit FAFSA. *Unit head:* Dr. Susan Kattelus, Head, 734-487-3320, Fax: 734-482-0806, E-mail: susan.kattelus@emich.edu.

Eastern University, Graduate Business Programs, St. Davids, PA 19087-3696. Offers business administration (MBA), including accounting, economics, finance, management, marketing; economic development (MBA, MS); nonprofit management (MBA, MS); M Div/MBA; M Div/

MS. Part-time and evening/weekend programs available. *Degree requirements:* For master's, thesis (for some programs). *Entrance requirements:* For master's, GMAT (MBA), minimum GPA of 2.5. *Expenses: Contact institution. Faculty research:* Micro-level economic development, China welfare and economic development, macroethics, micro- and macro-level economic development in transitional economics, organizational effectiveness.

East Tennessee State University, School of Graduate Studies, College of Business and Technology, Department of Accountancy, Johnson City, TN 37614. Offers M Acc. *Accreditation:* AACSB. Part-time and evening/weekend programs available. *Degree requirements:* For master's, comprehensive exam. *Entrance requirements:* For master's, GMAT, minimum GPA of 2.5. Additional exam requirements/recommendations for international students: Required—TOEFL (minimum score 550 paper-based; 213 computer-based). *Faculty research:* Financial accounting, taxation, auditing, management accounting.

Elmhurst College, Graduate Programs, Program in Professional Accountancy, Elmhurst, IL 60126-3296. Offers MPA. Part-time and evening/weekend programs available. *Faculty:* 4 full-time (1 woman), 5 part-time/adjunct (1 woman). *Students:* Average age 28. 12 applicants, 58% accepted, 6 enrolled. In 2006, 4 degrees awarded. *Median time to degree:* Master's–2 years part-time. *Entrance requirements:* For master's, 3 recommendations. Additional exam requirements/recommendations for international students: Required—TOEFL (minimum score 550 paper-based; 213 computer-based). *Application deadline:* Applications are processed on a rolling basis. Application fee: $25. Electronic applications accepted. *Expenses:* Tuition: Part-time $781 per hour. Required fees: $75 per hour. Part-time tuition and fees vary according to course load and student level. *Financial support:* In 2006–07, 2 students received support. Federal Work-Study and scholarships/grants available. Support available to part-time students. Financial award application deadline: 6/1; financial award applicants required to submit FAFSA. *Application contact:* Elizabeth D. Kuebler, Director of Adult and Graduate Admission, 630-617-3069, Fax: 630-617-5501, E-mail: betsyk@elmhurst.edu.

Emory University, Roberto C. Goizueta Business School, Doctoral Programs in Business, Atlanta, GA 30322-1100. Offers accounting (PhD); finance (PhD); information systems (PhD); marketing (PhD); organization and management (PhD). *Degree requirements:* For doctorate, thesis/dissertation, comprehensive exam. *Entrance requirements:* Additional exam requirements/recommendations for international students: Required—TOEFL (minimum score 600 paper-based; 250 computer-based). Electronic applications accepted. *Expenses:* Tuition: Full-time $30,246. *Faculty research:* Financial markets, banking, corporate disclosure, investor relations, marketing strategy.

Fairfield University, Charles F. Dolan School of Business, Fairfield, CT 06824-5195. Offers accounting (MBA, MS, CAS); finance (MBA, MS, CAS); general management (MBA); human resource management (MBA, CAS); information systems and operations (MBA); information systems and operations management (CAS); international business (MBA, CAS); marketing (MBA, CAS); taxation (MBA, MS, CAS). *Accreditation:* AACSB. Part-time and evening/weekend programs available. *Faculty:* 43 full-time (17 women), 2 part-time/adjunct (1 woman). *Students:* 65 full-time (31 women), 125 part-time (54 women); includes 4 Asian Americans or Pacific Islanders, 4 Hispanic Americans, 22 international. Average age 27. 99 applicants, 45% accepted, 38 enrolled. In 2006, 78 degrees awarded. *Degree requirements:* For master's, registration. *Entrance requirements:* For master's, GMAT, 2 letters of reference, resumé. Additional exam requirements/recommendations for international students: Required—TOEFL (minimum score 550 paper-based; 213 computer-based; 79 iBT). *Application deadline:* For fall admission, 8/15 priority date for domestic students, 5/15 priority date for international students; for spring admission, 11/15 priority date for domestic students, 10/15 priority date for international students. Applications are processed on a rolling basis. Application fee: $55. Electronic applications accepted. *Expenses: Contact institution. Financial support:* Unspecified assistantships available. *Faculty research:* Optimal investment strategies, organization structure, international finance, strategic management, customer behavior. *Unit head:* Dr. Norman A. Solomon, Dean, 203-254-4000 Ext. 4070, Fax: 203-254-4105, E-mail: nsolomon@mail.fairfield.edu. *Application contact:* Marianne Gumpper, Director of Graduate and Continuing Studies Admissions, 203-254-4184, Fax: 203-254-4073, E-mail: gradadmis@mail.fairfield.edu.

See Close-Up on page 271.

Fairleigh Dickinson University, College at Florham, Silberman College of Business, Department of Accounting, Law, and Tax, Program in Accounting, Madison, NJ 07940-1099. Offers MS. *Students:* 31 full-time (12 women), 50 part-time (27 women), 6 international. Average age 30. 34 applicants, 71% accepted, 24 enrolled. In 2006, 24 degrees awarded. *Entrance requirements:* For master's, GMAT. *Application deadline:* Applications are processed on a rolling basis. Application fee: $40.

Fairleigh Dickinson University, Metropolitan Campus, Silberman College of Business, Department of Accounting, Law, and Tax, Program in Accounting, Teaneck, NJ 07666-1914. Offers MS, Certificate. *Students:* 34 full-time (25 women), 32 part-time (14 women), 24 international. Average age 30. 49 applicants, 69% accepted, 21 enrolled. In 2006, 22 degrees awarded. *Application deadline:* Applications are processed on a rolling basis. Application fee: $40. *Faculty research:* Corporate accounting, legal issues. *Unit head:* Dr. Robert Greenfield, Dean, Silberman College of Business, 201-692-2000.

Fitchburg State College, Division of Graduate and Continuing Education, Program in Business Administration, Fitchburg, MA 01420-2697. Offers accounting (MBA); human resource management (MBA); management (MBA). Part-time and evening/weekend programs available. *Students:* 42 full-time (8 women), 36 part-time (19 women); includes 13 minority (6 African Americans, 3 Asian Americans or Pacific Islanders, 4 Hispanic Americans), 25 international. Average age 31. 51 applicants, 98% accepted, 41 enrolled. In 2006, 47 degrees awarded. *Entrance requirements:* For master's, GMAT, minimum GPA of 2.8, letters of recommendation, resumé. Additional exam requirements/recommendations for international students: Required—TOEFL (minimum score 550 paper-based; 213 computer-based; 79 iBT). *Application deadline:* Applications are processed on a rolling basis. Application fee: $25 ($50 for international students). *Expenses:* Tuition, state resident: part-time $150 per credit. Tuition, nonresident: part-time $150 per credit. Required fees: $90 per credit. *Financial support:* In 2006–07, research assistantships with partial tuition reimbursements (averaging $5,500 per year); Federal Work-Study, scholarships/grants, and unspecified assistantships also available. Support available to part-time students. Financial award application deadline: 3/1; financial award applicants required to submit FAFSA. *Unit head:* Joseph McAloon, Chair, 978-665-3745, Fax: 978-665-3658, E-mail: gce@fsc.edu. *Application contact:* Director of Admissions, 978-665-3144, Fax: 978-665-4540, E-mail: admissions@fsc.edu.

Florida Agricultural and Mechanical University, Division of Graduate Studies, Research, and Continuing Education, School of Business and Industry, Tallahassee, FL 32307-3200. Offers accounting (MBA); finance (MBA); management information systems (MBA); marketing (MBA). *Degree requirements:* For master's, residency. *Entrance requirements:* For master's, GMAT, minimum GPA of 3.0.

Florida Atlantic University, College of Business, Department of Management, International Business and Entrepreneurship, Boca Raton, FL 33431-0991. Offers business administration (Exec MBA, MBA), including accounting (MBA), electronic commerce (MBA), finance (MBA), financial planning (MBA), global entrepreneurship (MBA), health administration (MBA), international business (MBA), marketing (MBA), operations management (MBA), real estate (MBA), sport management (MBA). *Faculty:* 64 full-time (17 women), 15 part-time/adjunct (3 women). *Students:* 215 full-time (89 women), 365 part-time (189 women); includes 150 minority (49 African Americans, 2 American Indian/Alaska Native, 36 Asian Americans or Pacific Islanders, 63 Hispanic Americans), 54 international. Average age 32. 414 applicants, 55% accepted, 167 enrolled. In 2006, 196 master's awarded. *Degree requirements:* For master's, thesis optional. *Entrance requirements:* For master's, GMAT, minimum GPA of 3.0. Additional exam requirements/recommendations for international students: Required—TOEFL (minimum score 600 paper-based; 250 computer-based). *Application deadline:* For fall admission, 7/1 priority date for domestic students, 2/15 priority date for international students; for winter admission, 11/1 priority date for domestic students, 8/15 priority date for international students; for spring admission, 4/1 priority date for domestic students, 1/15 priority date for international students. Applications are processed on a rolling basis. Application fee: $30. Electronic applications accepted. *Expenses:* Tuition, area resident: Full-time $4,394. Tuition, nonresident: full-time $16,441. *Financial support:* Research assistantships, teaching assistantships, career-related internships or fieldwork, Federal Work-Study, institutionally sponsored loans, tuition waivers (partial), and unspecified assistantships available. Support available to part-time students. Financial award application deadline: 3/1; financial award applicants required to submit FAFSA. *Unit head:* Dr. Brenda Richey, Head, 561-297-3194, E-mail: brichey@fau.edu. *Application contact:* Fredrick G. Taylor, Graduate Adviser, 561-297-2768, Fax: 561-297-1315, E-mail: mba@fau.edu.

Florida Atlantic University, College of Business, School of Accounting, Boca Raton, FL 33431-0991. Offers M Ac, M Tax. Part-time and evening/weekend programs available. Post-baccalaureate distance learning degree programs offered (minimal on-campus study). *Faculty:* 19 full-time (6 women). *Students:* 54 full-time (29 women), 204 part-time (111 women); includes 69 minority (24 African Americans, 13 Asian Americans or Pacific Islanders, 32 Hispanic Americans), 9 international. Average age 33. 132 applicants, 59% accepted, 56 enrolled. In 2006, 78 degrees awarded. *Degree requirements:* For master's, thesis optional. *Entrance requirements:* For master's, GMAT, BS in accounting or equivalent, minimum GPA of 3.0 in accounting. Additional exam requirements/recommendations for international students: Required—TOEFL (minimum score 600 paper-based; 250 computer-based). *Application deadline:* For fall admission, 2/1 priority date for domestic students, 2/15 priority date for international students; for winter admission, 11/1 priority date for domestic students, 8/15 priority date for international students; for spring admission, 4/1 priority date for domestic students, 1/15 priority date for international students. Applications are processed on a rolling basis. Application fee: $30. *Expenses:* Tuition, area resident: Full-time $4,394. Tuition, nonresident: full-time $16,441. *Financial support:* In 2006–07, 1 student received support, including 1 research assistantship with partial tuition reimbursement available (averaging $6,000 per year), teaching assistantships (averaging $12,000 per year); fellowships, career-related internships or fieldwork, Federal Work-Study, institutionally sponsored loans, scholarships/grants, and tuition waivers (partial) also available. Support available to part-time students. Financial award application deadline: 3/1. *Faculty research:* Systems and computer applications, accounting theory, information systems. *Unit head:* Dr. Carl Borgia, Director, 561-297-3636, Fax: 561-297-7023, E-mail: borgiac@fau.edu. *Application contact:* Fredrick G. Taylor, Graduate Adviser, 561-297-2768, Fax: 561-297-1315, E-mail: mba@fau.edu.

Florida Gulf Coast University, College of Business, Program in Accounting and Taxation, Fort Myers, FL 33965-6565. Offers MS. Part-time and evening/weekend programs available. *Faculty:* 51 full-time (14 women), 18 part-time/adjunct (0 women). *Students:* 24 full-time (17 women), 13 part-time (9 women); includes 7 minority (1 Asian American or Pacific Islander, 6 Hispanic Americans). Average age 29. 25 applicants, 76% accepted, 13 enrolled. In 2006, 12 degrees awarded. *Degree requirements:* For master's, thesis or alternative. *Entrance requirements:* For master's, GMAT, minimum GPA of 3.0. Additional exam requirements/recommendations for international students: Required—TOEFL (minimum score 550 paper-based; 213 computer-based). *Application deadline:* For fall admission, 7/1 priority date for domestic students; for spring admission, 11/1 for domestic students. Applications are processed on a rolling basis. Application fee: $30. Electronic applications accepted. *Expenses:* Tuition, state resident: full-time $4,326. Tuition, nonresident: full-time $18,523. Required fees: $1,211. One-time fee: $5 full-time. *Faculty research:* Stock petitions, mergers and acquisitions, deferred taxes, fraud and accounting regulations, graphical reporting practices. *Unit head:* Dr. Ara Volkan, Chair, 239-590-7380, Fax: 239-590-7330, E-mail: avolkan@fgcu.edu. *Application contact:* Carol Burnette, Associate Dean, 239-590-7350, Fax: 239-590-7330, E-mail: burnette@fgcu.edu.

Florida International University, Alvah H. Chapman, Jr. Graduate School of Business, School of Accounting, Program in Accounting, Miami, FL 33199. Offers M Acc. *Accreditation:* AACSB. Part-time and evening/weekend programs available. *Students:* 22 full-time (12 women), 42 part-time (22 women); includes 45 minority (4 African Americans, 2 Asian Americans or Pacific Islanders, 39 Hispanic Americans), 5 international. Average age 30. 102 applicants, 20% accepted, 20 enrolled. In 2006, 57 degrees awarded. *Entrance requirements:* For master's, GMAT, minimum AACSB index of 1000, minimum GPA of 3.0. Additional exam requirements/recommendations for international students: Required—TOEFL. *Application deadline:* For fall admission, 4/1 priority date for domestic students; for spring admission, 10/1 for domestic students. Applications are processed on a rolling basis. Application fee: $25. *Expenses:* Tuition, state resident: part-time $249 per credit hour. Tuition, nonresident: part-time $753 per credit hour. Tuition and fees vary according to program. *Faculty research:* Financial and managerial accounting. *Unit head:* Dr. Christos Koulamas, Acting Director, School of Accounting, 305-348-2830, Fax: 305-348-4126, E-mail: christos.koulamas@fiu.edu.

Florida Metropolitan University–South Orlando Campus, Program in Business Administration, Orlando, FL 32819. Offers accounting (MBA); general management (MBA); human resources (MBA); international management (MBA).

Florida Metropolitan University–Tampa Campus, Department of Business Administration, Tampa, FL 33614-5899. Offers accounting (MBA); human resources (MBA); international business (MBA). Part-time and evening/weekend programs available. *Degree requirements:* For master's, thesis optional. *Entrance requirements:* For master's, GMAT or GRE, minimum GPA of 3.0.

Florida Southern College, Program in Business Administration, Lakeland, FL 33801-5698. Offers accounting (MBA); business administration (MBA); international business (MBA). Part-time and evening/weekend programs available. *Faculty:* 12 full-time (2 women). *Students:* Average age 31. 15 applicants, 80% accepted, 8 enrolled. In 2006, 9 degrees awarded. *Entrance requirements:* For master's, GMAT or GRE General Test, minimum GPA of 2.75. Additional exam requirements/recommendations for international students: Required—TOEFL (minimum score 550 paper-based). *Application deadline:* For fall admission, 8/1 for domestic students; for spring admission, 12/1 for domestic students. Applications are processed on a rolling basis. Application fee: $30. *Expenses:* Tuition: Part-time $250 per credit hour. Required fees: $10 per term. Tuition and fees vary according to program. *Financial support:* In 2006–07, 9 students received support. Scholarships/grants available. Support available to part-time students. Financial award applicants required to submit FAFSA. *Unit head:* Dr. Larry Ross, Program Coordinator, 863-680-4285, Fax: 863-680-4355, E-mail: lross@flsouthern.edu. *Application contact:* Craig Story, Evening Program Director, 863-680-6276, Fax: 863-680-4205, E-mail: cstory@flsouthern.edu.

Florida State University, Graduate Studies, College of Business, Tallahassee, FL 32306. Offers accounting (M Acc), including accounting information systems, assurance services, corporate accounting, taxation; business administration (MBA, PhD), including accounting (PhD), finance (PhD), information and management science (PhD), management (PhD), marketing (PhD), risk and insurance (PhD); insurance (MSM); management information systems (MS); JD/MBA. *Accreditation:* AACSB. Part-time and evening/weekend programs available. Postbaccalaureate distance learning degree programs offered (no on-campus study). *Faculty:* 107 full-time (26 women), 21 part-time/adjunct (2 women). *Students:* 145 full-time (62 women), 444 part-time (143 women); includes 147 minority (58 African Americans, 3 American Indian/Alaska Native, 45 Asian Americans or Pacific Islanders, 41 Hispanic Americans). Average age 29. 789 applicants, 50% accepted, 321 enrolled. In 2006, 263 master's, 19 doctorates awarded. Terminal master's awarded for partial completion of doctoral program. *Degree requirements:* For master's, registration; for doctorate, thesis/dissertation, comprehensive exam, registration. *Entrance requirements:* For master's, GMAT, substantial work experience (MBA, MS), minimum GPA of 3.0, letters of recommendation; for doctorate, GMAT, minimum graduate GPA of 3.5, letters of recommendation. Additional exam requirements/recommendations for international students: Required—TOEFL (minimum score 600 paper-based; 250 computer-based). *Application deadline:* For fall admission, 5/1 for domestic and international students; for spring admission, 10/1 for domestic students, 9/1 for international students. Applications are processed on a rolling basis. Application fee: $30. Electronic applications accepted. *Expenses:* Tuition, state resident: full-time $5,822; part-time $243 per credit hour. Tuition, nonresident: full-time $20,976; part-time $874 per credit hour. Tuition and fees vary according to program. *Financial support:* In 2006–07, 126 students received support, including 40 fellowships with partial tuition reimbursements available (averaging $4,600 per year), 37 research assistantships with partial tuition reimbursements available (averaging $4,600 per year), 49 teaching assistantships with partial tuition reimbursements available (averaging $10,500 per year); unspecified assistantships also available. Financial award application deadline: 1/1. Total annual research expenditures: $1.5 million. *Unit head:* Dr. Caryn Beck-Duolley, Dean, 850-644-3090, Fax: 850-644-0915. *Application contact:* Lisa Beverly, Coordinator, Graduate Programs Admissions, 850-644-6458, Fax: 850-644-0588, E-mail: lbeverly@cob.fsu.edu.

Fontbonne University, Graduate Programs, Department of Business Administration, Program in Accounting, St. Louis, MO 63105-3098. Offers MS. *Faculty:* 5 part-time/adjunct (4 women). *Students:* Average age 36. *Expenses:* Tuition: Full-time $4,890; part-time $489 per credit. Required fees: $160; $76 per credit. Full-time tuition and fees vary according to course load and program. *Financial support:* Application deadline: 4/1; *Unit head:* Dr. Linda Maurer, Dean of Business, 314-889-1423, Fax: 314-889-1451, E-mail: lmaurer@fontbonne.edu.

Fordham University, Graduate School of Business, New York, NY 10023. Offers accounting (MBA); communications and media management (MBA); finance (MBA, MS); information systems (MBA, MS); management systems (MBA); marketing (MBA); media management (MS); taxation (MS); JD/MBA; MBA/MIM; MS/MBA. *Accreditation:* AACSB. Part-time and evening/weekend programs available. *Faculty:* 87 full-time, 41 part-time/adjunct. *Students:* 345 full-time (132 women), 1,183 part-time (448 women); includes 238 minority (59 African Americans, 1 American Indian/Alaska Native, 116 Asian Americans or Pacific Islanders, 62 Hispanic Americans), 77 international. 1,081 applicants, 65% accepted, 422 enrolled. In 2006, 454 degrees awarded. *Entrance requirements:* For master's, GMAT. Additional exam requirements/recommendations for international students: Required—TOEFL (minimum score 600 paper-based; 250 computer-based). *Application deadline:* For fall admission, 6/1 priority date for domestic students, 5/1 priority date for international students; for winter admission, 11/1 priority date for domestic students, 10/1 priority date for international students; for spring admission, 3/1 priority date for domestic students, 2/1 priority date for international students. Applications are processed on a rolling basis. Application fee: $65. Electronic applications accepted. *Expenses: Contact institution. Financial support:* In 2006–07, 7 fellowships (averaging $27,000 per year), 128 research assistantships were awarded; career-related internships or fieldwork, institutionally sponsored loans, scholarships/grants, and unspecified assistantships also available. Support available to part-time students. Financial award application deadline: 5/1; financial award applicants required to submit FAFSA. *Unit head:* Dr. Howard Tuckman, Dean, 212-636-6165, Fax: 212-307-1779, E-mail: tuckman@fordham.edu. *Application contact:* Frank Fletcher, Director of Admissions and Financial Aid, 212-636-6200, Fax: 212-636-7076, E-mail: admissionsgb@fordham.edu.

Fort Hays State University, Graduate School, College of Business and Leadership, Department of Management and Marketing, Hays, KS 67601-4099. Offers accounting (MBA); management (MBA). *Faculty:* 19 full-time (1 woman). *Students:* 14 full-time (6 women), 8 part-time (3 women); includes 10 minority (all Asian Americans or Pacific Islanders) Average age 31. 39 applicants, 59% accepted. In 2006, 18 degrees awarded. *Degree requirements:* For master's, thesis optional. *Entrance requirements:* For master's, GMAT. Additional exam requirements/recommendations for international students: Required—TOEFL (minimum score 550 paper-based; 213 computer-based). *Application deadline:* For fall admission, 7/1 priority date for domestic students. Applications are processed on a rolling basis. Application fee: $35. Electronic applications accepted. *Financial support:* In 2006–07, 5 teaching assistantships (averaging $5,000 per year) were awarded; research assistantships, institutionally sponsored loans and tuition waivers (full) also available. Support available to part-time students. *Faculty research:* Organizational behavior and performance appraisal, data processing, international marketing. *Unit head:* Dr. Micol Maughan, Chair, 785-628-5877.

Gannon University, School of Graduate Studies, College of Humanities, Business, and Education, School of Business, Program in Accounting, Erie, PA 16541-0001. Offers Certificate. Part-time and evening/weekend programs available. *Students:* Average age 49. *Entrance requirements:* For degree, GMAT. Additional exam requirements/recommendations for international students: Required—TOEFL (minimum score 500 paper-based; 173 computer-based). *Application deadline:* Applications are processed on a rolling basis. Application fee: $25. *Expenses:* Tuition: Full-time $12,240; part-time $680 per credit. Required fees: $496; $16 per credit. Tuition and fees vary according to course load, degree level, campus/location and program. *Financial support:* Application deadline: 7/1; *Application contact:* Debra Meszaros, Director of Graduate Recruitment, 814-871-5819, Fax: 814-871-5827, E-mail: cfal@gannon.edu.

The George Washington University, School of Business, Department of Accountancy, Washington, DC 20052. Offers M Accy, MBA, PhD. *Accreditation:* AACSB. Part-time and evening/weekend programs available. *Degree requirements:* For doctorate, thesis/dissertation. *Entrance requirements:* For master's, GMAT; for doctorate, GMAT or GRE. Additional exam requirements/recommendations for international students: Required—TOEFL. *Faculty research:* Management accounting and capital markets, financial accounting and the analytic hierarchy process, ethics and accounting, accounting information systems.

Georgia College & State University, Graduate School, The J. Whitney Bunting School of Business, Milledgeville, GA 31061. Offers accountancy (MACCT); business (MBA); information systems (MIS). *Accreditation:* AACSB. Part-time and evening/weekend programs available. Postbaccalaureate distance learning degree programs offered (no on-campus study). *Faculty:* 43 full-time (18 women). *Students:* 44 full-time (19 women), 139 part-time (71 women); includes 28 minority (19 African Americans, 6 Asian Americans or Pacific Islanders, 3 Hispanic Americans), 17 international. Average age 30. 135 applicants, 56% accepted, 42 enrolled. In 2006, 76 degrees awarded. *Entrance requirements:* For master's, GMAT. Additional exam requirements/recommendations for international students: Required—TOEFL (minimum score 500 paper-based; 173 computer-based). *Application deadline:* For fall admission, 7/1 priority date for domestic students; for spring admission, 11/15 priority date for domestic students. Applications are processed on a rolling basis. Application fee: $25. Electronic applications accepted. *Expenses:* Tuition, state resident: full-time $3,222; part-time $179 per credit hour. Tuition, nonresident: full-time $12,870; part-time $715 per credit hour. Required fees: $391 per semester. Tuition and fees vary according to course load. *Financial support:* In 2006–07, 24 research assistantships with tuition reimbursements were awarded; career-related internships or fieldwork, Federal Work-Study, and unspecified assistantships also available. Support available to part-time students. Financial award application deadline: 3/1; financial award applicants required to submit FAFSA. *Faculty research:* Artificial intelligence, international trade, business ethics, curriculum issues. *Unit head:* Dr. Faye Gilbert, Dean, 478-445-5497, E-mail: faye.gilbert@gcsu.edu. *Application contact:* Lynn Hanson, Director of Graduate Programs in Business, 478-445-5115, E-mail: lynn.hanson@gcsu.edu.

Georgia Institute of Technology, Graduate Studies and Research, College of Management, Program in Business Administration, Atlanta, GA 30332-0001. Offers accounting (MBA); e-commerce (Certificate); engineering entrepreneurship (MBA); entrepreneurship (Certificate); finance (MBA); information technology management (MBA); international business (MBA, Certificate); management of technology (Certificate); marketing (MBA); operations management (MBA); organizational behavior (MBA); strategic management (MBA). *Accreditation:* AACSB.

Accounting

Georgia Institute of Technology, Graduate Studies and Research, College of Management, Program in Management, Atlanta, GA 30332-0001. Offers accounting (PhD); finance (PhD); information technology management (PhD); marketing (PhD); operations management (PhD); organizational behavior (PhD); quantitative and computational finance (MS); strategic management (PhD). *Accreditation:* AACSB. *Degree requirements:* For doctorate, thesis/dissertation, oral exams, comprehensive exam. *Entrance requirements:* For master's and doctorate, GMAT. Additional exam requirements/recommendations for international students: Required—TOEFL. *Faculty research:* MIS, management of technology, international business, entrepreneurship, operations management.

Georgia Southern University, Jack N. Averitt College of Graduate Studies, College of Business Administration, School of Accountancy, Statesboro, GA 30460. Offers accounting (M Acc). *Accreditation:* AACSB. Part-time and evening/weekend programs available. *Students:* 44 full-time (27 women), 16 part-time (10 women); includes 12 minority (9 African Americans, 2 Asian Americans or Pacific Islanders, 1 Hispanic American), 12 international. Average age 26. 35 applicants, 77% accepted, 17 enrolled. In 2006, 37 degrees awarded. *Entrance requirements:* For master's, GMAT. Additional exam requirements/recommendations for international students: Required—TOEFL (minimum score 550 paper-based; 213 computer-based). *Application deadline:* For fall admission, 3/1 priority date for domestic students, 3/1 for international students; for spring admission, 10/1 priority date for domestic students, 10/1 for international students. Applications are processed on a rolling basis. Application fee: $50. Electronic applications accepted. *Financial support:* In 2006–07, 46 students received support, including research assistantships with partial tuition reimbursements available (averaging $5,500 per year), teaching assistantships with partial tuition reimbursements available (averaging $5,500 per year); career-related internships or fieldwork, Federal Work-Study, scholarships/grants, tuition waivers (partial), and unspecified assistantships also available. Support available to part-time students. Financial award application deadline: 4/15; financial award applicants required to submit FAFSA. *Faculty research:* Applied business research in management, marketing finance, economics, accounting, systems research. *Unit head:* Dr. Charles Harter, Director, 912-681-5678, Fax: 912-681-0105, E-mail: charter@georgiasouthern.edu. *Application contact:* 912-681-5384, Fax: 912-681-0740, E-mail: gradadmissions@georgiasouthern.edu.

Georgia State University, J. Mack Robinson College of Business, Program in General Business Administration, Atlanta, GA 30303-3083. Offers accounting/information systems (MBA); enterprise risk management (MBA); general business (MBA); general business administration (EMBA, PMBA); information systems consulting (MBA); information systems risk management (MBA); international business and information technology (MBA); international entrepreneurship (MBA); MBA/JD. *Accreditation:* AACSB. Part-time and evening/weekend programs available. *Faculty:* 1 (woman) full-time. *Students:* 183 full-time (83 women), 212 part-time (57 women); includes 118 minority (73 African Americans, 36 Asian Americans or Pacific Islanders, 9 Hispanic Americans), 42 international. 294 applicants, 74% accepted, 182 enrolled. In 2006, 98 degrees awarded. *Entrance requirements:* For master's, GMAT. Additional exam requirements/recommendations for international students: Required—TOEFL (minimum score 610 paper-based; 255 computer-based; 101 iBT). *Application deadline:* For fall admission, 5/1 for domestic students, 2/1 for international students; for spring admission, 10/15 for domestic students, 5/1 for international students. Applications are processed on a rolling basis. Application fee: $50. Electronic applications accepted. *Financial support:* Research assistantships, tuition waivers (partial) available. Support available to part-time students. Financial award application deadline: 5/1; financial award applicants required to submit FAFSA. *Application contact:* Graduate Student and Alumni Services, 404-463-4568, Fax: 404-651-2721, E-mail: mastersadmissions@gsu.edu.

Georgia State University, J. Mack Robinson College of Business, School of Accountancy, Program in Accountancy, Atlanta, GA 30303-3083. Offers MBA, MPA, PhD, Certificate. *Accreditation:* AACSB. *Students:* 55 full-time (38 women), 58 part-time (27 women); includes 21 minority (6 African Americans, 1 American Indian/Alaska Native, 12 Asian Americans or Pacific Islanders, 2 Hispanic Americans), 19 international. 98 applicants, 47% accepted, 29 enrolled. In 2006, 34 master's, 2 doctorates awarded. *Degree requirements:* For doctorate, thesis/dissertation. *Entrance requirements:* For master's and doctorate, GMAT. Additional exam requirements/recommendations for international students: Required—TOEFL (minimum score 610 paper-based; 255 computer-based; 101 iBT). *Application deadline:* For fall admission, 5/1 for domestic students, 2/1 for international students; for spring admission, 10/15 for domestic students, 5/1 for international students. Applications are processed on a rolling basis. Application fee: $50. Electronic applications accepted. *Application contact:* Eric M. North, Faculty Advisor, 404-651-2611, Fax: 404-651-1033, E-mail: accenn@langate.gsu.edu.

Golden Gate University, Ageno School of Business, San Francisco, CA 94105-2968. Offers accounting (M Ac, MBA); business administration (EMBA, MBA, DBA); finance (MBA, MS, Certificate); financial planning (MS, Certificate); human resource management (MBA, MS); human resources management (Certificate); information technology (MBA); information technology management (MS, Certificate); integrated marketing and communications (MS, Certificate); international business (MBA); management (MBA); marketing (MBA, MS, Certificate); operations management (Certificate); psychology (MA, Certificate); public relations (MS, Certificate); JD/MBA. Part-time and evening/weekend programs available. *Students:* 355 full-time (192 women), 977 part-time (465 women); includes 447 minority (85 African Americans, 5 American Indian/Alaska Native, 274 Asian Americans or Pacific Islanders, 83 Hispanic Americans), 226 international. Average age 34. 548 applicants, 74% accepted, 201 enrolled. In 2006, 545 master's, 21 doctorates awarded. *Degree requirements:* For doctorate, thesis/dissertation. *Entrance requirements:* For master's, GMAT (MBA), minimum GPA of 2.5 (MS). Additional exam requirements/recommendations for international students: Required—TOEFL. *Application deadline:* Applications are processed on a rolling basis. Application fee: $55 ($90 for international students). *Financial support:* Career-related internships or fieldwork, Federal Work-Study, and institutionally sponsored loans available. Support available to part-time students. Financial award applicants required to submit FAFSA. *Unit head:* Terry Connelly, Dean, 415-442-6519, Fax: 415-442-5369. *Application contact:* Enrollment Services, 415-442-7800, Fax: 415-442-7807, E-mail: info@ggu.edu.

Golden Gate University, School of Accounting, San Francisco, CA 94105-2968. Offers M Ac, Graduate Certificate. *Students:* 57 full-time (33 women), 116 part-time (78 women); includes 55 minority (6 African Americans, 2 American Indian/Alaska Native, 41 Asian Americans or Pacific Islanders, 6 Hispanic Americans), 35 international. Average age 33. 65 applicants, 82% accepted, 43 enrolled.Application fee: $55 ($90 for international students).

Gonzaga University, School of Business Administration, Spokane, WA 99258. Offers M Acc, MBA, JD/M Acc, JD/MBA. *Accreditation:* AACSB. Part-time and evening/weekend programs available. *Faculty:* 24 full-time (1 woman). *Students:* 67 full-time (25 women), 134 part-time (51 women); includes 25 minority (1 African American, 14 American Indian/Alaska Native, 5 Asian Americans or Pacific Islanders, 5 Hispanic Americans), 10 international. Average age 31. In 2006, 88 degrees awarded. *Entrance requirements:* For master's, GMAT. Additional exam requirements/recommendations for international students: Required—TOEFL. *Application deadline:* For fall admission, 7/20 priority date for domestic students; for spring admission, 11/1 for domestic students. Applications are processed on a rolling basis. Application fee: $40. *Expenses:* Tuition: Full-time $10,620; part-time $590 per credit. *Financial support:* Teaching assistantships, Federal Work-Study available. Support available to part-time students. Financial award application deadline: 3/1. *Unit head:* Dr. Clarence H. Barnes, Dean, 509-328-4220 Ext. 5502.

Governors State University, College of Business and Public Administration, Program in Accounting, University Park, IL 60466-0975. Offers MS. *Students:* 13 full-time, 23 part-time. Average age 31. *Entrance requirements:* For master's, GMAT. *Application deadline:* For fall admission, 7/15 priority date for domestic students; for spring admission, 11/10 for domestic students. Applications are processed on a rolling basis. Application fee: $25. *Expenses:* Tuition, state resident: full-time $4,104; part-time $171 per hour. Tuition, nonresident: part-time $513 per hour. *Financial support:* Application deadline: 5/1.

Graduate School and University Center of the City University of New York, Graduate Studies, Program in Business, New York, NY 10016-4039. Offers accounting (PhD); behavioral science (PhD); finance (PhD); management planning systems (PhD). *Faculty:* 66 full-time (5 women). *Students:* 55 full-time (27 women); includes 7 minority (2 African Americans, 1 American Indian/Alaska Native, 2 Asian Americans or Pacific Islanders, 2 Hispanic Americans), 26 international. Average age 33. 74 applicants, 32% accepted, 11 enrolled. In 2006, 9 degrees awarded. *Degree requirements:* For doctorate, thesis/dissertation. *Entrance requirements:* For doctorate, GMAT, writing sample (15 pages). Additional exam requirements/recommendations for international students: Required—TOEFL. *Application deadline:* For fall admission, 1/15 for domestic students. Application fee: $125. Electronic applications accepted. *Financial support:* In 2006–07, 40 fellowships, 5 teaching assistantships were awarded; research assistantships, career-related internships or fieldwork, Federal Work-Study, institutionally sponsored loans, and tuition waivers (full and partial) also available. Financial award application deadline: 2/1; financial award applicants required to submit FAFSA. *Unit head:* Dr. Joseph Weintrop, Executive Officer, 646-312-3092, Fax: 646-312-3031.

Grand Valley State University, Seidman College of Business, Program in Accounting, Allendale, MI 49401-9403. Offers MSA. *Accreditation:* AACSB. Part-time and evening/weekend programs available. *Faculty:* 5 full-time (0 women). *Students:* 43 full-time (22 women), 50 part-time (28 women); includes 8 minority (6 Asian Americans or Pacific Islanders, 2 Hispanic Americans), 5 international. Average age 30. 31 applicants, 94% accepted, 24 enrolled. In 2006, 23 degrees awarded. *Degree requirements:* For master's, comprehensive exam. *Entrance requirements:* For master's, GMAT. Additional exam requirements/recommendations for international students: Required—TOEFL. *Application deadline:* For fall admission, 8/1 priority date for domestic students, 5/1 priority date for international students; for winter admission, 11/1 priority date for domestic and international students; for spring admission, 4/1 priority date for domestic students, 3/1 priority date for international students. Applications are processed on a rolling basis. Application fee: $30. *Expenses:* Tuition, state resident: full-time $5,850; part-time $325 per credit. Tuition, nonresident: full-time $10,800; part-time $600 per credit. Tuition and fees vary according to course load. *Financial support:* In 2006–07, 26 students received support, including 14 research assistantships with full and partial tuition reimbursements available (averaging $2,000 per year); Federal Work-Study, scholarships/grants, and unspecified assistantships also available. Support available to part-time students. Financial award application deadline: 2/15; financial award applicants required to submit FAFSA. *Faculty research:* Public trust, capacity measurement, theoretical capacity, economic order quantity. *Unit head:* Dr. Steve Goldberg, Director, 616-331-7190, Fax: 616-331-7389, E-mail: goldbers@gvsu.edu. *Application contact:* Claudia J. Bajema, Director, Graduate Business Programs, 616-331-7387, Fax: 616-331-7389, E-mail: bajemac@gvsu.edu.

Hawai'i Pacific University, College of Business Administration, Honolulu, HI 96813. Offers accounting/CPA (MBA); communication (MBA); e-business (MBA); economics (MBA); finance (MBA); human resource management (MBA); information systems (MBA); international business (MBA); management (MBA); marketing (MBA); organizational change (MBA); travel industry management (MBA). Part-time and evening/weekend programs available. *Faculty:* 40 full-time (16 women), 30 part-time/adjunct (10 women). *Students:* 320 full-time (150 women), 205 part-time (95 women); includes 168 minority (17 African Americans, 7 American Indian/Alaska Native, 137 Asian Americans or Pacific Islanders, 7 Hispanic Americans), 232 international. Average age 31. 279 applicants, 67% accepted, 166 enrolled. In 2006, 172 degrees awarded. *Degree requirements:* For master's, thesis. *Entrance requirements:* For master's, GMAT. Additional exam requirements/recommendations for international students: Recommended—TOEFL (minimum score 550 paper-based; 213 computer-based), TWE (minimum score 5). *Application deadline:* For fall admission, 2/15 priority date for domestic students; for spring admission, 10/15 priority date for domestic students. Applications are processed on a rolling basis. Application fee: $50. Electronic applications accepted. *Expenses:* Tuition: Full-time $10,080; part-time $560 per credit. *Financial support:* In 2006–07, 118 students received support; research assistantships, career-related internships or fieldwork, Federal Work-Study, scholarships/grants, and unspecified assistantships available. Support available to part-time students. Financial award application deadline: 3/1; financial award applicants required to submit FAFSA. *Faculty research:* Statistical control process as used by management, studies in comparative cross-cultural management styles, not-for-profit management. *Unit head:* Dr. Charles Steilen, Dean, 808-544-9301, Fax: 808-544-0283, E-mail: csteilen@hpu.edu. *Application contact:* Danny Lam, Assistant Director of Graduate Admissions, 808-544-1135, Fax: 808-544-0280, E-mail: graduate@hpu.edu.

See Close-Up on page 275.

HEC Montreal, School of Business Administration, Diploma Programs in Administration, Program in Public Accountancy, Montréal, QC H3T 2A7, Canada. Offers Diploma. All courses are given in French. Part-time programs available. *Students:* 181 full-time (89 women), 27 part-time (15 women). In 2006, 140 degrees awarded. *Degree requirements:* For Diploma, one foreign language. *Entrance requirements:* For degree, bachelor's degree in accounting. *Application deadline:* For spring admission, 2/15 for domestic and international students. Application fee: $60 Canadian dollars. Electronic applications accepted. Tuition and fees charges are reported in Canadian dollars. *Expenses:* Tuition, nonresident: part-time $56 Canadian dollars per credit. Required fees: $30 Canadian dollars per semester. *Financial support:* Scholarships/grants available. *Application contact:* Lyne Heroux, Administrative Director, 514-340-6139, Fax: 514-340-5640, E-mail: lyne.heroux@hec.ca.

HEC Montreal, School of Business Administration, Master of Science Programs in Administration, Program in Controllership, Montréal, QC H3T 2A7, Canada. Offers M Sc. All courses are given in French. Part-time programs available. *Degree requirements:* For master's, one foreign language, thesis. Application fee: $60 Canadian dollars. Electronic applications accepted. Tuition and fees charges are reported in Canadian dollars. *Expenses:* Tuition, nonresident: part-time $56 Canadian dollars per credit. Required fees: $30 Canadian dollars per semester. *Financial support:* Fellowships, research assistantships, teaching assistantships, scholarships/grants available. *Application contact:* Francine Blais, Administrative Director, 514-340-6112, Fax: 514-340-6411, E-mail: francine.blais@hec.ca.

Hendrix College, Program in Accounting, Conway, AR 72032-3080. Offers MA. Part-time programs available. *Faculty:* 5 full-time (1 woman), 1 part-time/adjunct (0 women). *Students:* 8 full-time (6 women). Average age 22. 8 applicants, 100% accepted, 8 enrolled. In 2006, 10 degrees awarded. *Entrance requirements:* For master's, GMAT. Additional exam requirements/recommendations for international students: Required—TOEFL. *Application deadline:* For fall admission, 2/1 priority date for domestic and international students. Applications are processed on a rolling basis. Application fee: $50. *Expenses:* Tuition: Full-time $18,742. *Financial support:* In 2006–07, 5 students received support, including 1 teaching assistantship with partial tuition reimbursement available (averaging $600 per year); career-related internships or fieldwork, Federal Work-Study, scholarships/grants, and tuition waivers (partial) also available. Financial award application deadline: 2/1; financial award applicants required to submit FAFSA. *Faculty research:* Meta-analysis, regulatory entities. *Unit head:* Prof. Stephen W. Kerr, Professor of Economics and Business, 501-329-6811, Fax: 501-450-1400, E-mail: kerr@hendrix.edu.

Hofstra University, Frank G. Zarb School of Business, Department of Accounting, Taxation and Legal Studies, Hempstead, NY 11549. Offers accounting (MBA, MS); taxation (MBA, MS). Part-time and evening/weekend programs available. *Faculty:* 8 full-time (2 women), 4 part-time/adjunct (1 woman). *Students:* 27 full-time (11 women), 43 part-time (21 women); includes 9 minority (3 African Americans, 4 Asian Americans or Pacific Islanders, 2 Hispanic Americans), 7 international. Average age 29. 54 applicants, 85% accepted, 20 enrolled. In 2006, 16 degrees awarded. *Degree requirements:* For master's, thesis (for some programs). *Entrance requirements:* For master's, GMAT, 2 letters of recommendation, resumé, essay. Additional exam requirements/recommendations for international students: Required—TOEFL (minimum score 550 paper-based; 213 computer-based). *Application deadline:* Applications are processed on a rolling basis. Application fee: $60. Electronic applications accepted. *Expenses:* Tuition: Full-time $13,320; part-time $740 per credit. Required fees: $930; $155 per term. *Financial support:* In 2006–07, 12 students received support, including 9 fellowships with tuition reimbursements available (averaging $6,821 per year); research assistantships with full and partial tuition reimbursements available, Federal Work-Study, scholarships/grants, tuition waivers (full and partial), and unspecified assistantships also available. Financial award applicants required to submit FAFSA. *Faculty research:* Impact of Sarbanes-Oaxley, law on various accounting functions, SEC retreat from SEC fraud investigation, corporate ownership structures, international auditing standards, constitutional questions such as Graves Amendment. *Unit head:* Dr. Nathan S. Slavin, Chairperson, 516-463-5690, Fax: 516-463-4834, E-mail: nathan.s.slavin@hofstra.edu. *Application contact:* Carol Drummer, Dean of Graduate Admissions, 516-463-4876, Fax: 516-463-4664, E-mail: gradstudent@hofstra.edu.

Houston Baptist University, College of Business and Economics, Program in Accounting, Houston, TX 77074-3298. Offers MACCT. *Degree requirements:* For master's, registration. *Entrance requirements:* For master's, GMAT with a minimum 3.5 AWA. Additional exam requirements/recommendations for international students: Required—TOEFL (minimum score 550 paper-based; 213 computer-based).

Howard University, School of Business, Graduate Programs in Business, Washington, DC 20059-0002. Offers accounting (MBA); entrepreneurship (MBA); finance (MBA); information systems (MBA); international business (MBA); marketing (MBA); supply chain management (MBA); JD/MBA. *Accreditation:* AACSB. Part-time and evening/weekend programs available. Postbaccalaureate distance learning degree programs offered (no on-campus study). *Entrance requirements:* For master's, GMAT, minimum 1 year post undergraduate work experience, resumé, 3 letters of recommendation, advanced college algebra. Additional exam requirements/recommendations for international students: Required—TOEFL. *Faculty research:* Marketing research in multi-ethnic populations, U.S. trade policies and international relations, risk management (finance).

Hunter College of the City University of New York, Graduate School, School of Arts and Sciences, Department of Economics, Program in Accounting, New York, NY 10021-5085. Offers MS. *Faculty:* 28 part-time/adjunct (14 women). *Students:* 1 full-time (0 women), 5 part-time (4 women); includes 2 minority (1 Asian American or Pacific Islander, 1 Hispanic American). Average age 28. 20 applicants, 40% accepted, 6 enrolled. *Application deadline:* For fall admission, 4/1 for domestic students, 2/1 for international students; for spring admission, 11/1 for domestic students, 9/1 for international students. Application fee: $125. *Expenses:* Tuition, state resident: part-time $270 per credit. Tuition, nonresident: part-time $500 per credit. Required fees: $45 per semester. *Application contact:* Avi Livenson, Director, 212-772-5394, E-mail: alivenson@hunter.cuny.edu.

Illinois State University, Graduate School, College of Business, Department of Accounting, Normal, IL 61790-2200. Offers MPA, MS. *Accreditation:* AACSB. *Faculty:* 14 full-time (4 women). *Students:* 40 full-time (18 women), 6 part-time (1 woman); includes 1 minority (African American), 6 international. 53 applicants, 70% accepted. In 2006, 26 degrees awarded. *Degree requirements:* For master's, comprehensive exam. *Entrance requirements:* For master's, GMAT, minimum GPA of 2.75 in last 60 hours of course work. Additional exam requirements/recommendations for international students: Required—TOEFL. *Application deadline:* Applications are processed on a rolling basis. Application fee: $40. *Expenses:* Tuition, state resident: full-time $3,330; part-time $185 per credit hour. Tuition, nonresident: full-time $6,948; part-time $438 per credit hour. Required fees: $1,259; $52 per credit hour. *Financial support:* In 2006–07, 16 research assistantships (averaging $5,375 per year) were awarded; Federal Work-Study, institutionally sponsored loans, and tuition waivers (full) also available. Financial award application deadline: 4/1. *Unit head:* Dr. Jerry McKean, Acting Chair, 309-438-7651.

Indiana Tech, Program in Business Administration, Fort Wayne, IN 46803-1297. Offers accounting (MBA); human resources (MBA); management (MBA); marketing (MBA). Part-time and evening/weekend programs available. *Entrance requirements:* For master's, minimum undergraduate GPA of 2.5, GMAT or 2 years of work experience. Additional exam requirements/recommendations for international students: Required—TOEFL (minimum score 550 paper-based). Electronic applications accepted.

Indiana University Northwest, School of Business and Economics, Gary, IN 46408-1197. Offers accountancy (M Acc); accounting (Certificate); business administration (MBA). *Accreditation:* AACSB. Part-time and evening/weekend programs available. *Faculty:* 5 full-time (0 women). *Students:* 11 full-time (7 women), 72 part-time (38 women); includes 19 minority (10 African Americans, 1 Asian American or Pacific Islander, 8 Hispanic Americans). Average age 32. In 2006, 39 degrees awarded. *Degree requirements:* For master's, registration. *Entrance requirements:* For master's, GMAT, letter of recommendation. *Application deadline:* For fall admission, 7/15 priority date for domestic students; for spring admission, 11/15 for domestic students. Applications are processed on a rolling basis. Application fee: $25. *Expenses: Contact institution.* Tuition and fees vary according to course load, campus/location and program. *Financial support:* In 2006–07, 9 students received support. Federal Work-Study, institutionally sponsored loans, and unspecified assistantships available. Support available to part-time students. Financial award application deadline: 7/15. *Faculty research:* International finance, wellness in the workplace, handicapped employment, MIS, regional economic forecasting. *Unit head:* Anna Rominger, Dean, 219-980-6636, Fax: 219-980-6916, E-mail: iunbiz@iun.edu. *Application contact:* John Gibson, Director of Graduate Program, 219-980-6500, Fax: 219-980-6916, E-mail: jagibson@iun.edu.

Indiana University South Bend, School of Business and Economics, South Bend, IN 46634-7111. Offers accounting (MSA); business administration (MBA); management of information technologies (MS). Part-time and evening/weekend programs available. *Faculty:* 17 full-time (2 women), 3 part-time/adjunct (1 woman). *Students:* 69 full-time (39 women), 118 part-time (43 women); includes 13 minority (5 African Americans, 4 Asian Americans or Pacific Islanders, 4 Hispanic Americans), 55 international. Average age 31. 49 applicants, 100% accepted, 47 enrolled. In 2006, 51 degrees awarded. *Entrance requirements:* For master's, GMAT. Additional exam requirements/recommendations for international students: Required—TOEFL (minimum score 550 paper-based; 213 computer-based). *Application deadline:* For fall admission, 7/1 priority date for domestic and international students; for spring admission, 11/1 priority date for domestic and international students. Applications are processed on a rolling basis. Application fee: $45 ($55 for international students). *Expenses: Contact institution. Financial support:* Federal Work-Study and institutionally sponsored loans available. Support available to part-time students. Financial award applicants required to submit FAFSA. *Faculty research:* Financial accounting, consumer research, capital budgeting research, business strategy research. *Unit head:* Dr. P. N. Saksena, Assistant Dean, Director of Graduate Studies, 574-520-4456, Fax: 574-520-4866, E-mail: psakena@iusb.edu. *Application contact:* Sharon Peterson, Secretary—Graduate Business, 574-520-4138, Fax: 574-520-4866, E-mail: speterso@iusb.edu.

Indiana University Southeast, School of Business, New Albany, IN 47150-6405. Offers accounting (Certificate); business administration (MBA); economics (Certificate); finance (Certificate); general business (Certificate); information and operations management (Certificate); management and marketing (Certificate); strategic finance (MS). *Accreditation:* AACSB. *Faculty:* 11 full-time (2 women). *Students:* 10 full-time (4 women), 201 part-time (65 women); includes 12 minority (2 African Americans, 8 Asian Americans or Pacific Islanders, 2 Hispanic Americans), 5 international. Average age 31. In 2006, 60 degrees awarded. *Degree requirements:* For master's, community service. *Entrance requirements:* For master's, GMAT, work experience. Additional exam requirements/recommendations for international students: Required—TOEFL. Application fee: $35. *Expenses: Contact institution.* Tuition and fees vary according to course load, campus/location and program. *Unit head:* Chris Bjornson, Dean, 812-941-2362, Fax: 812-941-2672. *Application contact:* Dr. Jay White, Director of Graduate Business Programs, 812-941-2364, Fax: 812-941-2581, E-mail: jwhite04@ius.edu.

Indiana Wesleyan University, College of Adult and Professional Studies, Program in Business Administration, Marion, IN 46953-4974. Offers accounting (MBA); applied management (MBA); health care management (MBA). Evening/weekend programs available. Postbaccalaureate distance learning degree programs offered (no on-campus study). *Faculty:* 13 full-time (1 woman), 162 part-time/adjunct (31 women). *Students:* 1,163 full-time. Average age 34. In 2006, 792 degrees awarded. *Degree requirements:* For master's, applied management project. *Entrance requirements:* For master's, minimum GPA of 2.5, related 3 years full time work experience, math/statistics (3 hours or proficiency exam). Additional exam requirements/recommendations for international students: Required—TOEFL (minimum score 550 paper-based; 213 computer-based). *Application deadline:* Applications are processed on a rolling basis. Application fee: $25. Electronic applications accepted. *Expenses:* Tuition: Full-time $16,000; part-time $400 per credit. Required fees: $3,000. Tuition and fees vary according to degree level, campus/location and program. *Financial support:* Applicants required to submit FAFSA. *Unit head:* Dr. Jim Kraai, Director, 765-677-2882, Fax: 765-677-2023, E-mail: jim.kraai@indwes.edu. *Application contact:* Kris Douglas, Marketing Manager, 800-234-5327, Fax: 765-674-8028, E-mail: kris.douglas@apollogrp.org.

Inter American University of Puerto Rico, Metropolitan Campus, Graduate Programs, Faculty of Economics and Administrative Sciences, Program in Accounting, San Juan, PR 00919-1293. Offers MBA. *Degree requirements:* For master's, comprehensive exam. *Entrance requirements:* For master's, GRE or EXADEP, interview. Electronic applications accepted.

Inter American University of Puerto Rico, Ponce Campus, Graduate School, Mercedita, PR 00715-1602. Offers accounting (MBA); biology (M Ed); chemistry (M Ed); criminal justice (MA); elementary education (M Ed); English as a Second Language (M Ed); finance (MBA); history (M Ed); human resources (MBA); mathematics (M Ed); Spanish (M Ed); trade (MBA). *Entrance requirements:* For master's, minimum GPA of 2.5.

Inter American University of Puerto Rico, San Germán Campus, Graduate Studies Center, Graduate Program in Business Administration, San Germán, PR 00683-5008. Offers accounting (MBA); finance (MBA); human resources (MBA, PhD); industrial relations (MBA); international business (PhD); labor relations (PhD); management information systems (MBA); marketing (MBA); quality organizational design (MBA). Part-time and evening/weekend programs available. *Faculty:* 12 full-time, 4 part-time/adjunct. *Students:* 265. Average age 27. In 2006, 67 master's, 1 doctorate awarded. *Degree requirements:* For master's, comprehensive exam. *Entrance requirements:* For master's, GRE General Test or EXADEP, minimum GPA of 3.0. *Application deadline:* For fall admission, 4/30 priority date for domestic students; for spring admission, 11/15 for domestic students. Applications are processed on a rolling basis. Application fee: $31. *Expenses:* Tuition: Part-time $175 per credit. Required fees: $238 per semester. Tuition and fees vary according to degree level. *Financial support:* Teaching assistantships, Federal Work-Study and unspecified assistantships available. *Application contact:* Prof. Duay Rivera, Graduate Coordinator, 787-264-1912 Ext. 7218, Fax: 787-892-7510, E-mail: durivera@sg.inter.edu.

Iowa State University of Science and Technology, Graduate College, College of Business, Department of Accounting, Ames, IA 50011. Offers M Acc. *Accreditation:* AACSB. *Faculty:* 12 full-time, 1 part-time/adjunct. *Students:* 31 full-time (19 women), 15 part-time (8 women); includes 1 minority (Asian American or Pacific Islander), 18 international. 32 applicants, 63% accepted, 17 enrolled. In 2006, 22 degrees awarded. *Degree requirements:* For master's, thesis or alternative. *Entrance requirements:* For master's, GMAT, resumé. Additional exam requirements/recommendations for international students: Required—TOEFL (minimum score 600 paper-based; 250 computer-based; 100 iBT), IELTS (minimum score 7). *Application deadline:* For fall admission, 7/15 priority date for domestic and international students; for spring admission, 11/15 priority date for domestic and international students. Application fee: $30 ($70 for international students). Electronic applications accepted. *Expenses:* Tuition, state resident: full-time $5,936; part-time $330 per credit. Tuition, nonresident: full-time $16,350; part-time $330 per credit. *Financial support:* In 2006–07, 7 research assistantships with full and partial tuition reimbursements (averaging $16,566 per year), 2 teaching assistantships (averaging $17,232 per year) were awarded; career-related internships or fieldwork, scholarships/grants, health care benefits, and unspecified assistantships also available. *Unit head:* Dr. Marvin Bouillon, Chair, 515-294-8118, E-mail: busgrad@iastate.edu.

Ithaca College, Graduate Studies, School of Business, Program in Professional Accountancy, Ithaca, NY 14850-7020. Offers MBA. Part-time programs available. *Faculty:* 4 full-time (2 women). *Students:* 10 full-time (6 women); includes 2 minority (1 African American, 1 Hispanic American). Average age 22. 16 applicants, 63% accepted, 10 enrolled. *Degree requirements:* For master's, registration. *Entrance requirements:* For master's, GMAT, minimum GPA of 3.0. Additional exam requirements/recommendations for international students: Required—TOEFL (minimum score 550 paper-based; 213 computer-based). *Application deadline:* For fall admission, 8/1 for domestic students; for spring admission, 12/1 for domestic students. Application fee: $40. *Expenses: Contact institution. Financial support:* In 2006–07, 10 students received support, including 3 fellowships (averaging $4,688 per year); Federal Work-Study, institutionally sponsored loans, and scholarships/grants also available. Support available to part-time students. Financial award application deadline: 4/15; financial award applicants required to submit FAFSA. *Application contact:* Dr. Eric Lewis, Coordinator, 607-274-1279, Fax: 607-274-1152, E-mail: elewis@ithaca.edu.

Jackson State University, Graduate School, School of Business, Department of Accounting, Jackson, MS 39217. Offers MPA. Part-time and evening/weekend programs available. *Faculty:* 4 full-time (0 women). *Students:* 9 full-time (7 women), 11 part-time (8 women); includes 12 minority (all African Americans), 5 international. In 2006, 6 degrees awarded. *Degree requirements:* For master's, comprehensive exam. *Entrance requirements:* For master's, GRE General Test, GMAT. Additional exam requirements/recommendations for international students: Required—TOEFL. *Application deadline:* For fall admission, 3/1 priority date for domestic students; for spring admission, 10/1 for domestic students. Applications are processed on a rolling basis. Application fee: $20. *Financial support:* Career-related internships or fieldwork, Federal Work-Study, and tuition waivers (full and partial) available. Support available to part-time students. Financial award application deadline: 3/1. *Unit head:* Dr. Jean Claude Assad, Director, 601-979-4326, Fax: 601-979-1205, E-mail: jean-claude.assad@jsums.edu. *Application contact:* Curtis Gore, Director of Graduate Admissions, 601-979-2455, Fax: 601-974-4325, E-mail: cgore@ccaix.jsums.edu.

James Madison University, College of Graduate and Outreach Programs, College of Business, Program in Accounting, Harrisonburg, VA 22807. Offers MS. *Accreditation:* AACSB. Part-time and evening/weekend programs available. *Students:* 55 full-time (24 women), 5 part-time (1 woman); includes 7 minority (1 African American, 6 Asian Americans or Pacific Islanders), 2 international. Average age 27. In 2006, 22 degrees awarded. *Entrance requirements:* For master's, GMAT or successful completion of all four parts of the CPA exam. Additional exam requirements/recommendations for international students: Required—TOEFL. *Application deadline:* For fall admission, 5/1 priority date for domestic students; for spring admission, 9/1 priority date for domestic students. Applications are processed on a rolling basis. Application fee: $55. Electronic applications accepted. *Expenses:* Tuition, state resident: full-time $6,336; part-time $264 per credit hour. Tuition, nonresident: full-time $17,832; part-time $743 per credit hour. *Financial support:* In 2006–07, 19 students received support. Federal Work-Study and unspecified assistantships available. Financial award application deadline: 3/1; financial award applicants required to submit FAFSA. *Faculty research:* Controllership, government accounting. *Unit head:* Paul A. Copley, Academic Unit Head, 540-568-3081.

John Carroll University, Graduate School, John M. and Mary Jo Boler School of Business, University Heights, OH 44118-4581. Offers accountancy (MS); business (MBA). *Accreditation:* AACSB. Part-time and evening/weekend programs available. *Faculty:* 33 full-time (6 women), 2 part-time/adjunct (0 women). *Students:* 31 full-time (13 women), 171 part-time (72 women); includes 14 minority (12 African Americans, 1 Asian American or Pacific Islander, 1 Hispanic American). Average age 29. 62 applicants, 81% accepted, 36 enrolled. In 2006, 91

Accounting

John Carroll University (continued)

degrees awarded. *Entrance requirements:* For master's, GMAT. Additional exam requirements/recommendations for international students: Required—TOEFL (minimum score 550 paper-based; 213 computer-based). *Application deadline:* Applications are processed on a rolling basis. Application fee: $25 ($35 for international students). *Expenses: Contact institution.* Tuition and fees vary according to program. *Financial support:* In 2006–07, 6 research assistantships with full tuition reimbursements (averaging $8,000 per year) were awarded; scholarships/grants and unspecified assistantships also available. Financial award application deadline: 3/15; financial award applicants required to submit FAFSA. *Faculty research:* Accounting, economics and finance, management, marketing and logistics. *Unit head:* Dr. Karen Schuele, Associate Dean, 216-397-4606, Fax: 216-397-1728, E-mail: kschuele@jcu.edu. *Application contact:* Gayle T. Bruno-Gannon, Assistant to the Dean, 216-397-1970, Fax: 216-397-1728, E-mail: ggannon@jcu.edu.

Johnson & Wales University, The Alan Shawn Feinstein Graduate School, Program in Global Business, Concentration in Accounting, Providence, RI 02903-3703. Offers MBA. Part-time and evening/weekend programs available. *Faculty:* 11 full-time (3 women), 9 part-time/adjunct (0 women). *Students:* 41 full-time (20 women), 11 part-time (7 women); includes 4 minority (3 African Americans, 1 Asian American or Pacific Islander), 21 international. Average age 32. In 2006, 15 degrees awarded. *Entrance requirements:* For master's, GMAT (recommended), minimum GPA of 2.75. Additional exam requirements/recommendations for international students: Required—TOEFL (paper-based 550; computer-based 210) or IELTS recommended. *Application deadline:* For fall admission, 8/15 priority date for domestic students, 6/28 priority date for international students; for winter admission, 11/10 priority date for domestic students, 9/20 priority date for international students; for spring admission, 2/15 priority date for domestic students, 12/20 priority date for international students. Applications are processed on a rolling basis. Application fee: $0. Electronic applications accepted. *Financial support:* Unspecified assistantships available. Financial award application deadline: 5/1. *Faculty research:* Applying new technology. *Unit head:* Dr. Kevin Fountain, Unit Head, 401-598-4738, Fax: 401-598-1162, E-mail: kfountain@jwu.edu. *Application contact:* Dr. Allan G. Freedman, Director of Graduate Admissions, 401-598-1015, Fax: 401-598-1286, E-mail: gradadm@jwu.edu.

Jones International University, Graduate School of Business Administration, Centennial, CO 80112. Offers accounting (MBA); business communication (MABC); entrepreneurship (MABC, MBA); finance (MBA); global enterprise management (MBA); health care management (MBA); information security management (MBA); information technology management (MBA); leadership and influence (MABC); leading the customer-driven organization (MABC); negotiation and conflict management (MBA); project management (MABC, MBA). Program only offered online. Part-time and evening/weekend programs available. Postbaccalaureate distance learning degree programs offered (no on-campus study). *Degree requirements:* For master's, capstone project. *Entrance requirements:* For master's, minimum cumulative GPA of 2.5. Additional exam requirements/recommendations for international students: Recommended—TOEFL (minimum score 550 paper-based; 213 computer-based). Electronic applications accepted.

Kansas State University, Graduate School, College of Business Administration, Department of Accounting, Manhattan, KS 66506. Offers M Acc. *Accreditation:* AACSB. *Faculty:* 7 full-time (1 woman). *Students:* 72 full-time (46 women), 3 part-time (all women); includes 1 minority (American Indian/Alaska Native), 2 international. Average age 25. 45 applicants, 91% accepted, 24 enrolled. In 2006, 46 degrees awarded. *Degree requirements:* For master's, comprehensive exam. *Entrance requirements:* For master's, GMAT, minimum undergraduate GPA of 3.0. Additional exam requirements/recommendations for international students: Required—TOEFL (minimum score 550 paper-based; 213 computer-based). *Application deadline:* For fall admission, 7/1 for domestic students, 2/1 for international students; for spring admission, 12/1 for domestic students, 8/1 for international students. Applications are processed on a rolling basis. Application fee: $50 ($60 for international students). *Expenses:* Tuition, state resident: full-time $6,352; part-time $240 per credit hour. Tuition, nonresident: full-time $14,296; part-time $571 per credit hour. Required fees: $585. *Financial support:* In 2006–07, 4 teaching assistantships with full and partial tuition reimbursements (averaging $8,400 per year) were awarded; research assistantships with partial tuition reimbursements, institutionally sponsored loans and scholarships/grants also available. Support available to part-time students. Financial award application deadline: 3/1; financial award applicants required to submit FAFSA. *Faculty research:* Accounting education, accounting ethics, capital markets (empirical/archival), research in tax and financial reporting, behavioral research in accounting. *Unit head:* Richard Ott, Head, 785-532-6184, Fax: 785-532-5959, E-mail: rlo@ksu.edu. *Application contact:* Jeff Katz, Director, 785-532-7451, E-mail: jkatz@ksu.edu.

Kean University, College of Business and Public Administration, Program in Accounting, Union, NJ 07083. Offers MS. Part-time and evening/weekend programs available. *Faculty:* 9 full-time (2 women). *Students:* 29 full-time (16 women), 59 part-time (32 women); includes 37 minority (9 African Americans, 19 Asian Americans or Pacific Islanders, 9 Hispanic Americans), 13 international. Average age 32. 33 applicants, 88% accepted, 21 enrolled. In 2006, 42 degrees awarded. *Entrance requirements:* For master's, GMAT, 2 letters of recommendation, interview, minimum GPA of 3.0. *Application deadline:* For fall admission, 5/1 for domestic students; for spring admission, 11/1 for domestic students. Application fee: $60 ($150 for international students). *Expenses:* Tuition, state resident: full-time $8,856; part-time $369 per credit. Tuition, nonresident: full-time $11,256; part-time $469 per credit. *Financial support:* In 2006–07, 5 research assistantships with full tuition reimbursements (averaging $3,217 per year) were awarded. *Unit head:* Dr. Eric Carlsen, Program Coordinator, 908-737-4104, E-mail: ecarlsen@kean.edu. *Application contact:* Joanne Morris, Director of Graduate Admissions, 908-737-3355, Fax: 908-737-3354, E-mail: grad-adm@kean.edu.

Kennesaw State University, Michael J. Coles College of Business, Program in Accounting, Kennesaw, GA 30144-5591. Offers M Acc. Part-time and evening/weekend programs available. *Students:* 61 full-time (29 women), 84 part-time (57 women); includes 28 minority (13 African Americans, 1 American Indian/Alaska Native, 12 Asian Americans or Pacific Islanders, 2 Hispanic Americans), 23 international. 57 applicants, 81% accepted, 34 enrolled. In 2006, 22 degrees awarded. *Entrance requirements:* Additional exam requirements/recommendations for international students: Required—TOEFL (minimum score 550 paper-based; 213 computer-based; 80 iBT), IELTS (minimum score 6). *Application deadline:* For fall admission, 6/15 for domestic students; for winter admission, 11/15 for domestic students; for spring admission, 4/15 for domestic students. Applications are processed on a rolling basis. Application fee: $50. Electronic applications accepted. *Expenses:* Tuition, state resident: full-time $3,044; part-time $127 per semester hour. Tuition, nonresident: full-time $12,172; part-time $508 per semester hour. Required fees: $353 per semester. Full-time tuition and fees vary according to campus/location and program. *Financial support:* Unspecified assistantships available. *Unit head:* Dr. Sher True, Director, 770-423-6087, E-mail: strue@kennesaw.edu. *Application contact:* Vilma Marquez, Admissions Counselor, 770-420-4377, Fax: 770-423-6885, E-mail: vmarquez@kennesaw.edu.

Kent State University, Graduate School of Management, Doctoral Program in Accounting, Kent, OH 44242-0001. Offers PhD. *Faculty:* 8 full-time (2 women). *Students:* 11 full-time (6 women), 7 international. Average age 34. 10 applicants, 20% accepted, 0 enrolled. In 2006, 1 degree awarded. *Degree requirements:* For doctorate, thesis/dissertation, oral defense, comprehensive exam. *Entrance requirements:* For doctorate, GMAT. Additional exam requirements/recommendations for international students: Required—TOEFL (minimum score 600 paper-based; 250 computer-based). *Application deadline:* For fall admission, 2/1 for domestic students, 1/1 for international students. Application fee: $30. Electronic applications accepted. *Financial support:* In 2006–07, 7 students received support, including fellowships with full tuition reimbursements available (averaging $15,000 per year), 7 teaching assistantships with full tuition reimbursements available (averaging $15,000 per year); Federal Work-Study and tuition waivers (full) also available. Financial award application deadline: 2/1; financial award applicants required to submit FAFSA. *Faculty research:* Information economics, capital management, use of accounting information, curriculum design. *Unit head:* Dr. Richard E. Brown, Chair, 330-672-2545, Fax: 330-672-2548, E-mail: rbrown1@kent.edu. *Application contact:* Felecia A. Urbanek, Coordinator, Graduate Programs, 330-672-2282, Fax: 330-672-7303, E-mail: gradbus@bsa3.kent.edu.

Kent State University, Graduate School of Management, Master's Program in Accounting, Kent, OH 44242-0001. Offers MS. Part-time programs available. *Faculty:* 11 full-time (3 women). *Students:* 40 full-time (24 women), 9 part-time (5 women), 15 international. Average age 26. 35 applicants, 89% accepted, 18 enrolled. In 2006, 20 degrees awarded. *Degree requirements:* For master's, internship. *Entrance requirements:* For master's, GMAT, minimum GPA of 2.75. Additional exam requirements/recommendations for international students: Required—TOEFL (minimum score 550 paper-based; 213 computer-based). *Application deadline:* For fall admission, 4/1 priority date for domestic students; for spring admission, 12/1 for domestic students. Applications are processed on a rolling basis. Application fee: $30. Electronic applications accepted. *Financial support:* In 2006–07, 14 students received support, including 14 research assistantships with full tuition reimbursements available (averaging $3,250 per year); Federal Work-Study and tuition waivers (full) also available. Financial award application deadline: 4/1; financial award applicants required to submit FAFSA. *Faculty research:* Financial accounting, managerial accounting, auditing, systems, nonprofit. *Unit head:* Dr. Richard E. Brown, Chair, 330-672-2545, Fax: 330-672-2548, E-mail: rbrown1@kent.edu. *Application contact:* Louise M. Ditchey, Director, 330-672-2282, Fax: 330-672-7303, E-mail: gradbus@bsa3.kent.edu.

Lamar University, College of Graduate Studies, College of Business, Beaumont, TX 77710. Offers accounting (MBA); experiential business and Entrepreneurship (MBA); financial management (MBA); healthcare administration (MBA); information systems (MBA); management (MBA). *Accreditation:* AACSB. Part-time and evening/weekend programs available. *Faculty:* 20 full-time (8 women), 2 part-time/adjunct (1 woman). *Students:* 55 full-time (27 women), 45 part-time (20 women); includes 17 minority (9 African Americans, 4 Asian Americans or Pacific Islanders, 4 Hispanic Americans), 14 international. Average age 29. 131 applicants, 34% accepted, 29 enrolled. In 2006, 29 degrees awarded. *Degree requirements:* For master's, thesis optional. *Entrance requirements:* For master's, GMAT. Additional exam requirements/recommendations for international students: Required—TOEFL (minimum score 525 paper-based; 197 computer-based). *Application deadline:* For fall admission, 3/15 priority date for domestic students; for spring admission, 10/1 priority date for domestic students. Applications are processed on a rolling basis. Application fee: $25 ($50 for international students). *Expenses:* Tuition, nonresident: part-time $33 per hour. Required fees: $43 per hour. $110 per semester. *Financial support:* In 2006–07, 12 students received support, including 4 research assistantships with partial tuition reimbursements available; fellowships with tuition reimbursements available, career-related internships or fieldwork, Federal Work-Study, institutionally sponsored loans, scholarships/grants, and tuition waivers (partial) also available. Support available to part-time students. Financial award application deadline: 4/1; financial award applicants required to submit FAFSA. *Faculty research:* Marketing, finance, quantitative methods, MIS, legal, environmental. Total annual research expenditures: $26,000. *Unit head:* Dr. Enrique R. Venta, Dean, 409-880-8604, Fax: 409-880-8088, E-mail: henry.venta@lamar.edu. *Application contact:* Dr. Brad Mayer, Professor and Associate Dean, 409-880-2383, Fax: 409-880-8605, E-mail: bradley.mayer@lamar.edu.

Lehigh University, College of Business and Economics, Department of Accounting, Bethlehem, PA 18015-3094. Offers accounting and information analysis (MS). *Accreditation:* AACSB. *Faculty:* 12 full-time (2 women), 3 part-time/adjunct (0 women). *Students:* 22 full-time (7 women), 2 part-time (1 woman); includes 2 minority (both Asian Americans or Pacific Islanders), 7 international. Average age 25. 71 applicants, 68% accepted, 18 enrolled. In 2006, 26 degrees awarded. *Entrance requirements:* For master's, GMAT. Additional exam requirements/recommendations for international students: Required—TOEFL (minimum score 600 paper-based; 250 computer-based). *Application deadline:* For fall admission, 5/1 for domestic and international students. Applications are processed on a rolling basis. Application fee: $60. Electronic applications accepted. *Expenses: Contact institution. Financial support:* In 2006–07, 4 research assistantships with partial tuition reimbursements (averaging $1,000 per year) were awarded; scholarships/grants and tuition waivers (partial) also available. Financial award application deadline: 1/15. *Faculty research:* Behavioral accounting, internal control, information systems, supply chain management, financial accounting. *Unit head:* Dr. Jack W. Paul, Director, 610-758-4452, Fax: 610-758-6429, E-mail: jwp1@lehigh.edu. *Application contact:* Mary- Theresa Taglang, Director of Graduate Programs, 610-758-5285, Fax: 610-758-5283, E-mail: mtt4@lehigh.edu.

See Close-Up on page 453.

Lehman College of the City University of New York, Division of Natural and Social Sciences, Department of Economics and Accounting, Bronx, NY 10468-1589. Offers accounting (MS). *Entrance requirements:* For master's, GMAT.

Lincoln University, School of Graduate Studies and Continuing Education, College of Business and Professional Studies, Department of Business and Economics, Jefferson City, MO 65102. Offers business administration (MBA), including accounting, entrepreneurship, management, public administration and policy. *Accreditation:* ACBSP. Part-time and evening/weekend programs available. *Faculty:* 7 part-time/adjunct (2 women). *Students:* 39 full-time (26 women), 23 part-time (14 women); includes 18 minority (17 African Americans, 1 American Indian/Alaska Native), 24 international. Average age 31. 28 applicants, 96% accepted, 14 enrolled. In 2006, 31 degrees awarded. *Degree requirements:* For master's, portfolio, thesis optional. *Entrance requirements:* For master's, GMAT. Additional exam requirements/recommendations for international students: Required—TOEFL (minimum score 500 paper-based; 173 computer-based; 61 iBT). *Application deadline:* For fall admission, 7/1 priority date for domestic and international students; for spring admission, 12/1 priority date for domestic and international students. Applications are processed on a rolling basis. Application fee: $17. *Expenses:* Tuition, state resident: part-time $189 per credit hour. Tuition, nonresident: part-time $351 per credit hour. Required fees: $15 per credit hour. $20 per semester. *Financial support:* Federal Work-Study and scholarships/grants available. Financial award application deadline: 4/1; financial award applicants required to submit FAFSA. *Unit head:* Dr. Ogugua Anunoby, Department Head, 573-681-5487, Fax: 573-681-6085, E-mail: anunobyo@lincolnu.edu.

Lindenwood University, Graduate Programs, Division of Management, St. Charles, MO 63301-1695. Offers accounting (MBA, MS); business administration (MBA); entrepreneurial studies (MBA); finance (MBA, MS); human resource management (MBA); human resources (MS); international business (MBA, MS); management (MBA, MS); management information systems (MBA, MS); managing business to business (MA); managing human resources (MA); managing international business (MA); managing investment management (MA); managing leadership (MA); managing marketing (MA); managing organizational behavior (MA); managing sales (MA); managing, training and development (MA); marketing (MBA, MS); nonprofit administration (MA); public management (MBA, MS); sport management (MA). Part-time and evening/weekend programs available. *Faculty:* 38 full-time (15 women), 20 part-time/adjunct (5 women). *Students:* 177 full-time (78 women), 138 part-time (67 women); includes 43 minority (27 African Americans, 4 American Indian/Alaska Native, 6 Asian Americans or Pacific Islanders, 6 Hispanic Americans), 73 international. Average age 30. In 2006, 159 degrees awarded. *Degree requirements:* For master's, thesis (for some programs). *Entrance requirements:* For master's, interview, minimum GPA of 3.0. Additional exam requirements/recommendations for international students: Required—TOEFL (minimum score 550 paper-based; 173 computer-based). *Application deadline:* For fall admission, 7/30 priority date for domestic students, 9/30 priority date for international students; for winter admission, 12/30 priority date for domestic and international students; for spring admission, 3/30 priority date for domestic and international students. Applications are processed on a rolling basis. Application fee: $30 ($100 for international students). Electronic applications accepted. *Expenses:* Tuition: Part-time $340 per credit hour. Tuition and fees vary according to course level, course load, degree level and program. *Financial support:* Career-related internships or fieldwork, Federal Work-Study, institutionally sponsored loans, and tuition waivers (partial) available. Financial award application deadline: 6/30; financial award applicants required to submit FAFSA. *Unit head:* Ed Morris, Dean, 636-949-4832, Fax: 636-949-4910, E-mail: emorris@lindenwood.edu. *Application contact:* Brett Barger, Dean Adult, Corporate and Graduate Admissions, 636-949-4366, Fax: 636-949-4109, E-mail: bbarger@lindenwood.edu.

Lipscomb University, MBA Program, Nashville, TN 37204-3951. Offers accounting (MBA); business administration (general) (MBA); conflict management (MBA); financial services (MBA); healthcare management (MBA); leadership (MBA); nonprofit management (MBA). *Accreditation:* ACBSP. Part-time and evening/weekend programs available. *Faculty:* 11 full-time (3 women), 6 part-time/adjunct (0 women). *Students:* 18 full-time (6 women), 50 part-time (23 women); includes 5 minority (4 African Americans, 1 American Indian/Alaska Native), 2 international. Average age 30. 48 applicants, 73% accepted, 27 enrolled. In 2006, 30 degrees awarded. *Median time to degree:* Master's–1 year full-time, 2.3 years part-time. *Entrance requirements:* For master's, GMAT, interview, 2 references, resumé. Additional exam requirements/recommendations for international students: Required—TOEFL (minimum score 570 paper-based; 230 computer-based). *Application deadline:* For fall admission, 7/1 for domestic students, 2/1 for international students; for winter admission, 12/1 for domestic students, 6/1 for international students. Applications are processed on a rolling basis. Application fee: $50 ($75 for international students). Electronic applications accepted. *Expenses: Contact institution. Financial support:* In 2006–07, 25 students received support. Career-related internships or fieldwork, Federal Work-Study, scholarships/grants, tuition waivers (partial), and unspecified assistantships available. Support available to part-time students. Financial award application deadline: 7/1; financial award applicants required to submit FAFSA. *Faculty research:* Impact of spirituality on organization commitment; leadership; psychological empowerment; training. *Unit head:* Dr. Steven K. Yoho, Associate Dean of Graduate Business Studies, 615-966-1833, Fax: 615-966-1818, E-mail: steven.yoho@lipscomb.edu. *Application contact:* Jackie Cash, MBA Assistant, 615-966-1833, Fax: 615-966-1818, E-mail: jackie.cash@lipscomb.edu.

Lipscomb University, Program in Accountancy, Nashville, TN 37204-3951. Offers M Acc. Part-time and evening/weekend programs available. *Entrance requirements:* For master's, GMAT, 2 references, interview. Application fee: $50 ($75 for international students). *Expenses:* Contact institution. *Financial support:* Career-related internships or fieldwork, Federal Work-Study, scholarships/grants, and tuition waivers available. Support available to part-time students. Financial award application deadline: 7/1. *Faculty research:* Internal auditing, ethics and fraud. *Unit head:* Dr. Perry Moore, Director of MACC Program, 615-966-5795, Fax: 615-966-1818, E-mail: perry.moore@lipscomb.edu. *Application contact:* Jackie Cash, Graduate Business Program Assistant, 615-966-1833, Fax: 615-966-1818, E-mail: jackie.cash@lipscomb.edu.

Long Island University, Brooklyn Campus, School of Business, Public Administration and Information Sciences, Program in Accountancy, Taxation and Law, Brooklyn, NY 11201-8423. Offers accounting (MS); taxation (MS). Part-time and evening/weekend programs available. *Entrance requirements:* For master's, GMAT or GRE General Test, 2 letters of recommendation. Additional exam requirements/recommendations for international students: Required—TOEFL (minimum score 500 paper-based; 173 computer-based). Electronic applications accepted.

Long Island University, C.W. Post Campus, College of Management, School of Business, Brookville, NY 11548-1300. Offers accounting and taxation (Certificate); business administration (Certificate); finance (MBA, Certificate); general business administration (MBA); international business (MBA, Certificate); management (MBA, Certificate); management information systems (MBA, Certificate); marketing (MBA, Certificate). *Accreditation:* AACSB. Part-time and evening/weekend programs available. *Entrance requirements:* For master's, GMAT, resumé, minimum GPA of 3.0, 2 letters of recommendation. Additional exam requirements/recommendations for international students: Required—TOEFL (minimum score 527 paper-based; 197 computer-based). Electronic applications accepted. *Faculty research:* Financial markets, consumer behavior.

Long Island University, C.W. Post Campus, College of Management, School of Professional Accountancy, Brookville, NY 11548-1300. Offers accounting (MS); taxation (MS). Part-time and evening/weekend programs available. *Entrance requirements:* For master's, GMAT, minimum GPA of 2.5, BS in accounting from accredited college or university. Electronic applications accepted. *Faculty research:* International taxation.

Louisiana State University and Agricultural and Mechanical College, Graduate School, E. J. Ourso College of Business, Department of Accounting, Baton Rouge, LA 70803. Offers MS, PhD. *Faculty:* 17 full-time (4 women). *Students:* 48 full-time (35 women), 13 part-time (9 women); includes 6 minority (1 African American, 3 Asian Americans or Pacific Islanders, 2 Hispanic Americans), 7 international. Average age 26. 36 applicants, 11% accepted, 4 enrolled. In 2006, 46 master's, 2 doctorates awarded. *Degree requirements:* For doctorate, thesis/dissertation. *Entrance requirements:* For master's, GMAT, minimum GPA of 3.2; for doctorate, GMAT, minimum GPA of 3.4. Additional exam requirements/recommendations for international students: Required—TOEFL (minimum score 550 paper-based; 213 computer-based; 79 iBT). *Application deadline:* For fall admission, 1/25 priority date for domestic students, 5/15 for international students; for spring admission, 10/15 for international students. Applications are processed on a rolling basis. Application fee: $25. Electronic applications accepted. *Financial support:* In 2006–07, 1 research assistantship with full and partial tuition reimbursement (averaging $5,400 per year), 17 teaching assistantships with full and partial tuition reimbursements (averaging $7,983 per year) were awarded; fellowships, Federal Work-Study, scholarships/grants, tuition waivers (full and partial), and unspecified assistantships also available. Support available to part-time students. Financial award application deadline: 4/15; financial award applicants required to submit FAFSA. *Faculty research:* Financial accounting, auditing fraud. Total annual research expenditures: $3,505. *Unit head:* Dr. Barbara Apostolu, Chair, 225-578-6202, Fax: 225-578-6201, E-mail: acapos@lsu.edu. *Application contact:* Dr. Nick Apostolou, M.S. Program Advisor, 225-578-6211, Fax: 225-578-6201, E-mail: acnicha@lsu.edu.

Louisiana Tech University, Graduate School, College of Administration and Business, School of Professional Accountancy, Ruston, LA 71272. Offers MBA, MPA, DBA. *Accreditation:* AACSB. Part-time programs available. *Degree requirements:* For doctorate, thesis/dissertation. *Entrance requirements:* For master's and doctorate, GMAT.

Loyola University Chicago, Graduate School of Business, Accountancy Department, Chicago, IL 60611-2196. Offers MS, MSA. *Accreditation:* AACSB. Part-time and evening/weekend programs available. *Faculty:* 10 full-time (2 women). *Students:* 32 full-time (17 women), 28 part-time (17 women); includes 11 minority (4 African Americans, 7 Asian Americans or Pacific Islanders). In 2006, 16 degrees awarded. *Entrance requirements:* For master's, GMAT, letters of recommendation, personal statement. Additional exam requirements/recommendations for international students: Required—TOEFL (minimum score 550 paper-based; 213 computer-based; 80 iBT). *Application deadline:* For fall admission, 7/1 for domestic and international students; for winter admission, 9/1 for domestic and international students; for spring admission, 1/3 for domestic and international students. Applications are processed on a rolling basis. Application fee: $50. Electronic applications accepted. *Financial support:* In 2006–07, 2 students received support, including 1 research assistantship with partial tuition reimbursement available (averaging $5,000 per year). Financial award application deadline: 3/15; financial award applicants required to submit FAFSA. *Faculty research:* Financial disclosure, web-based accounting issues, activities-based costing. *Unit head:* Dr. Brian Stanko, Chair, 312-915-7106, Fax: 312-915-7224, E-mail: bstanko@luc.edu. *Application contact:* Olivia Heath, Enrollment Advisor, 312-915-8908, Fax: 312-915-7207, E-mail: oheath@luc.edu.

Marquette University, Graduate School, College of Business Administration, Program in Accounting, Milwaukee, WI 53201-1881. Offers MSA. *Accreditation:* AACSB. *Faculty:* 9 full-time (3 women), 3 part-time/adjunct (1 woman). *Students:* 19 full-time (12 women), 4 part-time (1 woman); includes 2 minority (both Asian Americans or Pacific Islanders), 1 international. Average age 25. 37 applicants, 78% accepted, 14 enrolled. In 2006, 18

degrees awarded. *Entrance requirements:* For master's, GMAT. *Unit head:* Dr. Michael Akers, Chair. *Application contact:* James Trebby, Information Contact.

Maryville University of Saint Louis, The John E. Simon School of Business, St. Louis, MO 63141-7299. Offers accounting (MBA, PGC); business studies (PGC); e-business (MBA, PGC); management (MBA, PGC); marketing (MBA, PGC). *Accreditation:* ACBSP. Part-time and evening/weekend programs available. *Students:* 34 full-time (23 women), 162 part-time (101 women); includes 9 African Americans, 8 Asian Americans or Pacific Islanders, 2 international. Average age 31. 56 applicants, 96% accepted, 38 enrolled. In 2006, 89 degrees awarded. *Entrance requirements:* For master's, GMAT (unless applicant possesses a graduate degree or an undergraduate degree in business with a minimum GPA of 3.0), minimum AACSB index of 950. Additional exam requirements/recommendations for international students: Required—TOEFL (minimum score 550 paper-based). *Application deadline:* Applications are processed on a rolling basis. Application fee: $35 ($50 for international students). Electronic applications accepted. *Expenses:* Tuition: Full-time $17,800; part-time $555 per credit. Required fees: $55 per semester. Tuition and fees vary according to degree level and program. *Financial support:* Career-related internships or fieldwork, Federal Work-Study, tuition waivers (partial), and campus employment available. Financial award application deadline: 7/31; financial award applicants required to submit FAFSA. *Faculty research:* International business, e-business, strategic planning, interpersonal management skills, financial analysis. *Unit head:* Dr. Pamela Horwitz, Dean, 314-529-9418, Fax: 314-529-9975, E-mail: horwitz@maryville.edu. *Application contact:* Kathy Dougherty, Director of MBA Admissions and Enrollment, 314-529-9382, Fax: 314-529-9975, E-mail: business@marville.edu.

McGill University, Faculty of Graduate and Postdoctoral Studies, Desautels Faculty of Management, Montréal, QC H3A 2T5, Canada. Offers administration (PhD); entrepreneurial studies (MBA); finance (MBA); general management (Post Master's Certificate); information systems (MBA); international business (exchange program) (MBA); international Master's program in practicing management (MM); management (MBA); management for development (MBA); manufacturing management (MMM); marketing (MBA); operations management (MBA); public accountancy (Diploma); strategic management (MBA); MBA/LL B; MD/MBA. Part-time programs available. *Entrance requirements:* For master's, GMAT, minimum undergraduate GPA of 3.0, 2 years work experience; for doctorate, GMAT or GRE General Test, 2 letters of recommendation, preferably by professors in chosen field of specialization; for other advanced degree, 2 years of work experience, MBA, minimum GPA of 3.0 (Post-MBA Certificate). Additional exam requirements/recommendations for international students: Required—TOEFL (minimum score 600 paper-based; 250 computer-based), IELTS (minimum score 7). Electronic applications accepted. Expenses: Contact institution. *Faculty research:* Social innovation, leadership, strategy.

Mercer University, Graduate Studies, Macon Campus, School of Music, Macon, GA 31207-0003. Offers choral conducting (MM); church music (MM); performance (MM). *Faculty:* 1 full-time (0 women). *Students:* 11 full-time (5 women), 3 part-time (2 women); includes 2 minority (both African Americans), 1 international. Average age 32. In 2006, 1 degree awarded. *Degree requirements:* For master's, recitals. *Entrance requirements:* For master's, GRE, audition. Application fee: $50. *Unit head:* John E. Simons, Director of Graduate Studies, 478-301-4012, E-mail: simons_je@mercer.edu. *Application contact:* Gina Cook Nelson, Director of Admissions, 478-301-2307, E-mail: nelson_gc@mercer.edu.

Miami University, Graduate School, Richard T. Farmer School of Business Administration, Department of Accountancy, Oxford, OH 45056. Offers M Acc. *Accreditation:* AACSB. Part-time programs available. *Degree requirements:* For master's, final exam. *Entrance requirements:* For master's, GMAT, minimum undergraduate GPA of 3.0 during previous 2 years or 2.75 overall. Additional exam requirements/recommendations for international students: Required—TOEFL (minimum score 550 paper-based; 213 computer-based), TWE (minimum score 4).

Michigan State University, The Graduate School, Eli Broad Graduate School of Management, Department of Accounting and Information Systems, East Lansing, MI 48824. Offers accounting (MS); business administration (PhD). *Accreditation:* AACSB. *Faculty:* 27 full-time (9 women). *Students:* 189 full-time (93 women), 15 part-time (9 women); includes 17 minority (5 African Americans, 11 Asian Americans or Pacific Islanders, 1 Hispanic American), 35 international. Average age 24. 318 applicants, 44% accepted. In 2006, 131 master's, 2 doctorates awarded. *Entrance requirements:* Additional exam requirements/recommendations for international students: Required—TOEFL. *Application deadline:* Applications are processed on a rolling basis. Electronic applications accepted. *Expenses:* Tuition, state resident: part-time $346 per credit hour. Tuition, nonresident: part-time $730 per credit hour. Tuition and fees vary according to program. *Financial support:* In 2006–07, 8 fellowships with tuition reimbursements, 13 research assistantships with tuition reimbursements (averaging $12,159 per year), 8 teaching assistantships with tuition reimbursements (averaging $11,236 per year) were awarded. Total annual research expenditures: $129,357. *Unit head:* Dr. Kathy J. Petroni, Acting Chairperson, 517-423-2924, Fax: 517-423-1101, E-mail: petroni@bus.msu.edu. *Application contact:* Program Information, E-mail: msacct@bus.msu.edu.

Middle Tennessee State University, College of Graduate Studies, College of Business, Department of Accounting, Murfreesboro, TN 37132. Offers accounting (MS); information systems (MS). *Accreditation:* AACSB. Part-time and evening/weekend programs available. Postbaccalaureate distance learning degree programs offered. *Faculty:* 11 full-time (4 women). *Students:* 22 full-time (8 women), 81 part-time (47 women); includes 16 minority (5 African Americans, 11 Asian Americans or Pacific Islanders). Average age 30. 28 applicants, 100% accepted. In 2006, 29 degrees awarded. *Entrance requirements:* For master's, GMAT. Additional exam requirements/recommendations for international students: Required—TOEFL (minimum score 525 paper-based; 195 computer-based). *Application deadline:* For fall admission, 8/1 priority date for domestic students. Applications are processed on a rolling basis. Application fee: $25. Electronic applications accepted. *Financial support:* In 2006–07, 5 students received support. Institutionally sponsored loans available. Support available to part-time students. Financial award application deadline: 5/1; financial award applicants required to submit FAFSA. *Unit head:* Dr. Paula Thomas, Chair, 615-898-5655, Fax: 615-898-5045, E-mail: pbthomas@mtsu.edu.

Millsaps College, Else School of Management, Jackson, MS 39210-0001. Offers accounting (M Acc); business administration (MBA). *Accreditation:* AACSB. Part-time programs available. *Faculty:* 16 full-time (6 women), 1 part-time/adjunct (0 women). *Students:* 40 full-time (21 women), 41 part-time (21 women); includes 8 minority (6 African Americans, 1 Asian American or Pacific Islander, 1 Hispanic American), 5 international. Average age 26. 109 applicants, 76% accepted, 45 enrolled. In 2006, 31 degrees awarded. *Entrance requirements:* For master's, GMAT. Additional exam requirements/recommendations for international students: Required—TOEFL. *Application deadline:* For fall admission, 7/1 priority date for domestic students; for spring admission, 11/15 priority date for domestic students. Applications are processed on a rolling basis. Application fee: $25. Electronic applications accepted. *Expenses:* Tuition: Part-time $816 per hour. *Financial support:* In 2006–07, research assistantships (averaging $2,500 per year); career-related internships or fieldwork, Federal Work-Study, institutionally sponsored loans, scholarships/grants, and tuition waivers (partial) also available. Support available to part-time students. Financial award application deadline: 7/1; financial award applicants required to submit FAFSA. *Faculty research:* Ethics, audit independence, satisfaction with assurance services, political business cycles. *Unit head:* Howard L McMillan, Dean, 601-974-1250, Fax: 601-974-1260. *Application contact:* Dr. Bill Brisler, Associate Director of Graduate Business Admissions, 601-974-1277, Fax: 601-974-1260, E-mail: mbamacc@millsaps.edu.

Minnesota State University Mankato, College of Graduate Studies, College of Business, Mankato, MN 56001. Offers accounting and business law (MBA); finance (MBA); management (MBA); marketing and international business (MBA). *Accreditation:* AACSB. *Students:* 8 full-time (3 women), 32 part-time (13 women). *Entrance requirements:* For master's, GMAT, 2 letters of reference. Additional exam requirements/recommendations for international students: Required—TOEFL. *Application deadline:* For fall admission, 6/1 for domestic students; for

Accounting

Minnesota State University Mankato (continued)
spring admission, 10/1 for domestic students. Electronic applications accepted. *Unit head:* Scott Johnson, Dean, 507-389-5420.

Mississippi College, Graduate School, School of Business, Clinton, MS 39058. Offers accounting (Certificate); business administration (MBA), including accounting; business education (M Ed); JD/MBA. *Accreditation:* ACBSP. Part-time and evening/weekend programs available. *Faculty:* 12 full-time (2 women), 1 part-time/adjunct (0 women). *Students:* 55 full-time (28 women), 111 part-time (58 women); includes 41 minority (35 African Americans, 6 Asian Americans or Pacific Islanders), 32 international. Average age 29. In 2006, 45 master's, 5 other advanced degrees awarded. *Degree requirements:* For master's, thesis optional. *Entrance requirements:* For master's, GMAT, minimum GPA of 2.5, 24 hours of undergraduate course work in business. Additional exam requirements/recommendations for international students: Recommended—IELTS. *Application deadline:* For fall admission, 8/15 priority date for domestic students. Applications are processed on a rolling basis. Application fee: $25. Electronic applications accepted. *Expenses:* Tuition: Full-time $7,290; part-time $405 per hour. Required fees: $150 per term. Tuition and fees vary according to campus/location and program. *Financial support:* Federal Work-Study and unspecified assistantships available. Support available to part-time students. Financial award application deadline: 4/1; financial award applicants required to submit FAFSA. *Unit head:* Dr. Marcelo Eduardo, Dean, 601-925-3420, E-mail: eduardo@mc.edu.

Mississippi State University, College of Business and Industry, Graduate Studies in Business, Mississippi State, MS 39762. Offers business administration (MBA, PhD), including accounting (PhD), business information systems (PhD), finance (PhD), management (PhD), marketing (PhD); project management (MBA). *Accreditation:* AACSB. Part-time and evening/weekend programs available. Postbaccalaureate distance learning degree programs offered. *Faculty:* 66 full-time (18 women), 18 part-time/adjunct (9 women). *Students:* 143 full-time (52 women), 159 part-time (52 women); includes 30 minority (24 African Americans, 1 American Indian/Alaska Native, 2 Asian Americans or Pacific Islanders, 3 Hispanic Americans), 35 international. Average age 30. 605 applicants, 34% accepted, 142 enrolled. In 2006, 107 master's, 10 doctorates awarded. Terminal master's awarded for partial completion of doctoral program. *Degree requirements:* For doctorate, thesis/dissertation. *Entrance requirements:* For master's, GMAT, minimum GPA of 3.0 in last 60 hours of course work; for doctorate, GMAT, minimum GPA of 2.75 in last 60 undergraduate hours, 3.25 in last 60 graduate hours. Additional exam requirements/recommendations for international students: Required—TOEFL. *Application deadline:* For fall admission, 7/1 for domestic students; for spring admission, 11/1 for domestic students. Applications are processed on a rolling basis. Application fee: $30. Electronic applications accepted. *Expenses:* Tuition, state resident: full-time $4,550; part-time $253 per hour. Tuition, nonresident: full-time $10,552; part-time $584 per hour. International tuition: $10,882 full-time. Tuition and fees vary according to course load. *Financial support:* In 2006–07, 29 teaching assistantships with full tuition reimbursements (averaging $10,778 per year) were awarded; research assistantships with full tuition reimbursements, Federal Work-Study, institutionally sponsored loans, and unspecified assistantships also available. Financial award applicants required to submit FAFSA. *Unit head:* Dr. Barbara Spencer, Director, 662-325-1891, Fax: 662-325-8161, E-mail: gsb@cobilan.msstate.edu. *Application contact:* Dr. Phil Bonfanti, Director of Admissions, 662-325-4104, Fax: 662-325-8872, E-mail: admit@msstate.edu.

Mississippi State University, College of Business and Industry, School of Accountancy, Mississippi State, MS 39762. Offers MPA, MTX. *Accreditation:* AACSB. *Faculty:* 9 full-time (4 women), 4 part-time/adjunct (1 woman). *Students:* 47 full-time (20 women), 4 part-time (3 women); includes 4 minority (all African Americans), 7 international. Average age 24. 28 applicants, 75% accepted, 18 enrolled. In 2006, 26 degrees awarded. *Degree requirements:* For master's, comprehensive exam. *Entrance requirements:* For master's, GMAT, minimum GPA of 2.75, 3.0 in last 60 hours of course work, 2.75 in upper accounting. Additional exam requirements/recommendations for international students: Required—TOEFL. *Application deadline:* For fall admission, 7/1 for domestic students; for spring admission, 11/1 for domestic students. Applications are processed on a rolling basis. Application fee: $30. *Expenses:* Tuition, state resident: full-time $4,550; part-time $253 per hour. Tuition, nonresident: full-time $10,552; part-time $584 per hour. International tuition: $10,882 full-time. Tuition and fees vary according to course load. *Financial support:* Research assistantships with tuition reimbursements, teaching assistantships with partial tuition reimbursements, career-related internships or fieldwork, Federal Work-Study, institutionally sponsored loans, and unspecified assistantships available. Support available to part-time students. Financial award applicants required to submit FAFSA. *Faculty research:* Income tax, financial accounting system, managerial accounting, auditing. *Unit head:* Dr. Clyde Herring, Interim Director, 662-325-3710, Fax: 662-325-1646, E-mail: cherring@cobilan.msstate.edu. *Application contact:* Dr. Phil Bonfanti, Director of Admissions, 662-325-4104, Fax: 662-325-8872, E-mail: admit@msstate.edu.

Missouri State University, Graduate College, College of Business Administration, School of Accountancy, Springfield, MO 65804-0094. Offers M Acc. *Accreditation:* AACSB. Part-time and evening/weekend programs available. Postbaccalaureate distance learning degree programs offered (minimal on-campus study). *Faculty:* 16 full-time (4 women). *Students:* 58 full-time (34 women), 23 part-time (11 women); includes 3 minority (2 Asian Americans or Pacific Islanders, 1 Hispanic American), 15 international. Average age 29. 24 applicants, 63% accepted, 11 enrolled. In 2006, 40 degrees awarded. *Entrance requirements:* For master's, GMAT, minimum GPA of 2.75. Additional exam requirements/recommendations for international students: Required—TOEFL (minimum score 550 paper-based; 213 computer-based; 79 iBT). *Application deadline:* For fall admission, 7/20 priority date for domestic students; for spring admission, 12/20 priority date for domestic students. Applications are processed on a rolling basis. Application fee: $35. Electronic applications accepted. *Expenses:* Tuition, state resident: full-time $3,582; part-time $199 per credit hour. Tuition, nonresident: full-time $6,984; part-time $199 per credit hour. Required fees: $548. Full-time tuition and fees vary according to course level, course load, program and reciprocity agreements. *Financial support:* In 2006–07, 1 research assistantship with full tuition reimbursement (averaging $6,780 per year) was awarded; teaching assistantships with full tuition reimbursements, career-related internships or fieldwork, Federal Work-Study, institutionally sponsored loans, scholarships/grants, tuition waivers (partial), and unspecified assistantships also available. Support available to part-time students. Financial award application deadline: 3/31; financial award applicants required to submit FAFSA. *Faculty research:* Financial, managerial, tax, systems accounting, auditing, accounting education. *Unit head:* Dr. John R. Williams, Director, 417-836-5414, Fax: 417-836-6337, E-mail: accountancy@missouristate.edu.

Monmouth University, Graduate School, School of Business Administration, West Long Branch, NJ 07764-1898. Offers accounting (MBA); business administration (MBA); health care management (MBA, Certificate). *Accreditation:* AACSB. Part-time and evening/weekend programs available. *Faculty:* 30 full-time (11 women), 3 part-time/adjunct (1 woman). *Students:* 36 full-time (18 women), 198 part-time (88 women); includes 22 minority (9 African Americans, 1 American Indian/Alaska Native, 6 Asian Americans or Pacific Islanders, 6 Hispanic Americans), 12 international. Average age 30. 123 applicants, 89% accepted, 54 enrolled. In 2006, 74 degrees awarded. *Degree requirements:* For master's, capstone course. *Entrance requirements:* For master's, GMAT, minimum GPA of 3.0 in major, 2.75 overall. Additional exam requirements/recommendations for international students: Required—TOEFL (minimum score 550 paper-based; 213 computer-based; 79 iBT), IELTS (minimum score 5), MELAB 77, Cambridge A, B, C. *Application deadline:* For fall admission, 7/15 priority date for domestic students, 6/1 for international students; for spring admission, 11/15 priority date for domestic students, 11/1 for international students. Applications are processed on a rolling basis. Application fee: $50. Electronic applications accepted. *Expenses:* Tuition: Full-time $12,780; part-time $710 per credit. Required fees: $628; $314 per term. *Financial support:* In 2006–07, 126 fellowships (averaging $1,459 per year), 12 research assistantships (averaging $8,362 per year) were awarded; career-related internships or fieldwork, scholarships/grants, tuition waivers (partial), and unspecified assistantships also available. Support available to part-time students. Financial award application deadline: 3/1; financial award applicants required to submit FAFSA. *Faculty research:* Information technology and marketing, behavioral research in accounting, human resources, management of technology. *Unit head:* Donald Smith, Program Director, 732-571-7536, Fax: 732-263-5517, E-mail: dsmith@monmouth.edu. *Application contact:* Kevin Roane, Director, Office of Graduate Admission, 732-571-3452, Fax: 732-263-5123, E-mail: gradadm@monmouth.edu.

Montana State University, College of Graduate Studies, College of Business, Bozeman, MT 59717. Offers professional accountancy (MP Ac). *Accreditation:* AACSB. Part-time programs available. *Faculty:* 29 full-time (9 women), 21 part-time/adjunct (10 women). *Students:* 31 full-time (17 women), 2 part-time (both women); includes 2 minority (1 Asian American or Pacific Islander, 1 Hispanic American), 2 international. Average age 25. 16 applicants, 88% accepted, 13 enrolled. In 2006, 41 degrees awarded. *Degree requirements:* For master's, comprehensive exam, registration. *Entrance requirements:* For master's, GRE General Test. Additional exam requirements/recommendations for international students: Required—TOEFL (minimum score 550 paper-based; 213 computer-based). *Application deadline:* For fall admission, 7/15 priority date for domestic students, 5/15 priority date for international students; for spring admission, 12/1 priority date for domestic students, 10/1 priority date for international students. Applications are processed on a rolling basis. Application fee: $30. Electronic applications accepted. *Expenses:* Tuition, state resident: full-time $5,113. Tuition, nonresident: full-time $12,501. *Financial support:* In 2006–07, 5 teaching assistantships with partial tuition reimbursements (averaging $4,108 per year) were awarded; career-related internships or fieldwork, scholarships/grants, and unspecified assistantships also available. Financial award application deadline: 3/1; financial award applicants required to submit FAFSA. *Faculty research:* Tax research, fraud detection, performance measurement, audit evaluation, management control. Total annual research expenditures: $154,431. *Unit head:* Dr. Richard J. Semenik, Dean, College of Business, 406-994-4421, Fax: 406-994-6206, E-mail: semenik@montana.edu.

Montclair State University, The Graduate School, School of Business, Department of Accounting, Law and Taxation, Montclair, NJ 07043-1624. Offers accounting (MBA). Part-time and evening/weekend programs available. *Faculty:* 14 full-time (5 women), 10 part-time/adjunct (3 women). *Students:* 14 full-time (8 women), 52 part-time (30 women); includes 12 minority (2 African Americans, 6 Asian Americans or Pacific Islanders, 4 Hispanic Americans), 5 international. 24 applicants, 88% accepted, 18 enrolled. In 2006, 22 degrees awarded. *Entrance requirements:* For master's, GMAT, 2 letters of recommendation, resumé. Additional exam requirements/recommendations for international students: Required—TOEFL (minimum score 83 computer-based). *Application deadline:* For fall admission, 6/1 for international students; for spring admission, 10/1 for international students. Applications are processed on a rolling basis. Application fee: $60. Electronic applications accepted. *Expenses:* Tuition, state resident: part-time $450 per credit. Tuition, nonresident: part-time $682 per credit. Tuition and fees vary according to degree level and program. *Financial support:* In 2006–07, 3 research assistantships with full tuition reimbursements (averaging $7,000 per year) were awarded; Federal Work-Study and scholarships/grants also available. Support available to part-time students. Financial award application deadline: 3/1; financial award applicants required to submit FAFSA. *Unit head:* Prof. Frank Aquilino, Head, 973-655-4174. *Application contact:* Dr. Eileen Kaplan, Adviser, 973-655-7469, E-mail: kaplane@mail.montclair.edu.

Murray State University, College of Business and Public Affairs, Master of Professional Accountancy (MPAC) Program, Murray, KY 42071. Offers MPAC. Part-time programs available. *Faculty:* 7 full-time (2 women), 1 part-time/adjunct (0 women). *Students:* 22 full-time (15 women), 1 (woman) part-time; includes 1 minority (Asian American or Pacific Islander), 2 international. Average age 24. 8 applicants, 100% accepted, 8 enrolled. In 2006, 7 degrees awarded. *Degree requirements:* For master's, thesis. *Entrance requirements:* For master's, GMAT or GRE. Additional exam requirements/recommendations for international students: Required—TOEFL (minimum score 525 paper-based; 197 computer-based). *Application deadline:* For fall admission, 6/30 priority date for domestic and international students; for winter admission, 10/30 priority date for domestic and international students; for spring admission, 3/30 priority date for domestic and international students. Applications are processed on a rolling basis. Application fee: $25. *Financial support:* In 2006–07, 16 students received support, including 4 research assistantships (averaging $4,000 per year); career-related internships or fieldwork, Federal Work-Study, scholarships/grants, and unspecified assistantships also available. Financial award application deadline: 2/1; financial award applicants required to submit FAFSA. *Faculty research:* Corporate governance, information systems innovations, public finances, accounting education. *Unit head:* Dr. Tommy Stambaugh, Graduate Coordinator, 270-809-3169, Fax: 270-809-3922, E-mail: tommy.stambaugh@murraystate.edu.

National University, Academic Affairs, School of Business and Management, Department of Finance, Accounting and Economics, La Jolla, CA 92037-1011. Offers finance (MS); finance, accounting, and economics (EMBA, MBA); taxation (MS). Part-time and evening/weekend programs available. Postbaccalaureate distance learning degree programs offered (no on-campus study). *Faculty:* 11 full-time (1 woman), 114 part-time/adjunct (30 women). *Students:* 382 full-time (166 women), 694 part-time (302 women); includes 375 minority (91 African Americans, 5 American Indian/Alaska Native, 167 Asian Americans or Pacific Islanders, 112 Hispanic Americans), 144 international. Average age 34. 689 applicants, 577 enrolled. In 2006, 289 degrees awarded. *Degree requirements:* For master's, thesis. *Entrance requirements:* For master's, interview, minimum GPA of 2.5. Additional exam requirements/recommendations for international students: Required—TOEFL (minimum score 550 paper-based; 213 computer-based; 80 iBT), IELTS (minimum score 6). *Application deadline:* Applications are processed on a rolling basis. Application fee: $60 ($65 for international students). Electronic applications accepted. *Expenses:* Tuition: Full-time $7,722; part-time $286 per unit. One-time fee: $60. *Financial support:* Career-related internships or fieldwork, institutionally sponsored loans, scholarships/grants, and tuition waivers (partial) available. Support available to part-time students. Financial award application deadline: 6/30; financial award applicants required to submit FAFSA. *Unit head:* Donald A. Schwartz, Chair and Associate Professor, 858-642-8420, E-mail: dschwartz@nu.edu. *Application contact:* Dominick Giovanniello, Associate Regional Dean—San Diego, 800-NAT-UNIV, Fax: 858-642-8709, E-mail: dgiovann@nu.edu.

New Jersey City University, Graduate and Continuing Education, College of Professional Studies, Department of Business Administration, Jersey City, NJ 07305-1597. Offers accounting (MS); finance (MS). *Accreditation:* ACBSP. Evening/weekend programs available. *Faculty:* 9. *Students:* 2 full-time (1 woman), 33 part-time (10 women); includes 10 minority (3 African Americans, 4 Asian Americans or Pacific Islanders, 3 Hispanic Americans), 2 international. Average age 35. In 2006, 6 degrees awarded. *Application deadline:* For fall admission, 8/1 priority date for domestic students; for spring admission, 12/1 for domestic students. Applications are processed on a rolling basis. Application fee: $0. *Expenses:* Tuition, state resident: full-time $7,038; part-time $391 per credit. Tuition, nonresident: full-time $12,510; part-time $695 per credit. Required fees: $65 per credit. *Financial support:* Career-related internships or fieldwork and unspecified assistantships available. *Unit head:* Dr. Marilyn Ettinger, Head, 201-200-3353, E-mail: mettinger@njcu.edu.

New Mexico State University, Graduate School, College of Business, Department of Accounting and Information Systems, Las Cruces, NM 88003-8001. Offers M Acct. *Accreditation:* AACSB. Part-time programs available. *Faculty:* 9 full-time (3 women). *Students:* 29 full-time (13 women), 13 part-time (10 women); includes 15 minority (2 African Americans, 13 Hispanic Americans), 4 international. Average age 30. 19 applicants, 74% accepted. In 2006, 17 degrees awarded. *Degree requirements:* For master's, thesis optional. *Entrance requirements:* For master's, GMAT, minimum undergraduate accounting GPA of 2.85. Additional exam requirements/recommendations for international students: Required—TOEFL (minimum score 530 paper-based; 197 computer-based). *Application deadline:* For fall admission, 7/1 priority date for domestic students; for spring admission, 11/1 priority date for domestic students. Applications are processed on a rolling basis. Application fee: $30 ($50 for international students). Electronic applications accepted. *Financial support:* In 2006–07, 13 teaching assistantships were awarded; fellowships, research assistantships, career-related internships or fieldwork, Federal Work-Study, and health care benefits also available. Support available to part-time students. Financial award application deadline: 3/1. *Faculty research:* Taxation, financial accounting, managerial accounting, accounting systems, accounting education. *Unit head:* Dr. Larry Tunnell, Head, 505-646-4904, Fax: 505-646-1552, E-mail: ltunnell@nmsv.edu. *Application contact:* Dr. Cindy L. Seipel, Master of Accountancy Director, 505-646-5206, Fax: 505-646-1552, E-mail: cseipel@nmsu.edu.

New York Institute of Technology, Ellis College, Old Westbury, NY 11568. Offers accounting and information systems (MBA); e-commerce (MBA); finance (MBA); global management (MBA); healthcare administration (MBA); human resources management (MBA); leadership (MBA); management of information systems (MBA); management of technology (MBA); marketing (MBA); professional accounting (MBA); project management (MBA); risk management (MBA); strategy and economics (MBA). Ellis College is a collaboration between New York Institute of Technology and UNext online learning company. Part-time and evening/weekend programs available. Postbaccalaureate distance learning degree programs offered (no on-campus study). *Entrance requirements:* For master's, interview. Additional exam requirements/recommendations for international students: Required—TOEFL (minimum score 550 paper-based; 213 computer-based). Electronic applications accepted. *Expenses:* Tuition: Full-time $16,800; part-time $700 per credit.

New York Institute of Technology, Graduate Division, School of Management, Program in Business Administration, Old Westbury, NY 11568-8000. Offers accounting (Advanced Certificate); business administration (MBA); finance (Advanced Certificate); international business (Advanced Certificate); management of information systems (Advanced Certificate); marketing (Advanced Certificate). Part-time and evening/weekend programs available. *Students:* 481 full-time (120 women), 1,300 part-time (670 women); includes 297 minority (153 African Americans, 6 American Indian/Alaska Native, 81 Asian Americans or Pacific Islanders, 57 Hispanic Americans), 215 international. Average age 29. 1,049 applicants, 87% accepted, 137 enrolled. In 2006, 917 degrees awarded. *Degree requirements:* For master's, thesis (for some programs). *Entrance requirements:* For master's, minimum QPA of 2.85. Additional exam requirements/recommendations for international students: Required—TOEFL (minimum score 550 paper-based; 213 computer-based). *Application deadline:* For fall admission, 7/1 priority date for domestic students; for spring admission, 12/1 priority date for domestic students. Applications are processed on a rolling basis. Application fee: $50. Electronic applications accepted. *Expenses:* Tuition: Full-time $16,800; part-time $700 per credit. *Financial support:* Fellowships, research assistantships with partial tuition reimbursements, institutionally sponsored loans, tuition waivers (full and partial), and unspecified assistantships available. Support available to part-time students. Financial award applicants required to submit FAFSA. *Faculty research:* Instructor performance appraisal; relationship between TOEFL, GMAT, GRE, and performance in foreign students. *Unit head:* Dr. Gurumurthy Kalyanuram, Director, 516-686-7972, E-mail: gkalyana@nyit.edu. *Application contact:* Jacquelyn Nealon, Dean of Admissions and Financial Aid, 516-686-7925, Fax: 516-686-7613, E-mail: jnealon@nyit.edu.

New York University, Leonard N. Stern School of Business, Department of Accounting, New York, NY 10012-1019. Offers MBA, PhD. *Expenses:* Tuition: Part-time $1,080 per unit. Required fees: $56 per unit. $329 per term. Tuition and fees vary according to program. *Faculty research:* Earnings management and financial analysis effectiveness and accounting policy, value-relevance of financial reporting, intangibles-related reporting and analysis, equity.

North Carolina State University, Graduate School, College of Management, Department of Accounting, Raleigh, NC 27695. Offers MAC. *Degree requirements:* For master's, thesis optional. *Entrance requirements:* For master's, GMAT. Additional exam requirements/recommendations for international students: Required—TOEFL. Electronic applications accepted. *Faculty research:* Financial reporting issues using positive economic models and empirical studies of human behavior related to accounting decisions.

Northeastern Illinois University, Graduate College, College of Business and Management, Chicago, IL 60625-4699. Offers accounting (MBA); finance (MBA); management (MBA); marketing (MBA). Part-time and evening/weekend programs available. *Faculty:* 24 full-time (3 women), 13 part-time/adjunct (4 women). *Students:* 24 full-time (12 women), 40 part-time (16 women); includes 15 minority (4 African Americans, 8 Asian Americans or Pacific Islanders, 3 Hispanic Americans), 21 international. Average age 31. 23 applicants, 91% accepted. In 2006, 13 degrees awarded. *Degree requirements:* For master's, thesis optional. *Entrance requirements:* For master's, GMAT, minimum GPA of 2.75. Additional exam requirements/recommendations for international students: Required—TOEFL. *Application deadline:* For fall admission, 4/1 priority date for domestic students; for spring admission, 8/15 for domestic students. Applications are processed on a rolling basis. Application fee: $25. *Financial support:* In 2006–07, 20 students received support, including 8 research assistantships with full tuition reimbursements available (averaging $6,600 per year); career-related internships or fieldwork, Federal Work-Study, institutionally sponsored loans, and tuition waivers (full and partial) also available. Support available to part-time students. *Faculty research:* Perception of accountants and non-accountants toward future of the accounting industry, asynchronous learning outcomes, cost and efficiency of financial markets, impact of deregulation on airline industry, analysis of derivational instruments.

Northeastern State University, Graduate College, College of Business and Technology, Program in Accounting and Financial Analysis, Tahlequah, OK 74464-2399. Offers MS. Part-time and evening/weekend programs available. *Students:* 4 full-time (all women), 73 part-time (45 women); includes 20 minority (4 African Americans, 13 American Indian/Alaska Native, 2 Asian Americans or Pacific Islanders, 1 Hispanic American), 4 international. In 2006, 2 degrees awarded. *Entrance requirements:* For master's, GMAT. Additional exam requirements/recommendations for international students: Required—TOEFL (minimum score 213 computer-based). *Application deadline:* For fall admission, 6/1 priority date for domestic students. Applications are processed on a rolling basis. Application fee: $0 ($25 for international students). Electronic applications accepted. *Unit head:* Dr. Todd Jackson, Coordinator, 918-456-5511 Ext. 2939, E-mail: jacksongt@nsuok.edu.

Northeastern University, Graduate School of Business Administration, Graduate School of Professional Accounting, Boston, MA 02115-5096. Offers MST, CAGS, JD/MS/MBA, MS/MBA. *Faculty:* 16 full-time (6 women). *Students:* 61 full-time (31 women), 69 part-time (37 women). Average age 32. 205 applicants, 72% accepted. In 2006, 80 degrees awarded. *Entrance requirements:* For master's, GMAT, interview. Additional exam requirements/recommendations for international students: Required—TOEFL. *Application deadline:* For fall admission, 4/1 for domestic students, 1/15 for international students. Applications are processed on a rolling basis. Application fee: $100. Electronic applications accepted. *Expenses: Contact institution. Financial support:* Career-related internships or fieldwork, Federal Work-Study, institutionally sponsored loans, and scholarships/grants available. Support available to part-time students. Financial award application deadline: 3/1; financial award applicants required to submit FAFSA. *Unit head:* Annarita Meeker, Director, 617-373-4621.

Northern Illinois University, Graduate School, College of Business, Department of Accountancy, De Kalb, IL 60115-2854. Offers MAS, MST. *Accreditation:* AACSB. Part-time and evening/weekend programs available. *Faculty:* 14 full-time (4 women). *Students:* 121 full-time (59 women), 111 part-time (64 women); includes 39 minority (6 African Americans, 24 Asian Americans or Pacific Islanders, 9 Hispanic Americans), 20 international. Average age 29. 122 applicants, 66% accepted, 45 enrolled. In 2006, 128 degrees awarded. *Degree requirements:* For master's, thesis optional. *Entrance requirements:* For master's, GMAT, minimum GPA of 2.75. Additional exam requirements/recommendations for international students: Required—TOEFL (minimum score 550 paper-based; 213 computer-based). *Application deadline:* For fall admission, 4/1 priority date for domestic students, 5/1 for international students; for spring admission, 9/15 priority date for domestic students, 10/1 for international students. Applications are processed on a rolling basis. Application fee: $30. Electronic applications accepted. *Financial support:* In 2006–07, 29 research assistantships with full tuition reimbursements, 9 teaching assistantships with full tuition reimbursements were awarded; fellowships with full tuition reimbursements, career-related internships or fieldwork, Federal Work-Study, scholarships/grants, tuition waivers (full), and unspecified assistantships also available. Support available to part-time students. Financial award applicants required to submit FAFSA. *Faculty research:* Accounting fraud, governmental accounting, corporate income tax planning, auditing, ethics. *Unit head:* Dr. James C. Young, Chair, 815-753-1250, Fax: 815-753-8515. *Application contact:* Dr. John Simon, Graduate Adviser, 815-753-6203.

Northern Kentucky University, Office of Graduate Programs, College of Business, Program in Accountancy, Highland Heights, KY 41099. Offers M Acc. Part-time and evening/weekend programs available. *Faculty:* 5 full-time (1 woman). *Students:* 11 full-time (4 women), 46 part-time (22 women); includes 4 minority (3 African Americans, 1 Asian American or Pacific Islander), 3 international. Average age 31. 25 applicants, 84% accepted, 14 enrolled. In 2006, 17 degrees awarded. *Entrance requirements:* For master's, GMAT, minimum GPA of 2.5. Additional exam requirements/recommendations for international students: Required—TOEFL (minimum score 550 paper-based; 213 computer-based; 79 iBT), Michigan (must be taken at NKU). *Application deadline:* For fall admission, 8/1 priority date for domestic students, 6/1 for international students; for spring admission, 12/1 priority date for domestic students, 10/1 for international students. Applications are processed on a rolling basis. Application fee: $30. Electronic applications accepted. *Financial support:* In 2006–07, 27 students received support. Unspecified assistantships available. *Unit head:* Robert Salyer, Director, 859-572-5164, Fax: 859-572-6177, E-mail: salyerb@nku.edu. *Application contact:* Dr. Peg Griffin, Director of Graduate Programs, 859-572-1555, Fax: 859-572-6670, E-mail: gradprog@nku.edu.

Northwestern University, The Graduate School, Kellogg School of Management, Department of Accounting Information and Management, Evanston, IL 60208. Offers accounting (PhD). Admissions and degree offered through The Graduate School. *Degree requirements:* For doctorate, thesis/dissertation, comprehensive exam, registration. *Entrance requirements:* For doctorate, GMAT or GRE General Test. Additional exam requirements/recommendations for international students: Required—TOEFL. Electronic applications accepted. *Faculty research:* Managerial and financial accounting theory, financial accounting/theory, managerial accounting and performance measurement, international accounting, joint cost allocation.

Northwest Missouri State University, Graduate School, Melvin and Valorie Booth College of Business and Professional Studies, Program in Accounting, Maryville, MO 64468-6001. Offers MBA. *Faculty:* 15 full-time (2 women). *Students:* 2 full-time (1 woman), 3 part-time (2 women). 3 applicants, 67% accepted, 0 enrolled. In 2006, 2 degrees awarded. *Degree requirements:* For master's, comprehensive exam. *Entrance requirements:* For master's, GMAT, minimum GPA of 2.5. Additional exam requirements/recommendations for international students: Required—TOEFL (minimum score 550 paper-based; 213 computer-based). *Application deadline:* For fall admission, 7/1 for domestic and international students; for spring admission, 12/1 for domestic students, 11/15 for international students. Applications are processed on a rolling basis. Application fee: $0 ($50 for international students). Electronic applications accepted. *Financial support:* In 2006–07, 3 research assistantships with full tuition reimbursements (averaging $6,000 per year) were awarded. Financial award application deadline: 3/1; financial award applicants required to submit FAFSA. *Unit head:* Dr. Rahnl Wood, Head, 660-562-1759. *Application contact:* Dr. Frances Shipley, Dean of Graduate School, 660-562-1145, Fax: 660-562-1096, E-mail: gradsch@nwmissouri.edu.

Notre Dame College, Graduate Studies, South Euclid, OH 44121-4293. Offers accounting (Certificate); creative critical thinking (M Ed); financial services management (Certificate); information systems (Certificate); learning disabilities (M Ed); management (Certificate); paralegal (Certificate); pastoral ministry (Certificate); reading (M Ed); teacher education (Certificate). Part-time and evening/weekend programs available. *Degree requirements:* For master's, thesis. *Entrance requirements:* For master's, GRE General Test, MAT, minimum GPA of 2.75, valid teaching certificate. *Faculty research:* Cognitive psychology, teaching critical thinking in the classroom.

Nova Southeastern University, H. Wayne Huizenga School of Business and Entrepreneurship, Master's Program in Accounting, Fort Lauderdale, FL 33314-7796. Offers M Acc. Part-time and evening/weekend programs available. Postbaccalaureate distance learning degree programs offered. *Students:* 19 full-time (11 women), 292 part-time (198 women); includes 182 minority (89 African Americans, 21 Asian Americans or Pacific Islanders, 72 Hispanic Americans), 16 international. 30 applicants, 73% accepted. In 2006, 47 degrees awarded. *Degree requirements:* For master's, thesis or alternative. *Entrance requirements:* For master's, GMAT, GRE General Test, undergraduate degree in accounting, work experience. *Application deadline:* For fall admission, 8/15 for domestic students; for spring admission, 2/10 for domestic students. Applications are processed on a rolling basis. Application fee: $50. *Financial support:* Federal Work-Study and scholarships/grants available. Support available to part-time students. *Unit head:* Dr. Walter Moore, Chair and Professor for Accounting Programs, 954-262-5101, Fax: 954-262-3822, E-mail: moore@huizenga.nova.edu. *Application contact:* Aimee Fernandez, Assistant Director, 954-262-5019, Fax: 954-262-3822, E-mail: aimeefernandez@huizenga.nova.edu.

See Close-Up on page 295.

Nyack College, Graduate and Professional Programs, School of Business, Nyack, NY 10960-3698. Offers accounting (MBA); business administration (MBA). Evening/weekend programs available. *Degree requirements:* For master's, thesis. *Entrance requirements:* For master's, GMAT (may be waived based on business experience), minimum GPA of 3.0. Expenses: Contact institution.

Oakland University, Graduate Study and Lifelong Learning, School of Business Administration, Department of Accounting and Finance, Rochester, MI 48309-4401. Offers accounting (M Acc, Certificate); finance (Certificate). *Faculty:* 10 full-time (1 woman). *Students:* 20 full-time (5 women), 25 part-time (11 women); includes 3 minority (2 African Americans, 1 Asian American or Pacific Islander), 6 international. Average age 29. 18 applicants, 100% accepted, 14 enrolled. In 2006, 21 master's, 1 Certificate awarded. Application fee: $35. *Expenses:* Tuition, state resident: full-time $9,936; part-time $414 per credit. Tuition, nonresident: full-time $17,202; part-time $716 per credit. *Unit head:* Mohinder Parkash, Interim Chair, 248-370-4288, Fax: 248-370-4604.

The Ohio State University, Graduate School, Max M. Fisher College of Business, Department of Accounting and Management Information Systems, Columbus, OH 43210. Offers M Acc, MA, PhD. *Accreditation:* AACSB. *Faculty:* 25. *Students:* 102 full-time (45 women), 5 part-time (3 women); includes 9 minority (1 African American, 1 American Indian/Alaska Native, 7 Asian Americans or Pacific Islanders), 26 international. In 2006, 9 master's, 2 doctorates awarded. Terminal master's awarded for partial completion of doctoral program. *Degree requirements:* For doctorate, thesis/dissertation. *Entrance requirements:* For master's and doctorate, GMAT or GRE. Additional exam requirements/recommendations for international students: Required—TOEFL (minimum score 600 paper-based; 250 computer-based). *Application deadline:* For fall admission, 8/15 priority date for domestic students, 7/1 priority date for international students; for winter admission, 12/1 priority date for domestic students, 11/1 priority date for international students; for spring admission, 3/1 priority date for domestic students, 2/1 priority date for international students. Applications are processed on a rolling basis. Application fee: $40 ($50 for international students). Electronic applications accepted. *Expenses:* Tuition, state resident: full-time $9,438. Tuition, nonresident: full-time $22,791. Tuition and fees vary according to course load, campus/location and program. *Financial support:* Fellowships, research assistantships, teaching assistantships, career-related internships or fieldwork, Federal Work-Study, and institutionally sponsored loans available. Support available to part-time students. *Faculty research:* Artificial intelligence, protocol analysis, database design in decision-supporting systems. *Unit head:* Annette Beatty, Graduate Studies Committee Chair, 614-292-2081, Fax: 614-292-2118, E-mail: beatty.86@osu.edu. *Application contact:* 614-292-9444, Fax: 614-292-3895, E-mail: domestic.grad@osu.edu.

Accounting

Oklahoma City University, Meinders School of Business, Program in Accounting, Oklahoma City, OK 73106-1402. Offers MSA. Part-time and evening/weekend programs available. *Faculty:* 4 full-time (2 women). *Students:* 12 full-time (7 women), 9 part-time (6 women); includes 5 minority (1 African American, 4 Asian Americans or Pacific Islanders), 4 international. Average age 31. 10 applicants, 80% accepted. In 2006, 14 degrees awarded. *Entrance requirements:* Additional exam requirements/recommendations for international students: Required—TOEFL (minimum score 510 paper-based). *Application deadline:* For fall admission, 8/22 for domestic students; for spring admission, 1/15 for domestic students. Applications are processed on a rolling basis. Application fee: $30 ($70 for international students). *Financial support:* Fellowships with partial tuition reimbursements, career-related internships or fieldwork, Federal Work-Study, institutionally sponsored loans, and tuition waivers (partial) available. Support available to part-time students. Financial award application deadline: 8/1; financial award applicants required to submit FAFSA. *Faculty research:* Financial accounting, auditing, tax. *Unit head:* Dr. Jacci Rodgers, Coordinator, 405-208-5047, Fax: 405-208-5356, E-mail: gadmissions@okcu.edu. *Application contact:* Leslie McKenzie, Director, Graduate Admissions, 800-633-7242, Fax: 405-208-5356, E-mail: gadmissions@okcu.edu.

Oklahoma State University, William S. Spears School of Business, Department of Management Science and Information Systems, Stillwater, OK 74078. Offers management information systems (PhD); management information systems/accounting information systems (MS); management science (PhD); operations management (PhD); telecommunications management (MS, PhD). *Faculty:* 17 full-time (3 women), 1 part-time/adjunct (0 women). *Students:* 64 full-time (15 women), 66 part-time (15 women); includes 6 minority (2 American Indian/Alaska Native, 3 Asian Americans or Pacific Islanders, 1 Hispanic American), 77 international. Average age 31. 144 applicants, 55% accepted, 35 enrolled. In 2006, 62 master's, 1 doctorate awarded. *Degree requirements:* For doctorate, thesis/dissertation. *Entrance requirements:* For master's and doctorate, GMAT. *Application deadline:* For fall admission, 3/1 priority date for international students; for spring admission, 8/1 priority date for international students. Applications are processed on a rolling basis. Application fee: $40 ($75 for international students). Electronic applications accepted. *Expenses:* Tuition, state resident: part-time $146 per credit hour. Tuition, nonresident: part-time $516 per credit hour. Required fees: $44 per credit hour. Tuition and fees vary according to program. *Financial support:* In 2006–07, 2 research assistantships (averaging $4,620 per year), 19 teaching assistantships (averaging $7,334 per year) were awarded; career-related internships or fieldwork, Federal Work-Study, scholarships/grants, health care benefits, and unspecified assistantships also available. Support available to part-time students. *Unit head:* Dr. Rick Wilson, Head, 405-744-5084.

Oklahoma State University, William S. Spears School of Business, School of Accounting, Stillwater, OK 74078. Offers MS, PhD. *Accreditation:* AACSB. *Faculty:* 20 full-time (7 women). *Students:* 53 full-time (27 women), 16 part-time (8 women); includes 9 minority (1 African American, 8 American Indian/Alaska Native), 19 international. Average age 28. 79 applicants, 35% accepted, 20 enrolled. In 2006, 37 degrees awarded. *Degree requirements:* For doctorate, thesis/dissertation. *Entrance requirements:* For master's and doctorate, GMAT, minimum GPA of 3.25. Additional exam requirements/recommendations for international students: Required—TOEFL. *Application deadline:* For fall admission, 7/1 priority date for domestic students, 3/1 priority date for international students; for spring admission, 8/1 priority date for international students. Applications are processed on a rolling basis. Application fee: $40 ($75 for international students). Electronic applications accepted. *Expenses:* Tuition, state resident: part-time $146 per credit hour. Tuition, nonresident: part-time $516 per credit hour. Required fees: $44 per credit hour. Tuition and fees vary according to program. *Financial support:* In 2006–07, 6 research assistantships (averaging $18,667 per year), 24 teaching assistantships (averaging $7,908 per year) were awarded; career-related internships or fieldwork, Federal Work-Study, scholarships/grants, health care benefits, tuition waivers (partial), and unspecified assistantships also available. Support available to part-time students. Financial award application deadline: 3/1. *Faculty research:* International accounting, accounting education, cost-management, taxation, oil and gas. *Unit head:* Dr. Don Hansen, Head, 405-744-5123.

Old Dominion University, College of Business and Public Administration, Program in Accounting, Norfolk, VA 23529. Offers MS. *Accreditation:* AACSB. Part-time and evening/weekend programs available. *Faculty:* 8 full-time (2 women). *Students:* 4 full-time (2 women), 27 part-time (16 women); includes 3 minority (2 African Americans, 1 Asian American or Pacific Islander), 4 international. Average age 32. 40 applicants, 83% accepted. In 2006, 12 degrees awarded. *Degree requirements:* For master's, study tracks. *Entrance requirements:* For master's, GMAT, minimum GPA of 3.0. Additional exam requirements/recommendations for international students: Required—TOEFL (minimum score 550 paper-based). *Application deadline:* For fall admission, 7/1 priority date for domestic students, 4/15 priority date for international students; for spring admission, 11/1 priority date for domestic students, 10/1 priority date for international students. Applications are processed on a rolling basis. Application fee: $40. *Expenses:* Tuition, area resident: Part-time $285 per credit hour. Tuition, nonresident: part-time $715 per credit hour. Required fees: $94 per semester. *Financial support:* In 2006–07, 10 students received support, including 5 research assistantships with partial tuition reimbursements available (averaging $7,500 per year); career-related internships or fieldwork, tuition waivers (partial), and unspecified assistantships also available. Support available to part-time students. Financial award application deadline: 2/15; financial award applicants required to submit FAFSA. *Faculty research:* Assurance services, international accounting, strategic costing, business valuation. *Unit head:* Dr. Otto B. Martinson, Graduate Program Director, 757-683-3505, Fax: 757-683-5639, E-mail: acctgpd@odu.edu.

Oral Roberts University, School of Business, Tulsa, OK 74171-0001. Offers accounting (MBA); finance (MBA); international business (MBA); management (MBA); marketing (MBA); non-profit management (M Man, MBA); organizational dynamics (M Man); sales marketing (M Man). *Accreditation:* ACBSP. Part-time programs available. Postbaccalaureate distance learning degree programs offered (minimal on-campus study). *Faculty:* 9 full-time (2 women), 4 part-time/adjunct (2 women). *Students:* 33 full-time (18 women), 67 part-time (28 women); includes 28 minority (17 African Americans, 3 American Indian/Alaska Native, 6 Asian Americans or Pacific Islanders, 2 Hispanic Americans), 15 international. Average age 29. 69 applicants, 84% accepted, 33 enrolled. In 2006, 21 degrees awarded. *Degree requirements:* For master's, thesis optional. *Entrance requirements:* For master's, minimum GPA of 3.0. Additional exam requirements/recommendations for international students: Required—TOEFL (minimum score 550 paper-based; 213 computer-based). *Application deadline:* For fall admission, 7/1 priority date for domestic students, 5/1 priority date for international students; for spring admission, 12/1 priority date for domestic students, 10/1 priority date for international students. Applications are processed on a rolling basis. Application fee: $35. *Expenses:* *Contact institution.* *Financial support:* In 2006–07, 9 research assistantships (averaging $3,600 per year) were awarded; scholarships/grants and unspecified assistantships also available. Financial award application deadline: 6/1; financial award applicants required to submit FAFSA. *Faculty research:* Non-profit, international business and marketing. *Unit head:* Dr. Mark Lewandowski, Dean, 918-495-7040, Fax: 918-495-7876, E-mail: mlewandowski@oru.edu. *Application contact:* 918-495-6989, Fax: 918-495-7965, E-mail: alsc@oru.edu.

Pace University, Lubin School of Business, Accounting Program, New York, NY 10038. Offers managerial accounting (MBA); public accounting (MBA, MS). *Accreditation:* AACSB. Part-time and evening/weekend programs available. *Faculty:* 17 full-time, 2 part-time/adjunct. *Students:* 39 full-time (26 women), 97 part-time (47 women); includes 34 minority (3 African Americans, 24 Asian Americans or Pacific Islanders, 7 Hispanic Americans), 24 international. Average age 28. 145 applicants, 61% accepted, 35 enrolled. In 2006, 100 degrees awarded. *Entrance requirements:* For master's, GMAT. *Application deadline:* For fall admission, 7/31 priority date for domestic students; for spring admission, 11/30 for domestic students. Applications are processed on a rolling basis. Application fee: $65. Electronic applications accepted. *Expenses:* Tuition: Part-time $890 per credit. *Financial support:* Research assistantships, career-related internships or fieldwork and Federal Work-Study available. Support available to part-time students. Financial award applicants required to submit FAFSA. *Unit head:* Dr. Rudolph Jacob, Chairperson, 212-346-1960. *Application contact:* Joanna Broda, Director of Admissions, 212-346-1652, Fax: 212-346-1585, E-mail: gradnyc@pace.edu.

Pacific States University, College of Business, Los Angeles, CA 90006. Offers accounting (MBA); business administration (DBA); finance (MBA); international business (MBA); management of information technology (MBA); real estate management (MBA). Part-time and evening/weekend programs available. Postbaccalaureate distance learning degree programs offered (no on-campus study). *Faculty:* 3 full-time (0 women), 11 part-time/adjunct (0 women). *Students:* 106 full-time (47 women); includes 10 minority (all Asian Americans or Pacific Islanders), 96 international. Average age 32. 36 applicants, 81% accepted, 26 enrolled. In 2006, 68 degrees awarded. *Entrance requirements:* For master's, minimum undergraduate GPA of 2.5 during last 90 hours of course work. Additional exam requirements/recommendations for international students: Required—TOEFL (minimum score 133 computer-based). *Application deadline:* For fall admission, 8/15 priority date for domestic students; for winter admission, 10/15 priority date for domestic students; for spring admission, 1/15 priority date for domestic students. Applications are processed on a rolling basis. Application fee: $100. *Expenses:* Tuition: Full-time $6,360. Required fees: $1,080. Full-time tuition and fees vary according to course load and degree level. *Financial support:* Fellowships, research assistantships, teaching assistantships, scholarships/grants available. Financial award applicants required to submit FAFSA. *Unit head:* Dr. Kamol Somvichian, Director, 888-200-0383, Fax: 323-731-2383, E-mail: admission@psuca.edu. *Application contact:* Marina Miller, Assistant Director of Admissions, 323-731-2383 Ext. 11, Fax: 323-731-7276, E-mail: admissions@psuca.edu.

Penn State University Park, Graduate School, The Mary Jean and Frank P. Smeal College of Business Administration, State College, University Park, PA 16802-1503. Offers accounting (PhD); business administration (MBA); finance (PhD); management and organization (PhD); management science/operations/logistics (PhD); marketing (PhD); real estate (PhD); supply chain and information systems (PhD). *Students:* 287 full-time (79 women), 5 part-time (2 women); includes 39 minority (22 African Americans, 11 Asian Americans or Pacific Islanders, 6 Hispanic Americans), 93 international. Average age 31. 841 applicants, 31% accepted, 150 enrolled. In 2006, 107 master's, 11 doctorates awarded. *Expenses:* *Contact institution.* *Financial support:* In 2006–07, 1 fellowship, 11 research assistantships, 143 teaching assistantships were awarded. Financial award applicants required to submit FAFSA. *Unit head:* Dr. Kenneth B. Thomas, Dean, 814-863-0448, Fax: 814-865-7064, E-mail: j2t@psu.edu.

Pittsburg State University, Graduate School, Kelce College of Business, Department of Accounting, Pittsburg, KS 66762. Offers MBA. *Students:* 41. *Degree requirements:* For master's, thesis or alternative. *Entrance requirements:* For master's, GMAT. *Application deadline:* For fall admission, 7/1 for domestic students. Application fee: $35 ($60 for international students). *Expenses:* Tuition, state resident: full-time $2,144; part-time $181 per credit hour. Tuition, nonresident: full-time $5,273; part-time $442 per credit hour. Tuition and fees vary according to course load and campus/location. *Financial support:* In 2006–07, teaching assistantships (averaging $5,000 per year); research assistantships, career-related internships or fieldwork, Federal Work-Study, and unspecified assistantships also available. Financial award application deadline: 3/1. *Faculty research:* Accountant's legal liability, computer audit. *Unit head:* Dr. David O'Bryan, Interim Chairperson, 620-235-4566. *Application contact:* Jamie Vanderbeck, Assistant Director, 620-235-4223, Fax: 620-235-4219, E-mail: jvanderb@pittstate.edu.

Pontifical Catholic University of Puerto Rico, College of Business Administration, Ponce, PR 00717-0777. Offers accounting (MBA); business administration (PhD); finance (MBA); general business (MBA); human resources (MBA); international business (MBA); management (MBA); management information systems (MBA); marketing (MBA); office administration (MBA). Part-time and evening/weekend programs available. *Degree requirements:* For master's, thesis/dissertation; for doctorate, thesis/dissertation, comprehensive exam. *Entrance requirements:* For master's, GRE, interview, minimum GPA of 2.75; for doctorate, 2 letters of recommendation, 2 years experience in a related field, interview.

Prairie View A&M University, Graduate School, College of Business, Prairie View, TX 77446-0519. Offers accounting (MS); general business administration (MBA). *Accreditation:* AACSB. Evening/weekend programs available. *Faculty:* 30 full-time (7 women), 7 part-time/adjunct (2 women). *Students:* 10 full-time (6 women), 124 part-time (72 women); includes 118 minority (107 African Americans, 1 American Indian/Alaska Native, 8 Asian Americans or Pacific Islanders, 2 Hispanic Americans), 6 international. Average age 30. 76 applicants, 29% accepted. In 2006, 36 degrees awarded. *Degree requirements:* For master's, registration. *Entrance requirements:* For master's, GMAT, minimum GPA of 2.45. Additional exam requirements/recommendations for international students: Required—TOEFL. *Application deadline:* For fall admission, 7/1 priority date for domestic students, 6/1 priority date for international students; for spring admission, 11/1 priority date for domestic students, 10/1 priority date for international students. Applications are processed on a rolling basis. Application fee: $50. *Financial support:* In 2006–07, 4 research assistantships (averaging $1,500 per year) were awarded; career-related internships or fieldwork, Federal Work-Study, institutionally sponsored loans, and tuition waivers (partial) also available. Support available to part-time students. Financial award application deadline: 4/1; financial award applicants required to submit FAFSA. *Faculty research:* Operations management, international finance, marketing strategy, accounting theory, human resource management. Total annual research expenditures: $25,000. *Unit head:* John W. Dyck, Dean, 936-261-9217, Fax: 936-261-9232, E-mail: john_dyck@pvamo.edu. *Application contact:* Crystal Allen, Assistant to the Dean, 936-261-9237, Fax: 936-261-9241, E-mail: cjallen@pvamu.edu.

Purdue University, Graduate School, Krannert School of Management, Department of Management, West Lafayette, IN 47907. Offers accounting (PhD); business administration (MBA); finance (PhD); management information systems (PhD); marketing (PhD); operations management (PhD); quantitative methods (PhD); strategic management (PhD). *Students:* 56 full-time (21 women); includes 5 minority (3 Asian Americans or Pacific Islanders, 2 Hispanic Americans), 41 international. Average age 30. 421 applicants, 7% accepted, 19 enrolled. In 2006, 11 degrees awarded. *Median time to degree:* Doctorate–5 years full-time. Of those who began their doctoral program in fall 1998, 98% received their degree in 8 years or less. *Degree requirements:* For doctorate, thesis/dissertation, comprehensive exam, registration. *Entrance requirements:* For master's and doctorate, GMAT. Additional exam requirements/recommendations for international students: Required—TOEFL (minimum score 575 paper-based; 233 computer-based; 77 iBT), IELTS (minimum score 7). *Application deadline:* For fall admission, 2/15 for domestic and international students. Application fee: $55. Electronic applications accepted. *Financial support:* In 2006–07, 7 fellowships with partial tuition reimbursements (averaging $16,800 per year), 79 research assistantships with partial tuition reimbursements (averaging $16,800 per year), 8 teaching assistantships with partial tuition reimbursements (averaging $16,800 per year) were awarded; scholarships/grants and unspecified assistantships also available. Financial award application deadline: 2/15; financial award applicants required to submit FAFSA. *Faculty research:* Corporate finance, international business, enterprise integration. *Unit head:* Dr. John M. Barron, Head, 765-494-4451, Fax: 765-494-1526. *Application contact:* Kelly Felty, Assistant Director of Administration for Doctoral Programs, 765-494-4375, Fax: 765-494-1526, E-mail: phd@krannert.purdue.edu.

Purdue University Calumet, Graduate School, School of Management, Hammond, IN 46323-2094. Offers accountancy (M Acc); business administration (MBA). Part-time and evening/weekend programs available. *Entrance requirements:* For master's, GMAT. Additional exam requirements/recommendations for international students: Required—TOEFL. Electronic applications accepted.

Queens College of the City University of New York, Division of Graduate Studies, Social Science Division, Department of Accounting, Flushing, NY 11367-1597. Offers MS. *Faculty:* 19 full-time (1 woman). *Students:* 3 full-time (2 women), 63 part-time (38 women). 59 applicants, 83% accepted, 37 enrolled. In 2006, 17 degrees awarded. Application fee: $125. *Unit head:* Israel Blumenfrucht, Chairperson, 718-997-5070, E-mail: israel_blumenfrucht@qc.edu. *Applica-*

tion contact: Mario Caruso, Director of Graduate Admissions, 718-997-5200, Fax: 718-997-5193, E-mail: graduate_admissions@qc.edu.

Quinnipiac University, School of Business, Program in Accounting, Hamden, CT 06518-1940. Offers MS. Part-time and evening/weekend programs available. *Faculty:* 5 full-time (2 women), 5 part-time/adjunct (2 women). *Students:* 11 full-time (5 women), 11 part-time (5 women); includes 3 minority (1 African American, 1 Asian American or Pacific Islander, 1 Hispanic American), 2 international. Average age 25. 28 applicants, 75% accepted, 12 enrolled. In 2006, 18 degrees awarded. *Median time to degree:* Master's–1 year full-time, 2 years part-time. *Entrance requirements:* For master's, GMAT, BS in accounting or prerequisite course work in accounting. Additional exam requirements/recommendations for international students: Required—TOEFL (minimum score 575 paper-based; 233 computer-based; 90 iBT), IELTS (minimum score 7). *Application deadline:* For fall admission, 7/30 priority date for domestic students, 5/30 priority date for international students; for spring admission, 12/15 priority date for domestic students, 10/15 priority date for international students. Applications are processed on a rolling basis. Application fee: $45. Electronic applications accepted. *Expenses:* Tuition: Part-time $675 per credit. Required fees: $30 per credit. *Financial support:* Tuition waivers (partial) and unspecified assistantships available. Support available to part-time students. Financial award application deadline: 4/15; financial award applicants required to submit FAFSA. *Faculty research:* Financial reporting and disclosures, taxation research, accounting research. *Unit head:* Dr. Donn Johnson, Director, 203-582-8205, Fax: 203-582-8664, E-mail: donn.johnson@quinnipiac.edu. *Application contact:* 800-462-1944, Fax: 203-582-3443, E-mail: graduate@quinnipiac.edu.

See Close-Up on page 311.

Regis University, School for Professional Studies, Program in Business, Denver, CO 80221-1099. Offers accounting (MS); business administration (MBA); finance (MBA); finance and accounting (MBA); international business (MBA); marketing (MBA); operations management (MBA); organization leadership (MS); project management (Certificate); technical management (Certificate). Offered at Colorado Springs Campus, Northwest Denver Campus, Southeast Denver Campus, Fort Collins Campus, Broomfield Campus, Henderson (Nevada) Campus, and Summerlin (Nevada) Campus. Part-time and evening/weekend programs available. Postbaccalaureate distance learning degree programs offered (no on-campus study). *Faculty:* 16 full-time (4 women), 82 part-time/adjunct (22 women). *Students:* 1,770 (834 women). Average age 36. In 2006, 560 degrees awarded. *Degree requirements:* For master's, capstone project, thesis optional. *Entrance requirements:* For master's, GMAT, interview, 2 years of full-time business work experience; for Certificate, GMAT. Additional exam requirements/recommendations for international students: Required—TOEFL or university-based test. *Application deadline:* For fall admission, 8/22 for domestic and international students; for winter admission, 1/2 for domestic and international students; for spring admission, 4/30 for domestic and international students. Applications are processed on a rolling basis. Application fee: $75. Electronic applications accepted. *Financial support:* Federal Work-Study available. Support available to part-time students. Financial award applicants required to submit FAFSA. *Unit head:* Dr. Michael Goess, Chair, 303-458-4302, Fax: 303-964-5538. *Application contact:* 800-677-9270 Ext. 4080, Fax: 303-964-5538, E-mail: masters@regis.edu.

Rhode Island College, School of Graduate Studies, School of Management, Department of Accounting and Computer Information Systems, Providence, RI 02908-1991. Offers accounting (MP Ac); personal financial planning (MP Ac). Part-time and evening/weekend programs available. *Faculty:* 9 full-time (3 women). *Students:* 2 full-time (both women), 13 part-time (6 women); includes 1 African American, 1 international. Average age 37. In 2006, 8 degrees awarded. *Application deadline:* For fall admission, 4/1 for domestic students; for spring admission, 11/1 for domestic students. Applications are processed on a rolling basis. Application fee: $50. *Expenses:* Tuition, state resident: part-time $244 per credit. Tuition, nonresident: part-time $512 per credit. Required fees: $12 per credit. $66 per term. Tuition and fees vary according to degree level, program and reciprocity agreements. *Financial support:* Federal Work-Study, scholarships/grants, and health care benefits available. Support available to part-time students. Financial award application deadline: 5/15; financial award applicants required to submit FAFSA. *Unit head:* Dr. David Filipek, Chairperson, 401-456-8036, E-mail: dfilipek@ric.edu.

Rhodes College, Department of Economics/Business Administration, Memphis, TN 38112-1690. Offers accounting (MS). Part-time programs available. *Entrance requirements:* For master's, GMAT.

Rider University, College of Business Administration, Program in Accountancy, Lawrenceville, NJ 08648-3001. Offers M Acc. *Accreditation:* AACSB. *Faculty:* 5 full-time (3 women), 1 part-time/adjunct (0 women). *Students:* 20 full-time (11 women), 37 part-time (20 women); includes 11 minority (2 African Americans, 9 Asian Americans or Pacific Islanders), 13 international. Average age 28. 31 applicants, 65% accepted, 18 enrolled. In 2006, 21 degrees awarded. *Entrance requirements:* For master's, GMAT, resumé. Additional exam requirements/recommendations for international students: Required—TOEFL (minimum score 550 paper-based; 213 computer-based). *Application deadline:* For fall admission, 8/1 priority date for domestic students, 6/1 priority date for international students; for spring admission, 12/1 priority date for domestic students, 11/1 priority date for international students. Applications are processed on a rolling basis. Application fee: $50. Electronic applications accepted. *Expenses:* Tuition: Part-time $525 per credit. Required fees: $35 per course. $30 per semester. *Financial support:* In 2006–07, 26 students received support. Career-related internships or fieldwork, Federal Work-Study, institutionally sponsored loans, and unspecified assistantships available. Support available to part-time students. Financial award applicants required to submit FAFSA. *Faculty research:* Financial reporting, corporate governance, information technology, ethics, pedagogy. *Unit head:* Dr. Marge O'Reilly-Allen, Chairperson, 609-895-3505, Fax: 609-896-5304. *Application contact:* Jamie L Mitchell, Director of Graduate Admissions, 609-896-5036, Fax: 609-895-5680, E-mail: jmitchell@rider.edu.

See Close-Up on page 315.

Robert Morris University, Graduate Studies, School of Business, Moon Township, PA 15108-1189. Offers accounting (MS); business administration and management (MBA); finance (MS); human resource management (MS); nonprofit management (MS); sport management (MS); taxation (MS). Part-time and evening/weekend programs available. *Faculty:* 27 full-time (12 women), 6 part-time/adjunct (1 woman). *Students:* Average age 31. 253 applicants, 59% accepted, 103 enrolled. In 2006, 139 degrees awarded. *Entrance requirements:* For master's, GMAT, letters of recommendation. Additional exam requirements/recommendations for international students: Required—TOEFL (minimum score 550 paper-based; 213 computer-based). *Application deadline:* For fall admission, 7/1 priority date for domestic and international students; for spring admission, 11/1 priority date for domestic and international students. Applications are processed on a rolling basis. Application fee: $35. Electronic applications accepted. *Expenses:* Tuition: Part-time $580 per credit. Part-time tuition and fees vary according to degree level and program. *Financial support:* Research assistantships with partial tuition reimbursements, Federal Work-Study, institutionally sponsored loans, and unspecified assistantships available. Support available to part-time students. Financial award application deadline: 5/1; financial award applicants required to submit FAFSA. *Unit head:* Dr. Derya A. Jacobs, Dean, 412-262-8451, Fax: 412-262-8494, E-mail: jacobs@rmu.edu. *Application contact:* Kellie L. Laurenzi, Dean of Enrollment, 412-262-8235, Fax: 412-299-2425, E-mail: laurenzi@rmu.edu.

Rochester Institute of Technology, Graduate Enrollment Services, E. Philip Saunders College of Business, Department of Business Administration, Program in Accounting, Rochester, NY 14623-5603. Offers MBA, MS. *Students:* 10 full-time (5 women), 5 part-time (2 women); includes 3 minority (2 African Americans, 1 Asian American or Pacific Islander), 2 international. 22 applicants, 59% accepted, 9 enrolled. In 2006, 5 degrees awarded. *Entrance requirements:* For master's, GMAT, minimum GPA of 2.5. *Application deadline:* For fall admission, 3/1 priority date for domestic students. Applications are processed on a rolling basis. Application fee: $50. *Expenses:* Tuition: Full-time $28,491; part-time $800 per credit. Required fees: $201. *Financial support:* Research assistantships, career-related internships or fieldwork available. *Application contact:* Brian O'Neil, Associate Dean, 585-475-7784, E-mail: boneil@cob.rit.edu.

Roosevelt University, Graduate Division, Walter E. Heller College of Business Administration, Program in Accounting, Chicago, IL 60605-1394. Offers MSA. Part-time and evening/weekend programs available. *Students:* 12 full-time (7 women), 66 part-time (39 women); includes 32 minority (12 African Americans, 12 Asian Americans or Pacific Islanders, 8 Hispanic Americans), 4 international. Average age 32. 72 applicants, 82% accepted, 56 enrolled. In 2006, 32 degrees awarded. *Entrance requirements:* For master's, GMAT. *Application deadline:* For fall admission, 6/1 priority date for domestic students. Applications are processed on a rolling basis. Application fee: $25 ($35 for international students). *Financial support:* Application deadline: 2/15. *Unit head:* Deborah Pavelka, Director, 847-619-4865, E-mail: dpavelka@roosevelt.edu. *Application contact:* Joanne Canyon-Heller, Coordinator of Graduate Admission, 877-APPLY RU, Fax: 312-281-3356, E-mail: applyru@roosevelt.edu.

Rutgers, The State University of New Jersey, Newark, Graduate School, Program in Management, Newark, NJ 07102. Offers accounting (PhD); accounting information systems (PhD); computer information systems (PhD); finance (PhD); information technology (PhD); international business (PhD); management science (PhD); marketing (PhD); organization management (PhD). *Accreditation:* AACSB. *Faculty:* 101 full-time (16 women), 3 part-time/adjunct (1 woman). *Students:* 60 full-time (29 women), 32 part-time (17 women); includes 57 minority (6 African Americans, 49 Asian Americans or Pacific Islanders, 2 Hispanic Americans). 279 applicants, 13% accepted, 32 enrolled. In 2006, 10 degrees awarded. *Degree requirements:* For doctorate, thesis/dissertation, cumulative exams. *Entrance requirements:* For doctorate, GMAT or GRE, minimum undergraduate B average. Additional exam requirements/recommendations for international students: Required—TOEFL. *Application deadline:* For fall admission, 4/1 for domestic students; for spring admission, 11/1 for domestic students. Applications are processed on a rolling basis. Application fee: $50. Electronic applications accepted. *Financial support:* In 2006–07, 8 fellowships with full and partial tuition reimbursements (averaging $18,000 per year), 7 research assistantships with full tuition reimbursements (averaging $18,347 per year), teaching assistantships with full tuition reimbursements (averaging $18,347 per year) were awarded; institutionally sponsored loans and tuition waivers (full and partial) also available. Support available to part-time students. Financial award application deadline: 2/15. *Faculty research:* Technology management, leadership and teams, consumer behavior, financial and markets, logistics. *Unit head:* Dr. Glenn Shafer, Director, 973-353-1604, Fax: 973-353-5691, E-mail: gshafer@rbs.rutgers.edu. *Application contact:* Goncalo Filipe, Senior Academic Coordinator, 973-353-1002, Fax: 973-353-5691, E-mail: gfilipe@rbsmail.rutgers.edu.

Rutgers, The State University of New Jersey, Newark, Rutgers Business School: Graduate Programs-Newark/New Brunswick, Department of Accounting and Information Systems, Newark, NJ 07102. Offers professional accounting (MBA). *Accreditation:* AACSB. *Entrance requirements:* For master's, GMAT. Additional exam requirements/recommendations for international students: Required—TOEFL. Electronic applications accepted.

Rutgers, The State University of New Jersey, Newark, Rutgers Business School: Graduate Programs-Newark/New Brunswick, Doctoral Programs in Business, Newark, NJ 07102. Offers accounting (PhD); accounting information systems (PhD); finance (PhD); individualized study (PhD); information technology (PhD); international business (PhD); management science (PhD); organizational management (PhD); supply chain management (PhD).

Rutgers, The State University of New Jersey, Newark, Rutgers Business School: Graduate Programs-Newark/New Brunswick, Master of Accountancy in Governmental Accounting Program, Newark, NJ 07102. Offers government financial management (Certificate); governmental accounting (M Accy). *Accreditation:* AACSB. Postbaccalaureate distance learning degree programs offered.

St. Ambrose University, College of Business, Program in Accounting, Davenport, IA 52803-2898. Offers M Ac. Part-time and evening/weekend programs available. *Faculty:* 3 full-time (2 women), 2 part-time/adjunct (1 woman). *Students:* 6 full-time (2 women), 17 part-time (15 women); includes 2 minority (both Asian Americans or Pacific Islanders), 3 international. Average age 32. 24 applicants, 67% accepted, 11 enrolled. In 2006, 11 degrees awarded. *Degree requirements:* For master's, thesis or alternative, capstone seminar, comprehensive exam (for some programs), registration. *Entrance requirements:* For master's, GMAT. *Application deadline:* For fall admission, 8/15 priority date for domestic students; for winter admission, 12/15 priority date for domestic students; for spring admission, 1/1 priority date for domestic students. Applications are processed on a rolling basis. Application fee: $25. Electronic applications accepted. *Financial support:* In 2006–07, 9 students received support, including 1 research assistantship with partial tuition reimbursement available; career-related internships or fieldwork, tuition waivers (partial), and unspecified assistantships also available. Support available to part-time students. Financial award application deadline: 3/15; financial award applicants required to submit FAFSA. *Unit head:* Lewis Marx, Director, 563-333-6186, Fax: 563-333-6243. *Application contact:* Elizabeth Berridge, Director of Graduate Student Recruitment, 563-333-6271, Fax: 563-333-6268, E-mail: berridgeelizabethb@sau.edu.

St. Bonaventure University, School of Graduate Studies, School of Business, St. Bonaventure, NY 14778-2284. Offers accounting (Adv C); accounting and finance (MBA); finance (Adv C); management (Adv C); management and marketing (MBA); marketing (Adv C); professional leadership (Adv C). *Accreditation:* AACSB. Part-time and evening/weekend programs available. *Entrance requirements:* For master's, GMAT. Additional exam requirements/recommendations for international students: Required—TOEFL. *Faculty research:* Stock options, small business, market relationships, auditing, taxes.

St. Edward's University, School of Management and Business, Area of Business Administration, Austin, TX 78704. Offers accounting (MBA); business management (MBA); entrepreneurship (MBA, Certificate); finance—general (MBA, Certificate); global business (MBA, Certificate); human resource management (MBA, Certificate); management information systems (MBA, Certificate); marketing (MBA, Certificate); operations management (MBA, Certificate); personal financial planner (MBA, Certificate); sports management (MBA). Part-time and evening/weekend programs available. *Students:* 32 full-time (16 women), 394 part-time (195 women); includes 117 minority (23 African Americans, 2 American Indian/Alaska Native, 28 Asian Americans or Pacific Islanders, 64 Hispanic Americans), 21 international. Average age 33. 121 applicants, 74% accepted, 72 enrolled. In 2006, 142 degrees awarded. *Degree requirements:* For master's, minimum 24 resident hours. *Entrance requirements:* For master's, GMAT or GRE General Test, minimum GPA of 2.75 in last 60 hours of course work. Additional exam requirements/recommendations for international students: Required—TOEFL (minimum score 550 paper-based; 213 computer-based; 79 iBT). *Application deadline:* For fall admission, 8/1 for domestic students, 7/1 for international students; for spring admission, 12/1 for domestic students, 11/1 for international students. Applications are processed on a rolling basis. Application fee: $45 ($50 for international students). Electronic applications accepted. *Expenses:* Tuition: Full-time $11,682; part-time $649 per credit hour. Full-time tuition and fees vary according to course load and program. *Financial support:* In 2006–07, 4 students received support. Scholarships/grants available. Financial award applicants required to submit FAFSA. *Faculty research:* Operations management, minority entrepreneurship, globalization, professional services marketing. *Unit head:* Dr. Dianne Hill, Director, 512-428-1295, Fax: 512-448-8492, E-mail: dianneh@stedwards.edu. *Application contact:* Natalia Quintanilla, Graduate Admissions Coordinator, 512-233-1697, Fax: 512-428-1032, E-mail: nataliaq@stedwards.edu.

St. John's University, The Peter J. Tobin College of Business, Department of Accounting and Taxation, Program in Accounting, Queens, NY 11439. Offers MBA, MS, Adv C. *Accreditation:* AACSB. Part-time and evening/weekend programs available. *Faculty:* 20 full-time (6 women), 18 part-time/adjunct (4 women). *Students:* 34 full-time (19 women), 81 part-time (42 women);

Accounting

St. John's University (continued)

includes 37 minority (4 African Americans, 21 Asian Americans or Pacific Islanders, 12 Hispanic Americans), 44 international. Average age 27. 104 applicants, 81% accepted, 33 enrolled. In 2006, 69 degrees awarded. *Degree requirements:* For master's, thesis optional. *Entrance requirements:* For master's, GMAT, minimum GPA of 3.0. Additional exam requirements/recommendations for international students: Required—TOEFL (minimum score 500 paper-based; 173 computer-based). *Application deadline:* For fall admission, 5/1 priority date for domestic and international students; for spring admission, 11/1 priority date for domestic and international students. Applications are processed on a rolling basis. Application fee: $40. Electronic applications accepted. *Expenses: Contact institution.* Tuition and fees vary according to program. *Financial support:* Research assistantships available. Support available to part-time students. Financial award application deadline: 3/1; financial award applicants required to submit FAFSA. *Unit head:* Dr. Adrian Fitzsimons, Chair, 718-990-6460, Fax: 718-380-3803, E-mail: fitzsima@stjohns.edu. *Application contact:* Nicole T. Bryan, Assistant Dean, 718-990-2599, Fax: 718-990-5242, E-mail: mbaadmissions@stjohns.edu.

St. Joseph's College, New York, Graduate Programs, Program in Business, Field of Accounting, Brooklyn, NY 11205-3688. Offers MBA.

See Close-Up on page 317.

St. Joseph's College, Suffolk Campus, Program in Accounting, Patchogue, NY 11772-2399. Offers MBA.

Saint Joseph's University, Erivan K. Haub School of Business, Professional MBA Program, Program in Accounting, Philadelphia, PA 19131-1395. Offers MBA. *Accreditation:* AACSB. Part-time and evening/weekend programs available. *Faculty:* 3 full-time (0 women), 2 part-time/adjunct (0 women). *Students:* 3 full-time (0 women), 23 part-time (8 women); includes 5 minority (3 African Americans, 1 Asian American or Pacific Islander, 1 Hispanic American), 2 international. Average age 28. In 2006, 6 degrees awarded. *Entrance requirements:* For master's, GMAT, 2 letters of recommendation, resumé. Additional exam requirements/recommendations for international students: Required—TOEFL (minimum score 550 paper-based; 213 computer-based). *Application deadline:* For fall admission, 7/15 for domestic students, 4/15 for international students; for spring admission, 11/15 for domestic students, 10/15 for international students. Applications are processed on a rolling basis. Application fee: $35. *Financial support:* In 2006–07, 1 research assistantship with partial tuition reimbursement (averaging $2,000 per year) was awarded; unspecified assistantships also available. Financial award application deadline: 5/1. *Unit head:* Joseph Ragan, Chair, 610-660-1654, E-mail: jragan@sju.edu.

Saint Leo University, Graduate Business Studies, Saint Leo, FL 33574-6665. Offers accounting (MBA); business (MBA); criminal justice (MBA); human resource administration (MBA); information security management (MBA); sport business (MBA). Part-time and evening/weekend programs available. Postbaccalaureate distance learning degree programs offered (no on-campus study). *Faculty:* 17 full-time (5 women), 24 part-time/adjunct (6 women). *Students:* 298 full-time (187 women), 368 part-time (215 women); includes 195 minority (132 African Americans, 3 American Indian/Alaska Native, 23 Asian Americans or Pacific Islanders, 37 Hispanic Americans), 6 international. Average age 36. 863 applicants, 59% accepted, 282 enrolled. In 2006, 156 degrees awarded. *Degree requirements:* For master's, thesis. *Entrance requirements:* For master's, GMAT, 5 years of professional work experience, resumé, 2 letters of recommendation. Additional exam requirements/recommendations for international students: Required—TOEFL (minimum score 550 paper-based; 213 computer-based). *Application deadline:* For fall admission, 7/1 priority date for domestic students; for spring admission, 11/12 priority date for domestic students. Applications are processed on a rolling basis. Application fee: $45. Electronic applications accepted. *Expenses: Contact institution. Financial support:* In 2006–07, 39 students received support. Career-related internships or fieldwork, Federal Work-Study, and scholarships/grants available. Support available to part-time students. Financial award application deadline: 3/1; financial award applicants required to submit FAFSA. *Unit head:* Dr. Robert Robertson, Director, 352-588-8758, Fax: 352-588-8912, E-mail: mba@saintleo.edu. *Application contact:* Scott Cathcart, Vice President of Enrollment, 800-707-8846, Fax: 352-588-7873, E-mail: grad.admission@saintleo.edu.

Saint Louis University, Graduate School, John Cook School of Business, Department of Accounting, St. Louis, MO 63103-2097. Offers M Acct, MBA. Part-time and evening/weekend programs available. *Faculty:* 11 full-time (5 women), 1 part-time/adjunct (0 women). *Students:* 29 full-time (11 women), 7 part-time (5 women); includes 1 minority (Asian American or Pacific Islander), 2 international. Average age 24. 55 applicants, 71% accepted, 26 enrolled. In 2006, 14 degrees awarded. *Entrance requirements:* For master's, GMAT. Additional exam requirements/recommendations for international students: Required—TOEFL (minimum score 525 paper-based; 194 computer-based). *Application deadline:* For fall admission, 4/15 priority date for domestic students, 4/15 for international students. Applications are processed on a rolling basis. Application fee: $90. *Expenses: Contact institution. Financial support:* In 2006–07, 19 students received support. Federal Work-Study, scholarships/grants, traineeships, health care benefits, and unspecified assistantships available. Support available to part-time students. Financial award application deadline: 6/1; financial award applicants required to submit FAFSA. *Unit head:* Dr. Ananth Seetharaman, Chairperson, 314-977-3828, Fax: 314-977-1473, E-mail: acas@slu.edu.

St. Mary's University of San Antonio, Graduate School, Bill Greehey School of Business, Program in Accounting, San Antonio, TX 78228-8507. Offers taxation (M Acc). Part-time programs available. Postbaccalaureate distance learning degree programs offered (minimal on-campus study). *Faculty:* 3 full-time (1 woman). *Students:* 1 full-time (0 women), 13 part-time (10 women); includes 7 minority (1 African American, 6 Hispanic Americans), 1 international. Average age 31. In 2006, 3 degrees awarded. *Degree requirements:* For master's, registration. *Entrance requirements:* For master's, GMAT. Additional exam requirements/recommendations for international students: Required—TOEFL (minimum score 550 paper-based; 213 computer-based). *Application deadline:* Applications are processed on a rolling basis. Application fee: $30. Electronic applications accepted. *Expenses:* Tuition: Full-time $10,890; part-time $605 per hour. Required fees: $500. Tuition and fees vary according to degree level. *Financial support:* Career-related internships or fieldwork, Federal Work-Study, institutionally sponsored loans, scholarships/grants, health care benefits, and unspecified assistantships available. Financial award application deadline: 3/31; financial award applicants required to submit FAFSA. *Unit head:* Dr. Mark Persellin, Graduate Program Director, 210-436-3708, Fax: 210-436-3620.

Saint Peter's College, Program in Accountancy, Jersey City, NJ 07306-5997. Offers MS, Certificate, MBA/MS. Part-time and evening/weekend programs available. *Entrance requirements:* For master's, GMAT or MAT. *Faculty research:* Taxation, international business and finance, decision support and expert systems.

St. Thomas University, School of Graduate Studies, Department of Management, Miami Gardens, FL 33054-6459. Offers accounting (MBA); general management (MSM, Certificate); health management (MBA, MSM, Certificate); human resource management (MBA, MSM, Certificate); international business (MBA, MIB, MSM, Certificate); justice administration (MSM, Certificate); management accounting (MSM, Certificate); public management (MSM, Certificate). Part-time and evening/weekend programs available. *Degree requirements:* For master's, comprehensive exam. *Entrance requirements:* For master's, interview, minimum GPA of 3.0 or GMAT. Additional exam requirements/recommendations for international students: Required—TOEFL. Electronic applications accepted.

Saint Vincent College, Program in Accounting, Latrobe, PA 15650-2690. Offers MS. *Accreditation:* ACBSP. Part-time and evening/weekend programs available. *Entrance requirements:* For master's, GRE (if undergraduate GPA is below 3.0). Additional exam requirements/recommendations for international students: Required—TOEFL (minimum score 550 paper-based; 213 computer-based).

San Diego State University, Graduate and Research Affairs, College of Business Administration, School of Accountancy, San Diego, CA 92182. Offers MS. *Accreditation:* AACSB. *Students:* 43 full-time (25 women), 75 part-time (46 women); includes 20 minority (1 African American, 1 American Indian/Alaska Native, 12 Asian Americans or Pacific Islanders, 6 Hispanic Americans), 27 international. Average age 30. 126 applicants, 64% accepted, 20 enrolled. In 2006, 51 degrees awarded. *Degree requirements:* For master's, thesis or alternative. *Entrance requirements:* For master's, GMAT, resumé, letters of reference. Additional exam requirements/recommendations for international students: Required—TOEFL. *Application deadline:* For fall admission, 4/15 for domestic and international students; for spring admission, 11/1 for domestic students, 10/1 for international students. Applications are processed on a rolling basis. Application fee: $55. Electronic applications accepted. *Financial support:* In 2006–07, 12 teaching assistantships were awarded. Financial award applicants required to submit FAFSA. *Unit head:* Sharon Lightner, Director, 619-594-5070, Fax: 619-594-3675. *Application contact:* Information Contact, E-mail: sdsumba@mail.sdsu.edu.

San Jose State University, Graduate Studies and Research, Lucas Graduate School of Business, Program in Accounting, San Jose, CA 95192-0001. Offers MS. *Students:* 26 full-time (18 women); includes 10 minority (8 Asian Americans or Pacific Islanders, 2 Hispanic Americans), 11 international. Average age 32. 97 applicants, 41% accepted, 26 enrolled. In 2006, 29 degrees awarded. *Degree requirements:* For master's, thesis or alternative, comprehensive exam. *Entrance requirements:* For master's, GMAT, minimum GPA of 3.0. *Application deadline:* For fall admission, 6/29 for domestic students; for spring admission, 11/30 for domestic students. Applications are processed on a rolling basis. Application fee: $59. Electronic applications accepted. *Financial support:* Applicants required to submit FAFSA. *Unit head:* Bill Donnelly, Chair, 408-924-3493, Fax: 408-924-3463.

Seattle University, Albers School of Business and Economics, Program in Professional Accounting, Seattle, WA 98122-1090. Offers MPAC. *Faculty:* 8 full-time (2 women), 1 part-time/adjunct (0 women). *Students:* 23 full-time (15 women), 29 part-time (20 women); includes 10 minority (1 African American, 9 Asian Americans or Pacific Islanders), 13 international. Average age 27. 23 applicants, 52% accepted, 9 enrolled. In 2006, 1 degree awarded. *Entrance requirements:* For master's, GMAT, minimum GPA of 3.0, 1 year related experience. Additional exam requirements/recommendations for international students: Required—TOEFL. *Application deadline:* For fall admission, 8/20 priority date for domestic students; for winter admission, 11/20 for domestic students; for spring admission, 2/20 priority date for domestic students. Applications are processed on a rolling basis. Application fee: $55. *Financial support:* Career-related internships or fieldwork and Federal Work-Study available. Support available to part-time students. *Unit head:* Dr. Susan Weihrich, Program Director, 206-296-5690, E-mail: weihrich@seattleu.edu. *Application contact:* Janet Shandley, Associate Dean of Graduate Admissions, 206-296-5900, Fax: 206-298-5656, E-mail: grad_admissions@seattleu.edu.

Seton Hall University, Stillman School of Business, Department of Accounting, South Orange, NJ 07079-2692. Offers accounting (MS); professional accounting (MS). Part-time programs available. *Faculty:* 10 full-time (3 women), 2 part-time/adjunct (0 women). *Students:* 5 full-time (1 woman), 31 part-time (15 women). Average age 24. 42 applicants, 52% accepted, 15 enrolled. In 2006, 21 degrees awarded. *Median time to degree:* Master's–1 year full-time, 1.6 years part-time. *Degree requirements:* For master's, registration. *Entrance requirements:* For master's, GMAT, minimum GPA of 2.75. Additional exam requirements/recommendations for international students: Required—TOEFL (minimum score 550 paper-based; 213 computer-based). *Application deadline:* For fall admission, 6/1 priority date for domestic students, 5/1 for international students; for spring admission, 11/1 for domestic students, 10/1 for international students. Applications are processed on a rolling basis. Application fee: $75 ($100 for international students). Electronic applications accepted. *Financial support:* In 2006–07, 2 students received support, including research assistantships with full and partial tuition reimbursements available (averaging $5,400 per year); career-related internships or fieldwork, Federal Work-Study, scholarships/grants, and unspecified assistantships also available. Support available to part-time students. Financial award application deadline: 6/1; financial award applicants required to submit FAFSA. *Faculty research:* Voluntary disclosure, international accounting, pension and retirement accounting, ethics in financial reporting. *Unit head:* Dr. David Gelb, Chair of Accounting Dept., 973-761-9235, Fax: 973-761-9217, E-mail: gelbdavi@shu.edu. *Application contact:* Catherine Bianchi, Director of Graduate Admissions, 973-761-9220, Fax: 973-761-9208, E-mail: bianchca@shu.edu.

Seton Hall University, Stillman School of Business, Programs in Business Administration, South Orange, NJ 07079-2697. Offers accounting (MBA); finance (MBA); financial markets, institutions and instruments (MBA); healthcare management (MBA); information systems (MBA); international business (MBA); management (MBA); marketing (MBA); pharmaceutical management (MBA); sport management (MBA). Part-time and evening/weekend programs available. *Faculty:* 57 full-time (13 women), 30 part-time/adjunct (3 women). *Students:* 57 full-time (16 women), 180 part-time (57 women); includes 9 African Americans, 10 Asian Americans or Pacific Islanders, 7 Hispanic Americans. Average age 29. 195 applicants, 47% accepted, 48 enrolled. In 2006, 144 degrees awarded. *Median time to degree:* Master's–1.6 years full-time, 2.3 years part-time. *Degree requirements:* For master's, 20 hours of community service (Social Responsibility Project). *Entrance requirements:* For master's, GMAT, minimum GPA of 2.75. Additional exam requirements/recommendations for international students: Required—TOEFL (minimum score 550 paper-based; 213 computer-based). *Application deadline:* For fall admission, 6/1 priority date for domestic students; for spring admission, 11/1 priority date for domestic students. Applications are processed on a rolling basis. Application fee: $75 ($100 for international students). Electronic applications accepted. *Financial support:* In 2006–07, 40 students received support, including research assistantships with full and partial tuition reimbursements available (averaging $5,400 per year); career-related internships or fieldwork, Federal Work-Study, scholarships/grants, and unspecified assistantships also available. Support available to part-time students. Financial award application deadline: 6/1; financial award applicants required to submit FAFSA. *Faculty research:* Financial, hedge funds, international business, legal issues, disclosure and branding. *Unit head:* Dr. Joyce A. Strawser, Associate Dean for Undergraduate and MBA Curricula, 973-761-9225, Fax: 973-761-9217, E-mail: strawsjo@shu.edu. *Application contact:* Catherine Bianchi, Director of Graduate Admissions, 973-761-9220, Fax: 973-761-9208, E-mail: biancha@shu.edu.

Southeastern University, College of Graduate Studies, Program in Accounting, Washington, DC 20024-2788. Offers MBA. Part-time and evening/weekend programs available. *Entrance requirements:* Additional exam requirements/recommendations for international students: Required—TOEFL.

Southeast Missouri State University, School of Graduate Studies, Harrison College of Business, Cape Girardeau, MO 63701-4799. Offers accounting (MBA); environmental management (MBA); finance (MBA); general management (MBA); health administration (MBA); industrial management (MBA); international business (MBA). *Accreditation:* AACSB. Part-time and evening/weekend programs available. Postbaccalaureate distance learning degree programs offered (no on-campus study). *Faculty:* 33 full-time (10 women). *Students:* 35 full-time (18 women), 40 part-time (24 women); includes 5 minority (2 African Americans, 3 Asian Americans or Pacific Islanders), 9 international. Average age 27. 35 applicants, 86% accepted. In 2006, 23 degrees awarded. *Degree requirements:* For master's, applied research project. *Entrance requirements:* For master's, GMAT, minimum undergraduate GPA of 2.5. Additional exam requirements/recommendations for international students: Required—TOEFL (minimum score 550 paper-based; 213 computer-based). *Application deadline:* For fall admission, 8/1 for domestic students, 4/1 for international students; for spring admission, 11/21 for domestic students, 10/1 for international students. Applications are processed on a rolling basis. Application fee: $20 ($100 for international students). *Financial support:* In 2006–07, 54 students received support, including 31 research assistantships with full tuition reimbursements available (averaging $7,100 per year); career-related internships or fieldwork and unspecified assistantships also available. Financial award applicants required to submit FAFSA. *Unit head:* Dr. Kenneth Heischmidt, Director MBA Program, 573-651-2912, Fax: 573-651-5032, E-mail:

kheischmidt@semo.edu. *Application contact:* Marsha L. Arant, Senior Administrative Assistant, Office of Graduate Studies, 573-651-2192, Fax: 573-651-2001, E-mail: marant@semo.edu.

Southern Adventist University, School of Business and Management, Collegedale, TN 37315-0370. Offers accounting (MBA); administration (MS); financial services (MFS); health care administration (MBA); human resource management (MBA); management (MBA); marketing (MBA). Part-time and evening/weekend programs available. Postbaccalaureate distance learning degree programs offered (no on-campus study). *Faculty:* 7 full-time (0 women), 2 part-time/adjunct (1 woman). *Students:* 18 full-time (8 women), 66 part-time (37 women); includes 15 minority (6 African Americans, 7 Asian Americans or Pacific Islanders, 2 Hispanic Americans). Average age 35. 32 applicants, 84% accepted, 24 enrolled. In 2006, 11 degrees awarded. *Entrance requirements:* For master's, GMAT. Additional exam requirements/recommendations for international students: Required—TOEFL. *Application deadline:* For fall admission, 8/1 priority date for domestic students, 7/1 for international students; for winter admission, 12/1 priority date for domestic students, 11/1 for international students; for spring admission, 4/1 priority date for domestic students, 3/1 for international students. Applications are processed on a rolling basis. Application fee: $25. Electronic applications accepted. *Financial support:* In 2006–07, 32 students received support. Scholarships/grants available. Financial award application deadline: 9/1; financial award applicants required to submit FAFSA. *Unit head:* Dr. Don Van Ornam, Dean, 423-236-2750, Fax: 423-236-1527, E-mail: dvanorna@southern.edu. *Application contact:* Linda Wilhelm, Admissions Coordinator, 423-236-2751, Fax: 423-236-1527, E-mail: sbm@southern.edu.

Southern Illinois University Carbondale, Graduate School, College of Business and Administration, School of Accountancy, Carbondale, IL 62901-4701. Offers M Acc, PhD, JD/M Acc. *Accreditation:* AACSB. Part-time programs available. *Faculty:* 10 full-time (1 woman). *Students:* 27 full-time (16 women), 11 part-time (6 women); includes 3 minority (1 African American, 1 Asian American or Pacific Islander, 1 Hispanic American), 14 international. 29 applicants, 59% accepted, 4 enrolled. In 2006, 23 degrees awarded. *Degree requirements:* For doctorate, thesis/dissertation. *Entrance requirements:* For master's, GMAT, minimum GPA of 2.7; for doctorate, GMAT, minimum graduate GPA of 3.25. Additional exam requirements/recommendations for international students: Required—TOEFL. *Application deadline:* For fall admission, 6/15 priority date for domestic students. Applications are processed on a rolling basis. Application fee: $20. *Financial support:* In 2006–07, 15 students received support, including 6 research assistantships with full tuition reimbursements available, 6 teaching assistantships with full tuition reimbursements available; fellowships with full tuition reimbursements available, Federal Work-Study and institutionally sponsored loans also available. Support available to part-time students. Financial award application deadline: 4/1. *Faculty research:* Not-for-profit accounting, SEC regulations, computers and accounting education, taxation. *Unit head:* Dr. Marcus Odom, Director, 618-453-2289, E-mail: modom@cba.siu.edu. *Application contact:* Jeri Novara, Administrative Clerk, 618-453-1400, E-mail: jnovara@cba.siu.edu.

Southern Illinois University Edwardsville, Graduate Studies and Research, School of Business, Department of Accounting, Edwardsville, IL 62026-0001. Offers MSA. *Accreditation:* AACSB. Part-time and evening/weekend programs available. *Faculty:* 7 full-time (2 women). *Students:* 10 full-time (7 women), 10 part-time (4 women). Average age 33. 13 applicants, 77% accepted. In 2006, 19 degrees awarded. *Degree requirements:* For master's, thesis or alternative, final exam. *Entrance requirements:* For master's, GMAT. Additional exam requirements/recommendations for international students: Required—TOEFL. *Application deadline:* For fall admission, 7/20 for domestic students, 6/1 for international students; for spring admission, 12/14 for domestic students, 10/1 for international students. Application fee: $30. Electronic applications accepted. *Financial support:* Fellowships with full tuition reimbursements, research assistantships with full tuition reimbursements, teaching assistantships with full tuition reimbursements, Federal Work-Study, institutionally sponsored loans, and unspecified assistantships available. Support available to part-time students. Financial award application deadline: 3/1; financial award applicants required to submit FAFSA. *Unit head:* Dr. Michael Costigan, Chair, 618-650-2633, E-mail: mcostig@siue.edu.

Southern Methodist University, Cox School of Business, Program in Accounting, Dallas, TX 75275. Offers MSA. Part-time programs available. *Faculty:* 11 full-time (4 women), 6 part-time/adjunct (3 women). *Students:* 42 full-time (19 women), 4 part-time (2 women); includes 12 minority (2 African Americans, 9 Asian Americans or Pacific Islanders, 1 Hispanic American), 3 international. Average age 23. 65 applicants, 57% accepted. In 2006, 44 degrees awarded. *Entrance requirements:* For master's, GMAT. Additional exam requirements/recommendations for international students: Required—TOEFL. *Application deadline:* For fall admission, 5/15 priority date for domestic students; for winter admission, 11/30 for domestic students. Application fee: $75. *Expenses:* Contact institution. *Financial support:* In 2006–07, 17 students received support, including 17 fellowships (averaging $3,800 per year); scholarships/grants and tuition waivers (partial) also available. Financial award application deadline: 5/15. *Faculty research:* Capital markets, taxation, business combinations, intangibles accounting, accounting history. *Unit head:* Joseph Magliolo, Head, 214-768-1678, Fax: 214-768-4099, E-mail: jmagliol@mail.cox.smu.edu. *Application contact:* Jeffrey R. Austin, Coordinator, 214-768-3630, Fax: 214-768-4099, E-mail: jraustin@mail.cox.smu.edu.

Southern New Hampshire University, School of Business, Manchester, NH 03106-1045. Offers accounting (MS); business administration (MBA, Certificate), including accounting (Certificate), business administration (MBA), finance (Certificate), forensic accounting (Certificate), human resources management (Certificate), international business (Certificate), international sport management (Certificate), leadership of not for profit organizations (Certificate), marketing (Certificate), operations management (Certificate), sport management (Certificate), taxation (Certificate); finance (MS); hospitality and tourism leadership (Certificate); information technology (MS, Certificate); information technology/international business (Certificate); integrated marketing communications (Certificate); international business (MS, DBA); marketing (MS); operations and project management (MS); organizational leadership (MS); project management (Certificate); sport management (MS); MBA/Certificate. *Accreditation:* ACBSP. Part-time and evening/weekend programs available. Postbaccalaureate distance learning degree programs offered (no on-campus study). *Faculty:* 45 full-time, 75 part-time/adjunct. *Students:* 427 full-time (184 women), 774 part-time (428 women). Average age 32. In 2006, 682 master's, 1 doctorate awarded. Terminal master's awarded for partial completion of doctoral program. *Degree requirements:* For master's, one foreign language, thesis or alternative, comprehensive exam (for some programs); for doctorate, one foreign language, thesis/dissertation, comprehensive exam. *Entrance requirements:* For master's, minimum GPA of 2.5; for doctorate, GMAT. Additional exam requirements/recommendations for international students: Required—TOEFL (minimum score 500 paper-based). *Application deadline:* Applications are processed on a rolling basis. Application fee: $25. Electronic applications accepted. *Financial support:* Career-related internships or fieldwork, Federal Work-Study, institutionally sponsored loans, tuition waivers (partial), and unspecified assistantships available. Support available to part-time students. Financial award applicants required to submit FAFSA. *Unit head:* Dr. Martin Bradley, Dean, 603-644-3102, Fax: 603-644-3144, E-mail: m.bradley@snhu.edu. *Application contact:* Scott Durand, Director of Graduate Enrollment Services, 603-644-3102 Ext. 3338, Fax: 603-644-3144, E-mail: s.durand@snhu.edu.

See Close-Up on page 325.

Southern University and Agricultural and Mechanical College, Graduate School, College of Business, School of Accountancy, Baton Rouge, LA 70813. Offers MPA. *Degree requirements:* For master's, comprehensive exam. *Entrance requirements:* For master's, GMAT. Additional exam requirements/recommendations for international students: Required—TOEFL. *Faculty research:* Accounting theory, auditing, governmental and non-profit accounting.

Southern Utah University, School of Business, Program in Accounting, Cedar City, UT 84720-2498. Offers M Acc. Part-time programs available. *Faculty:* 5 full-time (0 women). *Students:* 22 full-time (6 women), 17 part-time (6 women); includes 1 minority (Asian American or Pacific Islander) Average age 27. 43 applicants, 81% accepted. In 2006, 23 degrees awarded. *Application deadline:* For fall admission, 8/1 priority date for domestic students. Applications are processed on a rolling basis. Application fee: $50. *Expenses:* Contact institution. Tuition and fees vary according to program. *Financial support:* In 2006–07, 5 research assistantships with full tuition reimbursements (averaging $4,916 per year) were awarded; career-related internships or fieldwork, institutionally sponsored loans, tuition waivers (full and partial), and unspecified assistantships also available. *Faculty research:* Cost accounting, intermediate accounting text, GAAP policy, statements on Standards for Accounting and Review Services (SSARS). *Application contact:* Paula Alger, Curriculum Coordinator and Adviser, 435-865-8157, Fax: 435-586-5493, E-mail: alger@suu.edu.

Southwestern Adventist University, Business Department, Graduate Program, Keene, TX 76059. Offers accounting (MBA). Part-time and evening/weekend programs available. *Degree requirements:* For master's, capstone course. *Entrance requirements:* For master's, GMAT, GRE General Test.

State University of New York at Binghamton, Graduate School, School of Management, Program in Accounting, Binghamton, NY 13902-6000. Offers MS, PhD. Evening/weekend programs available. *Students:* 34 full-time (24 women), 1 part-time; includes 5 minority (all Asian Americans or Pacific Islanders), 20 international. Average age 28. 65 applicants, 62% accepted. In 2006, 13 degrees awarded. *Degree requirements:* For doctorate, thesis/dissertation. *Entrance requirements:* For master's and doctorate, GMAT. Additional exam requirements/recommendations for international students: Required—TOEFL. *Application deadline:* For fall admission, 4/15 priority date for domestic students, 1/15 priority date for international students; for spring admission, 11/1 for domestic students, 10/1 priority date for international students. Applications are processed on a rolling basis. Application fee: $60. Electronic applications accepted. *Financial support:* In 2006–07, 5 students received support, including 5 teaching assistantships with full tuition reimbursements available (averaging $5,940 per year); fellowships, research assistantships, career-related internships or fieldwork, Federal Work-Study, institutionally sponsored loans, and unspecified assistantships also available. Support available to part-time students. Financial award application deadline: 2/15. *Unit head:* John Barden, Professor, 607-777-2306, E-mail: jbarden@binghamton.edu.

State University of New York at Fredonia, Graduate Studies, Department of Business Administration, Fredonia, NY 14063-1136. Offers accounting (MS). *Faculty:* 2 full-time (0 women). In 2006, 1 degree awarded. *Application deadline:* For fall admission, 8/5 for domestic students; for spring admission, 12/1 for domestic students. Application fee: $50. *Expenses:* Tuition, state resident: full-time $6,900; part-time $288 per credit hour. Tuition, nonresident: full-time $10,920; part-time $455 per credit hour. Required fees: $1,132; $47 per credit hour. *Financial support:* In 2006–07, 1 teaching assistantship (averaging $6,500 per year) was awarded; research assistantships, career-related internships or fieldwork and tuition waivers (full and partial) also available. Support available to part-time students. *Unit head:* Dr. Mojtaba Seyedian, Chair, 716-673-4603, E-mail: mojtaba.seyedian@fredonia.edu.

State University of New York at New Paltz, Graduate School, School of Business, New Paltz, NY 12561. Offers business administration (MBA); public accountancy (MBA). Part-time and evening/weekend programs available. *Faculty:* 25 full-time (6 women), 4 part-time/adjunct (1 woman). *Students:* 58 full-time (29 women), 48 part-time (24 women); includes 17 minority (3 African Americans, 11 Asian Americans or Pacific Islanders, 3 Hispanic Americans), 31 international. Average age 30. In 2006, 51 degrees awarded. *Entrance requirements:* For master's, GMAT, minimum GPA of 3.0. Additional exam requirements/recommendations for international students: Required—TOEFL (minimum score 550 paper-based; 213 computer-based; 80 iBT). *Application deadline:* For fall admission, 5/15 priority date for domestic students, 5/15 for international students; for spring admission, 11/15 for domestic and international students. Applications are processed on a rolling basis. Application fee: $50. Electronic applications accepted. *Expenses:* Contact institution. *Financial support:* In 2006–07, 14 students received support, including 8 research assistantships with partial tuition reimbursements available (averaging $5,000 per year), 1 teaching assistantship with partial tuition reimbursement available (averaging $5,000 per year). *Unit head:* Dr. Hadi Salavitabar, Dean, 845-257-3720, E-mail: mba@newpaltz.edu. *Application contact:* Rania Al-Haddad, Coordinator, 845-257-2968, E-mail: mba@newpaltz.edu.

State University of New York College at Old Westbury, Program in Accounting, Old Westbury, NY 11568-0210. Offers accounting (MS); taxation and finance (MS). Part-time and evening/weekend programs available. *Faculty:* 7 full-time (2 women), 2 part-time/adjunct (0 women). *Students:* 22 full-time (9 women), 17 part-time (12 women); includes 7 minority (3 African Americans, 3 Asian Americans or Pacific Islanders, 1 Hispanic American), 2 international. Average age 33. 37 applicants, 35% accepted, 10 enrolled. In 2006, 9 degrees awarded. *Entrance requirements:* For master's, GMAT, 2 letters of recommendation. Additional exam requirements/recommendations for international students: Required—TOEFL (minimum score 550 paper-based; 213 computer-based). *Application deadline:* For fall admission, 6/15 priority date for domestic students; for spring admission, 11/15 priority date for domestic students. Applications are processed on a rolling basis. Application fee: $50. Electronic applications accepted. *Expenses:* Tuition, state resident: full-time $6,900; part-time $288 per credit. Tuition, nonresident: full-time $10,920; part-time $455 per credit. Required fees: $491; $56 per credit. Part-time tuition and fees vary according to course load. *Faculty research:* Corporate governance, asset pricing, corporate finance, hedge funds, net-for-front accounting. *Unit head:* Dr. James M. Fornaro, Director of Graduate Business Programs, 516-876-2883, E-mail: fornaroj@oldwestbury.edu. *Application contact:* Philip D'Angelo, Graduate Admissions Office, 516-876-3073, E-mail: enroll@oldwestbury.edu.

See Close-Up on page 457.

State University of New York Institute of Technology, School of Business, Program in Accountancy, Utica, NY 13504-3050. Offers MS. Part-time and evening/weekend programs available. Postbaccalaureate distance learning degree programs offered (no on-campus study). *Faculty:* 5 full-time (2 women). *Students:* 14 full-time (8 women), 29 part-time (17 women); includes 1 African American, 6 Asian Americans or Pacific Islanders, 1 Hispanic American, 1 international. *Degree requirements:* For master's, capstone courses. *Entrance requirements:* For master's, GMAT, minimum GPA of 3.0, letters of recommendation. Additional exam requirements/recommendations for international students: Required—TOEFL (minimum score 550 paper-based; 213 computer-based). *Application deadline:* For fall admission, 6/15 priority date for domestic students. Applications are processed on a rolling basis. Application fee: $50. *Expenses:* Tuition, state resident: full-time $3,452; part-time $288 per credit hour. Tuition, nonresident: full-time $10,920; part-time $455 per credit hour. Required fees: $927; $38 per credit hour. *Financial support:* In 2006–07, 1 research assistantship (averaging $7,500 per year) was awarded; career-related internships or fieldwork, Federal Work-Study, scholarships/grants, health care benefits, and unspecified assistantships also available. Financial award application deadline: 6/1; financial award applicants required to submit FAFSA. *Faculty research:* Cash flows, accounting earnings, stock price analysis. *Unit head:* Dr. Hoseoup Lee, Unit Head, 315-792-7130. *Application contact:* Marybeth Lyons, Director of Admissions, 315-792-7500, Fax: 315-792-7837, E-mail: smbl@sunyit.edu.

Stephen F. Austin State University, Graduate School, College of Business, Program in Professional Accountancy, Nacogdoches, TX 75962. Offers MPAC. Students admitted at the undergraduate level. *Degree requirements:* For master's, comprehensive exam. *Entrance requirements:* For master's, GMAT. Additional exam requirements/recommendations for international students: Required—TOEFL.

Stetson University, School of Business Administration, Program in Accounting, DeLand, FL 32723. Offers M Acc. *Accreditation:* AACSB. Part-time programs available. *Students:* 12 full-time (6 women), 7 part-time (4 women); includes 3 minority (2 African Americans, 1 Hispanic American), 2 international. Average age 26. In 2006, 8 degrees awarded. *Entrance requirements:* For master's, GMAT. *Application deadline:* For fall admission, 7/1 for domestic students. Application fee: $25. *Financial support:* In 2006–07, 3 research assistantships were

Accounting

Stetson University *(continued)*
awarded; Federal Work-Study and institutionally sponsored loans also available. Support available to part-time students. Financial award application deadline: 3/15. *Unit head:* Dr. Frank DeZoort, Director, 386-822-7410. *Application contact:* Jeanne Bosco, Administrative Assistant, 386-822-7410, Fax: 386-822-7413, E-mail: jbosco@stetson.edu.

Stonehill College, Program in Accounting, Easton, MA 02357-5510. Offers accountancy (MSA). Part-time programs available. *Faculty:* 9 full-time (3 women). *Students:* 10 full-time (7 women), 5 part-time (3 women); includes 3 minority (1 African American, 1 Asian American or Pacific Islander, 1 Hispanic American). Average age 28. 13 applicants, 100% accepted, 7 enrolled. In 2006, 18 degrees awarded. *Degree requirements:* For master's, registration. *Entrance requirements:* For master's, GMAT, letters of reference. Additional exam requirements/recommendations for international students: Required—TOEFL. *Application deadline:* For fall admission, 3/1 for domestic and international students; for spring admission, 10/1 for domestic and international students. Application fee: $50. *Expenses:* Tuition: Full-time $27,330; part-time $2,733 per course. Required fees: $25 per semester. Part-time tuition and fees vary according to course load. *Financial support:* Career-related internships or fieldwork, Federal Work-Study, scholarships/grants, and health care benefits available. Support available to part-time students. Financial award application deadline: 3/15; financial award applicants required to submit FAFSA. *Faculty research:* Accounting information systems, accounting education, cross-cultural management, outsourcing stock market reaction to accounting information. *Unit head:* Richard J. Anderson, Director, 508-565-1224, E-mail: jranderson@stonehill.edu. *Application contact:* Brian P. Murphy, Dean of Admissions and Enrollment, 508-565-1373, Fax: 508-565-1545, E-mail: admissions@stonehill.edu.

Stratford University, Graduate Programs, Falls Church, VA 22043. Offers business administration (MBA); enterprise business management (MS); entrepreneurial business (MS); information systems (MS); software engineering (MS). Part-time and evening/weekend programs available. Postbaccalaureate distance learning degree programs offered (minimal on-campus study). *Entrance requirements:* Additional exam requirements/recommendations for international students: Required—TOEFL (minimum score 500 paper-based). Electronic applications accepted.

Strayer University, Graduate Studies, Washington, DC 20005-2603. Offers accounting (MS); business administration (MBA); communications technology (MS); information systems (MS); management information systems (MS). Part-time and evening/weekend programs available. Postbaccalaureate distance learning degree programs offered (minimal on-campus study). *Degree requirements:* For master's, thesis. *Entrance requirements:* For master's, GMAT, GRE General Test, bachelor's degree from an accredited college or university, minimum undergraduate GPA of 2.75. Electronic applications accepted.

Suffolk University, College of Arts and Sciences, Department of Education and Human Services, Program in Adult and Organizational Learning, Boston, MA 02108-2770. Offers adult and organizational learning (MS); human resources (MS, CAGS); instructional design (CAGS); organizational development (CAGS); organizational learning (CAGS). Part-time and evening/weekend programs available. *Entrance requirements:* For master's, GRE General Test or MAT. *Application deadline:* For fall admission, 6/15 priority date for domestic students, 6/15 for international students; for spring admission, 11/15 priority date for domestic students, 11/15 for international students. Applications are processed on a rolling basis. Application fee: $35. *Financial support:* Fellowships available. Financial award application deadline: 4/1. *Faculty research:* Adult training methods, adult learning theory, instructional design, learning and teaching styles, systems thinking. *Unit head:* Dr. Christine M. Westphal, Graduate Program Director, 617-994-6455, Fax: 617-722-9440, E-mail: cwestphal@suffolk.edu. *Application contact:* Judith Reynolds, Director of Graduate Admissions, 617-573-8302, Fax: 617-523-0116, E-mail: grad.admission@suffolk.edu.

Suffolk University, Sawyer Business School, Department of Accounting, Boston, MA 02108-2770. Offers accounting (MSA, GDPA); taxation (MST); GDPA/MST; MBA/GDPA; MBA/MSA; MBA/MST. *Accreditation:* AACSB. Part-time and evening/weekend programs available. *Faculty:* 17 full-time (4 women), 7 part-time/adjunct (6 women). *Students:* 39 full-time (28 women), 187 part-time (95 women); includes 27 minority (11 African Americans, 15 Asian Americans or Pacific Islanders, 1 Hispanic American), 45 international. Average age 30. 129 applicants, 84% accepted, 68 enrolled. In 2006, 46 master's, 3 other advanced degrees awarded. *Entrance requirements:* For master's, GMAT. Additional exam requirements/recommendations for international students: Required—TOEFL (minimum score 550 paper-based; 213 computer-based; 80 iBT). *Application deadline:* For fall admission, 6/15 priority date for domestic students, 6/15 for international students; for spring admission, 11/1 priority date for domestic students, 11/1 for international students. Applications are processed on a rolling basis. Application fee: $50. Electronic applications accepted. *Expenses: Contact institution. Financial support:* In 2006–07, 73 fellowships with full and partial tuition reimbursements (averaging $15,118 per year) were awarded; career-related internships or fieldwork, Federal Work-Study, and institutionally sponsored loans also available. Support available to part-time students. Financial award application deadline: 4/1; financial award applicants required to submit CSS PROFILE. *Faculty research:* Tax policy, tax research, decision making in accounting, accounting information systems, capital markets and strategic planning. *Unit head:* Dr. Morris McInnes, Chair, 617-573-8339, Fax: 617-573-8345, E-mail: mmcinnes@suffolk.edu. *Application contact:* Judith Reynolds, Director of Graduate Admissions, 617-573-8302, Fax: 617-523-0116, E-mail: grad.admission@suffolk.edu.

Swedish Institute, College of Health Sciences, Graduate Program, New York, NY 10001-6700. Offers acupuncture (MS). *Accreditation:* ACAOM. Part-time and evening/weekend programs available. *Faculty:* 6 full-time (4 women), 32 part-time/adjunct (16 women). *Students:* 71 full-time (48 women), 40 part-time (29 women); includes 30 minority (3 African Americans, 19 Asian Americans or Pacific Islanders, 8 Hispanic Americans). Average age 36. 36 applicants, 67% accepted, 20 enrolled. In 2006, 19 degrees awarded. *Median time to degree:* Master's–3 years full-time, 5 years part-time. *Entrance requirements:* Additional exam requirements/recommendations for international students: Required—TOEFL (minimum score 72 iBT). *Application deadline:* For fall admission, 11/9 priority date for domestic and international students; for winter admission, 7/13 priority date for domestic and international students. Application fee: $50. *Expenses:* Tuition: Full-time $8,700. Required fees: $180. One-time fee: $50 full-time. Tuition and fees vary according to class time, course load and student level. *Financial support:* In 2006–07, 3 teaching assistantships with full and partial tuition reimbursements were awarded.

Syracuse University, Martin J. Whitman School of Management, PhD Program in Business Administration, Syracuse, NY 13244. Offers accounting (PhD); finance (PhD); management information systems (PhD); managerial statistics (PhD); marketing (PhD); operations management (PhD); organizational behavior (PhD); strategy and human resources (PhD); supply chain management (PhD). *Faculty:* 71 full-time (16 women), 2 part-time/adjunct (1 woman). *Students:* 34 full-time (10 women); includes 1 minority (African American), 24 international. Average age 31. 89 applicants, 8% accepted, 4 enrolled. In 2006, 8 degrees awarded. *Degree requirements:* For doctorate, thesis/dissertation, summer research paper, comprehensive exam, registration. *Entrance requirements:* For doctorate, GMAT, 3 recommendations. Additional exam requirements/recommendations for international students: Required—TOEFL (minimum score 600 paper-based; 250 computer-based; 100 iBT). *Application deadline:* For fall admission, 1/30 priority date for domestic students. Applications are processed on a rolling basis. Application fee: $75. Electronic applications accepted. *Expenses:* Tuition: Full-time $16,920; part-time $940 per credit hour. Required fees: $930; $930 per year. *Financial support:* In 2006–07, 1 fellowship with full tuition reimbursement (averaging $19,000 per year), 26 teaching assistantships with full tuition reimbursements (averaging $16,500 per year) were awarded; research assistantships with full tuition reimbursements, health care benefits and unspecified assistantships also available. Financial award application deadline: 1/30. *Faculty research:* Marketing models, market microstructure, supply chain, auditing, corporate governance. *Unit head:* Dr. Ravi Dharwadkar, Director of the PhD Program, 315-443-3386, E-mail: rdharwad@syr.edu. *Application contact:* Shannon Hiemstra, Assistant Director for PhD and Research Programs, 315-443-3549, Fax: 315-443-3671, E-mail: srhiemst@syr.edu.

Syracuse University, Martin J. Whitman School of Management, Program in Accounting, Syracuse, NY 13244. Offers MS Acct, JD/MS Acct. Postbaccalaureate distance learning degree programs offered (minimal on-campus study). *Faculty:* 71 full-time (16 women), 2 part-time/adjunct (1 woman). *Students:* 9 full-time (4 women), 4 part-time (1 woman), 4 international. 59 applicants, 17% accepted, 7 enrolled. In 2006, 4 degrees awarded. *Degree requirements:* For master's, registration. *Entrance requirements:* For master's, GMAT, 2 letters of recommendation, bachelor's degree in accounting. Additional exam requirements/recommendations for international students: Required—TOEFL (minimum score 600 paper-based; 250 computer-based; 100 iBT). *Application deadline:* For fall admission, 1/15 priority date for domestic and international students; for winter admission, 11/1 for domestic and international students. Applications are processed on a rolling basis. Application fee: $75. Electronic applications accepted. *Expenses:* Tuition: Full-time $16,920; part-time $940 per credit hour. Required fees: $930; $930 per year. *Financial support:* In 2006–07, 5 students received support; fellowships with full tuition reimbursements available, teaching assistantships with partial tuition reimbursements available, career-related internships or fieldwork, scholarships/grants, and tuition waivers (partial) available. Financial award application deadline: 3/1. *Unit head:* Dr. Ravi Shukla, Associate Dean for MBA and MS Programs, 315-443-3576, Fax: 315-443-9517, E-mail: rkshukla@syr.edu. *Application contact:* Carol J. Swanberg, Director of Graduate Admissions and Financial Aid, 315-443-9214, Fax: 315-443-9517, E-mail: mbainfo@syr.edu.

Syracuse University, Martin J. Whitman School of Management, Program in Business Administration, Syracuse, NY 13244. Offers accounting (MBA); entrepreneurship (MBA); finance (MBA); marketing (MBA); supply chain management (MBA). Part-time programs available. Postbaccalaureate distance learning degree programs offered (minimal on-campus study). *Faculty:* 71 full-time (16 women), 2 part-time/adjunct (1 woman). *Students:* 70 full-time (21 women), 279 part-time (84 women); includes 83 minority (44 African Americans, 33 Asian Americans or Pacific Islanders, 6 Hispanic Americans), 36 international. Average age 27. 227 applicants, 37% accepted, 27 enrolled. In 2006, 140 degrees awarded. *Degree requirements:* For master's, registration. *Entrance requirements:* For master's, GMAT, 2 letters of recommendation, bachelor's degree. Additional exam requirements/recommendations for international students: Required—TOEFL (minimum score 600 paper-based; 250 computer-based; 100 iBT). *Application deadline:* For fall admission, 1/15 priority date for domestic and international students. Applications are processed on a rolling basis. Application fee: $75. Electronic applications accepted. *Expenses:* Tuition: Full-time $16,920; part-time $940 per credit hour. Required fees: $930; $930 per year. *Financial support:* In 2006–07, 17 students received support; fellowships with full and partial tuition reimbursements available, teaching assistantships with partial tuition reimbursements available, career-related internships or fieldwork, scholarships/grants, tuition waivers (partial), unspecified assistantships, and paid hourly positions available. Support available to part-time students. Financial award application deadline: 3/1. *Unit head:* Dr. Ravi Shukla, Associate Dean for MBA and MS Programs, 315-443-3576, Fax: 315-443-9517, E-mail: rkshukla@syr.edu. *Application contact:* Carol J. Swanberg, Director of Graduate Admissions and Financial Aid, 315-443-9214, Fax: 315-443-9517, E-mail: mbainfo@syr.edu.

Tabor College, Graduate Program, Hillsboro, KS 67063. Offers accounting (MBA). Program offered at the Wichita campus only.

Tarleton State University, College of Graduate Studies, College of Business Administration, Department of Accounting, Finance and Economics, Stephenville, TX 76402. Offers business administration (MBA). Part-time and evening/weekend programs available. *Faculty:* 10 full-time (1 woman), 1 (woman) part-time/adjunct. *Students:* 50 full-time (30 women), 138 part-time (74 women); includes 41 minority (28 African Americans, 3 Asian Americans or Pacific Islanders, 10 Hispanic Americans), 19 international. Average age 35. *Entrance requirements:* For master's, GRE or GMAT, minimum GPA of 3.0. *Application deadline:* For fall admission, 8/5 priority date for domestic students; for spring admission, 12/1 priority date for domestic students. Applications are processed on a rolling basis. Electronic applications accepted. *Financial support:* Research assistantships, teaching assistantships available. *Unit head:* Dr. Sue Cullers, Head, 254-968-9913.

Temple University, Graduate School, Fox School of Business and Management, Doctoral Programs in Business, Philadelphia, PA 19122-6096. Offers accounting (PhD); economics (PhD); finance (PhD); general and strategic management (PhD); healthcare management (PhD); human resource administration (PhD); international business administration (PhD); management information systems (PhD); management science/operations research (PhD); marketing (PhD); risk, insurance, and health-care management (PhD); statistics (PhD); tourism (PhD). *Accreditation:* AACSB. *Entrance requirements:* For doctorate, GRE General Test, minimum GPA of 3.0, master's degree. Additional exam requirements/recommendations for international students: Required—TOEFL. *Expenses:* Tuition, state resident: full-time $12,264; part-time $511 per credit. Tuition, nonresident: full-time $17,904; part-time $746 per credit. Required fees: $84 per course. Tuition and fees vary according to program.

Temple University, Graduate School, Fox School of Business and Management, Masters Programs in Business, MBA Programs, Philadelphia, PA 19122-6096. Offers accounting (MBA); business administration (EMBA, MBA); e-business (MBA); economics (MBA); finance (MBA); general and strategic management (MBA); healthcare management (MBA); human resource administration (MBA); international business (IMBA); management information systems (MBA); management science/operations management (MBA); marketing (MBA); risk management and insurance (MBA); statistics (MBA). EMBA offered in Philadelphia, PA and Tokyo, Japan. *Accreditation:* AACSB. *Entrance requirements:* For master's, GMAT, minimum undergraduate GPA of 3.0. Additional exam requirements/recommendations for international students: Required—TOEFL. *Expenses:* Tuition, state resident: full-time $12,264; part-time $511 per credit. Tuition, nonresident: full-time $17,904; part-time $746 per credit. Required fees: $84 per course. Tuition and fees vary according to program.

Temple University, Graduate School, Fox School of Business and Management, Masters Programs in Business, MS Programs, Philadelphia, PA 19122-6096. Offers accounting and financial management (MS); actuarial science (MS); e-business (MS); finance (MS); healthcare financial management (MS); human resource administration (MS); management information systems (MS); management science/operations management (MS); marketing (MS); statistics (MS). *Accreditation:* AACSB. *Entrance requirements:* For master's, GRE General Test, minimum undergraduate GPA of 3.0. Additional exam requirements/recommendations for international students: Required—TOEFL. *Expenses:* Tuition, state resident: full-time $12,264; part-time $511 per credit. Tuition, nonresident: full-time $17,904; part-time $746 per credit. Required fees: $84 per course. Tuition and fees vary according to program.

Texas A&M International University, Office of Graduate Studies and Research, College of Business Administration, Division of International Banking and Finance Studies, Laredo, TX 78041-1900. Offers accounting (MP Acc); international banking (MBA). *Faculty:* 9 full-time (1 woman), 2 part-time/adjunct (0 women). *Students:* 23 full-time (8 women), 21 part-time (7 women); includes 28 minority (all Hispanic Americans), 1 international. Average age 28. 25 applicants, 68% accepted, 16 enrolled. In 2006, 25 degrees awarded. *Entrance requirements:* For master's, GMAT or GRE General Test. Additional exam requirements/recommendations for international students: Required—TOEFL (minimum score 550 paper-based; 213 computer-based). *Application deadline:* For fall admission, 7/15 priority date for domestic students; for spring admission, 11/12 for domestic students. Applications are processed on a rolling basis. Application fee: $25. *Expenses:* Tuition, state resident: full-time $1,580. Tuition, nonresident: full-time $5,432. Required fees: $3,808. *Financial support:* In 2006–07, 21 students received support. *Unit head:* Dr. Antonio Rodriguez, Chair, 956-326-2490, Fax: 956-326-2481. *Application contact:* Imelda Lopez, Graduate Admissions Counselor, 956-326-2485, Fax: 956-326-2459, E-mail: lopez@tamiu.edu.

Texas A&M University, Mays Business School, Department of Accounting, College Station, TX 77843. Offers MS, PhD. *Accreditation:* AACSB. *Faculty:* 35 full-time (13 women), 2 part-time/adjunct (1 woman). *Students:* 143 full-time (82 women). Average age 27. In 2006, 116 master's, 1 doctorate awarded. Terminal master's awarded for partial completion of doctoral program. *Degree requirements:* For master's, comprehensive exam; for doctorate, thesis/dissertation. *Entrance requirements:* For master's, GMAT; for doctorate, GMAT or GRE General Test. Additional exam requirements/recommendations for international students: Required—TOEFL. *Application deadline:* For fall admission, 3/1 priority date for domestic students; for spring admission, 8/1 for domestic students. Applications are processed on a rolling basis. Application fee: $50 ($75 for international students). *Expenses:* Tuition, state resident: full-time $4,697. Tuition, nonresident: full-time $11,297. Required fees: $2,272. *Financial support:* In 2006–07, 100 students received support; fellowships, research assistantships, teaching assistantships, career-related internships or fieldwork and institutionally sponsored loans available. Financial award application deadline: 2/1. *Faculty research:* Financial reporting, taxation management, decision making, accounting information systems, government accounting. *Unit head:* Dr. James J. Benjamin, Head, 979-845-5014. *Application contact:* Dr. R. Austin Daily, Adviser, 979-862-1944, E-mail: rad@tamu.edu.

Texas A&M University–Corpus Christi, Graduate Studies and Research, College of Business, Corpus Christi, TX 78412-5503. Offers accounting (M Acc); health care administration (MBA); international business (MBA). *Accreditation:* AACSB. Part-time and evening/weekend programs available. *Degree requirements:* For master's, thesis (for some programs), comprehensive exam, registration. *Entrance requirements:* For master's, GMAT. Additional exam requirements/recommendations for international students: Required—TOEFL. Electronic applications accepted.

Texas A&M University–Texarkana, Graduate Studies and Research, College of Business, Texarkana, TX 75505-5518. Offers accounting (MSA); business administration (MBA, MS). Part-time and evening/weekend programs available. *Students:* 178. Average age 32. 81 applicants, 91% accepted. In 2006, 87 degrees awarded. *Degree requirements:* For master's, thesis or alternative. *Entrance requirements:* For master's, minimum GPA of 2.5 in last 60 hours of bachelor's degree. Additional exam requirements/recommendations for international students: Required—TOEFL. *Application deadline:* For fall admission, 7/15 priority date for domestic students; for spring admission, 12/1 priority date for domestic students. Applications are processed on a rolling basis. Application fee: $0 ($25 for international students). Electronic applications accepted. *Expenses:* Tuition, state resident: part-time $112 per credit hour. Tuition, nonresident: part-time $387 per credit hour. Required fees: $8 per credit hour. $8 per term. *Financial support:* Career-related internships or fieldwork and scholarships/grants available. Financial award application deadline: 3/1; financial award applicants required to submit FAFSA. *Unit head:* Dr. Edward Bashaw, Dean, 903-223-3106, E-mail: edward.bashaw@tamut.edu. *Application contact:* Patricia E. Black, Director of Admissions and Registrar, 903-223-3068, Fax: 903-223-3140, E-mail: pat.black@tamut.edu.

Texas Christian University, M. J. Neeley School of Business, Program in Accounting, Fort Worth, TX 76129-0002. Offers M Ac. *Accreditation:* AACSB. *Entrance requirements:* For master's, GMAT, 6 hours of course work in economics, 3 hours of course work in college algebra. Additional exam requirements/recommendations for international students: Required—TOEFL. *Application deadline:* For fall admission, 4/30 priority date for domestic students. Applications are processed on a rolling basis. Application fee: $50. *Expenses:* Tuition: Part-time $800 per credit hour. *Financial support:* Application deadline: 5/1. *Unit head:* Dr. Bob Vigeland, Chairperson, 817-257-7223. *Application contact:* Peggy Conway, Director, MBA Admissions, 817-257-7531, Fax: 817-257-6431, E-mail: mbainfo@tcu.edu.

Texas State University-San Marcos, Graduate School, Emmett & Miriam McCoy College of Business Administration, Program in Accounting, San Marcos, TX 78666. Offers M Acy. Part-time programs available. *Faculty:* 8 full-time (5 women). *Students:* 97 full-time (48 women), 44 part-time (29 women); includes 37 minority (5 African Americans, 1 American Indian/Alaska Native, 14 Asian Americans or Pacific Islanders, 17 Hispanic Americans), 14 international. Average age 28. 44 applicants, 93% accepted, 36 enrolled. In 2006, 42 degrees awarded. *Degree requirements:* For master's, comprehensive exam. *Entrance requirements:* For master's, GMAT, minimum GPA of 2.0 in last 60 hours of undergraduate work. *Application deadline:* For fall admission, 6/1 for domestic and international students; for spring admission, 10/1 for domestic and international students. Applications are processed on a rolling basis. Application fee: $40 ($90 for international students). *Financial support:* In 2006–07, 78 students received support, including 3 research assistantships (averaging $4,977 per year), 8 teaching assistantships (averaging $5,161 per year); Federal Work-Study and institutionally sponsored loans also available. Support available to part-time students. Financial award application deadline: 4/1; financial award applicants required to submit FAFSA. *Faculty research:* Tax and estate planning, foreign exchange risk. *Unit head:* Dr. Robert Davis, Associate Dean, 512-245-3692, Fax: 512-245-7973, E-mail: rd23@txstate.edu.

Texas Tech University, Jerry S. Rawls College of Business Administration, Area of Accounting, Lubbock, TX 79409. Offers accounting (PhD); audit/financial reporting (MSA); JD/MSA. *Accreditation:* AACSB. Part-time programs available. *Faculty:* 13 full-time (3 women). *Students:* 114 full-time (58 women); includes 8 minority (2 American Indian/Alaska Native, 2 Asian Americans or Pacific Islanders, 4 Hispanic Americans), 6 international. Average age 24. 99 applicants, 73% accepted, 69 enrolled. In 2006, 54 master's, 3 doctorates awarded. Terminal master's awarded for partial completion of doctoral program. *Degree requirements:* For master's, capstone course; for doctorate, thesis/dissertation, qualifying exams, comprehensive exam, registration. *Entrance requirements:* For master's and doctorate, GMAT, holistic profile of academic credentials. Additional exam requirements/recommendations for international students: Required—TOEFL (minimum score 550 paper-based; 213 computer-based; 79 iBT). *Application deadline:* For fall admission, 7/1 priority date for domestic students, 3/1 priority date for international students; for spring admission, 11/1 priority date for domestic students, 9/1 priority date for international students. Applications are processed on a rolling basis. Application fee: $50 ($60 for international students). Electronic applications accepted. *Expenses:* Tuition, state resident: full-time $4,440. Tuition, nonresident: full-time $11,040. Required fees: $2,136. *Financial support:* In 2006–07, 10 research assistantships (averaging $8,000 per year), 7 teaching assistantships (averaging $16,930 per year) were awarded; fellowships, career-related internships or fieldwork, Federal Work-Study, scholarships/grants, health care benefits, and unspecified assistantships also available. Financial award applicants required to submit FAFSA. *Faculty research:* Governmental and nonprofit accounting, managerial and financial accounting. *Unit head:* Dr. Linda Nichols, Area Coordinator, 806-742-1541, Fax: 806-742-3182, E-mail: linda.nichols@ttu.edu. *Application contact:* Cynthia D. Barnes, Director, Graduate Services Center, 806-742-3184, Fax: 806-742-3958, E-mail: ba_grad@ttu.edu.

Towson University, Joint University of Baltimore/Towson University (UB/Towson) MBA Program, Program in Accounting and Business Advisory Services, Towson, MD 21252-0001. Offers MS. *Accreditation:* AACSB. Part-time and evening/weekend programs available. *Students:* 15 full-time (10 women), 18 part-time (15 women); includes 2 African Americans, 2 Asian Americans or Pacific Islanders, 9 international. 31 applicants, 52% accepted, 10 enrolled. In 2006, 4 degrees awarded. *Entrance requirements:* For master's, GMAT, GRE General Test, minimum GPA of 3.0. *Application deadline:* Applications are processed on a rolling basis. Application fee: $50. Electronic applications accepted. *Expenses:* Tuition, state resident: part-time $275 per unit. Tuition, nonresident: part-time $577 per unit. Required fees: $72 per unit. *Unit head:* Martin Freedman, Graduate Program Director, 410-704-4143, E-mail: mfreedman@towson.edu. *Application contact:* 410-704-2501, Fax: 410-704-4675, E-mail: grads@towson.edu.

Trinity University, Department of Business Administration, San Antonio, TX 78212-7200. Offers accounting (MS). *Accreditation:* AACSB. Part-time programs available. *Faculty:* 4 full-time (2 women). *Students:* 21 full-time (13 women), 2 part-time (1 woman); includes 4 minority (all Hispanic Americans), 1 international. Average age 23. In 2006, 27 degrees awarded. *Entrance requirements:* For master's, GMAT, minimum GPA of 3.0, course work in accounting and business law. *Application deadline:* For fall admission, 2/1 priority date for domestic students. Application fee: $40. *Financial support:* In 2006–07, 12 research assistantships were awarded. Financial award application deadline: 4/1. *Unit head:* Dr. Petrea K. Sandlin, Director of the Accounting Program, 210-999-7296, Fax: 210-999-8134, E-mail: psandlin@trinity.edu.

Truman State University, Graduate School, Division of Business and Accountancy, Program in Accountancy, Kirksville, MO 63501-4221. Offers accounting (M Ac). *Accreditation:* AACSB. *Degree requirements:* For master's, comprehensive exam. *Entrance requirements:* For master's, GMAT, minimum GPA of 3.0. Additional exam requirements/recommendations for international students: Required—TOEFL (minimum score 550 paper-based; 213 computer-based). Electronic applications accepted.

Universidad Central del Este, Graduate School, San Pedro de Macoris, Dominican Republic. Offers accounting (M Ad); administration (M Ad); architecture (M Arch); civil engineering (ME); electromechanical engineering (ME); human resources (M Ad); industrial engineering (ME); public health (MPH). *Entrance requirements:* For master's, letters of recommendation.

Universidad del Este, Graduate School, Carolina, PR 00983. Offers accounting (MBA); administration (M Ed); criminal justice and criminology (MA); education (M Ed); elementary education (M Ed); human resources (MBA); management (MBA); social work (MA); teaching English (M Ed); teaching Spanish (M Ed).

Universidad del Turabo, Graduate Programs, School in Business Administration, Program in Accounting, Gurabo, PR 00778-3030. Offers MBA. Part-time and evening/weekend programs available. *Entrance requirements:* For master's, GRE, EXADEP, interview.

Universidad Metropolitana, School of Business Administration, Program in Accounting, San Juan, PR 00928-1150. Offers MBA. Part-time programs available. *Degree requirements:* For master's, thesis or alternative. *Entrance requirements:* For master's, GMAT, PAEG, interview. Electronic applications accepted.

Universidad Metropolitana, School of Business Administration, Program in Public Accounting, San Juan, PR 00928-1150. Offers Certificate. Part-time programs available.

Universidad Nacional Pedro Henriquez Urena, Graduate School, Santo Domingo, Dominican Republic. Offers accounting and auditing (M Acct); animal production (M Agr); business administration (MBA, PhD); Caribbean tropical architecture (M Arch); conservation of monuments and cultural goods (M Arch); economics (M Econ); education (PhD); environmental engineering (MEE); horticulture (M Agr); hospital administration (PhD); humanities (PhD); international relations (MPS); management of natural resources (MNRM); project management (M Man, MPM); public administration (MPS); sanitary engineering (ME); social science (PhD); veterinary medicine (DVM).

Université de Sherbrooke, Faculty of Administration, Program in Accounting, Sherbrooke, QC J1K 2R1, Canada. Offers M Sc.

Université du Québec à Montréal, Graduate Programs, Program in Accounting, Montréal, QC H3C 3P8, Canada. Offers M Sc, MPA, Diploma. Part-time programs available. *Degree requirements:* For master's, thesis (for some programs). *Entrance requirements:* For master's, appropriate bachelor's degree or equivalent and proficiency in French.

Université du Québec à Trois-Rivières, Graduate Programs, Program in Accounting Science, Trois-Rivières, QC G9A 5H7, Canada. Offers DESS.

Université du Québec en Outaouais, Graduate Programs, Program in Accounting, Gatineau, QC J8X 3X7, Canada. Offers DESS. *Students:* 13 full-time, 1 part-time. *Application deadline:* For fall admission, 6/1 for domestic students, 3/1 for international students; for winter admission, 11/1 for domestic students, 10/1 for international students. Application fee: $30 Canadian dollars. *Unit head:* Pierre Charron, Director, 819-595-3900 Ext. 1755, Fax: 818-773-1760, E-mail: pierre.charron@uqo.ca. *Application contact:* Registrar's Office, 819-773-1850, Fax: 819-773-1835, E-mail: registraire@ugo.ca.

Université du Québec en Outaouais, Graduate Programs, Program in Executive Certified Management Accounting, Gatineau, QC J8X 3X7, Canada. Offers MBA, Diploma. *Students:* 64 full-time, 27 part-time. *Application deadline:* For fall admission, 6/1 priority date for domestic students, 3/1 for international students; for winter admission, 11/1 priority date for domestic students, 10/1 for international students. Application fee: $30. *Unit head:* Pierre Charron, Director, 819-595-3900 Ext. 1755, Fax: 818-773-1760, E-mail: pierre.charron@uqo.ca. *Application contact:* Registrar's Office, 819-773-1850, Fax: 819-773-1835, E-mail: registraire@ugo.ca.

Université Laval, Faculty of Administrative Sciences, Programs in Business Administration, Québec, QC G1K 7P4, Canada. Offers accounting (MBA); agri-food management (MBA); electronic business (MBA, Diploma); factory management and logistics (MBA); finance (MBA); firm management (MBA); information technology management (MBA); international management (MBA); management (MBA); management accounting (MBA, Diploma); marketing (MBA); modelization and organizational decision (MBA); occupational health and safety management (MBA); pharmacy management (MBA); technological entrepreneurship (Diploma). *Accreditation:* AACSB. Part-time and evening/weekend programs available. Postbaccalaureate distance learning degree programs offered (no on-campus study). *Entrance requirements:* For master's and Diploma, knowledge of French and English. Electronic applications accepted.

Université Laval, Faculty of Administrative Sciences, Programs in Public Accountancy, Québec, QC G1K 7P4, Canada. Offers MBA, Diploma. Part-time programs available. *Entrance requirements:* For master's and Diploma, knowledge of French and English. Electronic applications accepted.

University at Albany, State University of New York, School of Business, Department of Accounting, Albany, NY 12222-0001. Offers accounting (MS); taxation (MS). *Accreditation:* AACSB. *Students:* 75 full-time (41 women), 17 part-time (9 women). Average age 31. In 2006, 44 degrees awarded. *Degree requirements:* For master's, research project. *Entrance requirements:* For master's, GMAT. Additional exam requirements/recommendations for international students: Required—TOEFL (minimum score 550 paper-based; 213 computer-based). *Application deadline:* For fall admission, 3/1 priority date for domestic students, 4/1 for international students. Applications are processed on a rolling basis. Application fee: $75. Electronic applications accepted. *Expenses:* Tuition, state resident: full-time $6,900; part-time $288 per credit. Tuition, nonresident: full-time $10,920; part-time $455 per credit. Required fees: $1,139. *Financial support:* Application deadline: 4/1. *Faculty research:* Professional ethics, statistical analysis, cost management systems, accounting theory. *Unit head:* Saurva Dutta, Chair, 518-442-4978. *Application contact:* Michael DeRensis, Director, Graduate Admissions, 518-442-3980, Fax: 518-442-3922, E-mail: graduate@uamail.albany.edu.

University at Buffalo, the State University of New York, Graduate School, School of Management, Buffalo, NY 14260. Offers accounting (MS); business administration (MBA); finance (MS); information assurance (Certificate); management (PhD); management information systems (MS); supply chains and operations management (MS); Au D/MBA; JD/MBA; M Arch/MBA; MA/MBA; MD/MBA; MPH/MBA; MSW/MBA; Pharm D/MBA. *Accreditation:* AACSB. Part-time and evening/weekend programs available. *Faculty:* 65 full-time (18 women), 30 part-time/adjunct (3 women). *Students:* 493 full-time (192 women), 212 part-time (55 women); includes 53 minority (11 African Americans, 3 American Indian/Alaska Native, 31 Asian Americans or Pacific Islanders, 8 Hispanic Americans), 283 international. Average age 27. 1,058 applicants, 55% accepted, 369 enrolled. In 2006, 260 master's, 5 doctorates, 3 other advanced degrees awarded. *Degree requirements:* For doctorate, thesis/dissertation, comprehensive exam. *Entrance requirements:* For master's, GMAT, GRE General Test (all master's degrees except accounting); for doctorate, GMAT or GRE. Additional exam requirements/recommendations for

Accounting

University at Buffalo, the State University of New York (continued)
international students: Required—TOEFL (minimum score 230 computer-based). *Application deadline:* For fall admission, 6/1 priority date for domestic students, 3/1 priority date for international students. Applications are processed on a rolling basis. Application fee: $50. Electronic applications accepted. *Expenses: Contact institution. Financial support:* In 2006–07, 91 students received support, including 17 fellowships with full and partial tuition reimbursements available (averaging $3,917 per year), 38 research assistantships with full and partial tuition reimbursements available (averaging $11,907 per year), 26 teaching assistantships with full and partial tuition reimbursements available (averaging $7,571 per year); career-related internships or fieldwork, Federal Work-Study, institutionally sponsored loans, scholarships/grants, health care benefits, and unspecified assistantships also available. Financial award application deadline: 2/15; financial award applicants required to submit FAFSA. *Faculty research:* Information assurance, relationship marketing, global processes, credit analysis in banking, disaster mitigation and response. Total annual research expenditures: $330,551. *Unit head:* John M. Thomas, Dean, 716-645-3221, Fax: 716-645-5926, E-mail: jmthomas@buffalo.edu. *Application contact:* David W. Frasier, Administrative Director of Graduate Programs and Assistant Dean, 716-645-3204, Fax: 716-645-2341, E-mail: davidf@buffalo.edu.

The University of Akron, Graduate School, College of Business Administration, School of Accountancy, Akron, OH 44325. Offers accountancy (MS); accounting-information systems (MS); taxation (MT); JD/MT. *Accreditation:* AACSB. Part-time and evening/weekend programs available. *Faculty:* 7 full-time (1 woman), 9 part-time/adjunct (3 women). *Students:* 48 full-time (23 women), 68 part-time (35 women); includes 9 minority (2 African Americans, 4 Asian Americans or Pacific Islanders, 3 Hispanic Americans), 16 international. Average age 30. 57 applicants, 75% accepted, 31 enrolled. In 2006, 38 degrees awarded. *Entrance requirements:* For master's, GMAT, minimum GPA of 2.75. Additional exam requirements/recommendations for international students: Required—TOEFL (minimum score 550 paper-based; 213 computer-based; 79 iBT), Michigan English Language Assessment Battery. *Application deadline:* For fall admission, 8/15 for domestic students. Applications are processed on a rolling basis. Application fee: $30 ($40 for international students). Electronic applications accepted. *Expenses:* Tuition, state resident: full-time $6,164; part-time $342 per credit. Tuition, nonresident: full-time $10,575; part-time $588 per credit. Required fees: $806; $43 per credit. $12 per term. Tuition and fees vary according to course load, degree level and program. *Financial support:* In 2006–07, 14 research assistantships with full tuition reimbursements were awarded; teaching assistantships with full tuition reimbursements, career-related internships or fieldwork, Federal Work-Study, tuition waivers (partial), and unspecified assistantships also available. *Faculty research:* Financial reporting, auditing and assurance of financial information, business and information systems risk management, corporate governance and ethics, accounting education. *Unit head:* Dr. Thomas Calderon, Chair, 330-972-6099, E-mail: tcalderon@uakron.edu. *Application contact:* Dr. James Divoky, Director of Graduate Business Programs, 330-972-7043, Fax: 330-972-6588, E-mail: jdivoky@uakron.edu.

The University of Alabama, Graduate School, Manderson Graduate School of Business, Culverhouse School of Accountancy, Tuscaloosa, AL 35487. Offers accounting (M Acc, PhD); tax accounting (MTA). *Accreditation:* AACSB. *Faculty:* 13 full-time (3 women). *Students:* 74 full-time (42 women), 4 part-time (2 women); includes 3 minority (1 African American, 2 Asian Americans or Pacific Islanders), 4 international. Average age 23. In 2006, 96 degrees awarded. *Degree requirements:* For doctorate, thesis/dissertation. *Entrance requirements:* For master's and doctorate, GMAT, minimum GPA of 3.0. Additional exam requirements/recommendations for international students: Required—TOEFL. *Application deadline:* Applications are processed on a rolling basis. Electronic applications accepted. *Financial support:* In 2006–07, 4 fellowships with tuition reimbursements (averaging $14,000 per year), 18 research assistantships with tuition reimbursements, 20 teaching assistantships with tuition reimbursements were awarded; career-related internships or fieldwork, Federal Work-Study, institutionally sponsored loans, scholarships/grants, health care benefits, and unspecified assistantships also available. Financial award application deadline: 3/31. *Faculty research:* Governmental and hospital pensions, artificial intelligence, corporate disclosure, auditing, taxation. *Unit head:* Dr. Mary S. Stone, Director, 205-348-2915, Fax: 205-348-8453, E-mail: mstone@cba.ua.edu. *Application contact:* Sandy D. Davidson, Advisor, 205-348-8997, Fax: 205-348-8453, E-mail: sdavidso@cba.ua.edu.

The University of Alabama, Graduate School, Manderson Graduate School of Business, Department of Management and Marketing, Program in Management, Tuscaloosa, AL 35487. Offers accounting (MA, PhD); applied statistics (PhD); economics (MA, PhD); finance (MS, PhD); management (MA, PhD); operations management (MS, PhD); statistics (MS); tax accounting (MA). *Faculty:* 27 full-time (8 women), 2 part-time/adjunct (0 women). *Students:* Average age 29. 112 applicants, 36% accepted. In 2006, 20 master's, 1 doctorate awarded. Terminal master's awarded for partial completion of doctoral program. *Median time to degree:* Master's–2.4 years part-time; doctorate–4 years full-time, 2 years part-time. Of those who began their doctoral program in fall 1998, 100% received their degree in 8 years or less. *Degree requirements:* For master's, thesis (for some programs), formal project paper, comprehensive exam (for some programs), registration; for doctorate, thesis/dissertation, comprehensive exam, registration. *Entrance requirements:* For master's and doctorate, GMAT or GRE, minimum GPA of 3.0. Additional exam requirements/recommendations for international students: Required—TOEFL. *Application deadline:* For fall admission, 6/30 priority date for domestic students, 1/31 for international students. Applications are processed on a rolling basis. Application fee: $25. *Financial support:* In 2006–07, 5 fellowships (averaging $2,000 per year), 2 research assistantships (averaging $2,000 per year), 2 teaching assistantships (averaging $2,000 per year) were awarded. *Faculty research:* Relationship marketing, team building, e-commerce strategy, entrepreneurship, health care management, service marketing.

The University of Alabama in Huntsville, School of Graduate Studies, College of Administrative Science, Department of Accounting, Huntsville, AL 35899. Offers M Acc, Certificate. Part-time and evening/weekend programs available. *Faculty:* 5 full-time (1 woman), 1 (woman) part-time/adjunct. *Students:* 10 full-time (6 women), 24 part-time (13 women); includes 2 minority (1 African American, 1 Hispanic American), 5 international. Average age 32. 11 applicants, 91% accepted, 8 enrolled. In 2006, 11 master's, 6 other advanced degrees awarded. *Degree requirements:* For master's, thesis or alternative, comprehensive exam, registration. *Entrance requirements:* For master's, GMAT, minimum AACSB index of 1000. Additional exam requirements/recommendations for international students: Required—TOEFL (minimum score 550 paper-based; 213 computer-based). *Application deadline:* For fall admission, 8/10 for domestic students; for spring admission, 12/10 for domestic students. Application fee: $40. *Expenses:* Tuition, state resident: full-time $6,072; part-time $253 per credit hour. Tuition, nonresident: full-time $12,476; part-time $519 per credit hour. *Financial support:* Fellowships, research assistantships with full and partial tuition reimbursements, teaching assistantships with full and partial tuition reimbursements, career-related internships or fieldwork, Federal Work-Study, institutionally sponsored loans, scholarships/grants, health care benefits, and unspecified assistantships available. Support available to part-time students. Financial award application deadline: 4/1; financial award applicants required to submit FAFSA. *Unit head:* Dr. Dorla Evans, Chair, 256-824-6593, Fax: 256-824-6328, E-mail: macc@email.uah.edu.

University of Alberta, Faculty of Graduate Studies and Research, Doctoral Program in Business, Edmonton, AB T6G 2E1, Canada. Offers accounting (PhD); finance (PhD); human resources/industrial relations (PhD); management science (PhD); marketing (PhD); organizational analysis (PhD); MBA/PhD. *Accreditation:* AACSB. Part-time programs available. *Faculty:* 41 full-time (7 women), 1 part-time/adjunct (0 women). *Students:* 46 full-time (27 women), 5 part-time (3 women). Average age 34. 307 applicants, 7% accepted, 11 enrolled. In 2006, 2 degrees awarded. *Median time to degree:* Of those who began their doctoral program in fall 1998, 60% received their degree in 8 years or less. *Degree requirements:* For doctorate, thesis/dissertation, comprehensive exam. *Entrance requirements:* For doctorate, GMAT. Additional exam requirements/recommendations for international students: Required—TOEFL (minimum score 550 paper-based; 213 computer-based). *Application deadline:* For fall admission, 6/1 priority date for domestic students; for winter admission, 5/1 for domestic students. Application fee: $0. Electronic applications accepted. *Financial support:* In 2006–07, 29 students received support, including 11 fellowships with full tuition reimbursements available (averaging $17,000 per year); scholarships/grants and tuition waivers (partial) also available. *Faculty research:* Accounting, capital markets and corporate finance, organizational change and human resource management, marketing, strategic management. Total annual research expenditures: $7.7 million. *Unit head:* Dr. Mike Percy, Director, 780-492-2361, Fax: 780-492-3325, E-mail: busphd@ualberta.ca. *Application contact:* Jeanette Gosine, Program Coordinator, 780-492-2361, Fax: 780-492-3325, E-mail: busphd@ualberta.ca.

See Close-Up on page 335.

The University of Arizona, Graduate College, College of Business and Public Administration, Eller Graduate School of Management, Department of Accounting, Tucson, AZ 85721. Offers M Ac. *Accreditation:* AACSB. Part-time programs available. *Faculty:* 6 full-time (4 women), 2 part-time/adjunct (0 women). *Students:* 40 full-time (19 women), 7 part-time (4 women); includes 8 minority (1 American Indian/Alaska Native, 2 Asian Americans or Pacific Islanders, 5 Hispanic Americans), 6 international. Average age 27. 69 applicants, 55% accepted, 24 enrolled. In 2006, 34 degrees awarded. *Degree requirements:* For master's, 1 year residency. *Entrance requirements:* For master's, GMAT, minimum GPA of 3.0. Additional exam requirements/recommendations for international students: Required—TOEFL (minimum score 600 paper-based; 250 computer-based). *Application deadline:* For fall admission, 3/1 priority date for domestic students, 12/1 priority date for international students; for spring admission, 10/1 priority date for domestic students, 6/1 priority date for international students. Applications are processed on a rolling basis. Application fee: $50. Electronic applications accepted. *Expenses: Contact institution. Financial support:* In 2006–07, 2 teaching assistantships (averaging $5,000 per year) were awarded; fellowships, research assistantships, career-related internships or fieldwork, Federal Work-Study, scholarships/grants, tuition waivers (partial), and unspecified assistantships also available. Financial award application deadline: 3/15. *Faculty research:* Auditing, financial reporting and financial markets, taxation policy and markets, behavioral research in accounting. *Unit head:* Dr. Dan S. Dhaliwal, Head, 520-621-2146, Fax: 520-621-3742, E-mail: dhaliwal@eller.arizona.edu. *Application contact:* Carol Plagman, Programs Coordinator, 520-621-3712, Fax: 520-621-3742, E-mail: accounting@eller.arizona.edu.

University of Arkansas, Graduate School, Sam M. Walton College of Business Administration, Department of Accounting, Fayetteville, AR 72701-1201. Offers M Acc. *Accreditation:* AACSB. *Students:* 32 full-time (17 women), 7 part-time (5 women); includes 3 minority (1 African American, 1 Asian American or Pacific Islander, 1 Hispanic American), 3 international. 36 applicants, 81% accepted. In 2006, 21 degrees awarded. *Entrance requirements:* For master's, GMAT. Application fee: $40 ($50 for international students). *Financial support:* In 2006–07, 10 fellowships with tuition reimbursements, 16 research assistantships, 2 teaching assistantships were awarded; career-related internships or fieldwork and Federal Work-Study also available. Support available to part-time students. Financial award application deadline: 4/1; financial award applicants required to submit FAFSA. *Unit head:* Dr. Karen Pincus, Chair, 479-575-4051, Fax: 479-575-2863. *Application contact:* Marinus Bouwman, Graduate Coordinator, 479-575-6117, E-mail: mbouwman@walton.uark.edu.

University of Baltimore, Graduate School, Merrick School of Business, Department of Accounting, Baltimore, MD 21201-5779. Offers accounting and business advisory services (MS). Part-time and evening/weekend programs available. *Faculty:* 8 full-time (3 women), 7 part-time/adjunct (1 woman). *Students:* 19 full-time (11 women), 27 part-time (20 women); includes 6 minority (5 African Americans, 1 Asian American or Pacific Islander), 16 international. Average age 32. 15 applicants, 67% accepted, 8 enrolled. In 2006, 16 degrees awarded. *Entrance requirements:* For master's, GMAT. Additional exam requirements/recommendations for international students: Required—TOEFL (minimum score 550 paper-based; 213 computer-based). *Application deadline:* For fall admission, 8/1 priority date for domestic students, 6/1 for international students; for spring admission, 12/1 for domestic students, 11/1 for international students. Applications are processed on a rolling basis. Application fee: $45. Electronic applications accepted. *Expenses:* Tuition, state resident: full-time $5,322; part-time $591 per credit. Tuition, nonresident: full-time $7,527; part-time $830 per credit. *Financial support:* Career-related internships or fieldwork and Federal Work-Study available. Support available to part-time students. Financial award application deadline: 4/1; financial award applicants required to submit FAFSA. *Faculty research:* Health care, accounting and administration, managerial accounting, financial accounting theory, accounting information. Total annual research expenditures: $5,000. *Unit head:* Dr. Phil Korb, Chair, 410-837-4955, E-mail: pkorb@ubalt.edu. *Application contact:* Dean Dreibelbis, Assistant Director, Office of Graduate Admissions, 410-837-6565, Fax: 410-837-4793, E-mail: gradadmissions@ubalt.edu.

The University of British Columbia, Sauder School of Business, Doctoral Program in Commerce and Business Administration, Vancouver, BC V6T 1Z1, Canada. Offers accounting (PhD); finance (PhD); international business (PhD); management information systems (PhD); management science (PhD); marketing (PhD); organizational behavior (PhD); policy analysis and strategy (PhD); transportation and logistics (PhD); urban land economics (PhD). *Degree requirements:* For doctorate, thesis/dissertation, comprehensive exam. *Entrance requirements:* For doctorate, GMAT or GRE. Additional exam requirements/recommendations for international students: Required—TOEFL. Electronic applications accepted.

University of California, Berkeley, Graduate Division, Haas School of Business, Program in Business, Berkeley, CA 94720-1500. Offers accounting (PhD); business and public policy (PhD); finance (PhD); marketing (PhD); organizational behavior and industrial relations (PhD); real estate (PhD). *Accreditation:* AACSB. *Students:* 83 full-time (28 women); includes 17 minority (14 Asian Americans or Pacific Islanders, 3 Hispanic Americans), 33 international. Average age 30. 347 applicants, 16 enrolled. In 2006, 17 degrees awarded. *Median time to degree:* Of those who began their doctoral program in fall 1998, 88% received their degree in 8 years or less. *Degree requirements:* For doctorate, thesis/dissertation, oral exam, written preliminary exams, comprehensive exam. *Entrance requirements:* For doctorate, GMAT or GRE, minimum GPA of 3.0. Additional exam requirements/recommendations for international students: Required—TOEFL (minimum score 570 paper-based; 230 computer-based), IELTS (minimum score 7). *Application deadline:* For fall admission, 12/15 for domestic and international students. Application fee: $60 ($80 for international students). Electronic applications accepted. *Financial support:* Fellowships with full and partial tuition reimbursements, research assistantships with full and partial tuition reimbursements, teaching assistantships with full and partial tuition reimbursements, career-related internships or fieldwork, Federal Work-Study, scholarships/grants, health care benefits, tuition waivers (full), and unspecified assistantships available. Financial award application deadline: 12/15; financial award applicants required to submit FAFSA. *Unit head:* Miguel Villas-Boas, Director, 510-642-1409, Fax: 510-643-4255, E-mail: kimg@haas.berkeley.edu. *Application contact:* Kim Guilfoyle, Administrative Director, 510-642-3944, Fax: 510-643-4255, E-mail: kimg@haas.berkeley.edu.

University of Central Arkansas, Graduate School, College of Business Administration, Program in Accounting, Conway, AR 72035-0001. Offers M Acc. *Faculty:* 8 full-time (4 women). *Students:* 18 full-time (14 women), 5 part-time (all women); includes 1 minority (American Indian/Alaska Native), 3 international. 21 applicants, 100% accepted, 21 enrolled. In 2006, 17 degrees awarded. *Degree requirements:* For master's, capstone course. *Entrance requirements:* For master's, GMAT, minimum GPA of 2.7. Additional exam requirements/recommendations for international students: Required—TOEFL (minimum score 550 paper-based; 213 computer-based). *Application deadline:* For fall admission, 3/1 for domestic and international students; for spring admission, 10/1 for domestic and international students. Applications are processed on a rolling basis. Application fee: $25 ($40 for international students). *Expenses:* Tuition, state resident: full-time $4,194; part-time $233 per semester. Tuition, nonresident: full-time $5,963; part-time $429 per semester. International tuition: $6,162 full-time. Required fees: $65; $23 per semester. One-time fee: $65 part-time. *Financial support:* In 2006–07, 4 research assistantships with partial tuition reimbursements (averaging $5,000 per year) were awarded; career-related internships or fieldwork, Federal Work-Study, scholarships/grants, tuition waivers (partial), and unspecified assistantships also available. Support available to part-time students. Financial award application deadline: 2/15. *Unit head:* Dr. Patricia Mounce, Interim Chair, 501-450-5333, Fax: 501-450-5302. *Application contact:* Brenda Herring, Admissions Assistant, 501-450-5065, Fax: 501-450-5678, E-mail: bherring@uca.edu.

University of Central Florida, College of Business Administration, Kenneth G. Dixon School of Accounting, Orlando, FL 32816. Offers MSA, MST. *Accreditation:* AACSB. Part-time and evening/weekend programs available. *Faculty:* 26 full-time (14 women), 6 part-time/adjunct (2 women). *Students:* 77 full-time (50 women), 133 part-time (83 women); includes 34 minority (7 African Americans, 1 American Indian/Alaska Native, 15 Asian Americans or Pacific Islanders, 11 Hispanic Americans), 27 international. Average age 31. In 2006, 79 master's awarded. *Degree requirements:* For master's, comprehensive exam. *Entrance requirements:* For master's, GMAT, minimum GPA of 3.0 in last 60 hours. Additional exam requirements/recommendations for international students: Required—TOEFL. *Application deadline:* For fall admission, 6/15 priority date for domestic students; for spring admission, 11/1 priority date for domestic students. Electronic applications accepted. *Expenses:* Tuition, state resident: full-time $6,167; part-time $257 per credit hour. Tuition, nonresident: full-time $22,790; part-time $950 per credit hour. *Financial support:* In 2006–07, 2 fellowships with partial tuition reimbursements (averaging $5,000 per year), 20 research assistantships with partial tuition reimbursements (averaging $6,500 per year) were awarded; teaching assistantships with partial tuition reimbursements, career-related internships or fieldwork, Federal Work-Study, institutionally sponsored loans, tuition waivers (partial), and unspecified assistantships also available. Financial award application deadline: 3/1; financial award applicants required to submit FAFSA. *Unit head:* Dr. Robin J. Roberts, Director, 407-823-2876, E-mail: robin.roberts@bus.ucf.edu.

University of Central Missouri, The Graduate School, Harmon College of Business Administration, Department of Accounting, Warrensburg, MO 64093. Offers MA. *Accreditation:* AACSB. Part-time programs available. *Faculty:* 8 full-time (2 women). *Students:* 27 full-time (14 women), 1 part-time; includes 2 minority (both African Americans), 4 international. Average age 25. 15 applicants. In 2006, 14 degrees awarded. *Entrance requirements:* For master's, minimum GPA of 2.5. Additional exam requirements/recommendations for international students: Required—TOEFL (minimum score 500 paper-based; 173 computer-based). *Application deadline:* For fall admission, 6/1 priority date for domestic students, 5/1 priority date for international students; for spring admission, 10/1 priority date for domestic students, 10/1 for international students. Application fee: $30 ($50 for international students). *Expenses:* Tuition, state resident: full-time $5,448; part-time $227 per credit hour. Tuition, nonresident: full-time $10,896; part-time $454 per credit hour. Required fees: $336; $14 per credit hour. *Financial support:* In 2006–07, 7 students received support; teaching assistantships available. Financial award applicants required to submit FAFSA. *Faculty research:* Financial accounting standards; auditing, fraud auditing, Sarbanes-Oxley Impact; financial reporting and effect of various actions on stock prices; income tax issues; managerial accounting, practice and behavioral aspects. *Unit head:* Dr. Kenneth Stone, Acting Chair, 660-543-4245, Fax: 660-543-8885, E-mail: stone@ucmo.edu.

University of Cincinnati, Division of Research and Advanced Studies, College of Business, Department of Accounting, Cincinnati, OH 45221. Offers accounting (MBA); accounting management/organizational behavior (PhD); general accounting (MS); taxation (MS). MBA offered to full-time students only. Part-time and evening/weekend programs available. *Degree requirements:* For master's, capstone project (MBA); for doctorate, thesis/dissertation, comprehensive exam. *Entrance requirements:* For master's, GMAT, resumé, letters of recommendation; for doctorate, GMAT, GRE. Additional exam requirements/recommendations for international students: Required—TOEFL (minimum score 600 paper-based; 250 computer-based). Application fee: $40. Electronic applications accepted. *Expenses: Contact institution. Financial support:* Fellowships with full tuition reimbursements, research assistantships with full tuition reimbursements, teaching assistantships with full and partial tuition reimbursements, scholarships/grants and tuition waivers (full and partial) available. Financial award application deadline: 2/1; financial award applicants required to submit FAFSA. *Unit head:* Dr. Jens Stephen, Head, 513-556-7055.

University of Colorado at Boulder, Leeds School of Business, Doctoral Program in Business, Boulder, CO 80309. Offers accounting (PhD); finance (PhD); management (PhD); marketing (PhD). *Degree requirements:* For doctorate, thesis/dissertation, research internship. *Entrance requirements:* For doctorate, minimum undergraduate GPA of 3.2. *Application deadline:* For fall admission, 1/31 for domestic students, 1/15 for international students; for spring admission, 11/1 for domestic and international students. Application fee: $50 ($60 for international students). *Financial support:* Fellowships, research assistantships, teaching assistantships, career-related internships or fieldwork, Federal Work-Study, scholarships/grants, and unspecified assistantships available. Financial award application deadline: 3/1; financial award applicants required to submit FAFSA. *Unit head:* Kenneth Kozar, Associate Dean, 303-492-8347, Fax: 303-492-7676. *Application contact:* Information Contact, 303-492-4984, Fax: 303-492-5962, E-mail: leedsphd@colorado.edu.

University of Colorado at Colorado Springs, Graduate School, Graduate School of Business Administration, Colorado Springs, CO 80933-7150. Offers accounting (MBA); finance (MBA); general health care administration (MBA); information systems (MBA); international business management (MBA); marketing (MBA); service management/technology management (MBA). *Accreditation:* AACSB. Part-time and evening/weekend programs available. *Faculty:* 15 full-time (4 women), 4 part-time/adjunct (0 women). *Students:* 158 full-time (70 women), 290 part-time (87 women); includes 48 minority (11 African Americans, 1 American Indian/Alaska Native, 20 Asian Americans or Pacific Islanders, 16 Hispanic Americans), 7 international. Average age 33. 158 applicants, 75% accepted, 51 enrolled. In 2006, 119 degrees awarded. *Entrance requirements:* For master's, GMAT. *Application deadline:* For fall admission, 6/1 for domestic students; for spring admission, 11/1 for domestic students. Application fee: $60 ($75 for international students). *Expenses: Contact institution.* Tuition and fees vary according to course load, campus/location and program. *Financial support:* Career-related internships or fieldwork, Federal Work-Study, and institutionally sponsored loans available. Support available to part-time students. Financial award applicants required to submit FAFSA. *Faculty research:* Quality financial reporting, investments and corporate governance, group support systems, environmental and project management, customer relationship management. Total annual research expenditures: $99,250. *Unit head:* Dr. Venkateshwar Reddy, Dean, 719-262-3113, Fax: 719-262-3494, E-mail: vreddy@uccs.edu. *Application contact:* Amy DeLourenco, MBA Program Director, 719-262-3408, Fax: 719-262-3100, E-mail: busadvsr@uccs.edu.

University of Colorado at Denver and Health Sciences Center, Business School, Program in Accounting, Denver, CO 80217-3364. Offers MS. *Accreditation:* AACSB. Part-time and evening/weekend programs available. *Faculty:* 12 full-time (5 women). *Students:* 36 full-time (22 women), 87 part-time (53 women); includes 20 minority (7 African Americans, 1 American Indian/Alaska Native, 8 Asian Americans or Pacific Islanders, 4 Hispanic Americans), 11 international. Average age 29. 42 applicants, 55% accepted, 19 enrolled. In 2006, 41 degrees awarded. *Entrance requirements:* For master's, GMAT. Additional exam requirements/recommendations for international students: Required—TOEFL (minimum score 525 paper-based; 197 computer-based). *Application deadline:* For fall admission, 6/1 for domestic students, 3/15 for international students; for spring admission, 11/1 priority date for domestic students, 10/1 for international students. Applications are processed on a rolling basis. Application fee: $50 ($75 for international students). Electronic applications accepted. *Financial support:* Federal Work-Study, institutionally sponsored loans, and scholarships/grants available. Support available to part-time students. Financial award application deadline: 4/1; financial award applicants required to submit FAFSA. *Faculty research:* Transfer pricing, behavioral accounting, environmental accounting, health services, international auditing. *Unit head:* Bruce Neumann, Director, 303-556-5884, Fax: 303-556-5899, E-mail: bruce.neumann@cudenver.edu. *Application contact:* Shelly Townley, Admissions Coordinator, 303-556-5956, Fax: 303-556-5904, E-mail: shelly.townley@cudenver.edu.

University of Connecticut, Graduate School, School of Business, Field of Accounting, Storrs, CT 06269. Offers MS, PhD. *Accreditation:* AACSB. *Faculty:* 30 full-time (7 women). *Students:* 27 full-time (11 women), 148 part-time (69 women); includes 24 minority (5 African Americans, 1 American Indian/Alaska Native, 12 Asian Americans or Pacific Islanders, 6 Hispanic Americans), 5 international. Average age 25. 154 applicants, 81% accepted, 124 enrolled. In 2006, 77 degrees awarded. *Financial support:* Research assistantships available. *Unit head:* Andrew Rosman, Admissions Chairperson, 860-486-5891, Fax: 860-486-4838, E-mail: andrew.rosman@uconn.edu. *Application contact:* Margaret Sweeney, Administrative Assistant, 860-486-3860, Fax: 860-846-4838, E-mail: msacct@sba.uconn.edu.

University of Dallas, Graduate School of Management, Irving, TX 75062-4736. Offers accounting (MBA, MS); business management (MBA); corporate finance (MBA, MM); engineering management (MBA, MM); entrepreneurship (MBA, MM); financial services (MBA, MM); global business (MBA, MM); health services management (MBA, MM); human resource management (MBA, MM, MS); information assurance (MBA, MM, MS); information technology (MBA, MM, MS); information technology service management (MBA); IT service management (MS); marketing (MM); marketing management (MBA); not-for-profit management (MBA); organization development (MBA); project management (MBA, MM); sports and entertainment management (MBA, MM); strategic leadership (MBA); supply chain management (MBA); supply chain management and market logistics (MM); telecommunications management (MBA, MM). *Accreditation:* ACBSP. Part-time and evening/weekend programs available. Postbaccalaureate distance learning degree programs offered (no on-campus study). *Faculty:* 26 full-time (5 women), 85 part-time/adjunct (18 women). *Students:* 227 full-time (98 women), 1,160 part-time (446 women); includes 473 minority (209 African Americans, 3 American Indian/Alaska Native, 143 Asian Americans or Pacific Islanders, 118 Hispanic Americans), 224 international. Average age 34. 556 applicants, 86% accepted, 291 enrolled. In 2006, 476 degrees awarded. *Entrance requirements:* Additional exam requirements/recommendations for international students: Required—TOEFL. *Application deadline:* Applications are processed on a rolling basis. Application fee: $50. Electronic applications accepted. *Expenses: Contact institution. Financial support:* In 2006–07, 468 students received support. Scholarships/grants and unspecified assistantships available. Financial award application deadline: 2/15; financial award applicants required to submit FAFSA. *Unit head:* Dr. J. Lee Whittington, Dean, 972-721-5230. *Application contact:* Sarah Stivison, Director of Graduate Admissions, 972-721-5198, Fax: 972-721-4009, E-mail: admiss@gsm.udallas.edu.

University of Delaware, Alfred Lerner College of Business and Economics, Department of Accounting and Management Information Systems, Newark, DE 19716. Offers accounting (MS); information systems and technology management (MS). *Accreditation:* AACSB. Part-time and evening/weekend programs available. *Degree requirements:* For master's, thesis optional. *Entrance requirements:* For master's, GMAT. Additional exam requirements/recommendations for international students: Required—TOEFL (minimum score 550 paper-based; 213 computer-based). Electronic applications accepted. *Faculty research:* External reporting, managerial accounting, auditing information systems, taxation.

University of Denver, Daniels College of Business, School of Accountancy, Denver, CO 80208. Offers accountancy (M Acc); accounting (IMBA, MBA). *Accreditation:* AACSB. Part-time and evening/weekend programs available. *Faculty:* 12 full-time (4 women). *Students:* 17 full-time (7 women), 27 part-time (15 women); includes 2 minority (1 African American, 1 Asian American or Pacific Islander), 8 international. Average age 28. 66 applicants, 73% accepted. In 2006, 38 degrees awarded. *Entrance requirements:* For master's, GMAT. *Application deadline:* For fall admission, 1/15 priority date for domestic students. Applications are processed on a rolling basis. Application fee: $50. Electronic applications accepted. *Expenses:* Tuition: Full-time $29,628; part-time $823 per credit. *Financial support:* Career-related internships or fieldwork, Federal Work-Study, institutionally sponsored loans, and scholarships/grants available. Support available to part-time students. Financial award application deadline: 2/15; financial award applicants required to submit FAFSA. *Faculty research:* Management accounting, activity-based management, benchmarking, financial management and human services, derivatives. *Unit head:* Dr. Ronald Kucic, Director, 303-871-2017. *Application contact:* Information Contact, 303-871-3416, Fax: 303-871-4466, E-mail: daniels@du.edu.

University of Florida, Graduate School, Warrington College of Business Administration, Fisher School of Accounting, Gainesville, FL 32611. Offers M Acc, PhD, JD/M Acc. *Accreditation:* AACSB. Part-time programs available. *Faculty:* 13 full-time (4 women). *Students:* 189 (81 women); includes 33 minority (2 African Americans, 1 American Indian/Alaska Native, 15 Asian Americans or Pacific Islanders, 15 Hispanic Americans) 8 international. In 2006, 141 master's, 1 doctorate awarded. *Entrance requirements:* For master's, GMAT or GRE General Test, minimum GPA of 3.0. Additional exam requirements/recommendations for international students: Required—TOEFL (minimum score 550 paper-based; 213 computer-based). *Application deadline:* For fall admission, 6/1 for domestic students. Applications are processed on a rolling basis. Application fee: $30. Electronic applications accepted. *Expenses:* Tuition, state resident: full-time $6,827. Tuition, nonresident: full-time $21,951. Required fees: $999. *Financial support:* In 2006–07, 8 research assistantships (averaging $15,032 per year) were awarded; fellowships, teaching assistantships with partial tuition reimbursements, Federal Work-Study and unspecified assistantships also available. Support available to part-time students. *Faculty research:* Auditing/financial accounting, accounting systems, taxation. *Unit head:* Gary McGill, Associate Dean, 352-273-0200, Fax: 352-392-7962, E-mail: mcgill@ufl.edu. *Application contact:* Dominique A. Desantiago, Associate Director, 352-273-0200, Fax: 352-392-7962, E-mail: dom.desantiago@cba.ufl.edu.

University of Florida, Graduate School, Warrington College of Business Administration, Programs in Business Administration, Gainesville, FL 32611. Offers accounting (MBA); arts administration (MBA); business strategy and public policy (MBA); competitive strategy (MBA); decision and information sciences (MBA); electronic commerce (MBA); finance (MBA); general business (MBA); global management (MBA); Graham-Buffett security analysis (MBA); health administration (MBA); human resources management (MBA); international studies (MBA); Latin American business (MBA); management (MBA); marketing (MBA); sports administration (MBA); JD/MBA; MBA/MS; MBA/PhD; MBA/Pharm D; MD/MBA. *Accreditation:* AACSB. Part-time and evening/weekend programs available. Postbaccalaureate distance learning degree programs offered. *Faculty:* 14. *Students:* 950 (282 women); includes 189 minority (31 African Americans, 2 American Indian/Alaska Native, 66 Asian Americans or Pacific Islanders, 90 Hispanic Americans) 56 international. In 2006, 481 degrees awarded. *Entrance requirements:* For master's, GMAT, minimum GPA of 3.0, interview. Additional exam requirements/recommendations for international students: Required—TOEFL (minimum score 550 paper-based; 213 computer-based). *Application deadline:* For fall admission, 4/15 for domestic students; for winter admission, 10/15 priority date for domestic students; for spring admission, 2/15 for domestic students. Applications are processed on a rolling basis. Application fee: $30. Electronic applications accepted. *Expenses:* Tuition, state resident: full-time $6,827. Tuition, nonresident: full-time $21,951. Required fees: $999. *Financial support:* Fellowships, research assistantships, teaching assistantships, career-related internships or fieldwork, scholarships/grants, and unspecified assistantships available. Support available to part-time students. Financial award application deadline: 2/15; financial award applicants required to submit FAFSA. *Faculty research:* Accounting, finance, insurance, management, real estate and urban analysis marketing. *Unit head:* Alex Sevilla, Director, 352-392-7992 Ext. 1206. *Application contact:* Patrick Foran, Associate Director of Admissions, 352-392-7992 Ext. 282, Fax: 352-392-8791, E-mail: patrick.foran@cba.ufl.edu.

University of Georgia, Graduate School, Terry College of Business, J. M. Tull School of Accounting, Athens, GA 30602. Offers M Acc, JD/M Acc. *Accreditation:* AACSB. *Faculty:* 12 full-time (5 women). *Students:* 121 full-time (49 women), 2 part-time (1 woman); includes 9 minority (2 African Americans, 6 Asian Americans or Pacific Islanders, 1 Hispanic American), 9 international. 120 applicants, 54% accepted, 46 enrolled. In 2006, 81 degrees awarded. *Entrance requirements:* For master's, GMAT. *Application deadline:* For fall admission, 7/1 priority date for domestic students; for spring admission, 11/15 for domestic students. Applica-

Accounting

University of Georgia (continued)
tion fee: $50. Electronic applications accepted. *Financial support:* Fellowships, research assistantships, teaching assistantships, unspecified assistantships available. *Unit head:* Dr. Benjamin C. Ayers, Director, 706-542-3772, Fax: 706-542-3630, E-mail: bayers@uga.edu.

University of Hartford, Barney School of Business, Department of Accounting and Taxation, West Hartford, CT 06117-1599. Offers professional accounting (Certificate); taxation (MSAT). Part-time and evening/weekend programs available. *Faculty:* 8 full-time (5 women), 4 part-time/adjunct (0 women). *Students:* 16 full-time (9 women), 78 part-time (31 women); includes 9 minority (3 African Americans, 5 Asian Americans or Pacific Islanders, 1 Hispanic American), 5 international. Average age 35. 43 applicants, 70% accepted, 22 enrolled. In 2006, 52 degrees awarded. *Entrance requirements:* For master's, GMAT, 2 letters of recommendation, resumé. Additional exam requirements/recommendations for international students: Required—TOEFL (minimum score 550 paper-based; 213 computer-based). *Application deadline:* For fall admission, 7/1 for domestic students; for spring admission, 12/1 for domestic students. Applications are processed on a rolling basis. Application fee: $40 ($55 for international students). Electronic applications accepted. *Expenses:* Tuition: Part-time $515 per credit. Required fees: $200 per term. *Financial support:* In 2006–07, 6 research assistantships (averaging $5,145 per year) were awarded; career-related internships or fieldwork and unspecified assistantships also available. Financial award application deadline: 5/1. *Unit head:* Dr. Patricia Nodoushani, Chairman, 860-768-4346, Fax: 860-768-4398, E-mail: nodoushan@hartford.edu.

University of Hawaii at Manoa, Graduate Division, Shidler College of Business, Program in Accounting, Honolulu, HI 96822. Offers accounting (M Acc); accounting law (M Acc); information systems (M Acc); taxation (M Acc). Part-time programs available. *Faculty:* 10 full-time (3 women). *Students:* 38 full-time (21 women), 17 part-time (14 women); includes 14 minority (13 Asian Americans or Pacific Islanders, 1 Hispanic American), 5 international. Average age 32. 52 applicants, 60% accepted, 18 enrolled. In 2006, 38 degrees awarded. *Entrance requirements:* For master's, GMAT, bachelor's degree in accounting, minimum GPA of 3.0. Additional exam requirements/recommendations for international students: Required—TOEFL (minimum score 520 paper-based; 213 computer-based; 79 iBT). *Application deadline:* For fall admission, 5/1 for domestic students, 3/1 for international students; for spring admission, 9/1 for domestic and international students. Application fee: $50. *Financial support:* In 2006–07, 1 research assistantship (averaging $15,552 per year) was awarded; career-related internships or fieldwork, Federal Work-Study, and tuition waivers (full) also available. *Faculty research:* International accounting, current tax topics, insurance industry financial reporting, behavioral accounting, auditing. Total annual research expenditures: $15,000. *Application contact:* Jenny Teruya, Information Contact, 808-956-7118, Fax: 808-956-9888, E-mail: hamid@hawaii.edu.

University of Hawaii at Manoa, Graduate Division, Shidler College of Business, Program in International Management, Honolulu, HI 96822. Offers Asian finance (PhD); global information technology management (PhD); international accounting (PhD); international marketing (PhD); international organization and strategy (PhD). *Faculty:* 42 full-time (8 women). *Students:* 36 applicants, 19% accepted, 4 enrolled. In 2006, 5 degrees awarded. *Median time to degree:* Of those who began their doctoral program in fall 1998, 33% received their degree in 8 years or less. *Degree requirements:* For doctorate, thesis/dissertation, comprehensive exam. *Entrance requirements:* For doctorate, GMAT or GRE General Test, minimum GPA of 3.0. Additional exam requirements/recommendations for international students: Required—TOEFL (minimum score 600 paper-based; 250 computer-based; 100 iBT). *Application deadline:* For fall admission, 3/1 for domestic and international students. Application fee: $50. *Financial support:* In 2006–07, 16 research assistantships (averaging $18,198 per year), 3 teaching assistantships (averaging $14,958 per year) were awarded. Total annual research expenditures: $3.3 million. *Application contact:* Ting Bui, Information Contact, 808-956-6723, Fax: 808-956-2774.

University of Houston, Bauer College of Business, Accountancy and Taxation Program, Houston, TX 77204. Offers accountancy (M Acy); accounting (PhD). *Accreditation:* AACSB. Part-time and evening/weekend programs available. *Faculty:* 13 full-time (5 women), 14 part-time/adjunct (3 women). *Students:* 156 full-time (100 women), 78 part-time (39 women); includes 99 minority (6 African Americans, 78 Asian Americans or Pacific Islanders, 15 Hispanic Americans), 51 international. Average age 28. 106 applicants, 54% accepted, 53 enrolled. In 2006, 122 master's awarded. *Degree requirements:* For doctorate, thesis/dissertation, comprehensive exam. *Entrance requirements:* For master's, GMAT; for doctorate, GMAT or GRE. Additional exam requirements/recommendations for international students: Required—TOEFL. *Application deadline:* For fall admission, 5/1 for domestic students; for spring admission, 10/1 for domestic students. Applications are processed on a rolling basis. Application fee: $75 ($150 for international students). *Expenses:* Tuition, state resident: full-time $5,429; part-time $226 per credit. Tuition, nonresident: full-time $12,029; part-time $501 per credit. Required fees: $2,454. *Financial support:* In 2006–07, 1 fellowship with full tuition reimbursement (averaging $8,600 per year), 31 teaching assistantships with full tuition reimbursements (averaging $7,000 per year) were awarded; research assistantships with full tuition reimbursements, career-related internships or fieldwork, Federal Work-Study, institutionally sponsored loans, scholarships/grants, and unspecified assistantships also available. Support available to part-time students. Financial award application deadline: 3/10; financial award applicants required to submit FAFSA. *Faculty research:* Accountancy and taxation, finance, international business, management. *Unit head:* Dr. Gerald Lobo, Chairperson, 713-743-4821, Fax: 713-743-4828, E-mail: gjlobo@uh.edu. *Application contact:* 713-743-4900, Fax: 713-743-4942, E-mail: oss@uh.edu.

University of Houston–Clear Lake, School of Business, Program in Accounting, Houston, TX 77058-1098. Offers accounting (MS); professional accounting (MS). *Accreditation:* AACSB. Part-time and evening/weekend programs available. *Students:* 75 full-time, 33 part-time; includes 28 minority (8 African Americans, 13 Asian Americans or Pacific Islanders, 7 Hispanic Americans), 44 international. 92 applicants, 52% accepted, 31 enrolled. In 2006, 41 degrees awarded. *Degree requirements:* For master's, thesis optional. *Entrance requirements:* For master's, GMAT. Additional exam requirements/recommendations for international students: Required—TOEFL (minimum score 550 paper-based; 213 computer-based). *Application deadline:* For fall admission, 8/1 for domestic students, 6/1 for international students; for spring admission, 12/1 for domestic students, 10/1 for international students. Applications are processed on a rolling basis. Application fee: $35 ($75 for international students). Electronic applications accepted. *Financial support:* Career-related internships or fieldwork, Federal Work-Study, and scholarships/grants available. Support available to part-time students. Financial award application deadline: 5/1; financial award applicants required to submit FAFSA. *Unit head:* Dr. Barry Marks, Chair, 281-283-3214, E-mail: marks@uhcl.edu. *Application contact:* Janis S. Bigelow, Assistant Director of Admissions, Recruitment and Communications, 281-283-2540, Fax: 281-283-2530, E-mail: bigelow@uhcl.edu.

University of Idaho, College of Graduate Studies, College of Business and Economics, Department of Accounting, Moscow, ID 83844-2282. Offers M Acct. *Accreditation:* AACSB. *Students:* 14. Average age 28. In 2006, 16 degrees awarded. *Degree requirements:* For master's, comprehensive exam. *Entrance requirements:* For master's, minimum GPA of 3.0. *Application deadline:* For fall admission, 8/1 for domestic students; for spring admission, 12/15 for domestic students. Application fee: $55 ($60 for international students). *Expenses:* Tuition, nonresident: full-time $9,600; part-time $140 per credit. Required fees: $4,740; $227 per credit. *Financial support:* Research assistantships, teaching assistantships available. Financial award application deadline: 2/15. *Unit head:* Marla Kraut, Head, 208-885-7116, Fax: 208-885-2939.

University of Illinois at Chicago, Graduate College, Liautaud Graduate School of Business, Department of Accounting, Chicago, IL 60607-7128. Offers MS, MBA/MS. *Accreditation:* AACSB. Part-time programs available. *Entrance requirements:* For master's, GMAT, minimum GPA of 2.75. Additional exam requirements/recommendations for international students: Required—TOEFL. Electronic applications accepted. *Faculty research:* Governmental accounting, managerial accounting, auditing.

University of Illinois at Springfield, Graduate Programs, College of Business and Management, Program in Accountancy, Springfield, IL 62703-5407. Offers MA. Part-time and evening/weekend programs available. *Faculty:* 8 full-time (4 women), 1 part-time/adjunct (0 women). *Students:* 22 full-time (12 women), 57 part-time (39 women); includes 15 minority (6 African Americans, 1 American Indian/Alaska Native, 8 Asian Americans or Pacific Islanders), 8 international. Average age 31. 40 applicants, 68% accepted, 20 enrolled. In 2006, 20 degrees awarded. *Degree requirements:* For master's, project. *Entrance requirements:* For master's, minimum undergraduate GPA of 2.7 in accountancy. Additional exam requirements/recommendations for international students: Required—TOEFL (minimum score 550 paper-based; 213 computer-based). *Application deadline:* Applications are processed on a rolling basis. Application fee: $50 ($60 for international students). Electronic applications accepted. *Expenses:* Tuition, state resident: full-time $4,722; part-time $197 per credit hour. Tuition, nonresident: full-time $12,558; part-time $523 per credit hour. Required fees: $1,614; $8 per credit hour. $597 per term. *Financial support:* In 2006–07, research assistantships with full tuition reimbursements (averaging $7,425 per year), teaching assistantships with full tuition reimbursements (averaging $7,425 per year) were awarded; career-related internships or fieldwork, Federal Work-Study, scholarships/grants, health care benefits, and unspecified assistantships also available. Support available to part-time students. Financial award application deadline: 11/15; financial award applicants required to submit FAFSA. *Unit head:* Dr. Bonnie Moe, Program Administrator, 217-206-7905, Fax: 217-206-7543, E-mail: moe.bonnie@uis.edu.

University of Illinois at Urbana–Champaign, Graduate College, College of Business, Department of Accountancy, Champaign, IL 61820. Offers MAS, MAS/JD, MS, PhD. *Accreditation:* AACSB. *Faculty:* 21 full-time (5 women), 3 part-time/adjunct (0 women). *Students:* 284 full-time (142 women), 12 part-time (3 women); includes 45 minority (5 African Americans, 36 Asian Americans or Pacific Islanders, 4 Hispanic Americans), 101 international. 657 applicants, 51% accepted, 176 enrolled. In 2006, 241 master's, 3 doctorates awarded. *Degree requirements:* For doctorate, thesis/dissertation. *Entrance requirements:* For master's and doctorate, GMAT, minimum GPA of 3.0. *Application deadline:* Applications are processed on a rolling basis. Application fee: $50 ($60 for international students). Electronic applications accepted. *Financial support:* In 2006–07, 10 fellowships, 12 research assistantships, 74 teaching assistantships were awarded; tuition waivers (full and partial) also available. Financial award application deadline: 2/15. *Unit head:* Ira Soloman, Head, 217-333-2451, Fax: 217-244-0902, E-mail: isolomon@uiuc.edu. *Application contact:* Cindy Wood, Administrative Secretary, 217-333-4572, Fax: 217-244-0902, E-mail: ckwood@uiuc.edu.

The University of Iowa, Henry B. Tippie College of Business, Department of Accounting, Iowa City, IA 52242-1316. Offers accountancy (M Ac); business administration (PhD); JD/M Ac. *Accreditation:* AACSB. Part-time programs available. *Faculty:* 13 full-time (4 women). *Students:* 50 full-time (22 women); includes 2 minority (both Asian Americans or Pacific Islanders) Average age 25. 103 applicants, 49% accepted, 31 enrolled. In 2006, 40 degrees awarded. *Degree requirements:* For doctorate, thesis/dissertation, thesis defense, comprehensive exam, registration. *Entrance requirements:* For master's and doctorate, GMAT. Additional exam requirements/recommendations for international students: Required—TOEFL (minimum score 600 paper-based; 250 computer-based; 100 iBT). *Application deadline:* For fall admission, 7/15 for domestic students, 4/15 for international students; for spring admission, 12/1 for domestic students, 10/1 for international students. Application fee: $60 ($85 for international students). Electronic applications accepted. *Financial support:* In 2006–07, 44 students received support, including fellowships with full tuition reimbursements available (averaging $18,000 per year), research assistantships with partial tuition reimbursements available (averaging $15,736 per year), teaching assistantships with partial tuition reimbursements available (averaging $15,985 per year); career-related internships or fieldwork, Federal Work-Study, institutionally sponsored loans, scholarships/grants, and unspecified assistantships also available. Financial award applicants required to submit FAFSA. *Faculty research:* Auditing judgment and decision making; corporate financial reporting and capital markets; cost structure: analysis, estimation, and management; experimental and prediction economics; income taxes and interaction of financial and tax reporting systems. *Unit head:* Prof. W Bruce Johnson, Department Executive Officer, 319-335-0910, Fax: 319-335-1956. *Application contact:* Prof. Lynn M. Pringle, Director, Master of Accountancy Program, 319-335-0894, Fax: 319-335-1956, E-mail: lynn-pringle@uiowa.edu.

The University of Iowa, Henry B. Tippie College of Business, Henry B. Tippie School of Management, Iowa City, IA 52242-1316. Offers accounting (MBA); corporate finance (MBA); entrepreneurship (MBA); finance (MBA); individually designed concentration (MBA); investment management (MBA); management information systems (MBA); marketing (MBA); nonprofit management (MBA); operations management (MBA); strategic management and consulting (MBA); JD/MBA; MBA/MA; MBA/MD; MBA/MHA; MBA/MSN. *Accreditation:* AACSB. Part-time and evening/weekend programs available. *Faculty:* 94 full-time (23 women), 65 part-time/adjunct (21 women). *Students:* 230 full-time (67 women), 712 part-time (234 women); includes 62 minority (6 African Americans, 1 American Indian/Alaska Native, 43 Asian Americans or Pacific Islanders, 12 Hispanic Americans), 127 international. Average age 30. 431 applicants, 61% accepted, 217 enrolled. In 2006, 363 degrees awarded. *Median time to degree:* Master's–2 years full-time, 3.5 years part-time. *Degree requirements:* For master's, registration. *Entrance requirements:* For master's, GMAT, work experience. Additional exam requirements/recommendations for international students: Required—TOEFL (minimum score 600 paper-based; 250 computer-based; 100 iBT). *Application deadline:* For fall admission, 7/15 for domestic students, 4/15 for international students; for spring admission, 12/15 priority date for domestic students, 11/1 priority date for international students. Applications are processed on a rolling basis. Application fee: $60 ($85 for international students). Electronic applications accepted. *Expenses: Contact institution. Financial support:* In 2006–07, 72 fellowships (averaging $3,892 per year), 55 research assistantships with partial tuition reimbursements (averaging $10,260 per year) were awarded; career-related internships or fieldwork, Federal Work-Study, institutionally sponsored loans, scholarships/grants, health care benefits, and unspecified assistantships also available. Support available to part-time students. Financial award application deadline: 4/15; financial award applicants required to submit FAFSA. *Faculty research:* Capital markets, econometrics, optimization, investments and empirical corporate finance, Iowa electronic markets. *Unit head:* Prof. Gary J. Gaeth, Associate Dean, MBA Programs, 800-622-4692, Fax: 319-335-3604, E-mail: gary-gaeth@uiowa.edu. *Application contact:* Jodi Schafer, Director of Student Recruitment and Marketing, 319-335-0864, Fax: 319-335-3604, E-mail: jodi-schafer@uiowa.edu.

University of Kansas, Graduate Studies, School of Business, Program in Accounting and Information Systems, Lawrence, KS 66045. Offers MAIS. *Accreditation:* AACSB. *Faculty:* 14 full-time (4 women), 3 part-time/adjunct (1 woman). *Students:* 71 full-time (32 women), 8 part-time (6 women); includes 3 minority (1 African American, 2 Hispanic Americans), 5 international. Average age 24. 61 applicants, 87% accepted. In 2006, 58 degrees awarded. *Entrance requirements:* For master's, GMAT. Additional exam requirements/recommendations for international students: Required—TOEFL; Recommended—IELTS (minimum score 6). *Application deadline:* For fall admission, 1/15 priority date for domestic and international students; for spring admission, 11/1 for domestic students, 10/1 for international students. Applications are processed on a rolling basis. Application fee: $65. Electronic applications accepted. *Expenses:* Tuition, area resident: Part-time $227 per credit. Tuition, state resident: part-time $543 per credit. Tuition and fees vary according to course load, campus/location, program and reciprocity agreements. *Financial support:* Fellowships, research assistantships with partial tuition reimbursements, teaching assistantships with full and partial tuition reimbursements available. *Faculty research:* Audit; artificial intelligence; agency theory; compensation; production, regulation, and use of accounting information. *Unit head:* Dr. James A. Heintz, Director, Accounting and Information Systems, 785-864-4500, Fax: 785-864-5328, E-mail: jheintz@ku.edu. *Application contact:* Dee Steinle, Administative Director of Masters Programs, 785-864-7596, Fax: 785-864-5376, E-mail: dsteinle@ku.edu.

University of Kentucky, Graduate School, Gatton College of Business and Economics, Program in Accounting, Lexington, KY 40506-0032. Offers MSACC. *Accreditation:* AACSB.

Faculty: 13 full-time (4 women), 1 part-time/adjunct (0 women). *Students:* 23 full-time (11 women), 6 part-time (3 women); includes 3 minority (2 African Americans, 1 Asian American or Pacific Islander). Average age 25. 50 applicants, 62% accepted, 21 enrolled. In 2006, 15 degrees awarded. *Degree requirements:* For master's, comprehensive exam. *Entrance requirements:* For master's, GRE General Test, minimum undergraduate GPA of 2.75. Additional exam requirements/recommendations for international students: Required—TOEFL (minimum score 550 paper-based; 213 computer-based). *Application deadline:* For fall admission, 7/17 priority date for domestic students, 2/1 priority date for international students; for spring admission, 12/13 priority date for domestic students, 6/15 priority date for international students. Application fee: $40 ($55 for international students). Electronic applications accepted. *Expenses:* Tuition, state resident: full-time $7,670; part-time $401 per credit hour. Tuition, nonresident: full-time $16,158; part-time $873 per credit hour. *Financial support:* In 2006–07, 3 students received support, including 1 fellowship with full tuition reimbursement available, 2 teaching assistantships with full tuition reimbursements available (averaging $5,844 per year); research assistantships with full tuition reimbursements available, career-related internships or fieldwork, Federal Work-Study, institutionally sponsored loans, scholarships/grants, traineeships, health care benefits, tuition waivers (full), and unspecified assistantships also available. Support available to part-time students. Financial award application deadline: 3/15. *Faculty research:* Taxation, financial accounting and auditing, managerial accounting, not-for-profit accounting. *Unit head:* Dr. Dan Stone, Director of Graduate Studies, 859-257-3654, Fax: 859-323-3654. *Application contact:* Dr. Brian Jackson, Senior Associate Dean, 859-257-4667, Fax: 859-257-4676, E-mail: brian.jackson@uky.edu.

University of La Verne, College of Business and Public Management, Graduate Programs in Business Administration, La Verne, CA 91750-4443. Offers accounting (MBA); business (MBIT); executive management (MBA-EP); finance (MBA, MBA-EP); health services management (MBA); information technology (MBA, MBA-EP); international business (MBA, MBA-EP); leadership (MBA-EP); managed care (MBA); management (MBA, MBA-EP); marketing (MBA, MBA-EP). Part-time and evening/weekend programs available. *Faculty:* 15 full-time (7 women), 13 part-time/adjunct (7 women). *Students:* 277 full-time (133 women), 112 part-time (64 women); includes 144 minority (32 African Americans, 3 American Indian/Alaska Native, 70 Asian Americans or Pacific Islanders, 39 Hispanic Americans), 160 international. Average age 30. In 2006, 142 degrees awarded. *Entrance requirements:* For master's, minimum undergraduate GPA of 3.0, 2 letters of recommendation, resumé. Additional exam requirements/recommendations for international students: Required—TOEFL (minimum score 550 paper-based; 213 computer-based). *Application deadline:* Applications are processed on a rolling basis. Application fee: $50. *Expenses:* Contact institution. *Financial support:* Career-related internships or fieldwork, institutionally sponsored loans, and scholarships/grants available. Financial award application deadline: 3/2; financial award applicants required to submit FAFSA. *Unit head:* Dr. Ibrahim Helou, Chairperson, 909-593-3511 Ext. 4211, Fax: 909-392-2704, E-mail: heloua@ulv.edu. *Application contact:* Dr. Julius Walecki, Marketing Director, 909-593-3511 Ext. 4192, Fax: 909-392-2704, E-mail: cbpm@ulv.edu.

University of Lethbridge, School of Graduate Studies, Lethbridge, AB T1K 3M4, Canada. Offers accounting (MScM); addictions counseling (M Sc); agricultural biotechnology (M Sc); agricultural studies (M Sc, MA); anthropology (MA); archaeology (MA); art (MA); biochemistry (M Sc); biological sciences (M Sc); biomolecular science (PhD); biosystems and biodiversity (PhD); Canadian studies (MA); chemistry (M Sc); computer science (M Sc); computer science and geographical information science (M Sc); counseling psychology (M Ed); dramatic arts (MA); earth, space, and physical science (PhD); economics (MA); educational leadership (M Ed); English (MA); environmental science (M Sc); evolution and behavior (PhD); exercise science (M Sc); finance (MScM); French (MA); French/German (MA); French/Spanish (MA); general education (M Ed); general management (MScM); geography (M Sc, MA); German (MA); health sciences (M Sc, MA); history (MA); human resource management and labour relations (MScM); individualized multidisciplinary (M Sc, MA); information systems (MScM); international management (MScM); kinesiology (M Sc, MA); management (M Sc, MA); marketing (MScM); mathematics (M Sc); music (MA); Native American studies (MA); neuroscience (M Sc, PhD); new media (MA); nursing (M Sc); philosophy (MA); physics (M Sc); policy and strategy (MScM); political science (MA); psychology (M Sc, MA); religious studies (MA); sociology (MA); theoretical and computational science (PhD); urban and regional studies (MA). Part-time and evening/weekend programs available. *Students:* 200 full-time, 90 part-time. In 2006, 105 master's, 3 doctorates awarded. *Degree requirements:* For doctorate, thesis/dissertation, comprehensive exam. *Entrance requirements:* For master's, GMAT (M Sc management), bachelor's degree in related field, minimum GPA of 3.0 during previous 20 graded semester courses, 2 years teaching or related experience (M Ed); for doctorate, master's degree, minimum graduate GPA of 3.5. Additional exam requirements/recommendations for international students: Required—TOEFL. Application fee: $60 Canadian dollars. *Financial support:* Fellowships, research assistantships, teaching assistantships, scholarships/grants, health care benefits, and unspecified assistantships available. *Faculty research:* Movement and brain plasticity, gibberellin physiology, photosynthesis, carbon cycling, molecular properties of main-group ring components. *Unit head:* Dr. Jo-Anne Fiske, Interim Dean, 403-329-2121, Fax: 403-329-2097. *Application contact:* Kathy Schrage, Administrative Assistant, Office of the Academic Vice President, 403-329-2121, Fax: 403-329-2097, E-mail: inquiries@uleth.ca.

University of Louisville, Graduate School, College of Business, School of Accountancy, Louisville, KY 40292-0001. Offers MAC. *Accreditation:* AACSB. *Students:* 11 full-time (3 women), 19 part-time (10 women); includes 1 minority (Hispanic American), 4 international. Average age 29. In 2006, 12 degrees awarded. *Entrance requirements:* For master's, GMAT, 2 letters of reference. Application fee: $50. *Unit head:* Dr. William Stout, Director, 502-852-5847, Fax: 502-852-6072, E-mail: wdstou01@louisville.edu.

University of Maine, Graduate School, College of Business, Public Policy and Health, The Maine Business School, Orono, ME 04469. Offers accounting (MS); business administration (MBA). *Accreditation:* AACSB. Part-time and evening/weekend programs available. *Faculty:* 20. *Students:* 56 full-time (19 women), 25 part-time (15 women); includes 1 minority (Asian American or Pacific Islander), 15 international. Average age 29. 48 applicants, 56% accepted, 19 enrolled. In 2006, 38 degrees awarded. *Entrance requirements:* For master's, GMAT. Additional exam requirements/recommendations for international students: Required—TOEFL (minimum score 550 paper-based; 213 computer-based). *Application deadline:* For fall admission, 6/1 priority date for domestic and international students; for spring admission, 11/1 priority date for domestic and international students. Applications are processed on a rolling basis. Application fee: $50. Electronic applications accepted. *Expenses:* Contact institution. *Financial support:* In 2006–07, 16 students received support, including 4 research assistantships with tuition reimbursements available (averaging $11,000 per year); career-related internships or fieldwork, Federal Work-Study, institutionally sponsored loans, scholarships/grants, tuition waivers (full and partial), and unspecified assistantships also available. Financial award application deadline: 3/1. *Faculty research:* Entrepreneurship, investment management, international markets, decision support systems, strategic planning. *Unit head:* Richard A. Grant, Director of Graduate Programs, 207-581-1971, Fax: 207-581-1930, E-mail: mba@maine.edu. *Application contact:* Scott G. Delcourt, Associate Dean of the Graduate School, 207-581-3219, Fax: 207-581-3232, E-mail: graduate@maine.edu.

University of Mary Hardin-Baylor, College of Business, Graduate Studies in Business Administration, Belton, TX 76513. Offers accounting (MBA); management (MBA); sport management (MBA). Part-time and evening/weekend programs available. *Faculty:* 10 full-time (3 women), 3 part-time/adjunct (1 woman). *Students:* 4 full-time (2 women), 19 part-time (10 women); includes 3 minority (all Hispanic Americans) Average age 24. In 2006, 9 degrees awarded. *Degree requirements:* For master's, practicum. *Entrance requirements:* For master's, GMAT, minimum GPA of 3.0, work experience, interview. *Application deadline:* For fall admission, 6/1 priority date for domestic students; for spring admission, 11/1 for domestic students. Applications are processed on a rolling basis. Application fee: $35 ($135 for international students). Electronic applications accepted. *Expenses:* Tuition: Full-time $8,910; part-time $495 per hour. Required fees: $906; $47 per hour. $30 per term. Tuition and fees vary according to course load. *Financial support:* Federal Work-Study and scholarships (for some active duty military personnel only) available. Financial award applicants required to submit FAFSA. *Unit head:* Dr. Chrisann Merriman, Director, 254-295-4647, E-mail: chrisann.merriman@umhb.edu.

University of Maryland University College, Graduate School of Management and Technology, Program in Accounting and Financial Management, Adelphi, MD 20783. Offers MS, Certificate. Part-time and evening/weekend programs available. Postbaccalaureate distance learning degree programs offered (no on-campus study). *Students:* 31 full-time (18 women), 414 part-time (282 women); includes 212 minority (145 African Americans, 44 Asian Americans or Pacific Islanders, 23 Hispanic Americans), 12 international. Average age 35. 116 applicants, 100% accepted, 89 enrolled. In 2006, 51 master's, 4 other advanced degrees awarded. *Degree requirements:* For master's, thesis or alternative. *Application deadline:* Applications are processed on a rolling basis. Application fee: $50. Electronic applications accepted. *Financial support:* Federal Work-Study and scholarships/grants available. Support available to part-time students. Financial award application deadline: 6/1; financial award applicants required to submit FAFSA. *Unit head:* Dr. James Howard, 301-985-7200, Fax: 301-985-4611, E-mail: jhoward@umuc.edu. *Application contact:* Coordinator, Graduate Admissions, 301-985-7155, Fax: 301-985-7175, E-mail: gradinfo@umuc.edu.

University of Maryland University College, Graduate School of Management and Technology, Program in Accounting and Information Technology, Adelphi, MD 20783. Offers MS, Certificate. Part-time and evening/weekend programs available. Postbaccalaureate distance learning degree programs offered (no on-campus study). *Students:* 7 full-time (4 women), 186 part-time (117 women); includes 90 minority (68 African Americans, 15 Asian Americans or Pacific Islanders, 7 Hispanic Americans), 4 international. Average age 37. 39 applicants, 100% accepted, 29 enrolled. In 2006, 20 master's, 3 other advanced degrees awarded. *Degree requirements:* For master's, thesis or alternative. *Application deadline:* Applications are processed on a rolling basis. Application fee: $50. Electronic applications accepted. *Financial support:* Federal Work-Study and scholarships/grants available. Support available to part-time students. Financial award application deadline: 6/1; financial award applicants required to submit FAFSA. *Unit head:* Dr. James Howard, 301-985-7200, Fax: 301-985-4611, E-mail: jhoward@umuc.edu. *Application contact:* Coordinator, Graduate Admissions, 301-985-7155, Fax: 301-985-7175, E-mail: gradinfo@umuc.edu.

University of Massachusetts Amherst, Graduate School, Isenberg School of Management, Program in Accounting, Amherst, MA 01003. Offers MS. *Accreditation:* AACSB. *Faculty:* 1 (woman) full-time. *Students:* 56 full-time (37 women), 2 part-time (1 woman); includes 8 minority (6 Asian Americans or Pacific Islanders, 2 Hispanic Americans), 2 international. Average age 23. 77 applicants, 81% accepted, 57 enrolled. *Entrance requirements:* For master's, GMAT. Additional exam requirements/recommendations for international students: Required—TOEFL (minimum score 530 paper-based; 197 computer-based). *Application deadline:* For fall admission, 2/1 priority date for domestic and international students. Applications are processed on a rolling basis. Application fee: $40 ($65 for international students). Electronic applications accepted. *Expenses:* Tuition, state resident: full-time $2,640; part-time $110 per credit. Tuition, nonresident: full-time $9,936; part-time $414 per credit. Required fees: $8,969; $3,129 per term. One-time fee: $257 full-time. Tuition and fees vary according to class time, course load, campus/location and reciprocity agreements. *Financial support:* Fellowships with full tuition reimbursements, research assistantships with full tuition reimbursements, teaching assistantships with full tuition reimbursements, career-related internships or fieldwork, Federal Work-Study, scholarships/grants, traineeships, health care benefits, and unspecified assistantships available. Support available to part-time students. Financial award application deadline: 2/1. *Unit head:* James F. Smith, Director, 413-545-5645.

University of Massachusetts Dartmouth, Graduate School, Charlton College of Business, Program in Business Administration, North Dartmouth, MA 02747-2300. Offers accounting (Postbaccalaureate Certificate); business administration (MBA); e-commerce (PMC); finance (PMC); general management (PMC); leadership (PMC); management (Postbaccalaureate Certificate); marketing (PMC); supply chain management (PMC). *Accreditation:* AACSB. Part-time programs available. *Faculty:* 41 full-time (11 women), 22 part-time/adjunct (8 women). *Students:* 66 full-time (20 women), 111 part-time (54 women); includes 16 minority (5 African Americans, 6 Asian Americans or Pacific Islanders, 5 Hispanic Americans), 46 international. Average age 30. 167 applicants, 83% accepted, 83 enrolled. In 2006, 73 master's, 20 other advanced degrees awarded. *Entrance requirements:* For master's, GMAT, resumé, letters of recommendation. Additional exam requirements/recommendations for international students: Required—TOEFL (minimum score 500 paper-based). *Application deadline:* For fall admission, 6/1 for domestic students, 4/1 for international students; for spring admission, 10/1 for domestic students, 8/1 for international students. Application fee: $40 ($60 for international students). Electronic applications accepted. *Expenses:* Tuition, state resident: full-time $2,071; part-time $86 per credit. Tuition, nonresident: full-time $8,099; part-time $337 per credit. *Financial support:* In 2006–07, 2 research assistantships with full tuition reimbursements (averaging $11,985 per year), 6 teaching assistantships with full tuition reimbursements (averaging $7,200 per year) were awarded; Federal Work-Study and unspecified assistantships also available. Support available to part-time students. Financial award application deadline: 3/1; financial award applicants required to submit FAFSA. *Faculty research:* Organizational identity dynamics in strategic alliances and partnerships, market analysis in cranberry industry, consumer choice modeling. Total annual research expenditures: $508,000. *Unit head:* Matthew Roy, Assistant Dean, 508-999-8409, Fax: 508-999-8776, E-mail: mroy@umassd.edu. *Application contact:* Carol Novo, Graduate Admissions Officer, 508-999-8604, Fax: 508-999-8183, E-mail: graduate@umassd.edu.

University of Memphis, Graduate School, Fogelman College of Business and Economics, Program in Business Administration, Memphis, TN 38152. Offers accounting (MBA, PhD); economics (MBA, PhD); executive business administration (MBA); finance (PhD); finance, insurance, and real estate (MBA, MS); international business administration (MBA); management (MBA, MS, PhD); management information systems (MBA, MS, PhD); management science (MBA); marketing (MBA, MS); marketing and supply chain management (PhD); real estate development (MS); JD/MBA. *Accreditation:* AACSB. *Faculty:* 84 full-time (14 women), 3 part-time/adjunct (0 women). *Students:* 222 full-time (92 women), 163 part-time (52 women); includes 62 minority (43 African Americans, 14 Asian Americans or Pacific Islanders, 5 Hispanic Americans), 119 international. Average age 29. In 2006, 196 master's, 12 doctorates awarded. *Degree requirements:* For master's, comprehensive exam; for doctorate, thesis/dissertation, comprehensive exam. *Entrance requirements:* For master's, GMAT, resumé; for doctorate, GMAT, interview, minimum GPA of 3.4, resumé, letter of recommendation. Additional exam requirements/recommendations for international students: Required—TOEFL (minimum score 550 paper-based; 220 computer-based). *Application deadline:* For fall admission, 8/1 for domestic students; for spring admission, 12/1 for domestic students. Application fee: $25 ($50 for international students). *Financial support:* Research assistantships with full tuition reimbursements, teaching assistantships, career-related internships or fieldwork, scholarships/grants, and unspecified assistantships available. Financial award application deadline: 3/1. *Faculty research:* Competitive business strategy, finance microstructures, supply chain management innovations, health care economics, litigation risks and corporate audits. Total annual research expenditures: $2.7 million. *Application contact:* Dr. Carol V. Danehower, Associate Dean for Programs, 901-678-5402, Fax: 901-678-3579, E-mail: fcbegp@memphis.edu.

University of Memphis, Graduate School, Fogelman College of Business and Economics, School of Accountancy, Memphis, TN 38152. Offers accounting (MS); accounting systems (MS); taxation (MS). *Accreditation:* AACSB. *Faculty:* 15 full-time (1 woman). *Students:* 25 full-time (15 women), 22 part-time (12 women); includes 13 minority (10 African Americans, 2 Asian Americans or Pacific Islanders, 1 Hispanic American), 12 international. Average age 29. 33 applicants, 79% accepted. In 2006, 16 degrees awarded. *Degree requirements:* For master's, comprehensive exam. *Entrance requirements:* For master's, GMAT. *Application*

Accounting

University of Memphis (continued)
deadline: For fall admission, 8/1 for domestic students; for spring admission, 12/1 for domestic students. Application fee: $25 ($50 for international students). *Financial support:* In 2006–07, 11 students received support, including 5 research assistantships with full tuition reimbursements available (averaging $20,000 per year); teaching assistantships, scholarships/grants also available. Financial award application deadline: 3/1. *Faculty research:* Financial accounting, corporate governance, EDP auditing, evolution of system analysis, investor behavior and investment decisions. *Unit head:* Dr. Kenneth Lambert, Chair, 901-678-4569, Fax: 901-678-2685, E-mail: klambert@memphis.edu. *Application contact:* Dr. Coy A. Jones, Interim Associate Dean for Academic Programs, 901-678-4649, Fax: 901-678-4705, E-mail: fcbegp@memphis.edu.

University of Miami, Graduate School, School of Business Administration, Department of Accounting, Coral Gables, FL 33124. Offers professional accounting (MP Acc); taxation (MS Tax). *Accreditation:* AACSB. Part-time and evening/weekend programs available. *Faculty:* 9 full-time (3 women), 2 part-time/adjunct (0 women). *Students:* 26 full-time (18 women), 12 part-time (5 women); includes 12 minority (4 Asian Americans or Pacific Islanders, 8 Hispanic Americans), 4 international. Average age 24. 52 applicants, 62% accepted, 21 enrolled. In 2006, 35 degrees awarded. *Entrance requirements:* For master's, GMAT or CPA exam. Additional exam requirements/recommendations for international students: Required—TOEFL. *Application deadline:* For fall admission, 7/30 priority date for domestic students; for spring admission, 11/30 priority date for domestic students. Applications are processed on a rolling basis. Application fee: $50. Electronic applications accepted. *Financial support:* In 2006–07, 7 students received support, including 2 research assistantships (averaging $3,000 per year); fellowships, institutionally sponsored loans, scholarships/grants, and unspecified assistantships also available. Financial award application deadline: 3/1. *Faculty research:* Financial reporting, audit risk, public policy and taxation issues, government accounting and public choice, corporate governance. *Unit head:* Dr. Kay W. Tatum, Chairperson, 305-284-6903, Fax: 305-284-5737, E-mail: ktatum@miami.edu. *Application contact:* Willie Risby-Hannah, Administrative Assistant, 305-284-5428, Fax: 305-284-5737, E-mail: wrisby@miami.edu.

University of Miami, Graduate School, School of Business Administration, Program in Business Administration, Coral Gables, FL 33124. Offers accounting (MBA); computer information systems (MBA); executive and professional (MBA), including international business, management; finance (MBA); international business (MBA); management (MBA); management science (MBA); marketing (MBA); professional management (MSPM); JD/MBA; MBA/MSIE. *Accreditation:* AACSB. Evening/weekend programs available. *Faculty:* 105 full-time (25 women). *Students:* 734 full-time (269 women), 19 part-time (4 women); includes 194 minority (24 African Americans, 1 American Indian/Alaska Native, 23 Asian Americans or Pacific Islanders, 146 Hispanic Americans), 115 international. Average age 31. 453 applicants, 71% accepted, 152 enrolled. In 2006, 394 degrees awarded. *Degree requirements:* For master's, comprehensive exam, registration. *Entrance requirements:* For master's, GMAT. Additional exam requirements/recommendations for international students: Required—TOEFL (minimum score 550 paper-based; 213 computer-based; 59 iBT). *Application deadline:* For fall admission, 7/30 priority date for domestic students, 6/30 priority date for international students; for spring admission, 12/31 priority date for domestic students, 10/31 priority date for international students. Applications are processed on a rolling basis. Application fee: $50. Electronic applications accepted. *Financial support:* In 2006–07, 418 students received support, including 19 fellowships with partial tuition reimbursements available; unspecified assistantships also available. Financial award application deadline: 3/1; financial award applicants required to submit FAFSA. *Faculty research:* Leadership, e-commerce, supply chain management. *Unit head:* Daniela Mu±iz, Associate Director, Graduate Business Programs, 305-284-4626, Fax: 305-284-1878, E-mail: dmuniz@miami.edu. *Application contact:* David S. Green, Director of Graduate Business Recruiting and Admissions, 305-284-4607, Fax: 305-284-1878, E-mail: mba@miami.edu.

University of Michigan–Dearborn, School of Management, Dearborn, MI 48128-1491. Offers accounting (MS); finance (MS); management (MBA); MBA/MHSA; MBA/MSE; MBA/MSF. *Accreditation:* AACSB. Part-time and evening/weekend programs available. Postbaccalaureate distance learning degree programs offered (no on-campus study). *Degree requirements:* For master's, registration. *Entrance requirements:* For master's, GMAT, 2 years of work experience (MBA); course work in computer applications, statistics, and pre-calculus or finite mathematics. Additional exam requirements/recommendations for international students: Required—TOEFL (minimum score 560 paper-based; 220 computer-based). Expenses: Contact institution. *Faculty research:* Cultural diversity, buyer-supplier relations, error detection in data, economic evolution.

University of Minnesota, Twin Cities Campus, Carlson School of Management, Carlson Full-time MBA Program, Minneapolis, MN 55455-0213. Offers accounting (MBA); entrepreneurship (MBA); finance (MBA); healthcare management (MBA); information and decision sciences (MBA); international business (MBA); marketing and logistics management (MBA); operations and management science (MBA); strategic management and organization (MBA); supply chain management (MBA); JD/MBA; MD/MBA; MHA/MBA. *Accreditation:* AACSB. *Faculty:* 125 full-time (27 women), 120 part-time/adjunct. *Students:* 218 full-time (70 women); includes 18 minority (4 African Americans, 1 American Indian/Alaska Native, 10 Asian Americans or Pacific Islanders, 3 Hispanic Americans), 86 international. Average age 28. 418 applicants, 53% accepted, 124 enrolled. In 2006, 105 degrees awarded. *Median time to degree:* Master's–2 years full-time. *Entrance requirements:* For master's, GMAT. Additional exam requirements/recommendations for international students: Required—TOEFL (minimum score 580 paper-based; 240 computer-based), IELTS. *Application deadline:* For fall admission, 4/15 for domestic students, 2/15 for international students. Application fee: $60 ($90 for international students). Electronic applications accepted. *Expenses: Contact institution.* Full-time tuition and fees vary according to class time, course load, program, reciprocity agreements and student level. *Financial support:* In 2006–07, 131 students received support, including 127 fellowships with full and partial tuition reimbursements available (averaging $20,000 per year); research assistantships with partial tuition reimbursements available, teaching assistantships with partial tuition reimbursements available, career-related internships or fieldwork, Federal Work-Study, institutionally sponsored loans, scholarships/grants, health care benefits, tuition waivers (full and partial), and unspecified assistantships also available. Support available to part-time students. Financial award application deadline: 2/15; financial award applicants required to submit FAFSA. *Faculty research:* IT, strategy, marketing, finance, quality management. *Unit head:* Kathryn J. Carlson, MBA Programs and Executive Education, 612-624-2039, Fax: 612-625-1012, E-mail: fulltimeembainfo@csom.umn.edu. *Application contact:* Jeffrey Bieganek, Director, Admissions and Business Development, MBA Programs and Executive Education, 612-625-6558, Fax: 612-625-1012, E-mail: full-timembainfo@csom.umn.edu.

University of Minnesota, Twin Cities Campus, Carlson School of Management, Doctoral Program in Business Administration, Minneapolis, MN 55455-0213. Offers accounting (PhD); finance (PhD); information and decision sciences (PhD); marketing and logistics management (PhD); operations and management science (PhD); strategic management and organization (PhD). *Faculty:* 109 full-time (26 women). *Students:* 90 full-time (30 women); includes 9 minority (5 African Americans, 1 Asian American or Pacific Islander, 3 Hispanic Americans), 60 international. Average age 30. 325 applicants, 8% accepted, 17 enrolled. In 2006, 16 degrees awarded. *Median time to degree:* Of those who began their doctoral program in fall 1998, 61% received their degree in 8 years or less. *Degree requirements:* For doctorate, thesis/dissertation, written and oral preliminary exams, comprehensive exam, registration. *Entrance requirements:* For doctorate, GMAT, GRE General Test, International must submit a TOEFL or IELT. Additional exam requirements/recommendations for international students: Required—TOEFL (minimum score 600 paper-based; 250 computer-based; 100 iBT), IELTS (minimum score 8), TOEFL (paper-based 600, computer-based 250) or IELTS (7.5). *Application deadline:* For fall admission, 12/30 for domestic students, 12/30 priority date for international students. Applications are processed on a rolling basis. Application fee: $55 ($75 for international students). Electronic applications accepted. *Expenses:* Tuition, state resident: full-time $9,302; part-time $775 per credit. Tuition, nonresident: full-time $16,400; part-time $1,367 per credit. Full-time tuition and fees vary according to class time, course load, program, reciprocity agreements and student level. *Financial support:* In 2006–07, 67 students received support, including fellowships with full tuition reimbursements available (averaging $11,000 per year), research assistantships with full tuition reimbursements available (averaging $6,000 per year), teaching assistantships with full tuition reimbursements available (averaging $6,000 per year); institutionally sponsored loans, scholarships/grants, health care benefits, and unspecified assistantships also available. Financial award application deadline: 12/31. *Faculty research:* Corporate strategy, international business, corporate finances, entrepreneurship, quality management, marketing, information and decision science, operations and accounting. Total annual research expenditures: $300,000. *Unit head:* Dr. Paul E. Johnson, Director of Graduate Studies and PhD Program Director, 612-624-5570, Fax: 612-624-8221, E-mail: pjohnson@csom.umn.edu. *Application contact:* Earlene Bronson, Assistant Director, PhD Program, 612-624-0875, Fax: 612-624-8221, E-mail: ebronson@csom.umn.edu.

University of Minnesota, Twin Cities Campus, Carlson School of Management, Master's Program in Accountancy, Minneapolis, MN 55455-0213. Offers M Acc. *Accreditation:* AACSB. *Students:* 28 full-time (16 women); includes 9 minority (all Asian Americans or Pacific Islanders) Average age 23. 38 applicants, 76% accepted, 28 enrolled. *Entrance requirements:* For master's, GMAT, letters of recommendation. Additional exam requirements/recommendations for international students: Required—TOEFL (minimum score 550 paper-based; 213 computer-based). *Application deadline:* For spring admission, 10/15 priority date for domestic and international students. Applications are processed on a rolling basis. Application fee: $55 ($75 for international students). Electronic applications accepted. *Expenses: Contact institution.* *Financial support:* In 2006–07, 8 fellowships (averaging $1,625 per year), 12 teaching assistantships with partial tuition reimbursements (averaging $5,600 per year) were awarded. *Unit head:* Larry Kallio, Program Director, 612-624-9818, Fax: 612-626-7795, E-mail: lkallio@csom.umn.edu. *Application contact:* JoAnn Ash, Administrator, 612-624-3320, Fax: 612-626-7795, E-mail: jash@csom.umn.edu.

University of Mississippi, Graduate School, School of Accountancy, Oxford, University, MS 38677. Offers accountancy (M Acc, PhD); taxation accounting (M Tax). *Accreditation:* AACSB. *Faculty:* 11 full-time (4 women), 1 part-time/adjunct (0 women). *Students:* 76 full-time (34 women), 25 part-time (13 women); includes 9 minority (7 African Americans, 1 American Indian/Alaska Native, 1 Asian American or Pacific Islander), 6 international. 116 applicants, 78% accepted, 72 enrolled. In 2006, 62 master's, 3 doctorates awarded. *Degree requirements:* For doctorate, thesis/dissertation. *Entrance requirements:* For master's, GMAT, minimum GPA of 3.0; for doctorate, GMAT. Additional exam requirements/recommendations for international students: Required—TOEFL. *Application deadline:* For fall admission, 4/1 for domestic students; for spring admission, 10/1 for domestic students. Applications are processed on a rolling basis. Application fee: $25. *Expenses:* Tuition, state resident: full-time $4,602; part-time $256 per credit hour. Tuition, nonresident: full-time $10,566; part-time $587 per credit hour. *Financial support:* Scholarships/grants available. Financial award application deadline: 3/1; financial award applicants required to submit FAFSA. *Unit head:* Dr. Mark Wilder, Interim Dean, 662-915-7468, Fax: 662-915-7483, E-mail: acwilder@olemiss.edu.

University of Missouri–Columbia, Graduate School, College of Business, School of Accountancy, Columbia, MO 65211. Offers M Acc, PhD. *Accreditation:* AACSB. Part-time programs available. *Faculty:* 17 full-time (6 women). *Students:* 130 full-time (59 women), 4 part-time (3 women); includes 8 minority (2 African Americans, 5 Asian Americans or Pacific Islanders, 1 Hispanic American), 7 international. In 2006, 98 master's, 1 doctorate awarded. *Degree requirements:* For master's, thesis or alternative; for doctorate, thesis/dissertation. *Entrance requirements:* For master's and doctorate, GMAT, minimum GPA of 3.0. *Application deadline:* For fall admission, 2/1 priority date for domestic students. Applications are processed on a rolling basis. Application fee: $45 ($60 for international students). *Financial support:* Fellowships, research assistantships, teaching assistantships, institutionally sponsored loans available. *Unit head:* Dr. Jere R. Francis, Director of Graduate Studies, 573-882-5156, E-mail: francisjr@missouri.edu.

University of Missouri–Kansas City, Henry W. Bloch School of Business and Public Administration, Kansas City, MO 64110-2499. Offers accounting (MS); business administration (MBA); public affairs (MPA, PhD); JD/MBA; LL M/MPA. *Accreditation:* AACSB; NASPAA. Part-time and evening/weekend programs available. *Faculty:* 42 full-time (11 women), 16 part-time/adjunct (7 women). *Students:* 201 full-time (104 women), 395 part-time (177 women); includes 80 minority (41 African Americans, 5 American Indian/Alaska Native, 21 Asian Americans or Pacific Islanders, 13 Hispanic Americans), 41 international. Average age 30. 464 applicants, 63% accepted, 226 enrolled. In 2006, 186 degrees awarded. Terminal master's awarded for partial completion of doctoral program. *Entrance requirements:* For master's, GMAT, GRE, 2 writing essays, 2 references and support of employer; for doctorate, GRE, minimum GPA of 3.0. Additional exam requirements/recommendations for international students: Required—TOEFL. *Application deadline:* For fall admission, 5/1 priority date for domestic students, 4/1 priority date for international students; for winter admission, 10/1 priority date for domestic students, 9/1 priority date for international students. Applications are processed on a rolling basis. Application fee: $35 ($50 for international students). Electronic applications accepted. *Expenses:* Tuition, state resident: full-time $4,975; part-time $276 per credit. Tuition, nonresident: full-time $12,847; part-time $713 per credit. Required fees: $595; $595 per year. *Financial support:* In 2006–07, 407 students received support, including 26 research assistantships with partial tuition reimbursements available (averaging $10,483 per year), 3 teaching assistantships with partial tuition reimbursements available (averaging $11,080 per year); fellowships, career-related internships or fieldwork, Federal Work-Study, institutionally sponsored loans, scholarships/grants, tuition waivers (full and partial), and unspecified assistantships also available. Support available to part-time students. Financial award application deadline: 3/1; financial award applicants required to submit FAFSA. *Faculty research:* Entrepreneurship, finance, non-profit, risk management. Total annual research expenditures: $803,340. *Unit head:* Dr. O. Homer Erekson, Dean, 816-235-2204, Fax: 816-235-2206, E-mail: ereksonh@umkc.edu. *Application contact:* 816-235-1111, E-mail: admit@umkc.edu.

University of Missouri–St. Louis, College of Business Administration, Program in Accounting, St. Louis, MO 63121. Offers M Acc. *Accreditation:* AACSB. Part-time and evening/weekend programs available. *Faculty:* 8 full-time (4 women). *Students:* 25 full-time (17 women), 27 part-time (11 women); includes 3 minority (all Asian Americans or Pacific Islanders), 8 international. Average age 28. In 2006, 18 degrees awarded. *Entrance requirements:* For master's, GMAT, 2 letters of recommendation. Additional exam requirements/recommendations for international students: Required—TOEFL (minimum score 550 paper-based; 213 computer-based). *Application deadline:* For fall admission, 7/1 for domestic students; for spring admission, 11/1 for domestic students. Applications are processed on a rolling basis. Application fee: $35 ($40 for international students). Electronic applications accepted. *Expenses:* Tuition, state resident: part-time $332 per credit hour. Tuition, nonresident: part-time $770 per credit hour. *Financial support:* Research assistantships, teaching assistantships, career-related internships or fieldwork, Federal Work-Study, and institutionally sponsored loans available. Support available to part-time students. Financial award application deadline: 4/1; financial award applicants required to submit FAFSA. *Faculty research:* Accounting information in contracts, financial reporting issues, empirical valuation issues. *Application contact:* 314-516-5458, Fax: 314-516-6996, E-mail: gradadm@umsl.edu.

University of Missouri–St. Louis, College of Business Administration, Program in Business Administration, St. Louis, MO 63121. Offers accounting (MBA); business administration (Certificate); finance (MBA); human resource management (Certificate); logistics and supply chain management (MBA, Certificate); management (MBA); marketing (MBA); marketing management (Certificate); operations (MBA); quantitative management science (MBA); telecommunications management (Certificate). *Accreditation:* AACSB. Part-time and evening/weekend programs available. *Faculty:* 26 full-time (6 women), 2 part-time/adjunct (0 women). *Students:* 242 full-time (156 women), 186 part-time (123 women); includes 48 minority (17 African

Americans, 1 American Indian/Alaska Native, 27 Asian Americans or Pacific Islanders, 3 Hispanic Americans), 96 international. Average age 33. In 2006, 138 degrees awarded. *Entrance requirements:* For master's, GMAT, 2 letters of recommendation. Additional exam requirements/recommendations for international students: Required—TOEFL (minimum score 550 paper-based; 213 computer-based). *Application deadline:* For fall admission, 7/1 for domestic students; for spring admission, 11/1 for domestic students. Applications are processed on a rolling basis. Application fee: $35 ($40 for international students). Electronic applications accepted. *Expenses:* Tuition, state resident: part-time $332 per credit hour. Tuition, nonresident: part-time $770 per credit hour. *Financial support:* Research assistantships with full and partial tuition reimbursements, teaching assistantships with full and partial tuition reimbursements, career-related internships or fieldwork, Federal Work-Study, and institutionally sponsored loans available. Support available to part-time students. Financial award application deadline: 4/1; financial award applicants required to submit FAFSA. *Faculty research:* Human resources, strategic management, marketing strategy, consumer behavior product development, advertising. *Application contact:* 314-516-5458, Fax: 314-516-6996, E-mail: gradadm@umsl.edu.

The University of Montana, Graduate School, School of Business Administration, Department of Accounting and Finance, Missoula, MT 59812-0002. Offers accounting (M Acct). *Accreditation:* AACSB. *Degree requirements:* For master's, thesis optional. *Entrance requirements:* For master's, GMAT. Additional exam requirements/recommendations for international students: Required—TOEFL (minimum score 580 paper-based; 237 computer-based). *Faculty research:* Income tax, financial markets, nonprofit accounting, accounting information systems, auditing.

University of Nebraska at Omaha, Graduate Studies and Research, College of Business Administration, Department of Accounting, Omaha, NE 68182. Offers M Acc. Part-time and evening/weekend programs available. *Faculty:* 9 full-time (2 women). *Students:* 4 full-time (2 women), 14 part-time (8 women); includes 2 minority (1 African American, 1 Asian American or Pacific Islander), 2 international. Average age 26. 13 applicants, 54% accepted, 5 enrolled. In 2006, 9 degrees awarded. *Degree requirements:* For master's, comprehensive exam. *Entrance requirements:* For master's, GMAT, minimum GPA of 3.0, resumé. Additional exam requirements/recommendations for international students: Required—TOEFL (minimum score 600 paper-based; 213 computer-based; 100 iBT). *Application deadline:* For fall admission, 5/1 priority date for domestic students; for spring admission, 12/1 priority date for domestic students. Applications are processed on a rolling basis. Application fee: $45. Electronic applications accepted. *Financial support:* In 2006–07, 9 students received support; research assistantships with tuition reimbursements available, Federal Work-Study, institutionally sponsored loans, scholarships/grants, tuition waivers (partial), and unspecified assistantships available. Support available to part-time students. Financial award application deadline: 3/1; financial award applicants required to submit FAFSA. *Unit head:* Dr. Jack Armitage, Chairperson, 402-554-3650.

University of Nebraska–Lincoln, Graduate College, College of Business Administration, Interdepartmental Area of Business, Lincoln, NE 68588. Offers accountancy (PhD); business (MBA); finance (MA, PhD), including business; management (MA, PhD), including business; marketing (MA, PhD), including business; JD/MA; JD/MBA; M Arch/MBA. *Accreditation:* AACSB. Part-time programs available. Postbaccalaureate distance learning degree programs offered. *Degree requirements:* For doctorate, thesis/dissertation, comprehensive exam. *Entrance requirements:* For master's and doctorate, GMAT. Additional exam requirements/recommendations for international students: Required—TOEFL (minimum score 550 paper-based; 213 computer-based). Electronic applications accepted.

University of Nebraska–Lincoln, Graduate College, College of Business Administration, School of Accountancy, Lincoln, NE 68588. Offers MPA, PhD, JD/MPA. *Accreditation:* AACSB. *Entrance requirements:* For master's, GMAT. Additional exam requirements/recommendations for international students: Required—TOEFL (minimum score 550 paper-based; 213 computer-based). Electronic applications accepted. *Faculty research:* Auditing, financial accounting, managerial accounting, capital markets, tax accounting.

University of Nevada, Las Vegas, Graduate College, College of Business, Department of Accounting, Las Vegas, NV 89154-9900. Offers MS. *Accreditation:* AACSB. Part-time and evening/weekend programs available. *Faculty:* 11 full-time (3 women), 5 part-time/adjunct (0 women). *Students:* 42 full-time (25 women), 33 part-time (20 women); includes 20 minority (2 African Americans, 16 Asian Americans or Pacific Islanders, 2 Hispanic Americans), 13 international. 68 applicants, 65% accepted, 31 enrolled. In 2006, 23 degrees awarded. *Entrance requirements:* For master's, GMAT, minimum GPA of 3.0 or 2.75 with an accounting degree. Additional exam requirements/recommendations for international students: Required—TOEFL (minimum score 550 paper-based; 213 computer-based; 80 iBT). *Application deadline:* For fall admission, 6/15 for domestic students, 5/1 for international students; for spring admission, 11/15 for domestic students, 10/1 for international students. Application fee: $60 ($75 for international students). Electronic applications accepted. *Financial support:* In 2006–07, 3 research assistantships with partial tuition reimbursements (averaging $10,000 per year) were awarded; teaching assistantships with partial tuition reimbursements, career-related internships or fieldwork, Federal Work-Study, institutionally sponsored loans, scholarships/grants, health care benefits, and unspecified assistantships also available. Support available to part-time students. Financial award application deadline: 3/1. *Unit head:* Dr. Paulette Tandy, Chair, 702-895-1559. *Application contact:* Graduate College Admissions Evaluator, 702-895-3320, Fax: 702-895-4180, E-mail: gradcollege@unlv.edu.

University of Nevada, Reno, Graduate School, College of Business Administration, Department of Accounting and Information Systems, Reno, NV 89557. Offers M Acc. *Accreditation:* AACSB. *Faculty:* 12. *Students:* 5 full-time (4 women), 14 part-time (9 women); includes 2 minority (1 Asian American or Pacific Islander, 1 Hispanic American), 3 international. Average age 32. 8 applicants, 38% accepted, 2 enrolled. In 2006, 16 degrees awarded. *Entrance requirements:* For master's, GMAT, minimum GPA of 2.75. Additional exam requirements/recommendations for international students: Required—TOEFL. *Application deadline:* For fall admission, 3/1 priority date for domestic students; for spring admission, 11/1 for domestic students. Application fee: $60 ($95 for international students). *Financial support:* Research assistantships, teaching assistantships available. *Unit head:* Dr. John Mills, Graduate Program Director, 775-784-6884.

University of New Hampshire, Graduate School, Whittemore School of Business and Economics, Department of Accounting and Finance, Durham, NH 03824. Offers accounting (MS). Part-time programs available. *Faculty:* 8 full-time. *Students:* 14 full-time (9 women), 3 part-time (all women); includes 1 minority (Asian American or Pacific Islander), 3 international. Average age 29. 26 applicants, 81% accepted, 15 enrolled. In 2006, 12 degrees awarded. *Entrance requirements:* For master's, GMAT. Additional exam requirements/recommendations for international students: Required—TOEFL (minimum score 550 paper-based; 213 computer-based). *Application deadline:* For fall admission, 4/1 priority date for domestic students, 4/1 for international students; for winter admission, 12/1 priority date for domestic students. Applications are processed on a rolling basis. Application fee: $60. *Expenses:* Tuition, state resident: full-time $8,540; part-time $474 per credit hour. Tuition, nonresident: full-time $20,990; part-time $862 per credit hour. Required fees: $1,343; $356 per term. Tuition and fees vary according to course load, program and reciprocity agreements. *Financial support:* In 2006–07, 1 fellowship, 1 teaching assistantship were awarded; research assistantships. Financial award application deadline: 2/15. *Unit head:* Dr. Ahmad Etebari, Chairperson, 603-862-3359, E-mail: ahmad.etebari@unh.edu. *Application contact:* Ginette Couture, Administrative Assistant, 603-862-3388, E-mail: wsbe.grad@unh.edu.

See Close-Up on page 459.

University of New Haven, Graduate School, School of Business, Program in Accounting, West Haven, CT 06516-1916. Offers financial accounting (MS); managerial accounting (MS); taxation (MS). *Degree requirements:* For master's, thesis.

University of New Haven, Graduate School, School of Business, Program in Business Administration, West Haven, CT 06516-1916. Offers accounting (MBA); business policy and strategy (MBA); finance (MBA); health care management (MBA); human resources management (MBA); international business (MBA); marketing (MBA); public relations (MBA); sports management (MBA); technology management (MBA); MBA/MPA; MBA/MSIE. Part-time and evening/weekend programs available. *Degree requirements:* For master's, thesis or alternative. *Entrance requirements:* For master's, GMAT.

University of New Mexico, Robert O. Anderson Graduate School of Management, Program in Accounting, Albuquerque, NM 87131-2039. Offers accounting (M Acc, MBA); tax accounting (MBA). *Accreditation:* AACSB. Part-time and evening/weekend programs available. *Entrance requirements:* For master's, GMAT. Additional exam requirements/recommendations for international students: Required—TOEFL (minimum score 550 paper-based; 213 computer-based). *Faculty research:* Critical accounting, accounting pedagogy, theory, taxation.

University of New Orleans, Graduate School, College of Business Administration, Department of Accounting, Program in Accounting, New Orleans, LA 70148. Offers MS. *Accreditation:* AACSB. Part-time and evening/weekend programs available. *Students:* 40 (23 women). Average age 30. In 2006, 20 degrees awarded. *Degree requirements:* For master's, thesis optional. *Entrance requirements:* For master's, GMAT. Additional exam requirements/recommendations for international students: Required—TOEFL (minimum score 550 paper-based; 213 computer-based). *Application deadline:* For fall admission, 7/1 priority date for domestic students, 6/1 for international students; for spring admission, 11/15 priority date for domestic students, 10/1 for international students. Applications are processed on a rolling basis. Application fee: $40. Electronic applications accepted. *Financial support:* Research assistantships, Federal Work-Study available. Financial award application deadline: 3/15; financial award applicants required to submit FAFSA. *Application contact:* Dr. Gordon Hosch, Graduate Coordinator, 504-280-6438, Fax: 504-280-5430, E-mail: gahosch@uno.edu.

The University of North Carolina at Chapel Hill, Kenan-Flagler Business School, Accounting Program, Chapel Hill, NC 27599. Offers MAC. *Entrance requirements:* For master's, GMAT. Additional exam requirements/recommendations for international students: Required—TOEFL. Expenses: Contact institution. *Faculty research:* Corporate taxation, international taxation, financial accounting, corporate governance, strategy.

The University of North Carolina at Chapel Hill, Kenan-Flagler Business School, Doctoral Program in Business Administration, Chapel Hill, NC 27599. Offers accounting (PhD); finance (PhD); marketing (PhD); operations management (PhD); organizational behavior (PhD); strategy (PhD). *Accreditation:* AACSB. *Degree requirements:* For doctorate, thesis/dissertation. *Entrance requirements:* For doctorate, GMAT or GRE General Test. Electronic applications accepted. Expenses: Contact institution.

The University of North Carolina at Charlotte, Graduate School, Belk College of Business Administration, Department of Accounting, Charlotte, NC 28223-0001. Offers M Acc. *Accreditation:* AACSB. *Faculty:* 10 full-time (3 women). *Students:* 31 full-time (17 women), 60 part-time (29 women); includes 9 minority (4 African Americans, 4 Asian Americans or Pacific Islanders, 1 Hispanic American), 5 international. Average age 29. 98 applicants, 59% accepted, 44 enrolled. In 2006, 42 degrees awarded. *Entrance requirements:* For master's, GMAT, minimum GPA of 3.0 in undergraduate major, 2.8 overall. Additional exam requirements/recommendations for international students: Required—TOEFL (minimum score 557 paper-based; 220 computer-based). *Application deadline:* For fall admission, 7/15 for domestic students, 5/1 for international students; for spring admission, 11/15 for domestic students, 10/1 for international students. Applications are processed on a rolling basis. Application fee: $55. Electronic applications accepted. *Expenses:* Tuition, state resident: full-time $2,719; part-time $170 per credit. Tuition, nonresident: full-time $12,926; part-time $808 per credit. Required fees: $1,555. *Financial support:* In 2006–07, 12 teaching assistantships (averaging $5,334 per year) were awarded; fellowships, research assistantships, career-related internships or fieldwork, Federal Work-Study, institutionally sponsored loans, scholarships/grants, and unspecified assistantships also available. Support available to part-time students. Financial award application deadline: 4/1; financial award applicants required to submit FAFSA. *Faculty research:* Corporate financial reporting trends, use of latest software for accounting and business applications, latest developments in federal and international taxation. *Unit head:* Dr. Casper Wiggins, Chair, 704-687-3620, Fax: 704-687-6938, E-mail: cwiggins@email.uncc.edu. *Application contact:* Kathy B. Giddings, Director of Graduate Admissions, 704-687-3366, Fax: 704-687-3279, E-mail: gradadm@email.uncc.edu.

The University of North Carolina at Greensboro, Graduate School, Bryan School of Business and Economics, Department of Accounting, Greensboro, NC 27412-5001. Offers accounting (MS); accounting systems (MS); financial accounting and reporting (MS); financial analysis (PMC); tax concentration (MS). *Accreditation:* AACSB. *Faculty:* 12 full-time (2 women). *Students:* 86 full-time (46 women), 16 part-time (8 women); includes 34 minority (17 African Americans, 1 American Indian/Alaska Native, 16 Asian Americans or Pacific Islanders). 50 applicants, 22% accepted. *Entrance requirements:* For master's, GMAT, GRE General Test, previous course work in accounting and business. Additional exam requirements/recommendations for international students: Required—TOEFL. *Application deadline:* For fall admission, 7/1 priority date for domestic students; for spring admission, 11/1 for domestic students. Applications are processed on a rolling basis. Application fee: $45. Electronic applications accepted. *Expenses:* Tuition, state resident: full-time $2,692. Tuition, nonresident: full-time $13,742. *Financial support:* In 2006–07, 17 students received support; fellowships with full tuition reimbursements available, research assistantships with full tuition reimbursements available, career-related internships or fieldwork, Federal Work-Study, scholarships/grants, and traineeships available. Support available to part-time students. *Unit head:* Dr. Edward Arrington, Head, 336-334-5647, Fax: 336-334-4706, E-mail: cearring@uncg.edu. *Application contact:* Michelle Harkleroad, Director of Graduate Admissions, 336-334-4884, Fax: 336-334-4424, E-mail: mbharkle@uncg.edu.

The University of North Carolina Wilmington, School of Business, Program in Accountancy, Wilmington, NC 28403-3297. Offers MSA. *Students:* 55 full-time (25 women); includes 6 minority (4 African Americans, 1 American Indian/Alaska Native, 1 Asian American or Pacific Islander). Average age 25. 99 applicants, 60% accepted, 55 enrolled. In 2006, 61 degrees awarded. *Degree requirements:* For master's, portfolio project. *Entrance requirements:* For master's, GMAT. *Application deadline:* For fall admission, 5/1 for domestic students. Applications are processed on a rolling basis. Application fee: $45. *Financial support:* In 2006–07, 24 teaching assistantships were awarded; career-related internships or fieldwork and Federal Work-Study also available. Support available to part-time students. Financial award application deadline: 3/15. *Unit head:* Dr. Daniel Ivancevich, Director, 910-962-7681, Fax: 910-962-3663, E-mail: ivancevichd@uncw.edu. *Application contact:* Dr. Robert D. Roer, Dean, Graduate School, 910-962-4117, Fax: 910-962-3787, E-mail: roer@uncw.edu.

University of Northern Iowa, Graduate College, College of Business Administration, Program in Accounting, Cedar Falls, IA 50614. Offers M Acc. *Students:* 19 full-time (10 women), 3 part-time (2 women), 2 international. 20 applicants, 85% accepted, 9 enrolled. In 2006, 19 degrees awarded. *Entrance requirements:* For master's, GMAT. Additional exam requirements/recommendations for international students: Required—TOEFL (minimum score 500 paper-based; 180 computer-based; 61 iBT). *Application deadline:* For fall admission, 8/1 priority date for domestic students. Applications are processed on a rolling basis. Application fee: $30 ($50 for international students). *Expenses:* Tuition, state resident: full-time $5,936. Tuition, nonresident: full-time $14,074. *Financial support:* Application deadline: 2/1. *Unit head:* Dr. Martha Wartick, Acting Head, 319-273-2394, Fax: 319-273-2922, E-mail: marty.wartick@uni.edu.

University of Northern Virginia, Graduate Programs, Manassas, VA 20109. Offers accountancy (MS); accounting (MBA); business administration (DBA); computer science (MS); counseling education (M Ed); early childhood education (M Ed); educational communication and instructional technology (M Ed); educational leadership (M Ed); finance (MBA); information systems technol-

Accounting

University of Northern Virginia (continued)
ogy (MS); management (MBA); marketing (MBA); project management (MBA); public administration (MPA); teaching English to speakers of other languages (M Ed). Part-time and evening/weekend programs available. Postbaccalaureate distance learning degree programs offered (no on-campus study). *Degree requirements:* For doctorate, thesis/dissertation, comprehensive exam, registration. *Entrance requirements:* Additional exam requirements/recommendations for international students: Required—TOEFL (minimum score 550 paper-based; 230 computer-based), IELTS (minimum score 6). Electronic applications accepted.

University of North Florida, Coggin College of Business, Department of Accounting and Finance, Jacksonville, FL 32224-2645. Offers accounting (M Acct). *Accreditation:* AACSB. Part-time and evening/weekend programs available. *Faculty:* 19 full-time (2 women). *Students:* 27 full-time (15 women), 63 part-time (38 women); includes 11 minority (6 African Americans, 5 Asian Americans or Pacific Islanders), 6 international. Average age 31. 53 applicants, 43% accepted, 17 enrolled. In 2006, 28 degrees awarded. *Entrance requirements:* For master's, GMAT, minimum GPA of 3.0 in last 60 hours. Additional exam requirements/recommendations for international students: Required—TOEFL (minimum score 550 paper-based; 213 computer-based). *Application deadline:* For fall admission, 7/6 priority date for domestic students, 5/1 for international students; for spring admission, 11/1 priority date for domestic students, 10/1 for international students. Applications are processed on a rolling basis. Application fee: $30. Electronic applications accepted. *Expenses:* Tuition, state resident: full-time $4,948; part-time $206 per semester hour. Tuition, nonresident: full-time $19,140; part-time $408 per semester hour. *Financial support:* In 2006–07, 25 students received support; teaching assistantships, career-related internships or fieldwork, Federal Work-Study, and tuition waivers (partial) available. Support available to part-time students. Financial award application deadline: 4/1; financial award applicants required to submit FAFSA. *Faculty research:* Enterprise-wide risk management, accounting input in the strategic planning process, accounting information systems, taxation issues in lawsuits and damage awards, database design. Total annual research expenditures: $99,395. *Unit head:* Dr. Charles Calhoun, Chair, 904-620-2630, Fax: 904-620-3861, E-mail: ccalhoun@unf.edu.

University of North Texas, Robert B. Toulouse School of Graduate Studies, College of Business Administration, Department of Accounting, Denton, TX 76203. Offers MS, PhD. *Accreditation:* AACSB. Part-time programs available. *Faculty:* 18 full-time (6 women). *Students:* 59 full-time (25 women), 59 part-time (25 women); includes 25 minority (7 African Americans, 8 Asian Americans or Pacific Islanders, 10 Hispanic Americans), 13 international. Average age 28. 89 applicants, 85% accepted, 13 enrolled. In 2006, 42 master's, 1 doctorate awarded. *Degree requirements:* For doctorate, thesis/dissertation. *Entrance requirements:* For master's, GMAT; for doctorate, GMAT or GRE General Test. Additional exam requirements/recommendations for international students: Required—TOEFL (minimum score 550 paper-based; 213 computer-based). *Application deadline:* For fall admission, 7/15 for domestic students; for spring admission, 12/1 for domestic students. Applications are processed on a rolling basis. Application fee: $50 ($75 for international students). *Expenses:* Tuition, state resident: full-time $3,573; part-time $198 per credit. Tuition, nonresident: full-time $8,577; part-time $476 per credit. Required fees: $1,258; $126 per credit. One-time fee: $150 full-time. Tuition and fees vary according to course load. *Financial support:* Teaching assistantships, career-related internships or fieldwork, Federal Work-Study, and institutionally sponsored loans available. Financial award application deadline: 2/1. *Faculty research:* Taxation and accounting problems of extractive industries, problems and issues in public interest areas, public sector empirical studies, historical perspective for accounting issues, behavioral issues in taxation and auditing. *Unit head:* Dr. O. Finley Graves, Chair, 940-565-3080, Fax: 940-565-3803, E-mail: gravesf@unt.edu. *Application contact:* Denise Galubenski, Graduate Adviser, 940-565-3027, Fax: 940-565-3803, E-mail: galubens@coloaf.unt.edu.

University of Notre Dame, Mendoza College of Business, Program in Accountancy, Notre Dame, IN 46556. Offers MS. *Accreditation:* AACSB. *Faculty:* 35 full-time (5 women), 11 part-time/adjunct (1 woman). *Students:* 108 full-time (35 women); includes 5 minority (4 Asian Americans or Pacific Islanders, 1 Hispanic American), 16 international. Average age 23. 295 applicants, 46% accepted, 108 enrolled. In 2006, 71 degrees awarded. *Entrance requirements:* For master's, GMAT. Additional exam requirements/recommendations for international students: Required—TOEFL (minimum score 630 paper-based; 267 computer-based; 109 iBT). *Application deadline:* For fall admission, 11/1 for domestic and international students; for spring admission, 5/12 for domestic and international students. Applications are processed on a rolling basis. Application fee: $50 ($100 for international students). Electronic applications accepted. *Financial support:* In 2006–07, 104 students received support, including 98 fellowships (averaging $13,000 per year); scholarships/grants and unspecified assistantships also available. Financial award application deadline: 2/28; financial award applicants required to submit FAFSA. *Faculty research:* Stock valuation, accounting information in decision-making, choice of accounting method, taxes cost on capital. *Unit head:* Linda N. Espahbodi, Director, 574-631-9732, Fax: 574-631-5300, E-mail: msacct.1@nd.edu. *Application contact:* Helen High, Program Manager, 574-631-6499, Fax: 574-631-5300, E-mail: msacct.1@nd.edu.

See Close-Up on page 355.

University of Oklahoma, Graduate College, Michael F. Price College of Business, School of Accounting, Norman, OK 73019-0390. Offers M Acc. *Accreditation:* AACSB. Part-time programs available. *Faculty:* 16 full-time (7 women), 1 (woman) part-time/adjunct. *Students:* 59 full-time (30 women), 14 part-time (3 women); includes 7 minority (5 American Indian/Alaska Native, 1 Asian American or Pacific Islander, 1 Hispanic American), 10 international. 19 applicants, 63% accepted, 9 enrolled. In 2006, 30 degrees awarded. Terminal master's awarded for partial completion of doctoral program. *Degree requirements:* For master's, comprehensive exam. *Entrance requirements:* For master's, GMAT, minimum GPA of 3.0 in last 60 hours. Additional exam requirements/recommendations for international students: Required—TOEFL (minimum score 550 paper-based; 213 computer-based). *Application deadline:* For fall admission, 4/1 for domestic and international students; for spring admission, 11/1 for domestic students, 9/1 for international students. Applications are processed on a rolling basis. Application fee: $40 ($90 for international students). *Expenses:* Tuition, state resident: full-time $3,180; part-time $133 per credit hour. Tuition, nonresident: full-time $11,347; part-time $473 per credit hour. Required fees: $1,729; $62 per credit hour. $117 per semester. Tuition and fees vary according to course load and program. *Financial support:* In 2006–07, 20 students received support, including 6 research assistantships with partial tuition reimbursements available (averaging $14,162 per year), 7 teaching assistantships with partial tuition reimbursements available (averaging $14,916 per year); career-related internships or fieldwork, scholarships/grants, health care benefits, and unspecified assistantships also available. Financial award application deadline: 4/1; financial award applicants required to submit FAFSA. *Faculty research:* Tax auditing ethics and fraud capital markets, judgement and decision making, financial accounting. *Unit head:* Dr. Frances L. Ayres, Director, 405-325-4221, Fax: 405-325-7348, E-mail: fayres@ou.edu. *Application contact:* Jim Smith, Academic Counselor, 405-325-3744, Fax: 405-325-7753, E-mail: jlsmith@ou.edu.

University of Oregon, Graduate School, Charles H. Lundquist College of Business, Department of Accounting, Eugene, OR 97403. Offers M Actg, PhD. *Accreditation:* AACSB. Part-time programs available. *Students:* 39 full-time (18 women), 1 (woman) part-time; includes 4 minority (1 Asian American or Pacific Islander, 3 Hispanic Americans), 10 international. 60 applicants, 62% accepted. In 2006, 1 degree awarded. *Degree requirements:* For doctorate, thesis/dissertation, 2 comprehensive exams. *Entrance requirements:* For master's, GMAT, minimum GPA of 3.0, bachelor's degree in accounting or equivalent; for doctorate, GMAT. Additional exam requirements/recommendations for international students: Required—TOEFL. Application fee: $50. *Financial support:* In 2006–07, 6 teaching assistantships were awarded; career-related internships or fieldwork and Federal Work-Study also available. *Faculty research:* Empirical financial accounting, effects of regulation on accounting standards, use of protocol analysis as a research methodology in accounting. *Unit head:* David Guenther, Head, 541-346-5127. *Application contact:* Perri McGee, Admissions Contact, 541-346-1462, E-mail: perone@uoregon.edu.

University of Pennsylvania, Wharton School, Accounting Department, Philadelphia, PA 19104. Offers MBA, PhD. Terminal master's awarded for partial completion of doctoral program. *Degree requirements:* For doctorate, thesis/dissertation. *Entrance requirements:* For master's, GMAT; for doctorate, GMAT or GRE. *Faculty research:* Financial reporting, information disclosure, performance measurement, executive compensation, corporate governance.

University of Phoenix–Augusta Campus, College of Graduate Business and Management, Augusta, GA 30909-4583. Offers accounting (MBA); business and management (MBA, MM); global management (MBA); human resources management (MBA, MM); marketing (MBA); public administration (MBA, MM).

University of Phoenix–Austin Campus, College of Graduate Business and Management, Austin, TX 78759. Offers accounting (MBA); business and management (MBA); e-business (MBA); global management (MBA); human resources management (MBA, MM); management (MM); marketing (MBA); public administration (MBA).

University of Phoenix–Bay Area Campus, John Sperling School of Business, College of Graduate Business and Management, Pleasanton, CA 94588-3677. Offers accounting (MBA); business administration (MBA); global management (MBA); human resource management (MBA); marketing (MBA); public administration (MBA). Evening/weekend programs available. *Faculty:* 30 full-time (3 women), 390 part-time/adjunct (106 women). *Students:* 523 full-time (279 women); includes 185 minority (40 African Americans, 2 American Indian/Alaska Native, 110 Asian Americans or Pacific Islanders, 33 Hispanic Americans), 84 international. Average age 37. In 2006, 205 degrees awarded. *Degree requirements:* For master's, thesis (for some programs), registration. *Entrance requirements:* For master's, minimum undergraduate GPA of 3.0, 3 years of work experience. Additional exam requirements/recommendations for international students: Required—TOEFL (minimum score 550 paper-based; 213 computer-based; 79 iBT). *Application deadline:* Applications are processed on a rolling basis. Application fee: $45. Electronic applications accepted. *Expenses:* Tuition: Full-time $12,648. Required fees: $760. *Financial support:* Institutionally sponsored loans and scholarships/grants available. Financial award applicants required to submit FAFSA. *Unit head:* Dr. Brian Lindquist, Associate Vice President and Dean/Executive Director, 408-557-1221, E-mail: brian.lindquist@phoenix.edu. *Application contact:* Chair, 408-435-8500, Fax: 408-435-8250.

University of Phoenix–Central Florida Campus, John Sperling School of Business, College of Graduate Business and Management, Maitland, FL 32751-7057. Offers accounting (MBA); business administration (MBA); business and management (MM); global management (MBA); management (MM); marketing (MBA). Evening/weekend programs available. *Faculty:* 50 full-time (11 women), 136 part-time/adjunct (32 women). *Students:* 440 full-time (265 women); includes 175 minority (102 African Americans, 4 American Indian/Alaska Native, 16 Asian Americans or Pacific Islanders, 53 Hispanic Americans), 38 international. Average age 36. In 2006, 149 degrees awarded. *Degree requirements:* For master's, thesis (for some programs), registration. *Entrance requirements:* For master's, minimum undergraduate GPA of 3.0, 3 years work experience. Additional exam requirements/recommendations for international students: Required—TOEFL (minimum score 550 paper-based; 213 computer-based; 79 iBT). *Application deadline:* Applications are processed on a rolling basis. Application fee: $45. Electronic applications accepted. *Expenses:* Tuition: Full-time $9,450. Required fees: $760. *Financial support:* Institutionally sponsored loans and scholarships/grants available. Financial award applicants required to submit FAFSA. *Unit head:* Dr. Brian Lindquist, Associate Vice President and Dean/Executive Director, 480-557-1221, E-mail: brian.lindquist@phoenix.edu. *Application contact:* Chair, 407-667-0555, Fax: 407-667-0560.

University of Phoenix–Central Valley Campus, College of Graduate Business and Management, Fresno, CA 93720. Offers accounting (MBA); business administration (MBA); global management (MBA); human resources management (MBA); management (MM); marketing (MBA); public administration (MBA).

University of Phoenix–Charlotte Campus, John Sperling School of Business, College of Graduate Business and Management, Charlotte, NC 28273-3409. Offers accounting (MBA); administration (MBA); global management (MBA). Evening/weekend programs available. *Faculty:* 18 full-time (2 women), 111 part-time/adjunct (33 women). *Students:* 423 full-time (272 women); includes 221 minority (211 African Americans, 6 Asian Americans or Pacific Islanders, 4 Hispanic Americans), 21 international. Average age 36. In 2006, 78 degrees awarded. *Degree requirements:* For master's, thesis (for some programs), registration. *Entrance requirements:* For master's, minimum undergraduate GPA of 3.0, 3 years work experience. Additional exam requirements/recommendations for international students: Required—TOEFL (minimum score 550 paper-based; 213 computer-based; 79 iBT). *Application deadline:* Applications are processed on a rolling basis. Application fee: $45. Electronic applications accepted. *Expenses:* Tuition: Full-time $10,320. Required fees: $760. *Financial support:* Institutionally sponsored loans and scholarships/grants available. Financial award applicants required to submit FAFSA. *Unit head:* Dr. Brian Lindquist, Associate Vice President and Dean/Executive Director, 480-557-1221, E-mail: brian.lindquist@phoenix.edu. *Application contact:* College Chair, 704-504-5409, Fax: 704-504-5360.

University of Phoenix–Chattanooga Campus, College of Graduate Business and Management, Chattanooga, TN 37421-3707. Offers accounting (MBA); business and management (MBA); global management (MBA); human resources management (MBA, MM); management (MM); marketing (MBA); public administration (MBA, MM).

University of Phoenix–Cleveland Campus, John Sperling School of Business, College of Graduate Business and Management, Independence, OH 44131-2194. Offers accounting (MBA); business administration (MBA); global management (MBA); human resources management (MM); management (MM); marketing (MBA); public administration (MBA, MM). Evening/weekend programs available. *Faculty:* 10 full-time (1 woman), 68 part-time/adjunct (16 women). *Students:* 178 full-time (107 women); includes 115 minority (66 African Americans, 1 American Indian/Alaska Native, 5 Asian Americans or Pacific Islanders, 43 Hispanic Americans), 9 international. Average age 37. In 2006, 25 degrees awarded. *Degree requirements:* For master's, thesis (for some programs), registration. *Entrance requirements:* For master's, minimum undergraduate GPA of 3.0, 3 years of work experience. Additional exam requirements/recommendations for international students: Required—TOEFL (minimum score 550 paper-based; 213 computer-based; 79 iBT). *Application deadline:* Applications are processed on a rolling basis. Application fee: $45. Electronic applications accepted. *Expenses:* Tuition: Full-time $11,608. Required fees: $760. *Financial support:* Institutionally sponsored loans and scholarships/grants available. Financial award applicants required to submit FAFSA. *Unit head:* Dr. Brian Lindquist, Associate Vice President and Dean/Executive Director, 480-557-1221, E-mail: brian.linquist@phoenix.edu. *Application contact:* Chair, 216-447-8807, Fax: 216-447-9144.

University of Phoenix–Columbus Georgia Campus, John Sperling School of Business, College of Graduate Business and Management, Columbus, GA 31904-6321. Offers accounting (MBA); administration (MBA); global management (MBA); human resource management (MBA); marketing (MBA); public administration (MBA). Evening/weekend programs available. *Faculty:* 11 full-time (1 woman), 53 part-time/adjunct (15 women). *Students:* 52 full-time (35 women); includes 27 minority (22 African Americans, 1 Asian American or Pacific Islander, 4 Hispanic Americans). Average age 37. In 2006, 10 degrees awarded. *Degree requirements:* For master's, thesis (for some programs), registration. *Entrance requirements:* For master's, minimum undergraduate GPA of 3.0, 3 years of work experience. Additional exam requirements/recommendations for international students: Required—TOEFL (minimum score 550 paper-based; 213 computer-based; 79 iBT). *Application deadline:* Applications are processed on a rolling basis. Application fee: $45. Electronic applications accepted. *Expenses:* Tuition: Full-time $10,200. Required fees: $760. *Financial support:* Institutionally sponsored loans and scholarships/grants available. Financial award applicants required to submit FAFSA. *Unit head:* Dr. Brian Lindquist, Associate Vice President/Dean/Executive Director, 480-557-1221, E-mail: brian.lindquist@phoenix.edu. *Application contact:* College Chair, 706-320-1262.

University of Phoenix–Dallas Campus, John Sperling School of Business, College of Graduate Business and Management, Dallas, TX 75251-2009. Offers accounting (MBA); administration (MBA); human resources management (MBA, MM); management (MM); marketing (MBA); public administration (MBA, MM). Evening/weekend programs available. *Faculty:* 27 full-time (5 women), 130 part-time/adjunct (34 women). *Students:* 517 full-time (320 women); includes 217 minority (166 African Americans, 7 American Indian/Alaska Native, 11 Asian Americans or Pacific Islanders, 33 Hispanic Americans), 68 international. Average age 37. In 2006, 127 degrees awarded. *Degree requirements:* For master's, thesis (for some programs), registration. *Entrance requirements:* For master's, 3 years of work experience, minimum undergraduate GPA of 3.0. Additional exam requirements/recommendations for international students: Required—TOEFL (minimum score 550 paper-based; 213 computer-based; 79 iBT). *Application deadline:* Applications are processed on a rolling basis. Application fee: $45. Electronic applications accepted. *Expenses:* Tuition: Full-time $11,832. Required fees: $760. *Financial support:* Institutionally sponsored loans and scholarships/grants available. Financial award applicants required to submit FAFSA. *Unit head:* Dr. Brian Lindquist, Associate Vice President and Dean/Executive Director, 480-557-1221, E-mail: brian.lindquist@phoenix.edu. *Application contact:* Chair, 972-385-1055, Fax: 972-385-1700.

University of Phoenix–Denver Campus, John Sperling School of Business, College of Graduate Business and Management, Lone Tree, CO 80124-5453. Offers accounting (MBA); business administration (MBA); e-business (MBA); global management (MBA); human resources management (MBA, MM); management (MM); marketing (MBA); public administration (MBA, MM). Evening/weekend programs available. *Faculty:* 63 full-time (22 women), 254 part-time/adjunct (56 women). *Students:* 289 full-time (139 women); includes 59 minority (25 African Americans, 1 American Indian/Alaska Native, 9 Asian Americans or Pacific Islanders, 24 Hispanic Americans), 20 international. Average age 37. In 2006, 93 degrees awarded. *Degree requirements:* For master's, thesis (for some programs), registration. *Entrance requirements:* For master's, minimum undergraduate GPA of 3.0, 3 years work experience. Additional exam requirements/recommendations for international students: Required—TOEFL (minimum score 550 paper-based; 213 computer-based; 79 iBT). *Application deadline:* Applications are processed on a rolling basis. Application fee: $45. Electronic applications accepted. *Expenses:* Tuition: Full-time $10,032. Required fees: $760. *Financial support:* Institutionally sponsored loans and scholarships/grants available. Financial award applicants required to submit FAFSA. *Unit head:* Dr. Brian Lindquist, Associate Vice President and Dean/Executive Director, 480-557-1221, E-mail: brian.lindquist@phoenix.edu. *Application contact:* Chair, 303-694-9093, Fax: 303-662-0911.

University of Phoenix–Des Moines Campus, College of Graduate Business and Management, Des Moines, IA 50266. Offers accounting (MBA); business administration (MBA); global management (MBA); human resources management (MBA, MM); management (MM); marketing (MBA); public administration (MBA, MM).

University of Phoenix–Detroit Campus, College of Graduate Business and Management, Southfield, MI 48076. Offers accounting (MBA); business administration (MBA); e-business (MBA); global management (MBA); human resources management (MBA, MM); management (MM); marketing (MBA); public administration (MBA).

University of Phoenix–Fort Lauderdale Campus, John Sperling School of Business, College of Graduate Business and Management, Fort Lauderdale, FL 33309. Offers accounting (MBA); business administration (MBA); global management (MBA); human resource management (MBA); human resources management (MM); management (MM); marketing (MBA); public administration (MBA). Evening/weekend programs available. *Faculty:* 31 full-time (13 women), 117 part-time/adjunct (33 women). *Students:* 433 full-time (273 women); includes 196 minority (113 African Americans, 3 American Indian/Alaska Native, 8 Asian Americans or Pacific Islanders, 72 Hispanic Americans), 64 international. Average age 38. In 2006, 112 degrees awarded. *Degree requirements:* For master's, thesis (for some programs), registration. *Entrance requirements:* For master's, minimum undergraduate GPA of 3.0, 3 years work experience. Additional exam requirements/recommendations for international students: Required—TOEFL (minimum score 550 paper-based; 213 computer-based; 79 iBT). *Application deadline:* Applications are processed on a rolling basis. Application fee: $45. Electronic applications accepted. *Expenses:* Tuition: Full-time $9,450. Required fees: $760. *Financial support:* Institutionally sponsored loans and scholarships/grants available. Financial award applicants required to submit FAFSA. *Unit head:* Dr. Brian Linquist, Associate V.P. & Dean/Executive Director, 480-557-1221, E-mail: brian.linquist@phoenix.edu. *Application contact:* Chair, 954-382-5303, Fax: 954-382-5304.

University of Phoenix–Harrisburg Campus, College of Graduate Business and Management, Harrisburg, PA 17112. Offers accounting (MBA); business and management (MBA); glboal management (MBA); human resources management (MBA, MM); management (MM); marketing (MBA); public administration (MBA, MM).

University of Phoenix–Hawaii Campus, John Sperling School of Business, College of Graduate Business and Management, Honolulu, HI 96813-4317. Offers accounting (MBA); business administration (MBA); global management (MBA); human resources management (MBA, MM); management (MM); marketing (MBA); public administration (MBA, MM). Evening/weekend programs available. *Faculty:* 17 full-time (4 women), 92 part-time/adjunct (23 women). *Students:* 72 full-time (39 women); includes 18 minority (3 African Americans, 13 Asian Americans or Pacific Islanders, 2 Hispanic Americans), 30 international. Average age 37. In 2006, 20 master's awarded. *Degree requirements:* For master's, thesis (for some programs), registration. *Entrance requirements:* For master's, minimum undergraduate GPA of 3.0, 3 years of work experience. Additional exam requirements/recommendations for international students: Required—TOEFL (minimum score 550 paper-based; 213 computer-based; 79 iBT). *Application deadline:* Applications are processed on a rolling basis. Application fee: $45. Electronic applications accepted. *Expenses:* Tuition: Full-time $11,520. Required fees: $760. *Financial support:* Institutionally sponsored loans and scholarships/grants available. Financial award applicants required to submit FAFSA. *Unit head:* Dr. Brian Lindquist, Associate Vice President and Dean/Executive Director, 480-557-1221, E-mail: brian.lindquist@phoenix.edu. *Application contact:* Chair, 808-536-2686, Fax: 808-536-3848.

University of Phoenix–Idaho Campus, John Sperling School of Business, College of Graduate Business and Management, Meridian, ID 83642-3014. Offers accounting (MBA); administration (MBA); management (MM). Evening/weekend programs available. *Faculty:* 7 full-time (0 women), 52 part-time/adjunct (12 women). *Students:* 104 full-time (34 women); includes 6 minority (1 African American, 2 Asian Americans or Pacific Islanders, 3 Hispanic Americans), 11 international. Average age 35. In 2006, 22 degrees awarded. *Degree requirements:* For master's, thesis (for some programs), registration. *Entrance requirements:* For master's, 3 years of work experience, minimum undergraduate GPA of 3.0. Additional exam requirements/recommendations for international students: Required—TOEFL (minimum score 550 paper-based; 213 computer-based). *Application deadline:* Applications are processed on a rolling basis. Application fee: $45. Electronic applications accepted. *Expenses:* Tuition: Full-time $9,104. *Financial support:* Institutionally sponsored loans and scholarships/grants available. Financial award applicants required to submit FAFSA. *Unit head:* Dr. Brian Lindquist, Dean, 480-557-1221, E-mail: brian.lindquist@phoenix.edu. *Application contact:* Chair, 208-888-1505, Fax: 208-888-4775.

University of Phoenix–Jersey City Campus, College of Graduate Business and Management, Jersey City, NJ 07310. Offers accounting (MBA); business and management (MBA); global management (MBA); human resources management (MBA, MM); management (MM); marketing (MBA); public administration (MBA, MM).

University of Phoenix–Madison Campus, College of Graduate Business and Management, Madison, WI 53718-2416. Offers accounting (MBA); business and management (MBA, MM); e-business (MBA); global management (MBA); human resources management (MBA, MM); marketing (MBA); public administration (MBA).

University of Phoenix–Memphis Campus, College of Graduate Business and Management, Cordova, TN 38018. Offers acounting (MBA); business and management (MBA); e-business (MBA); global management (MBA); human resources management (MBA, MM); marketing (MBA); public administration (MBA, MM).

University of Phoenix–Minneapolis/St. Louis Park Campus, College of Graduate Business and Management, St. Louis Park, MN 55426. Offers accounting (MBA); business administration (MBA); global management (MBA); human resources management (MBA); marketing (MBA).

University of Phoenix—Northern Nevada Campus, College of Graduate Business and Management, Reno, NV 89511. Offers accounting (MBA); business and management (MBA); global management (MBA); human resources management (MBA, MM); management (MM); marketing (MBA); public administration (MBA, MM).

University of Phoenix–Northern Virginia Campus, College of Graduate Business and Management, Reston, VA 20190. Offers accounting (MBA); business administration (MBA); e-business (MBA); global management (MBA); human resources management (MBA, MM); management (MM); marketing (MBA); public administration (MBA).

University of Phoenix–North Florida Campus, John Sperling School of Business, College of Graduate Business and Management, Jacksonville, FL 32216-0959. Offers accounting (MBA); business administration (MBA); global management (MBA); human resources management (MBA, MM); management (MM); marketing (MBA); public administration (MBA). Evening/weekend programs available. *Faculty:* 40 full-time (15 women), 105 part-time/adjunct (25 women). *Students:* 392 full-time (237 women); includes 135 minority (117 African Americans, 1 American Indian/Alaska Native, 12 Asian Americans or Pacific Islanders, 5 Hispanic Americans), 20 international. Average age 31. In 2006, 134 degrees awarded. *Degree requirements:* For master's, thesis (for some programs), registration. *Entrance requirements:* For master's, minimum undergraduate GPA of 3.0, 3 years work experience. Additional exam requirements/recommendations for international students: Required—TOEFL (minimum score 550 paper-based; 213 computer-based; 79 iBT). *Application deadline:* Applications are processed on a rolling basis. Application fee: $45. Electronic applications accepted. *Financial support:* Institutionally sponsored loans available. Financial award applicants required to submit FAFSA. *Unit head:* Dr. Brian Lindquist, Associate Vice President and Dean/Executive Director, 480-557-1221, E-mail: brian.lindquist@phoenix.edu. *Application contact:* Chair, 904-636-6645, Fax: 904-636-0998.

University of Phoenix–Northwest Arkansas Campus, College of Graduate Business and Management, Rogers, AR 72756-9615. Offers accounting (MBA); business and management (MBA); global management (MBA); human resources management (MBA, MM); management (MM); marketing (MBA); public administration (MBA, MM).

University of Phoenix–Omaha Campus, College of Graduate Business and Management, Omaha, NE 68154-5240. Offers accounting (MBA); business and management (MBA); global management (MBA); human resources management (MM); human resources managemetn (MBA); management (MM); marketing (MBA); public administration (MM); public adminstration (MBA).

University of Phoenix Online Campus, John Sperling School of Business, College of Graduate Business and Management, Phoenix, AZ 85034-7209. Offers accounting (MBA); administration (MBA); global management (MBA); human resources management (MBA); management (MM); marketing (MBA); public administration (MBA, MM). Evening/weekend programs available. *Faculty:* 25 full-time (15 women), 4,861 part-time/adjunct (1,504 women). *Students:* 17,914 full-time (10,655 women); includes 4,983 minority (3,259 African Americans, 113 American Indian/Alaska Native, 651 Asian Americans or Pacific Islanders, 960 Hispanic Americans), 1,805 international. Average age 36. In 2006, 1,740 master's awarded. *Degree requirements:* For master's, thesis (for some programs), registration. *Entrance requirements:* For master's, 3 years of work experience, minimum undergraduate GPA of 3.0. Additional exam requirements/recommendations for international students: Required—TOEFL (minimum score 550 paper-based; 213 computer-based; 79 iBT). *Application deadline:* Applications are processed on a rolling basis. Application fee: $45. Electronic applications accepted. *Expenses:* Tuition: Full-time $12,664. Required fees: $760. *Financial support:* Institutionally sponsored loans and scholarships/grants available. Financial award applicants required to submit FAFSA. *Unit head:* Brian Lindquist, Dean/Executive Director and Associate Vice President, 480-557-1221, E-mail: brian.lindquist@phoenix.edu. *Application contact:* Brian Lindquist, Dean/Executive Director and Associate Vice President, 480-557-1221, E-mail: brian.lindquist@phoenix.edu.

University of Phoenix–Oregon Campus, The John Sperling School of Business, College of Graduate Business and Management, Tigard, OR 97223. Offers accounting (MBA); business administration (MBA); global management (MBA); human resource management (MM); human resources management (MBA); management (MM). Evening/weekend programs available. *Faculty:* 28 full-time (4 women), 104 part-time/adjunct (24 women). *Students:* 241 full-time (103 women); includes 31 minority (7 African Americans, 4 American Indian/Alaska Native, 14 Asian Americans or Pacific Islanders, 6 Hispanic Americans), 21 international. Average age 39. In 2006, 66 degrees awarded. *Degree requirements:* For master's, thesis (for some programs), registration. *Entrance requirements:* For master's, minimum undergraduate GPA of 3.0, 3 years of work experience. Additional exam requirements/recommendations for international students: Required—TOEFL (minimum score 550 paper-based; 213 computer-based; 79 iBT). *Application deadline:* Applications are processed on a rolling basis. Application fee: $45. Electronic applications accepted. *Expenses:* Tuition: Full-time $10,200. Required fees: $760. *Financial support:* Institutionally sponsored loans and scholarships/grants available. Financial award applicants required to submit FAFSA. *Unit head:* Dr. Brian Lindquist, Associate Vice President and Dean/Executive Director, 480-557-1221, E-mail: brian.lindquist@phoenix.edu. *Application contact:* Chair, 503-403-2900, Fax: 503-670-0614.

University of Phoenix–Pittsburgh Campus, John Sperling School of Business, College of Graduate Business and Management, Pittsburgh, PA 15276. Offers accounting (MBA); business administration (MBA); global management (MBA); human resource management (MBA); human resources management (MM); management (MM); marketing (MBA); public administration (MBA, MM). Evening/weekend programs available. *Faculty:* 19 full-time (6 women), 49 part-time/adjunct (13 women). *Students:* 84 full-time (43 women); includes 16 minority (13 African Americans, 2 Asian Americans or Pacific Islanders, 1 Hispanic American), 4 international. Average age 37. In 2006, 35 degrees awarded. *Degree requirements:* For master's, thesis (for some programs), registration. *Entrance requirements:* For master's, minimum undergraduate GPA of 3.0, 3 years work experience. Additional exam requirements/recommendations for international students: Required—TOEFL (minimum score 550 paper-based; 213 computer-based; 79 iBT). *Application deadline:* Applications are processed on a rolling basis. Application fee: $45. Electronic applications accepted. *Expenses:* Tuition: Full-time $13,560. Required fees: $760. *Financial support:* Institutionally sponsored loans and scholarships/grants available. Financial award applicants required to submit FAFSA. *Unit head:* Dr. Brian Lindquist, Associate Vice President and Dean/Executive Director, 480-551-1221, E-mail: brian.lindquist@phoenix.edu. *Application contact:* College Chair, 412-747-9000, Fax: 412-747-0676.

University of Phoenix–Puerto Rico Campus, John Sperling School of Business, College of Graduate Business and Management, Guaynabo, PR 00968. Offers accounting (MBA); business administration (MBA); global management (MBA); human resource management (MBA); marketing (MBA). Evening/weekend programs available. *Faculty:* 19 full-time (8 women), 73 part-time/adjunct (25 women). *Students:* 1,122 full-time (671 women); includes 636 minority (2 African Americans, 3 American Indian/Alaska Native, 3 Asian Americans or Pacific Islanders,

Accounting

University of Phoenix–Puerto Rico Campus *(continued)*
628 Hispanic Americans), 31 international. Average age 34. In 2006, 281 degrees awarded. *Degree requirements:* For master's, thesis (for some programs), registration. *Entrance requirements:* For master's, minimum undergraduate GPA of 3.0, 3 years work experience. Additional exam requirements/recommendations for international students: Required—TOEFL (minimum score 550 paper-based; 213 computer-based; 79 iBT). *Application deadline:* Applications are processed on a rolling basis. Application fee: $45. Electronic applications accepted. *Expenses:* Tuition: Full-time $5,816. Required fees: $760. *Financial support:* Institutionally sponsored loans and scholarships/grants available. Financial award applicants required to submit FAFSA. *Unit head:* Dr. Brian Lindquist, Associate Vice President and Dean/Executive Director, 480-557-1221, E-mail: brian.lindquist@phoenix.edu. *Application contact:* Chair, 787-931-5400, Fax: 787-931-1510.

University of Phoenix–Raleigh Campus, College of Graduate Business and Management, Raleigh, NC 27606. Offers accounting (MBA); business administration (MBA); e-business (MBA); global management (MBA).

University of Phoenix–Renton Learning Center, College of Graduate Business and Management, Renton, WA 98005. Offers accounting (MBA); business and management (MBA, MM); global management (MBA); human resources management (MBA, MM); marketing (MBA); public administration (MBA, MM).

University of Phoenix–Richmond Campus, John Sperling School of Business, College of Graduate Business and Management, Richmond, VA 23230. Offers accounting (MBA); business administration (MBA); global management (MBA); human resources management (MBA, MM); management (MM); marketing (MBA); public administration (MBA, MM). Evening/weekend programs available. *Faculty:* 6 full-time (4 women), 60 part-time/adjunct (7 women). *Students:* 103 full-time (73 women); includes 42 minority (38 African Americans, 1 American Indian/Alaska Native, 2 Asian Americans or Pacific Islanders, 1 Hispanic American), 10 international. Average age 36. In 2006, 1 degree awarded. *Degree requirements:* For master's, thesis (for some programs), registration. *Entrance requirements:* For master's, minimum undergraduate GPA 3.0, 3 years work experience. Additional exam requirements/recommendations for international students: Required—TOEFL (minimum score 550 paper-based; 213 computer-based; 79 iBT). *Application deadline:* Applications are processed on a rolling basis. Application fee: $45. Electronic applications accepted. *Financial support:* Institutionally sponsored loans and scholarships/grants available. Financial award applicants required to submit FAFSA. *Unit head:* Dr. Brian Lindquist, Associate Vice President/Dean, 480-557-1221, E-mail: brian.lindquist@phoenix.edu. *Application contact:* Chair, 804-288-3390.

University of Phoenix–Sacramento Valley Campus, John Sperling School of Business, College of Graduate Business and Management, Sacramento, CA 95833-3632. Offers accounting (MBA); business administration (MBA); global management (MBA); human resources management (MBA); marketing (MBA); public administration (MBA). Evening/weekend programs available. *Faculty:* 36 full-time (19 women), 291 part-time/adjunct (83 women). *Students:* 395 full-time (197 women); includes 120 minority (62 African Americans, 2 American Indian/Alaska Native, 32 Asian Americans or Pacific Islanders, 24 Hispanic Americans), 34 international. Average age 37. In 2006, 138 master's awarded. *Degree requirements:* For master's, thesis (for some programs), registration. *Entrance requirements:* For master's, minimum undergraduate GPA of 3.0, 3 years work experience. Additional exam requirements/recommendations for international students: Required—TOEFL (minimum score 550 paper-based; 213 computer-based; 79 iBT). *Application deadline:* Applications are processed on a rolling basis. Application fee: $45. Electronic applications accepted. *Expenses:* Tuition: Full-time $12,024. Required fees: $760. *Financial support:* Institutionally sponsored loans and scholarships/grants available. Financial award applicants required to submit FAFSA. *Unit head:* Dr. Brian Lindquist, Associate Vice President and Dean/Executive Director, 480-557-1221, E-mail: brian.lindquist@phoenix.edu. *Application contact:* Campus College Chair, 916-923-2107, Fax: 916-923-3914.

University of Phoenix–San Antonio Campus, College of Graduate Business and Management, San Antonio, TX 78230. Offers accounting (MBA); business and management (MBA); e-business (MBA); global management (MBA); human resources management (MBA, MM); management (MM); marketing (MBA); public administration (MBA, MM).

University of Phoenix–Savannah Campus, College of Graduate Business and Management, Savannah, GA 31405-7400. Offers accounting (MBA); business administration (MBA); business and management (MM); global management (MBA); human resources management (MBA, MM); marketing (MBA); public administration (MBA, MM).

University of Phoenix–Southern Arizona Campus, John Sperling School of Business, College of Graduate Business and Management, Tucson, AZ 85712-2732. Offers accounting (MBA); business administration (MBA); global management (MBA); management (MM). Evening/weekend programs available. *Faculty:* 29 full-time (13 women), 207 part-time/adjunct (40 women). *Students:* 412 full-time (205 women); includes 107 minority (23 African Americans, 7 American Indian/Alaska Native, 10 Asian Americans or Pacific Islanders, 67 Hispanic Americans), 24 international. Average age 36. In 2006, 141 degrees awarded. *Degree requirements:* For master's, thesis (for some programs), registration. *Entrance requirements:* For master's, minimum undergraduate GPA of 3.0, 3 years of work experience. Additional exam requirements/recommendations for international students: Required—TOEFL (minimum score 550 paper-based; 213 computer-based; 79 iBT). *Application deadline:* Applications are processed on a rolling basis. Application fee: $45. Electronic applications accepted. *Expenses:* Tuition: Full-time $8,669. Required fees: $760. *Financial support:* Institutionally sponsored loans and scholarships/grants available. Financial award applicants required to submit FAFSA. *Unit head:* Dr. Brian Lindquist, Associate Vice President and Dean/Executive Director, 480-557-1221, E-mail: brian.lindquist@phoenix.edu. *Application contact:* Campus College Chair, 520-881-6512, Fax: 520-795-6177.

University of Phoenix–Southern California Campus, John Sperling School of Business, College of Graduate Business and Management, Costa Mesa, CA 92626. Offers accounting (MBA); business administration (MBA); business and management (MM); human resource management (MBA); marketing (MBA). Evening/weekend programs available. *Faculty:* 47 full-time (13 women), 513 part-time/adjunct (138 women). *Students:* 1,491 full-time (852 women); includes 558 minority (233 African Americans, 7 American Indian/Alaska Native, 124 Asian Americans or Pacific Islanders, 194 Hispanic Americans), 116 international. Average age 38. In 2006, 401 degrees awarded. *Degree requirements:* For master's, thesis (for some programs), registration. *Entrance requirements:* For master's, minimum undergraduate GPA of 3.0, 3 years work experience. Additional exam requirements/recommendations for international students: Required—TOEFL (minimum score 550 paper-based; 213 computer-based; 79 iBT). *Application deadline:* Applications are processed on a rolling basis. Application fee: $45. Electronic applications accepted. *Expenses:* Tuition: Full-time $13,512. Required fees: $760. *Financial support:* Institutionally sponsored loans and scholarships/grants available. Financial award applicants required to submit FAFSA. *Unit head:* Dr. Brian Lindquist, Associate Vice President and Dean/Executive Director, 480-557-1221, E-mail: brian.lindquist@phoenix.edu. *Application contact:* Campus College Chair, 714-378-1878, Fax: 714-378-5875.

University of Phoenix–Springfield Campus, College of Graduate Business and Management, Springfield, MO 65804-7211. Offers accounting (MBA); business and management (MBA); global management (MBA); human resources management (MBA, MM); management (MM); marketing (MBA); public administration (MBA, MM).

University of Phoenix–West Michigan Campus, The John Sperling School of Business, College of Graduate Business and Management, Walker, MI 49544. Offers accounting (MBA); business administration (MBA); global management (MBA); human resource management (MBA). Evening/weekend programs available. *Faculty:* 26 full-time (0 women), 95 part-

time/adjunct (42 women). *Students:* 124 full-time (62 women); includes 16 minority (15 African Americans, 1 Hispanic American), 4 international. Average age 37. In 2006, 50 degrees awarded. *Degree requirements:* For master's, thesis (for some programs), registration. *Entrance requirements:* For master's, minimum undergraduate GPA of 3.0, 3 years work experience. Additional exam requirements/recommendations for international students: Required—TOEFL (minimum score 550 paper-based; 213 computer-based; 79 iBT). *Application deadline:* Applications are processed on a rolling basis. Application fee: $45. Electronic applications accepted. *Expenses:* Tuition: Full-time $12,043. Required fees: $760. *Financial support:* Institutionally sponsored loans and scholarships/grants available. Financial award applicants required to submit FAFSA. *Unit head:* Dr. Brian Lindquist, Associate Vice President and Dean/Executive Director, 480-557-1221, E-mail: brian.lindquist@phoenix.edu. *Application contact:* Chair, 888-345-9699, Fax: 616-784-5300.

University of Rhode Island, Graduate School, College of Business Administration, Program in Accounting, Kingston, RI 02881. Offers MS. *Accreditation:* AACSB. In 2006, 12 degrees awarded. *Application deadline:* For fall admission, 4/15 priority date for domestic students. Applications are processed on a rolling basis. Application fee: $35. *Expenses:* Tuition, state resident: full-time $6,032; part-time $335 per credit. Tuition, nonresident: full-time $17,288; part-time $960 per credit. Required fees: $65 per credit. $30 per semester. One-time fee: $80 part-time.

University of St. Thomas, Graduate Studies, Opus College of Business, Program in Accountancy, St. Paul, MN 55105-1096. Offers MS. *Faculty:* 8 full-time (3 women), 1 part-time/adjunct (0 women). *Students:* 12 full-time (7 women), 5 international. Average age 25. 26 applicants, 77% accepted, 12 enrolled. In 2006, 16 degrees awarded. *Median time to degree:* Master's–1 year full-time. *Entrance requirements:* For master's, GMAT. Additional exam requirements/recommendations for international students: Required—TOEFL. *Application deadline:* For fall admission, 10/12 priority date for domestic and international students; for winter admission, 1/25 priority date for domestic and international students; for spring admission, 5/9 for domestic and international students. Applications are processed on a rolling basis. Application fee: $30. *Expenses: Contact institution. Financial support:* Scholarships/grants available. Financial award application deadline: 7/1; financial award applicants required to submit FAFSA. *Unit head:* Dr. Janice M. Raffield, Director, 651-962-4113, Fax: 651-962-4141, E-mail: jmraffield@stthomas.edu. *Application contact:* Cathy C. Davis, Program Coordinator, 651-962-4114, Fax: 651-962-4141, E-mail: ccdavis@stthomas.edu.

University of San Diego, School of Business Administration, San Diego, CA 92110-2492. Offers accounting and financial management (MS); business administration (MBA); executive leadership (MSEL); global leadership (MSGL); international business administration (IMBA); real estate (MSRE); supply chain management (MS, Certificate); taxation (MS); JD/IMBA; JD/MBA; MBA/MSIT; MBA/MSN; MBA/MSRE. *Accreditation:* AACSB. Part-time and evening/weekend programs available. *Faculty:* 35 full-time (10 women), 18 part-time/adjunct (4 women). *Students:* 187 full-time (76 women), 265 part-time (89 women); includes 55 minority (5 African Americans, 1 American Indian/Alaska Native, 32 Asian Americans or Pacific Islanders, 17 Hispanic Americans), 45 international. Average age 32. 517 applicants, 66% accepted, 187 enrolled. In 2006, 256 degrees awarded. *Entrance requirements:* For master's, GMAT, minimum GPA of 3.0, minimum 2 years of full-time work experience. Additional exam requirements/recommendations for international students: Required—TOEFL (minimum score 580 paper-based; 237 computer-based), TWE. *Application deadline:* For fall admission, 5/1 priority date for domestic students; for spring admission, 11/15 priority date for domestic students. Applications are processed on a rolling basis. Application fee: $45. Electronic applications accepted. *Financial support:* Career-related internships or fieldwork, Federal Work-Study, institutionally sponsored loans, scholarships/grants, tuition waivers (partial), and unspecified assistantships available. Support available to part-time students. Financial award application deadline: 5/1; financial award applicants required to submit FAFSA. *Faculty research:* Business management, production, purchasing, quantitative methods, accounting. *Unit head:* Dr. Andy Allen, Interim Dean, 619-260-4886, E-mail: sbadean@sandiego.edu. *Application contact:* Stephen Pultz, Director of Admissions, 619-260-4524, Fax: 619-260-4158, E-mail: grads@sandiego.edu.

University of Saskatchewan, College of Graduate Studies and Research, College of Commerce, Department of Accounting, Saskatoon, SK S7N 5A2, Canada. Offers M Sc, MP Acc. Part-time programs available. *Degree requirements:* For master's, thesis (for some programs), registration. *Entrance requirements:* For master's, GMAT. Additional exam requirements/recommendations for international students: Required—TOEFL.

The University of Scranton, Graduate School, Program in Business Administration, Scranton, PA 18510. Offers accounting (MBA); enterprise management technology (MBA); finance (MBA); general business administration (MBA); international business (MBA); management information systems (MBA); marketing (MBA); operations management (MBA). *Accreditation:* AACSB. Part-time and evening/weekend programs available. *Faculty:* 34 full-time (8 women). *Students:* 39 full-time (11 women), 54 part-time (15 women); includes 3 minority (1 American Indian/Alaska Native, 2 Hispanic Americans), 31 international. Average age 28. 58 applicants, 83% accepted. In 2006, 52 degrees awarded. *Degree requirements:* For master's, capstone experience. *Entrance requirements:* For master's, GMAT, minimum GPA of 2.75. Additional exam requirements/recommendations for international students: Required—TOEFL (minimum score 500 paper-based; 173 computer-based), IELTS (minimum score 6). *Application deadline:* Applications are processed on a rolling basis. Application fee: $50. *Expenses:* Tuition: Part-time $684 per credit. Required fees: $25 per term. *Financial support:* In 2006–07, 11 teaching assistantships with full tuition reimbursements (averaging $5,600 per year) were awarded; fellowships, career-related internships or fieldwork, Federal Work-Study, and unspecified assistantships also available. Support available to part-time students. Financial award application deadline: 3/1. *Faculty research:* Financial markets, strategic impact of total quality management, internal accounting controls, consumer preference, information systems and the Internet. *Unit head:* Dr. Murli Rajan, Director, 570-941-4043, Fax: 570-941-4342.

University of South Alabama, Graduate School, Mitchell College of Business, Program in Accounting, Mobile, AL 36688-0002. Offers M Acct. Part-time and evening/weekend programs available. *Faculty:* 5 full-time (2 women). *Students:* 17 full-time (10 women), 7 part-time (all women); includes 1 minority (African American), 4 international. 26 applicants, 62% accepted, 7 enrolled. In 2006, 7 degrees awarded. *Degree requirements:* For master's, comprehensive exam. *Entrance requirements:* For master's, GMAT, minimum undergraduate GPA of 3.0. *Application deadline:* For fall admission, 9/1 priority date for domestic students. Applications are processed on a rolling basis. Application fee: $25. *Financial support:* Available to part-time students. Application deadline: 4/1. *Unit head:* Dr. Mark A. Segal, Chair, 251-460-6144.

University of South Carolina, The Graduate School, The Darla Moore School of Business, Accountancy Program, Columbia, SC 29208. Offers business measurement and assurance (M Acc); JD/M Acc. *Accreditation:* AACSB. Part-time programs available. *Degree requirements:* For master's, comprehensive exam. *Entrance requirements:* For master's, GMAT. Additional exam requirements/recommendations for international students: Required—TOEFL (minimum score 600 paper-based; 250 computer-based). Electronic applications accepted. *Faculty research:* Judgment modeling, international accounting, accounting information systems, behavioral accounting, cost/management accounting.

The University of South Dakota, Graduate School, School of Business, Department of Accounting, Vermillion, SD 57069-2390. Offers professional accountancy (MP Acc); JD/MP Acc. Part-time programs available. Postbaccalaureate distance learning degree programs offered. *Faculty:* 5 full-time (1 woman), 4 part-time/adjunct (3 women). *Students:* 47 (32 women). In 2006, 20 degrees awarded. *Degree requirements:* For master's, comprehensive exam. *Entrance requirements:* For master's, GMAT, minimum GPA of 2.7. Additional exam requirements/recommendations for international students: Required—TOEFL (minimum score 550 paper-based; 213 computer-based; 79 iBT). *Application deadline:* For fall admission, 7/15 priority date for domestic students; for spring admission, 11/15 priority date for domestic students. Applications are processed on a rolling basis. Application fee: $35. Electronic applications accepted. *Expenses:* Tuition, state resident: part-time $120 per credit hour. Tuition, nonresident: part-time $355 per credit hour. Required fees: $90 per credit hour. *Financial support:* In 2006–07, research assistantships with partial tuition reimbursements (averaging $4,626 per year), teaching assistantships with partial tuition reimbursements (averaging $4,626 per year) were awarded; Federal Work-Study and unspecified assistantships also available. Financial award applicants required to submit FAFSA. *Unit head:* Dr. Jon R. Carpenter, Director of Graduate Studies, 605-677-5232, Fax: 605-677-5058, E-mail: mpa@usd.edu.

University of Southern California, Graduate School, Marshall School of Business, Leventhal School of Accounting, Program in Accounting, Los Angeles, CA 90089. Offers M Acc. *Accreditation:* AACSB. *Students:* 70 full-time (38 women); includes 26 minority (1 African American, 20 Asian Americans or Pacific Islanders, 5 Hispanic Americans), 18 international. In 2006, 72 degrees awarded. *Entrance requirements:* For master's, GMAT. *Application deadline:* For fall admission, 12/1 priority date for domestic students. Application fee: $85. *Expenses:* Tuition: Full-time $33,314; part-time $1,121 per credit. Required fees: $522. Full-time tuition and fees vary according to program. *Financial support:* Fellowships, research assistantships, teaching assistantships, Federal Work-Study, institutionally sponsored loans, and scholarships/grants available. Support available to part-time students. Financial award application deadline: 2/15; financial award applicants required to submit FAFSA. *Unit head:* Shirley Maxey, Director, 213-740-4839, E-mail: acc100@marshall.usc.edu.

University of Southern Indiana, Graduate Studies, College of Business, Program in Accountancy, Evansville, IN 47712-3590. Offers MSA. *Accreditation:* AACSB. Part-time and evening/weekend programs available. *Faculty:* 2 full-time (0 women). *Students:* Average age 37. In 2006, 2 degrees awarded. *Entrance requirements:* For master's, GMAT, minimum GPA of 2.5, resumé. Additional exam requirements/recommendations for international students: Required—TOEFL (minimum score 500 paper-based; 173 computer-based). *Application deadline:* For fall admission, 8/15 for domestic students, 3/1 priority date for international students. Application fee: $25. *Expenses:* Tuition, state resident: full-time $3,888; part-time $216 per credit hour. Tuition, nonresident: full-time $7,688; part-time $426 per credit hour. Required fees: $220; $23 per term. Tuition and fees vary according to course load and reciprocity agreements. *Financial support:* Federal Work-Study, scholarships/grants, tuition waivers (full and partial), and unspecified assistantships available. Financial award application deadline: 3/1; financial award applicants required to submit FAFSA. *Unit head:* Dr. Brian L. McGuire, Director, 812-464-7031, Fax: 812-464-1956, E-mail: bmcguire@usi.edu.

University of Southern Maine, School of Business, Portland, ME 04104-9300. Offers accounting (MSA); business administration (MBA); JD/MBA; MBA/MSA; MBA/MSN; MS/MBA. *Accreditation:* AACSB. Part-time and evening/weekend programs available. *Faculty:* 20 full-time (4 women). *Students:* 43 full-time (26 women), 117 part-time (45 women); includes 8 minority (1 American Indian/Alaska Native, 7 Asian Americans or Pacific Islanders), 2 international. Average age 32. 77 applicants, 82% accepted, 54 enrolled. In 2006, 32 degrees awarded. *Degree requirements:* For master's, registration. *Entrance requirements:* For master's, GMAT, minimum AACSB index of 1100. Additional exam requirements/recommendations for international students: Required—TOEFL (minimum score 550 paper-based; 213 computer-based; 79 iBT). *Application deadline:* For fall admission, 8/1 priority date for domestic students, 5/1 priority date for international students; for spring admission, 12/1 priority date for domestic students, 9/1 priority date for international students. Applications are processed on a rolling basis. Application fee: $50. Electronic applications accepted. *Expenses:* Tuition, state resident: full-time $4,860; part-time $270 per credit hour. Tuition, nonresident: full-time $13,572; part-time $754 per credit hour. Required fees: $222 per semester. Tuition and fees vary according to course load. *Financial support:* In 2006–07, 108 students received support, including 3 research assistantships with partial tuition reimbursements available (averaging $9,000 per year), 3 teaching assistantships with partial tuition reimbursements available (averaging $9,000 per year); career-related internships or fieldwork, Federal Work-Study, scholarships/grants, tuition waivers (full and partial), and unspecified assistantships also available. Support available to part-time students. Financial award application deadline: 2/15; financial award applicants required to submit FAFSA. *Faculty research:* Economic development, MIS, real options, system dynamics, simulation. *Unit head:* James B. Shaffer, Dean, 207-780-4020, Fax: 207-780-4662, E-mail: jshaffer@usm.maine.edu. *Application contact:* Alice B. Cash, Graduate Programs Director, 207-780-4184, Fax: 207-780-4662, E-mail: acash@usm.maine.edu.

University of Southern Mississippi, Graduate School, College of Business, School of Accountancy and Information Systems, Hattiesburg, MS 39406-0001. Offers accountancy (MPA). *Accreditation:* AACSB. Part-time and evening/weekend programs available. *Faculty:* 16 full-time (4 women). *Students:* 15 full-time (9 women), 4 part-time (3 women); includes 2 minority (both African Americans), 2 international. Average age 28. 17 applicants, 59% accepted, 9 enrolled. In 2006, 15 degrees awarded. *Degree requirements:* For master's, comprehensive exam, registration. *Entrance requirements:* For master's, GMAT. Additional exam requirements/recommendations for international students: Required—TOEFL. *Application deadline:* For fall admission, 7/15 priority date for domestic students, 7/15 for international students; for spring admission, 11/15 priority date for domestic students, 11/15 for international students. Applications are processed on a rolling basis. Application fee: $25 ($30 for international students). Electronic applications accepted. *Financial support:* In 2006–07, 8 research assistantships with full tuition reimbursements (averaging $5,400 per year) were awarded; Federal Work-Study and institutionally sponsored loans also available. Support available to part-time students. Financial award application deadline: 3/15. *Faculty research:* Bank liquidity, subchapter S corporations, internal auditing, governmental accounting, inflation accounting. *Unit head:* Dr. Stan Lewis, Interim Director, 601-266-4322, Fax: 601-266-4639. *Application contact:* Dr. Francis Daniel, Graduate Coordinator, 601-266-4664, Fax: 601-266-5814.

University of South Florida, Graduate School, College of Business Administration, School of Accounting, Tampa, FL 33620-9951. Offers M Acc. *Accreditation:* AACSB. Part-time and evening/weekend programs available. *Faculty:* 12 full-time (5 women), 2 part-time/adjunct (1 woman). *Students:* 34 full-time (19 women), 29 part-time (16 women); includes 11 minority (3 African Americans, 8 Hispanic Americans), 6 international. 63 applicants, 41% accepted, 21 enrolled. In 2006, 33 degrees awarded. *Degree requirements:* For master's, comprehensive exam. *Entrance requirements:* For master's, GMAT, minimum GPA of 3.0 in upper-level accounting course work in last 5 years. Additional exam requirements/recommendations for international students: Required—TOEFL (minimum score 550 paper-based; 213 computer-based). *Application deadline:* For fall admission, 6/1 for domestic students, 1/2 for international students; for spring admission, 10/15 for domestic students, 7/1 for international students. Application fee: $30. *Financial support:* Health care benefits and unspecified assistantships available. Financial award applicants required to submit FAFSA. *Unit head:* Dr. Robert Keith, Chairperson, 813-974-4186, Fax: 813-974-6528, E-mail: rkeith@coba.usf.edu. *Application contact:* Dr. William Parrott, Program Coordinator, 813-974-6736, Fax: 813-974-6528, E-mail: wparrott@coba.usf.edu.

The University of Tampa, John H. Sykes College of Business, Tampa, FL 33606-1490. Offers accounting (MBA, MS); economics (MBA); entrepreneurship (MBA); finance (MBA, MS); information systems management (MBA); innovation management (MS); international business (MBA); management (MBA); marketing (MBA, MS). *Accreditation:* AACSB. Part-time and evening/weekend programs available. *Faculty:* 39 full-time (9 women), 1 part-time/adjunct (0 women). *Students:* 143 full-time (52 women), 381 part-time (158 women); includes 78 minority (18 African Americans, 3 American Indian/Alaska Native, 19 Asian Americans or Pacific Islanders, 38 Hispanic Americans), 89 international. Average age 31. 486 applicants, 56% accepted, 231 enrolled. In 2006, 127 degrees awarded. *Median time to degree:* Master's–1.8 years full-time, 2.8 years part-time. *Entrance requirements:* For master's, GMAT. Additional exam requirements/recommendations for international students: Required—TOEFL (minimum score 577 paper-based; 230 computer-based; 90 iBT). *Application deadline:* For fall admission, 2/15 priority date for domestic students, 6/15 for international students; for spring admission, 12/15 for domestic students, 11/15 for international students. Applications are processed on a rolling basis. Application fee: $40. Electronic applications accepted. *Expenses:* Tuition: Part-time $426 per credit hour. Required fees: $35 per year. *Financial support:* In 2006–07, 57 students received support, including 57 research assistantships with tuition reimbursements available (averaging $3,000 per year); career-related internships or fieldwork and unspecified assistantships also available. Support available to part-time students. Financial award applicants required to submit FAFSA. *Faculty research:* Industrial organization and antitrust, artificial intelligence, corporate quality, leadership, ethics, quality. *Unit head:* Dr. William L. Rhey, Dean Graduate Studies, 813-253-6211, Fax: 813-259-5403, E-mail: wrhey@ut.edu. *Application contact:* Fernals Nolasco, Director of Graduate Studies, 813-253-6211, Fax: 813-259-5403, E-mail: fnolasco@ut.edu.

The University of Tennessee, Graduate School, College of Business Administration, Department of Accounting, Knoxville, TN 37996. Offers accounting (M Acc), including assurance; systems (M Acc); taxation (M Acc). *Accreditation:* AACSB. *Students:* 57 (35 women); includes 2 African Americans, 2 Asian Americans or Pacific Islanders 1 international. In 2006, 63 degrees awarded. *Degree requirements:* For master's, thesis or alternative. *Entrance requirements:* For master's, GMAT, minimum GPA of 2.7. Additional exam requirements/recommendations for international students: Required—TOEFL. *Application deadline:* For fall admission, 2/1 priority date for domestic students. Applications are processed on a rolling basis. Application fee: $35. Electronic applications accepted. *Expenses:* Tuition, state resident: full-time $5,574. Tuition, nonresident: full-time $16,840. Required fees: $792. *Financial support:* In 2006–07, 2 fellowships, 32 teaching assistantships were awarded; research assistantships, Federal Work-Study and institutionally sponsored loans also available. Financial award application deadline: 2/1; financial award applicants required to submit FAFSA. *Unit head:* Dr. Keith Stanga, Head, 865-974-1750, Fax: 865-974-4631, E-mail: kstanga@utk.edu. *Application contact:* Dr. Richard Townsend, Graduate Representative, 865-974-1750, E-mail: rtownsen@utk.edu.

The University of Tennessee, Graduate School, College of Business Administration, Program in Business Administration, Knoxville, TN 37996. Offers accounting (PhD); finance (MBA, PhD); logistics and transportation (MBA, PhD); management (PhD); marketing (MBA, PhD); operations management (MBA); professional business administration (MBA); statistics (PhD); JD/MBA; MS/MBA. *Accreditation:* AACSB. Postbaccalaureate distance learning degree programs offered. *Students:* 344 (105 women); includes 42 minority (20 African Americans, 4 American Indian/Alaska Native, 9 Asian Americans or Pacific Islanders, 9 Hispanic Americans) 49 international. In 2006, 169 master's, 9 doctorates awarded. *Degree requirements:* For master's, thesis or alternative; for doctorate, thesis/dissertation. *Entrance requirements:* For master's and doctorate, GMAT, minimum GPA of 2.7. Additional exam requirements/recommendations for international students: Required—TOEFL. *Application deadline:* For fall admission, 2/1 priority date for domestic students. Application fee: $35. Electronic applications accepted. *Expenses:* Tuition, state resident: full-time $5,574. Tuition, nonresident: full-time $16,840. Required fees: $792. *Financial support:* In 2006–07, 6 fellowships, 3 research assistantships, 35 teaching assistantships were awarded; career-related internships or fieldwork, Federal Work-Study, institutionally sponsored loans, and unspecified assistantships also available. Financial award application deadline: 2/1; financial award applicants required to submit FAFSA. *Unit head:* Dr. Sarah Gardial, Assistant Dean, 865-974-5033, Fax: 865-974-3826, E-mail: sgardial@utk.edu. *Application contact:* Donna Potts, Graduate Representative, 865-974-5033, Fax: 865-974-3826, E-mail: dpotts@utk.edu.

The University of Tennessee at Chattanooga, Graduate School, College of Business Administration, Program in Accountancy, Chattanooga, TN 37403-2598. Offers M Acc. *Accreditation:* AACSB. Part-time and evening/weekend programs available. *Faculty:* 10 full-time (3 women), 1 (woman) part-time/adjunct. *Students:* 10 full-time (5 women), 22 part-time (12 women); includes 5 minority (2 African Americans, 3 Asian Americans or Pacific Islanders). Average age 31. 20 applicants, 85% accepted, 10 enrolled. In 2006, 7 degrees awarded. *Entrance requirements:* For master's, GMAT. *Application deadline:* For fall admission, 8/1 priority date for domestic students; for spring admission, 12/1 priority date for domestic students. Applications are processed on a rolling basis. Application fee: $30. *Expenses:* Tuition, state resident: full-time $5,434; part-time $339 per hour. Tuition, nonresident: full-time $14,830; part-time $861 per hour. Required fees: $940; $178 per hour. *Financial support:* Fellowships, research assistantships, Federal Work-Study and institutionally sponsored loans available. Support available to part-time students. Financial award application deadline: 4/1; financial award applicants required to submit FAFSA. *Faculty research:* Performance measurement; auditing; income taxation; corporate efficiency; portfolio management and performance. *Unit head:* Dr. Kaye Sheridan, Head, 423-425-4770, Fax: 423-425-5255, E-mail: kaye-Sheridan@utc.edu. *Application contact:* Dr. Deborah E. Arfken, Dean of Graduate Studies, 423-425-4666, Fax: 423-425-5223, E-mail: deborah-arfken@utc.edu.

The University of Tennessee at Martin, Graduate Programs, College of Business and Public Affairs, Program in Accountancy, Martin, TN 38238-1000. Offers M Ac. Part-time programs available. Postbaccalaureate distance learning degree programs offered (no on-campus study). *Students:* 13 (8 women). In 2006, 13 degrees awarded. *Degree requirements:* For master's, comprehensive exam. *Entrance requirements:* For master's, GMAT, minimum GPA of 2.5, resumé. Additional exam requirements/recommendations for international students: Required—TOEFL (minimum score 525 paper-based; 197 computer-based). *Application deadline:* For fall admission, 8/1 priority date for domestic students, 8/1 for international students; for spring admission, 1/1 priority date for domestic students, 1/1 for international students. Applications are processed on a rolling basis. Application fee: $25 ($50 for international students). Electronic applications accepted. *Expenses:* Tuition, state resident: part-time $303 per credit hour. Tuition, nonresident: part-time $829 per credit hour. *Financial support:* In 2006–07, 1 student received support; research assistantships with full tuition reimbursements available, teaching assistantships with full tuition reimbursements available, scholarships/grants, tuition waivers (partial), and unspecified assistantships available. Financial award application deadline: 3/1. *Faculty research:* Managerial, financial, tax, nonprofit, and systems accounting; auditing. *Unit head:* Dr. Kevin Hammond, Coordinator, 731-881-7236, Fax: 731-881-7241, E-mail: bagrad@utm.edu.

The University of Texas at Arlington, Graduate School, College of Business Administration, Department of Accounting, Arlington, TX 76019. Offers accounting (MP Acc, MS); taxation (MS). Part-time and evening/weekend programs available. *Faculty:* 12 full-time (2 women). *Students:* 83 full-time (52 women), 120 part-time (59 women); includes 49 minority (8 African Americans, 23 Asian Americans or Pacific Islanders, 18 Hispanic Americans), 43 international. 124 applicants, 87% accepted, 74 enrolled. In 2006, 48 degrees awarded. *Degree requirements:* For master's, thesis optional. *Entrance requirements:* For master's, GMAT. Additional exam requirements/recommendations for international students: Required—TOEFL (minimum score 550 paper-based; 213 computer-based). *Application deadline:* For fall admission, 6/15 for domestic students. Applications are processed on a rolling basis. Application fee: $35 ($50 for international students). *Expenses:* Tuition, state resident: full-time $5,528. Tuition, nonresident: full-time $10,478. International tuition: $10,608 full-time. *Financial support:* In 2006–07, 2 fellowships (averaging $1,000 per year), 10 teaching assistantships (averaging $10,000 per year) were awarded; research assistantships, career-related internships or fieldwork, scholarships/grants, and unspecified assistantships also available. Financial award application deadline: 6/1; financial award applicants required to submit FAFSA. *Unit head:* Dr. Larry Walther, Chair, 817-272-3481, Fax: 817-282-5793, E-mail: walther@uta.edu. *Application contact:* Carly S. Andrews, Graduate Advisor, 817-272-3047, Fax: 817-272-5793, E-mail: graduate.accounting.advisor@uta.edu.

The University of Texas at Arlington, Graduate School, College of Business Administration, Program in Business Administration, Arlington, TX 76019. Offers accounting (PhD); business administration (PhD); business statistics (PhD); finance (MBA); information systems (MBA, PhD); management (MBA); management sciences (MBA); marketing (MBA, PhD); real estate (MBA). *Accreditation:* AACSB. Part-time and evening/weekend programs available.

Accounting

The University of Texas at Arlington (continued)

Postbaccalaureate distance learning degree programs offered (no on-campus study). *Faculty:* 1 full-time (0 women). *Students:* 156 full-time (60 women), 319 part-time (110 women); includes 123 minority (38 African Americans, 4 American Indian/Alaska Native, 52 Asian Americans or Pacific Islanders, 29 Hispanic Americans), 88 international. 502 applicants, 85% accepted, 199 enrolled. In 2006, 417 master's, 11 doctorates awarded. Terminal master's awarded for partial completion of doctoral program. *Degree requirements:* For master's, thesis optional; for doctorate, thesis/dissertation. *Entrance requirements:* For master's, GMAT; for doctorate, GMAT, minimum GPA of 3.0 (undergraduate), 3.4 (graduate); 30 hours of graduate course work. Additional exam requirements/recommendations for international students: Required—TOEFL (minimum score 550 paper-based; 213 computer-based). *Application deadline:* For fall admission, 6/15 for domestic students, 4/1 for international students; for spring admission, 10/15 for domestic students, 9/1 for international students. Applications are processed on a rolling basis. Application fee: $35 ($50 for international students). Electronic applications accepted. *Expenses:* Tuition, state resident: full-time $5,528. Tuition, nonresident: full-time $10,478. International tuition: $10,608 full-time. *Financial support:* In 2006–07, 1 fellowship (averaging $1,000 per year), 14 research assistantships (averaging $6,432 per year) were awarded; teaching assistantships, career-related internships or fieldwork, scholarships/grants, and unspecified assistantships also available. Financial award application deadline: 6/1; financial award applicants required to submit FAFSA. *Application contact:* Dr. Mike West, Assistant Dean, 817-272-1287, Fax: 817-272-5799, E-mail: mpwest@uta.edu.

See Close-Up on page 363.

The University of Texas at Austin, Graduate School, McCombs School of Business, Department of Accounting, Austin, TX 78712-1111. Offers MPA, PhD. *Accreditation:* AACSB. *Degree requirements:* For doctorate, thesis/dissertation, comprehensive exam. *Entrance requirements:* For master's and doctorate, GMAT. Additional exam requirements/recommendations for international students: Required—TOEFL. Electronic applications accepted.

The University of Texas at Dallas, School of Management, Program in Accounting and Information Management, Richardson, TX 75083-0688. Offers MS. *Accreditation:* AACSB. *Faculty:* 19 full-time (4 women). *Students:* 124 full-time (64 women), 268 part-time (149 women); includes 139 minority (31 African Americans, 81 Asian Americans or Pacific Islanders, 27 Hispanic Americans), 88 international. Average age 31. 471 applicants, 87% accepted, 261 enrolled. In 2006, 160 degrees awarded. *Entrance requirements:* For master's, GMAT. Additional exam requirements/recommendations for international students: Required—TOEFL (minimum score 550 paper-based; 213 computer-based). *Application deadline:* For fall admission, 7/15 for domestic students; for spring admission, 11/15 for domestic students. Applications are processed on a rolling basis. Application fee: $50 ($100 for international students). Electronic applications accepted. *Financial support:* In 2006–07, 3 research assistantships with tuition reimbursements (averaging $9,000 per year), 1 teaching assistantship with tuition reimbursement (averaging $9,550 per year) were awarded; fellowships, career-related internships or fieldwork, Federal Work-Study, institutionally sponsored loans, and scholarships/grants also available. Support available to part-time students. Financial award application deadline: 4/30; financial award applicants required to submit FAFSA. *Unit head:* Dr. Mark C Anderson, Area Coordinator, 972-883-2056, Fax: 972-883-6823, E-mail: mark.anderson@utdallas.edu. *Application contact:* David B. Ritchey, Director of Advising, 972-883-2701, Fax: 972-883-6425, E-mail: davidr@utdallas.edu.

See Close-Up on page 365.

The University of Texas at El Paso, Graduate School, College of Business Administration, Department of Accounting, El Paso, TX 79968-0001. Offers MACY. *Accreditation:* AACSB. Part-time and evening/weekend programs available. *Entrance requirements:* For master's, GMAT, minimum GPA of 2.7. Additional exam requirements/recommendations for international students: Required—TOEFL. Electronic applications accepted. *Faculty research:* International accounting, tax, not-for-profit accounting.

The University of Texas at San Antonio, College of Business, Department of Accounting, San Antonio, TX 78249-0617. Offers accounting (MS, PhD); management accounting (MBA); taxation (MBA, MT). *Accreditation:* AACSB. Part-time and evening/weekend programs available. *Faculty:* 9 full-time (2 women), 4 part-time/adjunct (1 woman). *Students:* 34 full-time (21 women), 78 part-time (46 women); includes 33 minority (4 Asian Americans or Pacific Islanders, 29 Hispanic Americans), 12 international. Average age 29. 57 applicants, 68% accepted, 36 enrolled. In 2006, 34 degrees awarded. *Degree requirements:* For master's, thesis optional. *Entrance requirements:* For master's, GMAT. Additional exam requirements/recommendations for international students: Required—TOEFL (minimum score 500 paper-based; 173 computer-based). *Application deadline:* For fall admission, 7/1 for domestic students, 4/1 for international students; for spring admission, 11/1 for domestic students, 9/1 for international students. Application fee: $45 ($80 for international students). *Expenses:* Tuition, state resident: full-time $1,730; part-time $192 per credit hour. Tuition, nonresident: full-time $6,680; part-time $742 per credit hour. Required fees: $733; $308,359 per credit hour. *Financial support:* In 2006–07, 2 research assistantships (averaging $20,800 per year), 6 teaching assistantships (averaging $15,600 per year) were awarded; career-related internships or fieldwork, Federal Work-Study, scholarships/grants, and unspecified assistantships also available. Support available to part-time students. Total annual research expenditures: $192,833. *Unit head:* Dr. James E. Groff, Interim Chair, 210-458-5239, Fax: 210-458-4322, E-mail: james.groff@utsa.edu.

The University of Texas of the Permian Basin, Office of Graduate Studies, School of Business, Program in Accountancy, Odessa, TX 79762-0001. Offers MPA. *Degree requirements:* For master's, registration. *Entrance requirements:* For master's, GMAT. Additional exam requirements/recommendations for international students: Required—TOEFL (minimum score 550 paper-based; 213 computer-based).

The University of Toledo, College of Graduate Studies, College of Business Administration, Department of Accounting, Toledo, OH 43606-3390. Offers accounting (MBA, MS Acct, MSA). Part-time and evening/weekend programs available. *Faculty:* 2 full-time (1 woman), 6 part-time/adjunct (0 women). *Students:* 29 full-time (12 women), 17 part-time (10 women), 5 international. Average age 27. 41 applicants, 63% accepted, 18 enrolled. In 2006, 23 degrees awarded. *Entrance requirements:* For master's, GMAT. Additional exam requirements/recommendations for international students: Required—TOEFL. *Application deadline:* For fall admission, 8/1 priority date for domestic students. Applications are processed on a rolling basis. Application fee: $45. *Financial support:* In 2006–07, 7 research assistantships with full tuition reimbursements (averaging $3,750 per year) were awarded; teaching assistantships with tuition reimbursements, career-related internships or fieldwork, Federal Work-Study, institutionally sponsored loans, and tuition waivers (full) also available. Support available to part-time students. Financial award application deadline: 4/1; financial award applicants required to submit FAFSA. *Faculty research:* Estate gift tax, audit and legal liability, corporate tax, accounting information systems. Total annual research expenditures: $10,000. *Unit head:* Dr. Diana Franz, Chair, 419-530-4264, E-mail: diana.franz@utoledo.edu.

University of Toronto, School of Graduate Studies, Social Sciences Division, Faculty of Management, Toronto, ON M5S 1A1, Canada. Offers EMBA, MBA, MMPA, PhD, JD/MBA, MBA/MA, MBA/MN. *Accreditation:* AACSB. Part-time and evening/weekend programs available. *Degree requirements:* For doctorate, thesis/dissertation. *Entrance requirements:* For master's, GMAT (MBA, MMPA; for EMBA: only applicants without an undergraduate degree), minimum mid-B average in final undergraduate year (MMPA, MBA), 2 years of full-time work experiences (MBA), 8 years work experience preferred (EMBA), 2-3 letters of reference; for doctorate, GMAT, minimum B+ average, master's degree in business administration, 2-3 letters of reference. Expenses: Contact institution. *Faculty research:* Natural resources, organizational behavior, finance.

University of Utah, The Graduate School, David Eccles School of Business, School of Accounting and Information Systems, Salt Lake City, UT 84112-1107. Offers M Pr A, PhD. *Accreditation:* AACSB. *Faculty:* 18 full-time (7 women), 4 part-time/adjunct (0 women). *Students:* 47 full-time (12 women), 4 part-time (1 woman); includes 3 minority (1 African American, 1 Asian American or Pacific Islander, 1 Hispanic American), 1 international. Average age 26. 111 applicants, 60% accepted, 32 enrolled. In 2006, 44 degrees awarded. *Degree requirements:* For doctorate, thesis/dissertation, oral qualifying exams, written qualifying exams. *Entrance requirements:* For master's, GMAT, minimum undergraduate GPA of 3.0; for doctorate, GMAT. Additional exam requirements/recommendations for international students: Required—TOEFL (minimum score 600 paper-based; 250 computer-based). *Application deadline:* For fall admission, 4/2 priority date for domestic students, 4/2 for international students. Application fee: $45 ($65 for international students). Electronic applications accepted. *Expenses:* Tuition, state resident: full-time $3,208. Tuition, nonresident: full-time $11,326. Required fees: $608. Tuition and fees vary according to class time and program. *Financial support:* In 2006–07, fellowships with partial tuition reimbursements (averaging $5,250 per year), teaching assistantships with partial tuition reimbursements (averaging $5,600 per year) were awarded; research assistantships, Federal Work-Study and tuition waivers (full) also available. Financial award application deadline: 2/15. *Faculty research:* Auditing, taxation, information systems, financial accounting, accounting theory. Total annual research expenditures: $145,098. *Unit head:* Bob Allen, Chair, 801-581-7208, Fax: 801-581-3666, E-mail: bob.allen@business.utah.edu. *Application contact:* Kanita Lipjankic, Advisor, 801-581-3016, Fax: 801-581-3666, E-mail: kanita.lipjankic@business.utah.edu.

University of Virginia, McIntire School of Commerce, Program in Accounting, Charlottesville, VA 22903. Offers MS. *Accreditation:* AACSB. *Students:* 56 full-time (30 women), 54 part-time (24 women); includes 5 minority (2 African Americans, 3 Hispanic Americans), 20 international. Average age 22. In 2006, 102 degrees awarded. *Entrance requirements:* For master's, GMAT. Additional exam requirements/recommendations for international students: Required—TOEFL. *Application deadline:* For fall admission, 2/15 for domestic students. Applications are processed on a rolling basis. Application fee: $60. Electronic applications accepted. *Financial support:* Fellowships, Federal Work-Study available. Financial award applicants required to submit FAFSA. *Application contact:* Peter A. Todd, Associate Dean for Graduate Programs, 434-243-8988, E-mail: mcintiregrad@virginia.edu.

University of Washington, Graduate School, Business School, Seattle, WA 98195-3200. Offers auditing and assurance (MP Acc); business (PhD); evening part-time (MBA); executive (MBA); full time (MBA); global (MBA); global executive (MBA); taxation (MP Acc); technology management (MBA); JD/MBA; MBA/MAIS; MBA/MHA. *Accreditation:* AACSB. Part-time and evening/weekend programs available. *Degree requirements:* For master's, registration; for doctorate, thesis/dissertation, comprehensive exam, registration. *Entrance requirements:* For master's, GMAT; for doctorate, GMAT, GRE. Additional exam requirements/recommendations for international students: Required—TOEFL (minimum score 600 paper-based; 250 computer-based). Electronic applications accepted. Expenses: Contact institution.

University of Waterloo, Graduate Studies, Faculty of Arts, School of Accountancy, Waterloo, ON N2L 3G1, Canada. Offers accounting (M Acc, PhD); finance (M Acc); taxation (M Tax). *Faculty:* 29 full-time (8 women), 3 part-time/adjunct (1 woman). *Students:* 100. 199 applicants, 24% accepted, 29 enrolled. In 2006, 133 master's, 1 doctorate awarded. *Degree requirements:* For master's, thesis or alternative; for doctorate, thesis/dissertation. *Entrance requirements:* For master's, honors degree, minimum B average, resumé; for doctorate, GMAT, master's degree, minimum A- average, resumé. Additional exam requirements/recommendations for international students: Required—TOEFL, TWE. *Application deadline:* For fall admission, 1/31 for domestic students. Application fee: $75 Canadian dollars. *Expenses: Contact institution. Faculty research:* Auditing, management accounting. *Unit head:* Dr. Alister Mason, Director, 519-888-4567 Ext. 33732, Fax: 519-888-7262, E-mail: amason@uwaterloo.ca. *Application contact:* Dr. Alan Macnaughton, Graduate Officer, 519-888-4567 Ext. 35776, Fax: 519-888-7562.

The University of Western Ontario, Richard Ivey School of Business, London, ON N6A 3K7, Canada. Offers biotechnology stream (MBA); business (EMBA, PhD); certified management accountant (MBA); China business stream (MBA); entrepreneurship (MBA); finance stream (MBA); LL B/MBA. Part-time and evening/weekend programs available. *Degree requirements:* For master's, thesis (for some programs); for doctorate, thesis/dissertation. *Entrance requirements:* For master's, GMAT, 3 years of full-time work experience, interview; for doctorate, GMAT. Additional exam requirements/recommendations for international students: Required—TOEFL. Electronic applications accepted. *Faculty research:* Strategy, organizational behavior, international business, finance, operations management.

University of West Florida, College of Business, Department of Accounting, Pensacola, FL 32514-5750. Offers MA. Part-time and evening/weekend programs available. *Faculty:* 10 full-time (1 woman), 2 part-time/adjunct (both women). *Students:* 18 full-time (10 women), 20 part-time (12 women); includes 10 minority (1 African American, 6 Asian Americans or Pacific Islanders, 3 Hispanic Americans). Average age 30. 23 applicants, 65% accepted, 14 enrolled. In 2006, 22 degrees awarded. *Entrance requirements:* For master's, GMAT. Additional exam requirements/recommendations for international students: Required—TOEFL (minimum score 550 paper-based; 213 computer-based). *Application deadline:* For fall admission, 6/30 priority date for domestic students, 5/15 for international students; for spring admission, 11/1 for domestic students, 10/1 for international students. Application fee: $30. *Expenses:* Tuition, state resident: full-time $5,871; part-time $245 per credit hour. Tuition, nonresident: full-time $21,241; part-time $885 per credit hour. *Financial support:* In 2006–07, 9 fellowships (averaging $500 per year), 2 research assistantships with partial tuition reimbursements (averaging $7,000 per year) were awarded; Federal Work-Study also available. Support available to part-time students. Financial award application deadline: 4/15; financial award applicants required to submit FAFSA. *Faculty research:* Audit risk, tax legislation, product costing, bank core deposit intangibles, financial reporting. *Unit head:* Dr. Chula G. King, Chairperson, 850-474-2717.

University of West Georgia, Graduate School, Richards College of Business, Department of Accounting and Finance, Carrollton, GA 30118. Offers MP Acc. *Accreditation:* AACSB. Part-time and evening/weekend programs available. *Faculty:* 8 full-time (2 women). *Students:* 9 full-time (6 women), 11 part-time (6 women); includes 2 minority (1 African American, 1 Asian American or Pacific Islander), 6 international. Average age 29. 25 applicants, 68% accepted, 8 enrolled. In 2006, 3 degrees awarded. *Degree requirements:* For master's, comprehensive exam. *Entrance requirements:* For master's, GMAT, minimum GPA of 2.5. Additional exam requirements/recommendations for international students: Required—TOEFL (minimum score 550 paper-based; 213 computer-based). *Application deadline:* For fall admission, 7/1 priority date for domestic students, 6/4 for international students; for spring admission, 11/1 for domestic students, 10/4 for international students. Application fee: $20. Electronic applications accepted. *Expenses:* Tuition, state resident: full-time $2,286; part-time $127 per credit. Tuition, nonresident: full-time $9,144; part-time $508 per credit. Required fees: $494; $27 per credit. $121 per semester. *Financial support:* In 2006–07, 1 student received support, including 1 research assistantship with full tuition reimbursement available (averaging $4,500 per year); tuition waivers (partial) also available. Financial award application deadline: 7/1; financial award applicants required to submit FAFSA. *Faculty research:* Taxpayer insolvency, non-gap financial measures, deferred taxes, financial accounting issues. Total annual research expenditures: $40,000. *Unit head:* Dr. James R. Colley, Interim Chair, 678-839-6469, Fax: 678-839-5041, E-mail: jcolley@westga.edu. *Application contact:* Dr. Charles W. Clark, Chair, 678-839-6508, E-mail: cclark@westga.edu.

University of Wisconsin–Madison, Graduate School, School of Business, Program in Accounting and Information Systems, Madison, WI 53706-1380. Offers PhD. *Accreditation:* AACSB. *Students:* 10 full-time (5 women), 2 international. Average age 33. 58 applicants, 7% accepted, 2 enrolled. In 2006, 3 degrees awarded. *Median time to degree:* Of those who began their doctoral program in fall 1998, 100% received their degree in 8 years or less. *Entrance requirements:* For doctorate, GMAT or GRE. Additional exam requirements/recommendations for international students: Required—TOEFL (minimum score 600 paper-based; 250 computer-based). *Application deadline:* For fall admission, 1/6 priority date for domestic and international students. Applications are processed on a rolling basis. Electronic applications accepted. *Financial support:* In 2006–07, 10 students received support, including fellowships with full tuition reimbursements available (averaging $16,110 per year), research assistantships with full tuition reimbursements available (averaging $13,502 per year), 10 teaching assistantships with full tuition reimbursements available (averaging $13,686 per year); Federal Work-Study, institutionally sponsored loans, scholarships/grants, health care benefits, and unspecified assistantships also available. Financial award application deadline: 1/6. *Faculty research:* Auditing, financial reporting, economic theory, strategy, computer models. *Unit head:* Dr. Jon Davis, Chair, 608-263-4264. *Application contact:* Belle Heberling, PhD Coordinator, 608-262-3749, Fax: 608-890-0180, E-mail: phd@bus.wisc.edu.

University of Wisconsin–Whitewater, School of Graduate Studies, College of Business and Economics, Department of Accounting, Whitewater, WI 53190-1790. Offers MPA. Part-time and evening/weekend programs available. Postbaccalaureate distance learning degree programs offered (no on-campus study). *Students:* 66 full-time (34 women), 21 part-time (13 women); includes 11 minority (1 African American, 8 Asian Americans or Pacific Islanders, 2 Hispanic Americans). Average age 26. 33 applicants, 70% accepted, 17 enrolled. In 2006, 68 degrees awarded. *Degree requirements:* For master's, thesis or alternative. *Entrance requirements:* For master's, GMAT, minimum AACSB index of 1000, minimum GPA of 2.75. Additional exam requirements/recommendations for international students: Required—TOEFL (minimum score 550 paper-based; 213 computer-based). *Application deadline:* For fall admission, 7/15 priority date for domestic students, 7/15 for international students; for spring admission, 12/1 priority date for domestic students, 12/1 for international students. Applications are processed on a rolling basis. Application fee: $45. Electronic applications accepted. *Expenses:* Tuition, state resident: full-time $3,311. Tuition, nonresident: full-time $8,616. Required fees: $368 per credit. *Financial support:* In 2006–07, 1 research assistantship (averaging $9,384 per year) was awarded; Federal Work-Study, unspecified assistantships, and out of state fee waiver also available. Support available to part-time students. Financial award application deadline: 3/15; financial award applicants required to submit FAFSA. *Faculty research:* Laws/economy/quality of life; tax, accounting and public policy. *Unit head:* Dr. Donald Zahn, Associate Dean, 262-472-1945, Fax: 262-472-4863, E-mail: zahnd@uww.edu.

University of Wyoming, Graduate School, College of Business, Program in Accounting, Laramie, WY 82070. Offers MS. *Faculty:* 8 full-time (4 women). *Students:* 18 full-time (14 women), 4 part-time (3 women), 3 international. Average age 27. 32 applicants, 91% accepted, 14 enrolled. In 2006, 12 degrees awarded. *Degree requirements:* For master's, thesis optional. *Entrance requirements:* For master's, GMAT/GRE, minimum GPA of 3.0. Additional exam requirements/recommendations for international students: Required—TOEFL (minimum score 525 paper-based; 197 computer-based). *Application deadline:* For fall admission, 4/1 priority date for domestic and international students; for spring admission, 10/15 priority date for domestic and international students. Applications are processed on a rolling basis. Application fee: $50. Electronic applications accepted. *Financial support:* In 2006–07, 7 students received support, including 5 research assistantships with partial tuition reimbursements available (averaging $5,192 per year), 2 teaching assistantships with partial tuition reimbursements available (averaging $5,192 per year); unspecified assistantships also available. Financial award application deadline: 2/1; financial award applicants required to submit FAFSA. *Faculty research:* Taxation, accounting education, assessment, not-for-profit accounting, fraud examination. *Unit head:* Penne L. Ainsworth, Professor and Chairperson, 307-766-3167, Fax: 307-766-4028, E-mail: acctdept@uwyo.edu. *Application contact:* Richard G. Elmendorf, Professor/Director, 307-766-3962, Fax: 307-766-4028, E-mail: msacctg@uwyo.edu.

Upper Iowa University, Online Master's Programs, Fayette, IA 52142-1857. Offers accounting (MBA); corporate financial management (MBA); global business (MBA); health and human services (MPA); homeland security (MPA); human resources management (MBA); justice administration (MPA); organizational development (MBA); public personnel management (MPA); quality management (MBA). MBA also available at Madison, Wisconsin campus. Part-time and evening/weekend programs available. Postbaccalaureate distance learning degree programs offered (no on-campus study). *Degree requirements:* For master's, research project. *Entrance requirements:* For master's, GMAT, GRE, or minimum GPA of 2.7 during last 60 hours. Additional exam requirements/recommendations for international students: Required—TOEFL (minimum score 570 paper-based; 230 computer-based). Electronic applications accepted. *Faculty research:* Total quality management, CQI, teams, organization culture and climate, management.

Utah State University, School of Graduate Studies, College of Business, School of Accountancy, Logan, UT 84322. Offers M Acc. *Accreditation:* AACSB. Part-time programs available. *Faculty:* 13 full-time (2 women), 2 part-time/adjunct (0 women). *Students:* 54 full-time (23 women), 1 (woman) part-time, 8 international. Average age 28. 92 applicants, 87% accepted, 50 enrolled. In 2006, 38 degrees awarded. *Degree requirements:* For master's, registration. *Entrance requirements:* For master's, GMAT, minimum GPA of 3.0, transcripts, 3 recommendation letters. Additional exam requirements/recommendations for international students: Required—TOEFL. *Application deadline:* For fall admission, 3/1 for domestic and international students; for spring admission, 10/1 for domestic and international students. Applications are processed on a rolling basis. Application fee: $50 ($60 for international students). *Financial support:* In 2006–07, 15 students received support, including 5 fellowships with partial tuition reimbursements available (averaging $2,500 per year), 10 teaching assistantships with partial tuition reimbursements available (averaging $2,800 per year); research assistantships with partial tuition reimbursements available, career-related internships or fieldwork, tuition waivers (full), and unspecified assistantships also available. Financial award application deadline: 3/1. *Faculty research:* Relationship theory, enterprise systems, just in time/loan, reported earnings measures, accounting education. Total annual research expenditures: $3,000. *Unit head:* Richard L. Jenson, Department Head and Director, 435-797-2335, Fax: 435-797-1475, E-mail: rjenson@cc.usu.edu. *Application contact:* Mary Ann Clark, Assistant to the Department Head, 435-797-2330, Fax: 435-797-1475, E-mail: maryann.clark@usu.edu.

Utica College, Program in Accountancy, Utica, NY 13502-4892. Offers MBA. Part-time and evening/weekend programs available. *Faculty:* 7 full-time (0 women). *Students:* 1 full-time (0 women), 8 part-time (3 women); includes 1 minority (African American) 10 applicants, 80% accepted, 7 enrolled. *Entrance requirements:* For master's, BS, minimum GPA of 3.0. Additional exam requirements/recommendations for international students: Required—TOEFL (minimum score 550 paper-based; 213 computer-based). *Application deadline:* Applications are processed on a rolling basis. Application fee: $50. Electronic applications accepted. *Expenses:* Tuition: Full-time $20,480; part-time $550 per credit hour. Required fees: $310; $50 per term. Tuition and fees vary according to course load, degree level and program. *Financial support:* In 2006–07, 6 students received support. Career-related internships or fieldwork, scholarships/grants, tuition waivers (partial), and unspecified assistantships available. Support available to part-time students. Financial award application deadline: 3/15; financial award applicants required to submit FAFSA. *Unit head:* Dr. Hartwell Herring, Director, MBA, 315-792-3335, E-mail: hherring@utica.edu. *Application contact:* John D. Rowe, Director of Graduate Admissions, 315-792-3824, Fax: 315-792-3003, E-mail: jrowe@utica.edu.

Villanova University, Villanova School of Business, Master of Accountancy Program, Villanova, PA 19085-1699. Offers M Ac. *Accreditation:* AACSB. *Faculty:* 9 full-time (2 women). *Students:* Average age 23. 45 applicants, 69% accepted, 20 enrolled. In 2006, 27 degrees awarded. *Entrance requirements:* Additional exam requirements/recommendations for international students: Required—TOEFL (minimum score 600 paper-based; 250 computer-based; 100 iBT). *Application deadline:* For spring admission, 3/31 for domestic and international students. Applications are processed on a rolling basis. Application fee: $50. *Expenses:* Tuition: Part-time $565 per credit. *Financial support:* Career-related internships or fieldwork available. Financial award application deadline: 3/31. *Unit head:* Simone L. Pollard, Director of Graduate Business, 610-519-4336, Fax: 610-519-6273, E-mail: simone.pollard@villanova.edu. *Application contact:* Maureen Piotti, Coordinator, Graduate Business Programs, 610-519-5456, Fax: 610-519-6273, E-mail: maureen.piotti@villanova.edu.

Virginia Commonwealth University, Graduate School, School of Business, Program in Accounting, Richmond, VA 23284-9005. Offers accountancy (M Acc, MBA, MS, PhD); tax (MS). *Accreditation:* AACSB. *Faculty:* 12 full-time (3 women). *Students:* 23 full-time (8 women), 26 part-time (16 women); includes 12 minority (9 African Americans, 3 Asian Americans or Pacific Islanders), 10 international. 38 applicants, 89% accepted. In 2006, 2 master's, 3 doctorates awarded. *Degree requirements:* For doctorate, thesis/dissertation. *Entrance requirements:* For master's, GMAT; for doctorate, GMAT, relevant work experience. *Application deadline:* For fall admission, 7/15 for domestic students; for spring admission, 11/15 for domestic students. Applications are processed on a rolling basis. Application fee: $50. *Financial support:* Fellowships, research assistantships, teaching assistantships, Federal Work-Study, institutionally sponsored loans, and tuition waivers (full and partial) available. Financial award application deadline: 3/15. *Unit head:* Dr. Ruth W. Epps, Chair, 804-828-1608, Fax: 804-828-1719, E-mail: rwepps@vcu.edu. *Application contact:* Tracy Green, Graduate Program Director, 804-828-1741, Fax: 804-828-7174, E-mail: tsgreen@vcu.edu.

See Close-Up on page 463.

Virginia Polytechnic Institute and State University, Graduate School, Pamplin College of Business, Department of Accounting and Information Systems, Blacksburg, VA 24061. Offers MACIS, PhD. *Accreditation:* AACSB. *Faculty:* 24 full-time (8 women), 1 part-time/adjunct (0 women). *Students:* 92 full-time (50 women), 11 part-time (6 women); includes 16 minority (2 African Americans, 1 American Indian/Alaska Native, 11 Asian Americans or Pacific Islanders, 2 Hispanic Americans), 22 international. Average age 27. 115 applicants, 70% accepted, 57 enrolled. In 2006, 53 master's, 5 doctorates awarded. *Entrance requirements:* For master's and doctorate, GMAT. Additional exam requirements/recommendations for international students: Required—TOEFL (minimum score 620 paper-based; 260 computer-based). *Application deadline:* For fall admission, 5/15 for international students; for spring admission, 10/15 for international students. Applications are processed on a rolling basis. Application fee: $45. Electronic applications accepted. *Expenses:* Tuition, state resident: full-time $7,017; part-time $390 per credit hour. Tuition, nonresident: full-time $12,414; part-time $690 per credit hour. International tuition: $11,296 full-time. Required fees: $1,523; $256 per term. *Financial support:* In 2006–07, 1 research assistantship (averaging $2,285 per year), 10 teaching assistantships with full tuition reimbursements (averaging $13,761 per year) were awarded; career-related internships or fieldwork, Federal Work-Study, scholarships/grants, and unspecified assistantships also available. Financial award application deadline:4/1. *Faculty research:* Financial accounting, international accounting, management accounting. *Unit head:* Dr. Robert M. Brown, Head, 540-231-6591, Fax: 540-231-2511, E-mail: acis@vt.edu. *Application contact:* Arnita Perfater, Information Contact, 540-231-6592, Fax: 540-231-2511, E-mail: arnita@vt.edu.

See Close-Up on page 467.

Wagner College, Division of Graduate Studies, Department of Business Administration, Program in Accounting, Staten Island, NY 10301-4495. Offers MS. Part-time programs available. *Faculty:* 3 full-time (2 women), 1 part-time/adjunct (0 women). *Students:* 13 full-time (7 women), 4 part-time (all women). 15 applicants, 87% accepted, 13 enrolled. In 2006, 10 degrees awarded. *Degree requirements:* For master's, thesis. *Entrance requirements:* For master's, bachelor's degree in accounting or business with a concentration in accounting. Additional exam requirements/recommendations for international students: Required—TOEFL (minimum score 550 paper-based; 217 computer-based). *Application deadline:* For fall admission, 8/1 priority date for domestic students, 6/30 priority date for international students; for spring admission, 12/10 priority date for domestic students, 11/15 for international students. Applications are processed on a rolling basis. Application fee: $50 ($85 for international students). *Expenses:* Tuition: Full-time $15,120; part-time $840 per credit. *Financial support:* Fellowships, unspecified assistantships available. Financial award applicants required to submit FAFSA. *Unit head:* Prof. Margaret Horan, Director, 718-390-3437. *Application contact:* Susan Rosenberg, Office of Graduate Studies, 718-390-3411, Fax: 718-390-3456, E-mail: graduate@wagner.edu.

Wake Forest University, Graduate School, Department of Accountancy, Winston-Salem, NC 27109. Offers MSA. *Accreditation:* AACSB. *Faculty:* 12 full-time (3 women). *Students:* 65 full-time (26 women), 1 (woman) part-time; includes 3 minority (2 African Americans, 1 Asian American or Pacific Islander), 4 international. Average age 23. 106 applicants, 58% accepted, 53 enrolled. In 2006, 56 degrees awarded. *Degree requirements:* For master's, one foreign language, registration. *Entrance requirements:* For master's, GMAT. Additional exam requirements/recommendations for international students: Required—TOEFL (minimum score 213 computer-based). *Application deadline:* For fall admission, 1/15 for domestic and international students. Application fee: $45 ($55 for international students). Electronic applications accepted. *Financial support:* In 2006–07, 62 students received support, including 1 research assistantship with full tuition reimbursement available (averaging $6,000 per year), 14 teaching assistantships with full tuition reimbursements available (averaging $6,000 per year); scholarships/grants and tuition waivers (full and partial) also available. Financial award application deadline: 1/15; financial award applicants required to submit FAFSA. *Unit head:* Dr. Yvonne Hinson, Director, 336-758-5113, Fax: 336-758-6133, E-mail: hinsonyl@wfu.edu.

Walsh College of Accountancy and Business Administration, Graduate Programs, Program in Accountancy, Troy, MI 48007-7006. Offers MSPA. Part-time and evening/weekend programs available. *Faculty:* 3 full-time (1 woman), 6 part-time/adjunct (2 women). *Students:* 22 full-time (9 women), 188 part-time (107 women). Average age 32. 84 applicants, 92% accepted, 77 enrolled. In 2006, 45 degrees awarded. *Degree requirements:* For master's, thesis optional. *Entrance requirements:* For master's, minimum GPA of 2.75, previous course work in business. Additional exam requirements/recommendations for international students: Required—TOEFL. *Application deadline:* For fall admission, 8/24 priority date for domestic students; for winter admission, 1/1 priority date for domestic students; for spring admission, 4/1 priority date for domestic students. Applications are processed on a rolling basis. Application fee: $25. Electronic applications accepted. *Expenses:* Tuition: Part-time $435 per hour. Required fees: $119 per semester. One-time fee: $50. *Financial support:* Available to part-time students. Application deadline: 6/30. *Unit head:* Rick Bershbeck, Director, 248-823-1345, Fax: 248-689-0920. *Application contact:* Karen Mahaffy, Director of Admissions and Academic Advising, 248-823-1610, Fax: 248-689-0938, E-mail: kmahaffy@walshcollege.edu.

Washington State University, Graduate School, College of Business, Department of Accounting and Business Law, Pullman, WA 99164. Offers accounting and information systems (M Acc); accounting and taxation (M Acc). *Accreditation:* AACSB. *Faculty:* 10 full-time (2 women). *Students:* 17 full-time (8 women), 2 part-time, 4 international. Average age 27. 63 applicants, 41% accepted, 10 enrolled. In 2006, 18 degrees awarded. *Degree requirements:* For master's, thesis (for some programs), oral exam, research paper, comprehensive exam (for some programs). *Entrance requirements:* For master's, GMAT, minimum GPA of 3.0, 3 letters of recommendation. Additional exam requirements/recommendations for international students: Required—TOEFL (minimum score 580 paper-based; 237 computer-based). *Application deadline:* For fall admission, 3/1 priority date for domestic students, 3/1 for international students; for spring admission, 7/1 for international students. Applications are processed on a rolling basis. Application fee: $50. Electronic applications accepted. *Expenses:* Tuition, state resident: full-time $7,066. Tuition, nonresident: full-time $17,204. *Financial support:* In 2006–07, 19 students received support, including 1 fellowship (averaging $5,500 per year), research assistantships (averaging $13,917 per year), 8 teaching assistantships with tuition reimbursements available (averaging $13,056 per year); Federal Work-Study, institutionally sponsored loans, tuition waivers (partial), and teaching associateships also available. Financial award application deadline: 3/1. *Faculty research:* Ethics, taxation, auditing. Total annual research expenditures: $11,753. *Unit head:* Dr. Robert R. Greenberg, Chair, 509-335-8541, Fax: 509-

Accounting

Washington State University (continued)
335-4275. *Application contact:* Graduate School Admissions, 800-GRADWSU, Fax: 509-335-1949, E-mail: gradsch@wsu.edu.

Washington State University, Graduate School, College of Business, Graduate Programs in Business, Pullman, WA 99164. Offers accounting and business law (M Acc); business administration (MBA, PhD), including accounting (PhD), finance (PhD), management and operations (PhD), management information systems (PhD), marketing (PhD); JD/MBA. *Accreditation:* AACSB. *Faculty:* 38. *Students:* 105 full-time (39 women), 14 part-time (5 women); includes 3 minority (1 American Indian/Alaska Native, 2 Asian Americans or Pacific Islanders), 62 international. Average age 30. 328 applicants, 32% accepted, 43 enrolled. In 2006, 56 master's, 8 doctorates awarded. *Degree requirements:* For master's, thesis (for some programs), final presentation, comprehensive exam (for some programs); for doctorate, thesis/dissertation, oral and written exams, comprehensive exam. *Entrance requirements:* For master's and doctorate, GMAT, minimum GPA of 3.0, 3 letters of recommendation. Additional exam requirements/recommendations for international students: Required—TOEFL. *Application deadline:* For fall admission, 3/1 priority date for domestic students, 3/1 for international students; for spring admission, 6/1 priority date for domestic students, 6/1 for international students. Applications are processed on a rolling basis. Application fee: $50. Electronic applications accepted. *Expenses:* Tuition, state resident: full-time $7,066. Tuition, nonresident: full-time $17,204. *Financial support:* In 2006–07, 102 students received support, including 9 fellowships (averaging $6,000 per year), 8 research assistantships with full and partial tuition reimbursements available (averaging $13,917 per year), 75 teaching assistantships with full and partial tuition reimbursements available (averaging $13,056 per year); career-related internships or fieldwork, Federal Work-Study, institutionally sponsored loans, health care benefits, tuition waivers (partial), unspecified assistantships, and teaching associateships also available. Financial award application deadline: 4/1. *Unit head:* Dr. Charles Munson, Associate Dean, 509-335-1193, E-mail: mba@wsu.edu. *Application contact:* Graduate School Admissions, 800-GRADWSU, Fax: 509-335-1949, E-mail: gradsch@wsu.edu.

Washington University in St. Louis, John M. Olin School of Business, Program in Accounting and Finance, St. Louis, MO 63130-4899. Offers accounting (MS); finance (MS). Part-time programs available. *Faculty:* 66 full-time, 39 part-time/adjunct. *Students:* 59 full-time. 170 applicants, 58% accepted, 57 enrolled. In 2006, 18 degrees awarded. *Entrance requirements:* For master's, GMAT or GRE. Additional exam requirements/recommendations for international students: Required—TOEFL. *Application deadline:* For fall admission, 3/15 for domestic and international students. Application fee: $80. *Expenses:* Contact institution. *Financial support:* Applicants required to submit FAFSA. *Unit head:* Joseph Peter Fox, Associate Dean and Director of MBA Programs, 314-935-6322, Fax: 314-935-4464, E-mail: fox@wustl.edu.

Wayne State College, School of Natural and Social Sciences, Department of Health, Human Performance and Sport, Wayne, NE 68787. Offers exercise science (MSE); organization management (MSE), including sport and recreation management. Part-time and evening/weekend programs available. *Faculty:* 6 part-time/adjunct (2 women). *Students:* 15 full-time (3 women), 6 part-time (1 woman); includes 3 minority (all African Americans), 2 international. Average age 27. In 2006, 11 degrees awarded. *Degree requirements:* For master's, thesis optional. *Entrance requirements:* For master's, GRE General Test, minimum GPA of 3.0. Additional exam requirements/recommendations for international students: Required—TOEFL (minimum score 550 paper-based; 213 computer-based). *Application deadline:* Applications are processed on a rolling basis. Application fee: $30. Electronic applications accepted. *Expenses:* Tuition, state resident: full-time $3,114; part-time $130 per credit hour. Tuition, nonresident: full-time $6,228; part-time $260 per credit hour. Required fees: $894; $37 per credit hour. Tuition and fees vary according to course load. *Financial support:* In 2006–07, 3 teaching assistantships with full tuition reimbursements (averaging $4,000 per year) were awarded; career-related internships or fieldwork also available. Financial award applicants required to submit FAFSA. *Unit head:* Dr. Kevin Hill, Dean, 402-375-7030.

Wayne State University, School of Business Administration, Detroit, MI 48202. Offers accounting (MS); business administration (MBA, PhD); interdisciplinary studies (PhD); taxation (MS); JD/MBA. *Accreditation:* AACSB. Part-time and evening/weekend programs available. *Faculty:* 64 full-time (11 women), 5 part-time/adjunct (1 woman). *Students:* 218 full-time (92 women), 1,021 part-time (446 women); includes 313 minority (179 African Americans, 2 American Indian/Alaska Native, 111 Asian Americans or Pacific Islanders, 21 Hispanic Americans), 153 international. Average age 30. 526 applicants, 73% accepted, 276 enrolled. In 2006, 386 degrees awarded. *Degree requirements:* For master's, thesis optional. *Entrance requirements:* For master's, GMAT. Additional exam requirements/recommendations for international students: Required—TOEFL (minimum score 550 paper-based; 213 computer-based); Recommended—TWE (minimum score 6). *Application deadline:* For fall admission, 8/1 for domestic students, 6/1 for international students; for winter admission, 10/1 for international students; for spring admission, 4/1 for domestic students, 2/1 for international students. Applications are processed on a rolling basis. Application fee: $30 ($50 for international students). Electronic applications accepted. *Financial support:* In 2006–07, 10 research assistantships (averaging $13,222 per year) were awarded; career-related internships or fieldwork, Federal Work-Study, and scholarships/grants also available. Support available to part-time students. Financial award applicants required to submit FAFSA. *Faculty research:* Corporate financial valuation, strategic advertising, information technology effectiveness, financial accounting and taxation, organizational performance and effectiveness. Total annual research expenditures: $188,100. *Unit head:* Dr. Richard Gabrys, Dean, 313-577-4501, Fax: 313-577-4557, E-mail: az4994@wayne.edu. *Application contact:* Linda Zaddach, Assistant Dean, 313-577-4510, E-mail: l.s.zaddach@wayne.edu.

See Close-Up on page 373.

Webber International University, Graduate School of Business, Babson Park, FL 33827-0096. Offers accounting (MBA); management (MBA); sports management (MBA). Part-time and evening/weekend programs available. *Degree requirements:* For master's, thesis or alternative. *Entrance requirements:* For master's, previous course work in financial and managerial accounting. Additional exam requirements/recommendations for international students: Required—TOEFL. *Faculty research:* Finance strategy, market research, investments, intranet.

See Close-Up on page 375.

Weber State University, John B. Goddard School of Business and Economics, School of Accountancy, Ogden, UT 84408-1001. Offers M Acc. *Accreditation:* AACSB. Part-time programs available. *Faculty:* 8 full-time (0 women), 2 part-time/adjunct (0 women). *Students:* 34 full-time (9 women), 18 part-time (6 women); includes 2 minority (both Asian Americans or Pacific Islanders), 1 international. Average age 28. 46 applicants, 89% accepted, 31 enrolled. In 2006, 50 degrees awarded. *Entrance requirements:* For master's, GMAT. *Application deadline:* For fall admission, 3/1 priority date for domestic students; for spring admission, 10/1 priority date for domestic students. Applications are processed on a rolling basis. Application fee: $30 ($45 for international students). *Expenses:* Tuition, state resident: full-time $3,950; part-time $203 per semester. Tuition, nonresident: full-time $10,371; part-time $518 per semester. Required fees: $544; $24 per semester. Tuition and fees vary according to course load and program. *Financial support:* In 2006–07, 21 students received support. Federal Work-Study, institutionally sponsored loans, scholarships/grants, and tuition waivers (full and partial) available. Financial award application deadline: 3/1. *Faculty research:* Taxation, financial accounting, auditing, managerial accounting, accounting education. *Unit head:* Dr. Larry A. Deppe, Chair, 801-626-7837, Fax: 801-626-7423, E-mail: ldeppe1@weber.edu. *Application contact:* Dr. Kevin McBeth, Graduate Coordinator, 801-626-6989, Fax: 801-626-7423, E-mail: kmcbeth@weber.edu.

Western Carolina University, Graduate School, College of Business, Program in Accountancy, Cullowhee, NC 28723. Offers M Ac. Part-time and evening/weekend programs available. *Entrance requirements:* For master's, GRE General Test or GMAT. Additional exam requirements/recommendations for international students: Required—TOEFL (minimum score 550 paper-based; 213 computer-based).

Western Connecticut State University, Division of Graduate Studies, Ancell School of Business, Program in Business Administration, Danbury, CT 06810-6885. Offers accounting (MBA); business administration (MBA). Part-time and evening/weekend programs available. *Faculty:* 12 full-time (3 women), 1 part-time/adjunct (0 women). *Students:* 2 full-time (1 woman), 57 part-time (23 women); includes 7 minority (1 African American, 5 Asian Americans or Pacific Islanders, 1 Hispanic American), 1 international. Average age 32. In 2006, 23 degrees awarded. *Entrance requirements:* For master's, GMAT. *Application deadline:* For fall admission, 8/1 priority date for domestic students. Applications are processed on a rolling basis. Application fee: $40. *Financial support:* Fellowships, career-related internships or fieldwork available. Support available to part-time students. Financial award application deadline: 5/1; financial award applicants required to submit FAFSA. *Unit head:* Dr. Fred Tesch, Professor, 203-837-8654. *Application contact:* Chris Shankle, Associate Director of Graduate Admissions, 203-837-8244, Fax: 203-837-8338, E-mail: shanklec@wcsu.edu.

Western Illinois University, School of Graduate Studies, College of Business and Technology, Department of Accountancy, Macomb, IL 61455-1390. Offers M Acct. *Accreditation:* AACSB. Part-time programs available. *Students:* 13 full-time (5 women), 3 part-time (2 women), 5 international. Average age 26. 7 applicants, 71% accepted. In 2006, 6 degrees awarded. *Degree requirements:* For master's, thesis or alternative. *Entrance requirements:* For master's, GMAT, minimum GPA of 2.75. Additional exam requirements/recommendations for international students: Required—TOEFL (minimum score 550 paper-based; 213 computer-based; 80 iBT). *Application deadline:* Applications are processed on a rolling basis. Application fee: $30. Electronic applications accepted. *Expenses:* Tuition, state resident: part-time $200 per credit hour. Tuition, nonresident: part-time $400 per credit hour. *Financial support:* In 2006–07, 7 students received support, including 7 research assistantships with full tuition reimbursements available (averaging $6,568 per year). Financial award applicants required to submit FAFSA. *Unit head:* Dr. John Elfrink, Chairperson, 309-298-1152. *Application contact:* Dr. Barbara Baily, Director of Graduate Studies/Associate Provost, 309-298-1806, Fax: 309-298-2345, E-mail: grad-office@wiu.edu.

Western Michigan University, Graduate College, Haworth College of Business, Department of Accountancy, Kalamazoo, MI 49008-5202. Offers MSA. *Accreditation:* AACSB. *Entrance requirements:* For master's, GMAT.

Western New England College, School of Business, Program in Accounting, Springfield, MA 01119. Offers MSA. Part-time and evening/weekend programs available. *Entrance requirements:* For master's, GMAT, 2 letters of reference.

West Texas A&M University, College of Business, Department of Accounting, Economics, and Finance, Program in Accounting, Canyon, TX 79016-0001. Offers MP Acc. Part-time and evening/weekend programs available. Postbaccalaureate distance learning degree programs offered (minimal on-campus study). *Degree requirements:* For master's, thesis optional. *Entrance requirements:* For master's, GMAT. Additional exam requirements/recommendations for international students: Required—TOEFL (minimum score 550 paper-based). Electronic applications accepted. *Faculty research:* Texas economy, service learnings, small business, entrepreneurship, corporation conversion.

West Texas A&M University, College of Business, Department of Accounting, Economics, and Finance, Program in Accounting/Business Administration, Canyon, TX 79016-0001. Offers professional accounting (MPA). Integrated program that allows students to enter program as undergraduates; after bachelor's degree in business administration is earned they progress into graduate accounting phase. Part-time programs available. Postbaccalaureate distance learning degree programs offered (minimal on-campus study). *Degree requirements:* For master's, registration. *Entrance requirements:* For master's, GMAT. Additional exam requirements/recommendations for international students: Required—TOEFL (minimum score 550 paper-based). Electronic applications accepted.

West Virginia University, College of Business and Economics, Division of Accounting, Morgantown, WV 26506. Offers MPA. *Accreditation:* AACSB. Part-time and evening/weekend programs available. *Faculty:* 9 full-time (2 women), 6 part-time/adjunct (4 women). *Students:* 39 full-time (14 women), 4 part-time (3 women); includes 5 minority (1 African American, 1 American Indian/Alaska Native, 2 Asian Americans or Pacific Islanders, 1 Hispanic American), 4 international. Average age 25. 47 applicants, 87% accepted, 32 enrolled. In 2006, 42 degrees awarded. *Entrance requirements:* For master's, GMAT, BS in accounting or equivalent, minimum GPA of 3.0. Additional exam requirements/recommendations for international students: Required—TOEFL. *Application deadline:* For fall admission, 6/30 priority date for domestic students; for spring admission, 11/15 for domestic students. Applications are processed on a rolling basis. Application fee: $50. Electronic applications accepted. *Expenses:* Tuition, state resident: full-time $4,926; part-time $276 per credit hour. Tuition, nonresident: full-time $14,278; part-time $796 per credit hour. Tuition and fees vary according to program. *Financial support:* In 2006–07, 30 students received support, including 2 research assistantships, 1 teaching assistantship; Federal Work-Study, institutionally sponsored loans, and unspecified assistantships also available. Financial award application deadline: 2/1; financial award applicants required to submit FAFSA. *Faculty research:* Financial reporting, government/not-for-profit accounting, information systems/technology, forensic accounting, internal control. Total annual research expenditures: $156,549. *Unit head:* Prof. Timothy Pearson, Director, 304-293-7847, Fax: 304-293-0635, E-mail: timothy.pearson@mail.wvu.edu. *Application contact:* Dr. Cyril Logar, Associate Dean/Interim Director for Graduate Programs, 304-293-7956, Fax: 304-293-5652, E-mail: cyril.logar@mail.wvu.edu.

Wheeling Jesuit University, Department of Business, Wheeling, WV 26003-6295. Offers accounting (MS); business administration (MBA). Part-time and evening/weekend programs available. *Faculty:* 6 full-time (0 women). *Students:* 19 full-time (5 women), 28 part-time (15 women), 2 international. Average age 31. 31 applicants, 97% accepted, 23 enrolled. In 2006, 18 degrees awarded. *Entrance requirements:* For master's, GMAT, minimum undergraduate GPA of 2.8. Additional exam requirements/recommendations for international students: Required—TOEFL (minimum score 600 paper-based; 250 computer-based; 80 iBT). *Application deadline:* For fall admission, 8/1 priority date for domestic students, 8/1 for international students; for spring admission, 12/15 priority date for domestic students, 12/15 for international students. Applications are processed on a rolling basis. Application fee: $25. Electronic applications accepted. *Expenses:* Tuition: Full-time $8,910; part-time $405 per credit hour. Required fees: $105 per semester. One-time fee: $380 full-time. Full-time tuition and fees vary according to course load, degree level and program. *Financial support:* In 2006–07, 38 students received support. Career-related internships or fieldwork, Federal Work-Study, and unspecified assistantships available. Financial award application deadline: 8/1; financial award applicants required to submit FAFSA. *Faculty research:* Forensic economics, philosophic economics, consumer behavior, international business, economic development. *Unit head:* Dr. Edward W Younkins, Director, 304-243-2255, Fax: 304-243-8703, E-mail: younkins@wju.edu. *Application contact:* Becky Forney, Associate Dean of Adult Education, 304-243-2250, Fax: 304-243-4441, E-mail: bforney@wju.edu.

Wichita State University, Graduate School, W. Frank Barton School of Business, School of Accountancy, Wichita, KS 67260. Offers professional accountancy (MPA). *Accreditation:* AACSB. Part-time and evening/weekend programs available. *Entrance requirements:* For master's, GMAT, minimum AACSB index of 1100, minimum GPA of 2.75. Additional exam requirements/recommendations for international students: Required—TOEFL. Electronic applications accepted. *Faculty research:* Professional standards, behavioral issues, social accounting, taxation, auditing issues.

Widener University, School of Business Administration, Program in Accounting Information Systems, Chester, PA 19013-5792. Offers MS. Part-time and evening/weekend programs available. *Entrance requirements:* For master's, Certified Management Accountant Exam, Certified Public Accountant Exam, or GMAT, minimum GPA of 2.5. Electronic applications accepted.

Wilkes University, Graduate Studies and Continued Learning, Jay S. Sidhu School of Business and Leadership, Wilkes-Barre, PA 18766-0002. Offers accounting (MBA); entrepreneurship (MBA); finance (MBA); human resource management (MBA); international business (MBA); management (MBA); marketing (MBA). *Accreditation:* ACBSP. Part-time and evening/weekend programs available. *Students:* 30 full-time (16 women), 149 part-time (73 women); includes 5 minority (1 African American, 2 Asian Americans or Pacific Islanders, 2 Hispanic Americans), 4 international. Average age 30. In 2006, 48 degrees awarded. *Entrance requirements:* For master's, GMAT. Additional exam requirements/recommendations for international students: Required—TOEFL (minimum score 500 paper-based; 173 computer-based). *Application deadline:* Applications are processed on a rolling basis. Application fee: $40. *Expenses: Contact institution. Financial support:* Federal Work-Study and unspecified assistantships available. Financial award application deadline: 3/1; financial award applicants required to submit FAFSA. *Unit head:* Dr. Paul Browne, Dean, 570-408-4701, Fax: 570-408-4700, E-mail: paul.browne@wilkes.edu. *Application contact:* Kathleen Houlihan, Director of Graduate Studies, 570-408-3235, Fax: 570-408-7846, E-mail: kathleen.houlihan@wilkes.edu.

Worcester State College, Graduate Studies, Program in Management, Worcester, MA 01602-2597. Offers accounting (MS); organizational leadership (MS). *Students:* 1 (woman) full-time, 14 part-time (8 women), 4 international. Average age 28. 20 applicants, 80% accepted, 12 enrolled. *Expenses:* Tuition, state resident: full-time $4,518; part-time $251 per credit hour. Tuition, nonresident: full-time $4,518; part-time $251 per credit hour. *Unit head:* Dr. Lauri Dahlin, Coordinator, 508-929-8094.

Wright State University, School of Graduate Studies, Raj Soin College of Business, Department of Accountancy, Accountancy Program, Dayton, OH 45435. Offers M Acc. *Unit head:* Dr. Susan S. Lightle, Director, 937-775-4169, Fax: 937-775-2310, E-mail: susan.lightle@wright.edu.

Yale University, Yale School of Management and Graduate School of Arts and Sciences, Doctoral Program in Management, New Haven, CT 06520. Offers accounting (PhD); financial economics (PhD); marketing (PhD). *Accreditation:* AACSB. *Faculty:* 55 full-time (7 women). *Students:* 25 full-time (6 women); includes 2 minority (both Asian Americans or Pacific Islanders), 20 international. Average age 28. 300 applicants, 4% accepted. In 2006, 6 doctorates awarded. *Degree requirements:* For doctorate, thesis/dissertation, comprehensive exam. *Entrance requirements:* For doctorate, GMAT or GRE General Test. Additional exam requirements/recommendations for international students: Required—TOEFL, IELTS. *Application deadline:* For fall admission, 1/2 for domestic and international students. Application fee: $85. Electronic applications accepted. *Expenses: Contact institution. Financial support:* Fellowships with full tuition reimbursements, research assistantships with full tuition reimbursements, teaching assistantships with full tuition reimbursements, institutionally sponsored loans, scholarships/grants, and health care benefits available. Financial award application deadline: 1/2. *Faculty research:* Pricing of options and futures, term structure of interest rates, use of accounting numbers in debt contracts, product differentiation, e-commerce and marketing, behavioral finance. *Unit head:* Mary Ellen Nichols, Registrar, 203-432-3955, Fax: 203-432-0342, E-mail: maryellen.nichols@yale.edu.

Youngstown State University, Graduate School, Warren P. Williamson Jr. College of Business Administration, Department of Accounting and Finance, Youngstown, OH 44555-0001. Offers accounting (MBA); finance (MBA). *Accreditation:* AACSB. Part-time and evening/weekend programs available. *Degree requirements:* For master's, thesis optional. *Entrance requirements:* For master's, GMAT, minimum GPA of 2.7. Additional exam requirements/recommendations for international students: Required—TOEFL. *Faculty research:* Taxation and compliance, capital markets, accounting information systems, accounting theory, tax and government accounting.

Finance and Banking

Adelphi University, School of Business, Department of Accounting, Finance and Economics, Garden City, NY 11530-0701. Offers accounting (MBA); finance (MBA, MS). Part-time and evening/weekend programs available. *Students:* 1 (woman) full-time, 8 part-time (4 women); includes 3 minority (1 African American, 1 American Indian/Alaska Native, 1 Asian American or Pacific Islander), 4 international. Average age 39. In 2006, 9 degrees awarded. *Entrance requirements:* For master's, GMAT, 2 letters of recommendation. Additional exam requirements/recommendations for international students: Required—TOEFL (minimum score 550 paper-based; 213 computer-based). *Application deadline:* For fall admission, 5/1 for international students; for spring admission, 12/1 for international students. Applications are processed on a rolling basis. Application fee: $50. Electronic applications accepted. *Financial support:* Research assistantships with full and partial tuition reimbursements, career-related internships or fieldwork, Federal Work-Study, institutionally sponsored loans, scholarships/grants, and unspecified assistantships available. Financial award application deadline: 3/1; financial award applicants required to submit FAFSA. *Faculty research:* Capital market, executive compensation, business ethics, classical value theory, labor economics. *Unit head:* Dr. Bruce Swensen, Chairperson, 516-877-4655, E-mail: swensen@adelphi.edu. *Application contact:* Christine Murphy, Director of Admissions, 516-877-3050, Fax: 516-877-3039, E-mail: graduateadmissions@adelphi.edu.

Alabama Agricultural and Mechanical University, School of Graduate Studies, School of Business, Department of Economics and Finance, Huntsville, AL 35811. Offers MS. Evening/weekend programs available. *Faculty:* 6 full-time (2 women). In 2006, 2 degrees awarded. *Degree requirements:* For master's, comprehensive exam. *Entrance requirements:* For master's, GRE General Test, minimum undergraduate GPA of 2.5. Additional exam requirements/recommendations for international students: Required—TOEFL. *Application deadline:* For fall admission, 5/1 for domestic students. Applications are processed on a rolling basis. Application fee: $25. Electronic applications accepted. *Financial support:* In 2006–07, 1 teaching assistantship with tuition reimbursement (averaging $9,000 per year) was awarded; career-related internships or fieldwork also available. Financial award application deadline: 4/1. *Faculty research:* Energy, banking, financial management, agricultural economics, sports economics. *Unit head:* Dr. Eric Rahimian, Chair, 256-372-5294, Fax: 256-372-5874.

Alaska Pacific University, Graduate Programs, Business Administration Department, Program in Business Administration, Anchorage, AK 99508-4672. Offers business administration (MBA); global finance (MBA); health services administration (MBA). Part-time and evening/weekend programs available. *Faculty:* 6 full-time (3 women), 4 part-time/adjunct (1 woman). *Students:* 5 full-time (3 women), 46 part-time (25 women); includes 16 minority (2 African Americans, 11 American Indian/Alaska Native, 3 Asian Americans or Pacific Islanders), 1 international. Average age 37. In 2006, 11 degrees awarded. *Degree requirements:* For master's, capstone course. *Entrance requirements:* For master's, GMAT or GRE, minimum GPA of 3.0. *Application deadline:* For fall admission, 4/1 priority date for domestic students; for spring admission, 12/15 for domestic students. Applications are processed on a rolling basis. Application fee: $25. *Expenses:* Tuition: Part-time $550 per credit hour. Required fees: $100 per semester. Tuition and fees vary according to program. *Financial support:* In 2006–07, fellowships (averaging $6,300 per year), 6 research assistantships (averaging $4,112 per year) were awarded; career-related internships or fieldwork and Federal Work-Study also available. Support available to part-time students. Financial award application deadline: 4/15. *Unit head:* Dr. Tracy Stewart, Director, 907-564-8358, Fax: 907-562-4276, E-mail: tstewart@alaskapacific.edu.

Alliant International University–San Diego, Marshall Goldsmith School of Management, Business and Management Division, San Diego, CA 92131-1799. Offers business administration (MBA); information and technology management (DBA); international business (MIBA, DBA), including finance (DBA), marketing (DBA); strategic business (DBA); sustainable management (MBA). Part-time and evening/weekend programs available. *Students:* 87 full-time (22 women), 51 part-time (17 women); includes 27 minority (8 African Americans, 2 American Indian/Alaska Native, 8 Asian Americans or Pacific Islanders, 9 Hispanic Americans), 68 international. Average age 32. 104 applicants, 66% accepted, 40 enrolled. *Degree requirements:* For doctorate, thesis/dissertation. *Entrance requirements:* For master's, GMAT, minimum GPA of 3.0; for doctorate, GMAT, minimum GPA of 3.3. Additional exam requirements/recommendations for international students: Required—TOEFL (minimum score 550 paper-based; 213 computer-based), TWE (minimum score 5). *Application deadline:* For fall admission, 8/1 priority date for domestic and international students; for spring admission, 12/1 priority date for domestic and international students. Applications are processed on a rolling basis. Application fee: $55. Electronic applications accepted. *Expenses:* Tuition: Part-time $825 per unit. Tuition and fees vary according to course load, degree level and program. *Financial support:* Research assistantships, teaching assistantships, career-related internships or fieldwork, Federal Work-Study, institutionally sponsored loans, scholarships/grants, and tuition waivers (partial) available. Support available to part-time students. Financial award application deadline: 2/15; financial award applicants required to submit FAFSA. *Faculty research:* Consumer behavior, international business, strategic management, information systems. *Unit head:* Dr. Fred Phillips, Associate Dean, 866-825-5426, Fax: 855-635-4739, E-mail: admissions@alliant.edu. *Application contact:* Alliant International University Central Contact Center, 866-U-ALLIANT, Fax: 858-635-4555, E-mail: admissions@alliant.edu.

See Close-Up on page 203.

The American College, Richard D. Irwin Graduate School, Bryn Mawr, PA 19010-2105. Offers MSFS. Part-time and evening/weekend programs available. Postbaccalaureate distance learning degree programs offered (minimal on-campus study). *Faculty:* 19 full-time (1 woman), 9 part-time/adjunct (1 woman). *Students:* 130 applicants, 92% accepted. In 2006, 79 degrees awarded. *Application deadline:* Applications are processed on a rolling basis. Application fee: $300. Electronic applications accepted. *Faculty research:* Retirement counseling, social security, aging, family composition, inflation. *Unit head:* Dr. Walter Woerheide, Executive Vice President and Dean, 610-526-1398, Fax: 610-526-1359, E-mail: walt.woerheide@theamericancollege.edu. *Application contact:* Joanne F. Patterson, Associate Director of Graduate Administration, 610-526-1366, Fax: 610-526-1359, E-mail: joanne.patterson@theamericancollege.edu.

American College of Thessaloniki, Department of Business Administration, Pylea, Greece. Offers banking and finance (MBA); entrepreneurship (MBA, Certificate); finance (Certificate); management (MBA, Certificate); marketing (MBA, Certificate). Part-time and evening/weekend programs available. *Faculty:* 6 full-time (1 woman), 10 part-time/adjunct (4 women). *Students:* 9 full-time (6 women), 39 part-time (24 women), 22 international. 36 applicants, 97% accepted, 26 enrolled. In 2006, 25 degrees awarded. *Degree requirements:* For master's, thesis, registration. *Application deadline:* For fall admission, 9/30 priority date for domestic students; for spring admission, 1/31 priority date for domestic students. Applications are processed on a rolling basis. Application fee: $70. Electronic applications accepted. *Expenses:* Tuition: Full-time $10,560; part-time $660 per course. Part-time tuition and fees vary according to course load. *Unit head:* Dr. Nikolaos Kourkoumelis, Chair, Business Division, E-mail: nikolaos@act.edu. *Application contact:* Vasilis Blatsas, Coordinator of Business Programs and MBA Advisor, 30-310-398206 Ext. 206.

American InterContinental University, Program in International Business, Weston, FL 33326. Offers accounting and finance (MBA); human resource management (MBA); management (MBA); marketing (MBA). Part-time and evening/weekend programs available. Postbaccalaureate distance learning degree programs offered. *Faculty:* 3 full-time (0 women), 2 part-time/adjunct (0 women). *Students:* 87 full-time (51 women), 7 part-time (4 women); includes 62 minority (42 African Americans, 1 American Indian/Alaska Native, 1 Asian American or Pacific Islander, 18 Hispanic Americans), 5 international. Average age 34. In 2006, 51 degrees awarded. *Application deadline:* Applications are processed on a rolling basis. Application fee: $50. Electronic applications accepted. *Financial support:* Federal Work-Study and scholarships/grants available. Financial award application deadline: 1/15; financial award applicants required to submit FAFSA. *Unit head:* Dr. David Kalichavan, Acting Dean, School of Business, 954-446-6100, Fax: 954-446-6393, E-mail: dkalichavan@aiufl.edu.

American InterContinental University Buckhead Campus, Program in Business Administration, Atlanta, GA 30326-1016. Offers accounting and finance (MBA); management (MBA); marketing (MBA). Evening/weekend programs available. Postbaccalaureate distance learning degree programs offered. *Faculty:* 2 full-time (1 woman), 1 part-time/adjunct (0 women). *Students:* 19 full-time (16 women); includes 1 minority (African American) Average age 28. 10 applicants, 60% accepted, 5 enrolled. In 2006, 25 degrees awarded. *Median time to degree:* Master's–1 year full-time. *Entrance requirements:* For master's, minimum cumulative undergraduate GPA of 2.0. Additional exam requirements/recommendations for international students: Required—TOEFL (minimum score 530 paper-based; 230 computer-based). *Application deadline:* Applications are processed on a rolling basis. Application fee: $50. Electronic applications accepted. *Financial support:* In 2006–07, 14 students received support. Career-related internships or fieldwork, Federal Work-Study, institutionally sponsored loans, and scholarships/grants available. Financial award applicants required to submit FAFSA. *Faculty research:* Leadership management, international advertising. *Unit head:* Dr. Sonia Heywood, Dean of Business, 404-965-5764, Fax: 404-965-5957, E-mail: sonia.heywood@buckhead.aiuniv.edu. *Application contact:* Mike Betz, Vice President Admissions and Marketing, 404-965-5719, Fax: 404-965-5997, E-mail: mbetz@aiuniv.edu.

American InterContinental University Online, Program in Business Administration, Hoffman Estates, IL 60192. Offers accounting and finance (MBA); healthcare management (MBA); human resource management (MBA); international business (MBA); management (MBA); marketing (MBA); operations management (MBA); organizational psychology and development (MBA); project management (MBA). Evening/weekend programs available. Postbaccalaureate distance learning degree programs offered (no on-campus study). *Entrance requirements:* Additional exam requirements/recommendations for international students: Required—TOEFL (minimum score 550 paper-based; 213 computer-based). *Application deadline:* Applications are processed on a rolling basis. Application fee: $50. Electronic applications accepted. *Financial support:* Institutionally sponsored loans and scholarships/grants available. Financial award applicants required to submit FAFSA. *Unit head:* Kerri J

Finance and Banking

American InterContinental University Online (continued)
Holloway, Vice President of Academic Affairs, 847-851-5000 Ext. 15399, Fax: 847-586-6309, E-mail: kholloway@aivonline.edu. *Application contact:* 877-701-3800, E-mail: info@aiuonline.edu.

American University, Kogod School of Business, Department of Finance, Program in Finance, Washington, DC 20016-8001. Offers MBA. Part-time and evening/weekend programs available. *Students:* 31 full-time (10 women), 44 part-time (14 women); includes 18 minority (5 African Americans, 7 Asian Americans or Pacific Islanders, 6 Hispanic Americans), 18 international. Average age 30. In 2006, 55 degrees awarded. *Entrance requirements:* For master's, GMAT. Additional exam requirements/recommendations for international students: Required—TOEFL. *Application deadline:* For fall admission, 2/1 priority date for domestic students; for spring admission, 10/1 priority date for domestic students. Applications are processed on a rolling basis. Application fee: $50. *Expenses:* Tuition: Full-time $18,864; part-time $1,048 per credit. Required fees: $380. Tuition and fees vary according to program. *Financial support:* In 2006–07, 15 students received support; fellowships, research assistantships with partial tuition reimbursements available, career-related internships or fieldwork, Federal Work-Study, institutionally sponsored loans, and tuition waivers (partial) available. Support available to part-time students. Financial award application deadline: 2/1. *Faculty research:* Development finance, market microstructure, international investment, real estate finance, quantitative modeling.

American University, School of Public Affairs, Department of Public Administration, Washington, DC 20016-8001. Offers organization development (MSOD); organizational change (Certificate); public administration (MPA, PhD); public financial management (Certificate); public management (Certificate); public policy (MPP). Part-time and evening/weekend programs available. *Faculty:* 15 full-time (6 women), 13 part-time/adjunct (6 women). *Students:* 127 full-time (77 women), 223 part-time (142 women); includes 69 minority (44 African Americans, 1 American Indian/Alaska Native, 12 Asian Americans or Pacific Islanders, 12 Hispanic Americans), 33 international. Average age 32. 635 applicants, 66% accepted, 107 enrolled. In 2006, 187 master's, 5 doctorates, 5 other advanced degrees awarded. *Degree requirements:* For master's, comprehensive exam; for doctorate, thesis/dissertation, comprehensive exam. *Entrance requirements:* For master's and doctorate, GRE General Test. Additional exam requirements/recommendations for international students: Required—TOEFL (minimum score 550 paper-based; 213 computer-based). *Application deadline:* For fall admission, 2/1 for domestic students; for spring admission, 10/1 for domestic students. Application fee: $50. *Expenses:* Tuition: Full-time $18,864; part-time $1,048 per credit. Required fees: $380. Tuition and fees vary according to program. *Financial support:* Fellowships, research assistantships, teaching assistantships, career-related internships or fieldwork, Federal Work-Study, and institutionally sponsored loans available. Financial award application deadline: 2/1. *Faculty research:* Urban management, conservation politics, state and local budgeting, tax policy. *Unit head:* Dr. Howard Mc Curdy, Chair, 202-885-6236.

The American University of Paris, Graduate Programs, Paris, France. Offers finance (MSF); global communications (MAGC); international affairs, conflict resolution and civil society development (MA); Middle Eastern and Islamic studies (MA); public administration (MPA). *Faculty:* 2 full-time (1 woman), 8 part-time/adjunct (2 women). *Students:* 72 full-time (47 women). 71 applicants, 92% accepted, 34 enrolled. *Degree requirements:* For master's, thesis, registration. *Entrance requirements:* For master's, minimum undergraduate GPA of 3.0. *Application deadline:* For fall admission, 4/15 priority date for international students; for spring admission, 11/15 priority date for international students. Applications are processed on a rolling basis. Application fee: $75. Tuition charges are reported in euros. *Expenses:* Tuition: Full-time 22,200 euros. *Financial support:* In 2006–07, 25 students received support. Scholarships/grants available. Financial award applicants required to submit FAFSA. *Unit head:* Gerardo Della Paolera, President, 331-40620739, E-mail: gerry@aup.edu. *Application contact:* Lynn Richardson, International Admissions Counselor, 33-140620720, Fax: 33-147053432, E-mail: lynn.richardson@aup.edu.

Andrew Jackson University, Brian Tracy College of Business and Entrepreneurship, Birmingham, AL 35244. Offers entrepreneurship (MBA); finance (MBA); health services management (MBA); hospitality and tourism management (MBA); human resource management (MBA); international business (MBA); management (MBA); marketing (MBA). Part-time and evening/weekend programs available. Postbaccalaureate distance learning degree programs offered (no on-campus study). *Faculty:* 13 part-time/adjunct (1 woman). *Students:* Average age 40. In 2006, 6 degrees awarded. *Entrance requirements:* For master's, course work in calculus, statistics. Additional exam requirements/recommendations for international students: Required—TOEFL (minimum score 550 paper-based; 213 computer-based). *Application deadline:* Applications are processed on a rolling basis. Application fee: $75. *Expenses:* Tuition: Part-time $705 per course. *Application contact:* Betty Howell, Director of Student Affairs, 205-871-9288 Ext. 108, Fax: 205-871-9294, E-mail: bhowell@aju.edu.

Andrews University, School of Graduate Studies, School of Business, Department of Accounting, Economics and Finance, Berrien Springs, MI 49104. Offers MBA, MSA.

Argosy University, Atlanta Campus, College of Business, Atlanta, GA 30328. Offers accounting (DBA); customized professional concentration (MBA, DBA); finance (MBA); healthcare administration (MBA); information systems (DBA); information systems management (MBA); international business (MBA, DBA); management (MBA, DBA); marketing (MBA, DBA). Part-time programs available. *Students:* 53 full-time (38 women), 35 part-time (28 women); includes 73 minority (66 African Americans, 3 Asian Americans or Pacific Islanders, 4 Hispanic Americans). *Degree requirements:* For master's, comprehensive exam (for some programs), registration; for doctorate, thesis/dissertation, comprehensive exam, registration. *Entrance requirements:* For master's, minimum undergraduate GPA of 3.0; for doctorate, master's degree, minimum GPA of 3.0. Additional exam requirements/recommendations for international students: Required—TOEFL. *Application deadline:* For fall admission, 7/1 priority date for domestic students, 6/1 for international students; for spring admission, 11/1 priority date for domestic students, 10/1 for international students. Applications are processed on a rolling basis. Application fee: $50. Electronic applications accepted. *Financial support:* Applicants required to submit FAFSA. *Unit head:* Dr. Robert A. Berg, Department Chair, 770-407-1042, E-mail: rberg@argosy.edu. *Application contact:* Christa Holton, Director of Admissions, 770-671-1200 Ext. 1014, Fax: 770-671-9050, E-mail: cholton@argosy.edu.

See Close-Up on page 207.

Argosy University, Chicago Campus, College of Business, Chicago, IL 60603. Offers accounting (DBA); customized professional concentration (MBA, DBA); finance (MBA); healthcare administration (MBA); information systems (DBA); information systems management (MBA); international business (MBA, DBA); management (MBA, DBA); marketing (MBA, DBA). Part-time and evening/weekend programs available. *Faculty:* 2 full-time (both women), 4 part-time/adjunct (3 women). *Students:* 52 full-time (30 women), 18 part-time (7 women); includes 37 minority (24 African Americans, 7 Asian Americans or Pacific Islanders, 6 Hispanic Americans). Average age 37. 32 applicants, 81% accepted, 25 enrolled. In 2006, 9 master's, 2 doctorates awarded. *Entrance requirements:* For master's and doctorate, minimum GPA of 3.0. Additional exam requirements/recommendations for international students: Required—TOEFL (minimum score 550 paper-based; 213 computer-based). *Application deadline:* For fall admission, 2/28 for domestic and international students; for spring admission, 10/30 for domestic and international students. Applications are processed on a rolling basis. Application fee: $50. Electronic applications accepted. *Financial support:* In 2006–07, 3 students received support. Scholarships/grants available. Financial award application deadline: 4/1. *Unit head:* Dr. Cynthia Scarlett, Associate Head, 800-626-4123, Fax: 212-727-7750, E-mail: cscarlett@argosy.edu. *Application contact:* Ashley Delaney, Director of Admissions, 800-626-4123, Fax: 312-777-7750, E-mail: argosyadmissions@argosy.edu.

See Close-Up on page 209.

Argosy University, Denver Campus, College of Business, Denver, CO 80203. Offers accounting (DBA); customized professional concentraion (DBA); customized professional concentration (MBA); finance (MBA); healthcare administration (MBA); information systems (DBA); information systems management (MBA); international business (MBA, DBA); management (MBA, MSM, DBA); marketing (MBA, DBA).

See Close-Up on page 213.

Argosy University, Hawai'i Campus, College of Business, Honolulu, HI 96813. Offers accounting (DBA); customized professional concentration (MBA, DBA); finance (MBA, Certificate); healthcare administration (MBA, Certificate); information systems (DBA); information systems management (MBA, Certificate); international business (MBA, DBA, Certificate); management (MBA, DBA); marketing (MBA, DBA, Certificate). Evening/weekend programs available. *Faculty:* 12 part-time/adjunct (2 women). *Students:* 3 full-time (2 women), 1 part-time; includes 2 minority (1 Asian American or Pacific Islander, 1 Hispanic American). 6 applicants, 67% accepted, 3 enrolled. *Degree requirements:* For master's, capstone project. *Entrance requirements:* For master's, minimum GPA of 3.0 in last 60 hours. Additional exam requirements/recommendations for international students: Required—TOEFL (minimum score 550 paper-based; 213 computer-based). *Application deadline:* For fall admission, 1/15 priority date for domestic students; for spring admission, 10/15 for domestic students. Applications are processed on a rolling basis. Application fee: $50. *Financial support:* Teaching assistantships, Federal Work-Study and scholarships/grants available. Support available to part-time students. *Unit head:* Lisa Parker, Interim Chair, College of Business and Information Technology, 888-323-2777, Fax: 808-536-5505, E-mail: lparker@argosy.edu. *Application contact:* Cherie Andrade, Director of Admissions, 888-323-2777, Fax: 808-536-5505, E-mail: candrade@argosy.edu.

See Close-Up on page 215.

Argosy University, Inland Empire Campus, College of Business, San Bernardino, CA 92408. Offers accounting (DBA); customized professional concentration (MBA, DBA); finance (MBA); healthcare administration (MBA); information systems (DBA); information systems management (MBA); international business (MBA, DBA); management (DBA); mangement (MBA); marketing (MBA, DBA).

See Close-Up on page 217.

Argosy University, Orange County Campus, College of Business, Santa Ana, CA 92704. Offers accounting (DBA, Adv C); customized professional concentration (MBA, DBA); finance (MBA, Certificate); healthcare administration (MBA, Certificate); information systems (DBA, Adv C); information systems management (MBA); international business (MBA, DBA, Adv C, Certificate); management (MBA, MSM, DBA, EDBA); mangement (Adv C); marketing (MBA, DBA, Adv C, Certificate); organizational leadership (Ed D); public administration (MBA, Certificate). Part-time and evening/weekend programs available. *Faculty:* 4 full-time (1 woman), 20 part-time/adjunct (7 women). *Students:* 163 full-time (64 women), 41 part-time (16 women). Average age 42. 72 applicants, 51 enrolled. In 2006, 6 master's, 23 doctorates awarded. *Degree requirements:* For doctorate, thesis/dissertation, preliminary and final dissertation defense, comprehensive exam. *Entrance requirements:* For master's, minimum GPA of 3.0 in final 2 years of course work, 3 letters of recommendation, resumé; for doctorate, minimum GPA of 3.0 in graduate study, 3 letters of recommendation, resumé. Additional exam requirements/recommendations for international students: Required—TOEFL. *Application deadline:* Applications are processed on a rolling basis. Application fee: $50. Electronic applications accepted. *Financial support:* Federal Work-Study, institutionally sponsored loans, and scholarships/grants available. Support available to part-time students. Financial award applicants required to submit FAFSA. *Faculty research:* Crisis management, leadership in organizations, finance, business systems. *Unit head:* Dr. Ray London, Dean, 800-716-9598, Fax: 714-437-1284, E-mail: auocadmissions@argosy.edu. *Application contact:* Mark Betz, Director of Admissions, 800-716-9598, Fax: 714-437-1697, E-mail: mbetz@argosy.edu.

See Close-Up on page 221.

Argosy University, Phoenix Campus, College of Business, Phoenix, AZ 85021. Offers accounting (DBA); customized professional concentration (MBA, DBA); finance (MBA); healthcare administration (MBA); information systems (DBA); information systems management (MBA); international business (MBA, DBA); management (MBA, DBA); marketing (MBA, DBA). Part-time and evening/weekend programs available. *Faculty:* 1 full-time (0 women). *Students:* 7 full-time (4 women); includes 2 minority (1 African American, 1 Hispanic American). *Entrance requirements:* For doctorate, master's degree. Additional exam requirements/recommendations for international students: Required—TOEFL (minimum score 550 paper-based; 213 computer-based). Application fee: $50. *Financial support:* In 2006–07, 2 students received support. Federal Work-Study, institutionally sponsored loans, and scholarships/grants available. Support available to part-time students. Financial award applicants required to submit FAFSA. *Unit head:* Dr. Gary Berg, Program Chair, 866-216-2777, Fax: 602-216-2601. *Application contact:* Andy Hughes, Director of Admissions, 866-216-2777 Ext. 3110, Fax: 602-216-2601, E-mail: ahughes@argosyu.edu.

See Close-Up on page 223.

Argosy University, San Diego Campus, College of Business, San Diego, CA 92108. Offers accounting (DBA); customized professional concentration (MBA, DBA); finance (MBA); information systems (DBA); information systems management (MBA); international business (MBA, DBA); management (MBA, MSM, DBA); marketing (MBA, DBA); public administration (MBA).

See Close-Up on page 225.

Argosy University, San Francisco Bay Area Campus, College of Business, Point Richmond, CA 94804-3547. Offers accounting (DBA); corporate compliance (MBA); customized professional concentration (MBA, DBA); finance (MBA); healthcare administration (MBA); information systems (DBA); information systems management (MBA); international business (MBA, DBA); management (MBA, MSM, DBA); marketing (MBA, DBA). Part-time and evening/weekend programs available. *Faculty:* 2 full-time (0 women), 9 part-time/adjunct (0 women). *Students:* 29 full-time (8 women), 9 part-time (2 women); includes 30 minority (5 African Americans, 24 Asian Americans or Pacific Islanders, 1 Hispanic American). 21 applicants, 76% accepted, 13 enrolled. In 2006, 3 master's, 2 doctorates awarded. *Degree requirements:* For master's, capstone project; for doctorate, thesis/dissertation, comprehensive exam, registration. *Entrance requirements:* For master's, minimum GPA of 3.0; for doctorate, MBA or minimum GPA of 3.0. Additional exam requirements/recommendations for international students: Required—TOEFL (minimum score 550 paper-based; 213 computer-based). *Application deadline:* For fall admission, 7/1 priority date for domestic and international students; for winter admission, 11/1 priority date for domestic and international students; for spring admission, 4/1 priority date for domestic and international students. Applications are processed on a rolling basis. Application fee: $50. Electronic applications accepted. *Financial support:* Federal Work-Study and scholarships/grants available. Support available to part-time students. Financial award applicants required to submit FAFSA. *Unit head:* Dr. Anthony Martinez, Department Chair, Business and Information Technology, 866-215-0277, Fax: 510-215-0299, E-mail: amartinez@argosy.edu. *Application contact:* John Vincent Stofan, Director of Admissions, 866-215-2727 Ext. 205, Fax: 510-215-0299, E-mail: jstofan@argosyu.edu.

See Close-Up on page 227.

Argosy University, Santa Monica Campus, College of Business, Santa Monica, CA 90405. Offers accounting (DBA); customized professional concentration (MBA, DBA); finance (MBA); healthcare administration (MBA); information systems (DBA); information systems management (MBA); international business (MBA, DBA); management (MBA, MS, MSM, DBA); marketing (MBA, DBA).

See Close-Up on page 229.

Argosy University, Sarasota Campus, College of Business, Sarasota, FL 34235-8246. Offers accounting (DBA, Adv C); customized professional concentration (MBA, DBA); finance (MBA, Certificate); healtcare administration (Certificate); healthcare administration (MBA); information systems (DBA, Adv C); information systems management (MBA, Certificate); international business (MBA, DBA, Adv C, Certificate); management (MBA, MSM, DBA); mangement (Adv C); marketing (MBA, DBA, Adv C, Certificate). Part-time and evening/weekend programs available. Postbaccalaureate distance learning degree programs offered (minimal on-campus study). *Faculty:* 6 full-time (3 women), 13 part-time/adjunct (5 women). *Students:* 71 applicants, 92% accepted, 64 enrolled. In 2006, 7 master's, 30 doctorates awarded. *Degree requirements:* For doctorate, thesis/dissertation, comprehensive exam. *Entrance requirements:* For master's, minimum GPA of 3.0; for doctorate, minimum undergraduate GPA of 3.0. Additional exam requirements/recommendations for international students: Required—TOEFL. *Application deadline:* Applications are processed on a rolling basis. Application fee: $50. Electronic applications accepted. *Financial support:* Federal Work-Study and scholarships/grants available. Support available to part-time students. Financial award application deadline: 4/1; financial award applicants required to submit FAFSA. *Unit head:* Dr. Kathleen Cornett, Dean, 800-331-5995, Fax: 941-379-9464, E-mail: kcornett@argosy.edu. *Application contact:* Admissions Representative, 800-331-5995 Ext. 221, Fax: 941-379-5964.

See Close-Up on page 231.

Argosy University, Schaumburg Campus, College of Business, Schaumburg, IL 60173-5403. Offers accounting (DBA, Adv C); corporate compliance (MBA); customized professional concentration (MBA, DBA); finance (MBA, Certificate); healthcare administration (MBA, Certificate); information systems (DBA, Adv C); information systems management (MBA, Certificate); international business (MBA, DBA, Adv C, Certificate); management (MBA, DBA, Adv C, Certificate); marketing (MBA, DBA, Adv C, Certificate). Part-time and evening/weekend programs available. *Faculty:* 1 (woman) full-time, 7 part-time/adjunct (0 women). *Students:* 36 full-time, 23 part-time. 13 applicants, 69% accepted, 9 enrolled. In 2006, 5 master's, 4 doctorates awarded. *Degree requirements:* For doctorate, thesis/dissertation, comprehensive exam. *Entrance requirements:* For master's and doctorate, minimum GPA of 3.0. Additional exam requirements/recommendations for international students: Required—TOEFL. *Application deadline:* For fall admission, 3/15 priority date for domestic and international students; for spring admission, 10/15 priority date for domestic and international students. Applications are processed on a rolling basis. Application fee: $50. Electronic applications accepted. *Expenses: Contact institution. Financial support:* Federal Work-Study and scholarships/grants available. *Unit head:* Dr. Harriet Kandelman, Dean, 866-290-2777, Fax: 847-548-6159, E-mail: agrosyadmissions@argosy.edu. *Application contact:* Jamal Scott, Director of Admissions, 847-598-6159, Fax: 630-598-6191, E-mail: jscott@argosy.edu.

See Close-Up on page 233.

Argosy University, Seattle Campus, College of Business, Seattle, WA 98121. Offers accounting (DBA); customized professional concentration (MBA, DBA); finance (MBA); healthcare administration (MBA); information systems (DBA); information systems management (MBA); international business (MBA, DBA); management (MSM, DBA); mangement (MBA); marketing (MBA, DBA). Part-time and evening/weekend programs available. *Students:* 1 applicant, 100% accepted, 1 enrolled. In 2006, 1 degree awarded. *Degree requirements:* For master's, capstone experience; for doctorate, thesis/dissertation, comprehensive exam (for some programs). *Entrance requirements:* For master's, minimum GPA of 3.0 in last 2 years or cumulative of 2.7; for doctorate, minimum GPA of 3.0. Additional exam requirements/recommendations for international students: Required—TOEFL (minimum score 550 paper-based; 213 computer-based). *Application deadline:* For fall admission, 4/15 priority date for domestic students, 4/15 for international students; for winter admission, 10/15 priority date for domestic students. Applications are processed on a rolling basis. Application fee: $50. Electronic applications accepted. *Expenses: Contact institution. Financial support:* Federal Work-Study and unspecified assistantships available. Support available to part-time students. Financial award applicants required to submit FAFSA. *Unit head:* Dr. Kylene Quinn, Chair, 206-393-3543, Fax: 206-283-5777, E-mail: kquinn@argosy.edu. *Application contact:* Heather Simpson, Director of Admissions, 866-283-4500, Fax: 206-283-5777, E-mail: hsimpson@argosy.edu.

See Close-Up on page 235.

Argosy University, Tampa Campus, College of Business, Tampa, FL 33614. Offers accounting (DBA); customized professional concentration (MBA, DBA); finance (MBA, Certificate); healthcare administration (MBA, Certificate); information systems (DBA); information systems management (MBA); international business (MBA, DBA, Certificate); management (MBA, MSM, DBA); marketing (MBA, DBA, Certificate); public administration (MBA). *Entrance requirements:* For doctorate, minimum GPA of 3.0. *Unit head:* Dr. Andrew Ghillyer, Dean, 813-393-5270, E-mail: aghillyer@argosy.edu.

See Close-Up on page 237.

Argosy University, Twin Cities Campus, College of Business, Eagan, MN 55121. Offers accounting (DBA); corporate compliance (MBA); customized professional certification (DBA); customized professional concentration (MBA); finance (MBA); healthcare administration (MBA); information systems (DBA); information systems management (MBA); international business (MBA, DBA); management (MBA, MSM, DBA, EDBA); marketing (MBA, DBA). Part-time and evening/weekend programs available. *Faculty:* 1 (woman) full-time, 20 part-time/adjunct (6 women). *Students:* 47 full-time (23 women), 20 part-time (11 women); includes 21 minority (10 African Americans, 1 American Indian/Alaska Native, 9 Asian Americans or Pacific Islanders, 1 Hispanic American). Average age 39. 72 applicants, 76% accepted, 45 enrolled. In 2006, 6 degrees awarded. *Degree requirements:* For doctorate, thesis/dissertation, comprehensive exam. *Entrance requirements:* For master's, 3 letters of recommendation, bachelor's degree in a related field, minimum undergraduate GPA of 3.0, resumé; for doctorate, 3 letters of recommendation, master's degree in a related field, minimum GPA of 3.0, resumé. Additional exam requirements/recommendations for international students: Required—TOEFL (minimum score 550 paper-based; 213 computer-based). *Application deadline:* For fall admission, 5/15 priority date for domestic students, 5/15 for international students; for spring admission, 10/15 priority date for domestic students, 10/15 for international students. Applications are processed on a rolling basis. Application fee: $50. Electronic applications accepted. *Financial support:* In 2006–07, 3 fellowships with partial tuition reimbursements, 3 teaching assistantships with partial tuition reimbursements were awarded; Federal Work-Study and scholarships/grants also available. Financial award applicants required to submit FAFSA. *Unit head:* Dr. Paula King, Department Head, 651-846-3377, E-mail: pking@argosy.edu. *Application contact:* Jennifer Radke, 2nd Director of Graduate Admissions, 651-846-3300, Fax: 651-994-7954, E-mail: tcadmissions@argosy.edu.

See Close-Up on page 239.

Argosy University, Washington DC Campus, College of Business, Arlington, VA 22209. Offers accounting (DBA); customized professional concentration (MBA, DBA); finance (MBA); healthcare administration (MBA); information systems (DBA); information systems management (MBA); international business (MBA, DBA); international business marketing (Graduate Certificate); management (MBA, DBA); marketing (MBA, DBA). *Faculty:* 1 full-time (0 women), 5 part-time/adjunct (2 women). *Students:* 5 full-time (4 women), 4 part-time (1 woman); includes 4 minority (3 African Americans, 1 Asian American or Pacific Islander). 21 applicants, 86% accepted. *Degree requirements:* For master's, thesis (for some programs), comprehensive exam (for some programs); for doctorate, thesis/dissertation, comprehensive exam. *Entrance requirements:* For master's and doctorate, minimum GPA of 3.0. Additional exam requirements/recommendations for international students: Required—TOEFL (minimum score 550 paper-based; 213 computer-based). *Application deadline:* For fall admission, 6/15 priority date for domestic students; for spring admission, 10/15 priority date for domestic students. Application fee: $50. *Financial support:* Federal Work-Study and scholarships/grants available. Financial award applicants required to submit FAFSA. *Unit head:* Dr. Colleen Logan, Academic Affairs Officer, 866-703-2777, Fax: 703-521-5850, E-mail: dcadmissions@argosy.edu. *Application contact:* Emily Peck, Director of Admissions, 866-703-2777 Ext. 5851, Fax: 703-526-5850, E-mail: dcadmissions@argosy.edu.

See Close-Up on page 241.

Arizona State University, Division of Graduate Studies, W.P. Carey School of Business, Program in Business Administration, Tempe, AZ 85287. Offers accountancy (PhD); business administration (MBA); finance (PhD); health services research (PhD); information management (PhD); management (PhD); marketing (PhD); supply chain management (PhD); JD/MBA; MBA/M Arch; MBA/MHSM. MBA/MIM offered jointly with Thunderbird, The American Graduate School of International Management and Groupe Ecole Supéieure de Commerce, Toulouse, France. *Accreditation:* AACSB. *Degree requirements:* For master's, thesis optional; for doctorate, thesis/dissertation. *Entrance requirements:* For master's, GMAT.

Auburn University, Graduate School, College of Business, Department of Finance, Auburn University, AL 36849. Offers MS. *Faculty:* 10 full-time (2 women). *Students:* 14 full-time (9 women), 2 part-time (both women); includes 2 minority (both African Americans), 3 international. Average age 27. 34 applicants, 50% accepted, 12 enrolled. In 2006, 4 degrees awarded. Application fee: $25 ($50 for international students). *Expenses:* Tuition, state resident: full-time $5,000. Tuition, nonresident: full-time $15,000. Required fees: $416. Tuition and fees vary according to program. *Unit head:* Dr. John S. Janera, Head, 334-844-5344. *Application contact:* Dr. Joe Pittman, Interim Dean of the Graduate School, 334-844-4700.

Avila University, School of Business, Kansas City, MO 64145-1698. Offers accounting (MBA); finance (MBA); general management (MBA); health care administration (MBA); international business (MBA); management information systems (MBA); marketing (MBA). Part-time and evening/weekend programs available. *Faculty:* 8 full-time (4 women), 17 part-time/adjunct (4 women). *Students:* 31 full-time (19 women), 165 part-time (96 women); includes 18 minority (14 African Americans, 1 American Indian/Alaska Native, 3 Hispanic Americans), 16 international. Average age 32. 77 applicants, 81% accepted, 62 enrolled. In 2006, 54 degrees awarded. *Degree requirements:* For master's, capstone course. *Entrance requirements:* For master's, GMAT, minimum GPA of 3.0. Additional exam requirements/recommendations for international students: Required—TOEFL (minimum score 550 paper-based). *Application deadline:* For fall admission, 7/30 priority date for domestic students; for winter admission, 11/30 priority date for domestic students; for spring admission, 2/28 priority date for domestic students. Applications are processed on a rolling basis. Application fee: $20. Electronic applications accepted. *Expenses:* Tuition: Full-time $7,470; part-time $415 per credit. *Financial support:* In 2006–07, 78 students received support. Career-related internships or fieldwork available. Support available to part-time students. Financial award applicants required to submit FAFSA. *Faculty research:* Leadership characteristics, financial hedging, group dynamics. *Unit head:* Dr. Richard Woodall, Dean, 816-501-3798, Fax: 816-501-2463. *Application contact:* JoAnna Giffin, MBA Admissions Director, 816-501-3601, Fax: 816-501-2463, E-mail: joanna.giffin@avila.edu.

Baker College Center for Graduate Studies, Programs in Business, Flint, MI 48507-9843. Offers accounting (MBA); computer information systems (MBA); finance (MBA); general business (MBA); health and recreation services management (MBA); health care management (MBA); human resource management (MBA); industrial management (MBA); international business (MBA); leadership (MBA); marketing (MBA). MBA in health and recreation services management enrollment limited to international students. Part-time and evening/weekend programs available. *Faculty:* 15 full-time (6 women), 425 part-time/adjunct (200 women). *Students:* 370 full-time (190 women), 1,060 part-time (560 women); includes 372 minority (205 African Americans, 27 American Indian/Alaska Native, 66 Asian Americans or Pacific Islanders, 74 Hispanic Americans), 30 international. Average age 38. 780 applicants, 85% accepted, 567 enrolled. In 2006, 202 degrees awarded. *Degree requirements:* For master's, portfolio. *Entrance requirements:* For master's, 3 years of work experience, minimum undergraduate GPA of 2.5, writing sample, letters of recommendation. Additional exam requirements/recommendations for international students: Required—TOEFL (minimum score 550 paper-based; 213 computer-based). *Application deadline:* For fall admission, 8/6 priority date for domestic students; for winter admission, 12/15 priority date for domestic students; for spring admission, 2/15 priority date for domestic students. Applications are processed on a rolling basis. Application fee: $25. Electronic applications accepted. *Expenses:* Tuition: Full-time $7,200; part-time $300 per credit hour. *Financial support:* In 2006–07, 410 students received support. Scholarships/grants available. Support available to part-time students. Financial award applicants required to submit FAFSA. *Unit head:* Dr. Michael Heberling, President, 800-469-3165, Fax: 810-766-4399, E-mail: heberling@baker.edu. *Application contact:* Chuck J. Gurden, Vice President for Graduate and Online Admissions, 800-469-3165, Fax: 810-766-2051, E-mail: chuck@baker.edu.

Barry University, Andreas School of Business, Graduate Certificate Programs, Miami Shores, FL 33161-6695. Offers finance (Certificate); health services administration (Certificate); international business (Certificate); management (Certificate); management information systems (Certificate); marketing (Certificate). *Application contact:* Dave Fletcher, Director of Graduate Admissions, 305-899-3113, Fax: 305-899-2971, E-mail: dfletcher@mail.barry.edu.

Bayamón Central University, Graduate Programs, Program in Business Administration, Bayamón, PR 00960-1725. Offers accounting (MBA); finance (MBA); general business (MBA); management (MBA); management of security and protection (MBA); marketing (MBA). Part-time and evening/weekend programs available. *Degree requirements:* For master's, comprehensive exam (for some programs), registration (for some programs). *Entrance requirements:* For master's, EXADEP, bachelor's degree in business or related field.

Bentley College, The Elkin B. McCallum Graduate School of Business, Program in Finance, Waltham, MA 02452-4705. Offers MSF. Part-time and evening/weekend programs available. *Faculty:* 25 full-time (8 women), 6 part-time/adjunct (1 woman). *Students:* 32 full-time (9 women), 53 part-time (13 women); includes 13 minority (2 African Americans, 9 Asian Americans or Pacific Islanders, 2 Hispanic Americans), 16 international. Average age 27. 94 applicants, 68% accepted, 32 enrolled. In 2006, 18 degrees awarded. *Entrance requirements:* For master's, GMAT. Additional exam requirements/recommendations for international students: Required—TOEFL (minimum score 600 paper-based; 250 computer-based). *Application deadline:* For fall admission, 6/1 priority date for domestic students, 3/1 priority date for international students; for spring admission, 11/1 priority date for domestic and international students. Applications are processed on a rolling basis. Application fee: $50. Electronic applications accepted. *Expenses:* Tuition: Full-time $28,440; part-time $2,844 per course. Required fees: $404; $105 per year. *Financial support:* Research assistantships, scholarships/grants, tuition waivers, and unspecified assistantships available. Financial award application deadline: 4/12; financial award applicants required to submit CSS PROFILE or FAFSA. *Faculty research:* Large investments and project finance, quantitative finance and market risk, emerging market financial systems, credit risk in financial markets, risk management. *Unit head:* Philipp Uhlmann, Head, 781-891-3175. *Application contact:* Sharon Hill, Director of Graduate Admissions, 781-891-2108, Fax: 781-891-2464, E-mail: shill@bentley.edu.

Bentley College, The Elkin B. McCallum Graduate School of Business, Program in Financial Planning, Waltham, MA 02452-4705. Offers MSFP. Part-time and evening/weekend programs available. *Faculty:* 13 full-time (3 women), 16 part-time/adjunct (7 women). *Students:* 13 full-time (4 women), 53 part-time (25 women); includes 4 minority (2 African Americans, 1 American Indian/Alaska Native, 1 Asian American or Pacific Islander), 4 international. Average age 32. 28 applicants, 89% accepted, 25 enrolled. In 2006, 10 degrees awarded. *Entrance requirements:* For master's, GMAT. Additional exam requirements/recommendations for international students: Required—TOEFL (minimum score 600 paper-based; 250 computer-based). *Application deadline:* For fall admission, 6/1 priority date for domestic students, 3/1 priority date for international students; for spring admission, 11/1 priority date for domestic and international students. Applications are processed on a rolling basis. Application fee: $50. Electronic applications accepted. *Expenses:* Tuition: Full-time $28,440; part-time $2,844 per course. Required

Finance and Banking

Bentley College (continued)

fees: $404; $105 per year. *Financial support:* Research assistantships, scholarships/grants, tuition waivers, and unspecified assistantships available. Financial award application deadline: 4/12; financial award applicants required to submit CSS PROFILE or FAFSA. *Faculty research:* International financial planning, compensation and benefits, retirement planning. *Unit head:* John Lynch, Director, 781-891-2624, E-mail: jlynch@bentley.edu. *Application contact:* Sharon Hill, Director of Graduate Admissions, 781-891-2108, Fax: 781-891-2464, E-mail: shill@bentley.edu.

Bernard M. Baruch College of the City University of New York, Zicklin School of Business, Department of Economics and Finance, Program in Finance, New York, NY 10010-5585. Offers MBA, MS, PhD. Part-time and evening/weekend programs available. *Faculty:* 51 full-time (10 women), 45 part-time/adjunct (5 women). *Students:* 170 full-time (61 women), 349 part-time (101 women); includes 160 minority (25 African Americans, 2 American Indian/Alaska Native, 110 Asian Americans or Pacific Islanders, 23 Hispanic Americans). In 2006, 267 degrees awarded. *Degree requirements:* For doctorate, thesis/dissertation, comprehensive exam. *Entrance requirements:* For master's, GMAT, 2 letters of recommendation, resumé, 2 years of work experience; for doctorate, GMAT. Additional exam requirements/recommendations for international students: Required—TOEFL (minimum score 590 paper-based; 243 computer-based), TWE (minimum score 5). *Application deadline:* For fall admission, 5/31 for domestic students, 4/30 for international students; for spring admission, 10/31 for domestic and international students. Application fee: $125. *Financial support:* Fellowships, research assistantships, teaching assistantships, career-related internships or fieldwork, Federal Work-Study, and unspecified assistantships available. Financial award application deadline: 4/30; financial award applicants required to submit FAFSA. *Application contact:* Frances Murphy, Office of Graduate Admissions, 646-312-1300, Fax: 646-312-1301, E-mail: zicklingradadmissions@baruch.cuny.edu.

Bernard M. Baruch College of the City University of New York, Zicklin School of Business, Zicklin Executive Programs, Executive Program in Finance, New York, NY 10010-5585. Offers MS. Evening/weekend programs available. *Faculty:* 9 full-time (1 woman), 2 part-time/adjunct (0 women). *Students:* 41 full-time (19 women); includes 17 minority (6 African Americans, 8 Asian Americans or Pacific Islanders, 3 Hispanic Americans), 1 international. Average age 34. 60 applicants, 75% accepted, 38 enrolled. In 2006, 30 degrees awarded. *Entrance requirements:* For master's, personal interview, work experience. *Application deadline:* For fall admission, 5/15 priority date for domestic students, 5/15 for international students. Applications are processed on a rolling basis. Application fee: $125. *Expenses: Contact institution. Financial support:* Applicants required to submit FAFSA. *Faculty research:* Corporate finance, investments, options, securities, system risk. *Unit head:* Chris Koutsoutis, Director, 646-312-3100, Fax: 646-312-3101, E-mail: chris_koutsoutis@baruch.cuny.edu. *Application contact:* Chris Koutsoutis, Director, 646-312-3100, Fax: 646-312-3101, E-mail: chris_koutsoutis@baruch.cuny.edu.

Boston College, The Carroll School of Management, Graduate Finance Programs, Chestnut Hill, MA 02467-3800. Offers MSF, PhD, MBA/MSF. Part-time programs available. *Faculty:* 10 full-time (1 woman), 6 part-time/adjunct (0 women). *Students:* 85 full-time (33 women), 97 part-time (27 women); includes 20 minority (4 African Americans, 12 Asian Americans or Pacific Islanders, 4 Hispanic Americans), 53 international. Average age 26. 226 applicants, 35% accepted, 36 enrolled. In 2006, 84 master's, 5 doctorates awarded. *Degree requirements:* For doctorate, thesis/dissertation. *Entrance requirements:* For master's, GMAT, resumé, recommendations; for doctorate, GMAT or GRE, curriculum vitae, recommendations. Additional exam requirements/recommendations for international students: Required—TOEFL (minimum score 600 paper-based; 250 computer-based; 100 iBT). *Application deadline:* For fall admission, 3/15 for domestic and international students; for spring admission, 10/15 for domestic and international students. Application fee: $100. Electronic applications accepted. *Financial support:* Fellowships with partial tuition reimbursements, research assistantships with tuition reimbursements, teaching assistantships with tuition reimbursements, Federal Work-Study, scholarships/grants, and unspecified assistantships available. Financial award application deadline: 3/1; financial award applicants required to submit FAFSA. *Faculty research:* Security and derivative markets, financial institutions, corporate finance and capital markets, market macrostructure, investments, portfolio analysis. *Unit head:* Peter DiCarlo, Director, 617-552-3997, Fax: 617-552-8078, E-mail: gradfin@bc.edu. *Application contact:* Shelley A. Burt, Director of Graduate Enrollment, 617-552-3920, Fax: 617-552-8078, E-mail: bcmba@bc.edu.

Boston University, Graduate School of Arts and Sciences, Department of Mathematics and Statistics, Boston, MA 02215. Offers mathematical finance (MA); mathematics (MA, PhD). *Students:* 80 full-time (29 women), 8 part-time (2 women); includes 8 minority (1 African American, 5 Asian Americans or Pacific Islanders, 2 Hispanic Americans), 57 international. Average age 26. 269 applicants, 29% accepted, 38 enrolled. In 2006, 29 master's, 6 doctorates awarded. Terminal master's awarded for partial completion of doctoral program. *Degree requirements:* For master's, one foreign language, comprehensive exam, registration; for doctorate, one foreign language, thesis/dissertation, comprehensive exam, registration. *Entrance requirements:* For master's and doctorate, GRE General Test, GRE Subject Test, 3 letters of recommendation. Additional exam requirements/recommendations for international students: Required—TOEFL (minimum score 600 paper-based; 250 computer-based). *Application deadline:* For fall admission, 1/15 for domestic and international students; for spring admission, 10/15 for domestic and international students. Application fee: $70. *Expenses:* Tuition: Full-time $33,330; part-time $1,042 per credit. Required fees: $462; $40. *Financial support:* In 2006–07, 58 students received support, including 4 fellowships with full tuition reimbursements available (averaging $16,500 per year), 17 research assistantships with full tuition reimbursements available (averaging $16,000 per year), 26 teaching assistantships with full tuition reimbursements available (averaging $16,000 per year); Federal Work-Study and scholarships/grants also available. Support available to part-time students. Financial award application deadline: 1/15; financial award applicants required to submit FAFSA. *Unit head:* Ralph D'Agostino, Chairman, 617-353-2767, Fax: 617-353-8100, E-mail: ralph@bu.edu. *Application contact:* Angela M. Silva, Staff Coordinator, 617-353-2560, Fax: 617-353-8100, E-mail: amsilva@bu.edu.

Boston University, Metropolitan College (Continuing Education), Program in Administrative Studies, Boston, MA 02215. Offers banking and financial management (MSM); business continuity in emergency management (MSM); economics development and tourism management (MSAS); electronic commerce, systems, and technology (MSAS); financial economics (MSAS); human resource management (MSM); innovation and technology (MSAS); insurance management (MSM); international market management (MSM); multinational commerce (MSAS); project management (MSM). *Accreditation:* AACSB. Part-time and evening/weekend programs available. *Faculty:* 9 full-time (0 women), 51 part-time/adjunct (8 women). *Students:* 105 full-time (40 women), 171 part-time (65 women); includes 27 minority (5 African Americans, 18 Asian Americans or Pacific Islanders, 4 Hispanic Americans), 125 international. Average age 29. In 2006, 310 degrees awarded. *Degree requirements:* For master's, thesis optional. *Entrance requirements:* For master's, 1 year of work experience, minimum GPA of 3.0. Additional exam requirements/recommendations for international students: Required—TOEFL (minimum score 560 paper-based; 220 computer-based). *Application deadline:* Applications are processed on a rolling basis. Application fee: $65. *Expenses:* Tuition: Full-time $33,330; part-time $1,042 per credit. Required fees: $462; $40. *Financial support:* In 2006–07, 15 students received support, including research assistantships (averaging $10,000 per year); career-related internships or fieldwork and Federal Work-Study also available. *Faculty research:* International business, innovative process. *Unit head:* Dr. Kip Becker, Chairman, 617-353-3016, E-mail: adminsc@bu.edu. *Application contact:* Lucille Dicker, Administrative Sciences Department, 617-353-3016, E-mail: adminsc@bu.edu.

Boston University, School of Law, Boston, MA 02215. Offers American law (LL M); banking law (LL M); intellectual property law (LL M); law (JD); taxation (LL M); JD/LL M; JD/MA; JD/MBA; JD/MPH; JD/MS; JD/MSW. *Accreditation:* ABA. Part-time and evening/weekend programs available. *Faculty:* 69 full-time (21 women), 72 part-time/adjunct (20 women). *Students:* 987 full-time (495 women), 103 part-time (52 women); includes 195 minority (38 African Americans, 2 American Indian/Alaska Native, 125 Asian Americans or Pacific Islanders, 30 Hispanic Americans), 132 international. Average age 27. 7,265 applicants, 19% accepted, 285 enrolled. In 2006, 262 JDs, 162 master's awarded. *Degree requirements:* For JD, thesis, research project resulting in a paper; for master's, thesis (for some programs). *Entrance requirements:* For JD, LSAT; for master's, JD. Additional exam requirements/recommendations for international students: Required—TOEFL (minimum score 600 paper-based; 250 computer-based). *Application deadline:* For fall admission, 3/1 for domestic and international students. Applications are processed on a rolling basis. Application fee: $60. Electronic applications accepted. *Expenses:* Tuition: Full-time $33,330; part-time $1,042 per credit. Required fees: $462; $40. *Financial support:* In 2006–07, 681 students received support. Career-related internships or fieldwork, Federal Work-Study, institutionally sponsored loans, and scholarships/grants available. Financial award application deadline: 3/1; financial award applicants required to submit CSS PROFILE or FAFSA. *Faculty research:* Litigation and dispute resolution, intellectual property law, business organizations and finance law, international law, health law. *Unit head:* Maureen O'Rourke, Interim Dean, 617-353-3112, Fax: 617-353-7400. *Application contact:* Joan Horgan, Director of Admissions and Financial Aid, 617-353-3100, Fax: 617-353-0578, E-mail: bulawadm@bu.edu.

Boston University, School of Management, Program in Investment Management, Boston, MA 02215. Offers MSIM. Part-time and evening/weekend programs available. *Faculty:* 7 full-time (0 women), 2 part-time/adjunct (0 women). *Students:* 48 applicants, 75% accepted, 30 enrolled. In 2006, 22 degrees awarded. *Entrance requirements:* For master's, GMAT. *Application deadline:* For spring admission, 11/15 for domestic students. Applications are processed on a rolling basis. Application fee: $100. Electronic applications accepted. *Expenses:* Tuition: Full-time $33,330; part-time $1,042 per credit. Required fees: $462; $40. *Financial support:* Career-related internships or fieldwork, Federal Work-Study, and institutionally sponsored loans available. Support available to part-time students. Financial award applicants required to submit FAFSA. *Faculty research:* Behavioral finance, computational finance, risk management, portfolio management, derivatives. *Unit head:* Scott Stewart, Director, 617-353-2353, Fax: 617-353-6667, E-mail: msim@bu.edu. *Application contact:* Hayden Estrada, Assistant Dean, Admissions, 617-353-2670, Fax: 617-353-7368, E-mail: mba@bu.edu.

Brandeis University, International Business School, Waltham, MA 02454-9110. Offers finance (MSF); international business (MBAi); international economics and finance (MA, PhD); international finance/international economics (MBAi). Part-time and evening/weekend programs available. Terminal master's awarded for partial completion of doctoral program. *Degree requirements:* For master's, one foreign language; for doctorate, thesis/dissertation. *Entrance requirements:* For master's, GMAT or GRE General Test (MA), GMAT (MBAi and MSF); for doctorate, GRE General Test. Additional exam requirements/recommendations for international students: Required—TOEFL (minimum score 600 paper-based; 250 computer-based), IELTS (minimum score 7). Electronic applications accepted. *Faculty research:* International finance and business, trade policy, macroeconomics, Asian economic issues, developmental economics.

Bridgewater State College, School of Graduate Studies, School of Business, Department of Accounting and Finance, Bridgewater, MA 02325-0001. Offers MSM. Part-time and evening/weekend programs available. *Entrance requirements:* For master's, GMAT. *Application deadline:* For fall admission, 3/1 priority date for domestic students; for spring admission, 10/1 priority date for domestic students. Application fee: $50. *Financial support:* Health care benefits and unspecified assistantships available. Support available to part-time students. *Application contact:* Dr. Raymond Charles Guillette, Assistant Dean School of Graduate Studies, 508-531-2919, Fax: 508-531-6162, E-mail: rguillette@bridgew.edu.

Bryant University, Graduate School, Graduate School of Business, Programs in Business Administration, Smithfield, RI 02917-1284. Offers accounting (MBA, CAGS); computer information systems (MBA, CAGS); e-strategy (MBA, CAGS); finance (MBA, CAGS); general business (MBA); management (MBA, CAGS); marketing (MBA, CAGS); operations management (MBA). *Accreditation:* AACSB. *Faculty:* 49 full-time (13 women), 2 part-time/adjunct (0 women). *Students:* 143 applicants, 41% accepted, 46 enrolled. In 2006, 106 master's, 10 other advanced degrees awarded. *Entrance requirements:* For master's, GMAT, letter of recommendation, resumé; for CAGS, GMAT, resumé. Additional exam requirements/recommendations for international students: Required—TOEFL (minimum score 580 paper-based; 237 computer-based). *Application deadline:* For fall admission, 7/15 for domestic students, 4/1 for international students; for spring admission, 11/15 for domestic and international students. Application fee: $80. *Expenses:* Tuition: Part-time $1,998 per course. *Financial support:* Research assistantships with full tuition reimbursements, unspecified assistantships available. Financial award applicants required to submit FAFSA. *Unit head:* Kristopher T. Sullivan, Assistant Dean of the Graduate School, 401-232-6230, Fax: 401-232-6494, E-mail: gradprog@bryant.edu.

California Lutheran University, Graduate Studies, School of Business, Thousand Oaks, CA 91360-2787. Offers finance (MBA); healthcare management (MBA); international business (MBA); management information systems (MBA); marketing (MBA); organizational behavior (MBA); small business/entrepreneurship (MBA). Evening/weekend programs available. *Entrance requirements:* For master's, GMAT, interview, minimum GPA of 3.0. Expenses: Contact institution.

California State University, East Bay, Academic Programs and Graduate Studies, College of Business and Economics, Department of Management and Finance, Option in Finance, Hayward, CA 94542-3000. Offers MBA. Part-time and evening/weekend programs available. *Degree requirements:* For master's, comprehensive exam or thesis. *Entrance requirements:* For master's, GMAT, minimum GPA of 2.75. Additional exam requirements/recommendations for international students: Required—TOEFL (minimum score 550 paper-based; 213 computer-based). *Application deadline:* For fall admission, 5/31 for domestic students, 4/30 for international students; for winter admission, 9/30 for domestic and international students; for spring admission, 12/31 for domestic students, 11/30 for international students. Application fee: $55. *Financial support:* Career-related internships or fieldwork, Federal Work-Study, and institutionally sponsored loans available. Support available to part-time students. Financial award application deadline: 3/2. *Unit head:* Surendra Pradhan, Graduate Adviser, 510-885-2601, E-mail: surenda.pradham@csueastbay.edu. *Application contact:* Doris Duncan, Director of Graduate Programs, 510-885-3364, Fax: 510-885-2176, E-mail: doris.duncan@csueastbay.edu.

California State University, Fullerton, Graduate Studies, College of Business and Economics, Department of Finance, Fullerton, CA 92834-9480. Offers MBA. Part-time and evening/weekend programs available. *Students:* 31 full-time (17 women), 72 part-time (22 women); includes 37 minority (1 African American, 32 Asian Americans or Pacific Islanders, 4 Hispanic Americans), 29 international. Average age 28. 78 applicants, 51% accepted, 27 enrolled. In 2006, 29 degrees awarded. *Degree requirements:* For master's, project or thesis. *Entrance requirements:* For master's, GMAT, minimum AACSB index of 950. Application fee: $55. *Expenses:* Tuition, nonresident: part-time $339 per unit. Required fees: $1,155 per semester. *Financial support:* Teaching assistantships, Federal Work-Study, institutionally sponsored loans, and scholarships/grants available. Support available to part-time students. Financial award application deadline: 3/1. *Unit head:* Dr. Mark Stohs, Chair, 714-278-2217. *Application contact:* Robert Miyake, Assistant Dean, 714-278-2211.

California State University, Los Angeles, Graduate Studies, College of Business and Economics, Major in Business Administration, Department of Finance and Law, Los Angeles, CA 90032-8530. Offers finance and banking (MBA, MS). Part-time and evening/weekend programs available. *Faculty:* 3 full-time (0 women). *Students:* 8 full-time (3 women), 30 part-time (13 women); includes 16 minority (1 African American, 11 Asian Americans or Pacific Islanders, 4 Hispanic Americans), 14 international. *Degree requirements:* For master's, comprehensive exam (MBA), thesis (MS). *Entrance requirements:* For master's, GMAT, minimum GPA of 2.5 during previous 2 years of course work. Additional exam requirements/recommendations for international students: Required—TOEFL. *Application deadline:* For fall admission, 6/30 for domestic students; for spring admission, 11/30 for domestic students. Applications are processed on a rolling basis. Application fee: $55. *Expenses:* Tuition, nonresident: part-time $226 per unit. *Financial support:* Career-related internships or fieldwork and Federal Work-Study available. Support available to part-time students. Financial award application deadline: 3/1. *Unit head:* Dr. Hsing Fang, Chair, 323-343-2870, Fax: 323-343-2885.

California State University, Stanislaus, Graduate School, College of Business Administration, Turlock, CA 95382. Offers business administration (MBA); international finance (MSBA). *Accreditation:* AACSB. Part-time and evening/weekend programs available. *Degree requirements:* For master's, thesis or alternative, comprehensive exam. *Entrance requirements:* For master's, GMAT, minimum GPA of 2.5. Additional exam requirements/recommendations for international students: Required—TOEFL (minimum score 550 paper-based; 213 computer-based).

Capella University, School of Business and Technology, Minneapolis, MN 55402. Offers accounting (MBA), including system design and programming; business (Certificate), including human resource management (MS, PhD, Certificate), information technology management (MS, PhD, Certificate), leadership (MBA, MS, PhD, Certificate); finance (MBA); general business (MBA); health care management (MBA); information technology (MS, Certificate), including general information technology (MS), information security, network architecture and design (MS), professional projects management (Certificate), project management and leadership (MS), system design and development (MS),); information technology management (MBA); marketing (MBA); organization and management (MBA, MS, PhD), including general business (PhD), general organization and management (MBA, MS), human resource management (MS, PhD, Certificate), information technology management (MS, PhD, Certificate), leadership (MBA, MS, PhD, Certificate); project management (MBA). Part-time and evening/weekend programs available. Postbaccalaureate distance learning degree programs offered (minimal on-campus study). Terminal master's awarded for partial completion of doctoral program. *Degree requirements:* For master's, integrative project, thesis optional; for doctorate, thesis/dissertation, comprehensive exam, registration. *Entrance requirements:* Additional exam requirements/recommendations for international students: Required—TOEFL (minimum score 550 paper-based; 213 computer-based), TWE (minimum score 4). Electronic applications accepted. *Faculty research:* Business policies: strategic, corporate, and financial management; interplay of technological, organizational and social change.

Cardean University, MBA Program, Chicago, IL 60606-7204. Offers accounting and information systems (MBA); e-commerce (MBA); finance (MBA); global management (MBA); health care administration (MBA); human resources management (MBA); leadership (MBA); management of information systems (MBA); management of technology (MBA); marketing (MBA); professional accounting (MBA); project management (MBA); risk management (MBA); strategy and economics (MBA). Part-time and evening/weekend programs available. Postbaccalaureate distance learning degree programs offered (no on-campus study). *Entrance requirements:* Additional exam requirements/recommendations for international students: Required—TOEFL (minimum score 550 paper-based; 213 computer-based).

Cardinal Stritch University, College of Business and Management, Programs in Management for Adults, Milwaukee, WI 53217-3985. Offers business administration (MBA); financial services (MS); health care executives (MBA); management (MS). Part-time and evening/weekend programs available.

Carnegie Mellon University, Tepper School of Business, Program in Finance, Pittsburgh, PA 15213-3891. Offers PhD. *Degree requirements:* For doctorate, thesis/dissertation. *Entrance requirements:* For doctorate, GRE General Test.

Case Western Reserve University, Weatherhead School of Management, Department of Banking and Finance, Cleveland, OH 44106. Offers MBA. *Faculty:* 11 full-time (1 woman), 1 part-time/adjunct (0 women). *Students:* 184 full-time (81 women), 235 part-time (73 women); includes 15 minority (6 African Americans, 9 Asian Americans or Pacific Islanders), 74 international. In 2006, 203 degrees awarded. *Entrance requirements:* For master's, GMAT. *Application deadline:* For fall admission, 4/15 priority date for domestic students. Application fee: $50. *Faculty research:* Monetary and fiscal policy, corporate finance, future markets, derivative pricing, capital market efficiency. *Unit head:* Peter Ritchken, Chair, 216-368-2040, Fax: 216-368-5548, E-mail: phr@po.cwru.edu. *Application contact:* Deborah L Bibb, Professional Program Director, 216-368-6702, Fax: 216-368-4776, E-mail: clg3@po.cwru.edu.

Case Western Reserve University, Weatherhead School of Management, Department of Operations, Cleveland, OH 44106. Offers management (MS, MSM), including finance (MS), information systems (MS), marketing (MS), operations research, quality management (MS), supply chain (MSM); management for liberal arts graduates (MSM); operations research (PhD); MBA/MSM. Part-time programs available. *Faculty:* 12 full-time (1 woman), 2 part-time/adjunct (1 woman). *Students:* 32 full-time (8 women), 6 part-time (1 woman), 21 international. Average age 28. In 2006, 28 master's, 4 doctorates awarded. *Degree requirements:* For doctorate, thesis/dissertation. *Entrance requirements:* For master's, GRE General Test; for doctorate, GMAT, GRE General Test. *Application deadline:* For fall admission, 4/15 priority date for domestic students. Applications are processed on a rolling basis. Application fee: $50. *Financial support:* Tuition waivers (full and partial) available. Financial award application deadline: 5/1. *Faculty research:* Mathematical finance, mathematical programming, scheduling, stochastic optimization, environmental/energy models. *Unit head:* Kamlesh Mathur, Chairman, 216-368-3857, E-mail: kamlesh.mathur@case.edu.

Central European University, CEU Business School, Budapest, Hungary. Offers finance (MBA); general management (MBA); information technology (M Sc); information technology management (MBA); management (EMBA); marketing (MBA); real estate management (MBA). Part-time and evening/weekend programs available. *Faculty:* 15 full-time (3 women), 30 part-time/adjunct (9 women). *Students:* 47 full-time (18 women), 158 part-time (22 women). Average age 32. 450 applicants, 43% accepted, 160 enrolled. In 2006, 77 degrees awarded. *Entrance requirements:* For master's, GMAT. Additional exam requirements/recommendations for international students: Required—TOEFL (minimum score 570 paper-based; 230 computer-based). *Application deadline:* For fall admission, 5/22 priority date for domestic students, 5/22 for international students; for winter admission, 11/13 priority date for domestic students, 11/13 for international students. Applications are processed on a rolling basis. Application fee: $0. Electronic applications accepted. *Financial support:* In 2006–07, 4 students received support, including research assistantships with partial tuition reimbursements available (averaging $3,800 per year); tuition waivers (partial) and GMAT-based tuition fee discounts also available. *Faculty research:* Social and ethical business, marketing. Total annual research expenditures: 11,000 euros. *Unit head:* Dr. Paul Garrison, Dean and Managing Director, 36-18875050, Fax: 36-18875001, E-mail: garrisonp@ceubusiness.com. *Application contact:* Tunde Hegedus, MBA Program Manager, 36-18875060, Fax: 36-18875133, E-mail: mba@ceubusiness.com.

Central Michigan University, College of Graduate Studies, College of Business Administration, Department of Finance and Law, Mount Pleasant, MI 48859. Offers MBA. *Degree requirements:* For master's, thesis or alternative, registration. *Entrance requirements:* For master's, GMAT. *Faculty research:* Investments, commercial banking, financial management.

Charleston Southern University, Program in Business, Charleston, SC 29423-8087. Offers accounting (MBA); finance (MBA); health care administration (MBA); information systems (MBA); organizational development (MBA). Part-time and evening/weekend programs available. *Degree requirements:* For master's, thesis optional. *Entrance requirements:* For master's, GMAT. *Faculty research:* Economic forecasting.

Christian Brothers University, Graduate Programs, School of Business, Memphis, TN 38104-5581. Offers business (MBA); executive leadership (MAEL); financial planning (Certificate); project management (Certificate). Part-time and evening/weekend programs available. *Faculty:* 8 full-time (3 women), 1 part-time/adjunct (0 women). *Students:* 13 full-time (1 woman), 88 part-time (38 women); includes 21 minority (18 African Americans, 2 Asian Americans or

Pacific Islanders, 1 Hispanic American), 4 international. Average age 33. In 2006, 69 degrees awarded. *Entrance requirements:* For master's, GMAT. Additional exam requirements/recommendations for international students: Required—TOEFL. *Application deadline:* Applications are processed on a rolling basis. Application fee: $25. *Financial support:* Institutionally sponsored loans available. Support available to part-time students. *Faculty research:* Business ethics. *Unit head:* Dr. Mike R. Ryan, Dean, 901-321-3316. *Application contact:* Dr. Bevalee B. Pray, Director, Graduate Business Programs, 901-321-3319, Fax: 901-321-3494.

City University, Graduate Division, School of Management, Bellevue, WA 98005. Offers accounting (MBA); C++ programming (Certificate); computer systems—C++ programming (MS); computer systems—individualized study (MS); computer systems—web programming in e-commerce (MS); computer systems-web development (MS); financial management (MBA, Certificate); general management (MBA, MPA, Certificate); general management-Europe (MBA); human resource management (MPA); individualized study (MBA); information systems (MBA, Certificate); management—general management (MA); management—human resource management (MA); management—individualized study (MA); marketing (MBA, Certificate); personal financial planning (MBA, Certificate); project management (MBA, MS, Certificate); technology management (MS, Certificate); web development (Certificate); web programming in e-commerce (Certificate). Part-time and evening/weekend programs available. Post-baccalaureate distance learning degree programs offered (no on-campus study). *Entrance requirements:* Additional exam requirements/recommendations for international students: Required—TOEFL (minimum score 540 paper-based; 207 computer-based); Recommended—IELTS. Electronic applications accepted.

Clark Atlanta University, School of Business Administration, Department of Finance, Atlanta, GA 30314. Offers MBA. *Accreditation:* AACSB. Part-time programs available. *Entrance requirements:* For master's, GMAT.

Clark University, Graduate School, Graduate School of Management, Business Administration Program, Worcester, MA 01610-1477. Offers accounting (MBA); finance (MBA); global business (MBA); health care management (MBA); management (MBA); management of information technology (MBA); marketing (MBA). *Accreditation:* AACSB. Part-time and evening/weekend programs available. *Students:* 122 full-time (64 women), 113 part-time (42 women); includes 18 minority (3 African Americans, 9 Asian Americans or Pacific Islanders, 6 Hispanic Americans), 115 international. Average age 29. 235 applicants, 78% accepted, 80 enrolled. In 2006, 109 degrees awarded. *Degree requirements:* For master's, thesis optional. *Application deadline:* For fall admission, 6/1 priority date for domestic students; for spring admission, 12/1 priority date for domestic students. Applications are processed on a rolling basis. Application fee: $50. Electronic applications accepted. *Financial support:* In 2006–07, research assistantships with partial tuition reimbursements (averaging $6,000 per year), teaching assistantships with partial tuition reimbursements (averaging $6,000 per year) were awarded; fellowships with full and partial tuition reimbursements, career-related internships or fieldwork, Federal Work-Study, institutionally sponsored loans, and tuition waivers (partial) also available. Support available to part-time students. Financial award application deadline: 5/31. *Faculty research:* Organizational development, accounting, marketing, finance, human resource management. *Application contact:* Patricia Tollo, Admissions Director, 508-793-7406, Fax: 508-793-8822, E-mail: clarkmba@clarku.edu.

See Close-Up on page 257.

Clark University, Graduate School, Graduate School of Management, Program in Finance, Worcester, MA 01610-1477. Offers MSF. *Students:* 39 full-time (24 women), 12 part-time (5 women); includes 2 minority (1 African American, 1 Hispanic American), 42 international. Average age 28. 107 applicants, 89% accepted, 30 enrolled. In 2006, 13 degrees awarded. *Degree requirements:* For master's, thesis optional. *Application deadline:* For fall admission, 6/1 priority date for domestic students; for spring admission, 12/1 priority date for domestic students. Applications are processed on a rolling basis. Application fee: $50. Electronic applications accepted. *Financial support:* In 2006–07, research assistantships with partial tuition reimbursements (averaging $6,000 per year), teaching assistantships with partial tuition reimbursements (averaging $6,000 per year) were awarded; fellowships with full and partial tuition reimbursements, tuition waivers (partial) also available. Financial award application deadline: 5/31. *Application contact:* Patricia Tollo, Admissions Director, 508-793-7406, Fax: 508-793-8822, E-mail: clarkmba@clarku.edu.

See Close-Up on page 257.

Cleveland State University, College of Graduate Studies, Maxine Goodman Levin College of Urban Affairs, Program in Urban Planning, Design, and Development, Cleveland, OH 44115. Offers urban economic development (Certificate); urban planning, design, and development (MUPDD); urban real estate development and finance (Certificate); JD/MUPDD. *Accreditation:* ACSP. Part-time and evening/weekend programs available. *Faculty:* 25 full-time (10 women), 11 part-time/adjunct (3 women). *Students:* 25 full-time (10 women), 46 part-time (23 women); includes 13 minority (12 African Americans, 1 Asian American or Pacific Islander), 7 international. Average age 30. 63 applicants, 59% accepted, 20 enrolled. In 2006, 7 degrees awarded. *Degree requirements:* For master's, project or thesis. *Entrance requirements:* For master's, GRE General Test, minimum GPA of 3.0. Additional exam requirements/recommendations for international students: Required—TOEFL (minimum score 525 paper-based; 197 computer-based). *Application deadline:* For fall admission, 7/15 priority date for domestic students. Applications are processed on a rolling basis. Application fee: $30. *Financial support:* In 2006–07, 6 research assistantships with full and partial tuition reimbursements (averaging $6,960 per year) were awarded; teaching assistantships with full and partial tuition reimbursements, career-related internships or fieldwork, Federal Work-Study, tuition waivers (full and partial), and unspecified assistantships also available. Support available to part-time students. Financial award application deadline: 3/1. *Faculty research:* Community development, environmental issues. *Unit head:* Dr. Wendy A. Kellogg, Director, 216-687-5265, Fax: 216-687-9342, E-mail: wendy@urban.csuohio.edu. *Application contact:* Graduate Programs Coordinator, 216-523-7522, Fax: 216-687-5398, E-mail: gradprog@urban.csuohio.edu.

Cleveland State University, College of Graduate Studies, Nance College of Business Administration, Doctoral Programs in Business Administration, Cleveland, OH 44115. Offers business administration (DBA); finance (DBA); information systems (DBA); marketing (DBA); production/operations management (DBA). *Accreditation:* AACSB. In 2006, 3 degrees awarded. *Degree requirements:* For doctorate, thesis/dissertation. *Entrance requirements:* For doctorate, GMAT, MBA or equivalent. *Unit head:* Dr. Raj Shekhar G. Javalgi, Director, 216-687-3786, Fax: 216-687-9354, E-mail: r.javalgi@csuohio.edu.

Cleveland State University, College of Graduate Studies, Nance College of Business Administration, MBA Programs, Cleveland, OH 44115. Offers business statistics (MBA); finance (MBA); health care administration (MBA); marketing (MBA); operations management (MBA); JD/MBA; MSN/MBA. *Accreditation:* AACSB. Part-time and evening/weekend programs available. *Faculty:* 21 full-time (5 women), 10 part-time/adjunct (1 woman). *Students:* 276 full-time (119 women), 623 part-time (279 women); includes 120 minority (74 African Americans, 3 American Indian/Alaska Native, 32 Asian Americans or Pacific Islanders, 11 Hispanic Americans), 108 international. Average age 28. 530 applicants, 51% accepted, 146 enrolled. In 2006, 308 degrees awarded. *Entrance requirements:* For master's, GMAT or GRE. Additional exam requirements/recommendations for international students: Required—TOEFL (minimum score 525 paper-based; 197 computer-based). *Application deadline:* For fall admission, 7/15 priority date for domestic students, 5/15 for international students; for spring admission, 12/15 priority date for domestic students, 11/1 for international students. Applications are processed on a rolling basis. Application fee: $30. *Financial support:* In 2006–07, 45 research assistantships with full and partial tuition reimbursements (averaging $6,960 per year), 1 teaching assistantship with full and partial tuition reimbursement (averaging $7,800 per year) were awarded; tuition waivers (full) and unspecified assistantships also available. Financial award application deadline: 5/17; financial award applicants required to submit FAFSA. Total annual research

Finance and Banking

Cleveland State University (continued)

expenditures: $63,645. *Unit head:* Bruce Gottschalk, Associate Dean, 216-687-3730, Fax: 216-687-5311, E-mail: cbacsu@csuohio.edu. *Application contact:* Patricia Hite, Director, Academic Program Support, 216-687-6925, Fax: 216-687-6888, E-mail: p.hite@csuohio.edu.

College for Financial Planning, Program in Financial Planning, Greenwood Village, CO 80111. Offers finance (MS); financial analysis (MS); personal financial planning (MS). Part-time and evening/weekend programs available. Postbaccalaureate distance learning degree programs offered (no on-campus study). *Faculty:* 4 full-time (0 women), 6 part-time/adjunct (1 woman). *Students:* Average age 41. 250 applicants, 96% accepted. In 2006, 95 degrees awarded. *Degree requirements:* For master's, thesis. *Entrance requirements:* Additional exam requirements/recommendations for international students: Required—TOEFL (minimum score 550 paper-based; 213 computer-based). *Application deadline:* Applications are processed on a rolling basis. Application fee: $75. Electronic applications accepted. *Expenses:* Tuition: Full-time $4,275. One-time fee: $75 full-time. *Unit head:* Dr. Jesse B. Arman, Vice President, Academic Affairs, 303-220-4823, Fax: 303-220-4811, E-mail: jesse.arman@apollogrp.edu. *Application contact:* JuliAnna Sanchez, Senior Director of Enrollment, 303-220-4992, Fax: 303-220-1810, E-mail: julianna.sanchez@apollogrp.edu.

College of Santa Fe, Department of Business Administration, Santa Fe, NM 87505-7634. Offers finance (MBA); human resources (MBA). Program also available at Albuquerque campus. Part-time and evening/weekend programs available. *Entrance requirements:* For master's, minimum GPA of 3.0 in last 60 hours (preferred).

Columbia University, Graduate School of Business, Doctoral Program in Business, New York, NY 10027. Offers business (PhD), including accounting, decision, risk, and operations, finance and economics, management, marketing. *Accreditation:* AACSB. *Faculty:* 118 full-time (14 women), 106 part-time/adjunct (18 women). *Students:* 114 full-time (38 women); includes 3 Hispanic Americans, 96 international. Average age 27. 636 applicants, 6% accepted, 18 enrolled. In 2006, 15 degrees awarded. *Degree requirements:* For doctorate, thesis/dissertation, major field exam, research paper, thesis proposal, comprehensive exam, registration. *Entrance requirements:* For doctorate, GMAT, 2 letters of reference, resumé. Additional exam requirements/recommendations for international students: Required—TOEFL. *Application deadline:* For fall admission, 1/1 for domestic and international students. Application fee: $75. Electronic applications accepted. *Expenses: Contact institution. Financial support:* In 2006–07, fellowships with full tuition reimbursements (averaging $20,500 per year), research assistantships (averaging $4,000 per year) were awarded; teaching assistantships, career-related internships or fieldwork, institutionally sponsored loans, health care benefits, tuition waivers (full), and unspecified assistantships also available. *Unit head:* Elizabeth Elam Chang, Administrative Director, 212-854-2836, Fax: 212-932-2359, E-mail: phdinfo@gsb.columbia.edu.

Columbia University, Graduate School of Business, MBA Program, New York, NY 10027. Offers accounting (MBA); decision, risk, and operations (MBA); entrepreneurship (MBA); finance and economics (MBA); human resource management (MBA); international business (MBA); management (MBA); marketing (MBA); media (MBA); real estate (MBA); social enterprise (MBA); DDS/MBA; JD/MBA; MBA/MIA; MBA/MPH; MBA/MS; MD/MBA. *Faculty:* 118 full-time (14 women), 106 part-time/adjunct (18 women). *Students:* 1,242 full-time (428 women); includes 291 minority (65 African Americans, 5 American Indian/Alaska Native, 189 Asian Americans or Pacific Islanders, 32 Hispanic Americans), 392 international. Average age 28. 5,372 applicants, 17% accepted, 726 enrolled. In 2006, 682 degrees awarded. *Entrance requirements:* For master's, GMAT, 2 letters of recommendation. Additional exam requirements/recommendations for international students: Required—TOEFL. *Application deadline:* For fall admission, 4/20 for domestic students, 3/1 for international students; for spring admission, 10/12 for domestic and international students. Applications are processed on a rolling basis. Application fee: $215. Electronic applications accepted. *Financial support:* Fellowships, research assistantships, teaching assistantships, career-related internships or fieldwork, Federal Work-Study, institutionally sponsored loans, scholarships/grants, and unspecified assistantships available. Financial award applicants required to submit FAFSA. *Unit head:* Prof. Amir Ziv, Vice Dean of Students and the MBA Program, 212-854-3485, Fax: 212-932-0545, E-mail: az50@columbia.edu. *Application contact:* Linda B. Meehan, Assistant Dean of Admissions, 212-854-1961, Fax: 212-662-6754, E-mail: apply@claven.gsb.columbia.edu.

Concordia University Wisconsin, Graduate Programs, School of Business and Legal Studies, MBA Program, Mequon, WI 53097-2402. Offers finance (MBA); health care administration (MBA); human resource management (MBA); international business (MBA); international business-English/Chinese (MBA); management (MBA); management information services (MBA); managerial communications (MBA); marketing (MBA); public administration (MBA); risk management (MBA). Postbaccalaureate distance learning degree programs offered (minimal on-campus study). *Students:* 504 (249 women). In 2006, 110 degrees awarded. *Degree requirements:* For master's, thesis or alternative, comprehensive exam. *Entrance requirements:* Additional exam requirements/recommendations for international students: Required—TOEFL. *Application deadline:* For fall admission, 8/1 priority date for domestic students; for spring admission, 1/15 for domestic students. Applications are processed on a rolling basis. Application fee: $50. *Expenses: Contact institution. Financial support:* Application deadline: 8/1. *Unit head:* Dr. David Borst, Director, 262-243-4298, Fax: 262-243-4428, E-mail: david.borst@cuw.edu.

Cornell University, Graduate School, Graduate Field of Management, Ithaca, NY 14853-0001. Offers accounting (PhD); behavioral decision theory (PhD); finance (PhD); marketing (PhD); organizational behavior (PhD); production and operations management (PhD). *Accreditation:* AACSB. *Faculty:* 57 full-time (11 women). *Students:* 38 full-time (14 women); includes 2 minority (both Asian Americans or Pacific Islanders), 20 international. Average age 31. 457 applicants, 5% accepted, 8 enrolled. In 2006, 4 doctorates awarded. *Degree requirements:* For doctorate, thesis/dissertation, comprehensive exam. *Entrance requirements:* For doctorate, GMAT or GRE General Test. Additional exam requirements/recommendations for international students: Required—TOEFL (minimum score 600 paper-based; 250 computer-based). *Application deadline:* For fall admission, 1/3 for domestic students. Application fee: $60. Electronic applications accepted. *Expenses: Contact institution.* Full-time tuition and fees vary according to program. *Financial support:* In 2006–07, 37 students received support, including 2 fellowships with full tuition reimbursements available, 31 research assistantships with full tuition reimbursements available, 4 teaching assistantships with full tuition reimbursements available; institutionally sponsored loans, scholarships/grants, health care benefits, tuition waivers (full and partial), and unspecified assistantships also available. Financial award applicants required to submit FAFSA. *Faculty research:* Operations and manufacturing. *Unit head:* Director of Graduate Studies, 607-255-3669. *Application contact:* Graduate Field Assistant, 607-255-9431, E-mail: js_phd@cornell.edu.

Cornell University, Graduate School, Graduate Fields of Arts and Sciences, Field of Economics, Ithaca, NY 14853-0001. Offers applied economics (PhD); basic analytical economics (PhD); econometrics and economic statistics (PhD); economic development and planning (PhD); economic theory (PhD); industrial organization and control (PhD); international economics (PhD); labor economics (PhD); monetary and macroeconomics (PhD); public finance (PhD). *Faculty:* 64 full-time (10 women). *Students:* 108 full-time (39 women); includes 8 minority (4 African Americans, 3 Asian Americans or Pacific Islanders, 1 Hispanic American), 67 international. Average age 30. 575 applicants, 9% accepted, 20 enrolled. In 2006, 22 doctorates awarded. *Degree requirements:* For doctorate, thesis/dissertation, comprehensive exam. *Entrance requirements:* For doctorate, GRE General Test, 3 letters of recommendation. Additional exam requirements/recommendations for international students: Required—TOEFL (minimum score 550 paper-based; 213 computer-based). *Application deadline:* For fall admission, 1/15 priority date for domestic students. Application fee: $60. Electronic applications accepted. *Expenses:* Tuition: Full-time $32,800. Full-time tuition and fees vary according to program. *Financial support:* In 2006–07, 90 students received support, including 27 fellowships with full tuition reimbursements available, 13 research assistantships with full tuition reimbursements available, 50 teaching assistantships with full tuition reimbursements available; institutionally sponsored loans, scholarships/grants, health care benefits, tuition waivers (full and partial), and unspecified assistantships also available. Financial award applicants required to submit FAFSA. *Faculty research:* Learning and games, economics of education, political economy, transfer payments, time series and nonparametrics. *Unit head:* Director of Graduate Studies, 607-255-4893, Fax: 607-255-2818. *Application contact:* Graduate Field Assistant, 607-255-4893, Fax: 607-255-2818, E-mail: econ_phd@cornell.edu.

Dallas Baptist University, College of Adult Education, Professional Development Program, Dallas, TX 75211-9299. Offers accounting (MA); business (MA); church leadership (MA); corporate management (MA); counseling (MA); criminal justice (MA); English as a second language (MA); finance (MA); higher education (MA); leadership studies (MA); management (MA); management information systems (MA); marketing (MA); missions (MA). Part-time and evening/weekend programs available. *Faculty:* 49 full-time (21 women), 112 part-time/adjunct (46 women). *Students:* 31 full-time, 65 part-time. 51 applicants, 49% accepted, 15 enrolled. In 2006, 41 degrees awarded. Application fee: $25. *Expenses:* Tuition: Full-time $8,370; part-time $465 per credit hour. Required fees: $465 per credit hour. *Financial support:* Tuition waivers (full and partial) available. *Unit head:* Lynda Jackson, Director, 214-333-6830, Fax: 214-333-5558, E-mail: graduate@dbu.edu. *Application contact:* Kit P. Montgomery, Director of Graduate Programs, 214-333-5242, Fax: 214-333-5579, E-mail: graduate@dbu.edu.

Dallas Baptist University, Graduate School of Business, Business Administration Program, Dallas, TX 75211-9299. Offers accounting (MBA); business communication (MBA); conflict resolution management (MBA); e-business (MBA); entrepreneurship (MBA); finance (MBA); health care management (MBA); international business (MBA); management (MBA); management information systems (MBA); marketing (MBA); project management (MBA); technology and engineering management (MBA). *Accreditation:* ACBSP. Part-time and evening/weekend programs available. Postbaccalaureate distance learning degree programs offered (no on-campus study). *Faculty:* 49 full-time (21 women), 112 part-time/adjunct (46 women). *Students:* 103 full-time, 318 part-time. 226 applicants, 38% accepted. In 2006, 124 degrees awarded. *Entrance requirements:* For master's, GMAT, minimum GPA of 3.0. Additional exam requirements/recommendations for international students: Required—TOEFL. *Application deadline:* Applications are processed on a rolling basis. Application fee: $25. Electronic applications accepted. *Expenses:* Tuition: Full-time $8,370; part-time $465 per credit hour. Required fees: $465 per credit hour. *Financial support:* Career-related internships or fieldwork, Federal Work-Study, institutionally sponsored loans, scholarships/grants, and tuition waivers (full and partial) available. Support available to part-time students. *Faculty research:* Sports management, services marketing, retailing, strategic management, financial planning/investments. *Unit head:* Dr. Sandra S. Reid, Director, 214-333-5244, Fax: 214-333-5293, E-mail: graduate@dbu.edu. *Application contact:* Kit P. Montgomery, Director of Graduate Programs, 214-333-5242, Fax: 214-333-5579, E-mail: graduate@dbu.edu.

Davenport University, Sneden Graduate School, Warren, MI 48092-5209. Offers accounting (MBA); commerce (MBA); finance (MBA); health care management (MBA); human resources management (MBA); management (MBA). *Entrance requirements:* For master's, minimum undergraduate GPA of 2.7.

Davenport University, Sneden Graduate School, Dearborn, MI 48126-3799. Offers accounting (MBA); e-business (MBA); finance (MBA); global business (MBA); health care management (MBA); human resources management (MBA); management (MBA); marketing (MBA). Part-time and evening/weekend programs available. Postbaccalaureate distance learning degree programs offered (no on-campus study). *Entrance requirements:* For master's, minimum GPA of 2.7, previous course work in accounting and statistics. *Faculty research:* Accounting, international accounting, social and environmental accounting, finance.

DePaul University, Charles H. Kellstadt Graduate School of Business, Department of Finance, Chicago, IL 60604-2287. Offers behavioral finance (MBA); computational finance (MS); finance (MBA, MSF); financial analysis (MBA); financial management and control (MBA); international marketing and finance (MBA); managerial finance (MBA); real estate (MS); real estate finance and investment (MBA); strategy, execution and valuation (MBA). Part-time and evening/weekend programs available. *Faculty:* 21 full-time (3 women), 19 part-time/adjunct (1 woman). *Students:* 309 full-time (90 women), 212 part-time (57 women); includes 70 minority (14 African Americans, 41 Asian Americans or Pacific Islanders, 15 Hispanic Americans), 54 international. Average age 29. In 2006, 239 degrees awarded. *Entrance requirements:* For master's, GMAT, 2 letters of recommendation, resumé. Additional exam requirements/recommendations for international students: Required—TOEFL (minimum score 550 paper-based; 213 computer-based). *Application deadline:* For fall admission, 7/1 for domestic students; for winter admission, 10/1 for domestic students; for spring admission, 2/1 for domestic students. Applications are processed on a rolling basis. Application fee: $60. Electronic applications accepted. *Financial support:* In 2006–07, 8 students received support, including 6 research assistantships with partial tuition reimbursements available (averaging $5,100 per year). Support available to part-time students. Financial award application deadline: 4/1; financial award applicants required to submit FAFSA. *Faculty research:* Derivatives, valuation, international finance, real estate, corporate finance. *Unit head:* Ali M. Falemi, Professor and Chair, 312-362-8820, Fax: 312-362-6566. *Application contact:* Christopher E. Kinsella, Director of Cohort MBA Programs, 312-362-8810, Fax: 312-362-6677, E-mail: kgsb@depaul.edu.

DePaul University, Charles H. Kellstadt Graduate School of Business, School of Accountancy and Management Information Systems, Chicago, IL 60604-2287. Offers accountancy (M Acc, MSA); business information technology (MS); e-business (MBA, MS); financial management and control (MBA); management accounting (MBA); management information systems (MBA); taxation (MST). Part-time and evening/weekend programs available. *Faculty:* 30 full-time (9 women), 54 part-time/adjunct (7 women). *Students:* 127 full-time (53 women), 209 part-time (101 women); includes 53 minority (13 African Americans, 3 American Indian/Alaska Native, 28 Asian Americans or Pacific Islanders, 9 Hispanic Americans), 56 international. Average age 30. In 2006, 141 degrees awarded. *Entrance requirements:* For master's, GMAT, 2 letters of recommendation, resumé. Additional exam requirements/recommendations for international students: Required—TOEFL (minimum score 550 paper-based; 213 computer-based). *Application deadline:* For fall admission, 7/1 for domestic students; for winter admission, 10/1 for domestic students; for spring admission, 2/1 for domestic students. Applications are processed on a rolling basis. Application fee: $60. *Financial support:* In 2006–07, 7 research assistantships with full tuition reimbursements (averaging $4,100 per year) were awarded; institutionally sponsored loans also available. Financial award application deadline: 4/2. *Faculty research:* Tax policy, property transactions, stock options as compensation, standards setting, activity-based costing in health care. *Application contact:* Christopher E. Kinsella, Director of Cohort MBA Programs, 312-362-8810, Fax: 312-362-6677, E-mail: kgsb@depaul.edu.

DePaul University, School of Public Service, Chicago, IL 60604-2287. Offers financial administration management (Certificate); health administration (Certificate); health law and policy (MS); international public services (MS); metropolitan planning (Certificate); public administration (MS); public service management (MS), including association management, fundraising and philanthropy, healthcare administration, higher education administration, metropolitan planning, non-profit administration, public administration, public policy; public services (Certificate); JD/MS; MA/MS. Part-time and evening/weekend programs available. Postbaccalaureate distance learning degree programs offered (minimal on-campus study). *Faculty:* 11 full-time (2 women), 19 part-time/adjunct (16 women). *Students:* 195 full-time (146 women), 132 part-time (89 women); includes 114 minority (58 African Americans, 1 American Indian/Alaska Native, 27 Asian Americans or Pacific Islanders, 28 Hispanic Americans). 140 applicants, 96% accepted, 96 enrolled. In 2006, 89 degrees awarded. *Degree requirements:* For master's, thesis or integrative seminar. *Entrance requirements:* For master's, minimum GPA of 2.7. Additional exam requirements/recommendations for international students: Required—TOEFL (minimum score 550 paper-based; 213 computer-based; 80 iBT), IELTS (minimum score 7). *Application deadline:* Applications are processed on a rolling basis. Application fee: $25. Electronic applications accepted. *Financial support:* In 2006–07, 28 students received support, including 3 research assistantships with full tuition reimbursements available (averaging $7,000 per year); career-related internships or fieldwork, Federal Work-Study, institutionally sponsored loans, scholarships/grants, and tuition waivers (partial) also available. Support available to part-time students. Financial award application deadline: 7/1; financial award applicants required to submit FAFSA. *Faculty research:* Government financing, transportation, leadership, health care, volunteerism and organizational behavior, non-profit organizations. Total annual research expenditures: $20,000. *Unit head:* Dr. J. Patrick Murphy, Director, 312-362-5608, Fax: 312-362-5506, E-mail: jpmurphy@depaul.edu. *Application contact:* Megan B. Balderston, Director of Admissions and Marketing, 312-362-5565, Fax: 312-362-5506, E-mail: pubserv@depaul.edu.

DeVry University, Keller Graduate School of Management, Oakbrook Terrace, IL 60181. Offers accounting and financial management (MAFM); business administration (MBA); human resources management (MHRM); information systems management (MISM); network and communications management (MNCM); project management (MPM); public administration (MPA); telecommunications management (MTM). Part-time and evening/weekend programs available. Postbaccalaureate distance learning degree programs offered (no on-campus study). *Degree requirements:* For master's, business plan (MBA), capstone project (MHRM, MPM, MTM, MAFM). *Entrance requirements:* For master's, GMAT, GRE General Test, or institutional assessment, interview. Additional exam requirements/recommendations for international students: Required—TOEFL (minimum score 500 paper-based; 173 computer-based). Electronic applications accepted.

See Close-Up on page 265.

Dowling College, School of Business, Oakdale, NY 11769-1999. Offers aviation management (MBA, Certificate); banking and finance (MBA, Certificate); general management (MBA); public management (MBA, Certificate); total quality management (MBA, Certificate). Part-time and evening/weekend programs available. *Students:* 239 full-time (105 women), 566 part-time (273 women); includes 132 African Americans, 55 Asian Americans or Pacific Islanders, 48 Hispanic Americans, 3 international. Average age 31. 414 applicants, 82% accepted, 166 enrolled. In 2006, 471 master's, 1 other advanced degree awarded. *Degree requirements:* For master's, thesis optional. *Entrance requirements:* For master's, minimum GPA of 2.8, 2 letters of recommendation, courses in accounting and finance or seminar in accounting/finance, resumé. Additional exam requirements/recommendations for international students: Required—TOEFL (minimum score 550 paper-based). *Application deadline:* For fall admission, 9/1 priority date for domestic students; for winter admission, 1/1 priority date for domestic students; for spring admission, 2/1 priority date for domestic students. Applications are processed on a rolling basis. Application fee: $25. Electronic applications accepted. *Expenses:* Tuition: Full-time $16,008; part-time $667 per credit. Tuition and fees vary according to course load. *Financial support:* In 2006–07, 126 students received support, including 30 research assistantships (averaging $3,150 per year); career-related internships or fieldwork, Federal Work-Study, scholarships/grants, and unspecified assistantships also available. Support available to part-time students. Financial award application deadline: 6/30; financial award applicants required to submit FAFSA. *Faculty research:* International finance, computer applications, labor relations, executive development. *Unit head:* Dr. Elana Zolfo, Dean of the School of Business, 631-244-3190, Fax: 631-244-1018, E-mail: zdfoe@dowling.edu. *Application contact:* Franks S. Pizzardi, Director of Admissions Operations, 631-244-3227, Fax: 631-244-1059, E-mail: pizzardf@dowling.edu.

Drexel University, LeBow College of Business, Department of Finance, Philadelphia, PA 19104-2875. Offers MS. *Degree requirements:* For master's, seminar paper. *Entrance requirements:* For master's, GMAT, minimum GPA of 2.75. Additional exam requirements/recommendations for international students: Required—TOEFL. Electronic applications accepted. *Faculty research:* Investment analysis, portfolio mix, capital budgeting, banking and financial institutions, international finance.

Drexel University, LeBow College of Business, Program in Business Administration, Philadelphia, PA 19104-2875. Offers business administration (MBA, PhD, APC), including accounting (MBA, PhD), decision sciences (PhD), economics (MBA, PhD), finance (MBA, PhD), legal studies (MBA), management (MBA), marketing (MBA, PhD), organizational sciences (PhD), quantitative methods (MBA), strategic management (PhD). *Accreditation:* AACSB. Part-time and evening/weekend programs available. Postbaccalaureate distance learning degree programs offered (minimal on-campus study). Terminal master's awarded for partial completion of doctoral program. *Entrance requirements:* For master's, GMAT, minimum GPA of 2.75; for doctorate, GMAT. Additional exam requirements/recommendations for international students: Required—TOEFL. Electronic applications accepted. *Faculty research:* Decision support systems, individual and group behavior, operations research, techniques and strategy.

Eastern Michigan University, Graduate School, College of Business, Program in Business Administration, Ypsilanti, MI 48197. Offers business administration (MBA); e-business (MBA); enterprise business intelligence (MBA); entrepreneurship (MBA); finance (MBA); human resources (MBA); information systems (MBA); internal auditing (MBA); international business (MBA); nonprofit management (MBA); supply chain management (MBA). *Accreditation:* AACSB. Part-time and evening/weekend programs available. Postbaccalaureate distance learning degree programs offered (minimal on-campus study). *Students:* 98 full-time (36 women), 192 part-time (86 women); includes 50 minority (26 African Americans, 19 Asian Americans or Pacific Islanders, 5 Hispanic Americans), 76 international. Average age 29. In 2006, 109 degrees awarded. *Entrance requirements:* For master's, GMAT. Additional exam requirements/recommendations for international students: Required—TOEFL. *Application deadline:* For fall admission, 5/15 priority date for domestic students, 5/1 priority date for international students; for winter admission, 10/15 priority date for domestic students, 10/1 priority date for international students; for spring admission, 3/15 priority date for domestic students, 3/1 priority date for international students. Applications are processed on a rolling basis. Application fee: $35. *Expenses:* Tuition, state resident: part-time $341 per credit hour. Tuition, nonresident: full-time $16,104; part-time $671 per credit hour. Required fees: $816; $34 per credit hour. $40 per term. One-time fee: $82 full-time. Tuition and fees vary according to course level, course load, degree level and reciprocity agreements. *Financial support:* Fellowships, research assistantships with full tuition reimbursements, teaching assistantships with full tuition reimbursements, career-related internships or fieldwork, Federal Work-Study, institutionally sponsored loans, scholarships/grants, tuition waivers (partial), and unspecified assistantships available. Support available to part-time students. Financial award applicants required to submit FAFSA. *Unit head:* Dawn Gaymer, Assistant Dean, Graduate Business Programs, 734-487-4444, Fax: 734-483-1316, E-mail: dawn.malone@emich.edu. *Application contact:* K. Michelle Henry, Coordinator, 734-487-4444, Fax: 734-483-1316, E-mail: michelle.henry@emich.edu.

Eastern University, Graduate Business Programs, St. Davids, PA 19087-3696. Offers business administration (MBA), including accounting, economics, finance, management, marketing; economic development (MBA, MS); nonprofit management (MBA, MS); M Div/MBA; M Div/MS. Part-time and evening/weekend programs available. *Degree requirements:* For master's, thesis (for some programs). *Entrance requirements:* For master's, GMAT (MBA), minimum GPA of 2.5. Expenses: Contact institution. *Faculty research:* Micro-level economic development, China welfare and economic development, macroethics, micro- and macro-level economic development in transitional economics, organizational effectiveness.

East Tennessee State University, School of Graduate Studies, College of Business and Technology, Department of Economics, Finance, and Urban Studies, Johnson City, TN 37614. Offers city management (MCM); community development (MPM); general administration (MPM); municipal service management (MPM); urban and regional economic development (MPM); urban and regional planning (MPM). *Degree requirements:* For master's, internship, oral defense of thesis, research report. *Entrance requirements:* For master's, GRE General Test,

minimum GPA of 3.0. Additional exam requirements/recommendations for international students: Required—TOEFL (minimum score 550 paper-based; 213 computer-based).

Emory University, Roberto C. Goizueta Business School, Doctoral Programs in Business, Atlanta, GA 30322-1100. Offers accounting (PhD); finance (PhD); information systems (PhD); marketing (PhD); organization and management (PhD). *Degree requirements:* For doctorate, thesis/dissertation, comprehensive exam. *Entrance requirements:* Additional exam requirements/recommendations for international students: Required—TOEFL (minimum score 600 paper-based; 250 computer-based). Electronic applications accepted. *Expenses:* Tuition: Full-time $30,246. *Faculty research:* Financial markets, banking, corporate disclosure, investor relations, marketing strategy.

Fairfield University, Charles F. Dolan School of Business, Fairfield, CT 06824-5195. Offers accounting (MBA, MS, CAS); finance (MBA, MS, CAS); general management (MBA); human resource management (MBA, CAS); information systems and operations (MBA); information systems and operations management (CAS); international business (MBA, CAS); marketing (MBA, CAS); taxation (MBA, MS, CAS). *Accreditation:* AACSB. Part-time and evening/weekend programs available. *Faculty:* 43 full-time (17 women), 2 part-time/adjunct (1 woman). *Students:* 65 full-time (31 women), 125 part-time (54 women); includes 4 Asian Americans or Pacific Islanders, 4 Hispanic Americans, 22 international. Average age 27. 99 applicants, 45% accepted, 38 enrolled. In 2006, 78 degrees awarded. *Degree requirements:* For master's, registration. *Entrance requirements:* For master's, GMAT, 2 letters of reference, resumé. Additional exam requirements/recommendations for international students: Required—TOEFL (minimum score 550 paper-based; 213 computer-based; 79 iBT). *Application deadline:* For fall admission, 8/15 priority date for domestic students, 5/15 priority date for international students; for spring admission, 11/15 priority date for domestic students, 10/15 priority date for international students. Applications are processed on a rolling basis. Application fee: $55. Electronic applications accepted. *Expenses:* Contact institution. *Financial support:* Unspecified assistantships available. *Faculty research:* Optimal investment strategies, organization structure, international finance, strategic management, customer behavior. *Unit head:* Dr. Norman A. Solomon, Dean, 203-254-4000 Ext. 4070, Fax: 203-254-4105, E-mail: nsolomon@mail.fairfield.edu. *Application contact:* Marianne Gumpper, Director of Graduate and Continuing Studies Admissions, 203-254-4184, Fax: 203-254-4073, E-mail: gradadmis@mail.fairfield.edu.

See Close-Up on page 271.

Fairleigh Dickinson University, College at Florham, Silberman College of Business, Department of Economics, Finance, and International Business, Program in Finance, Madison, NJ 07940-1099. Offers MBA, Certificate. *Students:* 28 full-time (6 women), 67 part-time (30 women), 4 international. Average age 30. 39 applicants, 72% accepted, 25 enrolled. In 2006, 34 degrees awarded. *Application deadline:* Applications are processed on a rolling basis. Application fee: $40.

Fairleigh Dickinson University, Metropolitan Campus, Silberman College of Business, Department of Economics, Finance and International Business, Program in Finance, Teaneck, NJ 07666-1914. Offers MBA, Certificate. *Students:* 52 full-time (15 women), 24 part-time (10 women), 53 international. Average age 26. 78 applicants, 69% accepted, 23 enrolled. In 2006, 35 degrees awarded. *Application deadline:* Applications are processed on a rolling basis. Application fee: $40. *Unit head:* Dr. Evangelos Djimopoulos, Chairperson, Department of Economics, Finance and International Business, 201-692-2000.

Florida Agricultural and Mechanical University, Division of Graduate Studies, Research, and Continuing Education, School of Business and Industry, Tallahassee, FL 32307-3200. Offers accounting (MBA); finance (MBA); management information systems (MBA); marketing (MBA). *Degree requirements:* For master's, residency. *Entrance requirements:* For master's, GMAT, minimum GPA of 3.0.

Florida Atlantic University, College of Business, Department of Finance, Boca Raton, FL 33431-0991. Offers MS. *Faculty:* 14 full-time (4 women), 4 part-time/adjunct (0 women). *Students:* 1 full-time (0 women), 7 part-time (2 women). Average age 32. 1 applicant, 100% accepted, 1 enrolled. *Degree requirements:* For master's, thesis optional. *Entrance requirements:* For master's, GMAT or GRE, minimum GPA of 3.0. Additional exam requirements/recommendations for international students: Required—TOEFL (minimum score 600 paper-based; 250 computer-based). *Application deadline:* For fall admission, 7/1 priority date for domestic students, 2/15 priority date for international students; for winter admission, 11/1 priority date for domestic students, 8/15 priority date for international students; for spring admission, 4/1 priority date for domestic students, 1/15 priority date for international students. Applications are processed on a rolling basis. Application fee: $30. *Expenses:* Tuition, area resident: Full-time $4,394. Tuition, nonresident: full-time $16,441. *Unit head:* Dr. Emilio Zarruk, Chair, 561-297-3995.

Florida Atlantic University, College of Business, Department of Management, International Business and Entrepreneurship, Boca Raton, FL 33431-0991. Offers business administration (Exec MBA, MBA), including accounting (MBA), electronic commerce (MBA), finance (MBA), financial planning (MBA), global entrepreneurship (MBA), health administration (MBA), international business (MBA), marketing (MBA), operations management (MBA), real estate (MBA), sport management (MBA). *Faculty:* 64 full-time (17 women), 15 part-time/adjunct (3 women). *Students:* 215 full-time (89 women), 365 part-time (189 women); includes 150 minority (49 African Americans, 2 American Indian/Alaska Native, 36 Asian Americans or Pacific Islanders, 63 Hispanic Americans), 54 international. Average age 32. 414 applicants, 55% accepted, 167 enrolled. In 2006, 196 master's awarded. *Degree requirements:* For master's, thesis optional. *Entrance requirements:* For master's, GMAT, minimum GPA of 3.0. Additional exam requirements/recommendations for international students: Required—TOEFL (minimum score 600 paper-based; 250 computer-based). *Application deadline:* For fall admission, 7/1 priority date for domestic students, 2/15 priority date for international students; for winter admission, 11/1 priority date for domestic students, 8/15 priority date for international students; for spring admission, 4/1 priority date for domestic students, 1/15 priority date for international students. Applications are processed on a rolling basis. Application fee: $30. Electronic applications accepted. *Expenses:* Tuition, area resident: Full-time $4,394. Tuition, nonresident: full-time $16,441. *Financial support:* Research assistantships, teaching assistantships, career-related internships or fieldwork, Federal Work-Study, institutionally sponsored loans, tuition waivers (partial), and unspecified assistantships available. Support available to part-time students. Financial award application deadline: 3/1; financial award applicants required to submit FAFSA. *Unit head:* Dr. Brenda Richey, Head, 561-297-3194, E-mail: brichey@fau.edu. *Application contact:* Fredrick G. Taylor, Graduate Adviser, 561-297-2768, Fax: 561-297-1315, E-mail: mba@fau.edu.

Florida International University, Alvah H. Chapman, Jr. Graduate School of Business, Department of Finance, Miami, FL 33199. Offers MSF. Part-time and evening/weekend programs available. *Faculty:* 18 full-time (3 women). *Students:* 81 full-time (25 women), 12 part-time (3 women); includes 57 minority (9 African Americans, 2 Asian Americans or Pacific Islanders, 46 Hispanic Americans), 12 international. Average age 28. 150 applicants, 38% accepted, 33 enrolled. In 2006, 62 degrees awarded. *Entrance requirements:* For master's, GMAT, minimum AACSB index of 1000, minimum GPA of 3.0. Additional exam requirements/recommendations for international students: Required—TOEFL. *Application deadline:* For fall admission, 4/1 priority date for domestic students; for spring admission, 10/1 for domestic students. Applications are processed on a rolling basis. Application fee: $25. *Expenses:* Tuition, state resident: part-time $249 per credit hour. Tuition, nonresident: part-time $753 per credit hour. Tuition and fees vary according to program. *Unit head:* Dr. William Welch, Chairperson, 305-348-2680, Fax: 305-348-4245, E-mail: william.welch@fiu.edu.

Florida State University, Graduate Studies, College of Business, Tallahassee, FL 32306. Offers accounting (M Acc), including accounting information systems, assurance services, corporate accounting, taxation; business administration (MBA, PhD), including accounting

Finance and Banking

Florida State University (continued)
(PhD), finance (PhD), information and management science (PhD), management (PhD), marketing (PhD), risk and insurance (PhD); insurance (MSM); management information systems (MS); JD/MBA. *Accreditation:* AACSB. Part-time and evening/weekend programs available. Postbaccalaureate distance learning degree programs offered (no on-campus study). *Faculty:* 107 full-time (26 women), 21 part-time/adjunct (2 women). *Students:* 145 full-time (62 women), 444 part-time (143 women); includes 147 minority (58 African Americans, 3 American Indian/Alaska Native, 45 Asian Americans or Pacific Islanders, 41 Hispanic Americans). Average age 29. 789 applicants, 50% accepted, 321 enrolled. In 2006, 263 master's, 19 doctorates awarded. Terminal master's awarded for partial completion of doctoral program. *Degree requirements:* For master's, registration; for doctorate, thesis/dissertation, comprehensive exam, registration. *Entrance requirements:* For master's, GMAT, substantial work experience (MBA, MS), minimum GPA of 3.0, letters of recommendation; for doctorate, GMAT, minimum graduate GPA of 3.5, letters of recommendation. Additional exam requirements/recommendations for international students: Required—TOEFL (minimum score 600 paper-based; 250 computer-based). *Application deadline:* For fall admission, 5/1 for domestic and international students; for spring admission, 10/1 for domestic students, 9/1 for international students. Applications are processed on a rolling basis. Application fee: $30. Electronic applications accepted. *Expenses:* Tuition, state resident: full-time $5,822; part-time $243 per credit hour. Tuition, nonresident: full-time $20,976; part-time $874 per credit hour. Tuition and fees vary according to program. *Financial support:* In 2006–07, 126 students received support, including 40 fellowships with partial tuition reimbursements available (averaging $4,600 per year), 37 research assistantships with partial tuition reimbursements available (averaging $4,600 per year), 49 teaching assistantships with partial tuition reimbursements available (averaging $10,500 per year); unspecified assistantships also available. Financial award application deadline: 1/1. Total annual research expenditures: $1.5 million. *Unit head:* Dr. Caryn Beck-Duolley, Dean, 850-644-3090, Fax: 850-644-0915. *Application contact:* Lisa Beverly, Coordinator, Graduate Programs Admissions, 850-644-6458, Fax: 850-644-0588, E-mail: lbeverly@cob.fsu.edu.

Fordham University, Graduate School of Business, New York, NY 10023. Offers accounting (MBA); communications and media management (MBA); finance (MBA, MS); information systems (MBA, MS); management systems (MBA); marketing (MBA); media management (MS); taxation (MS); JD/MBA; MBA/MIM; MS/MBA. *Accreditation:* AACSB. Part-time and evening/weekend programs available. *Faculty:* 87 full-time, 41 part-time/adjunct. *Students:* 345 full-time (132 women), 1,183 part-time (448 women); includes 238 minority (59 African Americans, 1 American Indian/Alaska Native, 116 Asian Americans or Pacific Islanders, 62 Hispanic Americans), 77 international. 1,081 applicants, 65% accepted, 422 enrolled. In 2006, 454 degrees awarded. *Entrance requirements:* For master's, GMAT. Additional exam requirements/recommendations for international students: Required—TOEFL (minimum score 600 paper-based; 250 computer-based). *Application deadline:* For fall admission, 6/1 priority date for domestic students, 5/1 priority date for international students; for winter admission, 11/1 priority date for domestic students, 10/1 priority date for international students; for spring admission, 3/1 priority date for domestic students, 2/1 priority date for international students. Applications are processed on a rolling basis. Application fee: $65. Electronic applications accepted. *Expenses: Contact institution. Financial support:* In 2006–07, 7 fellowships (averaging $27,000 per year), 128 research assistantships were awarded; career-related internships or fieldwork, institutionally sponsored loans, scholarships/grants, and unspecified assistantships also available. Support available to part-time students. Financial award application deadline: 5/1; financial award applicants required to submit FAFSA. *Unit head:* Dr. Howard Tuckman, Dean, 212-636-6165, Fax: 212-307-1779, E-mail: tuckman@fordham.edu. *Application contact:* Frank Fletcher, Director of Admissions and Financial Aid, 212-636-6200, Fax: 212-636-7076, E-mail: admissionsgb@fordham.edu.

Gannon University, School of Graduate Studies, College of Humanities, Business, and Education, School of Business, Program in Finance, Erie, PA 16541-0001. Offers Certificate. Part-time and evening/weekend programs available. *Entrance requirements:* For degree, GMAT. Additional exam requirements/recommendations for international students: Required—TOEFL (minimum score 500 paper-based; 173 computer-based). *Application deadline:* Applications are processed on a rolling basis. Application fee: $25. *Expenses:* Tuition: Full-time $12,240; part-time $680 per credit. Required fees: $496; $16 per credit. Tuition and fees vary according to course load, degree level, campus/location and program. *Financial support:* Career-related internships or fieldwork available. Financial award application deadline: 7/1; financial award applicants required to submit FAFSA. *Application contact:* Debra Meszaros, Director of Graduate Recruitment, 814-871-5819, Fax: 814-871-5827, E-mail: cfal@gannon.edu.

The George Washington University, Columbian College of Arts and Sciences, School of Public Policy and Public Administration, Washington, DC 20052. Offers public policy (MA, MPP), including environmental and resource policy (MA), philosophy and social policy (MA), women's studies (MA); public policy and administration (PhD); public policy and public administration (MPA), including budget and public finance, federal policy, politics, and management, international development management, managing public organizations, managing state and local governments and urban policy, nonprofit management, policy analysis and evaluation, public administration; JD/MPP; MPA/JD; PhD/MPP. Part-time and evening/weekend programs available. *Degree requirements:* For doctorate, thesis/dissertation, general exam. *Entrance requirements:* For master's, GRE General Test, minimum GPA of 3.0; for doctorate, GRE General Test, interview, minimum GPA of 3.0. Additional exam requirements/recommendations for international students: Required—TOEFL (minimum score 550 paper-based; 213 computer-based). Electronic applications accepted.

The George Washington University, Columbian College of Arts and Sciences, School of Public Policy and Public Administration, Programs in Public Policy and Public Administration, Program in Budget and Public Finance, Washington, DC 20052. Offers MPA. Part-time and evening/weekend programs available. *Entrance requirements:* For master's, GRE General Test. Additional exam requirements/recommendations for international students: Required—TOEFL.

The George Washington University, School of Business, Department of Finance, Washington, DC 20052. Offers finance (MSF, PhD); finance and investments (MBA); real estate development (MBA). Part-time and evening/weekend programs available. *Degree requirements:* For doctorate, thesis/dissertation. *Entrance requirements:* For master's, GMAT; for doctorate, GMAT or GRE. Additional exam requirements/recommendations for international students: Required—TOEFL.

Georgia Institute of Technology, Graduate Studies and Research, College of Management, Program in Business Administration, Atlanta, GA 30332-0001. Offers accounting (MBA); e-commerce (Certificate); engineering entrepreneurship (MBA); entrepreneurship (Certificate); finance (MBA); information technology management (MBA); international business (MBA, Certificate); management of technology (Certificate); marketing (MBA); operations management (MBA); organizational behavior (MBA); strategic management (MBA). *Accreditation:* AACSB.

Georgia Institute of Technology, Graduate Studies and Research, College of Management, Program in Management, Atlanta, GA 30332-0001. Offers accounting (PhD); finance (PhD); information technology management (PhD); marketing (PhD); operations management (PhD); organizational behavior (PhD); quantitative and computational finance (MS); strategic management (PhD). *Accreditation:* AACSB. *Degree requirements:* For doctorate, thesis/dissertation, oral exams, comprehensive exam. *Entrance requirements:* For master's and doctorate, GMAT. Additional exam requirements/recommendations for international students: Required—TOEFL. *Faculty research:* MIS, management of technology, international business, entrepreneurship, operations management.

Georgia State University, J. Mack Robinson College of Business, Department of Finance, Atlanta, GA 30303-3083. Offers MBA, MS, PhD. Part-time and evening/weekend programs available. *Faculty:* 19 full-time (2 women), 2 part-time/adjunct (1 woman). *Students:* 70 full-time (22 women), 172 part-time (38 women); includes 48 minority (14 African Americans, 27 Asian Americans or Pacific Islanders, 7 Hispanic Americans), 37 international. Average age 30. 137 applicants, 42% accepted, 39 enrolled. In 2006, 101 master's, 6 doctorates awarded. Terminal master's awarded for partial completion of doctoral program. *Degree requirements:* For doctorate, thesis/dissertation. *Entrance requirements:* For master's and doctorate, GMAT. Additional exam requirements/recommendations for international students: Required—TOEFL (minimum score 610 paper-based; 255 computer-based; 101 iBT). *Application deadline:* For fall admission, 5/1 for domestic students, 2/1 for international students; for spring admission, 10/15 for domestic students, 5/1 for international students. Applications are processed on a rolling basis. Application fee: $50. Electronic applications accepted. *Financial support:* Fellowships, research assistantships, teaching assistantships, career-related internships or fieldwork and tuition waivers (partial) available. Support available to part-time students. Financial award applicants required to submit FAFSA. *Unit head:* Dr. Gerald D. Gay, Chair, 404-651-2628, Fax: 404-651-2630, E-mail: ggay@gsu.edu.

Georgia State University, J. Mack Robinson College of Business, Department of Risk Management and Insurance, Program in Personal Financial Planning, Atlanta, GA 30303-3083. Offers MS, Certificate. *Students:* 11 full-time (3 women), 25 part-time (9 women); includes 7 minority (6 African Americans, 1 Asian American or Pacific Islander), 3 international. 14 applicants, 79% accepted, 10 enrolled. In 2006, 12 degrees awarded. *Entrance requirements:* For master's, GMAT. Additional exam requirements/recommendations for international students: Required—TOEFL (minimum score 610 paper-based; 255 computer-based; 101 iBT). *Application deadline:* For fall admission, 5/1 for domestic students, 2/1 for international students; for spring admission, 10/15 for domestic students, 5/1 for international students. Applications are processed on a rolling basis. Application fee: $50. Electronic applications accepted. *Unit head:* Dr. Conrad Ciccotello, Faculty Advisor, 404-651-1711, Fax: 404-651-4219.

Golden Gate University, Ageno School of Business, San Francisco, CA 94105-2968. Offers accounting (M Ac, MBA); business administration (EMBA, MBA, DBA); finance (MBA, MS, Certificate); financial planning (MS, Certificate); human resource management (MBA, MS); human resources management (Certificate); information technology (MBA); information technology management (MS, Certificate); integrated marketing and communications (MS, Certificate); international business (MBA); management (MBA); marketing (MBA, MS, Certificate); operations management (Certificate); psychology (MA, Certificate); public relations (MS, Certificate); JD/MBA. Part-time and evening/weekend programs available. *Students:* 355 full-time (192 women), 977 part-time (465 women); includes 447 minority (85 African Americans, 5 American Indian/Alaska Native, 274 Asian Americans or Pacific Islanders, 83 Hispanic Americans), 226 international. Average age 34. 548 applicants, 74% accepted, 201 enrolled. In 2006, 545 master's, 21 doctorates awarded. *Degree requirements:* For doctorate, thesis/dissertation. *Entrance requirements:* For master's, GMAT (MBA), minimum GPA of 2.5 (MS). Additional exam requirements/recommendations for international students: Required—TOEFL. *Application deadline:* Applications are processed on a rolling basis. Application fee: $55 ($90 for international students). *Financial support:* Career-related internships or fieldwork, Federal Work-Study, and institutionally sponsored loans available. Support available to part-time students. Financial award applicants required to submit FAFSA. *Unit head:* Terry Connelly, Dean, 415-442-6519, Fax: 415-442-5369. *Application contact:* Enrollment Services, 415-442-7800, Fax: 415-442-7807, E-mail: info@ggu.edu.

Goldey-Beacom College, Graduate Program, Wilmington, DE 19808-1999. Offers business administration (MBA); financial management (MBA); human resource management (MBA); information technology (MBA); management (MM); marketing management (MBA). *Accreditation:* ACBSP. Part-time and evening/weekend programs available. *Entrance requirements:* For master's, GMAT, minimum GPA of 3.0. Additional exam requirements/recommendations for international students: Required—TOEFL (minimum score 525 paper-based; 195 computer-based). Electronic applications accepted.

Graduate School and University Center of the City University of New York, Graduate Studies, Program in Business, New York, NY 10016-4039. Offers accounting (PhD); behavioral science (PhD); finance (PhD); management planning systems (PhD). *Faculty:* 66 full-time (5 women). *Students:* 55 full-time (27 women); includes 7 minority (2 African Americans, 1 American Indian/Alaska Native, 2 Asian Americans or Pacific Islanders, 2 Hispanic Americans), 26 international. Average age 33. 74 applicants, 32% accepted, 11 enrolled. In 2006, 9 degrees awarded. *Degree requirements:* For doctorate, thesis/dissertation. *Entrance requirements:* For doctorate, GMAT, writing sample (15 pages). Additional exam requirements/recommendations for international students: Required—TOEFL. *Application deadline:* For fall admission, 1/15 for domestic students. Application fee: $125. Electronic applications accepted. *Financial support:* In 2006–07, 40 fellowships, 5 teaching assistantships were awarded; research assistantships, career-related internships or fieldwork, Federal Work-Study, institutionally sponsored loans, and tuition waivers (full and partial) also available. Financial award application deadline: 2/1; financial award applicants required to submit FAFSA. *Unit head:* Dr. Joseph Weintrop, Executive Officer, 646-312-3092, Fax: 646-312-3031.

Hawai'i Pacific University, College of Business Administration, Honolulu, HI 96813. Offers accounting/CPA (MBA); communication (MBA); e-business (MBA); economics (MBA); finance (MBA); human resource management (MBA); information systems (MBA); international business (MBA); management (MBA); marketing (MBA); organizational change (MBA); travel industry management (MBA). Part-time and evening/weekend programs available. *Faculty:* 40 full-time (16 women), 30 part-time/adjunct (10 women). *Students:* 320 full-time (150 women), 205 part-time (95 women); includes 168 minority (17 African Americans, 7 American Indian/Alaska Native, 137 Asian Americans or Pacific Islanders, 7 Hispanic Americans), 232 international. Average age 31. 279 applicants, 67% accepted, 166 enrolled. In 2006, 172 degrees awarded. *Degree requirements:* For master's, thesis. *Entrance requirements:* For master's, GMAT. Additional exam requirements/recommendations for international students: Recommended—TOEFL (minimum score 550 paper-based; 213 computer-based), TWE (minimum score 5). *Application deadline:* For fall admission, 2/15 priority date for domestic students; for spring admission, 10/15 priority date for domestic students. Applications are processed on a rolling basis. Application fee: $50. Electronic applications accepted. *Expenses:* Tuition: Full-time $10,080; part-time $560 per credit. *Financial support:* In 2006–07, 118 students received support; research assistantships, career-related internships or fieldwork, Federal Work-Study, scholarships/grants, and unspecified assistantships available. Support available to part-time students. Financial award application deadline: 3/1; financial award applicants required to submit FAFSA. *Faculty research:* Statistical control process as used by management, studies in comparative cross-cultural management styles, not-for-profit management. *Unit head:* Dr. Charles Steilen, Dean, 808-544-9301, Fax: 808-544-0283, E-mail: csteilen@hpu.edu. *Application contact:* Danny Lam, Assistant Director of Graduate Admissions, 808-544-1135, Fax: 808-544-0280, E-mail: graduate@hpu.edu.

See Close-Up on page 275.

HEC Montreal, School of Business Administration, Diploma Programs in Administration, Program in Private Wealth Management, Montréal, QC H3T 2A7, Canada. Offers Diploma. Part-time programs available. *Application deadline:* For fall admission, 5/15 for domestic students. Application fee: $60. Tuition and fees charges are reported in Canadian dollars. *Expenses:* Tuition, nonresident: part-time $56 Canadian dollars per credit. Required fees: $30 Canadian dollars per semester. *Application contact:* Francine Blais, Administrative Director, 514-340-6112, Fax: 514-340-6411, E-mail: francine.blais@hec.ca.

HEC Montreal, School of Business Administration, Master of Science Programs in Administration, Program in Applied Financial Economics, Montréal, QC H3T 2A7, Canada. Offers M Sc. Part-time programs available. *Degree requirements:* For master's, one foreign language, thesis. Application fee: $60 Canadian dollars. Electronic applications accepted. Tuition and fees charges are reported in Canadian dollars. *Expenses:* Tuition, nonresident: part-time $56 Canadian dollars per credit. Required fees: $30 Canadian dollars per semester. *Financial* *support:* Fellowships, research assistantships, teaching assistantships, scholarships/grants available. *Application contact:* Francine Blais, Administrative Director, 514-340-6112, Fax: 514-340-6411, E-mail: francine.blais@hec.ca.

HEC Montreal, School of Business Administration, Master of Science Programs in Administration, Program in Finance, Montréal, QC H3T 2A7, Canada. Offers M Sc. All courses are given in French. Part-time programs available. *Degree requirements:* For master's, one foreign language. Application fee: $60 Canadian dollars. Electronic applications accepted. Tuition and fees charges are reported in Canadian dollars. *Expenses:* Tuition, nonresident: part-time $56 Canadian dollars per credit. Required fees: $30 Canadian dollars per semester. *Financial support:* Fellowships, research assistantships, teaching assistantships, scholarships/grants available. *Application contact:* Francine Blais, Administrative Director, 514-340-6112, Fax: 514-340-6411, E-mail: francine.blais@hec.ca.

Hofstra University, Frank G. Zarb School of Business, Department of Finance, Hempstead, NY 11549. Offers finance (MBA, MS); quantitative finance (MS). Part-time programs available. *Faculty:* 8 full-time (1 woman), 1 part-time/adjunct (0 women). *Students:* 68 full-time (16 women), 90 part-time (28 women); includes 29 minority (10 African Americans, 13 Asian Americans or Pacific Islanders, 6 Hispanic Americans), 27 international. Average age 29. 88 applicants, 83% accepted, 35 enrolled. In 2006, 70 degrees awarded. *Degree requirements:* For master's, capstone course, core courses, 5 courses in finance. *Entrance requirements:* For master's, GMAT, 2 letters of recommendation, resumé, essay. Additional exam requirements/recommendations for international students: Required—TOEFL (minimum score 550 paper-based; 213 computer-based). *Application deadline:* Applications are processed on a rolling basis. Application fee: $60. Electronic applications accepted. *Expenses:* Tuition: Full-time $13,320; part-time $740 per credit. Required fees: $930; $155 per term. *Financial support:* In 2006–07, 39 students received support, including 30 fellowships with tuition reimbursements available (averaging $6,596 per year), 3 research assistantships with full and partial tuition reimbursements available (averaging $4,913 per year); scholarships/grants, tuition waivers (full and partial), and unspecified assistantships also available. Financial award applicants required to submit FAFSA. *Faculty research:* Corporate finance, financial institutions, real estate, investments, derivative markets. *Unit head:* Dr. Nancy W. White, Chairperson, 516-463-5699, Fax: 516-463-4834, E-mail: finnwh@hofstra.edu. *Application contact:* Carol Drummer, Dean of Graduate Admissions, 516-463-4876, Fax: 516-463-4664, E-mail: gradstudent@hofstra.edu.

Howard University, School of Business, Graduate Programs in Business, Washington, DC 20059-0002. Offers accounting (MBA); entrepreneurship (MBA); finance (MBA); information systems (MBA); international business (MBA); marketing (MBA); supply chain management (MBA); JD/MBA. *Accreditation:* AACSB. Part-time and evening/weekend programs available. Postbaccalaureate distance learning degree programs offered (no on-campus study). *Entrance requirements:* For master's, GMAT, minimum 1 year post undergraduate work experience, resumé, 3 letters of recommendation, advanced college algebra. Additional exam requirements/recommendations for international students: Required—TOEFL. *Faculty research:* Marketing research in multi-ethnic populations, U.S. trade policies and international relations, risk management (finance).

Huron University USA in London, Graduate Programs, Program in Business Administration, London, United Kingdom. Offers entrepreneurship (MBA); international business (MBA); international finance (MBA); marketing (MBA). Part-time programs available. *Degree requirements:* For master's, thesis, internship, comprehensive exam. *Entrance requirements:* Additional exam requirements/recommendations for international students: Required—TOEFL (minimum score 580 paper-based; 237 computer-based), TWE (minimum score 5). Electronic applications accepted.

Huron University USA in London, Graduate Programs, Program in Finance, London, United Kingdom. Offers MS. *Entrance requirements:* Additional exam requirements/recommendations for international students: Required—TOEFL (minimum score 580 paper-based; 237 computer-based), TWE (minimum score 5). Electronic applications accepted.

Illinois Institute of Technology, Chicago-Kent College of Law, Chicago, IL 60661-3691. Offers family law (LL M); financial services (LL M); international intellectual property (LL M); international law (LL M); law (JD); taxation (LL M); JD/LL M; JD/MBA; JD/MPA; JD/MPH; JD/MS. *Accreditation:* ABA. Part-time and evening/weekend programs available. *Faculty:* 61 full-time (20 women), 132 part-time/adjunct (34 women). *Students:* 827 full-time (395 women), 302 part-time (130 women); includes 221 minority (61 African Americans, 4 American Indian/Alaska Native, 95 Asian Americans or Pacific Islanders, 61 Hispanic Americans), 70 international. Average age 27. 3,510 applicants, 31% accepted, 307 enrolled. In 2006, 283 JDs, 28 master's awarded. *Entrance requirements:* LSAT, LSDAS. *Application deadline:* For fall admission, 3/1 priority date for domestic and international students. Applications are processed on a rolling basis. Application fee: $60. Electronic applications accepted. *Expenses:* Contact institution. Tuition and fees vary according to class time, course level, course load, program and student level. *Financial support:* In 2006–07, 573 students received support. Career-related internships or fieldwork, institutionally sponsored loans, scholarships/grants, and tuition waivers (full) available. Support available to part-time students. Financial award application deadline: 3/15; financial award applicants required to submit FAFSA. *Faculty research:* Constitutional law, bioethics, environmental law. Total annual research expenditures: $1.2 million. *Unit head:* Harold J. Krent, Dean, 312-906-5010, Fax: 312-906-5335, E-mail: hkrent@kentlaw.edu. *Application contact:* Nicole Vilches, Assistant Dean, 312-906-5020, Fax: 312-906-5274, E-mail: admit@kentlaw.edu.

Illinois Institute of Technology, Stuart School of Business, Program in Business Administration, Chicago, IL 60616-3793. Offers entrepreneurship (MBA); financial management (MBA); financial markets (MBA); healthcare management (MBA); information technology management (MBA); international business (MBA); management science (MBA); marketing (MBA); operations, quality, and technology management (MBA); strategic management of organizations (MBA); sustainable enterprise (MBA); JD/MBA; MBA/MS. *Accreditation:* AACSB. Part-time and evening/weekend programs available. *Faculty:* 13 full-time (1 woman), 9 part-time/adjunct (0 women). *Students:* 74 full-time (29 women), 42 part-time (16 women); includes 17 minority (5 African Americans, 11 Asian Americans or Pacific Islanders, 1 Hispanic American), 74 international. Average age 29. 247 applicants, 70% accepted, 51 enrolled. In 2006, 45 degrees awarded. *Entrance requirements:* For master's, GMAT. Additional exam requirements/recommendations for international students: Required—TOEFL (minimum score 600 paper-based; 250 computer-based). *Application deadline:* For fall admission, 8/15 priority date for domestic students, 7/1 for international students; for winter admission, 11/1 priority date for domestic students, 10/1 for international students; for spring admission, 1/1 priority date for domestic students, 1/1 for international students. Applications are processed on a rolling basis. Application fee: $75. Electronic applications accepted. *Expenses:* Contact institution. Tuition and fees vary according to class time, course level, course load, program and student level. *Financial support:* Career-related internships or fieldwork, Federal Work-Study, institutionally sponsored loans, scholarships/grants, traineeships, health care benefits, tuition waivers, and unspecified assistantships available. Support available to part-time students. Financial award applicants required to submit FAFSA. *Faculty research:* Knowledge management, healthcare management, sustainability in supply chain. *Unit head:* Dr. George P. Nassos, Interim Director, 312-906-6543, Fax: 312-906-6549, E-mail: george.nassos@iit.edu. *Application contact:* Brian Jansen, Director of Graduate Admissions, 312-906-6521, Fax: 312-906-6549, E-mail: admission@stuart.iit.edu.

Illinois Institute of Technology, Stuart School of Business, Program in Finance, Chicago, IL 60616-3793. Offers MS. Part-time and evening/weekend programs available. *Faculty:* 2 full-time (0 women), 5 part-time/adjunct (0 women). *Students:* 92 full-time (34 women), 19 part-time (1 woman); includes 4 minority (1 African American, 2 Asian Americans or Pacific Islanders, 1 Hispanic American), 95 international. Average age 27. 229 applicants, 31% accepted, 63 enrolled. In 2006, 24 degrees awarded. *Entrance requirements:* For master's, GMAT or GRE General Test. Additional exam requirements/recommendations for international students: Required—TOEFL (minimum score 600 paper-based; 250 computer-based). *Application deadline:* For fall admission, 8/15 priority date for domestic students, 7/1 for international students; for winter admission, 11/1 priority date for domestic students, 10/1 for international students; for spring admission, 1/1 priority date for domestic students, 1/1 for international students. Applications are processed on a rolling basis. Application fee: $75. Electronic applications accepted. *Expenses:* Contact institution. Tuition and fees vary according to class time, course level, course load, program and student level. *Financial support:* Career-related internships or fieldwork, Federal Work-Study, institutionally sponsored loans, scholarships/grants, traineeships, health care benefits, and unspecified assistantships available. Support available to part-time students. Financial award applicants required to submit FAFSA. *Faculty research:* Factor models for investment management, credit rating and credit risk management, hedge fund performance analysis, option trading and risk management, global asset allocation strategies. *Unit head:* John Bilson, Director, 312-906-6538, Fax: 312-906-6511, E-mail: john.bilson@iit.edu. *Application contact:* Brian Jansen, Director of Graduate Admissions, 312-906-6521, Fax: 312-906-6549, E-mail: admission@stuart.iit.edu.

Illinois Institute of Technology, Stuart School of Business, Program in Financial Markets, Chicago, IL 60616-3793. Offers MS, JD/MS. Part-time and evening/weekend programs available. *Faculty:* 4 full-time (0 women), 11 part-time/adjunct (1 woman). *Students:* 55 full-time (11 women), 71 part-time (4 women); includes 14 minority (all Asian Americans or Pacific Islanders), 57 international. Average age 29. In 2006, 45 master's awarded. *Entrance requirements:* For master's, GMAT or GRE General Test. Additional exam requirements/recommendations for international students: Required—TOEFL (minimum score 600 paper-based; 250 computer-based). *Application deadline:* For fall admission, 8/15 priority date for domestic students, 7/1 for international students; for winter admission, 11/1 priority date for domestic students, 10/1 for international students; for spring admission, 1/1 priority date for domestic students, 1/1 for international students. Applications are processed on a rolling basis. Application fee: $75. Electronic applications accepted. *Expenses:* Contact institution. Tuition and fees vary according to class time, course level, course load, program and student level. *Financial support:* Career-related internships or fieldwork, Federal Work-Study, institutionally sponsored loans, scholarships/grants, traineeships, health care benefits, and unspecified assistantships available. Support available to part-time students. Financial award applicants required to submit FAFSA. *Faculty research:* Performance analysis of hedge funds; product innovation in listed derivatives; structure, performance, and transformation of securities and derivatives exchanges. *Unit head:* Michael Gorham, Director, 312-906-6500, E-mail: gorham@stuart.iit.edu. *Application contact:* Brian Jansen, Director of Graduate Admissions, 312-906-6521, Fax: 312-906-6549, E-mail: admission@stuart.iit.edu.

Indiana University Southeast, School of Business, New Albany, IN 47150-6405. Offers accounting (Certificate); business administration (MBA); economics (Certificate); finance (Certificate); general business (Certificate); information and operations management (Certificate); management and marketing (Certificate); strategic finance (MS). *Accreditation:* AACSB. *Faculty:* 11 full-time (2 women). *Students:* 10 full-time (4 women), 201 part-time (65 women); includes 12 minority (2 African Americans, 8 Asian Americans or Pacific Islanders, 2 Hispanic Americans), 5 international. Average age 31. In 2006, 60 degrees awarded. *Degree requirements:* For master's, community service. *Entrance requirements:* For master's, GMAT, work experience. Additional exam requirements/recommendations for international students: Required—TOEFL. Application fee: $35. *Expenses:* Contact institution. Tuition and fees vary according to course load, campus/location and program. *Unit head:* Chris Bjornson, Dean, 812-941-2362, Fax: 812-941-2672. *Application contact:* Dr. Jay White, Director of Graduate Business Programs, 812-941-2364, Fax: 812-941-2581, E-mail: jwhite04@ius.edu.

Instituto Tecnologico de Santo Domingo, Graduate School, Santo Domingo, Dominican Republic. Offers corporate finance (M Mgmt); education (M Ed); engineering (M Eng), including data telecommunications, industrial engineering, sanitary and environmental engineering, structural engineering; environmental science (M En S); human resources administration (M Mgmt); management (M Mgmt); psychology (MA); social science (M Ed). *Entrance requirements:* For master's, birth certificate, minimum GPA of 2.0.

Instituto Tecnológico y de Estudios Superiores de Monterrey, Campus Central de Veracruz, Graduate Programs, Córdoba, Mexico. Offers administration (MA); administration of information technologies (MTI); computer sciences (MCC); education (MEE); educational institution administration (MAD); educational technology (MTE); electronic commerce (MCE); finance (MAF); humanistic studies (MEH); international business for Latin America (MNL); marketing (MMT); science (MCP); technology management (MTT). Part-time and evening/weekend programs available. Postbaccalaureate distance learning degree programs offered (minimal on-campus study). *Degree requirements:* For master's, thesis (for some programs). *Entrance requirements:* For master's, PAEP College Board. Electronic applications accepted.

Instituto Tecnológico y de Estudios Superiores de Monterrey, Campus Ciudad de México, Division of Business, Ciudad de Mexico, Mexico. Offers business administration (EMBA, MBA, PhD); economy (MBA); finance (MBA). Part-time and evening/weekend programs available. Postbaccalaureate distance learning degree programs offered (minimal on-campus study). *Entrance requirements:* For master's and doctorate, Instituto entrance exam. Additional exam requirements/recommendations for international students: Required—TOEFL.

Instituto Tecnológico y de Estudios Superiores de Monterrey, Campus Ciudad Juárez, Program in Financial Administration, Ciudad Juárez, Mexico. Offers MFA.

Instituto Tecnológico y de Estudios Superiores de Monterrey, Campus Ciudad Obregón, Program in Finance, Ciudad Obregón, Mexico. Offers MF.

Instituto Tecnológico y de Estudios Superiores de Monterrey, Campus Cuernavaca, Programs in Business Administration, Temixco, Mexico. Offers finance (MA); human resources management (MA); international business (MA); marketing (MA).

Instituto Tecnológico y de Estudios Superiores de Monterrey, Campus Estado de México, Professional and Graduate Division, Estado de Mexico, Mexico. Offers administration of information technologies (MITA); architecture (M Arch); business administration (GMBA, MBA); computer sciences (MCS, PhD); education (M Ed); educational institution administration (MAD); educational technology and innovation (PhD); electronic commerce (MEC); environmental systems (MS); finance (MAF); humanistic studies (MHS); information sciences and knowledge management (MISKM); information systems (MS); manufacturing systems (MS); marketing (MEM); quality systems and productivity (MS); science and materials engineering (PhD); telecommunications management (MTM). Part-time programs available. Postbaccalaureate distance learning degree programs offered (minimal on-campus study). *Degree requirements:* For master's, one foreign language, thesis (for some programs), registration; for doctorate, one foreign language, thesis/dissertation, registration (for some programs). *Entrance requirements:* For master's, E-PAEP 500, interview; for doctorate, E-PAEP 500, research proposal. Additional exam requirements/recommendations for international students: Required—TOEFL (minimum score 550 paper-based). *Faculty research:* Surface treatments by plasmas, mechanical properties, robotics, graphical computing, mechatronics security protocols.

Instituto Tecnológico y de Estudios Superiores de Monterrey, Campus Guadalajara, Program in Finance, Zapopan, Mexico. Offers MF. *Degree requirements:* For master's, one foreign language, thesis. *Entrance requirements:* For master's, ITESM admission test.

Instituto Tecnológico y de Estudios Superiores de Monterrey, Campus Irapuato, Graduate Programs, Irapuato, Mexico. Offers administration (MBA); administration of information technology (MAIT); administration of telecommunications (MAT); architecture (M Arch); computer science (MCS); education (M Ed); educational administration (MEA); educational innovation and technology (DEIT); educational technology (MET); electronic commerce (MBA); environmental administration and planning (MEAP); environmental systems (MES); finances (MBA); humanistic studies (MHS); international management for Latin American executives (MIMLAE);

Finance and Banking

Instituto Tecnológico y de Estudios Superiores de Monterrey, Campus Irapuato (continued)
library and information science (MLIS); manufacturing quality management (MMQM); marketing research (MBA).

Instituto Tecnológico y de Estudios Superiores de Monterrey, Campus Monterrey, Graduate School of Business Administration and Leadership, Program in Business Administration, Monterrey, Mexico. Offers business administration (MA, MBA); finance (M Sc); international business (M Sc); marketing (M Sc). Part-time programs available. *Degree requirements:* For master's, one foreign language, thesis. *Entrance requirements:* For master's, GMAT. Additional exam requirements/recommendations for international students: Required—TOEFL. *Faculty research:* Technology management, quality management, organizational theory and behavior.

Inter American University of Puerto Rico, Metropolitan Campus, Graduate Programs, Faculty of Economics and Administrative Sciences, Program in Finance, San Juan, PR 00919-1293. Offers MBA. *Degree requirements:* For master's, comprehensive exam. *Entrance requirements:* For master's, GRE or EXADEP, interview. Electronic applications accepted.

Inter American University of Puerto Rico, Ponce Campus, Graduate School, Mercedita, PR 00715-1602. Offers accounting (MBA); biology (M Ed); chemistry (M Ed); criminal justice (MA); elementary education (M Ed); English as a Second Language (M Ed); finance (MBA); history (M Ed); human resources (MBA); mathematics (M Ed); Spanish (M Ed); trade (MBA). *Entrance requirements:* For master's, minimum GPA of 2.5.

Inter American University of Puerto Rico, San Germán Campus, Graduate Studies Center, Graduate Program in Business Administration, San Germán, PR 00683-5008. Offers accounting (MBA); finance (MBA); human resources (MBA, PhD); industrial relations (MBA); international business (PhD); labor relations (PhD); management information systems (MBA); marketing (MBA); quality organizational design (MBA). Part-time and evening/weekend programs available. *Faculty:* 12 full-time, 4 part-time/adjunct. *Students:* 265. Average age 27. In 2006, 67 master's, 1 doctorate awarded. *Degree requirements:* For master's, comprehensive exam. *Entrance requirements:* For master's, GRE General Test or EXADEP, minimum GPA of 3.0. *Application deadline:* For fall admission, 4/30 priority date for domestic students; for spring admission, 11/15 for domestic students. Applications are processed on a rolling basis. Application fee: $31. *Expenses:* Tuition: Part-time $175 per credit. Required fees: $238 per semester. Tuition and fees vary according to degree level. *Financial support:* Teaching assistantships, Federal Work-Study and unspecified assistantships available. *Application contact:* Prof. Duay Rivera, Graduate Coordinator, 787-264-1912 Ext. 7218, Fax: 787-892-7510, E-mail: durivera@sg.inter.edu.

The International University of Monaco, Graduate Programs, Monte Carlo, Monaco. Offers entrepreneurship (EMBA, MBA); financial engineering (M Sc); international marketing (EMBA, MBA); luxury goods and services (EMBA, M Sc, MBA); wealth and asset management (EMBA, MBA). Part-time programs available. *Degree requirements:* For master's, applied research project. *Entrance requirements:* Additional exam requirements/recommendations for international students: Required—TOEFL (minimum score 550 paper-based; 213 computer-based), IELTS. Electronic applications accepted. *Faculty research:* Gaming, leadership, disintermediation.

Iona College, Hagan School of Business, Department of Finance, Business Economics and Legal Studies, New Rochelle, NY 10801-1890. Offers financial management (MBA, PMC). Part-time and evening/weekend programs available. *Faculty:* 8 full-time (2 women), 1 part-time/adjunct (0 women). *Students:* 14 full-time (5 women), 66 part-time (25 women); includes 9 minority (5 African Americans, 3 Asian Americans or Pacific Islanders, 1 Hispanic American), 3 international. Average age 31. 31 applicants, 87% accepted, 24 enrolled. In 2006, 52 degrees awarded. *Entrance requirements:* For master's, GMAT, 2 letters of recommendation. Additional exam requirements/recommendations for international students: Required—TOEFL (minimum score 550 paper-based; 213 computer-based). *Application deadline:* Applications are processed on a rolling basis. Application fee: $50. Electronic applications accepted. *Expenses:* Contact institution. *Financial support:* Scholarships/grants, tuition waivers (partial), and unspecified assistantships available. Support available to part-time students. *Faculty research:* Options, insurance financing, asset depreciation ranges, international finance, emerging markets. *Unit head:* Dr. Anand Shetty, Chairman, 914-633-2284, E-mail: ashetty@iona.edu. *Application contact:* Veronica Jarek-Prinz, Graduate Admissions, 914-633-2289, Fax: 914-633-2012, E-mail: vjarekprinz@iona.edu.

The Johns Hopkins University, Carey Business School, Department of Finance, Baltimore, MD 21218-2699. Offers finance (MS); financial management (Certificate); investments (Certificate). Part-time and evening/weekend programs available. *Students:* 56 full-time (25 women), 77 part-time (28 women); includes 13 minority (3 African Americans, 9 Asian Americans or Pacific Islanders, 1 Hispanic American), 3 international. Average age 32. 249 applicants, 56% accepted, 90 enrolled. In 2006, 47 master's, 8 other advanced degrees awarded. *Degree requirements:* For master's and Certificate, registration. *Entrance requirements:* For master's, GMAT or GRE (recommended), minimum GPA of 3.0, resumé, work experience, two letters of recommendation; for Certificate, minimum GPA of 3.0, resumé, work experience, two letters of recommendation. Additional exam requirements/recommendations for international students: Required—TOEFL (minimum score 600 paper-based; 250 computer-based; 100 iBT). *Application deadline:* For fall admission, 5/1 for international students; for spring admission, 10/15 for international students. Applications are processed on a rolling basis. Application fee: $60. *Expenses:* Tuition: Full-time $32,976. Tuition and fees vary according to degree level and program. *Financial support:* Scholarships/grants available. Support available to part-time students. Financial award application deadline: 6/1; financial award applicants required to submit FAFSA. *Unit head:* Dr. Ken Yook, Chair, 202-588-0683, Fax: 202-588-5192, E-mail: kyook@jhu.edu. *Application contact:* Robin Reed, Senior Academic Coordinator, 800-gotojhu, Fax: 410-872-1251, E-mail: onestop.admissions@jhu.edu.

Johnson & Wales University, The Alan Shawn Feinstein Graduate School, Certificate Programs, Providence, RI 02903-3703. Offers finance (CAGS); hospitality (CAGS); human resources management (CAGS). *Students:* 9 full-time (4 women), 2 part-time (both women); includes 1 African American, 8 international. Average age 29. *Unit head:* Thomas Rossi, Unit Head, 401-598-4738, E-mail: trossi@jwu.edu.

Johnson & Wales University, The Alan Shawn Feinstein Graduate School, Program in Global Business, Concentration in Financial Management, Providence, RI 02903-3703. Offers MBA. Part-time and evening/weekend programs available. *Students:* 131 full-time (51 women), 21 part-time (10 women); includes 10 minority (6 African Americans, 3 Asian Americans or Pacific Islanders, 1 Hispanic American), 101 international. Average age 28. In 2006, 54 degrees awarded. *Entrance requirements:* For master's, GMAT (recommended), minimum GPA of 2.75. Additional exam requirements/recommendations for international students: Required—TOEFL (paper-based 500; computer-based 210) or IELTS. *Application deadline:* For fall admission, 8/15 priority date for domestic students, 6/28 priority date for international students; for winter admission, 11/10 priority date for domestic students, 9/20 priority date for international students; for spring admission, 2/15 priority date for domestic students, 12/20 priority date for international students. Applications are processed on a rolling basis. Electronic applications accepted. *Financial support:* Unspecified assistantships available. Financial award application deadline: 5/1. *Unit head:* Dr. Kevin Fountain, Unit Head, 401-598-4738, Fax: 401-598-1162, E-mail: kfountain@jwu.edu. *Application contact:* Dr. Allan G. Freedman, Director of Graduate Admissions, 401-598-1015, Fax: 401-598-1286, E-mail: gradadm@jwu.edu.

Johnson & Wales University, The Alan Shawn Feinstein Graduate School, Program in Hospitality Administration, Concentration in Financial Management, Providence, RI 02903-3703. Offers MBA. *Students:* 19 full-time (7 women), 2 part-time (1 woman); includes 1 minority (Asian American or Pacific Islander), 14 international. Average age 26. *Unit head:* Thomas Rossi, Unit Head, 401-598-4738, E-mail: trossi@jwu.edu.

Jones International University, Graduate School of Business Administration, Centennial, CO 80112. Offers accounting (MBA); business communication (MABC); entrepreneurship (MABC, MBA); finance (MBA); global enterprise management (MBA); health care management (MBA); information security management (MBA); information technology management (MBA); leadership and influence (MABC); leading the customer-driven organization (MABC); negotiation and conflict management (MBA); project management (MABC, MBA). Program only offered online. Part-time and evening/weekend programs available. Postbaccalaureate distance learning degree programs offered (no on-campus study). *Degree requirements:* For master's, capstone project. *Entrance requirements:* For master's, minimum cumulative GPA of 2.5. Additional exam requirements/recommendations for international students: Recommended—TOEFL (minimum score 550 paper-based; 213 computer-based). Electronic applications accepted.

Kent State University, Graduate School of Management, Doctoral Program in Finance, Kent, OH 44242-0001. Offers PhD. *Faculty:* 6 full-time (2 women). *Students:* 14 full-time (5 women); includes 1 minority (African American), 8 international. Average age 35. 18 applicants, 33% accepted, 4 enrolled. In 2006, 2 degrees awarded. *Degree requirements:* For doctorate, thesis/dissertation, oral defense, comprehensive exam. *Entrance requirements:* For doctorate, GMAT. Additional exam requirements/recommendations for international students: Required—TOEFL (minimum score 600 paper-based; 250 computer-based). *Application deadline:* For fall admission, 2/1 for domestic students, 1/1 for international students. Application fee: $30. Electronic applications accepted. *Financial support:* In 2006–07, 9 students received support, including fellowships with full tuition reimbursements available (averaging $15,000 per year), 9 teaching assistantships with full tuition reimbursements available (averaging $15,000 per year); Federal Work-Study also available. Financial award application deadline: 2/1; financial award applicants required to submit FAFSA. *Faculty research:* Corporate finance, investments, international finance, futures and options, risk and insurance. *Unit head:* Dr. Mark E. Holder, Associate Professor, 330-672-2426, Fax: 330-672-9806, E-mail: mholder@kent.edu. *Application contact:* Felecia A. Urbanek, Coordinator, Graduate Programs, 330-672-2282, Fax: 330-672-7303, E-mail: gradbus@bsa3.kent.edu.

Lamar University, College of Graduate Studies, College of Business, Beaumont, TX 77710. Offers accounting (MBA); experiential business and Entrepreneurship (MBA); financial management (MBA); healthcare administration (MBA); information systems (MBA); management (MBA). *Accreditation:* AACSB. Part-time and evening/weekend programs available. *Faculty:* 20 full-time (8 women), 2 part-time/adjunct (1 woman). *Students:* 55 full-time (27 women), 45 part-time (20 women); includes 17 minority (9 African Americans, 4 Asian Americans or Pacific Islanders, 4 Hispanic Americans), 14 international. Average age 29. 131 applicants, 34% accepted, 29 enrolled. In 2006, 29 degrees awarded. *Degree requirements:* For master's, thesis optional. *Entrance requirements:* For master's, GMAT. Additional exam requirements/recommendations for international students: Required—TOEFL (minimum score 525 paper-based; 197 computer-based). *Application deadline:* For fall admission, 3/15 priority date for domestic students; for spring admission, 10/1 priority date for domestic students. Applications are processed on a rolling basis. Application fee: $25 ($50 for international students). *Expenses:* Tuition, nonresident: part-time $33 per hour. Required fees: $43 per hour. $110 per semester. *Financial support:* In 2006–07, 12 students received support, including 4 research assistantships with partial tuition reimbursements available; fellowships with tuition reimbursements available, career-related internships or fieldwork, Federal Work-Study, institutionally sponsored loans, scholarships/grants, and tuition waivers (partial) also available. Support available to part-time students. Financial award application deadline: 4/1; financial award applicants required to submit FAFSA. *Faculty research:* Marketing, finance, quantitative methods, MIS, legal, environmental. Total annual research expenditures: $26,000. *Unit head:* Dr. Enrique R. Venta, Dean, 409-880-8604, Fax: 409-880-8088, E-mail: henry.venta@lamar.edu. *Application contact:* Dr. Brad Mayer, Professor and Associate Dean, 409-880-2383, Fax: 409-880-8605, E-mail: bradley.mayer@lamar.edu.

Lehigh University, College of Business and Economics, Department of Finance, Bethlehem, PA 18015-3094. Offers analytical finance (MS); finance (MS). *Faculty:* 13 full-time (2 women), 2 part-time/adjunct (1 woman). *Students:* 12 full-time (1 woman), 24 part-time (6 women); includes 2 minority (both Asian Americans or Pacific Islanders), 10 international. Average age 22. 44 applicants, 75% accepted, 7 enrolled. In 2006, 20 degrees awarded. *Degree requirements:* For master's, capstone project. *Entrance requirements:* For master's, GMAT or GRE, bachelor's degree from a mathematically rigorous program, minimum GPA of 3.0. Additional exam requirements/recommendations for international students: Required—TOEFL (minimum score 600 paper-based; 250 computer-based). *Application deadline:* For fall admission, 7/15 for domestic students, 5/1 for international students. Applications are processed on a rolling basis. Application fee: $60. Electronic applications accepted. *Expenses:* Contact institution. *Unit head:* Richard Kish, Co-Director, 610-758-4205, E-mail: rjk7@lehigh.edu. *Application contact:* Mary- Theresa Taglang, Director of Graduate Programs, 610-758-5285, Fax: 610-758-5283, E-mail: mtt4@lehigh.edu.

See Close-Up on page 715.

Lindenwood University, Graduate Programs, Division of Management, St. Charles, MO 63301-1695. Offers accounting (MBA, MS); business administration (MBA); entrepreneurial studies (MBA); finance (MBA, MS); human resource management (MBA); human resources (MS); international business (MBA, MS); management (MBA, MS); management information systems (MBA, MS); managing business to business (MA); managing human resources (MA); managing international business (MA); managing investment management (MA); managing leadership (MA); managing marketing (MA); managing organizational behavior (MA); managing sales (MA); managing, training and development (MA); marketing (MBA, MS); nonprofit administration (MA); public management (MBA, MS); sport management (MA). Part-time and evening/weekend programs available. *Faculty:* 38 full-time (15 women), 20 part-time/adjunct (5 women). *Students:* 177 full-time (78 women), 138 part-time (67 women); includes 43 minority (27 African Americans, 4 American Indian/Alaska Native, 6 Asian Americans or Pacific Islanders, 6 Hispanic Americans), 73 international. Average age 30. In 2006, 159 degrees awarded. *Degree requirements:* For master's, thesis (for some programs). *Entrance requirements:* For master's, interview, minimum GPA of 3.0. Additional exam requirements/recommendations for international students: Required—TOEFL (minimum score 550 paper-based; 173 computer-based). *Application deadline:* For fall admission, 7/30 priority date for domestic students, 9/30 priority date for international students; for winter admission, 12/30 priority date for domestic and international students; for spring admission, 3/30 priority date for domestic and international students. Applications are processed on a rolling basis. Application fee: $30 ($100 for international students). Electronic applications accepted. *Expenses:* Tuition: Part-time $340 per credit hour. Tuition and fees vary according to course level, course load, degree level and program. *Financial support:* Career-related internships or fieldwork, Federal Work-Study, institutionally sponsored loans, and tuition waivers (partial) available. Financial award application deadline: 6/30; financial award applicants required to submit FAFSA. *Unit head:* Ed Morris, Dean, 636-949-4832, Fax: 636-949-4910, E-mail: emorris@lindenwood.edu. *Application contact:* Brett Barger, Dean Adult, Corporate and Graduate Admissions, 636-949-4366, Fax: 636-949-4109, E-mail: bbarger@lindenwood.edu.

Lipscomb University, MBA Program, Nashville, TN 37204-3951. Offers accounting (MBA); business administration (general) (MBA); conflict management (MBA); financial services (MBA); healthcare management (MBA); leadership (MBA); nonprofit management (MBA). *Accreditation:* ACBSP. Part-time and evening/weekend programs available. *Faculty:* 11 full-time (3 women), 6 part-time/adjunct (0 women). *Students:* 18 full-time (6 women), 50 part-time (23 women); includes 5 minority (4 African Americans, 1 American Indian/Alaska Native), 2 international. Average age 30. 48 applicants, 73% accepted, 27 enrolled. In 2006, 30 degrees awarded. *Median time to degree:* Master's–1 year full-time, 2.3 years part-time. *Entrance requirements:* For master's, GMAT, interview, 2 references, resumé. Additional exam requirements/recommendations for international students: Required—TOEFL (minimum score 570 paper-based; 230 computer-based). *Application deadline:* For fall admission, 7/1 for domestic students, 2/1 for international students; for winter admission, 12/1 for domestic students, 6/1 for international students. Applications are processed on a rolling basis. Application fee: $50 ($75 for international students). Electronic applications accepted. *Expenses: Contact institution. Financial support:* In 2006–07, 25 students received support. Career-related internships or fieldwork, Federal Work-Study, scholarships/grants, tuition waivers (partial), and unspecified assistantships available. Support available to part-time students. Financial award application deadline: 7/1; financial award applicants required to submit FAFSA. *Faculty research:* Impact of spirituality on organization commitment; leadership; psychological empowerment; training. *Unit head:* Dr. Steven K. Yoho, Associate Dean of Graduate Business Studies, 615-966-1833, Fax: 615-966-1818, E-mail: steven.yoho@lipscomb.edu. *Application contact:* Jackie Cash, MBA Assistant, 615-966-1833, Fax: 615-966-1818, E-mail: jackie.cash@lipscomb.edu.

Long Island University, C.W. Post Campus, College of Management, School of Business, Brookville, NY 11548-1300. Offers accounting and taxation (Certificate); business administration (Certificate); finance (MBA, Certificate); general business administration (MBA); international business (MBA, Certificate); management (MBA, Certificate); management information systems (MBA, Certificate); marketing (MBA, Certificate). *Accreditation:* AACSB. Part-time and evening/weekend programs available. *Entrance requirements:* For master's, GMAT, resumé, minimum GPA of 3.0, 2 letters of recommendation. Additional exam requirements/recommendations for international students: Required—TOEFL (minimum score 527 paper-based; 197 computer-based). Electronic applications accepted. *Faculty research:* Financial markets, consumer behavior.

Long Island University, Rockland Graduate Campus, Graduate School, Program in Health Administration, Orangeburg, NY 10962. Offers financial management (MPA); gerontology (Advanced Certificate); health administration (MPA); health services management (MPA); long term care administration (MPA); medical practice management (MPA); nonprofit management (MPA, Advanced Certificate). *Entrance requirements:* For master's, GRE General Test.

Louisiana State University and Agricultural and Mechanical College, Graduate School, E. J. Ourso College of Business, Department of Finance, Baton Rouge, LA 70803. Offers business administration (PhD), including finance; finance (MS). *Faculty:* 13 full-time (3 women), 2 part-time/adjunct (0 women). *Students:* 21 full-time (3 women), 4 part-time (1 woman); includes 1 African American, 11 international. Average age 30. 43 applicants, 37% accepted, 3 enrolled. In 2006, 11 master's, 2 doctorates awarded. *Degree requirements:* For master's, thesis or alternative; for doctorate, thesis/dissertation. *Entrance requirements:* For master's and doctorate, GMAT. Additional exam requirements/recommendations for international students: Required—TOEFL (minimum score 550 paper-based; 213 computer-based; 79 iBT). *Application deadline:* For fall admission, 1/25 priority date for domestic students, 5/15 for international students; for spring admission, 10/15 for international students. Applications are processed on a rolling basis. Application fee: $25. *Financial support:* In 2006–07, 12 students received support, including 5 research assistantships with full and partial tuition reimbursements available (averaging $12,400 per year), 5 teaching assistantships with full and partial tuition reimbursements available (averaging $12,000 per year); fellowships, career-related internships or fieldwork, Federal Work-Study, scholarships/grants, and unspecified assistantships also available. Support available to part-time students. Financial award application deadline: 4/1; financial award applicants required to submit FAFSA. *Faculty research:* Derivatives and risk management, capital structure, asset pricing, spatial statistics, financial institutions and underwriting. Total annual research expenditures: $16,562. *Unit head:* Dr. William R. Lane, Chair, 225-578-6367, Fax: 225-578-6366, E-mail: filane@lsu.edu.

Louisiana Tech University, Graduate School, College of Administration and Business, Department of Finance and Economics, Ruston, LA 71272. Offers business economics (MBA, DBA); finance (MBA, DBA). Part-time programs available. *Degree requirements:* For doctorate, thesis/dissertation. *Entrance requirements:* For master's and doctorate, GMAT.

Loyola College in Maryland, Graduate Programs, Sellinger School of Business and Management, Program in Business Administration, Baltimore, MD 21210-2699. Offers decision sciences (MBA); economics (MBA); finance (MBA); marketing/management (MBA). *Accreditation:* AACSB. Part-time and evening/weekend programs available. *Students:* 47 full-time (17 women), 733 part-time (315 women); includes 111 minority (59 African Americans, 1 American Indian/Alaska Native, 37 Asian Americans or Pacific Islanders, 14 Hispanic Americans), 19 international. Average age 31. In 2006, 215 degrees awarded. *Entrance requirements:* For master's, GMAT. Additional exam requirements/recommendations for international students: Required—TOEFL (minimum score 550 paper-based; 213 computer-based). *Application deadline:* For fall admission, 8/15 priority date for domestic students; for spring admission, 11/20 priority date for domestic students. Applications are processed on a rolling basis. Application fee: $50. *Financial support:* Applicants required to submit FAFSA. *Unit head:* Ann Attanasio, Director, 410-617-2308, E-mail: aattanasio@loyola.edu.

Loyola College in Maryland, Graduate Programs, Sellinger School of Business and Management, Program in Finance, Baltimore, MD 21210-2699. Offers MSF. Part-time and evening/weekend programs available. *Students:* 15 full-time (2 women), 66 part-time (16 women); includes 10 minority (2 African Americans, 4 Asian Americans or Pacific Islanders, 4 Hispanic Americans), 5 international. Average age 32. 73 applicants, 77% accepted, 40 enrolled. In 2006, 28 degrees awarded. *Entrance requirements:* For master's, GMAT. Additional exam requirements/recommendations for international students: Required—TOEFL (minimum score 550 paper-based; 213 computer-based). *Application deadline:* For fall admission, 8/15 priority date for domestic students; for spring admission, 11/20 priority date for domestic students. Applications are processed on a rolling basis. Application fee: $50. *Financial support:* Applicants required to submit FAFSA. *Unit head:* Dr. Lisa Fairchild, Chairman, 410-617-2681.

Marywood University, Academic Affairs, Insalaco College of Creative Arts and Management, Department of Business and Managerial Science, Emphasis in Finance and Investments, Scranton, PA 18509-1598. Offers MBA. Evening/weekend programs available. *Students:* 2 full-time (1 woman), 16 part-time (7 women); includes 1 minority (African American), 2 international. Average age 35. 6 applicants, 83% accepted. *Degree requirements:* For master's, comprehensive exam. *Entrance requirements:* For master's, GMAT. Additional exam requirements/recommendations for international students: Required—TOEFL (minimum score 550 paper-based; 213 computer-based). *Application deadline:* For fall admission, 4/15 priority date for domestic and international students; for spring admission, 11/15 priority date for domestic and international students. Applications are processed on a rolling basis. Application fee: $30. Electronic applications accepted. *Expenses:* Tuition: Part-time $672 per credit. Tuition and fees vary according to degree level, campus/location and program. *Financial support:* Research assistantships with tuition reimbursements, career-related internships or fieldwork, scholarships/grants, and tuition waivers (partial) available. Support available to part-time students. Financial award application deadline: 2/15; financial award applicants required to submit FAFSA. *Faculty research:* Accountant/auditor liability, corporate finance acquisitions and mergers, corporate bankruptcy. *Application contact:* Dr. Deborah M. Flynn, Coordinator of Graduate Advising (Enrollment Management), 570-348-6211, E-mail: flynn@ac.marywood.edu.

McGill University, Faculty of Graduate and Postdoctoral Studies, Desautels Faculty of Management, Montréal, QC H3A 2T5, Canada. Offers administration (PhD); entrepreneurial studies (MBA); finance (MBA); general management (Post Master's Certificate); information systems (MBA); international business (exchange program) (MBA); international Master's program in practicing management (MM); management (MBA); management for development (MBA); manufacturing management (MMM); marketing (MBA); operations management (MBA); public accountancy (Diploma); strategic management (MBA); MBA/LL B; MD/MBA. Part-time programs available. *Entrance requirements:* For master's, GMAT, minimum undergraduate GPA of 3.0, 2 years work experience; for doctorate, GMAT or GRE General Test, 2 letters of recommendation, preferably by professors in chosen field of specialization; for other advanced degree, 2 years of work experience, MBA, minimum GPA of 3.0 (Post-MBA Certificate). Additional exam requirements/recommendations for international students: Required—TOEFL (minimum score 600 paper-based; 250 computer-based), IELTS (minimum score 7). Electronic applications accepted. Expenses: Contact institution. *Faculty research:* Social innovation, leadership, strategy.

Mercy College, Division of Business and Accounting, Program in Banking, Dobbs Ferry, NY 10522-1189. Offers MS. Offered jointly with The Global Institute of Finance and Banking. Part-time and evening/weekend programs available. Postbaccalaureate distance learning degree programs offered (no on-campus study). *Students:* Average age 37. In 2006, 38 degrees awarded. *Degree requirements:* For master's, thesis. *Entrance requirements:* For master's, interview, letters of recommendation, 2 years of work experience. *Application deadline:* For fall admission, 2/1 for domestic students; for spring admission, 1/24 for domestic students. Applications are processed on a rolling basis. Application fee: $37. Electronic applications accepted. *Expenses: Contact institution.* Tuition and fees vary according to program. *Financial support:* In 2006–07, 20 students received support. *Unit head:* Robert Boccino, Director, 212-480-3200, Fax: 212-480-3705, E-mail: rboccino@mercy.edu. *Application contact:* Kathleen Jackson, Director of Admissions, 800-Mercy-NY, Fax: 914-674-7382, E-mail: admissions@mercy.edu.

Mercy College, Division of Business and Accounting, Program in Securities, Dobbs Ferry, NY 10522-1189. Offers MS. Offered jointly with The Global Institute of Finance and Banking. *Students:* 1 (woman) full-time, 8 part-time (6 women); includes 2 minority (both African Americans) Average age 37. In 2006, 11 degrees awarded. *Degree requirements:* For master's, research project. *Entrance requirements:* For master's, 2 years of relevant work experience, interview, resumé, letters of recommendation. *Application deadline:* Applications are processed on a rolling basis. Application fee: $37. Electronic applications accepted. *Expenses:* Tuition: Part-time $595 per credit. Required fees: $9 per credit. Tuition and fees vary according to program. *Unit head:* Robert Boccino, Director, 212-480-3200, Fax: 212-480-3705, E-mail: rboccino@mercy.edu. *Application contact:* Kathleen Jackson, Director of Admissions, 800-Mercy-NY, Fax: 914-674-7382, E-mail: admissions@mercy.edu.

Metropolitan State University, College of Management, St. Paul, MN 55106-5000. Offers finance (MBA); human resource management (MBA); information management (MMIS); international business (MBA); law enforcement (MPNA); management information systems (MBA); marketing (MBA); nonprofit management (MPNA); organizational studies (MBA); public administration (MPNA); purchasing management (MBA); systems management (MMIS). Part-time and evening/weekend programs available. *Degree requirements:* For master's, computer language (MMIS), thesis optional. *Entrance requirements:* For master's, GMAT (MBA), resumé. Additional exam requirements/recommendations for international students: Required—TOEFL (minimum score 550 paper-based; 213 computer-based). *Faculty research:* Yugoslav economic system, workers' cooperatives, participative management and job enrichment, global business systems.

Miami University, Graduate School, Richard T. Farmer School of Business Administration, Oxford, OH 45056. Offers accountancy (M Acc); business administration (MBA); economics (MA); finance (MBA); general management (MBA); management information systems (MBA); marketing (MBA); quality and process improvement (MBA). *Accreditation:* AACSB. Part-time programs available. *Entrance requirements:* For master's, GMAT, minimum undergraduate GPA of 3.0 during previous 2 years or 2.75 overall. Additional exam requirements/recommendations for international students: Required—TOEFL (minimum score 550 paper-based; 213 computer-based), TWE (minimum score 4).

Michigan State University, The Graduate School, Eli Broad Graduate School of Management, Department of Finance, East Lansing, MI 48824. Offers business administration (PhD); finance (MS). *Faculty:* 18 full-time (4 women), 1 part-time/adjunct (0 women). *Students:* 37 full-time (4 women), 1 part-time, 37 international. Average age 35. 20 applicants, 60% accepted. In 2006, 17 master's, 3 doctorates awarded. *Entrance requirements:* Additional exam requirements/recommendations for international students: Required—TOEFL. Electronic applications accepted. *Expenses:* Tuition, state resident: part-time $346 per credit hour. Tuition, nonresident: part-time $730 per credit hour. Tuition and fees vary according to program. *Financial support:* In 2006–07, 4 fellowships with tuition reimbursements, 9 research assistantships with tuition reimbursements (averaging $16,066 per year), 3 teaching assistantships with tuition reimbursements (averaging $19,293 per year) were awarded. *Unit head:* Dr. G. Geoffrey Booth, Chairperson, 517-353-1745, Fax: 517-432-1080, E-mail: boothg@bus.msu.edu. *Application contact:* Program Information, 517-353-1705, E-mail: fin@bus.msu.edu.

Middle Tennessee State University, College of Graduate Studies, College of Business, Department of Economics and Finance, Murfreesboro, TN 37132. Offers MA, PhD. Part-time and evening/weekend programs available. Postbaccalaureate distance learning degree programs offered. *Faculty:* 20 full-time (3 women), 1 part-time/adjunct (0 women). *Students:* 11 full-time (4 women), 33 part-time (15 women); includes 16 minority (4 African Americans, 12 Asian Americans or Pacific Islanders). Average age 30. 24 applicants, 75% accepted. In 2006, 17 degrees awarded. *Degree requirements:* For master's, thesis optional; for doctorate, thesis/dissertation, comprehensive exam. *Entrance requirements:* For master's and doctorate, GRE or MAT. Additional exam requirements/recommendations for international students: Required—TOEFL (minimum score 525 paper-based; 195 computer-based). *Application deadline:* For fall admission, 8/1 priority date for domestic students. Applications are processed on a rolling basis. Application fee: $25. Electronic applications accepted. *Financial support:* In 2006–07, 4 students received support. Application deadline: 5/1; *Unit head:* Dr. John Lee, Chair, 615-898-2520, Fax: 615-898-5596, E-mail: jlee@mtsu.edu.

Minnesota State University Mankato, College of Graduate Studies, College of Business, Mankato, MN 56001. Offers accounting and business law (MBA); finance (MBA); management (MBA); marketing and international business (MBA). *Accreditation:* AACSB. *Students:* 8 full-time (3 women), 32 part-time (13 women). *Entrance requirements:* For master's, GMAT, 2 letters of reference. Additional exam requirements/recommendations for international students: Required—TOEFL. *Application deadline:* For fall admission, 6/1 for domestic students; for spring admission, 10/1 for domestic students. Electronic applications accepted. *Unit head:* Scott Johnson, Dean, 507-389-5420.

Mississippi State University, College of Business and Industry, Department of Finance and Economics, Mississippi State, MS 39762. Offers applied economics (PhD); economics (MA); finance (MSBA). Part-time programs available. *Faculty:* 19 full-time (4 women), 5 part-time/adjunct (2 women). *Students:* 3 full-time (2 women), 1 international. Average age 24. 61 applicants, 21% accepted. In 2006, 3 master's, 1 doctorate awarded. Terminal master's awarded for partial completion of doctoral program. *Degree requirements:* For master's, thesis optional; for doctorate, thesis/dissertation, comprehensive exam, registration. *Entrance requirements:* For master's and doctorate, GMAT, GRE General Test. *Application deadline:* For fall admission, 7/1 for domestic students; for spring admission, 11/1 for domestic students. Applications are processed on a rolling basis. Application fee: $30. *Expenses:* Tuition, state resident: full-time $4,550; part-time $253 per hour. Tuition, nonresident: full-time $10,552; part-time $584 per hour. International tuition: $10,882 full-time. Tuition and fees vary according to course load. *Financial support:* In 2006–07, 1 teaching assistantship with tuition reimbursement (averaging $16,470 per year) was awarded; research assistantships with tuition reimbursements, Federal Work-Study, scholarships/grants, health care benefits, and unspecified assistantships also available. Financial award applicants required to submit FAFSA. *Faculty research:* Economics development, mergers, event studies, economic education, bank performance. Total annual research expenditures: $320,000. *Unit head:* Dr. Paul W. Grimes, Head, 662-325-2341, Fax: 662-325-1977, E-mail: pgrimes@cobilan.msstate.edu. *Application contact:* Dr. Phil Bonfanti, Director of Admissions, 662-325-4104, Fax: 662-325-8872, E-mail: admit@msstate.edu.

Mississippi State University, College of Business and Industry, Graduate Studies in Business, Mississippi State, MS 39762. Offers business administration (MBA, PhD), including accounting (PhD), business information systems (PhD), finance (PhD), management (PhD), marketing (PhD); project management (MBA). *Accreditation:* AACSB. Part-time and evening/weekend programs available. Postbaccalaureate distance learning degree programs offered.

Finance and Banking

Mississippi State University (continued)
Faculty: 66 full-time (18 women), 18 part-time/adjunct (9 women). *Students:* 143 full-time (52 women), 159 part-time (52 women); includes 30 minority (24 African Americans, 1 American Indian/Alaska Native, 2 Asian Americans or Pacific Islanders, 3 Hispanic Americans), 35 international. Average age 30. 605 applicants, 34% accepted, 142 enrolled. In 2006, 107 master's, 10 doctorates awarded. Terminal master's awarded for partial completion of doctoral program. *Degree requirements:* For doctorate, thesis/dissertation. *Entrance requirements:* For master's, GMAT, minimum GPA of 3.0 in last 60 hours of course work; for doctorate, GMAT, minimum GPA of 2.75 in last 60 undergraduate hours, 3.25 in last 60 graduate hours. Additional exam requirements/recommendations for international students: Required—TOEFL. *Application deadline:* For fall admission, 7/1 for domestic students; for spring admission, 11/1 for domestic students. Applications are processed on a rolling basis. Application fee: $30. Electronic applications accepted. *Expenses:* Tuition, state resident: full-time $4,550; part-time $253 per hour. Tuition, nonresident: full-time $10,552; part-time $584 per hour. International tuition: $10,882 full-time. Tuition and fees vary according to course load. *Financial support:* In 2006–07, 29 teaching assistantships with full tuition reimbursements (averaging $10,778 per year) were awarded; research assistantships with full tuition reimbursements, Federal Work-Study, institutionally sponsored loans, and unspecified assistantships also available. Financial award applicants required to submit FAFSA. *Unit head:* Dr. Barbara Spencer, Director, 662-325-1891, Fax: 662-325-8161, E-mail: gsb@cobilan.msstate.edu. *Application contact:* Dr. Phil Bonfanti, Director of Admissions, 662-325-4104, Fax: 662-325-8872, E-mail: admit@msstate.edu.

Montclair State University, The Graduate School, School of Business, Department of Economics and Finance, Montclair, NJ 07043-1624. Offers business economics (MBA); finance (MBA). Part-time and evening/weekend programs available. *Faculty:* 16 full-time (4 women), 4 part-time/adjunct (2 women). *Students:* 24 full-time (11 women), 70 part-time (24 women); includes 13 minority (4 African Americans, 6 Asian Americans or Pacific Islanders, 3 Hispanic Americans), 13 international. 59 applicants, 49% accepted, 22 enrolled. In 2006, 37 degrees awarded. *Entrance requirements:* For master's, GRE General Test, 2 letters of recommendation, resumé. Additional exam requirements/recommendations for international students: Required—TOEFL (minimum score 83 computer-based). *Application deadline:* For fall admission, 6/1 for international students; for spring admission, 10/1 for international students. Applications are processed on a rolling basis. Application fee: $60. Electronic applications accepted. *Expenses:* Tuition, state resident: part-time $450 per credit. Tuition, nonresident: part-time $682 per credit. Tuition and fees vary according to degree level and program. *Financial support:* In 2006–07, 3 research assistantships with full tuition reimbursements (averaging $7,000 per year) were awarded; Federal Work-Study, scholarships/grants, and unspecified assistantships also available. Support available to part-time students. Financial award application deadline: 3/1; financial award applicants required to submit FAFSA. *Unit head:* Dr. Sang-Hoon Kim, Chair, 973-655-5255, E-mail: kims@mail.montclair.edu. *Application contact:* Dr. Harold Flint, Adviser, 973-655-5255, E-mail: flinth@mail.montclair.edu.

Mount Saint Mary College, Division of Business, Newburgh, NY 12550-3494. Offers business (MBA); financial planning (MBA). Part-time and evening/weekend programs available. *Faculty:* 6 full-time (2 women), 4 part-time/adjunct (1 woman). *Students:* 20 full-time (13 women), 43 part-time (24 women); includes 20 minority (12 African Americans, 3 Asian Americans or Pacific Islanders, 5 Hispanic Americans). Average age 33. 23 applicants, 100% accepted, 22 enrolled. In 2006, 24 degrees awarded. *Degree requirements:* For master's, thesis. *Entrance requirements:* For master's, GMAT. *Application deadline:* Applications are processed on a rolling basis. Application fee: $35. *Expenses:* Tuition: Full-time $11,880; part-time $660 per credit. *Financial support:* In 2006–07, 8 students received support. Unspecified assistantships available. Financial award application deadline: 3/15. *Faculty research:* Financial reform, entrepreneurship and small business development, global business relations, technology's impact on business decision-making, college-assisted business education. *Unit head:* David R. Rant, Coordinator, 845-569-3124, Fax: 845-562-6762, E-mail: rant@msmc.edu. *Application contact:* Janice Banker, Secretary, 845-569-3582, Fax: 845-569-3885, E-mail: banker@msmc.edu.

National University, Academic Affairs, School of Business and Management, Department of Finance, Accounting and Economics, La Jolla, CA 92037-1011. Offers finance (MS); finance, accounting, and economics (EMBA, MBA); taxation (MS). Part-time and evening/weekend programs available. Postbaccalaureate distance learning degree programs offered (no on-campus study). *Faculty:* 11 full-time (1 woman), 114 part-time/adjunct (30 women). *Students:* 382 full-time (166 women), 694 part-time (302 women); includes 375 minority (91 African Americans, 5 American Indian/Alaska Native, 167 Asian Americans or Pacific Islanders, 112 Hispanic Americans), 144 international. Average age 34. 689 applicants, 577 enrolled. In 2006, 289 degrees awarded. *Degree requirements:* For master's, thesis. *Entrance requirements:* For master's, interview, minimum GPA of 2.5. Additional exam requirements/recommendations for international students: Required—TOEFL (minimum score 550 paper-based; 213 computer-based; 80 iBT), IELTS (minimum score 6). *Application deadline:* Applications are processed on a rolling basis. Application fee: $60 ($65 for international students). Electronic applications accepted. *Expenses:* Tuition: Full-time $7,722; part-time $286 per unit. One-time fee: $60. *Financial support:* Career-related internships or fieldwork, institutionally sponsored loans, scholarships/grants, and tuition waivers (partial) available. Support available to part-time students. Financial award application deadline: 6/30; financial award applicants required to submit FAFSA. *Unit head:* Donald A. Schwartz, Chair and Associate Professor, 858-642-8420, E-mail: dschwartz@nu.edu. *Application contact:* Dominick Giovanniello, Associate Regional Dean—San Diego, 800-NAT-UNIV, Fax: 858-642-8709, E-mail: dgiovann@nu.edu.

New Jersey City University, Graduate and Continuing Education, College of Professional Studies, Department of Business Administration, Jersey City, NJ 07305-1597. Offers accounting (MS); finance (MS). *Accreditation:* ACBSP. Evening/weekend programs available. *Faculty:* 9. *Students:* 2 full-time (1 woman), 33 part-time (10 women); includes 10 minority (3 African Americans, 4 Asian Americans or Pacific Islanders, 3 Hispanic Americans), 2 international. Average age 35. In 2006, 6 degrees awarded. *Application deadline:* For fall admission, 8/1 priority date for domestic students; for spring admission, 12/1 for domestic students. Applications are processed on a rolling basis. Application fee: $0. *Expenses:* Tuition, state resident: full-time $7,038; part-time $391 per credit. Tuition, nonresident: full-time $12,510; part-time $695 per credit. Required fees: $65 per credit. *Financial support:* Career-related internships or fieldwork and unspecified assistantships available. *Unit head:* Dr. Marilyn Ettinger, Head, 201-200-3353, E-mail: mettinger@njcu.edu.

New Mexico Highlands University, Graduate Studies, School of Business, Las Vegas, NM 87701. Offers business administration (MBA), including human resource management, international business, non-profit financial management. *Accreditation:* ACBSP. *Faculty:* 12 full-time (4 women), 1 part-time/adjunct (0 women). *Students:* 57 full-time (39 women), 103 part-time (69 women); includes 97 minority (1 African American, 26 American Indian/Alaska Native, 4 Asian Americans or Pacific Islanders, 66 Hispanic Americans), 17 international. Average age 35. 69 applicants, 84% accepted, 42 enrolled. In 2006, 29 degrees awarded. *Degree requirements:* For master's, thesis or alternative, comprehensive exam, registration. *Entrance requirements:* For master's, minimum undergraduate GPA of 3.0. Additional exam requirements/recommendations for international students: Required—TOEFL (minimum score 540 paper-based; 190 computer-based). *Application deadline:* For fall admission, 8/1 priority date for domestic students. Applications are processed on a rolling basis. Application fee: $15. *Expenses:* Tuition, state resident: part-time $101 per credit hour. Tuition, nonresident: part-time $101 per credit hour. *Financial support:* In 2006–07, 67 students received support, including 8 teaching assistantships with full and partial tuition reimbursements available (averaging $6,500 per year); career-related internships or fieldwork, Federal Work-Study, institutionally sponsored loans, scholarships/grants, tuition waivers (full and partial), and unspecified assistantships also available. Support available to part-time students. Financial award application deadline: 3/1; financial award applicants required to submit FAFSA. *Unit head:* Dr. William Taylor, Dean, 505-454-3344, Fax: 505-454-3354. *Application contact:* Diane Trujillo, Administrative Assistant Graduate Studies, 505-454-3266, Fax: 505-454-3558, E-mail: dtrujillo@nmhu.edu.

The New School: A University, The New School for General Studies, Program in International Affairs, New York, NY 10011. Offers global management, trade, and finance (MA, MS); international development (MA, MS); international media and communication (MA, MS); international politics and diplomacy (MA, MS); service, civic, and non-profit management (MS). Part-time programs available. *Students:* 159 full-time (104 women), 117 part-time (80 women); includes 62 minority (16 African Americans, 21 Asian Americans or Pacific Islanders, 25 Hispanic Americans), 45 international. Average age 30. In 2006, 92 degrees awarded. *Entrance requirements:* Additional exam requirements/recommendations for international students: Required—TOEFL (minimum score 600 paper-based; 250 computer-based; 100 iBT). *Application deadline:* For fall admission, 4/15 for domestic students; for spring admission, 10/15 for domestic students. Application fee: $50. *Financial support:* Fellowships with partial tuition reimbursements, research assistantships, teaching assistantships with partial tuition reimbursements, career-related internships or fieldwork, Federal Work-Study, scholarships/grants, tuition waivers (partial), and unspecified assistantships available. Support available to part-time students. Financial award application deadline: 3/1; financial award applicants required to submit FAFSA. *Unit head:* Dr. Michael Cohen, Director, 212-206-3524, Fax: 212-645-0661, E-mail: cohenm2@newschool.edu. *Application contact:* Gerianne Brusati, Associate Dean, Admissions and Student Services, 212-229-5630, Fax: 212-989-3887, E-mail: nsadmissions@newschool.edu.

The New School: A University, The New School for Social Research, Global Finance Program, New York, NY 10011. Offers MS. Application fee: $50. *Unit head:* Dr. Salih Neftei, Head, 212-229-5717 Ext. 3046, Fax: 212-229-5724, E-mail: sneftei@wwc.com. *Application contact:* Henry Watkins, Interim Director of Admissions, 809-523-5411, E-mail: gfadmit@newschool.edu.

New York Institute of Technology, Ellis College, Old Westbury, NY 11568. Offers accounting and information systems (MBA); e-commerce (MBA); finance (MBA); global management (MBA); healthcare administration (MBA); human resources management (MBA); leadership (MBA); management of information systems (MBA); management of technology (MBA); marketing (MBA); professional accounting (MBA); project management (MBA); risk management (MBA); strategy and economics (MBA). Ellis College is a collaboration between New York Institute of Technology and UNext online learning company. Part-time and evening/weekend programs available. Postbaccalaureate distance learning degree programs offered (no on-campus study). *Entrance requirements:* For master's, interview. Additional exam requirements/recommendations for international students: Required—TOEFL (minimum score 550 paper-based; 213 computer-based). Electronic applications accepted. *Expenses:* Tuition: Full-time $16,800; part-time $700 per credit.

New York Institute of Technology, Graduate Division, School of Management, Program in Business Administration, Old Westbury, NY 11568-8000. Offers accounting (Advanced Certificate); business administration (MBA); finance (Advanced Certificate); international business (Advanced Certificate); management of information systems (Advanced Certificate); marketing (Advanced Certificate). Part-time and evening/weekend programs available. *Students:* 481 full-time (120 women), 1,300 part-time (670 women); includes 297 minority (153 African Americans, 6 American Indian/Alaska Native, 81 Asian Americans or Pacific Islanders, 57 Hispanic Americans), 215 international. Average age 29. 1,049 applicants, 87% accepted, 137 enrolled. In 2006, 917 degrees awarded. *Degree requirements:* For master's, thesis (for some programs). *Entrance requirements:* For master's, minimum QPA of 2.85. Additional exam requirements/recommendations for international students: Required—TOEFL (minimum score 550 paper-based; 213 computer-based). *Application deadline:* For fall admission, 7/1 priority date for domestic students; for spring admission, 12/1 priority date for domestic students. Applications are processed on a rolling basis. Application fee: $50. Electronic applications accepted. *Expenses:* Tuition: Full-time $16,800; part-time $700 per credit. *Financial support:* Fellowships, research assistantships with partial tuition reimbursements, institutionally sponsored loans, tuition waivers (full and partial), and unspecified assistantships available. Support available to part-time students. Financial award applicants required to submit FAFSA. *Faculty research:* Instructor performance appraisal; relationship between TOEFL, GMAT, GRE, and performance in foreign students. *Unit head:* Dr. Gurumurthy Kalyanuram, Director, 516-686-7972, E-mail: gkalyana@nyit.edu. *Application contact:* Jacquelyn Nealon, Dean of Admissions and Financial Aid, 516-686-7925, Fax: 516-686-7613, E-mail: jnealon@nyit.edu.

New York University, Leonard N. Stern School of Business, Department of Finance, New York, NY 10012-1019. Offers MBA, PhD. *Expenses:* Tuition: Part-time $1,080 per unit. Required fees: $56 per unit. $329 per term. Tuition and fees vary according to program. *Faculty research:* Derivative securities, pricing of assets, credit risk, portfolio management, international finance.

New York University, Robert F. Wagner Graduate School of Public Service, Program in Public Administration, New York, NY 10012-1019. Offers public administration (PhD); public and nonprofit management and policy (MPA, Advanced Certificate), including developmental administration (Advanced Certificate), financial management and public finance, human resources management (Advanced Certificate), international administration (Advanced Certificate), management (MPA), management for public and nonprofit organizations (Advanced Certificate), public policy analysis, quantitative analysis and computer applications (Advanced Certificate), urban public policy (Advanced Certificate); JD/MPA; MBA/MPA; MPA/MA. *Accreditation:* NASPAA (one or more programs are accredited). Part-time and evening/weekend programs available. *Faculty:* 16 full-time (10 women), 42 part-time/adjunct (23 women). *Students:* 260 full-time (189 women), 246 part-time (182 women); includes 114 minority (40 African Americans, 2 American Indian/Alaska Native, 45 Asian Americans or Pacific Islanders, 27 Hispanic Americans), 44 international. Average age 28. 867 applicants, 60% accepted, 176 enrolled. In 2006, 209 master's, 5 doctorates awarded. *Degree requirements:* For master's, thesis or alternative, capstone/end event; for doctorate, one foreign language, thesis/dissertation. *Entrance requirements:* For master's, minimum undergraduate GPA of 3.0; for doctorate, GMAT or GRE General Test, minimum GPA of 3.5. Additional exam requirements/recommendations for international students: Required—TOEFL (minimum score 600 paper-based; 250 computer-based), TWE (minimum score 4). *Application deadline:* For fall admission, 6/1 for domestic students, 1/15 for international students; for spring admission, 11/15 for domestic students, 10/1 for international students. Applications are processed on a rolling basis. Application fee: $70. Electronic applications accepted. *Expenses: Contact institution.* Tuition and fees vary according to program. *Financial support:* In 2006–07, 142 fellowships (averaging $9,749 per year), 4 research assistantships with partial tuition reimbursements (averaging $15,000 per year) were awarded; career-related internships or fieldwork, Federal Work-Study, institutionally sponsored loans, scholarships/grants, health care benefits, and unspecified assistantships also available. Support available to part-time students. Financial award application deadline: 12/1; financial award applicants required to submit FAFSA. *Unit head:* Prof. Katherine O'Regan, Director, 212-998-7400, Fax: 212-995-4161. *Application contact:* Bethany Godsoe, Assistant Dean, Enrollment and Student Services, 212-998-7414, Fax: 212-995-4164, E-mail: wagner.admissions@nyu.edu.

Northeastern Illinois University, Graduate College, College of Business and Management, Chicago, IL 60625-4699. Offers accounting (MBA); finance (MBA); management (MBA); marketing (MBA). Part-time and evening/weekend programs available. *Faculty:* 24 full-time (3 women), 13 part-time/adjunct (4 women). *Students:* 24 full-time (12 women), 40 part-time (16 women); includes 15 minority (4 African Americans, 8 Asian Americans or Pacific Islanders, 3 Hispanic Americans), 21 international. Average age 31. 23 applicants, 91% accepted. In 2006, 13 degrees awarded. *Degree requirements:* For master's, thesis optional. *Entrance requirements:* For master's, GMAT, minimum GPA of 2.75. Additional exam requirements/recommendations for international students: Required—TOEFL. *Application deadline:* For fall admission, 4/1 priority date for domestic students; for spring admission, 8/15 for domestic students. Applications are processed on a rolling basis. Application fee: $25. *Financial support:* In 2006–07, 20 students received support, including 8 research assistantships with full tuition reimbursements available (averaging $6,600 per year); career-related internships or fieldwork, Federal Work-Study, institutionally sponsored loans, and tuition waivers (full and partial) also available. Support available to part-time students. *Faculty research:* Perception of accountants and non-accountants toward future of the accounting industry, asynchronous learning outcomes, cost and efficiency of financial markets, impact of deregulation on airline industry, analysis of derivational instruments.

Northeastern State University, Graduate College, College of Business and Technology, Program in Accounting and Financial Analysis, Tahlequah, OK 74464-2399. Offers MS. Part-time and evening/weekend programs available. *Students:* 4 full-time (all women), 73 part-time (45 women); includes 20 minority (4 African Americans, 13 American Indian/Alaska Native, 2 Asian Americans or Pacific Islanders, 1 Hispanic American), 4 international. In 2006, 2 degrees awarded. *Entrance requirements:* For master's, GMAT. Additional exam requirements/recommendations for international students: Required—TOEFL (minimum score 213 computer-based). *Application deadline:* For fall admission, 6/1 priority date for domestic students. Applications are processed on a rolling basis. Application fee: $0 ($25 for international students). Electronic applications accepted. *Unit head:* Dr. Todd Jackson, Coordinator, 918-456-5511 Ext. 2939, E-mail: jacksongt@nsuok.edu.

Northeastern University, Graduate School of Business Administration, Program in Finance, Boston, MA 02115-5096. Offers MSF. Part-time and evening/weekend programs available. *Faculty:* 21 full-time (4 women), 7 part-time/adjunct (1 woman). *Students:* Average age 30. 29 applicants, 59% accepted. In 2006, 24 degrees awarded. *Entrance requirements:* For master's, GMAT, bachelor's degree in business or economics. *Application deadline:* For fall admission, 4/1 for domestic students. Applications are processed on a rolling basis. Application fee: $100. Electronic applications accepted. *Financial support:* Institutionally sponsored loans available. Financial award application deadline: 2/1. *Faculty research:* Mergers and acquisitions, corporate bankruptcy, crisis management, risk management, financial markets, intermediation. *Unit head:* Florence LaForest, Manager, 617-373-5964, Fax: 617-373-8564.

Northwestern University, The Graduate School, Kellogg School of Management, Department of Finance, Evanston, IL 60208. Offers PhD. Admissions and degree offered through The Graduate School. *Degree requirements:* For doctorate, thesis/dissertation, comprehensive exam, registration. *Entrance requirements:* For doctorate, GMAT or GRE General Test, 2 years of undergraduate course work in mathematics. Additional exam requirements/recommendations for international students: Required—TOEFL. Electronic applications accepted. *Faculty research:* Corporate finance, asset pricing, international finance, micro-structure, empirical finance.

Notre Dame College, Graduate Studies, South Euclid, OH 44121-4293. Offers accounting (Certificate); creative critical thinking (M Ed); financial services management (Certificate); information systems (Certificate); learning disabilities (M Ed); management (Certificate); paralegal (Certificate); pastoral ministry (Certificate); reading (M Ed); teacher education (Certificate). Part-time and evening/weekend programs available. *Degree requirements:* For master's, thesis. *Entrance requirements:* For master's, GRE General Test, MAT, minimum GPA of 2.75, valid teaching certificate. *Faculty research:* Cognitive psychology, teaching critical thinking in the classroom.

Oakland University, Graduate Study and Lifelong Learning, School of Business Administration, Department of Accounting and Finance, Rochester, MI 48309-4401. Offers accounting (M Acc, Certificate); finance (Certificate). *Faculty:* 10 full-time (1 woman). *Students:* 20 full-time (5 women), 25 part-time (11 women); includes 3 minority (2 African Americans, 1 Asian American or Pacific Islander), 6 international. Average age 29. 18 applicants, 100% accepted, 14 enrolled. In 2006, 21 master's, 1 Certificate awarded. Application fee: $35. *Expenses:* Tuition, state resident: full-time $9,936; part-time $414 per credit. Tuition, nonresident: full-time $17,202; part-time $716 per credit. *Unit head:* Mohinder Parkash, Interim Chair, 248-370-4288, Fax: 248-370-4604.

The Ohio State University, Graduate School, Max M. Fisher College of Business, Program in Finance, Columbus, OH 43210. Offers MA, PhD. *Students:* 1 full-time (0 women). Average age 21. *Application deadline:* Applications are processed on a rolling basis. Application fee: $40 ($50 for international students). Electronic applications accepted. *Expenses:* Tuition, state resident: full-time $9,438. Tuition, nonresident: full-time $22,791. Tuition and fees vary according to course load, campus/location and program. *Application contact:* Graduate Admissions, 614-292-9444, Fax: 614-292-3895, E-mail: domestic.grad@osu.edu.

Ohio University, Graduate Studies, College of Arts and Sciences, Department of Economics, Athens, OH 45701-2979. Offers applied economics (MA); financial economics (MA). Evening/weekend programs available. *Faculty:* 15 full-time (3 women). *Students:* 31 full-time (16 women), 9 part-time (3 women); includes 2 minority (both American Indian/Alaska Native), 34 international. 94 applicants, 70% accepted, 21 enrolled. In 2006, 19 degrees awarded. *Degree requirements:* For master's, thesis or alternative. *Entrance requirements:* For master's, GRE or GMAT, minimum GPA of 3.0. Additional exam requirements/recommendations for international students: Required—TOEFL (minimum score 550 paper-based). *Application deadline:* For fall admission, 3/15 priority date for domestic students, 2/15 priority date for international students. Applications are processed on a rolling basis. Application fee: $45. *Financial support:* In 2006–07, 15 research assistantships with tuition reimbursements were awarded; Federal Work-Study, institutionally sponsored loans, scholarships/grants, and unspecified assistantships also available. Financial award application deadline: 3/15. *Faculty research:* Macroeconomics, public finance, international economics and finance, monetary theory, healthcare economics. *Unit head:* Dr. Roy Boyd, Chair, 740-593-2040, E-mail: boydr1@ohio.edu. *Application contact:* Dr. K. Doroodian, Graduate Chair, 740-593-2046, E-mail: doroodia@ohio.edu.

Oklahoma City University, Meinders School of Business, Program in Business Administration, Oklahoma City, OK 73106-1402. Offers finance (MBA); health administration (MBA); information technology (MBA); integrated marketing communications (MBA); international business (MBA); marketing (MBA); JD/MBA. *Accreditation:* ACBSP. Part-time and evening/weekend programs available. *Faculty:* 30 full-time (7 women), 24 part-time/adjunct (5 women). *Students:* 291 full-time (112 women), 186 part-time (68 women); includes 57 minority (27 African Americans, 9 American Indian/Alaska Native, 12 Asian Americans or Pacific Islanders, 9 Hispanic Americans), 218 international. Average age 27. In 2006, 341 degrees awarded. *Degree requirements:* For master's, comprehensive exam. *Entrance requirements:* For master's, minimum GPA of 2.5. Additional exam requirements/recommendations for international students: Required—TOEFL (minimum score 510 paper-based). *Application deadline:* For fall admission, 8/22 for domestic students; for spring admission, 1/15 for domestic students. Applications are processed on a rolling basis. Application fee: $30 ($70 for international students). *Financial support:* Fellowships with partial tuition reimbursements, career-related internships or fieldwork, Federal Work-Study, institutionally sponsored loans, and tuition waivers (partial) available. Support available to part-time students. Financial award application deadline: 8/1. *Faculty research:* Management information systems, international business strategies. *Unit head:* Dr. Mahmood Shandiz, Head, 405-208-5130, Fax: 405-208-5098, E-mail: mshandiz@okcu.edu. *Application contact:* Leslie McKenzie, Director, Graduate Admissions, 800-633-7242, Fax: 405-208-5356, E-mail: gadmissions@okcu.edu.

Oklahoma State University, William S. Spears School of Business, Department of Finance, Stillwater, OK 74078. Offers MBA, MSQFE, PhD. *Faculty:* 15 full-time (2 women), 4 part-time/adjunct (0 women). *Students:* 25 full-time (8 women), 10 part-time (2 women); includes 5 minority (2 African Americans, 1 American Indian/Alaska Native, 1 Asian American or Pacific Islander, 1 Hispanic American), 20 international. Average age 30. 87 applicants, 56% accepted, 18 enrolled. In 2006, 12 degrees awarded. *Degree requirements:* For doctorate, thesis/dissertation. *Entrance requirements:* For master's and doctorate, GMAT or GRE. Additional

exam requirements/recommendations for international students: Required—TOEFL. *Application deadline:* For fall admission, 2/1 priority date for domestic students, 3/1 priority date for international students; for spring admission, 8/1 priority date for international students. Applications are processed on a rolling basis. Application fee: $40 ($75 for international students). Electronic applications accepted. *Expenses:* Tuition, state resident: part-time $146 per credit hour. Tuition, nonresident: part-time $516 per credit hour. Required fees: $44 per credit hour. Tuition and fees vary according to program. *Financial support:* In 2006–07, 2 research assistantships (averaging $18,677 per year), 4 teaching assistantships (averaging $18,677 per year) were awarded; career-related internships or fieldwork, Federal Work-Study, scholarships/grants, tuition waivers (partial), and unspecified assistantships also available. Support available to part-time students. Financial award application deadline: 3/1. *Faculty research:* Corporate risk management, derivatives banking, investments and securities issuance, corporate governance, banking. *Unit head:* Dr. John Polonchek, Head, 405-624-5199.

Old Dominion University, College of Business and Public Administration, Doctoral Program in Business Administration, Norfolk, VA 23529. Offers finance (PhD); management (PhD); marketing (PhD). *Accreditation:* AACSB. *Faculty:* 20 full-time (2 women). *Students:* 21 full-time (7 women), 20 part-time (7 women); includes 4 minority (1 African American, 3 Asian Americans or Pacific Islanders), 28 international. Average age 35. 29 applicants, 59% accepted, 10 enrolled. In 2006, 5 degrees awarded. *Degree requirements:* For doctorate, thesis/dissertation, comprehensive exam. *Entrance requirements:* For doctorate, GMAT. Additional exam requirements/recommendations for international students: Required—TOEFL. *Application deadline:* For fall admission, 4/1 priority date for domestic and international students. Applications are processed on a rolling basis. Application fee: $40. Electronic applications accepted. *Expenses:* Tuition, area resident: Part-time $285 per credit hour. Tuition, nonresident: part-time $715 per credit hour. Required fees: $94 per semester. *Financial support:* In 2006–07, 11 research assistantships with full tuition reimbursements (averaging $11,500 per year), 9 teaching assistantships with full tuition reimbursements (averaging $11,500 per year) were awarded; fellowships, career-related internships or fieldwork and scholarships/grants also available. Financial award application deadline: 3/15; financial award applicants required to submit FAFSA. *Faculty research:* International business, buyer behavior, financial markets, strategy, operations research. *Unit head:* Dr. Sylvia C. Hudgins, Graduate Program Director, 757-683-3551, Fax: 757-683-4076, E-mail: shudgins@odu.edu.

See Close-Up on page 299.

Oral Roberts University, School of Business, Tulsa, OK 74171-0001. Offers accounting (MBA); finance (MBA); international business (MBA); management (MBA); marketing (MBA); non-profit management (M Man, MBA); organizational dynamics (M Man); sales marketing (M Man). *Accreditation:* ACBSP. Part-time programs available. Postbaccalaureate distance learning degree programs offered (minimal on-campus study). *Faculty:* 9 full-time (2 women), 4 part-time/adjunct (2 women). *Students:* 33 full-time (18 women), 67 part-time (28 women); includes 28 minority (17 African Americans, 3 American Indian/Alaska Native, 6 Asian Americans or Pacific Islanders, 2 Hispanic Americans), 15 international. Average age 29. 69 applicants, 84% accepted, 33 enrolled. In 2006, 21 degrees awarded. *Degree requirements:* For master's, thesis optional. *Entrance requirements:* For master's, minimum GPA of 3.0. Additional exam requirements/recommendations for international students: Required—TOEFL (minimum score 550 paper-based; 213 computer-based). *Application deadline:* For fall admission, 7/1 priority date for domestic students, 5/1 priority date for international students; for spring admission, 12/1 priority date for domestic students, 10/1 priority date for international students. Applications are processed on a rolling basis. Application fee: $35. *Expenses:* Contact institution. *Financial support:* In 2006–07, 9 research assistantships (averaging $3,600 per year) were awarded; scholarships/grants and unspecified assistantships also available. Financial award application deadline: 6/1; financial award applicants required to submit FAFSA. *Faculty research:* Non-profit, international business and marketing. *Unit head:* Dr. Mark Lewandowski, Dean, 918-495-7040, Fax: 918-495-7876, E-mail: mlewandowski@oru.edu. *Application contact:* 918-495-6989, Fax: 918-495-7965, E-mail: alsc@oru.edu.

Ottawa University, Graduate Studies-Arizona, Programs in Business, Ottawa, KS 66067-3399. Offers business administration (MBA); finance (MBA); human resources (MA, MBA); leadership (MBA); marketing (MBA). Programs offered in Mesa, Phoenix, Tempe and West Valley, AZ. Part-time and evening/weekend programs available. Postbaccalaureate distance learning degree programs offered. *Faculty:* 3 full-time (1 woman), 11 part-time/adjunct (3 women). *Students:* 5 full-time (1 woman), 125 part-time (73 women); includes 21 minority (7 African Americans, 1 American Indian/Alaska Native, 2 Asian Americans or Pacific Islanders, 11 Hispanic Americans), 5 international. Average age 39. In 2006, 42 degrees awarded. *Degree requirements:* For master's, thesis or alternative, registration. *Entrance requirements:* For master's, minimum undergraduate GPA of 3.0. Additional exam requirements/recommendations for international students: Required—TOEFL (minimum score 550 paper-based; 213 computer-based). *Application deadline:* For fall admission, 7/1 priority date for domestic students; for winter admission, 11/1 priority date for domestic students; for spring admission, 2/1 priority date for domestic students. Applications are processed on a rolling basis. Application fee: $50. Electronic applications accepted. *Unit head:* Dr. Tony Muscia, Director of Business Graduate Studies, 602-371-1188, E-mail: tony.muscia@ottawa.edu. *Application contact:* Sharon Lind, Advisement Assistant, 602-371-1188, Fax: 602-371-0035, E-mail: sharon.lind@ottawa.edu.

Our Lady of the Lake University of San Antonio, School of Business, San Antonio, TX 78207-4689. Offers general (MBA), including finance, international business, management; health care management (MBA). *Accreditation:* ACBSP. Part-time and evening/weekend programs available. *Degree requirements:* For master's, thesis optional. *Entrance requirements:* For master's, GMAT, GRE General Test, or MAT. Electronic applications accepted. *Faculty research:* International marketing, employee benefits, decision process.

Pace University, Lubin School of Business, Financial Management Program, New York, NY 10038. Offers banking and finance (MBA); corporate financial management (MBA); financial management (MBA); investment management (MBA, MS). Part-time and evening/weekend programs available. *Faculty:* 17 full-time, 9 part-time/adjunct. *Students:* 72 full-time (32 women), 344 part-time (126 women); includes 88 minority (18 African Americans, 54 Asian Americans or Pacific Islanders, 16 Hispanic Americans), 127 international. Average age 29. 375 applicants, 59% accepted, 88 enrolled. In 2006, 255 degrees awarded. *Entrance requirements:* For master's, GMAT. *Application deadline:* For fall admission, 7/31 priority date for domestic students; for spring admission, 11/30 for domestic students. Applications are processed on a rolling basis. Application fee: $65. Electronic applications accepted. *Expenses:* Tuition: Part-time $890 per credit. *Financial support:* Research assistantships, career-related internships or fieldwork, Federal Work-Study, and tuition waivers (full and partial) available. Support available to part-time students. Financial award application deadline: 8/15; financial award applicants required to submit FAFSA. *Unit head:* Dr. Edmund Mantell, Chairperson, 914-422-4165. *Application contact:* Joanna Broda, Director of Admissions, 212-346-1652, Fax: 212-346-1585, E-mail: gradnyc@pace.edu.

Pacific States University, College of Business, Los Angeles, CA 90006. Offers accounting (MBA); business administration (DBA); finance (MBA); international business (MBA); management of information technology (MBA); real estate management (MBA). Part-time and evening/weekend programs available. Postbaccalaureate distance learning degree programs offered (no on-campus study). *Faculty:* 3 full-time (0 women), 11 part-time/adjunct (0 women). *Students:* 106 full-time (47 women); includes 10 minority (all Asian Americans or Pacific Islanders), 96 international. Average age 32. 36 applicants, 81% accepted, 26 enrolled. In 2006, 68 degrees awarded. *Entrance requirements:* For master's, minimum undergraduate GPA of 2.5 during last 90 hours of course work. Additional exam requirements/recommendations for international students: Required—TOEFL (minimum score 133 computer-based). *Application deadline:* For fall admission, 8/15 priority date for domestic students; for winter admission, 10/15 priority date for domestic students; for spring admission, 1/15 priority date for domestic students. Applications are processed on a rolling basis. Application fee: $100. *Expenses:*

Finance and Banking

Pacific States University (continued)

Tuition: Full-time $6,360. Required fees: $1,080. Full-time tuition and fees vary according to course load and degree level. *Financial support:* Fellowships, research assistantships, teaching assistantships, scholarships/grants available. Financial award applicants required to submit FAFSA. *Unit head:* Dr. Kamol Somvichian, Director, 888-200-0383, Fax: 323-731-2383, E-mail: admission@psuca.edu. *Application contact:* Marina Miller, Assistant Director of Admissions, 323-731-2383 Ext. 11, Fax: 323-731-7276, E-mail: admissions@psuca.edu.

Penn State University Park, Graduate School, The Mary Jean and Frank P. Smeal College of Business Administration, State College, University Park, PA 16802-1503. Offers accounting (PhD); business administration (MBA); finance (PhD); management and organization (PhD); management science/operations/logistics (PhD); marketing (PhD); real estate (PhD); supply chain and information systems (PhD). *Students:* 287 full-time (79 women), 5 part-time (2 women); includes 39 minority (22 African Americans, 11 Asian Americans or Pacific Islanders, 6 Hispanic Americans), 93 international. Average age 31. 841 applicants, 31% accepted, 150 enrolled. In 2006, 107 master's, 11 doctorates awarded. *Expenses: Contact institution. Financial support:* In 2006–07, 1 fellowship, 11 research assistantships, 143 teaching assistantships were awarded. Financial award applicants required to submit FAFSA. *Unit head:* Dr. Kenneth B. Thomas, Dean, 814-863-0448, Fax: 814-865-7064, E-mail: j2t@psu.edu.

Philadelphia University, School of Business Administration, Program in Business Administration, Philadelphia, PA 19144-5497. Offers business administration (MBA); finance (MBA); health care management (MBA); international business (MBA); marketing (MBA); MBA/MS. Part-time and evening/weekend programs available. Postbaccalaureate distance learning degree programs offered (no on-campus study). *Faculty:* 10 full-time (2 women), 8 part-time/adjunct (0 women). *Students:* 43 full-time (24 women), 87 part-time (45 women); includes 3 Asian Americans or Pacific Islanders. 154 applicants, 56% accepted, 37 enrolled. In 2006, 85 degrees awarded. *Entrance requirements:* For master's, GMAT. Additional exam requirements/recommendations for international students: Required—TOEFL (minimum score 550 paper-based; 213 computer-based; 79 iBT). *Application deadline:* Applications are processed on a rolling basis. Application fee: $35. *Financial support:* In 2006–07, research assistantships with full tuition reimbursements (averaging $2,500 per year); career-related internships or fieldwork, Federal Work-Study, scholarships/grants, and unspecified assistantships also available. Support available to part-time students. Financial award applicants required to submit FAFSA. *Unit head:* MarySheila McDonald, Assistant Dean for Graduate Programs, 215-951-2950, Fax: 215-951-2653, E-mail: mcdonaldm@philau.edu. *Application contact:* Jack A. Klett, Director of Graduate Admissions, 215-951-2943, Fax: 215-951-2907, E-mail: gradadm@philau.edu.

Polytechnic University, Brooklyn Campus, Department of Finance and Risk Engineering, Brooklyn, NY 11201-2990. Offers financial engineering (MS, Advanced Certificate), including capital markets (MS), computational finance (MS), financial technology (MS); financial technology management (Advanced Certificate); risk management (Advanced Certificate). Part-time and evening/weekend programs available. *Students:* 114 full-time (29 women), 67 part-time (15 women); includes 21 minority (5 African Americans, 16 Asian Americans or Pacific Islanders), 85 international. Average age 32. 216 applicants, 87% accepted, 89 enrolled. In 2006, 35 degrees awarded. *Degree requirements:* For master's, thesis (for some programs), comprehensive exam (for some programs), registration. *Entrance requirements:* For master's, GMAT, minimum B average in undergraduate course work. Additional exam requirements/recommendations for international students: Required—TOEFL (minimum score 550 paper-based; 213 computer-based); Recommended—IELTS (minimum score 7). *Application deadline:* For fall admission, 7/15 priority date for domestic students, 4/1 priority date for international students; for spring admission, 12/15 priority date for domestic students, 10/1 priority date for international students. Applications are processed on a rolling basis. Application fee: $55. Electronic applications accepted. *Expenses:* Tuition: Full-time $17,784; part-time $988 per credit. *Financial support:* Applicants required to submit FAFSA. *Unit head:* Frederick Novomestky, Academic Director, 718-260-3436, Fax: 718-260-3874, E-mail: fnovomes@poly.edu.

Polytechnic University, Westchester Graduate Center, Graduate Programs, Department of Management, Major in Financial Engineering, Hawthorne, NY 10532-1507. Offers capital markets (MS); computational finance (MS); financial engineering (AC); financial technology (MS); financial technology management (AC); information management (AC). *Degree requirements:* For master's, thesis (for some programs), comprehensive exam (for some programs), registration. *Entrance requirements:* Additional exam requirements/recommendations for international students: Required—TOEFL (minimum score 550 paper-based; 213 computer-based); Recommended—IELTS (minimum score 7). *Application deadline:* For fall admission, 7/15 priority date for domestic students, 4/1 priority date for international students; for spring admission, 12/15 priority date for domestic students, 10/1 priority date for international students. Applications are processed on a rolling basis. Application fee: $55. Electronic applications accepted. *Expenses:* Tuition: Full-time $17,184; part-time $988 per credit. *Application contact:* Anthea Jeffrey, Graduate Admissions, 718-260-3200, Fax: 718-260-3624, E-mail: gradinfo@poly.edu.

Pontifical Catholic University of Puerto Rico, College of Business Administration, Ponce, PR 00717-0777. Offers accounting (MBA); business administration (PhD); finance (MBA); general business (MBA); human resources (MBA); international business (MBA); management (MBA); management information systems (MBA); marketing (MBA); office administration (MBA). Part-time and evening/weekend programs available. *Degree requirements:* For master's, thesis/dissertation; for doctorate, thesis/dissertation, comprehensive exam. *Entrance requirements:* For master's, GRE, interview, minimum GPA of 2.75; for doctorate, 2 letters of recommendation, 2 years experience in a related field, interview.

Pontificia Universidad Catolica Madre y Maestra, Graduate School, Santiago, Dominican Republic. Offers administration (M Adm, M Ed); architecture of interiors (M Arch); architecture of tourist lodgings (M Arch); construction administration (ME); convergent networks (ME); earthquake-resistant engineering (ME); environmental engineering (MEE); financial (M Mgmt); human resources (EMBA); international (M Mgmt); labor law and Social Security (M Mgmt); logistics management (ME); urban planning (M Urb). *Entrance requirements:* For master's, curriculum vitae, interview.

Portland State University, Graduate Studies, School of Business Administration, Program in Financial Analysis, Portland, OR 97207-0751. Offers MSFA. Part-time and evening/weekend programs available. *Students:* 26 full-time (13 women), 31 part-time (19 women); includes 10 minority (9 Asian Americans or Pacific Islanders, 1 Hispanic American), 11 international. Average age 30. 44 applicants, 86% accepted, 30 enrolled. In 2006, 44 degrees awarded. *Entrance requirements:* For master's, GMAT, minimum GPA of 2.75. Additional exam requirements/recommendations for international students: Required—TOEFL (minimum score 550 paper-based; 213 computer-based). *Application deadline:* For fall admission, 4/1 for domestic students, 3/1 for international students. Applications are processed on a rolling basis. Application fee: $50. *Expenses:* Tuition, state resident: full-time $6,426; part-time $238 per credit. Tuition, nonresident: full-time $11,016; part-time $408 per credit. Tuition and fees vary according to course load. *Financial support:* Research assistantships with full tuition reimbursements, career-related internships or fieldwork, Federal Work-Study, and scholarships/grants available. Financial award application deadline: 3/1; financial award applicants required to submit FAFSA. *Unit head:* Dr. John Settle, Coordinator, 503-725-3767, Fax: 503-725-5850.

Princeton University, Graduate School, Bendheim Center for Finance, Princeton, NJ 08544-1019. Offers M Fin. *Entrance requirements:* For master's, GRE General Test. Additional exam requirements/recommendations for international students: Required—TOEFL (minimum score 600 paper-based; 250 computer-based). Electronic applications accepted.

Purdue University, Graduate School, Krannert School of Management, Department of Management, West Lafayette, IN 47907. Offers accounting (PhD); business administration (MBA); finance (PhD); management information systems (PhD); marketing (PhD); operations management (PhD); quantitative methods (PhD); strategic management (PhD). *Students:* 56 full-time (21 women); includes 5 minority (3 Asian Americans or Pacific Islanders, 2 Hispanic Americans), 41 international. Average age 30. 421 applicants, 7% accepted, 19 enrolled. In 2006, 11 degrees awarded. *Median time to degree:* Doctorate–5 years full-time. Of those who began their doctoral program in fall 1998, 98% received their degree in 8 years or less. *Degree requirements:* For doctorate, thesis/dissertation, comprehensive exam, registration. *Entrance requirements:* For master's and doctorate, GMAT. Additional exam requirements/recommendations for international students: Required—TOEFL (minimum score 575 paper-based; 233 computer-based; 77 iBT), IELTS (minimum score 7). *Application deadline:* For fall admission, 2/15 for domestic and international students. Application fee: $55. Electronic applications accepted. *Financial support:* In 2006–07, 7 fellowships with partial tuition reimbursements (averaging $16,800 per year), 79 research assistantships with partial tuition reimbursements (averaging $16,800 per year), 8 teaching assistantships with partial tuition reimbursements (averaging $16,800 per year) were awarded; scholarships/grants and unspecified assistantships also available. Financial award application deadline: 2/15; financial award applicants required to submit FAFSA. *Faculty research:* Corporate finance, international business, enterprise integration. *Unit head:* Dr. John M. Barron, Head, 765-494-4451, Fax: 765-494-1526. *Application contact:* Kelly Felty, Assistant Director of Administration for Doctoral Programs, 765-494-4375, Fax: 765-494-1526, E-mail: phd@krannert.purdue.edu.

Quinnipiac University, School of Business, Program in Business Administration, Hamden, CT 06518-1940. Offers accounting (MBA); economics (MBA); finance (MBA); healthcare management (MBA); information systems management (MBA); international business (MBA); management (MBA); marketing (MBA); JD/MBA. *Accreditation:* AACSB. Part-time and evening/weekend programs available. *Faculty:* 16 full-time (2 women), 2 part-time/adjunct (1 woman). *Students:* 53 full-time (21 women), 112 part-time (48 women); includes 13 minority (2 African Americans, 1 American Indian/Alaska Native, 4 Asian Americans or Pacific Islanders, 6 Hispanic Americans), 7 international. Average age 26. 80 applicants, 65% accepted, 34 enrolled. In 2006, 73 degrees awarded. *Median time to degree:* Master's–1.5 years full-time, 2.5 years part-time. *Entrance requirements:* For master's, GMAT, minimum GPA of 3.0. Additional exam requirements/recommendations for international students: Required—TOEFL (minimum score 575 paper-based; 233 computer-based; 90 iBT), IELTS (minimum score 7). *Application deadline:* For fall admission, 7/30 priority date for domestic students, 5/30 priority date for international students; for spring admission, 12/15 priority date for domestic students, 10/15 priority date for international students. Applications are processed on a rolling basis. Application fee: $45. Electronic applications accepted. *Expenses:* Tuition: Part-time $675 per credit. Required fees: $30 per credit. *Financial support:* Tuition waivers (partial) and unspecified assistantships available. Support available to part-time students. Financial award application deadline: 4/15; financial award applicants required to submit FAFSA. *Faculty research:* Equity compensation, marketing relationships and public policy, corporate governance, international business. *Unit head:* Kevin B. Taylor, Director, 203-582-3676, Fax: 203-582-8664, E-mail: mba@quinnipiac.edu. *Application contact:* 800-462-1944, Fax: 203-582-3443, E-mail: graduate@quinnipiac.edu.

See Close-Up on page 311.

Regis University, School for Professional Studies, Program in Business, Denver, CO 80221-1099. Offers accounting (MS); business administration (MBA); finance (MBA); finance and accounting (MBA); international business (MBA); marketing (MBA); operations management (MBA); organization leadership (MS); project management (Certificate); technical management (Certificate). Offered at Colorado Springs Campus, Northwest Denver Campus, Southeast Denver Campus, Fort Collins Campus, Broomfield Campus, Henderson (Nevada) Campus, and Summerlin (Nevada) Campus. Part-time and evening/weekend programs available. Postbaccalaureate distance learning degree programs offered (no on-campus study). *Faculty:* 16 full-time (4 women), 82 part-time/adjunct (22 women). *Students:* 1,770 (834 women). Average age 36. In 2006, 560 degrees awarded. *Degree requirements:* For master's, capstone project, thesis optional. *Entrance requirements:* For master's, GMAT, interview, 2 years of full-time business work experience; for Certificate, GMAT. Additional exam requirements/recommendations for international students: Required—TOEFL or university-based test. *Application deadline:* For fall admission, 8/22 for domestic and international students; for winter admission, 1/2 for domestic and international students; for spring admission, 4/30 for domestic and international students. Applications are processed on a rolling basis. Application fee: $75. Electronic applications accepted. *Financial support:* Federal Work-Study available. Support available to part-time students. Financial award applicants required to submit FAFSA. *Unit head:* Dr. Michael Goess, Chair, 303-458-4302, Fax: 303-964-5538. *Application contact:* 800-677-9270 Ext. 4080, Fax: 303-964-5538, E-mail: masters@regis.edu.

Rensselaer Polytechnic Institute, Graduate School, Lally School of Management and Technology, Program in Management and Technology, Troy, NY 12180-3590. Offers finance (MBA, MS); financial technology (MS); management (PhD); management information systems (MBA, MS); new product development and marketing (MBA); new production and operations management (MS); product development and marketing (MS); production and operations management (MBA); technical commercialization (MS); technological entrepreneurship (MBA, MS). Part-time and evening/weekend programs available. Postbaccalaureate distance learning degree programs offered (no on-campus study). *Faculty:* 50 full-time (9 women), 1 part-time/adjunct (0 women). *Students:* 121 full-time (62 women), 525 part-time (184 women); includes 137 minority (43 African Americans, 60 Asian Americans or Pacific Islanders, 34 Hispanic Americans), 71 international. Average age 28. 416 applicants, 70% accepted, 240 enrolled. In 2006, 215 master's, 6 doctorates awarded. *Median time to degree:* Of those who began their doctoral program in fall 1998, 25% received their degree in 8 years or less. *Degree requirements:* For doctorate, thesis/dissertation. *Entrance requirements:* For master's, GMAT, resumé, 2 letters of recommendation; for doctorate, GMAT or GRE General Test, 2 letters of recommendation. Additional exam requirements/recommendations for international students: Required—TOEFL (minimum score 600 paper-based; 250 computer-based; 100 iBT); Recommended—IELTS (minimum score 7). *Application deadline:* For fall admission, 3/15 priority date for domestic and international students. Applications are processed on a rolling basis. Application fee: $75. Electronic applications accepted. *Expenses:* Tuition: Full-time $32,600; part-time $1,358 per credit. Required fees: $1,629. *Financial support:* In 2006–07, 48 students received support; fellowships with partial tuition reimbursements available, research assistantships with partial tuition reimbursements available, teaching assistantships with partial tuition reimbursements available, career-related internships or fieldwork, institutionally sponsored loans, and scholarships/grants available. Financial award application deadline: 3/15; financial award applicants required to submit FAFSA. *Faculty research:* Technological entrepreneurship, operations management, new product development and marketing, information systems, finance. Total annual research expenditures: $24,747. *Unit head:* Pedro Gonzalez, Director MBA/Admissons and Career Services, 518-276-2378, Fax: 518-276-2665, E-mail: gonzap3@rpi.edu. *Application contact:* Michele M. Martens, Manager of Graduate Programs, 518-276-6586, Fax: 518-276-2665, E-mail: martem@rpi.edu.

See Close-Up on page 313.

Rhode Island College, School of Graduate Studies, School of Management, Department of Accounting and Computer Information Systems, Providence, RI 02908-1991. Offers accounting (MP Ac); personal financial planning (MP Ac). Part-time and evening/weekend programs available. *Faculty:* 9 full-time (3 women). *Students:* 2 full-time (both women), 13 part-time (6 women); includes 1 African American, 1 international. Average age 37. In 2006, 8 degrees awarded. *Application deadline:* For fall admission, 4/1 for domestic students; for spring admission, 11/1 for domestic students. Applications are processed on a rolling basis. Application fee: $50. *Expenses:* Tuition, state resident: part-time $244 per credit. Tuition, nonresident: part-time $512 per credit. Required fees: $12 per credit. $66 per term. Tuition and fees vary according to degree level, program and reciprocity agreements. *Financial support:* Federal Work-Study, scholarships/grants, and health care benefits available. Support available to part-time students. Financial award application deadline: 5/15; financial award applicants required to submit FAFSA. *Unit head:* Dr. David Filipek, Chairperson, 401-456-8036, E-mail: dfilipek@ric.edu.

Robert Morris University, Graduate Studies, School of Business, Moon Township, PA 15108-1189. Offers accounting (MS); business administration and management (MBA); finance (MS); human resource management (MS); nonprofit management (MS); sport management (MS); taxation (MS). Part-time and evening/weekend programs available. *Faculty:* 27 full-time (12 women), 6 part-time/adjunct (1 woman). *Students:* Average age 31. 253 applicants, 59% accepted, 103 enrolled. In 2006, 139 degrees awarded. *Entrance requirements:* For master's, GMAT, letters of recommendation. Additional exam requirements/recommendations for international students: Required—TOEFL (minimum score 550 paper-based; 213 computer-based). *Application deadline:* For fall admission, 7/1 priority date for domestic and international students; for spring admission, 11/1 priority date for domestic and international students. Applications are processed on a rolling basis. Application fee: $35. Electronic applications accepted. *Expenses:* Tuition: Part-time $580 per credit. Part-time tuition and fees vary according to degree level and program. *Financial support:* Research assistantships with partial tuition reimbursements, Federal Work-Study, institutionally sponsored loans, and unspecified assistantships available. Support available to part-time students. Financial award application deadline: 5/1; financial award applicants required to submit FAFSA. *Unit head:* Dr. Derya A. Jacobs, Dean, 412-262-8451, Fax: 412-262-8494, E-mail: jacobs@rmu.edu. *Application contact:* Kellie L. Laurenzi, Dean of Enrollment, 412-262-8235, Fax: 412-299-2425, E-mail: laurenzi@rmu.edu.

Rochester Institute of Technology, Graduate Enrollment Services, E. Philip Saunders College of Business, Department of Business Administration, Program in Finance, Rochester, NY 14623-5603. Offers MS. *Students:* 11 full-time (4 women), 10 part-time (5 women); includes 1 minority (Asian American or Pacific Islander), 17 international. 66 applicants, 76% accepted, 11 enrolled. In 2006, 15 degrees awarded. *Entrance requirements:* For master's, GMAT, minimum GPA of 2.5. Additional exam requirements/recommendations for international students: Required—TOEFL (minimum score 580 paper-based; 237 computer-based; 92 iBT). *Application deadline:* For fall admission, 3/1 priority date for domestic students. Applications are processed on a rolling basis. Application fee: $50. *Expenses:* Tuition: Full-time $28,491; part-time $800 per credit. Required fees: $201. *Application contact:* Brian O'Neil, Associate Dean, 585-475-7784, E-mail: boneil@cob.rit.edu.

Rutgers, The State University of New Jersey, Newark, Graduate School, Program in Management, Newark, NJ 07102. Offers accounting (PhD); accounting information systems (PhD); computer information systems (PhD); finance (PhD); information technology (PhD); international business (PhD); management science (PhD); marketing (PhD); organization management (PhD). *Accreditation:* AACSB. *Faculty:* 101 full-time (16 women), 3 part-time/adjunct (1 woman). *Students:* 60 full-time (29 women), 32 part-time (17 women); includes 57 minority (6 African Americans, 49 Asian Americans or Pacific Islanders, 2 Hispanic Americans). 279 applicants, 13% accepted, 32 enrolled. In 2006, 10 degrees awarded. *Degree requirements:* For doctorate, thesis/dissertation, cumulative exams. *Entrance requirements:* For doctorate, GMAT or GRE, minimum undergraduate B average. Additional exam requirements/recommendations for international students: Required—TOEFL. *Application deadline:* For fall admission, 4/1 for domestic students; for spring admission, 11/1 for domestic students. Applications are processed on a rolling basis. Application fee: $50. Electronic applications accepted. *Financial support:* In 2006–07, 8 fellowships with full and partial tuition reimbursements (averaging $18,000 per year), 7 research assistantships with full tuition reimbursements (averaging $18,347 per year), teaching assistantships with full tuition reimbursements (averaging $18,347 per year) were awarded; institutionally sponsored loans and tuition waivers (full and partial) also available. Support available to part-time students. Financial award application deadline: 2/15. *Faculty research:* Technology management, leadership and teams, consumer behavior, financial and markets, logistics. *Unit head:* Dr. Glenn Shafer, Director, 973-353-1604, Fax: 973-353-5691, E-mail: gshafer@rbs.rutgers.edu. *Application contact:* Goncalo Filipe, Senior Academic Coordinator, 973-353-1002, Fax: 973-353-5691, E-mail: gfilipe@rbsmail.rutgers.edu.

Rutgers, The State University of New Jersey, Newark, Rutgers Business School: Graduate Programs-Newark/New Brunswick, Department of Finance and Economics, Newark, NJ 07102. Offers MBA, MQF. *Entrance requirements:* For master's, GMAT (MBA), GRE (MQF). Additional exam requirements/recommendations for international students: Required—TOEFL.

Rutgers, The State University of New Jersey, Newark, Rutgers Business School: Graduate Programs-Newark/New Brunswick, Doctoral Programs in Business, Newark, NJ 07102. Offers accounting (PhD); accounting information systems (PhD); finance (PhD); individualized study (PhD); information technology (PhD); international business (PhD); management science (PhD); organizational management (PhD); supply chain management (PhD).

Rutgers, The State University of New Jersey, Newark, Rutgers Business School: Graduate Programs-Newark/New Brunswick, Master of Accountancy in Governmental Accounting Program, Newark, NJ 07102. Offers government financial management (Certificate); governmental accounting (M Accy). *Accreditation:* AACSB. Postbaccalaureate distance learning degree programs offered.

Rutgers, The State University of New Jersey, New Brunswick, Graduate School, Program in Mathematics, New Brunswick, NJ 08901-1281. Offers applied mathematics (MS, PhD); math finance (MS); mathematics (MS, PhD). Part-time programs available. *Degree requirements:* For doctorate, one foreign language, thesis/dissertation, comprehensive exam. *Entrance requirements:* For master's and doctorate, GRE General Test, GRE Subject Test. Additional exam requirements/recommendations for international students: Required—TOEFL. *Faculty research:* Logic and set theory, number theory, mathematical physics, control theory, partial differential equations.

Sage Graduate School, Graduate School, Division of Management, Communications and Legal Studies, Program in Business Administration, Troy, NY 12180-4115. Offers business strategy (MBA); finance (MBA); human resources (MBA); marketing (MBA); JD/MBA; MBA/MS. Part-time and evening/weekend programs available. *Faculty:* 3 full-time (1 woman), 4 part-time/adjunct (2 women). *Students:* 9 full-time (5 women), 60 part-time (35 women); includes 10 minority (7 African Americans, 3 Hispanic Americans), 2 international. Average age 31. 58 applicants, 67% accepted, 27 enrolled. In 2006, 12 degrees awarded. *Entrance requirements:* For master's, minimum GPA of 2.75. Additional exam requirements/recommendations for international students: Required—TOEFL (minimum score 550 paper-based; 213 computer-based). *Application deadline:* Applications are processed on a rolling basis. Application fee: $40. *Expenses:* Tuition: Full-time $9,270; part-time $515 per credit hour. *Financial support:* Career-related internships or fieldwork, scholarships/grants, and unspecified assistantships available. Support available to part-time students. Financial award application deadline: 3/1; financial award applicants required to submit FAFSA. *Unit head:* Dr. David Kiner, Director, 518-292-1761, E-mail: kinerd@sage.edu. *Application contact:* Shannon K. Easton, Director of Graduate and Adult Admission, 518-244-2443, Fax: 518-244-6880, E-mail: sgsadm@sage.edu.

St. Bonaventure University, School of Graduate Studies, School of Business, St. Bonaventure, NY 14778-2284. Offers accounting (Adv C); accounting and finance (MBA); finance (Adv C); management (Adv C); management and marketing (MBA); marketing (Adv C); professional leadership (Adv C). *Accreditation:* AACSB. Part-time and evening/weekend programs available. *Entrance requirements:* For master's, GMAT. Additional exam requirements/recommendations for international students: Required—TOEFL. *Faculty research:* Stock options, small business, market relationships, auditing, taxes.

St. Cloud State University, School of Graduate Studies, G.R. Herberger College of Business, St. Cloud, MN 56301-4498. Offers management and finance (MBA), including finance; marketing and general business (MBA), including marketing. *Accreditation:* AACSB. Part-time and evening/weekend programs available. *Faculty:* 62 full-time (17 women), 4 part-time/adjunct (1 woman). *Students:* 35 full-time (11 women), 98 part-time (39 women); includes 9 minority (5 African Americans, 1 American Indian/Alaska Native, 3 Asian Americans or Pacific Islanders), 21 international. 67 applicants, 84% accepted. In 2006, 87 degrees awarded. *Degree requirements:* For master's, thesis or alternative. *Entrance requirements:* For master's, GMAT, minimum GPA of 2.75. Additional exam requirements/recommendations for international students: Required—MELAB; Recommended—TOEFL (minimum score 550 paper-based; 213 computer-based), IELTS (minimum score 7). *Application deadline:* For fall admission, 6/1 priority date for domestic students, 4/1 for international students; for spring admission, 10/1 priority date for domestic students, 8/1 for international students. Applications are processed on a rolling basis. Application fee: $35. Electronic applications accepted. *Expenses:* Contact institution. *Financial support:* Federal Work-Study, scholarships/grants, and unspecified assistantships available. Financial award application deadline: 3/1. *Unit head:* Dr. P.N. Subba, Graduate Director, 320-308-3212. *Application contact:* Linda Lou Krueger, School of Graduate Studies, 320-308-2113, Fax: 320-308-5371, E-mail: lekrueger@stcloudstate.edu.

St. Edward's University, School of Management and Business, Area of Business Administration, Austin, TX 78704. Offers accounting (MBA); business management (MBA); entrepreneurship (MBA, Certificate); finance—general (MBA, Certificate); global business (MBA, Certificate); human resource management (MBA, Certificate); management information systems (MBA, Certificate); marketing (MBA, Certificate); operations management (MBA, Certificate); personal financial planner (MBA, Certificate); sports management (MBA). Part-time and evening/weekend programs available. *Students:* 32 full-time (16 women), 394 part-time (195 women); includes 117 minority (23 African Americans, 2 American Indian/Alaska Native, 28 Asian Americans or Pacific Islanders, 64 Hispanic Americans), 21 international. Average age 33. 121 applicants, 74% accepted, 72 enrolled. In 2006, 142 degrees awarded. *Degree requirements:* For master's, minimum 24 resident hours. *Entrance requirements:* For master's, GMAT or GRE General Test, minimum GPA of 2.75 in last 60 hours of course work. Additional exam requirements/recommendations for international students: Required—TOEFL (minimum score 550 paper-based; 213 computer-based; 79 iBT). *Application deadline:* For fall admission, 8/1 for domestic students, 7/1 for international students; for spring admission, 12/1 for domestic students, 11/1 for international students. Applications are processed on a rolling basis. Application fee: $45 ($50 for international students). Electronic applications accepted. *Expenses:* Tuition: Full-time $11,682; part-time $649 per credit hour. Full-time tuition and fees vary according to course load and program. *Financial support:* In 2006–07, 4 students received support. Scholarships/grants available. Financial award applicants required to submit FAFSA. *Faculty research:* Operations management, minority entrepreneurship, globalization, professional services marketing. *Unit head:* Dr. Dianne Hill, Director, 512-428-1295, Fax: 512-448-8492, E-mail: dianneh@stedwards.edu. *Application contact:* Natalia Quintanilla, Graduate Admissions Coordinator, 512-233-1697, Fax: 512-428-1032, E-mail: nataliaq@stedwards.edu.

St. John's University, The Peter J. Tobin College of Business, Department of Economics and Finance, Program in Finance, Queens, NY 11439. Offers MBA, Adv C. Part-time and evening/weekend programs available. *Students:* 30 full-time (14 women), 105 part-time (37 women); includes 34 minority (16 African Americans, 11 Asian Americans or Pacific Islanders, 7 Hispanic Americans), 33 international. Average age 28. 135 applicants, 60% accepted, 0 enrolled. In 2006, 99 degrees awarded. *Degree requirements:* For master's, thesis optional. *Entrance requirements:* For master's, GMAT, minimum GPA of 3.0. Additional exam requirements/recommendations for international students: Required—TOEFL (minimum score 500 paper-based; 173 computer-based). *Application deadline:* For fall admission, 5/1 priority date for domestic and international students; for spring admission, 11/1 priority date for domestic and international students. Applications are processed on a rolling basis. Application fee: $40. Electronic applications accepted. *Expenses:* Contact institution. Tuition and fees vary according to program. *Financial support:* Research assistantships, scholarships/grants available. Support available to part-time students. Financial award application deadline: 3/1; financial award applicants required to submit FAFSA. *Application contact:* Nicole T. Bryan, Assistant Dean, 718-990-2599, Fax: 718-990-5242, E-mail: mbaadmissions@stjohns.edu.

Saint Joseph's University, Erivan K. Haub School of Business, Professional MBA Program, Program in Finance, Philadelphia, PA 19131-1395. Offers certified financial planner (Certificate); finance (MBA). Part-time and evening/weekend programs available. *Faculty:* 9 full-time (4 women), 5 part-time/adjunct (1 woman). *Students:* 22 full-time (5 women), 79 part-time (24 women); includes 9 minority (4 African Americans, 3 Asian Americans or Pacific Islanders, 2 Hispanic Americans), 15 international. Average age 28. In 2006, 53 degrees awarded. *Entrance requirements:* For master's, GMAT, 2 letters of recommendation. Additional exam requirements/recommendations for international students: Required—TOEFL (minimum score 550 paper-based; 213 computer-based). *Application deadline:* For fall admission, 7/15 for domestic students, 4/15 for international students; for spring admission, 11/15 for domestic students, 10/15 for international students. Applications are processed on a rolling basis. Application fee: $35. Electronic applications accepted. *Financial support:* In 2006–07, research assistantships with partial tuition reimbursements (averaging $2,000 per year); unspecified assistantships also available. Financial award application deadline: 2/1. *Unit head:* David Benglian, Director, 610-660-1671, Fax: 610-660-1599, E-mail: david.benglian@sju.edu.

Saint Joseph's University, Erivan K. Haub School of Business, Program in Financial Services, Philadelphia, PA 19131-1395. Offers MS. Part-time and evening/weekend programs available. *Faculty:* 11 full-time (1 woman), 11 part-time/adjunct (1 woman). *Students:* 5 full-time (2 women), 46 part-time (13 women); includes 9 minority (4 African Americans, 4 Asian Americans or Pacific Islanders, 1 Hispanic American), 4 international. Average age 31. In 2006, 14 degrees awarded. *Entrance requirements:* For master's, GMAT, 2 letters of recommendation, resumé. Additional exam requirements/recommendations for international students: Required—TOEFL (minimum score 550 paper-based; 213 computer-based). *Application deadline:* For fall admission, 7/15 priority date for domestic and international students; for spring admission, 11/15 priority date for domestic students, 10/15 priority date for international students. Applications are processed on a rolling basis. Application fee: $35. Electronic applications accepted. *Financial support:* Research assistantships, scholarships/grants and unspecified assistantships available. *Unit head:* David Benglian, Director, 610-660-1626, Fax: 610-660-1599, E-mail: david.benglia@sju.edu. *Application contact:* Information Contact, E-mail: msfs@sju.edu.

See Close-Up on page 455.

Saint Louis University, Graduate School, John Cook School of Business, Department of Finance, St. Louis, MO 63103-2097. Offers MBA, MSF. Part-time and evening/weekend programs available. *Faculty:* 7 full-time (1 woman), 1 part-time/adjunct (0 women). *Students:* 3 full-time (2 women), 21 part-time (7 women), 6 international. Average age 27. 45 applicants, 58% accepted, 8 enrolled. In 2006, 8 degrees awarded. *Degree requirements:* For master's, thesis. *Entrance requirements:* For master's, GMAT or GRE, letters of recommendation, resumé. Additional exam requirements/recommendations for international students: Required—TOEFL (minimum score 550 paper-based; 213 computer-based). *Application deadline:* For fall admission, 4/15 priority date for domestic and international students. Applications are processed on a rolling basis. Application fee: $90. Electronic applications accepted. *Expenses:* Contact institution. *Financial support:* Career-related internships or fieldwork, Federal Work-Study, traineeships, health care benefits, and unspecified assistantships available. Support available to part-time students. Financial award application deadline: 6/1; financial award applicants required to submit FAFSA. *Faculty research:* Market microstructure, corporate governance, banking, portfolio performance and asset allocation. *Unit head:* Dr. Brian L. Betker, Chairperson, 314-977-3858, E-mail: betkerhl@slu.edu.

Saint Mary's University of Minnesota, School of Graduate and Professional Programs, Program in Business Administration, Winona, MN 55987-1399. Offers business administration (MBA); executive business leadership (Certificate); finance manager (Certificate). *Unit head:* Dr. Karen Gulliver, Director, 612-728-5147, Fax: 612-728-5121, E-mail: kgulliver@smumn.edu.

Finance and Banking

St. Mary's University of San Antonio, Graduate School, Bill Greehey School of Business, MBA Program, San Antonio, TX 78228-8507. Offers finance (MBA); international business (MBA); management (MBA). *Faculty:* 17 full-time (6 women), 1 part-time/adjunct (0 women). *Students:* 19 full-time (9 women), 75 part-time (32 women); includes 38 minority (1 African American, 2 Asian Americans or Pacific Islanders, 35 Hispanic Americans), 3 international. Average age 29. In 2006, 34 degrees awarded. *Expenses:* Tuition: Full-time $10,890; part-time $605 per hour. Required fees: $500. Tuition and fees vary according to degree level. *Unit head:* Dr. Monica Parzinger, Director, 210-436-3708.

Saint Peter's College, MBA Programs, Jersey City, NJ 07306-5997. Offers finance (MBA); international business (MBA); management (MBA); management information systems (MBA); marketing (MBA); MBA/MS. Part-time and evening/weekend programs available. *Degree requirements:* For master's, exit presentation. *Entrance requirements:* For master's, GMAT or MAT. *Faculty research:* International finance, operations research, expert systems, networking, decision support systems.

St. Thomas Aquinas College, Division of Business Administration, Sparkill, NY 10976. Offers business administration (MBA); finance (MBA); management (MBA); marketing (MBA). Part-time and evening/weekend programs available. *Entrance requirements:* For master's, GMAT. Additional exam requirements/recommendations for international students: Required—TOEFL. Electronic applications accepted.

Saint Xavier University, Graduate Studies, Graham School of Management, Chicago, IL 60655-3105. Offers e-commerce (MBA); employee health benefits (Certificate); finance (MBA, MS); financial analysis and investments (MBA); financial planning (MBA, Certificate); financial trading and practice (MBA, Certificate); generalist/administration (MBA); health administration (MBA, MS); managed care (Certificate); management (MBA, MS); marketing (MBA); public and non-profit management (MBA); public health (MPH); service management (MBA); training and performance management (MBA); MBA/MS. *Accreditation:* ACBSP. Part-time and evening/weekend programs available. *Faculty:* 27. *Students:* 67 full-time (32 women), 291 part-time (152 women). Average age 35. In 2006, 61 degrees awarded. *Entrance requirements:* For master's, GMAT, minimum GPA of 3.0, 2 years of work experience. *Application deadline:* For fall admission, 8/15 for domestic students. Applications are processed on a rolling basis. Application fee: $35. Electronic applications accepted. *Expenses: Contact institution. Financial support:* Career-related internships or fieldwork available. Support available to part-time students. Financial award applicants required to submit FAFSA. *Unit head:* Dr. John Eber, Dean, 773-298-3601, Fax: 773-298-3601, E-mail: eber@sxu.edu. *Application contact:* Beth Gierach, Managing Director of Admission, 773-298-3053, Fax: 773-298-3076, E-mail: gierach@sxu.edu.

Sam Houston State University, College of Business Administration, Department of General Business and Finance, Huntsville, TX 77341. Offers finance (MS). *Faculty:* 11 full-time (2 women). *Students:* 95 full-time (40 women), 118 part-time (56 women); includes 37 minority (12 African Americans, 1 American Indian/Alaska Native, 6 Asian Americans or Pacific Islanders, 18 Hispanic Americans), 15 international. Average age 30. In 2006, 81 degrees awarded. *Entrance requirements:* For master's, GMAT. Application fee: $20. *Expenses:* Tuition, state resident: full-time $5,904; part-time $164 per semester hour. Tuition, nonresident: full-time $15,804; part-time $439 per semester hour. Required fees: $1,374; $462 per semester. *Unit head:* Dr. Joe James, Chair, 936-294-1278, Fax: 936-294-3074. *Application contact:* Dr. Leroy Ashorn, Advisor, 936-294-4040, E-mail: busgrad@shsu.edu.

San Diego State University, Graduate and Research Affairs, College of Business Administration, Department of Finance, San Diego, CA 92182. Offers MS. Part-time and evening/weekend programs available. *Students:* 33 full-time (20 women), 44 part-time (12 women); includes 12 minority (1 American Indian/Alaska Native, 6 Asian Americans or Pacific Islanders, 5 Hispanic Americans), 26 international. Average age 29. 65 applicants, 63% accepted, 21 enrolled. In 2006, 41 degrees awarded. *Degree requirements:* For master's, thesis or alternative. *Entrance requirements:* For master's, GMAT, resumé, letters of reference. Additional exam requirements/recommendations for international students: Required—TOEFL. *Application deadline:* For fall admission, 4/15 for domestic and international students; for spring admission, 11/1 for domestic students, 10/1 for international students. Applications are processed on a rolling basis. Application fee: $55. Electronic applications accepted. *Financial support:* In 2006–07, 10 teaching assistantships were awarded; fellowships, research assistantships, Federal Work-Study also available. Financial award applicants required to submit FAFSA. *Unit head:* Dr. Nikhil P. Varaiya, Chair, 619-594-5323, Fax: 619-594-1573, E-mail: nvaraiya@sciences.sdsu.edu. *Application contact:* Information Contact, E-mail: sdsumba@mail.sdsu.edu.

Schiller International University, MBA Programs, Florida, Largo, FL 33770. Offers financial planning (MBA); information technology (MBA); international business (MBA); international hotel and tourism management (MBA). Part-time and evening/weekend programs available. Postbaccalaureate distance learning degree programs offered (no on-campus study). *Faculty:* 5 full-time (0 women), 10 part-time/adjunct (1 woman). *Students:* 146. Average age 25. In 2006, 39 degrees awarded. *Degree requirements:* For master's, thesis optional. *Entrance requirements:* Additional exam requirements/recommendations for international students: Required—TOEFL (minimum score 550 paper-based; 213 computer-based). *Application deadline:* For fall admission, 8/1 priority date for domestic and international students; for spring admission, 12/1 priority date for domestic and international students. Applications are processed on a rolling basis. Application fee: $60. *Expenses:* Tuition: Full-time $17,920; part-time $1,420 per course. *Financial support:* Federal Work-Study, scholarships/grants, tuition waivers (partial), and unspecified assistantships available. Support available to part-time students. Financial award application deadline: 3/30; financial award applicants required to submit FAFSA. *Unit head:* Dr. Cathy Eberhart, Head, 727-736-5082, Fax: 727-734-0359. *Application contact:* Susan Russeff, Associate Director of Admissions, 727-736-5082, Fax: 727-734-0359, E-mail: admissions@schiller.edu.

Seattle University, Albers School of Business and Economics, Program in Finance, Seattle, WA 98122-1090. Offers MSF, Certificate, JD/MSF. Part-time and evening/weekend programs available. *Faculty:* 22 full-time (8 women), 1 (woman) part-time/adjunct. *Students:* 12 full-time (3 women), 58 part-time (12 women); includes 9 minority (1 African American, 8 Asian Americans or Pacific Islanders), 5 international. Average age 33. 53 applicants, 53% accepted, 24 enrolled. In 2006, 19 degrees awarded. *Entrance requirements:* For master's, GMAT, minimum GPA of 3.0, 1 year of related work experience. Additional exam requirements/recommendations for international students: Required—TOEFL. *Application deadline:* For fall admission, 8/20 priority date for domestic students; for winter admission, 11/20 for domestic students; for spring admission, 2/20 for domestic students. Applications are processed on a rolling basis. Application fee: $55. *Financial support:* Career-related internships or fieldwork and Federal Work-Study available. Support available to part-time students. Financial award applicants required to submit FAFSA. *Unit head:* Dr. Jot Yau, Chair, 206-296-5639, Fax: 206-296-5795, E-mail: jyau@seattleu.edu. *Application contact:* Janet Shandley, Associate Dean of Graduate Admissions, 206-296-5900, Fax: 206-298-5656, E-mail: grad_admissions@seattleu.edu.

Seton Hall University, Stillman School of Business, Programs in Business Administration, South Orange, NJ 07079-2697. Offers accounting (MBA); finance (MBA); financial markets, institutions and instruments (MBA); healthcare management (MBA); information systems (MBA); international business (MBA); management (MBA); marketing (MBA); pharmaceutical management (MBA); sport management (MBA). Part-time and evening/weekend programs available. *Faculty:* 57 full-time (13 women), 30 part-time/adjunct (3 women). *Students:* 57 full-time (16 women), 180 part-time (57 women); includes 9 African Americans, 10 Asian Americans or Pacific Islanders, 7 Hispanic Americans. Average age 29. 195 applicants, 47% accepted, 48 enrolled. In 2006, 144 degrees awarded. *Median time to degree:* Master's–1.6 years full-time, 2.3 years part-time. *Degree requirements:* For master's, 20 hours of community service (Social Responsibility Project). *Entrance requirements:* For master's, GMAT, minimum GPA of 2.75. Additional exam requirements/recommendations for international students: Required—TOEFL (minimum score 550 paper-based; 213 computer-based). *Application deadline:* For fall admission, 6/1 priority date for domestic students; for spring admission, 11/1 priority date for domestic students. Applications are processed on a rolling basis. Application fee: $75 ($100 for international students). Electronic applications accepted. *Financial support:* In 2006–07, 40 students received support, including research assistantships with full and partial tuition reimbursements available (averaging $5,400 per year); career-related internships or fieldwork, Federal Work-Study, scholarships/grants, and unspecified assistantships also available. Support available to part-time students. Financial award application deadline: 6/1; financial award applicants required to submit FAFSA. *Faculty research:* Financial, hedge funds, international business, legal issues, disclosure and branding. *Unit head:* Dr. Joyce A. Strawser, Associate Dean for Undergraduate and MBA Curricula, 973-761-9225, Fax: 973-761-9217, E-mail: strawsjo@shu.edu. *Application contact:* Catherine Bianchi, Director of Graduate Admissions, 973-761-9220, Fax: 973-761-9208, E-mail: biancha@shu.edu.

Southeastern University, College of Graduate Studies, Program in Financial Management, Washington, DC 20024-2788. Offers MBA. Part-time and evening/weekend programs available. *Entrance requirements:* Additional exam requirements/recommendations for international students: Required—TOEFL.

Southeast Missouri State University, School of Graduate Studies, Harrison College of Business, Cape Girardeau, MO 63701-4799. Offers accounting (MBA); environmental management (MBA); finance (MBA); general management (MBA); health administration (MBA); industrial management (MBA); international business (MBA). *Accreditation:* AACSB. Part-time and evening/weekend programs available. Postbaccalaureate distance learning degree programs offered (no on-campus study). *Faculty:* 33 full-time (10 women). *Students:* 35 full-time (18 women), 40 part-time (24 women); includes 5 minority (2 African Americans, 3 Asian Americans or Pacific Islanders), 9 international. Average age 27. 35 applicants, 86% accepted. In 2006, 23 degrees awarded. *Degree requirements:* For master's, applied research project. *Entrance requirements:* For master's, GMAT, minimum undergraduate GPA of 2.5. Additional exam requirements/recommendations for international students: Required—TOEFL (minimum score 550 paper-based; 213 computer-based). *Application deadline:* For fall admission, 8/1 for domestic students, 4/1 for international students; for spring admission, 11/21 for domestic students, 10/1 for international students. Applications are processed on a rolling basis. Application fee: $20 ($100 for international students). *Financial support:* In 2006–07, 54 students received support, including 31 research assistantships with full tuition reimbursements available (averaging $7,100 per year); career-related internships or fieldwork and unspecified assistantships also available. Financial award applicants required to submit FAFSA. *Unit head:* Dr. Kenneth Heischmidt, Director MBA Program, 573-651-2912, Fax: 573-651-5032, E-mail: kheischmidt@semo.edu. *Application contact:* Marsha L. Arant, Senior Administrative Assistant, Office of Graduate Studies, 573-651-2192, Fax: 573-651-2001, E-mail: marant@semo.edu.

Southern Adventist University, School of Business and Management, Collegedale, TN 37315-0370. Offers accounting (MBA); administration (MS); financial services (MFS); health care administration (MBA); human resource management (MBA); management (MBA); marketing (MBA). Part-time and evening/weekend programs available. Postbaccalaureate distance learning degree programs offered (no on-campus study). *Faculty:* 7 full-time (0 women), 2 part-time/adjunct (1 woman). *Students:* 18 full-time (8 women), 66 part-time (37 women); includes 15 minority (6 African Americans, 7 Asian Americans or Pacific Islanders, 2 Hispanic Americans). Average age 35. 32 applicants, 84% accepted, 24 enrolled. In 2006, 11 degrees awarded. *Entrance requirements:* For master's, GMAT. Additional exam requirements/recommendations for international students: Required—TOEFL. *Application deadline:* For fall admission, 8/1 priority date for domestic students, 7/1 for international students; for winter admission, 12/1 priority date for domestic students, 11/1 for international students; for spring admission, 4/1 priority date for domestic students, 3/1 for international students. Applications are processed on a rolling basis. Application fee: $25. Electronic applications accepted. *Financial support:* In 2006–07, 32 students received support. Scholarships/grants available. Financial award application deadline: 9/1; financial award applicants required to submit FAFSA. *Unit head:* Dr. Don Van Ornam, Dean, 423-236-2750, Fax: 423-236-1527, E-mail: dvanorna@southern.edu. *Application contact:* Linda Wilhelm, Admissions Coordinator, 423-236-2751, Fax: 423-236-1527, E-mail: sbm@southern.edu.

Southern Illinois University Edwardsville, Graduate Studies and Research, School of Business, Department of Economics and Finance, Edwardsville, IL 62026-0001. Offers MA, MS. Part-time and evening/weekend programs available. *Faculty:* 14 full-time (3 women). *Students:* 21 full-time (5 women), 17 part-time (6 women); includes 3 minority (2 African Americans, 1 Asian American or Pacific Islander), 14 international. Average age 33. 27 applicants, 56% accepted. In 2006, 12 degrees awarded. *Degree requirements:* For master's, thesis or alternative, final exam, portfolio. *Entrance requirements:* For master's, GMAT or GRE. Additional exam requirements/recommendations for international students: Required—TOEFL. *Application deadline:* For fall admission, 7/20 for domestic students, 6/1 for international students; for spring admission, 12/14 for domestic students, 10/1 for international students. Application fee: $30. Electronic applications accepted. *Financial support:* In 2006–07, 2 fellowships with full tuition reimbursements, 5 research assistantships with full tuition reimbursements were awarded; teaching assistantships with full tuition reimbursements, career-related internships or fieldwork, Federal Work-Study, institutionally sponsored loans, traineeships, and unspecified assistantships also available. Support available to part-time students. Financial award application deadline: 3/1; financial award applicants required to submit FAFSA. *Unit head:* Dr. Rik Hafer, Chair, 618-650-2542, E-mail: rhafer@siue.edu. *Application contact:* Dr. Donald Elliot, Director, 618-650-2542, E-mail: delliot@siue.edu.

Southern New Hampshire University, School of Business, Manchester, NH 03106-1045. Offers accounting (MS); business administration (MBA, Certificate), including accounting (Certificate), business administration (MBA), finance (Certificate), forensic accounting (Certificate), human resources management (Certificate), international business (Certificate), international sport management (Certificate), leadership of not for profit organizations (Certificate), marketing (Certificate), operations management (Certificate), sport management (Certificate), taxation (Certificate); finance (MS); hospitality and tourism leadership (Certificate); information technology (MS, Certificate); information technology/international business (Certificate); integrated marketing communications (Certificate); international business (MS, DBA); marketing (MS); operations and project management (MS); organizational leadership (MS); project management (Certificate); sport management (MS); MBA/Certificate. *Accreditation:* ACBSP. Part-time and evening/weekend programs available. Postbaccalaureate distance learning degree programs offered (no on-campus study). *Faculty:* 45 full-time, 75 part-time/adjunct. *Students:* 427 full-time (184 women), 774 part-time (428 women). Average age 32. In 2006, 682 master's, 1 doctorate awarded. Terminal master's awarded for partial completion of doctoral program. *Degree requirements:* For master's, one foreign language, thesis or alternative, comprehensive exam (for some programs); for doctorate, one foreign language, thesis/dissertation, comprehensive exam. *Entrance requirements:* For master's, minimum GPA of 2.5; for doctorate, GMAT. Additional exam requirements/recommendations for international students: Required—TOEFL (minimum score 500 paper-based). *Application deadline:* Applications are processed on a rolling basis. Application fee: $25. Electronic applications accepted. *Financial support:* Career-related internships or fieldwork, Federal Work-Study, institutionally sponsored loans, tuition waivers (partial), and unspecified assistantships available. Support available to part-time students. Financial award applicants required to submit FAFSA. *Unit head:* Dr. Martin Bradley, Dean, 603-644-3102, Fax: 603-644-3144, E-mail: m.bradley@snhu.edu. *Application contact:* Scott Durand, Director of Graduate Enrollment Services, 603-644-3102 Ext. 3338, Fax: 603-644-3144, E-mail: s.durand@snhu.edu.

See Close-Up on page 325.

State University of New York at Binghamton, Graduate School, School of Arts and Sciences, Department of Economics, Binghamton, NY 13902-6000. Offers economics (MA, PhD); economics and finance (MA, PhD). *Faculty:* 23 full-time (4 women), 4 part-time/adjunct (0 women). *Students:* 52 full-time (21 women), 7 part-time (2 women); includes 8 minority (3 African Americans, 3 Asian Americans or Pacific Islanders, 2 Hispanic Americans), 38 international. Average age 28. 212 applicants, 36% accepted. In 2006, 14 master's, 3 doctorates awarded. Terminal master's awarded for partial completion of doctoral program. *Degree requirements:* For doctorate, thesis/dissertation. *Entrance requirements:* For master's and doctorate, GRE General Test. Additional exam requirements/recommendations for international students: Required—TOEFL. *Application deadline:* For fall admission, 8/15 priority date for domestic students, 1/15 priority date for international students; for spring admission, 11/1 for domestic students, 10/1 priority date for international students. Applications are processed on a rolling basis. Application fee: $60. Electronic applications accepted. *Financial support:* In 2006–07, 5 fellowships with full tuition reimbursements (averaging $5,849 per year), 23 teaching assistantships with full tuition reimbursements (averaging $7,716 per year) were awarded; research assistantships, Federal Work-Study, institutionally sponsored loans, scholarships/grants, tuition waivers (full and partial), and unspecified assistantships also available. Financial award application deadline: 2/15. *Unit head:* Dr. Clifford Kern, Chairperson, 607-777-2228, E-mail: ckern@binghamton.edu.

Stevens Institute of Technology, Graduate School, Wesley J. Howe School of Technology Management, Program in Business Administration, Hoboken, NJ 07030. Offers engineering management (MBA); financial management (MBA); global technology management (MBA); information management (MBA); information technology in financial services (MBA); information technology in the pharmaceutical industry (MBA); information technology outsourcing (MBA); pharmaceutical technology management (MBA); project management (MBA); telecommunications management (MBA).

Stony Brook University, State University of New York, Graduate School, College of Business, Program in Business Administration, Stony Brook, NY 11794. Offers business administration (MBA); finance (Certificate). *Students:* 150 full-time (70 women), 58 part-time (23 women); includes 43 minority (7 African Americans, 24 Asian Americans or Pacific Islanders, 12 Hispanic Americans), 54 international. In 2006, 48 master's, 22 other advanced degrees awarded. Application fee: $60. *Expenses:* Tuition, state resident: full-time $6,900; part-time $288 per credit. Tuition, nonresident: full-time $10,920; part-time $455 per credit. *Application contact:* Dr. Jeff Casey, Director, Graduate Program, 631-632-7171, E-mail: jcasey@notes.cc.sunysb.edu.

See Close-Up on page 327.

Suffolk University, Sawyer Business School, Department of Public Administration, Boston, MA 02108-2770. Offers disability studies (MPA); health administration (MPA); nonprofit management (MPA); public administration (CASPA); public finance and human resources (MPA); state and local government (MPA); JD/MPA; MPA/MS. *Accreditation:* NASPAA (one or more programs are accredited). Part-time and evening/weekend programs available. *Faculty:* 11 full-time (4 women), 7 part-time/adjunct (4 women). *Students:* 40 full-time (25 women), 123 part-time (80 women); includes 22 minority (12 African Americans, 4 Asian Americans or Pacific Islanders, 6 Hispanic Americans), 9 international. Average age 31. 103 applicants, 87% accepted, 48 enrolled. In 2006, 65 degrees awarded. *Entrance requirements:* Additional exam requirements/recommendations for international students: Required—TOEFL (minimum score 550 paper-based; 213 computer-based; 80 iBT). *Application deadline:* For fall admission, 6/15 priority date for domestic students, 6/15 for international students; for spring admission, 11/1 priority date for domestic students, 11/1 for international students. Applications are processed on a rolling basis. Application fee: $50. Electronic applications accepted. *Expenses: Contact institution. Financial support:* In 2006–07, 55 fellowships with full and partial tuition reimbursements (averaging $8,817 per year) were awarded; career-related internships or fieldwork and Federal Work-Study also available. Support available to part-time students. Financial award application deadline: 4/1; financial award applicants required to submit FAFSA. *Faculty research:* Local government, health care, federal policy, mental health, HIV/AIDS. Total annual research expenditures: $200,000. *Unit head:* Dr. Rick Beineck, Chair, 617-573-8062, E-mail: rbeineck@suffolk.edu. *Application contact:* Judith Reynolds, Director of Graduate Admissions, 617-573-8302, Fax: 617-523-0116, E-mail: grad.admission@suffolk.edu.

Suffolk University, Sawyer Business School, Program in Finance, Boston, MA 02108-2770. Offers banking and financial services (MS); finance (MSF, CPASF); JD/MSF. *Accreditation:* AACSB. Part-time and evening/weekend programs available. *Faculty:* 15 full-time (2 women), 10 part-time/adjunct (1 woman). *Students:* Average age 29. 88 applicants, 65% accepted, 30 enrolled. In 2006, 30 degrees awarded. *Entrance requirements:* For master's, GMAT, interview. Additional exam requirements/recommendations for international students: Required—TOEFL (minimum score 550 paper-based; 213 computer-based; 80 iBT). *Application deadline:* For fall admission, 6/15 priority date for domestic students, 6/15 for international students; for spring admission, 11/1 priority date for domestic students, 11/1 for international students. Applications are processed on a rolling basis. Application fee: $50. Electronic applications accepted. *Expenses: Contact institution. Financial support:* In 2006–07, 12 students received support, including 12 fellowships (averaging $7,856 per year); career-related internships or fieldwork, Federal Work-Study, and institutionally sponsored loans also available. Support available to part-time students. Financial award application deadline: 4/1; financial award applicants required to submit FAFSA. *Faculty research:* Financial institutions, corporate finance, ownership structure, dividend policy, corporate restructuring. *Unit head:* Dr. Ki Han, Director of Graduate Programs in Finance, 617-573-8641, E-mail: msf@suffolk.edu. *Application contact:* Judith Reynolds, Director of Graduate Admissions, 617-573-8302, Fax: 617-523-0116, E-mail: grad.admission@suffolk.edu.

Syracuse University, Martin J. Whitman School of Management, PhD Program in Business Administration, Syracuse, NY 13244. Offers accounting (PhD); finance (PhD); management information systems (PhD); managerial statistics (PhD); marketing (PhD); operations management (PhD); organizational behavior (PhD); strategy and human resources (PhD); supply chain management (PhD). *Faculty:* 71 full-time (16 women), 2 part-time/adjunct (1 woman). *Students:* 34 full-time (10 women); includes 1 minority (African American), 24 international. Average age 31. 89 applicants, 8% accepted, 4 enrolled. In 2006, 8 degrees awarded. *Degree requirements:* For doctorate, thesis/dissertation, summer research paper, comprehensive exam, registration. *Entrance requirements:* For doctorate, GMAT, 3 recommendations. Additional exam requirements/recommendations for international students: Required—TOEFL (minimum score 600 paper-based; 250 computer-based; 100 iBT). *Application deadline:* For fall admission, 1/30 priority date for domestic students. Applications are processed on a rolling basis. Application fee: $75. Electronic applications accepted. *Expenses:* Tuition: Full-time $16,920; part-time $940 per credit hour. Required fees: $930; $930 per year. *Financial support:* In 2006–07, 1 fellowship with full tuition reimbursement (averaging $19,000 per year), 26 teaching assistantships with full tuition reimbursements (averaging $16,500 per year) were awarded; research assistantships with full tuition reimbursements, health care benefits and unspecified assistantships also available. Financial award application deadline: 1/30. *Faculty research:* Marketing models, market microstructure, supply chain, auditing, corporate governance. *Unit head:* Dr. Ravi Dharwadkar, Director of the PhD Program, 315-443-3386, E-mail: rdharwad@syr.edu. *Application contact:* Shannon Hiemstra, Assistant Director for PhD and Research Programs, 315-443-3549, Fax: 315-443-3671, E-mail: srhiemst@syr.edu.

Syracuse University, Martin J. Whitman School of Management, Program in Business Administration, Syracuse, NY 13244. Offers accounting (MBA); entrepreneurship (MBA); finance (MBA); marketing (MBA); supply chain management (MBA). Part-time programs available. Postbaccalaureate distance learning degree programs offered (minimal on-campus study). *Faculty:* 71 full-time (16 women), 2 part-time/adjunct (1 woman). *Students:* 70 full-time (21 women), 279 part-time (84 women); includes 83 minority (44 African Americans, 33 Asian Americans or Pacific Islanders, 6 Hispanic Americans), 36 international. Average age 27. 227 applicants, 37% accepted, 27 enrolled. In 2006, 140 degrees awarded. *Degree requirements:* For master's, registration. *Entrance requirements:* For master's, GMAT, 2 letters of recommendation, bachelor's degree. Additional exam requirements/recommendations for international students: Required—TOEFL (minimum score 600 paper-based; 250 computer-based; 100 iBT). *Application deadline:* For fall admission, 1/15 priority date for domestic and international students. Applications are processed on a rolling basis. Application fee: $75. Electronic applications accepted. *Expenses:* Tuition: Full-time $16,920; part-time $940 per credit hour. Required fees: $930; $930 per year. *Financial support:* In 2006–07, 17 students received support; fellowships with full and partial tuition reimbursements available, teaching assistantships with partial tuition reimbursements available, career-related internships or fieldwork, scholarships/grants, tuition waivers (partial), unspecified assistantships, and paid hourly positions available. Support available to part-time students. Financial award application deadline: 3/1. *Unit head:* Dr. Ravi Shukla, Associate Dean for MBA and MS Programs, 315-443-3576, Fax: 315-443-9517, E-mail: rkshukla@syr.edu. *Application contact:* Carol J. Swanberg, Director of Graduate Admissions and Financial Aid, 315-443-9214, Fax: 315-443-9517, E-mail: mbainfo@syr.edu.

Syracuse University, Martin J. Whitman School of Management, Program in Finance, Syracuse, NY 13244. Offers MSF, JD/MSF. *Faculty:* 71 full-time (16 women), 2 part-time/adjunct (1 woman). *Students:* 2 full-time (1 woman), 2 part-time, 2 international. 83 applicants, 4% accepted, 1 enrolled. In 2006, 2 degrees awarded. *Degree requirements:* For master's, registration. *Entrance requirements:* For master's, GMAT, 2 letters of recommendation, bachelor's degree in finance or economics. Additional exam requirements/recommendations for international students: Required—TOEFL (minimum score 600 paper-based; 250 computer-based; 100 iBT). *Application deadline:* For fall admission, 1/15 priority date for domestic and international students; for winter admission, 11/1 for domestic and international students. Applications are processed on a rolling basis. Application fee: $75. Electronic applications accepted. *Expenses:* Tuition: Full-time $16,920; part-time $940 per credit hour. Required fees: $930; $930 per year. *Financial support:* Career-related internships or fieldwork available. Financial award application deadline: 3/1. *Unit head:* Dr. Ravi Shukla, Associate Dean for MBA and MS Programs, 315-443-3576, Fax: 315-443-9517, E-mail: rkshukla@syr.edu. *Application contact:* Carol J. Swanberg, Director of Graduate Admissions and Financial Aid, 315-443-9214, Fax: 315-443-9517, E-mail: mbainfo@syr.edu.

Tarleton State University, College of Graduate Studies, College of Business Administration, Department of Accounting, Finance and Economics, Stephenville, TX 76402. Offers business administration (MBA). Part-time and evening/weekend programs available. *Faculty:* 10 full-time (1 woman), 1 (woman) part-time/adjunct. *Students:* 50 full-time (30 women), 138 part-time (74 women); includes 41 minority (28 African Americans, 3 Asian Americans or Pacific Islanders, 10 Hispanic Americans), 19 international. Average age 35. *Entrance requirements:* For master's, GRE or GMAT, minimum GPA of 3.0. *Application deadline:* For fall admission, 8/5 priority date for domestic students; for spring admission, 12/1 priority date for domestic students. Applications are processed on a rolling basis. Electronic applications accepted. *Financial support:* Research assistantships, teaching assistantships available. *Unit head:* Dr. Sue Cullers, Head, 254-968-9913.

Télé-université, Graduate Programs, Québec, QC G1K 9H5, Canada. Offers computer science (PhD); corporate finance (MS); distance learning (MS). Part-time programs available.

Temple University, Graduate School, Fox School of Business and Management, Doctoral Programs in Business, Philadelphia, PA 19122-6096. Offers accounting (PhD); economics (PhD); finance (PhD); general and strategic management (PhD); healthcare management (PhD); human resource administration (PhD); international business administration (PhD); management information systems (PhD); management science/operations research (PhD); marketing (PhD); risk, insurance, and health-care management (PhD); statistics (PhD); tourism (PhD). *Accreditation:* AACSB. *Entrance requirements:* For doctorate, GRE General Test, minimum GPA of 3.0, master's degree. Additional exam requirements/recommendations for international students: Required—TOEFL. *Expenses:* Tuition, state resident: full-time $12,264; part-time $511 per credit. Tuition, nonresident: full-time $17,904; part-time $746 per credit. Required fees: $84 per course. Tuition and fees vary according to program.

Temple University, Graduate School, Fox School of Business and Management, Masters Programs in Business, MBA Programs, Philadelphia, PA 19122-6096. Offers accounting (MBA); business administration (EMBA, MBA); e-business (MBA); economics (MBA); finance (MBA); general and strategic management (MBA); healthcare management (MBA); human resource administration (MBA); international business (IMBA); management information systems (MBA); management science/operations management (MBA); marketing (MBA); risk management and insurance (MBA); statistics (MBA). EMBA offered in Philadelphia, PA and Tokyo, Japan. *Accreditation:* AACSB. *Entrance requirements:* For master's, GMAT, minimum undergraduate GPA of 3.0. Additional exam requirements/recommendations for international students: Required—TOEFL. *Expenses:* Tuition, state resident: full-time $12,264; part-time $511 per credit. Tuition, nonresident: full-time $17,904; part-time $746 per credit. Required fees: $84 per course. Tuition and fees vary according to program.

Temple University, Graduate School, Fox School of Business and Management, Masters Programs in Business, MS Programs, Philadelphia, PA 19122-6096. Offers accounting and financial management (MS); actuarial science (MS); e-business (MS); finance (MS); healthcare financial management (MS); human resource administration (MS); management information systems (MS); management science/operations management (MS); marketing (MS); statistics (MS). *Accreditation:* AACSB. *Entrance requirements:* For master's, GRE General Test, minimum undergraduate GPA of 3.0. Additional exam requirements/recommendations for international students: Required—TOEFL. *Expenses:* Tuition, state resident: full-time $12,264; part-time $511 per credit. Tuition, nonresident: full-time $17,904; part-time $746 per credit. Required fees: $84 per course. Tuition and fees vary according to program.

Texas A&M International University, Office of Graduate Studies and Research, College of Business Administration, Division of International Banking and Finance Studies, Laredo, TX 78041-1900. Offers accounting (MP Acc); international banking (MBA). *Faculty:* 9 full-time (1 woman), 2 part-time/adjunct (0 women). *Students:* 23 full-time (8 women), 21 part-time (7 women); includes 28 minority (all Hispanic Americans), 1 international. Average age 28. 25 applicants, 68% accepted, 16 enrolled. In 2006, 25 degrees awarded. *Entrance requirements:* For master's, GMAT or GRE General Test. Additional exam requirements/recommendations for international students: Required—TOEFL (minimum score 550 paper-based; 213 computer-based). *Application deadline:* For fall admission, 7/15 priority date for domestic students; for spring admission, 11/12 for domestic students. Applications are processed on a rolling basis. Application fee: $25. *Expenses:* Tuition, state resident: full-time $1,580. Tuition, nonresident: full-time $5,432. Required fees: $3,808. *Financial support:* In 2006–07, 21 students received support. *Unit head:* Dr. Antonio Rodriguez, Chair, 956-326-2490, Fax: 956-326-2481. *Application contact:* Imelda Lopez, Graduate Admissions Counselor, 956-326-2485, Fax: 956-326-2459, E-mail: lopez@tamiu.edu.

Texas A&M University, Mays Business School, Department of Finance, College Station, TX 77843. Offers MS, PhD. *Faculty:* 24 full-time (3 women), 4 part-time/adjunct (1 woman). *Students:* 202 full-time (74 women). Average age 27. 110 applicants, 33% accepted. In 2006, 106 master's, 1 doctorate awarded. Terminal master's awarded for partial completion of doctoral program. *Degree requirements:* For master's, comprehensive exam; for doctorate, thesis/dissertation. *Entrance requirements:* For master's, GMAT; for doctorate, GMAT or GRE General Test. Additional exam requirements/recommendations for international students: Required—TOEFL. *Application deadline:* For fall admission, 3/1 priority date for domestic students; for spring admission, 8/1 for domestic students. Applications are processed on a rolling basis. Application fee: $50 ($75 for international students). *Expenses:* Tuition, state resident: full-time $4,697. Tuition, nonresident: full-time $11,297. Required fees: $2,272. *Financial support:* In 2006–07, 30 students received support; fellowships, research assistantships, teaching assistantships, career-related internships or fieldwork and institutionally sponsored loans available. Financial award application deadline: 2/1. *Unit head:* Dr. David Blackwell, Head, 979-845-3514, Fax: 979-845-3884. *Application contact:* Timothy Dye, Adviser, 979-845-3446, E-mail: tdye@tamu.edu.

Finance and Banking

Texas Tech University, Jerry S. Rawls College of Business Administration, Area of Finance, Lubbock, TX 79409. Offers MS, PhD. Part-time programs available. *Faculty:* 11 full-time (0 women). *Students:* 27 full-time (2 women); includes 1 minority (Asian American or Pacific Islander), 9 international. Average age 28. 41 applicants, 46% accepted, 13 enrolled. In 2006, 11 master's, 1 doctorate awarded. Terminal master's awarded for partial completion of doctoral program. *Degree requirements:* For master's, capstone course; for doctorate, thesis/dissertation, qualifying exams, comprehensive exam, registration. *Entrance requirements:* For master's and doctorate, GMAT, holistic review of academic credentials. Additional exam requirements/recommendations for international students: Required—TOEFL (minimum score 550 paper-based; 213 computer-based; 79 iBT). *Application deadline:* For fall admission, 7/1 priority date for domestic students, 3/1 priority date for international students; for spring admission, 11/1 priority date for domestic students, 9/1 priority date for international students. Applications are processed on a rolling basis. Application fee: $50 ($60 for international students). Electronic applications accepted. *Expenses:* Tuition, state resident: full-time $4,440. Tuition, nonresident: full-time $11,040. Required fees: $2,136. *Financial support:* In 2006–07, 6 research assistantships (averaging $8,000 per year), 7 teaching assistantships (averaging $16,930 per year) were awarded; Federal Work-Study and scholarships/grants also available. Support available to part-time students. Financial award applicants required to submit FAFSA. *Faculty research:* Portfolio theory, banking and financial institutions, corporate finance, securities and options futures. *Unit head:* Dr. Drew Winters, Area Coordinator, 806-742-3350, Fax: 806-742-2099, E-mail: drew.winters@ttu.edu. *Application contact:* Cynthia D. Barnes, Director, Graduate Services Center, 806-742-3184, Fax: 806-742-3958, E-mail: ba_grad@ttu.edu.

Texas Tech University, Jerry S. Rawls College of Business Administration, Programs in Business Administration, Lubbock, TX 79409. Offers agricultural business (MBA); entrepreneurship (MBA); finance (MBA); general business (MBA); health organization management (MBA); international business (MBA); management and leadership skills (MBA); management information systems (MBA); marketing (MBA); statistics (MBA); JD/MBA; MBA/M Arch; MBA/MA; MBA/MD; MBA/MS. Part-time and evening/weekend programs available. *Students:* 65 full-time (16 women), 347 part-time (121 women); includes 74 minority (5 African Americans, 5 American Indian/Alaska Native, 24 Asian Americans or Pacific Islanders, 40 Hispanic Americans), 24 international. Average age 25. 382 applicants, 82% accepted, 244 enrolled. In 2006, 150 degrees awarded. *Degree requirements:* For master's, capstone course. *Entrance requirements:* For master's, GMAT, holistic review of academic credentials. Additional exam requirements/recommendations for international students: Required—TOEFL (minimum score 550 paper-based; 213 computer-based; 79 iBT). *Application deadline:* For fall admission, 7/1 priority date for domestic students, 3/1 priority date for international students; for spring admission, 11/1 priority date for domestic students, 9/1 priority date for international students. Applications are processed on a rolling basis. Application fee: $50 ($60 for international students). Electronic applications accepted. *Expenses:* Tuition, state resident: full-time $4,440. Tuition, nonresident: full-time $11,040. Required fees: $2,136. *Financial support:* In 2006–07, 36 research assistantships (averaging $8,000 per year) were awarded; teaching assistantships, career-related internships or fieldwork, Federal Work-Study, scholarships/grants, health care benefits, and unspecified assistantships also available. Support available to part-time students. Financial award applicants required to submit FAFSA. *Unit head:* Dr. W. Jay Conover, Director, 806-742-1546, Fax: 806-742-3958, E-mail: jay.conover@ttu.edu. *Application contact:* Cynthia D. Barnes, Director, Graduate Services Center, 806-742-3184, Fax: 806-742-3958, E-mail: ba_grad@ttu.edu.

Touro University International, College of Business Administration, Program in Business Administration, Cypress, CA 90630. Offers business administration (PhD); conflict and negotiation management (MBA); criminal justice administration (MBA); entrepreneurship (MBA); finance (MBA); general management (MBA); human resource management (MBA); information technology management (MBA); international business (MBA); logistics management (MBA); public management (MBA); strategic leadership (MBA). Part-time and evening/weekend programs available. Postbaccalaureate distance learning degree programs offered (no on-campus study). In 2006, 631 master's, 30 doctorates awarded. *Degree requirements:* For doctorate, thesis/dissertation, defense of dissertation, comprehensive exam. *Entrance requirements:* For master's, minimum GPA of 3.0; for doctorate, minimum GPA of 3.4, curriculum vitae, course work in research methods or statistics. Additional exam requirements/recommendations for international students: Required—TOEFL (minimum score 550 paper-based). *Application deadline:* Applications are processed on a rolling basis. Application fee: $75. Electronic applications accepted. *Expenses:* Tuition: Part-time $300 per credit hour. Tuition and fees vary according to course level and program.

Union Graduate College, School of Management, Schenectady, NY 12308-3107. Offers business administration (MBA, Certificate); financial management (Certificate); general management (Certificate); health systems administration (MBA, Certificate); healthcare management (Certificate). *Accreditation:* AACSB. Part-time and evening/weekend programs available. *Students:* 94 full-time (48 women), 211 part-time (81 women); includes 32 minority (9 African Americans, 17 Asian Americans or Pacific Islanders, 6 Hispanic Americans), 23 international. Average age 27. 116 applicants, 72% accepted, 67 enrolled. In 2006, 58 master's, 2 other advanced degrees awarded. *Degree requirements:* For master's, internship, capstone course. *Entrance requirements:* For master's, GMAT, minimum GPA of 3.0, letters of recommendation. Additional exam requirements/recommendations for international students: Required—TOEFL (minimum score 550 paper-based; 213 computer-based). *Application deadline:* Applications are processed on a rolling basis. Application fee: $60. *Financial support:* Research assistantships, career-related internships or fieldwork, Federal Work-Study, scholarships/grants, health care benefits, and tuition waivers (partial) available. Support available to part-time students. Financial award applicants required to submit FAFSA. *Unit head:* Melvin Chudzik, Dean, 518-388-6447, Fax: 518-388-6754, E-mail: chudzikm@union.edu. *Application contact:* Rhonda Sheehan, Director of Graduate Admissions Registrar, 518-388-6238, Fax: 518-388-6686, E-mail: sheehanr@union.edu.

United States International University, School of Business Administration, Nairobi, Kenya. Offers finance (MBA); information technology management (MBA); integrated studies (MBA); management and organizational development (MS); marketing (MBA); strategic management (MBA). Part-time and evening/weekend programs available. *Degree requirements:* For master's, thesis, registration. *Entrance requirements:* For master's, GMAT, 2 letters of reference, resumé. Additional exam requirements/recommendations for international students: Required—TOEFL (minimum score 550 paper-based; 213 computer-based). *Faculty research:* Marketing in small business enterprises, total quality management in Kenya.

Universidad de las Americas, A.C., Program in Business Administration, Mexico City, Mexico. Offers finance (MBA); marketing research (MBA); production and quality (MBA).

Universidad de las Américas–Puebla, Division of Graduate Studies, School of Business Administration, Puebla, Mexico. Offers business administration (MBA); finance (M Adm). Part-time and evening/weekend programs available. *Degree requirements:* For master's, one foreign language, thesis. *Entrance requirements:* Additional exam requirements/recommendations for international students: Required—TOEFL. *Faculty research:* System dynamics, information technology, marketing, international business, strategic planning, quality.

Universidad de las Américas–Puebla, Division of Graduate Studies, School of Social Sciences, Program in Economics, Puebla, Mexico. Offers economics (MA); finance (M Adm). Part-time and evening/weekend programs available. *Degree requirements:* For master's, one foreign language, thesis. *Faculty research:* Economic models (mathematics), industrial organization, assets and values market.

Universidad Metropolitana, School of Business Administration, Program in Finance, San Juan, PR 00928-1150. Offers MBA.

Université de Sherbrooke, Faculty of Administration, Program in Finance, Sherbrooke, QC J1K 2R1, Canada. Offers M Sc.

Université du Québec à Montréal, Graduate Programs, Program in Finance, Montréal, QC H3C 3P8, Canada. Offers Diploma. Part-time programs available. *Entrance requirements:* For degree, appropriate bachelor's degree or equivalent, proficiency in French.

Université du Québec à Trois-Rivières, Graduate Programs, Program in Finance and Economic Finance, Trois-Rivières, QC G9A 5H7, Canada. Offers DESS.

Université du Québec en Outaouais, Graduate Programs, Program in Financial Services, Gatineau, QC J8X 3X7, Canada. Offers MBA, Diploma. *Students:* 32 full-time, 60 part-time, 5 international. *Application deadline:* For fall admission, 6/1 priority date for domestic students, 3/1 for international students; for winter admission, 11/1 priority date for domestic students, 10/1 for international students. Application fee: $30. *Unit head:* Jan Saint-Macary, Director, 819-773-1725, Fax: 819-773-1747, E-mail: jan.saint-macary@uqo.ca. *Application contact:* Registrar's Office, 819-773-1850, Fax: 819-773-1835, E-mail: registraire@uqo.ca.

Université Laval, Faculty of Administrative Sciences, Programs in Business Administration, Québec, QC G1K 7P4, Canada. Offers accounting (MBA); agri-food management (MBA); electronic business (MBA, Diploma); factory management and logistics (MBA); finance (MBA); firm management (MBA); information technology management (MBA); international management (MBA); management (MBA); management accounting (MBA, Diploma); marketing (MBA); modelization and organizational decision (MBA); occupational health and safety management (MBA); pharmacy management (MBA); technological entrepreneurship (Diploma). *Accreditation:* AACSB. Part-time and evening/weekend programs available. Postbaccalaureate distance learning degree programs offered (no on-campus study). *Entrance requirements:* For master's and Diploma, knowledge of French and English. Electronic applications accepted.

University at Albany, State University of New York, School of Business, Department of Finance, Albany, NY 12222-0001. Offers MBA. *Degree requirements:* For master's, field study project. *Entrance requirements:* For master's, GMAT. Additional exam requirements/recommendations for international students: Required—TOEFL (minimum score 550 paper-based; 213 computer-based). *Application deadline:* For fall admission, 3/1 priority date for domestic students, 4/1 for international students. Applications are processed on a rolling basis. Application fee: $75. Electronic applications accepted. *Expenses:* Tuition, state resident: full-time $6,900; part-time $288 per credit. Tuition, nonresident: full-time $10,920; part-time $455 per credit. Required fees: $1,139. *Financial support:* Application deadline: 4/1. *Faculty research:* Tax-exempt securities, public finance, financial engineering, international finance, investments management. *Unit head:* Rita Biswas, Chair, 518-442-4915. *Application contact:* Michael DeRensis, Director, Graduate Admissions, 518-442-3980, Fax: 518-442-3922, E-mail: graduate@uamail.albany.edu.

University at Buffalo, the State University of New York, Graduate School, School of Management, Buffalo, NY 14260. Offers accounting (MS); business administration (MBA); finance (MS); information assurance (Certificate); management (PhD); management information systems (MS); supply chains and operations management (MS); Au D/MBA; JD/MBA; M Arch/MBA; MA/MBA; MD/MBA; MPH/MBA; MSW/MBA; Pharm D/MBA. *Accreditation:* AACSB. Part-time and evening/weekend programs available. *Faculty:* 65 full-time (18 women), 30 part-time/adjunct (3 women). *Students:* 493 full-time (192 women), 212 part-time (55 women); includes 53 minority (11 African Americans, 3 American Indian/Alaska Native, 31 Asian Americans or Pacific Islanders, 8 Hispanic Americans), 283 international. Average age 27. 1,058 applicants, 55% accepted, 369 enrolled. In 2006, 260 master's, 5 doctorates, 3 other advanced degrees awarded. *Degree requirements:* For doctorate, thesis/dissertation, comprehensive exam. *Entrance requirements:* For master's, GMAT, GRE General Test (all master's degrees except accounting); for doctorate, GMAT or GRE. Additional exam requirements/recommendations for international students: Required—TOEFL (minimum score 230 computer-based). *Application deadline:* For fall admission, 6/1 priority date for domestic students, 3/1 priority date for international students. Applications are processed on a rolling basis. Application fee: $50. Electronic applications accepted. *Expenses:* Contact institution. *Financial support:* In 2006–07, 91 students received support, including 17 fellowships with full and partial tuition reimbursements available (averaging $3,917 per year), 38 research assistantships with full and partial tuition reimbursements available (averaging $11,907 per year), 26 teaching assistantships with full and partial tuition reimbursements available (averaging $7,571 per year); career-related internships or fieldwork, Federal Work-Study, institutionally sponsored loans, scholarships/grants, health care benefits, and unspecified assistantships also available. Financial award application deadline: 2/15; financial award applicants required to submit FAFSA. *Faculty research:* Information assurance, relationship marketing, global processes, credit analysis in banking, disaster mitigation and response. Total annual research expenditures: $330,551. *Unit head:* John M. Thomas, Dean, 716-645-3221, Fax: 716-645-5926, E-mail: jmthomas@buffalo.edu. *Application contact:* David W. Frasier, Administrative Director of Graduate Programs and Assistant Dean, 716-645-3204, Fax: 716-645-2341, E-mail: davidf@buffalo.edu.

The University of Akron, Graduate School, College of Business Administration, Department of Finance, Akron, OH 44325. Offers MBA, JD/MBA. Part-time and evening/weekend programs available. *Faculty:* 9 full-time (2 women), 2 part-time/adjunct (0 women). *Students:* 41 full-time (13 women), 32 part-time (8 women); includes 2 minority (1 African American, 1 Asian American or Pacific Islander), 24 international. Average age 28. 42 applicants, 69% accepted, 16 enrolled. In 2006, 23 master's awarded. *Entrance requirements:* For master's, GMAT, minimum GPA of 2.75. Additional exam requirements/recommendations for international students: Required—TOEFL (minimum score 550 paper-based; 213 computer-based; 79 iBT). *Application deadline:* For fall admission, 8/15 for domestic students. Applications are processed on a rolling basis. Application fee: $30 ($40 for international students). Electronic applications accepted. *Expenses:* Tuition, state resident: full-time $6,164; part-time $342 per credit. Tuition, nonresident: full-time $10,575; part-time $588 per credit. Required fees: $806; $43 per credit. $12 per term. Tuition and fees vary according to course load, degree level and program. *Financial support:* In 2006–07, 16 research assistantships with full tuition reimbursements, 1 teaching assistantship with full tuition reimbursement were awarded; tuition waivers (partial) also available. *Faculty research:* Corporate finance, financial markets and institutions, investment and equity market analysis, personal financial planning, real estate. *Unit head:* David A. Redle, Chair, 330-972-6329, E-mail: dredle@uakron.edu. *Application contact:* Dr. James Divoky, Director of Graduate Business Programs, 330-972-7043, Fax: 330-972-6588, E-mail: jdivoky@uakron.edu.

The University of Alabama, Graduate School, Manderson Graduate School of Business, Department of Management and Marketing, Program in Management, Tuscaloosa, AL 35487. Offers accounting (MA, PhD); applied statistics (PhD); economics (MA, PhD); finance (MS, PhD); management (MA, PhD); operations management (MS, PhD); statistics (MS); tax accounting (MA). *Faculty:* 27 full-time (8 women), 2 part-time/adjunct (0 women). *Students:* Average age 29. 112 applicants, 36% accepted. In 2006, 20 master's, 1 doctorate awarded. Terminal master's awarded for partial completion of doctoral program. *Median time to degree:* Master's–2.4 years part-time; doctorate–4 years full-time, 2 years part-time. Of those who began their doctoral program in fall 1998, 100% received their degree in 8 years or less. *Degree requirements:* For master's, thesis (for some programs), formal project paper, comprehensive exam (for some programs), registration; for doctorate, thesis/dissertation, comprehensive exam, registration. *Entrance requirements:* For master's and doctorate, GMAT or GRE, minimum GPA of 3.0. Additional exam requirements/recommendations for international students: Required—TOEFL. *Application deadline:* For fall admission, 6/30 priority date for domestic students, 1/31 for international students. Applications are processed on a rolling basis. Application fee: $25. *Financial support:* In 2006–07, 5 fellowships (averaging $2,000 per year), 2 research assistantships (averaging $2,000 per year), 2 teaching assistantships (averaging $2,000 per year) were awarded. *Faculty research:* Relationship marketing, team building, e-commerce strategy, entrepreneurship, health care management, service marketing.

The University of Alabama, Graduate School, Manderson Graduate School of Business, Economics, Finance and Legal Studies Department, Tuscaloosa, AL 35487. Offers economics (MA, PhD); finance (MS, PhD). *Faculty:* 25 full-time (2 women), 1 (woman) part-time/adjunct. *Students:* 56 full-time (15 women), 13 part-time (8 women); includes 5 minority (2 African Americans, 3 Asian Americans or Pacific Islanders), 28 international. Average age 28. 141 applicants, 43% accepted, 32 enrolled. In 2006, 19 master's, 4 doctorates awarded. Terminal master's awarded for partial completion of doctoral program. *Median time to degree:* Of those who began their doctoral program in fall 1998, 99% received their degree in 8 years or less. *Degree requirements:* For master's, thesis, comprehensive exam (MA), thesis (MSC), comprehensive exam. *Entrance requirements:* For master's, GMAT, GRE; for doctorate, GRE/GMAT. Additional exam requirements/recommendations for international students: Required—TOEFL (minimum score 550 paper-based; 213 computer-based). *Application deadline:* For fall admission, 7/1 priority date for domestic students, 1/15 for international students; for spring admission, 11/1 priority date for domestic students, 6/1 for international students. Applications are processed on a rolling basis. Application fee: $25. Electronic applications accepted. *Financial support:* In 2006–07, 5 fellowships (averaging $3,200 per year), 21 research assistantships with full and partial tuition reimbursements (averaging $11,000 per year), 16 teaching assistantships with full and partial tuition reimbursements (averaging $11,000 per year) were awarded; Federal Work-Study, institutionally sponsored loans, and unspecified assistantships also available. *Faculty research:* Taxation, futures market, monetary theory and policy, income distribution. *Unit head:* Prof. Billy P. Helms, Head, 205-348-8067, E-mail: bhelms@cba.ua.edu.

University of Alaska Fairbanks, School of Management, Department of Business Administration, Fairbanks, AK 99775-7520. Offers capital markets (MBA); general management (MBA). *Accreditation:* AACSB. Part-time programs available. *Faculty:* 9 full-time (2 women), 2 part-time/adjunct (1 woman). *Students:* 16 full-time (5 women), 8 part-time (7 women); includes 1 minority (Asian American or Pacific Islander), 6 international. Average age 33. 16 applicants, 56% accepted, 5 enrolled. In 2006, 7 degrees awarded. *Degree requirements:* For master's, thesis or alternative, comprehensive exam, registration. *Entrance requirements:* For master's, GMAT. Additional exam requirements/recommendations for international students: Required—TOEFL (minimum score 550 paper-based; 213 computer-based). *Application deadline:* For fall admission, 6/1 priority date for domestic students, 2/1 for international students; for spring admission, 10/15 priority date for domestic students, 9/1 for international students. Applications are processed on a rolling basis. Application fee: $50. Electronic applications accepted. *Financial support:* In 2006–07, 1 research assistantship with tuition reimbursement (averaging $4,800 per year), 5 teaching assistantships with tuition reimbursements (averaging $10,773 per year) were awarded; fellowships with tuition reimbursements, career-related internships or fieldwork, Federal Work-Study, and scholarships/grants also available. Financial award applicants required to submit FAFSA. *Faculty research:* Consumer behavior, portfolio theory, marketing, international finance and business, asset pricing. *Unit head:* Dr. Laura Milner, Director, MBA Program, 907-474-5294, Fax: 907-474-5219, E-mail: fflmm@uaf.edu.

University of Alberta, Faculty of Graduate Studies and Research, Department of Economics, Edmonton, AB T6G 2E1, Canada. Offers economics (MA, PhD); economics and finance (MA); environmental and natural resource economics (PhD). Part-time programs available. *Faculty:* 25 full-time (5 women), 3 part-time/adjunct (0 women). *Students:* 33 full-time (7 women), 7 part-time (3 women). Average age 26. 112 applicants, 58% accepted, 22 enrolled. In 2006, 8 master's, 1 doctorate awarded. *Degree requirements:* For doctorate, thesis/dissertation. *Entrance requirements:* For master's and doctorate, GRE. Additional exam requirements/recommendations for international students: Required—TOEFL. *Application deadline:* For fall admission, 6/15 for domestic students. Applications are processed on a rolling basis. *Financial support:* In 2006–07, 19 students received support, including 6 research assistantships with partial tuition reimbursements available (averaging $14,300 per year), 5 teaching assistantships with partial tuition reimbursements available (averaging $11,200 per year); career-related internships or fieldwork and scholarships/grants also available. Financial award application deadline: 3/1. *Faculty research:* Public finance, international trade, industrial organization, Pacific Rim economics, monetary economics. *Unit head:* Henry van Egteren, Graduate Coordinator, 780-492-7634, Fax: 780-492-3300. *Application contact:* Audrey Jackson, Graduate Program Administrator, 780-492-7634, Fax: 780-492-3300, E-mail: econapps@ualberta.ca.

University of Alberta, Faculty of Graduate Studies and Research, Doctoral Program in Business, Edmonton, AB T6G 2E1, Canada. Offers accounting (PhD); finance (PhD); human resources/industrial relations (PhD); management science (PhD); marketing (PhD); organizational analysis (PhD); MBA/PhD. *Accreditation:* AACSB. Part-time programs available. *Faculty:* 41 full-time (7 women), 1 part-time/adjunct (0 women). *Students:* 46 full-time (27 women), 5 part-time (3 women). Average age 34. 307 applicants, 7% accepted, 11 enrolled. In 2006, 2 degrees awarded. *Median time to degree:* Of those who began their doctoral program in fall 1998, 60% received their degree in 8 years or less. *Degree requirements:* For doctorate, thesis/dissertation, comprehensive exam. *Entrance requirements:* For doctorate, GMAT. Additional exam requirements/recommendations for international students: Required—TOEFL (minimum score 550 paper-based; 213 computer-based). *Application deadline:* For fall admission, 6/1 priority date for domestic students; for winter admission, 5/1 for domestic students. Application fee: $0. Electronic applications accepted. *Financial support:* In 2006–07, 29 students received support, including 11 fellowships with full tuition reimbursements available (averaging $17,000 per year); scholarships/grants and tuition waivers (partial) also available. *Faculty research:* Accounting, capital markets and corporate finance, organizational change and human resource management, marketing, strategic management. Total annual research expenditures: $7.7 million. *Unit head:* Dr. Mike Percy, Director, 780-492-2361, Fax: 780-492-3325, E-mail: busphd@ualberta.ca. *Application contact:* Jeanette Gosine, Program Coordinator, 780-492-2361, Fax: 780-492-3325, E-mail: busphd@ualberta.ca.

See Close-Up on page 335.

The University of Arizona, Graduate College, College of Business and Public Administration, Eller Graduate School of Management, Department of Finance, Tucson, AZ 85721. Offers MS, PhD. Part-time programs available. *Faculty:* 14 full-time (3 women). *Students:* 35 full-time (13 women), 2 part-time; includes 5 minority (all Asian Americans or Pacific Islanders), 20 international. Average age 27. 133 applicants, 56% accepted, 30 enrolled. In 2006, 24 master's, 3 doctorates awarded. Terminal master's awarded for partial completion of doctoral program. *Median time to degree:* Of those who began their doctoral program in fall 1998, 25% received their degree in 8 years or less. *Degree requirements:* For master's, project; for doctorate, thesis/dissertation, comprehensive exam, registration. *Entrance requirements:* For master's, GMAT, minimum GPA of 3.0; for doctorate, GMAT or GRE. Additional exam requirements/recommendations for international students: Required—TOEFL (minimum score 600 paper-based; 250 computer-based). *Application deadline:* For fall admission, 3/15 for domestic students, 12/1 for international students. Applications are processed on a rolling basis. Application fee: $50. *Expenses:* Contact institution. *Financial support:* In 2006–07, 11 students received support, including 1 research assistantship (averaging $16,000 per year), 8 teaching assistantships (averaging $16,000 per year); fellowships, tuition waivers (partial) and unspecified assistantships also available. Financial award application deadline: 3/15. *Faculty research:* Corporate finance, banking, investments, stock market. *Unit head:* Dr. Chris Lamoureux, Head, 520-621-7448, Fax: 520-621-1261, E-mail: lamoureu@lamfin.eller.arizona.edu. *Application contact:* Kay Ross, Program Coordinator, 520-621-1520, Fax: 520-621-1261, E-mail: kross@eller.arizona.edu.

University of Baltimore, Graduate School, Merrick School of Business, Department of Economics and Finance, Baltimore, MD 21201-5779. Offers business/finance (MS). Part-time and evening/weekend programs available. *Faculty:* 13 full-time (8 women), 4 part-time/adjunct (1 woman). *Students:* 8 full-time (6 women), 15 part-time (7 women); includes 1 minority (Asian American or Pacific Islander), 7 international. Average age 31. 20 applicants, 60% accepted, 7 enrolled. In 2006, 14 degrees awarded. *Entrance requirements:* For master's, GMAT. Additional exam requirements/recommendations for international students: Required—TOEFL (minimum score 550 paper-based; 213 computer-based). *Application deadline:* For fall admission, 8/1 priority date for domestic students, 6/1 for international students; for spring admission, 12/1 for domestic students, 11/1 for international students. Applications are processed on a rolling basis. Application fee: $45. Electronic applications accepted. *Expenses:* Tuition, state resident: full-time $5,322; part-time $591 per credit. Tuition, nonresident: full-time $7,527; part-time $830 per credit. *Financial support:* In 2006–07, 3 research assistantships were awarded; fellowships, career-related internships or fieldwork and Federal Work-Study also available. Support available to part-time students. Financial award application deadline: 4/1; financial award applicants required to submit FAFSA. *Faculty research:* International finance, corporate finance, health care, regional economics, small business. Total annual research expenditures: $105,000. *Unit head:* Dr. Deborah Ford, Chair, 410-837-4957, E-mail: dford@ubalt.edu. *Application contact:* Dean Dreibelbis, Assistant Director, Office of Graduate Admissions, 410-837-6565, Fax: 410-837-4793, E-mail: gradadmissions@ubalt.edu.

The University of British Columbia, Sauder School of Business, Doctoral Program in Commerce and Business Administration, Vancouver, BC V6T 1Z1, Canada. Offers accounting (PhD); finance (PhD); international business (PhD); management information systems (PhD); management science (PhD); marketing (PhD); organizational behavior (PhD); policy analysis and strategy (PhD); transportation and logistics (PhD); urban land economics (PhD). *Degree requirements:* For doctorate, thesis/dissertation, comprehensive exam. *Entrance requirements:* For doctorate, GMAT or GRE. Additional exam requirements/recommendations for international students: Required—TOEFL. Electronic applications accepted.

University of California, Berkeley, Graduate Division, Haas School of Business, Program in Business, Berkeley, CA 94720-1500. Offers accounting (PhD); business and public policy (PhD); finance (PhD); marketing (PhD); organizational behavior and industrial relations (PhD); real estate (PhD). *Accreditation:* AACSB. *Students:* 83 full-time (28 women); includes 17 minority (14 Asian Americans or Pacific Islanders, 3 Hispanic Americans), 33 international. Average age 30. 347 applicants, 16 enrolled. In 2006, 17 degrees awarded. *Median time to degree:* Of those who began their doctoral program in fall 1998, 88% received their degree in 8 years or less. *Degree requirements:* For doctorate, thesis/dissertation, oral exam, written preliminary exams, comprehensive exam. *Entrance requirements:* For doctorate, GMAT or GRE, minimum GPA of 3.0. Additional exam requirements/recommendations for international students: Required—TOEFL (minimum score 570 paper-based; 230 computer-based), IELTS (minimum score 7). *Application deadline:* For fall admission, 12/15 for domestic and international students. Application fee: $60 ($80 for international students). Electronic applications accepted. *Financial support:* Fellowships with full and partial tuition reimbursements, research assistantships with full and partial tuition reimbursements, teaching assistantships with full and partial tuition reimbursements, career-related internships or fieldwork, Federal Work-Study, scholarships/grants, health care benefits, tuition waivers (full), and unspecified assistantships available. Financial award application deadline: 12/15; financial award applicants required to submit FAFSA. *Unit head:* Miguel Villas-Boas, Director, 510-642-1409, Fax: 510-643-4255, E-mail: kimg@haas.berkeley.edu. *Application contact:* Kim Guilfoyle, Administrative Director, 510-642-3944, Fax: 510-643-4255, E-mail: kimg@haas.berkeley.edu.

University of Cincinnati, Division of Research and Advanced Studies, College of Business, Department of Finance, Cincinnati, OH 45221. Offers MBA, MS, PhD. Part-time and evening/weekend programs available. *Degree requirements:* For master's, thesis or alternative, capstone project; for doctorate, thesis/dissertation, comprehensive exam. *Entrance requirements:* For master's, GMAT, resumé, letters of recommendation; for doctorate, GMAT, GRE. Additional exam requirements/recommendations for international students: Required—TOEFL (minimum score 600 paper-based; 250 computer-based). Application fee: $40. Electronic applications accepted. *Expenses:* Contact institution. *Financial support:* Fellowships with full tuition reimbursements, research assistantships with full tuition reimbursements, scholarships/grants and tuition waivers (full and partial) available. Financial award application deadline: 2/1; financial award applicants required to submit FAFSA. *Unit head:* Dr. Steve Slezak, Head, 513-556-7023, Fax: 513-556-4891.

University of Colorado at Boulder, Leeds School of Business, Doctoral Program in Business, Boulder, CO 80309. Offers accounting (PhD); finance (PhD); management (PhD); marketing (PhD). *Degree requirements:* For doctorate, thesis/dissertation, research internship. *Entrance requirements:* For doctorate, minimum undergraduate GPA of 3.2. *Application deadline:* For fall admission, 1/31 for domestic students, 1/15 for international students; for spring admission, 11/1 for domestic and international students. Application fee: $50 ($60 for international students). *Financial support:* Fellowships, research assistantships, teaching assistantships, career-related internships or fieldwork, Federal Work-Study, scholarships/grants, and unspecified assistantships available. Financial award application deadline: 3/1; financial award applicants required to submit FAFSA. *Unit head:* Kenneth Kozar, Associate Dean, 303-492-8347, Fax: 303-492-7676. *Application contact:* Information Contact, 303-492-4984, Fax: 303-492-5962, E-mail: leedsphd@colorado.edu.

University of Colorado at Colorado Springs, Graduate School, Graduate School of Business Administration, Colorado Springs, CO 80933-7150. Offers accounting (MBA); finance (MBA); general health care administration (MBA); information systems (MBA); international business management (MBA); marketing (MBA); service management/technology management (MBA). *Accreditation:* AACSB. Part-time and evening/weekend programs available. *Faculty:* 15 full-time (4 women), 4 part-time/adjunct (0 women). *Students:* 158 full-time (70 women), 290 part-time (87 women); includes 48 minority (11 African Americans, 1 American Indian/Alaska Native, 20 Asian Americans or Pacific Islanders, 16 Hispanic Americans), 7 international. Average age 33. 158 applicants, 75% accepted, 51 enrolled. In 2006, 119 degrees awarded. *Entrance requirements:* For master's, GMAT. *Application deadline:* For fall admission, 6/1 for domestic students; for spring admission, 11/1 for domestic students. Application fee: $60 ($75 for international students). *Expenses:* Contact institution. Tuition and fees vary according to course load, campus/location and program. *Financial support:* Career-related internships or fieldwork, Federal Work-Study, and institutionally sponsored loans available. Support available to part-time students. Financial award applicants required to submit FAFSA. *Faculty research:* Quality financial reporting, investments and corporate governance, group support systems, environmental and project management, customer relationship management. Total annual research expenditures: $99,250. *Unit head:* Dr. Venkateshwar Reddy, Dean, 719-262-3113, Fax: 719-262-3494, E-mail: vreddy@uccs.edu. *Application contact:* Amy DeLourenco, MBA Program Director, 719-262-3408, Fax: 719-262-3100, E-mail: busadvsr@uccs.edu.

University of Colorado at Denver and Health Sciences Center, Business School, Program in Finance, Denver, CO 80217-3364. Offers MS. Part-time and evening/weekend programs available. *Faculty:* 13 full-time (5 women). *Students:* 30 full-time (11 women), 62 part-time (17 women); includes 8 minority (1 African American, 3 Asian Americans or Pacific Islanders, 4 Hispanic Americans), 24 international. Average age 27. 59 applicants, 42% accepted, 18 enrolled. In 2006, 59 degrees awarded. *Entrance requirements:* For master's, GMAT. Additional exam requirements/recommendations for international students: Required—TOEFL (minimum score 525 paper-based; 197 computer-based). *Application deadline:* For fall admission, 6/1 for domestic students, 3/15 for international students; for spring admission, 11/1 priority date for domestic students, 10/1 for international students. Applications are processed on a rolling basis. Application fee: $50 ($75 for international students). *Financial support:* Federal Work-Study, institutionally sponsored loans, and scholarships/grants available. Support available to part-time students. Financial award application deadline: 4/1; financial award applicants required to submit FAFSA. *Faculty research:* Corporate governance, debt maturity policies, regulation and financial markets, option management strategies. *Unit head:* James Morris, Director, 303-556-4370, Fax: 303-556-5899, E-mail: james.morris@cudenver.edu. *Application contact:* Shelly Townley, Admissions Coordinator, 303-556-5956, Fax: 303-556-5904, E-mail: shelly.townley@cudenver.edu.

University of Connecticut, Graduate School, College of Liberal Arts and Sciences, Department of Public Policy, Storrs, CT 06269. Offers nonprofit management (Graduate Certificate);

Finance and Banking

University of Connecticut (continued)

public administration (MPA); public financial management (Graduate Certificate); survey research (MA); JD/MPA; MPA/MSW. *Faculty:* 10 full-time (5 women). *Students:* 53 full-time (33 women), 26 part-time (14 women); includes 7 minority (3 African Americans, 2 American Indian/Alaska Native, 2 Asian Americans or Pacific Islanders), 5 international. Average age 28. 104 applicants, 52% accepted, 54 enrolled. In 2006, 24 master's, 7 other advanced degrees awarded. *Degree requirements:* For master's, comprehensive exam. *Entrance requirements:* For master's, GRE General Test. Additional exam requirements/recommendations for international students: Required—TOEFL (minimum score 550 paper-based; 213 computer-based). *Application deadline:* For fall admission, 2/1 priority date for domestic and international students; for spring admission, 11/1 for domestic students, 10/1 for international students. Applications are processed on a rolling basis. Application fee: $55. Electronic applications accepted. *Financial support:* In 2006–07, 15 research assistantships with full tuition reimbursements were awarded; teaching assistantships with full tuition reimbursements, Federal Work-Study, scholarships/grants, health care benefits, and unspecified assistantships also available. Financial award application deadline: 2/1; financial award applicants required to submit FAFSA. *Unit head:* Kenneth Dautrich, Chairperson, 860-486-2579, E-mail: dautrich@uconnvm.uconn.edu. *Application contact:* Valerie Rogers, Director, 860-570-9047, Fax: 860-486-3109, E-mail: msr@uconn.edu.

University of Connecticut, Graduate School, School of Business, Storrs, CT 06269. Offers accounting (MS, PhD); business administration (Exec MBA, MBA, PhD); finance (PhD); health care management and insurance studies (MBA); management (PhD); management consulting (MBA); marketing (PhD); marketing intelligence (MBA); MA/MBA; MBA/MSW. *Accreditation:* AACSB. *Faculty:* 70 full-time (14 women). *Students:* 378 full-time (126 women), 852 part-time (322 women); includes 154 minority (43 African Americans, 5 American Indian/Alaska Native, 71 Asian Americans or Pacific Islanders, 35 Hispanic Americans), 171 international. Average age 30. 632 applicants, 72% accepted, 452 enrolled. In 2006, 413 master's, 9 doctorates awarded. *Degree requirements:* For master's, comprehensive exam; for doctorate, thesis/dissertation. *Entrance requirements:* For master's and doctorate, GMAT. Additional exam requirements/recommendations for international students: Required—TOEFL (minimum score 550 paper-based; 213 computer-based). *Application deadline:* For fall admission, 2/1 priority date for domestic and international students; for spring admission, 11/1 for domestic students, 10/1 for international students. Applications are processed on a rolling basis. Electronic applications accepted. *Financial support:* In 2006–07, 107 research assistantships with full tuition reimbursements, 4 teaching assistantships with full tuition reimbursements were awarded; fellowships, career-related internships or fieldwork, Federal Work-Study, scholarships/grants, health care benefits, and unspecified assistantships also available. Financial award application deadline: 2/1; financial award applicants required to submit FAFSA. *Unit head:* William Curt Hunter, Dean, 860-486-2317, Fax: 860-846-0889, E-mail: william.hunter@uconn.edu. *Application contact:* Richard Dino, Admissions Chairperson, 860-486-4483, E-mail: rich.dino@uconn.edu.

See Close-Up on page 343.

University of Dallas, Graduate School of Management, Irving, TX 75062-4736. Offers accounting (MBA, MS); business management (MBA); corporate finance (MBA, MM); engineering management (MBA, MM); entrepreneurship (MBA, MM); financial services (MBA, MM); global business (MBA, MM); health services management (MBA, MM); human resource management (MBA, MM, MS); information assurance (MBA, MM, MS); information technology (MBA, MM, MS); information technology service management (MBA); IT service management (MS); marketing (MM); marketing management (MBA); not-for-profit management (MBA); organization development (MBA); project management (MBA, MM); sports and entertainment management (MBA, MM); strategic leadership (MBA); supply chain management (MBA); supply chain management and market logistics (MM); telecommunications management (MBA, MM). *Accreditation:* ACBSP. Part-time and evening/weekend programs available. Postbaccalaureate distance learning degree programs offered (no on-campus study). *Faculty:* 26 full-time (5 women), 85 part-time/adjunct (18 women). *Students:* 227 full-time (98 women), 1,160 part-time (446 women); includes 473 minority (209 African Americans, 3 American Indian/Alaska Native, 143 Asian Americans or Pacific Islanders, 118 Hispanic Americans), 224 international. Average age 34. 556 applicants, 86% accepted, 291 enrolled. In 2006, 476 degrees awarded. *Entrance requirements:* Additional exam requirements/recommendations for international students: Required—TOEFL. *Application deadline:* Applications are processed on a rolling basis. Application fee: $50. Electronic applications accepted. *Expenses:* Contact institution. *Financial support:* In 2006–07, 468 students received support. Scholarships/grants and unspecified assistantships available. Financial award application deadline: 2/15; financial award applicants required to submit FAFSA. *Unit head:* Dr. J. Lee Whittington, Dean, 972-721-5230. *Application contact:* Sarah Stivison, Director of Graduate Admissions, 972-721-5198, Fax: 972-721-4009, E-mail: admiss@gsm.udallas.edu.

University of Denver, Daniels College of Business, Department of Finance, Denver, CO 80208. Offers IMBA, MBA, MS. Part-time and evening/weekend programs available. *Faculty:* 10 full-time (1 woman). *Students:* 116 full-time (38 women), 102 part-time (20 women); includes 16 minority (1 African American, 1 American Indian/Alaska Native, 9 Asian Americans or Pacific Islanders, 5 Hispanic Americans), 72 international. Average age 27. 98 applicants, 79% accepted. In 2006, 121 degrees awarded. *Entrance requirements:* For master's, GMAT. *Application deadline:* For fall admission, 1/15 priority date for domestic students. Applications are processed on a rolling basis. Application fee: $50. Electronic applications accepted. *Expenses:* Tuition: Full-time $29,628; part-time $823 per credit. *Financial support:* Career-related internships or fieldwork, Federal Work-Study, institutionally sponsored loans, and scholarships/grants available. Support available to part-time students. Financial award application deadline: 2/15; financial award applicants required to submit FAFSA. *Unit head:* Dr. Maclyn Clouse, Chairman, 303-871-3320. *Application contact:* Information Contact, 303-871-3416, Fax: 303-871-4466, E-mail: daniels@du.edu.

The University of Findlay, Graduate and Professional Studies, MBA Program, Findlay, OH 45840-3653. Offers financial management (MBA); human resource management (MBA); international management (MBA); management (MBA); marketing (MBA); public management (MBA). Part-time and evening/weekend programs available. Postbaccalaureate distance learning degree programs offered (no on-campus study). *Faculty:* 16 full-time, 1 part-time/adjunct. *Students:* 80 full-time (26 women), 456 part-time (168 women); includes 20 minority (13 African Americans, 1 American Indian/Alaska Native, 4 Asian Americans or Pacific Islanders, 2 Hispanic Americans), 289 international. Average age 35. 208 applicants, 88% accepted, 181 enrolled. In 2006, 210 degrees awarded. *Degree requirements:* For master's, thesis, cumulative project. *Entrance requirements:* For master's, GMAT, minimum undergraduate GPA of 3.0 in last 60 hours of course work. Additional exam requirements/recommendations for international students: Required—TOEFL (minimum score 550 paper-based). *Application deadline:* Applications are processed on a rolling basis. Application fee: $25. Electronic applications accepted. *Expenses:* Contact institution. *Financial support:* In 2006–07, 1 student received support, including 1 teaching assistantship with full tuition reimbursement available (averaging $6,000 per year); unspecified assistantships also available. Financial award application deadline: 4/1; financial award applicants required to submit FAFSA. *Faculty research:* Health care management, operations and logistics management. *Unit head:* Dr. Paul Sears, Dean, 419-434-4704, Fax: 419-434-4822. *Application contact:* Heather Riffle, Director, Graduate and Special Programs, 419-434-4640, Fax: 419-434-5517, E-mail: riffle@findlay.edu.

University of Florida, Graduate School, Warrington College of Business Administration, Department of Finance, Insurance and Real Estate, Gainesville, FL 32611. Offers business administration (MS), including entrepreneurship, insurance, real estate and urban analysis, retailing; finance (PhD); financial services (Certificate); insurance (PhD); real estate and urban analysis (PhD); JD/MS. *Faculty:* 15 full-time (1 woman). *Students:* 69 (17 women); includes 14 minority (2 African Americans, 5 Asian Americans or Pacific Islanders, 7 Hispanic Americans) 12 international. In 2006, 54 master's, 1 doctorate awarded. Terminal master's awarded for partial completion of doctoral program. *Degree requirements:* For doctorate, thesis/dissertation. *Entrance requirements:* For master's, GMAT or GRE General Test, minimum GPA of 3.0 for last 60 hours of undergraduate degree, work experience (preferred); for doctorate, GMAT or GRE General Test, minimum GPA of 3.0. Additional exam requirements/recommendations for international students: Required—TOEFL (minimum score 550 paper-based; 213 computer-based). *Application deadline:* For fall admission, 5/1 priority date for domestic students. Applications are processed on a rolling basis. Application fee: $30. Electronic applications accepted. *Expenses:* Tuition, state resident: full-time $6,827. Tuition, nonresident: full-time $21,951. Required fees: $999. *Financial support:* In 2006–07, 10 research assistantships (averaging $23,562 per year), 1 teaching assistantship (averaging $40,989 per year) were awarded; fellowships, career-related internships or fieldwork, scholarships/grants, and unspecified assistantships also available. *Faculty research:* Financial management, financial markets and institutions, investments, risk and insurance, real estate development. *Unit head:* Dr. Michael D. Ryngaert, Chair, 352-392-9765, Fax: 352-392-0301, E-mail: michael.ryngaert@cba.ufl.edu. *Application contact:* Pamela De Michele, Director of Admissions and Student Services, 352-273-0310, Fax: 352-392-0301, E-mail: pam.demichele@cba.ufl.edu.

University of Florida, Graduate School, Warrington College of Business Administration, Programs in Business Administration, Gainesville, FL 32611. Offers accounting (MBA); arts administration (MBA); business strategy and public policy (MBA); competitive strategy (MBA); decision and information sciences (MBA); electronic commerce (MBA); finance (MBA); general business (MBA); global management (MBA); Graham-Buffett security analysis (MBA); health administration (MBA); human resources management (MBA); international studies (MBA); Latin American business (MBA); management (MBA); marketing (MBA); sports administration (MBA); JD/MBA; MBA/MS; MBA/PhD; MBA/Pharm D; MD/MBA. *Accreditation:* AACSB. Part-time and evening/weekend programs available. Postbaccalaureate distance learning degree programs offered. *Faculty:* 14. *Students:* 950 (282 women); includes 189 minority (31 African Americans, 2 American Indian/Alaska Native, 66 Asian Americans or Pacific Islanders, 90 Hispanic Americans) 56 international. In 2006, 481 degrees awarded. *Entrance requirements:* For master's, GMAT, minimum GPA of 3.0, interview. Additional exam requirements/recommendations for international students: Required—TOEFL (minimum score 550 paper-based; 213 computer-based). *Application deadline:* For fall admission, 4/15 for domestic students; for winter admission, 10/15 priority date for domestic students; for spring admission, 2/15 for domestic students. Applications are processed on a rolling basis. Application fee: $30. Electronic applications accepted. *Expenses:* Tuition, state resident: full-time $6,827. Tuition, nonresident: full-time $21,951. Required fees: $999. *Financial support:* Fellowships, research assistantships, teaching assistantships, career-related internships or fieldwork, scholarships/grants, and unspecified assistantships available. Support available to part-time students. Financial award application deadline: 2/15; financial award applicants required to submit FAFSA. *Faculty research:* Accounting, finance, insurance, management, real estate and urban analysis marketing. *Unit head:* Alex Sevilla, Director, 352-392-7992 Ext. 1206. *Application contact:* Patrick Foran, Associate Director of Admissions, 352-392-7992 Ext. 282, Fax: 352-392-8791, E-mail: patrick.foran@cba.ufl.edu.

University of Hawaii at Manoa, Graduate Division, Shidler College of Business, Program in Business Administration, Honolulu, HI 96822. Offers Asian business studies (MBA); Chinese business studies (MBA); decision sciences (MBA); entrepreneurship (MBA); finance (MBA); finance and banking (MBA); human resources management (MBA); information management (MBA); information technology (MBA); international business (MBA); Japanese business studies (MBA); marketing (MBA); organizational behavior (MBA); organizational management (MBA); real estate (MBA); student-designed track (MBA). *Accreditation:* AACSB. Part-time programs available. *Faculty:* 48 full-time (9 women). *Students:* 207 full-time (77 women), 158 part-time (60 women); includes 93 minority (2 African Americans, 1 American Indian/Alaska Native, 88 Asian Americans or Pacific Islanders, 2 Hispanic Americans), 58 international. Average age 33. 235 applicants, 55% accepted, 68 enrolled. In 2006, 147 degrees awarded. *Degree requirements:* For master's, thesis optional. *Entrance requirements:* For master's, GMAT, minimum GPA of 3.0. Additional exam requirements/recommendations for international students: Required—TOEFL (minimum score 500 paper-based; 173 computer-based; 61 iBT). *Application deadline:* For fall admission, 5/1 for domestic and international students; for spring admission, 9/1 for domestic and international students. Application fee: $50. *Financial support:* In 2006–07, 7 research assistantships (averaging $17,409 per year), 3 teaching assistantships (averaging $14,028 per year) were awarded. *Application contact:* Ting Bui, Information Contact, 808-956-5565, Fax: 808-956-6889.

University of Hawaii at Manoa, Graduate Division, Shidler College of Business, Program in International Management, Honolulu, HI 96822. Offers Asian finance (PhD); global information technology management (PhD); international accounting (PhD); international marketing (PhD); international organization and strategy (PhD). *Faculty:* 42 full-time (8 women). *Students:* 36 applicants, 19% accepted, 4 enrolled. In 2006, 5 degrees awarded. *Median time to degree:* Of those who began their doctoral program in fall 1998, 33% received their degree in 8 years or less. *Degree requirements:* For doctorate, thesis/dissertation, comprehensive exam. *Entrance requirements:* For doctorate, GMAT or GRE General Test, minimum GPA of 3.0. Additional exam requirements/recommendations for international students: Required—TOEFL (minimum score 600 paper-based; 250 computer-based; 100 iBT). *Application deadline:* For fall admission, 3/1 for domestic and international students. Application fee: $50. *Financial support:* In 2006–07, 16 research assistantships (averaging $18,198 per year), 3 teaching assistantships (averaging $14,958 per year) were awarded. Total annual research expenditures: $3.3 million. *Application contact:* Ting Bui, Information Contact, 808-956-6723, Fax: 808-956-2774.

University of Houston, Bauer College of Business, Finance Program, Houston, TX 77204. Offers MS. Part-time and evening/weekend programs available. *Faculty:* 11 full-time (2 women), 4 part-time/adjunct (2 women). *Students:* 39 full-time (16 women), 50 part-time (17 women); includes 23 minority (3 African Americans, 20 Asian Americans or Pacific Islanders), 37 international. Average age 30. 35 applicants, 66% accepted, 14 enrolled. In 2006, 10 master's awarded. *Entrance requirements:* For master's, GMAT. Additional exam requirements/recommendations for international students: Required—TOEFL. *Application deadline:* For fall admission, 5/1 for domestic students; for spring admission, 10/1 for domestic students. Applications are processed on a rolling basis. Application fee: $75 ($150 for international students). *Expenses:* Tuition, state resident: full-time $5,429; part-time $226 per credit. Tuition, nonresident: full-time $12,029; part-time $501 per credit. Required fees: $2,454. *Financial support:* In 2006–07, 3 fellowships with full tuition reimbursements (averaging $8,600 per year), 20 teaching assistantships with full tuition reimbursements (averaging $7,000 per year) were awarded; research assistantships with full tuition reimbursements, career-related internships or fieldwork, Federal Work-Study, institutionally sponsored loans, scholarships/grants, health care benefits, and unspecified assistantships also available. Support available to part-time students. Financial award application deadline: 3/10; financial award applicants required to submit FAFSA. *Faculty research:* Accountancy and taxation, finance, international business, management. *Unit head:* Dr. Praveen Kumar, Chairperson, 713-743-4772, E-mail: pkumar@uh.edu. *Application contact:* 713-743-4900, Fax: 713-743-4942, E-mail: oss@cba.uh.edu.

University of Houston–Clear Lake, School of Business, Program in Finance, Houston, TX 77058-1098. Offers MS. Part-time and evening/weekend programs available. *Students:* 36 full-time, 29 part-time; includes 14 minority (2 African Americans, 8 Asian Americans or Pacific Islanders, 4 Hispanic Americans), 31 international. 48 applicants, 69% accepted, 18 enrolled. In 2006, 22 degrees awarded. *Degree requirements:* For master's, thesis optional. *Entrance requirements:* For master's, GMAT. Additional exam requirements/recommendations for international students: Required—TOEFL (minimum score 550 paper-based; 213 computer-based). *Application deadline:* For fall admission, 8/1 for domestic students, 6/1 for international students; for spring admission, 12/1 for domestic students, 10/1 for international students. Applications are processed on a rolling basis. Application fee: $35 ($75 for international students). Electronic applications accepted. *Financial support:* Career-related internships or fieldwork, Federal Work-Study, institutionally sponsored loans, and scholarships/grants available. Support available to part-time students. Financial award application deadline: 5/1; financial award applicants required to submit FAFSA. *Unit head:* Dr. Ed R. Waller, Chair, 281-283-3206, E-mail: waller@uhcl.edu. *Application contact:* Janis S. Bigelow, Assistant Director of Admissions, Recruitment and Communications, 281-283-2540, Fax: 281-283-2530, E-mail: bigelow@uhcl.edu.

University of Illinois at Urbana–Champaign, Graduate College, College of Business, Department of Finance, Champaign, IL 61820. Offers MS, PhD. *Faculty:* 21 full-time (0 women), 3 part-time/adjunct (0 women). *Students:* 131 full-time (52 women), 7 part-time (1 woman); includes 7 minority (all Asian Americans or Pacific Islanders), 115 international. 585 applicants, 36% accepted, 29 enrolled. In 2006, 86 master's, 4 doctorates awarded. *Degree requirements:* For doctorate, thesis/dissertation. *Entrance requirements:* For master's, GRE General Test, 2 years of business experience, minimum GPA of 3.0; for doctorate, GMAT, GRE General Test, minimum GPA of 3.75. *Application deadline:* For fall admission, 2/16 for domestic students. Applications are processed on a rolling basis. Application fee: $50 ($60 for international students). Electronic applications accepted. *Financial support:* In 2006–07, 2 fellowships, 12 research assistantships, 5 teaching assistantships were awarded; tuition waivers (full and partial) also available. Financial award application deadline: 2/15. *Unit head:* David L. Ikenberry, Chair, 217-333-6396, Fax: 217-244-3102, E-mail: daveike@uiuc.edu. *Application contact:* Elizabeth Birnschein, Graduate Studies Secretary, 217-333-8153, Fax: 217-244-9867, E-mail: birnsche@uiuc.edu.

University of Indianapolis, Graduate Programs, School of Business, Graduate Business Programs, Indianapolis, IN 46227-3697. Offers business (EMBA); business administration (MBA); finance (Graduate Certificate); global supply chains management (Graduate Certificate); marketing (Graduate Certificate); organizational leadership (Graduate Certificate); technology management (Graduate Certificate). *Accreditation:* ACBSP. Part-time and evening/weekend programs available. *Faculty:* 6 full-time (2 women), 6 part-time/adjunct (1 woman). *Students:* 50 full-time (16 women), 92 part-time (32 women); includes 12 minority (4 African Americans, 7 Asian Americans or Pacific Islanders, 1 Hispanic American), 10 international. Average age 32. In 2006, 57 degrees awarded. *Entrance requirements:* For master's, GMAT, interview, minimum GPA of 2.8, 2 letters of recommendation, resumé. Additional exam requirements/recommendations for international students: Required—TOEFL (minimum score 550 paper-based; 213 computer-based). *Application deadline:* Applications are processed on a rolling basis. Application fee: $50. *Expenses:* Contact institution. *Financial support:* Federal Work-Study and unspecified assistantships available. Financial award application deadline: 5/1; financial award applicants required to submit FAFSA. *Faculty research:* Integration of microcomputers into decision making, communication skills, application of synthesized theories. *Unit head:* Dr. Matthew Will, Associate Dean, 317-788-3370, E-mail: mwill@uindy.edu.

The University of Iowa, Henry B. Tippie College of Business, Department of Finance, Iowa City, IA 52242-1316. Offers business administration (PhD). *Faculty:* 16 full-time (1 woman), 9 part-time/adjunct (1 woman). *Students:* 13 full-time (6 women), 9 international. Average age 29. 118 applicants, 5% accepted, 3 enrolled. In 2006, 1 degree awarded. *Degree requirements:* For doctorate, thesis/dissertation, thesis defense, comprehensive exam, registration. *Entrance requirements:* For doctorate, GMAT or GRE. Additional exam requirements/recommendations for international students: Required—TOEFL (minimum score 600 paper-based; 250 computer-based). *Application deadline:* For fall admission, 1/31 for domestic and international students. Applications are processed on a rolling basis. Application fee: $60 ($85 for international students). Electronic applications accepted. *Financial support:* In 2006–07, 12 students received support, including 1 fellowship with full tuition reimbursement available (averaging $20,000 per year), 11 teaching assistantships with full tuition reimbursements available (averaging $15,985 per year); institutionally sponsored loans, scholarships/grants, health care benefits, unspecified assistantships, and Department of Finance pays full tuition also available. Financial award application deadline: 1/31. *Faculty research:* Market microstructure, international finance, real estate finance, theoretical and empirical corporate finance, asset pricing theory, derivatives. *Unit head:* Prof. Paul Weller, Department Executive Officer, 319-335-0929, Fax: 319-335-3690, E-mail: paul-weller@uiowa.edu. *Application contact:* Renea L. Jay, PhD Program Coordinator, 319-335-0830, Fax: 319-335-1956, E-mail: renea-jay@uiowa.edu.

The University of Iowa, Henry B. Tippie College of Business, Henry B. Tippie School of Management, Iowa City, IA 52242-1316. Offers accounting (MBA); corporate finance (MBA); entrepreneurship (MBA); finance (MBA); individually designed concentration (MBA); investment management (MBA); management information systems (MBA); marketing (MBA); nonprofit management (MBA); operations management (MBA); strategic management and consulting (MBA); JD/MBA; MBA/MA; MBA/MD; MBA/MHA; MBA/MSN. *Accreditation:* AACSB. Part-time and evening/weekend programs available. *Faculty:* 94 full-time (23 women), 65 part-time/adjunct (21 women). *Students:* 230 full-time (67 women), 712 part-time (234 women); includes 62 minority (6 African Americans, 1 American Indian/Alaska Native, 43 Asian Americans or Pacific Islanders, 12 Hispanic Americans), 127 international. Average age 30. 431 applicants, 61% accepted, 217 enrolled. In 2006, 363 degrees awarded. *Median time to degree:* Master's–2 years full-time, 3.5 years part-time. *Degree requirements:* For master's, registration. *Entrance requirements:* For master's, GMAT, work experience. Additional exam requirements/recommendations for international students: Required—TOEFL (minimum score 600 paper-based; 250 computer-based; 100 iBT). *Application deadline:* For fall admission, 7/15 for domestic students, 4/15 for international students; for spring admission, 12/15 priority date for domestic students, 11/1 priority date for international students. Applications are processed on a rolling basis. Application fee: $60 ($85 for international students). Electronic applications accepted. *Expenses:* Contact institution. *Financial support:* In 2006–07, 72 fellowships (averaging $3,892 per year), 55 research assistantships with partial tuition reimbursements (averaging $10,260 per year) were awarded; career-related internships or fieldwork, Federal Work-Study, institutionally sponsored loans, scholarships/grants, health care benefits, and unspecified assistantships also available. Support available to part-time students. Financial award application deadline: 4/15; financial award applicants required to submit FAFSA. *Faculty research:* Capital markets, econometrics, optimization, investments and empirical corporate finance, Iowa electronic markets. *Unit head:* Prof. Gary J. Gaeth, Associate Dean, MBA Programs, 800-622-4692, Fax: 319-335-3604, E-mail: gary-gaeth@uiowa.edu. *Application contact:* Jodi Schafer, Director of Student Recruitment and Marketing, 319-335-0864, Fax: 319-335-3604, E-mail: jodi-schafer@uiowa.edu.

University of La Verne, College of Business and Public Management, Graduate Programs in Business Administration, La Verne, CA 91750-4443. Offers accounting (MBA); business (MBIT); executive management (MBA-EP); finance (MBA, MBA-EP); health services management (MBA); information technology (MBA, MBA-EP); international business (MBA, MBA-EP); leadership (MBA-EP); managed care (MBA); management (MBA, MBA-EP); marketing (MBA, MBA-EP). Part-time and evening/weekend programs available. *Faculty:* 15 full-time (7 women), 13 part-time/adjunct (7 women). *Students:* 277 full-time (133 women), 112 part-time (64 women); includes 144 minority (32 African Americans, 3 American Indian/Alaska Native, 70 Asian Americans or Pacific Islanders, 39 Hispanic Americans), 160 international. Average age 30. In 2006, 142 degrees awarded. *Entrance requirements:* For master's, minimum undergraduate GPA of 3.0, 2 letters of recommendation, resumé. Additional exam requirements/recommendations for international students: Required—TOEFL (minimum score 550 paper-based; 213 computer-based). *Application deadline:* Applications are processed on a rolling basis. Application fee: $50. *Expenses:* Contact institution. *Financial support:* Career-related internships or fieldwork, institutionally sponsored loans, and scholarships/grants available. Financial award application deadline: 3/2; financial award applicants required to submit FAFSA. *Unit head:* Dr. Ibrahim Helou, Chairperson, 909-593-3511 Ext. 4211, Fax: 909-392-2704, E-mail: heloua@ulv.edu. *Application contact:* Dr. Julius Walecki, Marketing Director, 909-593-3511 Ext. 4192, Fax: 909-392-2704, E-mail: cbpm@ulv.edu.

University of Lethbridge, School of Graduate Studies, Lethbridge, AB T1K 3M4, Canada. Offers accounting (MScM); addictions counseling (M Sc); agricultural biotechnology (M Sc); agricultural studies (M Sc, MA); anthropology (MA); archaeology (MA); art (MA); biochemistry (M Sc); biological sciences (M Sc); biomolecular science (PhD); biosystems and biodiversity (PhD); Canadian studies (MA); chemistry (M Sc); computer science (M Sc); computer science and geographical information science (M Sc); counseling psychology (M Ed); dramatic arts (MA); earth, space, and physical science (PhD); economics (MA); educational leadership (M Ed); English (MA); environmental science (M Sc); evolution and behavior (PhD); exercise science (M Sc); finance (MScM); French (MA); French/German (MA); French/Spanish (MA); general education (M Ed); general management (MScM); geography (M Sc, MA); German (MA); health sciences (M Sc, MA); history (MA); human resource management and labour relations (MScM); individualized multidisciplinary (M Sc, MA); information systems (MScM); international management (MScM); kinesiology (M Sc, MA); management (M Sc, MA); marketing (MScM); mathematics (M Sc); music (MA); Native American studies (MA); neuroscience (M Sc, PhD); new media (MA); nursing (M Sc); philosophy (MA); physics (M Sc); policy and strategy (MScM); political science (MA); psychology (M Sc, MA); religious studies (MA); sociology (MA); theoretical and computational science (PhD); urban and regional studies (MA). Part-time and evening/weekend programs available. *Students:* 200 full-time, 90 part-time. In 2006, 105 master's, 3 doctorates awarded. *Degree requirements:* For doctorate, thesis/dissertation, comprehensive exam. *Entrance requirements:* For master's, GMAT (M Sc management), bachelor's degree in related field, minimum GPA of 3.0 during previous 20 graded semester courses, 2 years teaching or related experience (M Ed); for doctorate, master's degree, minimum graduate GPA of 3.5. Additional exam requirements/recommendations for international students: Required—TOEFL. Application fee: $60 Canadian dollars. *Financial support:* Fellowships, research assistantships, teaching assistantships, scholarships/grants, health care benefits, and unspecified assistantships available. *Faculty research:* Movement and brain plasticity, gibberellin physiology, photosynthesis, carbon cycling, molecular properties of main-group ring components. *Unit head:* Dr. Jo-Anne Fiske, Interim Dean, 403-329-2121, Fax: 403-329-2097. *Application contact:* Kathy Schrage, Administrative Assistant, Office of the Academic Vice President, 403-329-2121, Fax: 403-329-2097, E-mail: inquiries@uleth.ca.

University of Maryland University College, Graduate School of Management and Technology, Program in Accounting and Financial Management, Adelphi, MD 20783. Offers MS, Certificate. Part-time and evening/weekend programs available. Postbaccalaureate distance learning degree programs offered (no on-campus study). *Students:* 31 full-time (18 women), 414 part-time (282 women); includes 212 minority (145 African Americans, 44 Asian Americans or Pacific Islanders, 23 Hispanic Americans), 12 international. Average age 35. 116 applicants, 100% accepted, 89 enrolled. In 2006, 51 master's, 4 other advanced degrees awarded. *Degree requirements:* For master's, thesis or alternative. *Application deadline:* Applications are processed on a rolling basis. Application fee: $50. Electronic applications accepted. *Financial support:* Federal Work-Study and scholarships/grants available. Support available to part-time students. Financial award application deadline: 6/1; financial award applicants required to submit FAFSA. *Unit head:* Dr. James Howard, 301-985-7200, Fax: 301-985-4611, E-mail: jhoward@umuc.edu. *Application contact:* Coordinator, Graduate Admissions, 301-985-7155, Fax: 301-985-7175, E-mail: gradinfo@umuc.edu.

University of Maryland University College, Graduate School of Management and Technology, Program in Financial Management and Information Systems, Adelphi, MD 20783. Offers MS, Certificate. Part-time and evening/weekend programs available. Postbaccalaureate distance learning degree programs offered (no on-campus study). *Students:* 3 full-time (1 woman), 74 part-time (40 women); includes 41 minority (31 African Americans, 7 Asian Americans or Pacific Islanders, 3 Hispanic Americans), 5 international. Average age 34. 42 applicants, 100% accepted, 35 enrolled. *Degree requirements:* For master's, thesis or alternative. *Application deadline:* Applications are processed on a rolling basis. Application fee: $50. Electronic applications accepted. *Financial support:* Federal Work-Study and scholarships/grants available. Support available to part-time students. Financial award application deadline: 6/1. *Unit head:* Dr. James Howard, 301-985-7200, Fax: 301-985-4611, E-mail: jhoward@umuc.edu. *Application contact:* Coordinator, Graduate Admissions, 301-985-7155, Fax: 301-985-7175, E-mail: gradinfo@umuc.edu.

University of Massachusetts Dartmouth, Graduate School, Charlton College of Business, Program in Business Administration, North Dartmouth, MA 02747-2300. Offers accounting (Postbaccalaureate Certificate); business administration (MBA); e-commerce (PMC); finance (PMC); general management (PMC); leadership (PMC); management (Postbaccalaureate Certificate); marketing (PMC); supply chain management (PMC). *Accreditation:* AACSB. Part-time programs available. *Faculty:* 41 full-time (11 women), 22 part-time/adjunct (8 women). *Students:* 66 full-time (20 women), 111 part-time (54 women); includes 16 minority (5 African Americans, 6 Asian Americans or Pacific Islanders, 5 Hispanic Americans), 46 international. Average age 30. 167 applicants, 83% accepted, 83 enrolled. In 2006, 73 master's, 20 other advanced degrees awarded. *Entrance requirements:* For master's, GMAT, resumé, letters of recommendation. Additional exam requirements/recommendations for international students: Required—TOEFL (minimum score 500 paper-based). *Application deadline:* For fall admission, 6/1 for domestic students, 4/1 for international students; for spring admission, 10/1 for domestic students, 8/1 for international students. Application fee: $40 ($60 for international students). Electronic applications accepted. *Expenses:* Tuition, state resident: full-time $2,071; part-time $86 per credit. Tuition, nonresident: full-time $8,099; part-time $337 per credit. *Financial support:* In 2006–07, 2 research assistantships with full tuition reimbursements (averaging $11,985 per year), 6 teaching assistantships with full tuition reimbursements (averaging $7,200 per year) were awarded; Federal Work-Study and unspecified assistantships also available. Support available to part-time students. Financial award application deadline: 3/1; financial award applicants required to submit FAFSA. *Faculty research:* Organizational identity dynamics in strategic alliances and partnerships, market analysis in cranberry industry, consumer choice modeling. Total annual research expenditures: $508,000. *Unit head:* Matthew Roy, Assistant Dean, 508-999-8409, Fax: 508-999-8776, E-mail: mroy@umassd.edu. *Application contact:* Carol Novo, Graduate Admissions Officer, 508-999-8604, Fax: 508-999-8183, E-mail: graduate@umassd.edu.

University of Memphis, Graduate School, Fogelman College of Business and Economics, Program in Business Administration, Memphis, TN 38152. Offers accounting (MBA, PhD); economics (MBA, PhD); executive business administration (MBA); finance (PhD); finance, insurance, and real estate (MBA, MS); international business administration (MBA); management (MBA, MS, PhD); management information systems (MBA, MS, PhD); management science (MBA); marketing (MBA, MS); marketing and supply chain management (PhD); real estate development (MS); JD/MBA. *Accreditation:* AACSB. *Faculty:* 84 full-time (14 women), 3 part-time/adjunct (0 women). *Students:* 222 full-time (92 women), 163 part-time (52 women); includes 62 minority (43 African Americans, 14 Asian Americans or Pacific Islanders, 5 Hispanic Americans), 119 international. Average age 29. In 2006, 196 master's, 12 doctorates awarded. *Degree requirements:* For master's, comprehensive exam; for doctorate, thesis/dissertation, comprehensive exam. *Entrance requirements:* For master's, GMAT, resumé; for doctorate, GMAT, interview, minimum GPA of 3.4, resumé, letter of recommendation. Additional exam requirements/recommendations for international students: Required—TOEFL (minimum score 550 paper-based; 220 computer-based). *Application deadline:* For fall admission, 8/1 for domestic students; for spring admission, 12/1 for domestic students. Application fee: $25 ($50 for international students). *Financial support:* Research assistantships with full tuition reimbursements, teaching assistantships, career-related internships or fieldwork, scholarships/grants, and unspecified assistantships available. Financial award application deadline: 3/1. *Faculty research:* Competitive business strategy, finance microstructures, supply chain management innovations, health care economics, litigation risks and corporate audits. Total annual research expenditures: $2.7 million. *Application contact:* Dr. Carol V. Danehower, Associate Dean for Programs, 901-678-5402, Fax: 901-678-3579, E-mail: fcbegp@memphis.edu.

University of Miami, Graduate School, School of Business Administration, Program in Business Administration, Coral Gables, FL 33124. Offers accounting (MBA); computer information systems (MBA); executive and professional (MBA), including international business, management; finance (MBA); international business (MBA); management (MBA); management science (MBA); marketing (MBA); professional management (MSPM); JD/MBA; MBA/MSIE.

Finance and Banking

University of Miami (continued)

Accreditation: AACSB. Evening/weekend programs available. *Faculty:* 105 full-time (25 women). *Students:* 734 full-time (269 women), 19 part-time (4 women); includes 194 minority (24 African Americans, 1 American Indian/Alaska Native, 23 Asian Americans or Pacific Islanders, 146 Hispanic Americans), 115 international. Average age 31. 453 applicants, 71% accepted, 152 enrolled. In 2006, 394 degrees awarded. *Degree requirements:* For master's, comprehensive exam, registration. *Entrance requirements:* For master's, GMAT. Additional exam requirements/recommendations for international students: Required—TOEFL (minimum score 550 paper-based; 213 computer-based; 59 iBT). *Application deadline:* For fall admission, 7/30 priority date for domestic students, 6/30 priority date for international students; for spring admission, 12/31 priority date for domestic students, 10/31 priority date for international students. Applications are processed on a rolling basis. Application fee: $50. Electronic applications accepted. *Financial support:* In 2006–07, 418 students received support, including 19 fellowships with partial tuition reimbursements available; unspecified assistantships also available. Financial award application deadline: 3/1; financial award applicants required to submit FAFSA. *Faculty research:* Leadership, e-commerce, supply chain management. *Unit head:* Daniela Mu±iz, Associate Director, Graduate Business Programs, 305-284-4626, Fax: 305-284-1878, E-mail: dmuniz@miami.edu. *Application contact:* David S. Green, Director of Graduate Business Recruiting and Admissions, 305-284-4607, Fax: 305-284-1878, E-mail: mba@miami.edu.

University of Michigan–Dearborn, School of Management, Dearborn, MI 48128-1491. Offers accounting (MS); finance (MS); management (MS); MBA/MHSA; MBA/MSE; MBA/MSF. *Accreditation:* AACSB. Part-time and evening/weekend programs available. Postbaccalaureate distance learning degree programs offered (no on-campus study). *Degree requirements:* For master's, registration. *Entrance requirements:* For master's, GMAT, 2 years of work experience (MBA); course work in computer applications, statistics, and pre-calculus or finite mathematics. Additional exam requirements/recommendations for international students: Required—TOEFL (minimum score 560 paper-based; 220 computer-based). Expenses: Contact institution. *Faculty research:* Cultural diversity, buyer-supplier relations, error detection in data, economic evolution.

University of Minnesota, Twin Cities Campus, Carlson School of Management, Carlson Full-time MBA Program, Minneapolis, MN 55455-0213. Offers accounting (MBA); entrepreneurship (MBA); finance (MBA); healthcare management (MBA); information and decision sciences (MBA); international business (MBA); marketing and logistics management (MBA); operations and management science (MBA); strategic management and organization (MBA); supply chain management (MBA); JD/MBA; MD/MBA; MHA/MBA. *Accreditation:* AACSB. *Faculty:* 125 full-time (27 women), 120 part-time/adjunct. *Students:* 218 full-time (70 women); includes 18 minority (4 African Americans, 1 American Indian/Alaska Native, 10 Asian Americans or Pacific Islanders, 3 Hispanic Americans), 86 international. Average age 28. 418 applicants, 53% accepted, 124 enrolled. In 2006, 105 degrees awarded. *Median time to degree:* Master's–2 years full-time. *Entrance requirements:* For master's, GMAT. Additional exam requirements/recommendations for international students: Required—TOEFL (minimum score 580 paper-based; 240 computer-based), IELTS. *Application deadline:* For fall admission, 4/15 for domestic students, 2/15 for international students. Application fee: $60 ($90 for international students). Electronic applications accepted. *Expenses: Contact institution.* Full-time tuition and fees vary according to class time, course load, program, reciprocity agreements and student level. *Financial support:* In 2006–07, 131 students received support, including 127 fellowships with full and partial tuition reimbursements available (averaging $20,000 per year); research assistantships with partial tuition reimbursements available, teaching assistantships with partial tuition reimbursements available, career-related internships or fieldwork, Federal Work-Study, institutionally sponsored loans, scholarships/grants, health care benefits, tuition waivers (full and partial), and unspecified assistantships also available. Support available to part-time students. Financial award application deadline: 2/15; financial award applicants required to submit FAFSA. *Faculty research:* IT, strategy, marketing, finance, quality management. *Unit head:* Kathryn J. Carlson, MBA Programs and Executive Education, 612-624-2039, Fax: 612-625-1012, E-mail: fulltimeembainfo@csom.umn.edu. *Application contact:* Jeffrey Bieganek, Director, Admissions and Business Development, MBA Programs and Executive Education, 612-625-6558, Fax: 612-625-1012, E-mail: full-timembainfo@csom.umn.edu.

University of Minnesota, Twin Cities Campus, Carlson School of Management, Doctoral Program in Business Administration, Minneapolis, MN 55455-0213. Offers accounting (PhD); finance (PhD); information and decision sciences (PhD); marketing and logistics management (PhD); operations and management science (PhD); strategic management and organization (PhD). *Faculty:* 109 full-time (26 women). *Students:* 90 full-time (30 women); includes 9 minority (5 African Americans, 1 Asian American or Pacific Islander, 3 Hispanic Americans), 60 international. Average age 30. 325 applicants, 8% accepted, 17 enrolled. In 2006, 16 degrees awarded. *Median time to degree:* Of those who began their doctoral program in fall 1998, 61% received their degree in 8 years or less. *Degree requirements:* For doctorate, thesis/dissertation, written and oral preliminary exams, comprehensive exam, registration. *Entrance requirements:* For doctorate, GMAT, GRE General Test, International must submit a TOEFL or IELT. Additional exam requirements/recommendations for international students: Required—TOEFL (minimum score 600 paper-based; 250 computer-based; 100 iBT), IELTS (minimum score 8), TOEFL (paper-based 600, computer-based 250) or IELTS (7.5). *Application deadline:* For fall admission, 12/30 for domestic students, 12/30 priority date for international students. Applications are processed on a rolling basis. Application fee: $55 ($75 for international students). Electronic applications accepted. *Expenses:* Tuition, state resident: full-time $9,302; part-time $775 per credit. Tuition, nonresident: full-time $16,400; part-time $1,367 per credit. Full-time tuition and fees vary according to class time, course load, program, reciprocity agreements and student level. *Financial support:* In 2006–07, 67 students received support, including fellowships with full tuition reimbursements available (averaging $11,000 per year), research assistantships with full tuition reimbursements available (averaging $6,000 per year), teaching assistantships with full tuition reimbursements available (averaging $6,000 per year); institutionally sponsored loans, scholarships/grants, health care benefits, and unspecified assistantships also available. Financial award application deadline: 12/31. *Faculty research:* Corporate strategy, international business, corporate finances, entrepreneurship, quality management, marketing, information and decision science, operations and accounting. Total annual research expenditures: $300,000. *Unit head:* Dr. Paul E. Johnson, Director of Graduate Studies and PhD Program Director, 612-624-5570, Fax: 612-624-8221, E-mail: pjohnson@csom.umn.edu. *Application contact:* Earlene Bronson, Assistant Director, PhD Program, 612-624-0875, Fax: 612-624-8221, E-mail: ebronson@csom.umn.edu.

University of Missouri–St. Louis, College of Business Administration, Program in Business Administration, St. Louis, MO 63121. Offers accounting (MBA); business administration (Certificate); finance (MBA); human resource management (Certificate); logistics and supply chain management (MBA, Certificate); management (MBA); marketing (MBA); marketing management (Certificate); operations (MBA); quantitative management science (MBA); telecommunications management (Certificate). *Accreditation:* AACSB. Part-time and evening/weekend programs available. *Faculty:* 26 full-time (6 women), 2 part-time/adjunct (0 women). *Students:* 242 full-time (156 women), 186 part-time (123 women); includes 48 minority (17 African Americans, 1 American Indian/Alaska Native, 27 Asian Americans or Pacific Islanders, 3 Hispanic Americans), 96 international. Average age 33. In 2006, 138 degrees awarded. *Entrance requirements:* For master's, GMAT, 2 letters of recommendation. Additional exam requirements/recommendations for international students: Required—TOEFL (minimum score 550 paper-based; 213 computer-based). *Application deadline:* For fall admission, 7/1 for domestic students; for spring admission, 11/1 for domestic students. Applications are processed on a rolling basis. Application fee: $35 ($40 for international students). Electronic applications accepted. *Expenses:* Tuition, state resident: part-time $332 per credit hour. Tuition, nonresident: part-time $770 per credit hour. *Financial support:* Research assistantships with full and partial tuition reimbursements, teaching assistantships with full and partial tuition reimbursements, career-related internships or fieldwork, Federal Work-Study, and institutionally sponsored loans available. Support available to part-time students. Financial award application deadline: 4/1; financial award applicants required to submit FAFSA. *Faculty research:* Human resources, strategic management, marketing strategy, consumer behavior product development, advertising. *Application contact:* 314-516-5458, Fax: 314-516-6996, E-mail: gradadm@umsl.edu.

University of Nebraska–Lincoln, Graduate College, College of Business Administration, Interdepartmental Area of Business, Department of Finance, Lincoln, NE 68588. Offers business (MA, PhD). *Degree requirements:* For doctorate, thesis/dissertation, comprehensive exam. *Entrance requirements:* For master's and doctorate, GMAT. Additional exam requirements/recommendations for international students: Required—TOEFL. Electronic applications accepted. *Faculty research:* Banking, investments, international finance, insurance, corporate finance.

University of Nevada, Reno, Graduate School, College of Business Administration, Department of Finance, Reno, NV 89557. Offers MS. *Students:* 2 full-time (0 women), 2 part-time, 3 international. Average age 26. *Entrance requirements:* For master's, GMAT. Additional exam requirements/recommendations for international students: Required—TOEFL. *Application deadline:* For fall admission, 3/15 for domestic students; for spring admission, 10/15 for domestic students. Application fee: $60 ($95 for international students). *Unit head:* Sheri Faircloth, Graduate Program Director, 775-682-9178, E-mail: fairclos@unr.nevada.edu.

University of New Haven, Graduate School, School of Business, Program in Business Administration, West Haven, CT 06516-1916. Offers accounting (MBA); business policy and strategy (MBA); finance (MBA); health care management (MBA); human resources management (MBA); international business (MBA); marketing (MBA); public relations (MBA); sports management (MBA); technology management (MBA); MBA/MPA; MBA/MSIE. Part-time and evening/weekend programs available. *Degree requirements:* For master's, thesis or alternative. *Entrance requirements:* For master's, GMAT.

University of New Haven, Graduate School, School of Business, Program in Finance and Financial Services, West Haven, CT 06516-1916. Offers MS.

University of New Mexico, Robert O. Anderson Graduate School of Management, Department of Financial, International and Technology Management, Albuquerque, NM 87131-1221. Offers financial management (MBA); international management (MBA); international management in Latin America (MBA); management of technology (MBA). Part-time and evening/weekend programs available. *Entrance requirements:* For master's, GMAT. Additional exam requirements/recommendations for international students: Required—TOEFL (minimum score 550 paper-based; 213 computer-based). *Faculty research:* Corporation finance, investments, applied macroeconomics, risk management and banking, international finance.

University of New Orleans, Graduate School, College of Business Administration, Department of Economics and Finance, New Orleans, LA 70148. Offers economics and finance (MS); financial economics (PhD). *Accreditation:* AACSB. *Students:* 33 (8 women). Average age 33. In 2006, 5 master's, 5 doctorates awarded. Terminal master's awarded for partial completion of doctoral program. *Degree requirements:* For master's, thesis optional; for doctorate, one foreign language, thesis/dissertation, general exams, comprehensive exam. *Entrance requirements:* For doctorate, GRE General Test, minimum GPA of 3.0. Additional exam requirements/recommendations for international students: Required—TOEFL (minimum score 550 paper-based; 213 computer-based). *Application deadline:* For fall admission, 7/1 priority date for domestic students, 6/1 for international students; for spring admission, 11/15 priority date for domestic students, 10/1 for international students. Applications are processed on a rolling basis. Application fee: $40. *Financial support:* Fellowships, research assistantships, teaching assistantships, Federal Work-Study available. Financial award application deadline: 5/15; financial award applicants required to submit FAFSA. *Faculty research:* Monetary economics, international economics, urban economics, real estate. *Unit head:* Dr. Walter Lane, Chairperson, 504-280-7145, Fax: 504-280-6397, E-mail: wlane@uno.edu. *Application contact:* Dr. Neal Maroney, Graduate Coordinator, 504-280-6896, Fax: 504-280-6397, E-mail: dfinec@uno.edu.

The University of North Carolina at Chapel Hill, Kenan-Flagler Business School, Doctoral Program in Business Administration, Chapel Hill, NC 27599. Offers accounting (PhD); finance (PhD); marketing (PhD); operations management (PhD); organizational behavior (PhD); strategy (PhD). *Accreditation:* AACSB. *Degree requirements:* For doctorate, thesis/dissertation. *Entrance requirements:* For doctorate, GMAT or GRE General Test. Electronic applications accepted. Expenses: Contact institution.

The University of North Carolina at Greensboro, Graduate School, Bryan School of Business and Economics, Department of Accounting, Greensboro, NC 27412-5001. Offers accounting (MS); accounting systems (MS); financial accounting and reporting (MS); financial analysis (PMC); tax concentration (MS). *Accreditation:* AACSB. *Faculty:* 12 full-time (2 women). *Students:* 86 full-time (46 women), 16 part-time (8 women); includes 34 minority (17 African Americans, 1 American Indian/Alaska Native, 16 Asian Americans or Pacific Islanders). 50 applicants, 22% accepted. *Entrance requirements:* For master's, GMAT, GRE General Test, previous course work in accounting and business. Additional exam requirements/recommendations for international students: Required—TOEFL. *Application deadline:* For fall admission, 7/1 priority date for domestic students; for spring admission, 11/1 for domestic students. Applications are processed on a rolling basis. Application fee: $45. Electronic applications accepted. *Expenses:* Tuition, state resident: full-time $2,692. Tuition, nonresident: full-time $13,742. *Financial support:* In 2006–07, 17 students received support; fellowships with full tuition reimbursements available, research assistantships with full tuition reimbursements available, career-related internships or fieldwork, Federal Work-Study, scholarships/grants, and traineeships available. Support available to part-time students. *Unit head:* Dr. Edward Arrington, Head, 336-334-5647, Fax: 336-334-4706, E-mail: cearring@uncg.edu. *Application contact:* Michelle Harkleroad, Director of Graduate Admissions, 336-334-4884, Fax: 336-334-4424, E-mail: mbharkle@uncg.edu.

University of Northern Virginia, Graduate Programs, Manassas, VA 20109. Offers accountancy (MS); accounting (MBA); business administration (DBA); computer science (MS); counseling education (M Ed); early childhood education (M Ed); educational communication and instructional technology (M Ed); educational leadership (M Ed); finance (MBA); information systems technology (MS); management (MBA); marketing (MBA); project management (MBA); public administration (MPA); teaching English to speakers of other languages (M Ed). Part-time and evening/weekend programs available. Postbaccalaureate distance learning degree programs offered (no on-campus study). *Degree requirements:* For doctorate, thesis/dissertation, comprehensive exam, registration. *Entrance requirements:* Additional exam requirements/recommendations for international students: Required—TOEFL (minimum score 550 paper-based; 230 computer-based), IELTS (minimum score 6). Electronic applications accepted.

University of North Texas, Robert B. Toulouse School of Graduate Studies, College of Business Administration, Department of Finance, Insurance, Real Estate, and Law, Denton, TX 76203. Offers banking (MBA, PhD); finance (MBA, PhD); finance, insurance, real estate, and law (MS); insurance (MBA); real estate (MBA). Part-time programs available. *Faculty:* 23 full-time (3 women). *Students:* 37 full-time (13 women), 69 part-time (21 women); includes 28 minority (11 African Americans, 2 American Indian/Alaska Native, 9 Asian Americans or Pacific Islanders, 6 Hispanic Americans), 24 international. Average age 27. 105 applicants, 78% accepted, 23 enrolled. In 2006, 51 master's, 3 doctorates awarded. *Degree requirements:* For doctorate, thesis/dissertation. *Entrance requirements:* For master's, GMAT; for doctorate, GMAT or GRE General Test. Additional exam requirements/recommendations for international students: Required—TOEFL (minimum score 550 paper-based; 213 computer-based). *Application deadline:* For fall admission, 7/15 for domestic students. Application fee: $50 ($75 for international students). *Expenses:* Tuition, state resident: full-time $3,573; part-time $198 per credit. Tuition, nonresident: full-time $8,577; part-time $476 per credit. Required fees: $1,258; $126 per credit. One-time fee: $150 full-time. Tuition and fees vary according to course load. *Financial support:* Fellowships, research assistantships, teaching assistantships, career-related internships or fieldwork available. Financial award application deadline: 4/1. *Faculty research:* Financial impact of regulation, risk management, financial instrument rating changes, taxes and valuation, bankruptcy. *Unit head:* Dr. Mazhar Siddiqi, Interim Chair, 940-369-7300, Fax: 940-565-4234, E-mail: siddiqi@unt.edu. *Application contact:* Dr. James A. Conover, Graduate Adviser, 940-565-3061, Fax: 940-565-4234, E-mail: conoverj@unt.edu.

University of Oregon, Graduate School, Charles H. Lundquist College of Business, Department of Finance, Eugene, OR 97403. Offers PhD. Part-time programs available. *Students:* 6 full-time (2 women); includes 1 minority (Asian American or Pacific Islander), 5 international. 39 applicants, 8% accepted. In 2006, 1 doctorate awarded. Terminal master's awarded for partial completion of doctoral program. *Degree requirements:* For doctorate, thesis/dissertation, 2 comprehensive exams. *Entrance requirements:* For doctorate, GMAT. Additional exam requirements/recommendations for international students: Required—TOEFL. *Application deadline:* For fall admission, 2/1 for domestic students. Application fee: $50. *Financial support:* Teaching assistantships, career-related internships or fieldwork and Federal Work-Study available. *Faculty research:* Changes in firm value in response to corporate takeovers and defenses, capital structure, regulatory changes, financial intermediaries. *Unit head:* M. Megan Partch, Head, 541-346-5126. *Application contact:* Perri McGee, Admissions Contact, 541-346-1462, E-mail: pcrone@uoregon.edu.

University of Ottawa, Faculty of Graduate and Postdoctoral Studies, Interdisciplinary Programs, Ottawa, ON K1N 6N5, Canada. Offers e-business (Certificate); e-commerce (Certificate); finance (Certificate); health services and policies research (Diploma); population health (PhD); population health risk assessment and management (Certificate); public management and governance (Certificate); systems science (Certificate).

University of Pennsylvania, Wharton School, Finance Department, Philadelphia, PA 19104. Offers MBA, PhD. *Degree requirements:* For doctorate, thesis/dissertation. *Entrance requirements:* For doctorate, GMAT or GRE. *Faculty research:* Corporate finance, investments, macroeconomics, international finance.

University of Puerto Rico, Mayagüez Campus, Graduate Studies, College of Business Administration, Mayagüez, PR 00681-9000. Offers business administration (MBA); finance (MBA); human resources (MBA); industrial management (MBA). Part-time and evening/weekend programs available. *Faculty:* 52 full-time (30 women). *Students:* 32 full-time (15 women), 52 part-time (37 women); includes 73 minority (all Hispanic Americans), 11 international. 47 applicants, 70% accepted, 24 enrolled. In 2006, 13 degrees awarded. *Degree requirements:* For master's, comprehensive exam. *Entrance requirements:* For master's, GMAT or EXADEP, bachelor's degree with courses in calculus, microeconomics, accounting and statistics. Additional exam requirements/recommendations for international students: Required—TOEFL (minimum score 500 paper-based; 173 computer-based). *Application deadline:* For fall admission, 2/15 for domestic and international students; for spring admission, 9/15 for domestic and international students. Applications are processed on a rolling basis. Application fee: $25. *Expenses:* Tuition, nonresident: full-time $4,655. Required fees: $210. One-time fee: $77 full-time. Part-time tuition and fees vary according to course load and reciprocity agreements. *Financial support:* In 2006–07, 10 students received support, including fellowships (averaging $12,000 per year), 7 research assistantships (averaging $15,000 per year), 3 teaching assistantships (averaging $8,500 per year); Federal Work-Study and institutionally sponsored loans also available. *Faculty research:* Organizational studies, management, accounting. Total annual research expenditures: $264,836. *Unit head:* Prof. Eva Quinñnones, Dean, 787-265-3800, Fax: 787-832-5320, E-mail: quinones-e@rigel.uprm.edu. *Application contact:* Dr. Yolanda Ruiz, Director, 787-265-3887, Fax: 787-832-5320, E-mail: yruiz@caribe.net.

University of Rhode Island, Graduate School, College of Business Administration, PhD Programs in Business Administration, Kingston, RI 02881. Offers finance (PhD); management (PhD); management sciences and information systems (PhD); marketing (PhD). *Expenses:* Tuition, state resident: full-time $6,032; part-time $335 per credit. Tuition, nonresident: full-time $17,288; part-time $960 per credit. Required fees: $65 per credit. $30 per semester. One-time fee: $80 part-time. *Application contact:* Dr. Laura Beauvais, Director of Graduate Programs, 401-874-4341.

University of San Diego, School of Business Administration, San Diego, CA 92110-2492. Offers accounting and financial management (MS); business administration (MBA); executive leadership (MSEL); global leadership (MSGL); international business administration (IMBA); real estate (MSRE); supply chain management (MS, Certificate); taxation (MS); JD/IMBA; JD/MBA; MBA/MSIT; MBA/MSN; MBA/MSRE. *Accreditation:* AACSB. Part-time and evening/weekend programs available. *Faculty:* 35 full-time (10 women), 18 part-time/adjunct (4 women). *Students:* 187 full-time (76 women), 265 part-time (89 women); includes 55 minority (5 African Americans, 1 American Indian/Alaska Native, 32 Asian Americans or Pacific Islanders, 17 Hispanic Americans), 45 international. Average age 32. 517 applicants, 66% accepted, 187 enrolled. In 2006, 256 degrees awarded. *Entrance requirements:* For master's, GMAT, minimum GPA of 3.0, minimum 2 years of full-time work experience. Additional exam requirements/recommendations for international students: Required—TOEFL (minimum score 580 paper-based; 237 computer-based), TWE. *Application deadline:* For fall admission, 5/1 priority date for domestic students; for spring admission, 11/15 priority date for domestic students. Applications are processed on a rolling basis. Application fee: $45. Electronic applications accepted. *Financial support:* Career-related internships or fieldwork, Federal Work-Study, institutionally sponsored loans, scholarships/grants, tuition waivers (partial), and unspecified assistantships available. Support available to part-time students. Financial award application deadline: 5/1; financial award applicants required to submit FAFSA. *Faculty research:* Business management, production, purchasing, quantitative methods, accounting. *Unit head:* Dr. Andy Allen, Interim Dean, 619-260-4886, E-mail: sbadean@sandiego.edu. *Application contact:* Stephen Pultz, Director of Admissions, 619-260-4524, Fax: 619-260-4158, E-mail: grads@sandiego.edu.

University of San Francisco, Masagung Graduate School of Management, Program in Business Administration, San Francisco, CA 94117-1080. Offers business economics (MBA); e-business (MBA); entrepreneurship (MBA); finance and banking (MBA); international business (MBA); management (MBA); marketing (MBA); telecommunications management and policy (MBA); JD/MBA; MSN/MBA. *Accreditation:* AACSB. *Faculty:* 27 full-time (4 women), 21 part-time/adjunct (7 women). *Students:* 191 full-time (73 women), 71 part-time (33 women); includes 51 minority (4 African Americans, 1 American Indian/Alaska Native, 35 Asian Americans or Pacific Islanders, 11 Hispanic Americans), 102 international. Average age 28. 373 applicants, 70% accepted, 106 enrolled. In 2006, 163 degrees awarded. *Entrance requirements:* For master's, GMAT, minimum undergraduate GPA of 3.2. Additional exam requirements/recommendations for international students: Required—TOEFL. *Application deadline:* For fall admission, 7/1 priority date for domestic students; for spring admission, 11/30 for domestic students. Applications are processed on a rolling basis. Application fee: $55 ($65 for international students). *Expenses:* Tuition: Full-time $17,370; part-time $965 per unit. Tuition and fees vary according to degree level, campus/location and program. *Financial support:* In 2006–07, 104 students received support; fellowships available. Financial award application deadline: 3/2; financial award applicants required to submit FAFSA. *Faculty research:* International financial markets, technology transfer licensing, international marketing, strategic planning. Total annual research expenditures: $50,000. *Unit head:* Carol Langlois, Director, 415-422-6314, Fax: 415-422-2502.

University of Saskatchewan, College of Graduate Studies and Research, College of Commerce, Department of Finance and Management Science, Saskatoon, SK S7N 5A2, Canada. Offers finance (M Sc). Part-time programs available. *Degree requirements:* For master's, thesis, registration. *Entrance requirements:* For master's, GMAT. Additional exam requirements/recommendations for international students: Required—TOEFL.

The University of Scranton, Graduate School, Program in Business Administration, Scranton, PA 18510. Offers accounting (MBA); enterprise management technology (MBA); finance (MBA); general business administration (MBA); international business (MBA); management information systems (MBA); marketing (MBA); operations management (MBA). *Accreditation:* AACSB. Part-time and evening/weekend programs available. *Faculty:* 34 full-time (8 women). *Students:* 39 full-time (11 women), 54 part-time (15 women); includes 3 minority (1 American Indian/Alaska Native, 2 Hispanic Americans), 31 international. Average age 28. 58 applicants, 83% accepted. In 2006, 52 degrees awarded. *Degree requirements:* For master's, capstone experience. *Entrance requirements:* For master's, GMAT, minimum GPA of 2.75. Additional exam requirements/recommendations for international students: Required—TOEFL (minimum score 500 paper-based; 173 computer-based), IELTS (minimum score 6). *Application deadline:* Applications are processed on a rolling basis. Application fee: $50. *Expenses:* Tuition: Part-time $684 per credit. Required fees: $25 per term. *Financial support:* In 2006–07, 11 teaching assistantships with full tuition reimbursements (averaging $5,600 per year) were awarded; fellowships, career-related internships or fieldwork, Federal Work-Study, and unspecified assistantships also available. Support available to part-time students. Financial award application deadline: 3/1. *Faculty research:* Financial markets, strategic impact of total quality management, internal accounting controls, consumer preference, information systems and the Internet. *Unit head:* Dr. Murli Rajan, Director, 570-941-4043, Fax: 570-941-4342.

University of Southern California, Graduate School, Marshall School of Business, Department of Finance and Business Economics, Los Angeles, CA 90089. Offers MBA. *Entrance requirements:* For master's, GMAT. *Application deadline:* For fall admission, 12/1 for domestic students. Application fee: $85. *Expenses:* Tuition: Full-time $33,314; part-time $1,121 per credit. Required fees: $522. Full-time tuition and fees vary according to program. *Financial support:* In 2006–07, research assistantships (averaging $18,500 per year), teaching assistantships (averaging $18,500 per year) were awarded; fellowships, Federal Work-Study and institutionally sponsored loans also available. Support available to part-time students. Financial award application deadline: 2/15; financial award applicants required to submit FAFSA. *Unit head:* Dr. Ayse Imrohoroglu, Chair, 213-740-6515, E-mail: fbe@usc.edu.

University of South Florida, Graduate School, College of Business Administration, School of Finance, Tampa, FL 33620-9951. Offers MS. *Faculty:* 14 full-time (2 women), 1 part-time/adjunct (0 women). *Students:* 3 applicants, 100% accepted, 2 enrolled. *Entrance requirements:* For master's, GMAT. Application fee: $30. *Financial support:* Application deadline: 6/30. Total annual research expenditures: $111,608. *Application contact:* MBA Program Staff, 813-974-3335, Fax: 813-974-4518, E-mail: mba@coba.usf.edu.

The University of Tampa, John H. Sykes College of Business, Tampa, FL 33606-1490. Offers accounting (MBA, MS); economics (MBA); entrepreneurship (MBA); finance (MBA, MS); information systems management (MBA); innovation management (MS); international business (MBA); management (MBA); marketing (MBA, MS). *Accreditation:* AACSB. Part-time and evening/weekend programs available. *Faculty:* 39 full-time (9 women), 1 part-time/adjunct (0 women). *Students:* 143 full-time (52 women), 381 part-time (158 women); includes 78 minority (18 African Americans, 3 American Indian/Alaska Native, 19 Asian Americans or Pacific Islanders, 38 Hispanic Americans), 89 international. Average age 31. 486 applicants, 59% accepted, 231 enrolled. In 2006, 127 degrees awarded. *Median time to degree:* Master's–1.8 years full-time, 2.8 years part-time. *Entrance requirements:* For master's, GMAT. Additional exam requirements/recommendations for international students: Required—TOEFL (minimum score 577 paper-based; 230 computer-based; 90 iBT). *Application deadline:* For fall admission, 2/15 priority date for domestic students, 6/15 for international students; for spring admission, 12/15 for domestic students, 11/15 for international students. Applications are processed on a rolling basis. Application fee: $40. Electronic applications accepted. *Expenses:* Tuition: Part-time $426 per credit hour. Required fees: $35 per year. *Financial support:* In 2006–07, 57 students received support, including 57 research assistantships with tuition reimbursements available (averaging $3,000 per year); career-related internships or fieldwork and unspecified assistantships also available. Support available to part-time students. Financial award applicants required to submit FAFSA. *Faculty research:* Industrial organization and antitrust, artificial intelligence, corporate quality, leadership, ethics, quality. *Unit head:* Dr. William L. Rhey, Dean Graduate Studies, 813-253-6211, Fax: 813-259-5403, E-mail: wrhey@ut.edu. *Application contact:* Fernals Nolasco, Director of Graduate Studies, 813-253-6211, Fax: 813-259-5403, E-mail: fnolasco@ut.edu.

The University of Tennessee, Graduate School, College of Business Administration, Program in Business Administration, Knoxville, TN 37996. Offers accounting (PhD); finance (MBA, PhD); logistics and transportation (MBA, PhD); management (PhD); marketing (MBA, PhD); operations management (MBA); professional business administration (MBA); statistics (PhD); JD/MBA; MS/MBA. *Accreditation:* AACSB. Postbaccalaureate distance learning degree programs offered. *Students:* 344 (105 women); includes 42 minority (20 African Americans, 4 American Indian/Alaska Native, 9 Asian Americans or Pacific Islanders, 9 Hispanic Americans) 49 international. In 2006, 169 master's, 9 doctorates awarded. *Degree requirements:* For master's, thesis or alternative; for doctorate, thesis/dissertation. *Entrance requirements:* For master's and doctorate, GMAT, minimum GPA of 2.7. Additional exam requirements/recommendations for international students: Required—TOEFL. *Application deadline:* For fall admission, 2/1 priority date for domestic students. Application fee: $35. Electronic applications accepted. *Expenses:* Tuition, state resident: full-time $5,574. Tuition, nonresident: full-time $16,840. Required fees: $792. *Financial support:* In 2006–07, 6 fellowships, 3 research assistantships, 35 teaching assistantships were awarded; career-related internships or fieldwork, Federal Work-Study, institutionally sponsored loans, and unspecified assistantships also available. Financial award application deadline: 2/1; financial award applicants required to submit FAFSA. *Unit head:* Dr. Sarah Gardial, Assistant Dean, 865-974-5033, Fax: 865-974-3826, E-mail: sgardial@utk.edu. *Application contact:* Donna Potts, Graduate Representative, 865-974-5033, Fax: 865-974-3826, E-mail: dpotts@utk.edu.

The University of Texas at Arlington, Graduate School, College of Business Administration, Program in Business Administration, Arlington, TX 76019. Offers accounting (PhD); business administration (PhD); business statistics (PhD); finance (MBA); information systems (MBA, PhD); management (MBA); management sciences (MBA); marketing (MBA, PhD); real estate (MBA). *Accreditation:* AACSB. Part-time and evening/weekend programs available. Postbaccalaureate distance learning degree programs offered (no on-campus study). *Faculty:* 1 full-time (0 women). *Students:* 156 full-time (60 women), 319 part-time (110 women); includes 123 minority (38 African Americans, 4 American Indian/Alaska Native, 52 Asian Americans or Pacific Islanders, 29 Hispanic Americans), 88 international. 502 applicants, 85% accepted, 199 enrolled. In 2006, 417 master's, 11 doctorates awarded. Terminal master's awarded for partial completion of doctoral program. *Degree requirements:* For master's, thesis optional; for doctorate, thesis/dissertation. *Entrance requirements:* For master's, GMAT; for doctorate, GMAT, minimum GPA of 3.0 (undergraduate), 3.4 (graduate); 30 hours of graduate course work. Additional exam requirements/recommendations for international students: Required—TOEFL (minimum score 550 paper-based; 213 computer-based). *Application deadline:* For fall admission, 6/15 for domestic students, 4/1 for international students; for spring admission, 10/15 for domestic students, 9/1 for international students. Applications are processed on a rolling basis. Application fee: $35 ($50 for international students). Electronic applications accepted. *Expenses:* Tuition, state resident: full-time $5,528. Tuition, nonresident: full-time $10,478. International tuition: $10,608 full-time. *Financial support:* In 2006–07, 1 fellowship (averaging $1,000 per year), 14 research assistantships (averaging $6,432 per year) were awarded; teaching assistantships, career-related internships or fieldwork, scholarships/grants, and unspecified assistantships also available. Financial award application deadline: 6/1; financial award applicants required to submit FAFSA. *Application contact:* Dr. Mike West, Assistant Dean, 817-272-1287, Fax: 817-272-5799, E-mail: mpwest@uta.edu.

See Close-Up on page 363.

The University of Texas at Austin, Graduate School, McCombs School of Business, Department of Finance, Austin, TX 78712-1111. Offers PhD. *Entrance requirements:* For doctorate, GMAT or GRE. Electronic applications accepted.

Finance and Banking

The University of Texas at San Antonio, College of Business, Department of Finance, San Antonio, TX 78249-0617. Offers business finance (MBA); finance (MS, PhD). Part-time and evening/weekend programs available. *Faculty:* 9 full-time (0 women). *Students:* 34 full-time (12 women), 64 part-time (18 women); includes 42 minority (2 African Americans, 12 Asian Americans or Pacific Islanders, 28 Hispanic Americans), 17 international. Average age 30. 58 applicants, 67% accepted, 37 enrolled. In 2006, 33 degrees awarded. *Degree requirements:* For master's, thesis optional. *Entrance requirements:* For master's, GMAT, minimum GPA of 3.0. Additional exam requirements/recommendations for international students: Required—TOEFL (minimum score 500 paper-based; 173 computer-based). *Application deadline:* For fall admission, 7/1 for domestic students, 4/1 for international students; for spring admission, 11/1 for domestic students, 9/1 for international students. Applications are processed on a rolling basis. Application fee: $45 ($85 for international students). Electronic applications accepted. *Expenses:* Tuition, state resident: full-time $1,730; part-time $192 per credit hour. Tuition, nonresident: full-time $6,680; part-time $742 per credit hour. Required fees: $733; $308,359 per credit hour. *Financial support:* In 2006–07, 1 research assistantship (averaging $21,840 per year), 8 teaching assistantships (averaging $15,600 per year) were awarded; career-related internships or fieldwork, Federal Work-Study, scholarships/grants, and unspecified assistantships also available. Support available to part-time students. Total annual research expenditures: $17,414. *Unit head:* Dr. Keith Fairchild, Chair, 210-458-5307, Fax: 210-458-5320, E-mail: kfairchild@utsa.edu.

University of the West, Department of Business Administration, Rosemead, CA 91770. Offers business administration (EMBA); finance (MBA); information technology and management (MBA); international business (MBA); nonprofit organization management (MBA). Part-time and evening/weekend programs available. *Entrance requirements:* Additional exam requirements/recommendations for international students: Required—TOEFL.

The University of Toledo, College of Graduate Studies, College of Business Administration, Department of Finance and Business Economics, Toledo, OH 43606-3390. Offers MBA. Evening/weekend programs available. *Faculty:* 2. *Students:* 37 full-time (17 women), 17 part-time (4 women); includes 2 minority (1 African American, 1 Hispanic American), 16 international. Average age 27. 36 applicants, 67% accepted, 15 enrolled. In 2006, 29 degrees awarded. *Degree requirements:* For master's, thesis or alternative. *Entrance requirements:* For master's, GMAT. Additional exam requirements/recommendations for international students: Required—TOEFL. *Application deadline:* For fall admission, 8/1 priority date for domestic students. Applications are processed on a rolling basis. Application fee: $45. *Financial support:* Research assistantships, career-related internships or fieldwork, Federal Work-Study, institutionally sponsored loans, scholarships/grants, tuition waivers (full), and administrative assistantships available. Support available to part-time students. Financial award application deadline: 4/1; financial award applicants required to submit FAFSA. *Faculty research:* Financial management, banking, international finance, investments. *Unit head:* Dr. Andrew Solocha, Chair, 419-530-2564.

University of Tulsa, Graduate School, College of Business Administration, Program in Finance, Tulsa, OK 74104-3189. Offers corporate finance (MS); investments and portfolio management (MS); risk management (MS). Part-time and evening/weekend programs available. *Faculty:* 7 full-time (0 women). *Students:* 18 full-time (5 women), 4 part-time (1 woman); includes 2 minority (1 American Indian/Alaska Native, 1 Hispanic American), 8 international. Average age 28. 42 applicants, 26% accepted, 8 enrolled. In 2006, 12 degrees awarded. *Median time to degree:* Master's–2 years full-time. *Degree requirements:* For master's, thesis optional. *Entrance requirements:* For master's, GMAT. Additional exam requirements/recommendations for international students: Required—TOEFL (minimum score 575 paper-based; 231 computer-based), IELTS (minimum score 7). *Application deadline:* Applications are processed on a rolling basis. Application fee: $40. Electronic applications accepted. *Expenses:* Tuition: Full-time $13,338; part-time $741 per credit hour. *Financial support:* In 2006–07, 9 students received support, including 9 teaching assistantships with full and partial tuition reimbursements available (averaging $10,125 per year); fellowships with full and partial tuition reimbursements available, career-related internships or fieldwork, Federal Work-Study, institutionally sponsored loans, scholarships/grants, tuition waivers (full and partial), and unspecified assistantships also available. Support available to part-time students. Financial award application deadline: 2/1; financial award applicants required to submit FAFSA. *Unit head:* Markham Collins, Associate Dean, 918-631-2783, Fax: 918-631-2142, E-mail: markham-collins@utulsa.edu.

See Close-Up on page 461.

University of Utah, The Graduate School, David Eccles School of Business, Department of Finance, Salt Lake City, UT 84112-1107. Offers MS, PhD. *Faculty:* 15 full-time (2 women), 2 part-time/adjunct (1 woman). *Students:* 20 full-time (9 women), 18 part-time (7 women); includes 4 minority (1 African American, 2 Asian Americans or Pacific Islanders, 1 Hispanic American), 8 international. Average age 28. 80 applicants, 60% accepted, 29 enrolled. In 2006, 15 degrees awarded. Terminal master's awarded for partial completion of doctoral program. *Degree requirements:* For master's, thesis; for doctorate, thesis/dissertation, oral qualifying exams, written qualifying exams, research paper. *Entrance requirements:* For master's, GMAT, minimum undergraduate GPA of 3.0; for doctorate, GMAT. Additional exam requirements/recommendations for international students: Required—TOEFL (minimum score 600 paper-based; 250 computer-based). *Application deadline:* For fall admission, 4/2 priority date for domestic students, 4/2 for international students. Application fee: $45 ($65 for international students). Electronic applications accepted. *Expenses:* Tuition, state resident: full-time $3,208. Tuition, nonresident: full-time $11,326. Required fees: $608. Tuition and fees vary according to class time and program. *Financial support:* In 2006–07, 7 students received support, including 7 teaching assistantships (averaging $7,950 per year); fellowships, research assistantships, tuition waivers (full and partial) also available. Financial award application deadline: 2/15; financial award applicants required to submit FAFSA. *Faculty research:* Investment, managerial finance, corporate finance, capital budgeting, risk management. Total annual research expenditures: $63,035. *Unit head:* Uri Loewenstein, Chair, 801-581-4419, Fax: 801-581-3956, E-mail: uri.lowenstein@business.utah.edu.

University of Waterloo, Graduate Studies, Faculty of Arts, School of Accountancy, Waterloo, ON N2L 3G1, Canada. Offers accounting (M Acc, PhD); finance (M Acc); taxation (M Tax). *Faculty:* 29 full-time (8 women), 3 part-time/adjunct (1 woman). *Students:* 100. 199 applicants, 24% accepted, 29 enrolled. In 2006, 133 master's, 1 doctorate awarded. *Degree requirements:* For master's, thesis or alternative; for doctorate, thesis/dissertation. *Entrance requirements:* For master's, honors degree, minimum B average, resumé; for doctorate, GMAT, master's degree, minimum A- average, resumé. Additional exam requirements/recommendations for international students: Required—TOEFL, TWE. *Application deadline:* For fall admission, 1/31 for domestic students. Application fee: $75 Canadian dollars. *Expenses:* Contact institution. *Faculty research:* Auditing, management accounting. *Unit head:* Dr. Alister Mason, Director, 519-888-4567 Ext. 33732, Fax: 519-888-7262, E-mail: amason@uwaterloo.ca. *Application contact:* Dr. Alan Macnaughton, Graduate Officer, 519-888-4567 Ext. 35776, Fax: 519-888-7562.

The University of Western Ontario, Richard Ivey School of Business, London, ON N6A 3K7, Canada. Offers biotechnology stream (MBA); business (EMBA, PhD); certified management accountant (MBA); China business stream (MBA); entrepreneurship (MBA); finance stream (MBA); LL B/MBA. Part-time and evening/weekend programs available. *Degree requirements:* For master's, thesis (for some programs); for doctorate, thesis/dissertation. *Entrance requirements:* For master's, GMAT, 3 years of full-time work experience, interview; for doctorate, GMAT. Additional exam requirements/recommendations for international students: Required—TOEFL. Electronic applications accepted. *Faculty research:* Strategy, organizational behavior, international business, finance, operations management.

University of Wisconsin–Madison, Graduate School, School of Business, Program in Finance, Investment, and Banking, Madison, WI 53706-1380. Offers finance, investment, and banking (PhD); international business (PhD). Evening/weekend programs available. *Students:* 9 full-time (5 women), 8 international. Average age 28. 113 applicants, 4% accepted, 4 enrolled. In 2006, 2 degrees awarded. *Entrance requirements:* For doctorate, GMAT or GRE. Additional exam requirements/recommendations for international students: Required—TOEFL (minimum score 600 paper-based; 250 computer-based). *Application deadline:* For fall admission, 1/6 priority date for domestic and international students. Applications are processed on a rolling basis. Application fee: $45. Electronic applications accepted. *Financial support:* In 2006–07, 9 students received support, including fellowships with partial tuition reimbursements available (averaging $16,110 per year), research assistantships with full tuition reimbursements available (averaging $13,502 per year), 8 teaching assistantships (averaging $13,686 per year); Federal Work-Study, institutionally sponsored loans, scholarships/grants, health care benefits, and unspecified assistantships also available. Financial award application deadline: 1/6; financial award applicants required to submit FAFSA. *Faculty research:* Banking and financial institutions, business cycles, investments, derivatives, corporate finance. *Unit head:* Dr. James P. Hodder, Chair, 608-262-8774, Fax: 608-265-4195, E-mail: jhodder@bus.wisc.edu. *Application contact:* Belle Heberling, PhD Coordinator, 608-262-3749, Fax: 608-890-0180, E-mail: phd@bus.wisc.edu.

University of Wisconsin–Madison, Graduate School, School of Business, Program in Quantitative Financial Management, Madison, WI 53706-1380. Offers MS. *Students:* 5 full-time (2 women), (all international). Average age 25. 69 applicants, 6% accepted, 3 enrolled. In 2006, 6 degrees awarded. *Degree requirements:* For master's, registration. *Entrance requirements:* For master's, GMAT or GRE. Additional exam requirements/recommendations for international students: Required—TOEFL. *Application deadline:* For fall admission, 4/15 for domestic students. Applications are processed on a rolling basis. Application fee: $45. Electronic applications accepted. *Financial support:* In 2006–07, 5 students received support, including 5 teaching assistantships with full tuition reimbursements available (averaging $8,411 per year); fellowships, research assistantships with full tuition reimbursements available, career-related internships or fieldwork, Federal Work-Study, institutionally sponsored loans, scholarships/grants, health care benefits, and unspecified assistantships also available. Financial award application deadline: 2/15. *Faculty research:* Capital markets, derivatives, financial markets, liquidity constraints. *Unit head:* Dr. James Hodder, Chair, 608-262-8774, Fax: 608-265-4195, E-mail: jhodder@bus.wisc.edu. *Application contact:* Belle Heberling, MS Coordinator, 608-262-3749, Fax: 608-890-0180, E-mail: ms@bus.wisc.edu.

University of Wisconsin–Madison, Graduate School, School of Business, Wisconsin Full-Time MBA Programs, Madison, WI 53706-1380. Offers applied corporate finance (MBA); applied security analysis (MBA); arts administration (MBA); brand and product management (MBA); entrepreneurial management (MBA); information systems (MBA); marketing research (MBA); operations and technology management (MBA); real estate (MBA); risk management and insurance (MBA); strategic human resource management (MBA); strategic management in the life and engineering sciences (MBA); supply chain management (MBA). *Faculty:* 84. *Students:* 231 full-time (74 women); includes 21 minority (10 African Americans, 5 Asian Americans or Pacific Islanders, 6 Hispanic Americans), 59 international. Average age 28. 405 applicants, 43% accepted, 121 enrolled. In 2006, 110 degrees awarded. *Entrance requirements:* For master's, GMAT, bachelors or equivalent degree, 2 years of work experience. Additional exam requirements/recommendations for international students: Required—TOEFL (minimum score 600 paper-based; 250 computer-based; 90 iBT). *Application deadline:* For fall admission, 11/1 for domestic and international students; for winter admission, 1/23 for domestic and international students; for spring admission, 3/26 for domestic and international students. Applications are processed on a rolling basis. Application fee: $45. Electronic applications accepted. *Financial support:* In 2006–07, 177 students received support, including 20 fellowships with full and partial tuition reimbursements available (averaging $16,566 per year), 105 research assistantships with full tuition reimbursements available (averaging $8,098 per year), 33 teaching assistantships with full tuition reimbursements available (averaging $10,112 per year); scholarships/grants, health care benefits, and unspecified assistantships also available. *Unit head:* Gary Lessuise, Assistant Dean, Masters Programs, 608-265-5102, Fax: 608-265-4192, E-mail: glessuise@bus.wisc.edu. *Application contact:* Betsy Kacizak, Director of Admissions and Financial Aid—Full Time MBA, 608-262-4000, Fax: 608-265-4192, E-mail: mba@bus.wisc.edu.

University of Wisconsin–Whitewater, School of Graduate Studies, College of Business and Economics, Program in Business Administration, Whitewater, WI 53190-1790. Offers finance (MBA); human resource management (MBA); information technology management (MBA); international business (MBA); management (MBA); marketing (MBA); operations and supply chain management (MBA); technology and training (MBA). *Accreditation:* AACSB. Part-time and evening/weekend programs available. Postbaccalaureate distance learning degree programs offered (no on-campus study). *Students:* 67 full-time (26 women), 331 part-time (136 women); includes 71 minority (20 African Americans, 40 Asian Americans or Pacific Islanders, 11 Hispanic Americans). Average age 28. 167 applicants, 62% accepted, 75 enrolled. In 2006, 141 degrees awarded. *Degree requirements:* For master's, thesis or alternative. *Entrance requirements:* For master's, GMAT, minimum AACSB index of 1000, minimum GPA of 2.75. Additional exam requirements/recommendations for international students: Required—TOEFL (minimum score 550 paper-based; 213 computer-based). *Application deadline:* For fall admission, 7/15 for domestic students, 7/15 priority date for international students; for spring admission, 12/1 for domestic and international students. Applications are processed on a rolling basis. Application fee: $45. Electronic applications accepted. *Expenses:* Tuition, state resident: full-time $3,311. Tuition, nonresident: full-time $8,616. Required fees: $368 per credit. *Financial support:* In 2006–07, 11 research assistantships (averaging $7,385 per year) were awarded; Federal Work-Study, unspecified assistantships, and out of state fee waiver also available. Support available to part-time students. Financial award application deadline: 3/15; financial award applicants required to submit FAFSA. *Faculty research:* Interface between social institutions and individual behavior, technology and innovation management, occupational mental health, workplace deviance and workplace romance. *Unit head:* Dr. Donald Zahn, Associate Dean, 262-472-1945, Fax: 262-472-4863, E-mail: zahnd@uww.edu.

University of Wyoming, Graduate School, College of Business, Department of Economics and Finance, Program in Economics and Finance, Laramie, WY 82070. Offers MS. *Application contact:* Abby Derr, Graduate Coordinator, 307-766-2175, Fax: 307-766-5090, E-mail: derra7@uwyo.edu.

University of Wyoming, Graduate School, College of Business, Department of Economics and Finance, Program in Finance, Laramie, WY 82070. Offers MS. Part-time programs available. *Faculty:* 4 full-time (0 women), 2 part-time/adjunct (0 women). *Students:* 7 full-time (2 women), 1 (woman) part-time, 3 international. Average age 25. 13 applicants, 15% accepted, 2 enrolled. In 2006, 7 degrees awarded. *Degree requirements:* For master's, thesis. *Entrance requirements:* For master's, GMAT, GRE, minimum GPA of 3.0. Additional exam requirements/recommendations for international students: Required—TOEFL (minimum score 525 paper-based; 197 computer-based). *Application deadline:* For fall admission, 3/1 for domestic students; for spring admission, 10/1 for domestic students. Applications are processed on a rolling basis. Application fee: $50. *Financial support:* In 2006–07, 2 research assistantships with partial tuition reimbursements (averaging $5,031 per year), 3 teaching assistantships with partial tuition reimbursements (averaging $5,031 per year) were awarded. Financial award application deadline: 3/1. *Faculty research:* Banking. *Application contact:* Abby Derr, Graduate Coordinator, 307-766-2175, Fax: 307-766-5090, E-mail: derra7@uwyo.edu.

Upper Iowa University, Online Master's Programs, Fayette, IA 52142-1857. Offers accounting (MBA); corporate financial management (MBA); global business (MBA); health and human services (MPA); homeland security (MPA); human resources management (MBA); justice administration (MPA); organizational development (MBA); public personnel management (MPA); quality management (MBA). MBA also available at Madison, Wisconsin campus. Part-time and evening/weekend programs available. Postbaccalaureate distance learning degree programs offered (no on-campus study). *Degree requirements:* For master's, research project. *Entrance* *requirements:* For master's, GMAT, GRE, or minimum GPA of 2.7 during last 60 hours. Additional exam requirements/recommendations for international students: Required—TOEFL (minimum score 570 paper-based; 230 computer-based). Electronic applications accepted. *Faculty research:* Total quality management, CQI, teams, organization culture and climate, management.

Vanderbilt University, Owen Graduate School of Management, Program in Finance, Nashville, TN 37240-1001. Offers MSF. *Faculty:* 25. *Students:* 21 full-time (6 women), 12 international. Average age 26. 169 applicants, 28% accepted, 19 enrolled. *Entrance requirements:* Additional exam requirements/recommendations for international students: Required—TOEFL. *Application deadline:* For fall admission, 11/15 priority date for domestic students; for winter admission, 1/15 priority date for domestic students; for spring admission, 3/1 priority date for domestic students. Application fee: $50. *Expenses:* Tuition: Full-time $24,462. Required fees: $2,515. One-time fee: $30 full-time. Full-time tuition and fees vary according to course load, degree level and program. *Financial support:* In 2006–07, 6 students received support. Scholarships/grants available. *Unit head:* Dr. Clifford Ball, Director, 615-322-2909, E-mail: cliff.ball@owen.vanderbilt.edu. *Application contact:* Amy Achterhof Johnson, Program Director, 615-322-6509, Fax: 615-343-1175, E-mail: amy.achterhof@owen.vanderbilt.edu.

Vanderbilt University, Owen Graduate School of Management and Graduate School, Program in Management, Nashville, TN 37240-1001. Offers finance (PhD); marketing (PhD); operations management (PhD); organization studies (PhD). PhD offered through the Graduate School. *Accreditation:* AACSB. *Faculty:* 46 full-time (8 women). *Students:* 19 full-time (6 women); includes 12 minority (all Asian Americans or Pacific Islanders) Average age 28. 169 applicants, 5% accepted, 5 enrolled. In 2006, 3 degrees awarded. *Median time to degree:* Doctorate–5 years full-time. Of those who began their doctoral program in fall 1998, 100% received their degree in 8 years or less. *Degree requirements:* For doctorate, thesis/dissertation, registration. *Entrance requirements:* For doctorate, GMAT or GRE. Additional exam requirements/recommendations for international students: Required—TOEFL. *Application deadline:* For fall admission, 1/15 priority date for domestic students; for spring admission, 3/15 for domestic students. Application fee: $0. Electronic applications accepted. *Expenses: Contact institution.* One-time fee: $30 full-time. Full-time tuition and fees vary according to course load, degree level and program. *Financial support:* In 2006–07, 19 students received support, including 4 fellowships with full tuition reimbursements available (averaging $20,500 per year); scholarships/grants, health care benefits, and tuition waivers (full and partial) also available. Financial award application deadline: 5/1. *Faculty research:* Financial marketing, operations, human resources. *Unit head:* Dr. Clifford Ball, Director, 615-322-2909, E-mail: cliff.ball@owen.vanderbilt.edu. *Application contact:* Janet Sisco, Information Contact, 615-322-5652, E-mail: janet.sisco@owen.vanderbilt.edu.

Villanova University, Villanova School of Business, Master of Science in Finance Program, Villanova, PA 19085-1699. Offers MS. *Faculty:* 8 full-time (1 woman). *Students:* 12 full-time (4 women); includes 1 Asian American or Pacific Islander. Average age 25. 30 applicants, 60% accepted, 12 enrolled. In 2006, 9 degrees awarded. *Entrance requirements:* Additional exam requirements/recommendations for international students: Required—TOEFL (minimum score 600 paper-based; 250 computer-based; 100 iBT). *Application deadline:* For spring admission, 3/31 for domestic and international students. Applications are processed on a rolling basis. Application fee: $50. Electronic applications accepted. *Expenses:* Tuition: Part-time $565 per credit. *Financial support:* Application deadline: 3/31. *Unit head:* Simone L. Pollard, Director of Graduate Business, 610-519-4336, Fax: 610-519-6273, E-mail: simone.pollard@villanova.edu. *Application contact:* Maureen Piotti, Coordinator, Graduate Business Programs, 610-519-5456, Fax: 610-519-6273, E-mail: maureen.piotti@villanova.edu.

Virginia Commonwealth University, Graduate School, School of Business, Program in Finance, Insurance, and Real Estate, Richmond, VA 23284-9005. Offers MS. *Faculty:* 11 full-time (0 women). *Students:* 2 full-time (0 women), 6 part-time (1 woman), 1 international. 5 applicants, 80% accepted, 3 enrolled. In 2006, 17 degrees awarded. *Entrance requirements:* For master's, GMAT. *Application deadline:* Applications are processed on a rolling basis. Application fee: $50. *Financial support:* Fellowships, research assistantships, teaching assistantships, Federal Work-Study, institutionally sponsored loans, and tuition waivers (full and partial) available. Financial award application deadline: 3/15. *Unit head:* Dr. David E. Upton, Acting Chair, 804-828-7169, Fax: 804-828-3972, E-mail: deupton@vcu.edu. *Application contact:* Tracy Green, Graduate Program Director, 804-828-1741, Fax: 804-828-7174, E-mail: tsgreen@vcu.edu.

Virginia Polytechnic Institute and State University, Graduate School, Pamplin College of Business, Department of Finance, Blacksburg, VA 24061. Offers business administration/finance (MS, PhD). *Faculty:* 21 full-time (1 woman). *Students:* 8 full-time (1 woman), 7 international. Average age 31. 19 applicants, 5% accepted, 1 enrolled. In 2006, 2 degrees awarded. *Entrance requirements:* For master's and doctorate, GMAT. Additional exam requirements/recommendations for international students: Required—TOEFL (minimum score 600 paper-based; 250 computer-based). *Application deadline:* For fall admission, 5/15 for international students; for spring admission, 10/15 for international students. Applications are processed on a rolling basis. Application fee: $45. Electronic applications accepted. *Expenses:* Tuition, state resident: full-time $7,017; part-time $390 per credit hour. Tuition, nonresident: full-time $12,414; part-time $690 per credit hour. International tuition: $11,296 full-time. Required fees: $1,523; $256 per term. *Financial support:* In 2006–07, 7 teaching assistantships with full tuition reimbursements (averaging $12,946 per year) were awarded; career-related internships or fieldwork, Federal Work-Study, scholarships/grants, and unspecified assistantships also available. Financial award application deadline: 1/15. *Faculty research:* Capital markets, corporate finance, investment banking, derivatives, international finance. *Unit head:* Dr. Vijay Singal, Head, 540-231-5904, Fax: 540-231-4487, E-mail: singal@vt.edu. *Application contact:* Leanne Brownlee, Information Contact, 540-231-5886, Fax: 540-231-4487, E-mail: lbrownle@vt.edu.

Wagner College, Division of Graduate Studies, Department of Business Administration, Program in Finance, Staten Island, NY 10301-4495. Offers MBA. Part-time and evening/weekend programs available. *Faculty:* 3 full-time (1 woman). *Students:* 11 full-time (8 women), 8 part-time (4 women); includes 3 minority (2 African Americans, 1 Asian American or Pacific Islander). 7 applicants, 86% accepted, 5 enrolled. In 2006, 16 degrees awarded. *Degree requirements:* For master's, thesis optional. *Entrance requirements:* For master's, GMAT, minimum GPA of 2.6, computer and math proficiency. *Application deadline:* For fall admission, 8/1 priority date for domestic students, 6/30 priority date for international students; for spring admission, 12/10 for domestic students, 11/15 for international students. Applications are processed on a rolling basis. Application fee: $50 ($85 for international students). *Expenses:* Tuition: Full-time $15,120; part-time $840 per credit. *Financial support:* Fellowships, tuition waivers (partial) and unspecified assistantships available. Financial award applicants required to submit FAFSA. *Application contact:* Susan Rosenberg, Office of Graduate Studies, 718-390-3106, Fax: 718-390-3456, E-mail: graduate@wagner.edu.

Walsh College of Accountancy and Business Administration, Graduate Programs, Program in Finance, Troy, MI 48007-7006. Offers MSF. Part-time and evening/weekend programs available. *Faculty:* 3 full-time (0 women), 18 part-time/adjunct (1 woman). *Students:* 15 full-time (5 women), 299 part-time (146 women). Average age 34. 78 applicants, 100% accepted, 78 enrolled. In 2006, 146 degrees awarded. *Entrance requirements:* For master's, minimum GPA of 2.75, previous course work in business. Additional exam requirements/recommendations for international students: Required—TOEFL. *Application deadline:* For fall admission, 8/24 priority date for domestic students; for winter admission, 1/1 priority date for domestic students; for spring admission, 4/1 priority date for domestic students. Applications are processed on a rolling basis. Application fee: $25. Electronic applications accepted. *Expenses:* Tuition: Part-time $435 per hour. Required fees: $119 per semester. One-time fee: $50. *Financial support:* Available to part-time students. Application deadline: 6/30. *Unit head:* Dr. Linda Wiechowski, Chair, 248-823-1265, Fax: 248-689-0920. *Application contact:* Karen Mahaffy, Director of Admissions and Academic Advising, 248-823-1610, Fax: 248-689-0938, E-mail: kmahaffy@walshcollege.edu.

Washington State University, Graduate School, College of Business, Department of Finance, Insurance and Real Estate, Pullman, WA 99164. Offers PhD. Application fee: $50. *Expenses:* Tuition, state resident: full-time $7,066. Tuition, nonresident: full-time $17,204. *Unit head:* Dr. Gene Lai, Chair.

Washington State University, Graduate School, College of Business, Graduate Programs in Business, Pullman, WA 99164. Offers accounting and business law (M Acc); business administration (MBA, PhD), including accounting (PhD), finance (PhD), management and operations (PhD), management information systems (PhD), marketing (PhD); JD/MBA. *Accreditation:* AACSB. *Faculty:* 38. *Students:* 105 full-time (39 women), 14 part-time (5 women); includes 3 minority (1 American Indian/Alaska Native, 2 Asian Americans or Pacific Islanders), 62 international. Average age 30. 328 applicants, 32% accepted, 43 enrolled. In 2006, 56 master's, 8 doctorates awarded. *Degree requirements:* For master's, thesis (for some programs), final presentation, comprehensive exam (for some programs); for doctorate, thesis/dissertation, oral and written exams, comprehensive exam. *Entrance requirements:* For master's and doctorate, GMAT, minimum GPA of 3.0, 3 letters of recommendation. Additional exam requirements/recommendations for international students: Required—TOEFL. *Application deadline:* For fall admission, 3/1 priority date for domestic students, 3/1 for international students; for spring admission, 6/1 priority date for domestic students, 6/1 for international students. Applications are processed on a rolling basis. Application fee: $50. Electronic applications accepted. *Expenses:* Tuition, state resident: full-time $7,066. Tuition, nonresident: full-time $17,204. *Financial support:* In 2006–07, 102 students received support, including 9 fellowships (averaging $6,000 per year), 8 research assistantships with full and partial tuition reimbursements available (averaging $13,917 per year), 75 teaching assistantships with full and partial tuition reimbursements available (averaging $13,056 per year); career-related internships or fieldwork, Federal Work-Study, institutionally sponsored loans, health care benefits, tuition waivers (partial), unspecified assistantships, and teaching associateships also available. Financial award application deadline: 4/1. *Unit head:* Dr. Charles Munson, Associate Dean, 509-335-1193, E-mail: mba@wsu.edu. *Application contact:* Graduate School Admissions, 800-GRADWSU, Fax: 509-335-1949, E-mail: gradsch@wsu.edu.

Washington University in St. Louis, John M. Olin School of Business, Program in Accounting and Finance, St. Louis, MO 63130-4899. Offers accounting (MS); finance (MS). Part-time programs available. *Faculty:* 66 full-time, 39 part-time/adjunct. *Students:* 59 full-time. 170 applicants, 58% accepted, 57 enrolled. In 2006, 18 degrees awarded. *Entrance requirements:* For master's, GMAT or GRE. Additional exam requirements/recommendations for international students: Required—TOEFL. *Application deadline:* For fall admission, 3/15 for domestic and international students. Application fee: $80. *Expenses: Contact institution. Financial support:* Applicants required to submit FAFSA. *Unit head:* Joseph Peter Fox, Associate Dean and Director of MBA Programs, 314-935-6322, Fax: 314-935-4464, E-mail: fox@wustl.edu.

Webster University, School of Business and Technology, Department of Business, St. Louis, MO 63119-3194. Offers business (MA); business and organizational security management (MBA); computer resources and information management (MBA); environmental management (MBA); finance (MA, MBA); health services management (MBA); human resources development (MBA); human resources management (MBA); international business (MA, MBA); management and leadership (MBA); marketing (MBA); procurement and acquisitions management (MBA); telecommunications management (MBA). Part-time and evening/weekend programs available. Postbaccalaureate distance learning degree programs offered (no on-campus study). *Students:* 1,205 full-time (629 women), 4,197 part-time (2,153 women); includes 2,005 minority (1,467 African Americans, 29 American Indian/Alaska Native, 212 Asian Americans or Pacific Islanders, 297 Hispanic Americans), 485 international. Average age 33. *Application deadline:* Applications are processed on a rolling basis. Application fee: $25 ($50 for international students). *Expenses:* Tuition: Full-time $8,820; part-time $490 per credit. Tuition and fees vary according to degree level, campus/location and program. *Financial support:* Federal Work-Study available. Support available to part-time students. Financial award application deadline: 4/1; financial award applicants required to submit FAFSA. *Unit head:* Bradford Scott, Chair, 314-961-2260 Ext. 7574, Fax: 314-968-7077, E-mail: buschair@webster.edu. *Application contact:* Director of Graduate and Evening Student Admissions, Fax: 314-968-7116, E-mail: gadmit@webster.edu.

West Chester University of Pennsylvania, Graduate Studies, School of Business and Public Affairs, Program in Business Administration, West Chester, PA 19383. Offers economics/finance (MBA); executive business administration (MBA); general business (MBA); management (MBA); technology and electronic commerce (MBA). *Accreditation:* AACSB. Part-time and evening/weekend programs available. *Students:* 2 full-time (1 woman), 68 part-time (19 women); includes 3 African Americans, 8 Asian Americans or Pacific Islanders, 2 Hispanic Americans, 5 international. Average age 34. 39 applicants, 77% accepted, 27 enrolled. In 2006, 41 degrees awarded. *Degree requirements:* For master's, thesis optional. *Entrance requirements:* For master's, GMAT, interview, minimum GPA of 3.0. *Application deadline:* For fall admission, 4/15 priority date for domestic students; for spring admission, 10/15 for domestic students. Applications are processed on a rolling basis. Application fee: $35. *Financial support:* In 2006–07, 4 research assistantships with full tuition reimbursements (averaging $5,000 per year) were awarded; unspecified assistantships also available. Support available to part-time students. Financial award application deadline: 2/15; financial award applicants required to submit FAFSA. *Unit head:* Dr. Pual Christ, Director, 610-436-2608, E-mail: pchrist@wcupa.edu. *Application contact:* Dr. Pual Christ, Graduate Coordinator, 610-436-2608, E-mail: mba@wcupa.edu.

Western International University, Graduate Programs in Business, Program in Finance, Phoenix, AZ 85021-2718. Offers MBA. Evening/weekend programs available. Postbaccalaureate distance learning degree programs offered (no on-campus study). *Faculty:* 238 part-time/adjunct (58 women). *Students:* 80 full-time (40 women); includes 23 minority (8 African Americans, 1 American Indian/Alaska Native, 4 Asian Americans or Pacific Islanders, 10 Hispanic Americans), 14 international. Average age 35. In 2006, 21 degrees awarded. *Degree requirements:* For master's, thesis, research project. *Entrance requirements:* For master's, minimum GPA of 2.75. *Application deadline:* Applications are processed on a rolling basis. Application fee: $85 ($100 for international students). *Expenses:* Tuition: Full-time $9,600; part-time $400 per credit. One-time fee: $85 full-time. *Financial support:* Career-related internships or fieldwork, institutionally sponsored loans, and scholarships/grants available. Support available to part-time students. Financial award applicants required to submit FAFSA. *Unit head:* Trish Ellenberg, Chair, 602-943-2311. *Application contact:* Karen Janitell, Director of Enrollment, 602-943-2311 Ext. 1063, Fax: 602-371-8637, E-mail: karen_janitell@apollogrp.edu.

West Texas A&M University, College of Business, Department of Accounting, Economics, and Finance, Program in Finance and Economics, Canyon, TX 79016-0001. Offers MS. Part-time and evening/weekend programs available. Postbaccalaureate distance learning degree programs offered (minimal on-campus study). *Degree requirements:* For master's, thesis optional. *Entrance requirements:* For master's, GMAT. Additional exam requirements/recommendations for international students: Required—TOEFL (minimum score 550 paper-based). Electronic applications accepted. *Faculty research:* International trade composition, cycle of poverty, trade effects in Asian countries, structural problems in Japanese economy, reform and the US sugar program-Nebraska.

Wilkes University, Graduate Studies and Continued Learning, Jay S. Sidhu School of Business and Leadership, Wilkes-Barre, PA 18766-0002. Offers accounting (MBA); entrepreneurship (MBA); finance (MBA); human resource management (MBA); international business (MBA); management (MBA); marketing (MBA). *Accreditation:* ACBSP. Part-time and evening/weekend programs available. *Students:* 30 full-time (16 women), 149 part-time (73 women);

Finance and Banking

Wilkes University (continued)

includes 5 minority (1 African American, 2 Asian Americans or Pacific Islanders, 2 Hispanic Americans), 4 international. Average age 30. In 2006, 48 degrees awarded. *Entrance requirements:* For master's, GMAT. Additional exam requirements/recommendations for international students: Required—TOEFL (minimum score 500 paper-based; 173 computer-based). *Application deadline:* Applications are processed on a rolling basis. Application fee: $40. *Expenses:* Contact institution. *Financial support:* Federal Work-Study and unspecified assistantships available. Financial award application deadline: 3/1; financial award applicants required to submit FAFSA. *Unit head:* Dr. Paul Browne, Dean, 570-408-4701, Fax: 570-408-4700, E-mail: paul.browne@wilkes.edu. *Application contact:* Kathleen Houlihan, Director of Graduate Studies, 570-408-3235, Fax: 570-408-7846, E-mail: kathleen.houlihan@wilkes.edu.

Wilmington College, Division of Business, New Castle, DE 19720-6491. Offers business administration (MBA); finance (MBA); health care administration (MBA, MS); human resource management (MS); management (MS); management information systems (MBA); organizational leadership (MS); public administration (MS); transportation and logistics (MBA, MS). Part-time and evening/weekend programs available. *Faculty:* 3 full-time (0 women). *Students:* 230 full-time (138 women), 432 part-time (274 women); includes 109 minority (98 African Americans, 1 American Indian/Alaska Native, 3 Asian Americans or Pacific Islanders, 7 Hispanic Americans). Average age 34. 229 applicants, 100% accepted, 156 enrolled. In 2006, 273 degrees awarded. *Entrance requirements:* Additional exam requirements/recommendations for international students: Required—TOEFL (minimum score 500 paper-based; 173 computer-based). *Application deadline:* Applications are processed on a rolling basis. Application fee: $25. *Financial support:* Applicants required to submit FAFSA. *Unit head:* Dr. Robert Edelson, Chair, 302-295-1147, Fax: 302-328-7021, E-mail: robert.e.edelson@wilmcoll.edu. *Application contact:* Chris Ferguson, Director of Admissions and Financial Aid, 302-328-9407 Ext. 256, Fax: 302-328-5164, E-mail: inquire@wilmcoll.edu.

Wright State University, School of Graduate Studies, Raj Soin College of Business, Department of Finance and Financial Services, Dayton, OH 45435. Offers finance (MBA); MBA/MS. *Students:* 19 full-time (5 women), 51 part-time (23 women). Average age 31. 37 applicants, 89% accepted. In 2006, 30 degrees awarded. *Entrance requirements:* For master's, GMAT, minimum AACSB index of 1000. Additional exam requirements/recommendations for international students: Required—TOEFL. Application fee: $25. *Financial support:* Fellowships, research assistantships, teaching assistantships, unspecified assistantships available. Support available to part-time students. Financial award applicants required to submit FAFSA. *Unit head:* Dr. Fall K. Ainina, Chair, 937-775-3671, Fax: 937-775-3545, E-mail: fall.ainina@wright.edu. *Application contact:* Mike Evans, Graduate Director, 937-775-2437, Fax: 937-775-3545, E-mail: michael.evans@wright.edu.

Xavier University, Williams College of Business, Master of Business Administration Program, Cincinnati, OH 45207. Offers business administration (Exec MBA, MBA); e-commerce (MBA); finance (MBA); international business (MBA); management information systems (MBA); marketing (MBA);); MBA/MHSA; MSN/MBA. *Accreditation:* AACSB. Part-time and evening/weekend programs available. *Faculty:* 59 full-time (22 women), 29 part-time/adjunct (8 women). *Students:* 227 full-time (66 women), 708 part-time (252 women); includes 99 minority (41 African Americans, 1 American Indian/Alaska Native, 43 Asian Americans or Pacific Islanders, 14 Hispanic Americans), 43 international. Average age 31. 486 applicants, 63% accepted, 229 enrolled. In 2006, 294 degrees awarded. *Entrance requirements:* For master's, GMAT, resumé. Additional exam requirements/recommendations for international students: Required—TOEFL (minimum score 550 paper-based; 213 computer-based; 79 iBT). *Application deadline:* For fall admission, 8/1 priority date for domestic students; 6/1 for international students; for winter admission, 12/1 priority date for domestic students; for spring admission, 4/1 priority date for domestic students, 10/1 for international students. Applications are processed on a rolling basis. Application fee: $35. Electronic applications accepted. *Expenses:* Contact institution. Part-time tuition and fees vary according to degree level, campus/location and program. *Financial support:* In 2006–07, 175 students received support, including 11 research assistantships with full and partial tuition reimbursements available; career-related internships or fieldwork, scholarships/grants, and tuition waivers (partial) also available. Support available to part-time students. Financial award application deadline: 4/30; financial award applicants required to submit FAFSA. *Faculty research:* Supply chain management, category management, data mining, off-shoring. *Unit head:* Dr. Raghu Tadepalli, Associate Dean, 513-745-3525, Fax: 513-745-2929, E-mail: tadepalli@xavier.edu. *Application contact:* Jennifer Bush, Executive Director, MBA Programs, 513-745-3525, Fax: 513-745-2929, E-mail: xumba@xavier.edu.

Yale University, Yale School of Management and Graduate School of Arts and Sciences, Doctoral Program in Management, New Haven, CT 06520. Offers accounting (PhD); financial economics (PhD); marketing (PhD). *Accreditation:* AACSB. *Faculty:* 55 full-time (7 women). *Students:* 25 full-time (6 women); includes 2 minority (both Asian Americans or Pacific Islanders), 20 international. Average age 28. 300 applicants, 4% accepted. In 2006, 6 doctorates awarded. *Degree requirements:* For doctorate, thesis/dissertation, comprehensive exam. *Entrance requirements:* For doctorate, GMAT or GRE General Test. Additional exam requirements/recommendations for international students: Required—TOEFL, IELTS. *Application deadline:* For fall admission, 1/2 for domestic and international students. Application fee: $85. Electronic applications accepted. *Expenses:* Contact institution. *Financial support:* Fellowships with full tuition reimbursements, research assistantships with full tuition reimbursements, teaching assistantships with full tuition reimbursements, institutionally sponsored loans, scholarships/grants, and health care benefits available. Financial award application deadline: 1/2. *Faculty research:* Pricing of options and futures, term structure of interest rates, use of accounting numbers in debt contracts, product differentiation, e-commerce and marketing, behavioral finance. *Unit head:* Mary Ellen Nichols, Registrar, 203-432-3955, Fax: 203-432-0342, E-mail: maryellen.nichols@yale.edu.

Youngstown State University, Graduate School, Warren P. Williamson Jr. College of Business Administration, Department of Accounting and Finance, Youngstown, OH 44555-0001. Offers accounting (MBA); finance (MBA). *Accreditation:* AACSB. Part-time and evening/weekend programs available. *Degree requirements:* For master's, thesis optional. *Entrance requirements:* For master's, GMAT, minimum GPA of 2.7. Additional exam requirements/recommendations for international students: Required—TOEFL. *Faculty research:* Taxation and compliance, capital markets, accounting information systems, accounting theory, tax and government accounting.

Investment Management

Boston University, School of Management, Program in Investment Management, Boston, MA 02215. Offers MSIM. Part-time and evening/weekend programs available. *Faculty:* 7 full-time (0 women), 2 part-time/adjunct (0 women). *Students:* 48 applicants, 75% accepted, 30 enrolled. In 2006, 22 degrees awarded. *Entrance requirements:* For master's, GMAT. *Application deadline:* For spring admission, 11/15 for domestic students. Applications are processed on a rolling basis. Application fee: $100. Electronic applications accepted. *Expenses:* Tuition: Full-time $33,330; part-time $1,042 per credit. Required fees: $462; $40. *Financial support:* Career-related internships or fieldwork, Federal Work-Study, and institutionally sponsored loans available. Support available to part-time students. Financial award applicants required to submit FAFSA. *Faculty research:* Behavioral finance, computational finance, risk management, portfolio management, derivatives. *Unit head:* Scott Stewart, Director, 617-353-2353, Fax: 617-353-6667, E-mail: msim@bu.edu. *Application contact:* Hayden Estrada, Assistant Dean, Admissions, 617-353-2670, Fax: 617-353-7368, E-mail: mba@bu.edu.

Concordia University, School of Graduate Studies, John Molson School of Business, Montréal, QC H3G 1M8, Canada. Offers administration (M Sc, Diploma); aviation management (Certificate, Diploma); business administration (MBA, UA Undergraduate Associate, PhD), including international aviation (UA Undergraduate Associate); chartered accountancy (Diploma); community organizational development (Certificate); event management and fundraising (Certificate); executive business administration (EMBA); investment management (Diploma); investment management option (MBA); management accounting (Certificate); management of healthcare organizations (Certificate); sport administration (Diploma). *Accreditation:* AACSB. Part-time and evening/weekend programs available. *Students:* 447 full-time (174 women), 448 part-time (206 women). 925 applicants, 59% accepted, 319 enrolled. In 2006, 183 master's, 6 doctorates, 62 other advanced degrees awarded. *Degree requirements:* For master's, one foreign language, thesis (for some programs), research project; for doctorate, one foreign language, thesis/dissertation; for other advanced degree, one foreign language. *Entrance requirements:* For master's and doctorate, GMAT. Additional exam requirements/recommendations for international students: Required—TOEFL. Application fee: $50. *Expenses:* Contact institution. *Financial support:* Fellowships, career-related internships or fieldwork available. *Faculty research:* General business, capital markets, international business. *Unit head:* Dr. Jerry Tomberlin, Dean, 514-848-2424 Ext. 2700, Fax: 514-848-4502. *Application contact:* Dr. Michel Magnan, Associate Dean, Graduate Programs, 514-848-2424 Ext. 4145, Fax: 514-848-4208.

Gannon University, School of Graduate Studies, College of Humanities, Business, and Education, School of Business, Program in Investments, Erie, PA 16541-0001. Offers Certificate. In 2006, 4 degrees awarded. *Entrance requirements:* Additional exam requirements/recommendations for international students: Required—TOEFL (minimum score 500 paper-based; 173 computer-based). *Application deadline:* Applications are processed on a rolling basis. *Expenses:* Tuition: Full-time $12,240; part-time $680 per credit. Required fees: $496; $16 per credit. Tuition and fees vary according to course load, degree level, campus/location and program. *Financial support:* Application deadline: 7/1; *Application contact:* Debra Meszaros, Director of Graduate Recruitment, 814-871-5819, Fax: 814-871-5827, E-mail: cfal@gannon.edu.

The George Washington University, School of Business, Department of Finance, Washington, DC 20052. Offers finance (MSF, PhD); finance and investments (MBA); real estate development (MBA). Part-time and evening/weekend programs available. *Degree requirements:* For doctorate, thesis/dissertation. *Entrance requirements:* For master's, GMAT; for doctorate, GMAT or GRE. Additional exam requirements/recommendations for international students: Required—TOEFL.

The Johns Hopkins University, Carey Business School, Department of Finance, Baltimore, MD 21218-2699. Offers finance (MS); financial management (Certificate); investments (Certificate). Part-time and evening/weekend programs available. *Students:* 56 full-time (25 women), 77 part-time (28 women); includes 13 minority (3 African Americans, 9 Asian Americans or Pacific Islanders, 1 Hispanic American), 3 international. Average age 32. 249 applicants, 56% accepted, 90 enrolled. In 2006, 47 master's, 8 other advanced degrees awarded. *Degree requirements:* For master's and Certificate, registration. *Entrance requirements:* For master's, GMAT or GRE (recommended), minimum GPA of 3.0, resumé, work experience, two letters of recommendation; for Certificate, minimum GPA of 3.0, resumé, work experience, two letters of recommendation. Additional exam requirements/recommendations for international students: Required—TOEFL (minimum score 600 paper-based; 250 computer-based; 100 iBT). *Application deadline:* For fall admission, 5/1 for international students; for spring admission, 10/15 for international students. Applications are processed on a rolling basis. Application fee: $60. *Expenses:* Tuition: Full-time $32,976. Tuition and fees vary according to degree level and program. *Financial support:* Scholarships/grants available. Support available to part-time students. Financial award application deadline: 6/1; financial award applicants required to submit FAFSA. *Unit head:* Dr. Ken Yook, Chair, 202-588-0683, Fax: 202-588-5192, E-mail: kyook@jhu.edu. *Application contact:* Robin Reed, Senior Academic Coordinator, 800-gotojhu, Fax: 410-872-1251, E-mail: onestop.admissions@jhu.edu.

Lindenwood University, Graduate Programs, Division of Management, St. Charles, MO 63301-1695. Offers accounting (MBA, MS); business administration (MBA); entrepreneurial studies (MBA); finance (MBA, MS); human resource management (MBA); human resources (MS); international business (MBA, MS); management (MBA, MS); management information systems (MBA, MS); managing business to business (MA); managing human resources (MA); managing international business (MA); managing investment management (MA); managing leadership (MA); managing marketing (MA); managing organizational behavior (MA); managing sales (MA); managing, training and development (MA); marketing (MBA, MS); nonprofit administration (MA); public management (MBA, MS); sport management (MA). Part-time and evening/weekend programs available. *Faculty:* 38 full-time (15 women), 20 part-time/adjunct (5 women). *Students:* 177 full-time (78 women), 138 part-time (67 women); includes 43 minority (27 African Americans, 4 American Indian/Alaska Native, 6 Asian Americans or Pacific Islanders, 6 Hispanic Americans), 73 international. Average age 30. In 2006, 159 degrees awarded. *Degree requirements:* For master's, thesis (for some programs). *Entrance requirements:* For master's, interview, minimum GPA of 3.0. Additional exam requirements/recommendations for international students: Required—TOEFL (minimum score 550 paper-based; 173 computer-based). *Application deadline:* For fall admission, 7/30 priority date for domestic students, 9/30 priority date for international students; for winter admission, 12/30 priority date for domestic and international students; for spring admission, 3/30 priority date for domestic and international students. Applications are processed on a rolling basis. Application fee: $30 ($100 for international students). Electronic applications accepted. *Expenses:* Tuition: Part-time $340 per credit hour. Tuition and fees vary according to course level, course load, degree level and program. *Financial support:* Career-related internships or fieldwork, Federal Work-Study, institutionally sponsored loans, and tuition waivers (partial) available. Financial award application deadline: 6/30; financial award applicants required to submit FAFSA. *Unit head:* Ed Morris, Dean, 636-949-4832, Fax: 636-949-4910, E-mail: emorris@lindenwood.edu. *Application contact:* Brett Barger, Dean Adult, Corporate and Graduate Admissions, 636-949-4366, Fax: 636-949-4109, E-mail: bbarger@lindenwood.edu.

Lynn University, College of Business and Management, Boca Raton, FL 33431-5598. Offers aviation management (MBA); financial valuation and investment management (MBA); global leadership (PhD); hospitality management (MBA); international business (MBA); marketing (MBA); mass communication and media management (MBA); sports and athletics administration (MBA). Part-time and evening/weekend programs available. Postbaccalaureate distance learning degree programs offered. *Faculty:* 13 full-time (5 women), 7 part-time/adjunct (3 women). *Students:* 71 full-time (37 women), 113 part-time (47 women); includes 35 minority (13 African Americans, 6 Asian Americans or Pacific Islanders, 16 Hispanic Americans), 55 international. Average age 32. 114 applicants, 88% accepted, 71 enrolled. In 2006, 83 master's, 9 doctorates awarded. *Degree requirements:* For master's, project; for doctorate, thesis/dissertation, qualifying paper. *Entrance requirements:* For master's, GMAT or GRE, minimum undergraduate GPA of 3.0, resumé, 2 letters of recommendation; for doctorate, GRE or GMAT, minimum graduate GPA of 3.25, resumé, 2 letters of recommendation. Additional exam requirements/recommendations for international students: Required—TOEFL (minimum score 550 paper-based; 213 computer-based). *Application deadline:* Applications are processed on a rolling basis. Application fee: $50. Electronic applications accepted. *Expenses:* Tuition: Full-time $26,200. Required fees: $1,500. Tuition and fees vary according to class time, course load and degree level. *Financial support:* In 2006–07, 160 students received support. Career-related internships or fieldwork, Federal Work-Study, institutionally sponsored loans, scholarships/grants, tuition waivers (full and partial), and unspecified assistantships available. Support available to part-time students. Financial award application deadline: 8/1; financial award applicants required to submit FAFSA. *Faculty research:* Labor relations, dynamic balance in leisure-time skills, ethics in athletics, hotel development. *Unit head:* Dr. Russell Boisjoly, Dean, 561-237-7458, Fax: 561-237-7014, E-mail: rboisjoly@lynn.edu. *Application contact:* Dr. Larissa Baia, Assistant Director of Graduate Admissions, 561-237-7916, Fax: 561-237-7100, E-mail: admissionpm@lynn.edu.

Marywood University, Academic Affairs, Insalaco College of Creative Arts and Management, Department of Business and Managerial Science, Emphasis in Finance and Investments, Scranton, PA 18509-1598. Offers MBA. Evening/weekend programs available. *Students:* 2 full-time (1 woman), 16 part-time (7 women); includes 1 minority (African American), 2 international. Average age 35. 6 applicants, 83% accepted. *Degree requirements:* For master's, comprehensive exam. *Entrance requirements:* For master's, GMAT. Additional exam requirements/recommendations for international students: Required—TOEFL (minimum score 550 paper-based; 213 computer-based). *Application deadline:* For fall admission, 4/15 priority date for domestic and international students; for spring admission, 11/15 priority date for domestic and international students. Applications are processed on a rolling basis. Application fee: $30. Electronic applications accepted. *Expenses:* Tuition: Part-time $672 per credit. Tuition and fees vary according to degree level, campus/location and program. *Financial support:* Research assistantships with tuition reimbursements, career-related internships or fieldwork, scholarships/grants, and tuition waivers (partial) available. Support available to part-time students. Financial award application deadline: 2/15; financial award applicants required to submit FAFSA. *Faculty research:* Accountant/auditor liability, corporate finance acquisitions and mergers, corporate bankruptcy. *Application contact:* Dr. Deborah M. Flynn, Coordinator of Graduate Advising (Enrollment Management), 570-348-6211, E-mail: flynn@ac.marywood.edu.

Pace University, Lubin School of Business, Financial Management Program, New York, NY 10038. Offers banking and finance (MBA); corporate financial management (MBA); financial management (MBA); investment management (MBA, MS). Part-time and evening/weekend programs available. *Faculty:* 17 full-time, 9 part-time/adjunct. *Students:* 72 full-time (32 women), 344 part-time (126 women); includes 88 minority (18 African Americans, 54 Asian Americans or Pacific Islanders, 16 Hispanic Americans), 127 international. Average age 29. 375 applicants, 59% accepted, 88 enrolled. In 2006, 255 degrees awarded. *Entrance requirements:* For master's, GMAT. *Application deadline:* For fall admission, 7/31 priority date for domestic students; for spring admission, 11/30 for domestic students. Applications are processed on a rolling basis. Application fee: $65. Electronic applications accepted. *Expenses:* Tuition: Part-time $890 per credit. *Financial support:* Research assistantships, career-related internships or fieldwork, Federal Work-Study, and tuition waivers (full and partial) available. Support available to part-time students. Financial award application deadline: 8/15; financial award applicants required to submit FAFSA. *Unit head:* Dr. Edmund Mantell, Chairperson, 914-422-4165. *Application contact:* Joanna Broda, Director of Admissions, 212-346-1652, Fax: 212-346-1585, E-mail: gradnyc@pace.edu.

Quinnipiac University, School of Business, Chartered Financial Analyst Program, Hamden, CT 06518-1940. Offers MBA. *Application deadline:* Applications are processed on a rolling basis. Electronic applications accepted. *Expenses:* Tuition: Part-time $675 per credit. Required fees: $30 per credit. *Application contact:* 800-462-1944, Fax: 203-582-3443, E-mail: graduate@quinnipiac.edu.

See Close-Up on page 311.

The University of Iowa, Henry B. Tippie College of Business, Henry B. Tippie School of Management, Iowa City, IA 52242-1316. Offers accounting (MBA); corporate finance (MBA); entrepreneurship (MBA); finance (MBA); individually designed concentration (MBA); investment management (MBA); management information systems (MBA); marketing (MBA); nonprofit management (MBA); operations management (MBA); strategic management and consulting (MBA); JD/MBA; MBA/MA; MBA/MD; MBA/MHA; MBA/MSN. *Accreditation:* AACSB. Part-time and evening/weekend programs available. *Faculty:* 94 full-time (23 women), 65 part-time/adjunct (21 women). *Students:* 230 full-time (67 women), 712 part-time (234 women); includes 62 minority (6 African Americans, 1 American Indian/Alaska Native, 43 Asian Americans or Pacific Islanders, 12 Hispanic Americans), 127 international. Average age 30. 431 applicants, 61% accepted, 217 enrolled. In 2006, 363 degrees awarded. *Median time to degree:* Master's–2 years full-time, 3.5 years part-time. *Degree requirements:* For master's, registration. *Entrance requirements:* For master's, GMAT, work experience. Additional exam requirements/recommendations for international students: Required—TOEFL (minimum score 600 paper-based; 250 computer-based; 100 iBT). *Application deadline:* For fall admission, 7/15 for domestic students, 4/15 for international students; for spring admission, 12/15 priority date for domestic students, 11/1 priority date for international students. Applications are processed on a rolling basis. Application fee: $60 ($85 for international students). Electronic applications accepted. *Expenses: Contact institution. Financial support:* In 2006–07, 72 fellowships (averaging $3,892 per year), 55 research assistantships with partial tuition reimbursements (averaging $10,260 per year) were awarded; career-related internships or fieldwork, Federal Work-Study, institutionally sponsored loans, scholarships/grants, health care benefits, and unspecified assistantships also available. Support available to part-time students. Financial award application deadline: 4/15; financial award applicants required to submit FAFSA. *Faculty research:* Capital markets, econometrics, optimization, investments and empirical corporate finance, Iowa electronic markets. *Unit head:* Prof. Gary J. Gaeth, Associate Dean, MBA Programs, 800-622-4692, Fax: 319-335-3604, E-mail: gary-gaeth@uiowa.edu. *Application contact:* Jodi Schafer, Director of Student Recruitment and Marketing, 319-335-0864, Fax: 319-335-3604, E-mail: jodi-schafer@uiowa.edu.

University of Tulsa, Graduate School, College of Business Administration, Program in Finance, Tulsa, OK 74104-3189. Offers corporate finance (MS); investments and portfolio management (MS); risk management (MS). Part-time and evening/weekend programs available. *Faculty:* 7 full-time (0 women). *Students:* 18 full-time (5 women), 4 part-time (1 woman); includes 2 minority (1 American Indian/Alaska Native, 1 Hispanic American), 8 international. Average age 28. 42 applicants, 26% accepted, 8 enrolled. In 2006, 12 degrees awarded. *Median time to degree:* Master's–2 years full-time. *Degree requirements:* For master's, thesis optional. *Entrance requirements:* For master's, GMAT. Additional exam requirements/recommendations for international students: Required—TOEFL (minimum score 575 paper-based; 231 computer-based), IELTS (minimum score 7). *Application deadline:* Applications are processed on a rolling basis. Application fee: $40. Electronic applications accepted. *Expenses:* Tuition: Full-time $13,338; part-time $741 per credit hour. *Financial support:* In 2006–07, 9 students received support, including 9 teaching assistantships with full and partial tuition reimbursements available (averaging $10,125 per year); fellowships with full and partial tuition reimbursements available, career-related internships or fieldwork, Federal Work-Study, institutionally sponsored loans, scholarships/grants, tuition waivers (full and partial), and unspecified assistantships also available. Support available to part-time students. Financial award application deadline: 2/1; financial award applicants required to submit FAFSA. *Unit head:* Markham Collins, Associate Dean, 918-631-2783, Fax: 918-631-2142, E-mail: markham-collins@utulsa.edu.

See Close-Up on page 461.

University of Wisconsin–Madison, Graduate School, School of Business, Program in Finance, Investment, and Banking, Madison, WI 53706-1380. Offers finance, investment, and banking (PhD); international business (PhD). Evening/weekend programs available. *Students:* 9 full-time (5 women), 8 international. Average age 28. 113 applicants, 4% accepted, 4 enrolled. In 2006, 2 degrees awarded. *Entrance requirements:* For doctorate, GMAT or GRE. Additional exam requirements/recommendations for international students: Required—TOEFL (minimum score 600 paper-based; 250 computer-based). *Application deadline:* For fall admission, 1/6 priority date for domestic and international students. Applications are processed on a rolling basis. Application fee: $45. Electronic applications accepted. *Financial support:* In 2006–07, 9 students received support, including fellowships with partial tuition reimbursements available (averaging $16,110 per year), research assistantships with full tuition reimbursements available (averaging $13,502 per year), 8 teaching assistantships (averaging $13,686 per year); Federal Work-Study, institutionally sponsored loans, scholarships/grants, health care benefits, and unspecified assistantships also available. Financial award application deadline: 1/6; financial award applicants required to submit FAFSA. *Faculty research:* Banking and financial institutions, business cycles, investments, derivatives, corporate finance. *Unit head:* Dr. James P. Hodder, Chair, 608-262-8774, Fax: 608-265-4195, E-mail: jhodder@bus.wisc.edu. *Application contact:* Belle Heberling, PhD Coordinator, 608-262-3749, Fax: 608-890-0180, E-mail: phd@bus.wisc.edu.

Taxation

American University, Kogod School of Business, Department of Accounting, Program in Taxation, Washington, DC 20016-8001. Offers MS. Part-time and evening/weekend programs available. *Students:* 3 full-time (all women), 88 part-time (45 women); includes 21 minority (10 African Americans, 10 Asian Americans or Pacific Islanders, 1 Hispanic American), 5 international. Average age 34. In 2006, 17 degrees awarded. *Entrance requirements:* For master's, GMAT or CPA. Additional exam requirements/recommendations for international students: Required—TOEFL. *Application deadline:* For fall admission, 2/1 priority date for domestic students; for spring admission, 10/1 priority date for domestic students. Applications are processed on a rolling basis. Application fee: $50. *Expenses:* Tuition: Full-time $18,864; part-time $1,048 per credit. Required fees: $380. Tuition and fees vary according to program. *Financial support:* Fellowships, career-related internships or fieldwork, Federal Work-Study, and institutionally sponsored loans available. Support available to part-time students. Financial award application deadline: 2/1. *Faculty research:* International transactions, corporate partnership, taxation, real estate, estate gift planning.

Bentley College, The Elkin B. McCallum Graduate School of Business, Program in Taxation, Waltham, MA 02452-4705. Offers MST. Part-time and evening/weekend programs available. Postbaccalaureate distance learning degree programs offered (minimal on-campus study). *Faculty:* 13 full-time (3 women), 16 part-time/adjunct (7 women). *Students:* 28 full-time (16 women), 166 part-time (91 women); includes 27 minority (4 African Americans, 19 Asian Americans or Pacific Islanders, 4 Hispanic Americans). Average age 31. 93 applicants, 90% accepted, 73 enrolled. In 2006, 28 degrees awarded. *Entrance requirements:* For master's, GMAT. Additional exam requirements/recommendations for international students: Required—TOEFL (minimum score 600 paper-based; 250 computer-based). *Application deadline:* For fall admission, 6/1 priority date for domestic students, 3/1 priority date for international students; for spring admission, 11/1 priority date for domestic and international students. Applications are processed on a rolling basis. Application fee: $50. Electronic applications accepted. *Expenses:* Tuition: Full-time $28,440; part-time $2,844 per course. Required fees: $404; $105 per year. *Financial support:* Research assistantships, scholarships/grants, tuition waivers, and unspecified assistantships available. Financial award application deadline: 4/12; financial award applicants required to submit CSS PROFILE or FAFSA. *Faculty research:* Taxation of intellectual property, tax dispute resolution, corporate tax planning and advocacy, estate and financial planning. *Unit head:* John Lynch, Director, 781-891-2624, E-mail: jlynch@bentley.edu. *Application contact:* Sharon Hill, Director of Graduate Admissions, 781-891-2108, Fax: 781-891-2464, E-mail: shill@bentley.edu.

Bernard M. Baruch College of the City University of New York, Zicklin School of Business, Department of Accounting, Program in Taxation, New York, NY 10010-5585. Offers MBA, MS. Part-time and evening/weekend programs available. *Faculty:* 33 full-time (9 women), 33 part-time/adjunct (6 women). *Students:* 22 full-time (10 women), 76 part-time (44 women); includes 48 minority (7 African Americans, 38 Asian Americans or Pacific Islanders, 3 Hispanic Americans). In 2006, 69 degrees awarded. *Entrance requirements:* For master's, GMAT, 2 letters of recommendation, resumé, 2 years of work experience. Additional exam requirements/recommendations for international students: Required—TOEFL (minimum score 590 paper-based; 243 computer-based), TWE. *Application deadline:* For fall admission, 5/31 for domestic students, 4/30 for international students; for spring admission, 10/31 for domestic and international students. Application fee: $125. *Financial support:* Fellowships, research assistantships, teaching assistantships, career-related internships or fieldwork, Federal Work-Study, scholarships/grants, and unspecified assistantships available. Financial award application deadline: 4/30; financial award applicants required to submit FAFSA. *Unit head:* Steven Melnik, Head, 646-312-3227, Fax: 646-312-3161, E-mail: steven_melnik@baruch.cuny.edu. *Application contact:* Frances Murphy, Office of Graduate Admissions, 646-312-1300, Fax: 646-312-1301, E-mail: zicklingradadmissions@baruch.cuny.edu.

See Close-Up on page 449.

Boise State University, Graduate College, College of Business and Economics, Program in Accountancy, Boise, ID 83725-0399. Offers accountancy (MSA); taxation (MSA). *Accreditation:* AACSB. Part-time programs available. *Faculty:* 8 full-time (0 women), 3 part-time/adjunct (1 woman). *Students:* 19 full-time (6 women), 33 part-time (22 women); includes 1 minority (Hispanic American), 2 international. Average age 35. 21 applicants, 86% accepted, 9 enrolled. In 2006, 20 degrees awarded. *Entrance requirements:* For master's, GMAT, minimum GPA of 3.0. Additional exam requirements/recommendations for international students: Required—TOEFL. *Application deadline:* For fall admission, 3/1 priority date for domestic students; for spring admission, 10/1 priority date for domestic students. Applications are processed on a rolling basis. Application fee: $0. Electronic applications accepted. *Financial support:* Career-related internships or fieldwork, Federal Work-Study, institutionally sponsored loans, and unspecified assistantships available. Support available to part-time students. Financial award application deadline: 3/1. *Unit head:* Dr. Kirk Smith, Director, 208-426-3180. *Application contact:* J. Renee Anchustegui, Coordinator, 208-426-3116, Fax: 208-426-1135, E-mail: ranchust@boisestate.edu.

Boston University, School of Law, Boston, MA 02215. Offers American law (LL M); banking law (LL M); intellectual property law (LL M); law (JD); taxation (LL M); JD/LL M; JD/MA;

Taxation

Boston University (continued)

JD/MBA; JD/MPH; JD/MS; JD/MSW. *Accreditation:* ABA. Part-time and evening/weekend programs available. *Faculty:* 69 full-time (21 women), 72 part-time/adjunct (20 women). *Students:* 987 full-time (495 women), 103 part-time (52 women); includes 195 minority (38 African Americans, 2 American Indian/Alaska Native, 125 Asian Americans or Pacific Islanders, 30 Hispanic Americans), 132 international. Average age 27. 7,265 applicants, 19% accepted, 285 enrolled. In 2006, 262 JDs, 162 master's awarded. *Degree requirements:* For JD, thesis, research project resulting in a paper; for master's, thesis (for some programs). *Entrance requirements:* For JD, LSAT; for master's, JD. Additional exam requirements/recommendations for international students: Required—TOEFL (minimum score 600 paper-based; 250 computer-based). *Application deadline:* For fall admission, 3/1 for domestic and international students. Applications are processed on a rolling basis. Application fee: $60. Electronic applications accepted. *Expenses:* Tuition: Full-time $33,330; part-time $1,042 per credit. Required fees: $462; $40. *Financial support:* In 2006–07, 681 students received support. Career-related internships or fieldwork, Federal Work-Study, institutionally sponsored loans, and scholarships/grants available. Financial award application deadline: 3/1; financial award applicants required to submit CSS PROFILE or FAFSA. *Faculty research:* Litigation and dispute resolution, intellectual property law, business organizations and finance law, international law, health law. *Unit head:* Maureen O'Rourke, Interim Dean, 617-353-3112, Fax: 617-353-7400. *Application contact:* Joan Horgan, Director of Admissions and Financial Aid, 617-353-3100, Fax: 617-353-0578, E-mail: bulawadm@bu.edu.

Bryant University, Graduate School, Graduate School of Business, Program in Taxation, Smithfield, RI 02917-1284. Offers MST, CAGS. Part-time and evening/weekend programs available. *Faculty:* 3 full-time (0 women), 7 part-time/adjunct (1 woman). *Students:* Average age 30. 21 applicants, 81% accepted, 13 enrolled. In 2006, 15 degrees awarded. *Entrance requirements:* For master's, GMAT, letter of recommendation, resumé; for CAGS, GMAT, resumé. Additional exam requirements/recommendations for international students: Required—TOEFL (minimum score 580 paper-based; 237 computer-based). *Application deadline:* For fall admission, 7/15 for domestic students, 4/1 for international students; for spring admission, 11/15 for domestic and international students. Applications are processed on a rolling basis. Application fee: $80. Electronic applications accepted. *Expenses:* Contact institution. *Financial support:* Applicants required to submit FAFSA. *Unit head:* Eugene A. Amelio, MST Coordinator, 401-232-6062, Fax: 401-232-6319, E-mail: eamelio@bryant.edu. *Application contact:* Kristopher T. Sullivan, Assistant Dean of the Graduate School, 401-232-6230, Fax: 401-232-6494, E-mail: gradprog@bryant.edu.

California Polytechnic State University, San Luis Obispo, Orfalea College of Business, San Luis Obispo, CA 93407. Offers business (MBA); industrial and technical studies (MS); taxation (MS Acct). *Accreditation:* AACSB. *Faculty:* 4 full-time (1 woman), 6 part-time/adjunct (0 women). *Students:* 51 full-time (14 women), 19 part-time (9 women); includes 4 minority (3 Asian Americans or Pacific Islanders, 1 Hispanic American), 4 international. 104 applicants, 49% accepted, 46 enrolled. In 2006, 42 degrees awarded. *Degree requirements:* For master's, thesis (for some programs). *Entrance requirements:* For master's, GMAT. Additional exam requirements/recommendations for international students: Required—TOEFL (minimum score 550 paper-based; 213 computer-based), TWE (minimum score 4.5). *Application deadline:* For fall admission, 7/1 for domestic students, 11/30 for international students. Applications are processed on a rolling basis. Application fee: $55. Electronic applications accepted. *Financial support:* Career-related internships or fieldwork, Federal Work-Study, institutionally sponsored loans, scholarships/grants, and unspecified assistantships available. Support available to part-time students. Financial award application deadline: 3/2; financial award applicants required to submit FAFSA. *Faculty research:* Management of high-tech firms, Pacific Rim, capital market structures, economics of environmental policy, marketing of services. *Unit head:* Dr. David P. Christy, Dean, 805-756-2705, Fax: 805-756-5452, E-mail: dchristy@calpoly.edu. *Application contact:* Dr. Chris Carr, Associate Dean, 805-756-2637, Fax: 805-756-0110, E-mail: ccarr@calpoly.edu.

California State University, East Bay, Academic Programs and Graduate Studies, College of Business and Economics, Department of Accounting and Computer Information Systems, Option in Taxation, Hayward, CA 94542-3000. Offers MBA, MS. Part-time and evening/weekend programs available. *Faculty:* 2 full-time (0 women), 1 (woman) part-time/adjunct. *Students:* 9 full-time, 27 part-time; includes 16 minority (1 African American, 14 Asian Americans or Pacific Islanders, 1 Hispanic American), 8 international. Average age 37. 14 applicants, 57% accepted, 6 enrolled. In 2006, 8 degrees awarded. *Degree requirements:* For master's, comprehensive exam or thesis. *Entrance requirements:* For master's, GMAT, minimum GPA of 2.75. Additional exam requirements/recommendations for international students: Required—TOEFL (minimum score 550 paper-based; 213 computer-based). *Application deadline:* For fall admission, 5/31 for domestic students, 4/30 for international students; for winter admission, 9/30 for domestic and international students; for spring admission, 12/31 for domestic students, 11/30 for international students. Application fee: $55. *Financial support:* Career-related internships or fieldwork, Federal Work-Study, and institutionally sponsored loans available. Support available to part-time students. Financial award application deadline: 3/2. *Unit head:* Gary McBride, Graduate Advisor, 510-885-3307, E-mail: gary.mcbride@csueastbay.edu. *Application contact:* Doris Duncan, Director of Graduate Programs, 510-885-3364, Fax: 510-885-2176, E-mail: doris.duncan@csueastbay.edu.

California State University, Fullerton, Graduate Studies, College of Business and Economics, Department of Accounting, Fullerton, CA 92834-9480. Offers accounting (MBA, MS); taxation (MS). *Accreditation:* AACSB. Part-time and evening/weekend programs available. *Students:* 85 full-time (54 women), 81 part-time (54 women); includes 76 minority (1 African American, 63 Asian Americans or Pacific Islanders, 12 Hispanic Americans), 41 international. Average age 30. 170 applicants, 61% accepted, 62 enrolled. In 2006, 27 degrees awarded. *Degree requirements:* For master's, thesis or alternative, project. *Entrance requirements:* For master's, GMAT, minimum AACSB index of 950. Application fee: $55. *Expenses:* Tuition, nonresident: part-time $339 per unit. Required fees: $1,155 per semester. *Financial support:* Teaching assistantships, Federal Work-Study, institutionally sponsored loans, and scholarships/grants available. Support available to part-time students. Financial award application deadline: 3/1. *Unit head:* Dr. Betty Chavis, Chair, 714-278-2225.

California State University, Los Angeles, Graduate Studies, College of Business and Economics, Department of Accounting, Los Angeles, CA 90032-8530. Offers accountancy (MS), including business taxation, financial accounting, information systems, management accounting; accounting (MBA). Part-time and evening/weekend programs available. *Faculty:* 6 full-time (0 women), 2 part-time/adjunct (0 women). *Students:* 45 full-time (36 women), 44 part-time (29 women); includes 40 minority (39 Asian Americans or Pacific Islanders, 1 Hispanic American), 37 international. In 2006, 25 degrees awarded. *Degree requirements:* For master's, comprehensive exam (MBA), thesis (MS). *Entrance requirements:* For master's, GMAT, minimum GPA of 2.5 during previous 2 years of course work. Additional exam requirements/recommendations for international students: Required—TOEFL. *Application deadline:* For fall admission, 6/30 for domestic students; for spring admission, 11/30 for domestic students. Applications are processed on a rolling basis. Application fee: $55. *Expenses:* Tuition, nonresident: part-time $226 per unit. *Financial support:* Career-related internships or fieldwork and Federal Work-Study available. Support available to part-time students. Financial award application deadline: 3/1. *Unit head:* Dr. Greg Kunkel, Chair, 323-343-2830, Fax: 323-343-6439.

Capital University, Law School, Program in Business Law and Taxation, Columbus, OH 43209-2394. Offers business (LL M); business and taxation (LL M); taxation (LL M); JD/LL M. Part-time and evening/weekend programs available. *Degree requirements:* For master's, thesis or alternative. *Entrance requirements:* For master's, previous course work in accounting, business law, and taxation. Additional exam requirements/recommendations for international students: Required—TOEFL (minimum score 600 paper-based; 250 computer-based). Electronic

applications accepted. *Expenses:* Tuition: Part-time $920 per credit. Part-time tuition and fees vary according to program.

Capital University, Law School, Program in Taxation, Columbus, OH 43209-2394. Offers taxation (MT). Part-time and evening/weekend programs available. *Degree requirements:* For master's, thesis or alternative. *Entrance requirements:* For master's, previous course work in accounting, business law, and taxation. Additional exam requirements/recommendations for international students: Required—TOEFL (minimum score 600 paper-based; 250 computer-based). Electronic applications accepted. Expenses: Contact institution. Part-time tuition and fees vary according to program.

Chapman University, Graduate Studies, School of Law, Orange, CA 92866. Offers law (JD); taxation (LL M); JD/MBA. *Accreditation:* ABA. Part-time and evening/weekend programs available. *Faculty:* 36 full-time (15 women), 30 part-time/adjunct (5 women). *Students:* 509 full-time (235 women), 75 part-time (36 women); includes 134 minority (5 African Americans, 3 American Indian/Alaska Native, 90 Asian Americans or Pacific Islanders, 36 Hispanic Americans), 7 international. Average age 26. 2,385 applicants, 33% accepted, 197 enrolled. In 2006, 181 JDs, 15 master's awarded. *Degree requirements:* For master's, registration. *Entrance requirements:* LSAT, minimum undergraduate GPA of 2.75. Additional exam requirements/recommendations for international students: Required—TOEFL (minimum score 600 paper-based). *Application deadline:* Applications are processed on a rolling basis. Application fee: $60. Electronic applications accepted. *Expenses:* Contact institution. *Financial support:* In 2006–07, 492 students received support; fellowships, Federal Work-Study available. Financial award application deadline: 6/30; financial award applicants required to submit FAFSA. *Unit head:* Dr. Parham Williams, Dean, 714-628-2500. *Application contact:* Demetrius L. Greer, Office of Admissions, 888-242-1913, E-mail: greer@chapman.edu.

Cleveland State University, College of Graduate Studies, Nance College of Business Administration, Department of Accounting, Cleveland, OH 44115. Offers financial accounting/audit (MAC); taxation (MAC). *Accreditation:* AACSB. Part-time and evening/weekend programs available. *Faculty:* 15 full-time (3 women), 3 part-time/adjunct (1 woman). *Students:* 23 full-time (13 women), 47 part-time (23 women); includes 14 minority (8 African Americans, 5 Asian Americans or Pacific Islanders, 1 Hispanic American), 17 international. Average age 31. 82 applicants, 56% accepted, 24 enrolled. In 2006, 30 degrees awarded. *Entrance requirements:* For master's, GMAT, minimum GPA of 2.75. Additional exam requirements/recommendations for international students: Required—TOEFL (minimum score 525 paper-based; 197 computer-based). *Application deadline:* For fall admission, 7/15 priority date for domestic students; for spring admission, 12/15 priority date for domestic students. Applications are processed on a rolling basis. Application fee: $30. *Financial support:* In 2006–07, 3 research assistantships with full and partial tuition reimbursements (averaging $6,960 per year) were awarded; career-related internships or fieldwork, Federal Work-Study, scholarships/grants, and unspecified assistantships also available. *Faculty research:* Internal auditing, computer auditing, accounting education, managerial accounting. *Unit head:* Dr. Dennis J. Gaffney, Chair, 216-687-4720, Fax: 216-687-9212, E-mail: dennis.gaffney@csuohio.edu. *Application contact:* Bruce Gottschalk, Associate Dean, 216-687-3730, Fax: 216-687-5311, E-mail: cbacsu@csuohio.edu.

DePaul University, Charles H. Kellstadt Graduate School of Business, School of Accountancy and Management Information Systems, Chicago, IL 60604-2287. Offers accountancy (M Acc, MSA); business information technology (MS); e-business (MBA, MS); financial management and control (MBA); management accounting (MBA); management information systems (MBA); taxation (MST). Part-time and evening/weekend programs available. *Faculty:* 30 full-time (9 women), 54 part-time/adjunct (7 women). *Students:* 127 full-time (53 women), 209 part-time (101 women); includes 53 minority (13 African Americans, 3 American Indian/Alaska Native, 28 Asian Americans or Pacific Islanders, 9 Hispanic Americans), 56 international. Average age 30. In 2006, 141 degrees awarded. *Entrance requirements:* For master's, GMAT, 2 letters of recommendation, resumé. Additional exam requirements/recommendations for international students: Required—TOEFL (minimum score 550 paper-based; 213 computer-based). *Application deadline:* For fall admission, 7/1 for domestic students; for winter admission, 10/1 for domestic students; for spring admission, 2/1 for domestic students. Applications are processed on a rolling basis. Application fee: $60. *Financial support:* In 2006–07, 7 research assistantships with full tuition reimbursements (averaging $4,100 per year) were awarded; institutionally sponsored loans also available. Financial award application deadline: 4/2. *Faculty research:* Tax policy, property transactions, stock options as compensation, standards setting, activity-based costing in health care. *Application contact:* Christopher E. Kinsella, Director of Cohort MBA Programs, 312-362-8810, Fax: 312-362-6677, E-mail: kgsb@depaul.edu.

Drexel University, LeBow College of Business, Department of Accounting, Program in Taxation, Philadelphia, PA 19104-2875. Offers MS. Part-time and evening/weekend programs available. *Entrance requirements:* For master's, GMAT, minimum GPA of 2.75. Additional exam requirements/recommendations for international students: Required—TOEFL. Electronic applications accepted. *Faculty research:* Individual retirement accounts, state taxation, fiscal planning.

Duquesne University, John F. Donahue Graduate School of Business, Pittsburgh, PA 15282-0001. Offers business administration (MBA); taxation (MS); JD/MBA; MBA/MA; MBA/MES; MBA/MHMS; MBA/MLLS; MBA/MS; MBA/MSN. *Accreditation:* AACSB. Part-time and evening/weekend programs available. *Faculty:* 50 full-time (5 women), 20 part-time/adjunct (5 women). *Students:* 110 full-time (49 women), 233 part-time (86 women); includes 26 minority (15 African Americans, 1 American Indian/Alaska Native, 1 Asian American or Pacific Islander, 9 Hispanic Americans), 31 international. Average age 31. 174 applicants, 69% accepted, 75 enrolled. In 2006, 146 degrees awarded. *Entrance requirements:* For master's, GMAT, letter of recommendation. Additional exam requirements/recommendations for international students: Required—TOEFL (minimum score 550 paper-based; 213 computer-based); Recommended—TWE. *Application deadline:* For fall admission, 6/1 priority date for domestic students, 6/1 for international students; for spring admission, 11/1 for domestic and international students. Applications are processed on a rolling basis. Application fee: $50. Electronic applications accepted. *Expenses:* Tuition: Part-time $723 per credit. Required fees: $71 per credit. Tuition and fees vary according to degree level and program. *Financial support:* In 2006–07, 31 students received support, including 27 research assistantships with partial tuition reimbursements available; career-related internships or fieldwork and unspecified assistantships also available. Support available to part-time students. Financial award application deadline: 7/1; financial award applicants required to submit FAFSA. *Faculty research:* International business, investment management, business ethics, technology management, supply chain management, business strategy, finance. *Unit head:* Alan R. Miciak, Dean, 412-396-5848, Fax: 412-396-5304, E-mail: miciak@duq.edu. *Application contact:* Dr. Patricia Moore, Assistant Director, 412-396-6276, Fax: 412-396-1726, E-mail: moorep@duq.edu.

See Close-Up on page 267.

Fairfield University, Charles F. Dolan School of Business, Fairfield, CT 06824-5195. Offers accounting (MBA, MS, CAS); finance (MBA, MS, CAS); general management (MBA); human resource management (MBA, CAS); information systems and operations (MBA); information systems and operations management (CAS); international business (MBA, CAS); marketing (MBA, CAS); taxation (MBA, MS, CAS). *Accreditation:* AACSB. Part-time and evening/weekend programs available. *Faculty:* 43 full-time (17 women), 2 part-time/adjunct (1 woman). *Students:* 65 full-time (31 women), 125 part-time (54 women); includes 4 Asian Americans or Pacific Islanders, 4 Hispanic Americans, 22 international. Average age 27. 99 applicants, 45% accepted, 38 enrolled. In 2006, 78 degrees awarded. *Degree requirements:* For master's, registration. *Entrance requirements:* For master's, GMAT, 2 letters of reference, resumé. Additional exam requirements/recommendations for international students: Required—TOEFL (minimum score 550 paper-based; 213 computer-based; 79 iBT). *Application deadline:* For fall admission, 8/15 priority date for domestic students, 5/15 priority date for international students; for spring admission, 11/15 priority date for domestic students, 10/15 priority date for international students. Applications are processed on a rolling basis. Application fee: $55. Electronic applications accepted. *Expenses:* *Contact institution.* *Financial support:* Unspecified assistantships available. *Faculty research:* Optimal investment strategies, organization structure, international finance, strategic management, customer behavior. *Unit head:* Dr. Norman A. Solomon, Dean, 203-254-4000 Ext. 4070, Fax: 203-254-4105, E-mail: nsolomon@mail.fairfield.edu. *Application contact:* Marianne Gumpper, Director of Graduate and Continuing Studies Admissions, 203-254-4184, Fax: 203-254-4073, E-mail: gradadmis@mail.fairfield.edu.

See Close-Up on page 271.

Fairleigh Dickinson University, College at Florham, Silberman College of Business, Department of Accounting, Law, and Tax, Program in Taxation, Madison, NJ 07940-1099. Offers MS, Certificate. *Students:* 5 full-time (3 women), 65 part-time (21 women), 5 international. Average age 34. 30 applicants, 83% accepted, 16 enrolled. In 2006, 19 degrees awarded. *Application deadline:* Applications are processed on a rolling basis. Application fee: $40.

Fairleigh Dickinson University, Metropolitan Campus, Silberman College of Business, Department of Accounting, Law, and Tax, Program in Taxation, Teaneck, NJ 07666-1914. Offers MS. *Students:* Average age 36. 2 applicants, 50% accepted, 0 enrolled. *Application deadline:* Applications are processed on a rolling basis. Application fee: $40. *Unit head:* Dr. Robert Greenfield, Dean, Silberman College of Business, 201-692-2000.

Florida Atlantic University, College of Business, School of Accounting, Program in Taxation, Boca Raton, FL 33431-0991. Offers M Tax. Part-time and evening/weekend programs available. Postbaccalaureate distance learning degree programs offered (minimal on-campus study). *Faculty:* 4 full-time (1 woman), 2 part-time/adjunct (0 women). *Students:* 6 full-time (3 women), 22 part-time (10 women); includes 11 minority (3 African Americans, 5 Asian Americans or Pacific Islanders, 3 Hispanic Americans), 1 international. Average age 33. 18 applicants, 28% accepted, 1 enrolled. In 2006, 12 degrees awarded. *Degree requirements:* For master's, thesis optional. *Entrance requirements:* For master's, GMAT, minimum GPA of 3.0. Additional exam requirements/recommendations for international students: Required—TOEFL (minimum score 600 paper-based; 250 computer-based). *Application deadline:* For fall admission, 7/15 priority date for domestic students, 2/15 priority date for international students; for winter admission, 11/1 priority date for domestic students, 8/15 priority date for international students; for spring admission, 4/1 priority date for domestic students, 1/15 priority date for international students. Applications are processed on a rolling basis. Application fee: $30. *Expenses:* Tuition, area resident: Full-time $4,394. Tuition, nonresident: full-time $16,441. *Financial support:* Career-related internships or fieldwork, Federal Work-Study, institutionally sponsored loans, scholarships/grants, tuition waivers (full and partial), and unspecified assistantships available. Support available to part-time students. Financial award application deadline: 3/1. *Application contact:* Fredrick G. Taylor, Graduate Adviser, 561-297-2768, Fax: 561-297-1315, E-mail: mba@fau.edu.

Florida Gulf Coast University, College of Business, Program in Accounting and Taxation, Fort Myers, FL 33965-6565. Offers MS. Part-time and evening/weekend programs available. *Faculty:* 51 full-time (14 women), 18 part-time/adjunct (0 women). *Students:* 24 full-time (17 women), 13 part-time (9 women); includes 7 minority (1 Asian American or Pacific Islander, 6 Hispanic Americans). Average age 29. 25 applicants, 76% accepted, 13 enrolled. In 2006, 12 degrees awarded. *Degree requirements:* For master's, thesis or alternative. *Entrance requirements:* For master's, GMAT, minimum GPA of 3.0. Additional exam requirements/recommendations for international students: Required—TOEFL (minimum score 550 paper-based; 213 computer-based). *Application deadline:* For fall admission, 7/1 priority date for domestic students; for spring admission, 11/1 for domestic students. Applications are processed on a rolling basis. Application fee: $30. Electronic applications accepted. *Expenses:* Tuition, state resident: full-time $4,326. Tuition, nonresident: full-time $18,523. Required fees: $1,211. One-time fee: $5 full-time. *Faculty research:* Stock petitions, mergers and acquisitions, deferred taxes, fraud and accounting regulations, graphical reporting practices. *Unit head:* Dr. Ara Volkan, Chair, 239-590-7380, Fax: 239-590-7330, E-mail: avolkan@fgcu.edu. *Application contact:* Carol Burnette, Associate Dean, 239-590-7350, Fax: 239-590-7330, E-mail: burnette@fgcu.edu.

Florida International University, Alvah H. Chapman, Jr. Graduate School of Business, School of Accounting, Program in Taxation, Miami, FL 33199. Offers MST. Part-time and evening/weekend programs available. *Students:* 23 full-time (12 women), 15 part-time (8 women); includes 32 minority (4 African Americans, 28 Hispanic Americans). Average age 30. 55 applicants, 45% accepted, 20 enrolled. In 2006, 36 degrees awarded. *Entrance requirements:* For master's, GMAT, minimum AACSB index of 1000, minimum GPA of 3.0. Additional exam requirements/recommendations for international students: Required—TOEFL. *Application deadline:* For fall admission, 4/1 priority date for domestic students; for spring admission, 10/1 for domestic students. Applications are processed on a rolling basis. Application fee: $25. *Expenses:* Tuition, state resident: part-time $249 per credit hour. Tuition, nonresident: part-time $753 per credit hour. Tuition and fees vary according to program. *Unit head:* Dr. Christos Koulamas, Acting Director, School of Accounting, 305-348-2830, Fax: 305-348-4126, E-mail: christos.koulamas@fiu.edu.

Florida State University, Graduate Studies, College of Business, Tallahassee, FL 32306. Offers accounting (M Acc), including accounting information systems, assurance services, corporate accounting, taxation; business administration (MBA, PhD), including accounting (PhD), finance (PhD), information and management science (PhD), management (PhD), marketing (PhD), risk and insurance (PhD); insurance (MSM); management information systems (MS); JD/MBA. *Accreditation:* AACSB. Part-time and evening/weekend programs available. Postbaccalaureate distance learning degree programs offered (no on-campus study). *Faculty:* 107 full-time (26 women), 21 part-time/adjunct (2 women). *Students:* 145 full-time (62 women), 444 part-time (143 women); includes 147 minority (58 African Americans, 3 American Indian/Alaska Native, 45 Asian Americans or Pacific Islanders, 41 Hispanic Americans). Average age 29. 789 applicants, 50% accepted, 321 enrolled. In 2006, 263 master's, 19 doctorates awarded. Terminal master's awarded for partial completion of doctoral program. *Degree requirements:* For master's, registration; for doctorate, thesis/dissertation, comprehensive exam, registration. *Entrance requirements:* For master's, GMAT, substantial work experience (MBA, MS), minimum GPA of 3.0, letters of recommendation; for doctorate, GMAT, minimum graduate GPA of 3.5, letters of recommendation. Additional exam requirements/recommendations for international students: Required—TOEFL (minimum score 600 paper-based; 250 computer-based). *Application deadline:* For fall admission, 5/1 for domestic and international students; for spring admission, 10/1 for domestic students, 9/1 for international students. Applications are processed on a rolling basis. Application fee: $30. Electronic applications accepted. *Expenses:* Tuition, state resident: full-time $5,822; part-time $243 per credit hour. Tuition, nonresident: full-time $20,976; part-time $874 per credit hour. Tuition and fees vary according to program. *Financial support:* In 2006–07, 126 students received support, including 40 fellowships with partial tuition reimbursements available (averaging $4,600 per year), 37 research assistantships with partial tuition reimbursements available (averaging $4,600 per year), 49 teaching assistantships with partial tuition reimbursements available (averaging $10,500 per year); unspecified assistantships also available. Financial award application deadline: 1/1. Total annual research expenditures: $1.5 million. *Unit head:* Dr. Caryn Beck-Dudley, Dean, 850-644-3090, Fax: 850-644-0915. *Application contact:* Lisa Beverly, Coordinator, Graduate Programs Admissions, 850-644-6458, Fax: 850-644-0588, E-mail: lbeverly@cob.fsu.edu.

Fontbonne University, Graduate Programs, Department of Business Administration, Program in Taxation, St. Louis, MO 63105-3098. Offers MST. Part-time and evening/weekend programs available. *Faculty:* 6 part-time/adjunct (0 women). *Students:* 2 full-time (1 woman), 17 part-time (13 women); includes 4 minority (all African Americans), 1 international. Average age 38. 3 applicants, 100% accepted, 2 enrolled. In 2006, 7 degrees awarded. *Entrance requirements:* For master's, minimum GPA of 2.5. *Application deadline:* For fall admission, 9/1 priority date for domestic students; for spring admission, 4/15 for domestic students. Applications are processed on a rolling basis. Application fee: $25. *Expenses:* Tuition: Full-time $4,890; part-time $489 per credit. Required fees: $160; $76 per credit. Full-time tuition and fees vary according to course load and program. *Financial support:* Application deadline: 4/1; *Unit head:* Dr. Linda Maurer, Dean of Business, 314-889-1423, Fax: 314-889-1451, E-mail: lmaurer@fontbonne.edu. *Application contact:* William D. Foster, Administrative Director, Business and Administration, 314-889-1418, Fax: 314-889-1451, E-mail: bfoster@fontbonne.edu.

Fordham University, Graduate School of Business, New York, NY 10023. Offers accounting (MBA); communications and media management (MBA); finance (MBA, MS); information systems (MBA, MS); management systems (MBA); marketing (MBA); media management (MS); taxation (MS); JD/MBA; MBA/MIM; MS/MBA. *Accreditation:* AACSB. Part-time and evening/weekend programs available. *Faculty:* 87 full-time, 41 part-time/adjunct. *Students:* 345 full-time (132 women), 1,183 part-time (448 women); includes 238 minority (59 African Americans, 1 American Indian/Alaska Native, 116 Asian Americans or Pacific Islanders, 62 Hispanic Americans), 77 international. 1,081 applicants, 65% accepted, 422 enrolled. In 2006, 454 degrees awarded. *Entrance requirements:* For master's, GMAT. Additional exam requirements/recommendations for international students: Required—TOEFL (minimum score 600 paper-based; 250 computer-based). *Application deadline:* For fall admission, 6/1 priority date for domestic students, 5/1 priority date for international students; for winter admission, 11/1 priority date for domestic students, 10/1 priority date for international students; for spring admission, 3/1 priority date for domestic students, 2/1 priority date for international students. Applications are processed on a rolling basis. Application fee: $65. Electronic applications accepted. *Expenses:* *Contact institution.* *Financial support:* In 2006–07, 7 fellowships (averaging $27,000 per year), 128 research assistantships were awarded; career-related internships or fieldwork, institutionally sponsored loans, scholarships/grants, and unspecified assistantships also available. Support available to part-time students. Financial award application deadline: 5/1; financial award applicants required to submit FAFSA. *Unit head:* Dr. Howard Tuckman, Dean, 212-636-6165, Fax: 212-307-1779, E-mail: tuckman@fordham.edu. *Application contact:* Frank Fletcher, Director of Admissions and Financial Aid, 212-636-6200, Fax: 212-636-7076, E-mail: admissionsgb@fordham.edu.

Georgetown University, Law Center, Washington, DC 20001. Offers advocacy (LL M); common law studies (LL M); general (LL M); international and comparative law (LL M); labor and employment law (LL M); law (JD, SJD); securities regulation (LL M); taxation (LL M); JD/MA; JD/MBA; JD/MPH; JD/MS; JD/PhD. *Accreditation:* ABA. Part-time and evening/weekend programs available. *Degree requirements:* For master's and doctorate, thesis/dissertation. *Entrance requirements:* For JD, LSAT; for master's and doctorate, JD, LL B, or first law degree earned in country of origin. Additional exam requirements/recommendations for international students: Required—TOEFL. Expenses: Contact institution. *Faculty research:* Constitutional law, legal history, jurisprudence.

Georgia State University, J. Mack Robinson College of Business, School of Accountancy, Program in Taxation, Atlanta, GA 30303-3083. Offers MTX. Part-time and evening/weekend programs available. *Students:* 22 full-time (12 women), 41 part-time (19 women); includes 12 minority (6 African Americans, 5 Asian Americans or Pacific Islanders, 1 Hispanic American), 2 international. 27 applicants, 63% accepted, 12 enrolled. In 2006, 24 degrees awarded. *Entrance requirements:* For master's, GMAT, GRE General Test or LSAT. Additional exam requirements/recommendations for international students: Required—TOEFL (minimum score 610 paper-based; 255 computer-based; 101 iBT). *Application deadline:* For fall admission, 5/1 for domestic students, 2/1 for international students; for spring admission, 10/15 for domestic students, 5/1 for international students. Applications are processed on a rolling basis. Application fee: $50. Electronic applications accepted. *Financial support:* Research assistantships, career-related internships or fieldwork and tuition waivers (partial) available. Support available to part-time students. Financial award application deadline: 5/1; financial award applicants required to submit FAFSA. *Unit head:* Dr. Tad Ransopher, Faculty Adviser, 404-651-4467, Fax: 404-651-1033, E-mail: acctdr@gsu.edu.

Golden Gate University, School of Law, San Francisco, CA 94105-2968. Offers environmental law (LL M); intellectual property law (LL M); international legal studies (LL M, SJD); law (JD); taxation (LL M); U.S. legal studies (LL M); JD/MBA; JD/PhD. *Accreditation:* ABA. Part-time and evening/weekend programs available. *Faculty:* 49 full-time (22 women), 68 part-time/adjunct (31 women). *Students:* 733 full-time (415 women), 345 part-time (196 women); includes 276 minority (47 African Americans, 4 American Indian/Alaska Native, 168 Asian Americans or Pacific Islanders, 57 Hispanic Americans), 74 international. Average age 28. 2,761 applicants, 49% accepted, 222 enrolled. In 2006, 168 JDs, 113 master's, 3 doctorates awarded. *Entrance requirements:* LSAT. Additional exam requirements/recommendations for international students: Required—TOEFL (minimum score 600 paper-based; 250 computer-based). *Application deadline:* For fall admission, 4/1 for domestic students, 4/15 for international students; for spring admission, 11/15 for international students. Applications are processed on a rolling basis. Application fee: $60. Electronic applications accepted. *Expenses:* *Contact institution.* *Financial support:* In 2006–07, 331 students received support, including 3 fellowships (averaging $36,000 per year), 60 research assistantships (averaging $2,400 per year), 30 teaching assistantships (averaging $2,400 per year); career-related internships or fieldwork, Federal Work-Study, institutionally sponsored loans, scholarships/grants, tuition waivers (full and partial), and unspecified assistantships also available. Support available to part-time students. Financial award application deadline: 3/1; financial award applicants required to submit FAFSA. *Faculty research:* International law, intellectual property law, environmental law, real estate, civil rights. *Unit head:* Frederic White, Dean, 415-442-6600, Fax: 415-442-6609. *Application contact:* Sherolyn Hurst, Director of Admissions, 415-442-6630, Fax: 415-442-6631, E-mail: lawadmit@ggu.edu.

Golden Gate University, School of Taxation, San Francisco, CA 94105-2968. Offers MS, Certificate. Part-time and evening/weekend programs available. *Students:* 54 full-time (29 women), 630 part-time (358 women); includes 211 minority (21 African Americans, 1 American Indian/Alaska Native, 159 Asian Americans or Pacific Islanders, 30 Hispanic Americans), 37 international. Average age 36. 281 applicants, 86% accepted, 149 enrolled. In 2006, 215 degrees awarded. *Entrance requirements:* For master's, minimum GPA of 3.0. Additional exam requirements/recommendations for international students: Required—TOEFL. *Application deadline:* For fall admission, 7/1 priority date for domestic students. Applications are processed on a rolling basis. Application fee: $55 ($90 for international students). *Expenses:* *Contact institution.* *Financial support:* Career-related internships or fieldwork, Federal Work-Study, and institutionally sponsored loans available. Support available to part-time students. Financial award applicants required to submit FAFSA. *Unit head:* Mary Canning, Dean, 415-442-7885. *Application contact:* Enrollment Services, 415-442-7800, Fax: 415-442-7807, E-mail: info@ggu.edu.

Grand Valley State University, Seidman College of Business, Program in Taxation, Allendale, MI 49401-9403. Offers MST. Part-time and evening/weekend programs available. *Faculty:* 2 full-time (0 women), 3 part-time/adjunct (0 women). *Students:* 6 full-time (2 women), 39 part-time (21 women), 1 international. Average age 31. 15 applicants, 80% accepted, 10 enrolled. In 2006, 11 degrees awarded. *Entrance requirements:* For master's, GMAT. Additional exam requirements/recommendations for international students: Required—TOEFL. *Application deadline:* For fall admission, 8/1 priority date for domestic students, 5/1 priority date for international students; for winter admission, 12/1 priority date for domestic students, 11/1 priority date for international students; for spring admission, 4/1 priority date for domestic students, 3/1 priority date for international students. Applications are processed on a rolling basis. Application fee: $30. Electronic applications accepted. *Expenses:* Tuition, state resident: full-time $5,850; part-time $325 per credit. Tuition, nonresident: full-time $10,800; part-time $600 per credit. Tuition and fees vary according to course load. *Financial support:* In 2006–07, 8 students received support; research assistantships, Federal Work-Study, institutionally sponsored loans, and unspecified assistantships available. Financial award application deadline: 2/15. *Faculty research:* Individual income taxation, state taxation, pass-through entities, estate and gift taxation, sale-leasebacks. *Unit head:* Dr. Steve Goldberg, Director, 616-331-

Taxation

Grand Valley State University (continued)
7190, Fax: 616-331-7389, E-mail: goldbers@gvsu.edu. *Application contact:* Claudia J. Bajema, Director, Graduate Business Programs, 616-331-7387, Fax: 616-331-7389, E-mail: bajemac@gvsu.edu.

HEC Montreal, School of Business Administration, Diploma Programs in Administration, Program in Taxation, Montréal, QC H3T 2A7, Canada. Offers LL M, Diploma. All courses are given in French. Part-time programs available. *Students:* 23 full-time (12 women), 82 part-time (36 women). In 2006, 16 master's, 7 Diplomas awarded. *Degree requirements:* For master's, one foreign language, thesis; for Diploma, one foreign language. *Entrance requirements:* For master's, diploma in taxation from HEC Montreal; for Diploma, work experience in Canadian taxation system. *Application deadline:* For fall admission, 4/1 for domestic and international students; for winter admission, 10/1 for domestic and international students. Application fee: $60 Canadian dollars. Electronic applications accepted. Tuition and fees charges are reported in Canadian dollars. *Expenses:* Tuition, nonresident: part-time $56 Canadian dollars per credit. Required fees: $30 Canadian dollars per semester. *Financial support:* Scholarships/grants available. *Application contact:* Francine Blais, Administrative Director, 514-340-6112, Fax: 514-340-6411, E-mail: francine.blais@hec.ca.

Hofstra University, Frank G. Zarb School of Business, Department of Accounting, Taxation and Legal Studies, Hempstead, NY 11549. Offers accounting (MBA, MS); taxation (MBA, MS). Part-time and evening/weekend programs available. *Faculty:* 8 full-time (2 women), 4 part-time/adjunct (1 woman). *Students:* 27 full-time (11 women), 43 part-time (21 women); includes 9 minority (3 African Americans, 4 Asian Americans or Pacific Islanders, 2 Hispanic Americans), 7 international. Average age 29. 54 applicants, 85% accepted, 20 enrolled. In 2006, 16 degrees awarded. *Degree requirements:* For master's, thesis (for some programs). *Entrance requirements:* For master's, GMAT, 2 letters of recommendation, resumé, essay. Additional exam requirements/recommendations for international students: Required—TOEFL (minimum score 550 paper-based; 213 computer-based). *Application deadline:* Applications are processed on a rolling basis. Application fee: $60. Electronic applications accepted. *Expenses:* Tuition: Full-time $13,320; part-time $740 per credit. Required fees: $930; $155 per term. *Financial support:* In 2006–07, 12 students received support, including 9 fellowships with tuition reimbursements available (averaging $6,821 per year); research assistantships with full and partial tuition reimbursements available, Federal Work-Study, scholarships/grants, tuition waivers (full and partial), and unspecified assistantships also available. Financial award applicants required to submit FAFSA. *Faculty research:* Impact of Sarbanes-Oaxley, law on various accounting functions, SEC retreat from SEC fraud investigation, corporate ownership structures, international auditing standards, constitutional questions such as Graves Amendment. *Unit head:* Dr. Nathan S. Slavin, Chairperson, 516-463-5690, Fax: 516-463-4834, E-mail: nathan.s.slavin@hofstra.edu. *Application contact:* Carol Drummer, Dean of Graduate Admissions, 516-463-4876, Fax: 516-463-4664, E-mail: gradstudent@hofstra.edu.

Illinois Institute of Technology, Chicago-Kent College of Law, Chicago, IL 60661-3691. Offers family law (LL M); financial services (LL M); international intellectual property (LL M); international law (LL M); law (JD); taxation (LL M); JD/LL M; JD/MBA; JD/MPA; JD/MPH; JD/MS. *Accreditation:* ABA. Part-time and evening/weekend programs available. *Faculty:* 61 full-time (20 women), 132 part-time/adjunct (34 women). *Students:* 827 full-time (395 women), 302 part-time (130 women); includes 221 minority (61 African Americans, 4 American Indian/Alaska Native, 95 Asian Americans or Pacific Islanders, 61 Hispanic Americans), 70 international. Average age 27. 3,510 applicants, 31% accepted, 307 enrolled. In 2006, 283 JDs, 28 master's awarded. *Entrance requirements:* LSAT, LSDAS. *Application deadline:* For fall admission, 3/1 priority date for domestic and international students. Applications are processed on a rolling basis. Application fee: $60. Electronic applications accepted. *Expenses: Contact institution.* Tuition and fees vary according to class time, course level, course load, program and student level. *Financial support:* In 2006–07, 573 students received support. Career-related internships or fieldwork, institutionally sponsored loans, scholarships/grants, and tuition waivers (full) available. Support available to part-time students. Financial award application deadline: 3/15; financial award applicants required to submit FAFSA. *Faculty research:* Constitutional law, bioethics, environmental law. Total annual research expenditures: $1.2 million. *Unit head:* Harold J. Krent, Dean, 312-906-5010, Fax: 312-906-5335, E-mail: hkrent@kentlaw.edu. *Application contact:* Nicole Vilches, Assistant Dean, 312-906-5020, Fax: 312-906-5274, E-mail: admit@kentlaw.edu.

John Marshall Law School, Graduate and Professional Programs, Chicago, IL 60604-3968. Offers comparative legal studies (LL M); employee benefits (LL M, MS); information technology (LL M, MS); intellectual property (LL M); international business and trade (LL M); law (JD); real estate (LL M, MS); taxation (LL M, MS); JD/LL M; JD/MA; JD/MBA; JD/MPA. *Accreditation:* ABA. Part-time and evening/weekend programs available. *Faculty:* 64 full-time (23 women), 113 part-time/adjunct (29 women). *Students:* 1,157 full-time (479 women), 421 part-time (187 women); includes 253 minority (76 African Americans, 10 American Indian/Alaska Native, 101 Asian Americans or Pacific Islanders, 66 Hispanic Americans), 48 international. Average age 27. 3,169 applicants, 37% accepted, 333 enrolled. In 2006, 347 JDs, 69 master's awarded. *Entrance requirements:* For JD, LSAT; for master's, JD. Additional exam requirements/recommendations for international students: Required—TOEFL. *Application deadline:* For fall admission, 3/1 priority date for domestic and international students; for spring admission, 10/15 priority date for domestic and international students. Applications are processed on a rolling basis. Application fee: $60. Electronic applications accepted. *Expenses: Contact institution. Financial support:* In 2006–07, 1,339 students received support. Scholarships/grants and tuition waivers (full and partial) available. Support available to part-time students. Financial award application deadline: 6/1; financial award applicants required to submit FAFSA. *Unit head:* John Corkery, Dean, 312-427-2737. *Application contact:* William B. Powers, Associate Dean of Admission and Student Affairs, 800-537-4280, Fax: 312-427-5136, E-mail: admission@jmls.edu.

Long Island University, Brooklyn Campus, School of Business, Public Administration and Information Sciences, Program in Accountancy, Taxation and Law, Brooklyn, NY 11201-8423. Offers accounting (MS); taxation (MS). Part-time and evening/weekend programs available. *Entrance requirements:* For master's, GMAT or GRE General Test, 2 letters of recommendation. Additional exam requirements/recommendations for international students: Required—TOEFL (minimum score 500 paper-based; 173 computer-based). Electronic applications accepted.

Long Island University, C.W. Post Campus, College of Management, School of Business, Brookville, NY 11548-1300. Offers accounting and taxation (Certificate); business administration (Certificate); finance (MBA, Certificate); general business administration (MBA); international business (MBA, Certificate); management (MBA, Certificate); management information systems (MBA, Certificate); marketing (MBA, Certificate). *Accreditation:* AACSB. Part-time and evening/weekend programs available. *Entrance requirements:* For master's, GMAT, resumé, minimum GPA of 3.0, 2 letters of recommendation. Additional exam requirements/recommendations for international students: Required—TOEFL (minimum score 527 paper-based; 197 computer-based). Electronic applications accepted. *Faculty research:* Financial markets, consumer behavior.

Long Island University, C.W. Post Campus, College of Management, School of Professional Accountancy, Program in Taxation, Brookville, NY 11548-1300. Offers MS. Part-time programs available. *Entrance requirements:* For master's, GMAT, minimum GPA of 2.5, BS in accounting from accredited college or university, 3 credits in business law and taxation. Electronic applications accepted. *Faculty research:* Reporting methods, specialized tax rules and regulations.

Loyola Marymount University, Loyola Law School, Los Angeles, CA 90015. Offers American law and international practice (LL M); law (JD); taxation (LL M); JD/MBA. *Accreditation:* ABA. Part-time and evening/weekend programs available. *Faculty:* 65 full-time (26 women), 61 part-time/adjunct (27 women). *Students:* 1,022 full-time, 343 part-time; includes 233 minority (55 African Americans, 8 American Indian/Alaska Native, 42 Asian Americans or Pacific Islanders, 128 Hispanic Americans), 20 international. Average age 23. 4,537 applicants, 30% accepted, 423 enrolled. In 2006, 419 JDs, 15 master's awarded. *Entrance requirements:* For JD, LSAT; for master's, JD (LLM). Additional exam requirements/recommendations for international students: Required—TOEFL. *Application deadline:* For fall admission, 2/1 priority date for domestic and international students. Applications are processed on a rolling basis. Application fee: $65. Electronic applications accepted. *Financial support:* In 2006–07, 246 students received support; research assistantships, Federal Work-Study and scholarships/grants available. Financial award application deadline: 3/15; financial award applicants required to submit FAFSA. *Unit head:* David W. Burcham, Dean, 213-736-1028, Fax: 213-487-6736, E-mail: david.burcham@lls.edu. *Application contact:* Janell Lundy Roberts, Assistant Dean, Admissions, 213-736-1074, Fax: 213-736-6523, E-mail: admissions@lls.edu.

Mississippi State University, College of Business and Industry, School of Accountancy, Mississippi State, MS 39762. Offers MPA, MTX. *Accreditation:* AACSB. *Faculty:* 9 full-time (4 women), 4 part-time/adjunct (1 woman). *Students:* 47 full-time (20 women), 4 part-time (3 women); includes 4 minority (all African Americans), 7 international. Average age 24. 28 applicants, 75% accepted, 18 enrolled. In 2006, 26 degrees awarded. *Degree requirements:* For master's, comprehensive exam. *Entrance requirements:* For master's, GMAT, minimum GPA of 2.75, 3.0 in last 60 hours of course work, 2.75 in upper accounting. Additional exam requirements/recommendations for international students: Required—TOEFL. *Application deadline:* For fall admission, 7/1 for domestic students; for spring admission, 11/1 for domestic students. Applications are processed on a rolling basis. Application fee: $30. *Expenses:* Tuition, state resident: full-time $4,550; part-time $253 per hour. Tuition, nonresident: full-time $10,552; part-time $584 per hour. International tuition: $10,882 full-time. Tuition and fees vary according to course load. *Financial support:* Research assistantships with tuition reimbursements, teaching assistantships with partial tuition reimbursements, career-related internships or fieldwork, Federal Work-Study, institutionally sponsored loans, and unspecified assistantships available. Support available to part-time students. Financial award applicants required to submit FAFSA. *Faculty research:* Income tax, financial accounting system, managerial accounting, auditing. *Unit head:* Dr. Clyde Herring, Interim Director, 662-325-3710, Fax: 662-325-1646, E-mail: cherring@cobilan.msstate.edu. *Application contact:* Dr. Phil Bonfanti, Director of Admissions, 662-325-4104, Fax: 662-325-8872, E-mail: admit@msstate.edu.

National University, Academic Affairs, School of Business and Management, Department of Finance, Accounting and Economics, La Jolla, CA 92037-1011. Offers finance (MS); finance, accounting, and economics (EMBA, MBA); taxation (MS). Part-time and evening/weekend programs available. Postbaccalaureate distance learning degree programs offered (no on-campus study). *Faculty:* 11 full-time (1 woman), 114 part-time/adjunct (30 women). *Students:* 382 full-time (166 women), 694 part-time (302 women); includes 375 minority (91 African Americans, 5 American Indian/Alaska Native, 167 Asian Americans or Pacific Islanders, 112 Hispanic Americans), 144 international. Average age 34. 689 applicants, 577 enrolled. In 2006, 289 degrees awarded. *Degree requirements:* For master's, thesis. *Entrance requirements:* For master's, interview, minimum GPA of 2.5. Additional exam requirements/recommendations for international students: Required—TOEFL (minimum score 550 paper-based; 213 computer-based; 80 iBT), IELTS (minimum score 6). *Application deadline:* Applications are processed on a rolling basis. Application fee: $60 ($65 for international students). Electronic applications accepted. *Expenses:* Tuition: Full-time $7,722; part-time $286 per unit. One-time fee: $60. *Financial support:* Career-related internships or fieldwork, institutionally sponsored loans, scholarships/grants, and tuition waivers (partial) available. Support available to part-time students. Financial award application deadline: 6/30; financial award applicants required to submit FAFSA. *Unit head:* Donald A. Schwartz, Chair and Associate Professor, 858-642-8420, E-mail: dschwartz@nu.edu. *Application contact:* Dominick Giovanniello, Associate Regional Dean—San Diego, 800-NAT-UNIV, Fax: 858-642-8709, E-mail: dgiovann@nu.edu.

New York Law School, Professional Program, New York, NY 10013. Offers law (JD); tax (LL M); JD/MBA. *Accreditation:* ABA. Part-time and evening/weekend programs available. *Faculty:* 76 full-time (28 women), 94 part-time/adjunct (36 women). *Students:* 1,168 full-time (629 women), 394 part-time (203 women); includes 355 minority (93 African Americans, 3 American Indian/Alaska Native, 142 Asian Americans or Pacific Islanders, 117 Hispanic Americans), 9 international. Average age 28. 5,557 applicants, 44% accepted, 549 enrolled. In 2006, 521 degrees awarded. *Entrance requirements:* LSAT, letters of recommendation, resumé. Additional exam requirements/recommendations for international students: Recommended—TOEFL (minimum score 600 paper-based; 250 computer-based). *Application deadline:* For fall admission, 4/1 priority date for domestic and international students. Applications are processed on a rolling basis. Application fee: $60. Electronic applications accepted. *Expenses:* Tuition: Full-time $38,535. Required fees: $809. Tuition and fees vary according to degree level and student level. *Financial support:* In 2006–07, 679 students received support, including 202 research assistantships (averaging $3,920 per year), 5 teaching assistantships (averaging $1,000 per year); career-related internships or fieldwork, Federal Work-Study, institutionally sponsored loans, and scholarships/grants also available. Support available to part-time students. Financial award application deadline: 4/2; financial award applicants required to submit FAFSA. *Unit head:* Richard A. Matasar, President and Dean, 212-431-2840, Fax: 212-219-3752, E-mail: rmatasar@nyls.edu. *Application contact:* William D. Perez, Assistant Dean for Admissions and Financial Aid, 212-431-2888, Fax: 212-966-1522, E-mail: wperez@nyls.edu.

New York University, School of Law, New York, NY 10012-1019. Offers law (JD, LL M, JSD); law and business (Advanced Certificate); tax (Advanced Certificate); JD/LL M; JD/MA; JD/MBA; JD/MPA; JD/MSW; JD/PhD. *Accreditation:* ABA. Part-time programs available. *Faculty:* 117 full-time (35 women), 64 part-time/adjunct (18 women). *Students:* 1,442 full-time (667 women); includes 345 minority (124 African Americans, 153 Asian Americans or Pacific Islanders, 68 Hispanic Americans), 53 international. 7,571 applicants, 448 enrolled. In 2006, 465 JDs, 472 master's, 6 doctorates awarded. *Entrance requirements:* LSAT. *Application deadline:* For fall admission, 2/1 for domestic students. Application fee: $85. Electronic applications accepted. *Expenses: Contact institution.* Tuition and fees vary according to program. *Financial support:* Fellowships, research assistantships, teaching assistantships, career-related internships or fieldwork, Federal Work-Study, institutionally sponsored loans, scholarships/grants, tuition waivers (partial), and loan repayment assistance available. Financial award application deadline: 4/15; financial award applicants required to submit FAFSA. *Faculty research:* Constitutional law, environmental law, corporate law, globalization of law, philosophy of law. *Unit head:* Richard L. Revesz, Dean, 212-998-6000, Fax: 212-995-3150. *Application contact:* Kenneth J. Kleinrock, Assistant Dean for Admissions, 212-998-6060, Fax: 212-995-4527.

Northeastern University, Graduate School of Business Administration, Graduate School of Professional Accounting, Program in Taxation, Boston, MA 02115-5096. Offers MST, CAGS. Part-time and evening/weekend programs available. *Faculty:* 2 full-time (0 women), 22 part-time/adjunct (1 woman). *Students:* 6 full-time (4 women), 67 part-time (36 women). Average age 35. 16 applicants, 69% accepted. In 2006, 23 degrees awarded. *Entrance requirements:* For master's, GMAT or CPA exam, interview, undergraduate business degree. *Application deadline:* For fall admission, 8/1 for domestic students; for winter admission, 11/15 for domestic students; for spring admission, 3/15 for domestic students. Applications are processed on a rolling basis. Application fee: $100. Electronic applications accepted. *Expenses: Contact institution. Financial support:* In 2006–07, 3 students received support; fellowships, research assistantships, teaching assistantships, career-related internships or fieldwork and institutionally sponsored loans available. Financial award application deadline: 3/1; financial award applicants required to submit FAFSA. *Faculty research:* Estate planning, taxpayer compliance.

Northern Illinois University, Graduate School, College of Business, Department of Accountancy, De Kalb, IL 60115-2854. Offers MAS, MST. *Accreditation:* AACSB. Part-time and evening/weekend programs available. *Faculty:* 14 full-time (4 women). *Students:* 121 full-time (59 women), 111 part-time (64 women); includes 39 minority (6 African Americans, 24 Asian Americans or Pacific Islanders, 9 Hispanic Americans), 20 international. Average age 29. 122 applicants, 66% accepted, 45 enrolled. In 2006, 128 degrees awarded. *Degree requirements:*

For master's, thesis optional. *Entrance requirements:* For master's, GMAT, minimum GPA of 2.75. Additional exam requirements/recommendations for international students: Required—TOEFL (minimum score 550 paper-based; 213 computer-based). *Application deadline:* For fall admission, 4/1 priority date for domestic students, 5/1 for international students; for spring admission, 9/15 priority date for domestic students, 10/1 for international students. Applications are processed on a rolling basis. Application fee: $30. Electronic applications accepted. *Financial support:* In 2006–07, 29 research assistantships with full tuition reimbursements, 9 teaching assistantships with full tuition reimbursements were awarded; fellowships with full tuition reimbursements, career-related internships or fieldwork, Federal Work-Study, scholarships/grants, tuition waivers (full), and unspecified assistantships also available. Support available to part-time students. Financial award applicants required to submit FAFSA. *Faculty research:* Accounting fraud, governmental accounting, corporate income tax planning, auditing, ethics. *Unit head:* Dr. James C. Young, Chair, 815-753-1250, Fax: 815-753-8515. *Application contact:* Dr. John Simon, Graduate Adviser, 815-753-6203.

Nova Southeastern University, H. Wayne Huizenga School of Business and Entrepreneurship, Program in Taxation, Fort Lauderdale, FL 33314-7796. Offers MT. Evening/weekend programs available. Postbaccalaureate distance learning degree programs offered. *Students:* 3 full-time (2 women), 71 part-time (44 women); includes 58 minority (33 African Americans, 1 American Indian/Alaska Native, 3 Asian Americans or Pacific Islanders, 21 Hispanic Americans). In 2006, 24 degrees awarded. *Entrance requirements:* Additional exam requirements/recommendations for international students: Required—TOEFL (minimum score 550 paper-based; 213 computer-based). Application fee: $50. *Unit head:* Dr. Walter Moore, Chair and Professor for Accounting Programs, 954-262-5101, Fax: 954-262-3822, E-mail: moore@huizenga.nova.edu. *Application contact:* Aimee Fernandez, Assistant Director, 954-262-5019, Fax: 954-262-3822, E-mail: aimeefernandez@huizenga.nova.edu.

See Close-Up on page 295.

Pace University, Lubin School of Business, Taxation Program, New York, NY 10038. Offers MBA, MS. Part-time and evening/weekend programs available. *Faculty:* 7 full-time, 8 part-time/adjunct. *Students:* Average age 33. 35 applicants, 74% accepted, 13 enrolled. In 2006, 20 degrees awarded. *Entrance requirements:* For master's, GMAT. *Application deadline:* For fall admission, 7/31 priority date for domestic students; for spring admission, 11/30 for domestic students. Applications are processed on a rolling basis. Application fee: $65. Electronic applications accepted. *Expenses:* Tuition: Part-time $890 per credit. *Financial support:* Research assistantships, career-related internships or fieldwork and Federal Work-Study available. Support available to part-time students. Financial award applicants required to submit FAFSA. *Unit head:* Dr. Walter Joyce, Chairperson, 212-346-1294. *Application contact:* Joanna Broda, Director of Admissions, 212-346-1652, Fax: 212-346-1585, E-mail: gradnyc@pace.edu.

Philadelphia University, School of Business Administration, Program in Taxation, Philadelphia, PA 19144-5497. Offers MS. Part-time and evening/weekend programs available. *Faculty:* 2 full-time (0 women), 4 part-time/adjunct (0 women). *Students:* 4 full-time (3 women), 30 part-time (13 women). 24 applicants, 46% accepted, 9 enrolled. In 2006, 19 degrees awarded. *Entrance requirements:* For master's, GMAT. Additional exam requirements/recommendations for international students: Required—TOEFL (minimum score 550 paper-based; 213 computer-based; 79 iBT). *Application deadline:* Applications are processed on a rolling basis. Application fee: $35. Electronic applications accepted. *Financial support:* In 2006–07, research assistantships with full tuition reimbursements (averaging $2,500 per year); career-related internships or fieldwork, Federal Work-Study, scholarships/grants, and unspecified assistantships also available. Support available to part-time students. Financial award applicants required to submit FAFSA. *Unit head:* MarySheila McDonald, Assistant Dean for Graduate Programs, 215-951-2950, Fax: 215-951-2653, E-mail: mcdonaldm@philau.edu. *Application contact:* Jack A. Klett, Director of Graduate Admissions, 215-951-2943, Fax: 215-951-2907, E-mail: gradadm@philau.edu.

Robert Morris University, Graduate Studies, School of Business, Moon Township, PA 15108-1189. Offers accounting (MS); business administration and management (MBA); finance (MS); human resource management (MS); nonprofit management (MS); sport management (MS); taxation (MS). Part-time and evening/weekend programs available. *Faculty:* 27 full-time (12 women), 6 part-time/adjunct (1 woman). *Students:* Average age 31. 253 applicants, 59% accepted, 103 enrolled. In 2006, 139 degrees awarded. *Entrance requirements:* For master's, GMAT, letters of recommendation. Additional exam requirements/recommendations for international students: Required—TOEFL (minimum score 550 paper-based; 213 computer-based). *Application deadline:* For fall admission, 7/1 priority date for domestic and international students; for spring admission, 11/1 priority date for domestic and international students. Applications are processed on a rolling basis. Application fee: $35. Electronic applications accepted. *Expenses:* Tuition: Part-time $580 per credit. Part-time tuition and fees vary according to degree level and program. *Financial support:* Research assistantships with partial tuition reimbursements, Federal Work-Study, institutionally sponsored loans, and unspecified assistantships available. Support available to part-time students. Financial award application deadline: 5/1; financial award applicants required to submit FAFSA. *Unit head:* Dr. Derya A. Jacobs, Dean, 412-262-8451, Fax: 412-262-8494, E-mail: jacobs@rmu.edu. *Application contact:* Kellie L. Laurenzi, Dean of Enrollment, 412-262-8235, Fax: 412-299-2425, E-mail: laurenzi@rmu.edu.

Rutgers, The State University of New Jersey, Newark, Rutgers Business School: Graduate Programs-Newark/New Brunswick, Master of Accountancy in Taxation Program, Newark, NJ 07102. Offers M Accy.

St. John's University, The Peter J. Tobin College of Business, Department of Accounting and Taxation, Program in Taxation, Queens, NY 11439. Offers MBA, MS, Adv C. Part-time and evening/weekend programs available. *Faculty:* 20 full-time (6 women), 18 part-time/adjunct (4 women). *Students:* 5 full-time (2 women), 42 part-time (22 women); includes 25 minority (7 African Americans, 14 Asian Americans or Pacific Islanders, 4 Hispanic Americans), 3 international. Average age 30. 29 applicants, 90% accepted, 23 enrolled. In 2006, 32 degrees awarded. *Degree requirements:* For master's, thesis optional. *Entrance requirements:* For master's, GMAT, minimum GPA of 3.0. Additional exam requirements/recommendations for international students: Required—TOEFL (minimum score 500 paper-based; 173 computer-based). *Application deadline:* For fall admission, 5/1 priority date for domestic and international students; for spring admission, 11/1 priority date for domestic and international students. Applications are processed on a rolling basis. Application fee: $40. Electronic applications accepted. *Expenses: Contact institution.* Tuition and fees vary according to program. *Financial support:* Research assistantships available. Support available to part-time students. Financial award application deadline: 3/1; financial award applicants required to submit FAFSA. *Unit head:* Dr. Adrian Fitzsimons, Chair, 718-990-6460, Fax: 718-380-3803, E-mail: fitzsima@stjohns.edu. *Application contact:* Nicole T. Bryan, Assistant Dean, 718-990-2599, Fax: 718-990-5242, E-mail: mbaadmissions@stjohns.edu.

St. Mary's University of San Antonio, Graduate School, Bill Greehey School of Business, Program in Accounting, San Antonio, TX 78228-8507. Offers taxation (M Acc). Part-time programs available. Postbaccalaureate distance learning degree programs offered (minimal on-campus study). *Faculty:* 3 full-time (1 woman). *Students:* 1 full-time (0 women), 13 part-time (10 women); includes 7 minority (1 African American, 6 Hispanic Americans), 1 international. Average age 31. In 2006, 3 degrees awarded. *Degree requirements:* For master's, registration. *Entrance requirements:* For master's, GMAT. Additional exam requirements/recommendations for international students: Required—TOEFL (minimum score 550 paper-based; 213 computer-based). *Application deadline:* Applications are processed on a rolling basis. Application fee: $30. Electronic applications accepted. *Expenses:* Tuition: Full-time $10,890; part-time $605 per hour. Required fees: $500. Tuition and fees vary according to degree level. *Financial support:* Career-related internships or fieldwork, Federal Work-Study, institutionally sponsored loans, scholarships/grants, health care benefits, and unspecified assistantships available. Financial award application deadline: 3/31; financial award applicants required to submit FAFSA. *Unit head:* Dr. Mark Persellin, Graduate Program Director, 210-436-3708, Fax: 210-436-3620.

St. Thomas University, School of Law, Miami, FL 33054-6459. Offers international human rights (LL M); international taxation (LL M); law (JD); JD/MBA; JD/MS. *Accreditation:* ABA. Postbaccalaureate distance learning degree programs offered (no on-campus study). *Degree requirements:* For master's, thesis (international taxation). *Entrance requirements:* LSAT. Electronic applications accepted. Expenses: Contact institution.

San Jose State University, Graduate Studies and Research, Lucas Graduate School of Business, Program in Taxation, San Jose, CA 95192-0001. Offers MS. *Students:* 39 applicants, 54% accepted, 0 enrolled. *Degree requirements:* For master's, thesis or alternative, comprehensive exam. *Entrance requirements:* For master's, GMAT, minimum GPA of 3.0. *Application deadline:* For fall admission, 6/29 for domestic students; for spring admission, 11/30 for domestic students. Applications are processed on a rolling basis. Application fee: $59. Electronic applications accepted. *Financial support:* Applicants required to submit FAFSA.

Seton Hall University, Stillman School of Business, Department of Taxation, South Orange, NJ 07079-2692. Offers MS. Part-time and evening/weekend programs available. *Faculty:* 3 full-time (0 women). *Students:* Average age 30. 25 applicants, 84% accepted, 13 enrolled. In 2006, 18 degrees awarded. *Median time to degree:* Master's–1.25 years full-time, 1.7 years part-time. *Degree requirements:* For master's, registration. *Entrance requirements:* For master's, GMAT or CPA license, minimum GPA of 2.75. Additional exam requirements/recommendations for international students: Required—TOEFL (minimum score 550 paper-based; 213 computer-based). *Application deadline:* For fall admission, 6/1 priority date for domestic students, 5/1 for international students; for spring admission, 11/1 priority date for domestic students, 10/1 for international students. Application fee: $75 ($100 for international students). Electronic applications accepted. *Expenses: Contact institution. Financial support:* In 2006–07, 3 students received support, including research assistantships with full tuition reimbursements available (averaging $5,400 per year); career-related internships or fieldwork, Federal Work-Study, scholarships/grants, health care benefits, and unspecified assistantships also available. Support available to part-time students. Financial award application deadline: 6/1; financial award applicants required to submit FAFSA. *Faculty research:* Issues affecting cost capitalization, estate valuation discounts, qualified terminable interest property elections, eastern European tax initiatives, realigning the capital structure of closely-held business enterprises. *Unit head:* Dr. Reed Easton, Chairperson, 973-761-9249, Fax: 973-761-9217, E-mail: eastonre@shu.edu. *Application contact:* Catherine Bianchi, Director of Graduate Admissions, 973-761-9220, Fax: 973-761-9208, E-mail: biancha@shu.edu.

Southeastern University, College of Graduate Studies, Program in Taxation, Washington, DC 20024-2788. Offers MS. Part-time and evening/weekend programs available. *Entrance requirements:* Additional exam requirements/recommendations for international students: Required—TOEFL.

Southern Methodist University, Dedman School of Law, Dallas, TX 75275-0110. Offers comparative and international law (LL M); law (JD, SJD); law-general (LL M); taxation (LL M); JD/MA; JD/MBA. *Accreditation:* ABA. Part-time and evening/weekend programs available. *Faculty:* 37 full-time (15 women), 27 part-time/adjunct (6 women). *Students:* 922 full-time (424 women), 76 part-time (34 women); includes 193 minority (44 African Americans, 8 American Indian/Alaska Native, 75 Asian Americans or Pacific Islanders, 66 Hispanic Americans), 46 international. Average age 27. 2,640 applicants, 23% accepted, 275 enrolled. In 2006, 261 JDs, 45 master's awarded. *Median time to degree:* 3 years full-time, 4 years part-time. *Degree requirements:* For JD, 30 hours of public service; for master's, thesis optional; for doctorate, thesis/dissertation. *Entrance requirements:* For JD, LSAT, 2 letters of recommendation, resumé, personal statement; for master's, JD (LL M in law, taxation), foreign law degree (LL M in comparative and international law); for doctorate, LL M. Additional exam requirements/recommendations for international students: Required—TOEFL (minimum score 575 paper-based; 233 computer-based). *Application deadline:* For fall admission, 2/15 priority date for domestic students. Applications are processed on a rolling basis. Application fee: $75. Electronic applications accepted. *Expenses: Contact institution. Financial support:* Career-related internships or fieldwork, Federal Work-Study, and scholarships/grants available. Financial award application deadline: 2/15; financial award applicants required to submit FAFSA. *Faculty research:* Corporate law, intellectual property, international law, commercial law, dispute resolution. *Unit head:* John B. Attanasio, Dean, 214-768-8999, Fax: 214-768-2182, E-mail: jba@mail.smu.edu. *Application contact:* Virginia Keehan, Assistant Dean for Admissions, 214-768-2550, Fax: 214-768-2549, E-mail: lawadmit@smu.edu.

Southern New Hampshire University, School of Business, Manchester, NH 03106-1045. Offers accounting (MS); business administration (MBA, Certificate), including accounting (Certificate), business administration (MBA), finance (Certificate), forensic accounting (Certificate), human resources management (Certificate), international business (Certificate), international sport management (Certificate), leadership of not for profit organizations (Certificate), marketing (Certificate), operations management (Certificate), sport management (Certificate), taxation (Certificate); finance (MS); hospitality and tourism leadership (Certificate); information technology (MS, Certificate); information technology/international business (Certificate); integrated marketing communications (Certificate); international business (MS, DBA); marketing (MS); operations and project management (MS); organizational leadership (MS); project management (Certificate); sport management (MS); MBA/Certificate. *Accreditation:* ACBSP. Part-time and evening/weekend programs available. Postbaccalaureate distance learning degree programs offered (no on-campus study). *Faculty:* 45 full-time, 75 part-time/adjunct. *Students:* 427 full-time (184 women), 774 part-time (428 women). Average age 32. In 2006, 682 master's, 1 doctorate awarded. Terminal master's awarded for partial completion of doctoral program. *Degree requirements:* For master's, one foreign language, thesis or alternative, comprehensive exam (for some programs); for doctorate, one foreign language, thesis/dissertation, comprehensive exam. *Entrance requirements:* For master's, minimum GPA of 2.5; for doctorate, GMAT. Additional exam requirements/recommendations for international students: Required—TOEFL (minimum score 500 paper-based). *Application deadline:* Applications are processed on a rolling basis. Application fee: $25. Electronic applications accepted. *Financial support:* Career-related internships or fieldwork, Federal Work-Study, institutionally sponsored loans, tuition waivers (partial), and unspecified assistantships available. Support available to part-time students. Financial award applicants required to submit FAFSA. *Unit head:* Dr. Martin Bradley, Dean, 603-644-3102, Fax: 603-644-3144, E-mail: m.bradley@snhu.edu. *Application contact:* Scott Durand, Director of Graduate Enrollment Services, 603-644-3102 Ext. 3338, Fax: 603-644-3144, E-mail: s.durand@snhu.edu.

See Close-Up on page 325.

State University of New York College at Old Westbury, Program in Accounting, Old Westbury, NY 11568-0210. Offers accounting (MS); taxation and finance (MS). Part-time and evening/weekend programs available. *Faculty:* 7 full-time (2 women), 2 part-time/adjunct (0 women). *Students:* 22 full-time (9 women), 17 part-time (12 women); includes 7 minority (3 African Americans, 3 Asian Americans or Pacific Islanders, 1 Hispanic American), 2 international. Average age 33. 37 applicants, 35% accepted, 10 enrolled. In 2006, 9 degrees awarded. *Entrance requirements:* For master's, GMAT, 2 letters of recommendation. Additional exam requirements/recommendations for international students: Required—TOEFL (minimum score 550 paper-based; 213 computer-based). *Application deadline:* For fall admission, 6/15 priority date for domestic students; for spring admission, 11/15 priority date for domestic students. Applications are processed on a rolling basis. Application fee: $50. Electronic applications accepted. *Expenses:* Tuition, state resident: full-time $6,900; part-time $288 per credit. Tuition, nonresident: full-time $10,920; part-time $455 per credit. Required fees: $491; $56 per credit. Part-time tuition and fees vary according to course load. *Faculty research:* Corporate governance, asset pricing, corporate finance, hedge funds, net-for-front accounting. *Unit head:* Dr. James M. Fornaro, Director of Graduate Business Programs, 516-876-2883, E-mail:

Taxation

State University of New York College at Old Westbury (continued)
fornaroj@oldwestbury.edu. *Application contact:* Philip D'Angelo, Graduate Admissions Office, 516-876-3073, E-mail: enroll@oldwestbury.edu.

See Close-Up on page 457.

Suffolk University, Sawyer Business School, Department of Accounting, Boston, MA 02108-2770. Offers accounting (MSA, GDPA); taxation (MST); GDPA/MST; MBA/GDPA; MBA/MSA; MBA/MST. *Accreditation:* AACSB. Part-time and evening/weekend programs available. *Faculty:* 17 full-time (4 women), 7 part-time/adjunct (6 women). *Students:* 39 full-time (28 women), 187 part-time (95 women); includes 27 minority (11 African Americans, 15 Asian Americans or Pacific Islanders, 1 Hispanic American), 45 international. Average age 30. 129 applicants, 84% accepted, 68 enrolled. In 2006, 46 master's, 3 other advanced degrees awarded. *Entrance requirements:* For master's, GMAT. Additional exam requirements/recommendations for international students: Required—TOEFL (minimum score 550 paper-based; 213 computer-based; 80 iBT). *Application deadline:* For fall admission, 6/15 priority date for domestic students, 6/15 for international students; for spring admission, 11/1 priority date for domestic students, 11/1 for international students. Applications are processed on a rolling basis. Application fee: $50. Electronic applications accepted. *Expenses:* Contact institution. *Financial support:* In 2006–07, 73 fellowships with full and partial tuition reimbursements (averaging $15,118 per year) were awarded; career-related internships or fieldwork, Federal Work-Study, and institutionally sponsored loans also available. Support available to part-time students. Financial award application deadline: 4/1; financial award applicants required to submit CSS PROFILE. *Faculty research:* Tax policy, tax research, decision making in accounting, accounting information systems, capital markets and strategic planning. *Unit head:* Dr. Morris McInnes, Chair, 617-573-8339, Fax: 617-573-8345, E-mail: mmcinnes@suffolk.edu. *Application contact:* Judith Reynolds, Director of Graduate Admissions, 617-573-8302, Fax: 617-523-0116, E-mail: grad.admission@suffolk.edu.

Temple University, James E. Beasley School of Law, Philadelphia, PA 19122. Offers law (JD); taxation (LL M); transnational law (LL M); trial advocacy (LL M); JD/LL M; JD/MBA. *Accreditation:* ABA. Part-time and evening/weekend programs available. *Degree requirements:* For first-professional, 87 credits, completion of professional responsibility course and two writing courses. *Entrance requirements:* LSAT. Electronic applications accepted. Expenses: Contact institution. Tuition and fees vary according to program. *Faculty research:* Public health law/AIDS, religious rights, sexual harassment, children's rights, products liability.

Université de Sherbrooke, Faculty of Administration, Program in Taxation, Sherbrooke, QC J1K 2R1, Canada. Offers M Tax, Diploma.

University at Albany, State University of New York, School of Business, Department of Accounting, Albany, NY 12222-0001. Offers accounting (MS); taxation (MS). *Accreditation:* AACSB. *Students:* 75 full-time (41 women), 17 part-time (9 women). Average age 31. In 2006, 44 degrees awarded. *Degree requirements:* For master's, research project. *Entrance requirements:* For master's, GMAT. Additional exam requirements/recommendations for international students: Required—TOEFL (minimum score 550 paper-based; 213 computer-based). *Application deadline:* For fall admission, 3/1 priority date for domestic students, 4/1 for international students. Applications are processed on a rolling basis. Application fee: $75. Electronic applications accepted. *Expenses:* Tuition, state resident: full-time $6,900; part-time $288 per credit. Tuition, nonresident: full-time $10,920; part-time $455 per credit. Required fees: $1,139. *Financial support:* Application deadline: 4/1. *Faculty research:* Professional ethics, statistical analysis, cost management systems, accounting theory. *Unit head:* Saurva Dutta, Chair, 518-442-4978. *Application contact:* Michael DeRensis, Director, Graduate Admissions, 518-442-3980, Fax: 518-442-3922, E-mail: graduate@uamail.albany.edu.

The University of Akron, Graduate School, College of Business Administration, School of Accountancy, Program in Taxation, Akron, OH 44325. Offers MT. *Students:* 12 full-time (5 women), 28 part-time (13 women); includes 3 minority (1 Asian American or Pacific Islander, 2 Hispanic Americans). Average age 30. 17 applicants, 76% accepted, 13 enrolled. In 2006, 10 degrees awarded. *Entrance requirements:* For master's, GMAT, minimum GPA of 2.75. Additional exam requirements/recommendations for international students: Required—TOEFL (minimum score 550 paper-based; 213 computer-based; 79 iBT). *Application deadline:* For fall admission, 8/15 for domestic students. Applications are processed on a rolling basis. Application fee: $30 ($40 for international students). Electronic applications accepted. *Expenses:* Tuition, state resident: full-time $6,164; part-time $342 per credit. Tuition, nonresident: full-time $10,575; part-time $588 per credit. Required fees: $806; $43 per credit. $12 per term. Tuition and fees vary according to course load, degree level and program. *Unit head:* Alvin Lieberman, Coordinator, 330-972-6229. *Application contact:* Dr. James Divoky, Director of Graduate Business Programs, 330-972-7043, Fax: 330-972-6588, E-mail: jdivoky@uakron.edu.

The University of Alabama, Graduate School, Manderson Graduate School of Business, Culverhouse School of Accountancy, Tuscaloosa, AL 35487. Offers accounting (M Acc, PhD); tax accounting (MTA). *Accreditation:* AACSB. *Faculty:* 13 full-time (3 women). *Students:* 74 full-time (42 women), 4 part-time (2 women); includes 3 minority (1 African American, 2 Asian Americans or Pacific Islanders), 4 international. Average age 23. In 2006, 96 degrees awarded. *Degree requirements:* For doctorate, thesis/dissertation. *Entrance requirements:* For master's and doctorate, GMAT, minimum GPA of 3.0. Additional exam requirements/recommendations for international students: Required—TOEFL. *Application deadline:* Applications are processed on a rolling basis. Electronic applications accepted. *Financial support:* In 2006–07, 4 fellowships with tuition reimbursements (averaging $14,000 per year), 18 research assistantships with tuition reimbursements, 20 teaching assistantships with tuition reimbursements were awarded; career-related internships or fieldwork, Federal Work-Study, institutionally sponsored loans, scholarships/grants, health care benefits, and unspecified assistantships also available. Financial award application deadline: 3/31. *Faculty research:* Governmental and hospital pensions, artificial intelligence, corporate disclosure, auditing, taxation. *Unit head:* Dr. Mary S. Stone, Director, 205-348-2915, Fax: 205-348-8453, E-mail: mstone@cba.ua.edu. *Application contact:* Sandy D. Davidson, Advisor, 205-348-8997, Fax: 205-348-8453, E-mail: sdavidso@cba.ua.edu.

The University of Alabama, Graduate School, Manderson Graduate School of Business, Department of Management and Marketing, Program in Management, Tuscaloosa, AL 35487. Offers accounting (MA, PhD); applied statistics (PhD); economics (MA, PhD); finance (MS, PhD); management (MA, PhD); operations management (MS, PhD); statistics (MS); tax accounting (MA). *Faculty:* 27 full-time (8 women), 2 part-time/adjunct (0 women). *Students:* Average age 29. 112 applicants, 36% accepted. In 2006, 20 master's, 1 doctorate awarded. Terminal master's awarded for partial completion of doctoral program. *Median time to degree:* Master's–2.4 years part-time; doctorate–4 years full-time, 2 years part-time. Of those who began their doctoral program in fall 1998, 100% received their degree in 8 years or less. *Degree requirements:* For master's, thesis (for some programs), formal project paper, comprehensive exam (for some programs), registration; for doctorate, thesis/dissertation, comprehensive exam, registration. *Entrance requirements:* For master's and doctorate, GMAT or GRE, minimum GPA of 3.0. Additional exam requirements/recommendations for international students: Required—TOEFL. *Application deadline:* For fall admission, 6/30 priority date for domestic students, 1/31 for international students. Applications are processed on a rolling basis. Application fee: $25. *Financial support:* In 2006–07, 5 fellowships (averaging $2,000 per year), 2 research assistantships (averaging $2,000 per year), 2 teaching assistantships (averaging $2,000 per year) were awarded. *Faculty research:* Relationship marketing, team building, e-commerce strategy, entrepreneurship, health care management, service marketing.

University of Baltimore, Graduate School, Merrick School of Business, Program in Taxation, Baltimore, MD 21201-5779. Offers MS. Part-time and evening/weekend programs available. *Faculty:* 8 full-time (3 women), 7 part-time/adjunct (1 woman). *Students:* 1 full-time (0 women), 40 part-time (19 women); includes 10 minority (5 African Americans, 5 Asian Americans or Pacific Islanders), 1 international. Average age 33. 21 applicants, 81% accepted, 13 enrolled. In 2006, 18 degrees awarded. *Entrance requirements:* For master's, GMAT, minimum GPA of 3.0. Additional exam requirements/recommendations for international students: Required—TOEFL (minimum score 550 paper-based; 213 computer-based). *Application deadline:* For fall admission, 8/1 priority date for domestic students, 6/1 for international students; for spring admission, 12/1 for domestic students, 11/1 for international students. Applications are processed on a rolling basis. Application fee: $35. *Expenses:* Contact institution. *Financial support:* Fellowships, research assistantships, career-related internships or fieldwork and Federal Work-Study available. Support available to part-time students. Financial award application deadline: 4/1; financial award applicants required to submit FAFSA. *Faculty research:* Taxation of not-for-profit entities. *Unit head:* Dr. Fred Brown, Chair, 410-837-4532, E-mail: brown@ubalt.edu. *Application contact:* Ray Frederick, Graduate Advisor, 410-837-4944, E-mail: rfrederick@ubalt.edu.

University of Baltimore, School of Law, Baltimore, MD 21201. Offers law (JD); taxation (LL M); JD/LL M; JD/MBA; JD/MPA; JD/MS; JD/PhD. *Accreditation:* ABA. Part-time and evening/weekend programs available. *Faculty:* 60 full-time (23 women), 92 part-time/adjunct (24 women). *Students:* 726 full-time, 306 part-time; includes 181 minority (106 African Americans, 5 American Indian/Alaska Native, 50 Asian Americans or Pacific Islanders, 20 Hispanic Americans), 7 international. Average age 27. 2,896 applicants, 41% accepted, 382 enrolled. In 2006, 276 degrees awarded. *Entrance requirements:* LSAT. *Application deadline:* For fall admission, 3/1 priority date for domestic students. Applications are processed on a rolling basis. Application fee: $60. Electronic applications accepted. *Expenses:* Contact institution. *Financial support:* In 2006–07, 650 students received support, including 27 teaching assistantships; research assistantships, career-related internships or fieldwork, Federal Work-Study, institutionally sponsored loans, and scholarships/grants also available. Support available to part-time students. Financial award application deadline: 4/1; financial award applicants required to submit FAFSA. *Faculty research:* Plain view doctrine, statute of limitations, bankruptcy, family law, international and comparative law. *Unit head:* Phillip J. Closius, Dean, 410-837-4458. *Application contact:* Mark Bell, Assistant Director of Law Admissions, 410-837-4464, Fax: 410-837-4450, E-mail: kbell@ubalt.edu.

University of Central Florida, College of Business Administration, Kenneth G. Dixon School of Accounting, Program in Taxation, Orlando, FL 32816. Offers MST. Part-time and evening/weekend programs available. *Students:* 14 full-time (10 women), 23 part-time (14 women); includes 8 minority (1 African American, 5 Asian Americans or Pacific Islanders, 2 Hispanic Americans), 2 international. In 2006, 30 degrees awarded. *Degree requirements:* For master's, comprehensive exam. *Entrance requirements:* For master's, GMAT, minimum GPA of 3.0 in last 60 hours of course work. Additional exam requirements/recommendations for international students: Required—TOEFL. *Application deadline:* For fall admission, 2/1 priority date for domestic students; for spring admission, 11/1 priority date for domestic students. Application fee: $30. Electronic applications accepted. *Expenses:* Tuition, state resident: full-time $6,167; part-time $257 per credit hour. Tuition, nonresident: full-time $22,790; part-time $950 per credit hour. *Financial support:* In 2006–07, 1 fellowship with partial tuition reimbursement (averaging $5,000 per year), 3 research assistantships with partial tuition reimbursements (averaging $5,600 per year) were awarded; teaching assistantships with partial tuition reimbursements, career-related internships or fieldwork, Federal Work-Study, institutionally sponsored loans, tuition waivers (partial), and unspecified assistantships also available. Financial award application deadline: 3/1; financial award applicants required to submit FAFSA. *Application contact:* Dr. Linda Savage, Coordinator, 407-823-5561, E-mail: lsavage@bus.ucf.edu.

University of Cincinnati, Division of Research and Advanced Studies, College of Business, Department of Accounting, Program in Taxation, Cincinnati, OH 45221. Offers MS. Part-time and evening/weekend programs available. *Degree requirements:* For master's, thesis or alternative. *Entrance requirements:* For master's, GMAT, resumé, letters of recommendation. Additional exam requirements/recommendations for international students: Required—TOEFL (minimum score 600 paper-based; 250 computer-based). Application fee: $40. *Expenses:* Contact institution. *Financial support:* Research assistantships with full and partial tuition reimbursements, teaching assistantships with full and partial tuition reimbursements, scholarships/grants, tuition waivers (full and partial), and unspecified assistantships available. Financial award application deadline: 2/15; financial award applicants required to submit FAFSA. *Unit head:* Dr. Jens Stephen, Head, Department of Accounting, 513-556-7055.

University of Denver, College of Law, Taxation Program, Denver, CO 80208. Offers LL M, MT. Part-time and evening/weekend programs available. *Faculty:* 3 full-time (0 women). *Students:* 55 full-time (23 women), 58 part-time (37 women); includes 19 minority (5 African Americans, 1 American Indian/Alaska Native, 8 Asian Americans or Pacific Islanders, 5 Hispanic Americans), 5 international. Average age 33. 117 applicants, 100% accepted. In 2006, 104 degrees awarded. *Entrance requirements:* For master's, LSAT, JD from an ABA approved institution. *Application deadline:* Applications are processed on a rolling basis. Application fee: $30. *Expenses:* Contact institution. *Financial support:* Federal Work-Study, institutionally sponsored loans, scholarships/grants, and tuition waivers (full and partial) available. Support available to part-time students. Financial award application deadline: 6/1; financial award applicants required to submit FAFSA. *Unit head:* Dr. Mark Vogel, Director, 303-871-6239. *Application contact:* Information Contact, 303-871-6239, Fax: 303-571-6358, E-mail: gtp@du.edu.

University of Florida, Levin College of Law, Gainesville, FL 32611. Offers comparative law (LL M); international taxation (LL M); law (JD); taxation (LL M, SJD). *Accreditation:* ABA. *Faculty:* 61 full-time (31 women), 46 part-time/adjunct (11 women). *Students:* 1,364 full-time (636 women); includes 281 minority (82 African Americans, 3 American Indian/Alaska Native, 68 Asian Americans or Pacific Islanders, 128 Hispanic Americans), 51 international. Average age 25. 2,535 applicants, 41% accepted, 447 enrolled. In 2006, 310 first professional degrees awarded. *Median time to degree:* 3 years full-time. *Degree requirements:* For first-professional, thesis or alternative. *Entrance requirements:* LSAT. Additional exam requirements/recommendations for international students: Required—TOEFL. *Application deadline:* For fall admission, 1/15 for domestic and international students. Applications are processed on a rolling basis. Application fee: $30. Electronic applications accepted. *Expenses:* Contact institution. *Financial support:* In 2006–07, 241 students received support, including 4 fellowships (averaging $3,655 per year); Federal Work-Study, institutionally sponsored loans, and scholarships/grants also available. Financial award application deadline: 4/1; financial award applicants required to submit FAFSA. *Faculty research:* Environmental and land use law, taxation, family law, international law, constitutional law. *Unit head:* Robert Jerry, Dean, 352-273-0600, Fax: 352-392-8727, E-mail: jerryr@law.ufl.edu. *Application contact:* J. Michael Patrick, Assistant Dean for Admissions, 352-273-0890, Fax: 352-392-4087, E-mail: patrick@law.ufl.edu.

University of Hartford, Barney School of Business, Department of Accounting and Taxation, West Hartford, CT 06117-1599. Offers professional accounting (Certificate); taxation (MSAT). Part-time and evening/weekend programs available. *Faculty:* 8 full-time (5 women), 4 part-time/adjunct (0 women). *Students:* 16 full-time (9 women), 78 part-time (31 women); includes 9 minority (3 African Americans, 5 Asian Americans or Pacific Islanders, 1 Hispanic American), 5 international. Average age 35. 43 applicants, 70% accepted, 22 enrolled. In 2006, 52 degrees awarded. *Entrance requirements:* For master's, GMAT, 2 letters of recommendation, resumé. Additional exam requirements/recommendations for international students: Required—TOEFL (minimum score 550 paper-based; 213 computer-based). *Application deadline:* For fall admission, 7/1 for domestic students; for spring admission, 12/1 for domestic students. Applications are processed on a rolling basis. Application fee: $40 ($55 for international students). Electronic applications accepted. *Expenses:* Tuition: Part-time $515 per credit. Required fees: $200 per term. *Financial support:* In 2006–07, 6 research assistantships (averaging $5,145 per year) were awarded; career-related internships or fieldwork and unspecified assistantships also available. Financial award application deadline: 5/1. *Unit head:* Dr. Patricia Nodoushani, Chairman, 860-768-4346, Fax: 860-768-4398, E-mail: nodoushan@hartford.edu.

University of Hawaii at Manoa, Graduate Division, Shidler College of Business, Program in Accounting, Honolulu, HI 96822. Offers accounting (M Acc); accounting law (M Acc); information systems (M Acc); taxation (M Acc). Part-time programs available. *Faculty:* 10 full-time (3 women). *Students:* 38 full-time (21 women), 17 part-time (14 women); includes 14 minority (13 Asian Americans or Pacific Islanders, 1 Hispanic American), 5 international. Average age 32. 52 applicants, 60% accepted, 18 enrolled. In 2006, 38 degrees awarded. *Entrance requirements:* For master's, GMAT, bachelor's degree in accounting, minimum GPA of 3.0. Additional exam requirements/recommendations for international students: Required—TOEFL (minimum score 520 paper-based; 213 computer-based; 79 iBT). *Application deadline:* For fall admission, 5/1 for domestic students, 3/1 for international students; for spring admission, 9/1 for domestic and international students. Application fee: $50. *Financial support:* In 2006–07, 1 research assistantship (averaging $15,552 per year) was awarded; career-related internships or fieldwork, Federal Work-Study, and tuition waivers (full) also available. *Faculty research:* International accounting, current tax topics, insurance industry financial reporting, behavioral accounting, auditing. Total annual research expenditures: $15,000. *Application contact:* Jenny Teruya, Information Contact, 808-956-7118, Fax: 808-956-9888, E-mail: hamid@hawaii.edu.

University of Memphis, Graduate School, Fogelman College of Business and Economics, School of Accountancy, Memphis, TN 38152. Offers accounting (MS); accounting systems (MS); taxation (MS). *Accreditation:* AACSB. *Faculty:* 15 full-time (1 woman). *Students:* 25 full-time (15 women), 22 part-time (12 women); includes 13 minority (10 African Americans, 2 Asian Americans or Pacific Islanders, 1 Hispanic American), 12 international. Average age 29. 33 applicants, 79% accepted. In 2006, 16 degrees awarded. *Degree requirements:* For master's, comprehensive exam. *Entrance requirements:* For master's, GMAT. *Application deadline:* For fall admission, 8/1 for domestic students; for spring admission, 12/1 for domestic students. Application fee: $25 ($50 for international students). *Financial support:* In 2006–07, 11 students received support, including 5 research assistantships with full tuition reimbursements available (averaging $20,000 per year); teaching assistantships, scholarships/grants also available. Financial award application deadline: 3/1. *Faculty research:* Financial accounting, corporate governance, EDP auditing, evolution of system analysis, investor behavior and investment decisions. *Unit head:* Dr. Kenneth Lambert, Chair, 901-678-4569, Fax: 901-678-2685, E-mail: klambert@memphis.edu. *Application contact:* Dr. Coy A. Jones, Interim Associate Dean for Academic Programs, 901-678-4649, Fax: 901-678-4705, E-mail: fcbegp@memphis.edu.

University of Miami, Graduate School, School of Business Administration, Department of Accounting, Coral Gables, FL 33124. Offers professional accounting (MP Acc); taxation (MS Tax). *Accreditation:* AACSB. Part-time and evening/weekend programs available. *Faculty:* 9 full-time (3 women), 2 part-time/adjunct (0 women). *Students:* 26 full-time (18 women), 12 part-time (5 women); includes 12 minority (4 Asian Americans or Pacific Islanders, 8 Hispanic Americans), 4 international. Average age 24. 52 applicants, 62% accepted, 21 enrolled. In 2006, 35 degrees awarded. *Entrance requirements:* For master's, GMAT or CPA exam. Additional exam requirements/recommendations for international students: Required—TOEFL. *Application deadline:* For fall admission, 7/30 priority date for domestic students; for spring admission, 11/30 priority date for domestic students. Applications are processed on a rolling basis. Application fee: $50. Electronic applications accepted. *Financial support:* In 2006–07, 7 students received support, including 2 research assistantships (averaging $3,000 per year); fellowships, institutionally sponsored loans, scholarships/grants, and unspecified assistantships also available. Financial award application deadline: 3/1. *Faculty research:* Financial reporting, audit risk, public policy and taxation issues, government accounting and public choice, corporate governance. *Unit head:* Dr. Kay W. Tatum, Chairperson, 305-284-6903, Fax: 305-284-5737, E-mail: ktatum@miami.edu. *Application contact:* Willie Risby-Hannah, Administrative Assistant, 305-284-5428, Fax: 305-284-5737, E-mail: wrisby@miami.edu.

University of Minnesota, Twin Cities Campus, Carlson School of Management, Master's Program in Business Taxation, Minneapolis, MN 55455-0213. Offers MBT. Part-time and evening/weekend programs available. *Faculty:* 4 full-time (0 women), 19 part-time/adjunct (2 women). *Students:* 19 full-time (11 women), 87 part-time (35 women); includes 28 minority (1 African American, 25 Asian Americans or Pacific Islanders, 2 Hispanic Americans). Average age 32. 58 applicants, 86% accepted, 42 enrolled. In 2006, 36 degrees awarded. *Entrance requirements:* For master's, GMAT or LSAT. Additional exam requirements/recommendations for international students: Required—TOEFL (minimum score 550 paper-based; 213 computer-based). *Application deadline:* For fall admission, 6/15 priority date for domestic and international students; for spring admission, 10/15 priority date for domestic and international students. Applications are processed on a rolling basis. Application fee: $55 ($75 for international students). Electronic applications accepted. *Expenses:* Contact institution. Full-time tuition and fees vary according to class time, course load, program, reciprocity agreements and student level. *Financial support:* In 2006–07, 3 fellowships (averaging $4,000 per year), 2 teaching assistantships with partial tuition reimbursements (averaging $5,000 per year) were awarded; career-related internships or fieldwork and institutionally sponsored loans also available. Financial award application deadline: 4/1; financial award applicants required to submit FAFSA. *Faculty research:* Partnership taxation, tax theory, corporate taxation. *Unit head:* Dr. Frederick R. Jacobs, Director, 612-624-7584, Fax: 612-626-7795, E-mail: fjacobs@csom.umn.edu. *Application contact:* JoAnn Ash, Administrator, 612-624-3320, Fax: 612-626-7795, E-mail: jash@csom.umn.edu.

University of Mississippi, Graduate School, School of Accountancy, Oxford, University, MS 38677. Offers accountancy (M Acc, PhD); taxation accounting (M Tax). *Accreditation:* AACSB. *Faculty:* 11 full-time (4 women), 1 part-time/adjunct (0 women). *Students:* 76 full-time (34 women), 25 part-time (13 women); includes 9 minority (7 African Americans, 1 American Indian/Alaska Native, 1 Asian American or Pacific Islander), 6 international. 116 applicants, 78% accepted, 72 enrolled. In 2006, 62 master's, 3 doctorates awarded. *Degree requirements:* For doctorate, thesis/dissertation. *Entrance requirements:* For master's, GMAT, minimum GPA of 3.0; for doctorate, GMAT. Additional exam requirements/recommendations for international students: Required—TOEFL. *Application deadline:* For fall admission, 4/1 for domestic students; for spring admission, 10/1 for domestic students. Applications are processed on a rolling basis. Application fee: $25. *Expenses:* Tuition, state resident: full-time $4,602; part-time $256 per credit hour. Tuition, nonresident: full-time $10,566; part-time $587 per credit hour. *Financial support:* Scholarships/grants available. Financial award application deadline: 3/1; financial award applicants required to submit FAFSA. *Unit head:* Dr. Mark Wilder, Interim Dean, 662-915-7468, Fax: 662-915-7483, E-mail: acwilder@olemiss.edu.

University of Missouri–Kansas City, School of Law, Kansas City, MO 64110-2499. Offers law (JD, LL M), including general (LL M), taxation (LL M); JD/LL M; JD/MBA; LL M/MPA. *Accreditation:* ABA. Part-time programs available. *Faculty:* 34 full-time (13 women). *Students:* 496 full-time (214 women), 41 part-time (20 women); includes 45 minority (15 African Americans, 3 American Indian/Alaska Native, 17 Asian Americans or Pacific Islanders, 10 Hispanic Americans), 6 international. Average age 27. 1,327 applicants, 40% accepted, 216 enrolled. In 2006, 156 JDs, 22 master's awarded. *Degree requirements:* For master's, thesis (general). *Entrance requirements:* For JD, LSAT; for master's, LSAT, minimum GPA of 3.0 (general), 2.7 (taxation). Additional exam requirements/recommendations for international students: Required—TOEFL. *Application deadline:* For fall admission, 4/1 priority date for domestic students. Applications are processed on a rolling basis. Application fee: $50. Electronic applications accepted. *Expenses:* Contact institution. *Financial support:* In 2006–07, 162 students received support, including 1 research assistantship (averaging $54,667 per year), 38 teaching assistantships with partial tuition reimbursements available (averaging $2,587 per year); fellowships with partial tuition reimbursements available, career-related internships or fieldwork, Federal Work-Study, institutionally sponsored loans, scholarships/grants, and tuition waivers (full and partial) also available. Support available to part-time students. *Faculty research:* Family and children's issues, litigation, estate planning, urban law, business, tax entrepreneurial law. *Unit head:* Ellen Y. Suni, Dean, 816-235-1677, Fax: 816-235-5276, E-mail: sunie@umkc.edu. *Application contact:* Debbie Brooks, Director of Admissions, 816-325-1644, Fax: 816-235-5276, E-mail: brooksdv@umkc.edu.

University of New Haven, Graduate School, School of Business, Program in Accounting, West Haven, CT 06516-1916. Offers financial accounting (MS); managerial accounting (MS); taxation (MS). *Degree requirements:* For master's, thesis.

University of New Haven, Graduate School, School of Business, Program in Taxation, West Haven, CT 06516-1916. Offers corporate taxation (MS); public taxation (MS). Part-time and evening/weekend programs available. *Degree requirements:* For master's, thesis or alternative.

University of New Mexico, Robert O. Anderson Graduate School of Management, Program in Accounting, Albuquerque, NM 87131-2039. Offers accounting (M Acc, MBA); tax accounting (MBA). *Accreditation:* AACSB. Part-time and evening/weekend programs available. *Entrance requirements:* For master's, GMAT. Additional exam requirements/recommendations for international students: Required—TOEFL (minimum score 550 paper-based; 213 computer-based). *Faculty research:* Critical accounting, accounting pedagogy, theory, taxation.

University of New Orleans, Graduate School, College of Business Administration, Department of Accounting, Program in Taxation, New Orleans, LA 70148. Offers MS. Part-time and evening/weekend programs available. *Students:* 16 (8 women). Average age 31. In 2006, 23 degrees awarded. *Degree requirements:* For master's, thesis optional. *Entrance requirements:* For master's, GMAT. Additional exam requirements/recommendations for international students: Required—TOEFL (minimum score 550 paper-based; 213 computer-based). *Application deadline:* For fall admission, 7/1 priority date for domestic students, 6/1 for international students; for spring admission, 11/15 priority date for domestic students, 10/1 for international students. Applications are processed on a rolling basis. Application fee: $40. Electronic applications accepted. *Financial support:* Research assistantships, Federal Work-Study available. Financial award application deadline: 5/15; financial award applicants required to submit FAFSA. *Application contact:* Dr. Gordon Hosch, Graduate Coordinator, 504-280-6438, Fax: 504-280-5430, E-mail: gahosch@uno.edu.

The University of North Carolina at Greensboro, Graduate School, Bryan School of Business and Economics, Department of Accounting, Greensboro, NC 27412-5001. Offers accounting (MS); accounting systems (MS); financial accounting and reporting (MS); financial analysis (PMC); tax concentration (MS). *Accreditation:* AACSB. *Faculty:* 12 full-time (2 women). *Students:* 86 full-time (46 women), 16 part-time (8 women); includes 34 minority (17 African Americans, 1 American Indian/Alaska Native, 16 Asian Americans or Pacific Islanders). 50 applicants, 22% accepted. *Entrance requirements:* For master's, GMAT, GRE General Test, previous course work in accounting and business. Additional exam requirements/recommendations for international students: Required—TOEFL. *Application deadline:* For fall admission, 7/1 priority date for domestic students; for spring admission, 11/1 for domestic students. Applications are processed on a rolling basis. Application fee: $45. Electronic applications accepted. *Expenses:* Tuition, state resident: full-time $2,692. Tuition, nonresident: full-time $13,742. *Financial support:* In 2006–07, 17 students received support; fellowships with full tuition reimbursements available, research assistantships with full tuition reimbursements available, career-related internships or fieldwork, Federal Work-Study, scholarships/grants, and traineeships available. Support available to part-time students. *Unit head:* Dr. Edward Arrington, Head, 336-334-5647, Fax: 336-334-4706, E-mail: cearring@uncg.edu. *Application contact:* Michelle Harkleroad, Director of Graduate Admissions, 336-334-4884, Fax: 336-334-4424, E-mail: mbharkle@uncg.edu.

University of San Diego, School of Business Administration, San Diego, CA 92110-2492. Offers accounting and financial management (MS); business administration (MBA); executive leadership (MSEL); global leadership (MSGL); international business administration (IMBA); real estate (MSRE); supply chain management (MS, Certificate); taxation (MS); JD/IMBA; JD/MBA; MBA/MSIT; MBA/MSN; MBA/MSRE. *Accreditation:* AACSB. Part-time and evening/weekend programs available. *Faculty:* 35 full-time (10 women), 18 part-time/adjunct (4 women). *Students:* 187 full-time (76 women), 265 part-time (89 women); includes 55 minority (5 African Americans, 1 American Indian/Alaska Native, 32 Asian Americans or Pacific Islanders, 17 Hispanic Americans), 45 international. Average age 32. 517 applicants, 66% accepted, 187 enrolled. In 2006, 256 degrees awarded. *Entrance requirements:* For master's, GMAT, minimum GPA of 3.0, minimum 2 years of full-time work experience. Additional exam requirements/recommendations for international students: Required—TOEFL (minimum score 580 paper-based; 237 computer-based), TWE. *Application deadline:* For fall admission, 5/1 priority date for domestic students; for spring admission, 11/15 priority date for domestic students. Applications are processed on a rolling basis. Application fee: $45. Electronic applications accepted. *Financial support:* Career-related internships or fieldwork, Federal Work-Study, institutionally sponsored loans, scholarships/grants, tuition waivers (partial), and unspecified assistantships available. Support available to part-time students. Financial award application deadline: 5/1; financial award applicants required to submit FAFSA. *Faculty research:* Business management, production, purchasing, quantitative methods, accounting. *Unit head:* Dr. Andy Allen, Interim Dean, 619-260-4886, E-mail: sbadean@sandiego.edu. *Application contact:* Stephen Pultz, Director of Admissions, 619-260-4524, Fax: 619-260-4158, E-mail: grads@sandiego.edu.

University of San Diego, School of Law, San Diego, CA 92110. Offers business and corporate law (LL M); comparative law (LL M); general studies (LL M); international law (LL M); law (JD); taxation (LL M, Diploma); JD/IMBA; JD/MA; JD/MBA. *Accreditation:* ABA. Part-time and evening/weekend programs available. *Faculty:* 53 full-time (20 women), 44 part-time/adjunct (9 women). *Students:* 796 full-time (363 women), 333 part-time (151 women); includes 324 minority (34 African Americans, 11 American Indian/Alaska Native, 165 Asian Americans or Pacific Islanders, 114 Hispanic Americans), 21 international. Average age 27. 4,818 applicants, 31% accepted, 342 enrolled. In 2006, 313 JDs, 59 master's awarded. *Entrance requirements:* For JD, LSAT; for master's, JD, LLB or equivalent from an ABA-accredited law school. Additional exam requirements/recommendations for international students: Required—TOEFL. *Application deadline:* For fall admission, 2/1 priority date for domestic students. Applications are processed on a rolling basis. Application fee: $50. Electronic applications accepted. *Expenses:* Contact institution. *Financial support:* In 2006–07, 60 research assistantships were awarded; career-related internships or fieldwork, Federal Work-Study, institutionally sponsored loans, and scholarships/grants also available. Support available to part-time students. Financial award application deadline: 3/1; financial award applicants required to submit FAFSA. *Unit head:* Kevin Cole, Dean, 619-260-2330, Fax: 619-260-2218. *Application contact:* Carl J. Eging, Director of Admissions and Financial Aid, 619-260-4528, Fax: 619-260-2218, E-mail: eging@sandiego.edu.

University of Southern California, Graduate School, Marshall School of Business, Leventhal School of Accounting, Program in Business Taxation, Los Angeles, CA 90089. Offers MBT, JD/MBT. *Students:* 42 full-time (21 women), 57 part-time (39 women); includes 49 minority (2 African Americans, 42 Asian Americans or Pacific Islanders, 5 Hispanic Americans), 14 international. In 2006, 44 degrees awarded. *Entrance requirements:* For master's, GMAT. *Application deadline:* For fall admission, 12/1 priority date for domestic students. Application fee: $85. *Expenses:* Tuition: Full-time $33,314; part-time $1,121 per credit. Required fees: $522. Full-time tuition and fees vary according to program. *Financial support:* In 2006–07, research assistantships (averaging $18,500 per year), teaching assistantships (averaging $18,500 per year) were awarded; fellowships, Federal Work-Study, institutionally sponsored loans, and scholarships/grants also available. Support available to part-time students. Financial award application deadline: 2/15; financial award applicants required to submit FAFSA. *Unit head:* Shirley Maxey, Director, 213-740-4839, E-mail: acc100@marshall.usc.edu.

The University of Texas at Arlington, Graduate School, College of Business Administration, Department of Accounting, Arlington, TX 76019. Offers accounting (MP Acc, MS); taxation (MS). Part-time and evening/weekend programs available. *Faculty:* 12 full-time (2 women). *Students:* 83 full-time (52 women), 120 part-time (59 women); includes 49 minority (8 African Americans, 23 Asian Americans or Pacific Islanders, 18 Hispanic Americans), 43 international. 124 applicants, 87% accepted, 74 enrolled. In 2006, 48 degrees awarded. *Degree requirements:* For master's, thesis optional. *Entrance requirements:* For master's, GMAT. Additional exam requirements/recommendations for international students: Required—TOEFL (minimum score 550 paper-based; 213 computer-based). *Application deadline:* For fall admission, 6/15 for domestic students. Applications are processed on a rolling basis. Application fee: $35 ($50 for

Taxation

The University of Texas at Arlington (continued)

international students). *Expenses:* Tuition, state resident: full-time $5,528. Tuition, nonresident: full-time $10,478. International tuition: $10,608 full-time. *Financial support:* In 2006–07, 2 fellowships (averaging $1,000 per year), 10 teaching assistantships (averaging $10,000 per year) were awarded; research assistantships, career-related internships or fieldwork, scholarships/grants, and unspecified assistantships also available. Financial award application deadline: 6/1; financial award applicants required to submit FAFSA. *Unit head:* Dr. Larry Walther, Chair, 817-272-3481, Fax: 817-282-5793, E-mail: walther@uta.edu. *Application contact:* Carly S. Andrews, Graduate Advisor, 817-272-3047, Fax: 817-272-5793, E-mail: graduate.accounting.advisor@uta.edu.

The University of Texas at San Antonio, College of Business, Department of Accounting, San Antonio, TX 78249-0617. Offers accounting (MS, PhD); management accounting (MBA); taxation (MBA, MT). *Accreditation:* AACSB. Part-time and evening/weekend programs available. *Faculty:* 9 full-time (2 women), 4 part-time/adjunct (1 woman). *Students:* 34 full-time (21 women), 78 part-time (46 women); includes 33 minority (4 Asian Americans or Pacific Islanders, 29 Hispanic Americans), 12 international. Average age 29. 57 applicants, 68% accepted, 36 enrolled. In 2006, 34 degrees awarded. *Degree requirements:* For master's, thesis optional. *Entrance requirements:* For master's, GMAT. Additional exam requirements/recommendations for international students: Required—TOEFL (minimum score 500 paper-based; 173 computer-based). *Application deadline:* For fall admission, 7/1 for domestic students, 4/1 for international students; for spring admission, 11/1 for domestic students, 9/1 for international students. Application fee: $45 ($80 for international students). *Expenses:* Tuition, state resident: full-time $1,730; part-time $192 per credit hour. Tuition, nonresident: full-time $6,680; part-time $742 per credit hour. Required fees: $733; $308,359 per credit hour. *Financial support:* In 2006–07, 2 research assistantships (averaging $20,800 per year), 6 teaching assistantships (averaging $15,600 per year) were awarded; career-related internships or fieldwork, Federal Work-Study, scholarships/grants, and unspecified assistantships also available. Support available to part-time students. Total annual research expenditures: $192,833. *Unit head:* Dr. James E. Groff, Interim Chair, 210-458-5239, Fax: 210-458-4322, E-mail: james.groff@utsa.edu.

University of the Sacred Heart, Graduate Programs, Department of Business Administration, Program in Taxation, San Juan, PR 00914-0383. Offers MBA. Part-time and evening/weekend programs available. *Degree requirements:* For master's, thesis. *Entrance requirements:* For master's, EXADEP, minimum undergraduate GPA of 2.75, interview.

University of Tulsa, Graduate School, College of Business Administration, Online Program in Taxation, Tulsa, OK 74104-3189. Offers M Tax. Part-time and evening/weekend programs available. Postbaccalaureate distance learning degree programs offered (no on-campus study). *Faculty:* 4 full-time (2 women), 1 part-time/adjunct (0 women). *Students:* 1 (woman) full-time, 48 part-time (23 women); includes 4 minority (2 African Americans, 1 American Indian/Alaska Native, 1 Hispanic American). Average age 38. 16 applicants, 69% accepted, 8 enrolled. In 2006, 18 degrees awarded. *Median time to degree:* Master's–2.5 years full-time. *Entrance requirements:* For master's, GMAT or LSAT. Additional exam requirements/recommendations for international students: Required—TOEFL (minimum score 575 paper-based; 231 computer-based), IELTS (minimum score 7). *Application deadline:* Applications are processed on a rolling basis. Application fee: $40. Electronic applications accepted. *Expenses:* Tuition: Full-time $13,338; part-time $741 per credit hour. *Financial support:* Research assistantships, teaching assistantships with partial tuition reimbursements, career-related internships or fieldwork, Federal Work-Study, institutionally sponsored loans, scholarships/grants, tuition waivers (full and partial), and unspecified assistantships available. Support available to part-time students. Financial award application deadline: 2/1; financial award applicants required to submit FAFSA. *Unit head:* Markham Collins, Associate Dean, 918-631-2783, Fax: 918-631-2142, E-mail: markham-collins@utulsa.edu. *Application contact:* Markham Collins, Associate Dean, 918-631-2783, Fax: 918-631-2142, E-mail: markham-collins@utulsa.edu.

University of Washington, Graduate School, Business School, Seattle, WA 98195-3200. Offers auditing and assurance (MP Acc); business (PhD); evening part-time (MBA); executive (MBA); full time (MBA); global (MBA); global executive (MBA); taxation (MP Acc); technology management (MBA); JD/MBA; MBA/MAIS; MBA/MHA. *Accreditation:* AACSB. Part-time and evening/weekend programs available. *Degree requirements:* For master's, registration; for doctorate, thesis/dissertation, comprehensive exam, registration. *Entrance requirements:* For master's, GMAT; for doctorate, GMAT, GRE. Additional exam requirements/recommendations for international students: Required—TOEFL (minimum score 600 paper-based; 250 computer-based). Electronic applications accepted. Expenses: Contact institution.

University of Washington, School of Law, Seattle, WA 98195-3020. Offers Asian law (LL M, PhD); intellectual property law and policy (LL M); law (JD); law of sustainable international development (LL M); taxation (LL M); JD/LL M; JD/MA; JD/MAIS; JD/MBA; JD/MPA; JD/MS; JD/PhD. *Accreditation:* ABA. *Degree requirements:* For master's and doctorate, thesis/dissertation. *Entrance requirements:* For JD, LSAT; for master's, language proficiency (LL M in Asian law). Additional exam requirements/recommendations for international students: Required—TOEFL. Expenses: Contact institution. *Faculty research:* Asian, international and comparative law, intellectual property law, health law, environmental law, taxation.

University of Waterloo, Graduate Studies, Faculty of Arts, School of Accountancy, Waterloo, ON N2L 3G1, Canada. Offers accounting (M Acc, PhD); finance (M Acc); taxation (M Tax). *Faculty:* 29 full-time (8 women), 3 part-time/adjunct (1 woman). *Students:* 100. 199 applicants, 24% accepted, 29 enrolled. In 2006, 133 master's, 1 doctorate awarded. *Degree requirements:* For master's, thesis or alternative; for doctorate, thesis/dissertation. *Entrance requirements:* For master's, honors degree, minimum B average, resumé; for doctorate, GMAT, master's degree, minimum A- average, resumé. Additional exam requirements/recommendations for international students: Required—TOEFL, TWE. *Application deadline:* For fall admission, 1/31 for domestic students. Application fee: $75 Canadian dollars. *Expenses:* Contact institution. *Faculty research:* Auditing, management accounting. *Unit head:* Dr. Alister Mason, Director, 519-888-4567 Ext. 33732, Fax: 519-888-7262, E-mail: amason@uwaterloo.ca. *Application contact:* Dr. Alan Macnaughton, Graduate Officer, 519-888-4567 Ext. 35776, Fax: 519-888-7562.

Villanova University, School of Law and Villanova School of Business, Tax Program, Villanova, PA 19085-1699. Offers LL M, JD/LL M. Part-time and evening/weekend programs available. *Faculty:* 5 full-time (2 women), 28 part-time/adjunct (4 women). *Students:* 21 full-time (11 women), 57 part-time (17 women); includes 6 minority (1 African American, 1 American Indian/Alaska Native, 3 Asian Americans or Pacific Islanders, 1 Hispanic American), 3 international. Average age 29. 60 applicants, 62% accepted, 19 enrolled. In 2006, 32 degrees awarded. *Entrance requirements:* For master's, JD (LL M). *Application deadline:* Applications are processed on a rolling basis. Application fee: $25. *Expenses:* Contact institution. *Financial support:* Research assistantships, career-related internships or fieldwork, Federal Work-Study, and unspecified assistantships available. Support available to part-time students. Financial award application deadline: 3/15; financial award applicants required to submit FAFSA. *Faculty research:* Taxation and estate planning, corporate tax planning, international taxation, state taxation. *Unit head:* Prof. Michael Mulroney, Director, Graduate Tax Program, 610-519-7043, Fax: 610-519-5362, E-mail: mulroney@law.villanova.edu. *Application contact:* Cindy R. Kesselman, Coordinator, 610-519-4533, Fax: 610-519-5362, E-mail: kesselman@law.villanova.edu.

Virginia Commonwealth University, Graduate School, School of Business, Program in Accounting, Richmond, VA 23284-9005. Offers accountancy (M Acc, MBA, MS, PhD); tax (MS). *Accreditation:* AACSB. *Faculty:* 12 full-time (3 women). *Students:* 23 full-time (8 women), 26 part-time (16 women); includes 12 minority (9 African Americans, 3 Asian Americans or Pacific Islanders), 10 international. 38 applicants, 89% accepted. In 2006, 2 master's, 3 doctorates awarded. *Degree requirements:* For doctorate, thesis/dissertation. *Entrance requirements:* For master's, GMAT; for doctorate, GMAT, relevant work experience. *Application deadline:* For fall admission, 7/15 for domestic students; for spring admission, 11/15 for domestic students. Applications are processed on a rolling basis. Application fee: $50. *Financial support:* Fellowships, research assistantships, teaching assistantships, Federal Work-Study, institutionally sponsored loans, and tuition waivers (full and partial) available. Financial award application deadline: 3/15. *Unit head:* Dr. Ruth W. Epps, Chair, 804-828-1608, Fax: 804-828-1719, E-mail: rwepps@vcu.edu. *Application contact:* Tracy Green, Graduate Program Director, 804-828-1741, Fax: 804-828-7174, E-mail: tsgreen@vcu.edu.

See Close-Up on page 463.

Virginia Commonwealth University, Graduate School, School of Business, Program in Taxation, Richmond, VA 23284-9005. Offers M Tax. *Students:* 2 full-time (1 woman), 13 part-time (11 women); includes 6 minority (4 African Americans, 2 Asian Americans or Pacific Islanders). In 2006, 3 degrees awarded. *Entrance requirements:* For master's, GMAT. *Application deadline:* For fall admission, 7/15 for domestic students; for spring admission, 11/15 for domestic students. Applications are processed on a rolling basis. Application fee: $50. *Financial support:* Fellowships, research assistantships, teaching assistantships, Federal Work-Study, institutionally sponsored loans, and tuition waivers (full and partial) available. Financial award application deadline: 3/15. *Unit head:* Wayne L. Edmunds, Coordinator, 804-828-7115. *Application contact:* Tracy Green, Graduate Program Director, 804-828-1741, Fax: 804-828-7174, E-mail: tsgreen@vcu.edu.

See Close-Up on page 465.

Walsh College of Accountancy and Business Administration, Graduate Programs, Program in Taxation, Troy, MI 48007-7006. Offers MST. Part-time and evening/weekend programs available. *Faculty:* 1 full-time (0 women), 19 part-time/adjunct (0 women). *Students:* 2 full-time (0 women), 130 part-time (69 women). Average age 35. 40 applicants, 93% accepted, 37 enrolled. In 2006, 39 degrees awarded. *Entrance requirements:* For master's, minimum GPA of 2.75, previous course work in individual income taxation and business. Additional exam requirements/recommendations for international students: Required—TOEFL. *Application deadline:* For fall admission, 8/24 priority date for domestic students; for winter admission, 1/1 priority date for domestic students; for spring admission, 4/1 priority date for domestic students. Applications are processed on a rolling basis. Application fee: $25. Electronic applications accepted. *Expenses:* Tuition: Part-time $435 per hour. Required fees: $119 per semester. One-time fee: $50. *Financial support:* Available to part-time students. Application deadline: 6/30. *Unit head:* Mark R. Solomon, Director, 248-823-1277, Fax: 248-689-0920, E-mail: msolomon@walshcollege.edu. *Application contact:* Karen Mahaffy, Director of Admissions and Academic Advising, 248-823-1610, Fax: 248-689-0938, E-mail: kmahaffy@walshcollege.edu.

Washington State University, Graduate School, College of Business, Department of Accounting and Business Law, Pullman, WA 99164. Offers accounting and information systems (M Acc); accounting and taxation (M Acc). *Accreditation:* AACSB. *Faculty:* 10 full-time (2 women). *Students:* 17 full-time (8 women), 2 part-time, 4 international. Average age 27. 63 applicants, 41% accepted, 10 enrolled. In 2006, 18 degrees awarded. *Degree requirements:* For master's, thesis (for some programs), oral exam, research paper, comprehensive exam (for some programs). *Entrance requirements:* For master's, GMAT, minimum GPA of 3.0, 3 letters of recommendation. Additional exam requirements/recommendations for international students: Required—TOEFL (minimum score 580 paper-based; 237 computer-based). *Application deadline:* For fall admission, 3/1 priority date for domestic students, 3/1 for international students; for spring admission, 7/1 for international students. Applications are processed on a rolling basis. Application fee: $50. Electronic applications accepted. *Expenses:* Tuition, state resident: full-time $7,066. Tuition, nonresident: full-time $17,204. *Financial support:* In 2006–07, 19 students received support, including 1 fellowship (averaging $5,500 per year), research assistantships (averaging $13,917 per year), 8 teaching assistantships with tuition reimbursements available (averaging $13,056 per year); Federal Work-Study, institutionally sponsored loans, tuition waivers (partial), and teaching associateships also available. Financial award application deadline: 3/1. *Faculty research:* Ethics, taxation, auditing. Total annual research expenditures: $11,753. *Unit head:* Dr. Robert R. Greenberg, Chair, 509-335-8541, Fax: 509-335-4275. *Application contact:* Graduate School Admissions, 800-GRADWSU, Fax: 509-335-1949, E-mail: gradsch@wsu.edu.

Wayne State University, School of Business Administration, Detroit, MI 48202. Offers accounting (MS); business administration (MBA, PhD); interdisciplinary studies (PhD); taxation (MS); JD/MBA. *Accreditation:* AACSB. Part-time and evening/weekend programs available. *Faculty:* 64 full-time (11 women), 5 part-time/adjunct (1 woman). *Students:* 218 full-time (92 women), 1,021 part-time (446 women); includes 313 minority (179 African Americans, 2 American Indian/Alaska Native, 111 Asian Americans or Pacific Islanders, 21 Hispanic Americans), 153 international. Average age 30. 526 applicants, 73% accepted, 276 enrolled. In 2006, 386 degrees awarded. *Degree requirements:* For master's, thesis optional. *Entrance requirements:* For master's, GMAT. Additional exam requirements/recommendations for international students: Required—TOEFL (minimum score 550 paper-based; 213 computer-based); Recommended—TWE (minimum score 6). *Application deadline:* For fall admission, 8/1 for domestic students, 6/1 for international students; for winter admission, 10/1 for international students; for spring admission, 4/1 for domestic students, 2/1 for international students. Applications are processed on a rolling basis. Application fee: $30 ($50 for international students). Electronic applications accepted. *Financial support:* In 2006–07, 10 research assistantships (averaging $13,222 per year) were awarded; career-related internships or fieldwork, Federal Work-Study, and scholarships/grants also available. Support available to part-time students. Financial award applicants required to submit FAFSA. *Faculty research:* Corporate financial valuation, strategic advertising, information technology effectiveness, financial accounting and taxation, organizational performance and effectiveness. Total annual research expenditures: $188,100. *Unit head:* Dr. Richard Gabrys, Dean, 313-577-4501, Fax: 313-577-4557, E-mail: az4994@wayne.edu. *Application contact:* Linda Zaddach, Assistant Dean, 313-577-4510, E-mail: l.s.zaddach@wayne.edu.

See Close-Up on page 373.

Widener University, School of Business Administration, Program in Taxation, Chester, PA 19013-5792. Offers MS. Part-time and evening/weekend programs available. *Entrance requirements:* For master's, Certified Public Accountant Exam or GMAT. Electronic applications accepted. *Faculty research:* Financial planning, taxation fraud.

William Howard Taft University, Graduate Programs, Bernard E. Witkin School of Law, Santa Ana, CA 92704. Offers American jurisprudence (LL M); law (JD); taxation (LL M).

William Howard Taft University, Graduate Programs, W. Edwards Deming School of Business, Santa Ana, CA 92704. Offers taxation (MS).

BERNARD M. BARUCH COLLEGE
OF THE CITY UNIVERSITY OF NEW YORK

Zicklin School of Business
Stan Ross Department of Accountancy
Master of Science in Taxation

Program of Study

The Master of Science (M.S.) in Taxation Program provides concentrated training in taxation. The program's goals are to prepare graduates for responsible positions in the area of taxation and, ultimately, for leadership in the marketplace. To accomplish these goals, the program combines advanced technical and research skills with the business and management fundamentals necessary for students to operate effectively as tax professionals and industry leaders. The program also provides the necessary background for students to interpret new developments and remain in the vanguard of the profession. The program satisfies the 150-hour CPA licensing requirement for eligible students.

The program is presented in a cohort style. Participants benefit by going through the program with a group of individuals who share practical business experience and bring their experience to bear on the development of theory. A more flexible program format is available as well. The M.S. in Taxation Program can be completed on a full- or part-time basis. Both formats involve taking courses in a carefully designed sequence, beginning in the fall semester, but students can customize their schedule in consultation with a faculty adviser. All of the courses for the degree program are scheduled in the evening.

The program requires 30 credit hours: 18 credit hours are required courses and 12 are electives, which are chosen from nine available 2- and 3-credit courses. Full-time students complete the program in one year, including two 4-week summer sessions. The full-time schedule involves taking 12 credits per semester and one 3-credit course in each of the summer sessions. Part-time students complete the program in two years, including one 4-week summer session each year. The part-time schedule consists of 6 credit hours per semester and one 3-credit course in the summer. All full- and part-time students must take TAX 9900 in their last summer session, which is a capstone course that requires a paper/project.

Research Facilities

One of Zicklin's greatest advantages is its modern, technologically advanced learning environment. With access to Baruch's new "vertical campus," state-of-the-art library and technology center, and one-of-a-kind simulated trading floor, Zicklin students have unmatched educational resources that enable them to compete successfully for leading positions in business and industry. The William and Anita Newman Library is one of the most technologically advanced facilities in New York. In addition to books and periodicals, the library maintains local area networks that provide access to information resources in CD-ROM format and to several hundred online databases through the Dow Jones News/Retrieval, LexisNexis, and Dialog services. Baruch College students and faculty and staff members also have access to the 4.5 million volumes in the CUNY library system and to the collections of the world-famous New York Public Library. The Baruch Computing and Technology Center provides more than 500 computer workstations with Web access and multimedia capability. Baruch's 800,000-square-foot Vertical Campus building features 102 classrooms, fourteen research labs, and thirty-six computer labs that are all fully equipped with state-of-the-art instructional technology.

Through its Center for Financial Integrity, which is located in the Stan Ross Department of Accountancy in the Zicklin School of Business, the College sponsors events exploring changes needed in corporate financial reporting and accounting standards, the repercussions for corporate audit committees, changes in the oversight of auditing firms, and the efficacy of class-action litigation. For many years, the accounting department has been host to the Critical Perspectives on Accounting Conference, which provides a forum for exploring critical research on emerging issues in accounting and auditing, bringing together interested faculty members, professionals, policy makers, accounting students, and others concerned with professional and regulatory issues in the corporate, university, government, and financial sectors.

Financial Aid

Merit-based graduate assistantships are awarded to qualified full-time master's students. The assistantships carry an annual stipend of $5000 and are renewable for one year; they do not include a tuition waiver. Financial aid also is available through a variety of state, federal, and College programs. International students are eligible to apply for graduate assistantships and College work-study.

Cost of Study

M.S. tuition for state residents in fall 2007 was $3200 per semester for full-time and $270 per credit for part-time study. For out-of-state residents and international students, tuition was $500 per credit.

Living and Housing Costs

Baruch College does not offer student housing at this time; students must provide for their own room and board. A single student should anticipate spending approximately $16,900 per year for housing, food, utilities, books, transportation, entertainment, and incidental expenses.

Student Group

Baruch College attracts students from New York, neighboring states, and abroad. In the traditional M.B.A. and M.S. programs, the Zicklin School enrolls approximately 600 full-time students, about half of whom are international students representing thirty-seven countries worldwide.

Location

Baruch College occupies five buildings in the Gramercy Park area of Manhattan, the heart of one of the world's most dynamic cultural and financial centers.

The College and The School

Baruch College has evolved from the innovative School of Business and Civic Administration, which was established in 1919 by the trustees of the City College of New York. The first master's degree program in business administration was offered by the School in 1920. The Zicklin School of Business is the largest collegiate school of business in the nation and one of the most academically prestigious. The Zicklin School has a full range of business degree programs that are nationally accredited and is one of a handful of business schools to be fully accredited in both business and accounting programs through the Ph.D. Zicklin is situated in the heart of Manhattan, the center of global business. The Stan Ross Department of Accountancy is one of the premier departments of the Zicklin School. The activities of the Department and its faculty members have a major impact on the business and financial communities and on the practice of accounting and taxation. Department sponsors include Ernst & Young, the Foundation for Accounting Practitioners, the Institute of Internal Auditors, M. R. Weiser and Company, and Richard A. Eisner and Company.

Applying

Although each application is considered individually, successful applicants must possess a baccalaureate degree from an accredited college and should have a GPA indicating achievement as well as impressive GMAT scores. Admission is for the fall only. Application forms and supporting documents may be downloaded from the Web site, or students can apply online. The application deadline is April 30 for international applicants and May 31 for domestic applicants. Further details are available on the School's Web site.

Correspondence and Information

Graduate Admissions
Zicklin School of Business
Baruch College
One Bernard Baruch Way, Box H-0820
New York, New York 10010-5518

Phone: 646-312-1300
Fax: 646-312-1301
E-mail: zicklingradadmissions@baruch.cuny.edu
Web site: http://www.zicklin.baruch.cuny.edu

Bernard M. Baruch College of the City University of New York

THE FACULTY AND THEIR RESEARCH

The faculty of the Zicklin School of Business is large, distinguished, and diverse. It includes noted scholars, authors, sought-after consultants, and master teachers who hold advanced degrees from such prestigious institutions as Harvard, MIT, Columbia, Stanford, Northwestern, Chicago, New York University, Cornell, Berkeley, Yale, Dartmouth, Michigan, UCLA, Indiana, Texas, Oxford, Princeton, Caltech, Duke, Georgetown, and other world-class universities.

Through their important work, the Zicklin School provides ideas and solutions for a rapidly changing global business environment. Among the many faculty members who are internationally recognized authorities in their fields are:

June O'Neill, Wollman Professor of Economics and Director of the Center for the Study of Business and Government at Baruch College. Served as the director of the U.S. Congressional Budget Office from 1995 to 1999.

Robert A. Schwartz, University Distinguished Professor of Economics and Finance. Expert in securities markets, microstructure, and the electronic call auction.

S. Prakash Sethi, University Distinguished Professor of Management. Consultant for Mattel Inc.; helped the company establish a worldwide code of conduct and monitoring plan.

Yoshihiro Tsurumi. Scholar in the fields of industrial policy, international transfer of technology, and global business and a leading consultant to many government and multinational firms and the International Monetary Fund.

Many faculty members are regularly called upon for expert commentary by such media outlets as the *Wall Street Journal*, the *Washington Post, Crain's New York Business, USA Today,* CNBC, and CNN.

THE CORE FACULTY

Masako N. Darrough, Professor and Chair of the Stan Ross Department of Accountancy; Ph.D. (economics), British Columbia, 1975. Dr. Darrough's areas of expertise lie in the strategic use of information within the firm and the capital markets. Her research has appeared in top-tier journals, including *Journal of Accounting Research, Journal of Business, International Public Management Journal, Journal of Political Economy, Journal of Accounting Research,* and *Accounting Review.*

Steven V. Melnik, Assistant Professor of Accountancy and Director of Taxation Program; B.B.A. (accounting), CUNY, Baruch, 1993; J.D., New York Law, 1999; LL.M. (taxation), NYU, 2000. Money laundering, tax evasion, audits of publicly held companies. Professor Melnik's professional career consisted of working as a Manager in the Regulatory Compliance Consulting and Audit Practices of Andersen, the Market Surveillance Department of the New York Stock Exchange, and the Controller's Group of Merrill Lynch. He researches and writes in areas of money laundering and tax evasion. He is editorial adviser to the *Journal of Accountancy* and *The Practicing CPA.* Melnik is a member of the Accounting Subgroup of the United States Treasury Department Bank Secrecy Act Advisory Group, the American Institute of CPAs (AICPA), and the American Bar Association. steven_melnik@baruch.cuny.edu

Hyman Gorenberg, Professor of Accountancy; J.D., Brooklyn Law; LL.M. (taxation), NYU; CPA. Professor Gorenberg has been on the faculty of Baruch College for more than forty years. A CPA and a member of the New York Bar Association, he is the author of numerous training manuals that are used by the American Institute of CPAs and has lectured nationally and internationally for the AICPA for many years.

CLEMSON UNIVERSITY

Master of Professional Accountancy

Program of Study

The School of Accountancy and Legal Studies at Clemson University offers the Master of Professional Accountancy (M.P.Acc.) degree. The program is designed to prepare the student for a career in professional accounting. Most graduates take a position in public accounting upon graduation. There are two areas of concentration: assurance and management services and taxation. The M.P.Acc. Program is a one-year program for full-time students. Some students complete the program on a part-time basis. The program consists of 33 hours (15 hours in the core and 18 hours in one of the two areas of concentration) and a self-study class, the professional exam review class. The professional exam review class is designed to prepare students for their upcoming CPA, CMA, or CIA professional exam.

Research Facilities

M.P.Acc. students in the taxation concentration have full access to two tax research databases: Commerce Clearing House's Tax Research Network and the Research Institute of America's Checkpoint. M.P.Acc. students in the assurance and management services concentration have full access to the Financial Accounting Research System.

Financial Aid

The School of Accountancy and Legal Studies currently offers eight graduate assistantships. Each assistantship pays the student $10 per hour for 10 hours of work a week providing grading and research assistance to professors. In addition, each assistantship provides for tuition and fee reduction. The school also offers two fellowships. The financial award for each fellowship varies, but it has been as much as $2800 for a full-time student's one year in the M.P.Acc. Program.

Cost of Study

Tuition for 2007–08 is $3641 per semester for in-state students and $7285 per semester for nonresidents. Off-campus rates are $330 per hour for in-state students and $660 per hour for nonresidents. Graduate assistants pay a flat fee of $950 per semester and $315 per summer session. Graduate fellows pay South Carolina resident fees.

Living and Housing Costs

On-campus housing is available; for more information, prospective students should visit http://www.housing.clemson.edu. The cost of living in Clemson is quite low compared to the national average. Students who choose to live off campus typically spend $300–$400 per month for rent, depending on location, amenities, and roommates.

Student Group

The program has approximately 30 students. Fifty percent of students are women. Eighty-four percent of students attend on a full-time basis, and 9 percent are international students.

Student Outcomes

Eighty percent of M.P.Acc. Program graduates accept positions with international, regional, and local public accounting firms. Other graduates take professional accounting positions in industry or education.

Location

Clemson is a small, beautiful college town near the Blue Ridge Mountains and Lake Hartwell in upstate South Carolina. The Upstate is one of the country's fastest-growing areas and is an important part of the I-85 corridor, a multistate area along Interstate 85 that runs from metro Atlanta to Richmond, Virginia, and encompasses Charlotte, North Carolina, and North Carolina's Research Triangle. Atlanta and Charlotte are each a 2-hour drive away. Many financial institutions and other industries have national headquarters in the Upstate, including Wachovia, Bank of America, BMW, Bon Secours St. Francis Health System, Bosch North America, Bowater, Charter Communications, Ernst & Young, Fluor Corporation, IBM, Microsoft, Michelin of North America, and many others.

The University

Clemson is classified by the Carnegie Foundation as an RU/H: Research University (high research activity), a category comprising just 10 percent of all graduate degree–granting universities in America. The University's mission is to fulfill the covenant between its founder and the people of South Carolina to establish a "high seminary of learning" through its responsibilities of teaching, research, and extended public service. The University has identified eight areas of academic emphasis that create collaborations that, in turn, help fulfill the University's mission.

Applying

Students must provide acceptable GPA and GMAT scores to enter the M.P.Acc. Program. Applicants may apply on the Web at http://www.grad.clemson.edu/p_apply.html. Applications with a $50 nonrefundable fee should be received no later than five weeks prior to registration. Every required item in support of the application must be on file by that date. Students are advised to contact the department for the deadlines of the program of proposed study.

Correspondence and Information

Dr. Thomas L. Dickens, M.P.Acc. Coordinator
301-B Sirrine Hall
Clemson University
Clemson, South Carolina 29634-1303
Phone: 864-656-4890
Fax: 864-656-48925
E-mail: dickent@clemson.edu
Web site: http://business.clemson.edu/Account/advising/aadvise.html

Clemson University

THE FACULTY AND THEIR RESEARCH

L. Stephen Cash, Professor; J.D., Tennessee. Law.
Thomas L. Dickens, Alumni Professor; Ph.D., Texas A&M. Accounting.
Roger K. Doost, Professor; D.P.A., Georgia. Accounting.
Richard B. Dull, Assistant Professor; Ph.D., Virginia Tech. Accounting information systems.
Frances L. Edwards, Associate Professor; J.D., Kansas. Law.
Daryl M. Guffey, Associate Professor; Ph.D., South Carolina. Business administration–accounting.
Frances A. Kennedy, Assistant Professor; Ph.D., North Texas. Accounting.
Jeffrey J. McMillan, Professor; Ph.D., South Carolina. Accounting.
Megan E. Mowrey, Assistant Professor; Ph.D., Iowa. Industrial relations and human resources.
Lisa A. Owens, Assistant Professor; Ph.D., Oklahoma State. Accounting.
Lydia Lancaster Folger Schleifer, Associate Professor; Ph.D., Georgia. Accounting.
Ralph E. Welton Jr., Academic Program Director; Ph.D., LSU. Accounting.
Alan J. Winters, Professor; Ph.D., Texas Tech. Accounting.

LEHIGH UNIVERSITY

College of Business and Economics
Master's in Accounting and Information Analysis

Program of Study

Dramatic changes in the way of conducting business in the twenty-first century produce unprecedented challenges in the preparation of future business leaders. As businesses decisively react to these new sets of demands in the workplace, a critical component of success is the need for reliable financial assessment of organizations and systems to enable proper decision making. The Master of Science in Accounting and Information Analysis (M.S.A.I.A.) program at Lehigh University develops the necessary decision-making skills by focusing on business solutions. Students learn how to use both information and technology to improve business processes and forge business solutions. In addition, the program provides the course work that accountants need, irrespective of their ultimate career objectives.

Focal points include understanding the business framework, exposure to business subjects in complementary areas, advanced communication skills, strategic use of technology, specialized accounting knowledge, consulting skills, advanced technical information systems, leadership, and globalization. Students may choose either a general degree that emphasizes assurance services or a degree with a concentration in a specialized area. Concentrations include consulting and business risk management, financial services, and strategic cost management.

An important and unique aspect of this program is partnering with professional firms. Public accounting firms, consulting organizations, and corporate partners lend their expertise by partnering with faculty members to teach the six core courses. These organizations also provide internships.

The Master of Science in Accounting and Information Analysis degree program accommodates all students with undergraduate degrees. Background courses available in a convenient link program provide the requisite accounting knowledge of nonaccounting majors.

This one-year, full-time, 30-hour degree program also fulfills the 150-hour CPA educational requirement that has been adopted by most states.

Research Facilities

The Rauch Business Center is a modern, professional environment for learning and teaching, including forty well-equipped classrooms, computer labs, auditoriums, and conference rooms. A new state-of-the-art wireless Financial Services Laboratory opened in fall 2004. This twenty-seven-seat classroom is designed to simulate a Wall Street trading environment. Along with books and journals, Lehigh's library system includes electronic databases and microfilm, computer software, and media collections. Via the campuswide integrated voice and data communication network, users can access the Internet, the libraries' online catalog, and hundreds of national and international electronic databases and can submit reference inquires, place orders, request media services, and request delivery of documents electronically. The campus network provides access to mainframe computers, the Integrated Library System, and other computers on campus. The Computing Center houses several mainframes and maintains hundreds of microcomputers in sites across the campus.

Financial Aid

Financial aid for graduate students is based on academic performance. Students interested in financial aid must file a complete application and be admitted to the College of Business and Economics M.S.A.I.A. program for the upcoming academic year. Financial aid is dispersed through graduate and research assistantships (which cover tuition and pay a stipend) for the academic year. Domestic students receive priority for financial aid.

The primary loan source for graduate students is the Federal Stafford Student Loan. Students must file the Free Application for Federal Student Aid (FAFSA), an institutional application, and their most recent 1040. Students may complete the FAFSA at http://www.fafsa.ed.gov.

Cost of Study

Tuition for the 2007–08 academic year for the M.S.A.I.A. program is $630 per credit hour. Full-time students are assessed a $150 technology fee each semester. Online courses also require a $100 technology fee.

Living and Housing Costs

Information on graduate student housing is available through the Department of Residential Services at 610-758-3500. On-campus housing costs range from $470 per month to $625 per month. Off-campus listings are also available through residential services. Students should budget approximately $33,000 per year in tuition and living expenses.

Student Group

There are currently 24 students in the M.S.A.I.A. program, 7 of whom are international students. A number of students hail from top colleges in the U.S. and abroad, including Lehigh University.

Location

Lehigh University, founded in 1865, consists of three distinctive, continuous areas, totaling more than 1,600 acres. Located 90 miles southwest of New York City and 50 miles north of Philadelphia, the Lehigh Valley is Pennsylvania's fourth-largest metropolitan area. Bethlehem, one of three principal cities of the Lehigh Valley, is a center of industry, high technology, culture, and education.

The University and The Program

Lehigh is one of approximately forty key target schools for recruiters of accounting students. This achievement is owed in no small measure to Lehigh's excellent faculty members, who are well known in their profession for both textbooks and scholarly work. A strong faculty provides substantial assurance that students will be successful in their professional careers. Lehigh accounting students are known throughout the accounting profession for their intelligence, pride in achievement, and outstanding work ethic. Many have gone on to become partners in public accounting and top management in many other types of organizations.

Applying

Candidates must have completed an undergraduate program at an accredited U.S. college or university. International students must have sixteen years of formal education, including four years at the university level. A TOEFL score is required of all applicants for whom English is not the native language. The credentials evaluated by the faculty admission committee include the candidate's undergraduate background, GMAT scores, personal essay, and letters of recommendation.

Lehigh evaluates applications on a rolling basis and usually notifies applicants of admissions decisions within three weeks of receiving a completed application. Deadlines for regular students are July 15 for fall semester, December 1 for spring semester, April 30 for summer session I, and June 15 for summer session II. Associate students (those who have conditional status) may apply up to two weeks before classes begin in any semester or summer session. The deadline for financial aid is January 15 for the upcoming academic year.

Correspondence and Information

Corinn McBride
Director of Recruitment and Admissions
Graduate Programs Office
College of Business and Economics
Lehigh University
621 Taylor Street
Bethlehem, Pennsylvania 18015
Phone: 610-758-5280
Fax: 610-758-5283
E-mail: business@lehigh.edu
Web site: http://www.lehigh.edu/business

Dr. James A. Largay III
Director M.S. in Accounting and Information Analysis
Rauch Business Center
Lehigh University
621 Taylor Street
Bethlehem, PA 18015
Phone: 610-758-3409
E-mail: jal3@lehigh.edu
Web site: http://www.lehigh.edu/msaccounting

Lehigh University

THE FACULTY AND THEIR RESEARCH

M.S.A.I.A. Faculty

Karen Collins, Associate Professor of Accounting; M.B.A., Salisbury State, 1984; Ph.D., Virginia Tech, 1988; CPA. Teaching areas: financial accounting, financial accounting theory, introduction to business. Research areas: behavioral accounting, behavioral aspects of public practice.

Robert C. Giambatista, Assistant Professor of Management; Ph.D., Wisconsin–Madison, 1999. Teaching areas: management, organizational behavior, decision-making, conflict and negotiation, philosophy of science (doctoral seminar), executive (interpersonal) skills. Research areas: diversity, individual and group decision-making, leadership.

Paul Gordon, Professor of Practice; M.B.A., Wisconsin–Madison; CPA. Teaching area: financial accounting.

Parveen P. Gupta, Frank L. McGee Professor of Accounting; M.B.A., Connecticut, 1983; Ph.D., Penn State, 1987. Teaching areas: corporate financial reporting; cost management, total quality management. Research areas: control systems, corporate governance.

James A. Hall, Associate Professor of Accounting; Ph.D., Oklahoma State, 1979. Teaching areas: accounting information systems, information systems auditing. Research areas: IS auditing and controls, computer fraud.

Michael G. Kolchin, Professor of Management and Chair, Department of Management and Marketing; D.B.A., Indiana, 1980. Teaching areas: organizational behavior, human resource management, supply chain management. Research areas: performance measurement, supply chain effectiveness, participation.

James A. Largay III, Professor of Accounting; Ph.D., Cornell, 1971; CPA. Teaching areas: financial accounting and reporting, financial statement analysis. Research areas: cash flow reporting, accounting for financial instruments, consolidated financial statements.

Jack W. Paul, Professor of Accounting; M.B.A., Ph.D., Lehigh. Teaching areas: management accounting, financial accounting, auditing. Research areas: auditing, management accounting.

Kenneth P. Sinclair, Professor of Accounting and Chair, Department of Accounting; Ph.D., Massachusetts, 1972. Teaching areas: managerial accounting, essentials of accounting Research areas: performance evaluation, human resource accounting.

College of Business and Economics Faculty

Mark R. Adams, Professor of Practice, Business Minor Program; M.B.A., Pittsburgh; J.D., Baltimore; CFA, CPA. Accounting, corporate reporting, finance, capita evaluations and investments.

Anne-Marie Anderson, Assistant Professor of Finance; M.B.A., Tulsa, 1998; Ph.D., Arizona, 2003. Corporate restructuring, mergers and acquisitions, valuation.

J. Richard Aronson, William L. Clayton Professor of Business and Economics and Director, Martindale Center for the Study of Private Enterprise; Ph.D., Clark, 1964. Tax and expenditure analysis, pension funds, municipal bond analysis, fiscal federalism.

Richard W. Barsness, Professor Emeritus; Ph.D., Minnesota, 1963. International business, corporate strategy in the airline industry.

John W. Bonge, Professor Emeritus; Ph.D., Northwestern, 1968. Business strategy and entrepreneurship.

Paul R. Brown, Professor of Accounting and Dean, College of Business and Economics; Ph.D., Texas at Austin. Financial statement analysis, FASB/SEC policy analysis, international reporting and analysis, earnings measurement and management, managing earnings expectations.

Stephen G. Buell, Professor; Ph.D., Lehigh, 1977. High-yield bonds, corporate bankruptcy.

Franklin J. Carter, Assistant Professor of Marketing; Ph.D., Carnegie Mellon, 1997. Business-to-business marketing, sales force management, diffusion of innovation.

Ravi Chitturi, Assistant Professor of Marketing; M.B.A., 1996, Ph.D., 2003, Texas at Austin. Technology and innovation, design and consumer emotions, brand value and marketing strategy.

Shin-Yi Chou, Assistant Professor of Economics; Ph.D., Duke, 1999. Health economics.

James A. Dearden, Professor; Ph.D., Penn State, 1987. Game theory, marketing science, institution design, microeconomics.

Mary E. Deily, Associate Professor; Ph.D., Harvard, 1985. Industrial organization, exit behavior, industries in transition.

Dale F. Falcinelli, Swartley Professor of Finance, Professor of Practice in Marketing and Management, and Chairman, vSeries Corporate Entrepreneurship; M.A., Lehigh, 1972. Contemporary marketing, business management policies, entrepreneurship, strategic business analysis.

James A. Greenleaf, Associate Professor; Ph.D., NYU, 1973. Portfolio management, derivative instruments, international investments, quantitative applications to investments.

Frank Gunter, Associate Professor; Ph.D., Johns Hopkins, 1985. Economies of Colombia, Iraq, China, and Latvia; capital flight; customs; unions.

Reetika Gupta, Assistant Professor of Marketing; Ph.D., CUNY, Baruch. Complexity in interactive consumption environments, consumer learning of new products.

Thomas J. Hyclak, Professor; Ph.D., Notre Dame, 1976. Labor market developments in transition economies, urban economic development.

Arthur E. King, Professor; Ph.D., Ohio State, 1976. Applied econometrics, comparative economics, economics of Central Europe.

Richard J. Kish, Professor; Ph.D., Florida, 1988. Fixed-income securities, efficient markets, international mergers.

Nevena T. Koukova, Assistant Professor of Marketing; Ph.D., Maryland, 2005. Pricing of digital products, bundling and unbundling of electronic content, and behavioral aspects of bundling; marketing strategy; consumer analysis; marketing research; principles of marketing; services marketing.

Robert Kuchta, Professor of Practice; M.S., NJIT, 1982. Marketing as a business.

James M. Maskulka, Associate Professor; D.B.A., Kent State, 1984. Marketing communications, branding, media.

Teresa McCarthy, Assistant Professor of Supply Chain Management; Ph.D., Tennessee, 2003. Role of marketing in demand management, demand planning and demand forecasting, market orientation and supply chain orientation, collaboration forecasting and sales force forecasting management, e-commerce demand management.

Judith A. McDonald, Associate Professor; Ph.D., Princeton, 1986. United States–Canada economic relations, external debt and tropical deforestation issues, pay equity, gender differences in starting salaries.

Matthew A. Melone, Associate Professor; J.D., Pennsylvania, 1993. Taxation, law and accounting, real estate law, partnership and LLC taxation.

Erin Moore, Assistant Professor of Accounting; Ph.D., Massachusetts, 2006; CPA. Earnings restatements, firm valuation.

Vincent G. Munley, Professor; Ph.D., SUNY at Binghamton, 1979. Political economy of state and local government finances.

David H. Myers, Professor of Practice; Ph.D., Washington (Seattle), 2001. Conditional performance measurement of mutual funds; pension funds, portfolio strategies, Japanese equity markets, international investing, stochastic programming applications for asset/liability management.

George A. Nation III, Professor; J.D., Villanova, 1983. Commercial lending law topics, environmental liability for lenders, promissory notes, guaranty and surety law, product liability.

Nandkumar Nayar, Professor and Hans Baer Chair in Finance; Ph.D., Iowa, 1988. Investment banking and financing methods, derivative securities, working capital management, tax issues, game theory modeling.

Anthony P. O'Brien, Professor; Ph.D., Berkeley, 1986. Business history, economic history, microeconomics.

Catherine A. Ridings, Assistant Professor; Ph.D., Drexel, 2000. Virtual communities, trust, e-commerce, management of technical personnel.

Heibatollah Sami, Eugene and Sue Mercy Professor of Accounting; Ph.D., Louisiana State, 1984. Impact of accounting information on capital markets, international accounting, auditing.

Michael D. Santoro, Associate Professor; Ph.D., Rutgers, 1998. Organizational strategy, entrepreneurship and intrapreneurship, sources of technological innovation, role of industry-university collaboration in advancing new technologies.

Theodore W. Schlie, Associate Professor; Ph.D., Northwestern, 1973. Advanced manufacturing and competitive strategy, globalization of industrial research and development, international competitiveness.

Susan A. Sherer, Kenan Professor of Information Technology Management, Business Information Systems Program Director, and Co-director for the Center for Value Chain Research; Ph.D., Pennsylvania, 1988. Software failure risk, management of software development, manufacturing networks, interorganizational information systems, strategic information systems, IT investment management.

K. Sivakumar, Arthur Tauck Professor of International Marketing and Logistics and Professor and Chairperson of Marketing; Ph.D., Syracuse, 1992. Pricing, international marketing, innovation management.

Quingjiu (Tom) Tao, Assistant Professor of Management; Ph.D., Pittsburgh, 2004. Strategic alliance in emerging market environments, institutions and firm behavior, first mover advantage in international market entry.

Larry W. Taylor, Professor; Ph.D., North Carolina, 1984. Specification testing for economic models, finite-sample issues in econometrics, econometric methodology, macroeconomic modeling, qualitative dependent variables.

Stephen F. Thode, Associate Professor and Director, Goodman Center for Real Estate Studies; D.B.A., Indiana, 1980. New mortgage products, mortgage pricing, affordable housing financing, taxation of real estate investments, real option pricing.

Robert J. Thornton, Charles W. MacFarlane Professor of Economics and Program Director; Ph.D., Illinois, 1970. Unionism and collective bargaining, public employment, labor market discrimination, forensic economics.

Robert J. Trent, Associate Professor and Program Director, Supply Chain Management Program; Ph.D., Michigan State, 1993. Cross-functional teams in purchasing.

Geraldo M. Vasconcellos, Allen DuBois Professor of Finance and Economics and Director, Business Minor Program; Ph.D., Illinois at Urbana-Champaign, 1986. Cross-border mergers and acquisitions foreign direct investment, international financial markets, privatizations, financial structure and development.

Todd A. Watkins, Associate Professor; Ph.D., Harvard, 1986. Technology and industrial policy, economics and management of innovation, defense and optoelectronics industries.

Samuel C. Weaver, Swartley Professor of Finance; Ph.D., Lehigh, 1985. Value-based management, performance metrics, capital evaluation, cost of capital, mergers and acquisitions.

Wenlong Weng, Assistant Professor; Ph.D., Stanford, 2001. Managerial economics, planning and decision making under uncertainty, real options, financial risk measurement and management.

Yuliang (Oliver) Yao, Assistant Professor of Business Information Systems; M.B.A., Rensselaer, 1997; Ph.D., Maryland, 2002. Supply chain management, electronic commerce, technology issues in supply chains, logistics modeling/simulation.

SAINT JOSEPH'S UNIVERSITY

Master of Science in Financial Services

Program of Study

Saint Joseph's University's Master of Science in Financial Services (M.S.F.S.)—the first of its kind in the Philadelphia area—provides professionals with the tools, theory, practice, and knowledge they need in the financial services industry. The students take courses from a variety of disciplines, including accounting, law, and ethics, and they gain additional knowledge in finance through course offerings in personal financial planning, actuarial studies, security analysis, mergers and acquisitions, and estate planning.

The goal of the program is to provide the educational background for graduates to successfully engage in professional financial planning services and financial analysis. It also provides interested students with the academic background to sit for professional certification exams in financial services. Six courses in the M.S.F.S. program satisfy the education requirement of the CFP® certification examination and have been registered as such by the CFP Board. Saint Joseph's University does not certify individuals to use the CERTIFIED FINANCIAL PLANNER™ and CFP® certification marks. CFP certification is granted only by Certified Financial Planner Board of Standards, Inc. to those persons who, in addition to completing an educational requirement such as this CFP Board Registered Program, have met its ethics, experience, and examination requirements. The curriculum is rich enough to also meet the needs of students pursuing careers in financial analysis and corporate finance. Saint Joseph's University recently established a tailor-made Wall Street trading room where students can experience firsthand exposure to financial concepts such as portfolio construction, risk management, and financial engineering. This facility—the newest technological addition to Mandeville Hall and the first of its kind in the Philadelphia region—is just another example of how real-time experiential learning is incorporated into the classroom.

The room's electronic ticker displays ongoing, real-time market activity and stock prices, while a tricolor board provides students with current financial information and graphics. The trading room at Saint Joseph's, designed by Trans-Lux Corporation, gives students the opportunity to apply and practice financial analysis and risk-management skills before entering the high-technology business arena. Students use both current and historical information in the classroom, which is the same information used by portfolio managers in their day-to-day business.

When graduates of Saint Joseph's University become practitioners, they can immediately use their experiences from the campus trading room in their professional careers. This technology ensures an effortless transition between the academic world and the professional world.

Research Facilities

Saint Joseph's University opened its newest building, Mandeville Hall, in 1998. This technologically advanced $25-million building is a three-story, 89,000-square-foot facility that houses the Erivan K. Haub School of Business, the Center for Food Marketing Research, and the Academy of Food Marketing. Included in the building are new classrooms, a lecture hall, seminar rooms, research facilities, computer labs, a 180-seat teletorium equipped for teleconferencing (with a translation booth for international presentations), faculty and administrative offices, and informational gathering spaces. Many of the teaching areas are highly innovative in concept and are equipped with interactive communication multimedia technology, which greatly enhances pedagogical possibilities.

One of the most innovative concepts consists of a suite of classrooms that includes two moot board rooms, a preparation seminar room, a video room, and meeting break-out rooms. These rooms are modeled after the moot court concept in law schools. They accommodate the teachings of real-world situations through dramatizations and analysis of interactive business negotiations. They are equipped with stepped, semicircular seating that surrounds a board room table. Video cameras are available to record sessions for later replay or for simultaneous projection to the teletorium or off-site locations around the globe.

The Francis A. Drexel Library contains a business collection of approximately 350,000 bound volumes, 1,400 periodical subscriptions, 840,500 microforms, more than 2,750 videos, and Fortune 500 annual reports. The business print collection also contains nearly half of the Harvard Core, a list of more than 3,500 books recommended by the Harvard Business School, and it serves as a selective depository for U.S. government documents. The library has an online public access catalog for searching its holdings and the holdings of other university libraries. The catalog is accessible from remote locations via the University's academic computer. There are 100 computer terminals available to Saint Joseph's students, and many online services are available to M.B.A. students. The Instructional Media Center (IMC) at Saint Joseph's University offers students assistance with presentation materials. The IMC has nearly 1,200 videotapes, which can be viewed in the IMC or signed out if needed as part of a presentation.

Services at the Career Development Center include individual career counseling, job search advising, access to alumni contact lists, and the career resource library, which contains occupational information, employer literature and directories, and current employment listings. Workshops are offered on resume writing, interviewing, and job search techniques. Graduating students can also participate in on-campus recruiting. In addition, job search assistance is available in the form of a resume referral program.

Financial Aid

Through guaranteed loan agreements with lending institutions and state agencies such as the Pennsylvania Higher Education Assistance Agency (PHEAA) and the New Jersey Department of Higher Education, students can secure long-term loans at a low-interest rate. The University initiates an electronic loan application and forwards it to its guarantor, the PHEAA. Federal Stafford Student Loans can be subsidized or unsubsidized. A student may borrow up to $18,500 per academic year. All full- or half-time students (at least 6 credits per semester) are eligible to apply for federal aid. Students may elect to finance part of their tuition through a deferred-payment program offered by the University.

Cost of Study

Tuition and fees for the 2007–08 academic year are $765 per credit hour.

Living and Housing Costs

Saint Joseph's University is located in the suburbs of Philadelphia, only 15 minutes from Center City. Off-campus apartments are available within walking distance of both the campus and the local train station.

Student Group

The M.S. degree in financial services has been in place since the fall of 2001. The program has attracted students from some of the areas top accounting and financial services firms. A majority of the students enrolled in this program hold an undergraduate degree in business or a related field, but it is not required. Students range from those who have just completed their undergraduate course work and seek an advanced degree in order to get an edge over the competition to those with several years of work experience in the field of financial services. Even students who have completed an M.B.A. come back to supplement that degree with a master's degree in financial services. Approximately 40 percent of the students entering this program have already earned a CFP®, CPA, CFA, or a master's degree.

Location

The University is located in eastern Pennsylvania in the suburbs of Philadelphia, only 15 minutes from downtown. An off-campus site at Ursinus College in Collegeville, Pennsylvania, is available for Saint Joseph's M.B.A. students residing or employed in the northern part of the greater Delaware Valley.

The University

Founded by the Society of Jesus in 1851, Saint Joseph's University advances the professional and personal ambitions of men and women by providing a demanding, yet supportive, educational experience. One of only 142 schools with a Phi Beta Kappa chapter and AACSB International business school accreditation, Saint Joseph's is home to 3,900 full-time undergraduates and 3,400 graduate, part-time, and doctoral students. Steeped in the 450-year Jesuit tradition of scholarship and service, the University strives to be recognized as the preeminent comprehensive Catholic university in the Northeast. Saint Joseph's Erivan K. Haub School of Business is the Philadelphia areas only college or university to appear in the top twenty of *U.S. News & World Report's* 2004 edition of *America's Best Graduate Schools* for part-time M.B.A. programs.

Applying

Applications are accepted on a rolling admission basis. Students applying to the Master of Science in Financial Services must have a baccalaureate degree from an accredited college or university. Applicants must submit an application, the application fee, official transcripts, an official GMAT score (waived for those with CFP®, CFA, CPA, or prior master's degree), two letters of recommendation, a resume, and a personal statement. International students must also submit TOEFL scores (for those whose native language is not English) and an affidavit of support. International applicants are required to submit an official course-by-course credentials evaluation of their undergraduate work. Students are strongly advised to register with World Education Services (WES). Deadlines for international students are July 15 for the fall, November 15 for spring, April 1 for summer session I, and May 15 for summer session II.

Correspondence and Information

David M. Benglian
Director of Graduate Programs in Finance, Human Resources, and Decision and System Sciences
Erivan K. Haub School of Business
Saint Joseph's University
5600 City Avenue
Philadelphia, Pennsylvania 19131-1395
Phone: 610-660-1626
E-mail: david.benglian@sju.edu
Web site: http://www.sju.edu/hsb/fsp

Saint Joseph's University

THE FACULTY

Accounting
Waqar I. Ghani, Associate Professor; Ph.D.

Decision and System Sciences
Vipul K. Gupta, Associate Professor; Ph.D.

Finance
Christopher Coyne, Associate Professor; M.B.A., Ph.D.
Morris Danileson, Associate Professor; M.B.A.; Ph.D.
Rajneesh Sharma, Assistant Professor; M.B.A.; M.M.M
Ahmet Tezel, Associate Professor; M.B.A.; Ph.D.

Management
David Steingard, Assistant Professor; Ph.D.
C. Ken Weidner, Assistant Professor; M.B.A., Ph.D.

Additional Faculty
Dr. Paul Foster
Dr. Jean Heck

STATE UNIVERSITY OF NEW YORK COLLEGE AT OLD WESTBURY

Programs in Accounting and Taxation

Programs of Study

The traditional role of accountants has been drastically altered by the rapidly changing and increasingly complex business environment of today. The evolution of new technologies, increased regulatory demands, and pace of global business demand accountants who can provide traditional services along with added value through nontraditional services and an expanded perspective. The graduate programs offered by the School of Business at SUNY College at Old Westbury were developed to answer that demand. Through the expertise of its faculty and innovation of its curriculum, Old Westbury offers a Master of Science (M.S.) in accounting and an M.S. in taxation that prepare both accounting and nonaccounting professionals to advance in or begin a wide range of careers in accounting and business.

The M.S. program in accounting prepares its graduates to lead in a financial world that is constantly impacted by the need for skilled professionals in assurance services, consulting services, financial planning, and information systems; the evolution of information technology; and the globalization of markets. With an emphasis on both analytical and professional skill building, the M.S. in accounting is the program of choice for professionals seeking the specialized preparation required in American business today. The program employs a curriculum that incorporates issues critical to today's professional practice of accounting, including the impact of information technology and globalization of markets, and a portfolio of skills in assurance services, consulting services, financial planning, and information systems. The objective of the accounting program is to provide the analytical skills and knowledge needed for public accounting and other branches of the profession.

The accounting M.S. program is divided into two tracks: a 36-credit program for those who hold a degree in accounting and a 58-credit program for those with undergraduate degrees in areas other than accounting. Students in both tracks take courses from both an analytical core sequence of courses and a professional core.

The M.S. in taxation expands the portfolio of skills of its students beyond financial accounting, preparing them to meet the growing demand of private, public, not-for-profit, and government organizations for professionals with up-to-date knowledge of federal, state, and International taxation issues. With an emphasis on both analytical and technical skill building, the M.S. in taxation is designed to provide the specialized preparation required in contemporary business today. Like the accounting degree program, students take courses from both an analytical core sequence and a professional core. Courses in the analytical core include Accounting Information Systems, Advanced Auditing and Assurance Services, and Taxation for Corporate Managers. The Professional core consists of such courses as Tax Ethics, Practice, & Procedures, Estate and Gift Taxation, and Tax and Accounting Research.

For each M.S. degree program, the College provides a full curriculum in the evening to accommodate working professionals, and occasionally classes are offered on Saturdays. In addition, through the school's three-semester scheduling, students who qualify can complete the program within one calendar year.

The School of Business provides students with many opportunities to participate in its voluntary internship program. Those who qualify may be placed in area businesses to work and learn for credit, thus gaining on-site practical knowledge and experience that is beneficial for future employment.

Research Facilities

Located in the Campus Center, the SUNY Old Westbury Library provides access to print, electronic, and media resources. The library's holdings include approximately 212,000 volumes, 900 periodical titles, and 8,200 audiovisual items. A variety of study and reading spaces are available for about 800 patrons.

Financial Aid

Applicants interested in applying for federal, state, and/or local financial assistance (grants, loans, and scholarships) must contact the Office of Financial Aid at 516-876-3222 or 3223 or via e-mail at finaid@oldwestbury.edu for the specific year's financial aid packet. Students must complete all the required applications by the suggested deadline dates. More information can be found online.

Cost of Study

Full-time tuition (12 or more credits) for New York State residents was $3450 in the 2006–07 academic year, whereas out-of-state students paid $5460. Fees totaled $245.50 for all full-time students. Tuition for part-time students was $288 per credit for residents and $455 per credit for nonresidents. All part-time students paid fees based on the total number of credits taken.

Living and Housing Costs

On-campus housing is available for full-time students only. The cost was $4151.50 per semester in 2006–07.

Student Group

The strength of the College's academic offerings has attracted the interest of what has become one of the most diverse student populations in the nation. Currently, the combined undergraduate and graduate student population at the College at Old Westbury numbers approximately 3,450 (75 percent full-time and 25 percent part-time). Sixty percent of students are women; 25 percent, African American; 7 percent, Asian American; 30 percent, Caucasian; 16 percent, Hispanic American; 0.1 percent, Native American; and 2 percent, international. Through this diversity, the College prepares its graduates to serve the world through their character and leadership.

Student Outcomes

In recent results, Old Westbury graduates taking the CPA exam for the first time scored higher than students from every other Long Island college and university, passing all the sections they took. Graduates with accounting degrees competitively qualify for positions in public accounting, private accounting, government, and not-for-profit organizations.

Location

Located on the historic north shore of New York's Long Island, the SUNY College at Old Westbury features a 604-acre campus of spectacular wooded and open land located just 20 miles from the center of New York City.

The College

The only public four-year arts, science, and business campus in Nassau County, Long Island, the College at Old Westbury is a community dedicated to learning and leadership. The curriculum at the College at Old Westbury is carefully designed to enable students to compete in the global economy or to pursue further studies at the finest graduate and professional schools. Offering instruction to the multicultural body of students is an equally diverse, internationally acclaimed faculty that has the highest percentage of Distinguished Teaching and Service Professors in the SUNY system. Old Westbury students learn from instructors who include a Pulitzer Prize–winning journalist, Fulbright Scholars, a Guggenheim Fellow, a CASE New York State Professor of the Year, and recent recipients of awards and research grants from such prestigious organizations as the National Institute of General Medical Sciences, the U.S. Department of Education, and the National Science Foundation.

Applying

Students must submit an application form, which can be completed online; downloaded, printed, and mailed; or obtained by phone, fax, or mail through the Graduate Admissions Office. No matter how a student applies, all supporting documentation and the $50 application fee must be sent by mail to the appropriate address. All applicants must submit an official copy of transcripts from every institution of higher education ever attended, an official GMAT exam score not more than two years old, a typed personal statement, and the completed recommendation form with two letters of recommendation, one from a professor and the other from an employer or business associate. Students who have not attended school for more than five years may submit two employer/business associate letters. Those who have not been employed may use two professor recommendations. Official scores on the Test of English as a Foreign Language (TOEFL) are also required of all international applicants whose native language is not English.

The application for admission and all documents must be submitted by the appropriate deadline, which, for the fall semester, is June 15. Incomplete applications are not processed for admission. Completed applications received after the deadline are processed on a space-available basis.

Correspondence and Information

For more information, students should contact:
Graduate Business Program
School of Business
Campus Center, Suite H213
State University of New York College at Old Westbury
Old Westbury, New York 11568-0210
Phone: 516-876-3446
Web site: http://www.oldwestbury.edu/

All application materials should be mailed to:
Office of Enrollment Services
Campus Center, Room I-202
State University of New York College at Old Westbury
P.O. Box 307
Old Westbury, New York 11568-0210
Phone: 516-876-3073
E-mail: enroll@oldwestbury.edu

State University of New York College at Old Westbury

THE FACULTY

The accounting faculty members are experienced educators with extensive knowledge in their areas of specialization, including public accounting, private industry, government, and not-for-profit organizations. Given the small class sizes, the accounting faculty members, who are readily available outside of the classroom, are able to maintain close working relationships with students.

Patrick O'Sullivan, Provost and Vice President for Academic Affairs; Ph.D., Fordham.
N.J. Delener, Dean of the School of Business; Ph.D., CUNY; M.B.A., NYU.

Anthony Barbera, Interim Assistant Vice President for Academic Affairs; M.B.A., CUNY, Baruch; CPA.
John Biondo, Associate Professor; M.B.A., Hofstra; CPA, PFS.
Rita Buttermilch, Associate Professor; M.S., LIU; CPA.
Tim Coville, Assistant Professor; M.B.A., NYU; CPA.
Madeline Crocitto, Associate Professor; Ph.D., CUNY; M.B.A., CUNY, Baruch.
Thomas Del Giudice, Associate Professor; Ph.D., Massachusetts Amherst.
Alireza Ebrahimi, Associate Professor; Ph.D., Polytechnic.
James Fornaro, Director of Graduate Programs; D.P.S., Pace; M.B.A., Adelphi; CPA, CMA.
Annette Forti, Professor; Ph.D., Fordham; M.B.A., NYU.
Marita Herbold, Visiting Assistant Professor; M.B.A., LIU, C.W. Post; J.D., Touro; CPA.
Wei (Alan) Jiang, Assistant Professor; Ph.D., Rutgers.
Maureen Keefe, Instructor; M.B.A., Columbia.
Lawrence Krause, Associate Professor; Ph.D., Massachusetts Amherst.
Peter Lucido, Assistant Professor; L.L.M., NYU; J.D., Fordham.
Albert Murphy, Assistant Professor; Ph.D., CUNY.
Barbara Olsen, Associate Professor, Ph.D., New School.
Christina Schweikert, Visiting Instructor; Ph.D. candidate, CUNY; M.S., NYIT.
Zhihong Shi, Assistant Professor; Ph.D., M.B.A., CUNY, Baruch.
Sirousse Tabriztchi, Associate Professor and Chair of Business, Economics, and Finance; Ph.D., M.B.A., Columbia; CPA.
Lynn Walsh, Associate Professor and Chair of Management, Marketing, and Information Systems; Ph.D., NYU.
Kenneth Winkelman, Assistant Professor; L.L.M., NYU; J.D., Hofstra; CPA.

UNIVERSITY OF NEW HAMPSHIRE

Whittemore School of Business and Economics
Master of Science in Accounting Program

Program of Study

The Whittemore School of Business and Economics offers a program of study leading to a Master of Science (M.S.) degree in accounting. The program can be completed in one year on a full-time basis. The principal requirement for the M.S. degree is 30 semester hours of graduate course work: six required courses and four electives. Options also exist for students without an undergraduate degree in accounting. During the first year, students take prerequisite work, and the second year students take master's level courses.

The M.S. program is designed to address the concerns of the accounting profession within the parameters of the Whittemore School's educational philosophy. The program emphasizes analytical communication skills while preserving the basic core of technical accounting knowledge. Students awarded the M.S. degree are competitively equipped to compete in the job market for accounting professionals.

Research Facilities

The University of New Hampshire (UNH) library houses more than 1.1 million volumes, 6,500 periodical subscriptions, and 1 million government documents that form the core of print materials. Electronic sources include EBSCOhost, which provides indexes to general, academic, and business periodicals; LexisNexis, which accesses a wide variety of full-text news and legal information; and PubMed, which contains 9 million citations of medical materials. The library provides access to a wide variety of materials, from medieval manuscripts to electronic data sets, from nineteenth-century novels to Web-based full-text documents, and from bound periodicals to electronic journals. For more information, students should visit http://www.library.unh.edu.

Financial Aid

Applicants with strong academic records may qualify for financial aid. Tuition scholarships are available, as are federally funded loans for those who qualify.

Cost of Study

Yearly tuition for the program in 2006–07 was $8540 for New Hampshire students. Nonresident tuition was $20,990. Mandatory yearly fees were $1926.

Living and Housing Costs

Babcock House, the graduate residence hall, provided single rooms at a cost of $5162 for the 2006–07 academic year. Students may remain in Babcock during the summer at reduced rates. Limited on-campus housing for married students is provided at Forest Park. Prices for efficiency and one- or two-bedroom apartments ranged from $640 to $848 per month. Off-campus housing is available in a wide range of prices. Applicants should visit the UNH Housing Web site at http://www.unh.edu/housing for further information.

Student Group

The University has an enrollment of 13,544 students, 2,481 of whom are graduate students; many are international students. The graduate program in accounting typically enrolls 15 to 20 students.

Location

Located 60 miles north of Boston, the University of New Hampshire occupies a picturesque 170-acre campus in the attractive New England town of Durham. It is only 10 miles from the Atlantic Ocean and 50 miles from the scenic lakes and mountains for which the state is well known.

The University and The School

The University of New Hampshire was founded in 1866. It serves as a cultural and scientific center for the area, with the New England Center, Space Science Center, and Paul Arts Center. The Whittemore School of Business and Economics, established in 1962 and one of six schools and colleges of the University, offers undergraduate as well as graduate degrees.

Applying

The program begins in the fall semester. An applicant for admission must submit the following materials directly to the Graduate School, Room 109, Thompson Hall, University of New Hampshire, in Durham: the official Graduate School application forms for admission to graduate study; two official transcripts showing the grades earned in all of the applicant's previous graduate and undergraduate academic work; three letters of recommendation, on Whittemore School recommendation forms, from persons in a position to judge the applicant's preparation for and ability to undertake graduate study; GMAT scores; and, for international applicants, TOEFL scores.

Candidates for the M.S. program have generally completed prerequisite courses at an accredited school in each of the following areas: taxation, intermediate financial accounting I and II, business law, auditing, and advanced managerial accounting. Candidates who may be lacking a course are still encouraged to apply. The admissions committee has some flexibility to adjust schedules to allow for provisional admission for individuals who demonstrate academic promise.

The application deadline is July 1. The application deadline for international students is April 1.

Correspondence and Information

Director, Graduate and Executive Programs
Whittemore School of Business and Economics
116 McConnell Hall
University of New Hampshire
15 College Road
Durham, New Hampshire 03824-3593

Phone: 603-862-1367
Fax: 603-862-4468
E-mail: wsbe.grad@unh.edu
Web site: http://wsbe.unh.edu/grad

University of New Hampshire

THE FACULTY AND THEIR RESEARCH

Business Administration

Carole K. Barnett, Associate Professor of Management; Ph.D., Michigan. Organizational leadership and learning, change and transformation, design and development, culture.

Clayton Barrows, Professor of Hospitality Management; Ed.D., Massachusetts. Food and beverage management, private club management.

Steven Bolander, Professor and Dean, Decision Sciences; D.B.A., Kent State. Planning and scheduling systems for process industries.

Brian Bolton, Assistant Professor of Finance; Ph.D., Colorado. Corporate governance, capital structure, financial econometrics, investments.

Ludwig Bstieler, Assistant Professor of Marketing; Ph.D., Innsbruck (Austria). Design and marketing of new products, market research methods.

Stephen Ciccone, Associate Professor of Finance; Ph.D., Florida State. Investments and international corporate governance.

Eleanne Solorzano Dowd, Associate Professor of Statistics; Ph.D., South Carolina. Nonparametric statistics, multiple comparisons, statistical computing, distribution theory, Bayesian inference.

Vanessa Urch Druskat, Associate Professor of Organizational Behavior and Management; Ph.D., Boston University. Work team effectiveness, team leader effectiveness, the influence of emotional competence on team effectiveness and on leader effectiveness, and effective leadership in public school systems.

Joseph F. Durocher, Associate Professor of Hospitality Management; Ph.D., Cornell. Food service management, restaurant and hotel design, computers in management and training, economic forecasting for the hospitality industry.

Ahmad Etebari, Professor and Chair, Accounting and Finance; Ph.D., North Texas State. Investments, corporate finance.

Ross Gittell, Professor of Business Administration; Ph.D., Harvard. Business, government and competition, regional and urban development, business and public policy.

Raymond J. Goodman Jr., Professor and Chair, Hospitality Management; Ph.D., Cornell. Human resources management: training and performance evaluation; retirement facilities planning, design, marketing, management and operations; lodging and restaurant industry indexing and forecasting.

Roger Grinde, Associate Professor and Associate Dean, Management Sciences; Ph.D., Penn State. Operations research, spreadsheet model auditing and control, mathematical modeling.

Charles W. Gross, Professor of Marketing; Ph.D., Colorado. International marketing, marketing planning and strategy, forecasting.

Khole Gwebu, Assistant Professor of Decision Sciences; Ph.D., Kent State. E-commerce, reverse auctions, agent-based simulations.

Afshad J. Irani, Associate Professor of Accounting and Academic Director, M.S. in Accounting; Ph.D., Penn State. Voluntary disclosure, earnings management, insider trading, SEC and FASB regulations.

Willliam Johnson, Assistant Professor of Finance; Ph.D., Michigan State. Initial public offerings, investment banking.

Fred R. Kaen, Professor of Finance and Co-Director, International Private Enterprise Center; Ph.D., Michigan. Financial management, international finance, corporate finance, corporate governance.

Allen M. Kaufman, Professor of Business Administration; Ph.D., Rutgers. Business-government relations, corporate strategy, business history.

Peter Lane, Associate Professor of Strategic Management and Technology; Ph.D., Connecticut. Strategy development processes, strategic alliances and joint ventures, technology and innovation management, intellectual capital management.

Jun Li, Assistant Professor of Strategic Management and Entrepreneurship; Ph.D., Texas A&M. Strategic leadership and governance in IPO-stage firms, new venture strategy and entrepreneurship, multinational corporations in transnational economies.

Michael J. Merenda, Professor of Strategic Management and Chair, Management and Marketing; Ph.D., Massachusetts Amherst. Strategic planning and management, entrepreneurship, international business and SME competitiveness.

Mehdi Mourali, Assistant Professor of Marketing; Ph.D., Oregon. Consumer behavior, behavioral decision-making, services marketing, and marketing research.

William Naumes, Associate Professor of Strategic Management; Ph.D., Stanford. International business, strategic management, entrepreneurship, ethics and values.

John Niser, Associate Professor of Hospitality Management; Ph.D., Anglia Polytechnic (UK).

Jeong Eun "John" Park, Assistant Professor of Marketing; Ph.D., Alabama. Marketing strategy, sales management, retail, organizational learning, outsourcing management, international marketing, cross-cultural study, U.S. and Asian countries.

Anthony Pescosolido, Assistant Professor of Organizational Behavior and Management; Ph.D., Case Western Reserve. Team dynamics, emotion in organizations, emergent leadership, team leadership.

Catherine Plante, Associate Professor of Accounting; Ph.D., Ohio State. Financial, governmental, and nonprofit accounting.

R. Dan Reid, Associate Professor of Operations Management; Ph.D., Ohio State. Production/operations management, purchasing, business logistics, supply chain management.

Richard Saavedra, Associate Professor of Organizational Behavior; Ph.D., Michigan. Workteam design and management, mood and behavior, social influence and comparison processes.

Udo Schlentrich, Associate Professor of Hospitality Management and Director, William Rosenberg International Center of Franchising; Ph.D., Strathclyde. Consumer marketing, international hospitality and tourism, franchising, finance and project development.

Christine Shea, Associate Professor of Technology and Operations Management; Ph.D., Western Ontario. Technology and operations management, managing innovation, nanotechnology.

Barry Shore, Professor of Information Systems and Academic Director, M.B.A. Programs; Ph.D., Wisconsin. Information systems, international management.

Jeffrey E. Sohl, Professor of Entrepreneurship and Decision Sciences and Director, Center for Venture Research; Ph.D., Maryland. Early stage equity financing of high-growth ventures, trends in the angel market, time series forecasting, entrepreneurship.

Stefanie Tate, Assistant Professor of Accounting; Ph.D., Michigan State. Auditing, nonprofit accounting, fraud.

A. R. Venkatachalam, Professor of Information Systems; Chair, Decision Sciences; and Director, Enterprise Integration Research Center; Ph.D., Alabama. MIS, artificial intelligence in business, global information management, electronic commerce, enterprise integration, information technology outsourcing, emerging technologies, technology management.

Mary Wagner, Instructor of Marketing; Ph.D. candidate, Michigan. Music in marketing, advertising, product placement, pricing context effects.

Craig Wood, Associate Professor of Operations Management; Ph.D., Ohio State. Production and operations management, operations strategy, total quality management, technology management, project management, supply chain management.

Emily Xu, Assistant Professor of Accounting; Ph.D., Massachusetts Amherst. Financial analysis, valuation models, financial reporting.

Honggeng Zhou, Assistant Professor of Decision Sciences; Ph.D., Ohio State. Supply chain management, information systems and technology management, production and operations management, operations strategy.

Economics

Reagan Baughman, Assistant Professor of Economics; Ph.D., Syracuse. Labor economics, public finance, health economics and policy.

Karen Smith Conway, Professor of Economics; Ph.D., North Carolina at Chapel Hill. Public economics, applied econometrics, labor supply, health economics.

Bruce T. Elmslie, Professor of Economics; Ph.D., Utah. International trade, history of economic thought, growth theory.

Richard W. England, Professor of Economics and Natural Resources; Ph.D., Michigan. Environmental policy, ecological economics, environmental management, property taxation, smart growth, land development, local economic development, state and local government finance.

Michael Goldberg, Associate Professor of Economics and Academic Director, Economics Program; Ph.D., NYU. International finance, macroeconomic theory, financial markets, expectations.

Marc W. Herold, Associate Professor of Economic Development and Women's Studies; Ph.D., Berkeley. Third World economic development, Brazil, women and development, international studies, postmodernism, economic systems, political economy, civilian casualties of war.

Ju-Chin Huang, Associate Professor of Economics; Ph.D., North Carolina State. Applied econometrics, environmental economics.

Robert D. Mohr, Assistant Professor of Economics; Ph.D., Texas at Austin. Environmental and natural resource economics, public finance.

Neil B. Niman, Associate Professor of Economics; Ph.D., Texas at Austin. Evolutionary economics, organizational economics, history of economic thought.

Torsten Schmidt, Associate Professor of Economics; Ph.D., Florida. Industrial organization, econometrics, microeconomic theory, economics of information and uncertainty.

Evangelos O. Simos, Professor and Chair, Economics; Ph.D., Northern Illinois. Macroeconomics, international trade and finance, modeling and forecasting, econometrics, economic growth, monetary theory and policy, international affairs.

James R. Wible, Professor of Economics; Ph.D., Penn State. Macroeconomics and monetary theory, economics of science and philosophy of science, law and economics.

Robert Woodward, Forrest D. McKerley Professor of Health Economics; Ph.D., Washington (St. Louis). Economics, health economics, pharmaco-economics, Medicare, health-care reform, transplantation economics.

UNIVERSITY OF TULSA

Master of Science in Finance

Program of Study

In conjunction with the Master of Science in Finance (M.S.F.) program, the University of Tulsa (TU) offers the following dual-degree programs: M.B.A./M.S.F., J.D./M.S.F., and M.S.F./M.S.A.M. (M.S. in Applied Mathematics). The dual-degree programs share between 9 and 12 hours, which significantly reduces the time required to earn two degrees. Each dual-degree program provides students with options in risk management, corporate finance, and investments and portfolio management.

The primary goal of the M.S.F. program is to provide a high-quality graduate business program concentrated in finance and directly related areas. The program furnishes new skills, analytical tools, and perspectives that serve as a sound foundation for financial decision making in an increasingly complex financial world. In particular, the M.S.F. curriculum is designed to provide a rigorous body of course work that reflects current financial theory and practice; provide each student with a knowledge of the primary areas of finance: corporate finance, investment/portfolio management, and risk management; provide each student with the quantitative and analytical skills necessary to work effectively in a rapidly changing financial world; and provide each student with an opportunity to develop specialized knowledge in one of the following areas: corporate finance, investments and portfolio management, and risk management.

The M.S.F. program prepares students for a professional career in a range of specialized areas, such as corporate finance, investments, portfolio management, and risk management. This program is designed for students who desire an opportunity for in-depth study of the sophisticated analytical techniques and market transactions that drive financial innovation. Curriculum options in corporate finance and investments and portfolio management are designed for students with an undergraduate degree in business administration, an M.B.A., or undergraduate or graduate degrees in other disciplines who desire to specialize in finance. The risk management option is designed for students with strong quantitative backgrounds, typically with undergraduate degrees in mathematics, statistics, the physical sciences, or engineering.

Contemporary finance, risk management, and financial engineering are ideal environments for the integration of applied mathematics and finance. The dual M.S.F./M.S.A.M. degree program capitalizes on this environment by combining an in-depth study of financial theory and application with a study of advanced applied mathematics. Graduates obtain a level of understanding of both finance and mathematics that gives them a competitive edge and prepares them to work on the very frontiers of finance.

In an increasingly competitive, complex, and global world, corporations desire individuals who are not only able to manage across all dimensions of a firm but also have an in-depth knowledge in a business discipline. The dual M.B.A./M.S.F. degree program meets this challenge by combining the broad graduate business degree with an in-depth specialized degree in finance. M.B.A./M.S.F. graduates acquire a unique set of skills that provide a competitive edge for both entry-level and executive leadership positions.

The increasing complexity of the financial world and the associated legal issues requires individuals who are well trained in both finance and law. The dual J.D./M.S.F. degree program meets this challenge by allowing students to combine the in-depth study of financial theory and application of the M.S.F. program with the legal aspects of financial decisions of a J.D. program. Graduates have a level of understanding of finance and law that allows them to operate at the highest levels.

Research Facilities

The Williams Risk Management Center (WRMC) serves as the heart of the M.S.F. research program. Its sophisticated workstations, real-time data feeds, databases, and state-of-the-art software provide an ideal environment for cutting-edge research. Students are able to apply classroom theories and test the most complex financial topics, including exotics options, portfolio optimization, and mergers and acquisition models. Some of the hardware and software in the WRMC includes twenty-two workstations, Bloomberg, Reuters, SAS, MATLAB, @Risk, and Compustat. Industry specialists help to team-teach some classes.

Financial Aid

Financial aid is available through graduate assistantships, corporate internships, and fellowships. Graduate assistantships pay for 9 credit hours of tuition per semester plus a stipend. Corporate internships allow students to apply their knowledge and skills to real-world problems while interacting with corporate leaders. Interns work year-round and go to school part-time. Compensation includes 50 percent tuition support plus competitive pay for hours worked. Approximately 25 percent of the students are corporate interns. Current internship sponsors include Williams, Nordam, Bank of Oklahoma, SemGroup, and Samson. All financial aid is awarded on a competitive basis.

Cost of Study

For 2007–08, tuition is $778 per credit hour. Other mandatory fees total about $200 per year. Books and supplies cost approximately $1000 per year.

Living and Housing Costs

Living expenses for the academic year (nine months) are estimated to be $14,000. This estimate covers room and board, transportation, and personal needs for a single student with no dependents. Campus apartments are available. Applications are required early in the calendar year for fall residency.

Student Group

The M.S.F. student body is very diverse. The 2006–07 class of 22 students included students from fifteen universities and six countries. The demographic breakdown of the class was 27 percent women and 36 percent international students. Their average GMAT score was 670. Undergraduate majors included engineering, history, computer science, mathematics, economics, statistics, chemistry, government, information systems, and business. Recent graduates with any of these backgrounds are encouraged to apply. Students with graduate degrees and/or work experience in mathematics, engineering, or physical sciences who desire a career change are welcome. Those who work in the financial world and recognize the need for additional training to remain competitive are encouraged to apply.

Location

The University of Tulsa features a residential campus in midtown Tulsa, Oklahoma. Tulsa's prominent industries include energy, telecommunications and data, finance, medicine, aerospace, transportation, and education, all of which present rich internship opportunities for students and employment opportunities for graduates.

Newsweek has named Tulsa one of ten "New Frontier" technology cities, and the *New York Times* declared Tulsa "a new economy hotbed." *Southern Living* magazine named Tulsa one of its five favorite Southern cities. The Tulsa metropolitan area has more than 840,000 residents and features cultural assets such as the Performing Arts Center, ballet, theater, symphony, opera, two nationally renowned museums, and cultural festivals such as Jazzfest, Mayfest, and Octoberfest. Professional sports in Tulsa include baseball, basketball, golf, hockey, arena football, and horse racing. The extensive River Parks development, 3 miles from the campus, has facilities for outdoor activities, jogging and bicycle trails, and an outdoor floating amphitheater.

The University

TU is a comprehensive, doctoral-degree-granting private university founded in 1894. Today, TU provides undergraduate, graduate, and professional education in the arts, humanities, sciences, business, education, engineering, law, nursing, and applied health sciences. Its current undergraduate enrollment is almost 2,800, with about 1,300 students in its graduate and law programs. Since 1995, TU students have received forty-one Goldwater Scholarships, twenty-seven National Science Foundation Graduate Fellowships, seven Department of Defense Fellowships, eight Truman Scholarships, six Fulbright Grants, five Morris K. Udall Scholarships, seven Phi Kappa Phi Graduate Fellowships, one Howard Hughes Medical Institute Fellowship, and four British Marshall Scholarships, the first of which was the first to be awarded in Oklahoma in twenty-eight years. TU ranks ninth in the nation for the number of National Merit Scholars—one of every ten freshmen.

Applying

The College offers rolling admission, allowing students to enter the M.S.F. program in the fall, spring, or summer terms. More information and online applications can be found at the Web site.

Correspondence and Information

Candace Sitzer, Admissions/Advising
College of Business Administration
University of Tulsa
600 South College Avenue
Tulsa, Oklahoma 74104-3189

Phone: 918-631-2242 or 2553
Fax: 918-631-2142
E-mail: graduate-business@utulsa.edu
Web site: http://www.cba.utulsa.edu/msfinance

University of Tulsa

THE FACULTY AND THEIR RESEARCH

Roger P. Bey, Professor of Finance and J. Bradley Oxley Chair; Ph.D., Penn State. Portfolio performance and revision, portfolio diversification and emerging markets, capital budgeting.

Richard C. Burgess, Professor of Finance; D.B.A., Kentucky. Global portfolio optimization, efficient markets, short selling models.

Wen-Chyuan Chiang, Professor of Operations Management; Ph.D., Texas at Austin. Supply-chain management, distribution and logistics, facility layout, AI applications to operations management problems.

J. Markham Collins, Professor of Finance and Associate Dean; Ph.D., Oklahoma. International business finance, international leasing.

Peyton Cook, Associate Professor of Mathematical Sciences; Ph.D., Oklahoma State. Bayesian statistical inference, time-series models, generalized linear models.

David Enke, Associate Professor of Finance and H. Michael and Laurie Krimbill Finance Fellow; Ph.D., Missouri–Rolla. Financial engineering, intelligent systems, financial forecasting.

Richard P. Gebhart, Applied Assistant Professor of Operations Management; J.D., Tulsa.

Larry J. Johnson, Associate Professor of Finance; D.B.A., Indiana. Option valuation, stochastic processes of energy commodities, emerging markets, short selling models.

Robert J. Monroe, Trustees Professor; D.B.A., Indiana. Financial institutions and markets, financial management.

Robert A. Russell, Collins Professor of Business Operations Management; Ph.D., Texas at Austin. Supply-chain management, logistics, vehicle routing and scheduling, metaheuristics optimization.

Timothy L. Urban, Collins Professor of Business Operations Management; Ph.D., Texas at Arlington. Mathematical modeling and development of solution methodologies for operations management systems, particularly in the areas of facility design and inventory control.

VIRGINIA COMMONWEALTH UNIVERSITY

Program in Accounting

Program of Study

The School of Business at Virginia Commonwealth University (VCU) offers the Master of Accountancy. The program provides students with the skills and knowledge necessary to be future leaders in the professional business community and the public sector. The graduate degree requires completion of ten graduate courses. There are four 600-level required accounting courses and six 600-level courses selected from the three tracks of interest (information systems, finance and auditing, or general business). Students can work with their advisers to identify a separate track of study in economics, international business, management, marketing, or another area negotiated with the faculty adviser. Depending upon the track of study selected, students may have to complete additional undergraduate prerequisites. The number of graduate electives that must be taken is the same, regardless of the area of study. Students must complete four graduate electives in the selected track, one graduate elective in accounting, and one graduate elective in accounting or the selected track.

The Master of Accountancy degree was most recently revised in the spring of 2000. The revision addresses a requirement that future candidates for the CPA exam must have completed at least 150 credit hours of college study to be eligible to sit for the examination. Most undergraduate students complete 120 credit hours as part of their bachelor's degrees. Students who intend to take the CPA examination are encouraged to consider earning the additional credit hours of study in the integrated Master of Accountancy program.

Research Facilities

VCU libraries provide a combined capacity of more than 1.7 million volumes and 10,200 periodical titles and an online bibliographic search service accessing hundreds of databases. In addition, the Virginia State and Richmond Public Libraries are within walking distance of both VCU campuses. Academic Computing provides a variety of microcomputer, minicomputer, and mainframe computing services to support the research and instructional endeavors of the faculty and students, including consultation, instruction, and computer acquisition.

Financial Aid

The School of Business offers a limited number of graduate assistantship positions to full-time students. Scholarship opportunities exist for graduate students after they have completed at least one semester of study. Students may apply for need-based assistance with the University's Financial Aid Office. Current information on financial aid programs, policies, and procedures is available at http://www.vcu.edu/enroll/finaid.

Cost of Study

For full-time study (9–15 credits) in 2007–08, Virginia residents pay tuition and fees of $4452 per semester; nonresidents, $8876 per semester. For part-time study, Virginia residents pay tuition and fees of $465 per hour; nonresidents, $954 per hour. Some programs require additional fees. On the Medical College of Virginia (MCV) campus, tuition, fees, and other expenses vary in the medicine, pharmacy, nurse anesthesia, dentistry, and School of Allied Health programs.

Living and Housing Costs

Graduate student housing is available on both the MCV campus and the academic campus of Virginia Commonwealth University. Many graduate students live in off-campus housing, which is reasonably priced and readily available in a variety of styles and settings in nearby residential areas or within easy commuting distance. On- and off-campus housing information is available on the Web at http://www.housing.vcu.edu/.

Student Group

VCU enrolls 30,452 students, 7,611 of whom are graduate students. More than 200 clubs and organizations reflect the diverse social, recreational, educational, political, and religious interests of the student body.

Location

Richmond is Virginia's capital and a major East Coast financial and manufacturing center that offers students a wide range of cultural, educational, and recreational activities. Richmond is located in central Virginia at the intersection of Interstates 95 and 64, 2 hours south of Washington, D.C., and nestled between the Blue Ridge Mountains and the Atlantic coast. The Richmond region is easily accessible by plane, car, and train. With nearly 1 million residents, the historic city of Richmond combines big-city offerings with small-town hospitality. Applicants are encouraged to explore http://www.visit.richmond.com/ for more information on the city.

The University

VCU is a state-supported coeducational university with a graduate school, a major teaching hospital, and twelve academic and professional units that offer fifty-two undergraduate, twenty-two postbaccalaureate certificate, sixty-five master's, six post-master's certificate, and twenty-nine Ph.D. programs. VCU also offers M.D., D.D.S., D.P.T., and Pharm.D. programs as well as cooperative degree programs with other major Virginia colleges and universities. VCU has one of the largest evening colleges in the United States. The academic campus is located in Richmond's historic Fan District. The health sciences campus and hospital are located 2 miles east in the downtown business district. A University bus service provides free intercampus transportation for faculty members and students.

With more than $211 million in annual research funding, Virginia Commonwealth University is classified as one of the nation's top research universities by the Carnegie Foundation for the Advancement of Teaching. More than 29,000 undergraduate, certificate, graduate, post-master's, professional, and doctoral students are enrolled in 162 academic programs, forty of which are unique in the commonwealth of Virginia. The faculty members represent the finest American and international graduate institutions and enhance the University's position among the important institutions of higher learning in the United States and the world via their work in the classroom, laboratory, studio, and clinic and in their scholarly publications.

Applying

Admission procedures and program requirements are detailed in the *Graduate Bulletin*. Application deadlines and materials, including the application and the *Graduate Bulletin*, are available online at the Graduate School Web site at http://www.graduate.vcu.edu. Virginia Commonwealth University is an equal opportunity/affirmative action institution providing access to education and employment without regard to age, race, color, national origin, gender, religion, sexual orientation, veteran's status, political affiliation, or disability.

Correspondence and Information

Jana P. McQuaid, Graduate Program Director
School of Business
Virginia Commonwealth University
1015 Floyd Avenue
Richmond, Virginia 23284-4000
Phone: 804-828-1595
E-mail: jpmcquaid@vcu.edu
Web site: http://www.gsib.bus.vcu.edu/index.html

Virginia Commonwealth University

THE FACULTY AND THEIR RESEARCH

Edward N. Coffman, Professor; D.B.A., George Washington. Financial accounting, accounting history.

Wayne Edmunds, Associate Professor; M.L.T., J.D., William and Mary; CPA.

Ruth W. Epps, Professor and Chair; Ph.D., Virginia Commonwealth; CPA. Governmental/not-for-profit accounting, corporate governance.

John O. Everett, Professor; Ph.D., Oklahoma State; CPA. Taxation, computer solutions to tax planning problems, tax policy issues.

Carolyn Norman, Assistant Professor; Ph.D., Texas A&M.

Philip R. Olds, Associate Professor; Ph.D., Georgia State; CPA. Accounting education.

Myung Park, Assistant Professor; Ph.D., Purdue. Capital market research, earnings management, fair-value accounting, and other topics in financial, managerial accounting, and accounting information systems.

Edward C. Spede, Associate Professor; Ph.D., Virginia Tech. Financial accounting, accounting education.

Roxanne Spindle, Associate Professor; Ph.D., Colorado; CPA. Public policy and the tax structure, individual tax planning.

Rasoul H. Tondkar, Professor; Ph.D., North Texas. International accounting.

Jayaraman Vijayakumur, Associate Professor; Ph.D., Pittsburgh. State and local government finances and accounting, capital markets, financial reporting, insider trading.

Benson Wier, Professor; Ph.D., Texas Tech; CPA. Behavioral facets of managerial accounting.

VIRGINIA COMMONWEALTH UNIVERSITY

Program in Taxation

Programs of Study

Virginia Commonwealth University (VCU), through the School of Business, offers the Master of Taxation (M.Tax.) to give existing tax professionals an opportunity to update and expand existing tax knowledge; the program also prepares students for entry-level positions in the field of taxation. The complexity and changing nature of tax law has created a need for specialists—individuals who can interpret tax law, convey its meaning, plan, and comply with myriad reporting requirements. The M.Tax. program includes a comprehensive study of tax laws and regulations, administrative practice and procedure, and tax research fundamentals. Students develop both technical knowledge and conceptual understanding within the field of taxation. Ethical considerations are stressed within the framework of individual courses. The curriculum is flexible and is designed for students with diverse undergraduate backgrounds. Three semester hours of tax accounting and a course in college algebra are prerequisites for the M.Tax. The program consists of one prerequisite course, three foundation courses, and ten courses distributed over core courses, restricted electives, and individual electives. A minimum of 30 hours of advanced graduate credit at the 600 level or higher is required of all students. There are two admission tracks—academic and professional. To be eligible for the latter, an applicant must be a CPA, a CMA, or an attorney and have at least two years of relevant work experience.

Research Facilities

VCU libraries provide a combined capacity of more than 1.7 million volumes and 10,200 periodical titles and an online bibliographic search service accessing hundreds of databases. In addition, the Virginia State and Richmond Public Libraries are within walking distance of both VCU campuses. Academic Computing provides a variety of microcomputer, minicomputer, and mainframe computing services to support the research and instructional endeavors of the faculty and students, including consultation, instruction, and computer acquisition.

Financial Aid

The School of Business offers a limited number of graduate assistantship positions to full-time students. Scholarship opportunities exist for graduate students after they have completed at least one semester of study. Students may apply for need-based assistance with the University's Financial Aid Office. Current information on financial aid programs, policies, and procedures is available at http://www.vcu.edu/enroll/finaid.

Cost of Study

For full-time study (9–15 credits) in 2007–08, Virginia residents pay tuition and fees of $4452 per semester; nonresidents, $8876 per semester. For part-time study, Virginia residents pay tuition and fees of $465 per hour; nonresidents, $954 per hour. Some programs require additional fees. On the Medical College of Virginia (MCV) campus, tuition, fees, and other expenses vary in the medicine, pharmacy, nurse anesthesia, dentistry, and School of Allied Health programs.

Living and Housing Costs

Graduate student housing is available on both the MCV campus and the academic campus of Virginia Commonwealth University. Many graduate students live in off-campus housing, which is reasonably priced and readily available in a variety of styles and settings in nearby residential areas or within easy commuting distance. On- and off-campus housing information is available on the Web at http://www.housing.vcu.edu/.

Student Group

VCU enrolls 30,452 students, 7,611 of whom are graduate students. More than 200 clubs and organizations reflect the diverse social, recreational, educational, political, and religious interests of the student body.

Location

Richmond is Virginia's capital and a major East Coast financial and manufacturing center that offers students a wide range of cultural, educational, and recreational activities. Richmond is located in central Virginia at the intersection of Interstates 95 and 64, 2 hours south of Washington, D.C., and nestled between the Blue Ridge Mountains and the Atlantic coast. The Richmond region is easily accessible by plane, car, and train. With nearly 1 million residents, the historic city of Richmond combines big-city offerings with small-town hospitality. Applicants are encouraged to explore http://www.visit.richmond.com/ for more information on the city.

The University

VCU is a state-supported coeducational university with a graduate school, a major teaching hospital, and twelve academic and professional units that offer fifty-two undergraduate, twenty-two postbaccalaureate certificate, sixty-five master's certificate, and twenty-nine Ph.D. programs. VCU also offers M.D., D.D.S., D.P.T., and Pharm.D. programs as well as cooperative degree programs with other major Virginia colleges and universities. VCU has one of the largest evening colleges in the United States. The academic campus is located in Richmond's historic Fan District. The health sciences campus and hospital are located 2 miles east in the downtown business district. A University bus service provides free intercampus transportation for faculty members and students.

With more than $211 million in annual research funding, Virginia Commonwealth University is classified as one of the nation's top research universities by the Carnegie Foundation for the Advancement of Teaching. More than 29,000 undergraduate, certificate, graduate, post-master's, professional, and doctoral students are enrolled in 162 academic programs, forty of which are unique in the commonwealth of Virginia. The faculty members represent the finest American and international graduate institutions and enhance the University's position among the important institutions of higher learning in the United States and the world via their work in the classroom, laboratory, studio, and clinic and in their scholarly publications.

Applying

Admission procedures and program requirements are detailed in the *Graduate Bulletin*. Application deadlines and materials, including the application and the *Graduate Bulletin*, are available online at the Graduate School Web site at http://www.graduate.vcu.edu. Virginia Commonwealth University is an equal opportunity/affirmative action institution providing access to education and employment without regard to age, race, color, national origin, gender, religion, sexual orientation, veteran's status, political affiliation, or disability.

Correspondence and Information

Jana P. McQuaid, Graduate Program Director
School of Business
Virginia Commonwealth University
1015 Floyd Avenue
Richmond, Virginia 23284-4000
Phone: 804-828-4622
E-mail: jpmcquaid@vcu.edu
Web site: http://www.gsib.vcu.edu

Virginia Commonwealth University

THE FACULTY AND THEIR RESEARCH

ACCOUNTING

Edward N. Coffman, Professor; D.B.A., George Washington. Financial accounting, accounting history.

Wayne Edmunds, Associate Professor; M.L.T., J.D., William and Mary; CPA.

Ruth W. Epps, Professor and Chair; Ph.D., Virginia Commonwealth; CPA. Governmental/not-for-profit accounting, corporate governance.

John O. Everett, Professor; Ph.D., Oklahoma State; CPA. Taxation, computer solutions to tax planning problems, tax policy issues.

Carolyn Norman, Assistant Professor; Ph.D., Texas A&M.

Philip R. Olds, Associate Professor; Ph.D., Georgia State; CPA. Accounting education.

Myung Park, Assistant Professor; Ph.D., Purdue. Capital market research, earnings management, fair-value accounting, and other topics in financial, managerial accounting, and accounting information systems.

Edward C. Spede, Associate Professor; Ph.D., Virginia Tech. Financial accounting, accounting education.

Roxanne Spindle, Associate Professor; Ph.D., Colorado; CPA. Public policy and the tax structure, individual tax planning.

Rasoul H. Tondkar, Professor; Ph.D., North Texas. International accounting.

Jayaraman Vijayakumur, Associate Professor; Ph.D., Pittsburgh. State and local government finances and accounting, capital markets, financial reporting, insider trading.

Benson Wier, Professor; Ph.D., Texas Tech; CPA. Behavioral facets of managerial accounting.

ECONOMICS

Douglas D. Davis, Professor; Ph.D., Indiana. Tools used by antitrust authorities for detecting collusion and for identifying problematic mergers.

David Harless, Professor; Ph.D., Indiana. Applied econometrics, health economics, behavior under risk and uncertainty.

George E. Hoffer, Professor; Ph.D., Virginia. Pricing and consumer topics related to the automobile industry.

Oleg Korenok, Assistant Professor; Ph.D., Rutgers. Prices and inflation: price/information stickiness (macroeconomics), price discovery (financial economics), price formation mechanisms (experimental economics).

Carol Scotese Lehr, Associate Professor; Ph.D., Penn State. Institutional aspects of economic development.

Edward L. Millner, Professor and Chair; Ph.D., North Carolina at Chapel Hill. Experimental economics, decision making in the face of uncertainty, economic analysis of business strategies and tactics.

Shannon K. Mitchell, Associate Professor; Ph.D., Virginia. Health care in developing countries, particularly AIDS in sub-Saharan Africa; development economics; and international trade theory.

Dennis M. O'Toole, Associate Professor; Ph.D., Ohio. Factors that lead college students to alter their enrollment behavior—switching between full-time, part-time, and stop-out status.

Steven P. Peterson, Director of Research, Virginia Retirement System; Ph.D., Indiana. Econometrics of financial markets, risk and distress models, neural networks, covariance misspecification in asset allocation.

Michael D. Pratt, Professor; Ph.D., Kansas. Experimental economics directed to public choice theory, controls for and analysis of risk aversion, industrial organization.

Laura Razzolini, Professor; Ph.D., Southern Methodist. Mechanism design and experimental economics.

Robert J. Reilly, Professor; Ph.D., Tennessee. Experimental economics, individual behavior under uncertainty, biodiversity and ecological economics, applied microeconomics.

Leslie S. Stratton, Associate Professor; Ph.D., MIT. Interaction between market and nonmarket activities, particularly as they influence market outcomes; undergraduate enrollment patterns.

James N. Wetzel, Professor; Ph.D., North Carolina. Environmental, urban, and managerial economics and public finance.

FINANCE, INSURANCE, AND REAL ESTATE

Etti Baranoff, Associate Professor; Ph.D., Texas. Insurance law and regulation, all coverages (personal and commercial lines), insurers' financial stability, alternative risk financing, risk management information systems (RMIS).

Kenneth N. Daniels, Professor; Ph.D., Connecticut. Municipal bonds, corporate finance, financial institutions, small-business development, financial economics of minorities.

David Downs, Professor and Alfred L. Blake Chair; Ph.D., North Carolina at Chapel Hill. Real estate finance and investment, issues relevant to institutional real estate investors, the implications of real estate regulation.

John Guthmann, Assistant Professor; Ph.D., New Mexico.

R. Michael McDonald, Associate Professor; Ed.D., Virginia Tech. Impediments to organizational change and the application of concept-mapping techniques to holistic problem analysis and strategic planning.

E. G. Miller, Senior Associate Dean; Ph.D., Alabama. Statistical applications in the insurance industry and insurance regulation.

Oghenovo Obrimah, Assistant Professor; Ph.D., Maryland.

Richard A. Phillips, Professor; Ph.D., North Carolina at Chapel Hill. Real estate finance and economics, housing economics, and economics of transportation and public policy.

Daniel P. Salandro, Associate Professor; Ph.D., Pittsburgh.

Tai S. Shin, Professor; Ph.D., Illinois. Corporate finance, investment, banking, and international finance.

David E. Upton, Professor and Chair; Ph.D., North Carolina. Security analysis, portfolio management, investments.

INFORMATION SYSTEMS

Peter Aiken, Associate Professor; Ph.D., George Mason.

Richard J. Coppins, Associate Professor; Ph.D., North Carolina State. Computer/network security and application of operations research techniques to problems related to computer systems.

Gupreet Dhillon, Professor; Ph.D., London. Information security, its right use, and the range of related ethical and philosophical issues.

George Kasper, Professor; Ph.D., SUNY at Buffalo. Computer-human interaction, decision-support systems.

Allen S. Lee, Professor; Ph.D., MIT. Qualitative, interpretive, and case research on information technology and organizations; communications; research methodologies in information systems research and the social sciences; action research.

Kweku-Muata (Noel) Osei-Bryson, Professor; Ph.D., Maryland, College Park. Data mining, database systems, expert systems, decision-support systems, group-support systems, multicriteria decision analysis, cluster analysis, integer programming, and parametric programming.

Richard T. Redmond, Associate Professor; D.B.A., Kent State. Software productivity, expert systems, applications of AI to business, database/imagebase design theory and compression theory.

John Sutherland, Professor; Ph.D., UCLA.

Heinz R. Weistroffer, Associate Professor; Ph.D., Free University of Berlin. Software engineering, decision support systems, conceptual modeling, portfolio decision making, economics of information technology.

James Wynne, Associate Professor; Ph.D., Nebraska–Lincoln. Software project management, software training and curriculum development, group-decision support systems, systems analysis and design.

MANAGEMENT

R. Jon Ackley, Associate Professor; Ed.D., Utah State. Applied statistics and quantitative methods.

Robert L. Andrews, Associate Professor; Ph.D., Virginia Tech. Applied statistics, decision analysis, quantitative methods.

Randolph T. Barker, Professor; Ph.D., Florida State. Multidimensional aspects of organizational communication including team leadership, listening, and strategy.

Charles M. Byles, Associate Professor; D.B.A., Kent State. Relationship between strategy and human resource management practices, differences in cognitive styles among managers in several countries.

George C. Canavos, Professor; Ph.D., Virginia Tech.

José Dulá, Associate Professor; Ph.D., Michigan.

Glenn H. Gilbreath, Professor and Chair; Ph.D., Alabama. Statistics and quality management.

George R. Gray, Ph.D., Alabama.

Ronald Humphrey, Associate Professor; Ph.D., Michigan. Cognitive and emotional processes in organizations, especially with regard to performance appraisals, personnel selection, assessment centers, group dynamics, and decision-making.

Iris W. Johnson, Ed.D., Virginia Tech.

Jeffrey Krug, Associate Professor; Ph.D., Indiana. Corporate strategy, mergers and acquisitions, corporate governance, top management teams, global strategy.

Ibrahim Kurtulus, Associate Professor; Ph.D., North Carolina at Chapel Hill. Purchasing, logistics, MRP, JIT, and resource-constrained scheduling.

Michael A. McDaniel, Professor; Ph.D., George Washington. Situational judgment tests, race and sex differences in work-related variables, effects of applicant faking on employment decisions and issues concerning older workers, applications of meta-analysis in the evaluation of personnel selection methods.

Marianne Miller, Associate Professor; Ph.D., Oregon. Employee recruitment, selection, and socialization; management of a diverse work force, particularly issues related to inclusion and accommodation of people with disabilities.

Elliott D. Minor III, Associate Professor; Ph.D., South Carolina.

Subhash C. Narula, Professor; Ph.D., Iowa.

Michael W. Pitts, Associate Professor; D.B.A., Tennessee. Strategic management process in former Soviet-type economic systems and competitive intelligence activities.

Anson Seers, Professor; Ph.D., Cincinnati. Work roles and relationships, including leadership, the development of effective teamwork, and employee motivation.

Randall G. Sleeth, Associate Professor; Ph.D., Massachusetts. Leadership processes, computer-mediated instruction.

Robert R. Trumble, Professor; Ph.D., Minnesota. Human resources, labor relations and strategic planning.

Larry Williams, Professor; Ph.D., Indiana. Application of structural equation methods to various substantive and methodological concerns in the field of organizational behavior.

Margaret Williams, Associate Professor; Ph.D., Indiana. Employee compensation programs, particularly employee reactions to benefits; work-life issues, with a particular emphasis on part-time or reduced load work at the managerial and professional levels and work-life issues in small organizations; leadership and motivation issues within organizations.

D. Robley Wood Jr., Professor; D.B.A., Tennessee. Characteristics of successful formal planning for the operations function of commercial banks.

MARKETING AND BUSINESS LAW

Deborah L. Cowles, Associate Professor; Ph.D., Arizona State. Relationship marketing (including database marketing), e-commerce (including retail and business-to-business), services marketing (including service quality, customer service, and customer satisfaction).

Frank J. Franzak, Associate Professor and Chair; Ph.D., Maryland. New product development, global marketing strategy, marketing of technology products, public policy issues, evaluation research methods.

Haeran Jae, Assistant Professor; Ph.D., Kentucky. Low-literate consumers, linguistically isolated consumers.

Michael W. Little, Associate Professor; Ph.D., Michigan State. Electronic retail/marketing on the World Wide Web.

Dennis R. McDermott, Associate Professor; Ph.D., Ohio State. Strategic marketing, marketing management, marketing education.

David J. Urban, Professor; Ph.D., Michigan. Customer satisfaction research, retailing, and distribution channel management.

Heiko de B. Wijnholds, Associate Professor; D.Com., South Africa. International marketing, marketing management, forensic marketing, forecasting.

Van R. Wood, Professor and Phillip Morris Chair in International Business; Ph.D., Oregon. International marketing/globalization (risk assessment, market development and management in international markets), marketing management (strategic planning and assessment).

VIRGINIA POLYTECHNIC INSTITUTE AND STATE UNIVERSITY

Department of Accounting and Information Systems

Programs of Study

The Department of Accounting and Information Systems in the Pamplin College of Business offers graduate programs leading to the Master of Accounting and Information Systems and the Doctor of Philosophy degrees. The Master of Accounting and Information Systems program is open to qualified students with a bachelor's degree in any discipline. Students without prior collegiate studies in accounting, information systems, and/or business administration, however, should expect to spend at least two years in the program in order to meet prerequisite course work. For those who have fulfilled the background requirements, the program consists of 30 semester hours (ten courses) and is usually completed in twelve to sixteen months. Students with background deficiencies may use graduate-level background courses to meet any nonaccounting elective course requirements.

The master's program is divided into two basic tracks: accounting and information systems. All accounting option master's students take seven courses in accounting and information systems, including global issues, mergers and acquisitions or governmental and not-for-profit accounting, strategic cost management, taxation of business entities, auditing theory, management information systems, and business law. The remaining three courses depend on the student's desired concentration and may be completed in income tax (tax research and concepts, corporate tax, and multijurisdictional tax), financial reporting (financial statement analysis and 6 hours of course work in finance), or information systems auditing (networks and telecommunications, information systems auditing and control, and information systems security).

Students choosing the information systems option take classes in advanced database management systems, information systems development, applied software development, Web-based applications and e-commerce, distributed processing and data communications, management information systems, global issues, and strategic cost management as well as two electives.

The Ph.D. program provides advanced graduate studies as preparation for a career in university research and teaching. The program's basic requirements call for course work in accounting and statistics and a support area, followed by completion of a dissertation. Areas of concentration are offered in financial accounting, managerial accounting, auditing, taxation, and information systems.

Research Facilities

The Department of Accounting and Information Systems is housed in Pamplin Hall, a modern building located near the center of the campus. Three computer laboratories are available for classroom and student use in the Pamplin College of Business. All campus facilities, including residence halls, are connected by more than 1,000 miles of fiber-optic cable providing voice, data, and video communications. Virginia Tech leads the nationally recognized Blacksburg Electronic Village project, connecting the town and campus with each other and the world.

Financial Aid

The Department offers graduate assistantships that carry stipends of $535 per month in 2007–08. The stipend permits the student to carry 12 hours of course work. Additional grants and scholarships are awarded by the Department, including fellowships from industrial and public accounting firms and Virginia state scholarships. A limited number of instructorships are available for doctoral students. Financial support is awarded on the basis of the applicant's grade record, GMAT scores, and letters of recommendation. Job opportunities for students' spouses are available in the community.

Cost of Study

Student fees in 2007–08 are $4493 per semester. Out-of-state graduate students who do not have an assistantship are required to pay an additional $3182.50 tuition fee per semester. Book costs average $500 per semester.

Living and Housing Costs

A wide variety of housing for graduate students is available at reasonable cost in Blacksburg and the surrounding area. In general, the cost of living is less than the national average. Limited on-campus housing is also available.

Student Group

Virginia Tech has an enrollment of approximately 28,000 students, including off-campus students, of whom 80 percent are undergraduate students. The University offers about 120 master's and doctoral programs through eight colleges. There are approximately 80 students in the Master of Accounting and Information Systems program and 12 students in the doctoral program in accounting and information systems.

Location

Virginia Tech is located in Blacksburg, Virginia, a rapidly growing town with a population of almost 30,000. The campus is nestled on a plain in the Appalachians, 2,100 feet above sea level. The surrounding area offers numerous recreational opportunities, including hiking, fishing, boating, camping, sightseeing, and mountain climbing.

The University

Virginia Polytechnic Institute and State University, Virginia's land-grant university, has grown since its founding in 1872 into the largest university in the state. Its recent history is one of rapid, well-planned growth in the size and quality of programs. The programs of the College of Business, of which the Department of Accounting and Information Systems is an integral part, are fully accredited by AACSB International–The Association to Advance Collegiate Schools of Business. In addition, both the undergraduate and master's degree programs in accounting have separate AACSB International accounting accreditation.

The University provides a large variety of activities that span from the arts (e.g., theater, orchestra, lecture-concert series, band) to club sports (e.g., skiing, soccer, lacrosse) to varsity intercollegiate athletics (e.g., football, basketball). High quality individuals attend and visit the University, including an extensive visiting scholar program.

Applying

Applications for admission to the master's and the doctoral programs in accounting and information systems can be made at any time. Applications should be submitted prior to March 15 of each year. Students may apply online at http://www.grads.vt.edu. The Graduate Management Admission Test (GMAT) is required for admission to the graduate programs in accounting and information systems. A minimum TOEFL score of 620 (paper-based test), 260 (computer-based test), or 105 (Internet-based test) is required.

Correspondence and Information

Master's and Ph.D. Committee
Department of Accounting and Information Systems
3007 Pamplin Hall (0101)
Pamplin College of Business
Virginia Polytechnic Institute and State University
Blacksburg, Virginia 24061
Phone: 540-231-6591
Web site: http://www.acis.pamplin.vt.edu

Virginia Polytechnic Institute and State University

THE FACULTY AND THEIR RESEARCH

Reza Barkhi, Ph.D., Ohio State, 1995. Information systems.
France Belanger, Ph.D., South Florida, 1997. Information systems.
Sudip Bhattacharjee, Ph.D., Massachusetts Amherst, 1997. Managerial accounting, information systems.
Robert M. Brown, Ph.D., Georgia State, 1977. Information systems, managerial accounting.
John A. Brozovsky, Ph.D., Colorado, 1990. Financial accounting, managerial accounting.
C. Bryan Cloyd, Ph.D., Indiana, 1992. Tax.
Weiguo "Patrick" Fan, Ph.D., Michigan, 2002. Information systems.
James O. Hicks Jr., Ph.D., Georgia State, 1976. Information systems, managerial accounting.
Sam A. Hicks, Ph.D., Wisconsin, 1976. Income tax, information systems.
J. Gregory Jenkins, Ph.D., Virginia Tech, 1998. Auditing.
Larry N. Killough, Ph.D., Missouri–Columbia, 1969. Managerial accounting.
John J. Maher, Ph.D., Penn State, 1985. Information systems, financial accounting.
Mitchell J. Oler, Ph.D., Washington (Seattle), 2006. Financial accounting.
Debra A. Salbador, Ph.D., South Carolina, 1993. Income tax.
W. Eugene Seago, J.D., Ph.D., Georgia, 1970. Income tax.
Tarun K. Sen, Ph.D., Iowa, 1985. Information systems.
Steven D. Sheetz, Ph.D., Colorado, 1996. Information systems.
C. J. Song, Ph.D., Michigan State, 2004. Financial accounting.
David P. Tegarden, Ph.D., Colorado, 1991. Information systems.
Linda Wallace, Ph.D., Georgia State, 2000. Information systems.
Lynette I. Wood, Ph.D., Indiana, 2003. Behavioral.
James A. Yardley, Ph.D., Illinois at Urbana-Champaign, 1986. Auditing.

An aerial view of the campus.

Section 3
Advertising and Public Relations

This section contains a directory of institutions offering graduate work in advertising and public relations. Additional information about programs listed in the directory but not augmented by an in-depth entry may be obtained by writing directly to the dean of a graduate school or chair of a department at the address given in the directory.

For programs offering related work, see also in this book Business Administration and Management and Marketing. In Book 2, see Communication and Media.

CONTENTS

Advertising and Public Relations

Academy of Art University, Graduate Program, School of Advertising, San Francisco, CA 94105-3410. Offers MFA. Part-time programs available. Postbaccalaureate distance learning degree programs offered (no on-campus study). *Faculty:* 4 full-time (2 women), 30 part-time/adjunct (11 women). *Students:* 95 full-time (47 women), 45 part-time (26 women); includes 8 African Americans, 10 Asian Americans or Pacific Islanders, 4 Hispanic Americans, 49 international. Average age 28. 44 applicants. In 2006, 26 degrees awarded. *Degree requirements:* For master's, thesis, final review. *Entrance requirements:* For master's, minimum GPA of 3.0, portfolio. *Application deadline:* For fall admission, 9/7 for domestic and international students; for spring admission, 2/2 for domestic and international students. Applications are processed on a rolling basis. Application fee: $100 ($500 for international students). Electronic applications accepted. *Expenses:* Tuition: Full-time $15,600; part-time $650 per unit. Required fees: $280. *Financial support:* In 2006–07, 78 students received support; fellowships, career-related internships or fieldwork and Federal Work-Study available. Support available to part-time students. Financial award application deadline: 8/10; financial award applicants required to submit FAFSA. *Unit head:* Melinda Mettler, Director, 800-544-ARTS, E-mail: mmettler@academyart.edu. *Application contact:* 800-544-ARTS, Fax: 415-263-4130, E-mail: info@academyart.edu.

Ball State University, Graduate School, College of Communication, Information, and Media, Department of Journalism, Muncie, IN 47306-1099. Offers journalism (MA); public relations (MA). *Faculty:* 14. *Students:* 41 full-time (29 women), 39 part-time (33 women); includes 7 minority (5 African Americans, 1 American Indian/Alaska Native, 1 Asian American or Pacific Islander), 19 international. Average age 26. 49 applicants, 69% accepted, 18 enrolled. In 2006, 30 degrees awarded. *Entrance requirements:* For master's, resumé. Application fee: $25 ($35 for international students). *Financial support:* In 2006–07, 3 research assistantships with full tuition reimbursements (averaging $7,326 per year), 14 teaching assistantships with full tuition reimbursements (averaging $7,326 per year) were awarded; career-related internships or fieldwork also available. Financial award application deadline: 3/1. *Faculty research:* Image studies, readership surveys, audience perception studies. *Unit head:* Marilyn Weaver, Chairperson, 765-285-8200, Fax: 765-285-7997, E-mail: mweaver@bsu.edu. *Application contact:* Dan Waechter, Information Contact, 765-285-8200, Fax: 765-285-7997, E-mail: dwaechter@bsu.edu.

Boston University, College of Communication, Department of Mass Communication, Advertising, and Public Relations, Boston, MA 02215. Offers advertising (MS); communication research (MS); communication studies (MS); public relations (MS); JD/MS. *Faculty:* 21 full-time, 28 part-time/adjunct. *Students:* 105 full-time (85 women), 51 part-time (38 women); includes 20 minority (4 African Americans, 10 Asian Americans or Pacific Islanders, 6 Hispanic Americans), 24 international. Average age 24. In 2006, 65 degrees awarded. *Degree requirements:* For master's, thesis. *Entrance requirements:* For master's, GRE General Test, samples of written work. Additional exam requirements/recommendations for international students: Required—TOEFL. *Application deadline:* For fall admission, 2/1 for domestic students. Application fee: $60. Electronic applications accepted. *Expenses:* Tuition: Full-time $33,330; part-time $1,042 per credit. Required fees: $462; $40. *Financial support:* Research assistantships, teaching assistantships with partial tuition reimbursements, career-related internships or fieldwork, Federal Work-Study, institutionally sponsored loans, scholarships/grants, and unspecified assistantships available. Support available to part-time students. Financial award application deadline: 2/1; financial award applicants required to submit FAFSA. *Unit head:* T. Barton Carter, Chairman, 617-353-3482, E-mail: comlaw@bu.edu. *Application contact:* William A. Taylor, Assistant Director, Graduate Services and Financial Aid, 617-353-3481, Fax: 617-358-0399, E-mail: comgrad@bu.edu.

Boston University, Metropolitan College (Continuing Education), Program in Advertising, Boston, MA 02215. Offers MS. Part-time programs available. *Faculty:* 4 part-time/adjunct (2 women). *Application deadline:* Applications are processed on a rolling basis. Application fee: $65. Electronic applications accepted. *Expenses:* Tuition: Full-time $33,330; part-time $1,042 per credit. Required fees: $462; $40. *Financial support:* Institutionally sponsored loans, tuition waivers (partial), and unspecified assistantships available. *Faculty research:* Communication and advertising. *Unit head:* Dr. Tobe Berkovitz, Associate Dean, 617-353-3447, E-mail: tobetv@bu.edu. *Application contact:* Dr. Tobe Berkovitz, Associate Dean, 617-353-3447, E-mail: tobetv@bu.edu.

California State University, Fullerton, Graduate Studies, College of Communications, Department of Communications, Fullerton, CA 92834-9480. Offers advertising (MA); communications (MA); journalism education (MA); news editorial (MA); photo communication (MA); public relations (MA); radio, television and film (MA); technical communication (MA). Part-time programs available. *Students:* 24 full-time (18 women), 34 part-time (21 women); includes 15 minority (2 African Americans, 5 Asian Americans or Pacific Islanders, 8 Hispanic Americans), 10 international. Average age 30. 159 applicants, 35% accepted, 21 enrolled. In 2006, 60 degrees awarded. *Degree requirements:* For master's, project or thesis. *Entrance requirements:* For master's, GRE General Test. Application fee: $55. *Expenses:* Tuition, nonresident: part-time $339 per unit. Required fees: $1,155 per semester. *Financial support:* Teaching assistantships, career-related internships or fieldwork, Federal Work-Study, institutionally sponsored loans, and scholarships/grants available. Support available to part-time students. Financial award application deadline: 3/1. *Unit head:* Dr. Tony Fellow, Chair, 714-278-3517. *Application contact:* Coordinator, 714-278-3832.

Colorado State University, Graduate School, College of Liberal Arts, Department of Journalism and Technical Communication, Fort Collins, CO 80523-0015. Offers technical communication (MS). Part-time programs available. *Faculty:* 16 full-time (6 women). *Students:* 17 full-time (4 women), 29 part-time (3 women); includes 8 minority (2 American Indian/Alaska Native, 1 Asian American or Pacific Islander, 5 Hispanic Americans), 2 international. Average age 35. 32 applicants, 63% accepted, 11 enrolled. In 2006, 35 degrees awarded. *Degree requirements:* For master's, thesis (for some programs), registration. *Entrance requirements:* For master's, GRE General Test, samples of written work, letters of recommendation, resumé or curriculum vita, 3 writing/communication projects. Additional exam requirements/recommendations for international students: Required—TOEFL (minimum score 600 paper-based; 250 computer-based). *Application deadline:* For fall admission, 4/1 priority date for domestic students, 4/1 for international students. Applications are processed on a rolling basis. Application fee: $50. Electronic applications accepted. *Expenses:* Tuition, state resident: full-time $4,248; part-time $236 per credit. Tuition, nonresident: full-time $15,642; part-time $869 per credit. Required fees: $66 per credit. Tuition and fees vary according to program. *Financial support:* In 2006–07, 18 students received support, including 1 fellowship with partial tuition reimbursement available (averaging $10,000 per year), 3 research assistantships with full and partial tuition reimbursements available (averaging $2,124 per year), 10 teaching assistantships with partial tuition reimbursements available (averaging $2,832 per year); career-related internships or fieldwork, Federal Work-Study, institutionally sponsored loans, scholarships/grants, and traineeships also available. Support available to part-time students. Financial award application deadline: 4/1. *Faculty research:* Technical/science communication, public relations, health/risk communication, web/new media technologies, environmental communication. Total annual research expenditures: $452,751. *Unit head:* Greg Luft, Chair, 970-491-6310, Fax: 970-491-2908. *Application contact:* Cindy Christen, Associate Professor and Graduate Program Coordinator, 970-491-6319, Fax: 970-491-2908, E-mail: cindy.christen@colostate.edu.

Emerson College, Graduate Studies, School of Communication, Department of Marketing Communication, Boston, MA 02116-4624. Offers global marketing communication and advertising (MA); health communication (MA); integrated marketing communication (MA). *Entrance requirements:* For master's, GRE General Test. Additional exam requirements/recommendations for international students: Required—TOEFL. Electronic applications accepted.

Golden Gate University, Ageno School of Business, San Francisco, CA 94105-2968. Offers accounting (M Ac, MBA); business administration (EMBA, MBA, DBA); finance (MBA, MS, Certificate); financial planning (MS, Certificate); human resource management (MBA, MS); human resources management (Certificate); information technology (MBA); information technology management (MS, Certificate); integrated marketing and communications (MS, Certificate); international business (MBA); management (MBA); marketing (MBA, MS, Certificate); operations management (Certificate); psychology (MA, Certificate); public relations (MS, Certificate); JD/MBA. Part-time and evening/weekend programs available. *Students:* 355 full-time (192 women), 977 part-time (465 women); includes 447 minority (85 African Americans, 5 American Indian/Alaska Native, 274 Asian Americans or Pacific Islanders, 83 Hispanic Americans), 226 international. Average age 34. 548 applicants, 74% accepted, 201 enrolled. In 2006, 545 master's, 21 doctorates awarded. *Degree requirements:* For doctorate, thesis/dissertation. *Entrance requirements:* For master's, GMAT (MBA), minimum GPA of 2.5 (MS). Additional exam requirements/recommendations for international students: Required—TOEFL. *Application deadline:* Applications are processed on a rolling basis. Application fee: $55 ($90 for international students). *Financial support:* Career-related internships or fieldwork, Federal Work-Study, and institutionally sponsored loans available. Support available to part-time students. Financial award applicants required to submit FAFSA. *Unit head:* Terry Connelly, Dean, 415-442-6519, Fax: 415-442-5369. *Application contact:* Enrollment Services, 415-442-7800, Fax: 415-442-7807, E-mail: info@ggu.edu.

Huron University USA in London, Graduate Programs, Program in Marketing, London, United Kingdom. Offers advertising (MA); marketing (MA); public relations (MA). *Entrance requirements:* Additional exam requirements/recommendations for international students: Required—TOEFL (minimum score 580 paper-based; 237 computer-based), TWE (minimum score 5). Electronic applications accepted.

Iona College, School of Arts and Science, Department of Mass Communication, New Rochelle, NY 10801-1890. Offers journalism (MS); public relations (MA). *Accreditation:* ACEJMC (one or more programs are accredited). Part-time and evening/weekend programs available. *Faculty:* 19 full-time (0 women), 15 part-time/adjunct (8 women). *Students:* 2 full-time (both women), 39 part-time (29 women); includes 8 minority (3 African Americans, 1 American Indian/Alaska Native, 4 Hispanic Americans), 3 international. Average age 29. 34 applicants, 59% accepted, 15 enrolled. In 2006, 22 degrees awarded. *Degree requirements:* For master's, comprehensive exam or thesis. *Entrance requirements:* For master's, GRE General Test, minimum GPA of 3.0. Additional exam requirements/recommendations for international students: Required—TOEFL (minimum score 550 paper-based; 213 computer-based). *Application deadline:* Applications are processed on a rolling basis. Application fee: $50. Electronic applications accepted. *Expenses:* Contact institution. *Financial support:* Career-related internships or fieldwork, tuition waivers (partial), and unspecified assistantships available. Support available to part-time students. *Faculty research:* Media ecology, new media, corporate communication, media images, organizational learning in public relations. *Unit head:* Dr. Orly Shachar, Chair, 914-633-2165, E-mail: oshachar@iona.edu. *Application contact:* Veronica Jarek-Prinz, Graduate Admissions, 914-633-2289, Fax: 914-633-2012, E-mail: vjarekprinz@iona.edu.

Marquette University, Graduate School, College of Communication, Milwaukee, WI 53201-1881. Offers advertising and public relations (MA); broadcasting and electronic communications (MA); communications studies (MA); journalism (MA); mass communications (MA); religious communications (MA); science, health and environmental communications (MA). *Accreditation:* ACEJMC. Part-time and evening/weekend programs available. *Faculty:* 33 full-time (17 women), 43 part-time/adjunct (25 women). *Students:* 29 full-time (19 women), 23 part-time (11 women); includes 5 minority (1 African American, 3 Asian Americans or Pacific Islanders, 1 Hispanic American), 11 international. Average age 29. 119 applicants, 54% accepted, 29 enrolled. In 2006, 17 degrees awarded. *Degree requirements:* For master's, comprehensive exam. *Entrance requirements:* For master's, GRE. Additional exam requirements/recommendations for international students: Required—TOEFL. Application fee: $40. *Financial support:* In 2006–07, 6 research assistantships, 12 teaching assistantships were awarded; career-related internships or fieldwork, Federal Work-Study, institutionally sponsored loans, scholarships/grants, and tuition waivers (full and partial) also available. Support available to part-time students. Financial award application deadline: 2/15. *Faculty research:* Urban journalism, gender and communication, intercultural communication, religious communication. Total annual research expenditures: $17,806. *Unit head:* Dr. Ana Garner, Dean, 414-288-3588, Fax: 414-288-1578.

Michigan State University, The Graduate School, College of Communication Arts and Sciences, Department of Advertising, Public Relations and Retailing, East Lansing, MI 48824. Offers advertising (MA); public relations (MA); retailing (MS, PhD). *Faculty:* 14 full-time (9 women). *Students:* 73 full-time (57 women), 16 part-time (13 women); includes 12 minority (7 African Americans, 5 Asian Americans or Pacific Islanders), 60 international. Average age 27. 165 applicants, 58% accepted. In 2006, 25 degrees awarded. *Entrance requirements:* Additional exam requirements/recommendations for international students: Required—TOEFL. Application fee: $50. Electronic applications accepted. *Expenses:* Tuition, state resident: part-time $346 per credit hour. Tuition, nonresident: part-time $730 per credit hour. Tuition and fees vary according to program. *Financial support:* In 2006–07, 5 fellowships with tuition reimbursements, 7 research assistantships with tuition reimbursements (averaging $12,578 per year), 8 teaching assistantships with tuition reimbursements (averaging $12,256 per year) were awarded; career-related internships or fieldwork, scholarships/grants, and unspecified assistantships also available. Total annual research expenditures: $87,285. *Unit head:* Dr. Richard T. Cole, Chairperson, 517-355-2314, Fax: 517-432-2589, E-mail: rcole1@msu.edu. *Application contact:* Pamela Brock, Graduate Secretary, 517-355-2314, Fax: 517-432-2589, E-mail: brockp@msu.edu.

Mississippi College, Graduate School, College of Arts and Sciences, School of Christian Studies and the Arts, Department of Communication, Clinton, MS 39058. Offers applied communication (MSC); public relations and corporate communication (MSC). Part-time programs available. *Faculty:* 3 full-time (0 women), 4 part-time/adjunct (1 woman). *Students:* 7 full-time (4 women), 9 part-time (8 women); includes 5 minority (all African Americans), 4 international. Average age 27. In 2006, 5 degrees awarded. *Degree requirements:* For master's, thesis optional. *Entrance requirements:* For master's, GRE or NTE, minimum GPA of 2.5. Additional exam requirements/recommendations for international students: Recommended—IELTS. *Application deadline:* For fall admission, 4/1 for domestic students. Applications are processed on a rolling basis. Application fee: $25. Electronic applications accepted. *Expenses:* Tuition: Full-time $7,290; part-time $405 per hour. Required fees: $150 per term. Tuition and fees vary according to campus/location and program. *Financial support:* Career-related internships or fieldwork, Federal Work-Study, and unspecified assistantships available. Support available to part-time students. Financial award application deadline: 4/1; financial award applicants required to submit FAFSA. *Unit head:* Dr. Cliff Fortenberry, Chair, 601-925-3457, E-mail: fortenbe@mc.edu.

Monmouth University, Graduate School, Department of Corporate and Public Communication, West Long Branch, NJ 07764-1898. Offers corporate and public communication (MA); human resources communication (Certificate); media studies (Certificate); public relations (Certificate). *Faculty:* 8 full-time (5 women). *Students:* 7 full-time (4 women), 43 part-time (33 women); includes 5 minority (1 African American, 2 Asian Americans or Pacific Islanders, 2 Hispanic Americans), 3 international. Average age 31. 33 applicants, 97% accepted, 14 enrolled. In 2006, 16 degrees awarded. *Degree requirements:* For master's, project. *Entrance requirements:* For master's, GRE, minimum GPA of 3.0 in major, 2.75 overall. Additional exam requirements/recommendations for international students: Required—TOEFL (minimum score 550 paper-based; 213 computer-based; 79 iBT), IELTS (minimum score 5), MELAB 77, Cambridge A, B, C. *Application deadline:* For fall admission, 7/15 priority date for domestic students, 6/1 for international students; for spring admission, 11/15 priority date for domestic students, 11/1 for international students. Applications are processed on a rolling basis. Application fee: $50. Electronic applications accepted. *Expenses:* Tuition: Full-time $12,780; part-time $710 per credit. Required fees: $628; $314 per term. *Financial support:* In 2006–07, 31 fellowships (averaging $1,706 per year), 9 research assistantships (averaging $6,536 per year) were awarded; scholarships/grants and unspecified assistantships also available. Support available to part-time students. Financial award application deadline: 3/1; financial award applicants required to submit FAFSA. *Faculty research:* Service learning, history of television, feminism and the media, executive communication, public relations pedagogy. *Unit head:* Dr. Eleanor Novek, Program Director, 732-263-5449, Fax: 732-571-3609, E-mail: enovek@monmouth.edu. *Application contact:* Kevin Roane, Director, Office of Graduate Admission, 732-571-3452, Fax: 732-263-5123, E-mail: gradadm@monmouth.edu.

Montana State University–Billings, College of Arts and Sciences, Department of Communication and Theater, Billings, MT 59101-0298. Offers public relations (MS). Part-time programs available. Postbaccalaureate distance learning degree programs offered. *Students:* 13. 12 applicants, 100% accepted, 12 enrolled. In 2006, 11 degrees awarded. *Degree requirements:* For master's, thesis optional. *Entrance requirements:* For master's, GRE General Test, minimum undergraduate GPA of 3.0, 3 letters of recommendation. *Application deadline:* For fall admission, 3/15 for domestic students; for spring admission, 10/15 for domestic students. Applications are processed on a rolling basis. Application fee: $40. *Expenses:* Tuition, state resident: full-time $4,599. Tuition, nonresident: full-time $10,786. *Financial support:* Teaching assistantships, career-related internships or fieldwork, Federal Work-Study, institutionally sponsored loans, and scholarships/grants available. Support available to part-time students. Financial award application deadline: 5/1; financial award applicants required to submit FAFSA. *Unit head:* Dr. Daniel Gross, Chair, 406-657-2178, E-mail: dgross@msubillings.edu. *Application contact:* David M. Sullivan, Graduate Studies Counselor, 406-657-2053, Fax: 406-657-2299, E-mail: dsullivan@msubillings.edu.

Montclair State University, The Graduate School, School of the Arts, Department of Communication Studies, Montclair, NJ 07043-1624. Offers organizational communication (MA); public relations (MA); speech communication (MA). Part-time and evening/weekend programs available. *Faculty:* 4 full-time (2 women), 41 part-time/adjunct (21 women). *Students:* 7 full-time (6 women), 18 part-time (12 women); includes 6 minority (5 African Americans, 1 Hispanic American), 3 international. 25 applicants, 28% accepted, 5 enrolled. In 2006, 2 degrees awarded. *Degree requirements:* For master's, comprehensive exam. *Entrance requirements:* For master's, GRE General Test, minimum GPA of 3.0; undergraduate degree or work in theatre, oral interpretation, speech communication, media, or broadcasting; 2 letters of recommendation. Additional exam requirements/recommendations for international students: Required—TOEFL (minimum score 83 computer-based). *Application deadline:* For fall admission, 6/1 for international students; for spring admission, 10/1 for international students. Applications are processed on a rolling basis. Application fee: $60. Electronic applications accepted. *Expenses:* Tuition, state resident: part-time $450 per credit. Tuition, nonresident: part-time $682 per credit. Tuition and fees vary according to degree level and program. *Financial support:* In 2006–07, 1 research assistantship with full tuition reimbursement (averaging $7,000 per year) was awarded; Federal Work-Study, scholarships/grants, and unspecified assistantships also available. Support available to part-time students. Financial award application deadline: 3/1; financial award applicants required to submit FAFSA. *Unit head:* Dr. Wayne Bond, Chairperson, 973-655-5214. *Application contact:* Dr. Michael Kent, Adviser, 973-655-5130, E-mail: kentm@mail.montclair.edu.

New York University, School of Continuing and Professional Studies, Center for Marketing, Program in Public Relations and Corporate Communications, New York, NY 10012-1019. Offers MS. Part-time programs available. *Faculty:* 1 full-time (0 women), 9 part-time/adjunct (2 women). *Students:* 20 full-time (17 women), 77 part-time (63 women); includes 25 minority (13 African Americans, 4 Asian Americans or Pacific Islanders, 8 Hispanic Americans), 12 international. Average age 27. 85 applicants, 58% accepted, 31 enrolled. *Degree requirements:* For master's, capstone project. *Entrance requirements:* For master's, GRE General Test or GMAT, related work experience, 2 letters of recommendation, resumé. Additional exam requirements/recommendations for international students: Required—TOEFL (minimum score 600 paper-based; 250 computer-based; 100 iBT), TWE. *Application deadline:* For fall admission, 3/15 priority date for domestic students, 3/15 for international students; for spring admission, 10/15 priority date for domestic students, 8/15 for international students. Applications are processed on a rolling basis. Application fee: $75. *Expenses:* Tuition: Part-time $1,080 per unit. Required fees: $56 per unit. $329 per term. Tuition and fees vary according to program. *Financial support:* In 2006–07, 34 students received support, including fellowships (averaging $922 per year); scholarships/grants also available. Financial award applicants required to submit FAFSA. *Unit head:* John Doorley, Director, 212-992-3600, Fax: 212-992-3650. *Application contact:* Helen Sapp, Assistant Director, 212-992-3600, Fax: 212-992-3676, E-mail: helen.sapp@nyu.edu.

Northwestern University, Medill School of Journalism, Integrated Marketing Communications Program, Evanston, IL 60208. Offers advertising/sales promotion (MSIMC); direct database and e-commerce marketing (MSIMC); general studies (MSIMC); public relations (MSIMC). Part-time programs available. *Entrance requirements:* For master's, GRE General Test or GMAT, full-time work experience (preferred). Additional exam requirements/recommendations for international students: Required—TOEFL. Electronic applications accepted. *Faculty research:* Data mining, business to business marketing, values in advertising, political advertising.

See Close-Up on page 655.

Rowan University, Graduate School, College of Communication, Program in Public Relations, Glassboro, NJ 08028-1701. Offers MA. Part-time and evening/weekend programs available. *Students:* 13 full-time (9 women), 10 part-time (7 women); includes 3 minority (2 African Americans, 1 Asian American or Pacific Islander). Average age 27. 12 applicants, 92% accepted, 11 enrolled. In 2006, 8 degrees awarded. *Degree requirements:* For master's, thesis, comprehensive exam. *Entrance requirements:* Additional exam requirements/recommendations for international students: Required—TOEFL. *Application deadline:* Applications are processed on a rolling basis. Application fee: $50. Electronic applications accepted. *Expenses:* Tuition, state resident: full-time $9,882; part-time $549 per credit. Tuition, nonresident: full-time $9,882; part-time $549 per credit. Tuition and fees vary according to degree level. *Financial support:* Career-related internships or fieldwork and unspecified assistantships available. Support available to part-time students. *Unit head:* Dr. J. Basso, Adviser, 856-256-4609, E-mail: basso@rowan.edu. *Application contact:* Chair, 856-256-4265.

Royal Roads University, Graduate Studies, School of Business, Victoria, BC V9B 5Y2, Canada. Offers digital technologies management (MBA); executive management (MBA), including global aviation management, knowledge management, leadership; human resources management (MBA); public relations and communications management (MBA). Postbaccalaureate distance learning degree programs offered (minimal on-campus study). *Degree requirements:* For master's, thesis. *Entrance requirements:* For master's, 5-7 years of related work experience. Additional exam requirements/recommendations for international students: Required—TOEFL (paper-based 570; computer-based 233) or IELTS (paper-based 7) (recommended). Electronic applications accepted. Expenses: Contact institution. *Faculty research:* Global venture analysis standards; computer assisted venture opportunity screening; teaching philosophies, instructions and methods.

San Diego State University, Graduate and Research Affairs, College of Professional Studies and Fine Arts, School of Communication, San Diego, CA 92182. Offers advertising and public relations (MA); critical-cultural studies (MA); interaction studies (MA); intercultural and international studies (MA); new media studies (MA); news and information studies (MA); telecommunications and media management (MA). *Students:* 31 full-time (14 women), 54 part-time (41 women); includes 13 minority (4 African Americans, 4 Asian Americans or Pacific Islanders, 5 Hispanic Americans), 6 international. 177 applicants, 37% accepted, 37 enrolled. In 2006, 39 degrees awarded. *Degree requirements:* For master's, thesis. *Entrance requirements:* For master's, GRE General Test, 3 letters of recommendation. Additional exam requirements/recommendations for international students: Required—TOEFL. *Application deadline:* For fall admission, 3/1 for domestic and international students; for spring admission, 10/1 for domestic and international students. Applications are processed on a rolling basis. Application fee: $55. Electronic applications accepted. *Financial support:* In 2006–07, 34 teaching assistantships were awarded; career-related internships or fieldwork and unspecified assistantships also available. Financial award applicants required to submit FAFSA. Total annual research expenditures: $153,598. *Unit head:* Diane Borden, Interim Director, 619-594-8098, Fax: 619-594-6246. *Application contact:* Patricia Geist-Martin, Information Contact, 619-594-4182, E-mail: pgeist@mail.sdsu.edu.

Savannah College of Art and Design, Graduate School, Program in Advertising Design, Savannah, GA 31402-3146. Offers MA, MFA. Part-time programs available. *Faculty:* 3 full-time (1 woman). *Students:* 30 full-time (19 women), 10 part-time (7 women); includes 6 minority (5 African Americans, 1 Hispanic American), 14 international. 56 applicants, 39% accepted, 14 enrolled. In 2006, 2 degrees awarded. *Degree requirements:* For master's, thesis, internships. *Entrance requirements:* For master's, interview, portfolio. Additional exam requirements/recommendations for international students: Required—TOEFL (minimum score 450 paper-based; 133 computer-based). *Application deadline:* For fall admission, 4/1 priority date for domestic and international students. Applications are processed on a rolling basis. Application fee: $50. Electronic applications accepted. *Expenses:* Tuition: Full-time $23,400; part-time $520 per credit. One-time fee: $500. *Financial support:* Fellowships, career-related internships or fieldwork, Federal Work-Study, and scholarships/grants available. Financial award application deadline: 4/1; financial award applicants required to submit FAFSA. *Unit head:* David Foote, Chair, 404-253-3144, Fax: 404-253-3254, E-mail: dfoote@scad.edu. *Application contact:* Darrell Tutchton, Director of Graduate and International Enrollment, 912-525-5961, Fax: 912-525-5985, E-mail: admission@scad.edu.

Syracuse University, Graduate School, S. I. Newhouse School of Public Communications, Department of Advertising, Syracuse, NY 13244. Offers MA. *Faculty:* 5 full-time (3 women), 5 part-time/adjunct (1 woman). *Students:* 15 full-time (7 women), 1 (woman) part-time; includes 2 Hispanic Americans, 5 international. 94 applicants, 47% accepted, 15 enrolled. *Degree requirements:* For master's, capstone course. *Entrance requirements:* For master's, GRE General Test. Additional exam requirements/recommendations for international students: Required—TOEFL (minimum score 600 paper-based; 250 computer-based). *Application deadline:* For fall admission, 2/1 for domestic and international students. Application fee: $65. Electronic applications accepted. *Expenses:* Tuition: Full-time $16,920; part-time $940 per credit hour. Required fees: $930; $930 per year. *Financial support:* Fellowships, research assistantships, teaching assistantships, Federal Work-Study and tuition waivers (partial) available. *Unit head:* Caria V. Lloyd, Chair, 315-443-1944, Fax: 315-443-3946, E-mail: pcgrad@syr.edu. *Application contact:* Graduate Records Office, 315-443-4039, Fax: 315-443-1834, E-mail: pcgrad@syr.edu.

Syracuse University, Graduate School, S. I. Newhouse School of Public Communications, Department of Public Relations, Program in Public Relations, Syracuse, NY 13244. Offers MS. *Students:* 30 full-time (26 women), 1 (woman) part-time; includes 4 minority (2 African Americans, 2 Hispanic Americans), 7 international. 121 applicants, 62% accepted, 31 enrolled. *Entrance requirements:* For master's, GRE General Test. Additional exam requirements/recommendations for international students: Required—TOEFL (minimum score 600 paper-based; 250 computer-based). *Application deadline:* For fall admission, 2/1 for domestic and international students. Application fee: $65. Electronic applications accepted. *Expenses:* Tuition: Full-time $16,920; part-time $940 per credit hour. Required fees: $930; $930 per year. *Application contact:* Graduate Records Office, 315-443-4039, Fax: 315-443-1834, E-mail: pcgrad@syr.edu.

Texas Christian University, College of Communication, Schieffer School of Journalism, Fort Worth, TX 76129-0002. Offers advertising/public relations (MS); news-editorial (MS). Part-time and evening/weekend programs available. *Degree requirements:* For master's, thesis, written exam. *Entrance requirements:* For master's, GRE General Test. Additional exam requirements/recommendations for international students: Required—TOEFL. *Application deadline:* For fall admission, 3/1 for domestic students; for spring admission, 12/1 for domestic students. Applications are processed on a rolling basis. Application fee: $0. *Expenses:* Tuition: Part-time $800 per credit hour. *Financial support:* Application deadline: 3/1. *Unit head:* Dr. Tommy Thomason, Director, 817-257-7425, E-mail: t.thomason@tcu.edu.

Towson University, Graduate School, Program in Strategic Public Relations and Integrated Communications, Towson, MD 21252-0001. Offers Certificate. Evening/weekend programs available. Postbaccalaureate distance learning degree programs offered (no on-campus study). *Students:* 6 full-time (5 women), 8 part-time (all women); includes 5 minority (all African Americans) In 2006, 5 degrees awarded. *Entrance requirements:* For degree, 24 credits in related course work, minimum GPA of 3.0. *Application deadline:* For fall admission, 1/15 for domestic students. Application fee: $50. Electronic applications accepted. *Expenses:* Tuition, state resident: part-time $275 per unit. Tuition, nonresident: part-time $577 per unit. Required fees: $72 per unit. *Financial support:* Fellowships, teaching assistantships, career-related internships or fieldwork, Federal Work-Study, and unspecified assistantships available. Support available to part-time students. Financial award application deadline: 4/1; financial award applicants required to submit FAFSA. *Unit head:* Meg Algren, Graduate Program Director, 410-704-5641, E-mail: malgren@towson.edu. *Application contact:* 410-704-2501, Fax: 410-704-4675, E-mail: grads@towson.edu.

Université Laval, Faculty of Letters, Program in Public Relations, Québec, QC G1K 7P4, Canada. Offers Diploma. Part-time and evening/weekend programs available. *Entrance requirements:* For degree, knowledge of French, comprehension of written English. Electronic applications accepted.

The University of Alabama, Graduate School, College of Communication and Information Sciences, Department of Advertising and Public Relations, Tuscaloosa, AL 35487. Offers MA. *Faculty:* 11 full-time (4 women). *Students:* 25 full-time (21 women), 2 part-time (both women); includes 3 minority (2 African Americans, 1 Hispanic American). Average age 24. 71 applicants, 48% accepted, 21 enrolled. In 2006, 15 degrees awarded. *Median time to degree:* Master's–1 year full-time, 1.8 years part-time. *Degree requirements:* For master's, thesis or alternative, comprehensive exam, registration. *Entrance requirements:* For master's, GRE General Test, minimum GPA of 3.0. Additional exam requirements/recommendations for international students: Required—TOEFL. *Application deadline:* For fall admission, 2/15 priority date for domestic students, 4/15 for international students. Applications are processed on a rolling basis. Application fee: $25. Electronic applications accepted. *Financial support:* In 2006–07, 3 research assistantships with tuition reimbursements (averaging $9,850 per year), 2 teaching assistantships with tuition reimbursements (averaging $9,850 per year) were awarded; career-related internships or fieldwork, Federal Work-Study, and institutionally sponsored loans also available. Financial award application deadline: 2/15. *Faculty research:* Advertising and public relations management, public opinion, political communication, advertising media, international communication. *Unit head:* Dr. Bruce Berger, Chair and Professor, 205-348-7692, Fax: 205-348-2401, E-mail: berger@apr.ua.edu. *Application contact:* Dr. Karla Gower, Graduate Coordinator, 205-348-0132, Fax: 205-348-2401, E-mail: gower@apr.ua.edu.

University of Colorado at Denver and Health Sciences Center, College of Liberal Arts and Sciences, Department of Communication, Denver, CO 80217-3364. Offers communication (MA); interactive media (Certificate); public relations (Certificate); technical and professional communication (Certificate); technical communication (MS); usability testing and interface design (Certificate). Part-time and evening/weekend programs available. *Faculty:* 9 full-time (4 women). *Students:* 7 full-time (6 women), 16 part-time (9 women); includes 4 minority (1 African American, 1 Asian American or Pacific Islander, 2 Hispanic Americans), 1 international. Average age 31. 12 applicants, 50% accepted, 2 enrolled. In 2006, 9 degrees awarded. *Degree requirements:* For master's, thesis or alternative, comprehensive exam, registration

Advertising and Public Relations

University of Colorado at Denver and Health Sciences Center (continued)
(for some programs). *Entrance requirements:* For master's, GRE General Test. Additional exam requirements/recommendations for international students: Required—TOEFL (minimum score 525 paper-based; 197 computer-based). *Application deadline:* For fall admission, 6/1 for domestic students. Applications are processed on a rolling basis. Application fee: $50 ($75 for international students). Electronic applications accepted. *Financial support:* Fellowships with partial tuition reimbursements, research assistantships with partial tuition reimbursements, teaching assistantships, Federal Work-Study and institutionally sponsored loans available. Financial award application deadline: 4/1; financial award applicants required to submit FAFSA. *Unit head:* Dr. Brenda J Allen, Chair, 303-556-6713, E-mail: brenda.j.allen@cudenver.edu.

University of Denver, Faculty of Arts and Humanities/Social Sciences, School of Communication, Department of Mass Communications, Denver, CO 80208. Offers advertising management (MS); digital media studies (MA); mass communications (MA); public relations (MS); video production (MA). Part-time programs available. *Faculty:* 14 full-time (8 women). *Students:* 5 full-time (2 women), 37 part-time (24 women); includes 4 minority (1 African American, 3 Hispanic Americans), 2 international. Average age 27. 97 applicants, 64% accepted. In 2006, 18 degrees awarded. *Degree requirements:* For master's, thesis (for some programs). *Entrance requirements:* For master's, GRE General Test. Additional exam requirements/recommendations for international students: Required—TOEFL, TWE. *Application deadline:* Applications are processed on a rolling basis. Application fee: $50. Electronic applications accepted. *Expenses:* Tuition: Full-time $29,628; part-time $823 per credit. *Financial support:* In 2006–07, 1 research assistantship with full and partial tuition reimbursement (averaging $6,000 per year), 4 teaching assistantships with full and partial tuition reimbursements (averaging $10,000 per year) were awarded; career-related internships or fieldwork, Federal Work-Study, institutionally sponsored loans, and scholarships/grants also available. Support available to part-time students. Financial award application deadline: 3/1; financial award applicants required to submit FAFSA. *Unit head:* Dr. Diane Waldman, Unit Head, 303-871-2166. *Application contact:* Information Contact, 303-871-2166, E-mail: mcomadm@du.edu.

University of Florida, Graduate School, College of Journalism and Communications, Department of Advertising, Gainesville, FL 32611. Offers M Adv. *Faculty:* 12 full-time (7 women). *Students:* 27 (20 women); includes 2 minority (both Asian Americans or Pacific Islanders) 13 international. In 2006, 8 degrees awarded. *Degree requirements:* For master's, thesis optional. *Entrance requirements:* For master's, GRE General Test, minimum GPA of 3.0. Additional exam requirements/recommendations for international students: Required—TOEFL (minimum score 550 paper-based; 213 computer-based). *Application deadline:* For fall admission, 6/1 priority date for domestic students. Applications are processed on a rolling basis. Application fee: $30. *Expenses:* Tuition, state resident: full-time $6,827. Tuition, nonresident: full-time $21,951. Required fees: $999. *Unit head:* Dr. John C. Sutherland, Chair, 352-392-9172, Fax: 352-846-3015, E-mail: jsutherland@jou.ufl.edu.

University of Florida, Graduate School, College of Journalism and Communications, Department of Public Relations, Gainesville, FL 32611. Offers MAMC. *Faculty:* 9 full-time (5 women). *Degree requirements:* For master's, thesis optional. *Entrance requirements:* For master's, GRE General Test, minimum GPA of 3.0. *Application deadline:* For fall admission, 6/1 priority date for domestic students. Applications are processed on a rolling basis. Application fee: $20. *Expenses:* Tuition, state resident: full-time $6,827. Tuition, nonresident: full-time $21,951. Required fees: $999. *Unit head:* Spiro K. Kiousis, Chair, 352-273-1220. *Application contact:* Dr. Linda C. Hon, Graduate Coordinator, 352-392-6522, Fax: 352-392-3952, E-mail: lhon@jou.ufl.edu.

University of Houston, College of Liberal Arts and Social Sciences, School of Communication, Houston, TX 77204. Offers mass communication studies (MA); public relations studies (MA); speech communication (MA). Part-time and evening/weekend programs available. *Faculty:* 8 full-time (3 women), 1 part-time/adjunct (0 women). *Students:* 42 full-time (31 women), 56 part-time (42 women); includes 39 minority (24 African Americans, 1 American Indian/Alaska Native, 4 Asian Americans or Pacific Islanders, 10 Hispanic Americans), 13 international. Average age 29. 62 applicants, 65% accepted, 23 enrolled. In 2006, 13 master's awarded. *Entrance requirements:* For master's, GRE General Test, minimum GPA of 3.0 in last 60 hours of course work. *Application deadline:* For fall admission, 7/3 priority date for domestic students. Applications are processed on a rolling basis. Application fee: $25 ($75 for international students). *Expenses:* Tuition, state resident: full-time $5,429; part-time $226 per credit. Tuition, nonresident: full-time $12,029; part-time $501 per credit. Required fees: $2,454. *Financial support:* In 2006–07, 3 fellowships with full tuition reimbursements (averaging $9,750 per year), 8 teaching assistantships with full tuition reimbursements (averaging $9,750 per year) were awarded; research assistantships with full tuition reimbursements, career-related internships or fieldwork, Federal Work-Study, institutionally sponsored loans, scholarships/grants, health care benefits, and unspecified assistantships also available. Support available to part-time students. Financial award application deadline: 3/10. *Faculty research:* Risk communication, relationship development, critical studies, corporate communication. *Unit head:* Beth Olson, Chairperson, 713-743-2873, Fax: 713-743-2876, E-mail: bolson@uh.edu. *Application contact:* Angela Parrish, Graduate Coordinator, 713-743-2873, Fax: 713-743-2876, E-mail: aparrish@bayou.uh.edu.

University of Illinois at Urbana–Champaign, Graduate College, College of Communications, Department of Advertising, Champaign, IL 61820. Offers MS. *Accreditation:* ACEJMC. *Faculty:* 7 full-time (3 women). *Students:* 26 full-time (18 women), 1 (woman) part-time; includes 5 minority (3 African Americans, 2 Asian Americans or Pacific Islanders), 10 international. 89 applicants, 33% accepted, 13 enrolled. In 2006, 17 degrees awarded. *Entrance requirements:* For master's, GMAT or GRE General Test, minimum GPA of 3.0. *Application deadline:* For fall admission, 2/15 priority date for domestic students. Applications are processed on a rolling basis. Application fee: $50 ($60 for international students). Electronic applications accepted. *Financial support:* In 2006–07, 1 research assistantship, 18 teaching assistantships were awarded; fellowships, tuition waivers (full and partial) also available. Financial award application deadline: 2/15. *Faculty research:* Consumer behavior, persuasive communication. *Unit head:* Norman Denzin, Interim Head, 217-333-1602, Fax: 217-244-3348, E-mail: n-denzin@uiuc.edu. *Application contact:* Cinda Robbins-Cornstubble, Administrative Secretary, 217-333-1602, Fax: 217-244-3348, E-mail: ccornstu@uiuc.edu.

University of Maryland, College Park, Graduate Studies, College of Arts and Humanities, Department of Communication, College Park, MD 20742. Offers MA, PhD. *Faculty:* 25 full-time (14 women), 3 part-time/adjunct (2 women). *Students:* 51 full-time (35 women), 6 part-time (4 women); includes 5 minority (4 African Americans, 1 Asian American or Pacific Islander), 12 international. 182 applicants, 16% accepted, 17 enrolled. In 2006, 7 master's, 6 doctorates awarded. *Degree requirements:* For master's, thesis optional; for doctorate, thesis/dissertation, comprehensive exam. *Entrance requirements:* For master's, GRE General Test, minimum GPA of 3.0, sample of scholarly writing, 3 letters of recommendation; for doctorate, GRE General Test. Additional exam requirements/recommendations for international students: Required—TOEFL. *Application deadline:* For fall admission, 2/1 for domestic and international students. Applications are processed on a rolling basis. Application fee: $60. Electronic applications accepted. *Financial support:* In 2006–07, 6 fellowships with full tuition reimbursements (averaging $7,844 per year), 44 teaching assistantships with tuition reimbursements (averaging $14,288 per year) were awarded; Federal Work-Study, scholarships/grants, and unspecified assistantships also available. Support available to part-time students. Financial award applicants required to submit FAFSA. *Faculty research:* Health communication, interpersonal communication, persuasion, intercultural communication, contemporary rhetoric theory. Total annual research expenditures: $58,984. *Unit head:* Dr. Edward L. Fink, Chairman, 301-405-0870, Fax: 301-314-9471, E-mail: elf@deans.umd.edu. *Application contact:* Dean of Graduate School, 301-405-4190, Fax: 301-314-9305.

University of Miami, Graduate School, School of Communication, Coral Gables, FL 33124. Offers communication (PhD); communication studies (MA); film studies (MA, PhD); motion pictures (MFA), including production, producing, and screenwriting; print journalism (MA); public relations (MA); Spanish language journalism (MA); television broadcast journalism (MA). *Accreditation:* ACEJMC. Part-time programs available. *Faculty:* 39 full-time (12 women). *Students:* 107 full-time (57 women), 24 part-time (15 women); includes 38 minority (10 African Americans, 3 Asian Americans or Pacific Islanders, 25 Hispanic Americans), 15 international. Average age 27. 330 applicants, 44% accepted, 64 enrolled. In 2006, 54 degrees awarded. *Degree requirements:* For master's, thesis (for some programs), comprehensive exam (for some programs); for doctorate, thesis/dissertation, comprehensive exam. *Entrance requirements:* For master's, GRE General Test; for doctorate, GRE General Test, master's thesis or scholarly research. Additional exam requirements/recommendations for international students: Required—TOEFL (minimum score 600 paper-based; 250 computer-based; 100 iBT). *Application deadline:* For fall admission, 12/15 priority date for domestic and international students. Applications are processed on a rolling basis. Application fee: $50. Electronic applications accepted. *Financial support:* In 2006–07, 8 teaching assistantships with full tuition reimbursements were awarded; fellowships with full tuition reimbursements, Federal Work-Study, institutionally sponsored loans, scholarships/grants, tuition waivers (partial), and unspecified assistantships also available. Financial award application deadline: 3/1; financial award applicants required to submit FAFSA. *Faculty research:* Communication studies, mass communication, international/interpersonal communication, film studies, journalism. *Unit head:* Dr. Sam L. Grogg, Dean, 305-284-3420, Fax: 305-284-2454, E-mail: sgrogg@miami.edu. *Application contact:* Dr. Leonardo C. Ferreira, Director of Graduate Studies, 305-284-3180, Fax: 305-284-8701, E-mail: lferreira@miami.edu.

University of New Haven, Graduate School, School of Business, Program in Business Administration, West Haven, CT 06516-1916. Offers accounting (MBA); business policy and strategy (MBA); finance (MBA); health care management (MBA); human resources management (MBA); international business (MBA); marketing (MBA); public relations (MBA); sports management (MBA); technology management (MBA); MBA/MPA; MBA/MSIE. Part-time and evening/weekend programs available. *Degree requirements:* For master's, thesis or alternative. *Entrance requirements:* For master's, GMAT.

University of Oklahoma, Graduate College, Gaylord College of Journalism and Mass Communication, Program in Journalism and Mass Communication, Norman, OK 73019-0390. Offers advertising and public relations (MA); information gathering and distribution (MA); mass communication management and policy (MA); professional writing (MA); telecommunication and new technology (MA). Part-time programs available. *Students:* 31 full-time (20 women), 48 part-time (28 women); includes 11 minority (2 African Americans, 4 American Indian/Alaska Native, 1 Asian American or Pacific Islander, 4 Hispanic Americans), 11 international. 23 applicants, 91% accepted, 17 enrolled. In 2006, 8 degrees awarded. Terminal master's awarded for partial completion of doctoral program. *Degree requirements:* For master's, thesis optional. *Entrance requirements:* For master's, GRE General Test, minimum GPA of 3.2, 9 hours of course work in journalism, course work in statistics. Additional exam requirements/recommendations for international students: Required—TOEFL (minimum score 600 paper-based; 250 computer-based), TWE (minimum score 5). *Application deadline:* For fall admission, 2/1 for domestic students, 4/1 for international students; for spring admission, 11/1 for domestic students, 9/1 for international students. Application fee: $40 ($90 for international students). *Expenses:* Tuition, state resident: full-time $3,180; part-time $133 per credit hour. Tuition, nonresident: full-time $11,347; part-time $473 per credit hour. Required fees: $1,729; $62 per credit hour. $117 per semester. Tuition and fees vary according to course load and program. *Financial support:* In 2006–07, 22 students received support. Career-related internships or fieldwork, institutionally sponsored loans, scholarships/grants, health care benefits, and unspecified assistantships available. *Faculty research:* Diversity in media, PR issues management, journalism ethics, advertising humor, media management. *Application contact:* Kelly Storm, Assistant to Graduate Director, 405-325-2722, Fax: 405-325-7565, E-mail: kstorm@ou.edu.

University of Southern California, Graduate School, Annenberg School for Communication, School of Journalism, Program in Strategic Public Relations, Los Angeles, CA 90089. Offers MA. *Students:* 58 full-time, 4 part-time; includes 19 minority (6 African Americans, 8 Asian Americans or Pacific Islanders, 5 Hispanic Americans), 10 international. 109 applicants, 43% accepted, 27 enrolled. In 2006, 35 degrees awarded. *Degree requirements:* For master's, comprehensive exam. *Entrance requirements:* For master's, GRE General Test, resumé, writing samples, letters of recommendation, statement of purpose. Additional exam requirements/recommendations for international students: Required—TOEFL (minimum score 280 computer-based; 114 iBT). *Application deadline:* For fall admission, 1/15 for domestic and international students. Application fee: $85. Electronic applications accepted. *Expenses:* Tuition: Full-time $33,314; part-time $1,121 per credit. Required fees: $522. Full-time tuition and fees vary according to program. *Financial support:* Career-related internships or fieldwork, Federal Work-Study, institutionally sponsored loans, scholarships/grants, health care benefits, and unspecified assistantships available. Support available to part-time students. Financial award application deadline: 1/15; financial award applicants required to submit FAFSA. *Unit head:* Jerry Swerling, Director, 310-456-8045, Fax: 213-740-8624, E-mail: jerry@swerling.net. *Application contact:* Allyson Hill.

University of Southern Mississippi, Graduate School, College of Arts and Letters, School of Mass Communication and Journalism, Hattiesburg, MS 39406-0001. Offers mass communication (MA, MS, PhD); public relations (MS). *Faculty:* 12 full-time (2 women). *Students:* 34 full-time (24 women), 36 part-time (21 women); includes 12 minority (10 African Americans, 2 Hispanic Americans), 6 international. Average age 32. 37 applicants, 51% accepted, 11 enrolled. In 2006, 12 master's, 6 doctorates awarded. *Degree requirements:* For master's, thesis optional; for doctorate, thesis/dissertation, comprehensive exam, registration. *Entrance requirements:* For master's, GRE General Test, minimum GPA of 3.0 in field of study, 2.75 in last 2 years; for doctorate, GRE General Test, minimum GPA of 3.5. Additional exam requirements/recommendations for international students: Required—TOEFL. *Application deadline:* For fall admission, 3/1 priority date for domestic students, 3/1 for international students. Applications are processed on a rolling basis. Application fee: $25 ($30 for international students). *Financial support:* In 2006–07, 18 students received support, including 11 teaching assistantships with full tuition reimbursements available (averaging $7,187 per year); fellowships with full tuition reimbursements available, research assistantships with full tuition reimbursements available, career-related internships or fieldwork, Federal Work-Study, and unspecified assistantships available. Financial award application deadline: 3/15. *Unit head:* Dr. Christopher Campbell, Director, 601-266-5650, Fax: 601-266-4263. *Application contact:* Dr. Gene Wiggins, Graduate Coordinator, 601-266-5650, Fax: 601-266-6473.

The University of Tennessee, Graduate School, College of Communication and Information, Knoxville, TN 37996. Offers advertising (MS, PhD); broadcasting (MS, PhD); communications (MS, PhD); information sciences (MS, PhD); journalism (MS, PhD); public relations (MS, PhD); speech communication (MS, PhD). *Accreditation:* ACEJMC (one or more programs are accredited at the [master's] level). Part-time and evening/weekend programs available. Postbaccalaureate distance learning degree programs offered (no on-campus study). *Faculty:* 63 full-time (35 women). *Students:* 118 full-time (85 women), 192 part-time (136 women); includes 24 minority (16 African Americans, 2 American Indian/Alaska Native, 5 Asian Americans or Pacific Islanders, 1 Hispanic American), 19 international. 153 applicants, 39% accepted. In 2006, 86 master's, 5 doctorates awarded. *Degree requirements:* For master's, thesis or alternative; for doctorate, thesis/dissertation. *Entrance requirements:* For master's and doctorate, GRE General Test, minimum GPA of 2.7. Additional exam requirements/recommendations for international students: Required—TOEFL. *Application deadline:* For fall admission, 2/1 priority date for domestic students. Applications are processed on a rolling basis. Application fee: $35. Electronic applications accepted. *Expenses:* Tuition, state resident: full-time $5,574. Tuition, nonresident: full-time $16,840. Required fees: $792. *Financial support:* In 2006–07, 1 fellowship, 1 research assistantship, 19 teaching assistantships were awarded; career-related internships or fieldwork, Federal Work-Study, institutionally sponsored loans, and unspecified assistantships also available. Financial award application deadline: 2/1; financial award applicants required to submit FAFSA. *Unit head:* Dr. Michael Wirth, Dean, 865-974-

3031, Fax: 865-974-3896. *Application contact:* Dr. Edward Caudill, Head, 865-974-6651, Fax: 865-974-3896, E-mail: ccaudill@utk.edu.

The University of Texas at Austin, Graduate School, College of Communication, Department of Advertising, Austin, TX 78712-1111. Offers MA, PhD. *Entrance requirements:* For master's and doctorate, GRE General Test. Electronic applications accepted. *Faculty research:* Interactive advertising, advertising laws and ethics, advertising creativity, media planning and modeling, international advertising.

University of the Sacred Heart, Graduate Programs, Department of Communication, Program in Advertising, San Juan, PR 00914-0383. Offers MA. *Degree requirements:* For master's, thesis.

University of the Sacred Heart, Graduate Programs, Department of Communication, Program in Public Relations, San Juan, PR 00914-0383. Offers MA. Part-time and evening/weekend programs available. *Degree requirements:* For master's, thesis. *Entrance requirements:* For master's, EXADEP, minimum undergraduate GPA of 2.75, interview.

University of Wisconsin–Stevens Point, College of Fine Arts and Communication, Division of Communication, Stevens Point, WI 54481-3897. Offers interpersonal communication (MA); mass communication (MA); organizational communication (MA); public relations (MA). Part-time programs available. *Faculty:* 13 full-time (5 women). *Students:* 4 full-time (3 women), 15 part-time (11 women); includes 1 minority (African American) In 2006, 7 degrees awarded. *Degree requirements:* For master's, thesis or alternative. *Entrance requirements:* For master's, GRE. Additional exam requirements/recommendations for international students: Required— TOEFL (minimum score 575 paper-based). *Application deadline:* For fall admission, 3/1 priority date for domestic students. Applications are processed on a rolling basis. Application fee: $45. *Expenses:* Tuition, state resident: full-time $5,910; part-time $328 per credit. Tuition, nonresident: full-time $16,520; part-time $918 per credit. Required fees: $756; $73 per credit. *Financial support:* In 2006–07, 9 teaching assistantships were awarded; career-related internships or fieldwork, Federal Work-Study, institutionally sponsored loans, and unspecified assistantships also available. Support available to part-time students. Financial award application deadline: 5/1; financial award applicants required to submit FAFSA. *Faculty research:* Communication theory and research, film history. *Unit head:* Dr. James Haney, Chair, 715-346-3409, E-mail: jhaney@uwsp.edu. *Application contact:* Dr. Chris Sadler, Graduate Coordinator, 715-346-3898, E-mail: csadler@uwsp.edu.

Virginia Commonwealth University, Graduate School, College of Humanities and Sciences, School of Mass Communications, Adcenter, Richmond, VA 23284-9005. Offers account management (MS); account planning (MS); art direction (MS); copywriting (MS); creative brand management (MS); creative media planning (MS). In 2006, 52 degrees awarded. *Degree requirements:* For master's, thesis optional. *Entrance requirements:* For master's, GRE General Test, interview, portfolio, screening test. Application fee: $50. *Financial support:* Career-related internships or fieldwork and Federal Work-Study available. Support available to part-time students.

Virginia Commonwealth University, Graduate School, College of Humanities and Sciences, School of Mass Communications, Program in Mass Communications, Richmond, VA 23284-9005. Offers scholastic journalism (MS); strategic public relations (MS). *Degree requirements:* For master's, thesis optional. *Entrance requirements:* For master's, GRE General Test. *Application deadline:* For fall admission, 7/1 for domestic students; for spring admission, 11/15 for domestic students. Applications are processed on a rolling basis. Application fee: $50. *Financial support:* Teaching assistantships, career-related internships or fieldwork, Federal Work-Study, institutionally sponsored loans, and tuition waivers (full and partial) available. Support available to part-time students. Financial award applicants required to submit FAFSA.

Wayne State University, College of Fine, Performing and Communication Arts, Department of Communication, Detroit, MI 48202. Offers communication studies (MA, PhD); public relations and organizational communication (MA); radio-TV-film (MA, PhD); speech communication (MA, PhD). *Faculty:* 25 full-time (10 women). *Students:* 64 full-time (43 women), 141 part-time (104 women); includes 64 minority (54 African Americans, 1 American Indian/Alaska Native, 2 Asian Americans or Pacific Islanders, 7 Hispanic Americans), 19 international. Average age 35. 84 applicants, 51% accepted, 30 enrolled. In 2006, 40 master's, 10 doctorates awarded. *Degree requirements:* For master's, thesis, essay, or comprehensive exam; for doctorate, thesis/dissertation. *Entrance requirements:* For master's, minimum GPA of 3.0; for doctorate, GRE, minimum GPA of 3.3. Additional exam requirements/recommendations for international students: Required—TOEFL (minimum score 550 paper-based; 213 computer-based); Recommended—TWE (minimum score 6). *Application deadline:* For fall admission, 4/1 for domestic students, 6/1 for international students; for winter admission, 10/1 for international students; for spring admission, 2/1 for international students. Applications are processed on a rolling basis. Application fee: $30 ($50 for international students). Electronic applications accepted. *Financial support:* In 2006–07, 22 students received support, including 17 teaching assistantships with tuition reimbursements available (averaging $12,447 per year); fellowships with tuition reimbursements available, research assistantships with tuition reimbursements available, career-related internships or fieldwork also available. Financial award application deadline: 2/1. *Faculty research:* Rhetorical theory and criticism; media history and criticism; argumentation; organizational communication and public relations; interpersonal, family, and health communication. *Unit head:* Dr. Matthew Seeger, Chair, 313-577-2959, Fax: 313-577-6300, E-mail: aa4331@wayne.edu. *Application contact:* Hayg Oshagan, Associate Professor, 313-577-0429, E-mail: ad4570@wayne.edu.

Webster University, School of Communications, Program in Advertising and Marketing Communications, St. Louis, MO 63119-3194. Offers MA. *Expenses:* Tuition: Full-time $8,820; part-time $490 per credit. Tuition and fees vary according to degree level, campus/location and program. *Unit head:* Susan Seymour, Director, 314-961-2660 Ext. 7527.

Webster University, School of Communications, Program in Public Relations, St. Louis, MO 63119-3194. Offers MA. *Expenses:* Tuition: Full-time $8,820; part-time $490 per credit. Tuition and fees vary according to degree level, campus/location and program. *Unit head:* Susan Seymour, Director, 314-961-2660 Ext. 7527.

Section 4
Electronic Commerce

This section contains a directory of institutions offering graduate work in electronic commerce. Additional information about programs listed in the directory but not augmented by an in-depth entry may be obtained by writing directly to the dean of a graduate school or chair of a department at the address given in the directory.

CONTENTS

Program Directory

Close-Ups

Electronic Commerce

Adelphi University, School of Business, Department of Management, Marketing, and Decision Sciences, Garden City, NY 11530-0701. Offers management information systems (MBA); management/human resource management (MBA); marketing/e-commerce (MBA). Part-time and evening/weekend programs available. *Students:* 67 full-time (34 women), 173 part-time (85 women); includes 44 minority (24 African Americans, 11 Asian Americans or Pacific Islanders, 9 Hispanic Americans), 49 international. Average age 31. In 2006, 122 degrees awarded. *Degree requirements:* For master's, capstone course. *Entrance requirements:* For master's, GMAT, 2 letters of recommendation. Additional exam requirements/recommendations for international students: Required—TOEFL. *Application deadline:* For fall admission, 5/1 for international students; for spring admission, 12/1 for international students. Applications are processed on a rolling basis. Application fee: $50. Electronic applications accepted. *Financial support:* Research assistantships with full and partial tuition reimbursements, career-related internships or fieldwork, Federal Work-Study, institutionally sponsored loans, scholarships/grants, and unspecified assistantships available. Financial award application deadline: 3/1; financial award applicants required to submit FAFSA. *Faculty research:* Supply chain management, distribution channels, productivity benchmark analysis, data envelopment analysis, financial portfolio analysis. *Unit head:* Dr. Allan Ashley, Chairperson, 516-877-4640, E-mail: ashley@adelphi.edu. *Application contact:* Christine Murphy, Director of Admissions, 516-877-3050, Fax: 516-877-3039, E-mail: graduateadmissions@adelphi.edu.

American University, Kogod School of Business, Department of Marketing, Program in Marketing Information and Technology, Washington, DC 20016-8001. Offers MBA. In 2006, 1 degree awarded. *Entrance requirements:* For master's, GMAT. *Expenses:* Tuition: Full-time $18,864; part-time $1,048 per credit. Required fees: $380. Tuition and fees vary according to program.

Arkansas State University, Graduate School, College of Business, Department of Computer and Information Technology, Jonesboro, State University, AR 72467. Offers business education (SCCT); business technology education (MSE); information systems and e-commerce (MS). Part-time programs available. *Faculty:* 6 full-time (1 woman), 1 part-time/adjunct (0 women). *Students:* 8 full-time (4 women), 17 part-time (13 women); includes 8 minority (all African Americans), 1 international. Average age 33. 13 applicants, 100% accepted, 13 enrolled. In 2006, 9 degrees awarded. *Degree requirements:* For master's and SCCT, thesis or alternative, comprehensive exam. *Entrance requirements:* For master's, GRE General Test or MAT, appropriate bachelor's degree, official transcript. Additional exam requirements/recommendations for international students: Required—TOEFL (minimum score 213 computer-based). *Application deadline:* Applications are processed on a rolling basis. Application fee: $30 ($40 for international students). Electronic applications accepted. *Expenses:* Contact institution. *Financial support:* Teaching assistantships, career-related internships or fieldwork and unspecified assistantships available. Financial award application deadline: 7/1; financial award applicants required to submit FAFSA. *Unit head:* Dr. John Seydel, Chair, 870-972-3416, Fax: 870-972-3417, E-mail: jseydel@astate.edu.

Boston University, Metropolitan College (Continuing Education), Program in Administrative Studies, Boston, MA 02215. Offers banking and financial management (MSM); business continuity in emergency management (MSM); economics development and tourism management (MSAS); electronic commerce, systems, and technology (MSAS); financial economics (MSAS); human resource management (MSM); innovation and technology (MSAS); insurance management (MSM); international market management (MSM); multinational commerce (MSAS); project management (MSM). *Accreditation:* AACSB. Part-time and evening/weekend programs available. *Faculty:* 9 full-time (0 women), 51 part-time/adjunct (8 women). *Students:* 105 full-time (40 women), 171 part-time (65 women); includes 27 minority (5 African Americans, 18 Asian Americans or Pacific Islanders, 4 Hispanic Americans), 125 international. Average age 29. In 2006, 310 degrees awarded. *Degree requirements:* For master's, thesis optional. *Entrance requirements:* For master's, 1 year of work experience, minimum GPA of 3.0. Additional exam requirements/recommendations for international students: Required—TOEFL (minimum score 560 paper-based; 220 computer-based). *Application deadline:* Applications are processed on a rolling basis. Application fee: $65. *Expenses:* Tuition: Full-time $33,330; part-time $1,042 per credit. Required fees: $462; $40. *Financial support:* In 2006–07, 15 students received support, including research assistantships (averaging $10,000 per year); career-related internships or fieldwork and Federal Work-Study also available. *Faculty research:* International business, innovative process. *Unit head:* Dr. Kip Becker, Chairman, 617-353-3016, E-mail: adminsc@bu.edu. *Application contact:* Lucille Dicker, Administrative Sciences Department, 617-353-3016, E-mail: adminsc@bu.edu.

Bryant University, Graduate School, Graduate School of Business, Programs in Business Administration, Smithfield, RI 02917-1284. Offers accounting (MBA, CAGS); computer information systems (MBA, CAGS); e-strategy (MBA, CAGS); finance (MBA, CAGS); general business (MBA); management (MBA, CAGS); marketing (MBA, CAGS); operations management (MBA). *Accreditation:* AACSB. *Faculty:* 49 full-time (13 women), 2 part-time/adjunct (0 women). *Students:* 143 applicants, 41% accepted, 46 enrolled. In 2006, 106 master's, 10 other advanced degrees awarded. *Entrance requirements:* For master's, GMAT, letter of recommendation, resumé; for CAGS, GMAT, resumé. Additional exam requirements/recommendations for international students: Required—TOEFL (minimum score 580 paper-based; 237 computer-based). *Application deadline:* For fall admission, 7/15 for domestic students, 4/1 for international students; for spring admission, 11/15 for domestic and international students. Application fee: $80. *Expenses:* Tuition: Part-time $1,998 per course. *Financial support:* Research assistantships with full tuition reimbursements, unspecified assistantships available. Financial award applicants required to submit FAFSA. *Unit head:* Kristopher T. Sullivan, Assistant Dean of the Graduate School, 401-232-6230, Fax: 401-232-6494, E-mail: gradprog@bryant.edu.

California State University, East Bay, Academic Programs and Graduate Studies, College of Business and Economics, Department of Accounting and Computer Information Systems, Hayward, CA 94542-3000. Offers accounting (MBA); computer information systems (MBA, MS), including business administration (MBA), computer information systems (MS); e-business (MBA); supply chain management (MBA); taxation (MBA, MS), including telecommunication (MBA); telecommunications (MS). Part-time and evening/weekend programs available. *Students:* 36. In 2006, 5 degrees awarded. *Degree requirements:* For master's, comprehensive exam or thesis. *Entrance requirements:* For master's, GMAT, minimum GPA of 2.75. Additional exam requirements/recommendations for international students: Required—TOEFL (minimum score 550 paper-based; 213 computer-based). *Application deadline:* For fall admission, 5/31 for domestic students, 4/30 for international students; for winter admission, 9/30 for domestic and international students; for spring admission, 12/31 for domestic students, 11/30 for international students. Application fee: $55. *Financial support:* Career-related internships or fieldwork, Federal Work-Study, and institutionally sponsored loans available. Support available to part-time students. Financial award application deadline: 3/2. *Unit head:* Dr. Christopher Lubwanna, Chair, 510-885-3397, Fax: 510-885-4796, E-mail: chris.lubwanna@csueastbay.edu. *Application contact:* Doris Duncan, Director of Graduate Programs, 510-885-3364, Fax: 510-885-2176, E-mail: doris.duncan@csueastbay.edu.

California State University, East Bay, Academic Programs and Graduate Studies, College of Business and Economics, Department of Management and Finance, Hayward, CA 94542-3000. Offers e-business (MBA); finance (MBA); human resources management (MBA); international business (MBA); management sciences (MBA); operations and material management (MBA); operations research (MBA); quantitative business methods (MS); strategic management (MBA); supply chain management (MBA). Part-time and evening/weekend programs available. *Faculty:* 37 full-time (7 women), 8 part-time/adjunct (3 women). *Students:* 204 full-time, 363 part-time; includes 234 minority (17 African Americans, 191 Asian Americans or Pacific Islanders, 26 Hispanic Americans), 158 international. Average age 32. 373 applicants, 43% accepted, 100 enrolled. In 2006, 281 degrees awarded. *Degree requirements:* For master's, comprehensive exam or thesis. *Entrance requirements:* For master's, GMAT, minimum GPA of 2.75. Additional exam requirements/recommendations for international students: Required—TOEFL (minimum score 550 paper-based; 213 computer-based). *Application deadline:* For fall admission, 5/31 for domestic students, 4/30 for international students; for winter admission, 9/30 for domestic and international students; for spring admission, 12/31 for domestic students, 11/30 for international students. Application fee: $55. *Financial support:* Career-related internships or fieldwork, Federal Work-Study, and institutionally sponsored loans available. Support available to part-time students. Financial award application deadline: 3/2. *Unit head:* Dr. Joyendu Bhadury, Chair, 510-885-3307, E-mail: joy.bhadury@csueastbay.edu. *Application contact:* Doris Duncan, Director of Graduate Programs, 510-885-3364, Fax: 510-885-2176, E-mail: doris.duncan@csueastbay.edu.

Cambridge College, Program in Management, Cambridge, MA 02138-5304. Offers e-commerce (M Mgt); management (M Mgt). Part-time and evening/weekend programs available. *Faculty:* 4 full-time (all women), 305 part-time/adjunct (167 women). *Students:* 362 full-time (207 women), 219 part-time (135 women); includes 203 minority (131 African Americans, 2 American Indian/Alaska Native, 22 Asian Americans or Pacific Islanders, 48 Hispanic Americans), 80 international. Average age 39. 160 applicants, 96% accepted, 126 enrolled. In 2006, 165 degrees awarded. *Degree requirements:* For master's, thesis. *Application deadline:* Applications are processed on a rolling basis. Application fee: $30. *Expenses:* Contact institution. One-time fee: $130 full-time. Tuition and fees vary according to degree level and program. *Financial support:* Teaching assistantships, career-related internships or fieldwork and Federal Work-Study available. Financial award applicants required to submit FAFSA. *Unit head:* Dr. Bill Hancock, Associate Dean, 617-873-0281, Fax: 617-349-3545. *Application contact:* Michael Travaghini, Director of Graduate Admissions, 617-868-1000 Ext. 1162, Fax: 617-349-3561, E-mail: admit@cambridgecollege.edu.

Cardean University, MBA Program, Chicago, IL 60606-7204. Offers accounting and information systems (MBA); e-commerce (MBA); finance (MBA); global management (MBA); health care administration (MBA); human resources management (MBA); leadership (MBA); management of information systems (MBA); management of technology (MBA); marketing (MBA); professional accounting (MBA); project management (MBA); risk management (MBA); strategy and economics (MBA). Part-time and evening/weekend programs available. Postbaccalaureate distance learning degree programs offered (no on-campus study). *Entrance requirements:* Additional exam requirements/recommendations for international students: Required—TOEFL (minimum score 550 paper-based; 213 computer-based).

Carnegie Mellon University, Tepper School of Business and School of Computer Science, Program in Electronic Commerce, Pittsburgh, PA 15213-3891. Offers MS. *Entrance requirements:* For master's, GRE General Test or GMAT. Additional exam requirements/recommendations for international students: Required—TOEFL.

City University, Graduate Division, School of Management, Bellevue, WA 98005. Offers accounting (MBA); C++ programming (Certificate); computer systems—C++ programming (MS); computer systems—individualized study (MS); computer systems—web programming in e-commerce (MS); computer systems-web development (MS); financial management (MBA, Certificate); general management (MBA, MPA, Certificate); general management-Europe (MBA); human resource management (MPA); individualized study (MBA); information systems (MBA, Certificate); management—general management (MA); management—human resource management (MA); management—individualized study (MA); marketing (MBA, Certificate); personal financial planning (MBA, Certificate); project management (MBA, MS, Certificate); technology management (MS, Certificate); web development (Certificate); web programming in e-commerce (Certificate). Part-time and evening/weekend programs available. Postbaccalaureate distance learning degree programs offered (no on-campus study). *Entrance requirements:* Additional exam requirements/recommendations for international students: Required—TOEFL (minimum score 540 paper-based; 207 computer-based); Recommended—IELTS. Electronic applications accepted.

Claremont Graduate University, Graduate Programs, School of Information Systems and Technology, Claremont, CA 91711-6160. Offers electronic commerce (MS, PhD); information systems (Certificate); knowledge management (MS, PhD); systems development (MS, PhD); telecommunications and networking (MS, PhD); MBA/MS. Part-time programs available. *Faculty:* 5 full-time (1 woman), 4 part-time/adjunct (0 women). *Students:* 68 full-time (22 women), 44 part-time (16 women); includes 32 minority (3 African Americans, 21 Asian Americans or Pacific Islanders, 8 Hispanic Americans), 28 international. Average age 37. In 2006, 13 master's, 7 doctorates awarded. *Degree requirements:* For doctorate, thesis/dissertation, portfolio, comprehensive exam. *Entrance requirements:* For master's and doctorate, GMAT, GRE General Test. *Application deadline:* For fall admission, 2/15 priority date for domestic students. Applications are processed on a rolling basis. Electronic applications accepted. *Financial support:* Fellowships, research assistantships, teaching assistantships, Federal Work-Study and institutionally sponsored loans available. Support available to part-time students. Financial award application deadline: 2/15; financial award applicants required to submit FAFSA. *Faculty research:* GPSS, man-machine interaction, organizational aspects of computing, implementation of information systems, information systems practice. *Unit head:* Lorne Olfman, Dean, 909-607-3035, Fax: 909-621-8564, E-mail: lorne.olfman@cgu.edu. *Application contact:* Go Yoshida, Director of Recruitment/Admissions, 909-621-3140, Fax: 909-621-8564, E-mail: go.yoshida@cgu.edu.

Clemson University, Graduate School, College of Business and Behavioral Science, Department of Management, Clemson, SC 29634. Offers electronic commerce (M E Com); management (MS, PhD). *Accreditation:* AACSB. Part-time programs available. *Faculty:* 29 full-time (6 women), 1 part-time/adjunct (0 women). *Students:* 22 full-time (4 women), 2 part-time; includes 3 minority (1 American Indian/Alaska Native, 2 Hispanic Americans), 13 international. Average age 25. 33 applicants, 21% accepted, 3 enrolled. In 2006, 4 master's, 2 doctorates awarded. Terminal master's awarded for partial completion of doctoral program. *Degree requirements:* For doctorate, thesis/dissertation. *Entrance requirements:* For master's, GMAT, GRE General Test, minimum GPA of 3.0; for doctorate, GRE General Test, minimum GPA of 3.5. Additional exam requirements/recommendations for international students: Required—TOEFL. *Application deadline:* For fall admission, 2/1 for domestic students, 4/15 for international students; for spring admission, 10/1 for domestic students, 9/15 for international students. Applications are processed on a rolling basis. Application fee: $50. *Expenses:* Tuition, state resident: full-time $8,812; part-time $450 per hour. Tuition, nonresident: full-time $18,036; part-time $760 per hour. Required fees: $474; $5 per term. *Financial support:* In 2006–07, 13 research assistantships were awarded; fellowships, teaching assistantships, institutionally sponsored loans also available. Financial award applicants required to submit FAFSA. *Faculty research:* Production/operations, strategic management, organizational behavior, management information systems. *Unit head:* Dr. Patricia Layton, Chair, 864-656-3303, Fax: 864-656-3304, E-mail: playton@clemson.edu.

Cleveland State University, College of Graduate Studies, Nance College of Business Administration, Department of Marketing, Cleveland, OH 44115. Offers data-driven marketing planning (Graduate Certificate); e-commerce (MBA); global business (Graduate Certificate); marketing (MBA, DBA). *Unit head:* Dr. Thomas W. Whipple, Chair, 216-687-4771, Fax: 216-687-9354, E-mail: t.whipple@csuohio.edu.

Columbia Southern University, MBA Program, Orange Beach, AL 36561. Offers electronic business and technology (MBA); healthcare management (MBA); human resources management (MBA); international management (MBA); marketing (MBA); project management (MBA); public administration (MBA); sport management (MBA). Part-time and evening/weekend programs available. Postbaccalaureate distance learning degree programs offered (no on-campus study). *Entrance requirements:* Additional exam requirements/recommendations for international students: Required—TOEFL. Electronic applications accepted.

Dalhousie University, Faculty of Graduate Studies, Faculty of Computer Science, Halifax, NS B3H 4R2, Canada. Offers computer science (MC Sc, PhD); electronic commerce (MEC). *Degree requirements:* For master's and doctorate, thesis/dissertation. *Entrance requirements:* Additional exam requirements/recommendations for international students: Required—TOEFL.

Dallas Baptist University, Graduate School of Business, Business Administration Program, Dallas, TX 75211-9299. Offers accounting (MBA); business communication (MBA); conflict resolution management (MBA); e-business (MBA); entrepreneurship (MBA); finance (MBA); health care management (MBA); international business (MBA); management (MBA); management information systems (MBA); marketing (MBA); project management (MBA); technology and engineering management (MBA). *Accreditation:* ACBSP. Part-time and evening/weekend programs available. Postbaccalaureate distance learning degree programs offered (no on-campus study). *Faculty:* 49 full-time (21 women), 112 part-time/adjunct (46 women). *Students:* 103 full-time, 318 part-time. 226 applicants, 38% accepted. In 2006, 124 degrees awarded. *Entrance requirements:* For master's, GMAT, minimum GPA of 3.0. Additional exam requirements/recommendations for international students: Required—TOEFL. *Application deadline:* Applications are processed on a rolling basis. Application fee: $25. Electronic applications accepted. *Expenses:* Tuition: Full-time $8,370; part-time $465 per credit hour. Required fees: $465 per credit hour. *Financial support:* Career-related internships or fieldwork, Federal Work-Study, institutionally sponsored loans, scholarships/grants, and tuition waivers (full and partial) available. Support available to part-time students. *Faculty research:* Sports management, services marketing, retailing, strategic management, financial planning/investments. *Unit head:* Dr. Sandra S. Reid, Director, 214-333-5244, Fax: 214-333-5293, E-mail: graduate@dbu.edu. *Application contact:* Kit P. Montgomery, Director of Graduate Programs, 214-333-5242, Fax: 214-333-5579, E-mail: graduate@dbu.edu.

Davenport University, Sneden Graduate School, Warren, MI 48092-5209. Offers accounting (MBA); commerce (MBA); finance (MBA); health care management (MBA); human resources management (MBA); management (MBA). *Entrance requirements:* For master's, minimum undergraduate GPA of 2.7.

Davenport University, Sneden Graduate School, Dearborn, MI 48126-3799. Offers accounting (MBA); e-business (MBA); finance (MBA); global business (MBA); health care management (MBA); human resources management (MBA); management (MBA); marketing (MBA). Part-time and evening/weekend programs available. Postbaccalaureate distance learning degree programs offered (no on-campus study). *Entrance requirements:* For master's, minimum GPA of 2.7, previous course work in accounting and statistics. *Faculty research:* Accounting, international accounting, social and environmental accounting, finance.

DePaul University, Charles H. Kellstadt Graduate School of Business, School of Accountancy and Management Information Systems, Chicago, IL 60604-2287. Offers accountancy (M Acc, MSA); business information technology (MS); e-business (MBA, MS); financial management and control (MBA); management accounting (MBA); management information systems (MBA); taxation (MST). Part-time and evening/weekend programs available. *Faculty:* 30 full-time (9 women), 54 part-time/adjunct (7 women). *Students:* 127 full-time (53 women), 209 part-time (101 women); includes 53 minority (13 African Americans, 3 American Indian/Alaska Native, 28 Asian Americans or Pacific Islanders, 9 Hispanic Americans), 56 international. Average age 30. In 2006, 141 degrees awarded. *Entrance requirements:* For master's, GMAT, 2 letters of recommendation, resumé. Additional exam requirements/recommendations for international students: Required—TOEFL (minimum score 550 paper-based; 213 computer-based). *Application deadline:* For fall admission, 7/1 for domestic students; for winter admission, 10/1 for domestic students; for spring admission, 2/1 for domestic students. Applications are processed on a rolling basis. Application fee: $60. *Financial support:* In 2006–07, 7 research assistantships with full tuition reimbursements (averaging $4,100 per year) were awarded; institutionally sponsored loans also available. Financial award application deadline: 4/2. *Faculty research:* Tax policy, property transactions, stock options as compensation, standards setting, activity-based costing in health care. *Application contact:* Christopher E. Kinsella, Director of Cohort MBA Programs, 312-362-8810, Fax: 312-362-6677, E-mail: kgsb@depaul.edu.

DePaul University, School of Computer Science, Telecommunications, and Information Systems, Chicago, IL 60604-2287. Offers business information technology (MS); computational finance (MS); computer graphics and animation (MS); computer science (MS, PhD); computer, information and network security (MS); digital cinema (MFA, MS); e-commerce technology (MS); human-computer interaction (MS); information systems (MS); information technology (MA); instructional technology systems (MS); software engineering (MS); telecommunication systems (MS); MA/JD; MS/JD. Part-time and evening/weekend programs available. Postbaccalaureate distance learning degree programs offered (no on-campus study). *Faculty:* 80 full-time (13 women), 133 part-time/adjunct (29 women). *Students:* 1,002 full-time (246 women), 995 part-time (263 women); includes 475 minority (185 African Americans, 3 American Indian/Alaska Native, 207 Asian Americans or Pacific Islanders, 80 Hispanic Americans), 329 international. Average age 31. 830 applicants, 80% accepted, 400 enrolled. In 2006, 514 master's, 4 doctorates awarded. *Degree requirements:* For master's, comprehensive exam (for some programs); for doctorate, thesis/dissertation, comprehensive exam. *Entrance requirements:* For doctorate, GRE, master's degree in computer science. Additional exam requirements/recommendations for international students: Required—TOEFL (minimum score 550 paper-based; 213 computer-based). *Application deadline:* For fall admission, 8/1 priority date for domestic and international students; for winter admission, 11/15 priority date for domestic and international students; for spring admission, 3/1 priority date for domestic and international students. Applications are processed on a rolling basis. Application fee: $25. Electronic applications accepted. *Expenses:* Contact institution. *Financial support:* In 2006–07, 63 teaching assistantships with full and partial tuition reimbursements (averaging $9,085 per year) were awarded; fellowships, research assistantships, Federal Work-Study, tuition waivers (full and partial), and unspecified assistantships also available. Support available to part-time students. Financial award application deadline: 4/1; financial award applicants required to submit FAFSA. *Faculty research:* Computer graphics, computer vision, information systems technology, computer network, programming. *Unit head:* Dr. David Miller, Dean, 312-362-8381, Fax: 312-362-5185. *Application contact:* Maureen Garvey, Information Contact, 312-362-8714, Fax: 312-362-5327, E-mail: mgarvey@cti.depaul.edu.

Eastern Michigan University, Graduate School, College of Business, Department of Marketing, Ypsilanti, MI 48197. Offers e-business (MBA); international business (MBA); supply chain management (MBA). Part-time and evening/weekend programs available. Postbaccalaureate distance learning degree programs offered (minimal on-campus study). *Entrance requirements:* For master's, GMAT. Additional exam requirements/recommendations for international students: Required—TOEFL. *Application deadline:* For fall admission, 5/15 priority date for domestic and international students; for winter admission, 10/15 priority date for domestic and international students; for spring admission, 3/15 priority date for domestic and international students. Applications are processed on a rolling basis. Application fee: $35. *Expenses:* Tuition, state resident: part-time $341 per credit hour. Tuition, nonresident: full-time $16,104; part-time $671 per credit hour. Required fees: $816; $34 per credit hour. $40 per term. One-time fee: $82 full-time. Tuition and fees vary according to course level, course load, degree level and reciprocity agreements. *Financial support:* Fellowships, research assistantships with full tuition reimbursements, teaching assistantships with full tuition reimbursements, career-related internships or fieldwork, Federal Work-Study, institutionally sponsored loans, scholarships/grants, tuition waivers (partial), and unspecified assistantships available. Support available to part-time students. Financial award applicants required to submit FAFSA. *Unit head:* Dr. Denise Tanguay, Interim Head, 734-487-3323. *Application contact:* Dr. Russ Merz, Department Coordinator, 734-487-1852, E-mail: russ.merz@emich.edu.

Eastern Michigan University, Graduate School, College of Business, Program in Business Administration, Ypsilanti, MI 48197. Offers business administration (MBA); e-business (MBA); enterprise business intelligence (MBA); entrepreneurship (MBA); finance (MBA); human resources (MBA); information systems (MBA); internal auditing (MBA); international business (MBA); nonprofit management (MBA); supply chain management (MBA). *Accreditation:* AACSB. Part-time and evening/weekend programs available. Postbaccalaureate distance learning degree programs offered (minimal on-campus study). *Students:* 98 full-time (36 women), 192 part-time (86 women); includes 50 minority (26 African Americans, 19 Asian Americans or Pacific Islanders, 5 Hispanic Americans), 76 international. Average age 29. In 2006, 109 degrees awarded. *Entrance requirements:* For master's, GMAT. Additional exam requirements/recommendations for international students: Required—TOEFL. *Application deadline:* For fall admission, 5/15 priority date for domestic students, 5/1 priority date for international students; for winter admission, 10/15 priority date for domestic students, 10/1 priority date for international students; for spring admission, 3/15 priority date for domestic students, 3/1 priority date for international students. Applications are processed on a rolling basis. Application fee: $35. *Expenses:* Tuition, state resident: part-time $341 per credit hour. Tuition, nonresident: full-time $16,104; part-time $671 per credit hour. Required fees: $816; $34 per credit hour. $40 per term. One-time fee: $82 full-time. Tuition and fees vary according to course level, course load, degree level and reciprocity agreements. *Financial support:* Fellowships, research assistantships with full tuition reimbursements, teaching assistantships with full tuition reimbursements, career-related internships or fieldwork, Federal Work-Study, institutionally sponsored loans, scholarships/grants, tuition waivers (partial), and unspecified assistantships available. Support available to part-time students. Financial award applicants required to submit FAFSA. *Unit head:* Dawn Gaymer, Assistant Dean, Graduate Business Programs, 734-487-4444, Fax: 734-483-1316, E-mail: dawn.malone@emich.edu. *Application contact:* K. Michelle Henry, Coordinator, 734-487-4444, Fax: 734-483-1316, E-mail: michelle.henry@emich.edu.

Fairleigh Dickinson University, Metropolitan Campus, University College: Arts, Sciences, and Professional Studies, School of Computer Sciences and Engineering, Program in E-Commerce, Teaneck, NJ 07666-1914. Offers MS. *Students:* 8 full-time (1 woman), 1 part-time, 8 international. Average age 28. 22 applicants, 68% accepted, 5 enrolled. *Application deadline:* Applications are processed on a rolling basis. Application fee: $40.

Ferris State University, College of Business, Big Rapids, MI 49307. Offers application development (MSISM); database administration (MSISM); e-business (MSISM); information systems (MBA); networking (MSISM); quality management (MBA); security (MSISM). Part-time and evening/weekend programs available. *Faculty:* 5 full-time (2 women), 2 part-time/adjunct (both women). *Students:* 35 full-time (12 women), 60 part-time (24 women); includes 5 minority (3 African Americans, 1 American Indian/Alaska Native, 1 Asian American or Pacific Islander), 13 international. Average age 34. 90 applicants, 72% accepted, 29 enrolled. In 2006, 40 degrees awarded. *Degree requirements:* For master's, thesis. *Entrance requirements:* For master's, GRE or GMAT, minimum GPA of 3.0 in CIS and business core, 2.75 overall; writing sample; 3 letters of reference; resumé. Additional exam requirements/recommendations for international students: Required—TOEFL (minimum score 500 paper-based; 173 computer-based). *Application deadline:* For fall admission, 7/1 priority date for domestic students, 6/15 for international students; for winter admission, 11/1 priority date for domestic students, 10/15 for international students; for spring admission, 3/1 priority date for domestic students, 2/15 for international students. Applications are processed on a rolling basis. Electronic applications accepted. *Expenses:* Tuition, state resident: part-time $355 per credit hour. Tuition, nonresident: part-time $687 per credit hour. *Financial support:* In 2006–07, 40 research assistantships, 10 teaching assistantships were awarded; career-related internships or fieldwork, Federal Work-Study, and unspecified assistantships also available. Support available to part-time students. Financial award applicants required to submit FAFSA. *Faculty research:* Quality improvement, client/server end-user computing, information management and policy, learning space/Lotus Notes, security. *Unit head:* Dr. Bill Boras, Department Chair, 231-591-2168, Fax: 231-591-2973, E-mail: cbgp@ferris.edu. *Application contact:* Shannon Yost, Department Secretary, 231-591-2168, Fax: 231-591-2973, E-mail: yosts@ferris.edu.

Florida Atlantic University, College of Business, Department of Management, International Business and Entrepreneurship, Boca Raton, FL 33431-0991. Offers business administration (Exec MBA, MBA), including accounting (MBA), electronic commerce (MBA), finance (MBA), financial planning (MBA), global entrepreneurship (MBA), health administration (MBA), international business (MBA), marketing (MBA), operations management (MBA), real estate (MBA), sport management (MBA). *Faculty:* 64 full-time (17 women), 15 part-time/adjunct (3 women). *Students:* 215 full-time (89 women), 365 part-time (189 women); includes 150 minority (49 African Americans, 2 American Indian/Alaska Native, 36 Asian Americans or Pacific Islanders, 63 Hispanic Americans), 54 international. Average age 32. 414 applicants, 55% accepted, 167 enrolled. In 2006, 196 master's awarded. *Degree requirements:* For master's, thesis optional. *Entrance requirements:* For master's, GMAT, minimum GPA of 3.0. Additional exam requirements/recommendations for international students: Required—TOEFL (minimum score 600 paper-based; 250 computer-based). *Application deadline:* For fall admission, 7/1 priority date for domestic students, 2/15 priority date for international students; for winter admission, 11/1 priority date for domestic students, 8/15 priority date for international students; for spring admission, 4/1 priority date for domestic students, 1/15 priority date for international students. Applications are processed on a rolling basis. Application fee: $30. Electronic applications accepted. *Expenses:* Tuition, area resident: Full-time $4,394. Tuition, nonresident: full-time $16,441. *Financial support:* Research assistantships, teaching assistantships, career-related internships or fieldwork, Federal Work-Study, institutionally sponsored loans, tuition waivers (partial), and unspecified assistantships available. Support available to part-time students. Financial award application deadline: 3/1; financial award applicants required to submit FAFSA. *Unit head:* Dr. Brenda Richey, Head, 561-297-3194, E-mail: brichey@fau.edu. *Application contact:* Fredrick G. Taylor, Graduate Adviser, 561-297-2768, Fax: 561-297-1315, E-mail: mba@fau.edu.

Florida Institute of Technology, Graduate Programs, University College, Melbourne, FL 32901-6975. Offers acquisition and contract management (MS, PMBA); aerospace engineering (MS); business administration (PMBA); computer information systems (MS); computer science (MS); e-business (PMBA); electrical engineering (MS); engineering management (MS); human resource management (PMBA); human resources management (MS); information systems (PMBA); logistics management (MS); management (MS), including acquisition and contract management, e-business, human resource management, information systems, logistics management, transportation management; materiel acquisition management (MS); mechanical engineering (MS); operations research (MS); project management (MS), including information systems, operations research; public administration (MPA); software engineering (MS); space systems (MS); space systems management (MS); systems management (MS), including information systems, operations research. Part-time and evening/weekend programs available. Postbaccalaureate distance learning degree programs offered (no on-campus study). *Faculty:* 11 full-time (4 women), 129 part-time/adjunct (17 women). *Students:* 78 full-time (34 women), 1,258 part-time (507 women); includes 384 minority (252 African Americans, 9 American Indian/Alaska Native, 58 Asian Americans or Pacific Islanders, 65 Hispanic Americans), 28 international. Average age 36. 629 applicants, 65% accepted, 320 enrolled. In 2006, 505 degrees awarded. *Degree requirements:* For master's, registration. *Entrance requirements:* For master's, minimum GPA of 3.0. Additional exam requirements/recommendations for international students: Required—TOEFL (minimum score 550 paper-based; 213 computer-based). *Application deadline:* Applications are processed on a rolling basis. Application fee: $50. Electronic applications accepted. *Expenses:* Tuition: Part-time $900 per credit. *Financial support:* Institutionally sponsored loans available. Financial award application deadline: 3/1; financial award applicants required to submit FAFSA. *Unit head:* Dr. Clifford Bragdon, Dean, 321-674-8821, Fax: 321-951-7694, E-mail: cbragdon@fit.edu. *Application contact:* Carolyn P. Farrior, Director of Graduate Admissions, 321-674-7118, Fax: 321-723-9468, E-mail: cfarrior@fit.edu.

Georgia Institute of Technology, Graduate Studies and Research, College of Management, Program in Business Administration, Atlanta, GA 30332-0001. Offers accounting (MBA); e-commerce (Certificate); engineering entrepreneurship (MBA); entrepreneurship (Certificate);

Electronic Commerce

Georgia Institute of Technology (continued)
finance (MBA); information technology management (MBA); international business (MBA, Certificate); management of technology (Certificate); marketing (MBA); operations management (MBA); organizational behavior (MBA); strategic management (MBA). *Accreditation:* AACSB.

Hawai'i Pacific University, College of Business Administration, Honolulu, HI 96813. Offers accounting/CPA (MBA); communication (MBA); e-business (MBA); economics (MBA); finance (MBA); human resource management (MBA); information systems (MBA); international business (MBA); management (MBA); marketing (MBA); organizational change (MBA); travel industry management (MBA). Part-time and evening/weekend programs available. *Faculty:* 40 full-time (16 women), 30 part-time/adjunct (10 women). *Students:* 320 full-time (150 women), 205 part-time (95 women); includes 168 minority (17 African Americans, 7 American Indian/Alaska Native, 137 Asian Americans or Pacific Islanders, 7 Hispanic Americans), 232 international. Average age 31. 279 applicants, 67% accepted, 166 enrolled. In 2006, 172 degrees awarded. *Degree requirements:* For master's, thesis. *Entrance requirements:* For master's, GMAT. Additional exam requirements/recommendations for international students: Recommended—TOEFL (minimum score 550 paper-based; 213 computer-based), TWE (minimum score 5). *Application deadline:* For fall admission, 2/15 priority date for domestic students; for spring admission, 10/15 priority date for domestic students. Applications are processed on a rolling basis. Application fee: $50. Electronic applications accepted. *Expenses:* Tuition: Full-time $10,080; part-time $560 per credit. *Financial support:* In 2006–07, 118 students received support; research assistantships, career-related internships or fieldwork, Federal Work-Study, scholarships/grants, and unspecified assistantships available. Support available to part-time students. Financial award application deadline: 3/1; financial award applicants required to submit FAFSA. *Faculty research:* Statistical control process as used by management, studies in comparative cross-cultural management styles, not-for-profit management. *Unit head:* Dr. Charles Steilen, Dean, 808-544-9301, Fax: 808-544-0283, E-mail: csteilen@hpu.edu. *Application contact:* Danny Lam, Assistant Director of Graduate Admissions, 808-544-1135, Fax: 808-544-0280, E-mail: graduate@hpu.edu.

See Close-Up on page 275.

HEC Montreal, School of Business Administration, Diploma Programs in Administration, Program in E-Business, Montréal, QC H3T 2A7, Canada. Offers Diploma. All courses are given in French. Part-time programs available. *Students:* 3 full-time (1 woman), 19 part-time (7 women). In 2006, 14 degrees awarded. *Degree requirements:* For Diploma, one foreign language. *Application deadline:* For fall admission, 4/15 for domestic and international students; for winter admission, 10/1 for domestic and international students. Application fee: $60 Canadian dollars. Electronic applications accepted. Tuition and fees charges are reported in Canadian dollars. *Expenses:* Tuition, nonresident: part-time $56 Canadian dollars per credit. Required fees: $30 Canadian dollars per semester. *Financial support:* Scholarships/grants available. *Application contact:* Francine Blais, Administrative Director, 514-340-6112, Fax: 514-340-6411, E-mail: francine.blais@hec.ca.

HEC Montreal, School of Business Administration, Program in Electronic Commerce, Montréal, QC H3T 2A7, Canada. Offers M Sc. *Students:* 14 full-time (8 women), 8 part-time (1 woman). In 2006, 8 degrees awarded. *Degree requirements:* For master's, one foreign language. *Entrance requirements:* For master's, bachelor's degree in law, management, information systems or related field. *Application deadline:* For fall admission, 4/1 for domestic and international students. Application fee: $60 Canadian dollars. Tuition and fees charges are reported in Canadian dollars. *Expenses:* Tuition, nonresident: part-time $56 Canadian dollars per credit. Required fees: $30 Canadian dollars per semester. *Unit head:* Veronika Kisfalvi, Director, 514-340-6205, Fax: 514-340-5640, E-mail: veronika.kisfalvi@hec.ca. *Application contact:* Francine Blais, Administrative Director, 514-340-6112, Fax: 514-340-6411, E-mail: francine.blais@hec.ca.

Instituto Tecnológico y de Estudios Superiores de Monterrey, Campus Central de Veracruz, Graduate Programs, Córdoba, Mexico. Offers administration (MA); administration of information technologies (MTI); computer sciences (MCC); education (MEE); educational institution administration (MAD); educational technology (MTE); electronic commerce (MCE); finance (MAF); humanistic studies (MEH); international business for Latin America (MNL); marketing (MMT); science (MCP); technology management (MTT). Part-time and evening/weekend programs available. Postbaccalaureate distance learning degree programs offered (minimal on-campus study). *Degree requirements:* For master's, thesis (for some programs). *Entrance requirements:* For master's, PAEP College Board. Electronic applications accepted.

Instituto Tecnológico y de Estudios Superiores de Monterrey, Campus Estado de México, Professional and Graduate Division, Estado de Mexico, Mexico. Offers administration of information technologies (MITA); architecture (M Arch); business administration (GMBA, MBA); computer sciences (MCS, PhD); education (M Ed); educational institution administration (MAD); educational technology and innovation (PhD); electronic commerce (MEC); environmental systems (MS); finance (MAF); humanistic studies (MHS); information sciences and knowledge management (MISKM); information systems (MS); manufacturing systems (MS); marketing (MEM); quality systems and productivity (MS); science and materials engineering (PhD); telecommunications management (MTM). Part-time programs available. Postbaccalaureate distance learning degree programs offered (minimal on-campus study). *Degree requirements:* For master's, one foreign language, thesis (for some programs), registration; for doctorate, one foreign language, thesis/dissertation, registration (for some programs). *Entrance requirements:* For master's, E-PAEP 500, interview; for doctorate, E-PAEP 500, research proposal. Additional exam requirements/recommendations for international students: Required—TOEFL (minimum score 550 paper-based). *Faculty research:* Surface treatments by plasmas, mechanical properties, robotics, graphical computing, mechatronics security protocols.

Instituto Tecnológico y de Estudios Superiores de Monterrey, Campus Irapuato, Graduate Programs, Irapuato, Mexico. Offers administration (MBA); administration of information technology (MAIT); administration of telecommunications (MAT); architecture (M Arch); computer science (MCS); education (M Ed); educational administration (MEA); educational innovation and technology (DEIT); educational technology (MET); electronic commerce (MBA); environmental administration and planning (MEAP); environmental systems (MES); finances (MBA); humanistic studies (MHS); international management for Latin American executives (MIMLAE); library and information science (MLIS); manufacturing quality management (MMQM); marketing research (MBA).

Inter American University of Puerto Rico, Bayamón Campus, Graduate School, Bayamón, PR 00957. Offers e-commerce (MBA); human resources (MBA). Part-time and evening/weekend programs available. *Faculty:* 7 full-time (1 woman), 2 part-time/adjunct (1 woman). *Students:* 11 full-time (10 women), 50 part-time (24 women); all Hispanic Americans *Entrance requirements:* For master's, EXADEP, GRE General Test, letters of recommendation. *Application deadline:* For fall admission, 7/1 for domestic students. Application fee: $31. *Expenses:* Tuition: Part-time $175 per credit. Required fees: $231 per semester. *Unit head:* Prof. Juan F. Martinez, Chancellor, 787-279-1912 Ext. 2295, Fax: 787-279-2205, E-mail: jmartinez@bc.inter.edu. *Application contact:* Carlos Alicea, Director of Admission, 787-279-1912 Ext. 2017, Fax: 787-279-2205, E-mail: calicea@bc.inter.edu.

International University in Geneva, MBA Program, Geneva, Switzerland. Offers e-commerce (MBA); human relations (MBA); international business (Exec MBA, MBA); marketing (MBA); organizational development (MBA); telecommunications (MBA). Part-time and evening/weekend programs available. *Degree requirements:* For master's, comprehensive exam, registration. *Entrance requirements:* For master's, GMAT. Additional exam requirements/recommendations for international students: Required—TOEFL. Electronic applications accepted.

Maryville University of Saint Louis, The John E. Simon School of Business, St. Louis, MO 63141-7299. Offers accounting (MBA, PGC); business studies (PGC); e-business (MBA, PGC); management (MBA, PGC); marketing (MBA, PGC). *Accreditation:* ACBSP. Part-time and evening/weekend programs available. *Students:* 34 full-time (23 women), 162 part-time (101 women); includes 9 African Americans, 8 Asian Americans or Pacific Islanders, 2 international. Average age 31. 56 applicants, 96% accepted, 38 enrolled. In 2006, 89 degrees awarded. *Entrance requirements:* For master's, GMAT (unless applicant possesses a graduate degree or an undergraduate degree in business with a minimum GPA of 3.0), minimum AACSB index of 950. Additional exam requirements/recommendations for international students: Required—TOEFL (minimum score 550 paper-based). *Application deadline:* Applications are processed on a rolling basis. Application fee: $35 ($50 for international students). Electronic applications accepted. *Expenses:* Tuition: Full-time $17,800; part-time $555 per credit. Required fees: $55 per semester. Tuition and fees vary according to degree level and program. *Financial support:* Career-related internships or fieldwork, Federal Work-Study, tuition waivers (partial), and campus employment available. Financial award application deadline: 7/31; financial award applicants required to submit FAFSA. *Faculty research:* International business, e-business, strategic planning, interpersonal management skills, financial analysis. *Unit head:* Dr. Pamela Horwitz, Dean, 314-529-9418, Fax: 314-529-9975, E-mail: horwitz@maryville.edu. *Application contact:* Kathy Dougherty, Director of MBA Admissions and Enrollment, 314-529-9382, Fax: 314-529-9975, E-mail: business@marville.edu.

Marywood University, Academic Affairs, Insalaco College of Creative Arts and Management, Department of Communication Arts, Program in Communication Arts, Scranton, PA 18509-1598. Offers corporate communication (Certificate); e-business (Certificate); health communication (Certificate); instructional technology (Certificate); interdisciplinary (MA); library science/information specialist (Certificate); media management (MA); production (MA). *Students:* 13 full-time (7 women), 14 part-time (6 women); includes 3 minority (1 African American, 2 Hispanic Americans), 1 international. Average age 28. In 2006, 3 degrees awarded. Application fee: $30. *Expenses:* Tuition: Part-time $672 per credit. Tuition and fees vary according to degree level, campus/location and program. *Application contact:* Dr. Deborah M. Flynn, Coordinator of Graduate Advising (Enrollment Management), 570-348-6211, E-mail: flynn@ac.marywood.edu.

Marywood University, Academic Affairs, Insalaco College of Creative Arts and Management, Department of Communication Arts, Program in Information Sciences, Scranton, PA 18509-1598. Offers corporate communication (MS); e-business (MS); health communication (MS); instructional technology (MS); library science/information science (MS). *Students:* 4 full-time (2 women), 18 part-time (16 women); includes 1 minority (African American) Average age 40.Application fee: $30. *Expenses:* Tuition: Part-time $672 per credit. Tuition and fees vary according to degree level, campus/location and program. *Application contact:* Dr. Deborah M. Flynn, Coordinator of Graduate Advising (Enrollment Management), 570-348-6211, E-mail: flynn@ac.marywood.edu.

Mercy College, Division of Mathematics and Computer Information Science, Program in Internet Business Systems, Dobbs Ferry, NY 10522-1189. Offers MS. *Students:* Average age 34. In 2006, 6 degrees awarded. *Entrance requirements:* For master's, 2 years of work experience, 2 letters of recommendation, interview, resumé. *Application deadline:* Applications are processed on a rolling basis. Application fee: $37. Electronic applications accepted. *Expenses:* Tuition: Part-time $595 per credit. Required fees: $9 per credit. Tuition and fees vary according to program. *Unit head:* John DiElsi, Director, 914-674-7306, Fax: 914-374-7518, E-mail: jdielsi@mercy.edu. *Application contact:* Kathleen Jackson, Director of Admissions, 800-Mercy-NY, Fax: 914-674-7382, E-mail: admissions@mercy.edu.

The National Graduate School of Quality Management, Program in Quality Systems Management, Falmouth, MA 02541. Offers e-commerce (MS); management (MS); six sigma (MS).

National University, Academic Affairs, School of Business and Management, Department of Management, Marketing and E-Business, La Jolla, CA 92037-1011. Offers e-business (MS); human resource management and organizational development (MA); management (MA); organizational leadership (MS). Part-time and evening/weekend programs available. Postbaccalaureate distance learning degree programs offered (no on-campus study). *Faculty:* 17 full-time (5 women), 209 part-time/adjunct (57 women). *Students:* 134 full-time (74 women), 244 part-time (119 women); includes 148 minority (55 African Americans, 4 American Indian/Alaska Native, 35 Asian Americans or Pacific Islanders, 54 Hispanic Americans), 19 international. Average age 38. 166 applicants, 143 enrolled. In 2006, 82 degrees awarded. *Degree requirements:* For master's, thesis. *Entrance requirements:* For master's, interview, minimum GPA of 2.5. Additional exam requirements/recommendations for international students: Required—TOEFL (minimum score 550 paper-based; 213 computer-based; 80 iBT), IELTS (minimum score 6). *Application deadline:* Applications are processed on a rolling basis. Application fee: $60 ($65 for international students). Electronic applications accepted. *Expenses:* Tuition: Full-time $7,722; part-time $286 per unit. One-time fee: $60. *Financial support:* Career-related internships or fieldwork, institutionally sponsored loans, scholarships/grants, and tuition waivers (partial) available. Support available to part-time students. Financial award application deadline: 6/30; financial award applicants required to submit FAFSA. *Unit head:* Dr. George Drops, Chair and Professor, 858-642-8438, Fax: 858-642-8406, E-mail: gdrops@nu.edu. *Application contact:* Dominick Giovanniello, Associate Regional Dean—San Diego, 800-NAT-UNIV, Fax: 858-642-8709, E-mail: dgiovann@nu.edu.

New York Institute of Technology, Ellis College, Old Westbury, NY 11568. Offers accounting and information systems (MBA); e-commerce (MBA); finance (MBA); global management (MBA); healthcare administration (MBA); human resources management (MBA); leadership (MBA); management of information systems (MBA); management of technology (MBA); marketing (MBA); professional accounting (MBA); project management (MBA); risk management (MBA); strategy and economics (MBA). Ellis College is a collaboration between New York Institute of Technology and UNext online learning company. Part-time and evening/weekend programs available. Postbaccalaureate distance learning degree programs offered (no on-campus study). *Entrance requirements:* For master's, interview. Additional exam requirements/recommendations for international students: Required—TOEFL (minimum score 550 paper-based; 213 computer-based). Electronic applications accepted. *Expenses:* Tuition: Full-time $16,800; part-time $700 per credit.

New York University, School of Continuing and Professional Studies, Center for Management, Graduate Programs in Management and Systems, New York, NY 10012-1019. Offers applied database technologies (MS); enterprise and risk management (Advanced Certificate); leadership and knowledge management (MS); management in the Internet E-conomy (MS); strategy and leadership (Advanced Certificate); systems management (MS). Part-time and evening/weekend programs available. Postbaccalaureate distance learning degree programs offered (no on-campus study). *Faculty:* 2 full-time (0 women), 9 part-time/adjunct (2 women). *Students:* 10 full-time (4 women), 200 part-time (64 women); includes 73 minority (26 African Americans, 36 Asian Americans or Pacific Islanders, 11 Hispanic Americans), 28 international. Average age 34. 64 applicants, 77% accepted, 28 enrolled. In 2006, 12 degrees awarded. *Degree requirements:* For master's, thesis, capstone project. *Entrance requirements:* For master's, GMAT or GRE General Test, work experience, resumé, 2 letters of recommendation. Additional exam requirements/recommendations for international students: Required—TOEFL (minimum score 600 paper-based; 250 computer-based), TWE. *Application deadline:* For fall admission, 3/15 priority date for domestic and international students; for spring admission, 10/15 priority date for domestic students, 8/15 priority date for international students. Applications are processed on a rolling basis. Application fee: $75. *Expenses:* Tuition: Part-time $1,080 per unit. Required fees: $56 per unit. $329 per term. Tuition and fees vary according to program. *Financial support:* In 2006–07, 87 students received support, including fellowships (averaging $1,009 per year); scholarships/grants also available. Support available to part-time students. Financial award application deadline: 3/1; financial award applicants required to submit FAFSA. *Faculty research:* Six sigma and TQ, business continuity, systems security, digital economy. *Application contact:* Helen Sapp, Assistant Director, 212-992-3600, Fax: 212-992-3676, E-mail: helen.sapp@nyu.edu.

See Close-Up on page 613.

Northwestern University, Medill School of Journalism, Integrated Marketing Communications Program, Evanston, IL 60208. Offers advertising/sales promotion (MSIMC); direct database and e-commerce marketing (MSIMC); general studies (MSIMC); public relations (MSIMC). Part-time programs available. *Entrance requirements:* For master's, GRE General Test or GMAT, full-time work experience (preferred). Additional exam requirements/recommendations for international students: Required—TOEFL. Electronic applications accepted. *Faculty research:* Data mining, business to business marketing, values in advertising, political advertising.

See Close-Up on page 655.

Regis University, School for Professional Studies, Program in Computer Information Technology, Denver, CO 80221-1099. Offers database administration with IBM DB2 (Certificate); database administration with Oracle (Certificate); database development (Certificate); database technologies (MSCIT); enterprise Java software development (Certificate); executive information technologies (Certificate); executive information technology (MSCIT); information assurance (Certificate); software engineering (MSCIT, Certificate); storage area networks (Certificate); systems engineering (MSCIT, Certificate). Offered at Boulder Campus, Northwest Denver Campus, Southeast Denver Campus, Fort Collins Campus, Colorado Springs Campus, and Broomfield Campus. Part-time and evening/weekend programs available. Postbaccalaureate distance learning degree programs offered (no on-campus study). *Faculty:* 5 full-time (1 woman), 84 part-time/adjunct (12 women). *Students:* Average age 36. In 2006, 166 degrees awarded. *Degree requirements:* For master's, thesis, final research project; for Certificate, final research project. *Entrance requirements:* For master's and Certificate, 2 years of related experience, resumé. Additional exam requirements/recommendations for international students: Required—TOEFL (minimum score 213 computer-based), TWE (minimum score 5), TOEFL or university-based test. *Application deadline:* For fall admission, 8/13 priority date for domestic students, 7/13 for international students; for winter admission, 10/8 priority date for domestic students, 9/8 for international students; for spring admission, 12/17 priority date for domestic students, 11/17 for international students. Applications are processed on a rolling basis. Application fee: $75. Electronic applications accepted. *Expenses: Contact institution. Financial support:* Federal Work-Study available. Support available to part-time students. Financial award applicants required to submit FAFSA. *Unit head:* Donald Archer, Chair, 303-458-4302, Fax: 303-964-5538. *Application contact:* 800-677-9270 Ext. 4080, Fax: 303-964-5538, E-mail: masters@regis.edu.

Rensselaer Polytechnic Institute, Graduate School, Lally School of Management and Technology, Program in Management and Technology, Troy, NY 12180-3590. Offers finance (MBA, MS); financial technology (MS); management (PhD); management information systems (MBA, MS); new product development and marketing (MBA); new production and operations management (MS); product development and marketing (MS); production and operations management (MBA); technical commercialization (MS); technological entrepreneurship (MBA, MS). Part-time and evening/weekend programs available. Postbaccalaureate distance learning degree programs offered (no on-campus study). *Faculty:* 50 full-time (9 women), 1 part-time/adjunct (0 women). *Students:* 121 full-time (62 women), 525 part-time (184 women); includes 137 minority (43 African Americans, 60 Asian Americans or Pacific Islanders, 34 Hispanic Americans), 71 international. Average age 28. 416 applicants, 70% accepted, 240 enrolled. In 2006, 215 master's, 6 doctorates awarded. *Median time to degree:* Of those who began their doctoral program in fall 1998, 25% received their degree in 8 years or less. *Degree requirements:* For doctorate, thesis/dissertation. *Entrance requirements:* For master's, GMAT, resumé, 2 letters of recommendation; for doctorate, GMAT or GRE General Test, 2 letters of recommendation. Additional exam requirements/recommendations for international students: Required—TOEFL (minimum score 600 paper-based; 250 computer-based; 100 iBT); Recommended—IELTS (minimum score 7). *Application deadline:* For fall admission, 3/15 priority date for domestic and international students. Applications are processed on a rolling basis. Application fee: $75. Electronic applications accepted. *Expenses:* Tuition: Full-time $32,600; part-time $1,358 per credit. Required fees: $1,629. *Financial support:* In 2006–07, 48 students received support; fellowships with partial tuition reimbursements available, research assistantships with partial tuition reimbursements available, teaching assistantships with partial tuition reimbursements available, career-related internships or fieldwork, institutionally sponsored loans, and scholarships/grants available. Financial award application deadline: 3/15; financial award applicants required to submit FAFSA. *Faculty research:* Technological entrepreneurship, operations management, new product development and marketing, information systems, finance. Total annual research expenditures: $24,747. *Unit head:* Pedro Gonzalez, Director MBA/Admissons and Career Services, 518-276-2378, Fax: 518-276-2665, E-mail: gonzap3@rpi.edu. *Application contact:* Michele M. Martens, Manager of Graduate Programs, 518-276-6586, Fax: 518-276-2665, E-mail: martem@rpi.edu.

See Close-Up on page 313.

Saint Joseph's University, Erivan K. Haub School of Business, Professional MBA Program, Philadelphia, PA 19131-1395. Offers accounting (MBA); decision and system sciences (MBA), including information systems; e-business (MBA); finance (MBA, Certificate), including certified financial planner (Certificate), finance (MBA); general business (MBA); health and medical services administration (MBA); human resource management (MBA); international business (MBA); international marketing (MBA); management (MBA); marketing (MBA); DO/MBA. Part-time and evening/weekend programs available. *Students:* 85 full-time, 440 part-time; includes 60 minority (27 African Americans, 14 Asian Americans or Pacific Islanders, 19 Hispanic Americans), 50 international. Average age 29. In 2006, 204 degrees awarded. *Entrance requirements:* For master's, GMAT, 2 letters of recommendation, resumé. Additional exam requirements/recommendations for international students: Required—TOEFL (minimum score 550 paper-based; 213 computer-based). *Application deadline:* For fall admission, 7/15 priority date for domestic students, 4/15 for international students; for spring admission, 11/15 priority date for domestic students, 10/15 for international students. Applications are processed on a rolling basis. Application fee: $35. Electronic applications accepted. *Expenses: Contact institution. Financial support:* In 2006–07, 3 research assistantships with full tuition reimbursements were awarded; unspecified assistantships also available. Financial award application deadline: 5/1. *Unit head:* Adele C. Foley, Associate Dean/Director, Graduate Business Programs, 610-660-1690, Fax: 610-660-1599, E-mail: sjumba@sju.edu. *Application contact:* Marla D. Gaglione, Assistant Director, Graduate Business Programs, 610-660-1695, Fax: 610-660-1599, E-mail: sjumba@sju.edu.

Saint Xavier University, Graduate Studies, Graham School of Management, Chicago, IL 60655-3105. Offers e-commerce (MBA); employee health benefits (Certificate); finance (MBA, MS); financial analysis and investments (MBA); financial planning (MBA, Certificate); financial trading and practice (MBA, Certificate); generalist/administration (MBA); health administration (MBA, MS); managed care (Certificate); management (MBA, MS); marketing (MBA); public and non-profit management (MBA); public health (MPH); service management (MBA); training and performance management (MBA); MBA/MS. *Accreditation:* ACBSP. Part-time and evening/weekend programs available. *Faculty:* 27. *Students:* 67 full-time (32 women), 291 part-time (152 women). Average age 35. In 2006, 61 degrees awarded. *Entrance requirements:* For master's, GMAT, minimum GPA of 3.0, 2 years of work experience. *Application deadline:* For fall admission, 8/15 for domestic students. Applications are processed on a rolling basis. Application fee: $35. Electronic applications accepted. *Expenses: Contact institution. Financial support:* Career-related internships or fieldwork available. Support available to part-time students. Financial award applicants required to submit FAFSA. *Unit head:* Dr. John Eber, Dean, 773-298-3601, Fax: 773-298-3601, E-mail: eber@sxu.edu. *Application contact:* Beth Gierach, Managing Director of Admission, 773-298-3053, Fax: 773-298-3076, E-mail: gierach@sxu.edu.

Stevens Institute of Technology, Graduate School, Wesley J. Howe School of Technology Management, Program in Information Systems, Hoboken, NJ 07030. Offers computer science (MS); e-commerce (MS, Certificate); entrepreneurial information technology (MS); global innovation management (MS); human resource management (MS); information management (MS, Certificate); information security (MS); information technology in financial services industry (MS); information technology in the pharmaceutical industry (MS); information technology outsourcing management (MS); integrated information architecture (MS); project management (MS, Certificate); quantitative software engineering (MS); systems engineering (MS); telecommunications management (MS). *Degree requirements:* For master's, thesis optional. *Entrance requirements:* For master's, GMAT, GRE General Test. Additional exam requirements/recommendations for international students: Required—TOEFL. Electronic applications accepted.

Temple University, Graduate School, Fox School of Business and Management, Masters Programs in Business, MBA Programs, Philadelphia, PA 19122-6096. Offers accounting (MBA); business administration (EMBA, MBA); e-business (MBA); economics (MBA); finance (MBA); general and strategic management (MBA); healthcare management (MBA); human resource administration (MBA); international business (IMBA); management information systems (MBA); management science/operations management (MBA); marketing (MBA); risk management and insurance (MBA); statistics (MBA). EMBA offered in Philadelphia, PA and Tokyo, Japan. *Accreditation:* AACSB. *Entrance requirements:* For master's, GMAT, minimum undergraduate GPA of 3.0. Additional exam requirements/recommendations for international students: Required—TOEFL. *Expenses:* Tuition, state resident: full-time $12,264; part-time $511 per credit. Tuition, nonresident: full-time $17,904; part-time $746 per credit. Required fees: $84 per course. Tuition and fees vary according to program.

Temple University, Graduate School, Fox School of Business and Management, Masters Programs in Business, MS Programs, Philadelphia, PA 19122-6096. Offers accounting and financial management (MS); actuarial science (MS); e-business (MS); finance (MS); healthcare financial management (MS); human resource administration (MS); management information systems (MS); management science/operations management (MS); marketing (MS); statistics (MS). *Accreditation:* AACSB. *Entrance requirements:* For master's, GRE General Test, minimum undergraduate GPA of 3.0. Additional exam requirements/recommendations for international students: Required—TOEFL. *Expenses:* Tuition, state resident: full-time $12,264; part-time $511 per credit. Tuition, nonresident: full-time $17,904; part-time $746 per credit. Required fees: $84 per course. Tuition and fees vary according to program.

Université Laval, Faculty of Administrative Sciences, Programs in Business Administration, Québec, QC G1K 7P4, Canada. Offers accounting (MBA); agri-food management (MBA); electronic business (MBA, Diploma); factory management and logistics (MBA); finance (MBA); firm management (MBA); information technology management (MBA); international management (MBA); management (MBA); management accounting (MBA, Diploma); marketing (MBA); modelization and organizational decision (MBA); occupational health and safety management (MBA); pharmacy management (MBA); technological entrepreneurship (Diploma). *Accreditation:* AACSB. Part-time and evening/weekend programs available. Postbaccalaureate distance learning degree programs offered (no on-campus study). *Entrance requirements:* For master's and Diploma, knowledge of French and English. Electronic applications accepted.

University at Buffalo, the State University of New York, Graduate School, College of Arts and Sciences, Department of Economics, Buffalo, NY 14260. Offers economics (MA, MS, PhD); financial economics (Certificate); health services (Certificate); information and Internet economics (Certificate); international economics (Certificate); law and regulation (Certificate); urban and regional economics (Certificate). *Faculty:* 18 full-time (2 women), 8 part-time/adjunct (1 woman). *Students:* 184 full-time (64 women), 16 part-time (5 women); includes 13 minority (3 African Americans, 9 Asian Americans or Pacific Islanders, 1 Hispanic American), 145 international. Average age 27. 403 applicants, 53% accepted, 85 enrolled. In 2006, 67 master's, 1 doctorate, 8 other advanced degrees awarded. Terminal master's awarded for partial completion of doctoral program. *Degree requirements:* For master's, theory exam, thesis optional; for doctorate, thesis/dissertation, field and theory exams. *Entrance requirements:* For master's and doctorate, GRE General Test. Additional exam requirements/recommendations for international students: Required—TOEFL (minimum score 550 paper-based; 213 computer-based). *Application deadline:* For fall admission, 1/15 priority date for domestic and international students; for spring admission, 11/1 priority date for domestic and international students. Applications are processed on a rolling basis. Application fee: $50. Electronic applications accepted. *Financial support:* In 2006–07, 26 students received support, including 13 fellowships with full tuition reimbursements available (averaging $2,115 per year), 1 research assistantship with full tuition reimbursement available (averaging $10,900 per year), 12 teaching assistantships with full tuition reimbursements available (averaging $10,900 per year); Federal Work-Study, health care benefits, and unspecified assistantships also available. Financial award application deadline: 1/15; financial award applicants required to submit FAFSA. *Faculty research:* International economics, econometrics, applied economics, urban economics, economic growth and development. *Unit head:* Dr. Isaac Ehrlich, Chair, 716-645-2121 Ext. 422, Fax: 716-645-2127, E-mail: mgtehrl@buffalo.edu. *Application contact:* Dr. Nagesh Revankar, Director of Graduate Studies, 716-645-2121 Ext. 428, Fax: 716-645-2127, E-mail: ecorevan@buffalo.edu.

The University of Akron, Graduate School, College of Business Administration, Department of Management, Program in Electronic Business, Akron, OH 44325. Offers MBA. *Students:* Average age 37. 1 applicant, 100% accepted, 0 enrolled. In 2006, 1 degree awarded. *Entrance requirements:* For master's, GMAT, minimum GPA of 2.75. Additional exam requirements/recommendations for international students: Required—TOEFL (minimum score 550 paper-based; 213 computer-based; 79 iBT). *Application deadline:* For fall admission, 8/15 for domestic students. Applications are processed on a rolling basis. Application fee: $30 ($40 for international students). Electronic applications accepted. *Expenses:* Tuition, state resident: full-time $6,164; part-time $342 per credit. Tuition, nonresident: full-time $10,575; part-time $588 per credit. Required fees: $806; $43 per credit. $12 per term. Tuition and fees vary according to course load, degree level and program. *Unit head:* Dr. B.S. Vijayaraman, Head, 330-972-5442, E-mail: bsv@uakron.edu. *Application contact:* Dr. James Divoky, Director of Graduate Business Programs, 330-972-7043, Fax: 330-972-6588, E-mail: jdivoky@uakron.edu.

University of Cincinnati, Division of Research and Advanced Studies, College of Business, Department of Information Systems, Cincinnati, OH 45221. Offers e-business (MBA); information systems (MBA, MS); MBA/MS. *Degree requirements:* For master's, thesis or alternative, capstone project (MBA). *Entrance requirements:* For master's, GMAT, GRE General Test (information systems), resumé, letters of recommendation. Additional exam requirements/recommendations for international students: Required—TOEFL (minimum score 600 paper-based; 250 computer-based). Application fee: $40. *Expenses: Contact institution. Financial support:* Fellowships, research assistantships, teaching assistantships with full and partial tuition reimbursements, scholarships/grants, tuition waivers (full and partial), and unspecified assistantships available. Financial award application deadline: 2/1; financial award applicants required to submit FAFSA. *Unit head:* Dr. Vivek Choudhury, Head, 513-556-7115, E-mail: vivek.choudhury@uc.edu.

University of Denver, Daniels College of Business, Department of Information Technology and Electronic Commerce, Denver, CO 80208. Offers IMBA, MBA. Part-time and evening/weekend programs available. *Faculty:* 8 full-time (2 women). *Students:* 11 full-time (3 women), 26 part-time (7 women); includes 5 minority (4 Asian Americans or Pacific Islanders, 1 Hispanic American), 8 international. Average age 30. 18 applicants, 72% accepted. In 2006, 34 degrees awarded. *Entrance requirements:* For master's, GMAT. *Application deadline:* For fall admission, 1/15 priority date for domestic students. Applications are processed on a rolling basis. Application fee: $50. Electronic applications accepted. *Expenses:* Tuition: Full-time $29,628; part-time $823 per credit. *Financial support:* Career-related internships or fieldwork, Federal Work-Study, institutionally sponsored loans, and scholarships/grants available. Support available to part-time students. Financial award application deadline: 2/15. *Faculty research:* Cross-cultural research in information systems, electronic commerce, distributed project management, strategic information systems, management of emerging technologies. *Unit head:* Dr. Dick Scudder, Chair, 303-871-2197. *Application contact:* Information Contact, 303-871-3416, Fax: 303-871-4466, E-mail: daniels@du.edu.

Electronic Commerce

University of Florida, Graduate School, Warrington College of Business Administration, Programs in Business Administration, Gainesville, FL 32611. Offers accounting (MBA); arts administration (MBA); business strategy and public policy (MBA); competitive strategy (MBA); decision and information sciences (MBA); electronic commerce (MBA); finance (MBA); general business (MBA); global management (MBA); Graham-Buffett security analysis (MBA); health administration (MBA); human resources management (MBA); international studies (MBA); Latin American business (MBA); management (MBA); marketing (MBA); sports administration (MBA); JD/MBA; MBA/MS; MBA/PhD; MBA/Pharm D; MD/MBA. *Accreditation:* AACSB. Part-time and evening/weekend programs available. Postbaccalaureate distance learning degree programs offered. *Faculty:* 14. *Students:* 950 (282 women); includes 189 minority (31 African Americans, 2 American Indian/Alaska Native, 66 Asian Americans or Pacific Islanders, 90 Hispanic Americans) 56 international. In 2006, 481 degrees awarded. *Entrance requirements:* For master's, GMAT, minimum GPA of 3.0, interview. Additional exam requirements/recommendations for international students: Required—TOEFL (minimum score 550 paper-based; 213 computer-based). *Application deadline:* For fall admission, 4/15 for domestic students; for winter admission, 10/15 priority date for domestic students; for spring admission, 2/15 for domestic students. Applications are processed on a rolling basis. Application fee: $30. Electronic applications accepted. *Expenses:* Tuition, state resident: full-time $6,827. Tuition, nonresident: full-time $21,951. Required fees: $999. *Financial support:* Fellowships, research assistantships, teaching assistantships, career-related internships or fieldwork, scholarships/grants, and unspecified assistantships available. Support available to part-time students. Financial award application deadline: 2/15; financial award applicants required to submit FAFSA. *Faculty research:* Accounting, finance, insurance, management, real estate and urban analysis marketing. *Unit head:* Alex Sevilla, Director, 352-392-7992 Ext. 1206. *Application contact:* Patrick Foran, Associate Director of Admissions, 352-392-7992 Ext. 282, Fax: 352-392-8791, E-mail: patrick.foran@cba.ufl.edu.

University of Massachusetts Dartmouth, Graduate School, Charlton College of Business, Program in Business Administration, North Dartmouth, MA 02747-2300. Offers accounting (Postbaccalaureate Certificate); business administration (MBA); e-commerce (PMC); finance (PMC); general management (PMC); leadership (PMC); management (Postbaccalaureate Certificate); marketing (PMC); supply chain management (PMC). *Accreditation:* AACSB. Part-time programs available. *Faculty:* 41 full-time (11 women), 22 part-time/adjunct (8 women). *Students:* 66 full-time (20 women), 111 part-time (54 women); includes 16 minority (5 African Americans, 6 Asian Americans or Pacific Islanders, 5 Hispanic Americans), 46 international. Average age 30. 167 applicants, 83% accepted, 83 enrolled. In 2006, 73 master's, 20 other advanced degrees awarded. *Entrance requirements:* For master's, GMAT, resumé, letters of recommendation. Additional exam requirements/recommendations for international students: Required—TOEFL (minimum score 500 paper-based). *Application deadline:* For fall admission, 6/1 for domestic students, 4/1 for international students; for spring admission, 10/1 for domestic students, 8/1 for international students. Application fee: $40 ($60 for international students). Electronic applications accepted. *Expenses:* Tuition, state resident: full-time $2,071; part-time $86 per credit. Tuition, nonresident: full-time $8,099; part-time $337 per credit. *Financial support:* In 2006–07, 2 research assistantships with full tuition reimbursements (averaging $11,985 per year), 6 teaching assistantships with full tuition reimbursements (averaging $7,200 per year) were awarded; Federal Work-Study and unspecified assistantships also available. Support available to part-time students. Financial award application deadline: 3/1; financial award applicants required to submit FAFSA. *Faculty research:* Organizational identity dynamics in strategic alliances and partnerships, market analysis in cranberry industry, consumer choice modeling. Total annual research expenditures: $508,000. *Unit head:* Matthew Roy, Assistant Dean, 508-999-8409, Fax: 508-999-8776, E-mail: mroy@umassd.edu. *Application contact:* Carol Novo, Graduate Admissions Officer, 508-999-8604, Fax: 508-999-8183, E-mail: graduate@umassd.edu.

University of New Brunswick Saint John, Faculty of Business, Saint John, NB E2L 4L5, Canada. Offers administration (MBA); electronic commerce (MBA); international business (MBA); natural resource management (MBA). Part-time programs available. *Degree requirements:* For master's, thesis optional. *Entrance requirements:* For master's, GMAT. Additional exam requirements/recommendations for international students: Required—TOEFL (minimum score 550 paper-based). Expenses: Contact institution.

University of Ottawa, Faculty of Graduate and Postdoctoral Studies, Interdisciplinary Programs, Ottawa, ON K1N 6N5, Canada. Offers e-business (Certificate); e-commerce (Certificate); finance (Certificate); health services and policies research (Diploma); population health (PhD); population health risk assessment and management (Certificate); public management and governance (Certificate); systems science (Certificate).

University of Ottawa, Faculty of Graduate and Postdoctoral Studies, Program in E-Business Technologies, Ottawa, ON K1N 6N5, Canada. Offers M Sc, MEBT. *Degree requirements:* For master's, thesis or alternative, project. *Entrance requirements:* For master's, honours degree or equivalent, minimum B average.

University of Phoenix–Austin Campus, College of Graduate Business and Management, Austin, TX 78759. Offers accounting (MBA); business and management (MBA); e-business (MBA); global management (MBA); human resources management (MBA, MM); management (MM); marketing (MBA); public administration (MBA).

University of Phoenix–Bay Area Campus, John Sperling School of Business, College of Information Systems and Technology, Pleasanton, CA 94588-3677. Offers e-business (MBA); technology management (MBA). Evening/weekend programs available. *Faculty:* 19 full-time (1 woman), 166 part-time/adjunct (35 women). *Students:* 94 full-time (19 women); includes 26 minority (4 African Americans, 18 Asian Americans or Pacific Islanders, 4 Hispanic Americans), 30 international. Average age 38. In 2006, 90 degrees awarded. *Degree requirements:* For master's, thesis (for some programs), registration. *Entrance requirements:* For master's, minimum undergraduate GPA of 3.0, 3 years of work experience. Additional exam requirements/recommendations for international students: Required—TOEFL (minimum score 550 paper-based; 213 computer-based; 79 iBT). *Application deadline:* Applications are processed on a rolling basis. Application fee: $45. Electronic applications accepted. *Expenses:* Tuition: Full-time $12,648. Required fees: $760. *Financial support:* Institutionally sponsored loans and scholarships/grants available. Financial award applicants required to submit FAFSA. *Unit head:* Dr. Adam Honea, Dean/Executive Director, 480-557-1659, E-mail: adam.honea@phoenix.edu. *Application contact:* Chair, 408-435-8500, Fax: 408-435-8250.

University of Phoenix–Chicago Campus, John Sperling School of Business, College of Information Systems and Technology, Schaumburg, IL 60173-4399. Offers e-business (MBA); information systems (MIS); management (MM); technology management (MBA). Evening/weekend programs available. *Faculty:* 4 full-time (3 women), 38 part-time/adjunct (8 women). *Students:* 10 full-time (4 women); includes 6 minority (1 African American, 3 Asian Americans or Pacific Islanders, 2 Hispanic Americans). Average age 37. In 2006, 19 degrees awarded. *Degree requirements:* For master's, thesis (for some programs), registration. *Entrance requirements:* For master's, 3 years of work experience, minimum undergraduate GPA of 3.0. Additional exam requirements/recommendations for international students: Required—TOEFL (minimum score 550 paper-based; 213 computer-based; 79 iBT). *Application deadline:* Applications are processed on a rolling basis. Application fee: $45. Electronic applications accepted. *Expenses:* Tuition: Full-time $12,120. Required fees: $760. *Financial support:* Institutionally sponsored loans and scholarships/grants available. Financial award applicants required to submit FAFSA. *Application contact:* Campus College Chair—Technology, 847-413-1922, Fax: 847-413-8706.

University of Phoenix–Cincinnati Campus, John Sperling School of Business, College of Information Systems and Technology, West Chester, OH 45069-4875. Offers electronic business (MBA); technology management (MBA). Evening/weekend programs available. *Degree requirements:* For master's, thesis (for some programs), registration. *Entrance requirements:* For master's, minimum undergraduate GPA of 2.5, 3 years of work experience. Additional exam requirements/recommendations for international students: Required—TOEFL (minimum score 550 paper-based; 213 computer-based; 79 iBT). *Application deadline:* Applications are processed on a rolling basis. Application fee: $45. Electronic applications accepted. *Expenses:* Tuition: Full-time $11,832. Required fees: $760. *Financial support:* Institutionally sponsored loans and scholarships/grants available. Financial award applicants required to submit FAFSA. *Unit head:* Dr. Adam Honea, Dean/Executive Director, 480-557-1659, E-mail: adam.honea@phoenix.edu. *Application contact:* College Chair, 513-772-9600.

University of Phoenix–Columbus Georgia Campus, John Sperling School of Business, College of Information Systems and Technology, Columbus, GA 31904-6321. Offers e-business (MBA); technology management (MBA). Evening/weekend programs available. *Faculty:* 6 full-time (0 women), 12 part-time/adjunct (4 women). *Students:* 8 full-time (2 women); includes 5 minority (all African Americans) Average age 44. In 2006, 10 degrees awarded. *Degree requirements:* For master's, thesis (for some programs), registration. *Entrance requirements:* For master's, minimum undergraduate GPA of 3.0, 3 years of work experience. Additional exam requirements/recommendations for international students: Required—TOEFL (minimum score 550 paper-based; 213 computer-based; 79 iBT). *Application deadline:* Applications are processed on a rolling basis. Application fee: $45. Electronic applications accepted. *Expenses:* Tuition: Full-time $10,200. Required fees: $760. *Financial support:* Institutionally sponsored loans and scholarships/grants available. Financial award applicants required to submit FAFSA. *Unit head:* Dr. Adam Honea, Dean/Executive Director, 480-557-1659, E-mail: adam.honea@phoenix.edu. *Application contact:* College Chair, 706-320-1262.

University of Phoenix–Dallas Campus, John Sperling School of Business, College of Information Systems and Technology, Dallas, TX 75251-2009. Offers e-business (MBA); technology management (MBA). Evening/weekend programs available. *Faculty:* 10 full-time (0 women), 32 part-time/adjunct (4 women). *Students:* 15 full-time (3 women); includes 3 minority (2 African Americans, 1 Asian American or Pacific Islander), 2 international. Average age 46. In 2006, 4 degrees awarded. *Degree requirements:* For master's, thesis (for some programs), registration. *Entrance requirements:* For master's, minimum undergraduate GPA of 3.0, 3 years of work experience. Additional exam requirements/recommendations for international students: Required—TOEFL (minimum score 550 paper-based; 213 computer-based; 79 iBT). *Application deadline:* Applications are processed on a rolling basis. Application fee: $45. Electronic applications accepted. *Expenses:* Tuition: Full-time $11,832. Required fees: $760. *Financial support:* Institutionally sponsored loans and scholarships/grants available. *Unit head:* Dr. Adam Honea, Dean, 480-557-1659, E-mail: adam.honea@phoenix.edu. *Application contact:* Campus College Chair, 972-385-1055, Fax: 972-385-1700.

University of Phoenix–Denver Campus, John Sperling School of Business, College of Graduate Business and Management, Lone Tree, CO 80124-5453. Offers accounting (MBA); business administration (MBA); e-business (MBA); global management (MBA); human resources management (MBA, MM); management (MM); marketing (MBA); public administration (MBA, MM). Evening/weekend programs available. *Faculty:* 63 full-time (22 women), 254 part-time/adjunct (56 women). *Students:* 289 full-time (139 women); includes 59 minority (25 African Americans, 1 American Indian/Alaska Native, 9 Asian Americans or Pacific Islanders, 24 Hispanic Americans), 20 international. Average age 37. In 2006, 93 degrees awarded. *Degree requirements:* For master's, thesis (for some programs), registration. *Entrance requirements:* For master's, minimum undergraduate GPA of 3.0, 3 years work experience. Additional exam requirements/recommendations for international students: Required—TOEFL (minimum score 550 paper-based; 213 computer-based; 79 iBT). *Application deadline:* Applications are processed on a rolling basis. Application fee: $45. Electronic applications accepted. *Expenses:* Tuition: Full-time $10,032. Required fees: $760. *Financial support:* Institutionally sponsored loans and scholarships/grants available. Financial award applicants required to submit FAFSA. *Unit head:* Dr. Brian Lindquist, Associate Vice President and Dean/Executive Director, 480-557-1221, E-mail: brian.lindquist@phoenix.edu. *Application contact:* Chair, 303-694-9093, Fax: 303-662-0911.

University of Phoenix–Denver Campus, John Sperling School of Business, College of Information Systems and Technology, Lone Tree, CO 80124-5453. Offers e-business (MBA); management (MIS); technology management (MBA). Evening/weekend programs available. *Faculty:* 26 full-time (9 women), 118 part-time/adjunct (25 women). *Students:* 7 full-time (2 women); includes 1 minority (Hispanic American) Average age 38. In 2006, 11 master's awarded. *Degree requirements:* For master's, thesis (for some programs), registration. *Entrance requirements:* For master's, minimum undergraduate GPA of 3.0, 3 years of work experience. Additional exam requirements/recommendations for international students: Required—TOEFL (minimum score 550 paper-based; 213 computer-based; 79 iBT). *Application deadline:* Applications are processed on a rolling basis. Application fee: $45. Electronic applications accepted. *Expenses:* Tuition: Full-time $10,032. Required fees: $760. *Financial support:* Institutionally sponsored loans and scholarships/grants available. Financial award applicants required to submit FAFSA. *Unit head:* Dr. Adam Honea, Dean/Executive Director, 480-557-1659, E-mail: adam.honea@phoenix.edu. *Application contact:* Chair, 303-694-9093, Fax: 303-662-0911.

University of Phoenix–Detroit Campus, College of Graduate Business and Management, Southfield, MI 48076. Offers accounting (MBA); business administration (MBA); e-business (MBA); global management (MBA); human resources management (MBA, MM); management (MM); marketing (MBA); public administration (MBA).

University of Phoenix–Houston Campus, John Sperling School of Business, College of Information Systems and Technology, Houston, TX 77079-2004. Offers e-business (MBA); technology management (MBA). Evening/weekend programs available. *Faculty:* 2 full-time (0 women), 52 part-time/adjunct (6 women). *Students:* 51 full-time (19 women); includes 27 minority (19 African Americans, 4 Asian Americans or Pacific Islanders, 4 Hispanic Americans), 5 international. Average age 41. *Degree requirements:* For master's, thesis, comprehensive exam (for some programs). *Entrance requirements:* For master's, minimum undergraduate GPA of 3.0, 3 years of work experience. Additional exam requirements/recommendations for international students: Required—TOEFL (minimum score 550 paper-based; 213 computer-based; 79 iBT). *Application deadline:* Applications are processed on a rolling basis. Application fee: $45. Electronic applications accepted. *Expenses:* Tuition: Full-time $11,832. Required fees: $760. *Financial support:* Institutionally sponsored loans available. *Unit head:* Dr. Adam Honea, Dean, 480-557-1659, E-mail: adam.honea@phoenix.edu. *Application contact:* Campus College Chair, 713-465-9966, Fax: 713-465-2686.

University of Phoenix–Louisville Campus, College of Graduate Business and Management, Louisville, KY 40223-3839. Offers business and management (MBA, MM); e-business (MBA).

University of Phoenix–Madison Campus, College of Graduate Business and Management, Madison, WI 53718-2416. Offers accounting (MBA); business and management (MBA, MM); e-business (MBA); global management (MBA); human resources management (MBA, MM); marketing (MBA); public administration (MBA).

University of Phoenix–Maryland Campus, John Sperling School of Business, College of Graduate Business and Management, Columbia, MD 21045-5424. Offers business administration (MBA); e-business (MBA); global management (MBA); human resources management (MBA, MM); marketing (MBA); public administration (MBA, MM). Evening/weekend programs available. *Faculty:* 22 full-time (6 women), 136 part-time/adjunct (35 women). *Students:* 357 full-time (223 women); includes 148 minority (128 African Americans, 2 American Indian/Alaska Native, 9 Asian Americans or Pacific Islanders, 9 Hispanic Americans), 38 international. Average age 37. In 2006, 111 master's awarded. *Degree requirements:* For master's, thesis (for some programs), registration. *Entrance requirements:* For master's, minimum undergraduate GPA of 3.0, 3 years of work experience. Additional exam requirements/recommendations for international students: Required—TOEFL (minimum score 550 paper-based; 213 computer-based; 79 iBT). *Application deadline:* Applications are processed on a rolling basis. Application fee: $45. Electronic applications accepted. *Expenses:* Tuition: Full-time $13,200.

Required fees: $760. *Financial support:* Institutionally sponsored loans and scholarships/grants available. Financial award applicants required to submit FAFSA. *Unit head:* Dr. Brian Lindquist, Associate Vice President and Dean/Executive Director, 480-557-1221, E-mail: brian.lindquist@phoenix.edu. *Application contact:* Chair, 410-872-9001, Fax: 410-536-5727.

University of Phoenix–Memphis Campus, College of Graduate Business and Management, Cordova, TN 38018. Offers acounting (MBA); business and management (MBA); e-business (MBA); global management (MBA); human resources management (MBA, MM); marketing (MBA); public administration (MBA, MM).

University of Phoenix–New Mexico Campus, John Sperling School of Business, College of Information Systems and Technology, Albuquerque, NM 87109-4645. Offers e-business (MBA); technology management (MBA). Evening/weekend programs available. *Faculty:* 7 full-time (2 women), 115 part-time/adjunct (14 women). *Students:* 20 full-time (8 women); includes 9 minority (1 Asian American or Pacific Islander, 8 Hispanic Americans). Average age 37. In 2006, 36 degrees awarded. *Degree requirements:* For master's, thesis (for some programs), registration. *Entrance requirements:* For master's, minimum undergraduate GPA of 3.0, 3 years of work experience. Additional exam requirements/recommendations for international students: Required—TOEFL (minimum score 550 paper-based; 213 computer-based; 79 iBT). *Application deadline:* Applications are processed on a rolling basis. Application fee: $45. Electronic applications accepted. *Expenses:* Tuition: Full-time $9,005. Required fees: $760. *Financial support:* Institutionally sponsored loans and scholarships/grants available. Financial award applicants required to submit FAFSA. *Unit head:* Dr. Adam Honea, Dean/Executive Director, 480-557-1659, E-mail: adam.honea@phoenix.edu. *Application contact:* Chair, 505-821-4800, Fax: 505-821-5551.

University of Phoenix–Northern Virginia Campus, College of Graduate Business and Management, Reston, VA 20190. Offers accounting (MBA); business administration (MBA); e-business (MBA); global management (MBA); human resources management (MBA, MM); management (MM); marketing (MBA); public administration (MBA).

University of Phoenix–Oklahoma City Campus, John Sperling School of Business, College of Information Systems and Technology, Oklahoma City, OK 73116-8244. Offers e-business (MBA); technology management (MBA). Evening/weekend programs available. *Faculty:* 4 full-time (0 women), 49 part-time/adjunct (6 women). *Students:* 2 full-time (0 women); includes 3 minority (2 American Indian/Alaska Native, 1 Hispanic American). Average age 39. In 2006, 10 degrees awarded. *Degree requirements:* For master's, thesis (for some programs), registration. *Entrance requirements:* For master's, minimum undergraduate GPA of 3.0, 3 years of work experience. Additional exam requirements/recommendations for international students: Required—TOEFL (minimum score 550 paper-based; 213 computer-based; 79 iBT). *Application deadline:* Applications are processed on a rolling basis. Application fee: $45. Electronic applications accepted. *Expenses:* Tuition: Full-time $10,608. Required fees: $760. *Financial support:* Institutionally sponsored loans and scholarships/grants available. Financial award applicants required to submit FAFSA. *Unit head:* Dr. Adam Honea, Provost/Dean, 480-557-1659, E-mail: adam.honea@phoenix.edu. *Application contact:* Chair, 405-842-8007, Fax: 405-841-3386.

University of Phoenix Online Campus, John Sperling School of Business, College of Information Systems and Technology, Phoenix, AZ 85034-7209. Offers e-business (MBA); management (MIS); technology management (MBA). Evening/weekend programs available. *Faculty:* 7 full-time (3 women), 2,317 part-time/adjunct (528 women). *Students:* 4,315 full-time (1,423 women); includes 967 minority (552 African Americans, 19 American Indian/Alaska Native, 222 Asian Americans or Pacific Islanders, 174 Hispanic Americans), 581 international. Average age 38. In 2006, 7359 degrees awarded. *Degree requirements:* For master's, thesis (for some programs), registration. *Entrance requirements:* For master's, 3 years of work experience, minimum undergraduate GPA of 3.0. Additional exam requirements/recommendations for international students: Required—TOEFL (minimum score 550 paper-based; 213 computer-based; 79 iBT). *Application deadline:* Applications are processed on a rolling basis. Application fee: $45. Electronic applications accepted. *Expenses:* Tuition: Full-time $12,664. Required fees: $760. *Financial support:* Institutionally sponsored loans and scholarships/grants available. Financial award applicants required to submit FAFSA. *Unit head:* Dr. Adam Honea, Dean/Executive Director, 480-557-1659, E-mail: adam.honea@phoenix.edu. *Application contact:* Dr. Adam Honea, Dean/Executive Director, 480-557-1659, E-mail: adam.honea@phoenix.edu.

University of Phoenix–Pittsburgh Campus, John Sperling School of Business, College of Information Systems and Technology, Pittsburgh, PA 15276. Offers e-business (MBA); information systems (MIS); technology management (MBA). Evening/weekend programs available. *Faculty:* 11 full-time (3 women), 21 part-time/adjunct (0 women). *Students:* 12 full-time (3 women); includes 3 minority (2 African Americans, 1 Asian American or Pacific Islander). Average age 36. In 2006, 8 degrees awarded. *Degree requirements:* For master's, thesis (for some programs), registration. *Entrance requirements:* For master's, minimum undergraduate GPA of 3.0, 3 years work experience. Additional exam requirements/recommendations for international students: Required—TOEFL (minimum score 550 paper-based; 213 computer-based; 79 iBT). *Application deadline:* Applications are processed on a rolling basis. Application fee: $45. Electronic applications accepted. *Expenses:* Tuition: Full-time $13,560. Required fees: $760. *Financial support:* Institutionally sponsored loans and scholarships/grants available. Financial award applicants required to submit FAFSA. *Unit head:* Dr. Adam Honea, Provost/Dean, Vice President Research and Development, 480-557-1659, E-mail: adam.honea@phoenix.edu. *Application contact:* Campus College Chair, 412-747-9000, Fax: 412-747-0676.

University of Phoenix–Raleigh Campus, College of Graduate Business and Management, Raleigh, NC 27606. Offers accounting (MBA); business administration (MBA); e-business (MBA); global management (MBA).

University of Phoenix–San Antonio Campus, College of Graduate Business and Management, San Antonio, TX 78230. Offers accounting (MBA); business and management (MBA); e-business (MBA); global management (MBA); human resources management (MBA, MM); management (MM); marketing (MBA); public administration (MBA, MM).

University of Phoenix–West Michigan Campus, The John Sperling School of Business, College of Information Systems and Technology, Walker, MI 49544. Offers e-business (MBA); technology management (MBA). Evening/weekend programs available. *Faculty:* 8 full-time (0 women), 26 part-time/adjunct (7 women). *Students:* 6 full-time (0 women); includes 1 minority (African American) Average age 33. In 2006, 11 master's awarded. *Degree requirements:* For master's, thesis (for some programs), registration. *Entrance requirements:* For master's, minimum undergraduate GPA of 3.0, 3 years of work experience. Additional exam requirements/recommendations for international students: Required—TOEFL (minimum score 550 paper-based; 213 computer-based; 79 iBT). *Application deadline:* Applications are processed on a rolling basis. Application fee: $45. Electronic applications accepted. *Expenses:* Tuition: Full-time $12,043. Required fees: $760. *Financial support:* Institutionally sponsored loans available. Financial award applicants required to submit FAFSA. *Unit head:* Dr. Adam Honea, Dean/Executive Director, 408-557-1659, E-mail: adam.honea@phoenix.edu. *Application contact:* Chair, 888-345-9699, Fax: 616-784-5300.

University of San Francisco, Masagung Graduate School of Management, Program in Business Administration, San Francisco, CA 94117-1080. Offers business economics (MBA); e-business (MBA); entrepreneurship (MBA); finance and banking (MBA); international business (MBA); management (MBA); marketing (MBA); telecommunications management and policy (MBA); JD/MBA; MSN/MBA. *Accreditation:* AACSB. *Faculty:* 27 full-time (4 women), 21 part-time/adjunct (7 women). *Students:* 191 full-time (73 women), 71 part-time (33 women); includes 51 minority (4 African Americans, 1 American Indian/Alaska Native, 35 Asian Americans or Pacific Islanders, 11 Hispanic Americans), 102 international. Average age 28. 373 applicants, 70% accepted, 106 enrolled. In 2006, 163 degrees awarded. *Entrance requirements:* For master's, GMAT, minimum undergraduate GPA of 3.2. Additional exam requirements/recommendations for international students: Required—TOEFL. *Application deadline:* For fall admission, 7/1 priority date for domestic students; for spring admission, 11/30 for domestic students. Applications are processed on a rolling basis. Application fee: $55 ($65 for international students). *Expenses:* Tuition: Full-time $17,370; part-time $965 per unit. Tuition and fees vary according to degree level, campus/location and program. *Financial support:* In 2006–07, 104 students received support; fellowships available. Financial award application deadline: 3/2; financial award applicants required to submit FAFSA. *Faculty research:* International financial markets, technology transfer licensing, international marketing, strategic planning. Total annual research expenditures: $50,000. *Unit head:* Carol Langlois, Director, 415-422-6314, Fax: 415-422-2502.

West Chester University of Pennsylvania, Graduate Studies, School of Business and Public Affairs, Program in Business Administration, West Chester, PA 19383. Offers economics/finance (MBA); executive business administration (MBA); general business (MBA); management (MBA); technology and electronic commerce (MBA). *Accreditation:* AACSB. Part-time and evening/weekend programs available. *Students:* 2 full-time (1 woman), 68 part-time (19 women); includes 3 African Americans, 8 Asian Americans or Pacific Islanders, 2 Hispanic Americans, 5 international. Average age 34. 39 applicants, 77% accepted, 27 enrolled. In 2006, 41 degrees awarded. *Degree requirements:* For master's, thesis optional. *Entrance requirements:* For master's, GMAT, interview, minimum GPA of 3.0. *Application deadline:* For fall admission, 4/15 priority date for domestic students; for spring admission, 10/15 for domestic students. Applications are processed on a rolling basis. Application fee: $35. *Financial support:* In 2006–07, 4 research assistantships with full tuition reimbursements (averaging $5,000 per year) were awarded; unspecified assistantships also available. Support available to part-time students. Financial award application deadline: 2/15; financial award applicants required to submit FAFSA. *Unit head:* Dr. Pual Christ, Director, 610-436-2608, E-mail: pchrist@wcupa.edu. *Application contact:* Dr. Pual Christ, Graduate Coordinator, 610-436-2608, E-mail: mba@wcupa.edu.

Xavier University, Williams College of Business, Master of Business Administration Program, Cincinnati, OH 45207. Offers business administration (Exec MBA, MBA); e-commerce (MBA); finance (MBA); international business (MBA); management information systems (MBA); marketing (MBA);); MBA/MHSA; MSN/MBA. *Accreditation:* AACSB. Part-time and evening/weekend programs available. *Faculty:* 59 full-time (22 women), 29 part-time/adjunct (8 women). *Students:* 227 full-time (66 women), 708 part-time (252 women); includes 99 minority (41 African Americans, 1 American Indian/Alaska Native, 43 Asian Americans or Pacific Islanders, 14 Hispanic Americans), 43 international. Average age 31. 486 applicants, 63% accepted, 229 enrolled. In 2006, 294 degrees awarded. *Entrance requirements:* For master's, GMAT, resumé. Additional exam requirements/recommendations for international students: Required—TOEFL (minimum score 550 paper-based; 213 computer-based; 79 iBT). *Application deadline:* For fall admission, 8/1 priority date for domestic students, 6/1 for international students; for winter admission, 12/1 priority date for domestic students; for spring admission, 4/1 priority date for domestic students, 10/1 for international students. Applications are processed on a rolling basis. Application fee: $35. Electronic applications accepted. *Expenses: Contact institution.* Part-time tuition and fees vary according to degree level, campus/location and program. *Financial support:* In 2006–07, 175 students received support, including 11 research assistantships with full and partial tuition reimbursements available; career-related internships or fieldwork, scholarships/grants, and tuition waivers (partial) also available. Support available to part-time students. Financial award application deadline: 4/30; financial award applicants required to submit FAFSA. *Faculty research:* Supply chain management, category management, data mining, off-shoring. *Unit head:* Dr. Raghu Tadepalli, Associate Dean, 513-745-3525, Fax: 513-745-2929, E-mail: tadepalli@xavier.edu. *Application contact:* Jennifer Bush, Executive Director, MBA Programs, 513-745-3525, Fax: 513-745-2929, E-mail: xumba@xavier.edu.

Section 5
Entrepreneurship

This section contains a directory of institutions offering graduate work in entrepreneurship, followed by in-depth entries submitted by institutions that chose to prepare detailed program descriptions. Additional information about programs listed in the directory but not augmented by an in-depth entry may be obtained by writing directly to the dean of a graduate school or chair of a department at the address given in the directory.

For programs offering related work, see also in this book Business Administration and Management, International Business, and Education (Business Education).

CONTENTS

Entrepreneurship

American College of Thessaloniki, Department of Business Administration, Pylea, Greece. Offers banking and finance (MBA); entrepreneurship (MBA, Certificate); finance (Certificate); management (MBA, Certificate); marketing (MBA, Certificate). Part-time and evening/weekend programs available. *Faculty:* 6 full-time (1 woman), 10 part-time/adjunct (4 women). *Students:* 9 full-time (6 women), 39 part-time (24 women), 22 international. 36 applicants, 97% accepted, 26 enrolled. In 2006, 25 degrees awarded. *Degree requirements:* For master's, thesis, registration. *Application deadline:* For fall admission, 9/30 priority date for domestic students; for spring admission, 1/31 priority date for domestic students. Applications are processed on a rolling basis. Application fee: $70. Electronic applications accepted. *Expenses:* Tuition: Full-time $10,560; part-time $660 per course. Part-time tuition and fees vary according to course load. *Unit head:* Dr. Nikolaos Kourkoumelis, Chair, Business Division, E-mail: nikolaos@act.edu. *Application contact:* Vasilis Blatsas, Coordinator of Business Programs and MBA Advisor, 30-310-398206 Ext. 206.

American University, Kogod School of Business, Department of Management, Program in Entrepreneurship and Management, Washington, DC 20016-8001. Offers MBA. *Students:* 14 full-time (5 women), 17 part-time (5 women); includes 12 minority (8 African Americans, 1 American Indian/Alaska Native, 2 Asian Americans or Pacific Islanders, 1 Hispanic American), 6 international. Average age 29. In 2006, 3 degrees awarded. *Entrance requirements:* For master's, GMAT. Additional exam requirements/recommendations for international students: Required—TOEFL. *Application deadline:* For fall admission, 2/1 priority date for domestic students; for spring admission, 10/1 priority date for domestic students. Applications are processed on a rolling basis. Application fee: $50. *Expenses:* Tuition: Full-time $18,864; part-time $1,048 per credit. Required fees: $380. Tuition and fees vary according to program. *Financial support:* Fellowships, research assistantships available. Financial award application deadline: 2/1.

Andrew Jackson University, Brian Tracy College of Business and Entrepreneurship, Birmingham, AL 35244. Offers entrepreneurship (MBA); finance (MBA); health services management (MBA); hospitality and tourism management (MBA); human resource management (MBA); international business (MBA); management (MBA); marketing (MBA). Part-time and evening/weekend programs available. Postbaccalaureate distance learning degree programs offered (no on-campus study). *Faculty:* 13 part-time/adjunct (1 woman). *Students:* Average age 40. In 2006, 6 degrees awarded. *Entrance requirements:* For master's, course work in calculus, statistics. Additional exam requirements/recommendations for international students: Required—TOEFL (minimum score 550 paper-based; 213 computer-based). *Application deadline:* Applications are processed on a rolling basis. Application fee: $75. *Expenses:* Tuition: Part-time $705 per course. *Application contact:* Betty Howell, Director of Student Affairs, 205-871-9288 Ext. 108, Fax: 205-871-9294, E-mail: bhowell@aju.edu.

Baldwin-Wallace College, Graduate Programs, Division of Business Administration, Program in Entrepreneurship, Berea, OH 44017-2088. Offers MBA. *Students:* 20 full-time (6 women), 9 part-time (2 women); includes 3 minority (2 African Americans, 1 Asian American or Pacific Islander). Average age 30. 8 applicants, 88% accepted, 7 enrolled. In 2006, 9 degrees awarded. *Application deadline:* For fall admission, 7/25 priority date for domestic students; for spring admission, 12/15 priority date for domestic students. Applications are processed on a rolling basis. Application fee: $25. Electronic applications accepted. *Expenses:* Tuition: Part-time $760 per credit hour. Tuition and fees vary according to program. *Unit head:* J. Peter Kelly, Director of MBA, Executive MBA and Human Resources Programs, 440-826-2391, Fax: 440-826-3868, E-mail: pkelly@bw.edu. *Application contact:* Winifred W. Gerhardt, Director of Admission for the Evening and Weekend College, 440-826-2222, Fax: 440-826-3830, E-mail: admission@bw.edu.

Bay Path College, Program in Entrepreneurial Thinking and Innovative Practices, Longmeadow, MA 01106-2292. Offers MBA. Part-time and evening/weekend programs available. *Entrance requirements:* Additional exam requirements/recommendations for international students: Recommended—TOEFL (minimum score 500 paper-based). Electronic applications accepted.

Bernard M. Baruch College of the City University of New York, Zicklin School of Business, Department of Management, New York, NY 10010-5585. Offers entrepreneurship (MBA); general management and policy (MBA); human resources management (MBA); management planning systems (PhD); management science (MBA); organization and policy studies (PhD); organizational behavior (MBA). Part-time and evening/weekend programs available. *Faculty:* 38 full-time (10 women), 41 part-time/adjunct (6 women). *Students:* 30 full-time (14 women), 117 part-time (52 women); includes 37 minority (17 African Americans, 14 Asian Americans or Pacific Islanders, 6 Hispanic Americans). In 2006, 39 master's, 1 doctorate awarded. *Degree requirements:* For doctorate, thesis/dissertation, comprehensive exam. *Entrance requirements:* For master's, GMAT, 2 letters of recommendation, resumé, 2 years of work experience; for doctorate, GMAT. Additional exam requirements/recommendations for international students: Required—TOEFL (minimum score 590 paper-based; 243 computer-based), TWE. *Application deadline:* For fall admission, 5/31 for domestic students, 4/30 for international students; for spring admission, 10/31 for domestic and international students. Application fee: $125. *Financial support:* Fellowships, research assistantships, teaching assistantships, career-related internships or fieldwork, Federal Work-Study, scholarships/grants, and unspecified assistantships available. Financial award application deadline: 4/30; financial award applicants required to submit FAFSA. *Unit head:* Harry M. Rosen, Chairman, 646-312-3620, Fax: 646-312-3621, E-mail: harry_rosen@baruch.cuny.edu. *Application contact:* Frances Murphy, Office of Graduate Admissions, 646-312-1300, Fax: 646-312-1301, E-mail: zicklingradadmissions@baruch.cuny.edu.

California Lutheran University, Graduate Studies, School of Business, Thousand Oaks, CA 91360-2787. Offers finance (MBA); healthcare management (MBA); international business (MBA); management information systems (MBA); marketing (MBA); organizational behavior (MBA); small business/entrepreneurship (MBA). Evening/weekend programs available. *Entrance requirements:* For master's, GMAT, interview, minimum GPA of 3.0. Expenses: Contact institution.

California State University, East Bay, Academic Programs and Graduate Studies, College of Business and Economics, Department of Marketing, Option in New Ventures/Small Business Management, Hayward, CA 94542-3000. Offers MBA. *Degree requirements:* For master's, comprehensive exam or thesis. *Entrance requirements:* For master's, GMAT, minimum GPA of 2.75. Additional exam requirements/recommendations for international students: Required—TOEFL (minimum score 550 paper-based; 213 computer-based). *Application deadline:* For fall admission, 5/31 for domestic students, 4/30 for international students; for winter admission, 9/30 for domestic and international students; for spring admission, 12/31 for domestic students, 11/30 for international students. Application fee: $55. *Financial support:* Application deadline: 3/2. *Unit head:* Dr. Ricardo Singson, Advisor, 510-885-3557, E-mail: ricardo.singson@csueastbay.edu. *Application contact:* Doris Duncan, Director of Graduate Programs, 510-885-3364, Fax: 510-885-2176, E-mail: doris.duncan@csueastbay.edu.

California State University, East Bay, Academic Programs and Graduate Studies, College of Business and Economics, Option in Entrepreneurship, Hayward, CA 94542-3000. Offers MBA. *Entrance requirements:* Additional exam requirements/recommendations for international students: Required—TOEFL (minimum score 550 paper-based; 213 computer-based). *Application deadline:* For fall admission, 5/31 for domestic students, 4/30 for international students; for winter admission, 9/30 for domestic and international students; for spring admission, 12/31 for domestic students, 11/30 for international students. *Unit head:* Norman Smothers, Advisor, 510-885-3797, E-mail: norman.smothers@csueastbay.edu. *Application contact:* Doris Duncan, Director of Graduate Programs, 510-885-3364, Fax: 510-885-2176, E-mail: doris.duncan@csueastbay.edu.

Cameron University, Office of Graduate Studies, Program in Entrepreneurial Studies, Lawton, OK 73505-6377. Offers MS. Part-time and evening/weekend programs available. Postbaccalaureate distance learning degree programs offered (no on-campus study). *Students:* 3 full-time (all women), 4 part-time (1 woman); all minorities (all African Americans) Average age 35. *Degree requirements:* For master's, comprehensive exam, registration. *Entrance requirements:* Additional exam requirements/recommendations for international students: Required—TOEFL (minimum score 550 paper-based; 213 computer-based). *Application deadline:* Applications are processed on a rolling basis. Application fee: $15 ($32 for international students). Electronic applications accepted. *Expenses:* Tuition, state resident: full-time $2,479; part-time $138 per credit hour. Tuition, nonresident: full-time $5,976; part-time $332 per credit hour. Tuition and fees vary according to campus/location. *Financial support:* In 2006–07, 5 research assistantships (averaging $3,600 per year), 1 teaching assistantship (averaging $1,280 per year) were awarded; career-related internships or fieldwork, Federal Work-Study, and unspecified assistantships also available. Support available to part-time students. Financial award application deadline: 4/15. *Faculty research:* Entrepreneurial competition, new venture creation, legal issues, electronic commerce. *Unit head:* Bernadette Lonzanida, Graduate Advisor, 580-581-2271, Fax: 580-591-8087, E-mail: bernadel@cameron.edu. *Application contact:* Teresa Enriquez, Graduate Admissions/Enrollment Coordinator, 580-581-2987, E-mail: teresae@cameron.edu.

Carlos Albizu University, Miami Campus, Graduate Programs, Miami, FL 33172-2209. Offers clinical psychology (Psy D); entrepreneurship (MBA); exceptional student education (MS); industrial/organizational psychology (MS); marriage and family therapy (MS); mental health counseling (MS); nonprofit management (MBA); organizational management (MBA); psychology (MS); school counseling (MS); teaching English as a second language (MS). *Accreditation:* APA. Part-time and evening/weekend programs available. Terminal master's awarded for partial completion of doctoral program. *Degree requirements:* For master's, one foreign language, comprehensive exam, integrative project (MBA), research project (MSESE); for doctorate, one foreign language, comprehensive exam, internship, doctoral project. *Entrance requirements:* For master's, 3 letters of recommendation, interview, minimum GPA of 3.0, resumé; for doctorate, 3 letters of recommendation, minimum GPA of 3.0, resumé, interview. *Faculty research:* Psychotherapy, forensic psychology, neuropsychology, marketing strategy, entrepreneurship.

Columbia University, Graduate School of Business, MBA Program, New York, NY 10027. Offers accounting (MBA); decision, risk, and operations (MBA); entrepreneurship (MBA); finance and economics (MBA); human resource management (MBA); international business (MBA); management (MBA); marketing (MBA); media (MBA); real estate (MBA); social enterprise (MBA); DDS/MBA; JD/MBA; MBA/MIA; MBA/MPH; MBA/MS; MD/MBA. *Faculty:* 118 full-time (14 women), 106 part-time/adjunct (18 women). *Students:* 1,242 full-time (428 women); includes 291 minority (65 African Americans, 5 American Indian/Alaska Native, 189 Asian Americans or Pacific Islanders, 32 Hispanic Americans), 392 international. Average age 28. 5,372 applicants, 17% accepted, 726 enrolled. In 2006, 682 degrees awarded. *Entrance requirements:* For master's, GMAT, 2 letters of recommendation. Additional exam requirements/recommendations for international students: Required—TOEFL. *Application deadline:* For fall admission, 4/20 for domestic students, 3/1 for international students; for spring admission, 10/12 for domestic and international students. Applications are processed on a rolling basis. Application fee: $215. Electronic applications accepted. *Financial support:* Fellowships, research assistantships, teaching assistantships, career-related internships or fieldwork, Federal Work-Study, institutionally sponsored loans, scholarships/grants, and unspecified assistantships available. Financial award applicants required to submit FAFSA. *Unit head:* Prof. Amir Ziv, Vice Dean of Students and the MBA Program, 212-854-3485, Fax: 212-932-0545, E-mail: az50@columbia.edu. *Application contact:* Linda B. Meehan, Assistant Dean of Admissions, 212-854-1961, Fax: 212-662-6754, E-mail: apply@claven.gsb.columbia.edu.

Concordia University, School of Business and Professional Studies, Program in Entrepreneurial Business Administration, Irvine, CA 92612-3299. Offers MBA. *Faculty:* 3 full-time, 5 part-time/adjunct. *Students:* 58 full-time (29 women), 1 (woman) part-time; includes 9 minority (2 African Americans, 5 Asian Americans or Pacific Islanders, 2 Hispanic Americans), 10 international. Average age 32. 29 applicants, 86% accepted, 23 enrolled. In 2006, 14 degrees awarded. *Degree requirements:* For master's, thesis or alternative. *Entrance requirements:* For master's, GMAT, 2 years of work experience. Additional exam requirements/recommendations for international students: Required—TOEFL (minimum score 550 paper-based; 213 computer-based). *Application deadline:* For fall admission, 7/1 for domestic students; for spring admission, 12/1 for domestic students. Applications are processed on a rolling basis. Application fee: $25 ($300 for international students). *Financial support:* Applicants required to submit FAFSA. Total annual research expenditures: $10,000. *Application contact:* Roberto Marquez, Coordinator of Graduate Enrollment, 949-854-8002 Ext. 1133, Fax: 949-854-6894, E-mail: roberto.marquez@cui.edu.

Dallas Baptist University, Graduate School of Business, Business Administration Program, Dallas, TX 75211-9299. Offers accounting (MBA); business communication (MBA); conflict resolution management (MBA); e-business (MBA); entrepreneurship (MBA); finance (MBA); health care management (MBA); international business (MBA); management (MBA); management information systems (MBA); marketing (MBA); project management (MBA); technology and engineering management (MBA). *Accreditation:* ACBSP. Part-time and evening/weekend programs available. Postbaccalaureate distance learning degree programs offered (no on-campus study). *Faculty:* 49 full-time (21 women), 112 part-time/adjunct (46 women). *Students:* 103 full-time, 318 part-time. 226 applicants, 38% accepted. In 2006, 124 degrees awarded. *Entrance requirements:* For master's, GMAT, minimum GPA of 3.0. Additional exam requirements/recommendations for international students: Required—TOEFL. *Application deadline:* Applications are processed on a rolling basis. Application fee: $25. Electronic applications accepted. *Expenses:* Tuition: Full-time $8,370; part-time $465 per credit hour. Required fees: $465 per credit hour. *Financial support:* Career-related internships or fieldwork, Federal Work-Study, institutionally sponsored loans, scholarships/grants, and tuition waivers (full and partial) available. Support available to part-time students. *Faculty research:* Sports management, services marketing, retailing, strategic management, financial planning/investments. *Unit head:* Dr. Sandra S. Reid, Director, 214-333-5244, Fax: 214-333-5293, E-mail: graduate@dbu.edu. *Application contact:* Kit P. Montgomery, Director of Graduate Programs, 214-333-5242, Fax: 214-333-5579, E-mail: graduate@dbu.edu.

DePaul University, Charles H. Kellstadt Graduate School of Business, Department of Management, Chicago, IL 60604-2287. Offers entrepreneurship (MBA); health sector management (MBA); human resource management (MBA, MSHR); leadership/change management (MBA); management planning and strategy (MBA); operations management (MBA). Part-time and evening/weekend programs available. *Faculty:* 36 full-time (7 women), 35 part-time/adjunct (16 women). *Students:* 173 full-time (71 women), 134 part-time (61 women); includes 60 minority (12 African Americans, 34 Asian Americans or Pacific Islanders, 14 Hispanic Americans), 13 international. Average age 31. In 2006, 112 degrees awarded. *Entrance requirements:* For master's, GMAT, GRE (MSHR), 2 letters of recommendation, resumé. Additional exam requirements/recommendations for international students: Required—TOEFL (minimum score 550 paper-based; 213 computer-based). *Application deadline:* For fall admission, 7/1 for domestic students; for winter admission, 10/1 for domestic students; for spring admission, 2/1 for domestic students. Applications are processed on a rolling basis. Application fee: $60. Electronic applications accepted. *Financial support:* Research assistantships available. Financial award application deadline: 4/1. *Faculty research:* Growth management, creativity and innovation, quality management and business process design, entrepreneurship. *Application contact:* Christopher E. Kinsella, Director of Cohort MBA Programs, 312-362-8810, Fax: 312-362-6677, E-mail: kgsb@depaul.edu.

Eastern Michigan University, Graduate School, College of Business, Program in Business Administration, Ypsilanti, MI 48197. Offers business administration (MBA); e-business (MBA); enterprise business intelligence (MBA); entrepreneurship (MBA); finance (MBA); human resources (MBA); information systems (MBA); internal auditing (MBA); international business (MBA); nonprofit management (MBA); supply chain management (MBA). *Accreditation:* AACSB. Part-time and evening/weekend programs available. Postbaccalaureate distance learning degree programs offered (minimal on-campus study). *Students:* 98 full-time (36 women), 192 part-time (86 women); includes 50 minority (26 African Americans, 19 Asian Americans or Pacific Islanders, 5 Hispanic Americans), 76 international. Average age 29. In 2006, 109 degrees awarded. *Entrance requirements:* For master's, GMAT. Additional exam requirements/recommendations for international students: Required—TOEFL. *Application deadline:* For fall admission, 5/15 priority date for domestic students, 5/1 priority date for international students; for winter admission, 10/15 priority date for domestic students, 10/1 priority date for international students; for spring admission, 3/15 priority date for domestic students, 3/1 priority date for international students. Applications are processed on a rolling basis. Application fee: $35. *Expenses:* Tuition, state resident: part-time $341 per credit hour. Tuition, nonresident: full-time $16,104; part-time $671 per credit hour. Required fees: $816; $34 per credit hour. $40 per term. One-time fee: $82 full-time. Tuition and fees vary according to course level, course load, degree level and reciprocity agreements. *Financial support:* Fellowships, research assistantships with full tuition reimbursements, teaching assistantships with full tuition reimbursements, career-related internships or fieldwork, Federal Work-Study, institutionally sponsored loans, scholarships/grants, tuition waivers (partial), and unspecified assistantships available. Support available to part-time students. Financial award applicants required to submit FAFSA. *Unit head:* Dawn Gaymer, Assistant Dean, Graduate Business Programs, 734-487-4444, Fax: 734-483-1316, E-mail: dawn.malone@emich.edu. *Application contact:* K. Michelle Henry, Coordinator, 734-487-4444, Fax: 734-483-1316, E-mail: michelle.henry@emich.edu.

Fairleigh Dickinson University, College at Florham, Silberman College of Business, Departments of Management, Marketing, and Entrepreneurial Studies, Program in Entrepreneurial Studies, Madison, NJ 07940-1099. Offers MBA, Certificate. *Students:* 6 full-time (1 woman), 6 part-time (2 women), 1 international. Average age 30. 3 applicants, 100% accepted. In 2006, 3 degrees awarded. *Application deadline:* Applications are processed on a rolling basis. Application fee: $40.

Fairleigh Dickinson University, Metropolitan Campus, Silberman College of Business, Departments of Management, Marketing, and Entrepreneurial Studies, Program in Entrepreneurial Studies, Teaneck, NJ 07666-1914. Offers MBA, Certificate. *Students:* 4 full-time (1 woman), 6 part-time (4 women), 2 international. Average age 28. 6 applicants, 83% accepted, 3 enrolled. In 2006, 5 degrees awarded. *Application deadline:* Applications are processed on a rolling basis. Application fee: $40. *Unit head:* Dr. Robert Greenfield, Dean, Silberman College of Business, 201-692-2000.

Felician College, Program in Business, Lodi, NJ 07644-2117. Offers innovation and entrepreneurship (MBA). Part-time and evening/weekend programs available. *Students:* 47. 28 applicants, 89% accepted, 24 enrolled. *Entrance requirements:* For master's, GMAT. *Application deadline:* Applications are processed on a rolling basis. Application fee: $40. *Expenses:* Tuition: Part-time $675 per credit. Tuition and fees vary according to program. *Unit head:* Dr. William Morgan, Dean, Division of Business and Management Services, 201-559-6140, E-mail: morganw@felician.edu. *Application contact:* Dominic DiGioacchino, Associate Director of Adult and Graduate Admission, 201-559-6097, Fax: 201-559-6138, E-mail: digioacchinod@felician.edu.

Florida Atlantic University, College of Business, Department of Management, International Business and Entrepreneurship, Boca Raton, FL 33431-0991. Offers business administration (Exec MBA, MBA), including accounting (MBA), electronic commerce (MBA), finance (MBA), financial planning (MBA), global entrepreneurship (MBA), health administration (MBA), international business (MBA), marketing (MBA), operations management (MBA), real estate (MBA), sport management (MBA). *Faculty:* 64 full-time (17 women), 15 part-time/adjunct (3 women). *Students:* 215 full-time (89 women), 365 part-time (189 women); includes 150 minority (49 African Americans, 2 American Indian/Alaska Native, 36 Asian Americans or Pacific Islanders, 63 Hispanic Americans), 54 international. Average age 32. 414 applicants, 55% accepted, 167 enrolled. In 2006, 196 master's awarded. *Degree requirements:* For master's, thesis optional. *Entrance requirements:* For master's, GMAT, minimum GPA of 3.0. Additional exam requirements/recommendations for international students: Required—TOEFL (minimum score 600 paper-based; 250 computer-based). *Application deadline:* For fall admission, 7/1 priority date for domestic students, 2/15 priority date for international students; for winter admission, 11/1 priority date for domestic students, 8/15 priority date for international students; for spring admission, 4/1 priority date for domestic students, 1/15 priority date for international students. Applications are processed on a rolling basis. Application fee: $30. Electronic applications accepted. *Expenses:* Tuition, area resident: Full-time $4,394. Tuition, nonresident: full-time $16,441. *Financial support:* Research assistantships, teaching assistantships, career-related internships or fieldwork, Federal Work-Study, institutionally sponsored loans, tuition waivers (partial), and unspecified assistantships available. Support available to part-time students. Financial award application deadline: 3/1; financial award applicants required to submit FAFSA. *Unit head:* Dr. Brenda Richey, Head, 561-297-3194, E-mail: brichey@fau.edu. *Application contact:* Fredrick G. Taylor, Graduate Adviser, 561-297-2768, Fax: 561-297-1315, E-mail: mba@fau.edu.

Georgia Institute of Technology, Graduate Studies and Research, College of Management, Program in Business Administration, Atlanta, GA 30332-0001. Offers accounting (MBA); e-commerce (Certificate); engineering entrepreneurship (MBA); entrepreneurship (Certificate); finance (MBA); information technology management (MBA); international business (MBA, Certificate); management of technology (Certificate); marketing (MBA); operations management (MBA); organizational behavior (MBA); strategic management (MBA). *Accreditation:* AACSB.

Georgia State University, J. Mack Robinson College of Business, Department of Managerial Sciences, Atlanta, GA 30303-3083. Offers business analysis (MBA, MS); entrepreneurship (MBA); human resources management (MBA, MS); management (MBA, PhD); operations management (MBA, MS, PhD); organization change (MS). Part-time and evening/weekend programs available. *Faculty:* 34 full-time (14 women). *Students:* 53 full-time (18 women), 177 part-time (61 women); includes 37 minority (21 African Americans, 11 Asian Americans or Pacific Islanders, 5 Hispanic Americans), 19 international. Average age 32. 68 applicants, 35% accepted, 20 enrolled. In 2006, 98 master's, 4 doctorates awarded. *Degree requirements:* For doctorate, thesis/dissertation. *Entrance requirements:* For master's and doctorate, GMAT. Additional exam requirements/recommendations for international students: Required—TOEFL (minimum score 610 paper-based; 255 computer-based; 101 iBT). *Application deadline:* For fall admission, 5/1 for domestic students, 2/1 for international students; for spring admission, 10/15 for domestic students, 5/1 for international students. Applications are processed on a rolling basis. Application fee: $50. Electronic applications accepted. *Unit head:* Dr. Todd J. Maurer, Chair, 404-651-3400, E-mail: tmaurer@gsu.edu.

Georgia State University, J. Mack Robinson College of Business, Program in General Business Administration, Atlanta, GA 30303-3083. Offers accounting/information systems (MBA); enterprise risk management (MBA); general business (MBA); general business administration (EMBA, PMBA); information systems consulting (MBA); information systems risk management (MBA); international business and information technology (MBA); international entrepreneurship (MBA); MBA/JD. *Accreditation:* AACSB. Part-time and evening/weekend programs available. *Faculty:* 1 (woman) full-time. *Students:* 183 full-time (83 women), 212 part-time (57 women); includes 118 minority (73 African Americans, 36 Asian Americans or Pacific Islanders, 9 Hispanic Americans), 42 international. 294 applicants, 74% accepted, 182 enrolled. In 2006, 98 degrees awarded. *Entrance requirements:* For master's, GMAT. Additional exam requirements/recommendations for international students: Required—TOEFL (minimum score 610 paper-based; 255 computer-based; 101 iBT). *Application deadline:* For fall admission, 5/1 for domestic students, 2/1 for international students; for spring admission, 10/15 for domestic students, 5/1 for international students. Applications are processed on a rolling basis. Application fee: $50. Electronic applications accepted. *Financial support:* Research assistantships, tuition waivers (partial) available. Support available to part-time students. Financial award application deadline: 5/1; financial award applicants required to submit FAFSA. *Application contact:* Graduate Student and Alumni Services, 404-463-4568, Fax: 404-651-2721, E-mail: mastersadmissions@gsu.edu.

Huron University USA in London, Graduate Programs, Program in Business Administration, London, United Kingdom. Offers entrepreneurship (MBA); international business (MBA); international finance (MBA); marketing (MBA). Part-time programs available. *Degree requirements:* For master's, thesis, internship, comprehensive exam. *Entrance requirements:* Additional exam requirements/recommendations for international students: Required—TOEFL (minimum score 580 paper-based; 237 computer-based), TWE (minimum score 5). Electronic applications accepted.

Illinois Institute of Technology, Stuart School of Business, Program in Business Administration, Chicago, IL 60616-3793. Offers entrepreneurship (MBA); financial management (MBA); financial markets (MBA); healthcare management (MBA); information technology management (MBA); international business (MBA); management science (MBA); marketing (MBA); operations, quality, and technology management (MBA); strategic management of organizations (MBA); sustainable enterprise (MBA); JD/MBA; MBA/MS. *Accreditation:* AACSB. Part-time and evening/weekend programs available. *Faculty:* 13 full-time (1 woman), 9 part-time/adjunct (0 women). *Students:* 74 full-time (29 women), 42 part-time (16 women); includes 17 minority (5 African Americans, 11 Asian Americans or Pacific Islanders, 1 Hispanic American), 74 international. Average age 29. 247 applicants, 70% accepted, 51 enrolled. In 2006, 45 degrees awarded. *Entrance requirements:* For master's, GMAT. Additional exam requirements/recommendations for international students: Required—TOEFL (minimum score 600 paper-based; 250 computer-based). *Application deadline:* For fall admission, 8/15 priority date for domestic students, 7/1 for international students; for winter admission, 11/1 priority date for domestic students, 10/1 for international students; for spring admission, 1/1 priority date for domestic students, 1/1 for international students. Applications are processed on a rolling basis. Application fee: $75. Electronic applications accepted. *Expenses: Contact institution.* Tuition and fees vary according to class time, course level, course load, program and student level. *Financial support:* Career-related internships or fieldwork, Federal Work-Study, institutionally sponsored loans, scholarships/grants, traineeships, health care benefits, tuition waivers, and unspecified assistantships available. Support available to part-time students. Financial award applicants required to submit FAFSA. *Faculty research:* Knowledge management, healthcare management, sustainability in supply chain. *Unit head:* Dr. George P. Nassos, Interim Director, 312-906-6543, Fax: 312-906-6549, E-mail: george.nassos@iit.edu. *Application contact:* Brian Jansen, Director of Graduate Admissions, 312-906-6521, Fax: 312-906-6549, E-mail: admission@stuart.iit.edu.

Inter American University of Puerto Rico, San Germán Campus, Graduate Studies Center, Graduate Program in Entrepreneurial and Managerial Development, San Germán, PR 00683-5008. Offers human resources (PhD); interregional and international business (PhD); labor relations (PhD). Part-time and evening/weekend programs available. *Faculty:* 12 full-time, 4 part-time/adjunct. *Students:* 52. Average age 41. In 2006, 1 degree awarded. *Degree requirements:* For doctorate, thesis/dissertation, comprehensive exam. *Entrance requirements:* For doctorate, EXADEP or GMAT, minimum graduate GPA of 3.25. *Application deadline:* For fall admission, 4/30 priority date for domestic students; for spring admission, 11/15 for domestic students. Applications are processed on a rolling basis. Application fee: $75. *Expenses:* Tuition: Part-time $175 per credit. Required fees: $238 per semester. Tuition and fees vary according to degree level. *Financial support:* Teaching assistantships available. *Application contact:* Dr. Carlos E. Irizarry, Director of Graduate Studies Center, 787-264-1912 Ext. 7357, Fax: 787-892-6350, E-mail: carlos.irizarry@sg.inter.edu.

The International University of Monaco, Graduate Programs, Monte Carlo, Monaco. Offers entrepreneurship (EMBA, MBA); financial engineering (M Sc); international marketing (EMBA, MBA); luxury goods and services (EMBA, M Sc, MBA); wealth and asset management (EMBA, MBA). Part-time programs available. *Degree requirements:* For master's, applied research project. *Entrance requirements:* Additional exam requirements/recommendations for international students: Required—TOEFL (minimum score 550 paper-based; 213 computer-based), IELTS. Electronic applications accepted. *Faculty research:* Gaming, leadership, disintermediation.

Jones International University, Graduate School of Business Administration, Centennial, CO 80112. Offers accounting (MBA); business communication (MABC); entrepreneurship (MABC, MBA); finance (MBA); global enterprise management (MBA); health care management (MBA); information security management (MBA); information technology management (MBA); leadership and influence (MABC); leading the customer-driven organization (MABC); negotiation and conflict management (MBA); project management (MABC, MBA). Program only offered online. Part-time and evening/weekend programs available. Postbaccalaureate distance learning degree programs offered (no on-campus study). *Degree requirements:* For master's, capstone project. *Entrance requirements:* For master's, minimum cumulative GPA of 2.5. Additional exam requirements/recommendations for international students: Recommended—TOEFL (minimum score 550 paper-based; 213 computer-based). Electronic applications accepted.

Lamar University, College of Graduate Studies, College of Business, Beaumont, TX 77710. Offers accounting (MBA); experiential business and Entrepreneurship (MBA); financial management (MBA); healthcare administration (MBA); information systems (MBA); management (MBA). *Accreditation:* AACSB. Part-time and evening/weekend programs available. *Faculty:* 20 full-time (8 women), 2 part-time/adjunct (1 woman). *Students:* 55 full-time (27 women), 45 part-time (20 women); includes 17 minority (9 African Americans, 4 Asian Americans or Pacific Islanders, 4 Hispanic Americans), 14 international. Average age 29. 131 applicants, 34% accepted, 29 enrolled. In 2006, 29 degrees awarded. *Degree requirements:* For master's, thesis optional. *Entrance requirements:* For master's, GMAT. Additional exam requirements/recommendations for international students: Required—TOEFL (minimum score 525 paper-based; 197 computer-based). *Application deadline:* For fall admission, 3/15 priority date for domestic students; for spring admission, 10/1 priority date for domestic students. Applications are processed on a rolling basis. Application fee: $25 ($50 for international students). *Expenses:* Tuition, nonresident: part-time $33 per hour. Required fees: $43 per hour. $110 per semester. *Financial support:* In 2006–07, 12 students received support, including 4 research assistantships with partial tuition reimbursements available; fellowships with tuition reimbursements available, career-related internships or fieldwork, Federal Work-Study, institutionally sponsored loans, scholarships/grants, and tuition waivers (partial) also available. Support available to part-time students. Financial award application deadline: 4/1; financial award applicants required to submit FAFSA. *Faculty research:* Marketing, finance, quantitative methods, MIS, legal, environmental. Total annual research expenditures: $26,000. *Unit head:* Dr. Enrique R. Venta, Dean, 409-880-8604, Fax: 409-880-8088, E-mail: henry.venta@lamar.edu. *Application contact:* Dr. Brad Mayer, Professor and Associate Dean, 409-880-2383, Fax: 409-880-8605, E-mail: bradley.mayer@lamar.edu.

Lincoln University, School of Graduate Studies and Continuing Education, College of Business and Professional Studies, Department of Business and Economics, Jefferson City, MO 65102. Offers business administration (MBA), including accounting, entrepreneurship, management, public administration and policy. *Accreditation:* ACBSP. Part-time and evening/weekend programs available. *Faculty:* 7 part-time/adjunct (2 women). *Students:* 39 full-time (26 women), 23 part-time (14 women); includes 18 minority (17 African Americans, 1 American Indian/Alaska Native), 24 international. Average age 31. 28 applicants, 96% accepted, 14 enrolled. In 2006, 31 degrees awarded. *Degree requirements:* For master's, portfolio, thesis optional. *Entrance requirements:* For master's, GMAT. Additional exam requirements/recommendations

Entrepreneurship

Lincoln University (continued)
for international students: Required—TOEFL (minimum score 500 paper-based; 173 computer-based; 61 iBT). *Application deadline:* For fall admission, 7/1 priority date for domestic and international students; for spring admission, 12/1 priority date for domestic and international students. Applications are processed on a rolling basis. Application fee: $17. *Expenses:* Tuition, state resident: part-time $189 per credit hour. Tuition, nonresident: part-time $351 per credit hour. Required fees: $15 per credit hour. $20 per semester. *Financial support:* Federal Work-Study and scholarships/grants available. Financial award application deadline: 4/1; financial award applicants required to submit FAFSA. *Unit head:* Dr. Ogugua Anunoby, Department Head, 573-681-5487, Fax: 573-681-6085, E-mail: anunobyo@lincolnu.edu.

Lindenwood University, Graduate Programs, Division of Management, St. Charles, MO 63301-1695. Offers accounting (MBA, MS); business administration (MBA); entrepreneurial studies (MBA); finance (MBA, MS); human resource management (MBA); human resources (MS); international business (MBA, MS); management (MBA, MS); management information systems (MBA, MS); managing business to business (MA); managing human resources (MA); managing international business (MA); managing investment management (MA); managing leadership (MA); managing marketing (MA); managing organizational behavior (MA); managing sales (MA); managing, training and development (MA); marketing (MBA, MS); nonprofit administration (MA); public management (MBA, MS); sport management (MA). Part-time and evening/weekend programs available. *Faculty:* 38 full-time (15 women), 20 part-time/adjunct (5 women). *Students:* 177 full-time (78 women), 138 part-time (67 women); includes 43 minority (27 African Americans, 4 American Indian/Alaska Native, 6 Asian Americans or Pacific Islanders, 6 Hispanic Americans), 73 international. Average age 30. In 2006, 159 degrees awarded. *Degree requirements:* For master's, thesis (for some programs). *Entrance requirements:* For master's, interview, minimum GPA of 3.0. Additional exam requirements/recommendations for international students: Required—TOEFL (minimum score 550 paper-based; 173 computer-based). *Application deadline:* For fall admission, 7/30 priority date for domestic students, 9/30 priority date for international students; for winter admission, 12/30 priority date for domestic and international students; for spring admission, 3/30 priority date for domestic and international students. Applications are processed on a rolling basis. Application fee: $30 ($100 for international students). Electronic applications accepted. *Expenses:* Tuition: Part-time $340 per credit hour. Tuition and fees vary according to course level, course load, degree level and program. *Financial support:* Career-related internships or fieldwork, Federal Work-Study, institutionally sponsored loans, and tuition waivers (partial) available. Financial award application deadline: 6/30; financial award applicants required to submit FAFSA. *Unit head:* Ed Morris, Dean, 636-949-4832, Fax: 636-949-4910, E-mail: emorris@lindenwood.edu. *Application contact:* Brett Barger, Dean Adult, Corporate and Graduate Admissions, 636-949-4366, Fax: 636-949-4109, E-mail: bbarger@lindenwood.edu.

McGill University, Faculty of Graduate and Postdoctoral Studies, Desautels Faculty of Management, Montréal, QC H3A 2T5, Canada. Offers administration (PhD); entrepreneurial studies (MBA); finance (MBA); general management (Post Master's Certificate); information systems (MBA); international business (exchange program) (MBA); international Master's program in practicing management (MM); management (MBA); management for development (MBA); manufacturing management (MMM); marketing (MBA); operations management (MBA); public accountancy (Diploma); strategic management (MBA); MBA/LL B; MD/MBA. Part-time programs available. *Entrance requirements:* For master's, GMAT, minimum undergraduate GPA of 3.0, 2 years work experience; for doctorate, GMAT or GRE General Test, 2 letters of recommendation, preferably by professors in chosen field of specialization; for other advanced degree, 2 years of work experience, MBA, minimum GPA of 3.0 (Post-MBA Certificate). Additional exam requirements/recommendations for international students: Required—TOEFL (minimum score 600 paper-based; 250 computer-based), IELTS (minimum score 7). Electronic applications accepted. Expenses: Contact institution. *Faculty research:* Social innovation, leadership, strategy.

Northeastern University, School of Technological Entrepreneurship, Boston, MA 02115-5096. Offers MS. *Faculty:* 6 full-time (0 women), 1 part-time/adjunct (0 women). *Students:* 11 full-time (3 women), 3 part-time. 26 applicants, 77% accepted. *Entrance requirements:* For master's, minimum GPA of 3.0. *Unit head:* Paul M. Zavracky, Dean, 617-373-2788, Fax: 617-373-7490, E-mail: ste@neu.edu.

Oakland University, Graduate Study and Lifelong Learning, School of Business Administration, Department of Management and Marketing, Rochester, MI 48309-4401. Offers business administration (MBA); entrepreneurship (Certificate); general management (Certificate); human resource management (Certificate); international business (Certificate); marketing (Certificate). *Faculty:* 9 full-time (3 women), 2 part-time/adjunct (both women). *Students:* 61 full-time (25 women), 416 part-time (137 women); includes 72 minority (14 African Americans, 1 American Indian/Alaska Native, 46 Asian Americans or Pacific Islanders, 11 Hispanic Americans), 45 international. Average age 31. 121 applicants, 88% accepted, 65 enrolled. In 2006, 163 degrees awarded. Application fee: $35. *Expenses:* Tuition, state resident: full-time $9,936; part-time $414 per credit. Tuition, nonresident: full-time $17,202; part-time $716 per credit. *Unit head:* Ravi Parameswaran, Chair, 238-370-3279, Fax: 249-370-4275.

Park University, College of Graduate and Professional Studies, Kansas City, MO 54105. Offers adult education (M Ed); at-risk students (M Ed); disaster and emergency management (MPA); educational administration (M Ed); entrepreneurship (MBA); general business (MBA); general education (M Ed); government/business relations (MPA); healthcare/services management (MBA, MPA); international business (MBA); K-12 certification (MAT); management information systems (MBA); management of information systems (MPA); middle school certification (MAT); multi-cultural education (M Ed); nonprofit management (MPA); public management (MPA); school law (M Ed); secondary school certification (MAT); special education (M Ed). Part-time and evening/weekend programs available. Postbaccalaureate distance learning degree programs offered (no on-campus study). *Degree requirements:* For master's, thesis (for some programs), comprehensive exam, registration. *Entrance requirements:* For master's, GRE, GMAT, teacher certification (M Ed). Additional exam requirements/recommendations for international students: Required—TOEFL (minimum score 550 paper-based). Electronic applications accepted. *Faculty research:* Literacy, leadership, brain based research, multicultural education, diversity.

Penn State Great Valley, Graduate Studies, Management Division, Malvern, PA 19355-1488. Offers biotechnology and health industry management (MBA); business administration (MBA); finance (M Fin); leadership development (MLD); new venture and entrepreneurial studies (MBA);).

Polytechnic University, Long Island Graduate Center, Graduate Programs, Department of Chemical and Biological Sciences, Melville, NY 11747. Offers bioinstrumentation (Certificate); biomedical engineering (MS, PhD); biomedical materials (Certificate); biotechnology (MS); biotechnology and entrepreneurship (MS); chemistry (MS, PhD), including chemistry (MS), materials chemistry (PhD). *Expenses:* Tuition: Full-time $17,184. *Unit head:* Prof. Bruce Garetz, Department Head.

Regent University, Graduate School, School of Global Leadership and Entrepreneurship, Virginia Beach, VA 23464-9800. Offers business administration (MBA); management (MA); organizational leadership (MA, PhD, Certificate); strategic foresight (MA); strategic leadership (DSL). Part-time programs available. Postbaccalaureate distance learning degree programs offered (minimal on-campus study). *Faculty:* 20 full-time (3 women), 36 part-time/adjunct (6 women). *Students:* 68 full-time (40 women), 482 part-time (170 women); includes 144 minority (110 African Americans, 6 American Indian/Alaska Native, 9 Asian Americans or Pacific Islanders, 19 Hispanic Americans), 37 international. Average age 40. 395 applicants, 37% accepted, 64 enrolled. In 2006, 100 master's, 69 doctorates awarded. *Degree requirements:* For master's, thesis or alternative, 3 credit hour culminating experience; for doctorate, thesis/dissertation. *Entrance requirements:* For master's, GRE, GMAT or MAT, minimum undergraduate GPA of 2.75, computer literacy survey, 2 recommendations, resumé; for doctorate, GRE, GMAT or MAT, sample of writing, minimum of 3 years of relevant experience, computer literacy survey, 2 recommendations, resumé; for Certificate, GRE, GMAT or MAT, writing sample. Additional exam requirements/recommendations for international students: Required—TOEFL (minimum score 577 paper-based; 233 computer-based). *Application deadline:* For fall admission, 5/1 priority date for domestic students; for spring admission, 10/1 priority date for domestic students. Applications are processed on a rolling basis. Application fee: $50. Electronic applications accepted. *Expenses: Contact institution. Financial support:* In 2006–07, 321 students received support. Scholarships/grants and tuition waivers (full and partial) available. Support available to part-time students. Financial award application deadline: 9/1. *Faculty research:* Servant leadership, ethics and values, telecommuting and family values, organizational communications, distance education. *Unit head:* Dr. Bruce Winston, Dean, 757-226-4306, Fax: 757-226-4634, E-mail: brucwin@regent.edu. *Application contact:* Althea Bishard, Registrar and Executive Director of Enrollment and Academic Services, 800-373-5504, Fax: 757-226-4381, E-mail: admissions@regent.edu.

Rensselaer Polytechnic Institute, Graduate School, Lally School of Management and Technology, Program in Management and Technology, Troy, NY 12180-3590. Offers finance (MBA, MS); financial technology (MS); management (PhD); management information systems (MBA, MS); new product development and marketing (MBA); new production and operations management (MS); product development and marketing (MS); production and operations management (MBA); technical commercialization (MS); technological entrepreneurship (MBA, MS). Part-time and evening/weekend programs available. Postbaccalaureate distance learning degree programs offered (no on-campus study). *Faculty:* 50 full-time (9 women), 1 part-time/adjunct (0 women). *Students:* 121 full-time (62 women), 525 part-time (184 women); includes 137 minority (43 African Americans, 60 Asian Americans or Pacific Islanders, 34 Hispanic Americans), 71 international. Average age 28. 416 applicants, 70% accepted, 240 enrolled. In 2006, 215 master's, 6 doctorates awarded. *Median time to degree:* Of those who began their doctoral program in fall 1998, 25% received their degree in 8 years or less. *Degree requirements:* For doctorate, thesis/dissertation. *Entrance requirements:* For master's, GMAT, resumé, 2 letters of recommendation; for doctorate, GMAT or GRE General Test, 2 letters of recommendation. Additional exam requirements/recommendations for international students: Required—TOEFL (minimum score 600 paper-based; 250 computer-based; 100 iBT); Recommended—IELTS (minimum score 7). *Application deadline:* For fall admission, 3/15 priority date for domestic and international students. Applications are processed on a rolling basis. Application fee: $75. Electronic applications accepted. *Expenses:* Tuition: Full-time $32,600; part-time $1,358 per credit. Required fees: $1,629. *Financial support:* In 2006–07, 48 students received support; fellowships with partial tuition reimbursements available, research assistantships with partial tuition reimbursements available, teaching assistantships with partial tuition reimbursements available, career-related internships or fieldwork, institutionally sponsored loans, and scholarships/grants available. Financial award application deadline: 3/15; financial award applicants required to submit FAFSA. *Faculty research:* Technological entrepreneurship, operations management, new product development and marketing, information systems, finance. Total annual research expenditures: $24,747. *Unit head:* Pedro Gonzalez, Director MBA/Admissons and Career Services, 518-276-2378, Fax: 518-276-2665, E-mail: gonzap3@rpi.edu. *Application contact:* Michele M. Martens, Manager of Graduate Programs, 518-276-6586, Fax: 518-276-2665, E-mail: martem@rpi.edu.

See Close-Up on page 313.

St. Edward's University, School of Management and Business, Area of Business Administration, Austin, TX 78704. Offers accounting (MBA); business management (MBA); entrepreneurship (MBA, Certificate); finance—general (MBA, Certificate); global business (MBA, Certificate); human resource management (MBA, Certificate); management information systems (MBA, Certificate); marketing (MBA, Certificate); operations management (MBA, Certificate); personal financial planner (MBA, Certificate); sports management (MBA). Part-time and evening/weekend programs available. *Students:* 32 full-time (16 women), 394 part-time (195 women); includes 117 minority (23 African Americans, 2 American Indian/Alaska Native, 28 Asian Americans or Pacific Islanders, 64 Hispanic Americans), 21 international. Average age 33. 121 applicants, 74% accepted, 72 enrolled. In 2006, 142 degrees awarded. *Degree requirements:* For master's, minimum 24 resident hours. *Entrance requirements:* For master's, GMAT or GRE General Test, minimum GPA of 2.75 in last 60 hours of course work. Additional exam requirements/recommendations for international students: Required—TOEFL (minimum score 550 paper-based; 213 computer-based; 79 iBT). *Application deadline:* For fall admission, 8/1 for domestic students, 7/1 for international students; for spring admission, 12/1 for domestic students, 11/1 for international students. Applications are processed on a rolling basis. Application fee: $45 ($50 for international students). Electronic applications accepted. *Expenses:* Tuition: Full-time $11,682; part-time $649 per credit hour. Full-time tuition and fees vary according to course load and program. *Financial support:* In 2006–07, 4 students received support. Scholarships/grants available. Financial award applicants required to submit FAFSA. *Faculty research:* Operations management, minority entrepreneurship, globalization, professional services marketing. *Unit head:* Dr. Dianne Hill, Director, 512-428-1295, Fax: 512-448-8492, E-mail: dianneh@stedwards.edu. *Application contact:* Natalia Quintanilla, Graduate Admissions Coordinator, 512-233-1697, Fax: 512-428-1032, E-mail: nataliaq@stedwards.edu.

San Diego State University, Graduate and Research Affairs, College of Business Administration, Department of Management, San Diego, CA 92182. Offers entrepreneurship (MS); human resources management (MS); management science (MS). Part-time and evening/weekend programs available. *Students:* 16 full-time (6 women), 23 part-time (13 women); includes 5 minority (4 Asian Americans or Pacific Islanders, 1 Hispanic American), 9 international. Average age 30. 24 applicants, 75% accepted, 6 enrolled. In 2006, 21 degrees awarded. *Degree requirements:* For master's, thesis or alternative. *Entrance requirements:* For master's, GMAT, resumé, letters of reference. Additional exam requirements/recommendations for international students: Required—TOEFL. *Application deadline:* For fall admission, 4/15 for domestic and international students; for spring admission, 11/1 for domestic students, 10/1 for international students. Applications are processed on a rolling basis. Application fee: $55. Electronic applications accepted. *Financial support:* In 2006–07, 14 teaching assistantships were awarded; fellowships, research assistantships, career-related internships or fieldwork also available. Financial award applicants required to submit FAFSA. Total annual research expenditures: $11,500. *Unit head:* Gangaram Singh, Chair, 619-594-5306, Fax: 619-594-3272. *Application contact:* Information Contact, E-mail: sdsumba@mail.sdsu.edu.

Simmons College, Simmons School of Management, Boston, MA 02115. Offers entrepreneurship (Certificate); management (MBA). Part-time and evening/weekend programs available. *Faculty:* 25 full-time (21 women), 8 part-time/adjunct (4 women). *Students:* 32 full-time (all women), 117 part-time (all women); includes 23 minority (14 African Americans, 7 Asian Americans or Pacific Islanders, 2 Hispanic Americans), 2 international. Average age 31. 98 applicants, 82% accepted, 53 enrolled. In 2006, 99 master's, 5 other advanced degrees awarded. *Entrance requirements:* For master's, GMAT, 3 letters of recommendation, minimum 2 years experience, resumé. Additional exam requirements/recommendations for international students: Required—TOEFL. *Application deadline:* For fall admission, 6/30 priority date for domestic and international students; for spring admission, 12/1 priority date for domestic students, 11/15 priority date for international students. Applications are processed on a rolling basis. Application fee: $75. Electronic applications accepted. *Expenses: Contact institution. Financial support:* Institutionally sponsored loans, scholarships/grants, and unspecified assistantships available. Support available to part-time students. Financial award application deadline: 3/1; financial award applicants required to submit FAFSA. *Faculty research:* Women, leadership, gender equity, organizational effectiveness, general management negotiations, entrepreneurship. *Unit head:* Dr. Deborah Merrill-Sands, Dean, 617-521-3827, Fax: 617-521-3881. *Application contact:* Denise Haile, Director of Admissions, 617-521-3840, Fax: 617-521-3880, E-mail: somadm@simmons.edu.

South Carolina State University, School of Graduate Studies, Department of Accounting, Agribusiness and Economics, Orangeburg, SC 29117-0001. Offers agribusiness (MS); agribusiness and entrepreneurship (MBA). Part-time and evening/weekend programs available. *Faculty:* 7 full-time (1 woman). *Students:* 7 full-time (3 women), 4 part-time (1 woman); includes 10 minority (all African Americans) Average age 26. 14 applicants, 43% accepted, 5 enrolled. In 2006, 1 degree awarded. *Degree requirements:* For master's, departmental qualifying exam, thesis optional. *Entrance requirements:* For master's, GMAT or GRE, minimum GPA of 2.8. *Application deadline:* For fall admission, 6/15 for domestic and international students; for spring admission, 11/1 for domestic and international students. Applications are processed on a rolling basis. Application fee: $25. Electronic applications accepted. *Expenses:* Tuition, state resident: full-time $7,278. Tuition, nonresident: full-time $14,322. *Financial support:* Fellowships, research assistantships, career-related internships or fieldwork, Federal Work-Study, and institutionally sponsored loans available. Financial award application deadline: 6/1. *Faculty research:* Small farm income and profitability, agricultural credit, aquaculture, low-input sustainable agriculture, rural development. *Unit head:* Dr. Haile M. Gebre-Selassie, Interim Chair, 803-536-8456, Fax: 803-533-3639, E-mail: selassie@scsu.edu. *Application contact:* Annette Hazzard-Jones, Program Coordinator II, 803-536-8809, Fax: 803-536-8812, E-mail: zs_ahazzard@scsu.edu.

Stevens Institute of Technology, Graduate School, Wesley J. Howe School of Technology Management, Program in Information Systems, Hoboken, NJ 07030. Offers computer science (MS); e-commerce (MS, Certificate); entrepreneurial information technology (MS); global innovation management (MS); human resource management (MS); information management (MS, Certificate); information security (MS); information technology in financial services industry (MS); information technology in the pharmaceutical industry (MS); information technology outsourcing management (MS); integrated information architecture (MS); project management (MS, Certificate); quantitative software engineering (MS); systems engineering (MS); telecommunications management (MS). *Degree requirements:* For master's, thesis optional. *Entrance requirements:* For master's, GMAT, GRE General Test. Additional exam requirements/recommendations for international students: Required—TOEFL. Electronic applications accepted.

Stratford University, Graduate Programs, Falls Church, VA 22043. Offers business administration (MBA); enterprise business management (MS); entrepreneurial business (MS); information systems (MS); software engineering (MS). Part-time and evening/weekend programs available. Postbaccalaureate distance learning degree programs offered (minimal on-campus study). *Entrance requirements:* Additional exam requirements/recommendations for international students: Required—TOEFL (minimum score 500 paper-based). Electronic applications accepted.

Syracuse University, Martin J. Whitman School of Management, Program in Business Administration, Syracuse, NY 13244. Offers accounting (MBA); entrepreneurship (MBA); finance (MBA); marketing (MBA); supply chain management (MBA). Part-time programs available. Postbaccalaureate distance learning degree programs offered (minimal on-campus study). *Faculty:* 71 full-time (16 women), 2 part-time/adjunct (1 woman). *Students:* 70 full-time (21 women), 279 part-time (84 women); includes 83 minority (44 African Americans, 33 Asian Americans or Pacific Islanders, 6 Hispanic Americans), 36 international. Average age 27. 227 applicants, 37% accepted, 27 enrolled. In 2006, 140 degrees awarded. *Degree requirements:* For master's, registration. *Entrance requirements:* For master's, GMAT, 2 letters of recommendation, bachelor's degree. Additional exam requirements/recommendations for international students: Required—TOEFL (minimum score 600 paper-based; 250 computer-based; 100 iBT). *Application deadline:* For fall admission, 1/15 priority date for domestic and international students. Applications are processed on a rolling basis. Application fee: $75. Electronic applications accepted. *Expenses:* Tuition: Full-time $16,920; part-time $940 per credit hour. Required fees: $930; $930 per year. *Financial support:* In 2006–07, 17 students received support; fellowships with full and partial tuition reimbursements available, teaching assistantships with partial tuition reimbursements available, career-related internships or fieldwork, scholarships/grants, tuition waivers (partial), unspecified assistantships, and paid hourly positions available. Support available to part-time students. Financial award application deadline: 3/1. *Unit head:* Dr. Ravi Shukla, Associate Dean for MBA and MS Programs, 315-443-3576, Fax: 315-443-9517, E-mail: rkshukla@syr.edu. *Application contact:* Carol J. Swanberg, Director of Graduate Admissions and Financial Aid, 315-443-9214, Fax: 315-443-9517, E-mail: mbainfo@syr.edu.

Texas Tech University, Jerry S. Rawls College of Business Administration, Programs in Business Administration, Lubbock, TX 79409. Offers agricultural business (MBA); entrepreneurship (MBA); finance (MBA); general business (MBA); health organization management (MBA); international business (MBA); management and leadership skills (MBA); management information systems (MBA); marketing (MBA); statistics (MBA); JD/MBA; MBA/M Arch; MBA/MA; MBA/MD; MBA/MS. Part-time and evening/weekend programs available. *Students:* 65 full-time (16 women), 347 part-time (121 women); includes 74 minority (5 African Americans, 5 American Indian/Alaska Native, 24 Asian Americans or Pacific Islanders, 40 Hispanic Americans), 24 international. Average age 25. 382 applicants, 82% accepted, 244 enrolled. In 2006, 150 degrees awarded. *Degree requirements:* For master's, capstone course. *Entrance requirements:* For master's, GMAT, holistic review of academic credentials. Additional exam requirements/recommendations for international students: Required—TOEFL (minimum score 550 paper-based; 213 computer-based; 79 iBT). *Application deadline:* For fall admission, 7/1 priority date for domestic students, 3/1 priority date for international students; for spring admission, 11/1 priority date for domestic students, 9/1 priority date for international students. Applications are processed on a rolling basis. Application fee: $50 ($60 for international students). Electronic applications accepted. *Expenses:* Tuition, state resident: full-time $4,440. Tuition, nonresident: full-time $11,040. Required fees: $2,136. *Financial support:* In 2006–07, 36 research assistantships (averaging $8,000 per year) were awarded; teaching assistantships, career-related internships or fieldwork, Federal Work-Study, scholarships/grants, health care benefits, and unspecified assistantships also available. Support available to part-time students. Financial award applicants required to submit FAFSA. *Unit head:* Dr. W. Jay Conover, Director, 806-742-1546, Fax: 806-742-3958, E-mail: jay.conover@ttu.edu. *Application contact:* Cynthia D. Barnes, Director, Graduate Services Center, 806-742-3184, Fax: 806-742-3958, E-mail: ba_grad@ttu.edu.

Université du Québec à Trois-Rivières, Graduate Programs, Program in Management of Small and Medium-Sized Enterprises and Their Environment, Trois-Rivières, QC G9A 5H7, Canada. Offers M Sc. Part-time programs available. *Degree requirements:* For master's, research report. *Entrance requirements:* For master's, appropriate bachelor's degree, proficiency in French.

Université Laval, Faculty of Administrative Sciences, Programs in Business Administration, Québec, QC G1K 7P4, Canada. Offers accounting (MBA); agri-food management (MBA); electronic business (MBA, Diploma); factory management and logistics (MBA); finance (MBA); firm management (MBA); information technology management (MBA); international management (MBA); management (MBA); management accounting (MBA, Diploma); marketing (MBA); modelization and organizational decision (MBA); occupational health and safety management (MBA); pharmacy management (MBA); technological entrepreneurship (Diploma). *Accreditation:* AACSB. Part-time and evening/weekend programs available. Postbaccalaureate distance learning degree programs offered (no on-campus study). *Entrance requirements:* For master's and Diploma, knowledge of French and English. Electronic applications accepted.

The University of Akron, Graduate School, College of Business Administration, Department of Management, Program in Entrepreneurship, Akron, OH 44325. Offers MBA. *Students:* 1 full-time (0 women), 2 part-time (1 woman), 1 international. Average age 28. 8 applicants, 63% accepted, 2 enrolled. In 2006, 1 degree awarded. *Entrance requirements:* For master's, GMAT, minimum GPA of 2.75. Additional exam requirements/recommendations for international students: Required—TOEFL (minimum score 550 paper-based; 213 computer-based; 79 iBT). *Application deadline:* For fall admission, 8/15 for domestic students. Applications are processed on a rolling basis. Application fee: $30 ($40 for international students). Electronic applications accepted. *Expenses:* Tuition, state resident: full-time $6,164; part-time $342 per credit. Tuition, nonresident: full-time $10,575; part-time $588 per credit. Required fees: $806; $43 per credit. $12 per term. Tuition and fees vary according to course load, degree level and program. *Financial support:* Research assistantships available. *Unit head:* Dr. Todd Finkle, Head, 330-972-8479, E-mail: finklet@uakron.edu.

University of Dallas, Graduate School of Management, Irving, TX 75062-4736. Offers accounting (MBA, MS); business management (MBA); corporate finance (MBA, MM); engineering management (MBA, MM); entrepreneurship (MBA, MM); financial services (MBA, MM); global business (MBA, MM); health services management (MBA, MM); human resource management (MBA, MM, MS); information assurance (MBA, MM, MS); information technology (MBA, MM, MS); information technology service management (MBA); IT service management (MS); marketing (MM); marketing management (MBA); not-for-profit management (MBA); organization development (MBA); project management (MBA, MM); sports and entertainment management (MBA, MM); strategic leadership (MBA); supply chain management (MBA); supply chain management and market logistics (MM); telecommunications management (MBA, MM). *Accreditation:* ACBSP. Part-time and evening/weekend programs available. Postbaccalaureate distance learning degree programs offered (no on-campus study). *Faculty:* 26 full-time (5 women), 85 part-time/adjunct (18 women). *Students:* 227 full-time (98 women), 1,160 part-time (446 women); includes 473 minority (209 African Americans, 3 American Indian/Alaska Native, 143 Asian Americans or Pacific Islanders, 118 Hispanic Americans), 224 international. Average age 34. 556 applicants, 86% accepted, 291 enrolled. In 2006, 476 degrees awarded. *Entrance requirements:* Additional exam requirements/recommendations for international students: Required—TOEFL. *Application deadline:* Applications are processed on a rolling basis. Application fee: $50. Electronic applications accepted. *Expenses:* Contact institution. *Financial support:* In 2006–07, 468 students received support. Scholarships/grants and unspecified assistantships available. Financial award application deadline: 2/15; financial award applicants required to submit FAFSA. *Unit head:* Dr. J. Lee Whittington, Dean, 972-721-5230. *Application contact:* Sarah Stivison, Director of Graduate Admissions, 972-721-5198, Fax: 972-721-4009, E-mail: admiss@gsm.udallas.edu.

University of Delaware, Alfred Lerner College of Business and Economics, Department of Economics, Newark, DE 19716. Offers economics (MA, MS, PhD); economics for entrepreneurship and educators (MA); MA/MBA. Part-time programs available. *Degree requirements:* For master's, thesis (for some programs), mathematics review exam, research project, comprehensive exam; for doctorate, thesis/dissertation, field exam, comprehensive exam. *Entrance requirements:* For master's, GMAT or GRE General Test, minimum GPA of 2.5; for doctorate, GRE General Test, minimum GPA of 3.5 in graduate economics course work. Additional exam requirements/recommendations for international students: Required—TOEFL (minimum score 550 paper-based; 225 computer-based). Electronic applications accepted. *Faculty research:* Applied quantitative economics, industrial organization, resource economics, monetary economics, labor economics.

University of Florida, Graduate School, Warrington College of Business Administration, Department of Finance, Insurance and Real Estate, Gainesville, FL 32611. Offers business administration (MS), including entrepreneurship, insurance, real estate and urban analysis, retailing; finance (PhD); financial services (Certificate); insurance (PhD); real estate and urban analysis (PhD); JD/MS. *Faculty:* 15 full-time (1 woman). *Students:* 69 (17 women); includes 14 minority (2 African Americans, 5 Asian Americans or Pacific Islanders, 7 Hispanic Americans) 12 international. In 2006, 54 master's, 1 doctorate awarded. Terminal master's awarded for partial completion of doctoral program. *Degree requirements:* For doctorate, thesis/dissertation. *Entrance requirements:* For master's, GMAT or GRE General Test, minimum GPA of 3.0 for last 60 hours of undergraduate degree, work experience (preferred); for doctorate, GMAT or GRE General Test, minimum GPA of 3.0. Additional exam requirements/recommendations for international students: Required—TOEFL (minimum score 550 paper-based; 213 computer-based). *Application deadline:* For fall admission, 5/1 priority date for domestic students. Applications are processed on a rolling basis. Application fee: $30. Electronic applications accepted. *Expenses:* Tuition, state resident: full-time $6,827. Tuition, nonresident: full-time $21,951. Required fees: $999. *Financial support:* In 2006–07, 10 research assistantships (averaging $23,562 per year), 1 teaching assistantship (averaging $40,989 per year) were awarded; fellowships, career-related internships or fieldwork, scholarships/grants, and unspecified assistantships also available. *Faculty research:* Financial management, financial markets and institutions, investments, risk and insurance, real estate development. *Unit head:* Dr. Michael D. Ryngaert, Chair, 352-392-9765, Fax: 352-392-0301, E-mail: michael.ryngaert@cba.ufl.edu. *Application contact:* Pamela De Michele, Director of Admissions and Student Services, 352-273-0310, Fax: 352-392-0301, E-mail: pam.demichele@cba.ufl.edu.

University of Hawaii at Manoa, Graduate Division, Shidler College of Business, Program in Business Administration, Honolulu, HI 96822. Offers Asian business studies (MBA); Chinese business studies (MBA); decision sciences (MBA); entrepreneurship (MBA); finance (MBA); finance and banking (MBA); human resources management (MBA); information management (MBA); information technology (MBA); international business (MBA); Japanese business studies (MBA); marketing (MBA); organizational behavior (MBA); organizational management (MBA); real estate (MBA); student-designed track (MBA). *Accreditation:* AACSB. Part-time programs available. *Faculty:* 48 full-time (9 women). *Students:* 207 full-time (77 women), 158 part-time (60 women); includes 93 minority (2 African Americans, 1 American Indian/Alaska Native, 88 Asian Americans or Pacific Islanders, 2 Hispanic Americans), 58 international. Average age 33. 235 applicants, 55% accepted, 68 enrolled. In 2006, 147 degrees awarded. *Degree requirements:* For master's, thesis optional. *Entrance requirements:* For master's, GMAT, minimum GPA of 3.0. Additional exam requirements/recommendations for international students: Required—TOEFL (minimum score 500 paper-based; 173 computer-based; 61 iBT). *Application deadline:* For fall admission, 5/1 for domestic and international students; for spring admission, 9/1 for domestic and international students. Application fee: $50. *Financial support:* In 2006–07, 7 research assistantships (averaging $17,409 per year), 3 teaching assistantships (averaging $14,028 per year) were awarded. *Application contact:* Ting Bui, Information Contact, 808-956-5565, Fax: 808-956-6889.

University of Houston, Bauer College of Business, Marketing and Entrepreneurship Program, Houston, TX 77204. Offers PhD. Part-time and evening/weekend programs available. *Faculty:* 7 full-time (0 women), 5 part-time/adjunct (0 women). *Students:* 13 full-time (6 women), 6 part-time (3 women); includes 6 minority (1 African American, 5 Asian Americans or Pacific Islanders), 5 international. Average age 31. *Degree requirements:* For doctorate, thesis/dissertation, comprehensive exam. *Entrance requirements:* For doctorate, GMAT or GRE. *Application deadline:* For fall admission, 5/1 for domestic students; for spring admission, 10/1 for domestic students. Applications are processed on a rolling basis. Application fee: $75 ($150 for international students). *Expenses:* Tuition, state resident: full-time $5,429; part-time $226 per credit. Tuition, nonresident: full-time $12,029; part-time $501 per credit. Required fees: $2,454. *Financial support:* In 2006–07, 12 teaching assistantships with full tuition reimbursements (averaging $7,000 per year) were awarded; fellowships with full tuition reimbursements, research assistantships with full tuition reimbursements, career-related internships or fieldwork, Federal Work-Study, institutionally sponsored loans, scholarships/grants, health care benefits, and unspecified assistantships also available. Support available to part-time students. Financial award application deadline: 3/10; financial award applicants required to submit FAFSA. *Faculty research:* Accountancy and taxation, finance, international business, management. *Unit head:* Dr. Ed Blair, Chair, 713-743-4555, E-mail: blair@uh.edu. *Application contact:* 713-743-4900, Fax: 713-743-4942, E-mail: oss@uh.edu.

The University of Iowa, Henry B. Tippie College of Business, Henry B. Tippie School of Management, Iowa City, IA 52242-1316. Offers accounting (MBA); corporate finance (MBA); entrepreneurship (MBA); finance (MBA); individually designed concentration (MBA); investment management (MBA); management information systems (MBA); marketing (MBA); nonprofit management (MBA); operations management (MBA); strategic management and consulting (MBA); JD/MBA; MBA/MA; MBA/MD; MBA/MHA; MBA/MSN. *Accreditation:* AACSB. Part-time and evening/weekend programs available. *Faculty:* 94 full-time (23 women), 65 part-time/

Entrepreneurship

The University of Iowa (continued)

adjunct (21 women). *Students:* 230 full-time (67 women), 712 part-time (234 women); includes 62 minority (6 African Americans, 1 American Indian/Alaska Native, 43 Asian Americans or Pacific Islanders, 12 Hispanic Americans), 127 international. Average age 30. 431 applicants, 61% accepted, 217 enrolled. In 2006, 363 degrees awarded. *Median time to degree:* Master's–2 years full-time, 3.5 years part-time. *Degree requirements:* For master's, registration. *Entrance requirements:* For master's, GMAT, work experience. Additional exam requirements/recommendations for international students: Required—TOEFL (minimum score 600 paper-based; 250 computer-based; 100 iBT). *Application deadline:* For fall admission, 7/15 for domestic students, 4/15 for international students; for spring admission, 12/15 priority date for domestic students, 11/1 priority date for international students. Applications are processed on a rolling basis. Application fee: $60 ($85 for international students). Electronic applications accepted. *Expenses: Contact institution. Financial support:* In 2006–07, 72 fellowships (averaging $3,892 per year), 55 research assistantships with partial tuition reimbursements (averaging $10,260 per year) were awarded; career-related internships or fieldwork, Federal Work-Study, institutionally sponsored loans, scholarships/grants, health care benefits, and unspecified assistantships also available. Support available to part-time students. Financial award application deadline: 4/15; financial award applicants required to submit FAFSA. *Faculty research:* Capital markets, econometrics, optimization, investments and empirical corporate finance, Iowa electronic markets. *Unit head:* Prof. Gary J. Gaeth, Associate Dean, MBA Programs, 800-622-4692, Fax: 319-335-3604, E-mail: gary-gaeth@uiowa.edu. *Application contact:* Jodi Schafer, Director of Student Recruitment and Marketing, 319-335-0864, Fax: 319-335-3604, E-mail: jodi-schafer@uiowa.edu.

University of Louisville, Graduate School, College of Business, Program in Entrepreneurship, Louisville, KY 40292-0001. Offers PhD. *Students:* 12 full-time (4 women); includes 1 minority (African American), 3 international. Average age 35. *Entrance requirements:* For doctorate, GMAT, 3 letters of recommendation, curriculum vitae. *Unit head:* Dr. James Fiet, Director, 502-852-4793, Fax: 502-852-7557, E-mail: jofiet01@louisville.edu.

University of Minnesota, Twin Cities Campus, Carlson School of Management, Carlson Full-time MBA Program, Minneapolis, MN 55455-0213. Offers accounting (MBA); entrepreneurship (MBA); finance (MBA); healthcare management (MBA); information and decision sciences (MBA); international business (MBA); marketing and logistics management (MBA); operations and management science (MBA); strategic management and organization (MBA); supply chain management (MBA); JD/MBA; MD/MBA; MHA/MBA. *Accreditation:* AACSB. *Faculty:* 125 full-time (27 women), 120 part-time/adjunct. *Students:* 218 full-time (70 women); includes 18 minority (4 African Americans, 1 American Indian/Alaska Native, 10 Asian Americans or Pacific Islanders, 3 Hispanic Americans), 86 international. Average age 28. 418 applicants, 53% accepted, 124 enrolled. In 2006, 105 degrees awarded. *Median time to degree:* Master's–2 years full-time. *Entrance requirements:* For master's, GMAT. Additional exam requirements/recommendations for international students: Required—TOEFL (minimum score 580 paper-based; 240 computer-based), IELTS. *Application deadline:* For fall admission, 4/15 for domestic students, 2/15 for international students. Application fee: $60 ($90 for international students). Electronic applications accepted. *Expenses: Contact institution.* Full-time tuition and fees vary according to class time, course load, program, reciprocity agreements and student level. *Financial support:* In 2006–07, 131 students received support, including 127 fellowships with full and partial tuition reimbursements available (averaging $20,000 per year); research assistantships with partial tuition reimbursements available, teaching assistantships with partial tuition reimbursements available, career-related internships or fieldwork, Federal Work-Study, institutionally sponsored loans, scholarships/grants, health care benefits, tuition waivers (full and partial), and unspecified assistantships also available. Support available to part-time students. Financial award application deadline: 2/15; financial award applicants required to submit FAFSA. *Faculty research:* IT, strategy, marketing, finance, quality management. *Unit head:* Kathryn J. Carlson, MBA Programs and Executive Education, 612-624-2039, Fax: 612-625-1012, E-mail: full-timembainfo@csom.umn.edu. *Application contact:* Jeffrey Bieganek, Director, Admissions and Business Development, MBA Programs and Executive Education, 612-625-6558, Fax: 612-625-1012, E-mail: full-timembainfo@csom.umn.edu.

University of San Francisco, Masagung Graduate School of Management, Program in Business Administration, San Francisco, CA 94117-1080. Offers business economics (MBA); e-business (MBA); entrepreneurship (MBA); finance and banking (MBA); international business (MBA); management (MBA); marketing (MBA); telecommunications management and policy (MBA); JD/MBA; MSN/MBA. *Accreditation:* AACSB. *Faculty:* 27 full-time (4 women), 21 part-time/adjunct (7 women). *Students:* 191 full-time (73 women), 71 part-time (33 women); includes 51 minority (4 African Americans, 1 American Indian/Alaska Native, 35 Asian Americans or Pacific Islanders, 11 Hispanic Americans), 102 international. Average age 28. 373 applicants, 70% accepted, 106 enrolled. In 2006, 163 degrees awarded. *Entrance requirements:* For master's, GMAT, minimum undergraduate GPA of 3.2. Additional exam requirements/recommendations for international students: Required—TOEFL. *Application deadline:* For fall admission, 7/1 priority date for domestic students; for spring admission, 11/30 for domestic students. Applications are processed on a rolling basis. Application fee: $55 ($65 for international students). *Expenses:* Tuition: Full-time $17,370; part-time $965 per unit. Tuition and fees vary according to degree level, campus/location and program. *Financial support:* In 2006–07, 104 students received support; fellowships available. Financial award application deadline: 3/2; financial award applicants required to submit FAFSA. *Faculty research:* International financial markets, technology transfer licensing, international marketing, strategic planning. Total annual research expenditures: $50,000. *Unit head:* Carol Langlois, Director, 415-422-6314, Fax: 415-422-2502.

University of South Florida, Center for Entrepreneurship, Tampa, FL 33620-9951. Offers MS, Graduate Certificate. Part-time and evening/weekend programs available. *Faculty:* 11 full-time (3 women). *Entrance requirements:* For master's, GMAT, GRE General Test, minimum undergraduate GPA of 3.0 in last 2 years. Additional exam requirements/recommendations for international students: Required—TOEFL (minimum score 550 paper-based; 213 computer-based). *Application deadline:* For fall admission, 3/15 for domestic students, 7/2 for international students; for spring admission, 10/15 for domestic students. Application fee: $30. *Financial support:* Applicants required to submit FAFSA. *Unit head:* Dr. Michael W. Fountain, Director, 813-974-7900, Fax: 813-974-7663, E-mail: fountain@coba.usf.edu.

The University of Tampa, John H. Sykes College of Business, Tampa, FL 33606-1490. Offers accounting (MBA, MS); economics (MBA); entrepreneurship (MBA); finance (MBA, MS); information systems management (MBA); innovation management (MS); international business (MBA); management (MBA); marketing (MBA, MS). *Accreditation:* AACSB. Part-time and evening/weekend programs available. *Faculty:* 39 full-time (9 women), 1 part-time/adjunct (0 women). *Students:* 143 full-time (52 women), 381 part-time (158 women); includes 78 minority (18 African Americans, 3 American Indian/Alaska Native, 19 Asian Americans or Pacific Islanders, 38 Hispanic Americans), 89 international. Average age 31. 486 applicants, 59% accepted, 231 enrolled. In 2006, 127 degrees awarded. *Median time to degree:* Master's–1.8 years full-time, 2.8 years part-time. *Entrance requirements:* For master's, GMAT. Additional exam requirements/recommendations for international students: Required—TOEFL (minimum score 577 paper-based; 230 computer-based; 90 iBT). *Application deadline:* For fall admission, 2/15 priority date for domestic students, 6/15 for international students; for spring admission, 12/15 for domestic students, 11/15 for international students. Applications are processed on a rolling basis. Application fee: $40. Electronic applications accepted. *Expenses:* Tuition: Part-time $426 per credit hour. Required fees: $35 per year. *Financial support:* In 2006–07, 57 students received support, including 57 research assistantships with tuition reimbursements available (averaging $3,000 per year); career-related internships or fieldwork and unspecified assistantships also available. Support available to part-time students. Financial award applicants required to submit FAFSA. *Faculty research:* Industrial organization and antitrust, artificial intelligence, corporate quality, leadership, ethics, quality. *Unit head:* Dr. William L. Rhey, Dean Graduate Studies, 813-253-6211, Fax: 813-259-5403, E-mail: wrhey@ut.edu. *Application contact:* Fernals Nolasco, Director of Graduate Studies, 813-253-6211, Fax: 813-259-5403, E-mail: fnolasco@ut.edu.

University of the Incarnate Word, School of Graduate Studies and Research, Dreeben School of Education, Programs in Education, San Antonio, TX 78209-6397. Offers adult education (M Ed, MA); diversity education (M Ed, MA); early childhood education (M Ed, MA); instructional technology (M Ed, MA); international education and entrepreneurship (PhD); kinesiology (M Ed, MA); mathematics education (PhD); organizational leadership (PhD); organizational learning (M Ed, MA); reading (M Ed, MA); special education (M Ed, MA). *Students:* 15 full-time (8 women), 179 part-time (117 women); includes 70 minority (20 African Americans, 1 American Indian/Alaska Native, 1 Asian American or Pacific Islander, 48 Hispanic Americans), 54 international. Average age 39. In 2006, 15 degrees awarded. Application fee: $20. *Expenses:* Tuition: Part-time $570 per credit hour. Required fees: $54 per credit hour. One-time fee: $195 part-time. Tuition and fees vary according to degree level. *Financial support:* Federal Work-Study and scholarships/grants available. *Unit head:* Dr. Richard Gray, Director, 210-829-3138, Fax: 210-829-3134, E-mail: gray@uiwtx.edu. *Application contact:* Andrea Cyterski-Acosta, Dean of Enrollment, 210-829-6005, Fax: 210-829-3921, E-mail: cyterski@uiwtx.edu.

University of Waterloo, Graduate Studies, Centre for Business, Entrepreneurship and Technology, Waterloo, ON N2L 3G1, Canada. Offers MBET. *Faculty:* 15 full-time. *Students:* 33 full-time (11 women). 57 applicants, 63% accepted, 23 enrolled. In 2006, 31 degrees awarded. *Degree requirements:* For master's, registration. *Entrance requirements:* For master's, honors degree. Additional exam requirements/recommendations for international students: Required—TOEFL (minimum score 550 paper-based; 213 computer-based), TWE. *Application deadline:* Applications are processed on a rolling basis. Application fee: $75. Electronic applications accepted. *Unit head:* Dr. Howard Armitage, Director, 519-888-4567 Ext. 35776, Fax: 519-888-7562, E-mail: howard@uwaterloo.ca. *Application contact:* Emily Stafford, Administrative Liaison and Support, 519-888-4567 Ext. 31167, Fax: 519-888-7562, E-mail: estaffor@uwaterloo.ca.

The University of Western Ontario, Richard Ivey School of Business, London, ON N6A 3K7, Canada. Offers biotechnology stream (MBA); business (EMBA, PhD); certified management accountant (MBA); China business stream (MBA); entrepreneurship (MBA); finance stream (MBA); LL B/MBA. Part-time and evening/weekend programs available. *Degree requirements:* For master's, thesis (for some programs); for doctorate, thesis/dissertation. *Entrance requirements:* For master's, GMAT, 3 years of full-time work experience, interview; for doctorate, GMAT. Additional exam requirements/recommendations for international students: Required—TOEFL. Electronic applications accepted. *Faculty research:* Strategy, organizational behavior, international business, finance, operations management.

University of Wisconsin–Madison, Graduate School, School of Business, Wisconsin Full-Time MBA Programs, Madison, WI 53706-1380. Offers applied corporate finance (MBA); applied security analysis (MBA); arts administration (MBA); brand and product management (MBA); entrepreneurial management (MBA); information systems (MBA); marketing research (MBA); operations and technology management (MBA); real estate (MBA); risk management and insurance (MBA); strategic human resource management (MBA); strategic management in the life and engineering sciences (MBA); supply chain management (MBA). *Faculty:* 84. *Students:* 231 full-time (74 women); includes 21 minority (10 African Americans, 5 Asian Americans or Pacific Islanders, 6 Hispanic Americans), 59 international. Average age 28. 405 applicants, 43% accepted, 121 enrolled. In 2006, 110 degrees awarded. *Entrance requirements:* For master's, GMAT, bachelors or equivalent degree, 2 years of work experience. Additional exam requirements/recommendations for international students: Required—TOEFL (minimum score 600 paper-based; 250 computer-based; 90 iBT). *Application deadline:* For fall admission, 11/1 for domestic and international students; for winter admission, 1/23 for domestic and international students; for spring admission, 3/26 for domestic and international students. Applications are processed on a rolling basis. Application fee: $45. Electronic applications accepted. *Financial support:* In 2006–07, 177 students received support, including 20 fellowships with full and partial tuition reimbursements available (averaging $16,566 per year), 105 research assistantships with full tuition reimbursements available (averaging $8,098 per year), 33 teaching assistantships with full tuition reimbursements available (averaging $10,112 per year); scholarships/grants, health care benefits, and unspecified assistantships also available. *Unit head:* Gary Lessuise, Assistant Dean, Masters Programs, 608-265-5102, Fax: 608-265-4192, E-mail: glessuise@bus.wisc.edu. *Application contact:* Betsy Kacizak, Director of Admissions and Financial Aid—Full Time MBA, 608-262-4000, Fax: 608-265-4192, E-mail: mba@bus.wisc.edu.

Western Carolina University, Graduate School, College of Arts and Sciences, Department of Chemistry and Physics, Program in Science and Entrepreneurship, Cullowhee, NC 28723. Offers PSM.

See Close-Up on page 489.

Western Carolina University, Graduate School, College of Business, Program in Entrepreneurship, Cullowhee, NC 28723. Offers ME. Part-time and evening/weekend programs available. Postbaccalaureate distance learning degree programs offered (no on-campus study). *Entrance requirements:* For master's, GMAT or GRE General Test. Additional exam requirements/recommendations for international students: Required—TOEFL (minimum score 550 paper-based; 213 computer-based).

Wilkes University, Graduate Studies and Continued Learning, Jay S. Sidhu School of Business and Leadership, Wilkes-Barre, PA 18766-0002. Offers accounting (MBA); entrepreneurship (MBA); finance (MBA); human resource management (MBA); international business (MBA); management (MBA); marketing (MBA). *Accreditation:* ACBSP. Part-time and evening/weekend programs available. *Students:* 30 full-time (16 women), 149 part-time (73 women); includes 5 minority (1 African American, 2 Asian Americans or Pacific Islanders, 2 Hispanic Americans), 4 international. Average age 30. In 2006, 48 degrees awarded. *Entrance requirements:* For master's, GMAT. Additional exam requirements/recommendations for international students: Required—TOEFL (minimum score 500 paper-based; 173 computer-based). *Application deadline:* Applications are processed on a rolling basis. Application fee: $40. *Expenses: Contact institution. Financial support:* Federal Work-Study and unspecified assistantships available. Financial award application deadline: 3/1; financial award applicants required to submit FAFSA. *Unit head:* Dr. Paul Browne, Dean, 570-408-4701, Fax: 570-408-4700, E-mail: paul.browne@wilkes.edu. *Application contact:* Kathleen Houlihan, Director of Graduate Studies, 570-408-3235, Fax: 570-408-7846, E-mail: kathleen.houlihan@wilkes.edu.

WESTERN CAROLINA UNIVERSITY

Master of Science in Science and Entrepreneurship

Program of Study

The Master of Science in science and entrepreneurship (SAE) at Western Carolina University (WCU) is designed to educate and support individuals who want to participate in technical innovation and small-business development. This 36-credit-hour program has a three-part curriculum covering the student's scientific area of interest, technical innovation and opportunity, and integrated business skills taught by entrepreneurs in the nationally recognized entrepreneurship program. Graduate courses are available in chemistry, biology, biotechnology, environmental science, and engineering. Students complete a technical internship, which could include working at a company or partnering with a faculty member or a business on a technical project. This experience serves as the basis for an original technical idea that the student refines toward degree completion. The capstone project is the culmination of the student's research of technical feasibility, market analysis, and business plan development. Students leave the program having executed the steps required to take a technical idea from early-stage development to business launch.

All students study with entrepreneurs in the College of Business during the first year and complete the required capstone project with independent research by the second year. The remaining scientific curriculum is selected by the student and approved by the program director. Graduate courses are offered in various fields of chemistry, biology, engineering, and mathematics. The program also addresses the interface of science and business with such topics as technical innovation and opportunity, intellectual property, and product development. The program is designed to be completed in two academic years for a full-time student. It is possible to finish in less time if all course requirements and independent work are completed through summer work or an increased course load. Part-time students can move through the program at a slower, more convenient pace. The SAE program is designed to be very hands on. Students will work on projects, often in teams, to reinforce principles presented in class. The capstone project revolves around an invention derived from the student or other sources, such as faculty members or business. These projects could be rooted in chemistry, biology, engineering, or any combination thereof. The program director guides the students and partners them with the appropriate mentors in science and business. Expertise from outside the University is heavily solicited. Students will develop excellent communication skills, research capabilities, and decision-making experience through practice. Students also complete the steps to investigating and positioning new ideas or products for success. These skills can be used in existing companies for marketing, product development and management, or to create a new business.

Research Facilities

Although this is not a research degree, students can use existing equipment on campus or partner with a research student who is conducting high-level technical work. Students have access to faculty members and equipment in the Departments of Chemistry and Biology. The Center for Integrated Technologies is also on campus and provides rapid prototyping for the development of small devices.

Financial Aid

This program belongs to the Academic Common Market; students from Alabama, Arkansas, Delaware, Florida, Georgia, Kentucky, Louisiana, Maryland, Mississippi, Oklahoma, South Carolina, Tennessee, Texas, Virginia, and West Virginia can apply to this program and pay North Carolina in-state tuition rates.

Graduate assistantships are available, and paid internships are possible. Scholarships are not currently available.

Cost of Study

For 2007–08, full-time residents of North Carolina pay tuition ($1086.50), required fees ($1211.50), room ($1330), and board ($900) that total $4528. Out-of-state students pay $5879 for tuition, $1211.50 for required fees, $1330 for room, $900 for board; the total cost is $9320.50. Students who enroll for 8 or fewer semester hours are considered part-time. Part-time tuition ranges from $335.58 (in-state) and $1534.08 (out-of-state) for 1 semester hour to $1326.48 (in-state) and $4921.48 (out-of-state) for 8 semester hours. Required fees are prorated for part-time students. Students should visit http://www.wcu.edu/259.asp for more information. Other costs, which vary for each student, include transportation, books, supplies, and personal items. Fees include the application fee ($40), late registration fee ($10), and graduation fee ($30).

Living and Housing Costs

Western Carolina University is a rural campus and has a relatively low cost of living and plenty of low-cost housing off campus.

Student Group

This program is looking for a small number of highly motivated students with a degree in science from an accredited institution. Students must have an interest in the interface between science and business.

Location

Surrounded by the Great Smoky and Blue Ridge Mountains, WCU's approximately 600-acre campus blends scenic beauty with convenient modern facilities. The result is a pleasant learning and living environment that fosters a healthy balance of work and play. Activities available in the area include hiking, fishing, camping, shopping, and dining. For a wider range of shopping and dining experiences, the city of Asheville is 50 miles from campus. At the heart of campus is the UC, which is the A. K. Hinds University Center, a place for students to meet, mingle, and take advantage of services designed to make college life just a little more pleasant—from WCU's movie theater to the very popular food court. Students also gather on the quad—a green space ideal for a sunny afternoon study break or an outdoor festival—and take time to stroll the pathways of the pedestrian-friendly campus. At WCU, students find activities to participate in year-round, including cheering on their Catamounts at sporting events or supporting local and world-known artists alike at the Fine and Performing Arts Center. There are also many diverse groups to be involved in that help foster leadership skills and provide contacts for career opportunities.

The University

Western Carolina University was founded in 1889 to bring higher education and career opportunities to the western region of North Carolina. A member of the University of North Carolina system, WCU now provides an education to more than 8,000 students from forty-six states and thirty-nine countries. WCU is accredited by the Commission on Colleges of the Southern Association of Colleges and Schools to award bachelor's, master's, education specialist, and doctoral degrees. The University also holds twenty-one special program accreditations and is a member of more than thirty state and national associations and organizations to which its professional programs are related.

Applying

Applicants must have a bachelor's degree in chemistry or biology from an accredited institution. GRE exam scores, undergraduate transcripts, and letters of recommendation are required. Other experience is considered for admission. Students may apply online through the WCU Web site or print out the application and mail it in. Official transcripts must be received from all schools previously attended before an admissions decision can be made. Once a complete application has been received, an admissions decision is made in four to six weeks.

Interested students should contact the program director for additional information or with questions.

Correspondence and Information

Dr. Jonathan Snover, Program Director
Master of Science in Science and Entrepreneurship
Department of Chemistry and Physics
Western Carolina University
Cullowhee, North Carolina 28723
Phone: 828-227-3683
Fax: 828-227-7393
E-mail: jsnover@wcu.edu
Web site: http://sae.wcu.edu

Western Carolina University

THE FACULTY AND THEIR RESEARCH

For more information regarding the research in progress in chemistry and physics at Western Carolina University and for more general information about the University, students should visit http://www.wcu.edu.

Section 6
Facilities Management

This section contains a directory of institutions offering graduate work in facilities management. Additional information about programs listed in the directory but not augmented by an in-depth entry may be obtained by writing directly to the dean of a graduate school or chair of a department at the address given in the directory.

For programs offering related work, see also in this book Business Administration and Management.

CONTENTS

Program Directory

Facilities Management

Cornell University, Graduate School, Graduate Fields of Human Ecology, Field of Design and Environmental Analysis, Ithaca, NY 14853-0001. Offers applied research in human-environment relations (MS); facilities planning and management (MS); housing and design (MS); human factors and ergonomics (MS); human-environment relations (MS); interior design (MA, MPS). *Faculty:* 13 full-time (5 women). *Students:* 20 full-time (14 women); includes 2 minority (1 Asian American or Pacific Islander, 1 Hispanic American), 9 international. Average age 28. 47 applicants, 45% accepted, 14 enrolled. In 2006, 8 degrees awarded. *Degree requirements:* For master's, thesis. *Entrance requirements:* For master's, GRE General Test, portfolio or slides of recent work; bachelor's degree in interior design, architecture or related design discipline; 2 letters of recommendation. Additional exam requirements/recommendations for international students: Required—TOEFL (minimum score 600 paper-based; 250 computer-based). *Application deadline:* For fall admission, 2/1 priority date for domestic students. Application fee: $60. Electronic applications accepted. *Expenses:* Tuition: Full-time $32,800. Full-time tuition and fees vary according to program. *Financial support:* In 2006–07, 12 students received support, including 2 fellowships with full tuition reimbursements available, 10 teaching assistantships with full tuition reimbursements available; research assistantships with full tuition reimbursements available, institutionally sponsored loans, scholarships/grants, health care benefits, tuition waivers (full and partial), and unspecified assistantships also available. Financial award applicants required to submit FAFSA. *Faculty research:* Facility planning and management, environmental psychology, housing, interior design, ergonomics and human factors. *Unit head:* Director of Graduate Studies, 607-255-2168, Fax: 607-255-0305. *Application contact:* Graduate Field Assistant, 607-255-2168, Fax: 607-255-0305, E-mail: deagrad@cornell.edu.

Indiana University of Pennsylvania, School of Graduate Studies and Research, College of Health and Human Services, Department of Health and Physical Education, Indiana, PA 15705-1087. Offers aquatics administration and facilities management (MS); exercise science (MS); sport management (MS); sport science (MS). Part-time programs available. *Faculty:* 8 full-time (4 women). *Students:* 33 full-time (17 women), 39 part-time (21 women); includes 3 minority (2 African Americans, 1 Asian American or Pacific Islander), 12 international. Average age 27. 75 applicants, 75% accepted. In 2006, 18 degrees awarded. *Degree requirements:* For master's, thesis optional. *Entrance requirements:* For master's, 2 letters of recommendation. Additional exam requirements/recommendations for international students: Required—TOEFL. *Application deadline:* For fall admission, 7/1 priority date for domestic students; for spring admission, 11/1 for domestic students. Applications are processed on a rolling basis. Application fee: $30. *Expenses:* Tuition, state resident: full-time $6,048; part-time $336 per credit. Tuition, nonresident: full-time $9,678; part-time $538 per credit. Required fees: $1,069; $148 per year. *Financial support:* In 2006–07, 6 research assistantships with full and partial tuition reimbursements (averaging $4,990 per year) were awarded. Financial award application deadline: 3/15; financial award applicants required to submit FAFSA. *Unit head:* Dr. Elaine Blair, Chairperson, 724-357-2770, E-mail: eblair@iup.edu.

Massachusetts Maritime Academy, Program in Facilities Management, Buzzards Bay, MA 02532-1803. Offers MS. *Entrance requirements:* For master's, GRE or GMAT, interview.

Pratt Institute, School of Architecture, Program in Facilities Management, Brooklyn, NY 11205-3899. Offers MS. *Faculty:* 1 (woman) full-time, 5 part-time/adjunct (0 women). *Students:* 16 full-time (9 women), 7 part-time (4 women); includes 7 minority (5 African Americans, 2 Hispanic Americans), 10 international. Average age 34. 4 applicants, 50% accepted, 2 enrolled. In 2006, 8 degrees awarded. *Degree requirements:* For master's, thesis. *Entrance requirements:* For master's, writing sample. Additional exam requirements/recommendations for international students: Required—TOEFL (minimum score 550 paper-based; 213 computer-based). *Application deadline:* For fall admission, 2/1 for domestic students; for spring admission, 10/1 for domestic students. Applications are processed on a rolling basis. Application fee: $40 ($90 for international students). Electronic applications accepted. *Expenses:* Tuition: Full-time $24,240. Tuition and fees vary according to course load and program. *Financial support:* In 2006–07, 3 research assistantships (averaging $2,500 per year) were awarded; fellowships, career-related internships or fieldwork, Federal Work-Study, institutionally sponsored loans, scholarships/grants, and unspecified assistantships also available. Support available to part-time students. Financial award application deadline: 2/1; financial award applicants required to submit FAFSA. *Faculty research:* Benchmarking, organizational studies, resource planning and management, computer-aided facilities management, value analysis. *Unit head:* Diane Kaufman Fredette, Chairperson, 212-647-7524, Fax: 212-367-2497, E-mail: fredette@pratt.edu. *Application contact:* Young Hah, Director of Graduate Admissions, 718-636-3683, Fax: 718-399-4242, E-mail: yhah@pratt.edu.

Southern Methodist University, School of Engineering, Department of Environmental and Civil Engineering, Dallas, TX 75275. Offers applied science (MS, PhD); civil engineering (MS, PhD); environmental engineering (MS); environmental science (MS), including environmental systems management, hazardous and waste materials management; facilities management (MS). Part-time and evening/weekend programs available. Postbaccalaureate distance learning degree programs offered (no on-campus study). *Faculty:* 5 full-time (0 women), 14 part-time/adjunct (0 women). *Students:* 10 full-time (3 women), 41 part-time (11 women); includes 11 minority (3 African Americans, 1 American Indian/Alaska Native, 2 Asian Americans or Pacific Islanders, 5 Hispanic Americans), 7 international. Average age 33. 21 applicants, 38% accepted, 4 enrolled. In 2006, 18 master's, 1 doctorate awarded. Terminal master's awarded for partial completion of doctoral program. *Degree requirements:* For master's, thesis optional; for doctorate, thesis/dissertation, oral and written qualifying exams. *Entrance requirements:* For master's, GRE General Test, minimum GPA of 3.0 in last 2 years; bachelor's degree in engineering, mathematics, or sciences; for doctorate, GRE, BS and MS in related field, minimum GPA of 3.3. Additional exam requirements/recommendations for international students: Required—TOEFL. *Application deadline:* For fall admission, 7/1 for domestic students, 5/15 for international students; for spring admission, 11/15 for domestic students, 9/1 for international students. Applications are processed on a rolling basis. Application fee: $75. *Financial support:* In 2006–07, 6 students received support, including 2 research assistantships with full tuition reimbursements available (averaging $18,000 per year), 3 teaching assistantships with full tuition reimbursements available (averaging $18,000 per year); career-related internships or fieldwork, tuition waivers (full and partial), and unspecified assistantships also available. *Faculty research:* Human and environmental health effects of endocrine disrupters, development of air pollution control systems for diesel engines, structural analysis and design, modeling and design of waste treatment systems. Total annual research expenditures: $100,000. *Unit head:* Dr. Bijan Mohraz, Chair, 214-768-3123, Fax: 214-768-2164, E-mail: bmohraz@engr.smu.edu. *Application contact:* Marc Valerin, Director of Graduate and Executive Admissions, 214-768-3042, E-mail: valerin@engr.smu.edu.

Université Laval, Faculty of Administrative Sciences, Programs in Business Administration, Québec, QC G1K 7P4, Canada. Offers accounting (MBA); agri-food management (MBA); electronic business (MBA, Diploma); factory management and logistics (MBA); finance (MBA); firm management (MBA); information technology management (MBA); international management (MBA); management (MBA); management accounting (MBA, Diploma); marketing (MBA); modelization and organizational decision (MBA); occupational health and safety management (MBA); pharmacy management (MBA); technological entrepreneurship (Diploma). *Accreditation:* AACSB. Part-time and evening/weekend programs available. Postbaccalaureate distance learning degree programs offered (no on-campus study). *Entrance requirements:* For master's and Diploma, knowledge of French and English. Electronic applications accepted.

Section 7
Hospitality Management

This section contains a directory of institutions offering graduate work in hospitality management, followed by in-depth entries submitted by institutions that chose to prepare detailed program descriptions. Additional information about programs listed in the directory but not augmented by an in-depth entry may be obtained by writing directly to the dean of a graduate school or chair of a department at the address given in the directory.

For programs offering related work, see also in this book Business Administration and Management, Advertising and Public Relations, and Health Services. In Book 4, see Agricultural and Food Sciences (Food Science and Technology).

CONTENTS

Program Directories

Close-Ups

Hospitality Management

Andrew Jackson University, Brian Tracy College of Business and Entrepreneurship, Birmingham, AL 35244. Offers entrepreneurship (MBA); finance (MBA); health services management (MBA); hospitality and tourism management (MBA); human resource management (MBA); international business (MBA); management (MBA); marketing (MBA). Part-time and evening/weekend programs available. Postbaccalaureate distance learning degree programs offered (no on-campus study). *Faculty:* 13 part-time/adjunct (1 woman). *Students:* Average age 40. In 2006, 6 degrees awarded. *Entrance requirements:* For master's, course work in calculus, statistics. Additional exam requirements/recommendations for international students: Required—TOEFL (minimum score 550 paper-based; 213 computer-based). *Application deadline:* Applications are processed on a rolling basis. Application fee: $75. *Expenses:* Tuition: Part-time $705 per course. *Application contact:* Betty Howell, Director of Student Affairs, 205-871-9288 Ext. 108, Fax: 205-871-9294, E-mail: bhowell@aju.edu.

Central Michigan University, College of Graduate Studies, College of Business Administration, Department of Marketing and Hospitality Services Administration, Mount Pleasant, MI 48859. Offers MBA. *Degree requirements:* For master's, thesis or alternative, registration. *Entrance requirements:* For master's, GMAT.

Central Michigan University, College of Graduate Studies, Program in Administration, Mount Pleasant, MI 48859. Offers general administration (MSA); health services administration (MSA); hospitality and tourism administration (MSA); human resource administration (MSA); information resource administration (MSA); international administration (MSA); leadership (MSA); organizational communications (MSA); public administration (MSA); recreation and park administration (MSA); software engineering (MSA); sports administration (MSA). *Accreditation:* AACSB. *Degree requirements:* For master's, thesis or alternative. *Entrance requirements:* For master's, minimum undergraduate GPA of 2.5.

See Close-Up on page 253.

Cornell University, Graduate School, Field of Hotel Administration, Ithaca, NY 14853-0001. Offers hospitality management (MMH); hotel administration (MS, PhD). *Faculty:* 43 full-time (12 women). *Students:* 67 full-time (36 women); includes 9 minority (1 American Indian/Alaska Native, 7 Asian Americans or Pacific Islanders, 1 Hispanic American); 38 international. Average age 30. In 2006, 82 master's, 2 doctorates awarded. Terminal master's awarded for partial completion of doctoral program. *Degree requirements:* For master's, thesis (MS); for doctorate, thesis/dissertation, comprehensive exam. *Entrance requirements:* For master's and doctorate, GMAT, 1 academic and 1 employer letter of recommendation, 2 interviews. Additional exam requirements/recommendations for international students: Required—TOEFL (minimum score 600 paper-based; 250 computer-based). *Application deadline:* For fall admission, 2/1 for domestic students. Application fee: $70. Electronic applications accepted. *Expenses:* Tuition: Full-time $32,800. Full-time tuition and fees vary according to program. *Financial support:* In 2006–07, 9 students received support, including 2 fellowships with full tuition reimbursements available, 7 teaching assistantships with full tuition reimbursements available; research assistantships with full tuition reimbursements available, institutionally sponsored loans, scholarships/grants, health care benefits, tuition waivers (full and partial), and unspecified assistantships also available. Financial award applicants required to submit FAFSA. *Faculty research:* Hospitality finance; property-asset management; real estate; management, strategy, and human resources; organizational communication. *Unit head:* Director of Graduate Studies, 607-255-7245. *Application contact:* Graduate Field Assistant, 607-255-6376, E-mail: mmh@cornell.edu.

Eastern Michigan University, Graduate School, College of Technology, School of Technology Studies, Program in Hotel and Restaurant Management, Ypsilanti, MI 48197. Offers MS. Part-time and evening/weekend programs available. Postbaccalaureate distance learning degree programs offered (minimal on-campus study). *Students:* Average age 37. *Entrance requirements:* Additional exam requirements/recommendations for international students: Required—TOEFL. *Application deadline:* For fall admission, 5/15 priority date for domestic students, 5/1 priority date for international students; for winter admission, 10/15 priority date for domestic students, 10/1 priority date for international students; for spring admission, 3/15 priority date for domestic students, 3/1 priority date for international students. Applications are processed on a rolling basis. Application fee: $35. *Expenses:* Tuition, state resident: part-time $341 per credit hour. Tuition, nonresident: full-time $16,104; part-time $671 per credit hour. Required fees: $816; $34 per credit hour. $40 per term. One-time fee: $82 full-time. Tuition and fees vary according to course level, course load, degree level and reciprocity agreements. *Financial support:* Fellowships, research assistantships with full tuition reimbursements, teaching assistantships with full tuition reimbursements, career-related internships or fieldwork, Federal Work-Study, institutionally sponsored loans, scholarships/grants, tuition waivers (partial), and unspecified assistantships available. Support available to part-time students. Financial award applicants required to submit FAFSA. *Unit head:* Dr. John Boyless, Director, School of Technology Studies, 734-487-1161, Fax: 734-487-7690, E-mail: john.boyless@emich.edu.

East Stroudsburg University of Pennsylvania, Graduate School, School of Professional Studies, Department of Hotel, Restaurant and Tourism Management, East Stroudsburg, PA 18301-2999. Offers management and leadership (MS). *Faculty:* 2 full-time (1 woman). *Students:* 1 (woman) full-time, 4 part-time (1 woman), 2 international. Average age 28. In 2006, 1 degree awarded. *Degree requirements:* For master's, comprehensive exam. *Entrance requirements:* For master's, GRE or GMAT, 3 letters of recommendation. Additional exam requirements/recommendations for international students: Required—TOEFL (minimum score 560 paper-based; 220 computer-based; 83 iBT). *Application deadline:* For fall admission, 7/31 priority date for domestic students, 5/1 priority date for international students; for spring admission, 11/30 for domestic students, 10/1 for international students. Applications are processed on a rolling basis. Application fee: $50. *Expenses:* Tuition, state resident: full-time $6,048; part-time $336 per credit. Tuition, nonresident: full-time $9,678; part-time $538 per credit. Required fees: $1,353; $67 per credit. One-time fee: $37 part-time. *Financial support:* In 2006–07, 1 research assistantship was awarded; Federal Work-Study and unspecified assistantships also available. Financial award application deadline: 3/1; financial award applicants required to submit FAFSA. *Unit head:* Dr. Al Moranville, Unit Head, 570-422-3049.

Endicott College, Van Loan School of Graduate and Professional Studies, Program in Hospitality Organizational Training and Management, Beverly, MA 01915-2096. Offers M Ed. *Faculty:* 5 part-time/adjunct (2 women). *Students:* 10 full-time (5 women). Average age 30. In 2006, 19 degrees awarded. *Degree requirements:* For master's, thesis, registration. *Entrance requirements:* For master's, letters of recommendation. *Expenses:* Tuition: Part-time $279 per credit. Tuition and fees vary according to program. *Unit head:* Dr. Jayanti Bandyopadhyay, Associate Dean of Graduate School, 978-232-2744, Fax: 978-232-3000, E-mail: jbandyop@endicott.edu. *Application contact:* Dr. Debbie Prince, Director GIHE, Bulle, Switzerland.

Fairleigh Dickinson University, College at Florham, Anthony J. Petrocelli College of Continuing Studies, International School of Hospitality and Tourism Management, Madison, NJ 07940-1099. Offers hospitality management studies (MS). *Students:* 7 full-time (3 women), 26 part-time (12 women), 1 international. Average age 32. 19 applicants, 100% accepted, 19 enrolled. In 2006, 11 degrees awarded. *Application deadline:* Applications are processed on a rolling basis. Application fee: $40.

See Close-Up on page 501.

Fairleigh Dickinson University, Metropolitan Campus, Anthony J. Petrocelli College of Continuing Studies, International School of Hospitality and Tourism Management, Program in Hospitality Management Studies, Teaneck, NJ 07666-1914. Offers MS. *Students:* 8 full-time (5 women), 17 part-time (10 women), 7 international. Average age 35. 13 applicants, 69% accepted. In 2006, 10 degrees awarded. *Application deadline:* Applications are processed on a rolling basis. Application fee: $40. *Unit head:* Dr. Richard Wisch, Director, International School of Hospitality and Tourism Management, 201-692-2000.

See Close-Up on page 501.

Florida International University, School of Hospitality Management, North Miami, FL 33181-3000. Offers hotel and food service management (MS). *Faculty:* 18 full-time (5 women), 2 part-time/adjunct (0 women). *Students:* 92 full-time (63 women), 49 part-time (25 women); includes 41 minority (14 African Americans, 5 Asian Americans or Pacific Islanders, 22 Hispanic Americans), 68 international. Average age 29. 82 applicants, 71% accepted, 27 enrolled. In 2006, 62 degrees awarded. *Entrance requirements:* For master's, GMAT or GRE, minimum GPA of 3.0. Additional exam requirements/recommendations for international students: Required—TOEFL. Application fee: $25. *Expenses:* Tuition, state resident: part-time $249 per credit hour. Tuition, nonresident: part-time $753 per credit hour. Tuition and fees vary according to program. *Unit head:* Dr. Joseph West, Dean, 305-919-4500, Fax: 305-919-4555, E-mail: jwest@fiu.edu.

The George Washington University, School of Business, Department of Tourism and Hospitality Management, Washington, DC 20052. Offers event management (MTA, Professional Certificate); sport management (MTA); tourism administration (MTA); tourism and hospitality management (MBA); tourism destination management (Professional Certificate). Part-time programs available. *Degree requirements:* For master's, thesis, comprehensive exam. *Entrance requirements:* For master's, GRE General Test. Additional exam requirements/recommendations for international students: Required—TOEFL. *Faculty research:* Tourism policy, tourism impact forecasting, geotourism.

Iowa State University of Science and Technology, Graduate College, College of Human Sciences, Department of Apparel, Education Studies, and Hospitality Management, Program in Foodservice and Lodging Management, Ames, IA 50011. Offers MFCS, MS, PhD. *Students:* 13 full-time (11 women), 22 part-time (19 women); includes 2 minority (both African Americans), 11 international. 23 applicants, 43% accepted, 6 enrolled. In 2006, 1 master's, 5 doctorates awarded. *Degree requirements:* For master's, thesis or alternative; for doctorate, thesis/dissertation. *Entrance requirements:* For master's and doctorate, GMAT or GRE General Test. Additional exam requirements/recommendations for international students: Required—TOEFL (paper-based 550; computer-based 213; iBT 80) or IELTS (6.5). *Application deadline:* For fall admission, 2/1 priority date for domestic and international students; for spring admission, 9/1 priority date for domestic and international students. Application fee: $30 ($70 for international students). Electronic applications accepted. *Expenses:* Tuition, state resident: full-time $5,936; part-time $330 per credit. Tuition, nonresident: full-time $16,350; part-time $330 per credit. *Financial support:* In 2006–07, 3 research assistantships with full and partial tuition reimbursements (averaging $16,314 per year), 6 teaching assistantships with partial tuition reimbursements (averaging $16,764 per year) were awarded; scholarships/grants also available. *Unit head:* Dr. Haemon Oh, Director of Graduate Education, 515-294-7409, E-mail: hmoh@iastate.edu.

Johnson & Wales University, The Alan Shawn Feinstein Graduate School, Certificate Programs, Providence, RI 02903-3703. Offers finance (CAGS); hospitality (CAGS); human resources management (CAGS). *Students:* 9 full-time (4 women), 2 part-time (both women); includes 1 African American, 8 international. Average age 29. *Unit head:* Thomas Rossi, Unit Head, 401-598-4738, E-mail: trossi@jwu.edu.

Johnson & Wales University, The Alan Shawn Feinstein Graduate School, Program in Hospitality Administration, Concentration in Event Leadership, Providence, RI 02903-3703. Offers MBA. Part-time and evening/weekend programs available. *Students:* 75 full-time (56 women), 5 part-time (all women); includes 3 minority (2 African Americans, 1 Hispanic American), 46 international. Average age 26. *Entrance requirements:* For master's, GMAT recommended, minimum GPA of 2.75. Additional exam requirements/recommendations for international students: Required—TOEFL (paper-based 550; computer-based 210) or IELTS. *Application deadline:* For fall admission, 3/15 priority date for domestic students, 6/28 priority date for international students; for winter admission, 11/10 priority date for domestic students, 9/20 priority date for international students; for spring admission, 2/15 priority date for domestic students, 12/20 priority date for international students. Applications are processed on a rolling basis. Electronic applications accepted. *Financial support:* Unspecified assistantships available. Financial award application deadline: 5/1. *Unit head:* Thomas Rossi, Unit Head, 401-598-4738, E-mail: trossi@jwu.edu. *Application contact:* Dr. Allan G. Freedman, Director of Graduate Admissions, 401-598-1015, Fax: 401-598-1286, E-mail: gradadm@jwu.edu.

Kansas State University, Graduate School, College of Human Ecology, Department of Hotel, Restaurant, Institutional Management, and Dietetics, Manhattan, KS 66506. Offers dietetics and administration (MS); food service and hospitality management (MS). Part-time programs available. *Faculty:* 3 full-time (2 women), 1 (woman) part-time/adjunct. *Students:* 46 full-time (28 women), 23 part-time (15 women); includes 11 minority (8 African Americans, 1 American Indian/Alaska Native, 2 Asian Americans or Pacific Islanders), 15 international. Average age 28. 12 applicants, 50% accepted, 6 enrolled. In 2006, 1 degree awarded. *Degree requirements:* For master's, thesis or alternative, residency. *Entrance requirements:* Additional exam requirements/recommendations for international students: Required—TOEFL. *Application deadline:* For fall admission, 2/1 priority date for domestic and international students; for spring admission, 8/1 for domestic students, 8/1 priority date for international students. Applications are processed on a rolling basis. Application fee: $30 ($55 for international students). Electronic applications accepted. *Expenses:* Tuition, state resident: full-time $6,352; part-time $240 per credit hour. Tuition, nonresident: full-time $14,296; part-time $571 per credit hour. Required fees: $585. *Financial support:* In 2006–07, 4 research assistantships (averaging $13,040 per year), 2 teaching assistantships with full and partial tuition reimbursements (averaging $9,000 per year) were awarded; Federal Work-Study, institutionally sponsored loans, and scholarships/grants also available. Support available to part-time students. Financial award application deadline: 3/1; financial award applicants required to submit FAFSA. *Faculty research:* Customer satisfaction, brand loyalty, food safety and biosecurity issues in foodservice operations, gerontology and the hospitality industry; education, training, and career development in dietetics and hospitality. Total annual research expenditures: $141,871. *Unit head:* Deborah Canter, Head, 785-532-5507, Fax: 785-532-5522, E-mail: canter@ksu.edu.

Kansas State University, Graduate School, College of Human Ecology, Program in Human Ecology, Manhattan, KS 66506. Offers apparel and textiles (PhD); family life education and consultation (PhD); food service, hospitality management, and administrative dietetics (PhD); institutional management (PhD); lifespan and human development (PhD); marriage and family therapy (PhD). *Students:* 47 full-time (31 women), 22 part-time (14 women); includes 13 minority (8 African Americans, 1 American Indian/Alaska Native, 3 Asian Americans or Pacific Islanders, 1 Hispanic American), 14 international. 39 applicants, 54% accepted, 6 enrolled. In 2006, 14 degrees awarded. *Application deadline:* For fall admission, 2/1 priority date for domestic and international students; for spring admission, 8/1 priority date for domestic and international students. Application fee: $30 ($55 for international students). *Expenses:* Tuition, state resident: full-time $6,352; part-time $240 per credit hour. Tuition, nonresident: full-time $14,296; part-time $571 per credit hour. Required fees: $585. Total annual research expenditures: $4.8 million. *Unit head:* Elizabeth McCullough, Director, 785-532-2284, Fax: 785-532-3796, E-mail: lizm@ksu.edu.

Lynn University, College of Business and Management, Boca Raton, FL 33431-5598. Offers aviation management (MBA); financial valuation and investment management (MBA); global leadership (PhD); hospitality management (MBA); international business (MBA); marketing (MBA); mass communication and media management (MBA); sports and athletics administration (MBA). Part-time and evening/weekend programs available. Postbaccalaureate distance learning degree programs offered. *Faculty:* 13 full-time (5 women), 7 part-time/adjunct (3 women). *Students:* 71 full-time (37 women), 113 part-time (47 women); includes 35 minority (13 African Americans, 6 Asian Americans or Pacific Islanders, 16 Hispanic Americans), 55 international. Average age 32. 114 applicants, 88% accepted, 71 enrolled. In 2006, 83 master's, 9 doctorates awarded. *Degree requirements:* For master's, project; for doctorate, thesis/dissertation, qualifying paper. *Entrance requirements:* For master's, GMAT or GRE, minimum undergraduate GPA of 3.0, resumé, 2 letters of recommendation; for doctorate, GRE or GMAT, minimum graduate GPA of 3.25, resumé, 2 letters of recommendation. Additional exam requirements/recommendations for international students: Required—TOEFL (minimum score 550 paper-based; 213 computer-based). *Application deadline:* Applications are processed on a rolling basis. Application fee: $50. Electronic applications accepted. *Expenses:* Tuition: Full-time $26,200. Required fees: $1,500. Tuition and fees vary according to class time, course load and degree level. *Financial support:* In 2006–07, 160 students received support. Career-related internships or fieldwork, Federal Work-Study, institutionally sponsored loans, scholarships/grants, tuition waivers (full and partial), and unspecified assistantships available. Support available to part-time students. Financial award application deadline: 8/1; financial award applicants required to submit FAFSA. *Faculty research:* Labor relations, dynamic balance in leisure-time skills, ethics in athletics, hotel development. *Unit head:* Dr. Russell Boisjoly, Dean, 561-237-7458, Fax: 561-237-7014, E-mail: rboisjoly@lynn.edu. *Application contact:* Dr. Larissa Baia, Assistant Director of Graduate Admissions, 561-237-7916, Fax: 561-237-7100, E-mail: admissionpm@lynn.edu.

Michigan State University, The Graduate School, Eli Broad Graduate School of Management, The School of Hospitality Business, East Lansing, MI 48824. Offers food service management (MS); hospitality business (MS). *Faculty:* 10 full-time (1 woman), 1 part-time/adjunct (0 women). *Students:* 16 full-time (9 women), 3 part-time (2 women); includes 1 minority (African American), 12 international. Average age 27. 31 applicants, 48% accepted. In 2006, 12 degrees awarded. *Degree requirements:* For master's, research project. *Entrance requirements:* For master's, GRE General Test, minimum GPA of 3.0 in last 2 years of undergraduate course work, working knowledge of computers, resumé, 3 letters of recommendation, specified college-level coursework or work experience. Additional exam requirements/recommendations for international students: Required—TOEFL (minimum score 580 paper-based; 237 computer-based). *Application deadline:* For fall admission, 12/27 priority date for domestic students. Application fee: $50. Electronic applications accepted. *Expenses:* Tuition, state resident: part-time $346 per credit hour. Tuition, nonresident: part-time $730 per credit hour. Tuition and fees vary according to program. *Financial support:* In 2006–07, 1 fellowship with tuition reimbursement (averaging $2,500 per year), 2 research assistantships with tuition reimbursements (averaging $10,877 per year) were awarded; career-related internships or fieldwork, Federal Work-Study, scholarships/grants, and unspecified assistantships also available. Support available to part-time students. *Faculty research:* Corporate food service management, entrepreneurial and food service management, hospitality business. Total annual research expenditures: $2,500. *Unit head:* Dr. Ronald F. Cichy, Director, 517-355-5080, Fax: 517-432-1170, E-mail: cichy@msu.edu. *Application contact:* Program Information, 517-353-9211, E-mail: mshb@bus.msu.edu.

See Close-Up on page 503.

New York University, School of Continuing and Professional Studies, Tisch Center for Hospitality, Tourism and Sports Management, Program in Hospitality Industry Studies, New York, NY 10012-1019. Offers hospitality industry studies (MS, Advanced Certificate). Part-time and evening/weekend programs available. Postbaccalaureate distance learning degree programs offered (minimal on-campus study). *Faculty:* 5 full-time (2 women), 24 part-time/adjunct (6 women). *Students:* 18 full-time (11 women), 39 part-time (24 women); includes 17 minority (2 African Americans, 11 Asian Americans or Pacific Islanders, 4 Hispanic Americans), 17 international. Average age 31. 45 applicants, 56% accepted, 16 enrolled. In 2006, 8 master's, 1 other advanced degree awarded. *Degree requirements:* For master's, thesis, comprehensive exam (for some programs). *Entrance requirements:* For master's, GMAT or GRE General Test, 1 year of work experience. Additional exam requirements/recommendations for international students: Required—TOEFL (minimum score 600 paper-based; 250 computer-based; 100 iBT), TWE. *Application deadline:* For fall admission, 3/15 priority date for domestic and international students; for spring admission, 10/15 priority date for domestic students, 8/15 priority date for international students. Applications are processed on a rolling basis. Application fee: $75. *Expenses:* Tuition: Part-time $1,080 per unit. Required fees: $56 per unit. $329 per term. Tuition and fees vary according to program. *Financial support:* In 2006–07, fellowships (averaging $33,338 per year); research assistantships, career-related internships or fieldwork, Federal Work-Study, institutionally sponsored loans, and scholarships/grants also available. Support available to part-time students. Financial award application deadline: 3/1; financial award applicants required to submit FAFSA. *Faculty research:* Hotel statistics, hotel investments, and revenue management; hospitality work force issues; internet distribution channels. *Unit head:* Dr. Mark M. Warner, Director, Graduate Programs, 212-998-9107, Fax: 212-995-4676, E-mail: mmw4@nyu.edu.

See Close-Up on page 505.

New York University, Steinhardt School of Culture, Education and Human Development, Department of Nutrition, Food Studies, and Public Health, Program in Food Studies and Food Management, New York, NY 10012-1019. Offers food management (MA); food studies (MA); food studies and food management (PhD). Part-time and evening/weekend programs available. *Faculty:* 4 full-time (3 women). *Students:* 23 full-time (22 women), 66 part-time (56 women); includes 15 minority (3 African Americans, 7 Asian Americans or Pacific Islanders, 5 Hispanic Americans), 15 international. 39 applicants, 92% accepted, 31 enrolled. In 2006, 19 master's, 1 doctorate awarded. *Degree requirements:* For master's, thesis (for some programs); for doctorate, thesis/dissertation. *Entrance requirements:* For doctorate, GRE General Test, interview. Additional exam requirements/recommendations for international students: Required—TOEFL. *Application deadline:* For fall admission, 1/15 priority date for domestic students, 1/15 for international students; for spring admission, 11/1 for domestic and international students. Applications are processed on a rolling basis. Application fee: $50. *Expenses:* Tuition: Part-time $1,080 per unit. Required fees: $56 per unit. $329 per term. Tuition and fees vary according to program. *Financial support:* Fellowships with full and partial tuition reimbursements, career-related internships or fieldwork, Federal Work-Study, scholarships/grants, tuition waivers (partial), and unspecified assistantships available. Financial award application deadline: 2/1; financial award applicants required to submit FAFSA. *Faculty research:* Cultural and social history of food, food service systems, recipe modification, discourses of dieting, nutrition and health. *Unit head:* Dr. Jennifer Berg, Director, 212-998-5580, Fax: 212-995-4194. *Application contact:* 212-998-5030, Fax: 212-995-4328, E-mail: steinhardt.gradadmissions@nyu.edu.

The Ohio State University, Graduate School, College of Education and Human Ecology, Department of Human Nutrition, Columbus, OH 43210. Offers food service management (MS, PhD); foods (MS, PhD); nutrition (MS, PhD). *Accreditation:* ADtA. *Faculty:* 18. *Students:* 13 full-time (12 women), 5 part-time (4 women); includes 1 minority (Asian American or Pacific Islander), 1 international. Average age 27. 17 applicants, 76% accepted, 4 enrolled. In 2006, 6 master's, 2 doctorates awarded. *Degree requirements:* For master's, thesis optional; for doctorate, thesis/dissertation. *Entrance requirements:* For master's and doctorate, GRE General Test. Additional exam requirements/recommendations for international students: Required—TOEFL (minimum score 577 paper-based; 233 computer-based). *Application deadline:* For fall admission, 8/15 priority date for domestic students, 7/1 priority date for international students; for winter admission, 12/1 priority date for domestic students, 11/1 priority date for international students; for spring admission, 3/1 priority date for domestic students, 2/1 priority date for international students. Applications are processed on a rolling basis. Application fee: $40 ($50 for international students). Electronic applications accepted. *Expenses:* Tuition, state resident: full-time $9,438. Tuition, nonresident: full-time $22,791. Tuition and fees vary according to course load, campus/location and program. *Financial support:* Fellowships, research assistantships, teaching assistantships, Federal Work-Study and institutionally sponsored loans available. Support available to part-time students. *Unit head:* Martha A. Belury, Graduate Services Committee Chair, 614-292-4485, Fax: 614-292-2531, E-mail: belury.1@osu.edu. *Application contact:* 614-292-9444, Fax: 614-292-3895, E-mail: domestic.grad@osu.edu.

The Ohio State University, Graduate School, College of Education and Human Ecology, Program in Hospitality Management, Columbus, OH 43210. Offers MS, PhD. *Students:* 6 full-time (5 women), 3 part-time (2 women); includes 1 minority (African American), 5 international. Average age 33. 17 applicants, 29% accepted, 2 enrolled. In 2006, 2 degrees awarded. *Entrance requirements:* For master's and doctorate, GRE. *Application deadline:* Applications are processed on a rolling basis. Application fee: $40 ($50 for international students). Electronic applications accepted. *Expenses:* Tuition, state resident: full-time $9,438. Tuition, nonresident: full-time $22,791. Tuition and fees vary according to course load, campus/location and program. *Unit head:* Jay Kandampully, Graduate Studies Committee Chair, 614-688-4583, Fax: 614-292-2581, E-mail: kandampully.1@osu.edu. *Application contact:* Graduate Admissions, 614-292-94444, Fax: 614-292-3895, E-mail: domestic.grad@osu.edu.

Oklahoma State University, College of Human Environmental Sciences, School of Hotel and Restaurant Administration, Stillwater, OK 74078. Offers MS, PhD. *Faculty:* 10 full-time (2 women), 2 part-time/adjunct (0 women). *Students:* 26 full-time (15 women), 31 part-time (19 women); includes 3 minority (1 African American, 2 Asian Americans or Pacific Islanders), 42 international. Average age 35. 25 applicants, 20% accepted, 0 enrolled. In 2006, 8 master's, 2 doctorates awarded. *Degree requirements:* For master's and doctorate, thesis/dissertation. *Entrance requirements:* For master's and doctorate, GMAT or GRE. Additional exam requirements/recommendations for international students: Required—TOEFL. *Application deadline:* For fall admission, 7/1 priority date for domestic students, 3/1 priority date for international students; for spring admission, 8/1 priority date for international students. Applications are processed on a rolling basis. Application fee: $40 ($75 for international students). Electronic applications accepted. *Expenses:* Tuition, state resident: part-time $146 per credit hour. Tuition, nonresident: part-time $516 per credit hour. Required fees: $44 per credit hour. Tuition and fees vary according to program. *Financial support:* In 2006–07, 9 research assistantships (averaging $8,181 per year), 8 teaching assistantships (averaging $13,030 per year) were awarded; career-related internships or fieldwork, Federal Work-Study, scholarships/grants, health care benefits, tuition waivers (partial), and unspecified assistantships also available. Support available to part-time students. Financial award application deadline: 3/1. *Faculty research:* Hotel operations and management, restaurant/food service management, hospitality education, hospitality human resources management, tourism. *Unit head:* Dr. Bill Ryan, Interim Head, 405-744-6713.

Penn State University Park, Graduate School, College of Health and Human Development, School of Hospitality Management, Program in Hotel, Restaurant, and Institutional Management, State College, University Park, PA 16802-1503. Offers MHRIM, MS, PhD.

See Close-Up on page 1813.

Purdue University, Graduate School, College of Consumer and Family Sciences, Department of Hospitality and Tourism Management, West Lafayette, IN 47907. Offers MS, PhD. *Faculty:* 13 full-time (4 women), 2 part-time/adjunct (0 women). *Students:* 27 full-time (17 women), 9 part-time (7 women); includes 2 minority (1 African American, 1 Hispanic American), 26 international. Average age 28. 85 applicants, 40% accepted, 11 enrolled. In 2006, 15 master's, 3 doctorates awarded. *Degree requirements:* For master's and doctorate, thesis optional. *Entrance requirements:* For master's, GMAT or GRE, minimum GPA of 3.0; for doctorate, GMAT or GRE. Additional exam requirements/recommendations for international students: Required—TOEFL. *Application deadline:* For fall admission, 1/20 for domestic and international students; for spring admission, 9/20 for domestic and international students. Applications are processed on a rolling basis. Application fee: $55. Electronic applications accepted. *Financial support:* In 2006–07, 4 research assistantships, 14 teaching assistantships were awarded; career-related internships or fieldwork also available. Support available to part-time students. Financial award applicants required to submit FAFSA. *Faculty research:* Human resources, marketing, hotel and restaurant operations, food product and equipment development, tourism development. *Unit head:* Dr. Ray R. Kavanaugh, Head, 765-494-4643. *Application contact:* Dr. Janet S Bray, Graduate Director, 765-494-4984, Fax: 765-494-0327, E-mail: brayj@cgs.purdue.edu.

Rochester Institute of Technology, Graduate Enrollment Services, College of Applied Science and Technology, Department of Hospitality and Service Management, Program in Hospitality-Tourism Management, Rochester, NY 14623-5603. Offers MS. *Students:* 6 full-time (1 woman), 2 part-time (1 woman); includes 2 minority (1 African American, 1 Asian American or Pacific Islander), 4 international. 17 applicants, 88% accepted, 3 enrolled. In 2006, 1 degree awarded. *Entrance requirements:* For master's, minimum GPA of 3.0. *Application deadline:* For fall admission, 3/1 priority date for domestic students. Applications are processed on a rolling basis. Application fee: $50. *Expenses:* Tuition: Full-time $28,491; part-time $800 per credit. Required fees: $201. *Unit head:* Dr. James Jacobs, Head, 585-475-6017, E-mail: jwjism@rit.edu.

Rochester Institute of Technology, Graduate Enrollment Services, College of Applied Science and Technology, Department of Hospitality and Service Management, Program in Service Management, Rochester, NY 14623-5603. Offers MS. *Students:* 7 full-time (2 women), 26 part-time (12 women); includes 3 minority (2 African Americans, 1 Hispanic American), 16 international. 18 applicants, 33% accepted, 4 enrolled. In 2006, 20 degrees awarded. *Entrance requirements:* For master's, minimum GPA of 3.0. *Application deadline:* For fall admission, 3/1 priority date for domestic students. Applications are processed on a rolling basis. Application fee: $50. *Expenses:* Tuition: Full-time $28,491; part-time $800 per credit. Required fees: $201. *Unit head:* Dr. James Jacobs, Head, 585-475-6017, E-mail: jwjism@rit.edu.

Roosevelt University, Graduate Division, Evelyn T. Stone University College, Program in Hospitality Management, Chicago, IL 60605-1394. Offers MS. *Students:* 12 full-time (11 women), 40 part-time (31 women); includes 17 minority (12 African Americans, 4 Asian Americans or Pacific Islanders, 1 Hispanic American), 7 international. Average age 29. 48 applicants, 73% accepted, 30 enrolled. In 2006, 10 degrees awarded. *Degree requirements:* For master's, thesis. *Entrance requirements:* For master's, minimum GPA of 2.75, work experience. *Application deadline:* For fall admission, 6/1 priority date for domestic students. Applications are processed on a rolling basis. Application fee: $25 ($35 for international students). *Financial support:* Application deadline: 2/15. *Unit head:* Gerald Bober, Director, 312-281-3174. *Application contact:* Joanne Canyon-Heller, Coordinator of Graduate Admission, 877-APPLY RU, Fax: 312-281-3356, E-mail: applyru@roosevelt.edu.

Schiller International University, Graduate Programs, London, Program in International Hotel and Tourism Management, London, United Kingdom. Offers MA, MBA. Part-time and evening/weekend programs available. *Faculty:* 41. *Degree requirements:* For master's, GMAT before graduation, thesis optional. *Entrance requirements:* Additional exam requirements/recommendations for international students: Required—TOEFL (minimum score 550 paper-based; 213 computer-based). *Application deadline:* For fall admission, 8/1 priority date for domestic and international students; for spring admission, 12/1 priority date for domestic and international students. Applications are processed on a rolling basis. Application fee: $60. *Expenses:* Tuition: Full-time $20,306; part-time $1,601 per course. *Financial support:* Scholarships/grants available. Support available to part-time students. Financial award application deadline: 4/30; financial award applicants required to submit FAFSA. *Unit head:* Sally Bennett, Associate Director of Admissions, 207-928-1372, Fax: 207-620-1226, E-mail: admissions@schillerlondon.ac.uk. *Application contact:* Susan Russeff, Associate Director of Admissions, 727-736-5082, Fax: 727-734-0359, E-mail: admissions@schiller.edu.

Schiller International University, MBA Programs, Florida, Program in International Hotel and Tourism Management, Largo, FL 33770. Offers MBA. *Students:* 14 full-time, 9 part-time. *Degree requirements:* For master's, thesis optional. *Entrance requirements:* Additional exam

Hospitality Management

Schiller International University (continued)

requirements/recommendations for international students: Required—TOEFL (minimum score 550 paper-based; 213 computer-based). *Application deadline:* For fall admission, 8/1 priority date for domestic and international students; for spring admission, 12/1 priority date for domestic and international students. Applications are processed on a rolling basis. Application fee: $60. *Expenses:* Tuition: Full-time $17,920; part-time $1,420 per course. *Financial support:* Available to part-time students. Application deadline: 3/30; *Unit head:* Bryan Cummins, Director of School of Tourism and Hospitality Management, 727-736-5082 Ext. 251, Fax: 727-734-0359, E-mail: bryan_cummins@schiller.edu. *Application contact:* Susan Russeff, Associate Director of Admissions, 727-736-5082, Fax: 727-734-0359, E-mail: admissions@schiller.edu.

South Dakota State University, Graduate School, College of Family and Consumer Sciences, Department of Nutrition, Food Sciences and Hospitality, Brookings, SD 57007. Offers MFCS. Part-time programs available. *Faculty:* 7 full-time (2 women), 2 part-time/adjunct (1 woman). *Students:* 20 applicants, 85% accepted, 17 enrolled. In 2006, 8 degrees awarded. *Degree requirements:* For master's, thesis (for some programs), oral exam, comprehensive exam (for some programs). *Entrance requirements:* Additional exam requirements/recommendations for international students: Required—TOEFL (minimum score 525 paper-based). Application fee: $35. *Financial support:* In 2006–07, 10 research assistantships with partial tuition reimbursements (averaging $15,750 per year), 2 teaching assistantships with partial tuition reimbursements (averaging $15,750 per year) were awarded; Federal Work-Study, scholarships/grants, and unspecified assistantships also available. *Faculty research:* Food chemistry, bone density, functional food, nutrition education, nutrition biochemistry. *Unit head:* Dr. C.Y. Wang, Head, 605-688-5161, Fax: 605-688-5603, E-mail: cy.wang@sdstate.edu.

Southern New Hampshire University, School of Business, Manchester, NH 03106-1045. Offers accounting (MS); business administration (MBA, Certificate), including accounting (Certificate), business administration (MBA), finance (Certificate), forensic accounting (Certificate), human resources management (Certificate), international business (Certificate), international sport management (Certificate), leadership of not for profit organizations (Certificate), marketing (Certificate), operations management (Certificate), sport management (Certificate), taxation (Certificate); finance (MS); hospitality and tourism leadership (Certificate); information technology (MS, Certificate); information technology/international business (Certificate); integrated marketing communications (Certificate); international business (MS, DBA); marketing (MS); operations and project management (MS); organizational leadership (MS); project management (Certificate); sport management (MS); MBA/Certificate. *Accreditation:* ACBSP. Part-time and evening/weekend programs available. Postbaccalaureate distance learning degree programs offered (no on-campus study). *Faculty:* 45 full-time, 75 part-time/adjunct. *Students:* 427 full-time (184 women), 774 part-time (428 women). Average age 32. In 2006, 682 master's, 1 doctorate awarded. Terminal master's awarded for partial completion of doctoral program. *Degree requirements:* For master's, one foreign language, thesis or alternative, comprehensive exam (for some programs); for doctorate, one foreign language, thesis/dissertation, comprehensive exam. *Entrance requirements:* For master's, minimum GPA of 2.5; for doctorate, GMAT. Additional exam requirements/recommendations for international students: Required—TOEFL (minimum score 500 paper-based). *Application deadline:* Applications are processed on a rolling basis. Application fee: $25. Electronic applications accepted. *Financial support:* Career-related internships or fieldwork, Federal Work-Study, institutionally sponsored loans, tuition waivers (partial), and unspecified assistantships available. Support available to part-time students. Financial award applicants required to submit FAFSA. *Unit head:* Dr. Martin Bradley, Dean, 603-644-3102, Fax: 603-644-3144, E-mail: m.bradley@snhu.edu. *Application contact:* Scott Durand, Director of Graduate Enrollment Services, 603-644-3102 Ext. 3338, Fax: 603-644-3144, E-mail: s.durand@snhu.edu.

See Close-Up on page 325.

Temple University, Graduate School, School of Tourism and Hospitality Management, Program in Tourism and Hospitality Management, Philadelphia, PA 19122-6096. Offers MTHM. Part-time and evening/weekend programs available. *Faculty:* 3 full-time (0 women). *Students:* 12 full-time (8 women), 13 part-time (10 women); includes 2 minority (1 African American, 1 Asian American or Pacific Islander), 4 international. 55 applicants, 58% accepted, 12 enrolled. In 2006, 7 degrees awarded. *Entrance requirements:* For master's, GRE General Test or MAT, minimum of 2 years professional experience, minimum undergraduate GPA of 3.0. Additional exam requirements/recommendations for international students: Required—TOEFL (minimum score 550 paper-based; 213 computer-based; 79 iBT). *Application deadline:* For fall admission, 4/1 priority date for domestic students, 12/15 for international students; for spring admission, 9/30 priority date for domestic students, 8/1 for international students. Application fee: $50. Electronic applications accepted. *Expenses:* Tuition, state resident: full-time $12,264; part-time $511 per credit. Tuition, nonresident: full-time $17,904; part-time $746 per credit. Required fees: $84 per course. Tuition and fees vary according to program. *Financial support:* Teaching assistantships available. Financial award application deadline: 1/15; financial award applicants required to submit FAFSA. *Unit head:* Dr. Wesley Roehl, Director, 215-204-5861, E-mail: wroehl@temple.edu.

See Close-Up on page 507.

Texas Tech University, Graduate School, College of Human Sciences, Department of Nutrition, Hospitality, and Retailing, Program in Restaurant, Hotel, and Institutional Management, Lubbock, TX 79409. Offers hospitality administration (PhD); restaurant, hotel and institutional management (MS). Part-time programs available. Postbaccalaureate distance learning degree programs offered (minimal on-campus study). *Students:* 20 full-time (12 women), 4 part-time (1 woman); includes 3 minority (1 African American, 1 Asian American or Pacific Islander, 1 Hispanic American), 12 international. Average age 28. 21 applicants, 57% accepted, 8 enrolled. In 2006, 14 degrees awarded. *Degree requirements:* For master's, thesis optional; for doctorate, thesis/dissertation. *Entrance requirements:* For master's, GRE General Test; for doctorate, GRE. Additional exam requirements/recommendations for international students: Required—TOEFL (minimum score 550 paper-based; 213 computer-based). *Application deadline:* For fall admission, 3/1 priority date for international students; for spring admission, 11/1 priority date for international students. Applications are processed on a rolling basis. Application fee: $50 ($60 for international students). Electronic applications accepted. *Expenses:* Tuition, state resident: full-time $4,440. Tuition, nonresident: full-time $11,040. Required fees: $2,136. *Financial support:* Research assistantships with partial tuition reimbursements, teaching assistantships with partial tuition reimbursements, career-related internships or fieldwork, Federal Work-Study, institutionally sponsored loans, and scholarships/grants available. Support available to part-time students. Financial award application deadline: 4/15; financial award applicants required to submit FAFSA. *Faculty research:* Community engagement and food supply development and security, tourism, lodging and human resource management, rural tourism. *Unit head:* Dr. Lynn Huffman, Chairperson, 806-742-3068 Ext. 223, Fax: 806-742-3042, E-mail: lynn.huffman@ttu.edu. *Application contact:* Dr. Betty Stout, Graduate Advisor, Doctoral Program, 806-742-3068, Fax: 806-742-3042, E-mail: betty.stout@ttu.edu.

Texas Woman's University, Graduate School, College of Health Sciences, Department of Nutrition and Food Sciences, Denton, TX 76201. Offers exercise and sports nutrition (MS); food science (MS); institutional administration (MS); nutrition (MS, PhD). Part-time and evening/weekend programs available. *Students:* 69 full-time (62 women), 91 part-time (86 women); includes 37 minority (9 African Americans, 10 Asian Americans or Pacific Islanders, 18 Hispanic Americans), 28 international. Average age 29. In 2006, 29 degrees awarded. *Degree requirements:* For master's, comprehensive exam; for doctorate, thesis/dissertation, qualifying exam, comprehensive exam. *Entrance requirements:* For master's, GRE General Test, minimum GPA of 3.25, resumé; for doctorate, GRE General Test, minimum GPA of 3.5, 2 letters of reference. Additional exam requirements/recommendations for international students: Required—TOEFL (minimum score 550 paper-based; 213 computer-based; 79 iBT). *Application deadline:* For fall admission, 4/1 for international students; for spring admission, 8/1 for international students. Applications are processed on a rolling basis. Application fee: $30 ($50 for international students). Electronic applications accepted. *Expenses:* Tuition, area resident: Part-time $168 per unit. Tuition, state resident: full-time $4,369. Tuition, nonresident: full-time $9,373; part-time $443 per unit. Required fees: $20 per unit. $177 per term. *Financial support:* In 2006–07, 28 research assistantships (averaging $10,494 per year), 2 teaching assistantships (averaging $10,494 per year) were awarded; career-related internships or fieldwork, Federal Work-Study, institutionally sponsored loans, scholarships/grants, traineeships, health care benefits, and unspecified assistantships also available. Support available to part-time students. Financial award application deadline: 3/1; financial award applicants required to submit FAFSA. *Faculty research:* Food science, food safety, clinical nutrition, nutrition and cancer, weight management. *Unit head:* Dr. Chandan Prasad, Chair, 940-898-2636, Fax: 940-898-2634, E-mail: cprasad@mail.twu.edu. *Application contact:* Samuel Wheeler, Coordinator of Graduate Admissions, 940-898-3188, Fax: 940-898-3081, E-mail: wheelersr@twu.edu.

The University of Alabama, Graduate School, College of Human Environmental Sciences, Department of Human Nutrition and Hospitality Management, Tuscaloosa, AL 35487. Offers MSHES. Part-time programs available. Postbaccalaureate distance learning degree programs offered (no on-campus study). *Faculty:* 4 full-time (2 women), 1 (woman) part-time/adjunct. *Students:* 16 full-time (15 women), 39 part-time (38 women); includes 8 minority (4 African Americans, 2 Asian Americans or Pacific Islanders, 2 Hispanic Americans), 4 international. Average age 30. 27 applicants, 85% accepted, 18 enrolled. In 2006, 22 master's awarded. *Median time to degree:* Master's–1.6 years full-time, 2.4 years part-time. *Degree requirements:* For master's, thesis optional. *Entrance requirements:* For master's, minimum GPA of 3.0. Additional exam requirements/recommendations for international students: Required—TOEFL. *Application deadline:* For fall admission, 7/6 for domestic students. Applications are processed on a rolling basis. Application fee: $25. Electronic applications accepted. *Financial support:* In 2006–07, 4 students received support, including 2 research assistantships (averaging $8,100 per year), 2 teaching assistantships (averaging $8,100 per year); career-related internships or fieldwork also available. Financial award application deadline: 3/15. *Faculty research:* Fat determination of low-fat foods, maternal and child nutrition, obesity and eating disorders, community nutrition interventions. *Unit head:* Dr. Olivia W. Kendrick, Chair and Associate Professor, 205-348-6150, Fax: 205-348-3789, E-mail: okendric@ches.ua.edu.

University of Central Florida, Rosen College of Hospitality Management, Orlando, FL 32816. Offers hospitality and tourism management (MS). *Students:* 38 full-time (22 women), 38 part-time (31 women); includes 15 minority (5 African Americans, 3 Asian Americans or Pacific Islanders, 7 Hispanic Americans), 10 international. Average age 27. In 2006, 20 degrees awarded. *Degree requirements:* For master's, thesis or alternative. *Entrance requirements:* For master's, GMAT or GRE, minimum GPA of 3.0 in last 60 hours. Additional exam requirements/recommendations for international students: Required—TOEFL. *Application deadline:* For fall admission, 2/1 for domestic students. Application fee: $30. Electronic applications accepted. *Expenses:* Tuition, state resident: full-time $6,167; part-time $257 per credit hour. Tuition, nonresident: full-time $22,790; part-time $950 per credit hour. *Financial support:* In 2006–07, 1 fellowship with partial tuition reimbursement (averaging $5,000 per year), 19 research assistantships with partial tuition reimbursements (averaging $4,600 per year) were awarded. *Unit head:* Dr. Abraham C. Pizam, Dean, 407-903-8010, E-mail: apizam@mail.ucf.edu. *Application contact:* Dr. Paul Rompf, Coordinator, 407-903-8027, E-mail: prompf@mail.ucf.edu.

University of Delaware, College of Human Services, Education and Public Policy, Program in Hospitality Information Management, Newark, DE 19716. Offers MS. *Entrance requirements:* Additional exam requirements/recommendations for international students: Required—TOEFL (minimum score 550 paper-based; 213 computer-based). Electronic applications accepted. *Faculty research:* Foodservice, lodging and tourism management.

University of Guelph, Graduate Program Services, College of Management and Economics, Faculty of Management, Guelph, ON N1G 2W1, Canada. Offers business administration (MBA), including agribusiness management, hospitality and tourism management; leadership (MA). Part-time and evening/weekend programs available. Postbaccalaureate distance learning degree programs offered. *Entrance requirements:* For master's, minimum B average, minimum 3 years managerial experience. Additional exam requirements/recommendations for international students: Required—TOEFL (minimum score 550 paper-based; 213 computer-based). Electronic applications accepted. *Faculty research:* Marketing, operations management, business policy, financial management, organizational behavior.

University of Guelph, Graduate Program Services, College of Management and Economics, MBA Program, Guelph, ON N1G 2W1, Canada. Offers agribusiness management (MBA); hospitality and tourism management (MBA). Part-time and evening/weekend programs available. Postbaccalaureate distance learning degree programs offered (minimal on-campus study). *Faculty:* 37 full-time (10 women), 7 part-time/adjunct (0 women). *Students:* 79 full-time (32 women); includes 14 minority (2 African Americans, 12 Asian Americans or Pacific Islanders). Average age 34. 102 applicants, 65% accepted, 51 enrolled. In 2006, 23 degrees awarded. *Entrance requirements:* For master's, minimum B average, minimum of 3 years of managerial experience. Additional exam requirements/recommendations for international students: Required—TOEFL (minimum score 550 paper-based; 213 computer-based). *Application deadline:* For spring admission, 4/30 priority date for domestic and international students. Applications are processed on a rolling basis. Application fee: $150. Electronic applications accepted. *Financial support:* In 2006–07, 24 students received support, including 12 teaching assistantships (averaging $5,100 per year); scholarships/grants also available. *Faculty research:* Marketing, operations management, business policy, financial management, organizational behavior. *Unit head:* Prof. Geoff Smith, Assistant Dean, Executive Programs, 519-824-4120 Ext. 58855, Fax: 519-8838-0661, E-mail: gwsmith@uoguelph.ca. *Application contact:* Patti Lago, Manager, Graduate Programs (FOM), 519-824-4120 Ext. 56617, Fax: 519-836-0661, E-mail: plago@uoguelph.ca.

University of Houston, Conrad N. Hilton College of Hotel and Restaurant Management, Houston, TX 77204. Offers MHM, MS. Part-time and evening/weekend programs available. Postbaccalaureate distance learning degree programs offered (minimal on-campus study). *Faculty:* 11 full-time (4 women), 9 part-time/adjunct (2 women). *Students:* 38 full-time (28 women), 22 part-time (15 women); includes 12 minority (2 African Americans, 1 American Indian/Alaska Native, 6 Asian Americans or Pacific Islanders, 3 Hispanic Americans), 29 international. Average age 27. 34 applicants, 71% accepted, 12 enrolled. In 2006, 30 degrees awarded. *Degree requirements:* For master's, thesis, practical experience. *Entrance requirements:* For master's, GMAT or GRE General Test, resumé. Additional exam requirements/recommendations for international students: Required—TOEFL. *Application deadline:* For fall admission, 5/1 for domestic students; for spring admission, 10/1 for domestic students. Applications are processed on a rolling basis. Application fee: $25 ($75 for international students). Electronic applications accepted. *Expenses:* Tuition, state resident: full-time $5,429; part-time $226 per credit. Tuition, nonresident: full-time $12,029; part-time $501 per credit. Required fees: $2,454. *Financial support:* In 2006–07, 9 fellowships with full tuition reimbursements (averaging $9,200 per year), 1 research assistantship with full tuition reimbursement (averaging $9,200 per year), 10 teaching assistantships with full tuition reimbursements (averaging $9,200 per year) were awarded; career-related internships or fieldwork, Federal Work-Study, institutionally sponsored loans, scholarships/grants, health care benefits, and unspecified assistantships also available. Support available to part-time students. Financial award application deadline: 3/10. *Faculty research:* Catering, tourism, hospitality marketing, security and risk management, purchasing and financial information usage. *Unit head:* John Bowen, Dean, 713-743-0209, Fax: 713-743-2482, E-mail: jbowen@uh.edu. *Application contact:* Lilian Sutawan-Binns, Program Manager, 713-743-2457, Fax: 713-743-2591, E-mail: lbinns@uh.edu.

University of Kentucky, Graduate School, College of Agriculture, Program in Hospitality and Dietetic Administration, Lexington, KY 40506-0032. Offers MS. *Faculty:* 9 full-time (7 women). *Students:* 14 full-time (11 women), 2 part-time (both women); includes 2 minority (1 African American, 1 Hispanic American), 4 international. Average age 31. 10 applicants, 60% accepted,

5 enrolled. In 2006, 7 degrees awarded. *Degree requirements:* For master's, thesis optional. *Entrance requirements:* For master's, GRE General Test, minimum undergraduate GPA of 2.75. Additional exam requirements/recommendations for international students: Required—TOEFL (minimum score 550 paper-based; 213 computer-based). *Application deadline:* For fall admission, 7/17 priority date for domestic students, 2/1 priority date for international students; for spring admission, 12/13 priority date for domestic students, 6/15 priority date for international students. Application fee: $40 ($55 for international students). Electronic applications accepted. *Expenses:* Tuition, state resident: full-time $7,670; part-time $401 per credit hour. Tuition, nonresident: full-time $16,158; part-time $873 per credit hour. *Financial support:* In 2006–07, 1 fellowship with full tuition reimbursement (averaging $2,601 per year), 2 research assistantships with full tuition reimbursements (averaging $6,502 per year), 10 teaching assistantships with full tuition reimbursements (averaging $2,601 per year) were awarded; Federal Work-Study, scholarships/grants, traineeships, health care benefits, tuition waivers (partial), and unspecified assistantships also available. Support available to part-time students. Financial award application deadline: 3/15. *Unit head:* Dr. Lisa Gaetke, Director of Graduate Studies, 859-257-3829, Fax: 859-257-3707, E-mail: lisa.gaetke@uky.edu. *Application contact:* Dr. Brian Jackson, Senior Associate Dean, 859-257-4667, Fax: 859-257-4676, E-mail: brian.jackson@uky.edu.

University of Massachusetts Amherst, Graduate School, Isenberg School of Management, Department of Hospitality and Tourism Management, Amherst, MA 01003. Offers MS, MS/MBA. Part-time programs available. *Faculty:* 11 full-time (3 women). *Students:* 20 full-time (11 women), 5 part-time (1 woman); includes 2 minority (both Asian Americans or Pacific Islanders), 17 international. Average age 29. 30 applicants, 73% accepted, 7 enrolled. In 2006, 8 degrees awarded. *Degree requirements:* For master's, thesis optional. *Entrance requirements:* For master's, GMAT. Additional exam requirements/recommendations for international students: Required—TOEFL (minimum score 530 paper-based; 197 computer-based). *Application deadline:* For fall admission, 2/1 priority date for domestic and international students; for spring admission, 10/1 for domestic and international students. Applications are processed on a rolling basis. Application fee: $40 ($65 for international students). Electronic applications accepted. *Expenses:* Tuition, state resident: full-time $2,640; part-time $110 per credit. Tuition, nonresident: full-time $9,936; part-time $414 per credit. Required fees: $8,969; $3,129 per term. One-time fee: $257 full-time. Tuition and fees vary according to class time, course load, campus/location and reciprocity agreements. *Financial support:* In 2006–07, 16 teaching assistantships with full tuition reimbursements (averaging $5,970 per year) were awarded; fellowships with full tuition reimbursements, research assistantships with full tuition reimbursements, career-related internships or fieldwork, Federal Work-Study, scholarships/grants, traineeships, and unspecified assistantships also available. Support available to part-time students. Financial award application deadline: 2/1. *Unit head:* Dr. Rodney Warnick, Director, 413-645-1389, Fax: 413-545-1235, E-mail: warnick@ht.umass.edu.

University of Missouri–Columbia, Graduate School, College of Agriculture, Food and Natural Resources, Department of Food and Hospitality Systems, Columbia, MO 65211. Offers food science (MS, PhD); foods and food systems management (MS); human nutrition (MS). *Faculty:* 12 full-time (5 women). *Students:* 19 full-time (12 women), 11 part-time (3 women); includes 1 minority (Asian American or Pacific Islander), 22 international. In 2006, 5 master's, 1 doctorate awarded. Terminal master's awarded for partial completion of doctoral program. *Degree requirements:* For doctorate, thesis/dissertation. *Entrance requirements:* For master's and doctorate, GRE General Test, minimum GPA of 3.0. Additional exam requirements/recommendations for international students: Required—TOEFL (minimum score 550 paper-based; 213 computer-based). *Application deadline:* For fall admission, 4/1 priority date for domestic students. Applications are processed on a rolling basis. Application fee: $45 ($60 for international students). *Financial support:* Research assistantships, teaching assistantships, institutionally sponsored loans available. *Unit head:* Dr. Andrew D. Clarke, Director of Graduate Studies, 573-882-2610, E-mail: clarkea@missouri.edu.

University of Nevada, Las Vegas, Graduate College, William F. Harrah College of Hotel Administration, Program in Hotel Administration, Las Vegas, NV 89154-9900. Offers hospitality administration (MHA, PhD); hotel administration (MS). Part-time programs available. Postbaccalaureate distance learning degree programs offered. *Faculty:* 38 full-time (11 women), 11 part-time/adjunct (4 women). *Students:* 38 full-time (20 women), 45 part-time (22 women); includes 16 minority (3 African Americans, 8 American Indian/Alaska Native, 4 Asian Americans or Pacific Islanders, 1 Hispanic American), 19 international. 124 applicants, 30% accepted, 28 enrolled. In 2006, 56 master's, 7 doctorates awarded. *Degree requirements:* For master's, thesis (for some programs), professional paper, comprehensive exam; for doctorate, thesis/dissertation, dissertation defense, seminar, comprehensive exam. *Entrance requirements:* For master's, GMAT or GRE General Test, minimum GPA of 2.75 overall or 3.0 in last 2 years of course work, 1 year of work experience, resumé; for doctorate, GMAT, minimum graduate GPA of 3.0, resumé. Additional exam requirements/recommendations for international students: Required—TOEFL (minimum score 550 paper-based; 213 computer-based; 80 iBT). *Application deadline:* For fall admission, 6/15 for domestic students, 5/1 for international students; for spring admission, 10/1 for domestic and international students. Application fee: $60 ($75 for international students). Electronic applications accepted. *Financial support:* In 2006–07, 15 research assistantships with partial tuition reimbursements (averaging $11,500 per year), 2 teaching assistantships (averaging $11,000 per year) were awarded. Financial award application deadline: 3/1. *Unit head:* Gail Sammons, Chair, 702-895-3230, Fax: 702-895-4870. *Application contact:* Graduate College Admissions Evaluator, 702-895-3320, Fax: 702-895-4180, E-mail: gradcollege@unlv.edu.

University of New Haven, Graduate School, College of Arts and Sciences, School of Hotel, Restaurant, Tourism and Dietetics Administration, Program in Executive Tourism and Hospitality, West Haven, CT 06516-1916. Offers MS.

University of New Haven, Graduate School, College of Arts and Sciences, School of Hotel, Restaurant, Tourism and Dietetics Administration, Program in Tourism and Hospitality Management, West Haven, CT 06516-1916. Offers MS.

University of New Orleans, Graduate School, College of Business Administration, School of Hotel, Restaurant, and Tourism Administration, Program in Hospitality and Tourism Management, New Orleans, LA 70148. Offers MS. *Students:* 26 full-time (19 women), 14 part-time (11 women); includes 8 minority (5 African Americans, 3 Hispanic Americans), 5 international. Average age 28. 36 applicants, 94% accepted, 20 enrolled. *Entrance requirements:* Additional exam requirements/recommendations for international students: Required—TOEFL (minimum score 550 paper-based; 213 computer-based). *Application deadline:* For fall admission, 7/1 priority date for domestic students, 6/1 for international students; for spring admission, 11/15 priority date for domestic students, 10/1 for international students. Application fee: $20. *Financial support:* Application deadline: 5/15. *Unit head:* Dr. Harsha Chacko, Graduate Coordinator, 504-280-6821, Fax: 504-280-3189, E-mail: hrt@uno.edu. *Application contact:* Dr. George Fenich, 504-280-6957, Fax: 504-280-6693, E-mail: george.fenich@uno.edu.

University of North Texas, Robert B. Toulouse School of Graduate Studies, School of Merchandising and Hospitality Management, Denton, TX 76203. Offers hotel/restaurant management (MS); merchandising and fabric analytics (MS). Part-time programs available. *Faculty:* 19 full-time (14 women). *Students:* 24 full-time (19 women), 10 part-time (7 women); includes 16 minority (8 African Americans, 1 American Indian/Alaska Native, 4 Asian Americans or Pacific Islanders, 3 Hispanic Americans), 9 international. Average age 26. 43 applicants, 47% accepted, 12 enrolled. In 2006, 6 degrees awarded. *Degree requirements:* For master's, thesis or alternative, comprehensive exam. *Entrance requirements:* For master's, GRE General Test, minimum GPA of 2.8, course work in major area. Additional exam requirements/recommendations for international students: Recommended—TOEFL (minimum score 550 paper-based; 213 computer-based). *Application deadline:* For fall admission, 7/15 for domestic students. Application fee: $50 ($75 for international students). *Expenses:* Tuition, state resident: full-time $3,573; part-time $198 per credit. Tuition, nonresident: full-time $8,577; part-time $476 per credit. Required fees: $1,258; $126 per credit. One-time fee: $150 full-time. Tuition and fees vary according to course load. *Financial support:* Fellowships, research assistantships, teaching assistantships, career-related internships or fieldwork, Federal Work-Study, and institutionally sponsored loans available. Financial award application deadline: 4/1. *Faculty research:* Employee imaging, western wear, diversity in the workplace, leadership development, quality assessment. *Unit head:* Dr. Judith C. Forney, Dean, 940-565-2436, Fax: 940-565-4348, E-mail: forney@smhm.cmm.unt.edu. *Application contact:* Lynne Hale, Graduate Adviser, 940-565-3518, Fax: 940-565-4348, E-mail: lhale@unt.edu.

University of South Carolina, The Graduate School, College of Hospitality, Retail, and Sport Management, School of Hotel, Restaurant and Tourism Management, Columbia, SC 29208. Offers MHRTM. *Entrance requirements:* For master's, GMAT or GRE General Test, minimum GPA of 3.0, 2 letters of recommendation. Electronic applications accepted. *Faculty research:* Corporate strategy and management practices, sustainable tourism, club management, tourism technology, revenue management.

The University of Tennessee, Graduate School, College of Education, Health and Human Sciences, Department of Consumer and Industry Services Management, Program in Hotel, Restaurant, and Tourism Management, Knoxville, TN 37996. Offers hospitality management (MS); tourism (MS). Part-time programs available. *Students:* 32. Average age 24. 34 applicants, 53% accepted. *Degree requirements:* For master's, thesis or alternative. *Entrance requirements:* For master's, GRE General Test, minimum GPA of 2.7. Additional exam requirements/recommendations for international students: Required—TOEFL. *Application deadline:* For fall admission, 2/1 priority date for domestic students. Applications are processed on a rolling basis. Application fee: $35. Electronic applications accepted. *Expenses:* Tuition, state resident: full-time $5,574. Tuition, nonresident: full-time $16,840. Required fees: $792. *Financial support:* Career-related internships or fieldwork available. Financial award application deadline: 2/1; financial award applicants required to submit FAFSA. *Unit head:* Dr. Gene Hayes, Graduate Representative, 865-974-1288, E-mail: ghayes1@utk.edu.

Virginia Polytechnic Institute and State University, Graduate School, Pamplin College of Business, Department of Hospitality and Tourism Management, Blacksburg, VA 24061. Offers MS, PhD. *Faculty:* 11 full-time (3 women), 1 part-time/adjunct (0 women). *Students:* 24 full-time (12 women), 4 part-time (2 women); includes 1 minority (Asian American or Pacific Islander), 21 international. Average age 32. 38 applicants, 71% accepted, 9 enrolled. In 2006, 2 master's, 3 doctorates awarded. *Entrance requirements:* For master's and doctorate, GRE, GMAT. Additional exam requirements/recommendations for international students: Required—TOEFL (minimum score 600 paper-based; 250 computer-based). *Application deadline:* For fall admission, 5/15 for international students; for spring admission, 10/15 for international students. Applications are processed on a rolling basis. Application fee: $45. Electronic applications accepted. *Expenses:* Tuition, state resident: full-time $7,017; part-time $390 per credit hour. Tuition, nonresident: full-time $12,414; part-time $690 per credit hour. International tuition: $11,296 full-time. Required fees: $1,523; $256 per term. *Financial support:* In 2006–07, 10 teaching assistantships with full tuition reimbursements (averaging $9,606 per year) were awarded; career-related internships or fieldwork, Federal Work-Study, scholarships/grants, and unspecified assistantships also available. Financial award application deadline: 4/1. *Faculty research:* Human resource management, service management, marketing, strategy and finance tourist behavior. *Unit head:* Dr. Rick R. Perdue, Head, 540-231-3287, Fax: 540-231-8383, E-mail: perduerr@vt.edu. *Application contact:* Beth Weaver, Information Contact, 540-231-8429, Fax: 540-231-8313, E-mail: beweaver@vt.edu.

Travel and Tourism

Boston University, Metropolitan College (Continuing Education), Program in Administrative Studies, Boston, MA 02215. Offers banking and financial management (MSM); business continuity in emergency management (MSM); economics development and tourism management (MSAS); electronic commerce, systems, and technology (MSAS); financial economics (MSAS); human resource management (MSM); innovation and technology (MSAS); insurance management (MSM); international market management (MSM); multinational commerce (MSAS); project management (MSM). *Accreditation:* AACSB. Part-time and evening/weekend programs available. *Faculty:* 9 full-time (0 women), 51 part-time/adjunct (8 women). *Students:* 105 full-time (40 women), 171 part-time (65 women); includes 27 minority (5 African Americans, 18 Asian Americans or Pacific Islanders, 4 Hispanic Americans), 125 international. Average age 29. In 2006, 310 degrees awarded. *Degree requirements:* For master's, thesis optional. *Entrance requirements:* For master's, 1 year of work experience, minimum GPA of 3.0. Additional exam requirements/recommendations for international students: Required—TOEFL (minimum score 560 paper-based; 220 computer-based). *Application deadline:* Applications are processed on a rolling basis. Application fee: $65. *Expenses:* Tuition: Full-time $33,330; part-time $1,042 per credit. Required fees: $462; $40. *Financial support:* In 2006–07, 15 students received support, including research assistantships (averaging $10,000 per year); career-related internships or fieldwork and Federal Work-Study also available. *Faculty research:* International business, innovative process. *Unit head:* Dr. Kip Becker, Chairman, 617-353-3016, E-mail: adminsc@bu.edu. *Application contact:* Lucille Dicker, Administrative Sciences Department, 617-353-3016, E-mail: adminsc@bu.edu.

Clemson University, Graduate School, College of Health, Education, and Human Development, Department of Parks, Recreation, and Tourism Management, Clemson, SC 29634. Offers MPRTM, MS, PhD. Part-time programs available. *Faculty:* 20 full-time (7 women). *Students:* 44 full-time (26 women), 16 part-time (10 women); includes 1 minority (Hispanic American), 13 international. Average age 25. 60 applicants, 62% accepted, 20 enrolled. In 2006, 5 master's, 6 doctorates awarded. *Degree requirements:* For master's, thesis (for some programs); for doctorate, thesis/dissertation. *Entrance requirements:* For master's, GRE General Test, minimum undergraduate GPA of 3.0; for doctorate, GRE General Test, minimum graduate GPA of 3.0. Additional exam requirements/recommendations for international students: Required—TOEFL. *Application deadline:* For fall admission, 5/1 priority date for domestic students; for spring admission, 10/1 for domestic students. Application fee: $50. *Expenses:* Tuition, state resident: full-time $8,812; part-time $450 per hour. Tuition, nonresident: full-time $18,036; part-time $760 per hour. Required fees: $474; $5 per term. *Financial support:* Fellowships, research assistantships, teaching assistantships, career-related internships or fieldwork, tuition waivers (partial), and unspecified assistantships available. Financial award application deadline: 4/15; financial award applicants required to submit FAFSA. *Faculty research:* Recreation resource management, leisure behavior, therapeutic recreation, community leisure services. *Unit head:* Dr. Brett A Wright, Chair, 864-656-3036, Fax: 864-656-

Travel and Tourism

Clemson University (continued)

2226, E-mail: wright@clemson.edu. *Application contact:* Dr. Fran McGuire, Graduate Coordinator, 864-656-2183, Fax: 864-656-2226, E-mail: lefty@clemson.edu.

See Close-Ups on pages 2279 and 2281.

East Stroudsburg University of Pennsylvania, Graduate School, School of Professional Studies, Department of Hotel, Restaurant and Tourism Management, East Stroudsburg, PA 18301-2999. Offers management and leadership (MS). *Faculty:* 2 full-time (1 woman). *Students:* 1 (woman) full-time, 4 part-time (1 woman), 2 international. Average age 28. In 2006, 1 degree awarded. *Degree requirements:* For master's, comprehensive exam. *Entrance requirements:* For master's, GRE or GMAT, 3 letters of recommendation. Additional exam requirements/recommendations for international students: Required—TOEFL (minimum score 560 paper-based; 220 computer-based; 83 iBT). *Application deadline:* For fall admission, 7/31 priority date for domestic students, 5/1 priority date for international students; for spring admission, 11/30 for domestic students, 10/1 for international students. Applications are processed on a rolling basis. Application fee: $50. *Expenses:* Tuition, state resident: full-time $6,048; part-time $336 per credit. Tuition, nonresident: full-time $9,678; part-time $538 per credit. Required fees: $1,353; $67 per credit. One-time fee: $37 part-time. *Financial support:* In 2006–07, 1 research assistantship was awarded; Federal Work-Study and unspecified assistantships also available. Financial award application deadline: 3/1; financial award applicants required to submit FAFSA. *Unit head:* Dr. Al Moranville, Unit Head, 570-422-3049.

The George Washington University, School of Business, Department of Tourism and Hospitality Management, Washington, DC 20052. Offers event management (MTA, Professional Certificate); sport management (MTA); tourism administration (MTA); tourism and hospitality management (MBA); tourism destination management (Professional Certificate). Part-time programs available. *Degree requirements:* For master's, thesis, comprehensive exam. *Entrance requirements:* For master's, GRE General Test. Additional exam requirements/recommendations for international students: Required—TOEFL. *Faculty research:* Tourism policy, tourism impact forecasting, geotourism.

Indiana University–Purdue University Indianapolis, School of Physical Education and Tourism Management, Indianapolis, IN 46202-2896. Offers MS. *Faculty:* 4 full-time (2 women). *Students:* 8 full-time (6 women), 8 part-time (3 women); includes 3 minority (1 African American, 2 Asian Americans or Pacific Islanders), 1 international. Average age 30. In 2006, 5 degrees awarded. *Expenses:* Tuition, state resident: full-time $5,437; part-time $227 per credit hour. Tuition, nonresident: full-time $15,694; part-time $654 per credit hour. Required fees: $620. Tuition and fees vary according to course load, campus/location and program. *Financial support:* Career-related internships or fieldwork, Federal Work-Study, institutionally sponsored loans, and scholarships/grants available. Support available to part-time students. *Unit head:* P. Nicholas Kellum, Dean, 317-274-0606, Fax: 317-278-2041, E-mail: pkellum@iupui.edu.

New York University, School of Continuing and Professional Studies, Tisch Center for Hospitality, Tourism and Sports Management, Program in Tourism and Travel Management, New York, NY 10012-1019. Offers MS, Advanced Certificate. Part-time and evening/weekend programs available. Postbaccalaureate distance learning degree programs offered (minimal on-campus study). *Faculty:* 7 full-time (4 women), 14 part-time/adjunct (5 women). *Students:* 16 full-time (12 women), 15 part-time (11 women); includes 10 minority (4 African Americans, 2 Asian Americans or Pacific Islanders, 4 Hispanic Americans), 6 international. Average age 28. 26 applicants, 62% accepted, 7 enrolled. In 2006, 6 master's, 2 other advanced degrees awarded. *Entrance requirements:* For master's, GMAT or GRE General Test, 1 year of work experience. Additional exam requirements/recommendations for international students: Required—TOEFL (minimum score 600 paper-based; 250 computer-based; 100 iBT), TWE. *Application deadline:* For fall admission, 3/15 priority date for domestic and international students; for spring admission, 10/15 priority date for domestic students, 8/15 priority date for international students. Applications are processed on a rolling basis. Application fee: $75. *Expenses:* Tuition: Part-time $1,080 per unit. Required fees: $56 per unit. $329 per term. Tuition and fees vary according to program. *Financial support:* In 2006–07, 31 students received support, including fellowships (averaging $3,288 per year); research assistantships, career-related internships or fieldwork, Federal Work-Study, institutionally sponsored loans, and scholarships/grants also available. Support available to part-time students. Financial award application deadline: 3/1; financial award applicants required to submit FAFSA. *Faculty research:* Tourism planning for national parks and protected areas, leadership and organizational behavior issues.

See Close-Up on page 505.

North Carolina State University, Graduate School, College of Natural Resources, Department of Parks, Recreation and Tourism Management, Raleigh, NC 27695. Offers geographic information systems (MS); maintenance management (MRRA, MS); parks, recreation and tourism management (PhD); recreation planning (MRRA, MS); recreation resources administration/public administration (MRRA); recreation/park management (MRRA, MS); sports management (MRRA, MS); travel and tourism management (MS). *Degree requirements:* For master's, thesis (for some programs); for doctorate, thesis/dissertation. *Entrance requirements:* For master's and doctorate, GRE General Test. Additional exam requirements/recommendations for international students: Required—TOEFL. Electronic applications accepted. *Faculty research:* Tourism policy and development, spatial information systems, natural resource management, recreational sports management, park and recreation management.

Old Dominion University, Darden College of Education, Program in Physical Education, Recreation and Tourism Studies Emphasis, Norfolk, VA 23529. Offers MS Ed. Part-time and evening/weekend programs available. *Faculty:* 2 full-time (0 women). *Students:* 2 full-time (0 women), 4 part-time (all women); includes 1 minority (African American) Average age 28. 10 applicants, 60% accepted, 5 enrolled. In 2006, 1 degree awarded. *Degree requirements:* For master's, thesis or alternative, internship, research project, comprehensive exam. *Entrance requirements:* For master's, GRE, minimum GPA of 2.8 overall, 3.0 in major. Additional exam requirements/recommendations for international students: Required—TOEFL (minimum score 500 paper-based; 200 computer-based). *Application deadline:* For fall admission, 7/1 for domestic students; for spring admission, 11/1 for domestic students. Applications are processed on a rolling basis. Application fee: $40. *Expenses:* Tuition, area resident: Part-time $285 per credit hour. Tuition, nonresident: part-time $715 per credit hour. Required fees: $94 per semester. *Financial support:* In 2006–07, 1 student received support, including 1 research assistantship with partial tuition reimbursement available (averaging $9,000 per year); career-related internships or fieldwork and scholarships/grants also available. Financial award application deadline: 4/15; financial award applicants required to submit FAFSA. *Faculty research:* Ethnicity and recreation, recreation programming, recreation and resiliency, tourism development, dog parks, recreation and diabetes. Total annual research expenditures: $12,000. *Unit head:* Dr. Edward Lee Hill, Graduate Program Director, 757-683-4881, Fax: 757-683-4270, E-mail: ehill@odu.edu. *Application contact:* Dr. Edward Lee Hill, Graduate Program Director, 757-683-4881, Fax: 757-683-4270, E-mail: ehill@odu.edu.

Purdue University, Graduate School, College of Consumer and Family Sciences, Department of Hospitality and Tourism Management, West Lafayette, IN 47907. Offers MS, PhD. *Faculty:* 13 full-time (4 women), 2 part-time/adjunct (0 women). *Students:* 27 full-time (17 women), 9 part-time (7 women); includes 2 minority (1 African American, 1 Hispanic American), 26 international. Average age 28. 85 applicants, 40% accepted, 11 enrolled. In 2006, 15 master's, 3 doctorates awarded. *Degree requirements:* For master's and doctorate, thesis optional. *Entrance requirements:* For master's, GMAT or GRE, minimum GPA of 3.0; for doctorate, GMAT or GRE. Additional exam requirements/recommendations for international students: Required—TOEFL. *Application deadline:* For fall admission, 1/20 for domestic and international students; for spring admission, 9/20 for domestic and international students. Applications are processed on a rolling basis. Application fee: $55. Electronic applications accepted. *Financial support:* In 2006–07, 4 research assistantships, 14 teaching assistantships were awarded; career-related internships or fieldwork also available. Support available to part-time students. Financial award applicants required to submit FAFSA. *Faculty research:* Human resources, marketing, hotel and restaurant operations, food product and equipment development, tourism development. *Unit head:* Dr. Ray R. Kavanaugh, Head, 765-494-4643. *Application contact:* Dr. Janet S Bray, Graduate Director, 765-494-4984, Fax: 765-494-0327, E-mail: brayj@cgs.purdue.edu.

Rochester Institute of Technology, Graduate Enrollment Services, College of Applied Science and Technology, Department of Hospitality and Service Management, Program in Hospitality-Tourism Management, Rochester, NY 14623-5603. Offers MS. *Students:* 6 full-time (1 woman), 2 part-time (1 woman); includes 2 minority (1 African American, 1 Asian American or Pacific Islander), 4 international. 17 applicants, 88% accepted, 3 enrolled. In 2006, 1 degree awarded. *Entrance requirements:* For master's, minimum GPA of 3.0. *Application deadline:* For fall admission, 3/1 priority date for domestic students. Applications are processed on a rolling basis. Application fee: $50. *Expenses:* Tuition: Full-time $28,491; part-time $800 per credit. Required fees: $201. *Unit head:* Dr. James Jacobs, Head, 585-475-6017, E-mail: jwjism@rit.edu.

Rochester Institute of Technology, Graduate Enrollment Services, College of Applied Science and Technology, Department of Hospitality and Service Management, Program in Service Management, Rochester, NY 14623-5603. Offers MS. *Students:* 7 full-time (2 women), 26 part-time (12 women); includes 3 minority (2 African Americans, 1 Hispanic American), 16 international. 18 applicants, 33% accepted, 4 enrolled. In 2006, 20 degrees awarded. *Entrance requirements:* For master's, minimum GPA of 3.0. *Application deadline:* For fall admission, 3/1 priority date for domestic students. Applications are processed on a rolling basis. Application fee: $50. *Expenses:* Tuition: Full-time $28,491; part-time $800 per credit. Required fees: $201. *Unit head:* Dr. James Jacobs, Head, 585-475-6017, E-mail: jwjism@rit.edu.

Saint Xavier University, Graduate Studies, Graham School of Management, Chicago, IL 60655-3105. Offers e-commerce (MBA); employee health benefits (Certificate); finance (MBA, MS); financial analysis and investments (MBA); financial planning (MBA, Certificate); financial trading and practice (MBA, Certificate); generalist/administration (MBA); health administration (MBA, MS); managed care (Certificate); management (MBA, MS); marketing (MBA); public and non-profit management (MBA); public health (MPH); service management (MBA); training and performance management (MBA); MBA/MS. *Accreditation:* ACBSP. Part-time and evening/weekend programs available. *Faculty:* 27. *Students:* 67 full-time (32 women), 291 part-time (152 women). Average age 35. In 2006, 61 degrees awarded. *Entrance requirements:* For master's, GMAT, minimum GPA of 3.0, 2 years of work experience. *Application deadline:* For fall admission, 8/15 for domestic students. Applications are processed on a rolling basis. Application fee: $35. Electronic applications accepted. *Expenses:* Contact institution. *Financial support:* Career-related internships or fieldwork available. Support available to part-time students. Financial award applicants required to submit FAFSA. *Unit head:* Dr. John Eber, Dean, 773-298-3601, Fax: 773-298-3601, E-mail: eber@sxu.edu. *Application contact:* Beth Gierach, Managing Director of Admission, 773-298-3053, Fax: 773-298-3076, E-mail: gierach@sxu.edu.

Schiller International University, Graduate Programs, London, Program in International Hotel and Tourism Management, London, United Kingdom. Offers MA, MBA. Part-time and evening/weekend programs available. *Faculty:* 41. *Degree requirements:* For master's, GMAT before graduation, thesis optional. *Entrance requirements:* Additional exam requirements/recommendations for international students: Required—TOEFL (minimum score 550 paper-based; 213 computer-based). *Application deadline:* For fall admission, 8/1 priority date for domestic and international students; for spring admission, 12/1 priority date for domestic and international students. Applications are processed on a rolling basis. Application fee: $60. *Expenses:* Tuition: Full-time $20,306; part-time $1,601 per course. *Financial support:* Scholarships/grants available. Support available to part-time students. Financial award application deadline: 4/30; financial award applicants required to submit FAFSA. *Unit head:* Sally Bennett, Associate Director of Admissions, 207-928-1372, Fax: 207-620-1226, E-mail: admissions@schillerlondon.ac.uk. *Application contact:* Susan Russeff, Associate Director of Admissions, 727-736-5082, Fax: 727-734-0359, E-mail: admissions@schiller.edu.

Schiller International University, MBA Programs, Florida, Program in International Hotel and Tourism Management, Largo, FL 33770. Offers MBA. *Students:* 14 full-time, 9 part-time. *Degree requirements:* For master's, thesis optional. *Entrance requirements:* Additional exam requirements/recommendations for international students: Required—TOEFL (minimum score 550 paper-based; 213 computer-based). *Application deadline:* For fall admission, 8/1 priority date for domestic and international students; for spring admission, 12/1 priority date for domestic and international students. Applications are processed on a rolling basis. Application fee: $60. *Expenses:* Tuition: Full-time $17,920; part-time $1,420 per course. *Financial support:* Available to part-time students. Application deadline: 3/30; *Unit head:* Bryan Cummins, Director of School of Tourism and Hospitality Management, 727-736-5082 Ext. 251, Fax: 727-734-0359, E-mail: bryan_cummins@schiller.edu. *Application contact:* Susan Russeff, Associate Director of Admissions, 727-736-5082, Fax: 727-734-0359, E-mail: admissions@schiller.edu.

Temple University, Graduate School, Fox School of Business and Management, Doctoral Programs in Business, Philadelphia, PA 19122-6096. Offers accounting (PhD); economics (PhD); finance (PhD); general and strategic management (PhD); healthcare management (PhD); human resource administration (PhD); international business administration (PhD); management information systems (PhD); management science/operations research (PhD); marketing (PhD); risk, insurance, and health-care management (PhD); statistics (PhD); tourism (PhD). *Accreditation:* AACSB. *Entrance requirements:* For doctorate, GRE General Test, minimum GPA of 3.0, master's degree. Additional exam requirements/recommendations for international students: Required—TOEFL. *Expenses:* Tuition, state resident: full-time $12,264; part-time $511 per credit. Tuition, nonresident: full-time $17,904; part-time $746 per credit. Required fees: $84 per course. Tuition and fees vary according to program.

Temple University, Graduate School, School of Tourism and Hospitality Management, Program in Tourism and Hospitality Management, Philadelphia, PA 19122-6096. Offers MTHM. Part-time and evening/weekend programs available. *Faculty:* 3 full-time (0 women). *Students:* 12 full-time (8 women), 13 part-time (10 women); includes 2 minority (1 African American, 1 Asian American or Pacific Islander), 4 international. 55 applicants, 58% accepted, 12 enrolled. In 2006, 7 degrees awarded. *Entrance requirements:* For master's, GRE General Test or MAT, minimum of 2 years professional experience, minimum undergraduate GPA of 3.0. Additional exam requirements/recommendations for international students: Required—TOEFL (minimum score 550 paper-based; 213 computer-based; 79 iBT). *Application deadline:* For fall admission, 4/1 priority date for domestic students, 12/15 for international students; for spring admission, 9/30 priority date for domestic students, 8/1 for international students. Application fee: $50. Electronic applications accepted. *Expenses:* Tuition, state resident: full-time $12,264; part-time $511 per credit. Tuition, nonresident: full-time $17,904; part-time $746 per credit. Required fees: $84 per course. Tuition and fees vary according to program. *Financial support:* Teaching assistantships available. Financial award application deadline: 1/15; financial award applicants required to submit FAFSA. *Unit head:* Dr. Wesley Roehl, Director, 215-204-5861, E-mail: wroehl@temple.edu.

See Close-Up on page 507.

Université du Québec à Trois-Rivières, Graduate Programs, Program in Leisure, Culture and Tourism Sciences, Trois-Rivières, QC G9A 5H7, Canada. Offers MA, DESS. Part-time programs available. *Degree requirements:* For master's, thesis optional. *Entrance requirements:* For master's, appropriate bachelor's degree, proficiency in French.

University of Central Florida, Rosen College of Hospitality Management, Orlando, FL 32816. Offers hospitality and tourism management (MS). *Students:* 38 full-time (22 women), 38 part-time (31 women); includes 15 minority (5 African Americans, 3 Asian Americans or Pacific

Islanders, 7 Hispanic Americans), 10 international. Average age 27. In 2006, 20 degrees awarded. *Degree requirements:* For master's, thesis or alternative. *Entrance requirements:* For master's, GMAT or GRE, minimum GPA of 3.0 in last 60 hours. Additional exam requirements/recommendations for international students: Required—TOEFL. *Application deadline:* For fall admission, 2/1 for domestic students. Application fee: $30. Electronic applications accepted. *Expenses:* Tuition, state resident: full-time $6,167; part-time $257 per credit hour. Tuition, nonresident: full-time $22,790; part-time $950 per credit hour. *Financial support:* In 2006–07, 1 fellowship with partial tuition reimbursement (averaging $5,000 per year), 19 research assistantships with partial tuition reimbursements (averaging $4,600 per year) were awarded. *Unit head:* Dr. Abraham C. Pizam, Dean, 407-903-8010, E-mail: apizam@mail.ucf.edu. *Application contact:* Dr. Paul Rompf, Coordinator, 407-903-8027, E-mail: prompf@mail.ucf.edu.

University of Hawaii at Manoa, Graduate Division, School of Travel Industry Management, Honolulu, HI 96822. Offers MS. Part-time programs available. *Faculty:* 13 full-time (4 women). *Students:* 15 full-time (9 women), 4 part-time (all women); includes 2 minority (both Asian Americans or Pacific Islanders), 3 international. Average age 28. 46 applicants, 43% accepted, 5 enrolled. In 2006, 14 degrees awarded. *Degree requirements:* For master's, thesis optional. *Entrance requirements:* For master's, GRE General Test, minimum GPA of 3.0. Additional exam requirements/recommendations for international students: Required—TOEFL (minimum score 560 paper-based; 220 computer-based; 83 iBT). *Application deadline:* For fall admission, 3/1 for domestic and international students; for spring admission, 9/1 for domestic and international students. Applications are processed on a rolling basis. Application fee: $50. Electronic applications accepted. *Financial support:* In 2006–07, 4 fellowships with partial tuition reimbursements were awarded; career-related internships or fieldwork, scholarships/grants, tuition waivers (full and partial), and student assistantships also available. Financial award application deadline: 3/1. *Faculty research:* Travel information technology, tourism development and policy, transportation management and policy, hospitality management, sustainable tourism development. Total annual research expenditures: $261,275. *Application contact:* Harold Richins, Graduate Chair, 808-956-9840, Fax: 808-956-5378.

University of Massachusetts Amherst, Graduate School, Isenberg School of Management, Department of Hospitality and Tourism Management, Amherst, MA 01003. Offers MS, MS/MBA. Part-time programs available. *Faculty:* 11 full-time (3 women). *Students:* 20 full-time (11 women), 5 part-time (1 woman); includes 2 minority (both Asian Americans or Pacific Islanders), 17 international. Average age 29. 30 applicants, 73% accepted, 7 enrolled. In 2006, 8 degrees awarded. *Degree requirements:* For master's, thesis optional. *Entrance requirements:* For master's, GMAT. Additional exam requirements/recommendations for international students: Required—TOEFL (minimum score 530 paper-based; 197 computer-based). *Application deadline:* For fall admission, 2/1 priority date for domestic and international students; for spring admission, 10/1 for domestic and international students. Applications are processed on a rolling basis. Application fee: $40 ($65 for international students). Electronic applications accepted. *Expenses:* Tuition, state resident: full-time $2,640; part-time $110 per credit. Tuition, nonresident: full-time $9,936; part-time $414 per credit. Required fees: $8,969; $3,129 per term. One-time fee: $257 full-time. Tuition and fees vary according to class time, course load, campus/location and reciprocity agreements. *Financial support:* In 2006–07, 16 teaching assistantships with full tuition reimbursements (averaging $5,970 per year) were awarded; fellowships with full tuition reimbursements, research assistantships with full tuition reimbursements, career-related internships or fieldwork, Federal Work-Study, scholarships/grants, traineeships, and unspecified assistantships also available. Support available to part-time students. Financial award application deadline: 2/1. *Unit head:* Dr. Rodney Warnick, Director, 413-645-1389, Fax: 413-545-1235, E-mail: warnick@ht.umass.edu.

University of New Haven, Graduate School, College of Arts and Sciences, School of Hotel, Restaurant, Tourism and Dietetics Administration, Program in Executive Tourism and Hospitality, West Haven, CT 06516-1916. Offers MS.

University of New Haven, Graduate School, College of Arts and Sciences, School of Hotel, Restaurant, Tourism and Dietetics Administration, Program in Tourism and Hospitality Management, West Haven, CT 06516-1916. Offers MS.

University of New Orleans, Graduate School, College of Business Administration, School of Hotel, Restaurant, and Tourism Administration, Program in Hospitality and Tourism Management, New Orleans, LA 70148. Offers MS. *Students:* 26 full-time (19 women), 14 part-time (11 women); includes 8 minority (5 African Americans, 3 Hispanic Americans), 5 international. Average age 28. 36 applicants, 94% accepted, 20 enrolled. *Entrance requirements:* Additional exam requirements/recommendations for international students: Required—TOEFL (minimum score 550 paper-based; 213 computer-based). *Application deadline:* For fall admission, 7/1 priority date for domestic students, 6/1 for international students; for spring admission, 11/15 priority date for domestic students, 10/1 for international students. Application fee: $20. *Financial*

support: Application deadline: 5/15. *Unit head:* Dr. Harsha Chacko, Graduate Coordinator, 504-280-6821, Fax: 504-280-3189, E-mail: hrt@uno.edu. *Application contact:* Dr. George Fenich, 504-280-6957, Fax: 504-280-6693, E-mail: george.fenich@uno.edu.

University of South Carolina, The Graduate School, College of Hospitality, Retail, and Sport Management, School of Hotel, Restaurant and Tourism Management, Columbia, SC 29208. Offers MHRTM. *Entrance requirements:* For master's, GMAT or GRE General Test, minimum GPA of 3.0, 2 letters of recommendation. Electronic applications accepted. *Faculty research:* Corporate strategy and management practices, sustainable tourism, club management, tourism technology, revenue management.

The University of Tennessee, Graduate School, College of Education, Health and Human Sciences, Department of Consumer and Industry Services Management, Program in Hotel, Restaurant, and Tourism Management, Knoxville, TN 37996. Offers hospitality management (MS); tourism (MS). Part-time programs available. *Students:* 32. Average age 24. 34 applicants, 53% accepted. *Degree requirements:* For master's, thesis or alternative. *Entrance requirements:* For master's, GRE General Test, minimum GPA of 2.7. Additional exam requirements/recommendations for international students: Required—TOEFL. *Application deadline:* For fall admission, 2/1 priority date for domestic students. Applications are processed on a rolling basis. Application fee: $35. Electronic applications accepted. *Expenses:* Tuition, state resident: full-time $5,574. Tuition, nonresident: full-time $16,840. Required fees: $792. *Financial support:* Career-related internships or fieldwork available. Financial award application deadline: 2/1; financial award applicants required to submit FAFSA. *Unit head:* Dr. Gene Hayes, Graduate Representative, 865-974-1288, E-mail: ghayes1@utk.edu.

University of Waterloo, Graduate Studies, Faculty of Environmental Studies, Program in Local Economic Development/Tourism Policy and Planning, Waterloo, ON N2L 3G1, Canada. Offers MAES. Part-time programs available. *Degree requirements:* For master's, research paper. *Entrance requirements:* For master's, honors degree in related field, minimum B average. Additional exam requirements/recommendations for international students: Required—TOEFL, TWE. Electronic applications accepted. *Faculty research:* Urban and regional economics, regional economic development, strategic planning, environmental economics, economic geography.

Virginia Polytechnic Institute and State University, Graduate School, Pamplin College of Business, Department of Hospitality and Tourism Management, Blacksburg, VA 24061. Offers MS, PhD. *Faculty:* 11 full-time (3 women), 1 part-time/adjunct (0 women). *Students:* 24 full-time (12 women), 4 part-time (2 women); includes 1 minority (Asian American or Pacific Islander), 21 international. Average age 32. 38 applicants, 71% accepted, 9 enrolled. In 2006, 2 master's, 3 doctorates awarded. *Entrance requirements:* For master's and doctorate, GRE, GMAT. Additional exam requirements/recommendations for international students: Required—TOEFL (minimum score 600 paper-based; 250 computer-based). *Application deadline:* For fall admission, 5/15 for international students; for spring admission, 10/15 for international students. Applications are processed on a rolling basis. *Expenses:* Tuition, state resident: full-time $7,017; part-time $390 per credit hour. Tuition, nonresident: full-time $12,414; part-time $690 per credit hour. International tuition: $11,296 full-time. Required fees: $1,523; $256 per term. *Financial support:* In 2006–07, 10 teaching assistantships with full tuition reimbursements (averaging $9,606 per year) were awarded; career-related internships or fieldwork, Federal Work-Study, scholarships/grants, and unspecified assistantships also available. Financial award application deadline: 4/1. *Faculty research:* Human resource management, service management, marketing, strategy and finance tourist behavior. *Unit head:* Dr. Rick R. Perdue, Head, 540-231-3287, Fax: 540-231-8383, E-mail: perduerr@vt.edu. *Application contact:* Beth Weaver, Information Contact, 540-231-8429, Fax: 540-231-8313, E-mail: beweaver@vt.edu.

Western Illinois University, School of Graduate Studies, College of Education and Human Services, Department of Recreation, Park, and Tourism Administration, Macomb, IL 61455-1390. Offers MS. Part-time programs available. *Students:* 30 full-time (9 women), 4 part-time (3 women); includes 3 minority (1 African American, 2 Asian Americans or Pacific Islanders), 2 international. Average age 28. 30 applicants, 57% accepted. In 2006, 19 degrees awarded. *Degree requirements:* For master's, thesis or alternative. *Entrance requirements:* Additional exam requirements/recommendations for international students: Required—TOEFL (minimum score 550 paper-based; 213 computer-based; 80 iBT). *Application deadline:* Applications are processed on a rolling basis. Application fee: $30. Electronic applications accepted. *Expenses:* Tuition, state resident: part-time $200 per credit hour. Tuition, nonresident: part-time $400 per credit hour. *Financial support:* In 2006–07, 27 students received support, including 27 research assistantships with full tuition reimbursements available (averaging $6,568 per year). Financial award applicants required to submit FAFSA. *Unit head:* Dr. K. Dale Adkins, Chairperson, 309-298-1967. *Application contact:* Dr. Barbara Baily, Director of Graduate Studies/Associate Provost, 309-298-1806, Fax: 309-298-2345, E-mail: grad-office@wiu.edu.

THE LEADER IN GLOBAL EDUCATION

FAIRLEIGH
DICKINSON
UNIVERSITY

FAIRLEIGH DICKINSON UNIVERSITY

International School of Hospitality and Tourism Management

Programs of Study
Fairleigh Dickinson University's (FDU) International School of Hospitality and Tourism Management (ISHTM) is located in the largest hospitality destination in the world. Founded in 1942, it was the first four-year school in the New York metropolitan region to offer degrees in hospitality management. Today, it remains the only program of its kind in New Jersey.

The School's 36-credit Master of Science in hospitality management studies is structured to meet the career needs of adults working as managers, entrepreneurs, educators, and in other professional positions in the hospitality industry.

Graduate hospitality programs are offered at FDU's College at Florham (Madison, New Jersey) and Metropolitan Campus (Teaneck, New Jersey), as well as select statewide locations. Students can also attend classes at the University's facilities at Atlantic Cape Community College in Mays Landing (which offers a specialization in hospitality management). A culinary arts management specialization is also available through the University's on-site partnership with the Culinary Arts Institute at Hudson County Community College (HCCC) in Jersey City, New Jersey. The School also offers classes at Ocean County Community College and at Mercer County Community College.

For working adults seeking to enhance their careers by upgrading their professional skills, the program increases analytical, managerial, and leadership competencies and provides graduates with the requisite preparation for career advancement in various hospitality-related professional areas. To further enhance practical training, numerous hospitality facilities in New York City and New Jersey serve as hands-on laboratory facilities for fostering technical and management skills.

Research Facilities
The School provides extensive facilities to support education, research, and training in the hospitality industry. The Metropolitan Campus facility is located in a modern classroom building and features a 2,000-square-foot demonstration lab housing food production and dining areas, television cameras, teleconferencing equipment, and a suite of administrative and faculty offices.

Facilities at the College at Florham include Chaîne House, the U.S. headquarters of the Confrere de la Chaîne des Rôtisseurs, the world's oldest and most prestigious organization dedicated to promoting the culinary and hospitality arts. The 6,000-square-foot building is now the headquarters of FDU's International School of Hospitality and Tourism Management. Another special research and learning feature at the College at Florham is the Hamilton Park Hotel and Conference Center. A full partner with the School, it offers jobs and internship experiences, special classes and projects on-site, and hands-on laboratory experiences.

The Atlantic City site features modern offices and classrooms at Atlantic Cape Community College. This location offers students the opportunity to visit and interact with management of the many properties within the industry.

Students in the Jersey City culinary arts management program work in the Culinary Arts Building of Hudson County Community College. HCCC offers New Jersey's only accredited program by the Culinary Arts Federation.

Financial Aid
A limited number of research, honors research, teaching, and graduate administrative scholarships are available at Fairleigh Dickinson University.

An international scholarship program is offered for non-U.S., full-time graduate students. The University's application, available through the Office of International Admissions, evaluates the student on both academic merit and financial need.

Eligible domestic graduate students enrolled at least half-time may borrow up to a maximum of $20,500 annually in subsidized and unsubsidized loans under the Federal Stafford Student Loan program. In addition, the University offers a number of attractive flexible financing programs to its students.

Cost of Study
Tuition for master's-level studies in 2007–08 is $869 per credit for either full- or part-time students. An annual technology fee of $244 for part-time students or $304 for full-time students is also assessed.

Living and Housing Costs
The University currently offers only limited on-campus housing for graduate students, offered on a first-come, first-served basis. The annual costs at the Metropolitan Campus are $6420 for a standard double room and $3508 for the standard eleven-meal plan, which includes $300 in flex dollars. International students should contact the University's international student organizations for assistance in locating housing.

Student Group
Approximately 500 students are enrolled in the School, including students from Europe, Asia, Latin America, the Caribbean, Africa, and the U.S. Its students form strong personal and professional bonds, resulting in an invaluable worldwide network of more than 2,400 alumni members working in leadership positions in virtually every area of the hospitality industry.

Location
Located in the center of the world's largest hospitality/tourism market, the School's five locations are dedicated to using the resources the location offers in preparing students to assume key positions of responsibility in the industry following completion of their education.

The University and The School
The International School of Hospitality and Tourism Management has a unique relationship with the University. It was founded as one of the University's original programs primarily because of its location and is approaching its sixtieth anniversary. The School is the oldest postsecondary program in hospitality in the New York City metropolitan area.

Applying
Graduate candidates must be managers, business owners, or educators or in other professional positions related to the hospitality industry with at least three years of experience. Applicants must have a minimum undergraduate grade point average of 2.75 from an accredited college or university. Graduate Record Examinations (GRE) or Graduate Management Admission Test (GMAT) scores are not required.

For applicants whose native language is not English and who have not completed a baccalaureate degree in an English-language institution, a satisfactory score on the Test of English as a Foreign Language (TOEFL) is required.

Correspondence and Information
Office of International and Graduate Admissions
Metropolitan Campus
Fairleigh Dickinson University
1000 River Road, T-KB1-01
Teaneck, New Jersey 07666
Phone: 201-692-2554
Fax: 201-692-2506
E-mail: grad@fdu.edu
Web site: http://www.fdu.edu

Fairleigh Dickinson University

THE FACULTY

The faculty members of the International School of Hospitality and Tourism Management bring outstanding educational and practical credentials to the classroom. Students benefit from career-long acquired faculty insights into the School's specialized management programs in lodging, food service and culinary arts, and tourism.

Richard Wisch, Associate Professor, Associate Dean, and Director, International School of Hospitality and Tourism Management; Ed.D., Columbia. More than two decades of executive experience in the hospitality industry as well as nearly twenty-five years as a faculty member of the School and considered an expert in experiential education, active in both national and international educational associations and organizations.

Michelle Barto, Adjunct Faculty; Ed.D., Argosy/Sarasota. More than twenty-five years experience in higher education, ESL mentor, actively involved in teaching communications and research.

Robert Cohen, Adjunct Faculty; M.B.A., Pace; CPA. Vice president, Chase Manhattan Bank.

Mark Cosgrove, Adjunct Faculty; M.A.L.S.; Ed.D. candidate, Rutgers; Certified Hospitality Educator. Graduate of the Culinary Institute; chef, owner, educator.

Ray D'Amico, Adjunct Faculty; CPA. More than twenty years of experience in education, hospitality, and finance.

Chris Droussiotis, Adjunct Faculty; M.B.A., Fairleigh Dickinson; Certified Hospitality Educator. More than eighteen years of experience in executive management and finance.

Iris Gersh, Senior Lecturer and Director of the Jersey City Culinary Arts Management Program; M.B.A.; Ed.D. candidate, Seton Hall; Certified Hospitality Educator. More than eighteen years of industry experience with the Marriott Corporation, specializing in food and beverage management.

Mitchell Greene, Adjunct Faculty; M.B.A., Fairleigh Dickinson. More than twenty years in facilities management, including serving as director of operations for Madison Square Garden; vice president of facilities for the New York Racing Association, with responsibilities for Aqueduct, Belmont, and Saratoga race tracks; and vice president of the Jacob Javits Center.

Sandra Hayes, Adjunct Faculty; M.S.; Ed.D. candidate. Expertise in areas of organizational behavior and conflict resolution.

Ruth Hladyk, Adjunct Faculty and Assistant Director for Professional Development; M.S., Fairleigh Dickinson; Certified Hospitality Educator. More than twenty-five years of corporate industry experience.

Donald Hoover, Senior Lecturer; M.S., Fairleigh Dickinson. More than eighteen years of management experience in human resources with casino and industry resorts.

John Hughes, Associate Director; M.S., Fairleigh Dickinson; Ed.D. candidate; Certified Hospitality Educator. More than twenty-five years in the field with experience in operations management for hospitality industry organizations, serving as president and vice president of various operations.

Ronald Kapon, Adjunct Faculty; M.S., Columbia. More than forty years experience in the wine and spirits industry; managed a chain of wine and spirits retail stores; has taught wine classes at various institutions; currently serves as a vice president and codirector of the Tasters Guild, the largest wine educational organization in the U.S.; also well-known as a wine expert and journalist.

Craig Lazner, Adjunct Faculty; J.D., Seton Hall; Certified Hospitality Educator. Experience in a variety of management capacities at Marriott and Compass Group, a practicing attorney.

Jeffrey Martini, Adjunct Faculty; M.B.A., Fairleigh Dickinson. More than thirty years of experience in sales and marketing.

Robert Nochta, Adjunct Faculty; M.A., Montclair State. Director of Training and Development, Ritter Sysco Food Systems.

John Palsi, Adjunct Faculty; M.B.A., Fairleigh Dickinson. Has twenty years of executive experience in food and beverage with business and industry.

Aixa Ritz, Assistant Professor; Ed.D., Columbia; Certified Hospitality Educator. Actively involved in development and management of special interest, recreational, U.S., and international tourism; corporate travel management; and meeting planning for more than twenty-five years.

Lisa Ryan, Adjunct Faculty; M.S., Fairleigh Dickinson; Certified Hospitality Educator; Certified Hotel Administrator; Certified Meeting Professional. More than eighteen years of experience in hospitality management and executive training.

Joseph Tormey, Senior Lecturer; M.S., Fairleigh Dickinson; Certified Hospitality Educator; Certified Wine Educator. More than twenty years of industry and educational experience, a member of the American Wine Society.

Kirsten Tripodi, Senior Lecturer; M.P.S., Cornell; Ph.D. candidate, Seton Hall; Certified Hospitality Educator; Certified Wine Educator. More than twenty years of food and hospitality industry experience.

MICHIGAN STATE UNIVERSITY

The School of Hospitality Business
Hospitality Business and Foodservice Management Programs

Programs of Study

The mission of The School of Hospitality Business at Michigan State University (MSU) is to continually enhance The School's leadership position in hospitality business education through teaching, research, and service. The curriculum is unique because it integrates Eli Broad Graduate School of Business requirements with major courses in hospitality business.

As a highly ranked hospitality business school, The School offers an exceptionally well-crafted curriculum taught by innovative professors. The faculty includes leading textbook authors, sought-after consultants, and respected researchers. While the M.B.A. curriculum encourages dual concentration areas, the Master of Science (M.S.) curriculum options provide flexibility to meet many varied career goals.

The Master of Science in Hospitality Business Program prepares candidates for executive-level responsibilities in multiple segments of the hospitality industry. This intensive program focuses on a strong business core with a hospitality specialty course core and can be tailored to one's academic pursuits. The program provides flexibility and opportunities to choose education and career tracks in operations management, entrepreneurial ventures, training, education, research, and consulting. This 36-credit-hour Master of Science in hospitality business degree may be completed in two years on a full-time basis and in more than two years on a part-time basis.

The Michael L. Minor Master of Science in Foodservice Management Program equips candidates with an executive perspective for decision making while building skills that maximize their market value immediately upon graduation. It provides a contemporary forum for learning how to respond to competition with practical solutions and hands-on management. This program is ideal in a path toward earning a Ph.D. and becoming a hospitality educator. This program offers the opportunity to compete for funded graduate assistantships. This 30-credit-hour Master of Science in foodservice management degree may be completed in one year on a full-time basis and in fewer than two years on a part-time basis.

Research Facilities

Michigan State University's Gast Business Library is one of more than thirteen MSU libraries, containing electronic journals and periodicals, computing resources, and research centers and groups. The MSU libraries are a member of the Michigan Research Libraries Triangle (with the University of Michigan and Wayne State University) and the Committee on Institutional Cooperation (with the libraries at Northwestern, Ohio State, Penn State, and Purdue Universities and the Universities of Chicago, Illinois, Indiana, Iowa, Michigan, Wisconsin–Madison, and Minnesota). Information on Michigan State University research facilities, such as the MSU Library, MSU Special Collections, computing resources, and research centers and groups, can be found at http://www.msu.edu/research/.

Financial Aid

MSU offers a comprehensive financial assistance program, including scholarships and limited graduate assistantships. These are available upon application after establishing a minimum GPA. The Michael L. Minor Endowment supports M.S. students in foodservice management.

Cost of Study

Tuition is approximately $10,000 per year for full-time, in-state graduate students. Most students take 9–12 credits per semester. For a current estimate, prospective students should visit http://www.finaid.msu.edu/costs.asp.

Living and Housing Costs

There are three housing options: the Owen Graduate Center, University Apartments, or off-campus housing. For more information about Owen Graduate Center and University Apartments, students should contact the University Apartments and Residence Hall Assignments Office at 517-355-9550. Current listings of off-campus housing are available by contacting the Off-Campus Housing Office at 517-355-8303. Although there are no deadlines for housing applications, students are encouraged to apply as early as possible.

Student Group

In spring 2007, there were 20 students enrolled in the Master of Science programs and 2 in the graduate specialization. The student population is representative of the global nature of this industry, with individuals from South America, Asia, and the United States. Ninety percent of the students are full-time.

Location

Michigan State University's campus is a unique blend of the traditional and innovative within a parklike landscape. The Red Cedar River flows through the campus and sets the stage for springtime walks and summer concerts. North of the river's tree-lined banks and grassy slopes is the older, more traditional heart of the campus. The ivy-covered brick buildings house academic offices and the MSU Union and ten residence halls. Sweeping green lawns grace this area, accented by an arboretum of shade and flowering trees. South of the Red Cedar River are modern residence hall complexes, Spartan Stadium, the world's most powerful super-conducting cyclotron, the medical complex, and sophisticated scientific research laboratories as well as the Eppley Center and Business Complexes.

The University

As a pioneer land-grant institution and a respected research and teaching university, Michigan State University is committed to leadership and developing knowledge. MSU strives to discover practical uses for theoretical knowledge. In fostering both research and its applications, MSU continues to be a catalyst for positive intellectual, social, and technological change.

Applying

Admission to The School of Hospitality Business is selective. Master of Science degree applicants must meet the minimum GMAT or GRE scores and submit three letters of recommendation. International students must also submit TOEFL scores.

Correspondence and Information

Graduate Programs Coordinator
The School of Hospitality Business
Michigan State University
232 Eppley Center
East Lansing, Michigan 48824-1121

Phone: 517-353-9211
Fax: 517-432-1170
E-mail: mshb@bus.msu.edu
Web site: http://www.bus.msu.edu/shb/

Michigan State University

THE FACULTY AND THEIR RESEARCH

Jeffrey Beck, Ph.D., joined The School in July 2002. He has more than twenty years of experience in the lodging industry. His industry experience includes ten years with Marriott Hotels in various management positions. His interests are in hospitality marketing, sales management, meeting and event planning and marketing, and service experience and quality.

Carl P. Borchgrevink, Ph.D.; CFBE, is an authority on leader-member exchange research in the hospitality industry. He coordinates The School's International Hospitality Management Summer Program. His interests and areas of expertise include leader-member exchange, service management, service-employee persuasive influence, food and beverage operations and management, and menu language.

Ronald F. Cichy, M.B.A., Ph.D.; NCE, CHA, CHE, is the director and a professor of The School of Hospitality Business at Michigan State University, a position in which he has served at his alma mater since 1988. Cichy is a frequent speaker at annual conferences, meetings, and institutes for businesses ranging from Fortune 500 companies to the hospitality industry. His topics are both educational and entertaining. His insights come from decades of industry experience and working with top global service leaders. Cichy's work on four continents has developed managers and leaders, team builders and trainers, and helped businesses become high-performance organizations. His most recent book is *Managing Service in Food and Beverage Operations,* third edition, coauthored with Phil Hickey Jr., published in 2005. Cichy is recognized as a pioneer researcher on leadership qualities, keys, and secrets of hospitality leaders, both in the United States and Japan. His research has led to his identification as one of the top 50 most influential scholars in hospitality management.

Jeff Elsworth, Ph.D., joined The School in August 2001. His specialty areas are foodservice operations, food safety, media reporting issues, and hospitality wage determinants. He has written and won awards for several scholarly papers in these and other areas. He has also been a foodservice consultant, having served as a restaurant general manager and franchise trainer of managers for twenty years before entering academia.

Michael L. Kasavana, Ph.D.; CHTP, is the National Automatic Merchandising Association Professor in Hospitality Business. He is focused on hospitality information technology and has coauthored several texts, including *Managing Front Office Operations* and *Managing Computers in the Hospitality Industry.* He is an industry consultant, seminar leader, and industry adviser. He is a member of the HFTP Technology Hall of Fame and a FS/TEC Award Recipient.

Bonnie J. Knutson, Ph.D., is an authority on consumer trends and innovative marketing. With her wit and entertaining style, Bonnie is a frequent speaker at industry meetings nationally and abroad. She was named a national scholar by the National Advertising Foundation and is a winner of the Golden Key Teaching Excellence Award. She is also editor of the *Journal of Hospitality and Marketing.*

Jack D. Ninemeier, Ph.D.; CHA, is the author of *Planning and Control for Food and Beverage Operations,* an industry best seller. Ninemeier has published forty-two textbooks on food and beverage management, supervision, health care, and related topics. Areas of expertise include food and beverage management and supervision. He is the coordinator of the Club Managers Association of America's Business Management Institute III executive program.

James F. Rainey, J.D., has been a member of the MSU faculty for over forty years and served in the College of Business for nearly 24. As former associate dean for academic affairs his influence has touched thousands of business students, including those in The School. Most recently, he directed the M.B.A. program in the Eli Broad College of Business. For many years, he served as an adjunct professor in The School as well as teaching hospitality business law. He is currently The School's graduate programs' director, providing his special brand of leadership and insight to these important programs.

Kathryn A. Runyan, M.A., is the graduate programs' coordinator for The School of Hospitality Business. Her role is to help plan, develop, and implement policies for recruitment, retention, and advising of graduate students in the four graduate programs in The School. Her background in communications and counseling is beneficial as she provides assistance in the areas of academic advising, skill building, career development, and other supportive services to assist students in their pursuit of professional success.

Raymond S. Schmidgall, Ph.D.; CPA, is The School's Hilton Hotels Professor of Hospitality Financial Management. He has authored the highly acclaimed *Hospitality Industry Managerial Accounting* and *Financial Management for the Hospitality Industry* books, used around the world by both industry members and educators. He is a very active researcher and serves on numerous hospitality industry and educational association boards.

Michael P. Sciarini, Ph.D., was selected as an MSU Lilly Teaching Fellow in recognition of his commitment to undergraduate hospitality business education. His popular Introduction to the Hospitality Industry course combines an industry overview with career development tools. His research is focused on career development issues, career paths and succession planning for hotel managers, and other human resources issues.

Allan Sherwin, M.S.; CEC, CCE, FMP, is the Dr. Lewis J. and Mrs. Ruth E. Minor Chef-Professor Alumnus and returns to MSU with a wealth of industry and academic experience and oversees the culinary aspects of The School's bachelor's degree program, both of its Master of Science programs, executive education, and *Les Gourmets* and other special events.

A. J. Singh, Ph.D., is an Assistant Professor in The School of Hospitality Business. The focus of his teaching and research is lodging management systems and finance. His research on lodging operations and finance has been published in key academic and industry publications such as *Cornell Hotel and Restaurant Administration Quarterly, International Journal of Hospitality Management, Travel and Tourism Analyst, Journal of Lending and Credit Risk Management, Bottomline,* and *Lodging.*

NEW YORK UNIVERSITY

School of Continuing and Professional Studies
The Preston Robert Tisch Center for Hospitality, Tourism, and Sports Management

Programs of Study

The Preston Robert Tisch Center for Hospitality, Tourism, and Sports Management at New York University (NYU) offers six graduate programs: a Master of Science (M.S.) in hospitality industry studies, an M.S. in tourism and travel management, an M.S. in sports business, a graduate certificate in hospitality industry studies, a graduate certificate in tourism and travel management, and a graduate certificate in sports business. As a result of the increased complexities and burgeoning growth of the fields of hospitality, tourism, and sports management, the demand for professionals with advanced degrees is accelerating. The graduate programs at NYU feature the advanced knowledge and skills necessary to successfully compete in these global industries.

The graduate programs feature a multilayered learning environment that combines applied research, team projects, lectures by leading industry professionals, and conferences. The blending of classroom learning with a series of professional and business activities ensures an integrated educational experience. In concert with the unique location, the city is the classroom, and faculty members are professionals from all aspects of industry.

The Master of Science degree programs require 42 credits (fourteen courses, 3 credits each) of course work in a sequence of general core and concentration courses. Within the M.S. program in hospitality industry studies, there are four concentrations to select from: customer relationship management, hospitality investments, hotel operations, and revenue management. Within the M.S. program in tourism and travel management, there are four concentrations to choose from: customer relationship management, strategic marketing, tourism development, and tourism planning and analysis. The M.S. program in sports business offers two concentrations: finance and development and marketing and media. The Preston Robert Tisch Center for Hospitality, Tourism, and Sports Management continually reevaluates and updates all of its graduate programs in response to industry needs to provide the most up-to-date and relevant course of study.

Research Facilities

The Elmer Holmes Bobst Library and Study Center, one of the largest open-stack research libraries in the world, houses more than 3 million of NYU's nearly 4.4 million volumes. In addition to books, journals, and other print materials, the library provides access to many nonprint resources. These include microforms, databases, and other electronic resources that students can connect to from their home or residence hall; extensive video and audio collections; and a variety of computer equipment and software programs.

NYU's central source for computing, information, network, and telecommunications services is Information Technology Services (ITS). ITS maintains four large, modern computer labs with high-end Macintosh and Windows computers, laser printers, related multimedia equipment, and a wide variety of up-to-date software. The Client Services division of ITS provides comprehensive help with the materials and equipment available to students online, in person, and via telephone and e-mail.

Financial Aid

The Preston Robert Tisch Center for Hospitality, Tourism, and Sports Management offers financial aid in the form of scholarships to new and continuing domestic and international students. NYU's centralized Office of Financial Aid assists students with loan packages, and the NYU monthly payment plan enables students to spread out their tuition payments. For more information, students should visit http://www.nyu.edu/financial.aid.

Cost of Study

Tuition for part-time students for the 2007–08 academic year is $1266 per credit plus fees. For full-time students (10–12 credits per semester), the cost of tuition and related fees is $12,664 per semester. Fees vary somewhat by program. The Board of Trustees of New York University reserves the right to alter these costs without notice.

Living and Housing Costs

Graduate student housing is available on the University campus and is administered through the Office of Housing and Residence Life. However, students may choose to live off campus. NYU's Off-Campus Housing Office (OCHO) offers assistance to members of the NYU community in their search for non-University housing options. OCHO provides, exclusively to NYU students, listings of available locations for rent through private landlords, property managers, brokers, and real estate agents. Updated daily, these listings are accessible through OCHO's computer terminals or online for members of the NYU community.

Student Group

Academic year 2006–07 enrollment was 47 students in the M.S. program in hospitality industry studies, 18 students in the M.S. program in tourism and travel management, and 104 students in the M.S. program in sports business. The student population is representative of the global nature of the industry, with individuals from Europe, Asia, Africa, South America, and the Caribbean as well as the United States.

Location

New York University is located in the heart of Manhattan, surrounded by major attractions, accommodations, and entertainment. The Center's programs are ideally situated in New York City, which is universally recognized as the hospitality and tourism capital of the world. New York City is a focal point of the sports world and, as a result, is one of the best places to study the business of sports.

The University, The School, and The Center

NYU is a private university composed of fourteen schools and colleges. The University was founded in 1831, and the School of Continuing and Professional Studies was founded in 1934. The Preston Robert Tisch Center for Hospitality, Tourism, and Sports Management, which offers three master's degrees, three graduate certificates, two undergraduate degrees, summer intensive programs, and noncredit professional development courses, was established in 1995.

Applying

Admission to the 42-credit graduate programs is open to qualified applicants who hold a bachelor's degree from an accredited undergraduate institution. In addition, applicants are required to have three to five years of professional experience. For all graduate degree programs, students may apply for fall or spring admission, and application packages must include official transcripts of academic achievement from previous undergraduate and graduate course work, results of the GRE or GMAT, TOEFL score (for students whose native language is not English), business resumes, professional and academic recommendations, and a personal essay.

Correspondence and Information

For more information and an application package, students should contact:

Office of Admissions
Department of Graduate Studies
The Preston Robert Tisch Center for Hospitality, Tourism, and Sports Management
New York University
145 Fourth Avenue, Room 219
New York, New York 10003

Phone: 212-998-7200 Ext. 412
Fax: 212-995-4674
E-mail: scps.gradadmissions@nyu.edu
Web site: http://www.scps.nyu.edu/412

New York University

THE ADMINISTRATION

Robert S. Lapiner, Ph.D., Dean, School of Continuing and Professional Studies.

Lalia Rach, Ed.D., Divisional Dean, Clinical Professor, and HVS International Chair, Preston Robert Tisch Center for Hospitality, Tourism, and Sports Management, School of Continuing and Professional Studies.

Sandra Dove-Lowther, Ed.M., Associate Director, Graduate Programs, Preston Robert Tisch Center for Hospitality, Tourism, and Sports Management, School of Continuing and Professional Studies.

Mark M. Warner, D.P.A., Director and Clinical Professor, Graduate Programs, Preston Robert Tisch Center for Hospitality, Tourism, and Sports Management, School of Continuing and Professional Studies.

TEMPLE UNIVERSITY

School of Tourism and Hospitality Management

Programs of Study

The School of Tourism and Hospitality Management offers the Master of Tourism and Hospitality Management (M.T.H.M.) degree program and the Master of Education (Ed.M.) in Sport and Recreation Administration degree program. The M.T.H.M. degree program is designed to meet the growing demand for supervisors and administrators in the areas of tourism and hospitality management, hotel operations, event management, tourism planning, and international tourism. The Ed.M. degree program is designed to meet the growing demand for supervisors and administrators in the areas of sport management, sport administration, arena management, college athletics, sports governing bodies, marketing, ticketing, fund-raising, professional sports, amateur sports, intramurals, campus recreation, commercial recreation, public recreation and parks, resort management, voluntary agencies, private agencies, and leisure services. The curricula include courses in management, information technology, customer service, legal aspects, finance and fund-raising, marketing, and research methods. The strength of the programs lies in their internship opportunities, which are based on a nationwide network. Students work closely with their advisers, internship coordinators, and faculty mentors. The master's degree can be completed in one calendar year by full-time students or in two years by part-time students. The Ed.M. degree program offers four specialty options (thesis, project, comprehensive exam, and practicum), with requirements ranging from 30 to 39 semester hours. The 36-semester-hour M.T.H.M. degree program offers two specialty options (thesis and project). A Ph.D. in business administration with an emphasis in tourism is available in The Fox School of Business and Management. For more information on the Ph.D. program, prospective students should visit the Web site at http://www.fox.temple.edu/programs/phdba.

Research Facilities

The School of Tourism and Hospitality Management is the home of the National Laboratory for Tourism & *e*Commerce (NLT*e*C), under the direction of Dr. Daniel R. Fesenmaier. The National Laboratory for Tourism & *e*Commerce is multidisciplinary, multi-departmental, and multi-university. The primary mission of the National Laboratory for Tourism & *e*Commerce is to conduct and facilitate high-quality interdisciplinary and multidisciplinary research and development in those areas of tourism impacted by technology. To this end, the National Laboratory for Tourism & *e*Commerce provides a unique and powerful setting for scholars and practitioners to consider the nature and role of information technology in the tourism industry. Research by laboratory faculty and staff members and fellows include the following areas: advertising, business, communications, computer science, education, environmental studies, geography, management information systems, marketing, psychology, and urban and regional planning.

Financial Aid

The University offers financial aid through grants, loans, and work-study programs that are based on need, as calculated by Student Financial Services. The School of Tourism and Hospitality Management offers teaching and research assistantships, which include a stipend plus a tuition scholarship.

Cost of Study

Graduate tuition for 2006–07 was $511 per semester hour for Pennsylvania residents and $746 per semester hour for nonresidents; a $35 general activities fee, a $100 computer and technology fee, a $60 student health services fee, a $30 student recreation services fee, and a $25 student facilities fee are also required.

Living and Housing Costs

There is limited on-campus housing available for graduate students. Rooms, apartments, and houses are available for graduate students in the surrounding city and suburbs.

Student Group

The School of Tourism and Hospitality Management enrolls approximately 70 graduate students each year, about 50 percent of whom are women. Approximately half of the students are full-time. Generally, 10 percent are international students.

Student Outcomes

The rapid growth of travel, tourism, hospitality, sport, recreation, and leisure services has created a demand for qualified administrators who can plan, organize, and direct programs and facilities. The strength of the programs lies in the internship opportunities and professional placements. The master's programs place approximately 90 percent of their graduates directly in their field of study. Placements of recent graduate students from the Tourism and Hospitality Management program range from convention and tourism bureaus to hotels to event planning; recent graduates from the Sport and Recreation Administration program have been placed in college athletics, professional teams, arena management, and campus and municipal recreation.

Location

The Philadelphia region is among the country's most livable areas. A culturally diverse city, Philadelphia has many art museums, a symphony orchestra, and America's oldest zoo. There are professional sports teams in hockey, basketball, football, and baseball as well as college sports. Temple University's location provides access to outstanding internship sites and potential job placements in the region.

The University and The School

Temple University is one of the nation's senior comprehensive research institutions and enrolls more than 34,000 students in seventeen schools and colleges. Graduate students enjoy studying at Temple because it offers a culturally diverse campus life within an urban/metropolitan setting that is rich in vitality. Educators in the School of Tourism and Hospitality Management have been given the direct charge from industry leaders to prepare students so that they possess a wide variety of skills, including excellent human and conceptual skills and flexibility.

Applying

Students should apply by April 15 for the fall semester (December 15 for international students) and by September 30 for the spring semester (August 1 for international students). Applicants must have a minimum undergraduate grade point average of 3.0 and must submit three letters of recommendation, transcripts from all accredited institutions previously attended, Graduate Record Examinations (GRE) or Miller Analogies Test (MAT) scores, a 350- to 500-word statement of goals addressing the candidate's academic and professional objectives as well as strengths and weaknesses, and a resume detailing previous educational and work experience. Each of the admission criteria is weighted equally in reaching a final decision.

Correspondence and Information

Director of Graduate Programs
School of Tourism and Hospitality Management
1700 North Broad Street, Suite 412 (062-62)
Temple University
Philadelphia, Pennsylvania 19122
Phone: 215-204-8701
Fax: 215-204-8705
E-mail: sthm@temple.edu
Web site: http://www.temple.edu/sthm

Temple University

THE FACULTY AND THEIR RESEARCH

Elizabeth H. Barber, Associate Professor and Associate Dean; Ph.D., Iowa. Instructional design and professional preparation in related industries.

Debra K. Blair, Assistant Professor; Ed.D., Temple. Programming, special populations, and event management.

Daniel R. Fesenmaier, Professor and Director of the National Laboratory for Tourism & *e*Commerce; Ph.D., Western Ontario. Travel and tourism advertising, persuasive information systems, market information systems, adoption and use of technology by tourism organizations.

Joe J. Goldblatt, Professor and Executive Director for Professional Development Programs and Strategic Partnerships; Ed.D., George Washington. Event management, event tourism, event marketing, event risk management, and event leadership.

Clark Hu, Associate Professor; Ph.D., Purdue. Hospitality and tourism marketing and management, e-commerce in tourism and hospitality, tourism knowledge management, tourism demand modeling.

Michael W. Jackson, Professor; H.S.D., Indiana. Facility management, administration of sport.

Seoki Lee, Assistant Professor; Ph.D., Penn State. Hospitality accounting and finance, hotel valuation, hospitality cost-of-equity capital, hospitality capital structure, revenue management.

Bonnie L. Parkhouse, Professor; Ph.D., Minnesota. Sport management, fund-raising, gender equity, marketing of sport and recreation.

Wesley S. Roehl, Professor; Ph.D., Texas A&M. Impacts of tourism and legalized gambling, gambling behavior, economic geography of tourism and hospitality, risk perceptions and travel behavior.

Ira G. Shapiro, Professor and Chairperson; Ph.D., North Carolina at Chapel Hill. Philosophy, ethics, professional preparation in sport and recreation.

Ted Tedrick, Professor; Ph.D., Maryland. Leisure and aging, sport and recreation administration.

Section 8
Human Resources

This section contains a directory of institutions offering graduate work in human resources, followed by in-depth entries submitted by institutions that chose to prepare detailed program descriptions. Additional information about programs listed in the directory but not augmented by an in-depth entry may be obtained by writing directly to the dean of a graduate school or chair of a department at the address given in the directory.

For programs offering related work, see also in this book Business Administration and Management, Advertising and Public Relations, Hospitality Management, Industrial and Manufacturing Management, and Organizational Behavior. In Book 2, see Public, Regional, and Industrial Affairs (Industrial and Labor Relations).

CONTENTS

Human Resources Development

Abilene Christian University, Graduate School, College of Arts and Sciences, Department of Communication, Program in Organizational and Human Resource Development, Abilene, TX 79699-9100. Offers MS. Part-time and evening/weekend programs available. *Students:* 26 full-time (11 women), 23 part-time (13 women); includes 15 minority (7 African Americans, 1 Asian American or Pacific Islander, 7 Hispanic Americans), 3 international. 27 applicants, 78% accepted, 19 enrolled. In 2006, 18 degrees awarded. *Degree requirements:* For master's, comprehensive exam. *Entrance requirements:* For master's, GMAT, GRE General Test, or MAT. *Application deadline:* For fall admission, 4/1 priority date for domestic students; for spring admission, 11/1 for domestic students. Applications are processed on a rolling basis. Application fee: $40 ($45 for international students). Electronic applications accepted. *Expenses:* Tuition: Full-time $12,504; part-time $521 per hour. Required fees: $700; $34 per hour. *Financial support:* Federal Work-Study available. Support available to part-time students. Financial award application deadline: 4/1. *Application contact:* William Horn, Graduate Admissions Counselor, 325-674-2656, Fax: 325-674-6717, E-mail: gradinfo@acu.edu.

Amberton University, Graduate School, Program in Human Relations and Business, Garland, TX 75041-5595. Offers MA, MS. Part-time and evening/weekend programs available. *Faculty:* 4 full-time (3 women), 10 part-time/adjunct (5 women). *Students:* 100 full-time (50 women), 100 part-time (50 women); includes 75 minority (50 African Americans, 5 American Indian/Alaska Native, 5 Asian Americans or Pacific Islanders, 15 Hispanic Americans). Average age 35. In 2006, 50 degrees awarded. *Entrance requirements:* For master's, minimum GPA of 3.0. *Application deadline:* Applications are processed on a rolling basis. *Expenses:* Tuition: Full-time $4,800; part-time $600 per course. *Application contact:* Adviser, 972-279-6511 Ext. 180, Fax: 972-279-9773, E-mail: advisor@amberton.edu.

American International College, School of Psychology and Education, Center for Human Resource Development, Springfield, MA 01109-3189. Offers MA. Evening/weekend programs available. *Faculty:* 2 full-time (both women), 2 part-time/adjunct (1 woman). *Students:* 6 full-time (4 women), 4 part-time (3 women); includes 4 minority (2 African Americans, 2 Hispanic Americans). Average age 36. In 2006, 9 degrees awarded. *Degree requirements:* For master's, practicum, project. *Entrance requirements:* For master's, minimum B- average in undergraduate course work, writing sample. Additional exam requirements/recommendations for international students: Required—TOEFL. *Application deadline:* For fall admission, 7/1 priority date for domestic and international students; for spring admission, 12/1 priority date for domestic and international students. Applications are processed on a rolling basis. Application fee: $50. *Expenses:* Tuition: Part-time $585 per semester hour. Required fees: $100 per year. Full-time tuition and fees vary according to program. *Financial support:* Institutionally sponsored loans available. Financial award applicants required to submit FAFSA. *Faculty research:* Faculty development, teaching/training effectiveness. *Unit head:* Dr. Debra D. Anderson, Director, 413-205-3374, Fax: 413-205-3943, E-mail: debra.anderson@aic.edu. *Application contact:* Keshawn Dodds, Associate Director of Graduate Admissions, 413-205-3549, Fax: 413-205-3911, E-mail: keshawn.dodds@aic.edu.

Antioch University Los Angeles, Graduate Programs, Program in Organizational Management, Culver City, CA 90230. Offers human resource development (MA); leadership (MA); organizational development (MA). Part-time and evening/weekend programs available. *Entrance requirements:* For master's, interview. Additional exam requirements/recommendations for international students: Required—TOEFL. *Faculty research:* Systems thinking and chaos theory, technology and organizational structure, nonprofit management, power and empowerment.

Azusa Pacific University, School of Business and Management, Program in Human and Organizational Development, Azusa, CA 91702-7000. Offers MA. Part-time and evening/weekend programs available. *Students:* 2 full-time (both women), 14 part-time (11 women); includes 7 minority (2 African Americans, 2 Asian Americans or Pacific Islanders, 3 Hispanic Americans), 2 international. In 2006, 9 degrees awarded. *Degree requirements:* For master's, final project. *Entrance requirements:* For master's, minimum GPA of 3.0. *Application deadline:* For fall admission, 8/15 priority date for domestic students. Applications are processed on a rolling basis. Application fee: $45 ($65 for international students). *Expenses:* Tuition: Part-time $475 per credit.

Barry University, School of Education, Program in Human Resource Development and Administration, Miami Shores, FL 33161-6695. Offers MS. Part-time and evening/weekend programs available. *Students:* 13 full-time (11 women), 31 part-time (28 women); includes 23 minority (13 African Americans, 1 Asian American or Pacific Islander, 9 Hispanic Americans), 2 international. 4 applicants, 50% accepted, 1 enrolled. In 2006, 41 degrees awarded. *Degree requirements:* For master's, practicum. *Entrance requirements:* For master's, GRE General Test or MAT, minimum GPA of 3.0. *Application deadline:* For fall admission, 5/1 priority date for domestic students. Applications are processed on a rolling basis. Application fee: $30. Electronic applications accepted. *Unit head:* Dr. Betty Hubschman, Director, 305-899-3724, Fax: 305-899-4708, E-mail: bhubschman@mail.barry.edu. *Application contact:* Dave Fletcher, Director of Graduate Admissions, 305-899-3113, Fax: 305-899-2971, E-mail: dfletcher@mail.barry.edu.

Barry University, School of Education, Program in Leadership and Education, Miami Shores, FL 33161-6695. Offers educational technology (PhD); exceptional student education (PhD); higher education administration (PhD); human resource development (PhD); leadership (PhD). Part-time and evening/weekend programs available. *Students:* 15 full-time (7 women), 233 part-time (147 women); includes 97 minority (52 African Americans, 45 Hispanic Americans), 7 international. 58 applicants, 34% accepted, 18 enrolled. In 2006, 23 degrees awarded. *Degree requirements:* For doctorate, thesis/dissertation. *Entrance requirements:* For doctorate, GRE General Test, minimum GPA of 3.25. *Application deadline:* For fall admission, 5/1 priority date for domestic students. Applications are processed on a rolling basis. Application fee: $30. Electronic applications accepted. *Unit head:* Dr. Carmen McCrink, Director, 305-899-3702, Fax: 305-899-4708, E-mail: cmccrink@mail.barry.edu. *Application contact:* Dave Fletcher, Director of Graduate Admissions, 305-899-3113, Fax: 305-899-2971, E-mail: dfletcher@mail.barry.edu.

Bowie State University, Graduate Programs, Program in Human Resource Development, Bowie, MD 20715-9465. Offers MA. Part-time and evening/weekend programs available. *Faculty:* 4 full-time (3 women), 4 part-time/adjunct (2 women). *Students:* 22 full-time (18 women), 40 part-time (34 women); includes 61 minority (59 African Americans, 1 Asian American or Pacific Islander, 1 Hispanic American). Average age 31. 35 applicants, 100% accepted, 22 enrolled. In 2006, 30 degrees awarded. *Degree requirements:* For master's, research paper, thesis optional. *Entrance requirements:* For master's, minimum GPA of 2.5. *Application deadline:* For fall admission, 4/1 priority date for domestic and international students; for spring admission, 11/1 priority date for domestic and international students. Applications are processed on a rolling basis. Application fee: $40. Electronic applications accepted. *Expenses:* Tuition, state resident: full-time $7,344; part-time $306 per credit. Tuition, nonresident: full-time $14,304; part-time $396 per credit. Required fees: $1,078; $77 per credit. $539 per term. One-time fee: $40. *Financial support:* Career-related internships or fieldwork and institutionally sponsored loans available. Support available to part-time students. Financial award application deadline: 4/1. *Unit head:* Dr. Marsha Jackson, Coordinator, 301-860-3108, E-mail: mjackson@bowiestate.edu. *Application contact:* Angela Issac, Information Contact.

California State University, Sacramento, Graduate Studies, College of Business Administration, Program in Business Administration, Sacramento, CA 95819-6048. Offers business administration (MBA); human resources (MBA); urban land development (MBA). *Accreditation:* AACSB. Part-time programs available. *Students:* 26 full-time (16 women), 66 part-time (23 women); includes 20 minority (13 Asian Americans or Pacific Islanders, 7 Hispanic Americans), 6 international. Average age 30. 229 applicants, 69% accepted, 22 enrolled. *Degree requirements:* For master's, thesis or alternative, writing proficiency exam. *Entrance requirements:* For master's, GMAT. Additional exam requirements/recommendations for international students: Required—TOEFL. *Application deadline:* Applications are processed on a rolling basis. Application fee: $55. Electronic applications accepted. *Financial support:* Research assistantships, teaching assistantships, career-related internships or fieldwork and Federal Work-Study available. Support available to part-time students. Financial award application deadline: 3/1.

Clemson University, Graduate School, College of Health, Education, and Human Development, School of Education, Program in Human Resource Development, Clemson, SC 29634. Offers MHRD. Part-time programs available. *Students:* 17 full-time (11 women), 39 part-time (19 women); includes 10 minority (9 African Americans, 1 Hispanic American), 2 international. 33 applicants, 70% accepted, 21 enrolled. In 2006, 47 degrees awarded. *Entrance requirements:* For master's, GRE General Test. Additional exam requirements/recommendations for international students: Required—TOEFL. *Application deadline:* For fall admission, 6/1 for domestic students; for spring admission, 10/1 for domestic students. Application fee: $50. Electronic applications accepted. *Expenses:* Tuition, state resident: full-time $8,812; part-time $450 per hour. Tuition, nonresident: full-time $18,036; part-time $760 per hour. Required fees: $474; $5 per term. *Financial support:* Application deadline: 6/1; *Unit head:* Dr. Phil McGee, Coordinator, 864-250-8880, Fax: 864-250-8889, E-mail: pmcgee@clemson.edu.

See Close-Up on page 531.

The College of New Rochelle, Graduate School, Division of Human Services, Program in Career Development, New Rochelle, NY 10805-2308. Offers MS, Certificate. Part-time programs available. *Faculty:* 7 full-time (4 women), 6 part-time/adjunct (3 women). *Students:* 2 full-time (both women), 7 part-time (4 women); includes 4 minority (3 African Americans, 1 American Indian/Alaska Native). Average age 37. In 2006, 5 degrees awarded. *Degree requirements:* For master's, fieldwork, internship. *Entrance requirements:* For master's, interview, minimum GPA of 3.0, writing sample. *Application deadline:* For fall admission, 8/1 priority date for domestic students. Applications are processed on a rolling basis. Application fee: $35. *Expenses:* Tuition: Part-time $575 per credit. Required fees: $90 per term. *Financial support:* Scholarships/grants and unspecified assistantships available. *Faculty research:* Technology. *Unit head:* Dr. Marie Ribarich, Head, Division of Human Services, 914-654-5561, Fax: 914-654-5593, E-mail: mribarich@cnr.edu.

Florida International University, College of Education, Department of Educational Leadership and Policy Studies, Program in Adult Education in Human Resource Development, Miami, FL 33199. Offers Ed D. Part-time and evening/weekend programs available. *Faculty:* 2 full-time (1 woman), 3 part-time/adjunct (2 women). *Students:* 7 full-time (6 women), 31 part-time (23 women); includes 27 minority (13 African Americans, 4 Asian Americans or Pacific Islanders, 10 Hispanic Americans). Average age 44. 10 applicants, 30% accepted, 3 enrolled. In 2006, 4 degrees awarded. *Degree requirements:* For doctorate, thesis/dissertation, registration. *Entrance requirements:* For doctorate, GRE General Test. Additional exam requirements/recommendations for international students: Required—TOEFL (minimum score 550 paper-based; 213 computer-based; 80 iBT), IELTS (minimum score 6). *Application deadline:* For fall admission, 6/1 priority date for domestic students, 4/1 for international students; for winter admission, 10/1 priority date for domestic students, 9/1 for international students; for spring admission, 3/1 priority date for domestic students, 2/1 for international students. Applications are processed on a rolling basis. Application fee: $30. Electronic applications accepted. *Expenses:* Tuition, state resident: part-time $249 per credit hour. Tuition, nonresident: part-time $753 per credit hour. Tuition and fees vary according to program. *Financial support:* Fellowships, research assistantships with full and partial tuition reimbursements, teaching assistantships with full and partial tuition reimbursements, Federal Work-Study and tuition waivers (full and partial) available. Support available to part-time students. *Faculty research:* Adult education, family literacy, learning technologies. *Unit head:* Dr. Jonette Rocco, Assistant Professor, 305-348-6151, E-mail: rocco@fiu.edu. *Application contact:* Marisa Salazar, Student Recruiter, 305-348-3002, Fax: 305-348-3227, E-mail: marisa.salazar@fiu.edu.

Florida International University, College of Education, Department of Educational Leadership and Policy Studies, Program in Human Resource Development, Miami, FL 33199. Offers MS. Part-time and evening/weekend programs available. *Faculty:* 2 full-time (1 woman), 3 part-time/adjunct (2 women). *Students:* 9 full-time (all women), 15 part-time (all women); includes 18 minority (9 African Americans, 9 Hispanic Americans). Average age 33. 14 applicants, 64% accepted, 8 enrolled. In 2006, 8 degrees awarded. *Entrance requirements:* Additional exam requirements/recommendations for international students: Required—TOEFL (minimum score 550 paper-based; 213 computer-based; 80 iBT), IELTS (minimum score 6). *Application deadline:* For fall admission, 6/1 priority date for domestic students, 4/1 for international students; for winter admission, 10/1 priority date for domestic students, 9/1 for international students; for spring admission, 3/1 priority date for domestic students, 2/1 for international students. Applications are processed on a rolling basis. Application fee: $30. Electronic applications accepted. *Expenses:* Tuition, state resident: part-time $249 per credit hour. Tuition, nonresident: part-time $753 per credit hour. Tuition and fees vary according to program. *Financial support:* In 2006–07, 3 teaching assistantships were awarded; research assistantships. *Unit head:* Dr. Jonette Rocco, Assistant Professor, 305-348-6151, E-mail: rocco@fiu.edu. *Application contact:* Marisa Salazar, Student Recruiter, 305-348-3002, Fax: 305-348-3227, E-mail: marisa.salazar@fiu.edu.

Florida State University, Graduate Studies, College of Education, Department of Educational Leadership and Policy Studies, Program in Adult Education and Human Resource Development, Tallahassee, FL 32306. Offers MS, Ed D, PhD, Ed S. *Faculty:* 2 full-time (0 women). *Students:* 1 (woman) full-time, 27 part-time (22 women); includes 8 minority (6 African Americans, 1 Asian American or Pacific Islander, 1 Hispanic American). 30 applicants, 47% accepted, 13 enrolled. In 2006, 10 degrees awarded. *Degree requirements:* For master's and Ed S, thesis optional; for doctorate, thesis/dissertation, comprehensive exam. *Entrance requirements:* For master's, GRE General Test, minimum GPA of 3.0; for doctorate and Ed S, GRE General Test, minimum graduate GPA of 3.0. *Application deadline:* For fall admission, 7/1 priority date for domestic students; for spring admission, 11/1 for domestic students. Applications are processed on a rolling basis. Application fee: $30. *Expenses:* Tuition, state resident: full-time $5,822; part-time $243 per credit hour. Tuition, nonresident: full-time $20,976; part-time $874 per credit hour. Tuition and fees vary according to program. *Financial support:* Fellowships, research assistantships, teaching assistantships, career-related internships or fieldwork available. Financial award applicants required to submit FAFSA. *Unit head:* Dr. John Sample, Coordinator, 850-644-8176, Fax: 850-644-6401. *Application contact:* Jimmy Pastrano, Program Assistant, 850-644-6777, Fax: 850-644-1258, E-mail: pastrano@coe.fsu.edu.

Friends University, Graduate School, Division of Business, Technology, and Leadership, Program in Organization Development, Wichita, KS 67213. Offers MSOD. Evening/weekend programs available. *Faculty:* 1 full-time (0 women), 2 part-time/adjunct (both women). *Students:* 26 full-time. In 2006, 28 degrees awarded. *Entrance requirements:* Additional exam requirements/recommendations for international students: Required—TOEFL (minimum score 560 paper-based; 220 computer-based). *Application deadline:* For fall admission, 8/15 priority date for domestic students, 7/15 priority date for international students; for spring admission, 12/15 priority date for domestic students, 11/15 priority date for international students. Applications are processed on a rolling basis. Application fee: $45 ($65 for international students). Electronic applications accepted. *Unit head:* Dr. Jim Maddox, Director, 800-794-6945 Ext. 5639, E-mail: jmaddox@friends.edu. *Application contact:* Craig Davis, Director of Graduate Admissions, 800-794-6945 Ext. 5573, Fax: 316-295-5050, E-mail: cdavis@friends.edu.

The George Washington University, Graduate School of Education and Human Development, Department of Counseling/Human and Organizational Studies, Program in Human Resource Development, Washington, DC 20052. Offers MA Ed, Ed D, Ed S. *Degree requirements:* For master's and Ed S, comprehensive exam; for doctorate, thesis/dissertation, comprehensive exam. *Entrance requirements:* For master's, GRE General Test or MAT, minimum GPA of 2.75; for doctorate, GRE General Test or MAT, interview, minimum GPA of 3.3; for Ed S, GRE General Test or MAT, minimum GPA of 3.3. *Faculty research:* Organizational learning, program evaluation.

Illinois Institute of Technology, Graduate College, Institute of Psychology, Chicago, IL 60616-3793. Offers clinical psychology (PhD); industrial/organizational psychology (PhD); personnel/human resource development (MS); psychology (MS); rehabilitation counseling (MS); rehabilitation counseling education (PhD). *Accreditation:* APA (one or more programs are accredited); CORE. Evening/weekend programs available. *Faculty:* 14 full-time (8 women), 8 part-time/adjunct (6 women). *Students:* 111 full-time (84 women), 71 part-time (52 women); includes 43 minority (18 African Americans, 1 American Indian/Alaska Native, 13 Asian Americans or Pacific Islanders, 11 Hispanic Americans), 25 international. Average age 29. 290 applicants, 37% accepted, 32 enrolled. In 2006, 45 master's, 11 doctorates awarded. Terminal master's awarded for partial completion of doctoral program. *Degree requirements:* For master's, thesis (for some programs), comprehensive exam; for doctorate, thesis/dissertation, qualifying exams, comprehensive exam. *Entrance requirements:* For master's, GRE General Test, minimum GPA of 3.0; for doctorate, GRE General Test, minimum GPA of 3.2. Additional exam requirements/recommendations for international students: Required—TOEFL (minimum score 550 paper-based; 213 computer-based). *Application deadline:* For fall admission, 1/15 for domestic and international students. Application fee: $40. Electronic applications accepted. *Expenses:* Tuition: Full-time $13,086; part-time $727 per credit. Required fees: $7 per credit. $235 per term. Tuition and fees vary according to class time, course level, course load, program and student level. *Financial support:* In 2006–07, 107 fellowships with partial tuition reimbursements (averaging $1,038 per year), 3 research assistantships with partial tuition reimbursements (averaging $2,100 per year), 41 teaching assistantships with partial tuition reimbursements (averaging $2,345 per year) were awarded; career-related internships or fieldwork, Federal Work-Study, institutionally sponsored loans, scholarships/grants, traineeships, health care benefits, and unspecified assistantships also available. Support available to part-time students. Financial award applicants required to submit FAFSA. *Faculty research:* Stigma and mental illness, depression, couples communication, leadership, psychometric theory. Total annual research expenditures: $1 million. *Unit head:* Dr. M. Ellen Mitchell, Director, 312-567-3501, Fax: 312-567-3493, E-mail: mitchelle@itt.edu. *Application contact:* Application Contact, 312-567-3500, Fax: 312-567-3493, E-mail: psychology@iit.edu.

Indiana State University, School of Graduate Studies, College of Technology, Department of Industrial Technology Education, Terre Haute, IN 47809-1401. Offers career and technical education (MS); human resource development (MS); technology education (MS). *Accreditation:* NCATE. *Faculty:* 5 full-time (0 women), 1 part-time/adjunct (0 women). *Students:* 33 full-time (18 women), 120 part-time (70 women); includes 39 minority (29 African Americans, 6 Asian Americans or Pacific Islanders, 4 Hispanic Americans), 15 international. Average age 34. 70 applicants, 96% accepted, 35 enrolled. In 2006, 65 degrees awarded. *Entrance requirements:* For master's, bachelor's degree in industrial technology or related field. Additional exam requirements/recommendations for international students: Required—TOEFL. *Application deadline:* For fall admission, 7/1 priority date for domestic students; for spring admission, 11/1 priority date for domestic students. Applications are processed on a rolling basis. Application fee: $35. Electronic applications accepted. *Expenses:* Tuition, state resident: part-time $278 per credit. Tuition, nonresident: part-time $552 per credit. *Financial support:* In 2006–07, 6 research assistantships with partial tuition reimbursements (averaging $7,000 per year) were awarded; fellowships with partial tuition reimbursements, teaching assistantships with partial tuition reimbursements, institutionally sponsored loans and tuition waivers (partial) also available. Financial award application deadline: 3/1; financial award applicants required to submit FAFSA. *Unit head:* Dr. James Smallwood, Interim Chairperson, 812-237-2642.

Indiana Tech, Program in Business Administration, Fort Wayne, IN 46803-1297. Offers accounting (MBA); human resources (MBA); management (MBA); marketing (MBA). Part-time and evening/weekend programs available. *Entrance requirements:* For master's, minimum undergraduate GPA of 2.5, GMAT or 2 years of work experience. Additional exam requirements/recommendations for international students: Required—TOEFL (minimum score 550 paper-based). Electronic applications accepted.

Indiana University of Pennsylvania, School of Graduate Studies and Research, Eberly College of Business and Information Technology, Department of Technology Support and Training, Program in Business/Workforce Development, Indiana, PA 15705-1087. Offers M Ed. *Faculty:* 7 full-time (4 women). *Students:* 9 full-time (4 women), 23 part-time (15 women); includes 1 minority (African American), 1 international. Average age 33. 27 applicants, 48% accepted. In 2006, 14 degrees awarded. *Degree requirements:* For master's, thesis optional. *Entrance requirements:* For master's, 2 letters of recommendation. Additional exam requirements/recommendations for international students: Required—TOEFL. *Application deadline:* For fall admission, 7/1 priority date for domestic students; for spring admission, 11/1 for domestic students. Applications are processed on a rolling basis. Application fee: $30. *Expenses:* Tuition, state resident: full-time $6,048; part-time $336 per credit. Tuition, nonresident: full-time $9,678; part-time $538 per credit. Required fees: $1,069; $148 per year. *Financial support:* In 2006–07, 7 research assistantships with full and partial tuition reimbursements (averaging $1,372 per year) were awarded; career-related internships or fieldwork and Federal Work-Study also available. Support available to part-time students. Financial award application deadline: 3/15; financial award applicants required to submit FAFSA. *Unit head:* Dr. Dawn Woodland, Graduate Coordinator, 724-357-5736, E-mail: woodland@iup.edu.

Inter American University of Puerto Rico, Metropolitan Campus, Graduate Programs, Faculty of Economics and Administrative Sciences, Program in Human Resources, San Juan, PR 00919-1293. Offers MBA. *Degree requirements:* For master's, comprehensive exam. *Entrance requirements:* For master's, GRE or EXADEP, interview. Electronic applications accepted.

Inter American University of Puerto Rico, San Germán Campus, Graduate Studies Center, Graduate Program in Business Administration, San Germán, PR 00683-5008. Offers accounting (MBA); finance (MBA); human resources (MBA, PhD); industrial relations (MBA); international business (PhD); labor relations (PhD); management information systems (MBA); marketing (MBA); quality organizational design (MBA). Part-time and evening/weekend programs available. *Faculty:* 12 full-time, 4 part-time/adjunct. *Students:* 265. Average age 27. In 2006, 67 master's, 1 doctorate awarded. *Degree requirements:* For master's, comprehensive exam. *Entrance requirements:* For master's, GRE General Test or EXADEP, minimum GPA of 3.0. *Application deadline:* For fall admission, 4/30 priority date for domestic students; for spring admission, 11/15 for domestic students. Applications are processed on a rolling basis. Application fee: $31. *Expenses:* Tuition: Part-time $175 per credit. Required fees: $238 per semester. Tuition and fees vary according to degree level. *Financial support:* Teaching assistantships, Federal Work-Study and unspecified assistantships available. *Application contact:* Prof. Duay Rivera, Graduate Coordinator, 787-264-1912 Ext. 7218, Fax: 787-892-7510, E-mail: durivera@sg.inter.edu.

Iowa State University of Science and Technology, Graduate College, College of Human Sciences, Department of Educational Leadership and Policy Studies, Ames, IA 50011. Offers counselor education (M Ed, MS); educational administration (M Ed, MS); educational leadership (PhD); higher education (M Ed, MS); organizational learning and human resource development (M Ed, MS); research and evaluation (MS). *Faculty:* 19 full-time, 9 part-time/adjunct. *Students:* 82 full-time (53 women), 191 part-time (109 women); includes 40 minority (23 African Americans, 4 American Indian/Alaska Native, 5 Asian Americans or Pacific Islanders, 8 Hispanic Americans), 5 international. 156 applicants, 70% accepted, 76 enrolled. In 2006, 95 master's, 13 doctorates awarded. *Degree requirements:* For master's, thesis or alternative; for doctorate, thesis/dissertation. *Entrance requirements:* For doctorate, GRE General Test. Additional exam requirements/recommendations for international students: Required—TOEFL (paper-based 560; computer-based 220; iBT 79) or IELTS (6.0). *Application deadline:* For fall admission, 1/1 priority date for domestic and international students. Applications are processed on a rolling basis. Application fee: $30 ($70 for international students). Electronic applications accepted. *Expenses:* Tuition, state resident: full-time $5,936; part-time $330 per credit. Tuition, nonresident: full-time $16,350; part-time $330 per credit. *Financial support:* In 2006–07, 17 research assistantships with full and partial tuition reimbursements (averaging $16,419 per year) were awarded; fellowships, teaching assistantships with full and partial tuition reimbursements, scholarships/grants, health care benefits, and unspecified assistantships also available. *Unit head:* Dr. Laura Rendon, Chair, 515-294-7093, E-mail: lrendon@iastate.edu. *Application contact:* Dr. Daniel Robinson, Information Contact, 515-294-1241, E-mail: eldrshp@iastate.edu.

John F. Kennedy University, School of Management, Program in Career Development, Pleasant Hill, CA 94523-4817. Offers career coaching (Certificate); career development (MA, Certificate). Part-time and evening/weekend programs available. *Degree requirements:* For master's, thesis or alternative. *Entrance requirements:* For master's, interview. Additional exam requirements/recommendations for international students: Required—TOEFL.

The Johns Hopkins University, Carey Business School, Department of Management, Baltimore, MD 21218-2699. Offers leadership development (Certificate); organization development and strategic human resources (MS); skilled facilitator (Certificate). Part-time and evening/weekend programs available. *Students:* 44 full-time (30 women), 127 part-time (93 women); includes 52 minority (44 African Americans, 2 Asian Americans or Pacific Islanders, 6 Hispanic Americans), 3 international. Average age 33. 147 applicants, 82% accepted, 104 enrolled. In 2006, 33 master's, 44 other advanced degrees awarded. *Degree requirements:* For master's, project. *Entrance requirements:* For master's and Certificate, minimum GPA of 3.0, resumé, work experience, two letters of recommendation. Additional exam requirements/recommendations for international students: Required—TOEFL (minimum score 600 paper-based; 250 computer-based; 100 iBT). *Application deadline:* For fall admission, 5/1 for international students; for spring admission, 10/15 for international students. Applications are processed on a rolling basis. Application fee: $60. *Expenses:* Tuition: Full-time $32,976. Tuition and fees vary according to degree level and program. *Financial support:* Scholarships/grants available. Support available to part-time students. Financial award application deadline: 6/1; financial award applicants required to submit FAFSA. *Unit head:* Dr. Toni Ungaretti, Chair, 410-516-7190, Fax: 410-230-4257, E-mail: toni@jhu.edu. *Application contact:* Robin Reed, Senior Academic Coordinator, 800-gotojhu, Fax: 410-872-1251, E-mail: onestop.admissions@jhu.edu.

Johnson & Wales University, The Alan Shawn Feinstein Graduate School, Certificate Programs, Providence, RI 02903-3703. Offers finance (CAGS); hospitality (CAGS); human resources management (CAGS). *Students:* 9 full-time (4 women), 2 part-time (both women); includes 1 African American, 8 international. Average age 29.*Unit head:* Thomas Rossi, Unit Head, 401-598-4738, E-mail: trossi@jwu.edu.

Manhattanville College, Graduate Programs, Humanities and Social Sciences Programs, Program in Organization Development and Human Resources Management, Purchase, NY 10577-2132. Offers MS. Part-time and evening/weekend programs available. In 2006, 24 degrees awarded. *Degree requirements:* For master's, thesis. *Entrance requirements:* For master's, interview, 2 letters of recommendation. *Application deadline:* Applications are processed on a rolling basis. Application fee: $55. *Application contact:* Natalia Fernandez, Director of Admissions, 914-323-5418, E-mail: gps@myllle.edu.

Marquette University, Graduate School, College of Business Administration, Program in Human Resources, Milwaukee, WI 53201-1881. Offers MSHR. Part-time and evening/weekend programs available. *Faculty:* 4 full-time (3 women), 2 part-time/adjunct (1 woman). *Students:* 8 full-time (6 women), 20 part-time (17 women); includes 5 minority (3 African Americans, 1 Asian American or Pacific Islander, 1 Hispanic American), 1 international. Average age 31. 32 applicants, 91% accepted, 16 enrolled. In 2006, 12 degrees awarded. *Entrance requirements:* For master's, GMAT or GRE General Test. Additional exam requirements/recommendations for international students: Required—TOEFL. Application fee: $40. *Financial support:* Research assistantships, teaching assistantships, Federal Work-Study, institutionally sponsored loans, and tuition waivers (full and partial) available. Support available to part-time students. Financial award application deadline: 2/15. *Faculty research:* Diversity, mentoring. *Unit head:* Dr. Timothy Keaveny, Management Chair, 414-288-3643.

McDaniel College, Graduate and Professional Studies, Program in Human Resources Development, Westminster, MD 21157-4390. Offers MS. Part-time and evening/weekend programs available. *Degree requirements:* For master's, portfolio, internship. *Entrance requirements:* For master's, letters of reference (3). Additional exam requirements/recommendations for international students: Required—TOEFL (minimum score 213 computer-based).

Midwestern State University, Graduate Studies, College of Education, Program in Counseling, Wichita Falls, TX 76308. Offers general counseling (MA); human resource development (MA); school counseling (M Ed); training and development (MA). Part-time and evening/weekend programs available. *Faculty:* 11 full-time (7 women), 5 part-time/adjunct (4 women). *Students:* 14 full-time (12 women), 96 part-time (80 women); includes 8 minority (3 African Americans, 1 American Indian/Alaska Native, 1 Asian American or Pacific Islander, 3 Hispanic Americans), 3 international. Average age 36. 30 applicants, 73% accepted, 17 enrolled. In 2006, 29 degrees awarded. *Degree requirements:* For master's, thesis (for some programs), comprehensive exam. *Entrance requirements:* For master's, GRE General Test, MAT, or GMAT, valid teaching certificate (M Ed). Additional exam requirements/recommendations for international students: Required—TOEFL (minimum score 550 paper-based; 213 computer-based). *Application deadline:* For fall admission, 7/1 for domestic students, 4/1 for international students; for spring admission, 11/1 for domestic students, 8/1 for international students. Applications are processed on a rolling basis. Application fee: $35 ($50 for international students). Electronic applications accepted. *Financial support:* In 2006–07, 79 students received support, including 5 teaching assistantships with partial tuition reimbursements available (averaging $5,833 per year); career-related internships or fieldwork, Federal Work-Study, institutionally sponsored loans, scholarships/grants, tuition waivers (partial), and unspecified assistantships also available. Support available to part-time students. Financial award application deadline: 5/1; financial award applicants required to submit FAFSA. *Unit head:* Dr. Michaelle Kitchen, Chair, 940-397-4141, Fax: 940-397-4694, E-mail: michaelle.kitchen@mwsu.edu. *Application contact:* 800-842-1922, Fax: 940-397-4672, E-mail: admissions@mwsu.edu.

Mississippi State University, College of Education, Department of Instructional Systems, Leadership, and Workforce Development, Mississippi State, MS 39762. Offers instructional technology (MSIT); technology (MS, Ed D, PhD, Ed S); workforce education leadership (MS). *Faculty:* 20 full-time (7 women), 1 (woman) part-time/adjunct. *Students:* 48 full-time (30 women), 62 part-time (48 women); includes 54 minority (53 African Americans, 1 Hispanic American). Average age 34. 28 applicants, 75% accepted, 17 enrolled. In 2006, 65 master's, 8 doctorates awarded. *Degree requirements:* For master's, comprehensive oral or written exam, thesis optional; for doctorate, thesis/dissertation, comprehensive oral and written exam. *Entrance requirements:* For master's, GRE, minimum GPA of 2.75 in junior and senior courses; for doctorate, GRE. Additional exam requirements/recommendations for international students: Required—TOEFL. *Application deadline:* For fall admission, 7/1 for domestic students; for spring admission, 11/1 for domestic students. Applications are processed on a rolling basis. Application fee: $30. *Expenses:* Tuition, state resident: full-time $4,550; part-time $253 per hour. Tuition, nonresident: full-time $10,552; part-time $584 per hour. International tuition: $10,882 full-time. Tuition and fees vary according to course load. *Financial support:* In 2006–07, 6 teaching assistantships with full tuition reimbursements (averaging $8,923 per year) were awarded; Federal Work-Study, institutionally sponsored loans, and unspecified assistantships also available. Financial award applicants required to submit FAFSA. *Faculty research:* Computer technology, nontraditional students, interactive video, instructional technology, educational leadership. *Unit head:* Dr. Linda Cornelius, Interim Head, 662-325-2281, Fax:

Human Resources Development

Mississippi State University (continued)
662-325-7599, E-mail: lcornelius@colled.msstate.edu. *Application contact:* Dr. Phil Bonfanti, Director of Admissions, 662-325-4104, Fax: 662-325-8872, E-mail: admit@msstate.edu.

National-Louis University, College of Management and Business, Program in Human Resource Management and Development, Chicago, IL 60603. Offers MS. Part-time programs available. *Students:* 33 full-time (27 women), 2 part-time (1 woman); includes 30 minority (23 African Americans, 2 Asian Americans or Pacific Islanders, 5 Hispanic Americans). Average age 37. 59 applicants, 98% accepted. In 2006, 85 degrees awarded. *Entrance requirements:* For master's, college-administered critical thinking and writing skills test, minimum GPA of 3.0, resumé. *Application deadline:* Applications are processed on a rolling basis. Application fee: $25. *Expenses: Contact institution.* One-time fee: $40 full-time. *Financial support:* Federal Work-Study, institutionally sponsored loans, and scholarships/grants available. Support available to part-time students. Financial award applicants required to submit FAFSA. *Unit head:* Douglas Wuggazer, Assistant Professor, 630-874-4384, E-mail: dwuggazer@nl.edu. *Application contact:* David McCulloch, Vice President for University Services, 800-443-5522 Ext. 5127, Fax: 847-465-0593, E-mail: dmcc@wheeling1.nl.edu.

Naval Postgraduate School, Graduate Programs, School of Business and Public Policy, Monterey, CA 93943. Offers contract management (MS); defense-focused business administration (MBA); executive business administration (MBA); leadership and human resource development (MS); management (MS); program management (MS); systems engineering management (MS). Program only open to commissioned officers of the United States and friendly nations and selected United States federal civilian employees. *Accreditation:* AACSB; NASPAA. Part-time programs available. Postbaccalaureate distance learning degree programs offered (minimal on-campus study). *Degree requirements:* For master's, thesis.

New York University, School of Continuing and Professional Studies, Center for Management, Program in Human Resource Management and Development, New York, NY 10012-1019. Offers benefits and compensation (Advanced Certificate); executive coaching and organizational development (Advanced Certificate); human resource development (MS); human resource management (MS, Advanced Certificate); organizational effectiveness (MS). *Faculty:* 1 full-time (0 women), 4 part-time/adjunct (3 women). *Students:* 7 full-time (6 women), 73 part-time (60 women); includes 32 minority (8 African Americans, 11 Asian Americans or Pacific Islanders, 13 Hispanic Americans), 6 international. Average age 31. 64 applicants, 63% accepted, 22 enrolled. *Entrance requirements:* For master's, GRE General Test or GMAT, 2 letters of recommendation, related work experience, resumé. Additional exam requirements/recommendations for international students: Required—TOEFL (minimum score 600 paper-based; 250 computer-based; 100 iBT), TWE. *Application deadline:* Applications are processed on a rolling basis. Application fee: $75. *Expenses:* Tuition: Part-time $1,080 per unit. Required fees: $56 per unit. $329 per term. Tuition and fees vary according to program. *Financial support:* In 2006–07, fellowships (averaging $1,068 per year); career-related internships or fieldwork and scholarships/grants also available. Support available to part-time students. Financial award applicants required to submit FAFSA. *Unit head:* Dennis Garritan, Head, 212-992-3600, Fax: 212-992-3650, E-mail: dennis.garritan@nyu.edu. *Application contact:* Helen Sapp, Assistant Director, 212-992-3600, Fax: 212-992-3676, E-mail: helen.sapp@nyu.edu.

See Close-Up on page 533.

North Carolina Agricultural and Technical State University, Graduate School, School of Education, Department of Human Development and Services, Greensboro, NC 27411. Offers guidance and counseling (MS); human resources (MS). *Accreditation:* ACA. Part-time and evening/weekend programs available. *Degree requirements:* For master's, thesis, qualifying exam, comprehensive exam. *Entrance requirements:* For master's, GRE General Test, minimum GPA of 3.0.

Northeastern Illinois University, Graduate College, College of Education, Department of Educational Leadership and Development, Program in Human Resource Development, Chicago, IL 60625-4699. Offers MA. Part-time and evening/weekend programs available. *Faculty:* 25 full-time (11 women), 22 part-time/adjunct (8 women). *Students:* 5 full-time (3 women), 34 part-time (25 women); includes 11 African Americans, 3 Asian Americans or Pacific Islanders, 3 Hispanic Americans, 3 international. Average age 38. 11 applicants, 91% accepted. In 2006, 5 degrees awarded. *Degree requirements:* For master's, comprehensive papers. *Entrance requirements:* For master's, minimum GPA of 2.75, BA in human resource development. *Application deadline:* For fall admission, 4/1 priority date for domestic students; for spring admission, 8/15 for domestic students. Applications are processed on a rolling basis. Application fee: $25. *Financial support:* In 2006–07, 14 students received support, including research assistantships with full tuition reimbursements available (averaging $6,600 per year); career-related internships or fieldwork, Federal Work-Study, institutionally sponsored loans, and tuition waivers (full and partial) also available. Support available to part-time students. *Faculty research:* Analogics, development of expertise, case-based instruction, action science organizational development, theoretical model building.

Oakland University, Graduate Study and Lifelong Learning, School of Education and Human Services, Department of Human Resource Development, Rochester, MI 48309-4401. Offers MTD. *Faculty:* 3 full-time (2 women). *Students:* 24 full-time (18 women), 28 part-time (21 women); includes 12 minority (11 African Americans, 1 Hispanic American), 2 international. Average age 32. 33 applicants, 82% accepted, 25 enrolled. In 2006, 20 degrees awarded. *Entrance requirements:* For master's, minimum GPA of 3.0 for unconditional admission. Additional exam requirements/recommendations for international students: Required—TOEFL (minimum score 550 paper-based; 213 computer-based). *Application deadline:* For fall admission, 8/1 priority date for domestic students, 5/1 priority date for international students; for winter admission, 12/1 priority date for domestic students, 9/1 priority date for international students; for spring admission, 4/1 priority date for domestic students. Applications are processed on a rolling basis. Application fee: $35. Electronic applications accepted. *Expenses:* Tuition, state resident: full-time $9,936; part-time $414 per credit. Tuition, nonresident: full-time $17,202; part-time $716 per credit. *Financial support:* Application deadline: 3/1. *Unit head:* Dr. Michael P. Long, Chair, 248-370-4109, Fax: 248-370-4095, E-mail: mlong@oakland.edu.

Ottawa University, Graduate Studies-Kansas City, Overland Park, KS 66211. Offers business administration (MBA); human resources (MA). Part-time and evening/weekend programs available. Postbaccalaureate distance learning degree programs offered (minimal on-campus study). *Faculty:* 4 full-time (1 woman), 8 part-time/adjunct (4 women). *Students:* 4 full-time (all women), 63 part-time (42 women); includes 10 minority (7 African Americans, 2 Asian Americans or Pacific Islanders, 1 Hispanic American). Average age 37. In 2006, 30 degrees awarded. *Degree requirements:* For master's, thesis or alternative, registration. *Entrance requirements:* For master's, resumé, 3 letters of recommendation. Additional exam requirements/recommendations for international students: Required—TOEFL (minimum score 550 paper-based; 213 computer-based). *Application deadline:* Applications are processed on a rolling basis. Application fee: $65. Electronic applications accepted. *Expenses: Contact institution.* *Unit head:* Dr. W. A. Breytspraak, Director of Graduate Studies, 913-451-1431, Fax: 913-451-0806, E-mail: breytspraak@ottawa.edu. *Application contact:* Alisa Jones, Enrollment Coordinator, 913-451-1431, Fax: 913-451-0806, E-mail: alisa.jones@ottawa.edu.

Palm Beach Atlantic University, MacArthur School of Continuing Education, West Palm Beach, FL 33416-4708. Offers organizational leadership (MS). Part-time and evening/weekend programs available. *Faculty:* 5 full-time (3 women), 1 (woman) part-time/adjunct. *Students:* 10 full-time (8 women), 21 part-time (10 women); includes 13 minority (10 African Americans, 3 Hispanic Americans), 2 international. Average age 39. 21 applicants, 90% accepted, 16 enrolled. In 2006, 28 degrees awarded. *Degree requirements:* For master's, thesis optional. *Entrance requirements:* For master's, GRE, minimum GPA of 3.0. Additional exam requirements/recommendations for international students: Required—TOEFL (minimum score 550 paper-based; 213 computer-based). *Application deadline:* For fall admission, 7/15 priority date for domestic students; for spring admission, 11/15 priority date for domestic

students. Applications are processed on a rolling basis. Application fee: $35. Electronic applications accepted. *Expenses:* Tuition: Full-time $10,665; part-time $395 per credit. Required fees: $90 per semester. *Financial support:* Tuition waivers (partial) and unspecified assistantships available. Financial award applicants required to submit FAFSA. *Unit head:* Dr. Jim Laub, Dean, 561-803-2318, Fax: 561-803-2306, E-mail: jim_laub@pba.edu. *Application contact:* Laura A. Leinweber, Director of Graduate and Evening Admissions, 888-468-6722, Fax: 561-803-2115, E-mail: grad@pba.edu.

Penn State University Park, Graduate School, College of the Liberal Arts, Department of Labor Studies and Industrial Relations, State College, University Park, PA 16802-1503. Offers industrial relations and human resources (MS). *Unit head:* Dr. Paul Clark, Department Head, 814-865-5425, Fax: 814-863-3578, E-mail: pfc2@psu.edu. *Application contact:* Dr. Paul Clark, Department Head, 814-865-5425, Fax: 814-863-3578, E-mail: pfc2@psu.edu.

Pittsburg State University, Graduate School, College of Technology, Department of Graphics and Imaging Technologies and Technology Management, Pittsburg, KS 66762. Offers human resource development (MS); industrial education (Ed S); technology (MS), including printing management. *Faculty:* 3 full-time (0 women). *Students:* 59. *Degree requirements:* For master's, thesis or alternative. Application fee: $35 ($60 for international students). *Expenses:* Tuition, state resident: full-time $2,144; part-time $181 per credit hour. Tuition, nonresident: full-time $5,273; part-time $442 per credit hour. Tuition and fees vary according to course load and campus/location. *Financial support:* In 2006–07, teaching assistantships (averaging $5,000 per year); career-related internships or fieldwork also available. *Unit head:* Dr. Jesús Rodriguez, Chairperson, 620-235-4420. *Application contact:* Jamie Vanderbeck, Assistant Director, 620-235-4223, Fax: 620-235-4219, E-mail: jvanderb@pittstate.edu.

Pittsburg State University, Graduate School, College of Technology, Department of Technology Studies, Program in Human Resource Development and Technical Teacher Education, Pittsburg, KS 66762. Offers MS, Ed S. *Students:* 23. *Degree requirements:* For master's, thesis or alternative. Application fee: $30 ($60 for international students). *Expenses:* Tuition, state resident: full-time $2,144; part-time $181 per credit hour. Tuition, nonresident: full-time $5,273; part-time $442 per credit hour. Tuition and fees vary according to course load and campus/location. *Financial support:* Teaching assistantships, career-related internships or fieldwork and Federal Work-Study available. *Application contact:* Marvene Darraugh, Administrative Officer, 620-235-4220, Fax: 620-235-4219, E-mail: mdarraug@pittstate.edu.

Rochester Institute of Technology, Graduate Enrollment Services, College of Applied Science and Technology, Department of Hospitality and Service Management, Program in Human Resources Development, Rochester, NY 14623-5603. Offers MS, AC. *Students:* 8 full-time (all women), 19 part-time (16 women); includes 5 minority (2 African Americans, 2 Asian Americans or Pacific Islanders, 1 Hispanic American), 4 international. 18 applicants, 50% accepted, 5 enrolled. In 2006, 18 master's, 3 other advanced degrees awarded. *Entrance requirements:* For master's, minimum GPA of 3.0. *Application deadline:* For fall admission, 3/1 priority date for domestic students. Applications are processed on a rolling basis. Application fee: $50. *Expenses:* Tuition: Full-time $28,491; part-time $800 per credit. Required fees: $201.

Rollins College, Hamilton Holt School, Program in Human Resources, Winter Park, FL 32789-4499. Offers MA. Part-time and evening/weekend programs available. *Students:* 3 full-time (all women), 61 part-time (47 women); includes 15 minority (6 African Americans, 9 Hispanic Americans), 5 international. Average age 32. In 2006, 21 degrees awarded. *Degree requirements:* For master's, thesis optional. *Entrance requirements:* For master's, GMAT, GRE, or MAT, interview. Additional exam requirements/recommendations for international students: Required—TOEFL. *Application deadline:* For fall admission, 4/1 for domestic students; for winter admission, 12/1 for domestic students. Application fee: $50. Electronic applications accepted. *Expenses: Contact institution.* *Financial support:* Available to part-time students. *Unit head:* Dr. Donald Rogers, Director, 407-646-2348, E-mail: drogers@rollins.edu. *Application contact:* Claire Thiebault, Coordinator of Records and Registration, 407-646-2653, Fax: 407-646-1551, E-mail: cthiebault@rollins.edu.

Roosevelt University, Graduate Division, Evelyn T. Stone University College, Program in Training and Development, Chicago, IL 60605-1394. Offers MA. *Students:* 16 full-time (13 women), 127 part-time (108 women); includes 63 minority (58 African Americans, 1 American Indian/Alaska Native, 1 Asian American or Pacific Islander, 3 Hispanic Americans). Average age 40. 129 applicants, 53% accepted, 60 enrolled. In 2006, 27 degrees awarded. *Degree requirements:* For master's, thesis. *Entrance requirements:* For master's, minimum GPA of 2.75, relevant work experience. *Application deadline:* For fall admission, 6/1 priority date for domestic students. Applications are processed on a rolling basis. Application fee: $25 ($35 for international students). *Financial support:* Application deadline: 2/15. *Unit head:* Director, 312-281-3157. *Application contact:* Joanne Canyon-Heller, Coordinator of Graduate Admission, 877-APPLY RU, Fax: 312-281-3356, E-mail: applyru@roosevelt.edu.

St. John Fisher College, Office of the Provost, Human Resources Development Program, Rochester, NY 14618-3597. Offers MS. Part-time and evening/weekend programs available. *Faculty:* 1 full-time (0 women), 5 part-time/adjunct (3 women). *Students:* 12 full-time (10 women), 24 part-time (16 women); includes 5 African Americans, 4 Hispanic Americans. Average age 33. 15 applicants, 93% accepted, 12 enrolled. In 2006, 6 degrees awarded. *Degree requirements:* For master's, project, professional portfolio. *Entrance requirements:* For master's, minimum GPA of 3.0, 2 years of related work experience. Additional exam requirements/recommendations for international students: Required—TOEFL (minimum score 575 paper-based; 233 computer-based; 80 iBT). *Application deadline:* For fall admission, 7/1 for domestic students; for spring admission, 10/30 for domestic students. Applications are processed on a rolling basis. Application fee: $30. *Expenses:* Tuition: Part-time $615 per credit. Tuition and fees vary according to program. *Financial support:* Federal Work-Study and scholarships/grants available. Financial award application deadline: 2/15; financial award applicants required to submit FAFSA. *Faculty research:* Empowerment, leadership, group dynamics, team learning, project management. *Unit head:* Dr. Timothy M. Franz, Graduate Director, 585-385-8170, Fax: 585-385-7311, E-mail: tfranz@sjfc.edu. *Application contact:* Shannon Cleverley, Director of Graduate Admissions, 585-385-8161, Fax: 585-385-8344, E-mail: scleverley@sjfc.edu.

Salve Regina University, Graduate Studies, Program in Business Administration, Newport, RI 02840-4192. Offers business administration (MBA); business studies (Certificate); human resources management (Certificate); management (Certificate); organizational development (Certificate). Part-time and evening/weekend programs available. Postbaccalaureate distance learning degree programs offered (minimal on-campus study). *Faculty:* 1 (woman) full-time, 9 part-time/adjunct (2 women). *Students:* 21 full-time (6 women), 70 part-time (30 women); includes 1 minority (African American) Average age 35. 90 applicants, 70% accepted, 54 enrolled. In 2006, 42 degrees awarded. *Entrance requirements:* For master's, GMAT, GRE General Test, or MAT, 6 undergraduate credits each in accounting, economics, and quantitative analysts. Additional exam requirements/recommendations for international students: Required—TOEFL or IELTS. *Application deadline:* For fall admission, 3/15 priority date for domestic and international students; for spring admission, 9/15 priority date for domestic and international students. Applications are processed on a rolling basis. Application fee: $50. Electronic applications accepted. *Financial support:* Career-related internships or fieldwork and Federal Work-Study available. Support available to part-time students. Financial award application deadline: 3/1. *Unit head:* Dr. Myra Edelstein, Director, 401-341-2153, E-mail: edelstem@salve.edu. *Application contact:* Karen E. Johnson, Graduate Admissions Counselor, 401-341-2153, Fax: 401-341-2973, E-mail: johnsonke@salve.edu.

Siena Heights University, Graduate College, Program in Human Resource Development, Adrian, MI 49221-1796. Offers MA. Part-time and evening/weekend programs available. *Degree requirements:* For master's, thesis, internship, presentation, project. *Entrance requirements:* For master's, minimum GPA of 3.0, interview.

Southern New Hampshire University, School of Education, Manchester, NH 03106-1045. Offers business education (MS); child development (M Ed); computer technology education (Certificate); curriculum and instruction (M Ed); education (M Ed, CAS); elementary education (M Ed); general special education (Certificate); school business administrator (Certificate); school counseling (M Ed); school psychology (M Ed); secondary education (M Ed); training and development (Certificate). Part-time and evening/weekend programs available. Post-baccalaureate distance learning degree programs offered. *Faculty:* 6 full-time (3 women), 9 part-time/adjunct (7 women). *Students:* Average age 35. In 2006, 52 degrees awarded. *Degree requirements:* For master's, thesis or alternative, comprehensive exam (for some programs). *Entrance requirements:* For master's, GRE General Test or MAT, minimum GPA of 3.0. Additional exam requirements/recommendations for international students: Required—TOEFL (minimum score 550 paper-based; 213 computer-based). *Application deadline:* Applications are processed on a rolling basis. Application fee: $25. Electronic applications accepted. *Expenses: Contact institution. Financial support:* Institutionally sponsored loans available. Financial award applicants required to submit FAFSA. *Unit head:* Dr. Patrick J. Hartwick, Dean, 603-668-2211 Ext. 4698, Fax: 603-629-4673, E-mail: p.hartwick@snhu.edu. *Application contact:* Scott Durand, Director of Graduate Enrollment Services, 603-644-3102 Ext. 3338, Fax: 603-644-3144, E-mail: s.durand@snhu.edu.

Suffolk University, College of Arts and Sciences, Department of Education and Human Services, Program in Adult and Organizational Learning, Boston, MA 02108-2770. Offers adult and organizational learning (MS); human resources (MS, CAGS); instructional design (CAGS); organizational development (CAGS); organizational learning (CAGS). Part-time and evening/weekend programs available. *Entrance requirements:* For master's, GRE General Test or MAT. *Application deadline:* For fall admission, 6/15 priority date for domestic students, 6/15 for international students; for spring admission, 11/15 priority date for domestic students, 11/15 for international students. Applications are processed on a rolling basis. Application fee: $35. *Financial support:* Fellowships available. Financial award application deadline: 4/1. *Faculty research:* Adult training methods, adult learning theory, instructional design, learning and teaching styles, systems thinking. *Unit head:* Dr. Christine M. Westphal, Graduate Program Director, 617-994-6455, Fax: 617-722-9440, E-mail: cwestphal@suffolk.edu. *Application contact:* Judith Reynolds, Director of Graduate Admissions, 617-573-8302, Fax: 617-523-0116, E-mail: grad.admission@suffolk.edu.

Suffolk University, College of Arts and Sciences, Department of Education and Human Services, Program in Human Resources, Boston, MA 02108-2770. Offers MS, CAGS. Part-time and evening/weekend programs available. *Entrance requirements:* For master's, GRE General Test or MAT. *Application deadline:* For fall admission, 6/15 priority date for domestic students, 6/15 for international students; for spring admission, 11/15 priority date for domestic students, 11/15 for international students. Applications are processed on a rolling basis. Application fee: $35. *Financial support:* Fellowships, career-related internships or fieldwork, Federal Work-Study, and institutionally sponsored loans available. Support available to part-time students. Financial award application deadline: 4/1; financial award applicants required to submit FAFSA. *Unit head:* Dr. Christine M. Westphal, Director Human Resources, Learning and Performance Programs, 617-994-6455, Fax: 617-722-9440, E-mail: cwestphal@suffolk.edu. *Application contact:* Judith Reynolds, Director of Graduate Admissions, 617-573-8302, Fax: 617-523-0116, E-mail: grad.admission@suffolk.edu.

Syracuse University, Martin J. Whitman School of Management, PhD Program in Business Administration, Syracuse, NY 13244. Offers accounting (PhD); finance (PhD); management information systems (PhD); managerial statistics (PhD); marketing (PhD); operations management (PhD); organizational behavior (PhD); strategy and human resources (PhD); supply chain management (PhD). *Faculty:* 71 full-time (16 women), 2 part-time/adjunct (1 woman). *Students:* 34 full-time (10 women); includes 1 minority (African American), 24 international. Average age 31. 89 applicants, 8% accepted, 4 enrolled. In 2006, 8 degrees awarded. *Degree requirements:* For doctorate, thesis/dissertation, summer research paper, comprehensive exam, registration. *Entrance requirements:* For doctorate, GMAT, 3 recommendations. Additional exam requirements/recommendations for international students: Required—TOEFL (minimum score 600 paper-based; 250 computer-based; 100 iBT). *Application deadline:* For fall admission, 1/30 priority date for domestic students. Applications are processed on a rolling basis. Application fee: $75. Electronic applications accepted. *Expenses:* Tuition: Full-time $16,920; part-time $940 per credit hour. Required fees: $930; $930 per year. *Financial support:* In 2006–07, 1 fellowship with full tuition reimbursement (averaging $19,000 per year), 26 teaching assistantships with full tuition reimbursements (averaging $16,500 per year) were awarded; research assistantships with full tuition reimbursements, health care benefits and unspecified assistantships also available. Financial award application deadline: 1/30. *Faculty research:* Marketing models, market microstructure, supply chain, auditing, corporate governance. *Unit head:* Dr. Ravi Dharwadkar, Director of the PhD Program, 315-443-3386, E-mail: rdharwad@syr.edu. *Application contact:* Shannon Hiemstra, Assistant Director for PhD and Research Programs, 315-443-3549, Fax: 315-443-3671, E-mail: srhiemst@syr.edu.

Texas A&M University, College of Education and Human Development, Department of Educational Administration and Human Resource Development, College Station, TX 77843. Offers M Ed, MS, Ed D, PhD. *Accreditation:* NCATE. Part-time programs available. *Faculty:* 19 full-time (10 women), 4 part-time/adjunct (2 women). *Students:* 164 full-time (111 women), 289 part-time (185 women); includes 133 minority (50 African Americans, 2 American Indian/Alaska Native, 4 Asian Americans or Pacific Islanders, 77 Hispanic Americans), 31 international. Average age 37. 103 applicants, 68% accepted, 40 enrolled. In 2006, 47 master's, 26 doctorates awarded. *Degree requirements:* For master's, thesis optional; for doctorate, thesis/dissertation. *Entrance requirements:* For master's, GRE General Test, writing exam, interview, professional experience; for doctorate, GRE General Test, writing exam, interview/presentation, professional experience. Additional exam requirements/recommendations for international students: Required—TOEFL. *Application deadline:* For fall admission, 12/1 for domestic and international students; for spring admission, 8/15 for domestic and international students. Application fee: $50 ($75 for international students). Electronic applications accepted. *Expenses:* Tuition, state resident: full-time $4,697. Tuition, nonresident: full-time $11,297. Required fees: $2,272. *Financial support:* In 2006–07, fellowships (averaging $20,000 per year), research assistantships (averaging $12,000 per year) were awarded; career-related internships or fieldwork and institutionally sponsored loans also available. Support available to part-time students. Financial award application deadline: 3/1; financial award applicants required to submit FAFSA. *Faculty research:* Higher education administration, public school administration, student affairs. *Unit head:* Dr. Yvonna Lincoln, Head, 979-845-2716, Fax: 979-862-4347. *Application contact:* Joyce Nelson, Senior Academic Advisor, 979-847-9098, Fax: 979-862-4347, E-mail: jnelson@tamu.edu.

Towson University, Graduate School, Program in Human Resource Development, Towson, MD 21252-0001. Offers educational leadership (administrator I certification) (CAS); human resource development (MS). Part-time and evening/weekend programs available. *Faculty:* 10 full-time (5 women). *Students:* 45 full-time (37 women), 139 part-time (103 women); includes 45 minority (40 African Americans, 3 Asian Americans or Pacific Islanders, 2 Hispanic Americans), 10 international. 105 applicants, 74% accepted, 44 enrolled. In 2006, 51 degrees awarded. *Degree requirements:* For master's, comprehensive exam; for CAS, exam, internship. *Entrance requirements:* For master's, 2 letters of recommendation, minimum GPA of 3.0. Additional exam requirements/recommendations for international students: Required—TOEFL. *Application deadline:* Applications are processed on a rolling basis. Application fee: $50. Electronic applications accepted. *Expenses:* Tuition, state resident: part-time $275 per unit. Tuition, nonresident: part-time $577 per unit. Required fees: $72 per unit. *Financial support:* In 2006–07, 1 research assistantship with full and partial tuition reimbursement was awarded; career-related internships or fieldwork, Federal Work-Study, and unspecified assistantships also available. Financial award application deadline: 4/1; financial award applicants required to submit FAFSA. *Faculty research:* Workforce training and development. *Unit head:* Dr. Mark Arvisais, Graduate Program Director, 410-704-4661. *Application contact:* 410-704-2501, Fax: 410-704-4675, E-mail: grads@towson.edu.

Universidad Central del Este, Graduate School, San Pedro de Macoris, Dominican Republic. Offers accounting (M Ad); administration (M Ad); architecture (M Arch); civil engineering (ME); electromechanical engineering (ME); human resources (M Ad); industrial engineering (ME); public health (MPH). *Entrance requirements:* For master's, letters of recommendation.

University of Bridgeport, School of Education and Human Resources, Division of Human Resources, Bridgeport, CT 06604. Offers college student personnel (MS); community counseling (MS); human resource development (MS). Part-time and evening/weekend programs available. *Faculty:* 6 full-time (3 women), 14 part-time/adjunct (9 women). *Students:* 27 full-time (21 women), 76 part-time (59 women); includes 42 minority (30 African Americans, 1 American Indian/Alaska Native, 1 Asian American or Pacific Islander, 10 Hispanic Americans), 23 international. Average age 34. 84 applicants, 70% accepted, 37 enrolled. In 2006, 25 degrees awarded. *Degree requirements:* For master's, thesis optional. *Application deadline:* For fall admission, 8/1 priority date for domestic students; for spring admission, 12/1 priority date for domestic students. Applications are processed on a rolling basis. Application fee: $25 ($35 for international students). Electronic applications accepted. *Financial support:* In 2006–07, 27 students received support; fellowships, research assistantships, teaching assistantships, career-related internships or fieldwork, Federal Work-Study, and institutionally sponsored loans available. Support available to part-time students. Financial award application deadline: 6/1; financial award applicants required to submit FAFSA. *Faculty research:* Corporate elder care programs. *Unit head:* Dr. Joseph T. Cullen, Head, 203-576-4175.

University of Connecticut, Graduate School, Center for Continuing Studies, Program in Human Resource Management, Storrs, CT 06269. Offers labor relations (MPS); personnel (MPS). *Faculty:* 3 full-time (0 women). *Students:* 1 (woman) full-time, 36 part-time (28 women); includes 9 minority (5 African Americans, 4 Hispanic Americans), 1 international. Average age 35. 21 applicants, 48% accepted, 10 enrolled. In 2006, 1 degree awarded.

See Close-Up on page 539.

University of Illinois at Urbana–Champaign, Graduate College, College of Education, Department of Human Resource Education, Champaign, IL 61820. Offers Ed M, MA, MS, Ed D, PhD, CAS, MBA/M Ed. Part-time programs available. *Faculty:* 6 full-time (2 women), 3 part-time/adjunct (0 women). *Students:* 51 full-time (34 women), 138 part-time (96 women); includes 37 minority (24 African Americans, 11 Asian Americans or Pacific Islanders, 2 Hispanic Americans), 28 international. 82 applicants, 71% accepted, 57 enrolled. In 2006, 58 master's, 7 doctorates, 2 other advanced degrees awarded. *Degree requirements:* For master's, thesis (for some programs); for doctorate, thesis/dissertation. *Application deadline:* For fall admission, 5/15 for domestic students; for spring admission, 10/16 for domestic students. Applications are processed on a rolling basis. Application fee: $50 ($60 for international students). Electronic applications accepted. *Financial support:* In 2006–07, 2 fellowships, 10 research assistantships, 20 teaching assistantships were awarded; career-related internships or fieldwork and tuition waivers (full and partial) also available. Financial award application deadline: 2/15. *Unit head:* Scott D. Johnson, Interim Head, 217-333-0807, Fax: 217-244-5632, E-mail: sjohnson@uiuc.edu. *Application contact:* Laura Irle, Secretary, 217-333-0807, Fax: 217-244-5632, E-mail: lirle@uiuc.edu.

University of Louisville, Graduate School, College of Education and Human Development, Department of Leadership, Foundations and Human Resource Education, Program in Human Resource Education, Louisville, KY 40292-0001. Offers M Ed. *Accreditation:* NCATE. Part-time and evening/weekend programs available. *Students:* 23 full-time (13 women), 71 part-time (43 women); includes 8 minority (6 African Americans, 1 Asian American or Pacific Islander, 1 Hispanic American), 47 international. Average age 37. In 2006, 24 degrees awarded. *Degree requirements:* For master's, thesis. *Entrance requirements:* For master's, GRE General Test. *Application deadline:* Applications are processed on a rolling basis. Application fee: $50. Electronic applications accepted. *Financial support:* Research assistantships with full tuition reimbursements, career-related internships or fieldwork, Federal Work-Study, and scholarships/grants available. *Unit head:* Dr. Carolyn Rude-Parkins, Chair, 502-852-0609, Fax: 502-852-4653, E-mail: cparkins@louisville.edu.

University of Minnesota, Twin Cities Campus, Graduate School, College of Education and Human Development, Department of Work and Human Resource Education, Program in Human Resource Development, Minneapolis, MN 55455-0213. Offers M Ed, MA, Ed D, PhD, Certificate. *Students:* 36 full-time (25 women), 46 part-time (33 women); includes 11 minority (4 African Americans, 1 American Indian/Alaska Native, 4 Asian Americans or Pacific Islanders, 2 Hispanic Americans), 18 international. Average age 36. 48 applicants, 79% accepted, 34 enrolled. In 2006, 25 master's, 29 other advanced degrees awarded. *Expenses:* Tuition, state resident: full-time $9,302; part-time $775 per credit. Tuition, nonresident: full-time $16,400; part-time $1,367 per credit. Full-time tuition and fees vary according to class time, course load, program, reciprocity agreements and student level. *Application contact:* Dr. Mary Bents, Associate Dean, 612-625-6501, Fax: 612-626-1580, E-mail: mbents@tc.umn.edu.

University of Missouri–St. Louis, Graduate School, Program in Public Policy Administration, St. Louis, MO 63121. Offers health policy (MPPA); local government management (MPPA); managing human resources and organization (MPPA); nonprofit organization management (MPPA); nonprofit organization management and leadership (Certificate); policy research and analysis (MPPA); public sector human resources management (MPPA). *Accreditation:* NASPAA. Part-time and evening/weekend programs available. *Faculty:* 8 full-time (5 women), 5 part-time/adjunct (1 woman). *Students:* 21 full-time (13 women), 61 part-time (35 women); includes 22 minority (18 African Americans, 1 American Indian/Alaska Native, 2 Asian Americans or Pacific Islanders, 1 Hispanic American), 4 international. Average age 34. In 2006, 22 degrees awarded. *Entrance requirements:* For master's, 3 letters of recommendation. Additional exam requirements/recommendations for international students: Required—TOEFL (minimum score 550 paper-based; 213 computer-based). *Application deadline:* For fall admission, 7/15 priority date for domestic students; for spring admission, 12/15 priority date for domestic students. Applications are processed on a rolling basis. Application fee: $35 ($40 for international students). Electronic applications accepted. *Expenses:* Tuition, state resident: part-time $332 per credit hour. Tuition, nonresident: part-time $770 per credit hour. *Financial support:* In 2006–07, 2 research assistantships with full tuition reimbursements (averaging $14,100 per year) were awarded; teaching assistantships with partial tuition reimbursements, career-related internships or fieldwork also available. *Faculty research:* Urban policy, public finance, evaluation. *Unit head:* Brady Baybeck, Director, 314-516-5145, Fax: 314-516-5210, E-mail: baybeck@umsl.edu. *Application contact:* 314-516-5458, Fax: 314-516-6996, E-mail: gradadm@umsl.edu.

University of Regina, Faculty of Graduate Studies and Research, Faculty of Education, Department of Human Resources Development, Regina, SK S4S 0A2, Canada. Offers MHRD. Part-time programs available. *Faculty:* 2 full-time (1 woman). *Students:* 5 full-time (all women), 13 part-time (11 women). 8 applicants, 88% accepted. In 2006, 10 degrees awarded. *Degree requirements:* For master's, practicum, project, course-based thesis. *Entrance requirements:* Additional exam requirements/recommendations for international students: Required—TOEFL (minimum score 580 paper-based; 237 computer-based; 88 iBT). *Application deadline:* For fall admission, 2/15 for domestic students; for winter admission, 2/15 for domestic students; for spring admission, 2/15 for domestic students. Application fee: $60 ($100 for international students). *Financial support:* Fellowships, research assistantships, teaching assistantships available. Financial award application deadline: 6/15. *Application contact:* Vicki Minhinnick, Graduate Program Coordinator, 306-585-4506, Fax: 306-585-5387, E-mail: edgrad@uregina.ca.

The University of Scranton, Graduate School, Department of Health Administration and Human Resources, Program in Human Resources Administration, Scranton, PA 18510. Offers human resources (MS); human resources development (MS); organizational leadership (MS). Part-time and evening/weekend programs available. *Students:* 3 full-time (all women), 19 part-time (12 women); includes 1 minority (African American) Average age 34. 21 applicants,

Human Resources Development

The University of Scranton (continued)
100% accepted. In 2006, 19 degrees awarded. *Degree requirements:* For master's, capstone experience. *Entrance requirements:* For master's, minimum GPA of 2.75. Additional exam requirements/recommendations for international students: Required—TOEFL (minimum score 500 paper-based; 173 computer-based), IELTS (minimum score 6). *Application deadline:* Applications are processed on a rolling basis. Application fee: $50. *Expenses:* Tuition: Part-time $684 per credit. Required fees: $25 per term. *Financial support:* Fellowships, teaching assistantships, career-related internships or fieldwork, Federal Work-Study, and unspecified assistantships available. Support available to part-time students. Financial award application deadline: 3/1. *Unit head:* Dr. Terri Freeman Smith, Director, 570-941-6218.

The University of Tennessee, Graduate School, College of Business Administration, Program in Human Resource Development, Knoxville, TN 37996. Offers teacher licensure (MS); training and development (MS). Part-time programs available. *Faculty:* 15 full-time (2 women). *Students:* 20 (13 women); includes 1 African American. In 2006, 3 degrees awarded. *Degree requirements:* For master's, thesis. *Entrance requirements:* For master's, GRE General Test, minimum GPA of 2.7. *Application deadline:* For fall admission, 2/1 for domestic students. Application fee: $35. Electronic applications accepted. *Expenses:* Tuition, state resident: full-time $5,574. Tuition, nonresident: full-time $16,840. Required fees: $792. *Financial support:* In 2006–07, 9 teaching assistantships were awarded; fellowships, research assistantships, career-related internships or fieldwork, Federal Work-Study, institutionally sponsored loans, and unspecified assistantships also available. Financial award application deadline: 2/1; financial award applicants required to submit FAFSA. *Unit head:* Dr. Billie J. Collier, Interim Head, 865-974-5224, E-mail: bcollier@utk.edu. *Application contact:* Dr. Ernest Brewer, Graduate Representative, 865-974-8924, E-mail: ewbrewer@utk.edu.

The University of Texas at Austin, Graduate School, McCombs School of Business and College of Education, Program in Human Resource Development Leadership, Austin, TX 78712-1111. Offers MHRDL. *Entrance requirements:* For master's, GMAT or GRE, minimum GPA of 3.0.

The University of Texas at Tyler, Graduate Studies, College of Business and Technology, Department of Human Resource Development and Technology, Tyler, TX 75799-0001. Offers human resource development (MS); industrial distribution (MS); industrial safety (MS); industrial technology (MS); instructional technology (MS); technology systems (MS). Part-time and evening/weekend programs available. Postbaccalaureate distance learning degree programs offered (no on-campus study). *Degree requirements:* For master's, comprehensive exam. *Entrance requirements:* For master's, GRE General Test or MAT. Additional exam requirements/recommendations for international students: Required—TOEFL. Electronic applications accepted. *Expenses:* Tuition, state resident: part-time $50 per credit hour. Tuition, nonresident: part-time $328 per credit hour. Required fees: $107 per credit hour. $426 per term. *Faculty research:* Human resource development.

University of Wisconsin–Milwaukee, Graduate School, College of Letters and Sciences, Interdepartmental Program in Human Resources and Labor Relations, Milwaukee, WI 53201-0413. Offers MHRLR, Certificate. Part-time programs available. *Faculty:* 21 full-time (7 women). *Students:* 14 full-time (7 women), 35 part-time (28 women); includes 8 minority (4 African Americans, 2 American Indian/Alaska Native, 1 Asian American or Pacific Islander, 1 Hispanic American), 3 international. 49 applicants, 53% accepted, 15 enrolled. In 2006, 16 degrees awarded. *Entrance requirements:* For master's, GMAT or GRE General Test. *Application deadline:* For fall admission, 1/1 priority date for domestic students; for spring admission, 9/1 for domestic students. Applications are processed on a rolling basis. Application fee: $45 ($75 for international students). *Expenses:* Tuition, state resident: part-time $510 per credit. Tuition, nonresident: part-time $1,408 per credit. Tuition and fees vary according to program. *Financial support:* Fellowships, research assistantships, teaching assistantships, career-related internships or fieldwork available. Support available to part-time students. Financial award application deadline: 4/15. *Unit head:* Susan M. Donohue-Davies, Representative, 414-299-4009, Fax: 414-229-5915, E-mail: suedono@uwm.edu.

University of Wisconsin–Stout, Graduate School, College of Technology, Engineering, and Management, Program in Training and Development, Menomonie, WI 54751. Offers MS. Part-time programs available. *Faculty:* 8 full-time (3 women). *Students:* 29 full-time (16 women), 39 part-time (28 women); includes 5 minority (1 African American, 3 American Indian/Alaska Native, 1 Hispanic American), 7 international. Average age 34. 27 applicants, 85% accepted, 15 enrolled. In 2006, 29 degrees awarded. *Degree requirements:* For master's, thesis. *Entrance requirements:* For master's, minimum GPA of 2.75. Additional exam requirements/recommendations for international students: Required—TOEFL (minimum score 500 paper-based; 173 computer-based; 61 iBT). *Application deadline:* Applications are processed on a rolling basis. Application fee: $45. Electronic applications accepted. *Expenses:* Tuition, state resident: part-time $317 per credit. Tuition, nonresident: part-time $543 per credit. Tuition and fees vary according to reciprocity agreements. *Financial support:* In 2006–07, 2 research assistantships with partial tuition reimbursements (averaging $2,846 per year), 1 teaching assistantship (averaging $2,522 per year) were awarded; Federal Work-Study, scholarships/grants, tuition waivers (full and partial), and unspecified assistantships also available. Support available to part-time students. Financial award application deadline: 4/1; financial award applicants required to submit FAFSA. *Faculty research:* Organizational behavior, performance, learning and performance, strategic planning. *Unit head:* Dr. Katherine Lui, Director, 715-232-5634, E-mail: luik@uwstout.edu. *Application contact:* Anne E. Johnson, Graduate Student Evaluator, 715-232-1322, Fax: 715-232-2413, E-mail: johnsona@uwstout.edu.

Vanderbilt University, Peabody College, Department of Leadership and Organizations, Nashville, TN 37240-1001. Offers education policy (MPP); educational leadership and policy (Ed D); higher education (M Ed); higher education, leadership and policy (Ed D); human resource development (M Ed); international education policy and management (M Ed); organizational leadership (M Ed); school administration (M Ed). Part-time and evening/weekend programs available. *Faculty:* 21 full-time (6 women), 9 part-time/adjunct (3 women). *Students:* 131 full-time (88 women), 85 part-time (39 women); includes 35 minority (30 African Americans, 4 Asian Americans or Pacific Islanders, 1 Hispanic American), 11 international. Average age 31. 214 applicants, 63% accepted, 64 enrolled. In 2006, 43 master's, 12 doctorates awarded. *Median time to degree:* Of those who began their doctoral program in fall 1998, 62% received their degree in 8 years or less. *Degree requirements:* For master's, thesis optional; for doctorate, thesis/dissertation, qualifying exams, residency. *Entrance requirements:* For master's and doctorate, GRE General Test. Additional exam requirements/recommendations for international students: Required—TOEFL (minimum score 550 paper-based; 213 computer-based). *Application deadline:* For fall admission, 12/31 priority date for domestic and international students; for spring admission, 11/1 priority date for domestic and international students. Applications are processed on a rolling basis. Application fee: $0. Electronic applications accepted. *Expenses:* Tuition: Full-time $24,462. Required fees: $2,515. One-time fee: $30 full-time. Full-time tuition and fees vary according to course load, degree level and program. *Financial support:* In 2006–07, 90 students received support, including 50 fellowships with full and partial tuition reimbursements available, 38 research assistantships with full and partial tuition reimbursements available, 2 teaching assistantships with full and partial tuition reimbursements available; Federal Work-Study, institutionally sponsored loans, scholarships/grants, tuition waivers (partial), and unspecified assistantships also available. Support available to part-time students. Financial award application deadline: 2/1; financial award applicants required to submit FAFSA. *Faculty research:* Education policy, education finances, economics of education, education leadership and management, higher education leadership and policy; educator pay for performance. *Unit head:* James W. Guthrie, Chair, 615-322-8000, Fax: 615-343-7094, E-mail: james.w.guthrie@vanderbilt.edu. *Application contact:* Rosie Moody, Educational Coordinator, 615-322-8019, Fax: 615-343-7094, E-mail: rosie.moody@vanderbilt.edu.

Villanova University, Graduate School of Liberal Arts and Sciences, Department of Human Resource Development, Villanova, PA 19085-1699. Offers MS. Part-time and evening/

weekend programs available. *Faculty:* 3 full-time (1 woman), 8 part-time/adjunct (5 women). *Students:* 11 full-time (10 women), 44 part-time (32 women); includes 7 minority (2 African Americans, 4 Asian Americans or Pacific Islanders, 1 Hispanic American), 5 international. Average age 29. 33 applicants. In 2006, 46 degrees awarded. *Entrance requirements:* For master's, GRE General Test, minimum GPA of 3.0. *Application deadline:* For fall admission, 8/1 priority date for domestic students; for spring admission, 12/1 for domestic students. Applications are processed on a rolling basis. Application fee: $50. Electronic applications accepted. *Expenses:* Tuition: Part-time $565 per credit. *Financial support:* Fellowships, research assistantships, career-related internships or fieldwork and Federal Work-Study available. Financial award applicants required to submit FAFSA. *Unit head:* Dr. David F. Bush, Director, 610-519-4746, E-mail: david.bush@villanova.edu.

Virginia Commonwealth University, Graduate School, School of Education, Program in Adult and Organizational Learning, Richmond, VA 23284-9005. Offers adult literacy (M Ed); adults with disabilities (M Ed); human resource development (M Ed). *Accreditation:* NCATE. Part-time programs available. *Students:* 1 applicant, 0% accepted. In 2006, 14 degrees awarded. *Entrance requirements:* For master's, GRE General Test or MAT. *Application deadline:* For fall admission, 5/15 for domestic students; for spring admission, 11/15 for domestic students. Applications are processed on a rolling basis. Application fee: $50. *Financial support:* Career-related internships or fieldwork and Federal Work-Study available. Financial award application deadline: 3/1. *Faculty research:* Adult development and learning, program planning and evaluation. *Unit head:* James McMillan, Division Head, 804-828-1305. *Application contact:* Dr. Michael D. Davis, Director, Graduate Studies, 804-828-6530, Fax: 804-827-0676, E-mail: mddavis@vcu.edu.

See Close-Up on page 1279.

Virginia Polytechnic Institute and State University, Graduate School, College of Liberal Arts and Human Sciences, Department of Human Development, Blacksburg, VA 24061. Offers adult development and aging (MS, PhD); adult learning and human resource development (MS, PhD); child development (MS, PhD); family studies (MS, PhD); marriage and family therapy (MS, PhD). *Accreditation:* AAMFT/COAMFTE (one or more programs are accredited). *Faculty:* 23 full-time (17 women). *Students:* 54 full-time (43 women), 88 part-time (66 women); includes 27 minority (19 African Americans, 7 Asian Americans or Pacific Islanders, 1 Hispanic American), 9 international. Average age 37. 85 applicants, 45% accepted, 32 enrolled. In 2006, 27 master's, 17 doctorates awarded. *Entrance requirements:* For master's and doctorate, GRE General Test. Additional exam requirements/recommendations for international students: Required—TOEFL (minimum score 600 paper-based; 250 computer-based). *Application deadline:* For fall admission, 5/15 for international students; for spring admission, 10/15 for international students. Applications are processed on a rolling basis. Application fee: $45. Electronic applications accepted. *Expenses:* Tuition, state resident: full-time $7,017; part-time $390 per credit hour. Tuition, nonresident: full-time $12,414; part-time $690 per credit hour. International tuition: $11,296 full-time. Required fees: $1,523; $256 per term. *Financial support:* In 2006–07, 1 research assistantship with full tuition reimbursement, 16 teaching assistantships with full tuition reimbursements (averaging $9,911 per year) were awarded; career-related internships or fieldwork, Federal Work-Study, scholarships/grants, and unspecified assistantships also available. Financial award application deadline: 4/1. *Faculty research:* Stress management, children's play, dual-career families, social cognition, relationships of elderly. *Unit head:* Dr. Fred P. Piercy, Head, 540-231-4794, Fax: 540-231-7012, E-mail: piercy@vt.edu. *Application contact:* Kathy Surface, Information Contact, 540-231-6149, Fax: 540-231-7012, E-mail: ksurface@vt.edu.

Webster University, School of Business and Technology, Department of Business, St. Louis, MO 63119-3194. Offers business (MA); business and organizational security management (MBA); computer resources and information management (MBA); environmental management (MBA); finance (MA, MBA); health services management (MBA); human resources development (MBA); human resources management (MBA); international business (MA, MBA); management and leadership (MBA); marketing (MBA); procurement and acquisitions management (MBA); telecommunications management (MBA). Part-time and evening/weekend programs available. Postbaccalaureate distance learning degree programs offered (no on-campus study). *Students:* 1,205 full-time (629 women), 4,197 part-time (2,153 women); includes 2,005 minority (1,467 African Americans, 29 American Indian/Alaska Native, 212 Asian Americans or Pacific Islanders, 297 Hispanic Americans), 485 international. Average age 33. *Application deadline:* Applications are processed on a rolling basis. Application fee: $25 ($50 for international students). *Expenses:* Tuition: Full-time $8,820; part-time $490 per credit. Tuition and fees vary according to degree level, campus/location and program. *Financial support:* Federal Work-Study available. Support available to part-time students. Financial award application deadline: 4/1; financial award applicants required to submit FAFSA. *Unit head:* Bradford Scott, Chair, 314-961-2260 Ext. 7574, Fax: 314-968-7077, E-mail: buschair@webster.edu. *Application contact:* Director of Graduate and Evening Student Admissions, Fax: 314-968-7116, E-mail: gadmit@webster.edu.

Webster University, School of Business and Technology, Department of Management, St. Louis, MO 63119-3194. Offers business and organizational security management (MA); computer resources and information management (MA); environmental management (MS); health care management (MA); health services management (MA); human resources development (MA); human resources management (MA); management (DM); management and leadership (MA); marketing (MA); procurement and acquisitions management (MA); public administration (MA); quality management (MA); space systems operations management (MS); telecommunications management (MA). Part-time and evening/weekend programs available. Postbaccalaureate distance learning degree programs offered (no on-campus study). *Students:* 1,396 full-time (746 women), 4,727 part-time (2,579 women); includes 3,065 minority (2,374 African Americans, 45 American Indian/Alaska Native, 158 Asian Americans or Pacific Islanders, 488 Hispanic Americans), 128 international. Average age 37. In 2006, 9 degrees awarded. *Degree requirements:* For doctorate, thesis/dissertation, written exam. *Entrance requirements:* For doctorate, GMAT, 3 years of work experience, MBA. *Application deadline:* Applications are processed on a rolling basis. Application fee: $25 ($50 for international students). *Expenses:* Tuition: Full-time $8,820; part-time $490 per credit. Tuition and fees vary according to degree level, campus/location and program. *Financial support:* Federal Work-Study available. Support available to part-time students. Financial award application deadline: 4/1; financial award applicants required to submit FAFSA. *Unit head:* Jeffrey Haldeman, Chair, 314-961-2660 Ext. 7552, Fax: 314-968-7077, E-mail: mgtchair@webster.edu. *Application contact:* Director of Graduate and Evening Student Admissions, Fax: 314-968-7116, E-mail: gadmit@webster.edu.

Western Carolina University, Graduate School, College of Education and Allied Professions, Department of Human Services, Program in Human Resource Development, Cullowhee, NC 28723. Offers MS. Part-time and evening/weekend programs available. *Degree requirements:* For master's, comprehensive exam. *Entrance requirements:* For master's, GRE General Test. Additional exam requirements/recommendations for international students: Required—TOEFL (minimum score 550 paper-based; 213 computer-based).

Western Michigan University, Graduate College, College of Education, Department of Teaching, Learning, and Leadership, Kalamazoo, MI 49008-5202. Offers early childhood education (MA); education and professional development (MA); educational leadership (MA, Ed D, PhD, Ed S); educational technology (MA); elementary education (MA); human resources development (MA); middle school education (MA); reading (MA); socio-cultural foundations and educational thought (MA). *Degree requirements:* For doctorate and Ed S, thesis/dissertation, oral exams. *Entrance requirements:* For doctorate and Ed S, GRE General Test.

William Woods University, Graduate and Adult Studies, Fulton, MO 65251-1098. Offers administration (M Ed, Ed S); agribusiness (MBA); curriculum/instruction (M Ed); health management (MBA); human services (MBA); instructional leadership (Ed S). Evening/weekend programs available. *Faculty:* 38 full-time (14 women), 174 part-time/adjunct (50 women). *Students:* 1,944 full-time (1,230 women); includes 71 minority (43 African Americans, 16

American Indian/Alaska Native, 7 Asian Americans or Pacific Islanders, 5 Hispanic Americans), 41 international. 824 applicants, 86% accepted, 631 enrolled. In 2006, 919 master's, 112 other advanced degrees awarded. *Median time to degree:* Master's–1.5 years full-time; Ed S–1.5 years full-time. *Degree requirements:* For master's, capstone course (MBA), action research (M Ed); for Ed S, field experience. *Entrance requirements:* For master's, 2 recommendations, resumé, BA/BS; teaching certification (M Ed); course work in economics and accounting (MBA); for Ed S, M Ed, 2 letters of recommendation, resumé, teaching certification. Additional exam requirements/recommendations for international students: Required—TOEFL (minimum score 550 paper-based). *Application deadline:* Applications are processed on a rolling basis. Application fee: $25. Electronic applications accepted. *Expenses:* Tuition: Part-time $255 per credit hour. Tuition and fees vary according to program. *Financial support:* Institutionally sponsored loans available. Financial award applicants required to submit FAFSA. *Unit head:* Sean Siebert, Dean of Graduate and Adult Studies Enrollment Services, 573-592-4383, Fax: 573-592-1164. *Application contact:* Linda Rembish, Administrative Assistant, 800-995-3199, Fax: 573-592-1164, E-mail: cgas@williamwoods.edu.

Xavier University, College of Social Sciences, Health and Education, School of Education, Program in Human Resource Development, Cincinnati, OH 45207. Offers M Ed. Part-time and evening/weekend programs available. *Faculty:* 2 full-time (both women), 4 part-time/adjunct (1 woman). *Students:* 36 full-time (28 women), 38 part-time (30 women); includes 13 minority (12 African Americans, 1 American Indian/Alaska Native), 2 international. Average age 36. 61 applicants, 66% accepted, 37 enrolled. In 2006, 36 degrees awarded. *Entrance requirements:* For master's, MAT, GRE or GMAT, minimum GPA of 2.8, resumé, references. Additional exam requirements/recommendations for international students: Required—TOEFL (minimum score 550 paper-based; 213 computer-based; 79 iBT). *Application deadline:* For fall admission, 2/1 priority date for domestic students. Applications are processed on a rolling basis. Application fee: $35. Electronic applications accepted. *Expenses: Contact institution.* Part-time tuition and fees vary according to degree level, campus/location and program. *Financial support:* Teaching assistantships, scholarships/grants and unspecified assistantships available. Support available to part-time students. Financial award application deadline: 5/15; financial award applicants required to submit FAFSA. *Faculty research:* Graduate education, transfer of learning, organizational behavior. *Unit head:* Dr. Brenda Levya-Gardner, Director, 513-745-4287, Fax: 513-745-1048, E-mail: gardner@xavier.edu. *Application contact:* Roger Bosse, Interim Director of Graduate Studies, 513-745-3357, Fax: 513-745-1048, E-mail: bosse@xavier.edu.

Human Resources Management

Adelphi University, School of Business, Certificate Programs in Management, Garden City, NY 11530-0701. Offers human resource management (Certificate). Part-time and evening/weekend programs available. *Entrance requirements:* For degree, GMAT or master's degree. Additional exam requirements/recommendations for international students: Required—TOEFL (minimum score 550 paper-based; 213 computer-based). *Application deadline:* For fall admission, 5/1 for international students; for spring admission, 12/1 for international students. Applications are processed on a rolling basis. Application fee: $50. Electronic applications accepted. *Financial support:* Application deadline: 3/1; *Unit head:* Brian Rothschild, Assistant Dean, 516-877-4673, Fax: 516-877-4607, E-mail: rothschild@adelphi.edu. *Application contact:* Christine Murphy, Director of Admissions, 516-877-3050, Fax: 516-877-3039, E-mail: graduateadmissions@adelphi.edu.

Adelphi University, School of Business, Department of Management, Marketing, and Decision Sciences, Garden City, NY 11530-0701. Offers management information systems (MBA); management/human resource management (MBA); marketing/e-commerce (MBA). Part-time and evening/weekend programs available. *Students:* 67 full-time (34 women), 173 part-time (85 women); includes 44 minority (24 African Americans, 11 Asian Americans or Pacific Islanders, 9 Hispanic Americans), 49 international. Average age 31. In 2006, 122 degrees awarded. *Degree requirements:* For master's, capstone course. *Entrance requirements:* For master's, GMAT, 2 letters of recommendation. Additional exam requirements/recommendations for international students: Required—TOEFL. *Application deadline:* For fall admission, 5/1 for international students; for spring admission, 12/1 for international students. Applications are processed on a rolling basis. Application fee: $50. Electronic applications accepted. *Financial support:* Research assistantships with full and partial tuition reimbursements, career-related internships or fieldwork, Federal Work-Study, institutionally sponsored loans, scholarships/grants, and unspecified assistantships available. Financial award application deadline: 3/1; financial award applicants required to submit FAFSA. *Faculty research:* Supply chain management, distribution channels, productivity benchmark analysis, data envelopment analysis, financial portfolio analysis. *Unit head:* Dr. Allan Ashley, Chairperson, 516-877-4640, E-mail: ashley@adelphi.edu. *Application contact:* Christine Murphy, Director of Admissions, 516-877-3050, Fax: 516-877-3039, E-mail: graduateadmissions@adelphi.edu.

Alabama Agricultural and Mechanical University, School of Graduate Studies, School of Education, Department of Counseling and Special Education, Huntsville, AL 35811. Offers communicative disorders (M Ed, MS); psychology and counseling (MS, Ed S), including clinical psychology (MS), counseling and guidance, counseling psychology (MS), personnel management (MS), psychometry (MS), school psychology (MS); special education (M Ed, MS). *Accreditation:* CORE; NCATE. Part-time and evening/weekend programs available. *Faculty:* 4 full-time (3 women), 3 part-time/adjunct (1 woman). *Students:* 62 full-time (50 women), 121 part-time (93 women); includes 121 minority (113 African Americans, 2 American Indian/Alaska Native, 6 Hispanic Americans), 12 international. In 2006, 55 master's, 2 other advanced degrees awarded. *Degree requirements:* For master's, comprehensive exam. *Entrance requirements:* For master's, GRE General Test. *Application deadline:* For fall admission, 5/1 for domestic students. Application fee: $15 ($20 for international students). *Financial support:* Career-related internships or fieldwork available. Support available to part-time students. Financial award application deadline: 4/1. *Faculty research:* Increasing numbers of minorities in special education and speech-language pathology. Total annual research expenditures: $300,000. *Unit head:* Dr. Terry L. Douglas, Chair, 256-372-5533.

Albany State University, College of Arts and Sciences, Department of History, Political Science and Public Administration, Albany, GA 31705-2717. Offers community and economic development (MPA); criminal justice (MPA); fiscal management (MPA); general management (MPA); health administration and policy (MPA); human resources management (MPA); public policy (MPA); water resource management and policy (MPA). *Accreditation:* NASPAA. Part-time programs available. *Degree requirements:* For master's, thesis, comprehensive exam. *Entrance requirements:* For master's, GRE General Test, minimum GPA of 2.5. Electronic applications accepted. *Faculty research:* Transportation, urban affairs, political economy.

Amberton University, Graduate School, Program in Human Relations and Business, Garland, TX 75041-5595. Offers MA, MS. Part-time and evening/weekend programs available. *Faculty:* 4 full-time (3 women), 10 part-time/adjunct (5 women). *Students:* 100 full-time (50 women), 100 part-time (50 women); includes 75 minority (50 African Americans, 5 American Indian/Alaska Native, 5 Asian Americans or Pacific Islanders, 15 Hispanic Americans). Average age 35. In 2006, 50 degrees awarded. *Entrance requirements:* For master's, minimum GPA of 3.0. *Application deadline:* Applications are processed on a rolling basis. *Expenses:* Tuition: Full-time $4,800; part-time $600 per course. *Application contact:* Adviser, 972-279-6511 Ext. 180, Fax: 972-279-9773, E-mail: advisor@amberton.edu.

American InterContinental University, Program in International Business, Weston, FL 33326. Offers accounting and finance (MBA); human resource management (MBA); management (MBA); marketing (MBA). Part-time and evening/weekend programs available. Postbaccalaureate distance learning degree programs offered. *Faculty:* 3 full-time (0 women), 2 part-time/adjunct (0 women). *Students:* 87 full-time (51 women), 7 part-time (4 women); includes 62 minority (42 African Americans, 1 American Indian/Alaska Native, 1 Asian American or Pacific Islander, 18 Hispanic Americans), 5 international. Average age 34. In 2006, 51 degrees awarded. *Application deadline:* Applications are processed on a rolling basis. Application fee: $50. Electronic applications accepted. *Financial support:* Federal Work-Study and scholarships/grants available. Financial award application deadline: 1/15; financial award applicants required to submit FAFSA. *Unit head:* Dr. David Kalichavan, Acting Dean, School of Business, 954-446-6100, Fax: 954-446-6393, E-mail: dkalichavan@aiufl.edu.

American InterContinental University Online, Program in Business Administration, Hoffman Estates, IL 60192. Offers accounting and finance (MBA); healthcare management (MBA); human resource management (MBA); international business (MBA); management (MBA); marketing (MBA); operations management (MBA); organizational psychology and development (MBA); project management (MBA). Evening/weekend programs available. Postbaccalaureate distance learning degree programs offered (no on-campus study). *Entrance requirements:* Additional exam requirements/recommendations for international students: Required—TOEFL (minimum score 550 paper-based; 213 computer-based). *Application deadline:* Applications are processed on a rolling basis. Application fee: $50. Electronic applications accepted. *Financial support:* Institutionally sponsored loans and scholarships/grants available. Financial award applicants required to submit FAFSA. *Unit head:* Kerri J Holloway, Vice President of Academic Affairs, 847-851-5000 Ext. 15399, Fax: 847-586-6309, E-mail: kholloway@aivonline.edu. *Application contact:* 877-701-3800, E-mail: info@aiuonline.edu.

Andrew Jackson University, Brian Tracy College of Business and Entrepreneurship, Birmingham, AL 35244. Offers entrepreneurship (MBA); finance (MBA); health services management (MBA); hospitality and tourism management (MBA); human resource management (MBA); international business (MBA); management (MBA); marketing (MBA). Part-time and evening/weekend programs available. Postbaccalaureate distance learning degree programs offered (no on-campus study). *Faculty:* 13 part-time/adjunct (1 woman). *Students:* Average age 40. In 2006, 6 degrees awarded. *Entrance requirements:* For master's, course work in calculus, statistics. Additional exam requirements/recommendations for international students: Required—TOEFL (minimum score 550 paper-based; 213 computer-based). *Application deadline:* Applications are processed on a rolling basis. Application fee: $75. *Expenses:* Tuition: Part-time $705 per course. *Application contact:* Betty Howell, Director of Student Affairs, 205-871-9288 Ext. 108, Fax: 205-871-9294, E-mail: bhowell@aju.edu.

Auburn University, Graduate School, College of Business, Department of Management, Auburn University, AL 36849. Offers human resource management (PhD); management (MS, PhD); management information systems (MMIS, PhD). *Accreditation:* AACSB. Part-time programs available. *Faculty:* 27 full-time (4 women). *Students:* 27 full-time (6 women), 22 part-time (7 women); includes 5 minority (3 African Americans, 2 Asian Americans or Pacific Islanders), 6 international. Average age 32. 54 applicants, 35% accepted, 12 enrolled. In 2006, 17 master's, 8 doctorates awarded. *Degree requirements:* For master's, thesis (for some programs); for doctorate, thesis/dissertation. *Entrance requirements:* For master's, GMAT, GRE General Test (MS); for doctorate, GMAT, GRE General Test. Additional exam requirements/recommendations for international students: Required—TOEFL. *Application deadline:* For fall admission, 7/7 for domestic students; for spring admission, 11/24 for domestic students. Applications are processed on a rolling basis. Application fee: $25 ($50 for international students). Electronic applications accepted. *Expenses:* Tuition, state resident: full-time $5,000. Tuition, nonresident: full-time $15,000. Required fees: $416. Tuition and fees vary according to program. *Financial support:* Teaching assistantships, Federal Work-Study available. Support available to part-time students. Financial award application deadline: 3/15. *Unit head:* Dr. Sharon Oswald, Head, 334-844-4071. *Application contact:* Dr. Joe Pittman, Interim Dean of the Graduate School, 334-844-4700.

Baker College Center for Graduate Studies, Programs in Business, Flint, MI 48507-9843. Offers accounting (MBA); computer information systems (MBA); finance (MBA); general business (MBA); health and recreation services management (MBA); health care management (MBA); human resource management (MBA); industrial management (MBA); international business (MBA); leadership (MBA); marketing (MBA). MBA in health and recreation services management enrollment limited to international students. Part-time and evening/weekend programs available. *Faculty:* 15 full-time (6 women), 425 part-time/adjunct (200 women). *Students:* 370 full-time (190 women), 1,060 part-time (560 women); includes 372 minority (205 African Americans, 27 American Indian/Alaska Native, 66 Asian Americans or Pacific Islanders, 74 Hispanic Americans), 30 international. Average age 38. 780 applicants, 85% accepted, 567 enrolled. In 2006, 202 degrees awarded. *Degree requirements:* For master's, portfolio. *Entrance requirements:* For master's, 3 years of work experience, minimum undergraduate GPA of 2.5, writing sample, letters of recommendation. Additional exam requirements/recommendations for international students: Required—TOEFL (minimum score 550 paper-based; 213 computer-based). *Application deadline:* For fall admission, 8/6 priority date for domestic students; for winter admission, 12/15 priority date for domestic students; for spring admission, 2/15 priority date for domestic students. Applications are processed on a rolling basis. Application fee: $25. Electronic applications accepted. *Expenses:* Tuition: Full-time $7,200; part-time $300 per credit hour. *Financial support:* In 2006–07, 410 students received support. Scholarships/grants available. Support available to part-time students. Financial award applicants required to submit FAFSA. *Unit head:* Dr. Michael Heberling, President, 800-469-3165, Fax: 810-766-4399, E-mail: heberling@baker.edu. *Application contact:* Chuck J. Gurden, Vice President for Graduate and Online Admissions, 800-469-3165, Fax: 810-766-2051, E-mail: chuck@baker.edu.

Baldwin-Wallace College, Graduate Programs, Division of Business Administration, Program in Human Resources, Berea, OH 44017-2088. Offers MBA. *Students:* 15 full-time (13 women), 16 part-time (15 women); includes 4 minority (2 African Americans, 1 Asian American or Pacific Islander, 1 Hispanic American). Average age 33. 9 applicants, 78% accepted, 6 enrolled. In 2006, 5 degrees awarded. *Application deadline:* For fall admission, 7/25 priority date for domestic students; for spring admission, 12/15 priority date for domestic students. Applications are processed on a rolling basis. Application fee: $25. Electronic applications accepted. *Expenses:* Tuition: Part-time $760 per credit hour. Tuition and fees vary according to program. *Unit head:* J. Peter Kelly, Director of MBA, Executive MBA and Human Resources Programs, 440-826-2391, Fax: 440-826-3868, E-mail: pkelly@bw.edu.

Barry University, School of Education, Graduate Certificate Programs, Miami Shores, FL 33161-6695. Offers advanced teaching and learning with technology (Certificate); distance education (Certificate); higher education technology integration (Certificate); human resources: not for profit and religious organizations (Certificate); K-12 technology integration (Certificate). *Applica-*

Human Resources Management

Barry University (continued)

tion contact: Dave Fletcher, Director of Graduate Admissions, 305-899-3113, Fax: 305-899-2971, E-mail: dfletcher@mail.barry.edu.

Bernard M. Baruch College of the City University of New York, Zicklin School of Business, Department of Management, New York, NY 10010-5585. Offers entrepreneurship (MBA); general management and policy (MBA); human resources management (MBA); management planning systems (PhD); management science (MBA); organization and policy studies (PhD); organizational behavior (MBA). Part-time and evening/weekend programs available. *Faculty:* 38 full-time (10 women), 41 part-time/adjunct (6 women). *Students:* 30 full-time (14 women), 117 part-time (52 women); includes 37 minority (17 African Americans, 14 Asian Americans or Pacific Islanders, 6 Hispanic Americans). In 2006, 39 master's, 1 doctorate awarded. *Degree requirements:* For doctorate, thesis/dissertation, comprehensive exam. *Entrance requirements:* For master's, GMAT, 2 letters of recommendation, resumé, 2 years of work experience; for doctorate, GMAT. Additional exam requirements/recommendations for international students: Required—TOEFL (minimum score 590 paper-based; 243 computer-based), TWE. *Application deadline:* For fall admission, 5/31 for domestic students, 4/30 for international students; for spring admission, 10/31 for domestic and international students. Application fee: $125. *Financial support:* Fellowships, research assistantships, teaching assistantships, career-related internships or fieldwork, Federal Work-Study, scholarships/grants, and unspecified assistantships available. Financial award application deadline: 4/30; financial award applicants required to submit FAFSA. *Unit head:* Harry M. Rosen, Chairman, 646-312-3620, Fax: 646-312-3621, E-mail: harry_rosen@baruch.cuny.edu. *Application contact:* Frances Murphy, Office of Graduate Admissions, 646-312-1300, Fax: 646-312-1301, E-mail: zicklingradadmissions@baruch.cuny.edu.

Boston University, Metropolitan College (Continuing Education), Program in Administrative Studies, Boston, MA 02215. Offers banking and financial management (MSM); business continuity in emergency management (MSM); economics development and tourism management (MSAS); electronic commerce, systems, and technology (MSAS); financial economics (MSAS); human resource management (MSM); innovation and technology (MSAS); insurance management (MSM); international market management (MSM); multinational commerce (MSAS); project management (MSM). *Accreditation:* AACSB. Part-time and evening/weekend programs available. *Faculty:* 9 full-time (0 women), 51 part-time/adjunct (8 women). *Students:* 105 full-time (40 women), 171 part-time (65 women); includes 27 minority (5 African Americans, 18 Asian Americans or Pacific Islanders, 4 Hispanic Americans), 125 international. Average age 29. In 2006, 310 degrees awarded. *Degree requirements:* For master's, thesis optional. *Entrance requirements:* For master's, 1 year of work experience, minimum GPA of 3.0. Additional exam requirements/recommendations for international students: Required—TOEFL (minimum score 560 paper-based; 220 computer-based). *Application deadline:* Applications are processed on a rolling basis. Application fee: $65. *Expenses:* Tuition: Full-time $33,330; part-time $1,042 per credit. Required fees: $462; $40. *Financial support:* In 2006–07, 15 students received support, including research assistantships (averaging $10,000 per year); career-related internships or fieldwork and Federal Work-Study also available. *Faculty research:* International business, innovative process. *Unit head:* Dr. Kip Becker, Chairman, 617-353-3016, E-mail: adminsc@bu.edu. *Application contact:* Lucille Dicker, Administrative Sciences Department, 617-353-3016, E-mail: adminsc@bu.edu.

Boston University, School of Education, Department of Administration, Training, and Policy Studies, Program in Human Resource Education, Boston, MA 02215. Offers Ed M, CAGS. Part-time programs available. *Students:* 10 full-time (8 women), 8 part-time (6 women); includes 1 minority (Hispanic American), 1 international. Average age 36. 21 applicants, 67% accepted, 12 enrolled. *Degree requirements:* For master's, thesis optional. *Entrance requirements:* For master's and CAGS, GRE General Test or MAT. Additional exam requirements/recommendations for international students: Required—TOEFL. *Application deadline:* For fall admission, 2/15 priority date for domestic students; for winter admission, 11/1 priority date for domestic students. Applications are processed on a rolling basis. Application fee: $70. Electronic applications accepted. *Expenses:* Tuition: Full-time $33,330; part-time $1,042 per credit. Required fees: $462; $40. *Financial support:* Application deadline: 2/15; *Unit head:* Dr. Alan Gaynor, Coordinator, 617-353-3307, E-mail: agaynor@bu.edu. *Application contact:* 617-353-4237, Fax: 617-353-8937, E-mail: sedgrad@bu.edu.

Briar Cliff University, Program in Human Resource Management, Sioux City, IA 51104-0100. Offers MA. Part-time and evening/weekend programs available.

Buffalo State College, State University of New York, Graduate Studies and Research, Faculty of Applied Science and Education, Department of Educational Foundations, Program in Adult Education, Buffalo, NY 14222-1095. Offers adult education (MS, Certificate); human resources development (Certificate). Part-time and evening/weekend programs available. Postbaccalaureate distance learning degree programs offered (no on-campus study). *Degree requirements:* For master's, comprehensive exam. *Entrance requirements:* Additional exam requirements/recommendations for international students: Required—TOEFL (minimum score 550 paper-based; 213 computer-based).

California State University, East Bay, Academic Programs and Graduate Studies, College of Business and Economics, Department of Management and Finance, Option in Human Resources Management, Hayward, CA 94542-3000. Offers MBA. Part-time and evening/weekend programs available. *Degree requirements:* For master's, comprehensive exam or thesis. *Entrance requirements:* For master's, GMAT, minimum GPA of 2.75. Additional exam requirements/recommendations for international students: Required—TOEFL (minimum score 550 paper-based; 213 computer-based). *Application deadline:* For fall admission, 5/31 for domestic students, 4/30 for international students; for winter admission, 9/30 for domestic and international students; for spring admission, 11/30 for international students. Application fee: $55. *Financial support:* Application deadline: 3/2. *Unit head:* Dr. Asha Rao, Graduate Advisor, 510-885-4517, Fax: 510-885-2176, E-mail: asha.rao@csueastbay.edu. *Application contact:* Doris Duncan, Director of Graduate Programs, 510-885-3364, Fax: 510-885-2176, E-mail: doris.duncan@csueastbay.edu.

California State University, Sacramento, Graduate Studies, College of Business Administration, Program in Business Administration, Sacramento, CA 95819-6048. Offers business administration (MBA); human resources (MBA); urban land development (MBA). *Accreditation:* AACSB. Part-time programs available. *Students:* 26 full-time (16 women), 66 part-time (23 women); includes 20 minority (13 Asian Americans or Pacific Islanders, 7 Hispanic Americans), 6 international. Average age 30. 229 applicants, 69% accepted, 22 enrolled. *Degree requirements:* For master's, thesis or alternative, writing proficiency exam. *Entrance requirements:* For master's, GMAT. Additional exam requirements/recommendations for international students: Required—TOEFL. *Application deadline:* Applications are processed on a rolling basis. Application fee: $55. Electronic applications accepted. *Financial support:* Research assistantships, teaching assistantships, career-related internships or fieldwork and Federal Work-Study available. Support available to part-time students. Financial award application deadline: 3/1.

Capella University, School of Business and Technology, Minneapolis, MN 55402. Offers accounting (MBA), including system design and programming; business (Certificate), including human resource management (MS, PhD, Certificate), information technology management (MS, PhD, Certificate), leadership (MBA, MS, PhD, Certificate); finance (MBA); general business (MBA); health care management (MBA); information technology (MS, Certificate), including general information technology (MS), information security, network architecture and design (MS), professional projects management (Certificate), project management and leadership (MS), system design and development (MS),); information technology management (MBA); marketing (MBA); organization and management (MBA, MS, PhD), including general business (PhD), general organization and management (MBA, MS), human resource management (MS, PhD, Certificate), information technology management (MS, PhD, Certificate), leadership (MBA, MS, PhD, Certificate); project management (MBA). Part-time and evening/weekend programs available. Postbaccalaureate distance learning degree programs offered (minimal on-campus study). Terminal master's awarded for partial completion of doctoral program. *Degree requirements:* For master's, integrative project, thesis optional; for doctorate, thesis/dissertation, comprehensive exam, registration. *Entrance requirements:* Additional exam requirements/recommendations for international students: Required—TOEFL (minimum score 550 paper-based; 213 computer-based), TWE (minimum score 4). Electronic applications accepted. *Faculty research:* Business policies: strategic, corporate, and financial management; interplay of technological, organizational and social change.

Cardean University, MBA Program, Chicago, IL 60606-7204. Offers accounting and information systems (MBA); e-commerce (MBA); finance (MBA); global management (MBA); health care administration (MBA); human resources management (MBA); leadership (MBA); management of information systems (MBA); management of technology (MBA); marketing (MBA); professional accounting (MBA); project management (MBA); risk management (MBA); strategy and economics (MBA). Part-time and evening/weekend programs available. Postbaccalaureate distance learning degree programs offered (no on-campus study). *Entrance requirements:* Additional exam requirements/recommendations for international students: Required—TOEFL (minimum score 550 paper-based; 213 computer-based).

Caribbean University, Graduate School, Bayamón, PR 00960-0493. Offers accounting (MBA); administration and supervision (MA Ed); criminal justice (MA); curriculum and instruction (MA Ed); education (PhD); gerontology (MSN); human resources (MBA); museology, archiving and art history (MA Ed); neonatal pediatrics (MSN); physical education (MA Ed); special education (MA Ed). *Entrance requirements:* For master's, interview, minimum GPA of 2.5.

Case Western Reserve University, Weatherhead School of Management, Department of Marketing and Policy Studies, Division of Labor and Human Resource Policy, Cleveland, OH 44106. Offers MBA. Part-time and evening/weekend programs available. *Faculty:* 3 full-time (1 woman), 1 part-time/adjunct (0 women). *Students:* 6 full-time (4 women), 4 part-time (all women). Average age 28. In 2006, 10 degrees awarded. *Entrance requirements:* For master's, GMAT. *Application deadline:* For fall admission, 4/15 priority date for domestic students. Applications are processed on a rolling basis. Application fee: $50. *Financial support:* Career-related internships or fieldwork, Federal Work-Study, institutionally sponsored loans, and tuition waivers (full and partial) available. Financial award application deadline: 5/1. *Faculty research:* Strategic human resource management, negotiations and conflict management, human resources in high performance organizations, international human resources management, union management relations and collective bargaining. *Unit head:* Dr. Paul F. Gerhart, Head, 216-368-2045, E-mail: pfg2@po.cwru.edu.

Central Michigan University, Central Michigan University Off-Campus Programs, Program in Administration, Mount Pleasant, MI 48859. Offers acquisitions administration (MSA, Certificate); general administration (MSA, Certificate); health services administration (MSA, Certificate); human resources administration (MSA, Certificate); information resource management (MSA, Certificate); international administration (MSA, Certificate); leadership (MSA, Certificate); public administration (MSA, Certificate); software engineering administration (MSA, Certificate); vehicle design and manufacturing administration (MSA, Certificate). Part-time and evening/weekend programs available. Postbaccalaureate distance learning degree programs offered (no on-campus study). *Students:* Average age 38. *Entrance requirements:* For master's, minimum GPA of 2.7 in major. *Application deadline:* Applications are processed on a rolling basis. Application fee: $50. Electronic applications accepted. *Financial support:* Scholarships/grants available. Support available to part-time students. Financial award applicants required to submit FAFSA. *Unit head:* Dr. Peter G. Ross, Director, 989-774-6525, Fax: 989-774-2575, E-mail: ross1pg@cmich.edu. *Application contact:* 877-268-4636, E-mail: cmuoffcampus@cmich.edu.

Central Michigan University, College of Graduate Studies, Program in Administration, Mount Pleasant, MI 48859. Offers general administration (MSA); health services administration (MSA); hospitality and tourism administration (MSA); human resource administration (MSA); information resource administration (MSA); international administration (MSA); leadership (MSA); organizational communications (MSA); public administration (MSA); recreation and park administration (MSA); software engineering (MSA); sports administration (MSA). *Accreditation:* AACSB. *Degree requirements:* For master's, thesis or alternative. *Entrance requirements:* For master's, minimum undergraduate GPA of 2.5.

See Close-Up on page 253.

Chapman University, Graduate Studies, The George L. Argyros School of Business and Economics, Program in Human Resources Management, Orange, CA 92866. Offers human resources and management (MSHRM); human resources management (Certificate). Part-time and evening/weekend programs available. *Faculty:* 1 (woman) part-time/adjunct. *Students:* Average age 32. 15 applicants, 13% accepted, 0 enrolled. In 2006, 9 master's, 2 other advanced degrees awarded. *Degree requirements:* For master's, internship. *Entrance requirements:* For master's, GMAT or MAT, minimum GPA of 3.0, course work in statistics. Additional exam requirements/recommendations for international students: Required—TOEFL (minimum score 550 paper-based). *Application deadline:* For fall admission, 5/1 priority date for domestic and international students; for spring admission, 12/30 priority date for domestic and international students. Application fee: $55. Electronic applications accepted. *Expenses: Contact institution. Financial support:* In 2006–07, 15 students received support; fellowships, Federal Work-Study available. Financial award application deadline: 6/30; financial award applicants required to submit FAFSA. *Unit head:* Dr. Amy Hurley-Hanson, Chair, 714-628-7312, E-mail: ahurley@chapman.edu. *Application contact:* Debra Gonda, Coordinator, 714-638-7318, E-mail: gonda@chapman.edu.

City University, Graduate Division, School of Management, Bellevue, WA 98005. Offers accounting (MBA); C++ programming (Certificate); computer systems—C++ programming (MS); computer systems—individualized study (MS); computer systems—web programming in e-commerce (MS); computer systems-web development (MS); financial management (MBA, Certificate); general management (MBA, MPA, Certificate); general management-Europe (MBA); human resource management (MPA); individualized study (MBA); information systems (MBA, Certificate); management—general management (MA); management—human resource management (MA); management—individualized study (MA); marketing (MBA, Certificate); personal financial planning (MBA, Certificate); project management (MBA, MS, Certificate); technology management (MS, Certificate); web development (Certificate); web programming in e-commerce (Certificate). Part-time and evening/weekend programs available. Postbaccalaureate distance learning degree programs offered (no on-campus study). *Entrance requirements:* Additional exam requirements/recommendations for international students: Required—TOEFL (minimum score 540 paper-based; 207 computer-based); Recommended—IELTS. Electronic applications accepted.

Claremont Graduate University, Graduate Programs, School of Behavioral and Organizational Sciences, Program in Human Resources Design, Claremont, CA 91711-6160. Offers MS. Part-time and evening/weekend programs available. *Faculty:* 3 part-time/adjunct (0 women). *Students:* 19 full-time (15 women), 7 part-time (4 women); includes 11 minority (5 African Americans, 3 Asian Americans or Pacific Islanders, 3 Hispanic Americans), 4 international. Average age 30. In 2006, 11 degrees awarded. *Entrance requirements:* For master's, GMAT or GRE General Test. Additional exam requirements/recommendations for international students: Required—TOEFL (minimum score 550 paper-based; 213 computer-based). *Application deadline:* For fall admission, 2/15 priority date for domestic and international students; for spring admission, 11/15 for domestic and international students. Applications are processed on a rolling basis. Electronic applications accepted. *Financial support:* Fellowships, career-related internships or fieldwork, Federal Work-Study, and institutionally sponsored loans available. Support available to part-time students. Financial award application deadline: 2/15; financial award applicants required to submit FAFSA. *Unit head:* Katie Ear, Director, 909-607-3286,

Fax: 909-621-8905, E-mail: katie.ear@cgu.edu. *Application contact:* Carlos Mendez, Recruiter, 909-607-3286, Fax: 909-621-8905, E-mail: carlos.mendez@cgu.edu.

Clarkson University, Graduate School, School of Business, Program in Management Systems, Potsdam, NY 13699. Offers human resource management (MS); management information systems (MS); manufacturing management (MS). Part-time and evening/weekend programs available. *Students:* Average age 33. *Degree requirements:* For master's, project or thesis. *Entrance requirements:* For master's, GMAT, GRE General Test (highly recommended). Additional exam requirements/recommendations for international students: Required—TOEFL. *Application deadline:* For fall admission, 5/15 priority date for domestic students; for spring admission, 10/15 priority date for domestic students. Applications are processed on a rolling basis. Application fee: $25 ($35 for international students). Electronic applications accepted. *Expenses:* Tuition: Full-time $22,776; part-time $949 per credit. Required fees: $215. *Financial support:* Tuition waivers (partial) available. *Faculty research:* Management of technology planning and organizational development. *Application contact:* Dr. Farzad Mahmoodi, Director, 315-268-4281, Fax: 315-268-3810, E-mail: mahmoodi@clarkson.edu.

Cleveland State University, College of Graduate Studies, Nance College of Business Administration, Department of Management and Labor Relations, Cleveland, OH 44115. Offers labor relations and human resources (MLRHR). Part-time programs available. *Faculty:* 11 full-time (1 woman), 1 part-time/adjunct (0 women). *Students:* 19 full-time (13 women), 48 part-time (35 women); includes 11 minority (all African Americans), 7 international. Average age 30. 57 applicants, 60% accepted, 16 enrolled. In 2006, 22 degrees awarded. *Entrance requirements:* For master's, GMAT or GRE. Additional exam requirements/recommendations for international students: Required—TOEFL (minimum score 525 paper-based; 197 computer-based). *Application deadline:* For fall admission, 7/15 for domestic students; for spring admission, 12/15 for domestic students. Applications are processed on a rolling basis. Application fee: $30. Electronic applications accepted. *Financial support:* In 2006–07, 3 research assistantships with full and partial tuition reimbursements (averaging $6,960 per year) were awarded; career-related internships or fieldwork, tuition waivers (full), and unspecified assistantships also available. Financial award applicants required to submit FAFSA. *Unit head:* Dr. Jeffrey C. Susbauer, Chairperson, 216-687-4747, Fax: 216-687-4708, E-mail: j.susbauer@csuohio.edu.

College of Santa Fe, Department of Business Administration, Santa Fe, NM 87505-7634. Offers finance (MBA); human resources (MBA). Program also available at Albuquerque campus. Part-time and evening/weekend programs available. *Entrance requirements:* For master's, minimum GPA of 3.0 in last 60 hours (preferred).

Colorado Technical University, Graduate Studies, Program in Management, Colorado Springs, CO 80907-3896. Offers business administration (MBA); business management (MSM); business technology (MSM); database management (MSM); human resources management (MSM); information technology (MSM); logistics management (MSM); management (DM); organizational leadership (MSM); project management (MSM). Part-time and evening/weekend programs available. *Degree requirements:* For master's, thesis or alternative; for doctorate, thesis/dissertation. *Entrance requirements:* For doctorate, minimum graduate GPA of 3.0, 5 years of related work experience. *Faculty research:* Sexual harassment, performance evaluation, critical thinking.

Colorado Technical University Denver Campus, Programs in Business Administration and Management, Greenwood Village, CO 80111. Offers accounting (MBA); business administration (MBA); business administration and management (EMBA); business technology (MSM); database management (MSM); human resource management (MBA); information technology (MSM); project management (MSM); technology management (MBA). Part-time and evening/weekend programs available. *Degree requirements:* For master's, thesis or alternative. *Entrance requirements:* For master's, minimum undergraduate GPA of 3.0, resumé.

Colorado Technical University Sioux Falls Campus, Programs in Business Administration and Management, Sioux Falls, SD 57108. Offers business administration (MBA); business management (MSM); health science management (MSM); human resources management (MSM); information technology (MSM); organizational leadership (MSM); project management (MBA); technology management (MBA). Evening/weekend programs available. *Degree requirements:* For master's, thesis optional. *Entrance requirements:* For master's, minimum 2 years work experience, resumé.

Columbia Southern University, MBA Program, Orange Beach, AL 36561. Offers electronic business and technology (MBA); healthcare management (MBA); human resources management (MBA); international management (MBA); marketing (MBA); project management (MBA); public administration (MBA); sport management (MBA). Part-time and evening/weekend programs available. Postbaccalaureate distance learning degree programs offered (no on-campus study). *Entrance requirements:* Additional exam requirements/recommendations for international students: Required—TOEFL. Electronic applications accepted.

Columbia University, Graduate School of Business, MBA Program, New York, NY 10027. Offers accounting (MBA); decision, risk, and operations (MBA); entrepreneurship (MBA); finance and economics (MBA); human resource management (MBA); international business (MBA); management (MBA); marketing (MBA); media (MBA); real estate (MBA); social enterprise (MBA); DDS/MBA; JD/MBA; MBA/MIA; MBA/MPH; MBA/MS; MD/MBA. *Faculty:* 118 full-time (14 women), 106 part-time/adjunct (18 women). *Students:* 1,242 full-time (428 women); includes 291 minority (65 African Americans, 5 American Indian/Alaska Native, 189 Asian Americans or Pacific Islanders, 32 Hispanic Americans), 392 international. Average age 28. 5,372 applicants, 17% accepted, 726 enrolled. In 2006, 682 degrees awarded. *Entrance requirements:* For master's, GMAT, 2 letters of recommendation. Additional exam requirements/recommendations for international students: Required—TOEFL. *Application deadline:* For fall admission, 4/20 for domestic students, 3/1 for international students; for spring admission, 10/12 for domestic and international students. Applications are processed on a rolling basis. Application fee: $215. Electronic applications accepted. *Financial support:* Fellowships, research assistantships, teaching assistantships, career-related internships or fieldwork, Federal Work-Study, institutionally sponsored loans, scholarships/grants, and unspecified assistantships available. Financial award applicants required to submit FAFSA. *Unit head:* Prof. Amir Ziv, Vice Dean of Students and the MBA Program, 212-854-3485, Fax: 212-932-0545, E-mail: az50@columbia.edu. *Application contact:* Linda B. Meehan, Assistant Dean of Admissions, 212-854-1961, Fax: 212-662-6754, E-mail: apply@claven.gsb.columbia.edu.

Concordia University, St. Paul, College of Business and Organizational Leadership, St. Paul, MN 55104-5494. Offers business and organizational leadership (MBA); criminal justice (MAHS); human resources (MAOM); organizational management (MAOM). *Accreditation:* ACBSP. Evening/weekend programs available. Postbaccalaureate distance learning degree programs offered (minimal on-campus study). *Faculty:* 11 full-time (2 women), 18 part-time/adjunct (6 women). *Students:* 186 full-time (114 women); includes 26 minority (16 African Americans, 8 Asian Americans or Pacific Islanders, 2 Hispanic Americans), 1 international. Average age 33. In 2006, 92 degrees awarded. *Entrance requirements:* Additional exam requirements/recommendations for international students: Required—TOEFL. *Application deadline:* Applications are processed on a rolling basis. Application fee: $50. Electronic applications accepted. *Financial support:* Federal Work-Study and scholarships/grants available. Financial award applicants required to submit FAFSA. *Unit head:* Dr. Robert DeGregorio, Dean, 651-641-8845, Fax: 651-641-8807, E-mail: degregorio@csp.edu. *Application contact:* Kimberly Craig, Director of Graduate and Cohort Admission, 651-603-6223, Fax: 651-603-6320, E-mail: craig@csp.edu.

Concordia University Wisconsin, Graduate Programs, School of Business and Legal Studies, MBA Program, Mequon, WI 53097-2402. Offers finance (MBA); health care administration (MBA); human resource management (MBA); international business (MBA); international business-English/Chinese (MBA); management (MBA); management information services (MBA); managerial communications (MBA); marketing (MBA); public administration (MBA); risk management (MBA). Postbaccalaureate distance learning degree programs offered (minimal on-campus study). *Students:* 504 (249 women). In 2006, 110 degrees awarded. *Degree requirements:* For master's, thesis or alternative, comprehensive exam. *Entrance requirements:* Additional exam requirements/recommendations for international students: Required—TOEFL. *Application deadline:* For fall admission, 8/1 priority date for domestic students; for spring admission, 1/15 for domestic students. Applications are processed on a rolling basis. Application fee: $50. *Expenses: Contact institution. Financial support:* Application deadline: 8/1. *Unit head:* Dr. David Borst, Director, 262-243-4298, Fax: 262-243-4428, E-mail: david.borst@cuw.edu.

Cornell University, Graduate School, Graduate Fields of Industrial and Labor Relations, Ithaca, NY 14853-0001. Offers collective bargaining, labor law and labor history (MILR, MPS, MS, PhD); economic and social statistics (MILR); human resource studies (MILR, MPS, MS, PhD); industrial and labor relations problems (MILR, MPS, MS, PhD); international and comparative labor (MILR, MPS, MS, PhD); labor economics (MILR, MPS, MS, PhD); organizational behavior (MILR, MPS, MS, PhD); statistics (MPS, MS, PhD), including applied statistics (MPS), biometry (MS, PhD), decision theory (MS, PhD), economic and social statistics (MS, PhD), engineering statistics (MS, PhD), experimental design (MS, PhD), mathematical statistics (MS, PhD), probability (MS, PhD), sampling (MS, PhD), statistical computing (MS, PhD), stochastic processes (MS, PhD). *Faculty:* 50 full-time (11 women). *Students:* 127 full-time (75 women); includes 23 minority (10 African Americans, 7 Asian Americans or Pacific Islanders, 6 Hispanic Americans), 45 international. Average age 31. 214 applicants, 30% accepted, 51 enrolled. In 2006, 69 master's, 8 doctorates awarded. *Degree requirements:* For master's, thesis (MS); for doctorate, thesis/dissertation, teaching experience, comprehensive exam. *Entrance requirements:* For master's and doctorate, GMAT or GRE General Test, 2 academic recommendations. Additional exam requirements/recommendations for international students: Required—TOEFL (minimum score 550 paper-based; 213 computer-based). Application fee: $60. Electronic applications accepted. *Expenses: Contact institution.* Full-time tuition and fees vary according to program. *Financial support:* In 2006–07, 82 students received support, including 28 fellowships with full tuition reimbursements available, 27 research assistantships with full tuition reimbursements available, 27 teaching assistantships with full tuition reimbursements available; institutionally sponsored loans, scholarships/grants, health care benefits, tuition waivers (full and partial), and unspecified assistantships also available. Financial award applicants required to submit FAFSA. *Unit head:* Director of Graduate Studies, 607-255-1522. *Application contact:* Graduate Field Assistant, 607-255-1522, E-mail: ilrgradapplicant@cornell.edu.

Cumberland University, Program in Organizational Leadership and Human Relations Management, Lebanon, TN 37087-3408. Offers MS. Part-time and evening/weekend programs available. *Faculty:* 1 full-time (0 women), 3 part-time/adjunct (1 woman). *Students:* 2 full-time (1 woman), 14 part-time (4 women); includes 3 minority (all African Americans), 5 international. Average age 31. 4 applicants, 75% accepted, 3 enrolled. In 2006, 6 degrees awarded. *Degree requirements:* For master's, comprehensive exam, registration. *Entrance requirements:* For master's, MAT, 3 letters of recommendation. Additional exam requirements/recommendations for international students: Required—TOEFL (minimum score 500 paper-based; 173 computer-based). *Application deadline:* For fall admission, 8/1 priority date for domestic students. Application fee: $50. *Expenses:* Tuition: Full-time $10,890; part-time $605 per credit. *Financial support:* Scholarships/grants, tuition waivers (partial), and unspecified assistantships available. Financial award application deadline: 8/1; financial award applicants required to submit FAFSA. *Unit head:* Dr. William R. Cheatham, Associate Professor, Criminal Justice, 615-444-2562 Ext. 1276, Fax: 615-444-2569, E-mail: rcheatham@cumberland.edu.

Dallas Baptist University, Graduate School of Business, Management Program, Dallas, TX 75211-9299. Offers business communication (MA); conflict resolution management (MA); general management (MA); health care management (MA); human resource management (MA). Part-time and evening/weekend programs available. Postbaccalaureate distance learning degree programs offered (no on-campus study). *Faculty:* 49 full-time (21 women), 112 part-time/adjunct (46 women). *Students:* 46 full-time, 194 part-time. 96 applicants. In 2006, 77 degrees awarded. *Entrance requirements:* For master's, minimum GPA of 3.0. Additional exam requirements/recommendations for international students: Required—TOEFL. *Application deadline:* Applications are processed on a rolling basis. Application fee: $25. Electronic applications accepted. *Expenses:* Tuition: Full-time $8,370; part-time $465 per credit hour. Required fees: $465 per credit hour. *Financial support:* Federal Work-Study, institutionally sponsored loans, scholarships/grants, and tuition waivers (full and partial) available. Support available to part-time students. *Faculty research:* Organizational behavior, conflict personalities. *Unit head:* Connie F. Throne, Director of Organizational Management Program, 214-333-5244, Fax: 214-333-5579, E-mail: graduate@dbu.edu. *Application contact:* Kit P. Montgomery, Director of Graduate Programs, 214-333-5242, Fax: 214-333-5579, E-mail: graduate@dbu.edu.

Davenport University, Sneden Graduate School, Warren, MI 48092-5209. Offers accounting (MBA); commerce (MBA); finance (MBA); health care management (MBA); human resources management (MBA); management (MBA). *Entrance requirements:* For master's, minimum undergraduate GPA of 2.7.

Davenport University, Sneden Graduate School, Dearborn, MI 48126-3799. Offers accounting (MBA); e-business (MBA); finance (MBA); global business (MBA); health care management (MBA); human resources management (MBA); management (MBA); marketing (MBA). Part-time and evening/weekend programs available. Postbaccalaureate distance learning degree programs offered (no on-campus study). *Entrance requirements:* For master's, minimum GPA of 2.7, previous course work in accounting and statistics. *Faculty research:* Accounting, international accounting, social and environmental accounting, finance.

DePaul University, Charles H. Kellstadt Graduate School of Business, Department of Management, Chicago, IL 60604-2287. Offers entrepreneurship (MBA); health sector management (MBA); human resource management (MBA, MSHR); leadership/change management (MBA); management planning and strategy (MBA); operations management (MBA). Part-time and evening/weekend programs available. *Faculty:* 36 full-time (7 women), 35 part-time/adjunct (16 women). *Students:* 173 full-time (71 women), 134 part-time (61 women); includes 60 minority (12 African Americans, 34 Asian Americans or Pacific Islanders, 14 Hispanic Americans), 13 international. Average age 31. In 2006, 112 degrees awarded. *Entrance requirements:* For master's, GMAT, GRE (MSHR), 2 letters of recommendation, resumé. Additional exam requirements/recommendations for international students: Required—TOEFL (minimum score 550 paper-based; 213 computer-based). *Application deadline:* For fall admission, 7/1 for domestic students; for winter admission, 10/1 for domestic students; for spring admission, 2/1 for domestic students. Applications are processed on a rolling basis. Application fee: $60. Electronic applications accepted. *Financial support:* Research assistantships available. Financial award application deadline: 4/1. *Faculty research:* Growth management, creativity and innovation, quality management and business process design, entrepreneurship. *Application contact:* Christopher E. Kinsella, Director of Cohort MBA Programs, 312-362-8810, Fax: 312-362-6677, E-mail: kgsb@depaul.edu.

DeVry University, Keller Graduate School of Management, Oakbrook Terrace, IL 60181. Offers accounting and financial management (MAFM); business administration (MBA); human resources management (MHRM); information systems management (MISM); network and communications management (MNCM); project management (MPM); public administration (MPA); telecommunications management (MTM). Part-time and evening/weekend programs available. Postbaccalaureate distance learning degree programs offered (no on-campus study). *Degree requirements:* For master's, business plan (MBA), capstone project (MHRM, MPM, MTM, MAFM). *Entrance requirements:* For master's, GMAT, GRE General Test, or institutional assessment, interview. Additional exam requirements/recommendations for international students: Required—TOEFL (minimum score 500 paper-based; 173 computer-based). Electronic applications accepted.

See Close-Up on page 265.

Human Resources Management

East Central University, School of Graduate Studies, Department of Human Resources, Ada, OK 74820-6899. Offers administration (MSHR); counseling (MSHR); criminal justice (MSHR); rehabilitation counseling (MSHR). *Accreditation:* CORE. Part-time and evening/weekend programs available. *Faculty:* 7 part-time/adjunct (3 women). *Students:* 83 full-time (71 women), 103 part-time (73 women); includes 54 minority (11 African Americans, 38 American Indian/Alaska Native, 1 Asian American or Pacific Islander, 4 Hispanic Americans). Average age 37. 125 applicants, 90% accepted. In 2006, 60 degrees awarded. *Degree requirements:* For master's, thesis optional. *Entrance requirements:* For master's, GRE General Test, MAT, minimum GPA of 2.5. *Application deadline:* Applications are processed on a rolling basis. Application fee: $0 ($50 for international students). *Financial support:* In 2006–07, 1 teaching assistantship was awarded. *Unit head:* Dr. Steve Turner, Chairman, 580-332-8000 Ext. 481. *Application contact:* Juanita L. Pratt, Secretary, 580-310-5708, Fax: 580-282-8691, E-mail: jpratt@ecok.edu.

Eastern Michigan University, Graduate School, College of Business, Department of Management, Program in Human Resources Management and Organizational Development, Ypsilanti, MI 48197. Offers MSHROD. Part-time and evening/weekend programs available. Postbaccalaureate distance learning degree programs offered (minimal on-campus study). *Faculty:* 20 full-time (8 women). *Students:* 7 full-time (6 women), 65 part-time (46 women); includes 12 minority (4 African Americans, 7 Asian Americans or Pacific Islanders, 1 Hispanic American), 29 international. Average age 31. In 2006, 33 degrees awarded. *Degree requirements:* For master's, thesis optional. *Entrance requirements:* For master's, GMAT. Additional exam requirements/recommendations for international students: Required—TOEFL. *Application deadline:* For fall admission, 5/15 priority date for domestic and international students; for winter admission, 10/15 priority date for domestic and international students; for spring admission, 3/15 priority date for domestic and international students. Applications are processed on a rolling basis. Application fee: $35. *Expenses:* Tuition, state resident: part-time $341 per credit hour. Tuition, nonresident: full-time $16,104; part-time $671 per credit hour. Required fees: $816; $34 per credit hour. $40 per term. One-time fee: $82 full-time. Tuition and fees vary according to course level, course load, degree level and reciprocity agreements. *Financial support:* Fellowships, research assistantships with full tuition reimbursements, teaching assistantships with full tuition reimbursements, career-related internships or fieldwork, Federal Work-Study, institutionally sponsored loans, scholarships/grants, tuition waivers (partial), and unspecified assistantships available. Support available to part-time students. Financial award applicants required to submit FAFSA.

Eastern Michigan University, Graduate School, College of Business, Program in Business Administration, Ypsilanti, MI 48197. Offers business administration (MBA); e-business (MBA); enterprise business intelligence (MBA); entrepreneurship (MBA); finance (MBA); human resources (MBA); information systems (MBA); internal auditing (MBA); international business (MBA); nonprofit management (MBA); supply chain management (MBA). *Accreditation:* AACSB. Part-time and evening/weekend programs available. Postbaccalaureate distance learning degree programs offered (minimal on-campus study). *Students:* 98 full-time (36 women), 192 part-time (86 women); includes 50 minority (26 African Americans, 19 Asian Americans or Pacific Islanders, 5 Hispanic Americans), 76 international. Average age 29. In 2006, 109 degrees awarded. *Entrance requirements:* For master's, GMAT. Additional exam requirements/recommendations for international students: Required—TOEFL. *Application deadline:* For fall admission, 5/15 priority date for domestic students, 5/1 priority date for international students; for winter admission, 10/15 priority date for domestic students, 10/1 priority date for international students; for spring admission, 3/15 priority date for domestic students, 3/1 priority date for international students. Applications are processed on a rolling basis. Application fee: $35. *Expenses:* Tuition, state resident: part-time $341 per credit hour. Tuition, nonresident: full-time $16,104; part-time $671 per credit hour. Required fees: $816; $34 per credit hour. $40 per term. One-time fee: $82 full-time. Tuition and fees vary according to course level, course load, degree level and reciprocity agreements. *Financial support:* Fellowships, research assistantships with full tuition reimbursements, teaching assistantships with full tuition reimbursements, career-related internships or fieldwork, Federal Work-Study, institutionally sponsored loans, scholarships/grants, tuition waivers (partial), and unspecified assistantships available. Support available to part-time students. Financial award applicants required to submit FAFSA. *Unit head:* Dawn Gaymer, Assistant Dean, Graduate Business Programs, 734-487-4444, Fax: 734-483-1316, E-mail: dawn.malone@emich.edu. *Application contact:* K. Michelle Henry, Coordinator, 734-487-4444, Fax: 734-483-1316, E-mail: michelle.henry@emich.edu.

Emmanuel College, Graduate Programs, Program in Human Resource Management, Boston, MA 02115. Offers MS, Certificate. Part-time and evening/weekend programs available. *Faculty:* 22 part-time/adjunct (5 women). *Students:* Average age 32. 36 applicants, 58% accepted, 15 enrolled. In 2006, 18 master's, 2 other advanced degrees awarded. *Entrance requirements:* For master's, interview, resumé, 2 letters of recommendation, critical analysis essay, leadership statement; for Certificate, interview, resumé, letter of recommendation. Additional exam requirements/recommendations for international students: Required—TOEFL (minimum score 600 paper-based; 250 computer-based). *Application deadline:* For fall admission, 8/15 priority date for domestic students; for spring admission, 12/8 priority date for domestic students. Applications are processed on a rolling basis. Application fee: $50. Electronic applications accepted. *Expenses:* Tuition: Full-time $5,256. *Unit head:* Brian Minchello, Associate Director, Graduate and Professional Programs, 617-735-9928, Fax: 617-735-9708, E-mail: gpp@emmanuel.edu. *Application contact:* Kristin Balutis, Graduate Management Programs, 617-735-9859, Fax: 617-735-9708, E-mail: balutkr@emmanuel.edu.

Fairfield University, Charles F. Dolan School of Business, Fairfield, CT 06824-5195. Offers accounting (MBA, MS, CAS); finance (MBA, MS, CAS); general management (MBA); human resource management (MBA, CAS); information systems and operations (MBA); information systems and operations management (CAS); international business (MBA, CAS); marketing (MBA, CAS); taxation (MBA, MS, CAS). *Accreditation:* AACSB. Part-time and evening/weekend programs available. *Faculty:* 43 full-time (17 women), 2 part-time/adjunct (1 woman). *Students:* 65 full-time (31 women), 125 part-time (54 women); includes 4 Asian Americans or Pacific Islanders, 4 Hispanic Americans, 22 international. Average age 27. 99 applicants, 45% accepted, 38 enrolled. In 2006, 78 degrees awarded. *Degree requirements:* For master's, registration. *Entrance requirements:* For master's, GMAT, 2 letters of reference, resumé. Additional exam requirements/recommendations for international students: Required—TOEFL (minimum score 550 paper-based; 213 computer-based; 79 iBT). *Application deadline:* For fall admission, 8/15 priority date for domestic students, 5/15 priority date for international students; for spring admission, 11/15 priority date for domestic students, 10/15 priority date for international students. Applications are processed on a rolling basis. Application fee: $55. Electronic applications accepted. *Expenses: Contact institution. Financial support:* Unspecified assistantships available. *Faculty research:* Optimal investment strategies, organization structure, international finance, strategic management, customer behavior. *Unit head:* Dr. Norman A. Solomon, Dean, 203-254-4000 Ext. 4070, Fax: 203-254-4105, E-mail: nsolomon@mail.fairfield.edu. *Application contact:* Marianne Gumpper, Director of Graduate and Continuing Studies Admissions, 203-254-4184, Fax: 203-254-4073, E-mail: gradadmis@mail.fairfield.edu.

See Close-Up on page 271.

Fairleigh Dickinson University, College at Florham, Silberman College of Business, Center for Human Resource Management Studies, Program in Human Resource Management, Madison, NJ 07940-1099. Offers MBA, MA/MBA. *Students:* 6 full-time (3 women), 13 part-time (11 women). Average age 30. 13 applicants, 62% accepted, 4 enrolled. In 2006, 8 degrees awarded. *Application deadline:* Applications are processed on a rolling basis. Application fee: $40.

Fairleigh Dickinson University, Metropolitan Campus, Silberman College of Business, Center for Human Resources Management Studies, Program for Executives, Teaneck, NJ 07666-1914. Offers MBA. *Students:* 39 full-time (8 women), 15 part-time (2 women), 2 international. Average age 38. 37 applicants, 100% accepted, 23 enrolled. In 2006, 21 degrees awarded. *Application deadline:* Applications are processed on a rolling basis. Application fee: $40. *Unit head:* Dr. Robert Greenfield, Dean, Silberman College of Business, 201-692-2000.

Fairleigh Dickinson University, Metropolitan Campus, Silberman College of Business, Center for Human Resources Management Studies, Program in Human Resource Management, Teaneck, NJ 07666-1914. Offers MBA, Certificate. *Students:* 5 full-time (4 women), 9 part-time (7 women), 3 international. Average age 31. 11 applicants, 45% accepted, 2 enrolled. In 2006, 5 degrees awarded. *Application deadline:* Applications are processed on a rolling basis. Application fee: $40.

Fitchburg State College, Division of Graduate and Continuing Education, Program in Business Administration, Fitchburg, MA 01420-2697. Offers accounting (MBA); human resource management (MBA); management (MBA). Part-time and evening/weekend programs available. *Students:* 42 full-time (8 women), 36 part-time (19 women); includes 13 minority (6 African Americans, 3 Asian Americans or Pacific Islanders, 4 Hispanic Americans), 25 international. Average age 31. 51 applicants, 98% accepted, 41 enrolled. In 2006, 47 degrees awarded. *Entrance requirements:* For master's, GMAT, minimum GPA of 2.8, letters of recommendation, resumé. Additional exam requirements/recommendations for international students: Required—TOEFL (minimum score 550 paper-based; 213 computer-based; 79 iBT). *Application deadline:* Applications are processed on a rolling basis. Application fee: $25 ($50 for international students). *Expenses:* Tuition, state resident: part-time $150 per credit. Tuition, nonresident: part-time $150 per credit. Required fees: $90 per credit. *Financial support:* In 2006–07, research assistantships with partial tuition reimbursements (averaging $5,500 per year); Federal Work-Study, scholarships/grants, and unspecified assistantships also available. Support available to part-time students. Financial award application deadline: 3/1; financial award applicants required to submit FAFSA. *Unit head:* Joseph McAloon, Chair, 978-665-3745, Fax: 978-665-3658, E-mail: gce@fsc.edu. *Application contact:* Director of Admissions, 978-665-3144, Fax: 978-665-4540, E-mail: admissions@fsc.edu.

Florida Institute of Technology, Graduate Programs, University College, Melbourne, FL 32901-6975. Offers acquisition and contract management (MS, PMBA); aerospace engineering (MS); business administration (PMBA); computer information systems (MS); computer science (MS); e-business (PMBA); electrical engineering (MS); engineering management (MS); human resource management (PMBA); human resources management (MS); information systems (PMBA); logistics management (MS); management (MS), including acquisition and contract management, e-business, human resource management, information systems, logistics management, transportation management; materiel acquisition management (MS); mechanical engineering (MS); operations research (MS); project management (MS), including information systems, operations research; public administration (MPA); software engineering (MS); space systems (MS); space systems management (MS); systems management (MS), including information systems, operations research. Part-time and evening/weekend programs available. Postbaccalaureate distance learning degree programs offered (no on-campus study). *Faculty:* 11 full-time (4 women), 129 part-time/adjunct (17 women). *Students:* 78 full-time (34 women), 1,258 part-time (507 women); includes 384 minority (252 African Americans, 9 American Indian/Alaska Native, 58 Asian Americans or Pacific Islanders, 65 Hispanic Americans), 28 international. Average age 36. 629 applicants, 65% accepted, 320 enrolled. In 2006, 505 degrees awarded. *Degree requirements:* For master's, registration. *Entrance requirements:* For master's, minimum GPA of 3.0. Additional exam requirements/recommendations for international students: Required—TOEFL (minimum score 550 paper-based; 213 computer-based). *Application deadline:* Applications are processed on a rolling basis. Application fee: $50. Electronic applications accepted. *Expenses:* Tuition: Part-time $900 per credit. *Financial support:* Institutionally sponsored loans available. Financial award application deadline: 3/1; financial award applicants required to submit FAFSA. *Unit head:* Dr. Clifford Bragdon, Dean, 321-674-8821, Fax: 321-951-7694, E-mail: cbragdon@fit.edu. *Application contact:* Carolyn P. Farrior, Director of Graduate Admissions, 321-674-7118, Fax: 321-723-9468, E-mail: cfarrior@fit.edu.

Florida Metropolitan University–South Orlando Campus, Program in Business Administration, Orlando, FL 32819. Offers accounting (MBA); general management (MBA); human resources (MBA); international management (MBA).

Florida Metropolitan University–Tampa Campus, Department of Business Administration, Tampa, FL 33614-5899. Offers accounting (MBA); human resources (MBA); international business (MBA). Part-time and evening/weekend programs available. *Degree requirements:* For master's, thesis optional. *Entrance requirements:* For master's, GMAT or GRE, minimum GPA of 3.0.

Fordham University, Graduate School of Education, Division of Educational Leadership, Administration and Policy, New York, NY 10023. Offers administration and supervision (MSE, Adv C); administration and supervision for church leaders (PhD); educational administration and supervision (Ed D, PhD); human resource program administration (MS). *Accreditation:* NCATE. *Faculty:* 8 full-time (3 women), 20 part-time/adjunct (12 women). *Students:* 1 full-time (0 women), 229 part-time (174 women); includes 62 minority (23 African Americans, 12 Asian Americans or Pacific Islanders, 27 Hispanic Americans), 1 international. Average age 39. 144 applicants, 73% accepted, 82 enrolled. In 2006, 105 master's, 19 doctorates awarded. *Degree requirements:* For doctorate, thesis/dissertation. *Entrance requirements:* For doctorate, MAT, GRE General Test. Application fee: $65. *Financial support:* Career-related internships or fieldwork available. Financial award applicants required to submit FAFSA. *Unit head:* Dr. Gerald Cattaro, Chairperson, 212-636-6441.

Framingham State College, Division of Graduate and Continuing Education, Program in Human Resource Management, Framingham, MA 01701-9101. Offers MA. Part-time and evening/weekend programs available. *Faculty:* 2 full-time, 3 part-time/adjunct. *Students:* 24. In 2006, 15 degrees awarded. *Unit head:* Dr. Robert Wallace, Coordinator, 508-626-4888, Fax: 508-626-4030, E-mail: bwallace@frc.mass.edu. *Application contact:* 508-626-4550, Fax: 508-626-4030, E-mail: dgce@frc.mass.edu.

Gannon University, School of Graduate Studies, College of Humanities, Business, and Education, School of Business, Program in Human Resources Management, Erie, PA 16541-0001. Offers Certificate. Part-time and evening/weekend programs available. *Students:* Average age 39. 1 applicant, 100% accepted, 1 enrolled. *Entrance requirements:* For degree, GMAT. Additional exam requirements/recommendations for international students: Required—TOEFL (minimum score 500 paper-based; 173 computer-based). *Application deadline:* Applications are processed on a rolling basis. Application fee: $25. *Expenses:* Tuition: Full-time $12,240; part-time $680 per credit. Required fees: $496; $16 per credit. Tuition and fees vary according to course load, degree level, campus/location and program. *Financial support:* Application deadline: 7/1; *Application contact:* Debra Meszaros, Director of Graduate Recruitment, 814-871-5819, Fax: 814-871-5827, E-mail: cfal@gannon.edu.

George Mason University, School of Public Policy, Program in Organization Development and Knowledge Management, Fairfax, VA 22030. Offers MNPS. Part-time and evening/weekend programs available. *Faculty:* 48 full-time (8 women), 41 part-time/adjunct (6 women). *Students:* 78. 57 applicants, 74% accepted, 40 enrolled. In 2006, 8 degrees awarded. *Degree requirements:* For master's, thesis or alternative. *Entrance requirements:* For master's, minimum GPA of 3.0, 2 letters of recommendation, resumé, goals statement. Additional exam requirements/recommendations for international students: Required—TOEFL. *Application deadline:* For fall admission, 6/1 priority date for domestic students, 5/1 priority date for international students; for spring admission, 12/1 priority date for domestic and international students. Applications are processed on a rolling basis. Application fee: $60. Electronic applications accepted. *Expenses: Contact institution. Financial support:* Career-related internships or fieldwork, Federal Work-Study, scholarships/grants, tuition waivers (partial), and unspecified assistantships available. Support available to part-time students. Financial award application deadline: 3/1; financial award applicants required to submit FAFSA. *Unit head:* Dr. Ann Baker, Director,

703-993-8099, E-mail: spp@gmu.edu. *Application contact:* Leslie Metzger Levin, Director of Graduate Admissions, 703-993-8099, Fax: 703-993-4876, E-mail: lmetzger@gmu.edu.

The George Washington University, Columbian College of Arts and Sciences, Department of Organizational Sciences and Communication, Washington, DC 20052. Offers human resource management (MA); leadership and coaching (Certificate); organizational management (MA). Part-time and evening/weekend programs available. *Degree requirements:* For master's, comprehensive exam. *Entrance requirements:* For master's, GRE General Test, minimum GPA of 3.0; for Certificate, minimum GPA of 3.0. Additional exam requirements/recommendations for international students: Required—TOEFL (minimum score 500 paper-based). Electronic applications accepted.

See Close-Up on page 697.

The George Washington University, School of Business, Department of Management Science, Washington, DC 20052. Offers human resources management (MBA); information systems management (MBA); logistics, operations, and materials management (MBA); management and organization (PhD); management decision making (MBA, PhD); management information systems (MSIST); management of science, technology, and innovation (MBA); organizational behavior and development (MBA); project management (MS). *Accreditation:* AACSB. Part-time and evening/weekend programs available. *Degree requirements:* For doctorate, thesis/dissertation. *Entrance requirements:* For master's, GMAT; for doctorate, GMAT or GRE. Additional exam requirements/recommendations for international students: Required—TOEFL. *Faculty research:* Artificial intelligence, technological entrepreneurship, expert systems, strategic planning/management.

Georgia State University, J. Mack Robinson College of Business, Department of Managerial Sciences, Atlanta, GA 30303-3083. Offers business analysis (MBA, MS); entrepreneurship (MBA); human resources management (MBA, MS); management (MBA, PhD); operations management (MBA, MS, PhD); organization change (MS). Part-time and evening/weekend programs available. *Faculty:* 34 full-time (14 women). *Students:* 53 full-time (18 women), 177 part-time (61 women); includes 37 minority (21 African Americans, 11 Asian Americans or Pacific Islanders, 5 Hispanic Americans), 19 international. Average age 32. 68 applicants, 35% accepted, 20 enrolled. In 2006, 98 master's, 4 doctorates awarded. *Degree requirements:* For doctorate, thesis/dissertation. *Entrance requirements:* For master's and doctorate, GMAT. Additional exam requirements/recommendations for international students: Required—TOEFL (minimum score 610 paper-based; 255 computer-based; 101 iBT). *Application deadline:* For fall admission, 5/1 for domestic students, 2/1 for international students; for spring admission, 10/15 for domestic students, 5/1 for international students. Applications are processed on a rolling basis. Application fee: $50. Electronic applications accepted. *Unit head:* Dr. Todd J. Maurer, Chair, 404-651-3400, E-mail: tmaurer@gsu.edu.

Georgia State University, J. Mack Robinson College of Business, W. T. Beebe Institute of Personnel and Employee Relations, Atlanta, GA 30303-3083. Offers MBA, MS, PhD. Part-time and evening/weekend programs available. *Students:* 5 full-time (2 women), 21 part-time (19 women); includes 4 minority (3 African Americans, 1 Asian American or Pacific Islander), 2 international. Average age 32. 8 applicants, 75% accepted, 6 enrolled. In 2006, 13 master's, 1 doctorate awarded. Terminal master's awarded for partial completion of doctoral program. *Degree requirements:* For doctorate, thesis/dissertation. *Entrance requirements:* For master's and doctorate, GMAT. Additional exam requirements/recommendations for international students: Required—TOEFL (minimum score 610 paper-based; 255 computer-based; 101 iBT). *Application deadline:* For fall admission, 5/1 for domestic students, 2/1 for international students; for spring admission, 10/15 for domestic students, 5/1 for international students. Applications are processed on a rolling basis. Application fee: $50. *Financial support:* Fellowships, research assistantships, teaching assistantships, career-related internships or fieldwork and tuition waivers (partial) available. Support available to part-time students. Financial award applicants required to submit FAFSA. *Unit head:* Dr. Todd J. Maurer, Director, 404-651-2884, Fax: 404-651-1700. *Application contact:* Graduate Student and Alumni Services, 404-463-4568, Fax: 404-651-2721, E-mail: mastersadmissions@gsu.edu.

Golden Gate University, Ageno School of Business, San Francisco, CA 94105-2968. Offers accounting (M Ac, MBA); business administration (EMBA, MBA, DBA); finance (MBA, MS, Certificate); financial planning (MS, Certificate); human resource management (MBA, MS); human resources management (Certificate); information technology (MBA); information technology management (MS, Certificate); integrated marketing and communications (MS, Certificate); international business (MBA); management (MBA); marketing (MBA, MS, Certificate); operations management (Certificate); psychology (MA, Certificate); public relations (MS, Certificate); JD/MBA. Part-time and evening/weekend programs available. *Students:* 355 full-time (192 women), 977 part-time (465 women); includes 447 minority (85 African Americans, 5 American Indian/Alaska Native, 274 Asian Americans or Pacific Islanders, 83 Hispanic Americans), 226 international. Average age 34. 548 applicants, 74% accepted, 201 enrolled. In 2006, 545 master's, 21 doctorates awarded. *Degree requirements:* For doctorate, thesis/dissertation. *Entrance requirements:* For master's, GMAT (MBA), minimum GPA of 2.5 (MS). Additional exam requirements/recommendations for international students: Required—TOEFL. *Application deadline:* Applications are processed on a rolling basis. Application fee: $55 ($90 for international students). *Financial support:* Career-related internships or fieldwork, Federal Work-Study, and institutionally sponsored loans available. Support available to part-time students. Financial award applicants required to submit FAFSA. *Unit head:* Terry Connelly, Dean, 415-442-6519, Fax: 415-442-5369. *Application contact:* Enrollment Services, 415-442-7800, Fax: 415-442-7807, E-mail: info@ggu.edu.

Goldey-Beacom College, Graduate Program, Wilmington, DE 19808-1999. Offers business administration (MBA); financial management (MBA); human resource management (MBA); information technology (MBA); management (MM); marketing management (MBA). *Accreditation:* ACBSP. Part-time and evening/weekend programs available. *Entrance requirements:* For master's, GMAT, minimum GPA of 3.0. Additional exam requirements/recommendations for international students: Required—TOEFL (minimum score 525 paper-based; 195 computer-based). Electronic applications accepted.

Hawai'i Pacific University, College of Business Administration, Honolulu, HI 96813. Offers accounting/CPA (MBA); communication (MBA); e-business (MBA); economics (MBA); finance (MBA); human resource management (MBA); information systems (MBA); international business (MBA); management (MBA); marketing (MBA); organizational change (MBA); travel industry management (MBA). Part-time and evening/weekend programs available. *Faculty:* 40 full-time (16 women), 30 part-time/adjunct (10 women). *Students:* 320 full-time (150 women), 205 part-time (95 women); includes 168 minority (17 African Americans, 7 American Indian/Alaska Native, 137 Asian Americans or Pacific Islanders, 7 Hispanic Americans), 232 international. Average age 31. 279 applicants, 67% accepted, 166 enrolled. In 2006, 172 degrees awarded. *Degree requirements:* For master's, thesis. *Entrance requirements:* For master's, GMAT. Additional exam requirements/recommendations for international students: Recommended—TOEFL (minimum score 550 paper-based; 213 computer-based), TWE (minimum score 5). *Application deadline:* For fall admission, 2/15 priority date for domestic students; for spring admission, 10/15 priority date for domestic students. Applications are processed on a rolling basis. Application fee: $50. Electronic applications accepted. *Expenses:* Tuition: Full-time $10,080; part-time $560 per credit. *Financial support:* In 2006–07, 118 students received support; research assistantships, career-related internships or fieldwork, Federal Work-Study, scholarships/grants, and unspecified assistantships available. Support available to part-time students. Financial award application deadline: 3/1; financial award applicants required to submit FAFSA. *Faculty research:* Statistical control process as used by management, studies in comparative cross-cultural management styles, not-for-profit management. *Unit head:* Dr. Charles Steilen, Dean, 808-544-9301, Fax: 808-544-0283, E-mail: csteilen@hpu.edu. *Application contact:* Danny Lam, Assistant Director of Graduate Admissions, 808-544-1135, Fax: 808-544-0280, E-mail: graduate@hpu.edu.

See Close-Up on page 275.

Hawai'i Pacific University, College of Professional Studies, Honolulu, HI 96813. Offers global leadership and sustainable development (MA); human resource management (MA); information systems (MSIS); organizational change (MA). Part-time and evening/weekend programs available. *Faculty:* 15 full-time (2 women), 7 part-time/adjunct (2 women). *Students:* 118 full-time (56 women), 149 part-time (57 women); includes 101 minority (15 African Americans, 5 American Indian/Alaska Native, 70 Asian Americans or Pacific Islanders, 11 Hispanic Americans), 87 international. Average age 32. 188 applicants, 58% accepted, 67 enrolled. In 2006, 65 degrees awarded. *Degree requirements:* For master's, thesis. *Entrance requirements:* Additional exam requirements/recommendations for international students: Recommended—TOEFL (minimum score 550 paper-based; 213 computer-based), TWE (minimum score 5). *Application deadline:* For fall admission, 2/15 priority date for domestic students; for spring admission, 10/15 priority date for domestic students. Applications are processed on a rolling basis. Application fee: $50. Electronic applications accepted. *Expenses:* Tuition: Full-time $10,080; part-time $560 per credit. *Financial support:* In 2006–07, 54 students received support. Career-related internships or fieldwork, Federal Work-Study, scholarships/grants, and unspecified assistantships available. Support available to part-time students. Financial award application deadline: 3/1; financial award applicants required to submit FAFSA. *Unit head:* Dr. Gordon Jones, Dean, 808-544-1181, Fax: 808-544-0247, E-mail: gjones@hpu.edu. *Application contact:* Danny Lam, Assistant Director of Graduate Admissions, 808-544-1135, Fax: 808-544-0280, E-mail: graduate@hpu.edu.

HEC Montreal, School of Business Administration, Master of Science Programs in Administration, Program in Human Resources Management, Montréal, QC H3T 2A7, Canada. Offers M Sc. All courses are given in French. Part-time programs available. *Degree requirements:* For master's, one foreign language, thesis. Application fee: $60 Canadian dollars. Electronic applications accepted. Tuition and fees charges are reported in Canadian dollars. *Expenses:* Tuition, nonresident: part-time $56 Canadian dollars per credit. Required fees: $30 Canadian dollars per semester. *Financial support:* Fellowships, research assistantships, teaching assistantships, scholarships/grants available. *Application contact:* Francine Blais, Administrative Director, 514-340-6112, Fax: 514-340-6411, E-mail: francine.blais@hec.ca.

Hofstra University, Frank G. Zarb School of Business, Department of Management, Entrepreneurship and General Management, Hempstead, NY 11549. Offers health services management (MBA); human resource management (MS, Advanced Certificate); management (EMBA, MBA), including business administration (EMBA); quality management (MBA). Part-time and evening/weekend programs available. *Faculty:* 8 full-time (2 women), 1 part-time/adjunct (0 women). *Students:* 46 full-time (19 women), 238 part-time (114 women); includes 55 minority (20 African Americans, 25 Asian Americans or Pacific Islanders, 10 Hispanic Americans), 9 international. Average age 32. 183 applicants, 90% accepted, 117 enrolled. In 2006, 17 master's, 3 other advanced degrees awarded. *Degree requirements:* For master's, thesis optional. *Entrance requirements:* For master's, GMAT, 2 letters of recommendation, resumé, essay. Additional exam requirements/recommendations for international students: Required—TOEFL (minimum score 550 paper-based; 213 computer-based). *Application deadline:* Applications are processed on a rolling basis. Application fee: $60. Electronic applications accepted. *Expenses:* Tuition: Full-time $13,320; part-time $740 per credit. Required fees: $930; $155 per term. *Financial support:* In 2006–07, 25 students received support, including 17 fellowships with tuition reimbursements available (averaging $5,367 per year), 3 research assistantships with full and partial tuition reimbursements available (averaging $7,232 per year); tuition waivers (full and partial) and unspecified assistantships also available. Financial award applicants required to submit FAFSA. *Faculty research:* Business/personal ethics, stakeholders, whistle blowing and national/global labor practices; family business, entrepreneurship (for & non-profit); competition, innovation; risk taking, problem solving; and supple chain management, scheduling and health care industry. Total annual research expenditures: $24,000. *Unit head:* Dr. Mamdouh I. Farid, Chairperson, 516-463-5735, Fax: 516-463-4834, E-mail: mgbmif@hofstra.edu. *Application contact:* Carol Drummer, Dean of Graduate Admissions, 516-463-4876, Fax: 516-463-4664, E-mail: gradstudent@hofstra.edu.

Holy Family University, Graduate School, School of Business, Philadelphia, PA 19114-2094. Offers human resources management (MS); information systems management (MS). Part-time and evening/weekend programs available. *Degree requirements:* For master's, thesis optional. *Entrance requirements:* For master's, GMAT, GRE, or MAT, minimum GPA of 3.0.

Houston Baptist University, College of Business and Economics, Program in Human Resources Management, Houston, TX 77074-3298. Offers MSHRM. Part-time and evening/weekend programs available. *Degree requirements:* For master's, registration. *Entrance requirements:* For master's, GMAT, minimum GPA of 2.5. Additional exam requirements/recommendations for international students: Required—TOEFL (minimum score 550 paper-based; 213 computer-based). Expenses: Contact institution.

Indiana Tech, Program in Business Administration, Fort Wayne, IN 46803-1297. Offers accounting (MBA); human resources (MBA); management (MBA); marketing (MBA). Part-time and evening/weekend programs available. *Entrance requirements:* For master's, minimum undergraduate GPA of 2.5, GMAT or 2 years of work experience. Additional exam requirements/recommendations for international students: Required—TOEFL (minimum score 550 paper-based). Electronic applications accepted.

Instituto Tecnologico de Santo Domingo, Graduate School, Santo Domingo, Dominican Republic. Offers corporate finance (M Mgmt); education (M Ed); engineering (M Eng), including data telecommunications, industrial engineering, sanitary and environmental engineering, structural engineering; environmental science (M En S); human resources administration (M Mgmt); management (M Mgmt); psychology (MA); social science (M Ed). *Entrance requirements:* For master's, birth certificate, minimum GPA of 2.0.

Instituto Tecnológico y de Estudios Superiores de Monterrey, Campus Cuernavaca, Programs in Business Administration, Temixco, Mexico. Offers finance (MA); human resources management (MA); international business (MA); marketing (MA).

Inter American University of Puerto Rico, Bayamón Campus, Graduate School, Bayamón, PR 00957. Offers e-commerce (MBA); human resources (MBA). Part-time and evening/weekend programs available. *Faculty:* 7 full-time (1 woman), 2 part-time/adjunct (1 woman). *Students:* 11 full-time (10 women), 50 part-time (24 women); all Hispanic Americans *Entrance requirements:* For master's, EXADEP, GRE General Test, letters of recommendation. *Application deadline:* For fall admission, 7/1 for domestic students. Application fee: $31. *Expenses:* Tuition: Part-time $175 per credit. Required fees: $231 per semester. *Unit head:* Prof. Juan F. Martinez, Chancellor, 787-279-1912 Ext. 2295, Fax: 787-279-2205, E-mail: jmartinez@bc.inter.edu. *Application contact:* Carlos Alicea, Director of Admission, 787-279-1912 Ext. 2017, Fax: 787-279-2205, E-mail: calicea@bc.inter.edu.

Inter American University of Puerto Rico, Metropolitan Campus, Graduate Programs, Faculty of Economics and Administrative Sciences, Program in Human Resources, San Juan, PR 00919-1293. Offers MBA. *Degree requirements:* For master's, comprehensive exam. *Entrance requirements:* For master's, GRE or EXADEP, interview. Electronic applications accepted.

Inter American University of Puerto Rico, Ponce Campus, Graduate School, Mercedita, PR 00715-1602. Offers accounting (MBA); biology (M Ed); chemistry (M Ed); criminal justice (MA); elementary education (M Ed); English as a Second Language (M Ed); finance (MBA); history (M Ed); human resources (MBA); mathematics (M Ed); Spanish (M Ed); trade (MBA). *Entrance requirements:* For master's, minimum GPA of 2.5.

Inter American University of Puerto Rico, San Germán Campus, Graduate Studies Center, Graduate Program in Business Administration, San Germán, PR 00683-5008. Offers accounting (MBA); finance (MBA); human resources (MBA, PhD); industrial relations (MBA); international business (PhD); labor relations (PhD); management information systems (MBA); marketing (MBA); quality organizational design (MBA). Part-time and evening/weekend

Human Resources Management

Inter American University of Puerto Rico, San Germán Campus (continued)
programs available. *Faculty:* 12 full-time, 4 part-time/adjunct. *Students:* 265. Average age 27. In 2006, 67 master's, 1 doctorate awarded. *Degree requirements:* For master's, comprehensive exam. *Entrance requirements:* For master's, GRE General Test or EXADEP, minimum GPA of 3.0. *Application deadline:* For fall admission, 4/30 priority date for domestic students; for spring admission, 11/15 for domestic students. Applications are processed on a rolling basis. Application fee: $31. *Expenses:* Tuition: Part-time $175 per credit. Required fees: $238 per semester. Tuition and fees vary according to degree level. *Financial support:* Teaching assistantships, Federal Work-Study and unspecified assistantships available. *Application contact:* Prof. Duay Rivera, Graduate Coordinator, 787-264-1912 Ext. 7218, Fax: 787-892-7510, E-mail: durivera@sg.inter.edu.

Inter American University of Puerto Rico, San Germán Campus, Graduate Studies Center, Graduate Program in Entrepreneurial and Managerial Development, San Germán, PR 00683-5008. Offers human resources (PhD); interregional and international business (PhD); labor relations (PhD). Part-time and evening/weekend programs available. *Faculty:* 12 full-time, 4 part-time/adjunct. *Students:* 52. Average age 41. In 2006, 1 degree awarded. *Degree requirements:* For doctorate, thesis/dissertation, comprehensive exam. *Entrance requirements:* For doctorate, EXADEP or GMAT, minimum graduate GPA of 3.25. *Application deadline:* For fall admission, 4/30 priority date for domestic students; for spring admission, 11/15 for domestic students. Applications are processed on a rolling basis. Application fee: $75. *Expenses:* Tuition: Part-time $175 per credit. Required fees: $238 per semester. Tuition and fees vary according to degree level. *Financial support:* Teaching assistantships available. *Application contact:* Dr. Carlos E. Irizarry, Director of Graduate Studies Center, 787-264-1912 Ext. 7357, Fax: 787-892-6350, E-mail: carlos.irizarry@sg.inter.edu.

International College of the Cayman Islands, Graduate Program in Management, Newlands, Cayman Islands. Offers business administration (MBA); management (MS), including education, human resources. Part-time and evening/weekend programs available. *Degree requirements:* For master's, comprehensive exam. *Faculty research:* International human resources administration.

International University in Geneva, MBA Program, Geneva, Switzerland. Offers e-commerce (MBA); human relations (MBA); international business (Exec MBA, MBA); marketing (MBA); organizational development (MBA); telecommunications (MBA). Part-time and evening/weekend programs available. *Degree requirements:* For master's, comprehensive exam, registration. *Entrance requirements:* For master's, GMAT. Additional exam requirements/recommendations for international students: Required—TOEFL. Electronic applications accepted.

Iona College, Hagan School of Business, Department of Management and Business Administration, New Rochelle, NY 10801-1890. Offers human resource management (MBA, PMC); management (MBA, PMC). Part-time and evening/weekend programs available. *Faculty:* 5 full-time (0 women), 5 part-time/adjunct (1 woman). *Students:* 12 full-time (7 women), 72 part-time (38 women); includes 8 minority (7 African Americans, 1 Asian American or Pacific Islander), 4 international. Average age 31. 41 applicants, 78% accepted, 25 enrolled. In 2006, 40 master's, 1 other advanced degree awarded. *Entrance requirements:* For master's, GMAT, 2 letters of recommendation; for PMC, GMAT. Additional exam requirements/recommendations for international students: Required—TOEFL (minimum score 550 paper-based; 213 computer-based). *Application deadline:* Applications are processed on a rolling basis. Application fee: $50. Electronic applications accepted. *Expenses: Contact institution. Financial support:* Scholarships/grants, tuition waivers (partial), and unspecified assistantships available. Support available to part-time students. *Faculty research:* Information systems, strategic management, corporate values and ethics. *Unit head:* Dr. Ursula Witting–Berman, Chair, 914-633-2262, E-mail: uwitting-berman@iona.edu. *Application contact:* Veronica Jarek-Prinz, Graduate Admissions, 914-633-2289, Fax: 914-633-2012, E-mail: vjarekprinz@iona.edu.

La Roche College, School of Graduate Studies, Program in Human Resources Management, Pittsburgh, PA 15237-5898. Offers MS, Certificate. *Accreditation:* ACBSP. Part-time and evening/weekend programs available. *Faculty:* 2 full-time (both women), 9 part-time/adjunct (3 women). *Students:* 10 full-time (6 women), 40 part-time (34 women); includes 2 minority (both African Americans), 2 international. Average age 34. 15 applicants, 93% accepted, 12 enrolled. In 2006, 15 degrees awarded. *Median time to degree:* Master's–2 years full-time, 4 years part-time. *Entrance requirements:* For master's, GMAT, GRE or MAT, minimum GPA of 3.0 during previous 2 years. *Application deadline:* For fall admission, 8/15 priority date for domestic students; for spring admission, 12/15 priority date for domestic students. Applications are processed on a rolling basis. Application fee: $50. Electronic applications accepted. *Expenses:* Tuition: Full-time $9,900; part-time $550 per credit. Required fees: $14 per credit. *Financial support:* Unspecified assistantships available. Financial award application deadline: 3/31; financial award applicants required to submit FAFSA. *Faculty research:* Personnel administration, human resources development. *Unit head:* Dr. Jean Forti, Coordinator, 412-536-1193, Fax: 412-536-1179, E-mail: fortij1@laroche.edu. *Application contact:* Hope Schiffgens, Director of Admissions for Graduate and Continuing Education, 412-536-1266, Fax: 412-536-1283, E-mail: schombh1@laroche.edu.

Lindenwood University, Graduate Programs, Division of Management, St. Charles, MO 63301-1695. Offers accounting (MBA, MS); business administration (MBA); entrepreneurial studies (MBA); finance (MBA, MS); human resource management (MBA); human resources (MS); international business (MBA, MS); management (MBA, MS); management information systems (MBA, MS); managing business to business (MA); managing human resources (MA); managing international business (MA); managing investment management (MA); managing leadership (MA); managing marketing (MA); managing organizational behavior (MA); managing sales (MA); managing, training and development (MA); marketing (MBA, MS); nonprofit administration (MA); public management (MBA, MS); sport management (MA). Part-time and evening/weekend programs available. *Faculty:* 38 full-time (15 women), 20 part-time/adjunct (5 women). *Students:* 177 full-time (78 women), 138 part-time (67 women); includes 43 minority (27 African Americans, 4 American Indian/Alaska Native, 6 Asian Americans or Pacific Islanders, 6 Hispanic Americans), 73 international. Average age 30. In 2006, 159 degrees awarded. *Degree requirements:* For master's, thesis (for some programs). *Entrance requirements:* For master's, interview, minimum GPA of 3.0. Additional exam requirements/recommendations for international students: Required—TOEFL (minimum score 550 paper-based; 173 computer-based). *Application deadline:* For fall admission, 7/30 priority date for domestic students, 9/30 priority date for international students; for winter admission, 12/30 priority date for domestic and international students; for spring admission, 3/30 priority date for domestic and international students. Applications are processed on a rolling basis. Application fee: $30 ($100 for international students). Electronic applications accepted. *Expenses:* Tuition: Part-time $340 per credit hour. Tuition and fees vary according to course level, course load, degree level and program. *Financial support:* Career-related internships or fieldwork, Federal Work-Study, institutionally sponsored loans, and tuition waivers (partial) available. Financial award application deadline: 6/30; financial award applicants required to submit FAFSA. *Unit head:* Ed Morris, Dean, 636-949-4832, Fax: 636-949-4910, E-mail: emorris@lindenwood.edu. *Application contact:* Brett Barger, Dean Adult, Corporate and Graduate Admissions, 636-949-4366, Fax: 636-949-4109, E-mail: bbarger@lindenwood.edu.

Lindenwood University, Graduate Programs, Programs in Individualized Education, St. Charles, MO 63301-1695. Offers administration (MSA); business administration (MBA); communications (MA); criminal justice and administration (MS); gerontology (MA); health management (MS); human resource management (MS); management (MSA); marketing (MSA); writing (MFA). Part-time and evening/weekend programs available. *Faculty:* 18 full-time (9 women), 50 part-time/adjunct (25 women). *Students:* 595 full-time (348 women), 55 part-time (37 women); includes 176 minority (163 African Americans, 1 American Indian/Alaska Native, 5 Asian Americans or Pacific Islanders, 7 Hispanic Americans), 10 international. Average age 34. In 2006, 303 degrees awarded. *Degree requirements:* For master's, thesis. *Entrance requirements:* For master's, interview, minimum GPA of 3.0. Additional exam requirements/recommendations for international students: Required—TOEFL. *Application deadline:* For fall admission, 9/30 priority date for domestic and international students; for winter admission, 12/30 priority date for domestic and international students; for spring admission, 3/30 priority date for domestic and international students. Applications are processed on a rolling basis. Application fee: $30 ($100 for international students). *Expenses:* Tuition: Part-time $340 per credit hour. Tuition and fees vary according to course level, course load, degree level and program. *Financial support:* Career-related internships or fieldwork, institutionally sponsored loans, tuition waivers (partial), and unspecified assistantships available. Financial award application deadline: 6/30; financial award applicants required to submit FAFSA. *Unit head:* Dan Kemper, Dean of LCIE, 636-916-9125, E-mail: dkemper@lindenwood.edu. *Application contact:* Brett Barger, Dean, Adult, Corporate and Graduate Admissions, 636-949-4934, Fax: 636-949-4109, E-mail: adultadmissions@lindenwood.edu.

Long Island University, Brooklyn Campus, School of Business, Public Administration and Information Sciences, Program in Human Resources Management, Brooklyn, NY 11201-8423. Offers MS. *Entrance requirements:* For master's, GMAT or GRE, 2 letters of recommendation. Additional exam requirements/recommendations for international students: Required—TOEFL (minimum score 500 paper-based; 173 computer-based).

Loyola University Chicago, Graduate School of Business, Institute of Human Resources and Employee Relations, Chicago, IL 60611-2196. Offers MS, MSHR. Part-time programs available. *Faculty:* 6 full-time (3 women), 1 part-time/adjunct (0 women). *Students:* 12 full-time (7 women), 65 part-time (53 women); includes 24 minority (8 African Americans, 11 Asian Americans or Pacific Islanders, 5 Hispanic Americans). In 2006, 34 degrees awarded. *Entrance requirements:* For master's, GMAT or GRE General Test, personal statement, letters of recommendation. Additional exam requirements/recommendations for international students: Required—TOEFL (minimum score 550 paper-based; 213 computer-based; 80 iBT). *Application deadline:* For fall admission, 7/1 for domestic and international students; for winter admission, 9/1 for domestic and international students; for spring admission, 1/3 for domestic and international students. Applications are processed on a rolling basis. Application fee: $50. *Expenses: Contact institution. Financial support:* In 2006–07, 3 research assistantships were awarded; career-related internships or fieldwork and Federal Work-Study also available. Support available to part-time students. Financial award applicants required to submit FAFSA. *Faculty research:* Human resource management, labor relations, global human resource management, organizational development, compensation. *Unit head:* Dr. Arup Varma, Chair, 312-915-6595, Fax: 312-915-6231, E-mail: avarma@luc.edu. *Application contact:* Olivia Heath, Enrollment Advisor, 312-915-8908, Fax: 312-915-7207, E-mail: oheath@luc.edu.

Manhattanville College, Graduate Programs, Humanities and Social Sciences Programs, Program in Organization Development and Human Resources Management, Purchase, NY 10577-2132. Offers MS. Part-time and evening/weekend programs available. In 2006, 24 degrees awarded. *Degree requirements:* For master's, thesis. *Entrance requirements:* For master's, interview, 2 letters of recommendation. *Application deadline:* Applications are processed on a rolling basis. Application fee: $55. *Application contact:* Natalia Fernandez, Director of Admissions, 914-323-5418, E-mail: gps@mylllle.edu.

Marquette University, Graduate School, College of Business Administration, Program in Human Resources, Milwaukee, WI 53201-1881. Offers MSHR. Part-time and evening/weekend programs available. *Faculty:* 4 full-time (3 women), 2 part-time/adjunct (1 woman). *Students:* 8 full-time (6 women), 20 part-time (17 women); includes 5 minority (3 African Americans, 1 Asian American or Pacific Islander, 1 Hispanic American), 1 international. Average age 31. 32 applicants, 91% accepted, 16 enrolled. In 2006, 12 degrees awarded. *Entrance requirements:* For master's, GMAT or GRE General Test. Additional exam requirements/recommendations for international students: Required—TOEFL. Application fee: $40. *Financial support:* Research assistantships, teaching assistantships, Federal Work-Study, institutionally sponsored loans, and tuition waivers (full and partial) available. Support available to part-time students. Financial award application deadline: 2/15. *Faculty research:* Diversity, mentoring. *Unit head:* Dr. Timothy Keaveny, Management Chair, 414-288-3643.

Marshall University, Academic Affairs Division, Lewis College of Business, Graduate School of Management, Program in Human Resource Management, Huntington, WV 25755. Offers MS. Part-time and evening/weekend programs available. *Students:* 4 full-time (1 woman), 11 part-time (6 women); includes 1 minority (African American), 1 international. Average age 33. In 2006, 21 degrees awarded. *Degree requirements:* For master's, comprehensive assessment. *Entrance requirements:* For master's, GMAT or GRE General Test. *Application deadline:* Applications are processed on a rolling basis. Application fee: $40. *Financial support:* Tuition waivers (full) available. Support available to part-time students. Financial award applicants required to submit FAFSA. *Application contact:* Information Contact, 304-746-1900, Fax: 304-746-1902, E-mail: services@marshall.edu.

Marygrove College, Graduate Division, Human Resource Management Unit, Detroit, MI 48221-2599. Offers MA. *Entrance requirements:* For master's, interview, writing sample.

Marymount University, School of Business Administration, Program in Human Resource Management, Arlington, VA 22207-4299. Offers human resource management (MA, Certificate); instructional design (Certificate); organization development (Certificate). Part-time and evening/weekend programs available. *Faculty:* 5 full-time (3 women), 4 part-time/adjunct (3 women). *Students:* 12 full-time (9 women), 53 part-time (44 women); includes 22 minority (15 African Americans, 4 Asian Americans or Pacific Islanders, 3 Hispanic Americans), 7 international. Average age 32. 17 applicants, 100% accepted, 13 enrolled. In 2006, 29 master's, 3 other advanced degrees awarded. *Entrance requirements:* For master's, GMAT or GRE General Test, resumé, 2 letters of recommendation, interview; for Certificate, resumé. Additional exam requirements/recommendations for international students: Required—TOEFL (minimum score 600 paper-based; 250 computer-based). *Application deadline:* Applications are processed on a rolling basis. Application fee: $40. Electronic applications accepted. *Expenses:* Tuition: Full-time $11,160; part-time $620 per credit. Required fees: $113; $630 per credit. *Financial support:* Research assistantships with full tuition reimbursements, career-related internships or fieldwork, scholarships/grants, and unspecified assistantships available. Support available to part-time students. Financial award applicants required to submit FAFSA. *Unit head:* Dr. Virginia Bianco-Mathis, Director, 703-284-5957, Fax: 703-527-3830, E-mail: virginia.bianco-mathis@marymount.edu.

McMaster University, School of Graduate Studies, Faculty of Business, Program in Human Resources and Management, Hamilton, ON L8S 4M2, Canada. Offers MBA, PhD. Part-time programs available. *Faculty:* 10 full-time. *Students:* 13 full-time, 1 part-time. *Degree requirements:* For doctorate, thesis/dissertation, comprehensive exam. *Entrance requirements:* For master's, GMAT; for doctorate, GMAT or GRE, master's degree, minimum B+ average. Additional exam requirements/recommendations for international students: Required—TOEFL (minimum score 580 paper-based; 237 computer-based). *Application deadline:* For fall admission, 6/1 for domestic students. Application fee: $90. *Financial support:* In 2006–07, teaching assistantships (averaging $8,440 per year); career-related internships or fieldwork, Federal Work-Study, and scholarships/grants also available. *Faculty research:* Leadership, occupational mental health, work attitudes, human resources recruitment, change and stress management strategies. *Unit head:* Dr. N. C. Agarwal, Coordinator, 905-252-9140 Ext. 23953, Fax: 905-521-8995, E-mail: agarwal@mcmaster.ca.

Mercy College, Division of Business and Accounting, Program in Human Resource Management, Dobbs Ferry, NY 10522-1189. Offers MS. Part-time and evening/weekend programs available. *Students:* 6 full-time (all women), 61 part-time (53 women); includes 36 minority (23 African Americans, 13 Hispanic Americans), 5 international. Average age 32. In 2006, 23 degrees awarded. *Degree requirements:* For master's, thesis. *Entrance requirements:* For master's, GMAT, interview, letters of reference. *Application deadline:* For fall admission, 8/15 priority date for domestic students; for spring admission, 2/15 for domestic students. Applications are processed on a rolling basis. Application fee: $37. Electronic applications accepted. *Expenses:* Tuition: Part-time $595 per credit. Required fees: $9 per credit. Tuition and fees vary according to program. *Financial support:* Research assistantships, career-related internships or fieldwork and Federal Work-Study available. Support available to part-time students. *Faculty research:* Team building, motivation, leadership, training. *Unit head:* Fred Collett, Coordinator of Graduate Admissions, 914-674-7632, Fax: 914-674-7945, E-mail: hrm@mercy.edu. *Application contact:* Fred Collett, Coordinator of Graduate Admissions, 914-674-7632, Fax: 914-674-7945, E-mail: hrm@mercy.edu.

Metropolitan State University, College of Management, St. Paul, MN 55106-5000. Offers finance (MBA); human resource management (MBA); information management (MMIS); international business (MBA); law enforcement (MPNA); management information systems (MBA); marketing (MBA); nonprofit management (MPNA); organizational studies (MBA); public administration (MPNA); purchasing management (MBA); systems management (MMIS). Part-time and evening/weekend programs available. *Degree requirements:* For master's, computer language (MMIS), thesis optional. *Entrance requirements:* For master's, GMAT (MBA), resumé. Additional exam requirements/recommendations for international students: Required—TOEFL (minimum score 550 paper-based; 213 computer-based). *Faculty research:* Yugoslav economic system, workers' cooperatives, participative management and job enrichment, global business systems.

Michigan State University, The Graduate School, College of Social Science, School of Labor and Industrial Relations, East Lansing, MI 48824. Offers human resources and labor relations (MLRHR); industrial relations and human resources (PhD). *Faculty:* 17 full-time (5 women). *Students:* 82 full-time (45 women), 23 part-time (20 women); includes 22 minority (9 African Americans, 1 American Indian/Alaska Native, 7 Asian Americans or Pacific Islanders, 5 Hispanic Americans), 18 international. Average age 26. 166 applicants, 60% accepted. In 2006, 57 degrees awarded. *Entrance requirements:* Additional exam requirements/recommendations for international students: Required—TOEFL. *Application deadline:* For fall admission, 12/27 priority date for domestic students. Application fee: $50. *Expenses:* Tuition, state resident: part-time $346 per credit hour. Tuition, nonresident: part-time $730 per credit hour. Tuition and fees vary according to program. *Financial support:* In 2006–07, 4 fellowships, 21 research assistantships with tuition reimbursements (averaging $13,937 per year), 1 teaching assistantship with tuition reimbursement (averaging $12,222 per year) were awarded. Total annual research expenditures: $175,165. *Unit head:* Prof. Theodore H. Curry, II, Director, 517-355-1801, Fax: 517-355-7656, E-mail: curryt@msu.edu. *Application contact:* Annette Bacon, Graduate Program Administrator, 517-355-3285, Fax: 517-355-7656, E-mail: graduate@lir.msu.edu.

National-Louis University, College of Management and Business, Program in Human Resource Management and Development, Chicago, IL 60603. Offers MS. Part-time programs available. *Students:* 33 full-time (27 women), 2 part-time (1 woman); includes 30 minority (23 African Americans, 2 Asian Americans or Pacific Islanders, 5 Hispanic Americans). Average age 37. 59 applicants, 98% accepted. In 2006, 85 degrees awarded. *Entrance requirements:* For master's, college-administered critical thinking and writing skills test, minimum GPA of 3.0, resumé. *Application deadline:* Applications are processed on a rolling basis. Application fee: $25. *Expenses:* Contact institution. One-time fee: $40 full-time. *Financial support:* Federal Work-Study, institutionally sponsored loans, and scholarships/grants available. Support available to part-time students. Financial award applicants required to submit FAFSA. *Unit head:* Douglas Wuggazer, Assistant Professor, 630-874-4384, E-mail: dwuggazer@nl.edu. *Application contact:* David McCulloch, Vice President for University Services, 800-443-5522 Ext. 5127, Fax: 847-465-0593, E-mail: dmcc@wheeling1.nl.edu.

Nazareth College of Rochester, Graduate Studies, Department of Business, Program in Human Resource Management, Rochester, NY 14618-3790. Offers MS. *Faculty:* 1 full-time (0 women), 2 part-time/adjunct (0 women). *Students:* 2 full-time (both women), 20 part-time (all women); includes 7 minority (4 African Americans, 1 American Indian/Alaska Native, 2 Asian Americans or Pacific Islanders). 11 applicants, 100% accepted, 11 enrolled. *Entrance requirements:* For master's, minimum GPA of 3.0. *Application deadline:* For fall admission, 8/1 for domestic students; for spring admission, 11/1 for domestic students. Application fee: $40. *Financial support:* Research assistantships with partial tuition reimbursements available. Financial award application deadline: 3/1; financial award applicants required to submit FAFSA. *Application contact:* Judith G. Baker, Director, Graduate Admissions, 585-389-2050, Fax: 585-389-2817, E-mail: gradstudies@naz.edu.

New Mexico Highlands University, Graduate Studies, School of Business, Las Vegas, NM 87701. Offers business administration (MBA), including human resource management, international business, non-profit financial management. *Accreditation:* ACBSP. *Faculty:* 12 full-time (4 women), 1 part-time/adjunct (0 women). *Students:* 57 full-time (39 women), 103 part-time (69 women); includes 97 minority (1 African American, 26 American Indian/Alaska Native, 4 Asian Americans or Pacific Islanders, 66 Hispanic Americans), 17 international. Average age 35. 69 applicants, 84% accepted, 42 enrolled. In 2006, 29 degrees awarded. *Degree requirements:* For master's, thesis or alternative, comprehensive exam, registration. *Entrance requirements:* For master's, minimum undergraduate GPA of 3.0. Additional exam requirements/recommendations for international students: Required—TOEFL (minimum score 540 paper-based; 190 computer-based). *Application deadline:* For fall admission, 8/1 priority date for domestic students. Applications are processed on a rolling basis. Application fee: $15. *Expenses:* Tuition, state resident: part-time $101 per credit hour. Tuition, nonresident: part-time $101 per credit hour. *Financial support:* In 2006–07, 67 students received support, including 8 teaching assistantships with full and partial tuition reimbursements available (averaging $6,500 per year); career-related internships or fieldwork, Federal Work-Study, institutionally sponsored loans, scholarships/grants, tuition waivers (full and partial), and unspecified assistantships also available. Support available to part-time students. Financial award application deadline: 3/1; financial award applicants required to submit FAFSA. *Unit head:* Dr. William Taylor, Dean, 505-454-3344, Fax: 505-454-3354. *Application contact:* Diane Trujillo, Administrative Assistant Graduate Studies, 505-454-3266, Fax: 505-454-3558, E-mail: dtrujillo@nmhu.edu.

The New School: A University, Milano The New School for Management and Urban Policy, Program in Human Resources Management, New York, NY 10011. Offers MS, Adv C. Part-time and evening/weekend programs available. *Students:* 11 full-time (10 women), 64 part-time (52 women); includes 35 minority (18 African Americans, 3 Asian Americans or Pacific Islanders, 14 Hispanic Americans), 8 international. Average age 31. In 2006, 40 degrees awarded. *Degree requirements:* For master's, thesis. *Entrance requirements:* For master's, interview. *Application deadline:* For fall admission, 8/1 priority date for domestic students; for winter admission, 1/15 priority date for domestic students. Applications are processed on a rolling basis. Application fee: $50. *Financial support:* Research assistantships, career-related internships or fieldwork, Federal Work-Study, scholarships/grants, and tuition waivers (full and partial) available. Support available to part-time students. Financial award application deadline: 3/1; financial award applicants required to submit FAFSA. *Faculty research:* Organization, management, leadership development, training and development. *Unit head:* Dr. Mark Lipton, Chair, 212-229-5400 Ext. 1611, Fax: 212-229-5335, E-mail: lipton@newschool.edu. *Application contact:* Peter King, Director of Admissions, 212-229-5400, Fax: 212-229-5354, E-mail: kingp@newschool.edu.

New York Institute of Technology, Ellis College, Old Westbury, NY 11568. Offers accounting and information systems (MBA); e-commerce (MBA); finance (MBA); global management (MBA); healthcare administration (MBA); human resources management (MBA); leadership (MBA); management of information systems (MBA); management of technology (MBA); marketing (MBA); professional accounting (MBA); project management (MBA); risk management (MBA); strategy and economics (MBA). Ellis College is a collaboration between New York Institute of Technology and UNext online learning company. Part-time and evening/weekend programs available. Postbaccalaureate distance learning degree programs offered (no on-campus study). *Entrance requirements:* For master's, interview. Additional exam requirements/recommendations for international students: Required—TOEFL (minimum score 550 paper-based; 213 computer-based). Electronic applications accepted. *Expenses:* Tuition: Full-time $16,800; part-time $700 per credit.

New York Institute of Technology, Graduate Division, School of Management, Program in Human Resources Management and Labor Relations, Old Westbury, NY 11568-8000. Offers human resources administration (Advanced Certificate); human resources management and labor relations (MS); labor relations (Advanced Certificate). Part-time and evening/weekend programs available. *Students:* 20 full-time (16 women), 66 part-time (47 women); includes 24 minority (15 African Americans, 7 Asian Americans or Pacific Islanders, 2 Hispanic Americans), 11 international. Average age 32. 45 applicants, 76% accepted, 22 enrolled. In 2006, 41 master's, 1 other advanced degree awarded. *Degree requirements:* For master's, thesis optional. *Entrance requirements:* For master's, GRE, minimum QPA of 2.85, interview, 2 letters of recommendation. *Application deadline:* For fall admission, 7/1 priority date for domestic students; for spring admission, 12/1 priority date for domestic students. Applications are processed on a rolling basis. Application fee: $50. Electronic applications accepted. *Expenses:* Tuition: Full-time $16,800; part-time $700 per credit. *Financial support:* Fellowships, research assistantships, career-related internships or fieldwork, institutionally sponsored loans, and tuition waivers (full and partial) available. Support available to part-time students. Financial award applicants required to submit FAFSA. *Faculty research:* Ethics in industrial relations, employee relations, public sector labor relations, benefits. *Unit head:* Dr. Richard Dibble, Chair, 516-686-7722. *Application contact:* Jacquelyn Nealon, Dean of Admissions and Financial Aid, 516-686-7925, Fax: 516-686-7613, E-mail: jnealon@nyit.edu.

New York University, Robert F. Wagner Graduate School of Public Service, Program in Public Administration, New York, NY 10012-1019. Offers public administration (PhD); public and nonprofit management and policy (MPA, Advanced Certificate), including developmental administration (Advanced Certificate), financial management and public finance, human resources management (Advanced Certificate), international administration (Advanced Certificate), management (MPA), management for public and nonprofit organizations (Advanced Certificate), public policy analysis, quantitative analysis and computer applications (Advanced Certificate), urban public policy (Advanced Certificate); JD/MPA; MBA/MPA; MPA/MA. *Accreditation:* NASPAA (one or more programs are accredited). Part-time and evening/weekend programs available. *Faculty:* 16 full-time (10 women), 42 part-time/adjunct (23 women). *Students:* 260 full-time (189 women), 246 part-time (182 women); includes 114 minority (40 African Americans, 2 American Indian/Alaska Native, 45 Asian Americans or Pacific Islanders, 27 Hispanic Americans), 44 international. Average age 28. 867 applicants, 60% accepted, 176 enrolled. In 2006, 209 master's, 5 doctorates awarded. *Degree requirements:* For master's, thesis or alternative, capstone/end event; for doctorate, one foreign language, thesis/dissertation. *Entrance requirements:* For master's, minimum undergraduate GPA of 3.0; for doctorate, GMAT or GRE General Test, minimum GPA of 3.5. Additional exam requirements/recommendations for international students: Required—TOEFL (minimum score 600 paper-based; 250 computer-based), TWE (minimum score 4). *Application deadline:* For fall admission, 6/1 for domestic students, 1/15 for international students; for spring admission, 11/15 for domestic students, 10/1 for international students. Applications are processed on a rolling basis. Application fee: $70. Electronic applications accepted. *Expenses:* Contact institution. Tuition and fees vary according to program. *Financial support:* In 2006–07, 142 fellowships (averaging $9,749 per year), 4 research assistantships with partial tuition reimbursements (averaging $15,000 per year) were awarded; career-related internships or fieldwork, Federal Work-Study, institutionally sponsored loans, scholarships/grants, health care benefits, and unspecified assistantships also available. Support available to part-time students. Financial award application deadline: 12/1; financial award applicants required to submit FAFSA. *Unit head:* Prof. Katherine O'Regan, Director, 212-998-7400, Fax: 212-995-4161. *Application contact:* Bethany Godsoe, Assistant Dean, Enrollment and Student Services, 212-998-7414, Fax: 212-995-4164, E-mail: wagner.admissions@nyu.edu.

New York University, School of Continuing and Professional Studies, Center for Management, Program in Human Resource Management and Development, New York, NY 10012-1019. Offers benefits and compensation (Advanced Certificate); executive coaching and organizational development (Advanced Certificate); human resource development (MS); human resource management (MS, Advanced Certificate); organizational effectiveness (MS). *Faculty:* 1 full-time (0 women), 4 part-time/adjunct (3 women). *Students:* 7 full-time (6 women), 73 part-time (60 women); includes 32 minority (8 African Americans, 11 Asian Americans or Pacific Islanders, 13 Hispanic Americans), 6 international. Average age 31. 64 applicants, 63% accepted, 22 enrolled. *Entrance requirements:* For master's, GRE General Test or GMAT, 2 letters of recommendation, related work experience, resumé. Additional exam requirements/recommendations for international students: Required—TOEFL (minimum score 600 paper-based; 250 computer-based; 100 iBT), TWE. *Application deadline:* Applications are processed on a rolling basis. Application fee: $75. *Expenses:* Tuition: Part-time $1,080 per unit. Required fees: $56 per unit. $329 per term. Tuition and fees vary according to program. *Financial support:* In 2006–07, fellowships (averaging $1,068 per year); career-related internships or fieldwork and scholarships/grants also available. Support available to part-time students. Financial award applicants required to submit FAFSA. *Unit head:* Dennis Garritan, Head, 212-992-3600, Fax: 212-992-3650, E-mail: dennis.garritan@nyu.edu. *Application contact:* Helen Sapp, Assistant Director, 212-992-3600, Fax: 212-992-3676, E-mail: helen.sapp@nyu.edu.

See Close-Up on page 533.

North Carolina Agricultural and Technical State University, Graduate School, School of Education, Department of Human Development and Services, Greensboro, NC 27411. Offers guidance and counseling (MS); human resources (MS). *Accreditation:* ACA. Part-time and evening/weekend programs available. *Degree requirements:* For master's, thesis, qualifying exam, comprehensive exam. *Entrance requirements:* For master's, GRE General Test, minimum GPA of 3.0.

Nova Southeastern University, H. Wayne Huizenga School of Business and Entrepreneurship, Master's Program in Human Resources Management, Fort Lauderdale, FL 33314-7796. Offers MSHRM. Part-time and evening/weekend programs available. *Faculty:* 3 full-time (1 woman), 19 part-time/adjunct (6 women). *Students:* 12 full-time (11 women), 208 part-time (178 women); includes 150 minority (104 African Americans, 3 Asian Americans or Pacific Islanders, 43 Hispanic Americans), 24 international. 22 applicants, 91% accepted. In 2006, 80 degrees awarded. *Degree requirements:* For master's, thesis or alternative. *Entrance requirements:* For master's, GMAT, GRE General Test, work experience. *Application deadline:* For fall admission, 8/15 for domestic students; for spring admission, 2/10 for domestic students. Applications are processed on a rolling basis. Application fee: $50. *Financial support:* Federal Work-Study and scholarships/grants available. Support available to part-time students. *Unit head:* Steve Harvey, Assistant Dean, 954-262-5047, Fax: 954-262-3829, E-mail: harvey@nsu.nova.edu. *Application contact:* Karen Goldberg, Assistant Director, 954-262-5039, Fax: 954-262-3822, E-mail: karen@nova.edu.

See Close-Up on page 295.

Oakland University, Graduate Study and Lifelong Learning, School of Business Administration, Department of Management and Marketing, Rochester, MI 48309-4401. Offers business administration (MBA); entrepreneurship (Certificate); general management (Certificate); human resource management (Certificate); international business (Certificate); marketing (Certificate). *Faculty:* 9 full-time (3 women), 2 part-time/adjunct (both women). *Students:* 61 full-time (25 women), 416 part-time (137 women); includes 72 minority (14 African Americans, 1 American Indian/Alaska Native, 46 Asian Americans or Pacific Islanders, 11 Hispanic Americans), 45 international. Average age 31. 121 applicants, 88% accepted, 65 enrolled. In 2006, 163 degrees awarded. Application fee: $35. *Expenses:* Tuition, state resident: full-time $9,936; part-time $414 per credit. Tuition, nonresident: full-time $17,202; part-time $716 per credit. *Unit head:* Ravi Parameswaran, Chair, 238-370-3279, Fax: 249-370-4275.

The Ohio State University, Graduate School, Max M. Fisher College of Business, Program in Labor and Human Resources, Columbus, OH 43210. Offers MLHR, PhD. *Faculty:* 28.

Human Resources Management

The Ohio State University (continued)

Students: 67 full-time (52 women), 38 part-time (30 women); includes 18 minority (9 African Americans, 3 American Indian/Alaska Native, 4 Asian Americans or Pacific Islanders, 2 Hispanic Americans), 18 international. 76 applicants, 86% accepted, 17 enrolled. In 2006, 37 master's, 1 doctorate awarded. *Degree requirements:* For master's, thesis optional; for doctorate, thesis/dissertation. *Entrance requirements:* For master's and doctorate, GRE General Test. Additional exam requirements/recommendations for international students: Recommended—TOEFL (minimum score 600 paper-based; 250 computer-based). *Application deadline:* For fall admission, 8/15 priority date for domestic students, 7/1 priority date for international students; for winter admission, 12/1 priority date for domestic students, 11/1 priority date for international students; for spring admission, 3/1 priority date for domestic students, 2/1 priority date for international students. Applications are processed on a rolling basis. Application fee: $40 ($50 for international students). Electronic applications accepted. *Expenses:* Tuition, state resident: full-time $9,438. Tuition, nonresident: full-time $22,791. Tuition and fees vary according to course load, campus/location and program. *Financial support:* Fellowships, research assistantships, teaching assistantships, Federal Work-Study and institutionally sponsored loans available. Support available to part-time students. *Unit head:* Robert L. Heneman, Graduate Studies Committee Chair, 614-292-4587, Fax: 614-292-9006, E-mail: heneman.1@osu.edu. *Application contact:* 614-292-9444, Fax: 614-292-3895, E-mail: domestic.grad@osu.edu.

Ottawa University, Graduate Studies-Arizona, Programs in Business, Ottawa, KS 66067-3399. Offers business administration (MBA); finance (MBA); human resources (MA, MBA); leadership (MBA); marketing (MBA). Programs offered in Mesa, Phoenix, Tempe and West Valley, AZ. Part-time and evening/weekend programs available. Postbaccalaureate distance learning degree programs offered. *Faculty:* 3 full-time (1 woman), 11 part-time/adjunct (3 women). *Students:* 5 full-time (1 woman), 125 part-time (73 women); includes 21 minority (7 African Americans, 1 American Indian/Alaska Native, 2 Asian Americans or Pacific Islanders, 11 Hispanic Americans), 5 international. Average age 39. In 2006, 42 degrees awarded. *Degree requirements:* For master's, thesis or alternative, registration. *Entrance requirements:* For master's, minimum undergraduate GPA of 3.0. Additional exam requirements/recommendations for international students: Required—TOEFL (minimum score 550 paper-based; 213 computer-based). *Application deadline:* For fall admission, 7/1 priority date for domestic students; for winter admission, 11/1 priority date for domestic students; for spring admission, 2/1 priority date for domestic students. Applications are processed on a rolling basis. Application fee: $50. Electronic applications accepted. *Unit head:* Dr. Tony Muscia, Director of Business Graduate Studies, 602-371-1188, E-mail: tony.muscia@ottawa.edu. *Application contact:* Sharon Lind, Advisement Assistant, 602-371-1188, Fax: 602-371-0035, E-mail: sharon.lind@ottawa.edu.

Pontifical Catholic University of Puerto Rico, College of Business Administration, Ponce, PR 00717-0777. Offers accounting (MBA); business administration (PhD); finance (MBA); general business (MBA); human resources (MBA); international business (MBA); management (MBA); management information systems (MBA); marketing (MBA); office administration (MBA). Part-time and evening/weekend programs available. *Degree requirements:* For master's, thesis/dissertation; for doctorate, thesis/dissertation, comprehensive exam. *Entrance requirements:* For master's, GRE, interview, minimum GPA of 2.75; for doctorate, 2 letters of recommendation, 2 years experience in a related field, interview.

Pontificia Universidad Catolica Madre y Maestra, Graduate School, Santiago, Dominican Republic. Offers administration (M Adm, M Ed); architecture of interiors (M Arch); architecture of tourist lodgings (M Arch); construction administration (ME); convergent networks (ME); earthquake-resistant engineering (ME); environmental engineering (MEE); financial (M Mgmt); human resources (EMBA); international (M Mgmt); labor law and Social Security (M Mgmt); logistics management (ME); urban planning (M Urb). *Entrance requirements:* For master's, curriculum vitae, interview.

Purdue University, Graduate School, Krannert School of Management, Department of Organizational Behavior and Human Resource Management, West Lafayette, IN 47907. Offers PhD. *Students:* 8 full-time (4 women); includes 1 minority (American Indian/Alaska Native), 4 international. Average age 26. 102 applicants, 2% accepted, 2 enrolled. In 2006, 2 degrees awarded. *Median time to degree:* Doctorate–4 years part-time. Of those who began their doctoral program in fall 1998, 100% received their degree in 8 years or less. *Degree requirements:* For doctorate, thesis/dissertation, comprehensive exam, registration. *Entrance requirements:* For doctorate, GMAT, GRE General Test. Additional exam requirements/recommendations for international students: Required—TOEFL (minimum score 575 paper-based; 233 computer-based; 77 iBT), IELTS (minimum score 7). *Application deadline:* For fall admission, 2/15 for domestic and international students. Application fee: $55. Electronic applications accepted. *Financial support:* In 2006–07, 8 students received support, including fellowships with partial tuition reimbursements available (averaging $16,800 per year), 6 research assistantships with partial tuition reimbursements available (averaging $16,800 per year), 2 teaching assistantships with partial tuition reimbursements available (averaging $16,800 per year); scholarships/grants and unspecified assistantships also available. Financial award application deadline: 2/15; financial award applicants required to submit FAFSA. *Faculty research:* Promotion and career development, organizational trust, leadership, negotiations, compensation and organizational rewards. *Unit head:* Dr. John M. Barron, Head, 765-494-4451, Fax: 765-494-1526. *Application contact:* Kelly Felty, Assistant Director of Administration for Doctoral Programs, 765-494-4375, Fax: 765-494-1526, E-mail: phd@krannert.purdue.edu.

Purdue University, Graduate School, Krannert School of Management, Program in Organizational Behavior and Human Resource Management, West Lafayette, IN 47907. Offers human resource management (MS). *Faculty:* 9 full-time (1 woman). *Students:* 49 full-time (32 women); includes 11 minority (7 African Americans, 1 Asian American or Pacific Islander, 3 Hispanic Americans), 14 international. Average age 28. 90 applicants, 50% accepted, 32 enrolled. In 2006, 25 degrees awarded. *Entrance requirements:* For master's, GMAT. Additional exam requirements/recommendations for international students: Required—TOEFL. *Application deadline:* For fall admission, 11/1 priority date for domestic students, 12/1 priority date for international students; for winter admission, 2/1 priority date for domestic students, 2/1 for international students; for spring admission, 5/1 priority date for domestic students. Applications are processed on a rolling basis. Application fee: $55. Electronic applications accepted. *Expenses: Contact institution. Financial support:* Fellowships with partial tuition reimbursements, research assistantships with partial tuition reimbursements, teaching assistantships with partial tuition reimbursements, career-related internships or fieldwork, tuition waivers (partial), and unspecified assistantships available. *Unit head:* Charles R. Johnson, Director, 765-496-3668, Fax: 765-494-9841, E-mail: cjohnson@mgmt.purdue.edu. *Application contact:* Carmen Castro-Rivera, Director of Admissions, 765-494-0773, Fax: 765-494-9841, E-mail: ccastror@purdue.edu.

Regis University, School for Professional Studies, Program in Organization Leadership, Denver, CO 80221-1099. Offers computer information technology (MSOL); executive international management (Certificate); executive leadership (Certificate); human resource management (MSOL); organizational leadership (MSOL); project leadership and management (MSOL, Certificate); strategic business (Certificate); strategic human resource (Certificate). Offered at Boulder Campus, Fort Collins Campus, Northwest Denver Campus, Southeast Denver Campus, Colorado Springs Campus, and Broomfield Campus. Part-time and evening/weekend programs available. Postbaccalaureate distance learning degree programs offered. *Faculty:* 55. *Students:* Average age 35. In 2006, 61 degrees awarded. *Median time to degree:* Master's–3 years full-time. *Degree requirements:* For master's, capstone course; for Certificate, final research project. *Entrance requirements:* For master's, 3 years of management-related experience, resumé. Additional exam requirements/recommendations for international students: Required—TOEFL, TWE (minimum score 5), TOEFL or university-based test. *Application deadline:* For fall admission, 8/13 priority date for domestic students, 7/13 for international students; for winter admission, 10/8 priority date for domestic students, 9/8 for international students; for spring admission, 12/17 priority date for domestic students, 11/11 for international students. Applications are processed on a rolling basis. Application fee: $75. Electronic applications accepted. *Expenses: Contact institution. Financial support:* Federal Work-Study available. Support available to part-time students. Financial award applicants required to submit FAFSA. *Faculty research:* Organizational behavior, leadership, change, quality control, global economics. *Unit head:* Dr. Donna VanDusen, Chair, 303-458-4302, Fax: 303-964-5538. *Application contact:* 800-677-9270, Fax: 303-964-5538, E-mail: masters@regis.edu.

Rivier College, School of Graduate Studies, Department of Business Administration, Nashua, NH 03060-5086. Offers business administration (MBA); health care administration (MBA); human resources management (MS); organizational leadership (EMBA). Part-time and evening/weekend programs available. *Faculty:* 4 full-time (2 women), 21 part-time/adjunct (6 women). *Students:* 12 full-time (10 women), 60 part-time (35 women); includes 7 minority (2 African Americans, 2 Asian Americans or Pacific Islanders, 3 Hispanic Americans), 6 international. Average age 36. In 2006, 37 degrees awarded. *Degree requirements:* For master's, registration. *Application deadline:* Applications are processed on a rolling basis. Application fee: $25. *Financial support:* Available to part-time students. Application deadline: 2/1; *Unit head:* Maria Matarazzo, Division Chair, 603-897-8532, Fax: 603-897-8885, E-mail: mmatarazzo@rivier.edu. *Application contact:* Diane Monahan, Director of Graduate Admissions, 603-897-8129, Fax: 603-897-8810, E-mail: gradadm@rivier.edu.

Robert Morris University, Graduate Studies, School of Business, Moon Township, PA 15108-1189. Offers accounting (MS); business administration and management (MBA); finance (MS); human resource management (MS); nonprofit management (MS); sport management (MS); taxation (MS). Part-time and evening/weekend programs available. *Faculty:* 27 full-time (12 women), 6 part-time/adjunct (1 woman). *Students:* Average age 31. 253 applicants, 59% accepted, 103 enrolled. In 2006, 139 degrees awarded. *Entrance requirements:* For master's, GMAT, letters of recommendation. Additional exam requirements/recommendations for international students: Required—TOEFL (minimum score 550 paper-based; 213 computer-based). *Application deadline:* For fall admission, 7/1 priority date for domestic and international students; for spring admission, 11/1 priority date for domestic and international students. Applications are processed on a rolling basis. Application fee: $35. Electronic applications accepted. *Expenses:* Tuition: Part-time $580 per credit. Part-time tuition and fees vary according to degree level and program. *Financial support:* Research assistantships with partial tuition reimbursements, Federal Work-Study, institutionally sponsored loans, and unspecified assistantships available. Support available to part-time students. Financial award application deadline: 5/1; financial award applicants required to submit FAFSA. *Unit head:* Dr. Derya A. Jacobs, Dean, 412-262-8451, Fax: 412-262-8494, E-mail: jacobs@rmu.edu. *Application contact:* Kellie L. Laurenzi, Dean of Enrollment, 412-262-8235, Fax: 412-299-2425, E-mail: laurenzi@rmu.edu.

Rollins College, Hamilton Holt School, Program in Human Resources, Winter Park, FL 32789-4499. Offers MA. Part-time and evening/weekend programs available. *Students:* 3 full-time (all women), 61 part-time (47 women); includes 15 minority (6 African Americans, 9 Hispanic Americans), 5 international. Average age 32. In 2006, 21 degrees awarded. *Degree requirements:* For master's, thesis optional. *Entrance requirements:* For master's, GMAT, GRE, or MAT, interview. Additional exam requirements/recommendations for international students: Required—TOEFL. *Application deadline:* For fall admission, 4/1 for domestic students; for winter admission, 12/1 for domestic students. Application fee: $50. Electronic applications accepted. *Expenses: Contact institution. Financial support:* Available to part-time students. *Unit head:* Dr. Donald Rogers, Director, 407-646-2348, E-mail: drogers@rollins.edu. *Application contact:* Claire Thiebault, Coordinator of Records and Registration, 407-646-2653, Fax: 407-646-1551, E-mail: cthiebault@rollins.edu.

Roosevelt University, Graduate Division, Walter E. Heller College of Business Administration, Program in Human Resource Management, Chicago, IL 60605-1394. Offers MSHRM. *Students:* 8 full-time (7 women), 88 part-time (71 women); includes 39 minority (34 African Americans, 5 Hispanic Americans). Average age 35. 51 applicants, 67% accepted, 29 enrolled. In 2006, 39 degrees awarded. *Unit head:* Ralph Haug, Director, 847-619-4853, Fax: 847-619-4852. *Application contact:* Joanne Canyon-Heller, Coordinator of Graduate Admission, 877-APPLY RU, Fax: 312-281-3356, E-mail: applyru@roosevelt.edu.

Royal Roads University, Graduate Studies, School of Business, Victoria, BC V9B 5Y2, Canada. Offers digital technologies management (MBA); executive management (MBA), including global aviation management, knowledge management, leadership; human resources management (MBA); public relations and communications management (MBA). Postbaccalaureate distance learning degree programs offered (minimal on-campus study). *Degree requirements:* For master's, thesis. *Entrance requirements:* For master's, 5-7 years of related work experience. Additional exam requirements/recommendations for international students: Required—TOEFL (paper-based 570; computer-based 233) or IELTS (paper-based 7) (recommended). Electronic applications accepted. Expenses: Contact institution. *Faculty research:* Global venture analysis standards; computer assisted venture opportunity screening; teaching philosophies, instructions and methods.

Rutgers, The State University of New Jersey, Newark, Graduate School, Program in Public Administration, Newark, NJ 07102. Offers health care administration (MPA); human resources administration (MPA); public administration (PhD); public management (MPA); public policy analysis (MPA); urban systems and issues (MPA). *Accreditation:* NASPAA (one or more programs are accredited). Part-time and evening/weekend programs available. *Faculty:* 12 full-time (4 women). *Students:* 66 full-time (39 women), 202 part-time (114 women); includes 154 minority (93 African Americans, 1 American Indian/Alaska Native, 36 Asian Americans or Pacific Islanders, 24 Hispanic Americans). 252 applicants, 60% accepted, 71 enrolled. In 2006, 57 master's, 8 doctorates awarded. *Degree requirements:* For master's, thesis or alternative, comprehensive exam; for doctorate, thesis/dissertation. *Entrance requirements:* For master's, GRE, minimum undergraduate B average; for doctorate, GRE, MPA, minimum B average. *Application deadline:* For fall admission, 7/1 priority date for domestic students; for spring admission, 12/1 for domestic students. Applications are processed on a rolling basis. Application fee: $50. Electronic applications accepted. *Financial support:* In 2006–07, 5 fellowships with full tuition reimbursements (averaging $18,000 per year), 2 research assistantships (averaging $18,347 per year), 11 teaching assistantships with full tuition reimbursements (averaging $18,347 per year) were awarded; career-related internships or fieldwork also available. Support available to part-time students. Financial award application deadline: 3/1. *Faculty research:* Government finance, municipal and state government, public productivity. *Unit head:* Dr. Marc Holzer, Chairman and Director, 973-353-5093 Ext. 23, E-mail: mholzer@andromeda.rutgers.edu. *Application contact:* Gail Daniels, Contact, 201-973-5093 Ext. 11, E-mail: gaild@andromeda.rutgers.edu.

Rutgers, The State University of New Jersey, New Brunswick, Graduate School, Program in Industrial Relations and Human Resources, New Brunswick, NJ 08901-1281. Offers PhD. *Degree requirements:* For doctorate, thesis/dissertation, comprehensive exam. *Entrance requirements:* For doctorate, GMAT, GRE. Electronic applications accepted. *Faculty research:* Strategic human resource management, international human resource management, labor economics, collective bargaining, teams and diversity.

See Close-Up on page 535.

Rutgers, The State University of New Jersey, New Brunswick, School of Management and Labor Relations, Program in Human Resource Management, New Brunswick, NJ 08901-1281. Offers MHRM. Part-time and evening/weekend programs available. *Entrance requirements:* For master's, GMAT or GRE General Test, 3 letters of recommendation. Additional exam requirements/recommendations for international students: Required—TOEFL (minimum score 575 paper-based; 233 computer-based). Electronic applications accepted. Expenses: Contact institution. *Faculty research:* Human resource policy and planning, employee ownership and profit sharing, compensation and appraisal of performance, law and public policy, computers and decision making.

See Close-Up on page 535.

Sage Graduate School, Graduate School, Division of Management, Communications and Legal Studies, Program in Business Administration, Troy, NY 12180-4115. Offers business strategy (MBA); finance (MBA); human resources (MBA); marketing (MBA); JD/MBA; MBA/MS. Part-time and evening/weekend programs available. *Faculty:* 3 full-time (1 woman), 4 part-time/adjunct (2 women). *Students:* 9 full-time (5 women), 60 part-time (35 women); includes 10 minority (7 African Americans, 3 Hispanic Americans), 2 international. Average age 31. 58 applicants, 67% accepted, 27 enrolled. In 2006, 12 degrees awarded. *Entrance requirements:* For master's, minimum GPA of 2.75. Additional exam requirements/recommendations for international students: Required—TOEFL (minimum score 550 paper-based; 213 computer-based). *Application deadline:* Applications are processed on a rolling basis. Application fee: $40. *Expenses:* Tuition: Full-time $9,270; part-time $515 per credit hour. *Financial support:* Career-related internships or fieldwork, scholarships/grants, and unspecified assistantships available. Support available to part-time students. Financial award application deadline: 3/1; financial award applicants required to submit FAFSA. *Unit head:* Dr. David Kiner, Director, 518-292-1761, E-mail: kinerd@sage.edu. *Application contact:* Shannon K. Easton, Director of Graduate and Adult Admission, 518-244-2443, Fax: 518-244-6880, E-mail: sgsadm@sage.edu.

St. Ambrose University, College of Business, Program in Business Administration, Davenport, IA 52803-2898. Offers business administration (DBA); health care (MBA); human resources (MBA). *Accreditation:* ACBSP. Part-time and evening/weekend programs available. *Faculty:* 29 full-time (4 women), 24 part-time/adjunct (5 women). *Students:* 99 full-time (47 women), 352 part-time (164 women); includes 48 minority (28 African Americans, 6 Asian Americans or Pacific Islanders, 14 Hispanic Americans), 16 international. Average age 35. 201 applicants, 84% accepted, 112 enrolled. In 2006, 119 master's, 5 doctorates awarded. *Degree requirements:* For master's, thesis or alternative, capstone seminar, comprehensive exam (for some programs), registration; for doctorate, thesis/dissertation, oral and written exams, comprehensive exam, registration. *Entrance requirements:* For master's, GMAT; for doctorate, GMAT, master's degree. Additional exam requirements/recommendations for international students: Required—TOEFL. *Application deadline:* For fall admission, 8/15 priority date for domestic students; for winter admission, 12/15 for domestic students; for spring admission, 1/1 for domestic students. Applications are processed on a rolling basis. Application fee: $25. Electronic applications accepted. *Expenses:* Contact institution. *Financial support:* In 2006–07, 338 students received support, including 8 research assistantships with partial tuition reimbursements available; career-related internships or fieldwork, scholarships/grants, tuition waivers (partial), and unspecified assistantships also available. Support available to part-time students. Financial award application deadline: 3/15; financial award applicants required to submit FAFSA. *Unit head:* Allison S. Ambrose, Director of MBA Academic Services, 563-333-6155, Fax: 563-333-6243, E-mail: ambroseallisons@sau.edu. *Application contact:* Elizabeth Berridge, Director of Graduate Student Recruitment, 563-333-6271, Fax: 563-333-6268, E-mail: berridgeelizabethb@sau.edu.

St. Edward's University, School of Management and Business, Area of Business Administration, Austin, TX 78704. Offers accounting (MBA); business management (MBA); entrepreneurship (MBA, Certificate); finance—general (MBA, Certificate); global business (MBA, Certificate); human resource management (MBA, Certificate); management information systems (MBA, Certificate); marketing (MBA, Certificate); operations management (MBA, Certificate); personal financial planner (MBA, Certificate); sports management (MBA). Part-time and evening/weekend programs available. *Students:* 32 full-time (16 women), 394 part-time (195 women); includes 117 minority (23 African Americans, 2 American Indian/Alaska Native, 28 Asian Americans or Pacific Islanders, 64 Hispanic Americans), 21 international. Average age 33. 121 applicants, 74% accepted, 72 enrolled. In 2006, 142 degrees awarded. *Degree requirements:* For master's, minimum 24 resident hours. *Entrance requirements:* For master's, GMAT or GRE General Test, minimum GPA of 2.75 in last 60 hours of course work. Additional exam requirements/recommendations for international students: Required—TOEFL (minimum score 550 paper-based; 213 computer-based; 79 iBT). *Application deadline:* For fall admission, 8/1 for domestic students, 7/1 for international students; for spring admission, 12/1 for domestic students, 11/1 for international students. Applications are processed on a rolling basis. Application fee: $45 ($50 for international students). Electronic applications accepted. *Expenses:* Tuition: Full-time $11,682; part-time $649 per credit hour. Full-time tuition and fees vary according to course load and program. *Financial support:* In 2006–07, 4 students received support. Scholarships/grants available. Financial award applicants required to submit FAFSA. *Faculty research:* Operations management, minority entrepreneurship, globalization, professional services marketing. *Unit head:* Dr. Dianne Hill, Director, 512-428-1295, Fax: 512-448-8492, E-mail: dianneh@stedwards.edu. *Application contact:* Natalia Quintanilla, Graduate Admissions Coordinator, 512-233-1697, Fax: 512-428-1032, E-mail: nataliaq@stedwards.edu.

St. Edward's University, School of Management and Business, Program in Human Services, Austin, TX 78704. Offers conflict resolution (Certificate); human services (MA), including administration, conflict resolution, human resource management, sports management; sports management (Certificate). Part-time and evening/weekend programs available. *Students:* 9 full-time (8 women), 46 part-time (34 women); includes 19 minority (4 African Americans, 2 Asian Americans or Pacific Islanders, 13 Hispanic Americans), 2 international. Average age 34. 43 applicants, 84% accepted, 28 enrolled. In 2006, 28 degrees awarded. *Degree requirements:* For master's, minimum 24 resident hours. *Entrance requirements:* For master's, GRE General Test, GMAT, minimum GPA of 2.75 in last 60 hours of course work. Additional exam requirements/recommendations for international students: Required—TOEFL (minimum score 550 paper-based; 213 computer-based; 79 iBT). *Application deadline:* For fall admission, 8/1 for domestic students, 7/1 for international students; for spring admission, 12/1 for domestic students, 11/1 for international students. Applications are processed on a rolling basis. Application fee: $45 ($50 for international students). Electronic applications accepted. *Expenses:* Tuition: Full-time $11,682; part-time $649 per credit hour. Full-time tuition and fees vary according to course load and program. *Financial support:* In 2006–07, 4 students received support. Scholarships/grants available. Financial award applicants required to submit FAFSA. *Faculty research:* Leadership development, organizational management, public policy, emotional intelligence. *Unit head:* Dr. Constance D Porter, Director, 512-416-5827, Fax: 512-448-8492, E-mail: constanp@stedwards.edu. *Application contact:* Kay L. Arnold, Graduate Admissions Coordinator, 512-233-1636, Fax: 512-428-1032, E-mail: kayla@stedwards.edu.

Saint Francis University, Graduate School of Business and Human Resource Management, Human Resource Management Program, Loretto, PA 15940-0600. Offers MHRM. Part-time and evening/weekend programs available. *Faculty:* 31. *Students:* 5 full-time (4 women), 55 part-time (37 women); includes 5 minority (all African Americans) Average age 32. 20 applicants, 100% accepted, 17 enrolled. In 2006, 24 degrees awarded. *Degree requirements:* For master's, research paper. *Entrance requirements:* For master's, minimum GPA of 2.75, 2 letters of recommendation. Additional exam requirements/recommendations for international students: Required—TOEFL (minimum score 550 paper-based; 213 computer-based; 57 iBT). *Application deadline:* For fall admission, 8/1 priority date for domestic and international students; for spring admission, 12/1 priority date for domestic and international students. Applications are processed on a rolling basis. Application fee: $30. *Expenses:* Contact institution. *Financial support:* Fellowships with partial tuition reimbursements, unspecified assistantships available. *Faculty research:* Management selection and development, FMLA interpretation. Total annual research expenditures: $5,850. *Application contact:* Roxane Hogue, Coordinator, Graduate Business Programs, 814-472-3026, Fax: 814-472-3369, E-mail: rhogue@franics.edu.

St. Joseph's College, Suffolk Campus, Program in Management, Patchogue, NY 11772-2399. Offers health care (AC); health care management (MS); human resource management (AC); human resources management (MS); organizational management (MS).

Saint Joseph's University, Erivan K. Haub School of Business, Professional MBA Program, Program in Human Resource Management, Philadelphia, PA 19131-1395. Offers MBA. Part-time and evening/weekend programs available. *Students:* 2 full-time (both women), 36 part-time (29 women); includes 7 minority (6 African Americans, 1 Hispanic American), 1 international. Average age 38. In 2006, 4 degrees awarded. *Entrance requirements:* For master's, GMAT, 2 letters of recommendation, resumé. Additional exam requirements/recommendations for international students: Required—TOEFL (minimum score 550 paper-based; 213 computer-based). *Application deadline:* For fall admission, 7/15 for domestic students, 4/15 for international students; for spring admission, 11/15 for domestic students, 10/15 for international students. Applications are processed on a rolling basis. Application fee: $35. *Financial support:* Research assistantships available. *Unit head:* Dr. Elizabeth Doherty, Chair, 610-660-1987, E-mail: doherty@sju.edu.

Saint Joseph's University, Erivan K. Haub School of Business, Program in Human Resource Management, Philadelphia, PA 19131-1395. Offers MS. Part-time and evening/weekend programs available. *Faculty:* 8 full-time (2 women). *Entrance requirements:* For master's, MAT, GRE, or GMAT, 2 letters of recommendation, resumé. Additional exam requirements/recommendations for international students: Required—TOEFL. *Application deadline:* For fall admission, 7/15 for international students; for spring admission, 11/15 for international students. Applications are processed on a rolling basis. Application fee: $35. Electronic applications accepted. *Financial support:* Research assistantships with full tuition reimbursements available. *Unit head:* David Benglian, Director, 610-660-1626, Fax: 610-660-1599, E-mail: david.benglia@sju.edu. *Application contact:* Information Contact, E-mail: mshrm@sju.edu.

See Close-Up on page 537.

Saint Leo University, Graduate Business Studies, Saint Leo, FL 33574-6665. Offers accounting (MBA); business (MBA); criminal justice (MBA); human resource administration (MBA); information security management (MBA); sport business (MBA). Part-time and evening/weekend programs available. Postbaccalaureate distance learning degree programs offered (no on-campus study). *Faculty:* 17 full-time (5 women), 24 part-time/adjunct (6 women). *Students:* 298 full-time (187 women), 368 part-time (215 women); includes 195 minority (132 African Americans, 3 American Indian/Alaska Native, 23 Asian Americans or Pacific Islanders, 37 Hispanic Americans), 6 international. Average age 36. 863 applicants, 59% accepted, 282 enrolled. In 2006, 156 degrees awarded. *Degree requirements:* For master's, thesis. *Entrance requirements:* For master's, GMAT, 5 years of professional work experience, resumé, 2 letters of recommendation. Additional exam requirements/recommendations for international students: Required—TOEFL (minimum score 550 paper-based; 213 computer-based). *Application deadline:* For fall admission, 7/1 priority date for domestic students; for spring admission, 11/12 priority date for domestic students. Applications are processed on a rolling basis. Application fee: $45. Electronic applications accepted. *Expenses:* Contact institution. *Financial support:* In 2006–07, 39 students received support. Career-related internships or fieldwork, Federal Work-Study, and scholarships/grants available. Support available to part-time students. Financial award application deadline: 3/1; financial award applicants required to submit FAFSA. *Unit head:* Dr. Robert Robertson, Director, 352-588-8758, Fax: 352-588-8912, E-mail: mba@saintleo.edu. *Application contact:* Scott Cathcart, Vice President of Enrollment, 800-707-8846, Fax: 352-588-7873, E-mail: grad.admission@saintleo.edu.

Saint Mary's University of Minnesota, School of Graduate and Professional Programs, Program in Human Resource Management, Winona, MN 55987-1399. Offers MA. *Unit head:* Dr. Gerald Ellis, Director, 612-728-5178, E-mail: gellis@smumn.edu.

St. Thomas University, School of Graduate Studies, Department of Management, Miami Gardens, FL 33054-6459. Offers accounting (MBA); general management (MSM, Certificate); health management (MBA, MSM, Certificate); human resource management (MBA, MSM, Certificate); international business (MBA, MIB, MSM, Certificate); justice administration (MSM, Certificate); management accounting (MSM, Certificate); public management (MSM, Certificate). Part-time and evening/weekend programs available. *Degree requirements:* For master's, comprehensive exam. *Entrance requirements:* For master's, interview, minimum GPA of 3.0 or GMAT. Additional exam requirements/recommendations for international students: Required—TOEFL. Electronic applications accepted.

Salve Regina University, Graduate Studies, Program in Business Administration, Newport, RI 02840-4192. Offers business administration (MBA); business studies (Certificate); human resources management (Certificate); management (Certificate); organizational development (Certificate). Part-time and evening/weekend programs available. Postbaccalaureate distance learning degree programs offered (minimal on-campus study). *Faculty:* 1 (woman) full-time, 9 part-time/adjunct (2 women). *Students:* 21 full-time (6 women), 70 part-time (30 women); includes 1 minority (African American) Average age 35. 90 applicants, 70% accepted, 54 enrolled. In 2006, 42 degrees awarded. *Entrance requirements:* For master's, GMAT, GRE General Test, or MAT, 6 undergraduate credits each in accounting, economics, and quantitative analysts. Additional exam requirements/recommendations for international students: Required—TOEFL or IELTS. *Application deadline:* For fall admission, 3/15 priority date for domestic and international students; for spring admission, 9/15 priority date for domestic and international students. Applications are processed on a rolling basis. Application fee: $50. Electronic applications accepted. *Financial support:* Career-related internships or fieldwork and Federal Work-Study available. Support available to part-time students. Financial award application deadline: 3/1. *Unit head:* Dr. Myra Edelstein, Director, 401-341-2153, E-mail: edelstem@salve.edu. *Application contact:* Karen E. Johnson, Graduate Admissions Counselor, 401-341-2153, Fax: 401-341-2973, E-mail: johnsonke@salve.edu.

San Diego State University, Graduate and Research Affairs, College of Business Administration, Department of Management, San Diego, CA 92182. Offers entrepreneurship (MS); human resources management (MS); management science (MS). Part-time and evening/weekend programs available. *Students:* 16 full-time (6 women), 23 part-time (13 women); includes 5 minority (4 Asian Americans or Pacific Islanders, 1 Hispanic American), 9 international. Average age 30. 24 applicants, 75% accepted, 6 enrolled. In 2006, 21 degrees awarded. *Degree requirements:* For master's, thesis or alternative. *Entrance requirements:* For master's, GMAT, resumé, letters of reference. Additional exam requirements/recommendations for international students: Required—TOEFL. *Application deadline:* For fall admission, 4/15 for domestic and international students; for spring admission, 11/1 for domestic students, 10/1 for international students. Applications are processed on a rolling basis. Application fee: $55. Electronic applications accepted. *Financial support:* In 2006–07, 14 teaching assistantships were awarded; fellowships, research assistantships, career-related internships or fieldwork also available. Financial award applicants required to submit FAFSA. Total annual research expenditures: $11,500. *Unit head:* Gangaram Singh, Chair, 619-594-5306, Fax: 619-594-3272. *Application contact:* Information Contact, E-mail: sdsumba@mail.sdsu.edu.

Southern Adventist University, School of Business and Management, Collegedale, TN 37315-0370. Offers accounting (MBA); administration (MS); financial services (MFS); health care administration (MBA); human resource management (MBA); management (MBA); marketing (MBA). Part-time and evening/weekend programs available. Postbaccalaureate distance learning degree programs offered (no on-campus study). *Faculty:* 7 full-time (0 women), 2 part-time/adjunct (1 woman). *Students:* 18 full-time (8 women), 66 part-time (37 women); includes 15 minority (6 African Americans, 7 Asian Americans or Pacific Islanders, 2 Hispanic Americans). Average age 35. 32 applicants, 84% accepted, 24 enrolled. In 2006, 11 degrees awarded. *Entrance requirements:* For master's, GMAT. Additional exam requirements/recommendations for international students: Required—TOEFL. *Application deadline:* For fall admission, 8/1 priority date for domestic students, 7/1 for international students; for winter admission, 12/1 priority date for domestic students, 11/1 for international students; for spring admission, 4/1 priority date for domestic students, 3/1 for international students. Applications are processed on a rolling basis. Application fee: $25. Electronic applications accepted. *Financial support:* In 2006–07, 32 students received support. Scholarships/grants available. Financial award application deadline: 9/1; financial award applicants required to submit FAFSA.

Human Resources Management

Southern Adventist University (continued)
Unit head: Dr. Don Van Ornam, Dean, 423-236-2750, Fax: 423-236-1527, E-mail: dvanorna@southern.edu. *Application contact:* Linda Wilhelm, Admissions Coordinator, 423-236-2751, Fax: 423-236-1527, E-mail: sbm@southern.edu.

Southern New Hampshire University, School of Business, Manchester, NH 03106-1045. Offers accounting (MS); business administration (MBA, Certificate), including accounting (Certificate), business administration (MBA), finance (Certificate), forensic accounting (Certificate), human resources management (Certificate), international business (Certificate), international sport management (Certificate), leadership of not for profit organizations (Certificate), marketing (Certificate), operations management (Certificate), sport management (Certificate), taxation (Certificate); finance (MS); hospitality and tourism leadership (Certificate); information technology (MS, Certificate); information technology/international business (Certificate); integrated marketing communications (Certificate); international business (MS, DBA); marketing (MS); operations and project management (MS); organizational leadership (MS); project management (Certificate); sport management (MS); MBA/Certificate. *Accreditation:* ACBSP. Part-time and evening/weekend programs available. Postbaccalaureate distance learning degree programs offered (no on-campus study). *Faculty:* 45 full-time, 75 part-time/adjunct. *Students:* 427 full-time (184 women), 774 part-time (428 women). Average age 32. In 2006, 682 master's, 1 doctorate awarded. Terminal master's awarded for partial completion of doctoral program. *Degree requirements:* For master's, one foreign language, thesis or alternative, comprehensive exam (for some programs); for doctorate, one foreign language, thesis/dissertation, comprehensive exam. *Entrance requirements:* For master's, minimum GPA of 2.5; for doctorate, GMAT. Additional exam requirements/recommendations for international students: Required—TOEFL (minimum score 500 paper-based). *Application deadline:* Applications are processed on a rolling basis. Application fee: $25. Electronic applications accepted. *Financial support:* Career-related internships or fieldwork, Federal Work-Study, institutionally sponsored loans, tuition waivers (partial), and unspecified assistantships available. Support available to part-time students. Financial award applicants required to submit FAFSA. *Unit head:* Dr. Martin Bradley, Dean, 603-644-3102, Fax: 603-644-3144, E-mail: m.bradley@snhu.edu. *Application contact:* Scott Durand, Director of Graduate Enrollment Services, 603-644-3102 Ext. 3338, Fax: 603-644-3144, E-mail: s.durand@snhu.edu.

See Close-Up on page 325.

Stevens Institute of Technology, Graduate School, Wesley J. Howe School of Technology Management, Program in Information Systems, Hoboken, NJ 07030. Offers computer science (MS); e-commerce (MS, Certificate); entrepreneurial information technology (MS); global innovation management (MS); human resource management (MS); information management (MS, Certificate); information security (MS); information technology in financial services industry (MS); information technology in the pharmaceutical industry (MS); information technology outsourcing management (MS); integrated information architecture (MS); project management (MS, Certificate); quantitative software engineering (MS); systems engineering (MS); telecommunications management (MS). *Degree requirements:* For master's, thesis optional. *Entrance requirements:* For master's, GMAT, GRE General Test. Additional exam requirements/recommendations for international students: Required—TOEFL. Electronic applications accepted.

Stevens Institute of Technology, Graduate School, Wesley J. Howe School of Technology Management, Program in Management, Hoboken, NJ 07030. Offers general management (MS); global innovation management (MS); human resource management (MS); information management (MS); project management (MS); technology commercialization (MS); technology management (MS). Part-time programs available. *Degree requirements:* For master's, thesis optional. *Entrance requirements:* For master's, GMAT, GRE General Test. Additional exam requirements/recommendations for international students: Required—TOEFL. Electronic applications accepted. *Faculty research:* Industrial economics.

Stony Brook University, State University of New York, School of Professional Development, Stony Brook, NY 11794. Offers adolescence education: mathematics (Certificate); biology 7-12 (MAT); chemistry-grade 7-12 (MAT); coaching (Certificate); computer integrated engineering (Certificate); cultural studies (Certificate); earth science-grade 7-12 (MAT); educational computing (Advanced Certificate, Certificate); English-grade 7-12 (MAT); environmental and waste management (MS, Advanced Certificate); environmental systems management (Certificate); environmental/occupational health and safety (Certificate); French-grade 7-12 (MAT); German-grade 7-12 (MAT); human resource management (Certificate); industrial management (Certificate); information systems management (Certificate); Italian-grade 7-12 (MAT); liberal studies (MA); liberal studies online (MA); Long Island regional studies (Certificate); operation research (Certificate); physics-grade 7-12 (MAT); Russian-grade 7-12 (MAT); school administration and supervision (Certificate); school district administration (Certificate); social science and the professions (MPS), including human resources management, labor management, public affairs, waste management; social studies 7-12 (MAT); waste management (Certificate); women's studies (Certificate). Part-time and evening/weekend programs available. Postbaccalaureate distance learning degree programs offered. *Faculty:* 1 full-time (0 women), 118 part-time/adjunct (45 women). *Students:* 322 full-time (202 women), 1,188 part-time (728 women); includes 164 minority (69 African Americans, 2 American Indian/Alaska Native, 29 Asian Americans or Pacific Islanders, 64 Hispanic Americans), 11 international. Average age 28. In 2006, 738 master's, 405 other advanced degrees awarded. *Degree requirements:* For master's, one foreign language, thesis or alternative. *Application deadline:* Applications are processed on a rolling basis. Application fee: $62. *Expenses:* Tuition, state resident: full-time $6,900; part-time $288 per credit. Tuition, nonresident: full-time $10,920; part-time $455 per credit. *Financial support:* In 2006-07, 5 teaching assistantships were awarded; fellowships, research assistantships, career-related internships or fieldwork also available. Support available to part-time students. *Unit head:* Dr. Paul J. Edelson, Dean, 631-632-7052, Fax: 631-632-9046, E-mail: paul.edelson@sunysb.edu. *Application contact:* Sandra Romansky, Director of Admissions and Advisement, 631-632-7050, Fax: 631-632-9046, E-mail: sandra.romansky@sunysb.edu.

Suffolk University, Sawyer Business School, Department of Public Administration, Boston, MA 02108-2770. Offers disability studies (MPA); health administration (MPA); nonprofit management (MPA); public administration (CASPA); public finance and human resources (MPA); state and local government (MPA); JD/MPA; MPA/MS. *Accreditation:* NASPAA (one or more programs are accredited). Part-time and evening/weekend programs available. *Faculty:* 11 full-time (4 women), 7 part-time/adjunct (4 women). *Students:* 40 full-time (25 women), 123 part-time (80 women); includes 22 minority (12 African Americans, 4 Asian Americans or Pacific Islanders, 6 Hispanic Americans), 9 international. Average age 31. 103 applicants, 87% accepted, 48 enrolled. In 2006, 65 degrees awarded. *Entrance requirements:* Additional exam requirements/recommendations for international students: Required—TOEFL (minimum score 550 paper-based; 213 computer-based; 80 iBT). *Application deadline:* For fall admission, 6/15 priority date for domestic students, 6/15 for international students; for spring admission, 11/1 priority date for domestic students, 11/1 for international students. Applications are processed on a rolling basis. Application fee: $50. Electronic applications accepted. *Expenses: Contact institution. Financial support:* In 2006-07, 55 fellowships with full and partial tuition reimbursements (averaging $8,817 per year) were awarded; career-related internships or fieldwork and Federal Work-Study also available. Support available to part-time students. Financial award application deadline: 4/1; financial award applicants required to submit FAFSA. *Faculty research:* Local government, health care, federal policy, mental health, HIV/AIDS. Total annual research expenditures: $200,000. *Unit head:* Dr. Rick Beinecke, Chair, 617-573-8062, E-mail: rbeineck@suffolk.edu. *Application contact:* Judith Reynolds, Director of Graduate Admissions, 617-573-8302, Fax: 617-523-0116, E-mail: grad.admission@suffolk.edu.

Tarleton State University, College of Graduate Studies, College of Business Administration, Department of Management, Marketing, and Administrative Systems, Stephenville, TX 76402. Offers human resource management (MS). Part-time and evening/weekend programs available. Postbaccalaureate distance learning degree programs offered. *Faculty:* 24 full-time (8

women), 6 part-time/adjunct (2 women). *Students:* 10 full-time (8 women), 45 part-time (39 women); includes 20 minority (12 African Americans, 1 American Indian/Alaska Native, 1 Asian American or Pacific Islander, 6 Hispanic Americans), 2 international. Average age 36. In 2006, 72 degrees awarded. *Entrance requirements:* For master's, GRE, minimum GPA of 3.0. Additional exam requirements/recommendations for international students: Required—TOEFL. *Application deadline:* For fall admission, 8/5 priority date for domestic students; for spring admission, 12/1 priority date for domestic students. *Financial support:* Research assistantships, teaching assistantships, Federal Work-Study, scholarships/grants, and unspecified assistantships available. *Unit head:* Dr. Samuel Hazen, Head, 254-968-9277.

Temple University, Graduate School, Fox School of Business and Management, Doctoral Programs in Business, Philadelphia, PA 19122-6096. Offers accounting (PhD); economics (PhD); finance (PhD); general and strategic management (PhD); healthcare management (PhD); human resource administration (PhD); international business administration (PhD); management information systems (PhD); management science/operations research (PhD); marketing (PhD); risk, insurance, and health-care management (PhD); statistics (PhD); tourism (PhD). *Accreditation:* AACSB. *Entrance requirements:* For doctorate, GRE General Test, minimum GPA of 3.0, master's degree. Additional exam requirements/recommendations for international students: Required—TOEFL. *Expenses:* Tuition, state resident: full-time $12,264; part-time $511 per credit. Tuition, nonresident: full-time $17,904; part-time $746 per credit. Required fees: $84 per course. Tuition and fees vary according to program.

Temple University, Graduate School, Fox School of Business and Management, Masters Programs in Business, MBA Programs, Philadelphia, PA 19122-6096. Offers accounting (MBA); business administration (EMBA, MBA); e-business (MBA); economics (MBA); finance (MBA); general and strategic management (MBA); healthcare management (MBA); human resource administration (MBA); international business (IMBA); management information systems (MBA); management science/operations management (MBA); marketing (MBA); risk management and insurance (MBA); statistics (MBA). EMBA offered in Philadelphia, PA and Tokyo, Japan. *Accreditation:* AACSB. *Entrance requirements:* For master's, GMAT, minimum undergraduate GPA of 3.0. Additional exam requirements/recommendations for international students: Required—TOEFL. *Expenses:* Tuition, state resident: full-time $12,264; part-time $511 per credit. Tuition, nonresident: full-time $17,904; part-time $746 per credit. Required fees: $84 per course. Tuition and fees vary according to program.

Temple University, Graduate School, Fox School of Business and Management, Masters Programs in Business, MS Programs, Philadelphia, PA 19122-6096. Offers accounting and financial management (MS); actuarial science (MS); e-business (MS); finance (MS); healthcare financial management (MS); human resource administration (MS); management information systems (MS); management science/operations management (MS); marketing (MS); statistics (MS). *Accreditation:* AACSB. *Entrance requirements:* For master's, GRE General Test, minimum undergraduate GPA of 3.0. Additional exam requirements/recommendations for international students: Required—TOEFL. *Expenses:* Tuition, state resident: full-time $12,264; part-time $511 per credit. Tuition, nonresident: full-time $17,904; part-time $746 per credit. Required fees: $84 per course. Tuition and fees vary according to program.

Texas A&M University, Mays Business School, Department of Management, College Station, TX 77843. Offers human resource management (MS); management (PhD). *Faculty:* 32 full-time (10 women), 9 part-time/adjunct (2 women). *Students:* 60 full-time (37 women). Average age 31. 76 applicants, 28% accepted. In 2006, 19 master's, 3 doctorates awarded. Terminal master's awarded for partial completion of doctoral program. *Degree requirements:* For master's, comprehensive exam; for doctorate, thesis/dissertation. *Entrance requirements:* For master's, GMAT or GRE; for doctorate, GMAT or GRE General Test. Additional exam requirements/recommendations for international students: Required—TOEFL. *Application deadline:* For fall admission, 3/1 priority date for domestic students; for spring admission, 8/1 for domestic students. Applications are processed on a rolling basis. Application fee: $50 ($75 for international students). *Expenses:* Tuition, state resident: full-time $4,697. Tuition, nonresident: full-time $11,297. Required fees: $2,272. *Financial support:* In 2006-07, 25 students received support; fellowships, research assistantships, teaching assistantships, career-related internships or fieldwork and institutionally sponsored loans available. Financial award application deadline: 2/1. *Faculty research:* Strategic and human resource management, business and public policy, organizational behavior, organizational theory. *Unit head:* Dr. Duane Ireland, Head, 979-845-4851, Fax: 979-845-9641. *Application contact:* Kristi Mora, Information Contact, 979-845-4045.

Thomas College, Graduate School, Programs in Business, Waterville, ME 04901-5097. Offers business (MBA); computer technology education (MS); education (MS); human resource management (MBA). Part-time and evening/weekend programs available. *Entrance requirements:* For master's, GMAT or minimum GPA of 3.3 in first 3 graduate-level courses, GRE or minimum GPA of 3.3 in first 3 graduate-level courses, MAT or minimum GPA of 3.3 in first 3 graduate-level courses.

Thomas Edison State College, Heavin School of Arts and Sciences, Program in Liberal Studies, Trenton, NJ 08608-1176. Offers human resource management (MALS); online learning and teaching (MALS); organizational leadership (MALS). Part-time programs available. Postbaccalaureate distance learning degree programs offered (no on-campus study). *Students:* Average age 45. 34 applicants, 25 enrolled. In 2006, 12 degrees awarded. *Degree requirements:* For master's, capstone project. *Entrance requirements:* Additional exam requirements/recommendations for international students: Required—TOEFL (minimum score 550 paper-based; 213 computer-based). *Application deadline:* For fall admission, 8/15 priority date for domestic and international students; for winter admission, 11/15 priority date for domestic and international students; for spring admission, 2/15 priority date for domestic and international students. Applications are processed on a rolling basis. Application fee: $75. Electronic applications accepted. *Expenses:* Tuition, nonresident: part-time $422 per credit. Part-time tuition and fees vary according to program. *Financial support:* Applicants required to submit FAFSA. *Unit head:* Dr. Esther Taitsman, Director of Graduate School, 609-984-1168, Fax: 609-633-8593, E-mail: graduateschool@tesc.edu. *Application contact:* Renee San Giacomo, Director of Admissions, 888-442-8372, Fax: 609-984-8447, E-mail: admissions@tesc.edu.

Thomas Edison State College, School of Business and Management, Program in Human Resources Management, Trenton, NJ 08608-1176. Offers MSHRM. Part-time programs available. Postbaccalaureate distance learning degree programs offered (no on-campus study). *Students:* Average age 39. 18 applicants, 100% accepted, 18 enrolled. In 2006, 2 degrees awarded. *Degree requirements:* For master's, final project/capstone project. *Entrance requirements:* Additional exam requirements/recommendations for international students: Required—TOEFL (minimum score 550 paper-based; 213 computer-based). *Application deadline:* For fall admission, 8/15 priority date for domestic and international students; for winter admission, 11/15 priority date for domestic and international students; for spring admission, 2/15 priority date for domestic and international students. Applications are processed on a rolling basis. Application fee: $75. Electronic applications accepted. *Expenses:* Tuition, nonresident: part-time $422 per credit. Part-time tuition and fees vary according to program. *Financial support:* Applicants required to submit FAFSA. *Application contact:* Renee San Giacomo, Director of Admissions, 888-442-8372, Fax: 609-984-8447, E-mail: admissions@tesc.edu.

Thomas Edison State College, School of Business and Management, Program in Management, Trenton, NJ 08608-1176. Offers human resource management (MSM); online learning and teaching (MSM); organizational leadership (MSM); public sector auditing (MSM); public service leadership (MSM). Part-time programs available. Postbaccalaureate distance learning degree programs offered (minimal on-campus study). *Students:* Average age 42. 77 applicants, 60 enrolled. In 2006, 55 degrees awarded. *Degree requirements:* For master's, capstone/thesis, applied project. *Entrance requirements:* For master's, 3-5 years of work experience. Additional exam requirements/recommendations for international students: Required—TOEFL (minimum score 550 paper-based; 213 computer-based). *Application *deadline:* For fall admission, 8/15 priority date for domestic and international students; for winter admission, 11/15 priority date for domestic and international students; for spring admission, 2/15 priority date for domestic and international students. Applications are processed on a rolling basis. Application fee: $75. Electronic applications accepted. *Expenses:* Tuition, nonresident: part-time $422 per credit. Part-time tuition and fees vary according to program. *Financial support:* Applicants required to submit FAFSA. *Application contact:* Renee San Giacomo, Director of Admissions, 888-442-8372, Fax: 609-984-8447, E-mail: admissions@tesc.edu.

Touro University International, College of Business Administration, Program in Business Administration, Cypress, CA 90630. Offers business administration (PhD); conflict and negotiation management (MBA); criminal justice administration (MBA); entrepreneurship (MBA); finance (MBA); general management (MBA); human resource management (MBA); information technology management (MBA); international business (MBA); logistics management (MBA); public management (MBA); strategic leadership (MBA). Part-time and evening/weekend programs available. Postbaccalaureate distance learning degree programs offered (no on-campus study). In 2006, 631 master's, 30 doctorates awarded. *Degree requirements:* For doctorate, thesis/dissertation, defense of dissertation, comprehensive exam. *Entrance requirements:* For master's, minimum GPA of 3.0; for doctorate, minimum GPA of 3.4, curriculum vitae, course work in research methods or statistics. Additional exam requirements/recommendations for international students: Required—TOEFL (minimum score 550 paper-based). *Application deadline:* Applications are processed on a rolling basis. Application fee: $75. Electronic applications accepted. *Expenses:* Tuition: Part-time $300 per credit hour. Tuition and fees vary according to course level and program.

Trinity (Washington) University, School of Professional Studies, Washington, DC 20017-1094. Offers business administration (MBA); communication (MA); information security management (MS); organizational management (MSA), including federal program management, human resource management, nonprofit management, organizational development, public and community health. Part-time and evening/weekend programs available. *Degree requirements:* For master's, thesis (for some programs), capstone project (MSA). *Entrance requirements:* For master's, minimum GPA of 2.5. Additional exam requirements/recommendations for international students: Required—TOEFL (minimum score 550 paper-based; 213 computer-based).

Troy University, Graduate School, College of Business, Troy, AL 36082. Offers business administration (EMBA, MBA); human resource management (MS); management (MS, MSM). *Accreditation:* ACBSP. Part-time and evening/weekend programs available. Postbaccalaureate distance learning degree programs offered. *Students:* 1,274 full-time (604 women), 1,592 part-time (818 women); includes 1,615 minority (1,410 African Americans, 13 American Indian/Alaska Native, 97 Asian Americans or Pacific Islanders, 95 Hispanic Americans). Average age 33. In 2006, 1148 degrees awarded. *Degree requirements:* For master's, thesis or alternative, registration. *Entrance requirements:* For master's, GMAT, GRE General Test, minimum GPA of 2.5. Additional exam requirements/recommendations for international students: Required—TOEFL (minimum score 523 paper-based; 200 computer-based). *Application deadline:* Applications are processed on a rolling basis. Application fee: $50. Electronic applications accepted. *Expenses:* Tuition, state resident: full-time $4,368; part-time $182 per hour. Tuition, nonresident: full-time $8,736; part-time $364 per hour. Required fees: $50 per term. *Financial support:* In 2006–07, 5 research assistantships were awarded; career-related internships or fieldwork also available. Support available to part-time students. Financial award applicants required to submit FAFSA. *Faculty research:* Public accounting, investment, employee relations, networking, supply chain management. *Unit head:* Dr. Don Hines, Dean, 334-670-3143, Fax: 334-670-3708, E-mail: dhines@troy.edu. *Application contact:* Brenda K. Campbell, Director of Graduate Admissions, 334-670-3178, Fax: 334-670-3733, E-mail: bcamp@troy.edu.

Troy University, Graduate School, Program in Human Resources Management, Troy, AL 36082. Offers MS. Part-time and evening/weekend programs available. *Students:* 176 full-time (130 women), 462 part-time (335 women); includes 438 minority (408 African Americans, 1 American Indian/Alaska Native, 12 Asian Americans or Pacific Islanders, 17 Hispanic Americans). Average age 34. In 2006, 218 degrees awarded. *Degree requirements:* For master's, thesis or alternative, registration. *Entrance requirements:* Additional exam requirements/recommendations for international students: Required—TOEFL (minimum score 523 paper-based; 200 computer-based). *Application deadline:* Applications are processed on a rolling basis. Application fee: $50. *Expenses:* Tuition, state resident: full-time $4,368; part-time $182 per hour. Tuition, nonresident: full-time $8,736; part-time $364 per hour. Required fees: $50 per term. *Unit head:* Dr. Charles Durham, Associate Professor of Management, 334-241-9727, E-mail: cdurham@tsum.edu. *Application contact:* Brenda K. Campbell, Director of Graduate Admissions, 334-670-3178, Fax: 334-670-3733, E-mail: bcamp@troy.edu.

Universidad del Este, Graduate School, Carolina, PR 00983. Offers accounting (MBA); administration (M Ed); criminal justice and criminology (MA); education (M Ed); elementary education (M Ed); human resources (MBA); management (MBA); social work (MA); teaching English (M Ed); teaching Spanish (M Ed).

Universidad Metropolitana, School of Business Administration, Program in Human Resources Management, San Juan, PR 00928-1150. Offers MBA. Part-time programs available.

University at Albany, State University of New York, School of Business, Department of Management, Albany, NY 12222-0001. Offers human resource systems (MBA). *Degree requirements:* For master's, field study project. *Entrance requirements:* For master's, GMAT. Additional exam requirements/recommendations for international students: Required—TOEFL (minimum score 550 paper-based; 213 computer-based). *Application deadline:* For fall admission, 3/1 priority date for domestic students, 4/1 for international students. Applications are processed on a rolling basis. Application fee: $75. Electronic applications accepted. *Expenses:* Tuition, state resident: full-time $6,900; part-time $288 per credit. Tuition, nonresident: full-time $10,920; part-time $455 per credit. Required fees: $1,139. *Financial support:* Application deadline: 4/1. *Faculty research:* Leadership, strategic management, performance appraisal, franchising, job satisfaction. *Unit head:* Cecilia Falbe, Chair, 518-442-4966. *Application contact:* Michael DeRensis, Director, Graduate Admissions, 518-442-3980, Fax: 518-442-3922, E-mail: graduate@uamail.albany.edu.

University at Buffalo, the State University of New York, Graduate School, Graduate School of Education, Department of Educational Leadership and Policy, Buffalo, NY 14260. Offers educational administration (Ed M, Ed D, PhD); general education (Ed M); higher education (PhD); higher education administration (Ed M); school business and human resource administration (Certificate); social foundations (PhD); specialist in education administration (Certificate). Part-time and evening/weekend programs available. *Faculty:* 12 full-time (7 women), 6 part-time/adjunct (3 women). *Students:* 107 full-time (73 women), 141 part-time (89 women); includes 50 minority (35 African Americans, 1 American Indian/Alaska Native, 7 Asian Americans or Pacific Islanders, 7 Hispanic Americans), 25 international. Average age 37. 262 applicants, 36% accepted, 58 enrolled. In 2006, 28 master's, 17 doctorates, 12 other advanced degrees awarded. Terminal master's awarded for partial completion of doctoral program. *Median time to degree:* Master's–2 years full-time, 4 years part-time; doctorate–4 years full-time, 6 years part-time; Certificate–2 years part-time. *Degree requirements:* For master's, thesis optional; for doctorate, thesis/dissertation, comprehensive exam, registration. *Entrance requirements:* For doctorate, GRE General Test or MAT, writing sample. Additional exam requirements/recommendations for international students: Required—TOEFL (minimum score 550 paper-based; 213 computer-based). *Application deadline:* For fall admission, 3/1 priority date for domestic students, 3/1 for international students; for spring admission, 11/15 priority date for domestic students, 10/1 for international students. Applications are processed on a rolling basis. Application fee: $50. Electronic applications accepted. *Financial support:* In 2006–07, 50 students received support, including 1 fellowship with full tuition reimbursement available (averaging $10,000 per year), 10 research assistantships with full tuition reimbursements available (averaging $9,000 per year); career-related internships or fieldwork, Federal Work-Study, institutionally sponsored loans, health care benefits, tuition waivers (full and partial), and unspecified assistantships also available. Financial award application deadline: 3/15; financial award applicants required to submit FAFSA. *Faculty research:* Academic collective bargaining, faculty governance, educational technology, educational policy studies, multicultural issues. Total annual research expenditures: $326,191. *Unit head:* Dr. William C. Barba, Chairman, 716-645-2471 Ext. 1097, Fax: 716-645-2481, E-mail: barba@buffalo.edu. *Application contact:* Bonnie Fisher, Secretary, 716-645-2110 Ext. 1255, Fax: 716-645-2481, E-mail: brfisher@buffalo.edu.

The University of Akron, Graduate School, College of Business Administration, Department of Management, Program in Management-Human Resources, Akron, OH 44325. Offers MSM. *Students:* 6 full-time (2 women), 3 part-time (all women); includes 1 minority (African American), 1 international. Average age 28. 14 applicants, 64% accepted, 5 enrolled. In 2006, 2 degrees awarded. *Entrance requirements:* For master's, GMAT, minimum GPA of 2.75. Additional exam requirements/recommendations for international students: Required—TOEFL (minimum score 550 paper-based; 213 computer-based; 79 iBT). *Application deadline:* For fall admission, 8/15 for domestic students. Applications are processed on a rolling basis. Application fee: $30 ($40 for international students). Electronic applications accepted. *Expenses:* Tuition, state resident: full-time $6,164; part-time $342 per credit. Tuition, nonresident: full-time $10,575; part-time $588 per credit. Required fees: $806; $43 per credit. $12 per term. Tuition and fees vary according to course load, degree level and program.

The University of Alabama in Huntsville, School of Graduate Studies, College of Administrative Science, Department of Management, Huntsville, AL 35899. Offers human resource management (Certificate); management (MS, MSM). *Accreditation:* AACSB. Part-time and evening/weekend programs available. *Faculty:* 7 full-time (2 women), 6 part-time/adjunct (5 women). *Students:* 9 full-time (5 women), 63 part-time (29 women); includes 11 minority (3 African Americans, 2 American Indian/Alaska Native, 4 Asian Americans or Pacific Islanders, 2 Hispanic Americans), 4 international. Average age 32. 36 applicants, 83% accepted, 23 enrolled. In 2006, 36 master's, 2 other advanced degrees awarded. *Degree requirements:* For master's, thesis or alternative, comprehensive exam, registration. *Entrance requirements:* For master's, GMAT, minimum AACSB index of 1000. Additional exam requirements/recommendations for international students: Required—TOEFL (minimum score 550 paper-based; 213 computer-based). *Application deadline:* For fall admission, 8/10 for domestic students; for spring admission, 12/10 for domestic students. Application fee: $40. *Expenses:* Tuition, state resident: full-time $6,072; part-time $253 per credit hour. Tuition, nonresident: full-time $12,476; part-time $519 per credit hour. *Financial support:* Research assistantships, teaching assistantships with full and partial tuition reimbursements, career-related internships or fieldwork, Federal Work-Study, institutionally sponsored loans, scholarships/grants, health care benefits, and unspecified assistantships available. Support available to part-time students. Financial award application deadline: 4/1; financial award applicants required to submit FAFSA. *Unit head:* Dr. James Simpson, Chair, 256-824-6408, Fax: 256-824-7571, E-mail: msmprog@email.uah.edu.

University of Connecticut, Graduate School, Center for Continuing Studies, Program in Human Resource Management, Storrs, CT 06269. Offers labor relations (MPS); personnel (MPS). *Faculty:* 3 full-time (0 women). *Students:* 1 (woman) full-time, 36 part-time (28 women); includes 9 minority (5 African Americans, 4 Hispanic Americans), 1 international. Average age 35. 21 applicants, 48% accepted, 10 enrolled. In 2006, 1 degree awarded.

See Close-Up on page 539.

University of Dallas, Graduate School of Management, Irving, TX 75062-4736. Offers accounting (MBA, MS); business management (MBA); corporate finance (MBA, MM); engineering management (MBA, MM); entrepreneurship (MBA, MM); financial services (MBA, MM); global business (MBA, MM); health services management (MBA, MM); human resource management (MBA, MM, MS); information assurance (MBA, MM, MS); information technology (MBA, MM, MS); information technology service management (MBA); IT service management (MS); marketing (MM); marketing management (MBA); not-for-profit management (MBA); organization development (MBA); project management (MBA, MM); sports and entertainment management (MBA, MM); strategic leadership (MBA); supply chain management (MBA); supply chain management and market logistics (MM); telecommunications management (MBA, MM). *Accreditation:* ACBSP. Part-time and evening/weekend programs available. Postbaccalaureate distance learning degree programs offered (no on-campus study). *Faculty:* 26 full-time (5 women), 85 part-time/adjunct (18 women). *Students:* 227 full-time (98 women), 1,160 part-time (446 women); includes 473 minority (209 African Americans, 3 American Indian/Alaska Native, 143 Asian Americans or Pacific Islanders, 118 Hispanic Americans), 224 international. Average age 34. 556 applicants, 86% accepted, 291 enrolled. In 2006, 476 degrees awarded. *Entrance requirements:* Additional exam requirements/recommendations for international students: Required—TOEFL. *Application deadline:* Applications are processed on a rolling basis. Application fee: $50. Electronic applications accepted. *Expenses:* Contact institution. *Financial support:* In 2006–07, 468 students received support. Scholarships/grants and unspecified assistantships available. Financial award application deadline: 2/15; financial award applicants required to submit FAFSA. *Unit head:* Dr. J. Lee Whittington, Dean, 972-721-5230. *Application contact:* Sarah Stivison, Director of Graduate Admissions, 972-721-5198, Fax: 972-721-4009, E-mail: admiss@gsm.udallas.edu.

University of Denver, University College, Denver, CO 80208. Offers applied communication (MAS, MPS); computer information systems (MAS); environmental policy and management (MAS); geographic information systems (MAS); human resource administration (MPS); knowledge and information technologies (MAS); liberal studies (MLS); modern languages (MLS); organizational leadership (MPS); technology management (MAS); telecommunications (MAS). Part-time and evening/weekend programs available. Postbaccalaureate distance learning degree programs offered (no on-campus study). *Students:* 57 full-time (28 women), 453 part-time (253 women); includes 84 minority (37 African Americans, 1 American Indian/Alaska Native, 21 Asian Americans or Pacific Islanders, 25 Hispanic Americans), 39 international. Average age 26. 159 applicants, 84% accepted. In 2006, 171 master's awarded. *Entrance requirements:* Additional exam requirements/recommendations for international students: Required—TOEFL (minimum score 550 paper-based; 213 computer-based). *Application deadline:* Applications are processed on a rolling basis. Application fee: $75. Electronic applications accepted. *Expenses:* Contact institution. *Financial support:* Applicants required to submit FAFSA. *Unit head:* Dr. James Davis, Dean, 303-871-2291, Fax: 303-871-4047, E-mail: jdavis@du.edu. *Application contact:* Information Contact, 303-871-3069.

The University of Findlay, Graduate and Professional Studies, MBA Program, Findlay, OH 45840-3653. Offers financial management (MBA); human resource management (MBA); international management (MBA); management (MBA); marketing (MBA); public management (MBA). Part-time and evening/weekend programs available. Postbaccalaureate distance learning degree programs offered (no on-campus study). *Faculty:* 16 full-time, 1 part-time/adjunct. *Students:* 80 full-time (26 women), 456 part-time (168 women); includes 20 minority (13 African Americans, 1 American Indian/Alaska Native, 4 Asian Americans or Pacific Islanders, 2 Hispanic Americans), 289 international. Average age 35. 208 applicants, 88% accepted, 181 enrolled. In 2006, 210 degrees awarded. *Degree requirements:* For master's, thesis, cumulative project. *Entrance requirements:* For master's, GMAT, minimum undergraduate GPA of 3.0 in last 60 hours of course work. Additional exam requirements/recommendations for international students: Required—TOEFL (minimum score 550 paper-based). *Application deadline:* Applications are processed on a rolling basis. Application fee: $25. Electronic applications accepted. *Expenses:* Contact institution. *Financial support:* In 2006–07, 1 student received support, including 1 teaching assistantship with full tuition reimbursement available (averaging $6,000 per year); unspecified assistantships also available. Financial award application deadline: 4/1; financial award applicants required to submit FAFSA. *Faculty research:* Health care management, operations and logistics management. *Unit head:* Dr. Paul Sears,

Human Resources Management

The University of Findlay (continued)
Dean, 419-434-4704, Fax: 419-434-4822. *Application contact:* Heather Riffle, Director, Graduate and Special Programs, 419-434-4640, Fax: 419-434-5517, E-mail: riffle@findlay.edu.

University of Florida, Graduate School, Warrington College of Business Administration, Programs in Business Administration, Gainesville, FL 32611. Offers accounting (MBA); arts administration (MBA); business strategy and public policy (MBA); competitive strategy (MBA); decision and information sciences (MBA); electronic commerce (MBA); finance (MBA); general business (MBA); global management (MBA); Graham-Buffett security analysis (MBA); health administration (MBA); human resources management (MBA); international studies (MBA); Latin American business (MBA); management (MBA); marketing (MBA); sports administration (MBA); JD/MBA; MBA/MS; MBA/PhD; MBA/Pharm D; MD/MBA. *Accreditation:* AACSB. Part-time and evening/weekend programs available. Postbaccalaureate distance learning degree programs offered. *Faculty:* 14. *Students:* 950 (282 women); includes 189 minority (31 African Americans, 2 American Indian/Alaska Native, 66 Asian Americans or Pacific Islanders, 90 Hispanic Americans) 56 international. In 2006, 481 degrees awarded. *Entrance requirements:* For master's, GMAT, minimum GPA of 3.0, interview. Additional exam requirements/recommendations for international students: Required—TOEFL (minimum score 550 paper-based; 213 computer-based). *Application deadline:* For fall admission, 4/15 for domestic students; for winter admission, 10/15 priority date for domestic students; for spring admission, 2/15 for domestic students. Applications are processed on a rolling basis. Application fee: $30. Electronic applications accepted. *Expenses:* Tuition, state resident: full-time $6,827. Tuition, nonresident: full-time $21,951. Required fees: $999. *Financial support:* Fellowships, research assistantships, teaching assistantships, career-related internships or fieldwork, scholarships/grants, and unspecified assistantships available. Support available to part-time students. Financial award application deadline: 2/15; financial award applicants required to submit FAFSA. *Faculty research:* Accounting, finance, insurance, management, real estate and urban analysis marketing. *Unit head:* Alex Sevilla, Director, 352-392-7992 Ext. 1206. *Application contact:* Patrick Foran, Associate Director of Admissions, 352-392-7992 Ext. 282, Fax: 352-392-8791, E-mail: patrick.foran@cba.ufl.edu.

University of Hawaii at Manoa, Graduate Division, Shidler College of Business, Program in Business Administration, Honolulu, HI 96822. Offers Asian business studies (MBA); Chinese business studies (MBA); decision sciences (MBA); entrepreneurship (MBA); finance (MBA); finance and banking (MBA); human resources management (MBA); information management (MBA); information technology (MBA); international business (MBA); Japanese business studies (MBA); marketing (MBA); organizational behavior (MBA); organizational management (MBA); real estate (MBA); student-designed track (MBA). *Accreditation:* AACSB. Part-time programs available. *Faculty:* 48 full-time (9 women). *Students:* 207 full-time (77 women), 158 part-time (60 women); includes 93 minority (2 African Americans, 1 American Indian/Alaska Native, 88 Asian Americans or Pacific Islanders, 2 Hispanic Americans), 58 international. Average age 33. 235 applicants, 55% accepted, 68 enrolled. In 2006, 147 degrees awarded. *Degree requirements:* For master's, thesis optional. *Entrance requirements:* For master's, GMAT, minimum GPA of 3.0. Additional exam requirements/recommendations for international students: Required—TOEFL (minimum score 500 paper-based; 173 computer-based; 61 iBT). *Application deadline:* For fall admission, 5/1 for domestic and international students; for spring admission, 9/1 for domestic and international students. Application fee: $50. *Financial support:* In 2006–07, 7 research assistantships (averaging $17,409 per year), 3 teaching assistantships (averaging $14,028 per year) were awarded. *Application contact:* Ting Bui, Information Contact, 808-956-5565, Fax: 808-956-6889.

University of Hawaii at Manoa, Graduate Division, Shidler College of Business, Program in Human Resources Management, Honolulu, HI 96822. Offers MHRM. *Students:* 30 full-time (22 women), 1 (woman) part-time; includes 7 minority (all Asian Americans or Pacific Islanders), 1 international. 36 applicants, 78% accepted, 9 enrolled. In 2006, 1 degree awarded. *Entrance requirements:* Additional exam requirements/recommendations for international students: Required—TOEFL (minimum score 600 paper-based; 250 computer-based; 100 iBT). *Application deadline:* For fall admission, 7/1 for domestic and international students. Application fee: $50. *Financial support:* In 2006–07, 29 research assistantships (averaging $17,351 per year), 5 teaching assistantships (averaging $14,285 per year) were awarded. *Application contact:* Elaine Bailey, Information Contact, 808-956-5104, Fax: 808-956-2774.

University of Houston–Clear Lake, School of Business, Program in Administrative Science, Houston, TX 77058-1098. Offers environmental management (MS); human resource management (MA). *Accreditation:* CAHME (one or more programs are accredited). Part-time and evening/weekend programs available. *Students:* 15 full-time, 21 part-time; includes 8 minority (3 African Americans, 3 Asian Americans or Pacific Islanders, 2 Hispanic Americans), 4 international. 45 applicants, 36% accepted, 9 enrolled. In 2006, 9 degrees awarded. *Degree requirements:* For master's, thesis optional. *Entrance requirements:* For master's, GMAT. Additional exam requirements/recommendations for international students: Required—TOEFL (minimum score 550 paper-based; 213 computer-based). *Application deadline:* For fall admission, 8/1 for domestic students, 6/1 for international students; for spring admission, 12/1 for domestic students, 10/1 for international students. Applications are processed on a rolling basis. Application fee: $35 ($75 for international students). Electronic applications accepted. *Financial support:* Fellowships, research assistantships, teaching assistantships, career-related internships or fieldwork, Federal Work-Study, institutionally sponsored loans, and scholarships/grants available. Support available to part-time students. Financial award application deadline: 5/1; financial award applicants required to submit FAFSA. *Unit head:* Dr. Lou White, Chair, 281-283-3238, Fax: 281-283-3951, E-mail: whitel@uhcl.edu. *Application contact:* Janis S. Bigelow, Assistant Director of Admissions, Recruitment and Communications, 281-283-2540, Fax: 281-283-2530, E-mail: bigelow@uhcl.edu.

University of Illinois at Urbana–Champaign, Graduate College, Institute of Labor and Industrial Relations, Program in Human Resources, Champaign, IL 61820. Offers MHRIR, PhD. Part-time programs available. Terminal master's awarded for partial completion of doctoral program. *Degree requirements:* For doctorate, thesis/dissertation. *Entrance requirements:* For master's, GRE General Test, minimum GPA of 3.0; for doctorate, GRE General Test, research experience. Application fee: $50 ($60 for international students). Electronic applications accepted. *Financial support:* Fellowships, research assistantships, teaching assistantships, career-related internships or fieldwork, Federal Work-Study, scholarships/grants, and tuition waivers (full) available. Support available to part-time students. Financial award application deadline: 2/1. *Unit head:* Kevin Hallock, Director, 217-333-0981, Fax: 217-244-9290, E-mail: hallock@uiuc.edu. *Application contact:* Becky Barker, Graduate Admissions, 217-333-2381, Fax: 217-244-9290, E-mail: ebarker@uiuc.edu.

See Close-Up on page 541.

University of Lethbridge, School of Graduate Studies, Lethbridge, AB T1K 3M4, Canada. Offers accounting (MScM); addictions counseling (M Sc); agricultural biotechnology (M Sc); agricultural studies (M Sc, MA); anthropology (MA); archaeology (MA); art (MA); biochemistry (M Sc); biological sciences (M Sc); biomolecular science (PhD); biosystems and biodiversity (PhD); Canadian studies (MA); chemistry (M Sc); computer science (M Sc); computer science and geographical information science (M Sc); counseling psychology (M Ed); dramatic arts (MA); earth, space, and physical science (PhD); economics (MA); educational leadership (M Ed); English (MA); environmental science (M Sc); evolution and behavior (PhD); exercise science (M Sc); finance (MScM); French (MA); French/German (MA); French/Spanish (MA); general education (M Ed); general management (MScM); geography (M Sc, MA); German (MA); health sciences (M Sc, MA); history (MA); human resource management and labour relations (MScM); individualized multidisciplinary (M Sc, MA); information systems (MScM); international management (MScM); kinesiology (M Sc, MA); management (M Sc, MA); marketing (MScM); mathematics (M Sc); music (MA); Native American studies (MA); neuroscience (M Sc, PhD); new media (MA); nursing (M Sc); philosophy (MA); physics (M Sc); policy and strategy (MScM); political science (MA); psychology (M Sc, MA); religious studies (MA); sociology (MA); theoretical and computational science (PhD); urban and regional studies (MA). Part-time and evening/weekend programs available. *Students:* 200 full-time, 90 part-time. In 2006, 105 master's, 3 doctorates awarded. *Degree requirements:* For doctorate, thesis/dissertation, comprehensive exam. *Entrance requirements:* For master's, GMAT (M Sc management), bachelor's degree in related field, minimum GPA of 3.0 during previous 20 graded semester courses, 2 years teaching or related experience (M Ed); for doctorate, master's degree, minimum graduate GPA of 3.5. Additional exam requirements/recommendations for international students: Required—TOEFL. Application fee: $60 Canadian dollars. *Financial support:* Fellowships, research assistantships, teaching assistantships, scholarships/grants, health care benefits, and unspecified assistantships available. *Faculty research:* Movement and brain plasticity, gibberellin physiology, photosynthesis, carbon cycling, molecular properties of main-group ring components. *Unit head:* Dr. Jo-Anne Fiske, Interim Dean, 403-329-2121, Fax: 403-329-2097. *Application contact:* Kathy Schrage, Administrative Assistant, Office of the Academic Vice President, 403-329-2121, Fax: 403-329-2097, E-mail: inquiries@uleth.ca.

University of Minnesota, Twin Cities Campus, Carlson School of Management, Program in Human Resources and Industrial Relations, Minneapolis, MN 55455-0213. Offers MA, PhD. *Accreditation:* AACSB. Part-time and evening/weekend programs available. *Faculty:* 16 full-time (5 women), 8 part-time/adjunct (3 women). *Students:* 154 full-time (91 women), 74 part-time (58 women); includes 18 minority (9 African Americans, 7 Asian Americans or Pacific Islanders, 2 Hispanic Americans), 74 international. Average age 26. 163 applicants, 87% accepted, 70 enrolled. In 2006, 90 master's, 4 doctorates awarded. Terminal master's awarded for partial completion of doctoral program. *Degree requirements:* For master's, thesis optional; for doctorate, thesis/dissertation. *Entrance requirements:* For master's, GMAT or GRE General Test; for doctorate, GRE General Test. Additional exam requirements/recommendations for international students: Required—TOEFL (minimum score 580 paper-based). *Application deadline:* For fall admission, 6/15 for domestic and international students; for spring admission, 10/15 for domestic and international students. Applications are processed on a rolling basis. Application fee: $55 ($75 for international students). *Expenses: Contact institution.* Full-time tuition and fees vary according to class time, course load, program, reciprocity agreements and student level. *Financial support:* In 2006–07, 39 fellowships with partial tuition reimbursements (averaging $5,000 per year), 17 research assistantships with full and partial tuition reimbursements (averaging $10,300 per year), 7 teaching assistantships with full tuition reimbursements (averaging $7,500 per year) were awarded; career-related internships or fieldwork, Federal Work-Study, institutionally sponsored loans, and tuition waivers (full and partial) also available. Support available to part-time students. Financial award application deadline: 2/1. *Faculty research:* Staffing, training, and development; compensation and benefits; organization theory; collective bargaining. Total annual research expenditures: $200,000. *Unit head:* John Budd, Director of Graduate Studies, 612-624-0357, Fax: 612-624-8360, E-mail: jbudd@csom.umn.edu. *Application contact:* Laura Simpson, Admissions Coordinator, 612-624-5704, Fax: 612-624-8360, E-mail: lsimpson@csom.umn.edu.

See Close-Up on page 543.

University of Missouri–St. Louis, College of Business Administration, Program in Business Administration, St. Louis, MO 63121. Offers accounting (MBA); business administration (Certificate); finance (MBA); human resource management (Certificate); logistics and supply chain management (MBA, Certificate); management (MBA); marketing (MBA); marketing management (Certificate); operations (MBA); quantitative management science (MBA); telecommunications management (Certificate). *Accreditation:* AACSB. Part-time and evening/weekend programs available. *Faculty:* 26 full-time (6 women), 2 part-time/adjunct (0 women). *Students:* 242 full-time (156 women), 186 part-time (123 women); includes 48 minority (17 African Americans, 1 American Indian/Alaska Native, 27 Asian Americans or Pacific Islanders, 3 Hispanic Americans), 96 international. Average age 33. In 2006, 138 degrees awarded. *Entrance requirements:* For master's, GMAT, 2 letters of recommendation. Additional exam requirements/recommendations for international students: Required—TOEFL (minimum score 550 paper-based; 213 computer-based). *Application deadline:* For fall admission, 7/1 for domestic students; for spring admission, 11/1 for domestic students. Applications are processed on a rolling basis. Application fee: $35 ($40 for international students). Electronic applications accepted. *Expenses:* Tuition, state resident: part-time $332 per credit hour. Tuition, nonresident: part-time $770 per credit hour. *Financial support:* Research assistantships with full and partial tuition reimbursements, teaching assistantships with full and partial tuition reimbursements, career-related internships or fieldwork, Federal Work-Study, and institutionally sponsored loans available. Support available to part-time students. Financial award application deadline: 4/1; financial award applicants required to submit FAFSA. *Faculty research:* Human resources, strategic management, marketing strategy, consumer behavior product development, advertising. *Application contact:* 314-516-5458, Fax: 314-516-6996, E-mail: gradadm@umsl.edu.

University of Missouri–St. Louis, Graduate School, Program in Public Policy Administration, St. Louis, MO 63121. Offers health policy (MPPA); local government management (MPPA); managing human resources and organization (MPPA); nonprofit organization management (MPPA); nonprofit organization management and leadership (Certificate); policy research and analysis (MPPA); public sector human resources management (MPPA). *Accreditation:* NASPAA. Part-time and evening/weekend programs available. *Faculty:* 8 full-time (5 women), 5 part-time/adjunct (1 woman). *Students:* 21 full-time (13 women), 61 part-time (35 women); includes 22 minority (18 African Americans, 1 American Indian/Alaska Native, 2 Asian Americans or Pacific Islanders, 1 Hispanic American), 4 international. Average age 34. In 2006, 22 degrees awarded. *Entrance requirements:* For master's, 3 letters of recommendation. Additional exam requirements/recommendations for international students: Required—TOEFL (minimum score 550 paper-based; 213 computer-based). *Application deadline:* For fall admission, 7/15 priority date for domestic students; for spring admission, 12/15 priority date for domestic students. Applications are processed on a rolling basis. Application fee: $35 ($40 for international students). Electronic applications accepted. *Expenses:* Tuition, state resident: part-time $332 per credit hour. Tuition, nonresident: part-time $770 per credit hour. *Financial support:* In 2006–07, 2 research assistantships with full tuition reimbursements (averaging $14,100 per year) were awarded; teaching assistantships with partial tuition reimbursements, career-related internships or fieldwork also available. *Faculty research:* Urban policy, public finance, evaluation. *Unit head:* Brady Baybeck, Director, 314-516-5145, Fax: 314-516-5210, E-mail: baybeck@umsl.edu. *Application contact:* 314-516-5458, Fax: 314-516-6996, E-mail: gradadm@umsl.edu.

University of New Haven, Graduate School, School of Business, Program in Business Administration, West Haven, CT 06516-1916. Offers accounting (MBA); business policy and strategy (MBA); finance (MBA); health care management (MBA); human resources management (MBA); international business (MBA); marketing (MBA); public relations (MBA); sports management (MBA); technology management (MBA); MBA/MPA; MBA/MSIE. Part-time and evening/weekend programs available. *Degree requirements:* For master's, thesis or alternative. *Entrance requirements:* For master's, GMAT.

University of New Haven, Graduate School, School of Business, Program in Public Administration, West Haven, CT 06516-1916. Offers health care management (MPA); personnel and labor relations (MPA); MBA/MPA. Part-time and evening/weekend programs available. *Degree requirements:* For master's, thesis or alternative.

University of New Mexico, Robert O. Anderson Graduate School of Management, Department of Organizational Studies, Albuquerque, NM 87131-2039. Offers human resources management (MBA); policy and planning (MBA). Part-time and evening/weekend programs available. *Entrance requirements:* For master's, GMAT. Additional exam requirements/recommendations for international students: Required—TOEFL (minimum score 550 paper-based; 213 computer-based).

University of Phoenix–Atlanta Campus, John Sperling School of Business, College of Graduate Business and Management, Sandy Springs, GA 30350-4153. Offers business administration (MBA); global management (MBA); human resources management (MBA); management (MM). Evening/weekend programs available. *Faculty:* 25 full-time (15 women), 151 part-time/adjunct (31 women). *Students:* 605 full-time (375 women); includes 323 minority (303 African Americans, 1 American Indian/Alaska Native, 10 Asian Americans or Pacific Islanders, 9 Hispanic Americans), 22 international. Average age 36. In 2006, 156 degrees awarded. *Degree requirements:* For master's, thesis (for some programs), registration. *Entrance requirements:* For master's, minimum undergraduate GPA of 3.0, 3 years of work experience. Additional exam requirements/recommendations for international students: Required—TOEFL (minimum score 550 paper-based; 213 computer-based; 79 iBT). *Application deadline:* Applications are processed on a rolling basis. *Expenses:* Tuition: Full-time $10,560. Required fees: $760. *Financial support:* Institutionally sponsored loans and scholarships/grants available. Financial award applicants required to submit FAFSA. *Unit head:* Dr. Brian Lindquist, Associate Vice President and Dean/Executive Director, 480-557-1221, E-mail: brian.lindquist@phoenix.edu. *Application contact:* Chair, 678-731-0555, Fax: 678-731-9666.

University of Phoenix–Augusta Campus, College of Graduate Business and Management, Augusta, GA 30909-4583. Offers accounting (MBA); business and management (MBA, MM); global management (MBA); human resources management (MBA, MM); marketing (MBA); public administration (MBA, MM).

University of Phoenix–Austin Campus, College of Graduate Business and Management, Austin, TX 78759. Offers accounting (MBA); business and management (MBA); e-business (MBA); global management (MBA); human resources management (MBA, MM); management (MM); marketing (MBA); public administration (MBA).

University of Phoenix–Bay Area Campus, John Sperling School of Business, College of Graduate Business and Management, Pleasanton, CA 94588-3677. Offers accounting (MBA); business administration (MBA); global management (MBA); human resource management (MBA); marketing (MBA); public administration (MBA). Evening/weekend programs available. *Faculty:* 30 full-time (3 women), 390 part-time/adjunct (106 women). *Students:* 523 full-time (279 women); includes 185 minority (40 African Americans, 2 American Indian/Alaska Native, 110 Asian Americans or Pacific Islanders, 33 Hispanic Americans), 84 international. Average age 37. In 2006, 205 degrees awarded. *Degree requirements:* For master's, thesis (for some programs), registration. *Entrance requirements:* For master's, minimum undergraduate GPA of 3.0, 3 years of work experience. Additional exam requirements/recommendations for international students: Required—TOEFL (minimum score 550 paper-based; 213 computer-based; 79 iBT). *Application deadline:* Applications are processed on a rolling basis. Application fee: $45. Electronic applications accepted. *Expenses:* Tuition: Full-time $12,648. Required fees: $760. *Financial support:* Institutionally sponsored loans and scholarships/grants available. Financial award applicants required to submit FAFSA. *Unit head:* Dr. Brian Lindquist, Associate Vice President and Dean/Executive Director, 408-557-1221, E-mail: brian.lindquist@phoenix.edu. *Application contact:* Chair, 408-435-8500, Fax: 408-435-8250.

University of Phoenix–Central Valley Campus, College of Graduate Business and Management, Fresno, CA 93720. Offers accounting (MBA); business administration (MBA); global management (MBA); human resources management (MBA); management (MM); marketing (MBA); public administration (MBA).

University of Phoenix–Chattanooga Campus, College of Graduate Business and Management, Chattanooga, TN 37421-3707. Offers accounting (MBA); business and management (MBA); global management (MBA); human resources management (MBA, MM); management (MM); marketing (MBA); public administration (MBA, MM).

University of Phoenix–Cheyenne Campus, College of Graduate Business and Management, Cheyenne, WY 82009. Offers business and management (MM); global management (MBA); human resources management (MBA, MM); marketing (MBA); public administration (MBA, MM).

University of Phoenix–Cleveland Campus, John Sperling School of Business, College of Graduate Business and Management, Independence, OH 44131-2194. Offers accounting (MBA); business administration (MBA); global management (MBA); human resources management (MM); management (MM); marketing (MBA); public administration (MBA, MM). Evening/weekend programs available. *Faculty:* 10 full-time (1 woman), 68 part-time/adjunct (16 women). *Students:* 178 full-time (107 women); includes 115 minority (66 African Americans, 1 American Indian/Alaska Native, 5 Asian Americans or Pacific Islanders, 43 Hispanic Americans), 9 international. Average age 37. In 2006, 25 degrees awarded. *Degree requirements:* For master's, thesis (for some programs), registration. *Entrance requirements:* For master's, minimum undergraduate GPA of 3.0, 3 years of work experience. Additional exam requirements/recommendations for international students: Required—TOEFL (minimum score 550 paper-based; 213 computer-based; 79 iBT). *Application deadline:* Applications are processed on a rolling basis. Application fee: $45. Electronic applications accepted. *Expenses:* Tuition: Full-time $11,608. Required fees: $760. *Financial support:* Institutionally sponsored loans and scholarships/grants available. Financial award applicants required to submit FAFSA. *Unit head:* Dr. Brian Lindquist, Associate Vice President and Dean/Executive Director, 480-557-1221, E-mail: brian.linquist@phoenix.edu. *Application contact:* Chair, 216-447-8807, Fax: 216-447-9144.

University of Phoenix–Columbus Georgia Campus, John Sperling School of Business, College of Graduate Business and Management, Columbus, GA 31904-6321. Offers accounting (MBA); administration (MBA); global management (MBA); human resource management (MBA); marketing (MBA); public administration (MBA). Evening/weekend programs available. *Faculty:* 11 full-time (1 woman), 53 part-time/adjunct (15 women). *Students:* 52 full-time (35 women); includes 27 minority (22 African Americans, 1 Asian American or Pacific Islander, 4 Hispanic Americans). Average age 37. In 2006, 10 degrees awarded. *Degree requirements:* For master's, thesis (for some programs), registration. *Entrance requirements:* For master's, minimum undergraduate GPA of 3.0, 3 years of work experience. Additional exam requirements/recommendations for international students: Required—TOEFL (minimum score 550 paper-based; 213 computer-based; 79 iBT). *Application deadline:* Applications are processed on a rolling basis. Application fee: $45. Electronic applications accepted. *Expenses:* Tuition: Full-time $10,200. Required fees: $760. *Financial support:* Institutionally sponsored loans and scholarships/grants available. Financial award applicants required to submit FAFSA. *Unit head:* Dr. Brian Lindquist, Associate Vice President/Dean/Executive Director, 480-557-1221, E-mail: brian.lindquist@phoenix.edu. *Application contact:* College Chair, 706-320-1262.

University of Phoenix–Dallas Campus, John Sperling School of Business, College of Graduate Business and Management, Dallas, TX 75251-2009. Offers accounting (MBA); administration (MBA); human resources management (MBA, MM); management (MM); marketing (MBA); public administration (MBA, MM). Evening/weekend programs available. *Faculty:* 27 full-time (5 women), 130 part-time/adjunct (34 women). *Students:* 517 full-time (320 women); includes 217 minority (166 African Americans, 7 American Indian/Alaska Native, 11 Asian Americans or Pacific Islanders, 33 Hispanic Americans), 68 international. Average age 37. In 2006, 127 degrees awarded. *Degree requirements:* For master's, thesis (for some programs), registration. *Entrance requirements:* For master's, 3 years of work experience, minimum undergraduate GPA of 3.0. Additional exam requirements/recommendations for international students: Required—TOEFL (minimum score 550 paper-based; 213 computer-based; 79 iBT). *Application deadline:* Applications are processed on a rolling basis. Application fee: $45. Electronic applications accepted. *Expenses:* Tuition: Full-time $11,832. Required fees: $760. *Financial support:* Institutionally sponsored loans and scholarships/grants available. Financial award applicants required to submit FAFSA. *Unit head:* Dr. Brian Lindquist, Associate Vice President and Dean/Executive Director, 480-557-1221, E-mail: brian.lindquist@phoenix.edu. *Application contact:* Chair, 972-385-1055, Fax: 972-385-1700.

University of Phoenix–Denver Campus, John Sperling School of Business, College of Graduate Business and Management, Lone Tree, CO 80124-5453. Offers accounting (MBA); business administration (MBA); e-business (MBA); global management (MBA); human resources management (MBA, MM); management (MM); marketing (MBA); public administration (MBA, MM). Evening/weekend programs available. *Faculty:* 63 full-time (22 women), 254 part-time/adjunct (56 women). *Students:* 289 full-time (139 women); includes 59 minority (25 African Americans, 1 American Indian/Alaska Native, 9 Asian Americans or Pacific Islanders, 24 Hispanic Americans), 20 international. Average age 37. In 2006, 93 degrees awarded. *Degree requirements:* For master's, thesis (for some programs), registration. *Entrance requirements:* For master's, minimum undergraduate GPA of 3.0, 3 years work experience. Additional exam requirements/recommendations for international students: Required—TOEFL (minimum score 550 paper-based; 213 computer-based; 79 iBT). *Application deadline:* Applications are processed on a rolling basis. Application fee: $45. Electronic applications accepted. *Expenses:* Tuition: Full-time $10,032. Required fees: $760. *Financial support:* Institutionally sponsored loans and scholarships/grants available. Financial award applicants required to submit FAFSA. *Unit head:* Dr. Brian Lindquist, Associate Vice President and Dean/Executive Director, 480-557-1221, E-mail: brian.lindquist@phoenix.edu. *Application contact:* Chair, 303-694-9093, Fax: 303-662-0911.

University of Phoenix–Des Moines Campus, College of Graduate Business and Management, Des Moines, IA 50266. Offers accounting (MBA); business administration (MBA); global management (MBA); human resources management (MBA, MM); management (MM); marketing (MBA); public administration (MBA, MM).

University of Phoenix–Detroit Campus, College of Graduate Business and Management, Southfield, MI 48076. Offers accounting (MBA); business administration (MBA); e-business (MBA); global management (MBA); human resources management (MBA, MM); management (MM); marketing (MBA); public administration (MBA).

University of Phoenix–Fort Lauderdale Campus, John Sperling School of Business, College of Graduate Business and Management, Fort Lauderdale, FL 33309. Offers accounting (MBA); business administration (MBA); global management (MBA); human resource management (MBA); human resources management (MM); management (MM); marketing (MBA); public administration (MBA). Evening/weekend programs available. *Faculty:* 31 full-time (13 women), 117 part-time/adjunct (33 women). *Students:* 433 full-time (273 women); includes 196 minority (113 African Americans, 3 American Indian/Alaska Native, 8 Asian Americans or Pacific Islanders, 72 Hispanic Americans), 64 international. Average age 38. In 2006, 112 degrees awarded. *Degree requirements:* For master's, thesis (for some programs), registration. *Entrance requirements:* For master's, minimum undergraduate GPA of 3.0, 3 years work experience. Additional exam requirements/recommendations for international students: Required—TOEFL (minimum score 550 paper-based; 213 computer-based; 79 iBT). *Application deadline:* Applications are processed on a rolling basis. Application fee: $45. Electronic applications accepted. *Expenses:* Tuition: Full-time $9,450. Required fees: $760. *Financial support:* Institutionally sponsored loans and scholarships/grants available. Financial award applicants required to submit FAFSA. *Unit head:* Dr. Brian Linquist, Associate V.P. & Dean/Executive Director, 480-557-1221, E-mail: brian.linquist@phoenix.edu. *Application contact:* Chair, 954-382-5303, Fax: 954-382-5304.

University of Phoenix–Harrisburg Campus, College of Graduate Business and Management, Harrisburg, PA 17112. Offers accounting (MBA); business and management (MBA); glboal management (MBA); human resources management (MBA, MM); management (MM); marketing (MBA); public administration (MBA, MM).

University of Phoenix–Hawaii Campus, John Sperling School of Business, College of Graduate Business and Management, Honolulu, HI 96813-4317. Offers accounting (MBA); business administration (MBA); global management (MBA); human resources management (MBA, MM); management (MM); marketing (MBA); public administration (MBA, MM). Evening/weekend programs available. *Faculty:* 17 full-time (4 women), 92 part-time/adjunct (23 women). *Students:* 72 full-time (39 women); includes 18 minority (3 African Americans, 13 Asian Americans or Pacific Islanders, 2 Hispanic Americans), 30 international. Average age 37. In 2006, 20 master's awarded. *Degree requirements:* For master's, thesis (for some programs), registration. *Entrance requirements:* For master's, minimum undergraduate GPA of 3.0, 3 years of work experience. Additional exam requirements/recommendations for international students: Required—TOEFL (minimum score 550 paper-based; 213 computer-based; 79 iBT). *Application deadline:* Applications are processed on a rolling basis. Application fee: $45. Electronic applications accepted. *Expenses:* Tuition: Full-time $11,520. Required fees: $760. *Financial support:* Institutionally sponsored loans and scholarships/grants available. Financial award applicants required to submit FAFSA. *Unit head:* Dr. Brian Lindquist, Associate Vice President and Dean/Executive Director, 480-557-1221, E-mail: brian.lindquist@phoenix.edu. *Application contact:* Chair, 808-536-2686, Fax: 808-536-3848.

University of Phoenix–Houston Campus, John Sperling School of Business, College of Graduate Business and Management, Houston, TX 77079-2004. Offers business administration (MBA); global management (MBA); human resources management (MBA); public administration (MBA). Evening/weekend programs available. *Faculty:* 28 full-time (9 women), 149 part-time/adjunct (43 women). *Students:* 666 full-time (417 women); includes 350 minority (274 African Americans, 1 American Indian/Alaska Native, 34 Asian Americans or Pacific Islanders, 41 Hispanic Americans), 45 international. Average age 37. In 2006, 244 degrees awarded. *Degree requirements:* For master's, thesis (for some programs), registration. *Entrance requirements:* For master's, 3 years of work experience, minimum undergraduate GPA of 3.0. Additional exam requirements/recommendations for international students: Required—TOEFL (minimum score 550 paper-based; 213 computer-based; 79 iBT). *Application deadline:* Applications are processed on a rolling basis. Application fee: $45. Electronic applications accepted. *Expenses:* Tuition: Full-time $11,832. Required fees: $760. *Financial support:* Institutionally sponsored loans available. Financial award applicants required to submit FAFSA. *Unit head:* Dr. Brian Lindquist, Associate Vice President and Dean/Executive Director, 480-557-1221, E-mail: brian.lindquist@phoenix.edu. *Application contact:* 713-465-9966, Fax: 713-465-2686.

University of Phoenix–Jersey City Campus, College of Graduate Business and Management, Jersey City, NJ 07310. Offers accounting (MBA); business and management (MBA); global management (MBA); human resources management (MBA, MM); management (MM); marketing (MBA); public administration (MBA, MM).

University of Phoenix–Louisiana Campus, John Sperling School of Business, College of Graduate Business and Management, Metairie, LA 70001-2082. Offers business administration (MBA); human resource management (MBA, MM); public administration (MBA). Evening/weekend programs available. *Faculty:* 14 full-time (6 women), 123 part-time/adjunct (40 women). *Students:* 445 full-time (325 women); includes 225 minority (218 African Americans, 6 Asian Americans or Pacific Islanders, 1 Hispanic American), 38 international. Average age 35. In 2006, 126 degrees awarded. *Degree requirements:* For master's, thesis (for some programs), registration. *Entrance requirements:* For master's, minimum undergraduate GPA of 3.0, 3 years work experience. Additional exam requirements/recommendations for international students: Required—TOEFL (minimum score 550 paper-based; 213 computer-based; 79 iBT). *Application deadline:* Applications are processed on a rolling basis. Application fee: $45. Electronic applications accepted. *Expenses:* Tuition: Full-time $11,832. Required fees: $760. *Financial support:* Institutionally sponsored loans and scholarships/grants available. Financial award applicants required to submit FAFSA. *Unit head:* Dr. Brian Lindquist, Associate Vice President and Dean/Executive Director, 480-557-1221, E-mail: brian.linguist@phoenix.edu. *Application contact:* Chair, 504-461-8852, Fax: 504-464-6373.

University of Phoenix–Madison Campus, College of Graduate Business and Management, Madison, WI 53718-2416. Offers accounting (MBA); business and management (MBA, MM); e-business (MBA); global management (MBA); human resources management (MBA, MM); marketing (MBA); public administration (MBA).

Human Resources Management

University of Phoenix–Maryland Campus, John Sperling School of Business, College of Graduate Business and Management, Columbia, MD 21045-5424. Offers business administration (MBA); e-business (MBA); global management (MBA); human resources management (MBA, MM); marketing (MBA); public administration (MBA, MM). Evening/weekend programs available. *Faculty:* 22 full-time (6 women), 136 part-time/adjunct (35 women). *Students:* 357 full-time (223 women); includes 148 minority (128 African Americans, 2 American Indian/Alaska Native, 9 Asian Americans or Pacific Islanders, 9 Hispanic Americans), 38 international. Average age 37. In 2006, 111 master's awarded. *Degree requirements:* For master's, thesis (for some programs), registration. *Entrance requirements:* For master's, minimum undergraduate GPA of 3.0, 3 years of work experience. Additional exam requirements/recommendations for international students: Required—TOEFL (minimum score 550 paper-based; 213 computer-based; 79 iBT). *Application deadline:* Applications are processed on a rolling basis. Application fee: $45. Electronic applications accepted. *Expenses:* Tuition: Full-time $13,200. Required fees: $760. *Financial support:* Institutionally sponsored loans and scholarships/grants available. Financial award applicants required to submit FAFSA. *Unit head:* Dr. Brian Lindquist, Associate Vice President and Dean/Executive Director, 480-557-1221, E-mail: brian.lindquist@phoenix.edu. *Application contact:* Chair, 410-872-9001, Fax: 410-536-5727.

University of Phoenix–Memphis Campus, College of Graduate Business and Management, Cordova, TN 38018. Offers acounting (MBA); business and management (MBA); e-business (MBA); global management (MBA); human resources management (MBA, MM); marketing (MBA); public administration (MBA, MM).

University of Phoenix–Minneapolis/St. Louis Park Campus, College of Graduate Business and Management, St. Louis Park, MN 55426. Offers accounting (MBA); business administration (MBA); global management (MBA); human resources management (MBA); marketing (MBA).

University of Phoenix–Nashville Campus, John Sperling School of Business, College of Graduate Business and Management, Nashville, TN 37214-5048. Offers business administration (MBA); human resource management (MBA); management (MM). Evening/weekend programs available. *Faculty:* 29 full-time (2 women), 66 part-time/adjunct (20 women). *Students:* 246 full-time (145 women); includes 95 minority (90 African Americans, 1 American Indian/Alaska Native, 1 Asian American or Pacific Islander, 3 Hispanic Americans), 7 international. Average age 36. In 2006, 61 degrees awarded. *Degree requirements:* For master's, thesis (for some programs), registration. *Entrance requirements:* For master's, minimum undergraduate GPA of 3.0, 3 years of work experience. Additional exam requirements/recommendations for international students: Required—TOEFL (minimum score 550 paper-based; 213 computer-based; 79 iBT). *Application deadline:* Applications are processed on a rolling basis. Application fee: $45. Electronic applications accepted. *Expenses:* Tuition: Full-time $10,104. Required fees: $760. *Financial support:* Institutionally sponsored loans and scholarships/grants available. Financial award applicants required to submit FAFSA. *Unit head:* Dr. Brian Lindquist, Associate Vice President and Dean/Executive Director, 480-557-1221. *Application contact:* Chair, 615-872-0188.

University of Phoenix–New Mexico Campus, John Sperling School of Business, College of Graduate Business and Management, Albuquerque, NM 87109-4645. Offers business administration (MBA); global management (MBA); human resource management (MBA). Evening/weekend programs available. *Faculty:* 25 full-time (6 women), 305 part-time/adjunct (77 women). *Students:* 507 full-time (273 women); includes 235 minority (12 African Americans, 9 American Indian/Alaska Native, 7 Asian Americans or Pacific Islanders, 207 Hispanic Americans), 21 international. Average age 37. In 2006, 129 degrees awarded. *Degree requirements:* For master's, thesis (for some programs), registration. *Entrance requirements:* For master's, 3 years of work experience, minimum undergraduate GPA of 3.0. Additional exam requirements/recommendations for international students: Required—TOEFL (minimum score 550 paper-based; 213 computer-based; 79 iBT). *Application deadline:* Applications are processed on a rolling basis. Application fee: $45. Electronic applications accepted. *Expenses:* Tuition: Full-time $9,005. Required fees: $760. *Financial support:* Institutionally sponsored loans and scholarships/grants available. Financial award applicants required to submit FAFSA. *Unit head:* Dr. Brian Lindquist, Associate Vice President and Dean/Executive Director, 480-557-1221, E-mail: brian.lindquist@phoenix.edu. *Application contact:* Graduate Business Chair, 505-821-4800, Fax: 505-821-5551.

University of Phoenix—Northern Nevada Campus, College of Graduate Business and Management, Reno, NV 89511. Offers accounting (MBA); business and management (MBA); global management (MBA); human resources management (MBA, MM); management (MM); marketing (MBA); public administration (MBA, MM).

University of Phoenix–Northern Virginia Campus, College of Graduate Business and Management, Reston, VA 20190. Offers accounting (MBA); business administration (MBA); e-business (MBA); global management (MBA); human resources management (MBA, MM); management (MM); marketing (MBA); public administration (MBA).

University of Phoenix–North Florida Campus, John Sperling School of Business, College of Graduate Business and Management, Jacksonville, FL 32216-0959. Offers accounting (MBA); business administration (MBA); global management (MBA); human resources management (MBA, MM); management (MM); marketing (MBA); public administration (MBA). Evening/weekend programs available. *Faculty:* 40 full-time (15 women), 105 part-time/adjunct (25 women). *Students:* 392 full-time (237 women); includes 135 minority (117 African Americans, 1 American Indian/Alaska Native, 12 Asian Americans or Pacific Islanders, 5 Hispanic Americans), 20 international. Average age 31. In 2006, 134 degrees awarded. *Degree requirements:* For master's, thesis (for some programs), registration. *Entrance requirements:* For master's, minimum undergraduate GPA of 3.0, 3 years work experience. Additional exam requirements/recommendations for international students: Required—TOEFL (minimum score 550 paper-based; 213 computer-based; 79 iBT). *Application deadline:* Applications are processed on a rolling basis. Application fee: $45. Electronic applications accepted. *Financial support:* Institutionally sponsored loans available. Financial award applicants required to submit FAFSA. *Unit head:* Dr. Brian Lindquist, Associate Vice President and Dean/Executive Director, 480-557-1221, E-mail: brian.lindquist@phoenix.edu. *Application contact:* Chair, 904-636-6645, Fax: 904-636-0998.

University of Phoenix–Northwest Arkansas Campus, College of Graduate Business and Management, Rogers, AR 72756-9615. Offers accounting (MBA); business and management (MBA); global management (MBA); human resources management (MBA, MM); management (MM); marketing (MBA); public administration (MBA, MM).

University of Phoenix–Northwest Indiana, College of Graduate Business and Management, Merrillville, IN 46410. Offers business and management (MBA, MM); human resources management (MM); public administration (MBA, MM).

University of Phoenix–Oklahoma City Campus, John Sperling School of Business, College of Graduate Business and Management, Oklahoma City, OK 73116-8244. Offers business administration (MBA); business and management (MM); human resource management (MBA). Evening/weekend programs available. *Faculty:* 10 full-time (0 women), 135 part-time/adjunct (33 women). *Students:* 150 full-time (92 women); includes 45 minority (32 African Americans, 3 American Indian/Alaska Native, 4 Asian Americans or Pacific Islanders, 6 Hispanic Americans), 12 international. Average age 37. In 2006, 41 degrees awarded. *Degree requirements:* For master's, thesis (for some programs), registration. *Entrance requirements:* For master's, minimum undergraduate GPA of 3.0, 3 years of work experience. Additional exam requirements/recommendations for international students: Required—TOEFL (minimum score 550 paper-based; 213 computer-based; 79 iBT). *Application deadline:* Applications are processed on a rolling basis. Application fee: $45. Electronic applications accepted. *Expenses:* Tuition: Full-time $10,608. Required fees: $760. *Financial support:* Institutionally sponsored loans and scholarships/grants available. Financial award applicants required to submit FAFSA. *Unit head:* Dr. Brian Lindquist, Associate Vice President and Dean/Executive Director, 480-557-1221, E-mail: brian.lindquist@phoenix.edu. *Application contact:* Chair, 405-842-8007, Fax: 405-841-3386.

University of Phoenix–Omaha Campus, College of Graduate Business and Management, Omaha, NE 68154-5240. Offers accounting (MBA); business and management (MBA); global management (MBA); human resources management (MM); human resources managemetn (MBA); management (MM); marketing (MBA); public administration (MM); public adminstration (MBA).

University of Phoenix Online Campus, John Sperling School of Business, College of Graduate Business and Management, Phoenix, AZ 85034-7209. Offers accounting (MBA); administration (MBA); global management (MBA); human resources management (MBA); management (MM); marketing (MBA); public administration (MBA, MM). Evening/weekend programs available. *Faculty:* 25 full-time (15 women), 4,861 part-time/adjunct (1,504 women). *Students:* 17,914 full-time (10,655 women); includes 4,983 minority (3,259 African Americans, 113 American Indian/Alaska Native, 651 Asian Americans or Pacific Islanders, 960 Hispanic Americans), 1,805 international. Average age 36. In 2006, 1,740 master's awarded. *Degree requirements:* For master's, thesis (for some programs), registration. *Entrance requirements:* For master's, 3 years of work experience, minimum undergraduate GPA of 3.0. Additional exam requirements/recommendations for international students: Required—TOEFL (minimum score 550 paper-based; 213 computer-based; 79 iBT). *Application deadline:* Applications are processed on a rolling basis. Application fee: $45. Electronic applications accepted. *Expenses:* Tuition: Full-time $12,664. Required fees: $760. *Financial support:* Institutionally sponsored loans and scholarships/grants available. Financial award applicants required to submit FAFSA. *Unit head:* Brian Lindquist, Dean/Executive Director and Associate Vice President, 480-557-1221, E-mail: brian.lindquist@phoenix.edu. *Application contact:* Brian Lindquist, Dean/Executive Director and Associate Vice President, 480-557-1221, E-mail: brian.lindquist@phoenix.edu.

University of Phoenix–Oregon Campus, The John Sperling School of Business, College of Graduate Business and Management, Tigard, OR 97223. Offers accounting (MBA); business administration (MBA); global management (MBA); human resource management (MM); human resources management (MBA); management (MM). Evening/weekend programs available. *Faculty:* 28 full-time (4 women), 104 part-time/adjunct (24 women). *Students:* 241 full-time (103 women); includes 31 minority (7 African Americans, 4 American Indian/Alaska Native, 14 Asian Americans or Pacific Islanders, 6 Hispanic Americans), 21 international. Average age 39. In 2006, 66 degrees awarded. *Degree requirements:* For master's, thesis (for some programs), registration. *Entrance requirements:* For master's, minimum undergraduate GPA of 3.0, 3 years of work experience. Additional exam requirements/recommendations for international students: Required—TOEFL (minimum score 550 paper-based; 213 computer-based; 79 iBT). *Application deadline:* Applications are processed on a rolling basis. Application fee: $45. Electronic applications accepted. *Expenses:* Tuition: Full-time $10,200. Required fees: $760. *Financial support:* Institutionally sponsored loans and scholarships/grants available. Financial award applicants required to submit FAFSA. *Unit head:* Dr. Brian Lindquist, Associate Vice President and Dean/Executive Director, 480-557-1221, E-mail: brian.lindquist@phoenix.edu. *Application contact:* Chair, 503-403-2900, Fax: 503-670-0614.

University of Phoenix–Pittsburgh Campus, John Sperling School of Business, College of Graduate Business and Management, Pittsburgh, PA 15276. Offers accounting (MBA); business administration (MBA); global management (MBA); human resource management (MBA); human resources management (MM); management (MM); marketing (MBA); public administration (MBA, MM). Evening/weekend programs available. *Faculty:* 19 full-time (6 women), 49 part-time/adjunct (13 women). *Students:* 84 full-time (43 women); includes 16 minority (13 African Americans, 2 Asian Americans or Pacific Islanders, 1 Hispanic American), 4 international. Average age 37. In 2006, 35 degrees awarded. *Degree requirements:* For master's, thesis (for some programs), registration. *Entrance requirements:* For master's, minimum undergraduate GPA of 3.0, 3 years work experience. Additional exam requirements/recommendations for international students: Required—TOEFL (minimum score 550 paper-based; 213 computer-based; 79 iBT). *Application deadline:* Applications are processed on a rolling basis. Application fee: $45. Electronic applications accepted. *Expenses:* Tuition: Full-time $13,560. Required fees: $760. *Financial support:* Institutionally sponsored loans and scholarships/grants available. Financial award applicants required to submit FAFSA. *Unit head:* Dr. Brian Lindquist, Associate Vice President and Dean/Executive Director, 480-551-1221, E-mail: brian.lindquist@phoenix.edu. *Application contact:* College Chair, 412-747-9000, Fax: 412-747-0676.

University of Phoenix–Puerto Rico Campus, John Sperling School of Business, College of Graduate Business and Management, Guaynabo, PR 00968. Offers accounting (MBA); business administration (MBA); global management (MBA); human resource management (MBA); marketing (MBA). Evening/weekend programs available. *Faculty:* 19 full-time (8 women), 73 part-time/adjunct (25 women). *Students:* 1,122 full-time (671 women); includes 636 minority (2 African Americans, 3 American Indian/Alaska Native, 3 Asian Americans or Pacific Islanders, 628 Hispanic Americans), 31 international. Average age 34. In 2006, 281 degrees awarded. *Degree requirements:* For master's, thesis (for some programs), registration. *Entrance requirements:* For master's, minimum undergraduate GPA of 3.0, 3 years work experience. Additional exam requirements/recommendations for international students: Required—TOEFL (minimum score 550 paper-based; 213 computer-based; 79 iBT). *Application deadline:* Applications are processed on a rolling basis. Application fee: $45. Electronic applications accepted. *Expenses:* Tuition: Full-time $5,816. Required fees: $760. *Financial support:* Institutionally sponsored loans and scholarships/grants available. Financial award applicants required to submit FAFSA. *Unit head:* Dr. Brian Lindquist, Associate Vice President and Dean/Executive Director, 480-557-1221, E-mail: brian.lindquist@phoenix.edu. *Application contact:* Chair, 787-931-5400, Fax: 787-931-1510.

University of Phoenix–Renton Learning Center, College of Graduate Business and Management, Renton, WA 98005. Offers accounting (MBA); business and management (MBA, MM); global management (MBA); human resources management (MBA, MM); marketing (MBA); public administration (MBA, MM).

University of Phoenix–Richmond Campus, John Sperling School of Business, College of Graduate Business and Management, Richmond, VA 23230. Offers accounting (MBA); business administration (MBA); global management (MBA); human resources management (MBA, MM); management (MM); marketing (MBA); public administration (MBA, MM). Evening/weekend programs available. *Faculty:* 6 full-time (4 women), 60 part-time/adjunct (7 women). *Students:* 103 full-time (73 women); includes 42 minority (38 African Americans, 1 American Indian/Alaska Native, 2 Asian Americans or Pacific Islanders, 1 Hispanic American), 10 international. Average age 36. In 2006, 1 degree awarded. *Degree requirements:* For master's, thesis (for some programs), registration. *Entrance requirements:* For master's, minimum undergraduate GPA 3.0, 3 years work experience. Additional exam requirements/recommendations for international students: Required—TOEFL (minimum score 550 paper-based; 213 computer-based; 79 iBT). *Application deadline:* Applications are processed on a rolling basis. Application fee: $45. Electronic applications accepted. *Financial support:* Institutionally sponsored loans and scholarships/grants available. Financial award applicants required to submit FAFSA. *Unit head:* Dr. Brian Lindquist, Associate Vice President/Dean, 480-557-1221, E-mail: brian.lindquist@phoenix.edu. *Application contact:* Chair, 804-288-3390.

University of Phoenix–Sacramento Valley Campus, John Sperling School of Business, College of Graduate Business and Management, Sacramento, CA 95833-3632. Offers accounting (MBA); business administration (MBA); global management (MBA); human resources management (MBA); marketing (MBA); public administration (MBA). Evening/weekend programs available. *Faculty:* 36 full-time (19 women), 291 part-time/adjunct (83 women). *Students:* 395 full-time (197 women); includes 120 minority (62 African Americans, 2 American Indian/Alaska Native, 32 Asian Americans or Pacific Islanders, 24 Hispanic Americans), 34 international. Average age 37. In 2006, 138 master's awarded. *Degree requirements:* For master's, thesis (for some programs), registration. *Entrance requirements:* For master's, minimum undergraduate GPA of 3.0, 3 years work experience. Additional exam requirements/recommendations for international students: Required—TOEFL (minimum score 550 paper-based; 213 computer-based; 79 iBT). *Application deadline:* Applications are processed on a rolling basis. Application fee: $45. Electronic applications accepted. *Expenses:* Tuition: Full-time $12,024. Required fees: $760. *Financial support:* Institutionally sponsored loans and scholarships/grants available. Financial award applicants required to submit FAFSA. *Unit head:* Dr. Brian Lindquist, Associate Vice President and Dean/Executive Director, 480-557-1221, E-mail: brian.lindquist@phoenix.edu. *Application contact:* Campus College Chair, 916-923-2107, Fax: 916-923-3914.

University of Phoenix–San Antonio Campus, College of Graduate Business and Management, San Antonio, TX 78230. Offers accounting (MBA); business and management (MBA); e-business (MBA); global management (MBA); human resources management (MBA, MM); management (MM); marketing (MBA); public administration (MBA, MM).

University of Phoenix–Savannah Campus, College of Graduate Business and Management, Savannah, GA 31405-7400. Offers accounting (MBA); business administration (MBA); business and management (MM); global management (MBA); human resources management (MBA, MM); marketing (MBA); public administration (MBA, MM).

University of Phoenix–Southern California Campus, John Sperling School of Business, College of Graduate Business and Management, Costa Mesa, CA 92626. Offers accounting (MBA); business administration (MBA); business and management (MM); human resource management (MBA); marketing (MBA). Evening/weekend programs available. *Faculty:* 47 full-time (13 women), 513 part-time/adjunct (138 women). *Students:* 1,491 full-time (852 women); includes 558 minority (233 African Americans, 7 American Indian/Alaska Native, 124 Asian Americans or Pacific Islanders, 194 Hispanic Americans), 116 international. Average age 38. In 2006, 401 degrees awarded. *Degree requirements:* For master's, thesis (for some programs), registration. *Entrance requirements:* For master's, minimum undergraduate GPA of 3.0, 3 years work experience. Additional exam requirements/recommendations for international students: Required—TOEFL (minimum score 550 paper-based; 213 computer-based; 79 iBT). *Application deadline:* Applications are processed on a rolling basis. Application fee: $45. Electronic applications accepted. *Expenses:* Tuition: Full-time $13,512. Required fees: $760. *Financial support:* Institutionally sponsored loans and scholarships/grants available. Financial award applicants required to submit FAFSA. *Unit head:* Dr. Brian Lindquist, Associate Vice President and Dean/Executive Director, 480-557-1221, E-mail: brian.lindquist@phoenix.edu. *Application contact:* Campus College Chair, 714-378-1878, Fax: 714-378-5875.

University of Phoenix–Springfield Campus, College of Graduate Business and Management, Springfield, MO 65804-7211. Offers accounting (MBA); business and management (MBA); global management (MBA); human resources management (MBA, MM); management (MM); marketing (MBA); public administration (MBA, MM).

University of Phoenix–West Florida Campus, The John Sperling School of Business, College of Graduate Business and Management, Temple Terrace, FL 33637. Offers business administration (MBA); global management (MBA); human resource management (MBA); human resources management (MM); management (MM); marketing (MBA); public administration (MBA). Evening/weekend programs available. *Faculty:* 39 full-time (19 women), 145 part-time/adjunct (45 women). *Students:* 475 full-time (272 women); includes 150 minority (98 African Americans, 4 American Indian/Alaska Native, 9 Asian Americans or Pacific Islanders, 39 Hispanic Americans), 43 international. Average age 36. In 2006, 165 degrees awarded. *Degree requirements:* For master's, thesis (for some programs), registration. *Entrance requirements:* For master's, 3 years of work experience, minimum undergraduate GPA of 3.0. Additional exam requirements/recommendations for international students: Required—TOEFL (minimum score 550 paper-based; 213 computer-based; 79 iBT). *Application deadline:* Applications are processed on a rolling basis. Application fee: $45. Electronic applications accepted. *Expenses:* Tuition: Full-time $9,450. Required fees: $760. *Financial support:* Institutionally sponsored loans and scholarships/grants available. Financial award applicants required to submit FAFSA. *Unit head:* Dr. Brian Lindquist, Associate Vice President and Dean/Executive Director, 480-557-1221, E-mail: brian.lindquist@phoenix.edu. *Application contact:* Chair, 813-626-7911, Fax: 813-977-1449.

University of Phoenix–West Michigan Campus, The John Sperling School of Business, College of Graduate Business and Management, Walker, MI 49544. Offers accounting (MBA); business administration (MBA); global management (MBA); human resource management (MBA). Evening/weekend programs available. *Faculty:* 26 full-time (0 women), 95 part-time/adjunct (42 women). *Students:* 124 full-time (62 women); includes 16 minority (15 African Americans, 1 Hispanic American), 4 international. Average age 37. In 2006, 50 degrees awarded. *Degree requirements:* For master's, thesis (for some programs), registration. *Entrance requirements:* For master's, minimum undergraduate GPA of 3.0, 3 years work experience. Additional exam requirements/recommendations for international students: Required—TOEFL (minimum score 550 paper-based; 213 computer-based; 79 iBT). *Application deadline:* Applications are processed on a rolling basis. Application fee: $45. Electronic applications accepted. *Expenses:* Tuition: Full-time $12,043. Required fees: $760. *Financial support:* Institutionally sponsored loans and scholarships/grants available. Financial award applicants required to submit FAFSA. *Unit head:* Dr. Brian Lindquist, Associate Vice President and Dean/Executive Director, 480-557-1221, E-mail: brian.lindquist@phoenix.edu. *Application contact:* Chair, 888-345-9699, Fax: 616-784-5300.

University of Puerto Rico, Mayagüez Campus, Graduate Studies, College of Business Administration, Mayagüez, PR 00681-9000. Offers business administration (MBA); finance (MBA); human resources (MBA); industrial management (MBA). Part-time and evening/weekend programs available. *Faculty:* 52 full-time (30 women). *Students:* 32 full-time (15 women), 52 part-time (37 women); includes 73 minority (all Hispanic Americans), 11 international. 47 applicants, 70% accepted, 24 enrolled. In 2006, 13 degrees awarded. *Degree requirements:* For master's, comprehensive exam. *Entrance requirements:* For master's, GMAT or EXADEP, bachelor's degree with courses in calculus, microeconomics, accounting and statistics. Additional exam requirements/recommendations for international students: Required—TOEFL (minimum score 500 paper-based; 173 computer-based). *Application deadline:* For fall admission, 2/15 for domestic and international students; for spring admission, 9/15 for domestic and international students. Applications are processed on a rolling basis. Application fee: $25. *Expenses:* Tuition, nonresident: full-time $4,655. Required fees: $210. One-time fee: $77 full-time. Part-time tuition and fees vary according to course load and reciprocity agreements. *Financial support:* In 2006–07, 10 students received support, including fellowships (averaging $12,000 per year), 7 research assistantships (averaging $15,000 per year), 3 teaching assistantships (averaging $8,500 per year); Federal Work-Study and institutionally sponsored loans also available. *Faculty research:* Organizational studies, management, accounting. Total annual research expenditures: $264,836. *Unit head:* Prof. Eva Quinnnones, Dean, 787-265-3800, Fax: 787-832-5320, E-mail: quinones-e@rigel.uprm.edu. *Application contact:* Dr. Yolanda Ruiz, Director, 787-265-3887, Fax: 787-832-5320, E-mail: yruiz@caribe.net.

University of Regina, Faculty of Graduate Studies and Research, Kenneth Levene Graduate School of Business, Program in Human Resources Management, Regina, SK S4S 0A2, Canada. Offers MHRM, Master's Certificate. *Faculty:* 24 full-time (5 women), 3 part-time/adjunct (0 women). *Students:* 11 full-time (8 women), 24 part-time (13 women). 36 applicants, 83% accepted. In 2006, 9 degrees awarded. *Degree requirements:* For master's, project. *Entrance requirements:* For master's, 2 years of relevant work experience. Additional exam requirements/recommendations for international students: Required—TOEFL (minimum score 580 paper-based; 237 computer-based). *Application deadline:* Applications are processed on a rolling basis. Application fee: $60 ($100 for international students). Electronic applications accepted. *Expenses:* Contact institution. *Financial support:* Application deadline: 6/15. *Unit head:* Dr. Jack Ito, Professor, 306-585-4714, Fax: 306-585-4805, E-mail: jack.ito@uregina.ca.

University of Rhode Island, Graduate School, Labor Research Center, Kingston, RI 02881. Offers human resources (MS); labor relations (MS). Part-time and evening/weekend programs available. *Students:* Average age 32. In 2006, 4 degrees awarded. *Degree requirements:* For master's, core exams. *Entrance requirements:* For master's, GMAT, GRE, or MAT. *Application deadline:* For fall admission, 4/15 priority date for domestic students; for spring admission, 11/15 for domestic students. Applications are processed on a rolling basis. Application fee: $35. *Expenses:* Tuition, state resident: full-time $6,032; part-time $335 per credit. Tuition, nonresident: full-time $17,288; part-time $960 per credit. Required fees: $65 per credit. $30 per semester. One-time fee: $80 part-time. *Financial support:* Fellowships, research assistantships, teaching assistantships, career-related internships or fieldwork, Federal Work-Study, institutionally sponsored loans, and tuition waivers (full and partial) available. Support available to part-time students. *Unit head:* Dr. Richard Scholl, Director, 401-874-4347.

The University of Scranton, Graduate School, Department of Health Administration and Human Resources, Program in Human Resources Administration, Scranton, PA 18510. Offers human resources (MS); human resources development (MS); organizational leadership (MS). Part-time and evening/weekend programs available. *Students:* 3 full-time (all women), 19 part-time (12 women); includes 1 minority (African American) Average age 34. 21 applicants, 100% accepted. In 2006, 19 degrees awarded. *Degree requirements:* For master's, capstone experience. *Entrance requirements:* For master's, minimum GPA of 2.75. Additional exam requirements/recommendations for international students: Required—TOEFL (minimum score 500 paper-based; 173 computer-based), IELTS (minimum score 6). *Application deadline:* Applications are processed on a rolling basis. Application fee: $50. *Expenses:* Tuition: Part-time $684 per credit. Required fees: $25 per term. *Financial support:* Fellowships, teaching assistantships, career-related internships or fieldwork, Federal Work-Study, and unspecified assistantships available. Support available to part-time students. Financial award application deadline: 3/1. *Unit head:* Dr. Terri Freeman Smith, Director, 570-941-6218.

University of South Carolina, The Graduate School, The Darla Moore School of Business, Human Resources Program, Columbia, SC 29208. Offers MHR, JD/MHR. Part-time programs available. *Degree requirements:* For master's, internship, thesis optional. *Entrance requirements:* For master's, GMAT or GRE, minimum GPA of 3.0. Additional exam requirements/recommendations for international students: Required—TOEFL (minimum score 600 paper-based; 250 computer-based). Electronic applications accepted. *Faculty research:* Performance appraisal, work values, grievance systems, union formation, group behavior.

The University of Texas at Arlington, Graduate School, College of Business Administration, Department of Management, Arlington, TX 76019. Offers human resources (MSHRM). Part-time and evening/weekend programs available. *Faculty:* 11 full-time (2 women), 1 part-time/adjunct (0 women). *Students:* 24 full-time (13 women), 20 part-time (15 women); includes 11 minority (8 African Americans, 2 Asian Americans or Pacific Islanders, 1 Hispanic American), 10 international. 22 applicants, 77% accepted, 10 enrolled. In 2006, 5 degrees awarded. *Degree requirements:* For master's, thesis optional. *Entrance requirements:* For master's, GMAT. Additional exam requirements/recommendations for international students: Required—TOEFL (minimum score 550 paper-based; 213 computer-based). *Application deadline:* For fall admission, 6/15 priority date for domestic students. Applications are processed on a rolling basis. Application fee: $35 ($50 for international students). *Expenses:* Tuition, state resident: full-time $5,528. Tuition, nonresident: full-time $10,478. International tuition: $10,608 full-time. *Financial support:* In 2006–07, 4 fellowships (averaging $1,000 per year), 1 research assistantship (averaging $3,600 per year), 12 teaching assistantships (averaging $10,000 per year) were awarded; career-related internships or fieldwork, scholarships/grants, and unspecified assistantships also available. Support available to part-time students. Financial award application deadline: 6/1; financial award applicants required to submit FAFSA. *Faculty research:* Compensations, training, diversity, strategic human resources. *Unit head:* Dr. Jeffrey McGee, Chair, 817-272-3166, Fax: 817-272-3122, E-mail: jmcgee@uta.edu. *Application contact:* Rebecca Neilson, Graduate Advisor, 817-272-3166, Fax: 817-272-3122, E-mail: neilson@uta.edu.

University of the Sacred Heart, Graduate Programs, Department of Business Administration, Program in Human Resource Management, San Juan, PR 00914-0383. Offers MBA. Part-time and evening/weekend programs available. *Degree requirements:* For master's, thesis. *Entrance requirements:* For master's, EXADEP, minimum undergraduate GPA of 2.75, interview.

The University of Toledo, College of Graduate Studies, College of Business Administration, Department of Management, Program in Human Resource Management, Toledo, OH 43606-3390. Offers MBA. *Students:* 5 full-time (all women), 11 part-time (7 women); includes 2 minority (1 African American, 1 Hispanic American), 1 international. Average age 28. 10 applicants, 40% accepted, 2 enrolled. In 2006, 7 degrees awarded. *Entrance requirements:* For master's, GMAT. Application fee: $45. *Unit head:* David Chatfield, Chair, 419-530-2775, E-mail: david.chatfield@utoledo.edu. *Application contact:* Elissa Teal, Director, 419-530-2775, Fax: 419-530-7260, E-mail: elissa.teal@utoledo.edu.

University of Wisconsin–Madison, Graduate School, School of Business, Program in Management and Human Resources, Madison, WI 53706-1380. Offers international business (PhD); management and human resources (PhD). *Students:* 14 full-time (5 women); includes 2 minority (1 African American, 1 American Indian/Alaska Native), 6 international. Average age 35. 43 applicants, 5% accepted, 1 enrolled. In 2006, 3 degrees awarded. *Median time to degree:* Of those who began their doctoral program in fall 1998, 93% received their degree in 8 years or less. *Entrance requirements:* For doctorate, GMAT or GRE. Additional exam requirements/recommendations for international students: Required—TOEFL (minimum score 600 paper-based; 250 computer-based). *Application deadline:* For fall admission, 1/6 priority date for domestic and international students. Applications are processed on a rolling basis. Application fee: $45. Electronic applications accepted. *Financial support:* In 2006–07, fellowships with tuition reimbursements (averaging $16,110 per year), 4 research assistantships with full tuition reimbursements (averaging $13,502 per year), 10 teaching assistantships with full tuition reimbursements (averaging $13,686 per year) were awarded; Federal Work-Study, institutionally sponsored loans, scholarships/grants, health care benefits, and unspecified assistantships also available. Financial award application deadline: 1/6; financial award applicants required to submit FAFSA. *Faculty research:* Employee compensation, performance for work groups, small business management, venture financing, arts industry. *Unit head:* Dr. Randall Dunham, Chair, 608-265-2120, E-mail: rdunham@bus.wisc.edu. *Application contact:* Belle Heberling, PhD Coordinator, 608-262-3749, Fax: 608-890-0180, E-mail: phd@bus.wisc.edu.

University of Wisconsin–Madison, Graduate School, School of Business, Wisconsin Full-Time MBA Programs, Madison, WI 53706-1380. Offers applied corporate finance (MBA); applied security analysis (MBA); arts administration (MBA); brand and product management (MBA); entrepreneurial management (MBA); information systems (MBA); marketing research (MBA); operations and technology management (MBA); real estate (MBA); risk management and insurance (MBA); strategic human resource management (MBA); strategic management in the life and engineering sciences (MBA); supply chain management (MBA). *Faculty:* 84. *Students:* 231 full-time (74 women); includes 21 minority (10 African Americans, 5 Asian Americans or Pacific Islanders, 6 Hispanic Americans), 59 international. Average age 28. 405 applicants, 43% accepted, 121 enrolled. In 2006, 110 degrees awarded. *Entrance requirements:* For master's, GMAT, bachelors or equivalent degree, 2 years of work experience. Additional exam requirements/recommendations for international students: Required—TOEFL (minimum score 600 paper-based; 250 computer-based; 90 iBT). *Application deadline:* For fall admission, 11/1 for domestic and international students; for winter admission, 1/23 for domestic and international students; for spring admission, 3/26 for domestic and international students. Applications are processed on a rolling basis. Application fee: $45. Electronic applications accepted. *Financial support:* In 2006–07, 177 students received support, including 20 fellowships with full and partial tuition reimbursements available (averaging $16,566 per year), 105 research assistantships with full tuition reimbursements available (averaging $8,098 per year), 33 teaching assistantships with full tuition reimbursements available (averaging $10,112 per year); scholarships/grants, health care benefits, and unspecified assistantships also avail-

Human Resources Management

University of Wisconsin–Madison (continued)

able. *Unit head:* Gary Lessuise, Assistant Dean, Masters Programs, 608-265-5102, Fax: 608-265-4192, E-mail: glessuise@bus.wisc.edu. *Application contact:* Betsy Kacizak, Director of Admissions and Financial Aid—Full Time MBA, 608-262-4000, Fax: 608-265-4192, E-mail: mba@bus.wisc.edu.

University of Wisconsin–Whitewater, School of Graduate Studies, College of Business and Economics, Program in Business Administration, Whitewater, WI 53190-1790. Offers finance (MBA); human resource management (MBA); information technology management (MBA); international business (MBA); management (MBA); marketing (MBA); operations and supply chain management (MBA); technology and training (MBA). *Accreditation:* AACSB. Part-time and evening/weekend programs available. Postbaccalaureate distance learning degree programs offered (no on-campus study). *Students:* 67 full-time (26 women), 331 part-time (136 women); includes 71 minority (20 African Americans, 40 Asian Americans or Pacific Islanders, 11 Hispanic Americans). Average age 28. 167 applicants, 62% accepted, 75 enrolled. In 2006, 141 degrees awarded. *Degree requirements:* For master's, thesis or alternative. *Entrance requirements:* For master's, GMAT, minimum AACSB index of 1000, minimum GPA of 2.75. Additional exam requirements/recommendations for international students: Required—TOEFL (minimum score 550 paper-based; 213 computer-based). *Application deadline:* For fall admission, 7/15 for domestic students, 7/15 priority date for international students; for spring admission, 12/1 for domestic and international students. Applications are processed on a rolling basis. Application fee: $45. Electronic applications accepted. *Expenses:* Tuition, state resident: full-time $3,311. Tuition, nonresident: full-time $8,616. Required fees: $368 per credit. *Financial support:* In 2006–07, 11 research assistantships (averaging $7,385 per year) were awarded; Federal Work-Study, unspecified assistantships, and out of state fee waiver also available. Support available to part-time students. Financial award application deadline: 3/15; financial award applicants required to submit FAFSA. *Faculty research:* Interface between social institutions and individual behavior, technology and innovation management, occupational mental health, workplace deviance and workplace romance. *Unit head:* Dr. Donald Zahn, Associate Dean, 262-472-1945, Fax: 262-472-4863, E-mail: zahnd@uww.edu.

Upper Iowa University, Online Master's Programs, Fayette, IA 52142-1857. Offers accounting (MBA); corporate financial management (MBA); global business (MBA); health and human services (MPA); homeland security (MPA); human resources management (MBA); justice administration (MPA); organizational development (MPA); public personnel management (MPA); quality management (MBA). MBA also available at Madison, Wisconsin campus. Part-time and evening/weekend programs available. Postbaccalaureate distance learning degree programs offered (no on-campus study). *Degree requirements:* For master's, research project. *Entrance requirements:* For master's, GMAT, GRE, or minimum GPA of 2.7 during last 60 hours. Additional exam requirements/recommendations for international students: Required—TOEFL (minimum score 570 paper-based; 230 computer-based). Electronic applications accepted. *Faculty research:* Total quality management, CQI, teams, organization culture and climate, management.

Utah State University, School of Graduate Studies, College of Business, Program in Human Resource Management, Logan, UT 84322. Offers MS. Part-time and evening/weekend programs available. Postbaccalaureate distance learning degree programs offered. *Faculty:* 21 full-time (4 women). *Students:* 4 full-time (1 woman), 1 (woman) part-time, 1 international. 1 applicant, 0% accepted. In 2006, 41 degrees awarded. *Entrance requirements:* For master's, GMAT or GRE, minimum GPA of 3.0. Additional exam requirements/recommendations for international students: Required—TOEFL. *Application deadline:* For fall admission, 3/15 for domestic students; for spring admission, 10/15 for domestic students. Applications are processed on a rolling basis. Application fee: $50 ($60 for international students). Electronic applications accepted. *Expenses: Contact institution. Financial support:* Fellowships with partial tuition reimbursements, research assistantships with partial tuition reimbursements, career-related internships or fieldwork, Federal Work-Study, and tuition waivers (partial) available. Financial award application deadline: 4/1. *Faculty research:* International human resources, aging workforce. *Unit head:* Glenn McEvoy, Head, 435-797-2375, Fax: 435-797-2364, E-mail: glenn.mcevoy@usu.edu. *Application contact:* Mary Jo Blahna, Graduate Advisor, 435-797-3736, Fax: 435-797-1091, E-mail: mblahn@b202.usu.edu.

Wayland Baptist University, Graduate Programs, Programs in Business Administration/Management, Plainview, TX 79072-6998. Offers general business (MBA); health care administration (MBA); human resource management (MBA); international management (MBA); management (MA, MBA), including human resource management (MA), organization management (MA); management information systems (MBA). Part-time and evening/weekend programs available. Postbaccalaureate distance learning degree programs offered (no on-campus study). *Faculty:* 3 full-time (0 women). *Students:* 1 full-time (0 women), 7 part-time (2 women); includes 1 minority (Hispanic American) Average age 28. 1 applicant, 100% accepted, 1 enrolled. In 2006, 2 degrees awarded. *Degree requirements:* For master's, capstone course. *Entrance requirements:* For master's, GMAT, GRE or MAT. Additional exam requirements/recommendations for international students: Required—TOEFL (minimum score 500 paper-based; 173 computer-based). *Application deadline:* Applications are processed on a rolling basis. Application fee: $35. *Expenses:* Tuition: Full-time $6,120; part-time $340 per credit hour. Required fees: $50 per term. *Financial support:* Federal Work-Study, institutionally sponsored loans, and scholarships/grants available. Support available to part-time students. Financial award application deadline: 5/1; financial award applicants required to submit FAFSA. *Unit head:* Dr. Otto Schacht, Chairman, 806-291-1020, Fax: 806-291-1957.

Webster University, School of Business and Technology, Department of Business, St. Louis, MO 63119-3194. Offers business (MA); business and organizational security management (MBA); computer resources and information management (MBA); environmental management (MBA); finance (MA, MBA); health services management (MBA); human resources development (MBA); human resources management (MBA); international business (MA, MBA); management and leadership (MBA); marketing (MBA); procurement and acquisitions management (MBA); telecommunications management (MBA). Part-time and evening/weekend programs available. Postbaccalaureate distance learning degree programs offered (no on-campus study). *Students:* 1,205 full-time (629 women), 4,197 part-time (2,153 women); includes 2,005 minority (1,467 African Americans, 29 American Indian/Alaska Native, 212 Asian Americans or Pacific Islanders, 297 Hispanic Americans), 485 international. Average age 33. *Application deadline:* Applications are processed on a rolling basis. Application fee: $25 ($50 for international students). *Expenses:* Tuition: Full-time $8,820; part-time $490 per credit. Tuition and fees vary according to degree level, campus/location and program. *Financial support:* Federal Work-Study available. Support available to part-time students. Financial award application deadline: 4/1; financial award applicants required to submit FAFSA. *Unit head:* Bradford Scott, Chair, 314-961-2260 Ext. 7574, Fax: 314-968-7077, E-mail: buschair@webster.edu. *Application contact:* Director of Graduate and Evening Student Admissions, Fax: 314-968-7116, E-mail: gadmit@webster.edu.

Webster University, School of Business and Technology, Department of Management, St. Louis, MO 63119-3194. Offers business and organizational security management (MA); computer resources and information management (MA); environmental management (MS); health care management (MA); health services management (MA); human resources development (MA); human resources management (MA); management (DM); management and leadership (MA); marketing (MA); procurement and acquisitions management (MA); public administration (MA); quality management (MA); space systems operations management (MS); telecommunications management (MA). Part-time and evening/weekend programs available. Postbaccalaureate distance learning degree programs offered (no on-campus study). *Students:* 1,396 full-time (746 women), 4,727 part-time (2,579 women); includes 3,065 minority (2,374 African Americans, 45 American Indian/Alaska Native, 158 Asian Americans or Pacific Islanders, 488 Hispanic Americans), 128 international. Average age 37. In 2006, 9 degrees awarded. *Degree requirements:* For doctorate, thesis/dissertation, written exam. *Entrance requirements:* For doctorate, GMAT, 3 years of work experience, MBA. *Application deadline:* Applications are processed on a rolling basis. Application fee: $25 ($50 for international students). *Expenses:* Tuition: Full-time $8,820; part-time $490 per credit. Tuition and fees vary according to degree level, campus/location and program. *Financial support:* Federal Work-Study available. Support available to part-time students. Financial award application deadline: 4/1; financial award applicants required to submit FAFSA. *Unit head:* Jeffrey Haldeman, Chair, 314-961-2660 Ext. 7552, Fax: 314-968-7077, E-mail: mgtchair@webster.edu. *Application contact:* Director of Graduate and Evening Student Admissions, Fax: 314-968-7116, E-mail: gadmit@webster.edu.

Widener University, School of Business Administration, Program in Human Resource Management, Chester, PA 19013-5792. Offers MHR, MS, Psy D/MHR. Part-time and evening/weekend programs available. *Entrance requirements:* For master's, GMAT, GRE, or MAT, minimum GPA of 2.5. Electronic applications accepted. *Faculty research:* Training and development, collective bargaining and arbitration, business communication.

Wilkes University, Graduate Studies and Continued Learning, Jay S. Sidhu School of Business and Leadership, Wilkes-Barre, PA 18766-0002. Offers accounting (MBA); entrepreneurship (MBA); finance (MBA); human resource management (MBA); international business (MBA); management (MBA); marketing (MBA). *Accreditation:* ACBSP. Part-time and evening/weekend programs available. *Students:* 30 full-time (16 women), 149 part-time (73 women); includes 5 minority (1 African American, 2 Asian Americans or Pacific Islanders, 2 Hispanic Americans), 4 international. Average age 30. In 2006, 48 degrees awarded. *Entrance requirements:* For master's, GMAT. Additional exam requirements/recommendations for international students: Required—TOEFL (minimum score 500 paper-based; 173 computer-based). *Application deadline:* Applications are processed on a rolling basis. Application fee: $40. *Expenses: Contact institution. Financial support:* Federal Work-Study and unspecified assistantships available. Financial award application deadline: 3/1; financial award applicants required to submit FAFSA. *Unit head:* Dr. Paul Browne, Dean, 570-408-4701, Fax: 570-408-4700, E-mail: paul.browne@wilkes.edu. *Application contact:* Kathleen Houlihan, Director of Graduate Studies, 570-408-3235, Fax: 570-408-7846, E-mail: kathleen.houlihan@wilkes.edu.

Wilmington College, Division of Business, New Castle, DE 19720-6491. Offers business administration (MBA); finance (MBA); health care administration (MBA, MS); human resource management (MS); management (MS); management information systems (MBA); organizational leadership (MS); public administration (MS); transportation and logistics (MBA, MS). Part-time and evening/weekend programs available. *Faculty:* 3 full-time (0 women). *Students:* 230 full-time (138 women), 432 part-time (274 women); includes 109 minority (98 African Americans, 1 American Indian/Alaska Native, 3 Asian Americans or Pacific Islanders, 7 Hispanic Americans). Average age 34. 229 applicants, 100% accepted, 156 enrolled. In 2006, 273 degrees awarded. *Entrance requirements:* Additional exam requirements/recommendations for international students: Required—TOEFL (minimum score 500 paper-based; 173 computer-based). *Application deadline:* Applications are processed on a rolling basis. Application fee: $25. *Financial support:* Applicants required to submit FAFSA. *Unit head:* Dr. Robert Edelson, Chair, 302-295-1147, Fax: 302-328-7021, E-mail: robert.e.edelson@wilmcoll.edu. *Application contact:* Chris Ferguson, Director of Admissions and Financial Aid, 302-328-9407 Ext. 256, Fax: 302-328-5164, E-mail: inquire@wilmcoll.edu.

York University, Faculty of Graduate Studies, Atkinson Faculty of Liberal and Professional Studies, Program in Human Resources Management, Toronto, ON M3J 1P3, Canada. Offers MHRM, PhD. Part-time programs available. *Faculty:* 18 full-time (6 women). *Students:* 136 applicants, 26% accepted, 35 enrolled. *Degree requirements:* For master's, thesis or alternative, registration. *Entrance requirements:* Additional exam requirements/recommendations for international students: Required—TOEFL (minimum score 600 paper-based; 250 computer-based). Application fee: $80. Electronic applications accepted. *Financial support:* In 2006–07, 4 fellowships (averaging $1,437 per year), 1 research assistantship (averaging $3,873 per year), 1 teaching assistantship (averaging $2,804 per year) were awarded. *Unit head:* Ken McBerg, Director, 416-736-2100 Ext. 33390.

CLEMSON UNIVERSITY

Master of Human Resource Development

Program of Study

The human resource field is a specialized blend of education, systems design, consulting, psychology, management, and sociology. The Master of Human Resource Development (M.H.R.D.) degree is designed to prepare training directors, human performance improvement (HPI) specialists, and consultants to work in business, industry, nonprofit, and the government.

HRD/HPI specialists commonly provide diagnostic and intervention strategies related to the areas of technical and interpersonal skills, management, human and organizational performance, and motivation. The Human Resource Development (HRD) Program is designed to involve and enhance human performance in the workplace. The program serves professionals working in the areas of service, manufacturing, construction, health occupations, graphic communications, transportation, loss control, quality control, information services, and personnel management.

The program is designed for professionals with three or more years of experience and is delivered in an interactive online format. The curriculum consists of twelve courses delivered over a two-year period in a cohort setting.

Financial Aid

The Federal Stafford Loan is the only form of federal aid available to graduate students through Clemson University's Financial Aid Office. For additional information on graduate financial aid, students should visit http://virtual.clemson.edu/groups/finaid/graduate.htm.

Cost of Study

Tuition for 2007–08 is $3641 per semester for in-state students and $7285 per semester for nonresidents. Off-campus rates are $330 per hour for in-state students and $660 per hour for nonresidents. Graduate assistants pay a flat fee of $950 per semester. Graduate fellows pay South Carolina resident fees.

Student Group

Of the students currently in the program, 57 percent are women, 70 percent are part-time students, and 97 percent are from the United States.

Student Outcomes

Graduates of the program are capable of utilizing contemporary instructional and human performance technologies and methodologies. Program participants gain valuable skills and knowledge that accelerate their careers.

Location

Clemson is a small, beautiful college town near the Blue Ridge Mountains and Lake Hartwell in upstate South Carolina. The Upstate is one of the country's fastest-growing areas and is the midpoint of the Charlotte-to-Atlanta I-85 corridor that runs from metro Atlanta to Richmond, Virginia, and encompasses Charlotte, North Carolina, and North Carolina's Research Triangle. Atlanta and Charlotte are each a 2-hour's drive away. Many financial institutions and other industries have national headquarters for a major presence in the Upstate, including Wachovia, Bank of America, BMW, Bon Secours St. Francis Health System, Bosch North America, Bowater, Charter Communications, Ernst and Young, Fluor Corporation, IBM, Microsoft, Michelin of North America, and many others.

The University

Clemson is classified by the Carnegie Foundation as an RU/H: Research University (high research activity), a category comprising just 10 percent of all graduate degree-granting universities in America. The University's mission is to fulfill the covenant between its founder and the people of South Carolina to establish a "high seminary of learning" through its responsibilities of teaching, research, and extended public service. The University has identified eight areas of academic emphasis that create collaborations that, in turn, help fulfill the University's mission.

Applying

Applicants may apply on the Web at http://www.grad.clemson.edu/p_apply.html. Applications with a $50 nonrefundable fee should be received no later than July 1. Every required item in support of the application must be on file by that date. Application packets are also available from the Graduate Admissions office.

Applicants should have a baccalaureate degree, with a preferred minimum GPA of 3.0. Applications must include a letter describing professional goals and two letters of reference. Applicants with less than five years of progressively responsible management/HRD experience must submit GRE scores. Applicants who possess five or more years of progressively responsible management/HRD experience may request a waiver or submit previously taken GRE scores older than two years.

Applicants must complete the online Keirsey™ Temperament Sorter®-II and Campbell™ Interest and Skill Survey®. Students should use the promotion code (CLEMS0323) to have their scores for both tests sent to the M.H.R.D. admissions committee at Clemson University. A nominal fee is charged for these tests. For more information, prospective students should visit the Web site at http://www.keirseycampbell.com/payment.html.

Correspondence and Information

David S. Fleming, Ph.D.
Graduate Coordinator
Eugene T. Moore School of Education
G-01 Tillman Hall
Clemson University
Clemson, South Carolina 29634-0702
Phone: 864-656-1881
Fax: 864-656-0311
E-mail: dflemin@clemson.edu
Web site: http://www.hehd.clemson.edu/schoolofed/g-hrd.htm

Clemson University

THE FACULTY AND THEIR RESEARCH

John R. Duncan, Assistant Professor; Ph.D., Illinois. Human Resource Development/Human Performance Improvement.

Clinton H. Isbell, Professor; Ed.D., Texas A&M, 1980. Industrial education.

Philip H. McGee, Assistant Professor and Program Coordinator; Ed.D., Indiana, 1978. Human Resource Development/Human Performance Improvement.

NEW YORK UNIVERSITY

School of Continuing and Professional Studies
Master of Science in Human Resource Management and Development

Programs of Study

The School of Continuing and Professional Studies at New York University (NYU) offers a Master of Science (M.S.) program in human resource management and development and graduate certificates in benefits and compensation, human resource management, and organizational and executive coaching. The M.S. program in human resource management and development has been created to fill the professional and academic gaps that exist today in the field of human resource management. The role of the human resource (HR) professional is evolving from one essentially based in transactions and services to one that is more strategically oriented. While HR professionals continue in the traditional functions of recruiting and hiring new employees, overseeing compensation and benefits, improving employee relations, and ensuring compliance with labor laws, they are also expected to be key contributors to the business strategy of the organization. That is why the cornerstone of the M.S. program in human resource management and development is strategy, which is integrated into every course and project. At its core, the program reinforces the philosophy that the most successful human resource professionals know how to create sustainable competitive advantage through people.

The graduate certificates are designed for two kinds of students: those who have earned a bachelor's degree and are interested in pursuing further graduate study, but without yet committing to a master's program, and those who hold a graduate degree but seek education in a career area or specialization within the human resources industry.

NYU faculty members are among the finest in academia—distinguished and expert practitioners in human resource management and development. They have excellent academic credentials and extensive practical expertise, and in many instances, they have significant experience teaching in graduate programs at other universities in the tristate area. They include current and former senior executives in human resource management, organizational development, training and facilitation, organizational behavior, coaching, and human capital strategies.

The 42-credit master's degree program can be completed part-time or full-time. The program consists of three phases: a required core course of study, four courses from one concentration and an elective course from another concentration, and the capstone project. Students choose from three concentrations: human resource development, human resource management, and organizational effectiveness. The curriculum for the M.S. program in human resource management and development is continually reevaluated and updated in response to industry needs to provide the most up-to-date and relevant course of study.

Research Facilities

The Elmer Holmes Bobst Library and Study Center, one of the largest open-stack research libraries in the world, houses more than 3 million of NYU's nearly 4.4 million volumes. In addition to books, journals, and other print materials, the library provides access to many nonprint resources. These include microforms, databases, and other electronic resources that students can connect to from their home or residence hall; extensive video and audio collections; and a variety of computer equipment and software programs.

NYU's central source for computing, information, network, and telecommunications services is Information Technology Services (ITS). ITS maintains four large, modern computer labs with high-end Macintosh and Windows computers, laser printers, multimedia equipment, and a wide variety of up-to-date software. The Client Services division of ITS provides comprehensive help with the materials and equipment available to students, online, in person, and via telephone and e-mail.

Financial Aid

There are many financial aid options to consider, including fellowships and low-interest educational loans. NYU's centralized Office of Financial Aid assists students with loan packages, scholarships, and the NYU monthly payment plan, which enables students to spread out their tuition payments. Department scholarships are also available. For more information, students should visit http://www.nyu.edu/financial.aid.

Cost of Study

Tuition for part-time students for the 2007–08 academic year is $1266 per credit plus fees. For full-time students (10–12 credits per semester), the cost of tuition and related fees is $12,664 per semester. Fees vary somewhat by program. The Board of Trustees of New York University reserves the right to alter these costs without notice.

Living and Housing Costs

Graduate student housing is available on the University campus and is administered through the Office of Housing and Residence Life. However, students may choose to live off campus. NYU's Off-Campus Housing Office (OCHO) offers assistance to members of the NYU community in their search for non-University housing options. OCHO provides, exclusively to NYU students, listings of available locations for rent through private landlords, property managers, brokers, and real estate agents. Updated daily, these listings are accessible through OCHO's computer terminals or online for members of the NYU community.

Student Group

In 2006–07, there were 91 students enrolled in the Master of Science program in human resource management and development. Part-time students accounted for 84 percent of those enrolled, and 81 percent of the students were women.

Location

The School of Continuing and Professional Studies' graduate programs in human resource management and development are housed at NYU's Midtown Center at 11 West 42nd Street, in the heart of Manhattan. Students who are interested in HR or in HR issues that are industry specific (such as health care, government, nonprofit, real estate, publishing, or marketing) find New York City to be a laboratory offering unparalleled experiences to help build their professional relationships.

The University, The School, and The Program

NYU is a private university composed of fourteen schools and colleges. The University was founded in 1831, and the School of Continuing and Professional Studies was founded in 1934. The Graduate Programs in Human Resource Management and Development were established in 2005.

Applying

Students may apply for fall or spring admission. Factors that are considered in evaluating an applicant include official transcripts of academic achievement in previous undergraduate and graduate course work, scores from the GRE or GMAT, TOEFL score (for international students whose native language is not English), the nature and extent of previous work experience, professional recommendations, and a statement of purpose.

Correspondence and Information

For more information and an application package, students should contact:

Office of Admissions
Graduate Programs in Human Resource Management and Development
New York University
145 Fourth Avenue, Room 219
New York, New York 10003

Phone: 212-998-7200 Ext. 727
Fax: 212-995-4674
E-mail: scps.gradadmissions@nyu.edu
Web site: http://www.scps.nyu.edu/727

New York University

THE ADMINISTRATION

Robert S. Lapiner, Ph.D., Dean, School of Continuing and Professional Studies.

Anthony R. Davidson, Ph.D., EDP; Divisional Dean, Director, and Clinical Professor, Division of Programs in Business, School of Continuing and Professional Studies.

Dennis Garritan, Ph.D., Academic Chair and Clinical Associate Professor, Graduate Programs in Human Resource Management and Development, Division of Programs in Business, School of Continuing and Professional Studies.

RUTGERS, THE STATE UNIVERSITY OF NEW JERSEY, NEW BRUNSWICK

Graduate Programs in Human Resource Management, Labor and Employment Relations

Programs of Study

The School of Management and Labor Relations (SMLR) offers a Ph.D. in industrial relations and human resources (IRHR), a Master of Human Resources Management (M.H.R.M.), and a Master of Labor and Employment Relations (M.L.E.R.).

The Ph.D. program is designed to prepare students for research careers in colleges, universities, and other relevant institutions. It normally consists of 48 credit hours of course work, 6 hours of master's thesis credits, and 18 credit hours of dissertation study. All students take two Ph.D. seminars, three courses to fulfill their interdisciplinary distributional requirements, a minimum of three statistics and research methods courses, and the Pro-Seminar. Most Ph.D. students are full-time but it is possible for an individual who is interested in a research career to pursue the degree on a less than full-time basis.

The M.H.R.M. degree, which requires 48 credits of course work, focuses on the strategic role of HRM in shaping and supporting the organization's business plan. It is a professional program integrating theory and practice, training students to become internal consultants and business partners. Students are accepted into the program on a full-time or part-time basis, and courses are scheduled in the late afternoon and evening for the convenience of working adults. The proximity of a wide variety of the nation's leading businesses provides excellent opportunities for internships, research, and eventual job placement. The program is also offered off-site at firms such as AT&T. The M.H.R.M. program offers a one-year option to high-level HR managers or professionals who meet the program's criteria.

The M.L.E.R. program, which requires 39 credits of course work, affords students the opportunity to explore the causes and consequences of changes in employment relations as well as to develop the professional skills necessary to function in their chosen fields. The program combines professional education in labor relations, organizational change, and employee diversity with a broad approach to the study of work and work-related issues. Students prepare to pursue careers in labor organizations, in labor relations for private and public-sector employers, or in government agencies that regulate employment.

Research Facilities

The School of Management and Labor Relations conducts programs of graduate instruction, research, and continuing professional education for both management and labor to further their understanding of human resources management, the process of labor relations, and public employment and training policy.

SMLR has a specialized library within the 3-million-volume University library system. The SMLR library provides access to leading journals, reporting services, and databases in industrial relations and human resources. Graduate students have access to the Rutgers Center for Computer and Information Services, which contains some of the most powerful and innovative computer equipment in the country. Students are encouraged to develop computer skills through courses that rely heavily on the computer and its application to human resource issues.

Financial Aid

Research and teaching assistantships are available on a competitive basis. There are also opportunities for paid employment and paid or unpaid internships in the New Jersey–New York–Pennsylvania area. Work-study programs and Federal Stafford Student Loans are offered by the Financial Aid Office. The University offers Graduate Scholar Awards, Garden State Fellowships, and Ralph J. Bunche Fellowships.

Cost of Study

State residents pursuing graduate full-time study without financial assistance from the University paid tuition and student fees totaling $13,399 for the 2005–06 academic year. Nonresidents and international students paid $19,643.80.

Living and Housing Costs

Dormitory housing for the 2005–06 academic year ranged from $5390 to $7196. A full meal plan for the academic year cost $3460. Off-campus housing is generally more costly.

Student Group

One to 4 students are admitted to the Ph.D. program each fall, about 150 students are enrolled in the M.H.R.M. program, and 90 are enrolled in the M.L.E.R. program. Two thirds are women. The average age is 31. Within the M.H.R.M. program, approximately 26 percent of the student population is diverse.

Student Outcomes

Because the programs provide students with a broad theoretical foundation and an impressive array of professional skills, graduates have consistently obtained excellent positions in a variety of organizations. Recent placements of IRHR doctoral students include the University of Illinois, Simon Fraser University, and Meredith College, among many others. Recent placements of SMLR master's students include IBM, Bristol-Myers Squibb, GE, Anheuser-Busch, Wyeth, L'Oreal, Johnson & Johnson, Chevron, Lockheed, American Express, Merck, Tyco, Ford, CWA, SEIU, and the National Labor Relations Board.

Location

New Brunswick, with a population of about 42,000, is located in central New Jersey at Exit 9 of the New Jersey Turnpike and along the New York–Philadelphia railroad line. It is approximately 35 miles from New York City. To the south lie Princeton, 16 miles away; Philadelphia, about 60 miles; and Washington, D.C., under 200 miles. The many educational, cultural, and recreational resources of the New York–Philadelphia region are easily accessible to the interested student, and Rutgers attracts many distinguished visitors, lecturers, and performing artists not always available to less favorably situated institutions.

The University

As a university strongly committed to graduate education and research, Rutgers, The State University of New Jersey, provides graduate programs of exceptional academic quality taught by a distinguished faculty. Chartered in 1766, Rutgers is now one of the nation's largest state university systems; enrollment at the New Brunswick, Newark, and Camden campuses is approximately 48,000 students.

Applying

The M.H.R.M. program is also offered at off-campus locations. For example, the program was recently extended to Jersey City, New Jersey, to attract more New Jersey and New York City HR leaders.

The M.H.R.M. and M.L.E.R. program application deadlines are February 1 for the summer session; March 1 (M.H.R.M.) and July 1 (M.L.E.R.) for the fall semester; and October 1 (M.H.R.M.) and December 1 (M.L.E.R.) for the spring semester. International students applying from abroad must submit application materials by July 1 for spring term and February 1 for fall term admission. The Ph.D. program deadline is February 1 for fall admission. The Graduate Record Examinations (GRE) General Test is required for the M.L.E.R. program unless the applicant's bachelor's degree is more than five years old. The GRE General Test or the Graduate Management Admissions Test is required for the M.H.R.M. program. The M.H.R.M. and M.L.E.R. programs have a rolling admission policy. Admission decisions are made by judgment, not formula, but successful applicants are expected to achieve competitive grades and scores and provide letters of recommendation that indicate potential for graduate study.

Correspondence and Information

Director
Graduate Programs in HRM and IRHR
Janice H. Levin Building
Rutgers, The State University of New Jersey
94 Rockafeller Road, Room 216
New Brunswick, New Jersey 08903
Phone: 732-445-5973
E-mail: mhrm@rci.rutgers.edu (master's)
　　　irhrphd@rci.rutgers.edu (Ph.D.)
Web site: http://www.smlr.rutgers.edu

Director
Graduate Program in Labor and Employment Relations
Labor Education Center
Rutgers, The State University of New Jersey
50 Labor Center Way
New Brunswick, New Jersey 08903
Phone: 732-932-8559
E-mail: mlirls@rci.rutgers.edu

Rutgers, The State University of New Jersey, New Brunswick

THE FACULTY

John R. Aiello, Ph.D., Michigan State.
Clayton P. Alderfer, Ph.D., Yale.
Robert C. Angelo, Ed.D. (educational policy), Rutgers.
Eileen Appelbaum, Ph.D. (economics), Pennsylvania.
Richard W. Beatty, Ph.D. (organizational behavior), Washington (St. Louis).
David Bensman, Director, Credit Programs in LSER; Ph.D. (history), Columbia.
Joseph R. Blasi, Ed.D. (sociology of organizations), Harvard.
Paula Caligiuri, Ph.D. (industrial/organizational psychology), Penn State.
Cary Cherniss, Ph.D., Yale.
Dorothy Sue Cobble, Ph.D. (history), Stanford.
Niki T. Dickerson, Ph.D. (sociology), Michigan.
Steven M. Director, Associate Dean; Ph.D. (management), Northwestern.
Adrienne Eaton, Director, Labor Extension; Ph.D. (industrial relations), Wisconsin.
Charles H. Fay, Chair, H.R.M.; Ph.D. (management and organization behavior), Washington (Seattle).
David Ferio, Director, M.H.R.M.; M.S. candidate, Stevens.
Janice Fine, Ph.D. (American politics, public policy, political economy), MIT.
David L. Finegold, Dean; D.Phil., Political Science, Oxford.
Constance Finlay, Director, James Carey Library; M.A. (library and information science), Chicago.
Stanley M. Gully, Ph.D. (industrial/organizational psychology), Michigan State.
Charles Heckscher, Ph.D. (sociology), Harvard.
Mark A. Huselid, Ph.D. (human resource management), SUNY at Buffalo.
Susan E. Jackson, Director, Ph.D. Program; Ph.D. (organizational and social psychology), Berkeley.
Jeffrey H. Keefe, Ph.D. (economics), Claremont.
Mark R. Killingsworth, D. Phil. (labor and human resources, discrimination), Oxford.
Douglas Kruse, Ph.D. (economics), Harvard.
Barbara A. Lee, Ph.D. (higher education administration), Ohio State; J.D., Georgetown.
David Lepak, Ph.D. (human resource management), Penn State.
Hui Liao, Ph.D. (human resources and industrial relations), Minnesota, Twin Cities.
Claudia G. Meer, Ed.D. (adult education), Rutgers.
Jean M. Phillips, Ph.D. (business management and organizational behavior), Michigan State.
William Rodgers III, Ph.D. (economics), Harvard.
Saul Rubinstein, Ph.D. (industrial relations and management), MIT; M.B.A., Ed.M., Harvard.
Randall S. Schuler, Ph.D. (organizational strategy and human resource management), Michigan State.
Lisa Schur, J.D., Northeastern; Ph.D. (labor law and employment law, work and disability), Berkeley.
James C. Sesil, Ph.D. (industrial relations and human resource management), London School of Economics.
Charles G. Tharp, Ph.D. (labor and industrial relations), Michigan State.
Carl Edward Van Horn, Ph.D., Ohio State.
Paula B. Voos, Chair, LSER; Ph.D. (economics), Harvard.
John D. Worrall, Ph.D., Rutgers.

SAINT JOSEPH'S UNIVERSITY

Master of Science in Human Resource Management

Program of Study

The Master of Science in Human Resource Management (M.S.H.R.M.) program is a specialized program designed to equip students with an advanced level of technical expertise in human resource management and the critical business and personal skills to make a positive impact on their organizations' effectiveness in diverse, dynamic, and increasingly competitive global environments. The program is appropriate for both human resource professionals seeking to deepen or supplement their skills, as well as individuals preparing for a career as a human resources generalist or in a specialized area of the field.

The M.S.H.R.M. program at Saint Joseph's University is consistent with leading-edge practice within the field of human resources and is designed to equip students with the ability to be a strategic partner with others in the organization, requiring the human resource manager to have a clear understanding of the organization's mission and strategy as well as an understanding of basic business practices; technical competence in the human resource function, which includes such areas as employee selection, compensation, legal requirements, pension, benefits, and employee/labor relations; competence in organization development technologies, requiring practical knowledge and ability in team building, organization design, negotiation, and reengineering as well as the ability to understand and implement emerging change methods and management technologies; and the ability to help an organization manage change effectively, requiring the human resource professional to have vision and leadership skills to move organizations in positive directions.

Students in the M.S.H.R.M. program are exposed to the latest applications and theories to add value to their organizations through their greatest asset, their people. The M.S.H.R.M. program combines the concepts of management, ethics, finance, and law with traditional human resource functional content (e.g., compensation, staffing, negotiation, and organizational development) and culminates with the capstone business policy course. The goal of the M.S.H.R.M. program is to enhance students' abilities to perform as strategic partners with their business colleagues in the traditional business disciplines of finance, marketing, and accounting. A broad array of electives allows students to develop expertise in specific areas of human resources, such as compensation or labor relations. Students may also take elective courses in the University's other graduate programs (e.g., health administration, psychology, education, and public safety and environmental policy).

Research Facilities

Saint Joseph's University opened its newest building, Mandeville Hall, in 1998. This technologically advanced, $25-million building is a three-story, 89,000-square-foot facility that houses the Erivan K. Haub School of Business, the Center for Food Marketing Research, and the Academy of Food Marketing. Included in the building are classrooms, a lecture hall, seminar rooms, research facilities, computer labs, a 180-seat teletorium equipped for teleconferencing (with a translation booth for international presentations), faculty and administrative offices, and informational gathering spaces. Many of the teaching areas are highly innovative in concept and are equipped with interactive communication multimedia technology, which greatly enhances pedagogical possibilities.

One of the most innovative concepts consists of a suite of classrooms that includes two moot board rooms, a preparation seminar room, a video room, and meeting breakout rooms. These rooms are modeled after the moot court concept in law schools. They accommodate the teachings of real-world situations through dramatizations and analysis of interactive business negotiations. They are equipped with stepped, semicircular seating that surrounds a boardroom table. Video cameras are available to record sessions for later replay or for simultaneous projection to the teletorium or off-site locations around the globe.

The Francis A. Drexel Library contains a business collection of approximately 350,000 bound volumes, 1,400 periodical subscriptions, 840,500 microforms, more than 2,750 videos, and Fortune 500 annual reports. The business print collection also contains nearly half of the Harvard Core, a list of more than 3,500 books recommended by the Harvard Business School, and it serves as a selective depository for U.S. government documents. The library has an online public-access catalog for searching its holdings and the holdings of other university libraries. The catalog is accessible from remote locations via the University's academic computer. There are 100 computer terminals available to Saint Joseph's students, and many online services are available to M.B.A. students. The Instructional Media Center (IMC) at Saint Joseph's University offers students assistance with presentation materials. The IMC has nearly 1,200 videotapes, which can be viewed in the IMC or signed out if needed as part of a presentation.

Services at the Career Development Center include individual career counseling, job search advising, access to alumni contact lists, and the career resource library, which contains occupational information, employer literature/directories, and current employment listings. Workshops are offered on resume writing, interviewing, and job search techniques. Graduating students can also participate in on-campus recruiting. In addition, job search assistance is available in the form of a resume referral program.

Financial Aid

Through guaranteed loan agreements with lending institutions and state agencies such as the Pennsylvania Higher Education Assistance Agency (PHEAA) and the New Jersey Department of Higher Education, students can secure long-term loans at a low interest rate. The University initiates an electronic loan application and forwards it to its guarantor, the PHEAA. Stafford loans can be subsidized or unsubsidized. A student may borrow up to $18,500 per academic year. All full- or half-time students (at least 6 credits per semester) are eligible to apply for federal aid. Students may elect to finance part of their tuition through a deferred-payment program offered by the University.

Cost of Study

Tuition and fees for the 2007–08 academic year are $765 per credit hour.

Living and Housing Costs

Off-campus apartments are available within walking distance of both the campus and the local train station.

Student Group

The Master of Science in Human Resource Management degree has been in place since 2001. Many students in this program are currently human resource professionals looking for an advanced degree to take their careers to the next level. There are some career changers and students who have joined the program just after completing their undergraduate studies. Students in this program hold a wide array of undergraduate degrees from business to sociology, psychology, and education.

Location

Saint Joseph's University is located in eastern Pennsylvania in the suburbs of Philadelphia, only 15 minutes from downtown Center City. An off-campus site at Ursinus College in Collegeville, Pennsylvania, is available for Saint Joseph's M.B.A. students residing or employed in the northern part of the greater Delaware Valley.

The University

Founded by the Society of Jesus in 1851, Saint Joseph's University advances the professional and personal ambitions of men and women by providing a demanding, yet supportive, educational experience. One of only 142 schools with a Phi Beta Kappa chapter and AACSB business school accreditation, Saint Joseph's is home to 3,900 full-time undergraduates and 3,400 graduate, part-time, and doctoral students. Steeped in the 450-year Jesuit tradition of scholarship and service, the University strives to be recognized as the preeminent comprehensive Catholic university in the Northeast.

Saint Joseph's Erivan K. Haub School of Business is the Philadelphia area's only college or university to appear in the top twenty of *U.S. News & World Report's 2004 America's Best Graduate Schools* issue for part-time M.B.A. programs.

Applying

Applications are accepted on a rolling admission basis. Students applying to the Master of Science in Human Resource Management must have a baccalaureate degree from an accredited college or university. Applicants must submit an application, the application fee, official transcripts, an official test score (GMAT, GRE, or MAT), two letters of recommendation, a resume, and a personal statement. International students must also submit TOEFL scores (for those whose native language is not English) and an affidavit of support. International applicants are required to submit an official course-by-course credentials evaluation of their undergraduate work. Students are strongly advised to register with World Education Services (WES). Application deadlines for international students are July 15 for the fall, November 15 for the spring, April 1 for summer session I, and May 15 for summer session II.

Correspondence and Information

David M. Benglian
Director of Graduate Programs in Finance, Human Resources, and Decision and System Sciences
Erivan K. Haub School of Business
Saint Joseph's University
5600 City Avenue
Philadelphia, Pennsylvania 19131-1395

Phone: 610-660-1626
E-mail: david.benglian@sju.edu
Web site: http://www.sju.edu/hsb/HR

Saint Joseph's University

THE FACULTY

Accounting
Waqar I. Ghani, Associate Professor; Ph.D.

Management
David Benglian, Lecturer, M.B.A.
Susan Givens-Skeaton, Assistant Professor; Ph.D.
John J. McCall, Professor of Philosophy and Management, Ph.D.
William McDevitt, Associate Professor; J.D.
Claire Simmers, Associate Professor; M.B.A., Ph.D.
David Steingard, Assistant Professor; Ph.D.
C. Ken Weidner, Assistant Professor; M.B.A., Ph.D.

UNIVERSITY OF CONNECTICUT

Center for Continuing Studies
Master of Professional Studies in Human Resource Management

Program of Study

The online Master of Professional Studies (M.P.S.) degree is specifically designed to meet the professional development needs of individuals who are currently working in the field of human resource management or who are interested in pursuing a career in human resource management. Those who do not have human resource management or supervisory experience are strongly encouraged to participate in an internship, which may be taken for course credit.

The M.P.S. in human resource management features two different tracks—labor relations and personnel. The program prepares graduates to manage human resources effectively in the dynamic legal, social, and economic environment currently found in organizations. Students develop skills and knowledge in all fields of HRM, including human resource strategy; employment and labor law; compensation and benefits; labor relations; dispute resolution; staffing; training and development; contract negotiation and administration; human resource information systems, occupational safety, and health; and managing organizational change. Emphasis is placed on integrating human resource management with the overall business strategy. Graduates are qualified for professional HRM positions in industry, labor organizations, and government.

The degree program requires 36 credits, 30 of which are course work, and 6 are a capstone project. Core courses include Organizational Behavior, Program Evaluation, Quantitative Analysis, Human Resources and Public Policy, Labor Relations and the Law, Strategic Management of Human Resources, and Managing Organizational Change. The capstone project demonstrates the student's ability to define, analyze, evaluate, and recommend actions or solutions to deal with a major issue, problem, or opportunity within HRM.

Research Facilities

With 2.5 million volumes, the University of Connecticut's library system holds the largest public collection of research materials in the state. More than 2 million volumes are shelved in the Babbidge Library, which also houses nearly 3 million units of microtext, 180,000 maps, 35,000 reference volumes, and subscriptions to about 5,000 current journals. The archives and special collections at the Dodd Research Center support the teaching, research, and public service missions of the University by acquiring, preserving, organizing, and providing access to original source materials.

Financial Aid

Financial aid based on need is available. United States citizens or permanent residents of the United States may apply for need-based financial aid, which includes Federal Stafford Loans (FSL), Federal Work-Study, and the University of Connecticut Tuition Remission Grant. Prospective students should visit the Web site at http://www.grad.uconn.edu/financial_aid.html for additional information. International students can obtain special scholarships from their governments or from international sources, such as USAID, World Bank, and other foundations.

Cost of Study

Fees for fall 2007 online courses in the M.P.S. program are $1581 for a 3-credit course, plus a $45 infrastructure fee.

Living and Housing Costs

Although this M.P.S. is an online program, housing on or near campus is available.

Student Group

The program is designed especially for working adults and graduates interested in human resource management as a profession.

Location

Both the University and the town of Storrs are the homes of several cultural attractions. Storrs and Stamford have several art galleries, and the University includes the Connecticut State Museum of Natural History, the William Benton Museum of Art, and the Connecticut Repertory Theatre. The campus is a 30-minute drive from Hartford and 55 minutes from Providence, Rhode Island.

The University and The Center

The University of Connecticut (UConn) is the state's flagship institution of higher learning. Founded in 1881, the University has grown to include thirteen schools and colleges at its main campus in Storrs, separate Schools of Law and Social Work in Hartford, five regional campuses throughout the state, and the Schools of Medicine and Dentistry at the UConn Health Center in Farmington. Designated a Carnegie Foundation Research University–Extensive, a distinction shared by fewer than 4 percent of America's higher education institutions, UConn has more than seventy focused research centers where faculty members, graduate students, and undergraduates explore everything from improving human health to enhancing public education and protecting the country's natural resources.

The Center for Continuing Studies offers high-quality programs and courses that address lifelong educational needs. In fall 2003, the Center introduced its first online master's degree program, the Master of Professional Studies, which now offers four fields of study in human resource management, humanitarian services administration, occupational safety and health management, and homeland security leadership.

Applying

All applicants must have completed a baccalaureate degree from a regionally accredited college or university and have a GPA greater than 3.0 for the last two years of study. Two years' relevant work experience is highly desirable. Applicants must submit an official college transcript, three letters of reference from faculty members or others who can address the candidate's potential for success, and a personal statement that describes the student's reasons for application and future plans. Nonnative speakers of English must submit a TOEFL score of at least 550 on the paper-based version and at least 213 for the computer-based version. GRE scores are not required. Students should apply at least eight weeks before the start of a semester, and applications are evaluated as soon as the student's file is complete. Applicants are notified shortly after the admissions committee has made its decision.

Correspondence and Information

Peter Diplock, Associate Director
Center for Continuing Studies
University of Connecticut
One Bishop Circle, Unit 4056
Storrs, Connecticut 06269-4056
Phone: 860-486-2915
E-mail: peter.diplock@uconn.edu
Web site: http://continuingstudies.uconn.edu/mps/programs/hrm.html

University of Connecticut

THE FACULTY

Rodney G. Allen, Assistant Professor; Ph.D.
Peter Diplock, Associate Professor; Ph.D.
Anthony Joseph, Professor; Ph.D.
Ruth Rosenbaum, Assistant Professor; Ph.D.
Mark E. Sullivan, Associate Professor; Ph.D.
Kathleen Sweet, Associate Professor; J.D.

UNIVERSITY OF ILLINOIS AT URBANA-CHAMPAIGN

Institute of Labor and Industrial Relations

Program of Study

The Institute of Labor and Industrial Relations (ILIR) at the University of Illinois at Urbana-Champaign is a graduate program offering both the Master of Human Resources and Industrial Relations (M.H.R.I.R.) and the Doctor of Philosophy (Ph.D.) in human resources and industrial relations. Human resource management and industrial/employment relations concerns itself with many diverse employee and employment issues. Career opportunities in business firms include human resource generalist, employment relations specialist, compensation and benefits analyst, training and development specialist, labor relations administrator, and other human resource functions. Employment opportunities with government agencies, educational institutions, municipalities, and union organizations offer other career alternatives.

Graduate work for the master's degree program includes twelve to fourteen courses (depending on the number of hours each course is worth) and usually takes three semesters to complete. Required courses in the master's program include employment relations systems, quantitative methods, and research methods. Students must also choose at least one class from the following four distribution requirements: Human Resource Management and Organizational Behavior, International Human Resources, Labor Markets and Employment, and Union-Management Relations and Labor Relations Policy. The student's electives are driven by his or her interests and professional goals.

Most students attend the Institute on a full-time basis and complete their M.H.R.I.R. degree in three semesters. In addition, most students obtain a summer internship to make use of the knowledge and skills gained in the classroom. Other program options include part-time enrollment and joint-degree programs with the College of Law or the College of Business.

Graduate work at the Ph.D. level leads primarily to academic research and teaching careers in business schools that teach human resource management or labor relations. The program can be completed in three to four years beyond the master's degree. The doctoral degree requires 48 hours of course work, including a thesis.

Research Facilities

The University Library's extensive collection contains more than 22 million items, including nearly 9.8 million volumes, over 13 million print and nonprint materials, and more than 90,000 periodicals and journals. The Institute's departmental library, housed in the ILIR building, has an extensive labor and human resource collection, with a responsive and informed staff. The computer laboratory is equipped with personal computers, networked for worldwide access by scholars and practitioners in the field.

Financial Aid

Extremely competitive financial aid awards are available from the Institute. Award recipients are selected on the basis of academic excellence. Fellowships that include full tuition and service-fee waiver or research assistantships are available to highly qualified students. Some fellowships sponsored by various organizations, corporations, and alumni funds are designated for students in a particular area of interest or from a minority group. Fellowships or assistantships combined with tuition and fee waivers from the Institute make up an entire aid package totaling between $28,200 and $42,500, depending on in-state versus out-of-state tuition. There is no separate form on which to apply for financial aid. For information on loans, grants, and need-based financial aid from the government or other University sources, students should contact the Student Financial Aid Office (620 East John Street, Champaign, Illinois 61820; telephone: 217-333-0100; Web: http://www.osfa.uiuc.edu). All students pursuing a Ph.D. are given a generous financial aid package, including financial support for travel to professional conferences.

Cost of Study

For the 2007–08 academic year, in-state tuition is $12,950 and out-of-state tuition is $21,290. Textbook expenses range from $800 to $1200 per year.

Living and Housing Costs

Graduate student housing includes two residence halls for 750 students and two University-owned apartment complexes for 975 students with families or for single graduate students. In 2007–08, graduate residence hall rates are $4282 to $5400 for a single room per person per year and $4098 to $4926 for a double room per person per year. The board contract for meal plans ranges from $1712 to $4784 per year. Students should contact the University Housing Office (telephone: 217-333-1752; e-mail: farmhouse@uiuc.edu) for more complete information. Privately owned on- or off-campus housing is abundant and available at similar or higher rates.

Student Group

The Institute strives to maintain a student body balanced in geographic, gender, and ethnic composition. At any one time, there are about 160 students enrolled in the master's program and 12–16 students enrolled in the doctoral program. In 2007–08, ILIR students came from seventy-five undergraduate institutions in eighteen states and seven other countries. Of the student body, 64 percent are women, 19 percent are members of minority groups, and 18 percent are international.

Student Outcomes

ILIR Career Services provides a wide variety of career development services, including presentations and workshops covering cover letters and resumes, interviewing skills, off-campus job searches, internship searches, job offer evaluation, and networking with alumni and employers; etiquette dinners and plant tours; and individual advising. The office sponsors on-campus recruiting throughout the academic year with representatives of numerous corporations, labor unions, and government agencies interviewing students for positions in human resources, labor relations, and governmental positions. Further career information is available from ILIR Career Services, Institute of Labor and Industrial Relations (241 ILIR, 504 East Armory Avenue, Champaign, Illinois 61820; telephone: 217-333-1534; Web site: http://iliruiuc.v2.iconnectuiuc.com/).

Leading employers of graduates include Danaher Corporation, ExxonMobil, Frito-Lay, General Electric, Northrup Grumman, Shell, and Yum Brands. The average salary for last year's graduating class was $69,903, with an average signing bonus of $7913 (not including relocation and housing allowances).

Location

The University is located in the twin cities of Urbana and Champaign, with a combined population of about 110,000. The University enhances the community through a large variety of performing arts and entertainment bookings, in addition to various museums and intramural and intercollegiate athletic facilities. The University is located 140 miles south of Chicago, 120 miles west of Indianapolis, and 170 miles north of St. Louis. Three interstate highways, several airlines, Amtrak, and an excellent mass-transit system serve the twin cities. The community has excellent public school and park systems and numerous shopping facilities.

The University

The University of Illinois at Urbana-Champaign, founded in 1867 as one of the original thirty-seven public land-grant institutions, today ranks among the world's finest universities. It offers more than 150 fields of study for its 28,000 undergraduates and over 100 disciplines for more than 10,000 graduate students.

Applying

Students enter the Institute with a wide range of social science backgrounds. Psychology, business administration, history, economics, political science, and speech communications are typical undergraduate areas of study. To be accepted to the Institute of Labor and Industrial Relations, students must meet the general entrance requirements of the Graduate College at the University of Illinois at Urbana-Champaign as well as the Institute's specific requirements. Entering students at ILIR have an average GPA of 3.5, based on the last 60 hours of undergraduate work.

Application deadlines are November 1 for spring semester enrollment and February 1 for fall semester enrollment. Applicants are notified by March 15 for fall admission and by December 1 for spring admission. All applicants must submit a completed application form plus the application fee, academic transcripts, three letters of professional and personal recommendation, and Graduate Record Examinations (GRE) or Graduate Management Admission Test (GMAT) scores. International students are required to submit scores of the Test of English as a Foreign Language (TOEFL).

Correspondence and Information

Becky Barker, Director of Student Services
Institute of Labor and Industrial Relations
University of Illinois at Urbana-Champaign
504 East Armory Avenue
Champaign, Illinois 61820
Phone: 217-333-1482
Fax: 217-244-9290
E-mail: ilir-admissions@ad.uiuc.edu
Web site: http://www.ilir.uiuc.edu

University of Illinois at Urbana-Champaign

THE FACULTY AND THEIR RESEARCH

Ruth V. Aguilera, Associate Professor of LIR and Business Administration; Ph.D., Harvard. Cross-national employment systems, international comparative business, corporate governance.

Steven K. Ashby, Clinical Associate Professor of LIR assigned to the Chicago Labor Education Program; Ph.D., Chicago. Labor movement and distance learning.

Betty J. Barrett, Clinical Assistant Professor of LIR and Engineering and Director, Social Technical Systems Program; Ph.D., Michigan State. Socio-technical systems, large-scale systems change, work systems.

Monica Bielski Boris, Assistant Professor of LIR, Labor Education Program; Ph.D., Rutgers. Women's issues in the labor movement; lesbian, gay, and transgender challenges and issues in American labor.

Kristine M. Brown, Assistant Professor of LIR and Economics; Ph.D., Berkeley. Retirement decisions, economics of aging, health economics.

Robert Bruno, Associate Professor of LIR and Head, Labor Education Program; Ph.D., NYU. Unions and political action, union democracy, working-class culture and consciousness.

Joel Cutcher-Gershenfeld, Professor and Dean of ILIR; Ph.D., MIT. New work systems, labor-management relations, negotiations and conflict resolution, organizational learning and change, public policy, economic development, engineering systems.

John C. Dencker, Assistant Professor of LIR; Ph.D., Harvard. Corporate reorganization and workforce reductions, labor markets and international human resource management.

Fritz Drasgow, Professor of LIR and Psychology; Ph.D., Illinois at Urbana-Champaign. Psychological measurement, computerized testing and sexual harassment.

Jeff Ericksen, Assistant Professor of LIR; Ph.D., Cornell. How organizations manage people to gain a competitive edge in changing environments.

Peter Feuille, Professor of LIR; Ph.D., Berkeley. Workplace disputed resolution; human resource practices in multinational firms, human resource practices and firm performance.

Wallace Hendricks, Professor Emeritus of LIR and Economics; Ph.D., Berkeley. Performance evaluations and statistical discrimination.

Edward J. Hertenstein, Assistant Professor of LIR, Labor Education Program; Ph.D., Illinois at Urbana-Champaign. Training and development, especially with distance learning technologies and collective bargaining.

Aparna Joshi, Assistant Professor of LIR; Ph.D., Rutgers. Work team diversity, and global cross-cultural teams.

Ron Laschever, Assistant Professor of LIR and Economics; Ph.D., Northwestern. How personal interaction in social networks affect labor market outcomes.

John Lawler, Professor of LIR; Ph.D., Berkeley. Human resource information systems, international human resource management.

Michael LeRoy, Professor of LIR and Law; J.D., North Carolina at Chapel Hill. Government regulation, collective bargaining, grievance arbitration.

Darren Lubotsky, Assistant Professor of LIR and Economics; Ph.D., Berkeley. Labor and health economics, econometrics.

Joseph J. Martocchio, Professor of LIR; Ph.D., Michigan State. Training effectiveness and evaluation, absence motivation and control policies, incentive compensation systems.

Greg Northcraft, Harry J. Gray Professor in Executive Leadership for Business Administration and Professor of LIR; Ph.D., Stanford. Conflict and negotiation behavior, diversity and performance in cross-functional teams.

Greg Oldham, C. Clinton Spivey Distinguished Professor of Business Administration, Professor of LIR, and Interim Dean, College of Business; Ph.D., Yale. Work design, employee creativity and innovation, spatial configuration of organizations.

Craig Olson, ILIR Alumni Professor; Ph.D., Wisconsin–Madison. Effects of human resources and human resource policies on organizational performance, impact of employer-provided health insurance on labor market behaviors, causes of the decline in employer-provided health insurance in the United States.

Deborah Rupp, Assistant Professor of LIR and Psychology; Ph.D., Colorado State. Antecedents and consequences of organizational justice, impact of job attitudes on task and contextual performance, use of assessment centers for both personal decision making and development.

Helena Worthen, Clinical Assistant Professor of LIR, Labor Education Program; Ph.D., Berkeley. Workforce development systems; ethnography of the workplace; implementation of the Workforce Investment Act, garment and textile unions.

UNIVERSITY
OF MINNESOTA

UNIVERSITY OF MINNESOTA, TWIN CITIES CAMPUS

Graduate Programs in Human Resources and Industrial Relations

Programs of Study

The University of Minnesota's Industrial Relations Center (IRC) offers nationally recognized M.A. and Ph.D. Graduate Programs in Human Resources and Industrial Relations (HRIR). Minnesota's HRIR graduate degree programs are structured around the core HRIR areas of staffing, training, and development; compensation and benefits; and labor relations and collective bargaining and are rooted in key concepts from the social and behavioral sciences and business, such as organizational behavior and theory, labor market analysis, leadership, and strategy. Research methods and quantitative analysis of employment problems and issues are also included. As part of the Carlson School of Management and the University of Minnesota, HRIR students have the resources of a leading business school and a world-class research university.

The M.A. is a professional degree program that prepares individuals for private- and public-sector careers in human resource management, labor relations, and related fields. Students receive a rigorous education in the major areas of HRIR and can also take M.B.A. and law courses. The M.A. degree is generally completed in two years on a full-time basis or three or more years on a part-time basis. Unlike programs taught by practitioners, Minnesota course work relates contemporary practices and the conceptual basis and analytical framework for a successful career of leadership. HRIR graduate students also have access to semester-length and short-term study-abroad programs. Recent HRIR graduate students have studied in France, Italy, Switzerland, Spain, Japan, Australia, New Zealand, and elsewhere.

The Ph.D. is a full-time research degree program that prepares individuals for academic careers in teaching and conducting research. Specialization in two areas of HRIR is required for Ph.D. candidates as is intensive course work in quantitative methods. A master's degree is not required, and the Ph.D. degree is generally completed in four to five years.

Research Facilities

Minnesota HRIR students benefit from state-of-the-art classroom, computing, and library facilities. The Industrial Relations Center Reference Room is one of a small number of comprehensive reference libraries specializing in HRIR. The Carlson School's Business Career Center assists students in their job searches across the country and around the world and manages on-campus interviewing.

Financial Aid

HRIR graduate assistantships, fellowships, and tuition waivers are awarded on a competitive basis. M.A. assistantships usually require 10 hours of work per week assisting with faculty members' research projects or with library reference services. Many M.A. students also find part-time internships with local companies during the school year, especially in their second year of study. Ph.D. students are supported with research and teaching assistantships and summer research funds so that they can pursue their degree on a full-time basis.

Cost of Study

For the 2006–07 academic year, annual tuition for full-time students was $11,694 for residents of Minnesota, Wisconsin, North Dakota, South Dakota, and Manitoba and was $21,320 for nonresidents. Technology and student services fees are approximately $1000 per year. Evening students pay by the credit ($680 per credit in 2006–07). Ph.D. students supported by assistantships receive full tuition waivers.

Living and Housing Costs

Graduate students live off campus in apartments that are adjacent to the University or in other parts of the Twin Cities. Additional information, including online apartment listings, can be found at http://www.housing.umn.edu/offcampus/.

Student Group

The graduate HRIR programs attract individuals from throughout the United States and the world. Minnesota's HRIR M.A. program is one of the largest in the country with 140 full-time and 80 part-time students. There is a strong commitment to diversity, and 15 percent of the students in the full-time M.A. program are members of minority groups. The Ph.D. program generally has 15–20 students. Entering HRIR students have undergraduate degrees in many subjects that range from fine arts to engineering. Common majors include psychology, economics, business, and political science. Previous work experience is desirable but not required.

Student Outcomes

Employment opportunities for Minnesota HRIR alumni are excellent. In the last three years, the placement rate has been more than 90 percent, with average salaries around $62,000. Companies that have hired recent graduates include Anheuser-Busch, Bristol-Myers Squibb, Chevron, Citigroup, ExxonMobil, Ford, General Electric, General Mills, Hewlett-Packard, Honeywell, IBM, Merck, Microsoft, Pepsi Bottling, Pfizer, and Target. Many graduates enter HR leadership development programs or become HR generalists, compensation analysts, staffing specialists, or labor relations representatives. Full-time students generally have an internship between the first and second years of study. The Ph.D. program focuses on academic/university placements, and recent graduates are at the University of Florida, Ohio State University, Rutgers University, and the University of Northern Iowa.

Location

The HRIR graduate programs are located in the Carlson School of Management, minutes from downtown Minneapolis and St. Paul. The Carlson School is a gateway between the academic and business worlds. Location in a vibrant business community (headquarters of eighteen Fortune 500 companies) and in a leading business school means that Minnesota HRIR students benefit from a blending of a rigorous education and practical experience found in few HRIR programs. The Twin Cities of Minneapolis and St. Paul are clean, safe, and affordable. The Twin Cities are home to nationally renowned theaters, orchestras, and museums as well as professional and collegiate sports teams. Numerous parks, lakes, and rivers provide ample recreational opportunities. A major airport facilitates convenient national travel and job interviewing.

The University

The University of Minnesota is the state's major university. The Twin Cities campus has more than 35,000 students and offers nearly 200 graduate fields of study. With a host of nationally recognized, highly ranked programs, the Twin Cities campus provides a world-class setting for learning and opportunities for collaboration with faculty members in pacesetting research and professional development. Faculty members and students at the University of Minnesota have been studying work and human resources for more than fifty years.

Applying

The application deadline for M.A. students to enter in the fall is June 15, and the spring deadline is October 15. To be considered for financial aid, students must apply by February 1. Ph.D. students who wish to begin in the fall must submit their application by January 1. Applicants must submit three letters of recommendations, a complete set of transcripts, a resume, GRE scores, and a clearly written statement of career interests, goals, and objectives. M.A. applicants may substitute GMAT scores for GRE scores.

Correspondence and Information

Laura Simpson, Admissions Coordinator
Industrial Relations Center
3-300 Carlson School of Management
University of Minnesota
321 19th Avenue South
Minneapolis, Minnesota 55455-0438
Phone: 612-624-5704
Fax: 612-624-8360
E-mail: simpson@csom.umn.edu
Web site: http://www.csom.umn.edu

University of Minnesota, Twin Cities Campus

THE FACULTY AND THEIR RESEARCH

Richard Arvey, Professor; Ph.D., Minnesota. Staffing, training and development, organizational behavior.

Ross Azevedo, Associate Professor; Ph.D., Cornell. Compensation systems, human resource planning and skills, collective bargaining and negotiation.

Avner Ben-Ner, Professor and Director; Ph.D., SUNY at Stony Brook. Organization theory, employee ownership, nonprofit organizations, transition economics.

Mario Bognanno, Professor; Ph.D., Iowa. Labor economics and policy, collective bargaining, conflict resolution, international industrial relations.

Joyce Bono, Assistant Professor of Psychology; Ph.D., Iowa. Leadership and the influence process, personality and individual differences, conflict, affective experiences at work.

John Budd, Professor; Ph.D., Princeton. Collective bargaining, labor economics, and labor policy.

John Campbell, Professor of Psychology; Ph.D., Minnesota. Psychometrics, intra-inter group processes, individual differences.

Michelle Duffy, Assistant Professor; Ph.D., Arkansas. Workplace antisocial behavior, employee stress and well-being, effects of intimate partner violence at work.

Zvi Eckstein, Professor of Economics; Ph.D., Minnesota. Immigrants and their transition to a new labor market, labor search models, labor market discrimination.

John Fossum, Professor; Ph.D., Michigan State. Compensation, organizational demography.

Theresa Glomb, Associate Professor; Ph.D., Illinois. Workplace aggression and emotions in organizations, sexual harassment, contingent workers, job attitudes and behaviors.

Maria Hanratty, Associate Professor of Public Affairs; Ph.D., Harvard. Economics of poverty, health economics.

Jo-Ida Hansen, Professor of Psychology; Ph.D., Minnesota. Counseling, vocational interest inventory construction, career development, cross-cultural interest measurement.

Morris Kleiner, Professor of Public Affairs; Ph.D., Illinois. Labor economics, collective bargaining.

Stephanie Lluis, Assistant Professor; Ph.D., Montreal. Wage dynamics and workers' occupational mobility, impact of organizational changes and HR practices on wage dispersion.

Brian McCall, Professor; Ph.D., Princeton. Applied econometrics, labor economics, economics of information.

Jeylan Mortimer, Professor of Sociology. Occupational choice, work and family linkages.

John Remington, Professor; Ph.D., Michigan. Collective bargaining, organizational research and planning, labor arbitration, labor education/labor studies.

Paul Sackett, Professor of Psychology; Ph.D., Ohio State. Personnel decision making, fairness in employment testing, counterproductivity in the workplace.

James Scoville, Professor; Ph.D., Harvard. International and comparative industrial relations, labor markets in developing countries.

Jason Shaw, Associate Professor; Ph.D., Arkansas. Workforce voluntary and involuntary turnover, compensation systems and workforce performance, personality/environment congruence issues.

Connie Wanberg, Professor; Ph.D., Iowa State. Unemployment, job-seeking behavior, career indecision, mentoring.

Yijang Wang, Professor; Ph.D., Harvard. Organization theory, Industrial organization economics, comparative economics, Chinese economic reform, Japanese management.

Mahmood Zaidi, Professor; Ph.D., California. Labor market analysis, wage-price inflation and incomes policies, international human resource management.

Section 9
Industrial and Manufacturing Management

This section contains a directory of institutions offering graduate work in industrial and manufacturing management. Additional information about programs listed in the directory but not augmented by an in-depth entry may be obtained by writing directly to the dean of a graduate school or chair of a department at the address given in the directory.

For programs offering related work, see also in this book Business Administration and Management and Human Resources. In Book 2, see Public, Regional, and Industrial Affairs (Industrial and Labor Relations).

CONTENTS

Industrial and Manufacturing Management

American InterContinental University Online, Program in Business Administration, Hoffman Estates, IL 60192. Offers accounting and finance (MBA); healthcare management (MBA); human resource management (MBA); international business (MBA); management (MBA); marketing (MBA); operations management (MBA); organizational psychology and development (MBA); project management (MBA). Evening/weekend programs available. Postbaccalaureate distance learning degree programs offered (no on-campus study). *Entrance requirements:* Additional exam requirements/recommendations for international students: Required—TOEFL (minimum score 550 paper-based; 213 computer-based). *Application deadline:* Applications are processed on a rolling basis. Application fee: $50. Electronic applications accepted. *Financial support:* Institutionally sponsored loans and scholarships/grants available. Financial award applicants required to submit FAFSA. *Unit head:* Kerri J Holloway, Vice President of Academic Affairs, 847-851-5000 Ext. 15399, Fax: 847-586-6309, E-mail: kholloway@aivonline.edu. *Application contact:* 877-701-3800, E-mail: info@aiuonline.edu.

Baker College Center for Graduate Studies, Programs in Business, Flint, MI 48507-9843. Offers accounting (MBA); computer information systems (MBA); finance (MBA); general business (MBA); health and recreation services management (MBA); health care management (MBA); human resource management (MBA); industrial management (MBA); international business (MBA); leadership (MBA); marketing (MBA). MBA in health and recreation services management enrollment limited to international students. Part-time and evening/weekend programs available. *Faculty:* 15 full-time (6 women), 425 part-time/adjunct (200 women). *Students:* 370 full-time (190 women), 1,060 part-time (560 women); includes 372 minority (205 African Americans, 27 American Indian/Alaska Native, 66 Asian Americans or Pacific Islanders, 74 Hispanic Americans), 30 international. Average age 38. 780 applicants, 85% accepted, 567 enrolled. In 2006, 202 degrees awarded. *Degree requirements:* For master's, portfolio. *Entrance requirements:* For master's, 3 years of work experience, minimum undergraduate GPA of 2.5, writing sample, letters of recommendation. Additional exam requirements/recommendations for international students: Required—TOEFL (minimum score 550 paper-based; 213 computer-based). *Application deadline:* For fall admission, 8/6 priority date for domestic students; for winter admission, 12/15 priority date for domestic students; for spring admission, 2/15 priority date for domestic students. Applications are processed on a rolling basis. Application fee: $25. Electronic applications accepted. *Expenses:* Tuition: Full-time $7,200; part-time $300 per credit hour. *Financial support:* In 2006–07, 410 students received support. Scholarships/grants available. Support available to part-time students. Financial award applicants required to submit FAFSA. *Unit head:* Dr. Michael Heberling, President, 800-469-3165, Fax: 810-766-4399, E-mail: heberling@baker.edu. *Application contact:* Chuck J. Gurden, Vice President for Graduate and Online Admissions, 800-469-3165, Fax: 810-766-2051, E-mail: chuck@baker.edu.

Boston University, School of Management, Doctorate in Business Administration Program, Boston, MA 02215. Offers accounting (DBA); information systems (DBA); management policy (DBA); marketing (DBA); operations management (DBA); organizational behavior (DBA). *Students:* 48 full-time (26 women); includes 4 minority (all Asian Americans or Pacific Islanders), 24 international. Average age 35. 120 applicants, 17% accepted, 10 enrolled. In 2006, 8 degrees awarded. *Degree requirements:* For doctorate, thesis/dissertation. *Entrance requirements:* For doctorate, GMAT or GRE General Test. *Application deadline:* For fall admission, 1/31 for domestic students. Application fee: $125. *Expenses:* Tuition: Full-time $33,330; part-time $1,042 per credit. Required fees: $462; $40. *Financial support:* Career-related internships or fieldwork, Federal Work-Study, institutionally sponsored loans, scholarships/grants, and tuition waivers available. Support available to part-time students. Financial award applicants required to submit FAFSA. *Unit head:* Dr. Sushil Vachani, Director, 617-353-4875, E-mail: dba@bu.edu. *Application contact:* Hayden Estrada, Assistant Dean, Admissions, 617-353-2670, Fax: 617-353-7368, E-mail: dba@bu.edu.

Bryant University, Graduate School, Graduate School of Business, Programs in Business Administration, Smithfield, RI 02917-1284. Offers accounting (MBA, CAGS); computer information systems (MBA, CAGS); e-strategy (MBA, CAGS); finance (MBA, CAGS); general business (MBA); management (MBA, CAGS); marketing (MBA, CAGS); operations management (MBA). *Accreditation:* AACSB. *Faculty:* 49 full-time (13 women), 2 part-time/adjunct (0 women). *Students:* 143 applicants, 41% accepted, 46 enrolled. In 2006, 106 master's, 10 other advanced degrees awarded. *Entrance requirements:* For master's, GMAT, letter of recommendation, resumé; for CAGS, GMAT, resumé. Additional exam requirements/recommendations for international students: Required—TOEFL (minimum score 580 paper-based; 237 computer-based). *Application deadline:* For fall admission, 7/15 for domestic students, 4/1 for international students; for spring admission, 11/15 for domestic and international students. Application fee: $80. *Expenses:* Tuition: Part-time $1,998 per course. *Financial support:* Research assistantships with full tuition reimbursements, unspecified assistantships available. Financial award applicants required to submit FAFSA. *Unit head:* Kristopher T. Sullivan, Assistant Dean of the Graduate School, 401-232-6230, Fax: 401-232-6494, E-mail: gradprog@bryant.edu.

California Polytechnic State University, San Luis Obispo, Orfalea College of Business, Department of Industrial and Technical Studies, San Luis Obispo, CA 93407. Offers MS. Part-time programs available. *Faculty:* 1 full-time (0 women), 2 part-time/adjunct (0 women). *Students:* 11 full-time (2 women), 3 part-time (1 woman), 2 international. 6 applicants, 100% accepted, 6 enrolled. In 2006, 13 degrees awarded. *Degree requirements:* For master's, thesis or alternative. *Entrance requirements:* For master's, GRE General Test or GMAT, minimum GPA of 2.8 in last 90 quarter units of course work, 2 letters of recommendation. Additional exam requirements/recommendations for international students: Required—TOEFL (minimum score 550 paper-based; 213 computer-based), TWE (minimum score 4.5). *Application deadline:* For fall admission, 7/1 for domestic students, 11/30 for international students. Applications are processed on a rolling basis. Application fee: $55. Electronic applications accepted. *Financial support:* Career-related internships or fieldwork, Federal Work-Study, institutionally sponsored loans, and scholarships/grants available. Support available to part-time students. Financial award application deadline: 3/2; financial award applicants required to submit FAFSA. *Unit head:* Dr. Lou Tornatzky, Associate Dean/Graduate Coordinator, 805-756-2676, Fax: 805-756-6111, E-mail: ltornatzk@calpoly.edu.

California State University, East Bay, Academic Programs and Graduate Studies, College of Business and Economics, Department of Management and Finance, Option in Operations and Material Management, Hayward, CA 94542-3000. Offers MBA. *Application contact:* Doris Duncan, Director of Graduate Programs, 510-885-3364, Fax: 510-885-2176, E-mail: doris.duncan@csueastbay.edu.

Carnegie Mellon University, Carnegie Institute of Technology and School of Design, Program in Product Development, Pittsburgh, PA 15213-3891. Offers MPD. *Entrance requirements:* For master's, GRE General Test, undergraduate degree in engineering, industrial design, or related fields, 3 letters of reference, 2 years of professional experience. Additional exam requirements/recommendations for international students: Required—TOEFL or TSE.

Carnegie Mellon University, College of Fine Arts, School of Design, Pittsburgh, PA 15213-3891. Offers communication planning and information design (M Des); design (PhD); design theory (PhD); interaction design (M Des); new product development (PhD); product development (MPD); typography and information design (PhD). *Accreditation:* NASAD.

Carnegie Mellon University, Tepper School of Business, Program in Management of Manufacturing and Automation, Pittsburgh, PA 15213-3891. Offers industrial administration (PhD); manufacturing (MOM). *Degree requirements:* For doctorate, thesis/dissertation. *Entrance requirements:* For master's, GMAT.

Case Western Reserve University, Weatherhead School of Management, Department of Operations, Cleveland, OH 44106. Offers management (MS, MSM), including finance (MS), information systems (MS), marketing (MS), operations research, quality management (MS), supply chain (MSM); management for liberal arts graduates (MSM); operations research (PhD); MBA/MSM. Part-time programs available. *Faculty:* 12 full-time (1 woman), 2 part-time/adjunct (1 woman). *Students:* 32 full-time (8 women), 6 part-time (1 woman), 21 international. Average age 28. In 2006, 28 master's, 4 doctorates awarded. *Degree requirements:* For doctorate, thesis/dissertation. *Entrance requirements:* For master's, GRE General Test; for doctorate, GMAT, GRE General Test. *Application deadline:* For fall admission, 4/15 priority date for domestic students. Applications are processed on a rolling basis. Application fee: $50. *Financial support:* Tuition waivers (full and partial) available. Financial award application deadline: 5/1. *Faculty research:* Mathematical finance, mathematical programming, scheduling, stochastic optimization, environmental/energy models. *Unit head:* Kamlesh Mathur, Chairman, 216-368-3857, E-mail: kamlesh.mathur@case.edu.

Central Michigan University, College of Graduate Studies, College of Science and Technology, Department of Engineering Technology, Mount Pleasant, MI 48859. Offers industrial education (MA); industrial management and technology (MA). *Degree requirements:* For master's, thesis or alternative, registration. *Entrance requirements:* For master's, 2 years of teaching experience, undergraduate major/minor in industrial engineering or related field (industrial education). *Faculty research:* Computer applications, manufacturing process control, automation, industrial activities.

Clarkson University, Graduate School, School of Business, Program in Management Systems, Potsdam, NY 13699. Offers human resource management (MS); management information systems (MS); manufacturing management (MS). Part-time and evening/weekend programs available. *Students:* Average age 33. *Degree requirements:* For master's, project or thesis. *Entrance requirements:* For master's, GMAT, GRE General Test (highly recommended). Additional exam requirements/recommendations for international students: Required—TOEFL. *Application deadline:* For fall admission, 5/15 priority date for domestic students; for spring admission, 10/15 priority date for domestic students. Applications are processed on a rolling basis. Application fee: $25 ($35 for international students). Electronic applications accepted. *Expenses:* Tuition: Full-time $22,776; part-time $949 per credit. Required fees: $215. *Financial support:* Tuition waivers (partial) available. *Faculty research:* Management of technology planning and organizational development. *Application contact:* Dr. Farzad Mahmoodi, Director, 315-268-4281, Fax: 315-268-3810, E-mail: mahmoodi@clarkson.edu.

Clemson University, Graduate School, College of Business and Behavioral Science, Department of Management, Clemson, SC 29634. Offers electronic commerce (M E Com); management (MS, PhD). *Accreditation:* AACSB. Part-time programs available. *Faculty:* 29 full-time (6 women), 1 part-time/adjunct (0 women). *Students:* 22 full-time (4 women), 2 part-time; includes 3 minority (1 American Indian/Alaska Native, 2 Hispanic Americans), 13 international. Average age 25. 33 applicants, 21% accepted, 3 enrolled. In 2006, 4 master's, 2 doctorates awarded. Terminal master's awarded for partial completion of doctoral program. *Degree requirements:* For doctorate, thesis/dissertation. *Entrance requirements:* For master's, GMAT, GRE General Test, minimum GPA of 3.0; for doctorate, GRE General Test, minimum GPA of 3.5. Additional exam requirements/recommendations for international students: Required—TOEFL. *Application deadline:* For fall admission, 2/1 for domestic students, 4/15 for international students; for spring admission, 10/1 for domestic students, 9/15 for international students. Applications are processed on a rolling basis. Application fee: $50. *Expenses:* Tuition, state resident: full-time $8,812; part-time $450 per hour. Tuition, nonresident: full-time $18,036; part-time $760 per hour. Required fees: $474; $5 per term. *Financial support:* In 2006–07, 13 research assistantships were awarded; fellowships, teaching assistantships, institutionally sponsored loans also available. Financial award applicants required to submit FAFSA. *Faculty research:* Production/operations, strategic management, organizational behavior, management information systems. *Unit head:* Dr. Patricia Layton, Chair, 864-656-3303, Fax: 864-656-3304, E-mail: playton@clemson.edu.

Cleveland State University, College of Graduate Studies, Nance College of Business Administration, Doctoral Programs in Business Administration, Cleveland, OH 44115. Offers business administration (DBA); finance (DBA); information systems (DBA); marketing (DBA); production/operations management (DBA). *Accreditation:* AACSB. In 2006, 3 degrees awarded. *Degree requirements:* For doctorate, thesis/dissertation. *Entrance requirements:* For doctorate, GMAT, MBA or equivalent. *Unit head:* Dr. Raj Shekhar G. Javalgi, Director, 216-687-3786, Fax: 216-687-9354, E-mail: r.javalgi@csuohio.edu.

DePaul University, Charles H. Kellstadt Graduate School of Business, Department of Management, Chicago, IL 60604-2287. Offers entrepreneurship (MBA); health sector management (MBA); human resource management (MBA, MSHR); leadership/change management (MBA); management planning and strategy (MBA); operations management (MBA). Part-time and evening/weekend programs available. *Faculty:* 36 full-time (7 women), 35 part-time/adjunct (16 women). *Students:* 173 full-time (71 women), 134 part-time (61 women); includes 60 minority (12 African Americans, 34 Asian Americans or Pacific Islanders, 14 Hispanic Americans), 13 international. Average age 31. In 2006, 112 degrees awarded. *Entrance requirements:* For master's, GMAT, GRE (MSHR), 2 letters of recommendation, resumé. Additional exam requirements/recommendations for international students: Required—TOEFL (minimum score 550 paper-based; 213 computer-based). *Application deadline:* For fall admission, 7/1 for domestic students; for winter admission, 10/1 for domestic students; for spring admission, 2/1 for domestic students. Applications are processed on a rolling basis. Application fee: $60. Electronic applications accepted. *Financial support:* Research assistantships available. Financial award application deadline: 4/1. *Faculty research:* Growth management, creativity and innovation, quality management and business process design, entrepreneurship. *Application contact:* Christopher E. Kinsella, Director of Cohort MBA Programs, 312-362-8810, Fax: 312-362-6677, E-mail: kgsb@depaul.edu.

Eastern Michigan University, Graduate School, College of Business, Department of Management, Ypsilanti, MI 48197. Offers human resources management and organizational development (MSHROD); management of human resources (MBA); management organizational development (MBA); production and operations management (MBA); strategic quality management (MBA). Part-time and evening/weekend programs available. Postbaccalaureate distance learning degree programs offered (minimal on-campus study). *Students:* Average age 29. *Degree requirements:* For master's, thesis optional. *Entrance requirements:* For master's, GMAT. Additional exam requirements/recommendations for international students: Required—TOEFL. *Application deadline:* For fall admission, 5/15 priority date for domestic and international students; for winter admission, 10/15 priority date for domestic and international students; for spring admission, 3/15 priority date for domestic and international students. Applications are processed on a rolling basis. Application fee: $35. *Expenses:* Tuition, state resident: part-time $341 per credit hour. Tuition, nonresident: full-time $16,104; part-time $671 per credit hour. Required fees: $816; $34 per credit hour. $40 per term. One-time fee: $82 full-time. Tuition and fees vary according to course level, course load, degree level and reciprocity agreements. *Financial support:* Fellowships, research assistantships with full tuition reimbursements, teaching assistantships with full tuition reimbursements, career-related internships or fieldwork, Federal Work-Study, institutionally sponsored loans, scholarships/grants, tuition waivers (partial), and unspecified assistantships available. Support available to part-time students. Financial award applicants required to submit FAFSA. *Unit head:* Dr. Fraya Wagner-Marsh, Head, 734-487-3240, Fax: 734-487-4100, E-mail: fraya.wagner@emich.edu.

Florida Institute of Technology, Graduate Programs, University College, Melbourne, FL 32901-6975. Offers acquisition and contract management (MS, PMBA); aerospace engineering (MS); business administration (PMBA); computer information systems (MS); computer science (MS);

e-business (PMBA); electrical engineering (MS); engineering management (MS); human resource management (PMBA); human resources management (MS); information systems (PMBA); logistics management (MS); management (MS), including acquisition and contract management, e-business, human resource management, information systems, logistics management, transportation management; materiel acquisition management (MS); mechanical engineering (MS); operations research (MS); project management (MS), including information systems, operations research; public administration (MPA); software engineering (MS); space systems (MS); space systems management (MS); systems management (MS), including information systems, operations research. Part-time and evening/weekend programs available. Postbaccalaureate distance learning degree programs offered (no on-campus study). *Faculty:* 11 full-time (4 women), 129 part-time/adjunct (17 women). *Students:* 78 full-time (34 women), 1,258 part-time (507 women); includes 384 minority (252 African Americans, 9 American Indian/Alaska Native, 58 Asian Americans or Pacific Islanders, 65 Hispanic Americans), 28 international. Average age 36. 629 applicants, 65% accepted, 320 enrolled. In 2006, 505 degrees awarded. *Degree requirements:* For master's, registration. *Entrance requirements:* For master's, minimum GPA of 3.0. Additional exam requirements/recommendations for international students: Required—TOEFL (minimum score 550 paper-based; 213 computer-based). *Application deadline:* Applications are processed on a rolling basis. Application fee: $50. Electronic applications accepted. *Expenses:* Tuition: Part-time $900 per credit. *Financial support:* Institutionally sponsored loans available. Financial award application deadline: 3/1; financial award applicants required to submit FAFSA. *Unit head:* Dr. Clifford Bragdon, Dean, 321-674-8821, Fax: 321-951-7694, E-mail: cbragdon@fit.edu. *Application contact:* Carolyn P. Farrior, Director of Graduate Admissions, 321-674-7118, Fax: 321-723-9468, E-mail: cfarrior@fit.edu.

Friends University, Graduate School, Division of Business, Technology, and Leadership, Program in Service/Production Management, Wichita, KS 67213. Offers MSPM. Evening/weekend programs available. *Faculty:* 1 part-time/adjunct (0 women). *Students:* 13 full-time. In 2006, 13 degrees awarded. *Entrance requirements:* Additional exam requirements/recommendations for international students: Required—TOEFL (minimum score 560 paper-based; 220 computer-based). *Application deadline:* For fall admission, 8/1 priority date for domestic students, 7/1 priority date for international students. Applications are processed on a rolling basis. Application fee: $45 ($65 for international students). Electronic applications accepted. *Unit head:* Dr. Farhad Tadayon, Director, 800-794-6945 Ext. 5647, Fax: 316-295-5040.

The George Washington University, School of Business, Department of Management Science, Program in Logistics, Operations, and Materials Management, Washington, DC 20052. Offers MBA. Part-time and evening/weekend programs available. *Entrance requirements:* For master's, GMAT. Additional exam requirements/recommendations for international students: Required—TOEFL.

HEC Montreal, School of Business Administration, Master of Science Programs in Administration, Program in Production and Operations Management, Montréal, QC H3T 2A7, Canada. Offers M Sc. All courses are given in French. Part-time programs available. *Degree requirements:* For master's, one foreign language, thesis. Application fee: $60 Canadian dollars. Electronic applications accepted. Tuition and fees charges are reported in Canadian dollars. *Expenses:* Tuition, nonresident: part-time $56 Canadian dollars per credit. Required fees: $30 Canadian dollars per semester. *Financial support:* Fellowships, research assistantships, teaching assistantships, scholarships/grants available. *Application contact:* Francine Blais, Administrative Director, 514-340-6112, Fax: 514-340-6411, E-mail: francine.blais@hec.ca.

Illinois Institute of Technology, Graduate College, Center for Professional Development, Program in Industrial Technology and Operations, Chicago, IL 60616-3793. Offers MITO. Part-time and evening/weekend programs available. Postbaccalaureate distance learning degree programs offered (no on-campus study). *Faculty:* 12 part-time/adjunct (1 woman). *Students:* 22 full-time (4 women), 30 part-time (8 women); includes 10 minority (3 African Americans, 5 Asian Americans or Pacific Islanders, 2 Hispanic Americans), 23 international. Average age 32. 46 applicants, 80% accepted. In 2006, 10 degrees awarded. *Entrance requirements:* For master's, minimum undergraduate GPA of 3.0. Additional exam requirements/recommendations for international students: Required—TOEFL (minimum score 550 paper-based; 213 computer-based). *Application deadline:* For fall admission, 5/1 for domestic and international students; for spring admission, 10/15 for domestic and international students. Applications are processed on a rolling basis. Application fee: $40. Electronic applications accepted. *Expenses:* Tuition: Full-time $13,086; part-time $727 per credit. Required fees: $7 per credit. $235 per term. Tuition and fees vary according to class time, course level, course load, program and student level. *Financial support:* In 2006–07, research assistantships (averaging $25,000 per year), teaching assistantships (averaging $1,000 per year) were awarded; career-related internships or fieldwork, Federal Work-Study, institutionally sponsored loans, scholarships/grants, traineeships, health care benefits, tuition waivers (partial), and unspecified assistantships also available. Support available to part-time students. Financial award applicants required to submit FAFSA. *Faculty research:* Industrial logistics, industrial facilities, manufacturing technology, entrepreneurship, energy options. *Unit head:* Keith E. McKee, Director, 312-567-3650, Fax: 312-567-3657, E-mail: mckee@itt.edu. *Application contact:* Morgan Frederick, Assistant Director of Graduate Communications, 866-472-3448, Fax: 312-567-3138, E-mail: inquiry.grad@iit.edu.

Indiana University Southeast, School of Business, New Albany, IN 47150-6405. Offers accounting (Certificate); business administration (MBA); economics (Certificate); finance (Certificate); general business (Certificate); information and operations management (Certificate); management and marketing (Certificate); strategic finance (MS). *Accreditation:* AACSB. *Faculty:* 11 full-time (2 women). *Students:* 10 full-time (4 women), 201 part-time (65 women); includes 12 minority (2 African Americans, 8 Asian Americans or Pacific Islanders, 2 Hispanic Americans), 5 international. Average age 31. In 2006, 60 degrees awarded. *Degree requirements:* For master's, community service. *Entrance requirements:* For master's, GMAT, work experience. Additional exam requirements/recommendations for international students: Required—TOEFL. Application fee: $35. *Expenses: Contact institution.* Tuition and fees vary according to course load, campus/location and program. *Unit head:* Chris Bjornson, Dean, 812-941-2362, Fax: 812-941-2672. *Application contact:* Dr. Jay White, Director of Graduate Business Programs, 812-941-2364, Fax: 812-941-2581, E-mail: jwhite04@ius.edu.

Instituto Tecnológico y de Estudios Superiores de Monterrey, Campus Estado de México, Professional and Graduate Division, Estado de Mexico, Mexico. Offers administration of information technologies (MITA); architecture (M Arch); business administration (GMBA, MBA); computer sciences (MCS, PhD); education (M Ed); educational institution administration (MAD); educational technology and innovation (PhD); electronic commerce (MEC); environmental systems (MS); finance (MAF); humanistic studies (MHS); information sciences and knowledge management (MISKM); information systems (MS); manufacturing systems (MS); marketing (MEM); quality systems and productivity (MS); science and materials engineering (PhD); telecommunications management (MTM). Part-time programs available. Postbaccalaureate distance learning degree programs offered (minimal on-campus study). *Degree requirements:* For master's, one foreign language, thesis (for some programs), registration; for doctorate, one foreign language, thesis/dissertation, registration (for some programs). *Entrance requirements:* For master's, E-PAEP 500, interview; for doctorate, E-PAEP 500, research proposal. Additional exam requirements/recommendations for international students: Required—TOEFL (minimum score 550 paper-based). *Faculty research:* Surface treatments by plasmas, mechanical properties, robotics, graphical computing, mechatronics security protocols.

Instituto Tecnológico y de Estudios Superiores de Monterrey, Campus Irapuato, Graduate Programs, Irapuato, Mexico. Offers administration (MBA); administration of information technology (MAIT); administration of telecommunications (MAT); architecture (M Arch); computer science (MCS); education (M Ed); educational administration (MEA); educational innovation and technology (DEIT); educational technology (MET); electronic commerce (MBA); environmental administration and planning (MEAP); environmental systems (MES); finances (MBA); humanistic studies (MHS); international management for Latin American executives (MIMLAE); library and information science (MLIS); manufacturing quality management (MMQM); marketing research (MBA).

Inter American University of Puerto Rico, Metropolitan Campus, Graduate Programs, Faculty of Economics and Administrative Sciences, Program in Industrial Management, San Juan, PR 00919-1293. Offers MBA. *Degree requirements:* For master's, comprehensive exam. *Entrance requirements:* For master's, GRE or EXADEP, interview. Electronic applications accepted.

Kettering University, Graduate School, Department of Business, Flint, MI 48504-4898. Offers business administration (MBA); engineering management (MSEM); information technology (MSIT); manufacturing management (MSMM); manufacturing operations (MSMO); operations management (MSOM). *Accreditation:* ACBSP. *Faculty:* 13 full-time (5 women), 8 part-time/adjunct (1 woman). *Students:* 10 full-time (4 women), 455 part-time (122 women); includes 108 minority (53 African Americans, 1 American Indian/Alaska Native, 11 Asian Americans or Pacific Islanders, 43 Hispanic Americans), 2 international. Average age 33. 142 applicants, 91% accepted, 90 enrolled. In 2006, 158 degrees awarded. *Entrance requirements:* Additional exam requirements/recommendations for international students: Required—TOEFL (minimum score 550 paper-based; 213 computer-based). *Application deadline:* For fall admission, 8/15 for domestic students, 4/1 for international students; for winter admission, 11/15 for domestic students; for spring admission, 2/15 for domestic students. Applications are processed on a rolling basis. Electronic applications accepted. *Expenses:* Tuition: Part-time $629 per credit. *Application contact:* Allison Fleming, Graduate Admissions Assistant, 810-762-7953, Fax: 810-762-9935, E-mail: afleming@kettering.edu.

Lawrence Technological University, College of Management, Southfield, MI 48075-1058. Offers business administration (MBA, DBA); information systems (MS); information technology (DM); operations management (MS). *Accreditation:* ACBSP. Part-time and evening/weekend programs available. *Faculty:* 11 full-time (4 women), 61 part-time/adjunct (13 women). *Students:* 47 full-time (20 women), 702 part-time (235 women); includes 285 minority (98 African Americans, 178 Asian Americans or Pacific Islanders, 9 Hispanic Americans), 15 international. Average age 34. 337 applicants, 90% accepted, 192 enrolled. In 2006, 281 degrees awarded. *Entrance requirements:* For master's, GMAT. Additional exam requirements/recommendations for international students: Required—TOEFL (minimum score 550 paper-based; 213 computer-based). *Application deadline:* For fall admission, 8/1 priority date for domestic students; for winter admission, 12/1 priority date for domestic students; for spring admission, 5/1 for domestic students. Applications are processed on a rolling basis. Application fee: $50. Electronic applications accepted. *Financial support:* Institutionally sponsored loans available. Support available to part-time students. Financial award application deadline: 3/1; financial award applicants required to submit FAFSA. *Unit head:* Dr. Lou DeGennaro, Dean, 248-204-3050, E-mail: degennaro@ltu.edu. *Application contact:* Jane Rohrback, Director of Admissions, 248-204-3160, Fax: 248-204-3188, E-mail: admissions@ltu.edu.

Marist College, Graduate Programs, School of Management, Poughkeepsie, NY 12601-1387. Offers business administration (MBA, Adv C), including business administration (MBA), executive leadership (Adv C), production management (Adv C); public administration (MPA); technology management (MS). Part-time and evening/weekend programs available. Postbaccalaureate distance learning degree programs offered (no on-campus study). *Faculty:* 18 full-time (8 women), 10 part-time/adjunct (5 women). *Students:* 24 full-time (11 women), 429 part-time (190 women); includes 60 minority (26 African Americans, 16 Asian Americans or Pacific Islanders, 18 Hispanic Americans), 9 international. Average age 35. 142 applicants, 86% accepted, 87 enrolled. In 2006, 134 master's, 2 other advanced degrees awarded. *Entrance requirements:* For master's, GMAT (MBA) GRE (MPA), resumé, letters of recommendation, official transcripts, essay. Additional exam requirements/recommendations for international students: Required—TOEFL (minimum score 550 paper-based; 213 computer-based; 80 iBT); Recommended—IELTS (minimum score 6). *Application deadline:* For fall admission, 7/1 for domestic students, 6/1 for international students; for spring admission, 12/15 for domestic students, 10/15 for international students. Applications are processed on a rolling basis. Application fee: $50. Electronic applications accepted. *Expenses:* Tuition: Full-time $11,340; part-time $630 per credit. Required fees: $60; $30 per semester. *Financial support:* In 2006–07, 131 students received support. Scholarships/grants available. Support available to part-time students. Financial award application deadline: 8/15; financial award applicants required to submit FAFSA. *Unit head:* Dr. Elmore R. Alexander, Interim Dean, 845-575-3225, E-mail: elmore.alexander@marist.edu. *Application contact:* Anu R. Ailawadhi, Director of Graduate Admissions, 845-575-3800, Fax: 845-575-3166, E-mail: graduate@marist.edu.

McGill University, Faculty of Graduate and Postdoctoral Studies, Desautels Faculty of Management, Montréal, QC H3A 2T5, Canada. Offers administration (PhD); entrepreneurial studies (MBA); finance (MBA); general management (Post Master's Certificate); information systems (MBA); international business (exchange program) (MBA); international Master's program in practicing management (MM); management (MBA); management for development (MBA); manufacturing management (MMM); marketing (MBA); operations management (MBA); public accountancy (Diploma); strategic management (MBA); MBA/LL B; MD/MBA. Part-time programs available. *Entrance requirements:* For master's, GMAT, minimum undergraduate GPA of 3.0, 2 years work experience; for doctorate, GMAT or GRE General Test, 2 letters of recommendation, preferably by professors in chosen field of specialization; for other advanced degree, 2 years of work experience, MBA, minimum GPA of 3.0 (Post-MBA Certificate). Additional exam requirements/recommendations for international students: Required—TOEFL (minimum score 600 paper-based; 250 computer-based), IELTS (minimum score 7). Electronic applications accepted. Expenses: Contact institution. *Faculty research:* Social innovation, leadership, strategy.

McGill University, Faculty of Graduate and Postdoctoral Studies, Faculty of Engineering, Department of Mechanical Engineering and Desautels Faculty of Management, Program in Manufacturing Management, Montréal, QC H3A 2T5, Canada. Offers MMM. Part-time and evening/weekend programs available. *Degree requirements:* For master's, thesis or alternative, industrial project. *Entrance requirements:* For master's, GMAT or GRE, B Eng or equivalent, minimum GPA of 3.0. Additional exam requirements/recommendations for international students: Required—TOEFL (minimum score 600 paper-based; 250 computer-based), IELTS (minimum score 7). Electronic applications accepted. Expenses: Contact institution.

Announcement: The intensive Master in Manufacturing Management (MMM) program, operated jointly by the Faculties of Engineering and Management, with practical industry participation, trains engineering, science, and operations management students in analyzing, planning, and optimizing manufacturing and supply chain operations, processes, and systems in a global context. For details, consult www.mcgill.ca/mmm.

Northeastern State University, Graduate College, College of Business and Technology, Program in Industrial Management, Tahlequah, OK 74464-2399. Offers MS. Part-time and evening/weekend programs available. *Faculty:* 3 full-time (0 women). *Students:* 1 (woman) full-time, 18 part-time (6 women); includes 7 minority (all American Indian/Alaska Native). In 2006, 3 degrees awarded. *Degree requirements:* For master's, synergistic experience. *Entrance requirements:* For master's, GRE, MAT, minimum GPA of 2.5. Additional exam requirements/recommendations for international students: Required—TOEFL (minimum score 213 computer-based). *Application deadline:* For fall admission, 6/1 priority date for domestic students. Applications are processed on a rolling basis. Application fee: $0 ($25 for international students). Electronic applications accepted. *Financial support:* Teaching assistantships, Federal Work-Study available. Financial award application deadline: 3/1. *Unit head:* Dr. Michael Turner, Chair, 918-456-5511 Ext. 2970, Fax: 918-458-2337, E-mail: turne003@nsuok.edu.

Northern Illinois University, Graduate School, College of Engineering and Engineering Technology, Department of Technology, De Kalb, IL 60115-2854. Offers industrial manage-

Industrial and Manufacturing Management

Northern Illinois University (continued)

ment (MS). Part-time and evening/weekend programs available. *Faculty:* 14 full-time (1 woman), 1 part-time/adjunct (0 women). *Students:* 20 full-time (5 women), 23 part-time (6 women); includes 14 minority (7 African Americans, 1 American Indian/Alaska Native, 3 Asian Americans or Pacific Islanders, 3 Hispanic Americans), 3 international. Average age 32. 30 applicants, 67% accepted, 16 enrolled. In 2006, 24 degrees awarded. *Degree requirements:* For master's, thesis optional. *Entrance requirements:* For master's, GRE General Test, minimum GPA of 2.75. Additional exam requirements/recommendations for international students: Required—TOEFL (minimum score 550 paper-based; 213 computer-based). *Application deadline:* For fall admission, 6/1 for domestic students, 5/1 for international students; for spring admission, 11/1 for domestic students, 10/1 for international students. Applications are processed on a rolling basis. Application fee: $30. Electronic applications accepted. *Financial support:* In 2006–07, 2 research assistantships with full tuition reimbursements, 14 teaching assistantships with full tuition reimbursements were awarded; fellowships with full tuition reimbursements, career-related internships or fieldwork, Federal Work-Study, scholarships/grants, tuition waivers (full), and unspecified assistantships also available. Support available to part-time students. Financial award applicants required to submit FAFSA. *Faculty research:* Digital control, intelligent systems, engineering graphic design, occupational safety, ergonomics. *Unit head:* Dr. Clifford Mirman, Chair, 815-753-1349, Fax: 815-753-3702, E-mail: mirman@ceet.niu.edu.

Oakland University, Graduate Study and Lifelong Learning, School of Business Administration, Department of Decision and Information Sciences, Rochester, MI 48309-4401. Offers information technology management (MS); management information systems (Certificate); production and operations management (Certificate). *Faculty:* 8 full-time (0 women), 1 part-time/adjunct (0 women). *Students:* 7 full-time (2 women), 31 part-time (7 women); includes 8 minority (1 African American, 6 Asian Americans or Pacific Islanders, 1 Hispanic American), 8 international. Average age 33. 7 applicants, 86% accepted, 5 enrolled. In 2006, 10 master's, 1 other advanced degree awarded. Application fee: $30. *Expenses:* Tuition, state resident: full-time $9,936; part-time $414 per credit. Tuition, nonresident: full-time $17,202; part-time $716 per credit. *Unit head:* Dr. Thomas Lauer, Chair, 248-370-3283, Fax: 248-370-4604.

Oklahoma State University, William S. Spears School of Business, Department of Management Science and Information Systems, Stillwater, OK 74078. Offers management information systems (PhD); management information systems/accounting information systems (MS); management science (PhD); operations management (PhD); telecommunications management (MS, PhD). *Faculty:* 17 full-time (3 women), 1 part-time/adjunct (0 women). *Students:* 64 full-time (15 women), 66 part-time (15 women); includes 6 minority (2 American Indian/Alaska Native, 3 Asian Americans or Pacific Islanders, 1 Hispanic American), 77 international. Average age 31. 144 applicants, 55% accepted, 35 enrolled. In 2006, 62 master's, 1 doctorate awarded. *Degree requirements:* For doctorate, thesis/dissertation. *Entrance requirements:* For master's and doctorate, GMAT. *Application deadline:* For fall admission, 3/1 priority date for international students; for spring admission, 8/1 priority date for international students. Applications are processed on a rolling basis. Application fee: $40 ($75 for international students). Electronic applications accepted. *Expenses:* Tuition, state resident: part-time $146 per credit hour. Tuition, nonresident: part-time $516 per credit hour. Required fees: $44 per credit hour. Tuition and fees vary according to program. *Financial support:* In 2006–07, 2 research assistantships (averaging $4,620 per year), 19 teaching assistantships (averaging $7,334 per year) were awarded; career-related internships or fieldwork, Federal Work-Study, scholarships/grants, health care benefits, and unspecified assistantships also available. Support available to part-time students. *Unit head:* Dr. Rick Wilson, Head, 405-744-5084.

Penn State University Park, Graduate School, Intercollege Graduate Programs, Intercollege Program in Quality and Manufacturing Management, State College, University Park, PA 16802-1503. Offers MMM. *Unit head:* Dr. Jose A. Ventura, Co-Director, 814-865-5802, Fax: 814-863-4745, E-mail: jav1@psu.edu.

Penn State University Park, Graduate School, The Mary Jean and Frank P. Smeal College of Business Administration, State College, University Park, PA 16802-1503. Offers accounting (PhD); business administration (MBA); finance (PhD); management and organization (PhD); management science/operations/logistics (PhD); marketing (PhD); real estate (PhD); supply chain and information systems (PhD). *Students:* 287 full-time (79 women), 5 part-time (2 women); includes 39 minority (22 African Americans, 11 Asian Americans or Pacific Islanders, 6 Hispanic Americans), 93 international. Average age 31. 841 applicants, 31% accepted, 150 enrolled. In 2006, 107 master's, 11 doctorates awarded. *Expenses: Contact institution. Financial support:* In 2006–07, 1 fellowship, 11 research assistantships, 143 teaching assistantships were awarded. Financial award applicants required to submit FAFSA. *Unit head:* Dr. Kenneth B. Thomas, Dean, 814-863-0448, Fax: 814-865-7064, E-mail: j2t@psu.edu.

Polytechnic University of Puerto Rico, Graduate School, Hato Rey, PR 00919. Offers business administration (MBA), including general studies, management of information systems, management of international enterprises; civil engineering (ME, MS); competitiveness manufacturing (MCM, MMC, MS); computer engineering (ME, MS); electrical engineering (ME, MS); engineering management (MEM); environmental management (MEPM); manufacturing engineering (ME, MS). Part-time and evening/weekend programs available. *Entrance requirements:* For master's, 3 letters of recommendation.

Portland State University, Graduate Studies, Maseeh College of Engineering and Computer Science, Department of Engineering and Technology Management, Portland, OR 97207-0751. Offers engineering and technology management (M Eng); engineering management (MS); manufacturing engineering (ME); manufacturing management (M Eng); systems science/engineering management (PhD); MS/MBA; MS/MS. Part-time and evening/weekend programs available. *Faculty:* 7 full-time (1 woman), 4 part-time/adjunct (0 women). *Students:* 32 full-time (8 women), 55 part-time (22 women); includes 10 minority (3 African Americans, 4 Asian Americans or Pacific Islanders, 3 Hispanic Americans), 56 international. Average age 31. 57 applicants, 95% accepted, 32 enrolled. In 2006, 33 master's, 2 doctorates awarded. *Degree requirements:* For master's, thesis optional; for doctorate, one foreign language, thesis/dissertation, oral and written exams. *Entrance requirements:* For master's, minimum GPA of 3.0 in upper-division course work or 2.75 overall; for doctorate, GRE General Test, GRE Subject Test, minimum GPA of 3.0 in upper-division course work. Additional exam requirements/recommendations for international students: Required—TOEFL (minimum score 550 paper-based; 213 computer-based). *Application deadline:* For fall admission, 6/15 for domestic and international students; for winter admission, 11/1 for domestic and international students; for spring admission, 2/1 for domestic and international students. Applications are processed on a rolling basis. Application fee: $50. *Expenses:* Tuition, state resident: full-time $6,426; part-time $238 per credit. Tuition, nonresident: full-time $11,016; part-time $408 per credit. Tuition and fees vary according to course load. *Financial support:* In 2006–07, 1 teaching assistantship with full tuition reimbursement (averaging $9,437 per year) was awarded; research assistantships with full tuition reimbursements, career-related internships or fieldwork, Federal Work-Study, scholarships/grants, and unspecified assistantships also available. Support available to part-time students. Financial award application deadline: 3/1; financial award applicants required to submit FAFSA. *Faculty research:* Scheduling, hierarchical decision modeling, operations research, knowledge-based information systems. Total annual research expenditures: $27,471. *Unit head:* Dr. Dundar Kocaglu, Chair, 503-725-4660, Fax: 503-725-4667.

Purdue University, Graduate School, Krannert School of Management, Department of Management, West Lafayette, IN 47907. Offers accounting (PhD); business administration (MBA); finance (PhD); management information systems (PhD); marketing (PhD); operations management (PhD); quantitative methods (PhD); strategic management (PhD). *Students:* 56 full-time (21 women); includes 5 minority (3 Asian Americans or Pacific Islanders, 2 Hispanic Americans), 41 international. Average age 30. 421 applicants, 7% accepted, 19 enrolled. In 2006, 11 degrees awarded. *Median time to degree:* Doctorate–5 years full-time. Of those who began their doctoral program in fall 1998, 98% received their degree in 8 years or less. *Degree requirements:* For doctorate, thesis/dissertation, comprehensive exam, registration. *Entrance requirements:* For master's and doctorate, GMAT. Additional exam requirements/recommendations for international students: Required—TOEFL (minimum score 575 paper-based; 233 computer-based; 77 iBT), IELTS (minimum score 7). *Application deadline:* For fall admission, 2/15 for domestic and international students. Application fee: $55. Electronic applications accepted. *Financial support:* In 2006–07, 7 fellowships with partial tuition reimbursements (averaging $16,800 per year), 79 research assistantships with partial tuition reimbursements (averaging $16,800 per year), 8 teaching assistantships with partial tuition reimbursements (averaging $16,800 per year) were awarded; scholarships/grants and unspecified assistantships also available. Financial award application deadline: 2/15; financial award applicants required to submit FAFSA. *Faculty research:* Corporate finance, international business, enterprise integration. *Unit head:* Dr. John M. Barron, Head, 765-494-4451, Fax: 765-494-1526. *Application contact:* Kelly Felty, Assistant Director of Administration for Doctoral Programs, 765-494-4375, Fax: 765-494-1526, E-mail: phd@krannert.purdue.edu.

Regis University, School for Professional Studies, Program in Business, Denver, CO 80221-1099. Offers accounting (MS); business administration (MBA); finance (MBA); finance and accounting (MBA); international business (MBA); marketing (MBA); operations management (MBA); organization leadership (MS); project management (Certificate); technical management (Certificate). Offered at Colorado Springs Campus, Northwest Denver Campus, Southeast Denver Campus, Fort Collins Campus, Broomfield Campus, Henderson (Nevada) Campus, and Summerlin (Nevada) Campus. Part-time and evening/weekend programs available. Postbaccalaureate distance learning degree programs offered (no on-campus study). *Faculty:* 16 full-time (4 women), 82 part-time/adjunct (22 women). *Students:* 1,770 (834 women). Average age 36. In 2006, 560 degrees awarded. *Degree requirements:* For master's, capstone project, thesis optional. *Entrance requirements:* For master's, GMAT, interview, 2 years of full-time business work experience; for Certificate, GMAT. Additional exam requirements/recommendations for international students: Required—TOEFL or university-based test. *Application deadline:* For fall admission, 8/22 for domestic and international students; for winter admission, 1/2 for domestic and international students; for spring admission, 4/30 for domestic and international students. Applications are processed on a rolling basis. Application fee: $75. Electronic applications accepted. *Financial support:* Federal Work-Study available. Support available to part-time students. Financial award applicants required to submit FAFSA. *Unit head:* Dr. Michael Goess, Chair, 303-458-4302, Fax: 303-964-5538. *Application contact:* 800-677-9270 Ext. 4080, Fax: 303-964-5538, E-mail: masters@regis.edu.

Rensselaer Polytechnic Institute, Graduate School, Lally School of Management and Technology, Program in Management and Technology, Troy, NY 12180-3590. Offers finance (MBA, MS); financial technology (MS); management (PhD); management information systems (MBA, MS); new product development and marketing (MBA); new production and operations management (MS); product development and marketing (MS); production and operations management (MBA); technical commercialization (MS); technological entrepreneurship (MBA, MS). Part-time and evening/weekend programs available. Postbaccalaureate distance learning degree programs offered (no on-campus study). *Faculty:* 50 full-time (9 women), 1 part-time/adjunct (0 women). *Students:* 121 full-time (62 women), 525 part-time (184 women); includes 137 minority (43 African Americans, 60 Asian Americans or Pacific Islanders, 34 Hispanic Americans), 71 international. Average age 28. 416 applicants, 70% accepted, 240 enrolled. In 2006, 215 master's, 6 doctorates awarded. *Median time to degree:* Of those who began their doctoral program in fall 1998, 25% received their degree in 8 years or less. *Degree requirements:* For doctorate, thesis/dissertation. *Entrance requirements:* For master's, GMAT, resumé, 2 letters of recommendation; for doctorate, GMAT or GRE General Test, 2 letters of recommendation. Additional exam requirements/recommendations for international students: Required—TOEFL (minimum score 600 paper-based; 250 computer-based; 100 iBT); Recommended—IELTS (minimum score 7). *Application deadline:* For fall admission, 3/15 priority date for domestic and international students. Applications are processed on a rolling basis. Application fee: $75. Electronic applications accepted. *Expenses:* Tuition: Full-time $32,600; part-time $1,358 per credit. Required fees: $1,629. *Financial support:* In 2006–07, 48 students received support; fellowships with partial tuition reimbursements available, research assistantships with partial tuition reimbursements available, teaching assistantships with partial tuition reimbursements available, career-related internships or fieldwork, institutionally sponsored loans, and scholarships/grants available. Financial award application deadline: 3/15; financial award applicants required to submit FAFSA. *Faculty research:* Technological entrepreneurship, operations management, new product development and marketing, information systems, finance. Total annual research expenditures: $24,747. *Unit head:* Pedro Gonzalez, Director MBA/Admissons and Career Services, 518-276-2378, Fax: 518-276-2665, E-mail: gonzap3@rpi.edu. *Application contact:* Michele M. Martens, Manager of Graduate Programs, 518-276-6586, Fax: 518-276-2665, E-mail: martem@rpi.edu.

See Close-Up on page 313.

Rochester Institute of Technology, Graduate Enrollment Services, College of Engineering, Department of Design, Development and Manufacturing, Program in Manufacturing Leadership, Rochester, NY 14623-5603. Offers MS. *Students:* 1 (woman) full-time, 22 part-time (6 women); includes 6 minority (2 African Americans, 1 Asian American or Pacific Islander, 3 Hispanic Americans). 15 applicants, 93% accepted, 14 enrolled. In 2006, 8 degrees awarded. *Entrance requirements:* For master's, GMAT, minimum GPA of 2.5. *Application deadline:* For fall admission, 3/1 priority date for domestic students. Applications are processed on a rolling basis. Application fee: $50. *Expenses:* Tuition: Full-time $28,491; part-time $800 per credit. Required fees: $201. *Unit head:* Mark Smith, Director, Department of Design, Development and Manufacturing, 585-475-7102, E-mail: mwspd21@rit.edu.

San Diego State University, Graduate and Research Affairs, College of Business Administration, Department of Information and Decision Systems, San Diego, CA 92182. Offers information and decision systems (MS); production and operations management (MS). Evening/weekend programs available. *Students:* 7 full-time (2 women), 15 part-time (5 women); includes 4 minority (3 Asian Americans or Pacific Islanders, 1 Hispanic American), 7 international. Average age 29. 15 applicants, 73% accepted, 7 enrolled. In 2006, 14 degrees awarded. *Degree requirements:* For master's, thesis or alternative. *Entrance requirements:* For master's, GMAT, resumé, letters of reference. Additional exam requirements/recommendations for international students: Required—TOEFL. *Application deadline:* For fall admission, 4/15 for domestic and international students; for spring admission, 11/1 for domestic students, 10/1 for international students. Applications are processed on a rolling basis. Application fee: $55. Electronic applications accepted. *Financial support:* In 2006–07, 21 teaching assistantships were awarded; fellowships, research assistantships also available. Financial award applicants required to submit FAFSA. Total annual research expenditures: $8,000. *Unit head:* Bruce Reinig, Chair, 619-594-5316, Fax: 619-594-3675. *Application contact:* Information Contact, E-mail: sdsumba@mail.sdsu.edu.

San Jose State University, Graduate Studies and Research, Lucas Graduate School of Business, Programs in Business Administration, San Jose, CA 95192-0001. Offers MBA. *Accreditation:* AACSB. *Students:* 39 full-time (11 women), 172 part-time (75 women); includes 92 minority (1 African American, 83 Asian Americans or Pacific Islanders, 8 Hispanic Americans), 38 international. Average age 32. 332 applicants, 34% accepted, 32 enrolled. In 2006, 159 degrees awarded. *Degree requirements:* For master's, thesis or alternative, comprehensive exam. *Entrance requirements:* For master's, GMAT, minimum GPA of 3.0. *Application deadline:* For fall admission, 6/29 for domestic students; for spring admission, 11/30 for domestic students. Applications are processed on a rolling basis. Application fee: $59. Electronic applications accepted. *Financial support:* Applicants required to submit FAFSA.

Southeastern Oklahoma State University, Graduate School, School of Arts and Sciences, Durant, OK 74701-0609. Offers technology (MT). Part-time and evening/weekend programs available. *Degree requirements:* For master's, thesis optional. *Entrance requirements:* For master's, minimum GPA of 3.0 in last 60 hours or 2.75 overall. Additional exam requirements/

recommendations for international students: Required—TOEFL (minimum score 550 paper-based; 213 computer-based). Electronic applications accepted.

Southeast Missouri State University, School of Graduate Studies, Harrison College of Business, Cape Girardeau, MO 63701-4799. Offers accounting (MBA); environmental management (MBA); finance (MBA); general management (MBA); health administration (MBA); industrial management (MBA); international business (MBA). *Accreditation:* AACSB. Part-time and evening/weekend programs available. Postbaccalaureate distance learning degree programs offered (no on-campus study). *Faculty:* 33 full-time (10 women). *Students:* 35 full-time (18 women), 40 part-time (24 women); includes 5 minority (2 African Americans, 3 Asian Americans or Pacific Islanders), 9 international. Average age 27. 35 applicants, 86% accepted. In 2006, 23 degrees awarded. *Degree requirements:* For master's, applied research project. *Entrance requirements:* For master's, GMAT, minimum undergraduate GPA of 2.5. Additional exam requirements/recommendations for international students: Required—TOEFL (minimum score 550 paper-based; 213 computer-based). *Application deadline:* For fall admission, 8/1 for domestic students, 4/1 for international students; for spring admission, 11/21 for domestic students, 10/1 for international students. Applications are processed on a rolling basis. Application fee: $20 ($100 for international students). *Financial support:* In 2006–07, 54 students received support, including 31 research assistantships with full tuition reimbursements available (averaging $7,100 per year); career-related internships or fieldwork and unspecified assistantships also available. Financial award applicants required to submit FAFSA. *Unit head:* Dr. Kenneth Heischmidt, Director MBA Program, 573-651-2912, Fax: 573-651-5032, E-mail: kheischmidt@semo.edu. *Application contact:* Marsha L. Arant, Senior Administrative Assistant, Office of Graduate Studies, 573-651-2192, Fax: 573-651-2001, E-mail: marant@semo.edu.

Southeast Missouri State University, School of Graduate Studies, School of Polytechnic Studies, Cape Girardeau, MO 63701-4799. Offers industrial management (MS). Part-time and evening/weekend programs available. Postbaccalaureate distance learning degree programs offered (no on-campus study). *Faculty:* 9 full-time (1 woman). *Students:* 6 full-time (1 woman), 21 part-time (3 women); includes 3 minority (all African Americans), 2 international. Average age 30. 10 applicants, 90% accepted. In 2006, 9 master's awarded. *Degree requirements:* For master's, thesis or alternative. *Entrance requirements:* For master's, minimum GPA of 2.7. Additional exam requirements/recommendations for international students: Required—TOEFL (minimum score 550 paper-based; 213 computer-based). *Application deadline:* For fall admission, 8/1 for domestic students, 4/1 for international students; for spring admission, 11/21 for domestic students, 10/1 for international students. Applications are processed on a rolling basis. Application fee: $20 ($100 for international students). *Financial support:* In 2006–07, 10 students received support, including 2 research assistantships with full tuition reimbursements available (averaging $7,100 per year), 5 teaching assistantships with full tuition reimbursements available (averaging $7,100 per year); unspecified assistantships also available. Financial award applicants required to submit FAFSA. *Faculty research:* Graphic communications, ISQ/Q5 9000, SAP (enterprise Resource Planning), automatic control systems. *Unit head:* Dr. Randall Shaw, Dean, 573-651-5915, Fax: 573-651-2827, E-mail: rshaw@semo.edu. *Application contact:* Marsha L. Arant, Senior Administrative Assistant, Office of Graduate Studies, 573-651-2192, Fax: 573-651-2001, E-mail: marant@semo.edu.

Stevens Institute of Technology, Graduate School, Charles V. Schaefer Jr. School of Engineering, Department of Mechanical Engineering, Program in Integrated Product Development, Hoboken, NJ 07030. Offers armament engineering (M Eng); computer and electrical engineering (M Eng); manufacturing technologies (M Eng); systems reliability and design (M Eng).

Stony Brook University, State University of New York, Graduate School, College of Business, W. Averell Harriman School for Management and Policy, Stony Brook, NY 11794. Offers business administration (MBA); industrial management (Certificate); management policy (MS); technology management (MS). Part-time and evening/weekend programs available. *Degree requirements:* For master's, internship. *Expenses:* Tuition, state resident: full-time $6,900; part-time $288 per credit. Tuition, nonresident: full-time $10,920; part-time $455 per credit. *Financial support:* Fellowships, research assistantships, teaching assistantships, career-related internships or fieldwork available.

Stony Brook University, State University of New York, School of Professional Development, Stony Brook, NY 11794. Offers adolescence education: mathematics (Certificate); biology 7-12 (MAT); chemistry-grade 7-12 (MAT); coaching (Certificate); computer integrated engineering (Certificate); cultural studies (Certificate); earth science-grade 7-12 (MAT); educational computing (Advanced Certificate, Certificate); English-grade 7-12 (MAT); environmental and waste management (MS, Advanced Certificate); environmental systems management (Certificate); environmental/occupational health and safety (Certificate); French-grade 7-12 (MAT); German-grade 7-12 (MAT); human resource management (Certificate); industrial management (Certificate); information systems management (Certificate); Italian-grade 7-12 (MAT); liberal studies (MA); liberal studies online (MA); Long Island regional studies (Certificate); operation research (Certificate); physics-grade 7-12 (MAT); Russian-grade 7-12 (MAT); school administration and supervision (Certificate); school district administration (Certificate); social science and the professions (MPS), including human resources management, labor management, public affairs, waste management; social studies 7-12 (MAT); waste management (Certificate); women's studies (Certificate). Part-time and evening/weekend programs available. Postbaccalaureate distance learning degree programs offered. *Faculty:* 1 full-time (0 women), 118 part-time/adjunct (45 women). *Students:* 322 full-time (202 women), 1,188 part-time (728 women); includes 164 minority (69 African Americans, 2 American Indian/Alaska Native, 29 Asian Americans or Pacific Islanders, 64 Hispanic Americans), 11 international. Average age 28. In 2006, 738 master's, 405 other advanced degrees awarded. *Degree requirements:* For master's, one foreign language, thesis or alternative. *Application deadline:* Applications are processed on a rolling basis. Application fee: $62. *Expenses:* Tuition, state resident: full-time $6,900; part-time $288 per credit. Tuition, nonresident: full-time $10,920; part-time $455 per credit. *Financial support:* In 2006–07, 5 teaching assistantships were awarded; fellowships, research assistantships, career-related internships or fieldwork also available. Support available to part-time students. *Unit head:* Dr. Paul J. Edelson, Dean, 631-632-7052, Fax: 631-632-9046, E-mail: paul.edelson@sunysb.edu. *Application contact:* Sandra Romansky, Director of Admissions and Advisement, 631-632-7050, Fax: 631-632-9046, E-mail: sandra.romansky@sunysb.edu.

Syracuse University, Martin J. Whitman School of Management, PhD Program in Business Administration, Syracuse, NY 13244. Offers accounting (PhD); finance (PhD); management information systems (PhD); managerial statistics (PhD); marketing (PhD); operations management (PhD); organizational behavior (PhD); strategy and human resources (PhD); supply chain management (PhD). *Faculty:* 71 full-time (16 women), 2 part-time/adjunct (1 woman). *Students:* 34 full-time (10 women); includes 1 minority (African American), 24 international. Average age 31. 89 applicants, 8% accepted, 4 enrolled. In 2006, 8 degrees awarded. *Degree requirements:* For doctorate, thesis/dissertation, summer research paper, comprehensive exam, registration. *Entrance requirements:* For doctorate, GMAT, 3 recommendations. Additional exam requirements/recommendations for international students: Required—TOEFL (minimum score 600 paper-based; 250 computer-based; 100 iBT). *Application deadline:* For fall admission, 1/30 priority date for domestic students. Applications are processed on a rolling basis. Application fee: $75. Electronic applications accepted. *Expenses:* Tuition: Full-time $16,920; part-time $940 per credit hour. Required fees: $930; $930 per year. *Financial support:* In 2006–07, 1 fellowship with full tuition reimbursement (averaging $19,000 per year), 26 teaching assistantships with full tuition reimbursements (averaging $16,500 per year) were awarded; research assistantships with full tuition reimbursements, health care benefits and unspecified assistantships also available. Financial award application deadline: 1/30. *Faculty research:* Marketing models, market microstructure, supply chain, auditing, corporate governance. *Unit head:* Dr. Ravi Dharwadkar, Director of the PhD Program, 315-443-3386, E-mail: rdharwad@syr.edu. *Application contact:* Shannon Hiemstra, Assistant Director for PhD and Research Programs, 315-443-3549, Fax: 315-443-3671, E-mail: srhiemst@syr.edu.

Texas A&M University, Mays Business School, Department of Information and Operations Management, College Station, TX 77843. Offers management information systems (MS, PhD); management science (PhD); production and operations management (PhD). *Faculty:* 21 full-time (5 women), 4 part-time/adjunct (0 women). *Students:* 173 full-time (66 women). Average age 31. In 2006, 74 master's, 3 doctorates awarded. Terminal master's awarded for partial completion of doctoral program. *Degree requirements:* For master's, comprehensive exam; for doctorate, thesis/dissertation. *Entrance requirements:* For master's, GMAT; for doctorate, GMAT or GRE General Test. Additional exam requirements/recommendations for international students: Required—TOEFL. *Application deadline:* For fall admission, 3/1 priority date for domestic students; for spring admission, 8/1 for domestic students. Applications are processed on a rolling basis. Application fee: $50 ($75 for international students). *Expenses:* Tuition, state resident: full-time $4,697. Tuition, nonresident: full-time $11,297. Required fees: $2,272. *Financial support:* In 2006–07, 51 students received support; fellowships, research assistantships, teaching assistantships, career-related internships or fieldwork, Federal Work-Study, and institutionally sponsored loans available. Financial award application deadline: 2/1. *Unit head:* Dr. E. Powell Robinson, Head, 979-846-1616. *Application contact:* Louise Darcey, Adviser, 979-845-0811, E-mail: msmisadvisor@tamu.edu.

Texas Tech University, Jerry S. Rawls College of Business Administration, Area of Information Systems and Quantitative Sciences, Lubbock, TX 79409. Offers business statistics (MS, PhD); health organization management (MS); management information systems (MS, PhD); production and operations management (MS, PhD). Part-time programs available. *Faculty:* 15 full-time (0 women). *Students:* 18 full-time (6 women), 6 part-time (1 woman); includes 2 minority (1 African American, 1 Hispanic American), 11 international. Average age 31. 32 applicants, 53% accepted, 11 enrolled. In 2006, 13 master's, 5 doctorates awarded. Terminal master's awarded for partial completion of doctoral program. *Degree requirements:* For master's, comprehensive exam or capstone course; for doctorate, thesis/dissertation, qualifying exams. *Entrance requirements:* For master's and doctorate, GMAT, holistic profile of academic credentials. Additional exam requirements/recommendations for international students: Required—TOEFL (minimum score 550 paper-based; 213 computer-based; 79 iBT). *Application deadline:* For fall admission, 7/1 priority date for domestic students, 3/1 priority date for international students; for spring admission, 11/1 priority date for domestic students, 9/1 priority date for international students. Applications are processed on a rolling basis. Application fee: $50 ($60 for international students). Electronic applications accepted. *Expenses:* Tuition, state resident: full-time $4,440. Tuition, nonresident: full-time $11,040. Required fees: $2,136. *Financial support:* In 2006–07, 2 research assistantships (averaging $8,000 per year), 9 teaching assistantships (averaging $16,930 per year) were awarded; Federal Work-Study, scholarships/grants, and unspecified assistantships also available. *Faculty research:* Database management systems, systems management and engineering, expert systems and adaptive knowledge-based sciences, statistical analysis and design. *Unit head:* Dr. James Hoffman, Area Coordinator, 806-742-3192, Fax: 806-742-3958, E-mail: james.hoffman@ttu.edu. *Application contact:* Cynthia D. Barnes, Director, Graduate Services Center, 806-742-3184, Fax: 806-742-3958, E-mail: ba_grad@ttu.edu.

Universidad de las Américas–Puebla, Division of Graduate Studies, School of Engineering, Program in Industrial Engineering, Puebla, Mexico. Offers industrial engineering (MS); production management (M Adm). Part-time and evening/weekend programs available. *Degree requirements:* For master's, one foreign language, thesis. *Faculty research:* Textile industry, quality control.

Universidad de las Américas–Puebla, Division of Graduate Studies, School of Engineering, Program in Manufacturing Administration, Puebla, Mexico. Offers MS. *Faculty research:* Operations research, construction.

University of Arkansas, Graduate School, College of Engineering, Department of Industrial Engineering, Program in Operations Management, Fayetteville, AR 72701-1201. Offers MS. Part-time and evening/weekend programs available. Postbaccalaureate distance learning degree programs offered. *Students:* 7 full-time (1 woman), 221 part-time (55 women); includes 60 minority (43 African Americans, 5 American Indian/Alaska Native, 6 Asian Americans or Pacific Islanders, 6 Hispanic Americans), 3 international. 190 applicants, 34% accepted. In 2006, 72 degrees awarded. *Degree requirements:* For master's, thesis optional. Application fee: $40 ($50 for international students). *Financial support:* Fellowships available. Financial award application deadline: 4/1. *Unit head:* Dr. Sandra Parker, Head, 479-575-2687, Fax: 479-575-8431, E-mail: scparke@engr.uark.edu. *Application contact:* Nancy Sloan, Program Manager, 479-575-7426, E-mail: ncsloan@engr.uark.edu.

University of Central Missouri, The Graduate School, College of Science and Technology, School of Technology, Warrensburg, MO 64093. Offers industrial management (MS). Part-time programs available. *Faculty:* 33 full-time (9 women). *Students:* 24 full-time (3 women), 35 part-time (3 women); includes 13 minority (6 African Americans, 6 Asian Americans or Pacific Islanders, 1 Hispanic American), 14 international. Average age 33. 18 applicants, 78% accepted, 13 enrolled. In 2006, 18 degrees awarded. *Degree requirements:* For master's, comprehensive exam. *Entrance requirements:* For master's, minimum GPA of 2.5; course work in mathematics, science, and technology. Additional exam requirements/recommendations for international students: Required—TOEFL (minimum score 500 paper-based; 173 computer-based). *Application deadline:* For fall admission, 6/1 priority date for domestic students, 5/1 priority date for international students; for spring admission, 10/1 priority date for domestic students, 10/1 for international students. Applications are processed on a rolling basis. Application fee: $30 ($50 for international students). *Expenses:* Tuition, state resident: full-time $5,448; part-time $227 per credit hour. Tuition, nonresident: full-time $10,896; part-time $454 per credit hour. Required fees: $336; $14 per credit hour. *Financial support:* In 2006–07, 5 students received support. Federal Work-Study, scholarships/grants, unspecified assistantships, and laboratory assistantships available. Support available to part-time students. Financial award application deadline: 3/1; financial award applicants required to submit FAFSA. *Faculty research:* Labor relations, collective bargaining, manufacturing. Total annual research expenditures: $400,000. *Unit head:* Dr. John Sutton, Chair, 660-543-4439, Fax: 660-543-4578, E-mail: sutton@ucmo.edu.

University of Cincinnati, Division of Research and Advanced Studies, College of Business, Department of Quantitative Analysis and Operations Management, Cincinnati, OH 45221. Offers operations management (MBA, PhD); quantitative analysis (MBA, MS, PhD). Part-time and evening/weekend programs available. *Degree requirements:* For master's, capstone project (MBA); for doctorate, thesis/dissertation. *Entrance requirements:* For master's, GMAT, GRE General Test (MS), resumé, letters of recommendation; for doctorate, GMAT, GRE General Test. Application fee: $40. Electronic applications accepted. *Expenses:* Contact institution. *Financial support:* Fellowships, research assistantships, teaching assistantships, scholarships/grants, tuition waivers (full and partial), and unspecified assistantships available. Financial award application deadline: 2/1; financial award applicants required to submit FAFSA. *Unit head:* Dr. Jeffrey D. Camm, Head, 513-556-7146, Fax: 513-556-5499.

The University of Iowa, Henry B. Tippie College of Business, Henry B. Tippie School of Management, Iowa City, IA 52242-1316. Offers accounting (MBA); corporate finance (MBA); entrepreneurship (MBA); finance (MBA); individually designed concentration (MBA); investment management (MBA); management information systems (MBA); marketing (MBA); nonprofit management (MBA); operations management (MBA); strategic management and consulting (MBA); JD/MBA; MBA/MA; MBA/MD; MBA/MHA; MBA/MSN. *Accreditation:* AACSB. Part-time and evening/weekend programs available. *Faculty:* 94 full-time (23 women), 65 part-time/adjunct (21 women). *Students:* 230 full-time (67 women), 712 part-time (234 women); includes 62 minority (6 African Americans, 1 American Indian/Alaska Native, 43 Asian Americans or Pacific Islanders, 12 Hispanic Americans), 127 international. Average age 30. 431 applicants, 61% accepted, 217 enrolled. In 2006, 363 degrees awarded. *Median time to degree:* Master's–2 years full-time, 3.5 years part-time. *Degree requirements:* For master's, registration. *Entrance requirements:* For master's, GMAT, work experience. Additional exam requirements/

The University of Iowa (continued)
recommendations for international students: Required—TOEFL (minimum score 600 paper-based; 250 computer-based; 100 iBT). *Application deadline:* For fall admission, 7/15 for domestic students, 4/15 for international students; for spring admission, 12/15 priority date for domestic students, 11/1 priority date for international students. Applications are processed on a rolling basis. Application fee: $60 ($85 for international students). Electronic applications accepted. *Expenses: Contact institution. Financial support:* In 2006–07, 72 fellowships (averaging $3,892 per year), 55 research assistantships with partial tuition reimbursements (averaging $10,260 per year) were awarded; career-related internships or fieldwork, Federal Work-Study, institutionally sponsored loans, scholarships/grants, health care benefits, and unspecified assistantships also available. Support available to part-time students. Financial award application deadline: 4/15; financial award applicants required to submit FAFSA. *Faculty research:* Capital markets, econometrics, optimization, investments and empirical corporate finance, Iowa electronic markets. *Unit head:* Prof. Gary J. Gaeth, Associate Dean, MBA Programs, 800-622-4692, Fax: 319-335-3604, E-mail: gary-gaeth@uiowa.edu. *Application contact:* Jodi Schafer, Director of Student Recruitment and Marketing, 319-335-0864, Fax: 319-335-3604, E-mail: jodi-schafer@uiowa.edu.

University of Massachusetts Lowell, Graduate School, College of Management, Program in Manufacturing Management, Lowell, MA 01854-2881. Offers MMS. Part-time and evening/weekend programs available. *Entrance requirements:* For master's, GMAT.

University of Minnesota, Twin Cities Campus, Carlson School of Management, Carlson Full-time MBA Program, Minneapolis, MN 55455-0213. Offers accounting (MBA); entrepreneurship (MBA); finance (MBA); healthcare management (MBA); information and decision sciences (MBA); international business (MBA); marketing and logistics management (MBA); operations and management science (MBA); strategic management and organization (MBA); supply chain management (MBA); JD/MBA; MD/MBA; MHA/MBA. *Accreditation:* AACSB. *Faculty:* 125 full-time (27 women), 120 part-time/adjunct. *Students:* 218 full-time (70 women); includes 18 minority (4 African Americans, 1 American Indian/Alaska Native, 10 Asian Americans or Pacific Islanders, 3 Hispanic Americans), 86 international. Average age 28. 418 applicants, 53% accepted, 124 enrolled. In 2006, 105 degrees awarded. *Median time to degree:* Master's–2 years full-time. *Entrance requirements:* For master's, GMAT. Additional exam requirements/recommendations for international students: Required—TOEFL (minimum score 580 paper-based; 240 computer-based), IELTS. *Application deadline:* For fall admission, 4/15 for domestic students, 2/15 for international students. Application fee: $60 ($90 for international students). Electronic applications accepted. *Expenses: Contact institution.* Full-time tuition and fees vary according to class time, course load, program, reciprocity agreements and student level. *Financial support:* In 2006–07, 131 students received support, including 127 fellowships with full and partial tuition reimbursements available (averaging $20,000 per year); research assistantships with partial tuition reimbursements available, teaching assistantships with partial tuition reimbursements available, career-related internships or fieldwork, Federal Work-Study, institutionally sponsored loans, scholarships/grants, health care benefits, tuition waivers (full and partial), and unspecified assistantships also available. Support available to part-time students. Financial award application deadline: 2/15; financial award applicants required to submit FAFSA. *Faculty research:* IT, strategy, marketing, finance, quality management. *Unit head:* Kathryn J. Carlson, MBA Programs and Executive Education, 612-624-2039, Fax: 612-625-1012, E-mail: full-timeembainfo@csom.umn.edu. *Application contact:* Jeffrey Bieganek, Director, Admissions and Business Development, MBA Programs and Executive Education, 612-625-6558, Fax: 612-625-1012, E-mail: full-timembainfo@csom.umn.edu.

University of Minnesota, Twin Cities Campus, Carlson School of Management, Doctoral Program in Business Administration, Minneapolis, MN 55455-0213. Offers accounting (PhD); finance (PhD); information and decision sciences (PhD); marketing and logistics management (PhD); operations and management science (PhD); strategic management and organization (PhD). *Faculty:* 109 full-time (26 women). *Students:* 90 full-time (30 women); includes 9 minority (5 African Americans, 1 Asian American or Pacific Islander, 3 Hispanic Americans), 60 international. Average age 30. 325 applicants, 8% accepted, 17 enrolled. In 2006, 16 degrees awarded. *Median time to degree:* Of those who began their doctoral program in fall 1998, 61% received their degree in 8 years or less. *Degree requirements:* For doctorate, thesis/dissertation, written and oral preliminary exams, comprehensive exam, registration. *Entrance requirements:* For doctorate, GMAT, GRE General Test, International must submit a TOEFL or IELT. Additional exam requirements/recommendations for international students: Required—TOEFL (minimum score 600 paper-based; 250 computer-based; 100 iBT), IELTS (minimum score 8), TOEFL (paper-based 600, computer-based 250) or IELTS (7.5). *Application deadline:* For fall admission, 12/30 for domestic students, 12/30 priority date for international students. Applications are processed on a rolling basis. Application fee: $55 ($75 for international students). Electronic applications accepted. *Expenses:* Tuition, state resident: full-time $9,302; part-time $775 per credit. Tuition, nonresident: full-time $16,400; part-time $1,367 per credit. Full-time tuition and fees vary according to class time, course load, program, reciprocity agreements and student level. *Financial support:* In 2006–07, 67 students received support, including fellowships with full tuition reimbursements available (averaging $11,000 per year), research assistantships with full tuition reimbursements available (averaging $6,000 per year), teaching assistantships with full tuition reimbursements available (averaging $6,000 per year); institutionally sponsored loans, scholarships/grants, health care benefits, and unspecified assistantships also available. Financial award application deadline: 12/31. *Faculty research:* Corporate strategy, international business, corporate finances, entrepreneurship, quality management, marketing, information and decision science, operations and accounting. Total annual research expenditures: $300,000. *Unit head:* Dr. Paul E. Johnson, Director of Graduate Studies and PhD Program Director, 612-624-5570, Fax: 612-624-8221, E-mail: pjohnson@csom.umn.edu. *Application contact:* Earlene Bronson, Assistant Director, PhD Program, 612-624-0875, Fax: 612-624-8221, E-mail: ebronson@csom.umn.edu.

University of Missouri–St. Louis, College of Business Administration, Program in Business Administration, St. Louis, MO 63121. Offers accounting (MBA); business administration (Certificate); finance (MBA); human resource management (Certificate); logistics and supply chain management (MBA, Certificate); management (MBA); marketing (MBA); marketing management (Certificate); operations (MBA); quantitative management science (MBA); telecommunications management (Certificate). *Accreditation:* AACSB. Part-time and evening/weekend programs available. *Faculty:* 26 full-time (6 women), 2 part-time/adjunct (0 women). *Students:* 242 full-time (156 women), 186 part-time (123 women); includes 48 minority (17 African Americans, 1 American Indian/Alaska Native, 27 Asian Americans or Pacific Islanders, 3 Hispanic Americans), 96 international. Average age 33. In 2006, 138 degrees awarded. *Entrance requirements:* For master's, GMAT, 2 letters of recommendation. Additional exam requirements/recommendations for international students: Required—TOEFL (minimum score 550 paper-based; 213 computer-based). *Application deadline:* For fall admission, 7/1 for domestic students; for spring admission, 11/1 for domestic students. Applications are processed on a rolling basis. Application fee: $35 ($40 for international students). Electronic applications accepted. *Expenses:* Tuition, state resident: part-time $332 per credit hour. Tuition, nonresident: part-time $770 per credit hour. *Financial support:* Research assistantships with full and partial tuition reimbursements, teaching assistantships with full and partial tuition reimbursements, career-related internships or fieldwork, Federal Work-Study, and institutionally sponsored loans available. Support available to part-time students. Financial award application deadline: 4/1; financial award applicants required to submit FAFSA. *Faculty research:* Human resources, strategic management, marketing strategy, consumer behavior product development, advertising. *Application contact:* 314-516-5458, Fax: 314-516-6996, E-mail: gradadm@umsl.edu.

University of North Dakota, Graduate School, College of Business and Public Administration, Department of Technology Education, Grand Forks, ND 58202. Offers MS. *Faculty:* 5 full-time (1 woman). *Students:* 1 (woman) full-time. *Degree requirements:* For master's, thesis or alternative, final exam, comprehensive exam. *Entrance requirements:* For master's, minimum GPA of 3.0. Additional exam requirements/recommendations for international students: Required—TOEFL (minimum score 550 paper-based; 213 computer-based; 79 iBT), IELTS (minimum score 6). *Application deadline:* For fall admission, 2/15 priority date for domestic and international students; for spring admission, 10/15 priority date for domestic and international students. Application fee: $35. Electronic applications accepted. *Expenses:* Tuition, state resident: full-time $5,650; part-time $214 per credit. Tuition, nonresident: full-time $14,248; part-time $572 per credit. Required fees: $1,008; $42 per credit. Tuition and fees vary according to reciprocity agreements. *Financial support:* In 2006–07, 1 student received support; fellowships, research assistantships, teaching assistantships with full tuition reimbursements available, Federal Work-Study, scholarships/grants, tuition waivers (full and partial), and unspecified assistantships available. Support available to part-time students. Financial award application deadline: 3/15; financial award applicants required to submit FAFSA. *Faculty research:* Graphic communications, photography, design, drafting, computers. *Unit head:* Dr. Ronald Holten, Graduate Director, 701-777-2249, Fax: 701-777-4320, E-mail: ronald_holten@nodak.edu. *Application contact:* Linda M. Baeza, Admissions Officer, 701-777-2945, Fax: 701-777-3619, E-mail: gradschool@mail.und.nodak.edu.

University of North Texas, Robert B. Toulouse School of Graduate Studies, College of Business Administration, Department of Management, Denton, TX 76203. Offers administrative management (MBA); management (EMBA, MBA); organization theory and policy (PhD); personnel and industrial relations (MBA, PhD); production/operations management (MBA, PhD). *Faculty:* 24 full-time (10 women). *Students:* 18 full-time (11 women), 51 part-time (22 women); includes 15 minority (7 African Americans, 1 American Indian/Alaska Native, 1 Asian American or Pacific Islander, 6 Hispanic Americans), 13 international. Average age 30. 54 applicants, 83% accepted, 9 enrolled. In 2006, 29 master's, 1 doctorate awarded. *Degree requirements:* For doctorate, thesis/dissertation. *Entrance requirements:* For master's, GMAT, relevant work experience; for doctorate, GMAT or GRE General Test, relevant work experience. Additional exam requirements/recommendations for international students: Required—TOEFL. *Application deadline:* For fall admission, 7/15 for domestic students. Application fee: $50 ($75 for international students). *Expenses:* Tuition, state resident: full-time $3,573; part-time $198 per credit. Tuition, nonresident: full-time $8,577; part-time $476 per credit. Required fees: $1,258; $126 per credit. One-time fee: $150 full-time. Tuition and fees vary according to course load. *Financial support:* Fellowships, teaching assistantships, Federal Work-Study available. Financial award application deadline: 4/1. *Unit head:* Dr. J. Lynn Johnson, Chair, 940-565-3140, Fax: 940-565-4394, E-mail: johnsonl@cobaf.coba.unt.edu. *Application contact:* Dr. Nancy Boyd-Lillie, Graduate Adviser, 940-565-3158, E-mail: boyd@cobaf.coba.unt.edu.

University of Puerto Rico, Mayagüez Campus, Graduate Studies, College of Business Administration, Mayagüez, PR 00681-9000. Offers business administration (MBA); finance (MBA); human resources (MBA); industrial management (MBA). Part-time and evening/weekend programs available. *Faculty:* 52 full-time (30 women). *Students:* 32 full-time (15 women), 52 part-time (37 women); includes 73 minority (all Hispanic Americans), 11 international. 47 applicants, 70% accepted, 24 enrolled. In 2006, 13 degrees awarded. *Degree requirements:* For master's, comprehensive exam. *Entrance requirements:* For master's, GMAT or EXADEP, bachelor's degree with courses in calculus, microeconomics, accounting and statistics. Additional exam requirements/recommendations for international students: Required—TOEFL (minimum score 500 paper-based; 173 computer-based). *Application deadline:* For fall admission, 2/15 for domestic and international students; for spring admission, 9/15 for domestic and international students. Applications are processed on a rolling basis. Application fee: $25. *Expenses:* Tuition, nonresident: full-time $4,655. Required fees: $210. One-time fee: $77 full-time. Part-time tuition and fees vary according to course load and reciprocity agreements. *Financial support:* In 2006–07, 10 students received support, including fellowships (averaging $12,000 per year), 7 research assistantships (averaging $15,000 per year), 3 teaching assistantships (averaging $8,500 per year); Federal Work-Study and institutionally sponsored loans also available. *Faculty research:* Organizational studies, management, accounting. Total annual research expenditures: $264,836. *Unit head:* Prof. Eva Quinñones, Dean, 787-265-3800, Fax: 787-832-5320, E-mail: quinones-e@rigel.uprm.edu. *Application contact:* Dr. Yolanda Ruiz, Director, 787-265-3887, Fax: 787-832-5320, E-mail: yruiz@caribe.net.

University of Rhode Island, Graduate School, College of Business Administration, Kingston, RI 02881. Offers accounting (MS); business administration (PhD), including finance, management, management science and information systems, marketing; finance (MBA); international business (MBA); international sports management (MBA); management (MBA); management science (MBA), including management information systems, manufacturing; marketing (MBA). *Accreditation:* AACSB. In 2006, 86 master's, 1 doctorate awarded. *Entrance requirements:* For master's and doctorate, GMAT. Additional exam requirements/recommendations for international students: Required—TOEFL. *Application deadline:* For fall admission, 4/15 priority date for domestic students. Applications are processed on a rolling basis. Application fee: $35. *Expenses:* Tuition, state resident: full-time $6,032; part-time $335 per credit. Tuition, nonresident: full-time $17,288; part-time $960 per credit. Required fees: $65 per credit. $30 per semester. One-time fee: $80 part-time. *Financial support:* Unspecified assistantships available. *Unit head:* Mark Higgins, Dean, 401-874-2337. *Application contact:* Dr. Laura Beauvais, Director of Graduate Programs, 401-874-4341.

University of St. Thomas, Graduate Studies, School of Engineering, St. Paul, MN 55105-1096. Offers engineering and technology management (Certificate); manufacturing systems (MS); manufacturing systems engineering (MMSE); systems engineering (MS); technology management (MS). *Accreditation:* ABET (one or more programs are accredited). *Faculty:* 1 full-time (0 women), 40 part-time/adjunct (0 women). *Students:* 2 full-time (0 women), 210 part-time (58 women); includes 22 minority (3 African Americans, 14 Asian Americans or Pacific Islanders, 5 Hispanic Americans), 23 international. Average age 33. 190 applicants, 94% accepted, 162 enrolled. In 2006, 41 master's, 47 other advanced degrees awarded. *Application deadline:* For fall admission, 8/1 priority date for domestic students; for spring admission, 1/1 priority date for domestic students. Applications are processed on a rolling basis. Application fee: $30. Electronic applications accepted. *Expenses: Contact institution. Financial support:* In 2006–07, 17 students received support, including 2 research assistantships (averaging $2,443 per year); fellowships, institutionally sponsored loans and scholarships/grants also available. Support available to part-time students. Financial award application deadline: 4/1; financial award applicants required to submit FAFSA. *Unit head:* Ron Bennett, Dean, 651-962-5756, Fax: 651-962-6419, E-mail: rjbennett@stthomas.edu. *Application contact:* Joyce A. Taylor, Student Services Coordinator, 651-962-5756, Fax: 651-962-6419, E-mail: technology@stthomas.edu.

University of Southern Indiana, Graduate Studies, College of Science and Engineering, Program in Industrial Management, Evansville, IN 47712-3590. Offers MS. Part-time and evening/weekend programs available. *Faculty:* 2 full-time (0 women). *Students:* Average age 34. 6 applicants, 100% accepted, 6 enrolled. In 2006, 3 master's awarded. *Degree requirements:* For master's, project. *Entrance requirements:* For master's, minimum GPA of 2.5, BS in engineering or engineering technology. Additional exam requirements/recommendations for international students: Required—TOEFL (minimum score 500 paper-based; 173 computer-based). *Application deadline:* For fall admission, 8/15 priority date for domestic students, 3/1 priority date for international students. Applications are processed on a rolling basis. Application fee: $25. *Expenses:* Tuition, state resident: full-time $3,888; part-time $216 per credit hour. Tuition, nonresident: full-time $7,688; part-time $426 per credit hour. Required fees: $220; $23 per term. Tuition and fees vary according to course load and reciprocity agreements. *Financial support:* In 2006–07, 1 student received support. Federal Work-Study, scholarships/grants, tuition waivers (full and partial), and unspecified assistantships available. Financial award application deadline: 3/1; financial award applicants required to submit FAFSA. *Unit head:* Dr. David E. Schultz, Director, 812-464-1881, E-mail: dschultz@usi.edu.

The University of Tennessee, Graduate School, College of Business Administration, Program in Business Administration, Knoxville, TN 37996. Offers accounting (PhD); finance (MBA, PhD); logistics and transportation (MBA, PhD); management (PhD); marketing (MBA, PhD);

operations management (MBA); professional business administration (MBA); statistics (PhD); JD/MBA; MS/MBA. *Accreditation:* AACSB. Postbaccalaureate distance learning degree programs offered. *Students:* 344 (105 women); includes 42 minority (20 African Americans, 4 American Indian/Alaska Native, 9 Asian Americans or Pacific Islanders, 9 Hispanic Americans) 49 international. In 2006, 169 master's, 9 doctorates awarded. *Degree requirements:* For master's, thesis or alternative; for doctorate, thesis/dissertation. *Entrance requirements:* For master's and doctorate, GMAT, minimum GPA of 2.7. Additional exam requirements/recommendations for international students: Required—TOEFL. *Application deadline:* For fall admission, 2/1 priority date for domestic students. Application fee: $35. Electronic applications accepted. *Expenses:* Tuition, state resident: full-time $5,574. Tuition, nonresident: full-time $16,840. Required fees: $792. *Financial support:* In 2006–07, 6 fellowships, 3 research assistantships, 35 teaching assistantships were awarded; career-related internships or fieldwork, Federal Work-Study, institutionally sponsored loans, and unspecified assistantships also available. Financial award application deadline: 2/1; financial award applicants required to submit FAFSA. *Unit head:* Dr. Sarah Gardial, Assistant Dean, 865-974-5033, Fax: 865-974-3826, E-mail: sgardial@utk.edu. *Application contact:* Donna Potts, Graduate Representative, 865-974-5033, Fax: 865-974-3826, E-mail: dpotts@utk.edu.

The University of Texas at Tyler, Graduate Studies, College of Business and Technology, Department of Human Resource Development and Technology, Tyler, TX 75799-0001. Offers human resource development (MS); industrial distribution (MS); industrial safety (MS); industrial technology (MS); instructional technology (MS); technology systems (MS). Part-time and evening/weekend programs available. Postbaccalaureate distance learning degree programs offered (no on-campus study). *Degree requirements:* For master's, comprehensive exam. *Entrance requirements:* For master's, GRE General Test or MAT. Additional exam requirements/recommendations for international students: Required—TOEFL. Electronic applications accepted. *Expenses:* Tuition, state resident: part-time $50 per credit hour. Tuition, nonresident: part-time $328 per credit hour. Required fees: $107 per credit hour. $426 per term. *Faculty research:* Human resource development.

The University of Toledo, College of Graduate Studies, College of Business Administration, Department of Information Systems, Marketing, E-Commerce, and Sales, Program in Manufacturing Management, Toledo, OH 43606-3390. Offers MBA, DME. *Students:* 11 full-time (4 women), 10 part-time (2 women); includes 1 minority (African American), 15 international. Average age 33. 18 applicants, 56% accepted, 3 enrolled. In 2006, 7 degrees awarded. *Degree requirements:* For doctorate, thesis/dissertation. *Entrance requirements:* For master's, GMAT. Additional exam requirements/recommendations for international students: Required—TOEFL. *Application deadline:* For fall admission, 8/1 priority date for domestic students. Applications are processed on a rolling basis. Application fee: $45. *Financial support:* Application deadline: 4/1. *Application contact:* Elissa Teal, Director, 419-530-2775, Fax: 419-530-7260, E-mail: elissa.teal@utoledo.edu.

University of Wisconsin–Madison, Graduate School, School of Business, Doctoral Program in Operations and Technology Management, Madison, WI 53706-1380. Offers PhD. *Students:* 8 full-time (2 women), 5 international. Average age 36. 42 applicants, 0% accepted. In 2006, 1 degree awarded. *Median time to degree:* Of those who began their doctoral program in fall 1998, 90% received their degree in 8 years or less. *Entrance requirements:* For doctorate, GMAT or GRE. Additional exam requirements/recommendations for international students: Required—TOEFL (minimum score 600 paper-based; 250 computer-based). *Application deadline:* For fall admission, 1/6 priority date for domestic and international students. Applications are processed on a rolling basis. Application fee: $45. Electronic applications accepted. *Financial support:* In 2006–07, 5 students received support, including 1 fellowship with full tuition reimbursement available (averaging $16,110 per year), research assistantships with full tuition reimbursements available (averaging $13,502 per year), 4 teaching assistantships with full tuition reimbursements available (averaging $13,686 per year); Federal Work-Study, institutionally sponsored loans, scholarships/grants, health care benefits, and unspecified assistantships also available. Financial award application deadline: 1/6; financial award applicants required to submit FAFSA. *Faculty research:* Supply-chain management, reorganization of the factory, creating continuous innovation, transportation economics, organizational economics. *Unit head:* Dr. James G. Morris, Chair, 608-262-1284, E-mail: jmorris@bus.wisc.edu. *Application contact:* Belle Heberling, PhD Coordinator, 608-262-3749, Fax: 608-890-0180, E-mail: phd@bus.wisc.edu.

Washington State University, Graduate School, College of Business, Graduate Programs in Business, Pullman, WA 99164. Offers accounting and business law (M Acc); business administration (MBA, PhD), including accounting (PhD), finance (PhD), management and operations (PhD), management information systems (PhD), marketing (PhD); JD/MBA. *Accreditation:* AACSB. *Faculty:* 38. *Students:* 105 full-time (39 women), 14 part-time (5 women); includes 3 minority (1 American Indian/Alaska Native, 2 Asian Americans or Pacific Islanders), 62 international. Average age 30. 328 applicants, 32% accepted, 43 enrolled. In 2006, 56 master's, 8 doctorates awarded. *Degree requirements:* For master's, thesis (for some programs), final presentation, comprehensive exam (for some programs); for doctorate, thesis/dissertation, oral and written exams, comprehensive exam. *Entrance requirements:* For master's and doctorate, GMAT, minimum GPA of 3.0, 3 letters of recommendation. Additional exam requirements/recommendations for international students: Required—TOEFL. *Application deadline:* For fall admission, 3/1 priority date for domestic students, 3/1 for international students; for spring admission, 6/1 priority date for domestic students, 6/1 for international students. Applications are processed on a rolling basis. Application fee: $50. Electronic applications accepted. *Expenses:* Tuition, state resident: full-time $7,066. Tuition, nonresident: full-time $17,204. *Financial support:* In 2006–07, 102 students received support, including 9 fellowships (averaging $6,000 per year), 8 research assistantships with full and partial tuition reimbursements available (averaging $13,917 per year), 75 teaching assistantships with full and partial tuition reimbursements available (averaging $13,056 per year); career-related internships or fieldwork, Federal Work-Study, institutionally sponsored loans, health care benefits, tuition waivers (partial), unspecified assistantships, and teaching associateships also available. Financial award application deadline: 4/1. *Unit head:* Dr. Charles Munson, Associate Dean, 509-335-1193, E-mail: mba@wsu.edu. *Application contact:* Graduate School Admissions, 800-GRADWSU, Fax: 509-335-1949, E-mail: gradsch@wsu.edu.

Section 10
Insurance and Actuarial Science

This section contains a directory of institutions offering graduate work in insurance and actuarial science. Additional information about programs listed in the directory but not augmented by an in-depth entry may be obtained by writing directly to the dean of a graduate school or chair of a department at the address given in the directory.

For programs offering related work, see also in this book Business Administration and Management.

CONTENTS

Program Directories

Actuarial Science

Ball State University, Graduate School, College of Sciences and Humanities, Department of Mathematical Sciences, Program in Actuarial Science, Muncie, IN 47306-1099. Offers MA. *Students:* 20 full-time (4 women), 3 part-time (2 women); includes 1 minority (Asian American or Pacific Islander), 10 international. Average age 27. 40 applicants, 85% accepted, 10 enrolled. In 2006, 10 degrees awarded. *Entrance requirements:* For master's, GMAT. Application fee: $25 ($35 for international students). *Financial support:* Research assistantships with full tuition reimbursements, teaching assistantships with full tuition reimbursements available. Financial award application deadline: 3/1. *Unit head:* Dr. W. Bart Frye, Director, 765-285-8681, Fax: 765-285-1721.

Boston University, Metropolitan College (Continuing Education), Department of Actuarial Science, Boston, MA 02215. Offers MS. Part-time and evening/weekend programs available. *Faculty:* 1 (woman) full-time, 8 part-time/adjunct (3 women). *Students:* 35 full-time (18 women), 30 part-time (15 women); includes 10 minority (2 African Americans, 8 Asian Americans or Pacific Islanders), 38 international. Average age 27. 84 applicants, 98% accepted, 32 enrolled. In 2006, 50 master's awarded. *Entrance requirements:* For master's, calculus I, II, III. Additional exam requirements/recommendations for international students: Required—TOEFL (minimum score 550 paper-based; 213 computer-based). *Application deadline:* For fall admission, 5/31 priority date for domestic students, 2/15 priority date for international students; for spring admission, 10/31 priority date for domestic students, 10/15 priority date for international students. Applications are processed on a rolling basis. Application fee: $60. *Expenses:* Tuition: Full-time $33,330; part-time $1,042 per credit. Required fees: $462; $40. *Financial support:* In 2006–07, 1 fellowship with tuition reimbursement (averaging $16,000 per year), 4 research assistantships with full tuition reimbursements (averaging $14,500 per year), 9 teaching assistantships (averaging $5,000 per year) were awarded; career-related internships or fieldwork, Federal Work-Study, institutionally sponsored loans, scholarships/grants, and unspecified assistantships also available. *Faculty research:* Survival models, life contingencies, numerical analysis, operations research, compound interest. *Unit head:* Lois K. Horwitz, Interim Chairman, 617-353-8758, Fax: 617-353-8757, E-mail: lhorwitz@math.bu.edu. *Application contact:* Katherine Coughlin, Administrative Coordinator, 617-353-8758, Fax: 617-353-8757, E-mail: actuary@bu.edu.

Central Connecticut State University, School of Graduate Studies, School of Arts and Sciences, Department of Mathematics, New Britain, CT 06050-4010. Offers mathematics (MA, MS, Certificate), including actuarial (MA), operations research (MA), statistics (MA). Part-time and evening/weekend programs available. *Faculty:* 29 full-time (9 women), 69 part-time/adjunct (35 women). *Students:* 16 full-time (5 women), 102 part-time (53 women); includes 13 minority (3 African Americans, 5 Asian Americans or Pacific Islanders, 5 Hispanic Americans), 6 international. Average age 35. 87 applicants, 68% accepted, 33 enrolled. In 2006, 17 master's, 10 other advanced degrees awarded. *Degree requirements:* For master's, thesis or alternative, comprehensive exam or special project. *Entrance requirements:* For master's, minimum GPA of 2.4, conditional admissions to the Data Mining Program. Additional exam requirements/recommendations for international students: Required—TOEFL. *Application deadline:* For fall admission, 7/1 for domestic students; for spring admission, 12/1 for domestic students. Applications are processed on a rolling basis. Application fee: $50. Electronic applications accepted. *Expenses:* Tuition, area resident: Full-time $3,970; part-time $380 per credit. Tuition, state resident: full-time $5,955; part-time $380 per credit. Tuition, nonresident: full-time $11,061; part-time $380 per credit. Required fees: $3,189. One-time fee: $62 part-time. Tuition and fees vary according to degree level and program. *Financial support:* In 2006–07, 4 students received support; research assistantships, career-related internships or fieldwork, Federal Work-Study, scholarships/grants, and unspecified assistantships available. Support available to part-time students. Financial award application deadline: 3/1; financial award applicants required to submit FAFSA. *Faculty research:* Statistics, actuarial mathematics, computer systems and engineering, computer programming techniques, operations research. *Unit head:* Dr. Timothy Craine, Chair, 860-832-2835.

Columbia University, School of Continuing Education, Program in Actuarial Science, New York, NY 10027. Offers MS. *Students:* 7 full-time (2 women), 16 part-time (10 women); includes 7 minority (1 African American, 6 Asian Americans or Pacific Islanders), 11 international. *Degree requirements:* For master's, knowledge of elementary economics. *Entrance requirements:* For master's, BA, minimum GPA of 3.0. Additional exam requirements/recommendations for international students: Required—American Language Program (ALP) placement test. *Application deadline:* For fall admission, 7/15 for domestic students; for spring admission, 11/11 for domestic students. Application fee: $50. *Unit head:* Paul McNeil, Head, 212-854-9699, E-mail: ce-info@columbia.edu. *Application contact:* 212-854-9666, E-mail: ce-advis@columbia.edu.

Georgia State University, J. Mack Robinson College of Business, Department of Risk Management and Insurance, Program in Actuarial Science, Atlanta, GA 30303-3083. Offers MAS, MBA. *Students:* 38 full-time (21 women), 6 part-time (2 women); includes 4 minority (all Asian Americans or Pacific Islanders), 26 international. 37 applicants, 76% accepted, 15 enrolled. In 2006, 19 degrees awarded. *Entrance requirements:* For master's, GMAT. Additional exam requirements/recommendations for international students: Required—TOEFL (minimum score 610 paper-based; 255 computer-based; 101 iBT). *Application deadline:* For fall admission, 5/1 for domestic students, 2/1 for international students; for spring admission, 10/15 for domestic students, 5/1 for international students. Applications are processed on a rolling basis. Application fee: $50. Electronic applications accepted. *Unit head:* Dr. Shaun Wang, Director, 404-651-2736, Fax: 404-651-4219, E-mail: shaunwang@gsu.edu.

Maryville University of Saint Louis, Actuarial Science Program, St. Louis, MO 63141-7299. Part-time programs available. *Students:* 5 full-time (1 woman), 8 part-time (4 women); includes 2 Asian Americans or Pacific Islanders, 2 international. Average age 26. *Entrance requirements:* Additional exam requirements/recommendations for international students: Required—TOEFL (minimum score 550 paper-based). Application fee: $35 ($50 for international students). *Expenses:* Tuition: Full-time $17,800; part-time $555 per credit. Required fees: $55 per semester. Tuition and fees vary according to degree level and program. *Financial support:* Applicants required to submit FAFSA. *Unit head:* Dr. Min Deng, Director, 314-529-9433.

Roosevelt University, Graduate Division, College of Arts and Sciences, Department of Science and Mathematics, Program in Mathematics, Chicago, IL 60605-1394. Offers mathematical sciences (MS), including actuarial science. Part-time and evening/weekend programs available. *Students:* 12 full-time (7 women), 20 part-time (8 women); includes 6 minority (2 African Americans, 2 Asian Americans or Pacific Islanders, 2 Hispanic Americans), 6 international. Average age 34. 44 applicants, 73% accepted, 27 enrolled. In 2006, 9 degrees awarded. *Application deadline:* For fall admission, 6/1 priority date for domestic students. Applications are processed on a rolling basis. Application fee: $25 ($35 for international students). *Financial support:* Research assistantships, career-related internships or fieldwork and tuition waivers (partial) available. Support available to part-time students. Financial award application deadline: 2/15. *Faculty research:* Statistics, mathematics education, finite groups, computers in mathematics. *Application contact:* Joanne Canyon-Heller, Coordinator of Graduate Admission, 877-APPLY RU, Fax: 312-281-3356, E-mail: applyru@roosevelt.edu.

St. John's University, The Peter J. Tobin College of Business, School of Risk Management and Actuarial Science, Queens, NY 11439. Offers MBA, MS. *Faculty:* 7 full-time (0 women), 5 part-time/adjunct (2 women). *Students:* 16 full-time (9 women), 33 part-time (18 women); includes 7 minority (2 African Americans, 2 Asian Americans or Pacific Islanders, 3 Hispanic Americans), 32 international. Average age 27. 68 applicants, 71% accepted, 24 enrolled. In 2006, 9 degrees awarded. *Entrance requirements:* For master's, GMAT, minimum undergraduate GPA of 3.0. Additional exam requirements/recommendations for international students: Required—TOEFL (minimum score 500 paper-based; 173 computer-based). *Application deadline:* For fall admission, 5/1 priority date for domestic and international students; for spring admission, 11/1 priority date for domestic and international students. Applications are processed on a rolling basis. Application fee: $40. Electronic applications accepted. *Expenses:* Contact institution. Tuition and fees vary according to program. *Financial support:* Research assistantships available. *Unit head:* Dr. Nicos Scordis, Chair, 212-277-5193, E-mail: scordisn@stjohns.edu. *Application contact:* Nicole T. Bryan, Assistant Dean, 718-990-2599, Fax: 718-990-5242, E-mail: mbaadmissions@stjohns.edu.

Temple University, Graduate School, Fox School of Business and Management, Masters Programs in Business, MS Programs, Philadelphia, PA 19122-6096. Offers accounting and financial management (MS); actuarial science (MS); e-business (MS); finance (MS); healthcare financial management (MS); human resource administration (MS); management information systems (MS); management science/operations management (MS); marketing (MS); statistics (MS). *Accreditation:* AACSB. *Entrance requirements:* For master's, GRE General Test, minimum undergraduate GPA of 3.0. Additional exam requirements/recommendations for international students: Required—TOEFL. *Expenses:* Tuition, state resident: full-time $12,264; part-time $511 per credit. Tuition, nonresident: full-time $17,904; part-time $746 per credit. Required fees: $84 per course. Tuition and fees vary according to program.

Université du Québec à Montréal, Graduate Programs, Program in Actuarial Sciences, Montréal, QC H3C 3P8, Canada. Offers Diploma. Part-time programs available. *Entrance requirements:* For degree, appropriate bachelor's degree or equivalent and proficiency in French.

University of Central Florida, College of Sciences, Department of Statistics and Actuarial Science, Orlando, FL 32816. Offers actuarial science (MS); data mining (MS, Certificate); statistical computing (MS). Part-time and evening/weekend programs available. *Faculty:* 14 full-time (3 women), 1 part-time/adjunct (0 women). *Students:* 32 full-time (18 women), 21 part-time (9 women); includes 10 minority (3 African Americans, 4 Asian Americans or Pacific Islanders, 3 Hispanic Americans), 21 international. 65 applicants, 71% accepted, 21 enrolled. In 2006, 12 master's, 2 other advanced degrees awarded. *Degree requirements:* For master's, comprehensive exam. *Entrance requirements:* For master's, GRE General Test, minimum GPA of 3.0 in last 60 hours. Additional exam requirements/recommendations for international students: Required—TOEFL. *Application deadline:* For fall admission, 7/15 for domestic students; for spring admission, 12/1 for domestic students. Application fee: $30. Electronic applications accepted. *Expenses:* Tuition, state resident: full-time $6,167; part-time $257 per credit hour. Tuition, nonresident: full-time $22,790; part-time $950 per credit hour. *Financial support:* In 2006–07, 2 research assistantships with partial tuition reimbursements (averaging $5,000 per year), 16 teaching assistantships with partial tuition reimbursements (averaging $12,400 per year) were awarded; fellowships with partial tuition reimbursements, career-related internships or fieldwork, Federal Work-Study, institutionally sponsored loans, tuition waivers (partial), and unspecified assistantships also available. Financial award application deadline: 3/1; financial award applicants required to submit FAFSA. *Faculty research:* Multivariate analysis, quality control, shrinkage estimation. *Unit head:* Dr. David Nickerson, Interim Chair, 407-823-2289, Fax: 407-823-5419, E-mail: nickerson@mail.ucf.edu. *Application contact:* Dr. James R. Schott, Graduate Coordinator, 407-823-3323, Fax: 407-823-5419, E-mail: jschott@pegasus.cc.ucf.edu.

University of Connecticut, Graduate School, College of Liberal Arts and Sciences, Department of Mathematics, Storrs, CT 06269. Offers applied financial mathematics (MS); mathematics (MS, PhD), including actuarial science, mathematics. *Faculty:* 43 full-time (5 women). *Students:* 106 full-time (36 women), 19 part-time (10 women); includes 15 minority (5 African Americans, 9 Asian Americans or Pacific Islanders, 1 Hispanic American), 63 international. Average age 27. 276 applicants, 38% accepted, 58 enrolled. In 2006, 47 master's, 2 doctorates awarded. *Degree requirements:* For doctorate, thesis/dissertation. *Entrance requirements:* For master's and doctorate, GRE General Test, GRE Subject Test. Additional exam requirements/recommendations for international students: Required—TOEFL (minimum score 550 paper-based; 213 computer-based). *Application deadline:* For fall admission, 2/1 priority date for domestic and international students; for spring admission, 11/1 for domestic students, 10/1 for international students. Applications are processed on a rolling basis. Application fee: $55. Electronic applications accepted. *Financial support:* In 2006–07, 14 research assistantships with full tuition reimbursements, 52 teaching assistantships with full tuition reimbursements were awarded; fellowships, Federal Work-Study, scholarships/grants, health care benefits, and unspecified assistantships also available. Financial award application deadline: 2/1; financial award applicants required to submit FAFSA. *Unit head:* Michael Neumann, Head, 860-486-1290, Fax: 860-486-4283. *Application contact:* Manuel Lerman, Chairperson, 860-486-1293, Fax: 860-486-4283, E-mail: manuel.lerman@uconn.edu.

University of Connecticut, Graduate School, College of Liberal Arts and Sciences, Department of Mathematics, Field of Mathematics, Program in Actuarial Science, Storrs, CT 06269. Offers MS, PhD. *Faculty:* 40 full-time (5 women). *Students:* 32 full-time (18 women), 8 part-time (7 women); includes 5 minority (3 African Americans, 2 Asian Americans or Pacific Islanders), 30 international. Average age 26. 90 applicants, 42% accepted, 25 enrolled. In 2006, 27 degrees awarded. *Degree requirements:* For master's, comprehensive exam. *Entrance requirements:* Additional exam requirements/recommendations for international students: Required—TOEFL (minimum score 550 paper-based; 213 computer-based). *Application deadline:* For fall admission, 2/1 priority date for domestic and international students; for spring admission, 11/1 for domestic students, 10/1 for international students. Applications are processed on a rolling basis. Application fee: $55. Electronic applications accepted. *Financial support:* In 2006–07, 3 research assistantships with full tuition reimbursements, 5 teaching assistantships with full tuition reimbursements were awarded; career-related internships or fieldwork, Federal Work-Study, scholarships/grants, health care benefits, and unspecified assistantships also available. Financial award application deadline: 2/1; financial award applicants required to submit FAFSA. *Unit head:* Charles Vinsonhaler, Chairperson, 860-486-3944, Fax: 860-486-4283, E-mail: charles.vinsonhaler@uconn.edu. *Application contact:* Sharon McDermott, Administrative Assistant, 860-486-6452, Fax: 860-486-4283, E-mail: gradadm@math.uconn.edu.

The University of Iowa, Graduate College, College of Liberal Arts and Sciences, Department of Statistics and Actuarial Science, Iowa City, IA 52242-1316. Offers MS, PhD. *Faculty:* 18 full-time, 2 part-time/adjunct. *Students:* 76 full-time (41 women), 26 part-time (9 women); includes 5 minority (1 African American, 3 Asian Americans or Pacific Islanders, 1 Hispanic American), 84 international. 225 applicants, 55% accepted, 28 enrolled. In 2006, 28 master's, 5 doctorates awarded. *Degree requirements:* For master's, exam, thesis optional; for doctorate, thesis/dissertation, comprehensive exam, registration. *Entrance requirements:* For master's and doctorate, GRE General Test, minimum GPA of 3.0. Additional exam requirements/recommendations for international students: Required—TOEFL (minimum score 550 paper-based; 213 computer-based; 81 iBT). *Application deadline:* Applications are processed on a rolling basis. Application fee: $60 ($85 for international students). Electronic applications accepted. *Financial support:* In 2006–07, 11 research assistantships with partial tuition reimbursements, 41 teaching assistantships with partial tuition reimbursements were awarded; fellowships also available. Financial award applicants required to submit FAFSA. *Unit head:* Luke Tierney, Chair, 319-335-0712, Fax: 319-335-3017.

University of Nebraska–Lincoln, Graduate College, College of Business Administration, Interdepartmental Area of Actuarial Science, Lincoln, NE 68588. Offers MS. *Entrance requirements:* For master's, Survey of Actuaries, GRE. Additional exam requirements/recommendations for international students: Required—TOEFL (minimum score 550 paper-based; 213 computer-based). Electronic applications accepted. *Faculty research:* Risk theory, pensions, actuarial finance, decision theory, stochastic calculus.

University of Waterloo, Graduate Studies, Faculty of Mathematics, Department of Statistics and Actuarial Science, Waterloo, ON N2L 3G1, Canada. Offers actuarial science (M Math, PhD); biostatistics (PhD); statistics (M Math, PhD); statistics-biostatistics (M Math); statistics-computing (M Math); statistics-finance (M Math). *Faculty:* 39 full-time (7 women), 22 part-time/adjunct (2 women). *Students:* 39 full-time (58 women), 22 part-time (2 women). 308 applicants, 23% accepted, 57 enrolled. In 2006, 45 master's, 6 doctorates awarded. *Degree requirements:* For master's, research paper or thesis; for doctorate, thesis/dissertation, comprehensive exam, registration. *Entrance requirements:* For master's, honors degree in field, minimum B+ average; for doctorate, master's degree, minimum B+ average. Additional exam requirements/recommendations for international students: Required—TOEFL (minimum score 600 paper-based; 250 computer-based; 90 iBT), TWE (minimum score 4.5). *Application deadline:* For spring admission, 12/1 priority date for domestic students, 10/1 priority date for international students. Applications are processed on a rolling basis. Application fee: $75 Canadian dollars. Electronic applications accepted. *Financial support:* In 2006–07, 30 teaching assistantships were awarded; fellowships, research assistantships, career-related internships or fieldwork and scholarships/grants also available. *Faculty research:* Data analysis, risk theory, inference, stochastic processes, quantitative finance. *Unit head:* Dr. D. E. Matthews, Chair, 519-888-4567 Ext. 5530, Fax: 519-746-1875, E-mail: dematthe@uwaterloo.ca. *Application contact:* M. Dufton, Graduate Studies Coordinator, 519-888-4567 Ext. 36532, Fax: 519-746-1875, E-mail: mdufton@math.uwaterloo.ca.

University of Wisconsin–Madison, Graduate School, School of Business, Program in Actuarial Science, Madison, WI 53706-1380. Offers MS. *Students:* 20 full-time (13 women), 18 international. Average age 25. 52 applicants, 37% accepted, 5 enrolled. In 2006, 10 degrees awarded. *Degree requirements:* For master's, registration. *Entrance requirements:* For master's, GMAT or GRE. Additional exam requirements/recommendations for international students: Required—TOEFL (minimum score 600 paper-based; 250 computer-based). *Application deadline:* For fall admission, 4/15 for domestic students. Applications are processed on a rolling basis. Application fee: $45. Electronic applications accepted. *Financial support:* In 2006–07, 4 students received support, including 4 teaching assistantships with full tuition reimbursements available (averaging $8,411 per year); fellowships, research assistantships with full tuition reimbursements available, Federal Work-Study, institutionally sponsored loans, scholarships/grants, and unspecified assistantships also available. Financial award application deadline: 2/15; financial award applicants required to submit FAFSA. *Faculty research:* Fuzzy logic, business forecasting, health insurance, international insurance. *Unit head:* Joan Schmit, Chair, 608-262-4240, E-mail: jschmit@bus.wisc.edu. *Application contact:* Belle Heberling, MS Coordinator, 608-262-3749, Fax: 608-890-0180, E-mail: ms@bus.wisc.edu.

Insurance

Florida State University, Graduate Studies, College of Business, Tallahassee, FL 32306. Offers accounting (M Acc), including accounting information systems, assurance services, corporate accounting, taxation; business administration (MBA, PhD), including accounting (PhD), finance (PhD), information and management science (PhD), management (PhD), marketing (PhD), risk and insurance (PhD); insurance (MSM); management information systems (MS); JD/MBA. *Accreditation:* AACSB. Part-time and evening/weekend programs available. Postbaccalaureate distance learning degree programs offered (no on-campus study). *Faculty:* 107 full-time (26 women), 21 part-time/adjunct (2 women). *Students:* 145 full-time (62 women), 444 part-time (143 women); includes 147 minority (58 African Americans, 3 American Indian/Alaska Native, 45 Asian Americans or Pacific Islanders, 41 Hispanic Americans). Average age 29. 789 applicants, 50% accepted, 321 enrolled. In 2006, 263 master's, 19 doctorates awarded. Terminal master's awarded for partial completion of doctoral program. *Degree requirements:* For master's, registration; for doctorate, thesis/dissertation, comprehensive exam, registration. *Entrance requirements:* For master's, GMAT, substantial work experience (MBA, MS), minimum GPA of 3.0, letters of recommendation; for doctorate, GMAT, minimum graduate GPA of 3.5, letters of recommendation. Additional exam requirements/recommendations for international students: Required—TOEFL (minimum score 600 paper-based; 250 computer-based). *Application deadline:* For fall admission, 5/1 for domestic and international students; for spring admission, 10/1 for domestic students, 9/1 for international students. Applications are processed on a rolling basis. Application fee: $30. Electronic applications accepted. *Expenses:* Tuition, state resident: full-time $5,822; part-time $243 per credit hour. Tuition, nonresident: full-time $20,976; part-time $874 per credit hour. Tuition and fees vary according to program. *Financial support:* In 2006–07, 126 students received support, including 40 fellowships with partial tuition reimbursements available (averaging $4,600 per year), 37 research assistantships with partial tuition reimbursements available (averaging $4,600 per year), 49 teaching assistantships with partial tuition reimbursements available (averaging $10,500 per year); unspecified assistantships also available. Financial award application deadline: 1/1. Total annual research expenditures: $1.5 million. *Unit head:* Dr. Caryn Beck-Duolley, Dean, 850-644-3090, Fax: 850-644-0915. *Application contact:* Lisa Beverly, Coordinator, Graduate Programs Admissions, 850-644-6458, Fax: 850-644-0588, E-mail: lbeverly@cob.fsu.edu.

Georgia State University, J. Mack Robinson College of Business, Department of Risk Management and Insurance, Program in Risk Management and Insurance, Atlanta, GA 30303-3083. Offers MBA, MS, PhD. *Students:* 39 full-time (19 women), 15 part-time (2 women); includes 7 minority (2 African Americans, 3 Asian Americans or Pacific Islanders, 2 Hispanic Americans), 29 international. 48 applicants, 25% accepted, 10 enrolled. In 2006, 20 master's, 3 doctorates awarded. *Degree requirements:* For doctorate, thesis/dissertation. *Entrance requirements:* For master's and doctorate, GMAT. Additional exam requirements/recommendations for international students: Required—TOEFL (minimum score 610 paper-based; 255 computer-based; 101 iBT). *Application deadline:* For fall admission, 5/1 for domestic students, 2/1 for international students; for spring admission, 10/15 for domestic students, 5/1 for international students. Applications are processed on a rolling basis. Application fee: $50. Electronic applications accepted. *Unit head:* Dr. William R. Feldhaus, Faculty Advisor, 404-651-2727, Fax: 404-651-4219, E-mail: feldhaus@gsu.edu.

St. John's University, The Peter J. Tobin College of Business, School of Risk Management and Actuarial Science, Queens, NY 11439. Offers MBA, MS. *Faculty:* 7 full-time (0 women), 5 part-time/adjunct (2 women). *Students:* 16 full-time (9 women), 33 part-time (18 women); includes 7 minority (2 African Americans, 2 Asian Americans or Pacific Islanders, 3 Hispanic Americans), 32 international. Average age 27. 68 applicants, 71% accepted, 24 enrolled. In 2006, 9 degrees awarded. *Entrance requirements:* For master's, GMAT, minimum undergraduate GPA of 3.0. Additional exam requirements/recommendations for international students: Required—TOEFL (minimum score 500 paper-based; 173 computer-based). *Application deadline:* For fall admission, 5/1 priority date for domestic and international students; for spring admission, 11/1 priority date for domestic and international students. Applications are processed on a rolling basis. Application fee: $40. Electronic applications accepted. *Expenses: Contact institution.* Tuition and fees vary according to program. *Financial support:* Research assistantships available. *Unit head:* Dr. Nicos Scordis, Chair, 212-277-5193, E-mail: scordisn@stjohns.edu. *Application contact:* Nicole T. Bryan, Assistant Dean, 718-990-2599, Fax: 718-990-5242, E-mail: mbaadmissions@stjohns.edu.

Temple University, Graduate School, Fox School of Business and Management, Doctoral Programs in Business, Philadelphia, PA 19122-6096. Offers accounting (PhD); economics (PhD); finance (PhD); general and strategic management (PhD); healthcare management (PhD); human resource administration (PhD); international business administration (PhD); management information systems (PhD); management science/operations research (PhD); marketing (PhD); risk, insurance, and health-care management (PhD); statistics (PhD); tourism (PhD). *Accreditation:* AACSB. *Entrance requirements:* For doctorate, GRE General Test, minimum GPA of 3.0, master's degree. Additional exam requirements/recommendations for international students: Required—TOEFL. *Expenses:* Tuition, state resident: full-time $12,264; part-time $511 per credit. Tuition, nonresident: full-time $17,904; part-time $746 per credit. Required fees: $84 per course. Tuition and fees vary according to program.

Temple University, Graduate School, Fox School of Business and Management, Masters Programs in Business, MBA Programs, Philadelphia, PA 19122-6096. Offers accounting (MBA); business administration (EMBA, MBA); e-business (MBA); economics (MBA); finance (MBA); general and strategic management (MBA); healthcare management (MBA); human resource administration (MBA); international business (IMBA); management information systems (MBA); management science/operations management (MBA); marketing (MBA); risk management and insurance (MBA); statistics (MBA). EMBA offered in Philadelphia, PA and Tokyo, Japan. *Accreditation:* AACSB. *Entrance requirements:* For master's, GMAT, minimum undergraduate GPA of 3.0. Additional exam requirements/recommendations for international students: Required—TOEFL. *Expenses:* Tuition, state resident: full-time $12,264; part-time $511 per credit. Tuition, nonresident: full-time $17,904; part-time $746 per credit. Required fees: $84 per course. Tuition and fees vary according to program.

University of Florida, Graduate School, Warrington College of Business Administration, Department of Finance, Insurance and Real Estate, Gainesville, FL 32611. Offers business administration (MS), including entrepreneurship, insurance, real estate and urban analysis, retailing; finance (PhD); financial services (Certificate); insurance (PhD); real estate and urban analysis (PhD); JD/MS. *Faculty:* 15 full-time (1 woman). *Students:* 69 (17 women); includes 14 minority (2 African Americans, 5 Asian Americans or Pacific Islanders, 7 Hispanic Americans) 12 international. In 2006, 54 master's, 1 doctorate awarded. Terminal master's awarded for partial completion of doctoral program. *Degree requirements:* For doctorate, thesis/dissertation. *Entrance requirements:* For master's, GMAT or GRE General Test, minimum GPA of 3.0 for last 60 hours of undergraduate degree, work experience (preferred); for doctorate, GMAT or GRE General Test, minimum GPA of 3.0. Additional exam requirements/recommendations for international students: Required—TOEFL (minimum score 550 paper-based; 213 computer-based). *Application deadline:* For fall admission, 5/1 priority date for domestic students. Applications are processed on a rolling basis. Application fee: $30. Electronic applications accepted. *Expenses:* Tuition, state resident: full-time $6,827. Tuition, nonresident: full-time $21,951. Required fees: $999. *Financial support:* In 2006–07, 10 research assistantships (averaging $23,562 per year), 1 teaching assistantship (averaging $40,989 per year) were awarded; fellowships, career-related internships or fieldwork, scholarships/grants, and unspecified assistantships also available. *Faculty research:* Financial management, financial markets and institutions, investments, risk and insurance, real estate development. *Unit head:* Dr. Michael D. Ryngaert, Chair, 352-392-9765, Fax: 352-392-0301, E-mail: michael.ryngaert@cba.ufl.edu. *Application contact:* Pamela De Michele, Director of Admissions and Student Services, 352-273-0310, Fax: 352-392-0301, E-mail: pam.demichele@cba.ufl.edu.

University of North Texas, Robert B. Toulouse School of Graduate Studies, College of Business Administration, Department of Finance, Insurance, Real Estate, and Law, Denton, TX 76203. Offers banking (MBA, PhD); finance (MBA, PhD); finance, insurance, real estate, and law (MS); insurance (MBA); real estate (MBA). Part-time programs available. *Faculty:* 23 full-time (3 women). *Students:* 37 full-time (13 women), 69 part-time (21 women); includes 28 minority (11 African Americans, 2 American Indian/Alaska Native, 9 Asian Americans or Pacific Islanders, 6 Hispanic Americans), 24 international. Average age 27. 105 applicants, 78% accepted, 23 enrolled. In 2006, 51 master's, 3 doctorates awarded. *Degree requirements:* For doctorate, thesis/dissertation. *Entrance requirements:* For master's, GMAT; for doctorate, GMAT or GRE General Test. Additional exam requirements/recommendations for international students: Required—TOEFL (minimum score 550 paper-based; 213 computer-based). *Application deadline:* For fall admission, 7/15 for domestic students. Application fee: $50 ($75 for international students). *Expenses:* Tuition, state resident: full-time $3,573; part-time $198 per credit. Tuition, nonresident: full-time $8,577; part-time $476 per credit. Required fees: $1,258; $126 per credit. One-time fee: $150 full-time. Tuition and fees vary according to course load. *Financial support:* Fellowships, research assistantships, teaching assistantships, career-related internships or fieldwork available. Financial award application deadline: 4/1. *Faculty research:* Financial impact of regulation, risk management, financial instrument rating changes, taxes and valuation, bankruptcy. *Unit head:* Dr. Mazhar Siddiqi, Interim Chair, 940-369-7300, Fax: 940-565-4234, E-mail: siddiqi@unt.edu. *Application contact:* Dr. James A. Conover, Graduate Adviser, 940-565-3061, Fax: 940-565-4234, E-mail: conoverj@unt.edu.

University of Pennsylvania, Wharton School, Insurance and Risk Management Department, Philadelphia, PA 19104. Offers AM, MBA, PhD. *Degree requirements:* For doctorate, thesis/dissertation. *Entrance requirements:* For master's, GMAT; for doctorate, GMAT or GRE. *Faculty research:* Fair rate of return in insurance economics of pension plans, insurance regulation, malpractice insurance, actuarial science, genetic testing and life insurance.

University of Wisconsin–Madison, Graduate School, School of Business, Program in Risk Management and Insurance, Madison, WI 53706-1380. Offers PhD. *Students:* 9 full-time (5 women); includes 2 minority (both African Americans), 7 international. Average age 31. 38 applicants, 8% accepted, 2 enrolled. In 2006, 1 degree awarded. Terminal master's awarded for partial completion of doctoral program. *Median time to degree:* Of those who began their doctoral program in fall 1998, 100% received their degree in 8 years or less. *Degree requirements:* For doctorate, thesis/dissertation. *Entrance requirements:* For doctorate, GMAT or GRE. Additional exam requirements/recommendations for international students: Required—TOEFL. *Application deadline:* For fall admission, 1/6 priority date for domestic and international students. Applications are processed on a rolling basis. Application fee: $45. Electronic applications accepted. *Financial support:* In 2006–07, fellowships with full tuition reimbursements (averaging $16,110 per year), 1 research assistantship with full tuition reimbursement (averaging $13,502 per year), 7 teaching assistantships (averaging $13,686 per year) were awarded; Federal Work-Study, institutionally sponsored loans, scholarships/grants, health care benefits, and unspecified assistantships also available. Financial award application deadline: 1/6; financial award applicants required to submit FAFSA. *Faculty research:* Superfund, health insurance, workers compensation, employee benefits, fuzzy logic. *Unit head:* Joan Schmit, Chair, 608-262-4240, E-mail: jschmit@bus.wisc.edu. *Application contact:* Belle Heberling, PhD Coordinator, 608-262-3749, Fax: 608-890-0180, E-mail: phd@bus.wisc.edu.

University of Wisconsin–Madison, Graduate School, School of Business, Wisconsin Full-Time MBA Programs, Madison, WI 53706-1380. Offers applied corporate finance (MBA); applied security analysis (MBA); arts administration (MBA); brand and product management (MBA); entrepreneurial management (MBA); information systems (MBA); marketing research (MBA); operations and technology management (MBA); real estate (MBA); risk management and insurance (MBA); strategic human resource management (MBA); strategic management in the life and engineering sciences (MBA); supply chain management (MBA). *Faculty:* 84. *Students:* 231 full-time (74 women); includes 21 minority (10 African Americans, 5 Asian

Insurance

University of Wisconsin–Madison (continued)

Americans or Pacific Islanders, 6 Hispanic Americans), 59 international. Average age 28. 405 applicants, 43% accepted, 121 enrolled. In 2006, 110 degrees awarded. *Entrance requirements:* For master's, GMAT, bachelors or equivalent degree, 2 years of work experience. Additional exam requirements/recommendations for international students: Required—TOEFL (minimum score 600 paper-based; 250 computer-based; 90 iBT). *Application deadline:* For fall admission, 11/1 for domestic and international students; for winter admission, 1/23 for domestic and international students; for spring admission, 3/26 for domestic and international students. Applications are processed on a rolling basis. Application fee: $45. Electronic applications accepted. *Financial support:* In 2006–07, 177 students received support, including 20 fellowships with full and partial tuition reimbursements available (averaging $16,566 per year), 105 research assistantships with full tuition reimbursements available (averaging $8,098 per year), 33 teaching assistantships with full tuition reimbursements available (averaging $10,112 per year); scholarships/grants, health care benefits, and unspecified assistantships also available. *Unit head:* Gary Lessuise, Assistant Dean, Masters Programs, 608-265-5102, Fax: 608-265-4192, E-mail: glessuise@bus.wisc.edu. *Application contact:* Betsy Kacizak, Director of Admissions and Financial Aid—Full Time MBA, 608-262-4000, Fax: 608-265-4192, E-mail: mba@bus.wisc.edu.

Virginia Commonwealth University, Graduate School, School of Business, Program in Finance, Insurance, and Real Estate, Richmond, VA 23284-9005. Offers MS. *Faculty:* 11 full-time (0 women). *Students:* 2 full-time (0 women), 6 part-time (1 woman), 1 international. 5 applicants, 80% accepted, 3 enrolled. In 2006, 17 degrees awarded. *Entrance requirements:* For master's, GMAT. *Application deadline:* Applications are processed on a rolling basis. Application fee: $50. *Financial support:* Fellowships, research assistantships, teaching assistantships, Federal Work-Study, institutionally sponsored loans, and tuition waivers (full and partial) available. Financial award application deadline: 3/15. *Unit head:* Dr. David E. Upton, Acting Chair, 804-828-7169, Fax: 804-828-3972, E-mail: deupton@vcu.edu. *Application contact:* Tracy Green, Graduate Program Director, 804-828-1741, Fax: 804-828-7174, E-mail: tsgreen@vcu.edu.

Washington State University, Graduate School, College of Business, Department of Finance, Insurance and Real Estate, Pullman, WA 99164. Offers PhD. Application fee: $50. *Expenses:* Tuition, state resident: full-time $7,066. Tuition, nonresident: full-time $17,204. *Unit head:* Dr. Gene Lai, Chair.

Section 11
International Business

This section contains a directory of institutions offering graduate work in international business, followed by in-depth entries submitted by institutions that chose to prepare detailed program descriptions. Additional information about programs listed in the directory but not augmented by an in-depth entry may be obtained by writing directly to the dean of a graduate school or chair of a department at the address given in the directory.

For programs offering related work, see also in this book Business Administration and Management, Entrepreneurship, Industrial and Manufacturing Management, and Organizational Behavior. In Book 2, see Political Science and International Affairs and Public, Regional, and Industrial Affairs.

CONTENTS

International Business

Alliant International University–México City, Marshall Goldsmith School of Management, Mexico City, Mexico. Offers international business administration (MIBA); international relations (MA). Part-time and evening/weekend programs available. *Faculty:* 1 full-time (0 women), 11 part-time/adjunct (3 women). *Students:* 15 full-time (7 women), 11 part-time (6 women); includes 4 minority (all Hispanic Americans), 10 international. Average age 25. 17 applicants, 41% accepted. *Entrance requirements:* For master's, GMAT, minimum GPA of 3.0. Additional exam requirements/recommendations for international students: Required—TOEFL (minimum score 550 paper-based; 213 computer-based), TWE (minimum score 5). *Application deadline:* For fall admission, 8/1 priority date for domestic and international students; for spring admission, 12/1 priority date for domestic and international students. Applications are processed on a rolling basis. Application fee: $55. Electronic applications accepted. *Expenses:* Tuition: Full-time $5,640; part-time $235 per unit. Required fees: $300; $150 per semester. *Financial support:* Research assistantships, teaching assistantships, career-related internships or fieldwork, Federal Work-Study, institutionally sponsored loans, and scholarships/grants available. Support available to part-time students. Financial award application deadline: 2/15; financial award applicants required to submit FAFSA. *Faculty research:* Environmental impact and business in Mexico. *Unit head:* Dr. Jim Goodrich, Dean, 525-5264-2187, Fax: 525-5264-2188, E-mail: admissions@alliant.edu. *Application contact:* Alliant International University Central Contact Center, 866-U-ALLIANT, Fax: 858-635-4555, E-mail: admissions@alliant.edu.

See Close-Up on page 203.

Alliant International University–San Diego, Marshall Goldsmith School of Management, Business and Management Division, San Diego, CA 92131-1799. Offers business administration (MBA); information and technology management (DBA); international business (MIBA, DBA), including finance (DBA), marketing (DBA); strategic business (DBA); sustainable management (MBA). Part-time and evening/weekend programs available. *Students:* 87 full-time (22 women), 51 part-time (17 women); includes 27 minority (8 African Americans, 2 American Indian/Alaska Native, 8 Asian Americans or Pacific Islanders, 9 Hispanic Americans), 68 international. Average age 32. 104 applicants, 66% accepted, 40 enrolled. *Degree requirements:* For doctorate, thesis/dissertation. *Entrance requirements:* For master's, GMAT, minimum GPA of 3.0; for doctorate, GMAT, minimum GPA of 3.3. Additional exam requirements/recommendations for international students: Required—TOEFL (minimum score 550 paper-based; 213 computer-based), TWE (minimum score 5). *Application deadline:* For fall admission, 8/1 priority date for domestic and international students; for spring admission, 12/1 priority date for domestic and international students. Applications are processed on a rolling basis. Application fee: $55. Electronic applications accepted. *Expenses:* Tuition: Part-time $825 per unit. Tuition and fees vary according to course load, degree level and program. *Financial support:* Research assistantships, teaching assistantships, career-related internships or fieldwork, Federal Work-Study, institutionally sponsored loans, scholarships/grants, and tuition waivers (partial) available. Support available to part-time students. Financial award application deadline: 2/15; financial award applicants required to submit FAFSA. *Faculty research:* Consumer behavior, international business, strategic management, information systems. *Unit head:* Dr. Fred Phillips, Associate Dean, 866-825-5426, Fax: 855-635-4739, E-mail: admissions@alliant.edu. *Application contact:* Alliant International University Central Contact Center, 866-U-ALLIANT, Fax: 858-635-4555, E-mail: admissions@alliant.edu.

See Close-Up on page 203.

American InterContinental University, Program in International Business, Weston, FL 33326. Offers accounting and finance (MBA); human resource management (MBA); management (MBA); marketing (MBA). Part-time and evening/weekend programs available. Postbaccalaureate distance learning degree programs offered. *Faculty:* 3 full-time (0 women), 2 part-time/adjunct (0 women). *Students:* 87 full-time (51 women), 7 part-time (4 women); includes 62 minority (42 African Americans, 1 American Indian/Alaska Native, 1 Asian American or Pacific Islander, 18 Hispanic Americans), 5 international. Average age 34. In 2006, 51 degrees awarded. *Application deadline:* Applications are processed on a rolling basis. Application fee: $50. Electronic applications accepted. *Financial support:* Federal Work-Study and scholarships/grants available. Financial award application deadline: 1/15; financial award applicants required to submit FAFSA. *Unit head:* Dr. David Kalichavan, Acting Dean, School of Business, 954-446-6100, Fax: 954-446-6393, E-mail: dkalichavan@aiufl.edu.

American InterContinental University Dunwoody Campus, Program in Global Technology Management, Atlanta, GA 30328. Offers MBA. Part-time and evening/weekend programs available. Postbaccalaureate distance learning degree programs offered. *Entrance requirements:* For master's, interview. Electronic applications accepted. *Faculty research:* E-commerce, service quality leadership, human resources management.

American InterContinental University-London, Program in Business Administration, London, United Kingdom. Offers international business (MBA). *Degree requirements:* For master's, thesis optional. *Entrance requirements:* For master's, interview, professional experience. Additional exam requirements/recommendations for international students: Required—TOEFL or IELTS recommended. Electronic applications accepted.

American InterContinental University Online, Program in Business Administration, Hoffman Estates, IL 60192. Offers accounting and finance (MBA); healthcare management (MBA); human resource management (MBA); international business (MBA); management (MBA); marketing (MBA); operations management (MBA); organizational psychology and development (MBA); project management (MBA). Evening/weekend programs available. Postbaccalaureate distance learning degree programs offered (no on-campus study). *Entrance requirements:* Additional exam requirements/recommendations for international students: Required—TOEFL (minimum score 550 paper-based; 213 computer-based). *Application deadline:* Applications are processed on a rolling basis. Application fee: $50. Electronic applications accepted. *Financial support:* Institutionally sponsored loans and scholarships/grants available. Financial award applicants required to submit FAFSA. *Unit head:* Kerri J Holloway, Vice President of Academic Affairs, 847-851-5000 Ext. 15399, Fax: 847-586-6309, E-mail: kholloway@aivonline.edu. *Application contact:* 877-701-3800, E-mail: info@aiuonline.edu.

American University, Kogod School of Business, Department of International Business, Washington, DC 20016-8001. Offers international finance (MBA); international management (MBA); international marketing (MBA). Part-time and evening/weekend programs available. *Faculty:* 12 full-time (3 women). *Students:* 23 full-time (7 women), 14 part-time (7 women); includes 5 minority (2 African Americans, 3 Asian Americans or Pacific Islanders), 11 international. Average age 29. In 2006, 29 degrees awarded. *Entrance requirements:* For master's, GMAT. Additional exam requirements/recommendations for international students: Required—TOEFL (minimum score 550 paper-based; 213 computer-based). *Application deadline:* For fall admission, 2/1 priority date for domestic students; for spring admission, 10/1 priority date for domestic students. Applications are processed on a rolling basis. Application fee: $50. *Expenses:* Tuition: Full-time $18,864; part-time $1,048 per credit. Required fees: $380. Tuition and fees vary according to program. *Financial support:* In 2006–07, 11 students received support; fellowships, research assistantships with partial tuition reimbursements available, career-related internships or fieldwork, Federal Work-Study, and institutionally sponsored loans available. Support available to part-time students. Financial award application deadline: 2/1; financial award applicants required to submit FAFSA. *Faculty research:* Financial risk in the multinational corporation, emerging security markets, import/export issues, joint ventures in China, Japanese management. *Unit head:* Dr. Dara Khambat, Chair, 202-885-1964.

American University, Kogod School of Business, Department of Management, Program in Management of Global Information Technology, Washington, DC 20016-8001. Offers MBA. Part-time and evening/weekend programs available. *Students:* 7 full-time (2 women), 11 part-time (3 women); includes 4 minority (2 African Americans, 1 Asian American or Pacific Islander, 1 Hispanic American), 4 international. Average age 30. In 2006, 6 degrees awarded. *Entrance requirements:* For master's, GMAT. Additional exam requirements/recommendations for international students: Required—TOEFL. *Application deadline:* For fall admission, 2/1 priority date for domestic students; for spring admission, 10/1 priority date for domestic students. Application fee: $50. *Expenses:* Tuition: Full-time $18,864; part-time $1,048 per credit. Required fees: $380. Tuition and fees vary according to program. *Financial support:* Fellowships, research assistantships, career-related internships or fieldwork, Federal Work-Study, and institutionally sponsored loans available. Support available to part-time students. Financial award application deadline: 2/1. *Faculty research:* Global electronic commerce, global software development terms, end-user computer, knowledge management, assessing value of IT.

The American University in Dubai, Program in International Business, Dubai, United Arab Emirates. Offers MBA. Part-time programs available. *Degree requirements:* For master's, thesis optional. *Entrance requirements:* For master's, GMAT, interview. Additional exam requirements/recommendations for international students: Required—TOEFL. Electronic applications accepted.

Andrew Jackson University, Brian Tracy College of Business and Entrepreneurship, Birmingham, AL 35244. Offers entrepreneurship (MBA); finance (MBA); health services management (MBA); hospitality and tourism management (MBA); human resource management (MBA); international business (MBA); management (MBA); marketing (MBA). Part-time and evening/weekend programs available. Postbaccalaureate distance learning degree programs offered (no on-campus study). *Faculty:* 13 part-time/adjunct (1 woman). *Students:* Average age 40. In 2006, 6 degrees awarded. *Entrance requirements:* For master's, course work in calculus, statistics. Additional exam requirements/recommendations for international students: Required—TOEFL (minimum score 550 paper-based; 213 computer-based). *Application deadline:* Applications are processed on a rolling basis. Application fee: $75. *Expenses:* Tuition: Part-time $705 per course. *Application contact:* Betty Howell, Director of Student Affairs, 205-871-9288 Ext. 108, Fax: 205-871-9294, E-mail: bhowell@aju.edu.

Argosy University, Atlanta Campus, College of Business, Atlanta, GA 30328. Offers accounting (DBA); customized professional concentration (MBA, DBA); finance (MBA); healthcare administration (MBA); information systems (DBA); information systems management (MBA); international business (MBA, DBA); management (MBA, DBA); marketing (MBA, DBA). Part-time programs available. *Students:* 53 full-time (38 women), 35 part-time (28 women); includes 73 minority (66 African Americans, 3 Asian Americans or Pacific Islanders, 4 Hispanic Americans). *Degree requirements:* For master's, comprehensive exam (for some programs), registration; for doctorate, thesis/dissertation, comprehensive exam, registration. *Entrance requirements:* For master's, minimum undergraduate GPA of 3.0; for doctorate, master's degree, minimum GPA of 3.0. Additional exam requirements/recommendations for international students: Required—TOEFL. *Application deadline:* For fall admission, 7/1 priority date for domestic students, 6/1 for international students; for spring admission, 11/1 priority date for domestic students, 10/1 for international students. Applications are processed on a rolling basis. Application fee: $50. Electronic applications accepted. *Financial support:* Applicants required to submit FAFSA. *Unit head:* Dr. Robert A. Berg, Department Chair, 770-407-1042, E-mail: rberg@argosy.edu. *Application contact:* Christa Holton, Director of Admissions, 770-671-1200 Ext. 1014, Fax: 770-671-9050, E-mail: cholton@argosy.edu.

See Close-Up on page 207.

Argosy University, Chicago Campus, College of Business, Chicago, IL 60603. Offers accounting (DBA); customized professional concentration (MBA, DBA); finance (MBA); healthcare administration (MBA); information systems (DBA); information systems management (MBA); international business (MBA, DBA); management (MBA, DBA); marketing (MBA, DBA). Part-time and evening/weekend programs available. *Faculty:* 2 full-time (both women), 4 part-time/adjunct (3 women). *Students:* 52 full-time (30 women), 18 part-time (7 women); includes 37 minority (24 African Americans, 7 Asian Americans or Pacific Islanders, 6 Hispanic Americans). Average age 37. 32 applicants, 81% accepted, 25 enrolled. In 2006, 9 master's, 2 doctorates awarded. *Entrance requirements:* For master's and doctorate, minimum GPA of 3.0. Additional exam requirements/recommendations for international students: Required—TOEFL (minimum score 550 paper-based; 213 computer-based). *Application deadline:* For fall admission, 2/28 for domestic and international students; for spring admission, 10/30 for domestic and international students. Applications are processed on a rolling basis. Application fee: $50. Electronic applications accepted. *Financial support:* In 2006–07, 3 students received support. Scholarships/grants available. Financial award application deadline: 4/1. *Unit head:* Dr. Cynthia Scarlett, Associate Head, 800-626-4123, Fax: 212-727-7750, E-mail: cscarlett@argosy.edu. *Application contact:* Ashley Delaney, Director of Admissions, 800-626-4123, Fax: 312-777-7750, E-mail: argosyadmissions@argosy.edu.

See Close-Up on page 209.

Argosy University, Denver Campus, College of Business, Denver, CO 80203. Offers accounting (DBA); customized professional concentraion (DBA); customized professional concentration (MBA); finance (MBA); healthcare administration (MBA); information systems (DBA); information systems management (MBA); international business (MBA, DBA); management (MBA, MSM, DBA); marketing (MBA, DBA).

See Close-Up on page 213.

Argosy University, Hawai'i Campus, College of Business, Honolulu, HI 96813. Offers accounting (DBA); customized professional concentration (MBA, DBA); finance (MBA, Certificate); healthcare administration (MBA, Certificate); information systems (DBA); information systems management (MBA, Certificate); international business (MBA, DBA, Certificate); management (MBA, DBA); marketing (MBA, DBA, Certificate). Evening/weekend programs available. *Faculty:* 12 part-time/adjunct (2 women). *Students:* 3 full-time (2 women), 1 part-time; includes 2 minority (1 Asian American or Pacific Islander, 1 Hispanic American). 6 applicants, 67% accepted, 3 enrolled. *Degree requirements:* For master's, capstone project. *Entrance requirements:* For master's, minimum GPA of 3.0 in last 60 hours. Additional exam requirements/recommendations for international students: Required—TOEFL (minimum score 550 paper-based; 213 computer-based). *Application deadline:* For fall admission, 1/15 priority date for domestic students; for spring admission, 10/15 for domestic students. Applications are processed on a rolling basis. Application fee: $50. *Financial support:* Teaching assistantships, Federal Work-Study and scholarships/grants available. Support available to part-time students. *Unit head:* Lisa Parker, Interim Chair, College of Business and Information Technology, 888-323-2777, Fax: 808-536-5505, E-mail: lparker@argosy.edu. *Application contact:* Cherie Andrade, Director of Admissions, 888-323-2777, Fax: 808-536-5505, E-mail: candrade@argosy.edu.

See Close-Up on page 215.

Argosy University, Inland Empire Campus, College of Business, San Bernardino, CA 92408. Offers accounting (DBA); customized professional concentration (MBA, DBA); finance (MBA); healthcare administration (MBA); information systems (DBA); information systems management (MBA); international business (MBA, DBA); management (DBA); mangement (MBA); marketing (MBA, DBA).

See Close-Up on page 217.

Argosy University, Nashville Campus, College of Business, Franklin, TN 37067-7226. Offers accounting (DBA); customized professional concentration (DBA); information systems

(DBA); international business (DBA); management (DBA); marketing (DBA). *Degree requirements:* For doctorate, thesis/dissertation, comprehensive exam.

See Close-Up on page 219.

Argosy University, Orange County Campus, College of Business, Santa Ana, CA 92704. Offers accounting (DBA, Adv C); customized professional concentration (MBA, DBA); finance (MBA, Certificate); healthcare administration (MBA, Certificate); information systems (DBA, Adv C); information systems management (MBA); international business (MBA, DBA, Adv C, Certificate); management (MBA, MSM, DBA, EDBA); mangement (Adv C); marketing (MBA, DBA, Adv C, Certificate); organizational leadership (Ed D); public administration (MBA, Certificate). Part-time and evening/weekend programs available. *Faculty:* 4 full-time (1 woman), 20 part-time/adjunct (7 women). *Students:* 163 full-time (64 women), 41 part-time (16 women). Average age 42. 72 applicants, 51 enrolled. In 2006, 6 master's, 23 doctorates awarded. *Degree requirements:* For doctorate, thesis/dissertation, preliminary and final dissertation defense, comprehensive exam. *Entrance requirements:* For master's, minimum GPA of 3.0 in final 2 years of course work, 3 letters of recommendation, resumé; for doctorate, minimum GPA of 3.0 in graduate study, 3 letters of recommendation, resumé. Additional exam requirements/recommendations for international students: Required—TOEFL. *Application deadline:* Applications are processed on a rolling basis. Application fee: $50. Electronic applications accepted. *Financial support:* Federal Work-Study, institutionally sponsored loans, and scholarships/grants available. Support available to part-time students. Financial award applicants required to submit FAFSA. *Faculty research:* Crisis management, leadership in organizations, finance, business systems. *Unit head:* Dr. Ray London, Dean, 800-716-9598, Fax: 714-437-1284, E-mail: auocadmissions@argosy.edu. *Application contact:* Mark Betz, Director of Admissions, 800-716-9598, Fax: 714-437-1697, E-mail: mbetz@argosy.edu.

See Close-Up on page 221.

Argosy University, Phoenix Campus, College of Business, Phoenix, AZ 85021. Offers accounting (DBA); customized professional concentration (MBA, DBA); finance (MBA); healthcare administration (MBA); information systems (DBA); information systems management (MBA); international business (MBA, DBA); management (MBA, DBA); marketing (MBA, DBA). Part-time and evening/weekend programs available. *Faculty:* 1 full-time (0 women). *Students:* 7 full-time (4 women); includes 2 minority (1 African American, 1 Hispanic American). *Entrance requirements:* For doctorate, master's degree. Additional exam requirements/recommendations for international students: Required—TOEFL (minimum score 550 paper-based; 213 computer-based). Application fee: $50. *Financial support:* In 2006–07, 2 students received support. Federal Work-Study, institutionally sponsored loans, and scholarships/grants available. Support available to part-time students. Financial award applicants required to submit FAFSA. *Unit head:* Dr. Gary Berg, Program Chair, 866-216-2777, Fax: 602-216-2601. *Application contact:* Andy Hughes, Director of Admissions, 866-216-2777 Ext. 3110, Fax: 602-216-2601, E-mail: ahughes@argosyu.edu.

See Close-Up on page 223.

Argosy University, San Diego Campus, College of Business, San Diego, CA 92108. Offers accounting (DBA); customized professional concentration (MBA, DBA); finance (MBA); information systems (DBA); information systems management (MBA); international business (MBA, DBA); management (MBA, MSM, DBA); marketing (MBA, DBA); public administration (MBA).

See Close-Up on page 225.

Argosy University, San Francisco Bay Area Campus, College of Business, Point Richmond, CA 94804-3547. Offers accounting (DBA); corporate compliance (MBA); customized professional concentration (MBA, DBA); finance (MBA); healthcare administration (MBA); information systems (DBA); information systems management (MBA); international business (MBA, DBA); management (MBA, MSM, DBA); marketing (MBA, DBA). Part-time and evening/weekend programs available. *Faculty:* 2 full-time (0 women), 9 part-time/adjunct (0 women). *Students:* 29 full-time (8 women), 9 part-time (2 women); includes 30 minority (5 African Americans, 24 Asian Americans or Pacific Islanders, 1 Hispanic American). 21 applicants, 76% accepted, 13 enrolled. In 2006, 3 master's, 2 doctorates awarded. *Degree requirements:* For master's, capstone project; for doctorate, thesis/dissertation, comprehensive exam, registration. *Entrance requirements:* For master's, minimum GPA of 3.0; for doctorate, MBA or minimum GPA of 3.0. Additional exam requirements/recommendations for international students: Required—TOEFL (minimum score 550 paper-based; 213 computer-based). *Application deadline:* For fall admission, 7/1 priority date for domestic and international students; for winter admission, 11/1 priority date for domestic and international students; for spring admission, 4/1 priority date for domestic and international students. Applications are processed on a rolling basis. Application fee: $50. Electronic applications accepted. *Financial support:* Federal Work-Study and scholarships/grants available. Support available to part-time students. Financial award applicants required to submit FAFSA. *Unit head:* Dr. Anthony Martinez, Department Chair, Business and Information Technology, 866-215-0277, Fax: 510-215-0299, E-mail: amartinez@argosy.edu. *Application contact:* John Vincent Stofan, Director of Admissions, 866-215-2727 Ext. 205, Fax: 510-215-0299, E-mail: jstofan@argosyu.edu.

See Close-Up on page 227.

Argosy University, Santa Monica Campus, College of Business, Santa Monica, CA 90405. Offers accounting (DBA); customized professional concentration (MBA, DBA); finance (MBA); healthcare administration (MBA); information systems (DBA); information systems management (MBA); international business (MBA, DBA); management (MBA, MS, MSM, DBA); marketing (MBA, DBA).

See Close-Up on page 229.

Argosy University, Sarasota Campus, College of Business, Sarasota, FL 34235-8246. Offers accounting (DBA, Adv C); customized professional concentration (MBA, DBA); finance (MBA, Certificate); healtcare administration (Certificate); healthcare administration (MBA); information systems (DBA, Adv C); information systems management (MBA, Certificate); international business (MBA, DBA, Adv C, Certificate); management (MBA, MSM, DBA); mangement (Adv C); marketing (MBA, DBA, Adv C, Certificate). Part-time and evening/weekend programs available. Postbaccalaureate distance learning degree programs offered (minimal on-campus study). *Faculty:* 6 full-time (3 women), 13 part-time/adjunct (5 women). *Students:* 71 applicants, 92% accepted, 64 enrolled. In 2006, 7 master's, 30 doctorates awarded. *Degree requirements:* For doctorate, thesis/dissertation, comprehensive exam. *Entrance requirements:* For master's, minimum GPA of 3.0; for doctorate, minimum undergraduate GPA of 3.0. Additional exam requirements/recommendations for international students: Required—TOEFL. *Application deadline:* Applications are processed on a rolling basis. Application fee: $50. Electronic applications accepted. *Financial support:* Federal Work-Study and scholarships/grants available. Support available to part-time students. Financial award application deadline: 4/1; financial award applicants required to submit FAFSA. *Unit head:* Dr. Kathleen Cornett, Dean, 800-331-5995, Fax: 941-379-9464, E-mail: kcornett@argosy.edu. *Application contact:* Admissions Representative, 800-331-5995 Ext. 221, Fax: 941-379-5964.

See Close-Up on page 231.

Argosy University, Schaumburg Campus, College of Business, Schaumburg, IL 60173-5403. Offers accounting (DBA, Adv C); corporate compliance (MBA); customized professional concentration (MBA, DBA); finance (MBA, Certificate); healthcare administration (MBA, Certificate); information systems (DBA, Adv C); information systems management (MBA, Certificate); international business (MBA, DBA, Adv C, Certificate); management (MBA, DBA, Adv C, Certificate); marketing (MBA, DBA, Adv C, Certificate). Part-time and evening/weekend programs available. *Faculty:* 1 (woman) full-time, 7 part-time/adjunct (0 women). *Students:* 36 full-time, 23 part-time. 13 applicants, 69% accepted, 9 enrolled. In 2006, 5 master's, 4 doctorates awarded. *Degree requirements:* For doctorate, thesis/dissertation, comprehensive exam. *Entrance requirements:* For master's and doctorate, minimum GPA of 3.0. Additional exam requirements/recommendations for international students: Required—TOEFL. *Application deadline:* For fall admission, 3/15 priority date for domestic and international students; for spring admission, 10/15 priority date for domestic and international students. Applications are processed on a rolling basis. Application fee: $50. Electronic applications accepted. *Expenses: Contact institution. Financial support:* Federal Work-Study and scholarships/grants available. *Unit head:* Dr. Harriet Kandelman, Dean, 866-290-2777, Fax: 847-548-6159, E-mail: agrosyadmissions@argosy.edu. *Application contact:* Jamal Scott, Director of Admissions, 847-598-6159, Fax: 630-598-6191, E-mail: jscott@argosy.edu.

See Close-Up on page 233.

Argosy University, Seattle Campus, College of Business, Seattle, WA 98121. Offers accounting (DBA); customized professional concentration (MBA, DBA); finance (MBA); healthcare administration (MBA); information systems (DBA); information systems management (MBA); international business (MBA, DBA); management (MSM, DBA); mangement (MBA); marketing (MBA, DBA). Part-time and evening/weekend programs available. *Students:* 1 applicant, 100% accepted, 1 enrolled. In 2006, 1 degree awarded. *Degree requirements:* For master's, capstone experience; for doctorate, thesis/dissertation, comprehensive exam (for some programs). *Entrance requirements:* For master's, minimum GPA of 3.0 in last 2 years or cumulative of 2.7; for doctorate, minimum GPA of 3.0. Additional exam requirements/recommendations for international students: Required—TOEFL (minimum score 550 paper-based; 213 computer-based). *Application deadline:* For fall admission, 4/15 priority date for domestic students, 4/15 for international students; for winter admission, 10/15 priority date for domestic students. Applications are processed on a rolling basis. Application fee: $50. Electronic applications accepted. *Expenses: Contact institution. Financial support:* Federal Work-Study and unspecified assistantships available. Support available to part-time students. Financial award applicants required to submit FAFSA. *Unit head:* Dr. Kylene Quinn, Chair, 206-393-3543, Fax: 206-283-5777, E-mail: kquinn@argosy.edu. *Application contact:* Heather Simpson, Director of Admissions, 866-283-4500, Fax: 206-283-5777, E-mail: hsimpson@argosy.edu.

See Close-Up on page 235.

Argosy University, Tampa Campus, College of Business, Tampa, FL 33614. Offers accounting (DBA); customized professional concentration (MBA, DBA); finance (MBA, Certificate); healthcare administration (MBA, Certificate); information systems (DBA); information systems management (MBA); international business (MBA, DBA, Certificate); management (MBA, MSM, DBA); marketing (MBA, DBA, Certificate); public administration (MBA). *Entrance requirements:* For doctorate, minimum GPA of 3.0. *Unit head:* Dr. Andrew Ghillyer, Dean, 813-393-5270, E-mail: aghillyer@argosy.edu.

See Close-Up on page 237.

Argosy University, Twin Cities Campus, College of Business, Eagan, MN 55121. Offers accounting (DBA); corporate compliance (MBA); customized professional certification (DBA); customized professional concentration (MBA); finance (MBA); healthcare administration (MBA); information systems (DBA); information systems management (MBA); international business (MBA, DBA); management (MBA, MSM, DBA, EDBA); marketing (MBA, DBA). Part-time and evening/weekend programs available. *Faculty:* 1 (woman) full-time, 20 part-time/adjunct (6 women). *Students:* 47 full-time (23 women), 20 part-time (11 women); includes 21 minority (10 African Americans, 1 American Indian/Alaska Native, 9 Asian Americans or Pacific Islanders, 1 Hispanic American). Average age 39. 72 applicants, 76% accepted, 45 enrolled. In 2006, 6 degrees awarded. *Degree requirements:* For doctorate, thesis/dissertation, comprehensive exam. *Entrance requirements:* For master's, 3 letters of recommendation, bachelor's degree in a related field, minimum undergraduate GPA of 3.0, resumé; for doctorate, 3 letters of recommendation, master's degree in a related field, minimum GPA of 3.0, resumé. Additional exam requirements/recommendations for international students: Required—TOEFL (minimum score 550 paper-based; 213 computer-based). *Application deadline:* For fall admission, 5/15 priority date for domestic students, 5/15 for international students; for spring admission, 10/15 priority date for domestic students, 10/15 for international students. Applications are processed on a rolling basis. Application fee: $50. Electronic applications accepted. *Financial support:* In 2006–07, 3 fellowships with partial tuition reimbursements, 3 teaching assistantships with partial tuition reimbursements were awarded; Federal Work-Study and scholarships/grants also available. Financial award applicants required to submit FAFSA. *Unit head:* Dr. Paula King, Department Head, 651-846-3377, E-mail: pking@argosy.edu. *Application contact:* Jennifer Radke, 2nd Director of Graduate Admissions, 651-846-3300, Fax: 651-994-7954, E-mail: tcadmissions@argosy.edu.

See Close-Up on page 239.

Argosy University, Washington DC Campus, College of Business, Arlington, VA 22209. Offers accounting (DBA); customized professional concentration (MBA, DBA); finance (MBA); healthcare administration (MBA); information systems (DBA); information systems management (MBA); international business (MBA, DBA); international business marketing (Graduate Certificate); management (MBA, DBA); marketing (MBA, DBA). *Faculty:* 1 full-time (0 women), 5 part-time/adjunct (2 women). *Students:* 5 full-time (4 women), 4 part-time (1 woman); includes 4 minority (3 African Americans, 1 Asian American or Pacific Islander). 21 applicants, 86% accepted. *Degree requirements:* For master's, thesis (for some programs), comprehensive exam (for some programs); for doctorate, thesis/dissertation, comprehensive exam. *Entrance requirements:* For master's and doctorate, minimum GPA of 3.0. Additional exam requirements/recommendations for international students: Required—TOEFL (minimum score 550 paper-based; 213 computer-based). *Application deadline:* For fall admission, 6/15 priority date for domestic students; for spring admission, 10/15 priority date for domestic students. Application fee: $50. *Financial support:* Federal Work-Study and scholarships/grants available. Financial award applicants required to submit FAFSA. *Unit head:* Dr. Colleen Logan, Academic Affairs Officer, 866-703-2777, Fax: 703-521-5850, E-mail: dcadmissions@argosy.edu. *Application contact:* Emily Peck, Director of Admissions, 866-703-2777 Ext. 5851, Fax: 703-526-5850, E-mail: dcadmissions@argosy.edu.

See Close-Up on page 241.

Avila University, School of Business, Kansas City, MO 64145-1698. Offers accounting (MBA); finance (MBA); general management (MBA); health care administration (MBA); international business (MBA); management information systems (MBA); marketing (MBA). Part-time and evening/weekend programs available. *Faculty:* 8 full-time (4 women), 17 part-time/adjunct (4 women). *Students:* 31 full-time (19 women), 165 part-time (96 women); includes 18 minority (14 African Americans, 1 American Indian/Alaska Native, 3 Hispanic Americans), 16 international. Average age 32. 77 applicants, 81% accepted, 62 enrolled. In 2006, 54 degrees awarded. *Degree requirements:* For master's, capstone course. *Entrance requirements:* For master's, GMAT, minimum GPA of 3.0. Additional exam requirements/recommendations for international students: Required—TOEFL (minimum score 550 paper-based). *Application deadline:* For fall admission, 7/30 priority date for domestic students; for winter admission, 11/30 priority date for domestic students; for spring admission, 2/28 priority date for domestic students. Applications are processed on a rolling basis. Application fee: $20. Electronic applications accepted. *Expenses:* Tuition: Full-time $7,470; part-time $415 per credit. *Financial support:* In 2006–07, 78 students received support. Career-related internships or fieldwork available. Support available to part-time students. Financial award applicants required to submit FAFSA. *Faculty research:* Leadership characteristics, financial hedging, group dynamics. *Unit head:* Dr. Richard Woodall, Dean, 816-501-3798, Fax: 816-501-2463. *Application contact:* JoAnna Giffin, MBA Admissions Director, 816-501-3601, Fax: 816-501-2463, E-mail: joanna.giffin@avila.edu.

Azusa Pacific University, School of Business and Management, Azusa, CA 91702-7000. Offers business administration (MBA); human and organizational development (MA); international business (MBA); strategic management (MBA). Part-time and evening/weekend programs available. *Faculty:* 3 full-time (0 women). *Students:* 24 full-time (11 women), 126 part-time (51 women); includes 50 minority (8 African Americans, 1 American Indian/Alaska

International Business

Azusa Pacific University (continued)
Native, 12 Asian Americans or Pacific Islanders, 29 Hispanic Americans), 24 international. Average age 31. In 2006, 54 degrees awarded. *Degree requirements:* For master's, thesis (for some programs), final project. *Entrance requirements:* For master's, GMAT, minimum GPA of 3.0. Additional exam requirements/recommendations for international students: Required—TOEFL (minimum score 600 paper-based). *Application deadline:* For fall admission, 8/15 priority date for domestic students. Applications are processed on a rolling basis. Application fee: $45 ($65 for international students). *Expenses: Contact institution. Financial support:* Scholarships/grants available. *Faculty research:* Gender issues, financial risk, leadership and ethics, marketing strategy. *Unit head:* Dr. Ilene Bezjian, Dean, 626-815-3090, Fax: 626-815-3802, E-mail: ibezjian@apu.edu.

Baker College Center for Graduate Studies, Programs in Business, Flint, MI 48507-9843. Offers accounting (MBA); computer information systems (MBA); finance (MBA); general business (MBA); health and recreation services management (MBA); health care management (MBA); human resource management (MBA); industrial management (MBA); international business (MBA); leadership (MBA); marketing (MBA). MBA in health and recreation services management enrollment limited to international students. Part-time and evening/weekend programs available. *Faculty:* 15 full-time (6 women), 425 part-time/adjunct (200 women). *Students:* 370 full-time (190 women), 1,060 part-time (560 women); includes 372 minority (205 African Americans, 27 American Indian/Alaska Native, 66 Asian Americans or Pacific Islanders, 74 Hispanic Americans), 30 international. Average age 38. 780 applicants, 85% accepted, 567 enrolled. In 2006, 202 degrees awarded. *Degree requirements:* For master's, portfolio. *Entrance requirements:* For master's, 3 years of work experience, minimum undergraduate GPA of 2.5, writing sample, letters of recommendation. Additional exam requirements/recommendations for international students: Required—TOEFL (minimum score 550 paper-based; 213 computer-based). *Application deadline:* For fall admission, 8/6 priority date for domestic students; for winter admission, 12/15 priority date for domestic students; for spring admission, 2/15 priority date for domestic students. Applications are processed on a rolling basis. Application fee: $25. Electronic applications accepted. *Expenses:* Tuition: Full-time $7,200; part-time $300 per credit hour. *Financial support:* In 2006–07, 410 students received support. Scholarships/grants available. Support available to part-time students. Financial award applicants required to submit FAFSA. *Unit head:* Dr. Michael Heberling, President, 800-469-3165, Fax: 810-766-4399, E-mail: heberling@baker.edu. *Application contact:* Chuck J. Gurden, Vice President for Graduate and Online Admissions, 800-469-3165, Fax: 810-766-2051, E-mail: chuck@baker.edu.

Baldwin-Wallace College, Graduate Programs, Division of Business Administration, MBA Program in International Management, Berea, OH 44017-2088. Offers MBA. Part-time and evening/weekend programs available. *Students:* 56 full-time (36 women), 17 part-time (11 women); includes 8 minority (4 African Americans, 1 Asian American or Pacific Islander, 3 Hispanic Americans), 16 international. Average age 32. 34 applicants, 82% accepted, 19 enrolled. In 2006, 32 degrees awarded. *Degree requirements:* For master's, one foreign language. *Entrance requirements:* For master's, GMAT, interview, work experience. Additional exam requirements/recommendations for international students: Required—TOEFL (minimum score 500 paper-based). *Application deadline:* For fall admission, 7/25 priority date for domestic students; for spring admission, 12/15 priority date for domestic students. Applications are processed on a rolling basis. Application fee: $25. Electronic applications accepted. *Expenses: Contact institution.* Tuition and fees vary according to program. *Financial support:* Career-related internships or fieldwork available. Support available to part-time students. Financial award applicants required to submit FAFSA. *Faculty research:* International finance, systems approach, international marketing. *Unit head:* Malcolm Watson, Director, 440-826-2196, Fax: 440-826-3868. *Application contact:* Winifred W. Gerhardt, Director of Admission for the Evening and Weekend College, 440-826-2222, Fax: 440-826-3830, E-mail: admission@bw.edu.

Barry University, Andreas School of Business, Graduate Certificate Programs, Miami Shores, FL 33161-6695. Offers finance (Certificate); health services administration (Certificate); international business (Certificate); management (Certificate); management information systems (Certificate); marketing (Certificate). *Application contact:* Dave Fletcher, Director of Graduate Admissions, 305-899-3113, Fax: 305-899-2971, E-mail: dfletcher@mail.barry.edu.

Baylor University, Graduate School, Hankamer School of Business, Department of International Management, Waco, TX 76798. Offers MBA, MBAIM, MIM. Part-time programs available. *Students:* 7 full-time (4 women); includes 2 minority (1 African American, 1 Hispanic American), 3 international. *Entrance requirements:* For master's, GRE General Test or GMAT. *Application deadline:* For fall admission, 8/1 for domestic students; for spring admission, 12/1 for domestic students. Applications are processed on a rolling basis. Application fee: $25. *Financial support:* Research assistantships, career-related internships or fieldwork, Federal Work-Study, and institutionally sponsored loans available. *Application contact:* Vicky Todd, Administrative Assistant, 254-710-3718, Fax: 254-710-1066, E-mail: mba@hsb.baylor.edu.

Bernard M. Baruch College of the City University of New York, Zicklin School of Business, International Executive Programs, New York, NY 10010-5585. Offers MBA. Part-time and evening/weekend programs available. *Faculty:* 8 full-time (1 woman), 12 part-time/adjunct (4 women). In 2006, 13 degrees awarded. *Entrance requirements:* For master's, GMAT, 2 letters of recommendation, resumé, 2 years of work experience. Additional exam requirements/recommendations for international students: Required—TOEFL (minimum score 590 paper-based; 243 computer-based), TWE (minimum score 5). *Application deadline:* For fall admission, 5/31 for domestic students, 4/30 for international students; for spring admission, 10/31 for domestic and international students. Application fee: $125. *Financial support:* Fellowships, research assistantships, teaching assistantships, career-related internships or fieldwork, Federal Work-Study, scholarships/grants, and unspecified assistantships available. Financial award application deadline: 4/30; financial award applicants required to submit FAFSA. *Unit head:* Auner Wolf, Executive Director, 646-212-3453, Fax: 646-312-2111, E-mail: auner_wolf@baruch.cuny.edu. *Application contact:* Ellen Snyder, Associate Director, 646-312-1117, Fax: 646-312-2116, E-mail: ellen_snyder@baruch.cuny.edu.

Boston University, Metropolitan College (Continuing Education), Program in Administrative Studies, Boston, MA 02215. Offers banking and financial management (MSM); business continuity in emergency management (MSM); economics development and tourism management (MSAS); electronic commerce, systems, and technology (MSAS); financial economics (MSAS); human resource management (MSM); innovation and technology (MSAS); insurance management (MSM); international market management (MSM); multinational commerce (MSAS); project management (MSM). *Accreditation:* AACSB. Part-time and evening/weekend programs available. *Faculty:* 9 full-time (0 women), 51 part-time/adjunct (8 women). *Students:* 105 full-time (40 women), 171 part-time (65 women); includes 27 minority (5 African Americans, 18 Asian Americans or Pacific Islanders, 4 Hispanic Americans), 125 international. Average age 29. In 2006, 310 degrees awarded. *Degree requirements:* For master's, thesis optional. *Entrance requirements:* For master's, 1 year of work experience, minimum GPA of 3.0. Additional exam requirements/recommendations for international students: Required—TOEFL (minimum score 560 paper-based; 220 computer-based). *Application deadline:* Applications are processed on a rolling basis. Application fee: $65. *Expenses:* Tuition: Full-time $33,330; part-time $1,042 per credit. Required fees: $462; $40. *Financial support:* In 2006–07, 15 students received support, including research assistantships (averaging $10,000 per year); career-related internships or fieldwork and Federal Work-Study also available. *Faculty research:* International business, innovative process. *Unit head:* Dr. Kip Becker, Chairman, 617-353-3016, E-mail: adminsc@bu.edu. *Application contact:* Lucille Dicker, Administrative Sciences Department, 617-353-3016, E-mail: adminsc@bu.edu.

Brandeis University, The Heller School for Social Policy and Management, Program in Sustainable International Development, Waltham, MA 02454-9110. Offers international development (MA); international health policy and management (MS); sustainable development (MA). *Degree requirements:* For master's, 2nd-year fieldwork or internship. *Entrance requirements:* Additional exam requirements/recommendations for international students: Required—TOEFL. Electronic applications accepted. Expenses: Contact institution. *Faculty research:* Water resource management, human rights, biosphere management, rural development, public policy and governance.

Brandeis University, International Business School, Waltham, MA 02454-9110. Offers finance (MSF); international business (MBAi); international economics and finance (MA, PhD); international finance/international economics (MBAi). Part-time and evening/weekend programs available. Terminal master's awarded for partial completion of doctoral program. *Degree requirements:* For master's, one foreign language; for doctorate, thesis/dissertation. *Entrance requirements:* For master's, GMAT or GRE General Test (MA), GMAT (MBAi and MSF); for doctorate, GRE General Test. Additional exam requirements/recommendations for international students: Required—TOEFL (minimum score 600 paper-based; 250 computer-based), IELTS (minimum score 7). Electronic applications accepted. *Faculty research:* International finance and business, trade policy, macroeconomics, Asian economic issues, developmental economics.

California Lutheran University, Graduate Studies, School of Business, Thousand Oaks, CA 91360-2787. Offers finance (MBA); healthcare management (MBA); international business (MBA); management information systems (MBA); marketing (MBA); organizational behavior (MBA); small business/entrepreneurship (MBA). Evening/weekend programs available. *Entrance requirements:* For master's, GMAT, interview, minimum GPA of 3.0. Expenses: Contact institution.

California State University, East Bay, Academic Programs and Graduate Studies, College of Business and Economics, Department of Management and Finance, Option in International Business, Hayward, CA 94542-3000. Offers MBA. Part-time and evening/weekend programs available. *Degree requirements:* For master's, comprehensive exam or thesis. *Entrance requirements:* For master's, GMAT, minimum GPA of 2.75. Additional exam requirements/recommendations for international students: Required—TOEFL (minimum score 550 paper-based; 213 computer-based). *Application deadline:* For fall admission, 5/31 for domestic students, 4/30 for international students; for winter admission, 9/30 for domestic and international students; for spring admission, 12/31 for domestic students, 11/30 for international students. Application fee: $55. *Financial support:* Career-related internships or fieldwork, Federal Work-Study, and institutionally sponsored loans available. Support available to part-time students. Financial award application deadline: 3/2. *Unit head:* Yi Jiang, Advisor, 510-885-3078, E-mail: yi.jiang@csueastbay.edu. *Application contact:* Doris Duncan, Director of Graduate Programs, 510-885-3364, Fax: 510-885-2176, E-mail: doris.duncan@csueastbay.edu.

California State University, Fullerton, Graduate Studies, College of Business and Economics, Department of Marketing, Fullerton, CA 92834-9480. Offers international business (MBA); marketing (MBA). Part-time and evening/weekend programs available. *Students:* 10 full-time (7 women), 19 part-time (10 women); includes 8 minority (1 African American, 5 Asian Americans or Pacific Islanders, 2 Hispanic Americans), 11 international. Average age 27. 57 applicants, 39% accepted, 12 enrolled. In 2006, 11 degrees awarded. *Degree requirements:* For master's, project or thesis. *Entrance requirements:* For master's, GMAT, minimum AACSB index of 950. Application fee: $55. *Expenses:* Tuition, nonresident: part-time $339 per unit. Required fees: $1,155 per semester. *Financial support:* Teaching assistantships, Federal Work-Study, institutionally sponsored loans, and scholarships/grants available. Support available to part-time students. Financial award application deadline: 3/1. *Unit head:* Dr. Irene Lange, Chair, 714-278-2223. *Application contact:* Robert Miyake, Assistant Dean, 714-278-2211.

California State University, Los Angeles, Graduate Studies, College of Business and Economics, Major in Business Administration, Department of Marketing, Los Angeles, CA 90032-8530. Offers international business (MBA, MS); marketing (MBA, MS). Part-time and evening/weekend programs available. *Faculty:* 2 full-time (both women). *Students:* 9 full-time (4 women), 13 part-time (8 women); includes 11 minority (3 African Americans, 7 Asian Americans or Pacific Islanders, 1 Hispanic American), 7 international. *Degree requirements:* For master's, comprehensive exam (MBA), thesis (MS). *Entrance requirements:* For master's, GMAT, minimum GPA of 2.5 during previous 2 years of course work. Additional exam requirements/recommendations for international students: Required—TOEFL. *Application deadline:* For fall admission, 6/30 for domestic students; for spring admission, 11/30 for domestic students. Applications are processed on a rolling basis. Application fee: $55. *Expenses:* Tuition, nonresident: part-time $226 per unit. *Financial support:* Career-related internships or fieldwork and Federal Work-Study available. Support available to part-time students. Financial award application deadline: 3/1. *Unit head:* Dr. Richard Kao, Chair, 323-343-2960, Fax: 323-343-5462.

Cardean University, MBA Program, Chicago, IL 60606-7204. Offers accounting and information systems (MBA); e-commerce (MBA); finance (MBA); global management (MBA); health care administration (MBA); human resources management (MBA); leadership (MBA); management of information systems (MBA); management of technology (MBA); marketing (MBA); professional accounting (MBA); project management (MBA); risk management (MBA); strategy and economics (MBA). Part-time and evening/weekend programs available. Postbaccalaureate distance learning degree programs offered (no on-campus study). *Entrance requirements:* Additional exam requirements/recommendations for international students: Required—TOEFL (minimum score 550 paper-based; 213 computer-based).

Central Connecticut State University, School of Graduate Studies, School of Business, Program in International Business Administration, New Britain, CT 06050-4010. Offers MBA. Part-time and evening/weekend programs available. *Students:* 11 full-time (7 women), 49 part-time (20 women); includes 5 minority (2 African Americans, 1 Asian American or Pacific Islander, 2 Hispanic Americans), 7 international. 26 applicants, 23% accepted, 6 enrolled. In 2006, 27 degrees awarded. *Degree requirements:* For master's, one foreign language, thesis or alternative, special project. *Entrance requirements:* For master's, GMAT, minimum GPA of 2.7. Additional exam requirements/recommendations for international students: Required—TOEFL. *Application deadline:* For fall admission, 7/1 for domestic students; for spring admission, 12/1 for domestic students. Applications are processed on a rolling basis. Application fee: $50. Electronic applications accepted. *Expenses:* Tuition, area resident: Full-time $3,970; part-time $380 per credit. Tuition, state resident: full-time $5,955; part-time $380 per credit. Tuition, nonresident: full-time $11,061; part-time $380 per credit. Required fees: $3,189. One-time fee: $62 part-time. Tuition and fees vary according to degree level and program. *Financial support:* Research assistantships, career-related internships or fieldwork, Federal Work-Study, scholarships/grants, and unspecified assistantships available. Support available to part-time students. Financial award application deadline: 3/1; financial award applicants required to submit FAFSA. *Faculty research:* Contemporary issues in international business and global perspectives, international markets and market planning. *Unit head:* Dr. Chris Galligan, Director, 860-832-3205.

Central European University, Graduate Studies, Department of Legal Studies, Budapest, Hungary. Offers comparative constitutional law (LL M); economic and legal studies (LL M, MA); human rights (LL M, MA); international business law (LL M); legal studies (SJD). *Faculty:* 7 full-time (2 women), 3 part-time/adjunct (1 woman). *Students:* 115 full-time (58 women). Average age 26. 579 applicants, 21% accepted, 88 enrolled. In 2006, 40 master's, 4 doctorates awarded. Terminal master's awarded for partial completion of doctoral program. *Median time to degree:* Of those who began their doctoral program in fall 1998, 75% received their degree in 8 years or less. *Degree requirements:* For master's, one foreign language, thesis/dissertation, registration; for doctorate, one foreign language, thesis/dissertation, comprehensive exam, registration. *Entrance requirements:* For master's and doctorate, LSAT, CEU admissions exams. Additional exam requirements/recommendations for international students: Required—TOEFL (minimum score 570 paper-based; 230 computer-based). *Application deadline:* For fall admission, 1/5 for domestic and international students. Application fee: $0. Electronic applications accepted. *Expenses: Contact institution. Financial support:* In 2006–07, 84 students received support, including 65 fellowships with full and partial tuition reimbursements available (averaging $5,000 per year); career-related internships or fieldwork, institutionally sponsored loans, scholarships/grants, and tuition waivers (full and partial) also available. Financial award application deadline: 1/5. *Faculty research:* Institutional, constitutional and human rights in European Union law, biomedical law and reproductive rights, data protection law, Islamic banking and finance. *Unit head:* Dr. Stefan Messmann, Head, 361-327-3274, Fax: 361-327-3198, E-mail: legalst@ceu.hu. *Application contact:* Maria Balla, Coordinator, 361-327-3204, Fax: 361-327-3198, E-mail: ballam@ceu.hu.

Central Michigan University, College of Graduate Studies, Program in Administration, Mount Pleasant, MI 48859. Offers general administration (MSA); health services administration (MSA); hospitality and tourism administration (MSA); human resource administration (MSA); information resource administration (MSA); international administration (MSA); leadership (MSA); organizational communications (MSA); public administration (MSA); recreation and park administration (MSA); software engineering (MSA); sports administration (MSA). *Accreditation:* AACSB. *Degree requirements:* For master's, thesis or alternative. *Entrance requirements:* For master's, minimum undergraduate GPA of 2.5.

See Close-Up on page 253.

City University, Graduate Division, School of Management, Bellevue, WA 98005. Offers accounting (MBA); C++ programming (Certificate); computer systems—C++ programming (MS); computer systems—individualized study (MS); computer systems—web programming in e-commerce (MS); computer systems-web development (MS); financial management (MBA, Certificate); general management (MBA, MPA, Certificate); general management-Europe (MBA); human resource management (MPA); individualized study (MBA); information systems (MBA, Certificate); management—general management (MA); management—human resource management (MA); management—individualized study (MA); marketing (MBA, Certificate); personal financial planning (MBA, Certificate); project management (MBA, MS, Certificate); technology management (MS, Certificate); web development (Certificate); web programming in e-commerce (Certificate). Part-time and evening/weekend programs available. Postbaccalaureate distance learning degree programs offered (no on-campus study). *Entrance requirements:* Additional exam requirements/recommendations for international students: Required—TOEFL (minimum score 540 paper-based; 207 computer-based); Recommended—IELTS. Electronic applications accepted.

Clark Atlanta University, School of International Affairs and Development, Atlanta, GA 30314. Offers international affairs and development (PhD); international business and development (MA); international development administration (MA); international development education and planning (MA); international relations (MA); regional studies (MA). *Degree requirements:* For master's, one foreign language, thesis; for doctorate, 2 foreign languages, thesis/dissertation. *Entrance requirements:* For master's, GRE General Test, minimum GPA of 2.5; for doctorate, GRE General Test, minimum graduate GPA of 3.0.

Clark University, Graduate School, Graduate School of Management, Business Administration Program, Worcester, MA 01610-1477. Offers accounting (MBA); finance (MBA); global business (MBA); health care management (MBA); management (MBA); management of information technology (MBA); marketing (MBA). *Accreditation:* AACSB. Part-time and evening/weekend programs available. *Students:* 122 full-time (64 women), 113 part-time (42 women); includes 18 minority (3 African Americans, 9 Asian Americans or Pacific Islanders, 6 Hispanic Americans), 115 international. Average age 29. 235 applicants, 78% accepted, 80 enrolled. In 2006, 109 degrees awarded. *Degree requirements:* For master's, thesis optional. *Application deadline:* For fall admission, 6/1 priority date for domestic students; for spring admission, 12/1 priority date for domestic students. Applications are processed on a rolling basis. Application fee: $50. Electronic applications accepted. *Financial support:* In 2006–07, research assistantships with partial tuition reimbursements (averaging $6,000 per year), teaching assistantships with partial tuition reimbursements (averaging $6,000 per year) were awarded; fellowships with full and partial tuition reimbursements, career-related internships or fieldwork, Federal Work-Study, institutionally sponsored loans, and tuition waivers (partial) also available. Support available to part-time students. Financial award application deadline: 5/31. *Faculty research:* Organizational development, accounting, marketing, finance, human resource management. *Application contact:* Patricia Tollo, Admissions Director, 508-793-7406, Fax: 508-793-8822, E-mail: clarkmba@clarku.edu.

See Close-Up on page 257.

Cleveland State University, College of Graduate Studies, Nance College of Business Administration, Department of Marketing, Cleveland, OH 44115. Offers data-driven marketing planning (Graduate Certificate); e-commerce (MBA); global business (Graduate Certificate); marketing (MBA, DBA). *Unit head:* Dr. Thomas W. Whipple, Chair, 216-687-4771, Fax: 216-687-9354, E-mail: t.whipple@csuohio.edu.

Columbia Southern University, MBA Program, Orange Beach, AL 36561. Offers electronic business and technology (MBA); healthcare management (MBA); human resources management (MBA); international management (MBA); marketing (MBA); project management (MBA); public administration (MBA); sport management (MBA). Part-time and evening/weekend programs available. Postbaccalaureate distance learning degree programs offered (no on-campus study). *Entrance requirements:* Additional exam requirements/recommendations for international students: Required—TOEFL. Electronic applications accepted.

Columbia University, Graduate School of Business, Executive MBA Global Program, New York, NY 10027. Offers EMBA. Program offered jointly with London Business School. *Faculty:* 118 full-time (14 women), 106 part-time/adjunct (18 women). *Students:* 70 full-time (17 women); includes 9 minority (7 Asian Americans or Pacific Islanders, 2 Hispanic Americans), 40 international. Average age 33. In 2006, 59 degrees awarded. *Entrance requirements:* For master's, GMAT, 2 letters of reference, interview, minimum 5 years of work experience. *Application deadline:* For spring admission, 2/1 for domestic and international students. Applications are processed on a rolling basis. Application fee: $170. Electronic applications accepted. *Expenses:* Contact institution. *Unit head:* Ethan R. Hanabury, Associate Dean of the Executive MBA Programs, 212-854-6019, Fax: 212-316-1473, E-mail: emba@columbia.edu. *Application contact:* Sidney Jackson, Director of Marketing and Admissions, 212-854-1183, Fax: 212-854-8998, E-mail: stj9@columbia.edu.

Columbia University, Graduate School of Business, MBA Program, New York, NY 10027. Offers accounting (MBA); decision, risk, and operations (MBA); entrepreneurship (MBA); finance and economics (MBA); human resource management (MBA); international business (MBA); management (MBA); marketing (MBA); media (MBA); real estate (MBA); social enterprise (MBA); DDS/MBA; JD/MBA; MBA/MIA; MBA/MPH; MBA/MS; MD/MBA. *Faculty:* 118 full-time (14 women), 106 part-time/adjunct (18 women). *Students:* 1,242 full-time (428 women); includes 291 minority (65 African Americans, 5 American Indian/Alaska Native, 189 Asian Americans or Pacific Islanders, 32 Hispanic Americans), 392 international. Average age 28. 5,372 applicants, 17% accepted, 726 enrolled. In 2006, 682 degrees awarded. *Entrance requirements:* For master's, GMAT, 2 letters of recommendation. Additional exam requirements/recommendations for international students: Required—TOEFL. *Application deadline:* For fall admission, 4/20 for domestic students, 3/1 for international students; for spring admission, 10/12 for domestic and international students. Applications are processed on a rolling basis. Application fee: $215. Electronic applications accepted. *Financial support:* Fellowships, research assistantships, teaching assistantships, career-related internships or fieldwork, Federal Work-Study, institutionally sponsored loans, scholarships/grants, and unspecified assistantships available. Financial award applicants required to submit FAFSA. *Unit head:* Prof. Amir Ziv, Vice Dean of Students and the MBA Program, 212-854-3485, Fax: 212-932-0545, E-mail: az50@columbia.edu. *Application contact:* Linda B. Meehan, Assistant Dean of Admissions, 212-854-1961, Fax: 212-662-6754, E-mail: apply@claven.gsb.columbia.edu.

Concordia University Wisconsin, Graduate Programs, School of Business and Legal Studies, MBA Program, Mequon, WI 53097-2402. Offers finance (MBA); health care administration (MBA); human resource management (MBA); international business (MBA); international

business-English/Chinese (MBA); management (MBA); management information services (MBA); managerial communications (MBA); marketing (MBA); public administration (MBA); risk management (MBA). Postbaccalaureate distance learning degree programs offered (minimal on-campus study). *Students:* 504 (249 women). In 2006, 110 degrees awarded. *Degree requirements:* For master's, thesis or alternative, comprehensive exam. *Entrance requirements:* Additional exam requirements/recommendations for international students: Required—TOEFL. *Application deadline:* For fall admission, 8/1 priority date for domestic students; for spring admission, 1/15 for domestic students. Applications are processed on a rolling basis. Application fee: $50. *Expenses:* Contact institution. *Financial support:* Application deadline: 8/1. *Unit head:* Dr. David Borst, Director, 262-243-4298, Fax: 262-243-4428, E-mail: david.borst@cuw.edu.

Daemen College, Department of Accounting and Information Systems, Amherst, NY 14226-3592. Offers global business (MS). Part-time and evening/weekend programs available. *Faculty:* 1 full-time (0 women), 2 part-time/adjunct (0 women). *Students:* 1 (woman) full-time, 3 part-time (1 woman). Average age 32. 5 applicants, 80% accepted, 4 enrolled. In 2006, 5 degrees awarded. *Degree requirements:* For master's, thesis. *Entrance requirements:* For master's, oral and written English proficiency exam, minimum undergraduate GPA of 3.0 in business program or GMAT, interview, 2 letters of recommendation. Additional exam requirements/recommendations for international students: Required—TOEFL (minimum score 500 paper-based; 173 computer-based). *Application deadline:* For fall admission, 3/1 priority date for domestic and international students; for spring admission, 10/1 priority date for domestic and international students. Applications are processed on a rolling basis. Application fee: $25. Electronic applications accepted. *Expenses:* Tuition: Full-time $11,700; part-time $650 per credit hour. Required fees: $15 per credit hour. Tuition and fees vary according to course load. *Financial support:* Federal Work-Study and institutionally sponsored loans available. Financial award application deadline: 2/15; financial award applicants required to submit FAFSA. *Faculty research:* Internationalization of small business, cultural influences on business practices, international human resource practices. *Unit head:* Dr. Linda J. Kuechler, Chair, 716-839-8398, Fax: 716-839-8261, E-mail: lkuechle@daemen.edu. *Application contact:* Karl Shallowhorn, Associate Director of Graduate Admissions, 716-839-8225, Fax: 716-839-8229, E-mail: kshallow@daemen.edu.

Dallas Baptist University, Graduate School of Business, Business Administration Program, Dallas, TX 75211-9299. Offers accounting (MBA); business communication (MBA); conflict resolution management (MBA); e-business (MBA); entrepreneurship (MBA); finance (MBA); health care management (MBA); international business (MBA); management (MBA); management information systems (MBA); marketing (MBA); project management (MBA); technology and engineering management (MBA). *Accreditation:* ACBSP. Part-time and evening/weekend programs available. Postbaccalaureate distance learning degree programs offered (no on-campus study). *Faculty:* 49 full-time (21 women), 112 part-time/adjunct (46 women). *Students:* 103 full-time, 318 part-time. 226 applicants, 38% accepted. In 2006, 124 degrees awarded. *Entrance requirements:* For master's, GMAT, minimum GPA of 3.0. Additional exam requirements/recommendations for international students: Required—TOEFL. *Application deadline:* Applications are processed on a rolling basis. Application fee: $25. Electronic applications accepted. *Expenses:* Tuition: Full-time $8,370; part-time $465 per credit hour. Required fees: $465 per credit hour. *Financial support:* Career-related internships or fieldwork, Federal Work-Study, institutionally sponsored loans, scholarships/grants, and tuition waivers (full and partial) available. Support available to part-time students. *Faculty research:* Sports management, services marketing, retailing, strategic management, financial planning/investments. *Unit head:* Dr. Sandra S. Reid, Director, 214-333-5244, Fax: 214-333-5293, E-mail: graduate@dbu.edu. *Application contact:* Kit P. Montgomery, Director of Graduate Programs, 214-333-5242, Fax: 214-333-5579, E-mail: graduate@dbu.edu.

Davenport University, Sneden Graduate School, Dearborn, MI 48126-3799. Offers accounting (MBA); e-business (MBA); finance (MBA); global business (MBA); health care management (MBA); human resources management (MBA); management (MBA); marketing (MBA). Part-time and evening/weekend programs available. Postbaccalaureate distance learning degree programs offered (no on-campus study). *Entrance requirements:* For master's, minimum GPA of 2.7, previous course work in accounting and statistics. *Faculty research:* Accounting, international accounting, social and environmental accounting, finance.

DePaul University, Charles H. Kellstadt Graduate School of Business and College of Liberal Arts and Sciences, Department of Economics, Chicago, IL 60604-2287. Offers applied economics (MBA); economics (MA); international business (MBA). Part-time and evening/weekend programs available. *Faculty:* 21 full-time (5 women), 8 part-time/adjunct (1 woman). *Students:* 34 full-time (10 women), 17 part-time (8 women); includes 8 minority (3 African Americans, 2 Asian Americans or Pacific Islanders, 3 Hispanic Americans), 7 international. Average age 29. 23 applicants, 83% accepted. In 2006, 7 master's awarded. *Degree requirements:* For master's, thesis optional. *Entrance requirements:* For master's, GMAT (MBA). Additional exam requirements/recommendations for international students: Required—TOEFL, GRE. *Application deadline:* For fall admission, 7/1 for domestic students; for winter admission, 10/1 for domestic students; for spring admission, 2/1 for domestic students. Applications are processed on a rolling basis. Application fee: $40. Electronic applications accepted. *Financial support:* In 2006–07, 3 students received support, including 2 research assistantships with partial tuition reimbursements available (averaging $9,999 per year). Support available to part-time students. *Faculty research:* Forensic economics, game theory sports, economics of education, banking in Poland and Thailand. *Unit head:* Dr. Michael S. Miller, Chairperson, 312-362-8477, Fax: 312-362-5452, E-mail: mmiller@depaul.edu. *Application contact:* Kavitha Chinthada, Director of Graduate Admissions, 773-325-7885, Fax: 773-325-7311, E-mail: kchintha@depaul.edu.

Dominican University of California, Graduate Programs, School of Business, Education and Leadership, Division of Business and International Studies, Program in Global Strategic Management, San Rafael, CA 94901-2298. Offers MBA. Part-time programs available. *Entrance requirements:* For master's, minimum GPA of 3.0. Additional exam requirements/recommendations for international students: Required—TOEFL (minimum score 550 paper-based; 213 computer-based). Electronic applications accepted.

Drury University, Breech School of Business Administration, Program in Business and International Management, Springfield, MO 65802. Offers MBA, MBA/MIM. *Entrance requirements:* For master's, GMAT. Additional exam requirements/recommendations for international students: Required—TOEFL.

D'Youville College, Department of Business, Buffalo, NY 14201-1084. Offers international business (MS). Part-time and evening/weekend programs available. *Faculty:* 9 full-time (2 women), 10 part-time/adjunct (4 women). *Students:* 47 full-time (34 women), 17 part-time (8 women); includes 15 minority (10 African Americans, 5 Hispanic Americans), 16 international. Average age 28. 63 applicants, 52% accepted, 17 enrolled. In 2006, 15 degrees awarded. *Degree requirements:* For master's, 2 foreign languages, registration. *Entrance requirements:* For master's, minimum GPA of 3.0. Additional exam requirements/recommendations for international students: Required—TOEFL (minimum score 500 paper-based; 173 computer-based). *Application deadline:* For fall admission, 5/1 priority date for international students; for spring admission, 9/1 priority date for international students. Applications are processed on a rolling basis. Application fee: $25. Electronic applications accepted. *Financial support:* In 2006–07, 1 research assistantship with partial tuition reimbursement (averaging $3,000 per year) was awarded; career-related internships or fieldwork, Federal Work-Study, and scholarships/grants also available. Support available to part-time students. Financial award application deadline: 3/1; financial award applicants required to submit FAFSA. *Unit head:* Dr. Kushnood Haq, Chair, 716-829-8123, Fax: 716-829-7760. *Application contact:* Linda Fisher, Graduate Admissions Director, 716-829-8400, Fax: 716-829-7900, E-mail: graduateadmissions@dyc.edu.

Eastern Michigan University, Graduate School, College of Arts and Sciences, Department of Foreign Languages and Bilingual Studies, Program in Language and International Trade,

International Business

Eastern Michigan University (continued)
Ypsilanti, MI 48197. Offers MA. Evening/weekend programs available. *Students:* 1 (woman) full-time, 3 part-time (2 women); includes 1 minority (African American) Average age 28. *Degree requirements:* For master's, one foreign language. *Entrance requirements:* Additional exam requirements/recommendations for international students: Required—TOEFL. *Application deadline:* For fall admission, 5/15 priority date for domestic students, 5/1 priority date for international students; for winter admission, 10/15 priority date for domestic students, 10/1 priority date for international students; for spring admission, 3/15 priority date for domestic students, 3/1 priority date for international students. Applications are processed on a rolling basis. Application fee: $35. *Expenses:* Tuition, state resident: part-time $341 per credit hour. Tuition, nonresident: full-time $16,104; part-time $671 per credit hour. Required fees: $816; $34 per credit hour. $40 per term. One-time fee: $82 full-time. Tuition and fees vary according to course level, course load, degree level and reciprocity agreements. *Financial support:* Fellowships, research assistantships with full tuition reimbursements, teaching assistantships with full tuition reimbursements, career-related internships or fieldwork, Federal Work-Study, institutionally sponsored loans, scholarships/grants, tuition waivers (partial), and unspecified assistantships available. Support available to part-time students. Financial award applicants required to submit FAFSA. *Application contact:* Dr. William Cline, Program Advisor, 734-487-2283, E-mail: william.cline@emich.edu.

Eastern Michigan University, Graduate School, College of Business, Department of Marketing, Ypsilanti, MI 48197. Offers e-business (MBA); international business (MBA); supply chain management (MBA). Part-time and evening/weekend programs available. Postbaccalaureate distance learning degree programs offered (minimal on-campus study). *Entrance requirements:* For master's, GMAT. Additional exam requirements/recommendations for international students: Required—TOEFL. *Application deadline:* For fall admission, 5/15 priority date for domestic and international students; for winter admission, 10/15 priority date for domestic and international students; for spring admission, 3/15 priority date for domestic and international students. Applications are processed on a rolling basis. Application fee: $35. *Expenses:* Tuition, state resident: part-time $341 per credit hour. Tuition, nonresident: full-time $16,104; part-time $671 per credit hour. Required fees: $816; $34 per credit hour. $40 per term. One-time fee: $82 full-time. Tuition and fees vary according to course level, course load, degree level and reciprocity agreements. *Financial support:* Fellowships, research assistantships with full tuition reimbursements, teaching assistantships with full tuition reimbursements, career-related internships or fieldwork, Federal Work-Study, institutionally sponsored loans, scholarships/grants, tuition waivers (partial), and unspecified assistantships available. Support available to part-time students. Financial award applicants required to submit FAFSA. *Unit head:* Dr. Denise Tanguay, Interim Head, 734-487-3323. *Application contact:* Dr. Russ Merz, Department Coordinator, 734-487-1852, E-mail: russ.merz@emich.edu.

Eastern Michigan University, Graduate School, College of Business, Program in Business Administration, Ypsilanti, MI 48197. Offers business administration (MBA); e-business (MBA); enterprise business intelligence (MBA); entrepreneurship (MBA); finance (MBA); human resources (MBA); information systems (MBA); internal auditing (MBA); international business (MBA); nonprofit management (MBA); supply chain management (MBA). *Accreditation:* AACSB. Part-time and evening/weekend programs available. Postbaccalaureate distance learning degree programs offered (minimal on-campus study). *Students:* 98 full-time (36 women), 192 part-time (86 women); includes 50 minority (26 African Americans, 19 Asian Americans or Pacific Islanders, 5 Hispanic Americans), 76 international. Average age 29. In 2006, 109 degrees awarded. *Entrance requirements:* For master's, GMAT. Additional exam requirements/recommendations for international students: Required—TOEFL. *Application deadline:* For fall admission, 5/15 priority date for domestic students, 5/1 priority date for international students; for winter admission, 10/15 priority date for domestic students, 10/1 priority date for international students; for spring admission, 3/15 priority date for domestic students, 3/1 priority date for international students. Applications are processed on a rolling basis. Application fee: $35. *Expenses:* Tuition, state resident: part-time $341 per credit hour. Tuition, nonresident: full-time $16,104; part-time $671 per credit hour. Required fees: $816; $34 per credit hour. $40 per term. One-time fee: $82 full-time. Tuition and fees vary according to course level, course load, degree level and reciprocity agreements. *Financial support:* Fellowships, research assistantships with full tuition reimbursements, teaching assistantships with full tuition reimbursements, career-related internships or fieldwork, Federal Work-Study, institutionally sponsored loans, scholarships/grants, tuition waivers (partial), and unspecified assistantships available. Support available to part-time students. Financial award applicants required to submit FAFSA. *Unit head:* Dawn Gaymer, Assistant Dean, Graduate Business Programs, 734-487-4444, Fax: 734-483-1316, E-mail: dawn.malone@emich.edu. *Application contact:* K. Michelle Henry, Coordinator, 734-487-4444, Fax: 734-483-1316, E-mail: michelle.henry@emich.edu.

Emerson College, Graduate Studies, School of Communication, Department of Marketing Communication, Program in Global Marketing Communication and Advertising, Boston, MA 02116-4624. Offers MA. *Entrance requirements:* For master's, GMAT or GRE General Test. Additional exam requirements/recommendations for international students: Required—TOEFL. Electronic applications accepted.

See Close-Up on page 579.

Fairfield University, Charles F. Dolan School of Business, Fairfield, CT 06824-5195. Offers accounting (MBA, MS, CAS); finance (MBA, MS, CAS); general management (MBA); human resource management (MBA, CAS); information systems and operations (MBA); information systems and operations management (CAS); international business (MBA, CAS); marketing (MBA, CAS); taxation (MBA, MS, CAS). *Accreditation:* AACSB. Part-time and evening/weekend programs available. *Faculty:* 43 full-time (17 women), 2 part-time/adjunct (1 woman). *Students:* 65 full-time (31 women), 125 part-time (54 women); includes 4 Asian Americans or Pacific Islanders, 4 Hispanic Americans, 22 international. Average age 27. 99 applicants, 45% accepted, 38 enrolled. In 2006, 78 degrees awarded. *Degree requirements:* For master's, registration. *Entrance requirements:* For master's, GMAT, 2 letters of reference, resumé. Additional exam requirements/recommendations for international students: Required—TOEFL (minimum score 550 paper-based; 213 computer-based; 79 iBT). *Application deadline:* For fall admission, 8/15 priority date for domestic students, 5/15 priority date for international students; for spring admission, 11/15 priority date for domestic students, 10/15 priority date for international students. Applications are processed on a rolling basis. Application fee: $55. Electronic applications accepted. *Expenses:* Contact institution. *Financial support:* Unspecified assistantships available. *Faculty research:* Optimal investment strategies, organization structure, international finance, strategic management, customer behavior. *Unit head:* Dr. Norman A. Solomon, Dean, 203-254-4000 Ext. 4070, Fax: 203-254-4105, E-mail: nsolomon@mail.fairfield.edu. *Application contact:* Marianne Gumpper, Director of Graduate and Continuing Studies Admissions, 203-254-4184, Fax: 203-254-4073, E-mail: gradadmis@mail.fairfield.edu.

See Close-Up on page 271.

Fairleigh Dickinson University, College at Florham, Silberman College of Business, Department of Economics, Finance, and International Business, Program in International Business, Madison, NJ 07940-1099. Offers MBA, Certificate. *Students:* 5 full-time (4 women), 5 part-time (1 woman). Average age 30. 15 applicants, 53% accepted, 5 enrolled. In 2006, 10 degrees awarded. *Application deadline:* Applications are processed on a rolling basis. Application fee: $40.

Fairleigh Dickinson University, Metropolitan Campus, Silberman College of Business, Department of Economics, Finance and International Business, Program in International Business, Teaneck, NJ 07666-1914. Offers MBA. *Students:* 8 full-time (2 women), 4 part-time (3 women), 8 international. Average age 30. 19 applicants, 58% accepted, 6 enrolled. In 2006, 7 degrees awarded. *Application deadline:* Applications are processed on a rolling basis. Application fee: $40.

Florida Atlantic University, College of Business, Department of Management, International Business and Entrepreneurship, Boca Raton, FL 33431-0991. Offers business administration (Exec MBA, MBA), including accounting (MBA), electronic commerce (MBA), finance (MBA), financial planning (MBA), global entrepreneurship (MBA), health administration (MBA), international business (MBA), marketing (MBA), operations management (MBA), real estate (MBA), sport management (MBA). *Faculty:* 64 full-time (17 women), 15 part-time/adjunct (3 women). *Students:* 215 full-time (89 women), 365 part-time (189 women); includes 150 minority (49 African Americans, 2 American Indian/Alaska Native, 36 Asian Americans or Pacific Islanders, 63 Hispanic Americans), 54 international. Average age 32. 414 applicants, 55% accepted, 167 enrolled. In 2006, 196 master's awarded. *Degree requirements:* For master's, thesis optional. *Entrance requirements:* For master's, GMAT, minimum GPA of 3.0. Additional exam requirements/recommendations for international students: Required—TOEFL (minimum score 600 paper-based; 250 computer-based). *Application deadline:* For fall admission, 7/1 priority date for domestic students, 2/15 priority date for international students; for winter admission, 11/1 priority date for domestic students, 8/15 priority date for international students; for spring admission, 4/1 priority date for domestic students, 1/15 priority date for international students. Applications are processed on a rolling basis. Application fee: $30. Electronic applications accepted. *Expenses:* Tuition, area resident: Full-time $4,394. Tuition, nonresident: full-time $16,441. *Financial support:* Research assistantships, teaching assistantships, career-related internships or fieldwork, Federal Work-Study, institutionally sponsored loans, tuition waivers (partial), and unspecified assistantships available. Support available to part-time students. Financial award application deadline: 3/1; financial award applicants required to submit FAFSA. *Unit head:* Dr. Brenda Richey, Head, 561-297-3194, E-mail: brichey@fau.edu. *Application contact:* Fredrick G. Taylor, Graduate Adviser, 561-297-2768, Fax: 561-297-1315, E-mail: mba@fau.edu.

Florida International University, Alvah H. Chapman, Jr. Graduate School of Business, Department of Management and International Business, Miami, FL 33199. Offers international business (MIB). Part-time and evening/weekend programs available. *Faculty:* 22 full-time (10 women). *Students:* 92 full-time (34 women), 44 part-time (20 women); includes 69 minority (10 African Americans, 7 Asian Americans or Pacific Islanders, 52 Hispanic Americans), 41 international. Average age 28. 196 applicants, 47% accepted, 60 enrolled. In 2006, 114 degrees awarded. *Entrance requirements:* For master's, GMAT, minimum AACSB index of 1000, minimum GPA of 3.0. Additional exam requirements/recommendations for international students: Required—TOEFL. *Application deadline:* For fall admission, 4/1 priority date for domestic students; for spring admission, 10/1 for domestic students. Applications are processed on a rolling basis. Application fee: $25. *Expenses:* Tuition, state resident: part-time $249 per credit hour. Tuition, nonresident: part-time $753 per credit hour. Tuition and fees vary according to program. *Financial support:* Research assistantships, teaching assistantships available. *Unit head:* Dr. Galen Kroeck, Chairperson, 305-348-2791, Fax: 305-348-6146, E-mail: kroeck@fiu.edu.

Florida Metropolitan University–South Orlando Campus, Program in Business Administration, Orlando, FL 32819. Offers accounting (MBA); general management (MBA); human resources (MBA); international management (MBA).

Florida Metropolitan University–Tampa Campus, Department of Business Administration, Tampa, FL 33614-5899. Offers accounting (MBA); human resources (MBA); international business (MBA). Part-time and evening/weekend programs available. *Degree requirements:* For master's, thesis optional. *Entrance requirements:* For master's, GMAT or GRE, minimum GPA of 3.0.

Florida Southern College, Program in Business Administration, Lakeland, FL 33801-5698. Offers accounting (MBA); business administration (MBA); international business (MBA). Part-time and evening/weekend programs available. *Faculty:* 12 full-time (2 women). *Students:* Average age 31. 15 applicants, 80% accepted, 8 enrolled. In 2006, 9 degrees awarded. *Entrance requirements:* For master's, GMAT or GRE General Test, minimum GPA of 2.75. Additional exam requirements/recommendations for international students: Required—TOEFL (minimum score 550 paper-based). *Application deadline:* For fall admission, 8/1 for domestic students; for spring admission, 12/1 for domestic students. Applications are processed on a rolling basis. Application fee: $30. *Expenses:* Tuition: Part-time $250 per credit hour. Required fees: $10 per term. Tuition and fees vary according to program. *Financial support:* In 2006–07, 9 students received support. Scholarships/grants available. Support available to part-time students. Financial award applicants required to submit FAFSA. *Unit head:* Dr. Larry Ross, Program Coordinator, 863-680-4285, Fax: 863-680-4355, E-mail: lross@flsouthern.edu. *Application contact:* Craig Story, Evening Program Director, 863-680-6276, Fax: 863-680-4205, E-mail: cstory@flsouthern.edu.

The George Washington University, Elliott School of International Affairs, Program in International Trade and Investment Policy, Washington, DC 20052. Offers MA, JD/MA, MBA/MA. Part-time and evening/weekend programs available. *Degree requirements:* For master's, one foreign language. *Entrance requirements:* For master's, GRE General Test, 2 years of a modern foreign language and 2 semesters of introductory economics. Additional exam requirements/recommendations for international students: Required—TOEFL. Electronic applications accepted.

The George Washington University, School of Business, Department of International Business, Washington, DC 20052. Offers MBA, PhD, MBA/MA. Part-time and evening/weekend programs available. *Degree requirements:* For doctorate, thesis/dissertation. *Entrance requirements:* For master's, GMAT; for doctorate, GMAT or GRE. Additional exam requirements/recommendations for international students: Required—TOEFL. *Faculty research:* International trade, competitiveness, business management.

Georgia Institute of Technology, Graduate Studies and Research, College of Management, Program in Business Administration, Atlanta, GA 30332-0001. Offers accounting (MBA); e-commerce (Certificate); engineering entrepreneurship (MBA); entrepreneurship (Certificate); finance (MBA); information technology management (MBA); international business (MBA, Certificate); management of technology (Certificate); marketing (MBA); operations management (MBA); organizational behavior (MBA); strategic management (MBA). *Accreditation:* AACSB.

Georgia State University, J. Mack Robinson College of Business, Institute of International Business, Atlanta, GA 30303-3083. Offers MBA, MIB, MIB/MAPOLS. Part-time and evening/weekend programs available. *Faculty:* 6 full-time (2 women). *Students:* 35 full-time (14 women), 63 part-time (27 women); includes 23 minority (12 African Americans, 6 Asian Americans or Pacific Islanders, 5 Hispanic Americans), 13 international. Average age 31. 30 applicants, 67% accepted, 14 enrolled. In 2006, 49 degrees awarded. *Entrance requirements:* For master's, GMAT. Additional exam requirements/recommendations for international students: Required—TOEFL (minimum score 610 paper-based; 255 computer-based; 101 iBT). *Application deadline:* For fall admission, 5/1 for domestic students, 2/1 for international students; for spring admission, 10/15 for domestic students, 5/1 for international students. Applications are processed on a rolling basis. Application fee: $50. Electronic applications accepted. *Financial support:* Fellowships, research assistantships, teaching assistantships, career-related internships or fieldwork and tuition waivers (partial) available. Support available to part-time students. Financial award application deadline: 5/1; financial award applicants required to submit FAFSA. *Unit head:* Dr. Joan Gabel, Director, 404-651-3877, Fax: 404-651-3498.

Georgia State University, J. Mack Robinson College of Business, Program in General Business Administration, Atlanta, GA 30303-3083. Offers accounting/information systems (MBA); enterprise risk management (MBA); general business (MBA); general business administration (EMBA, PMBA); information systems consulting (MBA); information systems risk management (MBA); international business and information technology (MBA); international entrepreneurship (MBA); MBA/JD. *Accreditation:* AACSB. Part-time and evening/weekend programs available. *Faculty:* 1 (woman) full-time. *Students:* 183 full-time (83 women), 212 part-time (57 women); includes 118 minority (73 African Americans, 36 Asian Americans or Pacific Islanders, 9 Hispanic Americans), 42 international. 294 applicants, 74% accepted, 182 enrolled. In 2006, 98 degrees awarded. *Entrance requirements:* For master's, GMAT. Additional exam requirements/recommendations for international students: Required—TOEFL (minimum score 610 paper-based; 255 computer-based; 101 iBT). *Application deadline:* For fall admission, 5/1 for domestic students, 2/1 for international students; for spring admission, 10/15 for domestic students, 5/1 for international students. Applications are processed on a rolling basis. Application fee: $50. Electronic applications accepted. *Financial support:* Research assistantships, tuition waivers (partial) available. Support available to part-time students. Financial award application deadline: 5/1; financial award applicants required to submit FAFSA. *Application contact:* Graduate Student and Alumni Services, 404-463-4568, Fax: 404-651-2721, E-mail: mastersadmissions@gsu.edu.

Golden Gate University, Ageno School of Business, San Francisco, CA 94105-2968. Offers accounting (M Ac, MBA); business administration (EMBA, MBA, DBA); finance (MBA, MS, Certificate); financial planning (MS, Certificate); human resource management (MBA, MS); human resources management (Certificate); information technology (MBA); information technology management (MS, Certificate); integrated marketing and communications (MS, Certificate); international business (MBA); management (MBA); marketing (MBA, MS, Certificate); operations management (Certificate); psychology (MA, Certificate); public relations (MS, Certificate); JD/MBA. Part-time and evening/weekend programs available. *Students:* 355 full-time (192 women), 977 part-time (465 women); includes 447 minority (85 African Americans, 5 American Indian/Alaska Native, 274 Asian Americans or Pacific Islanders, 83 Hispanic Americans), 226 international. Average age 34. 548 applicants, 74% accepted, 201 enrolled. In 2006, 545 master's, 21 doctorates awarded. *Degree requirements:* For doctorate, thesis/dissertation. *Entrance requirements:* For master's, GMAT (MBA), minimum GPA of 2.5 (MS). Additional exam requirements/recommendations for international students: Required—TOEFL. *Application deadline:* Applications are processed on a rolling basis. Application fee: $55 ($90 for international students). *Financial support:* Career-related internships or fieldwork, Federal Work-Study, and institutionally sponsored loans available. Support available to part-time students. Financial award applicants required to submit FAFSA. *Unit head:* Terry Connelly, Dean, 415-442-6519, Fax: 415-442-5369. *Application contact:* Enrollment Services, 415-442-7800, Fax: 415-442-7807, E-mail: info@ggu.edu.

Hawai'i Pacific University, College of Business Administration, Honolulu, HI 96813. Offers accounting/CPA (MBA); communication (MBA); e-business (MBA); economics (MBA); finance (MBA); human resource management (MBA); information systems (MBA); international business (MBA); management (MBA); marketing (MBA); organizational change (MBA); travel industry management (MBA). Part-time and evening/weekend programs available. *Faculty:* 40 full-time (16 women), 30 part-time/adjunct (10 women). *Students:* 320 full-time (150 women), 205 part-time (95 women); includes 168 minority (17 African Americans, 7 American Indian/Alaska Native, 137 Asian Americans or Pacific Islanders, 7 Hispanic Americans), 232 international. Average age 31. 279 applicants, 67% accepted, 166 enrolled. In 2006, 172 degrees awarded. *Degree requirements:* For master's, thesis. *Entrance requirements:* For master's, GMAT. Additional exam requirements/recommendations for international students: Recommended—TOEFL (minimum score 550 paper-based; 213 computer-based), TWE (minimum score 5). *Application deadline:* For fall admission, 2/15 priority date for domestic students; for spring admission, 10/15 priority date for domestic students. Applications are processed on a rolling basis. Application fee: $50. Electronic applications accepted. *Expenses:* Tuition: Full-time $10,080; part-time $560 per credit. *Financial support:* In 2006–07, 118 students received support; research assistantships, career-related internships or fieldwork, Federal Work-Study, scholarships/grants, and unspecified assistantships available. Support available to part-time students. Financial award application deadline: 3/1; financial award applicants required to submit FAFSA. *Faculty research:* Statistical control process as used by management, studies in comparative cross-cultural management styles, not-for-profit management. *Unit head:* Dr. Charles Steilen, Dean, 808-544-9301, Fax: 808-544-0283, E-mail: csteilen@hpu.edu. *Application contact:* Danny Lam, Assistant Director of Graduate Admissions, 808-544-1135, Fax: 808-544-0280, E-mail: graduate@hpu.edu.

See Close-Up on page 275.

HEC Montreal, School of Business Administration, Master of Science Programs in Administration, Program in International Business, Montréal, QC H3T 2A7, Canada. Offers M Sc. Tuition and fees charges are reported in Canadian dollars. *Expenses:* Tuition, nonresident: part-time $56 Canadian dollars per credit. Required fees: $30 Canadian dollars per semester. *Application contact:* Francine Blais, Administrative Director, 514-340-6112, Fax: 514-340-6411, E-mail: francine.blais@hec.ca.

HEC Montreal, School of Business Administration, Master of Science Programs in Administration, Program in International Management, Montréal, QC H3T 2A7, Canada. Offers M Sc. All courses are given in French. Part-time programs available. *Degree requirements:* For master's, one foreign language, thesis. Application fee: $60 Canadian dollars. Electronic applications accepted. Tuition and fees charges are reported in Canadian dollars. *Expenses:* Tuition, nonresident: part-time $56 Canadian dollars per credit. Required fees: $30 Canadian dollars per semester. *Financial support:* Fellowships, research assistantships, teaching assistantships, scholarships/grants available. *Application contact:* Francine Blais, Administrative Director, 514-340-6112, Fax: 514-340-6411, E-mail: francine.blais@hec.ca.

Hofstra University, Frank G. Zarb School of Business, Department of Marketing and International Business, Hempstead, NY 11549. Offers international business (MBA, MS, Advanced Certificate); marketing (MBA, MS, Advanced Certificate); marketing research (MS). Part-time and evening/weekend programs available. *Faculty:* 7 full-time (0 women), 2 part-time/adjunct (0 women). *Students:* 39 full-time (22 women), 48 part-time (27 women); includes 23 minority (7 African Americans, 10 Asian Americans or Pacific Islanders, 6 Hispanic Americans), 10 international. Average age 28. 75 applicants, 73% accepted, 27 enrolled. In 2006, 42 degrees awarded. *Degree requirements:* For master's, thesis (for some programs), capstone course for MBA. *Entrance requirements:* For master's, GMAT, 2 letters of recommendation, resumé, essay. Additional exam requirements/recommendations for international students: Required—TOEFL (minimum score 550 paper-based; 213 computer-based). *Application deadline:* Applications are processed on a rolling basis. Application fee: $60. Electronic applications accepted. *Expenses:* Tuition: Full-time $13,320; part-time $740 per credit. Required fees: $930; $155 per term. *Financial support:* In 2006–07, 24 students received support, including 13 fellowships with tuition reimbursements available (averaging $5,748 per year), 5 research assistantships with full and partial tuition reimbursements available (averaging $3,416 per year); tuition waivers (full and partial) also available. Financial award applicants required to submit FAFSA. *Faculty research:* Outsourcing, cross cultural consumer behavior, global alliances, retailing, web marketing. *Unit head:* Dr. Benny Barak, Chairperson, 516-463-5707, Fax: 516-463-4834, E-mail: mktbzb@hofstra.edu. *Application contact:* Carol Drummer, Dean of Graduate Admissions, 516-463-4876, Fax: 516-463-4664, E-mail: gradstudent@hofstra.edu.

Hope International University, School of Graduate Studies, Program in Business Administration, Fullerton, CA 92831-3138. Offers international development (MBA, MSM); nonprofit management (MBA). Part-time programs available. Postbaccalaureate distance learning degree programs offered (no on-campus study). *Faculty:* 1 full-time (0 women), 11 part-time/adjunct (0 women). *Students:* 25 full-time (15 women), 46 part-time (22 women); includes 41 minority (16 African Americans, 1 American Indian/Alaska Native, 19 Asian Americans or Pacific Islanders, 5 Hispanic Americans). Average age 29. 40 applicants, 75% accepted, 18 enrolled. In 2006, 11 degrees awarded. *Degree requirements:* For master's, thesis (for some programs), project. *Entrance requirements:* For master's, minimum GPA of 3.0. Additional exam requirements/recommendations for international students: Required—TOEFL (minimum score 550 paper-based; 213 computer-based; 86 iBT). *Application deadline:* Applications are processed on a rolling basis. Application fee: $75. Electronic applications accepted. *Expenses:* Contact institution. *Financial support:* In 2006–07, 10 fellowships were awarded; scholarships/grants also available. Support available to part-time students. *Unit head:* Dr. Lind W. Coop, Chair, 714-879-3901 Ext. 2264, Fax: 714-681-7450, E-mail: lwcoop@hiu.edu. *Application contact:* Annette Mativo, Assistant Director of Admissions, 714-879-3901 Ext. 2244, Fax: 714-681-7450, E-mail: anmativo@hiu.edu.

Howard University, School of Business, Graduate Programs in Business, Washington, DC 20059-0002. Offers accounting (MBA); entrepreneurship (MBA); finance (MBA); information systems (MBA); international business (MBA); marketing (MBA); supply chain management (MBA); JD/MBA. *Accreditation:* AACSB. Part-time and evening/weekend programs available. Postbaccalaureate distance learning degree programs offered (no on-campus study). *Entrance requirements:* For master's, GMAT, minimum 1 year post undergraduate work experience, resumé, 3 letters of recommendation, advanced college algebra. Additional exam requirements/recommendations for international students: Required—TOEFL. *Faculty research:* Marketing research in multi-ethnic populations, U.S. trade policies and international relations, risk management (finance).

Huron University USA in London, Graduate Programs, Program in Business Administration, London, United Kingdom. Offers entrepreneurship (MBA); international business (MBA); international finance (MBA); marketing (MBA). Part-time programs available. *Degree requirements:* For master's, thesis, internship, comprehensive exam. *Entrance requirements:* Additional exam requirements/recommendations for international students: Required—TOEFL (minimum score 580 paper-based; 237 computer-based), TWE (minimum score 5). Electronic applications accepted.

Illinois Institute of Technology, Stuart School of Business, Program in Business Administration, Chicago, IL 60616-3793. Offers entrepreneurship (MBA); financial management (MBA); financial markets (MBA); healthcare management (MBA); information technology management (MBA); international business (MBA); management science (MBA); marketing (MBA); operations, quality, and technology management (MBA); strategic management of organizations (MBA); sustainable enterprise (MBA); JD/MBA; MBA/MS. *Accreditation:* AACSB. Part-time and evening/weekend programs available. *Faculty:* 13 full-time (1 woman), 9 part-time/adjunct (0 women). *Students:* 74 full-time (29 women), 42 part-time (16 women); includes 17 minority (5 African Americans, 11 Asian Americans or Pacific Islanders, 1 Hispanic American), 74 international. Average age 29. 247 applicants, 70% accepted, 51 enrolled. In 2006, 45 degrees awarded. *Entrance requirements:* For master's, GMAT. Additional exam requirements/recommendations for international students: Required—TOEFL (minimum score 600 paper-based; 250 computer-based). *Application deadline:* For fall admission, 8/15 priority date for domestic students, 7/1 for international students; for winter admission, 11/1 priority date for domestic students, 10/1 for international students; for spring admission, 1/1 priority date for domestic students, 1/1 for international students. Applications are processed on a rolling basis. Application fee: $75. Electronic applications accepted. *Expenses:* Contact institution. Tuition and fees vary according to class time, course level, course load, program and student level. *Financial support:* Career-related internships or fieldwork, Federal Work-Study, institutionally sponsored loans, scholarships/grants, traineeships, health care benefits, tuition waivers, and unspecified assistantships available. Support available to part-time students. Financial award applicants required to submit FAFSA. *Faculty research:* Knowledge management, healthcare management, sustainability in supply chain. *Unit head:* Dr. George P. Nassos, Interim Director, 312-906-6543, Fax: 312-906-6549, E-mail: george.nassos@iit.edu. *Application contact:* Brian Jansen, Director of Graduate Admissions, 312-906-6521, Fax: 312-906-6549, E-mail: admission@stuart.iit.edu.

Instituto Tecnológico y de Estudios Superiores de Monterrey, Campus Central de Veracruz, Graduate Programs, Córdoba, Mexico. Offers administration (MA); administration of information technologies (MTI); computer sciences (MCC); education (MEE); educational institution administration (MAD); educational technology (MTE); electronic commerce (MCE); finance (MAF); humanistic studies (MEH); international business for Latin America (MNL); marketing (MMT); science (MCP); technology management (MTT). Part-time and evening/weekend programs available. Postbaccalaureate distance learning degree programs offered (minimal on-campus study). *Degree requirements:* For master's, thesis (for some programs). *Entrance requirements:* For master's, PAEP College Board. Electronic applications accepted.

Instituto Tecnológico y de Estudios Superiores de Monterrey, Campus Chihuahua, Graduate Programs, Chihuahua, Mexico. Offers computer systems engineering (Ingeniero); electrical engineering (Ingeniero); electromechanical engineering (Ingeniero); electronic engineering (Ingeniero); engineering administration (MEA); industrial engineering (MIE, Ingeniero); international trade (MIT); mechanical engineering (Ingeniero).

Instituto Tecnológico y de Estudios Superiores de Monterrey, Campus Ciudad de México, Virtual University Division, Ciudad de Mexico, Mexico. Offers administration of information technologies (MA); computer sciences (MA); education (MA, PhD); educational technology (MA); environmental engineering (MA); environmental systems (MA); humanistic studies (MA); industrial engineering (MA); international business for Latin America (MA); quality systems (MA); quality systems and productivity (MA). Part-time and evening/weekend programs available. Postbaccalaureate distance learning degree programs offered (minimal on-campus study). *Entrance requirements:* For master's and doctorate, Instituto entrance exam. Additional exam requirements/recommendations for international students: Required—TOEFL.

Instituto Tecnológico y de Estudios Superiores de Monterrey, Campus Cuernavaca, Programs in Business Administration, Temixco, Mexico. Offers finance (MA); human resources management (MA); international business (MA); marketing (MA).

Instituto Tecnológico y de Estudios Superiores de Monterrey, Campus Irapuato, Graduate Programs, Irapuato, Mexico. Offers administration (MBA); administration of information technology (MAIT); administration of telecommunications (MAT); architecture (M Arch); computer science (MCS); education (M Ed); educational administration (MEA); educational innovation and technology (DEIT); educational technology (MET); electronic commerce (MBA); environmental administration and planning (MEAP); environmental systems (MES); finances (MBA); humanistic studies (MHS); international management for Latin American executives (MIMLAE); library and information science (MLIS); manufacturing quality management (MMQM); marketing research (MBA).

Instituto Tecnológico y de Estudios Superiores de Monterrey, Campus Monterrey, Graduate School of Business Administration and Leadership, Program in Business Administration, Monterrey, Mexico. Offers business administration (MA, MBA); finance (M Sc); international business (M Sc); marketing (M Sc). Part-time programs available. *Degree requirements:* For master's, one foreign language, thesis. *Entrance requirements:* For master's, GMAT. Additional exam requirements/recommendations for international students: Required—TOEFL. *Faculty research:* Technology management, quality management, organizational theory and behavior.

Inter American University of Puerto Rico, Ponce Campus, Graduate School, Mercedita, PR 00715-1602. Offers accounting (MBA); biology (M Ed); chemistry (M Ed); criminal justice (MA); elementary education (M Ed); English as a Second Language (M Ed); finance (MBA); history (M Ed); human resources (MBA); mathematics (M Ed); Spanish (M Ed); trade (MBA). *Entrance requirements:* For master's, minimum GPA of 2.5.

Inter American University of Puerto Rico, San Germán Campus, Graduate Studies Center, Graduate Program in Business Administration, San Germán, PR 00683-5008. Offers accounting (MBA); finance (MBA); human resources (MBA, PhD); industrial relations (MBA); international business (PhD); labor relations (PhD); management information systems (MBA); marketing (MBA); quality organizational design (MBA). Part-time and evening/weekend programs available. *Faculty:* 12 full-time, 4 part-time/adjunct. *Students:* 265. Average age 27. In 2006, 67 master's, 1 doctorate awarded. *Degree requirements:* For master's, comprehensive exam. *Entrance requirements:* For master's, GRE General Test or EXADEP, minimum GPA of 3.0. *Application deadline:* For fall admission, 4/30 priority date for domestic students; for spring admission, 11/15 for domestic students. Applications are processed on a

International Business

Inter American University of Puerto Rico, San Germán Campus (continued)
rolling basis. Application fee: $31. *Expenses:* Tuition: Part-time $175 per credit. Required fees: $238 per semester. Tuition and fees vary according to degree level. *Financial support:* Teaching assistantships, Federal Work-Study and unspecified assistantships available. *Application contact:* Prof. Duay Rivera, Graduate Coordinator, 787-264-1912 Ext. 7218, Fax: 787-892-7510, E-mail: durivera@sg.inter.edu.

Inter American University of Puerto Rico, San Germán Campus, Graduate Studies Center, Graduate Program in Entrepreneurial and Managerial Development, San Germán, PR 00683-5008. Offers human resources (PhD); interregional and international business (PhD); labor relations (PhD). Part-time and evening/weekend programs available. *Faculty:* 12 full-time, 4 part-time/adjunct. *Students:* 52. Average age 41. In 2006, 1 degree awarded. *Degree requirements:* For doctorate, thesis/dissertation, comprehensive exam. *Entrance requirements:* For doctorate, EXADEP or GMAT, minimum graduate GPA of 3.25. *Application deadline:* For fall admission, 4/30 priority date for domestic students; for spring admission, 11/15 for domestic students. Applications are processed on a rolling basis. Application fee: $75. *Expenses:* Tuition: Part-time $175 per credit. Required fees: $238 per semester. Tuition and fees vary according to degree level. *Financial support:* Teaching assistantships available. *Application contact:* Dr. Carlos E. Irizarry, Director of Graduate Studies Center, 787-264-1912 Ext. 7357, Fax: 787-892-6350, E-mail: carlos.irizarry@sg.inter.edu.

International University in Geneva, MBA Program, Geneva, Switzerland. Offers e-commerce (MBA); human relations (MBA); international business (Exec MBA, MBA); marketing (MBA); organizational development (MBA); telecommunications (MBA). Part-time and evening/weekend programs available. *Degree requirements:* For master's, comprehensive exam, registration. *Entrance requirements:* For master's, GMAT. Additional exam requirements/recommendations for international students: Required—TOEFL. Electronic applications accepted.

The International University of Monaco, Graduate Programs, Monte Carlo, Monaco. Offers entrepreneurship (EMBA, MBA); financial engineering (M Sc); international marketing (EMBA, MBA); luxury goods and services (EMBA, M Sc, MBA); wealth and asset management (EMBA, MBA). Part-time programs available. *Degree requirements:* For master's, applied research project. *Entrance requirements:* Additional exam requirements/recommendations for international students: Required—TOEFL (minimum score 550 paper-based; 213 computer-based), IELTS. Electronic applications accepted. *Faculty research:* Gaming, leadership, disintermediation.

Iona College, Hagan School of Business, Department of Marketing and International Business, New Rochelle, NY 10801-1890. Offers international business (PMC); marketing (MBA). Part-time and evening/weekend programs available. *Faculty:* 4 full-time (2 women), 3 part-time/adjunct (0 women). *Students:* 4 full-time (all women), 36 part-time (23 women), 1 international. Average age 29. 10 applicants, 90% accepted, 9 enrolled. In 2006, 19 master's, 24 other advanced degrees awarded. *Entrance requirements:* For master's, GMAT, 2 letters of recommendation; for PMC, GMAT. Additional exam requirements/recommendations for international students: Required—TOEFL (minimum score 550 paper-based; 213 computer-based). *Application deadline:* Applications are processed on a rolling basis. Application fee: $50. Electronic applications accepted. *Expenses: Contact institution. Financial support:* Scholarships/grants, tuition waivers (partial), and unspecified assistantships available. Support available to part-time students. *Faculty research:* Business ethics, international retailing, mega-marketing, consumer behavior and consumer confidence. *Unit head:* Dr. Frederica E. Rudell, Chair, 914-637-2748, E-mail: frudell@iona.edu. *Application contact:* Veronica Jarek-Prinz, Graduate Admissions, 914-633-2289, Fax: 914-633-2012, E-mail: vjarekprinz@iona.edu.

John Marshall Law School, Graduate and Professional Programs, Chicago, IL 60604-3968. Offers comparative legal studies (LL M); employee benefits (LL M, MS); information technology (LL M, MS); intellectual property (LL M); international business and trade (LL M); law (JD); real estate (LL M, MS); taxation (LL M, MS); JD/LL M; JD/MA; JD/MBA; JD/MPA. *Accreditation:* ABA. Part-time and evening/weekend programs available. *Faculty:* 64 full-time (23 women), 113 part-time/adjunct (29 women). *Students:* 1,157 full-time (479 women), 421 part-time (187 women); includes 253 minority (76 African Americans, 10 American Indian/Alaska Native, 101 Asian Americans or Pacific Islanders, 66 Hispanic Americans), 48 international. Average age 27. 3,169 applicants, 37% accepted, 333 enrolled. In 2006, 347 JDs, 69 master's awarded. *Entrance requirements:* For JD, LSAT; for master's, JD. Additional exam requirements/recommendations for international students: Required—TOEFL. *Application deadline:* For fall admission, 3/1 priority date for domestic and international students; for spring admission, 10/15 priority date for domestic and international students. Applications are processed on a rolling basis. Application fee: $60. Electronic applications accepted. *Expenses: Contact institution. Financial support:* In 2006–07, 1,339 students received support. Scholarships/grants and tuition waivers (full and partial) available. Support available to part-time students. Financial award application deadline: 6/1; financial award applicants required to submit FAFSA. *Unit head:* John Corkery, Dean, 312-427-2737. *Application contact:* William B. Powers, Associate Dean of Admission and Student Affairs, 800-537-4280, Fax: 312-427-5136, E-mail: admission@jmls.edu.

Johnson & Wales University, The Alan Shawn Feinstein Graduate School, Program in Global Business, Providence, RI 02903-3703. Offers accounting (MBA); financial management (MBA); international trade (MBA); marketing (MBA); organizational leadership (MBA). Part-time and evening/weekend programs available. *Entrance requirements:* For master's, minimum GPA of 2.75. Additional exam requirements/recommendations for international students: Required—TOEFL (paper-based 550; computer-based 210) or IELTS recommended; Recommended—TWE. *Application deadline:* For fall admission, 8/15 priority date for domestic students, 6/28 priority date for international students; for winter admission, 11/10 priority date for domestic students, 9/20 priority date for international students; for spring admission, 2/5 priority date for domestic students, 12/20 priority date for international students. Applications are processed on a rolling basis. *Financial support:* Tuition waivers (partial) and unspecified assistantships available. Support available to part-time students. Financial award application deadline: 5/1. *Faculty research:* International banking, global economy, international trade, cultural differences. *Application contact:* Dr. Allan G. Freedman, Director of Graduate Admissions, 401-598-1015, Fax: 401-598-1286, E-mail: gradadm@jwu.edu.

Kean University, Nathan Weiss Graduate College, Program in Global Management, Union, NJ 07083. Offers MBA. *Faculty:* 3 full-time (0 women). *Students:* 22 full-time (13 women), 20 part-time (12 women); includes 20 minority (9 African Americans, 3 Asian Americans or Pacific Islanders, 8 Hispanic Americans), 8 international. Average age 32. 29 applicants, 97% accepted, 7 enrolled. *Degree requirements:* For master's, one foreign language. *Entrance requirements:* For master's, GMAT, minimum GPA of 3.0, 3 letters of recommendation, business prerequisites. *Application deadline:* For fall admission, 5/1 for domestic students; for spring admission, 11/1 for domestic students. Application fee: $60 ($150 for international students). Electronic applications accepted. *Expenses:* Tuition, state resident: full-time $8,856; part-time $369 per credit. Tuition, nonresident: full-time $11,256; part-time $469 per credit. *Financial support:* In 2006–07, 10 research assistantships with full tuition reimbursements (averaging $3,217 per year) were awarded. *Unit head:* Prof. David Shani, Program Coordinator, 908-737-7122, E-mail: dshani@kean.edu. *Application contact:* Joanne Morris, Director of Graduate Admissions, 908-737-3355, Fax: 908-737-3354, E-mail: grad-adm@kean.edu.

Lindenwood University, Graduate Programs, Division of Management, St. Charles, MO 63301-1695. Offers accounting (MBA, MS); business administration (MBA); entrepreneurial studies (MBA); finance (MBA, MS); human resource management (MBA); human resources (MS); international business (MBA, MS); management (MBA, MS); management information systems (MBA, MS); managing business to business (MA); managing human resources (MA); managing international business (MA); managing investment management (MA); managing leadership (MA); managing marketing (MA); managing organizational behavior (MA); managing sales (MA); managing, training and development (MA); marketing (MBA, MS); nonprofit administration (MA); public management (MBA, MS); sport management (MA). Part-time and evening/weekend programs available. *Faculty:* 38 full-time (15 women), 20 part-time/adjunct (5 women). *Students:* 177 full-time (78 women), 138 part-time (67 women); includes 43 minority (27 African Americans, 4 American Indian/Alaska Native, 6 Asian Americans or Pacific Islanders, 6 Hispanic Americans), 73 international. Average age 30. In 2006, 159 degrees awarded. *Degree requirements:* For master's, thesis (for some programs). *Entrance requirements:* For master's, interview, minimum GPA of 3.0. Additional exam requirements/recommendations for international students: Required—TOEFL (minimum score 550 paper-based; 173 computer-based). *Application deadline:* For fall admission, 7/30 priority date for domestic students, 9/30 priority date for international students; for winter admission, 12/30 priority date for domestic and international students; for spring admission, 3/30 priority date for domestic and international students. Applications are processed on a rolling basis. Application fee: $30 ($100 for international students). Electronic applications accepted. *Expenses:* Tuition: Part-time $340 per credit hour. Tuition and fees vary according to course level, course load, degree level and program. *Financial support:* Career-related internships or fieldwork, Federal Work-Study, institutionally sponsored loans, and tuition waivers (partial) available. Financial award application deadline: 6/30; financial award applicants required to submit FAFSA. *Unit head:* Ed Morris, Dean, 636-949-4832, Fax: 636-949-4910, E-mail: emorris@lindenwood.edu. *Application contact:* Brett Barger, Dean Adult, Corporate and Graduate Admissions, 636-949-4366, Fax: 636-949-4109, E-mail: bbarger@lindenwood.edu.

Long Island University, C.W. Post Campus, College of Management, School of Business, Brookville, NY 11548-1300. Offers accounting and taxation (Certificate); business administration (Certificate); finance (MBA, Certificate); general business administration (MBA); international business (MBA, Certificate); management (MBA, Certificate); management information systems (MBA, Certificate); marketing (MBA, Certificate). *Accreditation:* AACSB. Part-time and evening/weekend programs available. *Entrance requirements:* For master's, GMAT, resumé, minimum GPA of 3.0, 2 letters of recommendation. Additional exam requirements/recommendations for international students: Required—TOEFL (minimum score 527 paper-based; 197 computer-based). Electronic applications accepted. *Faculty research:* Financial markets, consumer behavior.

Lynn University, College of Business and Management, Boca Raton, FL 33431-5598. Offers aviation management (MBA); financial valuation and investment management (MBA); global leadership (PhD); hospitality management (MBA); international business (MBA); marketing (MBA); mass communication and media management (MBA); sports and athletics administration (MBA). Part-time and evening/weekend programs available. Postbaccalaureate distance learning degree programs offered. *Faculty:* 13 full-time (5 women), 7 part-time/adjunct (3 women). *Students:* 71 full-time (37 women), 113 part-time (47 women); includes 35 minority (13 African Americans, 6 Asian Americans or Pacific Islanders, 16 Hispanic Americans), 55 international. Average age 32. 114 applicants, 88% accepted, 71 enrolled. In 2006, 83 master's, 9 doctorates awarded. *Degree requirements:* For master's, project; for doctorate, thesis/dissertation, qualifying paper. *Entrance requirements:* For master's, GMAT or GRE, minimum undergraduate GPA of 3.0, resumé, 2 letters of recommendation; for doctorate, GRE or GMAT, minimum graduate GPA of 3.25, resumé, 2 letters of recommendation. Additional exam requirements/recommendations for international students: Required—TOEFL (minimum score 550 paper-based; 213 computer-based). *Application deadline:* Applications are processed on a rolling basis. Application fee: $50. Electronic applications accepted. *Expenses:* Tuition: Full-time $26,200. Required fees: $1,500. Tuition and fees vary according to class time, course load and degree level. *Financial support:* In 2006–07, 160 students received support. Career-related internships or fieldwork, Federal Work-Study, institutionally sponsored loans, scholarships/grants, tuition waivers (full and partial), and unspecified assistantships available. Support available to part-time students. Financial award application deadline: 8/1; financial award applicants required to submit FAFSA. *Faculty research:* Labor relations, dynamic balance in leisure-time skills, ethics in athletics, hotel development. *Unit head:* Dr. Russell Boisjoly, Dean, 561-237-7458, Fax: 561-237-7014, E-mail: rboisjoly@lynn.edu. *Application contact:* Dr. Larissa Baia, Assistant Director of Graduate Admissions, 561-237-7916, Fax: 561-237-7100, E-mail: admissionpm@lynn.edu.

Madonna University, School of Business, Livonia, MI 48150-1173. Offers business administration (MBA); international business (MSBA); leadership studies (MSBA); leadership studies in criminal justice (MSBA); quality and operations management (MSBA). Part-time and evening/weekend programs available. Postbaccalaureate distance learning degree programs offered (minimal on-campus study). *Faculty:* 12 full-time (3 women), 14 part-time/adjunct (3 women). *Students:* 34 full-time (21 women), 214 part-time (107 women); includes 26 minority (7 African Americans, 7 American Indian/Alaska Native, 4 Asian Americans or Pacific Islanders, 8 Hispanic Americans), 88 international. Average age 36. 60 applicants, 60% accepted. In 2006, 41 degrees awarded. *Degree requirements:* For master's, thesis (for some programs), foreign language proficiency (international business). *Entrance requirements:* For master's, GMAT, GRE General Test, minimum GPA of 3.0. *Application deadline:* For fall admission, 8/1 priority date for domestic students; for winter admission, 12/1 priority date for domestic students; for spring admission, 4/1 priority date for domestic students. Applications are processed on a rolling basis. Application fee: $25 ($200 for international students). Electronic applications accepted. *Financial support:* Career-related internships or fieldwork, institutionally sponsored loans, and scholarships/grants available. Support available to part-time students. *Faculty research:* Management, women in management, future studies. *Unit head:* Dr. Stuart Arends, Dean, 734-432-5366, Fax: 734-432-5364, E-mail: sarends@madonna.edu. *Application contact:* Sandra Kellums, Coordinator of Graduate Admissions and Records, 734-432-5667, Fax: 734-432-5862, E-mail: skellum@madonna.edu.

Maine Maritime Academy, Department of Graduate Studies, Program in Global Supply Chain Management, Castine, ME 04420. Offers MS, Certificate, Diploma. Part-time programs available. *Degree requirements:* For master's, capstone course. *Entrance requirements:* For master's, GMAT or GRE, letters of recommendation. Additional exam requirements/recommendations for international students: Required—TOEFL.

Maine Maritime Academy, Department of Graduate Studies, Program in International Business, Castine, ME 04420. Offers MS, Certificate, Diploma. Part-time programs available. *Degree requirements:* For master's, capstone course, thesis optional. *Entrance requirements:* Additional exam requirements/recommendations for international students: Required—TOEFL.

Manhattanville College, Graduate Programs, Humanities and Social Sciences Programs, Program in International Management, Purchase, NY 10577-2132. Offers MS. Application fee: $55. *Application contact:* Natalia Fernandez, Director of Admissions, 914-323-5418, E-mail: gps@mylllle.edu.

McGill University, Faculty of Graduate and Postdoctoral Studies, Desautels Faculty of Management, Montréal, QC H3A 2T5, Canada. Offers administration (PhD); entrepreneurial studies (MBA); finance (MBA); general management (Post Master's Certificate); information systems (MBA); international business (exchange program) (MBA); international Master's program in practicing management (MM); management (MBA); management for development (MBA); manufacturing management (MMM); marketing (MBA); operations management (MBA); public accountancy (Diploma); strategic management (MBA); MBA/LL B; MD/MBA. Part-time programs available. *Entrance requirements:* For master's, GMAT, minimum undergraduate GPA of 3.0, 2 years work experience; for doctorate, GMAT or GRE General Test, 2 letters of recommendation, preferably by professors in chosen field of specialization; for other advanced degree, 2 years of work experience, MBA, minimum GPA of 3.0 (Post-MBA Certificate). Additional exam requirements/recommendations for international students: Required—TOEFL (minimum score 600 paper-based; 250 computer-based), IELTS (minimum score 7). Electronic applications accepted. Expenses: Contact institution. *Faculty research:* Social innovation, leadership, strategy.

Metropolitan State University, College of Management, St. Paul, MN 55106-5000. Offers finance (MBA); human resource management (MBA); information management (MMIS); international business (MBA); law enforcement (MPNA); management information systems (MBA); marketing (MBA); nonprofit management (MPNA); organizational studies (MBA); public administration (MPNA); purchasing management (MBA); systems management (MMIS). Part-time and evening/weekend programs available. *Degree requirements:* For master's, computer language (MMIS), thesis optional. *Entrance requirements:* For master's, GMAT (MBA), resumé. Additional exam requirements/recommendations for international students: Required—TOEFL (minimum score 550 paper-based; 213 computer-based). *Faculty research:* Yugoslav economic system, workers' cooperatives, participative management and job enrichment, global business systems.

Minnesota State University Mankato, College of Graduate Studies, College of Business, Mankato, MN 56001. Offers accounting and business law (MBA); finance (MBA); management (MBA); marketing and international business (MBA). *Accreditation:* AACSB. *Students:* 8 full-time (3 women), 32 part-time (13 women). *Entrance requirements:* For master's, GMAT, 2 letters of reference. Additional exam requirements/recommendations for international students: Required—TOEFL. *Application deadline:* For fall admission, 6/1 for domestic students; for spring admission, 10/1 for domestic students. Electronic applications accepted. *Unit head:* Scott Johnson, Dean, 507-389-5420.

Montclair State University, The Graduate School, School of Business, Department of International Business, Montclair, NJ 07043-1624. Offers MBA. *Faculty:* 10 full-time (2 women), 3 part-time/adjunct (1 woman). *Students:* 4 full-time (3 women), 10 part-time (7 women); includes 1 minority (Hispanic American), 4 international. 15 applicants, 40% accepted, 4 enrolled. In 2006, 2 degrees awarded. *Degree requirements:* For master's, comprehensive project. *Entrance requirements:* For master's, GMAT, 2 letters of recommendation, resumé. Additional exam requirements/recommendations for international students: Required—TOEFL. *Application deadline:* For fall admission, 6/1 for international students; for spring admission, 10/1 for international students. Applications are processed on a rolling basis. Application fee: $60. Electronic applications accepted. *Expenses:* Tuition, state resident: part-time $450 per credit. Tuition, nonresident: part-time $682 per credit. Tuition and fees vary according to degree level and program. *Financial support:* In 2006–07, 3 research assistantships with full tuition reimbursements (averaging $7,000 per year) were awarded; Federal Work-Study, scholarships/grants, and unspecified assistantships also available. Support available to part-time students. Financial award application deadline: 3/1; financial award applicants required to submit FAFSA. *Unit head:* Dr. Chandana Chakraborty, Head, 973-655-4280. *Application contact:* Dr. Eileen Kaplan, Adviser, 973-655-7469, E-mail: kaplane@mail.montclair.edu.

Monterey Institute of International Studies, Fisher Graduate School of International Business, Monterey, CA 93940-2691. Offers MBA. *Accreditation:* AACSB. *Faculty:* 7 full-time (1 woman), 3 part-time/adjunct (0 women). *Students:* 68 full-time (31 women), 1 part-time; includes 12 minority (1 African American, 6 Asian Americans or Pacific Islanders, 5 Hispanic Americans), 19 international. Average age 28. 86 applicants, 94% accepted, 41 enrolled. In 2006, 43 degrees awarded. *Degree requirements:* For master's, one foreign language, thesis. *Entrance requirements:* For master's, GMAT, minimum GPA of 3.0, proficiency in a foreign language. Additional exam requirements/recommendations for international students: Required—TOEFL (minimum score 550 paper-based; 213 computer-based; 80 iBT). *Application deadline:* For fall admission, 3/15 priority date for domestic students; for spring admission, 10/1 priority date for domestic students. Applications are processed on a rolling basis. Application fee: $50. Electronic applications accepted. *Expenses:* Tuition: Full-time $26,500; part-time $1,200 per credit. Required fees: $200. *Financial support:* In 2006–07, 59 students received support, including 2 research assistantships with partial tuition reimbursements available (averaging $4,000 per year); career-related internships or fieldwork, Federal Work-Study, institutionally sponsored loans, scholarships/grants, tuition waivers (partial), and unspecified assistantships also available. Support available to part-time students. Financial award application deadline: 3/15; financial award applicants required to submit FAFSA. *Faculty research:* Cross-cultural consumer behavior, foreign direct investment, marketing and entrepreneurial orientation, political risk analysis and area studies, managing international human resources. *Unit head:* Dr. Ernest J. Scalberg, Dean, 831-647-4140, Fax: 831-647-6506, E-mail: fgsib@miis.edu. *Application contact:* 831-647-4123, Fax: 831-647-6405, E-mail: admit@miis.edu.

Monterey Institute of International Studies, Graduate School of International Policy Studies, Program in International Trade Policy, Monterey, CA 93940-2691. Offers MA. *Students:* 25 full-time (16 women), 4 part-time (2 women); includes 8 minority (2 African Americans, 5 Asian Americans or Pacific Islanders, 1 Hispanic American), 6 international. Average age 30. 18 applicants, 100% accepted, 11 enrolled. In 2006, 11 degrees awarded. *Degree requirements:* For master's, one foreign language. *Entrance requirements:* For master's, minimum GPA of 3.0, proficiency in a foreign language. Additional exam requirements/recommendations for international students: Required—TOEFL. *Application deadline:* For fall admission, 3/15 priority date for domestic students; for spring admission, 10/1 priority date for domestic students. Applications are processed on a rolling basis. Application fee: $50. Electronic applications accepted. *Expenses:* Tuition: Full-time $26,500; part-time $1,200 per credit. Required fees: $200. *Financial support:* Application deadline: 3/15. *Application contact:* 831-647-4123, Fax: 831-647-6405, E-mail: admit@miis.edu.

Newman University, School of Business, Wichita, KS 67213-2097. Offers international business (MBA); leadership (MBA); management (MBA); technology (MBA). Part-time programs available. *Faculty:* 6 full-time (2 women), 3 part-time/adjunct (1 woman). *Students:* 34 full-time (14 women), 76 part-time (30 women); includes 14 minority (6 African Americans, 1 American Indian/Alaska Native, 3 Asian Americans or Pacific Islanders, 4 Hispanic Americans), 31 international. Average age 31. 74 applicants, 80% accepted, 46 enrolled. In 2006, 76 degrees awarded. *Degree requirements:* For master's, thesis optional. *Entrance requirements:* For master's, interview; minimum GPA of 3.0; 3 letters of recommendation; course work in algebra, statistics, macroeconomics. Additional exam requirements/recommendations for international students: Required—TOEFL (minimum score 600 paper-based; 250 computer-based; 100 iBT). *Application deadline:* For fall admission, 8/1 priority date for domestic students; for winter admission, 1/1 priority date for domestic students; for spring admission, 1/1 priority date for domestic students. Applications are processed on a rolling basis. Application fee: $25 ($40 for international students). Electronic applications accepted. *Expenses: Contact institution. Financial support:* In 2006–07, 3 students received support. Federal Work-Study and tuition waivers available. Financial award application deadline: 8/15; financial award applicants required to submit FAFSA. *Unit head:* Dr. Joe Goetz, Dean, 316-942-4291 Ext. 2111, Fax: 316-942-4486, E-mail: goetzj@newmanu.edu. *Application contact:* Linda Kay Sabala, Director of Graduate Admissions, 316-942-4291 Ext. 2230, Fax: 316-942-4483, E-mail: sabalal@newmanu.edu.

New Mexico Highlands University, Graduate Studies, School of Business, Las Vegas, NM 87701. Offers business administration (MBA), including human resource management, international business, non-profit financial management. *Accreditation:* ACBSP. *Faculty:* 12 full-time (4 women), 1 part-time/adjunct (0 women). *Students:* 57 full-time (39 women), 103 part-time (69 women); includes 97 minority (1 African American, 26 American Indian/Alaska Native, 4 Asian Americans or Pacific Islanders, 66 Hispanic Americans), 17 international. Average age 35. 69 applicants, 84% accepted, 42 enrolled. In 2006, 29 degrees awarded. *Degree requirements:* For master's, thesis or alternative, comprehensive exam, registration. *Entrance requirements:* For master's, minimum undergraduate GPA of 3.0. Additional exam requirements/recommendations for international students: Required—TOEFL (minimum score 540 paper-based; 190 computer-based). *Application deadline:* For fall admission, 8/1 priority date for domestic students. Applications are processed on a rolling basis. Application fee: $15. *Expenses:* Tuition, state resident: part-time $101 per credit hour. Tuition, nonresident: part-time $101 per credit hour. *Financial support:* In 2006–07, 67 students received support, including 8 teaching assistantships with full and partial tuition reimbursements available (averaging $6,500 per year); career-related internships or fieldwork, Federal Work-Study, institutionally sponsored loans, scholarships/grants, tuition waivers (full and partial), and unspecified assistantships also available. Support available to part-time students. Financial award application deadline: 3/1; financial award applicants required to submit FAFSA. *Unit head:* Dr. William Taylor, Dean, 505-454-3344, Fax: 505-454-3354. *Application contact:* Diane Trujillo, Administrative Assistant Graduate Studies, 505-454-3266, Fax: 505-454-3558, E-mail: dtrujillo@nmhu.edu.

The New School: A University, The New School for General Studies, Program in International Affairs, New York, NY 10011. Offers global management, trade, and finance (MA, MS); international development (MA, MS); international media and communication (MA, MS); international politics and diplomacy (MA, MS); service, civic, and non-profit management (MS). Part-time programs available. *Students:* 159 full-time (104 women), 117 part-time (80 women); includes 62 minority (16 African Americans, 21 Asian Americans or Pacific Islanders, 25 Hispanic Americans), 45 international. Average age 30. In 2006, 92 degrees awarded. *Entrance requirements:* Additional exam requirements/recommendations for international students: Required—TOEFL (minimum score 600 paper-based; 250 computer-based; 100 iBT). *Application deadline:* For fall admission, 4/15 for domestic students; for spring admission, 10/15 for domestic students. Application fee: $50. *Financial support:* Fellowships with partial tuition reimbursements, research assistantships, teaching assistantships with partial tuition reimbursements, career-related internships or fieldwork, Federal Work-Study, scholarships/grants, tuition waivers (partial), and unspecified assistantships available. Support available to part-time students. Financial award application deadline: 3/1; financial award applicants required to submit FAFSA. *Unit head:* Dr. Michael Cohen, Director, 212-206-3524, Fax: 212-645-0661, E-mail: cohenm2@newschool.edu. *Application contact:* Gerianne Brusati, Associate Dean, Admissions and Student Services, 212-229-5630, Fax: 212-989-3887, E-mail: nsadmissions@newschool.edu.

New York Institute of Technology, Ellis College, Old Westbury, NY 11568. Offers accounting and information systems (MBA); e-commerce (MBA); finance (MBA); global management (MBA); healthcare administration (MBA); human resources management (MBA); leadership (MBA); management of information systems (MBA); management of technology (MBA); marketing (MBA); professional accounting (MBA); project management (MBA); risk management (MBA); strategy and economics (MBA). Ellis College is a collaboration between New York Institute of Technology and UNext online learning company. Part-time and evening/weekend programs available. Postbaccalaureate distance learning degree programs offered (no on-campus study). *Entrance requirements:* For master's, interview. Additional exam requirements/recommendations for international students: Required—TOEFL (minimum score 550 paper-based; 213 computer-based). Electronic applications accepted. *Expenses:* Tuition: Full-time $16,800; part-time $700 per credit.

New York Institute of Technology, Graduate Division, School of Management, Program in Business Administration, Old Westbury, NY 11568-8000. Offers accounting (Advanced Certificate); business administration (MBA); finance (Advanced Certificate); international business (Advanced Certificate); management of information systems (Advanced Certificate); marketing (Advanced Certificate). Part-time and evening/weekend programs available. *Students:* 481 full-time (120 women), 1,300 part-time (670 women); includes 297 minority (153 African Americans, 6 American Indian/Alaska Native, 81 Asian Americans or Pacific Islanders, 57 Hispanic Americans), 215 international. Average age 29. 1,049 applicants, 87% accepted, 137 enrolled. In 2006, 917 degrees awarded. *Degree requirements:* For master's, thesis (for some programs). *Entrance requirements:* For master's, minimum QPA of 2.85. Additional exam requirements/recommendations for international students: Required—TOEFL (minimum score 550 paper-based; 213 computer-based). *Application deadline:* For fall admission, 7/1 priority date for domestic students; for spring admission, 12/1 priority date for domestic students. Applications are processed on a rolling basis. Application fee: $50. Electronic applications accepted. *Expenses:* Tuition: Full-time $16,800; part-time $700 per credit. *Financial support:* Fellowships, research assistantships with partial tuition reimbursements, institutionally sponsored loans, tuition waivers (full and partial), and unspecified assistantships available. Support available to part-time students. Financial award applicants required to submit FAFSA. *Faculty research:* Instructor performance appraisal; relationship between TOEFL, GMAT, GRE, and performance in foreign students. *Unit head:* Dr. Gurumurthy Kalyanuram, Director, 516-686-7972, E-mail: gkalyana@nyit.edu. *Application contact:* Jacquelyn Nealon, Dean of Admissions and Financial Aid, 516-686-7925, Fax: 516-686-7613, E-mail: jnealon@nyit.edu.

New York University, Graduate School of Arts and Science, Department of Politics, New York, NY 10012-1019. Offers political campaign management (MA); politics (MA, PhD); JD/MA; MBA/MA. Part-time programs available. *Faculty:* 30 full-time (4 women), 24 part-time/adjunct. *Students:* 130 full-time (58 women), 44 part-time (30 women); includes 18 minority (2 African Americans, 9 Asian Americans or Pacific Islanders, 7 Hispanic Americans), 74 international. Average age 28. 469 applicants, 46% accepted, 84 enrolled. In 2006, 52 master's, 9 doctorates awarded. Terminal master's awarded for partial completion of doctoral program. *Degree requirements:* For master's, one foreign language, thesis or alternative; for doctorate, 2 foreign languages, thesis/dissertation, comprehensive exam. *Entrance requirements:* For master's, GRE General Test; for doctorate, GRE General Test, master's degree in political science, minimum GPA of 2.5. Additional exam requirements/recommendations for international students: Required—TOEFL. *Application deadline:* For fall admission, 12/15 priority date for domestic students. Application fee: $80. *Expenses:* Tuition: Part-time $1,080 per unit. Required fees: $56 per unit. $329 per term. Tuition and fees vary according to program. *Financial support:* Fellowships with tuition reimbursements, teaching assistantships with tuition reimbursements, career-related internships or fieldwork, Federal Work-Study, and institutionally sponsored loans available. Financial award application deadline: 12/15; financial award applicants required to submit FAFSA. *Faculty research:* Comparative politics, democratic theory and practice, rational choice, political economy; international relations. *Unit head:* Nathaniel Beck, Chair, 212-998-8500, Fax: 212-995-4184, E-mail: politics.program@nyu.edu. *Application contact:* Jonathan Nagler, Director of Graduate Studies, 212-998-8500, Fax: 212-995-4184, E-mail: politics.program@nyu.edu.

Nova Southeastern University, H. Wayne Huizenga School of Business and Entrepreneurship, Program in International Business Administration, Fort Lauderdale, FL 33314-7796. Offers MIBA, DIBA. Part-time and evening/weekend programs available. *Students:* 20 full-time (14 women), 154 part-time (100 women); includes 105 minority (28 African Americans, 1 American Indian/Alaska Native, 9 Asian Americans or Pacific Islanders, 67 Hispanic Americans), 31 international. In 2006, 51 master's, 6 doctorates awarded. *Degree requirements:* For master's and doctorate, field experience or internship. *Entrance requirements:* Additional exam requirements/recommendations for international students: Required—TOEFL, Michigan English Language Assessment Battery. *Application deadline:* For fall admission, 8/15 for domestic students; for spring admission, 2/10 for domestic students. Applications are processed on a rolling basis. Application fee: $50. *Financial support:* Career-related internships or fieldwork, Federal Work-Study, and scholarships/grants available. Support available to part-time students. *Unit head:* Steve Harvey, Assistant Dean, 954-262-5047, Fax: 954-262-3829, E-mail: harvey@nsu.nova.edu. *Application contact:* Karen Goldberg, Assistant Director, 954-262-5039, Fax: 954-262-3822, E-mail: karen@nova.edu.

See Close-Up on page 295.

Oakland University, Graduate Study and Lifelong Learning, School of Business Administration, Department of Management and Marketing, Rochester, MI 48309-4401. Offers business administration (MBA); entrepreneurship (Certificate); general management (Certificate); human resource management (Certificate); international business (Certificate); marketing (Certificate). *Faculty:* 9 full-time (3 women), 2 part-time/adjunct (both women). *Students:* 61 full-time (25 women), 416 part-time (137 women); includes 72 minority (14 African Americans, 1 American Indian/Alaska Native, 46 Asian Americans or Pacific Islanders, 11 Hispanic Americans), 45 international. Average age 31. 121 applicants, 88% accepted, 65 enrolled. In 2006, 163 degrees awarded. Application fee: $35. *Expenses:* Tuition, state resident: full-time $9,936; part-time $414 per credit. Tuition, nonresident: full-time $17,202; part-time $716 per credit. *Unit head:* Ravi Parameswaran, Chair, 238-370-3279, Fax: 249-370-4275.

International Business

Oklahoma City University, Meinders School of Business, Program in Business Administration, Oklahoma City, OK 73106-1402. Offers finance (MBA); health administration (MBA); information technology (MBA); integrated marketing communications (MBA); international business (MBA); marketing (MBA); JD/MBA. *Accreditation:* ACBSP. Part-time and evening/weekend programs available. *Faculty:* 30 full-time (7 women), 24 part-time/adjunct (5 women). *Students:* 291 full-time (112 women), 186 part-time (68 women); includes 57 minority (27 African Americans, 9 American Indian/Alaska Native, 12 Asian Americans or Pacific Islanders, 9 Hispanic Americans), 218 international. Average age 27. In 2006, 341 degrees awarded. *Degree requirements:* For master's, comprehensive exam. *Entrance requirements:* For master's, minimum GPA of 2.5. Additional exam requirements/recommendations for international students: Required—TOEFL (minimum score 510 paper-based). *Application deadline:* For fall admission, 8/22 for domestic students; for spring admission, 1/15 for domestic students. Applications are processed on a rolling basis. Application fee: $30 ($70 for international students). *Financial support:* Fellowships with partial tuition reimbursements, career-related internships or fieldwork, Federal Work-Study, institutionally sponsored loans, and tuition waivers (partial) available. Support available to part-time students. Financial award application deadline: 8/1. *Faculty research:* Management information systems, international business strategies. *Unit head:* Dr. Mahmood Shandiz, Head, 405-208-5130, Fax: 405-208-5098, E-mail: mshandiz@okcu.edu. *Application contact:* Leslie McKenzie, Director, Graduate Admissions, 800-633-7242, Fax: 405-208-5356, E-mail: gadmissions@okcu.edu.

Oral Roberts University, School of Business, Tulsa, OK 74171-0001. Offers accounting (MBA); finance (MBA); international business (MBA); management (MBA); marketing (MBA); non-profit management (M Man, MBA); organizational dynamics (M Man); sales marketing (M Man). *Accreditation:* ACBSP. Part-time programs available. Postbaccalaureate distance learning degree programs offered (minimal on-campus study). *Faculty:* 9 full-time (2 women), 4 part-time/adjunct (2 women). *Students:* 33 full-time (18 women), 67 part-time (28 women); includes 28 minority (17 African Americans, 3 American Indian/Alaska Native, 6 Asian Americans or Pacific Islanders, 2 Hispanic Americans), 15 international. Average age 29. 69 applicants, 84% accepted, 33 enrolled. In 2006, 21 degrees awarded. *Degree requirements:* For master's, thesis optional. *Entrance requirements:* For master's, minimum GPA of 3.0. Additional exam requirements/recommendations for international students: Required—TOEFL (minimum score 550 paper-based; 213 computer-based). *Application deadline:* For fall admission, 7/1 priority date for domestic students, 5/1 priority date for international students; for spring admission, 12/1 priority date for domestic students, 10/1 priority date for international students. Applications are processed on a rolling basis. Application fee: $35. *Expenses: Contact institution. Financial support:* In 2006–07, 9 research assistantships (averaging $3,600 per year) were awarded; scholarships/grants and unspecified assistantships also available. Financial award application deadline: 6/1; financial award applicants required to submit FAFSA. *Faculty research:* Non-profit, international business and marketing. *Unit head:* Dr. Mark Lewandowski, Dean, 918-495-7040, Fax: 918-495-7876, E-mail: mlewandowski@oru.edu. *Application contact:* 918-495-6989, Fax: 918-495-7965, E-mail: alsc@oru.edu.

Our Lady of the Lake University of San Antonio, School of Business, San Antonio, TX 78207-4689. Offers general (MBA), including finance, international business, management; health care management (MBA). *Accreditation:* ACBSP. Part-time and evening/weekend programs available. *Degree requirements:* For master's, thesis optional. *Entrance requirements:* For master's, GMAT, GRE General Test, or MAT. Electronic applications accepted. *Faculty research:* International marketing, employee benefits, decision process.

Pace University, Lubin School of Business, International Business Program, New York, NY 10038. Offers MBA. Part-time and evening/weekend programs available. *Students:* 11 full-time (4 women), 33 part-time (17 women); includes 9 minority (3 African Americans, 2 Asian Americans or Pacific Islanders, 4 Hispanic Americans), 17 international. Average age 30. 101 applicants, 50% accepted, 19 enrolled. In 2006, 16 degrees awarded. *Entrance requirements:* For master's, GMAT. *Application deadline:* For fall admission, 7/31 priority date for domestic students; for spring admission, 11/30 for domestic students. Applications are processed on a rolling basis. Application fee: $65. Electronic applications accepted. *Expenses:* Tuition: Part-time $890 per credit. *Financial support:* Research assistantships, career-related internships or fieldwork and Federal Work-Study available. Support available to part-time students. Financial award applicants required to submit FAFSA. *Unit head:* Dr. Lawrence Bridwell, Chairperson, 914-422-4165. *Application contact:* Joanna Broda, Director of Admissions, 212-346-1652, Fax: 212-346-1585, E-mail: gradnyc@pace.edu.

Pacific States University, College of Business, Los Angeles, CA 90006. Offers accounting (MBA); business administration (DBA); finance (MBA); international business (MBA); management of information technology (MBA); real estate management (MBA). Part-time and evening/weekend programs available. Postbaccalaureate distance learning degree programs offered (no on-campus study). *Faculty:* 3 full-time (0 women), 11 part-time/adjunct (0 women). *Students:* 106 full-time (47 women); includes 10 minority (all Asian Americans or Pacific Islanders), 96 international. Average age 32. 36 applicants, 81% accepted, 26 enrolled. In 2006, 68 degrees awarded. *Entrance requirements:* For master's, minimum undergraduate GPA of 2.5 during last 90 hours of course work. Additional exam requirements/recommendations for international students: Required—TOEFL (minimum score 133 computer-based). *Application deadline:* For fall admission, 8/15 priority date for domestic students; for winter admission, 10/15 priority date for domestic students; for spring admission, 1/15 priority date for domestic students. Applications are processed on a rolling basis. Application fee: $100. *Expenses:* Tuition: Full-time $6,360. Required fees: $1,080. Full-time tuition and fees vary according to course load and degree level. *Financial support:* Fellowships, research assistantships, teaching assistantships, scholarships/grants available. Financial award applicants required to submit FAFSA. *Unit head:* Dr. Kamol Somvichian, Director, 888-200-0383, Fax: 323-731-2383, E-mail: admission@psuca.edu. *Application contact:* Marina Miller, Assistant Director of Admissions, 323-731-2383 Ext. 11, Fax: 323-731-7276, E-mail: admissions@psuca.edu.

Park University, College of Graduate and Professional Studies, Kansas City, MO 54105. Offers adult education (M Ed); at-risk students (M Ed); disaster and emergency management (MPA); educational administration (M Ed); entrepreneurship (MBA); general business (MBA); general education (M Ed); government/business relations (MPA); healthcare/services management (MBA, MPA); international business (MBA); K-12 certification (MAT); management information systems (MBA); management of information systems (MPA); middle school certification (MAT); multi-cultural education (M Ed); nonprofit management (MPA); public management (MPA); school law (M Ed); secondary school certification (MAT); special education (M Ed). Part-time and evening/weekend programs available. Postbaccalaureate distance learning degree programs offered (no on-campus study). *Degree requirements:* For master's, thesis (for some programs), comprehensive exam, registration. *Entrance requirements:* For master's, GRE, GMAT, teacher certification (M Ed). Additional exam requirements/recommendations for international students: Required—TOEFL (minimum score 550 paper-based). Electronic applications accepted. *Faculty research:* Literacy, leadership, brain based research, multicultural education, diversity.

Pepperdine University, Malibu Graduate Business Programs, Malibu, CA 90263. Offers business administration (MBA); international business (MIB); JD/MBA. *Accreditation:* AACSB. *Faculty:* 10 full-time (4 women). *Students:* 241 full-time (111 women), 3 part-time; includes 34 minority (1 African American, 1 American Indian/Alaska Native, 24 Asian Americans or Pacific Islanders, 8 Hispanic Americans), 94 international. 627 applicants, 62% accepted, 164 enrolled. In 2006, 86 degrees awarded. *Degree requirements:* For master's, foreign language (MIB). *Entrance requirements:* For master's, GMAT, MAT, 2 letters of recommendation, resumé. Additional exam requirements/recommendations for international students: Required—TOEFL (minimum score 550 paper-based; 220 computer-based). *Application deadline:* For fall admission, 5/1 for domestic and international students. Applications are processed on a rolling basis. Application fee: $45. Electronic applications accepted. *Expenses: Contact institution.* Full-time tuition and fees vary according to program. *Financial support:* Career-related internships or fieldwork, institutionally sponsored loans, scholarships/grants, and unspecified assistantships available. Financial award application deadline: 6/1; financial award applicants required to submit FAFSA. *Unit head:* Dr. Mark Mallinger, Director, Full-Time Programs, 310-506-6962, Fax: 310-506-4126, E-mail: mark.mallinger@pepperdine.edu. *Application contact:* Paul E. Pinckley, Executive Director, Recruitment and Student Recruitment, 310-506-4858, Fax: 310-506-4126, E-mail: paul.pinckley@pepperdine.edu.

See Close-Up on page 305.

Philadelphia University, School of Business Administration, Program in Business Administration, Philadelphia, PA 19144-5497. Offers business administration (MBA); finance (MBA); health care management (MBA); international business (MBA); marketing (MBA); MBA/MS. Part-time and evening/weekend programs available. Postbaccalaureate distance learning degree programs offered (no on-campus study). *Faculty:* 10 full-time (2 women), 8 part-time/adjunct (0 women). *Students:* 43 full-time (24 women), 87 part-time (45 women); includes 3 Asian Americans or Pacific Islanders. 154 applicants, 56% accepted, 37 enrolled. In 2006, 85 degrees awarded. *Entrance requirements:* For master's, GMAT. Additional exam requirements/recommendations for international students: Required—TOEFL (minimum score 550 paper-based; 213 computer-based; 79 iBT). *Application deadline:* Applications are processed on a rolling basis. Application fee: $35. *Financial support:* In 2006–07, research assistantships with full tuition reimbursements (averaging $2,500 per year); career-related internships or fieldwork, Federal Work-Study, scholarships/grants, and unspecified assistantships also available. Support available to part-time students. Financial award applicants required to submit FAFSA. *Unit head:* MarySheila McDonald, Assistant Dean for Graduate Programs, 215-951-2950, Fax: 215-951-2653, E-mail: mcdonaldm@philau.edu. *Application contact:* Jack A. Klett, Director of Graduate Admissions, 215-951-2943, Fax: 215-951-2907, E-mail: gradadm@philau.edu.

Polytechnic University of Puerto Rico, Graduate School, Hato Rey, PR 00919. Offers business administration (MBA), including general studies, management of information systems, management of international enterprises; civil engineering (ME, MS); competitiveness manufacturing (MCM, MMC, MS); computer engineering (ME, MS); electrical engineering (ME, MS); engineering management (MEM); environmental management (MEPM); manufacturing engineering (ME, MS). Part-time and evening/weekend programs available. *Entrance requirements:* For master's, 3 letters of recommendation.

Pontifical Catholic University of Puerto Rico, College of Business Administration, Ponce, PR 00717-0777. Offers accounting (MBA); business administration (PhD); finance (MBA); general business (MBA); human resources (MBA); international business (MBA); management (MBA); management information systems (MBA); marketing (MBA); office administration (MBA). Part-time and evening/weekend programs available. *Degree requirements:* For master's, thesis/dissertation; for doctorate, thesis/dissertation, comprehensive exam. *Entrance requirements:* For master's, GRE, interview, minimum GPA of 2.75; for doctorate, 2 letters of recommendation, 2 years experience in a related field, interview.

Pontificia Universidad Catolica Madre y Maestra, Graduate School, Santiago, Dominican Republic. Offers administration (M Adm, M Ed); architecture of interiors (M Arch); architecture of tourist lodgings (M Arch); construction administration (ME); convergent networks (ME); earthquake-resistant engineering (ME); environmental engineering (MEE); financial (M Mgmt); human resources (EMBA); international (M Mgmt); labor law and Social Security (M Mgmt); logistics management (ME); urban planning (M Urb). *Entrance requirements:* For master's, curriculum vitae, interview.

Portland State University, Graduate Studies, School of Business Administration, Program in International Management, Portland, OR 97207-0751. Offers MIM. Part-time and evening/weekend programs available. *Students:* 66 full-time (28 women), 19 part-time (10 women); includes 13 minority (1 African American, 8 Asian Americans or Pacific Islanders, 4 Hispanic Americans), 20 international. Average age 29. 75 applicants, 99% accepted, 53 enrolled. In 2006, 40 degrees awarded. *Degree requirements:* For master's, field study trip to China and Japan. *Entrance requirements:* For master's, GMAT, minimum GPA of 2.75, resumé, 2 letters of recommendation. Additional exam requirements/recommendations for international students: Required—TOEFL (minimum score 550 paper-based; 213 computer-based). *Application deadline:* For fall admission, 4/1 priority date for domestic students, 3/1 for international students. Applications are processed on a rolling basis. Application fee: $50. *Expenses:* Tuition, state resident: full-time $6,426; part-time $238 per credit. Tuition, nonresident: full-time $11,016; part-time $408 per credit. Tuition and fees vary according to course load. *Financial support:* Research assistantships with tuition reimbursements, teaching assistantships, career-related internships or fieldwork, Federal Work-Study, and institutionally sponsored loans available. Support available to part-time students. Financial award application deadline: 3/1; financial award applicants required to submit FAFSA. *Unit head:* Dr. Sully Taylor, Director, 503-725-2275, Fax: 503-725-2290, E-mail: sullyt@sba.pdx.edu.

Purdue University, Graduate School, Krannert School of Management, Department of Industrial Administration (MSIA), West Lafayette, IN 47907. Offers MSIA. *Students:* 34 full-time (15 women); includes 3 minority (all Asian Americans or Pacific Islanders), 19 international. 71 applicants, 69% accepted, 31 enrolled. In 2006, 30 degrees awarded. *Entrance requirements:* For master's, GMAT. Additional exam requirements/recommendations for international students: Required—TOEFL. *Application deadline:* For fall admission, 11/1 priority date for domestic students, 12/1 priority date for international students; for winter admission, 1/1 for domestic students, 2/1 for international students; for spring admission, 5/1 for domestic students. Applications are processed on a rolling basis. Application fee: $55. Electronic applications accepted. *Expenses: Contact institution. Financial support:* Fellowships, research assistantships, teaching assistantships, career-related internships or fieldwork, tuition waivers (partial), and unspecified assistantships available. *Unit head:* Dr. John J. McConnell, Head, 765-494-5980. *Application contact:* Mari-Ellyn Brack, Graduate Contact for Admission, 765-494-0773, Fax: 765-494-9841, E-mail: masters@krannert.purdue.edu.

Quinnipiac University, School of Business, Program in Business Administration, Hamden, CT 06518-1940. Offers accounting (MBA); economics (MBA); finance (MBA); healthcare management (MBA); information systems management (MBA); international business (MBA); management (MBA); marketing (MBA); JD/MBA. *Accreditation:* AACSB. Part-time and evening/weekend programs available. *Faculty:* 16 full-time (2 women), 2 part-time/adjunct (1 woman). *Students:* 53 full-time (21 women), 112 part-time (48 women); includes 13 minority (2 African Americans, 1 American Indian/Alaska Native, 4 Asian Americans or Pacific Islanders, 6 Hispanic Americans), 7 international. Average age 26. 80 applicants, 65% accepted, 34 enrolled. In 2006, 73 degrees awarded. *Median time to degree:* Master's–1.5 years full-time, 2.5 years part-time. *Entrance requirements:* For master's, GMAT, minimum GPA of 3.0. Additional exam requirements/recommendations for international students: Required—TOEFL (minimum score 575 paper-based; 233 computer-based; 90 iBT), IELTS (minimum score 7). *Application deadline:* For fall admission, 7/30 priority date for domestic students, 5/30 priority date for international students; for spring admission, 12/15 priority date for domestic students, 10/15 priority date for international students. Applications are processed on a rolling basis. Application fee: $45. Electronic applications accepted. *Expenses:* Tuition: Part-time $675 per credit. Required fees: $30 per credit. *Financial support:* Tuition waivers (partial) and unspecified assistantships available. Support available to part-time students. Financial award application deadline: 4/15; financial award applicants required to submit FAFSA. *Faculty research:* Equity compensation, marketing relationships and public policy, corporate governance, international business. *Unit head:* Kevin B. Taylor, Director, 203-582-3676, Fax: 203-582-8664, E-mail: mba@quinnipiac.edu. *Application contact:* 800-462-1944, Fax: 203-582-3443, E-mail: graduate@quinnipiac.edu.

See Close-Up on page 311.

Regis University, School for Professional Studies, Program in Business, Denver, CO 80221-1099. Offers accounting (MS); business administration (MBA); finance (MBA); finance and accounting (MBA); international business (MBA); marketing (MBA); operations management (MBA); organization leadership (MS); project management (Certificate); technical management (Certificate). Offered at Colorado Springs Campus, Northwest Denver Campus, Southeast Denver Campus, Fort Collins Campus, Broomfield Campus, Henderson (Nevada) Campus, and Summerlin (Nevada) Campus. Part-time and evening/weekend programs available. Postbaccalaureate distance learning degree programs offered (no on-campus study). *Faculty:* 16 full-time (4 women), 82 part-time/adjunct (22 women). *Students:* 1,770 (834 women). Average age 36. In 2006, 560 degrees awarded. *Degree requirements:* For master's, capstone project, thesis optional. *Entrance requirements:* For master's, GMAT, interview, 2 years of full-time business work experience; for Certificate, GMAT. Additional exam requirements/recommendations for international students: Required—TOEFL or university-based test. *Application deadline:* For fall admission, 8/22 for domestic and international students; for winter admission, 1/2 for domestic and international students; for spring admission, 4/30 for domestic and international students. Applications are processed on a rolling basis. Application fee: $75. Electronic applications accepted. *Financial support:* Federal Work-Study available. Support available to part-time students. Financial award applicants required to submit FAFSA. *Unit head:* Dr. Michael Goess, Chair, 303-458-4302, Fax: 303-964-5538. *Application contact:* 800-677-9270 Ext. 4080, Fax: 303-964-5538, E-mail: masters@regis.edu.

Regis University, School for Professional Studies, Program in Organization Leadership, Denver, CO 80221-1099. Offers computer information technology (MSOL); executive international management (Certificate); executive leadership (Certificate); human resource management (MSOL); organizational leadership (MSOL); project leadership and management (MSOL, Certificate); strategic business (Certificate); strategic human resource (Certificate). Offered at Boulder Campus, Fort Collins Campus, Northwest Denver Campus, Southeast Denver Campus, Colorado Springs Campus, and Broomfield Campus. Part-time and evening/weekend programs available. Postbaccalaureate distance learning degree programs offered. *Faculty:* 55. *Students:* Average age 35. In 2006, 61 degrees awarded. *Median time to degree:* Master's–3 years full-time. *Degree requirements:* For master's, capstone course; for Certificate, final research project. *Entrance requirements:* For master's, 3 years of management-related experience, resumé. Additional exam requirements/recommendations for international students: Required—TOEFL, TWE (minimum score 5), TOEFL or university-based test. *Application deadline:* For fall admission, 8/13 priority date for domestic students, 7/13 for international students; for winter admission, 10/8 priority date for domestic students, 9/8 for international students; for spring admission, 12/17 priority date for domestic students, 11/11 for international students. Applications are processed on a rolling basis. Application fee: $75. Electronic applications accepted. *Expenses:* Contact institution. *Financial support:* Federal Work-Study available. Support available to part-time students. Financial award applicants required to submit FAFSA. *Faculty research:* Organizational behavior, leadership, change, quality control, global economics. *Unit head:* Dr. Donna VanDusen, Chair, 303-458-4302, Fax: 303-964-5538. *Application contact:* 800-677-9270, Fax: 303-964-5538, E-mail: masters@regis.edu.

Rochester Institute of Technology, Graduate Enrollment Services, E. Philip Saunders College of Business, Department of Business Administration, Program in Management, Rochester, NY 14623-5603. Offers MS. *Students:* 1 full-time (0 women), 2 part-time (1 woman); includes 1 minority (Asian American or Pacific Islander), 2 international. 9 applicants, 44% accepted, 3 enrolled. In 2006, 2 degrees awarded. *Entrance requirements:* For master's, GMAT, minimum GPA of 2.5. Additional exam requirements/recommendations for international students: Required—TOEFL (minimum score 580 paper-based; 237 computer-based; 92 iBT). *Application deadline:* For fall admission, 3/1 priority date for domestic students. Applications are processed on a rolling basis. Application fee: $50. *Expenses:* Tuition: Full-time $28,491; part-time $800 per credit. Required fees: $201. *Application contact:* Brian O'Neil, Associate Dean, 585-475-7784, E-mail: boneil@cob.rit.edu.

Roosevelt University, Graduate Division, Walter E. Heller College of Business Administration, Program in International Business, Chicago, IL 60605-1394. Offers MSIB. Part-time and evening/weekend programs available. *Students:* 3 full-time (all women), 11 part-time (8 women); includes 4 minority (2 African Americans, 1 Asian American or Pacific Islander, 1 Hispanic American), 2 international. Average age 32. 4 applicants, 50% accepted, 2 enrolled. In 2006, 4 degrees awarded. *Degree requirements:* For master's, one foreign language. *Entrance requirements:* For master's, GMAT. *Application deadline:* For fall admission, 6/1 priority date for domestic students. Applications are processed on a rolling basis. Application fee: $25 ($35 for international students). *Financial support:* Career-related internships or fieldwork, Federal Work-Study, and tuition waivers (partial) available. Financial award application deadline: 2/15. *Unit head:* Dr. Alan G. Krabbenhoft, Associate Dean and Director, 312-281-3342, E-mail: akrabben@acfsysv.roosevelt.edu. *Application contact:* Joanne Canyon-Heller, Coordinator of Graduate Admission, 877-APPLY RU, Fax: 312-281-3356, E-mail: applyru@roosevelt.edu.

Rutgers, The State University of New Jersey, Newark, Graduate School, Program in Management, Newark, NJ 07102. Offers accounting (PhD); accounting information systems (PhD); computer information systems (PhD); finance (PhD); information technology (PhD); international business (PhD); management science (PhD); marketing (PhD); organization management (PhD). *Accreditation:* AACSB. *Faculty:* 101 full-time (16 women), 3 part-time/adjunct (1 woman). *Students:* 60 full-time (29 women), 32 part-time (17 women); includes 57 minority (6 African Americans, 49 Asian Americans or Pacific Islanders, 2 Hispanic Americans). 279 applicants, 13% accepted, 32 enrolled. In 2006, 10 degrees awarded. *Degree requirements:* For doctorate, thesis/dissertation, cumulative exams. *Entrance requirements:* For doctorate, GMAT or GRE, minimum undergraduate B average. Additional exam requirements/recommendations for international students: Required—TOEFL. *Application deadline:* For fall admission, 4/1 for domestic students; for spring admission, 11/1 for domestic students. Applications are processed on a rolling basis. Application fee: $50. Electronic applications accepted. *Financial support:* In 2006–07, 8 fellowships with full and partial tuition reimbursements (averaging $18,000 per year), 7 research assistantships with full tuition reimbursements (averaging $18,347 per year), teaching assistantships with full tuition reimbursements (averaging $18,347 per year) were awarded; institutionally sponsored loans and tuition waivers (full and partial) also available. Support available to part-time students. Financial award application deadline: 2/15. *Faculty research:* Technology management, leadership and teams, consumer behavior, financial and markets, logistics. *Unit head:* Dr. Glenn Shafer, Director, 973-353-1604, Fax: 973-353-5691, E-mail: gshafer@rbs.rutgers.edu. *Application contact:* Goncalo Filipe, Senior Academic Coordinator, 973-353-1002, Fax: 973-353-5691, E-mail: gfilipe@rbsmail.rutgers.edu.

Rutgers, The State University of New Jersey, Newark, Rutgers Business School: Graduate Programs-Newark/New Brunswick, Department of Business Environment, Newark, NJ 07102. Offers MBA. *Entrance requirements:* For master's, GMAT. Additional exam requirements/recommendations for international students: Required—TOEFL.

Rutgers, The State University of New Jersey, Newark, Rutgers Business School: Graduate Programs-Newark/New Brunswick, Department of Management and Global Business, Newark, NJ 07102. Offers customized concentration (MBA); global business (MBA); management and business strategy (MBA). *Entrance requirements:* For master's, GMAT. Additional exam requirements/recommendations for international students: Required—TOEFL.

Rutgers, The State University of New Jersey, Newark, Rutgers Business School: Graduate Programs-Newark/New Brunswick, Doctoral Programs in Business, Newark, NJ 07102. Offers accounting (PhD); accounting information systems (PhD); finance (PhD); individualized study (PhD); information technology (PhD); international business (PhD); management science (PhD); organizational management (PhD); supply chain management (PhD).

St. Edward's University, School of Management and Business, Area of Business Administration, Austin, TX 78704. Offers accounting (MBA); business management (MBA); entrepreneurship (MBA, Certificate); finance—general (MBA, Certificate); global business (MBA, Certificate); human resource management (MBA, Certificate); management information systems (MBA, Certificate); marketing (MBA, Certificate); operations management (MBA, Certificate); personal financial planner (MBA, Certificate); sports management (MBA). Part-time and evening/weekend programs available. *Students:* 32 full-time (16 women), 394 part-time (195 women); includes 117 minority (23 African Americans, 2 American Indian/Alaska Native, 28 Asian Americans or Pacific Islanders, 64 Hispanic Americans), 21 international. Average age 33. 121 applicants, 74% accepted, 72 enrolled. In 2006, 142 degrees awarded. *Degree requirements:* For master's, minimum 24 resident hours. *Entrance requirements:* For master's, GMAT or GRE General Test, minimum GPA of 2.75 in last 60 hours of course work. Additional exam requirements/recommendations for international students: Required—TOEFL (minimum score 550 paper-based; 213 computer-based; 79 iBT). *Application deadline:* For fall admission, 8/1 for domestic students, 7/1 for international students; for spring admission, 12/1 for domestic students, 11/1 for international students. Applications are processed on a rolling basis. Application fee: $45 ($50 for international students). Electronic applications accepted. *Expenses:* Tuition: Full-time $11,682; part-time $649 per credit hour. Full-time tuition and fees vary according to course load and program. *Financial support:* In 2006–07, 4 students received support. Scholarships/grants available. Financial award applicants required to submit FAFSA. *Faculty research:* Operations management, minority entrepreneurship, globalization, professional services marketing. *Unit head:* Dr. Dianne Hill, Director, 512-428-1295, Fax: 512-448-8492, E-mail: dianneh@stedwards.edu. *Application contact:* Natalia Quintanilla, Graduate Admissions Coordinator, 512-233-1697, Fax: 512-428-1032, E-mail: nataliaq@stedwards.edu.

St. John's University, The Peter J. Tobin College of Business, Program in International Business, Queens, NY 11439. Offers MBA, Adv C. Part-time and evening/weekend programs available. *Students:* 11 full-time (4 women), 15 part-time (8 women); includes 3 minority (1 African American, 1 Asian American or Pacific Islander, 1 Hispanic American), 8 international. Average age 26. 61 applicants, 38% accepted, 0 enrolled. In 2006, 14 degrees awarded. *Degree requirements:* For master's, thesis optional. *Entrance requirements:* For master's, GMAT, minimum GPA of 3.0. Additional exam requirements/recommendations for international students: Required—TOEFL (minimum score 500 paper-based; 173 computer-based). *Application deadline:* For fall admission, 5/1 priority date for domestic and international students; for spring admission, 11/1 priority date for domestic and international students. Applications are processed on a rolling basis. Application fee: $40. Electronic applications accepted. *Expenses:* Contact institution. Tuition and fees vary according to program. *Financial support:* Research assistantships, scholarships/grants available. Support available to part-time students. Financial award application deadline: 3/1; financial award applicants required to submit FAFSA. *Unit head:* Dr. Nejdet Delener, Coordinator, 718-990-6764, E-mail: delenern@stjohns.edu. *Application contact:* Nicole T. Bryan, Assistant Dean, 718-990-2599, Fax: 718-990-5242, E-mail: mbaadmissions@stjohns.edu.

Saint Joseph's University, Erivan K. Haub School of Business, Professional MBA Program, Program in International Business, Philadelphia, PA 19131-1395. Offers MBA. Part-time and evening/weekend programs available. *Students:* 6 full-time (2 women), 13 part-time (8 women); includes 13 minority (2 African Americans, 11 Hispanic Americans), 4 international. Average age 30. In 2006, 3 degrees awarded. *Entrance requirements:* For master's, GMAT, 2 letters of recommendation, resumé. Additional exam requirements/recommendations for international students: Required—TOEFL (minimum score 550 paper-based; 213 computer-based). *Application deadline:* For fall admission, 7/15 priority date for domestic students, 4/15 priority date for international students; for spring admission, 11/15 priority date for domestic students, 10/15 priority date for international students. Applications are processed on a rolling basis. Application fee: $35. *Financial support:* Unspecified assistantships available. Financial award application deadline: 5/1. *Application contact:* Maria D. Gaglione, Assistant Director, Graduate Business Programs, 610-660-1695, Fax: 610-660-1599, E-mail: sjumba@sju.edu.

Saint Joseph's University, Erivan K. Haub School of Business, Professional MBA Program, Program in International Marketing, Philadelphia, PA 19131-1395. Offers MBA. Part-time and evening/weekend programs available. *Entrance requirements:* For master's, GMAT, 2 letters of recommendation, resumé. Additional exam requirements/recommendations for international students: Required—TOEFL. *Application deadline:* Applications are processed on a rolling basis. Application fee: $35. Electronic applications accepted. *Financial support:* Unspecified assistantships available. Financial award application deadline: 5/1. *Unit head:* Christine Kaczmar-Russo, Director, 610-660-1238, Fax: 610-660-3239, E-mail: ckaczmar@sju.edu.

Saint Joseph's University, Erivan K. Haub School of Business, Program in International Marketing, Philadelphia, PA 19131-1395. Offers MS. Part-time and evening/weekend programs available. *Faculty:* 3 full-time (1 woman), 3 part-time/adjunct (1 woman). *Students:* 22 full-time (11 women), 19 part-time (14 women); includes 6 minority (2 Asian Americans or Pacific Islanders, 4 Hispanic Americans), 5 international. Average age 26. In 2006, 17 degrees awarded. *Entrance requirements:* For master's, GMAT, 2 letters of recommendation, resumé. Additional exam requirements/recommendations for international students: Required—TOEFL (minimum score 550 paper-based; 213 computer-based). *Application deadline:* For fall admission, 7/15 priority date for domestic students; for spring admission, 11/15 for domestic students. Applications are processed on a rolling basis. Application fee: $35. Electronic applications accepted. *Financial support:* In 2006–07, 5 students received support, including research assistantships with partial tuition reimbursements available (averaging $2,000 per year); career-related internships or fieldwork, Federal Work-Study, institutionally sponsored loans, and unspecified assistantships also available. Financial award application deadline: 5/15; financial award applicants required to submit FAFSA. *Faculty research:* Export marketing, international marketing research, global marketing. *Unit head:* Christine Kaczmar-Russo, Director, 610-660-1238, Fax: 610-660-3239, E-mail: ckaczmar@sju.edu.

Saint Louis University, Graduate School, John Cook School of Business, Boeing Institute of International Business, St. Louis, MO 63103-2097. Offers business administration (PhD), including international business and marketing; executive international business (EMIB); international business (MBA). Part-time and evening/weekend programs available. *Faculty:* 5 full-time (1 woman), 2 part-time/adjunct (0 women). *Students:* 2 full-time (0 women), 46 part-time (18 women); includes 8 minority (3 African Americans, 3 Asian Americans or Pacific Islanders, 2 Hispanic Americans), 1 international. Average age 38. 31 applicants, 84% accepted, 26 enrolled. In 2006, 2 master's, 4 doctorates awarded. *Degree requirements:* For master's, thesis, study abroad. *Entrance requirements:* For master's, GMAT, work experience. Additional exam requirements/recommendations for international students: Required—TOEFL (minimum score 525 paper-based; 194 computer-based). *Application deadline:* Applications are processed on a rolling basis. Application fee: $90. *Expenses:* Contact institution. *Financial support:* In 2006–07, 21 students received support, including 5 teaching assistantships with full tuition reimbursements available (averaging $11,000 per year); Federal Work-Study, scholarships/grants, traineeships, health care benefits, and unspecified assistantships also available. Support available to part-time students. Financial award application deadline: 6/1; financial award applicants required to submit FAFSA. *Faculty research:* Foreign direct investment, technology transfer, emerging markets, Asian business, Latin American business. Total annual research expenditures: $60,000. *Unit head:* Dr. Seung H. Kim, Director, 314-977-3898, Fax: 314-977-7188, E-mail: kimsh@slu.edu. *Application contact:* Mary M. Aita, Program Coordinator, 314-977-3631, Fax: 314-977-7188, E-mail: emib@alu.edu.

Saint Mary's University of Minnesota, School of Graduate and Professional Programs, Program in International Business, Winona, MN 55987-1399. Offers MA. *Unit head:* Jay Skranka, Director, 507-457-6696, Fax: 612-728-5121, E-mail: jskranka@smumn.edu.

St. Mary's University of San Antonio, Graduate School, Bill Greehey School of Business, MBA Program, San Antonio, TX 78228-8507. Offers finance (MBA); international business (MBA); management (MBA). *Faculty:* 17 full-time (6 women), 1 part-time/adjunct (0 women). *Students:* 19 full-time (9 women), 75 part-time (32 women); includes 38 minority (1 African American, 2 Asian Americans or Pacific Islanders, 35 Hispanic Americans), 3 international. Average age 29. In 2006, 34 degrees awarded. *Expenses:* Tuition: Full-time $10,890; part-time $605 per hour. Required fees: $500. Tuition and fees vary according to degree level. *Unit head:* Dr. Monica Parzinger, Director, 210-436-3708.

Saint Peter's College, MBA Programs, Jersey City, NJ 07306-5997. Offers finance (MBA); international business (MBA); management (MBA); management information systems (MBA);

International Business

Saint Peter's College (continued)
marketing (MBA); MBA/MS. Part-time and evening/weekend programs available. *Degree requirements:* For master's, exit presentation. *Entrance requirements:* For master's, GMAT or MAT. *Faculty research:* International finance, operations research, expert systems, networking, decision support systems.

St. Thomas University, School of Graduate Studies, Department of Management, Miami Gardens, FL 33054-6459. Offers accounting (MBA); general management (MSM, Certificate); health management (MBA, MSM, Certificate); human resource management (MBA, MSM, Certificate); international business (MBA, MIB, MSM, Certificate); justice administration (MSM, Certificate); management accounting (MSM, Certificate); public management (MSM, Certificate). Part-time and evening/weekend programs available. *Degree requirements:* For master's, comprehensive exam. *Entrance requirements:* For master's, interview, minimum GPA of 3.0 or GMAT. Additional exam requirements/recommendations for international students: Required—TOEFL. Electronic applications accepted.

Salem International University, School of Business, Salem, WV 26426-0500. Offers information security (eMBA); international business (MBA). Part-time programs available. Postbaccalaureate distance learning degree programs offered (no on-campus study). *Faculty:* 8 full-time (2 women), 13 part-time/adjunct (4 women). *Students:* 50 full-time (22 women), 88 part-time (31 women); includes 1 minority (African American), 87 international. 9 applicants, 56% accepted, 5 enrolled. In 2006, 1 degree awarded. *Degree requirements:* For master's, registration. *Entrance requirements:* For master's, GRE or GMAT, minimum undergraduate GPA of 2.5, course work in business, resumé. Additional exam requirements/recommendations for international students: Required—TOEFL (minimum score 550 paper-based). *Application deadline:* For fall admission, 8/15 priority date for domestic and international students; for winter admission, 12/15 priority date for domestic and international students; for spring admission, 4/15 priority date for domestic and international students. Applications are processed on a rolling basis. Application fee: $25. Electronic applications accepted. *Expenses: Contact institution.* One-time fee: $25 part-time. Tuition and fees vary according to program. *Financial support:* In 2006–07, 1 student received support. Career-related internships or fieldwork, institutionally sponsored loans, and tuition waivers (partial) available. *Faculty research:* Organizational behavior strategy, marketing services. *Unit head:* Dean, 304-326-1609, Fax: 304-326-1246. *Application contact:* Thomas White, Director of Admissions, 304-326-1549, Fax: 304-326-1246, E-mail: admission@salemiu.edu.

San Diego State University, Graduate and Research Affairs, College of Business Administration, Program in International Business, San Diego, CA 92182. Offers MS. Evening/weekend programs available. *Students:* 16 full-time (5 women), 11 part-time (6 women); includes 4 minority (1 American Indian/Alaska Native, 1 Asian American or Pacific Islander, 2 Hispanic Americans), 12 international. Average age 29. 22 applicants, 91% accepted, 9 enrolled. In 2006, 24 degrees awarded. *Degree requirements:* For master's, thesis or alternative. *Entrance requirements:* For master's, GMAT, resumé, letters of reference. Additional exam requirements/recommendations for international students: Required—TOEFL. *Application deadline:* For fall admission, 4/15 priority date for domestic students; for spring admission, 11/1 for domestic students. Applications are processed on a rolling basis. Application fee: $55. Electronic applications accepted. *Financial support:* Career-related internships or fieldwork available. *Faculty research:* International management. *Unit head:* Steven Loughrin-Sacco, Co-Director, 619-594-3008, Fax: 619-594-7738, E-mail: loughrin@mail.sdsu.edu. *Application contact:* Information Contact, E-mail: sdsumba@mail.sdsu.edu.

Schiller International University, Graduate Programs, London, Program in International Business, London, United Kingdom. Offers international business (MBA); management of information technology (MBA). Part-time programs available. Postbaccalaureate distance learning degree programs offered (no on-campus study). *Students:* 46 full-time. Average age 23. *Degree requirements:* For master's, GMAT before graduation, thesis optional. *Entrance requirements:* Additional exam requirements/recommendations for international students: Required—TOEFL (minimum score 550 paper-based; 213 computer-based). *Application deadline:* For fall admission, 8/1 priority date for domestic and international students; for spring admission, 12/1 priority date for domestic and international students. Applications are processed on a rolling basis. Application fee: $60. *Expenses:* Tuition: Full-time $20,306; part-time $1,601 per course. *Financial support:* Career-related internships or fieldwork and scholarships/grants available. Support available to part-time students. Financial award application deadline: 3/30; financial award applicants required to submit FAFSA. *Unit head:* Dr. Elizabeth Nunn, Director, 44-207-928-1372, Fax: 44-207-620-1226, E-mail: admissions@schillerlondon.ac.uk. *Application contact:* Susan Russeff, Associate Director of Admissions, 727-736-5082, Fax: 727-734-0359, E-mail: admissions@schiller.edu.

Schiller International University, Graduate Programs, London, Program in International Management, London, United Kingdom. Offers MIM. Part-time programs available. *Students:* 5 full-time (2 women), 1 part-time. *Degree requirements:* For master's, thesis optional. *Entrance requirements:* Additional exam requirements/recommendations for international students: Required—TOEFL (minimum score 550 paper-based; 213 computer-based). *Application deadline:* For fall admission, 8/1 priority date for domestic and international students; for spring admission, 12/1 priority date for domestic and international students. Applications are processed on a rolling basis. Application fee: $50. *Expenses:* Tuition: Full-time $20,306; part-time $1,601 per course. *Financial support:* Application deadline: 3/30; *Unit head:* Peter Bell, Director, 207-928-1372, Fax: 207-620-1226, E-mail: admissions@schillerlondon.ac.uk. *Application contact:* Susan Russeff, Associate Director of Admissions, 727-736-5082, Fax: 727-734-0359, E-mail: admissions@schiller.edu.

Schiller International University, MBA Program, Madrid, Spain, Madrid, Spain. Offers international business (MBA). Part-time programs available. *Faculty:* 6 full-time, 4 part-time/adjunct. *Students:* 7 full-time, 3 part-time. Average age 28. *Degree requirements:* For master's, thesis optional. *Entrance requirements:* Additional exam requirements/recommendations for international students: Required—TOEFL (minimum score 550 paper-based; 213 computer-based). *Application deadline:* For fall admission, 8/1 priority date for domestic and international students; for spring admission, 12/1 priority date for domestic and international students. Applications are processed on a rolling basis. Application fee: $60. *Expenses:* Tuition: Full-time $20,958; part-time $1,652 per course. Tuition and fees vary according to degree level. *Financial support:* In 2006–07, 8 students received support. Career-related internships or fieldwork, scholarships/grants, tuition waivers (partial), and unspecified assistantships available. Support available to part-time students. Financial award application deadline: 3/30; financial award applicants required to submit FAFSA. *Unit head:* Lynn Bergunde, Adviser, 34-91-448-2488, Fax: 34-91-445-2110, E-mail: admissions@schillermadrid.edu. *Application contact:* Susan Russeff, Associate Director of Admissions, 727-736-5082, Fax: 727-734-0359, E-mail: admissions@schiller.edu.

Schiller International University, MBA Program Paris, France, Paris, France. Offers international business (MBA). Bilingual French/English MBA available for native French speakers. Part-time and evening/weekend programs available. *Faculty:* 5 full-time (1 woman), 10 part-time/adjunct (5 women). *Students:* 50. In 2006, 12 degrees awarded. *Degree requirements:* For master's, thesis or alternative, comprehensive exam, registration. *Entrance requirements:* Additional exam requirements/recommendations for international students: Required—TOEFL (minimum score 550 paper-based; 213 computer-based). *Application deadline:* For fall admission, 8/1 priority date for domestic and international students; for spring admission, 12/1 priority date for domestic and international students. Applications are processed on a rolling basis. Application fee: $60. Tuition charges are reported in euros. *Expenses:* Tuition: Full-time 21,812 euros; part-time 1,724 euros per course. Tuition and fees vary according to degree level. *Financial support:* In 2006–07, 14 students received support; teaching assistantships, scholarships/grants, tuition waivers (partial), and unspecified assistantships available. Support available to part-time students. Financial award application deadline: 3/30; financial award applicants required to submit FAFSA. *Unit head:* Hassan Mansoor, Adviser, 1-4538-5601, Fax: 1-4538-5430, E-mail: info-schiller@schillerparis.com. *Application contact:* Kamala Dontamsetti, Associate Director of Admissions, 813-736-5082 Ext. 240, Fax: 813-734-0359, E-mail: admissions@schiller.edu.

Schiller International University, MBA Programs, Florida, Program in International Business, Largo, FL 33770. Offers MBA. Part-time and evening/weekend programs available. Postbaccalaureate distance learning degree programs offered (no on-campus study). *Students:* 35 full-time, 36 part-time. Average age 25. *Degree requirements:* For master's, thesis optional. *Entrance requirements:* Additional exam requirements/recommendations for international students: Required—TOEFL (minimum score 550 paper-based; 213 computer-based). *Application deadline:* For fall admission, 8/1 priority date for domestic and international students; for spring admission, 12/1 priority date for domestic and international students. Applications are processed on a rolling basis. Application fee: $60. *Expenses:* Tuition: Full-time $17,920; part-time $1,420 per course. *Financial support:* Federal Work-Study, scholarships/grants, and tuition waivers (partial) available. Support available to part-time students. Financial award application deadline: 3/30; financial award applicants required to submit FAFSA. *Unit head:* Tom Evans, Director of International Business, 727-736-5082 Ext. 277, Fax: 727-736-6263, E-mail: tom_evans@schiller.edu. *Application contact:* Susan Russeff, Associate Director of Admissions, 727-736-5082, Fax: 727-734-0359, E-mail: admissions@schiller.edu.

Schiller International University, MBA Programs, Heidelberg, Germany, Heidelberg, Germany. Offers international business (MBA, MIM); management of information technology (MBA). Part-time and evening/weekend programs available. *Faculty:* 7 full-time (3 women), 14 part-time/adjunct (4 women). *Students:* 28 full-time, 4 part-time. Average age 28. In 2006, 15 degrees awarded. *Degree requirements:* For master's, thesis optional. *Entrance requirements:* Additional exam requirements/recommendations for international students: Required—TOEFL (minimum score 550 paper-based; 213 computer-based). *Application deadline:* For fall admission, 8/1 priority date for domestic and international students; for spring admission, 12/1 priority date for domestic and international students. Applications are processed on a rolling basis. Application fee: $60. Tuition charges are reported in euros. *Expenses:* Tuition: Full-time 20,938 euros; part-time 1,651 euros per course. *Financial support:* In 2006–07, 32 students received support. Scholarships/grants, tuition waivers (partial), and unspecified assistantships available. Support available to part-time students. Financial award application deadline: 3/30; financial award applicants required to submit FAFSA. *Faculty research:* Leadership, international economy, foreign direct investment. *Unit head:* Dr. Nicolle Macho, Director, 49-6221-458135, Fax: 49-6221-402703, E-mail: campus@siu-heidelberg.de. *Application contact:* Susan Russeff, Assistant Director of Admissions, 727-736-5082, Fax: 727-734-0359, E-mail: admissions@schiller.edu.

Schiller International University, MBA Program, Strasbourg, France Campus, Strasbourg, France. Offers international business (MBA). Part-time and evening/weekend programs available. Postbaccalaureate distance learning degree programs offered (no on-campus study). *Faculty:* 8. *Students:* Average age 28. In 2006, 13 degrees awarded. *Degree requirements:* For master's, GMAT before graduation, oral comprehensive exam or thesis. *Entrance requirements:* For master's, BBA. Additional exam requirements/recommendations for international students: Recommended—TOEFL (minimum score 550 paper-based; 213 computer-based). *Application deadline:* For fall admission, 8/1 priority date for domestic and international students; for spring admission, 12/1 priority date for domestic and international students. Applications are processed on a rolling basis. Application fee: $60. *Expenses:* Tuition: Part-time $1,282 per course. *Financial support:* Teaching assistantships, tuition waivers (partial) and unspecified assistantships available. Support available to part-time students. Financial award application deadline: 3/30; financial award applicants required to submit FAFSA. *Unit head:* Anne Zedler, Director, 33-3884-58464, Fax: 33-3884-58460, E-mail: siustrmba@aol.com. *Application contact:* Kamala Dontamsetti, Associate Director of Admissions, 727-736-5082 Ext. 240, Fax: 727-734-0359, E-mail: admissions@schiller.edu.

Schiller International University, American College of Switzerland, MBA Program, Leysin, Switzerland. Offers international business (MBA). Part-time programs available. Postbaccalaureate distance learning degree programs offered (no on-campus study). *Faculty:* 6. *Students:* 8 full-time. Average age 23. *Degree requirements:* For master's, thesis or alternative, comprehensive exam, registration. *Entrance requirements:* For master's, bachelor's degree in business or BA with specific core courses. Additional exam requirements/recommendations for international students: Recommended—TOEFL (minimum score 550 paper-based; 213 computer-based). *Application deadline:* For fall admission, 8/1 priority date for domestic and international students; for spring admission, 12/1 priority date for domestic and international students. Applications are processed on a rolling basis. Application fee: $60. *Expenses:* Tuition: Full-time $22,622; part-time $1,178 per course. *Financial support:* In 2006–07, 3 students received support, including teaching assistantships (averaging $6,895 per year); career-related internships or fieldwork, scholarships/grants, tuition waivers (partial), and unspecified assistantships also available. Support available to part-time students. Financial award application deadline: 4/1; financial award applicants required to submit FAFSA. *Unit head:* Nancy Carroll, Provost, 41-244930303, Fax: 41-244930300, E-mail: acs_provost@bluewin.ch. *Application contact:* Bethani Ann Delong Vehapi, Director of Admissions, 41-244930309, Fax: 41-244930300, E-mail: siuadmissions@bluewin.ch.

School for International Training, Graduate Programs, Master's Programs in Intercultural Service, Leadership, and Management, Brattleboro, VT 05302-0676. Offers conflict transformation (MA); intercultural service, leadership, and management (MA); international education (MA); management (MS); social justice in intercultural relations (MA); sustainable development (MA). Postbaccalaureate distance learning degree programs offered (minimal on-campus study). *Students:* 182 full-time (116 women), 298 part-time (215 women); includes 60 minority (27 African Americans, 1 American Indian/Alaska Native, 14 Asian Americans or Pacific Islanders, 18 Hispanic Americans), 96 international. Average age 30. 634 applicants, 73% accepted, 157 enrolled. In 2006, 84 master's awarded. *Degree requirements:* For master's, one foreign language, thesis. *Entrance requirements:* For master's, 3 letters of reference. Additional exam requirements/recommendations for international students: Required—TOEFL. *Application deadline:* Applications are processed on a rolling basis. Application fee: $50. *Expenses:* Tuition: Full-time $27,355; part-time $638 per credit hour. Required fees: $1,092. *Financial support:* Career-related internships or fieldwork, Federal Work-Study, institutionally sponsored loans, and scholarships/grants available. Financial award application deadline: 3/1; financial award applicants required to submit FAFSA. *Faculty research:* Intercultural communication, conflict resolution, advising and training, world issues, international business. *Unit head:* Marla Solomon, Graduate Dean, 802-258-3325, Fax: 802-258-3241, E-mail: marla.solomon@sit.edu. *Application contact:* Information Contact, 800-336-1616, Fax: 802-258-3500, E-mail: admissions@sit.edu.

Seton Hall University, Stillman School of Business, Department of International Business, South Orange, NJ 07079-2692. Offers MS, Certificate, MADIR/MSIB, MBA/MSIB. Part-time and evening/weekend programs available. *Faculty:* 3 full-time (0 women), 2 part-time/adjunct (0 women). *Students:* 10 full-time (4 women), 16 part-time (4 women); includes 8 minority (5 Asian Americans or Pacific Islanders, 3 Hispanic Americans). Average age 32. 21 applicants, 19% accepted, 3 enrolled. In 2006, 11 degrees awarded. *Median time to degree:* Master's–1.25 years full-time, 1.7 years part-time. *Degree requirements:* For master's, registration. *Entrance requirements:* For master's, GMAT (or 3 years international business experience), minimum GPA of 2.75; for Certificate, master's degree. Additional exam requirements/recommendations for international students: Required—TOEFL (minimum score 550 paper-based; 213 computer-based). *Application deadline:* For fall admission, 6/1 priority date for domestic students, 5/1 for international students; for spring admission, 11/1 for domestic students, 10/1 for international students. Applications are processed on a rolling basis. Application fee: $75 ($100 for international students). Electronic applications accepted. *Expenses: Contact institution. Financial support:* In 2006–07, 7 students received support, including 2 research assistantships (averaging $5,400 per year); career-related internships or fieldwork, Federal Work-Study, scholarships/grants, health care benefits, and unspecified assistantships also available. Support available to part-time students. Financial award application deadline: 6/1; financial award applicants required to submit FAFSA. *Faculty research:* International marketing, Asian financial markets, economics in eastern Europe and accounting in the Middle East. *Unit head:* Dr. Hector Lozada, Director, 973-761-9259, Fax: 973-761-9217, E-mail: lozadahe@shu.edu. *Application contact:* Catherine Bianchi, Director of Graduate Admissions, 973-761-9220, Fax: 973-761-9208, E-mail: biancha@shu.edu.

Seton Hall University, Stillman School of Business, Programs in Business Administration, South Orange, NJ 07079-2697. Offers accounting (MBA); finance (MBA); financial markets, institutions and instruments (MBA); healthcare management (MBA); information systems (MBA); international business (MBA); management (MBA); marketing (MBA); pharmaceutical management (MBA); sport management (MBA). Part-time and evening/weekend programs available. *Faculty:* 57 full-time (13 women), 30 part-time/adjunct (3 women). *Students:* 57 full-time (16 women), 180 part-time (57 women); includes 9 African Americans, 10 Asian Americans or Pacific Islanders, 7 Hispanic Americans. Average age 29. 195 applicants, 47% accepted, 48 enrolled. In 2006, 144 degrees awarded. *Median time to degree:* Master's–1.6 years full-time, 2.3 years part-time. *Degree requirements:* For master's, 20 hours of community service (Social Responsibility Project). *Entrance requirements:* For master's, GMAT, minimum GPA of 2.75. Additional exam requirements/recommendations for international students: Required—TOEFL (minimum score 550 paper-based; 213 computer-based). *Application deadline:* For fall admission, 6/1 priority date for domestic students; for spring admission, 11/1 priority date for domestic students. Applications are processed on a rolling basis. Application fee: $75 ($100 for international students). Electronic applications accepted. *Financial support:* In 2006–07, 40 students received support, including research assistantships with full and partial tuition reimbursements available (averaging $5,400 per year); career-related internships or fieldwork, Federal Work-Study, scholarships/grants, and unspecified assistantships also available. Support available to part-time students. Financial award application deadline: 6/1; financial award applicants required to submit FAFSA. *Faculty research:* Financial, hedge funds, international business, legal issues, disclosure and branding. *Unit head:* Dr. Joyce A. Strawser, Associate Dean for Undergraduate and MBA Curricula, 973-761-9225, Fax: 973-761-9217, E-mail: strawsjo@shu.edu. *Application contact:* Catherine Bianchi, Director of Graduate Admissions, 973-761-9220, Fax: 973-761-9208, E-mail: biancha@shu.edu.

Simon Fraser University, Graduate Studies, Faculty of Business Administration, Burnaby, BC V5A 1S6, Canada. Offers business administration (EMBA); decision support systems (MBA); international business (MBA); management, organization studies (MBA); marketing (MBA); MBA/MRM. *Accreditation:* AACSB. Postbaccalaureate distance learning degree programs offered. *Degree requirements:* For master's, thesis or written project. *Entrance requirements:* For master's, minimum GPA of 3.0. Additional exam requirements/recommendations for international students: Required—TOEFL. Expenses: Contact institution. *Faculty research:* Leadership, marketing and technology, wealth management.

Southeastern University, College of Graduate Studies, Program in Business Management, Washington, DC 20024-2788. Offers international management (MBA); management (MBA). Part-time and evening/weekend programs available. *Degree requirements:* For master's, thesis optional. *Entrance requirements:* Additional exam requirements/recommendations for international students: Required—TOEFL.

Southeast Missouri State University, School of Graduate Studies, Harrison College of Business, Cape Girardeau, MO 63701-4799. Offers accounting (MBA); environmental management (MBA); finance (MBA); general management (MBA); health administration (MBA); industrial management (MBA); international business (MBA). *Accreditation:* AACSB. Part-time and evening/weekend programs available. Postbaccalaureate distance learning degree programs offered (no on-campus study). *Faculty:* 33 full-time (10 women). *Students:* 35 full-time (18 women), 40 part-time (24 women); includes 5 minority (2 African Americans, 3 Asian Americans or Pacific Islanders), 9 international. Average age 27. 35 applicants, 86% accepted. In 2006, 23 degrees awarded. *Degree requirements:* For master's, applied research project. *Entrance requirements:* For master's, GMAT, minimum undergraduate GPA of 2.5. Additional exam requirements/recommendations for international students: Required—TOEFL (minimum score 550 paper-based; 213 computer-based). *Application deadline:* For fall admission, 8/1 for domestic students, 4/1 for international students; for spring admission, 11/21 for domestic students, 10/1 for international students. Applications are processed on a rolling basis. Application fee: $20 ($100 for international students). *Financial support:* In 2006–07, 54 students received support, including 31 research assistantships with full tuition reimbursements available (averaging $7,100 per year); career-related internships or fieldwork and unspecified assistantships also available. Financial award applicants required to submit FAFSA. *Unit head:* Dr. Kenneth Heischmidt, Director MBA Program, 573-651-2912, Fax: 573-651-5032, E-mail: kheischmidt@semo.edu. *Application contact:* Marsha L. Arant, Senior Administrative Assistant, Office of Graduate Studies, 573-651-2192, Fax: 573-651-2001, E-mail: marant@semo.edu.

Southern New Hampshire University, School of Business, Manchester, NH 03106-1045. Offers accounting (MS); business administration (MBA, Certificate), including accounting (Certificate), business administration (MBA), finance (Certificate), forensic accounting (Certificate), human resources management (Certificate), international business (Certificate), international sport management (Certificate), leadership of not for profit organizations (Certificate), marketing (Certificate), operations management (Certificate), sport management (Certificate), taxation (Certificate); finance (MS); hospitality and tourism leadership (Certificate); information technology (MS, Certificate); information technology/international business (Certificate); integrated marketing communications (Certificate); international business (MS, DBA); marketing (MS); operations and project management (MS); organizational leadership (MS); project management (Certificate); sport management (MS); MBA/Certificate. *Accreditation:* ACBSP. Part-time and evening/weekend programs available. Postbaccalaureate distance learning degree programs offered (no on-campus study). *Faculty:* 45 full-time, 75 part-time/adjunct. *Students:* 427 full-time (184 women), 774 part-time (428 women). Average age 32. In 2006, 682 master's, 1 doctorate awarded. Terminal master's awarded for partial completion of doctoral program. *Degree requirements:* For master's, one foreign language, thesis or alternative, comprehensive exam (for some programs); for doctorate, one foreign language, thesis/dissertation, comprehensive exam. *Entrance requirements:* For master's, minimum GPA of 2.5; for doctorate, GMAT. Additional exam requirements/recommendations for international students: Required—TOEFL (minimum score 500 paper-based). *Application deadline:* Applications are processed on a rolling basis. Application fee: $25. Electronic applications accepted. *Financial support:* Career-related internships or fieldwork, Federal Work-Study, institutionally sponsored loans, tuition waivers (partial), and unspecified assistantships available. Support available to part-time students. Financial award applicants required to submit FAFSA. *Unit head:* Dr. Martin Bradley, Dean, 603-644-3102, Fax: 603-644-3144, E-mail: m.bradley@snhu.edu. *Application contact:* Scott Durand, Director of Graduate Enrollment Services, 603-644-3102 Ext. 3338, Fax: 603-644-3144, E-mail: s.durand@snhu.edu.

See Close-Up on page 325.

Stevens Institute of Technology, Graduate School, Wesley J. Howe School of Technology Management, Program in Management, Hoboken, NJ 07030. Offers general management (MS); global innovation management (MS); human resource management (MS); information management (MS); project management (MS); technology commercialization (MS); technology management (MS). Part-time programs available. *Degree requirements:* For master's, thesis optional. *Entrance requirements:* For master's, GMAT, GRE General Test. Additional exam requirements/recommendations for international students: Required—TOEFL. Electronic applications accepted. *Faculty research:* Industrial economics.

Suffolk University, College of Arts and Sciences, Department of Economics, Boston, MA 02108-2770. Offers economic policy (MSEP); economics (PhD); international economics (MSIE); JD/MSIE. Part-time and evening/weekend programs available. *Faculty:* 12 full-time (4 women). *Students:* 20 full-time (6 women), 18 part-time (7 women); includes 12 minority (1 African American, 2 Asian Americans or Pacific Islanders, 9 Hispanic Americans), 19 international. Average age 29. 85 applicants, 68% accepted, 15 enrolled. In 2006, 7 degrees awarded. *Degree requirements:* For doctorate, thesis/dissertation, comprehensive exam. *Entrance requirements:* For master's, GRE General Test or GMAT; for doctorate, GRE, letters of recommendation. Additional exam requirements/recommendations for international students: Required—TOEFL (minimum score 550 paper-based; 213 computer-based; 80 iBT). *Application deadline:* For fall admission, 6/15 priority date for domestic students, 6/15 for international students; for spring admission, 11/1 priority date for domestic students, 11/1 for international students. Applications are processed on a rolling basis. Application fee: $35. Electronic applications accepted. *Expenses:* Contact institution. *Financial support:* In 2006–07, 27 fellowships with full and partial tuition reimbursements (averaging $18,541 per year) were awarded; career-related internships or fieldwork, Federal Work-Study, and institutionally sponsored loans also available. Support available to part-time students. Financial award application deadline: 4/1; financial award applicants required to submit FAFSA. *Faculty research:* Trade demands, fair tax, smoking, multinational firms, charitable giving. *Unit head:* Dr. David Tuerch, Director, 617-573-8670, Fax: 617-720-4272, E-mail: dtuerch@suffolk.edu. *Application contact:* Judith Reynolds, Director of Graduate Admissions, 617-573-8302, Fax: 617-523-0116, E-mail: grad.admission@suffolk.edu.

Sul Ross State University, School of Professional Studies, Department of Business Administration, Alpine, TX 79832. Offers international trade (MBA); management (MBA). Part-time and evening/weekend programs available. *Degree requirements:* For master's, thesis optional. *Entrance requirements:* For master's, GMAT or GRE General Test, minimum GPA of 2.5 in last 60 hours of undergraduate work. *Faculty research:* Cross-cultural comparisons, U.S.-Mexico management relations.

Temple University, Graduate School, Fox School of Business and Management, Doctoral Programs in Business, Philadelphia, PA 19122-6096. Offers accounting (PhD); economics (PhD); finance (PhD); general and strategic management (PhD); healthcare management (PhD); human resource administration (PhD); international business administration (PhD); management information systems (PhD); management science/operations research (PhD); marketing (PhD); risk, insurance, and health-care management (PhD); statistics (PhD); tourism (PhD). *Accreditation:* AACSB. *Entrance requirements:* For doctorate, GRE General Test, minimum GPA of 3.0, master's degree. Additional exam requirements/recommendations for international students: Required—TOEFL. *Expenses:* Tuition, state resident: full-time $12,264; part-time $511 per credit. Tuition, nonresident: full-time $17,904; part-time $746 per credit. Required fees: $84 per course. Tuition and fees vary according to program.

Temple University, Graduate School, Fox School of Business and Management, Masters Programs in Business, MBA Programs, Philadelphia, PA 19122-6096. Offers accounting (MBA); business administration (EMBA, MBA); e-business (MBA); economics (MBA); finance (MBA); general and strategic management (MBA); healthcare management (MBA); human resource administration (MBA); international business (IMBA); management information systems (MBA); management science/operations management (MBA); marketing (MBA); risk management and insurance (MBA); statistics (MBA). EMBA offered in Philadelphia, PA and Tokyo, Japan. *Accreditation:* AACSB. *Entrance requirements:* For master's, GMAT, minimum undergraduate GPA of 3.0. Additional exam requirements/recommendations for international students: Required—TOEFL. *Expenses:* Tuition, state resident: full-time $12,264; part-time $511 per credit. Tuition, nonresident: full-time $17,904; part-time $746 per credit. Required fees: $84 per course. Tuition and fees vary according to program.

Texas A&M International University, Office of Graduate Studies and Research, College of Business Administration, Division of International Business and Technology Studies, Laredo, TX 78041-1900. Offers information systems (MSIS); international trade (MBA). *Faculty:* 8 full-time (0 women), 1 part-time/adjunct (0 women). *Students:* 30 full-time (8 women), 14 part-time (5 women); includes 12 minority (all Hispanic Americans), 32 international. Average age 25. 81 applicants, 41% accepted, 20 enrolled. In 2006, 26 degrees awarded. *Degree requirements:* For master's, thesis (for some programs). *Entrance requirements:* For master's, GMAT or GRE General Test. Additional exam requirements/recommendations for international students: Required—TOEFL (minimum score 550 paper-based; 213 computer-based). *Application deadline:* For fall admission, 7/15 priority date for domestic students; for spring admission, 11/12 for domestic students. Applications are processed on a rolling basis. Application fee: $25. *Expenses:* Tuition, state resident: full-time $1,580. Tuition, nonresident: full-time $5,432. Required fees: $3,808. *Financial support:* In 2006–07, 33 students received support; fellowships, Federal Work-Study, institutionally sponsored loans, and scholarships/grants available. Support available to part-time students. *Unit head:* Dr. Ned Kock, Chair, 956-326-2521, Fax: 956-326-2494, E-mail: nedkock@tamiu.edu. *Application contact:* Imelda Lopez, Graduate Admissions Counselor, 956-326-2485, Fax: 956-326-2459, E-mail: lopez@tamiu.edu.

Texas A&M University–Corpus Christi, Graduate Studies and Research, College of Business, Corpus Christi, TX 78412-5503. Offers accounting (M Acc); health care administration (MBA); international business (MBA). *Accreditation:* AACSB. Part-time and evening/weekend programs available. *Degree requirements:* For master's, thesis (for some programs), comprehensive exam, registration. *Entrance requirements:* For master's, GMAT. Additional exam requirements/recommendations for international students: Required—TOEFL. Electronic applications accepted.

Texas Christian University, M. J. Neeley School of Business, Program in International Management, Fort Worth, TX 76129-0002. Offers MIM. *Expenses:* Tuition: Part-time $800 per credit hour. *Unit head:* Dr. Greg Stephens, Chairperson, 817-257-7548.

Texas Tech University, Jerry S. Rawls College of Business Administration, Programs in Business Administration, Lubbock, TX 79409. Offers agricultural business (MBA); entrepreneurship (MBA); finance (MBA); general business (MBA); health organization management (MBA); international business (MBA); management and leadership skills (MBA); management information systems (MBA); marketing (MBA); statistics (MBA); JD/MBA; MBA/M Arch; MBA/MA; MBA/MD; MBA/MS. Part-time and evening/weekend programs available. *Students:* 65 full-time (16 women), 347 part-time (121 women); includes 74 minority (5 African Americans, 5 American Indian/Alaska Native, 24 Asian Americans or Pacific Islanders, 40 Hispanic Americans), 24 international. Average age 25. 382 applicants, 82% accepted, 244 enrolled. In 2006, 150 degrees awarded. *Degree requirements:* For master's, capstone course. *Entrance requirements:* For master's, GMAT, holistic review of academic credentials. Additional exam requirements/recommendations for international students: Required—TOEFL (minimum score 550 paper-based; 213 computer-based; 79 iBT). *Application deadline:* For fall admission, 7/1 priority date for domestic students, 3/1 priority date for international students; for spring admission, 11/1 priority date for domestic students, 9/1 priority date for international students. Applications are processed on a rolling basis. Application fee: $50 ($60 for international students). Electronic applications accepted. *Expenses:* Tuition, state resident: full-time $4,440. Tuition, nonresident: full-time $11,040. Required fees: $2,136. *Financial support:* In 2006–07, 36 research assistantships (averaging $8,000 per year) were awarded; teaching assistantships, career-related internships or fieldwork, Federal Work-Study, scholarships/grants, health care benefits, and unspecified assistantships also available. Support available to part-time students. Financial award applicants required to submit FAFSA. *Unit head:* Dr. W. Jay Conover, Director, 806-742-1546, Fax: 806-742-3958, E-mail: jay.conover@ttu.edu. *Application contact:* Cynthia D. Barnes, Director, Graduate Services Center, 806-742-3184, Fax: 806-742-3958, E-mail: ba_grad@ttu.edu.

Thunderbird School of Global Management, Graduate Programs, Department of Corporate Learning, Program in Global Management–Arizona, Glendale, AZ 85306-6000. Offers MBA. Part-time and evening/weekend programs available. *Faculty:* 26 part-time/adjunct (7 women). *Students:* Average age 35. 77 applicants, 78% accepted, 50 enrolled. In 2006, 46 degrees awarded. *Degree requirements:* For master's, one foreign language. *Entrance requirements:* For master's, 8 years of full-time work experience, 3 years of management experience, company sponsorship, mid-management position. *Application deadline:* For fall admission, 5/15 priority date for domestic and international students. Applications are processed

International Business

Thunderbird School of Global Management (continued)

on a rolling basis. Application fee: $50. Electronic applications accepted. *Expenses: Contact institution.* One-time fee: $625 full-time. Part-time tuition and fees vary according to course load and program. *Financial support:* In 2006–07, 25 students received support. Application deadline: 6/7; *Unit head:* Dr. Dale L. Davison, Academic Director, Executive Degree Programs, 602-978-7739, Fax: 602-843-6143, E-mail: davisond@thunderbird.edu. *Application contact:* Barbara Carpenter, Senior Director, EMBA Program, 602-978-7921, Fax: 602-978-7463, E-mail: carpentb@thunderbird.edu.

Thunderbird School of Global Management, Graduate Programs, Department of Corporate Learning, Program in Global Management–Central and Eastern Europe, Glendale, AZ 85306-6000. Offers MBA. Part-time programs available. *Faculty:* 18 part-time/adjunct (3 women). *Students:* Average age 36. 22 applicants, 91% accepted, 20 enrolled. In 2006, 24 degrees awarded. *Entrance requirements:* For master's, 8 years of full-time work experience, 3 years of management experience. *Application deadline:* For fall admission, 9/30 priority date for domestic and international students. Applications are processed on a rolling basis. Electronic applications accepted. *Expenses:* Tuition: Full-time $36,630. Required fees: $1,220. One-time fee: $625 full-time. Part-time tuition and fees vary according to course load and program. *Financial support:* Applicants required to submit FAFSA. *Unit head:* Dr. Roe Goddard, Academic Director, Executive Degree Programs, 602-978-7739, Fax: 602-843-6143, E-mail: goddardr@thunderbird.edu. *Application contact:* Julie Cook, Senior Director, +33-450-316-778, Fax: +33-450-820-593, E-mail: cookj@thunderbird.edu.

Thunderbird School of Global Management, Graduate Programs, Department of Corporate Learning, Program in Global Management—Republic of Korea, Glendale, AZ 85306-6000. Offers MBA. *Expenses:* Tuition: Full-time $36,630. Required fees: $1,220. One-time fee: $625 full-time. Part-time tuition and fees vary according to course load and program. *Unit head:* Dr. Graeme Ronkine, Academic Director, Executive Degree Programs, 602-978-7000.

Thunderbird School of Global Management, Graduate Programs, Master's Programs in Global Management, Glendale, AZ 85306-6000. Offers global affairs and management (MA); global management (MS). *Accreditation:* AACSB. *Faculty:* 40 full-time (10 women), 3 part-time/adjunct (1 woman). *Degree requirements:* For master's, one foreign language. *Entrance requirements:* For master's, GMAT/GRE. Additional exam requirements/recommendations for international students: Required—TOEFL (minimum score 567 paper-based). Application fee: $125. *Expenses:* Tuition: Full-time $36,630. Required fees: $1,220. One-time fee: $625 full-time. Part-time tuition and fees vary according to course load and program. *Financial support:* Career-related internships or fieldwork, Federal Work-Study, scholarships/grants, and unspecified assistantships available. *Unit head:* Dr. Glenn Fong, Unit Head, 602-978-7000.

Thunderbird School of Global Management, Graduate Programs, Program in Global Business Administration for Latin American Managers, Glendale, AZ 85306-6000. Offers GMBA. Offered jointly with Instituto Technológico y de Estudios Superiores de Monterrey. Part-time and evening/weekend programs available. Postbaccalaureate distance learning degree programs offered. *Faculty:* 20 full-time (5 women). *Students:* Average age 29. 226 applicants, 91% accepted, 185 enrolled. In 2006, 145 degrees awarded. *Entrance requirements:* For master's, GMAT or PAEP (Pruebade Admisiona Estudios Posgrado), minimum GPA of 3.0, 2 years of work experience. Additional exam requirements/recommendations for international students: Required—TOEFL (minimum score 550 paper-based; 213 computer-based). *Application deadline:* For spring admission, 4/30 priority date for domestic and international students. Application fee: $250. *Expenses: Contact institution.* One-time fee: $625 full-time. Part-time tuition and fees vary according to course load and program. *Financial support:* In 2006–07, 110 students received support. Scholarships/grants available. Financial award application deadline: 4/30. *Faculty research:* Globalization impact on Latin American business, doing business in Latin America, international marketing in Latin America. *Unit head:* Dr. Bert Valencia, Vice President, 602-978-7534, Fax: 602-978-7729, E-mail: globalma@thunderbird.edu.

Thunderbird School of Global Management, Graduate Programs, Program in Global Business Administration On-Demand, Glendale, AZ 85306-6000. Offers GMBA. Part-time programs available. Postbaccalaureate distance learning degree programs offered (minimal on-campus study). *Faculty:* 40 full-time (10 women), 3 part-time/adjunct (1 woman). *Students:* Average age 31. *Degree requirements:* For master's, registration. *Entrance requirements:* For master's, GMAT. Additional exam requirements/recommendations for international students: Required—TOEFL. Application fee: $125. *Expenses:* Tuition: Full-time $36,630. Required fees: $1,220. One-time fee: $625 full-time. Part-time tuition and fees vary according to course load and program. *Financial support:* In 2006–07, 65 students received support. Scholarships/grants available. Financial award application deadline: 2/15. *Unit head:* Dr. Bert Valencia, Vice President, 602-978-7534, Fax: 602-978-7729, E-mail: globalmba@thunderbird.edu.

Thunderbird School of Global Management, Graduate Programs, Program in Global Management, Glendale, AZ 85306-6000. Offers MBA, MGM/MBA. *Faculty:* 40 full-time (10 women), 3 part-time/adjunct (1 woman). *Students:* 534 full-time (167 women); includes 59 minority (5 African Americans, 39 Asian Americans or Pacific Islanders, 15 Hispanic Americans), 239 international. Average age 28. In 2006, 423 degrees awarded. *Degree requirements:* For master's, one foreign language, registration. *Entrance requirements:* For master's, GMAT, 3 years of work experience. Additional exam requirements/recommendations for international students: Required—TOEFL (minimum score 600 paper-based; 250 computer-based). *Application deadline:* For fall admission, 8/1 priority date for domestic and international students; for spring admission, 12/15 priority date for domestic and international students. Applications are processed on a rolling basis. Application fee: $125. Electronic applications accepted. *Expenses:* Tuition: Full-time $36,630. Required fees: $1,220. One-time fee: $625 full-time. Part-time tuition and fees vary according to course load and program. *Financial support:* In 2006–07, 331 students received support. Federal Work-Study and scholarships/grants available. Support available to part-time students. Financial award application deadline: 2/15; financial award applicants required to submit FAFSA. *Unit head:* Dr. Olufemi Barbarinde, Associate Professor of International Studies and Director, MBA in Global Management, 602-978-7150, Fax: 602-843-6143, E-mail: babarif@thunderbird.edu. *Application contact:* Judy Johnson, Director of Admissions, 602-978-7210, Fax: 602-439-5432, E-mail: johnsonj@thunderbird.edu.

Touro University International, College of Business Administration, Program in Business Administration, Cypress, CA 90630. Offers business administration (PhD); conflict and negotiation management (MBA); criminal justice administration (MBA); entrepreneurship (MBA); finance (MBA); general management (MBA); human resource management (MBA); information technology management (MBA); international business (MBA); logistics management (MBA); public management (MBA); strategic leadership (MBA). Part-time and evening/weekend programs available. Postbaccalaureate distance learning degree programs offered (no on-campus study). In 2006, 631 master's, 30 doctorates awarded. *Degree requirements:* For doctorate, thesis/dissertation, defense of dissertation, comprehensive exam. *Entrance requirements:* For master's, minimum GPA of 3.0; for doctorate, minimum GPA of 3.4, curriculum vitae, course work in research methods or statistics. Additional exam requirements/recommendations for international students: Required—TOEFL (minimum score 550 paper-based). *Application deadline:* Applications are processed on a rolling basis. Application fee: $75. Electronic applications accepted. *Expenses:* Tuition: Part-time $300 per credit hour. Tuition and fees vary according to course level and program.

Tufts University, Fletcher School of Law and Diplomacy, Medford, MA 02155. Offers MA, MAHA, MALD, PhD, DVM/MA, JD/MALD, MALD/MA, MALD/MBA, MALD/MS, MD/MA. Postbaccalaureate distance learning degree programs offered (minimal on-campus study). *Faculty:* 34 full-time (7 women), 31 part-time/adjunct (8 women). *Students:* 527 full-time (268 women), 9 part-time (4 women); includes 61 minority (12 African Americans, 1 American Indian/Alaska Native, 32 Asian Americans or Pacific Islanders, 16 Hispanic Americans), 212 international. Average age 31. 1,605 applicants, 40% accepted, 234 enrolled. In 2006, 203 master's, 10 doctorates awarded. *Median time to degree:* Of those who began their doctoral program in fall 1998, 75% received their degree in 8 years or less. *Degree requirements:* For master's, one foreign language, thesis, registration; for doctorate, one foreign language, thesis/dissertation, dissertation defense, comprehensive exam, registration. *Entrance requirements:* For master's and doctorate, GMAT or GRE General Test. Additional exam requirements/recommendations for international students: Required—TOEFL (minimum score 600 paper-based; 250 computer-based; 100 iBT), IELTS (minimum score 7). *Application deadline:* For fall admission, 1/15 for domestic and international students; for spring admission, 10/15 for domestic and international students. Application fee: $65. Electronic applications accepted. *Expenses: Contact institution.* Tuition and fees vary according to degree level and program. *Financial support:* Federal Work-Study, institutionally sponsored loans, scholarships/grants, and tuition waivers (partial) available. Financial award application deadline: 1/15; financial award applicants required to submit FAFSA. *Faculty research:* Negotiation and conflict resolution, international organizations, international business and economic law, security studies, development economics. *Unit head:* Stephen W. Bosworth, Dean, 617-627-3050, Fax: 617-627-3712. *Application contact:* Laurie A. Hurley, Director of Admissions and Financial Aid, 617-627-2410, Fax: 617-627-3712, E-mail: fletcheradmissions@tufts.edu.

Universidad Autonoma de Guadalajara, Graduate Programs, Guadalajara, Mexico. Offers architecture (M Arch); computational science (MCC); education (Ed M, Ed D); international business (MIB); manufacturing systems (MMS); quality systems (MQS);).

Universidad Iberoamericana, Graduate School, Santo Domingo D.N., Dominican Republic. Offers dentistry (DMD); education (M Ed); international business (IMBA).

Universidad Metropolitana, School of Business Administration, Program in International Business, San Juan, PR 00928-1150. Offers MBA.

Université de Sherbrooke, Faculty of Administration, Program in International Business, Sherbrooke, QC J1K 2R1, Canada. Offers M Sc.

Université du Québec, École nationale d'administration publique, Graduate Program in Public Administration, Program in International Administration, Quebec, QC G1K 9E5, Canada. Offers MAP, Diploma. Part-time programs available. *Entrance requirements:* For degree, appropriate bachelor's degree, proficiency in French.

Université Laval, Faculty of Administrative Sciences, Programs in Business Administration, Québec, QC G1K 7P4, Canada. Offers accounting (MBA); agri-food management (MBA); electronic business (MBA, Diploma); factory management and logistics (MBA); finance (MBA); firm management (MBA); information technology management (MBA); international management (MBA); management (MBA); management accounting (MBA, Diploma); marketing (MBA); modelization and organizational decision (MBA); occupational health and safety management (MBA); pharmacy management (MBA); technological entrepreneurship (Diploma). *Accreditation:* AACSB. Part-time and evening/weekend programs available. Postbaccalaureate distance learning degree programs offered (no on-campus study). *Entrance requirements:* For master's and Diploma, knowledge of French and English. Electronic applications accepted.

The University of Akron, Graduate School, College of Business Administration, Department of Marketing, Akron, OH 44325. Offers international business (MBA); international business for international executive (MBA); strategic marketing (MBA); JD/MBA. Part-time and evening/weekend programs available. *Faculty:* 10 full-time (2 women), 10 part-time/adjunct (2 women). *Students:* 16 full-time (8 women), 21 part-time (10 women); includes 2 minority (1 African American, 1 Asian American or Pacific Islander), 7 international. Average age 30. 34 applicants, 85% accepted, 11 enrolled. In 2006, 15 degrees awarded. *Entrance requirements:* For master's, GMAT, minimum GPA of 2.75. Additional exam requirements/recommendations for international students: Required—TOEFL (minimum score 550 paper-based; 213 computer-based; 79 iBT). *Application deadline:* For fall admission, 8/15 for domestic students. Applications are processed on a rolling basis. Application fee: $30 ($40 for international students). Electronic applications accepted. *Expenses:* Tuition, state resident: full-time $6,164; part-time $342 per credit. Tuition, nonresident: full-time $10,575; part-time $588 per credit. Required fees: $806; $43 per credit. $12 per term. Tuition and fees vary according to course load, degree level and program. *Financial support:* In 2006–07, 10 research assistantships with full tuition reimbursements, 1 teaching assistantship with full tuition reimbursement were awarded; tuition waivers (partial) also available. *Faculty research:* Professional selling, sales management, direct interactive marketing, marketing strategy, international business. *Unit head:* Dr. Dale M. Lewison, Chair, 330-972-5758, E-mail: dlewison@uakron.edu. *Application contact:* Dr. James Divoky, Director of Graduate Business Programs, 330-972-7043, Fax: 330-972-6588, E-mail: jdivoky@uakron.edu.

The University of Akron, Graduate School, College of Business Administration, Program in International Business, Akron, OH 44325. Offers MBA, JD/MBA. Part-time and evening/weekend programs available. *Students:* 4 full-time (2 women), 7 part-time (5 women), 4 international. Average age 33. 15 applicants, 53% accepted, 2 enrolled. In 2006, 12 degrees awarded. *Degree requirements:* For master's, foreign language cross-cultural option. *Entrance requirements:* For master's, GMAT, minimum GPA of 2.75. Additional exam requirements/recommendations for international students: Required—TOEFL (minimum score 550 paper-based; 213 computer-based; 79 iBT). *Application deadline:* For fall admission, 8/15 for domestic students. Applications are processed on a rolling basis. Application fee: $30 ($40 for international students). Electronic applications accepted. *Expenses:* Tuition, state resident: full-time $6,164; part-time $342 per credit. Tuition, nonresident: full-time $10,575; part-time $588 per credit. Required fees: $806; $43 per credit. $12 per term. Tuition and fees vary according to course load, degree level and program. *Financial support:* In 2006–07, 6 research assistantships with full tuition reimbursements were awarded; fellowships, teaching assistantships, tuition waivers (partial) and unspecified assistantships also available. *Unit head:* Dr. Douglas Hausknecht, Head, 330-972-5892. *Application contact:* Dr. James Divoky, Director of Graduate Business Programs, 330-972-7043, Fax: 330-972-6588, E-mail: jdivoky@uakron.edu.

University of Alberta, Faculty of Graduate Studies and Research, Program in Business Administration, Edmonton, AB T6G 2E1, Canada. Offers international business (MBA); leisure and sport management (MBA); natural resources and energy (MBA); technology commercialization (MBA); MBA/LL B; MBA/M Ag; MBA/M Eng; MBA/MF; MBA/PhD. *Accreditation:* AACSB. Part-time and evening/weekend programs available. *Faculty:* 77 full-time, 20 part-time/adjunct. *Students:* 131 full-time (56 women), 109 part-time (51 women). Average age 29. 525 applicants, 30% accepted, 90 enrolled. In 2006, 114 degrees awarded. *Degree requirements:* For master's, thesis or alternative. *Entrance requirements:* For master's, GMAT. Additional exam requirements/recommendations for international students: Required—TOEFL (minimum score 600 paper-based; 250 computer-based). *Application deadline:* For fall admission, 4/30 priority date for domestic students, 4/30 for international students. Applications are processed on a rolling basis. Application fee: $0. Electronic applications accepted. *Financial support:* Fellowships, research assistantships, teaching assistantships, career-related internships or fieldwork, scholarships/grants, health care benefits, and unspecified assistantships available. *Faculty research:* Natural resources and energy/management and policy/family enterprise/international business/healthcare research management. Total annual research expenditures: $1 million. *Unit head:* Dr. Douglas Olsen, Associate Dean, 780-492-5412, Fax: 780-492-7825. *Application contact:* Joan A. White, Secretary, 780-492-3679, Fax: 780-492-2024, E-mail: mba@ualberta.ca.

The University of British Columbia, Sauder School of Business, Doctoral Program in Commerce and Business Administration, Vancouver, BC V6T 1Z1, Canada. Offers accounting (PhD); finance (PhD); international business (PhD); management information systems (PhD); management science (PhD); marketing (PhD); organizational behavior (PhD); policy analysis and strategy (PhD); transportation and logistics (PhD); urban land economics (PhD). *Degree requirements:* For doctorate, thesis/dissertation, comprehensive exam. *Entrance requirements:*

For doctorate, GMAT or GRE. Additional exam requirements/recommendations for international students: Required—TOEFL. Electronic applications accepted.

University of Chicago, Graduate School of Business, Executive MBA Program Asia, Singapore, IL 238466, Singapore. Offers MBA. Part-time programs available. *Faculty:* 127 full-time, 43 part-time/adjunct. *Students:* Average age 36. In 2006, 75 degrees awarded. *Entrance requirements:* For master's, interview, letter of company support, 3 letters of recommendation, resumé, essays, transcripts. Additional exam requirements/recommendations for international students: Required—TOEFL (minimum score 600 paper-based; 250 computer-based), IELTS. Application fee: $100. Electronic applications accepted. *Expenses: Contact institution.* One-time fee: $35 full-time. Full-time tuition and fees vary according to course load, degree level and program. *Faculty research:* Finance, marketing, international business, general management, strategy. *Unit head:* Beth Bader, Managing Director, 65-(68) 356482, Fax: 65-(68) 356483, E-mail: singapore.inquiries@chicagogsb.edu. *Application contact:* Information Contact, E-mail: singapore.inquiries@chicagogsb.edu.

University of Chicago, Graduate School of Business, Executive MBA Program Europe, London, IL EC2V 5HA, United Kingdom. Offers MBA. Part-time programs available. *Faculty:* 127 full-time, 43 part-time/adjunct. *Students:* Average age 35. In 2006, 62 degrees awarded. *Entrance requirements:* For master's, interview, 3 letters of recommendation, letter of company support, resumé. Additional exam requirements/recommendations for international students: Required—TOEFL (minimum score 600 paper-based; 250 computer-based), IELTS. Application fee: $100. Electronic applications accepted. *Expenses: Contact institution.* One-time fee: $35 full-time. Full-time tuition and fees vary according to course load, degree level and program. *Faculty research:* Finance, marketing, international business, general management, strategy. *Unit head:* Glenn Sykes, Managing Director, 44-20-7070-2220, E-mail: glenn.sykes@chicagogsb.edu. *Application contact:* Arnold Longboy, Director, Recruitment and Corporate Relations, 44-0 207 070 2224, E-mail: europeinquiries@chicagogsb.edu.

University of Chicago, Graduate School of Business, Executive MBA Program North America, Chicago, IL 60637-1513. Offers MBA. Part-time programs available. *Faculty:* 127 full-time, 43 part-time/adjunct. *Students:* Average age 37. In 2006, 87 degrees awarded. *Entrance requirements:* For master's, interview, company-sponsored letter, 3 letters of recommendation, resumé. Additional exam requirements/recommendations for international students: Required—TOEFL (minimum score 600 paper-based; 250 computer-based), IELTS. Application fee: $100. Electronic applications accepted. *Expenses: Contact institution.* One-time fee: $35 full-time. Full-time tuition and fees vary according to course load, degree level and program. *Faculty research:* Finance, marketing, international business, general management, strategy. *Unit head:* Patty Keegan, Managing Director, 312-464-8751, Fax: 312-464-8755, E-mail: patty.keegan@chicagogsb.edu. *Application contact:* Information Contact, 312-464-8750, Fax: 312-464-8755, E-mail: xp@chicagogsb.edu.

University of Chicago, Graduate School of Business, International MBA Program, Chicago, IL 60637-1513. Offers IMBA. *Accreditation:* AACSB. *Faculty:* 127 full-time, 43 part-time/adjunct. *Students:* Average age 28. *Degree requirements:* For master's, one foreign language. *Entrance requirements:* For master's, GMAT, 2 letters of recommendation, transcripts, essays, first must be admitted to full-time MBA program. Additional exam requirements/recommendations for international students: Required—TOEFL (minimum score 600 paper-based; 250 computer-based), IELTS. *Application deadline:* For fall admission, 10/18 priority date for domestic and international students; for winter admission, 1/10 for domestic and international students; for spring admission, 3/14 for domestic and international students. Application fee: $200. Electronic applications accepted. *Expenses:* Tuition: Full-time $34,920. Required fees: $612. One-time fee: $35 full-time. Full-time tuition and fees vary according to course load, degree level and program. *Financial support:* In 2006–07, 230 students received support, including 230 fellowships; scholarships/grants also available. *Unit head:* Stacey Kole, Deputy Dean, Full-Time Programs, 773-702-7121. *Application contact:* Kari Nysather, Associate Director, IMBA Program, 773-834-2480, E-mail: kari.nysather@chicagogsb.edu.

University of Colorado at Colorado Springs, Graduate School, Graduate School of Business Administration, Colorado Springs, CO 80933-7150. Offers accounting (MBA); finance (MBA); general health care administration (MBA); information systems (MBA); international business management (MBA); marketing (MBA); service management/technology management (MBA). *Accreditation:* AACSB. Part-time and evening/weekend programs available. *Faculty:* 15 full-time (4 women), 4 part-time/adjunct (0 women). *Students:* 158 full-time (70 women), 290 part-time (87 women); includes 48 minority (11 African Americans, 1 American Indian/Alaska Native, 20 Asian Americans or Pacific Islanders, 16 Hispanic Americans), 7 international. Average age 33. 158 applicants, 75% accepted, 51 enrolled. In 2006, 119 degrees awarded. *Entrance requirements:* For master's, GMAT. *Application deadline:* For fall admission, 6/1 for domestic students; for spring admission, 11/1 for domestic students. Application fee: $60 ($75 for international students). *Expenses: Contact institution.* Tuition and fees vary according to course load, campus/location and program. *Financial support:* Career-related internships or fieldwork, Federal Work-Study, and institutionally sponsored loans available. Support available to part-time students. Financial award applicants required to submit FAFSA. *Faculty research:* Quality financial reporting, investments and corporate governance, group support systems, environmental and project management, customer relationship management. Total annual research expenditures: $99,250. *Unit head:* Dr. Venkateshwar Reddy, Dean, 719-262-3113, Fax: 719-262-3494, E-mail: vreddy@uccs.edu. *Application contact:* Amy DeLourenco, MBA Program Director, 719-262-3408, Fax: 719-262-3100, E-mail: busadvsr@uccs.edu.

University of Colorado at Denver and Health Sciences Center, Business School, Program in International Business, Denver, CO 80217-3364. Offers MSIB. Part-time and evening/weekend programs available. *Faculty:* 2 full-time (0 women). *Students:* 25 full-time (15 women), 22 part-time (15 women); includes 5 minority (3 Asian Americans or Pacific Islanders, 2 Hispanic Americans), 10 international. Average age 25. 21 applicants, 71% accepted, 12 enrolled. In 2006, 14 degrees awarded. *Degree requirements:* For master's, one foreign language. *Entrance requirements:* For master's, GMAT. Additional exam requirements/recommendations for international students: Required—TOEFL (minimum score 525 paper-based; 197 computer-based). *Application deadline:* For fall admission, 6/1 for domestic students, 3/15 for international students; for spring admission, 11/1 priority date for domestic students, 10/1 for international students. Applications are processed on a rolling basis. Application fee: $50 ($75 for international students). Electronic applications accepted. *Financial support:* Federal Work-Study, institutionally sponsored loans, and scholarships/grants available. Support available to part-time students. Financial award application deadline: 4/1; financial award applicants required to submit FAFSA. *Unit head:* Manuel Serapio, Director, 303-556-5832, Fax: 303-556-5899, E-mail: mserapio@carbon.cudenver.edu. *Application contact:* Shelly Townley, Admissions Coordinator, 303-556-5956, Fax: 303-556-5904, E-mail: shelly.townley@cudenver.edu.

University of Dallas, Graduate School of Management, Irving, TX 75062-4736. Offers accounting (MBA, MS); business management (MBA); corporate finance (MBA, MM); engineering management (MBA, MM); entrepreneurship (MBA, MM); financial services (MBA, MM); global business (MBA, MM); health services management (MBA, MM); human resource management (MBA, MM, MS); information assurance (MBA, MM, MS); information technology (MBA, MM, MS); information technology service management (MBA); IT service management (MS); marketing (MM); marketing management (MBA); not-for-profit management (MBA); organization development (MBA); project management (MBA, MM); sports and entertainment management (MBA, MM); strategic leadership (MBA); supply chain management (MBA); supply chain management and market logistics (MM); telecommunications management (MBA, MM). *Accreditation:* ACBSP. Part-time and evening/weekend programs available. Postbaccalaureate distance learning degree programs offered (no on-campus study). *Faculty:* 26 full-time (5 women), 85 part-time/adjunct (18 women). *Students:* 227 full-time (98 women), 1,160 part-time (446 women); includes 473 minority (209 African Americans, 3 American Indian/Alaska Native, 143 Asian Americans or Pacific Islanders, 118 Hispanic Americans), 224 international. Average age 34. 556 applicants, 86% accepted, 291 enrolled. In 2006, 476 degrees awarded. *Entrance requirements:* Additional exam requirements/recommendations for international students: Required—TOEFL. *Application deadline:* Applications are processed on a rolling basis. Application fee: $50. Electronic applications accepted. *Expenses: Contact institution. Financial support:* In 2006–07, 468 students received support. Scholarships/grants and unspecified assistantships available. Financial award application deadline: 2/15; financial award applicants required to submit FAFSA. *Unit head:* Dr. J. Lee Whittington, Dean, 972-721-5230. *Application contact:* Sarah Stivison, Director of Graduate Admissions, 972-721-5198, Fax: 972-721-4009, E-mail: admiss@gsm.udallas.edu.

University of Denver, Daniels College of Business, Programs in International Business/Management, Denver, CO 80208. Offers IMBA, MBA. *Accreditation:* AACSB. *Students:* 24 full-time (15 women), 12 part-time (5 women); includes 6 minority (1 African American, 2 Asian Americans or Pacific Islanders, 3 Hispanic Americans), 2 international. Average age 28. 69 applicants, 74% accepted. In 2006, 34 degrees awarded. *Entrance requirements:* For master's, GMAT. *Application deadline:* For fall admission, 1/15 priority date for domestic students. Applications are processed on a rolling basis. Application fee: $50. Electronic applications accepted. *Expenses:* Tuition: Full-time $29,628; part-time $823 per credit. *Financial support:* Career-related internships or fieldwork, Federal Work-Study, institutionally sponsored loans, and scholarships/grants available. Support available to part-time students. Financial award application deadline: 2/15. *Unit head:* Director, 303-871-2210. *Application contact:* Information Contact, 303-871-3416, E-mail: daniels@du.edu.

The University of Findlay, Graduate and Professional Studies, MBA Program, Findlay, OH 45840-3653. Offers financial management (MBA); human resource management (MBA); international management (MBA); management (MBA); marketing (MBA); public management (MBA). Part-time and evening/weekend programs available. Postbaccalaureate distance learning degree programs offered (no on-campus study). *Faculty:* 16 full-time, 1 part-time/adjunct. *Students:* 80 full-time (26 women), 456 part-time (168 women); includes 20 minority (13 African Americans, 1 American Indian/Alaska Native, 4 Asian Americans or Pacific Islanders, 2 Hispanic Americans), 289 international. Average age 35. 208 applicants, 88% accepted, 181 enrolled. In 2006, 210 degrees awarded. *Degree requirements:* For master's, thesis, cumulative project. *Entrance requirements:* For master's, GMAT, minimum undergraduate GPA of 3.0 in last 60 hours of course work. Additional exam requirements/recommendations for international students: Required—TOEFL (minimum score 550 paper-based). *Application deadline:* Applications are processed on a rolling basis. Application fee: $25. Electronic applications accepted. *Expenses: Contact institution. Financial support:* In 2006–07, 1 student received support, including 1 teaching assistantship with full tuition reimbursement available (averaging $6,000 per year); unspecified assistantships also available. Financial award application deadline: 4/1; financial award applicants required to submit FAFSA. *Faculty research:* Health care management, operations and logistics management. *Unit head:* Dr. Paul Sears, Dean, 419-434-4704, Fax: 419-434-4822. *Application contact:* Heather Riffle, Director, Graduate and Special Programs, 419-434-4640, Fax: 419-434-5517, E-mail: riffle@findlay.edu.

University of Florida, Graduate School, Warrington College of Business Administration, Department of Management, Gainesville, FL 32611. Offers international business (MAIB); management (MS, PhD). *Accreditation:* AACSB. *Faculty:* 13 full-time (2 women). *Students:* 108 (55 women); includes 20 minority (3 African Americans, 7 Asian Americans or Pacific Islanders, 10 Hispanic Americans) 11 international. In 2006, 92 master's, 4 doctorates awarded. Terminal master's awarded for partial completion of doctoral program. *Degree requirements:* For master's and doctorate, thesis/dissertation. *Entrance requirements:* For master's and doctorate, GMAT or GRE General Test, minimum GPA of 3.0. Additional exam requirements/recommendations for international students: Required—TOEFL (minimum score 550 paper-based; 213 computer-based). *Application deadline:* For fall admission, 2/16 for domestic students. Applications are processed on a rolling basis. Application fee: $30. Electronic applications accepted. *Expenses:* Tuition, state resident: full-time $6,827. Tuition, nonresident: full-time $21,951. Required fees: $999. *Financial support:* In 2006–07, 6 research assistantships (averaging $19,959 per year), 4 teaching assistantships (averaging $21,479 per year) were awarded; fellowships, unspecified assistantships also available. *Faculty research:* Organizational behavior, organizational theory, strategy and business policy. *Unit head:* Dr. Larry A. DiMatteo, Chair, 352-392-0163, Fax: 352-392-6020, E-mail: larry.dimatteo@cba.ufl.edu. *Application contact:* Mary Cano, Coordinator of Student Affairs, 352-273-0341, Fax: 352-392-6020, E-mail: mary.cano@cba.ufl.edu.

University of Florida, Graduate School, Warrington College of Business Administration, Programs in Business Administration, Gainesville, FL 32611. Offers accounting (MBA); arts administration (MBA); business strategy and public policy (MBA); competitive strategy (MBA); decision and information sciences (MBA); electronic commerce (MBA); finance (MBA); general business (MBA); global management (MBA); Graham-Buffett security analysis (MBA); health administration (MBA); human resources management (MBA); international studies (MBA); Latin American business (MBA); management (MBA); marketing (MBA); sports administration (MBA); JD/MBA; MBA/MS; MBA/PhD; MBA/Pharm D; MD/MBA. *Accreditation:* AACSB. Part-time and evening/weekend programs available. Postbaccalaureate distance learning degree programs offered. *Faculty:* 14. *Students:* 950 (282 women); includes 189 minority (31 African Americans, 2 American Indian/Alaska Native, 66 Asian Americans or Pacific Islanders, 90 Hispanic Americans) 56 international. In 2006, 481 degrees awarded. *Entrance requirements:* For master's, GMAT, minimum GPA of 3.0, interview. Additional exam requirements/recommendations for international students: Required—TOEFL (minimum score 550 paper-based; 213 computer-based). *Application deadline:* For fall admission, 4/15 for domestic students; for winter admission, 10/15 priority date for domestic students; for spring admission, 2/15 for domestic students. Applications are processed on a rolling basis. Application fee: $30. Electronic applications accepted. *Expenses:* Tuition, state resident: full-time $6,827. Tuition, nonresident: full-time $21,951. Required fees: $999. *Financial support:* Fellowships, research assistantships, teaching assistantships, career-related internships or fieldwork, scholarships/grants, and unspecified assistantships available. Support available to part-time students. Financial award application deadline: 2/15; financial award applicants required to submit FAFSA. *Faculty research:* Accounting, finance, insurance, management, real estate and urban analysis marketing. *Unit head:* Alex Sevilla, Director, 352-392-7992 Ext. 1206. *Application contact:* Patrick Foran, Associate Director of Admissions, 352-392-7992 Ext. 282, Fax: 352-392-8791, E-mail: patrick.foran@cba.ufl.edu.

University of Florida, Levin College of Law, Gainesville, FL 32611. Offers comparative law (LL M); international taxation (LL M); law (JD); taxation (LL M, SJD). *Accreditation:* ABA. *Faculty:* 61 full-time (31 women), 46 part-time/adjunct (11 women). *Students:* 1,364 full-time (636 women); includes 281 minority (82 African Americans, 3 American Indian/Alaska Native, 68 Asian Americans or Pacific Islanders, 128 Hispanic Americans), 51 international. Average age 25. 2,535 applicants, 41% accepted, 447 enrolled. In 2006, 310 first professional degrees awarded. *Median time to degree:* 3 years full-time. *Degree requirements:* For first-professional, thesis or alternative. *Entrance requirements:* LSAT. Additional exam requirements/recommendations for international students: Required—TOEFL. *Application deadline:* For fall admission, 1/15 for domestic and international students. Applications are processed on a rolling basis. Application fee: $30. Electronic applications accepted. *Expenses: Contact institution. Financial support:* In 2006–07, 241 students received support, including 4 fellowships (averaging $3,655 per year); Federal Work-Study, institutionally sponsored loans, and scholarships/grants also available. Financial award application deadline: 4/1; financial award applicants required to submit FAFSA. *Faculty research:* Environmental and land use law, taxation, family law, international law, constitutional law. *Unit head:* Robert Jerry, Dean, 352-273-0600, Fax: 352-392-8727, E-mail: jerryr@law.ufl.edu. *Application contact:* J. Michael Patrick, Assistant Dean for Admissions, 352-273-0890, Fax: 352-392-4087, E-mail: patrick@law.ufl.edu.

University of Hawaii at Manoa, Graduate Division, Shidler College of Business, Program in Business Administration, Honolulu, HI 96822. Offers Asian business studies (MBA); Chinese business studies (MBA); decision sciences (MBA); entrepreneurship (MBA); finance (MBA);

International Business

University of Hawaii at Manoa (continued)
finance and banking (MBA); human resources management (MBA); information management (MBA); information technology (MBA); international business (MBA); Japanese business studies (MBA); marketing (MBA); organizational behavior (MBA); organizational management (MBA); real estate (MBA); student-designed track (MBA). *Accreditation:* AACSB. Part-time programs available. *Faculty:* 48 full-time (9 women). *Students:* 207 full-time (77 women), 158 part-time (60 women); includes 93 minority (2 African Americans, 1 American Indian/Alaska Native, 88 Asian Americans or Pacific Islanders, 2 Hispanic Americans), 58 international. Average age 33. 235 applicants, 55% accepted, 68 enrolled. In 2006, 147 degrees awarded. *Degree requirements:* For master's, thesis optional. *Entrance requirements:* For master's, GMAT, minimum GPA of 3.0. Additional exam requirements/recommendations for international students: Required—TOEFL (minimum score 500 paper-based; 173 computer-based; 61 iBT). *Application deadline:* For fall admission, 5/1 for domestic and international students; for spring admission, 9/1 for domestic and international students. Application fee: $50. *Financial support:* In 2006–07, 7 research assistantships (averaging $17,409 per year), 3 teaching assistantships (averaging $14,028 per year) were awarded. *Application contact:* Ting Bui, Information Contact, 808-956-5565, Fax: 808-956-6889.

University of Hawaii at Manoa, Graduate Division, Shidler College of Business, Program in International Management, Honolulu, HI 96822. Offers Asian finance (PhD); global information technology management (PhD); international accounting (PhD); international marketing (PhD); international organization and strategy (PhD). *Faculty:* 42 full-time (8 women). *Students:* 36 applicants, 19% accepted, 4 enrolled. In 2006, 5 degrees awarded. *Median time to degree:* Of those who began their doctoral program in fall 1998, 33% received their degree in 8 years or less. *Degree requirements:* For doctorate, thesis/dissertation, comprehensive exam. *Entrance requirements:* For doctorate, GMAT or GRE General Test, minimum GPA of 3.0. Additional exam requirements/recommendations for international students: Required—TOEFL (minimum score 600 paper-based; 250 computer-based; 100 iBT). *Application deadline:* For fall admission, 3/1 for domestic and international students. Application fee: $50. *Financial support:* In 2006–07, 16 research assistantships (averaging $18,198 per year), 3 teaching assistantships (averaging $14,958 per year) were awarded. Total annual research expenditures: $3.3 million. *Application contact:* Ting Bui, Information Contact, 808-956-6723, Fax: 808-956-2774.

University of Kentucky, Graduate School, Patterson School of Diplomacy and International Commerce, Lexington, KY 40506-0027. Offers MA. *Faculty:* 6 full-time (1 woman), 2 part-time/adjunct (0 women). *Students:* 72 full-time (35 women), 2 part-time (1 woman); includes 1 minority (African American), 16 international. Average age 26. 101 applicants, 51% accepted, 37 enrolled. In 2006, 32 degrees awarded. *Degree requirements:* For master's, one foreign language, comprehensive exam, 30 credit hours, statistics. *Entrance requirements:* For master's, GRE General Test, minimum undergraduate GPA of 3.0. Additional exam requirements/recommendations for international students: Required—TOEFL (minimum score 550 paper-based; 213 computer-based; 79 iBT). *Application deadline:* For fall admission, 2/1 for domestic students. Application fee: $40 ($55 for international students). Electronic applications accepted. *Expenses:* Tuition, state resident: full-time $7,670; part-time $401 per credit hour. Tuition, nonresident: full-time $16,158; part-time $873 per credit hour. *Financial support:* Over half of the incoming students received institutionally-sponsored financial assistance ranging from one-half of tuition up to $20,000 available. Financial award application deadline: 3/15; financial award applicants required to submit FAFSA. *Faculty research:* International relations, foreign and defense policy, cross-cultural negotiation, international science and technology, diplomacy, international economics and development, geopolitical modeling. Total annual research expenditures: $100,000. *Unit head:* Dr. Evan Hillebrand, Director of Graduate Studies, 859-257-6928, Fax: 859-257-4676, E-mail: evan.hillebrand@uky.edu. *Application contact:* Dr. Brian Jackson, Senior Associate Dean, 859-257-4667, Fax: 859-257-4676, E-mail: brian.jackson@uky.edu.

University of La Verne, College of Business and Public Management, Graduate Programs in Business Administration, La Verne, CA 91750-4443. Offers accounting (MBA); business (MBIT); executive management (MBA-EP); finance (MBA, MBA-EP); health services management (MBA); information technology (MBA, MBA-EP); international business (MBA, MBA-EP); leadership (MBA-EP); managed care (MBA); management (MBA, MBA-EP); marketing (MBA, MBA-EP). Part-time and evening/weekend programs available. *Faculty:* 15 full-time (7 women), 13 part-time/adjunct (7 women). *Students:* 277 full-time (133 women), 112 part-time (64 women); includes 144 minority (32 African Americans, 3 American Indian/Alaska Native, 70 Asian Americans or Pacific Islanders, 39 Hispanic Americans), 160 international. Average age 30. In 2006, 142 degrees awarded. *Entrance requirements:* For master's, minimum undergraduate GPA of 3.0, 2 letters of recommendation, resumé. Additional exam requirements/recommendations for international students: Required—TOEFL (minimum score 550 paper-based; 213 computer-based). *Application deadline:* Applications are processed on a rolling basis. Application fee: $50. *Expenses: Contact institution. Financial support:* Career-related internships or fieldwork, institutionally sponsored loans, and scholarships/grants available. Financial award application deadline: 3/2; financial award applicants required to submit FAFSA. *Unit head:* Dr. Ibrahim Helou, Chairperson, 909-593-3511 Ext. 4211, Fax: 909-392-2704, E-mail: heloua@ulv.edu. *Application contact:* Dr. Julius Walecki, Marketing Director, 909-593-3511 Ext. 4192, Fax: 909-392-2704, E-mail: cbpm@ulv.edu.

University of Lethbridge, School of Graduate Studies, Lethbridge, AB T1K 3M4, Canada. Offers accounting (MScM); addictions counseling (M Sc); agricultural biotechnology (M Sc); agricultural studies (M Sc, MA); anthropology (MA); archaeology (MA); art (MA); biochemistry (M Sc); biological sciences (M Sc); biomolecular science (PhD); biosystems and biodiversity (PhD); Canadian studies (MA); chemistry (M Sc); computer science (M Sc); computer science and geographical information science (M Sc); counseling psychology (M Ed); dramatic arts (MA); earth, space, and physical science (PhD); economics (MA); educational leadership (M Ed); English (MA); environmental science (M Sc); evolution and behavior (PhD); exercise science (M Sc); finance (MScM); French (MA); French/German (MA); French/Spanish (MA); general education (M Ed); general management (MScM); geography (M Sc, MA); German (MA); health sciences (M Sc, MA); history (MA); human resource management and labour relations (MScM); individualized multidisciplinary (M Sc, MA); information systems (MScM); international management (MScM); kinesiology (M Sc, MA); management (M Sc, MA); marketing (MScM); mathematics (M Sc); music (MA); Native American studies (MA); neuroscience (M Sc, PhD); new media (MA); nursing (M Sc); philosophy (MA); physics (M Sc); policy and strategy (MScM); political science (MA); psychology (M Sc, MA); religious studies (MA); sociology (MA); theoretical and computational science (PhD); urban and regional studies (MA). Part-time and evening/weekend programs available. *Students:* 200 full-time, 90 part-time. In 2006, 105 master's, 3 doctorates awarded. *Degree requirements:* For doctorate, thesis/dissertation, comprehensive exam. *Entrance requirements:* For master's, GMAT (M Sc management), bachelor's degree in related field, minimum GPA of 3.0 during previous 20 graded semester courses, 2 years teaching or related experience (M Ed); for doctorate, master's degree, minimum graduate GPA of 3.5. Additional exam requirements/recommendations for international students: Required—TOEFL. Application fee: $60 Canadian dollars. *Financial support:* Fellowships, research assistantships, teaching assistantships, scholarships/grants, health care benefits, and unspecified assistantships available. *Faculty research:* Movement and brain plasticity, gibberellin physiology, photosynthesis, carbon cycling, molecular properties of main-group ring components. *Unit head:* Dr. Jo-Anne Fiske, Interim Dean, 403-329-2121, Fax: 403-329-2097. *Application contact:* Kathy Schrage, Administrative Assistant, Office of the Academic Vice President, 403-329-2121, Fax: 403-329-2097, E-mail: inquiries@uleth.ca.

University of Maryland University College, Graduate School of Management and Technology, Program in International Management, Adelphi, MD 20783. Offers MIM, Certificate. Offered evenings and weekends only. Part-time and evening/weekend programs available. Postbaccalaureate distance learning degree programs offered (no on-campus study). *Students:* 17 full-time (7 women), 208 part-time (95 women); includes 94 minority (51 African Americans, 23 Asian Americans or Pacific Islanders, 20 Hispanic Americans), 11 international. Average age 34. 47 applicants, 100% accepted, 32 enrolled. In 2006, 55 master's, 9 other advanced degrees awarded. *Degree requirements:* For master's, thesis or alternative. *Application deadline:* Applications are processed on a rolling basis. Application fee: $50. Electronic applications accepted. *Financial support:* Federal Work-Study and scholarships/grants available. Support available to part-time students. Financial award application deadline: 6/1; financial award applicants required to submit FAFSA. *Unit head:* Dr. Theresa Marron-Grodsky, 301-985-7200, Fax: 301-985-4611, E-mail: tmarron-grodsky@umuc.edu. *Application contact:* Coordinator, Graduate Admissions, 301-985-7155, Fax: 301-985-7175, E-mail: gradinfo@umuc.edu.

University of Memphis, Graduate School, Fogelman College of Business and Economics, Program in Business Administration, International Master of Business Administration Program, Memphis, TN 38152. Offers MBA. *Faculty:* 8 full-time (3 women). In 2006, 17 degrees awarded. *Degree requirements:* For master's, comprehensive exam. *Entrance requirements:* For master's, GMAT, GRE General Test. *Application deadline:* For fall admission, 8/1 for domestic students; for spring admission, 12/1 for domestic students. Application fee: $25 ($50 for international students). *Faculty research:* Institutional trading in equity and bond markets, understanding market to book ratio in international markets using data stream, endnote software, economic integration and international conflict, statistical analysis of heuristic development. Total annual research expenditures: $10,000. *Unit head:* Dr. Ben L. Kedia, Director, 901-678-2038, Fax: 901-678-3678, E-mail: bkedia@memphis.edu. *Application contact:* Pat M. Taylor, Coordinator, 901-678-3499, Fax: 901-678-3678, E-mail: ptaylor@memphis.edu.

University of Miami, Graduate School, School of Business Administration, Program in Business Administration, Coral Gables, FL 33124. Offers accounting (MBA); computer information systems (MBA); executive and professional (MBA), including international business, management; finance (MBA); international business (MBA); management (MBA); management science (MBA); marketing (MBA); professional management (MSPM); JD/MBA; MBA/MSIE. *Accreditation:* AACSB. Evening/weekend programs available. *Faculty:* 105 full-time (25 women). *Students:* 734 full-time (269 women), 19 part-time (4 women); includes 194 minority (24 African Americans, 1 American Indian/Alaska Native, 23 Asian Americans or Pacific Islanders, 146 Hispanic Americans), 115 international. Average age 31. 453 applicants, 71% accepted, 152 enrolled. In 2006, 394 degrees awarded. *Degree requirements:* For master's, comprehensive exam, registration. *Entrance requirements:* For master's, GMAT. Additional exam requirements/recommendations for international students: Required—TOEFL (minimum score 550 paper-based; 213 computer-based; 59 iBT). *Application deadline:* For fall admission, 7/30 priority date for domestic students, 6/30 priority date for international students; for spring admission, 12/31 priority date for domestic students, 10/31 priority date for international students. Applications are processed on a rolling basis. Application fee: $50. Electronic applications accepted. *Financial support:* In 2006–07, 418 students received support, including 19 fellowships with partial tuition reimbursements available; unspecified assistantships also available. Financial award application deadline: 3/1; financial award applicants required to submit FAFSA. *Faculty research:* Leadership, e-commerce, supply chain management. *Unit head:* Daniela Mu±iz, Associate Director, Graduate Business Programs, 305-284-4626, Fax: 305-284-1878, E-mail: dmuniz@miami.edu. *Application contact:* David S. Green, Director of Graduate Business Recruiting and Admissions, 305-284-4607, Fax: 305-284-1878, E-mail: mba@miami.edu.

University of Minnesota, Twin Cities Campus, Carlson School of Management, Carlson Full-time MBA Program, Minneapolis, MN 55455-0213. Offers accounting (MBA); entrepreneurship (MBA); finance (MBA); healthcare management (MBA); information and decision sciences (MBA); international business (MBA); marketing and logistics management (MBA); operations and management science (MBA); strategic management and organization (MBA); supply chain management (MBA); JD/MBA; MD/MBA; MHA/MBA. *Accreditation:* AACSB. *Faculty:* 125 full-time (27 women), 120 part-time/adjunct. *Students:* 218 full-time (70 women); includes 18 minority (4 African Americans, 1 American Indian/Alaska Native, 10 Asian Americans or Pacific Islanders, 3 Hispanic Americans), 86 international. Average age 28. 418 applicants, 53% accepted, 124 enrolled. In 2006, 105 degrees awarded. *Median time to degree:* Master's–2 years full-time. *Entrance requirements:* For master's, GMAT. Additional exam requirements/recommendations for international students: Required—TOEFL (minimum score 580 paper-based; 240 computer-based), IELTS. *Application deadline:* For fall admission, 4/15 for domestic students, 2/15 for international students. Application fee: $60 ($90 for international students). Electronic applications accepted. *Expenses: Contact institution.* Full-time tuition and fees vary according to class time, course load, program, reciprocity agreements and student level. *Financial support:* In 2006–07, 131 students received support, including 127 fellowships with full and partial tuition reimbursements available (averaging $20,000 per year); research assistantships with partial tuition reimbursements available, teaching assistantships with partial tuition reimbursements available, career-related internships or fieldwork, Federal Work-Study, institutionally sponsored loans, scholarships/grants, health care benefits, tuition waivers (full and partial), and unspecified assistantships also available. Support available to part-time students. Financial award application deadline: 2/15; financial award applicants required to submit FAFSA. *Faculty research:* IT, strategy, marketing, finance, quality management. *Unit head:* Kathryn J. Carlson, MBA Programs and Executive Education, 612-624-2039, Fax: 612-625-1012, E-mail: fulltimeembainfo@csom.umn.edu. *Application contact:* Jeffrey Bieganek, Director, Admissions and Business Development, MBA Programs and Executive Education, 612-625-6558, Fax: 612-625-1012, E-mail: full-timembainfo@csom.umn.edu.

University of New Brunswick Saint John, Faculty of Business, Saint John, NB E2L 4L5, Canada. Offers administration (MBA); electronic commerce (MBA); international business (MBA); natural resource management (MBA). Part-time programs available. *Degree requirements:* For master's, thesis optional. *Entrance requirements:* For master's, GMAT. Additional exam requirements/recommendations for international students: Required—TOEFL (minimum score 550 paper-based). Expenses: Contact institution.

University of New Haven, Graduate School, School of Business, Program in Business Administration, West Haven, CT 06516-1916. Offers accounting (MBA); business policy and strategy (MBA); finance (MBA); health care management (MBA); human resources management (MBA); international business (MBA); marketing (MBA); public relations (MBA); sports management (MBA); technology management (MBA); MBA/MPA; MBA/MSIE. Part-time and evening/weekend programs available. *Degree requirements:* For master's, thesis or alternative. *Entrance requirements:* For master's, GMAT.

University of New Mexico, Robert O. Anderson Graduate School of Management, Department of Financial, International and Technology Management, Albuquerque, NM 87131-1221. Offers financial management (MBA); international management (MBA); international management in Latin America (MBA); management of technology (MBA). Part-time and evening/weekend programs available. *Entrance requirements:* For master's, GMAT. Additional exam requirements/recommendations for international students: Required—TOEFL (minimum score 550 paper-based; 213 computer-based). *Faculty research:* Corporation finance, investments, applied macroeconomics, risk management and banking, international finance.

University of Oklahoma, Graduate College, College of Arts and Sciences, School of International and Area Studies, Norman, OK 73019-0390. Offers international studies (MA), including global affairs, global management. Part-time programs available. *Faculty:* 1 (woman) full-time. *Students:* 5 full-time (2 women), 8 part-time (4 women); includes 2 minority (1 Asian American or Pacific Islander, 1 Hispanic American), 2 international. 12 applicants, 75% accepted, 4 enrolled. In 2006, 3 degrees awarded. *Degree requirements:* For master's, one foreign language, thesis optional. *Entrance requirements:* For master's, GMAT or GRE. Additional exam requirements/recommendations for international students: Required—TOEFL (minimum score 550 paper-based; 213 computer-based). *Application deadline:* For fall admission, 2/15 for domestic students, 4/1 for international students; for spring admission, 10/15 for domestic students, 9/1 for international students. Applications are processed on a rolling basis. Application fee: $40 ($90 for international students). *Expenses:* Tuition, state resident: full-time $3,180; part-time $133 per credit hour. Tuition, nonresident: full-time $11,347; part-time $473 per credit hour. Required fees: $1,729; $62 per credit hour. $117 per semester. Tuition and fees vary according to course load and program. *Financial support:* In 2006–07, 5 students received support, including 3 research assistantships (averaging $13,500 per year), teaching assistantships with partial tuition reimbursements available (averaging $13,500 per year); career-related internships or fieldwork, scholarships/grants, and unspecified assistantships also available. Financial award applicants required to submit FAFSA. *Faculty research:* International relations, comparative politics, international economics, global environmental affairs, contemporary history. Total annual research expenditures: $1,000. *Unit head:* Dr. Robert Cox, Director, 405-325-1584, Fax: 405-325-7738, E-mail: rhcox@ou.edu. *Application contact:* Mitchell P. Amirh, Associate Professor and Director of Graduate Studies, 405-325-8893, Fax: 405-325-0718, E-mail: mps@ou.edu.

University of Pennsylvania, School of Arts and Sciences and Wharton School, Joseph H. Lauder Institute of Management and International Studies, Philadelphia, PA 19104. Offers international studies (MA); management and international studies (MBA); MBA/MA. Applications made concurrently and separately to Lauder Institute and Wharton MBA program. *Students:* 118 full-time (27 women). Average age 27. 200 applicants, 36% accepted. In 2006, 57 degrees awarded. *Degree requirements:* For master's, one foreign language, thesis. *Entrance requirements:* For master's, GMAT, advanced proficiency in a non-native language. Additional exam requirements/recommendations for international students: Required—TOEFL. *Application deadline:* For fall admission, 10/12 for domestic students; for winter admission, 1/4 for domestic students. Electronic applications accepted. *Expenses: Contact institution. Financial support:* Fellowships with tuition reimbursements, career-related internships or fieldwork and scholarships/grants available. *Faculty research:* Finance, marketing, strategy, operations management, multinational management. *Unit head:* Dr. Richard J. Herring, Director, 215-898-1215. *Application contact:* Marcy R. Bevan, Directorof Admissions, 215-898-1215, Fax: 215-898-2067, E-mail: lauderinfo@wharton.upenn.edu.

University of Phoenix–Atlanta Campus, John Sperling School of Business, College of Graduate Business and Management, Sandy Springs, GA 30350-4153. Offers business administration (MBA); global management (MBA); human resources management (MBA); management (MM). Evening/weekend programs available. *Faculty:* 25 full-time (15 women), 151 part-time/adjunct (31 women). *Students:* 605 full-time (375 women); includes 323 minority (303 African Americans, 1 American Indian/Alaska Native, 10 Asian Americans or Pacific Islanders, 9 Hispanic Americans), 22 international. Average age 36. In 2006, 156 degrees awarded. *Degree requirements:* For master's, thesis (for some programs), registration. *Entrance requirements:* For master's, minimum undergraduate GPA of 3.0, 3 years of work experience. Additional exam requirements/recommendations for international students: Required—TOEFL (minimum score 550 paper-based; 213 computer-based; 79 iBT). *Application deadline:* Applications are processed on a rolling basis. *Expenses:* Tuition: Full-time $10,560. Required fees: $760. *Financial support:* Institutionally sponsored loans and scholarships/grants available. Financial award applicants required to submit FAFSA. *Unit head:* Dr. Brian Lindquist, Associate Vice President and Dean/Executive Director, 480-557-1221, E-mail: brian.lindquist@phoenix.edu. *Application contact:* Chair, 678-731-0555, Fax: 678-731-9666.

University of Phoenix–Augusta Campus, College of Graduate Business and Management, Augusta, GA 30909-4583. Offers accounting (MBA); business and management (MBA, MM); global management (MBA); human resources management (MBA, MM); marketing (MBA); public administration (MBA, MM).

University of Phoenix–Austin Campus, College of Graduate Business and Management, Austin, TX 78759. Offers accounting (MBA); business and management (MBA); e-business (MBA); global management (MBA); human resources management (MBA, MM); management (MM); marketing (MBA); public administration (MBA).

University of Phoenix–Bay Area Campus, John Sperling School of Business, College of Graduate Business and Management, Pleasanton, CA 94588-3677. Offers accounting (MBA); business administration (MBA); global management (MBA); human resource management (MBA); marketing (MBA); public administration (MBA). Evening/weekend programs available. *Faculty:* 30 full-time (3 women), 390 part-time/adjunct (106 women). *Students:* 523 full-time (279 women); includes 185 minority (40 African Americans, 2 American Indian/Alaska Native, 110 Asian Americans or Pacific Islanders, 33 Hispanic Americans), 84 international. Average age 37. In 2006, 205 degrees awarded. *Degree requirements:* For master's, thesis (for some programs), registration. *Entrance requirements:* For master's, minimum undergraduate GPA of 3.0, 3 years of work experience. Additional exam requirements/recommendations for international students: Required—TOEFL (minimum score 550 paper-based; 213 computer-based; 79 iBT). *Application deadline:* Applications are processed on a rolling basis. Application fee: $45. Electronic applications accepted. *Expenses:* Tuition: Full-time $12,648. Required fees: $760. *Financial support:* Institutionally sponsored loans and scholarships/grants available. Financial award applicants required to submit FAFSA. *Unit head:* Dr. Brian Lindquist, Associate Vice President and Dean/Executive Director, 408-557-1221, E-mail: brian.lindquist@phoenix.edu. *Application contact:* Chair, 408-435-8500, Fax: 408-435-8250.

University of Phoenix–Boston Campus, John Sperling School of Business, College of Graduate Business and Management, Braintree, MA 02184-4949. Offers administration (MBA); global management (MBA). Evening/weekend programs available. *Faculty:* 34 full-time (30 women), 126 part-time/adjunct (0 women). *Students:* 136 full-time (76 women). Average age 36. In 2006, 55 degrees awarded. *Degree requirements:* For master's, thesis (for some programs), registration. *Entrance requirements:* For master's, 3 years of work experience, minimum undergraduate GPA of 3.0. Additional exam requirements/recommendations for international students: Required—TOEFL (minimum score 550 paper-based; 213 computer-based; 79 iBT). *Application deadline:* Applications are processed on a rolling basis. Application fee: $45. *Expenses:* Tuition: Full-time $13,848. Required fees: $760. *Financial support:* Institutionally sponsored loans and scholarships/grants available. Financial award applicants required to submit FAFSA. *Unit head:* Dr. Brian Lindquist, Associate Vice President and Dean/Executive Director, 480-557-1221, E-mail: brian.lindquist@phoenix.edu. *Application contact:* Chair, 781-843-0844, Fax: 781-843-8646.

University of Phoenix–Burlington Learning Center, College of Graduate Business and Management, Burlington, MA 01803. Offers business and management (MBA); global management (MBA).

University of Phoenix–Central Florida Campus, John Sperling School of Business, College of Graduate Business and Management, Maitland, FL 32751-7057. Offers accounting (MBA); business administration (MBA); business and management (MM); global management (MBA); management (MM); marketing (MBA). Evening/weekend programs available. *Faculty:* 50 full-time (11 women), 136 part-time/adjunct (32 women). *Students:* 440 full-time (265 women); includes 175 minority (102 African Americans, 4 American Indian/Alaska Native, 16 Asian Americans or Pacific Islanders, 53 Hispanic Americans), 38 international. Average age 36. In 2006, 149 degrees awarded. *Degree requirements:* For master's, thesis (for some programs), registration. *Entrance requirements:* For master's, minimum undergraduate GPA of 3.0, 3 years work experience. Additional exam requirements/recommendations for international students: Required—TOEFL (minimum score 550 paper-based; 213 computer-based; 79 iBT). *Application deadline:* Applications are processed on a rolling basis. Application fee: $45. Electronic applications accepted. *Expenses:* Tuition: Full-time $9,450. Required fees: $760. *Financial support:* Institutionally sponsored loans and scholarships/grants available. Financial award applicants required to submit FAFSA. *Unit head:* Dr. Brian Lindquist, Associate Vice President and Dean/Executive Director, 480-557-1221, E-mail: brian.lindquist@phoenix.edu. *Application contact:* Chair, 407-667-0555, Fax: 407-667-0560.

University of Phoenix–Central Valley Campus, College of Graduate Business and Management, Fresno, CA 93720. Offers accounting (MBA); business administration (MBA); global management (MBA); human resources management (MBA); management (MM); marketing (MBA); public administration (MBA).

University of Phoenix–Charlotte Campus, John Sperling School of Business, College of Graduate Business and Management, Charlotte, NC 28273-3409. Offers accounting (MBA); administration (MBA); global management (MBA). Evening/weekend programs available. *Faculty:* 18 full-time (2 women), 111 part-time/adjunct (33 women). *Students:* 423 full-time (272 women); includes 221 minority (211 African Americans, 6 Asian Americans or Pacific Islanders, 4 Hispanic Americans), 21 international. Average age 36. In 2006, 78 degrees awarded. *Degree requirements:* For master's, thesis (for some programs), registration. *Entrance requirements:* For master's, minimum undergraduate GPA of 3.0, 3 years work experience. Additional exam requirements/recommendations for international students: Required—TOEFL (minimum score 550 paper-based; 213 computer-based; 79 iBT). *Application deadline:* Applications are processed on a rolling basis. Application fee: $45. Electronic applications accepted. *Expenses:* Tuition: Full-time $10,320. Required fees: $760. *Financial support:* Institutionally sponsored loans and scholarships/grants available. Financial award applicants required to submit FAFSA. *Unit head:* Dr. Brian Lindquist, Associate Vice President and Dean/Executive Director, 480-557-1221, E-mail: brian.lindquist@phoenix.edu. *Application contact:* College Chair, 704-504-5409, Fax: 704-504-5360.

University of Phoenix–Chattanooga Campus, College of Graduate Business and Management, Chattanooga, TN 37421-3707. Offers accounting (MBA); business and management (MBA); global management (MBA); human resources management (MBA, MM); management (MM); marketing (MBA); public administration (MBA, MM).

University of Phoenix–Cheyenne Campus, College of Graduate Business and Management, Cheyenne, WY 82009. Offers business and management (MM); global management (MBA); human resources management (MBA, MM); marketing (MBA); public administration (MBA, MM).

University of Phoenix–Chicago Campus, John Sperling School of Business, College of Graduate Business and Management, Schaumburg, IL 60173-4399. Offers administration (MBA); global management (MBA); information systems (MIS); management (MM). Evening/weekend programs available. *Faculty:* 39 full-time (12 women), 109 part-time/adjunct (28 women). *Students:* 259 full-time (156 women); includes 99 minority (69 African Americans, 1 American Indian/Alaska Native, 17 Asian Americans or Pacific Islanders, 12 Hispanic Americans), 21 international. Average age 37. In 2006, 91 degrees awarded. *Degree requirements:* For master's, thesis (for some programs), registration. *Entrance requirements:* For master's, minimum undergraduate GPA of 3.0, 3 years of work experience. Additional exam requirements/recommendations for international students: Required—TOEFL (minimum score 550 paper-based; 213 computer-based; 79 iBT). *Application deadline:* Applications are processed on a rolling basis. Application fee: $45. Electronic applications accepted. *Expenses:* Tuition: Full-time $12,120. Required fees: $760. *Financial support:* Institutionally sponsored loans and scholarships/grants available. Financial award applicants required to submit FAFSA. *Unit head:* Dr. Brian Lindquist, Associate Vice President and Dean/Executive Director, 480-557-1221, E-mail: brian.lindquist@phoenix.edu. *Application contact:* Campus College Chair—Graduate Business, 847-413-1922, Fax: 847-413-8706.

University of Phoenix–Cleveland Campus, John Sperling School of Business, College of Graduate Business and Management, Independence, OH 44131-2194. Offers accounting (MBA); business administration (MBA); global management (MBA); human resources management (MM); management (MM); marketing (MBA); public administration (MBA, MM). Evening/weekend programs available. *Faculty:* 10 full-time (1 woman), 68 part-time/adjunct (16 women). *Students:* 178 full-time (107 women); includes 115 minority (66 African Americans, 1 American Indian/Alaska Native, 5 Asian Americans or Pacific Islanders, 43 Hispanic Americans), 9 international. Average age 37. In 2006, 25 degrees awarded. *Degree requirements:* For master's, thesis (for some programs), registration. *Entrance requirements:* For master's, minimum undergraduate GPA of 3.0, 3 years of work experience. Additional exam requirements/recommendations for international students: Required—TOEFL (minimum score 550 paper-based; 213 computer-based; 79 iBT). *Application deadline:* Applications are processed on a rolling basis. Application fee: $45. Electronic applications accepted. *Expenses:* Tuition: Full-time $11,608. Required fees: $760. *Financial support:* Institutionally sponsored loans and scholarships/grants available. Financial award applicants required to submit FAFSA. *Unit head:* Dr. Brian Lindquist, Associate Vice President and Dean/Executive Director, 480-557-1221, E-mail: brian.linquist@phoenix.edu. *Application contact:* Chair, 216-447-8807, Fax: 216-447-9144.

University of Phoenix–Columbus Georgia Campus, John Sperling School of Business, College of Graduate Business and Management, Columbus, GA 31904-6321. Offers accounting (MBA); administration (MBA); global management (MBA); human resource management (MBA); marketing (MBA); public administration (MBA). Evening/weekend programs available. *Faculty:* 11 full-time (1 woman), 53 part-time/adjunct (15 women). *Students:* 52 full-time (35 women); includes 27 minority (22 African Americans, 1 Asian American or Pacific Islander, 4 Hispanic Americans). Average age 37. In 2006, 10 degrees awarded. *Degree requirements:* For master's, thesis (for some programs), registration. *Entrance requirements:* For master's, minimum undergraduate GPA of 3.0, 3 years of work experience. Additional exam requirements/recommendations for international students: Required—TOEFL (minimum score 550 paper-based; 213 computer-based; 79 iBT). *Application deadline:* Applications are processed on a rolling basis. Application fee: $45. Electronic applications accepted. *Expenses:* Tuition: Full-time $10,200. Required fees: $760. *Financial support:* Institutionally sponsored loans and scholarships/grants available. Financial award applicants required to submit FAFSA. *Unit head:* Dr. Brian Lindquist, Associate Vice President/Dean/Executive Director, 480-557-1221, E-mail: brian.lindquist@phoenix.edu. *Application contact:* College Chair, 706-320-1262.

University of Phoenix–Denver Campus, John Sperling School of Business, College of Graduate Business and Management, Lone Tree, CO 80124-5453. Offers accounting (MBA); business administration (MBA); e-business (MBA); global management (MBA); human resources management (MBA, MM); management (MM); marketing (MBA); public administration (MBA, MM). Evening/weekend programs available. *Faculty:* 63 full-time (22 women), 254 part-time/adjunct (56 women). *Students:* 289 full-time (139 women); includes 59 minority (25 African Americans, 1 American Indian/Alaska Native, 9 Asian Americans or Pacific Islanders, 24 Hispanic Americans), 20 international. Average age 37. In 2006, 93 degrees awarded. *Degree requirements:* For master's, thesis (for some programs), registration. *Entrance requirements:* For master's, minimum undergraduate GPA of 3.0, 3 years work experience. Additional exam requirements/recommendations for international students: Required—TOEFL (minimum score 550 paper-based; 213 computer-based; 79 iBT). *Application deadline:* Applications are processed on a rolling basis. Application fee: $45. Electronic applications accepted. *Expenses:* Tuition: Full-time $10,032. Required fees: $760. *Financial support:* Institutionally sponsored loans and scholarships/grants available. Financial award applicants required to submit FAFSA. *Unit head:* Dr. Brian Lindquist, Associate Vice President and Dean/Executive Director, 480-557-1221, E-mail: brian.lindquist@phoenix.edu. *Application contact:* Chair, 303-694-9093, Fax: 303-662-0911.

University of Phoenix–Des Moines Campus, College of Graduate Business and Management, Des Moines, IA 50266. Offers accounting (MBA); business administration (MBA); global management (MBA); human resources management (MBA, MM); management (MM); marketing (MBA); public administration (MBA, MM).

University of Phoenix–Detroit Campus, College of Graduate Business and Management, Southfield, MI 48076. Offers accounting (MBA); business administration (MBA); e-business (MBA); global management (MBA); human resources management (MBA, MM); management (MM); marketing (MBA); public administration (MBA).

University of Phoenix–Fort Lauderdale Campus, John Sperling School of Business, College of Graduate Business and Management, Fort Lauderdale, FL 33309. Offers accounting (MBA); business administration (MBA); global management (MBA); human resource management (MBA); human resources management (MM); management (MM); marketing (MBA);

International Business

University of Phoenix–Fort Lauderdale Campus (continued)
public administration (MBA). Evening/weekend programs available. *Faculty:* 31 full-time (13 women), 117 part-time/adjunct (33 women). *Students:* 433 full-time (273 women); includes 196 minority (113 African Americans, 3 American Indian/Alaska Native, 8 Asian Americans or Pacific Islanders, 72 Hispanic Americans), 64 international. Average age 38. In 2006, 112 degrees awarded. *Degree requirements:* For master's, thesis (for some programs), registration. *Entrance requirements:* For master's, minimum undergraduate GPA of 3.0, 3 years work experience. Additional exam requirements/recommendations for international students: Required—TOEFL (minimum score 550 paper-based; 213 computer-based; 79 iBT). *Application deadline:* Applications are processed on a rolling basis. Application fee: $45. Electronic applications accepted. *Expenses:* Tuition: Full-time $9,450. Required fees: $760. *Financial support:* Institutionally sponsored loans and scholarships/grants available. Financial award applicants required to submit FAFSA. *Unit head:* Dr. Brian Linquist, Associate V.P. & Dean/Executive Director, 480-557-1221, E-mail: brian.linquist@phoenix.edu. *Application contact:* Chair, 954-382-5303, Fax: 954-382-5304.

University of Phoenix–Harrisburg Campus, College of Graduate Business and Management, Harrisburg, PA 17112. Offers accounting (MBA); business and management (MBA); glboal management (MBA); human resources management (MBA, MM); management (MM); marketing (MBA); public administration (MBA, MM).

University of Phoenix–Hawaii Campus, John Sperling School of Business, College of Graduate Business and Management, Honolulu, HI 96813-4317. Offers accounting (MBA); business administration (MBA); global management (MBA); human resources management (MBA, MM); management (MM); marketing (MBA); public administration (MBA, MM). Evening/weekend programs available. *Faculty:* 17 full-time (4 women), 92 part-time/adjunct (23 women). *Students:* 72 full-time (39 women); includes 18 minority (3 African Americans, 13 Asian Americans or Pacific Islanders, 2 Hispanic Americans), 30 international. Average age 37. In 2006, 20 master's awarded. *Degree requirements:* For master's, thesis (for some programs), registration. *Entrance requirements:* For master's, minimum undergraduate GPA of 3.0, 3 years of work experience. Additional exam requirements/recommendations for international students: Required—TOEFL (minimum score 550 paper-based; 213 computer-based; 79 iBT). *Application deadline:* Applications are processed on a rolling basis. Application fee: $45. Electronic applications accepted. *Expenses:* Tuition: Full-time $11,520. Required fees: $760. *Financial support:* Institutionally sponsored loans and scholarships/grants available. Financial award applicants required to submit FAFSA. *Unit head:* Dr. Brian Lindquist, Associate Vice President and Dean/Executive Director, 480-557-1221, E-mail: brian.lindquist@phoenix.edu. *Application contact:* Chair, 808-536-2686, Fax: 808-536-3848.

University of Phoenix–Houston Campus, John Sperling School of Business, College of Graduate Business and Management, Houston, TX 77079-2004. Offers business administration (MBA); global management (MBA); human resources management (MBA); public administration (MBA). Evening/weekend programs available. *Faculty:* 28 full-time (9 women), 149 part-time/adjunct (43 women). *Students:* 666 full-time (417 women); includes 350 minority (274 African Americans, 1 American Indian/Alaska Native, 34 Asian Americans or Pacific Islanders, 41 Hispanic Americans), 45 international. Average age 37. In 2006, 244 degrees awarded. *Degree requirements:* For master's, thesis (for some programs), registration. *Entrance requirements:* For master's, 3 years of work experience, minimum undergraduate GPA of 3.0. Additional exam requirements/recommendations for international students: Required—TOEFL (minimum score 550 paper-based; 213 computer-based; 79 iBT). *Application deadline:* Applications are processed on a rolling basis. Application fee: $45. Electronic applications accepted. *Expenses:* Tuition: Full-time $11,832. Required fees: $760. *Financial support:* Institutionally sponsored loans available. Financial award applicants required to submit FAFSA. *Unit head:* Dr. Brian Lindquist, Associate Vice President and Dean/Executive Director, 480-557-1221, E-mail: brian.lindquist@phoenix.edu. *Application contact:* 713-465-9966, Fax: 713-465-2686.

University of Phoenix–Jersey City Campus, College of Graduate Business and Management, Jersey City, NJ 07310. Offers accounting (MBA); business and management (MBA); global management (MBA); human resources management (MBA, MM); management (MM); marketing (MBA); public administration (MBA, MM).

University of Phoenix–Madison Campus, College of Graduate Business and Management, Madison, WI 53718-2416. Offers accounting (MBA); business and management (MBA, MM); e-business (MBA); global management (MBA); human resources management (MBA, MM); marketing (MBA); public administration (MBA).

University of Phoenix–Maryland Campus, John Sperling School of Business, College of Graduate Business and Management, Columbia, MD 21045-5424. Offers business administration (MBA); e-business (MBA); global management (MBA); human resources management (MBA, MM); marketing (MBA); public administration (MBA, MM). Evening/weekend programs available. *Faculty:* 22 full-time (6 women), 136 part-time/adjunct (35 women). *Students:* 357 full-time (223 women); includes 148 minority (128 African Americans, 2 American Indian/Alaska Native, 9 Asian Americans or Pacific Islanders, 9 Hispanic Americans), 38 international. Average age 37. In 2006, 111 master's awarded. *Degree requirements:* For master's, thesis (for some programs), registration. *Entrance requirements:* For master's, minimum undergraduate GPA of 3.0, 3 years of work experience. Additional exam requirements/recommendations for international students: Required—TOEFL (minimum score 550 paper-based; 213 computer-based; 79 iBT). *Application deadline:* Applications are processed on a rolling basis. Application fee: $45. Electronic applications accepted. *Expenses:* Tuition: Full-time $13,200. Required fees: $760. *Financial support:* Institutionally sponsored loans and scholarships/grants available. Financial award applicants required to submit FAFSA. *Unit head:* Dr. Brian Lindquist, Associate Vice President and Dean/Executive Director, 480-557-1221, E-mail: brian.lindquist@phoenix.edu. *Application contact:* Chair, 410-872-9001, Fax: 410-536-5727.

University of Phoenix–Memphis Campus, College of Graduate Business and Management, Cordova, TN 38018. Offers acounting (MBA); business and management (MBA); e-business (MBA); global management (MBA); human resources management (MBA, MM); marketing (MBA); public administration (MBA, MM).

University of Phoenix–Metro Detroit Campus, John Sperling School of Business, College of Graduate Business and Management, Troy, MI 48098-2623. Offers business administration (MBA); global management (MBA). Evening/weekend programs available. *Faculty:* 32 full-time (9 women), 223 part-time/adjunct (61 women). *Students:* 607 full-time (394 women); includes 267 minority (254 African Americans, 3 American Indian/Alaska Native, 7 Asian Americans or Pacific Islanders, 3 Hispanic Americans), 19 international. Average age 39. In 2006, 216 master's awarded. *Degree requirements:* For master's, thesis (for some programs), registration. *Entrance requirements:* For master's, minimum undergraduate GPA of 3.0, 3 years work experience. Additional exam requirements/recommendations for international students: Required—TOEFL (minimum score 550 paper-based; 213 computer-based; 79 iBT). *Application deadline:* Applications are processed on a rolling basis. Application fee: $45. Electronic applications accepted. *Expenses:* Tuition: Full-time $12,168. Required fees: $760. *Financial support:* Institutionally sponsored loans and scholarships/grants available. Financial award applicants required to submit FAFSA. *Unit head:* Dr. Brian Lindquist, Associate Vice President and Dean/Executive Director, 480-557-1221, E-mail: brian.lindquist@phoenix.edu. *Application contact:* Chair, 800-834-2438, Fax: 248-267-0147.

University of Phoenix–Minneapolis/St. Louis Park Campus, College of Graduate Business and Management, St. Louis Park, MN 55426. Offers accounting (MBA); business administration (MBA); global management (MBA); human resources management (MBA); marketing (MBA).

University of Phoenix–New Mexico Campus, John Sperling School of Business, College of Graduate Business and Management, Albuquerque, NM 87109-4645. Offers business administration (MBA); global management (MBA); human resource management (MBA). Evening/weekend programs available. *Faculty:* 25 full-time (6 women), 305 part-time/adjunct (77 women). *Students:* 507 full-time (273 women); includes 235 minority (12 African Americans, 9 American Indian/Alaska Native, 7 Asian Americans or Pacific Islanders, 207 Hispanic Americans), 21 international. Average age 37. In 2006, 129 degrees awarded. *Degree requirements:* For master's, thesis (for some programs), registration. *Entrance requirements:* For master's, 3 years of work experience, minimum undergraduate GPA of 3.0. Additional exam requirements/recommendations for international students: Required—TOEFL (minimum score 550 paper-based; 213 computer-based; 79 iBT). *Application deadline:* Applications are processed on a rolling basis. Application fee: $45. Electronic applications accepted. *Expenses:* Tuition: Full-time $9,005. Required fees: $760. *Financial support:* Institutionally sponsored loans and scholarships/grants available. Financial award applicants required to submit FAFSA. *Unit head:* Dr. Brian Lindquist, Associate Vice President and Dean/Executive Director, 480-557-1221, E-mail: brian.lindquist@phoenix.edu. *Application contact:* Graduate Business Chair, 505-821-4800, Fax: 505-821-5551.

University of Phoenix—Northern Nevada Campus, College of Graduate Business and Management, Reno, NV 89511. Offers accounting (MBA); business and management (MBA); global management (MBA); human resources management (MBA, MM); management (MM); marketing (MBA); public administration (MBA, MM).

University of Phoenix–Northern Virginia Campus, College of Graduate Business and Management, Reston, VA 20190. Offers accounting (MBA); business administration (MBA); e-business (MBA); global management (MBA); human resources management (MBA, MM); management (MM); marketing (MBA); public administration (MBA).

University of Phoenix–North Florida Campus, John Sperling School of Business, College of Graduate Business and Management, Jacksonville, FL 32216-0959. Offers accounting (MBA); business administration (MBA); global management (MBA); human resources management (MBA, MM); management (MM); marketing (MBA); public administration (MBA). Evening/weekend programs available. *Faculty:* 40 full-time (15 women), 105 part-time/adjunct (25 women). *Students:* 392 full-time (237 women); includes 135 minority (117 African Americans, 1 American Indian/Alaska Native, 12 Asian Americans or Pacific Islanders, 5 Hispanic Americans), 20 international. Average age 31. In 2006, 134 degrees awarded. *Degree requirements:* For master's, thesis (for some programs), registration. *Entrance requirements:* For master's, minimum undergraduate GPA of 3.0, 3 years work experience. Additional exam requirements/recommendations for international students: Required—TOEFL (minimum score 550 paper-based; 213 computer-based; 79 iBT). *Application deadline:* Applications are processed on a rolling basis. Application fee: $45. Electronic applications accepted. *Financial support:* Institutionally sponsored loans available. Financial award applicants required to submit FAFSA. *Unit head:* Dr. Brian Lindquist, Associate Vice President and Dean/Executive Director, 480-557-1221, E-mail: brian.lindquist@phoenix.edu. *Application contact:* Chair, 904-636-6645, Fax: 904-636-0998.

University of Phoenix–Northwest Arkansas Campus, College of Graduate Business and Management, Rogers, AR 72756-9615. Offers accounting (MBA); business and management (MBA); global management (MBA); human resources management (MBA, MM); management (MM); marketing (MBA); public administration (MBA, MM).

University of Phoenix–Omaha Campus, College of Graduate Business and Management, Omaha, NE 68154-5240. Offers accounting (MBA); business and management (MBA); global management (MBA); human resources management (MM); human resources managemetn (MBA); management (MM); marketing (MBA); public administration (MM); public adminstration (MBA).

University of Phoenix–Oregon Campus, The John Sperling School of Business, College of Graduate Business and Management, Tigard, OR 97223. Offers accounting (MBA); business administration (MBA); global management (MBA); human resource management (MM); human resources management (MBA); management (MM). Evening/weekend programs available. *Faculty:* 28 full-time (4 women), 104 part-time/adjunct (24 women). *Students:* 241 full-time (103 women); includes 31 minority (7 African Americans, 4 American Indian/Alaska Native, 14 Asian Americans or Pacific Islanders, 6 Hispanic Americans), 21 international. Average age 39. In 2006, 66 degrees awarded. *Degree requirements:* For master's, thesis (for some programs), registration. *Entrance requirements:* For master's, minimum undergraduate GPA of 3.0, 3 years of work experience. Additional exam requirements/recommendations for international students: Required—TOEFL (minimum score 550 paper-based; 213 computer-based; 79 iBT). *Application deadline:* Applications are processed on a rolling basis. Application fee: $45. Electronic applications accepted. *Expenses:* Tuition: Full-time $10,200. Required fees: $760. *Financial support:* Institutionally sponsored loans and scholarships/grants available. Financial award applicants required to submit FAFSA. *Unit head:* Dr. Brian Lindquist, Associate Vice President and Dean/Executive Director, 480-557-1221, E-mail: brian.lindquist@phoenix.edu. *Application contact:* Chair, 503-403-2900, Fax: 503-670-0614.

University of Phoenix–Philadelphia Campus, The John Sperling School of Business, College of Graduate Business and Management, Wayne, PA 19087-2121. Offers business administration (MBA); global management (MBA); management (MM). Evening/weekend programs available. *Faculty:* 21 full-time (4 women), 85 part-time/adjunct (19 women). *Students:* 271 full-time (160 women); includes 96 minority (86 African Americans, 3 American Indian/Alaska Native, 5 Asian Americans or Pacific Islanders, 2 Hispanic Americans), 18 international. Average age 36. In 2006, 102 degrees awarded. *Degree requirements:* For master's, thesis (for some programs), registration. *Entrance requirements:* For master's, minimum undergraduate GPA of 3.0, 3 years work experience. Additional exam requirements/recommendations for international students: Required—TOEFL (minimum score 550 paper-based; 213 computer-based; 79 iBT). *Application deadline:* Applications are processed on a rolling basis. Application fee: $45. Electronic applications accepted. *Expenses:* Tuition: Full-time $13,560. Required fees: $760. *Financial support:* Institutionally sponsored loans and scholarships/grants available. Financial award applicants required to submit FAFSA. *Unit head:* Dr. Brian Lindquist, Associate Vice President and Dean/Executive Director, 480-557-1221, E-mail: brian.lindquist@phoenix.edu. *Application contact:* Campus College Chair, 610-984-0880, Fax: 610-989-0881.

University of Phoenix–Pittsburgh Campus, John Sperling School of Business, College of Graduate Business and Management, Pittsburgh, PA 15276. Offers accounting (MBA); business administration (MBA); global management (MBA); human resource management (MBA); human resources management (MM); management (MM); marketing (MBA); public administration (MBA, MM). Evening/weekend programs available. *Faculty:* 19 full-time (6 women), 49 part-time/adjunct (13 women). *Students:* 84 full-time (43 women); includes 16 minority (13 African Americans, 2 Asian Americans or Pacific Islanders, 1 Hispanic American), 4 international. Average age 37. In 2006, 35 degrees awarded. *Degree requirements:* For master's, thesis (for some programs), registration. *Entrance requirements:* For master's, minimum undergraduate GPA of 3.0, 3 years work experience. Additional exam requirements/recommendations for international students: Required—TOEFL (minimum score 550 paper-based; 213 computer-based; 79 iBT). *Application deadline:* Applications are processed on a rolling basis. Application fee: $45. Electronic applications accepted. *Expenses:* Tuition: Full-time $13,560. Required fees: $760. *Financial support:* Institutionally sponsored loans and scholarships/grants available. Financial award applicants required to submit FAFSA. *Unit head:* Dr. Brian Lindquist, Associate Vice President and Dean/Executive Director, 480-551-1221, E-mail: brian.lindquist@phoenix.edu. *Application contact:* College Chair, 412-747-9000, Fax: 412-747-0676.

University of Phoenix–Puerto Rico Campus, John Sperling School of Business, College of Graduate Business and Management, Guaynabo, PR 00968. Offers accounting (MBA); business administration (MBA); global management (MBA); human resource management (MBA); marketing (MBA). Evening/weekend programs available. *Faculty:* 19 full-time (8 women), 73 part-time/adjunct (25 women). *Students:* 1,122 full-time (671 women); includes 636 minority (2 African Americans, 3 American Indian/Alaska Native, 3 Asian Americans or Pacific Islanders,

628 Hispanic Americans), 31 international. Average age 34. In 2006, 281 degrees awarded. *Degree requirements:* For master's, thesis (for some programs), registration. *Entrance requirements:* For master's, minimum undergraduate GPA of 3.0, 3 years work experience. Additional exam requirements/recommendations for international students: Required—TOEFL (minimum score 550 paper-based; 213 computer-based; 79 iBT). *Application deadline:* Applications are processed on a rolling basis. Application fee: $45. Electronic applications accepted. *Expenses:* Tuition: Full-time $5,816. Required fees: $760. *Financial support:* Institutionally sponsored loans and scholarships/grants available. Financial award applicants required to submit FAFSA. *Unit head:* Dr. Brian Lindquist, Associate Vice President and Dean/Executive Director, 480-557-1221, E-mail: brian.lindquist@phoenix.edu. *Application contact:* Chair, 787-931-5400, Fax: 787-931-1510.

University of Phoenix–Raleigh Campus, College of Graduate Business and Management, Raleigh, NC 27606. Offers accounting (MBA); business administration (MBA); e-business (MBA); global management (MBA).

University of Phoenix–Renton Learning Center, College of Graduate Business and Management, Renton, WA 98005. Offers accounting (MBA); business and management (MBA, MM); global management (MBA); human resources management (MBA, MM); marketing (MBA); public administration (MBA, MM).

University of Phoenix–Richmond Campus, John Sperling School of Business, College of Graduate Business and Management, Richmond, VA 23230. Offers accounting (MBA); business administration (MBA); global management (MBA); human resources management (MBA, MM); management (MM); marketing (MBA); public administration (MBA, MM). Evening/weekend programs available. *Faculty:* 6 full-time (4 women), 60 part-time/adjunct (7 women). *Students:* 103 full-time (73 women); includes 42 minority (38 African Americans, 1 American Indian/Alaska Native, 2 Asian Americans or Pacific Islanders, 1 Hispanic American), 10 international. Average age 36. In 2006, 1 degree awarded. *Degree requirements:* For master's, thesis (for some programs), registration. *Entrance requirements:* For master's, minimum undergraduate GPA 3.0, 3 years work experience. Additional exam requirements/recommendations for international students: Required—TOEFL (minimum score 550 paper-based; 213 computer-based; 79 iBT). *Application deadline:* Applications are processed on a rolling basis. Application fee: $45. Electronic applications accepted. *Financial support:* Institutionally sponsored loans and scholarships/grants available. Financial award applicants required to submit FAFSA. *Unit head:* Dr. Brian Lindquist, Associate Vice President/Dean, 480-557-1221, E-mail: brian.lindquist@phoenix.edu. *Application contact:* Chair, 804-288-3390.

University of Phoenix–Sacramento Valley Campus, John Sperling School of Business, College of Graduate Business and Management, Sacramento, CA 95833-3632. Offers accounting (MBA); business administration (MBA); global management (MBA); human resources management (MBA); marketing (MBA); public administration (MBA). Evening/weekend programs available. *Faculty:* 36 full-time (19 women), 291 part-time/adjunct (83 women). *Students:* 395 full-time (197 women); includes 120 minority (62 African Americans, 2 American Indian/Alaska Native, 32 Asian Americans or Pacific Islanders, 24 Hispanic Americans), 34 international. Average age 37. In 2006, 138 master's awarded. *Degree requirements:* For master's, thesis (for some programs), registration. *Entrance requirements:* For master's, minimum undergraduate GPA of 3.0, 3 years work experience. Additional exam requirements/recommendations for international students: Required—TOEFL (minimum score 550 paper-based; 213 computer-based; 79 iBT). *Application deadline:* Applications are processed on a rolling basis. Application fee: $45. Electronic applications accepted. *Expenses:* Tuition: Full-time $12,024. Required fees: $760. *Financial support:* Institutionally sponsored loans and scholarships/grants available. Financial award applicants required to submit FAFSA. *Unit head:* Dr. Brian Lindquist, Associate Vice President and Dean/Executive Director, 480-557-1221, E-mail: brian.lindquist@phoenix.edu. *Application contact:* Campus College Chair, 916-923-2107, Fax: 916-923-3914.

University of Phoenix–San Antonio Campus, College of Graduate Business and Management, San Antonio, TX 78230. Offers accounting (MBA); business and management (MBA); e-business (MBA); global management (MBA); human resources management (MBA, MM); management (MM); marketing (MBA); public administration (MBA, MM).

University of Phoenix–San Diego Campus, John Sperling School of Business, College of Graduate Business and Management, San Diego, CA 92123. Offers business administration (MBA); global management (MBA); management (MM). Evening/weekend programs available. *Faculty:* 39 full-time (4 women), 217 part-time/adjunct (39 women). *Students:* 437 full-time (211 women); includes 139 minority (32 African Americans, 2 American Indian/Alaska Native, 48 Asian Americans or Pacific Islanders, 57 Hispanic Americans), 24 international. Average age 36. In 2006, 127 degrees awarded. *Degree requirements:* For master's, thesis (for some programs), registration. *Entrance requirements:* For master's, 3 years of work experience, minimum undergraduate GPA of 3.0. Additional exam requirements/recommendations for international students: Required—TOEFL (minimum score 550 paper-based; 213 computer-based; 79 iBT). *Application deadline:* Applications are processed on a rolling basis. Application fee: $45. Electronic applications accepted. *Expenses:* Tuition: Full-time $11,419. Required fees: $760. *Financial support:* Institutionally sponsored loans and scholarships/grants available. Financial award applicants required to submit FAFSA. *Unit head:* Dr. Brian Lindquist, Associate Vice President and Dean/Executive Director, 480-557-1221, E-mail: brian.lindquist@phoenix.edu. *Application contact:* Campus Information Center, 888-UOP-INFO, Fax: 858-509-4399.

University of Phoenix–Savannah Campus, College of Graduate Business and Management, Savannah, GA 31405-7400. Offers accounting (MBA); business administration (MBA); business and management (MM); global management (MBA); human resources management (MBA, MM); marketing (MBA); public administration (MBA, MM).

University of Phoenix–Southern Arizona Campus, John Sperling School of Business, College of Graduate Business and Management, Tucson, AZ 85712-2732. Offers accounting (MBA); business administration (MBA); global management (MBA); management (MM). Evening/weekend programs available. *Faculty:* 29 full-time (13 women), 207 part-time/adjunct (40 women). *Students:* 412 full-time (205 women); includes 107 minority (23 African Americans, 7 American Indian/Alaska Native, 10 Asian Americans or Pacific Islanders, 67 Hispanic Americans), 24 international. Average age 36. In 2006, 141 degrees awarded. *Degree requirements:* For master's, thesis (for some programs), registration. *Entrance requirements:* For master's, minimum undergraduate GPA of 3.0, 3 years work experience. Additional exam requirements/recommendations for international students: Required—TOEFL (minimum score 550 paper-based; 213 computer-based; 79 iBT). *Application deadline:* Applications are processed on a rolling basis. Application fee: $45. Electronic applications accepted. *Expenses:* Tuition: Full-time $8,669. Required fees: $760. *Financial support:* Institutionally sponsored loans and scholarships/grants available. Financial award applicants required to submit FAFSA. *Unit head:* Dr. Brian Lindquist, Associate Vice President and Dean/Executive Director, 480-557-1221, E-mail: brian.lindquist@phoenix.edu. *Application contact:* Campus College Chair, 520-881-6512, Fax: 520-795-6177.

University of Phoenix–Springfield Campus, College of Graduate Business and Management, Springfield, MO 65804-7211. Offers accounting (MBA); business and management (MBA); global management (MBA); human resources management (MBA, MM); management (MM); marketing (MBA); public administration (MBA, MM).

University of Phoenix–West Florida Campus, The John Sperling School of Business, College of Graduate Business and Management, Temple Terrace, FL 33637. Offers business administration (MBA); global management (MBA); human resource management (MBA); human resources management (MM); management (MM); marketing (MBA); public administration (MBA). Evening/weekend programs available. *Faculty:* 39 full-time (19 women), 145 part-time/adjunct (45 women). *Students:* 475 full-time (272 women); includes 150 minority (98 African Americans, 4 American Indian/Alaska Native, 9 Asian Americans or Pacific Islanders, 39 Hispanic Americans), 43 international. Average age 36. In 2006, 165 degrees awarded. *Degree requirements:* For master's, thesis (for some programs), registration. *Entrance requirements:* For master's, 3 years of work experience, minimum undergraduate GPA of 3.0. Additional exam requirements/recommendations for international students: Required—TOEFL (minimum score 550 paper-based; 213 computer-based; 79 iBT). *Application deadline:* Applications are processed on a rolling basis. Application fee: $45. Electronic applications accepted. *Expenses:* Tuition: Full-time $9,450. Required fees: $760. *Financial support:* Institutionally sponsored loans and scholarships/grants available. Financial award applicants required to submit FAFSA. *Unit head:* Dr. Brian Lindquist, Associate Vice President and Dean/Executive Director, 480-557-1221, E-mail: brian.lindquist@phoenix.edu. *Application contact:* Chair, 813-626-7911, Fax: 813-977-1449.

University of Phoenix–West Michigan Campus, The John Sperling School of Business, College of Graduate Business and Management, Walker, MI 49544. Offers accounting (MBA); business administration (MBA); global management (MBA); human resource management (MBA). Evening/weekend programs available. *Faculty:* 26 full-time (0 women), 95 part-time/adjunct (42 women). *Students:* 124 full-time (62 women); includes 16 minority (15 African Americans, 1 Hispanic American), 4 international. Average age 37. In 2006, 50 degrees awarded. *Degree requirements:* For master's, thesis (for some programs), registration. *Entrance requirements:* For master's, minimum undergraduate GPA of 3.0, 3 years work experience. Additional exam requirements/recommendations for international students: Required—TOEFL (minimum score 550 paper-based; 213 computer-based; 79 iBT). *Application deadline:* Applications are processed on a rolling basis. Application fee: $45. Electronic applications accepted. *Expenses:* Tuition: Full-time $12,043. Required fees: $760. *Financial support:* Institutionally sponsored loans and scholarships/grants available. Financial award applicants required to submit FAFSA. *Unit head:* Dr. Brian Lindquist, Associate Vice President and Dean/Executive Director, 480-557-1221, E-mail: brian.lindquist@phoenix.edu. *Application contact:* Chair, 888-345-9699, Fax: 616-784-5300.

University of Pittsburgh, Joseph M. Katz Graduate School of Business, Augsburg Executive Fellows Program, Pittsburgh, PA 15260. Offers MBA. *Students:* 60 full-time (10 women), (all international). Average age 35. In 2006, 30 degrees awarded. *Degree requirements:* For master's, one foreign language. *Entrance requirements:* For master's, admission to the MBA program at the University of Augsburg. Additional exam requirements/recommendations for international students: Required—TOEFL (minimum score 220 computer-based). *Application deadline:* For spring admission, 7/1 priority date for international students. *Expenses:* Contact institution. *Unit head:* Dr. John Camillus, Executive Associate Dean, 412-648-1565, Fax: 412-648-1552, E-mail: camillus@katz.pitt.edu. *Application contact:* Beata Loch, Director, Special International Programs, 412-383-8835, Fax: 412-648-1552, E-mail: bloch@katz.pitt.edu.

University of Pittsburgh, Joseph M. Katz Graduate School of Business, Program in International Business, Pittsburgh, PA 15260. Offers MBA, MBA/MIB. *Students:* 2 full-time (1 woman), 1 (woman) part-time. Average age 26. 4 applicants, 50% accepted, 2 enrolled. *Degree requirements:* For master's, one foreign language. *Entrance requirements:* For master's, GMAT, foreign language proficiency. Additional exam requirements/recommendations for international students: Required—TOEFL. *Application deadline:* For fall admission, 4/15 priority date for domestic students. Applications are processed on a rolling basis. Application fee: $50. *Financial support:* Career-related internships or fieldwork, institutionally sponsored loans, scholarships/grants, and tuition waivers (partial) available. Financial award application deadline: 12/1. *Faculty research:* Foreign exchange risk management and trade flow pattern emergence post-NAFTA, equity market performance in emerging markets and international variation in compensation/incentive plans, comparative corporate guidance and financial disclosure practices in emerging markets. *Unit head:* Beata Loch, Director, Special International Programs, 412-383-8835, Fax: 412-648-1552, E-mail: bloch@katz.pitt.edu.

University of Regina, Faculty of Graduate Studies and Research, Kenneth Levene Graduate School of Business, Program in Business Administration, Regina, SK S4S 0A2, Canada. Offers business fundamentals (Master's Certificate); general management (Master's Certificate); international business (Master's Certificate). Part-time and evening/weekend programs available. *Faculty:* 24 full-time (5 women), 3 part-time/adjunct (0 women). *Students:* 55 full-time (19 women), 21 part-time (8 women). 68 applicants, 90% accepted. *Entrance requirements:* Additional exam requirements/recommendations for international students: Required—TOEFL (minimum score 580 paper-based; 237 computer-based; 88 iBT). *Application deadline:* Applications are processed on a rolling basis. Application fee: $60 ($100 for international students). Electronic applications accepted. *Expenses:* Contact institution. *Financial support:* Application deadline: 6/15. *Faculty research:* Accounting, finance, marketing, management science, operations management. *Unit head:* Dr. David Senkow, Professor, 306-585-4719, Fax: 306-585-4805, E-mail: david.senkow@uregina.ca.

University of Rhode Island, Graduate School, College of Business Administration, Kingston, RI 02881. Offers accounting (MS); business administration (PhD), including finance, management, management science and information systems, marketing; finance (MBA); international business (MBA); international sports management (MBA); management (MBA); management science (MBA), including management information systems, manufacturing; marketing (MBA). *Accreditation:* AACSB. In 2006, 86 master's, 1 doctorate awarded. *Entrance requirements:* For master's and doctorate, GMAT. Additional exam requirements/recommendations for international students: Required—TOEFL. *Application deadline:* For fall admission, 4/15 priority date for domestic students. Applications are processed on a rolling basis. Application fee: $35. *Expenses:* Tuition, state resident: full-time $6,032; part-time $335 per credit. Tuition, nonresident: full-time $17,288; part-time $960 per credit. Required fees: $65 per credit. $30 per semester. One-time fee: $80 part-time. *Financial support:* Unspecified assistantships available. *Unit head:* Mark Higgins, Dean, 401-874-2337. *Application contact:* Dr. Laura Beauvais, Director of Graduate Programs, 401-874-4341.

University of San Francisco, Masagung Graduate School of Management, Program in Business Administration, San Francisco, CA 94117-1080. Offers business economics (MBA); e-business (MBA); entrepreneurship (MBA); finance and banking (MBA); international business (MBA); management (MBA); marketing (MBA); telecommunications management and policy (MBA); JD/MBA; MSN/MBA. *Accreditation:* AACSB. *Faculty:* 27 full-time (4 women), 21 part-time/adjunct (7 women). *Students:* 191 full-time (73 women), 71 part-time (33 women); includes 51 minority (4 African Americans, 1 American Indian/Alaska Native, 35 Asian Americans or Pacific Islanders, 11 Hispanic Americans), 102 international. Average age 28. 373 applicants, 70% accepted, 106 enrolled. In 2006, 163 degrees awarded. *Entrance requirements:* For master's, GMAT, minimum undergraduate GPA of 3.2. Additional exam requirements/recommendations for international students: Required—TOEFL. *Application deadline:* For fall admission, 7/1 priority date for domestic students; for spring admission, 11/30 for domestic students. Applications are processed on a rolling basis. Application fee: $55 ($65 for international students). *Expenses:* Tuition: Full-time $17,370; part-time $965 per unit. Tuition and fees vary according to degree level, campus/location and program. *Financial support:* In 2006–07, 104 students received support; fellowships available. Financial award application deadline: 3/2; financial award applicants required to submit FAFSA. *Faculty research:* International financial markets, technology transfer licensing, international marketing, strategic planning. Total annual research expenditures: $50,000. *Unit head:* Carol Langlois, Director, 415-422-6314, Fax: 415-422-2502.

University of San Francisco, School of Law, Program in Law, San Francisco, CA 94117-1080. Offers intellectual property and technology law (LL M); international transactions and comparative law (LL M). *Faculty:* 16 full-time (6 women), 78 part-time/adjunct (32 women). *Students:* 5 full-time (3 women), 1 part-time, 2 international. Average age 31. 44 applicants, 66% accepted. In 2006, 6 degrees awarded. *Entrance requirements:* For master's, law degree from U.S. or foreign school (intellectual property and technology law), law degree from foreign school (international transactions and comparative law). Application fee: $60. *Expenses:* Tuition:

International Business

University of San Francisco (continued)
Full-time $17,370; part-time $965 per unit. Tuition and fees vary according to degree level, campus/location and program. *Financial support:* In 2006–07, 3 students received support. *Unit head:* Eldon Reiley, Director, Fax: 415-422-5440. *Application contact:* Program Assistant, 415-422-5100, E-mail: masterlaws@usfca.edu.

University of Saskatchewan, College of Graduate Studies and Research, College of Commerce, Program in Business Administration, Saskatoon, SK S7N 5A2, Canada. Offers agribusiness management (MBA); biotechnology management (MBA); health services management (MBA); indigenous management (MBA); international business management (MBA).

The University of Scranton, Graduate School, Program in Business Administration, Scranton, PA 18510. Offers accounting (MBA); enterprise management technology (MBA); finance (MBA); general business administration (MBA); international business (MBA); management information systems (MBA); marketing (MBA); operations management (MBA). *Accreditation:* AACSB. Part-time and evening/weekend programs available. *Faculty:* 34 full-time (8 women). *Students:* 39 full-time (11 women), 54 part-time (15 women); includes 3 minority (1 American Indian/Alaska Native, 2 Hispanic Americans), 31 international. Average age 28. 58 applicants, 83% accepted. In 2006, 52 degrees awarded. *Degree requirements:* For master's, capstone experience. *Entrance requirements:* For master's, GMAT, minimum GPA of 2.75. Additional exam requirements/recommendations for international students: Required—TOEFL (minimum score 500 paper-based; 173 computer-based), IELTS (minimum score 6). *Application deadline:* Applications are processed on a rolling basis. Application fee: $50. *Expenses:* Tuition: Part-time $684 per credit. Required fees: $25 per term. *Financial support:* In 2006–07, 11 teaching assistantships with full tuition reimbursements (averaging $5,600 per year) were awarded; fellowships, career-related internships or fieldwork, Federal Work-Study, and unspecified assistantships also available. Support available to part-time students. Financial award application deadline: 3/1. *Faculty research:* Financial markets, strategic impact of total quality management, internal accounting controls, consumer preference, information systems and the Internet. *Unit head:* Dr. Murli Rajan, Director, 570-941-4043, Fax: 570-941-4342.

University of South Carolina, The Graduate School, The Darla Moore School of Business, International Business Administration Program, Columbia, SC 29208. Offers IMBA. *Degree requirements:* For master's, one foreign language. *Entrance requirements:* For master's, GMAT, minimum GPA of 3.0, minimum two years of work experience. Additional exam requirements/recommendations for international students: Required—TOEFL (minimum score 600 paper-based; 250 computer-based). Electronic applications accepted.

University of Southern California, Graduate School, Marshall School of Business, International Business Education and Research (IBEAR) Program, Los Angeles, CA 90089. Offers international business (MBA). *Students:* 58 full-time (14 women), 1 (woman) part-time; includes 11 minority (1 African American, 10 Asian Americans or Pacific Islanders), 41 international. In 2006, 53 degrees awarded. *Degree requirements:* For master's, foreign language recommended. *Entrance requirements:* For master's, GMAT. Additional exam requirements/recommendations for international students: Required—TOEFL. *Application deadline:* For fall admission, 4/1 for domestic students. Applications are processed on a rolling basis. Application fee: $85. *Expenses:* Tuition: Full-time $33,314; part-time $1,121 per credit. Required fees: $522. Full-time tuition and fees vary according to program. *Financial support:* Fellowships, scholarships/grants available. *Faculty research:* Pacific Rim trade, international trade, international finance, international strategy. *Unit head:* Fujiko Terayama, Director, 213-740-7140, E-mail: ibearmba@marshall.usc.edu.

The University of Tampa, John H. Sykes College of Business, Tampa, FL 33606-1490. Offers accounting (MBA, MS); economics (MBA); entrepreneurship (MBA); finance (MBA, MS); information systems management (MBA); innovation management (MS); international business (MBA); management (MBA); marketing (MBA, MS). *Accreditation:* AACSB. Part-time and evening/weekend programs available. *Faculty:* 39 full-time (9 women), 1 part-time/adjunct (0 women). *Students:* 143 full-time (52 women), 381 part-time (158 women); includes 78 minority (18 African Americans, 3 American Indian/Alaska Native, 19 Asian Americans or Pacific Islanders, 38 Hispanic Americans), 89 international. Average age 31. 486 applicants, 59% accepted, 231 enrolled. In 2006, 127 degrees awarded. *Median time to degree:* Master's–1.8 years full-time, 2.8 years part-time. *Entrance requirements:* For master's, GMAT. Additional exam requirements/recommendations for international students: Required—TOEFL (minimum score 577 paper-based; 230 computer-based; 90 iBT). *Application deadline:* For fall admission, 2/15 priority date for domestic students, 6/15 for international students; for spring admission, 12/15 for domestic students, 11/15 for international students. Applications are processed on a rolling basis. Application fee: $40. Electronic applications accepted. *Expenses:* Tuition: Part-time $426 per credit hour. Required fees: $35 per year. *Financial support:* In 2006–07, 57 students received support, including 57 research assistantships with tuition reimbursements available (averaging $3,000 per year); career-related internships or fieldwork and unspecified assistantships also available. Support available to part-time students. Financial award applicants required to submit FAFSA. *Faculty research:* Industrial organization and antitrust, artificial intelligence, corporate quality, leadership, ethics, quality. *Unit head:* Dr. William L. Rhey, Dean Graduate Studies, 813-253-6211, Fax: 813-259-5403, E-mail: wrhey@ut.edu. *Application contact:* Fernals Nolasco, Director of Graduate Studies, 813-253-6211, Fax: 813-259-5403, E-mail: fnolasco@ut.edu.

The University of Texas at Dallas, School of Management, Program in International Management Studies, Richardson, TX 75083-0688. Offers MA, PhD. Part-time and evening/weekend programs available. *Faculty:* 10 full-time (3 women). *Students:* 13 full-time (8 women), 23 part-time (13 women); includes 16 minority (1 African American, 8 Asian Americans or Pacific Islanders, 7 Hispanic Americans), 10 international. Average age 33. 44 applicants, 50% accepted, 10 enrolled. In 2006, 12 master's, 4 doctorates awarded. *Degree requirements:* For doctorate, thesis/dissertation. *Entrance requirements:* For master's and doctorate, GMAT. Additional exam requirements/recommendations for international students: Required—TOEFL (minimum score 550 paper-based; 213 computer-based). *Application deadline:* For fall admission, 7/15 for domestic students; for spring admission, 11/15 for domestic students. Applications are processed on a rolling basis. Application fee: $50 ($100 for international students). Electronic applications accepted. *Financial support:* In 2006–07, 8 teaching assistantships with tuition reimbursements (averaging $14,625 per year) were awarded; fellowships, research assistantships, Federal Work-Study, institutionally sponsored loans, and scholarships/grants also available. Support available to part-time students. Financial award application deadline: 4/30; financial award applicants required to submit FAFSA. *Faculty research:* International accounting, international trade and finance, economic development, international economics. *Unit head:* Dr. George Barnes, Director, 972-883-2783, Fax: 972-883-2799, E-mail: gbarnes@utdallas.edu. *Application contact:* David B. Ritchey, Director of Advising, 972-883-2701, Fax: 972-883-6425, E-mail: davidr@utdallas.edu.

The University of Texas at San Antonio, College of Business, Department of Management, San Antonio, TX 78249-0617. Offers international business (MBA); management (PhD); management science (MBA). *Accreditation:* AACSB. Part-time and evening/weekend programs available. *Faculty:* 12 full-time (4 women), 7 part-time/adjunct (2 women). *Students:* 11 full-time (3 women), 15 part-time (3 women); includes 10 minority (1 African American, 5 Asian Americans or Pacific Islanders, 4 Hispanic Americans), 6 international. Average age 29. 17 applicants, 53% accepted, 8 enrolled. In 2006, 11 degrees awarded. *Degree requirements:* For master's, thesis optional. *Entrance requirements:* For master's, GMAT, minimum GPA of 3.0. Additional exam requirements/recommendations for international students: Required—TOEFL (minimum score 500 paper-based; 173 computer-based). *Application deadline:* For fall admission, 7/1 for domestic students, 4/1 for international students; for spring admission, 11/1 for domestic students, 9/1 for international students. Applications are processed on a rolling basis. Application fee: $45 ($80 for international students). Electronic applications accepted. *Expenses:* Tuition, state resident: full-time $1,730; part-time $192 per credit hour. Tuition, nonresident: full-time $6,680; part-time $742 per credit hour. Required fees: $733; $308,359 per credit hour. *Financial support:* In 2006–07, 3 research assistantships (averaging $20,800 per year), 5 teaching assistantships (averaging $15,600 per year) were awarded; career-related internships or fieldwork, Federal Work-Study, scholarships/grants, and unspecified assistantships also available. Support available to part-time students. *Unit head:* Dr. Robert L. Cardy, Chair, 210-458-7480, Fax: 210-458-6335, E-mail: robert.cardy@utsa.edu.

University of the Incarnate Word, School of Graduate Studies and Research, H-E-B School of Business and Administration, Programs in Administration, San Antonio, TX 78209-6397. Offers adult education (MAA); applied administration (MAA); communication arts (MAA); English (MAA); instructional technology (MAA); international business (Certificate); multidisciplinary sciences (MAA); nutrition (MAA); organizational development (MAA, Certificate); project management (Certificate); sports management (MAA); urban administration (MAA). *Students:* 1 (woman) full-time, 161 part-time (102 women); includes 17 African Americans, 1 American Indian/Alaska Native, 82 Hispanic Americans, 18 international. Average age 34. In 2006, 78 degrees awarded. *Entrance requirements:* For master's, GMAT, GRE, MAT. Additional exam requirements/recommendations for international students: Required—TOEFL. *Application deadline:* For fall admission, 8/15 priority date for domestic students; for spring admission, 12/31 for domestic students. Applications are processed on a rolling basis. Application fee: $20. *Expenses:* Tuition: Part-time $570 per credit hour. Required fees: $54 per credit hour. One-time fee: $195 part-time. Tuition and fees vary according to degree level. *Financial support:* Federal Work-Study and scholarships/grants available. *Unit head:* Dr. Dan Dominguez, MAA Director, 210-829-3180, Fax: 210-805-3564, E-mail: domingue@uiwtx.edu. *Application contact:* Andrea Cyterski-Acosta, Dean of Enrollment, 210-829-6005, Fax: 210-829-3921, E-mail: cyterski@uiwtx.edu.

University of the Incarnate Word, School of Graduate Studies and Research, H-E-B School of Business and Administration, Programs in Business Administration, San Antonio, TX 78209-6397. Offers international business (MBA); sports management (MBA); MBA/MSN. *Accreditation:* ACBSP. Part-time and evening/weekend programs available. *Students:* 19 full-time (13 women), 219 part-time (120 women); includes 123 minority (13 African Americans, 3 American Indian/Alaska Native, 4 Asian Americans or Pacific Islanders, 103 Hispanic Americans), 35 international. Average age 31. In 2006, 99 degrees awarded. *Entrance requirements:* For master's, GMAT. Additional exam requirements/recommendations for international students: Required—TOEFL. *Application deadline:* For fall admission, 8/15 priority date for domestic students; for spring admission, 12/31 for domestic students. Applications are processed on a rolling basis. Application fee: $20. *Expenses:* Tuition: Part-time $570 per credit hour. Required fees: $54 per credit hour. One-time fee: $195 part-time. Tuition and fees vary according to degree level. *Financial support:* Federal Work-Study, scholarships/grants, and tuition waivers (partial) available. Financial award application deadline: 5/31. *Faculty research:* Small business, Mexico/U.S. business, organizational development. *Unit head:* Dr. Connie Green, MBA Director, 210-829-3182, Fax: 210-805-3564, E-mail: greenc@uiwtx.edu. *Application contact:* Andrea Cyterski-Acosta, Dean of Enrollment, 210-829-6005, Fax: 210-829-3921, E-mail: cyterski@uiwtx.edu.

University of the West, Department of Business Administration, Rosemead, CA 91770. Offers business administration (EMBA); finance (MBA); information technology and management (MBA); international business (MBA); nonprofit organization management (MBA). Part-time and evening/weekend programs available. *Entrance requirements:* Additional exam requirements/recommendations for international students: Required—TOEFL.

The University of Toledo, College of Graduate Studies, College of Business Administration, Department of Marketing and International Business, Program in International Business, Toledo, OH 43606-3390. Offers MBA. *Students:* 18 full-time (11 women), 13 part-time (6 women); includes 3 minority (2 African Americans, 1 Hispanic American), 11 international. Average age 25. 18 applicants, 83% accepted, 9 enrolled. In 2006, 11 degrees awarded. *Entrance requirements:* For master's, GMAT. Application fee: $45. *Unit head:* David Chatfield, Chair, 419-530-2775, E-mail: david.chatfield@utoledo.edu. *Application contact:* Elissa Teal, Director, 419-530-2775, Fax: 419-530-7260, E-mail: elissa.teal@utoledo.edu.

University of Washington, Graduate School, Business School, Seattle, WA 98195-3200. Offers auditing and assurance (MP Acc); business (PhD); evening part-time (MBA); executive (MBA); full time (MBA); global (MBA); global executive (MBA); taxation (MP Acc); technology management (MBA); JD/MBA; MBA/MAIS; MBA/MHA. *Accreditation:* AACSB. Part-time and evening/weekend programs available. *Degree requirements:* For master's, registration; for doctorate, thesis/dissertation, comprehensive exam, registration. *Entrance requirements:* For master's, GMAT; for doctorate, GMAT, GRE. Additional exam requirements/recommendations for international students: Required—TOEFL (minimum score 600 paper-based; 250 computer-based). Electronic applications accepted. Expenses: Contact institution.

University of Washington, Graduate School, Interdisciplinary Graduate Program in Global Trade, Transportation, and Logistics Studies, Seattle, WA 98195. Offers Certificate.

University of Wisconsin–Whitewater, School of Graduate Studies, College of Business and Economics, Program in Business Administration, Whitewater, WI 53190-1790. Offers finance (MBA); human resource management (MBA); information technology management (MBA); international business (MBA); management (MBA); marketing (MBA); operations and supply chain management (MBA); technology and training (MBA). *Accreditation:* AACSB. Part-time and evening/weekend programs available. Postbaccalaureate distance learning degree programs offered (no on-campus study). *Students:* 67 full-time (26 women), 331 part-time (136 women); includes 71 minority (20 African Americans, 40 Asian Americans or Pacific Islanders, 11 Hispanic Americans). Average age 28. 167 applicants, 62% accepted, 75 enrolled. In 2006, 141 degrees awarded. *Degree requirements:* For master's, thesis or alternative. *Entrance requirements:* For master's, GMAT, minimum AACSB index of 1000, minimum GPA of 2.75. Additional exam requirements/recommendations for international students: Required—TOEFL (minimum score 550 paper-based; 213 computer-based). *Application deadline:* For fall admission, 7/15 for domestic students, 7/15 priority date for international students; for spring admission, 12/1 for domestic and international students. Applications are processed on a rolling basis. Application fee: $45. Electronic applications accepted. *Expenses:* Tuition, state resident: full-time $3,311. Tuition, nonresident: full-time $8,616. Required fees: $368 per credit. *Financial support:* In 2006–07, 11 research assistantships (averaging $7,385 per year) were awarded; Federal Work-Study, unspecified assistantships, and out of state fee waiver also available. Support available to part-time students. Financial award application deadline: 3/15; financial award applicants required to submit FAFSA. *Faculty research:* Interface between social institutions and individual behavior, technology and innovation management, occupational mental health, workplace deviance and workplace romance. *Unit head:* Dr. Donald Zahn, Associate Dean, 262-472-1945, Fax: 262-472-4863, E-mail: zahnd@uww.edu.

Upper Iowa University, Online Master's Programs, Fayette, IA 52142-1857. Offers accounting (MBA); corporate financial management (MBA); global business (MBA); health and human services (MPA); homeland security (MPA); human resources management (MBA); justice administration (MPA); organizational development (MBA); public personnel management (MPA); quality management (MBA). MBA also available at Madison, Wisconsin campus. Part-time and evening/weekend programs available. Postbaccalaureate distance learning degree programs offered (no on-campus study). *Degree requirements:* For master's, research project. *Entrance requirements:* For master's, GMAT, GRE, or minimum GPA of 2.7 during last 60 hours. Additional exam requirements/recommendations for international students: Required—TOEFL (minimum score 570 paper-based; 230 computer-based). Electronic applications accepted. *Faculty research:* Total quality management, CQI, teams, organization culture and climate, management.

Valparaiso University, Graduate Division, Program in International Commerce and Policy, Valparaiso, IN 46383. Offers MS, JD/MS. Part-time and evening/weekend programs available. *Students:* 29 full-time (12 women), 10 part-time (7 women); includes 6 minority (2 African Americans, 1 American Indian/Alaska Native, 3 Hispanic Americans), 19 international. Average age 25. In 2006, 28 degrees awarded. *Entrance requirements:* For master's, minimum

GPA of 3.0. Additional exam requirements/recommendations for international students: Required—TOEFL (minimum score 575 paper-based; 230 computer-based). *Application deadline:* Applications are processed on a rolling basis. Application fee: $30 ($50 for international students). Electronic applications accepted. *Expenses:* Tuition: Part-time $390 per credit hour. Required fees: $60 per term. Tuition and fees vary according to program. *Financial support:* Available to part-time students. Applicants required to submit FAFSA. *Application contact:* Jamie Haney, Coordinator of Recruitment Activities, 219-464-5313, Fax: 219-464-5381, E-mail: jamie.haney@valpo.edu.

Wagner College, Division of Graduate Studies, Department of Business Administration, Program in International Business, Staten Island, NY 10301-4495. Offers MBA. Part-time and evening/weekend programs available. *Faculty:* 1 full-time (0 women), 1 part-time/adjunct (0 women). *Students:* 2 full-time (1 woman), 2 part-time; all minorities (3 Asian Americans or Pacific Islanders, 1 Hispanic American). In 2006, 1 degree awarded. *Degree requirements:* For master's, thesis optional. *Entrance requirements:* For master's, GMAT, minimum GPA of 2.6. *Application deadline:* For fall admission, 8/1 priority date for domestic students, 6/30 priority date for international students; for spring admission, 12/10 for domestic students, 11/15 for international students. Applications are processed on a rolling basis. Application fee: $50 ($80 for international students). *Expenses:* Tuition: Full-time $15,120; part-time $840 per credit. *Financial support:* Fellowships, tuition waivers (partial) and unspecified assistantships available. Financial award applicants required to submit FAFSA. *Application contact:* Susan Rosenberg, Office of Graduate Studies, 718-390-3106, Fax: 718-390-3456, E-mail: graduate@wagner.edu.

Washington State University, Graduate School, College of Agricultural, Human, and Natural Resource Sciences, School of Economic Sciences, Department of Economics, Pullman, WA 99164. Offers applied economics (MA); economics (MA, PhD); international business economics (Certificate). *Faculty:* 16 full-time (1 woman). *Students:* 45 full-time (15 women), 8 part-time (5 women), 24 international. Average age 30. 135 applicants, 21% accepted, 16 enrolled. In 2006, 7 master's, 8 doctorates awarded. *Degree requirements:* For master's, thesis (for some programs), oral exam, comprehensive exam (for some programs); for doctorate, thesis/dissertation, oral exam, written exam, field exams, comprehensive exam. *Entrance requirements:* For master's, GRE General Test, minimum GPA of 3.0; for doctorate, GRE General Test or GMAT, minimum GPA of 3.0. Additional exam requirements/recommendations for international students: Required—TOEFL. *Application deadline:* For fall admission, 3/1 priority date for domestic students. Applications are processed on a rolling basis. Application fee: $50. *Expenses:* Tuition, state resident: full-time $7,066. Tuition, nonresident: full-time $17,204. *Financial support:* In 2006–07, research assistantships (averaging $13,917 per year), 13 teaching assistantships (averaging $13,506 per year) were awarded; career-related internships or fieldwork, Federal Work-Study, institutionally sponsored loans, tuition waivers (partial), and teaching associateships also available. Financial award application deadline: 4/1; financial award applicants required to submit FAFSA. *Faculty research:* Economic theory and quantitative methods, applied microeconomics. Total annual research expenditures: $80,141. *Unit head:* Dr. Charles Munson, Associate Dean, 509-335-1193, E-mail: mba@wsu.edu. *Application contact:* Graduate School Admissions, 800-GRADWSU, Fax: 509-335-1949, E-mail: gradsch@wsu.edu.

Wayland Baptist University, Graduate Programs, Programs in Business Administration/Management, Plainview, TX 79072-6998. Offers general business (MBA); health care administration (MBA); human resource management (MBA); international management (MBA); management (MA, MBA), including human resource management (MA), organization management (MA); management information systems (MBA). Part-time and evening/weekend programs available. Postbaccalaureate distance learning degree programs offered (no on-campus study). *Faculty:* 3 full-time (0 women). *Students:* 1 full-time (0 women), 7 part-time (2 women); includes 1 minority (Hispanic American) Average age 28. 1 applicant, 100% accepted, 1 enrolled. In 2006, 2 degrees awarded. *Degree requirements:* For master's, capstone course. *Entrance requirements:* For master's, GMAT, GRE or MAT. Additional exam requirements/recommendations for international students: Required—TOEFL (minimum score 500 paper-based; 173 computer-based). *Application deadline:* Applications are processed on a rolling basis. Application fee: $35. *Expenses:* Tuition: Full-time $6,120; part-time $340 per credit hour. Required fees: $50 per term. *Financial support:* Federal Work-Study, institutionally sponsored loans, and scholarships/grants available. Support available to part-time students. Financial award application deadline: 5/1; financial award applicants required to submit FAFSA. *Unit head:* Dr. Otto Schacht, Chairman, 806-291-1020, Fax: 806-291-1957.

Webster University, School of Business and Technology, Department of Business, St. Louis, MO 63119-3194. Offers business (MA); business and organizational security management (MBA); computer resources and information management (MBA); environmental management (MBA); finance (MA, MBA); health services management (MBA); human resources development (MBA); human resources management (MBA); international business (MA, MBA); management and leadership (MBA); marketing (MBA); procurement and acquisitions management (MBA); telecommunications management (MBA). Part-time and evening/weekend programs available. Postbaccalaureate distance learning degree programs offered (no on-campus study). *Students:* 1,205 full-time (629 women), 4,197 part-time (2,153 women); includes 2,005 minority (1,467 African Americans, 29 American Indian/Alaska Native, 212 Asian Americans or Pacific Islanders, 297 Hispanic Americans), 485 international. Average age 33. *Application deadline:* Applications are processed on a rolling basis. Application fee: $25 ($50 for international students). *Expenses:* Tuition: Full-time $8,820; part-time $490 per credit. Tuition and fees vary according to degree level, campus/location and program. *Financial support:* Federal Work-Study available. Support available to part-time students. Financial award application deadline: 4/1; financial award applicants required to submit FAFSA. *Unit head:* Bradford Scott, Chair, 314-961-2260 Ext. 7574, Fax: 314-968-7077, E-mail: buschair@webster.edu. *Application contact:* Director of Graduate and Evening Student Admissions, Fax: 314-968-7116, E-mail: gadmit@webster.edu.

Western International University, Graduate Programs in Business, Program in International Business, Phoenix, AZ 85021-2718. Offers MBA. Evening/weekend programs available. Postbaccalaureate distance learning degree programs offered (no on-campus study). *Faculty:* 233 part-time/adjunct (57 women). *Students:* 67 full-time (38 women); includes 19 minority (3 African Americans, 6 Asian Americans or Pacific Islanders, 10 Hispanic Americans), 19 international. Average age 35. In 2006, 17 degrees awarded. *Degree requirements:* For master's, thesis. *Entrance requirements:* For master's, minimum GPA of 2.75. *Application deadline:* Applications are processed on a rolling basis. Application fee: $85 ($100 for international students). *Expenses:* Tuition: Full-time $9,600; part-time $400 per credit. One-time fee: $85 full-time. *Financial support:* Career-related internships or fieldwork, institutionally sponsored loans, and scholarships/grants available. Support available to part-time students. Financial award applicants required to submit FAFSA. *Unit head:* Ched Yu, Chair, 602-943-2311. *Application contact:* Karen Janitell, Director of Enrollment, 602-943-2311 Ext. 1063, Fax: 602-371-8637, E-mail: karen_janitell@apollogrp.edu.

Whitworth University, School of Global Commerce and Management, Program in Business Administration, Spokane, WA 99251-0001. Offers business administration (MBA); international management (MBA). Part-time and evening/weekend programs available. *Faculty:* 4 full-time (3 women), 14 part-time/adjunct (11 women). *Students:* 13 full-time (8 women), 4 part-time (3 women); includes 1 Hispanic American, 2 international. 17 applicants, 65% accepted, 11 enrolled. *Entrance requirements:* For master's, GMAT, minimum GPA of 3.0, 2 letters of recommendation, resumé, completion of prerequisite courses in micro-economics, macro-economics, accounting, marketing, finance and statistics. Additional exam requirements/recommendations for international students: Required—TOEFL (minimum score 213 computer-based). *Application deadline:* For fall admission, 8/20 priority date for domestic students; for spring admission, 1/8 priority date for domestic students. Applications are processed on a rolling basis. Application fee: $35. *Financial support:* In 2006–07, 2 students received support; fellowships with tuition reimbursements available, career-related internships or fieldwork, Federal Work-Study, institutionally sponsored loans, and scholarships/grants available. Support available to part-time students. Financial award applicants required to submit FAFSA. *Faculty research:* International business (European, Central America and Asian topics), micro-finance, entrepreneurship. *Unit head:* 509-777-4606, Fax: 509-777-3723. *Application contact:* Bonnie Wakefield, Assistant Director, Graduate Studies in Business, 509-777-4606, Fax: 509-777-3723, E-mail: bwakefield@whitworth.edu.

Whitworth University, School of Global Commerce and Management, Program in International Management, Spokane, WA 99251-0001. Offers MIM. Part-time and evening/weekend programs available. *Faculty:* 4 full-time (3 women), 14 part-time/adjunct (11 women). *Students:* 11 full-time (4 women), 2 part-time (1 woman); includes 1 Asian American or Pacific Islander, 2 international. Average age 35. 8 applicants, 25% accepted. *Entrance requirements:* For master's, GRE, minimum GPA of 3.0, 2 letters of recommendation, resumé, completion of prerequisite courses in micro-economics, macro-economics, accounting, marketing and statistics. Additional exam requirements/recommendations for international students: Required—TOEFL (minimum score 213 computer-based). *Application deadline:* For fall admission, 8/20 priority date for domestic students; for spring admission, 1/8 priority date for domestic students. Applications are processed on a rolling basis. Application fee: $35. Electronic applications accepted. *Financial support:* In 2006–07, 6 students received support; fellowships with tuition reimbursements available, career-related internships or fieldwork, Federal Work-Study, institutionally sponsored loans, and scholarships/grants available. Support available to part-time students. Financial award application deadline: 3/1; financial award applicants required to submit FAFSA. *Faculty research:* International business (European, Central America and Asian topics), micro-finance, entrepreneurship, fraud. *Unit head:* 509-777-4606, Fax: 509-777-3723. *Application contact:* Bonnie Wakefield, Assistant Director, Graduate Studies in Business, 509-777-4606, Fax: 509-777-3723, E-mail: bwakefield@whitworth.edu.

Wilkes University, Graduate Studies and Continued Learning, Jay S. Sidhu School of Business and Leadership, Wilkes-Barre, PA 18766-0002. Offers accounting (MBA); entrepreneurship (MBA); finance (MBA); human resource management (MBA); international business (MBA); management (MBA); marketing (MBA). *Accreditation:* ACBSP. Part-time and evening/weekend programs available. *Students:* 30 full-time (16 women), 149 part-time (73 women); includes 5 minority (1 African American, 2 Asian Americans or Pacific Islanders, 2 Hispanic Americans), 4 international. Average age 30. In 2006, 48 degrees awarded. *Entrance requirements:* For master's, GMAT. Additional exam requirements/recommendations for international students: Required—TOEFL (minimum score 500 paper-based; 173 computer-based). *Application deadline:* Applications are processed on a rolling basis. Application fee: $40. *Expenses:* Contact institution. *Financial support:* Federal Work-Study and unspecified assistantships available. Financial award application deadline: 3/1; financial award applicants required to submit FAFSA. *Unit head:* Dr. Paul Browne, Dean, 570-408-4701, Fax: 570-408-4700, E-mail: paul.browne@wilkes.edu. *Application contact:* Kathleen Houlihan, Director of Graduate Studies, 570-408-3235, Fax: 570-408-7846, E-mail: kathleen.houlihan@wilkes.edu.

Wright State University, School of Graduate Studies, Raj Soin College of Business, Department of Management, Dayton, OH 45435. Offers flexible business (MBA); health care management (MBA); international business (MBA); management, innovation and change (MBA); project management (MBA); supply chain management (MBA); MBA/MS. *Students:* 47 full-time (22 women), 154 part-time (63 women). Average age 31. 40 applicants, 90% accepted. In 2006, 71 degrees awarded. *Entrance requirements:* For master's, GMAT, minimum AACSB index of 1000. Additional exam requirements/recommendations for international students: Required—TOEFL. Application fee: $25. *Financial support:* Fellowships, research assistantships, teaching assistantships, unspecified assistantships available. Support available to part-time students. Financial award applicants required to submit FAFSA. *Unit head:* Dr. Riad Ajami, Chair, 937-775-2375, Fax: 937-775-3545, E-mail: riad.ajami@wright.edu. *Application contact:* Michael Evans, Director of MBA Programs, 937-775-2437, Fax: 937-775-3545, E-mail: michael.evans@wright.edu.

Xavier University, Williams College of Business, Master of Business Administration Program, Cincinnati, OH 45207. Offers business administration (Exec MBA, MBA); e-commerce (MBA); finance (MBA); international business (MBA); management information systems (MBA); marketing (MBA);); MBA/MHSA; MSN/MBA. *Accreditation:* AACSB. Part-time and evening/weekend programs available. *Faculty:* 59 full-time (22 women), 29 part-time/adjunct (8 women). *Students:* 227 full-time (66 women), 708 part-time (252 women); includes 99 minority (41 African Americans, 1 American Indian/Alaska Native, 43 Asian Americans or Pacific Islanders, 14 Hispanic Americans), 43 international. Average age 31. 486 applicants, 63% accepted, 229 enrolled. In 2006, 294 degrees awarded. *Entrance requirements:* For master's, GMAT, resumé. Additional exam requirements/recommendations for international students: Required—TOEFL (minimum score 550 paper-based; 213 computer-based; 79 iBT). *Application deadline:* For fall admission, 8/1 priority date for domestic students, 6/1 for international students; for winter admission, 12/1 priority date for domestic students; for spring admission, 4/1 priority date for domestic students, 10/1 for international students. Applications are processed on a rolling basis. Application fee: $35. Electronic applications accepted. *Expenses:* Contact institution. Part-time tuition and fees vary according to degree level, campus/location and program. *Financial support:* In 2006–07, 175 students received support, including 11 research assistantships with full and partial tuition reimbursements available; career-related internships or fieldwork, scholarships/grants, and tuition waivers (partial) also available. Support available to part-time students. Financial award application deadline: 4/30; financial award applicants required to submit FAFSA. *Faculty research:* Supply chain management, category management, data mining, off-shoring. *Unit head:* Dr. Raghu Tadepalli, Associate Dean, 513-745-3525, Fax: 513-745-2929, E-mail: tadepalli@xavier.edu. *Application contact:* Jennifer Bush, Executive Director, MBA Programs, 513-745-3525, Fax: 513-745-2929, E-mail: xumba@xavier.edu.

EMERSON COLLEGE

School of Communication
Master of Arts in Global Marketing Communication & Advertising

Program of Study	Global marketing communication professionals are prepared to assist companies in establishing a worldwide presence and building brands that transcend national barriers, while simultaneously responding to the needs of consumers in particular local cultures.

Program of Study

Global marketing communication professionals are prepared to assist companies in establishing a worldwide presence and building brands that transcend national barriers, while simultaneously responding to the needs of consumers in particular local cultures.

Based on research and analysis within a cross-cultural framework, the Emerson College Master of Arts in Global Marketing Communication & Advertising (GMCA) program focuses on the strategic integration of advertising, public relations, branding, and direct and interactive marketing. Gaining a comprehensive understanding of the economic environment, partnerships, and cooperative strategies of the global market, students are prepared to manage the financial and strategic elements of marketing in a worldwide context.

The GMCA program is a one-year, full-time program in which all students move through the sequence of courses together as a cohort. The program culminates in a two-week capstone class during which students experience the process of an actual campaign pitch. As the final step of the program, Master of Arts (M.A.) degree candidates complete an internship at an organization anywhere in the world. Taking with them all that they have studied and learned, the internship is their opportunity to draw on real-world experience, classroom exercises, and their capstone.

For more information about Emerson's M.A. in Global Marketing Communication & Advertising Program, students should visit the Web site at http://admission.emerson.edu/admission/graduate/academics/gmca.cfm.

Research Facilities

The Emerson College library has more than 200,000 volumes, 20,000 journals (paper and electronic), 8,000 e-books, 10,000 nonprint materials, and 10,000 microforms in its collection that focuses on communication studies and the performing arts. Through membership in the Fenway Consortium, graduate students have access to more than 2 million volumes. Computer-assisted reference services provide bibliographic databases through Dialog, BRS, and other online services. The Online Computer Library Center is used for student research support.

M.A. candidates gain valuable hands-on experience in the Media Services Center, which provides students with access to approximately 2,400 films, videos, laser discs, and DVDs. The center is home to audio, video, and multimedia production facilities; a video studio; and several nonlinear editing suites comparable to those of any television studio in a major U.S. city. In addition, a marketing suite that opened in fall 2003 features a focus group room with an observation booth. There are also fully mediated classrooms.

Financial Aid

Emerson College offers several financial assistance programs that make an Emerson education possible: merit-based awards (domestic and international applicants), low-interest federal loans (domestic applicants only), Federal Work-Study (domestic applicants only), private loans (domestic and international applicants), Student Employment (domestic and international applicants), and alternative payment plans (domestic and international applicants). For detailed information, prospective students should visit the Office of Student Financial Services Web site at http://www.emerson.edu/financial_services.

Cost of Study

Tuition for the 2007–08 academic year is $840 per credit hour. Other fees vary and may apply.

Living and Housing Costs

Though on-campus housing is not available for its graduate students, the Emerson College Office of Off-Campus Student Services (http://www.emerson.edu/offcampus_housing/) offers assistance in finding housing, including local apartment listings, realtor lists, temporary accommodations, search tips, pertinent neighborhood information, a roommate networking service, and more. Costs for housing are comparable to those of rental properties available in larger East Coast cities.

Student Group

More than 950 graduate students representing forty-five states and sixty countries are enrolled in Emerson programs.

Student Outcomes

Graduates have found opportunities as account supervisors, marketing managers, and communication consultants in multinational corporations, international nonprofit organizations, and advertising agencies. Among recent employers are Avon, Disney, Greater Boston Convention Center and Visitors' Bureau, Levi Strauss, the National Geographic Society, and the United Nations.

Location

Situated in the heart of downtown Boston, Emerson offers access to the vast resources of a city that is home to the nation's finest educational institutions and an international hub of culture, media production, writing, publishing, communication, commerce, and medical innovation. Boston is a career launching pad for Emerson's students, many of whom intern or work at world-renowned organizations throughout the city. Emerson students from around the country and the world absorb the city's unique blend of local and global culture, and many find that Boston is an education in itself.

The College

Emerson College, founded in 1880 by Charles Wesley Emerson, has expanded upon its original mission of promoting the study of oratory and the performing arts by offering some of the nation's most distinctive graduate programs in communication.

Applying

Emerson's graduate programs welcome applicants from across the United States and around the world. Admission is competitive and selective. The College is looking for students whose academic and professional backgrounds, communication skills, and passion for the field meet the demands of their chosen program and promise a successful career.

The application deadline is March 1. Applications that are not complete by the final deadline are not reviewed by the admission committee. Applicants are responsible for ensuring the completion of their application. Application fees are nonrefundable; application forms and supporting materials become the property of the Office of Graduate Admission once they are sent to the office and are not returned.

All application materials, with the exception of GRE/GMAT test scores, must be submitted together in one package to ensure timely review. A complete application includes the application form (students may apply online or download the PDF version), the application fee ($60 for domestic applicants; $75 for international applicants), official transcripts from all colleges/universities previously attended, three letters of recommendation (by persons best able to assess academic and professional qualifications, including motivation and goals), GRE/GMAT test scores, two essay responses, and a professional resume.

Applicants whose native language is not English must provide evidence of English proficiency by submitting official TOEFL or IELTS test results. (Students from India and the Philippines are considered nonnative English speakers and are required to take the TOEFL.) Emerson College's school code for the TOEFL is 3367; no department code is needed. The minimum TOEFL score is 550 on the paper-based test (213 on the computer-based test or 80 on the Internet-based test). The minimum IELTS score is 6.5. Applicants who do not meet this requirement will not be reviewed for admission. For more information about these tests, students should visit http://www.toefl.org or http://www.ielts.org.

Decisions are made on complete applications within six to eight weeks. Deadlines for merit-based and federal aid applications for fall are March 1 and April 1, respectively. Students seeking additional information about financing their graduate education should visit http://www.emerson.edu/financial_services/info-grad.cfm/.

Correspondence and Information

Office of Graduate Admission
Emerson College
120 Boylston Street
Boston, Massachusetts 02116-4624

Phone: 617-824-8610
Fax: 617-824-8614
E-mail: gradapp@emerson.edu
Web site: http://admission.emerson.edu/admission/graduate

Emerson College

THE FACULTY AND THEIR RESEARCH

Joann M. Montepare, Chair of Marketing Communication and Associate Professor of Psychology; Ph.D., Brandeis. Dr. Montepare is a social-developmental psychologist who teaches courses in social psychology, developmental psychology, nonverbal communication, and face perception. Her research in person perception, emotion communication, and age-identity across the life span has been widely published in prominent journals such as the *Journal of Personality and Social Psychology, Developmental Psychology, Psychology and Aging, Advances in Experimental Social Psychology, Science,* and *Communication Research.* Dr. Montepare has also contributed to edited books such as *First Impressions, Ageism: Stereotyping and Prejudice Against Older Persons, The Social Psychology of Stigma,* and *Evolution and Social Psychology.* She is the Associate Editor for Special Issues for the *Journal of Nonverbal Behavior* and serves on the editorial board for the *Journal of Adult Development.*

Timothy Edgar, Graduate Program Director, Health Communication Program, and Associate Professor of Marketing Communication; Ph.D., Purdue. Dr. Edgar's professional career has been devoted to conducting quantitative and qualitative health-communication research on topics as diverse as HIV/AIDS, physical activity for adolescents, childhood and adult immunization, diabetes, epilepsy, and peptic ulcers. Prior to working at Emerson, Dr. Edgar was a Senior Study Director with Westat, a social science research firm in Rockville, Maryland. Dr. Edgar has also taught health communication and research methods at the University of Maryland, University of Wisconsin, and The George Washington University. Dr. Edgar has published widely in professional journals such as the *Journal of Health Communication, Health Education Research,* and *Health Communication,* and he has contributed to edited volumes such as *The Handbook of Health Communication.* He also co-edited the book, *AIDS: A Communication Perspective.* Dr. Edgar currently serves on the editorial board of *Health Communication,* and the *Journal of Health Communication.*

Thomas Vogel, Graduate Program Director, Global Marketing Communication and Advertising Program and Associate Professor of Marketing Communication; M.F.A., Academy of Fine Arts (Stuttgart). Mr. Vogel is a specialist in strategic communication on the Internet, online usability, and branding on the Internet. At the University of Applied Sciences in Wiesbaden, Germany, he was a Professor of Media Design in the Department of Media Management and also served as the Founding Dean from 1993 to 1999. Professor Vogel is an active public speaker, panelist, and consultant and is involved in special projects for the Internet, advertising, and multimedia. His current research focuses on the strategic design and usability aspects of interactive media, developing efficient experience design and online communication. He is also a founding partner of Mediaman, a German-based communications agency that specializes in integrated communication and advertising with a special focus on interactive communication. Formerly, he has worked as art director and creative director in New York City at Grey Advertising, Lois GGK, J. Walter Thompson, and Communication House.

Cathy Waters, Graduate Program Director, Integrated Marketing Communication Program and Executive-in-Residence; M.B.A., Boston College. Ms. Waters is a specialist in market analysis, forecasting, technical sales and sales management, personnel recruitment/development, and customer relations. Her career has spanned both the academic and professional worlds. Before coming to Emerson, she served on the faculty of Boston College's Carroll School of Management where she taught undergraduate and graduate courses in marketing, applied marketing management, product planning, and strategy as well as professional selling and sales management. Complementing her academic work is twelve years of experience in the corporate world with IMB where she held positions in sales and marketing management. Her combined expertise comes together in cases published in *Strategic Marketing Management Cases* and the *Journal of Business Research.*

William G. Anderson, Executive-in-Residence; M.B.A., Pennsylvania (Wharton). Mr. Anderson brings extensive, high-level experience to his teaching having worked for such corporations as Welch, Currier, Curry, Anderson, and Hill, Holliday, Connors, Cosmopulos. He has worked on major advertising assignments for brands, including Ameritech and Ocean Spray. At Emerson, Anderson collaborated to develop Marketing Finance for the IMC program and Financial and Strategic Context of Global Market Planning. His reputation for exceptional teaching has made his "Brands" classes very popular.

Karl Baehr, Executive-in-Residence; Ph.D., Regent University (Virginia). Dr. Baehr is a communication professional, scholar, and corporate leader whose career of more than twenty-five years is highlighted by a series of successes in new media and technology venture evolution, communication curriculum development, and pedagogy. He has extensive knowledge of mass media and Internet new media industries, marketing strategies and tactics, communication technologies and trends, broadcasting operations and management, audience research methods, distance education, and computer-mediated communication.

Silvia Hodges, Executive-in-Residence; Ph.D. candidate, Nottingham Trent (England). Ms. Hodges is a pioneer in legal marketing with expertise in continental European jurisdictions. Over the course of ten years as a communications and business development consultant, she has written several books and articles on law firm marketing. She is the founder of the Legal Marketing Italia network, writes a regular column on legal marketing for *Italia Ogg,* and has conducted professional seminars and workshops on legal marketing in Italy, Germany, England, and the United States. As a recipient of a scholarship from the German Department of Education and Research, she is completing her doctoral studies in law firm marketing with a special focus on marketing legal services to medium-size companies.

Abbott Ikeler, Executive-in-Residence; Ph.D., London. Dr. Ikeler taught literature and writing at Bowdoin College, University of Muenster, and Rhode Island College before entering the corporate world. His academic achievements include a Senior Fulbright Fellowship, a book on nineteenth-century aesthetics, and numerous articles on Victorian fiction. From the mid-1980s to 2001, he held public relations and advertising positions with three multinational organizations and a full-service agency. Immediately before coming to Emerson, Dr. Ikeler was Director of Communications and Public Affairs for the Internet and Networking Division of Motorola, a post he held for three years. The focus of his current research is global public relations, especially the impact of such nonmedia influencers as industry and financial analysts.

Julie C. Lellis, Instructor of Marketing Communication; Ph.D. candidate, North Carolina at Chapel Hill. Ms. Lellis brings experience teaching public relations issues and public relations writing, enhanced by service-learning practices in the classroom. Her award-winning research writing is influenced by her training in rehabilitation psychology and counseling coupled with mass communication and focuses on nonprofit communication about disability and chronic illness. She has worked in program development and clinical settings to aid adolescents. Her work has been presented at national and international conferences in public relations, mass media, and health communication.

Kristin Lieb, Instructor of Marketing Communication; Ph.D. candidate, Syracuse. Ms. Lieb's expertise combines executive experience in marketing and business development with scholarship in public communications. Her career has brought her from the interactive side of Newbury Comics to writing case studies for the Harvard Business School. She has served as the vice president for business development for Digital Media on Demand, Swap It, and Atomic Pop as well as consultant for America Online and UPS. She has been a freelance writer for *Billboard, Rolling Stone,* the *Boston Phoenix,* and the *Boston Globe.* Her research explores the branding of popular female celebrities and informs issues related to body image, gender, and aging.

Douglas Quintal, Executive-in-Residence; M.A., Emerson. Mr. Quintal specializes in entertainment marketing and teaches courses in integrated marketing communication, writing for marketing communication, advertising, and public relations. His professional experience includes work with Virgin Records, Hard Rock Café, Rogers and Cowen, Braithewaite and Katz, and the Charles Playhouse. He is on the Board of Directors for the Jennifer Stowers Quintal Education Foundation and is a member of the academic committee for the American Advertising Federation. He was the recipient of the 2007 Gold Key Honor Society Award for Outstanding Teaching. He is an avid musician and has opened for NoFX, Bad Religion, Rancid, and Blink 182.

James Rowean, Executive-in-Residence; M.A., Michigan State. Mr. Rowean brings twenty-five years of professional experience in advertising and marketing to his teaching of integrated marketing communication. A former account executive for Cronin/Wallwork Curry, Arnold Worldwide, and Campbell Ewald (Detroit), he also directed marketing for Dunkin' Donuts and Bread & Circus/Whole Foods Supermarkets. He has brand experience with Ocean Spray, Kimberly-Clark, Reebok, Timex, and Steinway Pianos. Rowean has been a guest lecturer at Boston University, New York University, and Boston College.

Tracy Worrell, Assistant Professor of Marketing Communication; Ph.D., Michigan State. Dr. Worrell is a rising scholar in the area of advertising, media, and health. Her timely work on television portrayals of weight, consumption, physical disability, and media impact has gained attention at national conferences and has been published in *Health Communication* and the *Journal of Creative Communications.* In addition to teaching core courses in human communication, she has taught courses in mass media, public relations, and public speaking. Her applied work in the television industry as a traffic manager, continuity director, and disc jockey complements her scholarly expertise.

Seounmi Han Youn, Assistant Professor of Marketing Communication; Ph.D., Minnesota. Dr. Youn has established a productive line of research focusing on the antecedents, correlates, and consequences of online consumer socialization among the young. In addition to presenting her work at national and international conferences, it has been featured in professional journals such as the *Journal of Advertising Research, Psychology and Marketing,* the *Journal of Interactive Advertising,* and the *Journal of Broadcasting and Electronic Media.* Dr. Youn's instruction in courses that deal with global applications and research methodology is enhanced by her industry experience with DongSeo Marketing Research in Seoul, Korea.

Section 12
Management Information Systems

This section contains a directory of institutions offering graduate work in management information systems, followed by in-depth entries submitted by institutions that chose to prepare detailed program descriptions. Additional information about programs listed in the directory but not augmented by an in-depth entry may be obtained by writing directly to the dean of a graduate school or chair of a department at the address given in the directory.

For programs offering related work, see also in this book Business Administration and Management. In Book 5, see Computer Science and Information Technology and Management of Engineering and Technology.

CONTENTS

Management Information Systems

Adelphi University, School of Business, Department of Management, Marketing, and Decision Sciences, Garden City, NY 11530-0701. Offers management information systems (MBA); management/human resource management (MBA); marketing/e-commerce (MBA). Part-time and evening/weekend programs available. *Students:* 67 full-time (34 women), 173 part-time (85 women); includes 44 minority (24 African Americans, 11 Asian Americans or Pacific Islanders, 9 Hispanic Americans), 49 international. Average age 31. In 2006, 122 degrees awarded. *Degree requirements:* For master's, capstone course. *Entrance requirements:* For master's, GMAT, 2 letters of recommendation. Additional exam requirements/recommendations for international students: Required—TOEFL. *Application deadline:* For fall admission, 5/1 for international students; for spring admission, 12/1 for international students. Applications are processed on a rolling basis. Application fee: $50. Electronic applications accepted. *Financial support:* Research assistantships with full and partial tuition reimbursements, career-related internships or fieldwork, Federal Work-Study, institutionally sponsored loans, scholarships/grants, and unspecified assistantships available. Financial award application deadline: 3/1; financial award applicants required to submit FAFSA. *Faculty research:* Supply chain management, distribution channels, productivity benchmark analysis, data envelopment analysis, financial portfolio analysis. *Unit head:* Dr. Allan Ashley, Chairperson, 516-877-4640, E-mail: ashley@adelphi.edu. *Application contact:* Christine Murphy, Director of Admissions, 516-877-3050, Fax: 516-877-3039, E-mail: graduateadmissions@adelphi.edu.

Air Force Institute of Technology, Graduate School of Engineering and Management, Department of Systems and Engineering Management, Dayton, OH 45433-7765. Offers cost analysis (MS); environmental and engineering management (MS); environmental engineering science (MS); information resource/systems management (MS). *Accreditation:* ABET. Part-time programs available. *Degree requirements:* For master's, thesis. *Entrance requirements:* For master's, GRE, GMAT, minimum GPA of 3.0.

Alliant International University–San Diego, Marshall Goldsmith School of Management, Business and Management Division, San Diego, CA 92131-1799. Offers business administration (MBA); information and technology management (DBA); international business (MIBA, DBA), including finance (DBA), marketing (DBA); strategic business (DBA); sustainable management (MBA). Part-time and evening/weekend programs available. *Students:* 87 full-time (22 women), 51 part-time (17 women); includes 27 minority (8 African Americans, 2 American Indian/Alaska Native, 8 Asian Americans or Pacific Islanders, 9 Hispanic Americans), 68 international. Average age 32. 104 applicants, 66% accepted, 40 enrolled. *Degree requirements:* For doctorate, thesis/dissertation. *Entrance requirements:* For master's, GMAT, minimum GPA of 3.0; for doctorate, GMAT, minimum GPA of 3.3. Additional exam requirements/recommendations for international students: Required—TOEFL (minimum score 550 paper-based; 213 computer-based), TWE (minimum score 5). *Application deadline:* For fall admission, 8/1 priority date for domestic and international students; for spring admission, 12/1 priority date for domestic and international students. Applications are processed on a rolling basis. Application fee: $55. Electronic applications accepted. *Expenses:* Tuition: Part-time $825 per unit. Tuition and fees vary according to course load, degree level and program. *Financial support:* Research assistantships, teaching assistantships, career-related internships or fieldwork, Federal Work-Study, institutionally sponsored loans, scholarships/grants, and tuition waivers (partial) available. Support available to part-time students. Financial award application deadline: 2/15; financial award applicants required to submit FAFSA. *Faculty research:* Consumer behavior, international business, strategic management, information systems. *Unit head:* Dr. Fred Phillips, Associate Dean, 866-825-5426, Fax: 855-635-4739, E-mail: admissions@alliant.edu. *Application contact:* Alliant International University Central Contact Center, 866-U-ALLIANT, Fax: 858-635-4555, E-mail: admissions@alliant.edu.

See Close-Up on page 203.

American InterContinental University, Program in Business Administration, Los Angeles, CA 90066. Offers business administration (MBA); global technology management (MBA). Part-time and evening/weekend programs available. Postbaccalaureate distance learning degree programs offered. *Faculty:* 5 full-time (0 women). *Students:* 44 full-time (19 women), 4 part-time (3 women); includes 6 minority (3 African Americans, 1 Asian American or Pacific Islander, 2 Hispanic Americans), 10 international. Average age 34. In 2006, 32 degrees awarded. *Entrance requirements:* For master's, interview, proof of Baccalaureate. Additional exam requirements/recommendations for international students: Required—TOEFL (minimum score 550 paper-based; 79 iBT), IELTS (minimum score 7). *Application deadline:* Applications are processed on a rolling basis. Application fee: $50. Electronic applications accepted. *Expenses:* Tuition: Full-time $26,400. *Financial support:* Institutionally sponsored loans, scholarships/grants, and health care benefits available. Support available to part-time students. Financial award applicants required to submit FAFSA. *Faculty research:* Organizational psychology management, marketing, economics, international relations. *Unit head:* Dr. James Carroll, Dean of School of Business, 310-302-2639, E-mail: james.carroll@la.aiuniv.edu. *Application contact:* Admissions Advisor, 310-302-2000, Fax: 310-302-2410.

American InterContinental University, Program in Information Technology, Los Angeles, CA 90066. Offers MIT. Part-time programs available. *Faculty:* 4 full-time (1 woman). *Students:* 8 full-time (3 women), 2 part-time (1 woman); includes 2 minority (both African Americans), 1 international. Average age 38. In 2006, 15 degrees awarded. *Entrance requirements:* For master's, interview. Additional exam requirements/recommendations for international students: Required—TOEFL (minimum score 550 paper-based; 79 iBT), IELTS (minimum score 7). *Application deadline:* Applications are processed on a rolling basis. Application fee: $50. Electronic applications accepted. *Expenses: Contact institution. Financial support:* Institutionally sponsored loans, scholarships/grants, and health care benefits available. Support available to part-time students. Financial award applicants required to submit FAFSA. *Faculty research:* Computer science, computer and systems science, information science, man and cybernetics. *Unit head:* Dr. Shantaram Vasikarla, Dean of Information Technology, 310-302-2646, E-mail: svasikarla@la.aiuniv.edu. *Application contact:* Admissions Advisor, Fax: 310-302-2001.

American InterContinental University Dunwoody Campus, Program in Information Technology, Atlanta, GA 30328. Offers MIT. Part-time and evening/weekend programs available. *Degree requirements:* For master's, technical proficiency demonstration. *Entrance requirements:* For master's, Computer Programmer Aptitude Battery Exam, interview. Electronic applications accepted. *Faculty research:* Operating systems, security issues, networks and routing, computer hardware.

American InterContinental University-London, Program in Information Technology, London, United Kingdom. Offers MIT. *Degree requirements:* For master's, thesis optional. *Entrance requirements:* For master's, interview, professional experience. Electronic applications accepted.

American Sentinel University, Graduate Programs, Englewood, CO 80112. Offers business administration (MBA); business intelligence (MS); computer science (MSCS); health information management (MS); healthcare (MBA); information systems (MSIS); nursing (MSN). Part-time and evening/weekend programs available. Postbaccalaureate distance learning degree programs offered (no on-campus study). *Faculty:* 40. *Students:* 400. Average age 36. In 2006, 47 degrees awarded. *Entrance requirements:* Additional exam requirements/recommendations for international students: Required—TOEFL (minimum score 600 paper-based; 215 computer-based). *Application deadline:* Applications are processed on a rolling basis. Application fee: $50. Electronic applications accepted. *Unit head:* Janette D. Marshall, Registrar, 800-729-2427 Ext. 2211, Fax: 205-326-3822, E-mail: jan.marshall@americansentinel.edu. *Application contact:* Natalie A. Nixon, Director of Admissions, 800-729-2427, Fax: 205-328-2229, E-mail: natalie.nixon@americansentinel.edu.

American University, Kogod School of Business, Department of Information Technology, Washington, DC 20016-8001. Offers information systems (MS, Certificate). *Faculty:* 10 full-time (2 women). *Students:* Average age 37. In 2006, 15 degrees awarded. *Expenses:* Tuition: Full-time $18,864; part-time $1,048 per credit. Required fees: $380. Tuition and fees vary according to program. *Unit head:* Dr. Erran Carmel, Chair, 202-885-1928.

American University, Kogod School of Business, Department of Management, Program in Management of Global Information Technology, Washington, DC 20016-8001. Offers MBA. Part-time and evening/weekend programs available. *Students:* 7 full-time (2 women), 11 part-time (3 women); includes 4 minority (2 African Americans, 1 Asian American or Pacific Islander, 1 Hispanic American), 4 international. Average age 30. In 2006, 6 degrees awarded. *Entrance requirements:* For master's, GMAT. Additional exam requirements/recommendations for international students: Required—TOEFL. *Application deadline:* For fall admission, 2/1 priority date for domestic students; for spring admission, 10/1 priority date for domestic students. Application fee: $50. *Expenses:* Tuition: Full-time $18,864; part-time $1,048 per credit. Required fees: $380. Tuition and fees vary according to program. *Financial support:* Fellowships, research assistantships, career-related internships or fieldwork, Federal Work-Study, and institutionally sponsored loans available. Support available to part-time students. Financial award application deadline: 2/1. *Faculty research:* Global electronic commerce, global software development terms, end-user computer, knowledge management, assessing value of IT.

American University, Kogod School of Business, Department of Marketing, Program in Marketing Information and Technology, Washington, DC 20016-8001. Offers MBA. In 2006, 1 degree awarded. *Entrance requirements:* For master's, GMAT. *Expenses:* Tuition: Full-time $18,864; part-time $1,048 per credit. Required fees: $380. Tuition and fees vary according to program.

Argosy University, Atlanta Campus, College of Business, Atlanta, GA 30328. Offers accounting (DBA); customized professional concentration (MBA, DBA); finance (MBA); healthcare administration (MBA); information systems (DBA); information systems management (MBA); international business (MBA, DBA); management (MBA, DBA); marketing (MBA, DBA). Part-time programs available. *Students:* 53 full-time (38 women), 35 part-time (28 women); includes 73 minority (66 African Americans, 3 Asian Americans or Pacific Islanders, 4 Hispanic Americans). *Degree requirements:* For master's, comprehensive exam (for some programs), registration; for doctorate, thesis/dissertation, comprehensive exam, registration. *Entrance requirements:* For master's, minimum undergraduate GPA of 3.0; for doctorate, master's degree, minimum GPA of 3.0. Additional exam requirements/recommendations for international students: Required—TOEFL. *Application deadline:* For fall admission, 7/1 priority date for domestic students, 6/1 for international students; for spring admission, 11/1 priority date for domestic students, 10/1 for international students. Applications are processed on a rolling basis. Application fee: $50. Electronic applications accepted. *Financial support:* Applicants required to submit FAFSA. *Unit head:* Dr. Robert A. Berg, Department Chair, 770-407-1042, E-mail: rberg@argosy.edu. *Application contact:* Christa Holton, Director of Admissions, 770-671-1200 Ext. 1014, Fax: 770-671-9050, E-mail: cholton@argosy.edu.

See Close-Up on page 207.

Argosy University, Chicago Campus, College of Business, Chicago, IL 60603. Offers accounting (DBA); customized professional concentration (MBA, DBA); finance (MBA); healthcare administration (MBA); information systems (DBA); information systems management (MBA); international business (MBA, DBA); management (MBA, DBA); marketing (MBA, DBA). Part-time and evening/weekend programs available. *Faculty:* 2 full-time (both women), 4 part-time/adjunct (3 women). *Students:* 52 full-time (30 women), 18 part-time (7 women); includes 37 minority (24 African Americans, 7 Asian Americans or Pacific Islanders, 6 Hispanic Americans). Average age 37. 32 applicants, 81% accepted, 25 enrolled. In 2006, 9 master's, 2 doctorates awarded. *Entrance requirements:* For master's and doctorate, minimum GPA of 3.0. Additional exam requirements/recommendations for international students: Required—TOEFL (minimum score 550 paper-based; 213 computer-based). *Application deadline:* For fall admission, 2/28 for domestic and international students; for spring admission, 10/30 for domestic and international students. Applications are processed on a rolling basis. Application fee: $50. Electronic applications accepted. *Financial support:* In 2006–07, 3 students received support. Scholarships/grants available. Financial award application deadline: 4/1. *Unit head:* Dr. Cynthia Scarlett, Associate Head, 800-626-4123, Fax: 212-727-7750, E-mail: cscarlett@argosy.edu. *Application contact:* Ashley Delaney, Director of Admissions, 800-626-4123, Fax: 312-777-7750, E-mail: argosyadmissions@argosy.edu.

See Close-Up on page 209.

Argosy University, Denver Campus, College of Business, Denver, CO 80203. Offers accounting (DBA); customized professional concentraion (DBA); customized professional concentration (MBA); finance (MBA); healthcare administration (MBA); information systems (DBA); information systems management (MBA); international business (MBA, DBA); management (MBA, MSM, DBA); marketing (MBA, DBA).

See Close-Up on page 213.

Argosy University, Hawai'i Campus, College of Business, Honolulu, HI 96813. Offers accounting (DBA); customized professional concentration (MBA, DBA); finance (MBA, Certificate); healthcare administration (MBA, Certificate); information systems (DBA); information systems management (MBA, Certificate); international business (MBA, DBA, Certificate); management (MBA, DBA); marketing (MBA, DBA, Certificate). Evening/weekend programs available. *Faculty:* 12 part-time/adjunct (2 women). *Students:* 3 full-time (2 women), 1 part-time; includes 2 minority (1 Asian American or Pacific Islander, 1 Hispanic American). 6 applicants, 67% accepted, 3 enrolled. *Degree requirements:* For master's, capstone project. *Entrance requirements:* For master's, minimum GPA of 3.0 in last 60 hours. Additional exam requirements/recommendations for international students: Required—TOEFL (minimum score 550 paper-based; 213 computer-based). *Application deadline:* For fall admission, 1/15 priority date for domestic students; for spring admission, 10/15 for domestic students. Applications are processed on a rolling basis. Application fee: $50. *Financial support:* Teaching assistantships, Federal Work-Study and scholarships/grants available. Support available to part-time students. *Unit head:* Lisa Parker, Interim Chair, College of Business and Information Technology, 888-323-2777, Fax: 808-536-5505, E-mail: lparker@argosy.edu. *Application contact:* Cherie Andrade, Director of Admissions, 888-323-2777, Fax: 808-536-5505, E-mail: candrade@argosy.edu.

See Close-Up on page 215.

Argosy University, Inland Empire Campus, College of Business, San Bernardino, CA 92408. Offers accounting (DBA); customized professional concentration (MBA, DBA); finance (MBA); healthcare administration (MBA); information systems (DBA); information systems management (MBA); international business (MBA, DBA); management (DBA); mangement (MBA); marketing (MBA, DBA).

See Close-Up on page 217.

Argosy University, Nashville Campus, College of Business, Franklin, TN 37067-7226. Offers accounting (DBA); customized professional concentration (DBA); information systems (DBA); international business (DBA); management (DBA); marketing (DBA). *Degree requirements:* For doctorate, thesis/dissertation, comprehensive exam.

See Close-Up on page 219.

Argosy University, Orange County Campus, College of Business, Santa Ana, CA 92704. Offers accounting (DBA, Adv C); customized professional concentration (MBA, DBA); finance

(MBA, Certificate); healthcare administration (MBA, Certificate); information systems (DBA, Adv C); information systems management (MBA); international business (MBA, DBA, Adv C, Certificate); management (MBA, MSM, DBA, EDBA); mangement (Adv C); marketing (MBA, DBA, Adv C, Certificate); organizational leadership (Ed D); public administration (MBA, Certificate). Part-time and evening/weekend programs available. *Faculty:* 4 full-time (1 woman), 20 part-time/adjunct (7 women). *Students:* 163 full-time (64 women), 41 part-time (16 women). Average age 42. 72 applicants, 51 enrolled. In 2006, 6 master's, 23 doctorates awarded. *Degree requirements:* For doctorate, thesis/dissertation, preliminary and final dissertation defense, comprehensive exam. *Entrance requirements:* For master's, minimum GPA of 3.0 in final 2 years of course work, 3 letters of recommendation, resumé; for doctorate, minimum GPA of 3.0 in graduate study, 3 letters of recommendation, resumé. Additional exam requirements/recommendations for international students: Required—TOEFL. *Application deadline:* Applications are processed on a rolling basis. Application fee: $50. Electronic applications accepted. *Financial support:* Federal Work-Study, institutionally sponsored loans, and scholarships/grants available. Support available to part-time students. Financial award applicants required to submit FAFSA. *Faculty research:* Crisis management, leadership in organizations, finance, business systems. *Unit head:* Dr. Ray London, Dean, 800-716-9598, Fax: 714-437-1284, E-mail: auocadmissions@argosy.edu. *Application contact:* Mark Betz, Director of Admissions, 800-716-9598, Fax: 714-437-1697, E-mail: mbetz@argosy.edu.

See Close-Up on page 221.

Argosy University, Phoenix Campus, College of Business, Phoenix, AZ 85021. Offers accounting (DBA); customized professional concentration (MBA, DBA); finance (MBA); healthcare administration (MBA); information systems (DBA); information systems management (MBA); international business (MBA, DBA); management (MBA, DBA); marketing (MBA, DBA). Part-time and evening/weekend programs available. *Faculty:* 1 full-time (0 women). *Students:* 7 full-time (4 women); includes 2 minority (1 African American, 1 Hispanic American). *Entrance requirements:* For doctorate, master's degree. Additional exam requirements/recommendations for international students: Required—TOEFL (minimum score 550 paper-based; 213 computer-based). Application fee: $50. *Financial support:* In 2006–07, 2 students received support. Federal Work-Study, institutionally sponsored loans, and scholarships/grants available. Support available to part-time students. Financial award applicants required to submit FAFSA. *Unit head:* Dr. Gary Berg, Program Chair, 866-216-2777, Fax: 602-216-2601. *Application contact:* Andy Hughes, Director of Admissions, 866-216-2777 Ext. 3110, Fax: 602-216-2601, E-mail: ahughes@argosyu.edu.

See Close-Up on page 223.

Argosy University, San Diego Campus, College of Business, San Diego, CA 92108. Offers accounting (DBA); customized professional concentration (MBA, DBA); finance (MBA); information systems (DBA); information systems management (MBA); international business (MBA, DBA); management (MBA, MSM, DBA); marketing (MBA, DBA); public administration (MBA).

See Close-Up on page 225.

Argosy University, San Francisco Bay Area Campus, College of Business, Point Richmond, CA 94804-3547. Offers accounting (DBA); corporate compliance (MBA); customized professional concentration (MBA, DBA); finance (MBA); healthcare administration (MBA); information systems (DBA); information systems management (MBA); international business (MBA, DBA); management (MBA, MSM, DBA); marketing (MBA, DBA). Part-time and evening/weekend programs available. *Faculty:* 2 full-time (0 women), 9 part-time/adjunct (0 women). *Students:* 29 full-time (8 women), 9 part-time (2 women); includes 30 minority (5 African Americans, 24 Asian Americans or Pacific Islanders, 1 Hispanic American). 21 applicants, 76% accepted, 13 enrolled. In 2006, 3 master's, 2 doctorates awarded. *Degree requirements:* For master's, capstone project; for doctorate, thesis/dissertation, comprehensive exam, registration. *Entrance requirements:* For master's, minimum GPA of 3.0; for doctorate, MBA or minimum GPA of 3.0. Additional exam requirements/recommendations for international students: Required—TOEFL (minimum score 550 paper-based; 213 computer-based). *Application deadline:* For fall admission, 7/1 priority date for domestic and international students; for winter admission, 11/1 priority date for domestic and international students; for spring admission, 4/1 priority date for domestic and international students. Applications are processed on a rolling basis. Application fee: $50. Electronic applications accepted. *Financial support:* Federal Work-Study and scholarships/grants available. Support available to part-time students. Financial award applicants required to submit FAFSA. *Unit head:* Dr. Anthony Martinez, Department Chair, Business and Information Technology, 866-215-0277, Fax: 510-215-0299, E-mail: amartinez@argosy.edu. *Application contact:* John Vincent Stofan, Director of Admissions, 866-215-2727 Ext. 205, Fax: 510-215-0299, E-mail: jstofan@argosy.edu.

See Close-Up on page 227.

Argosy University, Santa Monica Campus, College of Business, Santa Monica, CA 90405. Offers accounting (DBA); customized professional concentration (MBA, DBA); finance (MBA); healthcare administration (MBA); information systems (DBA); information systems management (MBA); international business (MBA, DBA); management (MBA, MS, MSM, DBA); marketing (MBA, DBA).

See Close-Up on page 229.

Argosy University, Sarasota Campus, College of Business, Sarasota, FL 34235-8246. Offers accounting (DBA, Adv C); customized professional concentration (MBA, DBA); finance (MBA, Certificate); healtcare administration (Certificate); healthcare administration (MBA); information systems (DBA, Adv C); information systems management (MBA, Certificate); international business (MBA, DBA, Adv C, Certificate); management (MBA, MSM, DBA); mangement (Adv C); marketing (MBA, DBA, Adv C, Certificate). Part-time and evening/weekend programs available. Postbaccalaureate distance learning degree programs offered (minimal on-campus study). *Faculty:* 6 full-time (3 women), 13 part-time/adjunct (5 women). *Students:* 71 applicants, 92% accepted, 64 enrolled. In 2006, 7 master's, 30 doctorates awarded. *Degree requirements:* For doctorate, thesis/dissertation, comprehensive exam. *Entrance requirements:* For master's, minimum GPA of 3.0; for doctorate, minimum undergraduate GPA of 3.0. Additional exam requirements/recommendations for international students: Required—TOEFL. *Application deadline:* Applications are processed on a rolling basis. Application fee: $50. Electronic applications accepted. *Financial support:* Federal Work-Study and scholarships/grants available. Support available to part-time students. Financial award application deadline: 4/1; financial award applicants required to submit FAFSA. *Unit head:* Dr. Kathleen Cornett, Dean, 800-331-5995, Fax: 941-379-9464, E-mail: kcornett@argosy.edu. *Application contact:* Admissions Representative, 800-331-5995 Ext. 221, Fax: 941-379-5964.

See Close-Up on page 231.

Argosy University, Schaumburg Campus, College of Business, Schaumburg, IL 60173-5403. Offers accounting (DBA, Adv C); corporate compliance (MBA); customized professional concentration (MBA, DBA); finance (MBA, Certificate); healthcare administration (MBA, Certificate); information systems (DBA, Adv C); information systems management (MBA, Certificate); international business (MBA, DBA, Adv C, Certificate); management (MBA, DBA, Adv C, Certificate); marketing (MBA, DBA, Adv C, Certificate). Part-time and evening/weekend programs available. *Faculty:* 1 (woman) full-time, 7 part-time/adjunct (0 women). *Students:* 36 full-time, 23 part-time. 13 applicants, 69% accepted, 9 enrolled. In 2006, 5 master's, 4 doctorates awarded. *Degree requirements:* For doctorate, thesis/dissertation, comprehensive exam. *Entrance requirements:* For master's and doctorate, minimum GPA of 3.0. Additional exam requirements/recommendations for international students: Required—TOEFL. *Application deadline:* For fall admission, 3/15 priority date for domestic and international students; for spring admission, 10/15 priority date for domestic and international students. Applications are processed on a rolling basis. Application fee: $50. Electronic applications accepted. *Expenses:* Contact institution. *Financial support:* Federal Work-Study and scholarships/grants available. *Unit head:* Dr. Harriet Kandelman, Dean, 866-290-2777, Fax: 847-548-6159, E-mail: agrosyadmissions@argosy.edu. *Application contact:* Jamal Scott, Director of Admissions, 847-598-6159, Fax: 630-598-6191, E-mail: jscott@argosy.edu.

See Close-Up on page 233.

Argosy University, Seattle Campus, College of Business, Seattle, WA 98121. Offers accounting (DBA); customized professional concentration (MBA, DBA); finance (MBA); healthcare administration (MBA); information systems (DBA); information systems management (MBA); international business (MBA, DBA); management (MSM, DBA); mangement (MBA); marketing (MBA, DBA). Part-time and evening/weekend programs available. *Students:* 1 applicant, 100% accepted, 1 enrolled. In 2006, 1 degree awarded. *Degree requirements:* For master's, capstone experience; for doctorate, thesis/dissertation, comprehensive exam (for some programs). *Entrance requirements:* For master's, minimum GPA of 3.0 in last 2 years or cumulative of 2.7; for doctorate, minimum GPA of 3.0. Additional exam requirements/recommendations for international students: Required—TOEFL (minimum score 550 paper-based; 213 computer-based). *Application deadline:* For fall admission, 4/15 priority date for domestic students, 4/15 for international students; for winter admission, 10/15 priority date for domestic students. Applications are processed on a rolling basis. Application fee: $50. Electronic applications accepted. *Expenses:* Contact institution. *Financial support:* Federal Work-Study and unspecified assistantships available. Support available to part-time students. Financial award applicants required to submit FAFSA. *Unit head:* Dr. Kylene Quinn, Chair, 206-393-3543, Fax: 206-283-5777, E-mail: kquinn@argosy.edu. *Application contact:* Heather Simpson, Director of Admissions, 866-283-4500, Fax: 206-283-5777, E-mail: hsimpson@argosy.edu.

See Close-Up on page 235.

Argosy University, Tampa Campus, College of Business, Tampa, FL 33614. Offers accounting (DBA); customized professional concentration (MBA, DBA); finance (MBA, Certificate); healthcare administration (MBA, Certificate); information systems (DBA); information systems management (MBA); international business (MBA, DBA, Certificate); management (MBA, MSM, DBA); marketing (MBA, DBA, Certificate); public administration (MBA). *Entrance requirements:* For doctorate, minimum GPA of 3.0. *Unit head:* Dr. Andrew Ghillyer, Dean, 813-393-5270, E-mail: aghillyer@argosy.edu.

See Close-Up on page 237.

Argosy University, Twin Cities Campus, College of Business, Eagan, MN 55121. Offers accounting (DBA); corporate compliance (MBA); customized professional certification (DBA); customized professional concentration (MBA); finance (MBA); healthcare administration (MBA); information systems (DBA); information systems management (MBA); international business (MBA, DBA); management (MBA, MSM, DBA, EDBA); marketing (MBA, DBA). Part-time and evening/weekend programs available. *Faculty:* 1 (woman) full-time, 20 part-time/adjunct (6 women). *Students:* 47 full-time (23 women), 20 part-time (11 women); includes 21 minority (10 African Americans, 1 American Indian/Alaska Native, 9 Asian Americans or Pacific Islanders, 1 Hispanic American). Average age 39. 72 applicants, 76% accepted, 45 enrolled. In 2006, 6 degrees awarded. *Degree requirements:* For doctorate, thesis/dissertation, comprehensive exam. *Entrance requirements:* For master's, 3 letters of recommendation, bachelor's degree in a related field, minimum undergraduate GPA of 3.0, resumé; for doctorate, 3 letters of recommendation, master's degree in a related field, minimum GPA of 3.0, resumé. Additional exam requirements/recommendations for international students: Required—TOEFL (minimum score 550 paper-based; 213 computer-based). *Application deadline:* For fall admission, 5/15 priority date for domestic students, 5/15 for international students; for spring admission, 10/15 priority date for domestic students, 10/15 for international students. Applications are processed on a rolling basis. Application fee: $50. Electronic applications accepted. *Financial support:* In 2006–07, 3 fellowships with partial tuition reimbursements, 3 teaching assistantships with partial tuition reimbursements were awarded; Federal Work-Study and scholarships/grants also available. Financial award applicants required to submit FAFSA. *Unit head:* Dr. Paula King, Department Head, 651-846-3377, E-mail: pking@argosy.edu. *Application contact:* Jennifer Radke, 2nd Director of Graduate Admissions, 651-846-3300, Fax: 651-994-7954, E-mail: tcadmissions@argosy.edu.

See Close-Up on page 239.

Argosy University, Washington DC Campus, College of Business, Arlington, VA 22209. Offers accounting (DBA); customized professional concentration (MBA, DBA); finance (MBA); healthcare administration (MBA); information systems (DBA); information systems management (MBA); international business (MBA, DBA); international business marketing (Graduate Certificate); management (MBA, DBA); marketing (MBA, DBA). *Faculty:* 1 full-time (0 women), 5 part-time/adjunct (2 women). *Students:* 5 full-time (4 women), 4 part-time (1 woman); includes 4 minority (3 African Americans, 1 Asian American or Pacific Islander). 21 applicants, 86% accepted. *Degree requirements:* For master's, thesis (for some programs), comprehensive exam (for some programs); for doctorate, thesis/dissertation, comprehensive exam. *Entrance requirements:* For master's and doctorate, minimum GPA of 3.0. Additional exam requirements/recommendations for international students: Required—TOEFL (minimum score 550 paper-based; 213 computer-based). *Application deadline:* For fall admission, 6/15 priority date for domestic students; for spring admission, 10/15 priority date for domestic students. Application fee: $50. *Financial support:* Federal Work-Study and scholarships/grants available. Financial award applicants required to submit FAFSA. *Unit head:* Dr. Colleen Logan, Academic Affairs Officer, 866-703-2777, Fax: 703-521-5850, E-mail: dcadmissions@argosy.edu. *Application contact:* Emily Peck, Director of Admissions, 866-703-2777 Ext. 5851, Fax: 703-526-5850, E-mail: dcadmissions@argosy.edu.

See Close-Up on page 241.

Arizona State University, Division of Graduate Studies, W.P. Carey School of Business, Department of Information Systems, Tempe, AZ 85287. Offers MS, MBA/MS.

Arizona State University, Division of Graduate Studies, W.P. Carey School of Business, Program in Business Administration, Tempe, AZ 85287. Offers accountancy (PhD); business administration (MBA); finance (PhD); health services research (PhD); information management (PhD); management (PhD); marketing (PhD); supply chain management (PhD); JD/MBA; MBA/M Arch; MBA/MHSM. MBA/MIM offered jointly with Thunderbird, The American Graduate School of International Management and Groupe Ecole Supéieure de Commerce, Toulouse, France. *Accreditation:* AACSB. *Degree requirements:* For master's, thesis optional; for doctorate, thesis/dissertation. *Entrance requirements:* For master's, GMAT.

Arizona State University, Division of Graduate Studies, W.P. Carey School of Business, School of Accountancy and Information Management, Tempe, AZ 85287. Offers M Tax, MAIS, MBA/M Tax, MBA/MAIS. *Accreditation:* AACSB. *Degree requirements:* For master's, thesis optional. *Entrance requirements:* For master's, GMAT.

Arizona State University at the Polytechnic Campus, College of Science and Technology, Department of Technology Management, Mesa, AZ 85212. Offers MS. Part-time and evening/weekend programs available. *Faculty:* 10 full-time (2 women). *Students:* 39 full-time (19 women), 181 part-time (76 women); includes 31 minority (6 African Americans, 6 American Indian/Alaska Native, 5 Asian Americans or Pacific Islanders, 14 Hispanic Americans), 20 international. Average age 36. 86 applicants, 88% accepted, 49 enrolled. In 2006, 28 degrees awarded. *Degree requirements:* For master's, thesis or applied project and oral defense. *Entrance requirements:* For master's, GRE, 30 semester hours in technology or high school equivalent; 16 semester hours of physical science and math; adequate technical preparation in a selected technology; resumé; industrial experience (strongly recommended); minimum GPA of 3.0. Additional exam requirements/recommendations for international students: Required—TOEFL (minimum score 550 paper-based; 213 computer-based; 83 iBT); Recommended—TWE. *Application deadline:* Applications are processed on a rolling basis. Application fee: $50. Electronic applications accepted. *Expenses:* Tuition, state resident: part-time $310 per credit hour. Tuition, nonresident: part-time $688 per credit hour. *Financial*

Management Information Systems

Arizona State University at the Polytechnic Campus (continued)
support: In 2006–07, 7 research assistantships with full and partial tuition reimbursements (averaging $9,316 per year) were awarded; teaching assistantships with full tuition reimbursements, career-related internships or fieldwork, Federal Work-Study, scholarships/grants, health care benefits, tuition waivers (full and partial), and unspecified assistantships also available. Support available to part-time students. Financial award application deadline: 3/1; financial award applicants required to submit FAFSA. *Faculty research:* Digital imaging, digital publishing, Internet development/e-commerce, information databases, multimedia, commercial digital photography, digital workflow, computer graphics modeling and animation, information design, sociotechnology, visual and technical literacy, environmental management, quality mgmt, project mgmt, international environmental, industrial ethics, hazardous materials, environmental chemistry. Total annual research expenditures: $407,295. *Unit head:* Dr. Thomas Schildgen, Chair, 480-727-1005, Fax: 480-727-1684, E-mail: ts@asu.edu.

Arkansas State University, Graduate School, College of Business, Department of Computer and Information Technology, Jonesboro, State University, AR 72467. Offers business education (SCCT); business technology education (MSE); information systems and e-commerce (MS). Part-time programs available. *Faculty:* 6 full-time (1 woman), 1 part-time/adjunct (0 women). *Students:* 8 full-time (4 women), 17 part-time (13 women); includes 8 minority (all African Americans), 1 international. Average age 33. 13 applicants, 100% accepted, 13 enrolled. In 2006, 9 degrees awarded. *Degree requirements:* For master's and SCCT, thesis or alternative, comprehensive exam. *Entrance requirements:* For master's, GRE General Test or MAT, appropriate bachelor's degree, official transcript. Additional exam requirements/recommendations for international students: Required—TOEFL (minimum score 213 computer-based). *Application deadline:* Applications are processed on a rolling basis. Application fee: $30 ($40 for international students). Electronic applications accepted. *Expenses: Contact institution. Financial support:* Teaching assistantships, career-related internships or fieldwork and unspecified assistantships available. Financial award application deadline: 7/1; financial award applicants required to submit FAFSA. *Unit head:* Dr. John Seydel, Chair, 870-972-3416, Fax: 870-972-3417, E-mail: jseydel@astate.edu.

Aspen University, Programs in Information Management, Denver, CO 80246. Offers information management (MS); information systems (Certificate). Part-time and evening/weekend programs available. Postbaccalaureate distance learning degree programs offered (no on-campus study). Electronic applications accepted.

Auburn University, Graduate School, College of Business, Department of Management, Auburn University, AL 36849. Offers human resource management (PhD); management (MS, PhD); management information systems (MMIS, PhD). *Accreditation:* AACSB. Part-time programs available. *Faculty:* 27 full-time (4 women). *Students:* 27 full-time (6 women), 22 part-time (7 women); includes 5 minority (3 African Americans, 2 Asian Americans or Pacific Islanders), 6 international. Average age 32. 54 applicants, 35% accepted, 12 enrolled. In 2006, 17 master's, 8 doctorates awarded. *Degree requirements:* For master's, thesis (for some programs); for doctorate, thesis/dissertation. *Entrance requirements:* For master's, GMAT, GRE General Test (MS); for doctorate, GMAT, GRE General Test. Additional exam requirements/recommendations for international students: Required—TOEFL. *Application deadline:* For fall admission, 7/7 for domestic students; for spring admission, 11/24 for domestic students. Applications are processed on a rolling basis. Application fee: $25 ($50 for international students). Electronic applications accepted. *Expenses:* Tuition, state resident: full-time $5,000. Tuition, nonresident: full-time $15,000. Required fees: $416. Tuition and fees vary according to program. *Financial support:* Teaching assistantships, Federal Work-Study available. Support available to part-time students. Financial award application deadline: 3/15. *Unit head:* Dr. Sharon Oswald, Head, 334-844-4071. *Application contact:* Dr. Joe Pittman, Interim Dean of the Graduate School, 334-844-4700.

Avila University, School of Business, Kansas City, MO 64145-1698. Offers accounting (MBA); finance (MBA); general management (MBA); health care administration (MBA); international business (MBA); management information systems (MBA); marketing (MBA). Part-time and evening/weekend programs available. *Faculty:* 8 full-time (4 women), 17 part-time/adjunct (4 women). *Students:* 31 full-time (19 women), 165 part-time (96 women); includes 18 minority (14 African Americans, 1 American Indian/Alaska Native, 3 Hispanic Americans), 16 international. Average age 32. 77 applicants, 81% accepted, 62 enrolled. In 2006, 54 degrees awarded. *Degree requirements:* For master's, capstone course. *Entrance requirements:* For master's, GMAT, minimum GPA of 3.0. Additional exam requirements/recommendations for international students: Required—TOEFL (minimum score 550 paper-based). *Application deadline:* For fall admission, 7/30 priority date for domestic students; for winter admission, 11/30 priority date for domestic students; for spring admission, 2/28 priority date for domestic students. Applications are processed on a rolling basis. Application fee: $20. Electronic applications accepted. *Expenses:* Tuition: Full-time $7,470; part-time $415 per credit. *Financial support:* In 2006–07, 78 students received support. Career-related internships or fieldwork available. Support available to part-time students. Financial award applicants required to submit FAFSA. *Faculty research:* Leadership characteristics, financial hedging, group dynamics. *Unit head:* Dr. Richard Woodall, Dean, 816-501-3798, Fax: 816-501-2463. *Application contact:* JoAnna Giffin, MBA Admissions Director, 816-501-3601, Fax: 816-501-2463, E-mail: joanna.giffin@avila.edu.

Baker College Center for Graduate Studies, Programs in Business, Flint, MI 48507-9843. Offers accounting (MBA); computer information systems (MBA); finance (MBA); general business (MBA); health and recreation services management (MBA); health care management (MBA); human resource management (MBA); industrial management (MBA); international business (MBA); leadership (MBA); marketing (MBA). MBA in health and recreation services management enrollment limited to international students. Part-time and evening/weekend programs available. *Faculty:* 15 full-time (6 women), 425 part-time/adjunct (200 women). *Students:* 370 full-time (190 women), 1,060 part-time (560 women); includes 372 minority (205 African Americans, 27 American Indian/Alaska Native, 66 Asian Americans or Pacific Islanders, 74 Hispanic Americans), 30 international. Average age 38. 780 applicants, 85% accepted, 567 enrolled. In 2006, 202 degrees awarded. *Degree requirements:* For master's, portfolio. *Entrance requirements:* For master's, 3 years of work experience, minimum undergraduate GPA of 2.5, writing sample, letters of recommendation. Additional exam requirements/recommendations for international students: Required—TOEFL (minimum score 550 paper-based; 213 computer-based). *Application deadline:* For fall admission, 8/6 priority date for domestic students; for winter admission, 12/15 priority date for domestic students; for spring admission, 2/15 priority date for domestic students. Applications are processed on a rolling basis. Application fee: $25. Electronic applications accepted. *Expenses:* Tuition: Full-time $7,200; part-time $300 per credit hour. *Financial support:* In 2006–07, 410 students received support. Scholarships/grants available. Support available to part-time students. Financial award applicants required to submit FAFSA. *Unit head:* Dr. Michael Heberling, President, 800-469-3165, Fax: 810-766-4399, E-mail: heberling@baker.edu. *Application contact:* Chuck J. Gurden, Vice President for Graduate and Online Admissions, 800-469-3165, Fax: 810-766-2051, E-mail: chuck@baker.edu.

Barry University, Andreas School of Business, Graduate Certificate Programs, Miami Shores, FL 33161-6695. Offers finance (Certificate); health services administration (Certificate); international business (Certificate); management (Certificate); management information systems (Certificate); marketing (Certificate). *Application contact:* Dave Fletcher, Director of Graduate Admissions, 305-899-3113, Fax: 305-899-2971, E-mail: dfletcher@mail.barry.edu.

Baylor University, Graduate School, Hankamer School of Business, Department of Information Systems, Waco, TX 76798. Offers information systems (MSIS); information systems management (MBA); MBA/MSIS. *Faculty:* 12 full-time (4 women). *Students:* 15 full-time (3 women), 7 part-time (3 women), 15 international. In 2006, 16 degrees awarded. *Entrance requirements:* For master's, GMAT. Additional exam requirements/recommendations for international students: Required—TOEFL. *Application deadline:* For fall admission, 8/1 for domestic students; for spring admission, 12/1 for domestic students. Applications are processed on a rolling basis. Application fee: $25. *Financial support:* Research assistantships, career-related internships or fieldwork and Federal Work-Study available. *Faculty research:* Computer personnel, group systems, information technology standards and infrastructure, international information systems, technology and the learning environment. *Unit head:* Dr. Jonathan Trower, Adviser, 254-710-4754, Fax: 254-710-1091, E-mail: jonathan_trower@baylor.edu. *Application contact:* Vicky Todd, Administrative Assistant, 254-710-3718, Fax: 254-710-1066, E-mail: mba@hsb.baylor.edu.

Bay Path College, Program in Communications and Information Management, Longmeadow, MA 01106-2292. Offers information management (MS); information systems (MS). Part-time and evening/weekend programs available. *Entrance requirements:* Additional exam requirements/recommendations for international students: Recommended—TOEFL (minimum score 500 paper-based). Electronic applications accepted.

Bellevue University, Graduate School, Program in Computer Information Systems, Bellevue, NE 68005-3098. Offers MS.

Benedictine University, Graduate Programs, Program in Management Information Systems, Lisle, IL 60532-0900. Offers MS, MBA/MS, MPH/MS. Part-time programs available. *Faculty:* 2 full-time (1 woman), 6 part-time/adjunct (1 woman). *Students:* 3 full-time (2 women), 12 part-time (6 women); includes 7 minority (4 African Americans, 3 Asian Americans or Pacific Islanders). Average age 36. 31 applicants, 97% accepted, 15 enrolled. In 2006, 10 degrees awarded. *Entrance requirements:* For master's, GMAT. Additional exam requirements/recommendations for international students: Required—TOEFL (minimum score 550 paper-based; 213 computer-based). *Application deadline:* For fall admission, 9/1 for domestic students; for winter admission, 12/1 for domestic students; for spring admission, 2/15 for domestic students. Applications are processed on a rolling basis. Application fee: $40. Electronic applications accepted. *Expenses:* Tuition: Full-time $12,150; part-time $450 per credit hour. *Financial support:* Career-related internships or fieldwork and health care benefits available. Support available to part-time students. *Faculty research:* Technology management, knowledge management, electronic commerce, information security. *Unit head:* Dr. Barbara Grabowski, Director, 630-829-6218, E-mail: bgrabowski@bea.edu. *Application contact:* Kari Gibbons, Director, Admissions, 630-829-6200, Fax: 630-829-6584, E-mail: kgibbons@ben.edu.

Bernard M. Baruch College of the City University of New York, Zicklin School of Business, Department of Statistics and Computer Information Systems, Program in Computer Information Systems, New York, NY 10010-5585. Offers MBA, MS, PhD. Part-time and evening/weekend programs available. *Faculty:* 32 full-time (7 women), 22 part-time/adjunct (5 women). *Students:* 16 full-time (5 women), 109 part-time (22 women); includes 48 minority (7 African Americans, 36 Asian Americans or Pacific Islanders, 5 Hispanic Americans). In 2006, 89 degrees awarded. Terminal master's awarded for partial completion of doctoral program. *Degree requirements:* For master's, thesis or alternative; for doctorate, thesis/dissertation, comprehensive exam. *Entrance requirements:* For master's, GMAT, 2 letters of recommendation, resumé, 2 years of work experience; for doctorate, GMAT. Additional exam requirements/recommendations for international students: Required—TOEFL (minimum score 590 paper-based; 243 computer-based), TWE (minimum score 5). *Application deadline:* For fall admission, 5/31 for domestic students, 4/30 for international students; for spring admission, 11/30 for domestic students, 10/31 for international students. Application fee: $125. *Financial support:* Fellowships, research assistantships, teaching assistantships, career-related internships or fieldwork, Federal Work-Study, scholarships/grants, and unspecified assistantships available. Financial award application deadline: 4/30; financial award applicants required to submit FAFSA. *Unit head:* Michael Palley, Head, 646-312-3362, Fax: 646-312-3351, E-mail: michael_palley@baruch.cuny.edu. *Application contact:* Frances Murphy, Office of Graduate Admissions, 646-312-1300, Fax: 646-312-1301, E-mail: zicklingradadmissions@baruch.cuny.edu.

Boise State University, Graduate College, College of Business and Economics, Program in Information Technology Management, Boise, ID 83725-0399. Offers MBA. Part-time programs available. *Students:* 1 full-time (0 women), 17 part-time (6 women); includes 1 minority (Hispanic American), 7 international. Average age 33. 6 applicants, 83% accepted, 0 enrolled. In 2006, 11 degrees awarded. *Entrance requirements:* For master's, GMAT, minimum GPA of 3.0. Additional exam requirements/recommendations for international students: Required—TOEFL. *Application deadline:* For fall admission, 3/1 priority date for domestic students; for spring admission, 10/1 priority date for domestic students. Applications are processed on a rolling basis. Application fee: $0. Electronic applications accepted. *Financial support:* Career-related internships or fieldwork, Federal Work-Study, institutionally sponsored loans, and unspecified assistantships available. Support available to part-time students. Financial award application deadline: 3/1. *Unit head:* Dr. Kirk Smith, Director, 208-426-3180. *Application contact:* J. Renee Anchustegui, Coordinator, 208-426-3116, Fax: 208-426-1135, E-mail: ranchust@boisestate.edu.

Boston University, School of Management, Doctorate in Business Administration Program, Boston, MA 02215. Offers accounting (DBA); information systems (DBA); management policy (DBA); marketing (DBA); operations management (DBA); organizational behavior (DBA). *Students:* 48 full-time (26 women); includes 4 minority (all Asian Americans or Pacific Islanders), 24 international. Average age 35. 120 applicants, 17% accepted, 10 enrolled. In 2006, 8 degrees awarded. *Degree requirements:* For doctorate, thesis/dissertation. *Entrance requirements:* For doctorate, GMAT or GRE General Test. *Application deadline:* For fall admission, 1/31 for domestic students. Application fee: $125. *Expenses:* Tuition: Full-time $33,330; part-time $1,042 per credit. Required fees: $462; $40. *Financial support:* Career-related internships or fieldwork, Federal Work-Study, institutionally sponsored loans, scholarships/grants, and tuition waivers available. Support available to part-time students. Financial award applicants required to submit FAFSA. *Unit head:* Dr. Sushil Vachani, Director, 617-353-4875, E-mail: dba@bu.edu. *Application contact:* Hayden Estrada, Assistant Dean, Admissions, 617-353-2670, Fax: 617-353-7368, E-mail: dba@bu.edu.

Bowie State University, Graduate Programs, Program in Management Information Systems, Bowie, MD 20715-9465. Offers information systems analyst (Certificate); management information systems (MS). Part-time and evening/weekend programs available. *Faculty:* 4 full-time (0 women). *Students:* 11 full-time (7 women), 37 part-time (13 women); includes 47 minority (45 African Americans, 2 Hispanic Americans), 1 international. Average age 33. 14 applicants, 86% accepted, 12 enrolled. In 2006, 42 degrees awarded. *Degree requirements:* For master's, research paper, thesis optional. *Entrance requirements:* For master's, minimum GPA of 2.5. *Application deadline:* For fall admission, 9/1 priority date for domestic students, 4/1 priority date for international students; for spring admission, 11/1 priority date for domestic and international students. Applications are processed on a rolling basis. Application fee: $40. Electronic applications accepted. *Expenses:* Tuition, state resident: full-time $7,344; part-time $306 per credit. Tuition, nonresident: full-time $14,304; part-time $396 per credit. Required fees: $1,078; $77 per credit. $539 per term. One-time fee: $40. *Financial support:* Career-related internships or fieldwork and institutionally sponsored loans available. Financial award application deadline: 4/1. *Unit head:* Dr. David Anyiwo, Coordinator, 301-860-3626, Fax: 301-860-3644, E-mail: danyiwo@bowiestate.edu. *Application contact:* Angela Issac, Information Contact.

Brigham Young University, Graduate Studies, Marriott School of Management, Information Systems Department, Provo, UT 84602-1001. Offers MISM. *Students:* 44 full-time (2 women); includes 2 minority (both Asian Americans or Pacific Islanders), 3 international. Average age 27. 68 applicants, 68% accepted, 42 enrolled. In 2006, 31 degrees awarded. *Entrance requirements:* For master's, GMAT, minimum GPA of 3.0 in last 60 hours of course work. Additional exam requirements/recommendations for international students: Required—TOEFL (minimum score 580 paper-based; 237 computer-based). *Application deadline:* For fall admission, 3/1 for domestic and international students. Application fee: $50. Electronic applications accepted. *Financial support:* In 2006–07, 44 students received support. Application deadline: 4/15. *Unit head:* Dr. Marshall B. Romney, Director, 801-422-5704, Fax: 801-422-

0573, E-mail: marshall_romney@byu.edu. *Application contact:* Julie Averett, Academic Advisor, 801-422-3951, Fax: 801-422-0621, E-mail: mism@byu.edu.

Bryant University, Graduate School, Graduate School of Business, Programs in Business Administration, Smithfield, RI 02917-1284. Offers accounting (MBA, CAGS); computer information systems (MBA, CAGS); e-strategy (MBA, CAGS); finance (MBA, CAGS); general business (MBA); management (MBA, CAGS); marketing (MBA, CAGS); operations management (MBA). *Accreditation:* AACSB. *Faculty:* 49 full-time (13 women), 2 part-time/adjunct (0 women). *Students:* 143 applicants, 41% accepted, 46 enrolled. In 2006, 106 master's, 10 other advanced degrees awarded. *Entrance requirements:* For master's, GMAT, letter of recommendation, resumé; for CAGS, GMAT, resumé. Additional exam requirements/recommendations for international students: Required—TOEFL (minimum score 580 paper-based; 237 computer-based). *Application deadline:* For fall admission, 7/15 for domestic students, 4/1 for international students; for spring admission, 11/15 for domestic and international students. Application fee: $80. *Expenses:* Tuition: Part-time $1,998 per course. *Financial support:* Research assistantships with full tuition reimbursements, unspecified assistantships available. Financial award applicants required to submit FAFSA. *Unit head:* Kristopher T. Sullivan, Assistant Dean of the Graduate School, 401-232-6230, Fax: 401-232-6494, E-mail: gradprog@bryant.edu.

California Lutheran University, Graduate Studies, School of Business, Thousand Oaks, CA 91360-2787. Offers finance (MBA); healthcare management (MBA); international business (MBA); management information systems (MBA); marketing (MBA); organizational behavior (MBA); small business/entrepreneurship (MBA). Evening/weekend programs available. *Entrance requirements:* For master's, GMAT, interview, minimum GPA of 3.0. Expenses: Contact institution.

California State University, East Bay, Academic Programs and Graduate Studies, College of Business and Economics, Department of Accounting and Computer Information Systems, Option in Computer Information Systems, Hayward, CA 94542-3000. Offers business administration (MBA); computer information systems (MS). Part-time and evening/weekend programs available. *Students:* 3 full-time (2 women), 11 part-time (5 women); includes 2 minority (both Asian Americans or Pacific Islanders), 5 international. Average age 32. *Degree requirements:* For master's, comprehensive exam or thesis. *Entrance requirements:* For master's, GMAT, minimum GPA of 2.75. Additional exam requirements/recommendations for international students: Required—TOEFL (minimum score 550 paper-based; 213 computer-based). *Application deadline:* For fall admission, 5/31 for domestic students, 4/30 for international students; for winter admission, 9/30 for domestic and international students; for spring admission, 12/31 for domestic students, 11/30 for international students. Application fee: $55. *Financial support:* Career-related internships or fieldwork, Federal Work-Study, and institutionally sponsored loans available. Support available to part-time students. Financial award application deadline: 3/2. *Unit head:* Doris Duncan, Director of Graduate Programs, 510-885-3364, Fax: 510-885-2176, E-mail: doris.duncan@csueastbay.edu.

California State University, Fullerton, Graduate Studies, College of Business and Economics, Department of Information Systems and Decision Sciences, Fullerton, CA 92834-9480. Offers management information systems (MS); management science (MBA, MS); operations research (MS); statistics (MS). Part-time and evening/weekend programs available. *Students:* 12 full-time (1 woman), 69 part-time (19 women); includes 27 minority (23 Asian Americans or Pacific Islanders, 4 Hispanic Americans), 9 international. Average age 33. 78 applicants, 51% accepted, 28 enrolled. In 2006, 21 degrees awarded. *Degree requirements:* For master's, project or thesis. *Entrance requirements:* For master's, GMAT, minimum AACSB index of 950. Application fee: $55. *Expenses:* Tuition, nonresident: part-time $339 per unit. Required fees: $1,155 per semester. *Financial support:* Teaching assistantships, Federal Work-Study, institutionally sponsored loans, and scholarships/grants available. Support available to part-time students. Financial award application deadline: 3/1. *Unit head:* Dr. Barry Pasternack, Chair, 714-278-2221.

California State University, Los Angeles, Graduate Studies, College of Business and Economics, Department of Information Systems, Los Angeles, CA 90032-8530. Offers business information systems (MBA); management (MS); management information systems (MS); office management (MBA). Part-time and evening/weekend programs available. *Faculty:* 6 full-time (0 women). *Students:* 8 full-time (4 women), 30 part-time (7 women); includes 24 minority (1 African American, 17 Asian Americans or Pacific Islanders, 6 Hispanic Americans), 6 international. In 2006, 12 degrees awarded. *Degree requirements:* For master's, comprehensive exam (MBA), thesis (MS). *Entrance requirements:* For master's, GMAT, minimum GPA of 2.5 during previous 2 years of course work. Additional exam requirements/recommendations for international students: Required—TOEFL. *Application deadline:* For fall admission, 6/30 for domestic students; for spring admission, 11/30 for domestic students. Applications are processed on a rolling basis. Application fee: $55. *Expenses:* Tuition, nonresident: part-time $226 per unit. *Financial support:* Career-related internships or fieldwork and Federal Work-Study available. Support available to part-time students. Financial award application deadline: 3/1. *Unit head:* Dr. Adam Huarng, Chair, 323-343-2983.

California State University, Los Angeles, Graduate Studies, College of Business and Economics, Major in Business Administration, Los Angeles, CA 90032-8530. Offers finance and law (MBA, MS), including finance and banking; information systems (MBA, MS), including business information systems (MBA), management (MS), management information systems (MS), office management (MBA); management (MBA, MS); marketing (MBA, MS), including international business, marketing. Part-time and evening/weekend programs available. *Students:* 64 full-time (32 women), 154 part-time (68 women); includes 111 minority (16 African Americans, 1 American Indian/Alaska Native, 69 Asian Americans or Pacific Islanders, 25 Hispanic Americans), 64 international. In 2006, 70 degrees awarded. *Entrance requirements:* For master's, GMAT, minimum GPA of 2.5 during previous 2 years of course work. Additional exam requirements/recommendations for international students: Required—TOEFL. *Application deadline:* For fall admission, 6/30 for domestic students; for spring admission, 11/30 for domestic students. Applications are processed on a rolling basis. Application fee: $55. *Expenses:* Tuition, nonresident: part-time $226 per unit. *Financial support:* Career-related internships or fieldwork and Federal Work-Study available. Support available to part-time students. Financial award application deadline: 3/1. *Unit head:* Dr. Giorgio Canarella, Head, 323-343-5156.

California State University, Monterey Bay, College of Science, Media Arts and Technology, School of Information Technology and Communication Design, Seaside, CA 93955-8001. Offers management and information technology (MSMIT). Part-time and evening/weekend programs available. *Degree requirements:* For master's, thesis or alternative. *Entrance requirements:* For master's, GRE or GMAT, 2 letters of recommendation, minimum GPA of 3.0. Additional exam requirements/recommendations for international students: Required—TOEFL (minimum score 550 paper-based; 213 computer-based). Electronic applications accepted. *Faculty research:* Electronic commerce, e-learning, knowledge management, international business, business and public policy.

California State University, Sacramento, Graduate Studies, College of Business Administration, Department of Management Information Science, Sacramento, CA 95819-6048. Offers MS. Part-time and evening/weekend programs available. *Students:* 7 full-time (2 women), 25 part-time (9 women); includes 13 minority (1 African American, 1 American Indian/Alaska Native, 7 Asian Americans or Pacific Islanders, 4 Hispanic Americans), 5 international. Average age 31. 23 applicants, 52% accepted, 6 enrolled. *Degree requirements:* For master's, thesis or alternative, writing proficiency exam. *Entrance requirements:* For master's, GMAT. Additional exam requirements/recommendations for international students: Required—TOEFL. *Application deadline:* Applications are processed on a rolling basis. Application fee: $55. Electronic applications accepted. *Financial support:* Research assistantships, teaching assistantships, career-related internships or fieldwork and Federal Work-Study available. Support available to part-time students. Financial award application deadline: 3/1. *Unit head:* Dr. Russell Ching, Chair, 916-278-6536, Fax: 916-278-6757.

Capella University, School of Business and Technology, Minneapolis, MN 55402. Offers accounting (MBA), including system design and programming; business (Certificate), including human resource management (MS, PhD, Certificate), information technology management (MS, PhD, Certificate), leadership (MBA, MS, PhD, Certificate); finance (MBA); general business (MBA); health care management (MBA); information technology (MS, Certificate), including general information technology (MS), information security, network architecture and design (MS), professional projects management (Certificate), project management and leadership (MS), system design and development (MS),); information technology management (MBA); marketing (MBA); organization and management (MBA, MS, PhD), including general business (PhD), general organization and management (MBA, MS), human resource management (MS, PhD, Certificate), information technology management (MS, PhD, Certificate), leadership (MBA, MS, PhD, Certificate); project management (MBA). Part-time and evening/weekend programs available. Postbaccalaureate distance learning degree programs offered (minimal on-campus study). Terminal master's awarded for partial completion of doctoral program. *Degree requirements:* For master's, integrative project, thesis optional; for doctorate, thesis/dissertation, comprehensive exam, registration. *Entrance requirements:* Additional exam requirements/recommendations for international students: Required—TOEFL (minimum score 550 paper-based; 213 computer-based), TWE (minimum score 4). Electronic applications accepted. *Faculty research:* Business policies: strategic, corporate, and financial management; interplay of technological, organizational and social change.

Capitol College, Graduate Programs, Laurel, MD 20708-9759. Offers business administration (MBA); computer science (MS); electrical engineering (MS); information and telecommunications systems management (MS); information architecture (MS); network security (MS). Part-time and evening/weekend programs available. Postbaccalaureate distance learning degree programs offered (no on-campus study). *Entrance requirements:* For master's, minimum GPA of 3.0. Electronic applications accepted.

Cardean University, MBA Program, Chicago, IL 60606-7204. Offers accounting and information systems (MBA); e-commerce (MBA); finance (MBA); global management (MBA); health care administration (MBA); human resources management (MBA); leadership (MBA); management of information systems (MBA); management of technology (MBA); marketing (MBA); professional accounting (MBA); project management (MBA); risk management (MBA); strategy and economics (MBA). Part-time and evening/weekend programs available. Postbaccalaureate distance learning degree programs offered (no on-campus study). *Entrance requirements:* Additional exam requirements/recommendations for international students: Required—TOEFL (minimum score 550 paper-based; 213 computer-based).

Carnegie Mellon University, H. John Heinz III School of Public Policy and Management, Program in Information Security Policy and Management, Pittsburgh, PA 15213-3891. Offers MSISPM.

Carnegie Mellon University, H. John Heinz III School of Public Policy and Management, Program in Information Systems Management, Pittsburgh, PA 15213-3891. Offers MISM.

Carnegie Mellon University, Tepper School of Business, Program in Information Systems, Pittsburgh, PA 15213-3891. Offers PhD. *Degree requirements:* For doctorate, thesis/dissertation. *Entrance requirements:* For doctorate, GRE General Test.

Case Western Reserve University, Weatherhead School of Management, Department of Information Systems, Cleveland, OH 44106. Offers MBA. Part-time and evening/weekend programs available. *Faculty:* 8 full-time (2 women), 2 part-time/adjunct (0 women). *Students:* 27 full-time (8 women), 21 part-time (11 women); includes 2 minority (both African Americans), 7 international. Average age 28. In 2006, 27 master's awarded. *Entrance requirements:* For master's, GMAT. *Application deadline:* For fall admission, 4/15 priority date for domestic students. Applications are processed on a rolling basis. Application fee: $50. *Financial support:* Career-related internships or fieldwork, Federal Work-Study, institutionally sponsored loans, and tuition waivers (full and partial) available. Financial award application deadline: 5/1. *Faculty research:* Decision support, business forecasting systems, design and use of information systems, artificial intelligence, executive information systems. *Unit head:* Fred Collopy, Chairman, 216-368-2144, Fax: 216-368-4776, E-mail: flc2@po.cwru.edu.

Case Western Reserve University, Weatherhead School of Management, Department of Operations, Cleveland, OH 44106. Offers management (MS, MSM), including finance (MS), information systems (MS), marketing (MS), operations research, quality management (MS), supply chain (MSM); management for liberal arts graduates (MSM); operations research (PhD); MBA/MSM. Part-time programs available. *Faculty:* 12 full-time (1 woman), 2 part-time/adjunct (1 woman). *Students:* 32 full-time (8 women), 6 part-time (1 woman), 21 international. Average age 28. In 2006, 28 master's, 4 doctorates awarded. *Degree requirements:* For doctorate, thesis/dissertation. *Entrance requirements:* For master's, GRE General Test; for doctorate, GMAT, GRE General Test. *Application deadline:* For fall admission, 4/15 priority date for domestic students. Applications are processed on a rolling basis. Application fee: $50. *Financial support:* Tuition waivers (full and partial) available. Financial award application deadline: 5/1. *Faculty research:* Mathematical finance, mathematical programming, scheduling, stochastic optimization, environmental/energy models. *Unit head:* Kamlesh Mathur, Chairman, 216-368-3857, E-mail: kamlesh.mathur@case.edu.

Central European University, CEU Business School, Budapest, Hungary. Offers finance (MBA); general management (MBA); information technology (M Sc); information technology management (MBA); management (EMBA); marketing (MBA); real estate management (MBA). Part-time and evening/weekend programs available. *Faculty:* 15 full-time (3 women), 30 part-time/adjunct (9 women). *Students:* 47 full-time (18 women), 158 part-time (22 women). Average age 32. 450 applicants, 43% accepted, 160 enrolled. In 2006, 77 degrees awarded. *Entrance requirements:* For master's, GMAT. Additional exam requirements/recommendations for international students: Required—TOEFL (minimum score 570 paper-based; 230 computer-based). *Application deadline:* For fall admission, 5/22 priority date for domestic students, 5/22 for international students; for winter admission, 11/13 priority date for domestic students, 11/13 for international students. Applications are processed on a rolling basis. Application fee: $0. Electronic applications accepted. *Financial support:* In 2006–07, 4 students received support, including research assistantships with partial tuition reimbursements available (averaging $3,800 per year); tuition waivers (partial) and GMAT-based tuition fee discounts also available. *Faculty research:* Social and ethical business, marketing. Total annual research expenditures: 11,000 euros. *Unit head:* Dr. Paul Garrison, Dean and Managing Director, 36-18875050, Fax: 36-18875001, E-mail: garrisonp@ceubusiness.com. *Application contact:* Tunde Hegedus, MBA Program Manager, 36-18875060, Fax: 36-18875133, E-mail: mba@ceubusiness.com.

Central Michigan University, Central Michigan University Off-Campus Programs, Program in Administration, Mount Pleasant, MI 48859. Offers acquisitions administration (MSA, Certificate); general administration (MSA, Certificate); health services administration (MSA, Certificate); human resources administration (MSA, Certificate); information resource management (MSA, Certificate); international administration (MSA, Certificate); leadership (MSA, Certificate); public administration (MSA, Certificate); software engineering administration (MSA, Certificate); vehicle design and manufacturing administration (MSA, Certificate). Part-time and evening/weekend programs available. Postbaccalaureate distance learning degree programs offered (no on-campus study). *Students:* Average age 38. *Entrance requirements:* For master's, minimum GPA of 2.7 in major. *Application deadline:* Applications are processed on a rolling basis. Application fee: $50. Electronic applications accepted. *Financial support:* Scholarships/grants available. Support available to part-time students. Financial award applicants required to submit FAFSA. *Unit head:* Dr. Peter G. Ross, Director, 989-774-6525, Fax: 989-774-2575, E-mail: ross1pg@cmich.edu. *Application contact:* 877-268-4636, E-mail: cmuoffcampus@cmich.edu.

Central Michigan University, College of Graduate Studies, College of Business Administration, Department of Business Information Systems, Mount Pleasant, MI 48859. Offers busi-

Management Information Systems

Central Michigan University (continued)
ness education (MBE); information systems (MS). *Degree requirements:* For master's, thesis or alternative, registration. *Entrance requirements:* For master's, GMAT or GRE (MBE). *Faculty research:* Business teacher education, office systems, management information systems, decision support systems.

See Close-Up on page 611.

Central Michigan University, College of Graduate Studies, Program in Administration, Mount Pleasant, MI 48859. Offers general administration (MSA); health services administration (MSA); hospitality and tourism administration (MSA); human resource administration (MSA); information resource administration (MSA); international administration (MSA); leadership (MSA); organizational communications (MSA); public administration (MSA); recreation and park administration (MSA); software engineering (MSA); sports administration (MSA). *Accreditation:* AACSB. *Degree requirements:* For master's, thesis or alternative. *Entrance requirements:* For master's, minimum undergraduate GPA of 2.5.

See Close-Up on page 253.

Charleston Southern University, Program in Business, Charleston, SC 29423-8087. Offers accounting (MBA); finance (MBA); health care administration (MBA); information systems (MBA); organizational development (MBA). Part-time and evening/weekend programs available. *Degree requirements:* For master's, thesis optional. *Entrance requirements:* For master's, GMAT. *Faculty research:* Economic forecasting.

City University, Graduate Division, School of Management, Bellevue, WA 98005. Offers accounting (MBA); C++ programming (Certificate); computer systems—C++ programming (MS); computer systems—individualized study (MS); computer systems—web programming in e-commerce (MS); computer systems-web development (MS); financial management (MBA, Certificate); general management (MBA, MPA, Certificate); general management-Europe (MBA); human resource management (MPA); individualized study (MBA); information systems (MBA, Certificate); management—general management (MA); management—human resource management (MA); management—individualized study (MA); marketing (MBA, Certificate); personal financial planning (MBA, Certificate); project management (MBA, MS, Certificate); technology management (MS, Certificate); web development (Certificate); web programming in e-commerce (Certificate). Part-time and evening/weekend programs available. Postbaccalaureate distance learning degree programs offered (no on-campus study). *Entrance requirements:* Additional exam requirements/recommendations for international students: Required—TOEFL (minimum score 540 paper-based; 207 computer-based); Recommended—IELTS. Electronic applications accepted.

Claremont Graduate University, Graduate Programs, School of Information Systems and Technology, Claremont, CA 91711-6160. Offers electronic commerce (MS, PhD); information systems (Certificate); knowledge management (MS, PhD); systems development (MS, PhD); telecommunications and networking (MS, PhD); MBA/MS. Part-time programs available. *Faculty:* 5 full-time (1 woman), 4 part-time/adjunct (0 women). *Students:* 68 full-time (22 women), 44 part-time (16 women); includes 32 minority (3 African Americans, 21 Asian Americans or Pacific Islanders, 8 Hispanic Americans), 28 international. Average age 37. In 2006, 13 master's, 7 doctorates awarded. *Degree requirements:* For doctorate, thesis/dissertation, portfolio, comprehensive exam. *Entrance requirements:* For master's and doctorate, GMAT, GRE General Test. *Application deadline:* For fall admission, 2/15 priority date for domestic students. Applications are processed on a rolling basis. Electronic applications accepted. *Financial support:* Fellowships, research assistantships, teaching assistantships, Federal Work-Study and institutionally sponsored loans available. Support available to part-time students. Financial award application deadline: 2/15; financial award applicants required to submit FAFSA. *Faculty research:* GPSS, man-machine interaction, organizational aspects of computing, implementation of information systems, information systems practice. *Unit head:* Lorne Olfman, Dean, 909-607-3035, Fax: 909-621-8564, E-mail: lorne.olfman@cgu.edu. *Application contact:* Go Yoshida, Director of Recruitment/Admissions, 909-621-3140, Fax: 909-621-8564, E-mail: go.yoshida@cgu.edu.

Clarkson University, Graduate School, School of Business, Program in Management Systems, Potsdam, NY 13699. Offers human resource management (MS); management information systems (MS); manufacturing management (MS). Part-time and evening/weekend programs available. *Students:* Average age 33. *Degree requirements:* For master's, project or thesis. *Entrance requirements:* For master's, GMAT, GRE General Test (highly recommended). Additional exam requirements/recommendations for international students: Required—TOEFL. *Application deadline:* For fall admission, 5/15 priority date for domestic students; for spring admission, 10/15 priority date for domestic students. Applications are processed on a rolling basis. Application fee: $25 ($35 for international students). Electronic applications accepted. *Expenses:* Tuition: Full-time $22,776; part-time $949 per credit. Required fees: $215. *Financial support:* Tuition waivers (partial) available. *Faculty research:* Management of technology planning and organizational development. *Application contact:* Dr. Farzad Mahmoodi, Director, 315-268-4281, Fax: 315-268-3810, E-mail: mahmoodi@clarkson.edu.

Clark University, Graduate School, Graduate School of Management, Business Administration Program, Worcester, MA 01610-1477. Offers accounting (MBA); finance (MBA); global business (MBA); health care management (MBA); management (MBA); management of information technology (MBA); marketing (MBA). *Accreditation:* AACSB. Part-time and evening/weekend programs available. *Students:* 122 full-time (64 women), 113 part-time (42 women); includes 18 minority (3 African Americans, 9 Asian Americans or Pacific Islanders, 6 Hispanic Americans), 115 international. Average age 29. 235 applicants, 78% accepted, 80 enrolled. In 2006, 109 degrees awarded. *Degree requirements:* For master's, thesis optional. *Application deadline:* For fall admission, 6/1 priority date for domestic students; for spring admission, 12/1 priority date for domestic students. Applications are processed on a rolling basis. Application fee: $50. Electronic applications accepted. *Financial support:* In 2006–07, research assistantships with partial tuition reimbursements (averaging $6,000 per year), teaching assistantships with partial tuition reimbursements (averaging $6,000 per year) were awarded; fellowships with full and partial tuition reimbursements, career-related internships or fieldwork, Federal Work-Study, institutionally sponsored loans, and tuition waivers (partial) also available. Support available to part-time students. Financial award application deadline: 5/31. *Faculty research:* Organizational development, accounting, marketing, finance, human resource management. *Application contact:* Patricia Tollo, Admissions Director, 508-793-7406, Fax: 508-793-8822, E-mail: clarkmba@clarku.edu.

See Close-Up on page 257.

Cleveland State University, College of Graduate Studies, Nance College of Business Administration, Department of Computer and Information Science, Cleveland, OH 44115. Offers computer information science (MS); information systems (DBA). Part-time and evening/weekend programs available. *Faculty:* 15 full-time (3 women), 2 part-time/adjunct (0 women). *Students:* 38 full-time (13 women), 109 part-time (26 women); includes 7 minority (1 African American, 5 Asian Americans or Pacific Islanders, 1 Hispanic American), 81 international. Average age 29. 246 applicants, 69% accepted, 47 enrolled. In 2006, 71 degrees awarded. *Degree requirements:* For master's, thesis optional; for doctorate, thesis/dissertation, comprehensive exam. *Entrance requirements:* For master's, GMAT or GRE, minimum GPA of 2.75; for doctorate, GMAT, MBA, MCIS or equivalent. Additional exam requirements/recommendations for international students: Required—TOEFL (minimum score 525 paper-based; 197 computer-based). *Application deadline:* For fall admission, 7/15 priority date for domestic students, 5/15 priority date for international students; for spring admission, 12/15 priority date for domestic students. Applications are processed on a rolling basis. Application fee: $30. Electronic applications accepted. *Financial support:* In 2006–07, 3 research assistantships with full tuition reimbursements (averaging $6,960 per year) were awarded; fellowships, teaching assistantships with full and partial tuition reimbursements, career-related internships or fieldwork, tuition waivers (full), and unspecified assistantships also available. *Faculty research:* Artificial intelligence, object oriented analysis, database design, software efficiency, distributed system. Total annual research expenditures: $9,040. *Unit head:* Dr. Santosh K. Misra, Chairman, 216-687-4760, Fax: 216-687-5448, E-mail: misra@csuohio.edu.

Cleveland State University, College of Graduate Studies, Nance College of Business Administration, Doctoral Programs in Business Administration, Cleveland, OH 44115. Offers business administration (DBA); finance (DBA); information systems (DBA); marketing (DBA); production/operations management (DBA). *Accreditation:* AACSB. In 2006, 3 degrees awarded. *Degree requirements:* For doctorate, thesis/dissertation. *Entrance requirements:* For doctorate, GMAT, MBA or equivalent. *Unit head:* Dr. Raj Shekhar G. Javalgi, Director, 216-687-3786, Fax: 216-687-9354, E-mail: r.javalgi@csuohio.edu.

The College of St. Scholastica, Graduate Studies, Department of Computer Information Systems, Duluth, MN 55811-4199. Offers MA. Part-time programs available. Postbaccalaureate distance learning degree programs offered (minimal on-campus study). *Faculty:* 1 full-time (0 women), 5 part-time/adjunct (0 women). *Students:* 3 full-time (0 women), 19 part-time (10 women); includes 2 minority (1 African American, 1 Asian American or Pacific Islander). Average age 37. 12 applicants, 92% accepted, 4 enrolled. *Degree requirements:* For master's, thesis. *Entrance requirements:* For master's, minimum GPA of 2.8. Additional exam requirements/recommendations for international students: Required—TOEFL (minimum score 550 paper-based; 213 computer-based; 79 iBT). *Application deadline:* For fall admission, 8/1 priority date for domestic students, 8/1 for international students; for spring admission, 11/15 priority date for domestic students, 11/15 for international students. Application fee: $50. *Expenses: Contact institution. Financial support:* In 2006–07, 15 students received support. Available to part-time students. Applicants required to submit FAFSA. *Faculty research:* Organization acceptance of software development methodologies. *Unit head:* Brandon Olson, Program Coordinator, 218-723-6199, E-mail: bolson@css.edu. *Application contact:* Tonya J. Roth, Graduate Recruitment Counselor, 218-723-6285, Fax: 218-733-2275, E-mail: gradstudies@css.edu.

Colorado State University, Graduate School, College of Business, Department of Computer Information Systems, Fort Collins, CO 80523-0015. Offers MSBA. Part-time programs available. *Faculty:* 13 full-time (3 women). *Students:* Average age 31. *Degree requirements:* For master's, thesis or alternative, project. *Entrance requirements:* For master's, GMAT, minimum GPA of 3.0. Additional exam requirements/recommendations for international students: Required—TOEFL (minimum score 565 paper-based; 227 computer-based; 86 iBT). *Application deadline:* For fall admission, 7/15 for domestic students, 4/1 for international students. Applications are processed on a rolling basis. Application fee: $50. Electronic applications accepted. *Expenses:* Tuition, state resident: full-time $4,248; part-time $236 per credit. Tuition, nonresident: full-time $15,642; part-time $869 per credit. Required fees: $66 per credit. Tuition and fees vary according to program. *Financial support:* In 2006–07, 1 fellowship (averaging $1,500 per year) was awarded; teaching assistantships with full and partial tuition reimbursements, career-related internships or fieldwork, Federal Work-Study, and traineeships also available. Support available to part-time students. Financial award application deadline: 3/1. *Faculty research:* Re-engineering, enterprise resource planning (ERP), security, decision-making, object-oriented design. Total annual research expenditures: $173,706. *Unit head:* Dr. John Plotnicki, Chair, 970-491-6203, Fax: 970-491-5205, E-mail: john.plotnicki@colostate.edu. *Application contact:* Dr. Susan Athey, Coordinator, 970-491-5322, Fax: 970-491-5205, E-mail: susan.athey@colostate.edu.

Colorado Technical University, Graduate Studies, Program in Management, Colorado Springs, CO 80907-3896. Offers business administration (MBA); business management (MSM); business technology (MSM); database management (MSM); human resources management (MSM); information technology (MSM); logistics management (MSM); management (DM); organizational leadership (MSM); project management (MSM). Part-time and evening/weekend programs available. *Degree requirements:* For master's, thesis or alternative; for doctorate, thesis/dissertation. *Entrance requirements:* For doctorate, minimum graduate GPA of 3.0, 5 years of related work experience. *Faculty research:* Sexual harassment, performance evaluation, critical thinking.

Colorado Technical University Denver Campus, Programs in Business Administration and Management, Greenwood Village, CO 80111. Offers accounting (MBA); business administration (MBA); business administration and management (EMBA); business technology (MSM); database management (MSM); human resource management (MBA); information technology (MSM); project management (MSM); technology management (MBA). Part-time and evening/weekend programs available. *Degree requirements:* For master's, thesis or alternative. *Entrance requirements:* For master's, minimum undergraduate GPA of 3.0, resumé.

Colorado Technical University Sioux Falls Campus, Programs in Business Administration and Management, Sioux Falls, SD 57108. Offers business administration (MBA); business management (MSM); health science management (MSM); human resources management (MSM); information technology (MSM); organizational leadership (MSM); project management (MBA); technology management (MBA). Evening/weekend programs available. *Degree requirements:* For master's, thesis optional. *Entrance requirements:* For master's, minimum 2 years work experience, resumé.

Concordia University Wisconsin, Graduate Programs, School of Business and Legal Studies, MBA Program, Mequon, WI 53097-2402. Offers finance (MBA); health care administration (MBA); human resource management (MBA); international business (MBA); international business-English/Chinese (MBA); management (MBA); management information services (MBA); managerial communications (MBA); marketing (MBA); public administration (MBA); risk management (MBA). Postbaccalaureate distance learning degree programs offered (minimal on-campus study). *Students:* 504 (249 women). In 2006, 110 degrees awarded. *Degree requirements:* For master's, thesis or alternative, comprehensive exam. *Entrance requirements:* Additional exam requirements/recommendations for international students: Required—TOEFL. *Application deadline:* For fall admission, 8/1 priority date for domestic students; for spring admission, 1/15 for domestic students. Applications are processed on a rolling basis. Application fee: $50. *Expenses: Contact institution. Financial support:* Application deadline: 8/1. *Unit head:* Dr. David Borst, Director, 262-243-4298, Fax: 262-243-4428, E-mail: david.borst@cuw.edu.

Creighton University, Graduate School, Eugene C. Eppley College of Business Administration, Omaha, NE 68178-0001. Offers business administration (MBA); information technology (MS); securities and portfolio management (MSAPM); JD/MBA; MBA/INR; MBA/MS-ITM; MBA/MSAPM; MS ITM/JD; Pharm D/MBA. *Accreditation:* AACSB. Part-time and evening/weekend programs available. *Faculty:* 13 full-time (3 women), 5 part-time/adjunct (3 women). *Students:* 26 full-time (9 women), 124 part-time (27 women); includes 17 minority (9 African Americans, 5 Asian Americans or Pacific Islanders, 3 Hispanic Americans), 19 international. Average age 27. 46 applicants, 100% accepted, 27 enrolled. In 2006, 65 degrees awarded. *Degree requirements:* For master's, thesis optional. *Entrance requirements:* For master's, GMAT, resumé, 2 letters of recommendation, financial statement. Additional exam requirements/recommendations for international students: Required—TOEFL (minimum score 550 paper-based; 213 computer-based; 80 iBT). *Application deadline:* For fall admission, 3/1 priority date for domestic students, 3/1 for international students; for spring admission, 10/1 priority date for domestic students, 10/1 for international students. Applications are processed on a rolling basis. Application fee: $40. Electronic applications accepted. *Expenses:* Tuition: Part-time $595 per credit hour. Required fees: $38 per semester. *Financial support:* In 2006–07, 8 research assistantships with full tuition reimbursements (averaging $8,400 per year) were awarded; career-related internships or fieldwork, tuition waivers (partial), and unspecified assistantships also available. Financial award application deadline: 3/1. *Faculty research:* Small business issues. *Unit head:* Dr. Ravi Nath, Director, 402-280-2439. *Application contact:* Gail Hafer, Coordinator, 402-280-2829, Fax: 402-280-2172, E-mail: ghafer@creighton.edu.

Dalhousie University, Faculty of Graduate Studies, Faculty of Management, School of Business Administration, Department of Information Technology, Halifax, NS B3H 4R2, Canada. Offers MBA. Part-time programs available. *Entrance requirements:* For master's, GMAT, minimum GPA of 3.0, resumé.

Dallas Baptist University, College of Adult Education, Professional Development Program, Dallas, TX 75211-9299. Offers accounting (MA); business (MA); church leadership (MA); corporate management (MA); counseling (MA); criminal justice (MA); English as a second language (MA); finance (MA); higher education (MA); leadership studies (MA); management (MA); management information systems (MA); marketing (MA); missions (MA). Part-time and evening/weekend programs available. *Faculty:* 49 full-time (21 women), 112 part-time/adjunct (46 women). *Students:* 31 full-time, 65 part-time. 51 applicants, 49% accepted, 15 enrolled. In 2006, 41 degrees awarded. Application fee: $25. *Expenses:* Tuition: Full-time $8,370; part-time $465 per credit hour. Required fees: $465 per credit hour. *Financial support:* Tuition waivers (full and partial) available. *Unit head:* Lynda Jackson, Director, 214-333-6830, Fax: 214-333-5558, E-mail: graduate@dbu.edu. *Application contact:* Kit P. Montgomery, Director of Graduate Programs, 214-333-5242, Fax: 214-333-5579, E-mail: graduate@dbu.edu.

Dallas Baptist University, Graduate School of Business, Business Administration Program, Dallas, TX 75211-9299. Offers accounting (MBA); business communication (MBA); conflict resolution management (MBA); e-business (MBA); entrepreneurship (MBA); finance (MBA); health care management (MBA); international business (MBA); management (MBA); management information systems (MBA); marketing (MBA); project management (MBA); technology and engineering management (MBA). *Accreditation:* ACBSP. Part-time and evening/weekend programs available. Postbaccalaureate distance learning degree programs offered (no on-campus study). *Faculty:* 49 full-time (21 women), 112 part-time/adjunct (46 women). *Students:* 103 full-time, 318 part-time. 226 applicants, 38% accepted. In 2006, 124 degrees awarded. *Entrance requirements:* For master's, GMAT, minimum GPA of 3.0. Additional exam requirements/recommendations for international students: Required—TOEFL. *Application deadline:* Applications are processed on a rolling basis. Application fee: $25. Electronic applications accepted. *Expenses:* Tuition: Full-time $8,370; part-time $465 per credit hour. Required fees: $465 per credit hour. *Financial support:* Career-related internships or fieldwork, Federal Work-Study, institutionally sponsored loans, scholarships/grants, and tuition waivers (full and partial) available. Support available to part-time students. *Faculty research:* Sports management, services marketing, retailing, strategic management, financial planning/investments. *Unit head:* Dr. Sandra S. Reid, Director, 214-333-5244, Fax: 214-333-5293, E-mail: graduate@dbu.edu. *Application contact:* Kit P. Montgomery, Director of Graduate Programs, 214-333-5242, Fax: 214-333-5579, E-mail: graduate@dbu.edu.

DePaul University, Charles H. Kellstadt Graduate School of Business, School of Accountancy and Management Information Systems, Chicago, IL 60604-2287. Offers accountancy (M Acc, MSA); business information technology (MS); e-business (MBA, MS); financial management and control (MBA); management accounting (MBA); management information systems (MBA); taxation (MST). Part-time and evening/weekend programs available. *Faculty:* 30 full-time (9 women), 54 part-time/adjunct (7 women). *Students:* 127 full-time (53 women), 209 part-time (101 women); includes 53 minority (13 African Americans, 3 American Indian/Alaska Native, 28 Asian Americans or Pacific Islanders, 9 Hispanic Americans), 56 international. Average age 30. In 2006, 141 degrees awarded. *Entrance requirements:* For master's, GMAT, 2 letters of recommendation, resumé. Additional exam requirements/recommendations for international students: Required—TOEFL (minimum score 550 paper-based; 213 computer-based). *Application deadline:* For fall admission, 7/1 for domestic students; for winter admission, 10/1 for domestic students; for spring admission, 2/1 for domestic students. Applications are processed on a rolling basis. Application fee: $60. *Financial support:* In 2006–07, 7 research assistantships with full tuition reimbursements (averaging $4,100 per year) were awarded; institutionally sponsored loans also available. Financial award application deadline: 4/2. *Faculty research:* Tax policy, property transactions, stock options as compensation, standards setting, activity-based costing in health care. *Application contact:* Christopher E. Kinsella, Director of Cohort MBA Programs, 312-362-8810, Fax: 312-362-6677, E-mail: kgsb@depaul.edu.

DePaul University, School of Computer Science, Telecommunications, and Information Systems, Chicago, IL 60604-2287. Offers business information technology (MS); computational finance (MS); computer graphics and animation (MS); computer science (MS, PhD); computer, information and network security (MS); digital cinema (MFA, MS); e-commerce technology (MS); human-computer interaction (MS); information systems (MS); information technology (MA); instructional technology systems (MS); software engineering (MS); telecommunication systems (MS); MA/JD; MS/JD. Part-time and evening/weekend programs available. Postbaccalaureate distance learning degree programs offered (no on-campus study). *Faculty:* 80 full-time (13 women), 133 part-time/adjunct (29 women). *Students:* 1,002 full-time (246 women), 995 part-time (263 women); includes 475 minority (185 African Americans, 3 American Indian/Alaska Native, 207 Asian Americans or Pacific Islanders, 80 Hispanic Americans), 329 international. Average age 31. 830 applicants, 80% accepted, 400 enrolled. In 2006, 514 master's, 4 doctorates awarded. *Degree requirements:* For master's, comprehensive exam (for some programs); for doctorate, thesis/dissertation, comprehensive exam. *Entrance requirements:* For doctorate, GRE, master's degree in computer science. Additional exam requirements/recommendations for international students: Required—TOEFL (minimum score 550 paper-based; 213 computer-based). *Application deadline:* For fall admission, 8/1 priority date for domestic and international students; for winter admission, 11/15 priority date for domestic and international students; for spring admission, 3/1 priority date for domestic and international students. Applications are processed on a rolling basis. Application fee: $25. Electronic applications accepted. *Expenses: Contact institution. Financial support:* In 2006–07, 63 teaching assistantships with full and partial tuition reimbursements (averaging $9,085 per year) were awarded; fellowships, research assistantships, Federal Work-Study, tuition waivers (full and partial), and unspecified assistantships also available. Support available to part-time students. Financial award application deadline: 4/1; financial award applicants required to submit FAFSA. *Faculty research:* Computer graphics, computer vision, information systems technology, computer network, programming. *Unit head:* Dr. David Miller, Dean, 312-362-8381, Fax: 312-362-5185. *Application contact:* Maureen Garvey, Information Contact, 312-362-8714, Fax: 312-362-5327, E-mail: mgarvey@cti.depaul.edu.

DeVry University, Keller Graduate School of Management, Oakbrook Terrace, IL 60181. Offers accounting and financial management (MAFM); business administration (MBA); human resources management (MHRM); information systems management (MISM); network and communications management (MNCM); project management (MPM); public administration (MPA); telecommunications management (MTM). Part-time and evening/weekend programs available. Postbaccalaureate distance learning degree programs offered (no on-campus study). *Degree requirements:* For master's, business plan (MBA), capstone project (MHRM, MPM, MTM, MAFM). *Entrance requirements:* For master's, GMAT, GRE General Test, or institutional assessment, interview. Additional exam requirements/recommendations for international students: Required—TOEFL (minimum score 500 paper-based; 173 computer-based). Electronic applications accepted.

See Close-Up on page 265.

Dominican University, Edward A. and Lois L. Brennan School of Business, River Forest, IL 60305-1099. Offers accounting (MSA); business administration (MBA); computer information systems (MSCIS); management information systems (MSMIS); organization management (MSOM); JD/MBA; MBA/MLIS. *Accreditation:* ACBSP. Part-time and evening/weekend programs available. *Faculty:* 12 full-time (4 women), 32 part-time/adjunct (9 women). *Students:* 171 full-time (46 women), 193 part-time (84 women); includes 26 minority (11 African Americans, 3 Asian Americans or Pacific Islanders, 12 Hispanic Americans), 173 international. Average age 30. 133 applicants, 98% accepted, 106 enrolled. In 2006, 118 degrees awarded. *Entrance requirements:* For master's, GMAT. Additional exam requirements/recommendations for international students: Required—TOEFL (minimum score 550 paper-based; 213 computer-based); Recommended—IELTS (minimum score 6). *Application deadline:* Applications are processed on a rolling basis. Application fee: $25. Electronic applications accepted. *Expenses: Contact institution.* Tuition and fees vary according to campus/location and program. *Financial support:* Career-related internships or fieldwork, tuition waivers (partial), and unspecified assistantships available. Support available to part-time students. Financial award applicants required to submit FAFSA. *Faculty research:* Entrepreneurship, small business finance, business ethics, marketing strategy. *Unit head:* Dr. Molly Burke, Dean, 708-524-6810, Fax: 708-524-6939, E-mail: burkemq@dom.edu. *Application contact:* Linda Puvogel, Assistant Dean for Graduate Business Programs, 708-524-6507, Fax: 708-524-6939, E-mail: lpuvogel@dom.edu.

East Carolina University, Graduate School, College of Technology and Computer Science, Department of Technology Systems, Greenville, NC 27858-4353. Offers computer network professional (Certificate); industrial technology (MS), including computer networking management, digital communications, industrial distribution and logistics, information security, manufacturing, performance improvement, planning; information assurance (Certificate); occupational safety (MS); technology management (PhD); Website developer (Certificate). *Students:* 27 full-time (8 women), 114 part-time (28 women); includes 34 minority (25 African Americans, 1 American Indian/Alaska Native, 3 Asian Americans or Pacific Islanders, 5 Hispanic Americans), 4 international. Average age 34. 53 applicants, 28% accepted, 13 enrolled. In 2006, 65 degrees awarded. *Entrance requirements:* For master's and Certificate, GRE General Test or MAT, minimum GPA of 2.5; for doctorate, GRE General Test, related work experience. *Application deadline:* For fall admission, 6/1 priority date for domestic students. Applications are processed on a rolling basis. Application fee: $50. *Financial support:* Application deadline: 6/1. *Unit head:* Dr. Andrew Jackson, Chair, 252-737-1468, Fax: 252-328-1618, E-mail: jacksona@ecu.edu. *Application contact:* Jenny Simpkins, Information Contact, 252-328-9653, Fax: 252-328-1618, E-mail: best@ecu.edu.

Eastern Michigan University, Graduate School, College of Business, Department of Computer Information Systems, Ypsilanti, MI 48197. Offers computer information systems (MBA); computer-based information systems (MSIS). Part-time and evening/weekend programs available. Postbaccalaureate distance learning degree programs offered (minimal on-campus study). *Faculty:* 14 full-time (1 woman). *Students:* 31 full-time (15 women), 27 part-time (9 women); includes 7 minority (1 African American, 6 Asian Americans or Pacific Islanders), 39 international. Average age 28. In 2006, 20 degrees awarded. *Entrance requirements:* For master's, GMAT. Additional exam requirements/recommendations for international students: Required—TOEFL. *Application deadline:* For fall admission, 5/15 priority date for domestic students, 5/1 priority date for international students; for winter admission, 10/15 priority date for domestic students, 10/1 priority date for international students; for spring admission, 3/15 priority date for domestic students, 3/1 priority date for international students. Applications are processed on a rolling basis. Application fee: $35. *Expenses:* Tuition, state resident: part-time $341 per credit hour. Tuition, nonresident: full-time $16,104; part-time $671 per credit hour. Required fees: $816; $34 per credit hour. $40 per term. One-time fee: $82 full-time. Tuition and fees vary according to course level, course load, degree level and reciprocity agreements. *Financial support:* Fellowships, research assistantships with full tuition reimbursements, teaching assistantships with full tuition reimbursements, career-related internships or fieldwork, Federal Work-Study, institutionally sponsored loans, scholarships/grants, tuition waivers (partial), and unspecified assistantships available. Support available to part-time students. Financial award applicants required to submit FAFSA. *Unit head:* Dr. Susan Kattelus, Interim Head, 734-487-2454, Fax: 734-487-1941, E-mail: susan.kattelus@emich.edu. *Application contact:* Dr. S. Imtiaz Ahmad, Program Coordinator, 734-487-2454, Fax: 734-487-1941, E-mail: imtiaz.ahmad@emich.edu.

Eastern Michigan University, Graduate School, College of Business, Program in Business Administration, Ypsilanti, MI 48197. Offers business administration (MBA); e-business (MBA); enterprise business intelligence (MBA); entrepreneurship (MBA); finance (MBA); human resources (MBA); information systems (MBA); internal auditing (MBA); international business (MBA); nonprofit management (MBA); supply chain management (MBA). *Accreditation:* AACSB. Part-time and evening/weekend programs available. Postbaccalaureate distance learning degree programs offered (minimal on-campus study). *Students:* 98 full-time (36 women), 192 part-time (86 women); includes 50 minority (26 African Americans, 19 Asian Americans or Pacific Islanders, 5 Hispanic Americans), 76 international. Average age 29. In 2006, 109 degrees awarded. *Entrance requirements:* For master's, GMAT. Additional exam requirements/recommendations for international students: Required—TOEFL. *Application deadline:* For fall admission, 5/15 priority date for domestic students, 5/1 priority date for international students; for winter admission, 10/15 priority date for domestic students, 10/1 priority date for international students; for spring admission, 3/15 priority date for domestic students, 3/1 priority date for international students. Applications are processed on a rolling basis. Application fee: $35. *Expenses:* Tuition, state resident: part-time $341 per credit hour. Tuition, nonresident: full-time $16,104; part-time $671 per credit hour. Required fees: $816; $34 per credit hour. $40 per term. One-time fee: $82 full-time. Tuition and fees vary according to course level, course load, degree level and reciprocity agreements. *Financial support:* Fellowships, research assistantships with full tuition reimbursements, teaching assistantships with full tuition reimbursements, career-related internships or fieldwork, Federal Work-Study, institutionally sponsored loans, scholarships/grants, tuition waivers (partial), and unspecified assistantships available. Support available to part-time students. Financial award applicants required to submit FAFSA. *Unit head:* Dawn Gaymer, Assistant Dean, Graduate Business Programs, 734-487-4444, Fax: 734-483-1316, E-mail: dawn.malone@emich.edu. *Application contact:* K. Michelle Henry, Coordinator, 734-487-4444, Fax: 734-483-1316, E-mail: michelle.henry@emich.edu.

Edinboro University of Pennsylvania, Graduate Studies and Research, School of Science, Management and Technology, Department of Mathematics and Computer Science, Program in Information Technology, Edinboro, PA 16444. Offers MS, Certificate. *Students:* 10 full-time (2 women), 8 part-time (2 women), 5 international. In 2006, 1 master's, 1 other advanced degree awarded. Application fee: $30. *Expenses:* Tuition, state resident: full-time $6,048; part-time $336 per credit. Tuition, nonresident: full-time $9,678; part-time $538 per credit. Required fees: $1,849; $42 per credit. *Financial support:* In 2006–07, 7 research assistantships with full and partial tuition reimbursements (averaging $3,850 per year) were awarded; Federal Work-Study, scholarships/grants, and unspecified assistantships also available. Support available to part-time students. Financial award application deadline: 2/15. *Unit head:* John Onderko, Unit Head, 814-732-2553, E-mail: jonderko@edinboro.edu. *Application contact:* Dr. R. Scott Baldwin, Dean, 814-732-2752, Fax: 814-732-2268, E-mail: sbaldwin@edinboro.edu.

Emory University, Roberto C. Goizueta Business School, Doctoral Programs in Business, Atlanta, GA 30322-1100. Offers accounting (PhD); finance (PhD); information systems (PhD); marketing (PhD); organization and management (PhD). *Degree requirements:* For doctorate, thesis/dissertation, comprehensive exam. *Entrance requirements:* Additional exam requirements/recommendations for international students: Required—TOEFL (minimum score 600 paper-based; 250 computer-based). Electronic applications accepted. *Expenses:* Tuition: Full-time $30,246. *Faculty research:* Financial markets, banking, corporate disclosure, investor relations, marketing strategy.

Fairfield University, Charles F. Dolan School of Business, Fairfield, CT 06824-5195. Offers accounting (MBA, MS, CAS); finance (MBA, MS, CAS); general management (MBA); human resource management (MBA, CAS); information systems and operations (MBA); information systems and operations management (CAS); international business (MBA, CAS); marketing (MBA, CAS); taxation (MBA, MS, CAS). *Accreditation:* AACSB. Part-time and evening/weekend programs available. *Faculty:* 43 full-time (17 women), 2 part-time/adjunct (1 woman). *Students:* 65 full-time (31 women), 125 part-time (54 women); includes 4 Asian Americans or Pacific Islanders, 4 Hispanic Americans, 22 international. Average age 27. 99 applicants, 45% accepted, 38 enrolled. In 2006, 78 degrees awarded. *Degree requirements:* For master's, registration. *Entrance requirements:* For master's, GMAT, 2 letters of reference, resumé. Additional exam requirements/recommendations for international students: Required—TOEFL

Management Information Systems

Fairfield University (continued)
(minimum score 550 paper-based; 213 computer-based; 79 iBT). *Application deadline:* For fall admission, 8/15 priority date for domestic students, 5/15 priority date for international students; for spring admission, 11/15 priority date for domestic students, 10/15 priority date for international students. Applications are processed on a rolling basis. Application fee: $55. Electronic applications accepted. *Expenses:* Contact institution. *Financial support:* Unspecified assistantships available. *Faculty research:* Optimal investment strategies, organization structure, international finance, strategic management, customer behavior. *Unit head:* Dr. Norman A. Solomon, Dean, 203-254-4000 Ext. 4070, Fax: 203-254-4105, E-mail: nsolomon@mail.fairfield.edu. *Application contact:* Marianne Gumpper, Director of Graduate and Continuing Studies Admissions, 203-254-4184, Fax: 203-254-4073, E-mail: gradadmis@mail.fairfield.edu.

See Close-Up on page 271.

Fairleigh Dickinson University, Metropolitan Campus, Silberman College of Business, Departments of Management, Marketing, and Entrepreneurial Studies, Program in Management, Teaneck, NJ 07666-1914. Offers management (MBA); management information systems (Certificate). *Accreditation:* AACSB. *Students:* 31 full-time (17 women), 20 part-time (8 women), 26 international. Average age 29. 101 applicants, 47% accepted, 20 enrolled. In 2006, 38 degrees awarded. *Application deadline:* Applications are processed on a rolling basis. Application fee: $40. *Unit head:* Dr. Robert Greenfield, Dean, Silberman College of Business, 201-692-2000.

Fairleigh Dickinson University, Metropolitan Campus, University College: Arts, Sciences, and Professional Studies, School of Computer Sciences and Engineering, Program in Management Information Systems, Teaneck, NJ 07666-1914. Offers MS. *Students:* 19 full-time (6 women), 14 part-time (5 women), 20 international. Average age 31. 54 applicants, 56% accepted, 6 enrolled. In 2006, 25 degrees awarded. *Application deadline:* Applications are processed on a rolling basis. Application fee: $40. *Unit head:* Dr. Alfredo Tan, Director, School of Computer Sciences and Engineering, 201-692-2000.

Ferris State University, College of Business, Big Rapids, MI 49307. Offers application development (MSISM); database administration (MSISM); e-business (MSISM); information systems (MBA); networking (MSISM); quality management (MBA); security (MSISM). Part-time and evening/weekend programs available. *Faculty:* 5 full-time (2 women), 2 part-time/adjunct (both women). *Students:* 35 full-time (12 women), 60 part-time (24 women); includes 5 minority (3 African Americans, 1 American Indian/Alaska Native, 1 Asian American or Pacific Islander), 13 international. Average age 34. 90 applicants, 72% accepted, 29 enrolled. In 2006, 40 degrees awarded. *Degree requirements:* For master's, thesis. *Entrance requirements:* For master's, GRE or GMAT, minimum GPA of 3.0 in CIS and business core, 2.75 overall; writing sample; 3 letters of reference; resumé. Additional exam requirements/recommendations for international students: Required—TOEFL (minimum score 500 paper-based; 173 computer-based). *Application deadline:* For fall admission, 7/1 priority date for domestic students, 6/15 for international students; for winter admission, 11/1 priority date for domestic students, 10/15 for international students; for spring admission, 3/1 priority date for domestic students, 2/15 for international students. Applications are processed on a rolling basis. Electronic applications accepted. *Expenses:* Tuition, state resident: part-time $355 per credit hour. Tuition, nonresident: part-time $687 per credit hour. *Financial support:* In 2006–07, 40 research assistantships, 10 teaching assistantships were awarded; career-related internships or fieldwork, Federal Work-Study, and unspecified assistantships also available. Support available to part-time students. Financial award applicants required to submit FAFSA. *Faculty research:* Quality improvement, client/server end-user computing, information management and policy, learning space/Lotus Notes, security. *Unit head:* Dr. Bill Boras, Department Chair, 231-591-2168, Fax: 231-591-2973, E-mail: cbgp@ferris.edu. *Application contact:* Shannon Yost, Department Secretary, 231-591-2168, Fax: 231-591-2973, E-mail: yosts@ferris.edu.

Florida Agricultural and Mechanical University, Division of Graduate Studies, Research, and Continuing Education, School of Business and Industry, Tallahassee, FL 32307-3200. Offers accounting (MBA); finance (MBA); management information systems (MBA); marketing (MBA). *Degree requirements:* For master's, residency. *Entrance requirements:* For master's, GMAT, minimum GPA of 3.0.

Florida Institute of Technology, Graduate Programs, University College, Melbourne, FL 32901-6975. Offers acquisition and contract management (MS, PMBA); aerospace engineering (MS); business administration (PMBA); computer information systems (MS); computer science (MS); e-business (PMBA); electrical engineering (MS); engineering management (MS); human resource management (PMBA); human resources management (MS); information systems (PMBA); logistics management (MS); management (MS), including acquisition and contract management, e-business, human resource management, information systems, logistics management, transportation management; materiel acquisition management (MS); mechanical engineering (MS); operations research (MS); project management (MS), including information systems, operations research; public administration (MPA); software engineering (MS); space systems (MS); space systems management (MS); systems management (MS), including information systems, operations research. Part-time and evening/weekend programs available. Postbaccalaureate distance learning degree programs offered (no on-campus study). *Faculty:* 11 full-time (4 women), 129 part-time/adjunct (17 women). *Students:* 78 full-time (34 women), 1,258 part-time (507 women); includes 384 minority (252 African Americans, 9 American Indian/Alaska Native, 58 Asian Americans or Pacific Islanders, 65 Hispanic Americans), 28 international. Average age 36. 629 applicants, 65% accepted, 320 enrolled. In 2006, 505 degrees awarded. *Degree requirements:* For master's, registration. *Entrance requirements:* For master's, minimum GPA of 3.0. Additional exam requirements/recommendations for international students: Required—TOEFL (minimum score 550 paper-based; 213 computer-based). *Application deadline:* Applications are processed on a rolling basis. Application fee: $50. Electronic applications accepted. *Expenses:* Tuition: Part-time $900 per credit. *Financial support:* Institutionally sponsored loans available. Financial award application deadline: 3/1; financial award applicants required to submit FAFSA. *Unit head:* Dr. Clifford Bragdon, Dean, 321-674-8821, Fax: 321-951-7694, E-mail: cbragdon@fit.edu. *Application contact:* Carolyn P. Farrior, Director of Graduate Admissions, 321-674-7118, Fax: 321-723-9468, E-mail: cfarrior@fit.edu.

Florida International University, Alvah H. Chapman, Jr. Graduate School of Business, Department of Decision Sciences and Information Systems, Miami, FL 33199. Offers PhD. Part-time and evening/weekend programs available. *Faculty:* 16 full-time (4 women). *Degree requirements:* For doctorate, thesis/dissertation. *Entrance requirements:* For doctorate, GMAT, minimum GPA of 3.0. Additional exam requirements/recommendations for international students: Required—TOEFL. *Application deadline:* For fall admission, 4/1 priority date for domestic students; for spring admission, 10/1 for domestic students. Applications are processed on a rolling basis. Application fee: $25. *Expenses:* Tuition, state resident: part-time $249 per credit hour. Tuition, nonresident: part-time $753 per credit hour. Tuition and fees vary according to program. *Unit head:* Dr. Christos Koulamas, Chairperson, 305-348-3309, Fax: 305-348-3278, E-mail: koulamas@fiu.edu.

Florida State University, Graduate Studies, College of Business, Tallahassee, FL 32306. Offers accounting (M Acc), including accounting information systems, assurance services, corporate accounting, taxation; business administration (MBA, PhD), including accounting (PhD), finance (PhD), information and management science (PhD), management (PhD), marketing (PhD), risk and insurance (PhD); insurance (MSM); management information systems (MS); JD/MBA. *Accreditation:* AACSB. Part-time and evening/weekend programs available. Postbaccalaureate distance learning degree programs offered (no on-campus study). *Faculty:* 107 full-time (26 women), 21 part-time/adjunct (2 women). *Students:* 145 full-time (62 women), 444 part-time (143 women); includes 147 minority (58 African Americans, 3 American Indian/Alaska Native, 45 Asian Americans or Pacific Islanders, 41 Hispanic Americans). Average age 29. 789 applicants, 50% accepted, 321 enrolled. In 2006, 263 master's, 19 doctorates awarded. Terminal master's awarded for partial completion of doctoral program. *Degree requirements:* For master's, registration; for doctorate, thesis/dissertation, comprehensive exam, registration. *Entrance requirements:* For master's, GMAT, substantial work experience (MBA, MS), minimum GPA of 3.0, letters of recommendation; for doctorate, GMAT, minimum graduate GPA of 3.5, letters of recommendation. Additional exam requirements/recommendations for international students: Required—TOEFL (minimum score 600 paper-based; 250 computer-based). *Application deadline:* For fall admission, 5/1 for domestic and international students; for spring admission, 10/1 for domestic students, 9/1 for international students. Applications are processed on a rolling basis. Application fee: $30. Electronic applications accepted. *Expenses:* Tuition, state resident: full-time $5,822; part-time $243 per credit hour. Tuition, nonresident: full-time $20,976; part-time $874 per credit hour. Tuition and fees vary according to program. *Financial support:* In 2006–07, 126 students received support, including 40 fellowships with partial tuition reimbursements available (averaging $4,600 per year), 37 research assistantships with partial tuition reimbursements available (averaging $4,600 per year), 49 teaching assistantships with partial tuition reimbursements available (averaging $10,500 per year); unspecified assistantships also available. Financial award application deadline: 1/1. Total annual research expenditures: $1.5 million. *Unit head:* Dr. Caryn Beck-Duolley, Dean, 850-644-3090, Fax: 850-644-0915. *Application contact:* Lisa Beverly, Coordinator, Graduate Programs Admissions, 850-644-6458, Fax: 850-644-0588, E-mail: lbeverly@cob.fsu.edu.

Fordham University, Graduate School of Business, New York, NY 10023. Offers accounting (MBA); communications and media management (MBA); finance (MBA, MS); information systems (MBA, MS); management systems (MBA); marketing (MBA); media management (MS); taxation (MS); JD/MBA; MBA/MIM; MS/MBA. *Accreditation:* AACSB. Part-time and evening/weekend programs available. *Faculty:* 87 full-time, 41 part-time/adjunct. *Students:* 345 full-time (132 women), 1,183 part-time (448 women); includes 238 minority (59 African Americans, 1 American Indian/Alaska Native, 116 Asian Americans or Pacific Islanders, 62 Hispanic Americans), 77 international. 1,081 applicants, 65% accepted, 422 enrolled. In 2006, 454 degrees awarded. *Entrance requirements:* For master's, GMAT. Additional exam requirements/recommendations for international students: Required—TOEFL (minimum score 600 paper-based; 250 computer-based). *Application deadline:* For fall admission, 6/1 priority date for domestic students, 5/1 priority date for international students; for winter admission, 11/1 priority date for domestic students, 10/1 priority date for international students; for spring admission, 3/1 priority date for domestic students, 2/1 priority date for international students. Applications are processed on a rolling basis. Application fee: $65. Electronic applications accepted. *Expenses:* Contact institution. *Financial support:* In 2006–07, 7 fellowships (averaging $27,000 per year), 128 research assistantships were awarded; career-related internships or fieldwork, institutionally sponsored loans, scholarships/grants, and unspecified assistantships also available. Support available to part-time students. Financial award application deadline: 5/1; financial award applicants required to submit FAFSA. *Unit head:* Dr. Howard Tuckman, Dean, 212-636-6165, Fax: 212-307-1779, E-mail: tuckman@fordham.edu. *Application contact:* Frank Fletcher, Director of Admissions and Financial Aid, 212-636-6200, Fax: 212-636-7076, E-mail: admissionsgb@fordham.edu.

Franklin Pierce University, Graduate Studies, Rindge, NH 03461-0060. Offers information technology management (MS); leadership (MBA); physical therapy (MS). *Accreditation:* APTA. Part-time and evening/weekend programs available. *Entrance requirements:* For master's, minimum GPA of 2.5. Additional exam requirements/recommendations for international students: Required—TOEFL (minimum score 550 paper-based; 195 computer-based). Electronic applications accepted.

Friends University, Graduate School, Division of Business, Technology, and Leadership, Program in Management Information Systems, Wichita, KS 67213. Offers MMIS. Evening/weekend programs available. *Faculty:* 2 full-time (1 woman), 2 part-time/adjunct (0 women). *Students:* 28 full-time. In 2006, 33 degrees awarded. *Entrance requirements:* Additional exam requirements/recommendations for international students: Required—TOEFL (minimum score 560 paper-based; 220 computer-based). *Application deadline:* For fall admission, 8/15 priority date for domestic students, 7/15 priority date for international students; for spring admission, 12/15 priority date for domestic students, 11/15 priority date for international students. Applications are processed on a rolling basis. Application fee: $45 ($65 for international students). Electronic applications accepted. *Unit head:* Dr. Mark Sanborn, Director, 800-794-6945 Ext. 5627, Fax: 316-295-5040. *Application contact:* Craig Davis, Director of Graduate Admissions, 800-794-6945 Ext. 5573, Fax: 316-295-5050, E-mail: cdavis@friends.edu.

The George Washington University, School of Business, Department of Management Science, Program in Management Information Systems, Washington, DC 20052. Offers MSIST. Part-time and evening/weekend programs available. *Entrance requirements:* For master's, GMAT. Additional exam requirements/recommendations for international students: Required—TOEFL. *Faculty research:* Expert systems, decision support systems.

Georgia College & State University, Graduate School, The J. Whitney Bunting School of Business, Milledgeville, GA 31061. Offers accountancy (MACCT); business (MBA); information systems (MIS). *Accreditation:* AACSB. Part-time and evening/weekend programs available. Postbaccalaureate distance learning degree programs offered (no on-campus study). *Faculty:* 43 full-time (18 women). *Students:* 44 full-time (19 women), 139 part-time (71 women); includes 28 minority (19 African Americans, 6 Asian Americans or Pacific Islanders, 3 Hispanic Americans), 17 international. Average age 30. 135 applicants, 56% accepted, 42 enrolled. In 2006, 76 degrees awarded. *Entrance requirements:* For master's, GMAT. Additional exam requirements/recommendations for international students: Required—TOEFL (minimum score 500 paper-based; 173 computer-based). *Application deadline:* For fall admission, 7/1 priority date for domestic students; for spring admission, 11/15 priority date for domestic students. Applications are processed on a rolling basis. Application fee: $25. Electronic applications accepted. *Expenses:* Tuition, state resident: full-time $3,222; part-time $179 per credit hour. Tuition, nonresident: full-time $12,870; part-time $715 per credit hour. Required fees: $391 per semester. Tuition and fees vary according to course load. *Financial support:* In 2006–07, 24 research assistantships with tuition reimbursements were awarded; career-related internships or fieldwork, Federal Work-Study, and unspecified assistantships also available. Support available to part-time students. Financial award application deadline: 3/1; financial award applicants required to submit FAFSA. *Faculty research:* Artificial intelligence, international trade, business ethics, curriculum issues. *Unit head:* Dr. Faye Gilbert, Dean, 478-445-5497, E-mail: faye.gilbert@gcsu.edu. *Application contact:* Lynn Hanson, Director of Graduate Programs in Business, 478-445-5115, E-mail: lynn.hanson@gcsu.edu.

Georgia Institute of Technology, Graduate Studies and Research, College of Management, Program in Business Administration, Atlanta, GA 30332-0001. Offers accounting (MBA); e-commerce (Certificate); engineering entrepreneurship (MBA); entrepreneurship (Certificate); finance (MBA); information technology management (MBA); international business (MBA, Certificate); management of technology (Certificate); marketing (MBA); operations management (MBA); organizational behavior (MBA); strategic management (MBA). *Accreditation:* AACSB.

Georgia Institute of Technology, Graduate Studies and Research, College of Management, Program in Management, Atlanta, GA 30332-0001. Offers accounting (PhD); finance (PhD); information technology management (PhD); marketing (PhD); operations management (PhD); organizational behavior (PhD); quantitative and computational finance (MS); strategic management (PhD). *Accreditation:* AACSB. *Degree requirements:* For doctorate, thesis/dissertation, oral exams, comprehensive exam. *Entrance requirements:* For master's and doctorate, GMAT. Additional exam requirements/recommendations for international students: Required—TOEFL. *Faculty research:* MIS, management of technology, international business, entrepreneurship, operations management.

Georgia State University, J. Mack Robinson College of Business, Department of Computer Information Systems, Atlanta, GA 30303-3083. Offers MBA, MSIS, PhD. Part-time and evening/weekend programs available. *Faculty:* 24 full-time (3 women). *Students:* 68 full-time (22 women), 58 part-time (13 women); includes 23 minority (10 African Americans, 12 Asian Americans or Pacific Islanders, 1 Hispanic American), 45 international. Average age 32. 110 applicants, 40% accepted, 22 enrolled. In 2006, 49 master's, 5 doctorates awarded. Terminal master's awarded for partial completion of doctoral program. *Degree requirements:* For doctorate, thesis/dissertation. *Entrance requirements:* For master's and doctorate, GMAT. Additional exam requirements/recommendations for international students: Required—TOEFL (minimum score 610 paper-based; 255 computer-based; 101 iBT). *Application deadline:* For fall admission, 5/1 for domestic students, 2/1 for international students; for spring admission, 10/15 for domestic students, 5/1 for international students. Applications are processed on a rolling basis. Application fee: $50. *Financial support:* Fellowships, research assistantships, teaching assistantships, career-related internships or fieldwork and tuition waivers (partial) available. Support available to part-time students. Financial award applicants required to submit FAFSA. *Unit head:* Dr. Mark Keil, Chair, 404-651-3830, Fax: 404-651-3842.

Georgia State University, J. Mack Robinson College of Business, Program in General Business Administration, Atlanta, GA 30303-3083. Offers accounting/information systems (MBA); enterprise risk management (MBA); general business (MBA); general business administration (EMBA, PMBA); information systems consulting (MBA); information systems risk management (MBA); international business and information technology (MBA); international entrepreneurship (MBA); MBA/JD. *Accreditation:* AACSB. Part-time and evening/weekend programs available. *Faculty:* 1 (woman) full-time. *Students:* 183 full-time (83 women), 212 part-time (57 women); includes 118 minority (73 African Americans, 36 Asian Americans or Pacific Islanders, 9 Hispanic Americans), 42 international. 294 applicants, 74% accepted, 182 enrolled. In 2006, 98 degrees awarded. *Entrance requirements:* For master's, GMAT. Additional exam requirements/recommendations for international students: Required—TOEFL (minimum score 610 paper-based; 255 computer-based; 101 iBT). *Application deadline:* For fall admission, 5/1 for domestic students, 2/1 for international students; for spring admission, 10/15 for domestic students, 5/1 for international students. Applications are processed on a rolling basis. Application fee: $50. Electronic applications accepted. *Financial support:* Research assistantships, tuition waivers (partial) available. Support available to part-time students. Financial award application deadline: 5/1; financial award applicants required to submit FAFSA. *Application contact:* Graduate Student and Alumni Services, 404-463-4568, Fax: 404-651-2721, E-mail: mastersadmissions@gsu.edu.

Golden Gate University, Ageno School of Business, San Francisco, CA 94105-2968. Offers accounting (M Ac, MBA); business administration (EMBA, MBA, DBA); finance (MBA, MS, Certificate); financial planning (MS, Certificate); human resource management (MBA, MS); human resources management (Certificate); information technology (MBA); information technology management (MS, Certificate); integrated marketing and communications (MS, Certificate); international business (MBA); management (MBA); marketing (MBA, MS, Certificate); operations management (Certificate); psychology (MA, Certificate); public relations (MS, Certificate); JD/MBA. Part-time and evening/weekend programs available. *Students:* 355 full-time (192 women), 977 part-time (465 women); includes 447 minority (85 African Americans, 5 American Indian/Alaska Native, 274 Asian Americans or Pacific Islanders, 83 Hispanic Americans), 226 international. Average age 34. 548 applicants, 74% accepted, 201 enrolled. In 2006, 545 master's, 21 doctorates awarded. *Degree requirements:* For doctorate, thesis/dissertation. *Entrance requirements:* For master's, GMAT (MBA), minimum GPA of 2.5 (MS). Additional exam requirements/recommendations for international students: Required—TOEFL. *Application deadline:* Applications are processed on a rolling basis. Application fee: $55 ($90 for international students). *Financial support:* Career-related internships or fieldwork, Federal Work-Study, and institutionally sponsored loans available. Support available to part-time students. Financial award applicants required to submit FAFSA. *Unit head:* Terry Connelly, Dean, 415-442-6519, Fax: 415-442-5369. *Application contact:* Enrollment Services, 415-442-7800, Fax: 415-442-7807, E-mail: info@ggu.edu.

Goldey-Beacom College, Graduate Program, Wilmington, DE 19808-1999. Offers business administration (MBA); financial management (MBA); human resource management (MBA); information technology (MBA); management (MM); marketing management (MBA). *Accreditation:* ACBSP. Part-time and evening/weekend programs available. *Entrance requirements:* For master's, GMAT, minimum GPA of 3.0. Additional exam requirements/recommendations for international students: Required—TOEFL (minimum score 525 paper-based; 195 computer-based). Electronic applications accepted.

Governors State University, College of Business and Public Administration, Program in Management Information Systems, University Park, IL 60466-0975. Offers MS. *Students:* 2 full-time, 20 part-time. Average age 35.Application fee: $25. *Expenses:* Tuition, state resident: full-time $4,104; part-time $171 per hour. Tuition, nonresident: part-time $513 per hour. *Application contact:* Dortha Brown, Adviser, 708-534-4391.

Graduate School and University Center of the City University of New York, Graduate Studies, Program in Business, New York, NY 10016-4039. Offers accounting (PhD); behavioral science (PhD); finance (PhD); management planning systems (PhD). *Faculty:* 66 full-time (5 women). *Students:* 55 full-time (27 women); includes 7 minority (2 African Americans, 1 American Indian/Alaska Native, 2 Asian Americans or Pacific Islanders, 2 Hispanic Americans), 26 international. Average age 33. 74 applicants, 32% accepted, 11 enrolled. In 2006, 9 degrees awarded. *Degree requirements:* For doctorate, thesis/dissertation. *Entrance requirements:* For doctorate, GMAT, writing sample (15 pages). Additional exam requirements/recommendations for international students: Required—TOEFL. *Application deadline:* For fall admission, 1/15 for domestic students. Application fee: $125. Electronic applications accepted. *Financial support:* In 2006–07, 40 fellowships, 5 teaching assistantships were awarded; research assistantships, career-related internships or fieldwork, Federal Work-Study, institutionally sponsored loans, and tuition waivers (full and partial) also available. Financial award application deadline: 2/1; financial award applicants required to submit FAFSA. *Unit head:* Dr. Joseph Weintrop, Executive Officer, 646-312-3092, Fax: 646-312-3031.

Grand Valley State University, Padnos College of Engineering and Computing, School of Computing and Information Systems, Allendale, MI 49401-9403. Offers computer information systems (MS), including database, distributed systems, management of information systems, object oriented systems, software engineering. Part-time and evening/weekend programs available. *Faculty:* 12 full-time (0 women). *Students:* 13 full-time (6 women), 57 part-time (14 women); includes 9 minority (2 African Americans, 7 Asian Americans or Pacific Islanders). Average age 32. 26 applicants, 96% accepted, 13 enrolled. In 2006, 33 degrees awarded. *Median time to degree:* Master's–1.5 years full-time, 3.5 years part-time. *Degree requirements:* For master's, thesis or alternative. *Entrance requirements:* For master's, GMAT or GRE General Test. Additional exam requirements/recommendations for international students: Required—TOEFL. *Application deadline:* For fall admission, 6/1 for international students; for winter admission, 9/1 for international students. Applications are processed on a rolling basis. Application fee: $30. Electronic applications accepted. *Expenses:* Tuition, state resident: full-time $5,850; part-time $325 per credit. Tuition, nonresident: full-time $10,800; part-time $600 per credit. Tuition and fees vary according to course load. *Financial support:* In 2006–07, 2 research assistantships with full and partial tuition reimbursements (averaging $8,000 per year) were awarded. *Faculty research:* Object technology, distributed computing, information systems management database, and software engineering. *Unit head:* Paul Leidig, Director, 616-331-2038, Fax: 616-331-2106, E-mail: leidigp@gvsu.edu. *Application contact:* D. Robert Adams, CIS Graduate Program Chair, 616-331-3885, Fax: 616-331-2106, E-mail: adams@cis.gvsu.edu.

Grantham University, College of Computer Science and Engineering Technology, Kansas City, MO 64153. Offers information management technology (MS); information technology (MS); project management (MS). Part-time and evening/weekend programs available. Postbaccalaureate distance learning degree programs offered (no on-campus study). *Students:* 177 full-time. Average age 36. *Entrance requirements:* Additional exam requirements/recommendations for international students: Required—TOEFL (minimum score 500 paper-based). *Application deadline:* Applications are processed on a rolling basis. Application fee: $0. Electronic applications accepted. *Financial support:* Institutionally sponsored loans and scholarships/grants available. *Application contact:* DeAnn Wandler, Director of Admissions, 800-955-2527, Fax: 816-595-5757, E-mail: admissions@grantham.edu.

Grantham University, Mark Skousen School of Business, Kansas City, MO 64153. Offers information management (MBA); project management (MBA). Part-time and evening/weekend programs available. Postbaccalaureate distance learning degree programs offered (no on-campus study). *Faculty:* 30. *Students:* 372 full-time. Average age 36. *Degree requirements:* For master's, thesis, registration. *Entrance requirements:* Additional exam requirements/recommendations for international students: Required—TOEFL (minimum score 500 paper-based). *Application deadline:* Applications are processed on a rolling basis. Application fee: $0. Electronic applications accepted. *Financial support:* Institutionally sponsored loans and scholarships/grants available. *Application contact:* DeAnn Wandler, Director of Admissions, 800-955-2527, Fax: 816-595-5757, E-mail: admissions@grantham.edu.

Harvard University, Business School, Doctoral Programs in Management, Boston, MA 02163. Offers business administration (DBA); business economics (PhD); health policy management (PhD); information and technology management (PhD); organizational behavior (PhD). *Degree requirements:* For doctorate, thesis/dissertation, comprehensive exam (for some programs). *Entrance requirements:* For doctorate, GRE General Test or GMAT. Additional exam requirements/recommendations for international students: Required—TOEFL. *Expenses:* Tuition: Full-time $30,275. Full-time tuition and fees vary according to program and student level.

Hawai'i Pacific University, College of Business Administration, Honolulu, HI 96813. Offers accounting/CPA (MBA); communication (MBA); e-business (MBA); economics (MBA); finance (MBA); human resource management (MBA); information systems (MBA); international business (MBA); management (MBA); marketing (MBA); organizational change (MBA); travel industry management (MBA). Part-time and evening/weekend programs available. *Faculty:* 40 full-time (16 women), 30 part-time/adjunct (10 women). *Students:* 320 full-time (150 women), 205 part-time (95 women); includes 168 minority (17 African Americans, 7 American Indian/Alaska Native, 137 Asian Americans or Pacific Islanders, 7 Hispanic Americans), 232 international. Average age 31. 279 applicants, 67% accepted, 166 enrolled. In 2006, 172 degrees awarded. *Degree requirements:* For master's, thesis. *Entrance requirements:* For master's, GMAT. Additional exam requirements/recommendations for international students: Recommended—TOEFL (minimum score 550 paper-based; 213 computer-based), TWE (minimum score 5). *Application deadline:* For fall admission, 2/15 priority date for domestic students; for spring admission, 10/15 priority date for domestic students. Applications are processed on a rolling basis. Application fee: $50. Electronic applications accepted. *Expenses:* Tuition: Full-time $10,080; part-time $560 per credit. *Financial support:* In 2006–07, 118 students received support; research assistantships, career-related internships or fieldwork, Federal Work-Study, scholarships/grants, and unspecified assistantships available. Support available to part-time students. Financial award application deadline: 3/1; financial award applicants required to submit FAFSA. *Faculty research:* Statistical control process as used by management, studies in comparative cross-cultural management styles, not-for-profit management. *Unit head:* Dr. Charles Steilen, Dean, 808-544-9301, Fax: 808-544-0283, E-mail: csteilen@hpu.edu. *Application contact:* Danny Lam, Assistant Director of Graduate Admissions, 808-544-1135, Fax: 808-544-0280, E-mail: graduate@hpu.edu.

See Close-Up on page 275.

Hawai'i Pacific University, College of Professional Studies, Honolulu, HI 96813. Offers global leadership and sustainable development (MA); human resource management (MA); information systems (MSIS); organizational change (MA). Part-time and evening/weekend programs available. *Faculty:* 15 full-time (2 women), 7 part-time/adjunct (2 women). *Students:* 118 full-time (56 women), 149 part-time (57 women); includes 101 minority (15 African Americans, 5 American Indian/Alaska Native, 70 Asian Americans or Pacific Islanders, 11 Hispanic Americans), 87 international. Average age 32. 188 applicants, 58% accepted, 67 enrolled. In 2006, 65 degrees awarded. *Degree requirements:* For master's, thesis. *Entrance requirements:* Additional exam requirements/recommendations for international students: Recommended—TOEFL (minimum score 550 paper-based; 213 computer-based), TWE (minimum score 5). *Application deadline:* For fall admission, 2/15 priority date for domestic students; for spring admission, 10/15 priority date for domestic students. Applications are processed on a rolling basis. Application fee: $50. Electronic applications accepted. *Expenses:* Tuition: Full-time $10,080; part-time $560 per credit. *Financial support:* In 2006–07, 54 students received support. Career-related internships or fieldwork, Federal Work-Study, scholarships/grants, and unspecified assistantships available. Support available to part-time students. Financial award application deadline: 3/1; financial award applicants required to submit FAFSA. *Unit head:* Dr. Gordon Jones, Dean, 808-544-1181, Fax: 808-544-0247, E-mail: gjones@hpu.edu. *Application contact:* Danny Lam, Assistant Director of Graduate Admissions, 808-544-1135, Fax: 808-544-0280, E-mail: graduate@hpu.edu.

HEC Montreal, School of Business Administration, Master of Science Programs in Administration, Program in Information Systems, Montréal, QC H3T 2A7, Canada. Offers M Sc. All courses are given in French. Part-time programs available. *Degree requirements:* For master's, one foreign language, thesis. Application fee: $60 Canadian dollars. Electronic applications accepted. Tuition and fees charges are reported in Canadian dollars. *Expenses:* Tuition, nonresident: part-time $56 Canadian dollars per credit. Required fees: $30 Canadian dollars per semester. *Financial support:* Fellowships, research assistantships, teaching assistantships, scholarships/grants available. *Application contact:* Francine Blais, Administrative Director, 514-340-6112, Fax: 514-340-6411, E-mail: francine.blais@hec.ca.

Hodges University, Graduate Programs, Naples, FL 34119. Offers business administration (MBA); computer information technology (MS); criminal justice (MCJ); education (MPS); information systems management (MIS); interdisciplinary (MPS); law (MPS); management (MSM); professional studies (MPS); psychology (MPS); public administration (MPA). Part-time and evening/weekend programs available. Postbaccalaureate distance learning degree programs offered (no on-campus study). *Faculty:* 17 full-time (4 women). *Students:* 35 full-time (22 women), 156 part-time (100 women); includes 52 minority (24 African Americans, 1 American Indian/Alaska Native, 4 Asian Americans or Pacific Islanders, 23 Hispanic Americans). Average age 32. In 2006, 101 degrees awarded. *Median time to degree:* Master's–1.5 years full-time, 2.5 years part-time. *Degree requirements:* For master's, comprehensive exam (for some programs), registration. *Entrance requirements:* For master's, in-house entrance exam. Application fee: $50. Electronic applications accepted. *Financial support:* Federal Work-Study and scholarships/grants available. Financial award applicants required to submit FAFSA. *Unit head:* Terry McMahan, President, 239-513-1122, Fax: 239-598-6253, E-mail: tmcmahan@internationalcollege.edu. *Application contact:* Rita Lampus, Vice President of Student Enrollment Management, 239-513-1122, Fax: 239-598-6253, E-mail: rlampus@internationalcollege.edu.

Hofstra University, Frank G. Zarb School of Business, Department of Business Computer Information Systems/Quantitative Methods, Hempstead, NY 11549. Offers business computer information systems (MBA); computer information systems (MS); quality management (MBA). Part-time and evening/weekend programs available. *Faculty:* 11 full-time (3 women). *Students:* 4 full-time (0 women), 26 part-time (6 women); includes 6 minority (1 African American, 5 Asian Americans or Pacific Islanders), 1 international. Average age 31. 14 applicants, 86% accepted, 8 enrolled. In 2006, 10 degrees awarded. *Degree requirements:* For master's, thesis or alternative, registration. *Entrance requirements:* For master's, GMAT, 2 letters of recommendation, resumé, essay. Additional exam requirements/recommendations for international students: Required—TOEFL (minimum score 550 paper-based; 213 computer-based). *Application deadline:* Applications are processed on a rolling basis. Application fee: $60. Electronic applications accepted. *Expenses:* Tuition: Full-time $13,320; part-time $740 per credit. Required fees: $930; $155 per term. *Financial support:* In 2006–07, 5 students received support, including 5 fellowships with tuition reimbursements available (averaging $10,844 per year);

Management Information Systems

Hofstra University (continued)
research assistantships with full and partial tuition reimbursements available, career-related internships or fieldwork, Federal Work-Study, scholarships/grants, tuition waivers (full and partial), and unspecified assistantships also available. Financial award applicants required to submit FAFSA. *Faculty research:* Decision support systems, econometrics-public issues, forecasting, LPT sizing-quality, enterprise planning systems-SAP. *Unit head:* Dr. John F. Affisco, Chairperson, 516-463-5362, E-mail: acsjfa@hofstra.edu. *Application contact:* Carol Drummer, Dean of Graduate Admissions, 516-463-4876, Fax: 516-463-4664, E-mail: gradstudent@hofstra.edu.

Holy Family University, Graduate School, School of Business, Philadelphia, PA 19114-2094. Offers human resources management (MS); information systems management (MS). Part-time and evening/weekend programs available. *Degree requirements:* For master's, thesis optional. *Entrance requirements:* For master's, GMAT, GRE, or MAT, minimum GPA of 3.0.

Howard University, School of Business, Graduate Programs in Business, Washington, DC 20059-0002. Offers accounting (MBA); entrepreneurship (MBA); finance (MBA); information systems (MBA); international business (MBA); marketing (MBA); supply chain management (MBA); JD/MBA. *Accreditation:* AACSB. Part-time and evening/weekend programs available. Postbaccalaureate distance learning degree programs offered (no on-campus study). *Entrance requirements:* For master's, GMAT, minimum 1 year post undergraduate work experience, resumé, 3 letters of recommendation, advanced college algebra. Additional exam requirements/recommendations for international students: Required—TOEFL. *Faculty research:* Marketing research in multi-ethnic populations, U.S. trade policies and international relations, risk management (finance).

Idaho State University, Office of Graduate Studies, College of Business, Pocatello, ID 83209. Offers business administration (MBA, Postbaccalaureate Certificate); computer information systems (MS, Postbaccalaureate Certificate). *Accreditation:* AACSB. Part-time and evening/weekend programs available. Postbaccalaureate distance learning degree programs offered (minimal on-campus study). *Faculty:* 26 full-time (4 women). *Students:* 55 full-time (11 women), 73 part-time (16 women); includes 3 minority (1 African American, 1 Asian American or Pacific Islander, 1 Hispanic American), 14 international. Average age 31. In 2006, 45 degrees awarded. *Degree requirements:* For master's, thesis (for some programs), comprehensive exam, registration; for Postbaccalaureate Certificate, thesis (for some programs), 6 hours of clerkship, comprehensive exam, registration. *Entrance requirements:* For master's, GMAT, GRE General Test, minimum GPA of 3.0, resumé outlining work experience, 2 letters of reference; for Postbaccalaureate Certificate, GMAT, GRE General Test, minimum upper level GPA of 3.0. Additional exam requirements/recommendations for international students: Required—TOEFL (minimum score 550 paper-based; 213 computer-based; 80 iBT). *Application deadline:* For fall admission, 7/1 for domestic students, 6/1 for international students; for spring admission, 12/1 for domestic students, 11/1 for international students. Applications are processed on a rolling basis. Application fee: $55. *Expenses:* Tuition, state resident: part-time $251 per credit. Tuition, nonresident: part-time $366 per credit. Tuition and fees vary according to degree level, program and reciprocity agreements. *Financial support:* In 2006–07, 9 teaching assistantships with full and partial tuition reimbursements (averaging $8,694 per year) were awarded; career-related internships or fieldwork, Federal Work-Study, traineeships, tuition waivers (full and partial), and unspecified assistantships also available. Support available to part-time students. Financial award application deadline: 1/1. *Faculty research:* Information assurance, computer information technology, finance management, marketing. Total annual research expenditures: $236,510. *Unit head:* Dr. William Stratton, Dean, 208-282-3585, Fax: 208-282-4367.

Illinois Institute of Technology, Graduate College, Center for Professional Development, Program in Information Technology and Management, Chicago, IL 60616-3793. Offers MITM. Part-time and evening/weekend programs available. Postbaccalaureate distance learning degree programs offered (no on-campus study). *Faculty:* 6 part-time/adjunct (0 women). *Students:* 95 full-time (24 women), 49 part-time (15 women); includes 27 minority (8 African Americans, 17 Asian Americans or Pacific Islanders, 2 Hispanic Americans), 92 international. Average age 28. 183 applicants, 77% accepted, 19 enrolled. In 2006, 35 master's awarded. *Entrance requirements:* For master's, minimum undergraduate GPA of 3.0. Additional exam requirements/recommendations for international students: Required—TOEFL (minimum score 550 paper-based; 213 computer-based). *Application deadline:* For fall admission, 5/1 for domestic and international students; for spring admission, 10/15 for domestic and international students. Applications are processed on a rolling basis. Application fee: $40. Electronic applications accepted. *Expenses:* Tuition: Full-time $13,086; part-time $727 per credit. Required fees: $7 per credit. $235 per term. Tuition and fees vary according to class time, course level, course load, program and student level. *Financial support:* In 2006–07, 10 fellowships with partial tuition reimbursements, 12 teaching assistantships with partial tuition reimbursements (averaging $3,000 per year) were awarded; career-related internships or fieldwork, Federal Work-Study, institutionally sponsored loans, scholarships/grants, health care benefits, and tuition waivers (partial) also available. Support available to part-time students. *Faculty research:* Information, computer and network security; computer forensics; voice over IP (VOIP) and telecommunications; web technologies; software engineering methodologies. *Application contact:* Barbara C. Kozi, Administrator, 630-682-6040, Fax: 630-682-6010, E-mail: kozi@iit.edu.

Illinois Institute of Technology, Graduate College, College of Science and Letters, Lewis Department of Humanities, Chicago, IL 60616-3793. Offers information architecture (MS); technical communication (PhD); technical communication and information design (MS). Part-time and evening/weekend programs available. *Faculty:* 14 full-time (5 women), 16 part-time/adjunct (11 women). *Students:* 14 full-time (7 women), 20 part-time (14 women); includes 12 minority (8 African Americans, 2 Asian Americans or Pacific Islanders, 2 Hispanic Americans), 8 international. Average age 32. 33 applicants, 70% accepted, 10 enrolled. In 2006, 5 master's, 1 doctorate awarded. *Degree requirements:* For master's, thesis or alternative, project, comprehensive exam; for doctorate, thesis/dissertation, qualifying exam, comprehensive exam. *Entrance requirements:* For master's, GRE General Test; for doctorate, GRE General Test, bachelor's degree in technical communication or other relevant field. Additional exam requirements/recommendations for international students: Required—TOEFL (minimum score 550 paper-based; 213 computer-based). *Application deadline:* For fall admission, 5/1 for domestic and international students; for spring admission, 10/15 for domestic and international students. Applications are processed on a rolling basis. Application fee: $40. Electronic applications accepted. *Expenses:* Tuition: Full-time $13,086; part-time $727 per credit. Required fees: $7 per credit. $235 per term. Tuition and fees vary according to class time, course level, course load, program and student level. *Financial support:* In 2006–07, 1 fellowship with full tuition reimbursement (averaging $12,000 per year), 15 teaching assistantships with partial tuition reimbursements (averaging $10,000 per year) were awarded; career-related internships or fieldwork, Federal Work-Study, institutionally sponsored loans, scholarships/grants, health care benefits, and tuition waivers (partial) also available. Support available to part-time students. Financial award applicants required to submit FAFSA. *Faculty research:* Discourse analysis, linguistics, readability, ethics in professions, instructional design, knowledge management, usability testing and evaluation. Total annual research expenditures: $22,435. *Unit head:* Kathryn Riley, Chair, 312-567-3566, Fax: 312-567-5187, E-mail: riley@iit.edu. *Application contact:* Morgan Frederick, Assistant Director of Graduate Communications, 866-472-3448, Fax: 312-567-3138, E-mail: inquiry.grad@iit.edu.

Illinois Institute of Technology, Stuart School of Business, Program in Business Administration, Chicago, IL 60616-3793. Offers entrepreneurship (MBA); financial management (MBA); financial markets (MBA); healthcare management (MBA); information technology management (MBA); international business (MBA); management science (MBA); marketing (MBA); operations, quality, and technology management (MBA); strategic management of organizations (MBA); sustainable enterprise (MBA); JD/MBA; MBA/MS. *Accreditation:* AACSB. Part-time and evening/weekend programs available. *Faculty:* 13 full-time (1 woman), 9 part-time/adjunct (0 women). *Students:* 74 full-time (29 women), 42 part-time (16 women); includes 17 minority (5 African Americans, 11 Asian Americans or Pacific Islanders, 1 Hispanic American), 74 international. Average age 29. 247 applicants, 70% accepted, 51 enrolled. In 2006, 45 degrees awarded. *Entrance requirements:* For master's, GMAT. Additional exam requirements/recommendations for international students: Required—TOEFL (minimum score 600 paper-based; 250 computer-based). *Application deadline:* For fall admission, 8/15 priority date for domestic students, 7/1 for international students; for winter admission, 11/1 priority date for domestic students, 10/1 for international students; for spring admission, 1/1 priority date for domestic students, 1/1 for international students. Applications are processed on a rolling basis. Application fee: $75. Electronic applications accepted. *Expenses: Contact institution.* Tuition and fees vary according to class time, course level, course load, program and student level. *Financial support:* Career-related internships or fieldwork, Federal Work-Study, institutionally sponsored loans, scholarships/grants, traineeships, health care benefits, tuition waivers, and unspecified assistantships available. Support available to part-time students. Financial award applicants required to submit FAFSA. *Faculty research:* Knowledge management, healthcare management, sustainability in supply chain. *Unit head:* Dr. George P. Nassos, Interim Director, 312-906-6543, Fax: 312-906-6549, E-mail: george.nassos@iit.edu. *Application contact:* Brian Jansen, Director of Graduate Admissions, 312-906-6521, Fax: 312-906-6549, E-mail: admission@stuart.iit.edu.

Illinois State University, Graduate School, College of Applied Science and Technology, School of Information Technology, Normal, IL 61790-2200. Offers MS. *Faculty:* 13 full-time (2 women). *Students:* 40 full-time (14 women), 24 part-time (6 women); includes 3 minority (all Asian Americans or Pacific Islanders), 43 international. 105 applicants, 60% accepted. In 2006, 31 degrees awarded. *Entrance requirements:* For master's, GRE General Test, minimum GPA of 3.0 in last 60 hours; proficiency in COBOL, FORTRAN, Pascal, or P12. *Application deadline:* Applications are processed on a rolling basis. Application fee: $40. *Expenses:* Tuition, state resident: full-time $3,330; part-time $185 per credit hour. Tuition, nonresident: full-time $6,948; part-time $438 per credit hour. Required fees: $1,259; $52 per credit hour. *Financial support:* In 2006–07, 17 teaching assistantships (averaging $4,204 per year) were awarded; fellowships, tuition waivers (full) and unspecified assistantships also available. Financial award application deadline: 4/1. *Faculty research:* Graduate practicum training in network support. Total annual research expenditures: $6,600. *Unit head:* Dr. Terry Dennis, Chairperson, 309-438-8338.

Indiana University South Bend, School of Business and Economics, South Bend, IN 46634-7111. Offers accounting (MSA); business administration (MBA); management of information technologies (MS). Part-time and evening/weekend programs available. *Faculty:* 17 full-time (2 women), 3 part-time/adjunct (1 woman). *Students:* 69 full-time (39 women), 118 part-time (43 women); includes 13 minority (5 African Americans, 4 Asian Americans or Pacific Islanders, 4 Hispanic Americans), 55 international. Average age 31. 49 applicants, 100% accepted, 47 enrolled. In 2006, 51 degrees awarded. *Entrance requirements:* For master's, GMAT. Additional exam requirements/recommendations for international students: Required—TOEFL (minimum score 550 paper-based; 213 computer-based). *Application deadline:* For fall admission, 7/1 priority date for domestic and international students; for spring admission, 11/1 priority date for domestic and international students. Applications are processed on a rolling basis. Application fee: $45 ($55 for international students). *Expenses: Contact institution. Financial support:* Federal Work-Study and institutionally sponsored loans available. Support available to part-time students. Financial award applicants required to submit FAFSA. *Faculty research:* Financial accounting, consumer research, capital budgeting research, business strategy research. *Unit head:* Dr. P. N. Saksena, Assistant Dean, Director of Graduate Studies, 574-520-4456, Fax: 574-520-4866, E-mail: psakena@iusb.edu. *Application contact:* Sharon Peterson, Secretary—Graduate Business, 574-520-4138, Fax: 574-520-4866, E-mail: speterso@iusb.edu.

Indiana University Southeast, School of Business, New Albany, IN 47150-6405. Offers accounting (Certificate); business administration (MBA); economics (Certificate); finance (Certificate); general business (Certificate); information and operations management (Certificate); management and marketing (Certificate); strategic finance (MS). *Accreditation:* AACSB. *Faculty:* 11 full-time (2 women). *Students:* 10 full-time (4 women), 201 part-time (65 women); includes 12 minority (2 African Americans, 8 Asian Americans or Pacific Islanders, 2 Hispanic Americans), 5 international. Average age 31. In 2006, 60 degrees awarded. *Degree requirements:* For master's, community service. *Entrance requirements:* For master's, GMAT, work experience. Additional exam requirements/recommendations for international students: Required—TOEFL. Application fee: $35. *Expenses: Contact institution.* Tuition and fees vary according to course load, campus/location and program. *Unit head:* Chris Bjornson, Dean, 812-941-2362, Fax: 812-941-2672. *Application contact:* Dr. Jay White, Director of Graduate Business Programs, 812-941-2364, Fax: 812-941-2581, E-mail: jwhite04@ius.edu.

Instituto Tecnológico y de Estudios Superiores de Monterrey, Campus Central de Veracruz, Graduate Programs, Córdoba, Mexico. Offers administration (MA); administration of information technologies (MTI); computer sciences (MCC); education (MEE); educational institution administration (MAD); educational technology (MTE); electronic commerce (MCE); finance (MAF); humanistic studies (MEH); international business for Latin America (MNL); marketing (MMT); science (MCP); technology management (MTT). Part-time and evening/weekend programs available. Postbaccalaureate distance learning degree programs offered (minimal on-campus study). *Degree requirements:* For master's, thesis (for some programs). *Entrance requirements:* For master's, PAEP College Board. Electronic applications accepted.

Instituto Tecnológico y de Estudios Superiores de Monterrey, Campus Ciudad de México, Virtual University Division, Ciudad de Mexico, Mexico. Offers administration of information technologies (MA); computer sciences (MA); education (MA, PhD); educational technology (MA); environmental engineering (MA); environmental systems (MA); humanistic studies (MA); industrial engineering (MA); international business for Latin America (MA); quality systems (MA); quality systems and productivity (MA). Part-time and evening/weekend programs available. Postbaccalaureate distance learning degree programs offered (minimal on-campus study). *Entrance requirements:* For master's and doctorate, Instituto entrance exam. Additional exam requirements/recommendations for international students: Required—TOEFL.

Instituto Tecnológico y de Estudios Superiores de Monterrey, Campus Ciudad Juárez, Program in Administration of Information Technology, Ciudad Juárez, Mexico. Offers MAIT.

Instituto Tecnológico y de Estudios Superiores de Monterrey, Campus Ciudad Obregón, Program in Administration of Information Technology, Ciudad Obregón, Mexico. Offers MATI.

Instituto Tecnológico y de Estudios Superiores de Monterrey, Campus Estado de México, Professional and Graduate Division, Estado de Mexico, Mexico. Offers administration of information technologies (MITA); architecture (M Arch); business administration (GMBA, MBA); computer sciences (MCS, PhD); education (M Ed); educational institution administration (MAD); educational technology and innovation (PhD); electronic commerce (MEC); environmental systems (MS); finance (MAF); humanistic studies (MHS); information sciences and knowledge management (MISKM); information systems (MS); manufacturing systems (MS); marketing (MEM); quality systems and productivity (MS); science and materials engineering (PhD); telecommunications management (MTM). Part-time programs available. Postbaccalaureate distance learning degree programs offered (minimal on-campus study). *Degree requirements:* For master's, one foreign language, thesis (for some programs), registration; for doctorate, one foreign language, thesis/dissertation, registration (for some programs). *Entrance requirements:* For master's, E-PAEP 500, interview; for doctorate, E-PAEP 500, research proposal. Additional exam requirements/recommendations for international students: Required—TOEFL (minimum score 550 paper-based). *Faculty research:* Surface treatments by plasmas, mechanical properties, robotics, graphical computing, mechatronics security protocols.

Instituto Tecnológico y de Estudios Superiores de Monterrey, Campus Irapuato, Graduate Programs, Irapuato, Mexico. Offers administration (MBA); administration of information technology (MAIT); administration of telecommunications (MAT); architecture (M Arch); computer science (MCS); education (M Ed); educational administration (MEA); educational innovation and technology (DEIT); educational technology (MET); electronic commerce (MBA); environmental administration and planning (MEAP); environmental systems (MES); finances (MBA); humanistic studies (MHS); international management for Latin American executives (MIMLAE); library and information science (MLIS); manufacturing quality management (MMQM); marketing research (MBA).

Instituto Tecnológico y de Estudios Superiores de Monterrey, Campus Laguna, Graduate School, Torreón, Mexico. Offers business administration (MBA); industrial engineering (MIE); management information systems (MS). Part-time programs available. *Entrance requirements:* For master's, GMAT. *Faculty research:* Computer communications from home to the University.

Inter American University of Puerto Rico, San Germán Campus, Graduate Studies Center, Graduate Program in Business Administration, San Germán, PR 00683-5008. Offers accounting (MBA); finance (MBA); human resources (MBA, PhD); industrial relations (MBA); international business (PhD); labor relations (PhD); management information systems (MBA); marketing (MBA); quality organizational design (MBA). Part-time and evening/weekend programs available. *Faculty:* 12 full-time, 4 part-time/adjunct. *Students:* 265. Average age 27. In 2006, 67 master's, 1 doctorate awarded. *Degree requirements:* For master's, comprehensive exam. *Entrance requirements:* For master's, GRE General Test or EXADEP, minimum GPA of 3.0. *Application deadline:* For fall admission, 4/30 priority date for domestic students; for spring admission, 11/15 for domestic students. Applications are processed on a rolling basis. Application fee: $31. *Expenses:* Tuition: Part-time $175 per credit. Required fees: $238 per semester. Tuition and fees vary according to degree level. *Financial support:* Teaching assistantships, Federal Work-Study and unspecified assistantships available. *Application contact:* Prof. Duay Rivera, Graduate Coordinator, 787-264-1912 Ext. 7218, Fax: 787-892-7510, E-mail: durivera@sg.inter.edu.

Iowa State University of Science and Technology, Graduate College, College of Business, Program in Logistics, Operations, and Management Information Systems, Ames, IA 50011. Offers information systems (MS). *Faculty:* 20 full-time. *Students:* 16 full-time (2 women), 8 part-time (1 woman); includes 5 minority (1 Asian American or Pacific Islander, 4 Hispanic Americans), 5 international. 26 applicants, 62% accepted, 8 enrolled. In 2006, 10 degrees awarded. *Degree requirements:* For master's, thesis or alternative. *Entrance requirements:* For master's, GMAT. Additional exam requirements/recommendations for international students: Required—TOEFL (paper-based 570; computer-based 230; iBT 88) or IELTS (7.0). *Application deadline:* For fall admission, 6/1 priority date for domestic students, 3/1 priority date for international students. Application fee: $30 ($70 for international students). Electronic applications accepted. *Expenses:* Tuition, state resident: full-time $5,936; part-time $330 per credit. Tuition, nonresident: full-time $16,350; part-time $330 per credit. *Financial support:* In 2006–07, 6 research assistantships with full and partial tuition reimbursements (averaging $16,623 per year), 2 teaching assistantships with full and partial tuition reimbursements (averaging $17,232 per year) were awarded; career-related internships or fieldwork, institutionally sponsored loans, scholarships/grants, health care benefits, and unspecified assistantships also available. *Unit head:* Dr. Richard Poist, Chair, 515-294-8118, E-mail: busgrad@iastate.edu. *Application contact:* Deb Johnson, Information Contact, 515-294-8118, E-mail: busgrad@iastate.edu.

John Marshall Law School, Graduate and Professional Programs, Chicago, IL 60604-3968. Offers comparative legal studies (LL M); employee benefits (LL M, MS); information technology (LL M, MS); intellectual property (LL M); international business and trade (LL M); law (JD); real estate (LL M, MS); taxation (LL M, MS); JD/LL M; JD/MA; JD/MBA; JD/MPA. *Accreditation:* ABA. Part-time and evening/weekend programs available. *Faculty:* 64 full-time (23 women), 113 part-time/adjunct (29 women). *Students:* 1,157 full-time (479 women), 421 part-time (187 women); includes 253 minority (76 African Americans, 10 American Indian/Alaska Native, 101 Asian Americans or Pacific Islanders, 66 Hispanic Americans), 48 international. Average age 27. 3,169 applicants, 37% accepted, 333 enrolled. In 2006, 347 JDs, 69 master's awarded. *Entrance requirements:* For JD, LSAT; for master's, JD. Additional exam requirements/recommendations for international students: Required—TOEFL. *Application deadline:* For fall admission, 3/1 priority date for domestic and international students; for spring admission, 10/15 priority date for domestic and international students. Applications are processed on a rolling basis. Application fee: $60. Electronic applications accepted. *Expenses:* Contact institution. *Financial support:* In 2006–07, 1,339 students received support. Scholarships/grants and tuition waivers (full and partial) available. Support available to part-time students. Financial award application deadline: 6/1; financial award applicants required to submit FAFSA. *Unit head:* John Corkery, Dean, 312-427-2737. *Application contact:* William B. Powers, Associate Dean of Admission and Student Affairs, 800-537-4280, Fax: 312-427-5136, E-mail: admission@jmls.edu.

The Johns Hopkins University, Carey Business School, Department of Information Technology, Baltimore, MD 21218-2699. Offers competitive intelligence (Certificate); information and telecommunication systems (Certificate); information security management (Certificate); information technology and telecommunication systems for business (MS); MBA/MSITS. Part-time and evening/weekend programs available. *Students:* 40 full-time (10 women), 322 part-time (100 women); includes 91 minority (42 African Americans, 3 American Indian/Alaska Native, 40 Asian Americans or Pacific Islanders, 6 Hispanic Americans), 1 international. Average age 32. 265 applicants, 81% accepted, 183 enrolled. In 2006, 116 master's, 56 other advanced degrees awarded. *Degree requirements:* For master's, project. *Entrance requirements:* For master's and Certificate, minimum GPA of 3.0, resumé, work experience, two letters of recommendation. Additional exam requirements/recommendations for international students: Required—TOEFL (minimum score 600 paper-based; 250 computer-based; 100 iBT). *Application deadline:* For fall admission, 5/1 for international students; for spring admission, 10/15 for international students. Applications are processed on a rolling basis. Application fee: $60. *Expenses:* Tuition: Full-time $32,976. Tuition and fees vary according to degree level and program. *Financial support:* Scholarships/grants available. Support available to part-time students. Financial award application deadline: 6/1; financial award applicants required to submit FAFSA. *Unit head:* Dr. Jim Novitzki, Chair, 301-294-7103, Fax: 301-315-2892. *Application contact:* Robin Reed, Senior Academic Coordinator, 800-gotojhu, Fax: 410-872-1251, E-mail: onestop.admissions@jhu.edu.

The Johns Hopkins University, Engineering and Applied Science Programs for Professionals, Part-time Program in Information Systems and Technology, Baltimore, MD 21218-2699. Offers MS. Part-time and evening/weekend programs available. *Faculty:* 8 part-time/adjunct (1 woman). In 2006, 64 degrees awarded. *Degree requirements:* For master's, registration. *Application deadline:* Applications are processed on a rolling basis. Application fee: $75. Electronic applications accepted. *Expenses:* Tuition: Full-time $32,976. Tuition and fees vary according to degree level and program. *Financial support:* Institutionally sponsored loans available. *Unit head:* Dr. Ralph D. Semmel, Program Chair, 410-540-2960, Fax: 410-579-8049. *Application contact:* Toni M. Riley, Director, Student Services, 410-540-2960, Fax: 410-579-8049, E-mail: triley4@jhu.edu.

Kean University, Nathan Weiss Graduate College, Program in Management Information Systems, Union, NJ 07083. Offers MSMIS. Part-time and evening/weekend programs available. *Faculty:* 3 full-time (0 women). *Students:* 13 full-time (7 women), 21 part-time (8 women); includes 14 minority (5 African Americans, 2 Asian Americans or Pacific Islanders, 7 Hispanic Americans), 9 international. Average age 33. 15 applicants, 87% accepted, 9 enrolled. In 2006, 18 degrees awarded. *Entrance requirements:* For master's, GMAT or GRE General Test if GPA is lower than 3.4, minimum GPA of 3.0, 2 letters of recommendation, 2 years of work experience, prerequisite courses. *Application deadline:* For fall admission, 5/1 for domestic students; for spring admission, 11/1 for domestic students. Application fee: $60 ($150 for international students). Electronic applications accepted. *Expenses:* Tuition, state resident: full-time $8,856; part-time $369 per credit. Tuition, nonresident: full-time $11,256; part-time $469 per credit. *Financial support:* In 2006–07, 9 research assistantships with full tuition reimbursements (averaging $3,217 per year) were awarded; career-related internships or fieldwork, institutionally sponsored loans, and unspecified assistantships also available. *Unit head:* Dr. Jack H. Ryder, Program Coordinator, 907-737-3798, E-mail: jryder@kean.edu. *Application contact:* Joanne Morris, Director of Graduate Admissions, 908-737-3355, Fax: 908-737-3354, E-mail: grad-adm@kean.edu.

Kent State University, Graduate School of Management, Doctoral Program in Management Systems, Kent, OH 44242-0001. Offers PhD. *Faculty:* 12 full-time (2 women). *Students:* 18 full-time (10 women); includes 1 minority (Asian American or Pacific Islander), 7 international. Average age 33. 9 applicants, 67% accepted, 2 enrolled. In 2006, 4 degrees awarded. *Degree requirements:* For doctorate, thesis/dissertation, oral defense, comprehensive exam. *Entrance requirements:* For doctorate, GMAT. Additional exam requirements/recommendations for international students: Required—TOEFL (minimum score 600 paper-based; 250 computer-based). *Application deadline:* For fall admission, 2/1 for domestic students, 1/1 for international students. Application fee: $30. Electronic applications accepted. *Financial support:* In 2006–07, 2 fellowships with full tuition reimbursements, 10 teaching assistantships with full tuition reimbursements (averaging $15,000 per year) were awarded; Federal Work-Study and tuition waivers also available. Financial award application deadline: 2/1; financial award applicants required to submit FAFSA. *Unit head:* Dr. O. Felix Offodile, Chair, 330-672-2750, Fax: 330-672-2953, E-mail: foffodil@kent.edu. *Application contact:* Felecia A. Urbanek, Coordinator, Graduate Programs, 330-672-2282, Fax: 330-672-7303, E-mail: gradbus@bsa3.kent.edu.

Lawrence Technological University, College of Management, Southfield, MI 48075-1058. Offers business administration (MBA, DBA); information systems (MS); information technology (DM); operations management (MS). *Accreditation:* ACBSP. Part-time and evening/weekend programs available. *Faculty:* 11 full-time (4 women), 61 part-time/adjunct (13 women). *Students:* 47 full-time (20 women), 702 part-time (235 women); includes 285 minority (98 African Americans, 178 Asian Americans or Pacific Islanders, 9 Hispanic Americans), 15 international. Average age 34. 337 applicants, 90% accepted, 192 enrolled. In 2006, 281 degrees awarded. *Entrance requirements:* For master's, GMAT. Additional exam requirements/recommendations for international students: Required—TOEFL (minimum score 550 paper-based; 213 computer-based). *Application deadline:* For fall admission, 8/1 priority date for domestic students; for winter admission, 12/1 priority date for domestic students; for spring admission, 5/1 for domestic students. Applications are processed on a rolling basis. Application fee: $50. Electronic applications accepted. *Financial support:* Institutionally sponsored loans available. Support available to part-time students. Financial award application deadline: 3/1; financial award applicants required to submit FAFSA. *Unit head:* Dr. Lou DeGennaro, Dean, 248-204-3050, E-mail: degennaro@ltu.edu. *Application contact:* Jane Rohrback, Director of Admissions, 248-204-3160, Fax: 248-204-3188, E-mail: admissions@ltu.edu.

Lindenwood University, Graduate Programs, Division of Management, St. Charles, MO 63301-1695. Offers accounting (MBA, MS); business administration (MBA); entrepreneurial studies (MBA); finance (MBA, MS); human resource management (MBA); human resources (MS); international business (MBA, MS); management (MBA, MS); management information systems (MBA, MS); managing business to business (MA); managing human resources (MA); managing international business (MA); managing investment management (MA); managing leadership (MA); managing marketing (MA); managing organizational behavior (MA); managing sales (MA); managing, training and development (MA); marketing (MBA, MS); nonprofit administration (MA); public management (MBA, MS); sport management (MA). Part-time and evening/weekend programs available. *Faculty:* 38 full-time (15 women), 20 part-time/adjunct (5 women). *Students:* 177 full-time (78 women), 138 part-time (67 women); includes 43 minority (27 African Americans, 4 American Indian/Alaska Native, 6 Asian Americans or Pacific Islanders, 6 Hispanic Americans), 73 international. Average age 30. In 2006, 159 degrees awarded. *Degree requirements:* For master's, thesis (for some programs). *Entrance requirements:* For master's, interview, minimum GPA of 3.0. Additional exam requirements/recommendations for international students: Required—TOEFL (minimum score 550 paper-based; 173 computer-based). *Application deadline:* For fall admission, 7/30 priority date for domestic students, 9/30 priority date for international students; for winter admission, 12/30 priority date for domestic and international students; for spring admission, 3/30 priority date for domestic and international students. Applications are processed on a rolling basis. Application fee: $30 ($100 for international students). Electronic applications accepted. *Expenses:* Tuition: Part-time $340 per credit hour. Tuition and fees vary according to course level, course load, degree level and program. *Financial support:* Career-related internships or fieldwork, Federal Work-Study, institutionally sponsored loans, and tuition waivers (partial) available. Financial award application deadline: 6/30; financial award applicants required to submit FAFSA. *Unit head:* Ed Morris, Dean, 636-949-4832, Fax: 636-949-4910, E-mail: emorris@lindenwood.edu. *Application contact:* Brett Barger, Dean Adult, Corporate and Graduate Admissions, 636-949-4366, Fax: 636-949-4109, E-mail: bbarger@lindenwood.edu.

Long Island University, C.W. Post Campus, College of Management, School of Business, Brookville, NY 11548-1300. Offers accounting and taxation (Certificate); business administration (Certificate); finance (MBA, Certificate); general business administration (MBA); international business (MBA, Certificate); management (MBA, Certificate); management information systems (MBA, Certificate); marketing (MBA, Certificate). *Accreditation:* AACSB. Part-time and evening/weekend programs available. *Entrance requirements:* For master's, GMAT, resumé, minimum GPA of 3.0, 2 letters of recommendation. Additional exam requirements/recommendations for international students: Required—TOEFL (minimum score 527 paper-based; 197 computer-based). Electronic applications accepted. *Faculty research:* Financial markets, consumer behavior.

Louisiana State University and Agricultural and Mechanical College, Graduate School, E. J. Ourso College of Business, Department of Information Systems and Decision Sciences, Baton Rouge, LA 70803. Offers information systems and decision sciences (MS, PhD). *Faculty:* 15 full-time (3 women). *Students:* 13 full-time (5 women), 9 part-time (2 women); includes 3 minority (2 African Americans, 1 Hispanic American), 10 international. Average age 34. 22 applicants, 18% accepted, 3 enrolled. In 2006, 8 master's, 1 doctorate awarded. Terminal master's awarded for partial completion of doctoral program. *Median time to degree:* Of those who began their doctoral program in fall 1998, 100% received their degree in 8 years or less. *Degree requirements:* For master's, thesis optional; for doctorate, thesis/dissertation, comprehensive exam, registration. *Entrance requirements:* For master's, GMAT or GRE General Test; for doctorate, GMAT or GRE. Additional exam requirements/recommendations for international students: Required—TOEFL (minimum score 550 paper-based; 213 computer-based; 79 iBT). *Application deadline:* For fall admission, 1/25 priority date for domestic students, 5/15 for international students; for spring admission, 10/15 for international students. Applications are processed on a rolling basis. Application fee: $25. Electronic applications accepted. *Financial support:* In 2006–07, 15 students received support, including 1 fellowship (averaging $29,539 per year), 10 research assistantships with full and partial tuition reimbursements available (averaging $18,000 per year), 2 teaching assistantships with full and partial tuition reimbursements available (averaging $20,000 per year); Federal Work-Study, institutionally sponsored loans, scholarships/grants, tuition waivers (full and partial), and unspecified assistantships also available. Support available to part-time students. Financial award applicants required to submit FAFSA. *Faculty research:* Healthcare informatics, outsourcing, information systems management, operations management. Total annual research expenditures: $657,590. *Unit head:* Dr. Helmut Schneider, Department Head, 225-578-2516, Fax: 225-578-2511, E-mail: hschnei@lsu.edu. *Application contact:* Dr. Rudy Hirschheim, Graduate Adviser, 225-578-2514, Fax: 225-578-2511, E-mail: rudy@lsu.edu.

Loyola University Chicago, Graduate School of Business, Information Systems and Operations Management Department, Chicago, IL 60611-2196. Offers information systems management (MS). Part-time and evening/weekend programs available. *Faculty:* 11 full-time (1 woman). *Students:* 7 full-time (2 women), 5 part-time (1 woman); includes 4 minority (2 African Americans, 2 Hispanic Americans). In 2006, 11 degrees awarded. *Entrance requirements:* For master's, GMAT, letters of recommendation, personal statement. Additional exam requirements/recommendations for international students: Required—TOEFL (minimum score 550 paper-

Management Information Systems

Loyola University Chicago (continued)

based; 213 computer-based; 80 iBT). *Application deadline:* For fall admission, 7/1 for domestic and international students; for winter admission, 9/1 for domestic and international students; for spring admission, 1/3 for domestic and international students. Applications are processed on a rolling basis. Application fee: $50. Electronic applications accepted. *Expenses: Contact institution. Financial support:* In 2006–07, 2 students received support, including research assistantships with partial tuition reimbursements available (averaging $5,000 per year). Financial award application deadline: 3/15; financial award applicants required to submit FAFSA. *Faculty research:* Strategic use of IT, database design data warehousing, e-business, applications of data mining. *Unit head:* Dr. Samuel Ramenofsky, Chair, 312-915-7051, Fax: 312-915-6231, E-mail: srameno@luc.edu. *Application contact:* Olivia Heath, Enrollment Advisor, 312-915-8908, Fax: 312-915-7207, E-mail: oheath@luc.edu.

Marist College, Graduate Programs, School of Computer Science and Mathematics, Poughkeepsie, NY 12601-1387. Offers information systems (MS, Adv C); software development (MS); technology management (MS). Part-time and evening/weekend programs available. Postbaccalaureate distance learning degree programs offered (minimal on-campus study). *Faculty:* 14 full-time (5 women). *Students:* 41 full-time (6 women), 70 part-time (21 women); includes 25 minority (10 African Americans, 3 American Indian/Alaska Native, 8 Asian Americans or Pacific Islanders, 4 Hispanic Americans), 38 international. Average age 31. 50 applicants, 92% accepted, 33 enrolled. In 2006, 48 master's, 3 other advanced degrees awarded. *Entrance requirements:* For master's, resumé, official transcripts, statement of purpose. Additional exam requirements/recommendations for international students: Required—TOEFL (minimum score 550 paper-based; 213 computer-based; 80 iBT); Recommended—IELTS (minimum score 6). *Application deadline:* For fall admission, 8/1 for domestic students, 6/1 for international students; for spring admission, 12/15 for domestic students, 10/15 for international students. Applications are processed on a rolling basis. Application fee: $50. Electronic applications accepted. *Expenses:* Tuition: Full-time $11,340; part-time $630 per credit. Required fees: $60; $30 per semester. *Financial support:* In 2006–07, 23 students received support. Scholarships/grants available. Support available to part-time students. Financial award application deadline: 8/15; financial award applicants required to submit FAFSA. *Faculty research:* Data quality, artificial intelligence, imaging, analysis of algorithms, distributed systems and applications. *Unit head:* Dr. Roger Norton, Dean, 845-575-3000, E-mail: roger.norton@marist.edu. *Application contact:* Anu R. Ailawadhi, Director of Graduate Admissions, 845-575-3800, Fax: 845-575-3166, E-mail: graduate@marist.edu.

Marymount University, School of Business Administration, Program in Information Management and Management Science, Arlington, VA 22207-4299. Offers health care informatics (Certificate); information systems (MS, Certificate); information systems program management (Certificate). Part-time and evening/weekend programs available. *Faculty:* 6 full-time (4 women), 2 part-time/adjunct (0 women). *Students:* 9 full-time (4 women), 29 part-time (6 women); includes 10 minority (7 African Americans, 3 Asian Americans or Pacific Islanders), 10 international. Average age 32. 13 applicants, 100% accepted, 9 enrolled. In 2006, 9 master's, 1 other advanced degree awarded. *Degree requirements:* For master's, thesis or alternative. *Entrance requirements:* For master's, GMAT or GRE General Test, interview, resumé; for Certificate, resumé. Additional exam requirements/recommendations for international students: Required—TOEFL (minimum score 600 paper-based; 250 computer-based). *Application deadline:* Applications are processed on a rolling basis. Application fee: $40. Electronic applications accepted. *Expenses:* Tuition: Full-time $11,160; part-time $620 per credit. Required fees: $113; $630 per credit. *Financial support:* Research assistantships with full tuition reimbursements, career-related internships or fieldwork, scholarships/grants, and unspecified assistantships available. Support available to part-time students. Financial award applicants required to submit FAFSA. *Unit head:* Dr. Diane Murphy, Chair, 703-284-5929, Fax: 703-527-3830, E-mail: diane.murphy@marymount.edu.

Marywood University, Academic Affairs, Insalaco College of Creative Arts and Management, Department of Business and Managerial Science, Emphasis in Management Information Systems, Scranton, PA 18509-1598. Offers MBA. Part-time and evening/weekend programs available. *Students:* Average age 34. In 2006, 5 degrees awarded. *Degree requirements:* For master's, comprehensive exam. *Entrance requirements:* For master's, GMAT. Additional exam requirements/recommendations for international students: Required—TOEFL (minimum score 550 paper-based; 213 computer-based). *Application deadline:* For fall admission, 4/15 priority date for domestic and international students; for spring admission, 11/15 priority date for domestic and international students. Applications are processed on a rolling basis. Application fee: $30. Electronic applications accepted. *Expenses:* Tuition: Part-time $672 per credit. Tuition and fees vary according to degree level, campus/location and program. *Financial support:* Research assistantships with tuition reimbursements, career-related internships or fieldwork, scholarships/grants, tuition waivers (partial), and unspecified assistantships available. Support available to part-time students. Financial award application deadline: 2/15; financial award applicants required to submit FAFSA. *Faculty research:* Systems design. *Application contact:* Dr. Deborah M. Flynn, Coordinator of Graduate Advising (Enrollment Management), 570-348-6211, E-mail: flynn@ac.marywood.edu.

Marywood University, Academic Affairs, Insalaco College of Creative Arts and Management, Department of Business and Managerial Science, Program in Management Information Systems, Scranton, PA 18509-1598. Offers MS. *Accreditation:* ACBSP. *Students:* Average age 35. In 2006, 15 degrees awarded. Application fee: $30. *Expenses:* Tuition: Part-time $672 per credit. Tuition and fees vary according to degree level, campus/location and program. *Application contact:* Dr. Deborah M. Flynn, Coordinator of Graduate Advising (Enrollment Management), 570-348-6211, E-mail: flynn@ac.marywood.edu.

See Close-Up on page 289.

McGill University, Faculty of Graduate and Postdoctoral Studies, Desautels Faculty of Management, Montréal, QC H3A 2T5, Canada. Offers administration (PhD); entrepreneurial studies (MBA); finance (MBA); general management (Post Master's Certificate); information systems (MBA); international business (exchange program) (MBA); international Master's program in practicing management (MM); management (MBA); management for development (MBA); manufacturing management (MMM); marketing (MBA); operations management (MBA); public accountancy (Diploma); strategic management (MBA); MBA/LL B; MD/MBA. Part-time programs available. *Entrance requirements:* For master's, GMAT, minimum undergraduate GPA of 3.0, 2 years work experience; for doctorate, GMAT or GRE General Test, 2 letters of recommendation, preferably by professors in chosen field of specialization; for other advanced degree, 2 years of work experience, MBA, minimum GPA of 3.0 (Post-MBA Certificate). Additional exam requirements/recommendations for international students: Required—TOEFL (minimum score 600 paper-based; 250 computer-based), IELTS (minimum score 7). Electronic applications accepted. Expenses: Contact institution. *Faculty research:* Social innovation, leadership, strategy.

McMaster University, School of Graduate Studies, Faculty of Business, Program in Management Science/Systems, Hamilton, ON L8S 4M2, Canada. Offers PhD. Part-time programs available. *Faculty:* 12 full-time. *Students:* 20 full-time. *Degree requirements:* For doctorate, thesis/dissertation, comprehensive exam. *Entrance requirements:* For doctorate, GMAT or GRE, master's degree, minimum B+ average. Additional exam requirements/recommendations for international students: Required—TOEFL (minimum score 580 paper-based; 237 computer-based). *Application deadline:* For fall admission, 6/1 for domestic students. Application fee: $90. *Financial support:* In 2006–07, teaching assistantships (averaging $8,440 per year); fellowships, research assistantships, scholarships/grants also available. *Faculty research:* Information systems, operations management, web-based decision support systems, web-based agents, financial engineering.

Metropolitan State University, College of Management, St. Paul, MN 55106-5000. Offers finance (MBA); human resource management (MBA); information management (MMIS); international business (MBA); law enforcement (MPNA); management information systems (MBA); marketing (MBA); nonprofit management (MPNA); organizational studies (MBA); public administration (MPNA); purchasing management (MBA); systems management (MMIS). Part-time and evening/weekend programs available. *Degree requirements:* For master's, computer language (MMIS), thesis optional. *Entrance requirements:* For master's, GMAT (MBA), resumé. Additional exam requirements/recommendations for international students: Required—TOEFL (minimum score 550 paper-based; 213 computer-based). *Faculty research:* Yugoslav economic system, workers' cooperatives, participative management and job enrichment, global business systems.

Miami University, Graduate School, Richard T. Farmer School of Business Administration, Oxford, OH 45056. Offers accountancy (M Acc); business administration (MBA); economics (MA); finance (MBA); general management (MBA); management information systems (MBA); marketing (MBA); quality and process improvement (MBA). *Accreditation:* AACSB. Part-time programs available. *Entrance requirements:* For master's, GMAT, minimum undergraduate GPA of 3.0 during previous 2 years or 2.75 overall. Additional exam requirements/recommendations for international students: Required—TOEFL (minimum score 550 paper-based; 213 computer-based), TWE (minimum score 4).

Michigan State University, The Graduate School, College of Communication Arts and Sciences, Department of Telecommunication, Information Studies, and Media, East Lansing, MI 48824. Offers MA. *Faculty:* 15 full-time (2 women). *Students:* 28 full-time (12 women), 15 part-time (3 women); includes 4 minority (2 African Americans, 2 Hispanic Americans), 15 international. Average age 26. 63 applicants, 46% accepted. In 2006, 27 degrees awarded. *Entrance requirements:* Additional exam requirements/recommendations for international students: Required—TOEFL. Electronic applications accepted. *Expenses:* Tuition, state resident: part-time $346 per credit hour. Tuition, nonresident: part-time $730 per credit hour. Tuition and fees vary according to program. *Financial support:* In 2006–07, 1 fellowship with tuition reimbursement, 5 research assistantships with tuition reimbursements (averaging $13,099 per year), 8 teaching assistantships with tuition reimbursements (averaging $12,231 per year) were awarded. Total annual research expenditures: $915,006. *Unit head:* Dr. Charles Steinfield, Chairperson, 517-355-8372, Fax: 517-355-1292, E-mail: steinfie@msu.edu. *Application contact:* Rachel Iseler, Academic Programs Coordinator, 517-432-3676, Fax: 517-355-1292, E-mail: tism@msu.edu.

Michigan State University, The Graduate School, Eli Broad Graduate School of Management, Department of Accounting and Information Systems, East Lansing, MI 48824. Offers accounting (MS); business administration (PhD). *Accreditation:* AACSB. *Faculty:* 27 full-time (9 women). *Students:* 189 full-time (93 women), 15 part-time (9 women); includes 17 minority (5 African Americans, 11 Asian Americans or Pacific Islanders, 1 Hispanic American), 35 international. Average age 24. 318 applicants, 44% accepted. In 2006, 131 master's, 2 doctorates awarded. *Entrance requirements:* Additional exam requirements/recommendations for international students: Required—TOEFL. *Application deadline:* Applications are processed on a rolling basis. Electronic applications accepted. *Expenses:* Tuition, state resident: part-time $346 per credit hour. Tuition, nonresident: part-time $730 per credit hour. Tuition and fees vary according to program. *Financial support:* In 2006–07, 8 fellowships with tuition reimbursements, 13 research assistantships with tuition reimbursements (averaging $12,159 per year), 8 teaching assistantships with tuition reimbursements (averaging $11,236 per year) were awarded. Total annual research expenditures: $129,357. *Unit head:* Dr. Kathy J. Petroni, Acting Chairperson, 517-423-2924, Fax: 517-423-1101, E-mail: petroni@bus.msu.edu. *Application contact:* Program Information, E-mail: msacct@bus.msu.edu.

Middle Tennessee State University, College of Graduate Studies, College of Business, Department of Accounting, Murfreesboro, TN 37132. Offers accounting (MS); information systems (MS). *Accreditation:* AACSB. Part-time and evening/weekend programs available. Postbaccalaureate distance learning degree programs offered. *Faculty:* 11 full-time (4 women). *Students:* 22 full-time (8 women), 81 part-time (47 women); includes 16 minority (5 African Americans, 11 Asian Americans or Pacific Islanders). Average age 30. 28 applicants, 100% accepted. In 2006, 29 degrees awarded. *Entrance requirements:* For master's, GMAT. Additional exam requirements/recommendations for international students: Required—TOEFL (minimum score 525 paper-based; 195 computer-based). *Application deadline:* For fall admission, 8/1 priority date for domestic students. Applications are processed on a rolling basis. Application fee: $25. Electronic applications accepted. *Financial support:* In 2006–07, 5 students received support. Institutionally sponsored loans available. Support available to part-time students. Financial award application deadline: 5/1; financial award applicants required to submit FAFSA. *Unit head:* Dr. Paula Thomas, Chair, 615-898-5655, Fax: 615-898-5045, E-mail: pbthomas@mtsu.edu.

Middle Tennessee State University, College of Graduate Studies, College of Business, Department of Computer Information Systems, Murfreesboro, TN 37132. Offers MS. Part-time and evening/weekend programs available. Postbaccalaureate distance learning degree programs offered. *Faculty:* 12 full-time (3 women). *Students:* Average age 32. 17 applicants, 94% accepted. *Entrance requirements:* For master's, GMAT. Additional exam requirements/recommendations for international students: Required—TOEFL (minimum score 525 paper-based; 195 computer-based). *Application deadline:* For fall admission, 8/1 priority date for domestic students. Applications are processed on a rolling basis. Application fee: $25. Electronic applications accepted. *Financial support:* In 2006–07, 6 students received support. Institutionally sponsored loans available. Support available to part-time students. Financial award application deadline: 5/1; financial award applicants required to submit FAFSA. *Faculty research:* Information technology assessment, information systems education, information technology job market, e-commerce, database technology. *Unit head:* Dr. Stanley Gambill, Head, 615-898-2362.

Minot State University, Graduate School, Information Systems Program, Minot, ND 58707-0002. Offers MSIS. *Students:* 20. *Unit head:* Dr. Linda Cresap, Dean, 701-858-3250, E-mail: linda.cresap@minotstateu.edu. *Application contact:* Brenda Anderson, Administrative Assistant, 701-858-3250, Fax: 701-858-4286, E-mail: brenda.anderson@minotstateu.edu.

Mississippi State University, College of Business and Industry, Department of Management and Information Systems, Mississippi State, MS 39762. Offers information systems (MSIS). Part-time programs available. *Faculty:* 19 full-time (6 women), 4 part-time/adjunct (3 women). *Students:* 34 applicants, 38% accepted, 8 enrolled. *Entrance requirements:* For master's, GMAT, minimum GPA of 3.0 in last 60 hours of course work. Additional exam requirements/recommendations for international students: Required—TOEFL. *Application deadline:* For fall admission, 7/1 for domestic students; for spring admission, 11/1 for domestic students. Applications are processed on a rolling basis. Application fee: $30. Electronic applications accepted. *Expenses:* Tuition, state resident: full-time $4,550; part-time $253 per hour. Tuition, nonresident: full-time $10,552; part-time $584 per hour. International tuition: $10,882 full-time. Tuition and fees vary according to course load. *Financial support:* Research assistantships with full tuition reimbursements, teaching assistantships, Federal Work-Study, institutionally sponsored loans, and unspecified assistantships available. Financial award applicants required to submit FAFSA. *Faculty research:* Electronic commerce, management of information technology. *Unit head:* Dr. Garry D. Smith, Head, 662-325-3928, Fax: 662-325-8651, E-mail: gsmith@cobilan.msstate.edu. *Application contact:* Dr. Phil Bonfanti, Director of Admissions, 662-325-4104, Fax: 662-325-8872, E-mail: admit@msstate.edu.

Missouri State University, Graduate College, College of Business Administration, Department of Computer Information Systems, Springfield, MO 65804-0094. Offers computer information systems (MS); secondary education (MS Ed), including business. Part-time and evening/weekend programs available. *Faculty:* 13 full-time (4 women). *Students:* 30 full-time (8 women), 9 part-time (7 women); includes 2 minority (1 African American, 1 Hispanic American), 2 international. Average age 35. 30 applicants, 40% accepted, 12 enrolled. In 2006, 11 degrees awarded. *Degree requirements:* For master's, thesis optional. *Entrance requirements:* For master's, GMAT, 3 years of work experience in computer information systems, minimum

GPA of 2.75 (MS), 9-12 teaching certification (MS Ed). Additional exam requirements/recommendations for international students: Required—TOEFL (minimum score 550 paper-based; 213 computer-based; 79 iBT), IELTS (minimum score 6). *Application deadline:* For fall admission, 7/20 priority date for domestic students; for spring admission, 12/20 priority date for domestic students. Applications are processed on a rolling basis. Application fee: $35. *Expenses:* Contact institution. Full-time tuition and fees vary according to course level, course load, program and reciprocity agreements. *Financial support:* Teaching assistantships with full tuition reimbursements, career-related internships or fieldwork, institutionally sponsored loans, scholarships/grants, tuition waivers (partial), and unspecified assistantships available. Support available to part-time students. Financial award application deadline: 3/31; financial award applicants required to submit FAFSA. *Unit head:* Dr. Jerry Chin, Head, 417-836-4131, Fax: 417-836-6907, E-mail: jerrychin@missouristate.edu.

Montclair State University, The Graduate School, School of Business, Department of Management Information Systems, Montclair, NJ 07043-1624. Offers management (MBA); management information systems (MBA). Part-time and evening/weekend programs available. *Faculty:* 23 full-time (5 women), 15 part-time/adjunct (7 women). *Students:* 5 full-time (3 women), 55 part-time (19 women); includes 13 minority (2 African Americans, 6 Asian Americans or Pacific Islanders, 5 Hispanic Americans), 6 international. 58 applicants, 38% accepted, 10 enrolled. In 2006, 23 degrees awarded. *Degree requirements:* For master's, comprehensive project. *Entrance requirements:* For master's, GMAT, 2 letters of recommendation, resumé. Additional exam requirements/recommendations for international students: Required—TOEFL (minimum score 83 computer-based). *Application deadline:* For fall admission, 6/1 for international students; for spring admission, 10/1 for international students. Applications are processed on a rolling basis. Application fee: $60. Electronic applications accepted. *Expenses:* Tuition, state resident: part-time $450 per credit. Tuition, nonresident: part-time $682 per credit. Tuition and fees vary according to degree level and program. *Financial support:* In 2006–07, 5 research assistantships (averaging $7,000 per year) were awarded; Federal Work-Study, scholarships/grants, and unspecified assistantships also available. Support available to part-time students. Financial award application deadline: 3/1; financial award applicants required to submit FAFSA. *Unit head:* Dr. Richard Peterson, Head, 973-655-4269. *Application contact:* Dr. Eileen Kaplan, Adviser, 973-655-7469, E-mail: kaplane@mail.montclair.edu.

Morehead State University, Graduate Programs, College of Business, Department of Information Systems, Morehead, KY 40351. Offers MSIS. *Faculty:* 10 full-time (3 women), 1 part-time/adjunct (0 women). *Students:* 9 full-time (1 woman), 14 part-time (6 women); includes 1 minority (Asian American or Pacific Islander), 1 international. Average age 32. *Entrance requirements:* For master's, GRE, GMAT. Additional exam requirements/recommendations for international students: Required—TOEFL (minimum score 525 paper-based). *Application deadline:* For fall admission, 8/1 for domestic and international students; for spring admission, 12/1 for domestic and international students. Applications are processed on a rolling basis. Electronic applications accepted. *Financial support:* In 2006–07, 5 teaching assistantships (averaging $6,000 per year) were awarded. *Unit head:* Dr. Betty Regan, Chair, 606-783-2730, Fax: 606-783-5025, E-mail: e.regan@moreheadstate.edu. *Application contact:* Michelle Barber, Graduate Admissions Counselor, 606-783-2039, Fax: 606-783-5061, E-mail: m.barber@moreheadstate.edu.

National University, Academic Affairs, School of Engineering and Technology, Department of Applied Engineering, La Jolla, CA 92037-1011. Offers database administration (MS); engineering management (MS); environmental engineering (MS); homeland security and safety engineering (MS); system engineering (MS); wireless communications (MS). Part-time and evening/weekend programs available. Postbaccalaureate distance learning degree programs offered (no on-campus study). *Faculty:* 6 full-time (0 women), 64 part-time/adjunct (11 women). *Students:* 35 full-time (6 women), 33 part-time (9 women); includes 21 minority (8 African Americans, 8 Asian Americans or Pacific Islanders, 5 Hispanic Americans), 12 international. Average age 37. 106 applicants. In 2006, 18 degrees awarded. *Degree requirements:* For master's, thesis. *Entrance requirements:* For master's, interview, minimum GPA of 2.5. Additional exam requirements/recommendations for international students: Required—TOEFL (minimum score 550 paper-based; 213 computer-based; 80 iBT), IELTS (minimum score 6). *Application deadline:* Applications are processed on a rolling basis. Application fee: $60 ($65 for international students). Electronic applications accepted. *Expenses:* Tuition: Full-time $7,722; part-time $286 per unit. One-time fee: $60. *Financial support:* Career-related internships or fieldwork, institutionally sponsored loans, scholarships/grants, and tuition waivers (partial) available. Support available to part-time students. Financial award application deadline: 6/30; financial award applicants required to submit FAFSA. *Unit head:* Dr. Shekar Viswanathan, Chair and Associate Professor, 858-642-8416, Fax: 858-642-8486, E-mail: sviswana@nu.edu. *Application contact:* Dominick Giovanniello, Associate Regional Dean—San Diego, 800-NAT-UNIV, Fax: 858-642-8709, E-mail: dgiovann@nu.edu.

National University, Academic Affairs, School of Engineering and Technology, Department of Computer Science and Information Systems, La Jolla, CA 92037-1011. Offers computer science (MS); information systems (MS); software engineering (MS); technology management (MS). Part-time and evening/weekend programs available. Postbaccalaureate distance learning degree programs offered (no on-campus study). *Faculty:* 8 full-time (1 woman), 101 part-time/adjunct (13 women). *Students:* 53 full-time (12 women), 83 part-time (19 women); includes 61 minority (13 African Americans, 1 American Indian/Alaska Native, 28 Asian Americans or Pacific Islanders, 19 Hispanic Americans), 13 international. Average age 35. 172 applicants, 120 enrolled. In 2006, 15 degrees awarded. *Degree requirements:* For master's, thesis. *Entrance requirements:* For master's, interview, minimum GPA of 2.5. Additional exam requirements/recommendations for international students: Required—TOEFL (minimum score 550 paper-based; 213 computer-based; 80 iBT), IELTS (minimum score 6). *Application deadline:* Applications are processed on a rolling basis. Application fee: $60 ($65 for international students). Electronic applications accepted. *Expenses:* Tuition: Full-time $7,722; part-time $286 per unit. One-time fee: $60. *Financial support:* Career-related internships or fieldwork, institutionally sponsored loans, scholarships/grants, and tuition waivers (partial) available. Support available to part-time students. Financial award application deadline: 6/30; financial award applicants required to submit FAFSA. *Unit head:* Dr. John Bugado, Interim Chair and Professor, 858-642-8407, Fax: 858-642-8489, E-mail: jbugado@nu.edu. *Application contact:* Dominick Giovanniello, Associate Regional Dean—San Diego, 800-NAT-UNIV, Fax: 858-642-8709, E-mail: dgiovann@nu.edu.

Naval Postgraduate School, Graduate Programs, Department of Information Sciences, Monterey, CA 93943. Offers information sciences (MS); knowledge superiority (MS, Certificate). Program open only to commissioned officers of the United States and friendly nations and selected United States federal civilian employees. Part-time programs available. *Degree requirements:* For master's, thesis.

Naval Postgraduate School, Graduate Programs, School of Business and Public Policy, Monterey, CA 93943. Offers contract management (MS); defense-focused business administration (MBA); executive business administration (MBA); leadership and human resource development (MS); management (MS); program management (MS); systems engineering management (MS). Program only open to commissioned officers of the United States and friendly nations and selected United States federal civilian employees. *Accreditation:* AACSB; NASPAA. Part-time programs available. Postbaccalaureate distance learning degree programs offered (minimal on-campus study). *Degree requirements:* For master's, thesis.

Newman University, School of Business, Wichita, KS 67213-2097. Offers international business (MBA); leadership (MBA); management (MBA); technology (MBA). Part-time programs available. *Faculty:* 6 full-time (2 women), 3 part-time/adjunct (1 woman). *Students:* 34 full-time (14 women), 76 part-time (30 women); includes 14 minority (6 African Americans, 1 American Indian/Alaska Native, 3 Asian Americans or Pacific Islanders, 4 Hispanic Americans), 31 international. Average age 31. 74 applicants, 80% accepted, 46 enrolled. In 2006, 76 degrees awarded. *Degree requirements:* For master's, thesis optional. *Entrance requirements:* For master's, interview; minimum GPA of 3.0; 3 letters of recommendation; course work in algebra, statistics, macroeconomics. Additional exam requirements/recommendations for international students: Required—TOEFL (minimum score 600 paper-based; 250 computer-based; 100 iBT). *Application deadline:* For fall admission, 8/1 priority date for domestic students; for winter admission, 1/1 priority date for domestic students; for spring admission, 1/1 priority date for domestic students. Applications are processed on a rolling basis. Application fee: $25 ($40 for international students). Electronic applications accepted. *Expenses:* Contact institution. *Financial support:* In 2006–07, 3 students received support. Federal Work-Study and tuition waivers available. Financial award application deadline: 8/15; financial award applicants required to submit FAFSA. *Unit head:* Dr. Joe Goetz, Dean, 316-942-4291 Ext. 2111, Fax: 316-942-4486, E-mail: goetzj@newmanu.edu. *Application contact:* Linda Kay Sabala, Director of Graduate Admissions, 316-942-4291 Ext. 2230, Fax: 316-942-4483, E-mail: sabalal@newmanu.edu.

New York Institute of Technology, Ellis College, Old Westbury, NY 11568. Offers accounting and information systems (MBA); e-commerce (MBA); finance (MBA); global management (MBA); healthcare administration (MBA); human resources management (MBA); leadership (MBA); management of information systems (MBA); management of technology (MBA); marketing (MBA); professional accounting (MBA); project management (MBA); risk management (MBA); strategy and economics (MBA). Ellis College is a collaboration between New York Institute of Technology and UNext online learning company. Part-time and evening/weekend programs available. Postbaccalaureate distance learning degree programs offered (no on-campus study). *Entrance requirements:* For master's, interview. Additional exam requirements/recommendations for international students: Required—TOEFL (minimum score 550 paper-based; 213 computer-based). Electronic applications accepted. *Expenses:* Tuition: Full-time $16,800; part-time $700 per credit.

New York Institute of Technology, Graduate Division, School of Management, Program in Business Administration, Old Westbury, NY 11568-8000. Offers accounting (Advanced Certificate); business administration (MBA); finance (Advanced Certificate); international business (Advanced Certificate); management of information systems (Advanced Certificate); marketing (Advanced Certificate). Part-time and evening/weekend programs available. *Students:* 481 full-time (120 women), 1,300 part-time (670 women); includes 297 minority (153 African Americans, 6 American Indian/Alaska Native, 81 Asian Americans or Pacific Islanders, 57 Hispanic Americans), 215 international. Average age 29. 1,049 applicants, 87% accepted, 137 enrolled. In 2006, 917 degrees awarded. *Degree requirements:* For master's, thesis (for some programs). *Entrance requirements:* For master's, minimum QPA of 2.85. Additional exam requirements/recommendations for international students: Required—TOEFL (minimum score 550 paper-based; 213 computer-based). *Application deadline:* For fall admission, 7/1 priority date for domestic students; for spring admission, 12/1 priority date for domestic students. Applications are processed on a rolling basis. Application fee: $50. Electronic applications accepted. *Expenses:* Tuition: Full-time $16,800; part-time $700 per credit. *Financial support:* Fellowships, research assistantships with partial tuition reimbursements, institutionally sponsored loans, tuition waivers (full and partial), and unspecified assistantships available. Support available to part-time students. Financial award applicants required to submit FAFSA. *Faculty research:* Instructor performance appraisal; relationship between TOEFL, GMAT, GRE, and performance in foreign students. *Unit head:* Dr. Gurumurthy Kalyanuram, Director, 516-686-7972, E-mail: gkalyana@nyit.edu. *Application contact:* Jacquelyn Nealon, Dean of Admissions and Financial Aid, 516-686-7925, Fax: 516-686-7613, E-mail: jnealon@nyit.edu.

New York University, Leonard N. Stern School of Business, Department of Information, Operations and Management Sciences, New York, NY 10012-1019. Offers information systems (MBA, PhD); operations management (MBA, PhD); statistics (MBA, PhD). *Expenses:* Tuition: Part-time $1,080 per unit. Required fees: $56 per unit. $329 per term. Tuition and fees vary according to program. *Faculty research:* Knowledge management, economics of information, computer-supported groups and communities financial information systems, data mining and business intelligence.

New York University, School of Continuing and Professional Studies, Center for Management, Graduate Programs in Management and Systems, New York, NY 10012-1019. Offers applied database technologies (MS); enterprise and risk management (Advanced Certificate); leadership and knowledge management (MS); management in the Internet E-conomy (MS); strategy and leadership (Advanced Certificate); systems management (MS). Part-time and evening/weekend programs available. Postbaccalaureate distance learning degree programs offered (no on-campus study). *Faculty:* 2 full-time (0 women), 9 part-time/adjunct (2 women). *Students:* 10 full-time (4 women), 200 part-time (64 women); includes 73 minority (26 African Americans, 36 Asian Americans or Pacific Islanders, 11 Hispanic Americans), 28 international. Average age 34. 64 applicants, 77% accepted, 28 enrolled. In 2006, 12 degrees awarded. *Degree requirements:* For master's, thesis, capstone project. *Entrance requirements:* For master's, GMAT or GRE General Test, work experience, resumé, 2 letters of recommendation. Additional exam requirements/recommendations for international students: Required—TOEFL (minimum score 600 paper-based; 250 computer-based), TWE. *Application deadline:* For fall admission, 3/15 priority date for domestic and international students; for spring admission, 10/15 priority date for domestic students, 8/15 priority date for international students. Applications are processed on a rolling basis. Application fee: $75. *Expenses:* Tuition: Part-time $1,080 per unit. Required fees: $56 per unit. $329 per term. Tuition and fees vary according to program. *Financial support:* In 2006–07, 87 students received support, including fellowships (averaging $1,009 per year); scholarships/grants also available. Support available to part-time students. Financial award application deadline: 3/1; financial award applicants required to submit FAFSA. *Faculty research:* Six sigma and TQ, business continuity, systems security, digital economy. *Application contact:* Helen Sapp, Assistant Director, 212-992-3600, Fax: 212-992-3676, E-mail: helen.sapp@nyu.edu.

See Close-Up on page 613.

New York University, School of Continuing and Professional Studies, Center for Management, Program in Information Technologies, New York, NY 10012-1019. Offers Advanced Certificate. Part-time and evening/weekend programs available. Postbaccalaureate distance learning degree programs offered (minimal on-campus study). *Faculty:* 2 full-time (0 women), 9 part-time/adjunct (2 women). *Students:* Average age 35. 21 applicants, 81% accepted, 12 enrolled. In 2006, 9 degrees awarded. *Degree requirements:* For Advanced Certificate, thesis. *Entrance requirements:* For degree, work-related experience. Additional exam requirements/recommendations for international students: Required—TOEFL (minimum score 600 paper-based; 250 computer-based; 100 iBT), TWE. *Application deadline:* For fall admission, 3/15 priority date for domestic students, 3/15 for international students; for spring admission, 10/15 priority date for domestic students, 8/15 for international students. Application fee: $75. *Expenses:* Tuition: Part-time $1,080 per unit. Required fees: $56 per unit. $329 per term. Tuition and fees vary according to program. *Financial support:* In 2006–07, 33 students received support, including fellowships (averaging $836 per year). Support available to part-time students. Financial award application deadline: 3/1. *Unit head:* Helen Sapp, Assistant Director, 212-992-3600, Fax: 212-992-3676, E-mail: helen.sapp@nyu.edu.

North Central College, Graduate Programs, Department of Business, Program in Management Information Systems, Naperville, IL 60566-7063. Offers MS. Part-time and evening/weekend programs available. *Degree requirements:* For master's, project. *Entrance requirements:* For master's, interview.

Northeastern University, College of Computer and Information Science, Boston, MA 02115-5096. Offers computer and information science (PhD); computer science (MS); health informatics (MS); information assurance (MS); telecommunication systems management (MS). Part-time and evening/weekend programs available. *Faculty:* 26 full-time (5 women), 5 part-time/adjunct (4 women). *Students:* 196 full-time (38 women), 38 part-time (9 women). Average age 28. 451 applicants, 55% accepted. In 2006, 49 master's, 4 doctorates awarded. Terminal master's awarded for partial completion of doctoral program. *Degree requirements:* For master's,

Management Information Systems

Northeastern University (continued)
thesis optional; for doctorate, thesis/dissertation, comprehensive exam. *Entrance requirements:* For master's and doctorate, GRE General Test. Additional exam requirements/recommendations for international students: Required—TOEFL. *Application deadline:* For fall admission, 7/15 for domestic students, 5/1 for international students; for spring admission, 11/30 for domestic students, 9/1 for international students. Applications are processed on a rolling basis. Application fee: $50. Electronic applications accepted. *Expenses: Contact institution. Financial support:* In 2006–07, 23 research assistantships with full tuition reimbursements (averaging $16,302 per year), 16 teaching assistantships with full tuition reimbursements (averaging $15,675 per year) were awarded; fellowships, career-related internships or fieldwork, Federal Work-Study, and institutionally sponsored loans also available. Financial award application deadline: 1/15. *Faculty research:* Programming languages, artificial intelligence, human-computer interaction, database management, network security. *Unit head:* Dr. Larry A. Finkelstein, Dean, 617-373-2462, Fax: 617-373-5121. *Application contact:* Dr. Agnes Chan, Associate Dean and Director of Graduate Program, 617-373-2462, Fax: 617-373-5121, E-mail: gradschool@ccs.neu.edu.

Northern Arizona University, Graduate College, College of Business Administration, Flagstaff, AZ 86011. Offers general management (MBA); management information systems (MBA). *Accreditation:* AACSB. Part-time programs available. *Entrance requirements:* For master's, GMAT. Expenses: Contact institution. *Faculty research:* Data processing applications to business situations and problems, accounting fraud, effects of sales tactics, self-efficacy and performance.

Northern Illinois University, Graduate School, College of Business, Department of Operations Management and Information Systems, De Kalb, IL 60115-2854. Offers management information systems (MS). Part-time programs available. *Faculty:* 11 full-time (3 women), 3 part-time/adjunct (0 women). *Students:* 13 full-time (1 woman), 27 part-time (12 women); includes 6 minority (2 African Americans, 1 Asian American or Pacific Islander, 3 Hispanic Americans), 3 international. Average age 31. 57 applicants, 47% accepted, 16 enrolled. In 2006, 33 degrees awarded. *Degree requirements:* For master's, computer language. *Entrance requirements:* For master's, GMAT, minimum GPA of 2.75. Additional exam requirements/recommendations for international students: Required—TOEFL (minimum score 550 paper-based; 213 computer-based). *Application deadline:* For fall admission, 6/1 for domestic students, 5/1 for international students; for spring admission, 11/1 for domestic students, 10/1 for international students. Applications are processed on a rolling basis. Application fee: $30. Electronic applications accepted. *Financial support:* In 2006–07, 15 research assistantships with full tuition reimbursements were awarded; fellowships with full tuition reimbursements, teaching assistantships with full tuition reimbursements, career-related internships or fieldwork, Federal Work-Study, scholarships/grants, tuition waivers (full), and unspecified assistantships also available. Support available to part-time students. Financial award applicants required to submit FAFSA. *Faculty research:* Affordability of homeownership, web portal competition intranet, electronic commerce, corporate-academic alliances. *Unit head:* Dr. Nancy Russo, Chair, 815-753-1185, Fax: 815-753-7460.

Northwestern University, The Graduate School, School of Communication, Department of Communication Studies, Communication Systems Strategy and Management Program, Evanston, IL 60208. Offers MSC. Part-time programs available. Electronic applications accepted.

Northwest Missouri State University, Graduate School, Melvin and Valorie Booth College of Business and Professional Studies, Program in Management Information Systems, Maryville, MO 64468-6001. Offers MBA. Part-time programs available. *Faculty:* 22 full-time (4 women). *Students:* 5 full-time (2 women), 1 (woman) part-time, (all international). 7 applicants, 71% accepted, 2 enrolled. In 2006, 4 degrees awarded. *Degree requirements:* For master's, comprehensive exam. *Entrance requirements:* For master's, GMAT, minimum GPA of 2.5. Additional exam requirements/recommendations for international students: Required—TOEFL (minimum score 550 paper-based; 213 computer-based). *Application deadline:* For fall admission, 7/1 for domestic and international students; for spring admission, 12/1 for domestic students, 11/15 for international students. Application fee: $0 ($50 for international students). *Financial support:* In 2006–07, 2 research assistantships with full tuition reimbursements (averaging $6,000 per year) were awarded. Financial award application deadline: 3/1; financial award applicants required to submit FAFSA. *Unit head:* Dr. Gary Ury, Head, 660-562-1185. *Application contact:* Dr. Frances Shipley, Dean of Graduate School, 660-562-1145, Fax: 660-562-1096, E-mail: gradsch@nwmissouri.edu.

Norwich University, School of Graduate Studies, Program in Information Assurance, Northfield, VT 05663. Offers MS. *Faculty:* 23 full-time (4 women). *Students:* 103 full-time (34 women). *Entrance requirements:* For master's, minimum undergraduate GPA of 2.75. Additional exam requirements/recommendations for international students: Required—TOEFL. *Application deadline:* For fall admission, 7/1 for domestic and international students; for winter admission, 11/1 for domestic and international students; for spring admission, 3/1 for domestic and international students. Application fee: $50. Electronic applications accepted. *Financial support:* Scholarships/grants available. Financial award applicants required to submit FAFSA. *Unit head:* Dr. Mich Kabay, Director, 802-485-2730, E-mail: mkabay@norwich.edu. *Application contact:* Elizabeth Templeton, Administrative Director, 802-485-2757, Fax: 802-485-2533, E-mail: etemplet@norwich.edu.

Notre Dame College, Graduate Studies, South Euclid, OH 44121-4293. Offers accounting (Certificate); creative critical thinking (M Ed); financial services management (Certificate); information systems (Certificate); learning disabilities (M Ed); management (Certificate); paralegal (Certificate); pastoral ministry (Certificate); reading (M Ed); teacher education (Certificate). Part-time and evening/weekend programs available. *Degree requirements:* For master's, thesis. *Entrance requirements:* For master's, GRE General Test, MAT, minimum GPA of 2.75, valid teaching certificate. *Faculty research:* Cognitive psychology, teaching critical thinking in the classroom.

Nova Southeastern University, Graduate School of Computer and Information Sciences, Program in Information Security, Fort Lauderdale, FL 33314-7796. Offers MS. *Students:* 1 (woman) full-time, 38 part-time (7 women); includes 16 minority (6 African Americans, 10 Hispanic Americans), 3 international. In 2006, 5 degrees awarded. *Application contact:* 954-262-2000, Fax: 954-262-3915, E-mail: scisinfo@nova.edu.

Nova Southeastern University, Graduate School of Computer and Information Sciences, Program in Information Systems, Fort Lauderdale, FL 33314-7796. Offers PhD. *Students:* 89 full-time (27 women), 136 part-time (42 women); includes 76 minority (47 African Americans, 13 Asian Americans or Pacific Islanders, 16 Hispanic Americans), 7 international. In 2006, 15 degrees awarded. *Application contact:* 954-262-2000, Fax: 954-262-3915, E-mail: scisinfo@nova.edu.

Nova Southeastern University, Graduate School of Computer and Information Sciences, Program in Management Information Systems, Fort Lauderdale, FL 33314-7796. Offers MS. Part-time and evening/weekend programs available. Postbaccalaureate distance learning degree programs offered (no on-campus study). *Students:* 21 full-time (5 women), 179 part-time (65 women); includes 97 minority (39 African Americans, 1 American Indian/Alaska Native, 12 Asian Americans or Pacific Islanders, 45 Hispanic Americans), 14 international. In 2006, 85 degrees awarded. *Degree requirements:* For master's, thesis optional. *Application deadline:* Applications are processed on a rolling basis. *Financial support:* Application deadline: 5/1; *Application contact:* 954-262-2000, Fax: 954-262-3915, E-mail: scisinfo@nova.edu.

Oakland University, Graduate Study and Lifelong Learning, School of Business Administration, Department of Decision and Information Sciences, Rochester, MI 48309-4401. Offers information technology management (MS); management information systems (Certificate); production and operations management (Certificate). *Faculty:* 8 full-time (0 women), 1 part-time/adjunct (0 women). *Students:* 7 full-time (2 women), 31 part-time (7 women); includes 8 minority (1 African American, 6 Asian Americans or Pacific Islanders, 1 Hispanic American), 8 international. Average age 33. 7 applicants, 86% accepted, 5 enrolled. In 2006, 10 master's, 1 other advanced degree awarded. Application fee: $30. *Expenses:* Tuition, state resident: full-time $9,936; part-time $414 per credit. Tuition, nonresident: full-time $17,202; part-time $716 per credit. *Unit head:* Dr. Thomas Lauer, Chair, 248-370-3283, Fax: 248-370-4604.

The Ohio State University, Graduate School, Max M. Fisher College of Business, Department of Accounting and Management Information Systems, Columbus, OH 43210. Offers M Acc, MA, PhD. *Accreditation:* AACSB. *Faculty:* 25. *Students:* 102 full-time (45 women), 5 part-time (3 women); includes 9 minority (1 African American, 1 American Indian/Alaska Native, 7 Asian Americans or Pacific Islanders), 26 international. In 2006, 9 master's, 2 doctorates awarded. Terminal master's awarded for partial completion of doctoral program. *Degree requirements:* For doctorate, thesis/dissertation. *Entrance requirements:* For master's and doctorate, GMAT or GRE. Additional exam requirements/recommendations for international students: Required—TOEFL (minimum score 600 paper-based; 250 computer-based). *Application deadline:* For fall admission, 8/15 priority date for domestic students, 7/1 priority date for international students; for winter admission, 12/1 priority date for domestic students, 11/1 priority date for international students; for spring admission, 3/1 priority date for domestic students, 2/1 priority date for international students. Applications are processed on a rolling basis. Application fee: $40 ($50 for international students). Electronic applications accepted. *Expenses:* Tuition, state resident: full-time $9,438. Tuition, nonresident: full-time $22,791. Tuition and fees vary according to course load, campus/location and program. *Financial support:* Fellowships, research assistantships, teaching assistantships, career-related internships or fieldwork, Federal Work-Study, and institutionally sponsored loans available. Support available to part-time students. *Faculty research:* Artificial intelligence, protocol analysis, database design in decision-supporting systems. *Unit head:* Annette Beatty, Graduate Studies Committee Chair, 614-292-2081, Fax: 614-292-2118, E-mail: beatty.86@osu.edu. *Application contact:* 614-292-9444, Fax: 614-292-3895, E-mail: domestic.grad@osu.edu.

Oklahoma City University, Meinders School of Business, Program in Business Administration, Oklahoma City, OK 73106-1402. Offers finance (MBA); health administration (MBA); information technology (MBA); integrated marketing communications (MBA); international business (MBA); marketing (MBA); JD/MBA. *Accreditation:* ACBSP. Part-time and evening/weekend programs available. *Faculty:* 30 full-time (7 women), 24 part-time/adjunct (5 women). *Students:* 291 full-time (112 women), 186 part-time (68 women); includes 57 minority (27 African Americans, 9 American Indian/Alaska Native, 12 Asian Americans or Pacific Islanders, 9 Hispanic Americans), 218 international. Average age 27. In 2006, 341 degrees awarded. *Degree requirements:* For master's, comprehensive exam. *Entrance requirements:* For master's, minimum GPA of 2.5. Additional exam requirements/recommendations for international students: Required—TOEFL (minimum score 510 paper-based). *Application deadline:* For fall admission, 8/22 for domestic students; for spring admission, 1/15 for domestic students. Applications are processed on a rolling basis. Application fee: $30 ($70 for international students). *Financial support:* Fellowships with partial tuition reimbursements, career-related internships or fieldwork, Federal Work-Study, institutionally sponsored loans, and tuition waivers (partial) available. Support available to part-time students. Financial award application deadline: 8/1. *Faculty research:* Management information systems, international business strategies. *Unit head:* Dr. Mahmood Shandiz, Head, 405-208-5130, Fax: 405-208-5098, E-mail: mshandiz@okcu.edu. *Application contact:* Leslie McKenzie, Director, Graduate Admissions, 800-633-7242, Fax: 405-208-5356, E-mail: gadmissions@okcu.edu.

Oklahoma State University, William S. Spears School of Business, Department of Management Science and Information Systems, Stillwater, OK 74078. Offers management information systems (PhD); management information systems/accounting information systems (MS); management science (PhD); operations management (PhD); telecommunications management (MS, PhD). *Faculty:* 17 full-time (3 women), 1 part-time/adjunct (0 women). *Students:* 64 full-time (15 women), 66 part-time (15 women); includes 6 minority (2 American Indian/Alaska Native, 3 Asian Americans or Pacific Islanders, 1 Hispanic American), 77 international. Average age 31. 144 applicants, 55% accepted, 35 enrolled. In 2006, 62 master's, 1 doctorate awarded. *Degree requirements:* For doctorate, thesis/dissertation. *Entrance requirements:* For master's and doctorate, GMAT. *Application deadline:* For fall admission, 3/1 priority date for international students; for spring admission, 8/1 priority date for international students. Applications are processed on a rolling basis. Application fee: $40 ($75 for international students). Electronic applications accepted. *Expenses:* Tuition, state resident: part-time $146 per credit hour. Tuition, nonresident: part-time $516 per credit hour. Required fees: $44 per credit hour. Tuition and fees vary according to program. *Financial support:* In 2006–07, 2 research assistantships (averaging $4,620 per year), 19 teaching assistantships (averaging $7,334 per year) were awarded; career-related internships or fieldwork, Federal Work-Study, scholarships/grants, health care benefits, and unspecified assistantships also available. Support available to part-time students. *Unit head:* Dr. Rick Wilson, Head, 405-744-5084.

Pace University, Lubin School of Business, Information Systems Program, New York, NY 10038. Offers MBA. Part-time and evening/weekend programs available. *Faculty:* 14 full-time. *Students:* 5 full-time (3 women), 39 part-time (11 women); includes 16 minority (3 African Americans, 9 Asian Americans or Pacific Islanders, 4 Hispanic Americans), 10 international. Average age 29. 30 applicants, 63% accepted, 6 enrolled. In 2006, 28 degrees awarded. *Entrance requirements:* For master's, GMAT. *Application deadline:* For fall admission, 7/31 priority date for domestic students; for spring admission, 11/30 for domestic students. Applications are processed on a rolling basis. Application fee: $65. Electronic applications accepted. *Expenses:* Tuition: Part-time $890 per credit. *Financial support:* Research assistantships, career-related internships or fieldwork and Federal Work-Study available. Support available to part-time students. Financial award applicants required to submit FAFSA. *Unit head:* Dr. John Molluzzo, Chair, 212-346-1780. *Application contact:* Joanna Broda, Director of Admissions, 212-346-1652, Fax: 212-346-1585, E-mail: gradnyc@pace.edu.

Pacific States University, College of Business, Los Angeles, CA 90006. Offers accounting (MBA); business administration (DBA); finance (MBA); international business (MBA); management of information technology (MBA); real estate management (MBA). Part-time and evening/weekend programs available. Postbaccalaureate distance learning degree programs offered (no on-campus study). *Faculty:* 3 full-time (0 women), 11 part-time/adjunct (0 women). *Students:* 106 full-time (47 women); includes 10 minority (all Asian Americans or Pacific Islanders), 96 international. Average age 32. 36 applicants, 81% accepted, 26 enrolled. In 2006, 68 degrees awarded. *Entrance requirements:* For master's, minimum undergraduate GPA of 2.5 during last 90 hours of course work. Additional exam requirements/recommendations for international students: Required—TOEFL (minimum score 133 computer-based). *Application deadline:* For fall admission, 8/15 priority date for domestic students; for winter admission, 10/15 priority date for domestic students; for spring admission, 1/15 priority date for domestic students. Applications are processed on a rolling basis. Application fee: $100. *Expenses:* Tuition: Full-time $6,360. Required fees: $1,080. Full-time tuition and fees vary according to course load and degree level. *Financial support:* Fellowships, research assistantships, teaching assistantships, scholarships/grants available. Financial award applicants required to submit FAFSA. *Unit head:* Dr. Kamol Somvichian, Director, 888-200-0383, Fax: 323-731-2383, E-mail: admission@psuca.edu. *Application contact:* Marina Miller, Assistant Director of Admissions, 323-731-2383 Ext. 11, Fax: 323-731-7276, E-mail: admissions@psuca.edu.

Pacific States University, College of Computer Science, Los Angeles, CA 90006. Offers computer science (MSCS); information systems (MSCS). Part-time and evening/weekend programs available. *Faculty:* 1 full-time (0 women), 3 part-time/adjunct (0 women). *Students:* 15 full-time (4 women); includes 2 minority (both Asian Americans or Pacific Islanders), 13 international. Average age 27. 11 applicants, 73% accepted, 6 enrolled. In 2006, 6 degrees awarded. *Entrance requirements:* For master's, bachelor's degree in physics, engineering, computer science, or applied mathematics; minimum undergraduate GPA of 2.5 during last 90 hours of course work. Additional exam requirements/recommendations for international students: Required—TOEFL (minimum score 133 computer-based). *Application deadline:* For fall admission, 8/15 priority date for domestic students; for winter admission, 10/15 priority date for domestic students; for spring admission, 1/15 priority date for domestic students. Applications are processed on a rolling basis. Application fee: $100. *Expenses:* Tuition: Full-time $6,360. Required fees: $1,080. Full-time tuition and fees vary according to course load and degree level. *Financial support:* Scholarships/grants available. Financial award applicants required to submit FAFSA. *Unit head:* Dr. Myung K. Yoo, Director, 888-200-0383, Fax: 323-731-7276, E-mail: admission@psuca.edu. *Application contact:* Namyoung Chah, Registrar, 323-731-2383, Fax: 323-731-7276, E-mail: registrar@psuca.edu.

Park University, College of Graduate and Professional Studies, Kansas City, MO 54105. Offers adult education (M Ed); at-risk students (M Ed); disaster and emergency management (MPA); educational administration (M Ed); entrepreneurship (MBA); general business (MBA); general education (M Ed); government/business relations (MPA); healthcare/services management (MBA, MPA); international business (MBA); K-12 certification (MAT); management information systems (MBA); management of information systems (MPA); middle school certification (MAT); multi-cultural education (M Ed); nonprofit management (MPA); public management (MPA); school law (M Ed); secondary school certification (MAT); special education (M Ed). Part-time and evening/weekend programs available. Postbaccalaureate distance learning degree programs offered (no on-campus study). *Degree requirements:* For master's, thesis (for some programs), comprehensive exam, registration. *Entrance requirements:* For master's, GRE, GMAT, teacher certification (M Ed). Additional exam requirements/recommendations for international students: Required—TOEFL (minimum score 550 paper-based). Electronic applications accepted. *Faculty research:* Literacy, leadership, brain based research, multicultural education, diversity.

Penn State Harrisburg, Graduate School, School of Business Administration, Middletown, PA 17057-4898. Offers business administration (MBA); information systems (MS); MBA/JD; MBA/PhD; MSIS/JD. *Entrance requirements:* For master's, GMAT. *Expenses:* Tuition, state resident: full-time $13,224; part-time $551 per credit. Tuition, nonresident: full-time $18,652; part-time $777 per credit. Required fees: $84 per semester. *Unit head:* Dr. Mukund S. Kulkarni, Professor, 717-948-6141, E-mail: msk5@psu.edu.

Penn State University Park, Graduate School, The Mary Jean and Frank P. Smeal College of Business Administration, State College, University Park, PA 16802-1503. Offers accounting (PhD); business administration (MBA); finance (PhD); management and organization (PhD); management science/operations/logistics (PhD); marketing (PhD); real estate (PhD); supply chain and information systems (PhD). *Students:* 287 full-time (79 women), 5 part-time (2 women); includes 39 minority (22 African Americans, 11 Asian Americans or Pacific Islanders, 6 Hispanic Americans), 93 international. Average age 31. 841 applicants, 31% accepted, 150 enrolled. In 2006, 107 master's, 11 doctorates awarded. *Expenses: Contact institution. Financial support:* In 2006–07, 1 fellowship, 11 research assistantships, 143 teaching assistantships were awarded. Financial award applicants required to submit FAFSA. *Unit head:* Dr. Kenneth B. Thomas, Dean, 814-863-0448, Fax: 814-865-7064, E-mail: j2t@psu.edu.

Polytechnic University, Westchester Graduate Center, Graduate Programs, Department of Management, Major in Financial Engineering, Hawthorne, NY 10532-1507. Offers capital markets (MS); computational finance (MS); financial engineering (AC); financial technology (MS); financial technology management (AC); information management (AC). *Degree requirements:* For master's, thesis (for some programs), comprehensive exam (for some programs), registration. *Entrance requirements:* Additional exam requirements/recommendations for international students: Required—TOEFL (minimum score 550 paper-based; 213 computer-based); Recommended—IELTS (minimum score 7). *Application deadline:* For fall admission, 7/15 priority date for domestic students, 4/1 priority date for international students; for spring admission, 12/15 priority date for domestic students, 10/1 priority date for international students. Applications are processed on a rolling basis. Application fee: $55. Electronic applications accepted. *Expenses:* Tuition: Full-time $17,184; part-time $988 per credit. *Application contact:* Anthea Jeffrey, Graduate Admissions, 718-260-3200, Fax: 718-260-3624, E-mail: gradinfo@poly.edu.

Pontifical Catholic University of Puerto Rico, College of Business Administration, Ponce, PR 00717-0777. Offers accounting (MBA); business administration (PhD); finance (MBA); general business (MBA); human resources (MBA); international business (MBA); management (MBA); management information systems (MBA); marketing (MBA); office administration (MBA). Part-time and evening/weekend programs available. *Degree requirements:* For master's, thesis/dissertation; for doctorate, thesis/dissertation, comprehensive exam. *Entrance requirements:* For master's, GRE, interview, minimum GPA of 2.75; for doctorate, 2 letters of recommendation, 2 years experience in a related field, interview.

Prairie View A&M University, Graduate School, College of Engineering, Prairie View, TX 77446-0519. Offers computer information systems (MSCIS); computer science (MSCS); electrical engineering (MSEE, PhDEE); engineering (MS Engr). Part-time and evening/weekend programs available. *Faculty:* 36 full-time (3 women). *Students:* 63 full-time (20 women), 27 part-time (5 women); includes 73 minority (57 African Americans, 14 Asian Americans or Pacific Islanders, 2 Hispanic Americans), 7 international. Average age 30. 86 applicants, 100% accepted, 86 enrolled. In 2006, 9 degrees awarded. *Degree requirements:* For master's, thesis optional; for doctorate, thesis/dissertation. *Entrance requirements:* For master's, GRE General Test, bachelor's degree in engineering from an ABET accredited institution; for doctorate, GRE. Additional exam requirements/recommendations for international students: Required—TOEFL (minimum score 550 paper-based). *Application deadline:* For fall admission, 7/1 priority date for domestic students, 6/1 priority date for international students; for spring admission, 11/1 priority date for domestic students, 10/1 priority date for international students. Applications are processed on a rolling basis. Application fee: $50. Electronic applications accepted. *Financial support:* In 2006–07, 12 fellowships with full tuition reimbursements (averaging $30,000 per year), 16 research assistantships (averaging $16,150 per year), 13 teaching assistantships (averaging $14,000 per year) were awarded; career-related internships or fieldwork, Federal Work-Study, institutionally sponsored loans, scholarships/grants, and tuition waivers (partial) also available. Support available to part-time students. Financial award application deadline: 3/1; financial award applicants required to submit FAFSA. *Faculty research:* Applied radiation research, lightweight structural materials and processing, thermal science, computational fluid dynamics, analog mixed signal. Total annual research expenditures: $3.8 million. *Unit head:* Dr. Milton R. Bryant, Dean, 936-261-9900, Fax: 936-261-9946, E-mail: m_bryant@pvamu.edu. *Application contact:* Dr. Shield B. Lin, Graduate Director, 936-857-4200, Fax: 936-857-4246, E-mail: shield_lin@pvamu.edu.

Purdue University, Graduate School, Krannert School of Management, Department of Management, West Lafayette, IN 47907. Offers accounting (PhD); business administration (MBA); finance (PhD); management information systems (PhD); marketing (PhD); operations management (PhD); quantitative methods (PhD); strategic management (PhD). *Students:* 56 full-time (21 women); includes 5 minority (3 Asian Americans or Pacific Islanders, 2 Hispanic Americans), 41 international. Average age 30. 421 applicants, 7% accepted, 19 enrolled. In 2006, 11 degrees awarded. *Median time to degree:* Doctorate–5 years full-time. Of those who began their doctoral program in fall 1998, 98% received their degree in 8 years or less. *Degree requirements:* For doctorate, thesis/dissertation, comprehensive exam, registration. *Entrance requirements:* For master's and doctorate, GMAT. Additional exam requirements/recommendations for international students: Required—TOEFL (minimum score 575 paper-based; 233 computer-based; 77 iBT), IELTS (minimum score 7). *Application deadline:* For fall admission, 2/15 for domestic and international students. Application fee: $55. Electronic applications accepted. *Financial support:* In 2006–07, 7 fellowships with partial tuition reimbursements (averaging $16,800 per year), 79 research assistantships with partial tuition reimbursements (averaging $16,800 per year), 8 teaching assistantships with partial tuition reimbursements (averaging $16,800 per year) were awarded; scholarships/grants and unspecified assistantships also available. Financial award application deadline: 2/15; financial award applicants required to submit FAFSA. *Faculty research:* Corporate finance, international business, enterprise integration. *Unit head:* Dr. John M. Barron, Head, 765-494-4451, Fax: 765-494-1526. *Application contact:* Kelly Felty, Assistant Director of Administration for Doctoral Programs, 765-494-4375, Fax: 765-494-1526, E-mail: phd@krannert.purdue.edu.

Quinnipiac University, School of Business, Program in Information Systems Management, Hamden, CT 06518-1940. Offers MS. *Faculty:* 4 full-time (1 woman), 1 part-time/adjunct (0 women). *Students:* 9 full-time (3 women), 31 part-time (9 women); includes 7 minority (3 African Americans, 4 Asian Americans or Pacific Islanders), 5 international. Average age 28. 17 applicants, 88% accepted, 13 enrolled. In 2006, 16 degrees awarded. *Median time to degree:* Master's–1.5 years full-time, 2.5 years part-time. *Entrance requirements:* For master's, minimum GPA of 2.75; course work in computer language programming, management, accounting foundation. Additional exam requirements/recommendations for international students: Required—TOEFL (minimum score 575 paper-based; 233 computer-based; 90 iBT), IELTS (minimum score 7). *Application deadline:* For fall admission, 7/30 priority date for domestic students, 5/30 priority date for international students; for spring admission, 12/15 priority date for domestic students, 10/15 priority date for international students. Applications are processed on a rolling basis. Application fee: $45. Electronic applications accepted. *Expenses:* Tuition: Part-time $675 per credit. Required fees: $30 per credit. *Financial support:* Tuition waivers (partial) and unspecified assistantships available. Support available to part-time students. Financial award application deadline: 4/15. *Faculty research:* Data management and warehousing, peer-to-peer counseling, decision support systems. *Unit head:* Dr. Bruce White, Director, 203-582-3386, Fax: 203-582-8664, E-mail: bruce.white@quinnipiac.edu. *Application contact:* 800-462-1944, Fax: 203-582-3443, E-mail: graduate@quinnipiac.edu.

See Close-Up on page 311.

Regis University, School for Professional Studies, Program in Computer Information Technology, Denver, CO 80221-1099. Offers database administration with IBM DB2 (Certificate); database administration with Oracle (Certificate); database development (Certificate); database technologies (MSCIT); enterprise Java software development (Certificate); executive information technologies (Certificate); executive information technology (MSCIT); information assurance (Certificate); software engineering (MSCIT, Certificate); storage area networks (Certificate); systems engineering (MSCIT, Certificate). Offered at Boulder Campus, Northwest Denver Campus, Southeast Denver Campus, Fort Collins Campus, Colorado Springs Campus, and Broomfield Campus. Part-time and evening/weekend programs available. Postbaccalaureate distance learning degree programs offered (no on-campus study). *Faculty:* 5 full-time (1 woman), 84 part-time/adjunct (12 women). *Students:* Average age 36. In 2006, 166 degrees awarded. *Degree requirements:* For master's, thesis, final research project; for Certificate, final research project. *Entrance requirements:* For master's and Certificate, 2 years of related experience, resumé. Additional exam requirements/recommendations for international students: Required—TOEFL (minimum score 213 computer-based), TWE (minimum score 5), TOEFL or university-based test. *Application deadline:* For fall admission, 8/13 priority date for domestic students, 7/13 for international students; for winter admission, 10/8 priority date for domestic students, 9/8 for international students; for spring admission, 12/17 priority date for domestic students, 11/17 for international students. Applications are processed on a rolling basis. Application fee: $75. Electronic applications accepted. *Expenses: Contact institution. Financial support:* Federal Work-Study available. Support available to part-time students. Financial award applicants required to submit FAFSA. *Unit head:* Donald Archer, Chair, 303-458-4302, Fax: 303-964-5538. *Application contact:* 800-677-9270 Ext. 4080, Fax: 303-964-5538, E-mail: masters@regis.edu.

Rensselaer Polytechnic Institute, Graduate School, Lally School of Management and Technology, Program in Management and Technology, Troy, NY 12180-3590. Offers finance (MBA, MS); financial technology (MS); management (PhD); management information systems (MBA, MS); new product development and marketing (MBA); new production and operations management (MS); product development and marketing (MS); production and operations management (MBA); technical commercialization (MS); technological entrepreneurship (MBA, MS). Part-time and evening/weekend programs available. Postbaccalaureate distance learning degree programs offered (no on-campus study). *Faculty:* 50 full-time (9 women), 1 part-time/adjunct (0 women). *Students:* 121 full-time (62 women), 525 part-time (184 women); includes 137 minority (43 African Americans, 60 Asian Americans or Pacific Islanders, 34 Hispanic Americans), 71 international. Average age 28. 416 applicants, 70% accepted, 240 enrolled. In 2006, 215 master's, 6 doctorates awarded. *Median time to degree:* Of those who began their doctoral program in fall 1998, 25% received their degree in 8 years or less. *Degree requirements:* For doctorate, thesis/dissertation. *Entrance requirements:* For master's, GMAT, resumé, 2 letters of recommendation; for doctorate, GMAT or GRE General Test, 2 letters of recommendation. Additional exam requirements/recommendations for international students: Required—TOEFL (minimum score 600 paper-based; 250 computer-based; 100 iBT); Recommended—IELTS (minimum score 7). *Application deadline:* For fall admission, 3/15 priority date for domestic and international students. Applications are processed on a rolling basis. Application fee: $75. Electronic applications accepted. *Expenses:* Tuition: Full-time $32,600; part-time $1,358 per credit. Required fees: $1,629. *Financial support:* In 2006–07, 48 students received support; fellowships with partial tuition reimbursements available, research assistantships with partial tuition reimbursements available, teaching assistantships with partial tuition reimbursements available, career-related internships or fieldwork, institutionally sponsored loans, and scholarships/grants available. Financial award application deadline: 3/15; financial award applicants required to submit FAFSA. *Faculty research:* Technological entrepreneurship, operations management, new product development and marketing, information systems, finance. Total annual research expenditures: $24,747. *Unit head:* Pedro Gonzalez, Director MBA/Admissons and Career Services, 518-276-2378, Fax: 518-276-2665, E-mail: gonzap3@rpi.edu. *Application contact:* Michele M. Martens, Manager of Graduate Programs, 518-276-6586, Fax: 518-276-2665, E-mail: martem@rpi.edu.

See Close-Up on page 313.

Rivier College, School of Graduate Studies, Department of Computer Information Systems, Nashua, NH 03060-5086. Offers MS. Part-time programs available. *Students:* 1 full-time (0 women), 2 part-time (1 woman). Average age 39. In 2006, 1 degree awarded. Application fee: $25. *Financial support:* Application deadline: 2/1; *Unit head:* Dr. Mihaela Sabin, Director, 603-888-1311, E-mail: msabin@rivier.edu. *Application contact:* Diane Monahan, Director of Graduate Admissions, 603-897-8129, Fax: 603-897-8810, E-mail: gradadm@rivier.edu.

Robert Morris University, Graduate Studies, School of Communications and Information Systems, Program in Computer and Information Systems, Moon Township, PA 15108-1189. Offers communications and information systems (MS); competitive intelligence systems (MS); information security and assurance (MS); information systems management (MS); Internet information systems (MS); IT project management (MS). Programs are part-time only. Part-time and evening/weekend programs available. *Faculty:* 21 full-time (6 women), 6 part-time/adjunct (2 women). *Students:* Average age 32. 163 applicants, 57% accepted, 76 enrolled. In 2006, 81 degrees awarded. *Entrance requirements:* For master's, letters of recommendation. Additional exam requirements/recommendations for international students: Required—TOEFL (minimum score 550 paper-based; 213 computer-based). *Application deadline:* For fall admission, 7/1 priority date for domestic and international students; for spring admission, 11/1 priority date for domestic and international students. Applications are processed on a rolling basis. Application fee: $35. Electronic applications accepted. *Expenses: Contact institution.* Part-time tuition and fees vary according to degree level and program. *Financial support:* Institutionally sponsored loans and unspecified assistantships available. Support available to part-time students. Financial award application deadline: 5/1; financial award applicants required to submit FAFSA. *Unit head:* Dr. David F. Wood, Department Head, 412-262-8393, Fax: 412-299-2481, E-mail: wood@rmu.edu. *Application contact:* Kellie L. Laurenzi, Dean of Enrollment, 412-262-8235, Fax: 412-299-2425, E-mail: laurenzi@rmu.edu.

Robert Morris University, Graduate Studies, School of Communications and Information Systems, Program in Information Systems and Communications, Moon Township, PA 15108-1189. Offers D Sc. Part-time and evening/weekend programs available. *Faculty:* 8 full-time (2

Management Information Systems

Robert Morris University (continued)

women). *Students:* Average age 41. 37 applicants, 68% accepted, 15 enrolled. In 2006, 6 degrees awarded. *Degree requirements:* For doctorate, thesis/dissertation. *Entrance requirements:* For doctorate, GRE or equivalent, employer letter of endorsement, interview. Additional exam requirements/recommendations for international students: Required—TOEFL (minimum score 550 paper-based; 213 computer-based). *Application deadline:* For fall admission, 8/1 priority date for domestic and international students. Applications are processed on a rolling basis. Application fee: $35. Electronic applications accepted. *Expenses: Contact institution.* Part-time tuition and fees vary according to degree level and program. *Financial support:* Application deadline: 5/1. *Unit head:* Dr. Frederick G. Kohun, Associate Dean, 412-262-8395, Fax: 412-299-2481, E-mail: kohun@rmu.edu. *Application contact:* Kellie L. Laurenzi, Dean of Enrollment, 412-262-8235, Fax: 412-299-2425, E-mail: laurenzi@rmu.edu.

Rochester Institute of Technology, Graduate Enrollment Services, Golisano College of Computing and Information Sciences, Department of Information Technology, Rochester, NY 14623-5603. Offers game design and development (MS); information technology (MS); interactive multimedia development (AC); learning and knowledge management systems (MS); software development and management (MS). *Students:* 75 full-time (15 women), 165 part-time (44 women); includes 38 minority (12 African Americans, 19 Asian Americans or Pacific Islanders, 7 Hispanic Americans), 49 international. 168 applicants, 68% accepted, 76 enrolled. In 2006, 83 master's, 1 other advanced degree awarded. *Entrance requirements:* For master's, minimum GPA of 3.0. Additional exam requirements/recommendations for international students: Required—TOEFL (minimum score 570 paper-based; 230 computer-based; 88 iBT), GRE. *Application deadline:* For fall admission, 3/1 priority date for domestic students. Applications are processed on a rolling basis. Application fee: $50. Electronic applications accepted. *Expenses:* Tuition: Full-time $28,491; part-time $800 per credit. Required fees: $201. *Unit head:* Jim Leone, Director, 585-475-6451, E-mail: leone@it.rit.edu. *Application contact:* Diane Bills, Graduate Coordinator, 585-475-6791, E-mail: dpb@it.rit.edu.

Rochester Institute of Technology, Graduate Enrollment Services, Golisano College of Computing and Information Sciences, Program in Networking and Systems Administration, Program in Security and Information Assurance, Rochester, NY 14623-5603. Offers MS. *Students:* 15 full-time (0 women), 7 part-time; includes 2 minority (1 African American, 1 Asian American or Pacific Islander), 4 international. 38 applicants, 71% accepted, 14 enrolled. *Expenses:* Tuition: Full-time $28,491; part-time $800 per credit. Required fees: $201.

Roosevelt University, Graduate Division, Walter E. Heller College of Business Administration, Program in Information Systems, Chicago, IL 60605-1394. Offers MSIS. Part-time and evening/weekend programs available. *Students:* 1 (woman) full-time, 29 part-time (15 women); includes 11 minority (5 African Americans, 2 Asian Americans or Pacific Islanders, 4 Hispanic Americans). Average age 36. 16 applicants, 38% accepted, 5 enrolled. In 2006, 13 degrees awarded. *Entrance requirements:* For master's, GMAT. *Application deadline:* For fall admission, 6/1 priority date for domestic students. Applications are processed on a rolling basis. Application fee: $25 ($35 for international students). *Financial support:* Application deadline: 2/15. *Unit head:* Joe Chan, Director, 847-619-4853, Fax: 847-619-4852. *Application contact:* Joanne Canyon-Heller, Coordinator of Graduate Admission, 877-APPLY RU, Fax: 312-281-3356, E-mail: applyru@roosevelt.edu.

Rutgers, The State University of New Jersey, Newark, Graduate School, Program in Management, Newark, NJ 07102. Offers accounting (PhD); accounting information systems (PhD); computer information systems (PhD); finance (PhD); information technology (PhD); international business (PhD); management science (PhD); marketing (PhD); organization management (PhD). *Accreditation:* AACSB. *Faculty:* 101 full-time (16 women), 3 part-time/adjunct (1 woman). *Students:* 60 full-time (29 women), 32 part-time (17 women); includes 57 minority (6 African Americans, 49 Asian Americans or Pacific Islanders, 2 Hispanic Americans). 279 applicants, 13% accepted, 32 enrolled. In 2006, 10 degrees awarded. *Degree requirements:* For doctorate, thesis/dissertation, cumulative exams. *Entrance requirements:* For doctorate, GMAT or GRE, minimum undergraduate B average. Additional exam requirements/recommendations for international students: Required—TOEFL. *Application deadline:* For fall admission, 4/1 for domestic students; for spring admission, 11/1 for domestic students. Applications are processed on a rolling basis. Application fee: $50. Electronic applications accepted. *Financial support:* In 2006–07, 8 fellowships with full and partial tuition reimbursements (averaging $18,000 per year), 7 research assistantships with full tuition reimbursements (averaging $18,347 per year), teaching assistantships with full tuition reimbursements (averaging $18,347 per year) were awarded; institutionally sponsored loans and tuition waivers (full and partial) also available. Support available to part-time students. Financial award application deadline: 2/15. *Faculty research:* Technology management, leadership and teams, consumer behavior, financial and markets, logistics. *Unit head:* Dr. Glenn Shafer, Director, 973-353-1604, Fax: 973-353-5691, E-mail: gshafer@rbs.rutgers.edu. *Application contact:* Goncalo Filipe, Senior Academic Coordinator, 973-353-1002, Fax: 973-353-5691, E-mail: gfilipe@rbsmail.rutgers.edu.

Rutgers, The State University of New Jersey, Newark, Rutgers Business School: Graduate Programs-Newark/New Brunswick, Department of Management Science and Information Systems, Newark, NJ 07102. Offers MBA. *Entrance requirements:* For master's, GMAT. Additional exam requirements/recommendations for international students: Required—TOEFL.

Rutgers, The State University of New Jersey, Newark, Rutgers Business School: Graduate Programs-Newark/New Brunswick, Doctoral Programs in Business, Newark, NJ 07102. Offers accounting (PhD); accounting information systems (PhD); finance (PhD); individualized study (PhD); information technology (PhD); international business (PhD); management science (PhD); organizational management (PhD); supply chain management (PhD).

Sacred Heart University, Graduate Studies, College of Arts and Sciences, Department of Computer Science and Information Technology, Fairfield, CT 06825-1000. Offers computer science (MS, CPS); information technology (MS, CPS); information technology and network security (CPS); interactive multimedia (CPS); Web development (CPS). Part-time and evening/weekend programs available. *Faculty:* 7 full-time (4 women). *Students:* 6 full-time (0 women), 70 part-time (31 women); includes 9 minority (3 African Americans, 2 American Indian/Alaska Native, 2 Asian Americans or Pacific Islanders, 2 Hispanic Americans), 15 international. Average age 33. 20 applicants, 85% accepted. In 2006, 18 degrees awarded. *Degree requirements:* For master's, thesis optional. *Entrance requirements:* Additional exam requirements/recommendations for international students: Required—TOEFL (minimum score 550 paper-based; 213 computer-based). *Application deadline:* Applications are processed on a rolling basis. Application fee: $50 ($100 for international students). Electronic applications accepted. *Expenses:* Tuition: Part-time $510 per credit. Required fees: $118 per term. Full-time tuition and fees vary according to degree level and program. *Financial support:* Career-related internships or fieldwork, institutionally sponsored loans, and unspecified assistantships available. Support available to part-time students. Financial award applicants required to submit FAFSA. *Faculty research:* Contemporary market software. *Unit head:* Domenick Pinto, Academic Director and Chairperson, 203-371-7789, Fax: 203-371-0506, E-mail: pintod@sacredheart.edu. *Application contact:* Information Contact, 203-365-7619, Fax: 203-365-4732.

St. Edward's University, School of Management and Business, Area of Business Administration, Austin, TX 78704. Offers accounting (MBA); business management (MBA); entrepreneurship (MBA, Certificate); finance—general (MBA, Certificate); global business (MBA, Certificate); human resource management (MBA, Certificate); management information systems (MBA, Certificate); marketing (MBA, Certificate); operations management (MBA, Certificate); personal financial planner (MBA, Certificate); sports management (MBA). Part-time and evening/weekend programs available. *Students:* 32 full-time (16 women), 394 part-time (195 women); includes 117 minority (23 African Americans, 2 American Indian/Alaska Native, 28 Asian Americans or Pacific Islanders, 64 Hispanic Americans), 21 international. Average age 33. 121 applicants, 74% accepted, 72 enrolled. In 2006, 142 degrees awarded. *Degree requirements:* For master's, minimum 24 resident hours. *Entrance requirements:* For master's, GMAT or GRE General Test, minimum GPA of 2.75 in last 60 hours of course work. Additional exam requirements/recommendations for international students: Required—TOEFL (minimum score 550 paper-based; 213 computer-based; 79 iBT). *Application deadline:* For fall admission, 8/1 for domestic students, 7/1 for international students; for spring admission, 12/1 for domestic students, 11/1 for international students. Applications are processed on a rolling basis. Application fee: $45 ($50 for international students). Electronic applications accepted. *Expenses:* Tuition: Full-time $11,682; part-time $649 per credit hour. Full-time tuition and fees vary according to course load and program. *Financial support:* In 2006–07, 4 students received support. Scholarships/grants available. Financial award applicants required to submit FAFSA. *Faculty research:* Operations management, minority entrepreneurship, globalization, professional services marketing. *Unit head:* Dr. Dianne Hill, Director, 512-428-1295, Fax: 512-448-8492, E-mail: dianneh@stedwards.edu. *Application contact:* Natalia Quintanilla, Graduate Admissions Coordinator, 512-233-1697, Fax: 512-428-1032, E-mail: nataliaq@stedwards.edu.

St. Edward's University, School of Management and Business, Program in Computer Information Systems, Austin, TX 78704. Offers MS. Part-time and evening/weekend programs available. *Students:* 4 full-time (1 woman), 55 part-time (13 women); includes 19 minority (4 African Americans, 4 Asian Americans or Pacific Islanders, 11 Hispanic Americans), 3 international. Average age 37. 14 applicants, 71% accepted, 10 enrolled. In 2006, 23 degrees awarded. *Degree requirements:* For master's, minimum 24 resident hours. *Entrance requirements:* For master's, GMAT or GRE General Test, minimum GPA of 2.75 in last 60 hours of course work. Additional exam requirements/recommendations for international students: Required—TOEFL (minimum score 550 paper-based; 213 computer-based; 79 iBT). *Application deadline:* For fall admission, 8/1 for domestic students, 7/1 for international students; for spring admission, 12/1 for domestic students, 11/1 for international students. Applications are processed on a rolling basis. Application fee: $45 ($50 for international students). Electronic applications accepted. *Expenses:* Tuition: Full-time $11,682; part-time $649 per credit hour. Full-time tuition and fees vary according to course load and program. *Financial support:* In 2006–07, 1 student received support. Scholarships/grants available. Financial award applicants required to submit FAFSA. *Faculty research:* System design. *Unit head:* Dr. Steven Crowl, Director, 512-428-1280, Fax: 512-428-8492, E-mail: stevenc@stedwards.edu. *Application contact:* Natalia Quintanilla, Graduate Admissions Coordinator, 512-233-1697, Fax: 512-428-1032, E-mail: nataliaq@stedwards.edu.

St. John's University, The Peter J. Tobin College of Business, Department of Computer Information Systems and Decision Sciences, Queens, NY 11439. Offers MBA, Adv C. Part-time and evening/weekend programs available. *Faculty:* 13 full-time (0 women), 5 part-time/adjunct (2 women). *Students:* 3 full-time (1 woman), 10 part-time (4 women); includes 5 minority (3 African Americans, 1 Asian American or Pacific Islander, 1 Hispanic American), 2 international. Average age 30. 19 applicants, 16% accepted, 0 enrolled. In 2006, 6 degrees awarded. *Degree requirements:* For master's, thesis optional. *Entrance requirements:* For master's, GMAT, minimum GPA of 3.0. Additional exam requirements/recommendations for international students: Required—TOEFL (minimum score 500 paper-based; 173 computer-based). *Application deadline:* For fall admission, 5/1 priority date for domestic and international students; for spring admission, 11/1 priority date for domestic and international students. Applications are processed on a rolling basis. Application fee: $40. Electronic applications accepted. *Expenses: Contact institution.* Tuition and fees vary according to program. *Financial support:* Research assistantships, scholarships/grants available. Support available to part-time students. Financial award application deadline: 3/1; financial award applicants required to submit FAFSA. *Unit head:* Dr. Victor Lu, Chair, 718-990-7382. *Application contact:* Nicole T. Bryan, Assistant Dean, 718-990-2599, Fax: 718-990-5242, E-mail: mbaadmissions@stjohns.edu.

Saint Joseph's University, Erivan K. Haub School of Business, Professional MBA Program, Program in Decision and System Sciences, Philadelphia, PA 19131-1395. Offers information systems (MBA). Part-time and evening/weekend programs available. *Faculty:* 4 full-time (1 woman), 5 part-time/adjunct (2 women). *Students:* 11 full-time (4 women), 14 part-time (6 women); includes 2 minority (1 African American, 1 Asian American or Pacific Islander), 11 international. Average age 28. In 2006, 6 degrees awarded. *Entrance requirements:* For master's, GMAT, 2 letters of recommendation, resumé. Additional exam requirements/recommendations for international students: Required—TOEFL. *Application deadline:* For fall admission, 7/15 for domestic students, 4/15 for international students; for spring admission, 11/15 for domestic students, 10/15 for international students. Applications are processed on a rolling basis. Application fee: $35. Electronic applications accepted. *Financial support:* In 2006–07, teaching assistantships with partial tuition reimbursements (averaging $2,500 per year); unspecified assistantships also available. Financial award application deadline: 5/1. *Unit head:* Dr. Richard Herschel, Chair, 610-660-1621, E-mail: herschel@sju.edu.

Saint Peter's College, MBA Programs, Jersey City, NJ 07306-5997. Offers finance (MBA); international business (MBA); management (MBA); management information systems (MBA); marketing (MBA); MBA/MS. Part-time and evening/weekend programs available. *Degree requirements:* For master's, exit presentation. *Entrance requirements:* For master's, GMAT or MAT. *Faculty research:* International finance, operations research, expert systems, networking, decision support systems.

San Diego State University, Graduate and Research Affairs, College of Business Administration, Department of Information and Decision Systems, San Diego, CA 92182. Offers information and decision systems (MS); production and operations management (MS). Evening/weekend programs available. *Students:* 7 full-time (2 women), 15 part-time (5 women); includes 4 minority (3 Asian Americans or Pacific Islanders, 1 Hispanic American), 7 international. Average age 29. 15 applicants, 73% accepted, 7 enrolled. In 2006, 14 degrees awarded. *Degree requirements:* For master's, thesis or alternative. *Entrance requirements:* For master's, GMAT, resumé, letters of reference. Additional exam requirements/recommendations for international students: Required—TOEFL. *Application deadline:* For fall admission, 4/15 for domestic and international students; for spring admission, 11/1 for domestic students, 10/1 for international students. Applications are processed on a rolling basis. Application fee: $55. Electronic applications accepted. *Financial support:* In 2006–07, 21 teaching assistantships were awarded; fellowships, research assistantships also available. Financial award applicants required to submit FAFSA. Total annual research expenditures: $8,000. *Unit head:* Bruce Reinig, Chair, 619-594-5316, Fax: 619-594-3675. *Application contact:* Information Contact, E-mail: sdsumba@mail.sdsu.edu.

San Jose State University, Graduate Studies and Research, Lucas Graduate School of Business, Programs in Business Administration, San Jose, CA 95192-0001. Offers MBA. *Accreditation:* AACSB. *Students:* 39 full-time (11 women), 172 part-time (75 women); includes 92 minority (1 African American, 83 Asian Americans or Pacific Islanders, 8 Hispanic Americans), 38 international. Average age 32. 332 applicants, 34% accepted, 32 enrolled. In 2006, 159 degrees awarded. *Degree requirements:* For master's, thesis or alternative, comprehensive exam. *Entrance requirements:* For master's, GMAT, minimum GPA of 3.0. *Application deadline:* For fall admission, 6/29 for domestic students; for spring admission, 11/30 for domestic students. Applications are processed on a rolling basis. Application fee: $59. Electronic applications accepted. *Financial support:* Applicants required to submit FAFSA.

Santa Clara University, Leavey School of Business, Program in Information Systems, Santa Clara, CA 95053. Offers MSIS. *Students:* 9 full-time (3 women), 41 part-time (8 women); includes 21 minority (2 American Indian/Alaska Native, 16 Asian Americans or Pacific Islanders, 3 Hispanic Americans), 12 international. Average age 30. 24 applicants, 79% accepted, 10 enrolled. *Entrance requirements:* For master's, GMAT or GRE. Additional exam requirements/recommendations for international students: Required—TOEFL. *Application deadline:* For fall admission, 6/1 for domestic students. Application fee: $75 ($100 for international students). *Expenses:* Tuition: Part-time $627 per unit. Tuition and fees vary according to program. *Financial support:* Scholarships/grants and unspecified assistantships available. Financial award application deadline: 3/1; financial award applicants required to submit FAFSA. *Unit head:* Dr. Manoochehr Ghiassi, Director, 408-554-4687.

Schiller International University, Graduate Programs, London, Program in International Business, London, United Kingdom. Offers international business (MBA); management of information technology (MBA). Part-time programs available. Postbaccalaureate distance learning degree programs offered (no on-campus study). *Students:* 46 full-time. Average age 23. *Degree requirements:* For master's, GMAT before graduation, thesis optional. *Entrance requirements:* Additional exam requirements/recommendations for international students: Required—TOEFL (minimum score 550 paper-based; 213 computer-based). *Application deadline:* For fall admission, 8/1 priority date for domestic and international students; for spring admission, 12/1 priority date for domestic and international students. Applications are processed on a rolling basis. Application fee: $60. *Expenses:* Tuition: Full-time $20,306; part-time $1,601 per course. *Financial support:* Career-related internships or fieldwork and scholarships/grants available. Support available to part-time students. Financial award application deadline: 3/30; financial award applicants required to submit FAFSA. *Unit head:* Dr. Elizabeth Nunn, Director, 44-207-928-1372, Fax: 44-207-620-1226, E-mail: admissions@schillerlondon.ac.uk. *Application contact:* Susan Russeff, Associate Director of Admissions, 727-736-5082, Fax: 727-734-0359, E-mail: admissions@schiller.edu.

Schiller International University, MBA Programs, Florida, Program in Information Technology, Largo, FL 33770. Offers MBA. *Students:* 7 full-time, 8 part-time. Average age 26. *Entrance requirements:* Additional exam requirements/recommendations for international students: Required—TOEFL. *Expenses:* Tuition: Full-time $17,920; part-time $1,420 per course. *Financial support:* Federal Work-Study, scholarships/grants, and tuition waivers (partial) available. *Unit head:* Tom Evans, Director, 727-736-5082 Ext. 277, Fax: 727-736-6263, E-mail: tom_evans@schiller.edu. *Application contact:* Susan Russeff, Associate Director of Admissions, 727-736-5082, Fax: 727-734-0359, E-mail: admissions@schiller.edu.

Schiller International University, MBA Programs, Heidelberg, Germany, Heidelberg, Germany. Offers international business (MBA, MIM); management of information technology (MBA). Part-time and evening/weekend programs available. *Faculty:* 7 full-time (3 women), 14 part-time/adjunct (4 women). *Students:* 28 full-time, 4 part-time. Average age 28. In 2006, 15 degrees awarded. *Degree requirements:* For master's, thesis optional. *Entrance requirements:* Additional exam requirements/recommendations for international students: Required—TOEFL (minimum score 550 paper-based; 213 computer-based). *Application deadline:* For fall admission, 8/1 priority date for domestic and international students; for spring admission, 12/1 priority date for domestic and international students. Applications are processed on a rolling basis. Application fee: $60. Tuition charges are reported in euros. *Expenses:* Tuition: Full-time 20,938 euros; part-time 1,651 euros per course. *Financial support:* In 2006–07, 32 students received support. Scholarships/grants, tuition waivers (partial), and unspecified assistantships available. Support available to part-time students. Financial award application deadline: 3/30; financial award applicants required to submit FAFSA. *Faculty research:* Leadership, international economy, foreign direct investment. *Unit head:* Dr. Nicolle Macho, Director, 49-6221-458135, Fax: 49-6221-402703, E-mail: campus@siu-heidelberg.de. *Application contact:* Susan Russeff, Assistant Director of Admissions, 727-736-5082, Fax: 727-734-0359, E-mail: admissions@schiller.edu.

Seattle Pacific University, Graduate School, School of Business and Economics, Program in Information Systems Management, Seattle, WA 98119-1997. Offers MS. *Students:* 1 (woman) full-time, 18 part-time (6 women); includes 2 minority (1 American Indian/Alaska Native, 1 Asian American or Pacific Islander), 1 international. 10 applicants, 80% accepted, 5 enrolled. In 2006, 15 degrees awarded. *Application contact:* Debbie Wysomierski, Assistant Graduate Director, 206-281-2753, Fax: 206-281-2733, E-mail: mba@spu.edu.

Seton Hall University, Stillman School of Business, Programs in Business Administration, South Orange, NJ 07079-2697. Offers accounting (MBA); finance (MBA); financial markets, institutions and instruments (MBA); healthcare management (MBA); information systems (MBA); international business (MBA); management (MBA); marketing (MBA); pharmaceutical management (MBA); sport management (MBA). Part-time and evening/weekend programs available. *Faculty:* 57 full-time (13 women), 30 part-time/adjunct (3 women). *Students:* 57 full-time (16 women), 180 part-time (57 women); includes 9 African Americans, 10 Asian Americans or Pacific Islanders, 7 Hispanic Americans. Average age 29. 195 applicants, 47% accepted, 48 enrolled. In 2006, 144 degrees awarded. *Median time to degree:* Master's–1.6 years full-time, 2.3 years part-time. *Degree requirements:* For master's, 20 hours of community service (Social Responsibility Project). *Entrance requirements:* For master's, GMAT, minimum GPA of 2.75. Additional exam requirements/recommendations for international students: Required—TOEFL (minimum score 550 paper-based; 213 computer-based). *Application deadline:* For fall admission, 6/1 priority date for domestic students; for spring admission, 11/1 priority date for domestic students. Applications are processed on a rolling basis. Application fee: $75 ($100 for international students). Electronic applications accepted. *Financial support:* In 2006–07, 40 students received support, including research assistantships with full and partial tuition reimbursements available (averaging $5,400 per year); career-related internships or fieldwork, Federal Work-Study, scholarships/grants, and unspecified assistantships also available. Support available to part-time students. Financial award application deadline: 6/1; financial award applicants required to submit FAFSA. *Faculty research:* Financial, hedge funds, international business, legal issues, disclosure and branding. *Unit head:* Dr. Joyce A. Strawser, Associate Dean for Undergraduate and MBA Curricula, 973-761-9225, Fax: 973-761-9217, E-mail: strawsjo@shu.edu. *Application contact:* Catherine Bianchi, Director of Graduate Admissions, 973-761-9220, Fax: 973-761-9208, E-mail: biancha@shu.edu.

Shenandoah University, Byrd School of Business, Winchester, VA 22601-5195. Offers business administration (MBA); health care management (Certificate); information systems and computer technology (Certificate). *Accreditation:* AACSB. Part-time and evening/weekend programs available. *Faculty:* 11 full-time (2 women), 1 part-time/adjunct (0 women). *Students:* 23 full-time (9 women), 10 part-time (3 women); includes 1 minority (Asian American or Pacific Islander), 7 international. Average age 29. 27 applicants, 59% accepted, 12 enrolled. In 2006, 23 degrees awarded. *Entrance requirements:* For master's, GMAT or GRE, 2 letters of recommendation, resumé. Additional exam requirements/recommendations for international students: Required—TOEFL (minimum score 527 paper-based; 197 computer-based; 71 IBT). *Application deadline:* Applications are processed on a rolling basis. Application fee: $30. Electronic applications accepted. *Expenses:* Tuition: Full-time $12,200; part-time $610 per credit. Required fees: $150. Full-time tuition and fees vary according to course load and program. *Financial support:* In 2006–07, 28 students received support, including 4 fellowships with partial tuition reimbursements available (averaging $1,518 per year), 8 teaching assistantships with partial tuition reimbursements available (averaging $4,278 per year); career-related internships or fieldwork, institutionally sponsored loans, and unspecified assistantships also available. Support available to part-time students. Financial award application deadline: 3/15; financial award applicants required to submit FAFSA. *Faculty research:* Business and economics, marketing. *Unit head:* Dr. Randy Boxx, Dean, 540-665-4572, Fax: 540-665-5437, E-mail: rboxx@su.edu. *Application contact:* David Anthony, Dean of Admissions, 540-665-4581, Fax: 540-665-4627, E-mail: admit@su.edu.

See Close-Up on page 321.

Simon Fraser University, Graduate Studies, Faculty of Business Administration, Burnaby, BC V5A 1S6, Canada. Offers business administration (EMBA); decision support systems (MBA); international business (MBA); management, organization studies (MBA); marketing (MBA); MBA/MRM. *Accreditation:* AACSB. Postbaccalaureate distance learning degree programs offered. *Degree requirements:* For master's, thesis or written project. *Entrance requirements:* For master's, minimum GPA of 3.0. Additional exam requirements/recommendations for international students: Required—TOEFL. Expenses: Contact institution. *Faculty research:* Leadership, marketing and technology, wealth management.

Southeastern University, College of Graduate Studies, Program in Management Information Systems, Washington, DC 20024-2788. Offers MBA. Part-time and evening/weekend programs available. *Entrance requirements:* Additional exam requirements/recommendations for international students: Required—TOEFL.

Southern Illinois University Edwardsville, Graduate Studies and Research, School of Business, Department of Computer Management and Information Systems, Edwardsville, IL 62026-0001. Offers MS. Part-time and evening/weekend programs available. *Faculty:* 8 full-time (4 women). *Students:* 7 full-time (1 woman), 19 part-time (6 women); includes 2 minority (both African Americans), 2 international. 23 applicants, 78% accepted. In 2006, 14 degrees awarded. *Degree requirements:* For master's, thesis or alternative, final exam. *Entrance requirements:* For master's, GMAT. Additional exam requirements/recommendations for international students: Required—TOEFL. *Application deadline:* For fall admission, 10/5 for domestic and international students. Application fee: $30. Electronic applications accepted. *Financial support:* Teaching assistantships with full tuition reimbursements available. *Unit head:* Dr. Susan Yager, Chair, 618-650-2433. *Application contact:* Dr. Jo Ellen Moore, Director, 618-650-5816, E-mail: joemoor@siue.edu.

Southern Illinois University Edwardsville, Graduate Studies and Research, School of Business, Program in Business Administration, Specialization in Management Information Systems, Edwardsville, IL 62026-0001. Offers MBA. Part-time programs available. *Students:* 2 full-time (1 woman), 20 part-time (5 women); includes 3 minority (1 American Indian/Alaska Native, 2 Asian Americans or Pacific Islanders), 2 international. Average age 33. 9 applicants, 56% accepted. In 2006, 14 degrees awarded. *Degree requirements:* For master's, thesis or alternative, final exam. *Entrance requirements:* For master's, GMAT. Additional exam requirements/recommendations for international students: Required—TOEFL. *Application deadline:* For fall admission, 7/20 for domestic students, 6/1 for international students; for spring admission, 12/14 for domestic students, 10/1 for international students. Application fee: $30. Electronic applications accepted. *Financial support:* Fellowships with full tuition reimbursements, research assistantships with full tuition reimbursements, teaching assistantships with full tuition reimbursements, career-related internships or fieldwork, Federal Work-Study, institutionally sponsored loans, traineeships, and unspecified assistantships available. Support available to part-time students. Financial award application deadline: 3/1; financial award applicants required to submit FAFSA.

Southern New Hampshire University, School of Business, Manchester, NH 03106-1045. Offers accounting (MS); business administration (MBA, Certificate), including accounting (Certificate), business administration (MBA), finance (Certificate), forensic accounting (Certificate), human resources management (Certificate), international business (Certificate), international sport management (Certificate), leadership of not for profit organizations (Certificate), marketing (Certificate), operations management (Certificate), sport management (Certificate), taxation (Certificate); finance (MS); hospitality and tourism leadership (Certificate); information technology (MS, Certificate); information technology/international business (Certificate); integrated marketing communications (Certificate); international business (MS, DBA); marketing (MS); operations and project management (MS); organizational leadership (MS); project management (Certificate); sport management (MS); MBA/Certificate. *Accreditation:* ACBSP. Part-time and evening/weekend programs available. Postbaccalaureate distance learning degree programs offered (no on-campus study). *Faculty:* 45 full-time, 75 part-time/adjunct. *Students:* 427 full-time (184 women), 774 part-time (428 women). Average age 32. In 2006, 682 master's, 1 doctorate awarded. Terminal master's awarded for partial completion of doctoral program. *Degree requirements:* For master's, one foreign language, thesis or alternative, comprehensive exam (for some programs); for doctorate, one foreign language, thesis/dissertation, comprehensive exam. *Entrance requirements:* For master's, minimum GPA of 2.5; for doctorate, GMAT. Additional exam requirements/recommendations for international students: Required—TOEFL (minimum score 500 paper-based). *Application deadline:* Applications are processed on a rolling basis. Application fee: $25. Electronic applications accepted. *Financial support:* Career-related internships or fieldwork, Federal Work-Study, institutionally sponsored loans, tuition waivers (partial), and unspecified assistantships available. Support available to part-time students. Financial award applicants required to submit FAFSA. *Unit head:* Dr. Martin Bradley, Dean, 603-644-3102, Fax: 603-644-3144, E-mail: m.bradley@snhu.edu. *Application contact:* Scott Durand, Director of Graduate Enrollment Services, 603-644-3102 Ext. 3338, Fax: 603-644-3144, E-mail: s.durand@snhu.edu.

See Close-Up on page 325.

Stevens Institute of Technology, Graduate School, Wesley J. Howe School of Technology Management, Doctoral Program in Technology Management, Hoboken, NJ 07030. Offers information management (PhD); technology management (PhD); telecommunications management (PhD). Part-time and evening/weekend programs available. Postbaccalaureate distance learning degree programs offered (minimal on-campus study). *Entrance requirements:* Additional exam requirements/recommendations for international students: Required—TOEFL. Electronic applications accepted.

Stevens Institute of Technology, Graduate School, Wesley J. Howe School of Technology Management, Program in Business Administration, Hoboken, NJ 07030. Offers engineering management (MBA); financial management (MBA); global technology management (MBA); information management (MBA); information technology in financial services (MBA); information technology in the pharmaceutical industry (MBA); information technology outsourcing (MBA); pharmaceutical technology management (MBA); project management (MBA); telecommunications management (MBA).

Stevens Institute of Technology, Graduate School, Wesley J. Howe School of Technology Management, Program in Information Systems, Hoboken, NJ 07030. Offers computer science (MS); e-commerce (MS, Certificate); entrepreneurial information technology (MS); global innovation management (MS); human resource management (MS); information management (MS, Certificate); information security (MS); information technology in financial services industry (MS); information technology in the pharmaceutical industry (MS); information technology outsourcing management (MS); integrated information architecture (MS); project management (MS, Certificate); quantitative software engineering (MS); systems engineering (MS); telecommunications management (MS). *Degree requirements:* For master's, thesis optional. *Entrance requirements:* For master's, GMAT, GRE General Test. Additional exam requirements/recommendations for international students: Required—TOEFL. Electronic applications accepted.

Stevens Institute of Technology, Graduate School, Wesley J. Howe School of Technology Management, Program in Management, Hoboken, NJ 07030. Offers general management (MS); global innovation management (MS); human resource management (MS); information management (MS); project management (MS); technology commercialization (MS); technology management (MS). Part-time programs available. *Degree requirements:* For master's, thesis optional. *Entrance requirements:* For master's, GMAT, GRE General Test. Additional exam requirements/recommendations for international students: Required—TOEFL. Electronic applications accepted. *Faculty research:* Industrial economics.

Stony Brook University, State University of New York, Graduate School, College of Engineering and Applied Sciences, Department of Computer Science, Stony Brook, NY 11794. Offers computer science (MS, PhD); information systems (Certificate); information systems engineering (MS); software engineering (Certificate). *Faculty:* 31 full-time (5 women), 1 part-time/adjunct (0 women). *Students:* 289 full-time (69 women), 17 part-time; includes 19 minority (1 African American, 15 Asian Americans or Pacific Islanders, 3 Hispanic Americans), 247 international. Average age 25. 1,025 applicants, 28% accepted. In 2006, 95 master's, 12 doctorates awarded. *Degree requirements:* For master's, thesis or alternative; for doctorate, thesis/dissertation, comprehensive exam. *Entrance requirements:* For master's and doctorate, GRE General Test. Additional exam requirements/recommendations for international students: Required—TOEFL. *Application deadline:* For fall admission, 1/15 for domestic students. Application fee: $60. *Expenses:* Tuition, state resident: full-time $6,900; part-time $288 per credit.

Management Information Systems

Stony Brook University, State University of New York (continued)
Tuition, nonresident: full-time $10,920; part-time $455 per credit. *Financial support:* In 2006–07, 4 fellowships, 88 research assistantships, 39 teaching assistantships were awarded. *Faculty research:* Artificial intelligence, computer architecture, database management systems, VLSI, operating systems. Total annual research expenditures: $3.9 million. *Unit head:* Dr. Arie Kaufman, Chairman, 631-632-8470. *Application contact:* Dr. Michael Kiefer, Director, 631-632-8443, Fax: 631-632-8334, E-mail: mkiefer@notes.cc.sunysb.edu.

Stony Brook University, State University of New York, School of Professional Development, Stony Brook, NY 11794. Offers adolescence education: mathematics (Certificate); biology 7-12 (MAT); chemistry-grade 7-12 (MAT); coaching (Certificate); computer integrated engineering (Certificate); cultural studies (Certificate); earth science-grade 7-12 (MAT); educational computing (Advanced Certificate, Certificate); English-grade 7-12 (MAT); environmental and waste management (MS, Advanced Certificate); environmental systems management (Certificate); environmental/occupational health and safety (Certificate); French-grade 7-12 (MAT); German-grade 7-12 (MAT); human resource management (Certificate); industrial management (Certificate); information systems management (Certificate); Italian-grade 7-12 (MAT); liberal studies (MA); liberal studies online (MA); Long Island regional studies (Certificate); operation research (Certificate); physics-grade 7-12 (MAT); Russian-grade 7-12 (MAT); school administration and supervision (Certificate); school district administration (Certificate); social science and the professions (MPS), including human resources management, labor management, public affairs, waste management; social studies 7-12 (MAT); waste management (Certificate); women's studies (Certificate). Part-time and evening/weekend programs available. Postbaccalaureate distance learning degree programs offered. *Faculty:* 1 full-time (0 women), 118 part-time/adjunct (45 women). *Students:* 322 full-time (202 women), 1,188 part-time (728 women); includes 164 minority (69 African Americans, 2 American Indian/Alaska Native, 29 Asian Americans or Pacific Islanders, 64 Hispanic Americans), 11 international. Average age 28. In 2006, 738 master's, 405 other advanced degrees awarded. *Degree requirements:* For master's, one foreign language, thesis or alternative. *Application deadline:* Applications are processed on a rolling basis. Application fee: $62. *Expenses:* Tuition, state resident: full-time $6,900; part-time $288 per credit. Tuition, nonresident: full-time $10,920; part-time $455 per credit. *Financial support:* In 2006–07, 5 teaching assistantships were awarded; fellowships, research assistantships, career-related internships or fieldwork also available. Support available to part-time students. *Unit head:* Dr. Paul J. Edelson, Dean, 631-632-7052, Fax: 631-632-9046, E-mail: paul.edelson@sunysb.edu. *Application contact:* Sandra Romansky, Director of Admissions and Advisement, 631-632-7050, Fax: 631-632-9046, E-mail: sandra.romansky@sunysb.edu.

Strayer University, Graduate Studies, Washington, DC 20005-2603. Offers accounting (MS); business administration (MBA); communications technology (MS); information systems (MS); management information systems (MS). Part-time and evening/weekend programs available. Postbaccalaureate distance learning degree programs offered (minimal on-campus study). *Degree requirements:* For master's, thesis. *Entrance requirements:* For master's, GMAT, GRE General Test, bachelor's degree from an accredited college or university, minimum undergraduate GPA of 2.75. Electronic applications accepted.

Syracuse University, Graduate School, School of Information Studies, Information Management Program, Syracuse, NY 13244. Offers MS, MS/CAS. Part-time and evening/weekend programs available. Postbaccalaureate distance learning degree programs offered (minimal on-campus study). *Students:* 124 full-time (43 women), 76 part-time (28 women); includes 33 minority (17 African Americans, 1 American Indian/Alaska Native, 10 Asian Americans or Pacific Islanders, 5 Hispanic Americans), 102 international. 211 applicants, 81% accepted, 63 enrolled. *Entrance requirements:* For master's, GRE General Test. *Application deadline:* For fall admission, 2/14 priority date for domestic students; for spring admission, 11/1 priority date for domestic students. Application fee: $65. Electronic applications accepted. *Expenses:* Tuition: Full-time $16,920; part-time $940 per credit hour. Required fees: $930; $930 per year. *Unit head:* Dr. Robert Heckman, Director, 315-443-4479, Fax: 315-443-6886, E-mail: rheckman@syr.edu. *Application contact:* Susan Corieri, Director of Enrollment Management, 315-443-6885, E-mail: ist@syr.edu.

See Close-Up on page 2135.

Syracuse University, Graduate School, School of Information Studies, Program in Information Security Management, Syracuse, NY 13244. Offers CAS. Part-time and evening/weekend programs available. Postbaccalaureate distance learning degree programs offered. *Students:* 1 (woman) full-time, 5 part-time (2 women), 1 international. 23 applicants, 91% accepted. *Application deadline:* For fall admission, 2/14 for domestic students. Application fee: $65. Electronic applications accepted. *Expenses:* Tuition: Full-time $16,920; part-time $940 per credit hour. Required fees: $930; $930 per year. *Unit head:* Jeffrey Stanton, Head, 315-443-2879, E-mail: jmstanto@syr.edu. *Application contact:* Susan Corieri, Director of Enrollment Management, 315-443-6885, E-mail: ist@syr.edu.

Syracuse University, Graduate School, School of Information Studies, Program in Information Systems and Telecommunications Management, Syracuse, NY 13244. Offers CAS. Part-time and evening/weekend programs available. Postbaccalaureate distance learning degree programs offered. *Students:* 4 full-time (1 woman), 15 part-time (6 women); includes 2 minority (1 African American, 1 Asian American or Pacific Islander), 3 international. 10 applicants, 80% accepted, 8 enrolled. *Application deadline:* For fall admission, 2/14 for domestic students. Application fee: $65. Electronic applications accepted. *Expenses:* Tuition: Full-time $16,920; part-time $940 per credit hour. Required fees: $930; $930 per year. *Unit head:* Dr. Bruce Kingma, Associate Dean, 315-443-7170. *Application contact:* Susan Corieri, Director of Enrollment Management, 315-443-6885, E-mail: ist@syr.edu.

See Close-Up on page 2135.

Syracuse University, Martin J. Whitman School of Management, PhD Program in Business Administration, Syracuse, NY 13244. Offers accounting (PhD); finance (PhD); management information systems (PhD); managerial statistics (PhD); marketing (PhD); operations management (PhD); organizational behavior (PhD); strategy and human resources (PhD); supply chain management (PhD). *Faculty:* 71 full-time (16 women), 2 part-time/adjunct (1 woman). *Students:* 34 full-time (10 women); includes 1 minority (African American), 24 international. Average age 31. 89 applicants, 8% accepted, 4 enrolled. In 2006, 8 degrees awarded. *Degree requirements:* For doctorate, thesis/dissertation, summer research paper, comprehensive exam, registration. *Entrance requirements:* For doctorate, GMAT, 3 recommendations. Additional exam requirements/recommendations for international students: Required—TOEFL (minimum score 600 paper-based; 250 computer-based; 100 iBT). *Application deadline:* For fall admission, 1/30 priority date for domestic students. Applications are processed on a rolling basis. Application fee: $75. Electronic applications accepted. *Expenses:* Tuition: Full-time $16,920; part-time $940 per credit hour. Required fees: $930; $930 per year. *Financial support:* In 2006–07, 1 fellowship with full tuition reimbursement (averaging $19,000 per year), 26 teaching assistantships with full tuition reimbursements (averaging $16,500 per year) were awarded; research assistantships with full tuition reimbursements, health care benefits and unspecified assistantships also available. Financial award application deadline: 1/30. *Faculty research:* Marketing models, market microstructure, supply chain, auditing, corporate governance. *Unit head:* Dr. Ravi Dharwadkar, Director of the PhD Program, 315-443-3386, E-mail: rdharwad@syr.edu. *Application contact:* Shannon Hiemstra, Assistant Director for PhD and Research Programs, 315-443-3549, Fax: 315-443-3671, E-mail: srhiemst@syr.edu.

Tarleton State University, College of Graduate Studies, College of Business Administration, Department of Computer Information Systems, Stephenville, TX 76402. Offers information systems (MS). Part-time and evening/weekend programs available. *Faculty:* 17 full-time (3 women), 4 part-time/adjunct (1 woman). *Students:* 26 full-time (8 women), 63 part-time (21 women); includes 26 minority (13 African Americans, 1 American Indian/Alaska Native, 6 Asian Americans or Pacific Islanders, 6 Hispanic Americans), 10 international. Average age 38. In

2006, 31 degrees awarded. *Entrance requirements:* For master's, GRE, minimum GPA of 3.0. *Application deadline:* For fall admission, 8/5 priority date for domestic students; for spring admission, 12/1 priority date for domestic students. Applications are processed on a rolling basis. Electronic applications accepted. *Financial support:* Research assistantships, teaching assistantships available. *Unit head:* Dr. Raja Iyer, Head, 254-968-9341, E-mail: iyer@tarleton.edu.

Temple University, Graduate School, Fox School of Business and Management, Doctoral Programs in Business, Philadelphia, PA 19122-6096. Offers accounting (PhD); economics (PhD); finance (PhD); general and strategic management (PhD); healthcare management (PhD); human resource administration (PhD); international business administration (PhD); management information systems (PhD); management science/operations research (PhD); marketing (PhD); risk, insurance, and health-care management (PhD); statistics (PhD); tourism (PhD). *Accreditation:* AACSB. *Entrance requirements:* For doctorate, GRE General Test, minimum GPA of 3.0, master's degree. Additional exam requirements/recommendations for international students: Required—TOEFL. *Expenses:* Tuition, state resident: full-time $12,264; part-time $511 per credit. Tuition, nonresident: full-time $17,904; part-time $746 per credit. Required fees: $84 per course. Tuition and fees vary according to program.

Temple University, Graduate School, Fox School of Business and Management, Masters Programs in Business, MBA Programs, Philadelphia, PA 19122-6096. Offers accounting (MBA); business administration (EMBA, MBA); e-business (MBA); economics (MBA); finance (MBA); general and strategic management (MBA); healthcare management (MBA); human resource administration (MBA); international business (IMBA); management information systems (MBA); management science/operations management (MBA); marketing (MBA); risk management and insurance (MBA); statistics (MBA). EMBA offered in Philadelphia, PA and Tokyo, Japan. *Accreditation:* AACSB. *Entrance requirements:* For master's, GMAT, minimum undergraduate GPA of 3.0. Additional exam requirements/recommendations for international students: Required—TOEFL. *Expenses:* Tuition, state resident: full-time $12,264; part-time $511 per credit. Tuition, nonresident: full-time $17,904; part-time $746 per credit. Required fees: $84 per course. Tuition and fees vary according to program.

Temple University, Graduate School, Fox School of Business and Management, Masters Programs in Business, MS Programs, Philadelphia, PA 19122-6096. Offers accounting and financial management (MS); actuarial science (MS); e-business (MS); finance (MS); healthcare financial management (MS); human resource administration (MS); management information systems (MS); management science/operations management (MS); marketing (MS); statistics (MS). *Accreditation:* AACSB. *Entrance requirements:* For master's, GRE General Test, minimum undergraduate GPA of 3.0. Additional exam requirements/recommendations for international students: Required—TOEFL. *Expenses:* Tuition, state resident: full-time $12,264; part-time $511 per credit. Tuition, nonresident: full-time $17,904; part-time $746 per credit. Required fees: $84 per course. Tuition and fees vary according to program.

Texas A&M International University, Office of Graduate Studies and Research, College of Business Administration, Division of International Business and Technology Studies, Laredo, TX 78041-1900. Offers information systems (MSIS); international trade (MBA). *Faculty:* 8 full-time (0 women), 1 part-time/adjunct (0 women). *Students:* 30 full-time (8 women), 14 part-time (5 women); includes 12 minority (all Hispanic Americans), 32 international. Average age 25. 81 applicants, 41% accepted, 20 enrolled. In 2006, 26 degrees awarded. *Degree requirements:* For master's, thesis (for some programs). *Entrance requirements:* For master's, GMAT or GRE General Test. Additional exam requirements/recommendations for international students: Required—TOEFL (minimum score 550 paper-based; 213 computer-based). *Application deadline:* For fall admission, 7/15 priority date for domestic students; for spring admission, 11/12 for domestic students. Applications are processed on a rolling basis. Application fee: $25. *Expenses:* Tuition, state resident: full-time $1,580. Tuition, nonresident: full-time $5,432. Required fees: $3,808. *Financial support:* In 2006–07, 33 students received support; fellowships, Federal Work-Study, institutionally sponsored loans, and scholarships/grants available. Support available to part-time students. *Unit head:* Dr. Ned Kock, Chair, 956-326-2521, Fax: 956-326-2494, E-mail: nedkock@tamiu.edu. *Application contact:* Imelda Lopez, Graduate Admissions Counselor, 956-326-2485, Fax: 956-326-2459, E-mail: lopez@tamiu.edu.

Texas A&M University, Mays Business School, Department of Information and Operations Management, College Station, TX 77843. Offers management information systems (MS, PhD); management science (PhD); production and operations management (PhD). *Faculty:* 21 full-time (5 women), 4 part-time/adjunct (0 women). *Students:* 173 full-time (66 women). Average age 31. In 2006, 74 master's, 3 doctorates awarded. Terminal master's awarded for partial completion of doctoral program. *Degree requirements:* For master's, comprehensive exam; for doctorate, thesis/dissertation. *Entrance requirements:* For master's, GMAT; for doctorate, GMAT or GRE General Test. Additional exam requirements/recommendations for international students: Required—TOEFL. *Application deadline:* For fall admission, 3/1 priority date for domestic students; for spring admission, 8/1 for domestic students. Applications are processed on a rolling basis. Application fee: $50 ($75 for international students). *Expenses:* Tuition, state resident: full-time $4,697. Tuition, nonresident: full-time $11,297. Required fees: $2,272. *Financial support:* In 2006–07, 51 students received support; fellowships, research assistantships, teaching assistantships, career-related internships or fieldwork, Federal Work-Study, and institutionally sponsored loans available. Financial award application deadline: 2/1. *Unit head:* Dr. E. Powell Robinson, Head, 979-846-1616. *Application contact:* Louise Darcey, Adviser, 979-845-0811, E-mail: msmisadvisor@tamu.edu.

Texas Tech University, Jerry S. Rawls College of Business Administration, Area of Information Systems and Quantitative Sciences, Lubbock, TX 79409. Offers business statistics (MS, PhD); health organization management (MS); management information systems (MS, PhD); production and operations management (MS, PhD). Part-time programs available. *Faculty:* 15 full-time (0 women). *Students:* 18 full-time (6 women), 6 part-time (1 woman); includes 2 minority (1 African American, 1 Hispanic American), 11 international. Average age 31. 32 applicants, 53% accepted, 11 enrolled. In 2006, 13 master's, 5 doctorates awarded. Terminal master's awarded for partial completion of doctoral program. *Degree requirements:* For master's, comprehensive exam or capstone course; for doctorate, thesis/dissertation, qualifying exams. *Entrance requirements:* For master's and doctorate, GMAT, holistic profile of academic credentials. Additional exam requirements/recommendations for international students: Required—TOEFL (minimum score 550 paper-based; 213 computer-based; 79 iBT). *Application deadline:* For fall admission, 7/1 priority date for domestic students, 3/1 priority date for international students; for spring admission, 11/1 priority date for domestic students, 9/1 priority date for international students. Applications are processed on a rolling basis. Application fee: $50 ($60 for international students). Electronic applications accepted. *Expenses:* Tuition, state resident: full-time $4,440. Tuition, nonresident: full-time $11,040. Required fees: $2,136. *Financial support:* In 2006–07, 2 research assistantships (averaging $8,000 per year), 9 teaching assistantships (averaging $16,930 per year) were awarded; Federal Work-Study, scholarships/grants, and unspecified assistantships also available. *Faculty research:* Database management systems, systems management and engineering, expert systems and adaptive knowledge-based sciences, statistical analysis and design. *Unit head:* Dr. James Hoffman, Area Coordinator, 806-742-3192, Fax: 806-742-3958, E-mail: james.hoffman@ttu.edu. *Application contact:* Cynthia D. Barnes, Director, Graduate Services Center, 806-742-3184, Fax: 806-742-3958, E-mail: ba_grad@ttu.edu.

Texas Tech University, Jerry S. Rawls College of Business Administration, Programs in Business Administration, Lubbock, TX 79409. Offers agricultural business (MBA); entrepreneurship (MBA); finance (MBA); general business (MBA); health organization management (MBA); international business (MBA); management and leadership skills (MBA); management information systems (MBA); marketing (MBA); statistics (MBA); JD/MBA; MBA/M Arch; MBA/MA; MBA/MD; MBA/MS. Part-time and evening/weekend programs available. *Students:* 65 full-time (16 women), 347 part-time (121 women); includes 74 minority (5 African Americans, 5 American Indian/Alaska Native, 24 Asian Americans or Pacific Islanders, 40 Hispanic Americans),

24 international. Average age 25. 382 applicants, 82% accepted, 244 enrolled. In 2006, 150 degrees awarded. *Degree requirements:* For master's, capstone course. *Entrance requirements:* For master's, GMAT, holistic review of academic credentials. Additional exam requirements/ recommendations for international students: Required—TOEFL (minimum score 550 paper-based; 213 computer-based; 79 iBT). *Application deadline:* For fall admission, 7/1 priority date for domestic students, 3/1 priority date for international students; for spring admission, 11/1 priority date for domestic students, 9/1 priority date for international students. Applications are processed on a rolling basis. Application fee: $50 ($60 for international students). Electronic applications accepted. *Expenses:* Tuition, state resident: full-time $4,440. Tuition, nonresident: full-time $11,040. Required fees: $2,136. *Financial support:* In 2006–07, 36 research assistantships (averaging $8,000 per year) were awarded; teaching assistantships, career-related internships or fieldwork, Federal Work-Study, scholarships/grants, health care benefits, and unspecified assistantships also available. Support available to part-time students. Financial award applicants required to submit FAFSA. *Unit head:* Dr. W. Jay Conover, Director, 806-742-1546, Fax: 806-742-3958, E-mail: jay.conover@ttu.edu. *Application contact:* Cynthia D. Barnes, Director, Graduate Services Center, 806-742-3184, Fax: 806-742-3958, E-mail: ba_grad@ttu.edu.

Touro University International, College of Business Administration, Program in Business Administration, Cypress, CA 90630. Offers business administration (PhD); conflict and negotiation management (MBA); criminal justice administration (MBA); entrepreneurship (MBA); finance (MBA); general management (MBA); human resource management (MBA); information technology management (MBA); international business (MBA); logistics management (MBA); public management (MBA); strategic leadership (MBA). Part-time and evening/weekend programs available. Postbaccalaureate distance learning degree programs offered (no on-campus study). In 2006, 631 master's, 30 doctorates awarded. *Degree requirements:* For doctorate, thesis/ dissertation, defense of dissertation, comprehensive exam. *Entrance requirements:* For master's, minimum GPA of 3.0; for doctorate, minimum GPA of 3.4, curriculum vitae, course work in research methods or statistics. Additional exam requirements/recommendations for international students: Required—TOEFL (minimum score 550 paper-based). *Application deadline:* Applications are processed on a rolling basis. Application fee: $75. Electronic applications accepted. *Expenses:* Tuition: Part-time $300 per credit hour. Tuition and fees vary according to course level and program.

Touro University International, College of Information Systems, Cypress, CA 90630. Offers business intelligence (Certificate); information systems (MS). Part-time and evening/weekend programs available. Postbaccalaureate distance learning degree programs offered (no on-campus study). In 2006, 129 degrees awarded. *Entrance requirements:* For master's, minimum GPA of 3.0, undergraduate degree completed within the past 5 years. Additional exam requirements/recommendations for international students: Required—TOEFL (minimum score 550 paper-based). *Expenses:* Tuition: Part-time $300 per credit hour. Tuition and fees vary according to course level and program. *Unit head:* Dr. Paul Watkins, Dean, 800-509-3901, Fax: 714-816-0367, E-mail: infocis@tourou.edu.

Towson University, Graduate School, Program in Applied Information Technology, Towson, MD 21252-0001. Offers applied information technology (MS, D Sc); information security and assurance (Certificate); information systems management (Certificate); Internet application development (Certificate); networking technologies (Certificate); software engineering (Certificate). *Students:* 44 full-time (13 women), 194 part-time (73 women); includes 46 African Americans, 17 Asian Americans or Pacific Islanders, 4 Hispanic Americans, 34 international. 74 applicants, 77% accepted, 29 enrolled. In 2006, 64 master's, 67 other advanced degrees awarded. *Entrance requirements:* For master's, minimum GPA of 3.0. Additional exam requirements/ recommendations for international students: Required—TOEFL (minimum score 550 paper-based). *Application deadline:* Applications are processed on a rolling basis. Application fee: $50. Electronic applications accepted. *Expenses:* Tuition, state resident: part-time $275 per unit. Tuition, nonresident: part-time $577 per unit. Required fees: $72 per unit. *Financial support:* Application deadline: 4/1. *Unit head:* Dr. Ali Behforooz, Graduate Program Director, 410-704-3035, Fax: 410-704-3868, E-mail: abehforooz@towson.edu. *Application contact:* 410-704-2501, Fax: 410-704-4675, E-mail: grads@towson.edu.

Towson University, Graduate School, Program in Information Systems Management, Towson, MD 21252-0001. Offers Certificate. Part-time and evening/weekend programs available. *Students:* 1; 1 African American. 1 applicant, 100% accepted, 0 enrolled. In 2006, 15 degrees awarded. Application fee: $50. Electronic applications accepted. *Expenses:* Tuition, state resident: part-time $275 per unit. Tuition, nonresident: part-time $577 per unit. Required fees: $72 per unit. *Financial support:* Application deadline: 4/1; *Unit head:* Dr. Ali Behforooz, Graduate Program Director, 410-704-3035, Fax: 410-704-3868, E-mail: abehforooz@towson.edu. *Application contact:* 410-704-2501, Fax: 410-704-4675, E-mail: grads@towson.edu.

United States International University, School of Business Administration, Nairobi, Kenya. Offers finance (MBA); information technology management (MBA); integrated studies (MBA); management and organizational development (MS); marketing (MBA); strategic management (MBA). Part-time and evening/weekend programs available. *Degree requirements:* For master's, thesis, registration. *Entrance requirements:* For master's, GMAT, 2 letters of reference, resumé. Additional exam requirements/recommendations for international students: Required—TOEFL (minimum score 550 paper-based; 213 computer-based). *Faculty research:* Marketing in small business enterprises, total quality management in Kenya.

Universidad del Turabo, Graduate Programs, School in Business Administration, Program in Management of Information Systems, Gurabo, PR 00778-3030. Offers DBA.

Université de Montréal, Faculty of Graduate Studies, Faculty of Arts and Sciences, Department of Computer Science and Operational Research, Montréal, QC H3C 3J7, Canada. Offers computer systems (M Sc, PhD); data processing (DESS). Part-time programs available. *Faculty:* 57 full-time (8 women), 8 part-time/adjunct (2 women). *Students:* 267 full-time (62 women), 16 part-time (5 women). 328 applicants, 23% accepted, 60 enrolled. In 2006, 48 master's, 7 doctorates, 12 other advanced degrees awarded. Terminal master's awarded for partial completion of doctoral program. *Degree requirements:* For master's, one foreign language, thesis; for doctorate, one foreign language, thesis/dissertation, general exam. *Entrance requirements:* For master's, B Sc in related field; for doctorate, MA or M Sc in related field. *Application deadline:* For fall admission, 2/1 priority date for domestic students; for winter admission, 11/1 priority date for domestic students; for spring admission, 2/1 priority date for domestic students. Application fee: $30. Electronic applications accepted. *Financial support:* Available to part-time students. Application deadline: 10/31. *Faculty research:* Optimization statistics, programming languages, telecommunications, theoretical computer science, artificial intelligence. *Unit head:* Jean Meunier, Chairperson, 514-343-7090, Fax: 514-343-5834. *Application contact:* Jean-Yves Potvin, Information Contact, 514-343-7093, Fax: 514-343-5834.

Université de Sherbrooke, Faculty of Administration, Program in Management Information Systems, Sherbrooke, QC J1K 2R1, Canada. Offers M Sc.

Université de Sherbrooke, Faculty of Sciences, Centre de Formation en Technologies de L'information, Sherbrooke, QC J1K 2R1, Canada. Offers M Sc, Diploma. Electronic applications accepted.

Université du Québec à Montréal, Graduate Programs, Program in Management Information Systems, Montréal, QC H3C 3P8, Canada. Offers M Sc, M Sc A. Part-time programs available. *Entrance requirements:* For master's, appropriate bachelor's degree or equivalent and proficiency in French.

Université Laval, Faculty of Administrative Sciences, Programs in Business Administration, Québec, QC G1K 7P4, Canada. Offers accounting (MBA); agri-food management (MBA); electronic business (MBA, Diploma); factory management and logistics (MBA); finance (MBA); firm management (MBA); information technology management (MBA); international management (MBA); management (MBA); management accounting (MBA, Diploma); marketing (MBA); modelization and organizational decision (MBA); occupational health and safety management (MBA); pharmacy management (MBA); technological entrepreneurship (Diploma). *Accreditation:* AACSB. Part-time and evening/weekend programs available. Postbaccalaureate distance learning degree programs offered (no on-campus study). *Entrance requirements:* For master's and Diploma, knowledge of French and English. Electronic applications accepted.

University at Buffalo, the State University of New York, Graduate School, School of Management, Buffalo, NY 14260. Offers accounting (MS); business administration (MBA); finance (MS); information assurance (Certificate); management (PhD); management information systems (MS); supply chains and operations management (MS); Au D/MBA; JD/MBA; M Arch/MBA; MA/MBA; MD/MBA; MPH/MBA; MSW/MBA; Pharm D/MBA. *Accreditation:* AACSB. Part-time and evening/weekend programs available. *Faculty:* 65 full-time (18 women), 30 part-time/adjunct (3 women). *Students:* 493 full-time (192 women), 212 part-time (55 women); includes 53 minority (11 African Americans, 3 American Indian/Alaska Native, 31 Asian Americans or Pacific Islanders, 8 Hispanic Americans), 283 international. Average age 27. 1,058 applicants, 55% accepted, 369 enrolled. In 2006, 260 master's, 5 doctorates, 3 other advanced degrees awarded. *Degree requirements:* For doctorate, thesis/dissertation, comprehensive exam. *Entrance requirements:* For master's, GMAT, GRE General Test (all master's degrees except accounting); for doctorate, GMAT or GRE. Additional exam requirements/recommendations for international students: Required—TOEFL (minimum score 230 computer-based). *Application deadline:* For fall admission, 6/1 priority date for domestic students, 3/1 priority date for international students. Applications are processed on a rolling basis. Application fee: $50. Electronic applications accepted. *Expenses:* Contact institution. *Financial support:* In 2006–07, 91 students received support, including 17 fellowships with full and partial tuition reimbursements available (averaging $3,917 per year), 38 research assistantships with full and partial tuition reimbursements available (averaging $11,907 per year), 26 teaching assistantships with full and partial tuition reimbursements available (averaging $7,571 per year); career-related internships or fieldwork, Federal Work-Study, institutionally sponsored loans, scholarships/ grants, health care benefits, and unspecified assistantships also available. Financial award application deadline: 2/15; financial award applicants required to submit FAFSA. *Faculty research:* Information assurance, relationship marketing, global processes, credit analysis in banking, disaster mitigation and response. Total annual research expenditures: $330,551. *Unit head:* John M. Thomas, Dean, 716-645-3221, Fax: 716-645-5926, E-mail: jmthomas@buffalo.edu. *Application contact:* David W. Frasier, Administrative Director of Graduate Programs and Assistant Dean, 716-645-3204, Fax: 716-645-2341, E-mail: davidf@buffalo.edu.

The University of Akron, Graduate School, College of Business Administration, Department of Management, Program in Management-Information Systems, Akron, OH 44325. Offers MSM. *Students:* 12 full-time (7 women), 10 part-time (3 women); includes 1 minority (Asian American or Pacific Islander), 13 international. Average age 29. 18 applicants, 50% accepted, 9 enrolled. In 2006, 6 degrees awarded. *Entrance requirements:* For master's, GMAT, minimum GPA of 2.75. Additional exam requirements/recommendations for international students: Required—TOEFL (minimum score 550 paper-based; 213 computer-based; 79 iBT). *Application deadline:* For fall admission, 8/15 for domestic students. Applications are processed on a rolling basis. Application fee: $30 ($40 for international students). Electronic applications accepted. *Expenses:* Tuition, state resident: full-time $6,164; part-time $342 per credit. Tuition, nonresident: full-time $10,575; part-time $588 per credit. Required fees: $806; $43 per credit. $12 per term. Tuition and fees vary according to course load, degree level and program. *Unit head:* Dr. B.S. Vijayaraman, Head, 330-972-5442, E-mail: bsv@uakron.edu.

The University of Alabama in Huntsville, School of Graduate Studies, College of Administrative Science, Department of Management Information Systems, Huntsville, AL 35899. Offers MSMIS, Certificate. Part-time and evening/weekend programs available. *Faculty:* 6 full-time (1 woman), 2 part-time/adjunct (0 women). *Students:* 9 full-time (5 women), 26 part-time (7 women); includes 1 American Indian/Alaska Native, 2 international. Average age 29. 19 applicants, 63% accepted, 11 enrolled. In 2006, 17 degrees awarded. *Degree requirements:* For master's, thesis or alternative, comprehensive exam, registration. *Entrance requirements:* For master's, GMAT, minimum AACSB index of 1000. Additional exam requirements/ recommendations for international students: Required—TOEFL (minimum score 550 paper-based; 213 computer-based). *Application deadline:* For fall admission, 8/10 for domestic students; for spring admission, 12/10 for domestic students. Application fee: $40. *Expenses:* Tuition, state resident: full-time $6,072; part-time $253 per credit hour. Tuition, nonresident: full-time $12,476; part-time $519 per credit hour. *Financial support:* In 2006–07, 2 students received support, including 2 fellowships (averaging $5,400 per year); research assistantships, teaching assistantships with full and partial tuition reimbursements available, career-related internships or fieldwork, Federal Work-Study, institutionally sponsored loans, scholarships/ grants, health care benefits, and unspecified assistantships also available. Support available to part-time students. Financial award application deadline: 4/1; financial award applicants required to submit FAFSA. *Unit head:* Dr. Allen W. Wilhite, Chair, 256-824-6591, Fax: 256-824-6328, E-mail: wilhitea@uah.edu.

The University of Alabama in Huntsville, School of Graduate Studies, Interdisciplinary Program in Information Assurance, Huntsville, AL 35899. Offers Certificate. Part-time and evening/weekend programs available. *Students:* 1 full-time (0 women), 18 part-time (5 women); includes 2 minority (both Hispanic Americans) 13 applicants, 100% accepted, 12 enrolled. *Entrance requirements:* For degree, GMAT. Additional exam requirements/recommendations for international students: Required—TOEFL (minimum score 550 paper-based; 213 computer-based). *Application deadline:* For fall admission, 8/10 priority date for domestic students, 6/1 priority date for international students; for spring admission, 12/10 priority date for domestic students, 10/1 priority date for international students. Application fee: $40. *Expenses:* Tuition, state resident: full-time $6,072; part-time $253 per credit hour. Tuition, nonresident: full-time $12,476; part-time $519 per credit hour. *Financial support:* Career-related internships or fieldwork, Federal Work-Study, institutionally sponsored loans, scholarships/grants, health care benefits, and unspecified assistantships available. Support available to part-time students. *Application contact:* Kathy Biggs, Manager, 256-824-6199, Fax: 256-824-6405, E-mail: deangrad@uah.edu.

The University of Arizona, Graduate College, College of Business and Public Administration, Eller Graduate School of Management, Department of Management Information Systems, Tucson, AZ 85721. Offers management (PhD); management information systems (MS). *Degree requirements:* For master's, thesis or alternative. *Entrance requirements:* For master's, GMAT, GRE General Test, minimum GPA of 3.0; for doctorate, GMAT, GRE, minimum GPA of 3.5. Additional exam requirements/recommendations for international students: Required—TOEFL. *Faculty research:* Group decision support systems, domestic and international computing issues, expert systems, data management and structures.

University of Arkansas, Graduate School, Sam M. Walton College of Business Administration, Department of Information Systems, Fayetteville, AR 72701-1201. Offers MIS. Part-time and evening/weekend programs available. *Students:* 13 full-time (7 women), 30 part-time (5 women); includes 5 minority (all Asian Americans or Pacific Islanders), 14 international. 27 applicants, 74% accepted. In 2006, 22 degrees awarded. *Entrance requirements:* For master's, GMAT. Application fee: $40 ($50 for international students). *Financial support:* In 2006–07, 8 fellowships with tuition reimbursements, 19 research assistantships, 5 teaching assistantships were awarded. Financial award application deadline: 4/1. *Unit head:* Fred Davis, Head, 479-575-4500. *Application contact:* Paul Cronan, Graduate Coordinator, 479-575-6130, E-mail: pcronan@walton.uark.edu.

University of Arkansas at Little Rock, Graduate School, College of Business Administration, Little Rock, AR 72204-1099. Offers business administration (MBA); management information system (MIS); JD/MBA. *Accreditation:* AACSB. Part-time and evening/weekend programs available. *Entrance requirements:* For master's, GMAT, minimum undergraduate GPA of 2.7. Additional exam requirements/recommendations for international students: Required—TOEFL (minimum score 525 paper-based; 195 computer-based).

Management Information Systems

University of Baltimore, Graduate School, Merrick School of Business, Department of Information and Quantitative Sciences, Baltimore, MD 21201-5779. Offers business/management information systems (MS). Part-time and evening/weekend programs available. *Faculty:* 11 full-time (3 women), 5 part-time/adjunct (0 women). *Students:* 2 full-time (1 woman), 4 part-time (1 woman); includes 2 minority (1 African American, 1 Asian American or Pacific Islander), 3 international. Average age 31. 38 applicants, 55% accepted. In 2006, 3 degrees awarded. *Entrance requirements:* For master's, GMAT. Additional exam requirements/recommendations for international students: Required—TOEFL (minimum score 550 paper-based; 213 computer-based). *Application deadline:* For fall admission, 8/1 priority date for domestic students, 6/1 for international students; for spring admission, 12/1 for domestic students, 11/1 for international students. Applications are processed on a rolling basis. Application fee: $30. Electronic applications accepted. *Expenses:* Tuition, state resident: full-time $5,322; part-time $591 per credit. Tuition, nonresident: full-time $7,527; part-time $830 per credit. *Financial support:* In 2006–07, 3 research assistantships were awarded; fellowships, career-related internships or fieldwork and Federal Work-Study also available. Support available to part-time students. Financial award application deadline: 4/1; financial award applicants required to submit FAFSA. *Faculty research:* Simulation and mathematical programming, health care information systems, Internet/World Wide Web, group decision making. Total annual research expenditures: $2,350. *Application contact:* Dean Dreibelbis, Assistant Director, Office of Graduate Admissions, 410-837-6565, Fax: 410-837-4793, E-mail: gradadmissions@ubalt.edu.

The University of British Columbia, Sauder School of Business, Doctoral Program in Commerce and Business Administration, Vancouver, BC V6T 1Z1, Canada. Offers accounting (PhD); finance (PhD); international business (PhD); management information systems (PhD); management science (PhD); marketing (PhD); organizational behavior (PhD); policy analysis and strategy (PhD); transportation and logistics (PhD); urban land economics (PhD). *Degree requirements:* For doctorate, thesis/dissertation, comprehensive exam. *Entrance requirements:* For doctorate, GMAT or GRE. Additional exam requirements/recommendations for international students: Required—TOEFL. Electronic applications accepted.

University of Central Florida, College of Business Administration, Department of Management Information Systems, Orlando, FL 32816. Offers MS. *Faculty:* 13 full-time (2 women), 1 (woman) part-time/adjunct. *Students:* 15 full-time (6 women), 46 part-time (12 women); includes 14 minority (2 African Americans, 5 Asian Americans or Pacific Islanders, 7 Hispanic Americans), 6 international. Average age 29. In 2006, 36 master's awarded. *Degree requirements:* For master's, thesis or alternative. *Entrance requirements:* For master's, GMAT or GRE General Test, minimum GPA of 3.0 in last 60 hours, letters of recommendation. Additional exam requirements/recommendations for international students: Required—TOEFL. *Application deadline:* For fall admission, 2/15 priority date for domestic students; for spring admission, 11/1 for domestic students. Application fee: $30. Electronic applications accepted. *Expenses:* Tuition, state resident: full-time $6,167; part-time $257 per credit hour. Tuition, nonresident: full-time $22,790; part-time $950 per credit hour. *Financial support:* In 2006–07, 3 research assistantships with partial tuition reimbursements (averaging $13,000 per year) were awarded; fellowships with partial tuition reimbursements, teaching assistantships with partial tuition reimbursements also available. *Unit head:* Dr. Paul Cheney, Chair, 407-823-3106, E-mail: paul.cheney@bus.ucf.edu.

University of Central Missouri, The Graduate School, Harmon College of Business Administration, Department of Computer Information Systems, Warrensburg, MO 64093. Offers information technology (MS). Part-time programs available. *Faculty:* 5 full-time (1 woman). *Students:* 30 full-time (2 women), 7 part-time (1 woman); includes 6 minority (1 African American, 5 Asian Americans or Pacific Islanders), 19 international. Average age 27. 14 applicants, 100% accepted, 14 enrolled. In 2006, 13 degrees awarded. *Degree requirements:* For master's, internship. *Entrance requirements:* For master's, GMAT or GRE, minimum undergraduate GPA of 2.5. Additional exam requirements/recommendations for international students: Required—TOEFL (minimum score 500 paper-based; 173 computer-based). *Application deadline:* For fall admission, 6/1 priority date for domestic students, 5/1 priority date for international students; for spring admission, 10/1 priority date for domestic students, 10/1 for international students. Applications are processed on a rolling basis. Application fee: $30 ($50 for international students). *Expenses:* Tuition, state resident: full-time $5,448; part-time $227 per credit hour. Tuition, nonresident: full-time $10,896; part-time $454 per credit hour. Required fees: $336; $14 per credit hour. *Financial support:* In 2006–07, 5 students received support. Career-related internships or fieldwork, Federal Work-Study, scholarships/grants, unspecified assistantships, and administrative and laboratory assistantships available. Support available to part-time students. Financial award application deadline: 3/1; financial award applicants required to submit FAFSA. *Faculty research:* Software engineering, network security, management information systems, e-commerce. *Unit head:* Dr. Mustafa Kamal, Chair, 660-543-4767, E-mail: kamal@ucmo.edu.

University of Cincinnati, Division of Research and Advanced Studies, College of Business, Department of Information Systems, Cincinnati, OH 45221. Offers e-business (MBA); information systems (MBA, MS); MBA/MS. *Degree requirements:* For master's, thesis or alternative, capstone project (MBA). *Entrance requirements:* For master's, GMAT, GRE General Test (information systems), resumé, letters of recommendation. Additional exam requirements/recommendations for international students: Required—TOEFL (minimum score 600 paper-based; 250 computer-based). Application fee: $40. *Expenses: Contact institution. Financial support:* Fellowships, research assistantships, teaching assistantships with full and partial tuition reimbursements, scholarships/grants, tuition waivers (full and partial), and unspecified assistantships available. Financial award application deadline: 2/1; financial award applicants required to submit FAFSA. *Unit head:* Dr. Vivek Choudhury, Head, 513-556-7115, E-mail: vivek.choudhury@uc.edu.

University of Colorado at Colorado Springs, Graduate School, Graduate School of Business Administration, Colorado Springs, CO 80933-7150. Offers accounting (MBA); finance (MBA); general health care administration (MBA); information systems (MBA); international business management (MBA); marketing (MBA); service management/technology management (MBA). *Accreditation:* AACSB. Part-time and evening/weekend programs available. *Faculty:* 15 full-time (4 women), 4 part-time/adjunct (0 women). *Students:* 158 full-time (70 women), 290 part-time (87 women); includes 48 minority (11 African Americans, 1 American Indian/Alaska Native, 20 Asian Americans or Pacific Islanders, 16 Hispanic Americans), 7 international. Average age 33. 158 applicants, 75% accepted, 51 enrolled. In 2006, 119 degrees awarded. *Entrance requirements:* For master's, GMAT. *Application deadline:* For fall admission, 6/1 for domestic students; for spring admission, 11/1 for domestic students. Application fee: $60 ($75 for international students). *Expenses: Contact institution.* Tuition and fees vary according to course load, campus/location and program. *Financial support:* Career-related internships or fieldwork, Federal Work-Study, and institutionally sponsored loans available. Support available to part-time students. Financial award applicants required to submit FAFSA. *Faculty research:* Quality financial reporting, investments and corporate governance, group support systems, environmental and project management, customer relationship management. Total annual research expenditures: $99,250. *Unit head:* Dr. Venkateshwar Reddy, Dean, 719-262-3113, Fax: 719-262-3494, E-mail: vreddy@uccs.edu. *Application contact:* Amy DeLourenco, MBA Program Director, 719-262-3408, Fax: 719-262-3100, E-mail: busadvsr@uccs.edu.

University of Colorado at Denver and Health Sciences Center, Business School, Program in Computer Science and Information Systems, Denver, CO 80217-3364. Offers PhD. *Students:* 4 full-time (1 woman), 13 part-time (4 women); includes 2 minority (both Asian Americans or Pacific Islanders), 6 international. 11 applicants, 73% accepted, 3 enrolled. *Degree requirements:* For doctorate, thesis/dissertation, comprehensive exam. *Entrance requirements:* For doctorate, GMAT or GRE General Test, minimum undergraduate GPA of 3.0, graduate 3.5; resumé. Additional exam requirements/recommendations for international students: Required—TOEFL (minimum score 525 paper-based; 197 computer-based). *Application deadline:* For fall admission, 6/1 for domestic students, 3/15 for international students; for spring admission, 11/1 for domestic students, 10/1 for international students. Application fee: $50 ($75 for international students). Electronic applications accepted. *Financial support:* Federal Work-Study, institutionally sponsored loans, and scholarships/grants available. Support available to part-time students. Financial award application deadline: 4/1; financial award applicants required to submit FAFSA. *Unit head:* Dr. Jahangir Karimi, Head, 303-556-5881, Fax: 303-556-5899, E-mail: jahangir.karimi@cudenver.edu. *Application contact:* Shelly Townley, Admissions Coordinator, 303-556-5956, Fax: 303-556-5904, E-mail: shelly.townley@cudenver.edu.

University of Colorado at Denver and Health Sciences Center, Business School, Program in Information Systems, Denver, CO 80217-3364. Offers MS. Part-time and evening/weekend programs available. *Students:* 7 full-time (3 women), 62 part-time (22 women); includes 15 minority (3 African Americans, 8 Asian Americans or Pacific Islanders, 4 Hispanic Americans), 12 international. Average age 30. 13 applicants, 69% accepted, 9 enrolled. In 2006, 20 degrees awarded. *Entrance requirements:* For master's, GMAT. Additional exam requirements/recommendations for international students: Required—TOEFL (minimum score 525 paper-based; 197 computer-based). *Application deadline:* For fall admission, 6/1 for domestic students, 3/15 for international students; for spring admission, 11/1 priority date for domestic students, 10/1 for international students. Applications are processed on a rolling basis. Application fee: $50 ($75 for international students). Electronic applications accepted. *Financial support:* Federal Work-Study, institutionally sponsored loans, and scholarships/grants available. Support available to part-time students. Financial award application deadline: 4/1; financial award applicants required to submit FAFSA. *Faculty research:* Human-computer interaction, expert systems, database management, electronic commerce, object-oriented software development. *Unit head:* Dr. Jahangir Karimi, Director, 303-556-5881, Fax: 303-556-5899, E-mail: jahangir.karimi@cudenver.edu. *Application contact:* Shelly Townley, Admissions Coordinator, 303-556-5956, Fax: 303-556-5904, E-mail: shelly.townley@cudenver.edu.

University of Dallas, Graduate School of Management, Irving, TX 75062-4736. Offers accounting (MBA, MS); business management (MBA); corporate finance (MBA, MM); engineering management (MBA, MM); entrepreneurship (MBA, MM); financial services (MBA, MM); global business (MBA, MM); health services management (MBA, MM); human resource management (MBA, MM, MS); information assurance (MBA, MM, MS); information technology (MBA, MM, MS); information technology service management (MBA); IT service management (MS); marketing (MM); marketing management (MBA); not-for-profit management (MBA); organization development (MBA); project management (MBA, MM); sports and entertainment management (MBA, MM); strategic leadership (MBA); supply chain management (MBA); supply chain management and market logistics (MM); telecommunications management (MBA, MM). *Accreditation:* ACBSP. Part-time and evening/weekend programs available. Postbaccalaureate distance learning degree programs offered (no on-campus study). *Faculty:* 26 full-time (5 women), 85 part-time/adjunct (18 women). *Students:* 227 full-time (98 women), 1,160 part-time (446 women); includes 473 minority (209 African Americans, 3 American Indian/Alaska Native, 143 Asian Americans or Pacific Islanders, 118 Hispanic Americans), 224 international. Average age 34. 556 applicants, 86% accepted, 291 enrolled. In 2006, 476 degrees awarded. *Entrance requirements:* Additional exam requirements/recommendations for international students: Required—TOEFL. *Application deadline:* Applications are processed on a rolling basis. Application fee: $50. Electronic applications accepted. *Expenses: Contact institution. Financial support:* In 2006–07, 468 students received support. Scholarships/grants and unspecified assistantships available. Financial award application deadline: 2/15; financial award applicants required to submit FAFSA. *Unit head:* Dr. J. Lee Whittington, Dean, 972-721-5230. *Application contact:* Sarah Stivison, Director of Graduate Admissions, 972-721-5198, Fax: 972-721-4009, E-mail: admiss@gsm.udallas.edu.

University of Delaware, Alfred Lerner College of Business and Economics, Department of Accounting and Management Information Systems and Department of Electrical and Computer Engineering, Program in Information Systems and Technology Management, Newark, DE 19716. Offers MS. Part-time and evening/weekend programs available. *Faculty:* 7 full-time (2 women). *Students:* Average age 28. 13 applicants, 62% accepted, 5 enrolled. In 2006, 5 degrees awarded. *Entrance requirements:* For master's, GRE or GMAT, 2 letters of recommendation, resumé, minimum GPA of 2.75. Additional exam requirements/recommendations for international students: Required—TOEFL (minimum score 600 paper-based; 250 computer-based). *Application deadline:* For fall admission, 5/1 priority date for domestic students, 5/1 for international students. Application fee: $60. *Financial support:* In 2006–07, 2 students received support, including 2 research assistantships with partial tuition reimbursements available (averaging $13,000 per year); career-related internships or fieldwork and tuition waivers (partial) also available. Financial award application deadline: 2/1; financial award applicants required to submit FAFSA. *Faculty research:* Security, developer trust, XML. Total annual research expenditures: $50,000. *Unit head:* Dr. Clinton White, Area Head, 302-831-6902, Fax: 302-831-4676, E-mail: whitec@lerner.udel.edu.

See Close-Up on page 615.

University of Denver, Daniels College of Business, Department of Information Technology and Electronic Commerce, Denver, CO 80208. Offers IMBA, MBA. Part-time and evening/weekend programs available. *Faculty:* 8 full-time (2 women). *Students:* 11 full-time (3 women), 26 part-time (7 women); includes 5 minority (4 Asian Americans or Pacific Islanders, 1 Hispanic American), 8 international. Average age 30. 18 applicants, 72% accepted. In 2006, 34 degrees awarded. *Entrance requirements:* For master's, GMAT. *Application deadline:* For fall admission, 1/15 priority date for domestic students. Applications are processed on a rolling basis. Application fee: $50. Electronic applications accepted. *Expenses:* Tuition: Full-time $29,628; part-time $823 per credit. *Financial support:* Career-related internships or fieldwork, Federal Work-Study, institutionally sponsored loans, and scholarships/grants available. Support available to part-time students. Financial award application deadline: 2/15. *Faculty research:* Cross-cultural research in information systems, electronic commerce, distributed project management, strategic information systems, management of emerging technologies. *Unit head:* Dr. Dick Scudder, Chair, 303-871-2197. *Application contact:* Information Contact, 303-871-3416, Fax: 303-871-4466, E-mail: daniels@du.edu.

University of Detroit Mercy, College of Business Administration, Program in Computer Information Systems, Detroit, MI 48221. Offers MSCIS. Part-time and evening/weekend programs available. *Faculty:* 3 full-time (1 woman). *Students:* 45 full-time (16 women), 45 part-time (28 women); includes 18 minority (all African Americans), 55 international. Average age 29. In 2006, 63 degrees awarded. *Degree requirements:* For master's, thesis or alternative. *Entrance requirements:* For master's, minimum GPA of 3.75. *Application deadline:* For fall admission, 8/1 priority date for domestic students. Applications are processed on a rolling basis. Application fee: $30 ($50 for international students). *Expenses:* Tuition: Full-time $15,750; part-time $875 per credit hour. Required fees: $570. *Financial support:* Research assistantships available. Financial award application deadline: 8/1. *Application contact:* Dr. Bonnie Naski, Coordinator for Graduate Programs, 313-993-1202, Fax: 313-993-1052, E-mail: mba@udmercy.edu.

University of Florida, Graduate School, Warrington College of Business Administration, Department of Information Systems and Operations Management, Gainesville, FL 32611. Offers decision and information sciences (MS, PhD); supply chain management (MS). *Faculty:* 13 full-time (2 women). *Students:* 118 (38 women); includes 22 minority (8 African Americans, 8 Asian Americans or Pacific Islanders, 6 Hispanic Americans) 38 international. In 2006, 5 degrees awarded. Terminal master's awarded for partial completion of doctoral program. *Degree requirements:* For doctorate, thesis/dissertation. *Entrance requirements:* For master's and doctorate, GMAT or GRE General Test, minimum GPA of 3.0. Additional exam requirements/recommendations for international students: Required—TOEFL (minimum score 550 paper-based; 213 computer-based). *Application deadline:* For fall admission, 2/16 priority date for domestic students. Applications are processed on a rolling basis. Application fee: $30. *Expenses:* Tuition, state resident: full-time $6,827. Tuition, nonresident: full-time $21,951. Required fees: $999. *Financial support:* In 2006–07, 1 research assistantship (averaging $20,376 per year), 10 teaching assistantships (averaging $18,437 per year) were awarded; fellowships, unspecified assistantships also available. *Faculty research:* Expert systems, nonconvex optimization, manufacturing management, production and operation management, telecommunication. *Unit head:* Dr. Asoo J. Vakharia, Chair, 352-392-8571, Fax: 352-392-5438, E-mail: asoov@ufl.edu. *Application contact:* Chandra Hardy, Coordinator, 352-846-1370, Fax: 352-392-5438, E-mail: chandra.hardy@cba.ufl.edu.

University of Hawaii at Manoa, Graduate Division, Colleges of Arts and Sciences, College of Social Sciences, School of Communications, Program in Telecommunication and Information Resource Management, Honolulu, HI 96822. Offers Graduate Certificate. *Students:* 7 applicants, 43% accepted, 2 enrolled. *Entrance requirements:* Additional exam requirements/recommendations for international students: Required—TOEFL (minimum score 500 paper-based; 173 computer-based; 61 iBT). *Application deadline:* For fall admission, 5/1 for domestic and international students; for spring admission, 10/1 for domestic and international students. Application fee: $50. *Application contact:* Don Wedemeyer, Information Contact, 808-956-2854, Fax: 808-956-5591.

University of Hawaii at Manoa, Graduate Division, Shidler College of Business, Program in Accounting, Honolulu, HI 96822. Offers accounting (M Acc); accounting law (M Acc); information systems (M Acc); taxation (M Acc). Part-time programs available. *Faculty:* 10 full-time (3 women). *Students:* 38 full-time (21 women), 17 part-time (14 women); includes 14 minority (13 Asian Americans or Pacific Islanders, 1 Hispanic American), 5 international. Average age 32. 52 applicants, 60% accepted, 18 enrolled. In 2006, 38 degrees awarded. *Entrance requirements:* For master's, GMAT, bachelor's degree in accounting, minimum GPA of 3.0. Additional exam requirements/recommendations for international students: Required—TOEFL (minimum score 520 paper-based; 213 computer-based; 79 iBT). *Application deadline:* For fall admission, 5/1 for domestic students, 3/1 for international students; for spring admission, 9/1 for domestic and international students. Application fee: $50. *Financial support:* In 2006–07, 1 research assistantship (averaging $15,552 per year) was awarded; career-related internships or fieldwork, Federal Work-Study, and tuition waivers (full) also available. *Faculty research:* International accounting, current tax topics, insurance industry financial reporting, behavioral accounting, auditing. Total annual research expenditures: $15,000. *Application contact:* Jenny Teruya, Information Contact, 808-956-7118, Fax: 808-956-9888, E-mail: hamid@hawaii.edu.

University of Hawaii at Manoa, Graduate Division, Shidler College of Business, Program in Business Administration, Honolulu, HI 96822. Offers Asian business studies (MBA); Chinese business studies (MBA); decision sciences (MBA); entrepreneurship (MBA); finance (MBA); finance and banking (MBA); human resources management (MBA); information management (MBA); information technology (MBA); international business (MBA); Japanese business studies (MBA); marketing (MBA); organizational behavior (MBA); organizational management (MBA); real estate (MBA); student-designed track (MBA). *Accreditation:* AACSB. Part-time programs available. *Faculty:* 48 full-time (9 women). *Students:* 207 full-time (77 women), 158 part-time (60 women); includes 93 minority (2 African Americans, 1 American Indian/Alaska Native, 88 Asian Americans or Pacific Islanders, 2 Hispanic Americans), 58 international. Average age 33. 235 applicants, 55% accepted, 68 enrolled. In 2006, 147 degrees awarded. *Degree requirements:* For master's, thesis optional. *Entrance requirements:* For master's, GMAT, minimum GPA of 3.0. Additional exam requirements/recommendations for international students: Required—TOEFL (minimum score 500 paper-based; 173 computer-based; 61 iBT). *Application deadline:* For fall admission, 5/1 for domestic and international students; for spring admission, 9/1 for domestic and international students. Application fee: $50. *Financial support:* In 2006–07, 7 research assistantships (averaging $17,409 per year), 3 teaching assistantships (averaging $14,028 per year) were awarded. *Application contact:* Ting Bui, Information Contact, 808-956-5565, Fax: 808-956-6889.

University of Hawaii at Manoa, Graduate Division, Shidler College of Business, Program in International Management, Honolulu, HI 96822. Offers Asian finance (PhD); global information technology management (PhD); international accounting (PhD); international marketing (PhD); international organization and strategy (PhD). *Faculty:* 42 full-time (8 women). *Students:* 36 applicants, 19% accepted, 4 enrolled. In 2006, 5 degrees awarded. *Median time to degree:* Of those who began their doctoral program in fall 1998, 33% received their degree in 8 years or less. *Degree requirements:* For doctorate, thesis/dissertation, comprehensive exam. *Entrance requirements:* For doctorate, GMAT or GRE General Test, minimum GPA of 3.0. Additional exam requirements/recommendations for international students: Required—TOEFL (minimum score 600 paper-based; 250 computer-based; 100 iBT). *Application deadline:* For fall admission, 3/1 for domestic and international students. Application fee: $50. *Financial support:* In 2006–07, 16 research assistantships (averaging $18,198 per year), 3 teaching assistantships (averaging $14,958 per year) were awarded. Total annual research expenditures: $3.3 million. *Application contact:* Ting Bui, Information Contact, 808-956-6723, Fax: 808-956-2774.

University of Houston–Clear Lake, School of Business, Program in Management Information Systems, Houston, TX 77058-1098. Offers MS. *Students:* 18 full-time, 28 part-time; includes 16 minority (5 African Americans, 6 Asian Americans or Pacific Islanders, 5 Hispanic Americans), 13 international. 49 applicants, 59% accepted, 14 enrolled. In 2006, 25 degrees awarded. *Entrance requirements:* For master's, GMAT. Additional exam requirements/recommendations for international students: Required—TOEFL (minimum score 550 paper-based; 213 computer-based). *Unit head:* Dr. Naveed Saleem, Professor, 281-283-3202, Fax: 281-283-3951, E-mail: saleem@uhcl.edu.

University of Illinois at Chicago, Graduate College, Liautaud Graduate School of Business, Department of Information and Decision Sciences, Chicago, IL 60607-7128. Offers management information systems (MS, PhD). Part-time and evening/weekend programs available. *Degree requirements:* For doctorate, thesis/dissertation. *Entrance requirements:* For doctorate, GMAT, minimum GPA of 2.75. Additional exam requirements/recommendations for international students: Required—TOEFL. Electronic applications accepted.

University of Illinois at Springfield, Graduate Programs, College of Business and Management, Program in Management Information Systems, Springfield, IL 62703-5407. Offers MS. Part-time and evening/weekend programs available. Postbaccalaureate distance learning degree programs offered (no on-campus study). *Faculty:* 8 full-time (1 woman), 1 (woman) part-time/adjunct. *Students:* 17 full-time (6 women), 125 part-time (35 women); includes 26 minority (11 African Americans, 1 American Indian/Alaska Native, 10 Asian Americans or Pacific Islanders, 4 Hispanic Americans), 12 international. Average age 37. 116 applicants, 55% accepted, 27 enrolled. In 2006, 45 degrees awarded. *Degree requirements:* For master's, project and closure seminar. *Entrance requirements:* For master's, GMAT or GRE General Test, course work in managerial and financial accountancy; 1 semester of course work in each productions/operations management, statistics, and college algebra or math. Additional exam requirements/recommendations for international students: Required—TOEFL (minimum score 550 paper-based; 213 computer-based). *Application deadline:* Applications are processed on a rolling basis. Application fee: $50 ($60 for international students). Electronic applications accepted. *Expenses:* Tuition, state resident: full-time $4,722; part-time $197 per credit hour. Tuition, nonresident: full-time $12,558; part-time $523 per credit hour. Required fees: $1,614; $8 per credit hour. $597 per term. *Financial support:* In 2006–07, research assistantships with full tuition reimbursements (averaging $7,425 per year), teaching assistantships with full tuition reimbursements (averaging $7,425 per year) were awarded; career-related internships or fieldwork, Federal Work-Study, scholarships/grants, health care benefits, and unspecified assistantships also available. Support available to part-time students. Financial award application deadline: 11/15; financial award applicants required to submit FAFSA. *Faculty research:* Web-based learning business processes, e-commerce, wide area artworks, data mining and knowledge discovery, data warehousing. *Unit head:* Rassule Hadidi, Program Administrator, 217-206-6067, Fax: 217-206-7543, E-mail: hadidi.rassule@uis.edu.

The University of Iowa, Henry B. Tippie College of Business, Henry B. Tippie School of Management, Iowa City, IA 52242-1316. Offers accounting (MBA); corporate finance (MBA); entrepreneurship (MBA); finance (MBA); individually designed concentration (MBA); investment management (MBA); management information systems (MBA); marketing (MBA); nonprofit management (MBA); operations management (MBA); strategic management and consulting (MBA); JD/MBA; MBA/MA; MBA/MD; MBA/MHA; MBA/MSN. *Accreditation:* AACSB. Part-time and evening/weekend programs available. *Faculty:* 94 full-time (23 women), 65 part-time/adjunct (21 women). *Students:* 230 full-time (67 women), 712 part-time (234 women); includes 62 minority (6 African Americans, 1 American Indian/Alaska Native, 43 Asian Americans or Pacific Islanders, 12 Hispanic Americans), 127 international. Average age 30. 431 applicants, 61% accepted, 217 enrolled. In 2006, 363 degrees awarded. *Median time to degree:* Master's–2 years full-time, 3.5 years part-time. *Degree requirements:* For master's, registration. *Entrance requirements:* For master's, GMAT, work experience. Additional exam requirements/recommendations for international students: Required—TOEFL (minimum score 600 paper-based; 250 computer-based; 100 iBT). *Application deadline:* For fall admission, 7/15 for domestic students, 4/15 for international students; for spring admission, 12/15 priority date for domestic students, 11/1 priority date for international students. Applications are processed on a rolling basis. Application fee: $60 ($85 for international students). Electronic applications accepted. *Expenses: Contact institution. Financial support:* In 2006–07, 72 fellowships (averaging $3,892 per year), 55 research assistantships with partial tuition reimbursements (averaging $10,260 per year) were awarded; career-related internships or fieldwork, Federal Work-Study, institutionally sponsored loans, scholarships/grants, health care benefits, and unspecified assistantships also available. Support available to part-time students. Financial award application deadline: 4/15; financial award applicants required to submit FAFSA. *Faculty research:* Capital markets, econometrics, optimization, investments and empirical corporate finance, Iowa electronic markets. *Unit head:* Prof. Gary J. Gaeth, Associate Dean, MBA Programs, 800-622-4692, Fax: 319-335-3604, E-mail: gary-gaeth@uiowa.edu. *Application contact:* Jodi Schafer, Director of Student Recruitment and Marketing, 319-335-0864, Fax: 319-335-3604, E-mail: jodi-schafer@uiowa.edu.

University of Kansas, Graduate Studies, School of Business, Program in Accounting and Information Systems, Lawrence, KS 66045. Offers MAIS. *Accreditation:* AACSB. *Faculty:* 14 full-time (4 women), 3 part-time/adjunct (1 woman). *Students:* 71 full-time (32 women), 8 part-time (6 women); includes 3 minority (1 African American, 2 Hispanic Americans), 5 international. Average age 24. 61 applicants, 87% accepted. In 2006, 58 degrees awarded. *Entrance requirements:* For master's, GMAT. Additional exam requirements/recommendations for international students: Required—TOEFL; Recommended—IELTS (minimum score 6). *Application deadline:* For fall admission, 1/15 priority date for domestic and international students; for spring admission, 11/1 for domestic students, 10/1 for international students. Applications are processed on a rolling basis. Application fee: $65. Electronic applications accepted. *Expenses:* Tuition, area resident: Part-time $227 per credit. Tuition, state resident: part-time $543 per credit. Tuition and fees vary according to course load, campus/location, program and reciprocity agreements. *Financial support:* Fellowships, research assistantships with partial tuition reimbursements, teaching assistantships with full and partial tuition reimbursements available. *Faculty research:* Audit; artificial intelligence; agency theory; compensation; production, regulation, and use of accounting information. *Unit head:* Dr. James A. Heintz, Director, Accounting and Information Systems, 785-864-4500, Fax: 785-864-5328, E-mail: jheintz@ku.edu. *Application contact:* Dee Steinle, Administative Director of Masters Programs, 785-864-7596, Fax: 785-864-5376, E-mail: dsteinle@ku.edu.

University of Kansas, Graduate Studies, School of Engineering, Department of Electrical Engineering and Computer Science, Lawrence, KS 66045. Offers computer engineering (MS); computer science (MS, PhD); electrical engineering (MS, DE, PhD); information technology (MS). Part-time programs available. *Faculty:* 37 full-time (4 women). *Students:* 117 full-time (23 women), 103 part-time (13 women); includes 13 minority (2 African Americans, 9 Asian Americans or Pacific Islanders, 2 Hispanic Americans), 111 international. Average age 27. 284 applicants, 49% accepted. In 2006, 58 master's, 6 doctorates awarded. Terminal master's awarded for partial completion of doctoral program. *Degree requirements:* For master's, exam, thesis optional; for doctorate, one foreign language, thesis/dissertation, qualifying exams, comprehensive exam. *Entrance requirements:* For master's, GRE, minimum GPA of 3.0; for doctorate, GRE, minimum GPA of 3.5. Additional exam requirements/recommendations for international students: Required—TOEFL (minimum score 600 paper-based; 250 computer-based; 100 iBT). *Application deadline:* For fall admission, 3/1 priority date for domestic students, 3/1 for international students; for spring admission, 10/1 priority date for domestic students, 10/1 for international students. Applications are processed on a rolling basis. Application fee: $55 ($60 for international students). Electronic applications accepted. *Expenses:* Tuition, area resident: Part-time $227 per credit. Tuition, state resident: part-time $543 per credit. Tuition and fees vary according to course load, campus/location, program and reciprocity agreements. *Financial support:* Fellowships, research assistantships with full and partial tuition reimbursements, teaching assistantships with full and partial tuition reimbursements, career-related internships or fieldwork, scholarships/grants, and unspecified assistantships available. Financial award application deadline: 1/1. *Faculty research:* Computer systems design, bioinformatics, communication systems and networking, interactive intelligent systems, radar systems and remote sensing. *Unit head:* Costas Tsatsoulis, Chairperson, 785-864-4620, Fax: 785-864-3226. *Application contact:* John M. Gauch, Graduate Director, 785-864-4487, Fax: 785-864-3226, E-mail: grad_admissions@eecs.ku.edu.

University of La Verne, College of Business and Public Management, Graduate Programs in Business Administration, La Verne, CA 91750-4443. Offers accounting (MBA); business (MBIT); executive management (MBA-EP); finance (MBA, MBA-EP); health services management (MBA); information technology (MBA, MBA-EP); international business (MBA, MBA-EP); leadership (MBA-EP); managed care (MBA); management (MBA, MBA-EP); marketing (MBA, MBA-EP). Part-time and evening/weekend programs available. *Faculty:* 15 full-time (7 women), 13 part-time/adjunct (7 women). *Students:* 277 full-time (133 women), 112 part-time (64 women); includes 144 minority (32 African Americans, 3 American Indian/Alaska Native, 70 Asian Americans or Pacific Islanders, 39 Hispanic Americans), 160 international. Average age 30. In 2006, 142 degrees awarded. *Entrance requirements:* For master's, minimum undergraduate GPA of 3.0, 2 letters of recommendation, resumé. Additional exam requirements/recommendations for international students: Required—TOEFL (minimum score 550 paper-based; 213 computer-based). *Application deadline:* Applications are processed on a rolling basis. Application fee: $50. *Expenses: Contact institution. Financial support:* Career-related internships or fieldwork, institutionally sponsored loans, and scholarships/grants available. Financial award application deadline: 3/2; financial award applicants required to submit FAFSA. *Unit head:* Dr. Ibrahim Helou, Chairperson, 909-593-3511 Ext. 4211, Fax: 909-392-2704, E-mail: heloua@ulv.edu. *Application contact:* Dr. Julius Walecki, Marketing Director, 909-593-3511 Ext. 4192, Fax: 909-392-2704, E-mail: cbpm@ulv.edu.

University of La Verne, Regional Campus Administration, Graduate Programs, Central Coast/Vandenberg Air Force Base Campuses, La Verne, CA 91750-4443. Offers business (MBA-EP), including health services management, information technology; health administration (MHA); leadership and management (MS). *Faculty:* 6 part-time/adjunct (0 women). *Students:* 14 full-time (5 women), 20 part-time (8 women); includes 7 minority (1 African American, 1 American Indian/Alaska Native, 5 Hispanic Americans). Average age 38. In 2006, 11 degrees awarded. *Entrance requirements:* For master's, 2 letters of recommendation, resumé. *Application deadline:* Applications are processed on a rolling basis. Application fee: $50. *Expenses: Contact institution. Financial support:* Institutionally sponsored loans available. Financial award application deadline: 3/2; financial award applicants required to submit FAFSA. *Unit head:* Kitt Vincent, Director, Central Coast Campus, 805-542-9690 Ext. 321, Fax: 805-542-9735, E-mail: vincentk@ulv.edu.

University of La Verne, Regional Campus Administration, Graduate Programs, Inland Empire Campus, Ranche Cucamonga, CA 91750-4443. Offers business (MBA-EP), including health services management, information technology, management, marketing; health administration (MHA); leadership and management (MS). *Faculty:* 2 full-time (1 woman), 8 part-time/adjunct (2 women). *Students:* 21 full-time (16 women), 32 part-time (18 women); includes 29 minority (13 African Americans, 1 American Indian/Alaska Native, 4 Asian Americans or Pacific Islanders, 11 Hispanic Americans). Average age 37. In 2006, 17 degrees awarded. *Entrance*

Management Information Systems

University of La Verne (continued)
requirements: For master's, 2 letters of recommendation, resumé. *Application deadline:* Applications are processed on a rolling basis. Application fee: $50. *Expenses: Contact institution. Financial support:* Institutionally sponsored loans available. Financial award application deadline: 3/2; financial award applicants required to submit FAFSA. *Unit head:* Jerry Ford, Director, 909-484-3858 Ext. 228, Fax: 909-484-9469, E-mail: fordj@ulv.edu.

University of La Verne, Regional Campus Administration, Graduate Programs, Kern County Campus, Bakersfield, CA 93301. Offers business (MBA-EP), including information technology, management, marketing; health administration (MHA); leadership and management (MS). *Faculty:* 4 part-time/adjunct (2 women). *Students:* 2 full-time (1 woman), 7 part-time (4 women); includes 2 minority (1 African American, 1 Hispanic American). Average age 37. In 2006, 4 degrees awarded. *Entrance requirements:* For master's, 2 letters of recommendation, resumé. *Application deadline:* Applications are processed on a rolling basis. Application fee: $50. *Expenses: Contact institution. Financial support:* Institutionally sponsored loans available. Financial award application deadline: 3/2; financial award applicants required to submit FAFSA. *Unit head:* Val Garcia, 661-328-1430, E-mail: vgarcia6@ulv.edu.

University of La Verne, Regional Campus Administration, Graduate Programs, Orange County Campus, Garden Grove, CA 92840. Offers business (MBA-EP), including health services management, information technology, management, marketing, supply chain management; health administration (MHA); leadership and management (MS); public administration (MPA). *Faculty:* 4 full-time (1 woman), 3 part-time/adjunct (1 woman). *Students:* 19 full-time (8 women), 64 part-time (29 women); includes 37 minority (4 African Americans, 2 American Indian/Alaska Native, 15 Asian Americans or Pacific Islanders, 16 Hispanic Americans). Average age 41. In 2006, 18 degrees awarded. *Entrance requirements:* For master's, 2 letters of recommendation, resumé. *Application deadline:* Applications are processed on a rolling basis. Application fee: $50. *Expenses: Contact institution. Financial support:* Institutionally sponsored loans available. Financial award application deadline: 3/2; financial award applicants required to submit FAFSA. *Unit head:* Pamela Bergovoy, Director, 714-534-4860, Fax: 714-534-4865, E-mail: bergovoy@ulv.edu.

University of La Verne, Regional Campus Administration, Graduate Programs, San Fernando Valley Campus, Burbank, CA 91505. Offers business (MBA-EP), including health services management, information technology, management, marketing; health administration (MHA); leadership and management (MS). *Faculty:* 3 full-time (2 women), 6 part-time/adjunct (2 women). *Students:* 24 full-time (12 women), 57 part-time (31 women); includes 42 minority (12 African Americans, 1 American Indian/Alaska Native, 9 Asian Americans or Pacific Islanders, 20 Hispanic Americans), 1 international. Average age 39. In 2006, 45 degrees awarded. *Entrance requirements:* For master's, 2 letters of recommendation, resumé. *Application deadline:* Applications are processed on a rolling basis. Application fee: $50. *Expenses: Contact institution. Financial support:* Institutionally sponsored loans available. Financial award application deadline: 3/2; financial award applicants required to submit FAFSA. *Unit head:* Nelly Kazman, Director, 818-846-4008 Ext. 26, Fax: 818-566-1047, E-mail: kazmann@ulv.edu.

University of La Verne, Regional Campus Administration, Graduate Programs, Ventura County/Point Mugu Naval Air Station Campuses, La Verne, CA 91750-4443. Offers business (MBA-EP), including health services management, information technology, management, marketing; business organizational management (MS); health administration (MHA); leadership and management (MS). *Faculty:* 2 full-time (0 women), 8 part-time/adjunct (1 woman). *Students:* 22 full-time (7 women), 29 part-time (16 women); includes 19 minority (4 African Americans, 7 Asian Americans or Pacific Islanders, 8 Hispanic Americans). Average age 40. In 2006, 26 degrees awarded. *Entrance requirements:* For master's, 2 letters of recommendation, resumé. Application fee: $50. *Expenses: Contact institution. Financial support:* Institutionally sponsored loans available. Financial award application deadline: 3/2; financial award applicants required to submit FAFSA. *Unit head:* Janet Meyer, Director, Ventura Campus, 805-981-8030 Ext. 225, Fax: 805-981-8033, E-mail: jmeyer2@ulv.edu.

University of Lethbridge, School of Graduate Studies, Lethbridge, AB T1K 3M4, Canada. Offers accounting (MScM); addictions counseling (M Sc); agricultural biotechnology (M Sc); agricultural studies (M Sc, MA); anthropology (MA); archaeology (MA); art (MA); biochemistry (M Sc); biological sciences (M Sc); biomolecular science (PhD); biosystems and biodiversity (PhD); Canadian studies (MA); chemistry (M Sc); computer science (M Sc); computer science and geographical information science (M Sc); counseling psychology (M Ed); dramatic arts (MA); earth, space, and physical science (PhD); economics (MA); educational leadership (M Ed); English (MA); environmental science (M Sc); evolution and behavior (PhD); exercise science (M Sc); finance (MScM); French (MA); French/German (MA); French/Spanish (MA); general education (M Ed); general management (MScM); geography (M Sc, MA); German (MA); health sciences (M Sc, MA); history (MA); human resource management and labour relations (MScM); individualized multidisciplinary (M Sc, MA); information systems (MScM); international management (MScM); kinesiology (M Sc, MA); management (M Sc, MA); marketing (MScM); mathematics (M Sc); music (MA); Native American studies (MA); neuroscience (M Sc, PhD); new media (MA); nursing (M Sc); philosophy (MA); physics (M Sc); policy and strategy (MScM); political science (MA); psychology (M Sc, MA); religious studies (MA); sociology (MA); theoretical and computational science (PhD); urban and regional studies (MA). Part-time and evening/weekend programs available. *Students:* 200 full-time, 90 part-time. In 2006, 105 master's, 3 doctorates awarded. *Degree requirements:* For doctorate, thesis/dissertation, comprehensive exam. *Entrance requirements:* For master's, GMAT (M Sc management), bachelor's degree in related field, minimum GPA of 3.0 during previous 20 graded semester courses, 2 years teaching or related experience (M Ed); for doctorate, master's degree, minimum graduate GPA of 3.5. Additional exam requirements/recommendations for international students: Required—TOEFL. Application fee: $60 Canadian dollars. *Financial support:* Fellowships, research assistantships, teaching assistantships, scholarships/grants, health care benefits, and unspecified assistantships available. *Faculty research:* Movement and brain plasticity, gibberellin physiology, photosynthesis, carbon cycling, molecular properties of main-group ring components. *Unit head:* Dr. Jo-Anne Fiske, Interim Dean, 403-329-2121, Fax: 403-329-2097. *Application contact:* Kathy Schrage, Administrative Assistant, Office of the Academic Vice President, 403-329-2121, Fax: 403-329-2097, E-mail: inquiries@uleth.ca.

University of Maine, Graduate School, Interdisciplinary Program in Information Systems, Orono, ME 04469. Offers MS. Part-time programs available. *Students:* 3 full-time (0 women), 5 part-time (2 women); includes 1 minority (American Indian/Alaska Native), 2 international. Average age 35. 5 applicants, 60% accepted, 2 enrolled. In 2006, 6 degrees awarded. *Entrance requirements:* For master's, GRE General Test or GMAT. Additional exam requirements/recommendations for international students: Required—TOEFL. *Application deadline:* For fall admission, 2/1 priority date for domestic students. Applications are processed on a rolling basis. Application fee: $50. Electronic applications accepted. *Financial support:* In 2006–07, 2 teaching assistantships with tuition reimbursements (averaging $9,010 per year) were awarded; Federal Work-Study also available.

University of Management and Technology, Program in Computer Science and Information Technology, Arlington, VA 22209. Offers computer science (MS); information technology (AC); information technology project management (MS, AC); management information systems (MS); multimedia technology (MS); software engineering (MS). Part-time and evening/weekend programs available. Postbaccalaureate distance learning degree programs offered (no on-campus study). *Entrance requirements:* For master's, 3 recommendations, current resumé. Additional exam requirements/recommendations for international students: Required—TOEFL (minimum score 550 paper-based; 213 computer-based). *Application deadline:* Applications are processed on a rolling basis. Application fee: $30. Electronic applications accepted. *Unit head:* Dr. C. Eric Kirkland, PMP, Vice President, 703-516-0035, Fax: 703-516-0985, E-mail: eric.kirkland@umtweb.edu.

University of Mary Hardin-Baylor, College of Business, Graduate Studies in Information Systems, Belton, TX 76513. Offers MS. Part-time and evening/weekend programs available. *Faculty:* 10 full-time (3 women), 3 part-time/adjunct (1 woman). *Students:* 1 full-time (0 women), 9 part-time (4 women); includes 3 minority (1 African American, 1 Asian American or Pacific Islander, 1 Hispanic American). Average age 24. In 2006, 2 degrees awarded. *Degree requirements:* For master's, practicum. *Entrance requirements:* For master's, GMAT, minimum GPA of 3.0, work experience, interview. *Application deadline:* For fall admission, 6/1 priority date for domestic students; for spring admission, 11/1 for domestic students. Applications are processed on a rolling basis. Application fee: $35 ($135 for international students). Electronic applications accepted. *Expenses:* Tuition: Full-time $8,910; part-time $495 per hour. Required fees: $906; $47 per hour. $30 per term. Tuition and fees vary according to course load. *Financial support:* Federal Work-Study and scholarships (for some active duty military personnel only) available. Support available to part-time students. Financial award applicants required to submit FAFSA. *Unit head:* Dr. Patrick Jaska, Director, 254-295-4654, E-mail: pjaska@umhb.edu.

University of Maryland University College, Graduate School of Management and Technology, Program in Financial Management and Information Systems, Adelphi, MD 20783. Offers MS, Certificate. Part-time and evening/weekend programs available. Postbaccalaureate distance learning degree programs offered (no on-campus study). *Students:* 3 full-time (1 woman), 74 part-time (40 women); includes 41 minority (31 African Americans, 7 Asian Americans or Pacific Islanders, 3 Hispanic Americans), 5 international. Average age 34. 42 applicants, 100% accepted, 35 enrolled. *Degree requirements:* For master's, thesis or alternative. *Application deadline:* Applications are processed on a rolling basis. Application fee: $50. Electronic applications accepted. *Financial support:* Federal Work-Study and scholarships/grants available. Support available to part-time students. Financial award application deadline: 6/1. *Unit head:* Dr. James Howard, 301-985-7200, Fax: 301-985-4611, E-mail: jhoward@umuc.edu. *Application contact:* Coordinator, Graduate Admissions, 301-985-7155, Fax: 301-985-7175, E-mail: gradinfo@umuc.edu.

University of Mary Washington, College of Graduate and Professional Studies, Fredericksburg, VA 22406-7239. Offers business administration (MBA); education (M Ed); management information systems (MSMIS). Part-time and evening/weekend programs available. *Faculty:* 25 full-time (17 women), 20 part-time/adjunct (10 women). *Students:* 121 full-time (92 women), 507 part-time (367 women); includes 95 minority (59 African Americans, 1 American Indian/Alaska Native, 10 Asian Americans or Pacific Islanders, 25 Hispanic Americans), 4 international. Average age 35. In 2006, 14 degrees awarded. *Entrance requirements:* For master's, GMAT (MBA), PRAXIS I (M Ed), minimum GPA of 3.0. Additional exam requirements/recommendations for international students: Required—TOEFL (minimum score 600 paper-based; 250 computer-based; 100 iBT). *Application deadline:* For fall admission, 6/1 priority date for domestic students, 6/1 for international students; for spring admission, 10/1 for domestic and international students. Application fee: $45. *Expenses:* Tuition, area resident: Part-time $275 per credit hour. Tuition, state resident: part-time $626 per credit. Required fees: $25 per term. One-time fee: $45 part-time. *Financial support:* In 2006–07, 46 students received support. Scholarships/grants available. Support available to part-time students. Financial award application deadline: 3/15; financial award applicants required to submit FAFSA. *Unit head:* Dr. Meta R. Braymer, Vice President for Graduate and Professional Studies and Dean of the Faculty, 540-286-8000, Fax: 540-286-8005, E-mail: mbraymer@umw.edu. *Application contact:* Mathew E. Mejia, Assistant Dean for Graduate and Professional Studies and Dean of the Faculty, 540-286-8017, Fax: 540-286-8085, E-mail: mmejia@umw.edu.

University of Memphis, Graduate School, Fogelman College of Business and Economics, Program in Business Administration, Memphis, TN 38152. Offers accounting (MBA, PhD); economics (MBA, PhD); executive business administration (MBA); finance (PhD); finance, insurance, and real estate (MBA, MS); international business administration (MBA); management (MBA, MS, PhD); management information systems (MBA, MS, PhD); management science (MBA); marketing (MBA, MS); marketing and supply chain management (PhD); real estate development (MS); JD/MBA. *Accreditation:* AACSB. *Faculty:* 84 full-time (14 women), 3 part-time/adjunct (0 women). *Students:* 222 full-time (92 women), 163 part-time (52 women); includes 62 minority (43 African Americans, 14 Asian Americans or Pacific Islanders, 5 Hispanic Americans), 119 international. Average age 29. In 2006, 196 master's, 12 doctorates awarded. *Degree requirements:* For master's, comprehensive exam; for doctorate, thesis/dissertation, comprehensive exam. *Entrance requirements:* For master's, GMAT, resumé; for doctorate, GMAT, interview, minimum GPA of 3.4, resumé, letter of recommendation. Additional exam requirements/recommendations for international students: Required—TOEFL (minimum score 550 paper-based; 220 computer-based). *Application deadline:* For fall admission, 8/1 for domestic students; for spring admission, 12/1 for domestic students. Application fee: $25 ($50 for international students). *Financial support:* Research assistantships with full tuition reimbursements, teaching assistantships, career-related internships or fieldwork, scholarships/grants, and unspecified assistantships available. Financial award application deadline: 3/1. *Faculty research:* Competitive business strategy, finance microstructures, supply chain management innovations, health care economics, litigation risks and corporate audits. Total annual research expenditures: $2.7 million. *Application contact:* Dr. Carol V. Danehower, Associate Dean for Programs, 901-678-5402, Fax: 901-678-3579, E-mail: fcbegp@memphis.edu.

University of Miami, Graduate School, School of Business Administration, Department of Computer Information Systems, Coral Gables, FL 33124. Offers MS. Part-time programs available. *Faculty:* 6 full-time (2 women). *Students:* 5 full-time (0 women), 11 part-time (3 women); includes 7 minority (4 Asian Americans or Pacific Islanders, 3 Hispanic Americans), 4 international. 14 applicants, 86% accepted, 6 enrolled. In 2006, 10 degrees awarded. *Entrance requirements:* For master's, GMAT or GRE. Additional exam requirements/recommendations for international students: Required—TOEFL. *Application deadline:* For fall admission, 6/30 priority date for domestic students; for spring admission, 10/31 priority date for domestic students. Applications are processed on a rolling basis. Application fee: $50. Electronic applications accepted. *Financial support:* In 2006–07, 5 research assistantships with partial tuition reimbursements were awarded; career-related internships or fieldwork, Federal Work-Study, institutionally sponsored loans, scholarships/grants, and unspecified assistantships also available. Financial award application deadline: 3/1. *Faculty research:* Database management, expert systems, systems analysis and design, information systems and strategic management, e-commerce. *Unit head:* Dr. Joel Stutz, Chairman, 305-284-6294, Fax: 305-284-5161, E-mail: jstutz@miami.edu. *Application contact:* David S. Green, Director of Graduate Business Recruiting and Admissions, 305-284-4607, Fax: 305-284-1878, E-mail: mba@miami.edu.

University of Miami, Graduate School, School of Business Administration, Program in Business Administration, Coral Gables, FL 33124. Offers accounting (MBA); computer information systems (MBA); executive and professional (MBA), including international business, management; finance (MBA); international business (MBA); management (MBA); management science (MBA); marketing (MBA); professional management (MSPM); JD/MBA; MBA/MSIE. *Accreditation:* AACSB. Evening/weekend programs available. *Faculty:* 105 full-time (25 women). *Students:* 734 full-time (269 women), 19 part-time (4 women); includes 194 minority (24 African Americans, 1 American Indian/Alaska Native, 23 Asian Americans or Pacific Islanders, 146 Hispanic Americans), 115 international. Average age 31. 453 applicants, 71% accepted, 152 enrolled. In 2006, 394 degrees awarded. *Degree requirements:* For master's, comprehensive exam, registration. *Entrance requirements:* For master's, GMAT. Additional exam requirements/recommendations for international students: Required—TOEFL (minimum score 550 paper-based; 213 computer-based; 59 iBT). *Application deadline:* For fall admission, 7/30 priority date for domestic students, 6/30 priority date for international students; for spring admission, 12/31 priority date for domestic students, 10/31 priority date for international students. Applications are processed on a rolling basis. Application fee: $50. Electronic applications accepted. *Financial support:* In 2006–07, 418 students received support, including 19 fellowships with partial tuition reimbursements available; unspecified assistantships also available. Financial award application deadline: 3/1; financial award applicants required to submit FAFSA. *Faculty research:* Leadership, e-commerce, supply chain management. *Unit head:* Daniela Mu±iz,

Associate Director, Graduate Business Programs, 305-284-4626, Fax: 305-284-1878, E-mail: dmuniz@miami.edu. *Application contact:* David S. Green, Director of Graduate Business Recruiting and Admissions, 305-284-4607, Fax: 305-284-1878, E-mail: mba@miami.edu.

University of Minnesota, Twin Cities Campus, Carlson School of Management, Carlson Full-time MBA Program, Minneapolis, MN 55455-0213. Offers accounting (MBA); entrepreneurship (MBA); finance (MBA); healthcare management (MBA); information and decision sciences (MBA); international business (MBA); marketing and logistics management (MBA); operations and management science (MBA); strategic management and organization (MBA); supply chain management (MBA); JD/MBA; MD/MBA; MHA/MBA. *Accreditation:* AACSB. *Faculty:* 125 full-time (27 women), 120 part-time/adjunct. *Students:* 218 full-time (70 women); includes 18 minority (4 African Americans, 1 American Indian/Alaska Native, 10 Asian Americans or Pacific Islanders, 3 Hispanic Americans), 86 international. Average age 28. 418 applicants, 53% accepted, 124 enrolled. In 2006, 105 degrees awarded. *Median time to degree:* Master's–2 years full-time. *Entrance requirements:* For master's, GMAT. Additional exam requirements/recommendations for international students: Required—TOEFL (minimum score 580 paper-based; 240 computer-based), IELTS. *Application deadline:* For fall admission, 4/15 for domestic students, 2/15 for international students. Application fee: $60 ($90 for international students). Electronic applications accepted. *Expenses:* Contact institution. Full-time tuition and fees vary according to class time, course load, program, reciprocity agreements and student level. *Financial support:* In 2006–07, 131 students received support, including 127 fellowships with full and partial tuition reimbursements available (averaging $20,000 per year); research assistantships with partial tuition reimbursements available, teaching assistantships with partial tuition reimbursements available, career-related internships or fieldwork, Federal Work-Study, institutionally sponsored loans, scholarships/grants, health care benefits, tuition waivers (full and partial), and unspecified assistantships also available. Support available to part-time students. Financial award application deadline: 2/15; financial award applicants required to submit FAFSA. *Faculty research:* IT, strategy, marketing, finance, quality management. *Unit head:* Kathryn J. Carlson, MBA Programs and Executive Education, 612-624-2039, Fax: 612-625-1012, E-mail: full-timeembainfo@csom.umn.edu. *Application contact:* Jeffrey Bieganek, Director, Admissions and Business Development, MBA Programs and Executive Education, 612-625-6558, Fax: 612-625-1012, E-mail: full-timembainfo@csom.umn.edu.

University of Minnesota, Twin Cities Campus, Carlson School of Management, Doctoral Program in Business Administration, Minneapolis, MN 55455-0213. Offers accounting (PhD); finance (PhD); information and decision sciences (PhD); marketing and logistics management (PhD); operations and management science (PhD); strategic management and organization (PhD). *Faculty:* 109 full-time (26 women). *Students:* 90 full-time (30 women); includes 9 minority (5 African Americans, 1 Asian American or Pacific Islander, 3 Hispanic Americans), 60 international. Average age 30. 325 applicants, 8% accepted, 17 enrolled. In 2006, 16 degrees awarded. *Median time to degree:* Of those who began their doctoral program in fall 1998, 61% received their degree in 8 years or less. *Degree requirements:* For doctorate, thesis/dissertation, written and oral preliminary exams, comprehensive exam, registration. *Entrance requirements:* For doctorate, GMAT, GRE General Test, International must submit a TOEFL or IELT. Additional exam requirements/recommendations for international students: Required—TOEFL (minimum score 600 paper-based; 250 computer-based; 100 iBT), IELTS (minimum score 8), TOEFL (paper-based 600, computer-based 250) or IELTS (7.5). *Application deadline:* For fall admission, 12/30 for domestic students, 12/30 priority date for international students. Applications are processed on a rolling basis. Application fee: $55 ($75 for international students). Electronic applications accepted. *Expenses:* Tuition, state resident: full-time $9,302; part-time $775 per credit. Tuition, nonresident: full-time $16,400; part-time $1,367 per credit. Full-time tuition and fees vary according to class time, course load, program, reciprocity agreements and student level. *Financial support:* In 2006–07, 67 students received support, including fellowships with full tuition reimbursements available (averaging $11,000 per year), research assistantships with full tuition reimbursements available (averaging $6,000 per year), teaching assistantships with full tuition reimbursements available (averaging $6,000 per year); institutionally sponsored loans, scholarships/grants, health care benefits, and unspecified assistantships also available. Financial award application deadline: 12/31. *Faculty research:* Corporate strategy, international business, corporate finances, entrepreneurship, quality management, marketing, information and decision science, operations and accounting. Total annual research expenditures: $300,000. *Unit head:* Dr. Paul E. Johnson, Director of Graduate Studies and PhD Program Director, 612-624-5570, Fax: 612-624-8221, E-mail: pjohnson@csom.umn.edu. *Application contact:* Earlene Bronson, Assistant Director, PhD Program, 612-624-0875, Fax: 612-624-8221, E-mail: ebronson@csom.umn.edu.

University of Mississippi, Graduate School, School of Business Administration, Oxford, University, MS 38677. Offers business administration (MBA, PhD); systems management (MS); JD/MBA. *Accreditation:* AACSB. *Faculty:* 44 full-time (13 women), 18 part-time/adjunct (5 women). *Students:* 62 full-time (19 women), 26 part-time (7 women); includes 2 Asian Americans or Pacific Islanders, 17 international. 203 applicants, 39% accepted, 55 enrolled. In 2006, 36 master's, 11 doctorates awarded. *Degree requirements:* For doctorate, thesis/dissertation. *Entrance requirements:* For master's, GMAT, minimum GPA of 3.0; for doctorate, GMAT. Additional exam requirements/recommendations for international students: Required—TOEFL. *Application deadline:* For fall admission, 2/1 for domestic students; for spring admission, 10/1 for domestic students. Applications are processed on a rolling basis. Application fee: $25. Electronic applications accepted. *Expenses:* Tuition, state resident: full-time $4,602; part-time $256 per credit hour. Tuition, nonresident: full-time $10,566; part-time $587 per credit hour. *Financial support:* Fellowships, career-related internships or fieldwork, scholarships/grants, tuition waivers (full), and unspecified assistantships available. Financial award application deadline: 3/1; financial award applicants required to submit FAFSA. *Unit head:* Dr. Brian Reithel, Dean, 662-915-5820, Fax: 662-915-5821, E-mail: breithel@bus.olemiss.edu.

University of Missouri–St. Louis, College of Business Administration, Program in Management Information Systems, St. Louis, MO 63121. Offers information systems (MSMIS, PhD); logistics and supply chain management (PhD). Part-time and evening/weekend programs available. *Faculty:* 8. *Students:* 8 full-time (1 woman), 25 part-time (6 women); includes 3 minority (1 African American, 2 Asian Americans or Pacific Islanders), 12 international. Average age 33. In 2006, 15 degrees awarded. *Entrance requirements:* For master's, GMAT, 2 letters of recommendation; for doctorate, GMAT or GRE, 3 letters of recommendation. Additional exam requirements/recommendations for international students: Required—TOEFL (minimum score 550 paper-based; 213 computer-based). *Application deadline:* For fall admission, 7/1 for domestic students; for spring admission, 11/1 for domestic students. Applications are processed on a rolling basis. Application fee: $35 ($40 for international students). Electronic applications accepted. *Expenses:* Tuition, state resident: part-time $332 per credit hour. Tuition, nonresident: part-time $770 per credit hour. *Financial support:* Career-related internships or fieldwork, Federal Work-Study, and institutionally sponsored loans available. Support available to part-time students. Financial award application deadline: 4/1; financial award applicants required to submit FAFSA. *Faculty research:* International information systems, telecommunications, systems development, information systems sourcing. *Application contact:* 314-516-5458, Fax: 314-516-6996, E-mail: gradadm@umsl.edu.

University of Nebraska at Omaha, Graduate Studies and Research, College of Information Science and Technology, Department of Information Systems and Quantitative Analysis, Omaha, NE 68182. Offers information technology (PhD); management information systems (MS). Part-time and evening/weekend programs available. *Faculty:* 15 full-time (7 women). *Students:* 42 full-time (9 women), 99 part-time (30 women); includes 17 minority (5 African Americans, 12 Asian Americans or Pacific Islanders), 43 international. Average age 33. 73 applicants, 49% accepted, 27 enrolled. In 2006, 31 master's, 2 doctorates awarded. *Degree requirements:* For master's, thesis (for some programs), comprehensive exam; for doctorate, thesis/dissertation, comprehensive exam. *Entrance requirements:* For master's, GMAT or GRE General Test; for doctorate, GMAT or GRE General Test, letters of recommendation. Additional exam requirements/recommendations for international students: Required—TOEFL (minimum score 575 paper-based; 230 computer-based; 89 iBT). *Application deadline:* For fall admission, 3/15 for domestic students; for spring admission, 10/1 for domestic students. Applications are processed on a rolling basis. Application fee: $45. Electronic applications accepted. *Financial support:* In 2006–07, 72 students received support; fellowships, research assistantships with tuition reimbursements available, teaching assistantships with tuition reimbursements available, career-related internships or fieldwork, Federal Work-Study, scholarships/grants, tuition waivers (partial), and unspecified assistantships available. Financial award application deadline: 3/1; financial award applicants required to submit FAFSA. *Unit head:* Dr. Deepak Khazanchi, Chairperson, 402-554-3770.

University of Nebraska–Lincoln, Graduate College, College of Agricultural Sciences and Natural Resources, Program in Mechanized Systems Management, Lincoln, NE 68588. Offers MS. *Degree requirements:* For master's, thesis optional. *Entrance requirements:* For master's, GRE General Test. Additional exam requirements/recommendations for international students: Required—TOEFL (minimum score 550 paper-based; 213 computer-based). Electronic applications accepted. *Faculty research:* Irrigation management, agricultural power and machinery systems, sensors and controls, food/industrial materials handling and processing systems.

University of Nevada, Las Vegas, Graduate College, College of Business, Department of Management Information Systems, Las Vegas, NV 89154-9900. Offers MS. *Faculty:* 6 full-time (0 women). *Students:* 9 full-time (4 women), 15 part-time (4 women); includes 5 minority (4 Asian Americans or Pacific Islanders, 1 Hispanic American), 4 international. 25 applicants, 48% accepted, 9 enrolled. *Entrance requirements:* Additional exam requirements/recommendations for international students: Required—TOEFL (minimum score 550 paper-based; 213 computer-based; 80 iBT). *Application deadline:* For fall admission, 6/15 for domestic students, 5/1 for international students; for spring admission, 11/15 for domestic students, 10/1 for international students. Application fee: $60 ($75 for international students). Electronic applications accepted. *Financial support:* In 2006–07, 4 research assistantships (averaging $10,000 per year) were awarded; career-related internships or fieldwork, Federal Work-Study, institutionally sponsored loans, scholarships/grants, health care benefits, and unspecified assistantships also available. Support available to part-time students. *Unit head:* Dr. Reza Torkzadeh, Chair, 702-895-3796, E-mail: mis@unlv.nevada.edu. *Application contact:* Graduate College Admissions Evaluator, 702-895-3320, Fax: 702-895-4180, E-mail: gradcollege@unlv.edu.

University of New Haven, Graduate School, Tagliatela College of Engineering, Program in Computer and Information Science, West Haven, CT 06516-1916. Offers applications software (MS); management information systems (MS); systems software (MS). Part-time and evening/weekend programs available. *Degree requirements:* For master's, thesis or alternative.

University of New Mexico, Robert O. Anderson Graduate School of Management, Department of Marketing, Information and Decision Sciences, Albuquerque, NM 87131-2039. Offers management information systems (MBA); marketing management (MBA); operations management (MBA). Part-time and evening/weekend programs available. *Entrance requirements:* For master's, GMAT. Additional exam requirements/recommendations for international students: Required—TOEFL (minimum score 550 paper-based; 213 computer-based).

The University of North Carolina at Chapel Hill, Kenan-Flagler Business School, Doctoral Program in Business Administration, Chapel Hill, NC 27599. Offers accounting (PhD); finance (PhD); marketing (PhD); operations management (PhD); organizational behavior (PhD); strategy (PhD). *Accreditation:* AACSB. *Degree requirements:* For doctorate, thesis/dissertation. *Entrance requirements:* For doctorate, GMAT or GRE General Test. Electronic applications accepted. Expenses: Contact institution.

The University of North Carolina at Greensboro, Graduate School, Bryan School of Business and Economics, Department of Information Systems and Operations Management, Greensboro, NC 27412-5001. Offers information systems (PhD); information technology (Certificate); information technology and management (MS); supply chain management (Certificate). *Faculty:* 14 full-time (2 women), 3 part-time/adjunct (2 women). *Students:* 27 full-time (12 women), 60 part-time (26 women); includes 21 minority (6 African Americans, 15 Asian Americans or Pacific Islanders). 60 applicants, 30% accepted. *Entrance requirements:* For master's, GMAT, GRE General Test. Additional exam requirements/recommendations for international students: Required—TOEFL. *Application deadline:* For fall admission, 7/1 priority date for domestic students; for spring admission, 11/1 for domestic students. Applications are processed on a rolling basis. Application fee: $45. Electronic applications accepted. *Expenses:* Tuition, state resident: full-time $2,692. Tuition, nonresident: full-time $13,742. *Unit head:* Dr. Kwasi Amoako-Gyampah, Head, 336-334-5666, Fax: 336-334-4083, E-mail: kwasi_amoako@uncg.edu. *Application contact:* Michelle Harkleroad, Director of Graduate Admissions, 336-334-4884, Fax: 336-334-4424, E-mail: mbharkle@uncg.edu.

University of Northern Virginia, Graduate Programs, Manassas, VA 20109. Offers accountancy (MS); accounting (MBA); business administration (DBA); computer science (MS); counseling education (M Ed); early childhood education (M Ed); educational communication and instructional technology (M Ed); educational leadership (M Ed); finance (MBA); information systems technology (MS); management (MBA); marketing (MBA); project management (MBA); public administration (MPA); teaching English to speakers of other languages (M Ed). Part-time and evening/weekend programs available. Postbaccalaureate distance learning degree programs offered (no on-campus study). *Degree requirements:* For doctorate, thesis/dissertation, comprehensive exam, registration. *Entrance requirements:* Additional exam requirements/recommendations for international students: Required—TOEFL (minimum score 550 paper-based; 230 computer-based), IELTS (minimum score 6). Electronic applications accepted.

University of North Texas, Robert B. Toulouse School of Graduate Studies, College of Business Administration, Department of Information Technology and Decision Sciences, Denton, TX 76203. Offers decision technologies (MS); information systems (PhD); information technology (MS); management science (PhD). Part-time and evening/weekend programs available. *Faculty:* 25 full-time (4 women). *Students:* 22 full-time (7 women), 19 part-time (2 women); includes 4 minority (3 African Americans, 1 Hispanic American), 21 international. Average age 31. 40 applicants, 83% accepted, 7 enrolled. In 2006, 15 master's, 2 doctorates awarded. *Degree requirements:* For doctorate, thesis/dissertation. *Entrance requirements:* For master's, GMAT; for doctorate, GMAT or GRE General Test. Additional exam requirements/recommendations for international students: Required—TOEFL (minimum score 550 paper-based; 213 computer-based). *Application deadline:* For fall admission, 7/15 for domestic students. Application fee: $50 ($75 for international students). *Expenses:* Tuition, state resident: full-time $3,573; part-time $198 per credit. Tuition, nonresident: full-time $8,577; part-time $476 per credit. Required fees: $1,258; $126 per credit. One-time fee: $150 full-time. Tuition and fees vary according to course load. *Financial support:* Fellowships, research assistantships, teaching assistantships, career-related internships or fieldwork and Federal Work-Study available. Financial award application deadline: 4/1. *Faculty research:* Databases, systems design, expert systems, applied statistics, quality and reliability management. *Unit head:* Dr. Marg Jones, Interim Chair, 940-565-3110, Fax: 940-565-4935, E-mail: jonesm@unt.edu. *Application contact:* Dr. Wayne Spence, Graduate Adviser, 940-565-3110, Fax: 940-565-4935, E-mail: spence@unt.edu.

University of Oklahoma, Graduate College, Gaylord College of Journalism and Mass Communication, Program in Journalism and Mass Communication, Norman, OK 73019-0390. Offers advertising and public relations (MA); information gathering and distribution (MA); mass communication management and policy (MA); professional writing (MA); telecommunication and new technology (MA). Part-time programs available. *Students:* 31 full-time (20 women), 48 part-time (28 women); includes 11 minority (2 African Americans, 4 American Indian/Alaska Native, 1 Asian American or Pacific Islander, 4 Hispanic Americans), 11 international. 23 applicants, 91% accepted, 17 enrolled. In 2006, 8 degrees awarded. Terminal master's awarded for partial completion of doctoral program. *Degree requirements:* For master's, thesis optional.

Management Information Systems

University of Oklahoma (continued)

Entrance requirements: For master's, GRE General Test, minimum GPA of 3.2, 9 hours of course work in journalism, course work in statistics. Additional exam requirements/recommendations for international students: Required—TOEFL (minimum score 600 paper-based; 250 computer-based), TWE (minimum score 5). *Application deadline:* For fall admission, 2/1 for domestic students, 4/1 for international students; for spring admission, 11/1 for domestic students, 9/1 for international students. Application fee: $40 ($90 for international students). *Expenses:* Tuition, state resident: full-time $3,180; part-time $133 per credit hour. Tuition, nonresident: full-time $11,347; part-time $473 per credit hour. Required fees: $1,729; $62 per credit hour. $117 per semester. Tuition and fees vary according to course load and program. *Financial support:* In 2006–07, 22 students received support. Career-related internships or fieldwork, institutionally sponsored loans, scholarships/grants, health care benefits, and unspecified assistantships available. *Faculty research:* Diversity in media, PR issues management, journalism ethics, advertising humor, media management. *Application contact:* Kelly Storm, Assistant to Graduate Director, 405-325-2722, Fax: 405-325-7565, E-mail: kstorm@ou.edu.

University of Oklahoma, Graduate College, Michael F. Price College of Business, Division of Management Information Systems, Norman, OK 73019-0390. Offers management (MS). Part-time and evening/weekend programs available. *Faculty:* 12 full-time (4 women). *Students:* 2 full-time (0 women), (both international). 8 applicants, 13% accepted, 1 enrolled. In 2006, 7 degrees awarded. *Entrance requirements:* Additional exam requirements/recommendations for international students: Required—TOEFL (minimum score 550 paper-based; 213 computer-based). *Application deadline:* For fall admission, 2/1 for domestic and international students; for spring admission, 11/1 for domestic students, 9/1 for international students. Applications are processed on a rolling basis. Application fee: $40 ($90 for international students). *Expenses:* Tuition, state resident: full-time $3,180; part-time $133 per credit hour. Tuition, nonresident: full-time $11,347; part-time $473 per credit hour. Required fees: $1,729; $62 per credit hour. $117 per semester. Tuition and fees vary according to course load and program. *Financial support:* In 2006–07, 6 research assistantships with full tuition reimbursements (averaging $12,450 per year), 4 teaching assistantships with full tuition reimbursements (averaging $16,272 per year) were awarded; Federal Work-Study, scholarships/grants, health care benefits, and unspecified assistantships also available. Financial award applicants required to submit FAFSA. *Faculty research:* Outsourcing and governance, virtual teams, systems analysis, data warehousing, project management. Total annual research expenditures: $26,022. *Unit head:* Lakshamanan Chidambaram, Director, 405-325-1957, Fax: 405-325-1957, E-mail: laku@ou.edu. *Application contact:* Jim Smith, Academic Counselor, 405-325-3744, Fax: 405-325-7753, E-mail: jlsmith@ou.edu.

University of Oregon, Graduate School, Interdisciplinary Program in Applied Information Management, Eugene, OR 97403. Offers MS. Part-time and evening/weekend programs available. *Students:* 2 applicants, 100% accepted. In 2006, 20 degrees awarded. *Degree requirements:* For master's, project. *Entrance requirements:* For master's, GMAT, GRE, or MAT. Additional exam requirements/recommendations for international students: Required—TOEFL. *Application deadline:* For winter admission, 10/1 for domestic students. Application fee: $50. Electronic applications accepted. *Expenses: Contact institution. Financial support:* Institutionally sponsored loans available. Support available to part-time students. Financial award application deadline: 2/1. *Faculty research:* Business management, information design. *Unit head:* Linda F. Ettinger, Director, 800-824-2714, E-mail: aim@continue.uoregon.edu. *Application contact:* Janet Cormack, Coordinator, 800-824-2714, Fax: 503-725-2289, E-mail: aim@continue.uoregon.edu.

University of Pennsylvania, Wharton School, Operations and Information Management Department, Philadelphia, PA 19104. Offers MBA, PhD. Terminal master's awarded for partial completion of doctoral program. *Degree requirements:* For master's and doctorate, thesis/dissertation, preliminary exams. *Entrance requirements:* For master's, GMAT, GRE; for doctorate, GRE. Electronic applications accepted. *Faculty research:* Supply chain management, operations research, economics of information systems, risk analysis, electronic commerce.

University of Phoenix–Atlanta Campus, John Sperling School of Business, College of Information Systems and Technology, Sandy Springs, GA 30350-4153. Offers information systems (MIS); technology management (MBA). Evening/weekend programs available. *Faculty:* 11 full-time (3 women), 52 part-time/adjunct (9 women). *Students:* 34 full-time (14 women); includes 21 minority (18 African Americans, 3 Asian Americans or Pacific Islanders), 4 international. Average age 37. In 2006, 22 degrees awarded. *Degree requirements:* For master's, thesis (for some programs), registration. *Entrance requirements:* For master's, 3 years of work experience, minimum undergraduate GPA of 3.0. Additional exam requirements/recommendations for international students: Required—TOEFL (minimum score 550 paper-based; 213 computer-based; 79 iBT). *Application deadline:* Applications are processed on a rolling basis. Application fee: $45. Electronic applications accepted. *Expenses:* Tuition: Full-time $10,560. Required fees: $760. *Financial support:* Institutionally sponsored loans and scholarships/grants available. Financial award applicants required to submit FAFSA. *Application contact:* Chair, 678-731-0555, Fax: 678-731-9666.

University of Phoenix–Augusta Campus, College of Information Systems and Technology, Augusta, GA 30909-4583. Offers information systems (MIS); technology management (MBA).

University of Phoenix–Austin Campus, College of Information Systems and Technology, Austin, TX 78759. Offers information systems (MIS); technology management (MBA).

University of Phoenix–Bay Area Campus, John Sperling School of Business, College of Information Systems and Technology, Pleasanton, CA 94588-3677. Offers e-business (MBA); technology management (MBA). Evening/weekend programs available. *Faculty:* 19 full-time (1 woman), 166 part-time/adjunct (35 women). *Students:* 94 full-time (19 women); includes 26 minority (4 African Americans, 18 Asian Americans or Pacific Islanders, 4 Hispanic Americans), 30 international. Average age 38. In 2006, 90 degrees awarded. *Degree requirements:* For master's, thesis (for some programs), registration. *Entrance requirements:* For master's, minimum undergraduate GPA of 3.0, 3 years of work experience. Additional exam requirements/recommendations for international students: Required—TOEFL (minimum score 550 paper-based; 213 computer-based; 79 iBT). *Application deadline:* Applications are processed on a rolling basis. Application fee: $45. Electronic applications accepted. *Expenses:* Tuition: Full-time $12,648. Required fees: $760. *Financial support:* Institutionally sponsored loans and scholarships/grants available. Financial award applicants required to submit FAFSA. *Unit head:* Dr. Adam Honea, Dean/Executive Director, 480-557-1659, E-mail: adam.honea@phoenix.edu. *Application contact:* Chair, 408-435-8500, Fax: 408-435-8250.

University of Phoenix–Boston Campus, John Sperling School of Business, College of Information Systems and Technology, Braintree, MA 02184-4949. Offers technology management (MBA). Evening/weekend programs available. *Faculty:* 62 part-time/adjunct (11 women). *Students:* 28 full-time (9 women); includes 4 minority (2 African Americans, 2 Asian Americans or Pacific Islanders), 3 international. Average age 40. In 2006, 10 degrees awarded. *Degree requirements:* For master's, thesis (for some programs), registration. *Entrance requirements:* For master's, minimum GPA of 3.0, 3 years of work experience. Additional exam requirements/recommendations for international students: Required—TOEFL (minimum score 550 paper-based; 213 computer-based; 79 iBT). *Application deadline:* Applications are processed on a rolling basis. Application fee: $45. Electronic applications accepted. *Expenses:* Tuition: Full-time $13,848. Required fees: $760. *Financial support:* Institutionally sponsored loans and scholarships/grants available. *Unit head:* Dr. Adam Honea, Dean and Executive Director, 480-557-1659, Fax: 480-929-7164, E-mail: adam.honea@phoenix.edu. *Application contact:* Campus College Chair, 781-843-0844.

University of Phoenix–Central Florida Campus, John Sperling School of Business, College of Information Systems and Technology, Maitland, FL 32751-7057. Offers management (MIS); technology management (MBA). Evening/weekend programs available. *Faculty:* 25 full-time (1 woman), 62 part-time/adjunct (9 women). *Students:* 1 full-time (0 women); minority (Asian American or Pacific Islander) Average age 39. In 2006, 24 degrees awarded. *Degree requirements:* For master's, thesis (for some programs), registration. *Entrance requirements:* For master's, minimum undergraduate GPA of 3.0, 3 years work experience. Additional exam requirements/recommendations for international students: Required—TOEFL (minimum score 550 paper-based; 213 computer-based; 79 iBT). *Application deadline:* Applications are processed on a rolling basis. Application fee: $45. Electronic applications accepted. *Expenses:* Tuition: Full-time $9,450. Required fees: $760. *Financial support:* Institutionally sponsored loans and scholarships/grants available. Financial award applicants required to submit FAFSA. *Application contact:* Chair, 407-667-0555, Fax: 407-667-0560.

University of Phoenix–Charlotte Campus, John Sperling School of Business, College of Information Systems and Technology, Charlotte, NC 28273-3409. Offers information systems (MIS); information systems management (MISM); technology management (MBA). Evening/weekend programs available. *Faculty:* 4 full-time (2 women), 51 part-time/adjunct (7 women). *Students:* 38 full-time (13 women); includes 14 minority (13 African Americans, 1 Hispanic American), 1 international. Average age 39. In 2006, 11 degrees awarded. *Degree requirements:* For master's, thesis (for some programs), registration. *Entrance requirements:* For master's, minimum undergraduate GPA of 3.0, 3 years work experience. Additional exam requirements/recommendations for international students: Required—TOEFL (minimum score 550 paper-based; 213 computer-based; 79 iBT). *Application deadline:* Applications are processed on a rolling basis. Application fee: $45. Electronic applications accepted. *Expenses:* Tuition: Full-time $10,320. Required fees: $760. *Financial support:* Institutionally sponsored loans and scholarships/grants available. Financial award applicants required to submit FAFSA. *Application contact:* College Chair, 704-504-5409, Fax: 704-504-5360.

University of Phoenix–Cheyenne Campus, College of Information Systems and Technology, Cheyenne, WY 82009. Offers information systems (MIS); technology management (MBA).

University of Phoenix–Chicago Campus, John Sperling School of Business, College of Information Systems and Technology, Schaumburg, IL 60173-4399. Offers e-business (MBA); information systems (MIS); management (MM); technology management (MBA). Evening/weekend programs available. *Faculty:* 4 full-time (3 women), 38 part-time/adjunct (8 women). *Students:* 10 full-time (4 women); includes 6 minority (1 African American, 3 Asian Americans or Pacific Islanders, 2 Hispanic Americans). Average age 37. In 2006, 19 degrees awarded. *Degree requirements:* For master's, thesis (for some programs), registration. *Entrance requirements:* For master's, 3 years of work experience, minimum undergraduate GPA of 3.0. Additional exam requirements/recommendations for international students: Required—TOEFL (minimum score 550 paper-based; 213 computer-based; 79 iBT). *Application deadline:* Applications are processed on a rolling basis. Application fee: $45. Electronic applications accepted. *Expenses:* Tuition: Full-time $12,120. Required fees: $760. *Financial support:* Institutionally sponsored loans and scholarships/grants available. Financial award applicants required to submit FAFSA. *Application contact:* Campus College Chair—Technology, 847-413-1922, Fax: 847-413-8706.

University of Phoenix–Cleveland Campus, John Sperling School of Business, College of Information Systems and Technology, Independence, OH 44131-2194. Offers information management (MIS); technology management (MBA). Evening/weekend programs available. *Faculty:* 7 full-time (0 women), 23 part-time/adjunct (8 women). *Students:* 1 (woman) full-time; minority (African American) Average age 32. *Degree requirements:* For master's, thesis (for some programs), registration. *Entrance requirements:* For master's, minimum undergraduate GPA of 3.0, 3 years of work experience. Additional exam requirements/recommendations for international students: Required—TOEFL (minimum score 550 paper-based; 213 computer-based; 79 iBT). *Application deadline:* Applications are processed on a rolling basis. Application fee: $45. Electronic applications accepted. *Expenses:* Tuition: Full-time $11,608. Required fees: $760. *Financial support:* Institutionally sponsored loans and scholarships/grants available. Financial award applicants required to submit FAFSA. *Unit head:* Dr. Adam Honea, Provost/Dean, Vice President Academic Research and Development, 480-557-1659, E-mail: adam.honea@phoenix.edu. *Application contact:* 216-447-8807, Fax: 216-447-9144.

University of Phoenix–Denver Campus, John Sperling School of Business, College of Information Systems and Technology, Lone Tree, CO 80124-5453. Offers e-business (MBA); management (MIS); technology management (MBA). Evening/weekend programs available. *Faculty:* 26 full-time (9 women), 118 part-time/adjunct (25 women). *Students:* 7 full-time (2 women); includes 1 minority (Hispanic American) Average age 38. In 2006, 11 master's awarded. *Degree requirements:* For master's, thesis (for some programs), registration. *Entrance requirements:* For master's, minimum undergraduate GPA of 3.0, 3 years of work experience. Additional exam requirements/recommendations for international students: Required—TOEFL (minimum score 550 paper-based; 213 computer-based; 79 iBT). *Application deadline:* Applications are processed on a rolling basis. Application fee: $45. Electronic applications accepted. *Expenses:* Tuition: Full-time $10,032. Required fees: $760. *Financial support:* Institutionally sponsored loans and scholarships/grants available. Financial award applicants required to submit FAFSA. *Unit head:* Dr. Adam Honea, Dean/Executive Director, 480-557-1659, E-mail: adam.honea@phoenix.edu. *Application contact:* Chair, 303-694-9093, Fax: 303-662-0911.

University of Phoenix–Des Moines Campus, College of Information Systems and Technology, Des Moines, IA 50266. Offers infomation systems and technology (MIS); technology management (MBA).

University of Phoenix–Detroit Campus, College of Information Systems and Technology, Southfield, MI 48076. Offers information systems (MIS); management (MIS); technology management (MBA).

University of Phoenix–Fort Lauderdale Campus, John Sperling School of Business, College of Information Systems and Technology, Fort Lauderdale, FL 33309. Offers management (MIS); technology management (MBA). Evening/weekend programs available. *Faculty:* 11 full-time (3 women), 53 part-time/adjunct (4 women). *Students:* 16 full-time (8 women); includes 9 minority (5 African Americans, 4 Hispanic Americans), 2 international. Average age 40. In 2006, 10 degrees awarded. *Degree requirements:* For master's, thesis (for some programs), registration. *Entrance requirements:* For master's, minimum undergraduate GPA of 3.0, 3 years of work experience. Additional exam requirements/recommendations for international students: Required—TOEFL (minimum score 550 paper-based; 213 computer-based; 79 iBT). *Application deadline:* Applications are processed on a rolling basis. Application fee: $45. Electronic applications accepted. *Expenses:* Tuition: Full-time $9,450. Required fees: $760. *Financial support:* Institutionally sponsored loans and scholarships/grants available. Financial award applicants required to submit FAFSA. *Application contact:* Chair, 954-382-5303, Fax: 954-382-5304.

University of Phoenix–Harrisburg Campus, College of Information Systems and Technology, Harrisburg, PA 17112. Offers information systems (MIS); technology management (MBA).

University of Phoenix–Hawaii Campus, John Sperling School of Business, College of Information Systems and Technology, Honolulu, HI 96813-4317. Offers management (MIS); technology management (MBA). Evening/weekend programs available. *Faculty:* 7 full-time (1 woman), 57 part-time/adjunct (7 women). *Students:* 16 full-time (3 women); includes 5 minority (2 African Americans, 3 Asian Americans or Pacific Islanders), 6 international. Average age 37. In 2006, 11 degrees awarded. *Degree requirements:* For master's, thesis (for some programs), registration. *Entrance requirements:* For master's, minimum undergraduate GPA of 3.0, 3 years of work experience. Additional exam requirements/recommendations for international students: Required—TOEFL (minimum score 550 paper-based; 213 computer-based; 79 iBT). *Application deadline:* Applications are processed on a rolling basis. Application fee: $45. Electronic applications accepted. *Expenses:* Tuition: Full-time $11,520. Required fees: $760. *Financial support:* Institutionally sponsored loans and scholarships/grants available. Financial award applicants required to submit FAFSA. *Unit head:* Dr. Adam Honea, Dean/Executive

Director, 480-557-1659, E-mail: adam.honea@phoenix.edu. *Application contact:* Chair, 808-536-2686, Fax: 808-536-3848.

University of Phoenix–Idaho Campus, John Sperling School of Business, College of Information Systems and Technology, Meridian, ID 83642-3014. Offers information systems (MIS); technology management (MBA). Evening/weekend programs available. *Faculty:* 4 full-time (0 women), 12 part-time/adjunct (3 women). *Students:* 1 full-time (0 women), 1 international. Average age 52. In 2006, 1 degree awarded. *Degree requirements:* For master's, thesis (for some programs), registration. *Entrance requirements:* For master's, minimum undergraduate GPA of 3.0, 3 years of work experience. Additional exam requirements/recommendations for international students: Required—TOEFL (minimum score 550 paper-based; 213 computer-based). *Application deadline:* Applications are processed on a rolling basis. Application fee: $45. Electronic applications accepted. *Expenses:* Tuition: Full-time $9,104. *Financial support:* Institutionally sponsored loans and scholarships/grants available. *Application contact:* College Chair, 208-888-1505, Fax: 208-888-4775.

University of Phoenix–Indianapolis Campus, John Sperling School of Business, College of Information Systems and Technology, Indianapolis, IN 46250-932. Offers information systems (MIS); technology management (MBA). Evening/weekend programs available. *Faculty:* 3 full-time (0 women), 41 part-time/adjunct (6 women). *Students:* 1 full-time (0 women), 1 international. Average age 39. In 2006, 1 degree awarded. *Degree requirements:* For master's, thesis (for some programs), registration. *Entrance requirements:* For master's, minimum undergraduate GPA of 3.0, 3 years of work experience. Additional exam requirements/recommendations for international students: Required—TOEFL (minimum score 550 paper-based; 213 computer-based). *Application deadline:* Applications are processed on a rolling basis. Application fee: $45. Electronic applications accepted. *Expenses:* Tuition: Full-time $10,320. Required fees: $760. *Financial support:* Institutionally sponsored loans and scholarships/grants available. Financial award applicants required to submit FAFSA. *Unit head:* Dr. Adam Honea, Dean/Executive Director, 480-557-1659, E-mail: adam.honea@phoenix.edu. *Application contact:* Chair, 317-585-8610.

University of Phoenix–Jersey City Campus, College of Information Systems and Technology, Jersey City, NJ 07310. Offers information systems (MIS); technology management (MBA).

University of Phoenix–Las Vegas Campus, John Sperling School of Business, College of Information Systems and Technology, Las Vegas, NV 89128. Offers information systems (MIS); technology management (MBA). Evening/weekend programs available. *Faculty:* 11 full-time (2 women), 64 part-time/adjunct (10 women). *Students:* 14 full-time (6 women); includes 4 minority (2 African Americans, 2 Hispanic Americans). Average age 37. In 2006, 13 degrees awarded. *Degree requirements:* For master's, thesis (for some programs), registration. *Entrance requirements:* For master's, minimum undergraduate GPA of 3.0, 3 years of work experience. Additional exam requirements/recommendations for international students: Required—TOEFL (minimum score 550 paper-based; 213 computer-based; 79 iBT). *Application deadline:* Applications are processed on a rolling basis. Application fee: $45. Electronic applications accepted. *Expenses:* Tuition: Full-time $9,576. Required fees: $760. *Financial support:* Institutionally sponsored loans and scholarships/grants available. Financial award applicants required to submit FAFSA. *Unit head:* Dr. Adam Honea, Dean/Executive Director, 480-557-1659, E-mail: adam.honea@phoenix.edu. *Application contact:* Chair, 702-638-7249, Fax: 702-638-8035.

University of Phoenix–Louisiana Campus, John Sperling School of Business, College of Information Systems and Technology, Metairie, LA 70001-2082. Offers information systems/management (MIS); technology management (MBA). Evening/weekend programs available. *Faculty:* 9 full-time (4 women), 56 part-time/adjunct (20 women). *Students:* 37 full-time (19 women); includes 14 minority (13 African Americans, 1 Asian American or Pacific Islander), 4 international. Average age 33. In 2006, 6 degrees awarded. *Degree requirements:* For master's, thesis (for some programs), registration. *Entrance requirements:* For master's, minimum undergraduate GPA of 3.0, 3 years work experience. Additional exam requirements/recommendations for international students: Required—TOEFL (minimum score 550 paper-based; 213 computer-based). *Application deadline:* Applications are processed on a rolling basis. Application fee: $45. Electronic applications accepted. *Expenses:* Tuition: Full-time $11,832. Required fees: $760. *Financial support:* Institutionally sponsored loans and scholarships/grants available. *Unit head:* Dr. Adam Honea, Dean, 480-557-1659, E-mail: adam.honea@phoenix.edu. *Application contact:* Campus College Chair, 504-461-8852, Fax: 504-464-6373.

University of Phoenix–Madison Campus, College of Information Systems and Technology, Madison, WI 53718-2416. Offers information systems (MIS); management (MIS); technology management (MBA).

University of Phoenix–Maryland Campus, John Sperling School of Business, College of Information Systems and Technology, Columbia, MD 21045-5424. Offers information systems (MIS); technology management (MBA). Evening/weekend programs available. *Faculty:* 11 full-time (5 women), 51 part-time/adjunct (7 women). *Students:* 31 full-time (17 women); includes 11 minority (all African Americans), 7 international. Average age 39. In 2006, 40 degrees awarded. *Degree requirements:* For master's, thesis (for some programs), registration. *Entrance requirements:* For master's, minimum undergraduate GPA of 3.0, 3 years of work experience. Additional exam requirements/recommendations for international students: Required—TOEFL (minimum score 550 paper-based; 213 computer-based; 79 iBT). *Application deadline:* Applications are processed on a rolling basis. Application fee: $45. Electronic applications accepted. *Expenses:* Tuition: Full-time $13,200. Required fees: $760. *Financial support:* Institutionally sponsored loans and scholarships/grants available. Financial award applicants required to submit FAFSA. *Unit head:* Dr. Adam Honea, Dean/Executive Director, 480-537-1659, E-mail: adam.honea@phoenix.edu. *Application contact:* Chair, 410-872-9001, Fax: 410-536-5727.

University of Phoenix–Memphis Campus, College of Information Systems and Technology, Cordova, TN 38018. Offers information systems (MIS); technology management (MBA).

University of Phoenix–Metro Detroit Campus, John Sperling School of Business, College of Information Systems and Technology, Troy, MI 48098-2623. Offers management (MIS); technology management (MBA). Evening/weekend programs available. *Faculty:* 20 full-time (5 women), 98 part-time/adjunct (18 women). *Students:* 49 full-time (20 women); includes 19 minority (17 African Americans, 2 Asian Americans or Pacific Islanders), 7 international. Average age 38. In 2006, 32 degrees awarded. *Degree requirements:* For master's, thesis (for some programs), registration. *Entrance requirements:* For master's, minimum undergraduate GPA of 3.0, 3 years work experience. Additional exam requirements/recommendations for international students: Required—TOEFL (minimum score 550 paper-based; 213 computer-based; 79 iBT). *Application deadline:* Applications are processed on a rolling basis. Application fee: $45. Electronic applications accepted. *Expenses:* Tuition: Full-time $12,168. Required fees: $760. *Financial support:* Institutionally sponsored loans and scholarships/grants available. Financial award applicants required to submit FAFSA. *Unit head:* Dr. Adam Honea, Dean/Executive Director, 480-557-1659, E-mail: adam.honea@phoenix.edu. *Application contact:* Chair, 800-834-2438, Fax: 248-267-0147.

University of Phoenix–Nashville Campus, John Sperling School of Business, College of Information Systems and Technology, Nashville, TN 37214-5048. Offers technology management (MBA). Evening/weekend programs available. *Faculty:* 15 full-time (0 women), 23 part-time/adjunct (5 women). *Students:* 34 full-time (16 women); includes 14 minority (13 African Americans, 1 Hispanic American), 1 international. Average age 34. In 2006, 10 degrees awarded. *Degree requirements:* For master's, thesis (for some programs), registration. *Entrance requirements:* For master's, 3 years of work experience, minimum undergraduate GPA of 3.0. Additional exam requirements/recommendations for international students: Required—TOEFL (minimum score 550 paper-based; 213 computer-based; 79 iBT). *Application deadline:* Applications are processed on a rolling basis. Application fee: $45. Electronic applications accepted. *Expenses:* Tuition: Full-time $10,104. Required fees: $760. *Financial support:* Institutionally sponsored loans and scholarships/grants available. Financial award applicants required to submit FAFSA. *Unit head:* Dr. Adam Honea, Dean/Executive Director, 480-557-1659, E-mail: adam.honea@phoenix.edu. *Application contact:* Chair, 615-872-0188.

University of Phoenix–New Mexico Campus, John Sperling School of Business, College of Information Systems and Technology, Albuquerque, NM 87109-4645. Offers e-business (MBA); technology management (MBA). Evening/weekend programs available. *Faculty:* 7 full-time (2 women), 115 part-time/adjunct (14 women). *Students:* 20 full-time (8 women); includes 9 minority (1 Asian American or Pacific Islander, 8 Hispanic Americans). Average age 37. In 2006, 36 degrees awarded. *Degree requirements:* For master's, thesis (for some programs), registration. *Entrance requirements:* For master's, minimum undergraduate GPA of 3.0, 3 years of work experience. Additional exam requirements/recommendations for international students: Required—TOEFL (minimum score 550 paper-based; 213 computer-based; 79 iBT). *Application deadline:* Applications are processed on a rolling basis. Application fee: $45. Electronic applications accepted. *Expenses:* Tuition: Full-time $9,005. Required fees: $760. *Financial support:* Institutionally sponsored loans and scholarships/grants available. Financial award applicants required to submit FAFSA. *Unit head:* Dr. Adam Honea, Dean/Executive Director, 480-557-1659, E-mail: adam.honea@phoenix.edu. *Application contact:* Chair, 505-821-4800, Fax: 505-821-5551.

University of Phoenix—Northern Nevada Campus, College of Information Systems and Technology, Reno, NV 89511. Offers information systems (MIS); technology management (MBA).

University of Phoenix–Northern Virginia Campus, College of Information Systems and Technology, Reston, VA 20190. Offers information systems and technology (MIS); management (MIS); technology management (MBA).

University of Phoenix–North Florida Campus, John Sperling School of Business, College of Information Systems and Technology, Jacksonville, FL 32216-0959. Offers information systems (MIS); management (MIS). Evening/weekend programs available. *Faculty:* 20 full-time (5 women), 50 part-time/adjunct (6 women). *Students:* 20 full-time (3 women); includes 4 minority (3 African Americans, 1 Asian American or Pacific Islander), 3 international. Average age 36. In 2006, 4 master's awarded. *Degree requirements:* For master's, thesis (for some programs), registration. *Entrance requirements:* For master's, minimum undergraduate GPA of 3.0, 3 years work experience. Additional exam requirements/recommendations for international students: Required—TOEFL (minimum score 550 paper-based; 213 computer-based; 79 iBT). *Application deadline:* Applications are processed on a rolling basis. Application fee: $45. Electronic applications accepted. *Financial support:* Institutionally sponsored loans and scholarships/grants available. Financial award applicants required to submit FAFSA. *Unit head:* Dr. Adam Honea, Dean, 480-557-1659, E-mail: adam.honea@phoenix.edu. *Application contact:* Chair, 904-636-6645, Fax: 904-636-0998.

University of Phoenix–Northwest Arkansas Campus, College of Information Systems and Technology, Rogers, AR 72756-9615. Offers information systems (MIS); technology management (MBA).

University of Phoenix–Northwest Indiana, College of Information Systems and Technology, Merrillville, IN 46410. Offers MIS.

University of Phoenix–Oklahoma City Campus, John Sperling School of Business, College of Information Systems and Technology, Oklahoma City, OK 73116-8244. Offers e-business (MBA); technology management (MBA). Evening/weekend programs available. *Faculty:* 4 full-time (0 women), 49 part-time/adjunct (6 women). *Students:* 2 full-time (0 women); includes 3 minority (2 American Indian/Alaska Native, 1 Hispanic American). Average age 39. In 2006, 10 degrees awarded. *Degree requirements:* For master's, thesis (for some programs), registration. *Entrance requirements:* For master's, minimum undergraduate GPA of 3.0, 3 years of work experience. Additional exam requirements/recommendations for international students: Required—TOEFL (minimum score 550 paper-based; 213 computer-based; 79 iBT). *Application deadline:* Applications are processed on a rolling basis. Application fee: $45. Electronic applications accepted. *Expenses:* Tuition: Full-time $10,608. Required fees: $760. *Financial support:* Institutionally sponsored loans and scholarships/grants available. Financial award applicants required to submit FAFSA. *Unit head:* Dr. Adam Honea, Provost/Dean, 480-557-1659, E-mail: adam.honea@phoenix.edu. *Application contact:* Chair, 405-842-8007, Fax: 405-841-3386.

University of Phoenix–Omaha Campus, College of Information Systems and Technology, Omaha, NE 68154-5240. Offers information systems (MIS); technology management (MBA).

University of Phoenix Online Campus, John Sperling School of Business, College of Information Systems and Technology, Phoenix, AZ 85034-7209. Offers e-business (MBA); management (MIS); technology management (MBA). Evening/weekend programs available. *Faculty:* 7 full-time (3 women), 2,317 part-time/adjunct (528 women). *Students:* 4,315 full-time (1,423 women); includes 967 minority (552 African Americans, 19 American Indian/Alaska Native, 222 Asian Americans or Pacific Islanders, 174 Hispanic Americans), 581 international. Average age 38. In 2006, 7359 degrees awarded. *Degree requirements:* For master's, thesis (for some programs), registration. *Entrance requirements:* For master's, 3 years of work experience, minimum undergraduate GPA of 3.0. Additional exam requirements/recommendations for international students: Required—TOEFL (minimum score 550 paper-based; 213 computer-based; 79 iBT). *Application deadline:* Applications are processed on a rolling basis. Application fee: $45. Electronic applications accepted. *Expenses:* Tuition: Full-time $12,664. Required fees: $760. *Financial support:* Institutionally sponsored loans and scholarships/grants available. Financial award applicants required to submit FAFSA. *Unit head:* Dr. Adam Honea, Dean/Executive Director, 480-557-1659, E-mail: adam.honea@phoenix.edu. *Application contact:* Dr. Adam Honea, Dean/Executive Director, 480-557-1659, E-mail: adam.honea@phoenix.edu.

University of Phoenix–Oregon Campus, The John Sperling School of Business, College of Information Systems and Technology, Tigard, OR 97223. Offers information systems (MIS); technology management (MBA). Evening/weekend programs available. *Faculty:* 10 full-time (0 women), 60 part-time/adjunct (12 women). *Students:* 22 full-time (7 women); includes 2 minority (both Hispanic Americans), 4 international. Average age 41. In 2006, 41 degrees awarded. *Degree requirements:* For master's, thesis (for some programs), registration. *Entrance requirements:* For master's, minimum undergraduate GPA of 2.5, 3 years work experience. Additional exam requirements/recommendations for international students: Required—TOEFL (minimum score 550 paper-based; 213 computer-based; 79 iBT). *Application deadline:* Applications are processed on a rolling basis. Application fee: $45. Electronic applications accepted. *Expenses:* Tuition: Full-time $10,200. Required fees: $760. *Financial support:* Institutionally sponsored loans and scholarships/grants available. Financial award applicants required to submit FAFSA. *Unit head:* Dr. Adam Honea, Provost/Dean, 480-557-1689, E-mail: adam.honea@phoenix.edu. *Application contact:* Chair, 503-403-2900, Fax: 503-670-0614.

University of Phoenix–Philadelphia Campus, The John Sperling School of Business, College of Information Systems and Technology, Wayne, PA 19087-2121. Offers information systems (MIS); technology management (MBA). Evening/weekend programs available. *Faculty:* 9 full-time (0 women), 34 part-time/adjunct (2 women). *Students:* 32 full-time (9 women); includes 14 minority (10 African Americans, 2 Asian Americans or Pacific Islanders, 2 Hispanic Americans), 2 international. Average age 39. In 2006, 16 degrees awarded. *Degree requirements:* For master's, thesis (for some programs), registration. *Entrance requirements:* For master's, 3 years of work experience, minimum undergraduate GPA of 3.0. Additional exam requirements/recommendations for international students: Required—TOEFL (minimum score 550 paper-based; 213 computer-based; 79 iBT). *Application deadline:* Applications are processed on a rolling basis. Application fee: $45. Electronic applications accepted. *Expenses:* Tuition: Full-time $13,560. Required fees: $760. *Financial support:* Institutionally sponsored

Management Information Systems

University of Phoenix–Philadelphia Campus (continued)
loans and scholarships/grants available. Financial award applicants required to submit FAFSA. *Unit head:* Dr. Adam Honea, Provost/Dean, Vice President Academic Research and Development, 480-557-1659, Fax: 480-929-7164, E-mail: adam.honea@phoenix.edu. *Application contact:* Campus College Chair, 610-984-0880, Fax: 610-989-0881.

University of Phoenix–Pittsburgh Campus, John Sperling School of Business, College of Information Systems and Technology, Pittsburgh, PA 15276. Offers e-business (MBA); information systems (MIS); technology management (MBA). Evening/weekend programs available. *Faculty:* 11 full-time (3 women), 21 part-time/adjunct (0 women). *Students:* 12 full-time (3 women); includes 3 minority (2 African Americans, 1 Asian American or Pacific Islander). Average age 36. In 2006, 8 degrees awarded. *Degree requirements:* For master's, thesis (for some programs), registration. *Entrance requirements:* For master's, minimum undergraduate GPA of 3.0, 3 years work experience. Additional exam requirements/recommendations for international students: Required—TOEFL (minimum score 550 paper-based; 213 computer-based; 79 iBT). *Application deadline:* Applications are processed on a rolling basis. Application fee: $45. Electronic applications accepted. *Expenses:* Tuition: Full-time $13,560. Required fees: $760. *Financial support:* Institutionally sponsored loans and scholarships/grants available. Financial award applicants required to submit FAFSA. *Unit head:* Dr. Adam Honea, Provost/Dean, Vice President Research and Development, 480-557-1659, E-mail: adam.honea@phoenix.edu. *Application contact:* Campus College Chair, 412-747-9000, Fax: 412-747-0676.

University of Phoenix–Raleigh Campus, College of Information Systems and Technology, Raleigh, NC 27606. Offers information systems and technology (MIS); management (MIS); technology management (MBA).

University of Phoenix–Renton Learning Center, College of Information Systems and Technology, Renton, WA 98005. Offers information systems (MIS); technology management (MBA).

University of Phoenix–Richmond Campus, John Sperling School of Business, College of Information Systems and Technology, Richmond, VA 23230. Offers information systems (MIS); technology management (MBA). Evening/weekend programs available. *Faculty:* 3 full-time (all women), 20 part-time/adjunct (2 women). *Students:* 6 full-time (3 women); includes 2 African Americans. Average age 42. *Degree requirements:* For master's, thesis (for some programs), registration. *Entrance requirements:* For master's, minimum undergraduate GPA 3.0, 3 years work experience. Additional exam requirements/recommendations for international students: Required—TOEFL (minimum score 500 paper-based; 213 computer-based; 79 iBT). *Application deadline:* Applications are processed on a rolling basis. Application fee: $45. Electronic applications accepted. *Financial support:* Institutionally sponsored loans and scholarships/grants available. Financial award applicants required to submit FAFSA. *Unit head:* Dr. Adam Honea, Provost, 480-557-1659, E-mail: adam.honea@phoenix.edu. *Application contact:* Chair, 804-288-3390.

University of Phoenix–Sacramento Valley Campus, John Sperling School of Business, College of Information Systems and Technology, Sacramento, CA 95833-3632. Offers management (MIS); technology management (MBA). Evening/weekend programs available. *Faculty:* 15 full-time (4 women), 144 part-time/adjunct (25 women). *Students:* 19 full-time (2 women); includes 8 minority (4 African Americans, 3 Asian Americans or Pacific Islanders, 1 Hispanic American), 2 international. Average age 41. In 2006, 22 degrees awarded. *Degree requirements:* For master's, thesis (for some programs), registration. *Entrance requirements:* For master's, minimum undergraduate GPA of 3.0, 3 years work experience. Additional exam requirements/recommendations for international students: Required—TOEFL (minimum score 550 paper-based; 213 computer-based; 79 iBT). *Application deadline:* Applications are processed on a rolling basis. Application fee: $45. Electronic applications accepted. *Expenses:* Tuition: Full-time $12,024. Required fees: $760. *Financial support:* Institutionally sponsored loans and scholarships/grants available. Financial award applicants required to submit FAFSA. *Unit head:* Dr. Adam Honea, Provost/Dean, Vice President Academic Research and Development, 480-557-1659, E-mail: adam.honea@phoenix.edu. *Application contact:* Campus College Chair, 916-923-2107, Fax: 916-923-3914.

University of Phoenix–St. Louis Campus, John Sperling School of Business, College of Information Systems and Technology, St. Louis, MO 63043-4828. Offers technology management (MBA). Evening/weekend programs available. *Faculty:* 7 full-time (2 women), 37 part-time/adjunct (11 women). *Degree requirements:* For master's, thesis (for some programs), registration. *Entrance requirements:* For master's, minimum undergraduate GPA of 3.0, 3 years of work experience. Additional exam requirements/recommendations for international students: Required—TOEFL (minimum score 550 paper-based; 213 computer-based). *Application deadline:* Applications are processed on a rolling basis. Application fee: $45. Electronic applications accepted. *Expenses:* Tuition: Full-time $11,832. Required fees: $762. *Financial support:* Institutionally sponsored loans available. Financial award applicants required to submit FAFSA. *Unit head:* Dr. Adam Honea, Dean/Executive Director, 480-557-1659, E-mail: adam.honea@phoenix.edu. *Application contact:* College Chair, 314-298-9755, Fax: 314-291-2901.

University of Phoenix–San Antonio Campus, College of Information Systems and Technology, San Antonio, TX 78230. Offers information systems (MIS); technology management (MBA).

University of Phoenix–San Diego Campus, John Sperling School of Business, College of Information Systems and Technology, San Diego, CA 92123. Offers management (MIS); technology management (MBA). Evening/weekend programs available. *Faculty:* 13 full-time (0 women), 133 part-time/adjunct (13 women). *Students:* 23 full-time (4 women); includes 3 minority (1 African American, 2 Hispanic Americans), 1 international. Average age 40. In 2006, 39 degrees awarded. *Degree requirements:* For master's, thesis (for some programs), registration. *Entrance requirements:* For master's, minimum undergraduate GPA of 3.0, 3 years work experience. Additional exam requirements/recommendations for international students: Required—TOEFL (minimum score 550 paper-based; 213 computer-based; 79 iBT). *Application deadline:* Applications are processed on a rolling basis. Application fee: $45. Electronic applications accepted. *Expenses:* Tuition: Full-time $11,419. Required fees: $760. *Financial support:* Institutionally sponsored loans and scholarships/grants available. Financial award applicants required to submit FAFSA. *Unit head:* Dr. Adam Honea, Provost/Dean, Vice President Academic Research and Development, 480-557-1659, E-mail: adam.honea@phoenix.edu. *Application contact:* Campus College Chair, 888-UOP-INFO, Fax: 858-509-4399.

University of Phoenix–Savannah Campus, College of Information Systems and Technology, Savannah, GA 31405-7400. Offers information systems and technology (MIS); technology management (MBA).

University of Phoenix–Southern Arizona Campus, John Sperling School of Business, College of Information Systems and Technology, Tucson, AZ 85712-2732. Offers information systems (MIS); technology management (MBA). Evening/weekend programs available. *Faculty:* 13 full-time (4 women), 120 part-time/adjunct (16 women). *Students:* 63 full-time (16 women); includes 16 minority (6 African Americans, 1 American Indian/Alaska Native, 1 Asian American or Pacific Islander, 8 Hispanic Americans), 7 international. Average age 37. In 2006, 68 degrees awarded. *Degree requirements:* For master's, thesis (for some programs), registration. *Entrance requirements:* For master's, minimum undergraduate GPA of 3.0, 3 years of work experience. Additional exam requirements/recommendations for international students: Required—TOEFL (minimum score 550 paper-based; 213 computer-based; 79 iBT). *Application deadline:* Applications are processed on a rolling basis. Application fee: $45. Electronic applications accepted. *Expenses:* Tuition: Full-time $8,669. Required fees: $760. *Financial support:* Institutionally sponsored loans and scholarships/grants available. Financial award applicants required to submit FAFSA. *Unit head:* Dr. Adam Honea, Provost/Dean, Vice President Academic Research and Development, 480-557-1659, E-mail: adam.honea@phoenix.edu. *Application contact:* Campus College Chair-Technology, 520-881-6512, Fax: 520-795-6177.

University of Phoenix–Southern California Campus, John Sperling School of Business, College of Information Systems and Technology, Costa Mesa, CA 92626. Offers technology management (MBA). Evening/weekend programs available. *Faculty:* 24 full-time (9 women), 278 part-time/adjunct (45 women). *Students:* 87 full-time (20 women); includes 25 minority (9 African Americans, 5 Asian Americans or Pacific Islanders, 11 Hispanic Americans), 12 international. Average age 39. In 2006, 60 degrees awarded. *Degree requirements:* For master's, thesis (for some programs), registration. *Entrance requirements:* For master's, minimum undergraduate GPA of 3.0, 3 years of work experience. Additional exam requirements/recommendations for international students: Required—TOEFL (minimum score 550 paper-based; 213 computer-based; 79 iBT). *Application deadline:* Applications are processed on a rolling basis. Application fee: $45. Electronic applications accepted. *Expenses:* Tuition: Full-time $13,512. Required fees: $760. *Financial support:* Institutionally sponsored loans and scholarships/grants available. Financial award applicants required to submit FAFSA. *Unit head:* Dr. Adam Honea, Provost/Dean, Vice President Research and Development, 480-557-1659, E-mail: adam.honea@phoenix.edu. *Application contact:* Campus College Chair, 714-378-1878.

University of Phoenix–Southern Colorado Campus, John Sperling School of Business, College of Information Systems and Technology, Colorado Springs, CO 80919-2335. Offers technology management (MBA). Evening/weekend programs available. *Faculty:* 4 full-time (0 women), 89 part-time/adjunct (20 women). *Students:* 1 full-time (0 women). Average age 25. In 2006, 6 degrees awarded. *Degree requirements:* For master's, thesis (for some programs), registration. *Entrance requirements:* For master's, minimum undergraduate GPA of 3.0, 3 years of work experience. Additional exam requirements/recommendations for international students: Required—TOEFL (minimum score 550 paper-based; 213 computer-based; 79 iBT). *Application deadline:* Applications are processed on a rolling basis. Application fee: $45. Electronic applications accepted. *Expenses:* Tuition: Full-time $10,291. Required fees: $760. *Financial support:* Institutionally sponsored loans and scholarships/grants available. Financial award applicants required to submit FAFSA. *Unit head:* Dr. Adam Honea, Provost/Dean, Vice President Academic Research and Development, 480-557-1659, E-mail: adam.honea@phoenix.edu. *Application contact:* Chair, 719-599-5282, Fax: 719-599-7973.

University of Phoenix–Springfield Campus, College of Information Systems and Technology, Springfield, MO 65804-7211. Offers information systems and technology (MIS); technology management (MBA).

University of Phoenix–Utah Campus, John Sperling School of Business, College of Information Systems and Technology, Salt Lake City, UT 84123-4617. Offers MIS. Evening/weekend programs available. *Faculty:* 27 full-time (1 woman), 64 part-time/adjunct (4 women). *Students:* 33 full-time (3 women); includes 1 minority (Asian American or Pacific Islander) Average age 32. In 2006, 15 degrees awarded. *Degree requirements:* For master's, thesis (for some programs), registration. *Entrance requirements:* For master's, minimum undergraduate GPA of 2.5, 3 years work experience. Additional exam requirements/recommendations for international students: Required—TOEFL (minimum score 550 paper-based; 213 computer-based; 79 iBT). *Application deadline:* Applications are processed on a rolling basis. Application fee: $45. Electronic applications accepted. *Expenses:* Tuition: Full-time $9,104. Required fees: $760. *Financial support:* Institutionally sponsored loans and scholarships/grants available. Financial award applicants required to submit FAFSA. *Unit head:* Dr. Adam Honea, Provost/Dean, Vice President Academic Research and Development, 480-557-1659, E-mail: adam.honea@phoenix.edu. *Application contact:* Chair, 801-263-1444, Fax: 801-269-9766.

University of Phoenix–Vancouver Campus, John Sperling School of Business, College of Information Systems and Technology, Burnaby, BC V5C 6G9, Canada. Offers technology management (MBA). Evening/weekend programs available. *Faculty:* 7. *Students:* 15 full-time (3 women); includes 5 minority (all Asian Americans or Pacific Islanders) Average age 35. In 2006, 4 degrees awarded. *Degree requirements:* For master's, thesis (for some programs), registration. *Entrance requirements:* For master's, minimum undergraduate GPA of 3.0, 3 years of work experience. Additional exam requirements/recommendations for international students: Required—TOEFL (minimum score 550 paper-based; 213 computer-based; 79 iBT). *Application deadline:* Applications are processed on a rolling basis. Application fee: $45. Electronic applications accepted. *Expenses:* Tuition: Full-time $12,840. Required fees: $760. *Financial support:* Institutionally sponsored loans and scholarships/grants available. *Unit head:* Dr. Adam Honea, Dean, 480-557-1659, E-mail: adam.honea@phoenix.edu. *Application contact:* Campus College Chair, 604-205-6999.

University of Phoenix–West Florida Campus, The John Sperling School of Business, College of Information Systems and Technology, Temple Terrace, FL 33637. Offers information systems and technology (MIS); technology management (MBA). Evening/weekend programs available. *Faculty:* 16 full-time (3 women), 79 part-time/adjunct (2 women). *Students:* 46 full-time (10 women); includes 18 minority (7 African Americans, 1 American Indian/Alaska Native, 3 Asian Americans or Pacific Islanders, 7 Hispanic Americans), 9 international. Average age 39. In 2006, 33 degrees awarded. *Degree requirements:* For master's, thesis (for some programs), registration. *Entrance requirements:* For master's, minimum undergraduate GPA of 3.0, 3 years work experience. Additional exam requirements/recommendations for international students: Required—TOEFL (minimum score 550 paper-based; 213 computer-based; 79 iBT). *Application deadline:* Applications are processed on a rolling basis. Application fee: $45. Electronic applications accepted. *Expenses:* Tuition: Full-time $9,450. Required fees: $760. *Financial support:* Institutionally sponsored loans and scholarships/grants available. Financial award applicants required to submit FAFSA. *Application contact:* Chair, 813-626-7911, Fax: 813-977-1449.

University of Phoenix–West Michigan Campus, The John Sperling School of Business, College of Information Systems and Technology, Walker, MI 49544. Offers e-business (MBA); technology management (MBA). Evening/weekend programs available. *Faculty:* 8 full-time (0 women), 26 part-time/adjunct (7 women). *Students:* 6 full-time (0 women); includes 1 minority (African American) Average age 33. In 2006, 11 master's awarded. *Degree requirements:* For master's, thesis (for some programs), registration. *Entrance requirements:* For master's, minimum undergraduate GPA of 3.0, 3 years of work experience. Additional exam requirements/recommendations for international students: Required—TOEFL (minimum score 550 paper-based; 213 computer-based; 79 iBT). *Application deadline:* Applications are processed on a rolling basis. Application fee: $45. Electronic applications accepted. *Expenses:* Tuition: Full-time $12,043. Required fees: $760. *Financial support:* Institutionally sponsored loans available. Financial award applicants required to submit FAFSA. *Unit head:* Dr. Adam Honea, Dean/Executive Director, 408-557-1659, E-mail: adam.honea@phoenix.edu. *Application contact:* Chair, 888-345-9699, Fax: 616-784-5300.

University of Phoenix–Wisconsin Campus, John Sperling School of Business, College of Information Systems and Technology, Brookfield, WI 53045-6608. Offers information systems (MIS); technology management (MBA). Evening/weekend programs available. *Faculty:* 4 full-time (2 women), 42 part-time/adjunct (11 women). *Students:* 2 full-time (0 women). Average age 46. In 2006, 11 degrees awarded. *Degree requirements:* For master's, thesis (for some programs), registration. *Entrance requirements:* For master's, 3 years of work experience, minimum undergraduate GPA of 3.0. Additional exam requirements/recommendations for international students: Required—TOEFL (minimum score 550 paper-based; 213 computer-based; 79 iBT). *Application deadline:* Applications are processed on a rolling basis. Application fee: $45. Electronic applications accepted. *Expenses:* Tuition: Full-time $10,944. Required fees: $760. *Financial support:* Institutionally sponsored loans available. Financial award applicants required to submit FAFSA. *Unit head:* Dr. Adam Honea, Provost, 480-557-1659, E-mail: adam.honea@phoenix.edu. *Application contact:* Chair, 262-785-0608, Fax: 262-785-0977.

University of Pittsburgh, Joseph M. Katz Graduate School of Business, Program in Management of Information Systems, Pittsburgh, PA 15260. Offers MS, MBA/MS. Part-time and evening/weekend programs available. *Faculty:* 9 full-time (1 woman). *Students:* 18 full-time (3 women), 17 part-time (1 woman); includes 3 minority (1 American Indian/Alaska Native, 1 Asian American or Pacific Islander, 1 Hispanic American). Average age 30. 35 applicants, 69% accepted, 15 enrolled. In 2006, 24 master's awarded. *Degree requirements:* For master's, thesis. *Entrance requirements:* For master's, GMAT. Additional exam requirements/recommendations for international students: Required—TOEFL. *Application deadline:* For fall admission, 3/1 for domestic students, 4/15 for international students. Application fee: $50. Electronic applications accepted. *Financial support:* In 2006–07, 3 students received support. Career-related internships or fieldwork, institutionally sponsored loans, scholarships/grants, and tuition waivers (full and partial) available. Financial award application deadline: 1/15; financial award applicants required to submit FAFSA. *Faculty research:* Software project management, knowledge management, human-computer interaction, electronic commerce, mis research methodology. Total annual research expenditures: $200,000. *Unit head:* Dr. Dennis F Galletta, Coordinator, 412-648-1699, Fax: 412-648-1693, E-mail: galletta@katz.pitt.edu. *Application contact:* Enrique Mu, Director, 412-648-2268, Fax: 412-648-1693, E-mail: enmu@katz.pitt.edu.

University of Redlands, School of Business, Redlands, CA 92373-0999. Offers business (MBA); information technology (MS); management (MA). Evening/weekend programs available. *Faculty:* 22 full-time, 138 part-time/adjunct. *Students:* 576 full-time (257 women); includes 247 minority (60 African Americans, 8 American Indian/Alaska Native, 54 Asian Americans or Pacific Islanders, 125 Hispanic Americans), 22 international. Average age 36. In 2006, 275 degrees awarded. *Entrance requirements:* For master's, minimum GPA of 3.0, 2 letters of recommendation. *Application deadline:* For fall admission, 9/1 priority date for domestic students; for spring admission, 2/1 priority date for domestic students. Applications are processed on a rolling basis. Application fee: $0. *Expenses:* Tuition: Part-time $584 per credit. Required fees: $20 per course. Full-time tuition and fees vary according to program. *Financial support:* Applicants required to submit FAFSA. *Faculty research:* Human resources management, educational leadership, humanities, teacher education. *Unit head:* Dr. Stuart Noble-Goodman, Interim Dean, 909-793-2121, Fax: 909-335-3400. *Application contact:* Kimmi Grulke, Campus Director, 885-999-9844, Fax: 909-335-5325, E-mail: schoolofbusiness@redlands.edu.

University of Rhode Island, Graduate School, College of Business Administration, PhD Programs in Business Administration, Kingston, RI 02881. Offers finance (PhD); management (PhD); management sciences and information systems (PhD); marketing (PhD). *Expenses:* Tuition, state resident: full-time $6,032; part-time $335 per credit. Tuition, nonresident: full-time $17,288; part-time $960 per credit. Required fees: $65 per credit. $30 per semester. One-time fee: $80 part-time. *Application contact:* Dr. Laura Beauvais, Director of Graduate Programs, 401-874-4341.

University of St. Thomas, Graduate Studies, Graduate Programs in Software, St. Paul, MN 55105-1096. Offers computer security (Certificate); information systems (MSDD, Certificate); software design and development (Certificate); software engineering (MS); software systems (MSS). *Faculty:* 6 full-time (0 women), 18 part-time/adjunct (1 woman). *Students:* Average age 34. 107 applicants, 100% accepted, 69 enrolled. In 2006, 121 master's, 16 other advanced degrees awarded. *Degree requirements:* For master's, thesis optional. *Application deadline:* For fall admission, 8/1 priority date for domestic students, 5/1 priority date for international students; for spring admission, 1/1 priority date for domestic students, 10/1 priority date for international students. Application fee: $30. *Expenses:* Contact institution. *Financial support:* In 2006–07, 139 students received support. Application deadline: 4/1. *Faculty research:* Distributed databases, fault tolerant computing, expert systems, bioinformatics. *Unit head:* Dr. Bhabani Misra, Director, 651-962-5508, Fax: 651-962-5543, E-mail: bsmisra@stthomas.edu. *Application contact:* Douglas J. Stubeda, Assistant Director, 651-962-5503, Fax: 651-962-5543, E-mail: djstubeda@stthomas.edu.

University of San Francisco, College of Professional Studies, Program in Information Systems, San Francisco, CA 94117-1080. Offers MS. Part-time and evening/weekend programs available. *Faculty:* 1 full-time (0 women), 16 part-time/adjunct (4 women). *Students:* 63 full-time (16 women); includes 25 minority (3 African Americans, 19 Asian Americans or Pacific Islanders, 3 Hispanic Americans), 8 international. Average age 36. 31 applicants, 77% accepted, 8 enrolled. In 2006, 28 degrees awarded. *Degree requirements:* For master's, thesis. *Entrance requirements:* For master's, minimum GPA of 3.0. Application fee: $55 ($65 for international students). *Expenses:* Tuition: Full-time $17,370; part-time $965 per unit. Tuition and fees vary according to degree level, campus/location and program. *Financial support:* In 2006–07, 29 students received support. Application deadline: 3/2. *Unit head:* Dr. Salomon Azhar, Director, 415-422-6952. *Application contact:* Advising Office, 415-422-6000.

The University of Scranton, Graduate School, Program in Business Administration, Scranton, PA 18510. Offers accounting (MBA); enterprise management technology (MBA); finance (MBA); general business administration (MBA); international business (MBA); management information systems (MBA); marketing (MBA); operations management (MBA). *Accreditation:* AACSB. Part-time and evening/weekend programs available. *Faculty:* 34 full-time (8 women). *Students:* 39 full-time (11 women), 54 part-time (15 women); includes 3 minority (1 American Indian/Alaska Native, 2 Hispanic Americans), 31 international. Average age 28. 58 applicants, 83% accepted. In 2006, 52 degrees awarded. *Degree requirements:* For master's, capstone experience. *Entrance requirements:* For master's, GMAT, minimum GPA of 2.75. Additional exam requirements/recommendations for international students: Required—TOEFL (minimum score 500 paper-based; 173 computer-based), IELTS (minimum score 6). *Application deadline:* Applications are processed on a rolling basis. Application fee: $50. *Expenses:* Tuition: Part-time $684 per credit. Required fees: $25 per term. *Financial support:* In 2006–07, 11 teaching assistantships with full tuition reimbursements (averaging $5,600 per year) were awarded; fellowships, career-related internships or fieldwork, Federal Work-Study, and unspecified assistantships also available. Support available to part-time students. Financial award application deadline: 3/1. *Faculty research:* Financial markets, strategic impact of total quality management, internal accounting controls, consumer preference, information systems and the Internet. *Unit head:* Dr. Murli Rajan, Director, 570-941-4043, Fax: 570-941-4342.

University of South Alabama, Graduate School, School of Computer and Information Sciences, Mobile, AL 36688-0002. Offers computer science (MS); information systems (MS). Part-time and evening/weekend programs available. *Faculty:* 12 full-time (1 woman). *Students:* 89 full-time (23 women), 12 part-time (3 women); includes 5 minority (all African Americans), 73 international. 231 applicants, 45% accepted, 26 enrolled. In 2006, 51 degrees awarded. *Degree requirements:* For master's, project, thesis optional. *Entrance requirements:* For master's, GRE General Test, minimum GPA of 2.5. *Application deadline:* For fall admission, 9/1 priority date for domestic students. Applications are processed on a rolling basis. Application fee: $25. *Financial support:* Research assistantships, career-related internships or fieldwork and institutionally sponsored loans available. Support available to part-time students. Financial award application deadline: 4/1. *Faculty research:* Numerical analysis, artificial intelligence, simulation, medical applications, software engineering. *Unit head:* Dr. David Feinstein, Dean, 251-460-6390.

University of Southern California, Graduate School, Marshall School of Business, Department of Information and Operations Management, Los Angeles, CA 90089. Offers MS. *Entrance requirements:* For master's, GMAT. *Expenses:* Tuition: Full-time $33,314; part-time $1,121 per credit. Required fees: $522. Full-time tuition and fees vary according to program. *Financial support:* Fellowships, research assistantships, teaching assistantships, Federal Work-Study, institutionally sponsored loans, and scholarships/grants available. Support available to part-time students. Financial award application deadline: 2/15; financial award applicants required to submit FAFSA. *Unit head:* Dr. Bert Steece, Chair, 213-740-0172.

University of Southern Mississippi, Graduate School, College of Business, School of Accountancy and Information Systems, Hattiesburg, MS 39406-0001. Offers accountancy (MPA). *Accreditation:* AACSB. Part-time and evening/weekend programs available. *Faculty:* 16 full-time (4 women). *Students:* 15 full-time (9 women), 4 part-time (3 women); includes 2 minority (both African Americans), 2 international. Average age 28. 17 applicants, 59% accepted, 9 enrolled. In 2006, 15 degrees awarded. *Degree requirements:* For master's, comprehensive exam, registration. *Entrance requirements:* For master's, GMAT. Additional exam requirements/recommendations for international students: Required—TOEFL. *Application deadline:* For fall admission, 7/15 priority date for domestic students, 7/15 for international students; for spring admission, 11/15 priority date for domestic students, 11/15 for international students. Applications are processed on a rolling basis. Application fee: $25 ($30 for international students). Electronic applications accepted. *Financial support:* In 2006–07, 8 research assistantships with full tuition reimbursements (averaging $5,400 per year) were awarded; Federal Work-Study and institutionally sponsored loans also available. Support available to part-time students. Financial award application deadline: 3/15. *Faculty research:* Bank liquidity, subchapter S corporations, internal auditing, governmental accounting, inflation accounting. *Unit head:* Dr. Stan Lewis, Interim Director, 601-266-4322, Fax: 601-266-4639. *Application contact:* Dr. Francis Daniel, Graduate Coordinator, 601-266-4664, Fax: 601-266-5814.

University of South Florida, Graduate School, College of Business Administration, Program in Information Systems and Decision Sciences, Tampa, FL 33620-9951. Offers management information systems (MS). *Faculty:* 17 full-time (2 women), 2 part-time/adjunct (0 women). *Students:* 26 full-time (9 women), 44 part-time (14 women); includes 14 minority (7 African Americans, 3 Asian Americans or Pacific Islanders, 4 Hispanic Americans), 23 international. 77 applicants, 66% accepted, 22 enrolled. In 2006, 38 degrees awarded. *Entrance requirements:* For master's, GMAT, minimum GPA of 3.0, industry experience. Additional exam requirements/recommendations for international students: Required—TOEFL (minimum score 550 paper-based; 213 computer-based). *Application deadline:* For fall admission, 6/1 for domestic students, 1/2 for international students. Applications are processed on a rolling basis. Application fee: $30. *Financial support:* Health care benefits and unspecified assistantships available. Total annual research expenditures: $99,012. *Unit head:* Dr. Stanley Birkin, Chairperson, 813-974-5524, Fax: 813-974-3030, E-mail: sbirkin@coba.usf.edu. *Application contact:* Mike Walters, Program Coordinator, 813-974-6776, Fax: 813-974-6749, E-mail: msmis@coba.usf.edu.

The University of Tampa, John H. Sykes College of Business, Tampa, FL 33606-1490. Offers accounting (MBA, MS); economics (MBA); entrepreneurship (MBA); finance (MBA, MS); information systems management (MBA); innovation management (MS); international business (MBA); management (MBA); marketing (MBA, MS). *Accreditation:* AACSB. Part-time and evening/weekend programs available. *Faculty:* 39 full-time (9 women), 1 part-time/adjunct (0 women). *Students:* 143 full-time (52 women), 381 part-time (158 women); includes 78 minority (18 African Americans, 3 American Indian/Alaska Native, 19 Asian Americans or Pacific Islanders, 38 Hispanic Americans), 89 international. Average age 31. 486 applicants, 59% accepted, 231 enrolled. In 2006, 127 degrees awarded. *Median time to degree:* Master's–1.8 years full-time, 2.8 years part-time. *Entrance requirements:* For master's, GMAT. Additional exam requirements/recommendations for international students: Required—TOEFL (minimum score 577 paper-based; 230 computer-based; 90 iBT). *Application deadline:* For fall admission, 2/15 priority date for domestic students, 6/15 for international students; for spring admission, 12/15 for domestic students, 11/15 for international students. Applications are processed on a rolling basis. Application fee: $40. Electronic applications accepted. *Expenses:* Tuition: Part-time $426 per credit hour. Required fees: $35 per year. *Financial support:* In 2006–07, 57 students received support, including 57 research assistantships with tuition reimbursements (averaging $3,000 per year); career-related internships or fieldwork and unspecified assistantships also available. Support available to part-time students. Financial award applicants required to submit FAFSA. *Faculty research:* Industrial organization and antitrust, artificial intelligence, corporate quality, leadership, ethics, quality. *Unit head:* Dr. William L. Rhey, Dean Graduate Studies, 813-253-6211, Fax: 813-259-5403, E-mail: wrhey@ut.edu. *Application contact:* Fernals Nolasco, Director of Graduate Studies, 813-253-6211, Fax: 813-259-5403, E-mail: fnolasco@ut.edu.

The University of Texas at Arlington, Graduate School, College of Business Administration, Department of Information Systems and Management Science, Arlington, TX 76019. Offers information systems (MS). Part-time and evening/weekend programs available. *Faculty:* 17 full-time (2 women). *Students:* 27 full-time (8 women), 21 part-time (4 women); includes 10 minority (1 African American, 9 Asian Americans or Pacific Islanders), 21 international. Average age 27. 41 applicants, 46% accepted, 12 enrolled. In 2006, 12 degrees awarded. *Degree requirements:* For master's, thesis optional. *Entrance requirements:* For master's, GMAT, minimum GPA of 3.0. Additional exam requirements/recommendations for international students: Required—TOEFL (minimum score 550 paper-based; 213 computer-based). *Application deadline:* For fall admission, 6/15 for domestic students, 4/11 for international students; for spring admission, 1/25 for international students. Applications are processed on a rolling basis. Application fee: $35 ($50 for international students). *Expenses:* Tuition, state resident: full-time $5,528. Tuition, nonresident: full-time $10,478. International tuition: $10,608 full-time. *Financial support:* In 2006–07, 5 fellowships (averaging $1,000 per year), 22 teaching assistantships (averaging $10,000 per year) were awarded; research assistantships, career-related internships or fieldwork and scholarships/grants also available. Support available to part-time students. Financial award application deadline: 6/1; financial award applicants required to submit FAFSA. *Faculty research:* Database modeling, strategic issues in information systems, simulations, production operations management. *Unit head:* Dr. R. C. Baker, Chair, 817-272-3502, Fax: 817-272-5801, E-mail: rcbaker@uta.edu. *Application contact:* Dr. Carolyn Davis, Graduate Adviser, 817-272-7399, Fax: 817-272-5801, E-mail: carolynd@exchange.uta.edu.

The University of Texas at Arlington, Graduate School, College of Business Administration, Program in Business Administration, Arlington, TX 76019. Offers accounting (PhD); business administration (PhD); business statistics (PhD); finance (MBA); information systems (MBA, PhD); management (MBA); management sciences (MBA); marketing (MBA, PhD); real estate (MBA). *Accreditation:* AACSB. Part-time and evening/weekend programs available. Postbaccalaureate distance learning degree programs offered (no on-campus study). *Faculty:* 1 full-time (0 women). *Students:* 156 full-time (60 women), 319 part-time (110 women); includes 123 minority (38 African Americans, 4 American Indian/Alaska Native, 52 Asian Americans or Pacific Islanders, 29 Hispanic Americans), 88 international. 502 applicants, 85% accepted, 199 enrolled. In 2006, 417 master's, 11 doctorates awarded. Terminal master's awarded for partial completion of doctoral program. *Degree requirements:* For master's, thesis optional; for doctorate, thesis/dissertation. *Entrance requirements:* For master's, GMAT; for doctorate, GMAT, minimum GPA of 3.0 (undergraduate), 3.4 (graduate); 30 hours of graduate course work. Additional exam requirements/recommendations for international students: Required—TOEFL (minimum score 550 paper-based; 213 computer-based). *Application deadline:* For fall admission, 6/15 for domestic students, 4/1 for international students; for spring admission, 10/15 for domestic students, 9/1 for international students. Applications are processed on a rolling basis. Application fee: $35 ($50 for international students). Electronic applications accepted. *Expenses:* Tuition, state resident: full-time $5,528. Tuition, nonresident: full-time $10,478. International tuition: $10,608 full-time. *Financial support:* In 2006–07, 1 fellowship (averaging $1,000 per year), 14 research assistantships (averaging $6,432 per year) were awarded; teaching assistantships, career-related internships or fieldwork, scholarships/grants, and unspecified assistantships also available. Financial award application deadline: 6/1; financial award applicants required to submit FAFSA. *Application contact:* Dr. Mike West, Assistant Dean, 817-272-1287, Fax: 817-272-5799, E-mail: mpwest@uta.edu.

See Close-Up on page 363.

The University of Texas at Austin, Graduate School, McCombs School of Business, Department of Management Sciences and Information Systems, Austin, TX 78712-1111. Offers PhD. *Degree requirements:* For doctorate, thesis/dissertation. *Entrance requirements:* For doctorate, GMAT or GRE. Electronic applications accepted. *Faculty research:* Stochastic processing and queuing, discrete nonlinear and large-scale optimization simulation, quality assurance logistics, distributed artificial intelligence, organizational modeling.

The University of Texas at Dallas, School of Management, Program in Accounting and Information Management, Richardson, TX 75083-0688. Offers MS. *Accreditation:* AACSB.

Management Information Systems

The University of Texas at Dallas (continued)

Faculty: 19 full-time (4 women). *Students:* 124 full-time (64 women), 268 part-time (149 women); includes 139 minority (31 African Americans, 81 Asian Americans or Pacific Islanders, 27 Hispanic Americans), 88 international. Average age 31. 471 applicants, 87% accepted, 261 enrolled. In 2006, 160 degrees awarded. *Entrance requirements:* For master's, GMAT. Additional exam requirements/recommendations for international students: Required—TOEFL (minimum score 550 paper-based; 213 computer-based). *Application deadline:* For fall admission, 7/15 for domestic students; for spring admission, 11/15 for domestic students. Applications are processed on a rolling basis. Application fee: $50 ($100 for international students). Electronic applications accepted. *Financial support:* In 2006–07, 3 research assistantships with tuition reimbursements (averaging $9,000 per year), 1 teaching assistantship with tuition reimbursement (averaging $9,550 per year) were awarded; fellowships, career-related internships or fieldwork, Federal Work-Study, institutionally sponsored loans, and scholarships/grants also available. Support available to part-time students. Financial award application deadline: 4/30; financial award applicants required to submit FAFSA. *Unit head:* Dr. Mark C Anderson, Area Coordinator, 972-883-2056, Fax: 972-883-6823, E-mail: mark.anderson@utdallas.edu. *Application contact:* David B. Ritchey, Director of Advising, 972-883-2701, Fax: 972-883-6425, E-mail: davidr@utdallas.edu.

See Close-Up on page 365.

The University of Texas at Dallas, School of Management, Program in Information Technology and Management, Richardson, TX 75083-0688. Offers MS. Part-time and evening/weekend programs available. *Faculty:* 21 full-time (1 woman), 3 part-time/adjunct (2 women). *Students:* 35 full-time (13 women), 47 part-time (9 women); includes 22 minority (3 African Americans, 10 Asian Americans or Pacific Islanders, 9 Hispanic Americans), 45 international. Average age 29. 99 applicants, 81% accepted, 26 enrolled. In 2006, 33 degrees awarded. *Degree requirements:* For master's, thesis optional. *Entrance requirements:* For master's, GMAT. Additional exam requirements/recommendations for international students: Required—TOEFL (minimum score 550 paper-based; 213 computer-based). *Application deadline:* Applications are processed on a rolling basis. Application fee: $50 ($100 for international students). Electronic applications accepted. *Financial support:* In 2006–07, 2 research assistantships (averaging $12,972 per year) were awarded; teaching assistantships, career-related internships or fieldwork, Federal Work-Study, institutionally sponsored loans, and scholarships/grants also available. Support available to part-time students. Financial award application deadline: 4/30; financial award applicants required to submit FAFSA. *Unit head:* Dr. Vijay Mookerjee, Coordinator, 972-883-4414, E-mail: vijaym@utdallas.edu. *Application contact:* David B. Ritchey, Director of Advising, 972-883-2701, Fax: 972-883-6425, E-mail: davidr@utdallas.edu.

The University of Texas at Dallas, School of Management, Program in Management and Administrative Sciences, Richardson, TX 75083-0688. Offers information technology and management (MS); management and administrative science (MS); medical management (MS). *Accreditation:* AACSB. Part-time and evening/weekend programs available. *Faculty:* 53 full-time (8 women), 4 part-time/adjunct (1 woman). *Students:* 67 full-time (25 women), 127 part-time (53 women); includes 46 minority (12 African Americans, 1 American Indian/Alaska Native, 27 Asian Americans or Pacific Islanders, 6 Hispanic Americans), 86 international. Average age 31. 140 applicants, 89% accepted, 74 enrolled. In 2006, 73 degrees awarded. *Degree requirements:* For master's, thesis optional. *Entrance requirements:* For master's, GMAT. Additional exam requirements/recommendations for international students: Required—TOEFL (minimum score 550 paper-based; 213 computer-based). *Application deadline:* Applications are processed on a rolling basis. Application fee: $50 ($100 for international students). Electronic applications accepted. *Financial support:* In 2006–07, 1 research assistantship with tuition reimbursement (averaging $9,000 per year), 22 teaching assistantships with tuition reimbursements (averaging $13,457 per year) were awarded; fellowships, career-related internships or fieldwork, Federal Work-Study, institutionally sponsored loans, and scholarships/grants also available. Support available to part-time students. Financial award application deadline: 4/30; financial award applicants required to submit FAFSA. *Faculty research:* Integrated and detailed knowledge of functional areas of management, as well as analytical tools for effective appraisal and decision making. *Unit head:* Dr. Diane McNulty, Associate Dean and College Master, 972-883-2705, Fax: 972-883-2799, E-mail: dmcnulty@utdallas.edu. *Application contact:* David B. Ritchey, Director of Advising, 972-883-2701, Fax: 972-883-6425, E-mail: davidr@utdallas.edu.

See Close-Up on page 365.

The University of Texas at San Antonio, College of Business, Department of Information Systems and Technology Management, San Antonio, TX 78249-0617. Offers information systems (MBA, PhD); information technology (MSIT); management technology (MSMOT). *Faculty:* 12 full-time (3 women), 4 part-time/adjunct (1 woman). *Students:* 20 full-time (5 women), 50 part-time (8 women); includes 26 minority (1 African American, 5 Asian Americans or Pacific Islanders, 20 Hispanic Americans), 11 international. Average age 32. 42 applicants, 88% accepted, 33 enrolled. In 2006, 45 degrees awarded. *Degree requirements:* For master's, thesis optional. *Entrance requirements:* For master's, GMAT, minimum GPA of 3.0. Additional exam requirements/recommendations for international students: Required—TOEFL (minimum score 500 paper-based; 173 computer-based). *Application deadline:* For fall admission, 7/1 for domestic students, 4/1 for international students; for spring admission, 11/1 for domestic students, 9/1 for international students. Applications are processed on a rolling basis. Application fee: $45 ($80 for international students). Electronic applications accepted. *Expenses:* Tuition, state resident: full-time $1,730; part-time $192 per credit hour. Tuition, nonresident: full-time $6,680; part-time $742 per credit hour. Required fees: $733; $308,359 per credit hour. *Financial support:* In 2006–07, 3 research assistantships (averaging $20,800 per year), 9 teaching assistantships (averaging $16,156 per year) were awarded; career-related internships or fieldwork, Federal Work-Study, scholarships/grants, and unspecified assistantships also available. Support available to part-time students. Total annual research expenditures: $258. *Unit head:* Dr. Glenn Dietrich, Chair, 210-458-5354, Fax: 210-458-6305, E-mail: gdietrich@utsa.edu.

The University of Texas–Pan American, College of Business Administration, Program in Computer Information Systems, Edinburg, TX 78541-2999. Offers MS, PhD. Evening/weekend programs available. Postbaccalaureate distance learning degree programs offered (no on-campus study). Terminal master's awarded for partial completion of doctoral program. *Degree requirements:* For master's, thesis optional; for doctorate, thesis/dissertation. *Expenses:* Tuition, state resident: full-time $2,577; part-time $143 per credit hour. Tuition, nonresident: full-time $7,527; part-time $418 per credit hour. Required fees: $561.

University of the Sacred Heart, Graduate Programs, Department of Business Administration, Program in Management Information Systems, San Juan, PR 00914-0383. Offers MBA. Part-time and evening/weekend programs available. *Degree requirements:* For master's, thesis. *Entrance requirements:* For master's, EXADEP, minimum undergraduate GPA of 2.75, interview.

University of the West, Department of Business Administration, Rosemead, CA 91770. Offers business administration (EMBA); finance (MBA); information technology and management (MBA); international business (MBA); nonprofit organization management (MBA). Part-time and evening/weekend programs available. *Entrance requirements:* Additional exam requirements/recommendations for international students: Required—TOEFL.

The University of Toledo, College of Graduate Studies, College of Business Administration, Department of Information Systems, Marketing, E-Commerce, and Sales, Program in Information Systems, Toledo, OH 43606-3390. Offers MBA. *Students:* 12 full-time (3 women), 14 part-time (2 women); includes 1 minority (African American), 10 international. Average age 28. 22 applicants, 86% accepted, 9 enrolled. In 2006, 8 degrees awarded. *Entrance requirements:* For master's, GMAT. *Application contact:* Graduate School Office, 419-530-4723, Fax: 419-530-4724, E-mail: gradsch@utnet.utoledo.edu.

The University of Toledo, College of Graduate Studies, College of Business Administration, Department of Information Systems, Marketing, E-Commerce, and Sales, Program in Operations Management, Toledo, OH 43606-3390. Offers MBA. *Students:* 5 full-time (1 woman), 9 part-time (1 woman), 3 international. Average age 30. 7 applicants, 71% accepted, 4 enrolled. In 2006, 8 degrees awarded. *Entrance requirements:* For master's, GMAT. *Application contact:* Graduate School Office, 419-530-4723, Fax: 419-530-4724, E-mail: gradsch@utnet.utoledo.edu.

University of Virginia, McIntire School of Commerce, Program in Management of Information Technology, Charlottesville, VA 22903. Offers MS. *Students:* 69 full-time (12 women), 1 part-time; includes 3 minority (1 African American, 2 Asian Americans or Pacific Islanders), 5 international. Average age 35. In 2006, 70 degrees awarded. *Entrance requirements:* For master's, GMAT. Additional exam requirements/recommendations for international students: Required—TOEFL. *Application deadline:* For fall admission, 2/15 for domestic students. Applications are processed on a rolling basis. Application fee: $60. Electronic applications accepted. *Expenses: Contact institution. Financial support:* Fellowships, Federal Work-Study available. Financial award applicants required to submit FAFSA. *Application contact:* Peter A. Todd, Associate Dean for Graduate Programs, 434-243-8988, E-mail: mcintiregrad@virginia.edu.

University of Wisconsin–Madison, Graduate School, School of Business, Doctoral Program in Operations and Technology Management, Madison, WI 53706-1380. Offers PhD. *Students:* 8 full-time (2 women), 5 international. Average age 36. 42 applicants, 0% accepted. In 2006, 1 degree awarded. *Median time to degree:* Of those who began their doctoral program in fall 1998, 90% received their degree in 8 years or less. *Entrance requirements:* For doctorate, GMAT or GRE. Additional exam requirements/recommendations for international students: Required—TOEFL (minimum score 600 paper-based; 250 computer-based). *Application deadline:* For fall admission, 1/6 priority date for domestic and international students. Applications are processed on a rolling basis. Application fee: $45. Electronic applications accepted. *Financial support:* In 2006–07, 5 students received support, including 1 fellowship with full tuition reimbursement available (averaging $16,110 per year), research assistantships with full tuition reimbursements available (averaging $13,502 per year), 4 teaching assistantships with full tuition reimbursements available (averaging $13,686 per year); Federal Work-Study, institutionally sponsored loans, scholarships/grants, health care benefits, and unspecified assistantships also available. Financial award application deadline: 1/6; financial award applicants required to submit FAFSA. *Faculty research:* Supply-chain management, reorganization of the factory, creating continuous innovation, transportation economics, organizational economics. *Unit head:* Dr. James G. Morris, Chair, 608-262-1284, E-mail: jmorris@bus.wisc.edu. *Application contact:* Belle Heberling, PhD Coordinator, 608-262-3749, Fax: 608-890-0180, E-mail: phd@bus.wisc.edu.

University of Wisconsin–Madison, Graduate School, School of Business, Program in Accounting and Information Systems, Madison, WI 53706-1380. Offers PhD. *Accreditation:* AACSB. *Students:* 10 full-time (5 women), 2 international. Average age 33. 58 applicants, 7% accepted, 2 enrolled. In 2006, 3 degrees awarded. *Median time to degree:* Of those who began their doctoral program in fall 1998, 100% received their degree in 8 years or less. *Entrance requirements:* For doctorate, GMAT or GRE. Additional exam requirements/recommendations for international students: Required—TOEFL (minimum score 600 paper-based; 250 computer-based). *Application deadline:* For fall admission, 1/6 priority date for domestic and international students. Applications are processed on a rolling basis. Electronic applications accepted. *Financial support:* In 2006–07, 10 students received support, including fellowships with full tuition reimbursements available (averaging $16,110 per year), research assistantships with full tuition reimbursements available (averaging $13,502 per year), 10 teaching assistantships with full tuition reimbursements available (averaging $13,686 per year); Federal Work-Study, institutionally sponsored loans, scholarships/grants, health care benefits, and unspecified assistantships also available. Financial award application deadline: 1/6. *Faculty research:* Auditing, financial reporting, economic theory, strategy, computer models. *Unit head:* Dr. Jon Davis, Chair, 608-263-4264. *Application contact:* Belle Heberling, PhD Coordinator, 608-262-3749, Fax: 608-890-0180, E-mail: phd@bus.wisc.edu.

University of Wisconsin–Madison, Graduate School, School of Business, Wisconsin Full-Time MBA Programs, Madison, WI 53706-1380. Offers applied corporate finance (MBA); applied security analysis (MBA); arts administration (MBA); brand and product management (MBA); entrepreneurial management (MBA); information systems (MBA); marketing research (MBA); operations and technology management (MBA); real estate (MBA); risk management and insurance (MBA); strategic human resource management (MBA); strategic management in the life and engineering sciences (MBA); supply chain management (MBA). *Faculty:* 84. *Students:* 231 full-time (74 women); includes 21 minority (10 African Americans, 5 Asian Americans or Pacific Islanders, 6 Hispanic Americans), 59 international. Average age 28. 405 applicants, 43% accepted, 121 enrolled. In 2006, 110 degrees awarded. *Entrance requirements:* For master's, GMAT, bachelors or equivalent degree, 2 years of work experience. Additional exam requirements/recommendations for international students: Required—TOEFL (minimum score 600 paper-based; 250 computer-based; 90 iBT). *Application deadline:* For fall admission, 11/1 for domestic and international students; for winter admission, 1/23 for domestic and international students; for spring admission, 3/26 for domestic and international students. Applications are processed on a rolling basis. Application fee: $45. Electronic applications accepted. *Financial support:* In 2006–07, 177 students received support, including 20 fellowships with full and partial tuition reimbursements available (averaging $16,566 per year), 105 research assistantships with full tuition reimbursements available (averaging $8,098 per year), 33 teaching assistantships with full tuition reimbursements available (averaging $10,112 per year); scholarships/grants, health care benefits, and unspecified assistantships also available. *Unit head:* Gary Lessuise, Assistant Dean, Masters Programs, 608-265-5102, Fax: 608-265-4192, E-mail: glessuise@bus.wisc.edu. *Application contact:* Betsy Kacizak, Director of Admissions and Financial Aid—Full Time MBA, 608-262-4000, Fax: 608-265-4192, E-mail: mba@bus.wisc.edu.

University of Wisconsin–Oshkosh, The School of Graduate Studies, College of Business Administration, Program in Information Systems, Oshkosh, WI 54901. Offers MS. Part-time programs available. *Degree requirements:* For master's, registration. *Entrance requirements:* For master's, GMAT, GRE, minimum undergraduate GPA of 2.75. Additional exam requirements/recommendations for international students: Required—TOEFL (minimum score 550 paper-based; 213 computer-based). Electronic applications accepted.

Utah State University, School of Graduate Studies, College of Business, Department of Business Information Systems, Logan, UT 84322. Offers business education (MS); business information systems (MS); business information systems and education (Ed D); education (PhD). Part-time programs available. *Faculty:* 11 full-time (2 women). *Students:* 29 full-time (4 women), 10 part-time (2 women); includes 1 minority (Hispanic American), 7 international. Average age 30. 37 applicants, 59% accepted, 19 enrolled. In 2006, 19 degrees awarded. Terminal master's awarded for partial completion of doctoral program. *Degree requirements:* For master's, thesis optional; for doctorate, thesis/dissertation. *Entrance requirements:* For master's, GMAT, minimum GPA of 3.2; for doctorate, GRE General Test, minimum GPA of 3.0. Additional exam requirements/recommendations for international students: Required—TOEFL. *Application deadline:* For fall admission, 6/6 priority date for domestic students, 6/1 for international students; for winter admission, 3/1 for domestic and international students; for spring admission, 10/1 for domestic and international students. Applications are processed on a rolling basis. Application fee: $50 ($60 for international students). *Financial support:* In 2006–07, 2 research assistantships with partial tuition reimbursements, 9 teaching assistantships with partial tuition reimbursements were awarded; fellowships with partial tuition reimbursements, career-related internships or fieldwork and Federal Work-Study also available. Financial award application deadline: 3/1. *Faculty research:* Oral and written communication, methods of teaching, CASE tools, object-oriented programming, decision support systems. Total annual research expenditures: $10,000. *Unit head:* Dr. Karen Forcht, Head, 435-797-2341, Fax:

435-797-2351. *Application contact:* Janet Bringhurst, Graduate Director, 435-797-2344, Fax: 435-797-2351, E-mail: janet.bringhurst@usu.edu.

Virginia Commonwealth University, Graduate School, School of Business, Program in Information Systems, Richmond, VA 23284-9005. Offers MS, PhD. *Faculty:* 13 full-time (3 women). *Students:* 26 full-time (6 women), 23 part-time (7 women); includes 7 minority (4 African Americans, 1 American Indian/Alaska Native, 2 Asian Americans or Pacific Islanders), 9 international. 27 applicants, 56% accepted, 10 enrolled. In 2006, 32 master's, 2 doctorates awarded. *Degree requirements:* For doctorate, thesis/dissertation. *Entrance requirements:* For master's, GMAT. *Application deadline:* Applications are processed on a rolling basis. Application fee: $50. *Financial support:* Fellowships, research assistantships, teaching assistantships, Federal Work-Study, institutionally sponsored loans, and tuition waivers (full and partial) available. Financial award application deadline: 3/15. *Unit head:* Dr. Richard Redmond, Chair, 804-828-7130, Fax: 804-828-3972, E-mail: rtredmon@vcu.edu. *Application contact:* Tracy Green, Graduate Program Director, 804-828-1741, Fax: 804-828-7174, E-mail: tsgreen@vcu.edu.

See Close-Up on page 617.

Virginia Polytechnic Institute and State University, Graduate School, Intercollege, Program in Information Technology, Blacksburg, VA 24061. Offers MIT. *Students:* 69 full-time (14 women), 258 part-time (55 women); includes 66 minority (16 African Americans, 1 American Indian/Alaska Native, 39 Asian Americans or Pacific Islanders, 10 Hispanic Americans), 79 international. Average age 33. 147 applicants, 86% accepted, 112 enrolled. In 2006, 125 degrees awarded. *Entrance requirements:* For master's, GRE. Additional exam requirements/recommendations for international students: Required—TOEFL (minimum score 550 paper-based; 213 computer-based). *Application deadline:* For fall admission, 5/15 for international students; for spring admission, 10/15 for international students. Applications are processed on a rolling basis. Application fee: $45. Electronic applications accepted. *Expenses:* Tuition, state resident: full-time $7,017; part-time $390 per credit hour. Tuition, nonresident: full-time $12,414; part-time $690 per credit hour. International tuition: $11,296 full-time. Required fees: $1,523; $256 per term. *Financial support:* Career-related internships or fieldwork, Federal Work-Study, scholarships/grants, and unspecified assistantships available. *Unit head:* Dr. Thomas T. Sheehan, Head, 703-238-8361, Fax: 540-231-8634, E-mail: thsheeha@vt.edu. *Application contact:* Shirin Naz Bahrami, Information Contact, 703-238-8397, Fax: 540-231-8364, E-mail: sbahrami@vt.edu.

Virginia Polytechnic Institute and State University, Graduate School, Pamplin College of Business, Department of Business Information Technology, Blacksburg, VA 24061. Offers business administration (PhD); business information technology (MS, PhD). *Faculty:* 23 full-time (7 women), 2 part-time/adjunct (0 women). *Students:* 3 full-time (1 woman), 2 part-time; includes 1 minority (African American), 2 international. Average age 30. 7 applicants. In 2006, 1 degree awarded. *Entrance requirements:* For master's and doctorate, GMAT. Additional exam requirements/recommendations for international students: Required—TOEFL (minimum score 600 paper-based; 250 computer-based). *Application deadline:* For fall admission, 5/15 for international students; for spring admission, 10/15 for international students. Applications are processed on a rolling basis. Application fee: $45. Electronic applications accepted. *Expenses:* Tuition, state resident: full-time $7,017; part-time $390 per credit hour. Tuition, nonresident: full-time $12,414; part-time $690 per credit hour. International tuition: $11,296 full-time. Required fees: $1,523; $256 per term. *Financial support:* In 2006–07, 4 teaching assistantships with full tuition reimbursements (averaging $15,538 per year) were awarded; career-related internships or fieldwork, Federal Work-Study, scholarships/grants, and unspecified assistantships also available. Financial award application deadline: 4/1. *Faculty research:* Mathematical programming, computer simulation, decision support systems, production/operations research, information technology. *Unit head:* Dr. Bernard W. Taylor, Head, 540-231-6596, Fax: 540-231-7916, E-mail: betaylo3@vt.edu. *Application contact:* Cliff Ragsdale, Information Contact, 540-231-4697, Fax: 540-231-7916, E-mail: cragsdal@vt.edu.

Walsh College of Accountancy and Business Administration, Graduate Programs, Program in Business Information Technology, Troy, MI 48007-7006. Offers MSBIT. *Faculty:* 2 full-time (1 woman), 8 part-time/adjunct (1 woman). *Students:* 10 full-time (1 woman), 233 part-time (103 women). 85 applicants, 91% accepted, 77 enrolled. In 2006, 88 degrees awarded. *Application deadline:* For fall admission, 8/24 priority date for domestic students; for winter admission, 1/1 priority date for domestic students; for spring admission, 4/1 priority date for domestic students. Application fee: $25. *Expenses:* Tuition: Part-time $435 per hour. Required fees: $119 per semester. One-time fee: $50. *Financial support:* Application deadline: 6/30; *Unit head:* Dr. Jeffrey Livermore, Chair, 248-823-1272, Fax: 248-689-0920. *Application contact:* Karen Mahaffy, Director of Admissions and Academic Advising, 248-823-1610, Fax: 248-689-0938, E-mail: kmahaffy@walshcollege.edu.

Washington State University, Graduate School, College of Business, Department of Accounting and Business Law, Pullman, WA 99164. Offers accounting and information systems (M Acc); accounting and taxation (M Acc). *Accreditation:* AACSB. *Faculty:* 10 full-time (2 women). *Students:* 17 full-time (8 women), 2 part-time, 4 international. Average age 27. 63 applicants, 41% accepted, 10 enrolled. In 2006, 18 degrees awarded. *Degree requirements:* For master's, thesis (for some programs), oral exam, research paper, comprehensive exam (for some programs). *Entrance requirements:* For master's, GMAT, minimum GPA of 3.0, 3 letters of recommendation. Additional exam requirements/recommendations for international students: Required—TOEFL (minimum score 580 paper-based; 237 computer-based). *Application deadline:* For fall admission, 3/1 priority date for domestic students, 3/1 for international students; for spring admission, 7/1 for international students. Applications are processed on a rolling basis. Application fee: $50. Electronic applications accepted. *Expenses:* Tuition, state resident: full-time $7,066. Tuition, nonresident: full-time $17,204. *Financial support:* In 2006–07, 19 students received support, including 1 fellowship (averaging $5,500 per year), research assistantships (averaging $13,917 per year), 8 teaching assistantships with tuition reimbursements available (averaging $13,056 per year); Federal Work-Study, institutionally sponsored loans, tuition waivers (partial), and teaching associateships also available. Financial award application deadline: 3/1. *Faculty research:* Ethics, taxation, auditing. Total annual research expenditures: $11,753. *Unit head:* Dr. Robert R. Greenberg, Chair, 509-335-8541, Fax: 509-335-4275. *Application contact:* Graduate School Admissions, 800-GRADWSU, Fax: 509-335-1949, E-mail: gradsch@wsu.edu.

Washington State University, Graduate School, College of Business, Graduate Programs in Business, Pullman, WA 99164. Offers accounting and business law (M Acc); business administration (MBA, PhD), including accounting (PhD), finance (PhD), management and operations (PhD), management information systems (PhD), marketing (PhD); JD/MBA. *Accreditation:* AACSB. *Faculty:* 38. *Students:* 105 full-time (39 women), 14 part-time (5 women); includes 3 minority (1 American Indian/Alaska Native, 2 Asian Americans or Pacific Islanders), 62 international. Average age 30. 328 applicants, 32% accepted, 43 enrolled. In 2006, 56 master's, 8 doctorates awarded. *Degree requirements:* For master's, thesis (for some programs), final presentation, comprehensive exam (for some programs); for doctorate, thesis/dissertation, oral and written exams, comprehensive exam. *Entrance requirements:* For master's and doctorate, GMAT, minimum GPA of 3.0, 3 letters of recommendation. Additional exam requirements/recommendations for international students: Required—TOEFL. *Application deadline:* For fall admission, 3/1 priority date for domestic students, 3/1 for international students; for spring admission, 6/1 priority date for domestic students, 6/1 for international students. Applications are processed on a rolling basis. Application fee: $50. Electronic applications accepted. *Expenses:* Tuition, state resident: full-time $7,066. Tuition, nonresident: full-time $17,204. *Financial support:* In 2006–07, 102 students received support, including 9 fellowships (averaging $6,000 per year), 8 research assistantships with full and partial tuition reimbursements available (averaging $13,917 per year), 75 teaching assistantships with full and partial tuition reimbursements available (averaging $13,056 per year); career-related internships or fieldwork, Federal Work-Study, institutionally sponsored loans, health care benefits, tuition waivers (partial), unspecified assistantships, and teaching associateships also available. Financial award application deadline: 4/1. *Unit head:* Dr. Charles Munson, Associate Dean, 509-335-1193, E-mail: mba@wsu.edu. *Application contact:* Graduate School Admissions, 800-GRADWSU, Fax: 509-335-1949, E-mail: gradsch@wsu.edu.

Wayland Baptist University, Graduate Programs, Programs in Business Administration/Management, Plainview, TX 79072-6998. Offers general business (MBA); health care administration (MBA); human resource management (MBA); international management (MBA); management (MA, MBA), including human resource management (MA), organization management (MA); management information systems (MBA). Part-time and evening/weekend programs available. Postbaccalaureate distance learning degree programs offered (no on-campus study). *Faculty:* 3 full-time (0 women). *Students:* 1 full-time (0 women), 7 part-time (2 women); includes 1 minority (Hispanic American) Average age 28. 1 applicant, 100% accepted, 1 enrolled. In 2006, 2 degrees awarded. *Degree requirements:* For master's, capstone course. *Entrance requirements:* For master's, GMAT, GRE or MAT. Additional exam requirements/recommendations for international students: Required—TOEFL (minimum score 500 paper-based; 173 computer-based). *Application deadline:* Applications are processed on a rolling basis. Application fee: $35. *Expenses:* Tuition: Full-time $6,120; part-time $340 per credit hour. Required fees: $50 per term. *Financial support:* Federal Work-Study, institutionally sponsored loans, and scholarships/grants available. Support available to part-time students. Financial award application deadline: 5/1; financial award applicants required to submit FAFSA. *Unit head:* Dr. Otto Schacht, Chairman, 806-291-1020, Fax: 806-291-1957.

Webster University, School of Business and Technology, Department of Business, St. Louis, MO 63119-3194. Offers business (MA); business and organizational security management (MBA); computer resources and information management (MBA); environmental management (MBA); finance (MA, MBA); health services management (MBA); human resources development (MBA); human resources management (MBA); international business (MA, MBA); management and leadership (MBA); marketing (MBA); procurement and acquisitions management (MBA); telecommunications management (MBA). Part-time and evening/weekend programs available. Postbaccalaureate distance learning degree programs offered (no on-campus study). *Students:* 1,205 full-time (629 women), 4,197 part-time (2,153 women); includes 2,005 minority (1,467 African Americans, 29 American Indian/Alaska Native, 212 Asian Americans or Pacific Islanders, 297 Hispanic Americans), 485 international. Average age 33. *Application deadline:* Applications are processed on a rolling basis. Application fee: $25 ($50 for international students). *Expenses:* Tuition: Full-time $8,820; part-time $490 per credit. Tuition and fees vary according to degree level, campus/location and program. *Financial support:* Federal Work-Study available. Support available to part-time students. Financial award application deadline: 4/1; financial award applicants required to submit FAFSA. *Unit head:* Bradford Scott, Chair, 314-961-2260 Ext. 7574, Fax: 314-968-7077, E-mail: buschair@webster.edu. *Application contact:* Director of Graduate and Evening Student Admissions, Fax: 314-968-7116, E-mail: gadmit@webster.edu.

Webster University, School of Business and Technology, Department of Management, St. Louis, MO 63119-3194. Offers business and organizational security management (MA); computer resources and information management (MA); environmental management (MS); health care management (MA); health services management (MA); human resources development (MA); human resources management (MA); management (DM); management and leadership (MA); marketing (MA); procurement and acquisitions management (MA); public administration (MA); quality management (MA); space systems operations management (MS); telecommunications management (MA). Part-time and evening/weekend programs available. Postbaccalaureate distance learning degree programs offered (no on-campus study). *Students:* 1,396 full-time (746 women), 4,727 part-time (2,579 women); includes 3,065 minority (2,374 African Americans, 45 American Indian/Alaska Native, 158 Asian Americans or Pacific Islanders, 488 Hispanic Americans), 128 international. Average age 37. In 2006, 9 degrees awarded. *Degree requirements:* For doctorate, thesis/dissertation, written exam. *Entrance requirements:* For doctorate, GMAT, 3 years of work experience, MBA. *Application deadline:* Applications are processed on a rolling basis. Application fee: $25 ($50 for international students). *Expenses:* Tuition: Full-time $8,820; part-time $490 per credit. Tuition and fees vary according to degree level, campus/location and program. *Financial support:* Federal Work-Study available. Support available to part-time students. Financial award application deadline: 4/1; financial award applicants required to submit FAFSA. *Unit head:* Jeffrey Haldeman, Chair, 314-961-2660 Ext. 7552, Fax: 314-968-7077, E-mail: mgtchair@webster.edu. *Application contact:* Director of Graduate and Evening Student Admissions, Fax: 314-968-7116, E-mail: gadmit@webster.edu.

Webster University, School of Business and Technology, Department of Mathematics and Computer Science, St. Louis, MO 63119-3194. Offers computer science/distributed systems (MS, Certificate). Part-time and evening/weekend programs available. *Students:* 2 full-time (1 woman), 66 part-time (19 women); includes 15 minority (6 African Americans, 5 Asian Americans or Pacific Islanders, 4 Hispanic Americans), 10 international. Average age 37. In 2006, 39 master's, 4 other advanced degrees awarded. *Entrance requirements:* For master's, 36 hours of graduate course work. *Application deadline:* Applications are processed on a rolling basis. Application fee: $25 ($50 for international students). *Expenses:* Tuition: Full-time $8,820; part-time $490 per credit. Tuition and fees vary according to degree level, campus/location and program. *Financial support:* Federal Work-Study available. Support available to part-time students. Financial award application deadline: 4/1; financial award applicants required to submit FAFSA. *Faculty research:* Databases, computer information systems networks, operating systems, computer architecture. *Unit head:* Al Cawns, Chair, 314-968-7127, Fax: 314-963-6050, E-mail: cawnsae@webster.edu. *Application contact:* Director of Graduate and Evening Student Admissions, Fax: 314-968-7116, E-mail: gadmit@webster.edu.

Western Governors University, Programs in Business, Salt Lake City, UT 84107. Offers information technology management (MBA); management and strategy (MBA); strategic leadership (MBA). Electronic applications accepted.

Western International University, Graduate Programs in Business, MBA Program in Information Technology, Phoenix, AZ 85021-2718. Offers MBA. Evening/weekend programs available. Postbaccalaureate distance learning degree programs offered (no on-campus study). *Faculty:* 237 part-time/adjunct (58 women). *Students:* 46 full-time (17 women); includes 9 minority (3 African Americans, 5 Asian Americans or Pacific Islanders, 1 Hispanic American), 9 international. Average age 33. In 2006, 15 degrees awarded. *Degree requirements:* For master's, thesis. *Entrance requirements:* For master's, minimum GPA of 2.75. *Application deadline:* Applications are processed on a rolling basis. Application fee: $85 ($100 for international students). *Expenses:* Tuition: Full-time $9,600; part-time $400 per credit. One-time fee: $85 full-time. *Financial support:* Career-related internships or fieldwork, institutionally sponsored loans, and scholarships/grants available. Support available to part-time students. Financial award applicants required to submit FAFSA. *Unit head:* Craig Horrocks, Chair, 602-943-2311. *Application contact:* Karen Janitell, Director of Enrollment, 602-943-2311 Ext. 1063, Fax: 602-371-8637, E-mail: karen_janitell@apollogrp.edu.

Western International University, Graduate Programs in Business, MS Program in Information Technology, Phoenix, AZ 85021-2718. Offers MS. Evening/weekend programs available. Postbaccalaureate distance learning degree programs offered (no on-campus study). *Students:* 11 full-time (2 women); includes 3 minority (1 African American, 1 Asian American or Pacific Islander, 1 Hispanic American), 2 international. Average age 33. In 2006, 10 degrees awarded. *Degree requirements:* For master's, thesis. *Entrance requirements:* For master's, minimum GPA of 2.75. *Application deadline:* Applications are processed on a rolling basis. Application fee: $85 ($100 for international students). *Expenses:* Tuition: Full-time $9,600; part-time $400 per credit. One-time fee: $85 full-time. *Financial support:* Career-related internships or fieldwork and scholarships/grants available. Support available to part-time students. Financial award applicants required to submit FAFSA. *Unit head:* Craig Horrocks, Chair, 602-943-2311. *Application contact:* Karen Janitell, Director of Enrollment, 602-943-2311 Ext. 1063, Fax: 602-371-8637, E-mail: karen_janitell@apollogrp.edu.

Management Information Systems

Western New England College, School of Engineering, Department of Electrical Engineering, Springfield, MA 01119. Offers computer and engineering information systems (MSEE); computer engineering (MSEE). Part-time and evening/weekend programs available. *Degree requirements:* For master's, thesis optional. *Entrance requirements:* For master's, GRE, bachelor's degree in engineering or related field. *Faculty research:* Superconductors, microwave cooking, computer voice output, digital filters, computer engineering.

Wilmington College, Division of Business, New Castle, DE 19720-6491. Offers business administration (MBA); finance (MBA); health care administration (MBA, MS); human resource management (MS); management (MS); management information systems (MBA); organizational leadership (MS); public administration (MS); transportation and logistics (MBA, MS). Part-time and evening/weekend programs available. *Faculty:* 3 full-time (0 women). *Students:* 230 full-time (138 women), 432 part-time (274 women); includes 109 minority (98 African Americans, 1 American Indian/Alaska Native, 3 Asian Americans or Pacific Islanders, 7 Hispanic Americans). Average age 34. 229 applicants, 100% accepted, 156 enrolled. In 2006, 273 degrees awarded. *Entrance requirements:* Additional exam requirements/recommendations for international students: Required—TOEFL (minimum score 500 paper-based; 173 computer-based). *Application deadline:* Applications are processed on a rolling basis. Application fee: $25. *Financial support:* Applicants required to submit FAFSA. *Unit head:* Dr. Robert Edelson, Chair, 302-295-1147, Fax: 302-328-7021, E-mail: robert.e.edelson@wilmcoll.edu. *Application contact:* Chris Ferguson, Director of Admissions and Financial Aid, 302-328-9407 Ext. 256, Fax: 302-328-5164, E-mail: inquire@wilmcoll.edu.

Wilmington College, Division of Information Technology and Advanced Communications, New Castle, DE 19720-6491. Offers corporate training (MS); information systems technologies (MS); Internet web design (MS); management information systems (MS). Part-time and evening/weekend programs available. *Students:* 21 full-time (10 women), 66 part-time (27 women); includes 11 minority (9 African Americans, 1 American Indian/Alaska Native, 1 Asian American or Pacific Islander). Average age 36. 28 applicants, 100% accepted, 19 enrolled. In 2006, 26 degrees awarded. *Entrance requirements:* Additional exam requirements/recommendations for international students: Required—TOEFL (minimum score 500 paper-based; 173 computer-based). Application fee: $25. *Unit head:* Dr. Jack Nold, Head, 302-328-9401 Ext. 254.

Winston-Salem State University, Program in Computer Science and Information Technology, Winston-Salem, NC 27110-0003. Offers MS. Part-time programs available. *Faculty:* 9 full-time (4 women). *Students:* 9 full-time (5 women), 14 part-time (3 women); includes 12 minority (9 African Americans, 2 Asian Americans or Pacific Islanders, 1 Hispanic American). 20 applicants, 35% accepted, 7 enrolled. In 2006, 5 degrees awarded. *Degree requirements:* For master's, thesis optional. *Entrance requirements:* For master's, GRE, resum[00e9]. *Application deadline:* For fall admission, 7/1 for domestic and international students; for spring admission, 11/1 for domestic and international students. Applications are processed on a rolling basis. Application fee: $40. Electronic applications accepted. *Expenses:* Tuition, state resident: full-time $2,010. Tuition, nonresident: full-time $10,502. Tuition and fees vary according to course load. *Financial support:* In 2006–07, 7 students received support, including 2 research assistantships (averaging $5,000 per year), 5 teaching assistantships (averaging $3,958 per year); career-related internships or fieldwork, institutionally sponsored loans, scholarships/grants, tuition waivers (partial), and unspecified assistantships also available. *Faculty research:* Artificial intelligence, network protocols, software engineering. *Unit head:* Dr. Elva Jones, Chair, 336-750-2485, Fax: 336-750-2499, E-mail: jonese@wssu.edu. *Application contact:* Graduate Studies and Research, 336-750-2102, Fax: 336-750-3042, E-mail: graduate@wssu.edu.

Worcester Polytechnic Institute, Graduate Studies and Enrollment, Department of Management, Program in Information Technology, Worcester, MA 01609-2280. Offers information security management (MS); information technology and entrepreneurship (MS); information technology applications development (MS); information technology project management (MS); manufacturing and service information technology applications (MS); marketing information technology applications (MS). Part-time and evening/weekend programs available. Post-baccalaureate distance learning degree programs offered (no on-campus study). *Faculty:* 12 full-time (6 women), 2 part-time/adjunct (1 woman). *Students:* 5 full-time (2 women), 11 part-time (1 woman); includes 1 minority (Asian American or Pacific Islander), 8 international. Average age 28. 37 applicants, 76% accepted, 10 enrolled. *Degree requirements:* For master's, thesis optional. *Entrance requirements:* For master's, GMAT or GRE. Additional exam

requirements/recommendations for international students: Required—TOEFL (minimum score 550 paper-based; 213 computer-based; 79 iBT), IELTS (minimum score 7). *Application deadline:* For fall admission, 6/1 priority date for domestic and international students; for spring admission, 10/15 priority date for domestic students, 10/1 priority date for international students. Applications are processed on a rolling basis. Application fee: $70. Electronic applications accepted. *Expenses:* Tuition: Part-time $1,042 per credit hour. Required fees: $1,009 per year. *Financial support:* In 2006–07, 5 students received support, including 3 research assistantships; career-related internships or fieldwork, Federal Work-Study, scholarships/grants, and unspecified assistantships also available. Financial award application deadline: 6/1; financial award applicants required to submit FAFSA. *Faculty research:* ERP implementation, improving web accessibility, information quality assessment, information quality assessment, website quality. Total annual research expenditures: $8,477. *Unit head:* Norm D. Wilkinson, Director, Graduate Management Programs, 508-831-5957, Fax: 508-831-5720, E-mail: nwilkins@wpi.edu.

See Close-Up on page 377.

Worcester Polytechnic Institute, Graduate Studies and Enrollment, Programs in Interdisciplinary Studies, Worcester, MA 01609-2280. Offers impact engineering (MS); manufacturing engineering management (MS); power systems management (MS); social science (PhD); systems engineering (MS); systems modeling (MS). Part-time and evening/weekend programs available. *Students:* 5 full-time (1 woman), 59 part-time (12 women); includes 4 minority (1 African American, 3 Asian Americans or Pacific Islanders), 3 international. 81 applicants, 85% accepted, 51 enrolled. In 2006, 19 degrees awarded. *Degree requirements:* For master's, thesis/dissertation; for doctorate, thesis/dissertation, comprehensive exam. *Entrance requirements:* For master's and doctorate, 3 letters of recommendation. Additional exam requirements/recommendations for international students: Required—TOEFL (minimum score 550 paper-based; 213 computer-based; 79 iBT), IELTS (minimum score 7). *Application deadline:* For fall admission, 1/15 priority date for domestic students; for spring admission, 10/15 priority date for domestic students. Application fee: $70. *Expenses:* Tuition: Part-time $1,042 per credit hour. Required fees: $1,009 per year. *Financial support:* In 2006–07, 1 student received support, including 1 research assistantship with full tuition reimbursement available; unspecified assistantships also available. Financial award application deadline: 1/15. *Unit head:* Dr. Fred J. Looft, Head, 508-831-5231, Fax: 508-831-5491, E-mail: fjlooft@wpi.edu. *Application contact:* Lynne Dougherty, Administrative Assistant, 508-831-5301, Fax: 508-831-5717, E-mail: lmd@wpi.edu.

Wright State University, School of Graduate Studies, Raj Soin College of Business, Department of Information Systems and Operations Management, Information Systems Program, Dayton, OH 45435. Offers MIS. *Unit head:* Dr. Martin H. Davis, Director.

Xavier University, Williams College of Business, Master of Business Administration Program, Cincinnati, OH 45207. Offers business administration (Exec MBA, MBA); e-commerce (MBA); finance (MBA); international business (MBA); management information systems (MBA); marketing (MBA);); MBA/MHSA; MSN/MBA. *Accreditation:* AACSB. Part-time and evening/weekend programs available. *Faculty:* 59 full-time (22 women), 29 part-time/adjunct (8 women). *Students:* 227 full-time (66 women), 708 part-time (252 women); includes 99 minority (41 African Americans, 1 American Indian/Alaska Native, 43 Asian Americans or Pacific Islanders, 14 Hispanic Americans), 43 international. Average age 31. 486 applicants, 63% accepted, 229 enrolled. In 2006, 294 degrees awarded. *Entrance requirements:* For master's, GMAT, resumé. Additional exam requirements/recommendations for international students: Required—TOEFL (minimum score 550 paper-based; 213 computer-based; 79 iBT). *Application deadline:* For fall admission, 8/1 priority date for domestic students, 6/1 for international students; for winter admission, 12/1 priority date for domestic students; for spring admission, 4/1 priority date for domestic students, 10/1 for international students. Applications are processed on a rolling basis. Application fee: $35. Electronic applications accepted. *Expenses: Contact institution.* Part-time tuition and fees vary according to degree level, campus/location and program. *Financial support:* In 2006–07, 175 students received support, including 11 research assistantships with full and partial tuition reimbursements available; career-related internships or fieldwork, scholarships/grants, and tuition waivers (partial) also available. Support available to part-time students. Financial award application deadline: 4/30; financial award applicants required to submit FAFSA. *Faculty research:* Supply chain management, category management, data mining, off-shoring. *Unit head:* Dr. Raghu Tadepalli, Associate Dean, 513-745-3525, Fax: 513-745-2929, E-mail: tadepalli@xavier.edu. *Application contact:* Jennifer Bush, Executive Director, MBA Programs, 513-745-3525, Fax: 513-745-2929, E-mail: xumba@xavier.edu.

CENTRAL MICHIGAN UNIVERSITY

Information Systems

Program of Study

Management information systems focus on how people use computers and systems to solve problems in business. Professionals in this area are in high demand as companies rely on such experts to help them stay current with technology and remain competitive in today's global marketplace.

The Master of Science degree in Information Systems (MSIS) program in the College of Business Administration at Central Michigan University (CMU) is designed for the student who does not have a bachelor's degree in information systems or a related computing field. Graduates are prepared for systems positions in business and industry. They are responsible for the completion of analysis and design of information systems, developing transaction processing systems and decision support systems, and applying appropriate methods in conducting systems research.

Students are required to complete a minimum of 30 graduate credits, pass a comprehensive examination, and satisfy a research requirement through completion of an applied project (Plan B). Required core courses include Systems Analysis and Design, Information Resources Management, Transaction Processing Systems, Database Management for Business Systems, and Decision Support Systems.

Each applicant, with MSIS director approval, must complete an area of concentration in one of three areas: enterprise software, systems applications, or general business.

Research Facilities

The University's library system includes off-campus library services, the Clarke Historical Library, and the main library, with numerous books and publications, electronic and paper journals, and access to several databases. There are three large public computer labs on campus that contain 400 PC and Mac workstations, and the Library offers more than 300 public workstations, which are distributed throughout the facility. A large selection of general software is available, including Adobe Photoshop, Microsoft Office, SPSS, SAS, and Minitab

Financial Aid

On-campus students whose research is accepted for publication or presentation are eligible for Publication and Presentation Grants worth up to $250. Research grants of up to $600 are awarded on the basis of proposals received by the Research Grants Committee. Nonresidents may pay resident tuition if they have undergraduate GPAs of 3.0 and GMAT scores of 600 or GRE scores of 560/600. In addition, students with an acceptable grade point average from Illinois, Indiana, Ohio, and Ontario, Canada, pay resident tuition.

Cost of Study

For the 2007–08 academic year, tuition is $388 per credit for Michigan residents and $719 per credit for out-of-state students.

Living and Housing Costs

Single-student and one- to three-bedroom family apartments are available in apartment complexes on campus. Rent includes electricity, gas, water, heat, telephone, cable TV, and other such services as the University deems appropriate. Off-campus housing is available from $250 per month, depending on the neighborhood, number of roommates, and size of the apartment.

Student Group

The program is designed to serve those individuals entering systems positions, those who wish to teach computer applications and information systems at community or two-year and four-year colleges, and those who plan to work with information systems in areas such as hospital administration and law enforcement.

Student Outcomes

Graduates are prepared for systems positions in business and industry and for teaching positions in community and four-year colleges. Graduates are able to complete the analysis and design of information systems, develop transaction-processing systems, develop decision-support systems using a fourth-generation language, apply appropriate research methods in conducting information systems research, and apply systems development concepts effectively to all phases of information systems development projects. A strength in the program is the business process engineering concentration that uses the leading enterprise software, SAP, as a teaching tool.

Location

Mt. Pleasant is located in Michigan's lower peninsula. The downtown district features specialty stores and boutiques of all types within walking distance of the campus. Thirteen golf courses are located within a 30-minute drive, while surrounding state preserves are frequented by local hunters. Eleven parks covering 300 acres—plus another 900 acres in Isabella County—offer venues for swimming, canoeing, hiking, camping, and cross-country skiing.

The University

Central Michigan University opened its doors in 1892 to formally train teachers in the state. Bachelor's degrees were first awarded in 1918, and graduate courses were first offered in 1938. Today, the University enrolls more than 28,000 students in more than 200 programs, leading to twenty-seven degrees at the bachelor's, master's, specialist's, and doctoral levels. The University's $50-million New Vision of Excellence Campaign is a broadly focused initiative to raise academic standards, strengthen discovery and creative activity, and enhance learning-environment facilities and technology.

Applying

To be considered for CMU College of Graduate Studies admission, an applicant must have a bachelor's degree from an accredited institution, a minimum undergraduate GPA of 2.7, and completed five prerequisite courses in computer competency, principles of accounting, managerial accounting, mathematics for business, and statistics. Applicants who have not satisfied these prerequisites are considered for conditional admission, but they must complete the prerequisites before beginning their graduate course work.

Admission to the MSIS program is competitive. To be considered for admission to the program, applicants must first meet the CMU College of Graduate Studies requirements listed above. Prospective students must submit an application form, official copies of undergraduate and graduate transcripts, a statement of purpose, and a $35 application fee ($45 for international students). International students must also submit a minimum TOEFL score of 550 (paper-based) or 213 (computer-based).

Prospective students should apply to the full-time on-campus program by March 1 for admission to the fall semester; however applications are accepted and reviewed after March 1. Applications for part-time admission should be sent at least six weeks prior to the start of the first semester of anticipated enrollment.

Correspondence and Information

To submit applications:
Graduate Admissions
College of Graduate Studies
Foust 100
Central Michigan University
Mount Pleasant, Michigan 48859

MSIS Program Information:
Karen Williamson
College of Graduate Studies
Foust 251
Central Michigan University
Mount Pleasant, Michigan 48859
Phone: 989-774-1910
Fax: 989-774-2372
E-mail: msis@cmich.edu
Web site: http://bis.cba.cmich.edu/msis

Central Michigan University

THE FACULTY AND THEIR RESEARCH

Frank Andera, Professor; Montana, 1980. Assessment of student satisfaction with SAP R/3 component courses, integration of ERP into undergraduate and graduate business curriculums.

James Cappel, Professor; Ph.D. (business computer information systems), North Texas, 1996. A scenario-based approach to improve team performance, evaluating e-learning, assessing responses to and success of e-mail marketing promotions, data-warehouse development and management.

Nancy Csapo, Professor; Ph.D. (adult and continuing education), Michigan State, 1994. Computer skills of college-bound high school graduates, team-based learning, preferred teaching methods of business faculty members and their students.

Roger Hayen, Professor; Ph.D. (management science), Colorado, 1972. Designing online lessons for Web-based course delivery, effects of group-decision support systems, using DSS for marketing decision making.

Monica Holmes, Professor; Ph.D., (business computer information systems), North Texas, 1995. Decision-support systems in information technology assimilation, issues in information systems, cross-cultural differences and information systems developer values.

Zhenyu Huang, Professor; Ph.D. (management information systems), Memphis, 2003. E-government in developing countries, improving efficiency of software testing without sacrificing quality, analysis of active-learning outcomes in large MIS courses, Internet EDI adoption.

Mark Hwang, Professor; Ph.D. (business computer information systems), North Texas, 1990. Enterprise resource planning systems integration, a neural fuzzy-system approach to assessing risk of earnings restatements, data-warehouse development and management.

Anil Kumar, Professor; Ph.D. (management information systems), Memphis, 1997. IS planning in nonprofit organizations, understanding role of information technology in global organizations.

James Scott, Professor; Ph.D. (management science), North Texas, 1979. Decision support systems in information technology, teaching high-tech in China, effectiveness of Web-based distance education.

Karl Smart, Professor; Ph.D. (English, rhetoric), Florida, 1989. Overcoming challenges of collaboration in business communication courses, impact of instructional methods and information technology on student learning styles, using instructional methods and information technology to promote collaboration among students, using customer data to drive documentation design decisions.

Susan Switzer, Professor; Ph.D. candidate (communications and business education). Computer skills of business students versus those of incoming freshman.

Russell Will, Professor; M.A. (history and philosophy), Notre Dame, 1974.

Hongjiang Xu, Professor; Ph.D. (information systems), Southern Queensland (Australia), 2004. Data quality and work alignment, understanding information quality in e-business, active-learning outcomes in large MIS courses.

NEW YORK UNIVERSITY

School of Continuing and Professional Studies
Master of Science in Management and Systems

Programs of Study	The School of Continuing and Professional Studies offers a Master of Science (M.S.) program in management and systems and graduate certificates in enterprise risk management, information technologies, and strategy and leadership.

The M.S. program in management and systems, offered online, on-site, or through a combination of both formats, is a unique interdisciplinary program that provides students with a solid understanding of traditional business disciplines and the cutting-edge information technology knowledge necessary to effectively manage in today's challenging business environment. Students are taught how to understand and maximize the role that information technology plays in formulating and implementing effective corporate strategy to maintain competitive advantage. They develop a deep understanding of the skills, techniques, and best practices of inspired creative leadership as well as the ability to align all of the discrete business units that make up the organization into one dynamic system. Many of the students are mid- to senior-level professionals employed in major corporations from around the world. The excellence of the students gives rise to an intensive peer-to-peer learning experience—a unique complement to the robust curriculum. Critical to the success of the international award-winning curriculum is a renowned faculty of academic scholars and industry leaders. Students graduate with a distinct advantage over the competition with specific knowledge that can be readily applied to business situations.

The 42-credit master's degree program can be completed on a part-time or full-time basis. The program consists of three phases: a required core course of study, a concentration, and the capstone project in which students choose the thesis research project or the applied project in their area of concentration. Students choose one of four concentrations: database technologies, enterprise risk management, strategy and leadership, or systems management. They also take one elective from one of the other concentrations. The curriculum for the M.S. program in management and systems is continually reevaluated and updated in response to industry needs to provide the most up-to-date and relevant course of study.

The graduate certificate in enterprise risk management defines and examines the types of risk. Course work provides a comprehensive approach to the challenges faced by managers where global data is readily available, risk is pervasive, regulations are ever-increasing, and the threat of disruption from potential crises is real.

The graduate certificate in information technologies focuses on managing database technologies through the development of the skills and knowledge of today's most widely used tools for gathering, storing, accessing, and utilizing information.

The graduate certificate in strategy and leadership addresses the need for managers and business leaders in the twenty-first century to understand how to set clear objectives with a competitive strategic advantage, motivate employees, and redevelop a culture of trust, integrity, and profit in the global, customer-centric marketplace. |
Research Facilities	Elmer Holmes Bobst Library and Study Center, one of the largest open-stack research libraries in the world, houses more than 3 million of NYU's nearly 4.4 million volumes. In addition to books, journals, and other print materials, the library provides access to many nonprint resources. These include microforms, databases, and other electronic resources that students can connect to from their homes or residence hall; extensive video and audio collections; and a variety of computer equipment and software programs.
Financial Aid	There are many financial aid options to consider, including fellowships and low-interest educational loans. NYU's centralized Office of Financial Aid assists students with loan packages, scholarships, and the NYU monthly payment plan, which enables students to spread out their tuition payments. Department scholarships are also available. For more information, students should visit http://www.nyu.edu/financial.aid.
Cost of Study	Tuition for the 2007–08 academic year is $1266 per credit plus fees. For full-time students (10–15 credits per semester), the cost of tuition and related fees is $12,664 per semester. Fees vary somewhat by program. The Board of Trustees of New York University reserves the right to alter these costs without notice.
Living and Housing Costs	Graduate student housing is available on the University campus and is administered through the Office of Housing and Residence Life. However, students may choose to live off campus. NYU's Off-Campus Housing Office (OCHO) offers assistance to members of the NYU community in their search for off-campus housing options. OCHO provides, exclusively to NYU students, listings of available locations for rent through private landlords, property managers, brokers, and real estate agents. Updated daily, these listings are accessible through OCHO's computer terminals or online for members of the NYU community.
Student Group	In 2006–07 there were 180 students enrolled in the M.S. program in management and systems. The median age was 32, and 70 percent of students were men. Part-time students accounted for 90 percent of those enrolled.
Location	The School of Continuing and Professional Studies' graduate programs in management and systems are housed at NYU's Midtown Center at 11 West 42nd Street, in the heart of Manhattan. For management and systems professionals, no other city comes close to the wide range of dynamic professional opportunities in New York City.
The University, The School, and The Program	NYU is a private university composed of fourteen schools and colleges. The University was founded in 1831 and the School of Continuing and Professional Studies in 1934. The graduate programs in management and systems were established in 1997.
Applying	Students may apply for fall or spring admission. Factors that are considered in evaluating an applicant include official transcripts of academic achievement in previous undergraduate and graduate course work, scores from the GRE or GMAT, TOEFL score (for international students whose native language is not English), the nature and extent of previous work experience, professional recommendations, and a statement of purpose.
Correspondence and Information	For more information and an application package, students should contact:

Office of Admissions
Graduate Programs in Management and Systems
New York University
145 Fourth Avenue, Room 219
New York, New York 10003
Phone: 212-998-7200 Ext. 415
Fax: 212-995-4674
E-mail: scps.gradadmissions@nyu.edu
Web site: http://www.scps.nyu.edu/415 |

New York University

THE ADMINISTRATION

Robert S. Lapiner, Ph.D., Dean, School of Continuing and Professional Studies.

Anthony R. Davidson, Ph.D., EDP; Divisional Dean, Director, and Clinical Professor, Division of Programs in Business, School of Continuing and Professional Studies.

Israel Moskowitz, M.S., Chair and Clinical Assistant Professor, Graduate Programs in Management and Systems, Division of Programs in Business, School of Continuing and Professional Studies.

ALFRED LERNER
COLLEGE OF
BUSINESS & ECONOMICS

UNIVERSITY OF DELAWARE

Alfred Lerner College of Business and Economics
Master of Science in Information Systems and Technology Management

Program of Study

The University of Delaware's Alfred Lerner College of Business and Economics offers a Master of Science in information systems and technology management (M.S. in IS&TM). The M.S. in IS&TM is a unique 36-credit interdisciplinary program that was jointly developed by the Alfred Lerner College of Business and Economics and the Department of Electrical and Computer Engineering. It provides students with a solid understanding of both information technology and the management processes needed to effectively manage in this dynamic environment and leverage information technology for the strategic benefit of the organization.

Because of the combination, the M.S. in IS&TM is primarily designed for two types of students: those with a background in business who want to move into a more technology-oriented role in their organization, and those with a background in a technical field who want to move into an IT/management role in their organization. Examples of the type of students with technical background appropriate for this degree include engineers, scientists, and those involved in biotechnology. Students with significant technical expertise and educational backgrounds in information technology (computer science undergraduates) may find the M.B.A. program a better fit for their needs.

The M.S. in IS&TM is designed to be completed on a part-time basis in two years and features two courses in telecommunications and networks as well as a speaker series of IT experts from firms such as J.P. Morgan Chase, AstraZeneca, and Deloitte & Touche, who discuss current issues and decision-making trends in information technology in their respective industries.

Research Facilities

The University library, a modem research facility with more than 2 million volumes and extensive electronic and database resources, is a member of the Association of Research Libraries and is a depository for U.S. government documents and patents.

All computing at the University is conducted over a high-speed, fiber-optic network connecting all buildings, laboratories, offices, and student housing on the campus. Also connected to the network are an array of computing resources ranging from NT servers to supercomputing clusters. The College offers a high-speed network, computing labs, computer classrooms, a variety of NT servers, an SAP environment, multimedia conferencing, and a behavioral research facility.

Financial Aid

Various financial aid packages are available to superior full-time graduate students. These include corporate assistantships, fellowships, graduate assistantships, and tuition grants, which are awarded on a competitive basis. Because the M.S. in IS&TM is a part-time program, assistantships, fellowships, and tuition grants are not available.

Cost of Study

The 2006–07 tuition for part-time study was $476 per credit hour for Delaware residents and $983 per credit hour for nonresident students.

Living and Housing Costs

Rental costs for shared occupancy in a graduate student complex were $450 per month in 2006–07. University and privately owned apartments, furnished and unfurnished, were available at costs ranging from $690 to $1200 per month.

Student Group

The M.S. in IS&TM program graduates its first students in May 2004; therefore, no group demographics are currently available.

Location

The University of Delaware is located in Newark, a suburban community of approximately 30,000. Newark is situated in the northwest corner of Delaware within 3 miles of the Pennsylvania and Maryland borders. It is located within easy driving distance of Philadelphia (45 miles), Baltimore (50 miles), Washington, D.C. (100 miles), and New York City (130 miles). Nearby Wilmington is a major center for credit banking and the chemical industry. More than 50 percent of all Fortune 500 companies are incorporated in Delaware. The College maintains strong ties with the corporate sector.

The University and The College

The University of Delaware, founded in 1743 as a small liberal arts school, was moved to Newark, where it became both a land-grant and a sea-grant college. It now ranks among the finest of the nation's medium-sized universities, with approximately 16,000 undergraduate and 3,000 graduate students. Included in the Alfred Lerner College of Business and Economics are the Departments of Accounting and MIS, Business Administration, Economics, and Finance. All accounting and business programs are accredited by AACSB International–The Association to Advance Collegiate Schools of Business. The MBNA Foundation and the company's executive committee have endowed the College of Business and Economics with $20 million in memory of former MBNA chairman and CEO, Alfred Lerner, who passed away in October 2002. In recognition of the endowment, the University has named the College the Alfred Lerner College of Business and Economics.

Applying

Students must submit official copies of all undergraduate and graduate transcripts, GMAT or GRE scores, and two letters of recommendation. A personal interview is also required for qualified applicants. All students whose native language is not English must have a minimum score of 600 on the TOEFL. Although there are no prerequisite courses, applicants are expected to possess basic skills in written and oral communication, mathematics, and computer usage.

Correspondence and Information

M.S. in IS&TM Program Admissions
Alfred Lerner College of Business and Economics
103 Alfred Lerner Hall
University of Delaware
Newark, Delaware 19716
Phone: 302-831-2221
Fax: 302-831-3329
E-mail: istm@udel.edu
Web site: http://www.istm.udel.edu

University of Delaware

THE FACULTY

Administration

Conrado (Bobby) Gempesaw, Dean, Alfred Lerner College of Business and Economics; Ph.D., Penn State.
Gloria Diodato, Assistant Dean, Graduate and Executive Programs, Alfred Lerner College of Business and Economics; M.B.A., Delaware.
Jeff Gillespie, Interim Chair of Accounting and MIS and Associate Professor; Ph.D., Virginia Tech.
Clinton E. White, Professor of Accounting and MIS and Head of MIS Faculty; D.B.A., Indiana.

Faculty

Dale A. Buckmaster, Professor of Accounting and MIS; Ph.D., Penn State; CPA.
Araya Debessay, Professor of Accounting; Ph.D., Penn State; CPA.
Andrea Everard, Assistant Professor of Accounting and MIS; Ph.D., Pittsburgh.
Guido L. Geerts, Associate Professor of Accounting and MIS; Ph.D., Free University of Brussels.
Thomas Hofferd, Assistant Professor of Accounting and MIS; Ph.D., Central Florida.
David Jenkins, Assistant Professor of Accounting and MIS; Ph.D., Maryland.
Scott K. Jones, Professor of Accounting and MIS; Ph.D., Drexel.
Gregory D. Kane, Associate Professor of Accounting and MIS; Ph.D., Virginia Tech; CPA.
Robert L. Paretta, Associate Professor of Accounting and MIS; Ph.D., Syracuse; CPA.
Neal Phillips, Assistant Professor of Accounting and MIS; J.D., Villanova.
Sheldon D. Pollack, Associate Professor of Accounting and MIS; J.D., Ph.D., Cornell.
Winifred Scott, Assistant Professor of Accounting and MIS; Ph.D., Florida State; CPA.
Mark Serva, Assistant Professor of Accounting and MIS; Ph.D., Texas at Austin.
Uma Velury, Assistant Professor of Accounting and MIS; Ph.D., South Carolina.
John H. Wragge, Associate Professor of Accounting and MIS and Faculty Director of Executive Education; Ph.D., Houston; CPA.

VIRGINIA COMMONWEALTH UNIVERSITY

Programs in Information Systems

Programs of Study

Virginia Commonwealth University (VCU), through the School of Business, offers a variety of programs in information systems. The M.S. in information systems is focused on the rapidly emerging area known as enterprise information systems (EIS). Graduates can take significant roles in planning, organizing, managing, designing, configuring, and implementing EIS systems using state-of-the-art technologies within organizations. The M.S. in information systems is available in both the traditional semester format and in an executive (alternate weekend) format. The executive program (fast-track executive M.S. in information systems) focuses on information technology management and is designed for students with six or more years of professional experience. There is a strong emphasis on the financial implications of information technology and business decisions, and leadership is the theme throughout the program. The traditional semester format program is intended to prepare students for senior-level positions—planning, organizing, managing, designing, configuring, and implementing information systems and using state-of-the-art technologies, methods, techniques, and tools. The program provides a graduate-level, technically oriented curriculum that focuses on the design and development of information systems to solve real-world problems.

In addition, students can pursue the Master of Business Administration with a concentration in information systems; the combined fast-track Master of Business Administration and Master of Science in information systems (M.S.), also available with a focus in information technology management; the Ph.D. in business with a concentration in information systems; or postbaccalaureate certificate programs in geographic information systems or planning information systems.

Research Facilities

Established in 1991 as an outreach vehicle for the Department of Information Systems at VCU, the Information Systems Research Institute (ISRI) facilitates professional education for current IT workers, technical assistance for specific business needs, and high-quality-applied research and practical real-world experience for faculty members and students. Through ISRI, department faculty members and students collaborate with industry to solve real problems through specific projects and custom training programs.

VCU libraries provide a combined capacity of more than 1.7 million volumes and 10,200 periodical titles and an online bibliographic search service accessing hundreds of databases. In addition, the Virginia State and Richmond Public Libraries are within walking distance of both VCU campuses. Academic Computing provides a variety of microcomputer, minicomputer, and mainframe computing services to support the research and instructional endeavors of the faculty and students, including consultation, instruction, and computer acquisition.

Financial Aid

The School of Business offers a limited number of graduate assistantship positions to full-time students. Scholarship opportunities exist for graduate students after they have completed at least one semester of study. Students may apply for need-based assistance with the University's Financial Aid Office. Current information on financial aid programs, policies, and procedures is available at http://www.vcu.edu/enroll/finaid.

Cost of Study

For full-time study (9–15 credits) in 2007–08, Virginia residents pay tuition and fees of $4452 per semester; nonresidents, $8876 per semester. For part-time study, Virginia residents pay tuition and fees of $465 per hour; nonresidents, $954 per hour. Some programs require additional fees. On the Medical College of Virginia (MCV) campus, tuition, fees, and other expenses vary in the medicine, pharmacy, nurse anesthesia, dentistry, and School of Allied Health programs.

Living and Housing Costs

Graduate student housing is available on both the MCV campus and the academic campus of Virginia Commonwealth University. Many graduate students live in off-campus housing, which is reasonably priced and readily available in a variety of styles and settings in nearby residential areas or within easy commuting distance. On- and off-campus housing information is available on the Web at http://www.housing.vcu.edu/.

Student Group

VCU enrolls 30,452 students, 7,611 of whom are graduate students. More than 200 clubs and organizations reflect the diverse social, recreational, educational, political, and religious interests of the student body.

Location

Richmond is Virginia's capital and a major East Coast financial and manufacturing center that offers students a wide range of cultural, educational, and recreational activities. Richmond is located in central Virginia at the intersection of Interstates 95 and 64, 2 hours south of Washington, D.C., and nestled between the Blue Ridge Mountains and the Atlantic coast. The Richmond region is easily accessible by plane, car, and train. With nearly 1 million residents, the historic city of Richmond combines big-city offerings with small-town hospitality. Applicants are encouraged to explore http://www.visit.richmond.com/ for more information on the city.

The University

VCU is a state-supported coeducational university with a graduate school, a major teaching hospital, and twelve academic and professional units that offer fifty-two undergraduate, twenty-two postbaccalaureate certificate, sixty-five master's, six post-master's certificate, and twenty-nine Ph.D. programs. VCU also offers M.D., D.D.S., D.P.T., and Pharm.D. programs as well as cooperative degree programs with other major Virginia colleges and universities. VCU has one of the largest evening colleges in the United States. The academic campus is located in Richmond's historic Fan District. The health sciences campus and hospital are located 2 miles east in the downtown business district. A University bus service provides free intercampus transportation for faculty members and students.

With more than $211 million in annual research funding, Virginia Commonwealth University is classified as one of the nation's top research universities by the Carnegie Foundation for the Advancement of Teaching. More than 29,000 undergraduate, certificate, graduate, post-master's, professional, and doctoral students are enrolled in 162 academic programs, forty of which are unique in the commonwealth of Virginia. The faculty members represent the finest American and international graduate institutions and enhance the University's position among the important institutions of higher learning in the United States and the world via their work in the classroom, laboratory, studio, and clinic and in their scholarly publications.

Applying

Admission procedures and program requirements are detailed in the *Graduate Bulletin.* Application deadlines and materials, including the application and the *Graduate Bulletin,* are available online at the Graduate School Web site at http://www.graduate.vcu.edu. Virginia Commonwealth University is an equal opportunity/affirmative action institution providing access to education and employment without regard to age, race, color, national origin, gender, religion, sexual orientation, veteran's status, political affiliation, or disability.

Correspondence and Information

Jana P. McQuaid, Graduate Program Director
Information Systems
School of Business
Virginia Commonwealth University
1015 Floyd Avenue
Richmond, Virginia 23284-4000
Phone: 804-828-4622
E-mail: jpmcquaid@vcu.edu
Web site: http://www.gsib.vcu.edu

Virginia Commonwealth University

THE FACULTY AND THEIR RESEARCH

Peter Aiken, Associate Professor; Ph.D., George Mason.

Measuring data management's maturity: A community's self-assessment. *IEEE Computer* 40(4):42–50, 2007. With Allen, Parker, and Mattia.

Richard J. Coppins, Associate Professor; Ph.D., North Carolina State. Computer/network security and application of operations research techniques to problems related to computer systems.

An improved suite of object-oriented measures. *J. Computer Inf. Syst.*, Fall 2005. With Neal and Weistroffer.

Gupreet Dhillon, Professor; Ph.D., London. Information security, its right use, and the range of related ethical and philosophical issues.

To opt-in, or to opt-out? That is the question. A case study. *J. Inf. Syst. Security* 2(2), 2006. With Chapman.

George Kasper, Professor; Ph.D., SUNY at Buffalo. Computer-human interaction, decision-support systems.

The accreditation process for IS programs in business schools. *J. Inf. Syst. Educ.* 16(2), July 2005. With Chandrashekar and Redmond.

Allen S. Lee, Professor; Ph.D., MIT. Qualitative, interpretive, and case research on information technology and organizations; communications; research methodologies in information systems research and the social sciences; action research.

Does the use of computer-based BPC tools contribute to redesign effectiveness? Insights from a hermeneutic study. *IEEE Trans. Eng. Manage.* 53(1):130–45, 2006. With Sarker.

Kweku-Muata (Noel) Osei-Bryson, Professor; Ph.D., Maryland, College Park. Data mining, database systems, expert systems, decision-support systems, group-support systems, multicriteria decision analysis, cluster analysis, integer programming, parametric programming.

An exploration of factors that impact individual performance in an ERP environment: An analysis using multiple analytical techniques. *Eur. J. Inf. Syst.* 15(6):556–68, 2006. With Kositanurit and Ngwenyama.

Richard T. Redmond, Associate Professor; D.B.A., Kent State. Software productivity, expert systems, applications of AI to business, database/imagebase design theory and compression theory.

A semantic approach to monitor business process performance. *Communications ACM* 48(12), December 2005. With Thomas, Yoon, Signh.

John Sutherland, Professor; Ph.D., UCLA.

Heinz R. Weistroffer, Associate Professor; Ph.D., Free University of Berlin. Software engineering, decision support systems, conceptual modeling, portfolio decision making, economics of information technology.

A conceptual model for integrative information systems security. *J. Inf. Syst. Security* 2(1):44–59, 2006. With Korzyk, Sutherland, and Weistroffer.

James Wynne, Associate Professor; Ph.D., Nebraska–Lincoln. Software project management, software training and curriculum development, group-decision support systems, systems analysis and design.

Section 13
Management Strategy and Policy

This section contains a directory of institutions offering graduate work in management strategy and policy. Additional information about programs listed in the directory but not augmented by an in-depth entry may be obtained by writing directly to the dean of a graduate school or chair of a department at the address given in the directory.

For programs offering related work, see also in this book Business Administration and Management. In Book 2, see Public, Regional, and Industrial Affairs (Public Administration and Public Policy).

CONTENTS

Program Directory

Close-Up

See:

Management Strategy and Policy

Alliant International University–San Diego, Marshall Goldsmith School of Management, Business and Management Division, San Diego, CA 92131-1799. Offers business administration (MBA); information and technology management (DBA); international business (MIBA, DBA), including finance (DBA), marketing (DBA); strategic business (DBA); sustainable management (MBA). Part-time and evening/weekend programs available. *Students:* 87 full-time (22 women), 51 part-time (17 women); includes 27 minority (8 African Americans, 2 American Indian/Alaska Native, 8 Asian Americans or Pacific Islanders, 9 Hispanic Americans), 68 international. Average age 32. 104 applicants, 66% accepted, 40 enrolled. *Degree requirements:* For doctorate, thesis/dissertation. *Entrance requirements:* For master's, GMAT, minimum GPA of 3.0; for doctorate, GMAT, minimum GPA of 3.3. Additional exam requirements/recommendations for international students: Required—TOEFL (minimum score 550 paper-based; 213 computer-based), TWE (minimum score 5). *Application deadline:* For fall admission, 8/1 priority date for domestic and international students; for spring admission, 12/1 priority date for domestic and international students. Applications are processed on a rolling basis. Application fee: $55. Electronic applications accepted. *Expenses:* Tuition: Part-time $825 per unit. Tuition and fees vary according to course load, degree level and program. *Financial support:* Research assistantships, teaching assistantships, career-related internships or fieldwork, Federal Work-Study, institutionally sponsored loans, scholarships/grants, and tuition waivers (partial) available. Support available to part-time students. Financial award application deadline: 2/15; financial award applicants required to submit FAFSA. *Faculty research:* Consumer behavior, international business, strategic management, information systems. *Unit head:* Dr. Fred Phillips, Associate Dean, 866-825-5426, Fax: 855-635-4739, E-mail: admissions@alliant.edu. *Application contact:* Alliant International University Central Contact Center, 866-U-ALLIANT, Fax: 858-635-4555, E-mail: admissions@alliant.edu.

See Close-Up on page 203.

Azusa Pacific University, School of Business and Management, Azusa, CA 91702-7000. Offers business administration (MBA); human and organizational development (MA); international business (MBA); strategic management (MBA). Part-time and evening/weekend programs available. *Faculty:* 3 full-time (0 women). *Students:* 24 full-time (11 women), 126 part-time (51 women); includes 50 minority (8 African Americans, 1 American Indian/Alaska Native, 12 Asian Americans or Pacific Islanders, 29 Hispanic Americans), 24 international. Average age 31. In 2006, 54 degrees awarded. *Degree requirements:* For master's, thesis (for some programs), final project. *Entrance requirements:* For master's, GMAT, minimum GPA of 3.0. Additional exam requirements/recommendations for international students: Required—TOEFL (minimum score 600 paper-based). *Application deadline:* For fall admission, 8/15 priority date for domestic students. Applications are processed on a rolling basis. Application fee: $45 ($65 for international students). *Expenses:* Contact institution. *Financial support:* Scholarships/grants available. *Faculty research:* Gender issues, financial risk, leadership and ethics, marketing strategy. *Unit head:* Dr. Ilene Bezjian, Dean, 626-815-3090, Fax: 626-815-3802, E-mail: ibezjian@apu.edu.

Bernard M. Baruch College of the City University of New York, Zicklin School of Business, Department of Management, New York, NY 10010-5585. Offers entrepreneurship (MBA); general management and policy (MBA); human resources management (MBA); management planning systems (PhD); management science (MBA); organization and policy studies (PhD); organizational behavior (MBA). Part-time and evening/weekend programs available. *Faculty:* 38 full-time (10 women), 41 part-time/adjunct (6 women). *Students:* 30 full-time (14 women), 117 part-time (52 women); includes 37 minority (17 African Americans, 14 Asian Americans or Pacific Islanders, 6 Hispanic Americans). In 2006, 39 master's, 1 doctorate awarded. *Degree requirements:* For doctorate, thesis/dissertation, comprehensive exam. *Entrance requirements:* For master's, GMAT, 2 letters of recommendation, resumé, 2 years of work experience; for doctorate, GMAT. Additional exam requirements/recommendations for international students: Required—TOEFL (minimum score 590 paper-based; 243 computer-based), TWE. *Application deadline:* For fall admission, 5/31 for domestic students, 4/30 for international students; for spring admission, 10/31 for domestic and international students. Application fee: $125. *Financial support:* Fellowships, research assistantships, teaching assistantships, career-related internships or fieldwork, Federal Work-Study, scholarships/grants, and unspecified assistantships available. Financial award application deadline: 4/30; financial award applicants required to submit FAFSA. *Unit head:* Harry M. Rosen, Chairman, 646-312-3620, Fax: 646-312-3621, E-mail: harry_rosen@baruch.cuny.edu. *Application contact:* Frances Murphy, Office of Graduate Admissions, 646-312-1300, Fax: 646-312-1301, E-mail: zicklingradadmissions@baruch.cuny.edu.

Brenau University, Graduate Programs, School of Business and Mass Communication, Gainesville, GA 30501. Offers accounting (MBA); healthcare management (MBA); leadership development (MBA); management (MBA); organizational development (MS). Part-time and evening/weekend programs available. Postbaccalaureate distance learning degree programs offered (no on-campus study). *Faculty:* 12 full-time (6 women), 16 part-time/adjunct (5 women). *Students:* 49 full-time (32 women), 148 part-time (89 women); includes 52 minority (45 African Americans, 2 Asian Americans or Pacific Islanders, 5 Hispanic Americans), 2 international. Average age 35. 222 applicants, 55% accepted, 111 enrolled. In 2006, 64 degrees awarded. *Degree requirements:* For master's, thesis (for some programs). *Entrance requirements:* For master's, GMAT, GRE General Test, or MAT, minimum undergraduate GPA of 3.0, faculty interview. Additional exam requirements/recommendations for international students: Required—TOEFL (minimum score 550 paper-based). *Application deadline:* Applications are processed on a rolling basis. Application fee: $30. Electronic applications accepted. *Expenses:* Contact institution. *Financial support:* Career-related internships or fieldwork available. Financial award application deadline: 7/15; financial award applicants required to submit FAFSA. *Faculty research:* International business, women in management entrepreneurship, simulations in business, Internet/online teaching in business, managerial leadership. *Unit head:* Dr. Bill Haney, Dean, 770-538-4707, Fax: 770-537-4701, E-mail: whaney@brenau.edu. *Application contact:* Nathan Goss, Admissions Coordinator, 770-534-6162, Fax: 770-538-4701, E-mail: ngoss@brenau.edu.

California State University, East Bay, Academic Programs and Graduate Studies, College of Business and Economics, Department of Management and Finance, Hayward, CA 94542-3000. Offers e-business (MBA); finance (MBA); human resources management (MBA); international business (MBA); management sciences (MBA); operations and material management (MBA); operations research (MBA); quantitative business methods (MS); strategic management (MBA); supply chain management (MBA). Part-time and evening/weekend programs available. *Faculty:* 37 full-time (7 women), 8 part-time/adjunct (3 women). *Students:* 204 full-time, 363 part-time; includes 234 minority (17 African Americans, 191 Asian Americans or Pacific Islanders, 26 Hispanic Americans), 158 international. Average age 32. 373 applicants, 43% accepted, 100 enrolled. In 2006, 281 degrees awarded. *Degree requirements:* For master's, comprehensive exam or thesis. *Entrance requirements:* For master's, GMAT, minimum GPA of 2.75. Additional exam requirements/recommendations for international students: Required—TOEFL (minimum score 550 paper-based; 213 computer-based). *Application deadline:* For fall admission, 5/31 for domestic students, 4/30 for international students; for winter admission, 9/30 for domestic and international students; for spring admission, 12/31 for domestic students, 11/30 for international students. Application fee: $55. *Financial support:* Career-related internships or fieldwork, Federal Work-Study, and institutionally sponsored loans available. Support available to part-time students. Financial award application deadline: 3/2. *Unit head:* Dr. Joyendu Bhadury, Chair, 510-885-3307, E-mail: joy.bhadury@csueastbay.edu. *Application contact:* Doris Duncan, Director of Graduate Programs, 510-885-3364, Fax: 510-885-2176, E-mail: doris.duncan@csueastbay.edu.

Cardean University, MBA Program, Chicago, IL 60606-7204. Offers accounting and information systems (MBA); e-commerce (MBA); finance (MBA); global management (MBA); health care administration (MBA); human resources management (MBA); leadership (MBA); management of information systems (MBA); management of technology (MBA); marketing (MBA); professional accounting (MBA); project management (MBA); risk management (MBA); strategy and economics (MBA). Part-time and evening/weekend programs available. Postbaccalaureate distance learning degree programs offered (no on-campus study). *Entrance requirements:* Additional exam requirements/recommendations for international students: Required—TOEFL (minimum score 550 paper-based; 213 computer-based).

Case Western Reserve University, Weatherhead School of Management, Department of Marketing and Policy Studies, Cleveland, OH 44106. Offers labor and human resource policy (MBA); management (MSM); management policy (MBA); marketing (MBA). Part-time and evening/weekend programs available. *Faculty:* 22 full-time (5 women), 4 part-time/adjunct (1 woman). *Students:* 131 full-time (62 women), 168 part-time (70 women); includes 18 minority (6 African Americans, 11 Asian Americans or Pacific Islanders, 1 Hispanic American), 32 international. Average age 28. In 2006, 183 degrees awarded. *Entrance requirements:* For master's, GMAT. *Application deadline:* For fall admission, 4/15 priority date for domestic students. Applications are processed on a rolling basis. Application fee: $50. *Financial support:* Career-related internships or fieldwork, Federal Work-Study, institutionally sponsored loans, and tuition waivers (full and partial) available. Financial award application deadline: 5/1. *Unit head:* Sayan Chatterjee, Chairman.

Claremont Graduate University, Graduate Programs, Peter F. Drucker and Masatoshi Ito Graduate School of Management, Program in Executive Management, Claremont, CA 91711-6160. Offers advanced management (MS); executive management (EMBA); leadership (Certificate); management (MA, PhD, Certificate); strategy (Certificate). *Accreditation:* AACSB. Part-time programs available. *Students:* 46 full-time (18 women), 61 part-time (22 women); includes 35 minority (6 African Americans, 1 American Indian/Alaska Native, 12 Asian Americans or Pacific Islanders, 16 Hispanic Americans), 8 international. Average age 45. In 2006, 17 master's, 1 doctorate, 22 other advanced degrees awarded. *Entrance requirements:* For master's, GMAT or GRE General Test (EMBA). *Application deadline:* For fall admission, 2/15 priority date for domestic students. Applications are processed on a rolling basis. Electronic applications accepted. *Financial support:* Federal Work-Study and institutionally sponsored loans available. Support available to part-time students. Financial award application deadline: 2/15; financial award applicants required to submit FAFSA. *Faculty research:* Strategy and leadership, brand management, cost management and control, organizational transformation, general management. *Unit head:* Christina Wassenaar, Director, 909-607-7812, Fax: 909-607-9104, E-mail: christina.wassenaar@cgu.edu. *Application contact:* Susan Townzen, Academic Advising, 909-607-7369, Fax: 909-607-9104, E-mail: susan.n.townzen@cgu.edu.

Clemson University, Graduate School, College of Business and Behavioral Science, Department of Management, Clemson, SC 29634. Offers electronic commerce (M E Com); management (MS, PhD). *Accreditation:* AACSB. Part-time programs available. *Faculty:* 29 full-time (6 women), 1 part-time/adjunct (0 women). *Students:* 22 full-time (4 women), 2 part-time; includes 3 minority (1 American Indian/Alaska Native, 2 Hispanic Americans), 13 international. Average age 25. 33 applicants, 21% accepted, 3 enrolled. In 2006, 4 master's, 2 doctorates awarded. Terminal master's awarded for partial completion of doctoral program. *Degree requirements:* For doctorate, thesis/dissertation. *Entrance requirements:* For master's, GMAT, GRE General Test, minimum GPA of 3.0; for doctorate, GRE General Test, minimum GPA of 3.5. Additional exam requirements/recommendations for international students: Required—TOEFL. *Application deadline:* For fall admission, 2/1 for domestic students, 4/15 for international students; for spring admission, 10/1 for domestic students, 9/15 for international students. Applications are processed on a rolling basis. Application fee: $50. *Expenses:* Tuition, state resident: full-time $8,812; part-time $450 per hour. Tuition, nonresident: full-time $18,036; part-time $760 per hour. Required fees: $474; $5 per term. *Financial support:* In 2006–07, 13 research assistantships were awarded; fellowships, teaching assistantships, institutionally sponsored loans also available. Financial award applicants required to submit FAFSA. *Faculty research:* Production/operations, strategic management, organizational behavior, management information systems. *Unit head:* Dr. Patricia Layton, Chair, 864-656-3303, Fax: 864-656-3304, E-mail: playton@clemson.edu.

DePaul University, Charles H. Kellstadt Graduate School of Business, Department of Management, Chicago, IL 60604-2287. Offers entrepreneurship (MBA); health sector management (MBA); human resource management (MBA, MSHR); leadership/change management (MBA); management planning and strategy (MBA); operations management (MBA). Part-time and evening/weekend programs available. *Faculty:* 36 full-time (7 women), 35 part-time/adjunct (16 women). *Students:* 173 full-time (71 women), 134 part-time (61 women); includes 60 minority (12 African Americans, 34 Asian Americans or Pacific Islanders, 14 Hispanic Americans), 13 international. Average age 31. In 2006, 112 degrees awarded. *Entrance requirements:* For master's, GMAT, GRE (MSHR), 2 letters of recommendation, resumé. Additional exam requirements/recommendations for international students: Required—TOEFL (minimum score 550 paper-based; 213 computer-based). *Application deadline:* For fall admission, 7/1 for domestic students; for winter admission, 10/1 for domestic students; for spring admission, 2/1 for domestic students. Applications are processed on a rolling basis. Application fee: $60. Electronic applications accepted. *Financial support:* Research assistantships available. Financial award application deadline: 4/1. *Faculty research:* Growth management, creativity and innovation, quality management and business process design, entrepreneurship. *Application contact:* Christopher E. Kinsella, Director of Cohort MBA Programs, 312-362-8810, Fax: 312-362-6677, E-mail: kgsb@depaul.edu.

DePaul University, Charles H. Kellstadt Graduate School of Business, Department of Marketing, Chicago, IL 60604-2287. Offers brand management (MBA); customer relationship management (MBA); integrated marketing communication (MBA); marketing analysis (MSMA); marketing and management (MBA); marketing strategy and analysis (MBA); marketing strategy and planning (MBA); new product management (MBA); sales leadership (MBA). Part-time and evening/weekend programs available. *Faculty:* 23 full-time (4 women), 15 part-time/adjunct (6 women). *Students:* 189 full-time (103 women), 126 part-time (68 women); includes 37 minority (18 African Americans, 14 Asian Americans or Pacific Islanders, 5 Hispanic Americans), 22 international. Average age 30. In 2006, 88 degrees awarded. *Degree requirements:* For master's, registration. *Entrance requirements:* For master's, GMAT, 2 letters of recommendation, resumé. Additional exam requirements/recommendations for international students: Required—TOEFL (minimum score 550 paper-based; 213 computer-based). *Application deadline:* For fall admission, 7/1 for domestic students; for winter admission, 10/1 for domestic students; for spring admission, 2/1 for domestic students. Applications are processed on a rolling basis. Application fee: $60. Electronic applications accepted. *Financial support:* In 2006–07, 6 research assistantships with partial tuition reimbursements (averaging $2,500 per year) were awarded. Financial award application deadline: 4/30. *Faculty research:* International and marketing role in developing economics, internet marketing, direct marketing, consumer behavior, new product development processes. Total annual research expenditures: $100,000. *Application contact:* Christopher E. Kinsella, Director of Cohort MBA Programs, 312-362-8810, Fax: 312-362-6677, E-mail: kgsb@depaul.edu.

Dominican University of California, Graduate Programs, School of Business, Education and Leadership, Division of Business and International Studies, Program in Strategic Leadership, San Rafael, CA 94901-2298. Offers MBA. Part-time and evening/weekend programs available. *Degree requirements:* For master's, thesis or alternative, practicum. *Entrance requirements:* For master's, minimum GPA of 3.0. Additional exam requirements/recommendations for international students: Required—TOEFL (minimum score 550 paper-based; 213 computer-based). Electronic applications accepted. Expenses: Contact institution.

Drexel University, LeBow College of Business, Program in Business Administration, Philadelphia, PA 19104-2875. Offers business administration (MBA, PhD, APC), including accounting (MBA, PhD), decision sciences (PhD), economics (MBA, PhD), finance (MBA, PhD), legal studies (MBA), management (MBA), marketing (MBA, PhD), organizational sciences (PhD), quantitative methods (MBA), strategic management (PhD). *Accreditation:* AACSB. Part-time and evening/weekend programs available. Postbaccalaureate distance learning degree programs offered (minimal on-campus study). Terminal master's awarded for partial completion of doctoral program. *Entrance requirements:* For master's, GMAT, minimum GPA of 2.75; for doctorate, GMAT. Additional exam requirements/recommendations for international students: Required—TOEFL. Electronic applications accepted. *Faculty research:* Decision support systems, individual and group behavior, operations research, techniques and strategy.

The George Washington University, School of Business, Department of Management Science, Program in Management Decision Making, Washington, DC 20052. Offers MBA, PhD. Part-time and evening/weekend programs available. *Degree requirements:* For doctorate, thesis/dissertation. *Entrance requirements:* For master's, GMAT; for doctorate, GMAT or GRE. Additional exam requirements/recommendations for international students: Required—TOEFL.

The George Washington University, School of Business, Department of Strategic Management and Public Policy, Washington, DC 20052. Offers business economics and public policy (MBA); strategic management and public policy (PhD). Part-time and evening/weekend programs available. *Degree requirements:* For doctorate, thesis/dissertation. *Entrance requirements:* For master's, GMAT; for doctorate, GMAT or GRE. Additional exam requirements/recommendations for international students: Required—TOEFL.

Georgia Institute of Technology, Graduate Studies and Research, College of Management, Program in Business Administration, Atlanta, GA 30332-0001. Offers accounting (MBA); e-commerce (Certificate); engineering entrepreneurship (MBA); entrepreneurship (Certificate); finance (MBA); information technology management (MBA); international business (MBA, Certificate); management of technology (Certificate); marketing (MBA); operations management (MBA); organizational behavior (MBA); strategic management (MBA). *Accreditation:* AACSB.

Georgia Institute of Technology, Graduate Studies and Research, College of Management, Program in Management, Atlanta, GA 30332-0001. Offers accounting (PhD); finance (PhD); information technology management (PhD); marketing (PhD); operations management (PhD); organizational behavior (PhD); quantitative and computational finance (MS); strategic management (PhD). *Accreditation:* AACSB. *Degree requirements:* For doctorate, thesis/dissertation, oral exams, comprehensive exam. *Entrance requirements:* For master's and doctorate, GMAT. Additional exam requirements/recommendations for international students: Required—TOEFL. *Faculty research:* MIS, management of technology, international business, entrepreneurship, operations management.

HEC Montreal, School of Business Administration, Master of Science Programs in Administration, Program in Business Intelligence, Montréal, QC H3T 2A7, Canada. Offers M Sc. All courses are given in French. Part-time programs available. *Degree requirements:* For master's, one foreign language, thesis. Application fee: $60 Canadian dollars. Electronic applications accepted. Tuition and fees charges are reported in Canadian dollars. *Expenses:* Tuition, nonresident: part-time $56 Canadian dollars per credit. Required fees: $30 Canadian dollars per semester. *Financial support:* Fellowships, research assistantships, teaching assistantships, scholarships/grants available. *Application contact:* Francine Blais, Administrative Director, 514-340-6112, Fax: 514-340-6411, E-mail: francine.blais@hec.ca.

Illinois Institute of Technology, Stuart School of Business, Program in Business Administration, Chicago, IL 60616-3793. Offers entrepreneurship (MBA); financial management (MBA); financial markets (MBA); healthcare management (MBA); information technology management (MBA); international business (MBA); management science (MBA); marketing (MBA); operations, quality, and technology management (MBA); strategic management of organizations (MBA); sustainable enterprise (MBA); JD/MBA; MBA/MS. *Accreditation:* AACSB. Part-time and evening/weekend programs available. *Faculty:* 13 full-time (1 woman), 9 part-time/adjunct (0 women). *Students:* 74 full-time (29 women), 42 part-time (16 women); includes 17 minority (5 African Americans, 11 Asian Americans or Pacific Islanders, 1 Hispanic American), 74 international. Average age 29. 247 applicants, 70% accepted, 51 enrolled. In 2006, 45 degrees awarded. *Entrance requirements:* For master's, GMAT. Additional exam requirements/recommendations for international students: Required—TOEFL (minimum score 600 paper-based; 250 computer-based). *Application deadline:* For fall admission, 8/15 priority date for domestic students, 7/1 for international students; for winter admission, 11/1 priority date for domestic students, 10/1 for international students; for spring admission, 1/1 priority date for domestic students, 1/1 for international students. Applications are processed on a rolling basis. Application fee: $75. Electronic applications accepted. *Expenses: Contact institution.* Tuition and fees vary according to class time, course level, course load, program and student level. *Financial support:* Career-related internships or fieldwork, Federal Work-Study, institutionally sponsored loans, scholarships/grants, traineeships, health care benefits, tuition waivers, and unspecified assistantships available. Support available to part-time students. Financial award applicants required to submit FAFSA. *Faculty research:* Knowledge management, healthcare management, sustainability in supply chain. *Unit head:* Dr. George P. Nassos, Interim Director, 312-906-6543, Fax: 312-906-6549, E-mail: george.nassos@iit.edu. *Application contact:* Brian Jansen, Director of Graduate Admissions, 312-906-6521, Fax: 312-906-6549, E-mail: admission@stuart.iit.edu.

Lamar University, College of Graduate Studies, College of Business, Beaumont, TX 77710. Offers accounting (MBA); experiential business and Entrepreneurship (MBA); financial management (MBA); healthcare administration (MBA); information systems (MBA); management (MBA). *Accreditation:* AACSB. Part-time and evening/weekend programs available. *Faculty:* 20 full-time (8 women), 2 part-time/adjunct (1 woman). *Students:* 55 full-time (27 women), 45 part-time (20 women); includes 17 minority (9 African Americans, 4 Asian Americans or Pacific Islanders, 4 Hispanic Americans), 14 international. Average age 29. 131 applicants, 34% accepted, 29 enrolled. In 2006, 29 degrees awarded. *Degree requirements:* For master's, thesis optional. *Entrance requirements:* For master's, GMAT. Additional exam requirements/recommendations for international students: Required—TOEFL (minimum score 525 paper-based; 197 computer-based). *Application deadline:* For fall admission, 3/15 priority date for domestic students; for spring admission, 10/1 priority date for domestic students. Applications are processed on a rolling basis. Application fee: $25 ($50 for international students). *Expenses:* Tuition, nonresident: part-time $33 per hour. Required fees: $43 per hour. $110 per semester. *Financial support:* In 2006–07, 12 students received support, including 4 research assistantships with partial tuition reimbursements available; fellowships with tuition reimbursements available, career-related internships or fieldwork, Federal Work-Study, institutionally sponsored loans, scholarships/grants, and tuition waivers (partial) also available. Support available to part-time students. Financial award application deadline: 4/1; financial award applicants required to submit FAFSA. *Faculty research:* Marketing, finance, quantitative methods, MIS, legal, environmental. Total annual research expenditures: $26,000. *Unit head:* Dr. Enrique R. Venta, Dean, 409-880-8604, Fax: 409-880-8088, E-mail: henry.venta@lamar.edu. *Application contact:* Dr. Brad Mayer, Professor and Associate Dean, 409-880-2383, Fax: 409-880-8605, E-mail: bradley.mayer@lamar.edu.

Manhattanville College, Graduate Programs, Humanities and Social Sciences Programs, Program in Leadership and Strategic Management, Purchase, NY 10577-2132. Offers MS. Part-time and evening/weekend programs available. In 2006, 9 degrees awarded. *Degree requirements:* For master's, thesis. *Entrance requirements:* For master's, 2 letters of recommendation, interview. *Application deadline:* Applications are processed on a rolling basis. Application fee: $55. *Financial support:* Scholarships/grants available. Financial award applicants required to submit FAFSA. *Application contact:* Natalia Fernandez, Director of Admissions, 914-323-5418, E-mail: gps@mylllle.edu.

McGill University, Faculty of Graduate and Postdoctoral Studies, Desautels Faculty of Management, Montréal, QC H3A 2T5, Canada. Offers administration (PhD); entrepreneurial studies (MBA); finance (MBA); general management (Post Master's Certificate); information systems (MBA); international business (exchange program) (MBA); international Master's program in practicing management (MM); management (MBA); management for development (MBA); manufacturing management (MMM); marketing (MBA); operations management (MBA); public accountancy (Diploma); strategic management (MBA); MBA/LL B; MD/MBA. Part-time programs available. *Entrance requirements:* For master's, GMAT, minimum undergraduate GPA of 3.0, 2 years work experience; for doctorate, GMAT or GRE General Test, 2 letters of recommendation, preferably by professors in chosen field of specialization; for other advanced degree, 2 years of work experience, MBA, minimum GPA of 3.0 (Post-MBA Certificate). Additional exam requirements/recommendations for international students: Required—TOEFL (minimum score 600 paper-based; 250 computer-based), IELTS (minimum score 7). Electronic applications accepted. Expenses: Contact institution. *Faculty research:* Social innovation, leadership, strategy.

Mountain State University, Graduate Studies, Program in Strategic Leadership, Beckley, WV 25802-9003. Offers MSSL. Part-time and evening/weekend programs available. Postbaccalaureate distance learning degree programs offered (no on-campus study). *Faculty:* 7 full-time (1 woman), 34 part-time/adjunct (9 women). *Students:* 248 full-time (105 women), 10 part-time (5 women); includes 59 minority (38 African Americans, 3 American Indian/Alaska Native, 3 Asian Americans or Pacific Islanders, 15 Hispanic Americans), 6 international. Average age 37. 368 applicants, 100% accepted, 243 enrolled. In 2006, 148 degrees awarded. *Median time to degree:* Master's–2 years full-time, 3 years part-time. *Degree requirements:* For master's, thesis or alternative. *Entrance requirements:* Additional exam requirements/recommendations for international students: Required—TOEFL (minimum score 550 paper-based; 213 computer-based); Recommended—IELTS (minimum score 7). *Application deadline:* For fall admission, 5/31 priority date for domestic and international students. Applications are processed on a rolling basis. Application fee: $25 ($50 for international students). Electronic applications accepted. *Expenses:* Tuition: Full-time $3,660; part-time $305 per credit. Tuition and fees vary according to course load and program. *Financial support:* In 2006–07, 1 research assistantship (averaging $1,200 per year) was awarded; Federal Work-Study, scholarships/grants, and unspecified assistantships also available. Support available to part-time students. Financial award applicants required to submit FAFSA. *Unit head:* Dr. William White, Dean, School of Leadership and Professional Development, 304-929-1658, Fax: 304-929-1637, E-mail: wwhite@mountainstate.edu. *Application contact:* Tammy Murphy, Online Recruiting Coordinator OL/SL, 304-929-1700, Fax: 304-929-1710, E-mail: tmurphy@mountainstate.edu.

Neumann College, Program in Strategic Leadership, Aston, PA 19014-1298. Offers MS. *Faculty:* 1 (woman) full-time, 4 part-time/adjunct (2 women). *Students:* Average age 41. 40 applicants, 100% accepted, 35 enrolled. In 2006, 55 degrees awarded. Application fee: $50. *Financial support:* Available to part-time students. Application deadline: 3/15; *Unit head:* Dr. Judith Stang, Coordinator, Division of Continuing Adult and Professional Studies, 610-361-5292, E-mail: stangj@neumann.edu. *Application contact:* Louise Bank, Assistant Director of Admissions, Graduate and Evening Programs, 610-558-5604, Fax: 610-459-1370, E-mail: bankl@neumann.edu.

New York Institute of Technology, Ellis College, Old Westbury, NY 11568. Offers accounting and information systems (MBA); e-commerce (MBA); finance (MBA); global management (MBA); healthcare administration (MBA); human resources management (MBA); leadership (MBA); management of information systems (MBA); management of technology (MBA); marketing (MBA); professional accounting (MBA); project management (MBA); risk management (MBA); strategy and economics (MBA). Ellis College is a collaboration between New York Institute of Technology and UNext online learning company. Part-time and evening/weekend programs available. Postbaccalaureate distance learning degree programs offered (no on-campus study). *Entrance requirements:* For master's, interview. Additional exam requirements/recommendations for international students: Required—TOEFL (minimum score 550 paper-based; 213 computer-based). Electronic applications accepted. *Expenses:* Tuition: Full-time $16,800; part-time $700 per credit.

New York University, Leonard N. Stern School of Business, Department of Management and Organizations, New York, NY 10012-1019. Offers management organizations (MBA); organization theory (PhD); organizational behavior (PhD); strategy (PhD). *Expenses:* Tuition: Part-time $1,080 per unit. Required fees: $56 per unit. $329 per term. Tuition and fees vary according to program. *Faculty research:* Strategic management, managerial cognition, interpersonal processes, conflict and negotiation.

Northwestern University, The Graduate School, Kellogg School of Management, Program in Managerial Economics and Strategy, Evanston, IL 60208. Offers PhD. Admissions and degree offered through The Graduate School. *Degree requirements:* For doctorate, thesis/dissertation, comprehensive exam, registration. *Entrance requirements:* For doctorate, GMAT or GRE General Test. Additional exam requirements/recommendations for international students: Required—TOEFL. Electronic applications accepted. *Faculty research:* Competitive strategy and organization, managerial economics, decision sciences, game theory, operations management.

Pace University, Lubin School of Business, Program in Management Science, New York, NY 10038. Offers management science (MBA); operations management (MBA). Part-time and evening/weekend programs available. *Faculty:* 24 full-time, 11 part-time/adjunct. *Students:* Average age 28. 5 applicants, 60% accepted, 1 enrolled. *Entrance requirements:* For master's, GMAT. *Application deadline:* For fall admission, 7/31 priority date for domestic students; for spring admission, 11/30 for domestic students. Applications are processed on a rolling basis. Application fee: $65. Electronic applications accepted. *Expenses:* Tuition: Part-time $890 per credit. *Financial support:* Research assistantships, career-related internships or fieldwork available. Support available to part-time students. Financial award applicants required to submit FAFSA. *Unit head:* Dr. Christian Madu, Chairperson, 212-346-1919. *Application contact:* Joanna Broda, Director of Admissions, 212-346-1652, Fax: 212-346-1585, E-mail: gradnyc@pace.edu.

Purdue University, Graduate School, Krannert School of Management, Department of Management, West Lafayette, IN 47907. Offers accounting (PhD); business administration (MBA); finance (PhD); management information systems (PhD); marketing (PhD); operations management (PhD); quantitative methods (PhD); strategic management (PhD). *Students:* 56 full-time (21 women); includes 5 minority (3 Asian Americans or Pacific Islanders, 2 Hispanic Americans), 41 international. Average age 30. 421 applicants, 7% accepted, 19 enrolled. In 2006, 11 degrees awarded. *Median time to degree:* Doctorate–5 years full-time. Of those who began their doctoral program in fall 1998, 98% received their degree in 8 years or less. *Degree requirements:* For doctorate, thesis/dissertation, comprehensive exam, registration. *Entrance requirements:* For master's and doctorate, GMAT. Additional exam requirements/recommendations for international students: Required—TOEFL (minimum score 575 paper-based; 233 computer-based; 77 iBT), IELTS (minimum score 7). *Application deadline:* For fall admission, 2/15 for domestic and international students. Application fee: $55. Electronic applications accepted. *Financial support:* In 2006–07, 7 fellowships with partial tuition reimbursements (averaging $16,800 per year), 79 research assistantships with partial tuition reimbursements (averaging $16,800 per year), 8 teaching assistantships with partial tuition reimbursements (averaging $16,800 per year) were awarded; scholarships/grants and unspecified assistantships also available. Financial award application deadline: 2/15; financial award applicants required to submit FAFSA. *Faculty research:* Corporate finance, international business, enterprise integration. *Unit head:* Dr. John M. Barron, Head, 765-494-4451, Fax: 765-494-1526. *Application contact:* Kelly Felty, Assistant Director of Administration for Doctoral Programs, 765-494-4375, Fax: 765-494-1526, E-mail: phd@krannert.purdue.edu.

Regent University, Graduate School, School of Global Leadership and Entrepreneurship, Virginia Beach, VA 23464-9800. Offers business administration (MBA); management (MA); organizational leadership (MA, PhD, Certificate); strategic foresight (MA); strategic leader-

Management Strategy and Policy

Regent University (continued)

ship (DSL). Part-time programs available. Postbaccalaureate distance learning degree programs offered (minimal on-campus study). *Faculty:* 20 full-time (3 women), 36 part-time/adjunct (6 women). *Students:* 68 full-time (40 women), 482 part-time (170 women); includes 144 minority (110 African Americans, 6 American Indian/Alaska Native, 9 Asian Americans or Pacific Islanders, 19 Hispanic Americans), 37 international. Average age 40. 395 applicants, 37% accepted, 64 enrolled. In 2006, 100 master's, 69 doctorates awarded. *Degree requirements:* For master's, thesis or alternative, 3 credit hour culminating experience; for doctorate, thesis/dissertation. *Entrance requirements:* For master's, GRE, GMAT or MAT, minimum undergraduate GPA of 2.75, computer literacy survey, 2 recommendations, resumé; for doctorate, GRE, GMAT or MAT, sample of writing, minimum of 3 years of relevant experience, computer literacy survey, 2 recommendations, resumé; for Certificate, GRE, GMAT or MAT, writing sample. Additional exam requirements/recommendations for international students: Required—TOEFL (minimum score 577 paper-based; 233 computer-based). *Application deadline:* For fall admission, 5/1 priority date for domestic students; for spring admission, 10/1 priority date for domestic students. Applications are processed on a rolling basis. Application fee: $50. Electronic applications accepted. *Expenses: Contact institution. Financial support:* In 2006–07, 321 students received support. Scholarships/grants and tuition waivers (full and partial) available. Support available to part-time students. Financial award application deadline: 9/1. *Faculty research:* Servant leadership, ethics and values, telecommuting and family values, organizational communications, distance education. *Unit head:* Dr. Bruce Winston, Dean, 757-226-4306, Fax: 757-226-4634, E-mail: brucwin@regent.edu. *Application contact:* Althea Bishard, Registrar and Executive Director of Enrollment and Academic Services, 800-373-5504, Fax: 757-226-4381, E-mail: admissions@regent.edu.

Roberts Wesleyan College, Division of Business, Rochester, NY 14624-1997. Offers nonprofit leadership (Certificate); strategic leadership (MS); strategic marketing (MS). Evening/weekend programs available. *Faculty:* 3 full-time (0 women), 13 part-time/adjunct (3 women). *Students:* 57 full-time (28 women). Average age 34. 45 applicants, 89% accepted. In 2006, 26 degrees awarded. *Degree requirements:* For master's, thesis or alternative. *Entrance requirements:* For master's, GMAT, minimum GPA of 2.75, verifiable work experience. *Application deadline:* Applications are processed on a rolling basis. Application fee: $35. *Expenses: Contact institution. Financial support:* In 2006–07, 15 students received support. Applicants required to submit FAFSA. *Unit head:* Dr. Steven Bovee, Chair, 716-594-6571, Fax: 716-594-6316, E-mail: bovees@roberts.edu.

Rutgers, The State University of New Jersey, Newark, Rutgers Business School: Graduate Programs-Newark/New Brunswick, Department of Management and Global Business, Newark, NJ 07102. Offers customized concentration (MBA); global business (MBA); management and business strategy (MBA). *Entrance requirements:* For master's, GMAT. Additional exam requirements/recommendations for international students: Required—TOEFL.

Sage Graduate School, Graduate School, Division of Management, Communications and Legal Studies, Program in Business Administration, Troy, NY 12180-4115. Offers business strategy (MBA); finance (MBA); human resources (MBA); marketing (MBA); JD/MBA; MBA/MS. Part-time and evening/weekend programs available. *Faculty:* 3 full-time (1 woman), 4 part-time/adjunct (2 women). *Students:* 9 full-time (5 women), 60 part-time (35 women); includes 10 minority (7 African Americans, 3 Hispanic Americans), 2 international. Average age 31. 58 applicants, 67% accepted, 27 enrolled. In 2006, 12 degrees awarded. *Entrance requirements:* For master's, minimum GPA of 2.75. Additional exam requirements/recommendations for international students: Required—TOEFL (minimum score 550 paper-based; 213 computer-based). *Application deadline:* Applications are processed on a rolling basis. Application fee: $40. *Expenses:* Tuition: Full-time $9,270; part-time $515 per credit hour. *Financial support:* Career-related internships or fieldwork, scholarships/grants, and unspecified assistantships available. Support available to part-time students. Financial award application deadline: 3/1; financial award applicants required to submit FAFSA. *Unit head:* Dr. David Kiner, Director, 518-292-1761, E-mail: kinerd@sage.edu. *Application contact:* Shannon K. Easton, Director of Graduate and Adult Admission, 518-244-2443, Fax: 518-244-6880, E-mail: sgsadm@sage.edu.

Saint Mary-of-the-Woods College, Program in Leadership Development, Saint Mary-of-the-Woods, IN 47876. Offers MLD.

Stevens Institute of Technology, Graduate School, Wesley J. Howe School of Technology Management, Program in Management, Hoboken, NJ 07030. Offers general management (MS); global innovation management (MS); human resource management (MS); information management (MS); project management (MS); technology commercialization (MS); technology management (MS). Part-time programs available. *Degree requirements:* For master's, thesis optional. *Entrance requirements:* For master's, GMAT, GRE General Test. Additional exam requirements/recommendations for international students: Required—TOEFL. Electronic applications accepted. *Faculty research:* Industrial economics.

Syracuse University, Martin J. Whitman School of Management, PhD Program in Business Administration, Syracuse, NY 13244. Offers accounting (PhD); finance (PhD); management information systems (PhD); managerial statistics (PhD); marketing (PhD); operations management (PhD); organizational behavior (PhD); strategy and human resources (PhD); supply chain management (PhD). *Faculty:* 71 full-time (16 women), 2 part-time/adjunct (1 woman). *Students:* 34 full-time (10 women); includes 1 minority (African American), 24 international. Average age 31. 89 applicants, 8% accepted, 4 enrolled. In 2006, 8 degrees awarded. *Degree requirements:* For doctorate, thesis/dissertation, summer research paper, comprehensive exam, registration. *Entrance requirements:* For doctorate, GMAT, 3 recommendations. Additional exam requirements/recommendations for international students: Required—TOEFL (minimum score 600 paper-based; 250 computer-based; 100 iBT). *Application deadline:* For fall admission, 1/30 priority date for domestic students. Applications are processed on a rolling basis. Application fee: $75. Electronic applications accepted. *Expenses:* Tuition: Full-time $16,920; part-time $940 per credit hour. Required fees: $930; $930 per year. *Financial support:* In 2006–07, 1 fellowship with full tuition reimbursement (averaging $19,000 per year), 26 teaching assistantships with full tuition reimbursements (averaging $16,500 per year) were awarded; research assistantships with full tuition reimbursements, health care benefits and unspecified assistantships also available. Financial award application deadline: 1/30. *Faculty research:* Marketing models, market microstructure, supply chain, auditing, corporate governance. *Unit head:* Dr. Ravi Dharwadkar, Director of the PhD Program, 315-443-3386, E-mail: rdharwad@syr.edu. *Application contact:* Shannon Hiemstra, Assistant Director for PhD and Research Programs, 315-443-3549, Fax: 315-443-3671, E-mail: srhiemst@syr.edu.

Temple University, Graduate School, Fox School of Business and Management, Doctoral Programs in Business, Philadelphia, PA 19122-6096. Offers accounting (PhD); economics (PhD); finance (PhD); general and strategic management (PhD); healthcare management (PhD); human resource administration (PhD); international business administration (PhD); management information systems (PhD); management science/operations research (PhD); marketing (PhD); risk, insurance, and health-care management (PhD); statistics (PhD); tourism (PhD). *Accreditation:* AACSB. *Entrance requirements:* For doctorate, GRE General Test, minimum GPA of 3.0, master's degree. Additional exam requirements/recommendations for international students: Required—TOEFL. *Expenses:* Tuition, state resident: full-time $12,264; part-time $511 per credit. Tuition, nonresident: full-time $17,904; part-time $746 per credit. Required fees: $84 per course. Tuition and fees vary according to program.

Temple University, Graduate School, Fox School of Business and Management, Masters Programs in Business, MBA Programs, Philadelphia, PA 19122-6096. Offers accounting (MBA); business administration (EMBA, MBA); e-business (MBA); economics (MBA); finance (MBA); general and strategic management (MBA); healthcare management (MBA); human resource administration (MBA); international business (IMBA); management information systems (MBA); management science/operations management (MBA); marketing (MBA); risk management and insurance (MBA); statistics (MBA). EMBA offered in Philadelphia, PA and Tokyo, Japan. *Accreditation:* AACSB. *Entrance requirements:* For master's, GMAT, minimum undergraduate GPA of 3.0. Additional exam requirements/recommendations for international students: Required—TOEFL. *Expenses:* Tuition, state resident: full-time $12,264; part-time $511 per credit. Tuition, nonresident: full-time $17,904; part-time $746 per credit. Required fees: $84 per course. Tuition and fees vary according to program.

Tennessee Technological University, Graduate School, Program of Professional Studies, Cookeville, TN 38505. Offers strategic leadership (MPS). *Students:* 1 (woman) full-time, 8 part-time (6 women); includes 1 minority (African American), 1 international. 12 applicants, 75% accepted, 8 enrolled. *Entrance requirements:* For master's, GRE. *Application deadline:* For fall admission, 3/1 priority date for domestic and international students; for spring admission, 8/1 priority date for domestic and international students. Application fee: $25 ($30 for international students). Electronic applications accepted. *Expenses:* Tuition, state resident: full-time $8,748; part-time $319 per hour. Tuition, nonresident: full-time $23,524; part-time $740 per hour. *Financial support:* Application deadline: 4/1. *Unit head:* Dr. Susan A. Elkins, Dean, School of Interdisciplinary Studies and Extended Education, 931-372-3394, Fax: 372-372-3499, E-mail: selkins@tntech.edu. *Application contact:* Dr. Francis Otuonye, Associate Vice President for Research and Graduate Studies, 931-372-3233.

Towson University, Graduate School, Program in Management and Leadership Development, Towson, MD 21252-0001. Offers Certificate. Part-time and evening/weekend programs available. *Students:* 6 full-time (all women), 7 part-time (all women); includes 10 minority (9 African Americans, 1 Hispanic American), 1 international. 9 applicants, 67% accepted, 6 enrolled. In 2006, 13 degrees awarded. Application fee: $50. *Expenses:* Tuition, state resident: part-time $275 per unit. Tuition, nonresident: part-time $577 per unit. Required fees: $72 per unit. *Unit head:* Dr. Mark Arvisais, Graduate Program Director, 410-704-4661. *Application contact:* The Graduate School, 410-704-2501, Fax: 410-704-9675, E-mail: grads@towson.edu.

Tufts University, Graduate School of Arts and Sciences, Graduate Certificate Programs, Program Evaluation Program, Medford, MA 02155. Offers Certificate. Part-time and evening/weekend programs available. *Students:* Average age 28. 1 applicant, 100% accepted, 0 enrolled. *Application deadline:* For fall admission, 8/15 priority date for domestic students; for spring admission, 12/12 priority date for domestic students. Applications are processed on a rolling basis. Application fee: $65. Electronic applications accepted. *Expenses: Contact institution.* Tuition and fees vary according to degree level and program. *Financial support:* Career-related internships or fieldwork available. Support available to part-time students. Financial award application deadline: 5/1; financial award applicants required to submit FAFSA. *Application contact:* Angela Foss, Program Administrator, 617-627-3395, Fax: 617-627-3016, E-mail: gradschool@ase.tufts.edu.

United States International University, School of Business Administration, Nairobi, Kenya. Offers finance (MBA); information technology management (MBA); integrated studies (MBA); management and organizational development (MS); marketing (MBA); strategic management (MBA). Part-time and evening/weekend programs available. *Degree requirements:* For master's, thesis, registration. *Entrance requirements:* For master's, GMAT, 2 letters of reference, resumé. Additional exam requirements/recommendations for international students: Required—TOEFL (minimum score 550 paper-based; 213 computer-based). *Faculty research:* Marketing in small business enterprises, total quality management in Kenya.

The University of Arizona, Graduate College, College of Business and Public Administration, Eller Graduate School of Management, Department of Management and Organizations, Tucson, AZ 85721. Offers management (MS, PhD). Evening/weekend programs available. *Faculty:* 13 full-time (3 women). *Students:* 8 full-time (2 women), 3 international. Average age 32. 14 applicants, 21% accepted, 1 enrolled. In 2006, 1 degree awarded. Terminal master's awarded for partial completion of doctoral program. *Median time to degree:* Doctorate–4 years full-time. Of those who began their doctoral program in fall 1998, 100% received their degree in 8 years or less. *Degree requirements:* For master's, thesis or alternative. *Entrance requirements:* For master's and doctorate, GMAT, GRE General Test, minimum GPA of 3.0. Additional exam requirements/recommendations for international students: Required—TOEFL (minimum score 550 paper-based; 244 computer-based). *Application deadline:* For fall admission, 1/15 priority date for domestic and international students. Application fee: $50. Electronic applications accepted. *Financial support:* In 2006–07, 8 research assistantships (averaging $17,100 per year) were awarded; fellowships, teaching assistantships, career-related internships or fieldwork, Federal Work-Study, institutionally sponsored loans, scholarships/grants, health care benefits, and tuition waivers (partial) also available. Financial award application deadline: 3/15. *Faculty research:* Organizational behavior, human resources, decision making, health economics and finance, immigration. *Unit head:* Dr. Stephen Gilliland, Head, 520-621-9324, E-mail: sgill@eller.arizona.edu. *Application contact:* Lori Topp, Administrative Assistant, 520-621-7463, Fax: 520-621-4171, E-mail: hopp@email.arizona.edu.

The University of British Columbia, Sauder School of Business, Doctoral Program in Commerce and Business Administration, Vancouver, BC V6T 1Z1, Canada. Offers accounting (PhD); finance (PhD); international business (PhD); management information systems (PhD); management science (PhD); marketing (PhD); organizational behavior (PhD); policy analysis and strategy (PhD); transportation and logistics (PhD); urban land economics (PhD). *Degree requirements:* For doctorate, thesis/dissertation, comprehensive exam. *Entrance requirements:* For doctorate, GMAT or GRE. Additional exam requirements/recommendations for international students: Required—TOEFL. Electronic applications accepted.

University of Calgary, Faculty of Graduate Studies, Centre for Military and Strategic Studies, Calgary, AB T2N 1N4, Canada. Offers MSS, PhD. PhD offered in special cases only. Part-time programs available. *Students:* 29 full-time (6 women), 20 part-time (8 women). Average age 28. 32 applicants, 31% accepted, 10 enrolled. In 2006, 4 master's, 1 doctorate awarded. *Median time to degree:* Of those who began their doctoral program in fall 1998, 100% received their degree in 8 years or less. *Degree requirements:* For master's, thesis/dissertation, registration; for doctorate, thesis/dissertation, comprehensive exam, registration. *Entrance requirements:* For master's, minimum GPA of 3.4. Additional exam requirements/recommendations for international students: Recommended—TOEFL (minimum score 550 paper-based). *Application deadline:* For fall admission, 1/15 for domestic and international students. Application fee: $100 ($130 for international students). *Faculty research:* Military history, Israeli studies, strategic studies, int'l relations, Arctic security. *Unit head:* Dr. David J. Bercuson, Director, 403-220-4038, E-mail: stratnet@ucalgary.ca. *Application contact:* Tracy Derksen, Graduate Program Administrator, 403-220-4038, Fax: 403-282-0594, E-mail: tjderkse@ucalgary.ca.

University of Dallas, Graduate School of Management, Irving, TX 75062-4736. Offers accounting (MBA, MS); business management (MBA); corporate finance (MBA, MM); engineering management (MBA, MM); entrepreneurship (MBA, MM); financial services (MBA, MM); global business (MBA, MM); health services management (MBA, MM); human resource management (MBA, MM, MS); information assurance (MBA, MM, MS); information technology (MBA, MM, MS); information technology service management (MBA); IT service management (MS); marketing (MM); marketing management (MBA); not-for-profit management (MBA); organization development (MBA); project management (MBA, MM); sports and entertainment management (MBA, MM); strategic leadership (MBA); supply chain management (MBA); supply chain management and market logistics (MM); telecommunications management (MBA, MM). *Accreditation:* ACBSP. Part-time and evening/weekend programs available. Postbaccalaureate distance learning degree programs offered (no on-campus study). *Faculty:* 26 full-time (5 women), 85 part-time/adjunct (18 women). *Students:* 227 full-time (98 women), 1,160 part-time (446 women); includes 473 minority (209 African Americans, 3 American Indian/Alaska Native, 143 Asian Americans or Pacific Islanders, 118 Hispanic Americans), 224 international. Average age 34. 556 applicants, 86% accepted, 291 enrolled. In 2006, 476 degrees awarded. *Entrance requirements:* Additional exam requirements/recommendations for international students: Required—TOEFL. *Application deadline:* Applications are processed on a rolling basis. Application fee: $50. Electronic applications accepted. *Expenses: Contact institution. Financial support:* In 2006–07, 468 students received support. Scholarships/grants and unspecified assistantships available. Financial award application deadline: 2/15; financial award applicants required to submit FAFSA. *Unit head:* Dr. J. Lee Whittington, Dean, 972-721-5230. *Application contact:* Sarah Stivison, Director of Graduate Admissions, 972-721-5198, Fax: 972-721-4009, E-mail: admiss@gsm.udallas.edu.

University of Florida, Graduate School, Warrington College of Business Administration, Programs in Business Administration, Gainesville, FL 32611. Offers accounting (MBA); arts administration (MBA); business strategy and public policy (MBA); competitive strategy (MBA); decision and information sciences (MBA); electronic commerce (MBA); finance (MBA); general business (MBA); global management (MBA); Graham-Buffett security analysis (MBA); health administration (MBA); human resources management (MBA); international studies (MBA); Latin American business (MBA); management (MBA); marketing (MBA); sports administration (MBA); JD/MBA; MBA/MS; MBA/PhD; MBA/Pharm D; MD/MBA. *Accreditation:* AACSB. Part-time and evening/weekend programs available. Postbaccalaureate distance learning degree programs offered. *Faculty:* 14. *Students:* 950 (282 women); includes 189 minority (31 African Americans, 2 American Indian/Alaska Native, 66 Asian Americans or Pacific Islanders, 90 Hispanic Americans) 56 international. In 2006, 481 degrees awarded. *Entrance requirements:* For master's, GMAT, minimum GPA of 3.0, interview. Additional exam requirements/recommendations for international students: Required—TOEFL (minimum score 550 paper-based; 213 computer-based). *Application deadline:* For fall admission, 4/15 for domestic students; for winter admission, 10/15 priority date for domestic students; for spring admission, 2/15 for domestic students. Applications are processed on a rolling basis. Application fee: $30. Electronic applications accepted. *Expenses:* Tuition, state resident: full-time $6,827. Tuition, nonresident: full-time $21,951. Required fees: $999. *Financial support:* Fellowships, research assistantships, teaching assistantships, career-related internships or fieldwork, scholarships/grants, and unspecified assistantships available. Support available to part-time students. Financial award application deadline: 2/15; financial award applicants required to submit FAFSA. *Faculty research:* Accounting, finance, insurance, management, real estate and urban analysis marketing. *Unit head:* Alex Sevilla, Director, 352-392-7992 Ext. 1206. *Application contact:* Patrick Foran, Associate Director of Admissions, 352-392-7992 Ext. 282, Fax: 352-392-8791, E-mail: patrick.foran@cba.ufl.edu.

The University of Iowa, Henry B. Tippie College of Business, Henry B. Tippie School of Management, Iowa City, IA 52242-1316. Offers accounting (MBA); corporate finance (MBA); entrepreneurship (MBA); finance (MBA); individually designed concentration (MBA); investment management (MBA); management information systems (MBA); marketing (MBA); nonprofit management (MBA); operations management (MBA); strategic management and consulting (MBA); JD/MBA; MBA/MA; MBA/MD; MBA/MHA; MBA/MSN. *Accreditation:* AACSB. Part-time and evening/weekend programs available. *Faculty:* 94 full-time (23 women), 65 part-time/adjunct (21 women). *Students:* 230 full-time (67 women), 712 part-time (234 women); includes 62 minority (6 African Americans, 1 American Indian/Alaska Native, 43 Asian Americans or Pacific Islanders, 12 Hispanic Americans), 127 international. Average age 30. 431 applicants, 61% accepted, 217 enrolled. In 2006, 363 degrees awarded. *Median time to degree:* Master's–2 years full-time, 3.5 years part-time. *Degree requirements:* For master's, registration. *Entrance requirements:* For master's, GMAT, work experience. Additional exam requirements/recommendations for international students: Required—TOEFL (minimum score 600 paper-based; 250 computer-based; 100 iBT). *Application deadline:* For fall admission, 7/15 for domestic students, 4/15 for international students; for spring admission, 12/15 priority date for domestic students, 11/1 priority date for international students. Applications are processed on a rolling basis. Application fee: $60 ($85 for international students). Electronic applications accepted. *Expenses: Contact institution. Financial support:* In 2006–07, 72 fellowships (averaging $3,892 per year), 55 research assistantships with partial tuition reimbursements (averaging $10,260 per year) were awarded; career-related internships or fieldwork, Federal Work-Study, institutionally sponsored loans, scholarships/grants, health care benefits, and unspecified assistantships also available. Support available to part-time students. Financial award application deadline: 4/15; financial award applicants required to submit FAFSA. *Faculty research:* Capital markets, econometrics, optimization, investments and empirical corporate finance, Iowa electronic markets. *Unit head:* Prof. Gary J. Gaeth, Associate Dean, MBA Programs, 800-622-4692, Fax: 319-335-3604, E-mail: gary-gaeth@uiowa.edu. *Application contact:* Jodi Schafer, Director of Student Recruitment and Marketing, 319-335-0864, Fax: 319-335-3604, E-mail: jodi-schafer@uiowa.edu.

University of Lethbridge, School of Graduate Studies, Lethbridge, AB T1K 3M4, Canada. Offers accounting (MScM); addictions counseling (M Sc); agricultural biotechnology (M Sc); agricultural studies (M Sc, MA); anthropology (MA); archaeology (MA); art (MA); biochemistry (M Sc); biological sciences (M Sc); biomolecular science (PhD); biosystems and biodiversity (PhD); Canadian studies (MA); chemistry (M Sc); computer science (M Sc); computer science and geographical information science (M Sc); counseling psychology (M Ed); dramatic arts (MA); earth, space, and physical science (PhD); economics (MA); educational leadership (M Ed); English (MA); environmental science (M Sc); evolution and behavior (PhD); exercise science (M Sc); finance (MScM); French (MA); French/German (MA); French/Spanish (MA); general education (M Ed); general management (MScM); geography (M Sc, MA); German (MA); health sciences (M Sc, MA); history (MA); human resource management and labour relations (MScM); individualized multidisciplinary (M Sc, MA); information systems (MScM); international management (MScM); kinesiology (M Sc, MA); management (M Sc, MA); marketing (MScM); mathematics (M Sc); music (MA); Native American studies (MA); neuroscience (M Sc, PhD); new media (MA); nursing (M Sc); philosophy (MA); physics (M Sc); policy and strategy (MScM); political science (MA); psychology (M Sc, MA); religious studies (MA); sociology (MA); theoretical and computational science (PhD); urban and regional studies (MA). Part-time and evening/weekend programs available. *Students:* 200 full-time, 90 part-time. In 2006, 105 master's, 3 doctorates awarded. *Degree requirements:* For doctorate, thesis/dissertation, comprehensive exam. *Entrance requirements:* For master's, GMAT (M Sc management), bachelor's degree in related field, minimum GPA of 3.0 during previous 20 graded semester courses, 2 years teaching or related experience (M Ed); for doctorate, master's degree, minimum graduate GPA of 3.5. Additional exam requirements/recommendations for international students: Required—TOEFL. Application fee: $60 Canadian dollars. *Financial support:* Fellowships, research assistantships, teaching assistantships, scholarships/grants, health care benefits, and unspecified assistantships available. *Faculty research:* Movement and brain plasticity, gibberellin physiology, photosynthesis, carbon cycling, molecular properties of main-group ring components. *Unit head:* Dr. Jo-Anne Fiske, Interim Dean, 403-329-2121, Fax: 403-329-2097. *Application contact:* Kathy Schrage, Administrative Assistant, Office of the Academic Vice President, 403-329-2121, Fax: 403-329-2097, E-mail: inquiries@uleth.ca.

University of Minnesota, Twin Cities Campus, Carlson School of Management, Carlson Full-time MBA Program, Minneapolis, MN 55455-0213. Offers accounting (MBA); entrepreneurship (MBA); finance (MBA); healthcare management (MBA); information and decision sciences (MBA); international business (MBA); marketing and logistics management (MBA); operations and management science (MBA); strategic management and organization (MBA); supply chain management (MBA); JD/MBA; MD/MBA; MHA/MBA. *Accreditation:* AACSB. *Faculty:* 125 full-time (27 women), 120 part-time/adjunct. *Students:* 218 full-time (70 women); includes 18 minority (4 African Americans, 1 American Indian/Alaska Native, 10 Asian Americans or Pacific Islanders, 3 Hispanic Americans), 86 international. Average age 28. 418 applicants, 53% accepted, 124 enrolled. In 2006, 105 degrees awarded. *Median time to degree:* Master's–2 years full-time. *Entrance requirements:* For master's, GMAT. Additional exam requirements/recommendations for international students: Required—TOEFL (minimum score 580 paper-based; 240 computer-based), IELTS. *Application deadline:* For fall admission, 4/15 for domestic students, 2/15 for international students. Application fee: $60 ($90 for international students). Electronic applications accepted. *Expenses: Contact institution.* Full-time tuition and fees vary according to class time, course load, program, reciprocity agreements and student level. *Financial support:* In 2006–07, 131 students received support, including 127 fellowships with full and partial tuition reimbursements available (averaging $20,000 per year); research assistantships with partial tuition reimbursements available, teaching assistantships with partial tuition reimbursements available, career-related internships or fieldwork, Federal Work-Study, institutionally sponsored loans, scholarships/grants, health care benefits, tuition waivers (full and partial), and unspecified assistantships also available. Support available to part-time students. Financial award application deadline: 2/15; financial award applicants required to submit FAFSA. *Faculty research:* IT, strategy, marketing, finance, quality management. *Unit head:* Kathryn J. Carlson, MBA Programs and Executive Education, 612-624-2039, Fax: 612-625-1012, E-mail: full-timeembainfo@csom.umn.edu. *Application contact:* Jeffrey Bieganek, Director, Admissions and Business Development, MBA Programs and Executive Education, 612-625-6558, Fax: 612-625-1012, E-mail: full-timembainfo@csom.umn.edu.

University of Minnesota, Twin Cities Campus, Carlson School of Management, Doctoral Program in Business Administration, Minneapolis, MN 55455-0213. Offers accounting (PhD); finance (PhD); information and decision sciences (PhD); marketing and logistics management (PhD); operations and management science (PhD); strategic management and organization (PhD). *Faculty:* 109 full-time (26 women). *Students:* 90 full-time (30 women); includes 9 minority (5 African Americans, 1 American Indian or Pacific Islander, 3 Hispanic Americans), 60 international. Average age 30. 325 applicants, 8% accepted, 17 enrolled. In 2006, 16 degrees awarded. *Median time to degree:* Of those who began their doctoral program in fall 1998, 61% received their degree in 8 years or less. *Degree requirements:* For doctorate, thesis/dissertation, written and oral preliminary exams, comprehensive exam, registration. *Entrance requirements:* For doctorate, GMAT, GRE General Test, International must submit a TOEFL or IELT. Additional exam requirements/recommendations for international students: Required—TOEFL (minimum score 600 paper-based; 250 computer-based; 100 iBT), IELTS (minimum score 8), TOEFL (paper-based 600, computer-based 250) or IELTS (7.5). *Application deadline:* For fall admission, 12/30 for domestic students, 12/30 priority date for international students. Applications are processed on a rolling basis. Application fee: $55 ($75 for international students). Electronic applications accepted. *Expenses:* Tuition, state resident: full-time $9,302; part-time $775 per credit. Tuition, nonresident: full-time $16,400; part-time $1,367 per credit. Full-time tuition and fees vary according to class time, course load, program, reciprocity agreements and student level. *Financial support:* In 2006–07, 67 students received support, including fellowships with full tuition reimbursements available (averaging $11,000 per year), research assistantships with full tuition reimbursements available (averaging $6,000 per year), teaching assistantships with full tuition reimbursements available (averaging $6,000 per year); institutionally sponsored loans, scholarships/grants, health care benefits, and unspecified assistantships also available. Financial award application deadline: 12/31. *Faculty research:* Corporate strategy, international business, corporate finances, entrepreneurship, quality management, marketing, information and decision science, operations and accounting. Total annual research expenditures: $300,000. *Unit head:* Dr. Paul E. Johnson, Director of Graduate Studies and PhD Program Director, 612-624-5570, Fax: 612-624-8221, E-mail: pjohnson@csom.umn.edu. *Application contact:* Earlene Bronson, Assistant Director, PhD Program, 612-624-0875, Fax: 612-624-8221, E-mail: ebronson@csom.umn.edu.

University of New Haven, Graduate School, School of Business, Program in Business Administration, West Haven, CT 06516-1916. Offers accounting (MBA); business policy and strategy (MBA); finance (MBA); health care management (MBA); human resources management (MBA); international business (MBA); marketing (MBA); public relations (MBA); sports management (MBA); technology management (MBA); MBA/MPA; MBA/MSIE. Part-time and evening/weekend programs available. *Degree requirements:* For master's, thesis or alternative. *Entrance requirements:* For master's, GMAT.

University of New Mexico, Robert O. Anderson Graduate School of Management, Department of Marketing, Information and Decision Sciences, Albuquerque, NM 87131-2039. Offers management information systems (MBA); marketing management (MBA); operations management (MBA). Part-time and evening/weekend programs available. *Entrance requirements:* For master's, GMAT. Additional exam requirements/recommendations for international students: Required—TOEFL (minimum score 550 paper-based; 213 computer-based).

University of New Mexico, Robert O. Anderson Graduate School of Management, Department of Organizational Studies, Albuquerque, NM 87131-2039. Offers human resources management (MBA); policy and planning (MBA). Part-time and evening/weekend programs available. *Entrance requirements:* For master's, GMAT. Additional exam requirements/recommendations for international students: Required—TOEFL (minimum score 550 paper-based; 213 computer-based).

The University of North Carolina at Chapel Hill, Kenan-Flagler Business School, Doctoral Program in Business Administration, Chapel Hill, NC 27599. Offers accounting (PhD); finance (PhD); marketing (PhD); operations management (PhD); organizational behavior (PhD); strategy (PhD). *Accreditation:* AACSB. *Degree requirements:* For doctorate, thesis/dissertation. *Entrance requirements:* For doctorate, GMAT or GRE General Test. Electronic applications accepted. Expenses: Contact institution.

University of North Texas, Robert B. Toulouse School of Graduate Studies, College of Business Administration, Department of Management, Denton, TX 76203. Offers administrative management (MBA); management (EMBA, MBA); organization theory and policy (PhD); personnel and industrial relations (MBA, PhD); production/operations management (MBA, PhD). *Faculty:* 24 full-time (10 women). *Students:* 18 full-time (11 women), 51 part-time (22 women); includes 15 minority (7 African Americans, 1 American Indian/Alaska Native, 1 Asian American or Pacific Islander, 6 Hispanic Americans), 13 international. Average age 30. 54 applicants, 83% accepted, 9 enrolled. In 2006, 29 master's, 1 doctorate awarded. *Degree requirements:* For doctorate, thesis/dissertation. *Entrance requirements:* For master's, GMAT, relevant work experience; for doctorate, GMAT or GRE General Test, relevant work experience. Additional exam requirements/recommendations for international students: Required—TOEFL. *Application deadline:* For fall admission, 7/15 for domestic students. Application fee: $50 ($75 for international students). *Expenses:* Tuition, state resident: full-time $3,573; part-time $198 per credit. Tuition, nonresident: full-time $8,577; part-time $476 per credit. Required fees: $1,258; $126 per credit. One-time fee: $150 full-time. Tuition and fees vary according to course load. *Financial support:* Fellowships, teaching assistantships, Federal Work-Study available. Financial award application deadline: 4/1. *Unit head:* Dr. J. Lynn Johnson, Chair, 940-565-3140, Fax: 940-565-4394, E-mail: johnsonl@cobaf.coba.unt.edu. *Application contact:* Dr. Nancy Boyd-Lillie, Graduate Adviser, 940-565-3158, E-mail: boyd@cobaf.coba.unt.edu.

University of Wisconsin–Madison, Graduate School, School of Business, Wisconsin Full-Time MBA Programs, Madison, WI 53706-1380. Offers applied corporate finance (MBA); applied security analysis (MBA); arts administration (MBA); brand and product management (MBA); entrepreneurial management (MBA); information systems (MBA); marketing research

Management Strategy and Policy

University of Wisconsin–Madison (continued)
(MBA); operations and technology management (MBA); real estate (MBA); risk management and insurance (MBA); strategic human resource management (MBA); strategic management in the life and engineering sciences (MBA); supply chain management (MBA). *Faculty:* 84. *Students:* 231 full-time (74 women); includes 21 minority (10 African Americans, 5 Asian Americans or Pacific Islanders, 6 Hispanic Americans), 59 international. Average age 28. 405 applicants, 43% accepted 121 enrolled. In 2006, 110 degrees awarded. *Entrance requirements:* For master's, GMAT, bachelors or equivalent degree, 2 years of work experience. Additional exam requirements/recommendations for international students: Required—TOEFL (minimum score 600 paper-based; 250 computer-based; 90 iBT). *Application deadline:* For fall admission, 11/1 for domestic and international students; for winter admission, 1/23 for domestic and international students; for spring admission, 3/26 for domestic and international students. Applications are processed on a rolling basis. Application fee: $45. Electronic applications accepted. *Financial support:* In 2006–07, 177 students received support, including 20 fellowships with full and partial tuition reimbursements available (averaging $16,566 per year), 105 research assistantships with full tuition reimbursements available (averaging $8,098 per year), 33 teaching assistantships with full tuition reimbursements available (averaging $10,112 per year); scholarships/grants, health care benefits, and unspecified assistantships also available. *Unit head:* Gary Lessuise, Assistant Dean, Masters Programs, 608-265-5102, Fax: 608-265-4192, E-mail: glessuise@bus.wisc.edu. *Application contact:* Betsy Kacizak, Director of Admissions and Financial Aid—Full Time MBA, 608-262-4000, Fax: 608-265-4192, E-mail: mba@bus.wisc.edu.

Western Governors University, Programs in Business, Salt Lake City, UT 84107. Offers information technology management (MBA); management and strategy (MBA); strategic leadership (MBA). Electronic applications accepted.

Western International University, Graduate Programs in Business, Program in Innovative Leadership, Phoenix, AZ 85021-2718. Offers MA. *Expenses:* Tuition: Full-time $9,600; part-time $400 per credit. One-time fee: $85 full-time. *Application contact:* Karen Janitell, Director of Enrollment, 602-943-2311 Ext. 1063, Fax: 602-371-8637, E-mail: karen_janitell@apollogrp.edu.

Section 14
Marketing

This section contains a directory of institutions offering graduate work in marketing, followed by in-depth entries submitted by institutions that chose to prepare detailed program descriptions. Additional information about programs listed in the directory but not augmented by an in-depth entry may be obtained by writing directly to the dean of a graduate school or chair of a department at the address given in the directory.

For programs offering related work, see also in this book Advertising and Public Relations, Business Administration and Management, and Hospitality Management. In Book 2, see Communication and Media and Public, Regional, and Industrial Affairs.

CONTENTS

Marketing

Adelphi University, School of Business, Department of Management, Marketing, and Decision Sciences, Garden City, NY 11530-0701. Offers management information systems (MBA); management/human resource management (MBA); marketing/e-commerce (MBA). Part-time and evening/weekend programs available. *Students:* 67 full-time (34 women), 173 part-time (85 women); includes 44 minority (24 African Americans, 11 Asian Americans or Pacific Islanders, 9 Hispanic Americans), 49 international. Average age 31. In 2006, 122 degrees awarded. *Degree requirements:* For master's, capstone course. *Entrance requirements:* For master's, GMAT, 2 letters of recommendation. Additional exam requirements/recommendations for international students: Required—TOEFL. *Application deadline:* For fall admission, 5/1 for international students; for spring admission, 12/1 for international students. Applications are processed on a rolling basis. Application fee: $50. Electronic applications accepted. *Financial support:* Research assistantships with full and partial tuition reimbursements, career-related internships or fieldwork, Federal Work-Study, institutionally sponsored loans, scholarships/grants, and unspecified assistantships available. Financial award application deadline: 3/1; financial award applicants required to submit FAFSA. *Faculty research:* Supply chain management, distribution channels, productivity benchmark analysis, data envelopment analysis, financial portfolio analysis. *Unit head:* Dr. Allan Ashley, Chairperson, 516-877-4640, E-mail: ashley@adelphi.edu. *Application contact:* Christine Murphy, Director of Admissions, 516-877-3050, Fax: 516-877-3039, E-mail: graduateadmissions@adelphi.edu.

Alabama Agricultural and Mechanical University, School of Graduate Studies, School of Business, Department of Management and Marketing, Huntsville, AL 35811. Offers MBA. Part-time and evening/weekend programs available. *Faculty:* 7 full-time (0 women), 1 part-time/adjunct (0 women). *Students:* 5 full-time (4 women), 9 part-time (4 women); all minorities (all African Americans) Average age 28. In 2006, 19 degrees awarded. *Degree requirements:* For master's, thesis optional. *Entrance requirements:* For master's, GMAT, minimum undergraduate GPA of 2.5. Additional exam requirements/recommendations for international students: Required—TOEFL. *Application deadline:* For fall admission, 5/1 priority date for domestic students. Applications are processed on a rolling basis. Application fee: $25. Electronic applications accepted. *Financial support:* Research assistantships, career-related internships or fieldwork, Federal Work-Study, and institutionally sponsored loans available. Financial award application deadline: 4/1. *Faculty research:* Consumer behavior of blacks, small business marketing, economics of education, China in transition, international economics. *Unit head:* Dr. Uchenna Elike, Chair, 256-372-5088. *Application contact:* Dr. Marsha D. Griffin, Coordinator, 256-372-5494.

Alliant International University–San Diego, Marshall Goldsmith School of Management, Business and Management Division, San Diego, CA 92131-1799. Offers business administration (MBA); information and technology management (DBA); international business (MIBA, DBA), including finance (DBA), marketing (DBA); strategic business (DBA); sustainable management (MBA). Part-time and evening/weekend programs available. *Students:* 87 full-time (22 women), 51 part-time (17 women); includes 27 minority (8 African Americans, 2 American Indian/Alaska Native, 8 Asian Americans or Pacific Islanders, 9 Hispanic Americans), 68 international. Average age 32. 104 applicants, 66% accepted, 40 enrolled. *Degree requirements:* For doctorate, thesis/dissertation. *Entrance requirements:* For master's, GMAT, minimum GPA of 3.0; for doctorate, GMAT, minimum GPA of 3.3. Additional exam requirements/recommendations for international students: Required—TOEFL (minimum score 550 paper-based; 213 computer-based), TWE (minimum score 5). *Application deadline:* For fall admission, 8/1 priority date for domestic and international students; for spring admission, 12/1 priority date for domestic and international students. Applications are processed on a rolling basis. Application fee: $55. Electronic applications accepted. *Expenses:* Tuition: Part-time $825 per unit. Tuition and fees vary according to course load, degree level and program. *Financial support:* Research assistantships, teaching assistantships, career-related internships or fieldwork, Federal Work-Study, institutionally sponsored loans, scholarships/grants, and tuition waivers (partial) available. Support available to part-time students. Financial award application deadline: 2/15; financial award applicants required to submit FAFSA. *Faculty research:* Consumer behavior, international business, strategic management, information systems. *Unit head:* Dr. Fred Phillips, Associate Dean, 866-825-5426, Fax: 855-635-4739, E-mail: admissions@alliant.edu. *Application contact:* Alliant International University Central Contact Center, 866-U-ALLIANT, Fax: 858-635-4555, E-mail: admissions@alliant.edu.

See Close-Up on page 203.

American College of Thessaloniki, Department of Business Administration, Pylea, Greece. Offers banking and finance (MBA); entrepreneurship (MBA, Certificate); finance (Certificate); management (MBA, Certificate); marketing (MBA, Certificate). Part-time and evening/weekend programs available. *Faculty:* 6 full-time (1 woman), 10 part-time/adjunct (4 women). *Students:* 9 full-time (6 women), 39 part-time (24 women), 22 international. 36 applicants, 97% accepted, 26 enrolled. In 2006, 25 degrees awarded. *Degree requirements:* For master's, thesis, registration. *Application deadline:* For fall admission, 9/30 priority date for domestic students; for spring admission, 1/31 priority date for domestic students. Applications are processed on a rolling basis. Application fee: $70. Electronic applications accepted. *Expenses:* Tuition: Full-time $10,560; part-time $660 per course. Part-time tuition and fees vary according to course load. *Unit head:* Dr. Nikolaos Kourkoumelis, Chair, Business Division, E-mail: nikolaos@act.edu. *Application contact:* Vasilis Blatsas, Coordinator of Business Programs and MBA Advisor, 30-310-398206 Ext. 206.

American InterContinental University, Program in International Business, Weston, FL 33326. Offers accounting and finance (MBA); human resource management (MBA); management (MBA); marketing (MBA). Part-time and evening/weekend programs available. Postbaccalaureate distance learning degree programs offered. *Faculty:* 3 full-time (0 women), 2 part-time/adjunct (0 women). *Students:* 87 full-time (51 women), 7 part-time (4 women); includes 62 minority (42 African Americans, 1 American Indian/Alaska Native, 1 Asian American or Pacific Islander, 18 Hispanic Americans), 5 international. Average age 34. In 2006, 51 degrees awarded. *Application deadline:* Applications are processed on a rolling basis. Application fee: $50. Electronic applications accepted. *Financial support:* Federal Work-Study and scholarships/grants available. Financial award application deadline: 1/15; financial award applicants required to submit FAFSA. *Unit head:* Dr. David Kalichavan, Acting Dean, School of Business, 954-446-6100, Fax: 954-446-6393, E-mail: dkalichavan@aiufl.edu.

American InterContinental University Buckhead Campus, Program in Business Administration, Atlanta, GA 30326-1016. Offers accounting and finance (MBA); management (MBA); marketing (MBA). Evening/weekend programs available. Postbaccalaureate distance learning degree programs offered. *Faculty:* 2 full-time (1 woman), 1 part-time/adjunct (0 women). *Students:* 19 full-time (16 women); includes 1 minority (African American) Average age 28. 10 applicants, 60% accepted, 5 enrolled. In 2006, 25 degrees awarded. *Median time to degree:* Master's–1 year full-time. *Entrance requirements:* For master's, minimum cumulative undergraduate GPA of 2.0. Additional exam requirements/recommendations for international students: Required—TOEFL (minimum score 530 paper-based; 230 computer-based). *Application deadline:* Applications are processed on a rolling basis. Application fee: $50. Electronic applications accepted. *Financial support:* In 2006–07, 14 students received support. Career-related internships or fieldwork, Federal Work-Study, institutionally sponsored loans, and scholarships/grants available. Financial award applicants required to submit FAFSA. *Faculty research:* Leadership management, international advertising. *Unit head:* Dr. Sonia Heywood, Dean of Business, 404-965-5764, Fax: 404-965-5957, E-mail: sonia.heywood@buckhead.aiuniv.edu. *Application contact:* Mike Betz, Vice President Admissions and Marketing, 404-965-5719, Fax: 404-965-5997, E-mail: mbetz@aiuniv.edu.

American InterContinental University Online, Program in Business Administration, Hoffman Estates, IL 60192. Offers accounting and finance (MBA); healthcare management (MBA);

human resource management (MBA); international business (MBA); management (MBA); marketing (MBA); operations management (MBA); organizational psychology and development (MBA); project management (MBA). Evening/weekend programs available. Postbaccalaureate distance learning degree programs offered (no on-campus study). *Entrance requirements:* Additional exam requirements/recommendations for international students: Required—TOEFL (minimum score 550 paper-based; 213 computer-based). *Application deadline:* Applications are processed on a rolling basis. Application fee: $50. Electronic applications accepted. *Financial support:* Institutionally sponsored loans and scholarships/grants available. Financial award applicants required to submit FAFSA. *Unit head:* Kerri J Holloway, Vice President of Academic Affairs, 847-851-5000 Ext. 15399, Fax: 847-586-6309, E-mail: kholloway@aivonline.edu. *Application contact:* 877-701-3800, E-mail: info@aiuonline.edu.

American University, Kogod School of Business, Department of Marketing, Program in Marketing, Washington, DC 20016-8001. Offers MBA. *Expenses:* Tuition: Full-time $18,864; part-time $1,048 per credit. Required fees: $380. Tuition and fees vary according to program.

American University, Kogod School of Business, Department of Marketing, Program in Marketing Management, Washington, DC 20016-8001. Offers MBA. *Students:* 12 full-time (11 women), 10 part-time (6 women); includes 1 minority (African American), 5 international. Average age 28. In 2006, 18 degrees awarded. *Expenses:* Tuition: Full-time $18,864; part-time $1,048 per credit. Required fees: $380. Tuition and fees vary according to program.

Andrew Jackson University, Brian Tracy College of Business and Entrepreneurship, Birmingham, AL 35244. Offers entrepreneurship (MBA); finance (MBA); health services management (MBA); hospitality and tourism management (MBA); human resource management (MBA); international business (MBA); management (MBA); marketing (MBA). Part-time and evening/weekend programs available. Postbaccalaureate distance learning degree programs offered (no on-campus study). *Faculty:* 13 part-time/adjunct (1 woman). *Students:* Average age 40. In 2006, 6 degrees awarded. *Entrance requirements:* For master's, course work in calculus, statistics. Additional exam requirements/recommendations for international students: Required—TOEFL (minimum score 550 paper-based; 213 computer-based). *Application deadline:* Applications are processed on a rolling basis. Application fee: $75. *Expenses:* Tuition: Part-time $705 per course. *Application contact:* Betty Howell, Director of Student Affairs, 205-871-9288 Ext. 108, Fax: 205-871-9294, E-mail: bhowell@aju.edu.

Andrews University, School of Graduate Studies, School of Business, Department of Management and Marketing, Berrien Springs, MI 49104. Offers MBA, MSA. *Entrance requirements:* For master's, GMAT. Additional exam requirements/recommendations for international students: Required—TOEFL.

Argosy University, Atlanta Campus, College of Business, Atlanta, GA 30328. Offers accounting (DBA); customized professional concentration (MBA, DBA); finance (MBA); healthcare administration (MBA); information systems (DBA); information systems management (MBA); international business (MBA, DBA); management (MBA, DBA); marketing (MBA, DBA). Part-time programs available. *Students:* 53 full-time (38 women), 35 part-time (28 women); includes 73 minority (66 African Americans, 3 Asian Americans or Pacific Islanders, 4 Hispanic Americans). *Degree requirements:* For master's, comprehensive exam (for some programs), registration; for doctorate, thesis/dissertation, comprehensive exam, registration. *Entrance requirements:* For master's, minimum undergraduate GPA of 3.0; for doctorate, master's degree, minimum GPA of 3.0. Additional exam requirements/recommendations for international students: Required—TOEFL. *Application deadline:* For fall admission, 7/1 priority date for domestic students, 6/1 for international students; for spring admission, 11/1 priority date for domestic students, 10/1 for international students. Applications are processed on a rolling basis. Application fee: $50. Electronic applications accepted. *Financial support:* Applicants required to submit FAFSA. *Unit head:* Dr. Robert A. Berg, Department Chair, 770-407-1042, E-mail: rberg@argosy.edu. *Application contact:* Christa Holton, Director of Admissions, 770-671-1200 Ext. 1014, Fax: 770-671-9050, E-mail: cholton@argosy.edu.

See Close-Up on page 207.

Argosy University, Chicago Campus, College of Business, Chicago, IL 60603. Offers accounting (DBA); customized professional concentration (MBA, DBA); finance (MBA); healthcare administration (MBA); information systems (DBA); information systems management (MBA); international business (MBA, DBA); management (MBA, DBA); marketing (MBA, DBA). Part-time and evening/weekend programs available. *Faculty:* 2 full-time (both women), 4 part-time/adjunct (3 women). *Students:* 52 full-time (30 women), 18 part-time (7 women); includes 37 minority (24 African Americans, 7 Asian Americans or Pacific Islanders, 6 Hispanic Americans). Average age 37. 32 applicants, 81% accepted, 25 enrolled. In 2006, 9 master's, 2 doctorates awarded. *Entrance requirements:* For master's and doctorate, minimum GPA of 3.0. Additional exam requirements/recommendations for international students: Required—TOEFL (minimum score 550 paper-based; 213 computer-based). *Application deadline:* For fall admission, 2/28 for domestic and international students; for spring admission, 10/30 for domestic and international students. Applications are processed on a rolling basis. Application fee: $50. Electronic applications accepted. *Financial support:* In 2006–07, 3 students received support. Scholarships/grants available. Financial award application deadline: 4/1. *Unit head:* Dr. Cynthia Scarlett, Associate Head, 800-626-4123, Fax: 212-727-7750, E-mail: cscarlett@argosy.edu. *Application contact:* Ashley Delaney, Director of Admissions, 800-626-4123, Fax: 312-777-7750, E-mail: argosyadmissions@argosy.edu.

See Close-Up on page 209.

Argosy University, Denver Campus, College of Business, Denver, CO 80203. Offers accounting (DBA); customized professional concentraion (DBA); customized professional concentration (MBA); finance (MBA); healthcare administration (MBA); information systems (DBA); information systems management (MBA); international business (MBA, DBA); management (MBA, MSM, DBA); marketing (MBA, DBA).

See Close-Up on page 213.

Argosy University, Hawai'i Campus, College of Business, Honolulu, HI 96813. Offers accounting (DBA); customized professional concentration (MBA, DBA); finance (MBA, Certificate); healthcare administration (MBA, Certificate); information systems (DBA); information systems management (MBA, Certificate); international business (MBA, DBA, Certificate); management (MBA, DBA); marketing (MBA, DBA, Certificate). Evening/weekend programs available. *Faculty:* 12 part-time/adjunct (2 women). *Students:* 3 full-time (2 women), 1 part-time; includes 2 minority (1 Asian American or Pacific Islander, 1 Hispanic American). 6 applicants, 67% accepted, 3 enrolled. *Degree requirements:* For master's, capstone project. *Entrance requirements:* For master's, minimum GPA of 3.0 in last 60 hours. Additional exam requirements/recommendations for international students: Required—TOEFL (minimum score 550 paper-based; 213 computer-based). *Application deadline:* For fall admission, 1/15 priority date for domestic students; for spring admission, 10/15 for domestic students. Applications are processed on a rolling basis. Application fee: $50. *Financial support:* Teaching assistantships, Federal Work-Study and scholarships/grants available. Support available to part-time students. *Unit head:* Lisa Parker, Interim Chair, College of Business and Information Technology, 888-323-2777, Fax: 808-536-5505, E-mail: lparker@argosy.edu. *Application contact:* Cherie Andrade, Director of Admissions, 888-323-2777, Fax: 808-536-5505, E-mail: candrade@argosy.edu.

See Close-Up on page 215.

Argosy University, Inland Empire Campus, College of Business, San Bernardino, CA 92408. Offers accounting (DBA); customized professional concentration (MBA, DBA); finance (MBA); healthcare administration (MBA); information systems (DBA); information systems management (MBA); international business (MBA, DBA); management (DBA); mangement (MBA); marketing (MBA, DBA).

See Close-Up on page 217.

Argosy University, Nashville Campus, College of Business, Franklin, TN 37067-7226. Offers accounting (DBA); customized professional concentration (DBA); information systems (DBA); international business (DBA); management (DBA); marketing (DBA). *Degree requirements:* For doctorate, thesis/dissertation, comprehensive exam.

See Close-Up on page 219.

Argosy University, Orange County Campus, College of Business, Santa Ana, CA 92704. Offers accounting (DBA, Adv C); customized professional concentration (MBA, DBA); finance (MBA, Certificate); healthcare administration (MBA, Certificate); information systems (DBA, Adv C); information systems management (MBA); international business (MBA, DBA, Adv C, Certificate); management (MBA, MSM, DBA, EDBA); mangement (Adv C); marketing (MBA, DBA, Adv C, Certificate); organizational leadership (Ed D); public administration (MBA, Certificate). Part-time and evening/weekend programs available. *Faculty:* 4 full-time (1 woman), 20 part-time/adjunct (7 women). *Students:* 163 full-time (64 women), 41 part-time (16 women). Average age 42. 72 applicants, 51 enrolled. In 2006, 6 master's, 23 doctorates awarded. *Degree requirements:* For doctorate, thesis/dissertation, preliminary and final dissertation defense, comprehensive exam. *Entrance requirements:* For master's, minimum GPA of 3.0 in final 2 years of course work, 3 letters of recommendation, resumé; for doctorate, minimum GPA of 3.0 in graduate study, 3 letters of recommendation, resumé. Additional exam requirements/recommendations for international students: Required—TOEFL. *Application deadline:* Applications are processed on a rolling basis. Application fee: $50. Electronic applications accepted. *Financial support:* Federal Work-Study, institutionally sponsored loans, and scholarships/grants available. Support available to part-time students. Financial award applicants required to submit FAFSA. *Faculty research:* Crisis management, leadership in organizations, finance, business systems. *Unit head:* Dr. Ray London, Dean, 800-716-9598, Fax: 714-437-1284, E-mail: auocadmissions@argosy.edu. *Application contact:* Mark Betz, Director of Admissions, 800-716-9598, Fax: 714-437-1697, E-mail: mbetz@argosy.edu.

See Close-Up on page 221.

Argosy University, Phoenix Campus, College of Business, Phoenix, AZ 85021. Offers accounting (DBA); customized professional concentration (MBA, DBA); finance (MBA); healthcare administration (MBA); information systems (DBA); information systems management (MBA); international business (MBA, DBA); management (MBA, DBA); marketing (MBA, DBA). Part-time and evening/weekend programs available. *Faculty:* 1 full-time (0 women). *Students:* 7 full-time (4 women); includes 2 minority (1 African American, 1 Hispanic American). *Entrance requirements:* For doctorate, master's degree. Additional exam requirements/recommendations for international students: Required—TOEFL (minimum score 550 paper-based; 213 computer-based). Application fee: $50. *Financial support:* In 2006–07, 2 students received support. Federal Work-Study, institutionally sponsored loans, and scholarships/grants available. Support available to part-time students. Financial award applicants required to submit FAFSA. *Unit head:* Dr. Gary Berg, Program Chair, 866-216-2777, Fax: 602-216-2601. *Application contact:* Andy Hughes, Director of Admissions, 866-216-2777 Ext. 3110, Fax: 602-216-2601, E-mail: ahughes@argosyu.edu.

See Close-Up on page 223.

Argosy University, San Diego Campus, College of Business, San Diego, CA 92108. Offers accounting (DBA); customized professional concentration (MBA, DBA); finance (MBA); information systems (DBA); information systems management (MBA); international business (MBA, DBA); management (MBA, MSM, DBA); marketing (MBA, DBA); public administration (MBA).

See Close-Up on page 225.

Argosy University, San Francisco Bay Area Campus, College of Business, Point Richmond, CA 94804-3547. Offers accounting (DBA); corporate compliance (MBA); customized professional concentration (MBA, DBA); finance (MBA); healthcare administration (MBA); information systems (DBA); information systems management (MBA); international business (MBA, DBA); management (MBA, MSM, DBA); marketing (MBA, DBA). Part-time and evening/weekend programs available. *Faculty:* 2 full-time (0 women), 9 part-time/adjunct (0 women). *Students:* 29 full-time (8 women), 9 part-time (2 women); includes 30 minority (5 African Americans, 24 Asian Americans or Pacific Islanders, 1 Hispanic American). 21 applicants, 76% accepted, 13 enrolled. In 2006, 3 master's, 2 doctorates awarded. *Degree requirements:* For master's, capstone project; for doctorate, thesis/dissertation, comprehensive exam, registration. *Entrance requirements:* For master's, minimum GPA of 3.0; for doctorate, MBA or minimum GPA of 3.0. Additional exam requirements/recommendations for international students: Required—TOEFL (minimum score 550 paper-based; 213 computer-based). *Application deadline:* For fall admission, 7/1 priority date for domestic and international students; for winter admission, 11/1 priority date for domestic and international students; for spring admission, 4/1 priority date for domestic and international students. Applications are processed on a rolling basis. Application fee: $50. Electronic applications accepted. *Financial support:* Federal Work-Study and scholarships/grants available. Support available to part-time students. Financial award applicants required to submit FAFSA. *Unit head:* Dr. Anthony Martinez, Department Chair, Business and Information Technology, 866-215-0277, Fax: 510-215-0299, E-mail: amartinez@argosy.edu. *Application contact:* John Vincent Stofan, Director of Admissions, 866-215-2727 Ext. 205, Fax: 510-215-0299, E-mail: jstofan@argosyu.edu.

See Close-Up on page 227.

Argosy University, Santa Monica Campus, College of Business, Santa Monica, CA 90405. Offers accounting (DBA); customized professional concentration (MBA, DBA); finance (MBA); healthcare administration (MBA); information systems (DBA); information systems management (MBA); international business (MBA, DBA); management (MBA, MS, MSM, DBA); marketing (MBA, DBA).

See Close-Up on page 229.

Argosy University, Sarasota Campus, College of Business, Sarasota, FL 34235-8246. Offers accounting (DBA, Adv C); customized professional concentration (MBA, DBA); finance (MBA, Certificate); healtcare administration (Certificate); healthcare administration (MBA); information systems (DBA, Adv C); information systems management (MBA, Certificate); international business (MBA, DBA, Adv C, Certificate); management (MBA, MSM, DBA); mangement (Adv C); marketing (MBA, DBA, Adv C, Certificate). Part-time and evening/weekend programs available. Postbaccalaureate distance learning degree programs offered (minimal on-campus study). *Faculty:* 6 full-time (3 women), 13 part-time/adjunct (5 women). *Students:* 71 applicants, 92% accepted, 64 enrolled. In 2006, 7 master's, 30 doctorates awarded. *Degree requirements:* For doctorate, thesis/dissertation, comprehensive exam. *Entrance requirements:* For master's, minimum GPA of 3.0; for doctorate, minimum undergraduate GPA of 3.0. Additional exam requirements/recommendations for international students: Required—TOEFL. *Application deadline:* Applications are processed on a rolling basis. Application fee: $50. Electronic applications accepted. *Financial support:* Federal Work-Study and scholarships/grants available. Support available to part-time students. Financial award application deadline: 4/1; financial award applicants required to submit FAFSA. *Unit head:* Dr. Kathleen Cornett, Dean, 800-331-5995, Fax: 941-379-9464, E-mail: kcornett@argosy.edu. *Application contact:* Admissions Representative, 800-331-5995 Ext. 221, Fax: 941-379-5964.

See Close-Up on page 231.

Argosy University, Schaumburg Campus, College of Business, Schaumburg, IL 60173-5403. Offers accounting (DBA, Adv C); corporate compliance (MBA); customized professional concentration (MBA, DBA); finance (MBA, Certificate); healthcare administration (MBA, Certificate); information systems (DBA, Adv C); information systems management (MBA, Certificate); international business (MBA, DBA, Adv C, Certificate); management (MBA, DBA, Adv C, Certificate); marketing (MBA, DBA, Adv C, Certificate). Part-time and evening/weekend programs available. *Faculty:* 1 (woman) full-time, 7 part-time/adjunct (0 women). *Students:* 36 full-time, 23 part-time. 13 applicants, 69% accepted, 9 enrolled. In 2006, 5 master's, 4 doctorates awarded. *Degree requirements:* For doctorate, thesis/dissertation, comprehensive exam. *Entrance requirements:* For master's and doctorate, minimum GPA of 3.0. Additional exam requirements/recommendations for international students: Required—TOEFL. *Application deadline:* For fall admission, 3/15 priority date for domestic and international students; for spring admission, 10/15 priority date for domestic and international students. Applications are processed on a rolling basis. Application fee: $50. Electronic applications accepted. *Expenses:* Contact institution. *Financial support:* Federal Work-Study and scholarships/grants available. *Unit head:* Dr. Harriet Kandelman, Dean, 866-290-2777, Fax: 847-548-6159, E-mail: agrosyadmissions@argosy.edu. *Application contact:* Jamal Scott, Director of Admissions, 847-598-6159, Fax: 630-598-6191, E-mail: jscott@argosy.edu.

See Close-Up on page 233.

Argosy University, Seattle Campus, College of Business, Seattle, WA 98121. Offers accounting (DBA); customized professional concentration (MBA, DBA); finance (MBA); healthcare administration (MBA); information systems (DBA); information systems management (MBA); international business (MBA, DBA); management (MSM, DBA); mangement (MBA); marketing (MBA, DBA). Part-time and evening/weekend programs available. *Students:* 1 applicant, 100% accepted, 1 enrolled. In 2006, 1 degree awarded. *Degree requirements:* For master's, capstone experience; for doctorate, thesis/dissertation, comprehensive exam (for some programs). *Entrance requirements:* For master's, minimum GPA of 3.0 in last 2 years or cumulative of 2.7; for doctorate, minimum GPA of 3.0. Additional exam requirements/recommendations for international students: Required—TOEFL (minimum score 550 paper-based; 213 computer-based). *Application deadline:* For fall admission, 4/15 priority date for domestic students, 4/15 for international students; for winter admission, 10/15 priority date for domestic students. Applications are processed on a rolling basis. Application fee: $50. Electronic applications accepted. *Expenses:* Contact institution. *Financial support:* Federal Work-Study and unspecified assistantships available. Support available to part-time students. Financial award applicants required to submit FAFSA. *Unit head:* Dr. Kylene Quinn, Chair, 206-393-3543, Fax: 206-283-5777, E-mail: kquinn@argosy.edu. *Application contact:* Heather Simpson, Director of Admissions, 866-283-4500, Fax: 206-283-5777, E-mail: hsimpson@argosy.edu.

See Close-Up on page 235.

Argosy University, Tampa Campus, College of Business, Tampa, FL 33614. Offers accounting (DBA); customized professional concentration (MBA, DBA); finance (MBA, Certificate); healthcare administration (MBA, Certificate); information systems (DBA); information systems management (MBA); international business (MBA, DBA, Certificate); management (MBA, MSM, DBA); marketing (MBA, DBA, Certificate); public administration (MBA). *Entrance requirements:* For doctorate, minimum GPA of 3.0. *Unit head:* Dr. Andrew Ghillyer, Dean, 813-393-5270, E-mail: aghillyer@argosy.edu.

See Close-Up on page 237.

Argosy University, Twin Cities Campus, College of Business, Eagan, MN 55121. Offers accounting (DBA); corporate compliance (MBA); customized professional certification (DBA); customized professional concentration (MBA); finance (MBA); healthcare administration (MBA); information systems (DBA); information systems management (MBA); international business (MBA, DBA); management (MBA, MSM, DBA, EDBA); marketing (MBA, DBA). Part-time and evening/weekend programs available. *Faculty:* 1 (woman) full-time, 20 part-time/adjunct (6 women). *Students:* 47 full-time (23 women), 20 part-time (11 women); includes 21 minority (10 African Americans, 1 American Indian/Alaska Native, 9 Asian Americans or Pacific Islanders, 1 Hispanic American). Average age 39. 72 applicants, 76% accepted, 45 enrolled. In 2006, 6 degrees awarded. *Degree requirements:* For doctorate, thesis/dissertation, comprehensive exam. *Entrance requirements:* For master's, 3 letters of recommendation, bachelor's degree in a related field, minimum undergraduate GPA of 3.0, resumé; for doctorate, 3 letters of recommendation, master's degree in a related field, minimum GPA of 3.0, resumé. Additional exam requirements/recommendations for international students: Required—TOEFL (minimum score 550 paper-based; 213 computer-based). *Application deadline:* For fall admission, 5/15 priority date for domestic students, 5/15 for international students; for spring admission, 10/15 priority date for domestic students, 10/15 for international students. Applications are processed on a rolling basis. Application fee: $50. Electronic applications accepted. *Financial support:* In 2006–07, 3 fellowships with partial tuition reimbursements, 3 teaching assistantships with partial tuition reimbursements were awarded; Federal Work-Study and scholarships/grants also available. Financial award applicants required to submit FAFSA. *Unit head:* Dr. Paula King, Department Head, 651-846-3377, E-mail: pking@argosy.edu. *Application contact:* Jennifer Radke, 2nd Director of Graduate Admissions, 651-846-3300, Fax: 651-994-7954, E-mail: tcadmissions@argosy.edu.

See Close-Up on page 239.

Argosy University, Washington DC Campus, College of Business, Arlington, VA 22209. Offers accounting (DBA); customized professional concentration (MBA, DBA); finance (MBA); healthcare administration (MBA); information systems (DBA); information systems management (MBA); international business (MBA, DBA); international business marketing (Graduate Certificate); management (MBA, DBA); marketing (MBA, DBA). *Faculty:* 1 full-time (0 women), 5 part-time/adjunct (2 women). *Students:* 5 full-time (4 women), 4 part-time (1 woman); includes 4 minority (3 African Americans, 1 Asian American or Pacific Islander). 21 applicants, 86% accepted. *Degree requirements:* For master's, thesis (for some programs), comprehensive exam (for some programs); for doctorate, thesis/dissertation, comprehensive exam. *Entrance requirements:* For master's and doctorate, minimum GPA of 3.0. Additional exam requirements/recommendations for international students: Required—TOEFL (minimum score 550 paper-based; 213 computer-based). *Application deadline:* For fall admission, 6/15 priority date for domestic students; for spring admission, 10/15 priority date for domestic students. Application fee: $50. *Financial support:* Federal Work-Study and scholarships/grants available. Financial award applicants required to submit FAFSA. *Unit head:* Dr. Colleen Logan, Academic Affairs Officer, 866-703-2777, Fax: 703-521-5850, E-mail: dcadmissions@argosy.edu. *Application contact:* Emily Peck, Director of Admissions, 866-703-2777 Ext. 5851, Fax: 703-526-5850, E-mail: dcadmissions@argosy.edu.

See Close-Up on page 241.

Arizona State University, Division of Graduate Studies, W.P. Carey School of Business, Program in Business Administration, Tempe, AZ 85287. Offers accountancy (PhD); business administration (MBA); finance (PhD); health services research (PhD); information management (PhD); management (PhD); marketing (PhD); supply chain management (PhD); JD/MBA; MBA/M Arch; MBA/MHSM. MBA/MIM offered jointly with Thunderbird, The American Graduate School of International Management and Groupe Ecole Supéieure de Commerce, Toulouse, France. *Accreditation:* AACSB. *Degree requirements:* For master's, thesis optional; for doctorate, thesis/dissertation. *Entrance requirements:* For master's, GMAT.

Avila University, School of Business, Kansas City, MO 64145-1698. Offers accounting (MBA); finance (MBA); general management (MBA); health care administration (MBA); international business (MBA); management information systems (MBA); marketing (MBA). Part-time and evening/weekend programs available. *Faculty:* 8 full-time (4 women), 17 part-time/adjunct (4 women). *Students:* 31 full-time (19 women), 165 part-time (96 women); includes 18 minority (14 African Americans, 1 American Indian/Alaska Native, 3 Hispanic Americans), 16 international. Average age 32. 77 applicants, 81% accepted, 62 enrolled. In 2006, 54 degrees awarded. *Degree requirements:* For master's, capstone course. *Entrance requirements:* For master's, GMAT, minimum GPA of 3.0. Additional exam requirements/recommendations for international students: Required—TOEFL (minimum score 550 paper-based). *Application deadline:* For fall

Marketing

Avila University (continued)
admission, 7/30 priority date for domestic students; for winter admission, 11/30 priority date for domestic students; for spring admission, 2/28 priority date for domestic students. Applications are processed on a rolling basis. Application fee: $20. Electronic applications accepted. *Expenses:* Tuition: Full-time $7,470; part-time $415 per credit. *Financial support:* In 2006–07, 78 students received support. Career-related internships or fieldwork available. Support available to part-time students. Financial award applicants required to submit FAFSA. *Faculty research:* Leadership characteristics, financial hedging, group dynamics. *Unit head:* Dr. Richard Woodall, Dean, 816-501-3798, Fax: 816-501-2463. *Application contact:* JoAnna Giffin, MBA Admissions Director, 816-501-3601, Fax: 816-501-2463, E-mail: joanna.giffin@avila.edu.

Baker College Center for Graduate Studies, Programs in Business, Flint, MI 48507-9843. Offers accounting (MBA); computer information systems (MBA); finance (MBA); general business (MBA); health and recreation services management (MBA); health care management (MBA); human resource management (MBA); industrial management (MBA); international business (MBA); leadership (MBA); marketing (MBA). MBA in health and recreation services management enrollment limited to international students. Part-time and evening/weekend programs available. *Faculty:* 15 full-time (6 women), 425 part-time/adjunct (200 women). *Students:* 370 full-time (190 women), 1,060 part-time (560 women); includes 372 minority (205 African Americans, 27 American Indian/Alaska Native, 66 Asian Americans or Pacific Islanders, 74 Hispanic Americans), 30 international. Average age 38. 780 applicants, 85% accepted, 567 enrolled. In 2006, 202 degrees awarded. *Degree requirements:* For master's, portfolio. *Entrance requirements:* For master's, 3 years of work experience, minimum undergraduate GPA of 2.5, writing sample, letters of recommendation. Additional exam requirements/recommendations for international students: Required—TOEFL (minimum score 550 paper-based; 213 computer-based). *Application deadline:* For fall admission, 8/6 priority date for domestic students; for winter admission, 12/15 priority date for domestic students; for spring admission, 2/15 priority date for domestic students. Applications are processed on a rolling basis. Application fee: $25. Electronic applications accepted. *Expenses:* Tuition: Full-time $7,200; part-time $300 per credit hour. *Financial support:* In 2006–07, 410 students received support. Scholarships/grants available. Support available to part-time students. Financial award applicants required to submit FAFSA. *Unit head:* Dr. Michael Heberling, President, 800-469-3165, Fax: 810-766-4399, E-mail: heberling@baker.edu. *Application contact:* Chuck J. Gurden, Vice President for Graduate and Online Admissions, 800-469-3165, Fax: 810-766-2051, E-mail: chuck@baker.edu.

Barry University, Andreas School of Business, Graduate Certificate Programs, Miami Shores, FL 33161-6695. Offers finance (Certificate); health services administration (Certificate); international business (Certificate); management (Certificate); management information systems (Certificate); marketing (Certificate). *Application contact:* Dave Fletcher, Director of Graduate Admissions, 305-899-3113, Fax: 305-899-2971, E-mail: dfletcher@mail.barry.edu.

Bayamón Central University, Graduate Programs, Program in Business Administration, Bayamón, PR 00960-1725. Offers accounting (MBA); finance (MBA); general business (MBA); management (MBA); management of security and protection (MBA); marketing (MBA). Part-time and evening/weekend programs available. *Degree requirements:* For master's, comprehensive exam (for some programs), registration (for some programs). *Entrance requirements:* For master's, EXADEP, bachelor's degree in business or related field.

Bentley College, The Elkin B. McCallum Graduate School of Business, Program in Marketing Analytics, Waltham, MA 02452-4705. Offers MSMA. Part-time and evening/weekend programs available. *Faculty:* 17 full-time (5 women), 8 part-time/adjunct (2 women). *Students:* 15 full-time (6 women), 11 part-time (7 women); includes 2 minority (1 Asian American or Pacific Islander, 1 Hispanic American), 5 international. Average age 26. 29 applicants, 72% accepted, 17 enrolled. In 2006, 6 degrees awarded. *Entrance requirements:* For master's, GMAT. Additional exam requirements/recommendations for international students: Required—TOEFL. *Application deadline:* For fall admission, 6/1 priority date for domestic students, 3/1 priority date for international students; for spring admission, 11/1 priority date for domestic and international students. Applications are processed on a rolling basis. Application fee: $50. Electronic applications accepted. *Expenses:* Tuition: Full-time $28,440; part-time $2,844 per course. Required fees: $404; $105 per year. *Financial support:* Research assistantships, scholarships/grants, tuition waivers, and unspecified assistantships available. Financial award application deadline: 4/12; financial award applicants required to submit CSS PROFILE or FAFSA. *Faculty research:* Customer relationship management, 'green" products, service marketing, creativity and marketing. *Unit head:* Andy Aylesworth, Director, 781-891-3149, E-mail: aaylesworth@bentley.edu. *Application contact:* Sharon Hill, Director of Graduate Admissions, 781-891-2108, Fax: 781-891-2464, E-mail: shill@bentley.edu.

Bernard M. Baruch College of the City University of New York, Zicklin School of Business, Department of Marketing, New York, NY 10010-5585. Offers MBA, MS, PhD. Part-time and evening/weekend programs available. *Faculty:* 29 full-time (6 women), 28 part-time/adjunct (6 women). *Students:* 72 full-time (40 women), 188 part-time (108 women); includes 40 minority (8 African Americans, 1 American Indian/Alaska Native, 31 Asian Americans or Pacific Islanders). In 2006, 320 master's, 1 doctorate awarded. *Degree requirements:* For doctorate, thesis/dissertation, comprehensive exam. *Entrance requirements:* For master's, GMAT, 2 letters of recommendation, resumé, 2 years of work experience; for doctorate, GMAT. Additional exam requirements/recommendations for international students: Required—TOEFL (minimum score 590 paper-based; 243 computer-based), TWE (minimum score 5). *Application deadline:* For fall admission, 5/31 for domestic students, 4/30 for international students; for spring admission, 10/31 for domestic and international students. Application fee: $125. *Financial support:* Fellowships, research assistantships, teaching assistantships, career-related internships or fieldwork, Federal Work-Study, scholarships/grants, and unspecified assistantships available. Financial award application deadline: 4/30; financial award applicants required to submit FAFSA. *Unit head:* Myung-Soo Lee, Chairman, 646-312-3288, E-mail: myung-soo_lee@baruch.cuny.edu. *Application contact:* Frances Murphy, Office of Graduate Admissions, 646-312-1300, Fax: 646-312-1301, E-mail: zicklingradadmissions@baruch.cuny.edu.

Boston University, School of Management, Doctorate in Business Administration Program, Boston, MA 02215. Offers accounting (DBA); information systems (DBA); management policy (DBA); marketing (DBA); operations management (DBA); organizational behavior (DBA). *Students:* 48 full-time (26 women); includes 4 minority (all Asian Americans or Pacific Islanders), 24 international. Average age 35. 120 applicants, 17% accepted, 10 enrolled. In 2006, 8 degrees awarded. *Degree requirements:* For doctorate, thesis/dissertation. *Entrance requirements:* For doctorate, GMAT or GRE General Test. *Application deadline:* For fall admission, 1/31 for domestic students. Application fee: $125. *Expenses:* Tuition: Full-time $33,330; part-time $1,042 per credit. Required fees: $462; $40. *Financial support:* Career-related internships or fieldwork, Federal Work-Study, institutionally sponsored loans, scholarships/grants, and tuition waivers available. Support available to part-time students. Financial award applicants required to submit FAFSA. *Unit head:* Dr. Sushil Vachani, Director, 617-353-4875, E-mail: dba@bu.edu. *Application contact:* Hayden Estrada, Assistant Dean, Admissions, 617-353-2670, Fax: 617-353-7368, E-mail: dba@bu.edu.

Bryant University, Graduate School, Graduate School of Business, Programs in Business Administration, Smithfield, RI 02917-1284. Offers accounting (MBA, CAGS); computer information systems (MBA, CAGS); e-strategy (MBA, CAGS); finance (MBA, CAGS); general business (MBA); management (MBA, CAGS); marketing (MBA, CAGS); operations management (MBA). *Accreditation:* AACSB. *Faculty:* 49 full-time (13 women), 2 part-time/adjunct (0 women). *Students:* 143 applicants, 41% accepted, 46 enrolled. In 2006, 106 master's, 10 other advanced degrees awarded. *Entrance requirements:* For master's, GMAT, letter of recommendation, resumé; for CAGS, GMAT, resumé. Additional exam requirements/recommendations for international students: Required—TOEFL (minimum score 580 paper-based; 237 computer-based). *Application deadline:* For fall admission, 7/15 for domestic students, 4/1 for international students; for spring admission, 11/15 for domestic and international students. Application fee: $80. *Expenses:* Tuition: Part-time $1,998 per course. *Financial support:* Research assistantships with full tuition reimbursements, unspecified assistantships available. Financial award applicants required to submit FAFSA. *Unit head:* Kristopher T. Sullivan, Assistant Dean of the Graduate School, 401-232-6230, Fax: 401-232-6494, E-mail: gradprog@bryant.edu.

California Lutheran University, Graduate Studies, School of Business, Thousand Oaks, CA 91360-2787. Offers finance (MBA); healthcare management (MBA); international business (MBA); management information systems (MBA); marketing (MBA); organizational behavior (MBA); small business/entrepreneurship (MBA). Evening/weekend programs available. *Entrance requirements:* For master's, GMAT, interview, minimum GPA of 3.0. Expenses: Contact institution.

California State University, East Bay, Academic Programs and Graduate Studies, College of Business and Economics, Department of Marketing, Option in Marketing Management, Hayward, CA 94542-3000. Offers MBA. Part-time and evening/weekend programs available. *Degree requirements:* For master's, comprehensive exam or thesis. *Entrance requirements:* For master's, GMAT, minimum GPA of 2.75. Additional exam requirements/recommendations for international students: Required—TOEFL (minimum score 550 paper-based; 213 computer-based). *Application deadline:* For fall admission, 5/31 for domestic students, 4/30 for international students; for winter admission, 9/30 for domestic and international students; for spring admission, 12/31 for domestic students, 11/30 for international students. Application fee: $55. *Financial support:* Application deadline: 3/2. *Unit head:* Cesar Maloles, Advisor, 510-885-2342, E-mail: cesar.maloles@csueastbay.edu. *Application contact:* Doris Duncan, Director of Graduate Programs, 510-885-3364, Fax: 510-885-2176, E-mail: doris.duncan@csueastbay.edu.

California State University, Fullerton, Graduate Studies, College of Business and Economics, Department of Marketing, Fullerton, CA 92834-9480. Offers international business (MBA); marketing (MBA). Part-time and evening/weekend programs available. *Students:* 10 full-time (7 women), 19 part-time (10 women); includes 8 minority (1 African American, 5 Asian Americans or Pacific Islanders, 2 Hispanic Americans), 11 international. Average age 27. 57 applicants, 39% accepted, 12 enrolled. In 2006, 11 degrees awarded. *Degree requirements:* For master's, project or thesis. *Entrance requirements:* For master's, GMAT, minimum AACSB index of 950. Application fee: $55. *Expenses:* Tuition, nonresident: part-time $339 per unit. Required fees: $1,155 per semester. *Financial support:* Teaching assistantships, Federal Work-Study, institutionally sponsored loans, and scholarships/grants available. Support available to part-time students. Financial award application deadline: 3/1. *Unit head:* Dr. Irene Lange, Chair, 714-278-2223. *Application contact:* Robert Miyake, Assistant Dean, 714-278-2211.

California State University, Los Angeles, Graduate Studies, College of Business and Economics, Major in Business Administration, Department of Marketing, Los Angeles, CA 90032-8530. Offers international business (MBA, MS); marketing (MBA, MS). Part-time and evening/weekend programs available. *Faculty:* 2 full-time (both women). *Students:* 9 full-time (4 women), 13 part-time (8 women); includes 11 minority (3 African Americans, 7 Asian Americans or Pacific Islanders, 1 Hispanic American), 7 international. *Degree requirements:* For master's, comprehensive exam (MBA), thesis (MS). *Entrance requirements:* For master's, GMAT, minimum GPA of 2.5 during previous 2 years of course work. Additional exam requirements/recommendations for international students: Required—TOEFL. *Application deadline:* For fall admission, 6/30 for domestic students; for spring admission, 11/30 for domestic students. Applications are processed on a rolling basis. Application fee: $55. *Expenses:* Tuition, nonresident: part-time $226 per unit. *Financial support:* Career-related internships or fieldwork and Federal Work-Study available. Support available to part-time students. Financial award application deadline: 3/1. *Unit head:* Dr. Richard Kao, Chair, 323-343-2960, Fax: 323-343-5462.

Canisius College, Graduate Division, Richard J. Wehle School of Business, Department of Management and Marketing, Buffalo, NY 14208-1098. Offers business administration (MBA). *Accreditation:* AACSB. *Faculty:* 32 full-time (6 women), 8 part-time/adjunct (2 women). *Students:* 68 full-time (21 women), 167 part-time (72 women); includes 24 minority (15 African Americans, 5 Asian Americans or Pacific Islanders, 4 Hispanic Americans), 19 international. Average age 29. In 2006, 81 degrees awarded. *Entrance requirements:* For master's, GMAT. *Application deadline:* For fall admission, 7/1 priority date for domestic students; for spring admission, 11/1 priority date for domestic students. Applications are processed on a rolling basis. Application fee: $25. *Expenses: Contact institution.* Tuition and fees vary according to program. *Financial support:* Research assistantships with partial tuition reimbursements, career-related internships or fieldwork, scholarships/grants, and unspecified assistantships available. Support available to part-time students. Financial award application deadline: 6/15; financial award applicants required to submit FAFSA. *Faculty research:* Risk aversion, information security, employee relations, urban finance, student expectations. *Unit head:* Dr. George Palumbo, Director, MBA Program, 716-888-2667, Fax: 716-888-3132, E-mail: palumbo@canisius.edu. *Application contact:* Laura McEwen, Director of Graduate Programs, 716-888-2140, Fax: 716-888-8211, E-mail: gradubus@canisius.edu.

Capella University, School of Business and Technology, Minneapolis, MN 55402. Offers accounting (MBA), including system design and programming; business (Certificate), including human resource management (MS, PhD, Certificate), information technology management (MS, PhD, Certificate), leadership (MBA, MS, PhD, Certificate); finance (MBA); general business (MBA); health care management (MBA); information technology (MS, Certificate), including general information technology (MS), information security, network architecture and design (MS), professional projects management (Certificate), project management and leadership (MS), system design and development (MS),); information technology management (MBA); marketing (MBA); organization and management (MBA, MS, PhD), including general business (PhD), general organization and management (MBA, MS), human resource management (MS, PhD, Certificate), information technology management (MS, PhD, Certificate), leadership (MBA, MS, PhD, Certificate); project management (MBA). Part-time and evening/weekend programs available. Postbaccalaureate distance learning degree programs offered (minimal on-campus study). Terminal master's awarded for partial completion of doctoral program. *Degree requirements:* For master's, integrative project, thesis optional; for doctorate, thesis/dissertation, comprehensive exam, registration. *Entrance requirements:* Additional exam requirements/recommendations for international students: Required—TOEFL (minimum score 550 paper-based; 213 computer-based), TWE (minimum score 4). Electronic applications accepted. *Faculty research:* Business policies: strategic, corporate, and financial management; interplay of technological, organizational and social change.

Cardean University, MBA Program, Chicago, IL 60606-7204. Offers accounting and information systems (MBA); e-commerce (MBA); finance (MBA); global management (MBA); health care administration (MBA); human resources management (MBA); leadership (MBA); management of information systems (MBA); management of technology (MBA); marketing (MBA); professional accounting (MBA); project management (MBA); risk management (MBA); strategy and economics (MBA). Part-time and evening/weekend programs available. Postbaccalaureate distance learning degree programs offered (no on-campus study). *Entrance requirements:* Additional exam requirements/recommendations for international students: Required—TOEFL (minimum score 550 paper-based; 213 computer-based).

Carnegie Mellon University, Tepper School of Business, Program in Marketing, Pittsburgh, PA 15213-3891. Offers PhD. *Degree requirements:* For doctorate, thesis/dissertation.

Case Western Reserve University, Weatherhead School of Management, Department of Marketing and Policy Studies, Division of Marketing, Cleveland, OH 44106. Offers MBA. *Faculty:* 7 full-time (3 women), 1 (woman) part-time/adjunct. *Students:* 82 full-time (39 women), 127 part-time (59 women); includes 13 minority (5 African Americans, 7 Asian Americans or Pacific Islanders, 1 Hispanic American), 27 international. Average age 28. In 2006, 116 degrees awarded. *Entrance requirements:* For master's, GMAT. *Application deadline:* For fall admission, 4/15 priority date for domestic students. Application fee: $50. *Financial support:*

Application deadline: 5/1. *Faculty research:* Consumer decision making, global marketing, brand equity management, supply chain management, industrial and new technology marketing. *Unit head:* Stan Cort, Head, 216-368-2038, E-mail: mxr8@po.cwru.edu.

Case Western Reserve University, Weatherhead School of Management, Department of Operations, Cleveland, OH 44106. Offers management (MS, MSM), including finance (MS), information systems (MS), marketing (MS), operations research, quality management (MS), supply chain (MSM); management for liberal arts graduates (MSM); operations research (PhD); MBA/MSM. Part-time programs available. *Faculty:* 12 full-time (1 woman), 2 part-time/adjunct (1 woman). *Students:* 32 full-time (8 women), 6 part-time (1 woman), 21 international. Average age 28. In 2006, 28 master's, 4 doctorates awarded. *Degree requirements:* For doctorate, thesis/dissertation. *Entrance requirements:* For master's, GRE General Test; for doctorate, GMAT, GRE General Test. *Application deadline:* For fall admission, 4/15 priority date for domestic students. Applications are processed on a rolling basis. Application fee: $50. *Financial support:* Tuition waivers (full and partial) available. Financial award application deadline: 5/1. *Faculty research:* Mathematical finance, mathematical programming, scheduling, stochastic optimization, environmental/energy models. *Unit head:* Kamlesh Mathur, Chairman, 216-368-3857, E-mail: kamlesh.mathur@case.edu.

Central European University, CEU Business School, Budapest, Hungary. Offers finance (MBA); general management (MBA); information technology (M Sc); information technology management (MBA); management (EMBA); marketing (MBA); real estate management (MBA). Part-time and evening/weekend programs available. *Faculty:* 15 full-time (3 women), 30 part-time/adjunct (9 women). *Students:* 47 full-time (18 women), 158 part-time (22 women). Average age 32. 450 applicants, 43% accepted, 160 enrolled. In 2006, 77 degrees awarded. *Entrance requirements:* For master's, GMAT. Additional exam requirements/recommendations for international students: Required—TOEFL (minimum score 570 paper-based; 230 computer-based). *Application deadline:* For fall admission, 5/22 priority date for domestic students, 5/22 for international students; for winter admission, 11/13 priority date for domestic students, 11/13 for international students. Applications are processed on a rolling basis. Application fee: $0. Electronic applications accepted. *Financial support:* In 2006–07, 4 students received support, including research assistantships with partial tuition reimbursements available (averaging $3,800 per year); tuition waivers (partial) and GMAT-based tuition fee discounts also available. *Faculty research:* Social and ethical business, marketing. Total annual research expenditures: 11,000 euros. *Unit head:* Dr. Paul Garrison, Dean and Managing Director, 36-18875050, Fax: 36-18875001, E-mail: garrisonp@ceubusiness.com. *Application contact:* Tunde Hegedus, MBA Program Manager, 36-18875060, Fax: 36-18875133, E-mail: mba@ceubusiness.com.

Central Michigan University, College of Graduate Studies, College of Business Administration, Department of Marketing and Hospitality Services Administration, Mount Pleasant, MI 48859. Offers MBA. *Degree requirements:* For master's, thesis or alternative, registration. *Entrance requirements:* For master's, GMAT.

City University, Graduate Division, School of Management, Bellevue, WA 98005. Offers accounting (MBA); C++ programming (Certificate); computer systems—C++ programming (MS); computer systems—individualized study (MS); computer systems—web programming in e-commerce (MS); computer systems-web development (MS); financial management (MBA, Certificate); general management (MBA, MPA, Certificate); general management-Europe (MBA); human resource management (MPA); individualized study (MBA); information systems (MBA, Certificate); management—general management (MA); management—human resource management (MA); management—individualized study (MA); marketing (MBA, Certificate); personal financial planning (MBA, Certificate); project management (MBA, MS, Certificate); technology management (MS, Certificate); web development (Certificate); web programming in e-commerce (Certificate). Part-time and evening/weekend programs available. Postbaccalaureate distance learning degree programs offered (no on-campus study). *Entrance requirements:* Additional exam requirements/recommendations for international students: Required—TOEFL (minimum score 540 paper-based; 207 computer-based); Recommended—IELTS. Electronic applications accepted.

Clark Atlanta University, School of Business Administration, Department of Marketing, Atlanta, GA 30314. Offers MBA. *Accreditation:* AACSB. Part-time programs available. *Entrance requirements:* For master's, GMAT.

Clark University, Graduate School, Graduate School of Management, Business Administration Program, Worcester, MA 01610-1477. Offers accounting (MBA); finance (MBA); global business (MBA); health care management (MBA); management (MBA); management of information technology (MBA); marketing (MBA). *Accreditation:* AACSB. Part-time and evening/weekend programs available. *Students:* 122 full-time (64 women), 113 part-time (42 women); includes 18 minority (3 African Americans, 9 Asian Americans or Pacific Islanders, 6 Hispanic Americans), 115 international. Average age 29. 235 applicants, 78% accepted, 80 enrolled. In 2006, 109 degrees awarded. *Degree requirements:* For master's, thesis optional. *Application deadline:* For fall admission, 6/1 priority date for domestic students; for spring admission, 12/1 priority date for domestic students. Applications are processed on a rolling basis. Application fee: $50. Electronic applications accepted. *Financial support:* In 2006–07, research assistantships with partial tuition reimbursements (averaging $6,000 per year), teaching assistantships with partial tuition reimbursements (averaging $6,000 per year) were awarded; fellowships with full and partial tuition reimbursements, career-related internships or fieldwork, Federal Work-Study, institutionally sponsored loans, and tuition waivers (partial) also available. Support available to part-time students. Financial award application deadline: 5/31. *Faculty research:* Organizational development, accounting, marketing, finance, human resource management. *Application contact:* Patricia Tollo, Admissions Director, 508-793-7406, Fax: 508-793-8822, E-mail: clarkmba@clarku.edu.

See Close-Up on page 257.

Clemson University, Graduate School, College of Business and Behavioral Science, Department of Marketing, Program in Marketing, Clemson, SC 29634. Offers MS. *Expenses:* Tuition, state resident: full-time $8,812; part-time $450 per hour. Tuition, nonresident: full-time $18,036; part-time $760 per hour. Required fees: $474; $5 per term. *Unit head:* Dr. John D. Mittelstaedt, Associate Professor, 864-656-5293, Fax: 864-656-0138, E-mail: jmittel@clemson.edu.

See Close-Up on page 649.

Cleveland State University, College of Graduate Studies, Nance College of Business Administration, Department of Marketing, Cleveland, OH 44115. Offers data-driven marketing planning (Graduate Certificate); e-commerce (MBA); global business (Graduate Certificate); marketing (MBA, DBA). *Unit head:* Dr. Thomas W. Whipple, Chair, 216-687-4771, Fax: 216-687-9354, E-mail: t.whipple@csuohio.edu.

Cleveland State University, College of Graduate Studies, Nance College of Business Administration, Doctoral Programs in Business Administration, Cleveland, OH 44115. Offers business administration (DBA); finance (DBA); information systems (DBA); marketing (DBA); production/operations management (DBA). *Accreditation:* AACSB. In 2006, 3 degrees awarded. *Degree requirements:* For doctorate, thesis/dissertation. *Entrance requirements:* For doctorate, GMAT, MBA or equivalent. *Unit head:* Dr. Raj Shekhar G. Javalgi, Director, 216-687-3786, Fax: 216-687-9354, E-mail: r.javalgi@csuohio.edu.

Columbia Southern University, MBA Program, Orange Beach, AL 36561. Offers electronic business and technology (MBA); healthcare management (MBA); human resources management (MBA); international management (MBA); marketing (MBA); project management (MBA); public administration (MBA); sport management (MBA). Part-time and evening/weekend programs available. Postbaccalaureate distance learning degree programs offered (no on-campus study). *Entrance requirements:* Additional exam requirements/recommendations for international students: Required—TOEFL. Electronic applications accepted.

Columbia University, Graduate School of Business, Doctoral Program in Business, New York, NY 10027. Offers business (PhD), including accounting, decision, risk, and operations, finance and economics, management, marketing. *Accreditation:* AACSB. *Faculty:* 118 full-time (14 women), 106 part-time/adjunct (18 women). *Students:* 114 full-time (38 women); includes 3 Hispanic Americans, 96 international. Average age 27. 636 applicants, 6% accepted, 18 enrolled. In 2006, 15 degrees awarded. *Degree requirements:* For doctorate, thesis/dissertation, major field exam, research paper, thesis proposal, comprehensive exam, registration. *Entrance requirements:* For doctorate, GMAT, 2 letters of reference, resumé. Additional exam requirements/recommendations for international students: Required—TOEFL. *Application deadline:* For fall admission, 1/1 for domestic and international students. Application fee: $75. Electronic applications accepted. *Expenses: Contact institution. Financial support:* In 2006–07, fellowships with full tuition reimbursements (averaging $20,500 per year), research assistantships (averaging $4,000 per year) were awarded; teaching assistantships, career-related internships or fieldwork, institutionally sponsored loans, health care benefits, tuition waivers (full), and unspecified assistantships also available. *Unit head:* Elizabeth Elam Chang, Administrative Director, 212-854-2836, Fax: 212-932-2359, E-mail: phdinfo@gsb.columbia.edu.

Columbia University, Graduate School of Business, MBA Program, New York, NY 10027. Offers accounting (MBA); decision, risk, and operations (MBA); entrepreneurship (MBA); finance and economics (MBA); human resource management (MBA); international business (MBA); management (MBA); marketing (MBA); media (MBA); real estate (MBA); social enterprise (MBA); DDS/MBA; JD/MBA; MBA/MIA; MBA/MPH; MBA/MS; MD/MBA. *Faculty:* 118 full-time (14 women), 106 part-time/adjunct (18 women). *Students:* 1,242 full-time (428 women); includes 291 minority (65 African Americans, 5 American Indian/Alaska Native, 189 Asian Americans or Pacific Islanders, 32 Hispanic Americans), 392 international. Average age 28. 5,372 applicants, 17% accepted, 726 enrolled. In 2006, 682 degrees awarded. *Entrance requirements:* For master's, GMAT, 2 letters of recommendation. Additional exam requirements/recommendations for international students: Required—TOEFL. *Application deadline:* For fall admission, 4/20 for domestic students, 3/1 for international students; for spring admission, 10/12 for domestic and international students. Applications are processed on a rolling basis. Application fee: $215. Electronic applications accepted. *Financial support:* Fellowships, research assistantships, teaching assistantships, career-related internships or fieldwork, Federal Work-Study, institutionally sponsored loans, scholarships/grants, and unspecified assistantships available. Financial award applicants required to submit FAFSA. *Unit head:* Prof. Amir Ziv, Vice Dean of Students and the MBA Program, 212-854-3485, Fax: 212-932-0545, E-mail: az50@columbia.edu. *Application contact:* Linda B. Meehan, Assistant Dean of Admissions, 212-854-1961, Fax: 212-662-6754, E-mail: apply@claven.gsb.columbia.edu.

Concordia University Wisconsin, Graduate Programs, School of Business and Legal Studies, MBA Program, Mequon, WI 53097-2402. Offers finance (MBA); health care administration (MBA); human resource management (MBA); international business (MBA); international business-English/Chinese (MBA); management (MBA); management information services (MBA); managerial communications (MBA); marketing (MBA); public administration (MBA); risk management (MBA). Postbaccalaureate distance learning degree programs offered (minimal on-campus study). *Students:* 504 (249 women). In 2006, 110 degrees awarded. *Degree requirements:* For master's, thesis or alternative, comprehensive exam. *Entrance requirements:* Additional exam requirements/recommendations for international students: Required—TOEFL. *Application deadline:* For fall admission, 8/1 priority date for domestic students; for spring admission, 1/15 for domestic students. Applications are processed on a rolling basis. Application fee: $50. *Expenses: Contact institution. Financial support:* Application deadline: 8/1. *Unit head:* Dr. David Borst, Director, 262-243-4298, Fax: 262-243-4428, E-mail: david.borst@cuw.edu.

Cornell University, Graduate School, Graduate Field of Management, Ithaca, NY 14853-0001. Offers accounting (PhD); behavioral decision theory (PhD); finance (PhD); marketing (PhD); organizational behavior (PhD); production and operations management (PhD). *Accreditation:* AACSB. *Faculty:* 57 full-time (11 women). *Students:* 38 full-time (14 women); includes 2 minority (both Asian Americans or Pacific Islanders), 20 international. Average age 31. 457 applicants, 5% accepted, 8 enrolled. In 2006, 4 doctorates awarded. *Degree requirements:* For doctorate, thesis/dissertation, comprehensive exam. *Entrance requirements:* For doctorate, GMAT or GRE General Test. Additional exam requirements/recommendations for international students: Required—TOEFL (minimum score 600 paper-based; 250 computer-based). *Application deadline:* For fall admission, 1/3 for domestic students. Application fee: $60. Electronic applications accepted. *Expenses: Contact institution.* Full-time tuition and fees vary according to program. *Financial support:* In 2006–07, 37 students received support, including 2 fellowships with full tuition reimbursements available, 31 research assistantships with full tuition reimbursements available, 4 teaching assistantships with full tuition reimbursements available; institutionally sponsored loans, scholarships/grants, health care benefits, tuition waivers (full and partial), and unspecified assistantships also available. Financial award applicants required to submit FAFSA. *Faculty research:* Operations and manufacturing. *Unit head:* Director of Graduate Studies, 607-255-3669. *Application contact:* Graduate Field Assistant, 607-255-9431, E-mail: js_phd@cornell.edu.

Dallas Baptist University, College of Adult Education, Professional Development Program, Dallas, TX 75211-9299. Offers accounting (MA); business (MA); church leadership (MA); corporate management (MA); counseling (MA); criminal justice (MA); English as a second language (MA); finance (MA); higher education (MA); leadership studies (MA); management (MA); management information systems (MA); marketing (MA); missions (MA). Part-time and evening/weekend programs available. *Faculty:* 49 full-time (21 women), 112 part-time/adjunct (46 women). *Students:* 31 full-time, 65 part-time. 51 applicants, 49% accepted, 15 enrolled. In 2006, 41 degrees awarded. Application fee: $25. *Expenses:* Tuition: Full-time $8,370; part-time $465 per credit hour. Required fees: $465 per credit hour. *Financial support:* Tuition waivers (full and partial) available. *Unit head:* Lynda Jackson, Director, 214-333-6830, Fax: 214-333-5558, E-mail: graduate@dbu.edu. *Application contact:* Kit P. Montgomery, Director of Graduate Programs, 214-333-5242, Fax: 214-333-5579, E-mail: graduate@dbu.edu.

Dallas Baptist University, Graduate School of Business, Business Administration Program, Dallas, TX 75211-9299. Offers accounting (MBA); business communication (MBA); conflict resolution management (MBA); e-business (MBA); entrepreneurship (MBA); finance (MBA); health care management (MBA); international business (MBA); management (MBA); management information systems (MBA); marketing (MBA); project management (MBA); technology and engineering management (MBA). *Accreditation:* ACBSP. Part-time and evening/weekend programs available. Postbaccalaureate distance learning degree programs offered (no on-campus study). *Faculty:* 49 full-time (21 women), 112 part-time/adjunct (46 women). *Students:* 103 full-time, 318 part-time. 226 applicants, 38% accepted. In 2006, 124 degrees awarded. *Entrance requirements:* For master's, GMAT, minimum GPA of 3.0. Additional exam requirements/recommendations for international students: Required—TOEFL. *Application deadline:* Applications are processed on a rolling basis. Application fee: $25. Electronic applications accepted. *Expenses:* Tuition: Full-time $8,370; part-time $465 per credit hour. Required fees: $465 per credit hour. *Financial support:* Career-related internships or fieldwork, Federal Work-Study, institutionally sponsored loans, scholarships/grants, and tuition waivers (full and partial) available. Support available to part-time students. *Faculty research:* Sports management, services marketing, retailing, strategic management, financial planning/investments. *Unit head:* Dr. Sandra S. Reid, Director, 214-333-5244, Fax: 214-333-5293, E-mail: graduate@dbu.edu. *Application contact:* Kit P. Montgomery, Director of Graduate Programs, 214-333-5242, Fax: 214-333-5579, E-mail: graduate@dbu.edu.

Davenport University, Sneden Graduate School, Dearborn, MI 48126-3799. Offers accounting (MBA); e-business (MBA); finance (MBA); global business (MBA); health care management (MBA); human resources management (MBA); management (MBA); marketing (MBA). Part-time and evening/weekend programs available. Postbaccalaureate distance learning degree programs offered (no on-campus study). *Entrance requirements:* For master's, minimum GPA

Marketing

Davenport University (continued)
of 2.7, previous course work in accounting and statistics. *Faculty research:* Accounting, international accounting, social and environmental accounting, finance.

Delta State University, Graduate Programs, College of Business, Division of Management, Marketing, and Business Administration, Cleveland, MS 38733-0001. Offers management (MBA); marketing (MBA). Part-time and evening/weekend programs available. *Entrance requirements:* For master's, GMAT. *Application deadline:* For fall admission, 8/1 priority date for domestic students; for spring admission, 12/1 priority date for domestic students. Applications are processed on a rolling basis. Application fee: $0. *Financial support:* In 2006–07, research assistantships (averaging $4,000 per year); career-related internships or fieldwork, Federal Work-Study, and institutionally sponsored loans also available. Support available to part-time students. Financial award application deadline: 6/1. *Unit head:* Dr. Cooper Johnson, Chair, 662-846-4190, Fax: 662-846-4232, E-mail: bcjohnsn@deltastate.edu.

DePaul University, Charles H. Kellstadt Graduate School of Business, Department of Marketing, Chicago, IL 60604-2287. Offers brand management (MBA); customer relationship management (MBA); integrated marketing communication (MBA); marketing analysis (MSMA); marketing and management (MBA); marketing strategy and analysis (MBA); marketing strategy and planning (MBA); new product management (MBA); sales leadership (MBA). Part-time and evening/weekend programs available. *Faculty:* 23 full-time (4 women), 15 part-time/adjunct (6 women). *Students:* 189 full-time (103 women), 126 part-time (68 women); includes 37 minority (18 African Americans, 14 Asian Americans or Pacific Islanders, 5 Hispanic Americans), 22 international. Average age 30. In 2006, 88 degrees awarded. *Degree requirements:* For master's, registration. *Entrance requirements:* For master's, GMAT, 2 letters of recommendation, resumé. Additional exam requirements/recommendations for international students: Required—TOEFL (minimum score 550 paper-based; 213 computer-based). *Application deadline:* For fall admission, 7/1 for domestic students; for winter admission, 10/1 for domestic students; for spring admission, 2/1 for domestic students. Applications are processed on a rolling basis. Application fee: $60. Electronic applications accepted. *Financial support:* In 2006–07, 6 research assistantships with partial tuition reimbursements (averaging $2,500 per year) were awarded. Financial award application deadline: 4/30. *Faculty research:* International and marketing role in developing economics, internet marketing, direct marketing, consumer behavior, new product development processes. Total annual research expenditures: $100,000. *Application contact:* Christopher E. Kinsella, Director of Cohort MBA Programs, 312-362-8810, Fax: 312-362-6677, E-mail: kgsb@depaul.edu.

Drexel University, LeBow College of Business, Department of Marketing, Philadelphia, PA 19104-2875. Offers MS. Part-time and evening/weekend programs available. *Entrance requirements:* For master's, GMAT, minimum GPA of 2.75. Additional exam requirements/recommendations for international students: Required—TOEFL. Electronic applications accepted. *Faculty research:* Multivariate analysis, new product development, marketing research, strategic planning, professional personal selling and sales management.

Drexel University, LeBow College of Business, Program in Business Administration, Philadelphia, PA 19104-2875. Offers business administration (MBA, PhD, APC), including accounting (MBA, PhD), decision sciences (PhD), economics (MBA, PhD), finance (MBA, PhD), legal studies (MBA), management (MBA), marketing (MBA, PhD), organizational sciences (PhD), quantitative methods (MBA), strategic management (PhD). *Accreditation:* AACSB. Part-time and evening/weekend programs available. Postbaccalaureate distance learning degree programs offered (minimal on-campus study). Terminal master's awarded for partial completion of doctoral program. *Entrance requirements:* For master's, GMAT, minimum GPA of 2.75; for doctorate, GMAT. Additional exam requirements/recommendations for international students: Required—TOEFL. Electronic applications accepted. *Faculty research:* Decision support systems, individual and group behavior, operations research, techniques and strategy.

Eastern Michigan University, Graduate School, College of Business, Department of Marketing, Ypsilanti, MI 48197. Offers e-business (MBA); international business (MBA); supply chain management (MBA). Part-time and evening/weekend programs available. Postbaccalaureate distance learning degree programs offered (minimal on-campus study). *Entrance requirements:* For master's, GMAT. Additional exam requirements/recommendations for international students: Required—TOEFL. *Application deadline:* For fall admission, 5/15 priority date for domestic and international students; for winter admission, 10/15 priority date for domestic and international students; for spring admission, 3/15 priority date for domestic and international students. Applications are processed on a rolling basis. Application fee: $35. *Expenses:* Tuition, state resident: part-time $341 per credit hour. Tuition, nonresident: full-time $16,104; part-time $671 per credit hour. Required fees: $816; $34 per credit hour. $40 per term. One-time fee: $82 full-time. Tuition and fees vary according to course level, course load, degree level and reciprocity agreements. *Financial support:* Fellowships, research assistantships with full tuition reimbursements, teaching assistantships with full tuition reimbursements, career-related internships or fieldwork, Federal Work-Study, institutionally sponsored loans, scholarships/grants, tuition waivers (partial), and unspecified assistantships available. Support available to part-time students. Financial award applicants required to submit FAFSA. *Unit head:* Dr. Denise Tanguay, Interim Head, 734-487-3323. *Application contact:* Dr. Russ Merz, Department Coordinator, 734-487-1852, E-mail: russ.merz@emich.edu.

Eastern University, Graduate Business Programs, St. Davids, PA 19087-3696. Offers business administration (MBA), including accounting, economics, finance, management, marketing; economic development (MBA, MS); nonprofit management (MBA, MS); M Div/MBA; M Div/MS. Part-time and evening/weekend programs available. *Degree requirements:* For master's, thesis (for some programs). *Entrance requirements:* For master's, GMAT (MBA), minimum GPA of 2.5. Expenses: Contact institution. *Faculty research:* Micro-level economic development, China welfare and economic development, macroethics, micro- and macro-level economic development in transitional economics, organizational effectiveness.

Emerson College, Graduate Studies, School of Communication, Department of Marketing Communication, Program in Integrated Marketing Communication, Boston, MA 02116-4624. Offers MA. Part-time programs available. *Entrance requirements:* For master's, GMAT or GRE General Test. Additional exam requirements/recommendations for international students: Required—TOEFL. Electronic applications accepted.

See Close-Up on page 651.

Emory University, Roberto C. Goizueta Business School, Doctoral Programs in Business, Atlanta, GA 30322-1100. Offers accounting (PhD); finance (PhD); information systems (PhD); marketing (PhD); organization and management (PhD). *Degree requirements:* For doctorate, thesis/dissertation, comprehensive exam. *Entrance requirements:* Additional exam requirements/recommendations for international students: Required—TOEFL (minimum score 600 paper-based; 250 computer-based). Electronic applications accepted. *Expenses:* Tuition: Full-time $30,246. *Faculty research:* Financial markets, banking, corporate disclosure, investor relations, marketing strategy.

Fairfield University, Charles F. Dolan School of Business, Fairfield, CT 06824-5195. Offers accounting (MBA, MS, CAS); finance (MBA, MS, CAS); general management (MBA); human resource management (MBA, CAS); information systems and operations (MBA); information systems and operations management (CAS); international business (MBA, CAS); marketing (MBA, CAS); taxation (MBA, MS, CAS). *Accreditation:* AACSB. Part-time and evening/weekend programs available. *Faculty:* 43 full-time (17 women), 2 part-time/adjunct (1 woman). *Students:* 65 full-time (31 women), 125 part-time (54 women); includes 4 Asian Americans or Pacific Islanders, 4 Hispanic Americans, 22 international. Average age 27. 99 applicants, 45% accepted, 38 enrolled. In 2006, 78 degrees awarded. *Degree requirements:* For master's, registration. *Entrance requirements:* For master's, GMAT, 2 letters of reference, resumé. Additional exam requirements/recommendations for international students: Required—TOEFL (minimum score 550 paper-based; 213 computer-based; 79 iBT). *Application deadline:* For fall admission, 8/15 priority date for domestic students, 5/15 priority date for international students; for spring admission, 11/15 priority date for domestic students, 10/15 priority date for international students. Applications are processed on a rolling basis. Application fee: $55. Electronic applications accepted. *Expenses: Contact institution. Financial support:* Unspecified assistantships available. *Faculty research:* Optimal investment strategies, organization structure, international finance, strategic management, customer behavior. *Unit head:* Dr. Norman A. Solomon, Dean, 203-254-4000 Ext. 4070, Fax: 203-254-4105, E-mail: nsolomon@mail.fairfield.edu. *Application contact:* Marianne Gumpper, Director of Graduate and Continuing Studies Admissions, 203-254-4184, Fax: 203-254-4073, E-mail: gradadmis@mail.fairfield.edu.

See Close-Up on page 271.

Fairleigh Dickinson University, College at Florham, Silberman College of Business, Departments of Management, Marketing, and Entrepreneurial Studies, Program in Marketing, Madison, NJ 07940-1099. Offers MBA, Certificate. *Students:* 14 full-time (8 women), 36 part-time (20 women), 4 international. Average age 31. 18 applicants, 67% accepted, 8 enrolled. In 2006, 13 degrees awarded. *Entrance requirements:* For master's, GMAT. *Application deadline:* Applications are processed on a rolling basis. Application fee: $40.

Fairleigh Dickinson University, Metropolitan Campus, Silberman College of Business, Departments of Management, Marketing, and Entrepreneurial Studies, Program in Marketing, Teaneck, NJ 07666-1914. Offers MBA, Certificate. *Students:* 16 full-time (8 women), 15 part-time (9 women), 11 international. Average age 27. 34 applicants, 38% accepted, 6 enrolled. In 2006, 10 degrees awarded. *Application deadline:* Applications are processed on a rolling basis. Application fee: $40.

Fashion Institute of Technology, School of Graduate Studies, Program in Cosmetics and Fragrance Marketing and Management, New York, NY 10001-5992. Offers MPS. *Students:* Average age 34. *Degree requirements:* For master's, capstone seminar. *Application deadline:* For fall admission, 2/15 priority date for domestic students. Application fee: $25. *Expenses:* Tuition, state resident: full-time $6,900; part-time $288 per credit. Tuition, nonresident: full-time $10,920; part-time $455 per credit. Required fees: $420; $30 per term. *Financial support:* In 2006–07, 7 students received support. Federal Work-Study and scholarships/grants available. Financial award applicants required to submit FAFSA. *Unit head:* Stephan Kanlian, Associate Chair, 212-217-5714, Fax: 212-217-5156, E-mail: kanliansim@aol.com. *Application contact:* Umilta Allsop, Administrative Assistant, 212-217-5716, Fax: 212-217-5156, E-mail: umilta_allsop@fitnyc.edu.

Florida Agricultural and Mechanical University, Division of Graduate Studies, Research, and Continuing Education, School of Business and Industry, Tallahassee, FL 32307-3200. Offers accounting (MBA); finance (MBA); management information systems (MBA); marketing (MBA). *Degree requirements:* For master's, residency. *Entrance requirements:* For master's, GMAT, minimum GPA of 3.0.

Florida Atlantic University, College of Business, Department of Management, International Business and Entrepreneurship, Boca Raton, FL 33431-0991. Offers business administration (Exec MBA, MBA), including accounting (MBA), electronic commerce (MBA), finance (MBA), financial planning (MBA), global entrepreneurship (MBA), health administration (MBA), international business (MBA), marketing (MBA), operations management (MBA), real estate (MBA), sport management (MBA). *Faculty:* 64 full-time (17 women), 15 part-time/adjunct (3 women). *Students:* 215 full-time (89 women), 365 part-time (189 women); includes 150 minority (49 African Americans, 2 American Indian/Alaska Native, 36 Asian Americans or Pacific Islanders, 63 Hispanic Americans), 54 international. Average age 32. 414 applicants, 55% accepted, 167 enrolled. In 2006, 196 master's awarded. *Degree requirements:* For master's, thesis optional. *Entrance requirements:* For master's, GMAT, minimum GPA of 3.0. Additional exam requirements/recommendations for international students: Required—TOEFL (minimum score 600 paper-based; 250 computer-based). *Application deadline:* For fall admission, 7/1 priority date for domestic students, 2/15 priority date for international students; for winter admission, 11/1 priority date for domestic students, 8/15 priority date for international students; for spring admission, 4/1 priority date for domestic students, 1/15 priority date for international students. Applications are processed on a rolling basis. Application fee: $30. Electronic applications accepted. *Expenses:* Tuition, area resident: Full-time $4,394. Tuition, nonresident: full-time $16,441. *Financial support:* Research assistantships, teaching assistantships, career-related internships or fieldwork, Federal Work-Study, institutionally sponsored loans, tuition waivers (partial), and unspecified assistantships available. Support available to part-time students. Financial award application deadline: 3/1; financial award applicants required to submit FAFSA. *Unit head:* Dr. Brenda Richey, Head, 561-297-3194, E-mail: brichey@fau.edu. *Application contact:* Fredrick G. Taylor, Graduate Adviser, 561-297-2768, Fax: 561-297-1315, E-mail: mba@fau.edu.

Florida State University, Graduate Studies, College of Business, Tallahassee, FL 32306. Offers accounting (M Acc), including accounting information systems, assurance services, corporate accounting, taxation; business administration (MBA, PhD), including accounting (PhD), finance (PhD), information and management science (PhD), management (PhD), marketing (PhD), risk and insurance (PhD); insurance (MSM); management information systems (MS); JD/MBA. *Accreditation:* AACSB. Part-time and evening/weekend programs available. Postbaccalaureate distance learning degree programs offered (no on-campus study). *Faculty:* 107 full-time (26 women), 21 part-time/adjunct (2 women). *Students:* 145 full-time (62 women), 444 part-time (143 women); includes 147 minority (58 African Americans, 3 American Indian/Alaska Native, 45 Asian Americans or Pacific Islanders, 41 Hispanic Americans). Average age 29. 789 applicants, 50% accepted, 321 enrolled. In 2006, 263 master's, 19 doctorates awarded. Terminal master's awarded for partial completion of doctoral program. *Degree requirements:* For master's, registration; for doctorate, thesis/dissertation, comprehensive exam, registration. *Entrance requirements:* For master's, GMAT, substantial work experience (MBA, MS), minimum GPA of 3.0, letters of recommendation; for doctorate, GMAT, minimum graduate GPA of 3.5, letters of recommendation. Additional exam requirements/recommendations for international students: Required—TOEFL (minimum score 600 paper-based; 250 computer-based). *Application deadline:* For fall admission, 5/1 for domestic and international students; for spring admission, 10/1 for domestic students, 9/1 for international students. Applications are processed on a rolling basis. Application fee: $30. Electronic applications accepted. *Expenses:* Tuition, state resident: full-time $5,822; part-time $243 per credit hour. Tuition, nonresident: full-time $20,976; part-time $874 per credit hour. Tuition and fees vary according to program. *Financial support:* In 2006–07, 126 students received support, including 40 fellowships with partial tuition reimbursements available (averaging $4,600 per year), 37 research assistantships with partial tuition reimbursements available (averaging $4,600 per year), 49 teaching assistantships with partial tuition reimbursements available (averaging $10,500 per year); unspecified assistantships also available. Financial award application deadline: 1/1. Total annual research expenditures: $1.5 million. *Unit head:* Dr. Caryn Beck-Dudley, Dean, 850-644-3090, Fax: 850-644-0915. *Application contact:* Lisa Beverly, Coordinator, Graduate Programs Admissions, 850-644-6458, Fax: 850-644-0588, E-mail: lbeverly@cob.fsu.edu.

Florida State University, Graduate Studies, College of Communication, Department of Communication, Tallahassee, FL 32306. Offers integrated marketing communication (MA, MS); mass communication (MA, MS, PhD); media and communication studies (MA, MS); speech communication (PhD). Part-time programs available. *Faculty:* 26 full-time (7 women), 2 part-time/adjunct (0 women). *Students:* 78 full-time (53 women), 106 part-time (60 women); includes 77 minority (28 African Americans, 1 American Indian/Alaska Native, 31 Asian Americans or Pacific Islanders, 17 Hispanic Americans), 4 international. 220 applicants, 45% accepted, 77 enrolled. In 2006, 72 master's, 9 doctorates awarded. *Median time to degree:* Of those who began their doctoral program in fall 1998, 67% received their degree in 8 years or less. *Degree requirements:* For master's, thesis (for some programs); for doctorate, thesis/dissertation, comprehensive exam. *Entrance requirements:* For master's, GRE General Test, minimum GPA of 3.0; for doctorate, GRE General Test, minimum GPA of 3.3 in graduate course work. Additional exam requirements/recommendations for international students: Required—TOEFL (minimum score 600 paper-based; 250 computer-based; 100 iBT). *Application deadline:* For fall admission, 2/1 priority date for domestic students; for winter admission, 11/1 priority date for domestic students. Applications are processed on a rolling basis. Application fee: $30. *Expenses:* Tuition, state resident: full-time $5,822; part-time $243 per credit hour. Tuition, nonresident: full-time $20,976; part-time $874 per credit hour. Tuition and fees vary according to program. *Financial support:* In 2006–07, 49 students received support, including 1 fellowship with full tuition reimbursement available, 8 research assistantships with full tuition reimbursements available (averaging $12,000 per year), 40 teaching assistantships with full tuition reimbursements available (averaging $4,200 per year); career-related internships or fieldwork, Federal Work-Study, institutionally sponsored loans, scholarships/grants, tuition waivers (partial), and unspecified assistantships also available. Support available to part-time students. Financial award application deadline: 2/1; financial award applicants required to submit FAFSA. *Faculty research:* Communication technology and policy, marketing communication, communication content and effect, new communication/information technologies. Total annual research expenditures: $264,208. *Unit head:* Dr. Stephen D. McDowell, Chairperson, 850-644-2276, Fax: 850-644-8642, E-mail: smcdowel@mailer.fsu.edu. *Application contact:* Chairperson, 850-644-8746, Fax: 850-644-8642, E-mail: smcdowel@mailer.fsu.edu.

Fordham University, Graduate School of Business, New York, NY 10023. Offers accounting (MBA); communications and media management (MBA); finance (MBA, MS); information systems (MBA, MS); management systems (MBA); marketing (MBA); media management (MS); taxation (MS); JD/MBA; MBA/MIM; MS/MBA. *Accreditation:* AACSB. Part-time and evening/weekend programs available. *Faculty:* 87 full-time, 41 part-time/adjunct. *Students:* 345 full-time (132 women), 1,183 part-time (448 women); includes 238 minority (59 African Americans, 1 American Indian/Alaska Native, 116 Asian Americans or Pacific Islanders, 62 Hispanic Americans), 77 international. 1,081 applicants, 65% accepted, 422 enrolled. In 2006, 454 degrees awarded. *Entrance requirements:* For master's, GMAT. Additional exam requirements/recommendations for international students: Required—TOEFL (minimum score 600 paper-based; 250 computer-based). *Application deadline:* For fall admission, 6/1 priority date for domestic students, 5/1 priority date for international students; for winter admission, 11/1 priority date for domestic students, 10/1 priority date for international students; for spring admission, 3/1 priority date for domestic students, 2/1 priority date for international students. Applications are processed on a rolling basis. Application fee: $65. Electronic applications accepted. *Expenses: Contact institution. Financial support:* In 2006–07, 7 fellowships (averaging $27,000 per year), 128 research assistantships were awarded; career-related internships or fieldwork, institutionally sponsored loans, scholarships/grants, and unspecified assistantships also available. Support available to part-time students. Financial award application deadline: 5/1; financial award applicants required to submit FAFSA. *Unit head:* Dr. Howard Tuckman, Dean, 212-636-6165, Fax: 212-307-1779, E-mail: tuckman@fordham.edu. *Application contact:* Frank Fletcher, Director of Admissions and Financial Aid, 212-636-6200, Fax: 212-636-7076, E-mail: admissionsgb@fordham.edu.

Franklin University, Marketing and Communications Program, Columbus, OH 43215-5399. Offers MS. Part-time and evening/weekend programs available. *Faculty:* 1 full-time (0 women), 7 part-time/adjunct (1 woman). *Students:* 83 full-time (58 women), 13 part-time (10 women); includes 23 minority (21 African Americans, 2 Asian Americans or Pacific Islanders), 7 international. Average age 34. In 2006, 20 degrees awarded. *Degree requirements:* For master's, thesis or alternative, registration. *Entrance requirements:* For master's, minimum undergraduate GPA of 2.75, undergraduate course work in marketing and statistics. Additional exam requirements/recommendations for international students: Required—TOEFL (minimum score 600 paper-based; 232 computer-based). *Application deadline:* For fall admission, 8/15 priority date for domestic students; for winter admission, 12/20 priority date for domestic students; for spring admission, 4/4 priority date for domestic students. Applications are processed on a rolling basis. Application fee: $30. Electronic applications accepted. *Expenses:* Tuition: Full-time $7,110; part-time $395 per credit hour. Tuition and fees vary according to campus/location and program. *Financial support:* In 2006–07, 50 students received support. Application deadline: 6/30. *Unit head:* Dr. Doug Ross, Program Chair, 614-947-6149. *Application contact:* Graduate Services Office, 614-797-4700, Fax: 614-224-7723, E-mail: gradschl@franklin.edu.

Gannon University, School of Graduate Studies, College of Humanities, Business, and Education, School of Business, Program in Marketing, Erie, PA 16541-0001. Offers Certificate. Part-time and evening/weekend programs available. *Entrance requirements:* For degree, GMAT. Additional exam requirements/recommendations for international students: Required—TOEFL (minimum score 500 paper-based; 173 computer-based). *Application deadline:* Applications are processed on a rolling basis. Application fee: $25. *Expenses:* Tuition: Full-time $12,240; part-time $680 per credit. Required fees: $496; $16 per credit. Tuition and fees vary according to course load, degree level, campus/location and program. *Financial support:* Application deadline: 7/1; *Application contact:* Debra Meszaros, Director of Graduate Recruitment, 814-871-5819, Fax: 814-871-5827, E-mail: cfal@gannon.edu.

The George Washington University, School of Business, Department of Marketing, Washington, DC 20052. Offers MBA, PhD. Part-time and evening/weekend programs available. *Degree requirements:* For doctorate, thesis/dissertation. *Entrance requirements:* For master's, GMAT; for doctorate, GMAT or GRE. Additional exam requirements/recommendations for international students: Required—TOEFL. *Faculty research:* Strategic marketing, marketing and public policy, marketing management.

Georgia Institute of Technology, Graduate Studies and Research, College of Management, Program in Business Administration, Atlanta, GA 30332-0001. Offers accounting (MBA); e-commerce (Certificate); engineering entrepreneurship (MBA); entrepreneurship (Certificate); finance (MBA); information technology management (MBA); international business (MBA, Certificate); management of technology (Certificate); marketing (MBA); operations management (MBA); organizational behavior (MBA); strategic management (MBA). *Accreditation:* AACSB.

Georgia Institute of Technology, Graduate Studies and Research, College of Management, Program in Management, Atlanta, GA 30332-0001. Offers accounting (PhD); finance (PhD); information technology management (PhD); marketing (PhD); operations management (PhD); organizational behavior (PhD); quantitative and computational finance (MS); strategic management (PhD). *Accreditation:* AACSB. *Degree requirements:* For doctorate, thesis/dissertation, oral exams, comprehensive exam. *Entrance requirements:* For master's and doctorate, GMAT. Additional exam requirements/recommendations for international students: Required—TOEFL. *Faculty research:* MIS, management of technology, international business, entrepreneurship, operations management.

Georgia State University, J. Mack Robinson College of Business, Department of Marketing, Atlanta, GA 30303-3083. Offers MBA, MS, PhD. Part-time and evening/weekend programs available. *Faculty:* 26 full-time (12 women), 2 part-time/adjunct (1 woman). *Students:* 50 full-time (26 women), 97 part-time (48 women); includes 23 minority (14 African Americans, 8 Asian Americans or Pacific Islanders, 1 Hispanic American), 19 international. Average age 31. 83 applicants, 48% accepted, 27 enrolled. In 2006, 58 degrees awarded. Terminal master's awarded for partial completion of doctoral program. *Degree requirements:* For doctorate, thesis/dissertation. *Entrance requirements:* For master's and doctorate, GMAT. Additional exam requirements/recommendations for international students: Required—TOEFL (minimum score 610 paper-based; 255 computer-based; 101 iBT). *Application deadline:* For fall admission, 5/1 for domestic students, 2/1 for international students; for spring admission, 10/15 for domestic students, 5/1 for international students. Applications are processed on a rolling basis. Application fee: $50. Electronic applications accepted. *Financial support:* Fellowships, research assistantships, teaching assistantships, career-related internships or fieldwork and tuition waivers (partial) available. Support available to part-time students. Financial award applicants required to submit FAFSA. *Unit head:* Dr. Edward Rigdon, Chair, 404-651-4180, Fax: 404-651-4198, E-mail: erigdon@gsu.edu. *Application contact:* Dr. Bruce Pilling, Director of Graduate Studies, 404-651-2740, Fax: 404-651-4198, E-mail: bpilling@gsu.edu.

Golden Gate University, Ageno School of Business, San Francisco, CA 94105-2968. Offers accounting (M Ac, MBA); business administration (EMBA, MBA, DBA); finance (MBA, MS, Certificate); financial planning (MS, Certificate); human resource management (MBA, MS); human resources management (Certificate); information technology (MBA); information technology management (MS, Certificate); integrated marketing and communications (MS, Certificate); international business (MBA); management (MBA); marketing (MBA, MS, Certificate); operations management (Certificate); psychology (MA, Certificate); public relations (MS, Certificate); JD/MBA. Part-time and evening/weekend programs available. *Students:* 355 full-time (192 women), 977 part-time (465 women); includes 447 minority (85 African Americans, 5 American Indian/Alaska Native, 274 Asian Americans or Pacific Islanders, 83 Hispanic Americans), 226 international. Average age 34. 548 applicants, 74% accepted, 201 enrolled. In 2006, 545 master's, 21 doctorates awarded. *Degree requirements:* For doctorate, thesis/dissertation. *Entrance requirements:* For master's, GMAT (MBA), minimum GPA of 2.5 (MS). Additional exam requirements/recommendations for international students: Required—TOEFL. *Application deadline:* Applications are processed on a rolling basis. Application fee: $55 ($90 for international students). *Financial support:* Career-related internships or fieldwork, Federal Work-Study, and institutionally sponsored loans available. Support available to part-time students. Financial award applicants required to submit FAFSA. *Unit head:* Terry Connelly, Dean, 415-442-6519, Fax: 415-442-5369. *Application contact:* Enrollment Services, 415-442-7800, Fax: 415-442-7807, E-mail: info@ggu.edu.

Goldey-Beacom College, Graduate Program, Wilmington, DE 19808-1999. Offers business administration (MBA); financial management (MBA); human resource management (MBA); information technology (MBA); management (MM); marketing management (MBA). *Accreditation:* ACBSP. Part-time and evening/weekend programs available. *Entrance requirements:* For master's, GMAT, minimum GPA of 3.0. Additional exam requirements/recommendations for international students: Required—TOEFL (minimum score 525 paper-based; 195 computer-based). Electronic applications accepted.

Hawai'i Pacific University, College of Business Administration, Honolulu, HI 96813. Offers accounting/CPA (MBA); communication (MBA); e-business (MBA); economics (MBA); finance (MBA); human resource management (MBA); information systems (MBA); international business (MBA); management (MBA); marketing (MBA); organizational change (MBA); travel industry management (MBA). Part-time and evening/weekend programs available. *Faculty:* 40 full-time (16 women), 30 part-time/adjunct (10 women). *Students:* 320 full-time (150 women), 205 part-time (95 women); includes 168 minority (17 African Americans, 7 American Indian/Alaska Native, 137 Asian Americans or Pacific Islanders, 7 Hispanic Americans), 232 international. Average age 31. 279 applicants, 67% accepted, 166 enrolled. In 2006, 172 degrees awarded. *Degree requirements:* For master's, thesis. *Entrance requirements:* For master's, GMAT. Additional exam requirements/recommendations for international students: Recommended—TOEFL (minimum score 550 paper-based; 213 computer-based), TWE (minimum score 5). *Application deadline:* For fall admission, 2/15 priority date for domestic students; for spring admission, 10/15 priority date for domestic students. Applications are processed on a rolling basis. Application fee: $50. Electronic applications accepted. *Expenses:* Tuition: Full-time $10,080; part-time $560 per credit. *Financial support:* In 2006–07, 118 students received support; research assistantships, career-related internships or fieldwork, Federal Work-Study, scholarships/grants, and unspecified assistantships available. Support available to part-time students. Financial award application deadline: 3/1; financial award applicants required to submit FAFSA. *Faculty research:* Statistical control process as used by management, studies in comparative cross-cultural management styles, not-for-profit management. *Unit head:* Dr. Charles Steilen, Dean, 808-544-9301, Fax: 808-544-0283, E-mail: csteilen@hpu.edu. *Application contact:* Danny Lam, Assistant Director of Graduate Admissions, 808-544-1135, Fax: 808-544-0280, E-mail: graduate@hpu.edu.

See Close-Up on page 275.

HEC Montreal, School of Business Administration, Master of Science Programs in Administration, Program in Marketing, Montréal, QC H3T 2A7, Canada. Offers M Sc. All courses are given in French. Part-time programs available. *Degree requirements:* For master's, one foreign language, thesis. Application fee: $60 Canadian dollars. Electronic applications accepted. Tuition and fees charges are reported in Canadian dollars. *Expenses:* Tuition, nonresident: part-time $56 Canadian dollars per credit. Required fees: $30 Canadian dollars per semester. *Financial support:* Fellowships, research assistantships, teaching assistantships, scholarships/grants available. *Application contact:* Francine Blais, Administrative Director, 514-340-6112, Fax: 514-340-6411, E-mail: francine.blais@hec.ca.

Hofstra University, Frank G. Zarb School of Business, Department of Marketing and International Business, Hempstead, NY 11549. Offers international business (MBA, MS, Advanced Certificate); marketing (MBA, MS, Advanced Certificate); marketing research (MS). Part-time and evening/weekend programs available. *Faculty:* 7 full-time (0 women), 2 part-time/adjunct (0 women). *Students:* 39 full-time (22 women), 48 part-time (27 women); includes 23 minority (7 African Americans, 10 Asian Americans or Pacific Islanders, 6 Hispanic Americans), 10 international. Average age 28. 75 applicants, 73% accepted, 27 enrolled. In 2006, 42 degrees awarded. *Degree requirements:* For master's, thesis (for some programs), capstone course for MBA. *Entrance requirements:* For master's, GMAT, 2 letters of recommendation, resumé, essay. Additional exam requirements/recommendations for international students: Required—TOEFL (minimum score 550 paper-based; 213 computer-based). *Application deadline:* Applications are processed on a rolling basis. Application fee: $60. Electronic applications accepted. *Expenses:* Tuition: Full-time $13,320; part-time $740 per credit. Required fees: $930; $155 per term. *Financial support:* In 2006–07, 24 students received support, including 13 fellowships with tuition reimbursements available (averaging $5,748 per year), 5 research assistantships with full and partial tuition reimbursements available (averaging $3,416 per year); tuition waivers (full and partial) also available. Financial award applicants required to submit FAFSA. *Faculty research:* Outsourcing, cross cultural consumer behavior, global alliances, retailing, web marketing. *Unit head:* Dr. Benny Barak, Chairperson, 516-463-5707, Fax: 516-463-4834, E-mail: mktbzb@hofstra.edu. *Application contact:* Carol Drummer, Dean of Graduate Admissions, 516-463-4876, Fax: 516-463-4664, E-mail: gradstudent@hofstra.edu.

Howard University, School of Business, Graduate Programs in Business, Washington, DC 20059-0002. Offers accounting (MBA); entrepreneurship (MBA); finance (MBA); information systems (MBA); international business (MBA); marketing (MBA); supply chain management (MBA); JD/MBA. *Accreditation:* AACSB. Part-time and evening/weekend programs available. Postbaccalaureate distance learning degree programs offered (no on-campus study). *Entrance requirements:* For master's, GMAT, minimum 1 year post undergraduate work experience, resumé, 3 letters of recommendation, advanced college algebra. Additional exam requirements/recommendations for international students: Required—TOEFL. *Faculty research:* Marketing research in multi-ethnic populations, U.S. trade policies and international relations, risk management (finance).

Huron University USA in London, Graduate Programs, Program in Business Administration, London, United Kingdom. Offers entrepreneurship (MBA); international business (MBA); international finance (MBA); marketing (MBA). Part-time programs available. *Degree requirements:* For master's, thesis, internship, comprehensive exam. *Entrance requirements:* Additional exam requirements/recommendations for international students: Required—TOEFL (minimum score 580 paper-based; 237 computer-based), TWE (minimum score 5). Electronic applications accepted.

Huron University USA in London, Graduate Programs, Program in Marketing, London, United Kingdom. Offers advertising (MA); marketing (MA); public relations (MA). *Entrance requirements:* Additional exam requirements/recommendations for international students:

Marketing

Huron University USA in London (continued)
Required—TOEFL (minimum score 580 paper-based; 237 computer-based), TWE (minimum score 5). Electronic applications accepted.

Illinois Institute of Technology, Stuart School of Business, Program in Business Administration, Chicago, IL 60616-3793. Offers entrepreneurship (MBA); financial management (MBA); financial markets (MBA); healthcare management (MBA); information technology management (MBA); international business (MBA); management science (MBA); marketing (MBA); operations, quality, and technology management (MBA); strategic management of organizations (MBA); sustainable enterprise (MBA); JD/MBA; MBA/MS. *Accreditation:* AACSB. Part-time and evening/weekend programs available. *Faculty:* 13 full-time (1 woman), 9 part-time/adjunct (0 women). *Students:* 74 full-time (29 women), 42 part-time (16 women); includes 17 minority (5 African Americans, 11 Asian Americans or Pacific Islanders, 1 Hispanic American), 74 international. Average age 29. 247 applicants, 70% accepted, 51 enrolled. In 2006, 45 degrees awarded. *Entrance requirements:* For master's, GMAT. Additional exam requirements/recommendations for international students: Required—TOEFL (minimum score 600 paper-based; 250 computer-based). *Application deadline:* For fall admission, 8/15 priority date for domestic students, 7/1 for international students; for winter admission, 11/1 priority date for domestic students, 10/1 for international students; for spring admission, 1/1 priority date for domestic students, 1/1 for international students. Applications are processed on a rolling basis. Application fee: $75. Electronic applications accepted. *Expenses: Contact institution.* Tuition and fees vary according to class time, course level, course load, program and student level. *Financial support:* Career-related internships or fieldwork, Federal Work-Study, institutionally sponsored loans, scholarships/grants, traineeships, health care benefits, tuition waivers, and unspecified assistantships available. Support available to part-time students. Financial award applicants required to submit FAFSA. *Faculty research:* Knowledge management, healthcare management, sustainability in supply chain. *Unit head:* Dr. George P. Nassos, Interim Director, 312-906-6543, Fax: 312-906-6549, E-mail: george.nassos@iit.edu. *Application contact:* Brian Jansen, Director of Graduate Admissions, 312-906-6521, Fax: 312-906-6549, E-mail: admission@stuart.iit.edu.

Illinois Institute of Technology, Stuart School of Business, Program in Marketing Communication, Chicago, IL 60616-3793. Offers MS. Part-time and evening/weekend programs available. *Faculty:* 1 full-time (0 women), 10 part-time/adjunct (3 women). *Students:* 36 full-time (27 women), 8 part-time (5 women); includes 1 minority (African American), 37 international. Average age 27. 62 applicants, 35% accepted, 16 enrolled. In 2006, 26 degrees awarded. *Entrance requirements:* For master's, GMAT or GRE General Test. Additional exam requirements/recommendations for international students: Required—TOEFL (minimum score 550 paper-based; 213 computer-based). *Application deadline:* For fall admission, 8/15 priority date for domestic students, 7/1 for international students; for winter admission, 11/1 priority date for domestic students, 10/1 for international students; for spring admission, 1/1 priority date for domestic students, 1/1 for international students. Applications are processed on a rolling basis. Application fee: $75. Electronic applications accepted. *Expenses: Contact institution.* Tuition and fees vary according to class time, course level, course load, program and student level. *Financial support:* Career-related internships or fieldwork, Federal Work-Study, institutionally sponsored loans, scholarships/grants, traineeships, health care benefits, tuition waivers (full and partial), and unspecified assistantships available. Support available to part-time students. Financial award applicants required to submit FAFSA. *Unit head:* Sanford Bredine, Associate Director, 312-906-6540, Fax: 312-906-6549, E-mail: bredine@stuart.iit.edu. *Application contact:* Brian Jansen, Director of Graduate Admissions, 312-906-6521, Fax: 312-906-6549, E-mail: admission@stuart.iit.edu.

Indiana Tech, Program in Business Administration, Fort Wayne, IN 46803-1297. Offers accounting (MBA); human resources (MBA); management (MBA); marketing (MBA). Part-time and evening/weekend programs available. *Entrance requirements:* For master's, minimum undergraduate GPA of 2.5, GMAT or 2 years of work experience. Additional exam requirements/recommendations for international students: Required—TOEFL (minimum score 550 paper-based). Electronic applications accepted.

Indiana University Southeast, School of Business, New Albany, IN 47150-6405. Offers accounting (Certificate); business administration (MBA); economics (Certificate); finance (Certificate); general business (Certificate); information and operations management (Certificate); management and marketing (Certificate); strategic finance (MS). *Accreditation:* AACSB. *Faculty:* 11 full-time (2 women). *Students:* 10 full-time (4 women), 201 part-time (65 women); includes 12 minority (2 African Americans, 8 Asian Americans or Pacific Islanders, 2 Hispanic Americans), 5 international. Average age 31. In 2006, 60 degrees awarded. *Degree requirements:* For master's, community service. *Entrance requirements:* For master's, GMAT, work experience. Additional exam requirements/recommendations for international students: Required—TOEFL. Application fee: $35. *Expenses: Contact institution.* Tuition and fees vary according to course load, campus/location and program. *Unit head:* Chris Bjornson, Dean, 812-941-2362, Fax: 812-941-2672. *Application contact:* Dr. Jay White, Director of Graduate Business Programs, 812-941-2364, Fax: 812-941-2581, E-mail: jwhite04@ius.edu.

Instituto Tecnológico y de Estudios Superiores de Monterrey, Campus Central de Veracruz, Graduate Programs, Córdoba, Mexico. Offers administration (MA); administration of information technologies (MTI); computer sciences (MCC); education (MEE); educational institution administration (MAD); educational technology (MTE); electronic commerce (MCE); finance (MAF); humanistic studies (MEH); international business for Latin America (MNL); marketing (MMT); science (MCP); technology management (MTT). Part-time and evening/weekend programs available. Postbaccalaureate distance learning degree programs offered (minimal on-campus study). *Degree requirements:* For master's, thesis (for some programs). *Entrance requirements:* For master's, PAEP College Board. Electronic applications accepted.

Instituto Tecnológico y de Estudios Superiores de Monterrey, Campus Ciudad Obregón, Program in Marketing Technology, Ciudad Obregón, Mexico. Offers MMT.

Instituto Tecnológico y de Estudios Superiores de Monterrey, Campus Cuernavaca, Programs in Business Administration, Temixco, Mexico. Offers finance (MA); human resources management (MA); international business (MA); marketing (MA).

Instituto Tecnológico y de Estudios Superiores de Monterrey, Campus Estado de México, Professional and Graduate Division, Estado de Mexico, Mexico. Offers administration of information technologies (MITA); architecture (M Arch); business administration (GMBA, MBA); computer sciences (MCS, PhD); education (M Ed); educational institution administration (MAD); educational technology and innovation (PhD); electronic commerce (MEC); environmental systems (MS); finance (MAF); humanistic studies (MHS); information sciences and knowledge management (MISKM); information systems (MS); manufacturing systems (MS); marketing (MEM); quality systems and productivity (MS); science and materials engineering (PhD); telecommunications management (MTM). Part-time programs available. Postbaccalaureate distance learning degree programs offered (minimal on-campus study). *Degree requirements:* For master's, one foreign language, thesis (for some programs), registration; for doctorate, one foreign language, thesis/dissertation, registration (for some programs). *Entrance requirements:* For master's, E-PAEP 500, interview; for doctorate, E-PAEP 500, research proposal. Additional exam requirements/recommendations for international students: Required—TOEFL (minimum score 550 paper-based). *Faculty research:* Surface treatments by plasmas, mechanical properties, robotics, graphical computing, mechatronics security protocols.

Instituto Tecnológico y de Estudios Superiores de Monterrey, Campus Monterrey, Graduate School of Business Administration and Leadership, Program in Business Administration, Monterrey, Mexico. Offers business administration (MA, MBA); finance (M Sc); international business (M Sc); marketing (M Sc). Part-time programs available. *Degree requirements:* For master's, one foreign language, thesis. *Entrance requirements:* For master's, GMAT. Additional exam requirements/recommendations for international students: Required—TOEFL. *Faculty research:* Technology management, quality management, organizational theory and behavior.

Inter American University of Puerto Rico, Metropolitan Campus, Graduate Programs, Faculty of Economics and Administrative Sciences, Program in Marketing, San Juan, PR 00919-1293. Offers MBA. *Degree requirements:* For master's, comprehensive exam. *Entrance requirements:* For master's, GRE or EXADEP, interview. Electronic applications accepted.

Inter American University of Puerto Rico, San Germán Campus, Graduate Studies Center, Graduate Program in Business Administration, San Germán, PR 00683-5008. Offers accounting (MBA); finance (MBA); human resources (MBA, PhD); industrial relations (MBA); international business (PhD); labor relations (PhD); management information systems (MBA); marketing (MBA); quality organizational design (MBA). Part-time and evening/weekend programs available. *Faculty:* 12 full-time, 4 part-time/adjunct. *Students:* 265. Average age 27. In 2006, 67 master's, 1 doctorate awarded. *Degree requirements:* For master's, comprehensive exam. *Entrance requirements:* For master's, GRE General Test or EXADEP, minimum GPA of 3.0. *Application deadline:* For fall admission, 4/30 priority date for domestic students; for spring admission, 11/15 for domestic students. Applications are processed on a rolling basis. Application fee: $31. *Expenses:* Tuition: Part-time $175 per credit. Required fees: $238 per semester. Tuition and fees vary according to degree level. *Financial support:* Teaching assistantships, Federal Work-Study and unspecified assistantships available. *Application contact:* Prof. Duay Rivera, Graduate Coordinator, 787-264-1912 Ext. 7218, Fax: 787-892-7510, E-mail: durivera@sg.inter.edu.

International University in Geneva, MBA Program, Geneva, Switzerland. Offers e-commerce (MBA); human relations (MBA); international business (Exec MBA, MBA); marketing (MBA); organizational development (MBA); telecommunications (MBA). Part-time and evening/weekend programs available. *Degree requirements:* For master's, comprehensive exam, registration. *Entrance requirements:* For master's, GMAT. Additional exam requirements/recommendations for international students: Required—TOEFL. Electronic applications accepted.

The International University of Monaco, Graduate Programs, Monte Carlo, Monaco. Offers entrepreneurship (EMBA, MBA); financial engineering (M Sc); international marketing (EMBA, MBA); luxury goods and services (EMBA, M Sc, MBA); wealth and asset management (EMBA, MBA). Part-time programs available. *Degree requirements:* For master's, applied research project. *Entrance requirements:* Additional exam requirements/recommendations for international students: Required—TOEFL (minimum score 550 paper-based; 213 computer-based), IELTS. Electronic applications accepted. *Faculty research:* Gaming, leadership, disintermediation.

Iona College, Hagan School of Business, Department of Marketing and International Business, New Rochelle, NY 10801-1890. Offers international business (PMC); marketing (MBA). Part-time and evening/weekend programs available. *Faculty:* 4 full-time (2 women), 3 part-time/adjunct (0 women). *Students:* 4 full-time (all women), 36 part-time (23 women), 1 international. Average age 29. 10 applicants, 90% accepted, 9 enrolled. In 2006, 19 master's, 24 other advanced degrees awarded. *Entrance requirements:* For master's, GMAT, 2 letters of recommendation; for PMC, GMAT. Additional exam requirements/recommendations for international students: Required—TOEFL (minimum score 550 paper-based; 213 computer-based). *Application deadline:* Applications are processed on a rolling basis. Application fee: $50. Electronic applications accepted. *Expenses: Contact institution. Financial support:* Scholarships/grants, tuition waivers (partial), and unspecified assistantships available. Support available to part-time students. *Faculty research:* Business ethics, international retailing, mega-marketing, consumer behavior and consumer confidence. *Unit head:* Dr. Frederica E. Rudell, Chair, 914-637-2748, E-mail: frudell@iona.edu. *Application contact:* Veronica Jarek-Prinz, Graduate Admissions, 914-633-2289, Fax: 914-633-2012, E-mail: vjarekprinz@iona.edu.

The Johns Hopkins University, Carey Business School, Department of Marketing, Baltimore, MD 21218-2699. Offers MS. Part-time and evening/weekend programs available. *Students:* 22 full-time (13 women), 81 part-time (58 women); includes 11 minority (9 African Americans, 2 Hispanic Americans), 1 international. Average age 31. 90 applicants, 58% accepted, 34 enrolled. In 2006, 11 degrees awarded. *Degree requirements:* For master's, research project. *Entrance requirements:* For master's, minimum GPA of 3.0, resumé, work experience, two letters of recommendation. Additional exam requirements/recommendations for international students: Required—TOEFL (minimum score 600 paper-based; 250 computer-based; 100 iBT). *Application deadline:* For fall admission, 5/1 for international students; for spring admission, 10/15 for international students. Applications are processed on a rolling basis. Application fee: $60. *Expenses:* Tuition: Full-time $32,976. Tuition and fees vary according to degree level and program. *Financial support:* Scholarships/grants available. Support available to part-time students. Financial award application deadline: 6/1; financial award applicants required to submit FAFSA. *Application contact:* Robin Reed, Senior Academic Coordinator, 800-gotojhu, Fax: 410-872-1251, E-mail: onestop.admissions@jhu.edu.

Johnson & Wales University, The Alan Shawn Feinstein Graduate School, Program in Global Business, Concentration in Marketing, Providence, RI 02903-3703. Offers MBA. Part-time and evening/weekend programs available. *Students:* 99 full-time (59 women), 23 part-time (18 women); includes 10 minority (7 African Americans, 2 Asian Americans or Pacific Islanders, 1 Hispanic American), 79 international. Average age 27. In 2006, 56 degrees awarded. *Entrance requirements:* For master's, GMAT recommended, minimum GPA of 2.75. Additional exam requirements/recommendations for international students: Required—TOEFL (paper-based 550; computer-based 210) or IELTS. *Application deadline:* For fall admission, 8/15 priority date for domestic students, 6/28 priority date for international students; for winter admission, 11/10 priority date for domestic students, 9/20 priority date for international students; for spring admission, 2/15 priority date for domestic students, 12/20 priority date for international students. Applications are processed on a rolling basis. Electronic applications accepted. *Financial support:* Unspecified assistantships available. Financial award application deadline: 5/1. *Unit head:* Dr. Gary Gray, Unit Head, 401-598-4738, Fax: 401-598-1286, E-mail: ggray@jwu.edu. *Application contact:* Dr. Allan G. Freedman, Director of Graduate Admissions, 401-598-1015, Fax: 401-598-1286, E-mail: gradadm@jwu.edu.

Johnson & Wales University, The Alan Shawn Feinstein Graduate School, Program in Hospitality Administration, Concentration in Marketing, Providence, RI 02903-3703. Offers MBA. *Students:* 65 full-time (32 women), 8 part-time (3 women); includes 2 minority (1 African American, 1 Asian American or Pacific Islander), 51 international. Average age 28. In 2006, 16 degrees awarded. *Unit head:* Thomas Rossi, Unit Head, 401-598-4738, E-mail: trossi@jwu.edu.

Kent State University, Graduate School of Management, Doctoral Program in Marketing, Kent, OH 44242-0001. Offers PhD. *Faculty:* 11 full-time (3 women). *Students:* 9 full-time (6 women), 7 international. Average age 33. 14 applicants, 43% accepted, 4 enrolled. In 2006, 1 degree awarded. *Degree requirements:* For doctorate, thesis/dissertation, oral defense, comprehensive exam. *Entrance requirements:* For doctorate, GMAT. Additional exam requirements/recommendations for international students: Required—TOEFL (minimum score 600 paper-based; 250 computer-based). *Application deadline:* For fall admission, 2/1 for domestic students, 1/1 for international students. Application fee: $30. Electronic applications accepted. *Financial support:* In 2006–07, teaching assistantships with full tuition reimbursements (averaging $15,000 per year); fellowships with full tuition reimbursements, Federal Work-Study also available. Financial award application deadline: 2/1; financial award applicants required to submit FAFSA. *Faculty research:* Advertising effects, satisfaction, international marketing, high-tech marketing, personality and consumer behavior. *Unit head:* Dr. Richard H Kolbe, Chair, 330-672-2170, Fax: 330-672-5006, E-mail: rkolbe@kent.edu. *Application contact:* Felecia A. Urbanek, Coordinator, Graduate Programs, 330-672-2282, Fax: 330-672-7303, E-mail: gradbus@bsa3.kent.edu.

Lasell College, Program in Management, Newton, MA 02466-2709. Offers elder care administration (MS); elder care marketing (MS); management (MS); marketing (MS). Part-time and evening/weekend programs available. *Entrance requirements:* Additional exam requirements/recommendations for international students: Required—TOEFL (minimum score 500 paper-based). Electronic applications accepted.

See Close-Up on page 281.

Lindenwood University, Graduate Programs, Division of Management, St. Charles, MO 63301-1695. Offers accounting (MBA, MS); business administration (MBA); entrepreneurial studies (MBA); finance (MBA, MS); human resource management (MBA); human resources (MS); international business (MBA, MS); management (MBA, MS); management information systems (MBA, MS); managing business to business (MA); managing human resources (MA); managing international business (MA); managing investment management (MA); managing leadership (MA); managing marketing (MA); managing organizational behavior (MA); managing sales (MA); managing, training and development (MA); marketing (MBA, MS); nonprofit administration (MA); public management (MBA, MS); sport management (MA). Part-time and evening/weekend programs available. *Faculty:* 38 full-time (15 women), 20 part-time/adjunct (5 women). *Students:* 177 full-time (78 women), 138 part-time (67 women); includes 43 minority (27 African Americans, 4 American Indian/Alaska Native, 6 Asian Americans or Pacific Islanders, 6 Hispanic Americans), 73 international. Average age 30. In 2006, 159 degrees awarded. *Degree requirements:* For master's, thesis (for some programs). *Entrance requirements:* For master's, interview, minimum GPA of 3.0. Additional exam requirements/recommendations for international students: Required—TOEFL (minimum score 550 paper-based; 173 computer-based). *Application deadline:* For fall admission, 7/30 priority date for domestic students, 9/30 priority date for international students; for winter admission, 12/30 priority date for domestic and international students; for spring admission, 3/30 priority date for domestic and international students. Applications are processed on a rolling basis. Application fee: $30 ($100 for international students). Electronic applications accepted. *Expenses:* Tuition: Part-time $340 per credit hour. Tuition and fees vary according to course level, course load, degree level and program. *Financial support:* Career-related internships or fieldwork, Federal Work-Study, institutionally sponsored loans, and tuition waivers (partial) available. Financial award application deadline: 6/30; financial award applicants required to submit FAFSA. *Unit head:* Ed Morris, Dean, 636-949-4832, Fax: 636-949-4910, E-mail: emorris@lindenwood.edu. *Application contact:* Brett Barger, Dean Adult, Corporate and Graduate Admissions, 636-949-4366, Fax: 636-949-4109, E-mail: bbarger@lindenwood.edu.

Lindenwood University, Graduate Programs, Programs in Individualized Education, St. Charles, MO 63301-1695. Offers administration (MSA); business administration (MBA); communications (MA); criminal justice and administration (MS); gerontology (MA); health management (MS); human resource management (MS); management (MSA); marketing (MSA); writing (MFA). Part-time and evening/weekend programs available. *Faculty:* 18 full-time (9 women), 50 part-time/adjunct (25 women). *Students:* 595 full-time (348 women), 55 part-time (37 women); includes 176 minority (163 African Americans, 1 American Indian/Alaska Native, 5 Asian Americans or Pacific Islanders, 7 Hispanic Americans), 10 international. Average age 34. In 2006, 303 degrees awarded. *Degree requirements:* For master's, thesis. *Entrance requirements:* For master's, interview, minimum GPA of 3.0. Additional exam requirements/recommendations for international students: Required—TOEFL. *Application deadline:* For fall admission, 9/30 priority date for domestic and international students; for winter admission, 12/30 priority date for domestic and international students; for spring admission, 3/30 priority date for domestic and international students. Applications are processed on a rolling basis. Application fee: $30 ($100 for international students). *Expenses:* Tuition: Part-time $340 per credit hour. Tuition and fees vary according to course level, course load, degree level and program. *Financial support:* Career-related internships or fieldwork, institutionally sponsored loans, tuition waivers (partial), and unspecified assistantships available. Financial award application deadline: 6/30; financial award applicants required to submit FAFSA. *Unit head:* Dan Kemper, Dean of LCIE, 636-916-9125, E-mail: dkemper@lindenwood.edu. *Application contact:* Brett Barger, Dean, Adult, Corporate and Graduate Admissions, 636-949-4934, Fax: 636-949-4109, E-mail: adultadmissions@lindenwood.edu.

Long Island University, C.W. Post Campus, College of Management, School of Business, Brookville, NY 11548-1300. Offers accounting and taxation (Certificate); business administration (Certificate); finance (MBA, Certificate); general business administration (MBA); international business (MBA, Certificate); management (MBA, Certificate); management information systems (MBA, Certificate); marketing (MBA, Certificate). *Accreditation:* AACSB. Part-time and evening/weekend programs available. *Entrance requirements:* For master's, GMAT, resumé, minimum GPA of 3.0, 2 letters of recommendation. Additional exam requirements/recommendations for international students: Required—TOEFL (minimum score 527 paper-based; 197 computer-based). Electronic applications accepted. *Faculty research:* Financial markets, consumer behavior.

Louisiana State University and Agricultural and Mechanical College, Graduate School, E. J. Ourso College of Business, Department of Marketing, Baton Rouge, LA 70803. Offers business administration (PhD), including marketing. Part-time programs available. *Faculty:* 9 full-time (2 women). *Students:* 10 full-time (6 women), 3 part-time (1 woman), 8 international. Average age 33. 16 applicants, 38% accepted, 4 enrolled. In 2006, 3 degrees awarded. *Degree requirements:* For doctorate, thesis/dissertation. *Entrance requirements:* Additional exam requirements/recommendations for international students: Required—TOEFL (minimum score 550 paper-based; 213 computer-based; 79 iBT). *Application deadline:* For fall admission, 1/25 priority date for domestic students, 5/15 for international students; for spring admission, 10/15 for international students. Applications are processed on a rolling basis. Application fee: $25. Electronic applications accepted. *Financial support:* In 2006–07, 10 students received support, including 9 teaching assistantships with full and partial tuition reimbursements available (averaging $16,533 per year); fellowships, research assistantships with partial tuition reimbursements available, career-related internships or fieldwork, Federal Work-Study, institutionally sponsored loans, scholarships/grants, and unspecified assistantships also available. Support available to part-time students. Financial award applicants required to submit FAFSA. *Faculty research:* Consumer behavior, marketing strategy, global marketing, e-commerce, branding/brand equity. *Unit head:* Dr. Alvin C. Burns, Chair, 225-578-8786, Fax: 225-578-8616, E-mail: alburns@lsu.edu. *Application contact:* Dr. William C. Black, Graduate Adviser, 225-578-8403, Fax: 225-578-8616, E-mail: wcblack@lsu.edu.

Louisiana Tech University, Graduate School, College of Administration and Business, Department of Management and Marketing, Ruston, LA 71272. Offers management (MBA, DBA); marketing (MBA, DBA). Part-time programs available. *Degree requirements:* For doctorate, thesis/dissertation. *Entrance requirements:* For master's and doctorate, GMAT.

Loyola College in Maryland, Graduate Programs, Sellinger School of Business and Management, Program in Business Administration, Baltimore, MD 21210-2699. Offers decision sciences (MBA); economics (MBA); finance (MBA); marketing/management (MBA). *Accreditation:* AACSB. Part-time and evening/weekend programs available. *Students:* 47 full-time (17 women), 733 part-time (315 women); includes 111 minority (59 African Americans, 1 American Indian/Alaska Native, 37 Asian Americans or Pacific Islanders, 14 Hispanic Americans), 19 international. Average age 31. In 2006, 215 degrees awarded. *Entrance requirements:* For master's, GMAT. Additional exam requirements/recommendations for international students: Required—TOEFL (minimum score 550 paper-based; 213 computer-based). *Application deadline:* For fall admission, 8/15 priority date for domestic students; for spring admission, 11/20 priority date for domestic students. Applications are processed on a rolling basis. Application fee: $50. *Financial support:* Applicants required to submit FAFSA. *Unit head:* Ann Attanasio, Director, 410-617-2308, E-mail: aattanasio@loyola.edu.

Loyola University Chicago, Graduate School of Business, Marketing Department, Chicago, IL 60611-2196. Offers integrated marketing communications (MS); marketing (MSIMC). Part-time and evening/weekend programs available. *Faculty:* 8 full-time (4 women), 6 part-time/adjunct (4 women). *Students:* 15 full-time (11 women), 53 part-time (30 women); includes 13 minority (7 African Americans, 4 Asian Americans or Pacific Islanders, 2 Hispanic Americans). In 2006, 11 degrees awarded. *Entrance requirements:* For master's, GMAT, letters of recommendation, personal statement. Additional exam requirements/recommendations for international students: Required—TOEFL (minimum score 550 paper-based; 213 computer-based; 80 iBT). *Application deadline:* For fall admission, 7/1 for domestic and international students; for winter admission, 9/1 for domestic and international students; for spring admission, 1/3 for domestic and international students. Applications are processed on a rolling basis. Application fee: $50. Electronic applications accepted. *Expenses:* Contact institution. *Financial support:* In 2006–07, 2 students received support, including research assistantships with partial tuition reimbursements available (averaging $5,000 per year); teaching assistantships, career-related internships or fieldwork also available. Support available to part-time students. Financial award application deadline: 3/15; financial award applicants required to submit FAFSA. *Faculty research:* Web performance metrics, new venture marketing strategies over consumption, benefit segmentation strategies. *Unit head:* Dr. Raymond Benton, Chair, E-mail: rbenton@luc.edu. *Application contact:* Olivia Heath, Enrollment Advisor, 312-915-8908, Fax: 312-915-7207, E-mail: oheath@luc.edu.

Lynn University, College of Business and Management, Boca Raton, FL 33431-5598. Offers aviation management (MBA); financial valuation and investment management (MBA); global leadership (PhD); hospitality management (MBA); international business (MBA); marketing (MBA); mass communication and media management (MBA); sports and athletics administration (MBA). Part-time and evening/weekend programs available. Postbaccalaureate distance learning degree programs offered. *Faculty:* 13 full-time (5 women), 7 part-time/adjunct (3 women). *Students:* 71 full-time (37 women), 113 part-time (47 women); includes 35 minority (13 African Americans, 6 Asian Americans or Pacific Islanders, 16 Hispanic Americans), 55 international. Average age 32. 114 applicants, 88% accepted, 71 enrolled. In 2006, 83 master's, 9 doctorates awarded. *Degree requirements:* For master's, project; for doctorate, thesis/dissertation, qualifying paper. *Entrance requirements:* For master's, GMAT or GRE, minimum undergraduate GPA of 3.0, resumé, 2 letters of recommendation; for doctorate, GRE or GMAT, minimum graduate GPA of 3.25, resumé, 2 letters of recommendation. Additional exam requirements/recommendations for international students: Required—TOEFL (minimum score 550 paper-based; 213 computer-based). *Application deadline:* Applications are processed on a rolling basis. Application fee: $50. Electronic applications accepted. *Expenses:* Tuition: Full-time $26,200. Required fees: $1,500. Tuition and fees vary according to class time, course load and degree level. *Financial support:* In 2006–07, 160 students received support. Career-related internships or fieldwork, Federal Work-Study, institutionally sponsored loans, scholarships/grants, tuition waivers (full and partial), and unspecified assistantships available. Support available to part-time students. Financial award application deadline: 8/1; financial award applicants required to submit FAFSA. *Faculty research:* Labor relations, dynamic balance in leisure-time skills, ethics in athletics, hotel development. *Unit head:* Dr. Russell Boisjoly, Dean, 561-237-7458, Fax: 561-237-7014, E-mail: rboisjoly@lynn.edu. *Application contact:* Dr. Larissa Baia, Assistant Director of Graduate Admissions, 561-237-7916, Fax: 561-237-7100, E-mail: admissionpm@lynn.edu.

Manhattanville College, Graduate Programs, Humanities and Social Sciences Programs, Program in Integrated Marketing Communications, Purchase, NY 10577-2132. Offers MS. Application fee: $55. *Application contact:* Natalia Fernandez, Director of Admissions, 914-323-5418, E-mail: gps@myllle.edu.

Maryville University of Saint Louis, The John E. Simon School of Business, St. Louis, MO 63141-7299. Offers accounting (MBA, PGC); business studies (PGC); e-business (MBA, PGC); management (MBA, PGC); marketing (MBA, PGC). *Accreditation:* ACBSP. Part-time and evening/weekend programs available. *Students:* 34 full-time (23 women), 162 part-time (101 women); includes 9 African Americans, 8 Asian Americans or Pacific Islanders, 2 international. Average age 31. 56 applicants, 96% accepted, 38 enrolled. In 2006, 89 degrees awarded. *Entrance requirements:* For master's, GMAT (unless applicant possesses a graduate degree or an undergaduate degree in business with a minimum GPA of 3.0), minimum AACSB index of 950. Additional exam requirements/recommendations for international students: Required—TOEFL (minimum score 550 paper-based). *Application deadline:* Applications are processed on a rolling basis. Application fee: $35 ($50 for international students). Electronic applications accepted. *Expenses:* Tuition: Full-time $17,800; part-time $555 per credit. Required fees: $55 per semester. Tuition and fees vary according to degree level and program. *Financial support:* Career-related internships or fieldwork, Federal Work-Study, tuition waivers (partial), and campus employment available. Financial award application deadline: 7/31; financial award applicants required to submit FAFSA. *Faculty research:* International business, e-business, strategic planning, interpersonal management skills, financial analysis. *Unit head:* Dr. Pamela Horwitz, Dean, 314-529-9418, Fax: 314-529-9975, E-mail: horwitz@maryville.edu. *Application contact:* Kathy Dougherty, Director of MBA Admissions and Enrollment, 314-529-9382, Fax: 314-529-9975, E-mail: business@marville.edu.

McGill University, Faculty of Graduate and Postdoctoral Studies, Desautels Faculty of Management, Montréal, QC H3A 2T5, Canada. Offers administration (PhD); entrepreneurial studies (MBA); finance (MBA); general management (Post Master's Certificate); information systems (MBA); international business (exchange program) (MBA); international Master's program in practicing management (MM); management (MBA); management for development (MBA); manufacturing management (MMM); marketing (MBA); operations management (MBA); public accountancy (Diploma); strategic management (MBA); MBA/LL B; MD/MBA. Part-time programs available. *Entrance requirements:* For master's, GMAT, minimum undergraduate GPA of 3.0, 2 years work experience; for doctorate, GMAT or GRE General Test, 2 letters of recommendation, preferably by professors in chosen field of specialization; for other advanced degree, 2 years of work experience, MBA, minimum GPA of 3.0 (Post-MBA Certificate). Additional exam requirements/recommendations for international students: Required—TOEFL (minimum score 600 paper-based; 250 computer-based), IELTS (minimum score 7). Electronic applications accepted. Expenses: Contact institution. *Faculty research:* Social innovation, leadership, strategy.

Mercy College, Division of Business and Accounting, Program in Direct Marketing, Dobbs Ferry, NY 10522-1189. Offers MS. *Students:* Average age 32. In 2006, 12 degrees awarded. *Degree requirements:* For master's, capstone project. *Entrance requirements:* For master's, interview, 2 years of work experience, letters of recommendation. *Application deadline:* Applications are processed on a rolling basis. Application fee: $37. Electronic applications accepted. *Expenses:* Tuition: Part-time $595 per credit. Required fees: $9 per credit. Tuition and fees vary according to program. *Unit head:* Walter Neff, Director, 914-674-7479, Fax: 914-734-1129, E-mail: wneff@mercy.edu. *Application contact:* Kathleen Jackson, Director of Admissions, 800-Mercy-NY, Fax: 914-674-7382, E-mail: admissions@mercy.edu.

Metropolitan State University, College of Management, St. Paul, MN 55106-5000. Offers finance (MBA); human resource management (MBA); information management (MMIS); international business (MBA); law enforcement (MPNA); management information systems (MBA); marketing (MBA); nonprofit management (MPNA); organizational studies (MBA); public administration (MPNA); purchasing management (MBA); systems management (MMIS). Part-time and evening/weekend programs available. *Degree requirements:* For master's, computer language (MMIS), thesis optional. *Entrance requirements:* For master's, GMAT (MBA), resumé. Additional exam requirements/recommendations for international students: Required—TOEFL (minimum score 550 paper-based; 213 computer-based). *Faculty research:* Yugoslav economic system, workers' cooperatives, participative management and job enrichment, global business systems.

Miami University, Graduate School, Richard T. Farmer School of Business Administration, Oxford, OH 45056. Offers accountancy (M Acc); business administration (MBA); economics (MA); finance (MBA); general management (MBA); management information systems (MBA); marketing (MBA); quality and process improvement (MBA). *Accreditation:* AACSB. Part-time

Marketing

Miami University (continued)

programs available. *Entrance requirements:* For master's, GMAT, minimum undergraduate GPA of 3.0 during previous 2 years or 2.75 overall. Additional exam requirements/recommendations for international students: Required—TOEFL (minimum score 550 paper-based; 213 computer-based), TWE (minimum score 4).

Michigan State University, The Graduate School, Eli Broad Graduate School of Management, Department of Marketing and Supply Chain Management, East Lansing, MI 48824. Offers business administration (PhD); manufacturing and engineering management (MS); supply chain management (MS). Part-time programs available. *Faculty:* 32 full-time (3 women). *Students:* 34 full-time (10 women), 35 part-time (10 women); includes 8 minority (5 African Americans, 1 American Indian/Alaska Native, 1 Asian American or Pacific Islander, 1 Hispanic American), 16 international. Average age 33. 65 applicants, 14% accepted. In 2006, 22 master's, 7 doctorates awarded. *Degree requirements:* For master's, field study, research project; for doctorate, thesis/dissertation, oral defense of dissertation proposal and dissertation, comprehensive exam. *Entrance requirements:* For master's, GMAT, bachelor's degree in related field, letters of recommendation, 2-3 years of work experience, minimum GPA of 3.0 in last 2 years of undergraduate course work; for doctorate, GMAT or GRE, letters of recommendation. Additional exam requirements/recommendations for international students: Required—TOEFL. Electronic applications accepted. *Expenses: Contact institution.* Tuition and fees vary according to program. *Financial support:* In 2006–07, 5 fellowships with tuition reimbursements, 23 research assistantships with tuition reimbursements (averaging $14,743 per year), 4 teaching assistantships with tuition reimbursements (averaging $12,000 per year) were awarded. Total annual research expenditures: $485,815. *Unit head:* Dr. Robert W. Nason, Chairperson, 517-355-2240, Fax: 517-432-1112, E-mail: nason@msu.edu. *Application contact:* Program Information, 517-353-6381, E-mail: mslogs@bus.msu.edu.

Middle Tennessee State University, College of Graduate Studies, College of Business, Department of Management and Marketing, Murfreesboro, TN 37132. Offers MBA. *Accreditation:* AACSB. Part-time and evening/weekend programs available. Postbaccalaureate distance learning degree programs offered. *Faculty:* 18 full-time (4 women). *Students:* 67 full-time (22 women), 235 part-time (108 women); includes 68 minority (37 African Americans, 24 Asian Americans or Pacific Islanders, 7 Hispanic Americans). Average age 28. 103 applicants, 100% accepted. In 2006, 113 degrees awarded. *Degree requirements:* For master's, comprehensive exam. *Entrance requirements:* For master's, GMAT. Additional exam requirements/recommendations for international students: Required—TOEFL (minimum score 525 paper-based; 195 computer-based). *Application deadline:* For fall admission, 8/1 priority date for domestic students. Applications are processed on a rolling basis. Application fee: $25. Electronic applications accepted. *Financial support:* In 2006–07, 6 students received support. Institutionally sponsored loans available. Support available to part-time students. Financial award application deadline: 5/1; financial award applicants required to submit FAFSA. *Faculty research:* International business, business strategy, organizational culture/leadership, consumer behavior, services marketing. *Unit head:* Dr. Jill Austin, Chair, 615-898-2736, Fax: 615-898-5308, E-mail: jaustin@mtsu.edu.

Minnesota State University Mankato, College of Graduate Studies, College of Business, Mankato, MN 56001. Offers accounting and business law (MBA); finance (MBA); management (MBA); marketing and international business (MBA). *Accreditation:* AACSB. *Students:* 8 full-time (3 women), 32 part-time (13 women). *Entrance requirements:* For master's, GMAT, 2 letters of reference. Additional exam requirements/recommendations for international students: Required—TOEFL. *Application deadline:* For fall admission, 6/1 for domestic students; for spring admission, 10/1 for domestic students. Electronic applications accepted. *Unit head:* Scott Johnson, Dean, 507-389-5420.

Mississippi State University, College of Business and Industry, Graduate Studies in Business, Mississippi State, MS 39762. Offers business administration (MBA, PhD), including accounting (PhD), business information systems (PhD), finance (PhD), management (PhD), marketing (PhD); project management (MBA). *Accreditation:* AACSB. Part-time and evening/weekend programs available. Postbaccalaureate distance learning degree programs offered. *Faculty:* 66 full-time (18 women), 18 part-time/adjunct (9 women). *Students:* 143 full-time (52 women), 159 part-time (52 women); includes 30 minority (24 African Americans, 1 American Indian/Alaska Native, 2 Asian Americans or Pacific Islanders, 3 Hispanic Americans), 35 international. Average age 30. 605 applicants, 34% accepted, 142 enrolled. In 2006, 107 master's, 10 doctorates awarded. Terminal master's awarded for partial completion of doctoral program. *Degree requirements:* For doctorate, thesis/dissertation. *Entrance requirements:* For master's, GMAT, minimum GPA of 3.0 in last 60 hours of course work; for doctorate, GMAT, minimum GPA of 2.75 in last 60 undergraduate hours, 3.25 in last 60 graduate hours. Additional exam requirements/recommendations for international students: Required—TOEFL. *Application deadline:* For fall admission, 7/1 for domestic students; for spring admission, 11/1 for domestic students. Applications are processed on a rolling basis. Application fee: $30. Electronic applications accepted. *Expenses:* Tuition, state resident: full-time $4,550; part-time $253 per hour. Tuition, nonresident: full-time $10,552; part-time $584 per hour. International tuition: $10,882 full-time. Tuition and fees vary according to course load. *Financial support:* In 2006–07, 29 teaching assistantships with full tuition reimbursements (averaging $10,778 per year) were awarded; research assistantships with full tuition reimbursements, Federal Work-Study, institutionally sponsored loans, and unspecified assistantships also available. Financial award applicants required to submit FAFSA. *Unit head:* Dr. Barbara Spencer, Director, 662-325-1891, Fax: 662-325-8161, E-mail: gsb@cobilan.msstate.edu. *Application contact:* Dr. Phil Bonfanti, Director of Admissions, 662-325-4104, Fax: 662-325-8872, E-mail: admit@msstate.edu.

Montclair State University, The Graduate School, School of Business, Department of Marketing, Montclair, NJ 07043-1624. Offers MBA. Part-time and evening/weekend programs available. *Faculty:* 10 full-time (3 women), 2 part-time/adjunct (0 women). *Students:* 6 full-time (5 women), 28 part-time (16 women); includes 6 minority (1 American Indian/Alaska Native, 2 Asian Americans or Pacific Islanders, 3 Hispanic Americans), 3 international. 16 applicants, 31% accepted, 4 enrolled. In 2006, 16 degrees awarded. *Entrance requirements:* For master's, GMAT, 2 letters of recommendation, resumé. Additional exam requirements/recommendations for international students: Required—TOEFL (minimum score 83 computer-based). *Application deadline:* For fall admission, 6/1 for international students; for spring admission, 10/1 for international students. Applications are processed on a rolling basis. Application fee: $60. Electronic applications accepted. *Expenses:* Tuition, state resident: part-time $450 per credit. Tuition, nonresident: part-time $682 per credit. Tuition and fees vary according to degree level and program. *Financial support:* In 2006–07, 3 research assistantships with tuition reimbursements (averaging $7,000 per year) were awarded; Federal Work-Study, scholarships/grants, and unspecified assistantships also available. Support available to part-time students. Financial award application deadline: 3/1; financial award applicants required to submit FAFSA. *Unit head:* Dr. John McGuiness, Head, 973-655-4254. *Application contact:* Dr. Eileen Kaplan, Adviser, 973-655-7469, E-mail: kaplane@mail.montclair.edu.

New Mexico State University, Graduate School, College of Business, Department of Marketing, Las Cruces, NM 88003-8001. Offers business administration (PhD), including marketing. *Faculty:* 6 full-time (2 women). *Students:* 8 full-time (3 women), 5 international. Average age 34. 10 applicants, 50% accepted. *Degree requirements:* For doctorate, thesis/dissertation, comprehensive exam, registration. *Entrance requirements:* For doctorate, GMAT. Additional exam requirements/recommendations for international students: Required—TOEFL. *Application deadline:* For fall admission, 3/9 priority date for domestic and international students. *Financial support:* In 2006–07, 8 teaching assistantships were awarded; health care benefits also available. *Unit head:* Dr. Gerald M. Hampton, Head, 505-646-1444, Fax: 505-646-1498, E-mail: ghampton@nmsu.edu.

New York Institute of Technology, Ellis College, Old Westbury, NY 11568. Offers accounting and information systems (MBA); e-commerce (MBA); finance (MBA); global management (MBA); healthcare administration (MBA); human resources management (MBA); leadership (MBA); management of information systems (MBA); management of technology (MBA); marketing (MBA); professional accounting (MBA); project management (MBA); risk management (MBA); strategy and economics (MBA). Ellis College is a collaboration between New York Institute of Technology and UNext online learning company. Part-time and evening/weekend programs available. Postbaccalaureate distance learning degree programs offered (no on-campus study). *Entrance requirements:* For master's, interview. Additional exam requirements/recommendations for international students: Required—TOEFL (minimum score 550 paper-based; 213 computer-based). Electronic applications accepted. *Expenses:* Tuition: Full-time $16,800; part-time $700 per credit.

New York Institute of Technology, Graduate Division, School of Management, Program in Business Administration, Old Westbury, NY 11568-8000. Offers accounting (Advanced Certificate); business administration (MBA); finance (Advanced Certificate); international business (Advanced Certificate); management of information systems (Advanced Certificate); marketing (Advanced Certificate). Part-time and evening/weekend programs available. *Students:* 481 full-time (120 women), 1,300 part-time (670 women); includes 297 minority (153 African Americans, 6 American Indian/Alaska Native, 81 Asian Americans or Pacific Islanders, 57 Hispanic Americans), 215 international. Average age 29. 1,049 applicants, 87% accepted, 137 enrolled. In 2006, 917 degrees awarded. *Degree requirements:* For master's, thesis (for some programs). *Entrance requirements:* For master's, minimum QPA of 2.85. Additional exam requirements/recommendations for international students: Required—TOEFL (minimum score 550 paper-based; 213 computer-based). *Application deadline:* For fall admission, 7/1 priority date for domestic students; for spring admission, 12/1 priority date for domestic students. Applications are processed on a rolling basis. Application fee: $50. Electronic applications accepted. *Expenses:* Tuition: Full-time $16,800; part-time $700 per credit. *Financial support:* Fellowships, research assistantships with partial tuition reimbursements, institutionally sponsored loans, tuition waivers (full and partial), and unspecified assistantships available. Support available to part-time students. Financial award applicants required to submit FAFSA. *Faculty research:* Instructor performance appraisal; relationship between TOEFL, GMAT, GRE, and performance in foreign students. *Unit head:* Dr. Gurumurthy Kalyanuram, Director, 516-686-7972, E-mail: gkalyana@nyit.edu. *Application contact:* Jacquelyn Nealon, Dean of Admissions and Financial Aid, 516-686-7925, Fax: 516-686-7613, E-mail: jnealon@nyit.edu.

New York University, Leonard N. Stern School of Business, Department of Marketing, New York, NY 10012-1019. Offers entertainment, media and technology (MBA); general marketing (MBA); marketing (PhD); product management (MBA). *Expenses:* Tuition: Part-time $1,080 per unit. Required fees: $56 per unit. $329 per term. Tuition and fees vary according to program.

New York University, School of Continuing and Professional Studies, Center for Marketing, New York, NY 10012-1019. Offers direct and interactive marketing (MS); public relations and corporate communications (MS, Advanced Certificate), including corporate training (Advanced Certificate). Part-time programs available. *Faculty:* 1 full-time (0 women), 11 part-time/adjunct (3 women). *Students:* 20 full-time (16 women), 65 part-time (41 women); includes 15 minority (4 African Americans, 7 Asian Americans or Pacific Islanders, 4 Hispanic Americans), 22 international. Average age 30. 95 applicants, 27% accepted, 16 enrolled. In 2006, 11 degrees awarded. *Degree requirements:* For master's, thesis, capstone project, comprehensive exam. *Entrance requirements:* For master's, GRE General Test or GMAT, work experience, resumé, 2 letters of recommendation. Additional exam requirements/recommendations for international students: Required—TOEFL (minimum score 600 paper-based; 250 computer-based; 100 iBT), TWE. *Application deadline:* For fall admission, 3/15 priority date for domestic students, 4/1 priority date for international students; for spring admission, 10/15 priority date for domestic students, 8/15 priority date for international students. Applications are processed on a rolling basis. Application fee: $75. *Expenses:* Tuition: Part-time $1,080 per unit. Required fees: $56 per unit. $329 per term. Tuition and fees vary according to program. *Financial support:* In 2006–07, 80 students received support, including fellowships (averaging $1,547 per year); career-related internships or fieldwork and scholarships/grants also available. Support available to part-time students. Financial award application deadline: 3/1; financial award applicants required to submit FAFSA. *Faculty research:* Branding, database marketing, consumer behavior, customer loyalty/CRM and customer acquisition models. *Unit head:* Dr. Marjorie Kalter, Director, 212-992-3221, Fax: 212-992-3377, E-mail: mk99@nyu.edu. *Application contact:* Fadia Saint-Juste, Program Coordinator, 212-992-3221, Fax: 212-992-3377, E-mail: fs20@nyu.edu.

See Close-Up on page 653.

Northeastern Illinois University, Graduate College, College of Business and Management, Chicago, IL 60625-4699. Offers accounting (MBA); finance (MBA); management (MBA); marketing (MBA). Part-time and evening/weekend programs available. *Faculty:* 24 full-time (3 women), 13 part-time/adjunct (4 women). *Students:* 24 full-time (12 women), 40 part-time (16 women); includes 15 minority (4 African Americans, 8 Asian Americans or Pacific Islanders, 3 Hispanic Americans), 21 international. Average age 31. 23 applicants, 91% accepted. In 2006, 13 degrees awarded. *Degree requirements:* For master's, thesis optional. *Entrance requirements:* For master's, GMAT, minimum GPA of 2.75. Additional exam requirements/recommendations for international students: Required—TOEFL. *Application deadline:* For fall admission, 4/1 priority date for domestic students; for spring admission, 8/15 for domestic students. Applications are processed on a rolling basis. Application fee: $25. *Financial support:* In 2006–07, 20 students received support, including 8 research assistantships with full tuition reimbursements available (averaging $6,600 per year); career-related internships or fieldwork, Federal Work-Study, institutionally sponsored loans, and tuition waivers (full and partial) also available. Support available to part-time students. *Faculty research:* Perception of accountants and non-accountants toward future of the accounting industry, asynchronous learning outcomes, cost and efficiency of financial markets, impact of deregulation on airline industry, analysis of derivational instruments.

Northwestern University, The Graduate School, Kellogg School of Management, Department of Marketing, Evanston, IL 60208. Offers PhD. Admissions and degree offered through The Graduate School. *Degree requirements:* For doctorate, thesis/dissertation, comprehensive exam, registration. *Entrance requirements:* For doctorate, GMAT or GRE General Test. Additional exam requirements/recommendations for international students: Required—TOEFL. Electronic applications accepted. *Faculty research:* Choice models, database and high-tech marketing, consumer information processing, ethnographic analysis of consumption, psychometric analysis of consumer behavior.

Northwestern University, Medill School of Journalism, Integrated Marketing Communications Program, Evanston, IL 60208. Offers advertising/sales promotion (MSIMC); direct database and e-commerce marketing (MSIMC); general studies (MSIMC); public relations (MSIMC). Part-time programs available. *Entrance requirements:* For master's, GRE General Test or GMAT, full-time work experience (preferred). Additional exam requirements/recommendations for international students: Required—TOEFL. Electronic applications accepted. *Faculty research:* Data mining, business to business marketing, values in advertising, political advertising.

See Close-Up on page 655.

Oakland University, Graduate Study and Lifelong Learning, School of Business Administration, Department of Management and Marketing, Rochester, MI 48309-4401. Offers business administration (MBA); entrepreneurship (Certificate); general management (Certificate); human resource management (Certificate); international business (Certificate); marketing (Certificate). *Faculty:* 9 full-time (3 women), 2 part-time/adjunct (both women). *Students:* 61 full-time (25 women), 416 part-time (137 women); includes 72 minority (14 African Americans, 1 American Indian/Alaska Native, 46 Asian Americans or Pacific Islanders, 11 Hispanic Americans), 45 international. Average age 31. 121 applicants, 88% accepted, 65 enrolled. In 2006, 163 degrees awarded. Application fee: $35. *Expenses:* Tuition, state resident: full-time $9,936;

part-time $414 per credit. Tuition, nonresident: full-time $17,202; part-time $716 per credit. *Unit head:* Ravi Parameswaran, Chair, 238-370-3279, Fax: 249-370-4275.

Oklahoma City University, Meinders School of Business, Program in Business Administration, Oklahoma City, OK 73106-1402. Offers finance (MBA); health administration (MBA); information technology (MBA); integrated marketing communications (MBA); international business (MBA); marketing (MBA); JD/MBA. *Accreditation:* ACBSP. Part-time and evening/weekend programs available. *Faculty:* 30 full-time (7 women), 24 part-time/adjunct (5 women). *Students:* 291 full-time (112 women), 186 part-time (68 women); includes 57 minority (27 African Americans, 9 American Indian/Alaska Native, 12 Asian Americans or Pacific Islanders, 9 Hispanic Americans), 218 international. Average age 27. In 2006, 341 degrees awarded. *Degree requirements:* For master's, comprehensive exam. *Entrance requirements:* For master's, minimum GPA of 2.5. Additional exam requirements/recommendations for international students: Required—TOEFL (minimum score 510 paper-based). *Application deadline:* For fall admission, 8/22 for domestic students; for spring admission, 1/15 for domestic students. Applications are processed on a rolling basis. Application fee: $30 ($70 for international students). *Financial support:* Fellowships with partial tuition reimbursements, career-related internships or fieldwork, Federal Work-Study, institutionally sponsored loans, and tuition waivers (partial) available. Support available to part-time students. Financial award application deadline: 8/1. *Faculty research:* Management information systems, international business strategies. *Unit head:* Dr. Mahmood Shandiz, Head, 405-208-5130, Fax: 405-208-5098, E-mail: mshandiz@okcu.edu. *Application contact:* Leslie McKenzie, Director, Graduate Admissions, 800-633-7242, Fax: 405-208-5356, E-mail: gadmissions@okcu.edu.

Oklahoma State University, William S. Spears School of Business, Department of Marketing, Stillwater, OK 74078. Offers MBA, PhD. *Faculty:* 18 full-time (3 women), 9 part-time/adjunct (4 women). *Students:* 5 full-time (1 woman), 9 part-time (1 woman); includes 1 minority (American Indian/Alaska Native), 6 international. Average age 30. *Degree requirements:* For doctorate, thesis/dissertation. *Entrance requirements:* For master's and doctorate, GMAT. Additional exam requirements/recommendations for international students: Required—TOEFL. *Application deadline:* For fall admission, 7/1 priority date for domestic students, 3/1 priority date for international students; for spring admission, 8/1 priority date for international students. Applications are processed on a rolling basis. Application fee: $40 ($75 for international students). Electronic applications accepted. *Expenses:* Tuition, state resident: part-time $146 per credit hour. Tuition, nonresident: part-time $516 per credit hour. Required fees: $44 per credit hour. Tuition and fees vary according to program. *Financial support:* In 2006–07, research assistantships (averaging $18,667 per year), 8 teaching assistantships (averaging $18,667 per year) were awarded; career-related internships or fieldwork, Federal Work-Study, scholarships/grants, health care benefits, tuition waivers (partial), and unspecified assistantships also available. Support available to part-time students. Financial award application deadline: 3/1. *Faculty research:* Decision making (consumer, managerial, cross-functional), communication effects, services marketing, public policy and marketing, corporate image. *Unit head:* Dr. Joshua L. Wiener, Head, 405-744-5192.

Old Dominion University, College of Business and Public Administration, Doctoral Program in Business Administration, Norfolk, VA 23529. Offers finance (PhD); management (PhD); marketing (PhD). *Accreditation:* AACSB. *Faculty:* 20 full-time (2 women). *Students:* 21 full-time (7 women), 20 part-time (7 women); includes 4 minority (1 African American, 3 Asian Americans or Pacific Islanders), 28 international. Average age 35. 29 applicants, 59% accepted, 10 enrolled. In 2006, 5 degrees awarded. *Degree requirements:* For doctorate, thesis/dissertation, comprehensive exam. *Entrance requirements:* For doctorate, GMAT. Additional exam requirements/recommendations for international students: Required—TOEFL. *Application deadline:* For fall admission, 4/1 priority date for domestic and international students. Applications are processed on a rolling basis. Application fee: $40. Electronic applications accepted. *Expenses:* Tuition, area resident: Part-time $285 per credit hour. Tuition, nonresident: part-time $715 per credit hour. Required fees: $94 per semester. *Financial support:* In 2006–07, 11 research assistantships with full tuition reimbursements (averaging $11,500 per year), 9 teaching assistantships with full tuition reimbursements (averaging $11,500 per year) were awarded; fellowships, career-related internships or fieldwork and scholarships/grants also available. Financial award application deadline: 3/15; financial award applicants required to submit FAFSA. *Faculty research:* International business, buyer behavior, financial markets, strategy, operations research. *Unit head:* Dr. Sylvia C. Hudgins, Graduate Program Director, 757-683-3551, Fax: 757-683-4076, E-mail: shudgins@odu.edu.

See Close-Up on page 299.

Oral Roberts University, School of Business, Tulsa, OK 74171-0001. Offers accounting (MBA); finance (MBA); international business (MBA); management (MBA); marketing (MBA); non-profit management (M Man, MBA); organizational dynamics (M Man); sales marketing (M Man). *Accreditation:* ACBSP. Part-time programs available. Postbaccalaureate distance learning degree programs offered (minimal on-campus study). *Faculty:* 9 full-time (2 women), 4 part-time/adjunct (2 women). *Students:* 33 full-time (18 women), 67 part-time (28 women); includes 28 minority (17 African Americans, 3 American Indian/Alaska Native, 6 Asian Americans or Pacific Islanders, 2 Hispanic Americans), 15 international. Average age 29. 69 applicants, 84% accepted, 33 enrolled. In 2006, 21 degrees awarded. *Degree requirements:* For master's, thesis optional. *Entrance requirements:* For master's, minimum GPA of 3.0. Additional exam requirements/recommendations for international students: Required—TOEFL (minimum score 550 paper-based; 213 computer-based). *Application deadline:* For fall admission, 7/1 priority date for domestic students, 5/1 priority date for international students; for spring admission, 12/1 priority date for domestic students, 10/1 priority date for international students. Applications are processed on a rolling basis. Application fee: $35. *Expenses: Contact institution. Financial support:* In 2006–07, 9 research assistantships (averaging $3,600 per year) were awarded; scholarships/grants and unspecified assistantships also available. Financial award application deadline: 6/1; financial award applicants required to submit FAFSA. *Faculty research:* Non-profit, international business and marketing. *Unit head:* Dr. Mark Lewandowski, Dean, 918-495-7040, Fax: 918-495-7876, E-mail: mlewandowski@oru.edu. *Application contact:* 918-495-6989, Fax: 918-495-7965, E-mail: alsc@oru.edu.

Ottawa University, Graduate Studies-Arizona, Programs in Business, Ottawa, KS 66067-3399. Offers business administration (MBA); finance (MBA); human resources (MA, MBA); leadership (MBA); marketing (MBA). Programs offered in Mesa, Phoenix, Tempe and West Valley, AZ. Part-time and evening/weekend programs available. Postbaccalaureate distance learning degree programs offered. *Faculty:* 3 full-time (1 woman), 11 part-time/adjunct (3 women). *Students:* 5 full-time (1 woman), 125 part-time (73 women); includes 21 minority (7 African Americans, 1 American Indian/Alaska Native, 2 Asian Americans or Pacific Islanders, 11 Hispanic Americans), 5 international. Average age 39. In 2006, 42 degrees awarded. *Degree requirements:* For master's, thesis or alternative, registration. *Entrance requirements:* For master's, minimum undergraduate GPA of 3.0. Additional exam requirements/recommendations for international students: Required—TOEFL (minimum score 550 paper-based; 213 computer-based). *Application deadline:* For fall admission, 7/1 priority date for domestic students; for winter admission, 11/1 priority date for domestic students; for spring admission, 2/1 priority date for domestic students. Applications are processed on a rolling basis. Application fee: $50. Electronic applications accepted. *Unit head:* Dr. Tony Muscia, Director of Business Graduate Studies, 602-371-1188, E-mail: tony.muscia@ottawa.edu. *Application contact:* Sharon Lind, Advisement Assistant, 602-371-1188, Fax: 602-371-0035, E-mail: sharon.lind@ottawa.edu.

Pace University, Lubin School of Business, Marketing Program, New York, NY 10038. Offers marketing management (MBA); marketing research (MBA). Part-time and evening/weekend programs available. *Faculty:* 8 full-time, 12 part-time/adjunct. *Students:* 25 full-time (15 women), 86 part-time (46 women); includes 16 minority (3 African Americans, 8 Asian Americans or Pacific Islanders, 5 Hispanic Americans), 39 international. Average age 28. 180 applicants, 54% accepted, 38 enrolled. In 2006, 53 degrees awarded. *Entrance requirements:* For master's, GMAT. *Application deadline:* For fall admission, 7/31 priority date for domestic students; for spring admission, 11/30 for domestic students. Applications are processed on a rolling basis. Application fee: $65. Electronic applications accepted. *Expenses:* Tuition: Part-time $890 per credit. *Financial support:* Research assistantships, career-related internships or fieldwork and Federal Work-Study available. Support available to part-time students. Financial award applicants required to submit FAFSA. *Unit head:* Dr. Martin Topol, Chairperson, 212-346-1827. *Application contact:* Joanna Broda, Director of Admissions, 212-346-1652, Fax: 212-346-1585, E-mail: gradnyc@pace.edu.

Penn State University Park, Graduate School, The Mary Jean and Frank P. Smeal College of Business Administration, State College, University Park, PA 16802-1503. Offers accounting (PhD); business administration (MBA); finance (PhD); management and organization (PhD); management science/operations/logistics (PhD); marketing (PhD); real estate (PhD); supply chain and information systems (PhD). *Students:* 287 full-time (79 women), 5 part-time (2 women); includes 39 minority (22 African Americans, 11 Asian Americans or Pacific Islanders, 6 Hispanic Americans), 93 international. Average age 31. 841 applicants, 31% accepted, 150 enrolled. In 2006, 107 master's, 11 doctorates awarded. *Expenses: Contact institution. Financial support:* In 2006–07, 1 fellowship, 11 research assistantships, 143 teaching assistantships were awarded. Financial award applicants required to submit FAFSA. *Unit head:* Dr. Kenneth B. Thomas, Dean, 814-863-0448, Fax: 814-865-7064, E-mail: j2t@psu.edu.

Philadelphia University, School of Business Administration, Program in Business Administration, Philadelphia, PA 19144-5497. Offers business administration (MBA); finance (MBA); health care management (MBA); international business (MBA); marketing (MBA); MBA/MS. Part-time and evening/weekend programs available. Postbaccalaureate distance learning degree programs offered (no on-campus study). *Faculty:* 10 full-time (2 women), 8 part-time/adjunct (0 women). *Students:* 43 full-time (24 women), 87 part-time (45 women); includes 3 Asian Americans or Pacific Islanders. 154 applicants, 56% accepted, 37 enrolled. In 2006, 85 degrees awarded. *Entrance requirements:* For master's, GMAT. Additional exam requirements/recommendations for international students: Required—TOEFL (minimum score 550 paper-based; 213 computer-based; 79 iBT). *Application deadline:* Applications are processed on a rolling basis. Application fee: $35. *Financial support:* In 2006–07, research assistantships with full tuition reimbursements (averaging $2,500 per year); career-related internships or fieldwork, Federal Work-Study, scholarships/grants, and unspecified assistantships also available. Support available to part-time students. Financial award applicants required to submit FAFSA. *Unit head:* MarySheila McDonald, Assistant Dean for Graduate Programs, 215-951-2950, Fax: 215-951-2653, E-mail: mcdonaldm@philau.edu. *Application contact:* Jack A. Klett, Director of Graduate Admissions, 215-951-2943, Fax: 215-951-2907, E-mail: gradadm@philau.edu.

Pontifical Catholic University of Puerto Rico, College of Business Administration, Ponce, PR 00717-0777. Offers accounting (MBA); business administration (PhD); finance (MBA); general business (MBA); human resources (MBA); international business (MBA); management (MBA); management information systems (MBA); marketing (MBA); office administration (MBA). Part-time and evening/weekend programs available. *Degree requirements:* For master's, thesis/dissertation; for doctorate, thesis/dissertation, comprehensive exam. *Entrance requirements:* For master's, GRE, interview, minimum GPA of 2.75; for doctorate, 2 letters of recommendation, 2 years experience in a related field, interview.

Purdue University, Graduate School, Krannert School of Management, Department of Management, West Lafayette, IN 47907. Offers accounting (PhD); business administration (MBA); finance (PhD); management information systems (PhD); marketing (PhD); operations management (PhD); quantitative methods (PhD); strategic management (PhD). *Students:* 56 full-time (21 women); includes 5 minority (3 Asian Americans or Pacific Islanders, 2 Hispanic Americans), 41 international. Average age 30. 421 applicants, 7% accepted, 19 enrolled. In 2006, 11 degrees awarded. *Median time to degree:* Doctorate–5 years full-time. Of those who began their doctoral program in fall 1998, 98% received their degree in 8 years or less. *Degree requirements:* For doctorate, thesis/dissertation, comprehensive exam, registration. *Entrance requirements:* For master's and doctorate, GMAT. Additional exam requirements/recommendations for international students: Required—TOEFL (minimum score 575 paper-based; 233 computer-based; 77 iBT), IELTS (minimum score 7). *Application deadline:* For fall admission, 2/15 for domestic and international students. Application fee: $55. Electronic applications accepted. *Financial support:* In 2006–07, 7 fellowships with partial tuition reimbursements (averaging $16,800 per year), 79 research assistantships with partial tuition reimbursements (averaging $16,800 per year), 8 teaching assistantships with partial tuition reimbursements (averaging $16,800 per year) were awarded; scholarships/grants and unspecified assistantships also available. Financial award application deadline: 2/15; financial award applicants required to submit FAFSA. *Faculty research:* Corporate finance, international business, enterprise integration. *Unit head:* Dr. John M. Barron, Head, 765-494-4451, Fax: 765-494-1526. *Application contact:* Kelly Felty, Assistant Director of Administration for Doctoral Programs, 765-494-4375, Fax: 765-494-1526, E-mail: phd@krannert.purdue.edu.

Quinnipiac University, School of Business, Program in Business Administration, Hamden, CT 06518-1940. Offers accounting (MBA); economics (MBA); finance (MBA); healthcare management (MBA); information systems management (MBA); international business (MBA); management (MBA); marketing (MBA); JD/MBA. *Accreditation:* AACSB. Part-time and evening/weekend programs available. *Faculty:* 16 full-time (2 women), 2 part-time/adjunct (1 woman). *Students:* 53 full-time (21 women), 112 part-time (48 women); includes 13 minority (2 African Americans, 1 American Indian/Alaska Native, 4 Asian Americans or Pacific Islanders, 6 Hispanic Americans), 7 international. Average age 26. 80 applicants, 65% accepted, 34 enrolled. In 2006, 73 degrees awarded. *Median time to degree:* Master's–1.5 years full-time, 2.5 years part-time. *Entrance requirements:* For master's, GMAT, minimum GPA of 3.0. Additional exam requirements/recommendations for international students: Required—TOEFL (minimum score 575 paper-based; 233 computer-based; 90 iBT), IELTS (minimum score 7). *Application deadline:* For fall admission, 7/30 priority date for domestic students, 5/30 priority date for international students; for spring admission, 12/15 priority date for domestic students, 10/15 priority date for international students. Applications are processed on a rolling basis. Application fee: $45. Electronic applications accepted. *Expenses:* Tuition: Part-time $675 per credit. Required fees: $30 per credit. *Financial support:* Tuition waivers (partial) and unspecified assistantships available. Support available to part-time students. Financial award application deadline: 4/15; financial award applicants required to submit FAFSA. *Faculty research:* Equity compensation, marketing relationships and public policy, corporate governance, international business. *Unit head:* Kevin B. Taylor, Director, 203-582-3676, Fax: 203-582-8664, E-mail: mba@quinnipiac.edu. *Application contact:* 800-462-1944, Fax: 203-582-3443, E-mail: graduate@quinnipiac.edu.

See Close-Up on page 311.

Regis University, School for Professional Studies, Program in Business, Denver, CO 80221-1099. Offers accounting (MS); business administration (MBA); finance (MBA); finance and accounting (MBA); international business (MBA); marketing (MBA); operations management (MBA); organization leadership (MS); project management (Certificate); technical management (Certificate). Offered at Colorado Springs Campus, Northwest Denver Campus, Southeast Denver Campus, Fort Collins Campus, Broomfield Campus, Henderson (Nevada) Campus, and Summerlin (Nevada) Campus. Part-time and evening/weekend programs available. Postbaccalaureate distance learning degree programs offered (no on-campus study). *Faculty:* 16 full-time (4 women), 82 part-time/adjunct (22 women). *Students:* 1,770 (834 women). Average age 36. In 2006, 560 degrees awarded. *Degree requirements:* For master's, capstone project, thesis optional. *Entrance requirements:* For master's, GMAT, interview, 2 years of full-time business work experience; for Certificate, GMAT. Additional exam requirements/recommendations for international students: Required—TOEFL or university-based test. *Application deadline:* For fall admission, 8/22 for domestic and international students; for winter admission, 1/2 for domestic and international students; for spring admission, 4/30 for domestic and international students. Applications are processed on a rolling basis. Application fee: $75. Electronic applications accepted. *Financial support:* Federal Work-Study available. Support

Regis University (continued)

available to part-time students. Financial award applicants required to submit FAFSA. *Unit head:* Dr. Michael Goess, Chair, 303-458-4302, Fax: 303-964-5538. *Application contact:* 800-677-9270 Ext. 4080, Fax: 303-964-5538, E-mail: masters@regis.edu.

Rensselaer Polytechnic Institute, Graduate School, Lally School of Management and Technology, Program in Management and Technology, Troy, NY 12180-3590. Offers finance (MBA, MS); financial technology (MS); management (PhD); management information systems (MBA, MS); new product development and marketing (MBA); new production and operations management (MS); product development and marketing (MS); production and operations management (MBA); technical commercialization (MS); technological entrepreneurship (MBA, MS). Part-time and evening/weekend programs available. Postbaccalaureate distance learning degree programs offered (no on-campus study). *Faculty:* 50 full-time (9 women), 1 part-time/adjunct (0 women). *Students:* 121 full-time (62 women), 525 part-time (184 women); includes 137 minority (43 African Americans, 60 Asian Americans or Pacific Islanders, 34 Hispanic Americans), 71 international. Average age 28. 416 applicants, 70% accepted, 240 enrolled. In 2006, 215 master's, 6 doctorates awarded. *Median time to degree:* Of those who began their doctoral program in fall 1998, 25% received their degree in 8 years or less. *Degree requirements:* For doctorate, thesis/dissertation. *Entrance requirements:* For master's, GMAT, resumé, 2 letters of recommendation; for doctorate, GMAT or GRE General Test, 2 letters of recommendation. Additional exam requirements/recommendations for international students: Required—TOEFL (minimum score 600 paper-based; 250 computer-based; 100 iBT); Recommended—IELTS (minimum score 7). *Application deadline:* For fall admission, 3/15 priority date for domestic and international students. Applications are processed on a rolling basis. Application fee: $75. Electronic applications accepted. *Expenses:* Tuition: Full-time $32,600; part-time $1,358 per credit. Required fees: $1,629. *Financial support:* In 2006–07, 48 students received support; fellowships with partial tuition reimbursements available, research assistantships with partial tuition reimbursements available, teaching assistantships with partial tuition reimbursements available, career-related internships or fieldwork, institutionally sponsored loans, and scholarships/grants available. Financial award application deadline: 3/15; financial award applicants required to submit FAFSA. *Faculty research:* Technological entrepreneurship, operations management, new product development and marketing, information systems, finance. Total annual research expenditures: $24,747. *Unit head:* Pedro Gonzalez, Director MBA/Admissons and Career Services, 518-276-2378, Fax: 518-276-2665, E-mail: gonzap3@rpi.edu. *Application contact:* Michele M. Martens, Manager of Graduate Programs, 518-276-6586, Fax: 518-276-2665, E-mail: martem@rpi.edu.

See Close-Up on page 313.

Roberts Wesleyan College, Division of Business, Rochester, NY 14624-1997. Offers nonprofit leadership (Certificate); strategic leadership (MS); strategic marketing (MS). Evening/weekend programs available. *Faculty:* 3 full-time (0 women), 13 part-time/adjunct (3 women). *Students:* 57 full-time (28 women). Average age 34. 45 applicants, 89% accepted. In 2006, 26 degrees awarded. *Degree requirements:* For master's, thesis or alternative. *Entrance requirements:* For master's, GMAT, minimum GPA of 2.75, verifiable work experience. *Application deadline:* Applications are processed on a rolling basis. Application fee: $35. *Expenses: Contact institution. Financial support:* In 2006–07, 15 students received support. Applicants required to submit FAFSA. *Unit head:* Dr. Steven Bovee, Chair, 716-594-6571, Fax: 716-594-6316, E-mail: bovees@roberts.edu.

Rutgers, The State University of New Jersey, Newark, Graduate School, Program in Management, Newark, NJ 07102. Offers accounting (PhD); accounting information systems (PhD); computer information systems (PhD); finance (PhD); information technology (PhD); international business (PhD); management science (PhD); marketing (PhD); organization management (PhD). *Accreditation:* AACSB. *Faculty:* 101 full-time (16 women), 3 part-time/adjunct (1 woman). *Students:* 60 full-time (29 women), 32 part-time (17 women); includes 57 minority (6 African Americans, 49 Asian Americans or Pacific Islanders, 2 Hispanic Americans). 279 applicants, 13% accepted, 32 enrolled. In 2006, 10 degrees awarded. *Degree requirements:* For doctorate, thesis/dissertation, cumulative exams. *Entrance requirements:* For doctorate, GMAT or GRE, minimum undergraduate B average. Additional exam requirements/recommendations for international students: Required—TOEFL. *Application deadline:* For fall admission, 4/1 for domestic students; for spring admission, 11/1 for domestic students. Applications are processed on a rolling basis. Application fee: $50. Electronic applications accepted. *Financial support:* In 2006–07, 8 fellowships with full and partial tuition reimbursements (averaging $18,000 per year), 7 research assistantships with full tuition reimbursements (averaging $18,347 per year), teaching assistantships with full tuition reimbursements (averaging $18,347 per year) were awarded; institutionally sponsored loans and tuition waivers (full and partial) also available. Support available to part-time students. Financial award application deadline: 2/15. *Faculty research:* Technology management, leadership and teams, consumer behavior, financial and markets, logistics. *Unit head:* Dr. Glenn Shafer, Director, 973-353-1604, Fax: 973-353-5691, E-mail: gshafer@rbs.rutgers.edu. *Application contact:* Goncalo Filipe, Senior Academic Coordinator, 973-353-1002, Fax: 973-353-5691, E-mail: gfilipe@rbsmail.rutgers.edu.

Rutgers, The State University of New Jersey, Newark, Rutgers Business School: Graduate Programs-Newark/New Brunswick, Department of Marketing, Newark, NJ 07102. Offers MBA. *Entrance requirements:* For master's, GMAT. Additional exam requirements/recommendations for international students: Required—TOEFL.

Sage Graduate School, Graduate School, Division of Management, Communications and Legal Studies, Program in Business Administration, Troy, NY 12180-4115. Offers business strategy (MBA); finance (MBA); human resources (MBA); marketing (MBA); JD/MBA; MBA/MS. Part-time and evening/weekend programs available. *Faculty:* 3 full-time (1 woman), 4 part-time/adjunct (2 women). *Students:* 9 full-time (5 women), 60 part-time (35 women); includes 10 minority (7 African Americans, 3 Hispanic Americans), 2 international. Average age 31. 58 applicants, 67% accepted, 27 enrolled. In 2006, 12 degrees awarded. *Entrance requirements:* For master's, minimum GPA of 2.75. Additional exam requirements/recommendations for international students: Required—TOEFL (minimum score 550 paper-based; 213 computer-based). *Application deadline:* Applications are processed on a rolling basis. Application fee: $40. *Expenses:* Tuition: Full-time $9,270; part-time $515 per credit hour. *Financial support:* Career-related internships or fieldwork, scholarships/grants, and unspecified assistantships available. Support available to part-time students. Financial award application deadline: 3/1; financial award applicants required to submit FAFSA. *Unit head:* Dr. David Kiner, Director, 518-292-1761, E-mail: kinerd@sage.edu. *Application contact:* Shannon K. Easton, Director of Graduate and Adult Admission, 518-244-2443, Fax: 518-244-6880, E-mail: sgsadm@sage.edu.

St. Bonaventure University, School of Graduate Studies, School of Business, St. Bonaventure, NY 14778-2284. Offers accounting (Adv C); accounting and finance (MBA); finance (Adv C); management (Adv C); management and marketing (MBA); marketing (Adv C); professional leadership (Adv C). *Accreditation:* AACSB. Part-time and evening/weekend programs available. *Entrance requirements:* For master's, GMAT. Additional exam requirements/recommendations for international students: Required—TOEFL. *Faculty research:* Stock options, small business, market relationships, auditing, taxes.

St. Cloud State University, School of Graduate Studies, G.R. Herberger College of Business, St. Cloud, MN 56301-4498. Offers management and finance (MBA), including finance; marketing and general business (MBA), including marketing. *Accreditation:* AACSB. Part-time and evening/weekend programs available. *Faculty:* 62 full-time (17 women), 4 part-time/adjunct (1 woman). *Students:* 35 full-time (11 women), 98 part-time (39 women); includes 9 minority (5 African Americans, 1 American Indian/Alaska Native, 3 Asian Americans or Pacific Islanders), 21 international. 67 applicants, 84% accepted. In 2006, 87 degrees awarded. *Degree requirements:* For master's, thesis or alternative. *Entrance requirements:* For master's, GMAT, minimum GPA of 2.75. Additional exam requirements/recommendations for international students: Required—MELAB; Recommended—TOEFL (minimum score 550 paper-based; 213 computer-based), IELTS (minimum score 7). *Application deadline:* For fall admission, 6/1 priority date for domestic students, 4/1 for international students; for spring admission, 10/1 priority date for domestic students, 8/1 for international students. Applications are processed on a rolling basis. Application fee: $35. Electronic applications accepted. *Expenses: Contact institution. Financial support:* Federal Work-Study, scholarships/grants, and unspecified assistantships available. Financial award application deadline: 3/1. *Unit head:* Dr. P.N. Subba, Graduate Director, 320-308-3212. *Application contact:* Linda Lou Krueger, School of Graduate Studies, 320-308-2113, Fax: 320-308-5371, E-mail: lekrueger@stcloudstate.edu.

St. Edward's University, School of Management and Business, Area of Business Administration, Austin, TX 78704. Offers accounting (MBA); business management (MBA); entrepreneurship (MBA, Certificate); finance—general (MBA, Certificate); global business (MBA, Certificate); human resource management (MBA, Certificate); management information systems (MBA, Certificate); marketing (MBA, Certificate); operations management (MBA, Certificate); personal financial planner (MBA, Certificate); sports management (MBA). Part-time and evening/weekend programs available. *Students:* 32 full-time (16 women), 394 part-time (195 women); includes 117 minority (23 African Americans, 2 American Indian/Alaska Native, 28 Asian Americans or Pacific Islanders, 64 Hispanic Americans), 21 international. Average age 33. 121 applicants, 74% accepted, 72 enrolled. In 2006, 142 degrees awarded. *Degree requirements:* For master's, minimum 24 resident hours. *Entrance requirements:* For master's, GMAT or GRE General Test, minimum GPA of 2.75 in last 60 hours of course work. Additional exam requirements/recommendations for international students: Required—TOEFL (minimum score 550 paper-based; 213 computer-based; 79 iBT). *Application deadline:* For fall admission, 8/1 for domestic students, 7/1 for international students; for spring admission, 12/1 for domestic students, 11/1 for international students. Applications are processed on a rolling basis. Application fee: $45 ($50 for international students). Electronic applications accepted. *Expenses:* Tuition: Full-time $11,682; part-time $649 per credit hour. Full-time tuition and fees vary according to course load and program. *Financial support:* In 2006–07, 4 students received support. Scholarships/grants available. Financial award applicants required to submit FAFSA. *Faculty research:* Operations management, minority entrepreneurship, globalization, professional services marketing. *Unit head:* Dr. Dianne Hill, Director, 512-428-1295, Fax: 512-448-8492, E-mail: dianneh@stedwards.edu. *Application contact:* Natalia Quintanilla, Graduate Admissions Coordinator, 512-233-1697, Fax: 512-428-1032, E-mail: nataliaq@stedwards.edu.

St. John's University, The Peter J. Tobin College of Business, Department of Marketing, Queens, NY 11439. Offers MBA, Adv C. Part-time and evening/weekend programs available. *Faculty:* 9 full-time (2 women), 4 part-time/adjunct (0 women). *Students:* 32 full-time (18 women), 42 part-time (20 women); includes 10 minority (4 African Americans, 3 Asian Americans or Pacific Islanders, 3 Hispanic Americans), 29 international. Average age 26. 100 applicants, 45% accepted, 0 enrolled. In 2006, 36 degrees awarded. *Degree requirements:* For master's, thesis optional. *Entrance requirements:* For master's, GMAT, minimum GPA of 3.0. Additional exam requirements/recommendations for international students: Required—TOEFL (minimum score 500 paper-based; 173 computer-based). *Application deadline:* For fall admission, 5/1 priority date for domestic and international students; for spring admission, 11/1 priority date for domestic and international students. Applications are processed on a rolling basis. Application fee: $40. Electronic applications accepted. *Expenses: Contact institution.* Tuition and fees vary according to program. *Financial support:* Research assistantships, scholarships/grants available. Support available to part-time students. Financial award application deadline: 3/1; financial award applicants required to submit FAFSA. *Unit head:* Dr. John Dobbins, Chair, 718-990-6391, E-mail: dobbinsj@stjohns.edu. *Application contact:* Nicole T. Bryan, Assistant Dean, 718-990-2599, Fax: 718-990-5242, E-mail: mbaadmissions@stjohns.edu.

Saint Joseph's University, Erivan K. Haub School of Business, Executive Master's in Food Marketing Program, Philadelphia, PA 19131-1395. Offers MBA, MS. Part-time and evening/weekend programs available. *Faculty:* 5 full-time (1 woman), 5 part-time/adjunct (0 women). *Students:* 1 full-time (0 women), 54 part-time (23 women); includes 2 African Americans, 3 Asian Americans or Pacific Islanders, 1 Hispanic American. Average age 36. In 2006, 18 degrees awarded. *Entrance requirements:* For master's, 4 years of industry experience, interview or GMAT, 2 letters of recommendation, resumé. Additional exam requirements/recommendations for international students: Required—TOEFL (minimum score 550 paper-based; 213 computer-based). *Application deadline:* For fall admission, 7/15 priority date for domestic students, 4/15 for international students; for spring admission, 11/15 priority date for domestic students, 10/15 for international students. Applications are processed on a rolling basis. Application fee: $65. Electronic applications accepted. *Financial support:* In 2006–07, 1 student received support, including research assistantships with partial tuition reimbursements available (averaging $4,000 per year), teaching assistantships (averaging $4,000 per year); fellowships, institutionally sponsored loans, tuition waivers (partial), and unspecified assistantships also available. Financial award applicants required to submit FAFSA. *Faculty research:* Marketing strategy, obesity, business ethics, bio-defense, international food marketing. *Unit head:* Christine Hartmann, Director, 610-660-1659, Fax: 610-660-3153, E-mail: chartman@sju.edu. *Application contact:* Amanda McCabe, Program Administrator, 610-660-3151, Fax: 610-660-3153, E-mail: amccabe@sju.edu.

Saint Joseph's University, Erivan K. Haub School of Business, Executive Pharmaceutical Marketing MBA Program, Philadelphia, PA 19131-1395. Offers MBA, Post Master's Certificate. Part-time and evening/weekend programs available. Postbaccalaureate distance learning degree programs offered (minimal on-campus study). *Faculty:* 3 full-time (1 woman), 5 part-time/adjunct (1 woman). *Students:* 2 full-time (0 women), 114 part-time (53 women); includes 13 African Americans, 3 Hispanic Americans, 1 international. Average age 36. 125 applicants, 92% accepted, 115 enrolled. In 2006, 38 degrees awarded. *Entrance requirements:* For master's, GMAT, 4 years of industry experience, letter of recommendation, resumé. Additional exam requirements/recommendations for international students: Required—TOEFL (minimum score 550 paper-based; 213 computer-based). *Application deadline:* For fall admission, 7/15 for domestic students, 4/15 for international students; for spring admission, 11/15 for domestic students, 10/15 for international students. Applications are processed on a rolling basis. Application fee: $65. Electronic applications accepted. *Financial support:* In 2006–07, 4 students received support. Tuition waivers (partial) available. Financial award applicants required to submit FAFSA. *Faculty research:* Pharmaceutical strategy, internet and pharmaceuticals, pharmaceutical promotion. *Unit head:* Terese W. Waldron, Director, 610-660-3150, Fax: 610-660-5160, E-mail: twaldron@sju.edu. *Application contact:* Christine Anderson, Administrator, 610-660-3157, Fax: 610-660-3160.

See Close-Up on page 657.

Saint Joseph's University, Erivan K. Haub School of Business, Professional MBA Program, Program in International Marketing, Philadelphia, PA 19131-1395. Offers MBA. Part-time and evening/weekend programs available. *Entrance requirements:* For master's, GMAT, 2 letters of recommendation, resumé. Additional exam requirements/recommendations for international students: Required—TOEFL. *Application deadline:* Applications are processed on a rolling basis. Application fee: $35. Electronic applications accepted. *Financial support:* Unspecified assistantships available. Financial award application deadline: 5/1. *Unit head:* Christine Kaczmar-Russo, Director, 610-660-1238, Fax: 610-660-3239, E-mail: ckaczmar@sju.edu.

Saint Joseph's University, Erivan K. Haub School of Business, Professional MBA Program, Program in Marketing, Philadelphia, PA 19131-1395. Offers MBA. Part-time and evening/weekend programs available. *Faculty:* 3 full-time (1 woman), 3 part-time/adjunct (1 woman). *Students:* 6 full-time (3 women), 43 part-time (30 women); includes 6 minority (4 African Americans, 1 Asian American or Pacific Islander, 1 Hispanic American), 3 international. Average age 29. In 2006, 11 degrees awarded. *Entrance requirements:* For master's, GMAT, 2 letters of recommendation, resumé. Additional exam requirements/recommendations for international students: Required—TOEFL (minimum score 550 paper-based; 213 computer-based). *Application deadline:* For fall admission, 7/15 for domestic students, 4/15 for international students; for spring admission, 11/15 for domestic students, 10/15 for international students. Applications are processed on a rolling basis. Application fee: $35. *Financial support:* In 2006–07, research assistantships with partial tuition reimbursements (averaging $2,000 per year); unspecified assistantships also available. Financial award application deadline: 5/1. *Unit head:* Dr. Diane Phillips, Chair, 610-660-3232.

Saint Joseph's University, Erivan K. Haub School of Business, Program in International Marketing, Philadelphia, PA 19131-1395. Offers MS. Part-time and evening/weekend programs available. *Faculty:* 3 full-time (1 woman), 3 part-time/adjunct (1 woman). *Students:* 22 full-time (11 women), 19 part-time (14 women); includes 6 minority (2 Asian Americans or Pacific Islanders, 4 Hispanic Americans), 5 international. Average age 26. In 2006, 17 degrees awarded. *Entrance requirements:* For master's, GMAT, 2 letters of recommendation, resumé. Additional exam requirements/recommendations for international students: Required—TOEFL (minimum score 550 paper-based; 213 computer-based). *Application deadline:* For fall admission, 7/15 priority date for domestic students; for spring admission, 11/15 for domestic students. Applications are processed on a rolling basis. Application fee: $35. Electronic applications accepted. *Financial support:* In 2006–07, 5 students received support, including research assistantships with partial tuition reimbursements available (averaging $2,000 per year); career-related internships or fieldwork, Federal Work-Study, institutionally sponsored loans, and unspecified assistantships also available. Financial award application deadline: 5/15; financial award applicants required to submit FAFSA. *Faculty research:* Export marketing, international marketing research, global marketing. *Unit head:* Christine Kaczmar-Russo, Director, 610-660-1238, Fax: 610-660-3239, E-mail: ckaczmar@sju.edu.

Saint Peter's College, MBA Programs, Jersey City, NJ 07306-5997. Offers finance (MBA); international business (MBA); management (MBA); management information systems (MBA); marketing (MBA); MBA/MS. Part-time and evening/weekend programs available. *Degree requirements:* For master's, exit presentation. *Entrance requirements:* For master's, GMAT or MAT. *Faculty research:* International finance, operations research, expert systems, networking, decision support systems.

St. Thomas Aquinas College, Division of Business Administration, Sparkill, NY 10976. Offers business administration (MBA); finance (MBA); management (MBA); marketing (MBA). Part-time and evening/weekend programs available. *Entrance requirements:* For master's, GMAT. Additional exam requirements/recommendations for international students: Required—TOEFL. Electronic applications accepted.

Saint Xavier University, Graduate Studies, Graham School of Management, Chicago, IL 60655-3105. Offers e-commerce (MBA); employee health benefits (Certificate); finance (MBA, MS); financial analysis and investments (MBA); financial planning (MBA, Certificate); financial trading and practice (MBA, Certificate); generalist/administration (MBA); health administration (MBA, MS); managed care (Certificate); management (MBA, MS); marketing (MBA); public and non-profit management (MBA); public health (MPH); service management (MBA); training and performance management (MBA); MBA/MS. *Accreditation:* ACBSP. Part-time and evening/weekend programs available. *Faculty:* 27. *Students:* 67 full-time (32 women), 291 part-time (152 women). Average age 35. In 2006, 61 degrees awarded. *Entrance requirements:* For master's, GMAT, minimum GPA of 3.0, 2 years of work experience. *Application deadline:* For fall admission, 8/15 for domestic students. Applications are processed on a rolling basis. Application fee: $35. Electronic applications accepted. *Expenses:* Contact institution. *Financial support:* Career-related internships or fieldwork available. Support available to part-time students. Financial award applicants required to submit FAFSA. *Unit head:* Dr. John Eber, Dean, 773-298-3601, Fax: 773-298-3601, E-mail: eber@sxu.edu. *Application contact:* Beth Gierach, Managing Director of Admission, 773-298-3053, Fax: 773-298-3076, E-mail: gierach@sxu.edu.

San Diego State University, Graduate and Research Affairs, College of Business Administration, Department of Marketing, San Diego, CA 92182. Offers MS. Part-time and evening/weekend programs available. *Students:* 39 full-time (29 women), 21 part-time (14 women); includes 5 minority (1 American Indian/Alaska Native, 3 Asian Americans or Pacific Islanders, 1 Hispanic American), 23 international. Average age 30. 39 applicants, 69% accepted, 13 enrolled. In 2006, 20 degrees awarded. *Degree requirements:* For master's, thesis or alternative. *Entrance requirements:* For master's, GMAT, resumé, letters of reference. Additional exam requirements/recommendations for international students: Required—TOEFL. *Application deadline:* For fall admission, 4/15 for domestic and international students; for spring admission, 11/1 for domestic students, 10/1 for international students. Applications are processed on a rolling basis. Application fee: $55. Electronic applications accepted. *Financial support:* In 2006–07, 7 teaching assistantships were awarded; fellowships, research assistantships, career-related internships or fieldwork also available. Financial award applicants required to submit FAFSA. Total annual research expenditures: $22,000. *Unit head:* George E. Belch, Chair, 619-594-5317, Fax: 619-594-1573, E-mail: gbelch@mail.sdsu.edu. *Application contact:* Information Contact, E-mail: sdsumba@mail.sdsu.edu.

Seton Hall University, Stillman School of Business, Programs in Business Administration, South Orange, NJ 07079-2697. Offers accounting (MBA); finance (MBA); financial markets, institutions and instruments (MBA); healthcare management (MBA); information systems (MBA); international business (MBA); management (MBA); marketing (MBA); pharmaceutical management (MBA); sport management (MBA). Part-time and evening/weekend programs available. *Faculty:* 57 full-time (13 women), 30 part-time/adjunct (3 women). *Students:* 57 full-time (16 women), 180 part-time (57 women); includes 9 African Americans, 10 Asian Americans or Pacific Islanders, 7 Hispanic Americans. Average age 29. 195 applicants, 47% accepted, 48 enrolled. In 2006, 144 degrees awarded. *Median time to degree:* Master's–1.6 years full-time, 2.3 years part-time. *Degree requirements:* For master's, 20 hours of community service (Social Responsibility Project). *Entrance requirements:* For master's, GMAT, minimum GPA of 2.75. Additional exam requirements/recommendations for international students: Required—TOEFL (minimum score 550 paper-based; 213 computer-based). *Application deadline:* For fall admission, 6/1 priority date for domestic students; for spring admission, 11/1 priority date for domestic students. Applications are processed on a rolling basis. Application fee: $75 ($100 for international students). Electronic applications accepted. *Financial support:* In 2006–07, 40 students received support, including research assistantships with full and partial tuition reimbursements available (averaging $5,400 per year); career-related internships or fieldwork, Federal Work-Study, scholarships/grants, and unspecified assistantships also available. Support available to part-time students. Financial award application deadline: 6/1; financial award applicants required to submit FAFSA. *Faculty research:* Financial, hedge funds, international business, legal issues, disclosure and branding. *Unit head:* Dr. Joyce A. Strawser, Associate Dean for Undergraduate and MBA Curricula, 973-761-9225, Fax: 973-761-9217, E-mail: strawsjo@shu.edu. *Application contact:* Catherine Bianchi, Director of Graduate Admissions, 973-761-9220, Fax: 973-761-9208, E-mail: biancha@shu.edu.

Simon Fraser University, Graduate Studies, Faculty of Business Administration, Burnaby, BC V5A 1S6, Canada. Offers business administration (EMBA); decision support systems (MBA); international business (MBA); management, organization studies (MBA); marketing (MBA); MBA/MRM. *Accreditation:* AACSB. Postbaccalaureate distance learning degree programs offered. *Degree requirements:* For master's, thesis or written project. *Entrance requirements:* For master's, minimum GPA of 3.0. Additional exam requirements/recommendations for international students: Required—TOEFL. Expenses: Contact institution. *Faculty research:* Leadership, marketing and technology, wealth management.

Southeastern University, College of Graduate Studies, Program in Marketing, Washington, DC 20024-2788. Offers MBA. Part-time and evening/weekend programs available. *Entrance requirements:* Additional exam requirements/recommendations for international students: Required—TOEFL.

Southern Adventist University, School of Business and Management, Collegedale, TN 37315-0370. Offers accounting (MBA); administration (MS); financial services (MFS); health care administration (MBA); human resource management (MBA); management (MBA); marketing (MBA). Part-time and evening/weekend programs available. Postbaccalaureate distance learning degree programs offered (no on-campus study). *Faculty:* 7 full-time (0 women), 2 part-time/adjunct (1 woman). *Students:* 18 full-time (8 women), 66 part-time (37 women); includes 15 minority (6 African Americans, 7 Asian Americans or Pacific Islanders, 2 Hispanic Americans). Average age 35. 32 applicants, 84% accepted, 24 enrolled. In 2006, 11 degrees awarded. *Entrance requirements:* For master's, GMAT. Additional exam requirements/recommendations for international students: Required—TOEFL. *Application deadline:* For fall admission, 8/1 priority date for domestic students, 7/1 for international students; for winter admission, 12/1 priority date for domestic students, 11/1 for international students; for spring admission, 4/1 priority date for domestic students, 3/1 for international students. Applications are processed on a rolling basis. Application fee: $25. Electronic applications accepted. *Financial support:* In 2006–07, 32 students received support. Scholarships/grants available. Financial award application deadline: 9/1; financial award applicants required to submit FAFSA. *Unit head:* Dr. Don Van Ornam, Dean, 423-236-2750, Fax: 423-236-1527, E-mail: dvanorna@southern.edu. *Application contact:* Linda Wilhelm, Admissions Coordinator, 423-236-2751, Fax: 423-236-1527, E-mail: sbm@southern.edu.

Southern New Hampshire University, School of Business, Manchester, NH 03106-1045. Offers accounting (MS); business administration (MBA, Certificate), including accounting (Certificate), business administration (MBA), finance (Certificate), forensic accounting (Certificate), human resources management (Certificate), international business (Certificate), international sport management (Certificate), leadership of not for profit organizations (Certificate), marketing (Certificate), operations management (Certificate), sport management (Certificate), taxation (Certificate); finance (MS); hospitality and tourism leadership (Certificate); information technology (MS, Certificate); information technology/international business (Certificate); integrated marketing communications (Certificate); international business (MS, DBA); marketing (MS); operations and project management (MS); organizational leadership (MS); project management (Certificate); sport management (MS); MBA/Certificate. *Accreditation:* ACBSP. Part-time and evening/weekend programs available. Postbaccalaureate distance learning degree programs offered (no on-campus study). *Faculty:* 45 full-time, 75 part-time/adjunct. *Students:* 427 full-time (184 women), 774 part-time (428 women). Average age 32. In 2006, 682 master's, 1 doctorate awarded. Terminal master's awarded for partial completion of doctoral program. *Degree requirements:* For master's, one foreign language, thesis or alternative, comprehensive exam (for some programs); for doctorate, one foreign language, thesis/dissertation, comprehensive exam. *Entrance requirements:* For master's, minimum GPA of 2.5; for doctorate, GMAT. Additional exam requirements/recommendations for international students: Required—TOEFL (minimum score 500 paper-based). *Application deadline:* Applications are processed on a rolling basis. Application fee: $25. Electronic applications accepted. *Financial support:* Career-related internships or fieldwork, Federal Work-Study, institutionally sponsored loans, tuition waivers (partial), and unspecified assistantships available. Support available to part-time students. Financial award applicants required to submit FAFSA. *Unit head:* Dr. Martin Bradley, Dean, 603-644-3102, Fax: 603-644-3144, E-mail: m.bradley@snhu.edu. *Application contact:* Scott Durand, Director of Graduate Enrollment Services, 603-644-3102 Ext. 3338, Fax: 603-644-3144, E-mail: s.durand@snhu.edu.

See Close-Up on page 325.

Stephen F. Austin State University, Graduate School, College of Business, Program in Business Administration, Nacogdoches, TX 75962. Offers business (MBA); management and marketing (MBA). *Accreditation:* AACSB. Part-time and evening/weekend programs available. *Degree requirements:* For master's, comprehensive exam. *Entrance requirements:* For master's, GMAT, minimum AACSB index of 1000. Additional exam requirements/recommendations for international students: Required—TOEFL (minimum score 550 paper-based; 213 computer-based). *Faculty research:* Strategic implications, information search, multinational firms, philosophical guidance.

Syracuse University, Martin J. Whitman School of Management, PhD Program in Business Administration, Syracuse, NY 13244. Offers accounting (PhD); finance (PhD); management information systems (PhD); managerial statistics (PhD); marketing (PhD); operations management (PhD); organizational behavior (PhD); strategy and human resources (PhD); supply chain management (PhD). *Faculty:* 71 full-time (16 women), 2 part-time/adjunct (1 woman). *Students:* 34 full-time (10 women); includes 1 minority (African American), 24 international. Average age 31. 89 applicants, 8% accepted, 4 enrolled. In 2006, 8 degrees awarded. *Degree requirements:* For doctorate, thesis/dissertation, summer research paper, comprehensive exam, registration. *Entrance requirements:* For doctorate, GMAT, 3 recommendations. Additional exam requirements/recommendations for international students: Required—TOEFL (minimum score 600 paper-based; 250 computer-based; 100 iBT). *Application deadline:* For fall admission, 1/30 priority date for domestic students. Applications are processed on a rolling basis. Application fee: $75. Electronic applications accepted. *Expenses:* Tuition: Full-time $16,920; part-time $940 per credit hour. Required fees: $930; $930 per year. *Financial support:* In 2006–07, 1 fellowship with full tuition reimbursement (averaging $19,000 per year), 26 teaching assistantships with full tuition reimbursements (averaging $16,500 per year) were awarded; research assistantships with full tuition reimbursements, health care benefits and unspecified assistantships also available. Financial award application deadline: 1/30. *Faculty research:* Marketing models, market microstructure, supply chain, auditing, corporate governance. *Unit head:* Dr. Ravi Dharwadkar, Director of the PhD Program, 315-443-3386, E-mail: rdharwad@syr.edu. *Application contact:* Shannon Hiemstra, Assistant Director for PhD and Research Programs, 315-443-3549, Fax: 315-443-3671, E-mail: srhiemst@syr.edu.

Syracuse University, Martin J. Whitman School of Management, Program in Business Administration, Syracuse, NY 13244. Offers accounting (MBA); entrepreneurship (MBA); finance (MBA); marketing (MBA); supply chain management (MBA). Part-time programs available. Postbaccalaureate distance learning degree programs offered (minimal on-campus study). *Faculty:* 71 full-time (16 women), 2 part-time/adjunct (1 woman). *Students:* 70 full-time (21 women), 279 part-time (84 women); includes 83 minority (44 African Americans, 33 Asian Americans or Pacific Islanders, 6 Hispanic Americans), 36 international. Average age 27. 227 applicants, 37% accepted, 27 enrolled. In 2006, 140 degrees awarded. *Degree requirements:* For master's, registration. *Entrance requirements:* For master's, GMAT, 2 letters of recommendation, bachelor's degree. Additional exam requirements/recommendations for international students: Required—TOEFL (minimum score 600 paper-based; 250 computer-based; 100 iBT). *Application deadline:* For fall admission, 1/15 priority date for domestic and international students. Applications are processed on a rolling basis. Application fee: $75. Electronic applications accepted. *Expenses:* Tuition: Full-time $16,920; part-time $940 per credit hour. Required fees: $930; $930 per year. *Financial support:* In 2006–07, 17 students received support; fellowships with full and partial tuition reimbursements available, teaching assistantships with partial tuition reimbursements available, career-related internships or fieldwork, scholarships/grants, tuition waivers (partial), unspecified assistantships, and paid hourly positions available. Support available to part-time students. Financial award application deadline: 3/1. *Unit head:* Dr. Ravi Shukla, Associate Dean for MBA and MS Programs, 315-443-3576, Fax: 315-443-9517, E-mail: rkshukla@syr.edu. *Application contact:* Carol J. Swanberg, Director of Graduate Admissions and Financial Aid, 315-443-9214, Fax: 315-443-9517, E-mail: mbainfo@syr.edu.

Temple University, Graduate School, Fox School of Business and Management, Doctoral Programs in Business, Philadelphia, PA 19122-6096. Offers accounting (PhD); economics (PhD); finance (PhD); general and strategic management (PhD); healthcare management (PhD); human resource administration (PhD); international business administration (PhD); management information systems (PhD); management science/operations research (PhD); marketing (PhD); risk, insurance, and health-care management (PhD); statistics (PhD); tourism (PhD). *Accreditation:* AACSB. *Entrance requirements:* For doctorate, GRE General Test,

Marketing

Temple University (continued)
minimum GPA of 3.0, master's degree. Additional exam requirements/recommendations for international students: Required—TOEFL. *Expenses:* Tuition, state resident: full-time $12,264; part-time $511 per credit. Tuition, nonresident: full-time $17,904; part-time $746 per credit. Required fees: $84 per course. Tuition and fees vary according to program.

Temple University, Graduate School, Fox School of Business and Management, Masters Programs in Business, MBA Programs, Philadelphia, PA 19122-6096. Offers accounting (MBA); business administration (EMBA, MBA); e-business (MBA); economics (MBA); finance (MBA); general and strategic management (MBA); healthcare management (MBA); human resource administration (MBA); international business (IMBA); management information systems (MBA); management science/operations management (MBA); marketing (MBA); risk management and insurance (MBA); statistics (MBA). EMBA offered in Philadelphia, PA and Tokyo, Japan. *Accreditation:* AACSB. *Entrance requirements:* For master's, GMAT, minimum undergraduate GPA of 3.0. Additional exam requirements/recommendations for international students: Required—TOEFL. *Expenses:* Tuition, state resident: full-time $12,264; part-time $511 per credit. Tuition, nonresident: full-time $17,904; part-time $746 per credit. Required fees: $84 per course. Tuition and fees vary according to program.

Temple University, Graduate School, Fox School of Business and Management, Masters Programs in Business, MS Programs, Philadelphia, PA 19122-6096. Offers accounting and financial management (MS); actuarial science (MS); e-business (MS); finance (MS); healthcare financial management (MS); human resource administration (MS); management information systems (MS); management science/operations management (MS); marketing (MS); statistics (MS). *Accreditation:* AACSB. *Entrance requirements:* For master's, GRE General Test, minimum undergraduate GPA of 3.0. Additional exam requirements/recommendations for international students: Required—TOEFL. *Expenses:* Tuition, state resident: full-time $12,264; part-time $511 per credit. Tuition, nonresident: full-time $17,904; part-time $746 per credit. Required fees: $84 per course. Tuition and fees vary according to program.

Texas A&M University, Mays Business School, Department of Marketing, College Station, TX 77843. Offers MS, PhD. *Faculty:* 20 full-time (3 women), 1 (woman) part-time/adjunct. *Students:* 63 full-time (33 women). Average age 30. 53 applicants, 25% accepted. In 2006, 23 master's, 2 doctorates awarded. Terminal master's awarded for partial completion of doctoral program. *Degree requirements:* For master's, comprehensive exam; for doctorate, thesis/dissertation. *Entrance requirements:* For master's, GMAT; for doctorate, GMAT or GRE General Test. Additional exam requirements/recommendations for international students: Required—TOEFL. *Application deadline:* For fall admission, 3/1 priority date for domestic students. Applications are processed on a rolling basis. Application fee: $50 ($75 for international students). *Expenses:* Tuition, state resident: full-time $4,697. Tuition, nonresident: full-time $11,297. Required fees: $2,272. *Financial support:* In 2006–07, 16 students received support; fellowships, research assistantships, teaching assistantships, career-related internships or fieldwork and institutionally sponsored loans available. Financial award application deadline: 2/1. *Faculty research:* Consumer behavior, innovation and product management, international marketing, marketing management and strategy, services marketing. *Unit head:* Dr. Jeff Conant, Head, 979-845-0824. *Application contact:* Stephen W. McDaniel, Adviser, 979-845-5801, E-mail: s-mcdaniel@tamu.edu.

Texas Tech University, Jerry S. Rawls College of Business Administration, Area of Marketing and International Business, Lubbock, TX 79409. Offers marketing (PhD). Part-time programs available. *Faculty:* 12 full-time (2 women). *Students:* 6 full-time (2 women); includes 2 minority (1 Asian American or Pacific Islander, 1 Hispanic American), 2 international. Average age 33. 7 applicants, 29% accepted, 2 enrolled. In 2006, 1 degree awarded. *Degree requirements:* For doctorate, thesis/dissertation, qualifying exams. *Entrance requirements:* For doctorate, GMAT, holistic profile of academic credentials. Additional exam requirements/recommendations for international students: Required—TOEFL (minimum score 550 paper-based; 213 computer-based; 79 iBT). *Application deadline:* For fall admission, 7/1 priority date for domestic students, 3/1 priority date for international students; for spring admission, 11/1 priority date for domestic students, 9/1 priority date for international students. Applications are processed on a rolling basis. Application fee: $50 ($60 for international students). Electronic applications accepted. *Expenses:* Tuition, state resident: full-time $4,440. Tuition, nonresident: full-time $11,040. Required fees: $2,136. *Financial support:* In 2006–07, 4 research assistantships (averaging $8,000 per year), 3 teaching assistantships (averaging $16,930 per year) were awarded; Federal Work-Study and scholarships/grants also available. *Faculty research:* Consumer behavior, macromarketing, marketing strategy and strategic planning. *Unit head:* Dr. Debra Laveric, Area Coordinator, 806-742-3953, Fax: 806-742-2199, E-mail: debbie.laveric@ttu.edu. *Application contact:* Cynthia D. Barnes, Director, Graduate Services Center, 806-742-3184, Fax: 806-742-3958, E-mail: ba_grad@ttu.edu.

Texas Tech University, Jerry S. Rawls College of Business Administration, Programs in Business Administration, Lubbock, TX 79409. Offers agricultural business (MBA); entrepreneurship (MBA); finance (MBA); general business (MBA); health organization management (MBA); international business (MBA); management and leadership skills (MBA); management information systems (MBA); marketing (MBA); statistics (MBA); JD/MBA; MBA/M Arch; MBA/MA; MBA/MD; MBA/MS. Part-time and evening/weekend programs available. *Students:* 65 full-time (16 women), 347 part-time (121 women); includes 74 minority (5 African Americans, 5 American Indian/Alaska Native, 24 Asian Americans or Pacific Islanders, 40 Hispanic Americans), 24 international. Average age 25. 382 applicants, 82% accepted, 244 enrolled. In 2006, 150 degrees awarded. *Degree requirements:* For master's, capstone course. *Entrance requirements:* For master's, GMAT, holistic review of academic credentials. Additional exam requirements/recommendations for international students: Required—TOEFL (minimum score 550 paper-based; 213 computer-based; 79 iBT). *Application deadline:* For fall admission, 7/1 priority date for domestic students, 3/1 priority date for international students; for spring admission, 11/1 priority date for domestic students, 9/1 priority date for international students. Applications are processed on a rolling basis. Application fee: $50 ($60 for international students). Electronic applications accepted. *Expenses:* Tuition, state resident: full-time $4,440. Tuition, nonresident: full-time $11,040. Required fees: $2,136. *Financial support:* In 2006–07, 36 research assistantships (averaging $8,000 per year) were awarded; teaching assistantships, career-related internships or fieldwork, Federal Work-Study, scholarships/grants, health care benefits, and unspecified assistantships also available. Support available to part-time students. Financial award applicants required to submit FAFSA. *Unit head:* Dr. W. Jay Conover, Director, 806-742-1546, Fax: 806-742-3958, E-mail: jay.conover@ttu.edu. *Application contact:* Cynthia D. Barnes, Director, Graduate Services Center, 806-742-3184, Fax: 806-742-3958, E-mail: ba_grad@ttu.edu.

United States International University, School of Business Administration, Nairobi, Kenya. Offers finance (MBA); information technology management (MBA); integrated studies (MBA); management and organizational development (MS); marketing (MBA); strategic management (MBA). Part-time and evening/weekend programs available. *Degree requirements:* For master's, thesis, registration. *Entrance requirements:* For master's, GMAT, 2 letters of reference, resumé. Additional exam requirements/recommendations for international students: Required—TOEFL (minimum score 550 paper-based; 213 computer-based). *Faculty research:* Marketing in small business enterprises, total quality management in Kenya.

Universidad del Turabo, Graduate Programs, School in Business Administration, Program in Marketing, Gurabo, PR 00778-3030. Offers MBA. Part-time and evening/weekend programs available. *Entrance requirements:* For master's, GRE, EXADEP, interview.

Universidad Metropolitana, School of Business Administration, Program in Marketing, San Juan, PR 00928-1150. Offers MBA. Part-time programs available. *Degree requirements:* For master's, thesis or alternative. *Entrance requirements:* For master's, GMAT, PAEG, interview. Electronic applications accepted.

Université de Sherbrooke, Faculty of Administration, Program in Marketing, Sherbrooke, QC J1K 2R1, Canada. Offers M Sc.

Université Laval, Faculty of Administrative Sciences, Programs in Business Administration, Québec, QC G1K 7P4, Canada. Offers accounting (MBA); agri-food management (MBA); electronic business (MBA, Diploma); factory management and logistics (MBA); finance (MBA); firm management (MBA); information technology management (MBA); international management (MBA); management (MBA); management accounting (MBA, Diploma); marketing (MBA); modelization and organizational decision (MBA); occupational health and safety management (MBA); pharmacy management (MBA); technological entrepreneurship (Diploma). *Accreditation:* AACSB. Part-time and evening/weekend programs available. Postbaccalaureate distance learning degree programs offered (no on-campus study). *Entrance requirements:* For master's and Diploma, knowledge of French and English. Electronic applications accepted.

University at Albany, State University of New York, School of Business, Department of Marketing, Albany, NY 12222-0001. Offers MBA. *Degree requirements:* For master's, field study project. *Entrance requirements:* For master's, GMAT. Additional exam requirements/recommendations for international students: Required—TOEFL (minimum score 550 paper-based; 213 computer-based). *Application deadline:* For fall admission, 3/1 priority date for domestic students, 4/1 for international students. Applications are processed on a rolling basis. Application fee: $75. Electronic applications accepted. *Expenses:* Tuition, state resident: full-time $6,900; part-time $288 per credit. Tuition, nonresident: full-time $10,920; part-time $455 per credit. Required fees: $1,139. *Financial support:* Application deadline: 4/1. *Faculty research:* Sales management, buyer-seller interaction, family decision making, sociological influence on consumption, health promotion. *Unit head:* William D. Danko, Chair, 518-442-4965. *Application contact:* Michael DeRensis, Director, Graduate Admissions, 518-442-3980, Fax: 518-442-3922, E-mail: graduate@uamail.albany.edu.

The University of Akron, Graduate School, College of Business Administration, Department of Marketing, Akron, OH 44325. Offers international business (MBA); international business for international executive (MBA); strategic marketing (MBA); JD/MBA. Part-time and evening/weekend programs available. *Faculty:* 10 full-time (2 women), 10 part-time/adjunct (2 women). *Students:* 16 full-time (8 women), 21 part-time (10 women); includes 2 minority (1 African American, 1 Asian American or Pacific Islander), 7 international. Average age 30. 34 applicants, 85% accepted, 11 enrolled. In 2006, 15 degrees awarded. *Entrance requirements:* For master's, GMAT, minimum GPA of 2.75. Additional exam requirements/recommendations for international students: Required—TOEFL (minimum score 550 paper-based; 213 computer-based; 79 iBT). *Application deadline:* For fall admission, 8/15 for domestic students. Applications are processed on a rolling basis. Application fee: $30 ($40 for international students). Electronic applications accepted. *Expenses:* Tuition, state resident: full-time $6,164; part-time $342 per credit. Tuition, nonresident: full-time $10,575; part-time $588 per credit. Required fees: $806; $43 per credit. $12 per term. Tuition and fees vary according to course load, degree level and program. *Financial support:* In 2006–07, 10 research assistantships with full tuition reimbursements, 1 teaching assistantship with full tuition reimbursement were awarded; tuition waivers (partial) also available. *Faculty research:* Professional selling, sales management, direct interactive marketing, marketing strategy, international business. *Unit head:* Dr. Dale M. Lewison, Chair, 330-972-5758, E-mail: dlewison@uakron.edu. *Application contact:* Dr. James Divoky, Director of Graduate Business Programs, 330-972-7043, Fax: 330-972-6588, E-mail: jdivoky@uakron.edu.

The University of Alabama, Graduate School, Manderson Graduate School of Business, Department of Management and Marketing, Program in Marketing, Tuscaloosa, AL 35487. Offers MS, PhD. *Accreditation:* AACSB. *Faculty:* 27 full-time (8 women), 2 part-time/adjunct (0 women). *Students:* 20 full-time (11 women); includes 2 minority (both African Americans), 2 international. Average age 29. 112 applicants, 36% accepted. In 2006, 20 master's, 1 doctorate awarded. Terminal master's awarded for partial completion of doctoral program. *Median time to degree:* Of those who began their doctoral program in fall 1998, 100% received their degree in 8 years or less. *Degree requirements:* For master's, internship; for doctorate, thesis/dissertation, comprehensive exam. *Entrance requirements:* For master's, GRE or GMAT; for doctorate, GRE or GMAT, minimum GPA of 3.0. Additional exam requirements/recommendations for international students: Required—TOEFL (minimum score 660 paper-based). *Application deadline:* For fall admission, 4/1 priority date for domestic and international students; for spring admission, 2/1 priority date for domestic and international students. Applications are processed on a rolling basis. Application fee: $25. Electronic applications accepted. *Financial support:* In 2006–07, fellowships with partial tuition reimbursements (averaging $15,000 per year), research assistantships with full and partial tuition reimbursements (averaging $25,000 per year), teaching assistantships with full tuition reimbursements (averaging $20,000 per year) were awarded; scholarships/grants, health care benefits, and unspecified assistantships also available. *Faculty research:* Relationship marketing, team building, e-commerce strategy, entrepreneurship, health care management, services marketing. *Unit head:* Dr. Robert M. Morgan, Department Head, 205-348-6183, Fax: 205-348-6695, E-mail: rmorgan@cba.ua.edu. *Application contact:* Carolyn Rhodes, Office Associate II, 205-348-6183, Fax: 205-348-6095, E-mail: crhodes@cba.ua.edu.

University of Alberta, Faculty of Graduate Studies and Research, Doctoral Program in Business, Edmonton, AB T6G 2E1, Canada. Offers accounting (PhD); finance (PhD); human resources/industrial relations (PhD); management science (PhD); marketing (PhD); organizational analysis (PhD); MBA/PhD. *Accreditation:* AACSB. Part-time programs available. *Faculty:* 41 full-time (7 women), 1 part-time/adjunct (0 women). *Students:* 46 full-time (27 women), 5 part-time (3 women). Average age 34. 307 applicants, 7% accepted, 11 enrolled. In 2006, 2 degrees awarded. *Median time to degree:* Of those who began their doctoral program in fall 1998, 60% received their degree in 8 years or less. *Degree requirements:* For doctorate, thesis/dissertation, comprehensive exam. *Entrance requirements:* For doctorate, GMAT. Additional exam requirements/recommendations for international students: Required—TOEFL (minimum score 550 paper-based; 213 computer-based). *Application deadline:* For fall admission, 6/1 priority date for domestic students; for winter admission, 5/1 for domestic students. Application fee: $0. Electronic applications accepted. *Financial support:* In 2006–07, 29 students received support, including 11 fellowships with full tuition reimbursements available (averaging $17,000 per year); scholarships/grants and tuition waivers (partial) also available. *Faculty research:* Accounting, capital markets and corporate finance, organizational change and human resource management, marketing, strategic management. Total annual research expenditures: $7.7 million. *Unit head:* Dr. Mike Percy, Director, 780-492-2361, Fax: 780-492-3325, E-mail: busphd@ualberta.ca. *Application contact:* Jeanette Gosine, Program Coordinator, 780-492-2361, Fax: 780-492-3325, E-mail: busphd@ualberta.ca.

See Close-Up on page 335.

The University of Arizona, Graduate College, College of Business and Public Administration, Eller Graduate School of Management, Department of Marketing, Tucson, AZ 85721. Offers PhD. *Faculty:* 8 full-time (5 women), 1 part-time/adjunct (0 women). *Students:* 10 full-time (5 women); includes 1 minority (Hispanic American), 2 international. Average age 30. 25 applicants, 12% accepted, 3 enrolled. In 2006, 3 degrees awarded. *Degree requirements:* For doctorate, thesis/dissertation, comprehensive exam, registration. *Entrance requirements:* For doctorate, GMAT or GRE General Test, minimum GPA of 3.0. Additional exam requirements/recommendations for international students: Required—TOEFL. *Application deadline:* For fall admission, 12/1 priority date for domestic students, 12/1 for international students. Applications are processed on a rolling basis. Application fee: $50. *Financial support:* In 2006–07, 10 students received support, including 2 research assistantships with full and partial tuition reimbursements available (averaging $18,000 per year), 4 teaching assistantships with full and partial tuition reimbursements available (averaging $18,000 per year); fellowships, career-related internships or fieldwork, Federal Work-Study, scholarships/grants, health care benefits, tuition waivers (partial), and unspecified assistantships also available. Financial award application deadline: 2/1. *Faculty research:* Consumer behavior, customer relationship management, research methods, brand strategy, public policy. *Unit head:* Dr. Robert F. Lusch, Head, 520-621-7480, Fax: 520-621-7483. *Application contact:* Audrey L. Hambleton, Graduate Secretary, 520-621-1321, Fax: 520-621-7483.

University of Baltimore, Graduate School, Merrick School of Business, Department of Marketing, Baltimore, MD 21201-5779. Offers business/marketing and venturing (MS). Part-time and evening/weekend programs available. *Students:* 2 (1 woman). Average age 26. 3 applicants, 67% accepted, 0 enrolled. *Entrance requirements:* For master's, GMAT. Additional exam requirements/recommendations for international students: Required—TOEFL (minimum score 550 paper-based; 213 computer-based). *Application deadline:* For fall admission, 8/1 priority date for domestic students, 6/1 for international students; for spring admission, 12/1 for domestic students, 11/1 for international students. Applications are processed on a rolling basis. Application fee: $30. Electronic applications accepted. *Expenses:* Tuition, state resident: full-time $5,322; part-time $591 per credit. Tuition, nonresident: full-time $7,527; part-time $830 per credit. *Financial support:* Application deadline: 4/1; Total annual research expenditures: $30,000. *Unit head:* Dr. Michael Laric, Adviser, E-mail: mlaric@ubalt.edu. *Application contact:* Dean Dreibelbis, Assistant Director, Office of Graduate Admissions, 410-837-6565, Fax: 410-837-4793, E-mail: gradadmissions@ubalt.edu.

The University of British Columbia, Sauder School of Business, Doctoral Program in Commerce and Business Administration, Vancouver, BC V6T 1Z1, Canada. Offers accounting (PhD); finance (PhD); international business (PhD); management information systems (PhD); management science (PhD); marketing (PhD); organizational behavior (PhD); policy analysis and strategy (PhD); transportation and logistics (PhD); urban land economics (PhD). *Degree requirements:* For doctorate, thesis/dissertation, comprehensive exam. *Entrance requirements:* For doctorate, GMAT or GRE. Additional exam requirements/recommendations for international students: Required—TOEFL. Electronic applications accepted.

University of California, Berkeley, Graduate Division, Haas School of Business, Program in Business, Berkeley, CA 94720-1500. Offers accounting (PhD); business and public policy (PhD); finance (PhD); marketing (PhD); organizational behavior and industrial relations (PhD); real estate (PhD). *Accreditation:* AACSB. *Students:* 83 full-time (28 women); includes 17 minority (14 Asian Americans or Pacific Islanders, 3 Hispanic Americans), 33 international. Average age 30. 347 applicants, 16 enrolled. In 2006, 17 degrees awarded. *Median time to degree:* Of those who began their doctoral program in fall 1998, 88% received their degree in 8 years or less. *Degree requirements:* For doctorate, thesis/dissertation, oral exam, written preliminary exams, comprehensive exam. *Entrance requirements:* For doctorate, GMAT or GRE, minimum GPA of 3.0. Additional exam requirements/recommendations for international students: Required—TOEFL (minimum score 570 paper-based; 230 computer-based), IELTS (minimum score 7). *Application deadline:* For fall admission, 12/15 for domestic and international students. Application fee: $60 ($80 for international students). Electronic applications accepted. *Financial support:* Fellowships with full and partial tuition reimbursements, research assistantships with full and partial tuition reimbursements, teaching assistantships with full and partial tuition reimbursements, career-related internships or fieldwork, Federal Work-Study, scholarships/grants, health care benefits, tuition waivers (full), and unspecified assistantships available. Financial award application deadline: 12/15; financial award applicants required to submit FAFSA. *Unit head:* Miguel Villas-Boas, Director, 510-642-1409, Fax: 510-643-4255, E-mail: kimg@haas.berkeley.edu. *Application contact:* Kim Guilfoyle, Administrative Director, 510-642-3944, Fax: 510-643-4255, E-mail: kimg@haas.berkeley.edu.

University of Cincinnati, Division of Research and Advanced Studies, College of Business, Department of Marketing, Cincinnati, OH 45221. Offers MBA, MS, PhD. Part-time and evening/weekend programs available. *Degree requirements:* For master's, capstone project; for doctorate, thesis/dissertation. *Entrance requirements:* For master's, GMAT, resumé, letters of recommendation; for doctorate, GMAT, GRE. Application fee: $40. Electronic applications accepted. *Expenses: Contact institution. Financial support:* Fellowships with full tuition reimbursements, research assistantships with full tuition reimbursements, scholarships/grants and tuition waivers (full and partial) available. Financial award application deadline: 2/1; financial award applicants required to submit FAFSA. *Unit head:* Dr. Karen Machleit, Head, 513-556-7102, Fax: 513-556-4891, E-mail: karen.machleit@uc.edu.

University of Colorado at Boulder, Leeds School of Business, Doctoral Program in Business, Boulder, CO 80309. Offers accounting (PhD); finance (PhD); management (PhD); marketing (PhD). *Degree requirements:* For doctorate, thesis/dissertation, research internship. *Entrance requirements:* For doctorate, minimum undergraduate GPA of 3.2. *Application deadline:* For fall admission, 1/31 for domestic students, 1/15 for international students; for spring admission, 11/1 for domestic and international students. Application fee: $50 ($60 for international students). *Financial support:* Fellowships, research assistantships, teaching assistantships, career-related internships or fieldwork, Federal Work-Study, scholarships/grants, and unspecified assistantships available. Financial award application deadline: 3/1; financial award applicants required to submit FAFSA. *Unit head:* Kenneth Kozar, Associate Dean, 303-492-8347, Fax: 303-492-7676. *Application contact:* Information Contact, 303-492-4984, Fax: 303-492-5962, E-mail: leedsphd@colorado.edu.

University of Colorado at Colorado Springs, Graduate School, Graduate School of Business Administration, Colorado Springs, CO 80933-7150. Offers accounting (MBA); finance (MBA); general health care administration (MBA); information systems (MBA); international business management (MBA); marketing (MBA); service management/technology management (MBA). *Accreditation:* AACSB. Part-time and evening/weekend programs available. *Faculty:* 15 full-time (4 women), 4 part-time/adjunct (0 women). *Students:* 158 full-time (70 women), 290 part-time (87 women); includes 48 minority (11 African Americans, 1 American Indian/Alaska Native, 20 Asian Americans or Pacific Islanders, 16 Hispanic Americans), 7 international. Average age 33. 158 applicants, 75% accepted, 51 enrolled. In 2006, 119 degrees awarded. *Entrance requirements:* For master's, GMAT. *Application deadline:* For fall admission, 6/1 for domestic students; for spring admission, 11/1 for domestic students. Application fee: $60 ($75 for international students). *Expenses: Contact institution.* Tuition and fees vary according to course load, campus/location and program. *Financial support:* Career-related internships or fieldwork, Federal Work-Study, and institutionally sponsored loans available. Support available to part-time students. Financial award applicants required to submit FAFSA. *Faculty research:* Quality financial reporting, investments and corporate governance, group support systems, environmental and project management, customer relationship management. Total annual research expenditures: $99,250. *Unit head:* Dr. Venkateshwar Reddy, Dean, 719-262-3113, Fax: 719-262-3494, E-mail: vreddy@uccs.edu. *Application contact:* Amy DeLourenco, MBA Program Director, 719-262-3408, Fax: 719-262-3100, E-mail: busadvsr@uccs.edu.

University of Colorado at Denver and Health Sciences Center, Business School, Program in Marketing, Denver, CO 80217-3364. Offers MS. Part-time and evening/weekend programs available. *Faculty:* 8 full-time (4 women). *Students:* 10 full-time (6 women), 26 part-time (17 women); includes 1 minority (Hispanic American), 10 international. Average age 24. 21 applicants, 67% accepted, 13 enrolled. In 2006, 29 degrees awarded. *Entrance requirements:* For master's, GMAT. Additional exam requirements/recommendations for international students: Required—TOEFL (minimum score 525 paper-based; 197 computer-based). *Application deadline:* For fall admission, 6/1 priority date for domestic students, 3/15 for international students; for spring admission, 11/1 priority date for domestic students, 10/1 for international students. Applications are processed on a rolling basis. Application fee: $50 ($75 for international students). Electronic applications accepted. *Financial support:* Federal Work-Study, institutionally sponsored loans, and scholarships/grants available. Support available to part-time students. Financial award application deadline: 4/1; financial award applicants required to submit FAFSA. *Unit head:* David Forlani, Director, 303-556-6616, Fax: 303-556-5899, E-mail: david.forlani@cudenver.edu. *Application contact:* Shelly Townley, Admissions Coordinator, 303-556-5956, Fax: 303-556-5904, E-mail: shelly.townley@cudenver.edu.

University of Connecticut, Graduate School, School of Business, Storrs, CT 06269. Offers accounting (MS, PhD); business administration (Exec MBA, MBA, PhD); finance (PhD); health care management and insurance studies (MBA); management (PhD); management consulting (MBA); marketing (PhD); marketing intelligence (MBA); MA/MBA; MBA/MSW. *Accreditation:* AACSB. *Faculty:* 70 full-time (14 women). *Students:* 378 full-time (126 women), 852 part-time (322 women); includes 154 minority (43 African Americans, 5 American Indian/Alaska Native, 71 Asian Americans or Pacific Islanders, 35 Hispanic Americans), 171 international. Average age 30. 632 applicants, 72% accepted, 452 enrolled. In 2006, 413 master's, 9 doctorates awarded. *Degree requirements:* For master's, comprehensive exam; for doctorate, thesis/dissertation. *Entrance requirements:* For master's and doctorate, GMAT. Additional exam requirements/recommendations for international students: Required—TOEFL (minimum score 550 paper-based; 213 computer-based). *Application deadline:* For fall admission, 2/1 priority date for domestic and international students; for spring admission, 11/1 for domestic students, 10/1 for international students. Applications are processed on a rolling basis. Electronic applications accepted. *Financial support:* In 2006–07, 107 research assistantships with full tuition reimbursements, 4 teaching assistantships with full tuition reimbursements were awarded; fellowships, career-related internships or fieldwork, Federal Work-Study, scholarships/grants, health care benefits, and unspecified assistantships also available. Financial award application deadline: 2/1; financial award applicants required to submit FAFSA. *Unit head:* William Curt Hunter, Dean, 860-486-2317, Fax: 860-846-0889, E-mail: william.hunter@uconn.edu. *Application contact:* Richard Dino, Admissions Chairperson, 860-486-4483, E-mail: rich.dino@uconn.edu.

See Close-Up on page 343.

University of Dallas, Graduate School of Management, Irving, TX 75062-4736. Offers accounting (MBA, MS); business management (MBA); corporate finance (MBA, MM); engineering management (MBA, MM); entrepreneurship (MBA, MM); financial services (MBA, MM); global business (MBA, MM); health services management (MBA, MM); human resource management (MBA, MM, MS); information assurance (MBA, MM, MS); information technology (MBA, MM, MS); information technology service management (MBA); IT service management (MS); marketing (MM); marketing management (MBA); not-for-profit management (MBA); organization development (MBA); project management (MBA, MM); sports and entertainment management (MBA, MM); strategic leadership (MBA); supply chain management (MBA); supply chain management and market logistics (MM); telecommunications management (MBA, MM). *Accreditation:* ACBSP. Part-time and evening/weekend programs available. Postbaccalaureate distance learning degree programs offered (no on-campus study). *Faculty:* 26 full-time (5 women), 85 part-time/adjunct (18 women). *Students:* 227 full-time (98 women), 1,160 part-time (446 women); includes 473 minority (209 African Americans, 3 American Indian/Alaska Native, 143 Asian Americans or Pacific Islanders, 118 Hispanic Americans), 224 international. Average age 34. 556 applicants, 86% accepted, 291 enrolled. In 2006, 476 degrees awarded. *Entrance requirements:* Additional exam requirements/recommendations for international students: Required—TOEFL. *Application deadline:* Applications are processed on a rolling basis. Application fee: $50. Electronic applications accepted. *Expenses: Contact institution. Financial support:* In 2006–07, 468 students received support. Scholarships/grants and unspecified assistantships available. Financial award application deadline: 2/15; financial award applicants required to submit FAFSA. *Unit head:* Dr. J. Lee Whittington, Dean, 972-721-5230. *Application contact:* Sarah Stivison, Director of Graduate Admissions, 972-721-5198, Fax: 972-721-4009, E-mail: admiss@gsm.udallas.edu.

University of Denver, Daniels College of Business, Department of Marketing, Denver, CO 80208. Offers IMBA, MBA, MS. Part-time and evening/weekend programs available. *Faculty:* 10 full-time (3 women). *Students:* 72 full-time (34 women), 63 part-time (30 women); includes 11 minority (1 African American, 7 Asian Americans or Pacific Islanders, 3 Hispanic Americans), 38 international. Average age 27. 44 applicants, 64% accepted. In 2006, 36 degrees awarded. *Entrance requirements:* For master's, GMAT. *Application deadline:* For fall admission, 1/15 priority date for domestic students. Applications are processed on a rolling basis. Application fee: $50. Electronic applications accepted. *Expenses:* Tuition: Full-time $29,628; part-time $823 per credit. *Financial support:* In 2006–07, 30 students received support. Career-related internships or fieldwork, Federal Work-Study, institutionally sponsored loans, and scholarships/grants available. Support available to part-time students. Financial award application deadline: 2/15; financial award applicants required to submit FAFSA. *Faculty research:* Social policy issues in marketing, price bundling, marketing to the disabled, marketing to the elderly, international marketing and logistics. *Unit head:* Dr. Steve Hartley, Chair, 303-871-2144. *Application contact:* Information Contact, 303-871-3416, Fax: 303-871-4466, E-mail: daniels@du.edu.

The University of Findlay, Graduate and Professional Studies, MBA Program, Findlay, OH 45840-3653. Offers financial management (MBA); human resource management (MBA); international management (MBA); management (MBA); marketing (MBA); public management (MBA). Part-time and evening/weekend programs available. Postbaccalaureate distance learning degree programs offered (no on-campus study). *Faculty:* 16 full-time, 1 part-time/adjunct. *Students:* 80 full-time (26 women), 456 part-time (168 women); includes 20 minority (13 African Americans, 1 American Indian/Alaska Native, 4 Asian Americans or Pacific Islanders, 2 Hispanic Americans), 289 international. Average age 35. 208 applicants, 88% accepted, 181 enrolled. In 2006, 210 degrees awarded. *Degree requirements:* For master's, thesis, cumulative project. *Entrance requirements:* For master's, GMAT, minimum undergraduate GPA of 3.0 in last 60 hours of course work. Additional exam requirements/recommendations for international students: Required—TOEFL (minimum score 550 paper-based). *Application deadline:* Applications are processed on a rolling basis. Application fee: $25. Electronic applications accepted. *Expenses: Contact institution. Financial support:* In 2006–07, 1 student received support, including 1 teaching assistantship with full tuition reimbursement available (averaging $6,000 per year); unspecified assistantships also available. Financial award application deadline: 4/1; financial award applicants required to submit FAFSA. *Faculty research:* Health care management, operations and logistics management. *Unit head:* Dr. Paul Sears, Dean, 419-434-4704, Fax: 419-434-4822. *Application contact:* Heather Riffle, Director, Graduate and Special Programs, 419-434-4640, Fax: 419-434-5517, E-mail: riffle@findlay.edu.

University of Florida, Graduate School, Warrington College of Business Administration, Department of Marketing, Gainesville, FL 32611. Offers MS, PhD. *Faculty:* 14 full-time (2 women). *Students:* 15 (3 women); includes 2 minority (1 Asian American or Pacific Islander, 1 Hispanic American) 7 international. In 2006, 3 master's, 3 doctorates awarded. Terminal master's awarded for partial completion of doctoral program. *Degree requirements:* For master's, thesis optional; for doctorate, thesis/dissertation. *Entrance requirements:* For master's and doctorate, GMAT or GRE General Test, minimum GPA of 3.0. Additional exam requirements/recommendations for international students: Required—TOEFL (minimum score 550 paper-based; 213 computer-based). *Application deadline:* For fall admission, 2/16 for domestic students. Applications are processed on a rolling basis. Application fee: $30. Electronic applications accepted. *Expenses:* Tuition, state resident: full-time $6,827. Tuition, nonresident: full-time $21,951. Required fees: $999. *Financial support:* In 2006–07, 9 research assistantships (averaging $24,413 per year) were awarded; fellowships, teaching assistantships, career-related internships or fieldwork, institutionally sponsored loans, and unspecified assistantships also available. Financial award application deadline: 2/10. *Faculty research:* Consumer behavior, advertising and sales promotion, sales management, pricing and retailing, mathematical models of marketing phenomena. *Unit head:* Dr. Joseph W. Alba, Chair, 352-392-0161 Ext. 1251, Fax: 352-846-0457, E-mail: joe.alba@cba.ufl.edu. *Application contact:* Dr. Chris Janiszewski, Coordinator, 352-392-0161 Ext. 1240, Fax: 352-846-0457, E-mail: chris.janiszewski@cba.ufl.edu.

University of Florida, Graduate School, Warrington College of Business Administration, Programs in Business Administration, Gainesville, FL 32611. Offers accounting (MBA); arts administration (MBA); business strategy and public policy (MBA); competitive strategy (MBA); decision and information sciences (MBA); electronic commerce (MBA); finance (MBA); general

Marketing

University of Florida (continued)

business (MBA); global management (MBA); Graham-Buffett security analysis (MBA); health administration (MBA); human resources management (MBA); international studies (MBA); Latin American business (MBA); management (MBA); marketing (MBA); sports administration (MBA); JD/MBA; MBA/MS; MBA/PhD; MBA/Pharm D; MD/MBA. *Accreditation:* AACSB. Part-time and evening/weekend programs available. Postbaccalaureate distance learning degree programs offered. *Faculty:* 14. *Students:* 950 (282 women); includes 189 minority (31 African Americans, 2 American Indian/Alaska Native, 66 Asian Americans or Pacific Islanders, 90 Hispanic Americans) 56 international. In 2006, 481 degrees awarded. *Entrance requirements:* For master's, GMAT, minimum GPA of 3.0, interview. Additional exam requirements/recommendations for international students: Required—TOEFL (minimum score 550 paper-based; 213 computer-based). *Application deadline:* For fall admission, 4/15 for domestic students; for winter admission, 10/15 priority date for domestic students; for spring admission, 2/15 for domestic students. Applications are processed on a rolling basis. Application fee: $30. Electronic applications accepted. *Expenses:* Tuition, state resident: full-time $6,827. Tuition, nonresident: full-time $21,951. Required fees: $999. *Financial support:* Fellowships, research assistantships, teaching assistantships, career-related internships or fieldwork, scholarships/grants, and unspecified assistantships available. Support available to part-time students. Financial award application deadline: 2/15; financial award applicants required to submit FAFSA. *Faculty research:* Accounting, finance, insurance, management, real estate and urban analysis marketing. *Unit head:* Alex Sevilla, Director, 352-392-7992 Ext. 1206. *Application contact:* Patrick Foran, Associate Director of Admissions, 352-392-7992 Ext. 282, Fax: 352-392-8791, E-mail: patrick.foran@cba.ufl.edu.

University of Georgia, Graduate School, Terry College of Business, Program in Marketing, Athens, GA 30602. Offers MMR. *Faculty:* 8 full-time (1 woman). *Students:* 19 full-time (11 women); includes 4 minority (all Asian Americans or Pacific Islanders), 7 international. In 2006, 16 degrees awarded. *Entrance requirements:* For master's, GMAT or GRE General Test. *Application deadline:* For fall admission, 7/1 priority date for domestic students; for spring admission, 11/15 for domestic students. Application fee: $50. Electronic applications accepted. *Financial support:* Research assistantships available. *Unit head:* Dr. Rajiv Grover, Head, 706-542-2123, Fax: 706-542-3738, E-mail: rgrover@terry.uga.edu. *Application contact:* Dr. Srinivas K. Reddy, Graduate Coordinator, 706-542-3759, Fax: 706-542-3738, E-mail: mmr@terry.uga.edu.

University of Hawaii at Manoa, Graduate Division, Shidler College of Business, Program in Business Administration, Honolulu, HI 96822. Offers Asian business studies (MBA); Chinese business studies (MBA); decision sciences (MBA); entrepreneurship (MBA); finance (MBA); finance and banking (MBA); human resources management (MBA); information management (MBA); information technology (MBA); international business (MBA); Japanese business studies (MBA); marketing (MBA); organizational behavior (MBA); organizational management (MBA); real estate (MBA); student-designed track (MBA). *Accreditation:* AACSB. Part-time programs available. *Faculty:* 48 full-time (9 women). *Students:* 207 full-time (77 women), 158 part-time (60 women); includes 93 minority (2 African Americans, 1 American Indian/Alaska Native, 88 Asian Americans or Pacific Islanders, 2 Hispanic Americans), 58 international. Average age 33. 235 applicants, 55% accepted, 68 enrolled. In 2006, 147 degrees awarded. *Degree requirements:* For master's, thesis optional. *Entrance requirements:* For master's, GMAT, minimum GPA of 3.0. Additional exam requirements/recommendations for international students: Required—TOEFL (minimum score 500 paper-based; 173 computer-based; 61 iBT). *Application deadline:* For fall admission, 5/1 for domestic and international students; for spring admission, 9/1 for domestic and international students. Application fee: $50. *Financial support:* In 2006–07, 7 research assistantships (averaging $17,409 per year), 3 teaching assistantships (averaging $14,028 per year) were awarded. *Application contact:* Ting Bui, Information Contact, 808-956-5565, Fax: 808-956-6889.

University of Hawaii at Manoa, Graduate Division, Shidler College of Business, Program in International Management, Honolulu, HI 96822. Offers Asian finance (PhD); global information technology management (PhD); international accounting (PhD); international marketing (PhD); international organization and strategy (PhD). *Faculty:* 42 full-time (8 women). *Students:* 36 applicants, 19% accepted, 4 enrolled. In 2006, 5 degrees awarded. *Median time to degree:* Of those who began their doctoral program in fall 1998, 33% received their degree in 8 years or less. *Degree requirements:* For doctorate, thesis/dissertation, comprehensive exam. *Entrance requirements:* For doctorate, GMAT or GRE General Test, minimum GPA of 3.0. Additional exam requirements/recommendations for international students: Required—TOEFL (minimum score 600 paper-based; 250 computer-based; 100 iBT). *Application deadline:* For fall admission, 3/1 for domestic and international students. Application fee: $50. *Financial support:* In 2006–07, 16 research assistantships (averaging $18,198 per year), 3 teaching assistantships (averaging $14,958 per year) were awarded. Total annual research expenditures: $3.3 million. *Application contact:* Ting Bui, Information Contact, 808-956-6723, Fax: 808-956-2774.

University of Houston, Bauer College of Business, Marketing and Entrepreneurship Program, Houston, TX 77204. Offers PhD. Part-time and evening/weekend programs available. *Faculty:* 7 full-time (0 women), 5 part-time/adjunct (0 women). *Students:* 13 full-time (6 women), 6 part-time (3 women); includes 6 minority (1 African American, 5 Asian Americans or Pacific Islanders), 5 international. Average age 31. *Degree requirements:* For doctorate, thesis/dissertation, comprehensive exam. *Entrance requirements:* For doctorate, GMAT or GRE. *Application deadline:* For fall admission, 5/1 for domestic students; for spring admission, 10/1 for domestic students. Applications are processed on a rolling basis. Application fee: $75 ($150 for international students). *Expenses:* Tuition, state resident: full-time $5,429; part-time $226 per credit. Tuition, nonresident: full-time $12,029; part-time $501 per credit. Required fees: $2,454. *Financial support:* In 2006–07, 12 teaching assistantships with full tuition reimbursements (averaging $7,000 per year) were awarded; fellowships with full tuition reimbursements, research assistantships with full tuition reimbursements, career-related internships or fieldwork, Federal Work-Study, institutionally sponsored loans, scholarships/grants, health care benefits, and unspecified assistantships also available. Support available to part-time students. Financial award application deadline: 3/10; financial award applicants required to submit FAFSA. *Faculty research:* Accountancy and taxation, finance, international business, management. *Unit head:* Dr. Ed Blair, Chair, 713-743-4555, E-mail: blair@uh.edu. *Application contact:* 713-743-4900, Fax: 713-743-4942, E-mail: oss@uh.edu.

University of Indianapolis, Graduate Programs, School of Business, Graduate Business Programs, Indianapolis, IN 46227-3697. Offers business (EMBA); business administration (MBA); finance (Graduate Certificate); global supply chains management (Graduate Certificate); marketing (Graduate Certificate); organizational leadership (Graduate Certificate); technology management (Graduate Certificate). *Accreditation:* ACBSP. Part-time and evening/weekend programs available. *Faculty:* 6 full-time (2 women), 6 part-time/adjunct (1 woman). *Students:* 50 full-time (16 women), 92 part-time (32 women); includes 12 minority (4 African Americans, 7 Asian Americans or Pacific Islanders, 1 Hispanic American), 10 international. Average age 32. In 2006, 57 degrees awarded. *Entrance requirements:* For master's, GMAT, interview, minimum GPA of 2.8, 2 letters of recommendation, resumé. Additional exam requirements/recommendations for international students: Required—TOEFL (minimum score 550 paper-based; 213 computer-based). *Application deadline:* Applications are processed on a rolling basis. Application fee: $50. *Expenses:* Contact institution. *Financial support:* Federal Work-Study and unspecified assistantships available. Financial award application deadline: 5/1; financial award applicants required to submit FAFSA. *Faculty research:* Integration of microcomputers into decision making, communication skills, application of synthesized theories. *Unit head:* Dr. Matthew Will, Associate Dean, 317-788-3370, E-mail: mwill@uindy.edu.

The University of Iowa, Henry B. Tippie College of Business, Department of Marketing, Iowa City, IA 52242-1316. Offers business administration (PhD). *Faculty:* 14 full-time (4 women), 5 part-time/adjunct (1 woman). *Students:* 9 full-time (4 women); includes 1 minority (Asian American or Pacific Islander), 7 international. Average age 29. 17 applicants, 12% accepted, 1

enrolled. In 2006, 1 degree awarded. *Degree requirements:* For doctorate, thesis/dissertation, thesis defense, comprehensive exam, registration. *Entrance requirements:* For doctorate, GMAT or GRE, minimum undergraduate GPA of 2.7. Additional exam requirements/recommendations for international students: Required—TOEFL (minimum score 600 paper-based). *Application deadline:* For fall admission, 1/15 for domestic and international students. Application fee: $60 ($85 for international students). Electronic applications accepted. *Financial support:* In 2006–07, 9 students received support, including 9 teaching assistantships with full tuition reimbursements available (averaging $15,985 per year); institutionally sponsored loans, scholarships/grants, health care benefits, unspecified assistantships, and Department of Marketing pays full tuition also available. Financial award application deadline: 1/15. Total annual research expenditures: $85,000. *Unit head:* Prof. Catherine A. Cole, Department Executive Officer, 319-335-1013, Fax: 319-335-1956, E-mail: cathy-cole@uiowa.edu. *Application contact:* Renea L. Jay, PhD Program Coordinator, 319-335-0830, Fax: 319-335-1956, E-mail: renea-jay@uiowa.edu.

The University of Iowa, Henry B. Tippie College of Business, Henry B. Tippie School of Management, Iowa City, IA 52242-1316. Offers accounting (MBA); corporate finance (MBA); entrepreneurship (MBA); finance (MBA); individually designed concentration (MBA); investment management (MBA); management information systems (MBA); marketing (MBA); nonprofit management (MBA); operations management (MBA); strategic management and consulting (MBA); JD/MBA; MBA/MA; MBA/MD; MBA/MHA; MBA/MSN. *Accreditation:* AACSB. Part-time and evening/weekend programs available. *Faculty:* 94 full-time (23 women), 65 part-time/adjunct (21 women). *Students:* 230 full-time (67 women), 712 part-time (234 women); includes 62 minority (6 African Americans, 1 American Indian/Alaska Native, 43 Asian Americans or Pacific Islanders, 12 Hispanic Americans), 127 international. Average age 30. 431 applicants, 61% accepted, 217 enrolled. In 2006, 363 degrees awarded. *Median time to degree:* Master's—2 years full-time, 3.5 years part-time. *Degree requirements:* For master's, registration. *Entrance requirements:* For master's, GMAT, work experience. Additional exam requirements/recommendations for international students: Required—TOEFL (minimum score 600 paper-based; 250 computer-based; 100 iBT). *Application deadline:* For fall admission, 7/15 for domestic students, 4/15 for international students; for spring admission, 12/15 priority date for domestic students, 11/1 priority date for international students. Applications are processed on a rolling basis. Application fee: $60 ($85 for international students). Electronic applications accepted. *Expenses:* Contact institution. *Financial support:* In 2006–07, 72 fellowships (averaging $3,892 per year), 55 research assistantships with partial tuition reimbursements (averaging $10,260 per year) were awarded; career-related internships or fieldwork, Federal Work-Study, institutionally sponsored loans, scholarships/grants, health care benefits, and unspecified assistantships also available. Support available to part-time students. Financial award application deadline: 4/15; financial award applicants required to submit FAFSA. *Faculty research:* Capital markets, econometrics, optimization, investments and empirical corporate finance, Iowa electronic markets. *Unit head:* Prof. Gary J. Gaeth, Associate Dean, MBA Programs, 800-622-4692, Fax: 319-335-3604, E-mail: gary-gaeth@uiowa.edu. *Application contact:* Jodi Schafer, Director of Student Recruitment and Marketing, 319-335-0864, Fax: 319-335-3604, E-mail: jodi-schafer@uiowa.edu.

University of La Verne, College of Business and Public Management, Graduate Programs in Business Administration, La Verne, CA 91750-4443. Offers accounting (MBA); business (MBIT); executive management (MBA-EP); finance (MBA, MBA-EP); health services management (MBA); information technology (MBA, MBA-EP); international business (MBA, MBA-EP); leadership (MBA-EP); managed care (MBA); management (MBA, MBA-EP); marketing (MBA, MBA-EP). Part-time and evening/weekend programs available. *Faculty:* 15 full-time (7 women), 13 part-time/adjunct (7 women). *Students:* 277 full-time (133 women), 112 part-time (64 women); includes 144 minority (32 African Americans, 3 American Indian/Alaska Native, 70 Asian Americans or Pacific Islanders, 39 Hispanic Americans), 160 international. Average age 30. In 2006, 142 degrees awarded. *Entrance requirements:* For master's, minimum undergraduate GPA of 3.0, 2 letters of recommendation, resumé. Additional exam requirements/recommendations for international students: Required—TOEFL (minimum score 550 paper-based; 213 computer-based). *Application deadline:* Applications are processed on a rolling basis. Application fee: $50. *Expenses:* Contact institution. *Financial support:* Career-related internships or fieldwork, institutionally sponsored loans, and scholarships/grants available. Financial award application deadline: 3/2; financial award applicants required to submit FAFSA. *Unit head:* Dr. Ibrahim Helou, Chairperson, 909-593-3511 Ext. 4211, Fax: 909-392-2704, E-mail: heloua@ulv.edu. *Application contact:* Dr. Julius Walecki, Marketing Director, 909-593-3511 Ext. 4192, Fax: 909-392-2704, E-mail: cbpm@ulv.edu.

University of La Verne, Regional Campus Administration, Graduate Programs, Inland Empire Campus, Ranche Cucamonga, CA 91750-4443. Offers business (MBA-EP), including health services management, information technology, management, marketing; health administration (MHA); leadership and management (MS). *Faculty:* 2 full-time (1 woman), 8 part-time/adjunct (2 women). *Students:* 21 full-time (16 women), 32 part-time (18 women); includes 29 minority (13 African Americans, 1 American Indian/Alaska Native, 4 Asian Americans or Pacific Islanders, 11 Hispanic Americans). Average age 37. In 2006, 17 degrees awarded. *Entrance requirements:* For master's, 2 letters of recommendation, resumé. *Application deadline:* Applications are processed on a rolling basis. Application fee: $50. *Expenses:* Contact institution. *Financial support:* Institutionally sponsored loans available. Financial award application deadline: 3/2; financial award applicants required to submit FAFSA. *Unit head:* Jerry Ford, Director, 909-484-3858 Ext. 228, Fax: 909-484-9469, E-mail: fordj@ulv.edu.

University of La Verne, Regional Campus Administration, Graduate Programs, Kern County Campus, Bakersfield, CA 93301. Offers business (MBA-EP), including information technology, management, marketing; health administration (MHA); leadership and management (MS). *Faculty:* 4 part-time/adjunct (2 women). *Students:* 2 full-time (1 woman), 7 part-time (4 women); includes 2 minority (1 African American, 1 Hispanic American). Average age 37. In 2006, 4 degrees awarded. *Entrance requirements:* For master's, 2 letters of recommendation, resumé. *Application deadline:* Applications are processed on a rolling basis. Application fee: $50. *Expenses:* Contact institution. *Financial support:* Institutionally sponsored loans available. Financial award application deadline: 3/2; financial award applicants required to submit FAFSA. *Unit head:* Val Garcia, 661-328-1430, E-mail: vgarcia6@ulv.edu.

University of La Verne, Regional Campus Administration, Graduate Programs, Orange County Campus, Garden Grove, CA 92840. Offers business (MBA-EP), including health services management, information technology, management, marketing, supply chain management; health administration (MHA); leadership and management (MS); public administration (MPA). *Faculty:* 4 full-time (1 woman), 3 part-time/adjunct (1 woman). *Students:* 19 full-time (8 women), 64 part-time (29 women); includes 37 minority (4 African Americans, 2 American Indian/Alaska Native, 15 Asian Americans or Pacific Islanders, 16 Hispanic Americans). Average age 41. In 2006, 18 degrees awarded. *Entrance requirements:* For master's, 2 letters of recommendation, resumé. *Application deadline:* Applications are processed on a rolling basis. Application fee: $50. *Expenses:* Contact institution. *Financial support:* Institutionally sponsored loans available. Financial award application deadline: 3/2; financial award applicants required to submit FAFSA. *Unit head:* Pamela Bergovoy, Director, 714-534-4860, Fax: 714-534-4865, E-mail: bergovoy@ulv.edu.

University of La Verne, Regional Campus Administration, Graduate Programs, San Fernando Valley Campus, Burbank, CA 91505. Offers business (MBA-EP), including health services management, information technology, management, marketing; health administration (MHA); leadership and management (MS). *Faculty:* 3 full-time (2 women), 6 part-time/adjunct (2 women). *Students:* 24 full-time (12 women), 57 part-time (31 women); includes 42 minority (12 African Americans, 1 American Indian/Alaska Native, 9 Asian Americans or Pacific Islanders, 20 Hispanic Americans), 1 international. Average age 39. In 2006, 45 degrees awarded. *Entrance requirements:* For master's, 2 letters of recommendation, resumé. *Application deadline:* Applications are processed on a rolling basis. Application fee: $50. *Expenses:* Contact institution. *Financial support:* Institutionally sponsored loans available. Financial award application deadline:

3/2; financial award applicants required to submit FAFSA. *Unit head:* Nelly Kazman, Director, 818-846-4008 Ext. 26, Fax: 818-566-1047, E-mail: kazmann@ulv.edu.

University of La Verne, Regional Campus Administration, Graduate Programs, Ventura County/ Point Mugu Naval Air Station Campuses, La Verne, CA 91750-4443. Offers business (MBA-EP), including health services management, information technology, management, marketing; business organizational management (MS); health administration (MHA); leadership and management (MS). *Faculty:* 2 full-time (0 women), 8 part-time/adjunct (1 woman). *Students:* 22 full-time (7 women), 29 part-time (16 women); includes 19 minority (4 African Americans, 7 Asian Americans or Pacific Islanders, 8 Hispanic Americans). Average age 40. In 2006, 26 degrees awarded. *Entrance requirements:* For master's, 2 letters of recommendation, resumé. Application fee: $50. *Expenses: Contact institution. Financial support:* Institutionally sponsored loans available. Financial award application deadline: 3/2; financial award applicants required to submit FAFSA. *Unit head:* Janet Meyer, Director, Ventura Campus, 805-981-8030 Ext. 225, Fax: 805-981-8033, E-mail: jmeyer2@ulv.edu.

University of Massachusetts Dartmouth, Graduate School, Charlton College of Business, Program in Business Administration, North Dartmouth, MA 02747-2300. Offers accounting (Postbaccalaureate Certificate); business administration (MBA); e-commerce (PMC); finance (PMC); general management (PMC); leadership (PMC); management (Postbaccalaureate Certificate); marketing (PMC); supply chain management (PMC). *Accreditation:* AACSB. Part-time programs available. *Faculty:* 41 full-time (11 women), 22 part-time/adjunct (8 women). *Students:* 66 full-time (20 women), 111 part-time (54 women); includes 16 minority (5 African Americans, 6 Asian Americans or Pacific Islanders, 5 Hispanic Americans), 46 international. Average age 30. 167 applicants, 83% accepted, 83 enrolled. In 2006, 73 master's, 20 other advanced degrees awarded. *Entrance requirements:* For master's, GMAT, resumé, letters of recommendation. Additional exam requirements/recommendations for international students: Required—TOEFL (minimum score 500 paper-based). *Application deadline:* For fall admission, 6/1 for domestic students, 4/1 for international students; for spring admission, 10/1 for domestic students, 8/1 for international students. Application fee: $40 ($60 for international students). Electronic applications accepted. *Expenses:* Tuition, state resident: full-time $2,071; part-time $86 per credit. Tuition, nonresident: full-time $8,099; part-time $337 per credit. *Financial support:* In 2006–07, 2 research assistantships with full tuition reimbursements (averaging $11,985 per year), 6 teaching assistantships with full tuition reimbursements (averaging $7,200 per year) were awarded; Federal Work-Study and unspecified assistantships also available. Support available to part-time students. Financial award application deadline: 3/1; financial award applicants required to submit FAFSA. *Faculty research:* Organizational identity dynamics in strategic alliances and partnerships, market analysis in cranberry industry, consumer choice modeling. Total annual research expenditures: $508,000. *Unit head:* Matthew Roy, Assistant Dean, 508-999-8409, Fax: 508-999-8776, E-mail: mroy@umassd.edu. *Application contact:* Carol Novo, Graduate Admissions Officer, 508-999-8604, Fax: 508-999-8183, E-mail: graduate@umassd.edu.

University of Memphis, Graduate School, Fogelman College of Business and Economics, Program in Business Administration, Memphis, TN 38152. Offers accounting (MBA, PhD); economics (MBA, PhD); executive business administration (MBA); finance (PhD); finance, insurance, and real estate (MBA, MS); international business administration (MBA); management (MBA, MS, PhD); management information systems (MBA, MS, PhD); management science (MBA); marketing (MBA, MS); marketing and supply chain management (PhD); real estate development (MS); JD/MBA. *Accreditation:* AACSB. *Faculty:* 84 full-time (14 women), 3 part-time/adjunct (0 women). *Students:* 222 full-time (92 women), 163 part-time (52 women); includes 62 minority (43 African Americans, 14 Asian Americans or Pacific Islanders, 5 Hispanic Americans), 119 international. Average age 29. In 2006, 196 master's, 12 doctorates awarded. *Degree requirements:* For master's, comprehensive exam; for doctorate, thesis/dissertation, comprehensive exam. *Entrance requirements:* For master's, GMAT, resumé; for doctorate, GMAT, interview, minimum GPA of 3.4, resumé, letter of recommendation. Additional exam requirements/recommendations for international students: Required—TOEFL (minimum score 550 paper-based; 220 computer-based). *Application deadline:* For fall admission, 8/1 for domestic students; for spring admission, 12/1 for domestic students. Application fee: $25 ($50 for international students). *Financial support:* Research assistantships with full tuition reimbursements, teaching assistantships, career-related internships or fieldwork, scholarships/grants, and unspecified assistantships available. Financial award application deadline: 3/1. *Faculty research:* Competitive business strategy, finance microstructures, supply chain management innovations, health care economics, litigation risks and corporate audits. Total annual research expenditures: $2.7 million. *Application contact:* Dr. Carol V. Danehower, Associate Dean for Programs, 901-678-5402, Fax: 901-678-3579, E-mail: fcbegp@memphis.edu.

University of Miami, Graduate School, School of Business Administration, Program in Business Administration, Coral Gables, FL 33124. Offers accounting (MBA); computer information systems (MBA); executive and professional (MBA), including international business, management; finance (MBA); international business (MBA); management (MBA); management science (MBA); marketing (MBA); professional management (MSPM); JD/MBA; MBA/MSIE. *Accreditation:* AACSB. Evening/weekend programs available. *Faculty:* 105 full-time (25 women). *Students:* 734 full-time (269 women), 19 part-time (4 women); includes 194 minority (24 African Americans, 1 American Indian/Alaska Native, 23 Asian Americans or Pacific Islanders, 146 Hispanic Americans), 115 international. Average age 31. 453 applicants, 71% accepted, 152 enrolled. In 2006, 394 degrees awarded. *Degree requirements:* For master's, comprehensive exam, registration. *Entrance requirements:* For master's, GMAT. Additional exam requirements/ recommendations for international students: Required—TOEFL (minimum score 550 paper-based; 213 computer-based; 59 iBT). *Application deadline:* For fall admission, 7/30 priority date for domestic students, 6/30 priority date for international students; for spring admission, 12/31 priority date for domestic students, 10/31 priority date for international students. Applications are processed on a rolling basis. Application fee: $50. Electronic applications accepted. *Financial support:* In 2006–07, 418 students received support, including 19 fellowships with partial tuition reimbursements available; unspecified assistantships also available. Financial award application deadline: 3/1; financial award applicants required to submit FAFSA. *Faculty research:* Leadership, e-commerce, supply chain management. *Unit head:* Daniela Mu±iz, Associate Director, Graduate Business Programs, 305-284-4626, Fax: 305-284-1878, E-mail: dmuniz@miami.edu. *Application contact:* David S. Green, Director of Graduate Business Recruiting and Admissions, 305-284-4607, Fax: 305-284-1878, E-mail: mba@miami.edu.

University of Minnesota, Twin Cities Campus, Carlson School of Management, Carlson Full-time MBA Program, Minneapolis, MN 55455-0213. Offers accounting (MBA); entrepreneurship (MBA); finance (MBA); healthcare management (MBA); information and decision sciences (MBA); international business (MBA); marketing and logistics management (MBA); operations and management science (MBA); strategic management and organization (MBA); supply chain management (MBA); JD/MBA; MD/MBA; MHA/MBA. *Accreditation:* AACSB. *Faculty:* 125 full-time (27 women), 120 part-time/adjunct. *Students:* 218 full-time (70 women); includes 18 minority (4 African Americans, 1 American Indian/Alaska Native, 10 Asian Americans or Pacific Islanders, 3 Hispanic Americans), 86 international. Average age 28. 418 applicants, 53% accepted, 124 enrolled. In 2006, 105 degrees awarded. *Median time to degree:* Master's–2 years full-time. *Entrance requirements:* For master's, GMAT. Additional exam requirements/ recommendations for international students: Required—TOEFL (minimum score 580 paper-based; 240 computer-based), IELTS. *Application deadline:* For fall admission, 4/15 for domestic students, 2/15 for international students. Application fee: $60 ($90 for international students). Electronic applications accepted. *Expenses: Contact institution.* Full-time tuition and fees vary according to class time, course load, program, reciprocity agreements and student level. *Financial support:* In 2006–07, 131 students received support, including 127 fellowships with full and partial tuition reimbursements available (averaging $20,000 per year); research assistantships with partial tuition reimbursements available, teaching assistantships with partial tuition reimbursements available, career-related internships or fieldwork, Federal Work-Study, institutionally sponsored loans, scholarships/grants, health care benefits, tuition waivers (full and partial), and unspecified assistantships also available. Support available to part-time students. Financial award application deadline: 2/15; financial award applicants required to submit FAFSA. *Faculty research:* IT, strategy, marketing, finance, quality management. *Unit head:* Kathryn J. Carlson, MBA Programs and Executive Education, 612-624-2039, Fax: 612-625-1012, E-mail: full-timeembainfo@csom.umn.edu. *Application contact:* Jeffrey Bieganek, Director, Admissions and Business Development, MBA Programs and Executive Education, 612-625-6558, Fax: 612-625-1012, E-mail: full-timembainfo@csom.umn.edu.

University of Minnesota, Twin Cities Campus, Carlson School of Management, Doctoral Program in Business Administration, Minneapolis, MN 55455-0213. Offers accounting (PhD); finance (PhD); information and decision sciences (PhD); marketing and logistics management (PhD); operations and management science (PhD); strategic management and organization (PhD). *Faculty:* 109 full-time (26 women). *Students:* 90 full-time (30 women); includes 9 minority (5 African Americans, 1 Asian American or Pacific Islander, 3 Hispanic Americans), 60 international. Average age 30. 325 applicants, 8% accepted, 17 enrolled. In 2006, 16 degrees awarded. *Median time to degree:* Of those who began their doctoral program in fall 1998, 61% received their degree in 8 years or less. *Degree requirements:* For doctorate, thesis/dissertation, written and oral preliminary exams, comprehensive exam, registration. *Entrance requirements:* For doctorate, GMAT, GRE General Test, International must submit a TOEFL or IELT. Additional exam requirements/recommendations for international students: Required—TOEFL (minimum score 600 paper-based; 250 computer-based; 100 iBT), IELTS (minimum score 8), TOEFL (paper-based 600, computer-based 250) or IELTS (7.5). *Application deadline:* For fall admission, 12/30 for domestic students, 12/30 priority date for international students. Applications are processed on a rolling basis. Application fee: $55 ($75 for international students). Electronic applications accepted. *Expenses:* Tuition, state resident: full-time $9,302; part-time $775 per credit. Tuition, nonresident: full-time $16,400; part-time $1,367 per credit. Full-time tuition and fees vary according to class time, course load, program, reciprocity agreements and student level. *Financial support:* In 2006–07, 67 students received support, including fellowships with full tuition reimbursements available (averaging $11,000 per year), research assistantships with full tuition reimbursements available (averaging $6,000 per year), teaching assistantships with full tuition reimbursements available (averaging $6,000 per year); institutionally sponsored loans, scholarships/grants, health care benefits, and unspecified assistantships also available. Financial award application deadline: 12/31. *Faculty research:* Corporate strategy, international business, corporate finances, entrepreneurship, quality management, marketing, information and decision science, operations and accounting. Total annual research expenditures: $300,000. *Unit head:* Dr. Paul E. Johnson, Director of Graduate Studies and PhD Program Director, 612-624-5570, Fax: 612-624-8221, E-mail: pjohnson@csom.umn.edu. *Application contact:* Earlene Bronson, Assistant Director, PhD Program, 612-624-0875, Fax: 612-624-8221, E-mail: ebronson@csom.umn.edu.

University of Missouri–St. Louis, College of Business Administration, Program in Business Administration, St. Louis, MO 63121. Offers accounting (MBA); business administration (Certificate); finance (MBA); human resource management (Certificate); logistics and supply chain management (MBA, Certificate); management (MBA); marketing (MBA); marketing management (Certificate); operations (MBA); quantitative management science (MBA); telecommunications management (Certificate). *Accreditation:* AACSB. Part-time and evening/weekend programs available. *Faculty:* 26 full-time (6 women), 2 part-time/adjunct (0 women). *Students:* 242 full-time (156 women), 186 part-time (123 women); includes 48 minority (17 African Americans, 1 American Indian/Alaska Native, 27 Asian Americans or Pacific Islanders, 3 Hispanic Americans), 96 international. Average age 33. In 2006, 138 degrees awarded. *Entrance requirements:* For master's, GMAT, 2 letters of recommendation. Additional exam requirements/recommendations for international students: Required—TOEFL (minimum score 550 paper-based; 213 computer-based). *Application deadline:* For fall admission, 7/1 for domestic students; for spring admission, 11/1 for domestic students. Applications are processed on a rolling basis. Application fee: $35 ($40 for international students). Electronic applications accepted. *Expenses:* Tuition, state resident: part-time $332 per credit hour. Tuition, nonresident: part-time $770 per credit hour. *Financial support:* Research assistantships with full and partial tuition reimbursements, teaching assistantships with full and partial tuition reimbursements, career-related internships or fieldwork, Federal Work-Study, and institutionally sponsored loans available. Support available to part-time students. Financial award application deadline: 4/1; financial award applicants required to submit FAFSA. *Faculty research:* Human resources, strategic management, marketing strategy, consumer behavior product development, advertising. *Application contact:* 314-516-5458, Fax: 314-516-6996, E-mail: gradadm@umsl.edu.

University of Nebraska–Lincoln, Graduate College, College of Business Administration, Interdepartmental Area of Business, Department of Marketing, Lincoln, NE 68588. Offers business (MA, PhD). *Degree requirements:* For doctorate, thesis/dissertation, comprehensive exam. *Entrance requirements:* For master's and doctorate, GMAT. Additional exam requirements/ recommendations for international students: Required—TOEFL. Electronic applications accepted. *Faculty research:* Channel information, marketing research methodology, sales management, cross-cultural marketing, impact of new technology.

University of New Brunswick Fredericton, School of Graduate Studies, Faculty of Forestry and Environmental Management, Fredericton, NB E3B 6C2, Canada. Offers ecological foundations of forest management (PhD); forest engineering (M Sc FE, MFE); forest products marketing (MBA); forest resources (M Sc F, MF, PhD). Part-time programs available. *Faculty:* 34 full-time (4 women). *Students:* 87 full-time (34 women), 22 part-time (8 women). In 2006, 13 master's, 5 doctorates awarded. *Degree requirements:* For master's and doctorate, thesis/ dissertation. *Entrance requirements:* For master's and doctorate, minimum GPA of 3.0. Additional exam requirements/recommendations for international students: Required—TOEFL (minimum score 580 paper-based), TWE (minimum score 4). *Application deadline:* For fall admission, 3/1 priority date for domestic students. Applications are processed on a rolling basis. Application fee: $50 Canadian dollars. *Financial support:* In 2006–07, 55 research assistantships, 17 teaching assistantships were awarded; fellowships also available. *Faculty research:* Genetics; soils; tree improvement, development, reproduction, physiology, and biotechnology; insect ecology; entomology. *Unit head:* Dr. John Kershaw, Director of Graduate Studies, 506-453-4933, Fax: 506-453-3538, E-mail: kershaw@unb.ca. *Application contact:* Faith Sharpe, Graduate Secretary, 506-458-7520, Fax: 506-453-3538, E-mail: fsharpe@unb.ca.

University of New Haven, Graduate School, School of Business, Program in Business Administration, West Haven, CT 06516-1916. Offers accounting (MBA); business policy and strategy (MBA); finance (MBA); health care management (MBA); human resources management (MBA); international business (MBA); marketing (MBA); public relations (MBA); sports management (MBA); technology management (MBA); MBA/MPA; MBA/MSIE. Part-time and evening/weekend programs available. *Degree requirements:* For master's, thesis or alternative. *Entrance requirements:* For master's, GMAT.

University of New Mexico, Robert O. Anderson Graduate School of Management, Department of Marketing, Information and Decision Sciences, Albuquerque, NM 87131-2039. Offers management information systems (MBA); marketing management (MBA); operations management (MBA). Part-time and evening/weekend programs available. *Entrance requirements:* For master's, GMAT. Additional exam requirements/recommendations for international students: Required—TOEFL (minimum score 550 paper-based; 213 computer-based).

The University of North Carolina at Chapel Hill, Kenan-Flagler Business School, Doctoral Program in Business Administration, Chapel Hill, NC 27599. Offers accounting (PhD); finance (PhD); marketing (PhD); operations management (PhD); organizational behavior (PhD); strategy (PhD). *Accreditation:* AACSB. *Degree requirements:* For doctorate, thesis/dissertation. *Entrance requirements:* For doctorate, GMAT or GRE General Test. Electronic applications accepted. Expenses: Contact institution.

The University of North Carolina at Charlotte, Graduate School, Belk College of Business Administration, Program in Sports Marketing Management, Charlotte, NC 28223-0001. Offers MS. *Expenses:* Tuition, state resident: full-time $2,719; part-time $170 per credit.

Marketing

The University of North Carolina at Charlotte (continued)
Tuition, nonresident: full-time $12,926; part-time $808 per credit. Required fees: $1,555. *Application contact:* Kathy B. Giddings, Director of Graduate Admissions, 704-687-3366, Fax: 704-687-3279, E-mail: gradadm@email.uncc.edu.

The University of North Carolina at Greensboro, Graduate School, School of Human Environmental Sciences, Department of Consumer, Apparel, and Retail Studies, Greensboro, NC 27412-5001. Offers MS, PhD. *Faculty:* 6 full-time (4 women). *Students:* 18 full-time (16 women), 2 part-time (1 woman); includes 11 minority (3 African Americans, 7 Asian Americans or Pacific Islanders, 1 Hispanic American). 20 applicants, 35% accepted. *Degree requirements:* For master's, one foreign language; for doctorate, one foreign language, thesis/dissertation. *Entrance requirements:* For master's and doctorate, GRE General Test. Additional exam requirements/recommendations for international students: Required—TOEFL. *Application deadline:* For fall admission, 7/1 priority date for domestic students; for spring admission, 11/1 for domestic students. Applications are processed on a rolling basis. Application fee: $45. Electronic applications accepted. *Expenses:* Tuition, state resident: full-time $2,692. Tuition, nonresident: full-time $13,742. *Financial support:* Fellowships with full tuition reimbursements, research assistantships with full tuition reimbursements, teaching assistantships with full tuition reimbursements available. *Faculty research:* Impact of phosphate removal, protective clothing for pesticide workers, fabric hand: subjective and objective measurements. *Unit head:* Dr. Gwendolyn O'Neal, Chair, 336-334-5472, Fax: 336-334-5614, E-mail: gsoneal@uncg.edu. *Application contact:* Michelle Harkleroad, Director of Graduate Admissions, 336-334-4884, Fax: 336-334-4424, E-mail: mbharkle@uncg.edu.

University of Northern Virginia, Graduate Programs, Manassas, VA 20109. Offers accountancy (MS); accounting (MBA); business administration (DBA); computer science (MS); counseling education (M Ed); early childhood education (M Ed); educational communication and instructional technology (M Ed); educational leadership (M Ed); finance (MBA); information systems technology (MS); management (MBA); marketing (MBA); project management (MBA); public administration (MPA); teaching English to speakers of other languages (M Ed). Part-time and evening/weekend programs available. Postbaccalaureate distance learning degree programs offered (no on-campus study). *Degree requirements:* For doctorate, thesis/dissertation, comprehensive exam, registration. *Entrance requirements:* Additional exam requirements/recommendations for international students: Required—TOEFL (minimum score 550 paper-based; 230 computer-based), IELTS (minimum score 6). Electronic applications accepted.

University of North Texas, Robert B. Toulouse School of Graduate Studies, College of Business Administration, Department of Marketing and Logistics, Denton, TX 76203. Offers MBA, PhD. Part-time programs available. *Faculty:* 18 full-time (1 woman). *Students:* 13 full-time (2 women), 25 part-time (11 women); includes 2 minority (1 Asian American or Pacific Islander, 1 Hispanic American), 13 international. Average age 30. 39 applicants, 87% accepted, 5 enrolled. In 2006, 15 master's, 2 doctorates awarded. *Degree requirements:* For doctorate, thesis/dissertation. *Entrance requirements:* For master's and doctorate, GMAT. Additional exam requirements/recommendations for international students: Required—TOEFL. *Application deadline:* For fall admission, 7/15 priority date for domestic students; for spring admission, 10/15 for domestic students. Applications are processed on a rolling basis. Application fee: $50 ($75 for international students). *Expenses:* Tuition, state resident: full-time $3,573; part-time $198 per credit. Tuition, nonresident: full-time $8,577; part-time $476 per credit. Required fees: $1,258; $126 per credit. One-time fee: $150 full-time. Tuition and fees vary according to course load. *Financial support:* Fellowships, teaching assistantships, career-related internships or fieldwork, Federal Work-Study, and institutionally sponsored loans available. Financial award application deadline: 4/1. *Faculty research:* Promotion, distribution channels, international distribution, sales management, consumer behavior. *Unit head:* Dr. Harold D. Strutton, Chair, 940-565-3120, Fax: 940-565-3837, E-mail: strutton@unt.edu. *Application contact:* Dr. John Crawford, Graduate Adviser, 940-565-3120, Fax: 940-565-3837, E-mail: crawford@unt.edu.

University of Oregon, Graduate School, Charles H. Lundquist College of Business, Department of Marketing, Eugene, OR 97403. Offers PhD. Part-time programs available. *Students:* 10 full-time (3 women); includes 1 minority (Asian American or Pacific Islander), 3 international. 2 applicants, 100% accepted. *Degree requirements:* For doctorate, thesis/dissertation, 2 comprehensive exams. *Entrance requirements:* For doctorate, GMAT. Additional exam requirements/recommendations for international students: Required—TOEFL. *Application deadline:* For fall admission, 2/1 for domestic students. Application fee: $50. *Financial support:* In 2006–07, 7 teaching assistantships were awarded; career-related internships or fieldwork and Federal Work-Study also available. *Faculty research:* Consumer behavior, marketing research, international marketing, marketing management, price quality. *Unit head:* Dennis Howard, Head, 541-346-3352. *Application contact:* Perri McGee, Admissions Contact, 541-346-1462, E-mail: pcrone@uoregon.edu.

University of Pennsylvania, Wharton School, Marketing Department, Philadelphia, PA 19104. Offers MBA, PhD. Terminal master's awarded for partial completion of doctoral program. *Degree requirements:* For master's, thesis optional; for doctorate, thesis/dissertation, registration. *Entrance requirements:* For doctorate, GMAT or GRE. *Faculty research:* Scanner data, consumer preferences, decision-making theory, modeling for marketing and e-business.

University of Phoenix–Augusta Campus, College of Graduate Business and Management, Augusta, GA 30909-4583. Offers accounting (MBA); business and management (MBA, MM); global management (MBA); human resources management (MBA, MM); marketing (MBA); public administration (MBA, MM).

University of Phoenix–Austin Campus, College of Graduate Business and Management, Austin, TX 78759. Offers accounting (MBA); business and management (MBA); e-business (MBA); global management (MBA); human resources management (MBA, MM); management (MM); marketing (MBA); public administration (MBA).

University of Phoenix–Bay Area Campus, John Sperling School of Business, College of Graduate Business and Management, Pleasanton, CA 94588-3677. Offers accounting (MBA); business administration (MBA); global management (MBA); human resource management (MBA); marketing (MBA); public administration (MBA). Evening/weekend programs available. *Faculty:* 30 full-time (3 women), 390 part-time/adjunct (106 women). *Students:* 523 full-time (279 women); includes 185 minority (40 African Americans, 2 American Indian/Alaska Native, 110 Asian Americans or Pacific Islanders, 33 Hispanic Americans), 84 international. Average age 37. In 2006, 205 degrees awarded. *Degree requirements:* For master's, thesis (for some programs), registration. *Entrance requirements:* For master's, minimum undergraduate GPA of 3.0, 3 years of work experience. Additional exam requirements/recommendations for international students: Required—TOEFL (minimum score 550 paper-based; 213 computer-based; 79 iBT). *Application deadline:* Applications are processed on a rolling basis. Application fee: $45. Electronic applications accepted. *Expenses:* Tuition: Full-time $12,648. Required fees: $760. *Financial support:* Institutionally sponsored loans and scholarships/grants available. Financial award applicants required to submit FAFSA. *Unit head:* Dr. Brian Lindquist, Associate Vice President and Dean/Executive Director, 408-557-1221, E-mail: brian.lindquist@phoenix.edu. *Application contact:* Chair, 408-435-8500, Fax: 408-435-8250.

University of Phoenix–Central Florida Campus, John Sperling School of Business, College of Graduate Business and Management, Maitland, FL 32751-7057. Offers accounting (MBA); business administration (MBA); business and management (MM); global management (MBA); management (MM); marketing (MBA). Evening/weekend programs available. *Faculty:* 50 full-time (11 women), 136 part-time/adjunct (32 women). *Students:* 440 full-time (265 women); includes 175 minority (102 African Americans, 4 American Indian/Alaska Native, 16 Asian Americans or Pacific Islanders, 53 Hispanic Americans), 38 international. Average age 36. In 2006, 149 degrees awarded. *Degree requirements:* For master's, thesis (for some programs), registration. *Entrance requirements:* For master's, minimum undergraduate GPA of 3.0, 3

years work experience. Additional exam requirements/recommendations for international students: Required—TOEFL (minimum score 550 paper-based; 213 computer-based; 79 iBT). *Application deadline:* Applications are processed on a rolling basis. Application fee: $45. Electronic applications accepted. *Expenses:* Tuition: Full-time $9,450. Required fees: $760. *Financial support:* Institutionally sponsored loans and scholarships/grants available. Financial award applicants required to submit FAFSA. *Unit head:* Dr. Brian Lindquist, Associate Vice President and Dean/Executive Director, 480-557-1221, E-mail: brian.lindquist@phoenix.edu. *Application contact:* Chair, 407-667-0555, Fax: 407-667-0560.

University of Phoenix–Central Valley Campus, College of Graduate Business and Management, Fresno, CA 93720. Offers accounting (MBA); business administration (MBA); global management (MBA); human resources management (MBA); management (MM); marketing (MBA); public administration (MBA).

University of Phoenix–Chattanooga Campus, College of Graduate Business and Management, Chattanooga, TN 37421-3707. Offers accounting (MBA); business and management (MBA); global management (MBA); human resources management (MBA, MM); management (MM); marketing (MBA); public administration (MBA, MM).

University of Phoenix–Cheyenne Campus, College of Graduate Business and Management, Cheyenne, WY 82009. Offers business and management (MM); global management (MBA); human resources management (MBA, MM); marketing (MBA); public administration (MBA, MM).

University of Phoenix–Cleveland Campus, John Sperling School of Business, College of Graduate Business and Management, Independence, OH 44131-2194. Offers accounting (MBA); business administration (MBA); global management (MBA); human resources management (MM); management (MM); marketing (MBA); public administration (MBA, MM). Evening/weekend programs available. *Faculty:* 10 full-time (1 woman), 68 part-time/adjunct (16 women). *Students:* 178 full-time (107 women); includes 115 minority (66 African Americans, 1 American Indian/Alaska Native, 5 Asian Americans or Pacific Islanders, 43 Hispanic Americans), 9 international. Average age 37. In 2006, 25 degrees awarded. *Degree requirements:* For master's, thesis (for some programs), registration. *Entrance requirements:* For master's, minimum undergraduate GPA of 3.0, 3 years of work experience. Additional exam requirements/recommendations for international students: Required—TOEFL (minimum score 550 paper-based; 213 computer-based; 79 iBT). *Application deadline:* Applications are processed on a rolling basis. Application fee: $45. Electronic applications accepted. *Expenses:* Tuition: Full-time $11,608. Required fees: $760. *Financial support:* Institutionally sponsored loans and scholarships/grants available. Financial award applicants required to submit FAFSA. *Unit head:* Dr. Brian Lindquist, Associate Vice President and Dean/Executive Director, 480-557-1221, E-mail: brian.linquist@phoenix.edu. *Application contact:* Chair, 216-447-8807, Fax: 216-447-9144.

University of Phoenix–Columbus Georgia Campus, John Sperling School of Business, College of Graduate Business and Management, Columbus, GA 31904-6321. Offers accounting (MBA); administration (MBA); global management (MBA); human resource management (MBA); marketing (MBA); public administration (MBA). Evening/weekend programs available. *Faculty:* 11 full-time (1 woman), 53 part-time/adjunct (15 women). *Students:* 52 full-time (35 women); includes 27 minority (22 African Americans, 1 Asian American or Pacific Islander, 4 Hispanic Americans). Average age 37. In 2006, 10 degrees awarded. *Degree requirements:* For master's, thesis (for some programs), registration. *Entrance requirements:* For master's, minimum undergraduate GPA of 3.0, 3 years of work experience. Additional exam requirements/recommendations for international students: Required—TOEFL (minimum score 550 paper-based; 213 computer-based; 79 iBT). *Application deadline:* Applications are processed on a rolling basis. Application fee: $45. Electronic applications accepted. *Expenses:* Tuition: Full-time $10,200. Required fees: $760. *Financial support:* Institutionally sponsored loans and scholarships/grants available. Financial award applicants required to submit FAFSA. *Unit head:* Dr. Brian Lindquist, Associate Vice President/Dean/Executive Director, 480-557-1221, E-mail: brian.lindquist@phoenix.edu. *Application contact:* College Chair, 706-320-1262.

University of Phoenix–Columbus Ohio Campus, John Sperling School of Business, College of Graduate Business and Management, Columbus, OH 43240-4032. Offers administration (MBA); marketing (MBA). Evening/weekend programs available. *Faculty:* 12 full-time (5 women), 27 part-time/adjunct (3 women). *Students:* 145 full-time (88 women); includes 40 minority (36 African Americans, 3 Asian Americans or Pacific Islanders, 1 Hispanic American), 6 international. Average age 37. In 2006, 40 degrees awarded. *Degree requirements:* For master's, thesis (for some programs), registration. *Entrance requirements:* For master's, minimum undergraduate GPA of 3.0, 3 years of work experience. Additional exam requirements/recommendations for international students: Required—TOEFL (minimum score 550 paper-based; 213 computer-based; 79 iBT). *Application deadline:* Applications are processed on a rolling basis. Application fee: $45. Electronic applications accepted. *Expenses:* Tuition: Full-time $11,832. Required fees: $760. *Financial support:* Institutionally sponsored loans and scholarships/grants available. Financial award applicants required to submit FAFSA. *Unit head:* Dr. Brian Lindquist, Associate Vice President and Dean/Executive Director, 480-557-1221, E-mail: brian.lindquist@phoenix.edu.

University of Phoenix–Dallas Campus, John Sperling School of Business, College of Graduate Business and Management, Dallas, TX 75251-2009. Offers accounting (MBA); administration (MBA); human resources management (MBA, MM); management (MM); marketing (MBA); public administration (MBA, MM). Evening/weekend programs available. *Faculty:* 27 full-time (5 women), 130 part-time/adjunct (34 women). *Students:* 517 full-time (320 women); includes 217 minority (166 African Americans, 7 American Indian/Alaska Native, 11 Asian Americans or Pacific Islanders, 33 Hispanic Americans), 68 international. Average age 37. In 2006, 127 degrees awarded. *Degree requirements:* For master's, thesis (for some programs), registration. *Entrance requirements:* For master's, 3 years of work experience, minimum undergraduate GPA of 3.0. Additional exam requirements/recommendations for international students: Required—TOEFL (minimum score 550 paper-based; 213 computer-based; 79 iBT). *Application deadline:* Applications are processed on a rolling basis. Application fee: $45. Electronic applications accepted. *Expenses:* Tuition: Full-time $11,832. Required fees: $760. *Financial support:* Institutionally sponsored loans and scholarships/grants available. Financial award applicants required to submit FAFSA. *Unit head:* Dr. Brian Lindquist, Associate Vice President and Dean/Executive Director, 480-557-1221, E-mail: brian.lindquist@phoenix.edu. *Application contact:* Chair, 972-385-1055, Fax: 972-385-1700.

University of Phoenix–Denver Campus, John Sperling School of Business, College of Graduate Business and Management, Lone Tree, CO 80124-5453. Offers accounting (MBA); business administration (MBA); e-business (MBA); global management (MBA); human resources management (MBA, MM); management (MM); marketing (MBA); public administration (MBA, MM). Evening/weekend programs available. *Faculty:* 63 full-time (22 women), 254 part-time/adjunct (56 women). *Students:* 289 full-time (139 women); includes 59 minority (25 African Americans, 1 American Indian/Alaska Native, 9 Asian Americans or Pacific Islanders, 24 Hispanic Americans), 20 international. Average age 37. In 2006, 93 degrees awarded. *Degree requirements:* For master's, thesis (for some programs), registration. *Entrance requirements:* For master's, minimum undergraduate GPA of 3.0, 3 years work experience. Additional exam requirements/recommendations for international students: Required—TOEFL (minimum score 550 paper-based; 213 computer-based; 79 iBT). *Application deadline:* Applications are processed on a rolling basis. Application fee: $45. Electronic applications accepted. *Expenses:* Tuition: Full-time $10,032. Required fees: $760. *Financial support:* Institutionally sponsored loans and scholarships/grants available. Financial award applicants required to submit FAFSA. *Unit head:* Dr. Brian Lindquist, Associate Vice President and Dean/Executive Director, 480-557-1221, E-mail: brian.lindquist@phoenix.edu. *Application contact:* Chair, 303-694-9093, Fax: 303-662-0911.

University of Phoenix–Des Moines Campus, College of Graduate Business and Management, Des Moines, IA 50266. Offers accounting (MBA); business administration (MBA); global management (MBA); human resources management (MBA, MM); management (MM); marketing (MBA); public administration (MBA, MM).

University of Phoenix–Detroit Campus, College of Graduate Business and Management, Southfield, MI 48076. Offers accounting (MBA); business administration (MBA); e-business (MBA); global management (MBA); human resources management (MBA, MM); management (MM); marketing (MBA); public administration (MBA).

University of Phoenix–Fort Lauderdale Campus, John Sperling School of Business, College of Graduate Business and Management, Fort Lauderdale, FL 33309. Offers accounting (MBA); business administration (MBA); global management (MBA); human resource management (MBA); human resources management (MM); management (MM); marketing (MBA); public administration (MBA). Evening/weekend programs available. *Faculty:* 31 full-time (13 women), 117 part-time/adjunct (33 women). *Students:* 433 full-time (273 women); includes 196 minority (113 African Americans, 3 American Indian/Alaska Native, 8 Asian Americans or Pacific Islanders, 72 Hispanic Americans), 64 international. Average age 38. In 2006, 112 degrees awarded. *Degree requirements:* For master's, thesis (for some programs), registration. *Entrance requirements:* For master's, minimum undergraduate GPA of 3.0, 3 years work experience. Additional exam requirements/recommendations for international students: Required—TOEFL (minimum score 550 paper-based; 213 computer-based; 79 iBT). *Application deadline:* Applications are processed on a rolling basis. Application fee: $45. Electronic applications accepted. *Expenses:* Tuition: Full-time $9,450. Required fees: $760. *Financial support:* Institutionally sponsored loans and scholarships/grants available. Financial award applicants required to submit FAFSA. *Unit head:* Dr. Brian Linquist, Associate V.P. & Dean/Executive Director, 480-557-1221, E-mail: brian.linquist@phoenix.edu. *Application contact:* Chair, 954-382-5303, Fax: 954-382-5304.

University of Phoenix–Harrisburg Campus, College of Graduate Business and Management, Harrisburg, PA 17112. Offers accounting (MBA); business and management (MBA); glboal management (MBA); human resources management (MBA, MM); management (MM); marketing (MBA); public administration (MBA, MM).

University of Phoenix–Hawaii Campus, John Sperling School of Business, College of Graduate Business and Management, Honolulu, HI 96813-4317. Offers accounting (MBA); business administration (MBA); global management (MBA); human resources management (MBA, MM); management (MM); marketing (MBA); public administration (MBA, MM). Evening/weekend programs available. *Faculty:* 17 full-time (4 women), 92 part-time/adjunct (23 women). *Students:* 72 full-time (39 women); includes 18 minority (3 African Americans, 13 Asian Americans or Pacific Islanders, 2 Hispanic Americans), 30 international. Average age 37. In 2006, 20 master's awarded. *Degree requirements:* For master's, thesis (for some programs), registration. *Entrance requirements:* For master's, minimum undergraduate GPA of 3.0, 3 years of work experience. Additional exam requirements/recommendations for international students: Required—TOEFL (minimum score 550 paper-based; 213 computer-based; 79 iBT). *Application deadline:* Applications are processed on a rolling basis. Application fee: $45. Electronic applications accepted. *Expenses:* Tuition: Full-time $11,520. Required fees: $760. *Financial support:* Institutionally sponsored loans and scholarships/grants available. Financial award applicants required to submit FAFSA. *Unit head:* Dr. Brian Lindquist, Associate Vice President and Dean/Executive Director, 480-557-1221, E-mail: brian.lindquist@phoenix.edu. *Application contact:* Chair, 808-536-2686, Fax: 808-536-3848.

University of Phoenix–Jersey City Campus, College of Graduate Business and Management, Jersey City, NJ 07310. Offers accounting (MBA); business and management (MBA); global management (MBA); human resources management (MBA, MM); management (MM); marketing (MBA); public administration (MBA, MM).

University of Phoenix–Madison Campus, College of Graduate Business and Management, Madison, WI 53718-2416. Offers accounting (MBA); business and management (MBA, MM); e-business (MBA); global management (MBA); human resources management (MBA, MM); marketing (MBA); public administration (MBA).

University of Phoenix–Maryland Campus, John Sperling School of Business, College of Graduate Business and Management, Columbia, MD 21045-5424. Offers business administration (MBA); e-business (MBA); global management (MBA); human resources management (MBA, MM); marketing (MBA); public administration (MBA, MM). Evening/weekend programs available. *Faculty:* 22 full-time (6 women), 136 part-time/adjunct (35 women). *Students:* 357 full-time (223 women); includes 148 minority (128 African Americans, 2 American Indian/Alaska Native, 9 Asian Americans or Pacific Islanders, 9 Hispanic Americans), 38 international. Average age 37. In 2006, 111 master's awarded. *Degree requirements:* For master's, thesis (for some programs), registration. *Entrance requirements:* For master's, minimum undergraduate GPA of 3.0, 3 years of work experience. Additional exam requirements/recommendations for international students: Required—TOEFL (minimum score 550 paper-based; 213 computer-based; 79 iBT). *Application deadline:* Applications are processed on a rolling basis. Application fee: $45. Electronic applications accepted. *Expenses:* Tuition: Full-time $13,200. Required fees: $760. *Financial support:* Institutionally sponsored loans and scholarships/grants available. Financial award applicants required to submit FAFSA. *Unit head:* Dr. Brian Lindquist, Associate Vice President and Dean/Executive Director, 480-557-1221, E-mail: brian.lindquist@phoenix.edu. *Application contact:* Chair, 410-872-9001, Fax: 410-536-5727.

University of Phoenix–Memphis Campus, College of Graduate Business and Management, Cordova, TN 38018. Offers accounting (MBA); business and management (MBA); e-business (MBA); global management (MBA); human resources management (MBA, MM); marketing (MBA); public administration (MBA, MM).

University of Phoenix–Minneapolis/St. Louis Park Campus, College of Graduate Business and Management, St. Louis Park, MN 55426. Offers accounting (MBA); business administration (MBA); global management (MBA); human resources management (MBA); marketing (MBA).

University of Phoenix—Northern Nevada Campus, College of Graduate Business and Management, Reno, NV 89511. Offers accounting (MBA); business and management (MBA); global management (MBA); human resources management (MBA, MM); management (MM); marketing (MBA); public administration (MBA, MM).

University of Phoenix–Northern Virginia Campus, College of Graduate Business and Management, Reston, VA 20190. Offers accounting (MBA); business administration (MBA); e-business (MBA); global management (MBA); human resources management (MBA, MM); management (MM); marketing (MBA); public administration (MBA).

University of Phoenix–North Florida Campus, John Sperling School of Business, College of Graduate Business and Management, Jacksonville, FL 32216-0959. Offers accounting (MBA); business administration (MBA); global management (MBA); human resources management (MBA, MM); management (MM); marketing (MBA); public administration (MBA). Evening/weekend programs available. *Faculty:* 40 full-time (15 women), 105 part-time/adjunct (25 women). *Students:* 392 full-time (237 women); includes 135 minority (117 African Americans, 1 American Indian/Alaska Native, 12 Asian Americans or Pacific Islanders, 5 Hispanic Americans), 20 international. Average age 31. In 2006, 134 degrees awarded. *Degree requirements:* For master's, thesis (for some programs), registration. *Entrance requirements:* For master's, minimum undergraduate GPA of 3.0, 3 years work experience. Additional exam requirements/recommendations for international students: Required—TOEFL (minimum score 550 paper-based; 213 computer-based; 79 iBT). *Application deadline:* Applications are processed on a rolling basis. Application fee: $45. Electronic applications accepted. *Financial support:* Institutionally sponsored loans available. Financial award applicants required to submit FAFSA. *Unit head:* Dr. Brian Lindquist, Associate Vice President and Dean/Executive Director, 480-557-1221, E-mail: brian.lindquist@phoenix.edu. *Application contact:* Chair, 904-636-6645, Fax: 904-636-0998.

University of Phoenix–Northwest Arkansas Campus, College of Graduate Business and Management, Rogers, AR 72756-9615. Offers accounting (MBA); business and management (MBA); global management (MBA); human resources management (MBA, MM); management (MM); marketing (MBA); public administration (MBA, MM).

University of Phoenix–Omaha Campus, College of Graduate Business and Management, Omaha, NE 68154-5240. Offers accounting (MBA); business and management (MBA); global management (MBA); human resources management (MM); human resources managemetn (MBA); management (MM); marketing (MBA); public administration (MM); public adminstration (MBA).

University of Phoenix Online Campus, John Sperling School of Business, College of Graduate Business and Management, Phoenix, AZ 85034-7209. Offers accounting (MBA); administration (MBA); global management (MBA); human resources management (MBA); management (MM); marketing (MBA); public administration (MBA, MM). Evening/weekend programs available. *Faculty:* 25 full-time (15 women), 4,861 part-time/adjunct (1,504 women). *Students:* 17,914 full-time (10,655 women); includes 4,983 minority (3,259 African Americans, 113 American Indian/Alaska Native, 651 Asian Americans or Pacific Islanders, 960 Hispanic Americans), 1,805 international. Average age 36. In 2006, 1,740 master's awarded. *Degree requirements:* For master's, thesis (for some programs), registration. *Entrance requirements:* For master's, 3 years of work experience, minimum undergraduate GPA of 3.0. Additional exam requirements/recommendations for international students: Required—TOEFL (minimum score 550 paper-based; 213 computer-based; 79 iBT). *Application deadline:* Applications are processed on a rolling basis. Application fee: $45. Electronic applications accepted. *Expenses:* Tuition: Full-time $12,664. Required fees: $760. *Financial support:* Institutionally sponsored loans and scholarships/grants available. Financial award applicants required to submit FAFSA. *Unit head:* Brian Lindquist, Dean/Executive Director and Associate Vice President, 480-557-1221, E-mail: brian.lindquist@phoenix.edu. *Application contact:* Brian Lindquist, Dean/Executive Director and Associate Vice President, 480-557-1221, E-mail: brian.lindquist@phoenix.edu.

University of Phoenix–Pittsburgh Campus, John Sperling School of Business, College of Graduate Business and Management, Pittsburgh, PA 15276. Offers accounting (MBA); business administration (MBA); global management (MBA); human resource management (MBA); human resources management (MM); management (MM); marketing (MBA); public administration (MBA, MM). Evening/weekend programs available. *Faculty:* 19 full-time (6 women), 49 part-time/adjunct (13 women). *Students:* 84 full-time (43 women); includes 16 minority (13 African Americans, 2 Asian Americans or Pacific Islanders, 1 Hispanic American), 4 international. Average age 37. In 2006, 35 degrees awarded. *Degree requirements:* For master's, thesis (for some programs), registration. *Entrance requirements:* For master's, minimum undergraduate GPA of 3.0, 3 years work experience. Additional exam requirements/recommendations for international students: Required—TOEFL (minimum score 550 paper-based; 213 computer-based; 79 iBT). *Application deadline:* Applications are processed on a rolling basis. Application fee: $45. Electronic applications accepted. *Expenses:* Tuition: Full-time $13,560. Required fees: $760. *Financial support:* Institutionally sponsored loans and scholarships/grants available. Financial award applicants required to submit FAFSA. *Unit head:* Dr. Brian Lindquist, Associate Vice President and Dean/Executive Director, 480-551-1221, E-mail: brian.lindquist@phoenix.edu. *Application contact:* College Chair, 412-747-9000, Fax: 412-747-0676.

University of Phoenix–Puerto Rico Campus, John Sperling School of Business, College of Graduate Business and Management, Guaynabo, PR 00968. Offers accounting (MBA); business administration (MBA); global management (MBA); human resource management (MBA); marketing (MBA). Evening/weekend programs available. *Faculty:* 19 full-time (8 women), 73 part-time/adjunct (25 women). *Students:* 1,122 full-time (671 women); includes 636 minority (2 African Americans, 3 American Indian/Alaska Native, 3 Asian Americans or Pacific Islanders, 628 Hispanic Americans), 31 international. Average age 34. In 2006, 281 degrees awarded. *Degree requirements:* For master's, thesis (for some programs), registration. *Entrance requirements:* For master's, minimum undergraduate GPA of 3.0, 3 years work experience. Additional exam requirements/recommendations for international students: Required—TOEFL (minimum score 550 paper-based; 213 computer-based; 79 iBT). *Application deadline:* Applications are processed on a rolling basis. Application fee: $45. Electronic applications accepted. *Expenses:* Tuition: Full-time $5,816. Required fees: $760. *Financial support:* Institutionally sponsored loans and scholarships/grants available. Financial award applicants required to submit FAFSA. *Unit head:* Dr. Brian Lindquist, Associate Vice President and Dean/Executive Director, 480-557-1221, E-mail: brian.lindquist@phoenix.edu. *Application contact:* Chair, 787-931-5400, Fax: 787-931-1510.

University of Phoenix–Renton Learning Center, College of Graduate Business and Management, Renton, WA 98005. Offers accounting (MBA); business and management (MBA, MM); global management (MBA); human resources management (MBA, MM); marketing (MBA); public administration (MBA, MM).

University of Phoenix–Richmond Campus, John Sperling School of Business, College of Graduate Business and Management, Richmond, VA 23230. Offers accounting (MBA); business administration (MBA); global management (MBA); human resources management (MBA, MM); management (MM); marketing (MBA); public administration (MBA, MM). Evening/weekend programs available. *Faculty:* 6 full-time (4 women), 60 part-time/adjunct (7 women). *Students:* 103 full-time (73 women); includes 42 minority (38 African Americans, 1 American Indian/Alaska Native, 2 Asian Americans or Pacific Islanders, 1 Hispanic American), 10 international. Average age 36. In 2006, 1 degree awarded. *Degree requirements:* For master's, thesis (for some programs), registration. *Entrance requirements:* For master's, minimum undergraduate GPA 3.0, 3 years work experience. Additional exam requirements/recommendations for international students: Required—TOEFL (minimum score 550 paper-based; 213 computer-based; 79 iBT). *Application deadline:* Applications are processed on a rolling basis. Application fee: $45. Electronic applications accepted. *Financial support:* Institutionally sponsored loans and scholarships/grants available. Financial award applicants required to submit FAFSA. *Unit head:* Dr. Brian Lindquist, Associate Vice President/Dean, 480-557-1221, E-mail: brian.lindquist@phoenix.edu. *Application contact:* Chair, 804-288-3390.

University of Phoenix–Sacramento Valley Campus, John Sperling School of Business, College of Graduate Business and Management, Sacramento, CA 95833-3632. Offers accounting (MBA); business administration (MBA); global management (MBA); human resources management (MBA); marketing (MBA); public administration (MBA). Evening/weekend programs available. *Faculty:* 36 full-time (19 women), 291 part-time/adjunct (83 women). *Students:* 395 full-time (197 women); includes 120 minority (62 African Americans, 2 American Indian/Alaska Native, 32 Asian Americans or Pacific Islanders, 24 Hispanic Americans), 34 international. Average age 37. In 2006, 138 master's awarded. *Degree requirements:* For master's, thesis (for some programs), registration. *Entrance requirements:* For master's, minimum undergraduate GPA of 3.0, 3 years work experience. Additional exam requirements/recommendations for international students: Required—TOEFL (minimum score 550 paper-based; 213 computer-based; 79 iBT). *Application deadline:* Applications are processed on a rolling basis. Application fee: $45. Electronic applications accepted. *Expenses:* Tuition: Full-time $12,024. Required fees: $760. *Financial support:* Institutionally sponsored loans and scholarships/grants available. Financial award applicants required to submit FAFSA. *Unit head:* Dr. Brian Lindquist, Associate Vice President and Dean/Executive Director, 480-557-1221, E-mail: brian.lindquist@phoenix.edu. *Application contact:* Campus College Chair, 916-923-2107, Fax: 916-923-3914.

University of Phoenix–San Antonio Campus, College of Graduate Business and Management, San Antonio, TX 78230. Offers accounting (MBA); business and management

Marketing

University of Phoenix–San Antonio Campus (continued)
(MBA); e-business (MBA); global management (MBA); human resources management (MBA, MM); management (MM); marketing (MBA); public administration (MBA, MM).

University of Phoenix–Savannah Campus, College of Graduate Business and Management, Savannah, GA 31405-7400. Offers accounting (MBA); business administration (MBA); business and management (MM); global management (MBA); human resources management (MBA, MM); marketing (MBA); public administration (MBA, MM).

University of Phoenix–Southern California Campus, John Sperling School of Business, College of Graduate Business and Management, Costa Mesa, CA 92626. Offers accounting (MBA); business administration (MBA); business and management (MM); human resource management (MBA); marketing (MBA). Evening/weekend programs available. *Faculty:* 47 full-time (13 women), 513 part-time/adjunct (138 women). *Students:* 1,491 full-time (852 women); includes 558 minority (233 African Americans, 7 American Indian/Alaska Native, 124 Asian Americans or Pacific Islanders, 194 Hispanic Americans), 116 international. Average age 38. In 2006, 401 degrees awarded. *Degree requirements:* For master's, thesis (for some programs), registration. *Entrance requirements:* For master's, minimum undergraduate GPA of 3.0, 3 years work experience. Additional exam requirements/recommendations for international students: Required—TOEFL (minimum score 550 paper-based; 213 computer-based; 79 iBT). *Application deadline:* Applications are processed on a rolling basis. Application fee: $45. Electronic applications accepted. *Expenses:* Tuition: Full-time $13,512. Required fees: $760. *Financial support:* Institutionally sponsored loans and scholarships/grants available. Financial award applicants required to submit FAFSA. *Unit head:* Dr. Brian Lindquist, Associate Vice President and Dean/Executive Director, 480-557-1221, E-mail: brian.lindquist@phoenix.edu. *Application contact:* Campus College Chair, 714-378-1878, Fax: 714-378-5875.

University of Phoenix–Springfield Campus, College of Graduate Business and Management, Springfield, MO 65804-7211. Offers accounting (MBA); business and management (MBA); global management (MBA); human resources management (MBA, MM); management (MM); marketing (MBA); public administration (MBA, MM).

University of Phoenix–West Florida Campus, The John Sperling School of Business, College of Graduate Business and Management, Temple Terrace, FL 33637. Offers business administration (MBA); global management (MBA); human resource management (MBA); human resources management (MM); management (MM); marketing (MBA); public administration (MBA). Evening/weekend programs available. *Faculty:* 39 full-time (19 women), 145 part-time/adjunct (45 women). *Students:* 475 full-time (272 women); includes 150 minority (98 African Americans, 4 American Indian/Alaska Native, 9 Asian Americans or Pacific Islanders, 39 Hispanic Americans), 43 international. Average age 36. In 2006, 165 degrees awarded. *Degree requirements:* For master's, thesis (for some programs), registration. *Entrance requirements:* For master's, 3 years of work experience, minimum undergraduate GPA of 3.0. Additional exam requirements/recommendations for international students: Required—TOEFL (minimum score 550 paper-based; 213 computer-based; 79 iBT). *Application deadline:* Applications are processed on a rolling basis. Application fee: $45. Electronic applications accepted. *Expenses:* Tuition: Full-time $9,450. Required fees: $760. *Financial support:* Institutionally sponsored loans and scholarships/grants available. Financial award applicants required to submit FAFSA. *Unit head:* Dr. Brian Lindquist, Associate Vice President and Dean/Executive Director, 480-557-1221, E-mail: brian.lindquist@phoenix.edu. *Application contact:* Chair, 813-626-7911, Fax: 813-977-1449.

University of Rhode Island, Graduate School, College of Business Administration, PhD Programs in Business Administration, Kingston, RI 02881. Offers finance (PhD); management (PhD); management sciences and information systems (PhD); marketing (PhD). *Expenses:* Tuition, state resident: full-time $6,032; part-time $335 per credit. Tuition, nonresident: full-time $17,288; part-time $960 per credit. Required fees: $65 per credit. $30 per semester. One-time fee: $80 part-time. *Application contact:* Dr. Laura Beauvais, Director of Graduate Programs, 401-874-4341.

University of San Francisco, Masagung Graduate School of Management, Program in Business Administration, San Francisco, CA 94117-1080. Offers business economics (MBA); e-business (MBA); entrepreneurship (MBA); finance and banking (MBA); international business (MBA); management (MBA); marketing (MBA); telecommunications management and policy (MBA); JD/MBA; MSN/MBA. *Accreditation:* AACSB. *Faculty:* 27 full-time (4 women), 21 part-time/adjunct (7 women). *Students:* 191 full-time (73 women), 71 part-time (33 women); includes 51 minority (4 African Americans, 1 American Indian/Alaska Native, 35 Asian Americans or Pacific Islanders, 11 Hispanic Americans), 102 international. Average age 28. 373 applicants, 70% accepted, 106 enrolled. In 2006, 163 degrees awarded. *Entrance requirements:* For master's, GMAT, minimum undergraduate GPA of 3.2. Additional exam requirements/recommendations for international students: Required—TOEFL. *Application deadline:* For fall admission, 7/1 priority date for domestic students; for spring admission, 11/30 for domestic students. Applications are processed on a rolling basis. Application fee: $55 ($65 for international students). *Expenses:* Tuition: Full-time $17,370; part-time $965 per unit. Tuition and fees vary according to degree level, campus/location and program. *Financial support:* In 2006–07, 104 students received support; fellowships available. Financial award application deadline: 3/2; financial award applicants required to submit FAFSA. *Faculty research:* International financial markets, technology transfer licensing, international marketing, strategic planning. Total annual research expenditures: $50,000. *Unit head:* Carol Langlois, Director, 415-422-6314, Fax: 415-422-2502.

University of Saskatchewan, College of Graduate Studies and Research, College of Commerce, Department of Management and Marketing, Saskatoon, SK S7N 5A2, Canada. Offers marketing (M Sc). Part-time programs available. *Degree requirements:* For master's, thesis, registration. *Entrance requirements:* For master's, GMAT. Additional exam requirements/recommendations for international students: Required—TOEFL.

The University of Scranton, Graduate School, Program in Business Administration, Scranton, PA 18510. Offers accounting (MBA); enterprise management technology (MBA); finance (MBA); general business administration (MBA); international business (MBA); management information systems (MBA); marketing (MBA); operations management (MBA). *Accreditation:* AACSB. Part-time and evening/weekend programs available. *Faculty:* 34 full-time (8 women). *Students:* 39 full-time (11 women), 54 part-time (15 women); includes 3 minority (1 American Indian/Alaska Native, 2 Hispanic Americans), 31 international. Average age 28. 58 applicants, 83% accepted. In 2006, 52 degrees awarded. *Degree requirements:* For master's, capstone experience. *Entrance requirements:* For master's, GMAT, minimum GPA of 2.75. Additional exam requirements/recommendations for international students: Required—TOEFL (minimum score 500 paper-based; 173 computer-based), IELTS (minimum score 6). *Application deadline:* Applications are processed on a rolling basis. Application fee: $50. *Expenses:* Tuition: Part-time $684 per credit. Required fees: $25 per term. *Financial support:* In 2006–07, 11 teaching assistantships with full tuition reimbursements (averaging $5,600 per year) were awarded; fellowships, career-related internships or fieldwork, Federal Work-Study, and unspecified assistantships also available. Support available to part-time students. Financial award application deadline: 3/1. *Faculty research:* Financial markets, strategic impact of total quality management, internal accounting controls, consumer preference, information systems and the Internet. *Unit head:* Dr. Murli Rajan, Director, 570-941-4043, Fax: 570-941-4342.

The University of Tampa, John H. Sykes College of Business, Tampa, FL 33606-1490. Offers accounting (MBA, MS); economics (MBA); entrepreneurship (MBA); finance (MBA, MS); information systems management (MBA); innovation management (MS); international business (MBA); management (MBA); marketing (MBA, MS). *Accreditation:* AACSB. Part-time and evening/weekend programs available. *Faculty:* 39 full-time (9 women), 1 part-time/adjunct (0 women). *Students:* 143 full-time (52 women), 381 part-time (158 women); includes 78 minority (18 African Americans, 3 American Indian/Alaska Native, 19 Asian Americans or Pacific Islanders, 38 Hispanic Americans), 89 international. Average age 31. 486 applicants, 59% accepted, 231 enrolled. In 2006, 127 degrees awarded. *Median time to degree:* Master's–1.8 years full-time, 2.8 years part-time. *Entrance requirements:* For master's, GMAT. Additional exam requirements/recommendations for international students: Required—TOEFL (minimum score 577 paper-based; 230 computer-based; 90 iBT). *Application deadline:* For fall admission, 2/15 priority date for domestic students, 6/15 for international students; for spring admission, 12/15 for domestic students, 11/15 for international students. Applications are processed on a rolling basis. Application fee: $40. Electronic applications accepted. *Expenses:* Tuition: Part-time $426 per credit hour. Required fees: $35 per year. *Financial support:* In 2006–07, 57 students received support, including 57 research assistantships with tuition reimbursements available (averaging $3,000 per year); career-related internships or fieldwork and unspecified assistantships also available. Support available to part-time students. Financial award applicants required to submit FAFSA. *Faculty research:* Industrial organization and antitrust, artificial intelligence, corporate quality, leadership, ethics, quality. *Unit head:* Dr. William L. Rhey, Dean Graduate Studies, 813-253-6211, Fax: 813-259-5403, E-mail: wrhey@ut.edu. *Application contact:* Fernals Nolasco, Director of Graduate Studies, 813-253-6211, Fax: 813-259-5403, E-mail: fnolasco@ut.edu.

The University of Tennessee, Graduate School, College of Business Administration, Program in Business Administration, Knoxville, TN 37996. Offers accounting (PhD); finance (MBA, PhD); logistics and transportation (MBA, PhD); management (PhD); marketing (MBA, PhD); operations management (MBA); professional business administration (MBA); statistics (PhD); JD/MBA; MS/MBA. *Accreditation:* AACSB. Postbaccalaureate distance learning degree programs offered. *Students:* 344 (105 women); includes 42 minority (20 African Americans, 4 American Indian/Alaska Native, 9 Asian Americans or Pacific Islanders, 9 Hispanic Americans) 49 international. In 2006, 169 master's, 9 doctorates awarded. *Degree requirements:* For master's, thesis or alternative; for doctorate, thesis/dissertation. *Entrance requirements:* For master's and doctorate, GMAT, minimum GPA of 2.7. Additional exam requirements/recommendations for international students: Required—TOEFL. *Application deadline:* For fall admission, 2/1 priority date for domestic students. Application fee: $35. Electronic applications accepted. *Expenses:* Tuition, state resident: full-time $5,574. Tuition, nonresident: full-time $16,840. Required fees: $792. *Financial support:* In 2006–07, 6 fellowships, 3 research assistantships, 35 teaching assistantships were awarded; career-related internships or fieldwork, Federal Work-Study, institutionally sponsored loans, and unspecified assistantships also available. Financial award application deadline: 2/1; financial award applicants required to submit FAFSA. *Unit head:* Dr. Sarah Gardial, Assistant Dean, 865-974-5033, Fax: 865-974-3826, E-mail: sgardial@utk.edu. *Application contact:* Donna Potts, Graduate Representative, 865-974-5033, Fax: 865-974-3826, E-mail: dpotts@utk.edu.

The University of Texas at Arlington, Graduate School, College of Business Administration, Program in Business Administration, Arlington, TX 76019. Offers accounting (PhD); business administration (PhD); business statistics (PhD); finance (MBA); information systems (MBA, PhD); management (MBA); management sciences (MBA); marketing (MBA, PhD); real estate (MBA). *Accreditation:* AACSB. Part-time and evening/weekend programs available. Postbaccalaureate distance learning degree programs offered (no on-campus study). *Faculty:* 1 full-time (0 women). *Students:* 156 full-time (60 women), 319 part-time (110 women); includes 123 minority (38 African Americans, 4 American Indian/Alaska Native, 52 Asian Americans or Pacific Islanders, 29 Hispanic Americans), 88 international. 502 applicants, 85% accepted, 199 enrolled. In 2006, 417 master's, 11 doctorates awarded. Terminal master's awarded for partial completion of doctoral program. *Degree requirements:* For master's, thesis optional; for doctorate, thesis/dissertation. *Entrance requirements:* For master's, GMAT; for doctorate, GMAT, minimum GPA of 3.0 (undergraduate), 3.4 (graduate); 30 hours of graduate course work. Additional exam requirements/recommendations for international students: Required—TOEFL (minimum score 550 paper-based; 213 computer-based). *Application deadline:* For fall admission, 6/15 for domestic students, 4/1 for international students; for spring admission, 10/15 for domestic students, 9/1 for international students. Applications are processed on a rolling basis. Application fee: $35 ($50 for international students). Electronic applications accepted. *Expenses:* Tuition, state resident: full-time $5,528. Tuition, nonresident: full-time $10,478. International tuition: $10,608 full-time. *Financial support:* In 2006–07, 1 fellowship (averaging $1,000 per year), 14 research assistantships (averaging $6,432 per year) were awarded; teaching assistantships, career-related internships or fieldwork, scholarships/grants, and unspecified assistantships also available. Financial award application deadline: 6/1; financial award applicants required to submit FAFSA. *Application contact:* Dr. Mike West, Assistant Dean, 817-272-1287, Fax: 817-272-5799, E-mail: mpwest@uta.edu.

See Close-Up on page 363.

The University of Texas at Austin, Graduate School, McCombs School of Business, Department of Marketing Administration, Austin, TX 78712-1111. Offers PhD. *Degree requirements:* For doctorate, thesis/dissertation, comprehensive exam. *Entrance requirements:* For doctorate, GMAT or GRE. Electronic applications accepted. *Faculty research:* Internet marketing, strategic marketing, buy behavior.

The University of Texas at San Antonio, College of Business, Department of Marketing, San Antonio, TX 78249-0617. Offers marketing management (MBA). Part-time and evening/weekend programs available. *Faculty:* 7 full-time (1 woman), 2 part-time/adjunct (0 women). *Students:* 19 full-time (9 women), 28 part-time (16 women); includes 17 minority (4 African Americans, 3 Asian Americans or Pacific Islanders, 10 Hispanic Americans), 11 international. Average age 27. 35 applicants, 63% accepted, 21 enrolled. In 2006, 19 degrees awarded. *Degree requirements:* For master's, thesis optional. *Entrance requirements:* For master's, GMAT, minimum GPA of 3.0. Additional exam requirements/recommendations for international students: Required—TOEFL (minimum score 500 paper-based; 173 computer-based). *Application deadline:* For fall admission, 7/1 for domestic students, 4/1 for international students; for spring admission, 11/1 for domestic students, 9/1 for international students. Applications are processed on a rolling basis. Application fee: $45 ($80 for international students). Electronic applications accepted. *Expenses:* Tuition, state resident: full-time $1,730; part-time $192 per credit hour. Tuition, nonresident: full-time $6,680; part-time $742 per credit hour. Required fees: $733; $308,359 per credit hour. *Financial support:* In 2006–07, 1 research assistantship (averaging $20,800 per year), 10 teaching assistantships (averaging $15,600 per year) were awarded; career-related internships or fieldwork, Federal Work-Study, scholarships/grants, and unspecified assistantships also available. Support available to part-time students. *Unit head:* Dr. Joel Saegert, Chair, 210-458-5375, Fax: 210-458-6335, E-mail: jsaegert@utsa.edu.

University of the Sacred Heart, Graduate Programs, Department of Business Administration, Program in Marketing, San Juan, PR 00914-0383. Offers MBA. Part-time and evening/weekend programs available. *Degree requirements:* For master's, thesis. *Entrance requirements:* For master's, EXADEP, minimum undergraduate GPA of 2.75, interview.

The University of Toledo, College of Graduate Studies, College of Business Administration, Department of Marketing and International Business, Program in Marketing, Toledo, OH 43606-3390. Offers MBA. *Students:* 14 full-time (5 women), 19 part-time (8 women); includes 2 minority (both African Americans), 10 international. Average age 26. 36 applicants, 39%

accepted, 9 enrolled. In 2006, 15 degrees awarded. *Entrance requirements:* For master's, GMAT, minimum GPA of 2.7. Additional exam requirements/recommendations for international students: Required—TOEFL. *Application deadline:* For fall admission, 8/1 priority date for domestic students. Applications are processed on a rolling basis. Electronic applications accepted. *Financial support:* Application deadline: 4/1. *Application contact:* Dr. Bruce Kuhlman, MBA Director, 419-530-2775, Fax: 419-530-7260, E-mail: mba0001@uoft01.utoledo.edu.

University of Wisconsin–Whitewater, School of Graduate Studies, College of Business and Economics, Program in Business Administration, Whitewater, WI 53190-1790. Offers finance (MBA); human resource management (MBA); information technology management (MBA); international business (MBA); management (MBA); marketing (MBA); operations and supply chain management (MBA); technology and training (MBA). *Accreditation:* AACSB. Part-time and evening/weekend programs available. Postbaccalaureate distance learning degree programs offered (no on-campus study). *Students:* 67 full-time (26 women), 331 part-time (136 women); includes 71 minority (20 African Americans, 40 Asian Americans or Pacific Islanders, 11 Hispanic Americans). Average age 28. 167 applicants, 62% accepted, 75 enrolled. In 2006, 141 degrees awarded. *Degree requirements:* For master's, thesis or alternative. *Entrance requirements:* For master's, GMAT, minimum AACSB index of 1000, minimum GPA of 2.75. Additional exam requirements/recommendations for international students: Required—TOEFL (minimum score 550 paper-based; 213 computer-based). *Application deadline:* For fall admission, 7/15 for domestic students, 7/15 priority date for international students; for spring admission, 12/1 for domestic and international students. Applications are processed on a rolling basis. Application fee: $45. Electronic applications accepted. *Expenses:* Tuition, state resident: full-time $3,311. Tuition, nonresident: full-time $8,616. Required fees: $368 per credit. *Financial support:* In 2006–07, 11 research assistantships (averaging $7,385 per year) were awarded; Federal Work-Study, unspecified assistantships, and out of state fee waiver also available. Support available to part-time students. Financial award application deadline: 3/15; financial award applicants required to submit FAFSA. *Faculty research:* Interface between social institutions and individual behavior, technology and innovation management, occupational mental health, workplace deviance and workplace romance. *Unit head:* Dr. Donald Zahn, Associate Dean, 262-472-1945, Fax: 262-472-4863, E-mail: zahnd@uww.edu.

Vanderbilt University, Owen Graduate School of Management and Graduate School, Program in Management, Nashville, TN 37240-1001. Offers finance (PhD); marketing (PhD); operations management (PhD); organization studies (PhD). PhD offered through the Graduate School. *Accreditation:* AACSB. *Faculty:* 46 full-time (8 women). *Students:* 19 full-time (6 women); includes 12 minority (all Asian Americans or Pacific Islanders) Average age 28. 169 applicants, 5% accepted, 5 enrolled. In 2006, 3 degrees awarded. *Median time to degree:* Doctorate–5 years full-time. Of those who began their doctoral program in fall 1998, 100% received their degree in 8 years or less. *Degree requirements:* For doctorate, thesis/dissertation, registration. *Entrance requirements:* For doctorate, GMAT or GRE. Additional exam requirements/recommendations for international students: Required—TOEFL. *Application deadline:* For fall admission, 1/15 priority date for domestic students; for spring admission, 3/15 for domestic students. Application fee: $0. Electronic applications accepted. *Expenses: Contact institution.* One-time fee: $30 full-time. Full-time tuition and fees vary according to course load, degree level and program. *Financial support:* In 2006–07, 19 students received support, including 4 fellowships with full tuition reimbursements available (averaging $20,500 per year); scholarships/grants, health care benefits, and tuition waivers (full and partial) also available. Financial award application deadline: 5/1. *Faculty research:* Financial marketing, operations, human resources. *Unit head:* Dr. Clifford Ball, Director, 615-322-2909, E-mail: cliff.ball@owen.vanderbilt.edu. *Application contact:* Janet Sisco, Information Contact, 615-322-5652, E-mail: janet.sisco@owen.vanderbilt.edu.

Virginia Commonwealth University, Graduate School, School of Business, Program in Marketing and Business Law, Richmond, VA 23284-9005. Offers Certificate. *Faculty:* 9 full-time (3 women). *Students:* 4 full-time (all women), 13 part-time (7 women); includes 3 minority (2 African Americans, 1 Asian American or Pacific Islander), 2 international. *Application deadline:* Applications are processed on a rolling basis. Application fee: $50. *Financial support:* Fellowships, research assistantships, teaching assistantships, Federal Work-Study, institutionally sponsored loans, and tuition waivers (full and partial) available. Financial award application deadline: 3/15. *Unit head:* Dr. Frank Franzak, Chair, 804-828-7090, Fax: 804-828-1602, E-mail: fjfranza@vcu.edu. *Application contact:* Tracy Green, Graduate Program Director, 804-828-1741, Fax: 804-828-7174, E-mail: tsgreen@vcu.edu.

Virginia Polytechnic Institute and State University, Graduate School, Pamplin College of Business, Department of Marketing, Blacksburg, VA 24061. Offers business administration/marketing (MS, PhD). *Faculty:* 13 full-time (7 women). *Students:* 8 full-time (6 women); includes 1 minority (Asian American or Pacific Islander), 5 international. Average age 30. 14 applicants, 21% accepted, 1 enrolled. In 2006, 1 degree awarded. *Entrance requirements:* For master's and doctorate, GMAT. Additional exam requirements/recommendations for international students: Required—TOEFL (minimum score 600 paper-based; 250 computer-based). *Application deadline:* For fall admission, 5/15 for international students; for spring admission, 10/15 for international students. Applications are processed on a rolling basis. Application fee: $45. Electronic applications accepted. *Expenses:* Tuition, state resident: full-time $7,017; part-time $390 per credit hour. Tuition, nonresident: full-time $12,414; part-time $690 per credit hour. International tuition: $11,296 full-time. Required fees: $1,523; $256 per term. *Financial support:* In 2006–07, 8 teaching assistantships with full tuition reimbursements (averaging $12,165 per year) were awarded; research assistantships with full tuition reimbursements, career-related internships or fieldwork, Federal Work-Study, scholarships/grants, and unspecified assistantships also available. Financial award application deadline:4/1. *Faculty research:* Consumer behavior, marketing research, channels of distribution, advertising, marketing strategy. *Unit head:* Dr. Kent Nakamoto, Head, 540-231-6949, Fax: 540-231-4487, E-mail: nakamoto@vt.edu. *Application contact:* Tina Harvey, Information Contact, 540-231-5708, Fax: 540-231-4487, E-mail: tharvey@vt.edu.

Wagner College, Division of Graduate Studies, Department of Business Administration, Program in Marketing, Staten Island, NY 10301-4495. Offers MBA. Part-time and evening/weekend programs available. *Faculty:* 1 full-time (0 women), 1 part-time/adjunct (0 women). *Students:* 14 full-time (8 women), 7 part-time (4 women); includes 3 minority (1 African American, 1 Asian American or Pacific Islander, 1 Hispanic American). 13 applicants, 92% accepted, 11 enrolled. In 2006, 16 degrees awarded. *Degree requirements:* For master's, thesis optional. *Entrance requirements:* For master's, GMAT, minimum GPA of 2.6. Additional exam requirements/recommendations for international students: Required—TOEFL (minimum score 550 paper-based; 217 computer-based). *Application deadline:* For fall admission, 8/1 priority date for domestic students, 6/30 for international students; for spring admission, 12/10 for domestic students, 11/15 for international students. Applications are processed on a rolling basis. Application fee: $50 ($80 for international students). *Expenses:* Tuition: Full-time $15,120; part-time $840 per credit. *Financial support:* Fellowships, tuition waivers (partial) and unspecified assistantships available. Financial award applicants required to submit FAFSA. *Application contact:* Susan Rosenberg, Office of Graduate Studies, 718-390-3106, Fax: 718-390-3456, E-mail: graduate@wagner.edu.

Washington State University, Graduate School, College of Business, Graduate Programs in Business, Pullman, WA 99164. Offers accounting and business law (M Acc); business administration (MBA, PhD), including accounting (PhD), finance (PhD), management and operations (PhD), management information systems (PhD), marketing (PhD); JD/MBA. *Accreditation:* AACSB. *Faculty:* 38. *Students:* 105 full-time (39 women), 14 part-time (5 women); includes 3 minority (1 American Indian/Alaska Native, 2 Asian Americans or Pacific Islanders), 62 international. Average age 30. 328 applicants, 32% accepted, 43 enrolled. In 2006, 56 master's, 8 doctorates awarded. *Degree requirements:* For master's, thesis (for some programs), final presentation, comprehensive exam (for some programs); for doctorate, thesis/dissertation, oral and written exams, comprehensive exam. *Entrance requirements:* For master's and doctorate, GMAT, minimum GPA of 3.0, 3 letters of recommendation. Additional exam requirements/recommendations for international students: Required—TOEFL. *Application deadline:* For fall admission, 3/1 priority date for domestic students, 3/1 for international students; for spring admission, 6/1 priority date for domestic students, 6/1 for international students. Applications are processed on a rolling basis. Application fee: $50. Electronic applications accepted. *Expenses:* Tuition, state resident: full-time $7,066. Tuition, nonresident: full-time $17,204. *Financial support:* In 2006–07, 102 students received support, including 9 fellowships (averaging $6,000 per year), 8 research assistantships with full and partial tuition reimbursements available (averaging $13,917 per year), 75 teaching assistantships with full and partial tuition reimbursements available (averaging $13,056 per year); career-related internships or fieldwork, Federal Work-Study, institutionally sponsored loans, health care benefits, tuition waivers (partial), unspecified assistantships, and teaching associateships also available. Financial award application deadline: 4/1. *Unit head:* Dr. Charles Munson, Associate Dean, 509-335-1193, E-mail: mba@wsu.edu. *Application contact:* Graduate School Admissions, 800-GRADWSU, Fax: 509-335-1949, E-mail: gradsch@wsu.edu.

Webster University, School of Business and Technology, Department of Business, St. Louis, MO 63119-3194. Offers business (MA); business and organizational security management (MBA); computer resources and information management (MBA); environmental management (MBA); finance (MA, MBA); health services management (MBA); human resources development (MBA); human resources management (MBA); international business (MA, MBA); management and leadership (MBA); marketing (MBA); procurement and acquisitions management (MBA); telecommunications management (MBA). Part-time and evening/weekend programs available. Postbaccalaureate distance learning degree programs offered (no on-campus study). *Students:* 1,205 full-time (629 women), 4,197 part-time (2,153 women); includes 2,005 minority (1,467 African Americans, 29 American Indian/Alaska Native, 212 Asian Americans or Pacific Islanders, 297 Hispanic Americans), 485 international. Average age 33. *Application deadline:* Applications are processed on a rolling basis. Application fee: $25 ($50 for international students). *Expenses:* Tuition: Full-time $8,820; part-time $490 per credit. Tuition and fees vary according to degree level, campus/location and program. *Financial support:* Federal Work-Study available. Support available to part-time students. Financial award application deadline: 4/1; financial award applicants required to submit FAFSA. *Unit head:* Bradford Scott, Chair, 314-961-2260 Ext. 7574, Fax: 314-968-7077, E-mail: buschair@webster.edu. *Application contact:* Director of Graduate and Evening Student Admissions, Fax: 314-968-7116, E-mail: gadmit@webster.edu.

Webster University, School of Business and Technology, Department of Management, St. Louis, MO 63119-3194. Offers business and organizational security management (MA); computer resources and information management (MA); environmental management (MS); health care management (MA); health services management (MA); human resources development (MA); human resources management (MA); management (DM); management and leadership (MA); marketing (MA); procurement and acquisitions management (MA); public administration (MA); quality management (MA); space systems operations management (MS); telecommunications management (MA). Part-time and evening/weekend programs available. Postbaccalaureate distance learning degree programs offered (no on-campus study). *Students:* 1,396 full-time (746 women), 4,727 part-time (2,579 women); includes 3,065 minority (2,374 African Americans, 45 American Indian/Alaska Native, 158 Asian Americans or Pacific Islanders, 488 Hispanic Americans), 128 international. Average age 37. In 2006, 9 degrees awarded. *Degree requirements:* For doctorate, thesis/dissertation, written exam. *Entrance requirements:* For doctorate, GMAT, 3 years of work experience, MBA. *Application deadline:* Applications are processed on a rolling basis. Application fee: $25 ($50 for international students). *Expenses:* Tuition: Full-time $8,820; part-time $490 per credit. Tuition and fees vary according to degree level, campus/location and program. *Financial support:* Federal Work-Study available. Support available to part-time students. Financial award application deadline: 4/1; financial award applicants required to submit FAFSA. *Unit head:* Jeffrey Haldeman, Chair, 314-961-2660 Ext. 7552, Fax: 314-968-7077, E-mail: mgtchair@webster.edu. *Application contact:* Director of Graduate and Evening Student Admissions, Fax: 314-968-7116, E-mail: gadmit@webster.edu.

Western International University, Graduate Programs in Business, Program in Marketing, Phoenix, AZ 85021-2718. Offers MBA. Evening/weekend programs available. Postbaccalaureate distance learning degree programs offered (no on-campus study). *Faculty:* 238 part-time/adjunct. *Students:* 71 full-time (35 women); includes 18 minority (3 African Americans, 9 Asian Americans or Pacific Islanders, 6 Hispanic Americans), 13 international. Average age 35. In 2006, 31 degrees awarded. *Degree requirements:* For master's, thesis. *Entrance requirements:* For master's, minimum GPA of 2.75. *Application deadline:* Applications are processed on a rolling basis. Application fee: $85 ($100 for international students). *Expenses:* Tuition: Full-time $9,600; part-time $400 per credit. One-time fee: $85 full-time. *Financial support:* Career-related internships or fieldwork, institutionally sponsored loans, and scholarships/grants available. Support available to part-time students. Financial award applicants required to submit FAFSA. *Unit head:* Dr. Gary Witt, Chair, 602-943-2311. *Application contact:* Karen Janitell, Director of Enrollment, 602-943-2311 Ext. 1063, Fax: 602-371-8637, E-mail: karen_janitell@apollogrp.edu.

West Virginia University, Perley Isaac Reed School of Journalism, Program in Integrated Marketing Communications, Morgantown, WV 26506. Offers MS. Part-time programs available. Postbaccalaureate distance learning degree programs offered (no on-campus study). *Students:* 50 full-time (37 women), 112 part-time (72 women); includes 23 minority (13 African Americans, 2 American Indian/Alaska Native, 3 Asian Americans or Pacific Islanders, 5 Hispanic Americans), 2 international. Average age 32. 113 applicants, 81% accepted, 69 enrolled. In 2006, 22 degrees awarded. *Entrance requirements:* For master's, GRE or GMAT. Additional exam requirements/recommendations for international students: Required—TOEFL. *Application deadline:* For fall admission, 6/15 priority date for domestic and international students; for spring admission, 10/15 priority date for domestic and international students. Applications are processed on a rolling basis. Application fee: $50. *Expenses:* Tuition, state resident: full-time $4,926; part-time $276 per credit hour. Tuition, nonresident: full-time $14,278; part-time $796 per credit hour. Tuition and fees vary according to program. *Financial support:* In 2006–07, 84 students received support. *Unit head:* Chad Mezera, Marketing Director, 304-293-3505 Ext. 5415, Fax: 304-293-3072, E-mail: chad.mezera@mail.wvu.edu.

Wilkes University, Graduate Studies and Continued Learning, Jay S. Sidhu School of Business and Leadership, Wilkes-Barre, PA 18766-0002. Offers accounting (MBA); entrepreneurship (MBA); finance (MBA); human resource management (MBA); international business (MBA); management (MBA); marketing (MBA). *Accreditation:* ACBSP. Part-time and evening/weekend programs available. *Students:* 30 full-time (16 women), 149 part-time (73 women); includes 5 minority (1 African American, 2 Asian Americans or Pacific Islanders, 2 Hispanic Americans), 4 international. Average age 30. In 2006, 48 degrees awarded. *Entrance requirements:* For master's, GMAT. Additional exam requirements/recommendations for international students: Required—TOEFL (minimum score 500 paper-based; 173 computer-based). *Application deadline:* Applications are processed on a rolling basis. Application fee: $40. *Expenses: Contact institution. Financial support:* Federal Work-Study and unspecified assistantships available. Financial award application deadline: 3/1; financial award applicants required to submit FAFSA. *Unit head:* Dr. Paul Browne, Dean, 570-408-4701, Fax: 570-408-4700, E-mail: paul.browne@wilkes.edu. *Application contact:* Kathleen Houlihan, Director of Graduate Studies, 570-408-3235, Fax: 570-408-7846, E-mail: kathleen.houlihan@wilkes.edu.

Marketing

Worcester Polytechnic Institute, Graduate Studies and Enrollment, Department of Management, Worcester, MA 01609-2280. Offers customized management (Certificate); information security management (Certificate); information technology (MS, Certificate), including information security management (MS), information technology and applications development (MS), information technology and entrepreneurship (MS), information technology project management (MS), manufacturing and service information technology applications (MS), marketing information technology applications (MS); management of technology (Certificate); marketing and technological innovation (MS); operations design and leadership (MS), including process design, supply chain management; technology (MBA); technology marketing (Certificate). *Accreditation:* AACSB. Part-time and evening/weekend programs available. Postbaccalaureate distance learning degree programs offered (no on-campus study). *Faculty:* 21 full-time (9 women), 5 part-time/adjunct (2 women). *Students:* 23 full-time (8 women), 178 part-time (48 women); includes 21 minority (2 African Americans, 2 American Indian/Alaska Native, 14 Asian Americans or Pacific Islanders, 3 Hispanic Americans), 30 international. Average age 32. 85 applicants, 76% accepted, 34 enrolled. In 2006, 31 degrees awarded. *Median time to degree:* Master's–2 years full-time, 4 years part-time. *Degree requirements:* For master's, thesis optional. *Entrance requirements:* For master's, GMAT (MBA), GMAT or GRE General Test (MS), 3 letters of recommendation, statement of purpose. Additional exam requirements/recommendations for international students: Required—TOEFL (minimum score 550 paper-based; 213 computer-based; 79 iBT), IELTS (minimum score 7). *Application deadline:* For fall admission, 6/1 priority date for domestic and international students; for spring admission, 10/15 priority date for domestic students, 10/1 priority date for international students. Applications are processed on a rolling basis. Application fee: $70. Electronic applications accepted. *Expenses:* Tuition: Part-time $1,042 per credit hour. Required fees: $1,009 per year. *Financial support:* In 2006–07, 10 students received support, including 1 research assistantship with full tuition reimbursement available; fellowships with full tuition reimbursements available, career-related internships or fieldwork, institutionally sponsored loans, scholarships/grants, and unspecified assistantships also available. Financial award application deadline: 6/1. *Faculty research:* Organizational aesthetics, resistance in organizations, dynamics of product innovation, economic approaches to productivity, corporate earnings forecasts and value relevance. Total annual research expenditures: $125,538. *Unit head:* Dr. McRae C. Banks, Head, 508-831-5218, Fax: 508-831-5720, E-mail: macb@wpi.edu. *Application contact:* Norm D. Wilkinson, Director, Graduate Management Programs, 508-831-5957, Fax: 508-831-5720, E-mail: nwilkins@wpi.edu.

See Close-Up on page 377.

Wright State University, School of Graduate Studies, Raj Soin College of Business, Department of Marketing, Dayton, OH 45435. Offers MBA, MBA/MS. *Students:* 10 full-time (6 women), 14 part-time (6 women). Average age 32. 29 applicants, 86% accepted. In 2006, 8 degrees awarded. *Entrance requirements:* For master's, GMAT, minimum AACSB index of 1000. Additional exam requirements/recommendations for international students: Required—TOEFL. Application fee: $25. *Financial support:* Fellowships, research assistantships, teaching assistantships, unspecified assistantships available. Support available to part-time students. Financial award applicants required to submit FAFSA. *Unit head:* Dr. James M. Munch, Chair, 937-775-4929, Fax: 937-775-3545, E-mail: james.munch@wright.edu. *Application contact:* Michael Evans, Director of MBA Programs, 937-775-2437, Fax: 937-775-3545, E-mail: michael.evans@wright.edu.

Xavier University, Williams College of Business, Master of Business Administration Program, Cincinnati, OH 45207. Offers business administration (Exec MBA, MBA); e-commerce (MBA); finance (MBA); international business (MBA); management information systems (MBA); marketing (MBA);); MBA/MHSA; MSN/MBA. *Accreditation:* AACSB. Part-time and evening/weekend programs available. *Faculty:* 59 full-time (22 women), 29 part-time/adjunct (8 women). *Students:* 227 full-time (66 women), 708 part-time (252 women); includes 99 minority (41 African Americans, 1 American Indian/Alaska Native, 43 Asian Americans or Pacific Islanders, 14 Hispanic Americans), 43 international. Average age 31. 486 applicants, 63% accepted, 229 enrolled. In 2006, 294 degrees awarded. *Entrance requirements:* For master's, GMAT, resumé. Additional exam requirements/recommendations for international students: Required—TOEFL (minimum score 550 paper-based; 213 computer-based; 79 iBT). *Application deadline:* For fall admission, 8/1 priority date for domestic students, 6/1 for international students; for winter admission, 12/1 priority date for domestic students; for spring admission, 4/1 priority date for domestic students, 10/1 for international students. Applications are processed on a rolling basis. Application fee: $35. Electronic applications accepted. *Expenses:* Contact institution. Part-time tuition and fees vary according to degree level, campus/location and program. *Financial support:* In 2006–07, 175 students received support, including 11 research assistantships with full and partial tuition reimbursements available; career-related internships or fieldwork, scholarships/grants, and tuition waivers (partial) also available. Support available to part-time students. Financial award application deadline: 4/30; financial award applicants required to submit FAFSA. *Faculty research:* Supply chain management, category management, data mining, off-shoring. *Unit head:* Dr. Raghu Tadepalli, Associate Dean, 513-745-3525, Fax: 513-745-2929, E-mail: tadepalli@xavier.edu. *Application contact:* Jennifer Bush, Executive Director, MBA Programs, 513-745-3525, Fax: 513-745-2929, E-mail: xumba@xavier.edu.

Yale University, Yale School of Management and Graduate School of Arts and Sciences, Doctoral Program in Management, New Haven, CT 06520. Offers accounting (PhD); financial economics (PhD); marketing (PhD). *Accreditation:* AACSB. *Faculty:* 55 full-time (7 women). *Students:* 25 full-time (6 women); includes 2 minority (both Asian Americans or Pacific Islanders), 20 international. Average age 28. 300 applicants, 4% accepted. In 2006, 6 doctorates awarded. *Degree requirements:* For doctorate, thesis/dissertation, comprehensive exam. *Entrance requirements:* For doctorate, GMAT or GRE General Test. Additional exam requirements/recommendations for international students: Required—TOEFL, IELTS. *Application deadline:* For fall admission, 1/2 for domestic and international students. Application fee: $85. Electronic applications accepted. *Expenses:* Contact institution. *Financial support:* Fellowships with full tuition reimbursements, research assistantships with full tuition reimbursements, teaching assistantships with full tuition reimbursements, institutionally sponsored loans, scholarships/grants, and health care benefits available. Financial award application deadline: 1/2. *Faculty research:* Pricing of options and futures, term structure of interest rates, use of accounting numbers in debt contracts, product differentiation, e-commerce and marketing, behavioral finance. *Unit head:* Mary Ellen Nichols, Registrar, 203-432-3955, Fax: 203-432-0342, E-mail: maryellen.nichols@yale.edu.

Youngstown State University, Graduate School, Warren P. Williamson Jr. College of Business Administration, Department of Marketing, Youngstown, OH 44555-0001. Offers MBA. Part-time and evening/weekend programs available. *Degree requirements:* For master's, thesis optional. *Entrance requirements:* For master's, GMAT, minimum GPA of 2.7. Additional exam requirements/recommendations for international students: Required—TOEFL. *Faculty research:* Media, international marketing, advanced marketing simulations, ethics in business.

Marketing Research

Hofstra University, Frank G. Zarb School of Business, Department of Marketing and International Business, Hempstead, NY 11549. Offers international business (MBA, MS, Advanced Certificate); marketing (MBA, MS, Advanced Certificate); marketing research (MS). Part-time and evening/weekend programs available. *Faculty:* 7 full-time (0 women), 2 part-time/adjunct (0 women). *Students:* 39 full-time (22 women), 48 part-time (27 women); includes 23 minority (7 African Americans, 10 Asian Americans or Pacific Islanders, 6 Hispanic Americans), 10 international. Average age 28. 75 applicants, 73% accepted, 27 enrolled. In 2006, 42 degrees awarded. *Degree requirements:* For master's, thesis (for some programs), capstone course for MBA. *Entrance requirements:* For master's, GMAT, 2 letters of recommendation, resumé, essay. Additional exam requirements/recommendations for international students: Required—TOEFL (minimum score 550 paper-based; 213 computer-based). *Application deadline:* Applications are processed on a rolling basis. Application fee: $60. Electronic applications accepted. *Expenses:* Tuition: Full-time $13,320; part-time $740 per credit. Required fees: $930; $155 per term. *Financial support:* In 2006–07, 24 students received support, including 13 fellowships with tuition reimbursements available (averaging $5,748 per year), 5 research assistantships with full and partial tuition reimbursements available (averaging $3,416 per year); tuition waivers (full and partial) also available. Financial award applicants required to submit FAFSA. *Faculty research:* Outsourcing, cross cultural consumer behavior, global alliances, retailing, web marketing. *Unit head:* Dr. Benny Barak, Chairperson, 516-463-5707, Fax: 516-463-4834, E-mail: mktbzb@hofstra.edu. *Application contact:* Carol Drummer, Dean of Graduate Admissions, 516-463-4876, Fax: 516-463-4664, E-mail: gradstudent@hofstra.edu.

Instituto Tecnológico y de Estudios Superiores de Monterrey, Campus Irapuato, Graduate Programs, Irapuato, Mexico. Offers administration (MBA); administration of information technology (MAIT); administration of telecommunications (MAT); architecture (M Arch); computer science (MCS); education (M Ed); educational administration (MEA); educational innovation and technology (DEIT); educational technology (MET); electronic commerce (MBA); environmental administration and planning (MEAP); environmental systems (MES); finances (MBA); humanistic studies (MHS); international management for Latin American executives (MIMLAE); library and information science (MLIS); manufacturing quality management (MMQM); marketing research (MBA).

Pace University, Lubin School of Business, Marketing Program, New York, NY 10038. Offers marketing management (MBA); marketing research (MBA). Part-time and evening/weekend programs available. *Faculty:* 8 full-time, 12 part-time/adjunct. *Students:* 25 full-time (15 women), 86 part-time (46 women); includes 16 minority (3 African Americans, 8 Asian Americans or Pacific Islanders, 5 Hispanic Americans), 39 international. Average age 28. 180 applicants, 54% accepted, 38 enrolled. In 2006, 53 degrees awarded. *Entrance requirements:* For master's, GMAT. *Application deadline:* For fall admission, 7/31 priority date for domestic students; for spring admission, 11/30 for domestic students. Applications are processed on a rolling basis. Application fee: $65. Electronic applications accepted. *Expenses:* Tuition: Part-time $890 per credit. *Financial support:* Research assistantships, career-related internships or fieldwork and Federal Work-Study available. Support available to part-time students. Financial award applicants required to submit FAFSA. *Unit head:* Dr. Martin Topol, Chairperson, 212-346-1827. *Application contact:* Joanna Broda, Director of Admissions, 212-346-1652, Fax: 212-346-1585, E-mail: gradnyc@pace.edu.

Southern Illinois University Edwardsville, Graduate Studies and Research, School of Business, Department of Management and Marketing, Edwardsville, IL 62026-0001. Offers marketing research (MMR). Part-time and evening/weekend programs available. *Faculty:* 14 full-time (4 women). *Students:* 10 full-time (3 women), 7 part-time (6 women); includes 1 minority (African American), 6 international. Average age 33. 15 applicants, 47% accepted. In 2006, 15 degrees awarded. *Degree requirements:* For master's, thesis or alternative, final exam. *Entrance requirements:* For master's, GMAT. Additional exam requirements/recommendations for international students: Required—TOEFL. *Application deadline:* For fall admission, 7/20 for domestic students, 6/1 for international students; for spring admission, 12/14 for domestic students, 10/1 for international students. Application fee: $30. Electronic applications accepted. *Financial support:* In 2006–07, 11 research assistantships with full tuition reimbursements were awarded; fellowships with full tuition reimbursements, teaching assistantships with full tuition reimbursements, career-related internships or fieldwork, Federal Work-Study, institutionally sponsored loans, traineeships, and unspecified assistantships also available. Support available to part-time students. Financial award application deadline: 3/1; financial award applicants required to submit FAFSA. *Unit head:* Dr. Joseph Michlitsch, Chair, 618-650-2750, E-mail: jmichli@siue.edu. *Application contact:* Dr. Madhav Segal, Program Director, 618-650-2601, E-mail: msegal@siue.edu.

Universidad de las Americas, A.C., Program in Business Administration, Mexico City, Mexico. Offers finance (MBA); marketing research (MBA); production and quality (MBA).

University of Georgia, Graduate School, Terry College of Business, Program in Marketing, Athens, GA 30602. Offers MMR. *Faculty:* 8 full-time (1 woman). *Students:* 19 full-time (11 women); includes 4 minority (all Asian Americans or Pacific Islanders), 7 international. In 2006, 16 degrees awarded. *Entrance requirements:* For master's, GMAT or GRE General Test. *Application deadline:* For fall admission, 7/1 priority date for domestic students; for spring admission, 11/15 for domestic students. Application fee: $50. Electronic applications accepted. *Financial support:* Research assistantships available. *Unit head:* Dr. Rajiv Grover, Head, 706-542-2123, Fax: 706-542-3738, E-mail: rgrover@terry.uga.edu. *Application contact:* Dr. Srinivas K. Reddy, Graduate Coordinator, 706-542-3759, Fax: 706-542-3738, E-mail: mmr@terry.uga.edu.

The University of Texas at Arlington, Graduate School, College of Business Administration, Department of Marketing, Arlington, TX 76019. Offers marketing research (MS). Part-time programs available. *Faculty:* 7 full-time (3 women), 1 part-time/adjunct (0 women). *Students:* 26 full-time (15 women), 22 part-time (16 women); includes 13 minority (1 African American, 10 Asian Americans or Pacific Islanders, 2 Hispanic Americans), 22 international. 21 applicants, 38% accepted, 7 enrolled. In 2006, 19 degrees awarded. *Entrance requirements:* For master's, GMAT. Additional exam requirements/recommendations for international students: Required—TOEFL (minimum score 550 paper-based; 213 computer-based). *Application deadline:* For fall admission, 6/15 for domestic students. Applications are processed on a rolling basis. Application fee: $35 ($50 for international students). Electronic applications accepted. *Expenses:* Tuition, state resident: full-time $5,528. Tuition, nonresident: full-time $10,478. International tuition: $10,608 full-time. *Financial support:* In 2006–07, 39 students received support, including 39 fellowships (averaging $1,000 per year), 8 teaching assistantships (averaging $10,000 per year); career-related internships or fieldwork, scholarships/grants, and unspecified assistantships also available. Support available to part-time students. Financial award application deadline: 6/1; financial award applicants required to submit FAFSA. *Faculty research:* Marketing strategy, marketing research, international marketing. Total annual research expenditures: $30,000. *Unit head:* Dr. Carl D. McDaniel, Chair, 817-272-2876, Fax: 817-272-2854, E-mail: mcdaniel@exchange.uta.edu. *Application contact:* Dr. John Bassler, Graduate Adviser, 817-272-2340, Fax: 817-272-2854, E-mail: msmr@uta.edu.

University of Wisconsin–Madison, Graduate School, School of Business, Wisconsin Full-Time MBA Programs, Madison, WI 53706-1380. Offers applied corporate finance (MBA); applied security analysis (MBA); arts administration (MBA); brand and product management (MBA); entrepreneurial management (MBA); information systems (MBA); marketing research (MBA); operations and technology management (MBA); real estate (MBA); risk management and insurance (MBA); strategic human resource management (MBA); strategic management in the life and engineering sciences (MBA); supply chain management (MBA). *Faculty:* 84. *Students:* 231 full-time (74 women); includes 21 minority (10 African Americans, 5 Asian Americans or Pacific Islanders, 6 Hispanic Americans), 59 international. Average age 28. 405 applicants, 43% accepted, 121 enrolled. In 2006, 110 degrees awarded. *Entrance requirements:* For master's, GMAT, bachelors or equivalent degree, 2 years of work experience. Additional exam requirements/recommendations for international students: Required—TOEFL (minimum score 600 paper-based; 250 computer-based; 90 iBT). *Application deadline:* For fall admission, 11/1 for domestic and international students; for winter admission, 1/23 for domestic and international students; for spring admission, 3/26 for domestic and international students. Applications are processed on a rolling basis. Application fee: $45. Electronic applications accepted. *Financial support:* In 2006–07, 177 students received support, including 20 fellowships with full and partial tuition reimbursements available (averaging $16,566 per year), 105 research assistantships with full tuition reimbursements available (averaging $8,098 per year), 33 teaching assistantships with full tuition reimbursements available (averaging $10,112 per year); scholarships/grants, health care benefits, and unspecified assistantships also available. *Unit head:* Gary Lessuise, Assistant Dean, Masters Programs, 608-265-5102, Fax: 608-265-4192, E-mail: glessuise@bus.wisc.edu. *Application contact:* Betsy Kacizak, Director of Admissions and Financial Aid—Full Time MBA, 608-262-4000, Fax: 608-265-4192, E-mail: mba@bus.wisc.edu.

CLEMSON UNIVERSITY

Master of Science in Marketing

Program of Study

The Department of Marketing at Clemson University offers the Master of Science (M.S.) degree in marketing, which is intended for students who are interested in advanced studies in analytical marketing.

The Master of Science in Marketing program is designed to advance students' knowledge and expertise in marketing theory and practice and prepare them for careers in marketing analysis, research, management, and scholarship. A coordinated curriculum of quantitative and analytical skills development, research methods, consumer analysis, and strategic-marketing analysis provides students with the necessary background to pursue careers in marketing research, analysis, and policy. It also serves as a platform for further education to prepare students for careers in academe. This is accomplished through rigorous course work and seminars and a major research project. This one-year master's degree program is designed to enhance the skills and training of students with prior academic and work experience in business.

The Master of Science in Marketing program requires successful completion of 30 credit hours of graduate marketing and related course work. Core courses are Statistical Methods I (4 hours), Marketing Research (3 hours), Quantitative Methods in Marketing (3 hours), Buyer Behavior (3 hours), Marketing Analysis and Strategy (3 hours), Seminar in Marketing Management (3 hours), Advanced Topics in Marketing (3 hours), Master's Project Research (5 hours), and Analytic Methods (3 hours).

Research Facilities

Students in the Master of Science in Marketing program at Clemson University have the opportunity to work on research teams in the Center for the Advancement of Marketing and Social Science (CAMSS), a collaborative partnership between Clemson University's Departments of Marketing and Sociology. CAMSS is a market-based, customer-focused initiative that seeks to connect business and nonprofit organizations with graduate students, undergraduate students, and faculty members through a research-focused approach to solving customer-defined problems. CAMSS provides unique educational experiences and training opportunities for Master of Science in Marketing students, while contributing to organizations and to the Clemson brand. Recent clients of CAMSS include Greased Lighting, Marsh and Associates, the Greater Greenville Chamber of Commerce, the South Carolina Department of Insurance, and the South Carolina Department of Transportation. Supervisory Board members represent organizations such as the Southern Company, Duke Energy, International Paper, Dow Chemical, and Ely Lilly and Co.

Financial Aid

A limited number of assistantships are available for qualified students. In addition, there are opportunities to assist in the Center for the Advancement of Marketing and Social Science and for teaching assistants to the Department of Marketing.

Cost of Study

Tuition for 2007–08 is $3641 per semester for in-state students and $7285 per semester for nonresidents. Off-campus rates were $330 per hour for in-state students and $660 per hour for nonresidents. Graduate assistants paid a flat fee of $950 per semester and $304 per summer session. Graduate fellows pay South Carolina resident fees.

Living and Housing Costs

Comfortable and economical housing is available in the Clemson area; most students pay rent of $300 or more depending on where they live, whether they share a home with roommates, etc. The cost of living in Clemson is quite low compared to the national average.

Student Outcomes

Jobs in marketing and survey research are numerous and expanding, according to the Bureau of Labor Statistics. Positions in this field doubled between 1996 and 2000, and again between 2000 and 2002. In the last decade, two major forces have changed the nature of employment in the United States. First, the information revolution has changed how firms use data to understand and manage customer demand. The use of credit cards, bank and grocery cards, online shopping, and customer databases generated by sales and inquiries have created a wealth of consumer information and offer advantages to those who can evaluate and assess consumer preferences, sentiments, and consumption patterns. In a knowledge-driven economy, the ability to use these kinds of information to better serve customers is a competitive advantage. Second, global competition has placed a premium on jobs that can improve the likely success of new products, more effectively target consumers' wants and needs, minimize inventory levels, and reduce the costs of advertising. This is what market and survey researchers are charged to do. These jobs will be central to success in the economy of the twenty-first century. The Master of Science in Marketing program is designed to prepare students to participate in this important and exciting field. In addition, a growing shortage of qualified faculty members in marketing make the M.S. in marketing the ideal preparation for students wishing to pursue Ph.D.'s in marketing—a necessary qualification for careers as college or university professors in marketing.

Location

Clemson is a small, beautiful college town in upstate South Carolina. The Upstate is one of the country's fastest-growing areas and is an important part of the I-85 Corridor, a multistate area along Interstate 85 that runs from the metro Atlanta area (home to nearly 5 million people) to Richmond, Virginia, and encompasses Charlotte, North Carolina (the second-largest financial center in the U.S.), as well as North Carolina's Research Triangle. Atlanta and Charlotte are each within a 2-hour drive.

Many financial institutions have regional offices located in the Upstate, including Wachovia and Bank of America. Other major industries of commerce in the Upstate include the auto industry, health care, and pharmaceuticals. Corporations based in or with a major presence in the Upstate include BMW, Bon Secours St. Francis Health System, Bosch North America, Bowater, Charter Communications, Ernst and Young, Fluor Corporation, IBM, Microsoft, and Michelin of North America.

The University

Clemson is classified by the Carnegie Foundation as a Research University (High Research Activity), a category comprising just 10 percent of all graduate degree–granting universities in America. The University's mission is to fulfill the covenant between its founder and the people of South Carolina to establish a "high seminary of learning" through its responsibilities of teaching, research, and extended public service. The University has identified eight areas of academic emphasis that create collaborations that, in turn, help fulfill the University's mission.

Applying

Applicants should have an undergraduate degree in business from an accredited college or university. In addition, it is preferred that incoming students have some professional work experience. Students applying to the Master of Science in Marketing program who are not graduates of an AACSB-accredited college or school of business administration are required to demonstrate successful completion of 3 hours of collegiate microeconomics, 6 hours of calculus, and a junior-level course in marketing or the equivalent to be considered for the program. Ideal candidates should have a minimum undergraduate GPA of 3.0 and a GMAT score of at least 600.

Applications are available online at http://www.grad.clemson.edu/p_apply.html. Applications, along with a $50 nonrefundable fee, should be received no later than five weeks prior to registration. All supporting documentation, including transcripts, GMAT scores, and letters of recommendation, must be received for full consideration of application. Students are encouraged to apply as early as possible for the best funding opportunities.

Correspondence and Information

Dr. John D Mittelstaedt
Department of Marketing
College of Business and Behavioral Science
Clemson University
Clemson, South Carolina 29634-1325

Phone: 864-656-5293
Fax: 864-656-0138
E-mail: jmittel@clemson.edu
Web site: http://business.clemson.edu/Market/

Clemson University

THE FACULTY AND THEIR RESEARCH

The faculty of the Department of Marketing includes 15 scholars who are recognized for their expertise in consumer behavior, marketing research, advertising research, services marketing, public policy, marketing ethics, electronic commerce, macromarketing, and marketing strategy. Faculty members include editors and former editors of leading journals in the field, officers in major international marketing societies, and principal and co-principal investigators on more than $500,000 in funded research. They include:

Les Carlson, Professor; Ph.D., Nebraska. Advertising; former editor, *Journal of Advertising.*

Michael Dorsch, Associate Professor; Ph.D., Arkansas. Marketing research, strategy; former editor, *Journal of Marketing Theory and Practice.*

Charles Duke, Professor; Ph.D., Texas at Arlington. New product development, international marketing, consumer decision making; associate editor, *Journal of Marketing Education.*

Roger Gomes, Associate Professor; Ph.D., Virginia Tech. Business to business, international marketing.

Stephen Grove, Professor; Ph.D., Oklahoma State. Services marketing.

Christopher Hopkins, Assistant Professor; Ph.D., Mississippi State. E-commerce, marketing research.

Scott A. Jones, Assistant Professor; Ph.D., Oregon. Entrepreneurship, sports marketing, consumer behavior.

William E. Kilbourne, Professor; Ph.D., Houston. Marketing research, international marketing, macromarketing; section editor, *Journal of Macromarketing.*

Patricia Knowles, Associate Professor; Ph.D., Bowling Green State. Non-profit marketing, consumer behavior.

Mary LaForge, Associate Professor; Ph.D., Georgia. Consumer behavior.

John D. Mittelstaedt, Associate Professor; Ph.D., Iowa. International marketing, macromarketing, consumer decision making.

Jesse N. Moore, Associate Professor; Ph.D., South Florida. Professional selling, sales management.

Gregory Pickett, Professor and Chair; Ph.D., Oklahoma State. Services marketing, sport marketing, sales management.

Mary Anne Raymond, Professor, Ph.D., Georgia. Marketing strategy.

EMERSON COLLEGE

School of Communication
Master of Arts in Integrated Marketing Communication

Program of Study

As Integrated Marketing Communication (IMC) practitioners, Emerson graduates are vital to the future of business. Developing creative, strategic communication plans, they are responsible for establishing dialogue between the providers of a product or service and their respective consumers or markets.

Master of Arts (M.A.) degree candidates learn to integrate advertising, public relations, direct/database marketing, sales, brand management, and e-communication to cultivate successful long-term relationships with customers. More focused than an M.B.A. and more comprehensive than an advertising degree, the Emerson College M.A. in Integrated Marketing Communication Program prepares students for career success in roles such as agency executive, brand manager, public relations director, or strategic communication consultant.

For more information about Emerson's M.A. in Integrated Marketing Communication Program, students should visit the Web site at http://admission.emerson.edu/admission/graduate/academics/imc.cfm.

Research Facilities

The Emerson College library has more than 200,000 volumes, 20,000 journals (paper and electronic), 8,000 e-books, 10,000 nonprint materials, and 10,000 microforms in its collection that focuses on communication studies and the performing arts. Through membership in the Fenway Consortium, graduate students have access to more than 2 million volumes. Computer-assisted reference services provide bibliographic databases through Dialog, BRS, and other online services. The Online Computer Library Center is used for student research support.

M.A. candidates gain valuable hands-on experience in the Media Services Center, which provides students with access to approximately 2,400 films, videos, laser discs, and DVDs. The center is home to audio, video, and multimedia production facilities; a video studio; and several nonlinear editing suites comparable to those of any television studio in a major U.S. city. In addition, a marketing suite that opened in fall 2003 features a focus group room with an observation booth. There are also fully mediated classrooms.

Financial Aid

Emerson College offers several financial assistance programs that make graduate education possible: merit-based awards (domestic and international applicants), low-interest federal loans (domestic applicants only), Federal Work-Study (domestic applicants only), private loans (domestic and international applicants), Student Employment (domestic and international applicants), and alternative payment plans (domestic and international applicants). For detailed information, prospective students should visit the Office of Student Financial Services Web site at http://www.emerson.edu/financial_services/info-grad.cfm.

Cost of Study

Tuition for the 2007–08 academic year is $840 per credit hour. Other fees vary and may apply.

Living and Housing Costs

Though on-campus housing is not available for its graduate students, the Emerson College Office of Off-Campus Student Services (http://www.emerson.edu/offcampus_housing/) offers assistance in finding housing, including local apartment listings, realtor lists, temporary accommodations, search tips, pertinent neighborhood information, a roommate networking service, and more. Costs for housing are comparable to those of rental properties available in larger East Coast cities.

Student Group

More than 950 graduate students representing forty-five states and sixty countries are enrolled in Emerson programs.

Student Outcomes

Graduates take positions in multinational corporations, advertising firms, insurance and financial institutions, not-for-profit and health-care organizations, and government agencies. Among recent employers are Accenture, Avid, Blue Cross & Blue Shield, the Boeing Company, Fidelity Investments, Forrester Research, the Four Seasons Hotel, Grey Advertising, IBM, Macy's, McCann-Erickson, the U.S. Tennis Association, and the Weber Group.

Location

Situated in the heart of downtown Boston, Emerson offers access to the vast resources of a city that is home to the nation's finest educational institutions and an international hub of culture, media production, writing, publishing, communication, commerce, and medical innovation. Boston is a career launching pad for Emerson's students, many of whom intern or work at world-renowned organizations throughout the city. Emerson students from around the country and the world absorb the city's unique blend of local and global culture, and many find that Boston is an education in itself.

The College

Emerson College, founded in 1880 by Charles Wesley Emerson, has expanded upon its original mission of promoting the study of oratory and the performing arts by offering some of the nation's most distinctive graduate programs in communication.

Applying

Emerson's graduate programs welcome applicants from across the United States and around the world. Admission is competitive and selective. The College is looking for students whose academic and professional backgrounds, communication skills, and passion for the field meet the demands of their chosen program and promise a successful career.

The application deadline is June 1 for domestic applicants and May 1 for international applicants. Applications that are not complete by the final deadline are not reviewed by the admission committee. Applicants are responsible for ensuring the completion of their application. Application fees are nonrefundable; application forms and supporting materials become the property of the Office of Graduate Admission once they are sent to the office and are not returned.

All application materials, with the exception of GRE/GMAT test scores, must be submitted together in one package to ensure timely review. A complete application includes the application form (students may apply online or download the PDF version), the application fee ($60 for domestic applicants; $75 for international applicants), official transcripts from all colleges/universities previously attended, three sealed letters of recommendation (by persons best able to assess academic and professional qualifications, including motivation and goals), GRE/GMAT test scores, an essay, and a professional resume.

Applicants whose native language is not English must provide evidence of English proficiency by submitting official TOEFL or IELTS test results. (Students from India and the Philippines are considered nonnative English speakers and are required to take the TOEFL.) Emerson College's school code for the TOEFL is 3367; no department code is needed. The minimum TOEFL score is 550 on the paper-based test (213 on the computer-based test or 80 on the Internet-based test). The minimum IELTS score is 6.5. Applicants who do not meet this requirement will not be reviewed for admission. For more information about these tests, students should visit http://www.toefl.org or http://www.ielts.org.

Decisions are made on complete applications within six to eight weeks. Deadlines for merit-based and federal aid applications for fall are March 1 and April 1, respectively. Students seeking additional information about financing their graduate education should visit http://www.emerson.edu/financial_services/info-grad.cfm/.

Correspondence and Information

Office of Graduate Admission
Emerson College
120 Boylston Street
Boston, Massachusetts 02116-4624

Phone: 617-824-8610
Fax: 617-824-8614
E-mail: gradapp@emerson.edu
Web site: http://admission.emerson.edu/admission/graduate

Emerson College

THE FACULTY AND THEIR RESEARCH

Joann Montepare, Chair of Marketing Communication and Associate Professor of Psychology; Ph.D., Brandeis. Dr. Montepare is a social-developmental psychologist who teaches courses in social psychology, developmental psychology, nonverbal communication, and face perception. Her research in person perception, emotion communication, and age-identity across the life span has been widely published in prominent journals such as the *Journal of Personality and Social Psychology, Developmental Psychology, Psychology and Aging, Advances in Experimental Social Psychology, Science*, and *Communication Research*. Dr. Montepare has also contributed to edited books such as *First Impressions, Ageism: Stereotyping and Prejudice Against Older Persons, The Social Psychology of Stigma*, and *Evolution and Social Psychology*. She is the Associate Editor for Special Issues for the *Journal of Nonverbal Behavior* and serves on the editorial board for the *Journal of Adult Development*.

Cathy Waters, Graduate Program Director, Integrated Marketing Communication Program and Executive-in-Residence; M.B.A., Boston College. Ms. Waters is a specialist in market analysis, forecasting, technical sales and sales management, personnel recruitment/development, and customer relations. Her career has spanned both the academic and professional worlds. Before coming to Emerson, she served on the faculty of Boston College's Carroll School of Management where she taught undergraduate and graduate courses in marketing, applied marketing management, product planning, and strategy as well as professional selling and sales management. Complementing her academic work is twelve years of experience in the corporate world with IMB where she held positions in sales and marketing management. Her combined expertise comes together in cases published in *Strategic Marketing Management Cases* and the *Journal of Business Research*.

Timothy Edgar, Graduate Program Director, Health Communication Program, and Associate Professor of Marketing Communication; Ph.D., Purdue. Dr. Edgar's professional career has been devoted to conducting quantitative and qualitative health-communication research on topics as diverse as HIV/AIDS, physical activity for adolescents, childhood and adult immunization, diabetes, epilepsy, and peptic ulcers. Prior to working at Emerson, Dr. Edgar was a Senior Study Director with Westat, a social science research firm in Rockville, Maryland. Dr. Edgar has also taught health communication and research methods at the University of Maryland, University of Wisconsin, and The George Washington University. Dr. Edgar has published widely in professional journals such as the *Journal of Health Communication, Health Education Research*, and *Health Communication*, and he has contributed to edited volumes such as *The Handbook of Health Communication*. He also co-edited the book, *AIDS: A Communication Perspective*. Dr. Edgar currently serves on the editorial board of *Health Communication*, and the *Journal of Health Communication*.

Thomas Vogel, Graduate Program Director, Global Marketing Communication and Advertising Program and Associate Professor of Marketing Communication; M.F.A., Academy of Fine Arts (Stuttgart). Mr. Vogel is a specialist in strategic communication on the Internet, online usability, and branding on the Internet. At the University of Applied Sciences in Wiesbaden, Germany, he was a Professor of Media Design in the Department of Media Management and also served as the Founding Dean from 1993 to 1999. Professor Vogel is an active public speaker, panelist, and consultant and is involved in special projects for the Internet, advertising, and multimedia. His current research focuses on the strategic design and usability aspects of interactive media, developing efficient experience design and online communication. He is also a founding partner of Mediaman, a German-based communications agency that specializes in integrated communication and advertising with a special focus on interactive communication. Formerly, he has worked as art director and creative director in New York City at Grey Advertising, Lois GGK, J. Walter Thompson, and Communication House.

William G. Anderson, Executive-in-Residence; M.B.A., Pennsylvania (Wharton). Mr. Anderson brings extensive, high-level experience to his teaching having worked for such corporations as Welch, Currier, Curry, Anderson, and Hill, Holliday, Connors, Cosmopulos. He has worked on major advertising assignments for brands, including Ameritech and Ocean Spray. At Emerson, Anderson collaborated to develop Marketing Finance for the IMC program and Financial and Strategic Context of Global Market Planning. His reputation for exceptional teaching has made his "Brands" classes very popular.

Karl Baehr, Executive-in-Residence; Ph.D., Regent University (Virginia). Dr. Baehr is a communication professional, scholar, and corporate leader whose career of more than twenty-five years is highlighted by a series of successes in new media and technology venture evolution, communication curriculum development, and pedagogy. He has extensive knowledge of mass media and Internet new media industries, marketing strategies and tactics, communication technologies and trends, broadcasting operations and management, audience research methods, distance education, and computer-mediated communication. He is also the director of the undergraduate program in entrepreneurial studies at Emerson College.

Silvia Hodges, Executive-in-Residence; Ph.D. candidate, Nottingham Trent (England). Ms. Hodges is a pioneer in legal marketing with expertise in continental European jurisdictions. Over the course of ten years as a communications and business development consultant, she has written several books and articles on law firm marketing. She is the founder of the Legal Marketing Italia network, writes a regular column on legal marketing for *Italia Ogg*, and has conducted professional seminars and workshops on legal marketing in Italy, Germany, England, and the United States. As a recipient of a scholarship from the German Department of Education and Research, she is completing her doctoral studies in law firm marketing with a special focus on marketing legal services to medium-size companies.

Abbott Ikeler, Executive-in-Residence; Ph.D., London. Dr. Ikeler taught literature and writing at Bowdoin College, University of Muenster, and Rhode Island College before entering the corporate world. His academic achievements include a Senior Fulbright Fellowship, a book on nineteenth-century aesthetics, and numerous articles on Victorian fiction. From the mid-1980s to 2001, he held public relations and advertising positions with three multinational organizations and a full-service agency. Immediately before coming to Emerson, Dr. Ikeler was Director of Communications and Public Affairs for the Internet and Networking Division of Motorola, a post he held for three years. The focus of his current research is global public relations, especially the impact of such nonmedia influencers as industry and financial analysts.

Julie C. Lellis, Instructor of Marketing Communication; Ph.D. candidate, North Carolina at Chapel Hill. Ms. Lellis brings experience teaching public relations issues and public relations writing, enhanced by service-learning practices in the classroom. Her award-winning research writing is influenced by her training in rehabilitation psychology and counseling coupled with mass communication and focuses on nonprofit communication about disability and chronic illness. She has worked in program development and clinical settings to aid adolescents. Her work has been presented at national and international conferences in public relations, mass media, and health communication.

Kristin Lieb, Instructor of Marketing Communication; Ph.D. candidate, Syracuse. Ms. Lieb's expertise combines executive experience in marketing and business development with scholarship in public communications. Her career has brought her from the interactive side of Newbury Comics to writing case studies for the Harvard Business School. She has served as the vice president for business development for Digital Media on Demand, Swap It, and Atomic Pop as well as consultant for America Online and UPS. She has been a freelance writer for *Billboard, Rolling Stone*, the *Boston Phoenix*, and the *Boston Globe*. Her research explores the branding of popular female celebrities and informs issues related to body image, gender, and aging.

Doug Quintal, Lecturer and Internship Coordinator; M.A., Emerson. Mr. Quintal's interests are in integrated marketing communication, writing for marketing and management communication, principles of public relations, and entertainment marketing. He has been PR consultant for a private individual taking on a national tax preparation corporation, as seen on *Dateline* and featured in the *Boston Globe* and the *Wall Street Journal*.

James Rowean, Executive-in-Residence; M.A., Michigan State. Mr. Rowean brings twenty-five years of professional experience in advertising and marketing to his teaching of integrated marketing communication. A former account executive for Cronin/Wallwork Curry, Arnold Worldwide, and Campbell Ewald (Detroit), he also directed marketing for Dunkin' Donuts and Bread & Circus/Whole Foods Supermarkets. He has brand experience with Ocean Spray, Kimberly-Clark, Reebok, Timex, and Steinway Pianos. Rowean has been a guest lecturer at Boston University, New York University, and Boston College.

Tracy Worrell, Assistant Professor of Marketing Communication; Ph.D., Michigan State. Dr. Worrell is a rising scholar in the area of advertising, media, and health. Her timely work on television portrayals of weight, consumption, physical disability, and media impact has gained attention at national conferences and has been published in *Health Communication* and the *Journal of Creative Communications*. In addition to teaching core courses in human communication, she has taught courses in mass media, public relations, and public speaking. Her applied work in the television industry as a traffic manager, continuity director, and disc jockey complements her scholarly expertise.

Seounmi Han Youn, Assistant Professor of Marketing Communication; Ph.D., Minnesota. Dr. Youn has established a productive line of research focusing on the antecedents, correlates, and consequences of online consumer socialization among the young. In addition to presenting her work at national and international conferences, it has been featured in professional journals such as the *Journal of Advertising Research, Psychology and Marketing*, the *Journal of Interactive Advertising*, and the *Journal of Broadcasting and Electronic Media*. Dr. Youn's instruction in courses that deal with global applications and research methodology is enhanced by her industry experience with DongSeo Marketing Research in Seoul, Korea.

NEW YORK UNIVERSITY

School of Continuing and Professional Studies
Master of Science in Direct and Interactive Marketing

Program of Study

The Master of Science program in direct and interactive marketing at New York University's (NYU) School of Continuing and Professional Studies prepares marketing professionals to take on significant management responsibilities in companies that use interactive and direct marketing to acquire and loyalize customers. Such responsibilities include product management, customer-relationship management (CRM), subscription/club marketing, catalog marketing, database management, e-commerce marketing, digital media, database analysis, advertising-agency account management, database management, media management, creative management, and strategic planning. Direct and interactive marketing methodologies and application are taught in every course. From database marketing to Web advertising and CRM, this management-focused program offers students a respected credential and a remarkable set of skills to help accelerate their careers.

Graduates of the master's program leave with a thorough understanding of the management, business, and leadership skills required to be successful in companies that use direct and interactive marketing to sell consumer products and services, to sell business products and services, and to increase return on investment (ROI) from their customers.

Renown faculty members—leading academics and distinguished marketing executives—bring strong industry knowledge and passion to all they teach. A master's from NYU represents the finest education available, one that is current in its teachings, demanding in its academic approach, and relevant in its application to the real world.

For the Master of Science degree, students must complete 42 credits of graduate course work. The curriculum consists of six required foundation courses, six required core competency courses, one elective, and a master's project. Some degree candidates complete the program full-time in two years; others study part-time over a period of two to five years. Courses are offered in the evenings at the NYU Midtown Center on 42nd Street. The curriculum for the M.S. program in direct and interactive marketing is continually reevaluated and updated in response to industry needs to provide the most up-to-date and relevant course of study.

Research Facilities

The Elmer Holmes Bobst Library and Study Center, one of the largest open-stack research libraries in the world, houses more than 3 million of NYU's nearly 4.4 million volumes. In addition to books, journals, and other print materials, the library provides access to many nonprint resources. These include microforms, databases, and other electronic resources that students can connect to from their home or residence hall; extensive video and audio collections; and a variety of computer equipment and software programs.

NYU's central source for computing, information, network, and telecommunications services is Information Technology Services (ITS). ITS maintains four large, modern computer labs with high-end Macintosh and Windows computers, laser printers, multimedia equipment, and a wide variety of up-to-date software. The Client Services division of ITS provides comprehensive help with the materials and equipment available to students online, in person, and via telephone and e-mail.

Financial Aid

There are many financial aid options to consider, including low-interest educational loans. NYU's centralized Office of Financial Aid assists students with loan packages, scholarships, and the NYU monthly payment plan, which enables students to spread out their tuition payments. Department scholarships are also available. For more information, students should visit http://www.nyu.edu/financial.aid.

Cost of Study

Tuition for part-time students for the 2007–08 academic year is $1266 per credit plus fees. For full-time students (10–12 credits per semester), the cost of tuition and related fees is $12,664 per semester. Fees vary somewhat by program. The Board of Trustees of New York University reserves the right to alter these costs without notice.

Living and Housing Costs

Graduate student housing is available on the University campus and is administered through the Office of Housing and Residence Life. However, students may choose to live off campus. NYU's Off-Campus Housing Office (OCHO) offers assistance to members of the NYU community in their search for non-University housing options. OCHO provides, exclusively to NYU students, listings of available locations for rent through private landlords, property managers, brokers, and real estate agents. Updated daily, these listings are accessible through OCHO's computer terminals or online for members of the NYU community.

Student Group

As of the spring 2007 semester, the student body numbered approximately 83 graduate students. Nearly 80 percent of the students work full-time and attend classes part-time. Eligible full-time students have internships at major companies to supplement classroom learning with experience. There is a student club that organizes events with VIP guest speakers from major companies, a resume book for student placement in internships and full-time positions, and an active alumni chapter that sponsors networking events.

Location

The School of Continuing and Professional Studies' Master of Science program in direct and interactive marketing is housed at NYU's Midtown Center, 11 West 42nd Street in Manhattan. New York City is considered to be the center of the direct marketing industry in North America.

The University, The School, and The Program

NYU is a private university, composed of fourteen schools and colleges. The University was founded in 1831 and the School of Continuing and Professional Studies in 1934. NYU is among the country's academic pioneers in the study of direct and interactive marketing. The School began offering marketing courses in the late 1960s, when direct response marketing was still in its infancy. As the field grew, so too did NYU's commitment. The Master of Science program in direct and interactive marketing was established in 1997. Today the master's program continues its tradition of innovation and is one of the most renowned graduate programs of its kind in this industry.

Applying

Students may apply for fall or spring admission. Matriculated students may take summer courses. Factors that are considered in evaluating an applicant include official transcripts of academic achievement in previous undergraduate and graduate course work, scores from the GRE or GMAT, TOEFL score (for international students whose native language is not English), the nature and extent of previous work experience, professional recommendations, and a statement of purpose.

Correspondence and Information

For more information and an application package, students should contact:

Office of Admissions
Master of Science in Direct and Interactive Marketing
New York University
145 Fourth Avenue, Room 219
New York, New York 10003

Phone: 212-998-7200 Ext. 410
Fax: 212-995-4674
E-mail: scps.gradadmissions@nyu.edu
Web site: http://www.scps.nyu.edu/410

New York University

THE ADMINISTRATION

Robert S. Lapiner, Ph.D., Dean, School of Continuing and Professional Studies.

Anthony R. Davidson, Ph.D., EDP; Divisional Dean, Director, and Clinical Professor, Division of Programs in Business, School of Continuing and Professional Studies.

Marjorie Kalter, Ph.D., Director and Clinical Professor, Graduate Programs in Direct and Interactive Marketing, Division of Programs in Business, School of Continuing and Professional Studies.

NORTHWESTERN UNIVERSITY

Medill School
Integrated Marketing Communications

Programs of Study

Medill offers the Master of Science in Integrated Marketing Communications (MSIMC) Program, the first such degree in the country. Taking a data-driven, customer-centric approach, the program teaches students how to develop and use consumer insights to drive marketing communications programs across various media platforms, with measurable results.

Courses include market research and statistics and marketing management and finance, as well as IMC strategy and tactics, database marketing and analysis, consumer insight, and media economics and technology. Electives include advertising/sales promotions, public relations, customer contact and data mining, marketing mix planning and analysis, building brand equity, and customer loyalty.

This innovative curriculum gives students the expertise to assess markets through advanced marketing research methods and database segmentation. Students also develop communication skills that measurably improve profitability and success, addressing every segment of an audience with a distinctive, persuasive message. The explosion of the Internet has accelerated the need for talented people who understand how to use data to drive marketing decisions, to build interactive relationships, and to apply winning customer relationship management strategies. This program is designed to prepare students to provide this highly desired skill set.

Advertising/sales promotion courses emphasize the strategic thinking that produces great advertising and promotions. Students learn media planning, marketing strategies, research techniques, and managerial decision making. Direct, database, and e-commerce marketing courses provide hands-on training in today's technology-oriented, data-gathering techniques and teach how to implement strategies to reach target audiences. Public relations courses concentrate on aligning public relations more closely with marketing and management functions to persuasively communicate with customers and all stakeholders, including investors, employees, and the media.

The full-time MSIMC program is fifteen months in length and begins in September. Students spend one quarter working on real-world marketing communications projects for Fortune 500 companies, communications agencies, or smaller emerging firms. The part-time MSIMC program is designed for working professionals. Students take two evening classes per quarter and typically earn their degree in two years.

The MSIMC program differs from the traditional M.B.A. by preparing students specifically for the future of marketing communications, which requires in-depth research and interdisciplinary work in addition to practical training.

Research Facilities

The full resources of Northwestern University are available to Medill students, including libraries, which hold more than 3 million volumes and 1,000 international and domestic newspapers. Northwestern's libraries offer a wide range of research information, including current information in print, on electronic resources that are also accessible from home, and a multimedia development center for creating projects with sound, video, and graphics. Northwestern is one of 137 members of the Center for Research Libraries through which students can receive infrequently used materials. Medill also maintains a resource library that features an excellent selection of books, newspapers, reference materials, magazines, online services, and periodicals that are pertinent to the communications industry.

Financial Aid

Eighty percent of Medill's full-time students receive some form of financial assistance. Financial aid packages comprise a combination of loans, federal work-study awards, and grants or scholarships. The amount of the financial aid package is primarily based on the student's eligibility and current financial need, as well as the availability of grant, scholarship, federal work-study, and loan funds. Merit scholarships are also awarded at the time of admission of the application.

Cost of Study

For the 2007–08 academic year, full-time program tuition is $11,688 per quarter for MSIMC students. Other estimated quarterly costs include $934 for books, $630 for transportation, and $1300 for personal expenses. The part-time program is $3815 per course for the 2007–08 academic year. Instead of a residency, part-time students take a practicum course involving real-world style marketing issues or projects.

Living and Housing Costs

For students wishing to live on campus, graduate housing is readily available on the Evanston campus. Off-campus apartments are plentiful in both Evanston and Chicago and vary in price. Estimated costs for room and board are $18,456 for twelve months.

Student Group

Enrollment in the full-time MSIMC program is about 85 students per year. These individuals come from colleges and universities that span the globe. The average age of the students is 26. Most have full-time work experience. Currently, about 90 percent of MSIMC program graduates find employment in corporate marketing departments, agencies, or nonprofit organizations. The part-time program enrolls 35 students per year.

Location

Medill's full-time MSIMC program is located at Northwestern's main campus in Evanston, Illinois, in the McCormick Tribune Center, a state-of-the-art facility that opened in 2002. It is a few steps from Lake Michigan. Historic Evanston, Chicago's first suburb to the north, blends urban convenience with small-town charm, while nearby Chicago offers its prominence in the business and cultural world and in some of the nation's most progressive blue chip marketing and service companies. Courses in the part-time program are offered at Northwestern's downtown Chicago Loop location.

The University

Established May 31, 1851, Northwestern University is one of the nation's major private research universities. Some 7,500 undergraduates and 5,200 graduate and professional school students study full-time on the Evanston and Chicago campuses with 1,600 full- and part-time faculty members. Medill is one of eight schools located on Northwestern's Evanston campus. The others are the Weinberg College of Arts and Sciences, the School of Education and Social Policy, the Graduate School, the J. L. Kellogg Graduate School of Management, the School of Music, the School of Communication, and the Robert R. McCormick School of Engineering and Applied Science of the Technological Institute. The Chicago campus accommodates the Center for Nursing, the School of Law, the Feinberg School of Medicine, the School of Continuing Studies, and the McGaw Medical Center.

Applying

Medill seeks graduate students with outstanding academic ability and career potential, who demonstrate strong motivation and commitment to the field of marketing as their profession. Applicants are required to submit the application form, including essays, three letters of recommendation, transcripts from all postsecondary institutions attended, GRE or GMAT scores, a resume, and a $50 nonrefundable application fee. An on-campus, telephone, or alumni interview is required. International applicants whose first language is not English must submit TOEFL scores received within twelve months of applying. The priority application deadline for the full-time program is January 15. Early application is strongly encouraged. Notification is mailed on or before March 15. The priority application deadline for the part-time program is July 1.

Correspondence and Information

Office of Graduate Admissions and Financial Aid
Medill School
Northwestern University
1845 Sheridan Road
Evanston, Illinois 60208-2101

Phone: 847-491-5228
Fax: 847-467-7342
Web site: http://www.medill.northwestern.edu/

Northwestern University

THE FACULTY AND THEIR RESEARCH

Integrated Marketing Communications Faculty

Martin Block, Professor. Chair, Department of Advertising, Michigan State University; senior market analyst, Goodyear Tire & Rubber Company; author, *Analyzing Sales Promotion, Business-to-Business Marketing Research* and *Cable Advertising: New Ways to New Business.*

Clarke Caywood, Associate Professor and Director, Public Relations Sequence. Former legislative officer, attorney general; former assistant to governor; editor, *Handbook of Strategic Public Relations and Integrated Communications;* founder, *Journal of Integrated Communications.*

Tom Collinger, Associate Professor, Department Chair, and Associate Dean. Former senior vice president, Leo Burnett Company; former vice president, Ogilvy & Mather Direct.

John Greening, Associate Professor and Director, Advertising and Sales Promotion. Former executive vice president–managing partner, DDB Needham; senior vice president–group account director, DDB Needham Worldwide.

Tom Hayden, Senior Lecturer. Former general manager, executive vice president, Bozell Worldwide, Chicago, subsidiary of True North Communications; former vice president, group account supervisor, D'Arcy Masius Benton & Bowles; vice president, account supervisor, DDB Needham; account executive, Leo Burnett.

Geraldine R. Henderson, Associate Professor; Ph.D., Northwestern. Former faculty member of Duke University's Fuqua School of Business, Howard University's School of Business, and the University of Texas at Austin's College of Communication.

Edward Malthouse, Associate Professor. Specialist in data mining, market research, media marketing, and statistics.

Francis J. Mulhern, Associate Professor and Associate Dean; Ph.D., Texas at Austin. Former faculty member, Penn State School of Business; specialist in database analysis, time series, and forecasting.

Don Schultz, Professor. Former senior vice president, Tracy-Locke Advertising and Public Relations; founding editor, *Journal of Direct Marketing;* author, *Strategic Advertising Campaigns, Raising the Corporate Umbrella,* and *Integrated Global Communications.*

Edward Spiegel, Professor Emeritus and Associate Director of Residency Program. Former senior vice president of marketing and advertising and member of the board of directors, Spiegel Inc.

Jacquelyn Thomas, Associate Professor. Specialist in customer relationship management, strategic database marketing, measurement and modeling of customer equity.

Paul Wang, Associate Professor; Ph.D., Northwestern. Technical editor, *Journal of Direct Marketing;* coauthor, *Database Marketing;* research fellow, Newspaper Management Center, Northwestern University.

SAINT JOSEPH'S UNIVERSITY

SAINT JOSEPH'S UNIVERSITY

Executive Pharmaceutical Marketing M.B.A. Program

Programs of Study

The Saint Joseph's University (SJU) Executive Pharmaceutical Marketing M.B.A. Program strives to provide advanced education and developmental experiences for those employed in the pharmaceutical and biopharmaceutical industries. Highly qualified faculty members, complemented by domestic and international business and marketing experts, bring real-world leadership and experience into the classroom. The courses offer the students the opportunity to cultivate an understanding of the latest techniques for developing sophisticated research tools, innovative marketing plans, and effective methods for implementing and evaluating strategies for the changing business environment. Offering two unique formats, the Executive Pharmaceutical Marketing M.B.A. Program is at the leading edge of convenience-driven, innovative education.

The program held at ACE Center (formerly called Eagle Lodge) is tailored to fit the needs of the pharmaceutical industry professional by providing a modular format for the delivery of business concepts and skills specific to this industry. The self-paced curriculum offers the ultimate in flexibility, as students may complete their M.B.A. in as few as two years or as many as six years. Courses are offered in a Friday/Saturday executive format and are held at ACE Center in Lafayette Hill, Pennsylvania. A Post-M.B.A. Certificate for those industry professionals who have already earned their M.B.A. is also offered. Candidates for the Post-M.B.A. Certificate are required to complete nine courses in pharmaceutical marketing.

The On-Line Executive Pharmaceutical Marketing M.B.A. provides ultimate flexibility by eliminating time, space, and distance constraints. An exciting lockstep curriculum, coupled with state-of-the-art technology, provides students with the tools they require to excel in the pharmaceutical industry. This twenty-two-month program is structured around one course per month and four on-campus residencies. The online lockstep cohort program means students graduate in two years with the same peers who entered with them. The utilization of cyber-teams allows students to take advantage of the knowledge and experience of their fellow students.

Research Facilities

The Francis A. Drexel Library supports the academic programs of the University with a collection of 348,000 volumes. In addition, 1,400 current periodical subscriptions, 800,000 microforms, and more than 4,000 titles are available electronically. The Drexel Library has extensive business resources. The library also serves as a selective depository for U.S. government documents. Drexel Library provides access to a wide range of computerized databases via a local area network and individual computers within the building. All online databases are also available on the campus network and can be accessed from off campus with a University ID number and password. In addition, the library's World Wide Web home page contains a selective subject guide to resources on the Internet to assist users in their searching.

Financial Aid

Through guaranteed loan agreements with lending institutions and state agencies such as the Pennsylvania Higher Education Assistance Agency and the New Jersey Department of Higher Education, students can secure long-term loans at a low interest rate. An electronic loan application is initiated at the University and forwarded to PHEAA, the guarantor. Federal Stafford Student Loans are either subsidized or unsubsidized. A student may borrow up to $18,500 per academic year. All full- or half-time students (at least 6 credits per semester) are eligible to apply for federal aid. Students may elect to finance part of their tuition through a deferred payment program offered by the University.

Cost of Study

Tuition costs vary depending on the chosen format. Students enrolled in the Executive Pharmaceutical Marketing M.B.A. Program held at ACE Center are charged on a per-course basis. Total tuition fees for students enrolled in the On-Line Executive Pharmaceutical Marketing M.B.A. Program for the 2007–08 academic year are $66,600, including a nonrefundable deposit and a monthly online fee. These fees are subject to change.

Student Group

Students in the Executive Pharmaceutical Marketing M.B.A. Program represent a number of industries, including pharmaceutical sales, quality assurance, health care, clinical research, and product management. Many have up to ten years' working experience and maintained impressive grade point averages as undergraduates.

Location

The University is located in eastern Pennsylvania in the suburbs of Philadelphia, only 15 minutes from downtown. Pharmaceutical marketing courses are offered at ACE Center, located 15 minutes from the main campus.

The University

Founded by the Society of Jesus in 1851, Saint Joseph's University advances the professional and personal ambitions of men and women by providing a demanding, yet supportive, educational experience. One of only 142 schools with a Phi Beta Kappa chapter and AACSB International business school accreditation, Saint Joseph's is home to 3,900 full-time undergraduates and 3,400 graduate, part-time, and doctoral students. Steeped in the 450-year Jesuit tradition of scholarship and service, the University strives to be recognized as the preeminent comprehensive Catholic university in the Northeast.

Saint Joseph's University is the area's only college or university to appear among the top thirty part-time M.B.A. programs of *U.S. News & World Report's* 2005 America's Best Graduate Schools and one of the nation's most outstanding business schools, according to the Princeton's Review's most recent student survey-driven guidebook, *The Best of 143 Business Schools.*

Applying

Applications are accepted on a rolling admission basis. Students applying for admission to the Executive Pharmaceutical Marketing M.B.A. Program must have a baccalaureate degree from an accredited college or university and four years of pharmaceutical industry experience. Applicants must submit official transcripts, an application, and one letter of recommendation and submit official GMAT scores or have a personal interview. TOEFL scores and an affidavit of support are required for international students. To apply online, students should visit the Pharmaceutical Marketing Web site.

Correspondence and Information

Executive Pharmaceutical Marketing M.B.A.
Mandeville Hall, Room 387
Saint Joseph's University
5600 City Avenue
Philadelphia, Pennsylvania 19131
Phone: 610-660-1318
E-mail: patricia.rafferty@sju.edu
Web site: http://www.sju.edu/PHARMACEUTICAL_MARKETING

Saint Joseph's University

THE FACULTY

Joseph A. DiAngelo Jr., Ed.D., Dean, Erivan K. Haub School of Business.
Stephen J. Porth, Ph.D., Associate Dean, Erivan K. Haub School of Business.
Terese Waldron, M.S., Director, Executive Pharmaceutical Marketing M.B.A. Program, On-Line Executive Pharmaceutical Marketing M.B.A. Program.

University Faculty
Nancy Childs, Ph.D., Professor of Marketing.
Carolyn Choh Fleming, M.B.A., Visiting Lecturer.
Waqar I. Ghani, Ph.D., Associate Professor of Accounting.
Vipul K. Gupta, Ph.D., Assistant Professor of Information Systems.
Karen Hogan, Ph.D., Associate Professor of Finance and Chair, Department of Finance.
Thani Jambulingam, Ph.D., Assistant Professor of Pharmaceutical Marketing.
Ronald K. Klimberg, Ph.D., Associate Professor of Finance.
Joseph M. Larkin, Ph.D., Associate Professor of Accounting.
John J. McCall, Ph.D., Professor of Philosophy and Management.
Alfredo Mauri, Ph.D., Assistant Professor of Management.
Harold F. Rahmlow, Ph.D., Assistant Professor of Finance.
George Sillup, Ph.D., Assistant Professor of Management.
Claire Simmers, Ph.D., Assistant Professor of Management.
David S. Steingard, Ph.D., Assistant Professor of Management.
William L. Trombetta, Ph.D., Professor of Marketing.
George H. Webster, Jr., Ph.D., Associate Professor of Finance.
Ira Yermish, Ph.D., Assistant Professor of Information Systems.

Professional Faculty
Dan Delucca, Assistant Professor of Management.
Stephen Kanovsky, U.S. Corporate Compliance Officer, Sanofi-Aventis U.S.
Dolores Shank-Samiec, Senior Marketing Manager, e-Business Strategies & Solutions, Merck.
Dick Shute, Assistant Professor of Marketing.
Norm Smith, President, Viewpoint Consulting, Inc.

Section 15
Nonprofit Management

This section contains a directory of institutions offering graduate work in nonprofit management, followed by in-depth entries submitted by institutions that chose to prepare detailed program descriptions. Additional information about programs listed in the directory but not augmented by an in-depth entry may be obtained by writing directly to the dean of a graduate school or chair of a department at the address given in the directory.

For programs offering related work, see also in this book Accounting and Finance and Business Administration and Management. In Book 2, see Public, Regional, and Industrial Affairs.

CONTENTS

Program Directory

Close-Ups

Nonprofit Management

American Jewish University, Graduate School, David Lieber School of Graduate Studies, Program in Business Administration, Bel Air, CA 90077-1599. Offers general nonprofit administration (MBA); Jewish nonprofit administration (MBA). Part-time and evening/weekend programs available. *Degree requirements:* For master's, thesis, internship. *Entrance requirements:* For master's, GMAT or GRE General Test, interview, minimum undergraduate GPA of 3.0. Additional exam requirements/recommendations for international students: Required—TOEFL (minimum score 550 paper-based; 247 computer-based).

Azusa Pacific University, Haggard School of Theology, Program in Non-Profit Leadership and Theology, Azusa, CA 91702-7000. Offers Christian non-profit leadership (MA). In 2006, 1 degree awarded. Application fee: $45 ($65 for international students). *Expenses:* Tuition: Part-time $475 per credit.

Boston University, School of Management, Master of Business Administration Program, Boston, MA 02215. Offers advanced accounting (Certificate); general management (MBA); healthcare management (MBA); public and nonprofit management (MBA); JD/MBA; MBA/MA; MBA/MPH; MBA/MS; MBA/MSIS; MS/MBA. Part-time and evening/weekend programs available. *Faculty:* 104 full-time (21 women). *Students:* 299 full-time (114 women), 487 part-time (190 women); includes 124 minority (12 African Americans, 2 American Indian/Alaska Native, 94 Asian Americans or Pacific Islanders, 16 Hispanic Americans), 143 international. Average age 26. 1,482 applicants, 42% accepted, 300 enrolled. In 2006, 342 degrees awarded. *Entrance requirements:* For master's, GMAT. *Application deadline:* For fall admission, 5/1 for domestic students. Applications are processed on a rolling basis. Application fee: $125. Electronic applications accepted. *Expenses:* Tuition: Full-time $33,330; part-time $1,042 per credit. Required fees: $462; $40. *Financial support:* Career-related internships or fieldwork, Federal Work-Study, institutionally sponsored loans, and tuition waivers (partial) available. Support available to part-time students. Financial award applicants required to submit FAFSA. *Unit head:* Dr. John Chalykoff, Associate Dean, Academic Program, 617-353-4157, Fax: 617-353-5003, E-mail: chalykof@bu.edu. *Application contact:* Hayden Estrada, Assistant Dean, Admissions, 617-353-2670, Fax: 617-353-7368, E-mail: mba@bu.edu.

Capella University, School of Human Services, Minneapolis, MN 55402. Offers addictions counseling (Certificate); counseling studies (MS, PhD); criminal justice (MS, PhD, Certificate); diversity studies (Certificate); general human services (MS, PhD); health care administration (MS, PhD, Certificate); management of nonprofit agencies (MS, PhD, Certificate); marital, couple and family counseling/therapy (MS); marriage and family services (Certificate); mental health counseling (MS); professional counseling (Certificate); social and community services (MS, PhD, Certificate). Part-time and evening/weekend programs available. Postbaccalaureate distance learning degree programs offered (minimal on-campus study). Terminal master's awarded for partial completion of doctoral program. *Degree requirements:* For master's, integrative project, thesis optional; for doctorate, thesis/dissertation, comprehensive exam, registration. *Entrance requirements:* Additional exam requirements/recommendations for international students: Required—TOEFL (minimum score 550 paper-based; 213 computer-based), TWE (minimum score 4). Electronic applications accepted. *Faculty research:* Compulsive and addictive behaviors, substance abuse, assessment of psychopathology and neuropsychology.

Carlos Albizu University, Miami Campus, Graduate Programs, Miami, FL 33172-2209. Offers clinical psychology (Psy D); entrepreneurship (MBA); exceptional student education (MS); industrial/organizational psychology (MS); marriage and family therapy (MS); mental health counseling (MS); nonprofit management (MBA); organizational management (MBA); psychology (MS); school counseling (MS); teaching English as a second language (MS). *Accreditation:* APA. Part-time and evening/weekend programs available. Terminal master's awarded for partial completion of doctoral program. *Degree requirements:* For master's, one foreign language, comprehensive exam, integrative project (MBA), research project (MSESE); for doctorate, one foreign language, comprehensive exam, internship, doctoral project. *Entrance requirements:* For master's, 3 letters of recommendation, interview, minimum GPA of 3.0, resumé; for doctorate, 3 letters of recommendation, minimum GPA of 3.0, resumé, interview. *Faculty research:* Psychotherapy, forensic psychology, neuropsychology, marketing strategy, entrepreneurship.

Carlow University, School for Social Change, Pittsburgh, PA 15213-3165. Offers management of non-profit organization (MS); organizational influence (MS); professional counseling (MSPC); training and development (MS). Part-time and evening/weekend programs available. *Entrance requirements:* For master's, interview, minimum GPA of 3.0, resumé, 3 letters of recommendation, 1 year professional experience. Additional exam requirements/recommendations for international students: Required—TOEFL (minimum score 550 paper-based; 213 computer-based). Electronic applications accepted. *Faculty research:* Gender and leadership, cross cultural communications and leadership, organizational culture.

Case Western Reserve University, Weatherhead School of Management, Mandel Center for Nonprofit Organizations, Non-profit Organizations Program, Cleveland, OH 44106. Offers MNO, MNO/MSSA, CNM, JD/MNO, MSSA/MNO. Part-time and evening/weekend programs available. *Students:* 27 full-time (20 women), 17 part-time (15 women); includes 14 minority (11 African Americans, 1 Asian American or Pacific Islander, 2 Hispanic Americans). Average age 31. 71 applicants, 85% accepted, 44 enrolled. In 2006, 21 master's, 24 other advanced degrees awarded. *Entrance requirements:* For master's, GMAT, letters of recommendation, resumé. Additional exam requirements/recommendations for international students: Required—TOEFL (minimum score 550 paper-based; 213 computer-based). *Application deadline:* For fall admission, 6/1 priority date for domestic students; for spring admission, 12/1 priority date for domestic students. Applications are processed on a rolling basis. Application fee: $25. *Expenses:* Contact institution. *Financial support:* Institutionally sponsored loans and scholarships/grants available. Financial award applicants required to submit FAFSA. *Application contact:* Rebecca W Zirm, Director of Recruitment, 800-435-6669, E-mail: mcnoadmissions@case.edu.

See Close-Up on page 667.

Cleveland State University, College of Graduate Studies, Maxine Goodman Levin College of Urban Affairs, Program in Nonprofit Administration and Leadership, Cleveland, OH 44115. Offers MNAL. *Faculty:* 7. *Entrance requirements:* For master's, GRE, 2 letters of recommendation. *Financial support:* Fellowships, career-related internships or fieldwork, scholarships/grants, and unspecified assistantships available. *Unit head:* Dr. Stuart Mendel, Director, 216-687-6908, E-mail: stuart@urban.csuohio.edu. *Application contact:* Graduate Advisor, 216-523-7522, Fax: 216-687-5398, E-mail: gradprog@urban.csuohio.edu.

Cleveland State University, College of Graduate Studies, Maxine Goodman Levin College of Urban Affairs, Program in Public Administration, Cleveland, OH 44115. Offers geographic information systems (Certificate); local and urban management (Certificate); non-profit management (Certificate); public administration (MPA); JD/MPA. *Accreditation:* NASPAA. Part-time and evening/weekend programs available. *Faculty:* 25 full-time (10 women), 11 part-time/adjunct (3 women). *Students:* 36 full-time (17 women), 108 part-time (76 women); includes 46 minority (43 African Americans, 1 Asian American or Pacific Islander, 2 Hispanic Americans), 1 international. Average age 35. 96 applicants, 66% accepted, 37 enrolled. In 2006, 1 degree awarded. *Degree requirements:* For master's, internship or project, capstone course, thesis optional. *Entrance requirements:* For master's, GMAT or GRE General Test, minimum GPA of 3.0. Additional exam requirements/recommendations for international students: Required—TOEFL (minimum score 525 paper-based; 197 computer-based). *Application deadline:* For fall admission, 7/15 priority date for domestic students. Applications are processed on a rolling basis. Application fee: $30. *Financial support:* In 2006–07, 11 research assistantships with full and partial tuition reimbursements (averaging $4,960 per year) were awarded; career-related internships or fieldwork, institutionally sponsored loans, tuition waivers (full and partial), and unspecified assistantships also available. Financial award application deadline: 3/1. *Faculty research:* Health care, public works, public management, economic development. *Unit head:* Dr. Vera Vogelsang–Coombs, Director, 216-687-9223, Fax: 216-687-5398, E-mail: vera@urban.csuohio.edu. *Application contact:* Graduate Programs Coordinator, 216-523-7522, Fax: 216-687-5398, E-mail: gradprog@urban.csuohio.edu.

College of Notre Dame of Maryland, Graduate Studies, Program in Nonprofit Management, Baltimore, MD 21210-2476. Offers MA. Part-time and evening/weekend programs available. *Students:* 1 (woman) full-time, 30 part-time (24 women). *Degree requirements:* For master's, thesis optional. *Entrance requirements:* For master's, minimum GPA of 3.0. Additional exam requirements/recommendations for international students: Required—TOEFL (minimum score 500 paper-based; 173 computer-based; 61 iBT). *Application deadline:* For fall admission, 8/15 priority date for domestic students; for winter admission, 12/15 for domestic students; for spring admission, 1/15 for domestic students. Applications are processed on a rolling basis. Application fee: $40. Electronic applications accepted. *Financial support:* Application deadline: 6/30; *Unit head:* Dr. Ann Breihan, Head, 410-532-5554, Fax: 410-532-5333, E-mail: abreihan@ndm.edu. *Application contact:* Erica D. Jones, Graduate Admissions Coordinator, 410-532-5317, Fax: 410-532-5333, E-mail: gradadm@ndm.edu.

The College of Saint Rose, Graduate Studies, School of Business, Department of Not-for-Profit Management, Albany, NY 12203-1419. Offers Certificate. Part-time and evening/weekend programs available. *Entrance requirements:* For degree, minimum undergraduate GPA of 3.0 or GMAT. Additional exam requirements/recommendations for international students: Required—TOEFL (minimum score 550 paper-based; 213 computer-based). Electronic applications accepted.

Columbia University, School of Continuing Education, Program in Fundraising Management, New York, NY 10027. Offers MS. Part-time and evening/weekend programs available. *Faculty:* 9 part-time/adjunct (5 women). *Students:* Average age 27. 46 applicants, 70% accepted, 24 enrolled. *Degree requirements:* For master's, internship. *Entrance requirements:* Additional exam requirements/recommendations for international students: Required—American Language Program (ALP) placement test. *Application deadline:* For fall admission, 7/15 priority date for domestic students; for spring admission, 11/11 priority date for domestic students. Application fee: $50. Electronic applications accepted. *Faculty research:* Fundraising for annual campaigns, capital campaigns, nonprofit financial management, research for fundraising and planned giving. *Unit head:* Dr. Lucas G. Rubin, Director, 212-854-9699, E-mail: lr2008@columbia.edu. *Application contact:* Donia Allen, Program Coordinator, 212-854-3771, Fax: 212-854-5861, E-mail: da1.20@columbia.edu.

DePaul University, School of Public Service, Chicago, IL 60604-2287. Offers financial administration management (Certificate); health administration (Certificate); health law and policy (MS); international public services (MS); metropolitan planning (Certificate); public administration (MS); public service management (MS), including association management, fundraising and philanthropy, healthcare administration, higher education administration, metropolitan planning, non-profit administration, public administration, public policy; public services (Certificate); JD/MS; MA/MS. Part-time and evening/weekend programs available. Postbaccalaureate distance learning degree programs offered (minimal on-campus study). *Faculty:* 11 full-time (2 women), 19 part-time/adjunct (16 women). *Students:* 195 full-time (146 women), 132 part-time (89 women); includes 114 minority (58 African Americans, 1 American Indian/Alaska Native, 27 Asian Americans or Pacific Islanders, 28 Hispanic Americans). 140 applicants, 96% accepted, 96 enrolled. In 2006, 89 degrees awarded. *Degree requirements:* For master's, thesis or integrative seminar. *Entrance requirements:* For master's, minimum GPA of 2.7. Additional exam requirements/recommendations for international students: Required—TOEFL (minimum score 550 paper-based; 213 computer-based; 80 iBT), IELTS (minimum score 7). *Application deadline:* Applications are processed on a rolling basis. Application fee: $25. Electronic applications accepted. *Financial support:* In 2006–07, 28 students received support, including 3 research assistantships with full tuition reimbursements available (averaging $7,000 per year); career-related internships or fieldwork, Federal Work-Study, institutionally sponsored loans, scholarships/grants, and tuition waivers (partial) also available. Support available to part-time students. Financial award application deadline: 7/1; financial award applicants required to submit FAFSA. *Faculty research:* Government financing, transportation, leadership, health care, volunteerism and organizational behavior, non-profit organizations. Total annual research expenditures: $20,000. *Unit head:* Dr. J. Patrick Murphy, Director, 312-362-5608, Fax: 312-362-5506, E-mail: jpmurphy@depaul.edu. *Application contact:* Megan B. Balderston, Director of Admissions and Marketing, 312-362-5565, Fax: 312-362-5506, E-mail: pubserv@depaul.edu.

Eastern Michigan University, Graduate School, College of Business, Program in Business Administration, Ypsilanti, MI 48197. Offers business administration (MBA); e-business (MBA); enterprise business intelligence (MBA); entrepreneurship (MBA); finance (MBA); human resources (MBA); information systems (MBA); internal auditing (MBA); international business (MBA); nonprofit management (MBA); supply chain management (MBA). *Accreditation:* AACSB. Part-time and evening/weekend programs available. Postbaccalaureate distance learning degree programs offered (minimal on-campus study). *Students:* 98 full-time (36 women), 192 part-time (86 women); includes 50 minority (26 African Americans, 19 Asian Americans or Pacific Islanders, 5 Hispanic Americans), 76 international. Average age 29. In 2006, 109 degrees awarded. *Entrance requirements:* For master's, GMAT. Additional exam requirements/recommendations for international students: Required—TOEFL. *Application deadline:* For fall admission, 5/15 priority date for domestic students, 5/1 priority date for international students; for winter admission, 10/15 priority date for domestic students, 10/1 priority date for international students; for spring admission, 3/15 priority date for domestic students, 3/1 priority date for international students. Applications are processed on a rolling basis. Application fee: $35. *Expenses:* Tuition, state resident: part-time $341 per credit hour. Tuition, nonresident: full-time $16,104; part-time $671 per credit hour. Required fees: $816; $34 per credit hour. $40 per term. One-time fee: $82 full-time. Tuition and fees vary according to course level, course load, degree level and reciprocity agreements. *Financial support:* Fellowships, research assistantships with full tuition reimbursements, teaching assistantships with full tuition reimbursements, career-related internships or fieldwork, Federal Work-Study, institutionally sponsored loans, scholarships/grants, tuition waivers (partial), and unspecified assistantships available. Support available to part-time students. Financial award applicants required to submit FAFSA. *Unit head:* Dawn Gaymer, Assistant Dean, Graduate Business Programs, 734-487-4444, Fax: 734-483-1316, E-mail: dawn.malone@emich.edu. *Application contact:* K. Michelle Henry, Coordinator, 734-487-4444, Fax: 734-483-1316, E-mail: michelle.henry@emich.edu.

Eastern University, Graduate Business Programs, Program in Nonprofit Management, St. Davids, PA 19087-3696. Offers MBA, MS. *Entrance requirements:* For master's, GMAT (MBA), minimum GPA of 2.5.

Fairleigh Dickinson University, Metropolitan Campus, Anthony J. Petrocelli College of Continuing Studies, Public Administration Institute, Teaneck, NJ 07666-1914. Offers public administration (MPA, Certificate); public non-profit management (Certificate). *Students:* 82 full-time (39 women), 95 part-time (51 women), 48 international. Average age 35. 147 applicants, 87% accepted, 55 enrolled. In 2006, 35 degrees awarded. *Application deadline:* Applications are processed on a rolling basis. Application fee: $40. *Unit head:* Dr. William Roberts, Director, 201-692-2000.

Florida Atlantic University, College of Architecture, Urban and Public Affairs, School of Public Administration, Program in Nonprofit Management, Boca Raton, FL 33431-0991. Offers MNM. *Faculty:* 3 full-time (1 woman), 1 (woman) part-time/adjunct. *Students:* 2 full-time (1 woman), 6 part-time (all women); includes 4 minority (3 African Americans, 1 Asian American or Pacific Islander). Average age 36. 9 applicants, 22% accepted, 1 enrolled. In 2006, 7 degrees awarded. *Degree requirements:* For master's, thesis optional. *Entrance requirements:*

For master's, GRE, minimum GPA of 3.0. Additional exam requirements/recommendations for international students: Required—TOEFL. *Application deadline:* For fall admission, 7/1 priority date for domestic students; for spring admission, 10/27 priority date for domestic students. Application fee: $30. *Expenses:* Tuition, area resident: Full-time $4,394. Tuition, nonresident: full-time $16,441. *Financial support:* Career-related internships or fieldwork and institutionally sponsored loans available. *Faculty research:* Governance, nonprofit management, resource development, public and private nonprofit enterprise, accounting for government. *Application contact:* Dr. Ron Nyhan, Professor and Coordinator, 954-762-5664, E-mail: rcnyhan@fau.edu.

The George Washington University, Columbian College of Arts and Sciences, School of Public Policy and Public Administration, Programs in Public Policy and Public Administration, Washington, DC 20052. Offers budget and public finance (MPA); federal policy, politics, and management (MPA); international development management (MPA); managing public organizations (MPA); managing state and local governments and urban policy (MPA); nonprofit management (MPA); policy analysis and evaluation (MPA); public administration (MPA). *Accreditation:* NASPAA. Part-time programs available. *Entrance requirements:* For master's, GRE General Test. Additional exam requirements/recommendations for international students: Required—TOEFL. *Faculty research:* Regulatory reform, policy and program evaluation, ethics and public management, managing not-for-profits, policy making in the White House and Congress.

Hamline University, Graduate School of Management, St. Paul, MN 55104-1284. Offers management (MAM); nonprofit management (MANM); public administration (MAPA); JD/MAM; JD/MANM; JD/MAPA. Part-time and evening/weekend programs available. *Faculty:* 10 full-time (5 women), 29 part-time/adjunct (13 women). *Students:* 184 full-time (101 women), 145 part-time (87 women); includes 29 minority (14 African Americans, 2 American Indian/Alaska Native, 9 Asian Americans or Pacific Islanders, 4 Hispanic Americans), 65 international. Average age 33. 145 applicants, 72% accepted, 86 enrolled. In 2006, 92 master's awarded. *Degree requirements:* For master's, thesis/dissertation. *Entrance requirements:* For master's, personal statement, c.v., official transcripts, letters of recommendation, writing sample. Additional exam requirements/recommendations for international students: Required—TOEFL (minimum score 550 paper-based; 213 computer-based). *Application deadline:* For fall admission, 3/30 priority date for domestic students. Applications are processed on a rolling basis. Application fee: $30. Electronic applications accepted. *Expenses:* Tuition: Full-time $5,104; part-time $319 per credit. One-time fee: $175. Tuition and fees vary according to course load, degree level and program. *Financial support:* Federal Work-Study available. Financial award applicants required to submit FAFSA. *Unit head:* Julian Schuster, Dean, 651-523-2335, Fax: 651-523-3098, E-mail: jschuster01@hamline.edu. *Application contact:* Rae A. Lenway, Director Graduate Recruitment and Admission, 651-523-2592, Fax: 458, E-mail: rlenway01@hamline.edu.

High Point University, Norcross Graduate School, High Point, NC 27262-3598. Offers business administration (MBA); educational leadership (M Ed); elementary education (M Ed); history (MA); nonprofit organizations (MPA); special education (M Ed); sport studies (MS). *Accreditation:* ACBSP; NCATE. Part-time and evening/weekend programs available. *Faculty:* 31 full-time (11 women), 1 part-time/adjunct (0 women). *Students:* 49 full-time (29 women), 202 part-time (130 women); includes 72 minority (66 African Americans, 1 American Indian/Alaska Native, 2 Asian Americans or Pacific Islanders, 3 Hispanic Americans), 11 international. Average age 33. 171 applicants, 71% accepted, 94 enrolled. In 2006, 95 degrees awarded. *Degree requirements:* For master's, thesis (for some programs), comprehensive exam (for some programs), registration. *Entrance requirements:* For master's, GMAT (MBA), GRE, MAT, minimum GPA of 3.0. Additional exam requirements/recommendations for international students: Required—TOEFL (minimum score 550 paper-based). *Application deadline:* For fall admission, 4/15 priority date for domestic and international students; for spring admission, 10/15 priority date for domestic and international students. Applications are processed on a rolling basis. Application fee: $50. Electronic applications accepted. *Expenses:* Tuition: Full-time $9,270; part-time $1,545 per course. *Financial support:* In 2006–07, 190 students received support. Federal Work-Study, scholarships/grants, and unspecified assistantships available. Support available to part-time students. Financial award application deadline: 3/1; financial award applicants required to submit FAFSA. *Application contact:* Dr. Alberta Haynes Herron, Dean of Norcross Graduate School, 336-841-9198, Fax: 336-888-6378, E-mail: aherron@highpoint.edu.

Hope International University, School of Graduate Studies, Program in Business Administration, Fullerton, CA 92831-3138. Offers international development (MBA, MSM); nonprofit management (MBA). Part-time programs available. Postbaccalaureate distance learning degree programs offered (no on-campus study). *Faculty:* 1 full-time (0 women), 11 part-time/adjunct (0 women). *Students:* 25 full-time (15 women), 46 part-time (22 women); includes 41 minority (16 African Americans, 1 American Indian/Alaska Native, 19 Asian Americans or Pacific Islanders, 5 Hispanic Americans). Average age 29. 40 applicants, 75% accepted, 18 enrolled. In 2006, 11 degrees awarded. *Degree requirements:* For master's, thesis (for some programs), project. *Entrance requirements:* For master's, minimum GPA of 3.0. Additional exam requirements/recommendations for international students: Required—TOEFL (minimum score 550 paper-based; 213 computer-based; 86 iBT). *Application deadline:* Applications are processed on a rolling basis. Application fee: $75. Electronic applications accepted. *Expenses: Contact institution. Financial support:* In 2006–07, 10 fellowships were awarded; scholarships/grants also available. Support available to part-time students. *Unit head:* Dr. Lind W. Coop, Chair, 714-879-3901 Ext. 2264, Fax: 714-681-7450, E-mail: lwcoop@hiu.edu. *Application contact:* Annette Mativo, Assistant Director of Admissions, 714-879-3901 Ext. 2244, Fax: 714-681-7450, E-mail: anmativo@hiu.edu.

Illinois Institute of Technology, Graduate College, College of Science and Letters, Department of Social Sciences, Chicago, IL 60616-3793. Offers nonprofit management (MPA); public administration (MPA); public safety and crisis management (MPA); JD/MPA; MBA/MPA. Part-time and evening/weekend programs available. *Faculty:* 10 full-time (3 women), 10 part-time/adjunct (3 women). *Students:* 29 full-time (18 women), 40 part-time (23 women); includes 23 minority (17 African Americans, 1 American Indian/Alaska Native, 1 Asian American or Pacific Islander, 4 Hispanic Americans), 24 international. Average age 35. 116 applicants, 91% accepted, 45 enrolled. In 2006, 65 degrees awarded. *Degree requirements:* For master's, capstone course (practicum). *Entrance requirements:* For master's, minimum undergraduate GPA of 3.0, 2 letters of recommendation. Additional exam requirements/recommendations for international students: Required—TOEFL (minimum score 550 paper-based; 213 computer-based). *Application deadline:* For fall admission, 5/1 for domestic and international students; for spring admission, 10/15 for domestic and international students. Applications are processed on a rolling basis. Application fee: $40. Electronic applications accepted. *Expenses:* Tuition: Full-time $13,086; part-time $727 per credit. Required fees: $7 per credit. $235 per term. Tuition and fees vary according to class time, course level, course load, program and student level. *Financial support:* Federal Work-Study, institutionally sponsored loans, scholarships/grants, and health care benefits available. Support available to part-time students. Financial award applicants required to submit FAFSA. *Faculty research:* Science policy, city management, urban politics, urban ethnography, social impact of science and technology. *Unit head:* Dr. Ullica C. Segerstrale, Chair, 312-567-5134, Fax: 312-567-6821, E-mail: segerstrale@iit.edu. *Application contact:* Lawerence Ruffolo, Assistant Director, Graduate Program in Public Administration, 312-906-5197, Fax: 312-906-5199, E-mail: ruffolo@iit.edu.

Indiana University Bloomington, School of Public and Environmental Affairs, Public Affairs Programs, Bloomington, IN 47405-7000. Offers nonprofit management (Certificate); public affairs (MPA, PhD); public management (Certificate); public policy (PhD); JD/MPA; MPA/MA; MPA/MIS; MPA/MLS; MSES/MPA. *Accreditation:* NASPAA (one or more programs are accredited). Part-time programs available. Terminal master's awarded for partial completion of doctoral program. *Degree requirements:* For doctorate, thesis/dissertation. *Entrance requirements:* For master's, GMAT or GRE, LSAT; for doctorate, GRE General Test. *Application deadline:* For fall admission, 2/1 priority date for domestic students, 1/15 for international students; for spring admission, 9/1 for international students. Applications are processed on a rolling basis. Application fee: $50 ($60 for international students). *Financial support:* Fellowships, research assistantships, teaching assistantships, career-related internships or fieldwork, Federal Work-Study, institutionally sponsored loans, and unspecified assistantships available. Financial award application deadline: 2/1; financial award applicants required to submit FAFSA. *Faculty research:* Comparative and international affairs, environmental policy and resource management, policy analysis, public finance, public management, urban management, nonprofit management. *Application contact:* Charles A. Johnson, Coordinator of Student Recruitment, 800-765-7755, Fax: 812-855-7802, E-mail: speainfo@indiana.edu.

Indiana University Northwest, School of Public and Environmental Affairs, Gary, IN 46408-1197. Offers criminal justice (MPA); environmental affairs (Certificate); health services administration (MPA); human services administration (MPA); nonprofit management (Certificate); public administration (MPA); public management (MPA, Certificate). *Accreditation:* NASPAA (one or more programs are accredited). Part-time programs available. *Faculty:* 5 full-time (3 women). *Students:* 16 full-time (12 women), 118 part-time (92 women); includes 89 minority (76 African Americans, 1 Asian American or Pacific Islander, 12 Hispanic Americans). Average age 39. In 2006, 30 master's, 31 other advanced degrees awarded. *Degree requirements:* For master's, registration. *Entrance requirements:* For master's, GRE General Test or GMAT, letters of recommendation. *Application deadline:* For fall admission, 8/15 priority date for domestic students. Applications are processed on a rolling basis. Application fee: $25. *Expenses:* Tuition, state resident: full-time $4,332; part-time $181 per credit hour. Tuition, nonresident: full-time $10,081; part-time $420 per credit hour. Tuition and fees vary according to course load, campus/location and program. *Financial support:* Career-related internships or fieldwork, Federal Work-Study, and tuition waivers (partial) available. Support available to part-time students. Financial award application deadline: 3/1. *Faculty research:* Employment in income security policies, evidence in criminal justice, equal employment law, social welfare policy and welfare reform, public finance in developing countries. *Unit head:* Karen Evans, Interim Assistant Dean/Division Director, 219-980-6695, Fax: 219-980-6737. *Application contact:* Sandra Hall Smith, Secretary, 219-980-6695, Fax: 219-980-6737, E-mail: shsmith@iun.edu.

Indiana University–Purdue University Indianapolis, School of Public and Environmental Affairs, Graduate Program in Public Affairs, Indianapolis, IN 46202-2896. Offers criminal justice (MPA); environmental management (MPA); nonprofit management (MPA); policy analysis (MPA); public management (MPA). *Accreditation:* NASPAA. Part-time and evening/weekend programs available. *Entrance requirements:* For master's, GRE General Test, minimum GPA of 3.0 (preferred). *Application deadline:* For fall admission, 7/15 priority date for domestic students; for spring admission, 11/15 for domestic students. Applications are processed on a rolling basis. Application fee: $50 ($60 for international students). *Expenses:* Tuition, state resident: full-time $5,437; part-time $227 per credit hour. Tuition, nonresident: full-time $15,694; part-time $654 per credit hour. Required fees: $620. Tuition and fees vary according to course load, campus/location and program. *Financial support:* Fellowships with full and partial tuition reimbursements, research assistantships with full and partial tuition reimbursements, career-related internships or fieldwork and Federal Work-Study available. Support available to part-time students. Financial award application deadline: 3/1. *Faculty research:* Workplace justice, ethics, crime and delinquency, economic development, water and air quality. *Unit head:* Dr. John Ottensmann, Director, 317-274-2631, E-mail: jottensmann@iupui.edu. *Application contact:* 317-274-4656, Fax: 317-274-5153, E-mail: infospea@iupui.edu.

Indiana University South Bend, School of Public and Environmental Affairs, South Bend, IN 46634-7111. Offers health systems administration and policy (MPA); health systems management (Certificate); nonprofit management (Certificate); public and community services administration and policy (MPA); public management (Certificate); urban affairs (Certificate). *Accreditation:* NASPAA. Part-time and evening/weekend programs available. *Faculty:* 4 full-time (1 woman). *Students:* 11 full-time (7 women), 36 part-time (29 women); includes 8 minority (5 African Americans, 1 Asian American or Pacific Islander, 2 Hispanic Americans), 3 international. Average age 34. In 2006, 27 degrees awarded. *Entrance requirements:* For master's, GRE General Test, minimum undergraduate GPA of 2.5. *Application deadline:* For fall admission, 7/1 priority date for domestic students; for spring admission, 11/1 for domestic students. Applications are processed on a rolling basis. *Expenses:* Tuition, state resident: full-time $4,450; part-time $185 per credit hour. Tuition, nonresident: full-time $10,954; part-time $456 per credit hour. Tuition and fees vary according to course load, campus/location and program. *Financial support:* Fellowships, research assistantships, career-related internships or fieldwork, Federal Work-Study, and institutionally sponsored loans available. Support available to part-time students. Financial award application deadline: 3/1; financial award applicants required to submit FAFSA. *Unit head:* Leda M. Hall, Dean, 574-520-4803.

John Carroll University, Graduate School, Program in Nonprofit Administration, University Heights, OH 44118-4581. Offers MA. Part-time and evening/weekend programs available. *Students:* 22 full-time (13 women), 2 part-time (1 woman); includes 1 minority (African American) 30 applicants, 93% accepted, 24 enrolled. *Degree requirements:* For master's, thesis optional. *Entrance requirements:* For master's, minimum GPA of 3.0. *Application deadline:* For fall admission, 7/15 priority date for domestic students; for winter admission, 11/1 priority date for domestic students; for spring admission, 5/1 priority date for domestic students. Application fee: $25 ($35 for international students). *Expenses:* Tuition: Full-time $9,675; part-time $645 per credit hour. Tuition and fees vary according to program. *Financial support:* In 2006–07, 1 research assistantship with full tuition reimbursement (averaging $8,700 per year) was awarded. *Unit head:* Dr. Duane A. Dukes, Coordinator of Nonprofit Administration Program, 216-397-4637, Fax: 216-397-1835, E-mail: dukes@jcu.edu.

Kean University, College of Business and Public Administration, Program in Public Administration, Union, NJ 07083. Offers criminal justice (MPA); environmental management (MPA); health services administration (MPA); non-profit management (MPA); public administration (MPA). *Accreditation:* NASPAA. Part-time and evening/weekend programs available. *Faculty:* 7 full-time (4 women). *Students:* 78 full-time (52 women), 101 part-time (62 women); includes 118 minority (84 African Americans, 9 Asian Americans or Pacific Islanders, 25 Hispanic Americans), 13 international. Average age 32. 76 applicants, 83% accepted, 40 enrolled. In 2006, 50 degrees awarded. *Degree requirements:* For master's, thesis, internship, research seminar. *Entrance requirements:* For master's, 2 letters of recommendation, interview. *Application deadline:* For fall admission, 5/1 for domestic students; for spring admission, 11/1 for domestic students. Application fee: $60 ($150 for international students). Electronic applications accepted. *Expenses:* Tuition, state resident: full-time $8,856; part-time $369 per credit. Tuition, nonresident: full-time $11,256; part-time $469 per credit. Required fees: $1,125; $94 per credit. *Financial support:* In 2006–07, 18 research assistantships with full tuition reimbursements (averaging $3,217 per year) were awarded; career-related internships or fieldwork, institutionally sponsored loans, and unspecified assistantships also available. Financial award application deadline: 5/1. *Faculty research:* Fiscal impact of New Federalism, New Jersey state and local government, computer application in public management. *Unit head:* Dr. Craig P. Donovan, Program Coordinator, 908-737-4307, E-mail: cpdonova@kean.edu. *Application contact:* Joanne Morris, Director of Graduate Admissions, 908-737-3355, Fax: 908-737-3354, E-mail: grad-adm@kean.edu.

Lindenwood University, Graduate Programs, Division of Management, St. Charles, MO 63301-1695. Offers accounting (MBA, MS); business administration (MBA); entrepreneurial studies (MBA); finance (MBA, MS); human resource management (MBA); human resources (MS); international business (MBA, MS); management (MBA, MS); management information systems (MBA, MS); managing business to business (MA); managing human resources (MA); managing international business (MA); managing investment management (MA); managing leadership (MA); managing marketing (MA); managing organizational behavior (MA); managing sales (MA); managing, training and development (MA); marketing (MBA, MS); nonprofit administration (MA); public management (MBA, MS); sport management (MA). Part-time and evening/weekend programs available. *Faculty:* 38 full-time (15 women), 20 part-time/adjunct (5 women). *Students:* 177 full-time (78 women), 138 part-time (67 women); includes 43 minority (27 African Americans, 4 American Indian/Alaska Native, 6 Asian Americans or Pacific Islanders, 6 Hispanic Americans), 73 international. Average age 30. In 2006, 159 degrees awarded.

Nonprofit Management

Lindenwood University (continued)
Degree requirements: For master's, thesis (for some programs). *Entrance requirements:* For master's, interview, minimum GPA of 3.0. Additional exam requirements/recommendations for international students: Required—TOEFL (minimum score 550 paper-based; 173 computer-based). *Application deadline:* For fall admission, 7/30 priority date for domestic students, 9/30 priority date for international students; for winter admission, 12/30 priority date for domestic and international students; for spring admission, 3/30 priority date for domestic and international students. Applications are processed on a rolling basis. Application fee: $30 ($100 for international students). Electronic applications accepted. *Expenses:* Tuition: Part-time $340 per credit hour. Tuition and fees vary according to course level, course load, degree level and program. *Financial support:* Career-related internships or fieldwork, Federal Work-Study, institutionally sponsored loans, and tuition waivers (partial) available. Financial award application deadline: 6/30; financial award applicants required to submit FAFSA. *Unit head:* Ed Morris, Dean, 636-949-4832, Fax: 636-949-4910, E-mail: emorris@lindenwood.edu. *Application contact:* Brett Barger, Dean Adult, Corporate and Graduate Admissions, 636-949-4366, Fax: 636-949-4109, E-mail: bbarger@lindenwood.edu.

Lipscomb University, MBA Program, Nashville, TN 37204-3951. Offers accounting (MBA); business administration (general) (MBA); conflict management (MBA); financial services (MBA); healthcare management (MBA); leadership (MBA); nonprofit management (MBA). *Accreditation:* ACBSP. Part-time and evening/weekend programs available. *Faculty:* 11 full-time (3 women), 6 part-time/adjunct (0 women). *Students:* 18 full-time (6 women), 50 part-time (23 women); includes 5 minority (4 African Americans, 1 American Indian/Alaska Native), 2 international. Average age 30. 48 applicants, 73% accepted, 27 enrolled. In 2006, 30 degrees awarded. *Median time to degree:* Master's–1 year full-time, 2.3 years part-time. *Entrance requirements:* For master's, GMAT, interview, 2 references, resumé. Additional exam requirements/recommendations for international students: Required—TOEFL (minimum score 570 paper-based; 230 computer-based). *Application deadline:* For fall admission, 7/1 for domestic students, 2/1 for international students; for winter admission, 12/1 for domestic students, 6/1 for international students. Applications are processed on a rolling basis. Application fee: $50 ($75 for international students). Electronic applications accepted. *Expenses:* Contact institution. *Financial support:* In 2006–07, 25 students received support. Career-related internships or fieldwork, Federal Work-Study, scholarships/grants, tuition waivers (partial), and unspecified assistantships available. Support available to part-time students. Financial award application deadline: 7/1; financial award applicants required to submit FAFSA. *Faculty research:* Impact of spirituality on organization commitment; leadership; psychological empowerment; training. *Unit head:* Dr. Steven K. Yoho, Associate Dean of Graduate Business Studies, 615-966-1833, Fax: 615-966-1818, E-mail: steven.yoho@lipscomb.edu. *Application contact:* Jackie Cash, MBA Assistant, 615-966-1833, Fax: 615-966-1818, E-mail: jackie.cash@lipscomb.edu.

Long Island University, C.W. Post Campus, College of Management, School of Public Service, Department of Health Care and Public Administration, Brookville, NY 11548-1300. Offers gerontology (Certificate); health care administration (MPA); health care administration/gerontology (MPA); nonprofit management (MPA, Certificate); public administration (MPA). *Accreditation:* NASPAA (one or more programs are accredited). Part-time and evening/weekend programs available. *Degree requirements:* For master's, thesis. *Entrance requirements:* For master's, GMAT, minimum GPA of 2.5; for Certificate, minimum GPA of 2.5. Electronic applications accepted. *Faculty research:* Critical issues in sexuality, social work in religious communities, gerontological social work.

Long Island University, Rockland Graduate Campus, Graduate School, Program in Health Administration, Orangeburg, NY 10962. Offers financial management (MPA); gerontology (Advanced Certificate); health administration (MPA); health services management (MPA); long term care administration (MPA); medical practice management (MPA); nonprofit management (MPA, Advanced Certificate). *Entrance requirements:* For master's, GRE General Test.

Metropolitan State University, College of Management, St. Paul, MN 55106-5000. Offers finance (MBA); human resource management (MBA); information management (MMIS); international business (MBA); law enforcement (MPNA); management information systems (MBA); marketing (MBA); nonprofit management (MPNA); organizational studies (MBA); public administration (MPNA); purchasing management (MBA); systems management (MMIS). Part-time and evening/weekend programs available. *Degree requirements:* For master's, computer language (MMIS), thesis optional. *Entrance requirements:* For master's, GMAT (MBA), resumé. Additional exam requirements/recommendations for international students: Required—TOEFL (minimum score 550 paper-based; 213 computer-based). *Faculty research:* Yugoslav economic system, workers' cooperatives, participative management and job enrichment, global business systems.

New England College, Program in Management, Henniker, NH 03242-3293. Offers healthcare administration (MS); nonprofit leadership (MS); organizational leadership (MS). Part-time and evening/weekend programs available. *Degree requirements:* For master's, independent research project. Electronic applications accepted.

New Mexico Highlands University, Graduate Studies, School of Business, Las Vegas, NM 87701. Offers business administration (MBA), including human resource management, international business, non-profit financial management. *Accreditation:* ACBSP. *Faculty:* 12 full-time (4 women), 1 part-time/adjunct (0 women). *Students:* 57 full-time (39 women), 103 part-time (69 women); includes 97 minority (1 African American, 26 American Indian/Alaska Native, 4 Asian Americans or Pacific Islanders, 66 Hispanic Americans), 17 international. Average age 35. 69 applicants, 84% accepted, 42 enrolled. In 2006, 29 degrees awarded. *Degree requirements:* For master's, thesis or alternative, comprehensive exam, registration. *Entrance requirements:* For master's, minimum undergraduate GPA of 3.0. Additional exam requirements/recommendations for international students: Required—TOEFL (minimum score 540 paper-based; 190 computer-based). *Application deadline:* For fall admission, 8/1 priority date for domestic students. Applications are processed on a rolling basis. Application fee: $15. *Expenses:* Tuition, state resident: part-time $101 per credit hour. Tuition, nonresident: part-time $101 per credit hour. *Financial support:* In 2006–07, 67 students received support, including 8 teaching assistantships with full and partial tuition reimbursements available (averaging $6,500 per year); career-related internships or fieldwork, Federal Work-Study, institutionally sponsored loans, scholarships/grants, tuition waivers (full and partial), and unspecified assistantships also available. Support available to part-time students. Financial award application deadline: 3/1; financial award applicants required to submit FAFSA. *Unit head:* Dr. William Taylor, Dean, 505-454-3344, Fax: 505-454-3354. *Application contact:* Diane Trujillo, Administrative Assistant Graduate Studies, 505-454-3266, Fax: 505-454-3558, E-mail: dtrujillo@nmhu.edu.

The New School: A University, Milano The New School for Management and Urban Policy, Program in Nonprofit Management, New York, NY 10011. Offers MS. Part-time and evening/weekend programs available. *Students:* 46 full-time (36 women), 82 part-time (57 women); includes 43 minority (21 African Americans, 1 American Indian/Alaska Native, 4 Asian Americans or Pacific Islanders, 17 Hispanic Americans), 5 international. Average age 32. In 2006, 47 degrees awarded. *Degree requirements:* For master's, thesis. *Entrance requirements:* For master's, interview. Additional exam requirements/recommendations for international students: Required—TOEFL (minimum score 600 paper-based; 250 computer-based; 100 iBT). *Application deadline:* For fall admission, 8/1 priority date for domestic students; for winter admission, 1/15 priority date for domestic students. Applications are processed on a rolling basis. Application fee: $50. *Financial support:* Fellowships, research assistantships, career-related internships or fieldwork, Federal Work-Study, scholarships/grants, and tuition waivers (full and partial) available. Support available to part-time students. Financial award application deadline: 3/1; financial award applicants required to submit FAFSA. *Faculty research:* Management of nonprofit organizations, fund raising in minority nonprofit organizations. *Unit head:* Dr. Mark Lipton, Chair, 212-229-5400 Ext. 1611, Fax: 212-229-5335, E-mail: lipton@newschool.edu. *Application contact:* Peter King, Director of Admissions, 212-229-5400, Fax: 212-229-5354, E-mail: kingp@newschool.edu.

See Close-Up on page 669.

The New School: A University, The New School for General Studies, Program in International Affairs, New York, NY 10011. Offers global management, trade, and finance (MA, MS); international development (MA, MS); international media and communication (MA, MS); international politics and diplomacy (MA, MS); service, civic, and non-profit management (MS). Part-time programs available. *Students:* 159 full-time (104 women), 117 part-time (80 women); includes 62 minority (16 African Americans, 21 Asian Americans or Pacific Islanders, 25 Hispanic Americans), 45 international. Average age 30. In 2006, 92 degrees awarded. *Entrance requirements:* Additional exam requirements/recommendations for international students: Required—TOEFL (minimum score 600 paper-based; 250 computer-based; 100 iBT). *Application deadline:* For fall admission, 4/15 for domestic students; for spring admission, 10/15 for domestic students. Application fee: $50. *Financial support:* Fellowships with partial tuition reimbursements, research assistantships, teaching assistantships with partial tuition reimbursements, career-related internships or fieldwork, Federal Work-Study, scholarships/grants, tuition waivers (partial), and unspecified assistantships available. Support available to part-time students. Financial award application deadline: 3/1; financial award applicants required to submit FAFSA. *Unit head:* Dr. Michael Cohen, Director, 212-206-3524, Fax: 212-645-0661, E-mail: cohenm2@newschool.edu. *Application contact:* Gerianne Brusati, Associate Dean, Admissions and Student Services, 212-229-5630, Fax: 212-989-3887, E-mail: nsadmissions@newschool.edu.

New York University, Robert F. Wagner Graduate School of Public Service, Program in Public Administration, New York, NY 10012-1019. Offers public administration (PhD); public and nonprofit management and policy (MPA, Advanced Certificate), including developmental administration (Advanced Certificate), financial management and public finance, human resources management (Advanced Certificate), international administration (Advanced Certificate), management (MPA), management for public and nonprofit organizations (Advanced Certificate), public policy analysis, quantitative analysis and computer applications (Advanced Certificate), urban public policy (Advanced Certificate); JD/MPA; MBA/MPA; MPA/MA. *Accreditation:* NASPAA (one or more programs are accredited). Part-time and evening/weekend programs available. *Faculty:* 16 full-time (10 women), 42 part-time/adjunct (23 women). *Students:* 260 full-time (189 women), 246 part-time (182 women); includes 114 minority (40 African Americans, 2 American Indian/Alaska Native, 45 Asian Americans or Pacific Islanders, 27 Hispanic Americans), 44 international. Average age 28. 867 applicants, 60% accepted, 176 enrolled. In 2006, 209 master's, 5 doctorates awarded. *Degree requirements:* For master's, thesis or alternative, capstone/end event; for doctorate, one foreign language, thesis/dissertation. *Entrance requirements:* For master's, minimum undergraduate GPA of 3.0; for doctorate, GMAT or GRE General Test, minimum GPA of 3.5. Additional exam requirements/recommendations for international students: Required—TOEFL (minimum score 600 paper-based; 250 computer-based), TWE (minimum score 4). *Application deadline:* For fall admission, 6/1 for domestic students, 1/15 for international students; for spring admission, 11/15 for domestic students, 10/1 for international students. Applications are processed on a rolling basis. Application fee: $70. Electronic applications accepted. *Expenses:* Contact institution. Tuition and fees vary according to program. *Financial support:* In 2006–07, 142 fellowships (averaging $9,749 per year), 4 research assistantships with partial tuition reimbursements (averaging $15,000 per year) were awarded; career-related internships or fieldwork, Federal Work-Study, institutionally sponsored loans, scholarships/grants, health care benefits, and unspecified assistantships also available. Support available to part-time students. Financial award application deadline: 12/1; financial award applicants required to submit FAFSA. *Unit head:* Prof. Katherine O'Regan, Director, 212-998-7400, Fax: 212-995-4161. *Application contact:* Bethany Godsoe, Assistant Dean, Enrollment and Student Services, 212-998-7414, Fax: 212-995-4164, E-mail: wagner.admissions@nyu.edu.

New York University, School of Continuing and Professional Studies, Program in Fundraising, New York, NY 10012-1019. Offers MS. Part-time and evening/weekend programs available. *Faculty:* 11 part-time/adjunct (6 women). *Students:* 1 full-time (0 women), 20 part-time (15 women); includes 6 minority (3 African Americans, 1 Asian American or Pacific Islander, 2 Hispanic Americans). Average age 38. 23 applicants, 96% accepted, 21 enrolled. *Degree requirements:* For master's, capstone project. *Entrance requirements:* For master's, GRE General Test or GMAT, related work experience, 2 letters of recommendation, resumé. Additional exam requirements/recommendations for international students: Required—TOEFL (minimum score 600 paper-based; 250 computer-based; 100 iBT), TWE. *Application deadline:* For fall admission, 6/1 priority date for domestic students; for spring admission, 10/15 priority date for domestic students. Applications are processed on a rolling basis. Application fee: $75. *Expenses:* Tuition: Part-time $1,080 per unit. Required fees: $56 per unit. $329 per term. Tuition and fees vary according to program. *Financial support:* Fellowships, scholarships/grants available. Financial award applicants required to submit FAFSA. *Unit head:* Lewis Brindle, Director, 212-998-6790, Fax: 212-995-4784, E-mail: lcb@nyu.edu.

See Close-Up on page 671.

North Central College, Graduate Programs, Department of Leadership Studies, Naperville, IL 60566-7063. Offers MLD. Part-time and evening/weekend programs available. *Degree requirements:* For master's, project. *Entrance requirements:* For master's, interview.

Northern Kentucky University, Office of Graduate Programs, College of Arts and Sciences, Highland Heights, KY 41099. Offers industrial psychology (Certificate); industrial-organizational psychology (MSIO); liberal studies (MALS); non-profit management (Certificate); occupational health psychology (Certificate); organizational psychology (Certificate); public administration (MPA). Part-time and evening/weekend programs available. *Students:* 32 full-time (20 women), 160 part-time (96 women); includes 20 minority (17 African Americans, 3 Asian Americans or Pacific Islanders), 3 international. Average age 33. 89 applicants, 61% accepted, 49 enrolled. In 2006, 34 master's awarded. *Degree requirements:* For master's, thesis (for some programs), comprehensive exam (for some programs), registration; for Certificate, thesis or alternative, registration. *Entrance requirements:* For master's, GRE, minimum GPA of 2.5. Additional exam requirements/recommendations for international students: Required—TOEFL (minimum score 550 paper-based; 213 computer-based; 79 iBT), Michigan (must be taken at NKU). *Application deadline:* For fall admission, 8/1 for domestic students, 6/1 for international students; for spring admission, 12/1 for domestic students, 10/1 for international students. Application fee: $30. *Expenses:* Tuition, state resident: full-time $5,274; part-time $293 per hour. Tuition, nonresident: full-time $10,314; part-time $573 per hour. Tuition and fees vary according to course load, program and reciprocity agreements. *Financial support:* In 2006–07, 99 students received support. Unspecified assistantships available. *Faculty research:* Robotic construction, foster care, opera, photography to promote social change. *Unit head:* Dr. Kevin Corcoran, Dean, 859-572-5494, Fax: 859-572-6185, E-mail: corcorank1@nku.edu. *Application contact:* Dr. Peg Griffin, Director of Graduate Programs, 859-572-1555, Fax: 859-572-6670, E-mail: gradprog@nku.edu.

Oral Roberts University, School of Business, Tulsa, OK 74171-0001. Offers accounting (MBA); finance (MBA); international business (MBA); management (MBA); marketing (MBA); non-profit management (M Man, MBA); organizational dynamics (M Man); sales marketing (M Man). *Accreditation:* ACBSP. Part-time programs available. Postbaccalaureate distance learning degree programs offered (minimal on-campus study). *Faculty:* 9 full-time (2 women), 4 part-time/adjunct (2 women). *Students:* 33 full-time (18 women), 67 part-time (28 women); includes 28 minority (17 African Americans, 3 American Indian/Alaska Native, 6 Asian Americans or Pacific Islanders, 2 Hispanic Americans), 15 international. Average age 29. 69 applicants, 84% accepted, 33 enrolled. In 2006, 21 degrees awarded. *Degree requirements:* For master's, thesis optional. *Entrance requirements:* For master's, minimum GPA of 3.0. Additional exam requirements/recommendations for international students: Required—TOEFL (minimum score 550 paper-based; 213 computer-based). *Application deadline:* For fall admission, 7/1 priority date for domestic students, 5/1 priority date for international students; for spring admission, 12/1 priority date for domestic students, 10/1 priority date for international students. Applications are processed on a rolling basis. Application fee: $35. *Expenses:* Contact institution. *Financial support:* In 2006–07, 9 research assistantships (averaging $3,600 per year) were awarded; scholarships/grants and unspecified assistantships also available. Financial award application deadline: 6/1; financial award applicants required to submit FAFSA. *Faculty research:* Non-profit, international business and marketing. *Unit head:* Dr. Mark Lewandowski, Dean, 918-495-7040, Fax: 918-495-7876, E-mail: mlewandowski@oru.edu. *Application contact:* 918-495-6989, Fax: 918-495-7965, E-mail: alsc@oru.edu.

Pace University, Dyson College of Arts and Sciences, Department of Public Administration, New York, NY 10038. Offers government management (MPA); health care administration (MPA); nonprofit management (MPA); JD/MPA. Offered at White Plains, NY location only. Part-time and evening/weekend programs available. *Faculty:* 4 full-time, 6 part-time/adjunct. *Students:* 31 full-time (19 women), 79 part-time (48 women); includes 45 minority (30 African Americans, 5 Asian Americans or Pacific Islanders, 10 Hispanic Americans), 4 international. Average age 34. 69 applicants, 74% accepted, 27 enrolled. In 2006, 38 degrees awarded. *Degree requirements:* For master's, capstone project. *Entrance requirements:* For master's, GRE General Test. *Application deadline:* For fall admission, 8/1 priority date for domestic students; for spring admission, 12/1 priority date for domestic students. Applications are processed on a rolling basis. Application fee: $65. Electronic applications accepted. *Expenses:* Tuition: Part-time $890 per credit. *Financial support:* Research assistantships, career-related internships or fieldwork, Federal Work-Study, and tuition waivers (partial) available. Support available to part-time students. Financial award applicants required to submit FAFSA. *Unit head:* Dr. Joseph Ryan, Chairperson, 914-422-4303. *Application contact:* Joanna Broda, Director of Admissions, 914-422-4283, Fax: 914-422-4287, E-mail: gradwp@pace.edu.

Park University, College of Graduate and Professional Studies, Kansas City, MO 54105. Offers adult education (M Ed); at-risk students (M Ed); disaster and emergency management (MPA); educational administration (M Ed); entrepreneurship (MBA); general business (MBA); general education (M Ed); government/business relations (MPA); healthcare/services management (MBA, MPA); international business (MBA); K-12 certification (MAT); management information systems (MBA); management of information systems (MPA); middle school certification (MAT); multi-cultural education (M Ed); nonprofit management (MPA); public management (MPA); school law (M Ed); secondary school certification (MAT); special education (M Ed). Part-time and evening/weekend programs available. Postbaccalaureate distance learning degree programs offered (no on-campus study). *Degree requirements:* For master's, thesis (for some programs), comprehensive exam, registration. *Entrance requirements:* For master's, GRE, GMAT, teacher certification (M Ed). Additional exam requirements/recommendations for international students: Required—TOEFL (minimum score 550 paper-based). Electronic applications accepted. *Faculty research:* Literacy, leadership, brain based research, multicultural education, diversity.

Regis University, School for Professional Studies, Program in Nonprofit Management, Denver, CO 80221-1099. Offers leadership (Certificate); nonprofit management (MNM); program management (Certificate); resource development (Certificate). Offered at Northwest Denver Campus and Southeast Denver Campus. Part-time and evening/weekend programs available. Postbaccalaureate distance learning degree programs offered (no on-campus study). *Faculty:* 68. *Students:* Average age 36. In 2006, 110 degrees awarded. *Degree requirements:* For master's and Certificate, final research project, thesis optional. *Entrance requirements:* For master's, 2 years of significant paid or volunteer experience in a nonprofit organization or 400-hour practicum in nonprofit sector; resumé, Admissions essays; for Certificate, 2 years of significant paid or volunteer experience in a nonprofit organization or 400-hour practicum in nonprofit sector; resumé. Additional exam requirements/recommendations for international students: Required—TOEFL, TWE (minimum score 5), TOEFL or university-based test. *Application deadline:* For fall admission, 8/6 priority date for domestic students, 7/6 priority date for international students; for winter admission, 10/1 priority date for domestic students, 9/1 priority date for international students; for spring admission, 12/14 priority date for domestic students, 11/14 priority date for international students. Applications are processed on a rolling basis. Application fee: $75. *Expenses:* Contact institution. *Financial support:* In 2006–07, 12 fellowships were awarded; career-related internships or fieldwork and Federal Work-Study also available. Support available to part-time students. Financial award applicants required to submit FAFSA. *Faculty research:* International nonprofits, enterprise, grass roots nonprofits, leadership. *Unit head:* Dr. Gary Smith, Chair, 303-458-4302, Fax: 303-964-5538. *Application contact:* 800-677-9270, Fax: 303-964-5538, E-mail: masters@regis.edu.

Robert Morris University, Graduate Studies, School of Business, Moon Township, PA 15108-1189. Offers accounting (MS); business administration and management (MBA); finance (MS); human resource management (MS); nonprofit management (MS); sport management (MS); taxation (MS). Part-time and evening/weekend programs available. *Faculty:* 27 full-time (12 women), 6 part-time/adjunct (1 woman). *Students:* Average age 31. 253 applicants, 59% accepted, 103 enrolled. In 2006, 139 degrees awarded. *Entrance requirements:* For master's, GMAT, letters of recommendation. Additional exam requirements/recommendations for international students: Required—TOEFL (minimum score 550 paper-based; 213 computer-based). *Application deadline:* For fall admission, 7/1 priority date for domestic and international students; for spring admission, 11/1 priority date for domestic and international students. Applications are processed on a rolling basis. Application fee: $35. Electronic applications accepted. *Expenses:* Tuition: Part-time $580 per credit. Part-time tuition and fees vary according to degree level and program. *Financial support:* Research assistantships with partial tuition reimbursements, Federal Work-Study, institutionally sponsored loans, and unspecified assistantships available. Support available to part-time students. Financial award application deadline: 5/1; financial award applicants required to submit FAFSA. *Unit head:* Dr. Derya A. Jacobs, Dean, 412-262-8451, Fax: 412-262-8494, E-mail: jacobs@rmu.edu. *Application contact:* Kellie L. Laurenzi, Dean of Enrollment, 412-262-8235, Fax: 412-299-2425, E-mail: laurenzi@rmu.edu.

Roberts Wesleyan College, Division of Business, Rochester, NY 14624-1997. Offers nonprofit leadership (Certificate); strategic leadership (MS); strategic marketing (MS). Evening/weekend programs available. *Faculty:* 3 full-time (0 women), 13 part-time/adjunct (3 women). *Students:* 57 full-time (28 women). Average age 34. 45 applicants, 89% accepted. In 2006, 26 degrees awarded. *Degree requirements:* For master's, thesis or alternative. *Entrance requirements:* For master's, GMAT, minimum GPA of 2.75, verifiable work experience. *Application deadline:* Applications are processed on a rolling basis. Application fee: $35. *Expenses:* Contact institution. *Financial support:* In 2006–07, 15 students received support. Applicants required to submit FAFSA. *Unit head:* Dr. Steven Bovee, Chair, 716-594-6571, Fax: 716-594-6316, E-mail: bovees@roberts.edu.

Rosemont College, Graduate School, Accelerated Program in Management, Rosemont, PA 19010-1699. Offers arts/culture/project management (MSM); criminal justice (MSM); not for profit (MSM); training and leadership (MSM). Part-time and evening/weekend programs available. *Degree requirements:* For master's, thesis or alternative. *Entrance requirements:* For master's, GRE or MAT. Expenses: Contact institution.

St. Cloud State University, School of Graduate Studies, College of Social Sciences, Department of Economics, Program in Public and Nonprofit Institutions, St. Cloud, MN 56301-4498. Offers MS. Part-time programs available. *Faculty:* 20 full-time (5 women), 1 part-time/adjunct (0 women). *Students:* 2 full-time (1 woman), 3 part-time (all women), 3 international. 5 applicants, 80% accepted. In 2006, 3 degrees awarded. *Degree requirements:* For master's, thesis or alternative. *Entrance requirements:* For master's, GRE General Test, minimum GPA of 2.75. Additional exam requirements/recommendations for international students: Required—MELAB; Recommended—TOEFL (minimum score 550 paper-based; 213 computer-based), IELTS (minimum score 7). *Application deadline:* For fall admission, 6/1 priority date for domestic students, 6/1 for international students; for spring admission, 10/1 priority date for domestic students, 10/1 for international students. Applications are processed on a rolling basis. Application fee: $35. Electronic applications accepted. *Financial support:* Federal Work-Study, scholarships/grants, and unspecified assistantships available. Financial award application deadline: 3/1. *Unit head:* Dr. Patricia Hughes, Coordinator, 320-308-2076, E-mail: pahughes@stcloudstate.edu. *Application contact:* Linda Lou Krueger, School of Graduate Studies, 320-308-2113, Fax: 320-308-5371, E-mail: lekrueger@stcloudstate.edu.

Saint Xavier University, Graduate Studies, Graham School of Management, Chicago, IL 60655-3105. Offers e-commerce (MBA); employee health benefits (Certificate); finance (MBA, MS); financial analysis and investments (MBA); financial planning (MBA, Certificate); financial trading and practice (MBA, Certificate); generalist/administration (MBA); health administration (MBA, MS); managed care (Certificate); management (MBA, MS); marketing (MBA); public and non-profit management (MBA); public health (MPH); service management (MBA); training and performance management (MBA); MBA/MS. *Accreditation:* ACBSP. Part-time and evening/weekend programs available. *Faculty:* 27. *Students:* 67 full-time (32 women), 291 part-time (152 women). Average age 35. In 2006, 61 degrees awarded. *Entrance requirements:* For master's, GMAT, minimum GPA of 3.0, 2 years of work experience. *Application deadline:* For fall admission, 8/15 for domestic students. Applications are processed on a rolling basis. Application fee: $35. Electronic applications accepted. *Expenses:* Contact institution. *Financial support:* Career-related internships or fieldwork available. Support available to part-time students. Financial award applicants required to submit FAFSA. *Unit head:* Dr. John Eber, Dean, 773-298-3601, Fax: 773-298-3601, E-mail: eber@sxu.edu. *Application contact:* Beth Gierach, Managing Director of Admission, 773-298-3053, Fax: 773-298-3076, E-mail: gierach@sxu.edu.

San Francisco State University, Division of Graduate Studies, College of Behavioral and Social Sciences, Public Administration Program, San Francisco, CA 94132-1722. Offers integrated and collaborative services (MPA); nonprofit administration (MPA); policy analysis (MPA); public management (MPA); urban administration (MPA). *Accreditation:* NASPAA. *Faculty:* 2 full-time (1 woman), 15 part-time/adjunct (4 women). *Students:* Average age 30. In 2006, 14 degrees awarded. *Degree requirements:* For master's, internship, project or thesis. *Entrance requirements:* For master's, GRE General Test, essay exam, minimum GPA of 3.0. *Application deadline:* For fall admission, 3/1 priority date for domestic students. Applications are processed on a rolling basis. Application fee: $55. *Financial support:* Application deadline: 3/1. *Faculty research:* Public and nonprofit budgeting, urban policy and politics, social service delivery for culturally diverse communities. *Unit head:* Dr. Genie Stowers, Director, 415-338-1846, Fax: 415-338-1980, E-mail: gstowers@sfsu.edu.

Seattle University, College of Arts and Sciences, The Center for Nonprofit and Social Enterprise Management, Seattle, WA 98122-1090. Offers MNPL. *Students:* 38 full-time (33 women), 40 part-time (29 women); includes 11 minority (2 African Americans, 5 Asian Americans or Pacific Islanders, 4 Hispanic Americans). Average age 37. In 2006, 14 degrees awarded. *Degree requirements:* For master's, thesis or alternative. *Entrance requirements:* For master's, interview, professional experience, minimum GPA of 3.0. *Application deadline:* For fall admission, 3/1 for domestic students. Application fee: $55. *Financial support:* Career-related internships or fieldwork and Federal Work-Study available. Support available to part-time students. Financial award applicants required to submit FAFSA. *Unit head:* Dr. Michael Bisesi, Director, 206-296-5435, Fax: 206-296-5997, E-mail: bisesim@seattleu.edu. *Application contact:* Janet Shandley, Associate Dean of Graduate Admissions, 206-296-5900, Fax: 206-298-5656, E-mail: grad_admissions@seattleu.edu.

Seton Hall University, College of Arts and Sciences, Department of Public and Healthcare Administration, South Orange, NJ 07079-2697. Offers arts administration (MPA); health policy and management (MPA); healthcare administration (MHA); nonprofit organization management (MPA); public service: leadership, governance, and policy (MPA). *Accreditation:* NASPAA. Part-time and evening/weekend programs available. Postbaccalaureate distance learning degree programs offered (minimal on-campus study). *Degree requirements:* For master's, research project. Electronic applications accepted.

See Close-Up on page 1815.

Southern New Hampshire University, School of Business, Manchester, NH 03106-1045. Offers accounting (MS); business administration (MBA, Certificate), including accounting (Certificate), business administration (MBA), finance (Certificate), forensic accounting (Certificate), human resources management (Certificate), international business (Certificate), international sport management (Certificate), leadership of not for profit organizations (Certificate), marketing (Certificate), operations management (Certificate), sport management (Certificate), taxation (Certificate); finance (MS); hospitality and tourism leadership (Certificate); information technology (MS, Certificate); information technology/international business (Certificate); integrated marketing communications (Certificate); international business (MS, DBA); marketing (MS); operations and project management (MS); organizational leadership (MS); project management (Certificate); sport management (MS); MBA/Certificate. *Accreditation:* ACBSP. Part-time and evening/weekend programs available. Postbaccalaureate distance learning degree programs offered (no on-campus study). *Faculty:* 45 full-time, 75 part-time/adjunct. *Students:* 427 full-time (184 women), 774 part-time (428 women). Average age 32. In 2006, 682 master's, 1 doctorate awarded. Terminal master's awarded for partial completion of doctoral program. *Degree requirements:* For master's, one foreign language, thesis or alternative, comprehensive exam (for some programs); for doctorate, one foreign language, thesis/dissertation, comprehensive exam. *Entrance requirements:* For master's, minimum GPA of 2.5; for doctorate, GMAT. Additional exam requirements/recommendations for international students: Required—TOEFL (minimum score 500 paper-based). *Application deadline:* Applications are processed on a rolling basis. Application fee: $25. Electronic applications accepted. *Financial support:* Career-related internships or fieldwork, Federal Work-Study, institutionally sponsored loans, tuition waivers (partial), and unspecified assistantships available. Support available to part-time students. Financial award applicants required to submit FAFSA. *Unit head:* Dr. Martin Bradley, Dean, 603-644-3102, Fax: 603-644-3144, E-mail: m.bradley@snhu.edu. *Application contact:* Scott Durand, Director of Graduate Enrollment Services, 603-644-3102 Ext. 3338, Fax: 603-644-3144, E-mail: s.durand@snhu.edu.

See Close-Up on page 325.

Spertus Institute of Jewish Studies, Graduate Programs, Program in Nonprofit Management, Chicago, IL 60605-1901. Offers MSNM. Part-time and evening/weekend programs available. *Faculty:* 35 part-time/adjunct (19 women). *Students:* Average age 32. In 2006, 42 degrees awarded. *Degree requirements:* For master's, one foreign language, thesis optional. *Entrance requirements:* For master's, interview, minimum GPA of 2.75, graduation from accredited undergraduate program. *Application deadline:* Applications are processed on a rolling basis. Application fee: $50. Electronic applications accepted. *Financial support:* In 2006–07, 112 students received support. Applicants required to submit FAFSA. *Unit head:* Dr. Lynda Crawford, Associate Dean, 312-322-1720, Fax: 312-994-5360, E-mail: lcrawford@spertus.edu. *Application contact:* Nadia Whiteside, Recruitment Manager, 312-322-1707, Fax: 312-922-6406, E-mail: mwhiteside@spertus.edu.

Suffolk University, Sawyer Business School, Department of Public Administration, Boston, MA 02108-2770. Offers disability studies (MPA); health administration (MPA); nonprofit management (MPA); public administration (CASPA); public finance and human resources (MPA); state and local government (MPA); JD/MPA; MPA/MS. *Accreditation:* NASPAA (one or more programs are accredited). Part-time and evening/weekend programs available. *Faculty:* 11 full-time (4 women), 7 part-time/adjunct (4 women). *Students:* 40 full-time (25 women), 123 part-time (80 women); includes 22 minority (12 African Americans, 4 Asian Americans or Pacific Islanders, 6 Hispanic Americans), 9 international. Average age 31. 103 applicants, 87% accepted, 48 enrolled. In 2006, 65 degrees awarded. *Entrance requirements:* Additional exam requirements/recommendations for international students: Required—TOEFL (minimum score 550 paper-based; 213 computer-based; 80 iBT). *Application deadline:* For fall admission, 6/15 priority

Nonprofit Management

Suffolk University (continued)
date for domestic students, 6/15 for international students; for spring admission, 11/1 priority date for domestic students, 11/1 for international students. Applications are processed on a rolling basis. Application fee: $50. Electronic applications accepted. *Expenses: Contact institution. Financial support:* In 2006–07, 55 fellowships with full and partial tuition reimbursements (averaging $8,817 per year) were awarded; career-related internships or fieldwork and Federal Work-Study also available. Support available to part-time students. Financial award application deadline: 4/1; financial award applicants required to submit FAFSA. *Faculty research:* Local government, health care, federal policy, mental health, HIV/AIDS. Total annual research expenditures: $200,000. *Unit head:* Dr. Rick Beinecke, Chair, 617-573-8062, E-mail: rbeineck@suffolk.edu. *Application contact:* Judith Reynolds, Director of Graduate Admissions, 617-573-8302, Fax: 617-523-0116, E-mail: grad.admission@suffolk.edu.

Trinity (Washington) University, School of Professional Studies, Washington, DC 20017-1094. Offers business administration (MBA); communication (MA); information security management (MS); organizational management (MSA), including federal program management, human resource management, nonprofit management, organizational development, public and community health. Part-time and evening/weekend programs available. *Degree requirements:* For master's, thesis (for some programs), capstone project (MSA). *Entrance requirements:* For master's, minimum GPA of 2.5. Additional exam requirements/recommendations for international students: Required—TOEFL (minimum score 550 paper-based; 213 computer-based).

Tufts University, Graduate School of Arts and Sciences, Graduate Certificate Programs, Management of Community Organizations Program, Medford, MA 02155. Offers Certificate. Part-time and evening/weekend programs available. *Students:* Average age 29. 1 applicant, 100% accepted, 1 enrolled. In 2006, 4 degrees awarded. *Application deadline:* For fall admission, 8/15 priority date for domestic students; for spring admission, 12/12 priority date for domestic students. Applications are processed on a rolling basis. Application fee: $65. Electronic applications accepted. *Expenses: Contact institution.* Tuition and fees vary according to degree level and program. *Financial support:* Career-related internships or fieldwork available. Support available to part-time students. Financial award application deadline: 5/1; financial award applicants required to submit FAFSA. *Application contact:* Angela Foss, Program Administrator, 617-627-3395, Fax: 617-627-3016, E-mail: gradschool@ase.tufts.edu.

University of Central Florida, College of Health and Public Affairs, Department of Public Administration, Orlando, FL 32816. Offers non-profit management (MNM, Certificate); public administration (MPA, Certificate); urban and regional planning (Certificate). *Accreditation:* NASPAA. Part-time and evening/weekend programs available. *Faculty:* 11 full-time (3 women). *Students:* 68 full-time (49 women), 160 part-time (105 women); includes 68 minority (36 African Americans, 1 American Indian/Alaska Native, 5 Asian Americans or Pacific Islanders, 26 Hispanic Americans), 3 international. In 2006, 49 master's, 20 other advanced degrees awarded. *Degree requirements:* For master's, thesis or alternative, research report, comprehensive exam. *Entrance requirements:* For master's, GRE General Test. *Application deadline:* For fall admission, 7/1 for domestic students; for spring admission, 12/1 for domestic students. Application fee: $30. Electronic applications accepted. *Expenses:* Tuition, state resident: full-time $6,167; part-time $257 per credit hour. Tuition, nonresident: full-time $22,790; part-time $950 per credit hour. *Financial support:* In 2006–07, 5 fellowships with partial tuition reimbursements (averaging $4,100 per year), 11 research assistantships with partial tuition reimbursements (averaging $6,000 per year) were awarded; teaching assistantships with partial tuition reimbursements, career-related internships or fieldwork, Federal Work-Study, institutionally sponsored loans, tuition waivers (partial), and unspecified assistantships also available. Financial award application deadline: 3/1; financial award applicants required to submit FAFSA. *Unit head:* Dr. MaryAnn Feldheim, Chair, 407-823-3693, Fax: 407-823-5651. *Application contact:* Dr. Ronnie Korosec, Coordinator, 407-523-2604, E-mail: rkorosec@mail.ucf.edu.

University of Connecticut, Graduate School, College of Liberal Arts and Sciences, Department of Public Policy, Storrs, CT 06269. Offers nonprofit management (Graduate Certificate); public administration (MPA); public financial management (Graduate Certificate); survey research (MA); JD/MPA; MPA/MSW. *Faculty:* 10 full-time (5 women). *Students:* 53 full-time (33 women), 26 part-time (14 women); includes 7 minority (3 African Americans, 2 American Indian/Alaska Native, 2 Asian Americans or Pacific Islanders), 5 international. Average age 28. 104 applicants, 52% accepted, 54 enrolled. In 2006, 24 master's, 7 other advanced degrees awarded. *Degree requirements:* For master's, comprehensive exam. *Entrance requirements:* For master's, GRE General Test. Additional exam requirements/recommendations for international students: Required—TOEFL (minimum score 550 paper-based; 213 computer-based). *Application deadline:* For fall admission, 2/1 priority date for domestic and international students; for spring admission, 11/1 for domestic students, 10/1 for international students. Applications are processed on a rolling basis. Application fee: $55. Electronic applications accepted. *Financial support:* In 2006–07, 15 research assistantships with full tuition reimbursements were awarded; teaching assistantships with full tuition reimbursements, Federal Work-Study, scholarships/grants, health care benefits, and unspecified assistantships also available. Financial award application deadline: 2/1; financial award applicants required to submit FAFSA. *Unit head:* Kenneth Dautrich, Chairperson, 860-486-2579, E-mail: dautrich@uconnvm.uconn.edu. *Application contact:* Valerie Rogers, Director, 860-570-9047, Fax: 860-486-3109, E-mail: msr@uconn.edu.

University of Dallas, Graduate School of Management, Irving, TX 75062-4736. Offers accounting (MBA, MS); business management (MBA); corporate finance (MBA, MM); engineering management (MBA, MM); entrepreneurship (MBA, MM); financial services (MBA, MM); global business (MBA, MM); health services management (MBA, MM); human resource management (MBA, MM, MS); information assurance (MBA, MM, MS); information technology (MBA, MM, MS); information technology service management (MBA); IT service management (MS); marketing (MM); marketing management (MBA); not-for-profit management (MBA); organization development (MBA); project management (MBA, MM); sports and entertainment management (MBA, MM); strategic leadership (MBA); supply chain management (MBA); supply chain management and market logistics (MM); telecommunications management (MBA, MM). *Accreditation:* ACBSP. Part-time and evening/weekend programs available. Postbaccalaureate distance learning degree programs offered (no on-campus study). *Faculty:* 26 full-time (5 women), 85 part-time/adjunct (18 women). *Students:* 227 full-time (98 women), 1,160 part-time (446 women); includes 473 minority (209 African Americans, 3 American Indian/Alaska Native, 143 Asian Americans or Pacific Islanders, 118 Hispanic Americans), 224 international. Average age 34. 556 applicants, 86% accepted, 291 enrolled. In 2006, 476 degrees awarded. *Entrance requirements:* Additional exam requirements/recommendations for international students: Required—TOEFL. *Application deadline:* Applications are processed on a rolling basis. Application fee: $50. Electronic applications accepted. *Expenses: Contact institution. Financial support:* In 2006–07, 468 students received support. Scholarships/grants and unspecified assistantships available. Financial award application deadline: 2/15; financial award applicants required to submit FAFSA. *Unit head:* Dr. J. Lee Whittington, Dean, 972-721-5230. *Application contact:* Sarah Stivison, Director of Graduate Admissions, 972-721-5198, Fax: 972-721-4009, E-mail: admiss@gsm.udallas.edu.

University of Delaware, College of Human Services, Education and Public Policy, School of Urban Affairs and Public Policy, Program in Urban Affairs and Public Policy, Newark, DE 19716. Offers community development and nonprofit leadership (MA); energy and environmental policy (MA); governance, planning and management (PhD); historic preservation (MA); social and urban policy (PhD); technology, environment and society (PhD). Part-time programs available. Terminal master's awarded for partial completion of doctoral program. *Degree requirements:* For master's, analytical paper or thesis; for doctorate, thesis/dissertation. *Entrance requirements:* For master's, GRE General Test, minimum GPA of 3.0; for doctorate, GRE General Test, minimum GPA of 3.5. Additional exam requirements/recommendations for international students: Required—TOEFL. Electronic applications accepted. *Faculty research:* Political economy; social policy analysis; technology and society; historic preservation; urban policy.

University of Georgia, Graduate School, School of Social Work, Institute for Non-Profit Organizations, Athens, GA 30602. Offers MA, Certificate. *Students:* 10 full-time (7 women), 3 part-time (all women); includes 2 minority (1 African American, 1 Asian American or Pacific Islander). 10 applicants, 90% accepted, 7 enrolled. In 2006, 6 degrees awarded. *Application deadline:* For fall admission, 7/1 priority date for domestic students; for spring admission, 11/15 for domestic students. Application fee: $50. *Unit head:* Dr. Thomas Holland, Director, 706-542-5463, E-mail: tholland@uga.edu.

University of Georgia, School of Public and International Affairs, Program in Public Administration and Policy, Athens, GA 30602. Offers non profit organization (MA); public administration (MPA, PhD). *Accreditation:* NASPAA (one or more programs are accredited). *Faculty:* 16 full-time (4 women), 1 part-time/adjunct (0 women). *Students:* 111 full-time (59 women), 59 part-time (37 women); includes 25 minority (19 African Americans, 1 American Indian/Alaska Native, 3 Asian Americans or Pacific Islanders, 2 Hispanic Americans), 16 international. 220 applicants, 45% accepted, 55 enrolled. In 2006, 59 master's, 4 doctorates awarded. *Degree requirements:* For master's, internship; for doctorate, thesis/dissertation. *Entrance requirements:* For master's and doctorate, GRE General Test. *Application deadline:* For fall admission, 7/1 priority date for domestic students; for spring admission, 11/15 for domestic students. Application fee: $50. Electronic applications accepted. *Financial support:* Fellowships, research assistantships, teaching assistantships, unspecified assistantships available. *Unit head:* Dr. Laurence J. O'Toole, Head, 706-542-2057, Fax: 706-542-4421, E-mail: cmsotool@uga.edu. *Application contact:* Dr. J. Edward Kellough, Graduate Coordinator, 706-542-2961, Fax: 706-542-4421, E-mail: kellough@uga.edu.

The University of Iowa, Henry B. Tippie College of Business, Henry B. Tippie School of Management, Iowa City, IA 52242-1316. Offers accounting (MBA); corporate finance (MBA); entrepreneurship (MBA); finance (MBA); individually designed concentration (MBA); investment management (MBA); management information systems (MBA); marketing (MBA); nonprofit management (MBA); operations management (MBA); strategic management and consulting (MBA); JD/MBA; MBA/MA; MBA/MD; MBA/MHA; MBA/MSN. *Accreditation:* AACSB. Part-time and evening/weekend programs available. *Faculty:* 94 full-time (23 women), 65 part-time/adjunct (21 women). *Students:* 230 full-time (67 women), 712 part-time (234 women); includes 62 minority (6 African Americans, 1 American Indian/Alaska Native, 43 Asian Americans or Pacific Islanders, 12 Hispanic Americans), 127 international. Average age 30. 431 applicants, 61% accepted, 217 enrolled. In 2006, 363 degrees awarded. *Median time to degree:* Master's–2 years full-time, 3.5 years part-time. *Degree requirements:* For master's, registration. *Entrance requirements:* For master's, GMAT, work experience. Additional exam requirements/recommendations for international students: Required—TOEFL (minimum score 600 paper-based; 250 computer-based; 100 iBT). *Application deadline:* For fall admission, 7/15 for domestic students, 4/15 for international students; for spring admission, 12/15 priority date for domestic students, 11/1 priority date for international students. Applications are processed on a rolling basis. Application fee: $60 ($85 for international students). Electronic applications accepted. *Expenses: Contact institution. Financial support:* In 2006–07, 72 fellowships (averaging $3,892 per year), 55 research assistantships with partial tuition reimbursements (averaging $10,260 per year) were awarded; career-related internships or fieldwork, Federal Work-Study, institutionally sponsored loans, scholarships/grants, health care benefits, and unspecified assistantships also available. Support available to part-time students. Financial award application deadline: 4/15; financial award applicants required to submit FAFSA. *Faculty research:* Capital markets, econometrics, optimization, investments and empirical corporate finance, Iowa electronic markets. *Unit head:* Prof. Gary J. Gaeth, Associate Dean, MBA Programs, 800-622-4692, Fax: 319-335-3604, E-mail: gary-gaeth@uiowa.edu. *Application contact:* Jodi Schafer, Director of Student Recruitment and Marketing, 319-335-0864, Fax: 319-335-3604, E-mail: jodi-schafer@uiowa.edu.

University of La Verne, College of Business and Public Management, Program in Organizational Management and Leadership, La Verne, CA 91750-4443. Offers leadership and management (MS); nonprofit management (Certificate); organizational leadership (Certificate). Part-time programs available. *Faculty:* 15 full-time (7 women), 13 part-time/adjunct (7 women). *Students:* 20 full-time (13 women), 40 part-time (25 women); includes 37 minority (5 African Americans, 5 American Indian/Alaska Native, 3 Asian Americans or Pacific Islanders, 24 Hispanic Americans), 2 international. Average age 35. In 2006, 21 degrees awarded. *Degree requirements:* For master's, thesis or research project. *Entrance requirements:* For master's, minimum undergraduate GPA of 2.75, 2 letters of recommendation, interview, resumé. Additional exam requirements/recommendations for international students: Required—TOEFL (minimum score 550 paper-based; 213 computer-based). *Application deadline:* Applications are processed on a rolling basis. Application fee: $50. *Expenses: Contact institution. Financial support:* Institutionally sponsored loans available. Financial award application deadline: 3/2; financial award applicants required to submit FAFSA. *Unit head:* Dr. Bernice Ledbetter, Chairperson, 909-593-3511 Ext. 4345, E-mail: bledbetter@ulv.edu. *Application contact:* Jo Nell Baker, Director, Graduate Admissions and Academic Services, 909-593-3511 Ext. 4244, Fax: 909-392-2761, E-mail: gradadmt@ulv.edu.

University of Maryland, Baltimore County, Graduate School, College of Arts, Humanities and Social Sciences, Department of Sociology and Anthropology, Baltimore, MD 21250. Offers applied sociology (MA, Postbaccalaureate Certificate), including applied sociology (MA), non-profit sector (Postbaccalaureate Certificate). Part-time and evening/weekend programs available. *Degree requirements:* For master's, thesis or alternative. *Entrance requirements:* For master's, GRE General Test, GRE Subject Test, minimum GPA of 3.0. Additional exam requirements/recommendations for international students: Required—TOEFL. *Application deadline:* For fall admission, 7/31 priority date for domestic students; for spring admission, 12/31 priority date for domestic students. Applications are processed on a rolling basis. Application fee: $50. Electronic applications accepted. *Expenses:* Tuition, state resident: part-time $412 per credit hour. Tuition, nonresident: part-time $681 per credit hour. Required fees: $91 per credit hour. One-time fee: $75 part-time. *Financial support:* Fellowships with full tuition reimbursements, research assistantships with full tuition reimbursements, teaching assistantships with full tuition reimbursements, tuition waivers (full) and unspecified assistantships available. Financial award application deadline: 2/1. *Faculty research:* Sociology of aging, gerontology, social stratification, medical sociology. *Unit head:* Dr. James E. Trela, Chairperson, 410-455-2076, Fax: 410-455-1154, E-mail: trela@umbc.edu. *Application contact:* Dr. William G. Rothstein, Director, 410-455-2078, Fax: 410-455-1154, E-mail: rothstei@umbc.edu.

University of Memphis, Graduate School, College of Arts and Sciences, School of Urban Affairs and Public Policy, Division of Public and Nonprofit Administration, Memphis, TN 38152. Offers nonprofit administration (MPA); public management and policy (MPA); urban management and planning (MPA). *Accreditation:* NASPAA. Part-time and evening/weekend programs available. *Faculty:* 6 full-time (3 women), 6 part-time/adjunct (2 women). *Students:* 15 full-time (7 women), 39 part-time (26 women); includes 24 minority (all African Americans), 2 international. Average age 33. 16 applicants, 15 enrolled. In 2006, 13 master's awarded. *Median time to degree:* Master's–2 years full-time, 3 years part-time. *Degree requirements:* For master's, thesis or alternative, internship, comprehensive exam. *Entrance requirements:* For master's, GRE General Test, GMAT, or MAT, minimum GPA of 3.0. *Application deadline:* For fall admission, 8/1 for domestic students; for spring admission, 12/1 for domestic students. Applications are processed on a rolling basis. Application fee: $25 ($50 for international students). *Financial support:* In 2006–07, 8 research assistantships with full tuition reimbursements (averaging $6,000 per year) were awarded; fellowships, career-related internships or fieldwork, Federal Work-Study, and scholarships/grants also available. Support available to part-time students. *Faculty research:* Nonprofit organization governance, local government management, community collaboration, urban problems, accountability. Total annual research expenditures: $75,000. *Unit head:* Dr. Dorothy Norris-Tirrell, Director, 901-678-3360, Fax: 901-678-2981, E-mail: dnrrstrr@memphis.edu. *Application contact:* Dr. Charles Menifield, Director of Admissions, 901-678-3369, Fax: 901-678-2981, E-mail: cmenifld@memphis.edu.

University of Michigan–Dearborn, School of Education, Division of Public Administration, Dearborn, MI 48128-1491. Offers educational administration (Certificate), including assistant principalship, central office administration, principalship; nonprofit leadership (Certificate); public administration (MPA). Part-time and evening/weekend programs available. *Entrance requirements:* For master's, GRE or minimum undergraduate GPA of 3.0. Additional exam requirements/recommendations for international students: Required—TOEFL, TWE. Electronic applications accepted. *Faculty research:* Federal, state, and local agency management; independent sector management; educational administration.

University of Missouri–St. Louis, Graduate School, Program in Public Policy Administration, St. Louis, MO 63121. Offers health policy (MPPA); local government management (MPPA); managing human resources and organization (MPPA); nonprofit organization management (MPPA); nonprofit organization management and leadership (Certificate); policy research and analysis (MPPA); public sector human resources management (MPPA). *Accreditation:* NASPAA. Part-time and evening/weekend programs available. *Faculty:* 8 full-time (5 women), 5 part-time/adjunct (1 woman). *Students:* 21 full-time (13 women), 61 part-time (35 women); includes 22 minority (18 African Americans, 1 American Indian/Alaska Native, 2 Asian Americans or Pacific Islanders, 1 Hispanic American), 4 international. Average age 34. In 2006, 22 degrees awarded. *Entrance requirements:* For master's, 3 letters of recommendation. Additional exam requirements/recommendations for international students: Required—TOEFL (minimum score 550 paper-based; 213 computer-based). *Application deadline:* For fall admission, 7/15 priority date for domestic students; for spring admission, 12/15 priority date for domestic students. Applications are processed on a rolling basis. Application fee: $35 ($40 for international students). Electronic applications accepted. *Expenses:* Tuition, state resident: part-time $332 per credit hour. Tuition, nonresident: part-time $770 per credit hour. *Financial support:* In 2006–07, 2 research assistantships with full tuition reimbursements (averaging $14,100 per year) were awarded; teaching assistantships with partial tuition reimbursements, career-related internships or fieldwork also available. *Faculty research:* Urban policy, public finance, evaluation. *Unit head:* Brady Baybeck, Director, 314-516-5145, Fax: 314-516-5210, E-mail: baybeck@umsl.edu. *Application contact:* 314-516-5458, Fax: 314-516-6996, E-mail: gradadm@umsl.edu.

The University of North Carolina at Greensboro, Graduate School, College of Arts and Sciences, Department of Political Science, Greensboro, NC 27412-5001. Offers nonprofit management (Certificate); public affairs (MPA); urban and economic development (Certificate). *Accreditation:* NASPAA. *Faculty:* 14 full-time (4 women). *Students:* 35 full-time (21 women), 28 part-time (20 women); includes 62 minority (13 African Americans, 1 American Indian/Alaska Native, 48 Hispanic Americans). 55 applicants, 27% accepted. *Degree requirements:* For master's, comprehensive exam. *Entrance requirements:* For master's, GRE General Test. Additional exam requirements/recommendations for international students: Required—TOEFL. *Application deadline:* For fall admission, 3/15 priority date for domestic students; for spring admission, 11/1 for domestic students. Applications are processed on a rolling basis. Electronic applications accepted. *Expenses:* Tuition, state resident: full-time $2,692. Tuition, nonresident: full-time $13,742. *Financial support:* In 2006–07, 19 students received support, including 4 research assistantships with full tuition reimbursements available; teaching assistantships with full tuition reimbursements available, career-related internships or fieldwork, Federal Work-Study, scholarships/grants, and traineeships also available. Support available to part-time students. *Faculty research:* U.S. Constitution, Canadian parliament, public management, ethical challenge of public service. *Unit head:* Dr. Ruth H. DeHoog, Head, 336-256-0511, Fax: 336-334-4315, E-mail: rhdehoog@uncg.edu. *Application contact:* Michelle Harkleroad, Director of Graduate Admissions, 336-334-4884, Fax: 336-334-4424, E-mail: mbharkle@uncg.edu.

University of Northern Iowa, Graduate College, Program in Philanthropy/Nonprofit Development, Cedar Falls, IA 50614. Offers MA. *Entrance requirements:* Additional exam requirements/recommendations for international students: Required—TOEFL (minimum score 500 paper-based; 180 computer-based; 61 iBT). *Application deadline:* Applications are processed on a rolling basis. Application fee: $30 ($50 for international students). Electronic applications accepted. *Expenses:* Tuition, state resident: full-time $5,936. Tuition, nonresident: full-time $14,074. *Financial support:* Application deadline: 2/1. *Unit head:* Dr. Christopher R. Edginton, Coordinator, 319-273-6475, Fax: 319-273-5958, E-mail: christopher.edginton@uni.edu.

University of Notre Dame, Mendoza College of Business, Program in Nonprofit Administration, Notre Dame, IN 46556. Offers MNA. *Accreditation:* AACSB. Part-time programs available. Postbaccalaureate distance learning degree programs offered (minimal on-campus study). *Faculty:* 10 full-time (0 women), 7 part-time/adjunct (5 women). *Students:* 4 full-time (3 women), 35 part-time (21 women); includes 5 minority (1 African American, 1 Asian American or Pacific Islander, 3 Hispanic Americans), 1 international. Average age 30. 38 applicants, 82% accepted, 21 enrolled. In 2006, 14 degrees awarded. *Degree requirements:* For master's, thesis. *Entrance requirements:* For master's, GRE General Test, work experience. Additional exam requirements/recommendations for international students: Required—TOEFL (minimum score 600 paper-based; 250 computer-based). *Application deadline:* For winter admission, 1/15 for domestic students; for spring admission, 3/31 for domestic students. Application fee: $50. Electronic applications accepted. *Expenses:* Contact institution. *Financial support:* In 2006–07, 7 students received support, including 7 fellowships (averaging $2,000 per year); institutionally sponsored loans and scholarships/grants also available. Support available to part-time students. *Unit head:* Thomas J. Harvey, Director, 574-631-7593, Fax: 574-631-6532, E-mail: harvey.18@nd.edu. *Application contact:* Kimberly M. Brennan, Program Manager, 574-631-3639, Fax: 574-631-6532, E-mail: brennan.53@nd.edu.

See Close-Up on page 355.

University of Pittsburgh, Graduate School of Public and International Affairs, Executive Programs in Public Policy and Management, Pittsburgh, PA 15260. Offers development planning (MPPM); international development (MPPM); international political economy (MPPM); international security studies (MPPM); management of non profit organizations (MPPM); metropolitan management and regional development (MPPM); policy analysis and evaluation (MPPM). Part-time programs available. *Faculty:* 35 full-time (11 women), 16 part-time/adjunct (9 women). *Students:* 15 full-time (4 women), 32 part-time (14 women); includes 5 minority (3 African Americans, 1 Asian American or Pacific Islander, 1 Hispanic American), 4 international. Average age 38. 25 applicants, 76% accepted, 16 enrolled. In 2006, 26 degrees awarded. *Degree requirements:* For master's, capstone seminar, thesis optional. *Entrance requirements:* For master's, 2 letters of recommendation, resumé. Additional exam requirements/recommendations for international students: Required—TOEFL (minimum score 600 paper-based; 250 computer-based), TWE (minimum score 4); Recommended—IELTS (minimum score 7). *Application deadline:* For fall admission, 5/1 priority date for domestic students, 2/1 for international students; for spring admission, 10/1 priority date for domestic students, 8/1 for international students. Applications are processed on a rolling basis. Application fee: $50. Electronic applications accepted. *Financial support:* In 2006–07, 4 students received support, including 4 fellowships (averaging $5,308 per year); institutionally sponsored loans and scholarships/grants also available. Support available to part-time students. Financial award application deadline: 2/1. *Faculty research:* Executive training and technical assistance for U.S. and international clients. Total annual research expenditures: $1.1 million. *Unit head:* Michele Garrity, Director, Executive Education, 412-648-7610, Fax: 412-648-2605, E-mail: garrity@birch.gspia.pitt.edu. *Application contact:* Maureen O'Malley, Admissions Counselor, 412-648-7640, Fax: 412-648-7641, E-mail: pronobis@birch.gspia.pitt.edu.

University of San Diego, School of Leadership and Education Sciences, Program in Leadership Studies, San Diego, CA 92110-2492. Offers educational leadership (M Ed); leadership studies (MA, PhD); nonprofit leadership and management (Certificate). Part-time programs available. *Faculty:* 6 full-time (4 women), 13 part-time/adjunct (8 women). *Students:* 16 full-time (10 women), 136 part-time (91 women); includes 39 minority (10 African Americans, 7 Asian Americans or Pacific Islanders, 22 Hispanic Americans), 7 international. Average age 38. 115 applicants, 64% accepted, 53 enrolled. In 2006, 38 master's, 8 doctorates awarded. *Degree requirements:* For master's, thesis (for some programs), portfolio; for doctorate, thesis/dissertation, comprehensive exam. *Entrance requirements:* For master's, minimum GPA of 3.0, interview; for doctorate, master's degree, minimum GPA of 3.5 (recommended), master's course work, interview, writing sample, resumé. Additional exam requirements/recommendations for international students: Required—TOEFL (minimum score 580 paper-based; 237 computer-based), TWE. *Application deadline:* For fall admission, 7/1 priority date for domestic students; for spring admission, 11/15 priority date for domestic students. Application fee: $45. Electronic applications accepted. *Financial support:* Career-related internships or fieldwork, Federal Work-Study, institutionally sponsored loans, tuition waivers (partial), unspecified assistantships, and stipends available. Support available to part-time students. Financial award application deadline: 5/1; financial award applicants required to submit FAFSA. *Unit head:* Dr. Edward DeRoche, Graduate Program Director, 619-260-2250, Fax: 619-260-6835, E-mail: deroche@sandiego.edu. *Application contact:* Stephen Pultz, Director of Admissions, 619-260-4524, Fax: 619-260-4158, E-mail: grads@sandiego.edu.

University of San Francisco, College of Professional Studies, Program in Nonprofit Administration, San Francisco, CA 94117-1080. Offers MNA. *Faculty:* 2 full-time (0 women), 14 part-time/adjunct (6 women). *Students:* 75 full-time (59 women); includes 15 minority (4 African Americans, 6 Asian Americans or Pacific Islanders, 5 Hispanic Americans), 2 international. Average age 34. 22 applicants, 82% accepted, 13 enrolled. In 2006, 22 degrees awarded. *Degree requirements:* For master's, thesis optional. *Entrance requirements:* For master's, minimum GPA of 3.0. Application fee: $55 ($65 for international students). *Expenses:* Tuition: Full-time $17,370; part-time $965 per unit. Tuition and fees vary according to degree level, campus/location and program. *Financial support:* In 2006–07, 42 students received support. Application deadline: 3/2; *Faculty research:* Philanthropy in ethnic communities. *Unit head:* Dr. Kathleen Fletcher, Director. *Application contact:* 415-422-6000.

University of Southern Maine, Edmund S. Muskie School of Public Service, Program in Public Policy and Management, Portland, ME 04104-9300. Offers child and family policy (Certificate); non-profit management (Certificate); public policy and management (MPPM); JD/MPPM. *Accreditation:* NASPAA. Part-time and evening/weekend programs available. Postbaccalaureate distance learning degree programs offered (minimal on-campus study). *Degree requirements:* For master's, thesis, capstone project, field experience. *Entrance requirements:* For master's, GRE General Test or LSAT. Additional exam requirements/recommendations for international students: Required—TOEFL. Electronic applications accepted. *Expenses:* Tuition, state resident: full-time $4,860; part-time $270 per credit hour. Tuition, nonresident: full-time $13,572; part-time $754 per credit hour. Required fees: $222 per semester. Tuition and fees vary according to course load. *Faculty research:* Sustainable communities, juvenile justice, program management, nonprofit management.

University of the Sacred Heart, Graduate Programs, Program in Nonprofit Organization, San Juan, PR 00914-0383. Offers MS.

University of the West, Department of Business Administration, Rosemead, CA 91770. Offers business administration (EMBA); finance (MBA); information technology and management (MBA); international business (MBA); nonprofit organization management (MBA). Part-time and evening/weekend programs available. *Entrance requirements:* Additional exam requirements/recommendations for international students: Required—TOEFL.

Virginia Commonwealth University, Graduate School, College of Humanities and Sciences, Program in Nonprofit Management, Richmond, VA 23284-9005. Offers Graduate Certificate.

See Close-Up on page 673.

Western Illinois University, School of Graduate Studies, College of Arts and Sciences, Department of Political Science, Macomb, IL 61455-1390. Offers political science (MA); public and non-profit management (Certificate). Part-time programs available. *Students:* 19 full-time (5 women), 8 part-time (2 women); includes 6 minority (4 African Americans, 2 Hispanic Americans), 10 international. Average age 30. 21 applicants, 48% accepted. In 2006, 4 degrees awarded. *Degree requirements:* For master's, thesis or alternative, comprehensive exam. *Entrance requirements:* For master's, minimum GPA of 2.75. Additional exam requirements/recommendations for international students: Required—TOEFL (minimum score 550 paper-based; 213 computer-based; 80 iBT). *Application deadline:* Applications are processed on a rolling basis. Electronic applications accepted. *Expenses:* Tuition, state resident: part-time $200 per credit hour. Tuition, nonresident: part-time $400 per credit hour. *Financial support:* In 2006–07, 12 students received support, including 12 research assistantships with full tuition reimbursements available (averaging $6,568 per year). Financial award applicants required to submit FAFSA. *Unit head:* Dr. Richard Hardy, Chairperson, 309-298-1055. *Application contact:* Dr. Barbara Baily, Director of Graduate Studies/Associate Provost, 309-298-1806, Fax: 309-298-2345, E-mail: grad-office@wiu.edu.

Willamette University, George H. Atkinson Graduate School of Management, Salem, OR 97301-3931. Offers business (MBA); government (MBA); not-for-profit management (MBA); JD/MBA. *Accreditation:* AACSB; NASPAA. Part-time programs available. *Faculty:* 15 full-time (3 women), 9 part-time/adjunct (2 women). *Students:* 116 full-time (38 women), 7 part-time (2 women); includes 15 minority (1 African American, 2 American Indian/Alaska Native, 8 Asian Americans or Pacific Islanders, 4 Hispanic Americans), 28 international. Average age 25. 101 applicants, 95% accepted, 50 enrolled. In 2006, 56 degrees awarded. *Median time to degree:* Master's–2 years full-time. *Entrance requirements:* For master's, GMAT or GRE. Additional exam requirements/recommendations for international students: Required—TOEFL (minimum score 570 paper-based; 230 computer-based; 88 iBT), Require TOEFL or IELTS. *Application deadline:* For fall admission, 1/9 priority date for domestic and international students; for winter admission, 3/1 priority date for domestic and international students; for spring admission, 5/1 priority date for domestic and international students. Applications are processed on a rolling basis. Application fee: $50. Electronic applications accepted. *Expenses:* Contact institution. *Financial support:* In 2006–07, 115 students received support, including 12 research assistantships (averaging $1,500 per year); teaching assistantships, career-related internships or fieldwork, Federal Work-Study, scholarships/grants, and unspecified assistantships also available. Financial award application deadline: 5/1; financial award applicants required to submit FAFSA. *Faculty research:* General management, finance, marketing, public management, human resources. *Unit head:* Debra J. Ringold, Interim Dean, 503-370-6440, Fax: 503-370-3011, E-mail: dringold@willamette.edu. *Application contact:* Judy O'Neill, Director of Admission, 503-370-6167, Fax: 503-370-3011, E-mail: joneill@willamette.edu.

Worcester State College, Graduate Studies, Program in Non-Profit Management, Worcester, MA 01602-2597. Offers MS. Part-time and evening/weekend programs available. *Students:* 6 full-time (3 women), 10 part-time (8 women); includes 1 minority (African American), 3 international. Average age 34. 19 applicants, 47% accepted, 2 enrolled. In 2006, 21 degrees awarded. *Degree requirements:* For master's, thesis optional. *Entrance requirements:* For master's, GRE General Test or MAT. Additional exam requirements/recommendations for international students: Required—TOEFL (minimum score 550 paper-based; 213 computer-based). *Application deadline:* Applications are processed on a rolling basis. Application fee: $30. *Expenses:* Tuition, state resident: full-time $4,518; part-time $251 per credit hour. Tuition, nonresident: full-time $4,518; part-time $251 per credit hour. *Financial support:* In 2006–07, 2 research assistantships with full tuition reimbursements (averaging $4,800 per year) were awarded; career-related internships or fieldwork, Federal Work-Study, institutionally sponsored loans, scholarships/grants, and unspecified assistantships also available. Support available to part-time students. Financial award application deadline: 3/1; financial award applicants required to submit FAFSA. *Faculty research:* Politics of human services, models of supervision. *Unit head:* Dr. Shiko Gathuo, Coordinator, 508-929-8892, Fax: 508-929-8144, E-mail: agathuo@worcester.edu. *Application contact:* Nicole Brown, Assistant Dean of Continuing Education, 508-929-8787, Fax: 508-929-8100, E-mail: nbrown@worcester.edu.

MANDEL CENTER FOR NONPROFIT ORGANIZATIONS

CASE WESTERN RESERVE UNIVERSITY

Mandel Center for Nonprofit Organizations

Programs of Study

Since 1987, the Mandel Center for Nonprofit Organizations has been the standard-setter in graduate education for executive leadership of nonprofit organizations in the United States. In that year, the Center instituted its credit-bearing Certificate in Nonprofit Management (CNM) program. Two years later, it established the groundbreaking Master of Nonprofit Organizations (M.N.O.) degree program. Students in the M.N.O. and CNM programs benefit from a multidisciplinary curriculum and faculty members drawn from the four partner schools of the Mandel Center: the Mandel School of Applied Social Sciences (MSASS), the Weatherhead School of Management, the School of Law, and the College of Arts and Sciences.

The Mandel Center began offering an expanded and enhanced version of its M.N.O. degree in 2000. The M.N.O. is a rigorous professional degree designed to prepare men and women for leadership across the full spectrum of nonprofits, including health and human services, fine and performing arts, cultural, educational, religious, community development, and environmental organizations. The revised curriculum focuses on four key areas of study: nonprofit purposes, traditions, and contexts; analytic thinking for nonprofit leaders; generating and managing resources for nonprofit organizations; and leading nonprofit organizations. Under the 60-credit-hour format, the number of required courses is reduced and the number of electives is increased, giving the student broad latitude to customize a program of study to meet professional interests and needs. The program may be pursued on a two-year full-time basis or on a part-time basis. Opportunities for externships, mentoring, and networking enable students to strengthen their ties to the world of practice while at the same time acquiring a solid academic foundation.

The Mandel Center also offers a 45-credit-hour Master of Nonprofit Organizations–Executive Option (M.N.O.–Executive Option) degree option. The M.N.O.–Executive Option is designed for nonprofit managers and practitioners with ten years of professional experience and five years of managerial and/or supervisory experience.

The CNM is a 15-credit-hour nondegree program for practitioners as well as for career changers seeking to enter the nonprofit field. Although it does carry graduate credit, the CNM is not a master's degree, nor is it intended for those seeking extensive graduate or professional course work. However, since courses for the CNM are drawn from the regular M.N.O. curriculum, students who perform successfully in the CNM program may apply to the M.N.O. If admission is granted, CNM course work is applied toward the master's degree.

The Mandel Center offers dual-degree and certificate programs in cooperation with MSASS, the Weatherhead School of Management, the School of Law, and the College of Arts and Sciences.

The Mandel Center, in partnership with the Weatherhead School of Management's Executive Doctor of Management (EDM) program, began in August 2000 to offer the nation's first practice-oriented, cross-sector, doctoral-level program for nonprofit leaders.

Research Facilities

Students have access to the libraries of the partner schools and the University library. These state-of-the-art facilities offer online access to a wide range of research materials and publications. The Mandel Center maintains a nonprofit reading room in the Lillian F. and Milford J. Harris Library of MSASS. The reading room contains a broad array of books and periodicals related to the nonprofit sector.

Financial Aid

The majority of Mandel Center students support their studies through a combination of loans, personal savings, and scholarships. The Mandel Center offers a variety of scholarships and other financial assistance for qualified students in the M.N.O. and CNM programs. The Mandel Scholarship is a full-tuition, merit-based scholarship for full-time master's degree applicants that is available each fall. The application deadline for fall 2007 is March 16, 2007. The Arthur Naparstek Memorial Scholarship is a full-tuition, merit-based scholarship for full-time master's degree applicants from outside the state of Ohio that is available each fall. The application deadline for fall 2007 is March 16, 2007. For other financial assistance opportunities, students should visit the Mandel Center's Web site at http://www.case.edu/mandelcenter/grad/finance/.

Cost of Study

Tuition for the 2006–07 academic year was $28,100 for full-time study and $1171 per credit hour for part-time study. A one-time application fee of $25 is also charged. Students accepted into one of the programs must make a nonrefundable tuition deposit of $150 to reserve a place in the entering class.

Living and Housing Costs

Off-campus housing costs between $500 and $1200 per month. (On-campus graduate housing is not available at this time.)

Student Group

The mean age of the 2006–07 class was 29. Seventy-six percent of these students are women, and 12 percent are people of color. An active student association plans activities among the students and faculty members and between students and nonprofit leaders in the Cleveland community.

Student Outcomes

The Mandel Center provides comprehensive support in career planning and job-search techniques for its students and alumni. Both students and alumni benefit from individualized attention and guidance throughout their careers.

Location

Cleveland provides a perfect laboratory for students who study nonprofit management. There are currently more than 3,000 nonprofit organizations in the city, building on a long tradition of innovative nonprofit activity. The attractive campus of Case Western Reserve University (Case) is located in University Circle, a 550-acre parklike concentration of more than forty cultural, medical, educational, religious, and social service institutions at the eastern end of the city of Cleveland. In addition to Case, University Circle includes Severance Hall (the home of the Cleveland Orchestra), the Cleveland Museum of Art, the Cleveland Institute of Art, the Cleveland Institute of Music, the Cleveland Museum of Natural History, the Cleveland Botanical Garden, and much more.

The University

Case Western Reserve University is one of the nation's leading independent research universities. Although its origins date back to 1826, the University in its present form is the result of the 1967 federation of Case Institute of Technology and Western Reserve University. The two institutions had shared adjacent campuses since the late nineteenth century and were involved in cooperative efforts for many years.

Applying

Applications are accepted for both fall and spring semesters. The application deadline for fall is the preceding June 1 and for spring, the preceding December 1. Admission to the M.N.O. program requires completion of the GMAT (this is not a requirement for the CNM) and proof of a baccalaureate degree. In addition, students must submit a completed application form, two letters of recommendation, an essay, a current resume, and official transcripts. International students must submit TOEFL scores.

Correspondence and Information

Rebecca W. Zirm, J.D.
Director of Recruitment
Case Western Reserve University
10900 Euclid Avenue
Cleveland, Ohio 44106-7167
Phone: 216-368-6025
        800-435-6669 (toll-free)
Fax: 216-368-6624
E-mail: mcnoadmissions@case.edu
Web site: http://www.case.edu/mandelcenter

Case Western Reserve University

MANDEL CENTER PROGRAM FACULTY

Diana Bilimoria, Associate Professor of Organizational Behavior, Weatherhead School of Management; Ph.D., Michigan.
Pranab Chatterjee, Grace Longwell Coyle Professor of Social Work, Mandel School of Applied Social Sciences; Ph.D., Chicago.
Laura Chisolm, Professor, School of Law; J.D., Case Western Reserve.
David Cooperrider, Professor of Organizational Behavior, Weatherhead School of Management; Ph.D., Case Western Reserve.
Claudia Coulton, Lillian F. Harris Professor of Urban Research and Social Change, Mandel School of Applied Social Sciences; Ph.D., Case Western Reserve.
Susan Lajoie Eagan, Mandel Professor, Mandel Center for Nonprofit Organizations; Ph.D., Harvard.
Steven Feldman, Associate Professor of Management Policy, Weatherhead School of Management; Ph.D., Pennsylvania.
Robert Fischer, Research Associate Professor, Mandel School of Applied Social Sciences; Ph.D., Vanderbilt.
David C. Hammack, Hiram C. Haydn Professor of History, College of Arts and Sciences; Ph.D., Columbia.
Sharon Milligan, Associate Professor, Mandel School of Applied Social Sciences; Ph.D., Pittsburgh.
Duncan Neuhauser, Professor of Epidemiology and Biostatistics and Charles Elton Blanchard, M.D. of Health Management Professor, School of Medicine; Ph.D., Chicago.
Myron Roomkin, Professor of Human Resources and Management Policy, Weatherhead School of Management; Ph.D., Wisconsin.
Paul Salipante Jr., Professor of Labor and Human Resource Policy, Weatherhead School of Management; Ph.D., Chicago.
Betty Vandenbosch, Associate Professor of Information Systems, Weatherhead School of Management; Ph.D., Western Ontario.
Joseph White, Luxemberg Family Professor of Public Policy and Chair, Department of Political Science, College of Arts and Sciences; Ph.D., Berkeley.

Emeritus Program Faculty

Arthur Blum, Grace Longwell Coyle Professor Emeritus, Mandel School of Applied Social Sciences; D.S.W., Western Reserve.
John Yankey, Leonard W. Mayo Professor Emeritus of Family and Child Welfare, Mandel School of Applied Social Sciences; Ph.D., Pittsburgh.

Associate Program Faculty

Steve Bullock, Adjunct Instructor, Mandel School of Applied Social Sciences; M.B.A., St. Thomas (Minnesota).
Susan Case, Associate Professor of Organizational Behavior, Weatherhead School of Management; Ph.D., SUNY at Buffalo.
Fred Collopy, Professor of Information Systems and Chair, Department of Information Systems, Weatherhead School of Management; Ph.D., Pennsylvania.
David Crampton, Assistant Professor of Social Work, Mandel School of Applied Social Sciences; Ph.D., Michigan.
Paul Feinberg, Adjunct Professor of Law, School of Law; LL.M., NYU.
Brian Gran, Assistant Professor of Sociology, College of Arts and Sciences; Ph.D., Northwestern.
Timothy Hagan, Distinguished Visiting Faculty of Public Affairs, Mandel School of Applied Social Sciences; B.A., Cleveland State.
Merl C. Hokenstad, Ralph S. and Dorothy P. Schmitt Professor, Mandel School of Applied Social Sciences; Ph.D., Brandeis.
Robert Lawry, Professor of Law, School of Law; J.D., Pennsylvania.
Miriam Levin, Associate Professor of History, College of Arts and Sciences; Ph.D., Massachusetts.
Roger Lohmann, Adjunct Instructor, Mandel School of Applied Social Sciences; Ph.D., Brandeis.
Kelly McMann, Assistant Professor of Political Science, College of Arts and Sciences; Ph.D., Michigan.
August Napoli Jr., Adjunct Instructor, Mandel School of Applied Social Sciences; B.A., Steubenville.
Mohan Reddy, Nancy and Joseph P. Keithley Professor of Technology Management, Associate Professor of Marketing, and Dean, Weatherhead School of Management; Ph.D., Case Western Reserve.
Judith Simpson, Adjunct Instructor, Mandel School of Applied Social Sciences; M.A., Goddard.
Louis Stokes, Distinguished Visiting Professor, Mandel School of Applied Social Sciences; J.D., Cleveland State.

Other Adjunct Instructors

Patricia Brandt, Part-Time Lecturer, Weatherhead School of Management; M.B.A., Case Western Reserve.
Patricia Choby, Adjunct Instructor, Mandel School of Applied Social Sciences; M.N.O., Case Western Reserve.
Barbara Clemenson, Adjunct Instructor, Weatherhead School of Management; M.Acc., Case Western Reserve.
Jennifer Johnson, Adjunct Instructor, Weatherhead School of Management; M.B.A., Case Western Reserve.
Jean Kilgore, Senior Lecturer, Weatherhead School of Management; Ph.D., Case Western Reserve.
Laura Maciag, Adjunct Instructor, Mandel School of Applied Social Sciences; M.N.O., Case Western Reserve.
Deborah O'Neil, Senior Lecturer, Weatherhead School of Management; Ph.D., Case Western Reserve.
Michele Seyranian, Adjunct Instructor, Mandel School of Applied Social Sciences; M.N.O., Case Western Reserve.
Janus Small, Adjunct Instructor, Mandel School of Applied Social Sciences; M.A., Cincinnati.

THE NEW SCHOOL
A UNIVERSITY

THE NEW SCHOOL: A UNIVERSITY

Milano The New School for Management and Urban Policy
Program in Nonprofit Management

Program of Study

The Program in Nonprofit Management at Milano The New School for Management and Urban Policy was founded in 1979 as one of the first academic programs in the United States to focus on the issues specific to nonprofit institutions. Today, the program continues to serve as a beacon and a pioneer in the nonprofit sector and to play an active role in the development of model research, curricula, and instructional materials as well as methods for nonprofit management programs worldwide. The program is consistently cited by national publications for offering top-tier nonprofit management training. It was cited as one of the five top nonprofit programs—and the only one in the New York City area—by the *Chronicle of Philanthropy* (January 2004).

Nonprofits operate in a global context, not in isolation or on just a local level. Students are exposed to the global environment in which nonprofits work and are trained to lead and run organizations of all sizes. The nonprofit management program builds skills in areas such as management of organizational change, leadership, coalition building, development, governance and advocacy, technological communications, marketing, finance, and results evaluation. In a hands-on approach to course work, students put the theory they study directly into practice by undertaking research and tasks for organizations that promote social change. The curriculum provides students with the knowledge and skills needed for effective management and leadership in the nonprofit sector in the United States and abroad.

To fulfill the required credits for this Master of Science degree, students structure a program comprising three components: a required schoolwide core of 12 credits, a required program core of 12 credits, and 18 credits of elective courses.

The four required schoolwide core courses equip students with basic analytic skills and an understanding of basic theories of management and organizational behavior. Students take one course from each of the following course groups: Managerial Economics or Economic Analysis, Quantitative Methods, Management and Organizational Behavior, and Policy Analysis or Analysis for Decision Making. The four required program core courses build on the knowledge and skill base developed in the schoolwide core and provide students with an understanding of key nonprofit management functions and issues while sharpening their analytic and decision-making capabilities. These courses are Theory and Practice of Nonprofit Management, Fundraising and Development, Financial Management in Nonprofit Organizations, and Advanced Seminar in Nonprofit Management. Students may work in consultation with an academic adviser to organize the six elective courses to suit their academic and professional interests and goals, drawing on the broad array of courses offered by the Program in Nonprofit Management, by other programs in the graduate school, and by other divisions of the University.

Research Facilities

The Center for New York City Affairs is a nonpartisan institute dedicated to advancing innovative public policies that strengthen neighborhoods, support families, and reduce urban poverty. Tools include rigorous analysis, research, candid public dialogue with stakeholders and opinion leaders, and strategic planning with government officials, nonprofit practitioners, and community residents. The center's original applied research and public seminars examine the politics of community change in local and state government and identify critical problems facing urban families and communities. The center's public programs offer community leaders and other participants the opportunity to meet powerful players in and around government and to learn about the context, the influential organizations, and other factors that define the policymaking landscape in New York City and urban America.

Financial Aid

Milano offers financial aid packages in the form of scholarships, fellowships, and loans. Financial aid awards are decided on a first-come, first-served basis, and applicants are encouraged to apply early to receive priority consideration. Financial aid award decisions are made after students are accepted at Milano. Applicants interested in obtaining financial aid should submit the Free Application for Federal Student Aid (FAFSA) or the Renewal Application for Federal Student Aid. More information is available from the Office of Financial Services at 212-229-8930.

Cost of Study

Tuition in 2006–07 was $1032 per credit, and fees were approximately $200 each term.

Living and Housing Costs

The University Housing Office maintains a comprehensive resource center with apartment listings. University-run apartments and residence halls are also available. The cost of housing, food, transportation, books, and living expenses averages $17,000 annually. For more information, students should go online to http://www.newschool.edu/studentservices.

Student Group

There are 151 students in the program; 52 attend on a full-time basis. Of these students, 118 are women, 54 are members of underrepresented groups, and 8 are international students.

Location

The New School's location in New York City gives students access to an abundance of resources. Students are encouraged to take advantage of the city's many museums, performance venues, and other cultural institutions, which are only a walk or a subway ride away. An extension of the classroom, the city also offers excellent professional and networking opportunities, and some classes require that students work with outside businesses to complete assignments—giving them unparalleled real-world experience. Internships and apprenticeships with leading New York City companies and organizations in every field are also available, and many students have moved on from internships to successful careers with those companies and organizations upon graduation.

The University and The School

The New School pioneered the idea of lifelong university-level education for adults. It was created for teachers and students from different backgrounds who were willing to take risks for their intellectual and political beliefs. Milano The New School for Management and Urban Policy trains leaders for the nonprofit, public, and private sectors with a measurable difference. The faculty blends theory with practice and progressive analysis with hands-on activism. Milano students work on local and global issues that affect organizations and urban communities—in New York City and around the world. The New School is accredited by the Commission on Higher Education of the Middle States Association of Colleges and Schools. A privately supported institution, The New School is chartered as a university by the Regents of the State of New York.

Applying

Students must submit the completed application form, the $50 application fee, official transcripts from all postsecondary institutions attended, a 300-word essay explaining their professional goals, two letters of recommendation, and a resume. Applications are reviewed on a rolling admissions basis. Although there is no specific deadline, applicants are strongly encouraged to apply by March 1 for the fall semester and by October 1 for the spring semester in order to take full advantage of financial aid and housing opportunities.

Correspondence and Information

Program in Nonprofit Management
Milano The New School for Management and Urban Policy
The New School
72 Fifth Avenue, 3rd Floor
New York, New York 10011

Phone: 212-229-5400
Fax: 212-229-5354
E-mail: milanoadmissions@newschool.edu
Web site: http://www.milano.newschool.edu

The New School: A University

THE FACULTY AND THEIR RESEARCH

Warren Balinsky, Associate Professor and Chair of Health Services Management; Ph.D., Case Western Reserve. Home health care and the applications of planning, development, marketing, and research to health services management and policy. Dr. Balinsky has written two books on home care; he has also written articles on various aspects of emergency preparedness, health care of the elderly, health-care reimbursement, health status indices, home care, pediatric health care, and the unequal distribution of medical personnel within the health-care system.

Robert Beauregard, Professor; Ph.D., Cornell. Urbanization in the United States, with particular focus on industrial urban decline after World War II and current problems posed by growth and decline in cities. Dr. Beauregard is currently working on *Writing Urban Theory*, a series of essays, and *Why Cities Endure*, a book investigating why some cities prosper while others do not. Dr. Beauregard teaches courses on the political economy of the city, urban redevelopment, neighborhood change, social theory, and research design.

Howard Berliner, Professor of Health Services Management and Director of Ph.D. in Public and Urban Policy Program; Sc.D., Johns Hopkins. Needs of vulnerable populations and access to health services for the uninsured. Dr. Berliner is the author of seven books, most recently *The Health Marketplace: New York City 1990–2010* with Ginzberg et al. He has also written numerous articles and reviews on health policy in academic and professional journals. Dr. Berliner served for two years as the assistant state health commissioner for New Jersey.

John Clinton, Visiting Assistant Professor; Ph.D., Fordham. Interprofessional collaboration. Dr. Clinton has served as corporation senior consultant on social responsibility at MetLife, senior vice president of the LightHouse for the Blind, and an administrator at NYU, Fordham University, and Hartwick College. He has been a consultant to foundations, nonprofit organizations, corporations, and higher education institutions.

Dennis Derryck, Professor of Professional Practice; Ph.D., Fordham. Innovative policies and strategies affecting the economic sustainability of nonprofit organizations. Dr. Derryck has held leadership positions in organizations involved in community economic development, operations and fiscal management, and research and policy analysis. He currently serves as chair of WE ACT for Environmental Justice and is vice chair of SoBro, the South Bronx Overall Economic Development Corporation.

Elizabeth Dickey, Professor; Ed.D., Massachusetts Amherst. Organizational behavior and leadership, with a psychosocial emphasis. Dr. Dickey is a developmental clinical psychologist. Between 1991 and 2005, she served as dean and then provost of The New School.

Peter Eisinger, Henry Cohen Professor; Ph.D., Yale. Urban politics and policy, state and local economic development, U.S. politics, state politics, federalism. Author of *Toward an End to Hunger in America*.

Alec Ian Gershberg, Associate Professor; Ph.D., Pennsylvania. School governance, education finance, decentralization in the developing world and in the United States, immigrant students in public schools in New York and California. Dr. Gershberg has conducted extensive research on Latin America—particularly Mexico, Nicaragua, and Ecuador—as well as on Egypt, Romania, and sub-Saharan Africa. He has been a frequent consultant to the World Bank, the Inter-American Development Bank, and the Urban Institute. Dr. Gershberg is the lead author of *Beyond Bilingual Education: New Immigrants and Public School Policies in California*.

Martin Greller, Professor and Associate Dean for Academic Affairs; Ph.D., Yale. Factors associated with career continuity for older workers, feedback systems in organizations as tools for increasing organizational effectiveness. Recent projects include an assessment of training needs for entry-level peace officers and a review of pay equity issues for a legislative body.

Darrick Hamilton, Assistant Professor; Ph.D., North Carolina at Chapel Hill. Ethnic and racial disparities in wealth, home ownership, and labor market outcomes. Dr. Hamilton's articles can be found in *African American Research Perspectives, American Economics Review, Applied Economics Letters, Challenge: The Magazine of Economic Affairs, Journal of Economic Psychology, Review of Black Political Economy, Social Science Quarterly, Southern Economics Journal,* and *Transforming Anthropology*.

David Howell, Professor; Ph.D., New School. Labor markets at the local, national, and international levels. Recent publications have examined the effects of immigration on the economic status of foreign and native-born workers in New York City, the nature of recent changes in skill requirements and the determinants of relative wage trends in the United States, and the extent to which labor market institutions and social policy explain patterns of unemployment in Europe and the United States. Dr. Howell is the editor of *Fighting Unemployment: The Limits of Free Market Orthodoxy*.

Mark Lipton, Professor of Management and Chair of Management; Ph.D., Massachusetts Amherst. Management, leadership, organizational strategy. Author of *Guiding Growth: How Vision Keeps Companies on Course*. Dr. Lipton's research and opinions on management and strategy have appeared in *Executive Excellence, Harvard Business Review, The Journal of Management Consulting, Optimize, Organization Development Journal,* and *Sloan Management Review*, among others.

Edwin Melendez, Professor; Ph.D., Massachusetts Amherst. Economics. Dr. Melendez was director of the Mauricio Gastón Institute for Latino Community Development and Public Policy at the University of Massachusetts Boston (1992–98) and director of the Community Development Research Center at the Milano Graduate School (1999–2004). He has worked as a consultant on employment, economic development, job creation, and small business for numerous government, community, and philanthropic foundations. Dr. Melendez has managed more than thirty-five research, outreach, and demonstration projects and supervised or collaborated with more than 60 researchers in projects that resulted in several books, special issues of academic journals, and other publications.

Aida Rodriguez, Professor of Professional Practice; Ph.D., Massachusetts. Leadership and effective management in the nonprofit sector. Formerly deputy director of the Equal Opportunity Division of the Rockefeller Foundation, Dr. Rodriguez now serves on various nonprofit boards, including One Economy, Inc.; Alliance for Nonprofit Management; and the Association for Public Policy Analysis and Management. Dr. Rodriguez is an adviser on philanthropic initiatives in the United States and in Latin America, including the Funders' Collaborative for Strong Latino Communities.

Bryna Sanger, Professor; Ph.D., Brandeis. Public policy and management, changes in service delivery and management systems induced by welfare reform in states and localities around the country. Former dean of the Robert J. Milano Graduate School of Management and Urban Policy, Dr. Sanger has worked in a wide range of policy and management areas, including city service delivery, welfare reform, leadership, innovation, and performance management. She recently led a research effort with the National Civic League on the experiences of cities that have developed exemplary performance measurement systems and that report to and engage citizens in their efforts. Her most recent book on this topic is entitled *The Welfare Marketplace: Privatization and Welfare Reform*.

Alex F. Schwartz, Associate Professor, Chair of Department of Urban Policy Analysis and Management, and Senior Research Associate, Community Development Research Center; Ph.D., Rutgers. Housing and community development, including affordable housing programs, community reinvestment, and community development corporations. Dr. Schwartz's most recent publication is *Housing Policy in the United States*. His research has also appeared in such journals as *Cityscape, Economic Development Quarterly, International Journal of Urban and Regional Research,* and the *Journal of Urban Affairs*.

Lisa J. Servon, Associate Professor and Associate Director of Community Development Research Center; Ph.D., Berkeley. Urban poverty, community development, economic development, gender issues. Dr. Servon recently coedited *Gender and Planning: A Reader* (with Susan Fainstein), which covers a range of planning and development fields, including transportation, land use, history, gender, housing, social justice, environmental design, race, and economic and community development. The book was selected as one of the Top 10 Books for 2006 by Planetizen, a public-interest information exchange for the urban planning, design, and development community.

Nidhi Srinivas, Assistant Professor of Nonprofit Management; Ph.D., McGill. Civil society, specifically management of nongovernmental organizations, and the transfer and transformation of management knowledge. Dr. Srinivas teaches courses in nonprofit management, international development, and strategic decision making. Courses he has developed include Managing Institutions for Development (part of the core curriculum in the graduate program in international affairs) and Civil Society and South Asia.

Antonin Wagner, Visiting Professor; Ph.D., Fribourg (Switzerland). Economics. From 1996 to 2000, Dr. Wagner was president of the International Society for Third Sector Research, the leading scholarly institution in the nonprofit field. He has served as a consultant on social security–related issues to the Swiss Federal Statistical Office and the World Bank in Washington. He is a member of the editorial board of several international journals and has published widely in English, German, and French on the welfare state and civil society.

Tatiana Wah, Assistant Professor; Ph.D., Rutgers. Regional and local economic development planning and developing nations, with a particular focus on small developing nations' economies. Dr. Wah's recent work is on transnational expatriate (immigrant) recovery and engagement programs of developing countries, particularly Haiti. She has been involved in community development work in the New York African American and Caribbean communities as a consultant, nonprofit administrator, and activist/advocate.

Mary R. Watson, Assistant Professor; Ph.D., Vanderbilt. Contemporary human capital issues in organizations, with particular emphasis on the social impact of labor market discontinuities. Dr. Watson teaches courses on management and organization behavior, human resources, social impact management, and globalization. She has a strong interest in cultural, racial, ethnic, and gender inequalities in the workplace and society. Dr. Watson's upcoming book (with Dr. Rikki Abzug), tentatively titled *Human Resources in Social Purpose Organizations*, is scheduled to be published by Jossey-Bass in 2007.

Part-Time Faculty

The part-time faculty members of Milano The New School for Management and Urban Policy are high-level executives and managers in the institutions and agencies for which they work and the organizations for which they volunteer. They bring to the classroom valuable insight into current management and policy issues from both their personal experience and relevant curriculum. For a current listing of part-time faculty members, students should visit the Faculty page of the Milano Web site at http://www.milano.newschool.edu.

NEW YORK UNIVERSITY

School of Continuing and Professional Studies
Master of Science in Fundraising

Program of Study	The Master of Science (M.S.) program in fundraising at New York University's (NYU) George H. Heyman, Jr. Center for Philanthropy and Fundraising gives professionals and career changers an important credential to advance in the rewarding and expanding field of fundraising. With more than 1.8 million nonprofit organizations in the U.S. having raised $245 billion last year alone, there has never been a better time to work in the fundraising arena. In response to both the needs of a growing profession and outstanding acceptance of the center's noncredit courses and certificate programs by working professionals, the NYU Heyman Center has developed its M.S. program in fundraising to offer further opportunities for professional growth and an expansion of knowledge, scholarship, and training in the field of fundraising and philanthropy.

Through scholarly and practical course work, the M.S. program in fundraising curriculum provides students with extensive knowledge in this field. Students study the history and philosophy of fundraising in the U.S. and why it is different from philanthropy abroad; the effects of globalization on philanthropy; the psychological reasons why people contribute to nonprofits; the state and federal laws that govern the operation of nonprofits; how boards are developed; the financial and statistical underpinning of fundraising analysis and reporting; the technological support systems necessary for an effective professional environment; the cultural and gender factors that influence giving; and the new opportunities and constraints that accompany globalization.

The high level of learning students experience in the classroom is the product of the world-class faculty members, many of whom are recognized scholars or have been senior development officers or executives with private foundations. Together with the Center's advisory board of distinguished fundraisers, foundation leaders, and private philanthropists, professors lead students in exploring the dynamics and strategies of fundraising and philanthropy through intelligent dialogue and debate.

For the M.S. degree, students must complete 42 to 44 credits of graduate course work. The program consists of three phases: a required core of courses; professional electives that students choose based on their academic and professional interests; and the capstone project (thesis project). Some degree candidates complete the program full-time in two years; others study part-time over a period of two to five years. The curriculum for the M.S. program in fundraising is continually reevaluated and updated in response to industry needs to provide the most up-to-date and relevant course of study.

Research Facilities
The Elmer Holmes Bobst Library and Study Center, one of the largest open-stack research libraries in the world, houses more than 3 million of NYU's nearly 4.4 million volumes. In addition to books, journals, and other print materials, the library provides access to many nonprint resources. These include microforms, databases, and other electronic resources that students can connect to from their home or residence hall; extensive video and audio collections; and a variety of computer equipment and software programs.

NYU's central source for computing, information, network, and telecommunications services is Information Technology Services (ITS). ITS maintains four large, modern computer labs with high-end Macintosh and Windows computers, laser printers, multimedia equipment, and a wide variety of up-to-date software. The Client Services division of ITS provides comprehensive help with the materials and equipment available to students online, in person, and via telephone and e-mail.

Financial Aid
There are many financial aid options to consider, including low-interest educational loans. NYU's centralized Office of Financial Aid assists students with loan packages, scholarships, and the NYU monthly payment plan, which enables students to spread out their tuition payments. For more information, students should visit http://www.nyu.edu/financial.aid.

Cost of Study
Tuition for part-time students for the 2007–08 academic year is $1266 per credit plus fees. For full-time students (10–12 credits per semester), the cost of tuition and related fees is $12,664 per semester. Fees vary somewhat by program. The Board of Trustees of New York University reserves the right to alter these costs without notice.

Living and Housing Costs
Graduate student housing is available on the University campus and is administered through the Office of Housing and Residence Life. However, students may choose to live off campus. NYU's Off-Campus Housing Office (OCHO) offers assistance to members of the NYU community in their search for non-University housing options. OCHO provides, exclusively to NYU students, listings of available locations for rent through private landlords, property managers, brokers, and real estate agents. Updated daily, these listings are accessible through OCHO's computer terminals or online for members of the NYU community.

Student Group
In 2006–07, there were 26 students enrolled in the Master of Science program in fundraising. The median age was 28, and 85 percent of the students were women. Part-time students accounted for 88 percent of those enrolled.

Location
The George H. Heyman, Jr. Center for Philanthropy and Fundraising is located at NYU's main campus, in the heart of Greenwich Village. Study takes place in New York City—one of the world's most vibrant philanthropic communities.

The University, The School, and The Center
NYU is a private university composed of fourteen schools and colleges. The University was founded in 1831 and the School of Continuing and Professional Studies in 1934. The George H. Heyman, Jr. Center for Philanthropy and Fundraising, which offers the Master of Science degree, noncredit courses, professional certificates, and summer intensive programs, was founded in 1999.

Applying
Students may apply for fall or spring admission. Factors that are considered in evaluating an applicant include official transcripts of academic achievement in previous undergraduate and graduate course work, scores from the GRE or GMAT, TOEFL score (for international students whose native language is not English), the nature and extent of previous work experience, professional recommendations, and a statement of purpose.

Correspondence and Information
For more information and an application package, students should contact:

Office of Admissions
Master of Science in Fundraising
New York University
145 Fourth Avenue, Room 219
New York, New York 10003

Phone: 212-998-7200 Ext. 778
Fax: 212-995-4674
E-mail: scps.gradadmissions@nyu.edu
Web site: http://www.scps.nyu.edu/778

New York University

THE ADMINISTRATION

Robert S. Lapiner, Ph.D., Dean, School of Continuing and Professional Studies.

Naomi Levine, J.S.D., Executive Director, George H. Heyman, Jr. Center for Philanthropy and Fundraising, School of Continuing and Professional Studies.

Lewis Brindle, M.A., Academic Director, George H. Heyman, Jr. Center for Philanthropy and Fundraising, School of Continuing and Professional Studies.

L. Jay Oliva, Ph.D., Honorary Chair, George H. Heyman, Jr. Center for Philanthropy and Fundraising, School of Continuing and Professional Studies; President Emeritus, New York University.

VIRGINIA COMMONWEALTH UNIVERSITY

Programs in Nonprofit Management

Programs of Study	Virginia Commonwealth University (VCU) offers a graduate certificate in nonprofit management, a postbaccalaureate program designed to enable practitioners principally in the nonprofit sector to acquire knowledge and skills in managing nonprofit organizations without pursuing a full master's degree. The certificate requires a total of 15 graduate credit hours—four courses in the graduate public administration program and one elective that may be public administration or from elsewhere within the school or University. The required courses are Principles of Nonprofit Management, Fund Development for Nonprofit Organizations, Financial Management for Nonprofit Organizations, and Nonprofit Law, Governance and Ethics.
	Through a cooperative arrangement with the L. Douglas Wilder School of Government and Public Affairs, M.S.W. students may also pursue the certificate. These students are required to complete three nonprofit courses: Fund Development for the Nonprofit Sector, Financial Management for Nonprofit Organizations, and Nonprofit Law, Governance and Ethics.
Research Facilities	VCU libraries provide a combined capacity of more than 1.7 million volumes and 10,200 periodical titles and an online bibliographic search service accessing hundreds of databases. In addition, the Virginia State and Richmond Public Libraries are within walking distance of both VCU campuses. Academic Computing provides a variety of microcomputer, minicomputer, and mainframe computing services to support the research and instructional endeavors of its faculty members and students, including consultation, instruction, and computer acquisition.
	The Center for Public Policy is a multidisciplinary policy studies organization with divisions that provide a wide variety of services, including professional and leadership training, survey design and implementation, economic research, transportation safety planning, and education policy analysis. The Office of Public Policy Training augments the public service mission of the Center for Public Policy by addressing the special training, research, and technical assistance needs of government and nonprofit organizations in the commonwealth. The office fulfills its missions by designing and arranging a variety of activities such as training programs, conferences, colloquia, seminars, technical consultations, data management and analysis, and survey research. The Commonwealth Education Policy Institute is a joint venture between the School of Education and Center for Public Policy. The institute is committed to the expansion of public dialogue and participation in the important issues facing K–12 public education. The institute provides research, analysis, training, and service to education policy makers, school systems, citizens, and the larger school community.
	The Survey and Evaluation Research Laboratory (SERL) conducts surveys and provides research and evaluation support for governmental units, public and private nonprofit agencies, and the mass media and for VCU's faculty and administration.
	The Virginia Center for Urban Development strives to enhance the development of Virginia's urban areas. The center's staff is available to conduct sophisticated statistical modeling, economic impact modeling using the IMPLAN model, and geo-mapping using Atlas Geographic Information System for business and government clients.
	The Grace E. Harris Leadership Institute helps to promote the development of current and emerging leaders in academic institutions; other public, private, and nonprofit organizations; and communities.
Financial Aid	The L. Douglas Wilder School of Government and Public Affairs offers a limited amount of financial assistance for graduate students, including teaching and research assistantships as well as scholarships and fellowships for tuition support. The Richmond area also provides ample opportunity for paid internships. Students may apply for need-based assistance with the University's Financial Aid Office. Current information on financial aid programs, policies, and procedures is available at http://www.vcu.edu/enroll/finaid.
Cost of Study	For full-time study (9–15 credits) in 2007–08, Virginia residents pay tuition and fees of $4452 per semester; nonresidents, $8876 per semester. For part-time study, Virginia residents pay tuition and fees of $465 per hour; nonresidents, $954 per hour. Some programs require additional fees. On the Medical College of Virginia (MCV) campus, tuition, fees, and other expenses vary in the medicine, pharmacy, nurse anesthesia, dentistry, and School of Allied Health programs.
Living and Housing Costs	Graduate student housing is available on both the MCV campus and the academic campus of Virginia Commonwealth University. Many graduate students live in off-campus housing, which is reasonably priced and readily available in a variety of styles and settings in nearby residential areas or within easy commuting distance. On- and off-campus housing information is available on the Web at http://www.housing.vcu.edu/.
Student Group	VCU enrolls 30,452 students, 7,611 of whom are graduate students. More than 200 clubs and organizations reflect the diverse social, recreational, educational, political, and religious interests of the student body.
Location	Richmond is Virginia's capital and a major East Coast financial and manufacturing center that offers students a wide range of cultural, educational, and recreational activities. Richmond is located in central Virginia at the intersection of Interstates 95 and 64, 2 hours south of Washington, D.C., and nestled between the Blue Ridge Mountains and the Atlantic coast. The Richmond region is easily accessible by plane, car, and train. With nearly 1 million residents, the historic city of Richmond combines big-city offerings with small-town hospitality. Applicants are encouraged to explore http://www.visit.richmond.com/ for more information on the city.
The University	VCU is a state-supported coeducational university with a graduate school, a major teaching hospital, and twelve academic and professional units that offer fifty-two undergraduate, twenty-two postbaccalaureate certificate, sixty-five master's, six post-master's certificate, and twenty-nine Ph.D. programs. VCU also offers M.D., D.D.S., D.P.T., and Pharm.D. programs as well as cooperative degree programs with other major Virginia colleges and universities. VCU has one of the largest evening colleges in the United States. The academic campus is located in Richmond's historic Fan District. The health sciences campus and hospital are located 2 miles east in the downtown business district. A University bus service provides free intercampus transportation for faculty members and students.
	With more than $211 million in annual research funding, Virginia Commonwealth University is classified as one of the nation's top research universities by the Carnegie Foundation for the Advancement of Teaching. More than 29,000 undergraduate, certificate, graduate, post-master's, professional, and doctoral students are enrolled in 162 academic programs, forty of which are unique in the commonwealth of Virginia. The faculty members represent the finest American and international graduate institutions and enhance the University's position among the important institutions of higher learning in the United States and the world via their work in the classroom, laboratory, studio, and clinic and in their scholarly publications.
Applying	Admission procedures and program requirements are detailed in the *Graduate Bulletin*. Application deadlines and materials, including the application and the *Graduate Bulletin*, are available online at the Graduate School Web site at http://www.graduate.vcu.edu. Virginia Commonwealth University is an equal opportunity/affirmative action institution providing access to education and employment without regard to age, race, color, national origin, gender, religion, sexual orientation, veteran's status, political affiliation, or disability.
Correspondence and Information	Janet Hutchinson, Coordinator Scherer Hall, Room 111 L. Douglas Wilder School of Government and Public Affairs Virginia Commonwealth University 923 West Franklin Street 923 West Franklin Street Richmond, Virginia 23284 Phone: 804-828-8041 E-mail: jhutch@vcu.edu Web site: http://www.pubapps.vcu.edu/gov/academics

Virginia Commonwealth University

THE FACULTY AND THEIR RESEARCH

John M. Aughenbaugh, Instructor; M.A., Virginia Tech. Administrative philosophy of retired Supreme Court Justice Byron White; judicialization of public administration management processes, particularly related to reform of public institutions; organizational dynamics of courts and their effect on public administration; application of performance measure for local government administration.

Deborah Brock, Assistant Professor and Associate Director for Operations; Ph.D., Virginia Commonwealth. Public human resource interests, job satisfaction, public financial management.

David Farmer, Professor; D.P.A., Nova.

Quintet: Introduction to post-traditional theory. *Int. J. Public Administration* 28(11&12):903–8, 2005.

Susan Gooden, Associate Professor; Ph.D., Syracuse. Social policy and social equity.

Examining the implementation of welfare reform by race: Do Blacks, Hispanics and Whites report similar experiences with welfare agencies? *Rev. Black Political Econ.* 32(2):27–53, 2004.

Farrah Stone Graham, Research Associate, Center for Public Policy; M.P.A., Virginia Commonwealth. Higher education policy, specifically issues of access and the college choice decision.

The energy policy act: A missed opportunity. *PA Times* 28(10), November 2005. With Flippen.

Robert D. Holsworth, Professor and Dean of the College of Humanities and Sciences; Ph.D., North Carolina at Chapel Hill. American politics and culture.

Janet R. Hutchinson, Director of the Public Administration Program in the L. Douglas Wilder School of Government and Public Affairs; Ph.D., Pittsburgh. Social policy affecting women, families, and children; issues of knowledge use and the dynamics of policy making in state and federal government.

Dale Jones, Associate Professor and Director of the National Homeland Security Project; Ph.D., Syracuse. Assessment of state government homeland security programs, interagency collaboration, and leadership and management for homeland security.

Michael D. Pratt, Professor; Ph.D., Kansas. Work in experimental economics directed to public choice theory, controls for and analysis of risk aversion, and industrial organization.

Mark C. Williams, Assistant Professor and Director of the Commonwealth Poll; Ph.D., Virginia Commonwealth. Research methods and statistics.

Blue Wooldridge, Associate Professor; D.P.A., USC. Strategies for increasing the effectiveness of management education and training, issues in privatization, trends in local government revenues, procedure and content of local government budgets, strategies to improve productivity, implications for public managers of the increased diversity of the workforce.

Preparing public administrators for an era of globalisation and decentralisation: A strategic-contingency approach. *Int. Rev. Administrative Sci.* 70(2):385–403, 2004.

Section 16
Organizational Studies

This section contains a directory of institutions offering graduate work in organizational studies, followed by in-depth entries submitted by institutions that chose to prepare detailed program descriptions. Additional information about programs listed in the directory but not augmented by an in-depth entry may be obtained by writing directly to the dean of a graduate school or chair of a department at the address given in the directory.

For programs offering related work, see also in this book Business Administration and Management, Human Resources, and Industrial and Manufacturing Management. In Book 2, see Communication and Media and Public, Regional, and Industrial Affairs.

CONTENTS

Organizational Behavior

Benedictine University, Graduate Programs, Program in Management and Organizational Behavior, Lisle, IL 60532-0900. Offers MS, MBA/MS, MPH/MS. Part-time and evening/weekend programs available. *Faculty:* 1 full-time (0 women), 15 part-time/adjunct (7 women). *Students:* 157 (88 women); includes 22 minority (20 African Americans, 2 Hispanic Americans) 2 international. Average age 40. 56 applicants, 96% accepted, 9 enrolled. In 2006, 49 degrees awarded. *Entrance requirements:* For master's, GMAT. Additional exam requirements/recommendations for international students: Required—TOEFL (minimum score 550 paper-based; 213 computer-based). *Application deadline:* For fall admission, 9/1 for domestic students; for winter admission, 12/1 for domestic students; for spring admission, 2/15 for domestic students. Applications are processed on a rolling basis. Application fee: $40. Electronic applications accepted. *Expenses:* Tuition: Full-time $12,150; part-time $450 per credit hour. *Financial support:* Career-related internships or fieldwork and health care benefits available. Support available to part-time students. *Faculty research:* Organizational change, transformation, development, learning organizations, career transitions for academics. *Unit head:* Dr. Peter F. Sorensen, Director, 630-829-6220, Fax: 630-960-1126, E-mail: psorensen@ben.edu. *Application contact:* Kari Gibbons, Director, Admissions, 630-829-6200, Fax: 630-829-6584, E-mail: kgibbons@ben.edu.

Bernard M. Baruch College of the City University of New York, Zicklin School of Business, Department of Management, New York, NY 10010-5585. Offers entrepreneurship (MBA); general management and policy (MBA); human resources management (MBA); management planning systems (PhD); management science (MBA); organization and policy studies (PhD); organizational behavior (MBA). Part-time and evening/weekend programs available. *Faculty:* 38 full-time (10 women), 41 part-time/adjunct (6 women). *Students:* 30 full-time (14 women), 117 part-time (52 women); includes 37 minority (17 African Americans, 14 Asian Americans or Pacific Islanders, 6 Hispanic Americans). In 2006, 39 master's, 1 doctorate awarded. *Degree requirements:* For doctorate, thesis/dissertation, comprehensive exam. *Entrance requirements:* For master's, GMAT, 2 letters of recommendation, resumé, 2 years of work experience; for doctorate, GMAT. Additional exam requirements/recommendations for international students: Required—TOEFL (minimum score 590 paper-based; 243 computer-based), TWE. *Application deadline:* For fall admission, 5/31 for domestic students, 4/30 for international students; for spring admission, 10/31 for domestic and international students. Application fee: $125. *Financial support:* Fellowships, research assistantships, teaching assistantships, career-related internships or fieldwork, Federal Work-Study, scholarships/grants, and unspecified assistantships available. Financial award application deadline: 4/30; financial award applicants required to submit FAFSA. *Unit head:* Harry M. Rosen, Chairman, 646-312-3620, Fax: 646-312-3621, E-mail: harry_rosen@baruch.cuny.edu. *Application contact:* Frances Murphy, Office of Graduate Admissions, 646-312-1300, Fax: 646-312-1301, E-mail: zicklingradadmissions@baruch.cuny.edu.

Boston College, The Carroll School of Management, Department of Organization Studies, Chestnut Hill, MA 02467-3800. Offers PhD. *Faculty:* 11 full-time (4 women). *Students:* 29 full-time (11 women); includes 2 minority (1 American Indian/Alaska Native, 1 Asian American or Pacific Islander), 6 international. Average age 32. 40 applicants, 10% accepted, 4 enrolled. In 2006, 4 doctorates awarded. *Degree requirements:* For doctorate, thesis/dissertation, teaching requirement, comprehensive exam. *Entrance requirements:* For doctorate, GMAT or GRE, letters of recommendation, resumé, transcripts. Additional exam requirements/recommendations for international students: Required—TOEFL. *Application deadline:* For spring admission, 2/1 for domestic and international students. Application fee: $50. *Financial support:* In 2006–07, 16 research assistantships with full tuition reimbursements (averaging $23,000 per year) were awarded. Financial award application deadline: 3/1; financial award applicants required to submit FAFSA. *Faculty research:* Organizational transformation, mergers and acquisitions, managerial effectiveness, organizational change, organizational structure. *Unit head:* Dr. Candace Jones, Associate Professor; PhD Program Chair. *Application contact:* Jean Passavant, Department Secretary, 617-552-0450, Fax: 617-552-4230, E-mail: jean.passavant@bc.edu.

Boston University, School of Management, Doctorate in Business Administration Program, Boston, MA 02215. Offers accounting (DBA); information systems (DBA); management policy (DBA); marketing (DBA); operations management (DBA); organizational behavior (DBA). *Students:* 48 full-time (26 women); includes 4 minority (all Asian Americans or Pacific Islanders), 24 international. Average age 35. 120 applicants, 17% accepted, 10 enrolled. In 2006, 8 degrees awarded. *Degree requirements:* For doctorate, thesis/dissertation. *Entrance requirements:* For doctorate, GMAT or GRE General Test. *Application deadline:* For fall admission, 1/31 for domestic students. Application fee: $125. *Expenses:* Tuition: Full-time $33,330; part-time $1,042 per credit. Required fees: $462; $40. *Financial support:* Career-related internships or fieldwork, Federal Work-Study, institutionally sponsored loans, scholarships/grants, and tuition waivers available. Support available to part-time students. Financial award applicants required to submit FAFSA. *Unit head:* Dr. Sushil Vachani, Director, 617-353-4875, E-mail: dba@bu.edu. *Application contact:* Hayden Estrada, Assistant Dean, Admissions, 617-353-2670, Fax: 617-353-7368, E-mail: dba@bu.edu.

California Lutheran University, Graduate Studies, School of Business, Thousand Oaks, CA 91360-2787. Offers finance (MBA); healthcare management (MBA); international business (MBA); management information systems (MBA); marketing (MBA); organizational behavior (MBA); small business/entrepreneurship (MBA). Evening/weekend programs available. *Entrance requirements:* For master's, GMAT, interview, minimum GPA of 3.0. Expenses: Contact institution.

Carnegie Mellon University, College of Humanities and Social Sciences, Department of Social and Decision Sciences, Pittsburgh, PA 15213-3891. Offers behavioral decision theory (PhD); organization science (PhD); social and decision science (PhD). Terminal master's awarded for partial completion of doctoral program. *Degree requirements:* For doctorate, thesis/dissertation, research paper, comprehensive exam. *Entrance requirements:* For doctorate, GRE General Test. Additional exam requirements/recommendations for international students: Required—TOEFL. Electronic applications accepted. *Faculty research:* Organization theory, political science, sociology, technology studies.

Carnegie Mellon University, Tepper School of Business, Organizational Behavior and Theory Program, Pittsburgh, PA 15213-3890. Offers PhD. *Degree requirements:* For doctorate, thesis/dissertation. *Entrance requirements:* For doctorate, GMAT or GRE General Test. Additional exam requirements/recommendations for international students: Required—TOEFL. *Faculty research:* Negotiation, organizational learning, interorganizational relations and strategy, group process and performance, communication process and electronic media, group goal setting, uncertainty in organizations, creation and effect of institutions and psychological contracts.

Case Western Reserve University, Weatherhead School of Management, Department of Organizational Behavior and Analysis, Cleveland, OH 44106. Offers MBA, MPOD, MS. Part-time and evening/weekend programs available. *Faculty:* 12 full-time (5 women), 4 part-time/adjunct (2 women). *Students:* 44 full-time (32 women), 13 part-time (9 women); includes 3 minority (1 African American, 1 American Indian/Alaska Native, 1 Hispanic American). Average age 28. In 2006, 47 master's awarded. *Entrance requirements:* For master's, GMAT. *Application deadline:* For fall admission, 4/15 priority date for domestic students. Applications are processed on a rolling basis. Application fee: $50. *Financial support:* Career-related internships or fieldwork, Federal Work-Study, institutionally sponsored loans, and tuition waivers (full and partial) available. Financial award application deadline: 5/1. *Faculty research:* Social innovation in global management, competency-based learning, life-long learning, organizational theory, organizational change. *Unit head:* David L. Cooperrider, Chairman, 216-368-2055, Fax: 216-368-4785, E-mail: reb2@po.cwru.edu. *Application contact:* Deborah L Bibb, Admissions Coordinator, 216-368-2030, Fax: 216-368-5548, E-mail: deborah.bibb@case.edu.

Columbia College, Graduate Programs, Department of Human Relations, Columbia, SC 29203-5998. Offers human behavior and conflict management (MA); interpersonal relations/conflict management (Certificate); organizational behavior/conflict management (Certificate). Part-time and evening/weekend programs available. Postbaccalaureate distance learning degree programs offered (minimal on-campus study). *Faculty:* 1 (woman) full-time, 3 part-time/adjunct (2 women). *Students:* Average age 40. 91 applicants, 64% accepted, 50 enrolled. In 2006, 21 degrees awarded. *Degree requirements:* For master's, thesis, practicum. *Entrance requirements:* For master's, GRE General Test, MAT, 2 letters of recommendation, valid teaching certificate, minimum GPA of 3.2. Additional exam requirements/recommendations for international students: Required—TOEFL. *Application deadline:* For fall admission, 7/15 priority date for domestic students, 7/15 for international students. Applications are processed on a rolling basis. Application fee: $50. Electronic applications accepted. *Expenses: Contact institution. Financial support:* Available to part-time students. Application deadline: 7/1; *Faculty research:* Envisioning and the resolution of conflict, environmental conflict resolution, crisis negotiation. *Unit head:* Dr. Elaine Ferraro, Chair, 803-786-3687, Fax: 803-786-3790, E-mail: eferraro@colacoll.edu. *Application contact:* Carolyn Emeneker, Director of Graduate School and Evening College Admissions, 803-786-3766, Fax: 803-786-3674, E-mail: emeneker@colacoll.edu.

Cornell University, Graduate School, Graduate Field of Management, Ithaca, NY 14853-0001. Offers accounting (PhD); behavioral decision theory (PhD); finance (PhD); marketing (PhD); organizational behavior (PhD); production and operations management (PhD). *Accreditation:* AACSB. *Faculty:* 57 full-time (11 women). *Students:* 38 full-time (14 women); includes 2 minority (both Asian Americans or Pacific Islanders), 20 international. Average age 31. 457 applicants, 5% accepted, 8 enrolled. In 2006, 4 doctorates awarded. *Degree requirements:* For doctorate, thesis/dissertation, comprehensive exam. *Entrance requirements:* For doctorate, GMAT or GRE General Test. Additional exam requirements/recommendations for international students: Required—TOEFL (minimum score 600 paper-based; 250 computer-based). *Application deadline:* For fall admission, 1/3 for domestic students. Application fee: $60. Electronic applications accepted. *Expenses: Contact institution.* Full-time tuition and fees vary according to program. *Financial support:* In 2006–07, 37 students received support, including 2 fellowships with full tuition reimbursements available, 31 research assistantships with full tuition reimbursements available, 4 teaching assistantships with full tuition reimbursements available; institutionally sponsored loans, scholarships/grants, health care benefits, tuition waivers (full and partial), and unspecified assistantships also available. Financial award applicants required to submit FAFSA. *Faculty research:* Operations and manufacturing. *Unit head:* Director of Graduate Studies, 607-255-3669. *Application contact:* Graduate Field Assistant, 607-255-9431, E-mail: js_phd@cornell.edu.

Cornell University, Graduate School, Graduate Fields of Industrial and Labor Relations, Ithaca, NY 14853-0001. Offers collective bargaining, labor law and labor history (MILR, MPS, MS, PhD); economic and social statistics (MILR); human resource studies (MILR, MPS, MS, PhD); industrial and labor relations problems (MILR, MPS, MS, PhD); international and comparative labor (MILR, MPS, MS, PhD); labor economics (MILR, MPS, MS, PhD); organizational behavior (MILR, MPS, MS, PhD); statistics (MPS, MS, PhD), including applied statistics (MPS), biometry (MS, PhD), decision theory (MS, PhD), economic and social statistics (MS, PhD), engineering statistics (MS, PhD), experimental design (MS, PhD), mathematical statistics (MS, PhD), probability (MS, PhD), sampling (MS, PhD), statistical computing (MS, PhD), stochastic processes (MS, PhD). *Faculty:* 50 full-time (11 women). *Students:* 127 full-time (75 women); includes 23 minority (10 African Americans, 7 Asian Americans or Pacific Islanders, 6 Hispanic Americans), 45 international. Average age 31. 214 applicants, 30% accepted, 51 enrolled. In 2006, 69 master's, 8 doctorates awarded. *Degree requirements:* For master's, thesis (MS); for doctorate, thesis/dissertation, teaching experience, comprehensive exam. *Entrance requirements:* For master's and doctorate, GMAT or GRE General Test, 2 academic recommendations. Additional exam requirements/recommendations for international students: Required—TOEFL (minimum score 550 paper-based; 213 computer-based). Application fee: $60. Electronic applications accepted. *Expenses: Contact institution.* Full-time tuition and fees vary according to program. *Financial support:* In 2006–07, 82 students received support, including 28 fellowships with full tuition reimbursements available, 27 research assistantships with full tuition reimbursements available, 27 teaching assistantships with full tuition reimbursements available; institutionally sponsored loans, scholarships/grants, health care benefits, tuition waivers (full and partial), and unspecified assistantships also available. Financial award applicants required to submit FAFSA. *Unit head:* Director of Graduate Studies, 607-255-1522. *Application contact:* Graduate Field Assistant, 607-255-1522, E-mail: ilrgradapplicant@cornell.edu.

Drexel University, LeBow College of Business, Program in Business Administration, Philadelphia, PA 19104-2875. Offers business administration (MBA, PhD, APC), including accounting (MBA, PhD), decision sciences (PhD), economics (MBA, PhD), finance (MBA, PhD), legal studies (MBA), management (MBA), marketing (MBA, PhD), organizational sciences (PhD), quantitative methods (MBA), strategic management (PhD). *Accreditation:* AACSB. Part-time and evening/weekend programs available. Postbaccalaureate distance learning degree programs offered (minimal on-campus study). Terminal master's awarded for partial completion of doctoral program. *Entrance requirements:* For master's, GMAT, minimum GPA of 2.75; for doctorate, GMAT. Additional exam requirements/recommendations for international students: Required—TOEFL. Electronic applications accepted. *Faculty research:* Decision support systems, individual and group behavior, operations research, techniques and strategy.

Fairleigh Dickinson University, College at Florham, Maxwell Becton College of Arts and Sciences, Department of Psychology, Program in Organizational Behavior, Madison, NJ 07940-1099. Offers organizational behavior (MA); organizational leadership (Certificate). *Students:* 2 full-time (both women), 15 part-time (8 women), 1 international. Average age 34. 2 applicants, 100% accepted, 1 enrolled. In 2006, 5 degrees awarded. Application fee: $40. *Unit head:* Dr. Diane Wentworth, Chairperson, Department of Psychology, 973-443-8548, Fax: 973-443-8562.

The George Washington University, School of Business, Department of Management Science, Washington, DC 20052. Offers human resources management (MBA); information systems management (MBA); logistics, operations, and materials management (MBA); management and organization (PhD); management decision making (MBA, PhD); management information systems (MSIST); management of science, technology, and innovation (MBA); organizational behavior and development (MBA); project management (MS). *Accreditation:* AACSB. Part-time and evening/weekend programs available. *Degree requirements:* For doctorate, thesis/dissertation. *Entrance requirements:* For master's, GMAT; for doctorate, GMAT or GRE. Additional exam requirements/recommendations for international students: Required—TOEFL. *Faculty research:* Artificial intelligence, technological entrepreneurship, expert systems, strategic planning/management.

Georgia Institute of Technology, Graduate Studies and Research, College of Management, Program in Business Administration, Atlanta, GA 30332-0001. Offers accounting (MBA); e-commerce (Certificate); engineering entrepreneurship (MBA); entrepreneurship (Certificate); finance (MBA); information technology management (MBA); international business (MBA, Certificate); management of technology (Certificate); marketing (MBA); operations management (MBA); organizational behavior (MBA); strategic management (MBA). *Accreditation:* AACSB.

Georgia Institute of Technology, Graduate Studies and Research, College of Management, Program in Management, Atlanta, GA 30332-0001. Offers accounting (PhD); finance (PhD); information technology management (PhD); marketing (PhD); operations management (PhD); organizational behavior (PhD); quantitative and computational finance (MS); strategic management (PhD). *Accreditation:* AACSB. *Degree requirements:* For doctorate, thesis/dissertation, oral exams, comprehensive exam. *Entrance requirements:* For master's and doctorate, GMAT. Additional exam requirements/recommendations for international students: Required—TOEFL.

Faculty research: MIS, management of technology, international business, entrepreneurship, operations management.

Graduate School and University Center of the City University of New York, Graduate Studies, Program in Business, New York, NY 10016-4039. Offers accounting (PhD); behavioral science (PhD); finance (PhD); management planning systems (PhD). *Faculty:* 66 full-time (5 women). *Students:* 55 full-time (27 women); includes 7 minority (2 African Americans, 1 American Indian/Alaska Native, 2 Asian Americans or Pacific Islanders, 2 Hispanic Americans), 26 international. Average age 33. 74 applicants, 32% accepted, 11 enrolled. In 2006, 9 degrees awarded. *Degree requirements:* For doctorate, thesis/dissertation. *Entrance requirements:* For doctorate, GMAT, writing sample (15 pages). Additional exam requirements/recommendations for international students: Required—TOEFL. *Application deadline:* For fall admission, 1/15 for domestic students. Application fee: $125. Electronic applications accepted. *Financial support:* In 2006–07, 40 fellowships, 5 teaching assistantships were awarded; research assistantships, career-related internships or fieldwork, Federal Work-Study, institutionally sponsored loans, and tuition waivers (full and partial) also available. Financial award application deadline: 2/1; financial award applicants required to submit FAFSA. *Unit head:* Dr. Joseph Weintrop, Executive Officer, 646-312-3092, Fax: 646-312-3031.

Harvard University, Business School, Doctoral Programs in Management, Boston, MA 02163. Offers business administration (DBA); business economics (PhD); health policy management (PhD); information and technology management (PhD); organizational behavior (PhD). *Degree requirements:* For doctorate, thesis/dissertation, comprehensive exam (for some programs). *Entrance requirements:* For doctorate, GRE General Test or GMAT. Additional exam requirements/recommendations for international students: Required—TOEFL. *Expenses:* Tuition: Full-time $30,275. Full-time tuition and fees vary according to program and student level.

Harvard University, Graduate School of Arts and Sciences and Doctoral Programs in Management, Committee on Organizational Behavior, Cambridge, MA 02138. Offers PhD. *Students:* 23 full-time (12 women). 115 applicants, 6% accepted. In 2006, 3 degrees awarded. *Entrance requirements:* For doctorate, GRE General Test or GMAT, major in psychology or sociology, course work in statistics or mathematics. Additional exam requirements/recommendations for international students: Required—TOEFL. *Application deadline:* For fall admission, 12/30 for domestic students. Application fee: $60. *Expenses:* Tuition: Full-time $30,275. Full-time tuition and fees vary according to program and student level. *Financial support:* Fellowships, research assistantships, teaching assistantships, career-related internships or fieldwork, Federal Work-Study, and institutionally sponsored loans available. Financial award application deadline: 12/30. *Unit head:* Deb Hoss, Financial and Student Services Manager, 617-495-6101. *Application contact:* Office of Admissions and Financial Aid, 617-495-5315.

John Jay College of Criminal Justice of the City University of New York, Graduate Studies, Programs in Criminal Justice, New York, NY 10019-1093. Offers criminal justice (MA, PhD); criminology and deviance (PhD); forensic psychology (PhD); forensic science (PhD); law and philosophy (PhD); organizational behavior (PhD); public policy (PhD). Part-time and evening/weekend programs available. Terminal master's awarded for partial completion of doctoral program. *Degree requirements:* For master's, thesis or alternative; for doctorate, one foreign language, thesis/dissertation. *Entrance requirements:* For master's, GRE General Test, minimum B average; for doctorate, GRE General Test. Additional exam requirements/recommendations for international students: Required—TOEFL (minimum score 500 paper-based; 173 computer-based).

Leadership Institute of Seattle, School of Applied Behavioral Science, Consulting and Coaching in Organizations Track, Kenmore, WA 98028-4966. Offers MA. *Faculty:* 10 full-time (6 women), 5 part-time/adjunct (2 women). *Students:* 48 full-time. Average age 40. 50 applicants, 98% accepted, 40 enrolled. In 2006, 19 degrees awarded. *Degree requirements:* For master's, thesis (for some programs), oral exams. *Entrance requirements:* For master's, bachelor's degree from an accredited college or university. *Application deadline:* Applications are processed on a rolling basis. Application fee: $65. *Expenses:* Tuition: Full-time $14,560. Required fees: $3,700. *Financial support:* In 2006–07, 32 students received support. Career-related internships or fieldwork, Federal Work-Study, and scholarships/grants available. Financial award applicants required to submit FAFSA. *Faculty research:* Cross-functional work teams, communication, management authority, employee influence, systems theory. *Unit head:* Dr. Shelley Drogin, Head, 425-939-8181, Fax: 425-939-8110, E-mail: sdrogin@lios.org. *Application contact:* Scott Harris, Director, Academic Admissions, 425-939-8124, Fax: 425-939-8110, E-mail: sharris@lios.org.

Lindenwood University, Graduate Programs, Division of Management, St. Charles, MO 63301-1695. Offers accounting (MBA, MS); business administration (MBA); entrepreneurial studies (MBA); finance (MBA, MS); human resource management (MBA); human resources (MS); international business (MBA, MS); management (MBA, MS); management information systems (MBA, MS); managing business to business (MA); managing human resources (MA); managing international business (MA); managing investment management (MA); managing leadership (MA); managing marketing (MA); managing organizational behavior (MA); managing sales (MA); managing, training and development (MA); marketing (MBA, MS); nonprofit administration (MA); public management (MBA, MS); sport management (MA). Part-time and evening/weekend programs available. *Faculty:* 38 full-time (15 women), 20 part-time/adjunct (5 women). *Students:* 177 full-time (78 women), 138 part-time (67 women); includes 43 minority (27 African Americans, 4 American Indian/Alaska Native, 6 Asian Americans or Pacific Islanders, 6 Hispanic Americans), 73 international. Average age 30. In 2006, 159 degrees awarded. *Degree requirements:* For master's, thesis (for some programs). *Entrance requirements:* For master's, interview, minimum GPA of 3.0. Additional exam requirements/recommendations for international students: Required—TOEFL (minimum score 550 paper-based; 173 computer-based). *Application deadline:* For fall admission, 7/30 priority date for domestic students, 9/30 priority date for international students; for winter admission, 12/30 priority date for domestic and international students; for spring admission, 3/30 priority date for domestic and international students. Applications are processed on a rolling basis. Application fee: $30 ($100 for international students). Electronic applications accepted. *Expenses:* Tuition: Part-time $340 per credit hour. Tuition and fees vary according to course level, course load, degree level and program. *Financial support:* Career-related internships or fieldwork, Federal Work-Study, institutionally sponsored loans, and tuition waivers (partial) available. Financial award application deadline: 6/30; financial award applicants required to submit FAFSA. *Unit head:* Ed Morris, Dean, 636-949-4832, Fax: 636-949-4910, E-mail: emorris@lindenwood.edu. *Application contact:* Brett Barger, Dean Adult, Corporate and Graduate Admissions, 636-949-4366, Fax: 636-949-4109, E-mail: bbarger@lindenwood.edu.

New York University, Leonard N. Stern School of Business, Department of Management and Organizations, New York, NY 10012-1019. Offers management organizations (MBA); organization theory (PhD); organizational behavior (PhD); strategy (PhD). *Expenses:* Tuition: Part-time $1,080 per unit. Required fees: $56 per unit. $329 per term. Tuition and fees vary according to program. *Faculty research:* Strategic management, managerial cognition, interpersonal processes, conflict and negotiation.

Northwestern University, The Graduate School, Interdepartmental Degree Programs and Kellogg School of Management, Program in Management and Organizations and Sociology, Evanston, IL 60208. Offers PhD. Program requires admission to both The Graduate School and the Kellogg Graduate School of Management. *Degree requirements:* For doctorate, thesis/dissertation, comprehensive exam, registration. *Entrance requirements:* For doctorate, GRE General Test. Additional exam requirements/recommendations for international students: Required—TOEFL. Electronic applications accepted. *Faculty research:* Strategic alliances and organizational competitiveness, institutional change and the information of industries, social capital and the creation of financial capital, negotiation, organizational networks, diversity.

Northwestern University, The Graduate School, School of Education and Social Policy, Program in Learning and Organizational Change, Evanston, IL 60208. Offers MS. Part-time and evening/weekend programs available. *Faculty:* 1 (woman) full-time, 17 part-time/adjunct (10 women). *Students:* 11 full-time (6 women), 48 part-time (38 women); includes 14 minority (8 African Americans, 5 Asian Americans or Pacific Islanders, 1 Hispanic American), 3 international. Average age 32. 36 applicants, 56% accepted, 19 enrolled. In 2006, 11 degrees awarded. *Median time to degree:* Master's–1.5 years full-time, 2.5 years part-time. *Degree requirements:* For master's, thesis, practicum. *Entrance requirements:* For master's, GRE/GMAT (recommended), letters of recommendation. Additional exam requirements/recommendations for international students: Required—TOEFL (minimum score 600 paper-based; 250 computer-based); Recommended—IELTS (minimum score 7). *Application deadline:* For fall admission, 8/1 priority date for domestic and international students; for winter admission, 12/1 priority date for domestic students; for spring admission, 3/1 priority date for domestic students. Applications are processed on a rolling basis. Application fee: $75. Electronic applications accepted. *Faculty research:* Strategic change, learning and performance in the workplace, leadership development, cognitive design, knowledge management. *Unit head:* Dr. Kimberly Scott, Director, 847-467-3102. *Application contact:* Leslie Zimmerman, Program Coordinator, 847-491-7376, Fax: 847-491-3957, E-mail: l-zimmerman@northwestern.edu.

Oral Roberts University, School of Business, Tulsa, OK 74171-0001. Offers accounting (MBA); finance (MBA); international business (MBA); management (MBA); marketing (MBA); non-profit management (M Man, MBA); organizational dynamics (M Man); sales marketing (M Man). *Accreditation:* ACBSP. Part-time programs available. Postbaccalaureate distance learning degree programs offered (minimal on-campus study). *Faculty:* 9 full-time (2 women), 4 part-time/adjunct (2 women). *Students:* 33 full-time (18 women), 67 part-time (28 women); includes 28 minority (17 African Americans, 3 American Indian/Alaska Native, 6 Asian Americans or Pacific Islanders, 2 Hispanic Americans), 15 international. Average age 29. 69 applicants, 84% accepted, 33 enrolled. In 2006, 21 degrees awarded. *Degree requirements:* For master's, thesis optional. *Entrance requirements:* For master's, minimum GPA of 3.0. Additional exam requirements/recommendations for international students: Required—TOEFL (minimum score 550 paper-based; 213 computer-based). *Application deadline:* For fall admission, 7/1 priority date for domestic students, 5/1 priority date for international students; for spring admission, 12/1 priority date for domestic students, 10/1 priority date for international students. Applications are processed on a rolling basis. Application fee: $35. *Expenses:* Contact institution. *Financial support:* In 2006–07, 9 research assistantships (averaging $3,600 per year) were awarded; scholarships/grants and unspecified assistantships also available. Financial award application deadline: 6/1; financial award applicants required to submit FAFSA. *Faculty research:* Non-profit, international business and marketing. *Unit head:* Dr. Mark Lewandowski, Dean, 918-495-7040, Fax: 918-495-7876, E-mail: mlewandowski@oru.edu. *Application contact:* 918-495-6989, Fax: 918-495-7965, E-mail: alsc@oru.edu.

Phillips Graduate Institute, Program in Marriage and Family Therapy, Organizational Behavior and School Counseling, Encino, CA 91316-1509. Offers marital and family therapy (MA); organizational consulting (MA); school counseling (MA). Evening/weekend programs available. *Degree requirements:* For master's, thesis, comprehensive exam. *Entrance requirements:* For master's, minimum GPA of 2.5. *Faculty research:* Integration of interpersonal psychological theory, systems approach, firsthand experiential learning.

Polytechnic University, Brooklyn Campus, Department of Management, Major in Organizational Behavior, Brooklyn, NY 11201-2990. Offers MS. Part-time and evening/weekend programs available. *Students:* 18 full-time (12 women), 19 part-time (17 women); includes 13 minority (11 African Americans, 2 Asian Americans or Pacific Islanders), 5 international. Average age 32. 52 applicants, 100% accepted, 15 enrolled. In 2006, 12 degrees awarded. *Degree requirements:* For master's, thesis (for some programs), comprehensive exam (for some programs), registration. *Entrance requirements:* For master's, GMAT, minimum B average in undergraduate course work. Additional exam requirements/recommendations for international students: Required—TOEFL (minimum score 550 paper-based; 213 computer-based); Recommended—IELTS (minimum score 7). *Application deadline:* For fall admission, 7/15 priority date for domestic students, 4/1 priority date for international students; for spring admission, 12/15 priority date for domestic students, 10/1 priority date for international students. Applications are processed on a rolling basis. Application fee: $55. Electronic applications accepted. *Expenses:* Tuition: Full-time $17,784; part-time $988 per credit. *Financial support:* Applicants required to submit FAFSA. *Unit head:* Harold Kaufman, Director, 718-260-3485, Fax: 718-260-3874, E-mail: hkaufman@poly.edu.

Purdue University, Graduate School, Krannert School of Management, Department of Organizational Behavior and Human Resource Management, West Lafayette, IN 47907. Offers PhD. *Students:* 8 full-time (4 women); includes 1 minority (American Indian/Alaska Native), 4 international. Average age 26. 102 applicants, 2% accepted, 2 enrolled. In 2006, 2 degrees awarded. *Median time to degree:* Doctorate–4 years part-time. Of those who began their doctoral program in fall 1998, 100% received their degree in 8 years or less. *Degree requirements:* For doctorate, thesis/dissertation, comprehensive exam, registration. *Entrance requirements:* For doctorate, GMAT, GRE General Test. Additional exam requirements/recommendations for international students: Required—TOEFL (minimum score 575 paper-based; 233 computer-based; 77 iBT), IELTS (minimum score 7). *Application deadline:* For fall admission, 2/15 for domestic and international students. Application fee: $55. Electronic applications accepted. *Financial support:* In 2006–07, 8 students received support, including fellowships with partial tuition reimbursements available (averaging $16,800 per year), 6 research assistantships with partial tuition reimbursements available (averaging $16,800 per year), 2 teaching assistantships with partial tuition reimbursements available (averaging $16,800 per year); scholarships/grants and unspecified assistantships also available. Financial award application deadline: 2/15; financial award applicants required to submit FAFSA. *Faculty research:* Promotion and career development, organizational trust, leadership, negotiations, compensation and organizational rewards. *Unit head:* Dr. John M. Barron, Head, 765-494-4451, Fax: 765-494-1526. *Application contact:* Kelly Felty, Assistant Director of Administration for Doctoral Programs, 765-494-4375, Fax: 765-494-1526, E-mail: phd@krannert.purdue.edu.

Purdue University, Graduate School, Krannert School of Management, Program in Organizational Behavior and Human Resource Management, West Lafayette, IN 47907. Offers human resource management (MS). *Faculty:* 9 full-time (1 woman). *Students:* 49 full-time (32 women); includes 11 minority (7 African Americans, 1 Asian American or Pacific Islander, 3 Hispanic Americans), 14 international. Average age 28. 90 applicants, 50% accepted, 32 enrolled. In 2006, 25 degrees awarded. *Entrance requirements:* For master's, GMAT. Additional exam requirements/recommendations for international students: Required—TOEFL. *Application deadline:* For fall admission, 11/1 priority date for domestic students, 12/1 priority date for international students; for winter admission, 2/1 priority date for domestic students, 2/1 for international students; for spring admission, 5/1 priority date for domestic students. Applications are processed on a rolling basis. Application fee: $55. Electronic applications accepted. *Expenses:* Contact institution. *Financial support:* Fellowships with partial tuition reimbursements, research assistantships with partial tuition reimbursements, teaching assistantships with partial tuition reimbursements, career-related internships or fieldwork, tuition waivers (partial), and unspecified assistantships available. *Unit head:* Charles R. Johnson, Director, 765-496-3668, Fax: 765-494-9841, E-mail: cjohnson@mgmt.purdue.edu. *Application contact:* Carmen Castro-Rivera, Director of Admissions, 765-494-0773, Fax: 765-494-9841, E-mail: ccastror@purdue.edu.

Regions University, Graduate and Professional Programs, Montgomery, AL 36117. Offers behavioral leadership and management (MA); biblical studies (MA, D Min, PhD); Christian ministry (M Div); family therapy (D Min, PhD); leadership and management (MS); marriage and family therapy (M Div, MA); ministerial leadership (M Div, MS); pastoral counseling (M Div, MS); practical theology (MA); professional counseling (M Div, MA). *Accreditation:* ATS. Part-time and evening/weekend programs available. Postbaccalaureate distance learning degree programs offered (no on-campus study). *Degree requirements:* For M Div, comprehensive exam (for some programs); for master's, one foreign language, thesis (for some programs), comprehensive exam (for some programs); for doctorate, thesis/dissertation, comprehensive

Organizational Behavior

Regions University (continued)
exam (for some programs). *Entrance requirements:* For M Div, master's, and doctorate, GRE General Test or MAT. Additional exam requirements/recommendations for international students: Required—TOEFL. Electronic applications accepted. *Faculty research:* Homiletics, hermeneutics, ancient Near Eastern history.

Saybrook Graduate School and Research Center, Program in Psychology, Human Science and Organizational Systems, San Francisco, CA 94111-1920. Offers human science (MA, PhD), including consciousness and spirituality, individualized (PhD), organizational systems, social transformation; organizational systems (MA, PhD), including individualized (PhD), organizational systems; psychology (MA, PhD), including consciousness and spirituality, health studies, humanistic and transpersonal psychology, individualized (PhD), licensure track (MA), organizational systems, police and public safety psychology (PhD), social transformation. Postbaccalaureate distance learning degree programs offered (minimal on-campus study). *Faculty:* 15 full-time (5 women), 83 part-time/adjunct (34 women). *Students:* 479 full-time (333 women); includes 62 minority (30 African Americans, 1 American Indian/Alaska Native, 13 Asian Americans or Pacific Islanders, 18 Hispanic Americans), 18 international. Average age 43. 280 applicants, 52% accepted, 105 enrolled. In 2006, 28 master's, 43 doctorates awarded. Terminal master's awarded for partial completion of doctoral program. *Degree requirements:* For master's, thesis or alternative; for doctorate, thesis/dissertation. *Entrance requirements:* Additional exam requirements/recommendations for international students: Required—TOEFL. *Application deadline:* For fall admission, 6/1 priority date for domestic students; for spring admission, 12/16 priority date for domestic students. Application fee: $50. Electronic applications accepted. *Financial support:* In 2006–07, 335 students received support. Scholarships/grants available. Financial award applicants required to submit FAFSA. *Faculty research:* Humanistic theory, health studies, organizational systems, consciousness and spirituality, social transformation. Total annual research expenditures: $90,000. *Unit head:* Lorne Buchman, President, 800-825-4480, Fax: 415-433-9271. *Application contact:* Director of Admissions, 800-825-4480, Fax: 415-433-9271, E-mail: admissions@saybrook.edu.

Silver Lake College, Division of Graduate Studies, Program in Management and Organizational Behavior, Manitowoc, WI 54220-9319. Offers MS. Part-time and evening/weekend programs available. Postbaccalaureate distance learning degree programs offered (minimal on-campus study). *Faculty:* 19 part-time/adjunct (8 women). *Students:* 15 full-time (13 women), 54 part-time (35 women). Average age 35. 30 applicants, 67% accepted, 15 enrolled. In 2006, 39 degrees awarded. *Degree requirements:* For master's, thesis optional. *Entrance requirements:* For master's, interview, minimum undergraduate GPA of 3.0, writing sample, two letters of recommendation. Additional exam requirements/recommendations for international students: Required—TOEFL. *Application deadline:* For fall admission, 8/1 priority date for domestic students; for spring admission, 12/1 priority date for domestic students. Applications are processed on a rolling basis. Application fee: $35. Electronic applications accepted. *Expenses:* Tuition: Full-time $6,120; part-time $340 per credit. *Financial support:* Career-related internships or fieldwork, Federal Work-Study, and scholarships/grants available. Support available to part-time students. Financial award applicants required to submit FAFSA. *Unit head:* Suzanne Lawrence, Director- MOB Program, 920-686-6198, Fax: 920-684-9734, E-mail: law@silver.sl.edu. *Application contact:* Jamie Grant, Associate Director- Admissions, 800-236-4752 Ext. 186, Fax: 920-684-7082, E-mail: jgrant@silver.sl.edu.

Syracuse University, Martin J. Whitman School of Management, PhD Program in Business Administration, Syracuse, NY 13244. Offers accounting (PhD); finance (PhD); management information systems (PhD); managerial statistics (PhD); marketing (PhD); operations management (PhD); organizational behavior (PhD); strategy and human resources (PhD); supply chain management (PhD). *Faculty:* 71 full-time (16 women), 2 part-time/adjunct (1 woman). *Students:* 34 full-time (10 women); includes 1 minority (African American), 24 international. Average age 31. 89 applicants, 8% accepted, 4 enrolled. In 2006, 8 degrees awarded. *Degree requirements:* For doctorate, thesis/dissertation, summer research paper, comprehensive exam, registration. *Entrance requirements:* For doctorate, GMAT, 3 recommendations. Additional exam requirements/recommendations for international students: Required—TOEFL (minimum score 600 paper-based; 250 computer-based; 100 iBT). *Application deadline:* For fall admission, 1/30 priority date for domestic students. Applications are processed on a rolling basis. Application fee: $75. Electronic applications accepted. *Expenses:* Tuition: Full-time $16,920; part-time $940 per credit hour. Required fees: $930; $930 per year. *Financial support:* In 2006–07, 1 fellowship with full tuition reimbursement (averaging $19,000 per year), 26 teaching assistantships with full tuition reimbursements (averaging $16,500 per year) were awarded; research assistantships with full tuition reimbursements, health care benefits and unspecified assistantships also available. Financial award application deadline: 1/30. *Faculty research:* Marketing models, market microstructure, supply chain, auditing, corporate governance. *Unit head:* Dr. Ravi Dharwadkar, Director of the PhD Program, 315-443-3386, E-mail: rdharwad@syr.edu. *Application contact:* Shannon Hiemstra, Assistant Director for PhD and Research Programs, 315-443-3549, Fax: 315-443-3671, E-mail: srhiemst@syr.edu.

Towson University, Graduate School, Program in Organizational Change, Towson, MD 21252-0001. Offers CAS. *Faculty:* 7 full-time (3 women), 3 part-time/adjunct (1 woman). *Students:* 2 full-time (both women), 54 part-time (39 women); includes 15 minority (12 African Americans, 2 Asian Americans or Pacific Islanders, 1 Hispanic American). 55 applicants, 64% accepted, 10 enrolled. In 2006, 13 degrees awarded. *Entrance requirements:* For degree, GRE or MAT, 2 letters of recommendation, minimum GPA of 3.5. Additional exam requirements/recommendations for international students: Required—TOEFL (minimum score 550 paper-based; 213 computer-based). *Application deadline:* Applications are processed on a rolling basis. Application fee: $50. Electronic applications accepted. *Expenses:* Tuition, state resident: part-time $275 per unit. Tuition, nonresident: part-time $577 per unit. Required fees: $72 per unit. *Faculty research:* Leadership, school administration, change, social responsibility. *Unit head:* Dr. Roxana Marie Della Vecchia, Assistant Dean, 410-704-2422, Fax: 410-704-2733, E-mail: rdellavecchia@towson.edu. *Application contact:* 410-704-2501, Fax: 410-704-4675, E-mail: grads@towson.edu.

Universidad de las Americas, A.C., Program in International Organizations and Institutions, Mexico City, Mexico. Offers MA.

Université de Sherbrooke, Faculty of Administration, Program in Organizational Change and Intervention, Sherbrooke, QC J1K 2R1, Canada. Offers M Sc.

The University of British Columbia, Sauder School of Business, Doctoral Program in Commerce and Business Administration, Vancouver, BC V6T 1Z1, Canada. Offers accounting (PhD); finance (PhD); international business (PhD); management information systems (PhD); management science (PhD); marketing (PhD); organizational behavior (PhD); policy analysis and strategy (PhD); transportation and logistics (PhD); urban land economics (PhD). *Degree requirements:* For doctorate, thesis/dissertation, comprehensive exam. *Entrance requirements:* For doctorate, GMAT or GRE. Additional exam requirements/recommendations for international students: Required—TOEFL. Electronic applications accepted.

University of California, Berkeley, Graduate Division, Haas School of Business, Program in Business, Berkeley, CA 94720-1500. Offers accounting (PhD); business and public policy (PhD); finance (PhD); marketing (PhD); organizational behavior and industrial relations (PhD); real estate (PhD). *Accreditation:* AACSB. *Students:* 83 full-time (28 women); includes 17 minority (14 Asian Americans or Pacific Islanders, 3 Hispanic Americans), 33 international. Average age 30. 347 applicants, 16 enrolled. In 2006, 17 degrees awarded. *Median time to degree:* Of those who began their doctoral program in fall 1998, 88% received their degree in 8 years or less. *Degree requirements:* For doctorate, thesis/dissertation, oral exam, written preliminary exams, comprehensive exam. *Entrance requirements:* For doctorate, GMAT or GRE, minimum GPA of 3.0. Additional exam requirements/recommendations for international students: Required—TOEFL (minimum score 570 paper-based; 230 computer-based), IELTS (minimum score 7). *Application deadline:* For fall admission, 12/15 for domestic and international students. Application fee: $60 ($80 for international students). Electronic applications accepted. *Financial support:* Fellowships with full and partial tuition reimbursements, research assistantships with full and partial tuition reimbursements, teaching assistantships with full and partial tuition reimbursements, career-related internships or fieldwork, Federal Work-Study, scholarships/grants, health care benefits, tuition waivers (full), and unspecified assistantships available. Financial award application deadline: 12/15; financial award applicants required to submit FAFSA. *Unit head:* Miguel Villas-Boas, Director, 510-642-1409, Fax: 510-643-4255, E-mail: kimg@haas.berkeley.edu. *Application contact:* Kim Guilfoyle, Administrative Director, 510-642-3944, Fax: 510-643-4255, E-mail: kimg@haas.berkeley.edu.

University of Hartford, College of Arts and Sciences, Department of Psychology, Program in Organizational Behavior, West Hartford, CT 06117-1599. Offers MS. Part-time and evening/weekend programs available. *Faculty:* 1 (woman) full-time, 1 part-time/adjunct (0 women). *Students:* 2 full-time (both women), 19 part-time (12 women); includes 4 minority (2 African Americans, 2 Hispanic Americans), 1 international. Average age 33. 16 applicants, 88% accepted, 8 enrolled. In 2006, 10 degrees awarded. *Entrance requirements:* Additional exam requirements/recommendations for international students: Required—TOEFL (minimum score 550 paper-based; 213 computer-based). *Application deadline:* For fall admission, 7/1 for domestic students; for spring admission, 12/1 for domestic students. Applications are processed on a rolling basis. Application fee: $40 ($55 for international students). Electronic applications accepted. *Financial support:* In 2006–07, 1 research assistantship (averaging $2,000 per year), 1 teaching assistantship (averaging $2,550 per year) were awarded. *Unit head:* Dr. Jack Powell, Director, 860-768-4720, E-mail: powell@hartford.edu. *Application contact:* Reneé Murphy, Assistant Director of Graduate Admissions, 860-768-4371, Fax: 860-768-5160, E-mail: gettoknow@hartford.edu.

University of Hawaii at Manoa, Graduate Division, Shidler College of Business, Program in Business Administration, Honolulu, HI 96822. Offers Asian business studies (MBA); Chinese business studies (MBA); decision sciences (MBA); entrepreneurship (MBA); finance (MBA); finance and banking (MBA); human resources management (MBA); information management (MBA); information technology (MBA); international business (MBA); Japanese business studies (MBA); marketing (MBA); organizational behavior (MBA); organizational management (MBA); real estate (MBA); student-designed track (MBA). *Accreditation:* AACSB. Part-time programs available. *Faculty:* 48 full-time (9 women). *Students:* 207 full-time (77 women), 158 part-time (60 women); includes 93 minority (2 African Americans, 1 American Indian/Alaska Native, 88 Asian Americans or Pacific Islanders, 2 Hispanic Americans), 58 international. Average age 33. 235 applicants, 55% accepted, 68 enrolled. In 2006, 147 degrees awarded. *Degree requirements:* For master's, thesis optional. *Entrance requirements:* For master's, GMAT, minimum GPA of 3.0. Additional exam requirements/recommendations for international students: Required—TOEFL (minimum score 500 paper-based; 173 computer-based; 61 iBT). *Application deadline:* For fall admission, 5/1 for domestic and international students; for spring admission, 9/1 for domestic and international students. Application fee: $50. *Financial support:* In 2006–07, 7 research assistantships (averaging $17,409 per year), 3 teaching assistantships (averaging $14,028 per year) were awarded. *Application contact:* Ting Bui, Information Contact, 808-956-5565, Fax: 808-956-6889.

The University of North Carolina at Chapel Hill, Kenan-Flagler Business School, Doctoral Program in Business Administration, Chapel Hill, NC 27599. Offers accounting (PhD); finance (PhD); marketing (PhD); operations management (PhD); organizational behavior (PhD); strategy (PhD). *Accreditation:* AACSB. *Degree requirements:* For doctorate, thesis/dissertation. *Entrance requirements:* For doctorate, GMAT or GRE General Test. Electronic applications accepted. Expenses: Contact institution.

University of Oklahoma, Graduate College, College of Arts and Sciences, Department of Psychology, Program in Organizational Dynamics, Norman, OK 73019-0390. Offers MS. Part-time and evening/weekend programs available. *Students:* 9 full-time (5 women), 29 part-time (16 women); includes 8 minority (3 African Americans, 1 American Indian/Alaska Native, 4 Hispanic Americans), 2 international. 12 applicants, 75% accepted, 7 enrolled. In 2006, 8 degrees awarded. *Entrance requirements:* For master's, minimum GPA of 3.0 in last 60 hours of undergraduate course work. Additional exam requirements/recommendations for international students: Required—TOEFL (minimum score 550 paper-based; 213 computer-based). *Application deadline:* For fall admission, 1/1 priority date for domestic students, 4/1 for international students; for spring admission, 11/1 for domestic students, 9/1 for international students. Applications are processed on a rolling basis. Application fee: $40 ($90 for international students). *Expenses:* Tuition, state resident: full-time $3,180; part-time $133 per credit hour. Tuition, nonresident: full-time $11,347; part-time $473 per credit hour. Required fees: $1,729; $62 per credit hour. $117 per semester. Tuition and fees vary according to course load and program. *Financial support:* Tuition waivers (full) and unspecified assistantships available. Financial award application deadline: 3/1; financial award applicants required to submit FAFSA. *Faculty research:* Interdisciplinary collaboration, shared leadership, meta-analysis of validity generalization, knowledge information. *Application contact:* Dr. Brigette Steinheider, Assistant Professor, 918-660-3476, Fax: 918-660-3490, E-mail: bsteinheider@ou.edu.

University of Pennsylvania, School of Arts and Sciences, Graduate Group in Organizational Dynamics, Philadelphia, PA 19104. Offers MS. Part-time and evening/weekend programs available. *Degree requirements:* For master's, thesis. Electronic applications accepted.

University of Saskatchewan, College of Graduate Studies and Research, College of Commerce, Department of Industrial Relations and Organizational Behavior, Saskatoon, SK S7N 5A2, Canada. Offers M Sc. Part-time programs available. *Degree requirements:* For master's, thesis, registration. *Entrance requirements:* For master's, GMAT. Additional exam requirements/recommendations for international students: Required—TOEFL.

Organizational Management

Adler Graduate School, Program in Adlerian Studies, Richfield, MN 55423. Offers art therapy specialization (MA); clinical counseling track (MA); coaching and consulting in organizations (Certificate); management consulting and organizational leadership (MA); marriage and family track (MA); non-clinical Adlerian studies track (MA); personal and professional life coaching (Certificate); school counseling (MA). Part-time and evening/weekend programs available. *Faculty:* 4 full-time (1 woman), 36 part-time/adjunct (21 women). *Students:* Average age 37. 48 applicants, 98% accepted, 46 enrolled. In 2006, 37 degrees awarded. *Degree requirements:* For master's, thesis or alternative, 500-700 hour internship, depending on license choice. *Entrance requirements:* For master's, minimum undergraduate GPA of 3.0, 12 credits of course work in psychology or related field. *Application deadline:* For fall admission, 10/1 priority date for domestic students; for winter admission, 1/1 priority date for domestic students; for spring admission, 4/1 priority date for domestic students. Applications are processed on a rolling basis. Application fee: $50. *Financial support:* In 2006–07, 121 students received support. Career-related internships or fieldwork and tuition waivers available. Support available to part-time students. Financial award applicants required to submit FAFSA. *Unit head:* Dr. Dennis Rislove, President, 612-861-7554 Ext. 106, Fax: 612-861-7559, E-mail: rislove@alfredadler.edu. *Application contact:* Evelyn B. Haas, Director of Student Services and Admissions, 612-861-7554 Ext. 103, Fax: 612-861-7559, E-mail: ev@alfredadler.edu.

American International College, School of Continuing Education and Graduate Studies, Program in Organization Development, Springfield, MA 01109-3189. Offers MSOD. Part-time and evening/weekend programs available. *Faculty:* 2 full-time (1 woman), 5 part-time/adjunct (3 women). *Students:* 1 full-time (0 women), 8 part-time (5 women); includes 2 minority (both African Americans) Average age 39. In 2006, 2 degrees awarded. *Degree requirements:* For master's, thesis (for some programs), project or research report, comprehensive exam (for some programs), registration. *Entrance requirements:* Additional exam requirements/recommendations for international students: Required—TOEFL. *Application deadline:* For fall admission, 7/1 priority date for domestic and international students; for spring admission, 12/1 for domestic students, 12/1 priority date for international students. Applications are processed on a rolling basis. Application fee: $50. Electronic applications accepted. *Expenses:* Tuition: Part-time $585 per semester hour. Required fees: $100 per year. Full-time tuition and fees vary according to program. *Financial support:* Career-related internships or fieldwork and unspecified assistantships available. Support available to part-time students. Financial award application deadline: 4/1; financial award applicants required to submit FAFSA. *Application contact:* Keshawn Dodds, Associate Director of Graduate Admissions, 413-205-3549, Fax: 413-205-3911, E-mail: keshawn.dodds@aic.edu.

American University, School of Public Affairs, Department of Public Administration, Program in Organization Development, Washington, DC 20016-8001. Offers MSOD. *Students:* 1 (woman) full-time, 61 part-time (46 women); includes 14 minority (11 African Americans, 2 Asian Americans or Pacific Islanders, 1 Hispanic American), 1 international. Average age 38. In 2006, 47 degrees awarded. *Degree requirements:* For master's, comprehensive exam. *Entrance requirements:* For master's, GRE General Test, 2 years of related professional experience. *Application deadline:* For fall admission, 2/1 for domestic students; for spring admission, 10/1 for domestic students. Application fee: $50. *Expenses:* Tuition: Full-time $18,864; part-time $1,048 per credit. Required fees: $380. Tuition and fees vary according to program. *Financial support:* Application deadline: 2/1.

Antioch University Los Angeles, Graduate Programs, Program in Organizational Management, Culver City, CA 90230. Offers human resource development (MA); leadership (MA); organizational development (MA). Part-time and evening/weekend programs available. *Entrance requirements:* For master's, interview. Additional exam requirements/recommendations for international students: Required—TOEFL. *Faculty research:* Systems thinking and chaos theory, technology and organizational structure, nonprofit management, power and empowerment.

Antioch University New England, Graduate School, Department of Organization and Management, Program in Organization Development, Keene, NH 03431-3552. Offers Certificate. *Faculty:* 3 full-time (1 woman), 5 part-time/adjunct (3 women). *Students:* Average age 30. *Expenses:* Tuition: Full-time $22,000. Tuition and fees vary according to program and student level. *Unit head:* Peter M. Smith, Director, 603-283-2424, Fax: 603-357-0718, E-mail: psmith@antiochne.edu. *Application contact:* Leatrice A. Oram, Co-Director of Admissions, 800-490-3310, Fax: 603-357-0718, E-mail: admissions@antiochne.edu.

Antioch University Santa Barbara, Program in Organizational Management, Santa Barbara, CA 93101-1581. Offers MA. Part-time and evening/weekend programs available. Postbaccalaureate distance learning degree programs offered (minimal on-campus study). *Faculty:* 16 full-time (11 women), 55 part-time/adjunct (21 women). *Students:* 14 full-time (10 women), 14 part-time (12 women); includes 8 minority (1 Asian American or Pacific Islander, 7 Hispanic Americans). In 2006, 12 degrees awarded. *Entrance requirements:* Additional exam requirements/recommendations for international students: Required—TOEFL (minimum score 550 paper-based; 213 computer-based). *Application deadline:* For fall admission, 8/6 priority date for domestic students; for winter admission, 11/5 priority date for domestic students. Applications are processed on a rolling basis. Application fee: $60 ($100 for international students). Electronic applications accepted. *Expenses:* Tuition: Part-time $515 per unit. Part-time tuition and fees vary according to course load and program. *Financial support:* Federal Work-Study available. Support available to part-time students. Financial award application deadline: 8/8; financial award applicants required to submit FAFSA. *Faculty research:* Multicultural communication, organizational change. *Unit head:* Dr. Esther Lopez-Mulnix, Chair, 805-962-8179 Ext. 328, Fax: 805-962-4786, E-mail: emulnix@antiochsb.edu. *Application contact:* Director of Admissions, 805-962-8179, Fax: 805-962-4786, E-mail: admissions@antiochsb.edu.

Antioch University Seattle, Graduate Programs, Center for Creative Change, Seattle, WA 98121-1814. Offers environment and community (MA); management (MS); organizational psychology (MA); strategic communications (MA); whole system design (MA). Evening/weekend programs available. Electronic applications accepted. Expenses: Contact institution.

Argosy University, Chicago Campus, College of Psychology and Behavioral Sciences, Program in Organizational Leadership, Chicago, IL 60603. Offers Ed D. *Students:* 27 full-time (16 women), 10 part-time (6 women); includes 17 African Americans. 11 applicants, 100% accepted, 11 enrolled. *Degree requirements:* For doctorate, thesis/dissertation. *Entrance requirements:* For doctorate, minimum GPA of 3.0. Additional exam requirements/recommendations for international students: Required—TOEFL (minimum score 550 paper-based; 213 computer-based). *Application deadline:* For fall admission, 2/28 for domestic and international students; for spring admission, 10/30 for domestic and international students. Applications are processed on a rolling basis. Application fee: $50. Electronic applications accepted. *Financial support:* In 2006–07, 30 students received support. Scholarships/grants available. Financial award application deadline: 4/1; financial award applicants required to submit FAFSA. *Unit head:* Michael Falotico, Head, 800-626-4123, Fax: 312-777-7750, E-mail: mfalotico@argosy.edu. *Application contact:* Ashley Delaney, Director of Admissions, 800-626-4123, Fax: 312-777-7750, E-mail: argosyadmissions@argosy.edu.

Argosy University, Denver Campus, College of Psychology and Behavioral Sciences, Denver, CO 80203. Offers clinical psychology (Psy D); community counseling (MA); counseling psychology (Ed D), including counselor education and supervision; counselor education and supervision (Ed D); forensic psychology (MA); organizational leadership (Ed D).

Argosy University, Hawai'i Campus, College of Psychology and Behavioral Sciences, Program in Organizational Leadership, Honolulu, HI 96813. Offers Ed D.

Argosy University, Orange County Campus, College of Business, Santa Ana, CA 92704. Offers accounting (DBA, Adv C); customized professional concentration (MBA, DBA); finance (MBA, Certificate); healthcare administration (MBA, Certificate); information systems (DBA, Adv C); information systems management (MBA); international business (MBA, DBA, Adv C, Certificate); management (MBA, MSM, DBA, EDBA); mangement (Adv C); marketing (MBA, DBA, Adv C, Certificate); organizational leadership (Ed D); public administration (MBA, Certificate). Part-time and evening/weekend programs available. *Faculty:* 4 full-time (1 woman), 20 part-time/adjunct (7 women). *Students:* 163 full-time (64 women), 41 part-time (16 women). Average age 42. 72 applicants, 51 enrolled. In 2006, 6 master's, 23 doctorates awarded. *Degree requirements:* For doctorate, thesis/dissertation, preliminary and final dissertation defense, comprehensive exam. *Entrance requirements:* For master's, minimum GPA of 3.0 in final 2 years of course work, 3 letters of recommendation, resumé; for doctorate, minimum GPA of 3.0 in graduate study, 3 letters of recommendation, resumé. Additional exam requirements/recommendations for international students: Required—TOEFL. *Application deadline:* Applications are processed on a rolling basis. Application fee: $50. Electronic applications accepted. *Financial support:* Federal Work-Study, institutionally sponsored loans, and scholarships/grants available. Support available to part-time students. Financial award applicants required to submit FAFSA. *Faculty research:* Crisis management, leadership in organizations, finance, business systems. *Unit head:* Dr. Ray London, Dean, 800-716-9598, Fax: 714-437-1284, E-mail: auocadmissions@argosy.edu. *Application contact:* Mark Betz, Director of Admissions, 800-716-9598, Fax: 714-437-1697, E-mail: mbetz@argosy.edu.

See Close-Up on page 221.

Argosy University, San Francisco Bay Area Campus, College of Psychology and Behavioral Sciences, Point Richmond, CA 94804-3547. Offers clinical psychology (MA, Psy D); counseling psychology (MA); forensic psychology (MA); organizational leadership (Ed D). *Accreditation:* APA (one or more programs are accredited). Part-time programs available. *Faculty:* 8 full-time (5 women), 5 part-time/adjunct (3 women). *Students:* 98 full-time (76 women), 57 part-time (41 women); includes 44 minority (8 African Americans, 3 American Indian/Alaska Native, 22 Asian Americans or Pacific Islanders, 11 Hispanic Americans). Average age 30. 230 applicants, 61% accepted, 59 enrolled. In 2006, 21 master's, 16 doctorates awarded. *Degree requirements:* For master's, comprehensive exam (for some programs), registration; for doctorate, thesis/dissertation, comprehensive exam, registration. *Entrance requirements:* For master's, minimum GPA of 3.0, letters of recommendation; for doctorate, minimum GPA of 3.25, letters of recommendation. Additional exam requirements/recommendations for international students: Required—TOEFL (minimum score 550 paper-based; 213 computer-based). *Application deadline:* For fall admission, 1/15 priority date for domestic students, 3/1 priority date for international students; for spring admission, 10/15 priority date for domestic students, 11/1 priority date for international students. Applications are processed on a rolling basis. Application fee: $50. Electronic applications accepted. *Financial support:* In 2006–07, teaching assistantships (averaging $1,200 per year); Federal Work-Study and scholarships/grants also available. Support available to part-time students. Financial award application deadline: 3/1; financial award applicants required to submit FAFSA. *Faculty research:* Consciousness studies, attitudes, non-verbal communication, substance abuse prevention, HIV/AIDS. *Unit head:* Dr. Andrea Morrison, Clinical Psychology Department Head, 866-215-2777, Fax: 510-215-0299, E-mail: argosyadmissions@argosy.edu. *Application contact:* John Vincent Stofan, Director, Admissions, 510-215-0277, Fax: 510-215-0299, E-mail: jstofan@argosy.edu.

Argosy University, Santa Monica Campus, College of Psychology and Behavioral Sciences, Santa Monica, CA 90405. Offers clinical psychology (MA); clinical psychology/marriage and family therapy (MA); counseling psychology (Ed D); counseling psychology/marriage and family therapy (MA); organizational leadership (Ed D).

Argosy University, Sarasota Campus, College of Psychology and Behavioral Sciences, Sarasota, FL 34235-8246. Offers clinical psychology (Psy D); community counseling (MA); counseling psychology (Ed D); counselor education and supervision (Ed D); forensic psychology (MA); marriage and family therapy (MA); mental health counseling (MA); organizational leadership (Ed D); pastoral community counseling (Ed D); school counseling (MA, Ed S); school psychology (MA). Part-time and evening/weekend programs available. Postbaccalaureate distance learning degree programs offered (minimal on-campus study). *Faculty:* 16 full-time (7 women), 38 part-time/adjunct (17 women). *Students:* 183 applicants, 75% accepted, 108 enrolled. In 2006, 14 master's, 24 doctorates awarded. *Degree requirements:* For master's, comprehensive exam (for some programs); for doctorate, thesis/dissertation, comprehensive exam. *Entrance requirements:* Additional exam requirements/recommendations for international students: Required—TOEFL. *Application deadline:* Applications are processed on a rolling basis. Application fee: $50. Electronic applications accepted. *Expenses: Contact institution. Financial support:* Federal Work-Study available. Support available to part-time students. Financial award application deadline: 4/1; financial award applicants required to submit FAFSA. *Unit head:* Dr. Douglas Riedmiller, Dean, 800-331-5995, Fax: 941-379-9464, E-mail: driedmiller@argosy.edu. *Application contact:* Admissions Representative, 800-331-5995 Ext. 221, Fax: 941-371-8910.

Argosy University, Schaumburg Campus, College of Psychology and Behavioral Sciences, Schaumburg, IL 60173-5403. Offers clinical health psychology (Post-Graduate Certificate); clinical psychology (MA, Psy D), including child and family psychology (Psy D), clinical health psychology (Psy D), diversity and multicultural psychology (Psy D), forensic psychology (Psy D); community counseling (MA); counseling psychology (Ed D), including counselor education and supervison; counselor education and supervision (Ed D); forensic psychology (MA, Post-Graduate Certificate); organizational leadership (Ed D); professional counseling (MA). *Accreditation:* ACA; APA. Evening/weekend programs available. *Students:* 273 full-time, 89 part-time. 220 applicants, 57% accepted, 83 enrolled. In 2006, 52 master's, 18 doctorates awarded. Terminal master's awarded for partial completion of doctoral program. *Degree requirements:* For master's, thesis, practicum; for doctorate, thesis/dissertation, internship, qualifying exam. *Entrance requirements:* For master's, 15 hours in psychology, interview, minimum GPA of 3.0; for doctorate, 15 hours in psychology, interview, minimum GPA of 3.25. Additional exam requirements/recommendations for international students: Required—TOEFL. *Application deadline:* For fall admission, 1/15 priority date for domestic and international students; for spring admission, 10/15 priority date for domestic and international students. Applications are processed on a rolling basis. Application fee: $50. Electronic applications accepted. *Financial support:* In 2006–07, 40 students received support, including 2 fellowships, 30 teaching assistantships; career-related internships or fieldwork, Federal Work-Study, and scholarships/grants also available. Support available to part-time students. *Unit head:* Dr. Jim Wasner, Dean, 866-290-2777, Fax: 847-598-6158, E-mail: argosyadmissions@argosy.edu. *Application contact:* Jamal Scott, Director of Admissions, 866-290-2777, Fax: 847-598-6191, E-mail: jscott@argosy.edu.

Argosy University, Tampa Campus, College of Psychology and Behavioral Sciences, Tampa, FL 33614. Offers clinical psychology (MA, Psy D), including child and adolescent psychology (MA), clinical psychology (Psy D), geropsychology (MA), marriage/couples and family therapy (MA), neuropsychology (MA); counselor education and supervision (Ed D); marriage and family therapy (MA); mental health counseling (MA); organizational leadership (Ed D); school counseling (MA).

Argosy University, Washington DC Campus, College of Psychology and Behavioral Sciences, Professional Programs in Psychology, Arlington, VA 22209. Offers clinical psychology (MA, Psy D, Postdoctoral Respecialization Certificate), including child and family psychology (Psy D), diversity and multicultural psychology (Psy D), forensic psychology (Psy D), health and neuropsychology (Psy D); community counseling (MA); counseling psychology (Ed D), including counselor education and supervision; forensic psychology (MA); organizational leader-

Organizational Management

Argosy University, Washington DC Campus (continued)
ship (Ed D). *Accreditation:* APA. Postbaccalaureate distance learning degree programs offered (minimal on-campus study). *Faculty:* 23 full-time (15 women), 51 part-time/adjunct (34 women). *Students:* 620 full-time (521 women), 209 part-time (173 women); includes 316 minority (239 African Americans, 5 American Indian/Alaska Native, 35 Asian Americans or Pacific Islanders, 37 Hispanic Americans). Average age 34. 518 applicants, 59% accepted, 193 enrolled. In 2006, 46 master's, 67 doctorates awarded. Terminal master's awarded for partial completion of doctoral program. *Median time to degree:* Of those who began their doctoral program in fall 1998, 62% received their degree in 8 years or less. *Degree requirements:* For master's, thesis (for some programs), practicum, comprehensive exam (for some programs); for doctorate, thesis/dissertation, internship, comprehensive exam. *Entrance requirements:* For master's, clinical experience, minimum GPA of 3.0; for doctorate, clinical experience, minimum GPA of 3.25. Additional exam requirements/recommendations for international students: Required—TOEFL (minimum score 550 paper-based; 213 computer-based). *Application deadline:* For fall admission, 1/15 priority date for domestic students. Applications are processed on a rolling basis. Application fee: $50. Electronic applications accepted. *Financial support:* In 2006–07, 462 students received support, including 2 fellowships with tuition reimbursements available (averaging $3,600 per year), 50 teaching assistantships with full and partial tuition reimbursements available (averaging $2,040 per year); research assistantships, career-related internships or fieldwork, Federal Work-Study, and scholarships/grants also available. Support available to part-time students. Financial award applicants required to submit FAFSA. *Faculty research:* Psychotherapy integration, minority health, forensic assessment, family violence, child maltreatment. Total annual research expenditures: $2,000. *Application contact:* Emily Peck, Director of Admissions, 866-703-2777 Ext. 5851, Fax: 703-526-5850, E-mail: dcadmissions@argosy.edu.

Athabasca University, Centre for Integrated Studies, Athabasca, AB T9S 3A3, Canada. Offers adult education (MA); community studies (MA); cultural studies (MA); educational studies (MA); global change (MA); work, organization, and leadership (MA). Part-time and evening/weekend programs available. Postbaccalaureate distance learning degree programs offered (no on-campus study). *Faculty:* 4 full-time (0 women), 50 part-time/adjunct (27 women). *Students:* Average age 39. 150 applicants, 87% accepted, 112 enrolled. In 2006, 40 degrees awarded. *Degree requirements:* For master's, project. *Entrance requirements:* For master's, 3- or 4-year BA. Additional exam requirements/recommendations for international students: Required—TOEFL or ENG 255 class (75) or Michigan English Language Assessment Battery (85) or IELTS (6.5) or CAEL (65); Recommended—TOEFL (minimum score 560 paper-based; 220 computer-based). *Application deadline:* For fall admission, 3/1 for domestic and international students; for winter admission, 10/1 for domestic and international students. Application fee: $65. Electronic applications accepted. *Faculty research:* Women's history, literature and culture studies, sustainable development, labor and education. *Unit head:* Dr. Derek Briton, Program Director, 780-675-6218, Fax: 780-675-6921, E-mail: derekb@athabascau.ca. *Application contact:* Derek Stovin, Program Administrator, 780-675-6236, Fax: 780-675-6921, E-mail: mais@athabascau.ca.

Augsburg College, Program in Leadership, Minneapolis, MN 55454-1351. Offers MA. Part-time and evening/weekend programs available. *Faculty:* 7 full-time (2 women), 2 part-time/adjunct (1 woman). *Students:* 22 full-time (14 women), 79 part-time (52 women); includes 13 minority (10 African Americans, 2 American Indian/Alaska Native, 1 Hispanic American). Average age 38. 213 applicants, 17% accepted, 31 enrolled. In 2006, 10 degrees awarded. *Degree requirements:* For master's, thesis or alternative. *Entrance requirements:* For master's, MAT, minimum GPA of 3.0. Additional exam requirements/recommendations for international students: Required—TOEFL (minimum score 600 paper-based; 250 computer-based). *Application deadline:* For fall admission, 8/9 priority date for domestic students; for winter admission, 12/15 for domestic students; for spring admission, 3/7 for domestic students. Applications are processed on a rolling basis. Application fee: $35. *Expenses:* Tuition: Full-time $10,584; part-time $1,764 per course. Required fees: $300; $35 per course. Tuition and fees vary according to program. *Financial support:* In 2006–07, 9 students received support. Available to part-time students. Application deadline: 8/1; *Faculty research:* Soviet leaders, artificial intelligence, homelessness. *Unit head:* Dr. Norma Noonan, Director, 612-330-1198, Fax: 612-330-1355, E-mail: noonan@augsburg.edu. *Application contact:* Patricia Park, Program Coordinator, 612-330-1150, E-mail: parkp@augsburg.edu.

Avila University, Program in Organizational Development, Kansas City, MO 64145-1698. Offers organizational development (MS); project management (Graduate Certificate). Part-time and evening/weekend programs available. *Faculty:* 3 full-time (2 women), 20 part-time/adjunct. *Students:* 75. Average age 33. In 2006, 5 degrees awarded. *Degree requirements:* For master's, thesis optional. *Entrance requirements:* For master's, letters of recommendation, minimum GPA of 3.0. Additional exam requirements/recommendations for international students: Required—TOEFL. *Application deadline:* Applications are processed on a rolling basis. Application fee: $0. Electronic applications accepted. *Expenses:* Tuition: Full-time $7,470; part-time $415 per credit. *Financial support:* Unspecified assistantships available. Support available to part-time students. Financial award applicants required to submit FAFSA. *Unit head:* Lacey Smith, Assistant Dean, 816-501-3737, Fax: 816-941-4650, E-mail: advantage@avila.edu.

See Close-Up on page 691.

Azusa Pacific University, School of Behavioral and Applied Sciences, Department of Higher Education and Organizational Leadership, Program in Leadership and Organizational Studies, Azusa, CA 91702-7000. Offers MLOS. In 2006, 28 degrees awarded. Application fee: $45 ($65 for international students). *Expenses:* Tuition: Part-time $475 per credit. *Unit head:* Dr. Dennis A. Sheridan, Director, Department of Higher Education and Organizational Leadership, 626-815-5485, Fax: 626-815-3868.

Azusa Pacific University, School of Behavioral and Applied Sciences, Department of Higher Education and Organizational Leadership, Program in Organizational Leadership, Azusa, CA 91702-7000. Offers MA. *Students:* 1 (woman) full-time, 120 part-time (58 women); includes 15 minority (3 African Americans, 6 Asian Americans or Pacific Islanders, 6 Hispanic Americans), 30 international. In 2006, 53 degrees awarded. *Expenses:* Tuition: Part-time $475 per credit. *Unit head:* Dr. Dennis A. Sheridan, Director, Department of Higher Education and Organizational Leadership, 626-815-5485, Fax: 626-815-3868.

Beacon University, Graduate Programs, Columbus, GA 31909. Offers cell church development (MAPM); counseling (MAC); counseling ministry (MAPM); military chaplaincy (MAPM); organizational leadership (MAPM); organizational leadership and management (MAOL); pastoral ministry (MAPM); theology (M Div, MABS).

Benedictine University, Graduate Programs, Program in Organizational Development, Lisle, IL 60532-0900. Offers PhD. Evening/weekend programs available. *Faculty:* 2 full-time (0 women), 2 part-time/adjunct (1 woman). *Students:* 40 (14 women); includes 5 minority (4 African Americans, 1 Asian American or Pacific Islander) 3 international. Average age 44. In 2006, 4 degrees awarded. *Degree requirements:* For doctorate, thesis/dissertation. *Entrance requirements:* Additional exam requirements/recommendations for international students: Required—TOEFL (minimum score 550 paper-based). *Application deadline:* For fall admission, 9/1 for domestic students; for winter admission, 12/1 for domestic students; for spring admission, 2/15 for domestic students. Application fee: $40. Electronic applications accepted. *Expenses:* Tuition: Full-time $12,150; part-time $450 per credit hour. *Financial support:* Career-related internships or fieldwork and health care benefits available. *Faculty research:* Change management, appreciative inquiry, innovation and organization design, global and international organization development, organization renewal. *Unit head:* Dr. Peter F. Sorensen, Director, 630-829-6220, Fax: 630-960-1126, E-mail: psorensen@ben.edu. *Application contact:* Kari Gibbons, Director, Admissions, 630-829-6200, Fax: 630-829-6584, E-mail: kgibbons@ben.edu.

Bernard M. Baruch College of the City University of New York, Zicklin School of Business, Department of Management, New York, NY 10010-5585. Offers entrepreneurship (MBA); general management and policy (MBA); human resources management (MBA); management planning systems (PhD); management science (MBA); organization and policy studies (PhD); organizational behavior (MBA). Part-time and evening/weekend programs available. *Faculty:* 38 full-time (10 women), 41 part-time/adjunct (6 women). *Students:* 30 full-time (14 women), 117 part-time (52 women); includes 37 minority (17 African Americans, 14 Asian Americans or Pacific Islanders, 6 Hispanic Americans). In 2006, 39 master's, 1 doctorate awarded. *Degree requirements:* For doctorate, thesis/dissertation, comprehensive exam. *Entrance requirements:* For master's, GMAT, 2 letters of recommendation, resumé, 2 years of work experience; for doctorate, GMAT. Additional exam requirements/recommendations for international students: Required—TOEFL (minimum score 590 paper-based; 243 computer-based), TWE. *Application deadline:* For fall admission, 5/31 for domestic students, 4/30 for international students; for spring admission, 10/31 for domestic and international students. Application fee: $125. *Financial support:* Fellowships, research assistantships, teaching assistantships, career-related internships or fieldwork, Federal Work-Study, scholarships/grants, and unspecified assistantships available. Financial award application deadline: 4/30; financial award applicants required to submit FAFSA. *Unit head:* Harry M. Rosen, Chairman, 646-312-3620, Fax: 646-312-3621, E-mail: harry_rosen@baruch.cuny.edu. *Application contact:* Frances Murphy, Office of Graduate Admissions, 646-312-1300, Fax: 646-312-1301, E-mail: zicklingradadmissions@baruch.cuny.edu.

Bethel University, Graduate School, Department of Organizational Leadership, St. Paul, MN 55112-6999. Offers MA. *Faculty:* 3 full-time (1 woman), 9 part-time/adjunct (3 women). *Students:* 96 full-time (51 women), 5 part-time (2 women); includes 8 minority (4 African Americans, 1 Asian American or Pacific Islander, 3 Hispanic Americans). Average age 38. In 2006, 23 degrees awarded. *Degree requirements:* For master's, thesis. *Entrance requirements:* For master's, interview, minimum GPA of 3.0, letters of reference. Additional exam requirements/recommendations for international students: Required—TOEFL (minimum score 550 paper-based; 213 computer-based). *Application deadline:* For fall admission, 6/1 priority date for domestic students; for winter admission, 11/15 priority date for domestic students. Application fee: $25. Electronic applications accepted. *Expenses:* Tuition: Part-time $395 per credit. Tuition and fees vary according to program. *Financial support:* Institutionally sponsored loans and scholarships/grants available. *Unit head:* Glori Sundberg, Director, 651-638-8000, Fax: 651-635-8004, E-mail: gs@bethel.edu. *Application contact:* Michael Price, Director of Admissions, 651-635-8000 Ext. 8017, Fax: 651-635-8004, E-mail: m_price@bethel.edu.

Biola University, School of Professional Studies, La Mirada, CA 90639-0001. Offers Christian apologetics (MA); organizational leadership (MA). Part-time and evening/weekend programs available. *Entrance requirements:* For master's, minimum undergraduate GPA of 3.0. Additional exam requirements/recommendations for international students: Required—TOEFL (minimum score 550 paper-based; 213 computer-based).

Bluffton University, Programs in Business, Bluffton, OH 45817. Offers business administration (MBA); organizational management (MA). Evening/weekend programs available. *Faculty:* 8 full-time (2 women), 4 part-time/adjunct (0 women). *Students:* 71 full-time (30 women), 10 part-time (5 women); includes 11 minority (8 African Americans, 2 Asian Americans or Pacific Islanders, 1 Hispanic American). Average age 37. 42 applicants, 100% accepted, 41 enrolled. In 2006, 43 degrees awarded. *Entrance requirements:* Additional exam requirements/recommendations for international students: Required—TOEFL. *Application deadline:* For fall admission, 7/31 priority date for domestic and international students. Applications are processed on a rolling basis. Application fee: $20. Electronic applications accepted. *Unit head:* Dr. George Lehman, Director of Graduate Programs in Business, 419-358-3302, E-mail: lehmang@bluffton.edu. *Application contact:* Betty Dills, Information Contact, 800-488-3257, Fax: 419-358-3399, E-mail: adulted@bluffton.edu.

Boston College, The Carroll School of Management, Department of Organization Studies, Chestnut Hill, MA 02467-3800. Offers PhD. *Faculty:* 11 full-time (4 women). *Students:* 29 full-time (11 women); includes 2 minority (1 American Indian/Alaska Native, 1 Asian American or Pacific Islander), 6 international. Average age 32. 40 applicants, 10% accepted, 4 enrolled. In 2006, 4 doctorates awarded. *Degree requirements:* For doctorate, thesis/dissertation, teaching requirement, comprehensive exam. *Entrance requirements:* For doctorate, GMAT or GRE, letters of recommendation, resumé, transcripts. Additional exam requirements/recommendations for international students: Required—TOEFL. *Application deadline:* For spring admission, 2/1 for domestic and international students. Application fee: $50. *Financial support:* In 2006–07, 16 research assistantships with full tuition reimbursements (averaging $23,000 per year) were awarded. Financial award application deadline: 3/1; financial award applicants required to submit FAFSA. *Faculty research:* Organizational transformation, mergers and acquisitions, managerial effectiveness, organizational change, organizational structure. *Unit head:* Dr. Candace Jones, Associate Professor; PhD Program Chair. *Application contact:* Jean Passavant, Department Secretary, 617-552-0450, Fax: 617-552-4230, E-mail: jean.passavant@bc.edu.

Bowling Green State University, Graduate College, College of Business Administration, Program in Organization Development, Bowling Green, OH 43403. Offers MOD. Part-time and evening/weekend programs available. *Faculty:* 16 full-time (9 women), 3 part-time/adjunct (2 women). *Students:* 15 full-time (11 women), 6 part-time (5 women); includes 2 minority (both African Americans), 2 international. Average age 29. 35 applicants, 14% accepted, 0 enrolled. In 2006, 31 degrees awarded. *Degree requirements:* For master's, thesis or alternative, internship. *Entrance requirements:* For master's, GMAT or GRE. Additional exam requirements/recommendations for international students: Required—TOEFL. *Application deadline:* Applications are processed on a rolling basis. Application fee: $30. Electronic applications accepted. *Expenses:* Tuition, state resident: part-time $535 per hour. Tuition, nonresident: part-time $884 per hour. *Financial support:* Research assistantships with full tuition reimbursements, teaching assistantships with full tuition reimbursements, career-related internships or fieldwork, Federal Work-Study, and unspecified assistantships available. Financial award applicants required to submit FAFSA. *Faculty research:* Charismatic leadership, self-managing work teams, knowledge workers, stress, effects of change processes. *Unit head:* Dr. James McFillen, Director, 419-372-2488. *Application contact:* Dr. Angie Stoller, Graduate Coordinator, 419-372-8139.

Brenau University, Graduate Programs, School of Business and Mass Communication, Gainesville, GA 30501. Offers accounting (MBA); healthcare management (MBA); leadership development (MBA); management (MBA); organizational development (MS). Part-time and evening/weekend programs available. Postbaccalaureate distance learning degree programs offered (no on-campus study). *Faculty:* 12 full-time (6 women), 16 part-time/adjunct (5 women). *Students:* 49 full-time (32 women), 148 part-time (89 women); includes 52 minority (45 African Americans, 2 Asian Americans or Pacific Islanders, 5 Hispanic Americans), 2 international. Average age 35. 222 applicants, 55% accepted, 111 enrolled. In 2006, 64 degrees awarded. *Degree requirements:* For master's, thesis (for some programs). *Entrance requirements:* For master's, GMAT, GRE General Test, or MAT, minimum undergraduate GPA of 3.0, faculty interview. Additional exam requirements/recommendations for international students: Required—TOEFL (minimum score 550 paper-based). *Application deadline:* Applications are processed on a rolling basis. Application fee: $30. Electronic applications accepted. *Expenses:* Contact institution. *Financial support:* Career-related internships or fieldwork available. Financial award application deadline: 7/15; financial award applicants required to submit FAFSA. *Faculty research:* International business, women in management entrepreneurship, simulations in business, Internet/online teaching in business, managerial leadership. *Unit head:* Dr. Bill Haney, Dean, 770-538-4707, Fax: 770-537-4701, E-mail: whaney@brenau.edu. *Application contact:* Nathan Goss, Admissions Coordinator, 770-534-6162, Fax: 770-538-4701, E-mail: ngoss@brenau.edu.

Briercrest Seminary, Graduate Programs, Program in Leadership and Management, Caronport, SK S0H 0S0, Canada. Offers organizational leadership (MA). Part-time programs available.

Faculty: 4 part-time/adjunct (0 women). *Students:* 1 full-time (0 women), 13 part-time (3 women). Average age 39. 10 applicants, 70% accepted, 4 enrolled. In 2006, 9 degrees awarded. *Degree requirements:* For master's, thesis optional. *Entrance requirements:* Additional exam requirements/recommendations for international students: Required—TOEFL (minimum score 550 paper-based; 213 computer-based). Application fee: $25. *Financial support:* Teaching assistantships available. *Unit head:* Dr. Dwayne Uglem, President, 306-756-3212, Fax: 306-756-5500, E-mail: duglem@briercrest.ca. *Application contact:* Kevin Weeks, Enrollment Management Officer, 306-756-3221, Fax: 306-756-5500, E-mail: kweeks@briercrest.ca.

Cabrini College, Graduate and Professional Studies, Radnor, PA 19087-3698. Offers biotechnology (Certificate); education (M Ed); educational leadership (Certificate); instructional systems technology (MS); organization leadership (MS); project management (Certificate). Part-time and evening/weekend programs available. *Faculty:* 11 full-time (7 women), 25 part-time/adjunct (11 women). *Students:* 91 full-time (63 women), 484 part-time (364 women); includes 43 minority (28 African Americans, 6 Asian Americans or Pacific Islanders, 9 Hispanic Americans), 6 international. Average age 32. In 2006, 143 degrees awarded. *Degree requirements:* For master's, thesis optional. *Entrance requirements:* For master's, GRE and/or MAT (in some cases), letter of recommendation, minimum GPA of 2.5. *Application deadline:* For fall admission, 7/29 priority date for domestic students; for spring admission, 12/9 for domestic students. Applications are processed on a rolling basis. Application fee: $50. Electronic applications accepted. *Expenses:* Tuition: Part-time $310 per credit. Required fees: $45 per term. Tuition and fees vary according to course load. *Financial support:* Career-related internships or fieldwork and unspecified assistantships available. Support available to part-time students. Financial award applicants required to submit FAFSA. *Faculty research:* Qualitative research in reading, ethnographic studies. *Unit head:* Dr. Michael W. Markowitz, Dean for Graduate and Professional Studies, 610-902-8501, Fax: 610-902-8522, E-mail: michael.w.markowitz@cabrini.edu. *Application contact:* Bruce D. Bryde, Director of Enrollment and Recruiting, 610-902-8291, Fax: 610-902-8522, E-mail: bruce.d.bryde@cabrini.edu.

Capella University, School of Business and Technology, Minneapolis, MN 55402. Offers accounting (MBA), including system design and programming; business (Certificate), including human resource management (MS, PhD, Certificate), information technology management (MS, PhD, Certificate), leadership (MBA, MS, PhD, Certificate); finance (MBA); general business (MBA); health care management (MBA); information technology (MS, Certificate), including general information technology (MS), information security, network architecture and design (MS), professional projects management (Certificate), project management and leadership (MS), system design and development (MS),); information technology management (MBA); marketing (MBA); organization and management (MBA, MS, PhD), including general business (PhD), general organization and management (MBA, MS), human resource management (MS, PhD, Certificate), information technology management (MS, PhD, Certificate), leadership (MBA, MS, PhD, Certificate); project management (MBA). Part-time and evening/weekend programs available. Postbaccalaureate distance learning degree programs offered (minimal on-campus study). Terminal master's awarded for partial completion of doctoral program. *Degree requirements:* For master's, integrative project, thesis optional; for doctorate, thesis/dissertation, comprehensive exam, registration. *Entrance requirements:* Additional exam requirements/recommendations for international students: Required—TOEFL (minimum score 550 paper-based; 213 computer-based), TWE (minimum score 4). Electronic applications accepted. *Faculty research:* Business policies: strategic, corporate, and financial management; interplay of technological, organizational and social change.

Cardean University, MBA Program, Chicago, IL 60606-7204. Offers accounting and information systems (MBA); e-commerce (MBA); finance (MBA); global management (MBA); health care administration (MBA); human resources management (MBA); leadership (MBA); management of information systems (MBA); management of technology (MBA); marketing (MBA); professional accounting (MBA); project management (MBA); risk management (MBA); strategy and economics (MBA). Part-time and evening/weekend programs available. Postbaccalaureate distance learning degree programs offered (no on-campus study). *Entrance requirements:* Additional exam requirements/recommendations for international students: Required—TOEFL (minimum score 550 paper-based; 213 computer-based).

Carlos Albizu University, Miami Campus, Graduate Programs, Miami, FL 33172-2209. Offers clinical psychology (Psy D); entrepreneurship (MBA); exceptional student education (MS); industrial/organizational psychology (MS); marriage and family therapy (MS); mental health counseling (MS); nonprofit management (MBA); organizational management (MBA); psychology (MS); school counseling (MS); teaching English as a second language (MS). *Accreditation:* APA. Part-time and evening/weekend programs available. Terminal master's awarded for partial completion of doctoral program. *Degree requirements:* For master's, one foreign language, comprehensive exam, integrative project (MBA), research project (MSESE); for doctorate, one foreign language, comprehensive exam, internship, doctoral project. *Entrance requirements:* For master's, 3 letters of recommendation, interview, minimum GPA of 3.0, resumé; for doctorate, 3 letters of recommendation, minimum GPA of 3.0, resumé, interview. *Faculty research:* Psychotherapy, forensic psychology, neuropsychology, marketing strategy, entrepreneurship.

Carlow University, School for Social Change, Pittsburgh, PA 15213-3165. Offers management of non-profit organization (MS); organizational influence (MS); professional counseling (MSPC); training and development (MS). Part-time and evening/weekend programs available. *Entrance requirements:* For master's, interview, minimum GPA of 3.0, resumé, 3 letters of recommendation, 1 year professional experience. Additional exam requirements/recommendations for international students: Required—TOEFL (minimum score 550 paper-based; 213 computer-based). Electronic applications accepted. *Faculty research:* Gender and leadership, cross cultural communications and leadership, organizational culture.

Carnegie Mellon University, College of Humanities and Social Sciences, Department of Social and Decision Sciences, Pittsburgh, PA 15213-3891. Offers behavioral decision theory (PhD); organization science (PhD); social and decision science (PhD). Terminal master's awarded for partial completion of doctoral program. *Degree requirements:* For doctorate, thesis/dissertation, research paper, comprehensive exam. *Entrance requirements:* For doctorate, GRE General Test. Additional exam requirements/recommendations for international students: Required—TOEFL. Electronic applications accepted. *Faculty research:* Organization theory, political science, sociology, technology studies.

Charleston Southern University, Program in Business, Charleston, SC 29423-8087. Offers accounting (MBA); finance (MBA); health care administration (MBA); information systems (MBA); organizational development (MBA). Part-time and evening/weekend programs available. *Degree requirements:* For master's, thesis optional. *Entrance requirements:* For master's, GMAT. *Faculty research:* Economic forecasting.

Chatham University, Program in Leadership and Organizational Transformation, Pittsburgh, PA 15232-2826. Offers MA. *Students:* 13 full-time (all women), 6 part-time (5 women). Average age 29. 21 applicants, 71% accepted, 14 enrolled. In 2006, 5 degrees awarded. *Entrance requirements:* For master's, resumé, 2 letters of recommendation. Additional exam requirements/recommendations for international students: Required—TOEFL (minimum score 600 paper-based; 250 computer-based; 100 iBT); Recommended—IELTS (minimum score 7). *Application deadline:* Applications are processed on a rolling basis. Application fee: $45. Electronic applications accepted. *Unit head:* Dr. Gloria Nouel, Director, 412-365-2766, E-mail: gnouel@chatham.edu. *Application contact:* Office of Graduate Admissions, 412-365-1825, Fax: 412-365-1609, E-mail: admissions@chatham.edu.

College Misericordia, College of Professional Studies and Social Sciences, Program in Organizational Management, Dallas, PA 18612-1098. Offers MS. Part-time and evening/weekend programs available. *Faculty:* 2 full-time (0 women), 11 part-time/adjunct (6 women). *Students:* Average age 36. 28 applicants, 89% accepted, 25 enrolled. In 2006, 22 degrees awarded. *Degree requirements:* For master's, thesis or alternative, practicum. *Entrance requirements:* For master's, GRE General Test or MAT, minimum GPA of 2.8. *Application deadline:* For fall admission, 8/1 priority date for domestic students. Applications are processed on a rolling basis. Application fee: $25. Electronic applications accepted. *Expenses:* Contact institution. *Financial support:* Career-related internships or fieldwork and scholarships/grants available. Support available to part-time students. Financial award application deadline: 6/30; financial award applicants required to submit FAFSA. *Unit head:* Dr. John Kachurick, Director, 570-674-6301, E-mail: jkachuri@misericordia.edu. *Application contact:* Larree Brown, Coordinator of Part-Time Undergraduate and Graduate Programs, 570-674-6451, Fax: 570-674-6232, E-mail: lbrown@misericordia.edu.

College of Mount St. Joseph, Multidisciplinary Program in Organizational Leadership, Cincinnati, OH 45233-1670. Offers MS. Part-time and evening/weekend programs available. *Faculty:* 6 full-time (2 women). *Students:* 1 full-time (0 women), 43 part-time (28 women); includes 6 minority (all African Americans) Average age 40. 11 applicants, 100% accepted, 10 enrolled. In 2006, 9 degrees awarded. *Degree requirements:* For master's, integrative project. *Entrance requirements:* For master's, minimum GPA of 3.0, interview, 3 years of work experience, 3 letters of reference, resumé. Additional exam requirements/recommendations for international students: Required—TOEFL (minimum score 560 paper-based; 220 computer-based). *Application deadline:* Applications are processed on a rolling basis. Application fee: $50. Electronic applications accepted. *Expenses:* Contact institution. *Financial support:* Application deadline: 6/1; *Faculty research:* Gender and cultural effects on management education, group identity formation, leadership skill development, methods for improving instructional effectiveness, technology-based productivity improvement. *Unit head:* Dr. Jim Brodzinski, Chair, 513-244-4917, Fax: 513-244-4270, E-mail: jim_brodzinski@mail.msj.edu. *Application contact:* Marilyn Hoskins, Assistant Director of Admissions for Graduate Recruitment, 513-244-4723, Fax: 513-244-4629, E-mail: marilyn_hoskins@mail.msg.edu.

College of St. Catherine, Graduate Programs, Program in Organizational Leadership, St. Paul, MN 55105-1789. Offers MA. Part-time and evening/weekend programs available. *Degree requirements:* For master's, thesis. *Entrance requirements:* For master's, GMAT, GRE General Test or MAT, 2 years of work experience, minimum GPA of 3.0. Additional exam requirements/recommendations for international students: Required—TOEFL. *Faculty research:* Ethics.

Colorado Technical University, Graduate Studies, Program in Management, Colorado Springs, CO 80907-3896. Offers business administration (MBA); business management (MSM); business technology (MSM); database management (MSM); human resources management (MSM); information technology (MSM); logistics management (MSM); management (DM); organizational leadership (MSM); project management (MSM). Part-time and evening/weekend programs available. *Degree requirements:* For master's, thesis or alternative; for doctorate, thesis/dissertation. *Entrance requirements:* For doctorate, minimum graduate GPA of 3.0, 5 years of related work experience. *Faculty research:* Sexual harassment, performance evaluation, critical thinking.

Colorado Technical University Sioux Falls Campus, Programs in Business Administration and Management, Sioux Falls, SD 57108. Offers business administration (MBA); business management (MSM); health science management (MSM); human resources management (MSM); information technology (MSM); organizational leadership (MSM); project management (MBA); technology management (MBA). Evening/weekend programs available. *Degree requirements:* For master's, thesis optional. *Entrance requirements:* For master's, minimum 2 years work experience, resumé.

Concordia University, Graduate Programs, Ann Arbor, MI 48105-2797. Offers educational leadership (MS); organizational leadership and administration (MS). Part-time and evening/weekend programs available. *Faculty:* 6 full-time (3 women), 56 part-time/adjunct (27 women). *Students:* 399 full-time (290 women), 8 part-time (4 women); includes 112 minority (97 African Americans, 3 American Indian/Alaska Native, 8 Asian Americans or Pacific Islanders, 4 Hispanic Americans). Average age 39. 542 applicants, 69% accepted, 349 enrolled. *Degree requirements:* For master's, thesis. *Entrance requirements:* Additional exam requirements/recommendations for international students: Required—TOEFL (minimum score 520 paper-based; 190 computer-based; 68 iBT); Recommended—IELTS, TWE. *Application deadline:* For fall admission, 9/7 priority date for domestic students, 8/15 priority date for international students; for winter admission, 1/18 priority date for domestic students, 12/15 priority date for international students; for spring admission, 5/10 priority date for domestic students, 4/15 priority date for international students. Applications are processed on a rolling basis. Application fee: $100. *Expenses:* Tuition: Full-time $7,020; part-time $390 per credit. Tuition and fees vary according to program. *Financial support:* In 2006–07, 263 students received support. Applicants required to submit FAFSA.

Concordia University, School of Graduate Studies, Faculty of Arts and Science, Department of Applied Human Sciences, Montréal, QC H3G 1M8, Canada. Offers human systems intervention (MA). *Students:* 19 full-time (16 women), 22 part-time (17 women). 48 applicants, 50% accepted, 21 enrolled. In 2006, 17 degrees awarded. *Degree requirements:* For master's, 2 week residential laboratory. *Entrance requirements:* For master's, 1 week residential laboratory, 2 full years of work experience. *Application deadline:* For fall admission, 3/1 for domestic students. Application fee: $50. *Financial support:* Fellowships, research assistantships available. Financial award application deadline: 2/1. *Faculty research:* Health promotion, adult learning and transitions, applications of group development and small group leadership, adolescent development, generational issues in immigrant families. *Unit head:* Dr. V. Mann-Feder, Chair, 514-848-2424 Ext. 2260, Fax: 514-848-5376. *Application contact:* Dr. James Gavin, Director, 514-848-2424 Ext. 2272, Fax: 514-848-2262.

Concordia University, St. Paul, College of Business and Organizational Leadership, St. Paul, MN 55104-5494. Offers business and organizational leadership (MBA); criminal justice (MAHS); human resources (MAOM); organizational management (MAOM). *Accreditation:* ACBSP. Evening/weekend programs available. Postbaccalaureate distance learning degree programs offered (minimal on-campus study). *Faculty:* 11 full-time (2 women), 18 part-time/adjunct (6 women). *Students:* 186 full-time (114 women); includes 26 minority (16 African Americans, 8 Asian Americans or Pacific Islanders, 2 Hispanic Americans), 1 international. Average age 33. In 2006, 92 degrees awarded. *Entrance requirements:* Additional exam requirements/recommendations for international students: Required—TOEFL. *Application deadline:* Applications are processed on a rolling basis. Application fee: $50. Electronic applications accepted. *Financial support:* Federal Work-Study and scholarships/grants available. Financial award applicants required to submit FAFSA. *Unit head:* Dr. Robert DeGregorio, Dean, 651-641-8845, Fax: 651-641-8807, E-mail: degregorio@csp.edu. *Application contact:* Kimberly Craig, Director of Graduate and Cohort Admission, 651-603-6223, Fax: 651-603-6320, E-mail: craig@csp.edu.

Cumberland University, Program in Organizational Leadership and Human Relations Management, Lebanon, TN 37087-3408. Offers MS. Part-time and evening/weekend programs available. *Faculty:* 1 full-time (0 women), 3 part-time/adjunct (1 woman). *Students:* 2 full-time (1 woman), 14 part-time (4 women); includes 3 minority (all African Americans), 5 international. Average age 31. 4 applicants, 75% accepted, 3 enrolled. In 2006, 6 degrees awarded. *Degree requirements:* For master's, comprehensive exam, registration. *Entrance requirements:* For master's, MAT, 3 letters of recommendation. Additional exam requirements/recommendations for international students: Required—TOEFL (minimum score 500 paper-based; 173 computer-based). *Application deadline:* For fall admission, 8/1 priority date for domestic students. Application fee: $50. *Expenses:* Tuition: Full-time $10,890; part-time $605 per credit. *Financial support:* Scholarships/grants, tuition waivers (partial), and unspecified assistantships available. Financial award application deadline: 8/1; financial award applicants required to submit FAFSA. *Unit head:* Dr. William R. Cheatham, Associate Professor, Criminal Justice, 615-444-2562 Ext. 1276, Fax: 615-444-2569, E-mail: rcheatham@cumberland.edu.

Defiance College, Program in Business and Organizational Leadership, Defiance, OH 43512-1610. Offers MBOL. Part-time and evening/weekend programs available. *Degree requirements:* For master's, thesis. *Entrance requirements:* For master's, minimum GPA of 2.5.

Organizational Management

Dominican University, Edward A. and Lois L. Brennan School of Business, River Forest, IL 60305-1099. Offers accounting (MSA); business administration (MBA); computer information systems (MSCIS); management information systems (MSMIS); organization management (MSOM); JD/MBA; MBA/MLIS. *Accreditation:* ACBSP. Part-time and evening/weekend programs available. *Faculty:* 12 full-time (4 women), 32 part-time/adjunct (9 women). *Students:* 171 full-time (46 women), 193 part-time (84 women); includes 26 minority (11 African Americans, 3 Asian Americans or Pacific Islanders, 12 Hispanic Americans), 173 international. Average age 30. 133 applicants, 98% accepted, 106 enrolled. In 2006, 118 degrees awarded. *Entrance requirements:* For master's, GMAT. Additional exam requirements/recommendations for international students: Required—TOEFL (minimum score 550 paper-based; 213 computer-based); Recommended—IELTS (minimum score 6). *Application deadline:* Applications are processed on a rolling basis. Application fee: $25. Electronic applications accepted. *Expenses: Contact institution.* Tuition and fees vary according to campus/location and program. *Financial support:* Career-related internships or fieldwork, tuition waivers (partial), and unspecified assistantships available. Support available to part-time students. Financial award applicants required to submit FAFSA. *Faculty research:* Entrepreneurship, small business finance, business ethics, marketing strategy. *Unit head:* Dr. Molly Burke, Dean, 708-524-6810, Fax: 708-524-6939, E-mail: burkemq@dom.edu. *Application contact:* Linda Puvogel, Assistant Dean for Graduate Business Programs, 708-524-6507, Fax: 708-524-6939, E-mail: lpuvogel@dom.edu.

Dominican University, Institute for Adult Learning, River Forest, IL 60305-1099. Offers MSOL. Part-time and evening/weekend programs available. *Faculty:* 5 part-time/adjunct (3 women). *Students:* 1 full-time (0 women), 17 part-time (14 women); includes 8 minority (5 African Americans, 3 Hispanic Americans). Average age 41. In 2006, 10 degrees awarded. *Entrance requirements:* Additional exam requirements/recommendations for international students: Required—TOEFL (minimum score 550 paper-based; 213 computer-based). *Application deadline:* Applications are processed on a rolling basis. Application fee: $25. *Expenses: Contact institution.* Tuition and fees vary according to campus/location and program. *Unit head:* Bryan J. Watkins, Executive Director, 708-714-9001, E-mail: bwatkins@dom.edu. *Application contact:* Lauren Kelleher, Associate Director of Marketing, 708-714-9003, Fax: 708-714-9126, E-mail: lkellehe@dom.edu.

Eastern Connecticut State University, School of Education and Professional Studies/ Graduate Division, Program in Organizational Management, Willimantic, CT 06226-2295. Offers MS. Part-time and evening/weekend programs available. *Faculty:* 5 full-time (1 woman), 1 part-time/adjunct (0 women). *Students:* 4 full-time (2 women), 48 part-time (28 women); includes 8 minority (6 African Americans, 1 Asian American or Pacific Islander, 1 Hispanic American), 2 international. Average age 39. 11 applicants, 100% accepted, 9 enrolled. In 2006, 17 degrees awarded. *Degree requirements:* For master's, comprehensive exam or thesis. *Entrance requirements:* For master's, minimum GPA of 2.7. Additional exam requirements/recommendations for international students: Required—TOEFL (minimum score 550 paper-based; 213 computer-based). *Application deadline:* For fall admission, 7/6 priority date for domestic and international students; for spring admission, 11/3 priority date for domestic and international students. Applications are processed on a rolling basis. Application fee: $50. *Expenses:* Tuition, state resident: full-time $3,970. Tuition, nonresident: full-time $11,061; part-time $336 per credit. Required fees: $35 per credit. *Financial support:* Teaching assistantships, career-related internships or fieldwork, scholarships/grants, and unspecified assistantships available. Support available to part-time students. Financial award application deadline: 3/15; financial award applicants required to submit FAFSA. *Unit head:* Dr. Elizabeth Scott, Advisor, 860-465-5366, Fax: 860-465-4459, E-mail: scotte@easternct.edu. *Application contact:* Dr. Tuesday L. Cooper, Associate Dean, 860-465-4543, Fax: 860-465-4538, E-mail: coopert@easternct.edu.

Eastern Michigan University, Graduate School, College of Business, Department of Management, Program in Human Resources Management and Organizational Development, Ypsilanti, MI 48197. Offers MSHROD. Part-time and evening/weekend programs available. Postbaccalaureate distance learning degree programs offered (minimal on-campus study). *Faculty:* 20 full-time (8 women). *Students:* 7 full-time (6 women), 65 part-time (46 women); includes 12 minority (4 African Americans, 7 Asian Americans or Pacific Islanders, 1 Hispanic American), 29 international. Average age 31. In 2006, 33 degrees awarded. *Degree requirements:* For master's, thesis optional. *Entrance requirements:* For master's, GMAT. Additional exam requirements/recommendations for international students: Required—TOEFL. *Application deadline:* For fall admission, 5/15 priority date for domestic and international students; for winter admission, 10/15 priority date for domestic and international students; for spring admission, 3/15 priority date for domestic and international students. Applications are processed on a rolling basis. Application fee: $35. *Expenses:* Tuition, state resident: part-time $341 per credit hour. Tuition, nonresident: full-time $16,104; part-time $671 per credit hour. Required fees: $816; $34 per credit hour. $40 per term. One-time fee: $82 full-time. Tuition and fees vary according to course level, course load, degree level and reciprocity agreements. *Financial support:* Fellowships, research assistantships with full tuition reimbursements, teaching assistantships with full tuition reimbursements, career-related internships or fieldwork, Federal Work-Study, institutionally sponsored loans, scholarships/grants, tuition waivers (partial), and unspecified assistantships available. Support available to part-time students. Financial award applicants required to submit FAFSA.

Eastern University, Office of Interdisciplinary Programs, Program in Organizational Leadership, St. Davids, PA 19087-3696. Offers PhD.

See Close-Up on page 693.

Emory University, Roberto C. Goizueta Business School, Doctoral Programs in Business, Atlanta, GA 30322-1100. Offers accounting (PhD); finance (PhD); information systems (PhD); marketing (PhD); organization and management (PhD). *Degree requirements:* For doctorate, thesis/dissertation, comprehensive exam. *Entrance requirements:* Additional exam requirements/recommendations for international students: Required—TOEFL (minimum score 600 paper-based; 250 computer-based). Electronic applications accepted. *Expenses:* Tuition: Full-time $30,246. *Faculty research:* Financial markets, banking, corporate disclosure, investor relations, marketing strategy.

Endicott College, Van Loan School of Graduate and Professional Studies, Program in International Education, Beverly, MA 01915-2096. Offers international education (M Ed); organizational management (M Ed). Part-time and evening/weekend programs available. Postbaccalaureate distance learning degree programs offered. *Faculty:* 2 part-time/adjunct (1 woman). *Students:* Average age 35. 23 applicants, 100% accepted, 23 enrolled. In 2006, 9 degrees awarded. *Degree requirements:* For master's, thesis, practicum. *Entrance requirements:* For master's, MAT or GRE, 2 letters of recommendation. *Application deadline:* For fall admission, 7/15 priority date for domestic students; for winter admission, 12/15 priority date for domestic students. Applications are processed on a rolling basis. Application fee: $50. *Expenses:* Tuition: Part-time $279 per credit. Tuition and fees vary according to program. *Financial support:* In 2006–07, 10 students received support. Career-related internships or fieldwork and scholarships/grants available. Financial award application deadline: 12/15. *Unit head:* Dr. April Burriss, Dean of School of International Studies, 978-232-2272, E-mail: aburriss@endicott.edu.

Endicott College, Van Loan School of Graduate and Professional Studies, Program in Organizational Management, Beverly, MA 01915-2096. Offers M Ed. Part-time and evening/weekend programs available. *Faculty:* 35 part-time/adjunct (10 women). *Students:* Average age 35. In 2006, 68 degrees awarded. *Degree requirements:* For master's, thesis. *Entrance requirements:* For master's, GRE or MAT, letters of recommendation. *Application deadline:* Applications are processed on a rolling basis. Application fee: $50. *Expenses:* Tuition: Part-time $279 per credit. Tuition and fees vary according to program. *Financial support:* Career-related internships or fieldwork, Federal Work-Study, institutionally sponsored loans, and tuition waivers (partial) available. *Unit head:* Dr. Jayanti Bandyopadhyay, Associate Dean of Graduate School,

978-232-2744, Fax: 978-232-3000, E-mail: jbandyop@endicott.edu. *Application contact:* Dr. Jayanti Bandyopadhyay, Associate Dean of Graduate School, 978-232-2744, Fax: 978-232-3000, E-mail: jbandyop@endicott.edu.

Evangel University, Organizational Leadership Program, Springfield, MO 65802-2191. Offers MOL. Part-time and evening/weekend programs available. *Faculty:* 4 full-time (2 women), 3 part-time/adjunct (2 women). *Students:* 20 full-time (8 women), 1 part-time; includes 1 minority (Hispanic American) Average age 35. 11 applicants, 100% accepted, 9 enrolled. *Degree requirements:* For master's, thesis, Capstone project, comprehensive exam. *Entrance requirements:* For master's, GMAT or GRE. Additional exam requirements/recommendations for international students: Required—TOEFL (minimum score 550 paper-based; 213 computer-based). *Application deadline:* For fall admission, 7/15 priority date for domestic and international students; for spring admission, 11/15 priority date for domestic and international students. Applications are processed on a rolling basis. Application fee: $25. *Financial support:* In 2006–07, 12 students received support. Career-related internships or fieldwork, institutionally sponsored loans, and scholarships/grants available. Support available to part-time students. Financial award application deadline: 3/1; financial award applicants required to submit FAFSA. *Unit head:* Dr. Jeff Fulks, Director of Graduate Studies, 417-865-2811 Ext. 8616, Fax: 417-575-5484, E-mail: fulksj@evangel.edu. *Application contact:* Charity H. Fahlstrom, Director of Graduate and Professional Studies Admissions, 417-865-2811 Ext. 1227, Fax: 417-575-5484.

Fairleigh Dickinson University, College at Florham, Maxwell Becton College of Arts and Sciences, Department of Psychology, Program in Organizational Behavior, Madison, NJ 07940-1099. Offers organizational behavior (MA); organizational leadership (Certificate). *Students:* 2 full-time (both women), 15 part-time (8 women), 1 international. Average age 34. 2 applicants, 100% accepted, 1 enrolled. In 2006, 5 degrees awarded. Application fee: $40. *Unit head:* Dr. Diane Wentworth, Chairperson, Department of Psychology, 973-443-8548, Fax: 973-443-8562.

Fielding Graduate University, Graduate Programs, School of Human and Organization Development, Santa Barbara, CA 93105-3538. Offers human and organizational systems (PhD); human development (PhD); integral studies (Certificate); organization management and development (MA). Evening/weekend programs available. *Faculty:* 26 full-time (11 women), 21 part-time/adjunct (5 women). *Students:* 526 full-time (353 women), 8 part-time (5 women); includes 119 minority (70 African Americans, 3 American Indian/Alaska Native, 22 Asian Americans or Pacific Islanders, 24 Hispanic Americans), 13 international. Average age 47. 148 applicants, 90% accepted, 97 enrolled. In 2006, 90 master's, 55 doctorates, 3 other advanced degrees awarded. *Median time to degree:* Master's–3 years full-time; doctorate–5.8 years full-time; Certificate–1.5 years part-time. *Degree requirements:* For doctorate, thesis/dissertation, comprehensive exam, registration. *Entrance requirements:* For doctorate, 2 letters of recommendation, writing sample, resumé, self-assessment statement. *Application deadline:* For fall admission, 3/1 for domestic and international students; for spring admission, 9/1 for domestic and international students. Application fee: $75. Electronic applications accepted. *Expenses: Contact institution. Financial support:* In 2006–07, 291 students received support, including 3 teaching assistantships (averaging $2,700 per year); career-related internships or fieldwork, institutionally sponsored loans, and scholarships/grants also available. Financial award application deadline: 3/1; financial award applicants required to submit FAFSA. *Unit head:* Dr. Charles McClintock, Dean, 805-898-2930, Fax: 805-687-4590, E-mail: cmcclintock@fielding.edu. *Application contact:* Carmen Kuchera, Admission Counselor, 800-340-1099, Fax: 805-687-9793, E-mail: ckuchera@fielding.edu.

See Close-Up on page 695.

Gannon University, School of Graduate Studies, College of Humanities, Business, and Education, School of Education, Program in Organizational Leadership, Erie, PA 16541-0001. Offers Certificate. *Expenses:* Tuition: Full-time $12,240; part-time $680 per credit. Required fees: $496; $16 per credit. Tuition and fees vary according to course load, degree level, campus/location and program. *Financial support:* Application deadline: 7/1; *Application contact:* Debra Meszaros, Director of Graduate Recruitment, 814-871-5819, Fax: 814-871-5827, E-mail: cfal@gannon.edu.

Geneva College, Program in Organizational Leadership, Beaver Falls, PA 15010-3599. Offers MS. Evening/weekend programs available. Terminal master's awarded for partial completion of doctoral program. *Degree requirements:* For master's, thesis. *Entrance requirements:* For master's, 3-5 years of professional experience, minimum GPA of 3.0 (preferred). Additional exam requirements/recommendations for international students: Required—TOEFL. Electronic applications accepted. *Faculty research:* Servant leadership.

George Fox University, Program in Organizational Leadership, Newberg, OR 97132-2697. Offers MAOL. Offered only in Boise, ID. Part-time and evening/weekend programs available. *Faculty:* 3 full-time (2 women), 2 part-time/adjunct (0 women). *Students:* 1 (woman) full-time, 22 part-time (9 women); includes 1 minority (Asian American or Pacific Islander), 1 international. Average age 38. 14 applicants, 86% accepted, 11 enrolled. In 2006, 9 degrees awarded. *Application deadline:* For fall admission, 7/1 for domestic students. Applications are processed on a rolling basis. Application fee: $40. Electronic applications accepted. *Expenses: Contact institution. Unit head:* Dr. Mary Olson, Director, 208-375-3900, Fax: 208-375-3564, E-mail: molson@georgefox.edu. *Application contact:* Kris Thompson, Admissions Counselor, 208-375-3900, E-mail: kthompson@georgefox.edu.

George Mason University, School of Public Policy, Program in Organization Development and Knowledge Management, Fairfax, VA 22030. Offers MNPS. Part-time and evening/weekend programs available. *Faculty:* 48 full-time (8 women), 41 part-time/adjunct (6 women). *Students:* 78. 57 applicants, 74% accepted, 40 enrolled. In 2006, 8 degrees awarded. *Degree requirements:* For master's, thesis or alternative. *Entrance requirements:* For master's, minimum GPA of 3.0, 2 letters of recommendation, resumé, goals statement. Additional exam requirements/recommendations for international students: Required—TOEFL. *Application deadline:* For fall admission, 6/1 priority date for domestic students, 5/1 priority date for international students; for spring admission, 12/1 priority date for domestic and international students. Applications are processed on a rolling basis. Application fee: $60. Electronic applications accepted. *Expenses: Contact institution. Financial support:* Career-related internships or fieldwork, Federal Work-Study, scholarships/grants, tuition waivers (partial), and unspecified assistantships available. Support available to part-time students. Financial award application deadline: 3/1; financial award applicants required to submit FAFSA. *Unit head:* Dr. Ann Baker, Director, 703-993-8099, E-mail: spp@gmu.edu. *Application contact:* Leslie Metzger Levin, Director of Graduate Admissions, 703-993-8099, Fax: 703-993-4876, E-mail: lmetzger@gmu.edu.

The George Washington University, Columbian College of Arts and Sciences, Department of Organizational Sciences and Communication, Washington, DC 20052. Offers human resource management (MA); leadership and coaching (Certificate); organizational management (MA). Part-time and evening/weekend programs available. *Degree requirements:* For master's, comprehensive exam. *Entrance requirements:* For master's, GRE General Test, minimum GPA of 3.0; for Certificate, minimum GPA of 3.0. Additional exam requirements/recommendations for international students: Required—TOEFL (minimum score 500 paper-based). Electronic applications accepted.

Announcement: The Department of Organizational Sciences and Communication at The George Washington University is founded on the philosophy that managerial and organizational success is closely tied to developing knowledge in strategy and change management, leadership and communication, and performance and talent management. These interlocking dimensions create a knowledge base critical for individual and organizational success.

See Close-Up on page 697.

Georgia State University, J. Mack Robinson College of Business, Department of Managerial Sciences, Atlanta, GA 30303-3083. Offers business analysis (MBA, MS); entrepreneurship

(MBA); human resources management (MBA, MS); management (MBA, PhD); operations management (MBA, MS, PhD); organization change (MS). Part-time and evening/weekend programs available. *Faculty:* 34 full-time (14 women). *Students:* 53 full-time (18 women), 177 part-time (61 women); includes 37 minority (21 African Americans, 11 Asian Americans or Pacific Islanders, 5 Hispanic Americans), 19 international. Average age 32. 68 applicants, 35% accepted, 20 enrolled. In 2006, 98 master's, 4 doctorates awarded. *Degree requirements:* For doctorate, thesis/dissertation. *Entrance requirements:* For master's and doctorate, GMAT. Additional exam requirements/recommendations for international students: Required—TOEFL (minimum score 610 paper-based; 255 computer-based; 101 iBT). *Application deadline:* For fall admission, 5/1 for domestic students, 2/1 for international students; for spring admission, 10/15 for domestic students, 5/1 for international students. Applications are processed on a rolling basis. Application fee: $50. Electronic applications accepted. *Unit head:* Dr. Todd J. Maurer, Chair, 404-651-3400, E-mail: tmaurer@gsu.edu.

Gonzaga University, School of Professional Studies, Program in Organizational Leadership, Spokane, WA 99258. Offers MOL. *Students:* 71 full-time (34 women), 524 part-time (273 women); includes 95 minority (35 African Americans, 9 American Indian/Alaska Native, 22 Asian Americans or Pacific Islanders, 29 Hispanic Americans), 3 international. Average age 37. In 2006, 66 degrees awarded. *Entrance requirements:* For master's, GRE General Test or MAT, minimum B average in undergraduate course work. Additional exam requirements/ recommendations for international students: Required—TOEFL. *Application deadline:* For fall admission, 7/20 priority date for domestic students; for spring admission, 11/1 for domestic students. Applications are processed on a rolling basis. Application fee: $40. *Expenses:* Tuition: Full-time $10,620; part-time $590 per credit. *Financial support:* Application deadline: 3/1. *Unit head:* Dr. Joseph Albert, Contact, 509-328-4220 Ext. 3564.

Hawai'i Pacific University, College of Business Administration, Honolulu, HI 96813. Offers accounting/CPA (MBA); communication (MBA); e-business (MBA); economics (MBA); finance (MBA); human resource management (MBA); information systems (MBA); international business (MBA); management (MBA); marketing (MBA); organizational change (MBA); travel industry management (MBA). Part-time and evening/weekend programs available. *Faculty:* 40 full-time (16 women), 30 part-time/adjunct (10 women). *Students:* 320 full-time (150 women), 205 part-time (95 women); includes 168 minority (17 African Americans, 7 American Indian/ Alaska Native, 137 Asian Americans or Pacific Islanders, 7 Hispanic Americans), 232 international. Average age 31. 279 applicants, 67% accepted, 166 enrolled. In 2006, 172 degrees awarded. *Degree requirements:* For master's, thesis. *Entrance requirements:* For master's, GMAT. Additional exam requirements/recommendations for international students: Recommended—TOEFL (minimum score 550 paper-based; 213 computer-based), TWE (minimum score 5). *Application deadline:* For fall admission, 2/15 priority date for domestic students; for spring admission, 10/15 priority date for domestic students. Applications are processed on a rolling basis. Application fee: $50. Electronic applications accepted. *Expenses:* Tuition: Full-time $10,080; part-time $560 per credit. *Financial support:* In 2006–07, 118 students received support; research assistantships, career-related internships or fieldwork, Federal Work-Study, scholarships/grants, and unspecified assistantships available. Support available to part-time students. Financial award application deadline: 3/1; financial award applicants required to submit FAFSA. *Faculty research:* Statistical control process as used by management, studies in comparative cross-cultural management styles, not-for-profit management. *Unit head:* Dr. Charles Steilen, Dean, 808-544-9301, Fax: 808-544-0283, E-mail: csteilen@ hpu.edu. *Application contact:* Danny Lam, Assistant Director of Graduate Admissions, 808-544-1135, Fax: 808-544-0280, E-mail: graduate@hpu.edu.

See Close-Up on page 275.

Hawai'i Pacific University, College of Professional Studies, Honolulu, HI 96813. Offers global leadership and sustainable development (MA); human resource management (MA); information systems (MSIS); organizational change (MA). Part-time and evening/weekend programs available. *Faculty:* 15 full-time (2 women), 7 part-time/adjunct (2 women). *Students:* 118 full-time (56 women), 149 part-time (57 women); includes 101 minority (15 African Americans, 5 American Indian/Alaska Native, 70 Asian Americans or Pacific Islanders, 11 Hispanic Americans), 87 international. Average age 32. 188 applicants, 58% accepted, 67 enrolled. In 2006, 65 degrees awarded. *Degree requirements:* For master's, thesis. *Entrance requirements:* Additional exam requirements/recommendations for international students: Recommended—TOEFL (minimum score 550 paper-based; 213 computer-based), TWE (minimum score 5). *Application deadline:* For fall admission, 2/15 priority date for domestic students; for spring admission, 10/15 priority date for domestic students. Applications are processed on a rolling basis. Application fee: $50. Electronic applications accepted. *Expenses:* Tuition: Full-time $10,080; part-time $560 per credit. *Financial support:* In 2006–07, 54 students received support. Career-related internships or fieldwork, Federal Work-Study, scholarships/grants, and unspecified assistantships available. Support available to part-time students. Financial award application deadline: 3/1; financial award applicants required to submit FAFSA. *Unit head:* Dr. Gordon Jones, Dean, 808-544-1181, Fax: 808-544-0247, E-mail: gjones@hpu.edu. *Application contact:* Danny Lam, Assistant Director of Graduate Admissions, 808-544-1135, Fax: 808-544-0280, E-mail: graduate@hpu.edu.

Immaculata University, College of Graduate Studies, Program in Organization Studies, Immaculata, PA 19345. Offers MA. Part-time and evening/weekend programs available. *Students:* Average age 35. 8 applicants, 75% accepted, 6 enrolled. In 2006, 7 degrees awarded. *Degree requirements:* For master's, thesis optional. *Entrance requirements:* For master's, GMAT, GRE General Test, MAT, minimum GPA of 3.0. *Application deadline:* Applications are processed on a rolling basis. Application fee: $35. Electronic applications accepted. *Financial support:* Application deadline: 5/1. *Unit head:* Dr. Janice Jacobs, Chair, 610-647-4400 Ext. 3452, Fax: 610-993-8550, E-mail: jjacobs@immaculata.edu. *Application contact:* 610-647-4400 Ext. 3211, Fax: 610-993-8550, E-mail: graduate@immaculata.edu.

Indiana University–Purdue University Fort Wayne, Division of Organizational Leadership and Supervision, Fort Wayne, IN 46805-1499. Offers MS. Part-time programs available. *Students:* 1 (woman) full-time, 9 part-time (7 women); includes 1 minority (African American) Average age 36. 16 applicants, 88% accepted, 10 enrolled. *Entrance requirements:* For master's, GRE or GMAT (if undergraduate GPA is below 3.0), current resumé, 2 recent letters of recommendation. Additional exam requirements/recommendations for international students: Required—TOEFL (minimum score 600 paper-based; 260 computer-based). *Application deadline:* For fall admission, 8/1 priority date for domestic students; for spring admission, 12/1 for domestic students. Applications are processed on a rolling basis. Application fee: $55. Electronic applications accepted. *Expenses:* Tuition, state resident: full-time $4,039; part-time $224 per credit. Tuition, nonresident: full-time $9,220; part-time $512 per credit. Required fees: $429; $24 per credit. Tuition and fees vary according to course load. *Financial support:* Scholarships/grants available. Support available to part-time students. Financial award application deadline: 3/1; financial award applicants required to submit FAFSA. *Faculty research:* Ethical issues in mentoring, career development. Total annual research expenditures: $2,000. *Unit head:* Dr. Kimberly McDonald, Chair, 260-481-6420, Fax: 260-481-6417, E-mail: mcdonalk@ ipfw.edu.

Indiana Wesleyan University, College of Graduate Studies, Department of Organizational Leadership, Marion, IN 46953-4974. Offers Ed D. Postbaccalaureate distance learning degree programs offered (minimal on-campus study). *Faculty:* 2 full-time (0 women). *Students:* 77 full-time (35 women); includes 19 minority (17 African Americans, 1 Asian American or Pacific Islander, 1 Hispanic American). Average age 45. *Expenses:* Tuition: Full-time $16,000; part-time $400 per credit. Required fees: $3,000. Tuition and fees vary according to degree level, campus/location and program. *Unit head:* Dr. Vern Ludden, Director, E-mail: vern.ludden@ indwes.edu. *Application contact:* David McMillan, Assistant Director of Enrollment Management, 765-677-2688, E-mail: david.mcmillan@indwes.edu.

International University in Geneva, MBA Program, Geneva, Switzerland. Offers e-commerce (MBA); human relations (MBA); international business (Exec MBA, MBA); marketing (MBA); organizational development (MBA); telecommunications (MBA). Part-time and evening/ weekend programs available. *Degree requirements:* For master's, comprehensive exam, registration. *Entrance requirements:* For master's, GMAT. Additional exam requirements/ recommendations for international students: Required—TOEFL. Electronic applications accepted.

John F. Kennedy University, School of Management, Program in Business Administration, Pleasant Hill, CA 94523-4817. Offers business administration (MBA); organizational leadership (Certificate). Part-time and evening/weekend programs available. *Degree requirements:* For master's, thesis or alternative. *Entrance requirements:* For master's, interview. Additional exam requirements/recommendations for international students: Required—TOEFL.

Johnson & Wales University, The Alan Shawn Feinstein Graduate School, Program in Global Business, Concentration in Organizational Leadership, Providence, RI 02903-3703. Offers MBA. Part-time and evening/weekend programs available. *Students:* 83 full-time (42 women), 58 part-time (30 women); includes 17 minority (7 African Americans, 7 Asian Americans or Pacific Islanders, 3 Hispanic Americans), 37 international. Average age 31. In 2006, 50 degrees awarded. *Entrance requirements:* For master's, GMAT recommended, minimum GPA of 2.75. Additional exam requirements/recommendations for international students: Required—TOEFL (paper-based 550; computer-based 210) or IELTS. *Application deadline:* For fall admission, 8/15 priority date for domestic students, 6/28 priority date for international students; for winter admission, 11/10 priority date for domestic students, 9/20 priority date for international students; for spring admission, 2/15 priority date for domestic students, 12/20 priority date for international students. Applications are processed on a rolling basis. Electronic applications accepted. *Financial support:* Unspecified assistantships available. Financial award application deadline: 5/1. *Unit head:* Dr. Frank Satterwaite, Unit Head. *Application contact:* Dr. Allan G. Freedman, Director of Graduate Admissions, 401-598-1015, Fax: 401-598-1286, E-mail: gradadm@jwu.edu.

Jones International University, Graduate School of Education, Centennial, CO 80112. Offers adult education (M Ed); corporate training and knowledge management (M Ed); curriculum and instruction (M Ed), including elementary teacher licensure, secondary teacher licensure; e-learning technology and design (M Ed); educational leadership and administration (M Ed); educational leadership and administration: principal and administrator licensure (M Ed); elementary curriculum instruction and assessment (M Ed); higher education leadership and administration (M Ed); K-12 instructional technology (M Ed); K-12 instructional technology: teacher licensure (M Ed); secondary curriculum instruction and assessment (M Ed); technology and design (M Ed). Part-time and evening/weekend programs available. Postbaccalaureate distance learning degree programs offered (no on-campus study). *Entrance requirements:* For master's, minimum cumulative GPA of 2.5. Additional exam requirements/recommendations for international students: Recommended—TOEFL (minimum score 550 paper-based; 213 computer-based). Electronic applications accepted.

Leadership Institute of Seattle, School of Applied Behavioral Science, Consulting and Coaching in Organizations Track, Kenmore, WA 98028-4966. Offers MA. *Faculty:* 10 full-time (6 women), 5 part-time/adjunct (2 women). *Students:* 48 full-time. Average age 40. 50 applicants, 98% accepted, 40 enrolled. In 2006, 19 degrees awarded. *Degree requirements:* For master's, thesis (for some programs), oral exams. *Entrance requirements:* For master's, bachelor's degree from an accredited college or university. *Application deadline:* Applications are processed on a rolling basis. Application fee: $65. *Expenses:* Tuition: Full-time $14,560. Required fees: $3,700. *Financial support:* In 2006–07, 32 students received support. Career-related internships or fieldwork, Federal Work-Study, and scholarships/grants available. Financial award applicants required to submit FAFSA. *Faculty research:* Cross-functional work teams, communication, management authority, employee influence, systems theory. *Unit head:* Dr. Shelley Drogin, Head, 425-939-8181, Fax: 425-939-8110, E-mail: sdrogin@lios.org. *Application contact:* Scott Harris, Director, Academic Admissions, 425-939-8124, Fax: 425-939-8110, E-mail: sharris@ lios.org.

Lehigh University, College of Business and Economics, Bethlehem, PA 18015-3094. Offers accounting (MS), including accounting and information analysis; business administration (MBA); economics (MS, PhD), including economics, health and bio-pharmaceutical economics (MS); entrepreneurship (Certificate); finance (MS), including analytical finance, finance; organizational leadership (Certificate); project management (Certificate); supply chain management (Certificate); MBA/E; MBA/M Ed. *Accreditation:* AACSB. Part-time and evening/weekend programs available. Postbaccalaureate distance learning degree programs offered (minimal on-campus study). *Faculty:* 64 full-time (14 women), 12 part-time/adjunct (0 women). *Students:* 87 full-time (25 women), 219 part-time (60 women); includes 34 minority (9 African Americans, 22 Asian Americans or Pacific Islanders, 3 Hispanic Americans), 56 international. 371 applicants, 69% accepted, 151 enrolled. In 2006, 103 master's, 2 doctorates awarded. Terminal master's awarded for partial completion of doctoral program. *Degree requirements:* For master's, thesis optional; for doctorate, thesis/dissertation, proposal defense, comprehensive exam. *Entrance requirements:* For master's, GMAT, GRE General Test; for doctorate, GMAT or GRE General Test. Additional exam requirements/recommendations for international students: Required—TOEFL (minimum score 600 paper-based; 250 computer-based). *Application deadline:* For fall admission, 7/15 for domestic students, 5/1 for international students; for spring admission, 12/1 for domestic and international students. Applications are processed on a rolling basis. Application fee: $60. Electronic applications accepted. *Expenses:* Contact institution. *Financial support:* In 2006–07, 2 fellowships with full tuition reimbursements (averaging $13,200 per year), 8 research assistantships with full and partial tuition reimbursements (averaging $1,000 per year), 13 teaching assistantships with full tuition reimbursements (averaging $13,200 per year) were awarded; career-related internships or fieldwork, scholarships/grants, health care benefits, tuition waivers (full and partial), and unspecified assistantships also available. Support available to part-time students. Financial award application deadline: 1/15. *Faculty research:* Public finance, energy, investments, activity-based costing, management information systems. *Unit head:* Michael G. Kolchin, Graduate Business Programs, 610-758-4450, Fax: 610-758-5283, E-mail: mgk1@lehigh.edu. *Application contact:* Mary- Theresa Taglang, Director of Graduate Programs, 610-758-5285, Fax: 610-758-5283, E-mail: mtt4@lehigh.edu.

See Close-Ups on pages 283, 285, and 1807.

Lewis University, College of Arts and Sciences, Program in Organizational Leadership, Romeoville, IL 60446. Offers higher education/student services (MA); organizational management (MA); public administration (MA); training and development (MA). Part-time and evening/ weekend programs available. *Entrance requirements:* For master's, bachelor's degree, at least 25 years of age, minimum of 3 years of work experience, minimum GPA of 3.0 (provisional admission possible), letter of recommendation, interview. Additional exam requirements/ recommendations for international students: Required—TOEFL (minimum score 550 paper-based; 213 computer-based). Electronic applications accepted.

Lindenwood University, Graduate Programs, Division of Management, St. Charles, MO 63301-1695. Offers accounting (MBA, MS); business administration (MBA); entrepreneurial studies (MBA); finance (MBA, MS); human resource management (MBA); human resources (MS); international business (MBA, MS); management (MBA, MS); management information systems (MBA, MS); managing business to business (MA); managing human resources (MA); managing international business (MA); managing investment management (MA); managing leadership (MA); managing marketing (MA); managing organizational behavior (MA); managing sales (MA); managing, training and development (MA); marketing (MBA, MS); nonprofit administration (MA); public management (MBA, MS); sport management (MA). Part-time and evening/weekend programs available. *Faculty:* 38 full-time (15 women), 20 part-time/adjunct (5 women). *Students:* 177 full-time (78 women), 138 part-time (67 women); includes 43 minority (27 African Americans, 4 American Indian/Alaska Native, 6 Asian Americans or Pacific Islanders, 6 Hispanic Americans), 73 international. Average age 30. In 2006, 159 degrees awarded. *Degree requirements:* For master's, thesis (for some programs). *Entrance requirements:* For master's, interview, minimum GPA of 3.0. Additional exam requirements/recommendations for international students: Required—TOEFL (minimum score 550 paper-based; 173 computer-

Organizational Management

Lindenwood University (continued)
based). *Application deadline:* For fall admission, 7/30 priority date for domestic students, 9/30 priority date for international students; for winter admission, 12/30 priority date for domestic and international students; for spring admission, 3/30 priority date for domestic and international students. Applications are processed on a rolling basis. Application fee: $30 ($100 for international students). Electronic applications accepted. *Expenses:* Tuition: Part-time $340 per credit hour. Tuition and fees vary according to course level, course load, degree level and program. *Financial support:* Career-related internships or fieldwork, Federal Work-Study, institutionally sponsored loans, and tuition waivers (partial) available. Financial award application deadline: 6/30; financial award applicants required to submit FAFSA. *Unit head:* Ed Morris, Dean, 636-949-4832, Fax: 636-949-4910, E-mail: emorris@lindenwood.edu. *Application contact:* Brett Barger, Dean Adult, Corporate and Graduate Admissions, 636-949-4366, Fax: 636-949-4109, E-mail: bbarger@lindenwood.edu.

Lourdes College, School of Graduate and Professional Studies, Program in Organizational Leadership, Sylvania, OH 43560-2898. Offers MOL. Evening/weekend programs available. *Entrance requirements:* Additional exam requirements/recommendations for international students: Required—TOEFL.

Manhattanville College, Graduate Programs, Humanities and Social Sciences Programs, Purchase, NY 10577-2132. Offers integrated marketing communications (MS); international management (MS); leadership and strategic management (MS); liberal studies (MA); management communications (MS); organization development and human resources management (MS); sports business management (MS); writing (MA). Part-time and evening/weekend programs available. *Students:* 15 full-time (6 women), 215 part-time (146 women); includes 21 minority (14 African Americans, 7 Hispanic Americans), 9 international. In 2006, 66 degrees awarded. *Degree requirements:* For master's, thesis. *Entrance requirements:* For master's, interview, 2 letters of recommendation. *Application deadline:* Applications are processed on a rolling basis. Application fee: $55. *Financial support:* Unspecified assistantships available. Financial award applicants required to submit FAFSA. *Unit head:* Sr. Ruth M. Dowd, Dean, School of Graduate and Professional Studies, 914-694-5483, Fax: 914-694-3488, E-mail: rdowd@mville.edu. *Application contact:* Natalia Fernandez, Director of Admissions, 914-323-5418, E-mail: gps@myllle.edu.

Marian College of Fond du Lac, Business Division, Fond du Lac, WI 54935-4699. Offers organizational leadership and quality (MS). Part-time and evening/weekend programs available. *Faculty:* 6 part-time/adjunct (0 women). *Students:* 1 full-time (0 women), 95 part-time (55 women); includes 7 minority (5 African Americans, 1 American Indian/Alaska Native, 1 Hispanic American). Average age 38. 44 applicants, 100% accepted, 44 enrolled. In 2006, 33 degrees awarded. *Degree requirements:* For master's, comprehensive group project. *Entrance requirements:* For master's, 3 years of managerial experience, minimum GPA of 2.75, letters of professional reference. *Application deadline:* Applications are processed on a rolling basis. Application fee: $25. Electronic applications accepted. *Expenses: Contact institution.* Tuition and fees vary according to degree level and program. *Financial support:* In 2006–07, 23 students received support. Institutionally sponsored loans available. Support available to part-time students. Financial award application deadline: 3/1; financial award applicants required to submit FAFSA. *Faculty research:* Organizational values, statistical decision making, learning organization, quality planning, customer research. *Unit head:* David McPhail, Dean of Lifelong Learning, 920-923-8760, Fax: 920-923-7167, E-mail: dmcphail@mariancollege.edu. *Application contact:* Tracy Qualman, Director of Marketing and Admission, 920-923-7159, Fax: 920-923-7167, E-mail: tqualmann@mariancollege.edu.

Medaille College, Program in Business Administration—Amherst, Buffalo, NY 14214-2695. Offers business administration (MBA); organizational leadership (MA). Evening/weekend programs available. *Faculty:* 4 full-time (1 woman), 30 part-time/adjunct (15 women). *Students:* 228 full-time (136 women); includes 64 minority (49 African Americans, 2 American Indian/Alaska Native, 2 Asian Americans or Pacific Islanders, 11 Hispanic Americans). Average age 36. 135 applicants, 96% accepted, 127 enrolled. In 2006, 86 degrees awarded. *Degree requirements:* For master's, thesis or alternative. *Entrance requirements:* For master's, GMAT, minimum undergraduate GPA of 2.7, 3 years of work experience. Additional exam requirements/recommendations for international students: Required—TOEFL (minimum score 550 paper-based; 213 computer-based). *Application deadline:* Applications are processed on a rolling basis. Application fee: $100. *Expenses: Contact institution.* Full-time tuition and fees vary according to program. *Financial support:* In 2006–07, 150 students received support. Federal Work-Study available. Financial award applicants required to submit FAFSA. *Unit head:* Jennifer Bavifard, Associate Dean for Special Programs, 716-631-1061 Ext. 150, Fax: 716-631-1380, E-mail: jbavifar@medaille.edu. *Application contact:* Susan Greenwald, Executive Director of Admissions, 716-635-5033 Ext. 2011, Fax: 716-631-1380, E-mail: sgreenwald@medaille.edu.

Medaille College, Program in Business Administration—Rochester, Buffalo, NY 14214-2695. Offers business administration (MBA); organizational leadership (MA). Evening/weekend programs available. *Faculty:* 3 full-time (2 women), 53 part-time/adjunct (27 women). *Students:* 46 full-time (32 women); includes 14 minority (9 African Americans, 5 Hispanic Americans). Average age 36. 31 applicants, 87% accepted, 25 enrolled. In 2006, 18 degrees awarded. *Degree requirements:* For master's, thesis or alternative. *Entrance requirements:* For master's, GMAT, 3 years of work experience, minimum undergraduate GPA of 2.7. Additional exam requirements/recommendations for international students: Required—TOEFL (minimum score 550 paper-based; 213 computer-based). *Application deadline:* Applications are processed on a rolling basis. Application fee: $100. *Expenses: Contact institution.* Full-time tuition and fees vary according to program. *Financial support:* In 2006–07, 34 students received support. Federal Work-Study available. Financial award applicants required to submit FAFSA. *Unit head:* Lorraine Beach-Horner, Branch Campus Director, 585-272-0030 Ext. 102, Fax: 585-273-0057, E-mail: lbeach-horner@medaille.edu. *Application contact:* Jane Rowlands, Marketing Support, 585-272-0030, Fax: 585-272-0057, E-mail: jrowlands@medaille.edu.

Mercy College, Division of Business and Accounting, Program in Organizational Leadership, Dobbs Ferry, NY 10522-1189. Offers MS. *Students:* 83 full-time (56 women), 5 part-time (2 women); includes 52 minority (36 African Americans, 2 Asian Americans or Pacific Islanders, 14 Hispanic Americans), 3 international. Average age 38. In 2006, 87 degrees awarded. *Entrance requirements:* For master's, interview, letters of reference. *Application deadline:* Applications are processed on a rolling basis. Application fee: $35. Electronic applications accepted. *Expenses:* Tuition: Part-time $595 per credit. Required fees: $9 per credit. Tuition and fees vary according to program. *Faculty research:* Organizational behavior, strategic management. *Unit head:* Benjamin Manjindo, Director, 212-615-3330, E-mail: bmanjindo@mercy.edu. *Application contact:* Kathleen Jackson, Director of Admissions, 800-Mercy-NY, Fax: 914-674-7382, E-mail: admissions@mercy.edu.

Mercyhurst College, Graduate Program, Program in Organizational Leadership, Erie, PA 16546. Offers MS, Certificate. Part-time and evening/weekend programs available. *Degree requirements:* For master's, thesis. *Entrance requirements:* For master's, GRE General Test or MAT, interview. Additional exam requirements/recommendations for international students: Required—TOEFL. Electronic applications accepted. *Faculty research:* Leadership training, organizational communication, leadership pedagogy.

Metropolitan State University, College of Management, St. Paul, MN 55106-5000. Offers finance (MBA); human resource management (MBA); information management (MMIS); international business (MBA); law enforcement (MPNA); management information systems (MBA); marketing (MBA); nonprofit management (MPNA); organizational studies (MBA); public administration (MPNA); purchasing management (MBA); systems management (MMIS). Part-time and evening/weekend programs available. *Degree requirements:* For master's, computer language (MMIS), thesis optional. *Entrance requirements:* For master's, GMAT (MBA), resumé. Additional exam requirements/recommendations for international students: Required—TOEFL (minimum score 550 paper-based; 213 computer-based). *Faculty research:* Yugoslav economic system, workers' cooperatives, participative management and job enrichment, global business systems.

National University, Academic Affairs, School of Business and Management, Department of Management, Marketing and E-Business, La Jolla, CA 92037-1011. Offers e-business (MS); human resource management and organizational development (MA); management (MA); organizational leadership (MS). Part-time and evening/weekend programs available. Postbaccalaureate distance learning degree programs offered (no on-campus study). *Faculty:* 17 full-time (5 women), 209 part-time/adjunct (57 women). *Students:* 134 full-time (74 women), 244 part-time (119 women); includes 148 minority (55 African Americans, 4 American Indian/Alaska Native, 35 Asian Americans or Pacific Islanders, 54 Hispanic Americans), 19 international. Average age 38. 166 applicants, 143 enrolled. In 2006, 82 degrees awarded. *Degree requirements:* For master's, thesis. *Entrance requirements:* For master's, interview, minimum GPA of 2.5. Additional exam requirements/recommendations for international students: Required—TOEFL (minimum score 550 paper-based; 213 computer-based; 80 iBT), IELTS (minimum score 6). *Application deadline:* Applications are processed on a rolling basis. Application fee: $60 ($65 for international students). Electronic applications accepted. *Expenses:* Tuition: Full-time $7,722; part-time $286 per unit. One-time fee: $60. *Financial support:* Career-related internships or fieldwork, institutionally sponsored loans, scholarships/grants, and tuition waivers (partial) available. Support available to part-time students. Financial award application deadline: 6/30; financial award applicants required to submit FAFSA. *Unit head:* Dr. George Drops, Chair and Professor, 858-642-8438, Fax: 858-642-8406, E-mail: gdrops@nu.edu. *Application contact:* Dominick Giovanniello, Associate Regional Dean—San Diego, 800-NAT-UNIV, Fax: 858-642-8709, E-mail: dgiovann@nu.edu.

New England College, Program in Management, Henniker, NH 03242-3293. Offers healthcare administration (MS); nonprofit leadership (MS); organizational leadership (MS). Part-time and evening/weekend programs available. *Degree requirements:* For master's, independent research project. Electronic applications accepted.

Newman University, School of Business, Wichita, KS 67213-2097. Offers international business (MBA); leadership (MBA); management (MBA); technology (MBA). Part-time programs available. *Faculty:* 6 full-time (2 women), 3 part-time/adjunct (1 woman). *Students:* 34 full-time (14 women), 76 part-time (30 women); includes 14 minority (6 African Americans, 1 American Indian/Alaska Native, 3 Asian Americans or Pacific Islanders, 4 Hispanic Americans), 31 international. Average age 31. 74 applicants, 80% accepted, 46 enrolled. In 2006, 76 degrees awarded. *Degree requirements:* For master's, thesis optional. *Entrance requirements:* For master's, interview; minimum GPA of 3.0; 3 letters of recommendation; course work in algebra, statistics, macroeconomics. Additional exam requirements/recommendations for international students: Required—TOEFL (minimum score 600 paper-based; 250 computer-based; 100 iBT). *Application deadline:* For fall admission, 8/1 priority date for domestic students; for winter admission, 1/1 priority date for domestic students; for spring admission, 1/1 priority date for domestic students. Applications are processed on a rolling basis. Application fee: $25 ($40 for international students). Electronic applications accepted. *Expenses: Contact institution. Financial support:* In 2006–07, 3 students received support. Federal Work-Study and tuition waivers available. Financial award application deadline: 8/15; financial award applicants required to submit FAFSA. *Unit head:* Dr. Joe Goetz, Dean, 316-942-4291 Ext. 2111, Fax: 316-942-4486, E-mail: goetzj@newmanu.edu. *Application contact:* Linda Kay Sabala, Director of Graduate Admissions, 316-942-4291 Ext. 2230, Fax: 316-942-4483, E-mail: sabalal@newmanu.edu.

The New School: A University, Milano The New School for Management and Urban Policy, Program in Organizational Change Management, New York, NY 10011. Offers MS. Part-time and evening/weekend programs available. *Students:* 15 full-time (10 women), 41 part-time (37 women); includes 18 minority (12 African Americans, 2 Asian Americans or Pacific Islanders, 4 Hispanic Americans), 5 international. Average age 36. In 2006, 9 degrees awarded. *Degree requirements:* For master's, thesis. *Entrance requirements:* For master's, 3 years of work experience, interview. Additional exam requirements/recommendations for international students: Required—TOEFL (minimum score 600 paper-based; 250 computer-based; 100 iBT). *Application deadline:* For fall admission, 8/1 priority date for domestic students; for spring admission, 1/15 priority date for domestic students. Application fee: $50. *Financial support:* Research assistantships available. Financial award application deadline: 3/1; financial award applicants required to submit FAFSA. *Unit head:* Dr. Mark Lipton, Chair, 212-229-5400 Ext. 1611, Fax: 212-229-5335, E-mail: lipton@newschool.edu. *Application contact:* Peter King, Director of Admissions, 212-229-5400, Fax: 212-229-5354, E-mail: kingp@newschool.edu.

See Close-Up on page 699.

New York University, Leonard N. Stern School of Business, Department of Management and Organizations, New York, NY 10012-1019. Offers management organizations (MBA); organization theory (PhD); organizational behavior (PhD); strategy (PhD). *Expenses:* Tuition: Part-time $1,080 per unit. Required fees: $56 per unit. $329 per term. Tuition and fees vary according to program. *Faculty research:* Strategic management, managerial cognition, interpersonal processes, conflict and negotiation.

Northern Kentucky University, Office of Graduate Programs, College of Business, Program in Executive Leadership and Organizational Change, Highland Heights, KY 41099. Offers MA. Part-time and evening/weekend programs available. *Faculty:* 5 full-time (2 women), 2 part-time/adjunct (both women). *Students:* 44 applicants, 66% accepted, 26 enrolled. *Entrance requirements:* For master's, minimum GPA of 2.5. Additional exam requirements/recommendations for international students: Required—TOEFL (minimum score 600 paper-based), Michigan (must be taken at NKU). *Application deadline:* For fall admission, 8/1 priority date for domestic students, 6/1 for international students; for spring admission, 12/1 priority date for domestic students, 10/1 for international students. Applications are processed on a rolling basis. Application fee: $30. Electronic applications accepted. *Financial support:* In 2006–07, 11 students received support. Unspecified assistantships available. *Faculty research:* Emotional and social intelligence, organizational changes, leadership, team work/ life issues. *Unit head:* Dr. Kenneth Rhee, Program Director, 859-572-6310, Fax: 859-572-5150, E-mail: rhee@nku.edu. *Application contact:* Dr. Peg Griffin, Director of Graduate Programs, 859-572-1555, Fax: 859-572-6670, E-mail: gradprog@nku.edu.

Northwestern University, The Graduate School, Kellogg School of Management, Department of Management and Organizations, Evanston, IL 60208. Offers PhD. Admissions and degree offered through The Graduate School. *Degree requirements:* For doctorate, thesis/dissertation, comprehensive exam, registration. *Entrance requirements:* For doctorate, GMAT or GRE General Test. Additional exam requirements/recommendations for international students: Required—TOEFL. Electronic applications accepted. *Faculty research:* Bargaining and negotiation, organizational design, decision making, organizational change, strategic alliances.

Northwestern University, The Graduate School, School of Education and Social Policy, Program in Learning and Organizational Change, Evanston, IL 60208. Offers MS. Part-time and evening/weekend programs available. *Faculty:* 1 (woman) full-time, 17 part-time/adjunct (10 women). *Students:* 11 full-time (6 women), 48 part-time (38 women); includes 14 minority (8 African Americans, 5 Asian Americans or Pacific Islanders, 1 Hispanic American), 3 international. Average age 32. 36 applicants, 56% accepted, 19 enrolled. In 2006, 11 degrees awarded. *Median time to degree:* Master's–1.5 years full-time, 2.5 years part-time. *Degree requirements:* For master's, thesis, practicum. *Entrance requirements:* For master's, GRE/GMAT (recommended), letters of recommendation. Additional exam requirements/recommendations for international students: Required—TOEFL (minimum score 600 paper-based; 250 computer-based); Recommended—IELTS (minimum score 7). *Application deadline:* For fall admission, 8/1 priority date for domestic and international students; for winter admission, 12/1 priority date for domestic students; for spring admission, 3/1 priority date for domestic students. Applications are processed on a rolling basis. Application fee: $75. Electronic applications accepted.

Faculty research: Strategic change, learning and performance in the workplace, leadership development, cognitive design, knowledge management. *Unit head:* Dr. Kimberly Scott, Director, 847-467-3102. *Application contact:* Leslie Zimmerman, Program Coordinator, 847-491-7376, Fax: 847-491-3957, E-mail: l-zimmerman@northwestern.edu.

Norwich University, School of Graduate Studies, Program in Organizational Leadership, Northfield, VT 05663. Offers MSOL. Postbaccalaureate distance learning degree programs offered. *Unit head:* Diane Ravenscroft, Unit Head, 802-485-2730.

Nova Southeastern University, Fischler School of Education and Human Services, Program in Education, Fort Lauderdale, FL 33314-7796. Offers educational leadership (Ed D); health care education (Ed D); higher education (Ed D); human serviced administration (Ed D); instructional leadership (Ed D); instructional technology distance education (Ed D); organizational leadership (Ed D); special education (Ed D); speech language pathology (Ed D). *Students:* 619 full-time (452 women), 615 part-time (473 women); includes 737 minority (616 African Americans, 2 American Indian/Alaska Native, 14 Asian Americans or Pacific Islanders, 105 Hispanic Americans), 8 international. Average age 38. 480 applicants, 83% accepted, 398 enrolled. *Degree requirements:* For doctorate, thesis/dissertation. *Entrance requirements:* For doctorate, MAT or GRE, master's degree, 2 letters of recommendation, work experience. Additional exam requirements/recommendations for international students: Required—TSE (recommended) with a minimum score of 50; Recommended—TOEFL (minimum score 550 paper-based; 213 computer-based), IELTS (minimum score 6). *Application deadline:* For fall admission, 8/11 priority date for domestic and international students; for winter admission, 12/28 priority date for domestic and international students; for spring admission, 4/22 priority date for domestic and international students. Applications are processed on a rolling basis. Application fee: $50. Electronic applications accepted. *Financial support:* In 2006–07, 2 fellowships (averaging $9,375 per year) were awarded; scholarships/grants and tuition waivers (full) also available. Support available to part-time students. Financial award application deadline: 1/7; financial award applicants required to submit FAFSA. *Unit head:* Dr. Karen D. Bowser, Associate Dean of Doctoral Programs, 954-262-8500, Fax: 954-262-3912, E-mail: bowserk@nova.edu. *Application contact:* Jennifer Quiñones Nottingham, Dean of Student Affairs, 800-986-3223 Ext. 8624, Fax: 954-262-3911, E-mail: jlquinon@nova.edu.

Nova Southeastern University, Fischler School of Education and Human Services, Program in Organizational Leadership, Fort Lauderdale, FL 33314-7796. Offers Ed D. Part-time and evening/weekend programs available. *Students:* 108 full-time (80 women), 622 part-time (467 women); includes 449 minority (392 African Americans, 2 American Indian/Alaska Native, 9 Asian Americans or Pacific Islanders, 46 Hispanic Americans), 33 international. 3 applicants, 67% accepted, 2 enrolled. In 2006, 21 degrees awarded. *Degree requirements:* For doctorate, thesis/dissertation. *Entrance requirements:* For doctorate, MAT or GRE, master's degree, minimum GPA of 3.0, letter of recommendation. Additional exam requirements/recommendations for international students: Recommended—TOEFL (minimum score 550 paper-based; 213 computer-based), IELTS (minimum score 6). *Application deadline:* For fall admission, 8/11 priority date for domestic and international students; for winter admission, 12/28 priority date for domestic and international students; for spring admission, 4/22 priority date for domestic and international students. Applications are processed on a rolling basis. Application fee: $50. Electronic applications accepted. *Financial support:* Tuition waivers (full) available. Financial award application deadline: 1/7; financial award applicants required to submit FAFSA. *Unit head:* Dr. Karen D. Bowser, Associate Dean of Doctoral Programs, 954-262-8500, Fax: 954-262-3912, E-mail: bowserk@nova.edu. *Application contact:* Jennifer Quiñones Nottingham, Dean of Student Affairs, 800-986-3223 Ext. 8624, Fax: 954-262-3911, E-mail: jlquinon@nova.edu.

Olivet Nazarene University, Program in Organizational Leadership, Bourbonnais, IL 60914-2271. Offers MOL.

Oxford Graduate School, Graduate Programs, Dayton, TN 37321-6736. Offers family life education (M Litt); organizational leadership in nonprofits (M Litt); religion and society (D Phil). *Expenses:* Tuition: Part-time $202 per credit hour. One-time fee: $415 part-time. Tuition and fees vary according to degree level and program.

Palm Beach Atlantic University, MacArthur School of Continuing Education, West Palm Beach, FL 33416-4708. Offers organizational leadership (MS). Part-time and evening/weekend programs available. *Faculty:* 5 full-time (3 women), 1 (woman) part-time/adjunct. *Students:* 10 full-time (8 women), 21 part-time (10 women); includes 13 minority (10 African Americans, 3 Hispanic Americans), 2 international. Average age 39. 21 applicants, 90% accepted, 16 enrolled. In 2006, 28 degrees awarded. *Degree requirements:* For master's, thesis optional. *Entrance requirements:* For master's, GRE, minimum GPA of 3.0. Additional exam requirements/recommendations for international students: Required—TOEFL (minimum score 550 paper-based; 213 computer-based). *Application deadline:* For fall admission, 7/15 priority date for domestic students; for spring admission, 11/15 priority date for domestic students. Applications are processed on a rolling basis. Application fee: $35. Electronic applications accepted. *Expenses:* Tuition: Full-time $10,665; part-time $395 per credit. Required fees: $90 per semester. *Financial support:* Tuition waivers (partial) and unspecified assistantships available. Financial award applicants required to submit FAFSA. *Unit head:* Dr. Jim Laub, Dean, 561-803-2318, Fax: 561-803-2306, E-mail: jim_laub@pba.edu. *Application contact:* Laura A. Leinweber, Director of Graduate and Evening Admissions, 888-468-6722, Fax: 561-803-2115, E-mail: grad@pba.edu.

Pepperdine University, The Graziadio School of Business and Management, Los Angeles, CA 90045. Offers business (MBA), including business administration; executive business administration (MBAA); organizational development (MSOD); technology management (MSTM). *Accreditation:* AACSB. Part-time and evening/weekend programs available. *Faculty:* 83 full-time (15 women), 47 part-time/adjunct (11 women). *Students:* 606 full-time (229 women), 766 part-time (301 women); includes 433 minority (43 African Americans, 6 American Indian/Alaska Native, 250 Asian Americans or Pacific Islanders, 134 Hispanic Americans), 54 international. 764 applicants, 71% accepted, 415 enrolled. In 2006, 681 degrees awarded. *Entrance requirements:* For master's, GMAT or MAT. Additional exam requirements/recommendations for international students: Required—TOEFL (minimum score 550 paper-based). *Application deadline:* For fall admission, 6/28 for domestic students. Applications are processed on a rolling basis. Application fee: $45. *Expenses: Contact institution. Financial support:* Career-related internships or fieldwork, institutionally sponsored loans, scholarships/grants, and unspecified assistantships available. Support available to part-time students. Financial award applicants required to submit FAFSA. *Unit head:* Dr. Linda A. Livingstone, Dean, 310-568-5689, Fax: 310-568-5766, E-mail: linda.livingstone@pepperdine.edu. *Application contact:* Darrell Eriksen, Director of Admission and Student Accounts, 310-568-5525, E-mail: darrell.eriksen@pepperdine.edu.

Pfeiffer University, Program in Business Administration, Misenheimer, NC 28109-0960. Offers business administration (MBA); organizational management (MS); MBA/MHA; MBA/MS. Part-time and evening/weekend programs available. Postbaccalaureate distance learning degree programs offered (minimal on-campus study). *Faculty:* 13 full-time (3 women), 15 part-time/adjunct (2 women). *Students:* 108 full-time (46 women), 395 part-time (248 women); includes 202 minority (182 African Americans, 9 Asian Americans or Pacific Islanders, 11 Hispanic Americans), 43 international. Average age 36. In 2006, 223 degrees awarded. *Entrance requirements:* For master's, GMAT, minimum GPA of 3.0. *Application deadline:* For fall admission, 8/21 for domestic students. Applications are processed on a rolling basis. Application fee: $75. *Expenses:* Tuition: Part-time $380 per semester hour. Tuition and fees vary according to campus/location. *Financial support:* Unspecified assistantships available. Support available to part-time students. Financial award applicants required to submit FAFSA. *Unit head:* Dr. Robert K. Spear, Director of the MBA Program, 704-521-9116 Ext. 244, Fax: 704-521-8617, E-mail: rks@pfeiffer.edu.

Pfeiffer University, Program in Organizational Change and Leadership, Misenheimer, NC 28109-0960. Offers MS, MBA/MS. *Faculty:* 7 full-time (3 women), 8 part-time/adjunct (2 women). *Students:* 24 full-time (15 women), 155 part-time (114 women); includes 80 minority (78 African Americans, 2 American Indian/Alaska Native), 10 international. Average age 38. In 2006, 50 degrees awarded. *Entrance requirements:* For master's, GRE or GMAT. Application fee: $75. *Expenses:* Tuition: Part-time $380 per semester hour. Tuition and fees vary according to campus/location. *Financial support:* Unspecified assistantships available. Support available to part-time students. Financial award applicants required to submit FAFSA. *Unit head:* Dr. Ron Hunady, Director, 704-521-9116 Ext. 224, E-mail: rhunady@pfeiffer.edu.

Philadelphia Biblical University, School of Business and Leadership, Langhorne, PA 19047-2990. Offers organizational leadership (MSOL). Part-time and evening/weekend programs available. *Faculty:* 1 full-time (0 women), 3 part-time/adjunct (1 woman). *Students:* Average age 40. 12 applicants, 75% accepted, 6 enrolled. In 2006, 12 degrees awarded. *Entrance requirements:* Additional exam requirements/recommendations for international students: Required—TOEFL (minimum score 550 paper-based; 213 computer-based). *Application deadline:* Applications are processed on a rolling basis. Application fee: $25. Electronic applications accepted. *Expenses:* Tuition: Full-time $8,820; part-time $490 per credit. *Financial support:* In 2006–07, 18 students received support. Scholarships/grants available. Support available to part-time students. Financial award applicants required to submit FAFSA. *Unit head:* Ron Ferner, Dean, 215-702-9260, Fax: 215-702-4248. *Application contact:* Binu Abraham, Assistant Director, Graduate Admissions, 800-572-2472, Fax: 215-702-4248, E-mail: babraham@pbu.edu.

Point Park University, School of Business, Pittsburgh, PA 15222-1984. Offers business (MBA); organizational leadership (MA). Part-time and evening/weekend programs available. *Faculty:* 13 full-time, 21 part-time/adjunct. *Students:* 133 full-time (72 women), 138 part-time (85 women); includes 60 minority (55 African Americans, 1 American Indian/Alaska Native, 2 Asian Americans or Pacific Islanders, 2 Hispanic Americans), 24 international. Average age 31. 269 applicants, 74% accepted, 140 enrolled. In 2006, 132 degrees awarded. *Entrance requirements:* For master's, minimum QPA of 2.75. Additional exam requirements/recommendations for international students: Required—TOEFL. *Application deadline:* Applications are processed on a rolling basis. Application fee: $30. Electronic applications accepted. *Expenses:* Tuition: Full-time $9,828; part-time $546 per credit. Required fees: $360; $20 per credit. *Financial support:* In 2006–07, 29 students received support, including 3 research assistantships with full tuition reimbursements available (averaging $5,400 per year); career-related internships or fieldwork and scholarships/grants also available. Support available to part-time students. Financial award application deadline: 5/1; financial award applicants required to submit FAFSA. *Faculty research:* Technology issues, foreign direct investment, multinational corporate issues, cross-cultural international organizations/administrations, regional integration issues. *Unit head:* Margaret Gilfillan, Interim Dean, 412-392-3942, Fax: 412-765-2570, E-mail: mgilfillan@pointpark.edu. *Application contact:* Kathryn B. Ballas, Director, Adult Enrollment, 412-392-3808, Fax: 412-392-6164, E-mail: kballas@pointpark.edu.

Regent University, Graduate School, School of Global Leadership and Entrepreneurship, Virginia Beach, VA 23464-9800. Offers business administration (MBA); management (MA); organizational leadership (MA, PhD, Certificate); strategic foresight (MA); strategic leadership (DSL). Part-time programs available. Postbaccalaureate distance learning degree programs offered (minimal on-campus study). *Faculty:* 20 full-time (3 women), 36 part-time/adjunct (6 women). *Students:* 68 full-time (40 women), 482 part-time (170 women); includes 144 minority (110 African Americans, 6 American Indian/Alaska Native, 9 Asian Americans or Pacific Islanders, 19 Hispanic Americans), 37 international. Average age 40. 395 applicants, 37% accepted, 64 enrolled. In 2006, 100 master's, 69 doctorates awarded. *Degree requirements:* For master's, thesis or alternative, 3 credit hour culminating experience; for doctorate, thesis/dissertation. *Entrance requirements:* For master's, GRE, GMAT or MAT, minimum undergraduate GPA of 2.75, computer literacy survey, 2 recommendations, resumé; for doctorate, GRE, GMAT or MAT, sample of writing, minimum of 3 years of relevant experience, computer literacy survey, 2 recommendations, resumé; for Certificate, GRE, GMAT or MAT, writing sample. Additional exam requirements/recommendations for international students: Required—TOEFL (minimum score 577 paper-based; 233 computer-based). *Application deadline:* For fall admission, 5/1 priority date for domestic students; for spring admission, 10/1 priority date for domestic students. Applications are processed on a rolling basis. Application fee: $50. Electronic applications accepted. *Expenses: Contact institution. Financial support:* In 2006–07, 321 students received support. Scholarships/grants and tuition waivers (full and partial) available. Support available to part-time students. Financial award application deadline: 9/1. *Faculty research:* Servant leadership, ethics and values, telecommuting and family values, organizational communications, distance education. *Unit head:* Dr. Bruce Winston, Dean, 757-226-4306, Fax: 757-226-4634, E-mail: brucwin@regent.edu. *Application contact:* Althea Bishard, Registrar and Executive Director of Enrollment and Academic Services, 800-373-5504, Fax: 757-226-4381, E-mail: admissions@regent.edu.

Regions University, Graduate and Professional Programs, Montgomery, AL 36117. Offers behavioral leadership and management (MA); biblical studies (MA, D Min, PhD); Christian ministry (M Div); family therapy (D Min, PhD); leadership and management (MS); marriage and family therapy (M Div, MA); ministerial leadership (M Div, MS); pastoral counseling (M Div, MS); practical theology (MA); professional counseling (M Div, MA). *Accreditation:* ATS. Part-time and evening/weekend programs available. Postbaccalaureate distance learning degree programs offered (no on-campus study). *Degree requirements:* For M Div, comprehensive exam (for some programs); for master's, one foreign language, thesis (for some programs), comprehensive exam (for some programs); for doctorate, thesis/dissertation, comprehensive exam (for some programs). *Entrance requirements:* For M Div, master's, and doctorate, GRE General Test or MAT. Additional exam requirements/recommendations for international students: Required—TOEFL. Electronic applications accepted. *Faculty research:* Homiletics, hermeneutics, ancient Near Eastern history.

Regis College, Department of Management and Leadership, Weston, MA 02493. Offers leadership and organizational change (MS). Part-time and evening/weekend programs available. *Faculty:* 1 full-time (0 women), 1 part-time/adjunct (0 women). *Students:* 1 (woman) full-time, 17 part-time (15 women); includes 3 minority (1 Asian American or Pacific Islander, 2 Hispanic Americans). Average age 36. 5 applicants, 100% accepted, 5 enrolled. In 2006, 9 degrees awarded. *Degree requirements:* For master's, thesis. *Entrance requirements:* For master's, GRE General Test. *Application deadline:* Applications are processed on a rolling basis. Application fee: $50. *Expenses:* Tuition: Full-time $23,680; part-time $665 per credit hour. *Financial support:* Applicants required to submit FAFSA. *Faculty research:* Leadership, service and learning, building high commitment organizations. *Unit head:* Dr. Phillip Jutras, Director, 781-768-7436, Fax: 781-768-7159, E-mail: phillip.jutras@regiscollege.edu.

Regis University, School for Professional Studies, Program in Business, Denver, CO 80221-1099. Offers accounting (MS); business administration (MBA); finance (MBA); finance and accounting (MBA); international business (MBA); marketing (MBA); operations management (MBA); organization leadership (MS); project management (Certificate); technical management (Certificate). Offered at Colorado Springs Campus, Northwest Denver Campus, Southeast Denver Campus, Fort Collins Campus, Broomfield Campus, Henderson (Nevada) Campus, and Summerlin (Nevada) Campus. Part-time and evening/weekend programs available. Postbaccalaureate distance learning degree programs offered (no on-campus study). *Faculty:* 16 full-time (4 women), 82 part-time/adjunct (22 women). *Students:* 1,770 (834 women). Average age 36. In 2006, 560 degrees awarded. *Degree requirements:* For master's, capstone project, thesis optional. *Entrance requirements:* For master's, GMAT, interview, 2 years of full-time business work experience; for Certificate, GMAT. Additional exam requirements/recommendations for international students: Required—TOEFL or university-based test. *Application deadline:* For fall admission, 8/22 for domestic and international students; for winter admission, 1/2 for domestic and international students; for spring admission, 4/30 for domestic and international students. Applications are processed on a rolling basis. Application fee: $75. Electronic applications accepted. *Financial support:* Federal Work-Study available. Support

Organizational Management

Regis University (continued)
available to part-time students. Financial award applicants required to submit FAFSA. *Unit head:* Dr. Michael Goess, Chair, 303-458-4302, Fax: 303-964-5538. *Application contact:* 800-677-9270 Ext. 4080, Fax: 303-964-5538, E-mail: masters@regis.edu.

Regis University, School for Professional Studies, Program in Organization Leadership, Denver, CO 80221-1099. Offers computer information technology (MSOL); executive international management (Certificate); executive leadership (Certificate); human resource management (MSOL); organizational leadership (MSOL); project leadership and management (MSOL, Certificate); strategic business (Certificate); strategic human resource (Certificate). Offered at Boulder Campus, Fort Collins Campus, Northwest Denver Campus, Southeast Denver Campus, Colorado Springs Campus, and Broomfield Campus. Part-time and evening/weekend programs available. Postbaccalaureate distance learning degree programs offered. *Faculty:* 55. *Students:* Average age 35. In 2006, 61 degrees awarded. *Median time to degree:* Master's–3 years full-time. *Degree requirements:* For master's, capstone course; for Certificate, final research project. *Entrance requirements:* For master's, 3 years of management-related experience, resumé. Additional exam requirements/recommendations for international students: Required—TOEFL, TWE (minimum score 5), TOEFL or university-based test. *Application deadline:* For fall admission, 8/13 priority date for domestic students, 7/13 for international students; for winter admission, 10/8 priority date for domestic students, 9/8 for international students; for spring admission, 12/17 priority date for domestic students, 11/11 for international students. Applications are processed on a rolling basis. Application fee: $75. Electronic applications accepted. *Expenses: Contact institution. Financial support:* Federal Work-Study available. Support available to part-time students. Financial award applicants required to submit FAFSA. *Faculty research:* Organizational behavior, leadership, change, quality control, global economics. *Unit head:* Dr. Donna VanDusen, Chair, 303-458-4302, Fax: 303-964-5538. *Application contact:* 800-677-9270, Fax: 303-964-5538, E-mail: masters@regis.edu.

Rider University, Department of Graduate Education, Leadership and Counseling, Program in Organizational Leadership, Lawrenceville, NJ 08648-3001. Offers MA. *Faculty:* 1 (woman) full-time, 4 part-time/adjunct (1 woman). *Students:* 12 full-time (8 women), 27 part-time (20 women); includes 14 minority (13 African Americans, 1 Hispanic American). Average age 31. 44 applicants, 84% accepted, 33 enrolled. In 2006, 12 degrees awarded. *Entrance requirements:* For master's, resumé. Application fee: $50. *Expenses:* Tuition: Part-time $525 per credit. Required fees: $35 per course. $30 per semester. *Financial support:* In 2006–07, 31 students received support. Career-related internships or fieldwork, Federal Work-Study, institutionally sponsored loans, and unspecified assistantships available. Support available to part-time students. Financial award applicants required to submit FAFSA. *Unit head:* Dr. Elizabeth Watson, Program Coordinator, 609-896-5353.

Rivier College, School of Graduate Studies, Department of Business Administration, Nashua, NH 03060-5086. Offers business administration (MBA); health care administration (MBA); human resources management (MS); organizational leadership (EMBA). Part-time and evening/weekend programs available. *Faculty:* 4 full-time (2 women), 21 part-time/adjunct (6 women). *Students:* 12 full-time (10 women), 60 part-time (35 women); includes 7 minority (2 African Americans, 2 Asian Americans or Pacific Islanders, 3 Hispanic Americans), 6 international. Average age 36. In 2006, 37 degrees awarded. *Degree requirements:* For master's, registration. *Application deadline:* Applications are processed on a rolling basis. Application fee: $25. *Financial support:* Available to part-time students. Application deadline: 2/1; *Unit head:* Maria Matarazzo, Division Chair, 603-897-8532, Fax: 603-897-8885, E-mail: mmatarazzo@rivier.edu. *Application contact:* Diane Monahan, Director of Graduate Admissions, 603-897-8129, Fax: 603-897-8810, E-mail: gradadm@rivier.edu.

Roosevelt University, Graduate Division, College of Education, Program in Educational Leadership and Organizational Change, Chicago, IL 60605-1394. Offers MA, Ed D. *Students:* 28 full-time (19 women), 97 part-time (58 women); includes 24 minority (21 African Americans, 2 Asian Americans or Pacific Islanders, 1 Hispanic American). Average age 38. 74 applicants, 59% accepted, 42 enrolled. In 2006, 23 master's, 7 doctorates awarded. *Unit head:* Dr. Susan Katz, Chair, 312-341-6498. *Application contact:* Joanne Canyon-Heller, Coordinator of Graduate Admission, 877-APPLY RU, Fax: 312-281-3356, E-mail: applyru@roosevelt.edu.

Royal Roads University, Graduate Studies, Organizational Leadership and Training Program, Victoria, BC V9B 5Y2, Canada. Offers distributed learning (MA); leadership and training (MA). Postbaccalaureate distance learning degree programs offered (minimal on-campus study). *Degree requirements:* For master's, thesis. *Entrance requirements:* For master's, 5-7 years of related work experience. Additional exam requirements/recommendations for international students: Required—TOEFL (paper-based 570; computer-based 233) or IELTS (paper-based 7) (recommended). Electronic applications accepted. Expenses: Contact institution. *Faculty research:* Approaches to leadership development, professional learning, problem-based learning, effective leadership styles, use of self-knowledge instruments in leadership development.

Rutgers, The State University of New Jersey, Newark, Rutgers Business School: Graduate Programs-Newark/New Brunswick, Doctoral Programs in Business, Newark, NJ 07102. Offers accounting (PhD); accounting information systems (PhD); finance (PhD); individualized study (PhD); information technology (PhD); international business (PhD); management science (PhD); organizational management (PhD); supply chain management (PhD).

Sage Graduate School, Graduate School, Division of Management, Communications and Legal Studies, Program in Organizational Management, Troy, NY 12180-4115. Offers MS. Part-time and evening/weekend programs available. *Faculty:* 3 full-time (1 woman), 4 part-time/adjunct (2 women). *Students:* Average age 33. 6 applicants, 67% accepted, 4 enrolled. In 2006, 11 degrees awarded. *Entrance requirements:* For master's, minimum GPA of 2.75. Additional exam requirements/recommendations for international students: Required—TOEFL (minimum score 550 paper-based; 213 computer-based). *Application deadline:* Applications are processed on a rolling basis. Application fee: $40. *Expenses:* Tuition: Full-time $9,270; part-time $515 per credit hour. *Financial support:* Career-related internships or fieldwork available. Support available to part-time students. Financial award application deadline: 3/1; financial award applicants required to submit FAFSA. *Application contact:* Shannon K. Easton, Director of Graduate and Adult Admission, 518-244-2443, Fax: 518-244-6880, E-mail: sgsadm@sage.edu.

St. Ambrose University, College of Arts and Sciences, Program in Leadership Studies, Davenport, IA 52803-2898. Offers MOL. Part-time and evening/weekend programs available. *Faculty:* 7 full-time (0 women), 5 part-time/adjunct (4 women). *Students:* 13 full-time (6 women), 84 part-time (50 women); includes 7 minority (3 African Americans, 4 Hispanic Americans). Average age 39. 30 applicants, 83% accepted, 25 enrolled. In 2006, 35 master's awarded. *Degree requirements:* For master's, thesis or alternative, integration projects, comprehensive exam (for some programs), registration. *Entrance requirements:* Additional exam requirements/recommendations for international students: Required—TOEFL. *Application deadline:* For fall admission, 8/15 priority date for domestic students; for winter admission, 12/15 priority date for domestic students; for spring admission, 1/1 priority date for domestic students. Applications are processed on a rolling basis. Application fee: $25. Electronic applications accepted. *Expenses: Contact institution. Financial support:* In 2006–07, 97 students received support. Tuition waivers (partial) available. Financial award application deadline: 3/15; financial award applicants required to submit FAFSA. *Unit head:* Dr. Ron O. Wastyn, Director, 563-333-6437, Fax: 563-333-6243, E-mail: wastynronaldo@sau.edu. *Application contact:* Elizabeth Berridge, Director of Graduate Student Recruitment, 563-333-6271, Fax: 563-333-6268, E-mail: berridgeelizabethb@sau.edu.

St. Edward's University, School of Management and Business, Program in Organizational Leadership and Ethics, Austin, TX 78704. Offers MS. Part-time and evening/weekend programs available. *Students:* 1 (woman) full-time, 57 part-time (31 women); includes 11 minority (4 African Americans, 1 American Indian/Alaska Native, 2 Asian Americans or Pacific Islanders, 4 Hispanic Americans). Average age 37. 34 applicants, 76% accepted, 21 enrolled. In 2006, 25 master's awarded. *Degree requirements:* For master's, minimum 24 hours in residence. *Entrance requirements:* For master's, GMAT or GRE General Test, minimum GPA of 2.75 in last 60 hours of course work. Additional exam requirements/recommendations for international students: Required—TOEFL (minimum score 550 paper-based; 213 computer-based; 79 iBT). *Application deadline:* For fall admission, 8/1 for domestic students, 7/1 for international students; for spring admission, 12/1 for domestic students, 11/1 for international students. Applications are processed on a rolling basis. Application fee: $45 ($50 for international students). Electronic applications accepted. *Expenses:* Tuition: Full-time $11,682; part-time $649 per credit hour. Full-time tuition and fees vary according to course load and program. *Financial support:* Scholarships/grants available. Financial award applicants required to submit FAFSA. *Faculty research:* Business ethics. *Unit head:* Dr. Tom Sechrest, Director, 512-637-1954, Fax: 512-448-8492, E-mail: thomasl@stedwards.edu. *Application contact:* Benjamin Jimenez, Recruiting Coordinator, 512-233-1694, Fax: 512-428-1032, E-mail: benjij@stedwards.edu.

St. Joseph's College, Suffolk Campus, Program in Management, Patchogue, NY 11772-2399. Offers health care (AC); health care management (MS); human resource management (AC); human resources management (MS); organizational management (MS).

Saint Joseph's University, College of Arts and Sciences, Department of Education, Philadelphia, PA 19131-1395. Offers educational leadership (Ed D); elementary education (MS); instructional technology (MS); professional education (MS); reading (MS); secondary education (MS); special education (MS); training and organizational development (MS, Certificate). Part-time and evening/weekend programs available. *Faculty:* 18 full-time (9 women), 67 part-time/adjunct (34 women). *Students:* 77 full-time (63 women), 551 part-time (417 women); includes 115 minority (94 African Americans, 2 American Indian/Alaska Native, 8 Asian Americans or Pacific Islanders, 11 Hispanic Americans), 12 international. In 2006, 286 master's, 5 doctorates awarded. *Entrance requirements:* For master's, 2 letters of recommendation, minimum GPA of 3.0; for doctorate, GRE/MAT, 2 letters of recommendation, resumé. Additional exam requirements/recommendations for international students: Required—TOEFL. *Application deadline:* For fall admission, 7/15 for domestic students. Application fee: $35. *Expenses: Contact institution. Financial support:* Fellowships, research assistantships, career-related internships or fieldwork and Federal Work-Study available. Support available to part-time students. *Unit head:* Dr. Encarnacion Rodriguez, Director of Graduate Education, 610-660-3348.

Saint Louis University, Graduate School, College of Public Service and Graduate School, Department of Public Policy Studies, St. Louis, MO 63103-2097. Offers geographic information systems (Certificate); organizational development (Certificate); public administration (MAPA); public policy analysis (PhD); urban affairs (MAUA); urban planning and real estate development (MUPRED). *Accreditation:* NASPAA. Part-time programs available. *Faculty:* 8 full-time (3 women), 3 part-time/adjunct (0 women). *Students:* 40 full-time (17 women), 58 part-time (27 women); includes 13 minority (9 African Americans, 1 Asian American or Pacific Islander, 3 Hispanic Americans), 3 international. Average age 32. 71 applicants, 90% accepted, 36 enrolled. In 2006, 15 master's, 2 doctorates awarded. *Degree requirements:* For master's, thesis (for some programs), comprehensive exam (for some programs), registration; for doctorate, thesis/dissertation, preliminary exams, comprehensive exam, registration. *Entrance requirements:* For master's and doctorate, GMAT, GRE General Test, or LSAT, letters of recommendation, resumé. Additional exam requirements/recommendations for international students: Required—TOEFL (minimum score 525 paper-based; 194 computer-based). *Application deadline:* For fall admission, 7/1 for domestic and international students; for spring admission, 11/1 for domestic and international students. Applications are processed on a rolling basis. Application fee: $40. *Expenses:* Tuition: Part-time $800 per credit hour. Required fees: $105 per semester. *Financial support:* In 2006–07, 36 students received support, including 9 teaching assistantships with full tuition reimbursements available (averaging $11,000 per year); Federal Work-Study, scholarships/grants, traineeships, health care benefits, tuition waivers, and unspecified assistantships also available. Support available to part-time students. Financial award application deadline: 6/1; financial award applicants required to submit FAFSA. *Faculty research:* Urban politics, brown fields, e-government, and administration, evaluation research, community development. *Unit head:* Dr. Robert A. Cropf, Chairperson, 314-977-3936, Fax: 314-977-3943, E-mail: cropfra@slu.edu. *Application contact:* Gary Behrman, Associate Dean of the Graduate School, 314-977-3827, E-mail: behrmang@slu.edu.

Saint Mary's University of Minnesota, School of Graduate and Professional Programs, Program in Organizational Leadership, Winona, MN 55987-1399. Offers MA. *Unit head:* Linda Frisbee, Unit Head, 612-728-5510, E-mail: lfrisbee@smumn.edu.

Saybrook Graduate School and Research Center, Program in Psychology, Human Science and Organizational Systems, San Francisco, CA 94111-1920. Offers human science (MA, PhD), including consciousness and spirituality, individualized (PhD), organizational systems, social transformation; organizational systems (MA, PhD), including individualized (PhD), organizational systems; psychology (MA, PhD), including consciousness and spirituality, health studies, humanistic and transpersonal psychology, individualized (PhD), licensure track (MA), organizational systems, police and public safety psychology (PhD), social transformation. Postbaccalaureate distance learning degree programs offered (minimal on-campus study). *Faculty:* 15 full-time (5 women), 83 part-time/adjunct (34 women). *Students:* 479 full-time (333 women); includes 62 minority (30 African Americans, 1 American Indian/Alaska Native, 13 Asian Americans or Pacific Islanders, 18 Hispanic Americans), 18 international. Average age 43. 280 applicants, 52% accepted, 105 enrolled. In 2006, 28 master's, 43 doctorates awarded. Terminal master's awarded for partial completion of doctoral program. *Degree requirements:* For master's, thesis or alternative; for doctorate, thesis/dissertation. *Entrance requirements:* Additional exam requirements/recommendations for international students: Required—TOEFL. *Application deadline:* For fall admission, 6/1 priority date for domestic students; for spring admission, 12/16 priority date for domestic students. Application fee: $50. Electronic applications accepted. *Financial support:* In 2006–07, 335 students received support. Scholarships/grants available. Financial award applicants required to submit FAFSA. *Faculty research:* Humanistic theory, health studies, organizational systems, consciousness and spirituality, social transformation. Total annual research expenditures: $90,000. *Unit head:* Lorne Buchman, President, 800-825-4480, Fax: 415-433-9271. *Application contact:* Director of Admissions, 800-825-4480, Fax: 415-433-9271, E-mail: admissions@saybrook.edu.

School for International Training, Graduate Programs, Master's Programs in Intercultural Service, Leadership, and Management, Program in Management, Brattleboro, VT 05302-0676. Offers MS. *Expenses:* Tuition: Full-time $27,355; part-time $638 per credit hour. Required fees: $1,092.

Seattle University, Albers School of Business and Economics, Center for Leadership Formation, Seattle, WA 98122-1090. Offers EMBA, Certificate. *Faculty:* 1 (woman) full-time. *Students:* 4 full-time (1 woman). Average age 42. *Unit head:* Dr. Marilyn Gist, Director, 206-296-5374, E-mail: gistm@seattleu.edu.

Shippensburg University of Pennsylvania, School of Graduate Studies, College of Arts and Sciences, Department of Sociology, Shippensburg, PA 17257-2299. Offers organizational development and leadership (MS). Part-time and evening/weekend programs available. *Faculty:* 3 full-time (all women). *Students:* 8 full-time (3 women), 26 part-time (17 women); includes 6 minority (5 African Americans, 1 American Indian/Alaska Native). Average age 32. 34 applicants, 68% accepted, 10 enrolled. In 2006, 16 degrees awarded. *Degree requirements:* For master's, internship or practicum, research paper or project. *Entrance requirements:* For master's, interview (if GPA less than 2.75), resumé or goals statement. Additional exam requirements/recommendations for international students: Required—TOEFL (minimum score 560 paper-based; 220 computer-based). *Application deadline:* For fall admission, 6/1 priority date for domestic students, 3/1 for international students; for spring admission, 11/1 priority date for domestic students, 7/1 for international students. Applications are processed on a rolling basis.

Application fee: $30. Electronic applications accepted. *Expenses:* Tuition, state resident: part-time $336 per credit. Tuition, nonresident: part-time $538 per credit. *Financial support:* In 2006–07, 5 research assistantships with full tuition reimbursements (averaging $3,125 per year) were awarded; career-related internships or fieldwork, scholarships/grants, and unspecified assistantships also available. Support available to part-time students. *Unit head:* Dr. Robert Pineda-Volk, Chairperson, 717-477-1735, Fax: 717-477-4011, E-mail: rwvolk@ship.edu. *Application contact:* Renee Payne, Associate Dean of Graduate Admissions, 717-477-1231, Fax: 717-477-4016, E-mail: rmpayn@ship.edu.

Southern New Hampshire University, School of Business, Manchester, NH 03106-1045. Offers accounting (MS); business administration (MBA, Certificate), including accounting (Certificate), business administration (MBA), finance (Certificate), forensic accounting (Certificate), human resources management (Certificate), international business (Certificate), international sport management (Certificate), leadership of not for profit organizations (Certificate), marketing (Certificate), operations management (Certificate), sport management (Certificate), taxation (Certificate); finance (MS); hospitality and tourism leadership (Certificate); information technology (MS, Certificate); information technology/international business (Certificate); integrated marketing communications (Certificate); international business (MS, DBA); marketing (MS); operations and project management (MS); organizational leadership (MS); project management (Certificate); sport management (MS); MBA/Certificate. *Accreditation:* ACBSP. Part-time and evening/weekend programs available. Postbaccalaureate distance learning degree programs offered (no on-campus study). *Faculty:* 45 full-time, 75 part-time/adjunct. *Students:* 427 full-time (184 women), 774 part-time (428 women). Average age 32. In 2006, 682 master's, 1 doctorate awarded. Terminal master's awarded for partial completion of doctoral program. *Degree requirements:* For master's, one foreign language, thesis or alternative, comprehensive exam (for some programs); for doctorate, one foreign language, thesis/dissertation, comprehensive exam. *Entrance requirements:* For master's, minimum GPA of 2.5; for doctorate, GMAT. Additional exam requirements/recommendations for international students: Required—TOEFL (minimum score 500 paper-based). *Application deadline:* Applications are processed on a rolling basis. Application fee: $25. Electronic applications accepted. *Financial support:* Career-related internships or fieldwork, Federal Work-Study, institutionally sponsored loans, tuition waivers (partial), and unspecified assistantships available. Support available to part-time students. Financial award applicants required to submit FAFSA. *Unit head:* Dr. Martin Bradley, Dean, 603-644-3102, Fax: 603-644-3144, E-mail: m.bradley@snhu.edu. *Application contact:* Scott Durand, Director of Graduate Enrollment Services, 603-644-3102 Ext. 3338, Fax: 603-644-3144, E-mail: s.durand@snhu.edu.

See Close-Up on page 325.

Spring Arbor University, School of Adult Studies, Spring Arbor, MI 49283-9799. Offers counseling (MAC); family studies (MAFS); organizational management (MAOM). Part-time and evening/weekend programs available. Postbaccalaureate distance learning degree programs offered (no on-campus study). *Faculty:* 1 full-time (0 women), 140 part-time/adjunct (59 women). *Students:* 575 full-time (443 women), 194 part-time (146 women); includes 161 minority (137 African Americans, 4 American Indian/Alaska Native, 2 Asian Americans or Pacific Islanders, 18 Hispanic Americans), 2 international. Average age 39. In 2006, 206 degrees awarded. *Entrance requirements:* For master's, minimum GPA of 3.0, interview, writing sample, 2 professional references. Additional exam requirements/recommendations for international students: Required—TOEFL (minimum score 550 paper-based; 220 computer-based). *Application deadline:* Applications are processed on a rolling basis. Application fee: $30. Electronic applications accepted. *Expenses:* Tuition: Full-time $4,200; part-time $350 per credit. Required fees: $140; $48 per term. Tuition and fees vary according to course load and program. *Financial support:* Scholarships/grants available. Support available to part-time students. Financial award applicants required to submit FAFSA. *Unit head:* Natalie Gianetti, Dean of Adult Studies, 517-750-1200 Ext. 1343, Fax: 517-750-6602, E-mail: gianetti@arbor.edu. *Application contact:* Dr. Carl Pavey, Director, Graduate Studies, School of Adult Studies, 517-750-1200 Ext. 1653, Fax: 517-750-6602, E-mail: cpavey@arbor.edu.

Thomas Edison State College, Heavin School of Arts and Sciences, Program in Liberal Studies, Trenton, NJ 08608-1176. Offers human resource management (MALS); online learning and teaching (MALS); organizational leadership (MALS). Part-time programs available. Postbaccalaureate distance learning degree programs offered (no on-campus study). *Students:* Average age 45. 34 applicants, 25 enrolled. In 2006, 12 degrees awarded. *Degree requirements:* For master's, capstone project. *Entrance requirements:* Additional exam requirements/recommendations for international students: Required—TOEFL (minimum score 550 paper-based; 213 computer-based). *Application deadline:* For fall admission, 8/15 priority date for domestic and international students; for winter admission, 11/15 priority date for domestic and international students; for spring admission, 2/15 priority date for domestic and international students. Applications are processed on a rolling basis. Application fee: $75. Electronic applications accepted. *Expenses:* Tuition, nonresident: part-time $422 per credit. Part-time tuition and fees vary according to program. *Financial support:* Applicants required to submit FAFSA. *Unit head:* Dr. Esther Taitsman, Director of Graduate School, 609-984-1168, Fax: 609-633-8593, E-mail: graduateschool@tesc.edu. *Application contact:* Renee San Giacomo, Director of Admissions, 888-442-8372, Fax: 609-984-8447, E-mail: admissions@tesc.edu.

Thomas Edison State College, School of Business and Management, Program in Management, Trenton, NJ 08608-1176. Offers human resource management (MSM); online learning and teaching (MSM); organizational leadership (MSM); public sector auditing (MSM); public service leadership (MSM). Part-time programs available. Postbaccalaureate distance learning degree programs offered (minimal on-campus study). *Students:* Average age 42. 77 applicants, 60 enrolled. In 2006, 55 degrees awarded. *Degree requirements:* For master's, capstone/thesis, applied project. *Entrance requirements:* For master's, 3-5 years of work experience. Additional exam requirements/recommendations for international students: Required—TOEFL (minimum score 550 paper-based; 213 computer-based). *Application deadline:* For fall admission, 8/15 priority date for domestic and international students; for winter admission, 11/15 priority date for domestic and international students; for spring admission, 2/15 priority date for domestic and international students. Applications are processed on a rolling basis. Application fee: $75. Electronic applications accepted. *Expenses:* Tuition, nonresident: part-time $422 per credit. Part-time tuition and fees vary according to program. *Financial support:* Applicants required to submit FAFSA. *Application contact:* Renee San Giacomo, Director of Admissions, 888-442-8372, Fax: 609-984-8447, E-mail: admissions@tesc.edu.

Trevecca Nazarene University, Graduate Division, School of Business and Management, Major in Management, Nashville, TN 37210-2877. Offers MSM. Evening/weekend programs available. *Students:* 83 full-time (44 women), 1 (woman) part-time; includes 20 minority (16 African Americans, 1 Asian American or Pacific Islander, 3 Hispanic Americans). In 2006, 10 degrees awarded. *Entrance requirements:* For master's, GMAT, proficiency exam (quantitative skills), minimum GPA of 2.5, resumé, 2 letters of recommendation, employer letter of recommendation, written business analysis. Additional exam requirements/recommendations for international students: Required—TOEFL (minimum score 500 paper-based; 173 computer-based). *Application deadline:* Applications are processed on a rolling basis. Application fee: $25. *Expenses: Contact institution.* Tuition and fees vary according to degree level and program. *Financial support:* Applicants required to submit FAFSA. *Unit head:* Dr. Ken Burger, Director, 615-248-1529, Fax: 615-248-1700, E-mail: management@trevecca.edu. *Application contact:* Marcus Lackey, Admissions Counselor, 615-248-1529, Fax: 615-248-1700, E-mail: management@trevecca.edu.

Trinity (Washington) University, School of Professional Studies, Washington, DC 20017-1094. Offers business administration (MBA); communication (MA); information security management (MS); organizational management (MSA), including federal program management, human resource management, nonprofit management, organizational development, public and community health. Part-time and evening/weekend programs available. *Degree requirements:* For master's, thesis (for some programs), capstone project (MSA). *Entrance requirements:* For master's, minimum GPA of 2.5. Additional exam requirements/recommendations for international students: Required—TOEFL (minimum score 550 paper-based; 213 computer-based).

Trinity Western University, Program in Leadership, Langley, BC V2Y 1Y1, Canada. Offers MA. Postbaccalaureate distance learning degree programs offered (minimal on-campus study). *Degree requirements:* For master's, major project. *Entrance requirements:* For master's, minimum GPA of 2.7. Additional exam requirements/recommendations for international students: Required—TOEFL (minimum score 600 paper-based; 250 computer-based). Expenses: Contact institution. *Faculty research:* Servant leadership.

Tusculum College, Graduate School, Program in Organizational Management, Greeneville, TN 37743-9997. Offers MAOM. *Degree requirements:* For master's, thesis or alternative. *Entrance requirements:* For master's, GMAT, GRE Subject Test, MAT, 3 years of work experience, minimum GPA of 2.75.

Université Laval, Faculty of Administrative Sciences, Programs in Business Administration, Québec, QC G1K 7P4, Canada. Offers accounting (MBA); agri-food management (MBA); electronic business (MBA, Diploma); factory management and logistics (MBA); finance (MBA); firm management (MBA); information technology management (MBA); international management (MBA); management (MBA); management accounting (MBA, Diploma); marketing (MBA); modelization and organizational decision (MBA); occupational health and safety management (MBA); pharmacy management (MBA); technological entrepreneurship (Diploma). *Accreditation:* AACSB. Part-time and evening/weekend programs available. Postbaccalaureate distance learning degree programs offered (no on-campus study). *Entrance requirements:* For master's and Diploma, knowledge of French and English. Electronic applications accepted.

University of Alberta, Faculty of Graduate Studies and Research, Doctoral Program in Business, Edmonton, AB T6G 2E1, Canada. Offers accounting (PhD); finance (PhD); human resources/industrial relations (PhD); management science (PhD); marketing (PhD); organizational analysis (PhD); MBA/PhD. *Accreditation:* AACSB. Part-time programs available. *Faculty:* 41 full-time (7 women), 1 part-time/adjunct (0 women). *Students:* 46 full-time (27 women), 5 part-time (3 women). Average age 34. 307 applicants, 7% accepted, 11 enrolled. In 2006, 2 degrees awarded. *Median time to degree:* Of those who began their doctoral program in fall 1998, 60% received their degree in 8 years or less. *Degree requirements:* For doctorate, thesis/dissertation, comprehensive exam. *Entrance requirements:* For doctorate, GMAT. Additional exam requirements/recommendations for international students: Required—TOEFL (minimum score 550 paper-based; 213 computer-based). *Application deadline:* For fall admission, 6/1 priority date for domestic students; for winter admission, 5/1 for domestic students. Application fee: $0. Electronic applications accepted. *Financial support:* In 2006–07, 29 students received support, including 11 fellowships with full tuition reimbursements available (averaging $17,000 per year); scholarships/grants and tuition waivers (partial) also available. *Faculty research:* Accounting, capital markets and corporate finance, organizational change and human resource management, marketing, strategic management. Total annual research expenditures: $7.7 million. *Unit head:* Dr. Mike Percy, Director, 780-492-2361, Fax: 780-492-3325, E-mail: busphd@ualberta.ca. *Application contact:* Jeanette Gosine, Program Coordinator, 780-492-2361, Fax: 780-492-3325, E-mail: busphd@ualberta.ca.

See Close-Up on page 335.

University of Cincinnati, Division of Research and Advanced Studies, McMicken College of Arts and Sciences, Center for Organizational Leadership, Cincinnati, OH 45221. Offers MALER. Part-time and evening/weekend programs available. *Faculty:* 2 full-time (1 woman), 12 part-time/adjunct (2 women). *Students:* 10 full-time (9 women), 43 part-time (38 women); includes 14 minority (12 African Americans, 1 Asian American or Pacific Islander, 1 Hispanic American). Average age 37. 15 applicants, 67% accepted, 7 enrolled. In 2006, 35 degrees awarded. *Entrance requirements:* For master's, GRE or GMAT. Additional exam requirements/recommendations for international students: Required—TOEFL (minimum score 520 paper-based; 190 computer-based; 68 iBT). *Application deadline:* For fall admission, 8/18 for domestic students; for winter admission, 12/1 for domestic students; for spring admission, 2/18 for domestic students. Applications are processed on a rolling basis. Application fee: $40. Electronic applications accepted. *Financial support:* In 2006–07, 5 students received support, including 1 research assistantship with tuition reimbursement available; teaching assistantships, scholarships/grants and tuition waivers (partial) also available. *Faculty research:* Leadership and diversity. *Unit head:* Dr. Joseph Gallo, Professor and Director, Center for Organizational Leadership, 513-556-2605, E-mail: joseph.gallo@uc.edu. *Application contact:* Tricia Yee, Program Coordinator, 513-556-2670, Fax: 513-556-2066, E-mail: tricia.yee@uc.edu.

University of Dallas, Graduate School of Management, Irving, TX 75062-4736. Offers accounting (MBA, MS); business management (MBA); corporate finance (MBA, MM); engineering management (MBA, MM); entrepreneurship (MBA, MM); financial services (MBA, MM); global business (MBA, MM); health services management (MBA, MM); human resource management (MBA, MM, MS); information assurance (MBA, MM, MS); information technology (MBA, MM, MS); information technology service management (MBA); IT service management (MS); marketing (MM); marketing management (MBA); not-for-profit management (MBA); organization development (MBA); project management (MBA, MM); sports and entertainment management (MBA, MM); strategic leadership (MBA); supply chain management (MBA); supply chain management and market logistics (MM); telecommunications management (MBA, MM). *Accreditation:* ACBSP. Part-time and evening/weekend programs available. Postbaccalaureate distance learning degree programs offered (no on-campus study). *Faculty:* 26 full-time (5 women), 85 part-time/adjunct (18 women). *Students:* 227 full-time (98 women), 1,160 part-time (446 women); includes 473 minority (209 African Americans, 3 American Indian/Alaska Native, 143 Asian Americans or Pacific Islanders, 118 Hispanic Americans), 224 international. Average age 34. 556 applicants, 86% accepted, 291 enrolled. In 2006, 476 degrees awarded. *Entrance requirements:* Additional exam requirements/recommendations for international students: Required—TOEFL. *Application deadline:* Applications are processed on a rolling basis. Application fee: $50. Electronic applications accepted. *Expenses: Contact institution.* *Financial support:* In 2006–07, 468 students received support. Scholarships/grants and unspecified assistantships available. Financial award application deadline: 2/15; financial award applicants required to submit FAFSA. *Unit head:* Dr. J. Lee Whittington, Dean, 972-721-5230. *Application contact:* Sarah Stivison, Director of Graduate Admissions, 972-721-5198, Fax: 972-721-4009, E-mail: admiss@gsm.udallas.edu.

University of Denver, University College, Denver, CO 80208. Offers applied communication (MAS, MPS); computer information systems (MAS); environmental policy and management (MAS); geographic information systems (MAS); human resource administration (MPS); knowledge and information technologies (MAS); liberal studies (MLS); modern languages (MLS); organizational leadership (MPS); technology management (MAS); telecommunications (MAS). Part-time and evening/weekend programs available. Postbaccalaureate distance learning degree programs offered (no on-campus study). *Students:* 57 full-time (28 women), 453 part-time (253 women); includes 84 minority (37 African Americans, 1 American Indian/Alaska Native, 21 Asian Americans or Pacific Islanders, 25 Hispanic Americans), 39 international. Average age 26. 159 applicants, 84% accepted. In 2006, 171 master's awarded. *Entrance requirements:* Additional exam requirements/recommendations for international students: Required—TOEFL (minimum score 550 paper-based; 213 computer-based). *Application deadline:* Applications are processed on a rolling basis. Application fee: $75. Electronic applications accepted. *Expenses: Contact institution.* *Financial support:* Applicants required to submit FAFSA. *Unit head:* Dr. James Davis, Dean, 303-871-2291, Fax: 303-871-4047, E-mail: jdavis@du.edu. *Application contact:* Information Contact, 303-871-3069.

University of Great Falls, Graduate Studies, Program in Human Services Administration, Great Falls, MT 59405. Offers organizational management (MS). Part-time and evening/weekend programs available. Postbaccalaureate distance learning degree programs offered

Organizational Management

University of Great Falls (continued)
(minimal on-campus study). *Faculty:* 2 full-time (both women), 4 part-time/adjunct (1 woman). *Students:* 2 full-time (1 woman), 2 part-time (both women); includes 2 minority (both American Indian/Alaska Native). Average age 37. 8 applicants, 88% accepted. In 2006, 4 degrees awarded. *Degree requirements:* For master's, thesis optional. *Entrance requirements:* For master's, GRE General Test or MAT, 3 letters of recommendation. Additional exam requirements/recommendations for international students: Required—TOEFL (minimum score 500 paper-based; 205 computer-based). *Application deadline:* For fall admission, 8/15 priority date for domestic students, 6/15 priority date for international students; for spring admission, 12/15 priority date for domestic students, 10/15 priority date for international students. Applications are processed on a rolling basis. Application fee: $50. Electronic applications accepted. *Financial support:* In 2006–07, 3 students received support. Career-related internships or fieldwork, Federal Work-Study, and institutionally sponsored loans available. Support available to part-time students. Financial award application deadline: 6/1; financial award applicants required to submit FAFSA. *Unit head:* Dr. Craig A. Ganster, Director, 406-791-5363, E-mail: cganster01@ugf.edu.

University of Hawaii at Manoa, Graduate Division, Shidler College of Business, Program in Business Administration, Honolulu, HI 96822. Offers Asian business studies (MBA); Chinese business studies (MBA); decision sciences (MBA); entrepreneurship (MBA); finance (MBA); finance and banking (MBA); human resources management (MBA); information management (MBA); information technology (MBA); international business (MBA); Japanese business studies (MBA); marketing (MBA); organizational behavior (MBA); organizational management (MBA); real estate (MBA); student-designed track (MBA). *Accreditation:* AACSB. Part-time programs available. *Faculty:* 48 full-time (9 women). *Students:* 207 full-time (77 women), 158 part-time (60 women); includes 93 minority (2 African Americans, 1 American Indian/Alaska Native, 88 Asian Americans or Pacific Islanders, 2 Hispanic Americans), 58 international. Average age 33. 235 applicants, 55% accepted, 68 enrolled. In 2006, 147 degrees awarded. *Degree requirements:* For master's, thesis optional. *Entrance requirements:* For master's, GMAT, minimum GPA of 3.0. Additional exam requirements/recommendations for international students: Required—TOEFL (minimum score 500 paper-based; 173 computer-based; 61 iBT). *Application deadline:* For fall admission, 5/1 for domestic and international students; for spring admission, 9/1 for domestic and international students. Application fee: $50. *Financial support:* In 2006–07, 7 research assistantships (averaging $17,409 per year), 3 teaching assistantships (averaging $14,028 per year) were awarded. *Application contact:* Ting Bui, Information Contact, 808-956-5565, Fax: 808-956-6889.

University of Hawaii at Manoa, Graduate Division, Shidler College of Business, Program in International Management, Honolulu, HI 96822. Offers Asian finance (PhD); global information technology management (PhD); international accounting (PhD); international marketing (PhD); international organization and strategy (PhD). *Faculty:* 42 full-time (8 women). *Students:* 36 applicants, 19% accepted, 4 enrolled. In 2006, 5 degrees awarded. *Median time to degree:* Of those who began their doctoral program in fall 1998, 33% received their degree in 8 years or less. *Degree requirements:* For doctorate, thesis/dissertation, comprehensive exam. *Entrance requirements:* For doctorate, GMAT or GRE General Test, minimum GPA of 3.0. Additional exam requirements/recommendations for international students: Required—TOEFL (minimum score 600 paper-based; 250 computer-based; 100 iBT). *Application deadline:* For fall admission, 3/1 for domestic and international students. Application fee: $50. *Financial support:* In 2006–07, 16 research assistantships (averaging $18,198 per year), 3 teaching assistantships (averaging $14,958 per year) were awarded. Total annual research expenditures: $3.3 million. *Application contact:* Ting Bui, Information Contact, 808-956-6723, Fax: 808-956-2774.

University of La Verne, College of Business and Public Management, Program in Organizational Management and Leadership, La Verne, CA 91750-4443. Offers leadership and management (MS); nonprofit management (Certificate); organizational leadership (Certificate). Part-time programs available. *Faculty:* 15 full-time (7 women), 13 part-time/adjunct (7 women). *Students:* 20 full-time (13 women), 40 part-time (25 women); includes 37 minority (5 African Americans, 5 American Indian/Alaska Native, 3 Asian Americans or Pacific Islanders, 24 Hispanic Americans), 2 international. Average age 35. In 2006, 21 degrees awarded. *Degree requirements:* For master's, thesis or research project. *Entrance requirements:* For master's, minimum undergraduate GPA of 2.75, 2 letters of recommendation, interview, resumé. Additional exam requirements/recommendations for international students: Required—TOEFL (minimum score 550 paper-based; 213 computer-based). *Application deadline:* Applications are processed on a rolling basis. Application fee: $50. *Expenses:* Contact institution. *Financial support:* Institutionally sponsored loans available. Financial award application deadline: 3/2; financial award applicants required to submit FAFSA. *Unit head:* Dr. Bernice Ledbetter, Chairperson, 909-593-3511 Ext. 4345, E-mail: bledbetter@ulv.edu. *Application contact:* Jo Nell Baker, Director, Graduate Admissions and Academic Services, 909-593-3511 Ext. 4244, Fax: 909-392-2761, E-mail: gradadmt@ulv.edu.

University of La Verne, College of Education and Organizational Leadership, Department of Organizational Leadership, La Verne, CA 91750-4443. Offers educational management (M Ed, Credential), including educational management (M Ed), preliminary administrative services (Credential), professional administrative services (Credential); organizational leadership (Ed D). Part-time programs available. *Faculty:* 14 full-time (8 women), 9 part-time/adjunct (8 women). *Students:* 183 full-time (124 women), 179 part-time (109 women); includes 111 minority (41 African Americans, 2 American Indian/Alaska Native, 13 Asian Americans or Pacific Islanders, 55 Hispanic Americans), 1 international. Average age 44. In 2006, 12 master's, 46 doctorates awarded. *Degree requirements:* For doctorate, thesis/dissertation. *Entrance requirements:* For doctorate, GRE or MAT, minimum GPA of 3.0 in graduate course work, resumé. Additional exam requirements/recommendations for international students: Required—TOEFL (minimum score 550 paper-based; 213 computer-based). *Application deadline:* Applications are processed on a rolling basis. Application fee: $50. *Expenses:* Contact institution. *Financial support:* Institutionally sponsored loans available. Financial award application deadline: 3/2; financial award applicants required to submit FAFSA. *Unit head:* Dr. Barbara Poling, Chairperson, 909-593-3511 Ext. 4380, Fax: 909-392-2700, E-mail: polingb@ulv.edu. *Application contact:* Jo Nell Baker, Director, Graduate Admissions and Academic Services, 909-593-3511 Ext. 4244, Fax: 909-392-2761, E-mail: gradadmt@ulv.edu.

University of La Verne, Regional Campus Administration, Graduate Programs, Central Coast/Vandenberg Air Force Base Campuses, La Verne, CA 91750-4443. Offers business (MBA-EP), including health services management, information technology; health administration (MHA); leadership and management (MS). *Faculty:* 6 part-time/adjunct (0 women). *Students:* 14 full-time (5 women), 20 part-time (8 women); includes 7 minority (1 African American, 1 American Indian/Alaska Native, 5 Hispanic Americans). Average age 38. In 2006, 11 degrees awarded. *Entrance requirements:* For master's, 2 letters of recommendation, resumé. *Application deadline:* Applications are processed on a rolling basis. Application fee: $50. *Expenses:* Contact institution. *Financial support:* Institutionally sponsored loans available. Financial award application deadline: 3/2; financial award applicants required to submit FAFSA. *Unit head:* Kitt Vincent, Director, Central Coast Campus, 805-542-9690 Ext. 321, Fax: 805-542-9735, E-mail: vincentk@ulv.edu.

University of La Verne, Regional Campus Administration, Graduate Programs, High Desert Campus, Victorville, CA 91750-4443. Offers business (MBA-EP); health administration (MHA); leadership and management (MS). *Faculty:* 2 part-time/adjunct (0 women). *Students:* 1 full-time (0 women), 13 part-time (7 women); includes 8 minority (5 African Americans, 1 American Indian/Alaska Native, 2 Hispanic Americans). Average age 41. In 2006, 1 degree awarded. *Entrance requirements:* For master's, 2 letters of recommendation, resumé. *Application deadline:* Applications are processed on a rolling basis. Application fee: $50. *Expenses:* Contact institution. *Financial support:* Application deadline: 3/2; *Unit head:* Teresa Anderson, Director, 760-843-0086, Fax: 760-843-9505, E-mail: tanderson7@ulv.edu.

University of La Verne, Regional Campus Administration, Graduate Programs, Inland Empire Campus, Ranche Cucamonga, CA 91750-4443. Offers business (MBA-EP), including health services management, information technology, management, marketing; health administration (MHA); leadership and management (MS). *Faculty:* 2 full-time (1 woman), 8 part-time/adjunct (2 women). *Students:* 21 full-time (16 women), 32 part-time (18 women); includes 29 minority (13 African Americans, 1 American Indian/Alaska Native, 4 Asian Americans or Pacific Islanders, 11 Hispanic Americans). Average age 37. In 2006, 17 degrees awarded. *Entrance requirements:* For master's, 2 letters of recommendation, resumé. *Application deadline:* Applications are processed on a rolling basis. Application fee: $50. *Expenses:* Contact institution. *Financial support:* Institutionally sponsored loans available. Financial award application deadline: 3/2; financial award applicants required to submit FAFSA. *Unit head:* Jerry Ford, Director, 909-484-3858 Ext. 228, Fax: 909-484-9469, E-mail: fordj@ulv.edu.

University of La Verne, Regional Campus Administration, Graduate Programs, Kern County Campus, Bakersfield, CA 93301. Offers business (MBA-EP), including information technology, management, marketing; health administration (MHA); leadership and management (MS). *Faculty:* 4 part-time/adjunct (2 women). *Students:* 2 full-time (1 woman), 7 part-time (4 women); includes 2 minority (1 African American, 1 Hispanic American). Average age 37. In 2006, 4 degrees awarded. *Entrance requirements:* For master's, 2 letters of recommendation, resumé. *Application deadline:* Applications are processed on a rolling basis. Application fee: $50. *Expenses:* Contact institution. *Financial support:* Institutionally sponsored loans available. Financial award application deadline: 3/2; financial award applicants required to submit FAFSA. *Unit head:* Val Garcia, 661-328-1430, E-mail: vgarcia6@ulv.edu.

University of La Verne, Regional Campus Administration, Graduate Programs, Ventura County/Point Mugu Naval Air Station Campuses, La Verne, CA 91750-4443. Offers business (MBA-EP), including health services management, information technology, management, marketing; business organizational management (MS); health administration (MHA); leadership and management (MS). *Faculty:* 2 full-time (0 women), 8 part-time/adjunct (1 woman). *Students:* 22 full-time (7 women), 29 part-time (16 women); includes 19 minority (4 African Americans, 7 Asian Americans or Pacific Islanders, 8 Hispanic Americans). Average age 40. In 2006, 26 degrees awarded. *Entrance requirements:* For master's, 2 letters of recommendation, resumé. Application fee: $50. *Expenses:* Contact institution. *Financial support:* Institutionally sponsored loans available. Financial award application deadline: 3/2; financial award applicants required to submit FAFSA. *Unit head:* Janet Meyer, Director, Ventura Campus, 805-981-8030 Ext. 225, Fax: 805-981-8033, E-mail: jmeyer2@ulv.edu.

University of Maryland Eastern Shore, Graduate Programs, Program in Organizational Leadership, Princess Anne, MD 21853-1299. Offers PhD. Evening/weekend programs available. *Faculty:* 1 full-time (0 women), 24 part-time/adjunct (7 women). *Students:* 29 full-time (18 women), 80 part-time (49 women); includes 76 minority (73 African Americans, 2 Asian Americans or Pacific Islanders, 1 Hispanic American), 1 international. Average age 40. 52 applicants, 63% accepted, 33 enrolled. In 2006, 7 degrees awarded. *Degree requirements:* For doctorate, thesis/dissertation, internship, comprehensive exam. *Entrance requirements:* For doctorate, interview, writing sample, successful record of employment or career in organization/profession. Additional exam requirements/recommendations for international students: Required—TOEFL (minimum score 213 computer-based). *Application deadline:* For fall admission, 3/1 for domestic and international students. Applications are processed on a rolling basis. Application fee: $30. Electronic applications accepted. *Financial support:* Career-related internships or fieldwork available. Financial award application deadline: 3/1; financial award applicants required to submit FAFSA. *Unit head:* Dr. Harry Hoffer, Director, 410-651-8361, Fax: 410-651-8414, E-mail: hehoffer@umes.edu. *Application contact:* Dr. Jay Bishop, Coordinator, 410-651-6581, Fax: 410-651-6584, E-mail: ijbishop@umes.edu.

University of Massachusetts Dartmouth, Graduate School, Charlton College of Business, Program in Business Administration, North Dartmouth, MA 02747-2300. Offers accounting (Postbaccalaureate Certificate); business administration (MBA); e-commerce (PMC); finance (PMC); general management (PMC); leadership (PMC); management (Postbaccalaureate Certificate); marketing (PMC); supply chain management (PMC). *Accreditation:* AACSB. Part-time programs available. *Faculty:* 41 full-time (11 women), 22 part-time/adjunct (8 women). *Students:* 66 full-time (20 women), 111 part-time (54 women); includes 16 minority (5 African Americans, 6 Asian Americans or Pacific Islanders, 5 Hispanic Americans), 46 international. Average age 30. 167 applicants, 83% accepted, 83 enrolled. In 2006, 73 master's, 20 other advanced degrees awarded. *Entrance requirements:* For master's, GMAT, resumé, letters of recommendation. Additional exam requirements/recommendations for international students: Required—TOEFL (minimum score 500 paper-based). *Application deadline:* For fall admission, 6/1 for domestic students, 4/1 for international students; for spring admission, 10/1 for domestic students, 8/1 for international students. Application fee: $40 ($60 for international students). Electronic applications accepted. *Expenses:* Tuition, state resident: full-time $2,071; part-time $86 per credit. Tuition, nonresident: full-time $8,099; part-time $337 per credit. *Financial support:* In 2006–07, 2 research assistantships with full tuition reimbursements (averaging $11,985 per year), 6 teaching assistantships with full tuition reimbursements (averaging $7,200 per year) were awarded; Federal Work-Study and unspecified assistantships also available. Support available to part-time students. Financial award application deadline: 3/1; financial award applicants required to submit FAFSA. *Faculty research:* Organizational identity dynamics in strategic alliances and partnerships, market analysis in cranberry industry, consumer choice modeling. Total annual research expenditures: $508,000. *Unit head:* Matthew Roy, Assistant Dean, 508-999-8409, Fax: 508-999-8776, E-mail: mroy@umassd.edu. *Application contact:* Carol Novo, Graduate Admissions Officer, 508-999-8604, Fax: 508-999-8183, E-mail: graduate@umassd.edu.

University of New Mexico, Robert O. Anderson Graduate School of Management, Department of Organizational Studies, Albuquerque, NM 87131-2039. Offers human resources management (MBA); policy and planning (MBA). Part-time and evening/weekend programs available. *Entrance requirements:* For master's, GMAT. Additional exam requirements/recommendations for international students: Required—TOEFL (minimum score 550 paper-based; 213 computer-based).

University of North Texas, Robert B. Toulouse School of Graduate Studies, College of Business Administration, Department of Management, Denton, TX 76203. Offers administrative management (MBA); management (EMBA, MBA); organization theory and policy (PhD); personnel and industrial relations (MBA, PhD); production/operations management (MBA, PhD). *Faculty:* 24 full-time (10 women). *Students:* 18 full-time (11 women), 51 part-time (22 women); includes 15 minority (7 African Americans, 1 American Indian/Alaska Native, 1 Asian American or Pacific Islander, 6 Hispanic Americans), 13 international. Average age 30. 54 applicants, 83% accepted, 9 enrolled. In 2006, 29 master's, 1 doctorate awarded. *Degree requirements:* For doctorate, thesis/dissertation. *Entrance requirements:* For master's, GMAT, relevant work experience; for doctorate, GMAT or GRE General Test, relevant work experience. Additional exam requirements/recommendations for international students: Required—TOEFL. *Application deadline:* For fall admission, 7/15 for domestic students. Application fee: $50 ($75 for international students). *Expenses:* Tuition, state resident: full-time $3,573; part-time $198 per credit. Tuition, nonresident: full-time $8,577; part-time $476 per credit. Required fees: $1,258; $126 per credit. One-time fee: $150 full-time. Tuition and fees vary according to course load. *Financial support:* Fellowships, teaching assistantships, Federal Work-Study available. Financial award application deadline: 4/1. *Unit head:* Dr. J. Lynn Johnson, Chair, 940-565-3140, Fax: 940-565-4394, E-mail: johnsonl@cobaf.coba.unt.edu. *Application contact:* Dr. Nancy Boyd-Lillie, Graduate Adviser, 940-565-3158, E-mail: boyd@cobaf.coba.unt.edu.

University of Pennsylvania, School of Arts and Sciences, Graduate Group in Organizational Dynamics, Philadelphia, PA 19104. Offers MS. Part-time and evening/weekend programs available. *Degree requirements:* For master's, thesis. Electronic applications accepted.

University of Phoenix Online Campus, School of Advanced Studies, Phoenix, AZ 85034-7209. Offers business administration (DBA); education (Ed D); health administration (DHA);

organizational management (DM). Evening/weekend programs available. *Faculty:* 36 full-time (13 women), 551 part-time/adjunct (224 women). *Students:* 4,544 full-time (2,756 women); includes 1,550 minority (1,136 African Americans, 32 American Indian/Alaska Native, 152 Asian Americans or Pacific Islanders, 230 Hispanic Americans), 378 international. Average age 44. In 2006, 210 degrees awarded. *Degree requirements:* For doctorate, thesis/dissertation. *Entrance requirements:* For doctorate, 3 letters of recommendation, minimum master's GPA of 3.0, 3 years professional work experience. Additional exam requirements/recommendations for international students: Required—TOEFL (minimum score 550 paper-based; 213 computer-based; 79 iBT). *Application deadline:* Applications are processed on a rolling basis. Application fee: $45. Electronic applications accepted. *Expenses:* Tuition: Full-time $12,664. Required fees: $760. *Financial support:* Institutionally sponsored loans and scholarships/grants available. Financial award applicants required to submit FAFSA. *Unit head:* Dr. Dawn Iwamoto, Dean/Executive Director, 480-557-3228, E-mail: dawn.iwamoto@phoenix.edu. *Application contact:* Information Contact, 800-697-8223.

University of St. Thomas, Graduate Studies, School of Education, Program in Organization Learning and Development, St. Paul, MN 55105-1096. Offers MA, Ed D, Certificate. Part-time and evening/weekend programs available. Postbaccalaureate distance learning degree programs offered (minimal on-campus study). *Faculty:* 4 full-time (2 women), 11 part-time/adjunct (7 women). *Students:* 2 full-time (both women), 149 part-time (107 women); includes 15 minority (10 African Americans, 4 Asian Americans or Pacific Islanders, 1 Hispanic American), 3 international. Average age 37. 50 applicants, 100% accepted, 50 enrolled. In 2006, 15 master's, 8 doctorates, 2 other advanced degrees awarded. *Degree requirements:* For master's and Certificate, registration; for doctorate, thesis/dissertation, comprehensive exam, registration. *Entrance requirements:* For master's, minimum GPA of 2.75, 3 letters of reference; for doctorate, MAT, minimum GPA of 3.5, interview; for Certificate, minimum graduate GPA of 3.25. Additional exam requirements/recommendations for international students: Required—TOEFL (minimum score 550 paper-based; 213 computer-based). *Application deadline:* For fall admission, 8/1 priority date for domestic and international students; for winter admission, 12/1 priority date for domestic students, 12/1 for international students; for spring admission, 12/1 priority date for domestic and international students. Applications are processed on a rolling basis. Application fee: $50. *Expenses: Contact institution. Financial support:* In 2006–07, 8 students received support, including 5 fellowships (averaging $2,000 per year), 3 research assistantships (averaging $1,000 per year); institutionally sponsored loans and scholarships/grants also available. Support available to part-time students. Financial award applicants required to submit FAFSA. *Faculty research:* Workplace conflict, physician leaders, entrepreneurship education, mentoring. Total annual research expenditures: $30,000. *Unit head:* Dr. John P. Conbere, Department Chair, 651-962-4456, Fax: 651-962-4169, E-mail: jpconbere@stthomas.edu. *Application contact:* Liz G. Knight, Department Coordinator, 651-962-4459, Fax: 651-962-4169, E-mail: egknight@stthomas.edu.

University of San Francisco, College of Professional Studies, Program in Organization Development, San Francisco, CA 94117-1080. Offers MS. Part-time and evening/weekend programs available. *Faculty:* 3 full-time (2 women), 15 part-time/adjunct (6 women). *Students:* 127 full-time (88 women); includes 43 minority (7 African Americans, 1 American Indian/Alaska Native, 17 Asian Americans or Pacific Islanders, 18 Hispanic Americans), 3 international. Average age 36. 42 applicants, 90% accepted, 24 enrolled. In 2006, 36 degrees awarded. *Degree requirements:* For master's, thesis. *Entrance requirements:* For master's, minimum GPA of 3.0. Application fee: $55 ($65 for international students). *Expenses:* Tuition: Full-time $17,370; part-time $965 per unit. Tuition and fees vary according to degree level, campus/location and program. *Financial support:* In 2006–07, 66 students received support. Application deadline: 3/2; *Unit head:* Dr. Sharon Wagner, Head. *Application contact:* 415-422-6000.

The University of Scranton, Graduate School, Department of Health Administration and Human Resources, Program in Human Resources Administration, Scranton, PA 18510. Offers human resources (MS); human resources development (MS); organizational leadership (MS). Part-time and evening/weekend programs available. *Students:* 3 full-time (all women), 19 part-time (12 women); includes 1 minority (African American) Average age 34. 21 applicants, 100% accepted. In 2006, 19 degrees awarded. *Degree requirements:* For master's, capstone experience. *Entrance requirements:* For master's, minimum GPA of 2.75. Additional exam requirements/recommendations for international students: Required—TOEFL (minimum score 500 paper-based; 173 computer-based), IELTS (minimum score 6). *Application deadline:* Applications are processed on a rolling basis. Application fee: $50. *Expenses:* Tuition: Part-time $684 per credit. Required fees: $25 per term. *Financial support:* Fellowships, teaching assistantships, career-related internships or fieldwork, Federal Work-Study, and unspecified assistantships available. Support available to part-time students. Financial award application deadline: 3/1. *Unit head:* Dr. Terri Freeman Smith, Director, 570-941-6218.

University of the Incarnate Word, School of Graduate Studies and Research, Dreeben School of Education, Programs in Education, San Antonio, TX 78209-6397. Offers adult education (M Ed, MA); diversity education (M Ed, MA); early childhood education (M Ed, MA); instructional technology (M Ed, MA); international education and entrepreneurship (PhD); kinesiology (M Ed, MA); mathematics education (PhD); organizational leadership (PhD); organizational learning (M Ed, MA); reading (M Ed, MA); special education (M Ed, MA). *Students:* 15 full-time (8 women), 179 part-time (117 women); includes 70 minority (20 African Americans, 1 American Indian/Alaska Native, 1 Asian American or Pacific Islander, 48 Hispanic Americans), 54 international. Average age 39. In 2006, 15 degrees awarded. Application fee: $20. *Expenses:* Tuition: Part-time $570 per credit hour. Required fees: $54 per credit hour. One-time fee: $195 part-time. Tuition and fees vary according to degree level. *Financial support:* Federal Work-Study and scholarships/grants available. *Unit head:* Dr. Richard Gray, Director, 210-829-3138, Fax: 210-829-3134, E-mail: gray@uiwtx.edu. *Application contact:* Andrea Cyterski-Acosta, Dean of Enrollment, 210-829-6005, Fax: 210-829-3921, E-mail: cyterski@uiwtx.edu.

University of the Incarnate Word, School of Graduate Studies and Research, H-E-B School of Business and Administration, Programs in Administration, San Antonio, TX 78209-6397. Offers adult education (MAA); applied administration (MAA); communication arts (MAA); English (MAA); instructional technology (MAA); international business (Certificate); multidisciplinary sciences (MAA); nutrition (MAA); organizational development (MAA, Certificate); project management (Certificate); sports management (MAA); urban administration (MAA). *Students:* 1 (woman) full-time, 161 part-time (102 women); includes 17 African Americans, 1 American Indian/Alaska Native, 82 Hispanic Americans, 18 international. Average age 34. In 2006, 78 degrees awarded. *Entrance requirements:* For master's, GMAT, GRE, MAT. Additional exam requirements/recommendations for international students: Required—TOEFL. *Application deadline:* For fall admission, 8/15 priority date for domestic students; for spring admission, 12/31 for domestic students. Applications are processed on a rolling basis. Application fee: $20. *Expenses:* Tuition: Part-time $570 per credit hour. Required fees: $54 per credit hour. One-time fee: $195 part-time. Tuition and fees vary according to degree level. *Financial support:* Federal Work-Study and scholarships/grants available. *Unit head:* Dr. Dan Dominguez, MAA Director, 210-829-3180, Fax: 210-805-3564, E-mail: domingue@uiwtx.edu. *Application contact:* Andrea Cyterski-Acosta, Dean of Enrollment, 210-829-6005, Fax: 210-829-3921, E-mail: cyterski@uiwtx.edu.

Upper Iowa University, Online Master's Programs, Fayette, IA 52142-1857. Offers accounting (MBA); corporate financial management (MBA); global business (MBA); health and human services (MPA); homeland security (MPA); human resources management (MBA); justice administration (MPA); organizational development (MBA); public personnel management (MPA); quality management (MBA). MBA also available at Madison, Wisconsin campus. Part-time and evening/weekend programs available. Postbaccalaureate distance learning degree programs offered (no on-campus study). *Degree requirements:* For master's, research project. *Entrance requirements:* For master's, GMAT, GRE, or minimum GPA of 2.7 during last 60 hours. Additional exam requirements/recommendations for international students: Required—TOEFL (minimum score 570 paper-based; 230 computer-based). Electronic applications accepted. *Faculty research:* Total quality management, CQI, teams, organization culture and climate, management.

Vanderbilt University, Owen Graduate School of Management and Graduate School, Program in Management, Nashville, TN 37240-1001. Offers finance (PhD); marketing (PhD); operations management (PhD); organization studies (PhD). PhD offered through the Graduate School. *Accreditation:* AACSB. *Faculty:* 46 full-time (8 women). *Students:* 19 full-time (6 women); includes 12 minority (all Asian Americans or Pacific Islanders) Average age 28. 169 applicants, 5% accepted, 5 enrolled. In 2006, 3 degrees awarded. *Median time to degree:* Doctorate–5 years full-time. Of those who began their doctoral program in fall 1998, 100% received their degree in 8 years or less. *Degree requirements:* For doctorate, thesis/dissertation, registration. *Entrance requirements:* For doctorate, GMAT or GRE. Additional exam requirements/recommendations for international students: Required—TOEFL. *Application deadline:* For fall admission, 1/15 priority date for domestic students; for spring admission, 3/15 for domestic students. Application fee: $0. Electronic applications accepted. *Expenses: Contact institution.* One-time fee: $30 full-time. Full-time tuition and fees vary according to course load, degree level and program. *Financial support:* In 2006–07, 19 students received support, including 4 fellowships with full tuition reimbursements available (averaging $20,500 per year); scholarships/grants, health care benefits, and tuition waivers (full and partial) also available. Financial award application deadline: 5/1. *Faculty research:* Financial marketing, operations, human resources. *Unit head:* Dr. Clifford Ball, Director, 615-322-2909, E-mail: cliff.ball@owen.vanderbilt.edu. *Application contact:* Janet Sisco, Information Contact, 615-322-5652, E-mail: janet.sisco@owen.vanderbilt.edu.

Vanderbilt University, Peabody College, Department of Leadership and Organizations, Nashville, TN 37240-1001. Offers education policy (MPP); educational leadership and policy (Ed D); higher education (M Ed); higher education, leadership and policy (Ed D); human resource development (M Ed); international education policy and management (M Ed); organizational leadership (M Ed); school administration (M Ed). Part-time and evening/weekend programs available. *Faculty:* 21 full-time (6 women), 9 part-time/adjunct (3 women). *Students:* 131 full-time (88 women), 85 part-time (39 women); includes 35 minority (30 African Americans, 4 Asian Americans or Pacific Islanders, 1 Hispanic American), 11 international. Average age 31. 214 applicants, 63% accepted, 64 enrolled. In 2006, 43 master's, 12 doctorates awarded. *Median time to degree:* Of those who began their doctoral program in fall 1998, 62% received their degree in 8 years or less. *Degree requirements:* For master's, thesis optional; for doctorate, thesis/dissertation, qualifying exams, residency. *Entrance requirements:* For master's and doctorate, GRE General Test. Additional exam requirements/recommendations for international students: Required—TOEFL (minimum score 550 paper-based; 213 computer-based). *Application deadline:* For fall admission, 12/31 priority date for domestic and international students; for spring admission, 11/1 priority date for domestic and international students. Applications are processed on a rolling basis. Application fee: $0. Electronic applications accepted. *Expenses:* Tuition: Full-time $24,462. Required fees: $2,515. One-time fee: $30 full-time. Full-time tuition and fees vary according to course load, degree level and program. *Financial support:* In 2006–07, 90 students received support, including 50 fellowships with full and partial tuition reimbursements available, 38 research assistantships with full and partial tuition reimbursements available, 2 teaching assistantships with full and partial tuition reimbursements available; Federal Work-Study, institutionally sponsored loans, scholarships/grants, tuition waivers (partial), and unspecified assistantships also available. Support available to part-time students. Financial award application deadline: 2/1; financial award applicants required to submit FAFSA. *Faculty research:* Education policy, education finances, economics of education, education leadership and management, higher education leadership and policy; educator pay for performance. *Unit head:* James W. Guthrie, Chair, 615-322-8000, Fax: 615-343-7094, E-mail: james.w.guthrie@vanderbilt.edu. *Application contact:* Rosie Moody, Educational Coordinator, 615-322-8019, Fax: 615-343-7094, E-mail: rosie.moody@vanderbilt.edu.

Wayland Baptist University, Graduate Programs, Programs in Business Administration/Management, Plainview, TX 79072-6998. Offers general business (MBA); health care administration (MBA); human resource management (MBA); international management (MBA); management (MA, MBA), including human resource management (MA), organization management (MA); management information systems (MBA). Part-time and evening/weekend programs available. Postbaccalaureate distance learning degree programs offered (no on-campus study). *Faculty:* 3 full-time (0 women). *Students:* 1 full-time (0 women), 7 part-time (2 women); includes 1 minority (Hispanic American) Average age 28. 1 applicant, 100% accepted, 1 enrolled. In 2006, 2 degrees awarded. *Degree requirements:* For master's, capstone course. *Entrance requirements:* For master's, GMAT, GRE or MAT. Additional exam requirements/recommendations for international students: Required—TOEFL (minimum score 500 paper-based; 173 computer-based). *Application deadline:* Applications are processed on a rolling basis. Application fee: $35. *Expenses:* Tuition: Full-time $6,120; part-time $340 per credit hour. Required fees: $50 per term. *Financial support:* Federal Work-Study, institutionally sponsored loans, and scholarships/grants available. Support available to part-time students. Financial award application deadline: 5/1; financial award applicants required to submit FAFSA. *Unit head:* Dr. Otto Schacht, Chairman, 806-291-1020, Fax: 806-291-1957.

Webster University, College of Arts and Sciences, Department of History, Politics and International Relations, Program in International Nongovernmental Organizations, St. Louis, MO 63119-3194. Offers MA. *Students:* 1 (woman) full-time, 4 part-time (all women). Average age 32. *Expenses:* Tuition: Full-time $8,820; part-time $490 per credit. Tuition and fees vary according to degree level, campus/location and program. *Unit head:* Kelly-Kate Pease, Director, 314-968-7083, E-mail: peasekk@webster.edu.

Wilmington College, Division of Business, New Castle, DE 19720-6491. Offers business administration (MBA); finance (MBA); health care administration (MBA, MS); human resource management (MS); management (MS); management information systems (MBA); organizational leadership (MS); public administration (MS); transportation and logistics (MBA, MS). Part-time and evening/weekend programs available. *Faculty:* 3 full-time (0 women). *Students:* 230 full-time (138 women), 432 part-time (274 women); includes 109 minority (98 African Americans, 1 American Indian/Alaska Native, 3 Asian Americans or Pacific Islanders, 7 Hispanic Americans). Average age 34. 229 applicants, 100% accepted, 156 enrolled. In 2006, 273 degrees awarded. *Entrance requirements:* Additional exam requirements/recommendations for international students: Required—TOEFL (minimum score 500 paper-based; 173 computer-based). *Application deadline:* Applications are processed on a rolling basis. Application fee: $25. *Financial support:* Applicants required to submit FAFSA. *Unit head:* Dr. Robert Edelson, Chair, 302-295-1147, Fax: 302-328-7021, E-mail: robert.e.edelson@wilmcoll.edu. *Application contact:* Chris Ferguson, Director of Admissions and Financial Aid, 302-328-9407 Ext. 256, Fax: 302-328-5164, E-mail: inquire@wilmcoll.edu.

Woodbury University, School of Business and Management, Program in Organizational Leadership, Burbank, CA 91504-1099. Offers MA. Evening/weekend programs available. *Faculty:* 4 part-time/adjunct (2 women). *Students:* 21 full-time (12 women); includes 2 African Americans, 5 Hispanic Americans. Average age 29. 34 applicants, 71% accepted, 21 enrolled. In 2006, 30 degrees awarded. *Entrance requirements:* For master's, GRE General Test (if GPA is below 2.5), 12-month cohort. *Application deadline:* For fall admission, 8/1 priority date for domestic students; for spring admission, 12/1 priority date for domestic students. Applications are processed on a rolling basis. Application fee: $35. *Expenses:* Tuition: Full-time $8,052; part-time $671 per unit. Tuition and fees vary according to course load and campus/location. *Financial support:* Application deadline: 7/15; *Application contact:* Mauro Diaz, Director of Admissions, 818-767-0888 Ext. 225, Fax: 818-767-0520, E-mail: maurodiaz@woodbury.edu.

Worcester Polytechnic Institute, Graduate Studies and Enrollment, Department of Management, Program in Operations Design and Leadership, Worcester, MA 01609-2280. Offers process design (MS); supply chain management (MS). Part-time and evening/weekend programs available. Postbaccalaureate distance learning degree programs offered (no on-campus study). *Faculty:* 11 full-time (6 women), 1 part-time/adjunct (0 women). *Students:* 4 full-time (2 women), 9 part-time (4 women), 3 international. Average age 32. 13 applicants, 85% accepted, 4 enrolled. In 2006, 2 degrees awarded. *Median time to degree:* Master's–1.5 years full-time, 3 years part-time. *Degree requirements:* For master's, thesis optional. *Entrance*

Organizational Management

Worcester Polytechnic Institute *(continued)*

requirements: For master's, GMAT or GRE. Additional exam requirements/recommendations for international students: Required—TOEFL (minimum score 550 paper-based; 213 computer-based; 79 iBT), IELTS (minimum score 7). *Application deadline:* For fall admission, 6/1 priority date for domestic and international students; for spring admission, 10/15 for domestic students, 10/1 priority date for international students. Applications are processed on a rolling basis. Application fee: $70. Electronic applications accepted. *Expenses:* Tuition: Part-time $1,042 per credit hour. Required fees: $1,009 per year. *Financial support:* In 2006–07, 3 students received support, including 2 research assistantships; career-related internships or fieldwork, Federal Work-Study, scholarships/grants, and unspecified assistantships also available. Financial award application deadline: 6/1; financial award applicants required to submit FAFSA. *Faculty research:*

Global sourcing and supply chain management, service operations modeling, health care operations and performance analysis, lean process deign. Total annual research expenditures: $117,061. *Unit head:* Norm D. Wilkinson, Director, Graduate Management Programs, 508-831-5957, Fax: 508-831-5720, E-mail: nwilkins@wpi.edu.

See Close-Up on page 377.

Worcester State College, Graduate Studies, Program in Management, Worcester, MA 01602-2597. Offers accounting (MS); organizational leadership (MS). *Students:* 1 (woman) full-time, 14 part-time (8 women), 4 international. Average age 28. 20 applicants, 80% accepted, 12 enrolled. *Expenses:* Tuition, state resident: full-time $4,518; part-time $251 per credit hour. Tuition, nonresident: full-time $4,518; part-time $251 per credit hour. *Unit head:* Dr. Lauri Dahlin, Coordinator, 508-929-8094.

AVILA UNIVERSITY

Program in Organizational Development

Program of Study	Avila University's Master of Science (M.S.) in organizational development helps students reach their career goals, providing them with skills to be on the leading edge. Students learn the tools to strategically motivate and manage individuals, teams, and organizations for effective change—skills useful in human resources, management, business, or consulting. Because the program is designed for working professionals, classes meet once a week, usually in the evenings, many students can complete the degree in less than two years.

The program consists of a 1-credit-hour introduction class, 22 hours of core requirements, 12 hours of course work in an area of concentration (organizational dynamics or project management), and a 3-credit-hour research project, for a total of 37 hours.

Graduate program faculty members believe that students graduating with a Master of Science degree should have a sound grasp of psychological theory and the methodologies that provide the foundation for effective organization interventions. In their capstone experience, students are given an option as to how they would like to articulate a theory to action. Students may write a thesis, which could address either a theoretical or an applied research issue, or they may invest in an applied internship project at an organization of their choice. The course instructor must approve all projects prior to enrollment in the course.

Research Facilities The Hooley-Bundschu Library is the information resource center for the campus. It houses a collection of more than 60,000 books, a current subscription list of 500 periodicals and newspapers, videotapes, CD-ROMs, DVDs, and the entire ERIC document collection on microfiche. The library is a member of MOBIUS, a statewide consortium of more than fifty academic libraries with a shared online catalog. The library subscribes to the online search services DIALOG and WESTLAW and provides student access to the bibliographic databases FirstSearch, ERIC, and the Modern Language Association. In addition, the library provides access to full-text and bibliographic databases, such as EBSCOhost, Academic Universe, Contemporary Women's Issues, NewsBank: Missouri Newspapers, the ABC-CLIO databases, ProQuest Psychology, and PsycArticles. There are study rooms available for faculty and student use. The library houses a computer lab with more than twenty PCs connected to the campus network, with e-mail and Internet access, Microsoft Office, and curriculum-related software, as well as digital camcorders, tripods, and software for class projects. Avila maintains several computer labs and classrooms to support teaching and learning. Labs have both PC and Macintosh computers, color monitors, and laser printers. Each computer lab facility is upgraded on a regular basis and is network supported, so students and faculty members can access specialty software, Internet resources, and Microsoft Office products.

Financial Aid Avila University believes that every student should choose a college based on the academic quality of the institution not the cost. Therefore, the University's goal is to use financial aid funds to make Avila an affordable choice for any student. The University provides financial aid funds to assist qualified students who would be unable to meet their university costs without such assistance. The University also offers significant additional institutional funds to recognize and encourage students who have superior academic records or demonstrate outstanding abilities. Students should contact the Financial Aid Office, located in Blasco Hall, for complete instructions on how to apply for all types of financial assistance (telephone: 816-501-3600; e-mail: financialaid@avila.edu).

Cost of Study Tuition is $415 per credit hour.

Living and Housing Costs Two residence halls provide 126 furnished double rooms. Each floor has a kitchen, laundry facilities, a lounge, and study rooms. Each room has free Internet access, cable, and local telephone service. On-campus housing ranges between $1375 and $2100. Meals plans range from $1000 to $1500.

Student Group There are 75 students enrolled in the program; the average age is 33.

Location Situated on 50 rolling acres in south Kansas City, Missouri, Avila University is just minutes off an interstate highway network and is convenient to Kansas City's many attractions. Kansas City, known as the City of Fountains, is home to more fountains than any city in the world except Rome. Many Fortune 500 companies also call Kansas City home.

The University Avila University is a Catholic coeducational university with liberal arts and professional programs. Avila University was founded in 1916 and is sponsored by the Sisters of St. Joseph of Carondelet. From its modest beginnings, Avila has become a flourishing comprehensive university offering a variety of degree programs. Founded as the College of St. Teresa, the college grew and expanded to a larger campus in 1963, when its name was changed to Avila to honor St. Teresa of Avila. In 2002, Avila College became Avila University, a name reflecting its growth and development as an institution of higher education. Avila University's commitment to excellence; to service of students and the community; to high-quality education of spirit, mind, and body; and to growth of the whole person is deeply rooted in its Catholic heritage and in the lives and beliefs of the founding Sisters of St. Joseph. Students and faculty and staff members provide a supportive, caring, yet challenging environment in which students receive close personalized attention, in a student-faculty ratio of 12:1.

Applying Applicants seeking admission to this program must have earned a bachelor's degree from an accredited institution and have a minimum GPA of 3.25 on a 4.0 scale for at least the last 60 hours of undergraduate course work. Students must submit the completed application, official transcripts, two letters of recommendation, a resume, and an essay. There are no deadlines for applications; students can start in the fall, spring, or summer semester. Should a student not meet the above stated admissions requirements, they are still encouraged to apply for provisional admittance.

Correspondence and Information
Lacey Smith, Assistant Dean
School of Professional Studies
Avila University
11901 Wornall Road
Kansas City, Missouri 64145-1698
Phone: 816-501-3737
Fax: 816-941-4650
E-mail: advantage@avila.edu
Web site: http://www.avila.edu/advantage/org.htm

Avila University

FACULTY AND STAFF

Steve Iliff, Dean. 816-501-3737; Steve.Iliff@Avila.edu.
Lacey Smith, Assistant Dean. 816-501-3737; Lacey.Smith@Avila.edu.
Kari Clevenger, Director of Admission and Marketing. 816-501-3675; Kari.Clevenger@Avila.edu.
Cathy Mahurin, Recruitment Representative. 816-501-2481; Cathy.Mahurin@Avila.edu.
Melanie DeFeo, Office Manager. 816-501-3737; Melanie.DeFeo@Avila.edu.

FACULTY

Nicki Alexopoulos
Randy Allen
Joe Barnhill
Ronnie Beach
Deb Belt
Betty Berg
Shari Blank
David Borcherding
Lisa Bowers
Rich Bradford
Rance Carlson
Lee Chiaramonte
Carol Cobb
Kevin Costello
Allison Darling
Amelia Davenport
Genevieve DelRosario
Mark Eaton
Paula Fremont
Ken Fuenshawsen
Karen Gaines
Shawnta Gantt
Cecilia Garrett
Phillip Gonsher
Brad Grabs
Robert Grady
Tim Hamilton
Betsy Hansbrough

Ira Harritt
Peggy Hinzman
Maria Hunt
Nancy Kennedy
Bob Larson
Teresa McClain
Carmela Meyer
Stacia Mitchell
Mary Patterson
Lora Rochelle
Mike Segalo
Jean Sheffer
Vicki Silvers-Gier
Elsje Smit
Jere Smith
Ray Smith
Marchita Stanton
Linda Strelluf
Jeff Sturgis
Loretta Summers
Dick Sumpter
Janet Sunderland
Carrie Surls
Billie Swaggart
George Townsend
Tom Turner
Margo Weatherby-Reynolds
Bart Whaley

EASTERN UNIVERSITY

Program in Organizational Leadership

Program of Study	The Ph.D. program in organizational leadership is an interdisciplinary program focused on the educational needs of leaders in business, education, and nonprofit management. Its mission is to equip professionals to effectively engage in the transformation of their organizations, communities, and society as practitioners and scholars. With this mission in mind, the program prepares its student to embrace the four different aspects of the transformational leader: the centered leader, the servant leader, the learning leader, and the visionary leader.
	The program synthesizes a mix of general leadership theory and practice while offering distinct concentrations in business leadership, education leadership, and nonprofit leadership. The core curriculum consists of eight courses in leadership theory and practice, research methodologies, management of organizations, and strategic management. From there, students choose from one of three concentrations.
	The business leadership concentration is designed primarily for those who have already earned an M.B.A. or its equivalent and do not need an introduction to the essential disciplines of business leadership. This concentration addresses practices and issues of concern to twenty-first century leaders. The focus is on the business leader as decision maker, consultant, and scholar. The program not only prepares the student to advance at work, but also enables a transition to consulting and scholarly roles.
	The educational leadership concentration is primarily for educational leaders aspiring to university administration or to the superintendency or other senior management roles in K–12 public systems or private schools. The Pennsylvania standards for certification for the K–12, known as the Letter of Eligibility, is integrated into the course work. Graduates are qualified for teaching and scholarship at the university level.
	The nonprofit leadership concentration is designed primarily for those who have already earned an advanced degree in business, leadership, nonprofits, public administration, social work, or health administration and wish to apply their knowledge to the nonprofit sector in which they are currently employed. The primary focus of this program is on the nonprofit leader as decision maker and scholar. Students enter the program in a cohort, completing a large portion of their studies with the same group of people. The program is delivered through a hybrid model of residencies, online discussions, and individualized instruction.
	Each fourteen-week term begins with a four-day residency (Wednesday evening through Saturday afternoon) of lectures, small-group sessions, and advising; students interact with faculty members and each other and are introduced to the two courses of the term. The residency is followed by ten weeks of significant online course work. The last two weeks of each term are devoted to a reading period during which assignments are completed and individual instruction is offered.
	The program takes three years of full-time course work followed by research for the dissertation. The calendar was designed to be sensitive to the working professional while maintaining the integrity of the Ph.D.-level work. To successfully complete the program, students must earn 60 credits, including 51 credits in core and concentration studies and 9 credits for the dissertation proposal, dissertation, and oral defense. Students must successfully complete comprehensive exams of the core curriculum in order to begin the dissertation proposal phase of the program.
Research Facilities	Warner Memorial Library, which has been rated A for size according to the Association of College and Research Libraries, has a collection of 275,000 items, including 626 current periodical titles in paper and microfiche; 13,000 electronic journal titles in online full-text format; more than 825,000 microforms, including a full collection of ERIC (the Educational Resource Information Center) titles; and 18,500 audio, video, and sound recordings. Over 65,000,000 books and 50 databases are available through FirstSearch, Interlibrary Loan, the Tri-State Library Cooperative, and the Pennsylvania Academic Library Consortium's E-Z Borrow, providing access to 35,000 journals and articles. Dissertation Abstracts, an important resource for Ph.D. students, is accessible, and the library staff is compiling an online reserve library where faculty members can request chapters of books and articles to be scanned and posted on Blackboard.
Financial Aid	The structure of this program qualifies students as being enrolled full-time and entitles them to all of the federal aid possibilities that entails. Doctoral students are eligible for Stafford Loans if they have not exhausted their financial aid opportunities in previous programs. Eastern University is committed to offering financial aid for students in need. For more information, interested students should consult Eastern's financial aid pages at http://www.eastern.edu/centers/finaid/index.shtml.
Cost of Study	Tuition for fall term 2007 is $4350 ($725 per credit) plus a $75 administrative fee that covers costs related to transcripts, technology, and the Wednesday evening meal at the beginning of each residency. Procedures for payment are detailed on the student account pages at http://www.eastern.edu/centers/sfs/index.shtml.
Living and Housing Costs	In 2007–08, students living on-campus spend $2275 per semester for basic housing (a single room costs an additional $430), a room with a semi-private bath costs $2635, and a suite or apartment costs $2830. Meal plans are also available; students pay $1840 per semester for twelve meals per week. Off-campus apartments rent for $850 to $950 per month, depending on size, location, and amenities. Other costs are estimated at $500 to $1000 for books and supplies and $600 to $1200 for transportation.
Student Group	The program is intended for students who expect to pursue this degree while continuing in their current responsibilities, including managers in business, educational administrators, nonprofit and community leaders, church and denominational leaders, and adjunct faculty members. Students are expected to have at least five years of professional practice in a leadership capacity and have taken graduate-level courses in statistics, research design, and finance.
Student Outcomes	Graduates of the program are prepared to continue in their current leadership positions or to advance in their careers. Many graduates are also prepared to teach organizational leadership or conduct scholarly research at the university level.
Location	Located just west of Philadelphia, St. Davids is part of Pennsylvania's Delaware County, the home of some of the region's most popular tourist attractions. The John Heinz Wildlife Refuge offers fishing, bird watching, and other activities for nature lovers. History buffs love visiting Valley Forge, Brandywine Battlefield, and other landmarks. St. Davids is also surrounded by shopping, dining, nightlife, and museums.
The University	Eastern University is a coeducational, comprehensive Christian university that integrates faith, reason, and justice to prepare students for thoughtful and productive lives of Christian faith and service. Founded in 1925 as a seminary school, Eastern currently offers fifty academic and preprofessional programs to 3,700 undergraduate, graduate, and seminary students. The University has a main campus in St. Davids but has other facilities throughout Pennsylvania and in West Virginia and Washington, D.C. Eastern is affiliated with the American Baptist Churches USA.
Applying	Applicants must submit a completed application; transcripts showing a graduate GPA of 3.0 or better; a current resume; three letters of recommendation, with at least one from an academic source; a four-page statement of purpose addressing personal and professional goals; official GRE or Miller Analogies Test (MAT) scores; a copy of a research thesis or other research project; a computer equipment and skills form; and a $75 application fee. Completed applications are due November 1 for the following September's cohort. The Admissions Committee issues decisions no later than January 15. Second- and third-round applications are reviewed as space is available. Once accepted into the program, students must submit a $150 deposit (deducted from tuition) and register for classes.
Correspondence and Information	Dr. David Greenhalgh, Program Director Eastern University 1300 Eagle Road St. Davids, Pennsylvania 19087-3696 Phone: 610-341-5800 E-mail: dgreenha@eastern.edu Web site: http://www.eastern.edu/academic/ccgps/oip/OLPhD.shtml

Eastern University

THE FACULTY

Anthony L. Blair, Associate Professor; Ph.D., Temple.
Darrell F. D. Boyd, Instructor; M.Div., Gordon-Conwell Theological Seminary.
Robert L. Muse, Assistant Professor; Th.M., Princeton Theological Seminary.
Rod Niner, Assistant Professor; D.Min., Trinity Evangelical Divinity School.
Miguel P. Pulido, Instructor; M.S.W., Temple.
Sheri L. Robinson, Assistant Professor; J.D., Temple.

FIELDING GRADUATE UNIVERSITY

School of Human & Organization Development

Programs of Study	The School of Human & Organization Development (HOD) offers doctoral (Ph.D.) degrees in human development and human and organizational systems and a master's (M.A.) degree in organization management and development.
	Advanced professional development courses and certificates are available in evidence-based coaching, organization management and development, and integral studies.
	Custom programs and courses for business, nonprofits, government agencies, education, and human services are available in the aforementioned areas as well as coaching and mentoring, community development, health-care systems and management, public administration, knowledge management, and conflict resolution and negotiation.
	Students in the Ph.D. programs are experienced professionals participating in a flexible, collaborative learning environment. They are encouraged to develop and direct their own learning plan, apply real-world experience, and collaborate with mentors and peers. Students pursue their course of study without relocating and participate in a variety of learning methods, including faculty member–facilitated face-to-face and virtual meetings, online seminars, research sessions, and national sessions. The learning model requires students to integrate theory, practice, and research and to apply their experience to the advancement of individuals, organizations, social systems, public policies, and communities.
	The organization management and development master's program affords students the opportunity to pursue their degree online and complete it in twenty months. While collaborating with faculty members and peer groups, students apply their professional experience to a curriculum that is dedicated to fostering new ways of leading and working within corporations, profit and nonprofit agencies, education, and government.
Research Facilities	Fielding's library services are designed to serve the complex needs of busy professionals by offering substantial research tools via the Web. The library collection and services include a database of Internet resources, a subsidized document delivery service, a catalog of available dissertations and electronic books, and access to numerous online library databases and journals.
Financial Aid	Fielding Graduate University participates in the Federal Stafford Student Loan program, which makes subsidized and unsubsidized loans available based on financial need. Fielding also participates in Veterans Assistance Programs. In 2006–07, Fielding Graduate University administered approximately $18 million in aid to about 75 percent of its graduate students.
Cost of Study	The 2007–08 tuition for the Ph.D. programs is $19,695. Tuition for the M.A. program is $5450 per term. Current tuition information can be found at http://www.fielding.edu/tuition.
Living and Housing Costs	Because Fielding Graduate University students work independently and live in various parts of the United States and beyond, costs in addition to tuition vary. Considerations include computer equipment, books and materials, travel to orientation sessions, and optional travel to research and national sessions and regional cluster meetings. There may be other costs related to a specific course of study.
Student Group	The Fielding Graduate University student community consists primarily of adult learners who have chosen a self-directed, independent learning program and are geographically dispersed, as are the members of the faculty. Fielding's total student population is more than 1,500. The 660 students in the School of Human & Organization Development are a diverse group of individuals who form a worldwide professional network. Fielding scholars are practitioners with varied experience in areas such as consulting, the corporate arena, profit and nonprofit agencies, education, and government. The average age of Fielding's HOD doctoral students is 47, with a range from 27 to 74 years of age. The average age of the organization management and development master's students is 38, with a range from 22 to 54.
Location	Fielding's administrative offices are located in Santa Barbara, California. The students and faculty members create a global Fielding community representing the United States and thirty-one countries. Attendance at an orientation and planning session meets the Ph.D. program residency requirements. Optional national sessions, research sessions, regional seminars, and cluster meetings, as well as virtual cluster meetings, are offered throughout the year.
The University	Founded in 1974, Fielding Graduate University is a global leader in graduate-level networked education for professionals. Fielding is dedicated to providing high-quality, accredited programs through a combination of face-to-face and online interactions between accomplished students and nationally recognized faculty members. The student-centered programs combine theory with practice and are designed to support flexible, independent learning and competency development. This flexibility allows students to apply their graduate studies to their professional work. The Fielding community is dedicated to lifelong learning, innovation, and change for individuals, communities, organizations, and social justice.
Applying	Students may enter the Ph.D. program in the School of Human & Organization Development twice a year (September and March). Master's degree students may enter in September, January, or May. Applicants must submit a $75 nonrefundable fee, an application form, and additional materials specific to their program of interest.
Correspondence and Information	Admission Office Fielding Graduate University 2112 Santa Barbara Street Santa Barbara, California 93105 Phone: 800-340-1099 (toll-free) E-mail: admission@fielding.edu Web site: http://www.fielding.edu

Fielding Graduate University

THE FACULTY

Ph.D. PROGRAM

Faculty
Charles McClintock, Ph.D., Dean.
Dottie Agger-Gupta, Ph.D., Associate Dean.
Katrina Rogers, Ph.D., Associate Dean.
Judith Stevens-Long, Ph.D., Associate Dean.

Richard P. Appelbaum, Ph.D.
Leonard Baca, Ed.D.
Frank Barrett, Ph.D.
Valerie Malhotra Bentz, Ph.D.
Marie Farrell, Ed.D.
Placido V. Gallegos, Ph.D.
Miguel G. Guilarte, Ph.D.
Matthews Hamabata, Ph.D.
Christine Ho, Ph.D.
Linda H. Lewis, Ed.D.
Milton Lopes, Ph.D.
Michael Manning, Ph.D.
Keith Melville, Ph.D.
Barbara Mink, Ed.D.
Stephen Murphy-Shigematsu, Ph.D.
Annabelle Nelson, Ph.D.
Margo Okazawa-Rey, Ed.D.
Thierry C. Pauchant, Ph.D.
W. Barnett Pearce, Ph.D.
Georgia A. Persons, Ph.D.
David Rehorick, Ph.D.
Steven A. Schapiro, Ed.D.
Charles Seashore, Ph.D.
Jeremy Shapiro, Ph.D.
Robert J. Silverman, Ph.D.
John H. Stanfield II, Ph.D.
Frederick Steier, Ph.D.

Adjunct and Consulting Faculty
Lita Furby, Ph.D.
Lenneal Henderson, Ph.D.
Gary Schulman, Ph.D.
Jerry Snow, Ph.D.
James Spickard, Ph.D.

MASTER'S PROGRAM
Candido Trujillo, Ph.D., Program Director.
Jim Beaubien, Ph.D.
Marcella Benson-Quaziena, Ph.D.
Sean Esbjorn Hargens, Ph.D.
Gary M. Fontaine, Ph.D.
Jeffrey Frakes, Ph.D.
Bo Gyllenpalm, Ph.D.
Barclay Hudson, Ed.D.
Dean S. Janoff, Ph.D.
Randy Martin, Ph.D.
Rena M. Palloff, Ph.D.
Dianne Stober, Ph.D.
Leni Wildflower, Ph.D.

THE GEORGE WASHINGTON UNIVERSITY

Department of Organizational Sciences & Communication

Programs of Study

The George Washington University (GWU) Department of Organizational Sciences & Communication hosts two graduate programs—a doctoral program in industrial and organizational psychology and master's programs in organizational sciences.

The Industrial/Organizational (I/O) Psychology Doctoral Program offers graduate training in areas such as personnel selection, training and development, work motivation, leadership, work teams, and organizational development. The program of study is designed in accordance with guidelines established by the Society for Industrial and Organizational Psychology (SIOP; Division 14, APA). A recent survey of graduate students placed GWU's I/O Psychology Doctoral Program first in terms of overall quality. For specific results, students should visit the Web site at http://www.siop.org/tip/backissues/July04/06kraiger.aspx.

The Organizational Sciences Program is part of the George Washington University Columbian College of Arts and Sciences and was founded in 1981. It draws from a broad range of resources within the University, including organizational management, psychology, communication, economics, and statistics. Organizational sciences ties managerial and executive success to the integration of knowledge in three key areas: strategy and change management, leadership and communication, and performance and talent management. The program is based on the premise that for individuals and organizations to succeed—whether they are in the for-profit, not-for-profit, government, military, service, or manufacturing sectors—they must be ready to think and act in the most effective ways possible.

The Organizational Sciences Program offers two-year M.A. degree programs in organizational sciences, with concentrations in both organizational management and human resources management, as well as a Certificate Program in Leadership Coaching. The program also offers an accelerated one-year M.A. Fellows Program in organizational sciences, with a concentration in organizational management (http://www.gwu.edu/~orgsci/fellows.htm). This is a lockstep program using cohort-learning principles, driven by cross-functional faculty members, and designed for experienced professionals. All master's programs incorporate a theory-to-practice model, while underscoring principles that encourage students to create their own areas of specialization.

Research Facilities

The George Washington University is a member of the Association of Research Libraries and the Washington Research Library Consortium (WRLC), which consists of eleven universities within the Washington metropolitan area. The library collections of the George Washington University are housed within Gelman Library and four other specialized libraries. The George Washington University Gelman Library contains more than 2 million volumes and over 18,000 serials, all supported by an extensive electronic database. ALADIN is the online electronic library resource of the WRLC; it contains a combined online catalog of seven member universities with more than 4.3 million records.

Financial Aid

The George Washington University is an eligible participant in Federal Stafford Student Loans and also has a GW Plan with preferred lenders that allows students to obtain up to 100 percent of the annual graduate education cost. For further information, students should visit http://www.gwu.edu/~fellows or http://www.gwired.gwu.edu/finaid.

Cost of Study

Those interested may contact the George Washington University Department of Organizational Sciences & Communication at 202-994-1878 for more information.

Living and Housing Costs

The University does not provide housing for graduate students. For housing information, students should visit http://www.gwu.edu/~gss/ and click on Student Life and Housing. Additional housing information is available at http://gwired.gwu.edu/cllc/. Living near GWU in a shared apartment costs approximately $9900 per academic year and $13,200 per calendar year.

Student Group

GWU promotes a group experience and values diversity, as domestic and international students and professionals from a variety of backgrounds (for-profit, not-for-profit, government, military, manufacturing, service, entrepreneurial) are welcomed. Most master's students are working full-time and studying part-time; most Ph.D. students are studying full-time.

Location

The University has three campuses, each hosting various combinations of degree programs. The Foggy Bottom Campus (600 21st Street, NW, Washington, D.C. 20052) is the main campus for the George Washington University. It is located in the heart of Washington and is housed in more than ninety buildings, all of which are within blocks of the White House, the John F. Kennedy Center for the Performing Arts, the State Department, the World Bank, the International Monetary Fund, and a host of federal agencies, museums, and galleries.

The Mount Vernon Campus (2100 Foxhall Road, NW, Washington, D.C. 20007) is located in a historic, wooded area within Washington and affords students the opportunity to study within a relaxed, spacious, and natural setting.

The Arlington, Virginia, Campus (3601 Wilson Boulevard, Arlington, Virginia 22201-2362) is located at the Virginia Square Metro Station and within the heart of a rapidly growing Arlington community.

The Department

The Department of Organizational Sciences & Communication (http://www.gwu.edu/~orgsci/) is part of the George Washington University's Columbian College of Arts and Sciences and is built on a program that was founded in 1981. The program draws from a broad range of resources within the University, including interdisciplinary courses in organizational management, psychology, communication, and economics.

Applying

In addition to the completed application form, applicants must have a bachelor's degree with a B average or better (3.0 on a 4.0 scale), official results from the Graduate Record Examinations General Test, official results from the Test of English as a Foreign Language (TOEFL) if English is not the applicant's official language or he or she does not hold a degree from an accredited U.S. institution, the $60 application fee, official transcripts from each college or university attended, two letters of recommendation, a statement of purpose (250 to 500 words), and a resume.

Students should apply online at http://www.columbian.gwu.edu/grad/index.php/id/44. The deadline for fall semester entrance is April 1; for spring semester it is October 1.

Correspondence and Information

David P. Costanza, Ph.D., Chair
Department of Organizational Sciences & Communication
The Columbian College of Arts and Sciences
The George Washington University
600 21st Street, NW
Washington D.C. 20052
Phone: 202-994-1878
Fax: 202-994-1881
E-mail: orgsci@gwu.edu
Web site: http://www.gwu.edu/~orgsci

The George Washington University

THE FACULTY

Full-Time Faculty

David P. Costanza, Associate Professor of Organizational Sciences and Industrial/Organizational Psychology and Chair, Department of Organizational Sciences & Communication; Ph.D., George Mason.

Andrew J. Critchfield, Assistant Professor of Communication; Ph.D., Howard.

Elizabeth B. Davis, Associate Professor and Program Director of Organizational Sciences; Ph.D., Pennsylvania (Wharton).

Gelaye Debebe, Assistant Professor of Organizational Sciences; Ph.D., Michigan.

Dana M. Glenn, Assistant Professor of Industrial/Organizational Psychology; Ph.D., Houston.

Jean C. Miller, Assistant Professor of Communication; Ph.D., Maryland, College Park.

Lynn R. Offermann, Professor of Psychology and Industrial/Organizational Psychology; Ph.D., Syracuse.

Nils Olsen, Assistant Professor of Organizational Sciences; Ph.D., North Carolina at Chapel Hill.

Nicholas L. Vasilopoulos, Associate Professor and Program Director of Industrial/Organizational Psychology; Ph.D., Stevens.

Clay Warren, Chauncey M. Depew Professor and Program Director of Communication; Ph.D., Colorado at Boulder.

Adjunct Faculty

Gary Bojes, Ph.D., Assistant Professorial Lecturer of Organizational Sciences.

Dede Bonner, Ed.D., Associate Professorial Lecturer of Organizational Sciences and Management Consultant, New Century Management, Inc.

Victoria Grady, Ph.D., Assistant Professorial Lecturer of Organizational Sciences.

Beth Hand, M.B.A., Assistant Professorial Lecturer of Organizational Sciences and President, Hand and Associates.

Eileen Hoffman, J.D., Professorial Lecturer of Organizational Sciences and Director, Office of Special Projects, Federal Mediation and Conciliation Service (FMCS).

David Koehn, Ph.D., Associate Professorial Lecturer of Organizational Sciences and Chief Learning Officer, McDonald Bradley.

Jean Claude Leon, Ph.D., Assistant Professorial Lecturer of Organizational Sciences and Assistant Professor of Business and Economics, Catholic University of America.

Mary Lippitt, Ph.D., Associate Professorial Lecturer of Organizational Sciences and President, Enterprise Management.

Govindan Nair, Associate Professorial Lecturer of Organizational Sciences and Senior Economist, World Bank.

Margaret New, Ed.D., Assistant Professorial Lecturer of Organizational Sciences and Executive Coach and Career Management Consultant, the Middleburg Group.

Jerome Paige, Ph.D., Assistant Professorial Lecturer of Organizational Sciences, Paige & Associates.

Maria Ramos, Ph.D., Assistant Professorial Lecturer of Organizational Sciences, Ramos & Associates.

Cynthia Roman, Ed.D., Assistant Professorial Lecturer of Organizational Sciences.

Trish Silber, M.B.A., Assistant Professorial Lecturer of Organizational Sciences and Partner, Catalyst Consulting Team.

William Smith, Ph.D., Associate Professorial Lecturer of Organizational Sciences and Founder and Director, Organizing for Development of an International Institute.

Armand Thieblot Jr., Ph.D., Professorial Lecturer of Organizational Sciences and President and Senior Consultant, A. J. Thieblot & Son/NCSDO.

Wayne Vick, M.B.A., Lecturer of Organizational Sciences and President, Vick Associates.

Diana Watts, Ph.D., Assistant Professorial Lecturer of Organizational Sciences.

Stephen Wehrenberg, Ph.D., Associate Professorial Lecturer of Organizational Sciences and Long-Range Manpower Planner, U.S. Coast Guard Headquarters.

THE NEW SCHOOL
A UNIVERSITY

THE NEW SCHOOL: A UNIVERSITY

Milano The New School for Management and Urban Policy
Program in Organizational Change Management

Program of Study

The Program in Organizational Change Management at Milano The New School for Management and Urban Policy is designed for those who wish to broaden their experience in organizational change management, either as line managers or change consultants, as well as those making a transition into the profession. In a commitment to individual professional development that is unique to Milano's program, students are assessed on their areas of competency, and the model is revisited as students move through the core curriculum to align competencies with skills.

The Master of Science degree is intended as a part-time program for students with a minimum of three years' work experience. The curriculum gives students the tools to implement planned change successfully at all levels—the individual, by changing behaviors through management leadership interventions; the group, through team building, reengineering work processes, and managing the diversity of group membership; and the organization, by articulating vision and ensuring that the organization's structure, culture, and people processes align with the vision. The curriculum develops competencies to support senior management's strategic change initiatives.

To fulfill the required 42 credits, students structure a program comprising three components: a required schoolwide core of 12 credits, a required program core of 18 credits (Foundations of Organizational Change; Organizational Assessment and Diagnosis; Group Processes, Facilitation, and Intervention; Organizational Change Interventions: Theory, Design, and Implementation; Managing the Consultant/Client Relationship; and Advanced Seminar in Organizational Change Management), and 12 credits of elective courses.

In addition to core and elective courses, the program offers a unique "laboratory-type" pedagogy, known as The Portfolio, in which a series of organizational change management courses lead students into increasingly complex organizational change situations with real clients. With the completion of the sequence, the student has a "portfolio" demonstrating a proven capacity for making serious contributions to the field.

Research Facilities

The Center for New York City Affairs is a nonpartisan institute dedicated to advancing innovative public policies that strengthen neighborhoods, support families, and reduce urban poverty. Tools include rigorous analysis, research, candid public dialogue with stakeholders and opinion leaders, and strategic planning with government officials, nonprofit practitioners, and community residents. The center's original applied research and public seminars examine the politics of community change in local and state government and identify critical problems facing urban families and communities. The center's public programs offer community leaders and other participants the opportunity to meet powerful players in and around government and to learn about the context, the influential organizations, and other factors that define the policymaking landscape in New York City and urban America.

Financial Aid

Milano offers financial aid packages in the form of scholarships, fellowships, and loans. Financial aid awards are decided on a first-come, first-served basis, and applicants are encouraged to apply early to receive priority consideration. Financial aid award decisions are made after students accepted at Milano. Applicants interested in obtaining financial aid should submit the Free Application for Federal Student Aid (FAFSA) or the Renewal Application for Federal Student Aid. More information is available from the Office of Financial Services at 212-229-8930.

Cost of Study

Tuition in 2006–07 was $1032 per credit, and fees were approximately $200 each term.

Living and Housing Costs

The University Housing Office maintains a comprehensive resource center with apartment listings. University-run apartments and residence halls are also available. The cost of housing, food, transportation, books, and living expenses averages $17,000 annually. For more information, students should go online to http://www.newschool.edu/studentservices.

Student Group

There are 55 students in the program; 7 attend on a full-time basis. Of these students, 47 are women, 16 are members of underrepresented groups, and 2 are international students.

Location

The New School's location in New York City gives students access to an abundance of resources. Students are encouraged to take advantage of the city's many museums, performance venues, and other cultural institutions, which are only a walk or a subway ride away. An extension of the classroom, the city also offers excellent professional and networking opportunities, and some classes require that students work with outside businesses to complete assignments—giving them unparalleled real-world experience. Internships and apprenticeships with leading New York City companies and organizations in every field are also available, and many students have moved on from internships to successful careers with those companies and organizations upon graduation.

The University and The School

The New School pioneered the idea of lifelong university-level education for adults. It was created for teachers and students from different backgrounds who were willing to take risks for their intellectual and political beliefs. Milano The New School for Management and Urban Policy trains leaders for the nonprofit, public, and private sectors with a measurable difference. The faculty blends theory with practice and progressive analysis with hands-on activism. Milano students work on local and global issues that affect organizations and urban communities—in New York City and around the world. The New School is accredited by the Commission on Higher Education of the Middle States Association of Colleges and Schools. A privately supported institution, The New School is chartered as a university by the Regents of the State of New York.

Applying

Students must submit the completed application form, the $50 application fee, official transcripts from all postsecondary institutions attended, a 300-word essay explaining their professional goals, two letters of recommendation, and a resume. Applications are reviewed on a rolling admissions basis. Although there is no specific deadline, applicants are strongly encouraged to apply by March 1 for the fall semester and by October 1 for the spring semester in order to take full advantage of financial aid and housing opportunities.

Correspondence and Information

Program in Organizational Change Management
Milano The New School for Management and Urban Policy
The New School
72 Fifth Avenue, 3rd Floor
New York, New York 10011
Phone: 212-229-5400
Fax: 212-229-5354
E-mail: milanoadmissions@newschool.edu
Web site: http://www.milano.newschool.edu

The New School: A University

THE FACULTY AND THEIR RESEARCH

Warren Balinsky, Associate Professor and Chair of Health Services Management; Ph.D., Case Western Reserve. Home health care and the applications of planning, development, marketing, and research to health services management and policy. Dr. Balinsky has written two books on home care; he has also written articles on various aspects of emergency preparedness, health care of the elderly, health-care reimbursement, health status indices, home care, pediatric health care, and the unequal distribution of medical personnel within the health-care system.

Robert Beauregard, Professor; Ph.D., Cornell. Urbanization in the United States, with particular focus on industrial urban decline after World War II and current problems posed by growth and decline in cities. Dr. Beauregard is currently working on *Writing Urban Theory,* a series of essays, and *Why Cities Endure,* a book investigating why some cities prosper while others do not. Dr. Beauregard teaches courses on the political economy of the city, urban redevelopment, neighborhood change, social theory, and research design.

Howard Berliner, Professor of Health Services Management and Director of Ph.D. in Public and Urban Policy Program; Sc.D., Johns Hopkins. Needs of vulnerable populations and access to health services for the uninsured. Dr. Berliner is the author of seven books, most recently *The Health Marketplace: New York City 1990–2010* with Ginzberg et al. He has also written numerous articles and reviews on health policy in academic and professional journals. Dr. Berliner served for two years as the assistant state health commissioner for New Jersey.

John Clinton, Visiting Assistant Professor; Ph.D., Fordham. Interprofessional collaboration. Dr. Clinton has served as corporation senior consultant on social responsibility at MetLife, senior vice president of the LightHouse for the Blind, and an administrator at NYU, Fordham University, and Hartwick College. He has been a consultant to foundations, nonprofit organizations, corporations, and higher education institutions.

Dennis Derryck, Professor of Professional Practice; Ph.D., Fordham. Innovative policies and strategies affecting the economic sustainability of nonprofit organizations. Dr. Derryck has held leadership positions in organizations involved in community economic development, operations and fiscal management, and research and policy analysis. He currently serves as chair of WE ACT for Environmental Justice and is vice chair of SoBro, the South Bronx Overall Economic Development Corporation.

Elizabeth Dickey, Professor; Ed.D., Massachusetts Amherst. Organizational behavior and leadership, with a psychosocial emphasis. Dr. Dickey is a developmental clinical psychologist. Between 1991 and 2005, she served as dean and then provost of The New School.

Peter Eisinger, Henry Cohen Professor; Ph.D., Yale. Urban politics and policy, state and local economic development, U.S. politics, state politics, federalism. Author of *Toward an End to Hunger in America.*

Alec Ian Gershberg, Associate Professor; Ph.D., Pennsylvania. School governance, education finance, decentralization in the developing world and in the United States, immigrant students in public schools in New York and California. Dr. Gershberg has conducted extensive research on Latin America—particularly Mexico, Nicaragua, and Ecuador—as well as on Egypt, Romania, and sub-Saharan Africa. He has been a frequent consultant to the World Bank, the Inter-American Development Bank, and the Urban Institute. Dr. Gershberg is the lead author of *Beyond Bilingual Education: New Immigrants and Public School Policies in California.*

Martin Greller, Professor and Associate Dean for Academic Affairs; Ph.D., Yale. Factors associated with career continuity for older workers, feedback systems in organizations as tools for increasing organizational effectiveness. Recent projects include an assessment of training needs for entry-level peace officers and a review of pay equity issues for a legislative body.

Darrick Hamilton, Assistant Professor; Ph.D., North Carolina at Chapel Hill. Ethnic and racial disparities in wealth, home ownership, and labor market outcomes. Dr. Hamilton's articles can be found in *African American Research Perspectives, American Economics Review, Applied Economics Letters, Challenge: The Magazine of Economic Affairs, Journal of Economic Psychology, Review of Black Political Economy, Social Science Quarterly, Southern Economics Journal,* and *Transforming Anthropology.*

David Howell, Professor; Ph.D., New School. Labor markets at the local, national, and international levels. Recent publications have examined the effects of immigration on the economic status of foreign and native-born workers in New York City, the nature of recent changes in skill requirements and the determinants of relative wage trends in the United States, and the extent to which labor market institutions and social policy explain patterns of unemployment in Europe and the United States. Dr. Howell is the editor of *Fighting Unemployment: The Limits of Free Market Orthodoxy.*

Mark Lipton, Professor of Management and Chair of Management; Ph.D., Massachusetts Amherst. Management, leadership, organizational strategy. Author of *Guiding Growth: How Vision Keeps Companies on Course.* Dr. Lipton's research and opinions on management and strategy have appeared in *Executive Excellence, Harvard Business Review, The Journal of Management Consulting, Optimize, Organization Development Journal,* and *Sloan Management Review,* among others.

Edwin Melendez, Professor; Ph.D., Massachusetts Amherst. Economics. Dr. Melendez was director of the Mauricio Gastón Institute for Latino Community Development and Public Policy at the University of Massachusetts Boston (1992–98) and director of the Community Development Research Center at the Milano Graduate School (1999–2004). He has worked as a consultant on employment, economic development, job creation, and small business for numerous government, community, and philanthropic foundations. Dr. Melendez has managed more than thirty-five research, outreach, and demonstration projects and supervised or collaborated with more than 60 researchers in projects that resulted in several books, special issues of academic journals, and other publications.

Aida Rodriguez, Professor of Professional Practice; Ph.D., Massachusetts. Leadership and effective management in the nonprofit sector. Formerly deputy director of the Equal Opportunity Division of the Rockefeller Foundation, Dr. Rodriguez now serves on various nonprofit boards, including One Economy, Inc.; Alliance for Nonprofit Management; and the Association for Public Policy Analysis and Management. Dr. Rodriguez is an adviser on philanthropic initiatives in the United States and in Latin America, including the Funders' Collaborative for Strong Latino Communities.

Bryna Sanger, Professor; Ph.D., Brandeis. Public policy and management, changes in service delivery and management systems induced by welfare reform in states and localities around the country. Former dean of the Robert J. Milano Graduate School of Management and Urban Policy, Dr. Sanger has worked in a wide range of policy and management areas, including city service delivery, welfare reform, leadership, innovation, and performance management. She recently led a research effort with the National Civic League on the experiences of cities that have developed exemplary performance measurement systems and that report to and engage citizens in their efforts. Her most recent book on this topic is entitled *The Welfare Marketplace: Privatization and Welfare Reform.*

Alex F. Schwartz, Associate Professor, Chair of Department of Urban Policy Analysis and Management, and Senior Research Associate, Community Development Research Center; Ph.D., Rutgers. Housing and community development, including affordable housing programs, community reinvestment, and community development corporations. Dr. Schwartz's most recent publication is *Housing Policy in the United States.* His research has also appeared in such journals as *Cityscape, Economic Development Quarterly, International Journal of Urban and Regional Research,* and the *Journal of Urban Affairs.*

Lisa J. Servon, Associate Professor and Associate Director of Community Development Research Center; Ph.D., Berkeley. Urban poverty, community development, economic development, gender issues. Dr. Servon recently coedited *Gender and Planning: A Reader* (with Susan Fainstein), which covers a range of planning and development fields, including transportation, land use, history, gender, housing, social justice, environmental design, race, and economic and community development. The book was selected as one of the Top 10 Books for 2006 by Planetizen, a public-interest information exchange for the urban planning, design, and development community.

Nidhi Srinivas, Assistant Professor of Nonprofit Management; Ph.D., McGill. Civil society, specifically management of nongovernmental organizations, and the transfer and transformation of management knowledge. Dr. Srinivas teaches courses on nonprofit management, international development, and strategic decision making. Courses he has developed include Managing Institutions for Development (part of the core curriculum in the graduate program in international affairs) and Civil Society and South Asia.

Antonin Wagner, Visiting Professor; Ph.D., Fribourg (Switzerland). Economics. From 1996 to 2000, Dr. Wagner was president of the International Society for Third Sector Research, the leading scholarly institution in the nonprofit field. He has served as a consultant on social security–related issues to the Swiss Federal Statistical Office and the World Bank in Washington. He is a member of the editorial board of several international journals and has published widely in English, German, and French on the welfare state and civil society.

Tatiana Wah, Assistant Professor; Ph.D., Rutgers. Regional and local economic development planning and developing nations, with a particular focus on small developing nations' economies. Dr. Wah's recent work is on transnational expatriate (immigrant) recovery and engagement programs of developing countries, particularly Haiti. She has been involved in community development work in the New York African American and Caribbean communities as a consultant, nonprofit administrator, and activist/advocate.

Mary R. Watson, Assistant Professor; Ph.D., Vanderbilt. Contemporary human capital issues in organizations, with particular emphasis on the social impact of labor market discontinuities. Dr. Watson teaches courses on management and organizational behavior, human resources, social impact management, and globalization. She has a strong interest in cultural, racial, ethnic, and gender inequalities in the workplace and society. Dr. Watson's upcoming book (with Dr. Rikki Abzug), tentatively titled *Human Resources in Social Purpose Organizations,* is scheduled to be published by Jossey-Bass in 2007.

Part-Time Faculty

The part-time faculty members of Milano The New School for Management and Urban Policy are high-level executives and managers in the institutions and agencies for which they work and the organizations for which they volunteer. They bring to the classroom valuable insight into current management and policy issues from both their personal experience and relevant curriculum. For a current listing of part-time faculty members, students should visit the Faculty page of the Milano Web site at http://www.milano.newschool.edu.

Section 17
Project Management

This section contains a directory of institutions offering graduate work in project management. Additional information about programs listed in the directory but not augmented by an in-depth entry may be obtained by writing directly to the dean of a graduate school or chair of a department at the address given in the directory.

For programs offering related work, see also in this book Business Administration and Management.

CONTENTS

Program Directory

Close-Ups

Project Management

American Graduate University, Program in Project Management, Covina, CA 91724. Offers MPM, Certificate. Part-time programs available. Postbaccalaureate distance learning degree programs offered (no on-campus study). *Faculty:* 2 full-time (1 woman), 12 part-time/adjunct (2 women). In 2006, 13 degrees awarded. *Entrance requirements:* For master's, 2 letters of recommendation, proctor designation. Additional exam requirements/recommendations for international students: Required—TOEFL. *Application deadline:* Applications are processed on a rolling basis. Application fee: $50. Electronic applications accepted. *Unit head:* Paul McDonald, President, 626-966-4576 Ext. 1006, E-mail: paulmcdonald@agu.edu. *Application contact:* Marie J. Sirney, Executive Vice President, 626-966-4576, Fax: 626-915-1709, E-mail: mariesirney@agu.edu.

American InterContinental University Online, Program in Business Administration, Hoffman Estates, IL 60192. Offers accounting and finance (MBA); healthcare management (MBA); human resource management (MBA); international business (MBA); management (MBA); marketing (MBA); operations management (MBA); organizational psychology and development (MBA); project management (MBA). Evening/weekend programs available. Postbaccalaureate distance learning degree programs offered (no on-campus study). *Entrance requirements:* Additional exam requirements/recommendations for international students: Required—TOEFL (minimum score 550 paper-based; 213 computer-based). *Application deadline:* Applications are processed on a rolling basis. Application fee: $50. Electronic applications accepted. *Financial support:* Institutionally sponsored loans and scholarships/grants available. Financial award applicants required to submit FAFSA. *Unit head:* Kerri J Holloway, Vice President of Academic Affairs, 847-851-5000 Ext. 15399, Fax: 847-586-6309, E-mail: kholloway@aivonline.edu. *Application contact:* 877-701-3800, E-mail: info@aiuonline.edu.

Aspen University, Program in Business Administration, Denver, CO 80246. Offers business administration (MBA); information management (MBA); project management (MBA, Certificate). Postbaccalaureate distance learning degree programs offered (no on-campus study). Electronic applications accepted.

Athabasca University, Centre for Innovative Management, Athabasca, AB T9S 3A3, Canada. Offers business administration (MBA); information technology management (MBA), including policing concentration; management (GDM); project management (MBA, GDM). Part-time and evening/weekend programs available. Postbaccalaureate distance learning degree programs offered (no on-campus study). *Faculty:* 11 full-time (7 women), 63 part-time/adjunct (18 women). *Students:* Average age 39. 264 applicants, 82% accepted, 184 enrolled. In 2006, 228 degrees awarded. *Degree requirements:* For master's, thesis or alternative, applied project. *Entrance requirements:* For master's, 3 -8 years of managerial experience, 3 years with undergraduate degree, 5 years managerial experience with professional designation, 8-10 years management experience (on exception). *Application deadline:* For fall admission, 6/15 for domestic and international students; for winter admission, 10/15 for domestic and international students; for spring admission, 2/15 for domestic and international students. Applications are processed on a rolling basis. Application fee: $165. Electronic applications accepted. *Expenses: Contact institution. Financial support:* In 2006–07, 34 students received support. Scholarships/grants available. *Faculty research:* Human resources, project management, operations research, information technology management, corporate stewardship, energy management. *Unit head:* Dr. Lindsay Redpath, Executive Director, 780-459-1144, Fax: 780-459-2093, E-mail: lindsayr@athabascau.ca. *Application contact:* Shannon LaRose, Customer Service Representative, 800-561-4650, Fax: 800-561-4660, E-mail: cimoffice@athabascau.ca.

Avila University, Program in Organizational Development, Kansas City, MO 64145-1698. Offers organizational development (MS); project management (Graduate Certificate). Part-time and evening/weekend programs available. *Faculty:* 3 full-time (2 women), 20 part-time/adjunct. *Students:* 75. Average age 33. In 2006, 5 degrees awarded. *Degree requirements:* For master's, thesis optional. *Entrance requirements:* For master's, letters of recommendation, minimum GPA of 3.0. Additional exam requirements/recommendations for international students: Required—TOEFL. *Application deadline:* Applications are processed on a rolling basis. Application fee: $0. Electronic applications accepted. *Expenses:* Tuition: Full-time $7,470; part-time $415 per credit. *Financial support:* Unspecified assistantships available. Support available to part-time students. Financial award applicants required to submit FAFSA. *Unit head:* Lacey Smith, Assistant Dean, 816-501-3737, Fax: 816-941-4650, E-mail: advantage@avila.edu.

See Close-Up on page 691.

Boston University, Metropolitan College (Continuing Education), Program in Administrative Studies, Boston, MA 02215. Offers banking and financial management (MSM); business continuity in emergency management (MSM); economics development and tourism management (MSAS); electronic commerce, systems, and technology (MSAS); financial economics (MSAS); human resource management (MSM); innovation and technology (MSAS); insurance management (MSM); international market management (MSM); multinational commerce (MSAS); project management (MSM). *Accreditation:* AACSB. Part-time and evening/weekend programs available. *Faculty:* 9 full-time (0 women), 51 part-time/adjunct (8 women). *Students:* 105 full-time (40 women), 171 part-time (65 women); includes 27 minority (5 African Americans, 18 Asian Americans or Pacific Islanders, 4 Hispanic Americans), 125 international. Average age 29. In 2006, 310 degrees awarded. *Degree requirements:* For master's, thesis optional. *Entrance requirements:* For master's, 1 year of work experience, minimum GPA of 3.0. Additional exam requirements/recommendations for international students: Required—TOEFL (minimum score 560 paper-based; 220 computer-based). *Application deadline:* Applications are processed on a rolling basis. Application fee: $65. *Expenses:* Tuition: Full-time $33,330; part-time $1,042 per credit. Required fees: $462; $40. *Financial support:* In 2006–07, 15 students received support, including research assistantships (averaging $10,000 per year); career-related internships or fieldwork and Federal Work-Study also available. *Faculty research:* International business, innovative process. *Unit head:* Dr. Kip Becker, Chairman, 617-353-3016, E-mail: adminsc@bu.edu. *Application contact:* Lucille Dicker, Administrative Sciences Department, 617-353-3016, E-mail: adminsc@bu.edu.

Cabrini College, Graduate and Professional Studies, Radnor, PA 19087-3698. Offers biotechnology (Certificate); education (M Ed); educational leadership (Certificate); instructional systems technology (MS); organization leadership (MS); project management (Certificate). Part-time and evening/weekend programs available. *Faculty:* 11 full-time (7 women), 25 part-time/adjunct (11 women). *Students:* 91 full-time (63 women), 484 part-time (364 women); includes 43 minority (28 African Americans, 6 Asian Americans or Pacific Islanders, 9 Hispanic Americans), 6 international. Average age 32. In 2006, 143 degrees awarded. *Degree requirements:* For master's, thesis optional. *Entrance requirements:* For master's, GRE and/or MAT (in some cases), letter of recommendation, minimum GPA of 2.5. *Application deadline:* For fall admission, 7/29 priority date for domestic students; for spring admission, 12/9 for domestic students. Applications are processed on a rolling basis. Application fee: $50. Electronic applications accepted. *Expenses:* Tuition: Part-time $310 per credit. Required fees: $45 per term. Tuition and fees vary according to course load. *Financial support:* Career-related internships or fieldwork and unspecified assistantships available. Support available to part-time students. Financial award applicants required to submit FAFSA. *Faculty research:* Qualitative research in reading, ethnographic studies. *Unit head:* Dr. Michael W. Markowitz, Dean for Graduate and Professional Studies, 610-902-8501, Fax: 610-902-8522, E-mail: michael.w.markowitz@cabrini.edu. *Application contact:* Bruce D. Bryde, Director of Enrollment and Recruiting, 610-902-8291, Fax: 610-902-8522, E-mail: bruce.d.bryde@cabrini.edu.

Capella University, School of Business and Technology, Minneapolis, MN 55402. Offers accounting (MBA), including system design and programming; business (Certificate), including human resource management (MS, PhD, Certificate), information technology management (MS, PhD, Certificate), leadership (MBA, MS, PhD, Certificate); finance (MBA); general business (MBA); health care management (MBA); information technology (MS, Certificate), including general information technology (MS), information security, network architecture and design (MS), professional projects management (Certificate), project management and leadership (MS), system design and development (MS),); information technology management (MBA); marketing (MBA); organization and management (MBA, MS, PhD), including general business (PhD), general organization and management (MBA, MS), human resource management (MS, PhD, Certificate), information technology management (MS, PhD, Certificate), leadership (MBA, MS, PhD, Certificate); project management (MBA). Part-time and evening/weekend programs available. Postbaccalaureate distance learning degree programs offered (minimal on-campus study). Terminal master's awarded for partial completion of doctoral program. *Degree requirements:* For master's, integrative project, thesis optional; for doctorate, thesis/dissertation, comprehensive exam, registration. *Entrance requirements:* Additional exam requirements/recommendations for international students: Required—TOEFL (minimum score 550 paper-based; 213 computer-based), TWE (minimum score 4). Electronic applications accepted. *Faculty research:* Business policies: strategic, corporate, and financial management; interplay of technological, organizational and social change.

Cardean University, MBA Program, Chicago, IL 60606-7204. Offers accounting and information systems (MBA); e-commerce (MBA); finance (MBA); global management (MBA); health care administration (MBA); human resources management (MBA); leadership (MBA); management of information systems (MBA); management of technology (MBA); marketing (MBA); professional accounting (MBA); project management (MBA); risk management (MBA); strategy and economics (MBA). Part-time and evening/weekend programs available. Postbaccalaureate distance learning degree programs offered (no on-campus study). *Entrance requirements:* Additional exam requirements/recommendations for international students: Required—TOEFL (minimum score 550 paper-based; 213 computer-based).

Christian Brothers University, Graduate Programs, School of Business, Memphis, TN 38104-5581. Offers business (MBA); executive leadership (MAEL); financial planning (Certificate); project management (Certificate). Part-time and evening/weekend programs available. *Faculty:* 8 full-time (3 women), 1 part-time/adjunct (0 women). *Students:* 13 full-time (1 woman), 88 part-time (38 women); includes 21 minority (18 African Americans, 2 Asian Americans or Pacific Islanders, 1 Hispanic American), 4 international. Average age 33. In 2006, 69 degrees awarded. *Entrance requirements:* For master's, GMAT. Additional exam requirements/recommendations for international students: Required—TOEFL. *Application deadline:* Applications are processed on a rolling basis. Application fee: $25. *Financial support:* Institutionally sponsored loans available. Support available to part-time students. *Faculty research:* Business ethics. *Unit head:* Dr. Mike R. Ryan, Dean, 901-321-3316. *Application contact:* Dr. Bevalee B. Pray, Director, Graduate Business Programs, 901-321-3319, Fax: 901-321-3494.

City University, Graduate Division, School of Management, Bellevue, WA 98005. Offers accounting (MBA); C++ programming (Certificate); computer systems—C++ programming (MS); computer systems—individualized study (MS); computer systems—web programming in e-commerce (MS); computer systems-web development (MS); financial management (MBA, Certificate); general management (MBA, MPA, Certificate); general management-Europe (MBA); human resource management (MPA); individualized study (MBA); information systems (MBA, Certificate); management—general management (MA); management—human resource management (MA); management—individualized study (MA); marketing (MBA, Certificate); personal financial planning (MBA, Certificate); project management (MBA, MS, Certificate); technology management (MS, Certificate); web development (Certificate); web programming in e-commerce (Certificate). Part-time and evening/weekend programs available. Postbaccalaureate distance learning degree programs offered (no on-campus study). *Entrance requirements:* Additional exam requirements/recommendations for international students: Required—TOEFL (minimum score 540 paper-based; 207 computer-based); Recommended—IELTS. Electronic applications accepted.

Colorado Technical University, Graduate Studies, Program in Computer Science, Colorado Springs, CO 80907-3896. Offers computer science (DCS); computer systems security (MSCS); software engineering (MSCS); software project management (MSCS). Part-time and evening/weekend programs available. *Degree requirements:* For master's, thesis or alternative; for doctorate, thesis/dissertation. *Entrance requirements:* For doctorate, minimum graduate GPA of 3.0, 5 years of related work experience. *Faculty research:* Software engineering, systems engineering.

Colorado Technical University, Graduate Studies, Program in Management, Colorado Springs, CO 80907-3896. Offers business administration (MBA); business management (MSM); business technology (MSM); database management (MSM); human resources management (MSM); information technology (MSM); logistics management (MSM); management (DM); organizational leadership (MSM); project management (MSM). Part-time and evening/weekend programs available. *Degree requirements:* For master's, thesis or alternative; for doctorate, thesis/dissertation. *Entrance requirements:* For doctorate, minimum graduate GPA of 3.0, 5 years of related work experience. *Faculty research:* Sexual harassment, performance evaluation, critical thinking.

Colorado Technical University Denver Campus, Program in Computer Science, Greenwood Village, CO 80111. Offers computer systems security (MSCS); software engineering (MSCS); software project management (MSCS). Part-time and evening/weekend programs available. *Degree requirements:* For master's, thesis or alternative. *Entrance requirements:* For master's, minimum undergraduate GPA of 3.0, resumé.

Colorado Technical University Denver Campus, Programs in Business Administration and Management, Greenwood Village, CO 80111. Offers accounting (MBA); business administration (MBA); business administration and management (EMBA); business technology (MSM); database management (MSM); human resource management (MBA); information technology (MSM); project management (MSM); technology management (MBA). Part-time and evening/weekend programs available. *Degree requirements:* For master's, thesis or alternative. *Entrance requirements:* For master's, minimum undergraduate GPA of 3.0, resumé.

Colorado Technical University Sioux Falls Campus, Programs in Business Administration and Management, Sioux Falls, SD 57108. Offers business administration (MBA); business management (MSM); health science management (MSM); human resources management (MSM); information technology (MSM); organizational leadership (MSM); project management (MBA); technology management (MBA). Evening/weekend programs available. *Degree requirements:* For master's, thesis optional. *Entrance requirements:* For master's, minimum 2 years work experience, resumé.

Dallas Baptist University, Graduate School of Business, Business Administration Program, Dallas, TX 75211-9299. Offers accounting (MBA); business communication (MBA); conflict resolution management (MBA); e-business (MBA); entrepreneurship (MBA); finance (MBA); health care management (MBA); international business (MBA); management (MBA); management information systems (MBA); marketing (MBA); project management (MBA); technology and engineering management (MBA). *Accreditation:* ACBSP. Part-time and evening/weekend programs available. Postbaccalaureate distance learning degree programs offered (no on-campus study). *Faculty:* 49 full-time (21 women), 112 part-time/adjunct (46 women). *Students:* 103 full-time, 318 part-time. 226 applicants, 38% accepted. In 2006, 124 degrees awarded. *Entrance requirements:* For master's, GMAT, minimum GPA of 3.0. Additional exam requirements/recommendations for international students: Required—TOEFL. *Application deadline:* Applications are processed on a rolling basis. Application fee: $25. Electronic applications accepted. *Expenses:* Tuition: Full-time $8,370; part-time $465 per credit hour. Required fees: $465 per credit hour. *Financial support:* Career-related internships or fieldwork, Federal Work-Study, institutionally sponsored loans, scholarships/grants, and tuition waivers (full and partial) available.

Support available to part-time students. *Faculty research:* Sports management, services marketing, retailing, strategic management, financial planning/investments. *Unit head:* Dr. Sandra S. Reid, Director, 214-333-5244, Fax: 214-333-5293, E-mail: graduate@dbu.edu. *Application contact:* Kit P. Montgomery, Director of Graduate Programs, 214-333-5242, Fax: 214-333-5579, E-mail: graduate@dbu.edu.

DeVry University, Keller Graduate School of Management, Oakbrook Terrace, IL 60181. Offers accounting and financial management (MAFM); business administration (MBA); human resources management (MHRM); information systems management (MISM); network and communications management (MNCM); project management (MPM); public administration (MPA); telecommunications management (MTM). Part-time and evening/weekend programs available. Postbaccalaureate distance learning degree programs offered (no on-campus study). *Degree requirements:* For master's, business plan (MBA), capstone project (MHRM, MPM, MTM, MAFM). *Entrance requirements:* For master's, GMAT, GRE General Test, or institutional assessment, interview. Additional exam requirements/recommendations for international students: Required—TOEFL (minimum score 500 paper-based; 173 computer-based). Electronic applications accepted.

See Close-Up on page 265.

The George Washington University, School of Business, Department of Management Science, Washington, DC 20052. Offers human resources management (MBA); information systems management (MBA); logistics, operations, and materials management (MBA); management and organization (PhD); management decision making (MBA, PhD); management information systems (MSIST); management of science, technology, and innovation (MBA); organizational behavior and development (MBA); project management (MS). *Accreditation:* AACSB. Part-time and evening/weekend programs available. *Degree requirements:* For doctorate, thesis/dissertation. *Entrance requirements:* For master's, GMAT; for doctorate, GMAT or GRE. Additional exam requirements/recommendations for international students: Required—TOEFL. *Faculty research:* Artificial intelligence, technological entrepreneurship, expert systems, strategic planning/management.

Grantham University, College of Computer Science and Engineering Technology, Kansas City, MO 64153. Offers information management technology (MS); information technology (MS); project management (MS). Part-time and evening/weekend programs available. Postbaccalaureate distance learning degree programs offered (no on-campus study). *Students:* 177 full-time. Average age 36. *Entrance requirements:* Additional exam requirements/recommendations for international students: Required—TOEFL (minimum score 500 paper-based). *Application deadline:* Applications are processed on a rolling basis. Application fee: $0. Electronic applications accepted. *Financial support:* Institutionally sponsored loans and scholarships/grants available. *Application contact:* DeAnn Wandler, Director of Admissions, 800-955-2527, Fax: 816-595-5757, E-mail: admissions@grantham.edu.

Grantham University, Mark Skousen School of Business, Kansas City, MO 64153. Offers information management (MBA); project management (MBA). Part-time and evening/weekend programs available. Postbaccalaureate distance learning degree programs offered (no on-campus study). *Faculty:* 30. *Students:* 372 full-time. Average age 36. *Degree requirements:* For master's, thesis, registration. *Entrance requirements:* Additional exam requirements/recommendations for international students: Required—TOEFL (minimum score 500 paper-based). *Application deadline:* Applications are processed on a rolling basis. Application fee: $0. Electronic applications accepted. *Financial support:* Institutionally sponsored loans and scholarships/grants available. *Application contact:* DeAnn Wandler, Director of Admissions, 800-955-2527, Fax: 816-595-5757, E-mail: admissions@grantham.edu.

Harrisburg University of Science and Technology, Graduate Studies, Program in Information Technology Project Management, Harrisburg, PA 17101. Offers MA.

Jones International University, Graduate School of Business Administration, Centennial, CO 80112. Offers accounting (MBA); business communication (MABC); entrepreneurship (MABC, MBA); finance (MBA); global enterprise management (MBA); health care management (MBA); information security management (MBA); information technology management (MBA); leadership and influence (MABC); leading the customer-driven organization (MABC); negotiation and conflict management (MBA); project management (MABC, MBA). Program only offered online. Part-time and evening/weekend programs available. Postbaccalaureate distance learning degree programs offered (no on-campus study). *Degree requirements:* For master's, capstone project. *Entrance requirements:* For master's, minimum cumulative GPA of 2.5. Additional exam requirements/recommendations for international students: Recommended—TOEFL (minimum score 550 paper-based; 213 computer-based). Electronic applications accepted.

Lehigh University, College of Business and Economics, Bethlehem, PA 18015-3094. Offers accounting (MS), including accounting and information analysis; business administration (MBA); economics (MS, PhD), including economics, health and bio-pharmaceutical economics (MS); entrepreneurship (Certificate); finance (MS), including analytical finance, finance; organizational leadership (Certificate); project management (Certificate); supply chain management (Certificate); MBA/E; MBA/M Ed. *Accreditation:* AACSB. Part-time and evening/weekend programs available. Postbaccalaureate distance learning degree programs offered (minimal on-campus study). *Faculty:* 64 full-time (14 women), 12 part-time/adjunct (0 women). *Students:* 87 full-time (25 women), 219 part-time (60 women); includes 34 minority (9 African Americans, 22 Asian Americans or Pacific Islanders, 3 Hispanic Americans), 56 international. 371 applicants, 69% accepted, 151 enrolled. In 2006, 103 master's, 2 doctorates awarded. Terminal master's awarded for partial completion of doctoral program. *Degree requirements:* For master's, thesis optional; for doctorate, thesis/dissertation, proposal defense, comprehensive exam. *Entrance requirements:* For master's, GMAT, GRE General Test; for doctorate, GMAT or GRE General Test. Additional exam requirements/recommendations for international students: Required—TOEFL (minimum score 600 paper-based; 250 computer-based). *Application deadline:* For fall admission, 7/15 for domestic students, 5/1 for international students; for spring admission, 12/1 for domestic and international students. Applications are processed on a rolling basis. Application fee: $60. Electronic applications accepted. *Expenses:* Contact institution. *Financial support:* In 2006–07, 2 fellowships with full tuition reimbursements (averaging $13,200 per year), 8 research assistantships with full and partial tuition reimbursements (averaging $1,000 per year), 13 teaching assistantships with full tuition reimbursements (averaging $13,200 per year) were awarded; career-related internships or fieldwork, scholarships/grants, health care benefits, tuition waivers (full and partial), and unspecified assistantships also available. Support available to part-time students. Financial award application deadline: 1/15. *Faculty research:* Public finance, energy, investments, activity-based costing, management information systems. *Unit head:* Michael G. Kolchin, Graduate Business Programs, 610-758-4450, Fax: 610-758-5283, E-mail: mgk1@lehigh.edu. *Application contact:* Mary- Theresa Taglang, Director of Graduate Programs, 610-758-5285, Fax: 610-758-5283, E-mail: mtt4@lehigh.edu.

See Close-Ups on pages 283, 285, and 1807.

Lehigh University, College of Education, Department of Education and Human Services, Program in Educational Technology, Bethlehem, PA 18015-3094. Offers educational technology (Ed D, PhD); instructional technology (MS); learning sciences and technology (PhD); project management (Certificate); technology use in schools (Certificate). Part-time and evening/weekend programs available. *Faculty:* 29 full-time (16 women), 17 part-time/adjunct (9 women). *Students:* 12 full-time (8 women), 32 part-time (18 women); includes 4 minority (2 African Americans, 1 Asian American or Pacific Islander, 1 Hispanic American), 10 international. 24 applicants, 58% accepted, 11 enrolled. In 2006, 9 degrees awarded. Terminal master's awarded for partial completion of doctoral program. *Degree requirements:* For doctorate, thesis/dissertation. *Entrance requirements:* For master's, minimum GPA of 3.0; for doctorate, GRE General Test or MAT, minimum graduate GPA of 3.0. Additional exam requirements/recommendations for international students: Required—TOEFL (minimum score 600 paper-based; 250 computer-based). *Application deadline:* Applications are processed on a rolling basis. Application fee: $60. Electronic applications accepted. *Financial support:* Career-related internships or fieldwork, Federal Work-Study, institutionally sponsored loans, scholarships/grants, and tuition waivers (full and partial) available. Financial award application deadline: 1/31. *Unit head:* Dr. H. Lynn Columba, Head, 610-758-3230, Fax: 610-758-3243, E-mail: hlc0@lehigh.edu.

Marymount University, School of Business Administration, Program in Management, Arlington, VA 22207-4299. Offers advanced leadership (Certificate); leading and managing change (Certificate); management (MS); management studies (Certificate); project management (Certificate). Part-time and evening/weekend programs available. *Students:* 2 full-time (1 woman), 20 part-time (13 women); includes 5 minority (4 African Americans, 1 Hispanic American), 1 international. Average age 38. 13 applicants, 100% accepted, 9 enrolled. In 2006, 5 master's, 4 other advanced degrees awarded. *Entrance requirements:* For master's, GRE or GMAT, resumé; for Certificate, resumé. Additional exam requirements/recommendations for international students: Required—TOEFL (minimum score 600 paper-based; 250 computer-based). *Application deadline:* Applications are processed on a rolling basis. Electronic applications accepted. *Expenses:* Tuition: Full-time $11,160; part-time $620 per credit. Required fees: $113; $630 per credit. *Financial support:* Research assistantships with full tuition reimbursements, career-related internships or fieldwork, scholarships/grants, and unspecified assistantships available. Support available to part-time students. Financial award applicants required to submit FAFSA. *Unit head:* Dr. Lorri Cooper, Director, 703-284-5950, Fax: 703-527-3830, E-mail: lorri.cooper@marymount.edu.

Mississippi State University, College of Business and Industry, Graduate Studies in Business, Mississippi State, MS 39762. Offers business administration (MBA, PhD), including accounting (PhD), business information systems (PhD), finance (PhD), management (PhD), marketing (PhD); project management (MBA). *Accreditation:* AACSB. Part-time and evening/weekend programs available. Postbaccalaureate distance learning degree programs offered. *Faculty:* 66 full-time (18 women), 18 part-time/adjunct (9 women). *Students:* 143 full-time (52 women), 159 part-time (52 women); includes 30 minority (24 African Americans, 1 American Indian/Alaska Native, 2 Asian Americans or Pacific Islanders, 3 Hispanic Americans), 35 international. Average age 30. 605 applicants, 34% accepted, 142 enrolled. In 2006, 107 master's, 10 doctorates awarded. Terminal master's awarded for partial completion of doctoral program. *Degree requirements:* For doctorate, thesis/dissertation. *Entrance requirements:* For master's, GMAT, minimum GPA of 3.0 in last 60 hours of course work; for doctorate, GMAT, minimum GPA of 2.75 in last 60 undergraduate hours, 3.25 in last 60 graduate hours. Additional exam requirements/recommendations for international students: Required—TOEFL. *Application deadline:* For fall admission, 7/1 for domestic students; for spring admission, 11/1 for domestic students. Applications are processed on a rolling basis. Application fee: $30. Electronic applications accepted. *Expenses:* Tuition, state resident: full-time $4,550; part-time $253 per hour. Tuition, nonresident: full-time $10,552; part-time $584 per hour. International tuition: $10,882 full-time. Tuition and fees vary according to course load. *Financial support:* In 2006–07, 29 teaching assistantships with full tuition reimbursements (averaging $10,778 per year) were awarded; research assistantships with full tuition reimbursements, Federal Work-Study, institutionally sponsored loans, and unspecified assistantships also available. Financial award applicants required to submit FAFSA. *Unit head:* Dr. Barbara Spencer, Director, 662-325-1891, Fax: 662-325-8161, E-mail: gsb@cobilan.msstate.edu. *Application contact:* Dr. Phil Bonfanti, Director of Admissions, 662-325-4104, Fax: 662-325-8872, E-mail: admit@msstate.edu.

Missouri State University, Graduate College, Interdisciplinary Program in Administrative Studies, Springfield, MO 65804-0094. Offers applied communication (MSAS); criminal justice (MSAS); environmental management (MSAS); project management (MSAS); sports management (MSAS). Part-time programs available. Postbaccalaureate distance learning degree programs offered (no on-campus study). *Students:* 9 full-time (4 women), 68 part-time (44 women); includes 2 minority (both African Americans), 3 international. Average age 35. 22 applicants, 86% accepted, 15 enrolled. In 2006, 29 degrees awarded. *Degree requirements:* For master's, thesis or alternative, comprehensive exam. *Entrance requirements:* For master's, GRE, GMAT, 3 years of work experience. Additional exam requirements/recommendations for international students: Required—TOEFL (minimum score 550 paper-based; 213 computer-based; 79 iBT). *Application deadline:* For fall admission, 7/20 priority date for domestic students; for spring admission, 12/20 priority date for domestic students. Applications are processed on a rolling basis. Application fee: $35. Electronic applications accepted. *Expenses:* Tuition, state resident: full-time $3,582; part-time $199 per credit hour. Tuition, nonresident: full-time $6,984; part-time $199 per credit hour. Required fees: $548. Full-time tuition and fees vary according to course level, course load, program and reciprocity agreements. *Financial support:* In 2006–07, 1 research assistantship (averaging $6,780 per year) was awarded; teaching assistantships, career-related internships or fieldwork, Federal Work-Study, institutionally sponsored loans, scholarships/grants, and unspecified assistantships also available. Support available to part-time students. Financial award application deadline: 3/31; financial award applicants required to submit FAFSA. *Unit head:* John Bourhis, Director, 417-836-6390, E-mail: johnbourhis@missouristate.edu.

Montana Tech of The University of Montana, Graduate School, Project Engineering and Management Program, Butte, MT 59701-8997. Offers MPEM. Part-time and evening/weekend programs available. Postbaccalaureate distance learning degree programs offered (no on-campus study). *Faculty:* 1 full-time (0 women), 7 part-time/adjunct (1 woman). *Students:* 5 full-time (2 women), 6 part-time (2 women); includes 1 minority (Hispanic American) 4 applicants, 75% accepted, 3 enrolled. In 2006, 4 degrees awarded. *Degree requirements:* For master's, comprehensive exam, registration. *Entrance requirements:* For master's, GRE General Test, minimum GPA of 3.0. Additional exam requirements/recommendations for international students: Required—TOEFL (minimum score 550 paper-based; 213 computer-based; 71 iBT). *Application deadline:* For fall admission, 4/1 priority date for domestic students, 3/1 priority date for international students; for spring admission, 10/1 priority date for domestic students, 7/1 priority date for international students. Applications are processed on a rolling basis. Application fee: $30. Electronic applications accepted. *Expenses:* Tuition, state resident: part-time $219 per credit. Tuition, nonresident: part-time $480 per credit. Required fees: $305 per credit. *Financial support:* Application deadline: 4/1. *Unit head:* Dr. Kumar Ganesan, Director, 406-496-4239, Fax: 406-496-4650, E-mail: kganesan@mtech.edu. *Application contact:* Cindy Dunstan, Administrator, Graduate School, 406-496-4304, Fax: 406-496-4710, E-mail: cdunstan@mtech.edu.

New York Institute of Technology, Ellis College, Old Westbury, NY 11568. Offers accounting and information systems (MBA); e-commerce (MBA); finance (MBA); global management (MBA); healthcare administration (MBA); human resources management (MBA); leadership (MBA); management of information systems (MBA); management of technology (MBA); marketing (MBA); professional accounting (MBA); project management (MBA); risk management (MBA); strategy and economics (MBA). Ellis College is a collaboration between New York Institute of Technology and UNext online learning company. Part-time and evening/weekend programs available. Postbaccalaureate distance learning degree programs offered (no on-campus study). *Entrance requirements:* For master's, interview. Additional exam requirements/recommendations for international students: Required—TOEFL (minimum score 550 paper-based; 213 computer-based). Electronic applications accepted. *Expenses:* Tuition: Full-time $16,800; part-time $700 per credit.

Northwestern University, McCormick School of Engineering and Applied Science, Department of Civil and Environmental Engineering, Program in Project Management, Evanston, IL 60208. Offers MPM. Part-time programs available. *Faculty:* 2 full-time (0 women), 23 part-time/adjunct (6 women). *Students:* 17 full-time (3 women), 41 part-time (10 women); includes 14 minority (4 African Americans, 4 Asian Americans or Pacific Islanders, 6 Hispanic Americans), 15 international. 30 applicants, 87% accepted, 21 enrolled. In 2006, 12 degrees awarded. *Degree requirements:* For master's, capstone report. *Entrance requirements:* Additional exam requirements/recommendations for international students: Required—TOEFL (minimum score 560 paper-based; 220 computer-based). *Application deadline:* For fall admission, 8/15 for

Project Management

Northwestern University (continued)
domestic students, 6/15 for international students; for winter admission, 11/15 for domestic students, 9/15 for international students; for spring admission, 2/15 for domestic students, 12/15 for international students. Applications are processed on a rolling basis. Application fee: $50. *Faculty research:* Construction management, environmental management, infrastructure management. *Unit head:* Prof. Raymond J. Krizek, Director, 847-491-4040, Fax: 847-491-4011, E-mail: rjkrizek@northwestern.edu. *Application contact:* Prof. Ahmad Hadavi, Associate Director, 847-467-3219, Fax: 847-491-4011, E-mail: a-hadavi@northwestern.edu.

Regis University, School for Professional Studies, Program in Business, Denver, CO 80221-1099. Offers accounting (MS); business administration (MBA); finance (MBA); finance and accounting (MBA); international business (MBA); marketing (MBA); operations management (MBA); organization leadership (MS); project management (Certificate); technical management (Certificate). Offered at Colorado Springs Campus, Northwest Denver Campus, Southeast Denver Campus, Fort Collins Campus, Broomfield Campus, Henderson (Nevada) Campus, and Summerlin (Nevada) Campus. Part-time and evening/weekend programs available. Postbaccalaureate distance learning degree programs offered (no on-campus study). *Faculty:* 16 full-time (4 women), 82 part-time/adjunct (22 women). *Students:* 1,770 (834 women). Average age 36. In 2006, 560 degrees awarded. *Degree requirements:* For master's, capstone project, thesis optional. *Entrance requirements:* For master's, GMAT, interview, 2 years of full-time business work experience; for Certificate, GMAT. Additional exam requirements/recommendations for international students: Required—TOEFL or university-based test. *Application deadline:* For fall admission, 8/22 for domestic and international students; for winter admission, 1/2 for domestic and international students; for spring admission, 4/30 for domestic and international students. Applications are processed on a rolling basis. Application fee: $75. Electronic applications accepted. *Financial support:* Federal Work-Study available. Support available to part-time students. Financial award applicants required to submit FAFSA. *Unit head:* Dr. Michael Goess, Chair, 303-458-4302, Fax: 303-964-5538. *Application contact:* 800-677-9270 Ext. 4080, Fax: 303-964-5538, E-mail: masters@regis.edu.

Regis University, School for Professional Studies, Program in Organization Leadership, Denver, CO 80221-1099. Offers computer information technology (MSOL); executive international management (Certificate); executive leadership (Certificate); human resource management (MSOL); organizational leadership (MSOL); project leadership and management (MSOL, Certificate); strategic business (Certificate); strategic human resource (Certificate). Offered at Boulder Campus, Fort Collins Campus, Northwest Denver Campus, Southeast Denver Campus, Colorado Springs Campus, and Broomfield Campus. Part-time and evening/weekend programs available. Postbaccalaureate distance learning degree programs offered. *Faculty:* 55. *Students:* Average age 35. In 2006, 61 degrees awarded. *Median time to degree:* Master's–3 years full-time. *Degree requirements:* For master's, capstone course; for Certificate, final research project. *Entrance requirements:* For master's, 3 years of management-related experience, resumé. Additional exam requirements/recommendations for international students: Required—TOEFL, TWE (minimum score 5), TOEFL or university-based test. *Application deadline:* For fall admission, 8/13 priority date for domestic students, 7/13 for international students; for winter admission, 10/8 priority date for domestic students, 9/8 for international students; for spring admission, 12/17 priority date for domestic students, 11/11 for international students. Applications are processed on a rolling basis. Application fee: $75. Electronic applications accepted. *Expenses: Contact institution. Financial support:* Federal Work-Study available. Support available to part-time students. Financial award applicants required to submit FAFSA. *Faculty research:* Organizational behavior, leadership, change, quality control, global economics. *Unit head:* Dr. Donna VanDusen, Chair, 303-458-4302, Fax: 303-964-5538. *Application contact:* 800-677-9270, Fax: 303-964-5538, E-mail: masters@regis.edu.

Rosemont College, Graduate School, Accelerated Program in Management, Rosemont, PA 19010-1699. Offers arts/culture/project management (MSM); criminal justice (MSM); not for profit (MSM); training and leadership (MSM). Part-time and evening/weekend programs available. *Degree requirements:* For master's, thesis or alternative. *Entrance requirements:* For master's, GRE or MAT. Expenses: Contact institution.

St. Edward's University, School of Management and Business, Program in Project Management, Austin, TX 78704. Offers MS. Part-time and evening/weekend programs available. *Students:* 1 (woman) full-time, 16 part-time (8 women); includes 9 minority (4 African Americans, 5 Hispanic Americans). Average age 37. 18 applicants, 94% accepted, 16 enrolled. *Degree requirements:* For master's, minimum 24 resident hours. *Entrance requirements:* For master's, GMAT or GRE General Test, minimum GPA of 2.75 in last 60 hours of course work. Additional exam requirements/recommendations for international students: Required—TOEFL (minimum score 550 paper-based; 213 computer-based; 79 iBT). *Application deadline:* For fall admission, 8/1 for domestic students, 7/1 for international students; for spring admission, 12/1 for domestic students, 11/1 for international students. Applications are processed on a rolling basis. Application fee: $45 ($50 for international students). Electronic applications accepted. *Expenses:* Tuition: Full-time $11,682; part-time $649 per credit hour. Full-time tuition and fees vary according to course load and program. *Financial support:* Scholarships/grants available. *Unit head:* Dr. John S. Loucks, Director, 512-448-8630, Fax: 512-448-8492, E-mail: johns1@stedwards.edu. *Application contact:* Benjamin Jimenez, Recruiting Coordinator, 512-233-1694, Fax: 512-428-1032, E-mail: benjij@stedwards.edu.

Saint Mary's University of Minnesota, School of Graduate and Professional Programs, Program in Project Management, Winona, MN 55987-1399. Offers MS. *Unit head:* Dr. Gerald Ellis, Director, 612-728-5178, E-mail: gellis@smumn.edu.

Southern New Hampshire University, School of Business, Manchester, NH 03106-1045. Offers accounting (MS); business administration (MBA, Certificate), including accounting (Certificate), business administration (MBA), finance (Certificate), forensic accounting (Certificate), human resources management (Certificate), international business (Certificate), international sport management (Certificate), leadership of not for profit organizations (Certificate), marketing (Certificate), operations management (Certificate), sport management (Certificate), taxation (Certificate); finance (MS); hospitality and tourism leadership (Certificate); information technology (MS, Certificate); information technology/international business (Certificate); integrated marketing communications (Certificate); international business (MS, DBA); marketing (MS); operations and project management (MS); organizational leadership (MS); project management (Certificate); sport management (MS); MBA/Certificate. *Accreditation:* ACBSP. Part-time and evening/weekend programs available. Postbaccalaureate distance learning degree programs offered (no on-campus study). *Faculty:* 45 full-time, 75 part-time/adjunct. *Students:* 427 full-time (184 women), 774 part-time (428 women). Average age 32. In 2006, 682 master's, 1 doctorate awarded. Terminal master's awarded for partial completion of doctoral program. *Degree requirements:* For master's, one foreign language, thesis or alternative, comprehensive exam (for some programs); for doctorate, one foreign language, thesis/dissertation, comprehensive exam. *Entrance requirements:* For master's, minimum GPA of 2.5; for doctorate, GMAT. Additional exam requirements/recommendations for international students: Required—TOEFL (minimum score 500 paper-based). *Application deadline:* Applications are processed on a rolling basis. Application fee: $25. Electronic applications accepted. *Financial support:* Career-related internships or fieldwork, Federal Work-Study, institutionally sponsored loans, tuition waivers (partial), and unspecified assistantships available. Support available to part-time students. Financial award applicants required to submit FAFSA. *Unit head:* Dr. Martin Bradley, Dean, 603-644-3102, Fax: 603-644-3144, E-mail: m.bradley@snhu.edu. *Application contact:* Scott Durand, Director of Graduate Enrollment Services, 603-644-3102 Ext. 3338, Fax: 603-644-3144, E-mail: s.durand@snhu.edu.

See Close-Up on page 325.

Stevens Institute of Technology, Graduate School, Wesley J. Howe School of Technology Management, Program in Business Administration, Hoboken, NJ 07030. Offers engineering management (MBA); financial management (MBA); global technology management (MBA); information management (MBA); information technology in financial services (MBA); information technology in the pharmaceutical industry (MBA); information technology outsourcing (MBA); pharmaceutical technology management (MBA); project management (MBA); telecommunications management (MBA).

Stevens Institute of Technology, Graduate School, Wesley J. Howe School of Technology Management, Program in Information Systems, Hoboken, NJ 07030. Offers computer science (MS); e-commerce (MS, Certificate); entrepreneurial information technology (MS); global innovation management (MS); human resource management (MS); information management (MS, Certificate); information security (MS); information technology in financial services industry (MS); information technology in the pharmaceutical industry (MS); information technology outsourcing management (MS); integrated information architecture (MS); project management (MS, Certificate); quantitative software engineering (MS); systems engineering (MS); telecommunications management (MS). *Degree requirements:* For master's, thesis optional. *Entrance requirements:* For master's, GMAT, GRE General Test. Additional exam requirements/recommendations for international students: Required—TOEFL. Electronic applications accepted.

Stevens Institute of Technology, Graduate School, Wesley J. Howe School of Technology Management, Program in Management, Hoboken, NJ 07030. Offers general management (MS); global innovation management (MS); human resource management (MS); information management (MS); project management (MS); technology commercialization (MS); technology management (MS). Part-time programs available. *Degree requirements:* For master's, thesis optional. *Entrance requirements:* For master's, GMAT, GRE General Test. Additional exam requirements/recommendations for international students: Required—TOEFL. Electronic applications accepted. *Faculty research:* Industrial economics.

Texas A&M University, College of Engineering, Zachry Department of Civil Engineering, College Station, TX 77843. Offers construction engineering and management (M Eng, MS, D Eng, PhD); environmental engineering (M Eng, MS, D Eng, PhD); geotechnical engineering (M Eng, MS, D Eng, PhD); materials engineering (M Eng, MS, D Eng, PhD); ocean engineering (M Eng, MS, D Eng, PhD); structural engineering (M Eng, MS, D Eng, PhD); transportation engineering (M Eng, MS, D Eng, PhD); water resources engineering (M Eng, MS, D Eng, PhD). Part-time programs available. *Faculty:* 50 full-time (6 women), 6 part-time/adjunct (1 woman). *Students:* 288 full-time (61 women), 38 part-time (5 women); includes 18 minority (2 African Americans, 1 American Indian/Alaska Native, 7 Asian Americans or Pacific Islanders, 8 Hispanic Americans), 209 international. Average age 29. 407 applicants, 67% accepted, 71 enrolled. In 2006, 82 master's, 16 doctorates awarded. *Degree requirements:* For master's, thesis (MS); for doctorate, dissertation (PhD), internship (D Eng). *Entrance requirements:* For master's and doctorate, GRE General Test. Additional exam requirements/recommendations for international students: Required—TOEFL. *Application deadline:* Applications are processed on a rolling basis. Application fee: $50 ($75 for international students). Electronic applications accepted. *Expenses:* Tuition, state resident: full-time $4,697. Tuition, nonresident: full-time $11,297. Required fees: $2,272. *Financial support:* In 2006–07, fellowships (averaging $4,500 per year), research assistantships (averaging $14,000 per year), teaching assistantships (averaging $14,400 per year) were awarded; career-related internships or fieldwork and institutionally sponsored loans also available. Financial award application deadline: 4/15; financial award applicants required to submit FAFSA. *Unit head:* Dr. Paul N. Roschke, Interim Head, 979-845-7435, Fax: 979-862-2800, E-mail: ce-grad@tamu.edu. *Application contact:* Dr. Peter B. Keating, Graduate Advisor, 979-845-2498, Fax: 979-862-2800, E-mail: ce-grad@tamu.edu.

Universidad Nacional Pedro Henriquez Urena, Graduate School, Santo Domingo, Dominican Republic. Offers accounting and auditing (M Acct); animal production (M Agr); business administration (MBA, PhD); Caribbean tropical architecture (M Arch); conservation of monuments and cultural goods (M Arch); economics (M Econ); education (PhD); environmental engineering (MEE); horticulture (M Agr); hospital administration (PhD); humanities (PhD); international relations (MPS); management of natural resources (MNRM); project management (M Man, MPM); public administration (MPS); sanitary engineering (ME); social science (PhD); veterinary medicine (DVM).

Université du Québec à Chicoutimi, Graduate Programs, Program in Project Management, Chicoutimi, QC G7H 2B1, Canada. Offers M Sc. Part-time programs available. *Entrance requirements:* For master's, appropriate bachelor's degree, proficiency in French.

Université du Québec à Montréal, Graduate Programs, Program in Project Management, Montréal, QC H3C 3P8, Canada. Offers MGP, Diploma. Part-time programs available. *Entrance requirements:* For master's and Diploma, appropriate bachelor's degree or equivalent, proficiency in French.

Université du Québec à Rimouski, Graduate Programs, Program in Project Management, Rimouski, QC G5L 3A1, Canada. Offers M Sc, Diploma. Part-time programs available. *Students:* 40 full-time, 25 part-time, 8 international. In 2006, 12 degrees awarded. *Entrance requirements:* For master's, proficiency in French, appropriate bachelor's degree. *Application deadline:* For fall admission, 5/1 priority date for domestic students. Application fee: $50. *Financial support:* Fellowships, research assistantships, teaching assistantships available. *Unit head:* Jean-Yves Lajoie, Director, 418-833-8800 Ext. 3237, Fax: 418-833-1113, E-mail: jean-yves_lajoie@uqar.ca. *Application contact:* Marc Berube, Office of Admissions, 418-724-1433, Fax: 418-724-1525, E-mail: marc_berube@uqar.ca.

Université du Québec à Trois-Rivières, Graduate Programs, Program in Project Management, Trois-Rivières, QC G9A 5H7, Canada. Offers M Sc, MGP, DESS. Part-time programs available. *Entrance requirements:* For master's, appropriate bachelor's degree, proficiency in French.

Université du Québec en Abitibi-Témiscamingue, Graduate Programs, Program in Project Management, Rouyn-Noranda, QC J9X 5E4, Canada. Offers M Sc. Part-time programs available. *Entrance requirements:* For master's, appropriate bachelor's degree, proficiency in French.

Université du Québec en Outaouais, Graduate Programs, Program in Project Management, Gatineau, QC J8X 3X7, Canada. Offers M Sc, MA, Diploma. Part-time programs available. *Students:* 150 full-time, 247 part-time, 48 international. *Entrance requirements:* For master's, appropriate bachelor's degree, proficiency in French. *Application deadline:* For fall admission, 6/1 priority date for domestic students, 3/1 for international students; for winter admission, 11/1 priority date for domestic students, 10/1 for international students. Application fee: $30 Canadian dollars. *Financial support:* Fellowships, research assistantships, teaching assistantships available. *Unit head:* Pierre-Paul Morin, Director, 819-595-3900 Ext. 1724, Fax: 819-773-1747, E-mail: pierre-paul.morin@uqo.ca. *Application contact:* Registrar's Office, 819-773-1850, Fax: 819-773-1835, E-mail: registraire@ugo.ca.

University of Alaska Anchorage, School of Engineering, Program in Project Management, Anchorage, AK 99508-8060. Offers MS. Part-time and evening/weekend programs available. Postbaccalaureate distance learning degree programs offered (no on-campus study). *Faculty:* 1 full-time (0 women), 6 part-time/adjunct (2 women). *Students:* 4 full-time (2 women), 31 part-time (8 women); includes 8 minority (2 African Americans, 1 American Indian/Alaska Native, 4 Asian Americans or Pacific Islanders, 1 Hispanic American), 1 international. 18 applicants, 17% accepted. In 2006, 6 degrees awarded. *Degree requirements:* For master's, thesis or alternative, case study and research project. *Entrance requirements:* For master's, two years of project management experience. Additional exam requirements/recommendations for international students: Required—TOEFL (minimum score 550 paper-based; 213 computer-based). *Application deadline:* For fall admission, 7/1 for domestic and international students; for spring admission, 11/1 for domestic and international students. Application fee: $45. *Expenses: Contact institution. Financial support:* In 2006–07, 2 research assistantships with full tuition reimbursements were awarded; Federal Work-Study, scholarships/grants, health care benefits, and unspecified assistantships also available. *Unit head:* Dr. Jang W. Ra, Chair,

907-786-1862, Fax: 907-786-1079, E-mail: afjwr@uaa.alaska.edu. *Application contact:* Mike Dorsey, Administrative Assistant, 907-786-1924, Fax: 907-786-1935, E-mail: anmld1@uaa.alaska.edu.

University of Dallas, Graduate School of Management, Irving, TX 75062-4736. Offers accounting (MBA, MS); business management (MBA); corporate finance (MBA, MM); engineering management (MBA, MM); entrepreneurship (MBA, MM); financial services (MBA, MM); global business (MBA, MM); health services management (MBA, MM); human resource management (MBA, MM, MS); information assurance (MBA, MM, MS); information technology (MBA, MM, MS); information technology service management (MBA); IT service management (MS); marketing (MM); marketing management (MBA); not-for-profit management (MBA); organization development (MBA); project management (MBA, MM); sports and entertainment management (MBA, MM); strategic leadership (MBA); supply chain management (MBA); supply chain management and market logistics (MM); telecommunications management (MBA, MM). *Accreditation:* ACBSP. Part-time and evening/weekend programs available. Postbaccalaureate distance learning degree programs offered (no on-campus study). *Faculty:* 26 full-time (5 women), 85 part-time/adjunct (18 women). *Students:* 227 full-time (98 women), 1,160 part-time (446 women); includes 473 minority (209 African Americans, 3 American Indian/Alaska Native, 143 Asian Americans or Pacific Islanders, 118 Hispanic Americans), 224 international. Average age 34. 556 applicants, 86% accepted, 291 enrolled. In 2006, 476 degrees awarded. *Entrance requirements:* Additional exam requirements/recommendations for international students: Required—TOEFL. *Application deadline:* Applications are processed on a rolling basis. Application fee: $50. Electronic applications accepted. *Expenses: Contact institution. Financial support:* In 2006–07, 468 students received support. Scholarships/grants and unspecified assistantships available. Financial award application deadline: 2/15; financial award applicants required to submit FAFSA. *Unit head:* Dr. J. Lee Whittington, Dean, 972-721-5230. *Application contact:* Sarah Stivison, Director of Graduate Admissions, 972-721-5198, Fax: 972-721-4009, E-mail: admiss@gsm.udallas.edu.

University of Management and Technology, Program in Business Administration, Arlington, VA 22209. Offers acquisition management (DBA); general management (MBA, DBA); project management (MBA, DBA). Part-time and evening/weekend programs available. Postbaccalaureate distance learning degree programs offered (no on-campus study). *Degree requirements:* For master's, comprehensive exam. *Entrance requirements:* For master's, 3 recommendations, current resumé. Additional exam requirements/recommendations for international students: Required—TOEFL (minimum score 550 paper-based; 213 computer-based). *Application deadline:* Applications are processed on a rolling basis. Application fee: $30. Electronic applications accepted. *Unit head:* Dr. J. Davidson Frame, Academic Dean, 703-516-0035 Ext. 25.

University of Management and Technology, Program in Computer Science and Information Technology, Arlington, VA 22209. Offers computer science (MS); information technology (AC); information technology project management (MS, AC); management information systems (MS); multimedia technology (MS); software engineering (MS). Part-time and evening/weekend programs available. Postbaccalaureate distance learning degree programs offered (no on-campus study). *Entrance requirements:* For master's, 3 recommendations, current resumé. Additional exam requirements/recommendations for international students: Required—TOEFL (minimum score 550 paper-based; 213 computer-based). *Application deadline:* Applications are processed on a rolling basis. Application fee: $30. Electronic applications accepted. *Unit head:* Dr. C. Eric Kirkland, PMP, Vice President, 703-516-0035, Fax: 703-516-0985, E-mail: eric.kirkland@umtweb.edu.

University of Management and Technology, Program in Management, Arlington, VA 22209. Offers acquisition management (MS, AC); management (MS); project management (MS, AC); public administration (MPA, MS, AC); public management (MS); telecommunications management (MS). Part-time and evening/weekend programs available. Postbaccalaureate distance learning degree programs offered (no on-campus study). *Entrance requirements:* For master's, 3 recommendations, current resumé. Additional exam requirements/recommendations for international students: Required—TOEFL (minimum score 550 paper-based; 213 computer-based). *Application deadline:* Applications are processed on a rolling basis. Application fee: $30. Electronic applications accepted. *Unit head:* Dr. J. Davidson Frame, Academic Dean, 703-516-0035 Ext. 25.

University of Northern Virginia, Graduate Programs, Manassas, VA 20109. Offers accountancy (MS); accounting (MBA); business administration (DBA); computer science (MS); counseling education (M Ed); early childhood education (M Ed); educational communication and instructional technology (M Ed); educational leadership (M Ed); finance (MBA); information systems technology (MS); management (MBA); marketing (MBA); project management (MBA); public administration (MPA); teaching English to speakers of other languages (M Ed). Part-time and evening/weekend programs available. Postbaccalaureate distance learning degree programs offered (no on-campus study). *Degree requirements:* For doctorate, thesis/dissertation, comprehensive exam, registration. *Entrance requirements:* Additional exam requirements/recommendations for international students: Required—TOEFL (minimum score 550 paper-based; 230 computer-based), IELTS (minimum score 6). Electronic applications accepted.

University of Ottawa, Faculty of Graduate and Postdoctoral Studies, Faculty of Engineering, Engineering Management Program, Ottawa, ON K1N 6N5, Canada. Offers engineering management (M Eng); information technology (Certificate); project management (Certificate). *Degree requirements:* For master's, thesis or alternative. *Entrance requirements:* For master's and Certificate, honors degree or equivalent, minimum B average. Electronic applications accepted.

University of San Francisco, College of Professional Studies, Program in Project Management, San Francisco, CA 94117-1080. Offers MS. *Faculty:* 1 (woman) full-time, 2 part-time/adjunct (both women). *Students:* 27 full-time (13 women); includes 13 minority (4 African Americans, 8 Asian Americans or Pacific Islanders, 1 Hispanic American), 3 international. Average age 36. 23 applicants, 91% accepted, 13 enrolled. *Expenses:* Tuition: Full-time $17,370; part-time $965 per unit. Tuition and fees vary according to degree level, campus/location and program. *Financial support:* In 2006–07, 18 students received support. *Unit head:* Dr. Linda Henderson, Director, 415-422-2592.

University of the Incarnate Word, School of Graduate Studies and Research, H-E-B School of Business and Administration, Programs in Administration, San Antonio, TX 78209-6397. Offers adult education (MAA); applied administration (MAA); communication arts (MAA); English (MAA); instructional technology (MAA); international business (Certificate); multidisciplinary sciences (MAA); nutrition (MAA); organizational development (MAA, Certificate); project management (Certificate); sports management (MAA); urban administration (MAA). *Students:* 1 (woman) full-time, 161 part-time (102 women); includes 17 African Americans, 1 American Indian/Alaska Native, 82 Hispanic Americans, 18 international. Average age 34. In 2006, 78 degrees awarded. *Entrance requirements:* For master's, GMAT, GRE, MAT. Additional exam requirements/recommendations for international students: Required—TOEFL. *Application deadline:* For fall admission, 8/15 priority date for domestic students; for spring admission, 12/31 for domestic students. Applications are processed on a rolling basis. Application fee: $20. *Expenses:* Tuition: Part-time $570 per credit hour. Required fees: $54 per credit hour. One-time fee: $195 part-time. Tuition and fees vary according to degree level. *Financial support:* Federal Work-Study and scholarships/grants available. *Unit head:* Dr. Dan Dominguez, MAA Director, 210-829-3180, Fax: 210-805-3564, E-mail: domingue@uiwtx.edu. *Application contact:* Andrea Cyterski-Acosta, Dean of Enrollment, 210-829-6005, Fax: 210-829-3921, E-mail: cyterski@uiwtx.edu.

University of Wisconsin–Platteville, School of Graduate Studies, Distance Learning Center, Online Program in Project Management, Platteville, WI 53818-3099. Offers MS. Part-time and evening/weekend programs available. Postbaccalaureate distance learning degree programs offered (no on-campus study). *Students:* 5 full-time (3 women), 147 part-time (62 women); includes 10 minority (8 African Americans, 2 Asian Americans or Pacific Islanders), 3 international. 53 applicants, 64% accepted. In 2006, 45 degrees awarded. *Degree requirements:* For master's, thesis or alternative. *Entrance requirements:* Additional exam requirements/recommendations for international students: Required—TOEFL (minimum score 500 paper-based; 173 computer-based). *Application deadline:* For fall admission, 7/1 priority date for domestic students; for spring admission, 11/1 priority date for domestic students. Applications are processed on a rolling basis. Application fee: $45. Electronic applications accepted. *Expenses:* Tuition, state resident: part-time $365 per credit. Tuition, nonresident: part-time $955 per credit. *Unit head:* William Haskins, Coordinator, 608-342-1961, Fax: 608-342-1466, E-mail: haskinsd@uwplatt.edu.

Western Carolina University, Graduate School, College of Business, Program in Project Management, Cullowhee, NC 28723. Offers MPM. Part-time and evening/weekend programs available. Postbaccalaureate distance learning degree programs offered (no on-campus study). *Entrance requirements:* For master's, GMAT. Additional exam requirements/recommendations for international students: Required—TOEFL (minimum score 550 paper-based; 213 computer-based).

Winthrop University, College of Business Administration, Program in Software Project Management, Rock Hill, SC 29733. Offers software development (MS); software project management (Certificate). *Faculty:* 3 full-time (1 woman). *Students:* 2 full-time (both women), 2 part-time; includes 1 minority (Hispanic American), 1 international. Average age 25. In 2006, 3 degrees awarded. *Expenses:* Tuition, state resident: full-time $9,148; part-time $383 per hour. Tuition, nonresident: full-time $16,864; part-time $704 per hour. *Unit head:* Peggy Hager, Director of Graduate Studies, 803-323-2408, E-mail: hagerp@winthrop.edu. *Application contact:* 800-411-7041, Fax: 803-323-2292, E-mail: graduatestu@winthrop.edu.

Worcester Polytechnic Institute, Graduate Studies and Enrollment, Department of Management, Program in Information Technology, Worcester, MA 01609-2280. Offers information security management (MS); information technology and entrepreneurship (MS); information technology applications development (MS); information technology project management (MS); manufacturing and service information technology applications (MS); marketing information technology applications (MS). Part-time and evening/weekend programs available. Postbaccalaureate distance learning degree programs offered (no on-campus study). *Faculty:* 12 full-time (6 women), 2 part-time/adjunct (1 woman). *Students:* 5 full-time (2 women), 11 part-time (1 woman); includes 1 minority (Asian American or Pacific Islander), 8 international. Average age 28. 37 applicants, 76% accepted, 10 enrolled. *Degree requirements:* For master's, thesis optional. *Entrance requirements:* For master's, GMAT or GRE. Additional exam requirements/recommendations for international students: Required—TOEFL (minimum score 550 paper-based; 213 computer-based; 79 iBT), IELTS (minimum score 7). *Application deadline:* For fall admission, 6/1 priority date for domestic and international students; for spring admission, 10/15 priority date for domestic students, 10/1 priority date for international students. Applications are processed on a rolling basis. Application fee: $70. Electronic applications accepted. *Expenses:* Tuition: Part-time $1,042 per credit hour. Required fees: $1,009 per year. *Financial support:* In 2006–07, 5 students received support, including 3 research assistantships; career-related internships or fieldwork, Federal Work-Study, scholarships/grants, and unspecified assistantships also available. Financial award application deadline: 6/1; financial award applicants required to submit FAFSA. *Faculty research:* ERP implementation, improving web accessibility, information quality assessment, information quality assessment, website quality. Total annual research expenditures: $8,477. *Unit head:* Norm D. Wilkinson, Director, Graduate Management Programs, 508-831-5957, Fax: 508-831-5720, E-mail: nwilkins@wpi.edu.

See Close-Up on page 377.

Wright State University, School of Graduate Studies, Raj Soin College of Business, Department of Management, Dayton, OH 45435. Offers flexible business (MBA); health care management (MBA); international business (MBA); management, innovation and change (MBA); project management (MBA); supply chain management (MBA); MBA/MS. *Students:* 47 full-time (22 women), 154 part-time (63 women). Average age 31. 40 applicants, 90% accepted. In 2006, 71 degrees awarded. *Entrance requirements:* For master's, GMAT, minimum AACSB index of 1000. Additional exam requirements/recommendations for international students: Required—TOEFL. Application fee: $25. *Financial support:* Fellowships, research assistantships, teaching assistantships, unspecified assistantships available. Support available to part-time students. Financial award applicants required to submit FAFSA. *Unit head:* Dr. Riad Ajami, Chair, 937-775-2375, Fax: 937-775-3545, E-mail: riad.ajami@wright.edu. *Application contact:* Michael Evans, Director of MBA Programs, 937-775-2437, Fax: 937-775-3545, E-mail: michael.evans@wright.edu.

Section 18
Quality Management

This section contains a directory of institutions offering graduate work in quality management. Additional information about programs listed in the directory but not augmented by an in-depth entry may be obtained by writing directly to the dean of a graduate school or chair of a department at the address given in the directory.

For programs offering related work, see also in this book Business Administration and Management.

CONTENTS

Program Directory

Quality Management

California State University, Dominguez Hills, College of Natural and Behavioral Science, Program in Quality Assurance, Carson, CA 90747-0001. Offers MS. Part-time and evening/weekend programs available. Postbaccalaureate distance learning degree programs offered (no on-campus study). *Faculty:* 18 part-time/adjunct (4 women). *Students:* 2 full-time (0 women), 229 part-time (80 women); includes 83 minority (23 African Americans, 2 American Indian/Alaska Native, 33 Asian Americans or Pacific Islanders, 25 Hispanic Americans), 28 international. Average age 41. 55 applicants, 82% accepted, 36 enrolled. In 2006, 31 degrees awarded. *Degree requirements:* For master's, thesis, registration. *Entrance requirements:* Additional exam requirements/recommendations for international students: Required—TOEFL. *Application deadline:* For fall admission, 4/1 priority date for domestic and international students; for winter admission, 3/1 priority date for domestic and international students; for spring admission, 12/1 priority date for domestic and international students. Application fee: $55. Electronic applications accepted. *Expenses: Contact institution. Faculty research:* Six sigma, lean thinking, risk management, quality management. *Unit head:* Coordinator, 310-243-3880. *Application contact:* Rodger Hamrick, Program Assistant, 310-243-3880, E-mail: rhamrick@csudh.edu.

Case Western Reserve University, Weatherhead School of Management, Department of Operations, Cleveland, OH 44106. Offers management (MS, MSM), including finance (MS), information systems (MS), marketing (MS), operations research, quality management (MS), supply chain (MSM); management for liberal arts graduates (MSM); operations research (PhD); MBA/MSM. Part-time programs available. *Faculty:* 12 full-time (1 woman), 2 part-time/adjunct (1 woman). *Students:* 32 full-time (8 women), 6 part-time (1 woman), 21 international. Average age 28. In 2006, 28 master's, 4 doctorates awarded. *Degree requirements:* For doctorate, thesis/dissertation. *Entrance requirements:* For master's, GRE General Test; for doctorate, GMAT, GRE General Test. *Application deadline:* For fall admission, 4/15 priority date for domestic students. Applications are processed on a rolling basis. Application fee: $50. *Financial support:* Tuition waivers (full and partial) available. Financial award application deadline: 5/1. *Faculty research:* Mathematical finance, mathematical programming, scheduling, stochastic optimization, environmental/energy models. *Unit head:* Kamlesh Mathur, Chairman, 216-368-3857, E-mail: kamlesh.mathur@case.edu.

Dowling College, School of Business, Oakdale, NY 11769-1999. Offers aviation management (MBA, Certificate); banking and finance (MBA, Certificate); general management (MBA); public management (MBA, Certificate); total quality management (MBA, Certificate). Part-time and evening/weekend programs available. *Students:* 239 full-time (105 women), 566 part-time (273 women); includes 132 African Americans, 55 Asian Americans or Pacific Islanders, 48 Hispanic Americans, 3 international. Average age 31. 414 applicants, 82% accepted, 166 enrolled. In 2006, 471 master's, 1 other advanced degree awarded. *Degree requirements:* For master's, thesis optional. *Entrance requirements:* For master's, minimum GPA of 2.8, 2 letters of recommendation, courses in accounting and finance or seminar in accounting/finance, resumé. Additional exam requirements/recommendations for international students: Required—TOEFL (minimum score 550 paper-based). *Application deadline:* For fall admission, 9/1 priority date for domestic students; for winter admission, 1/1 priority date for domestic students; for spring admission, 2/1 priority date for domestic students. Applications are processed on a rolling basis. Application fee: $25. Electronic applications accepted. *Expenses:* Tuition: Full-time $16,008; part-time $667 per credit. Tuition and fees vary according to course load. *Financial support:* In 2006–07, 126 students received support, including 30 research assistantships (averaging $3,150 per year); career-related internships or fieldwork, Federal Work-Study, scholarships/grants, and unspecified assistantships also available. Support available to part-time students. Financial award application deadline: 6/30; financial award applicants required to submit FAFSA. *Faculty research:* International finance, computer applications, labor relations, executive development. *Unit head:* Dr. Elana Zolfo, Dean of the School of Business, 631-244-3190, Fax: 631-244-1018, E-mail: zdfoe@dowling.edu. *Application contact:* Franks S. Pizzardi, Director of Admissions Operations, 631-244-3227, Fax: 631-244-1059, E-mail: pizzardf@dowling.edu.

Eastern Michigan University, Graduate School, College of Business, Department of Management, Ypsilanti, MI 48197. Offers human resources management and organizational development (MSHROD); management of human resources (MBA); management organizational development (MBA); production and operations management (MBA); strategic quality management (MBA). Part-time and evening/weekend programs available. Postbaccalaureate distance learning degree programs offered (minimal on-campus study). *Students:* Average age 29. *Degree requirements:* For master's, thesis optional. *Entrance requirements:* For master's, GMAT. Additional exam requirements/recommendations for international students: Required—TOEFL. *Application deadline:* For fall admission, 5/15 priority date for domestic and international students; for winter admission, 10/15 priority date for domestic and international students; for spring admission, 3/15 priority date for domestic and international students. Applications are processed on a rolling basis. Application fee: $35. *Expenses:* Tuition, state resident: part-time $341 per credit hour. Tuition, nonresident: full-time $16,104; part-time $671 per credit hour. Required fees: $816; $34 per credit hour. $40 per term. One-time fee: $82 full-time. Tuition and fees vary according to course level, course load, degree level and reciprocity agreements. *Financial support:* Fellowships, research assistantships with full tuition reimbursements, teaching assistantships with full tuition reimbursements, career-related internships or fieldwork, Federal Work-Study, institutionally sponsored loans, scholarships/grants, tuition waivers (partial), and unspecified assistantships available. Support available to part-time students. Financial award applicants required to submit FAFSA. *Unit head:* Dr. Fraya Wagner-Marsh, Head, 734-487-3240, Fax: 734-487-4100, E-mail: fraya.wagner@emich.edu.

Eastern Michigan University, Graduate School, College of Technology, School of Engineering Technology, Programs in Quality and Quality Management, Ypsilanti, MI 48197. Offers MS. Part-time and evening/weekend programs available. Postbaccalaureate distance learning degree programs offered (minimal on-campus study). *Students:* 1 (woman) full-time, 88 part-time (24 women); includes 16 minority (10 African Americans, 1 American Indian/Alaska Native, 4 Asian Americans or Pacific Islanders, 1 Hispanic American), 11 international. Average age 39. In 2006, 11 degrees awarded. *Entrance requirements:* Additional exam requirements/recommendations for international students: Required—TOEFL. *Application deadline:* For fall admission, 5/15 priority date for domestic students, 5/1 priority date for international students; for winter admission, 10/15 priority date for domestic students, 10/1 priority date for international students; for spring admission, 3/15 priority date for domestic students, 3/1 priority date for international students. Applications are processed on a rolling basis. Application fee: $35. *Expenses:* Tuition, state resident: part-time $341 per credit hour. Tuition, nonresident: full-time $16,104; part-time $671 per credit hour. Required fees: $816; $34 per credit hour. $40 per term. One-time fee: $82 full-time. Tuition and fees vary according to course level, course load, degree level and reciprocity agreements. *Financial support:* Fellowships, research assistantships with full tuition reimbursements, teaching assistantships with full tuition reimbursements, career-related internships or fieldwork, Federal Work-Study, institutionally sponsored loans, scholarships/grants, tuition waivers (partial), and unspecified assistantships available. Support available to part-time students. Financial award applicants required to submit FAFSA.

Ferris State University, College of Business, Big Rapids, MI 49307. Offers application development (MSISM); database administration (MSISM); e-business (MSISM); information systems (MBA); networking (MSISM); quality management (MBA); security (MSISM). Part-time and evening/weekend programs available. *Faculty:* 5 full-time (2 women), 2 part-time/adjunct (both women). *Students:* 35 full-time (12 women), 60 part-time (24 women); includes 5 minority (3 African Americans, 1 American Indian/Alaska Native, 1 Asian American or Pacific Islander), 13 international. Average age 34. 90 applicants, 72% accepted, 29 enrolled. In 2006, 40 degrees awarded. *Degree requirements:* For master's, thesis. *Entrance requirements:* For master's, GRE or GMAT, minimum GPA of 3.0 in CIS and business core, 2.75 overall; writing sample; 3 letters of reference; resumé. Additional exam requirements/recommendations for international students: Required—TOEFL (minimum score 500 paper-based; 173 computer-based). *Application deadline:* For fall admission, 7/1 priority date for domestic students, 6/15 for international students; for winter admission, 11/1 priority date for domestic students, 10/15 for international students; for spring admission, 3/1 priority date for domestic students, 2/15 for international students. Applications are processed on a rolling basis. Electronic applications accepted. *Expenses:* Tuition, state resident: part-time $355 per credit hour. Tuition, nonresident: part-time $687 per credit hour. *Financial support:* In 2006–07, 40 research assistantships, 10 teaching assistantships were awarded; career-related internships or fieldwork, Federal Work-Study, and unspecified assistantships also available. Support available to part-time students. Financial award applicants required to submit FAFSA. *Faculty research:* Quality improvement, client/server end-user computing, information management and policy, learning space/Lotus Notes, security. *Unit head:* Dr. Bill Boras, Department Chair, 231-591-2168, Fax: 231-591-2973, E-mail: cbgp@ferris.edu. *Application contact:* Shannon Yost, Department Secretary, 231-591-2168, Fax: 231-591-2973, E-mail: yosts@ferris.edu.

Hofstra University, Frank G. Zarb School of Business, Department of Business Computer Information Systems/Quantitative Methods, Hempstead, NY 11549. Offers business computer information systems (MBA); computer information systems (MS); quality management (MBA). Part-time and evening/weekend programs available. *Faculty:* 11 full-time (3 women). *Students:* 4 full-time (0 women), 26 part-time (6 women); includes 6 minority (1 African American, 5 Asian Americans or Pacific Islanders), 1 international. Average age 31. 14 applicants, 86% accepted, 8 enrolled. In 2006, 10 degrees awarded. *Degree requirements:* For master's, thesis or alternative, registration. *Entrance requirements:* For master's, GMAT, 2 letters of recommendation, resumé, essay. Additional exam requirements/recommendations for international students: Required—TOEFL (minimum score 550 paper-based; 213 computer-based). *Application deadline:* Applications are processed on a rolling basis. Application fee: $60. Electronic applications accepted. *Expenses:* Tuition: Full-time $13,320; part-time $740 per credit. Required fees: $930; $155 per term. *Financial support:* In 2006–07, 5 students received support, including 5 fellowships with tuition reimbursements available (averaging $10,844 per year); research assistantships with full and partial tuition reimbursements available, career-related internships or fieldwork, Federal Work-Study, scholarships/grants, tuition waivers (full and partial), and unspecified assistantships also available. Financial award applicants required to submit FAFSA. *Faculty research:* Decision support systems, econometrics-public issues, forecasting, LPT sizing-quality, enterprise planning systems-SAP. *Unit head:* Dr. John F. Affisco, Chairperson, 516-463-5362, E-mail: acsjfa@hofstra.edu. *Application contact:* Carol Drummer, Dean of Graduate Admissions, 516-463-4876, Fax: 516-463-4664, E-mail: gradstudent@hofstra.edu.

Hofstra University, Frank G. Zarb School of Business, Department of Management, Entrepreneurship and General Management, Hempstead, NY 11549. Offers health services management (MBA); human resource management (MS, Advanced Certificate); management (EMBA, MBA), including business administration (EMBA); quality management (MBA). Part-time and evening/weekend programs available. *Faculty:* 8 full-time (2 women), 1 part-time/adjunct (0 women). *Students:* 46 full-time (19 women), 238 part-time (114 women); includes 55 minority (20 African Americans, 25 Asian Americans or Pacific Islanders, 10 Hispanic Americans), 9 international. Average age 32. 183 applicants, 90% accepted, 117 enrolled. In 2006, 17 master's, 3 other advanced degrees awarded. *Degree requirements:* For master's, thesis optional. *Entrance requirements:* For master's, GMAT, 2 letters of recommendation, resumé, essay. Additional exam requirements/recommendations for international students: Required—TOEFL (minimum score 550 paper-based; 213 computer-based). *Application deadline:* Applications are processed on a rolling basis. Application fee: $60. Electronic applications accepted. *Expenses:* Tuition: Full-time $13,320; part-time $740 per credit. Required fees: $930; $155 per term. *Financial support:* In 2006–07, 25 students received support, including 17 fellowships with tuition reimbursements available (averaging $5,367 per year), 3 research assistantships with full and partial tuition reimbursements available (averaging $7,232 per year); tuition waivers (full and partial) and unspecified assistantships also available. Financial award applicants required to submit FAFSA. *Faculty research:* Business/personal ethics, stakeholders, whistle blowing and national/global labor practices; family business, entrepreneurship (for & non-profit); competition, innovation; risk taking, problem solving; and supple chain management, scheduling and health care industry. Total annual research expenditures: $24,000. *Unit head:* Dr. Mamdouh I. Farid, Chairperson, 516-463-5735, Fax: 516-463-4834, E-mail: mgbmif@hofstra.edu. *Application contact:* Carol Drummer, Dean of Graduate Admissions, 516-463-4876, Fax: 516-463-4664, E-mail: gradstudent@hofstra.edu.

Illinois Institute of Technology, Stuart School of Business, Program in Business Administration, Chicago, IL 60616-3793. Offers entrepreneurship (MBA); financial management (MBA); financial markets (MBA); healthcare management (MBA); information technology management (MBA); international business (MBA); management science (MBA); marketing (MBA); operations, quality, and technology management (MBA); strategic management of organizations (MBA); sustainable enterprise (MBA); JD/MBA; MBA/MS. *Accreditation:* AACSB. Part-time and evening/weekend programs available. *Faculty:* 13 full-time (1 woman), 9 part-time/adjunct (0 women). *Students:* 74 full-time (29 women), 42 part-time (16 women); includes 17 minority (5 African Americans, 11 Asian Americans or Pacific Islanders, 1 Hispanic American), 74 international. Average age 29. 247 applicants, 70% accepted, 51 enrolled. In 2006, 45 degrees awarded. *Entrance requirements:* For master's, GMAT. Additional exam requirements/recommendations for international students: Required—TOEFL (minimum score 600 paper-based; 250 computer-based). *Application deadline:* For fall admission, 8/15 priority date for domestic students, 7/1 for international students; for winter admission, 11/1 priority date for domestic students, 10/1 for international students; for spring admission, 1/1 priority date for domestic students, 1/1 for international students. Applications are processed on a rolling basis. Application fee: $75. Electronic applications accepted. *Expenses: Contact institution.* Tuition and fees vary according to class time, course level, course load, program and student level. *Financial support:* Career-related internships or fieldwork, Federal Work-Study, institutionally sponsored loans, scholarships/grants, traineeships, health care benefits, tuition waivers, and unspecified assistantships available. Support available to part-time students. Financial award applicants required to submit FAFSA. *Faculty research:* Knowledge management, healthcare management, sustainability in supply chain. *Unit head:* Dr. George P. Nassos, Interim Director, 312-906-6543, Fax: 312-906-6549, E-mail: george.nassos@iit.edu. *Application contact:* Brian Jansen, Director of Graduate Admissions, 312-906-6521, Fax: 312-906-6549, E-mail: admission@stuart.iit.edu.

Instituto Tecnológico y de Estudios Superiores de Monterrey, Campus Ciudad de México, Virtual University Division, Ciudad de Mexico, Mexico. Offers administration of information technologies (MA); computer sciences (MA); education (MA, PhD); educational technology (MA); environmental engineering (MA); environmental systems (MA); humanistic studies (MA); industrial engineering (MA); international business for Latin America (MA); quality systems (MA); quality systems and productivity (MA). Part-time and evening/weekend programs available. Postbaccalaureate distance learning degree programs offered (minimal on-campus study). *Entrance requirements:* For master's and doctorate, Instituto entrance exam. Additional exam requirements/recommendations for international students: Required—TOEFL.

Instituto Tecnológico y de Estudios Superiores de Monterrey, Campus Ciudad Juárez, Program in Quality Management, Ciudad Juárez, Mexico. Offers MQM.

Instituto Tecnológico y de Estudios Superiores de Monterrey, Campus Estado de México, Professional and Graduate Division, Estado de Mexico, Mexico. Offers administration of information technologies (MITA); architecture (M Arch); business administration (GMBA, MBA); computer sciences (MCS, PhD); education (M Ed); educational institution administration (MAD); educational technology and innovation (PhD); electronic commerce (MEC); environmental systems (MS); finance (MAF); humanistic studies (MHS); information sciences and knowledge management (MISKM); information systems (MS); manufacturing systems (MS); marketing (MEM); quality systems and productivity (MS); science and materials engineering (PhD); telecommunications management (MTM). Part-time programs available. Postbaccalaureate distance learning degree programs offered (minimal on-campus study). *Degree requirements:* For master's, one foreign language, thesis (for some programs), registration; for doctorate, one foreign language, thesis/dissertation, registration (for some programs). *Entrance requirements:* For master's, E-PAEP 500, interview; for doctorate, E-PAEP 500, research proposal. Additional exam requirements/recommendations for international students: Required—TOEFL (minimum score 550 paper-based). *Faculty research:* Surface treatments by plasmas, mechanical properties, robotics, graphical computing, mechatronics security protocols.

Instituto Tecnológico y de Estudios Superiores de Monterrey, Campus Irapuato, Graduate Programs, Irapuato, Mexico. Offers administration (MBA); administration of information technology (MAIT); administration of telecommunications (MAT); architecture (M Arch); computer science (MCS); education (M Ed); educational administration (MEA); educational innovation and technology (DEIT); educational technology (MET); electronic commerce (MBA); environmental administration and planning (MEAP); environmental systems (MES); finances (MBA); humanistic studies (MHS); international management for Latin American executives (MIMLAE); library and information science (MLIS); manufacturing quality management (MMQM); marketing research (MBA).

Madonna University, School of Business, Livonia, MI 48150-1173. Offers business administration (MBA); international business (MSBA); leadership studies (MSBA); leadership studies in criminal justice (MSBA); quality and operations management (MSBA). Part-time and evening/weekend programs available. Postbaccalaureate distance learning degree programs offered (minimal on-campus study). *Faculty:* 12 full-time (3 women), 14 part-time/adjunct (3 women). *Students:* 34 full-time (21 women), 214 part-time (107 women); includes 26 minority (7 African Americans, 7 American Indian/Alaska Native, 4 Asian Americans or Pacific Islanders, 8 Hispanic Americans), 88 international. Average age 36. 60 applicants, 60% accepted. In 2006, 41 degrees awarded. *Degree requirements:* For master's, thesis (for some programs), foreign language proficiency (international business). *Entrance requirements:* For master's, GMAT, GRE General Test, minimum GPA of 3.0. *Application deadline:* For fall admission, 8/1 priority date for domestic students; for winter admission, 12/1 priority date for domestic students; for spring admission, 4/1 priority date for domestic students. Applications are processed on a rolling basis. Application fee: $25 ($200 for international students). Electronic applications accepted. *Financial support:* Career-related internships or fieldwork, institutionally sponsored loans, and scholarships/grants available. Support available to part-time students. *Faculty research:* Management, women in management, future studies. *Unit head:* Dr. Stuart Arends, Dean, 734-432-5366, Fax: 734-432-5364, E-mail: sarends@madonna.edu. *Application contact:* Sandra Kellums, Coordinator of Graduate Admissions and Records, 734-432-5667, Fax: 734-432-5862, E-mail: skellum@madonna.edu.

Marian College of Fond du Lac, Business Division, Fond du Lac, WI 54935-4699. Offers organizational leadership and quality (MS). Part-time and evening/weekend programs available. *Faculty:* 6 part-time/adjunct (0 women). *Students:* 1 full-time (0 women), 95 part-time (55 women); includes 7 minority (5 African Americans, 1 American Indian/Alaska Native, 1 Hispanic American). Average age 38. 44 applicants, 100% accepted, 44 enrolled. In 2006, 33 degrees awarded. *Degree requirements:* For master's, comprehensive group project. *Entrance requirements:* For master's, 3 years of managerial experience, minimum GPA of 2.75, letters of professional reference. *Application deadline:* Applications are processed on a rolling basis. Application fee: $25. Electronic applications accepted. *Expenses: Contact institution.* Tuition and fees vary according to degree level and program. *Financial support:* In 2006–07, 23 students received support. Institutionally sponsored loans available. Support available to part-time students. Financial award application deadline: 3/1; financial award applicants required to submit FAFSA. *Faculty research:* Organizational values, statistical decision making, learning organization, quality planning, customer research. *Unit head:* David McPhail, Dean of Lifelong Learning, 920-923-8760, Fax: 920-923-7167, E-mail: dmcphail@mariancollege.edu. *Application contact:* Tracy Qualman, Director of Marketing and Admission, 920-923-7159, Fax: 920-923-7167, E-mail: tqualmann@mariancollege.edu.

The National Graduate School of Quality Management, Program in Quality Systems Management, Falmouth, MA 02541. Offers e-commerce (MS); management (MS); six sigma (MS).

Penn State University Park, Graduate School, Intercollege Graduate Programs, Intercollege Program in Quality and Manufacturing Management, State College, University Park, PA 16802-1503. Offers MMM. *Unit head:* Dr. Jose A. Ventura, Co-Director, 814-865-5802, Fax: 814-863-4745, E-mail: jav1@psu.edu.

Rutgers, The State University of New Jersey, New Brunswick, Graduate School, Program in Statistics, New Brunswick, NJ 08901-1281. Offers quality and productivity management (MS); statistics (MS, PhD), including biostatistics (PhD), data mining (PhD). Part-time programs available. Terminal master's awarded for partial completion of doctoral program. *Degree requirements:* For master's, essay, exam, non-thesis essay paper; for doctorate, one foreign language, thesis/dissertation, qualifying oral and written exams. *Entrance requirements:* For master's, GRE General Test; for doctorate, GRE General Test, GRE Subject Test (recommended). Additional exam requirements/recommendations for international students: Required—TOEFL (minimum score 550 paper-based; 213 computer-based). Electronic applications accepted. *Faculty research:* Probability, decision theory, linear models, multivariate statistics, statistical computing.

Saint Joseph's College of Maine, Program in Business Administration, Standish, ME 04084-5263. Offers quality leadership (MBA). Part-time programs available. *Faculty:* 15 part-time/adjunct (5 women). *Students:* Average age 40. 71 applicants, 93% accepted, 61 enrolled. *Entrance requirements:* For master's, 2 years work experience. *Expenses:* Tuition: Part-time $350 per credit. *Unit head:* Dr. Gregory Gull, Director, 207-893-7988, Fax: 207-892-7423, E-mail: ggull@sjcme.edu. *Application contact:* 800-752-4723, Fax: 207-892-7480, E-mail: info@sjcme.edu.

San Jose State University, Graduate Studies and Research, College of Engineering, Department of Technology, San Jose, CA 95192-0001. Offers quality assurance (MS). *Students:* 5 full-time (4 women), 10 part-time (5 women); includes 4 minority (all Asian Americans or Pacific Islanders), 6 international. Average age 36. 15 applicants, 87% accepted, 8 enrolled. In 2006, 2 degrees awarded. *Entrance requirements:* For master's, GRE. *Application deadline:* For fall admission, 6/29 for domestic students; for spring admission, 11/30 for domestic students. Applications are processed on a rolling basis. Application fee: $59. Electronic applications accepted. *Financial support:* Applicants required to submit FAFSA. *Unit head:* Patricia Backer, Chair, 408-924-3214, Fax: 408-924-3198. *Application contact:* Dr. Ali Zargar, Graduate Advisor, 408-924-3194, E-mail: azargar@email.sjsu.edu.

Southern Polytechnic State University, School of Engineering Technology and Management, Department of Industrial Engineering Technology, Marietta, GA 30060-2896. Offers quality assurance (MS); systems engineering (MS SEng). Part-time and evening/weekend programs available. Postbaccalaureate distance learning degree programs offered (minimal on-campus study). *Faculty:* 6 full-time (3 women), 3 part-time/adjunct (1 woman). *Students:* 11 full-time (7 women), 109 part-time (30 women); includes 34 minority (26 African Americans, 3 Asian Americans or Pacific Islanders, 5 Hispanic Americans), 16 international. Average age 39. 54 applicants, 70% accepted, 33 enrolled. In 2006, 24 degrees awarded. *Degree requirements:* For master's, thesis or alternative. *Entrance requirements:* For master's, 2 years full-time experience in industrial engineering field, 3 reference forms, minimum GPA of 2.7. Additional exam requirements/recommendations for international students: Required—TOEFL (minimum score 550 paper-based; 213 computer-based). *Application deadline:* For fall admission, 7/1 priority date for domestic students, 5/1 priority date for international students; for spring admission, 11/1 priority date for domestic students, 9/1 priority date for international students. Applications are processed on a rolling basis. Application fee: $20. Electronic applications accepted. *Expenses:* Tuition, state resident: part-time $422 per credit hour. Tuition, nonresident: part-time $835 per credit hour. *Financial support:* In 2006–07, 35 students received support, including 4 research assistantships with tuition reimbursements available (averaging $1,500 per year); career-related internships or fieldwork, scholarships/grants, and unspecified assistantships also available. Support available to part-time students. Financial award application deadline: 5/1; financial award applicants required to submit FAFSA. *Faculty research:* Robust design of experiments, pricing optimization models. *Unit head:* Dr. Ruston Hunt, Chair, 678-915-7243, Fax: 678-915-4991, E-mail: rhunt@spsu.edu. *Application contact:* Virginia A. Head, Director of Admissions, 678-915-4188, Fax: 678-915-7292, E-mail: vhead@spsu.edu.

Stevens Institute of Technology, Graduate School, Charles V. Schaefer Jr. School of Engineering, Department of Civil, Environmental, and Ocean Engineering, Program in Construction Management, Hoboken, NJ 07030. Offers construction accounting/estimating (Certificate); construction engineering (Certificate); construction law/disputes (Certificate); construction management (MS); construction/quality management (Certificate). *Degree requirements:* For master's, thesis optional. *Entrance requirements:* For master's, GMAT, GRE General Test. Additional exam requirements/recommendations for international students: Required—TOEFL. Electronic applications accepted.

Touro University International, College of Health Sciences, Program in Health Sciences, Cypress, CA 90630. Offers clinical research administration (MS, Certificate); emergency and disaster management (MS, Certificate); environmental health science (Certificate); health care administration (PhD); health care management (MS), including health informatics; health education (MS, Certificate); health informatics (Certificate); health sciences (PhD); international health (MS); international health: educator or researcher option (PhD); international health: practitioner option (PhD); law and expert witness studies (MS, Certificate); public health (MS); quality assurance (Certificate). Part-time and evening/weekend programs available. Postbaccalaureate distance learning degree programs offered (no on-campus study). In 2006, 322 master's, 21 doctorates awarded. *Degree requirements:* For doctorate, thesis/dissertation, defense of dissertation, comprehensive exam. *Entrance requirements:* For master's, minimum GPA of 3.0; for doctorate, minimum GPA of 3.4, curriculum vitae, course work in research methods or statistics. Additional exam requirements/recommendations for international students: Required—TOEFL (minimum score 550 paper-based). Application fee: $75. *Expenses:* Tuition: Part-time $300 per credit hour. Tuition and fees vary according to course level and program. *Unit head:* Dr. Edith Neumann, Vice President for Academic Affairs, College of Health Sciences, 714-816-0366 Ext. 2030, Fax: 714-226-9844, E-mail: eneumann@tourou.edu.

Universidad de las Americas, A.C., Program in Business Administration, Mexico City, Mexico. Offers finance (MBA); marketing research (MBA); production and quality (MBA).

University of Miami, Graduate School, School of Business Administration, Department of Management Science, Coral Gables, FL 33124. Offers management science (MS), including applied statistics, operations research, quality management. Part-time and evening/weekend programs available. Postbaccalaureate distance learning degree programs offered. *Faculty:* 9 full-time (1 woman). *Students:* 3 full-time (1 woman), 3 part-time (1 woman); includes 2 minority (both Asian Americans or Pacific Islanders), 1 international. Average age 36. 7 applicants, 71% accepted, 3 enrolled. In 2006, 1 degree awarded. *Degree requirements:* For master's, thesis optional. *Entrance requirements:* For master's, GRE General Test. Additional exam requirements/recommendations for international students: Required—TOEFL. *Application deadline:* For fall admission, 6/30 priority date for domestic students; for spring admission, 10/31 for domestic students. Applications are processed on a rolling basis. Application fee: $50. *Financial support:* Career-related internships or fieldwork and Federal Work-Study available. Financial award application deadline: 3/1. *Faculty research:* Mathematical programming, applied probability, logistics, statistical process control. Total annual research expenditures: $20,000. *Unit head:* Dr. Anuj Mehrotra, Chairman, 305-284-6595, Fax: 305-284-2321, E-mail: anuj@miami.edu. *Application contact:* Dr. Howard Gitlow, Director, 305-284-4296, Fax: 305-284-2321, E-mail: hgitlow@miami.edu.

Upper Iowa University, Online Master's Programs, Fayette, IA 52142-1857. Offers accounting (MBA); corporate financial management (MBA); global business (MBA); health and human services (MPA); homeland security (MPA); human resources management (MBA); justice administration (MPA); organizational development (MBA); public personnel management (MPA); quality management (MBA). MBA also available at Madison, Wisconsin campus. Part-time and evening/weekend programs available. Postbaccalaureate distance learning degree programs offered (no on-campus study). *Degree requirements:* For master's, research project. *Entrance requirements:* For master's, GMAT, GRE, or minimum GPA of 2.7 during last 60 hours. Additional exam requirements/recommendations for international students: Required—TOEFL (minimum score 570 paper-based; 230 computer-based). Electronic applications accepted. *Faculty research:* Total quality management, CQI, teams, organization culture and climate, management.

Webster University, School of Business and Technology, Department of Management, St. Louis, MO 63119-3194. Offers business and organizational security management (MA); computer resources and information management (MA); environmental management (MS); health care management (MA); health services management (MA); human resources development (MA); human resources management (MA); management (DM); management and leadership (MA); marketing (MA); procurement and acquisitions management (MA); public administration (MA); quality management (MA); space systems operations management (MS); telecommunications management (MA). Part-time and evening/weekend programs available. Postbaccalaureate distance learning degree programs offered (no on-campus study). *Students:* 1,396 full-time (746 women), 4,727 part-time (2,579 women); includes 3,065 minority (2,374 African Americans, 45 American Indian/Alaska Native, 158 Asian Americans or Pacific Islanders, 488 Hispanic Americans), 128 international. Average age 37. In 2006, 9 degrees awarded. *Degree requirements:* For doctorate, thesis/dissertation, written exam. *Entrance requirements:* For doctorate, GMAT, 3 years of work experience, MBA. *Application deadline:* Applications are processed on a rolling basis. Application fee: $25 ($50 for international students). *Expenses:* Tuition: Full-time $8,820; part-time $490 per credit. Tuition and fees vary according to degree level, campus/location and program. *Financial support:* Federal Work-Study available. Support available to part-time students. Financial award application deadline: 4/1; financial award applicants required to submit FAFSA. *Unit head:* Jeffrey Haldeman, Chair, 314-961-2660 Ext. 7552, Fax: 314-968-7077, E-mail: mgtchair@webster.edu. *Application contact:* Director of Graduate and Evening Student Admissions, Fax: 314-968-7116, E-mail: gadmit@webster.edu.

Section 19
Quantitative Analysis

This section contains a directory of institutions offering graduate work in quantitative analysis, followed by in-depth entries submitted by institutions that chose to prepare detailed program descriptions. Additional information about programs listed in the directory but not augmented by an in-depth entry may be obtained by writing directly to the dean of a graduate school or chair of a department at the address given in the directory.

For programs offering related work, see also in this book Business Administration and Management.

CONTENTS

Program Directory

Close-Ups

Quantitative Analysis

Bernard M. Baruch College of the City University of New York, Zicklin School of Business, Department of Statistics and Computer Information Systems, Program in Decision Sciences, New York, NY 10010-5585. Offers MBA, MS. Part-time and evening/weekend programs available. *Faculty:* 32 full-time (7 women), 22 part-time/adjunct (5 women). *Students:* 4 full-time (1 woman), 25 part-time (7 women); includes 10 minority (6 Asian Americans or Pacific Islanders, 4 Hispanic Americans). *Entrance requirements:* For master's, GMAT, 2 letters of recommendation, resumé, 2 years of work experience. Additional exam requirements/recommendations for international students: Required—TOEFL (minimum score 590 paper-based; 243 computer-based), TWE (minimum score 5). *Application deadline:* For fall admission, 5/31 for domestic students, 4/30 for international students; for spring admission, 10/31 for domestic and international students. Application fee: $125. *Financial support:* Fellowships, research assistantships, teaching assistantships, career-related internships or fieldwork, Federal Work-Study, scholarships/grants, and unspecified assistantships available. Financial award application deadline: 4/30; financial award applicants required to submit FAFSA. *Unit head:* Elsie Gottlieb, Head, 646-312-3380, Fax: 646-312-3351, E-mail: elsie_gottlieb@baruch.cuny.edu. *Application contact:* Frances Murphy, Office of Graduate Admissions, 646-312-1300, Fax: 646-312-1301, E-mail: zicklingradadmissions@baruch.cuny.edu.

California State University, East Bay, Academic Programs and Graduate Studies, College of Business and Economics, Department of Management and Finance, Option in Quantitative Business Methods, Hayward, CA 94542-3000. Offers MS. Part-time and evening/weekend programs available. *Degree requirements:* For master's, comprehensive exam or thesis. *Entrance requirements:* For master's, GMAT, minimum GPA of 2.75. *Application deadline:* For fall admission, 5/31 for domestic students, 4/30 for international students; for winter admission, 9/30 for domestic and international students; for spring admission, 12/31 for domestic students, 11/30 for international students. Application fee: $55. *Financial support:* Federal Work-Study and institutionally sponsored loans available. Support available to part-time students. Financial award application deadline: 3/2. *Unit head:* Doris Duncan, Director of Graduate Programs, 510-885-3364, Fax: 510-885-2176, E-mail: doris.duncan@csueastbay.edu.

Clark Atlanta University, School of Business Administration, Department of Decision Science, Atlanta, GA 30314. Offers MBA. Part-time programs available. *Entrance requirements:* For master's, GMAT.

Drexel University, LeBow College of Business, Department of Decision Sciences, Philadelphia, PA 19104-2875. Offers MS. *Entrance requirements:* For master's, GMAT, minimum GPA of 2.75. Additional exam requirements/recommendations for international students: Required—TOEFL. Electronic applications accepted.

Drexel University, LeBow College of Business, Program in Business Administration, Philadelphia, PA 19104-2875. Offers business administration (MBA, PhD, APC), including accounting (MBA, PhD), decision sciences (PhD), economics (MBA, PhD), finance (MBA, PhD), legal studies (MBA), management (MBA, PhD), marketing (MBA, PhD), organizational sciences (PhD), quantitative methods (MBA), strategic management (PhD). *Accreditation:* AACSB. Part-time and evening/weekend programs available. Postbaccalaureate distance learning degree programs offered (minimal on-campus study). Terminal master's awarded for partial completion of doctoral program. *Entrance requirements:* For master's, GMAT, minimum GPA of 2.75; for doctorate, GMAT. Additional exam requirements/recommendations for international students: Required—TOEFL. Electronic applications accepted. *Faculty research:* Decision support systems, individual and group behavior, operations research, techniques and strategy.

Hofstra University, Frank G. Zarb School of Business, Department of Business Computer Information Systems/Quantitative Methods, Hempstead, NY 11549. Offers business computer information systems (MBA); computer information systems (MS); quality management (MBA). Part-time and evening/weekend programs available. *Faculty:* 11 full-time (3 women). *Students:* 4 full-time (0 women), 26 part-time (6 women); includes 6 minority (1 African American, 5 Asian Americans or Pacific Islanders), 1 international. Average age 31. 14 applicants, 86% accepted, 8 enrolled. In 2006, 10 degrees awarded. *Degree requirements:* For master's, thesis or alternative, registration. *Entrance requirements:* For master's, GMAT, 2 letters of recommendation, resumé, essay. Additional exam requirements/recommendations for international students: Required—TOEFL (minimum score 550 paper-based; 213 computer-based). *Application deadline:* Applications are processed on a rolling basis. Application fee: $60. Electronic applications accepted. *Expenses:* Tuition: Full-time $13,320; part-time $740 per credit. Required fees: $930; $155 per term. *Financial support:* In 2006–07, 5 students received support, including 5 fellowships with tuition reimbursements available (averaging $10,844 per year); research assistantships with full and partial tuition reimbursements available, career-related internships or fieldwork, Federal Work-Study, scholarships/grants, tuition waivers (full and partial), and unspecified assistantships also available. Financial award applicants required to submit FAFSA. *Faculty research:* Decision support systems, econometrics-public issues, forecasting, LPT sizing-quality, enterprise planning systems-SAP. *Unit head:* Dr. John F. Affisco, Chairperson, 516-463-5362, E-mail: acsjfa@hofstra.edu. *Application contact:* Carol Drummer, Dean of Graduate Admissions, 516-463-4876, Fax: 516-463-4664, E-mail: gradstudent@hofstra.edu.

Lehigh University, College of Business and Economics, Department of Finance, Bethlehem, PA 18015-3094. Offers analytical finance (MS); finance (MS). *Faculty:* 13 full-time (2 women), 2 part-time/adjunct (1 woman). *Students:* 12 full-time (1 woman), 24 part-time (6 women); includes 2 minority (both Asian Americans or Pacific Islanders), 10 international. Average age 22. 44 applicants, 75% accepted, 7 enrolled. In 2006, 20 degrees awarded. *Degree requirements:* For master's, capstone project. *Entrance requirements:* For master's, GMAT or GRE, bachelor's degree from a mathematically rigorous program, minimum GPA of 3.0. Additional exam requirements/recommendations for international students: Required—TOEFL (minimum score 600 paper-based; 250 computer-based). *Application deadline:* For fall admission, 7/15 for domestic students, 5/1 for international students. Applications are processed on a rolling basis. Application fee: $60. Electronic applications accepted. *Expenses: Contact institution. Unit head:* Richard Kish, Co-Director, 610-758-4205, E-mail: rjk7@lehigh.edu. *Application contact:* Mary- Theresa Taglang, Director of Graduate Programs, 610-758-5285, Fax: 610-758-5283, E-mail: mtt4@lehigh.edu.

See Close-Up on page 715.

Loyola College in Maryland, Graduate Programs, Sellinger School of Business and Management, Program in Business Administration, Baltimore, MD 21210-2699. Offers decision sciences (MBA); economics (MBA); finance (MBA); marketing/management (MBA). *Accreditation:* AACSB. Part-time and evening/weekend programs available. *Students:* 47 full-time (17 women), 733 part-time (315 women); includes 111 minority (59 African Americans, 1 American Indian/Alaska Native, 37 Asian Americans or Pacific Islanders, 14 Hispanic Americans), 19 international. Average age 31. In 2006, 215 degrees awarded. *Entrance requirements:* For master's, GMAT. Additional exam requirements/recommendations for international students: Required—TOEFL (minimum score 550 paper-based; 213 computer-based). *Application deadline:* For fall admission, 8/15 priority date for domestic students; for spring admission, 11/20 priority date for domestic students. Applications are processed on a rolling basis. Application fee: $50. *Financial support:* Applicants required to submit FAFSA. *Unit head:* Ann Attanasio, Director, 410-617-2308, E-mail: aattanasio@loyola.edu.

New York University, Robert F. Wagner Graduate School of Public Service, Program in Public Administration, New York, NY 10012-1019. Offers public administration (PhD); public and nonprofit management and policy (MPA, Advanced Certificate), including developmental administration (Advanced Certificate), financial management and public finance, human resources management (Advanced Certificate), international administration (Advanced Certificate), management (MPA), management for public and nonprofit organizations (Advanced Certificate), public policy analysis, quantitative analysis and computer applications (Advanced Certificate), urban public policy (Advanced Certificate); JD/MPA; MBA/MPA; MPA/MA. *Accreditation:* NASPAA (one or more programs are accredited). Part-time and evening/weekend programs available. *Faculty:* 16 full-time (10 women), 42 part-time/adjunct (23 women). *Students:* 260 full-time (189 women), 246 part-time (182 women); includes 114 minority (40 African Americans, 2 American Indian/Alaska Native, 45 Asian Americans or Pacific Islanders, 27 Hispanic Americans), 44 international. Average age 28. 867 applicants, 60% accepted, 176 enrolled. In 2006, 209 master's, 5 doctorates awarded. *Degree requirements:* For master's, thesis or alternative, capstone/end event; for doctorate, one foreign language, thesis/dissertation. *Entrance requirements:* For master's, minimum undergraduate GPA of 3.0; for doctorate, GMAT or GRE General Test, minimum GPA of 3.5. Additional exam requirements/recommendations for international students: Required—TOEFL (minimum score 600 paper-based; 250 computer-based), TWE (minimum score 4). *Application deadline:* For fall admission, 6/1 for domestic students, 1/15 for international students; for spring admission, 11/15 for domestic students, 10/1 for international students. Applications are processed on a rolling basis. Application fee: $70. Electronic applications accepted. *Expenses: Contact institution.* Tuition and fees vary according to program. *Financial support:* In 2006–07, 142 fellowships (averaging $9,749 per year), 4 research assistantships with partial tuition reimbursements (averaging $15,000 per year) were awarded; career-related internships or fieldwork, Federal Work-Study, institutionally sponsored loans, scholarships/grants, health care benefits, and unspecified assistantships also available. Support available to part-time students. Financial award application deadline: 12/1; financial award applicants required to submit FAFSA. *Unit head:* Prof. Katherine O'Regan, Director, 212-998-7400, Fax: 212-995-4161. *Application contact:* Bethany Godsoe, Assistant Dean, Enrollment and Student Services, 212-998-7414, Fax: 212-995-4164, E-mail: wagner.admissions@nyu.edu.

Purdue University, Graduate School, Krannert School of Management, Department of Management, West Lafayette, IN 47907. Offers accounting (PhD); business administration (MBA); finance (PhD); management information systems (PhD); marketing (PhD); operations management (PhD); quantitative methods (PhD); strategic management (PhD). *Students:* 56 full-time (21 women); includes 5 minority (3 Asian Americans or Pacific Islanders, 2 Hispanic Americans), 41 international. Average age 30. 421 applicants, 7% accepted, 19 enrolled. In 2006, 11 degrees awarded. *Median time to degree:* Doctorate–5 years full-time. Of those who began their doctoral program in fall 1998, 98% received their degree in 8 years or less. *Degree requirements:* For doctorate, thesis/dissertation, comprehensive exam, registration. *Entrance requirements:* For master's and doctorate, GMAT. Additional exam requirements/recommendations for international students: Required—TOEFL (minimum score 575 paper-based; 233 computer-based; 77 iBT), IELTS (minimum score 7). *Application deadline:* For fall admission, 2/15 for domestic and international students. Application fee: $55. Electronic applications accepted. *Financial support:* In 2006–07, 7 fellowships with partial tuition reimbursements (averaging $16,800 per year), 79 research assistantships with partial tuition reimbursements (averaging $16,800 per year), 8 teaching assistantships with partial tuition reimbursements (averaging $16,800 per year) were awarded; scholarships/grants and unspecified assistantships also available. Financial award application deadline: 2/15; financial award applicants required to submit FAFSA. *Faculty research:* Corporate finance, international business, enterprise integration. *Unit head:* Dr. John M. Barron, Head, 765-494-4451, Fax: 765-494-1526. *Application contact:* Kelly Felty, Assistant Director of Administration for Doctoral Programs, 765-494-4375, Fax: 765-494-1526, E-mail: phd@krannert.purdue.edu.

St. John's University, The Peter J. Tobin College of Business, Department of Computer Information Systems and Decision Sciences, Queens, NY 11439. Offers MBA, Adv C. Part-time and evening/weekend programs available. *Faculty:* 13 full-time (0 women), 5 part-time/adjunct (2 women). *Students:* 3 full-time (1 woman), 10 part-time (4 women); includes 5 minority (3 African Americans, 1 Asian American or Pacific Islander, 1 Hispanic American), 2 international. Average age 30. 19 applicants, 16% accepted, 0 enrolled. In 2006, 6 degrees awarded. *Degree requirements:* For master's, thesis optional. *Entrance requirements:* For master's, GMAT, minimum GPA of 3.0. Additional exam requirements/recommendations for international students: Required—TOEFL (minimum score 500 paper-based; 173 computer-based). *Application deadline:* For fall admission, 5/1 priority date for domestic and international students; for spring admission, 11/1 priority date for domestic and international students. Applications are processed on a rolling basis. Application fee: $40. Electronic applications accepted. *Expenses: Contact institution.* Tuition and fees vary according to program. *Financial support:* Research assistantships, scholarships/grants available. Support available to part-time students. Financial award application deadline: 3/1; financial award applicants required to submit FAFSA. *Unit head:* Dr. Victor Lu, Chair, 718-990-7382. *Application contact:* Nicole T. Bryan, Assistant Dean, 718-990-2599, Fax: 718-990-5242, E-mail: mbaadmissions@stjohns.edu.

Saint Joseph's University, Erivan K. Haub School of Business, Professional MBA Program, Program in Decision and System Sciences, Philadelphia, PA 19131-1395. Offers information systems (MBA). Part-time and evening/weekend programs available. *Faculty:* 4 full-time (1 woman), 5 part-time/adjunct (2 women). *Students:* 11 full-time (4 women), 14 part-time (6 women); includes 2 minority (1 African American, 1 Asian American or Pacific Islander), 11 international. Average age 28. In 2006, 6 degrees awarded. *Entrance requirements:* For master's, GMAT, 2 letters of recommendation, resumé. Additional exam requirements/recommendations for international students: Required—TOEFL. *Application deadline:* For fall admission, 7/15 for domestic students, 4/15 for international students; for spring admission, 11/15 for domestic students, 10/15 for international students. Applications are processed on a rolling basis. Application fee: $35. Electronic applications accepted. *Financial support:* In 2006–07, teaching assistantships with partial tuition reimbursements (averaging $2,500 per year); unspecified assistantships also available. Financial award application deadline: 5/1. *Unit head:* Dr. Richard Herschel, Chair, 610-660-1621, E-mail: herschel@sju.edu.

Syracuse University, Martin J. Whitman School of Management, PhD Program in Business Administration, Syracuse, NY 13244. Offers accounting (PhD); finance (PhD); management information systems (PhD); managerial statistics (PhD); marketing (PhD); operations management (PhD); organizational behavior (PhD); strategy and human resources (PhD); supply chain management (PhD). *Faculty:* 71 full-time (16 women), 2 part-time/adjunct (1 woman). *Students:* 34 full-time (10 women); includes 1 minority (African American), 24 international. Average age 31. 89 applicants, 8% accepted, 4 enrolled. In 2006, 8 degrees awarded. *Degree requirements:* For doctorate, thesis/dissertation, summer research paper, comprehensive exam, registration. *Entrance requirements:* For doctorate, GMAT, 3 recommendations. Additional exam requirements/recommendations for international students: Required—TOEFL (minimum score 600 paper-based; 250 computer-based; 100 iBT). *Application deadline:* For fall admission, 1/30 priority date for domestic students. Applications are processed on a rolling basis. Application fee: $75. Electronic applications accepted. *Expenses:* Tuition: Full-time $16,920; part-time $940 per credit hour. Required fees: $930; $930 per year. *Financial support:* In 2006–07, 1 fellowship with full tuition reimbursement (averaging $19,000 per year), 26 teaching assistantships with full tuition reimbursements (averaging $16,500 per year) were awarded; research assistantships with full tuition reimbursements, health care benefits and unspecified assistantships also available. Financial award application deadline: 1/30. *Faculty research:* Marketing models, market microstructure, supply chain, auditing, corporate governance. *Unit head:* Dr. Ravi Dharwadkar, Director of the PhD Program, 315-443-3386, E-mail: rdharwad@syr.edu. *Application contact:* Shannon Hiemstra, Assistant Director for PhD and Research Programs, 315-443-3549, Fax: 315-443-3671, E-mail: srhiemst@syr.edu.

Texas Tech University, Jerry S. Rawls College of Business Administration, Area of Information Systems and Quantitative Sciences, Lubbock, TX 79409. Offers business statistics (MS, PhD); health organization management (MS); management information systems (MS, PhD); production and operations management (MS, PhD). Part-time programs available. *Faculty:* 15

full-time (0 women). *Students:* 18 full-time (6 women), 6 part-time (1 woman); includes 2 minority (1 African American, 1 Hispanic American), 11 international. Average age 31. 32 applicants, 53% accepted, 11 enrolled. In 2006, 13 master's, 5 doctorates awarded. Terminal master's awarded for partial completion of doctoral program. *Degree requirements:* For master's, comprehensive exam or capstone course; for doctorate, thesis/dissertation, qualifying exams. *Entrance requirements:* For master's and doctorate, GMAT, holistic profile of academic credentials. Additional exam requirements/recommendations for international students: Required—TOEFL (minimum score 550 paper-based; 213 computer-based; 79 iBT). *Application deadline:* For fall admission, 7/1 priority date for domestic students, 3/1 priority date for international students; for spring admission, 11/1 priority date for domestic students, 9/1 priority date for international students. Applications are processed on a rolling basis. Application fee: $50 ($60 for international students). Electronic applications accepted. *Expenses:* Tuition, state resident: full-time $4,440. Tuition, nonresident: full-time $11,040. Required fees: $2,136. *Financial support:* In 2006–07, 2 research assistantships (averaging $8,000 per year), 9 teaching assistantships (averaging $16,930 per year) were awarded; Federal Work-Study, scholarships/grants, and unspecified assistantships also available. *Faculty research:* Database management systems, systems management and engineering, expert systems and adaptive knowledge-based sciences, statistical analysis and design. *Unit head:* Dr. James Hoffman, Area Coordinator, 806-742-3192, Fax: 806-742-3958, E-mail: james.hoffman@ttu.edu. *Application contact:* Cynthia D. Barnes, Director, Graduate Services Center, 806-742-3184, Fax: 806-742-3958, E-mail: ba_grad@ttu.edu.

The University of British Columbia, Faculty of Arts and Faculty of Graduate Studies, Department of Psychology, Vancouver, BC V6T 1Z1, Canada. Offers behavioral neuroscience (MA, PhD); clinical psychology (MA, PhD); cognitive science (MA, PhD); developmental psychology (MA, PhD); forensic psychology (MA, PhD); health psychology (MA, PhD); quantitative methods (MA, PhD); social/personality psychology (MA, PhD). *Accreditation:* APA (one or more programs are accredited). *Faculty:* 47 full-time (18 women), 18 part-time/adjunct (14 women). *Students:* 95 full-time (66 women). Average age 29. 276 applicants, 9% accepted, 14 enrolled. In 2006, 17 master's, 8 doctorates awarded. Terminal master's awarded for partial completion of doctoral program. *Median time to degree:* Master's–2 years full-time; doctorate–4.2 years full-time. Of those who began their doctoral program in fall 1998, 92% received their degree in 8 years or less. *Degree requirements:* For master's, thesis/dissertation; for doctorate, thesis/dissertation, comprehensive exam, registration (for some programs). *Entrance requirements:* For master's and doctorate, GRE General Test, GRE Subject Test. Additional exam requirements/recommendations for international students: Required—TOEFL (minimum score 550 paper-based; 230 computer-based; 80 iBT). *Application deadline:* For fall admission, 1/15 for domestic and international students. Applications are processed on a rolling basis. Application fee: $90 Canadian dollars ($150 Canadian dollars for international students). Electronic applications accepted. *Financial support:* In 2006–07, 22 fellowships with full and partial tuition reimbursements (averaging $17,500 per year), 48 research assistantships with full and partial tuition reimbursements (averaging $5,000 per year), 81 teaching assistantships with full and partial tuition reimbursements (averaging $10,000 per year) were awarded; career-related internships or fieldwork, Federal Work-Study, institutionally sponsored loans, scholarships/grants, health care benefits, tuition waivers (full and partial), and unspecified assistantships also available. Financial award application deadline: 1/15. *Faculty research:* Clinical, developmental, social/personality, cognition, behavioral neuroscience. Total annual research expenditures: $6 million Canadian dollars. *Unit head:* Dr. Eric Eich, Head, 604-822-3078, Fax: 604-822-6923, E-mail: ee@psych.ubc.ca. *Application contact:* Rose Tam, Graduate Secretary, 604-822-3144, Fax: 604-822-6923, E-mail: gradsec@psych.ubc.ca.

University of California, Santa Barbara, Graduate Division, College of Letters and Sciences, Division of Mathematics, Life, and Physical Sciences, Department of Statistics and Applied Probability, Santa Barbara, CA 93106. Offers applied statistics (MA); mathematical and empirical finance (PhD); mathematical statistics (MA); quantitative methods in the social sciences (PhD); statistics and applied probability (PhD). *Students:* 43 full-time (15 women); includes 12 minority (1 African American, 8 Asian Americans or Pacific Islanders, 3 Hispanic Americans), 16 international. Average age 28. 97 applicants, 38% accepted, 13 enrolled. In 2006, 13 master's, 7 doctorates awarded. Terminal master's awarded for partial completion of doctoral program. *Median time to degree:* Master's–1.5 years full-time; doctorate–5.67 years full-time. Of those who began their doctoral program in fall 1998, 25% received their degree in 8 years or less. *Degree requirements:* For master's and doctorate, thesis/dissertation, comprehensive exam, registration. *Entrance requirements:* For master's and doctorate, GRE General Test. Additional exam requirements/recommendations for international students: Required—TOEFL (minimum score 550 paper-based; 213 computer-based; 80 iBT). *Application deadline:* For fall admission, 4/15 for domestic and international students; for winter admission, 11/15 for domestic and international students; for spring admission, 2/15 for domestic and international students. Applications are processed on a rolling basis. Application fee: $60. Electronic applications accepted. *Financial support:* In 2006–07, 1 fellowship with full tuition reimbursement (averaging $20,000 per year), 1 research assistantship with full tuition reimbursement (averaging $4,983 per year), 24 teaching assistantships with partial tuition reimbursements (averaging $11,165 per year) were awarded; health care benefits and tuition waivers (partial) also available. Financial award application deadline: 1/15; financial award applicants required to submit FAFSA. *Faculty research:* Bayesian methods, statistics including biostatistics, stochastic processes, probability, mathematical finance. *Unit head:* Dr. Raya E. Feldman, Chairman, 805-893-2826, Fax: 805-893-2334, E-mail: feldman@pstat.ucsb.edu. *Application contact:* Andrew V. Carter, Assistant Professor, 805-893-3299, Fax: 805-893-2334, E-mail: carter@pstat.ucsb.edu.

University of Cincinnati, Division of Research and Advanced Studies, College of Business, Department of Quantitative Analysis and Operations Management, Cincinnati, OH 45221. Offers operations management (MBA, PhD); quantitative analysis (MBA, MS, PhD). Part-time and evening/weekend programs available. *Degree requirements:* For master's, capstone project (MBA); for doctorate, thesis/dissertation. *Entrance requirements:* For master's, GMAT, GRE General Test (MS), resumé, letters of recommendation; for doctorate, GMAT, GRE General Test. Application fee: $40. Electronic applications accepted. *Expenses:* Contact institution. *Financial support:* Fellowships, research assistantships, teaching assistantships, scholarships/grants, tuition waivers (full and partial), and unspecified assistantships available. Financial award application deadline: 2/1; financial award applicants required to submit FAFSA. *Unit head:* Dr. Jeffrey D. Camm, Head, 513-556-7146, Fax: 513-556-5499.

University of Florida, Graduate School, Warrington College of Business Administration, Programs in Business Administration, Gainesville, FL 32611. Offers accounting (MBA); arts administration (MBA); business strategy and public policy (MBA); competitive strategy (MBA); decision and information sciences (MBA); electronic commerce (MBA); finance (MBA); general business (MBA); global management (MBA); Graham-Buffett security analysis (MBA); health administration (MBA); human resources management (MBA); international studies (MBA); Latin American business (MBA); management (MBA); marketing (MBA); sports administration (MBA); JD/MBA; MBA/MS; MBA/PhD; MBA/Pharm D; MD/MBA. *Accreditation:* AACSB. Part-time and evening/weekend programs available. Postbaccalaureate distance learning degree programs offered. *Faculty:* 14. *Students:* 950 (282 women); includes 189 minority (31 African Americans, 2 American Indian/Alaska Native, 66 Asian Americans or Pacific Islanders, 90 Hispanic Americans) 56 international. In 2006, 481 degrees awarded. *Entrance requirements:* For master's, GMAT, minimum GPA of 3.0, interview. Additional exam requirements/recommendations for international students: Required—TOEFL (minimum score 550 paper-based; 213 computer-based). *Application deadline:* For fall admission, 4/15 for domestic students; for winter admission, 10/15 priority date for domestic students; for spring admission, 2/15 for domestic students. Applications are processed on a rolling basis. Application fee: $30. Electronic applications accepted. *Expenses:* Tuition, state resident: full-time $6,827. Tuition, nonresident: full-time $21,951. Required fees: $999. *Financial support:* Fellowships, research assistantships, teaching assistantships, career-related internships or fieldwork, scholarships/grants, and unspecified assistantships available. Support available to part-time students.

Financial award application deadline: 2/15; financial award applicants required to submit FAFSA. *Faculty research:* Accounting, finance, insurance, management, real estate and urban analysis marketing. *Unit head:* Alex Sevilla, Director, 352-392-7992 Ext. 1206. *Application contact:* Patrick Foran, Associate Director of Admissions, 352-392-7992 Ext. 282, Fax: 352-392-8791, E-mail: patrick.foran@cba.ufl.edu.

University of Missouri–St. Louis, College of Business Administration, Program in Business Administration, St. Louis, MO 63121. Offers accounting (MBA); business administration (Certificate); finance (MBA); human resource management (Certificate); logistics and supply chain management (MBA, Certificate); management (MBA); marketing (MBA); marketing management (Certificate); operations (MBA); quantitative management science (MBA); telecommunications management (Certificate). *Accreditation:* AACSB. Part-time and evening/weekend programs available. *Faculty:* 26 full-time (6 women), 2 part-time/adjunct (0 women). *Students:* 242 full-time (156 women), 186 part-time (123 women); includes 48 minority (17 African Americans, 1 American Indian/Alaska Native, 27 Asian Americans or Pacific Islanders, 3 Hispanic Americans), 96 international. Average age 33. In 2006, 138 degrees awarded. *Entrance requirements:* For master's, GMAT, 2 letters of recommendation. Additional exam requirements/recommendations for international students: Required—TOEFL (minimum score 550 paper-based; 213 computer-based). *Application deadline:* For fall admission, 7/1 for domestic students; for spring admission, 11/1 for domestic students. Applications are processed on a rolling basis. Application fee: $35 ($40 for international students). Electronic applications accepted. *Expenses:* Tuition, state resident: part-time $332 per credit hour. Tuition, nonresident: part-time $770 per credit hour. *Financial support:* Research assistantships with full and partial tuition reimbursements, teaching assistantships with full and partial tuition reimbursements, career-related internships or fieldwork, Federal Work-Study, and institutionally sponsored loans available. Support available to part-time students. Financial award application deadline: 4/1; financial award applicants required to submit FAFSA. *Faculty research:* Human resources, strategic management, marketing strategy, consumer behavior product development, advertising. *Application contact:* 314-516-5458, Fax: 314-516-6996, E-mail: gradadm@umsl.edu.

University of North Texas, Robert B. Toulouse School of Graduate Studies, College of Business Administration, Department of Information Technology and Decision Sciences, Denton, TX 76203. Offers decision technologies (MS); information systems (PhD); information technology (MS); management science (PhD). Part-time and evening/weekend programs available. *Faculty:* 25 full-time (4 women). *Students:* 22 full-time (7 women), 19 part-time (2 women); includes 4 minority (3 African Americans, 1 Hispanic American), 21 international. Average age 31. 40 applicants, 83% accepted, 7 enrolled. In 2006, 15 master's, 2 doctorates awarded. *Degree requirements:* For doctorate, thesis/dissertation. *Entrance requirements:* For master's, GMAT; for doctorate, GMAT or GRE General Test. Additional exam requirements/recommendations for international students: Required—TOEFL (minimum score 550 paper-based; 213 computer-based). *Application deadline:* For fall admission, 7/15 for domestic students. Application fee: $50 ($75 for international students). *Expenses:* Tuition, state resident: full-time $3,573; part-time $198 per credit. Tuition, nonresident: full-time $8,577; part-time $476 per credit. Required fees: $1,258; $126 per credit. One-time fee: $150 full-time. Tuition and fees vary according to course load. *Financial support:* Fellowships, research assistantships, teaching assistantships, career-related internships or fieldwork and Federal Work-Study available. Financial award application deadline: 4/1. *Faculty research:* Databases, systems design, expert systems, applied statistics, quality and reliability management. *Unit head:* Dr. Marg Jones, Interim Chair, 940-565-3110, Fax: 940-565-4935, E-mail: jonesm@unt.edu. *Application contact:* Dr. Wayne Spence, Graduate Adviser, 940-565-3110, Fax: 940-565-4935, E-mail: spence@unt.edu.

University of Oregon, Graduate School, Charles H. Lundquist College of Business, Department of Decision Sciences, Eugene, OR 97403. Offers MA, MS. In 2006, 1 degree awarded. *Entrance requirements:* For master's, GMAT. *Application deadline:* For fall admission, 2/1 for domestic students. Application fee: $50. *Financial support:* Teaching assistantships, career-related internships or fieldwork and Federal Work-Study available. *Faculty research:* Time-series analysis, production scheduling, nonparametric methods, decision theory. *Unit head:* Sergio Koreisha, Head, 541-346-3377. *Application contact:* Perri McGee, Admissions Contact, 541-346-1462, E-mail: pcrone@uoregon.edu.

The University of Texas at Arlington, Graduate School, College of Business Administration, Department of Finance and Real Estate, Arlington, TX 76019. Offers quantitative finance (MS); real estate (MS). Part-time and evening/weekend programs available. *Faculty:* 13 full-time (3 women). *Students:* 43 full-time (11 women), 32 part-time (6 women); includes 18 minority (2 African Americans, 12 Asian Americans or Pacific Islanders, 4 Hispanic Americans), 21 international. 62 applicants, 76% accepted, 27 enrolled. In 2006, 12 degrees awarded. *Degree requirements:* For master's, thesis optional. *Entrance requirements:* For master's, GMAT, minimum GPA of 3.0. Additional exam requirements/recommendations for international students: Required—TOEFL (minimum score 550 paper-based; 213 computer-based). *Application deadline:* For fall admission, 6/15 priority date for domestic students. Applications are processed on a rolling basis. Application fee: $35 ($50 for international students). *Expenses:* Tuition, state resident: full-time $5,528. Tuition, nonresident: full-time $10,478. International tuition: $10,608 full-time. *Financial support:* In 2006–07, 3 fellowships (averaging $1,000 per year), 14 teaching assistantships (averaging $10,000 per year) were awarded; research assistantships, career-related internships or fieldwork, Federal Work-Study, and institutionally sponsored loans also available. Financial award application deadline: 6/1; financial award applicants required to submit FAFSA. *Unit head:* Dr. David Diltz, Chair, 817-272-3705, Fax: 817-272-2252, E-mail: diltz@uta.edu. *Application contact:* Dr. Scott Lowrance, Graduate Adviser, 817-272-3705, Fax: 817-272-2252, E-mail: realestate@uta.edu.

The University of Texas at Arlington, Graduate School, College of Business Administration, Program in Business Administration, Arlington, TX 76019. Offers accounting (PhD); business administration (PhD); business statistics (PhD); finance (MBA); information systems (MBA, PhD); management (MBA); management sciences (MBA); marketing (MBA, PhD); real estate (MBA). *Accreditation:* AACSB. Part-time and evening/weekend programs available. Postbaccalaureate distance learning degree programs offered (no on-campus study). *Faculty:* 1 full-time (0 women). *Students:* 156 full-time (60 women), 319 part-time (110 women); includes 123 minority (38 African Americans, 4 American Indian/Alaska Native, 52 Asian Americans or Pacific Islanders, 29 Hispanic Americans), 88 international. 502 applicants, 85% accepted, 199 enrolled. In 2006, 417 master's, 11 doctorates awarded. Terminal master's awarded for partial completion of doctoral program. *Degree requirements:* For master's, thesis optional; for doctorate, thesis/dissertation. *Entrance requirements:* For master's, GMAT; for doctorate, GMAT, minimum GPA of 3.0 (undergraduate), 3.4 (graduate); 30 hours of graduate course work. Additional exam requirements/recommendations for international students: Required—TOEFL (minimum score 550 paper-based; 213 computer-based). *Application deadline:* For fall admission, 6/15 for domestic students, 4/1 for international students; for spring admission, 10/15 for domestic students, 9/1 for international students. Applications are processed on a rolling basis. Application fee: $35 ($50 for international students). Electronic applications accepted. *Expenses:* Tuition, state resident: full-time $5,528. Tuition, nonresident: full-time $10,478. International tuition: $10,608 full-time. *Financial support:* In 2006–07, 1 fellowship (averaging $1,000 per year), 14 research assistantships (averaging $6,432 per year) were awarded; teaching assistantships, career-related internships or fieldwork, scholarships/grants, and unspecified assistantships also available. Financial award application deadline: 6/1; financial award applicants required to submit FAFSA. *Application contact:* Dr. Mike West, Assistant Dean, 817-272-1287, Fax: 817-272-5799, E-mail: mpwest@uta.edu.

See Close-Up on page 363.

Virginia Commonwealth University, Graduate School, School of Business, Program in Decision Sciences, Richmond, VA 23284-9005. Offers MBA. In 2006, 4 degrees awarded. *Entrance requirements:* For master's, GMAT. *Application deadline:* Applications are processed

Quantitative Analysis

Virginia Commonwealth University (continued)
on a rolling basis. Application fee: $50. *Financial support:* Fellowships, research assistantships, teaching assistantships, Federal Work-Study, institutionally sponsored loans, and tuition waivers (full and partial) available. Financial award application deadline: 3/15. *Unit head:* Dr. Glenn H. Gilbreath, Chair, 804-828-6468, Fax: 804-828-8884, E-mail: ghgilbre@vcu.edu. *Application contact:* Tracy Green, Graduate Program Director, 804-828-1741, Fax: 804-828-7174, E-mail: tsgreen@vcu.edu.

Walden University, Graduate Programs, School of Management, Minneapolis, MN 55401. Offers applied management and decision sciences (PhD). Part-time and evening/weekend programs available. Postbaccalaureate distance learning degree programs offered (minimal on-campus study). *Faculty:* 264. *Students:* 2,212 full-time (1,216 women), 752 part-time (390 women); includes 756 minority (626 African Americans, 11 American Indian/Alaska Native, 49 Asian Americans or Pacific Islanders, 70 Hispanic Americans), 22 international. Average age 40. 967 applicants, 83% accepted, 600 enrolled. In 2006, 267 master's, 55 doctorates awarded. *Degree requirements:* For doctorate, thesis/dissertation, brief dispersed residency sessions. *Entrance requirements:* For master's, minimum GPA of 3.0; for doctorate, 3 years of professional experience, master's degree. Additional exam requirements/recommendations for international students: Required—TOEFL (minimum score 550 paper-based; 213 computer-based), IELTS (minimum score 7). *Application deadline:* For fall admission, 8/15 priority date for domestic and international students; for winter admission, 11/15 priority date for domestic and international students; for spring admission, 12/15 priority date for domestic and international students. Applications are processed on a rolling basis. Application fee: $50. Electronic applications accepted. *Financial support:* In 2006–07, 1 fellowship with partial tuition reimbursement (averaging $750 per year) was awarded; scholarships/grants and tuition waivers (partial) also available. Support available to part-time students. Financial award application deadline: 6/1; financial award applicants required to submit FAFSA. *Faculty research:* International business, organizational behavior, entrepreneurship, economics, HR management. *Unit head:* Dr. Kathleen Simmons, Chair, 800-925-3368, Fax: 612-338-5092. *Application contact:* 866-4-WALDEN, Fax: 410-843-8780, E-mail: request@waldenu.edu.

LEHIGH UNIVERSITY

College of Business and Economics
Master of Science in Analytical Finance

Programs of Study	The field of analytical finance is a quickly emerging area of study that integrates finance, applied mathematics, computing, and engineering. It fulfills a market demand for specialists in financial firms who can bridge the gap between financial analysts and technical professionals. The Master of Science (M.S.) in analytical finance at Lehigh University—a joint program between the Department of Industrial and Systems Engineering and the Perella Department of Finance, with strong support from the Department of Mathematics—provides students with a rigorous education in advanced finance and quantitative financial analysis tools.
	The innovative curriculum provides key concepts in financial theory, mathematical finance, and engineering. The program explores and provides a concrete understanding of mathematics; hones quantitative modeling, computing, and IT skills; and introduces sophisticated financial and economic modeling, producing professionals instrumental in creating innovative solutions for real financial problems using state-of-the-art analytical techniques and computing technology. Continual hands-on experiences using the state-of-the-art wireless Financial Services Lab (FSL) give students the opportunity to work in a dynamic environment with real-time information. A highly interactive project provided by industry professionals rounds out the curriculum.
Research Facilities	The Financial Services Laboratory is a focal point for bringing together key constituent groups across the campus—undergraduate and graduate students, campus-wide faculty members, the corporate community, and alumni. The wireless, state-of-the-art laboratory allows students to test dynamic implementation of real-time data in a simulated environment and provides a practical learning experience.
	The College of Business and Economics (CBE) has a number of centers and institutes to provide greater research and academic opportunities for students and faculty members, which complement the scholarly activities of academic departments. Research centers and institutes include the E-Collaboration Research Center, the Iacocca Institute, the Martindale Center for the Study of Private Enterprise, the Murray H. Goodman Center for Real Estate Studies, the Musser Center for Entrepreneurship, the Rauch Center for Business Communication, the Small Business Development Center, and the Center for Value Chain Research.
Financial Aid	Financial aid is ordinarily available only for regular, full-time graduate students. Teaching assistantships, research assistantships, graduate assistantships, fellowships, and scholarships are academic awards made by individual academic departments. Several graduate assistantships unrelated to a particular area of study can be obtained by applying to the administrative offices. International students are also encouraged to apply for funding to outside sponsoring agencies and/or home governments.
Cost of Study	In 2007–08, tuition is $760 per credit hour.
Living and Housing Costs	Rental rates for on-campus graduate student apartments range from $470 per month plus utilities for an efficiency apartment to $625 per month plus utilities for a three-bedroom apartment.
Student Group	This highly quantitative degree attracts students from engineering, mathematics, and other quantitative areas.
Student Outcomes	The class of 2006 was fully employed within three months of graduation.
Location	Lehigh's picturesque 1,600-acre wooded campus is actually built into the side of what is affectionately known as "Old South Mountain" in historic Bethlehem, Pennsylvania. A little more than an hour's car ride from Philadelphia or New York City, Lehigh is located within the thriving economic and cultural corridor of the eastern United States.
The University and The College	Graduate study at Lehigh University revolves around a commitment to excellence in teaching and research that dates back to 1882, when the University first began awarding graduate degrees. Today, Lehigh graduate students across the University's four colleges enjoy the benefits of the institution's reputation as one of the most selective national universities in the country, including its state-of-the-art laboratories and research centers, well-equipped libraries, and vast technology resources.
	Lehigh's College of Business and Economics offers its graduate students a cutting-edge curriculum, which is designed to mirror business functions and decision making from the perspective of the firm as a whole. CBE graduates acquire the skills and abilities that are required of future leaders in an ever-changing business environment. Academic excellence, an outstanding faculty, and an unparalleled student body offer full- and part-time students an intellectually stimulating environment.
Applying	Applicants must have earned a baccalaureate from a mathematically rigorous program such as computer science, economics, engineering, mathematics, operations research, or the sciences (physics/chemistry). Four years of university-level study are necessary for entry into Lehigh University. Applicants must also have the proper background courses necessary to pursue the M.S. in analytical finance. An applicant is expected to have completed introduction to finance; corporate finance; investment and portfolio management; financial accounting; principles of economics; money, banking, and financial markets; statistics (including regression analysis); calculus (three terms); and linear algebra. Those without the proper background may receive a conditional offer of admission and are required to satisfactorily complete foundation course work prior to beginning regular M.S. course work.
	Applicants must submit a data sheet, a personal statement, a resume, GRE or GMAT scores, official transcripts from all universities attended, two letters of recommendation (professional or academic), and the $65 application fee. International applicants must submit Test of English as a Foreign Language (TOEFL) scores and must provide a financial guarantee to show sufficient funds for the first year of study.
	The recommended deadline is May 1, but applications are accepted until July 15. International applicants must apply by May 1. Admission decisions are made on a rolling basis, and applicants receive notice approximately two weeks after a complete application is made. Students begin the program in the summer or fall semester.
Correspondence and Information	Corinn McBride Director of Recruitment and Admissions College of Business and Economics Lehigh University 621 Taylor Street Bethlehem, Pennsylvania 18015 Phone: 610-758-5280 Fax: 610-758-5283 E-mail: business@lehigh.edu Web site: http://www3.lehigh.edu/business/cbegmsanalyticalfin.asp

Lehigh University

THE FACULTY AND THEIR RESEARCH

Mark R. Adams, Professor of Practice, Business Minor Program; M.B.A., Pittsburgh; J.D., Baltimore; CFA, CPA. Accounting, corporate reporting, finance, capital evaluations and investments.

Anne-Marie Anderson, Assistant Professor of Finance; M.B.A., Tulsa, 1998; Ph.D., Arizona, 2003. Corporate restructuring, mergers and acquisitions, valuation.

J. Richard Aronson, William L. Clayton Professor of Business and Economics and Director, Martindale Center for the Study of Private Enterprise; Ph.D., Clark, 1964. Tax and expenditure analysis, pension funds, municipal bond analysis, fiscal federalism.

Richard W. Barsness, Professor Emeritus; Ph.D., Minnesota, 1963. International business, corporate strategy in the airline industry.

John W. Bonge, Professor Emeritus; Ph.D., Northwestern, 1968. Business strategy and entrepreneurship.

Paul R. Brown, Professor of Accounting and Dean, College of Business and Economics; Ph.D., Texas at Austin. Financial statement analysis, FASB/SEC policy analysis, international reporting and analysis, earnings measurement and management, managing earnings expectations.

Stephen G. Buell, Professor; Ph.D., Lehigh, 1977. High-yield bonds, corporate bankruptcy.

Franklin J. Carter, Assistant Professor of Marketing; Ph.D., Carnegie Mellon, 1997. Business-to-business marketing, sales force management, diffusion of innovation.

Ravi Chitturi, Assistant Professor of Marketing; M.B.A., 1996, Ph.D., 2003, Texas at Austin. Technology and innovation, design and consumer emotions, brand value and marketing strategy.

Shin-Yi Chou, Assistant Professor of Economics; Ph.D., Duke, 1999. Health economics.

Karen M. Collins, Associate Professor; Ph.D., Virginia Tech, 1988. Behavioral dimensions of public accounting practice (including stress, turnover, and upward mobility of women), ethnic diversity.

James A. Dearden, Professor; Ph.D., Penn State, 1987. Game theory, marketing science, institution design, microeconomics.

Mary E. Deily, Associate Professor; Ph.D., Harvard, 1985. Industrial organization, exit behavior, industries in transition.

Dale F. Falcinelli, Swartley Professor of Finance, Professor of Practice in Marketing and Management, and Chairman, vSeries Corporate Entrepreneurship; M.A., Lehigh, 1972. Contemporary marketing, business management policies, entrepreneurship, strategic business analysis.

Robert C. Giambatista, Assistant Professor of Management; Ph.D., Wisconsin–Madison, 1999. Leadership, groups, decision making, diversity.

Paul Gordon, Professor of Practice; M.B.A., Wisconsin–Madison; CPA. Financial accounting.

James A. Greenleaf, Associate Professor; Ph.D., NYU, 1973. Portfolio management, derivative instruments, international investments, quantitative applications to investments.

Frank Gunter, Associate Professor; Ph.D., Johns Hopkins, 1985. Economies of Colombia, Iraq, China, and Latvia; capital flight; customs; unions.

Parveen P. Gupta, Frank L. McGee Professor of Accounting; Ph.D., Penn State, 1987. Process redesign through reengineering and benchmarking within manufacturing and service organizations; assessment of business risks and controls within the value chain; business valuation; financial analysis, corporate governance, and internal auditing.

Reetika Gupta, Assistant Professor of Marketing; Ph.D., CUNY, Baruch. Complexity in interactive consumption environments, consumer learning of new products.

James A. Hall, Associate Professor; Ph.D., Oklahoma State, 1979. Systems design, internal control of systems, computer systems auditing.

Thomas J. Hyclak, Professor; Ph.D., Notre Dame, 1976. Labor market developments in transition economies, urban economic development.

Arthur E. King, Professor; Ph.D., Ohio State, 1976. Applied econometrics, comparative economics, economics of Central Europe.

Richard J. Kish, Professor; Ph.D., Florida, 1988. Fixed-income securities, efficient markets, international mergers.

Michael D. Kolchin, Professor; D.B.A., Indiana, 1980. Comparative buying processes, purchasing education and training, purchasing effectiveness, supply chain management optimization.

Nevena T. Koukova, Assistant Professor of Marketing; Ph.D., Maryland, 2005. Pricing of digital products, bundling and unbundling of electronic content, and behavioral aspects of bundling; marketing strategy; consumer analysis; marketing research; principles of marketing; services marketing.

Robert Kuchta, Professor of Practice; M.S., NJIT, 1982. Marketing as a business.

James A. Largay, Professor; Ph.D., Cornell, 1971. Cash flow reporting, intercorporate investments, derivative financial investments.

James M. Maskulka, Associate Professor; D.B.A., Kent State, 1984. Marketing communications, branding, media.

Teresa McCarthy, Assistant Professor of Supply Chain Management; Ph.D., Tennessee, 2003. Role of marketing in demand management, demand planning and demand forecasting, market orientation and supply chain orientation, collaboration forecasting and sales force forecasting management, e-commerce demand management.

Judith A. McDonald, Associate Professor; Ph.D., Princeton, 1986. United States–Canada economic relations, external debt and tropical deforestation issues, pay equity, gender differences in starting salaries.

Matthew A. Melone, Associate Professor; J.D., Pennsylvania, 1993. Taxation, law and accounting, real estate law, partnership and LLC taxation.

Erin Moore, Assistant Professor of Accounting; Ph.D., Massachusetts, 2006; CPA. Earnings restatements, firm valuation.

Vincent G. Munley, Professor; Ph.D., SUNY at Binghamton, 1979. Political economy of state and local government finances.

David H. Myers, Professor of Practice; Ph.D., Washington (Seattle), 2001. Conditional performance measurement of mutual funds; pension funds, portfolio strategies, Japanese equity markets, international investing, stochastic programming applications for asset/liability management.

George A. Nation III, Professor; J.D., Villanova, 1983. Commercial lending law topics, environmental liability for lenders, promissory notes, guaranty and surety law, product liability.

Nandkumar Nayar, Professor and Hans Baer Chair in Finance; Ph.D., Iowa, 1988. Investment banking and financing methods, derivative securities, working capital management, tax issues, game theory modeling.

Anthony P. O'Brien, Professor; Ph.D., Berkeley, 1986. Business history, economic history, microeconomics.

John W. Paul, Professor; Ph.D., Lehigh, 1978. Audits of small businesses, audits of information systems, statistical sampling in auditing, cost allocation, activity-based costing.

Catherine M. Ridings, Assistant Professor; Ph.D., Drexel, 2000. Virtual communities, trust, e-commerce, management of technical personnel.

Heibatollah Sami, Eugene and Sue Mercy Professor of Accounting; Ph.D., Louisiana State, 1984. Impact of accounting information on capital markets, international accounting, auditing.

Michael D. Santoro, Associate Professor; Ph.D., Rutgers, 1998. Organizational strategy, entrepreneurship and intrapreneurship, sources of technological innovation, role of industry-university collaboration in advancing new technologies.

Theodore W. Schlie, Associate Professor; Ph.D., Northwestern, 1973. Advanced manufacturing and competitive strategy, globalization of industrial research and development, international competitiveness.

Susan A. Sherer, Kenan Professor of Information Technology Management, Business Information Systems Program Director, and Co-director for the Center for Value Chain Research; Ph.D., Pennsylvania, 1988. Software failure risk, management of software development, manufacturing networks, interorganizational information systems, strategic information systems, IT investment management.

Kenneth P. Sinclair, Professor and Accounting Department Chairman; Ph.D., Massachusetts, 1972. Performance evaluation, human resource accounting, case studies in managerial accounting.

K. Sivakumar, Arthur Tauck Professor of International Marketing and Logistics and Professor and Chairperson of Marketing; Ph.D., Syracuse, 1992. Pricing, international marketing, innovation management.

Quingjiu (Tom) Tao, Assistant Professor of Management; Ph.D., Pittsburgh, 2004. Strategic alliance in emerging market environments, institutions and firm behavior, first mover advantage in international market entry.

Larry W. Taylor, Professor; Ph.D., North Carolina, 1984. Specification testing for economic models, finite-sample issues in econometrics, econometric methodology, macroeconomic modeling, qualitative dependent variables.

Stephen F. Thode, Associate Professor and Director, Goodman Center for Real Estate Studies; D.B.A., Indiana, 1980. New mortgage products, mortgage pricing, affordable housing financing, taxation of real estate investments, real option pricing.

Robert J. Thornton, Charles W. MacFarlane Professor of Economics and Program Director; Ph.D., Illinois, 1970. Unionism and collective bargaining, public employment, labor market discrimination, forensic economics.

Robert J. Trent, Associate Professor and Program Director, Supply Chain Management Program; Ph.D., Michigan State, 1993. Cross-functional teams in purchasing.

Geraldo M. Vasconcellos, Allen DuBois Professor of Finance and Economics and Director, Business Minor Program; Ph.D., Illinois at Urbana-Champaign, 1986. Cross-border mergers and acquisitions foreign direct investment, international financial markets, privatizations, financial structure and development.

Todd A. Watkins, Associate Professor; Ph.D., Harvard, 1986. Technology and industrial policy, economics and management of innovation, defense and optoelectronics industries.

Samuel C. Weaver, Swartley Professor of Finance; Ph.D., Lehigh, 1985. Value-based management, performance metrics, capital evaluation, cost of capital, mergers and acquisitions.

Wenlong Weng, Assistant Professor; Ph.D., Stanford, 2001. Managerial economics, planning and decision making under uncertainty, real options, financial risk measurement and management.

Yuliang (Oliver) Yao, Assistant Professor of Business Information Systems; M.B.A., Rensselaer, 1997; Ph.D., Maryland, 2002. Supply chain management, electronic commerce, technology issues in supply chains, logistics modeling/simulation.

Section 20
Real Estate

This section contains a directory of institutions offering graduate work in real estate, followed by in-depth entries submitted by institutions that chose to prepare detailed program descriptions. Additional information about programs listed in the directory but not augmented by an in-depth entry may be obtained by writing directly to the dean of a graduate school or chair of a department at the address given in the directory.

For programs offering related work, see also in this book Business Administration and Management.

CONTENTS

Program Directory

Close-Ups

Real Estate

American University, Kogod School of Business, Department of Finance, Program in Real Estate, Washington, DC 20016-8001. Offers MBA. Part-time and evening/weekend programs available. *Students:* 8 full-time (2 women), 6 part-time (2 women); includes 6 minority (5 African Americans, 1 Hispanic American). Average age 29. In 2006, 13 degrees awarded. *Entrance requirements:* For master's, GMAT. Additional exam requirements/recommendations for international students: Required—TOEFL. *Application deadline:* For fall admission, 2/1 priority date for domestic students; for spring admission, 10/1 priority date for domestic students. Applications are processed on a rolling basis. Application fee: $50. *Expenses:* Tuition: Full-time $18,864; part-time $1,048 per credit. Required fees: $380. Tuition and fees vary according to program. *Financial support:* Fellowships, career-related internships or fieldwork, Federal Work-Study, and institutionally sponsored loans available. Support available to part-time students. Financial award application deadline: 2/1.

Bentley College, The Elkin B. McCallum Graduate School of Business, Program in Real Estate Management, Waltham, MA 02452-4705. Offers MSREM. Part-time and evening/weekend programs available. Postbaccalaureate distance learning degree programs offered (minimal on-campus study). *Students:* 8 full-time (4 women), 12 part-time (5 women); includes 1 minority (Asian American or Pacific Islander), 1 international. Average age 29. 28 applicants, 86% accepted, 16 enrolled. *Entrance requirements:* For master's, GMAT. Additional exam requirements/recommendations for international students: Required—TOEFL (minimum score 600 paper-based; 250 computer-based). *Application deadline:* For fall admission, 6/1 priority date for domestic students, 3/1 priority date for international students; for spring admission, 11/1 priority date for domestic and international students. Applications are processed on a rolling basis. Application fee: $50. Electronic applications accepted. *Expenses:* Tuition: Full-time $28,440; part-time $2,844 per course. Required fees: $404; $105 per year. *Financial support:* Research assistantships, scholarships/grants and unspecified assistantships available. Financial award application deadline: 4/12; financial award applicants required to submit CSS PROFILE or FAFSA. *Unit head:* David Milton, Unit Head, 781-891-2734. *Application contact:* Sharon Hill, Director of Graduate Admissions, 781-891-2108, Fax: 781-891-2464, E-mail: shill@bentley.edu.

California State University, Sacramento, Graduate Studies, College of Business Administration, Program in Business Administration, Sacramento, CA 95819-6048. Offers business administration (MBA); human resources (MBA); urban land development (MBA). *Accreditation:* AACSB. Part-time programs available. *Students:* 26 full-time (16 women), 66 part-time (23 women); includes 20 minority (13 Asian Americans or Pacific Islanders, 7 Hispanic Americans), 6 international. Average age 30. 229 applicants, 69% accepted, 22 enrolled. *Degree requirements:* For master's, thesis or alternative, writing proficiency exam. *Entrance requirements:* For master's, GMAT. Additional exam requirements/recommendations for international students: Required—TOEFL. *Application deadline:* Applications are processed on a rolling basis. Application fee: $55. Electronic applications accepted. *Financial support:* Research assistantships, teaching assistantships, career-related internships or fieldwork and Federal Work-Study available. Support available to part-time students. Financial award application deadline: 3/1.

Central European University, CEU Business School, Budapest, Hungary. Offers finance (MBA); general management (MBA); information technology (M Sc); information technology management (MBA); management (EMBA); marketing (MBA); real estate management (MBA). Part-time and evening/weekend programs available. *Faculty:* 15 full-time (3 women), 30 part-time/adjunct (9 women). *Students:* 47 full-time (18 women), 158 part-time (22 women). Average age 32. 450 applicants, 43% accepted, 160 enrolled. In 2006, 77 degrees awarded. *Entrance requirements:* For master's, GMAT. Additional exam requirements/recommendations for international students: Required—TOEFL (minimum score 570 paper-based; 230 computer-based). *Application deadline:* For fall admission, 5/22 priority date for domestic students, 5/22 for international students; for winter admission, 11/13 priority date for domestic students, 11/13 for international students. Applications are processed on a rolling basis. Application fee: $0. Electronic applications accepted. *Financial support:* In 2006–07, 4 students received support, including research assistantships with partial tuition reimbursements available (averaging $3,800 per year); tuition waivers (partial) and GMAT-based tuition fee discounts also available. *Faculty research:* Social and ethical business, marketing. Total annual research expenditures: 11,000 euros. *Unit head:* Dr. Paul Garrison, Dean and Managing Director, 36-18875050, Fax: 36-18875001, E-mail: garrisonp@ceubusiness.com. *Application contact:* Tunde Hegedus, MBA Program Manager, 36-18875060, Fax: 36-18875133, E-mail: mba@ceubusiness.com.

Clemson University, Graduate School, College of Architecture, Arts, and Humanities, Department of Planning and Landscape Architecture and College of Business and Behavioral Science, Program in Real Estate Development, Clemson, SC 29634. Offers MRED. *Students:* 30 full-time (4 women), 2 part-time; includes 4 minority (3 African Americans, 1 Hispanic American). 49 applicants, 65% accepted, 19 enrolled. In 2006, 6 degrees awarded. *Entrance requirements:* For master's, GRE or GMAT, 3 letters of recommendation. Additional exam requirements/recommendations for international students: Required—TOEFL (minimum score 600 paper-based). *Application deadline:* For fall admission, 2/1 for domestic students, 4/15 for international students. Application fee: $50. *Expenses:* Tuition, state resident: full-time $8,812; part-time $450 per hour. Tuition, nonresident: full-time $18,036; part-time $760 per hour. Required fees: $474; $5 per term. *Unit head:* Dr. Terry Farris, Coordinator, 864-656-3903, Fax: 864-656-0204, E-mail: jfarris@clemson.edu. *Application contact:* Admissions, 864-656-3926, Fax: 864-656-7519.

See Close-Up on page 723.

Clemson University, Graduate School, College of Business and Behavioral Science and Department of Planning and Landscape Architecture, Program in Real Estate Development, Clemson, SC 29634. Offers MRED. *Students:* 30 full-time (4 women), 2 part-time; includes 4 minority (3 African Americans, 1 Hispanic American). 49 applicants, 65% accepted, 17 enrolled. In 2006, 6 degrees awarded. *Entrance requirements:* For master's, GRE or GMAT, 3 letters of recommendation. Additional exam requirements/recommendations for international students: Required—TOEFL. *Application deadline:* For fall admission, 2/1 for domestic students, 4/15 for international students. Application fee: $50. *Expenses:* Tuition, state resident: full-time $8,812; part-time $450 per hour. Tuition, nonresident: full-time $18,036; part-time $760 per hour. Required fees: $474; $5 per term. *Unit head:* Dr. Terry Farris, Coordinator, 864-656-3903, Fax: 864-656-0204, E-mail: jfarris@clemson.edu.

See Close-Up on page 723.

Cleveland State University, College of Graduate Studies, Maxine Goodman Levin College of Urban Affairs, Program in Urban Planning, Design, and Development, Cleveland, OH 44115. Offers urban economic development (Certificate); urban planning, design, and development (MUPDD); urban real estate development and finance (Certificate); JD/MUPDD. *Accreditation:* ACSP. Part-time and evening/weekend programs available. *Faculty:* 25 full-time (10 women), 11 part-time/adjunct (3 women). *Students:* 25 full-time (10 women), 46 part-time (23 women); includes 13 minority (12 African Americans, 1 Asian American or Pacific Islander), 7 international. Average age 30. 63 applicants, 59% accepted, 20 enrolled. In 2006, 7 degrees awarded. *Degree requirements:* For master's, project or thesis. *Entrance requirements:* For master's, GRE General Test, minimum GPA of 3.0. Additional exam requirements/recommendations for international students: Required—TOEFL (minimum score 525 paper-based; 197 computer-based). *Application deadline:* For fall admission, 7/15 priority date for domestic students. Applications are processed on a rolling basis. Application fee: $30. *Financial support:* In 2006–07, 6 research assistantships with full and partial tuition reimbursements (averaging $6,960 per year) were awarded; teaching assistantships with full and partial tuition reimbursements, career-related internships or fieldwork, Federal Work-Study, tuition waivers (full and partial), and unspecified assistantships also available. Support available to part-time students. Financial award application deadline: 3/1. *Faculty research:* Community development, environmental issues. *Unit head:* Dr. Wendy A. Kellogg, Director, 216-687-5265, Fax: 216-687-9342, E-mail: wendy@urban.csuohio.edu. *Application contact:* Graduate Programs Coordinator, 216-523-7522, Fax: 216-687-5398, E-mail: gradprog@urban.csuohio.edu.

Columbia University, Graduate School of Architecture, Planning, and Preservation, Program in Real Estate Development, New York, NY 10027. Offers MS. *Degree requirements:* For master's, thesis, registration. *Entrance requirements:* For master's, GRE General Test.

Columbia University, Graduate School of Business, MBA Program, New York, NY 10027. Offers accounting (MBA); decision, risk, and operations (MBA); entrepreneurship (MBA); finance and economics (MBA); human resource management (MBA); international business (MBA); management (MBA); marketing (MBA); media (MBA); real estate (MBA); social enterprise (MBA); DDS/MBA; JD/MBA; MBA/MIA; MBA/MPH; MBA/MS; MD/MBA. *Faculty:* 118 full-time (14 women), 106 part-time/adjunct (18 women). *Students:* 1,242 full-time (428 women); includes 291 minority (65 African Americans, 5 American Indian/Alaska Native, 189 Asian Americans or Pacific Islanders, 32 Hispanic Americans), 392 international. Average age 28. 5,372 applicants, 17% accepted, 726 enrolled. In 2006, 682 degrees awarded. *Entrance requirements:* For master's, GMAT, 2 letters of recommendation. Additional exam requirements/recommendations for international students: Required—TOEFL. *Application deadline:* For fall admission, 4/20 for domestic students, 3/1 for international students; for spring admission, 10/12 for domestic and international students. Applications are processed on a rolling basis. Application fee: $215. Electronic applications accepted. *Financial support:* Fellowships, research assistantships, teaching assistantships, career-related internships or fieldwork, Federal Work-Study, institutionally sponsored loans, scholarships/grants, and unspecified assistantships available. Financial award applicants required to submit FAFSA. *Unit head:* Prof. Amir Ziv, Vice Dean of Students and the MBA Program, 212-854-3485, Fax: 212-932-0545, E-mail: az50@columbia.edu. *Application contact:* Linda B. Meehan, Assistant Dean of Admissions, 212-854-1961, Fax: 212-662-6754, E-mail: apply@claven.gsb.columbia.edu.

Cornell University, Graduate School, Graduate Fields of Architecture, Art and Planning, Field of Real Estate, Ithaca, NY 14853-0001. Offers MPSRE. *Faculty:* 20 full-time (1 woman). *Students:* 34 full-time (11 women); includes 4 minority (all Asian Americans or Pacific Islanders), 15 international. Average age 29. 52 applicants, 62% accepted, 18 enrolled. In 2006, 15 degrees awarded. *Degree requirements:* For master's, project paper. *Entrance requirements:* For master's, GMAT, 2 letters of recommendation, resumé. Additional exam requirements/recommendations for international students: Required—TOEFL (minimum score 600 paper-based; 250 computer-based). *Application deadline:* For fall admission, 1/15 for domestic students. Application fee: $60. Electronic applications accepted. *Expenses:* Tuition: Full-time $32,800. Full-time tuition and fees vary according to program. *Financial support:* In 2006–07, 15 students received support, including 1 fellowship with full tuition reimbursement available, 14 teaching assistantships with full tuition reimbursements available; research assistantships with full tuition reimbursements available, institutionally sponsored loans, scholarships/grants, health care benefits, and unspecified assistantships also available. Financial award applicants required to submit FAFSA. *Faculty research:* Smart growth, economic development, urban redevelopment, development financing, securitization of real estate. *Unit head:* Director of Graduate Studies, 607-255-7110, Fax: 607-255-0242. *Application contact:* Graduate Field Assistant, 607-255-7110, Fax: 607-255-0242, E-mail: real_estate@cornell.edu.

DePaul University, Charles H. Kellstadt Graduate School of Business, Department of Finance, Chicago, IL 60604-2287. Offers behavioral finance (MBA); computational finance (MS); finance (MBA, MSF); financial analysis (MBA); financial management and control (MBA); international marketing and finance (MBA); managerial finance (MBA); real estate (MS); real estate finance and investment (MBA); strategy, execution and valuation (MBA). Part-time and evening/weekend programs available. *Faculty:* 21 full-time (3 women), 19 part-time/adjunct (1 woman). *Students:* 309 full-time (90 women), 212 part-time (57 women); includes 70 minority (14 African Americans, 41 Asian Americans or Pacific Islanders, 15 Hispanic Americans), 54 international. Average age 29. In 2006, 239 degrees awarded. *Entrance requirements:* For master's, GMAT, 2 letters of recommendation, resumé. Additional exam requirements/recommendations for international students: Required—TOEFL (minimum score 550 paper-based; 213 computer-based). *Application deadline:* For fall admission, 7/1 for domestic students; for winter admission, 10/1 for domestic students; for spring admission, 2/1 for domestic students. Applications are processed on a rolling basis. Application fee: $60. Electronic applications accepted. *Financial support:* In 2006–07, 8 students received support, including 6 research assistantships with partial tuition reimbursements available (averaging $5,100 per year). Support available to part-time students. Financial award application deadline: 4/1; financial award applicants required to submit FAFSA. *Faculty research:* Derivatives, valuation, international finance, real estate, corporate finance. *Unit head:* Ali M. Falemi, Professor and Chair, 312-362-8820, Fax: 312-362-6566. *Application contact:* Christopher E. Kinsella, Director of Cohort MBA Programs, 312-362-8810, Fax: 312-362-6677, E-mail: kgsb@depaul.edu.

Florida Atlantic University, College of Business, Department of Management, International Business and Entrepreneurship, Boca Raton, FL 33431-0991. Offers business administration (Exec MBA, MBA), including accounting (MBA), electronic commerce (MBA), finance (MBA), financial planning (MBA), global entrepreneurship (MBA), health administration (MBA), international business (MBA), marketing (MBA), operations management (MBA), real estate (MBA), sport management (MBA). *Faculty:* 64 full-time (17 women), 15 part-time/adjunct (3 women). *Students:* 215 full-time (89 women), 365 part-time (189 women); includes 150 minority (49 African Americans, 2 American Indian/Alaska Native, 36 Asian Americans or Pacific Islanders, 63 Hispanic Americans), 54 international. Average age 32. 414 applicants, 55% accepted, 167 enrolled. In 2006, 196 master's awarded. *Degree requirements:* For master's, thesis optional. *Entrance requirements:* For master's, GMAT, minimum GPA of 3.0. Additional exam requirements/recommendations for international students: Required—TOEFL (minimum score 600 paper-based; 250 computer-based). *Application deadline:* For fall admission, 7/1 priority date for domestic students, 2/15 priority date for international students; for winter admission, 11/1 priority date for domestic students, 8/15 priority date for international students; for spring admission, 4/1 priority date for domestic students, 1/15 priority date for international students. Applications are processed on a rolling basis. Application fee: $30. Electronic applications accepted. *Expenses:* Tuition, area resident: Full-time $4,394. Tuition, nonresident: full-time $16,441. *Financial support:* Research assistantships, teaching assistantships, career-related internships or fieldwork, Federal Work-Study, institutionally sponsored loans, tuition waivers (partial), and unspecified assistantships available. Support available to part-time students. Financial award application deadline: 3/1; financial award applicants required to submit FAFSA. *Unit head:* Dr. Brenda Richey, Head, 561-297-3194, E-mail: brichey@fau.edu. *Application contact:* Fredrick G. Taylor, Graduate Adviser, 561-297-2768, Fax: 561-297-1315, E-mail: mba@fau.edu.

The George Washington University, School of Business, Department of Finance, Program in Real Estate Development, Washington, DC 20052. Offers MBA. Part-time and evening/weekend programs available. *Entrance requirements:* For master's, GMAT. Additional exam requirements/recommendations for international students: Required—TOEFL.

Georgia State University, J. Mack Robinson College of Business, Department of Real Estate, Atlanta, GA 30303-3083. Offers MBA, MSRE, PhD, Certificate. Part-time and evening/weekend programs available. *Faculty:* 7 full-time (1 woman). *Students:* 20 full-time (9 women), 41 part-time (9 women); includes 14 minority (9 African Americans, 4 Asian Americans or Pacific Islanders, 1 Hispanic American), 8 international. Average age 30. 38 applicants, 68% accepted, 17 enrolled. In 2006, 20 master's, 1 doctorate awarded. Terminal master's awarded for partial completion of doctoral program. *Degree requirements:* For doctorate, thesis/dissertation. *Entrance requirements:* For master's and doctorate, GMAT. Additional exam requirements/recommendations for international students: Required—TOEFL (minimum score 610 paper-based; 255 computer-based; 101 iBT). *Application deadline:* For fall admission, 5/1 for domestic students, 2/1 for international students; for spring admission, 10/15 for domestic students, 5/1 for international students. Applications are processed on a rolling basis. Application fee: $50. *Financial support:* Fellowships, research assistantships, teaching assistantships, career-related internships or fieldwork and tuition waivers (partial) available. Support available to part-time students. Financial award applicants required to submit FAFSA. *Unit head:* Dr. Julian Diaz, Interim Chair, 404-651-2760, Fax: 404-651-3396, E-mail: jdiaz@gsu.edu. *Application contact:* Dr. Alan J. Ziobrowski, Director of Graduate Studies, 404-651-4610, E-mail: aziobrowski@gsu.edu.

John Marshall Law School, Graduate and Professional Programs, Chicago, IL 60604-3968. Offers comparative legal studies (LL M); employee benefits (LL M, MS); information technology (LL M, MS); intellectual property (LL M); international business and trade (LL M); law (JD); real estate (LL M, MS); taxation (LL M, MS); JD/LL M; JD/MA; JD/MBA; JD/MPA. *Accreditation:* ABA. Part-time and evening/weekend programs available. *Faculty:* 64 full-time (23 women), 113 part-time/adjunct (29 women). *Students:* 1,157 full-time (479 women), 421 part-time (187 women); includes 253 minority (76 African Americans, 10 American Indian/Alaska Native, 101 Asian Americans or Pacific Islanders, 66 Hispanic Americans), 48 international. Average age 27. 3,169 applicants, 37% accepted, 333 enrolled. In 2006, 347 JDs, 69 master's awarded. *Entrance requirements:* For JD, LSAT; for master's, JD. Additional exam requirements/recommendations for international students: Required—TOEFL. *Application deadline:* For fall admission, 3/1 priority date for domestic and international students; for spring admission, 10/15 priority date for domestic and international students. Applications are processed on a rolling basis. Application fee: $60. Electronic applications accepted. *Expenses: Contact institution. Financial support:* In 2006–07, 1,339 students received support. Scholarships/grants and tuition waivers (full and partial) available. Support available to part-time students. Financial award application deadline: 6/1; financial award applicants required to submit FAFSA. *Unit head:* John Corkery, Dean, 312-427-2737. *Application contact:* William B. Powers, Associate Dean of Admission and Student Affairs, 800-537-4280, Fax: 312-427-5136, E-mail: admission@jmls.edu.

The Johns Hopkins University, Carey Business School, The Edward St. John Department of Real Estate, Baltimore, MD 21218-2699. Offers MS. Part-time and evening/weekend programs available. *Students:* 21 full-time (4 women), 124 part-time (38 women); includes 24 minority (14 African Americans, 6 Asian Americans or Pacific Islanders, 4 Hispanic Americans). Average age 32. 133 applicants, 53% accepted, 55 enrolled. In 2006, 39 degrees awarded. *Degree requirements:* For master's, project. *Entrance requirements:* For master's, GMAT, GRE, or LSAT (full-time only), minimum GPA of 3.0, resumé, work experience, two letters of recommendation. Additional exam requirements/recommendations for international students: Required—TOEFL (minimum score 600 paper-based; 250 computer-based; 100 iBT). *Application deadline:* For fall admission, 5/1 for international students; for spring admission, 10/15 for international students. Applications are processed on a rolling basis. Application fee: $60. *Expenses:* Tuition: Full-time $32,976. Tuition and fees vary according to degree level and program. *Financial support:* Scholarships/grants available. Support available to part-time students. Financial award application deadline: 6/1; financial award applicants required to submit FAFSA. *Unit head:* Dr. Michael Anikeeff, Chair, 410-516-0772, Fax: 410-659-8440. *Application contact:* Robin Reed, Senior Academic Coordinator, 800-gotojhu, Fax: 410-872-1251, E-mail: onestop.admissions@jhu.edu.

Massachusetts Institute of Technology, School of Architecture and Planning, Center for Real Estate, Cambridge, MA 02139-4307. Offers MSRED. *Faculty:* 8 full-time (3 women), 5 part-time/adjunct (0 women). *Students:* 29 full-time (7 women); includes 2 minority (both Asian Americans or Pacific Islanders), 9 international. Average age 29. In 2006, 36 degrees awarded. *Degree requirements:* For master's, thesis. *Entrance requirements:* For master's, GMAT. Additional exam requirements/recommendations for international students: Required—TOEFL. *Application deadline:* For fall admission, 2/15 for domestic students. Application fee: $70. Electronic applications accepted. *Expenses:* Tuition: Full-time $33,400; part-time $525 per unit. Required fees: $200. Part-time tuition and fees vary according to course load. *Financial support:* In 2006–07, 8 fellowships were awarded. *Faculty research:* Real estate finance, foreign investment, land use regulation, affordable housing, design. *Unit head:* David Geltner, Director, 617-253-5131, Fax: 617-258-6991. *Application contact:* Maria Vieira, Associate Director of Education, 617-253-4373.

New York University, School of Continuing and Professional Studies, Real Estate Institute, New York, NY 10012-1019. Offers construction management (MS, Advanced Certificate); real estate (MS, Advanced Certificate). Part-time and evening/weekend programs available. *Faculty:* 11 full-time (2 women), 105 part-time/adjunct (13 women). *Students:* 111 full-time (28 women), 650 part-time (182 women); includes 145 minority (42 African Americans, 62 Asian Americans or Pacific Islanders, 41 Hispanic Americans), 68 international. Average age 31. 375 applicants, 74% accepted, 184 enrolled. In 2006, 112 master's, 40 other advanced degrees awarded. *Degree requirements:* For master's, thesis, comprehensive exam (for some programs). *Entrance requirements:* For master's, GRE General Test or GMAT, 2 years of work experience, resumé, 2 letters of recommendation. Additional exam requirements/recommendations for international students: Required—TOEFL (minimum score 600 paper-based; 250 computer-based; 100 iBT), TWE. *Application deadline:* For fall admission, 3/15 priority date for domestic and international students; for spring admission, 10/15 priority date for domestic students, 8/15 priority date for international students. Applications are processed on a rolling basis. Application fee: $75. *Expenses:* Tuition: Part-time $1,080 per unit. Required fees: $56 per unit. $329 per term. Tuition and fees vary according to program. *Financial support:* In 2006–07, 455 students received support, including fellowships (averaging $1,255 per year); career-related internships or fieldwork and scholarships/grants also available. Support available to part-time students. Financial award application deadline: 3/1; financial award applicants required to submit FAFSA. *Faculty research:* Valuation, real estate capital markets, real estate investment trusts, regional economics. *Unit head:* D. Kenneth Patton, Associate Dean, 212-992-3335, Fax: 212-992-3686, E-mail: dkp2@nyu.edu. *Application contact:* Marcie Burros, Associate Director, 212-992-3335, Fax: 212-992-3686, E-mail: gradadmissions@nyu.edu.

See Close-Up on page 725.

Nova Southeastern University, H. Wayne Huizenga School of Business and Entrepreneurship, Program in Real Estate Development, Fort Lauderdale, FL 33314-7796. Offers MBA. *Entrance requirements:* Additional exam requirements/recommendations for international students: Required—TOEFL (minimum score 550 paper-based; 213 computer-based). Application fee: $50. *Unit head:* Steve Harvey, Assistant Dean, 954-262-5047, Fax: 954-262-3829, E-mail: harvey@nsu.nova.edu. *Application contact:* Karen Goldberg, Assistant Director, 800-672-7223, Fax: 954-262-3822, E-mail: karen@nova.edu.

Pacific States University, College of Business, Los Angeles, CA 90006. Offers accounting (MBA); business administration (DBA); finance (MBA); international business (MBA); management of information technology (MBA); real estate management (MBA). Part-time and evening/weekend programs available. Postbaccalaureate distance learning degree programs offered (no on-campus study). *Faculty:* 3 full-time (0 women), 11 part-time/adjunct (0 women). *Students:* 106 full-time (47 women); includes 10 minority (all Asian Americans or Pacific Islanders), 96 international. Average age 32. 36 applicants, 81% accepted, 26 enrolled. In 2006, 68 degrees awarded. *Entrance requirements:* For master's, minimum undergraduate GPA of 2.5 during last 90 hours of course work. Additional exam requirements/recommendations for international students: Required—TOEFL (minimum score 133 computer-based). *Application deadline:* For fall admission, 8/15 priority date for domestic students; for winter admission, 10/15 priority date for domestic students; for spring admission, 1/15 priority date for domestic students. Applications are processed on a rolling basis. Application fee: $100. *Expenses:* Tuition: Full-time $6,360. Required fees: $1,080. Full-time tuition and fees vary according to course load and degree level. *Financial support:* Fellowships, research assistantships, teaching assistantships, scholarships/grants available. Financial award applicants required to submit FAFSA. *Unit head:* Dr. Kamol Somvichian, Director, 888-200-0383, Fax: 323-731-2383, E-mail: admission@psuca.edu. *Application contact:* Marina Miller, Assistant Director of Admissions, 323-731-2383 Ext. 11, Fax: 323-731-7276, E-mail: admissions@psuca.edu.

Penn State University Park, Graduate School, The Mary Jean and Frank P. Smeal College of Business Administration, State College, University Park, PA 16802-1503. Offers accounting (PhD); business administration (MBA); finance (PhD); management and organization (PhD); management science/operations/logistics (PhD); marketing (PhD); real estate (PhD); supply chain and information systems (PhD). *Students:* 287 full-time (79 women), 5 part-time (2 women); includes 39 minority (22 African Americans, 11 Asian Americans or Pacific Islanders, 6 Hispanic Americans), 93 international. Average age 31. 841 applicants, 31% accepted, 150 enrolled. In 2006, 107 master's, 11 doctorates awarded. *Expenses: Contact institution. Financial support:* In 2006–07, 1 fellowship, 11 research assistantships, 143 teaching assistantships were awarded. Financial award applicants required to submit FAFSA. *Unit head:* Dr. Kenneth B. Thomas, Dean, 814-863-0448, Fax: 814-865-7064, E-mail: j2t@psu.edu.

Roosevelt University, Graduate Division, Walter E. Heller College of Business Administration, School of Real Estate, Chicago, IL 60605-1394. Offers commercial real estate development (Certificate); real estate (MBA, MS). *Students:* 3 full-time (0 women), 12 part-time (6 women); includes 4 minority (1 African American, 3 Hispanic Americans). 28 applicants, 75% accepted. *Unit head:* David Nickerson, Real Estate Chair, 312-281-3377, Fax: 312-281-3290. *Application contact:* Joanne Canyon-Heller, Coordinator of Graduate Admission, 877-APPLY RU, Fax: 312-281-3356, E-mail: applyru@roosevelt.edu.

Texas A&M University, Mays Business School, Real Estate Program, College Station, TX 77843. Offers MLERE. *Faculty:* 45 full-time (7 women). *Students:* 57 full-time (14 women). In 2006, 44 degrees awarded. *Entrance requirements:* For master's, GMAT or GRE. Additional exam requirements/recommendations for international students: Required—TOEFL. *Application deadline:* For fall admission, 3/1 for domestic students; for spring admission, 10/1 for domestic students. Application fee: $50 ($75 for international students). Electronic applications accepted. *Expenses:* Tuition, state resident: full-time $4,697. Tuition, nonresident: full-time $11,297. Required fees: $2,272. *Financial support:* Application deadline: 2/1. *Unit head:* Dr. David Blackwell, Head, 979-845-3514, Fax: 979-845-3884. *Application contact:* Cydney Donnell, Director, 979-845-3514, Fax: 979-458-4104.

University of California, Berkeley, Graduate Division, Haas School of Business, Program in Business, Berkeley, CA 94720-1500. Offers accounting (PhD); business and public policy (PhD); finance (PhD); marketing (PhD); organizational behavior and industrial relations (PhD); real estate (PhD). *Accreditation:* AACSB. *Students:* 83 full-time (28 women); includes 17 minority (14 Asian Americans or Pacific Islanders, 3 Hispanic Americans), 33 international. Average age 30. 347 applicants, 16 enrolled. In 2006, 17 degrees awarded. *Median time to degree:* Of those who began their doctoral program in fall 1998, 88% received their degree in 8 years or less. *Degree requirements:* For doctorate, thesis/dissertation, oral exam, written preliminary exams, comprehensive exam. *Entrance requirements:* For doctorate, GMAT or GRE, minimum GPA of 3.0. Additional exam requirements/recommendations for international students: Required—TOEFL (minimum score 570 paper-based; 230 computer-based), IELTS (minimum score 7). *Application deadline:* For fall admission, 12/15 for domestic and international students. Application fee: $60 ($80 for international students). Electronic applications accepted. *Financial support:* Fellowships with full and partial tuition reimbursements, research assistantships with full and partial tuition reimbursements, teaching assistantships with full and partial tuition reimbursements, career-related internships or fieldwork, Federal Work-Study, scholarships/grants, health care benefits, tuition waivers (full), and unspecified assistantships available. Financial award application deadline: 12/15; financial award applicants required to submit FAFSA. *Unit head:* Miguel Villas-Boas, Director, 510-642-1409, Fax: 510-643-4255, E-mail: kimg@haas.berkeley.edu. *Application contact:* Kim Guilfoyle, Administrative Director, 510-642-3944, Fax: 510-643-4255, E-mail: kimg@haas.berkeley.edu.

University of Denver, Daniels College of Business, School of Real Estate and Construction Management, Denver, CO 80208. Offers construction management (IMBA, MS); real estate (IMBA, MBA, MS). Part-time programs available. *Faculty:* 4 full-time (0 women). *Students:* 59 full-time (10 women), 84 part-time (17 women); includes 17 minority (5 African Americans, 1 American Indian/Alaska Native, 6 Asian Americans or Pacific Islanders, 5 Hispanic Americans), 14 international. Average age 31. 120 applicants, 88% accepted. In 2006, 52 degrees awarded. *Entrance requirements:* For master's, GMAT. *Application deadline:* For fall admission, 1/15 priority date for domestic students. Applications are processed on a rolling basis. Application fee: $50. Electronic applications accepted. *Expenses:* Tuition: Full-time $29,628; part-time $823 per credit. *Financial support:* In 2006–07, 70 students received support. Career-related internships or fieldwork, Federal Work-Study, institutionally sponsored loans, and scholarships/grants available. Support available to part-time students. Financial award application deadline: 2/15; financial award applicants required to submit FAFSA. *Unit head:* Dr. Mark Levine, Director, 303-871-2142. *Application contact:* Information Contact, 303-871-3416, Fax: 303-871-4466, E-mail: daniels@du.edu.

University of Florida, Graduate School, Warrington College of Business Administration, Department of Finance, Insurance and Real Estate, Gainesville, FL 32611. Offers business administration (MS), including entrepreneurship, insurance, real estate and urban analysis, retailing; finance (PhD); financial services (Certificate); insurance (PhD); real estate and urban analysis (PhD); JD/MS. *Faculty:* 15 full-time (1 woman). *Students:* 69 (17 women); includes 14 minority (2 African Americans, 5 Asian Americans or Pacific Islanders, 7 Hispanic Americans) 12 international. In 2006, 54 master's, 1 doctorate awarded. Terminal master's awarded for partial completion of doctoral program. *Degree requirements:* For doctorate, thesis/dissertation. *Entrance requirements:* For master's, GMAT or GRE General Test, minimum GPA of 3.0 for last 60 hours of undergraduate degree, work experience (preferred); for doctorate, GMAT or GRE General Test, minimum GPA of 3.0. Additional exam requirements/recommendations for international students: Required—TOEFL (minimum score 550 paper-based; 213 computer-based). *Application deadline:* For fall admission, 5/1 priority date for domestic students. Applications are processed on a rolling basis. Application fee: $30. Electronic applications accepted. *Expenses:* Tuition, state resident: full-time $6,827. Tuition, nonresident: full-time $21,951. Required fees: $999. *Financial support:* In 2006–07, 10 research assistantships (averaging $23,562 per year), 1 teaching assistantship (averaging $40,989 per year) were awarded; fellowships, career-related internships or fieldwork, scholarships/grants, and unspecified assistantships also available. *Faculty research:* Financial management, financial markets and institutions, investments, risk and insurance, real estate development. *Unit head:* Dr. Michael D. Ryngaert, Chair, 352-392-9765, Fax: 352-392-0301, E-mail: michael.ryngaert@cba.ufl.edu. *Application contact:* Pamela De Michele, Director of Admissions and Student Services, 352-273-0310, Fax: 352-392-0301, E-mail: pam.demichele@cba.ufl.edu.

Real Estate

University of Hawaii at Manoa, Graduate Division, Shidler College of Business, Program in Business Administration, Honolulu, HI 96822. Offers Asian business studies (MBA); Chinese business studies (MBA); decision sciences (MBA); entrepreneurship (MBA); finance (MBA); finance and banking (MBA); human resources management (MBA); information management (MBA); information technology (MBA); international business (MBA); Japanese business studies (MBA); marketing (MBA); organizational behavior (MBA); organizational management (MBA); real estate (MBA); student-designed track (MBA). *Accreditation:* AACSB. Part-time programs available. *Faculty:* 48 full-time (9 women). *Students:* 207 full-time (77 women), 158 part-time (60 women); includes 93 minority (2 African Americans, 1 American Indian/Alaska Native, 88 Asian Americans or Pacific Islanders, 2 Hispanic Americans), 58 international. Average age 33. 235 applicants, 55% accepted, 68 enrolled. In 2006, 147 degrees awarded. *Degree requirements:* For master's, thesis optional. *Entrance requirements:* For master's, GMAT, minimum GPA of 3.0. Additional exam requirements/recommendations for international students: Required—TOEFL (minimum score 500 paper-based; 173 computer-based; 61 iBT). *Application deadline:* For fall admission, 5/1 for domestic and international students; for spring admission, 9/1 for domestic and international students. Application fee: $50. *Financial support:* In 2006–07, 7 research assistantships (averaging $17,409 per year), 3 teaching assistantships (averaging $14,028 per year) were awarded. *Application contact:* Ting Bui, Information Contact, 808-956-5565, Fax: 808-956-6889.

University of Memphis, Graduate School, Fogelman College of Business and Economics, Program in Business Administration, Memphis, TN 38152. Offers accounting (MBA, PhD); economics (MBA, PhD); executive business administration (MBA); finance (PhD); finance, insurance, and real estate (MBA, MS); international business administration (MBA); management (MBA, MS, PhD); management information systems (MBA, MS, PhD); management science (MBA); marketing (MBA, MS); marketing and supply chain management (PhD); real estate development (MS); JD/MBA. *Accreditation:* AACSB. *Faculty:* 84 full-time (14 women), 3 part-time/adjunct (0 women). *Students:* 222 full-time (92 women), 163 part-time (52 women); includes 62 minority (43 African Americans, 14 Asian Americans or Pacific Islanders, 5 Hispanic Americans), 119 international. Average age 29. In 2006, 196 master's, 12 doctorates awarded. *Degree requirements:* For master's, comprehensive exam; for doctorate, thesis/dissertation, comprehensive exam. *Entrance requirements:* For master's, GMAT, resumé; for doctorate, GMAT, interview, minimum GPA of 3.4, resumé, letter of recommendation. Additional exam requirements/recommendations for international students: Required—TOEFL (minimum score 550 paper-based; 220 computer-based). *Application deadline:* For fall admission, 8/1 for domestic students; for spring admission, 12/1 for domestic students. Application fee: $25 ($50 for international students). *Financial support:* Research assistantships with full tuition reimbursements, teaching assistantships, career-related internships or fieldwork, scholarships/grants, and unspecified assistantships available. Financial award application deadline: 3/1. *Faculty research:* Competitive business strategy, finance microstructures, supply chain management innovations, health care economics, litigation risks and corporate audits. Total annual research expenditures: $2.7 million. *Application contact:* Dr. Carol V. Danehower, Associate Dean for Programs, 901-678-5402, Fax: 901-678-3579, E-mail: fcbegp@memphis.edu.

University of Michigan, A. Alfred Taubman College of Architecture and Urban Planning, Urban and Regional Planning Program, Ann Arbor, MI 48109. Offers real estate development (Certificate); urban planning (MUP); JD/MUP; M Arch/MUP; MBA/MUP; MLA/MUP; MPP/MUP. Offered through the Horace H. Rackham School of Graduate Studies; students in the Certificate program must either be currently enrolled in a graduate program or have earned a masters or PhD degree within the last five years. *Accreditation:* ACSP (one or more programs are accredited). *Degree requirements:* For master's, thesis or alternative. *Entrance requirements:* For master's, GRE General Test. Additional exam requirements/recommendations for international students: Required—TOEFL (minimum score 600 paper-based; 250 computer-based).

University of North Texas, Robert B. Toulouse School of Graduate Studies, College of Business Administration, Department of Finance, Insurance, Real Estate, and Law, Denton, TX 76203. Offers banking (MBA, PhD); finance (MBA, PhD); finance, insurance, real estate, and law (MS); insurance (MBA); real estate (MBA). Part-time programs available. *Faculty:* 23 full-time (3 women). *Students:* 37 full-time (13 women), 69 part-time (21 women); includes 28 minority (11 African Americans, 2 American Indian/Alaska Native, 9 Asian Americans or Pacific Islanders, 6 Hispanic Americans), 24 international. Average age 27. 105 applicants, 78% accepted, 23 enrolled. In 2006, 51 master's, 3 doctorates awarded. *Degree requirements:* For doctorate, thesis/dissertation. *Entrance requirements:* For master's, GMAT; for doctorate, GMAT or GRE General Test. Additional exam requirements/recommendations for international students: Required—TOEFL (minimum score 550 paper-based; 213 computer-based). *Application deadline:* For fall admission, 7/15 for domestic students. Application fee: $50 ($75 for international students). *Expenses:* Tuition, state resident: full-time $3,573; part-time $198 per credit. Tuition, nonresident: full-time $8,577; part-time $476 per credit. Required fees: $1,258; $126 per credit. One-time fee: $150 full-time. Tuition and fees vary according to course load. *Financial support:* Fellowships, research assistantships, teaching assistantships, career-related internships or fieldwork available. Financial award application deadline: 4/1. *Faculty research:* Financial impact of regulation, risk management, financial instrument rating changes, taxes and valuation, bankruptcy. *Unit head:* Dr. Mazhar Siddiqi, Interim Chair, 940-369-7300, Fax: 940-565-4234, E-mail: siddiqi@unt.edu. *Application contact:* Dr. James A. Conover, Graduate Adviser, 940-565-3061, Fax: 940-565-4234, E-mail: conoverj@unt.edu.

University of Pennsylvania, Wharton School, Real Estate Department, Philadelphia, PA 19104. Offers MBA, PhD. Terminal master's awarded for partial completion of doctoral program. *Degree requirements:* For doctorate, thesis/dissertation. *Entrance requirements:* For master's, GMAT; for doctorate, GRE General Test. *Faculty research:* Public economics and taxation economics and finance of real estate markets, economics of housing markets, real estate development.

University of St. Thomas, Graduate Studies, Opus College of Business, Program in Real Estate, St. Paul, MN 55105-1096. Offers MS. Part-time programs available. *Faculty:* 2 full-time (0 women). *Students:* Average age 46. In 2006, 4 degrees awarded. *Degree requirements:* For master's, thesis. *Entrance requirements:* For master's, GMAT or GRE General Test, MAT. Additional exam requirements/recommendations for international students: Required—TOEFL. *Application deadline:* For fall admission, 6/1 priority date for domestic students. Applications are processed on a rolling basis. Application fee: $30. Electronic applications accepted. *Financial support:* Fellowships, research assistantships, career-related internships or fieldwork, institutionally sponsored loans, and scholarships/grants available. Support available to part-time students. Financial award application deadline: 7/1; financial award applicants required to submit FAFSA. *Faculty research:* Business taxation, property taxation. *Application contact:* Dr. Thomas A. Musil, Director, 651-962-4263, Fax: 651-962-4125, E-mail: tamusil@stthomas.edu.

University of Southern California, Graduate School, School of Policy, Planning and Development, Program in Real Estate Development, Los Angeles, CA 90089. Offers MRED, JD/MRED, MBA/MRED. *Students:* 43 full-time (3 women), 20 part-time (4 women); includes 17 minority (1 African American, 11 Asian Americans or Pacific Islanders, 5 Hispanic Americans), 4 international. In 2006, 36 degrees awarded. *Entrance requirements:* For master's, GRE General Test. *Application deadline:* For fall admission, 12/1 priority date for domestic students. Application fee: $85. *Expenses:* Contact institution. Full-time tuition and fees vary according to program. *Financial support:* In 2006–07, research assistantships (averaging $18,500 per year), teaching assistantships (averaging $18,500 per year) were awarded; fellowships, Federal Work-Study and institutionally sponsored loans also available. Support available to part-time students. Financial award application deadline: 2/15; financial award applicants required to submit FAFSA. *Unit head:* Dr. Raphael Bostic, Director, 213-740-6844, E-mail: sppd@usc.edu.

The University of Texas at Arlington, Graduate School, College of Business Administration, Department of Finance and Real Estate, Arlington, TX 76019. Offers quantitative finance (MS); real estate (MS). Part-time and evening/weekend programs available. *Faculty:* 13 full-time (3 women). *Students:* 43 full-time (11 women), 32 part-time (6 women); includes 18 minority (2 African Americans, 12 Asian Americans or Pacific Islanders, 4 Hispanic Americans), 21 international. 62 applicants, 76% accepted, 27 enrolled. In 2006, 12 degrees awarded. *Degree requirements:* For master's, thesis optional. *Entrance requirements:* For master's, GMAT, minimum GPA of 3.0. Additional exam requirements/recommendations for international students: Required—TOEFL (minimum score 550 paper-based; 213 computer-based). *Application deadline:* For fall admission, 6/15 priority date for domestic students. Applications are processed on a rolling basis. Application fee: $35 ($50 for international students). *Expenses:* Tuition, state resident: full-time $5,528. Tuition, nonresident: full-time $10,478. International tuition: $10,608 full-time. *Financial support:* In 2006–07, 3 fellowships (averaging $1,000 per year), 14 teaching assistantships (averaging $10,000 per year) were awarded; research assistantships, career-related internships or fieldwork, Federal Work-Study, and institutionally sponsored loans also available. Financial award application deadline: 6/1; financial award applicants required to submit FAFSA. *Unit head:* Dr. David Diltz, Chair, 817-272-3705, Fax: 817-272-2252, E-mail: diltz@uta.edu. *Application contact:* Dr. Scott Lowrance, Graduate Adviser, 817-272-3705, Fax: 817-272-2252, E-mail: realestate@uta.edu.

The University of Texas at Arlington, Graduate School, College of Business Administration, Program in Business Administration, Arlington, TX 76019. Offers accounting (PhD); business administration (PhD); business statistics (PhD); finance (MBA); information systems (MBA, PhD); management (MBA); management sciences (MBA); marketing (MBA, PhD); real estate (MBA). *Accreditation:* AACSB. Part-time and evening/weekend programs available. Postbaccalaureate distance learning degree programs offered (no on-campus study). *Faculty:* 1 full-time (0 women). *Students:* 156 full-time (60 women), 319 part-time (110 women); includes 123 minority (38 African Americans, 4 American Indian/Alaska Native, 52 Asian Americans or Pacific Islanders, 29 Hispanic Americans), 88 international. 502 applicants, 85% accepted, 199 enrolled. In 2006, 417 master's, 11 doctorates awarded. Terminal master's awarded for partial completion of doctoral program. *Degree requirements:* For master's, thesis optional; for doctorate, thesis/dissertation. *Entrance requirements:* For master's, GMAT; for doctorate, GMAT, minimum GPA of 3.0 (undergraduate), 3.4 (graduate); 30 hours of graduate course work. Additional exam requirements/recommendations for international students: Required—TOEFL (minimum score 550 paper-based; 213 computer-based). *Application deadline:* For fall admission, 6/15 for domestic students, 4/1 for international students; for spring admission, 10/15 for domestic students, 9/1 for international students. Applications are processed on a rolling basis. Application fee: $35 ($50 for international students). Electronic applications accepted. *Expenses:* Tuition, state resident: full-time $5,528. Tuition, nonresident: full-time $10,478. International tuition: $10,608 full-time. *Financial support:* In 2006–07, 1 fellowship (averaging $1,000 per year), 14 research assistantships (averaging $6,432 per year) were awarded; teaching assistantships, career-related internships or fieldwork, scholarships/grants, and unspecified assistantships also available. Financial award application deadline: 6/1; financial award applicants required to submit FAFSA. *Application contact:* Dr. Mike West, Assistant Dean, 817-272-1287, Fax: 817-272-5799, E-mail: mpwest@uta.edu.

See Close-Up on page 363.

University of Wisconsin–Madison, Graduate School, School of Business, Program in Real Estate and Urban Land Economics, Madison, WI 53706-1380. Offers PhD. *Students:* 4 full-time (2 women), 3 international. Average age 27. 16 applicants, 13% accepted, 2 enrolled. In 2006, 4 degrees awarded. *Median time to degree:* Of those who began their doctoral program in fall 1998, 100% received their degree in 8 years or less. *Entrance requirements:* For doctorate, GMAT or GRE. Additional exam requirements/recommendations for international students: Required—TOEFL. *Application deadline:* For fall admission, 1/6 priority date for domestic and international students. Applications are processed on a rolling basis. Application fee: $45. Electronic applications accepted. *Financial support:* In 2006–07, 4 students received support, including fellowships with partial tuition reimbursements available (averaging $16,110 per year), research assistantships with full tuition reimbursements available (averaging $13,502 per year), 4 teaching assistantships with full tuition reimbursements available (averaging $13,686 per year); career-related internships or fieldwork, Federal Work-Study, institutionally sponsored loans, scholarships/grants, and unspecified assistantships also available. Financial award application deadline: 1/6; financial award applicants required to submit FAFSA. *Faculty research:* Real estate finance, real estate equity investments, zoning restructurings, home ownership, international real estate and public policy. *Unit head:* Dr. Stephen Malpezzi, Chair, 608-262-6007, Fax: 608-265-2738. *Application contact:* Belle Heberling, PhD Coordinator, 608-262-3749, Fax: 608-890-0180, E-mail: phd@bus.wisc.edu.

University of Wisconsin–Madison, Graduate School, School of Business, Wisconsin Full-Time MBA Programs, Madison, WI 53706-1380. Offers applied corporate finance (MBA); applied security analysis (MBA); arts administration (MBA); brand and product management (MBA); entrepreneurial management (MBA); information systems (MBA); marketing research (MBA); operations and technology management (MBA); real estate (MBA); risk management and insurance (MBA); strategic human resource management (MBA); strategic management in the life and engineering sciences (MBA); supply chain management (MBA). *Faculty:* 84. *Students:* 231 full-time (74 women); includes 21 minority (10 African Americans, 5 Asian Americans or Pacific Islanders, 6 Hispanic Americans), 59 international. Average age 28. 405 applicants, 43% accepted, 121 enrolled. In 2006, 110 degrees awarded. *Entrance requirements:* For master's, GMAT, bachelors or equivalent degree, 2 years of work experience. Additional exam requirements/recommendations for international students: Required—TOEFL (minimum score 600 paper-based; 250 computer-based; 90 iBT). *Application deadline:* For fall admission, 11/1 for domestic and international students; for winter admission, 1/23 for domestic and international students; for spring admission, 3/26 for domestic and international students. Applications are processed on a rolling basis. Application fee: $45. Electronic applications accepted. *Financial support:* In 2006–07, 177 students received support, including 20 fellowships with full and partial tuition reimbursements available (averaging $16,566 per year), 105 research assistantships with full tuition reimbursements available (averaging $8,098 per year), 33 teaching assistantships with full tuition reimbursements available (averaging $10,112 per year); scholarships/grants, health care benefits, and unspecified assistantships also available. *Unit head:* Gary Lessuise, Assistant Dean, Masters Programs, 608-265-5102, Fax: 608-265-4192, E-mail: glessuise@bus.wisc.edu. *Application contact:* Betsy Kacizak, Director of Admissions and Financial Aid—Full Time MBA, 608-262-4000, Fax: 608-265-4192, E-mail: mba@bus.wisc.edu.

Virginia Commonwealth University, Graduate School, School of Business, Program in Finance, Insurance, and Real Estate, Richmond, VA 23284-9005. Offers MS. *Faculty:* 11 full-time (0 women). *Students:* 2 full-time (0 women), 6 part-time (1 woman), 1 international. 5 applicants, 80% accepted, 3 enrolled. In 2006, 17 degrees awarded. *Entrance requirements:* For master's, GMAT. *Application deadline:* Applications are processed on a rolling basis. Application fee: $50. *Financial support:* Fellowships, research assistantships, teaching assistantships, Federal Work-Study, institutionally sponsored loans, and tuition waivers (full and partial) available. Financial award application deadline: 3/15. *Unit head:* Dr. David E. Upton, Acting Chair, 804-828-7169, Fax: 804-828-3972, E-mail: deupton@vcu.edu. *Application contact:* Tracy Green, Graduate Program Director, 804-828-1741, Fax: 804-828-7174, E-mail: tsgreen@vcu.edu.

Virginia Commonwealth University, Graduate School, School of Business, Program in Real Estate and Urban Land Development, Richmond, VA 23284-9005. Offers MS, Certificate. In 2006, 3 master's, 5 other advanced degrees awarded. *Entrance requirements:* For master's, GMAT. *Application deadline:* Applications are processed on a rolling basis. Application fee: $50.

Financial support: Fellowships, research assistantships, teaching assistantships, Federal Work-Study, institutionally sponsored loans, and tuition waivers (full and partial) available. Financial award application deadline: 3/15. *Unit head:* Dr. Richard Phillips, Acting Endowed Chair, 804-828-7188, Fax: 804-828-3972, E-mail: raphilli@vcu.edu. *Application contact:* Tracy Green, Graduate Program Director, 804-828-1741, Fax: 804-828-7174, E-mail: tsgreen@vcu.edu.

See Close-Up on page 727.

Washington State University, Graduate School, College of Business, Department of Finance, Insurance and Real Estate, Pullman, WA 99164. Offers PhD. Application fee: $50. *Expenses:* Tuition, state resident: full-time $7,066. Tuition, nonresident: full-time $17,204. *Unit head:* Dr. Gene Lai, Chair.

Woodbury University, School of Architecture, Burbank, CA 91504-1099. Offers real estate development (M Arch). *Faculty:* 7 part-time/adjunct (0 women). *Students:* 9 full-time (2 women); includes 5 minority (4 Asian Americans or Pacific Islanders, 1 Hispanic American). 14 applicants, 9 enrolled. In 2006, 6 degrees awarded. *Degree requirements:* For master's, thesis. *Entrance requirements:* For master's, 3 letters of recommendation, portfolio. Additional exam requirements/recommendations for international students: Required—TOEFL (minimum score 550 paper-based; 213 computer-based), IELTS (minimum score 7). *Application deadline:* For fall admission, 3/1 priority date for domestic and international students. Application fee: $60. *Expenses:* Contact institution. *Unit head:* Norman Millar, Chair, 318-767-0888 Ext. 130, Fax: 318-504-9320, E-mail: norman.millar@woodbury.edu. *Application contact:* Debra Abel, Administrative Director, 619-235-2900, Fax: 619-235-2901, E-mail: debra.abel@woodbury.edu.

Program of Study

The full-time, 54-credit, two-year professional Master of Real Estate Development (M.R.E.D.) Program is jointly offered by the Department of Planning and Landscape Architecture (administrative unit) in the College of Architecture, Arts, and Humanities and the Department of Finance in the College of Business and Behavioral Science, with required courses from business administration, finance, law, architecture, construction science and management, city and regional planning, and real estate development. Core courses include Introduction to Accounting and Finance, Real Estate Principles, Development Process, Human Settlement, Site Planning and Infrastructure, Building Design and Construction Principles, Investment, Valuation, Finance, Introduction to GIS, Market Analysis, Law, Real Estate Seminar Roundtable, Contractor Role in the Development Process, Personnel Management and Negotiations, Public-Private Partnership Development, Practicum in Commercial Development, and Practicum in Master Planned/Resort Communities. A two-week Maymester SC Coastal Real Estate Development Field Tour, studying developments in Myrtle Beach, Pawleys Island, Charleston, Beaufort, and Hilton Head, is required prior to the required ten-week supervised professional summer internship. Other regional field trips occur in Charlotte, Atlanta, and nearby areas. The M.R.E.D. program focuses on promoting an entire vision for a community through sustainable design, creative financing methods, place-making, and healthy communities. The program creates the educational opportunity for encouraging future development entrepreneurs to produce exciting, high-quality projects respecting environmental and economic sustainability, social consciousness, design excellence, and financial feasibility within the risk-reward framework. The complexities of the development process require future professionals to be trained from diverse disciplinary perspectives in order to take leadership positions in the development industry. The program specializes in mixed-use development and master-planned communities. The program primarily follows the principles of the Urban Land Institute (ULI), which acknowledges that development is a public-private partnership and that high-quality development requires integrating the perspectives of community, environment, and economics.

Research Facilities

Student study space, computer workstations, studios, and a lounge area are available. Lee Hall includes the School of Design and Building collection in the Emery Gunnin Library with more than 40,000 books, 85,000 slides, video recordings, and professional journals and periodicals, including the complete Hughes ULI Library Collection. Five student computing labs provide various software and hardware resources, including ESRI, ERDAS, and Trimble GIS and GPS software.

Financial Aid

Some first-year students obtain research analyst positions for 10 hours per week assisting professors in research at the Center for Real Estate Development. Second-year M.R.E.D. students may work two days each week during the academic year at a paid internship with a local real estate entity. Positions typically require interns to have transportation throughout the metro area (up to a 60-mile radius). The program requires a ten-week summer internship with a real estate business anywhere in the world. The program is establishing relationships with local chapters of real estate organizations to pursue scholarship opportunities. Limited program fellowships for exceptional students may also be available.

Cost of Study

Tuition costs for the M.R.E.D. program are different from the graduate school fee structure; they are structured to ensure the financial commitment for the program's national reputation and growth. No tuition waivers or reductions are provided, although research analyst positions are available. M.R.E.D. students pay the same tuition for both years of the program based upon the academic-year rate established for the year in which they enter the program. This includes tuition for the Maymester tour class and the summer internship. The Maymester class requires an additional $500 for travel expenses, including most meals. For the 2007–08 academic year, in-state and out-of-state tuition is $22,500. Tuition includes student memberships in ULI, NAIOP, and ICSC; a trip to the national Urban Land Institute Fall Conference; and other travel expenses to regional conferences or tours.

Living and Housing Costs

On-campus housing is available, although virtually all students live off campus; for information, prospective students should visit http://www.housing.clemson.edu. The cost of living in Clemson is quite low compared to the national average; students who choose to live off campus typically spend $350–$450 per month for rent, depending on location, amenities, roommates, and other factors.

Student Group

The program started in fall 2004 with 7 students (13 in 2005 and 18 in 2006), with a limit of 20 students annually. The program seeks an interdisciplinary student body whose members are entrepreneurial yet team-oriented. No specific bachelor's degree is required, although preference is given to related fields. Work experience is not required, although it is definitely preferred. The program is highly competitive.

The Student Real Estate Association sponsors a series of social and professional events. Students are active members of the Young Leaders group of the ULI and of the Congress for New Urbanism student chapter. The University employs a national executive search firm to assist students with resumes, interviewing, job placement with national firms, salary and compensation recommendations, and individual negotiations for the best position possible.

Student Outcomes

The program wants each student to become a visionary who serves as a craftsperson and designer of neighborhoods and community development, recognizing the role of the developer in guiding the different aspects of creating the built environment—political, economic, physical, environmental, legal, and sociological parameters. Clemson wants students to become great place makers—not just builders of projects.

Location

The Clemson campus is in the foothills of the Blue Ridge Mountains and adjacent to Lake Hartwell, a recreational lake with a 1,000-mile shoreline. Clemson is midway (approximately 2 hours) between Atlanta, Georgia, and Charlotte, North Carolina, in the Greenville-Spartanburg-Anderson metropolitan area of 1 million people. Mountain, lake, river, and coastal environments in the region are plentiful and serve as disparate laboratories for the study of development. The multitude of local firms that supply the architecture, engineering, planning, financing, appraisal/market research, legal, and construction needs for development also provide excellent opportunities for participation with the M.R.E.D. program. Because Clemson is near small and large communities, students can examine premier examples of new suburban development, central city redevelopment, neotraditional development/new urbanism, historic preservation/restoration, and master-planned/resort/retirement developments located in the nearby mountains and on the South Carolina coast. Students study the full array of development functions as well as product types, including residential, office, retail, industrial, hospitality, and institutional uses. New prototypes, as well as repositioning of underperforming real estate assets, are also examined. Many historic communities are in the region, including the leading city of historic preservation, Charleston, South Carolina. The nationally prominent resort/tourist destinations of Hilton Head Island and Myrtle Beach, 450 golf courses, and numerous master-planned communities are in the state. More than one third of the nation's new urbanist communities are in the Southeast, and premier examples of mixed-use development and redevelopment (including exceptional examples of brownfield redevelopment) abound in the region.

Clemson's location in the Greenville area offers many advantages to the students. The Interstate 85 corridor is a key transportation link that is encouraging major foreign investments. *Site Selection* magazine rated the Greenville metro area as number one in the United States for new and expanding international companies during the nineties. The *Harvard Business Review* states that the Greenville area has the highest international development per capita in the nation. The Clemson connection is even greater now with the development of the new Clemson-International Center for Automotive Research (Clemson-ICAR), a 400-acre automotive research park in Greenville that is sponsored by the University in conjunction with BMW, IBM, Microsoft, and Michelin. Students enjoy the sunny, four-season climate of Clemson with long spring and fall seasons. The climate is moderate, with an average temperature of 61 degrees.

The University

Clemson is classified by the Carnegie Foundation as an RU/H: Research University (high research activity), a category comprising just 10 percent of all graduate degree–granting universities in America. The University's mission is to fulfill the covenant between its founder and the people of South Carolina to establish a "high seminary of learning" through its responsibilities of teaching, research, and extended public service. The University has identified eight areas of academic emphasis that create collaborations that, in turn, help fulfill the University's mission.

Applying

Students may apply on the Web at http://www.grad.clemson.edu/p_apply.html. February 1 is the priority deadline. A specific bachelor's degree from an accredited institution is not required for admission, although priority is given to those from related disciplines. Completed applications are due February 1 for first-round admissions and priorities for any research analyst positions. Later applications may be accepted based on merit, number of applicants, and individual circumstances. Admission is allowed only in the fall semester due to class sequencing. Admission into the program is based on GRE scores (greater than 1240/5.0 are preferred) or GMAT scores (greater than 600/5.0 are preferred), three letters of recommendation, academic background and related transcript (a GPA of at least 3.0 on a 4.0 scale is preferred), resume, personal statement of objectives (600–1,500 words), and work experience, if any. International students should have exceptional TOEFL scores (greater than 600 is preferred).

Correspondence and Information

Dr. J. Terrence Farris, CRE, AICP, Program Director
Patty McNulty, Department Assistant
Master of Real Estate Development Program
Department of Planning and Landscape Architecture
121 Lee Hall, Box 340511
Clemson University
Clemson, South Carolina 29634-0511
Phone: 864-656-3926
Fax: 864-656-7519
E-mail: curealestate-l@clemson.edu
Web site: http://www.clemson.edu/caah/pla

Clemson University

THE FACULTY AND THEIR RESEARCH

Dennis C. Bausman, Assistant Professor of Construction Science and Management; Ph.D., Heriot-Watt; M.C.S.M., Clemson. Business strategic planning, financial management, business planning and project management.

Robert Benedict, Instructor of Environmental Design and Planning; M.B.A., Georgia; M.A., Goucher. Real estate development process and commercial development.

Cliff Ellis, Associate Professor; Ph.D., Berkeley; M.P.C.D., Colorado at Denver. Land-use planning, growth management, transportation planning, planning theory, urban design, metropolitan and regional planning, history of urban reform, history of city planning, community development.

J. Terrence Farris, Associate Professor, M.R.E.D. Program Director, and Director, Center for Real Estate Development; M.U.P., Ph.D., Michigan State; CRE, AICP. Real estate development process, market and feasibility analysis, housing and community development, public-private partnerships.

Anne Marie Jacques, Lecturer, School of Architecture; M.A., Clemson. Architectural design and building techniques.

Judson R. Jahn, Lecturer, School of Accounting and Legal Studies; J.D., Mercer; M.B.A., Clemson. Real estate and construction law.

Roger W. Liska, Professor, Department of Construction Science and Management; Ed.D., Georgia; M.S., Wayne State. Craftworker retention and total quality management.

Jeffrey J. McMillan, Professor of Accountancy; Ph.D., South Carolina. Financial accounting, behavioral, auditing, ethics, educational methods, market valuation.

Daniel J. Nadenicek, Professor and Chair, Department of Planning and Landscape Architecture; M.L.A., Minnesota; M.S., Mankato State. Community design, human settlements, landscape and urban planning history.

Jeff Randolph, Instructor, Department of Planning and Landscape Architecture; M.C.R.P., Clemson. New deal acquisition, project management, sales and marketing, support services for residential land development.

Stephen L. Sperry, Associate Professor of Planning; M.L.A., Harvard. Land-use planning, geographic information systems, database technology, spatial modeling, image processing, raster and vector technology.

Thomas Springer, Professor of Finance; Ph.D., M.B.A., Georgia. Real estate principles, real estate investment.

Neil G. Waller, Professor of Finance; Ph.D., Texas at Austin; MAI. Real estate finance, real estate valuation.

NEW YORK UNIVERSITY

School of Continuing and Professional Studies
Real Estate Institute

Programs of Study

New York University's (NYU) Real Estate Institute offers four graduate programs: the Master of Science (M.S.) in real estate, the graduate certificate in real estate, the M.S. in construction management, and the graduate certificate in construction management.

The investment-oriented M.S. program in real estate provides students with both the fundamental knowledge and the advanced technical and analytical skills for success across the spectrum of the real estate industry. Students get an in-depth immersion into the real estate industry and learn the mastery of the transaction, studying all phases of the real estate deal from initiation and deal analysis through negotiation and conclusion.

The management-oriented M.S. program in construction management integrates the construction process and theory with real-world applications. Students learn to effectively manage all components of a construction project and learn the broader business aspects, such as business development and managing a construction organization.

The graduate certificates are designed for two kinds of students: those who have earned a bachelor's degree and are interested in pursuing further graduate study without yet committing to a master's degree program and those holding a graduate degree but seeking education in a new area or specialization within the real estate or construction industries.

Courses are taught by a combination of full-time faculty members and adjunct faculty members who are active participants in the real estate and building industries. The program draws upon a faculty pool of approximately 250 lecturers and professors.

The master's degree programs require 42 credits (fourteen courses, 3 credits each) of course work in a sequence of tiered core and concentration courses. The M.S. program in real estate offers three concentrations to choose from: asset management, development, and finance and investment. The M.S. program in construction management offers two concentrations to select from: construction executive management and construction project management. The Real Estate Institute continually reevaluates and updates the curriculum of all its graduate programs in response to industry needs to provide the most up-to-date and relevant course of study.

Research Facilities

The Real Estate Institute draws upon the specialized resources of the Jack Brause Library, which is devoted exclusively to the subject matter of the building industry and is the most comprehensive facility of its kind, covering all aspects of the real estate and construction industries. The Elmer Holmes Bobst Library and Study Center, one of the largest open-stack research libraries in the world, houses more than 3 million of NYU's nearly 4.4 million volumes. In addition to books, journals, and other print materials, the library provides access to many nonprint resources. These include microforms, databases, and other electronic resources that students can connect to from their home or residence hall; extensive video and audio collections; and a variety of computer equipment and software programs.

Financial Aid

NYU's centralized Office of Financial Aid assists students with loan packages, and the NYU monthly payment plan enables students to spread out their tuition payments. For more information, students should visit http://www.nyu.edu/financial.aid. Merit scholarships are available for continuing students.

Cost of Study

Tuition for part-time students for the 2007–08 academic year is $1266 per credit plus fees. For full-time students (10–12 credits per semester), the cost of tuition and related fees is $12,664 per semester. Fees vary somewhat by program. The Board of Trustees of New York University reserves the right to alter these costs without notice.

Living and Housing Costs

Graduate student housing is available on the University campus and is administered through the Office of Housing and Residence Life; however, students may choose to live off campus. NYU's Off-Campus Housing Office (OCHO) offers assistance to members of the NYU community in their search for non-University housing options. OCHO provides, exclusively to NYU students, listings of available locations for rent through private landlords, property managers, brokers, and real estate agents. Updated daily, these listings are accessible through OCHO's computer terminals or online for members of the NYU community.

Student Group

In 2006–07, there were 434 students enrolled in the M.S. program in real estate. The median age was 29, and 73 percent of the students were men. There were 89 students enrolled in the M.S. program in construction management. The median age was 33, and 78 percent of the students were men.

Location

The Real Estate Institute is located at 11 West 42nd Street off Fifth Avenue in midtown Manhattan—close to shops, offices, theaters, and museums and directly across the street from the New York Public Library.

The University, The School, and The Institute

NYU is a private university composed of fourteen schools, colleges, and divisions. The University was founded in 1831 and the School of Continuing and Professional Studies in 1934. The Real Estate Institute, which offers two master's degrees, two graduate certificates, a bachelor's degree in real estate in conjunction with the Paul McGhee Division, and noncredit professional development courses, was established in 1966.

Applying

Students may apply for fall or spring admission. Factors that are considered in evaluating applicants include official transcripts of academic achievement in previous undergraduate and graduate course work, GRE or GMAT scores, TOEFL score (for students whose native language is not English), the nature and extent of previous work experience, letters of recommendation, and a statement of purpose.

Correspondence and Information

For more information and an application package, students should contact:

Office of Admissions
Department of Graduate Studies
The Real Estate Institute
New York University
145 Fourth Avenue, Room 219
New York, New York 10003

Phone: 212-998-7200 Ext. 414
Fax: 212-995-4674
E-mail: scps.gradadmissions@nyu.edu
Web site: http://www.scps.nyu.edu/414

New York University

THE ADMINISTRATION

Robert S. Lapiner, Ph.D., Dean, School of Continuing and Professional Studies.

D. Kenneth Patton, M.S., Divisional Dean, Clinical Professor, and Klara and Larry Silverstein Chair of Real Estate, School of Continuing and Professional Studies; NYU Real Estate Institute, School of Continuing and Professional Studies.

Marcie Burros, M.A., Associate Director, Graduate Programs, NYU Real Estate Institute, School of Continuing and Professional Studies.

Jennifer Monahan, B.A., Assistant Director, Graduate Programs, NYU Real Estate Institute, School of Continuing and Professional Studies.

Michael J. Rushman, M.R.P., J.D., Ph.D., Director of Academic Affairs and Clinical Associate Professor of Real Estate, Graduate Programs, NYU Real Estate Institute, School of Continuing and Professional Studies.

VIRGINIA COMMONWEALTH UNIVERSITY

Programs in Real Estate and Urban Land Development

Programs of Study

The School of Business at Virginia Commonwealth University (VCU) offers a Master of Science with a focus in real estate valuation. The program provides in-depth knowledge of one business discipline and allows students to develop and build technical skills. The real estate valuation concentration is one of only eight programs in the nation that satisfies the rigorous educational requirements of the Appraisal Institute's MAI designation. This concentration emphasizes real estate valuation while providing comprehensive education in related disciplines, so graduates' analytical skills and abilities to communicate with other professionals are greatly enhanced. Whenever possible, students are placed in internships with MAIs. Unless they were previously completed in an undergraduate program, students must complete up to 18 credit hours of foundational courses: Fundamentals of Accounting, Financial Concepts of Management, Statistical Elements of Quantitative Management, Fundamentals of the Legal Environment of Business, Concepts and Issues in Marketing, and Concepts in Economics. In addition, students take 30 credit hours in required core courses.

The Graduate Certificate in Real Estate and Land Development is designed for professionals who seek an opportunity for advanced study in real estate and are more interested in the focused knowledge obtainable than receipt of a graduate degree. The certificate provides students with the ability to advance their careers while receiving recognition for their academic accomplishment in the form of a graduate certificate. Many working professionals, especially those with undergraduate majors in liberal arts, find this program attractive, since they can concentrate their energies on a tightly focused curriculum without enrolling in a large number of prerequisite courses.

Research Facilities

VCU libraries provide a combined capacity of more than 1.7 million volumes and 10,200 periodical titles and an online bibliographic search service accessing hundreds of databases. In addition, the Virginia State and Richmond Public Libraries are within walking distance of both VCU campuses. Academic Computing provides a variety of microcomputer, minicomputer, and mainframe computing services to support the research and instructional endeavors of the faculty and students, including consultation, instruction, and computer acquisition.

Financial Aid

The School of Business offers a limited number of graduate assistantship positions to full-time students. Scholarship opportunities exist for graduate students after they have completed at least one semester of study. Students may apply for need-based assistance with the University's Financial Aid Office. Current information on financial aid programs, policies, and procedures is available at http://www.vcu.edu/enroll/finaid.

Cost of Study

For full-time study (9–15 credits) in 2007–08, Virginia residents pay tuition and fees of $4452 per semester; nonresidents, $8876 per semester. For part-time study, Virginia residents pay tuition and fees of $465 per hour; nonresidents, $954 per hour. Some programs require additional fees. On the Medical College of Virginia (MCV) campus, tuition, fees, and other expenses vary in the medicine, pharmacy, nurse anesthesia, dentistry, and School of Allied Health programs.

Living and Housing Costs

Graduate student housing is available on both the MCV campus and the academic campus of Virginia Commonwealth University. Many graduate students live in off-campus housing, which is reasonably priced and readily available in a variety of styles and settings in nearby residential areas or within easy commuting distance. On- and off-campus housing information is available on the Web at http://www.housing.vcu.edu/.

Student Group

VCU enrolls 30,452 students, 7,611 of whom are graduate students. More than 200 clubs and organizations reflect the diverse social, recreational, educational, political, and religious interests of the student body.

Location

Richmond is Virginia's capital and a major East Coast financial and manufacturing center that offers students a wide range of cultural, educational, and recreational activities. Richmond is located in central Virginia at the intersection of Interstates 95 and 64, 2 hours south of Washington, D.C., and nestled between the Blue Ridge Mountains and the Atlantic coast. The Richmond region is easily accessible by plane, car, and train. With nearly 1 million residents, the historic city of Richmond combines big-city offerings with small-town hospitality. Applicants are encouraged to explore http://www.visit.richmond.com/ for more information on the city.

The University

VCU is a state-supported coeducational university with a graduate school, a major teaching hospital, and twelve academic and professional units that offer fifty-two undergraduate, twenty-two postbaccalaureate certificate, sixty-five master's, six post-master's certificate, and twenty-nine Ph.D. programs. VCU also offers M.D., D.D.S., D.P.T., and Pharm.D. programs as well as cooperative degree programs with other major Virginia colleges and universities. VCU has one of the largest evening colleges in the United States. The academic campus is located in Richmond's historic Fan District. The health sciences campus and hospital are located 2 miles east in the downtown business district. A University bus service provides free intercampus transportation for faculty members and students.

With more than $211 million in annual research funding, Virginia Commonwealth University is classified as one of the nation's top research universities by the Carnegie Foundation for the Advancement of Teaching. More than 29,000 undergraduate, certificate, graduate, post-master's, professional, and doctoral students are enrolled in 162 academic programs, forty of which are unique in the commonwealth of Virginia. The faculty members represent the finest American and international graduate institutions and enhance the University's position among the important institutions of higher learning in the United States and the world via their work in the classroom, laboratory, studio, and clinic and in their scholarly publications.

Applying

Admission procedures and program requirements are detailed in the *Graduate Bulletin*. Application deadlines and materials, including the application and the *Graduate Bulletin*, are available online at the Graduate School Web site at http://www.graduate.vcu.edu. Virginia Commonwealth University is an equal opportunity/affirmative action institution providing access to education and employment without regard to age, race, color, national origin, gender, religion, sexual orientation, veteran's status, political affiliation, or disability.

Correspondence and Information

Jana P. McQuaid, Graduate Program Director
School of Business
Virginia Commonwealth University
1015 Floyd Avenue
Richmond, Virginia 23284-4000
Phone: 804-828-4622
E-mail: jpmcquaid@vcu.edu
Web site: http://www.gsib.vcu.edu

Virginia Commonwealth University

THE FACULTY AND THEIR RESEARCH

Etti Baranoff, Associate Professor; Ph.D., Texas. Insurance law and regulation, all coverages (personal and commercial lines), insurers' financial stability, alternative risk financing, risk management information systems (RMIS).

Risk management—A focus on holistic approach: Three years after September 11. *J. Insurance Regulation,* July 2004.

Kenneth N. Daniels, Professor; Ph.D., Connecticut, 1991. Municipal bonds, corporate finance, financial institutions, small-business development, financial economics of minorities.

The valuation impact of financial advisors: An empirical analysis of REIT mergers and acquisitions. *J. Real Estate Res.,* January–March 2007.

David Downs, Professor and Alfred L. Blake Chair; Ph.D., North Carolina at Chapel Hill. Real estate finance and investment, issues relevant to institutional real estate investors, the implications of real estate regulation.

On the quality of FFO forecasts. *J. Real Estate Res.* 28(3):257–74. With Güner.

John Guthmann, Assistant Professor; Ph.D., New Mexico.

R. Michael McDonald, Associate Professor; Ed.D., Virginia Tech. Impediments to organizational change and the application of concept-mapping techniques to holistic problem analysis and strategic planning.

E. G. Miller, Senior Associate Dean; Ph.D., Alabama. Statistical applications in the insurance industry and insurance regulation.

Oghenovo Obrimah, Assistant Professor; Ph.D., Maryland.

Richard A. Phillips, Associate Professor; Ph.D., North Carolina at Chapel Hill. Real estate finance and economics, housing economics, economics of transportation and public policy.

The conditional probability of foreclosure: An empirical analysis of defaulted residential mortgage loans. *Real Estate Economics* 32(4):571–87, Winter 2004.

Daniel P. Salandro, Associate Professor; Ph.D., Pittsburgh.

Tai S. Shin, Professor; Ph.D., Illinois. Corporate finance, investment, banking, international finance.

Financial Management, 4th ed. (Copley, 2007).

David E. Upton, Professor and Chair; Ph.D., North Carolina. Security analysis, portfolio management, investments.

Section 21
Transportation Management, Logistics, and Supply Chain Management

This section contains a directory of institutions offering graduate work in transportation management, logistics, and supply chain management, followed by in-depth entries submitted by institutions that chose to prepare detailed program descriptions. Additional information about programs listed in the directory but not augmented by an in-depth entry may be obtained by writing directly to the dean of a graduate school or chair of a department at the address given in the directory.

For programs offering related work, see also in this book Business Administration and Management.

CONTENTS

Program Directories

Close-Ups

Aviation Management

Concordia University, School of Graduate Studies, John Molson School of Business, Montréal, QC H3G 1M8, Canada. Offers administration (M Sc, Diploma); aviation management (Certificate, Diploma); business administration (MBA, UA Undergraduate Associate, PhD), including international aviation (UA Undergraduate Associate); chartered accountancy (Diploma); community organizational development (Certificate); event management and fundraising (Certificate); executive business administration (EMBA); investment management (Diploma); investment management option (MBA); management accounting (Certificate); management of healthcare organizations (Certificate); sport administration (Diploma). *Accreditation:* AACSB. Part-time and evening/weekend programs available. *Students:* 447 full-time (174 women), 448 part-time (206 women). 925 applicants, 59% accepted, 319 enrolled. In 2006, 183 master's, 6 doctorates, 62 other advanced degrees awarded. *Degree requirements:* For master's, one foreign language, thesis (for some programs), research project; for doctorate, one foreign language, thesis/dissertation; for other advanced degree, one foreign language. *Entrance requirements:* For master's and doctorate, GMAT. Additional exam requirements/recommendations for international students: Required—TOEFL. Application fee: $50. *Expenses:* Contact institution. *Financial support:* Fellowships, career-related internships or fieldwork available. *Faculty research:* General business, capital markets, international business. *Unit head:* Dr. Jerry Tomberlin, Dean, 514-848-2424 Ext. 2700, Fax: 514-848-4502. *Application contact:* Dr. Michel Magnan, Associate Dean, Graduate Programs, 514-848-2424 Ext. 4145, Fax: 514-848-4208.

Daniel Webster College, MBA Program for Aviation Professionals, Nashua, NH 03063-1300. Offers MBA. Postbaccalaureate distance learning degree programs offered.

Daniel Webster College–Portsmouth Campus, MBA Program for Aviation Professionals, Portsmouth, NH 03801. Offers applied management (MBA).

Delta State University, Graduate Programs, College of Business, Department of Commercial Aviation, Cleveland, MS 38733-0001. Offers MCA. Part-time and evening/weekend programs available. Postbaccalaureate distance learning degree programs offered (minimal on-campus study). *Degree requirements:* For master's, thesis or alternative. *Entrance requirements:* For master's, GMAT. *Application deadline:* For fall admission, 8/1 priority date for domestic students; for spring admission, 12/1 priority date for domestic students. Applications are processed on a rolling basis. Application fee: $0. *Financial support:* In 2006–07, research assistantships (averaging $4,000 per year); career-related internships or fieldwork, Federal Work-Study, and institutionally sponsored loans also available. Support available to part-time students. Financial award application deadline: 6/1. *Unit head:* Dr. Tommy Sledge, Chair, 662-846-4205, Fax: 662-846-4214, E-mail: tsledge@deltastate.edu.

Dowling College, School of Business, Oakdale, NY 11769-1999. Offers aviation management (MBA, Certificate); banking and finance (MBA, Certificate); general management (MBA); public management (MBA, Certificate); total quality management (MBA, Certificate). Part-time and evening/weekend programs available. *Students:* 239 full-time (105 women), 566 part-time (273 women); includes 132 African Americans, 55 Asian Americans or Pacific Islanders, 48 Hispanic Americans, 3 international. Average age 31. 414 applicants, 82% accepted, 166 enrolled. In 2006, 471 master's, 1 other advanced degree awarded. *Degree requirements:* For master's, thesis optional. *Entrance requirements:* For master's, minimum GPA of 2.8, 2 letters of recommendation, courses in accounting and finance or seminar in accounting/finance, resumé. Additional exam requirements/recommendations for international students: Required—TOEFL (minimum score 550 paper-based). *Application deadline:* For fall admission, 9/1 priority date for domestic students; for winter admission, 1/1 priority date for domestic students; for spring admission, 2/1 priority date for domestic students. Applications are processed on a rolling basis. Application fee: $25. Electronic applications accepted. *Expenses:* Tuition: Full-time $16,008; part-time $667 per credit. Tuition and fees vary according to course load. *Financial support:* In 2006–07, 126 students received support, including 30 research assistantships (averaging $3,150 per year); career-related internships or fieldwork, Federal Work-Study, scholarships/grants, and unspecified assistantships also available. Support available to part-time students. Financial award application deadline: 6/30; financial award applicants required to submit FAFSA. *Faculty research:* International finance, computer applications, labor relations, executive development. *Unit head:* Dr. Elana Zolfo, Dean of the School of Business, 631-244-3190, Fax: 631-244-1018, E-mail: zdfoe@dowling.edu. *Application contact:* Franks S. Pizzardi, Director of Admissions Operations, 631-244-3227, Fax: 631-244-1059, E-mail: pizzardf@dowling.edu.

Embry-Riddle Aeronautical University, Daytona Beach Campus Graduate Program, Department of Business Administration, Daytona Beach, FL 32114-3900. Offers business administration in aviation (MBAA). *Accreditation:* ACBSP. Part-time and evening/weekend programs available. *Students:* 74 full-time (17 women), 59 part-time (11 women); includes 16 minority (5 African Americans, 1 American Indian/Alaska Native, 5 Asian Americans or Pacific Islanders, 5 Hispanic Americans), 31 international. Average age 30. 46 applicants, 67% accepted, 22 enrolled. In 2006, 56 degrees awarded. *Degree requirements:* For master's, thesis or alternative. *Entrance requirements:* For master's, minimum GPA of 2.5. Additional exam requirements/recommendations for international students: Required—TOEFL. *Application deadline:* For fall admission, 8/1 priority date for domestic students; for spring admission, 12/1 priority date for domestic students. Applications are processed on a rolling basis. *Expenses:* Tuition: Full-time $12,240; part-time $1,020 per credit. *Financial support:* In 2006–07, 53 students received support, including 18 research assistantships with partial tuition reimbursements available (averaging $2,872 per year); fellowships with partial tuition reimbursements available, career-related internships or fieldwork, Federal Work-Study, and unspecified assistantships also available. Support available to part-time students. Financial award application deadline: 4/15; financial award applicants required to submit FAFSA. *Faculty research:* Aircraft safety operations analysis; energy consumption analysis; statistical analysis of general aviation accidents; airport funding strategies; industry assessment and marketing analysis for ENAER aerospace. Total annual research expenditures: $120,079. *Unit head:* Dr. Blaise Waguespack, Program Coordinator, 386-226-7235, Fax: 386-226-6696, E-mail: waguespb@erau.edu. *Application contact:* Tom Shea, Director, International and Graduate Admissions, 800-388-3728, Fax: 386-226-7070, E-mail: graduate.admissions@erau.edu.

Embry-Riddle Aeronautical University Worldwide, Worldwide Headquarters, Program in Management, Daytona Beach, FL 32114-3900. Offers MSM. Part-time and evening/weekend programs available. Postbaccalaureate distance learning degree programs offered. *Students:* 229 full-time (50 women), 275 part-time (76 women); includes 116 minority (47 African Americans, 6 American Indian/Alaska Native, 22 Asian Americans or Pacific Islanders, 41 Hispanic Americans), 10 international. Average age 35. 173 applicants, 71% accepted, 95 enrolled. In 2006, 108 degrees awarded. *Degree requirements:* For master's, thesis optional. *Entrance requirements:* For master's, GMAT. *Application deadline:* Applications are processed on a rolling basis. Application fee: $50. Electronic applications accepted. *Expenses:* Tuition: Full-time $7,800; part-time $325 per credit. *Financial support:* In 2006–07, 36 students received support. Applicants required to submit FAFSA. *Unit head:* Dr. Earl Wheeler, Chair, 904-284-5863, E-mail: wheel5ad@erau.edu. *Application contact:* Pam Thomas, Director of Enrollment Management, 386-226-6910, Fax: 386-226-6984, E-mail: ecinfo@erau.edu.

Lynn University, College of Business and Management, Boca Raton, FL 33431-5598. Offers aviation management (MBA); financial valuation and investment management (MBA); global leadership (PhD); hospitality management (MBA); international business (MBA); marketing (MBA); mass communication and media management (MBA); sports and athletics administration (MBA). Part-time and evening/weekend programs available. Postbaccalaureate distance learning degree programs offered. *Faculty:* 13 full-time (5 women), 7 part-time/adjunct (3 women). *Students:* 71 full-time (37 women), 113 part-time (47 women); includes 35 minority (13 African Americans, 6 Asian Americans or Pacific Islanders, 16 Hispanic Americans), 55 international. Average age 32. 114 applicants, 88% accepted, 71 enrolled. In 2006, 83 master's, 9 doctorates awarded. *Degree requirements:* For master's, project; for doctorate, thesis/dissertation, qualifying paper. *Entrance requirements:* For master's, GMAT or GRE, minimum undergraduate GPA of 3.0, resumé, 2 letters of recommendation; for doctorate, GRE or GMAT, minimum graduate GPA of 3.25, resumé, 2 letters of recommendation. Additional exam requirements/recommendations for international students: Required—TOEFL (minimum score 550 paper-based; 213 computer-based). *Application deadline:* Applications are processed on a rolling basis. Application fee: $50. Electronic applications accepted. *Expenses:* Tuition: Full-time $26,200. Required fees: $1,500. Tuition and fees vary according to class time, course load and degree level. *Financial support:* In 2006–07, 160 students received support. Career-related internships or fieldwork, Federal Work-Study, institutionally sponsored loans, scholarships/grants, tuition waivers (full and partial), and unspecified assistantships available. Support available to part-time students. Financial award application deadline: 8/1; financial award applicants required to submit FAFSA. *Faculty research:* Labor relations, dynamic balance in leisure-time skills, ethics in athletics, hotel development. *Unit head:* Dr. Russell Boisjoly, Dean, 561-237-7458, Fax: 561-237-7014, E-mail: rboisjoly@lynn.edu. *Application contact:* Dr. Larissa Baia, Assistant Director of Graduate Admissions, 561-237-7916, Fax: 561-237-7100, E-mail: admissionpm@lynn.edu.

Southeastern Oklahoma State University, Graduate School, Department of Aviation Science, Durant, OK 74701-0609. Offers aerospace administration (MS). Part-time and evening/weekend programs available. *Degree requirements:* For master's, registration. *Entrance requirements:* For master's, minimum GPA of 3.0 in last 60 hours or 2.75 overall. Electronic applications accepted.

Logistics

Air Force Institute of Technology, Graduate School of Engineering and Management, Department of Operational Sciences, Dayton, OH 45433-7765. Offers logistics management (MS); operations research (MS, PhD); space operations (MS). Part-time programs available. *Degree requirements:* For master's and doctorate, thesis/dissertation. *Entrance requirements:* For doctorate, GRE General Test, minimum GPA of 3.0, U.S. citizenship. *Faculty research:* Optimization, simulation, combat modeling and analysis, reliability and maintainability, resource scheduling.

American Public University System, AMU/APU Graduate Programs, Charles Town, WV 25414. Offers business administration (MBA); criminal justice (MA); emergency and disaster management (MA); environmental policy and management (MS); history (MA); homeland security (MA); humanities (MA); intelligence (MA Strategic Intelligence); international relations and conflict resolution (MA); management (MA); military history (MA); national security studies (MA); political science (MA); public administration (MA); public health (MA); security management (MA); space studies (MS); sports management (MA); transportation and logistics management (MA). Programs offered via distance learning only. Part-time and evening/weekend programs available. Postbaccalaureate distance learning degree programs offered (no on-campus study). *Faculty:* 10 full-time (3 women), 188 part-time/adjunct (57 women). *Students:* 498 full-time (104 women), 5,272 part-time (1,209 women). Average age 34. 6,574 applicants, 100% accepted, 3508 enrolled. In 2006, 358 degrees awarded. *Degree requirements:* For master's, comprehensive exam, registration. *Entrance requirements:* For master's, bachelor's degree or equivalent, minimum GPA of 2.7 in last 60 hours of course work. *Application deadline:* For fall admission, 9/1 priority date for domestic students; for winter admission, 1/1 priority date for domestic students; for spring admission, 5/1 priority date for domestic students. Applications are processed on a rolling basis. Application fee: $0. Electronic applications accepted. *Expenses:* Tuition: Full-time $4,950; part-time $275 per credit. One-time fee: $200 full-time. *Financial support:* Applicants required to submit FAFSA. *Faculty research:* Military history, criminal justice, management performance, national security. *Unit head:* Dr. Frank McCluskey, Provost, 877-468-6268, Fax: 304-724-3780. *Application contact:* Terry Grant, Director of Enrollment Management, 877-468-6268, Fax: 304-724-3780, E-mail: info@apus.edu.

Case Western Reserve University, School of Graduate Studies, The Case School of Engineering, Department of Electrical Engineering and Computer Science, Cleveland, OH 44106. Offers computer engineering (MS, PhD); computing and information science (MS, PhD); electrical engineering (MS, PhD); systems and control engineering (MS, PhD). Part-time and evening/weekend programs available. Postbaccalaureate distance learning degree programs offered (minimal on-campus study). *Faculty:* 35 full-time (2 women). *Students:* 90 full-time, 117 part-time. In 2006, 28 master's, 11 doctorates awarded. Terminal master's awarded for partial completion of doctoral program. *Degree requirements:* For master's, thesis; for doctorate, thesis/dissertation, qualifying exam, teaching experience. *Entrance requirements:* For master's and doctorate, GRE General Test. Additional exam requirements/recommendations for international students: Required—TOEFL. *Application deadline:* For fall admission, 2/1 for domestic students; for spring admission, 11/1 for domestic students. Applications are processed on a rolling basis. Application fee: $50. *Financial support:* Fellowships with full and partial tuition reimbursements, research assistantships with full and partial tuition reimbursements, teaching assistantships, career-related internships or fieldwork, Federal Work-Study, and institutionally sponsored loans available. Support available to part-time students. Financial award application deadline: 3/1; financial award applicants required to submit FAFSA. *Faculty research:* Applied artificial intelligence, automation, computer-aided design and testing of digital systems. Total annual research expenditures: $4.6 million. *Application contact:* Mark Doblekar, Graduate Coordinator, 216-368-4080, Fax: 216-368-2801, E-mail: mpd3@case.edu.

Colorado Technical University, Graduate Studies, Program in Management, Colorado Springs, CO 80907-3896. Offers business administration (MBA); business management (MSM); business technology (MSM); database management (MSM); human resources management (MSM); information technology (MSM); logistics management (MSM); management (DM); organizational leadership (MSM); project management (MSM). Part-time and evening/weekend programs available. *Degree requirements:* For master's, thesis or alternative; for doctorate, thesis/dissertation. *Entrance requirements:* For doctorate, minimum graduate GPA of 3.0, 5 years of related work experience. *Faculty research:* Sexual harassment, performance evaluation, critical thinking.

East Carolina University, Graduate School, College of Technology and Computer Science, Department of Technology Systems, Greenville, NC 27858-4353. Offers computer network professional (Certificate); industrial technology (MS), including computer networking management, digital communications, industrial distribution and logistics, information security, manufacturing, performance improvement, planning; information assurance (Certificate); occupational safety (MS); technology management (PhD); Website developer (Certificate). *Students:* 27 full-time (8 women), 114 part-time (28 women); includes 34 minority (25 African Americans, 1 American Indian/Alaska Native, 3 Asian Americans or Pacific Islanders, 5 Hispanic Americans), 4 international. Average age 34. 53 applicants, 28% accepted, 13 enrolled. In 2006, 65 degrees awarded. *Entrance requirements:* For master's and Certificate, GRE General Test or MAT, minimum GPA of 2.5; for doctorate, GRE General Test, related work experience. *Application deadline:* For fall admission, 6/1 priority date for domestic students. Applications are processed on a rolling basis. Application fee: $50. *Financial support:* Application deadline: 6/1. *Unit head:* Dr. Andrew Jackson, Chair, 252-737-1468, Fax: 252-328-1618, E-mail: jacksona@ecu.edu. *Application contact:* Jenny Simpkins, Information Contact, 252-328-9653, Fax: 252-328-1618, E-mail: best@ecu.edu.

Florida Institute of Technology, Graduate Programs, University College, Melbourne, FL 32901-6975. Offers acquisition and contract management (MS, PMBA); aerospace engineering (MS); business administration (PMBA); computer information systems (MS); computer science (MS); e-business (PMBA); electrical engineering (MS); engineering management (MS); human resource management (PMBA); human resources management (MS); information systems (PMBA); logistics management (MS); management (MS), including acquisition and contract management, e-business, human resource management, information systems, logistics management, transportation management; materiel acquisition management (MS); mechanical engineering (MS); operations research (MS); project management (MS), including information systems, operations research; public administration (MPA); software engineering (MS); space systems (MS); space systems management (MS); systems management (MS), including information systems, operations research. Part-time and evening/weekend programs available. Postbaccalaureate distance learning degree programs offered (no on-campus study). *Faculty:* 11 full-time (4 women), 129 part-time/adjunct (17 women). *Students:* 78 full-time (34 women), 1,258 part-time (507 women); includes 384 minority (252 African Americans, 9 American Indian/Alaska Native, 58 Asian Americans or Pacific Islanders, 65 Hispanic Americans), 28 international. Average age 36. 629 applicants, 65% accepted, 320 enrolled. In 2006, 505 degrees awarded. *Degree requirements:* For master's, registration. *Entrance requirements:* For master's, minimum GPA of 3.0. Additional exam requirements/recommendations for international students: Required—TOEFL (minimum score 550 paper-based; 213 computer-based). *Application deadline:* Applications are processed on a rolling basis. Application fee: $50. Electronic applications accepted. *Expenses:* Tuition: Part-time $900 per credit. *Financial support:* Institutionally sponsored loans available. Financial award application deadline: 3/1; financial award applicants required to submit FAFSA. *Unit head:* Dr. Clifford Bragdon, Dean, 321-674-8821, Fax: 321-951-7694, E-mail: cbragdon@fit.edu. *Application contact:* Carolyn P. Farrior, Director of Graduate Admissions, 321-674-7118, Fax: 321-723-9468, E-mail: cfarrior@fit.edu.

George Mason University, School of Public Policy, Program in Transportation Policy, Operations and Logistics, Fairfax, VA 22030. Offers MA. Part-time programs available. Postbaccalaureate distance learning degree programs offered (no on-campus study). *Faculty:* 48 full-time (8 women), 41 part-time/adjunct (6 women). *Students:* 5 full-time (2 women), 54 part-time (19 women); includes 4 minority (3 African Americans, 1 American Indian/Alaska Native), 2 international. 40 applicants, 68% accepted, 15 enrolled. In 2006, 21 degrees awarded. *Degree requirements:* For master's, thesis or alternative. *Entrance requirements:* For master's, minimum undergraduate GPA of 3.0, resumé, 2 letters of recommendation, goals statement. Additional exam requirements/recommendations for international students: Required—TOEFL. *Application deadline:* For fall admission, 6/1 priority date for domestic students, 5/1 priority date for international students; for spring admission, 12/1 priority date for domestic students, 11/1 priority date for international students. Applications are processed on a rolling basis. Application fee: $60. Electronic applications accepted. *Expenses: Contact institution. Financial support:* Career-related internships or fieldwork, Federal Work-Study, scholarships/grants, and tuition waivers (partial) available. Support available to part-time students. Financial award application deadline: 3/1; financial award applicants required to submit FAFSA. *Unit head:* Dr. Laurie Schintler, Director, 703-993-8099, E-mail: spp@gmu.edu. *Application contact:* Leslie Metzger Levin, Director of Graduate Admissions, 703-993-8099, Fax: 703-993-4876, E-mail: lmetzger@gmu.edu.

The George Washington University, School of Business, Department of Management Science, Program in Logistics, Operations, and Materials Management, Washington, DC 20052. Offers MBA. Part-time and evening/weekend programs available. *Entrance requirements:* For master's, GMAT. Additional exam requirements/recommendations for international students: Required—TOEFL.

Georgia College & State University, Graduate School, School of Liberal Arts and Sciences, Department of Government and Sociology, Logistics Education Center, Milledgeville, GA 31061. Offers logistics management (MSA); logistics systems (MSLS). Part-time and evening/weekend programs available. *Students:* 12 full-time (7 women), 58 part-time (28 women); includes 21 minority (17 African Americans, 1 Asian American or Pacific Islander, 3 Hispanic Americans). Average age 38. 22 applicants, 95% accepted, 18 enrolled. In 2006, 38 degrees awarded. *Entrance requirements:* For master's, MAT, GRE, GMAT or CSAT. Additional exam requirements/recommendations for international students: Required—TOEFL. *Application deadline:* For fall admission, 7/1 priority date for domestic students. Applications are processed on a rolling basis. Application fee: $25. Electronic applications accepted. *Expenses:* Tuition, state resident: full-time $3,222; part-time $179 per credit hour. Tuition, nonresident: full-time $12,870; part-time $715 per credit hour. Required fees: $391 per semester. Tuition and fees vary according to course load. *Financial support:* Application deadline: 3/1. *Unit head:* Glen Easterly, Director of Robins Center, Coordinator of Logistics Program, 478-327-7376, Fax: 478-923-2468, E-mail: glenn.easterly@gcsu.edu.

HEC Montreal, School of Business Administration, Master of Science Programs in Administration, Program in Logistics, Montréal, QC H3T 2A7, Canada. Offers M Sc. All courses are given in French. Part-time programs available. *Degree requirements:* For master's, one foreign language, thesis. Application fee: $60 Canadian dollars. Electronic applications accepted. Tuition and fees charges are reported in Canadian dollars. *Expenses:* Tuition, nonresident: part-time $56 Canadian dollars per credit. Required fees: $30 Canadian dollars per semester. *Financial support:* Fellowships, research assistantships, teaching assistantships, scholarships/grants available. *Application contact:* Francine Blais, Administrative Director, 514-340-6112, Fax: 514-340-6411, E-mail: francine.blais@hec.ca.

Maine Maritime Academy, Department of Graduate Studies, Program in Maritime Management, Castine, ME 04420. Offers MS, Certificate, Diploma. Part-time programs available. *Degree requirements:* For master's, capstone course, thesis optional. *Entrance requirements:* For master's, GMAT or GRE General Test, letters of recommendation. Additional exam requirements/recommendations for international students: Required—TOEFL. *Faculty research:* Human resources in maritime environment, management of organization change, economic analysis and maritime law.

Massachusetts Institute of Technology, School of Engineering, Engineering Systems Division, Cambridge, MA 02139-4307. Offers engineering and management (SM); engineering systems (SM, PhD); logistics (M Eng); technology and policy (SM); technology, management and policy (PhD); SM/MBA. *Faculty:* 1 full-time (0 women). *Students:* 254 full-time (55 women), 3 part-time (1 woman); includes 31 minority (6 African Americans, 1 American Indian/Alaska Native, 19 Asian Americans or Pacific Islanders, 5 Hispanic Americans), 84 international. Average age 31. 577 applicants, 37% accepted, 151 enrolled. In 2006, 124 master's, 9 doctorates awarded. *Degree requirements:* For master's, thesis/dissertation; for doctorate, thesis/dissertation, comprehensive exam. *Entrance requirements:* For master's and doctorate, GRE General Test. Additional exam requirements/recommendations for international students: Required—TOEFL (minimum score 610 paper-based; 255 computer-based; 103 iBT). Application fee: $70. *Expenses: Contact institution.* Part-time tuition and fees vary according to course load. *Financial support:* In 2006–07, 169 students received support, including 27 fellowships with tuition reimbursements available (averaging $10,091 per year), 87 research assistantships with tuition reimbursements available (averaging $20,543 per year), 9 teaching assistantships with tuition reimbursements available (averaging $16,331 per year); career-related internships or fieldwork, Federal Work-Study, institutionally sponsored loans, scholarships/grants, health care benefits, and unspecified assistantships also available. *Faculty research:* Systems and enterprise architecture; logistics; manufacturing; technology and policy; product development; transportation. Total annual research expenditures: $6.5 million. *Unit head:* Prof. Joel Moses, Acting Director, 617-253-9756, E-mail: esdinquiries@mit.edu. *Application contact:* Graduate Admissions, 617-253-1182, E-mail: esdgrad@mit.edu.

North Dakota State University, The Graduate School, College of Engineering and Architecture, Department of Civil Engineering, Fargo, ND 58105. Offers civil engineering (MS, PhD); environmental engineering (MS, PhD); natural resource management (MS, PhD); transportation and logistics (PhD). PhD in transportation and logistics offered jointly with Upper Great Plains Transportation Institute. Part-time programs available. Postbaccalaureate distance learning degree programs offered (minimal on-campus study). *Degree requirements:* For master's, thesis/dissertation; for doctorate, thesis/dissertation, comprehensive exam. *Entrance requirements:* Additional exam requirements/recommendations for international students: Required—TOEFL (minimum score 525 paper-based; 193 computer-based). *Application deadline:* For fall admission, 7/1 priority date for domestic students, 1/15 priority date for international students; for spring admission, 5/1 priority date for international students. Applications are processed on a rolling basis. Application fee: $45 ($60 for international students). *Financial support:* Fellowships with full tuition reimbursements, research assistantships with full tuition reimbursements, teaching assistantships with full tuition reimbursements, career-related internships or fieldwork, Federal Work-Study, and institutionally sponsored loans available. Support available to part-time students. Financial award application deadline: 1/15. *Faculty research:* Wastewater, solid waste, composites, nanotechnology. Total annual research expenditures: $800,000. *Unit head:* Dr. Dinesh R. Katti, Chair, 701-231-7244, Fax: 701-231-6185, E-mail: dinesh.katti@ndsu.edu. *Application contact:* Dr. Kalpana Katti, Associate Professor and Graduate Program Coordinator, 701-231-9504, Fax: 701-231-6185, E-mail: kalpana.katti@ndsu.edu.

North Dakota State University, The Graduate School, Interdisciplinary Program in Transportation and Logistics, Fargo, ND 58105. Offers PhD. *Entrance requirements:* For doctorate, 1 year of calculus, statistics and probability, minimum GPA of 3.0. Additional exam requirements/recommendations for international students: Required—TOEFL (minimum score 550 paper-based; 213 computer-based). *Application deadline:* For fall admission, 5/1 priority date for domestic students. Applications are processed on a rolling basis. Application fee: $35 ($50 for international students). *Financial support:* Research assistantships with full tuition reimbursements available. *Faculty research:* Supply chain optimization, spatial analysis of transportation networks, advanced traffic analysis, transportation demand, railroad/intermodal freight. *Unit head:* Dr. Denver Tolliver, Director, 701-231-7190, Fax: 701-231-1945, E-mail: denver.tolliver@ndsu.nodak.edu.

The Ohio State University, Graduate School, Max M. Fisher College of Business, Program in Business Logistics and Engineering, Columbus, OH 43210. Offers MBLE. *Students:* 17 full-time (8 women), 3 part-time (1 woman); includes 1 minority (Hispanic American), 17 international. Average age 27. 32 applicants, 66% accepted, 14 enrolled. In 2006, 2 degrees awarded. *Entrance requirements:* For master's, GRE or GMAT. Additional exam requirements/recommendations for international students: Required—TOEFL. *Application deadline:* Applications are processed on a rolling basis. Electronic applications accepted. *Expenses:* Tuition, state resident: full-time $9,438. Tuition, nonresident: full-time $22,791. Tuition and fees vary according to course load, campus/location and program. *Unit head:* Walter Zinn, Graduate Studies Committee Chair, 416-292-0797, Fax: 416-292-9006, E-mail: zinn.13@osu.edu. *Application contact:* Graduate Admissions, 614-292-9444, Fax: 614-292-3895, E-mail: domestic.grad@osu.edu.

Penn State University Park, Graduate School, The Mary Jean and Frank P. Smeal College of Business Administration, State College, University Park, PA 16802-1503. Offers accounting (PhD); business administration (MBA); finance (PhD); management and organization (PhD); management science/operations/logistics (PhD); marketing (PhD); real estate (PhD); supply chain and information systems (PhD). *Students:* 287 full-time (79 women), 5 part-time (2 women); includes 39 minority (22 African Americans, 11 Asian Americans or Pacific Islanders, 6 Hispanic Americans), 93 international. Average age 31. 841 applicants, 31% accepted, 150 enrolled. In 2006, 107 master's, 11 doctorates awarded. *Expenses: Contact institution. Financial support:* In 2006–07, 1 fellowship, 11 research assistantships, 143 teaching assistantships were awarded. Financial award applicants required to submit FAFSA. *Unit head:* Dr. Kenneth B. Thomas, Dean, 814-863-0448, Fax: 814-865-7064, E-mail: j2t@psu.edu.

Pontificia Universidad Catolica Madre y Maestra, Graduate School, Santiago, Dominican Republic. Offers administration (M Adm, M Ed); architecture of interiors (M Arch); architecture of tourist lodgings (M Arch); construction administration (ME); convergent networks (ME); earthquake-resistant engineering (ME); environmental engineering (MEE); financial (M Mgmt); human resources (EMBA); international (M Mgmt); labor law and Social Security (M Mgmt); logistics management (ME); urban planning (M Urb). *Entrance requirements:* For master's, curriculum vitae, interview.

Stevens Institute of Technology, Graduate School, Charles V. Schaefer Jr. School of Engineering, Department of Systems Engineering and Engineering Management, Program in Systems Design and Operational Effectiveness, Hoboken, NJ 07030. Offers M Eng.

Stevens Institute of Technology, Graduate School, Charles V. Schaefer Jr. School of Engineering, Department of Systems Engineering and Engineering Management, Program in Systems Engineering, Hoboken, NJ 07030. Offers agile systems engineering and design (Certificate); systems and supportability engineering (Certificate); systems engineering (M Eng, PhD); systems engineering and architecting (Certificate).

Touro University International, College of Business Administration, Program in Business Administration, Cypress, CA 90630. Offers business administration (PhD); conflict and negotiation management (MBA); criminal justice administration (MBA); entrepreneurship (MBA); finance (MBA); general management (MBA); human resource management (MBA); information technology management (MBA); international business (MBA); logistics management (MBA); public management (MBA); strategic leadership (MBA). Part-time and evening/weekend programs available. Postbaccalaureate distance learning degree programs offered (no on-campus study). In 2006, 631 master's, 30 doctorates awarded. *Degree requirements:* For doctorate, thesis/dissertation, defense of dissertation, comprehensive exam. *Entrance requirements:* For master's, minimum GPA of 3.0; for doctorate, minimum GPA of 3.4, curriculum vitae, course work in research methods or statistics. Additional exam requirements/recommendations for international students: Required—TOEFL (minimum score 550 paper-based). *Application deadline:* Applications are processed on a rolling basis. Application fee: $75. Electronic applications accepted. *Expenses:* Tuition: Part-time $300 per credit hour. Tuition and fees vary according to course level and program.

Universidad del Turabo, Graduate Programs, School in Business Administration, Program in Logistics and Materials Management, Gurabo, PR 00778-3030. Offers MBA. Part-time and evening/weekend programs available. *Entrance requirements:* For master's, GRE, EXADEP, interview.

University at Buffalo, the State University of New York, Graduate School, School of Management, Buffalo, NY 14260. Offers accounting (MS); business administration (MBA); finance (MS); information assurance (Certificate); management (PhD); management information systems (MS); supply chains and operations management (MS); Au D/MBA; JD/MBA;

Logistics

University at Buffalo, the State University of New York (continued)
M Arch/MBA; MA/MBA; MD/MBA; MPH/MBA; MSW/MBA; Pharm D/MBA. *Accreditation:* AACSB. Part-time and evening/weekend programs available. *Faculty:* 65 full-time (18 women), 30 part-time/adjunct (3 women). *Students:* 493 full-time (192 women), 212 part-time (55 women); includes 53 minority (11 African Americans, 3 American Indian/Alaska Native, 31 Asian Americans or Pacific Islanders, 8 Hispanic Americans), 283 international. Average age 27. 1,058 applicants, 55% accepted, 369 enrolled. In 2006, 260 master's, 5 doctorates, 3 other advanced degrees awarded. *Degree requirements:* For doctorate, thesis/dissertation, comprehensive exam. *Entrance requirements:* For master's, GMAT, GRE General Test (all master's degrees except accounting); for doctorate, GMAT or GRE. Additional exam requirements/recommendations for international students: Required—TOEFL (minimum score 230 computer-based). *Application deadline:* For fall admission, 6/1 priority date for domestic students, 3/1 priority date for international students. Applications are processed on a rolling basis. Application fee: $50. Electronic applications accepted. *Expenses: Contact institution. Financial support:* In 2006–07, 91 students received support, including 17 fellowships with full and partial tuition reimbursements available (averaging $3,917 per year), 38 research assistantships with full and partial tuition reimbursements available (averaging $11,907 per year), 26 teaching assistantships with full and partial tuition reimbursements available (averaging $7,571 per year); career-related internships or fieldwork, Federal Work-Study, institutionally sponsored loans, scholarships/grants, health care benefits, and unspecified assistantships also available. Financial award application deadline: 2/15; financial award applicants required to submit FAFSA. *Faculty research:* Information assurance, relationship marketing, global processes, credit analysis in banking, disaster mitigation and response. Total annual research expenditures: $330,551. *Unit head:* John M. Thomas, Dean, 716-645-3221, Fax: 716-645-5926, E-mail: jmthomas@buffalo.edu. *Application contact:* David W. Frasier, Administrative Director of Graduate Programs and Assistant Dean, 716-645-3204, Fax: 716-645-2341, E-mail: davidf@buffalo.edu.

University of Alaska Anchorage, College of Business and Public Policy, Program in Logistics, Anchorage, AK 99508-8060. Offers global supply chain management (MS); supply chain management (Certificate). Part-time and evening/weekend programs available. Postbaccalaureate distance learning degree programs offered (no on-campus study). *Students:* 3 full-time (1 woman), 9 part-time (3 women), 1 international. 12 applicants, 33% accepted, 4 enrolled. In 2006, 6 degrees awarded. *Degree requirements:* For master's, thesis or alternative, research project. *Entrance requirements:* Additional exam requirements/recommendations for international students: Required—TOEFL (minimum score 550 paper-based; 213 computer-based). *Application deadline:* For fall admission, 7/1 for domestic and international students; for spring admission, 11/1 for domestic and international students. Application fee: $45. *Expenses:* Tuition, state resident: part-time $268 per credit. Tuition, nonresident: part-time $547 per credit. Required fees: $124 per semester. Tuition and fees vary according to reciprocity agreements and student level. *Financial support:* Scholarships/grants, health care benefits, and unspecified assistantships available. Support available to part-time students. *Unit head:* Dr. Oliver Hedgepeth, Chair, 907-786-4116. *Application contact:* Pat Lee, CBPP Graduate Programs Assistant, 907-786-4101, Fax: 907-786-4119, E-mail: pat.lee@uaa.alaska.edu.

University of Arkansas, Graduate School, Sam M. Walton College of Business Administration, Department of Transportation and Logistics Management, Fayetteville, AR 72701-1201. Offers MTLM. Part-time programs available. *Students:* 1 (woman) full-time, 6 part-time (2 women); includes 1 minority (African American), 3 international. In 2006, 12 degrees awarded. Application fee: $40 ($50 for international students). *Financial support:* In 2006–07, 1 research assistantship was awarded; fellowships with tuition reimbursements, teaching assistantships also available. Financial award application deadline: 4/1. *Unit head:* Dr. Tom Jensen, Chair, 479-575-4055. *Application contact:* Matt Waller, Graduate Coordinator, 479-575-7334, E-mail: mwaller@walton.uark.edu.

University of Dallas, Graduate School of Management, Irving, TX 75062-4736. Offers accounting (MBA, MS); business management (MBA); corporate finance (MBA, MM); engineering management (MBA, MM); entrepreneurship (MBA, MM); financial services (MBA, MM); global business (MBA, MM); health services management (MBA, MM); human resource management (MBA, MM, MS); information assurance (MBA, MM, MS); information technology (MBA, MM, MS); information technology service management (MBA); IT service management (MS); marketing (MM); marketing management (MBA); not-for-profit management (MBA); organization development (MBA); project management (MBA, MM); sports and entertainment management (MBA, MM); strategic leadership (MBA); supply chain management (MBA); supply chain management and market logistics (MM); telecommunications management (MBA, MM). *Accreditation:* ACBSP. Part-time and evening/weekend programs available. Postbaccalaureate distance learning degree programs offered (no on-campus study). *Faculty:* 26 full-time (5 women), 85 part-time/adjunct (18 women). *Students:* 227 full-time (98 women), 1,160 part-time (446 women); includes 473 minority (209 African Americans, 3 American Indian/Alaska Native, 143 Asian Americans or Pacific Islanders, 118 Hispanic Americans), 224 international. Average age 34. 556 applicants, 86% accepted, 291 enrolled. In 2006, 476 degrees awarded. *Entrance requirements:* Additional exam requirements/recommendations for international students: Required—TOEFL. *Application deadline:* Applications are processed on a rolling basis. Application fee: $50. Electronic applications accepted. *Expenses: Contact institution. Financial support:* In 2006–07, 468 students received support. Scholarships/grants and unspecified assistantships available. Financial award application deadline: 2/15; financial award applicants required to submit FAFSA. *Unit head:* Dr. J. Lee Whittington, Dean, 972-721-5230. *Application contact:* Sarah Stivison, Director of Graduate Admissions, 972-721-5198, Fax: 972-721-4009, E-mail: admiss@gsm.udallas.edu.

University of Houston, College of Technology, Department of Information and Logistics Technology, Houston, TX 77204. Offers MS. *Faculty:* 3 full-time (0 women), 5 part-time/adjunct (1 woman). *Students:* 22 full-time (8 women), 24 part-time (4 women); includes 17 minority (3 African Americans, 6 Asian Americans or Pacific Islanders, 8 Hispanic Americans), 11 international. Average age 30. 20 applicants, 90% accepted, 10 enrolled. In 2006, 7 degrees awarded. *Expenses:* Tuition, state resident: full-time $5,429; part-time $226 per credit. Tuition, nonresident: full-time $12,029; part-time $501 per credit. Required fees: $2,454. *Unit head:* Michael Gibson, Chairperson, 713-743-5116, E-mail: mlgibson@uh.edu.

University of Minnesota, Twin Cities Campus, Carlson School of Management, Carlson Full-time MBA Program, Minneapolis, MN 55455-0213. Offers accounting (MBA); entrepreneurship (MBA); finance (MBA); healthcare management (MBA); information and decision sciences (MBA); international business (MBA); marketing and logistics management (MBA); operations and management science (MBA); strategic management and organization (MBA); supply chain management (MBA); JD/MBA; MD/MBA; MHA/MBA. *Accreditation:* AACSB. *Faculty:* 125 full-time (27 women), 120 part-time/adjunct. *Students:* 218 full-time (70 women); includes 18 minority (4 African Americans, 1 American Indian/Alaska Native, 10 Asian Americans or Pacific Islanders, 3 Hispanic Americans), 86 international. Average age 28. 418 applicants, 53% accepted, 124 enrolled. In 2006, 105 degrees awarded. *Median time to degree:* Master's–2 years full-time. *Entrance requirements:* For master's, GMAT. Additional exam requirements/recommendations for international students: Required—TOEFL (minimum score 580 paper-based; 240 computer-based), IELTS. *Application deadline:* For fall admission, 4/15 for domestic students, 2/15 for international students. Application fee: $60 ($90 for international students). Electronic applications accepted. *Expenses: Contact institution.* Full-time tuition and fees vary according to class time, course load, program, reciprocity agreements and student level. *Financial support:* In 2006–07, 131 students received support, including 127 fellowships with full and partial tuition reimbursements available (averaging $20,000 per year); research assistantships with partial tuition reimbursements available, teaching assistantships with partial tuition reimbursements available, career-related internships or fieldwork, Federal Work-Study, institutionally sponsored loans, scholarships/grants, health care benefits, tuition waivers (full and partial), and unspecified assistantships also available. Support available to part-time students. Financial award application deadline: 2/15; financial award applicants required to submit FAFSA. *Faculty research:* IT, strategy, marketing, finance, quality management. *Unit head:* Kathryn J. Carlson, MBA Programs and Executive Education, 612-624-2039, Fax: 612-625-1012, E-mail: full-timeembainfo@csom.umn.edu. *Application contact:* Jeffrey Bieganek, Director, Admissions and Business Development, MBA Programs and Executive Education, 612-625-6558, Fax: 612-625-1012, E-mail: full-timembainfo@csom.umn.edu.

University of Minnesota, Twin Cities Campus, Carlson School of Management, Doctoral Program in Business Administration, Minneapolis, MN 55455-0213. Offers accounting (PhD); finance (PhD); information and decision sciences (PhD); marketing and logistics management (PhD); operations and management science (PhD); strategic management and organization (PhD). *Faculty:* 109 full-time (26 women). *Students:* 90 full-time (30 women); includes 9 minority (5 African Americans, 1 Asian American or Pacific Islander, 3 Hispanic Americans), 60 international. Average age 30. 325 applicants, 8% accepted, 17 enrolled. In 2006, 16 degrees awarded. *Median time to degree:* Of those who began their doctoral program in fall 1998, 61% received their degree in 8 years or less. *Degree requirements:* For doctorate, thesis/dissertation, written and oral preliminary exams, comprehensive exam, registration. *Entrance requirements:* For doctorate, GMAT, GRE General Test, International must submit a TOEFL or IELT. Additional exam requirements/recommendations for international students: Required—TOEFL (minimum score 600 paper-based; 250 computer-based; 100 iBT), IELTS (minimum score 8), TOEFL (paper-based 600, computer-based 250) or IELTS (7.5). *Application deadline:* For fall admission, 12/30 for domestic students, 12/30 priority date for international students. Applications are processed on a rolling basis. Application fee: $55 ($75 for international students). Electronic applications accepted. *Expenses:* Tuition, state resident: full-time $9,302; part-time $775 per credit. Tuition, nonresident: full-time $16,400; part-time $1,367 per credit. Full-time tuition and fees vary according to class time, course load, program, reciprocity agreements and student level. *Financial support:* In 2006–07, 67 students received support, including fellowships with full tuition reimbursements available (averaging $11,000 per year), research assistantships with full tuition reimbursements available (averaging $6,000 per year), teaching assistantships with full tuition reimbursements available (averaging $6,000 per year); institutionally sponsored loans, scholarships/grants, health care benefits, and unspecified assistantships also available. Financial award application deadline: 12/31. *Faculty research:* Corporate strategy, international business, corporate finances, entrepreneurship, quality management, marketing, information and decision science, operations and accounting. Total annual research expenditures: $300,000. *Unit head:* Dr. Paul E. Johnson, Director of Graduate Studies and PhD Program Director, 612-624-5570, Fax: 612-624-8221, E-mail: pjohnson@csom.umn.edu. *Application contact:* Earlene Bronson, Assistant Director, PhD Program, 612-624-0875, Fax: 612-624-8221, E-mail: ebronson@csom.umn.edu.

University of Missouri–St. Louis, College of Business Administration, Program in Business Administration, St. Louis, MO 63121. Offers accounting (MBA); business administration (Certificate); finance (MBA); human resource management (Certificate); logistics and supply chain management (MBA, Certificate); management (MBA); marketing (MBA); marketing management (Certificate); operations (MBA); quantitative management science (MBA); telecommunications management (Certificate). *Accreditation:* AACSB. Part-time and evening/weekend programs available. *Faculty:* 26 full-time (6 women), 2 part-time/adjunct (0 women). *Students:* 242 full-time (156 women), 186 part-time (123 women); includes 48 minority (17 African Americans, 1 American Indian/Alaska Native, 27 Asian Americans or Pacific Islanders, 3 Hispanic Americans), 96 international. Average age 33. In 2006, 138 degrees awarded. *Entrance requirements:* For master's, GMAT, 2 letters of recommendation. Additional exam requirements/recommendations for international students: Required—TOEFL (minimum score 550 paper-based; 213 computer-based). *Application deadline:* For fall admission, 7/1 for domestic students; for spring admission, 11/1 for domestic students. Applications are processed on a rolling basis. Application fee: $35 ($40 for international students). Electronic applications accepted. *Expenses:* Tuition, state resident: part-time $332 per credit hour. Tuition, nonresident: part-time $770 per credit hour. *Financial support:* Research assistantships with full and partial tuition reimbursements, teaching assistantships with full and partial tuition reimbursements, career-related internships or fieldwork, Federal Work-Study, and institutionally sponsored loans available. Support available to part-time students. Financial award application deadline: 4/1; financial award applicants required to submit FAFSA. *Faculty research:* Human resources, strategic management, marketing strategy, consumer behavior product development, advertising. *Application contact:* 314-516-5458, Fax: 314-516-6996, E-mail: gradadm@umsl.edu.

University of Missouri–St. Louis, College of Business Administration, Program in Management Information Systems, St. Louis, MO 63121. Offers information systems (MSMIS, PhD); logistics and supply chain management (PhD). Part-time and evening/weekend programs available. *Faculty:* 8. *Students:* 8 full-time (1 woman), 25 part-time (6 women); includes 3 minority (1 African American, 2 Asian Americans or Pacific Islanders), 12 international. Average age 33. In 2006, 15 degrees awarded. *Entrance requirements:* For master's, GMAT, 2 letters of recommendation; for doctorate, GMAT or GRE, 3 letters of recommendation. Additional exam requirements/recommendations for international students: Required—TOEFL (minimum score 550 paper-based; 213 computer-based). *Application deadline:* For fall admission, 7/1 for domestic students; for spring admission, 11/1 for domestic students. Applications are processed on a rolling basis. Application fee: $35 ($40 for international students). Electronic applications accepted. *Expenses:* Tuition, state resident: part-time $332 per credit hour. Tuition, nonresident: part-time $770 per credit hour. *Financial support:* Career-related internships or fieldwork, Federal Work-Study, and institutionally sponsored loans available. Support available to part-time students. Financial award application deadline: 4/1; financial award applicants required to submit FAFSA. *Faculty research:* International information systems, telecommunications, systems development, information systems sourcing. *Application contact:* 314-516-5458, Fax: 314-516-6996, E-mail: gradadm@umsl.edu.

University of New Hampshire, Graduate School, College of Engineering and Physical Sciences, Department of Mechanical Engineering, Durham, NH 03824. Offers mechanical engineering (MS, PhD); systems design (PhD). Part-time programs available. *Faculty:* 12 full-time. *Students:* 20 full-time (4 women), 16 part-time (3 women); includes 2 minority (1 African American, 1 Asian American or Pacific Islander), 10 international. Average age 27. 25 applicants, 96% accepted, 13 enrolled. In 2006, 3 degrees awarded. *Degree requirements:* For master's, thesis or alternative; for doctorate, thesis/dissertation. *Entrance requirements:* For master's and doctorate, GRE. Additional exam requirements/recommendations for international students: Required—TOEFL (minimum score 550 paper-based; 213 computer-based). *Application deadline:* For fall admission, 4/1 priority date for domestic students, 4/1 for international students; for winter admission, 12/1 priority date for domestic students. Applications are processed on a rolling basis. Application fee: $60. Electronic applications accepted. *Expenses:* Tuition, state resident: full-time $8,540; part-time $474 per credit hour. Tuition, nonresident: full-time $20,990; part-time $862 per credit hour. Required fees: $1,343; $356 per term. Tuition and fees vary according to course load, program and reciprocity agreements. *Financial support:* In 2006–07, 11 research assistantships, 7 teaching assistantships were awarded; fellowships, Federal Work-Study, scholarships/grants, and tuition waivers (full and partial) also available. Support available to part-time students. Financial award application deadline: 2/15. *Faculty research:* Solid mechanics, dynamics, materials science, dynamic systems, automatic control. *Unit head:* Dr. Tozz Gross, Chairperson, 603-862-2445. *Application contact:* Tracey Harvery, Administrative Assistant, 603-862-1353, E-mail: mechanical.engineering@unh.edu.

University of New Haven, Graduate School, Tagliatela College of Engineering, Program in Industrial Engineering, West Haven, CT 06516-1916. Offers industrial engineering (MSIE); logistics (Certificate); MBA/MSIE. Part-time and evening/weekend programs available. *Degree requirements:* For master's, thesis or alternative. *Entrance requirements:* For master's, bachelor's degree in engineering.

The University of Tennessee, Graduate School, College of Business Administration, Program in Business Administration, Knoxville, TN 37996. Offers accounting (PhD); finance (MBA,

PhD); logistics and transportation (MBA, PhD); management (PhD); marketing (MBA, PhD); operations management (MBA); professional business administration (MBA); statistics (PhD); JD/MBA; MS/MBA. *Accreditation:* AACSB. Postbaccalaureate distance learning degree programs offered. *Students:* 344 (105 women); includes 42 minority (20 African Americans, 4 American Indian/Alaska Native, 9 Asian Americans or Pacific Islanders, 9 Hispanic Americans) 49 international. In 2006, 169 master's, 9 doctorates awarded. *Degree requirements:* For master's, thesis or alternative; for doctorate, thesis/dissertation. *Entrance requirements:* For master's and doctorate, GMAT, minimum GPA of 2.7. Additional exam requirements/recommendations for international students: Required—TOEFL. *Application deadline:* For fall admission, 2/1 priority date for domestic students. Application fee: $35. Electronic applications accepted. *Expenses:* Tuition, state resident: full-time $5,574. Tuition, nonresident: full-time $16,840. Required fees: $792. *Financial support:* In 2006–07, 6 fellowships, 3 research assistantships, 35 teaching assistantships were awarded; career-related internships or fieldwork, Federal Work-Study, institutionally sponsored loans, and unspecified assistantships also available. Financial award application deadline: 2/1; financial award applicants required to submit FAFSA. *Unit head:* Dr. Sarah Gardial, Assistant Dean, 865-974-5033, Fax: 865-974-3826, E-mail: sgardial@utk.edu. *Application contact:* Donna Potts, Graduate Representative, 865-974-5033, Fax: 865-974-3826, E-mail: dpotts@utk.edu.

The University of Texas at Arlington, Graduate School, College of Engineering, Department of Industrial and Manufacturing Systems Engineering, Program in Logistics, Arlington, TX 76019. Offers MS. *Students:* 9 full-time (2 women), 5 part-time (2 women); includes 2 minority (1 African American, 1 Hispanic American), 11 international. In 2006, 7 degrees awarded. *Degree requirements:* For master's, thesis optional. *Entrance requirements:* For master's, GRE, GMAT, minimum GPA of 3.0. Additional exam requirements/recommendations for international students: Required—TOEFL (minimum score 550 paper-based; 213 computer-based). *Application deadline:* For fall admission, 6/16 for domestic students. Application fee: $35 ($50 for international students). *Expenses:* Tuition, state resident: full-time $5,528. Tuition, nonresident: full-time $10,478. International tuition: $10,608 full-time. *Financial support:* Fellowships, research assistantships, teaching assistantships, career-related internships or fieldwork, Federal Work-Study, institutionally sponsored loans, scholarships/grants, and unspecified assistantships available. Financial award application deadline: 6/1; financial award applicants required to submit FAFSA. *Application contact:* Dr. Jamie Rogers, Graduate Advisor, 817-272-2495, Fax: 817-272-3406, E-mail: jrogers@uta.edu.

University of Washington, Graduate School, Interdisciplinary Graduate Program in Global Trade, Transportation, and Logistics Studies, Seattle, WA 98195. Offers Certificate.

Virginia Polytechnic Institute and State University, Graduate School, College of Engineering, Department of Electrical and Computer Engineering, Blacksburg, VA 24061. Offers computer engineering (M Eng, MS, PhD); electrical engineering (M Eng, MS, PhD). *Faculty:* 64 full-time (5 women). *Students:* 326 full-time (51 women), 129 part-time (15 women); includes 67 minority (15 African Americans, 2 American Indian/Alaska Native, 38 Asian Americans or Pacific Islanders, 12 Hispanic Americans), 201 international. Average age 29. 954 applicants, 17% accepted, 68 enrolled. In 2006, 105 master's, 33 doctorates awarded. *Entrance requirements:* For master's and doctorate, GRE General Test. Additional exam requirements/recommendations for international students: Required—TOEFL (minimum score 590 paper-based; 243 computer-based). *Application deadline:* For fall admission, 5/15 for international students; for spring admission, 10/15 for international students. Applications are processed on a rolling basis. Application fee: $45. Electronic applications accepted. *Financial support:* In 2006–07, 18 fellowships with full tuition reimbursements (averaging $10,667 per year), 137 research assistantships with full tuition reimbursements (averaging $17,307 per year), 50 teaching assistantships with full tuition reimbursements (averaging $14,930 per year) were awarded; career-related internships or fieldwork, Federal Work-Study, scholarships/grants, and unspecified assistantships also available. Financial award application deadline: 1/15. *Faculty research:* Electromagnetics, controls, electronics, power, communications. *Unit head:* Dr. James J. Thorp, Head, 540-231-7494, Fax: 540-231-3362. *Application contact:* Heather Robertson, Head, 540-231-7262, Fax: 540-231-3362, E-mail: vt.ece.gradadm@vt.edu.

Wilmington College, Division of Business, New Castle, DE 19720-6491. Offers business administration (MBA); finance (MBA); health care administration (MBA, MS); human resource management (MS); management (MS); management information systems (MBA); organizational leadership (MS); public administration (MS); transportation and logistics (MBA, MS). Part-time and evening/weekend programs available. *Faculty:* 3 full-time (0 women). *Students:* 230 full-time (138 women), 432 part-time (274 women); includes 109 minority (98 African Americans, 1 American Indian/Alaska Native, 3 Asian Americans or Pacific Islanders, 7 Hispanic Americans). Average age 34. 229 applicants, 100% accepted, 156 enrolled. In 2006, 273 degrees awarded. *Entrance requirements:* Additional exam requirements/recommendations for international students: Required—TOEFL (minimum score 500 paper-based; 173 computer-based). *Application deadline:* Applications are processed on a rolling basis. Application fee: $25. *Financial support:* Applicants required to submit FAFSA. *Unit head:* Dr. Robert Edelson, Chair, 302-295-1147, Fax: 302-328-7021, E-mail: robert.e.edelson@wilmcoll.edu. *Application contact:* Chris Ferguson, Director of Admissions and Financial Aid, 302-328-9407 Ext. 256, Fax: 302-328-5164, E-mail: inquire@wilmcoll.edu.

Wright State University, School of Graduate Studies, Raj Soin College of Business, Department of Information Systems and Operations Management, Logistics and Supply Chain Management Program, Dayton, OH 45435. Offers MS. *Application contact:* Michael Evans, Director of MBA Programs, 937-775-2437, Fax: 937-775-3545, E-mail: michael.evans@wright.edu.

Supply Chain Management

Arizona State University, Division of Graduate Studies, W.P. Carey School of Business, Program in Business Administration, Tempe, AZ 85287. Offers accountancy (PhD); business administration (MBA); finance (PhD); health services research (PhD); information management (PhD); management (PhD); marketing (PhD); supply chain management (PhD); JD/MBA; MBA/M Arch; MBA/MHSM. MBA/MIM offered jointly with Thunderbird, The American Graduate School of International Management and Groupe Ecole Supéieure de Commerce, Toulouse, France. *Accreditation:* AACSB. *Degree requirements:* For master's, thesis optional; for doctorate, thesis/dissertation. *Entrance requirements:* For master's, GMAT.

California State University, East Bay, Academic Programs and Graduate Studies, College of Business and Economics, Department of Accounting and Computer Information Systems, Hayward, CA 94542-3000. Offers accounting (MBA); computer information systems (MBA, MS), including business administration (MBA), computer information systems (MS); e-business (MBA); supply chain management (MBA); taxation (MBA, MS), including telecommunication (MBA); telecommunications (MS). Part-time and evening/weekend programs available. *Students:* 36. In 2006, 5 degrees awarded. *Degree requirements:* For master's, comprehensive exam or thesis. *Entrance requirements:* For master's, GMAT, minimum GPA of 2.75. Additional exam requirements/recommendations for international students: Required—TOEFL (minimum score 550 paper-based; 213 computer-based). *Application deadline:* For fall admission, 5/31 for domestic students, 4/30 for international students; for winter admission, 9/30 for domestic and international students; for spring admission, 12/31 for domestic students, 11/30 for international students. Application fee: $55. *Financial support:* Career-related internships or fieldwork, Federal Work-Study, and institutionally sponsored loans available. Support available to part-time students. Financial award application deadline: 3/2. *Unit head:* Dr. Christopher Lubwanna, Chair, 510-885-3397, Fax: 510-885-4796, E-mail: chris.lubwanna@csueastbay.edu. *Application contact:* Doris Duncan, Director of Graduate Programs, 510-885-3364, Fax: 510-885-2176, E-mail: doris.duncan@csueastbay.edu.

California State University, East Bay, Academic Programs and Graduate Studies, College of Business and Economics, Department of Management and Finance, Hayward, CA 94542-3000. Offers e-business (MBA); finance (MBA); human resources management (MBA); international business (MBA); management sciences (MBA); operations and material management (MBA); operations research (MBA); quantitative business methods (MS); strategic management (MBA); supply chain management (MBA). Part-time and evening/weekend programs available. *Faculty:* 37 full-time (7 women), 8 part-time/adjunct (3 women). *Students:* 204 full-time, 363 part-time; includes 234 minority (17 African Americans, 191 Asian Americans or Pacific Islanders, 26 Hispanic Americans), 158 international. Average age 32. 373 applicants, 43% accepted, 100 enrolled. In 2006, 281 degrees awarded. *Degree requirements:* For master's, comprehensive exam or thesis. *Entrance requirements:* For master's, GMAT, minimum GPA of 2.75. Additional exam requirements/recommendations for international students: Required—TOEFL (minimum score 550 paper-based; 213 computer-based). *Application deadline:* For fall admission, 5/31 for domestic students, 4/30 for international students; for winter admission, 9/30 for domestic and international students; for spring admission, 12/31 for domestic students, 11/30 for international students. Application fee: $55. *Financial support:* Career-related internships or fieldwork, Federal Work-Study, and institutionally sponsored loans available. Support available to part-time students. Financial award application deadline: 3/2. *Unit head:* Dr. Joyendu Bhadury, Chair, 510-885-3307, E-mail: joy.bhadury@csueastbay.edu. *Application contact:* Doris Duncan, Director of Graduate Programs, 510-885-3364, Fax: 510-885-2176, E-mail: doris.duncan@csueastbay.edu.

Case Western Reserve University, Weatherhead School of Management, Department of Operations, Management Program, Cleveland, OH 44106. Offers operations research (MSM); supply chain (MSM); MBA/MSM. *Accreditation:* AACSB. Part-time and evening/weekend programs available. *Faculty:* 10 full-time (2 women). *Students:* 27 full-time (8 women), 3 part-time (1 woman); includes 2 African Americans, 23 Asian Americans or Pacific Islanders, 1 Hispanic American. Average age 28. 46 applicants, 70% accepted, 13 enrolled. In 2006, 14 degrees awarded. *Degree requirements:* For master's, registration. *Entrance requirements:* For master's, GMAT or GRE, 3 letters of recommendation, resumé. Additional exam requirements/recommendations for international students: Required—TOEFL (minimum score 600 paper-based; 250 computer-based). *Application deadline:* For fall admission, 7/1 priority date for domestic and international students; for winter admission, 5/1 priority date for domestic students, 4/1 priority date for international students; for spring admission, 12/1 priority date for domestic students, 11/1 priority date for international students. Application fee: $50. *Financial support:* Career-related internships or fieldwork, institutionally sponsored loans, scholarships/grants, tuition waivers (partial), and unspecified assistantships available. Financial award application deadline: 3/1. *Faculty research:* Supply chain management, operations management, operations/finance interface optimization, scheduling. *Application contact:* Deborah L Bibb, Admissions Coordinator, 216-368-2030, Fax: 216-368-5548, E-mail: deborah.bibb@case.edu.

Eastern Michigan University, Graduate School, College of Business, Department of Marketing, Ypsilanti, MI 48197. Offers e-business (MBA); international business (MBA); supply chain management (MBA). Part-time and evening/weekend programs available. Postbaccalaureate distance learning degree programs offered (minimal on-campus study). *Entrance requirements:* For master's, GMAT. Additional exam requirements/recommendations for international students: Required—TOEFL. *Application deadline:* For fall admission, 5/15 priority date for domestic and international students; for winter admission, 10/15 priority date for domestic and international students; for spring admission, 3/15 priority date for domestic and international students. Applications are processed on a rolling basis. Application fee: $35. *Expenses:* Tuition, state resident: part-time $341 per credit hour. Tuition, nonresident: full-time $16,104; part-time $671 per credit hour. Required fees: $816; $34 per credit hour. $40 per term. One-time fee: $82 full-time. Tuition and fees vary according to course level, course load, degree level and reciprocity agreements. *Financial support:* Fellowships, research assistantships with full tuition reimbursements, teaching assistantships with full tuition reimbursements, career-related internships or fieldwork, Federal Work-Study, institutionally sponsored loans, scholarships/grants, tuition waivers (partial), and unspecified assistantships available. Support available to part-time students. Financial award applicants required to submit FAFSA. *Unit head:* Dr. Denise Tanguay, Interim Head, 734-487-3323. *Application contact:* Dr. Russ Merz, Department Coordinator, 734-487-1852, E-mail: russ.merz@emich.edu.

Eastern Michigan University, Graduate School, College of Business, Program in Business Administration, Ypsilanti, MI 48197. Offers business administration (MBA); e-business (MBA); enterprise business intelligence (MBA); entrepreneurship (MBA); finance (MBA); human resources (MBA); information systems (MBA); internal auditing (MBA); international business (MBA); nonprofit management (MBA); supply chain management (MBA). *Accreditation:* AACSB. Part-time and evening/weekend programs available. Postbaccalaureate distance learning degree programs offered (minimal on-campus study). *Students:* 98 full-time (36 women), 192 part-time (86 women); includes 50 minority (26 African Americans, 19 Asian Americans or Pacific Islanders, 5 Hispanic Americans), 76 international. Average age 29. In 2006, 109 degrees awarded. *Entrance requirements:* For master's, GMAT. Additional exam requirements/recommendations for international students: Required—TOEFL. *Application deadline:* For fall admission, 5/15 priority date for domestic students, 5/1 priority date for international students; for winter admission, 10/15 priority date for domestic students, 10/1 priority date for international students; for spring admission, 3/15 priority date for domestic students, 3/1 priority date for international students. Applications are processed on a rolling basis. Application fee: $35. *Expenses:* Tuition, state resident: part-time $341 per credit hour. Tuition, nonresident: full-time $16,104; part-time $671 per credit hour. Required fees: $816; $34 per credit hour. $40 per term. One-time fee: $82 full-time. Tuition and fees vary according to course level, course load, degree level and reciprocity agreements. *Financial support:* Fellowships, research assistantships with full tuition reimbursements, teaching assistantships with full tuition reimbursements, career-related internships or fieldwork, Federal Work-Study, institutionally sponsored loans, scholarships/grants, tuition waivers (partial), and unspecified assistantships available. Support available to part-time students. Financial award applicants required to submit FAFSA. *Unit head:* Dawn Gaymer, Assistant Dean, Graduate Business Programs, 734-487-4444, Fax: 734-483-1316, E-mail: dawn.malone@emich.edu. *Application contact:* K. Michelle Henry, Coordinator, 734-487-4444, Fax: 734-483-1316, E-mail: michelle.henry@emich.edu.

Elmhurst College, Graduate Programs, Program in Supply Chain Management, Elmhurst, IL 60126-3296. Offers MS. Part-time and evening/weekend programs available. *Faculty:* 2 full-time (0 women), 4 part-time/adjunct (0 women). *Students:* Average age 35. 35 applicants, 80% accepted, 22 enrolled. In 2006, 17 degrees awarded. *Median time to degree:* Master's–2 years part-time. *Entrance requirements:* For master's, 3 recommendations. Additional exam requirements/recommendations for international students: Required—TOEFL (minimum score 550 paper-based; 213 computer-based). *Application deadline:* Applications are processed on

Supply Chain Management

Elmhurst College (continued)

a rolling basis. Application fee: $25. Electronic applications accepted. *Expenses:* Tuition: Part-time $781 per hour. Required fees: $75 per hour. Part-time tuition and fees vary according to course load and student level. *Financial support:* In 2006–07, 2 students received support. Federal Work-Study and scholarships/grants available. Support available to part-time students. Financial award application deadline: 6/1; financial award applicants required to submit FAFSA. *Application contact:* Elizabeth D. Kuebler, Director of Adult and Graduate Admission, 630-617-3069, Fax: 630-617-5501, E-mail: betsyk@elmhurst.edu.

HEC Montreal, School of Business Administration, Diploma Programs in Administration, Program in Supply Chain Management, Montréal, QC H3T 2A7, Canada. Offers Diploma. Part-time programs available. *Students:* 20 full-time (4 women), 82 part-time (31 women). In 2006, 11 degrees awarded. *Degree requirements:* For Diploma, one foreign language. *Entrance requirements:* For degree, 2 years of working experience, letters of recommendation. *Application deadline:* For fall admission, 4/15 for domestic and international students; for winter admission, 10/1 for domestic and international students. Application fee: $60 Canadian dollars. Tuition and fees charges are reported in Canadian dollars. *Expenses:* Tuition, nonresident: part-time $56 Canadian dollars per credit. Required fees: $30 Canadian dollars per semester. *Application contact:* Francine Blais, Administrative Director, 514-340-6112, Fax: 514-340-6411, E-mail: francine.blais@hec.ca.

Howard University, School of Business, Graduate Programs in Business, Washington, DC 20059-0002. Offers accounting (MBA); entrepreneurship (MBA); finance (MBA); information systems (MBA); international business (MBA); marketing (MBA); supply chain management (MBA); JD/MBA. *Accreditation:* AACSB. Part-time and evening/weekend programs available. Postbaccalaureate distance learning degree programs offered (no on-campus study). *Entrance requirements:* For master's, GMAT, minimum 1 year post undergraduate work experience, resumé, 3 letters of recommendation, advanced college algebra. Additional exam requirements/recommendations for international students: Required—TOEFL. *Faculty research:* Marketing research in multi-ethnic populations, U.S. trade policies and international relations, risk management (finance).

Lehigh University, College of Business and Economics, Bethlehem, PA 18015-3094. Offers accounting (MS), including accounting and information analysis; business administration (MBA); economics (MS, PhD), including economics, health and bio-pharmaceutical economics (MS); entrepreneurship (Certificate); finance (MS), including analytical finance, finance; organizational leadership (Certificate); project management (Certificate); supply chain management (Certificate); MBA/E; MBA/M Ed. *Accreditation:* AACSB. Part-time and evening/weekend programs available. Postbaccalaureate distance learning degree programs offered (minimal on-campus study). *Faculty:* 64 full-time (14 women), 12 part-time/adjunct (0 women). *Students:* 87 full-time (25 women), 219 part-time (60 women); includes 34 minority (9 African Americans, 22 Asian Americans or Pacific Islanders, 3 Hispanic Americans), 56 international. 371 applicants, 69% accepted, 151 enrolled. In 2006, 103 master's, 2 doctorates awarded. Terminal master's awarded for partial completion of doctoral program. *Degree requirements:* For master's, thesis optional; for doctorate, thesis/dissertation, proposal defense, comprehensive exam. *Entrance requirements:* For master's, GMAT, GRE General Test; for doctorate, GMAT or GRE General Test. Additional exam requirements/recommendations for international students: Required—TOEFL (minimum score 600 paper-based; 250 computer-based). *Application deadline:* For fall admission, 7/15 for domestic students, 5/1 for international students; for spring admission, 12/1 for domestic and international students. Applications are processed on a rolling basis. Application fee: $60. Electronic applications accepted. *Expenses:* Contact institution. *Financial support:* In 2006–07, 2 fellowships with full tuition reimbursements (averaging $13,200 per year), 8 research assistantships with full and partial tuition reimbursements (averaging $1,000 per year), 13 teaching assistantships with full tuition reimbursements (averaging $13,200 per year) were awarded; career-related internships or fieldwork, scholarships/grants, health care benefits, tuition waivers (full and partial), and unspecified assistantships also available. Support available to part-time students. Financial award application deadline: 1/15. *Faculty research:* Public finance, energy, investments, activity-based costing, management information systems. *Unit head:* Michael G. Kolchin, Graduate Business Programs, 610-758-4450, Fax: 610-758-5283, E-mail: mgk1@lehigh.edu. *Application contact:* Mary- Theresa Taglang, Director of Graduate Programs, 610-758-5285, Fax: 610-758-5283, E-mail: mtt4@lehigh.edu.

See Close-Ups on pages 283, 285, and 1807.

Maine Maritime Academy, Department of Graduate Studies, Program in Global Supply Chain Management, Castine, ME 04420. Offers MS, Certificate, Diploma. Part-time programs available. *Degree requirements:* For master's, capstone course. *Entrance requirements:* For master's, GMAT or GRE, letters of recommendation. Additional exam requirements/recommendations for international students: Required—TOEFL.

Michigan State University, The Graduate School, Eli Broad Graduate School of Management, Department of Marketing and Supply Chain Management, East Lansing, MI 48824. Offers business administration (PhD); manufacturing and engineering management (MS); supply chain management (MS). Part-time programs available. *Faculty:* 32 full-time (3 women). *Students:* 34 full-time (10 women), 35 part-time (10 women); includes 8 minority (5 African Americans, 1 American Indian/Alaska Native, 1 Asian American or Pacific Islander, 1 Hispanic American), 16 international. Average age 33. 65 applicants, 14% accepted. In 2006, 22 master's, 7 doctorates awarded. *Degree requirements:* For master's, field study, research project; for doctorate, thesis/dissertation, oral defense of dissertation proposal and dissertation, comprehensive exam. *Entrance requirements:* For master's, GMAT, bachelor's degree in related field, letters of recommendation, 2-3 years of work experience, minimum GPA of 3.0 in last 2 years of undergraduate course work; for doctorate, GMAT or GRE, letters of recommendation. Additional exam requirements/recommendations for international students: Required—TOEFL. Electronic applications accepted. *Expenses:* Contact institution. Tuition and fees vary according to program. *Financial support:* In 2006–07, 5 fellowships with tuition reimbursements, 23 research assistantships with tuition reimbursements (averaging $14,743 per year), 4 teaching assistantships with tuition reimbursements (averaging $12,000 per year) were awarded. Total annual research expenditures: $485,815. *Unit head:* Dr. Robert W. Nason, Chairperson, 517-355-2240, Fax: 517-432-1112, E-mail: nason@msu.edu. *Application contact:* Program Information, 517-353-6381, E-mail: mslogs@bus.msu.edu.

North Carolina State University, Graduate School, College of Management, Program in Business Administration, Raleigh, NC 27695. Offers financial management (MBA); information technology management (MBA); marketing management (MBA); product innovation management (MBA); supply chain management (MBA); technology commercialization (MBA). *Accreditation:* AACSB. Part-time programs available. *Degree requirements:* For master's, thesis optional. *Entrance requirements:* For master's, GMAT. Additional exam requirements/recommendations for international students: Required—TOEFL. Electronic applications accepted. *Faculty research:* Manufacturing strategy, information systems, technology commercialization, managing research and development, historical stock returns.

Rutgers, The State University of New Jersey, Newark, Rutgers Business School: Graduate Programs-Newark/New Brunswick, Doctoral Programs in Business, Newark, NJ 07102. Offers accounting (PhD); accounting information systems (PhD); finance (PhD); individualized study (PhD); information technology (PhD); international business (PhD); management science (PhD); organizational management (PhD); supply chain management (PhD).

Syracuse University, Martin J. Whitman School of Management, PhD Program in Business Administration, Syracuse, NY 13244. Offers accounting (PhD); finance (PhD); management information systems (PhD); managerial statistics (PhD); marketing (PhD); operations management (PhD); organizational behavior (PhD); strategy and human resources (PhD); supply chain management (PhD). *Faculty:* 71 full-time (16 women), 2 part-time/adjunct (1 woman). *Students:* 34 full-time (10 women); includes 1 minority (African American), 24 international. Average age 31. 89 applicants, 8% accepted, 4 enrolled. In 2006, 8 degrees awarded. *Degree requirements:* For doctorate, thesis/dissertation, summer research paper, comprehensive exam, registration. *Entrance requirements:* For doctorate, GMAT, 3 recommendations. Additional exam requirements/recommendations for international students: Required—TOEFL (minimum score 600 paper-based; 250 computer-based; 100 iBT). *Application deadline:* For fall admission, 1/30 priority date for domestic students. Applications are processed on a rolling basis. Application fee: $75. Electronic applications accepted. *Expenses:* Tuition: Full-time $16,920; part-time $940 per credit hour. Required fees: $930; $930 per year. *Financial support:* In 2006–07, 1 fellowship with full tuition reimbursement (averaging $19,000 per year), 26 teaching assistantships with full tuition reimbursements (averaging $16,500 per year) were awarded; research assistantships with full tuition reimbursements, health care benefits and unspecified assistantships also available. Financial award application deadline: 1/30. *Faculty research:* Marketing models, market microstructure, supply chain, auditing, corporate governance. *Unit head:* Dr. Ravi Dharwadkar, Director of the PhD Program, 315-443-3386, E-mail: rdharwad@syr.edu. *Application contact:* Shannon Hiemstra, Assistant Director for PhD and Research Programs, 315-443-3549, Fax: 315-443-3671, E-mail: srhiemst@syr.edu.

Syracuse University, Martin J. Whitman School of Management, Program in Business Administration, Syracuse, NY 13244. Offers accounting (MBA); entrepreneurship (MBA); finance (MBA); marketing (MBA); supply chain management (MBA). Part-time programs available. Postbaccalaureate distance learning degree programs offered (minimal on-campus study). *Faculty:* 71 full-time (16 women), 2 part-time/adjunct (1 woman). *Students:* 70 full-time (21 women), 279 part-time (84 women); includes 83 minority (44 African Americans, 33 Asian Americans or Pacific Islanders, 6 Hispanic Americans), 36 international. Average age 27. 227 applicants, 37% accepted, 27 enrolled. In 2006, 140 degrees awarded. *Degree requirements:* For master's, registration. *Entrance requirements:* For master's, GMAT, 2 letters of recommendation, bachelor's degree. Additional exam requirements/recommendations for international students: Required—TOEFL (minimum score 600 paper-based; 250 computer-based; 100 iBT). *Application deadline:* For fall admission, 1/15 priority date for domestic and international students. Applications are processed on a rolling basis. Application fee: $75. Electronic applications accepted. *Expenses:* Tuition: Full-time $16,920; part-time $940 per credit hour. Required fees: $930; $930 per year. *Financial support:* In 2006–07, 17 students received support; fellowships with full and partial tuition reimbursements available, teaching assistantships with partial tuition reimbursements available, career-related internships or fieldwork, scholarships/grants, tuition waivers (partial), unspecified assistantships, and paid hourly positions available. Support available to part-time students. Financial award application deadline: 3/1. *Unit head:* Dr. Ravi Shukla, Associate Dean for MBA and MS Programs, 315-443-3576, Fax: 315-443-9517, E-mail: rkshukla@syr.edu. *Application contact:* Carol J. Swanberg, Director of Graduate Admissions and Financial Aid, 315-443-9214, Fax: 315-443-9517, E-mail: mbainfo@syr.edu.

The University of Akron, Graduate School, College of Business Administration, Department of Management, Program in Management-Supply Chain Management, Akron, OH 44325. Offers MSM. *Students:* 14 full-time (6 women), 8 part-time (1 woman), 13 international. Average age 28. 7 applicants, 100% accepted, 6 enrolled. In 2006, 1 degree awarded. *Entrance requirements:* Additional exam requirements/recommendations for international students: Required—TOEFL (minimum score 550 paper-based; 213 computer-based; 79 iBT). *Application deadline:* Applications are processed on a rolling basis. Application fee: $30 ($40 for international students). Electronic applications accepted. *Expenses:* Tuition, state resident: full-time $6,164; part-time $342 per credit. Tuition, nonresident: full-time $10,575; part-time $588 per credit. Required fees: $806; $43 per credit. $12 per term. Tuition and fees vary according to course load, degree level and program. *Application contact:* Dr. James Divoky, Director of Graduate Business Programs, 330-972-7043, Fax: 330-972-6588, E-mail: jdivoky@uakron.edu.

University of Dallas, Graduate School of Management, Irving, TX 75062-4736. Offers accounting (MBA, MS); business management (MBA); corporate finance (MBA, MM); engineering management (MBA, MM); entrepreneurship (MBA, MM); financial services (MBA, MM); global business (MBA, MM); health services management (MBA, MM); human resource management (MBA, MM, MS); information assurance (MBA, MM, MS); information technology (MBA, MM, MS); information technology service management (MBA); IT service management (MS); marketing (MM); marketing management (MBA); not-for-profit management (MBA); organization development (MBA); project management (MBA, MM); sports and entertainment management (MBA, MM); strategic leadership (MBA); supply chain management (MBA); supply chain management and market logistics (MM); telecommunications management (MBA, MM). *Accreditation:* ACBSP. Part-time and evening/weekend programs available. Postbaccalaureate distance learning degree programs offered (no on-campus study). *Faculty:* 26 full-time (5 women), 85 part-time/adjunct (18 women). *Students:* 227 full-time (98 women), 1,160 part-time (446 women); includes 473 minority (209 African Americans, 3 American Indian/Alaska Native, 143 Asian Americans or Pacific Islanders, 118 Hispanic Americans), 224 international. Average age 34. 556 applicants, 86% accepted, 291 enrolled. In 2006, 476 degrees awarded. *Entrance requirements:* Additional exam requirements/recommendations for international students: Required—TOEFL. *Application deadline:* Applications are processed on a rolling basis. Application fee: $50. Electronic applications accepted. *Expenses:* Contact institution. *Financial support:* In 2006–07, 468 students received support. Scholarships/grants and unspecified assistantships available. Financial award application deadline: 2/15; financial award applicants required to submit FAFSA. *Unit head:* Dr. J. Lee Whittington, Dean, 972-721-5230. *Application contact:* Sarah Stivison, Director of Graduate Admissions, 972-721-5198, Fax: 972-721-4009, E-mail: admiss@gsm.udallas.edu.

University of Florida, Graduate School, Warrington College of Business Administration, Department of Information Systems and Operations Management, Gainesville, FL 32611. Offers decision and information sciences (MS, PhD); supply chain management (MS). *Faculty:* 13 full-time (2 women). *Students:* 118 (38 women); includes 22 minority (8 African Americans, 8 Asian Americans or Pacific Islanders, 6 Hispanic Americans) 38 international. In 2006, 5 degrees awarded. Terminal master's awarded for partial completion of doctoral program. *Degree requirements:* For doctorate, thesis/dissertation. *Entrance requirements:* For master's and doctorate, GMAT or GRE General Test, minimum GPA of 3.0. Additional exam requirements/recommendations for international students: Required—TOEFL (minimum score 550 paper-based; 213 computer-based). *Application deadline:* For fall admission, 2/16 priority date for domestic students. Applications are processed on a rolling basis. Application fee: $30. *Expenses:* Tuition, state resident: full-time $6,827. Tuition, nonresident: full-time $21,951. Required fees: $999. *Financial support:* In 2006–07, 1 research assistantship (averaging $20,376 per year), 10 teaching assistantships (averaging $18,437 per year) were awarded; fellowships, unspecified assistantships also available. *Faculty research:* Expert systems, nonconvex optimization, manufacturing management, production and operation management, telecommunication. *Unit head:* Dr. Asoo J. Vakharia, Chair, 352-392-8571, Fax: 352-392-5438, E-mail: asoov@ufl.edu. *Application contact:* Chandra Hardy, Coordinator, 352-846-1370, Fax: 352-392-5438, E-mail: chandra.hardy@cba.ufl.edu.

University of Indianapolis, Graduate Programs, School of Business, Graduate Business Programs, Indianapolis, IN 46227-3697. Offers business (EMBA); business administration (MBA); finance (Graduate Certificate); global supply chains management (Graduate Certificate); marketing (Graduate Certificate); organizational leadership (Graduate Certificate); technology management (Graduate Certificate). *Accreditation:* ACBSP. Part-time and evening/weekend programs available. *Faculty:* 6 full-time (2 women), 6 part-time/adjunct (1 woman). *Students:* 50 full-time (16 women), 92 part-time (32 women); includes 12 minority (4 African Americans, 7 Asian Americans or Pacific Islanders, 1 Hispanic American), 10 international. Average age 32. In 2006, 57 degrees awarded. *Entrance requirements:* For master's, GMAT, interview, minimum GPA of 2.8, 2 letters of recommendation, resumé. Additional exam requirements/recommendations for international students: Required—TOEFL (minimum score 550 paper-based; 213 computer-based). *Application deadline:* Applications are processed on a rolling basis. Application fee: $50. *Expenses:* Contact institution. *Financial support:* Federal Work-Study and unspecified assistantships available. Financial award application deadline: 5/1;

financial award applicants required to submit FAFSA. *Faculty research:* Integration of microcomputers into decision making, communication skills, application of synthesized theories. *Unit head:* Dr. Matthew Will, Associate Dean, 317-788-3370, E-mail: mwill@uindy.edu.

University of La Verne, Regional Campus Administration, Graduate Programs, Orange County Campus, Garden Grove, CA 92840. Offers business (MBA-EP), including health services management, information technology, management, marketing, supply chain management; health administration (MHA); leadership and management (MS); public administration (MPA). *Faculty:* 4 full-time (1 woman), 3 part-time/adjunct (1 woman). *Students:* 19 full-time (8 women), 64 part-time (29 women); includes 37 minority (4 African Americans, 2 American Indian/Alaska Native, 15 Asian Americans or Pacific Islanders, 16 Hispanic Americans). Average age 41. In 2006, 18 degrees awarded. *Entrance requirements:* For master's, 2 letters of recommendation, resumé. *Application deadline:* Applications are processed on a rolling basis. Application fee: $50. *Expenses:* Contact institution. *Financial support:* Institutionally sponsored loans available. Financial award application deadline: 3/2; financial award applicants required to submit FAFSA. *Unit head:* Pamela Bergovoy, Director, 714-534-4860, Fax: 714-534-4865, E-mail: bergovoy@ulv.edu.

University of Massachusetts Dartmouth, Graduate School, Charlton College of Business, Program in Business Administration, North Dartmouth, MA 02747-2300. Offers accounting (Postbaccalaureate Certificate); business administration (MBA); e-commerce (PMC); finance (PMC); general management (PMC); leadership (PMC); management (Postbaccalaureate Certificate); marketing (PMC); supply chain management (PMC). *Accreditation:* AACSB. Part-time programs available. *Faculty:* 41 full-time (11 women), 22 part-time/adjunct (8 women). *Students:* 66 full-time (20 women), 111 part-time (54 women); includes 16 minority (5 African Americans, 6 Asian Americans or Pacific Islanders, 5 Hispanic Americans), 46 international. Average age 30. 167 applicants, 83% accepted, 83 enrolled. In 2006, 73 master's, 20 other advanced degrees awarded. *Entrance requirements:* For master's, GMAT, resumé, letters of recommendation. Additional exam requirements/recommendations for international students: Required—TOEFL (minimum score 500 paper-based). *Application deadline:* For fall admission, 6/1 for domestic students, 4/1 for international students; for spring admission, 10/1 for domestic students, 8/1 for international students. Application fee: $40 ($60 for international students). Electronic applications accepted. *Expenses:* Tuition, state resident: full-time $2,071; part-time $86 per credit. Tuition, nonresident: full-time $8,099; part-time $337 per credit. *Financial support:* In 2006–07, 2 research assistantships with full tuition reimbursements (averaging $11,985 per year), 6 teaching assistantships with full tuition reimbursements (averaging $7,200 per year) were awarded; Federal Work-Study and unspecified assistantships also available. Support available to part-time students. Financial award application deadline: 3/1; financial award applicants required to submit FAFSA. *Faculty research:* Organizational identity dynamics in strategic alliances and partnerships, market analysis in cranberry industry, consumer choice modeling. Total annual research expenditures: $508,000. *Unit head:* Matthew Roy, Assistant Dean, 508-999-8409, Fax: 508-999-8776, E-mail: mroy@umassd.edu. *Application contact:* Carol Novo, Graduate Admissions Officer, 508-999-8604, Fax: 508-999-8183, E-mail: graduate@umassd.edu.

University of Memphis, Graduate School, Fogelman College of Business and Economics, Program in Business Administration, Memphis, TN 38152. Offers accounting (MBA, PhD); economics (MBA, PhD); executive business administration (MBA); finance (PhD); finance, insurance, and real estate (MBA, MS); international business administration (MBA); management (MBA, MS, PhD); management information systems (MBA, MS, PhD); management science (MBA); marketing (MBA, MS); marketing and supply chain management (PhD); real estate development (MS); JD/MBA. *Accreditation:* AACSB. *Faculty:* 84 full-time (14 women), 3 part-time/adjunct (0 women). *Students:* 222 full-time (92 women), 163 part-time (52 women); includes 62 minority (43 African Americans, 14 Asian Americans or Pacific Islanders, 5 Hispanic Americans), 119 international. Average age 29. In 2006, 196 master's, 12 doctorates awarded. *Degree requirements:* For master's, comprehensive exam; for doctorate, thesis/dissertation, comprehensive exam. *Entrance requirements:* For master's, GMAT, resumé; for doctorate, GMAT, interview, minimum GPA of 3.4, resumé, letter of recommendation. Additional exam requirements/recommendations for international students: Required—TOEFL (minimum score 550 paper-based; 220 computer-based). *Application deadline:* For fall admission, 8/1 for domestic students; for spring admission, 12/1 for domestic students. Application fee: $25 ($50 for international students). *Financial support:* Research assistantships with full tuition reimbursements, teaching assistantships, career-related internships or fieldwork, scholarships/grants, and unspecified assistantships available. Financial award application deadline: 3/1. *Faculty research:* Competitive business strategy, finance microstructures, supply chain management innovations, health care economics, litigation risks and corporate audits. Total annual research expenditures: $2.7 million. *Application contact:* Dr. Carol V. Danehower, Associate Dean for Programs, 901-678-5402, Fax: 901-678-3579, E-mail: fcbegp@memphis.edu.

University of Minnesota, Twin Cities Campus, Carlson School of Management, Carlson Full-time MBA Program, Minneapolis, MN 55455-0213. Offers accounting (MBA); entrepreneurship (MBA); finance (MBA); healthcare management (MBA); information and decision sciences (MBA); international business (MBA); marketing and logistics management (MBA); operations and management science (MBA); strategic management and organization (MBA); supply chain management (MBA); JD/MBA; MD/MBA; MHA/MBA. *Accreditation:* AACSB. *Faculty:* 125 full-time (27 women), 120 part-time/adjunct. *Students:* 218 full-time (70 women); includes 18 minority (4 African Americans, 1 American Indian/Alaska Native, 10 Asian Americans or Pacific Islanders, 3 Hispanic Americans), 86 international. Average age 28. 418 applicants, 53% accepted, 124 enrolled. In 2006, 105 degrees awarded. *Median time to degree:* Master's–2 years full-time. *Entrance requirements:* For master's, GMAT. Additional exam requirements/recommendations for international students: Required—TOEFL (minimum score 580 paper-based; 240 computer-based), IELTS. *Application deadline:* For fall admission, 4/15 for domestic students, 2/15 for international students. Application fee: $60 ($90 for international students). Electronic applications accepted. *Expenses:* Contact institution. Full-time tuition and fees vary according to class time, course load, program, reciprocity agreements and student level. *Financial support:* In 2006–07, 131 students received support, including 127 fellowships with full and partial tuition reimbursements available (averaging $20,000 per year); research assistantships with partial tuition reimbursements available, teaching assistantships with partial tuition reimbursements available, career-related internships or fieldwork, Federal Work-Study, institutionally sponsored loans, scholarships/grants, health care benefits, tuition waivers (full and partial), and unspecified assistantships also available. Support available to part-time students. Financial award application deadline: 2/15; financial award applicants required to submit FAFSA. *Faculty research:* IT, strategy, marketing, finance, quality management. *Unit head:* Kathryn J. Carlson, MBA Programs and Executive Education, 612-624-2039, Fax: 612-625-1012, E-mail: fulltimeembainfo@csom.umn.edu. *Application contact:* Jeffrey Bieganek, Director, Admissions and Business Development, MBA Programs and Executive Education, 612-625-6558, Fax: 612-625-1012, E-mail: full-timembainfo@csom.umn.edu.

University of Missouri–St. Louis, College of Business Administration, Program in Business Administration, St. Louis, MO 63121. Offers accounting (MBA); business administration (Certificate); finance (MBA); human resource management (Certificate); logistics and supply chain management (MBA, Certificate); management (MBA); marketing (MBA); marketing management (Certificate); operations (MBA); quantitative management science (MBA); telecommunications management (Certificate). *Accreditation:* AACSB. Part-time and evening/weekend programs available. *Faculty:* 26 full-time (6 women), 2 part-time/adjunct (0 women). *Students:* 242 full-time (156 women), 186 part-time (123 women); includes 48 minority (17 African Americans, 1 American Indian/Alaska Native, 27 Asian Americans or Pacific Islanders, 3 Hispanic Americans), 96 international. Average age 33. In 2006, 138 degrees awarded. *Entrance requirements:* For master's, GMAT, 2 letters of recommendation. Additional exam requirements/recommendations for international students: Required—TOEFL (minimum score 550 paper-based; 213 computer-based). *Application deadline:* For fall admission, 7/1 for domestic students; for spring admission, 11/1 for domestic students. Applications are processed on a rolling basis. Application fee: $35 ($40 for international students). Electronic applications accepted. *Expenses:* Tuition, state resident: part-time $332 per credit hour. Tuition, nonresident: part-time $770 per credit hour. *Financial support:* Research assistantships with full and partial tuition reimbursements, teaching assistantships with full and partial tuition reimbursements, career-related internships or fieldwork, Federal Work-Study, and institutionally sponsored loans available. Support available to part-time students. Financial award application deadline: 4/1; financial award applicants required to submit FAFSA. *Faculty research:* Human resources, strategic management, marketing strategy, consumer behavior product development, advertising. *Application contact:* 314-516-5458, Fax: 314-516-6996, E-mail: gradadm@umsl.edu.

University of Missouri–St. Louis, College of Business Administration, Program in Management Information Systems, St. Louis, MO 63121. Offers information systems (MSMIS, PhD); logistics and supply chain management (PhD). Part-time and evening/weekend programs available. *Faculty:* 8. *Students:* 8 full-time (1 woman), 25 part-time (6 women); includes 3 minority (1 African American, 2 Asian Americans or Pacific Islanders), 12 international. Average age 33. In 2006, 15 degrees awarded. *Entrance requirements:* For master's, GMAT, 2 letters of recommendation; for doctorate, GMAT or GRE, 3 letters of recommendation. Additional exam requirements/recommendations for international students: Required—TOEFL (minimum score 550 paper-based; 213 computer-based). *Application deadline:* For fall admission, 7/1 for domestic students; for spring admission, 11/1 for domestic students. Applications are processed on a rolling basis. Application fee: $35 ($40 for international students). Electronic applications accepted. *Expenses:* Tuition, state resident: part-time $332 per credit hour. Tuition, nonresident: part-time $770 per credit hour. *Financial support:* Career-related internships or fieldwork, Federal Work-Study, and institutionally sponsored loans available. Support available to part-time students. Financial award application deadline: 4/1; financial award applicants required to submit FAFSA. *Faculty research:* International information systems, telecommunications, systems development, information systems sourcing. *Application contact:* 314-516-5458, Fax: 314-516-6996, E-mail: gradadm@umsl.edu.

The University of North Carolina at Greensboro, Graduate School, Bryan School of Business and Economics, Department of Information Systems and Operations Management, Greensboro, NC 27412-5001. Offers information systems (PhD); information technology (Certificate); information technology and management (MS); supply chain management (Certificate). *Faculty:* 14 full-time (2 women), 3 part-time/adjunct (2 women). *Students:* 27 full-time (12 women), 60 part-time (26 women); includes 21 minority (6 African Americans, 15 Asian Americans or Pacific Islanders). 60 applicants, 30% accepted. *Entrance requirements:* For master's, GMAT, GRE General Test. Additional exam requirements/recommendations for international students: Required—TOEFL. *Application deadline:* For fall admission, 7/1 priority date for domestic students; for spring admission, 11/1 for domestic students. Applications are processed on a rolling basis. Application fee: $45. Electronic applications accepted. *Expenses:* Tuition, state resident: full-time $2,692. Tuition, nonresident: full-time $13,742. *Unit head:* Dr. Kwasi Amoako-Gyampah, Head, 336-334-5666, Fax: 336-334-4083, E-mail: kwasi_amoako@uncg.edu. *Application contact:* Michelle Harkleroad, Director of Graduate Admissions, 336-334-4884, Fax: 336-334-4424, E-mail: mbharkle@uncg.edu.

University of San Diego, School of Business Administration, San Diego, CA 92110-2492. Offers accounting and financial management (MS); business administration (MBA); executive leadership (MSEL); global leadership (MSGL); international business administration (IMBA); real estate (MSRE); supply chain management (MS, Certificate); taxation (MS); JD/IMBA; JD/MBA; MBA/MSIT; MBA/MSN; MBA/MSRE. *Accreditation:* AACSB. Part-time and evening/weekend programs available. *Faculty:* 35 full-time (10 women), 18 part-time/adjunct (4 women). *Students:* 187 full-time (76 women), 265 part-time (89 women); includes 55 minority (5 African Americans, 1 American Indian/Alaska Native, 32 Asian Americans or Pacific Islanders, 17 Hispanic Americans), 45 international. Average age 32. 517 applicants, 66% accepted, 187 enrolled. In 2006, 256 degrees awarded. *Entrance requirements:* For master's, GMAT, minimum GPA of 3.0, minimum 2 years of full-time work experience. Additional exam requirements/recommendations for international students: Required—TOEFL (minimum score 580 paper-based; 237 computer-based), TWE. *Application deadline:* For fall admission, 5/1 priority date for domestic students; for spring admission, 11/15 priority date for domestic students. Applications are processed on a rolling basis. Application fee: $45. Electronic applications accepted. *Financial support:* Career-related internships or fieldwork, Federal Work-Study, institutionally sponsored loans, scholarships/grants, tuition waivers (partial), and unspecified assistantships available. Support available to part-time students. Financial award application deadline: 5/1; financial award applicants required to submit FAFSA. *Faculty research:* Business management, production, purchasing, quantitative methods, accounting. *Unit head:* Dr. Andy Allen, Interim Dean, 619-260-4886, E-mail: sbadean@sandiego.edu. *Application contact:* Stephen Pultz, Director of Admissions, 619-260-4524, Fax: 619-260-4158, E-mail: grads@sandiego.edu.

University of Wisconsin–Madison, Graduate School, School of Business, Wisconsin Full-Time MBA Programs, Madison, WI 53706-1380. Offers applied corporate finance (MBA); applied security analysis (MBA); arts administration (MBA); brand and product management (MBA); entrepreneurial management (MBA); information systems (MBA); marketing research (MBA); operations and technology management (MBA); real estate (MBA); risk management and insurance (MBA); strategic human resource management (MBA); strategic management in the life and engineering sciences (MBA); supply chain management (MBA). *Faculty:* 84. *Students:* 231 full-time (74 women); includes 21 minority (10 African Americans, 5 Asian Americans or Pacific Islanders, 6 Hispanic Americans), 59 international. Average age 28. 405 applicants, 43% accepted, 121 enrolled. In 2006, 110 degrees awarded. *Entrance requirements:* For master's, GMAT, bachelors or equivalent degree, 2 years of work experience. Additional exam requirements/recommendations for international students: Required—TOEFL (minimum score 600 paper-based; 250 computer-based; 90 iBT). *Application deadline:* For fall admission, 11/1 for domestic and international students; for winter admission, 1/23 for domestic and international students; for spring admission, 3/26 for domestic and international students. Applications are processed on a rolling basis. Application fee: $45. Electronic applications accepted. *Financial support:* In 2006–07, 177 students received support, including 20 fellowships with full and partial tuition reimbursements available (averaging $16,566 per year), 105 research assistantships with full tuition reimbursements available (averaging $8,098 per year), 33 teaching assistantships with full tuition reimbursements available (averaging $10,112 per year); scholarships/grants, health care benefits, and unspecified assistantships also available. *Unit head:* Gary Lessuise, Assistant Dean, Masters Programs, 608-265-5102, Fax: 608-265-4192, E-mail: glessuise@bus.wisc.edu. *Application contact:* Betsy Kacizak, Director of Admissions and Financial Aid—Full Time MBA, 608-262-4000, Fax: 608-265-4192, E-mail: mba@bus.wisc.edu.

University of Wisconsin–Whitewater, School of Graduate Studies, College of Business and Economics, Program in Business Administration, Whitewater, WI 53190-1790. Offers finance (MBA); human resource management (MBA); information technology management (MBA); international business (MBA); management (MBA); marketing (MBA); operations and supply chain management (MBA); technology and training (MBA). *Accreditation:* AACSB. Part-time and evening/weekend programs available. Postbaccalaureate distance learning degree programs offered (no on-campus study). *Students:* 67 full-time (26 women), 331 part-time (136 women); includes 71 minority (20 African Americans, 40 Asian Americans or Pacific Islanders, 11 Hispanic Americans). Average age 28. 167 applicants, 62% accepted, 75 enrolled. In 2006, 141 degrees awarded. *Degree requirements:* For master's, thesis or alternative. *Entrance requirements:* For master's, GMAT, minimum AACSB index of 1000, minimum GPA of 2.75. Additional exam requirements/recommendations for international students: Required—TOEFL (minimum score 550 paper-based; 213 computer-based). *Application deadline:* For fall admission, 7/15 for domestic students, 7/15 priority date for international students; for spring admission, 12/1 for domestic and international students. Applications are processed on a rolling basis. Application fee: $45. Electronic applications accepted. *Expenses:* Tuition, state resident: full-time $3,311. Tuition, nonresident: full-time $8,616. Required fees: $368 per credit. *Financial support:* In 2006–07, 11 research assistantships (averaging $7,385 per year)

Supply Chain Management

University of Wisconsin–Whitewater (continued)
were awarded; Federal Work-Study, unspecified assistantships, and out of state fee waiver also available. Support available to part-time students. Financial award application deadline: 3/15; financial award applicants required to submit FAFSA. *Faculty research:* Interface between social institutions and individual behavior, technology and innovation management, occupational mental health, workplace deviance and workplace romance. *Unit head:* Dr. Donald Zahn, Associate Dean, 262-472-1945, Fax: 262-472-4863, E-mail: zahnd@uww.edu.

Worcester Polytechnic Institute, Graduate Studies and Enrollment, Department of Management, Program in Operations Design and Leadership, Worcester, MA 01609-2280. Offers process design (MS); supply chain management (MS). Part-time and evening/weekend programs available. Postbaccalaureate distance learning degree programs offered (no on-campus study). *Faculty:* 11 full-time (6 women), 1 part-time/adjunct (0 women). *Students:* 4 full-time (2 women), 9 part-time (4 women), 3 international. Average age 32. 13 applicants, 85% accepted, 4 enrolled. In 2006, 2 degrees awarded. *Median time to degree:* Master's–1.5 years full-time, 3 years part-time. *Degree requirements:* For master's, thesis optional. *Entrance requirements:* For master's, GMAT or GRE. Additional exam requirements/recommendations for international students: Required—TOEFL (minimum score 550 paper-based; 213 computer-based; 79 iBT), IELTS (minimum score 7). *Application deadline:* For fall admission, 6/1 priority date for domestic and international students; for spring admission, 10/15 for domestic students, 10/1 priority date for international students. Applications are processed on a rolling basis. Application fee: $70. Electronic applications accepted. *Expenses:* Tuition: Part-time $1,042 per credit hour. Required fees: $1,009 per year. *Financial support:* In 2006–07, 3 students received support, including 2 research assistantships; career-related internships or fieldwork, Federal Work-Study, scholarships/grants, and unspecified assistantships also available. Financial award application deadline: 6/1; financial award applicants required to submit FAFSA. *Faculty research:* Global sourcing and supply chain management, service operations modeling, health care operations and performance analysis, lean process deign. Total annual research expenditures: $117,061. *Unit head:* Norm D. Wilkinson, Director, Graduate Management Programs, 508-831-5957, Fax: 508-831-5720, E-mail: nwilkins@wpi.edu.

See Close-Up on page 377.

Wright State University, School of Graduate Studies, Raj Soin College of Business, Department of Information Systems and Operations Management, Logistics and Supply Chain Management Program, Dayton, OH 45435. Offers MS. *Application contact:* Michael Evans, Director of MBA Programs, 937-775-2437, Fax: 937-775-3545, E-mail: michael.evans@wright.edu.

Wright State University, School of Graduate Studies, Raj Soin College of Business, Department of Management, Dayton, OH 45435. Offers flexible business (MBA); health care management (MBA); international business (MBA); management, innovation and change (MBA); project management (MBA); supply chain management (MBA); MBA/MS. *Students:* 47 full-time (22 women), 154 part-time (63 women). Average age 31. 40 applicants, 90% accepted. In 2006, 71 degrees awarded. *Entrance requirements:* For master's, GMAT, minimum AACSB index of 1000. Additional exam requirements/recommendations for international students: Required—TOEFL. Application fee: $25. *Financial support:* Fellowships, research assistantships, teaching assistantships, unspecified assistantships available. Support available to part-time students. Financial award applicants required to submit FAFSA. *Unit head:* Dr. Riad Ajami, Chair, 937-775-2375, Fax: 937-775-3545, E-mail: riad.ajami@wright.edu. *Application contact:* Michael Evans, Director of MBA Programs, 937-775-2437, Fax: 937-775-3545, E-mail: michael.evans@wright.edu.

Transportation Management

American Public University System, AMU/APU Graduate Programs, Charles Town, WV 25414. Offers business administration (MBA); criminal justice (MA); emergency and disaster management (MA); environmental policy and management (MS); history (MA); homeland security (MA); humanities (MA); intelligence (MA Strategic Intelligence); international relations and conflict resolution (MA); management (MA); military history (MA); national security studies (MA); political science (MA); public administration (MA); public health (MA); security management (MA); space studies (MS); sports management (MA); transportation and logistics management (MA). Programs offered via distance learning only. Part-time and evening/weekend programs available. Postbaccalaureate distance learning degree programs offered (no on-campus study). *Faculty:* 10 full-time (3 women), 188 part-time/adjunct (57 women). *Students:* 498 full-time (104 women), 5,272 part-time (1,209 women). Average age 34. 6,574 applicants, 100% accepted, 3508 enrolled. In 2006, 358 degrees awarded. *Degree requirements:* For master's, comprehensive exam, registration. *Entrance requirements:* For master's, bachelor's degree or equivalent, minimum GPA of 2.7 in last 60 hours of course work. *Application deadline:* For fall admission, 9/1 priority date for domestic students; for winter admission, 1/1 priority date for domestic students; for spring admission, 5/1 priority date for domestic students. Applications are processed on a rolling basis. Application fee: $0. Electronic applications accepted. *Expenses:* Tuition: Full-time $4,950; part-time $275 per credit. One-time fee: $200 full-time. *Financial support:* Applicants required to submit FAFSA. *Faculty research:* Military history, criminal justice, management performance, national security. *Unit head:* Dr. Frank McCluskey, Provost, 877-468-6268, Fax: 304-724-3780. *Application contact:* Terry Grant, Director of Enrollment Management, 877-468-6268, Fax: 304-724-3780, E-mail: info@apus.edu.

Arizona State University, Division of Graduate Studies, Interdisciplinary Program in Transportation Systems, Tempe, AZ 85287. Offers Certificate. Students must be enrolled in an appropriate degree program.

Arizona State University at the Polytechnic Campus, College of Science and Technology, Department of Aeronautical Management Technology, Mesa, AZ 85212. Offers MS. Part-time and evening/weekend programs available. *Faculty:* 3 full-time (1 woman). *Students:* 4 full-time (1 woman), 12 part-time (3 women); includes 2 minority (1 African American, 1 American Indian/Alaska Native), 5 international. Average age 32. 7 applicants, 100% accepted, 4 enrolled. In 2006, 6 degrees awarded. *Degree requirements:* For master's, thesis or applied project and oral defense. *Entrance requirements:* For master's, minimum GPA of 3.0, 30 semester hours in technology or equivalent, 16 hours of physical science and mathematics. Additional exam requirements/recommendations for international students: Required—TOEFL (minimum score 550 paper-based; 213 computer-based; 83 iBT); Recommended—TWE. *Application deadline:* Applications are processed on a rolling basis. Application fee: $50. Electronic applications accepted. *Expenses:* Tuition, state resident: part-time $310 per credit hour. Tuition, nonresident: part-time $688 per credit hour. *Financial support:* Research assistantships with full and partial tuition reimbursements, career-related internships or fieldwork, Federal Work-Study, scholarships/grants, health care benefits, tuition waivers (full and partial), and unspecified assistantships available. Support available to part-time students. Financial award application deadline: 3/1; financial award applicants required to submit FAFSA. *Faculty research:* Aviation training and education, human factors, aviation psychology, high altitude flight physiology, women in aviation, safety, aerospace medicine, metacognition, self regulation, learning strategies of pilots, aviation law, airline management. Total annual research expenditures: $14,451. *Unit head:* Dr. William K. McCurry, Chair, 480-727-1998, Fax: 480-727-1730, E-mail: mccurry@asu.edu.

Concordia University, School of Graduate Studies, John Molson School of Business, Montréal, QC H3G 1M8, Canada. Offers administration (M Sc, Diploma); aviation management (Certificate, Diploma); business administration (MBA, UA Undergraduate Associate, PhD), including international aviation (UA Undergraduate Associate); chartered accountancy (Diploma); community organizational development (Certificate); event management and fundraising (Certificate); executive business administration (EMBA); investment management (Diploma); investment management option (MBA); management accounting (Certificate); management of healthcare organizations (Certificate); sport administration (Diploma). *Accreditation:* AACSB. Part-time and evening/weekend programs available. *Students:* 447 full-time (174 women), 448 part-time (206 women). 925 applicants, 59% accepted, 319 enrolled. In 2006, 183 master's, 6 doctorates, 62 other advanced degrees awarded. *Degree requirements:* For master's, one foreign language, thesis (for some programs), research project; for doctorate, one foreign language, thesis/dissertation; for other advanced degree, one foreign language. *Entrance requirements:* For master's and doctorate, GMAT. Additional exam requirements/recommendations for international students: Required—TOEFL. Application fee: $50. *Expenses:* Contact institution. *Financial support:* Fellowships, career-related internships or fieldwork available. *Faculty research:* General business, capital markets, international business. *Unit head:* Dr. Jerry Tomberlin, Dean, 514-848-2424 Ext. 2700, Fax: 514-848-4502. *Application contact:* Dr. Michel Magnan, Associate Dean, Graduate Programs, 514-848-2424 Ext. 4145, Fax: 514-848-4208.

Florida Institute of Technology, Graduate Programs, University College, Melbourne, FL 32901-6975. Offers acquisition and contract management (MS, PMBA); aerospace engineering (MS); business administration (PMBA); computer information systems (MS); computer science (MS); e-business (PMBA); electrical engineering (MS); engineering management (MS); human resource management (PMBA); human resources management (MS); information systems (PMBA); logistics management (MS); management (MS), including acquisition and contract management, e-business, human resource management, information systems, logistics management, transportation management; materiel acquisition management (MS); mechanical engineering (MS); operations research (MS); project management (MS), including information systems, operations research; public administration (MPA); software engineering (MS); space systems (MS); space systems management (MS); systems management (MS), including information systems, operations research. Part-time and evening/weekend programs available. Postbaccalaureate distance learning degree programs offered (no on-campus study). *Faculty:* 11 full-time (4 women), 129 part-time/adjunct (17 women). *Students:* 78 full-time (34 women), 1,258 part-time (507 women); includes 384 minority (252 African Americans, 9 American Indian/Alaska Native, 58 Asian Americans or Pacific Islanders, 65 Hispanic Americans), 28 international. Average age 36. 629 applicants, 65% accepted, 320 enrolled. In 2006, 505 degrees awarded. *Degree requirements:* For master's, registration. *Entrance requirements:* For master's, minimum GPA of 3.0. Additional exam requirements/recommendations for international students: Required—TOEFL (minimum score 550 paper-based; 213 computer-based). *Application deadline:* Applications are processed on a rolling basis. Application fee: $50. Electronic applications accepted. *Expenses:* Tuition: Part-time $900 per credit. *Financial support:* Institutionally sponsored loans available. Financial award application deadline: 3/1; financial award applicants required to submit FAFSA. *Unit head:* Dr. Clifford Bragdon, Dean, 321-674-8821, Fax: 321-951-7694, E-mail: cbragdon@fit.edu. *Application contact:* Carolyn P. Farrior, Director of Graduate Admissions, 321-674-7118, Fax: 321-723-9468, E-mail: cfarrior@fit.edu.

George Mason University, School of Public Policy, Program in Transportation Policy, Operations and Logistics, Fairfax, VA 22030. Offers MA. Part-time programs available. Postbaccalaureate distance learning degree programs offered (no on-campus study). *Faculty:* 48 full-time (8 women), 41 part-time/adjunct (6 women). *Students:* 5 full-time (2 women), 54 part-time (19 women); includes 4 minority (3 African Americans, 1 American Indian/Alaska Native), 2 international. 40 applicants, 68% accepted, 15 enrolled. In 2006, 21 degrees awarded. *Degree requirements:* For master's, thesis or alternative. *Entrance requirements:* For master's, minimum undergraduate GPA of 3.0, resumé, 2 letters of recommendation, goals statement. Additional exam requirements/recommendations for international students: Required—TOEFL. *Application deadline:* For fall admission, 6/1 priority date for domestic students, 5/1 priority date for international students; for spring admission, 12/1 priority date for domestic students, 11/1 priority date for international students. Applications are processed on a rolling basis. Application fee: $60. Electronic applications accepted. *Expenses:* Contact institution. *Financial support:* Career-related internships or fieldwork, Federal Work-Study, scholarships/grants, and tuition waivers (partial) available. Support available to part-time students. Financial award application deadline: 3/1; financial award applicants required to submit FAFSA. *Unit head:* Dr. Laurie Schintler, Director, 703-993-8099, E-mail: spp@gmu.edu. *Application contact:* Leslie Metzger Levin, Director of Graduate Admissions, 703-993-8099, Fax: 703-993-4876, E-mail: lmetzger@gmu.edu.

Iowa State University of Science and Technology, Graduate College, College of Design, Department of Community and Regional Planning, Ames, IA 50011. Offers community and regional planning (MCRP); transportation (MS); M Arch/MCRP; MBA/MCRP; MCRP/MLA; MCRP/MPA. *Accreditation:* ACSP (one or more programs are accredited). Part-time programs available. *Faculty:* 11 full-time, 4 part-time/adjunct. *Students:* 25 full-time (12 women), 24 part-time (13 women); includes 6 minority (3 African Americans, 1 Asian American or Pacific Islander, 2 Hispanic Americans), 16 international. Average age 31. 32 applicants, 69% accepted, 13 enrolled. In 2006, 12 degrees awarded. *Degree requirements:* For master's, thesis or alternative. *Entrance requirements:* Additional exam requirements/recommendations for international students: Required—TOEFL (minimum score 550 paper-based; 213 computer-based; 79 iBT). *Application deadline:* For fall admission, 1/1 priority date for domestic and international students. Applications are processed on a rolling basis. Application fee: $30 ($70 for international students). Electronic applications accepted. *Expenses:* Tuition, state resident: full-time $5,936; part-time $330 per credit. Tuition, nonresident: full-time $16,350; part-time $330 per credit. *Financial support:* In 2006–07, 10 research assistantships with full and partial tuition reimbursements (averaging $17,532 per year), 8 teaching assistantships with full and partial tuition reimbursements (averaging $18,216 per year) were awarded; career-related internships or fieldwork, institutionally sponsored loans, tuition waivers (partial), and unspecified assistantships also available. Support available to part-time students. Financial award application deadline: 2/1; financial award applicants required to submit FAFSA. *Faculty research:* Economic development, housing, land use, geographic information systems planning in developing nations, regional and community revitalization, transportation planning in developing countries. *Unit head:* Dr. J. Timothy Keller, Chair, 515-294-5676, Fax: 515-294-2348, E-mail: landarch@iastate.edu. *Application contact:* Dr. David Valler, Director of Graduate Education, 515-294-8958, E-mail: crp@iastate.edu.

Iowa State University of Science and Technology, Graduate College, Interdisciplinary Programs, Program in Transportation, Ames, IA 50011. Offers MS. *Students:* 2 full-time (both women), 4 part-time (1 woman), 1 international. 7 applicants, 0% accepted. In 2006, 6 degrees awarded. *Degree requirements:* For master's, thesis. *Entrance requirements:* For master's, GMAT or GRE General Test. Additional exam requirements/recommendations for international students: Required—TOEFL (paper-based 550; computer-based 213; iBT 79) or IELTS (6.0). *Application deadline:* For fall admission, 7/15 priority date for domestic students,

3/15 priority date for international students. Application fee: $30 ($70 for international students). Electronic applications accepted. *Expenses:* Tuition, state resident: full-time $5,936; part-time $330 per credit. Tuition, nonresident: full-time $16,350; part-time $330 per credit. *Financial support:* In 2006–07, 1 research assistantship with full and partial tuition reimbursement (averaging $18,600 per year), 1 teaching assistantship (averaging $17,760 per year) were awarded; scholarships/grants, health care benefits, and unspecified assistantships also available. *Unit head:* Dr. David Plazak, Supervisory Committee Chair, 515-294-8103, Fax: 515-294-0467.

Maine Maritime Academy, Department of Graduate Studies, Program in Maritime Management, Castine, ME 04420. Offers MS, Certificate, Diploma. Part-time programs available. *Degree requirements:* For master's, capstone course, thesis optional. *Entrance requirements:* For master's, GMAT or GRE General Test, letters of recommendation. Additional exam requirements/recommendations for international students: Required—TOEFL. *Faculty research:* Human resources in maritime environment, management of organization change, economic analysis and maritime law.

McGill University, Faculty of Graduate and Postdoctoral Studies, Faculty of Engineering, School of Urban Planning, Montréal, QC H3A 2T5, Canada. Offers environmental planning (MUP); housing (MUP); transportation (MUP); urban planning (PhD); urban planning and design (MUP). Part-time programs available. *Degree requirements:* For master's, thesis/dissertation, registration; for doctorate, thesis/dissertation, comprehensive exam, registration. *Entrance requirements:* For master's, minimum GPA of 3.0; bachelor's degree or equivalent in anthropology, architecture, economics, engineering, environmental studies, geography, law, management, political science, social work, sociology or urban studies. Additional exam requirements/recommendations for international students: Required—TOEFL (minimum score 600 paper-based; 250 computer-based). Electronic applications accepted. *Faculty research:* Land-use planning and regulation; cities in the developing world; transportation planning; environmental planning and policy; geographic information systems.

Morgan State University, School of Graduate Studies, Clarence M. Mitchell, Jr. School of Engineering, Department of Transportation, Baltimore, MD 21251. Offers MS. Part-time and evening/weekend programs available. *Faculty:* 2 full-time (0 women). *Students:* 11. In 2006, 3 degrees awarded. *Degree requirements:* For master's, comprehensive exam or equivalent, thesis optional. *Entrance requirements:* For master's, minimum undergraduate GPA of 2.5. Additional exam requirements/recommendations for international students: Required—TOEFL (minimum score 550 paper-based; 213 computer-based). *Application deadline:* For fall admission, 2/1 priority date for domestic students; for spring admission, 10/1 priority date for domestic students. Applications are processed on a rolling basis. Application fee: $0. *Expenses:* Tuition, state resident: part-time $272 per credit. Tuition, nonresident: part-time $478 per credit. Required fees: $38 per credit. *Financial support:* Fellowships, research assistantships, career-related internships or fieldwork, Federal Work-Study, institutionally sponsored loans, scholarships/grants, health care benefits, and unspecified assistantships available. Support available to part-time students. Financial award application deadline: 2/1. *Faculty research:* Distributional impacts of congestion, pricing education and training for intelligent vehicle highway systems. Total annual research expenditures: $100,000. *Unit head:* Dr. Anthony Saka, Graduate Coordinator, 443-885-1871, Fax: 443-885-8324. *Application contact:* Dr. Maurice C. Taylor, Dean, 443-885-3185, Fax: 443-885-8226, E-mail: mctaylor@moac.morgan.edu.

New Jersey Institute of Technology, Office of Graduate Studies, Newark College of Engineering, Interdisciplinary Program in Transportation, Newark, NJ 07102. Offers MS, PhD. Part-time and evening/weekend programs available. *Faculty:* 2 part-time/adjunct (0 women). *Students:* 26 full-time (12 women), 19 part-time (3 women); includes 14 minority (4 African Americans, 8 Asian Americans or Pacific Islanders, 2 Hispanic Americans), 11 international. Average age 36. 43 applicants, 53% accepted, 12 enrolled. In 2006, 17 degrees awarded. Terminal master's awarded for partial completion of doctoral program. *Degree requirements:* For master's, thesis or alternative; for doctorate, thesis/dissertation, residency. *Entrance requirements:* For master's, GRE General Test; for doctorate, GRE General Test, minimum graduate GPA of 3.5. Additional exam requirements/recommendations for international students: Required—TOEFL (minimum score 550 paper-based; 213 computer-based). *Application deadline:* For fall admission, 6/5 priority date for domestic students; for spring admission, 10/15 for domestic students. Applications are processed on a rolling basis. Application fee: $60. Electronic applications accepted. *Expenses:* Tuition, state resident: full-time $11,896; part-time $648 per credit. Tuition, nonresident: full-time $16,900; part-time $892 per credit. Required fees: $336; $66 per credit. $168 per term. Tuition and fees vary according to course load. *Financial support:* Fellowships with full and partial tuition reimbursements, research assistantships with full and partial tuition reimbursements, teaching assistantships with full and partial tuition reimbursements, career-related internships or fieldwork, Federal Work-Study, institutionally sponsored loans, and unspecified assistantships available. Financial award application deadline: 3/15. *Faculty research:* Transportation planning, administration, and policy; intelligent vehicle highway systems; bridge maintenance. *Unit head:* Dr. Athanassios Bladikas, Director, 973-596-3653, Fax: 973-596-3652, E-mail: athanassios.bladikas@njit.edu. *Application contact:* Kathryn Kelly, Director of Admissions, 973-596-3300, Fax: 973-596-3461, E-mail: admissions@njit.edu.

North Dakota State University, The Graduate School, College of Engineering and Architecture, Department of Civil Engineering, Fargo, ND 58105. Offers civil engineering (MS, PhD); environmental engineering (MS, PhD); natural resource management (MS, PhD); transportation and logistics (PhD). PhD in transportation and logistics offered jointly with Upper Great Plains Transportation Institute. Part-time programs available. Postbaccalaureate distance learning degree programs offered (minimal on-campus study). *Degree requirements:* For master's, thesis/dissertation; for doctorate, thesis/dissertation, comprehensive exam. *Entrance requirements:* Additional exam requirements/recommendations for international students: Required—TOEFL (minimum score 525 paper-based; 193 computer-based). *Application deadline:* For fall admission, 7/1 priority date for domestic students, 1/15 priority date for international students; for spring admission, 5/1 priority date for international students. Applications are processed on a rolling basis. Application fee: $45 ($60 for international students). *Financial support:* Fellowships with full tuition reimbursements, research assistantships with full tuition reimbursements, teaching assistantships with full tuition reimbursements, career-related internships or fieldwork, Federal Work-Study, and institutionally sponsored loans available. Support available to part-time students. Financial award application deadline: 1/15. *Faculty research:* Wastewater, solid waste, composites, nanotechnology. Total annual research expenditures: $800,000. *Unit head:* Dr. Dinesh R. Katti, Chair, 701-231-7244, Fax: 701-231-6185, E-mail: dinesh.katti@ndsu.edu. *Application contact:* Dr. Kalpana Katti, Associate Professor and Graduate Program Coordinator, 701-231-9504, Fax: 701-231-6185, E-mail: kalpana.katti@ndsu.edu.

North Dakota State University, The Graduate School, Interdisciplinary Program in Transportation and Logistics, Fargo, ND 58105. Offers PhD. *Entrance requirements:* For doctorate, 1 year of calculus, statistics and probability, minimum GPA of 3.0. Additional exam requirements/recommendations for international students: Required—TOEFL (minimum score 550 paper-based; 213 computer-based). *Application deadline:* For fall admission, 5/1 priority date for domestic students. Applications are processed on a rolling basis. Application fee: $35 ($50 for international students). *Financial support:* Research assistantships with full tuition reimbursements available. *Faculty research:* Supply chain optimization, spatial analysis of transportation networks, advanced traffic analysis, transportation demand, railroad/intermodal freight. *Unit head:* Dr. Denver Tolliver, Director, 701-231-7190, Fax: 701-231-1945, E-mail: denver.tolliver@ndsu.nodak.edu.

Polytechnic University, Brooklyn Campus, Department of Civil Engineering, Major in Transportation Management, Brooklyn, NY 11201-2990. Offers MS. Part-time and evening/weekend programs available. *Students:* 1 full-time (0 women), 8 part-time (1 woman); includes 2 minority (both African Americans) Average age 32. 10 applicants, 40% accepted, 2 enrolled. In 2006, 5 degrees awarded. *Degree requirements:* For master's, thesis (for some programs), comprehensive exam (for some programs), registration. *Entrance requirements:* Additional exam requirements/recommendations for international students: Required—TOEFL (minimum score 550 paper-based; 213 computer-based); Recommended—IELTS (minimum score 7). *Application deadline:* For fall admission, 7/15 priority date for domestic students, 4/1 priority date for international students; for spring admission, 12/15 priority date for domestic students, 10/1 priority date for international students. Applications are processed on a rolling basis. Application fee: $55. Electronic applications accepted. *Expenses:* Tuition: Full-time $17,784; part-time $988 per credit. *Financial support:* Fellowships, research assistantships, teaching assistantships, institutionally sponsored loans available. Support available to part-time students. Financial award applicants required to submit FAFSA.

San Jose State University, Graduate Studies and Research, Lucas Graduate School of Business, Program in Transportation Management, San Jose, CA 95192-0001. Offers MS. Part-time and evening/weekend programs available. Postbaccalaureate distance learning degree programs offered (minimal on-campus study). *Students:* 5 applicants, 60% accepted, 0 enrolled. *Degree requirements:* For master's, thesis or alternative, comprehensive exam. *Entrance requirements:* For master's, GMAT, minimum GPA of 3.0. *Application deadline:* For fall admission, 6/29 priority date for domestic students; for spring admission, 11/30 for domestic students. Applications are processed on a rolling basis. Application fee: $59. Electronic applications accepted. *Financial support:* Applicants required to submit FAFSA. *Faculty research:* Surface intermodal transportation, economics, security. Total annual research expenditures: $100,000. *Unit head:* Dr. Peter J. Haas, Graduate Advisor, 408-924-5691, Fax: 408-924-3555.

State University of New York Maritime College, Program in International Transportation Management, Throggs Neck, NY 10465-4198. Offers MS. Part-time and evening/weekend programs available. *Degree requirements:* For master's, thesis. *Entrance requirements:* For master's, minimum GPA of 2.5. Additional exam requirements/recommendations for international students: Required—TOEFL. *Faculty research:* Ports, intermodal, shipping, logistics, port tax.

See Close-Up on page 739.

University at Buffalo, the State University of New York, Graduate School, College of Arts and Sciences, Department of Geography, Buffalo, NY 14260. Offers geographic information science (Certificate); geography (MA, MS, PhD); transportation and business geographics (Certificate); MA/MBA. *Faculty:* 16 full-time (5 women), 3 part-time/adjunct (0 women). *Students:* 76 full-time (23 women), 29 part-time (10 women); includes 10 minority (6 African Americans, 1 American Indian/Alaska Native, 2 Asian Americans or Pacific Islanders, 1 Hispanic American), 28 international. Average age 25. 160 applicants, 38% accepted, 20 enrolled. In 2006, 29 master's, 7 doctorates, 8 other advanced degrees awarded. *Degree requirements:* For master's, thesis (for some programs), project; for doctorate, thesis/dissertation, registration; for Certificate, portfolio. *Entrance requirements:* For master's, GRE General Test, minimum GPA of 2.9; for doctorate, GRE General Test, minimum GPA of 3.0. Additional exam requirements/recommendations for international students: Required—TOEFL (minimum score 550 paper-based; 213 computer-based; 79 iBT). *Application deadline:* For fall admission, 7/1 priority date for domestic students, 1/10 priority date for international students; for spring admission, 12/1 priority date for domestic students, 10/1 priority date for international students. Applications are processed on a rolling basis. Application fee: $50. Electronic applications accepted. *Financial support:* In 2006–07, 19 students received support, including 6 fellowships with full tuition reimbursements available (averaging $4,333 per year), 13 teaching assistantships with full tuition reimbursements available (averaging $11,489 per year); research assistantships, career-related internships or fieldwork, Federal Work-Study, institutionally sponsored loans, traineeships, health care benefits, and unspecified assistantships also available. Financial award application deadline: 1/10; financial award applicants required to submit FAFSA. *Faculty research:* International business and world trade, geographic information systems and cartography, transportation, urban and regional analysis, physical and environmental geography. Total annual research expenditures: $792,944. *Unit head:* Dr. Alan D. MacPherson, Chairman, 716-645-2722 Ext. 15, Fax: 716-645-2329, E-mail: geoadm@buffalo.edu. *Application contact:* Betsy Abraham, Graduate Secretary, 716-645-2722 Ext. 13, Fax: 716-645-2329, E-mail: babraham@buffalo.edu.

University of Arkansas, Graduate School, Sam M. Walton College of Business Administration, Department of Transportation and Logistics Management, Fayetteville, AR 72701-1201. Offers MTLM. Part-time programs available. *Students:* 1 (woman) full-time, 6 part-time (2 women); includes 1 minority (African American), 3 international. In 2006, 12 degrees awarded. Application fee: $40 ($50 for international students). *Financial support:* In 2006–07, 1 research assistantship was awarded; fellowships with tuition reimbursements, teaching assistantships also available. Financial award application deadline: 4/1. *Unit head:* Dr. Tom Jensen, Chair, 479-575-4055. *Application contact:* Matt Waller, Graduate Coordinator, 479-575-7334, E-mail: mwaller@walton.uark.edu.

The University of British Columbia, Sauder School of Business, Doctoral Program in Commerce and Business Administration, Vancouver, BC V6T 1Z1, Canada. Offers accounting (PhD); finance (PhD); international business (PhD); management information systems (PhD); management science (PhD); marketing (PhD); organizational behavior (PhD); policy analysis and strategy (PhD); transportation and logistics (PhD); urban land economics (PhD). *Degree requirements:* For doctorate, thesis/dissertation, comprehensive exam. *Entrance requirements:* For doctorate, GMAT or GRE. Additional exam requirements/recommendations for international students: Required—TOEFL. Electronic applications accepted.

University of California, Davis, College of Engineering, Graduate Group in Transportation Technology and Policy, Davis, CA 95616. Offers MS, PhD. Terminal master's awarded for partial completion of doctoral program. *Degree requirements:* For master's, thesis (for some programs), comprehensive exam (for some programs); for doctorate, thesis/dissertation. *Entrance requirements:* For master's, GRE General Test, minimum GPA of 3.0; for doctorate, GRE General Test, minimum GPA of 3.5. Additional exam requirements/recommendations for international students: Required—TOEFL (minimum score 550 paper-based; 213 computer-based). Electronic applications accepted.

University of Central Missouri, The Graduate School, College of Health and Human Services, Department of Safety Sciences, Warrensburg, MO 64093. Offers fire science (MS); human services/public services (Ed S); industrial hygiene (MS); industrial safety management (MS); loss control (MS); occupational safety management (MS); public safety (MS); security (MS); transportation safety (MS). *Accreditation:* ABET (one or more programs are accredited). Part-time programs available. *Faculty:* 18 full-time (3 women). *Students:* 14 full-time (4 women), 18 part-time (6 women); includes 6 minority (2 African Americans, 1 American Indian/Alaska Native, 3 Hispanic Americans), 1 international. Average age 36. 9 applicants, 78% accepted, 6 enrolled. In 2006, 6 degrees awarded. *Degree requirements:* For master's, comprehensive exam. *Entrance requirements:* For master's, GRE General Test, minimum GPA of 2.5, 15 hours of course work in related area; for Ed S, master's degree in related field. Additional exam requirements/recommendations for international students: Required—TOEFL (minimum score 500 paper-based; 173 computer-based). *Application deadline:* For fall admission, 6/1 priority date for domestic students, 5/1 priority date for international students; for spring admission, 10/1 priority date for domestic students, 10/1 for international students. Applications are processed on a rolling basis. Application fee: $30 ($50 for international students). *Expenses:* Tuition, state resident: full-time $5,448; part-time $227 per credit hour. Tuition, nonresident: full-time $10,896; part-time $454 per credit hour. Required fees: $336; $14 per credit hour. *Financial support:* In 2006–07, 5 students received support. Federal Work-Study, scholarships/grants, unspecified assistantships, and administrative and laboratory assistantships available. Support available to part-time students. Financial award application deadline: 3/1; financial award applicants required to submit FAFSA. *Faculty research:* Workplace and school safety, industrial hygiene assessment methods, lead and take-home toxins, rural emergency management, cultural aspects of safety, health, and the environment. Total annual research expenditures: $60,999. *Unit head:* Dr. Dennis Laster, Interim Chair, 660-543-4017, E-mail: laster@cmsu1.cmsu.edu.

Transportation Management

University of Denver, Graduate Studies, Intermodal Transportation Institute, Denver, CO 80208. Offers MS. *Students:* 35 full-time (10 women); includes 6 minority (2 Asian Americans or Pacific Islanders, 4 Hispanic Americans), 3 international. Average age 40. 19 applicants, 100% accepted. In 2006, 10 degrees awarded. Application fee: $0. *Expenses:* Tuition: Full-time $29,628; part-time $823 per credit. *Financial support:* Applicants required to submit FAFSA. Total annual research expenditures: $3,000. *Unit head:* Dr. Bill Zaranka, Director, 303-871-4146. *Application contact:* Cathy Johnson, Administrator, 308-871-4702, E-mail: du-iti@du.edu.

The University of Tennessee, Graduate School, College of Business Administration, Program in Business Administration, Knoxville, TN 37996. Offers accounting (PhD); finance (MBA, PhD); logistics and transportation (MBA, PhD); management (PhD); marketing (MBA, PhD); operations management (MBA); professional business administration (MBA); statistics (PhD); JD/MBA; MS/MBA. *Accreditation:* AACSB. Postbaccalaureate distance learning degree programs offered. *Students:* 344 (105 women); includes 42 minority (20 African Americans, 4 American Indian/Alaska Native, 9 Asian Americans or Pacific Islanders, 9 Hispanic Americans) 49 international. In 2006, 169 master's, 9 doctorates awarded. *Degree requirements:* For master's, thesis or alternative; for doctorate, thesis/dissertation. *Entrance requirements:* For master's and doctorate, GMAT, minimum GPA of 2.7. Additional exam requirements/recommendations for international students: Required—TOEFL. *Application deadline:* For fall admission, 2/1 priority date for domestic students. Application fee: $35. Electronic applications accepted. *Expenses:* Tuition, state resident: full-time $5,574. Tuition, nonresident: full-time $16,840. Required fees: $792. *Financial support:* In 2006–07, 6 fellowships, 3 research assistantships, 35 teaching assistantships were awarded; career-related internships or fieldwork, Federal Work-Study, institutionally sponsored loans, and unspecified assistantships also available. Financial award application deadline: 2/1; financial award applicants required to submit FAFSA. *Unit head:* Dr. Sarah Gardial, Assistant Dean, 865-974-5033, Fax: 865-974-3826, E-mail: sgardial@utk.edu. *Application contact:* Donna Potts, Graduate Representative, 865-974-5033, Fax: 865-974-3826, E-mail: dpotts@utk.edu.

University of Washington, Graduate School, Interdisciplinary Graduate Program in Global Trade, Transportation, and Logistics Studies, Seattle, WA 98195. Offers Certificate.

Wilmington College, Division of Business, New Castle, DE 19720-6491. Offers business administration (MBA); finance (MBA); health care administration (MBA, MS); human resource management (MS); management (MS); management information systems (MBA); organizational leadership (MS); public administration (MS); transportation and logistics (MBA, MS). Part-time and evening/weekend programs available. *Faculty:* 3 full-time (0 women). *Students:* 230 full-time (138 women), 432 part-time (274 women); includes 109 minority (98 African Americans, 1 American Indian/Alaska Native, 3 Asian Americans or Pacific Islanders, 7 Hispanic Americans). Average age 34. 229 applicants, 100% accepted, 156 enrolled. In 2006, 273 degrees awarded. *Entrance requirements:* Additional exam requirements/recommendations for international students: Required—TOEFL (minimum score 500 paper-based; 173 computer-based). *Application deadline:* Applications are processed on a rolling basis. Application fee: $25. *Financial support:* Applicants required to submit FAFSA. *Unit head:* Dr. Robert Edelson, Chair, 302-295-1147, Fax: 302-328-7021, E-mail: robert.e.edelson@wilmcoll.edu. *Application contact:* Chris Ferguson, Director of Admissions and Financial Aid, 302-328-9407 Ext. 256, Fax: 302-328-5164, E-mail: inquire@wilmcoll.edu.

STATE UNIVERSITY OF NEW YORK MARITIME COLLEGE

Program in International Transportation Management

Program of Study

Students in international transportation management are rewarded with exciting challenges, stimulating environments, and financial returns. Graduates enter the shipping and transportation industry with a skill set that guarantees rapid advancement. Those already in the industry raise their profile with qualifications that affirm and validate their abilities as leaders. Students are prepared for careers with any major maritime organization or for working independently.

Maritime College is now offering the Master of Science (M.S.) in international transportation management both online and in residence. In addition to the M.S., options are available to "Sea the World" and earn a 3rd Mates Deck License or receive a professional certification for supply chain management. This unique curriculum is a business degree specifically focused on the business of shipping, intermodal transportation, supply chain management, and security.

In the Graduate License option, students not only take the graduate courses with their contemporaries but also become a member of the Regiment and take marine transportation courses. License students enjoy a cruise in three consecutive summer sea terms. Each cruise is a two-month event that encompasses trips to both domestic and European seaports. License graduates become Coast Guard licensed 3rd Mate Deck Officers. Graduate courses are in late afternoon, evenings, and/or weekends. F1 visa students must comply with immigration laws relative to work. The License option is not available online.

Semesters begin late August and in again mid-January. For more information about the program, students should visit the Web site at http://www.sunymaritime.edu.

Research Facilities

The graduate program at SUNY Maritime College is affiliated with various regional and national research centers. The University Transportation Research Center (UTRC) Region II, established in 1987, is one of ten original national centers in recognition of transportation's key role in the nation's economy and in the quality of people's lives. UTRC/Region II represents New York, New Jersey, and Puerto Rico and functions as a consortium of twelve major universities throughout the region. The center, which is housed at the City College of New York, supports research, education, and technology transfer under the theme of "The New Paradigm of Transportation: Management Complexity and Change." The New York State Department of Transportation sponsors the Infrastructure Transportation Research Consortium. This regional consortium was established in 1996 and is housed at Cornell University. The consortium is made up of nine institutions. The Transportation Research Board (TRB) is a unit of the National Research Council, which serves the National Academy of Sciences and the National Academy of Engineering. TRB's mission is to promote innovations and progress in transportation by stimulating and conducting research, facilitating the dissemination of information, and encouraging the implementation of research results. The TRB has more than 4,000 members and operates through committees. The College's International Transportation Research Center (ITRC), which is affiliated with the graduate program, is responsible for competing for and executing transportation research projects. The ITRC was established in 1993 to provide the transportation industry, both private and public, with local, national, and international transportation research, regardless of mode of transportation.

Financial Aid

As a member of the State University of New York, the Maritime College participates in all state and federal aid programs as well as several private and campus-based programs of financial aid. Part-time or full-time positions at the College may be available for some students while completing their studies. In addition to work-study programs, graduate students have received scholarship money from the Connecticut Maritime Association, the SUNY Minority Graduate Fellowship Program, and the Alumni Association as well as several Fulbright Scholarships for international students.

Cost of Study

Because Maritime College is part of the State University system, tuition for international students and out-of-state students is dramatically less then other comparable major universities. State tuition is offered to those residing in states bordering the Atlantic Ocean. The State University of New York sets tuition. For the 2007–08 academic year, it is $3450 per semester for full-time in-region students and $5460 per semester for full-time out-of-region and international students. There is an international student health insurance fee of $951 per year and a technology fee of $267 per academic year.

Living and Housing Costs

The rent for each semester is based on two-bedroom occupancy for $2785 per semester. If space permits, a student may request a single bedroom at additional cost. Full information on current costs and fees is available by request. On-campus living, including all fees and rental charges, is approximately $600 per month.

Student Group

For the 2006–07 academic year, about 35 percent of the students were international students. The international students come from twenty-eight countries. Students come from varied backgrounds, and many have experience in international trade. SUNY Maritime College is an international school in one of the most cosmopolitan cities in the world.

Student Outcomes

The students have various career paths, but many fall into five broad categories of insurance and risk management, transportation operations, port and terminal operations, brokerage and finance, and shipboard operations. Recent graduates have entered positions in ship management, chartering operations, freight forwarding, bunker fuel brokerage, port operations, and marine insurance in the area of underwriting and brokerage. More information on recent graduates and their anticipated salaries is available on the graduate program's Web site.

Location

Maritime's beautiful location, on the banks of the East River and Long Island Sound, provides the student with the most scenic settings for campus life. The proximity to New York City places students in the middle of shipping, finance, chartering, insurance, and trade industries. The main campus is located in Throggs Neck, in the borough of the Bronx, New York City. Classes are given on the Bronx campus, with the exception of shipboard operations, which is given aboard the training ship *Empire State VI*. The Bronx campus occupies 55 scenic acres at the junction of the East River and Long Island Sound, conveniently located to New York City with all of the professional and recreational opportunities that one of the world's most cosmopolitan cities has to offer.

The College

The State University of New York Maritime College's impressive history began more than 125 years ago. In response to industry demand, more Americans were being encouraged to enter maritime careers. The governor of New York applied for a training ship, and, on December 14, 1874, the *USS St. Mary's* arrived in New York harbor and became the home of the first commercial maritime institution in the United States. The initial 26 students aboard the *St. Mary's*, known then as the New York Nautical School, became the first class of what has evolved into the State University of New York Maritime College. Maritime College is one of the State University of New York's sixty-four campuses and represented on the University's board of directors. The College has successfully competed for funded research and scholarships through this affiliation. Maritime students have been recognized for national awards of excellence.

Applying

Maritime College is friendly to veterans and welcomes service members and their family members alike. An official application form can be found online at http://www.sunymaritime.edu/1ngot/pdfs/graduateprogram/grad_application.pdf. All students must have a bachelor's degree; a grade point average of 3.0 is desirable, and all are required to submit a completed application, including official transcripts from all undergraduate institutions, GMAT scores, and a statement of purpose (short essay) describing career goals. Two letters of recommendation are required. There is no official application deadline; students are admitted in August, January, and May. International students are also required to submit an affidavit of financial support, a TOEFL score if their undergraduate degree was not granted in English, and transcript evaluations from World Education Services (http://www.wes.org).

Correspondence and Information

Robert L. Wolf
Director Graduate Admissions
State University of New York Maritime College
6 Pennyfield Avenue
Throggs Neck, New York 10465
Phone: 718-409-2258
      718-409-7285
Fax: 718-409-7359
E-mail: rwolf@sunymaritime.edu
Web site: http://www.sunymaritime.edu/Academics/GraduateProgram/

State University of New York Maritime College

THE FACULTY

Maritime College faculty members are members and/or affiliated members of the following Transportation Research Board committees: Transportation Education and Training, Transportation and Economic Development, Intermodal Freight Transportation, Port and Waterways, Inland Water Transportation, International Trade and Transportation, Transportation Economics, and Passenger Ferry Transportation.

Comdr. Joseph Ahlstrom, USNR, Adjunct Professor of Marine Transportation; M.S., SUNY Maritime College. Federal License, Master of Steam and Motor Vessels, any Gross Tons, Oceans; radar observer, general radio operator; arbitrator, NASD; past master, training ship *Empire State VI.*.

James Drogan, Lecturer in Management Information Systems and Intermodalism. Degrees and Certificates from SIU, Northwestern, MIT, and Harvard; formerly IBM lead executive for rail, intermodal, and logistics consulting.

Chang Q. Guan, Assistant Professor of Transportation/Logistics Management; D.B.A. candidate, CUNY Graduate Center. P.R.C. Third Mate License of Unlimited Gross Tonnage Upon Oceans.

Lars Gustafson, Assistant Professor of Insurance and Transportation; M.S., SUNY Maritime College. Federal Licenses: Third Mate of Steam and Motor Vessels of Unlimited Gross Tonnage Upon Oceans; Maritime Arbitrator, member of the Marine Insurance Claims Association, member of the General Average Association.

Jeffrey B. Hirsch, Adjunct Assistant Professor of Transportation; M.B.A., Johns Hopkins; M.S., NYU. Port and intermodal representative, U.S. Maritime Administration. Licensed merchant marine officer.

Larry Howard, Associate Professor; Ph.D., Washington (Seattle). Chair of the Department of Global Business and Transportation

Anthony Mavronicolas, Adjunct Assistant Professor of Law; J.D., Tulane. Member of the New York State, Massachusetts, and federal bars.

Riccardo R. Pellicciaro, Professor of Economics and Finance; Ph.D., Fordham. Financial economics.

Carl Selinger, Adjunct Assistant Professor of Aviation and Aviation Engineering; B.E., Cooper Union. Certificates: Highway Transportation, Yale University; American Society of Civil Engineers (ASCE); Institute of Transportation Engineers (ITE); and Women's Transportation Seminar (WTS).

Jeffrey A. Weiss, Associate Professor of Law and Transportation; J.D., Pace. Former director of the graduate program. Federal Licenses: Master of Freight and Towing Vessels of not more than 1,600 Gross Tons upon Oceans; Second Mate of Steam and Motor Vessels of Unlimited Gross Tonnage upon Oceans; member of the New York State and Federal Bars; maritime arbitrator; member of the Maritime Law Association of the United States. Teaching and research interests are in all aspects of maritime law.

Shmuel (Sam) Yahalom, Distinguished University Professor; Ph.D., Haifa (Israel). Former director of the graduate program; traffic officer at Haifa Airport; instructor, Israeli Air Force; teaches economics and quantitative analysis.

ACADEMIC AND PROFESSIONAL PROGRAMS IN EDUCATION

Section 22
Education

This section contains a directory of institutions offering graduate work in education, followed by in-depth entries submitted by institutions that chose to prepare detailed program descriptions. Additional information about programs listed in the directory but not augmented by an in-depth entry may be obtained by writing directly to the dean of a graduate school or chair of a department at the address given in the directory.

For programs offering related work, see also in this book Administration, Instruction, and Theory; Health-Related Professions; Instructional Levels; Leisure Studies and Recreation; Physical Education and Kinesiology; Special Focus; and Subject Areas; and in Book 2, Psychology and Counseling (School Psychology).

CONTENTS

Education—General

Abilene Christian University, Graduate School, College of Education and Human Services, Abilene, TX 79699-9100. Offers M Ed, MS, MSSW, Certificate. *Faculty:* 15 part-time/adjunct (11 women). *Students:* 38 full-time (32 women), 74 part-time (48 women); includes 10 minority (4 African Americans, 6 Hispanic Americans), 1 international. 128 applicants, 66% accepted, 76 enrolled. In 2006, 24 degrees awarded. *Degree requirements:* For master's, comprehensive exam. *Expenses:* Tuition: Full-time $12,504; part-time $521 per hour. Required fees: $700; $34 per hour. *Unit head:* Dr. Malesa Breeding, Dean, 325-674-2700, Fax: 325-674-2552, E-mail: breedingm@acu.edu. *Application contact:* William Horn, Graduate Admissions Counselor, 325-674-2656, Fax: 325-674-6717, E-mail: gradinfo@acu.edu.

Acadia University, Faculty of Professional Studies, School of Education, Wolfville, NS B4P 2R6, Canada. Offers counseling (M Ed); curriculum studies (M Ed), including cultural and media studies, inclusive education, learning and technology, science, math and technology; learning and technology (M Ed); organizational leadership (M Ed); special education (M Ed). Part-time and evening/weekend programs available. *Faculty:* 20 full-time (10 women). *Students:* 24 full-time (18 women), 152 part-time (121 women). In 2006, 101 master's awarded. *Degree requirements:* For master's, thesis optional. *Entrance requirements:* For master's, B Ed or the equivalent, minimum B average, 2 years of teaching or related experience. Additional exam requirements/recommendations for international students: Required—TOEFL (minimum score 580 paper-based; 237 computer-based). Application fee: $50. Electronic applications accepted. *Financial support:* In 2006–07, 7 teaching assistantships (averaging $4,000 per year) were awarded; research assistantships. Financial award application deadline: 2/1. *Application contact:* Sheila Langille, Secretary, 902-585-1229, Fax: 902-585-1071, E-mail: sheila.langille@acadiau.ca.

Adams State College, The Graduate School, Department of Teacher Education, Alamosa, CO 81102. Offers education (MA); special education (MA). *Accreditation:* Teacher Education Accreditation Council. Part-time programs available. Postbaccalaureate distance learning degree programs offered. *Degree requirements:* For master's, qualifying exam. *Entrance requirements:* For master's, GRE General Test or MAT, minimum undergraduate GPA of 3.0.

Adelphi University, School of Education, Garden City, NY 11530-0701. Offers MA, MS, DA, Certificate. *Accreditation:* NCATE. Part-time and evening/weekend programs available. *Faculty:* 62 full-time (43 women). *Students:* 432 full-time (379 women), 869 part-time (679 women); includes 186 minority (73 African Americans, 27 Asian Americans or Pacific Islanders, 86 Hispanic Americans), 6 international. Average age 30. 1,111 applicants, 53% accepted, 424 enrolled. In 2006, 599 master's, 9 other advanced degrees awarded. *Degree requirements:* For doctorate, one foreign language, thesis/dissertation, comprehensive exam. *Entrance requirements:* For master's, resumé, letters of recommendation, minimum cumulative GPA of 2.75; for doctorate, GRE General Test, 3 letters of recommendation, interview. Additional exam requirements/recommendations for international students: Required—TOEFL (minimum score 550 paper-based; 213 computer-based). *Application deadline:* Applications are processed on a rolling basis. Application fee: $50. Electronic applications accepted. *Financial support:* In 2006–07, 104 teaching assistantships (averaging $5,816 per year) were awarded; fellowships, research assistantships with full and partial tuition reimbursements, career-related internships or fieldwork, Federal Work-Study, institutionally sponsored loans, tuition waivers (full), and unspecified assistantships also available. Support available to part-time students. Financial award application deadline: 2/15; financial award applicants required to submit FAFSA. *Faculty research:* Multicultural and gender issues, psychometric assessment, quantitative research methods. *Unit head:* Dr. Ronald Feingold, Dean, 516-877-4100, E-mail: feingold@adelphi.edu. *Application contact:* Christine Murphy, Director of Admissions, 516-877-3050, Fax: 516-877-3039, E-mail: graduateadmissions@adelphi.edu.

See Close-Up on page 817.

Alabama Agricultural and Mechanical University, School of Graduate Studies, School of Education, Huntsville, AL 35811. Offers M Ed, MS, Ed S. *Accreditation:* NCATE. Part-time and evening/weekend programs available. *Faculty:* 36 full-time (18 women), 4 part-time/adjunct (1 woman). *Students:* 177 full-time (143 women), 376 part-time (284 women); includes 372 minority (355 African Americans, 2 American Indian/Alaska Native, 4 Asian Americans or Pacific Islanders, 11 Hispanic Americans), 22 international. In 2006, 94 degrees awarded. *Degree requirements:* For master's, comprehensive exam. *Entrance requirements:* For master's, GRE General Test. *Application deadline:* For fall admission, 5/1 for domestic students. Applications are processed on a rolling basis. Application fee: $25. Electronic applications accepted. *Financial support:* Fellowships, research assistantships, career-related internships or fieldwork, Federal Work-Study, institutionally sponsored loans, and traineeships available. Support available to part-time students. Financial award application deadline: 4/1. *Faculty research:* Speech defects, aging, blindness, multicultural education, learning styles. *Unit head:* Dr. John Vickers, Interim Dean, 256-372-5500.

Alabama State University, School of Graduate Studies, College of Education, Montgomery, AL 36101-0271. Offers M Ed, MS, Ed D, Ed S. *Accreditation:* NCATE. Part-time programs available. *Faculty:* 26 full-time (17 women), 22 part-time/adjunct (13 women). *Students:* 160 full-time (125 women), 739 part-time (581 women); includes 640 minority (635 African Americans, 1 American Indian/Alaska Native, 2 Asian Americans or Pacific Islanders, 2 Hispanic Americans), 4 international. In 2006, 201 master's, 7 other advanced degrees awarded. *Degree requirements:* For master's, comprehensive exam; for Ed S, thesis, comprehensive exam. *Entrance requirements:* For master's, GRE General Test, MAT, graduate writing competency test; for Ed S, graduate writing competency test, GRE, MAT. Additional exam requirements/recommendations for international students: Required—TOEFL (minimum score 500 paper-based; 173 computer-based). *Application deadline:* For fall admission, 7/15 for domestic students; for spring admission, 12/15 for domestic students. Applications are processed on a rolling basis. Application fee: $10. *Expenses:* Tuition, state resident: full-time $1,728; part-time $192 per hour. Tuition, nonresident: full-time $3,456; part-time $334 per hour. *Financial support:* In 2006–07, 2 research assistantships (averaging $9,450 per year) were awarded. *Faculty research:* Whole language instruction, African-American children's literature. *Unit head:* Dr. Katie Bell, Acting Dean, 334-229-4250, Fax: 334-229-4904.

Alaska Pacific University, Graduate Programs, Education Department, Program in Teaching, Anchorage, AK 99508-4672. Offers teaching (K-8) (MAT). *Faculty:* 3 full-time (2 women). *Students:* 10 full-time (8 women), 1 (woman) part-time. Average age 34. In 2006, 7 degrees awarded. *Degree requirements:* For master's, research project. *Entrance requirements:* For master's, GRE or MAT, PRAXIS, minimum GPA of 3.0. *Application deadline:* For fall admission, 4/15 for domestic students; for spring admission, 12/15 for domestic students. Applications are processed on a rolling basis. Application fee: $25. *Expenses:* Tuition: Part-time $550 per credit hour. Required fees: $100 per semester. Tuition and fees vary according to program. *Financial support:* Research assistantships, teaching assistantships, career-related internships or fieldwork and Federal Work-Study available. Support available to part-time students. Financial award application deadline: 4/15; financial award applicants required to submit FAFSA. *Unit head:* Dr. Theodore Munsch, Director, 907-564-8258, Fax: 907-564-8317, E-mail: edted@alaskapacific.edu. *Application contact:* Michael Warner, Director of Admissions, 907-564-8248, Fax: 907-564-8317, E-mail: mikew@alaskapacific.edu.

Albany State University, College of Education, Albany, GA 31705-2717. Offers M Ed, Certificate, Ed S. *Accreditation:* NCATE. Part-time programs available. *Degree requirements:* For master's, comprehensive exam. *Entrance requirements:* For master's, GRE General Test; for other advanced degree, GRE General Test, MAT. Electronic applications accepted. *Faculty research:* Science education-methods and achievement, special education-mainstreaming.

Albertson College of Idaho, Program in Teacher Education, Caldwell, ID 83605-4494. Offers MAT. *Faculty:* 3 full-time (2 women), 1 part-time/adjunct (0 women). *Students:* 29 full-time (23 women); includes 1 minority (Hispanic American) Average age 27. In 2006, 9 degrees awarded. *Degree requirements:* For master's, thesis. *Entrance requirements:* For master's, GRE, portfolio, minimum undergraduate GPA of 3.0, interview. *Application deadline:* For fall admission, 3/15 priority date for domestic students. *Expenses:* Tuition: Full-time $12,450; part-time $670 per credit. *Faculty research:* Discourse analysis, at risk youth, children's literature, research design, program evaluation. *Unit head:* Dr. Donald W. Burwell, Chair, 208-459-5222, E-mail: dburwell@albertson.edu.

Albright College, Department of Education—Graduate Division, Reading, PA 19612-5234. Offers early childhood education (MS); elementary education (MS); English as a second language (MA); general education (MA); special education (MS). Part-time and evening/weekend programs available. *Degree requirements:* For master's, thesis. *Entrance requirements:* For master's, GRE General Test or MAT, minimum undergraduate GPA of 3.0, 2 letters of recommendation, interview. Additional exam requirements/recommendations for international students: Recommended—TOEFL (minimum score 525 paper-based; 197 computer-based). Electronic applications accepted.

Alcorn State University, School of Graduate Studies, School of Psychology and Education, Alcorn State, MS 39096-7500. Offers agricultural education (MS Ed); elementary education (MS Ed, Ed S); guidance and counseling (MS Ed); industrial education (MS Ed); secondary education (MS Ed), including health and physical education; special education (MS Ed). *Accreditation:* NCATE. *Faculty:* 14 full-time (9 women), 21 part-time/adjunct (13 women). *Students:* 76 full-time (44 women), 271 part-time (226 women); includes 333 minority (all African Americans) In 2006, 119 degrees awarded. *Degree requirements:* For master's, thesis optional. *Application deadline:* For fall admission, 7/15 priority date for domestic students; for spring admission, 11/25 for domestic students. Applications are processed on a rolling basis. Application fee: $0 ($10 for international students). *Financial support:* Career-related internships or fieldwork available. Support available to part-time students. *Unit head:* Dr. Josephine M. Posey, Dean, 601-877-6141, Fax: 601-877-3867.

Alfred University, Graduate School, Division of Education, Alfred, NY 14802-1205. Offers counseling (MS Ed, CAS); literacy teacher (MS Ed). Part-time programs available. *Students:* 12 full-time (all women), 26 part-time (18 women). Average age 24. 62 applicants, 61% accepted, 30 enrolled. In 2006, 48 master's, 19 other advanced degrees awarded. *Entrance requirements:* For master's, LAST, Assessment of Teaching Skills (written), Content Specialty Test. Additional exam requirements/recommendations for international students: Required—TOEFL (minimum score 590 paper-based; 243 computer-based; 90 iBT), IELTS (minimum score 7). *Application deadline:* Applications are processed on a rolling basis. Application fee: $50. Electronic applications accepted. *Expenses:* Tuition: Full-time $29,600; part-time $630 per credit hour. Required fees: $850; $70 per semester. Tuition and fees vary according to program. *Financial support:* In 2006–07, 12 students received support, including research assistantships (averaging $14,225 per year); tuition waivers (partial) and unspecified assistantships also available. Financial award applicants required to submit FAFSA. *Faculty research:* Whole language, ethics in counseling and psychotherapy. *Unit head:* Dr. James Curl, Chair, 607-871-2219, E-mail: fcurl@alfred.edu. *Application contact:* Valerie Stephens, Coordinator of Graduate Admissions, 607-871-2141, Fax: 607-871-2198, E-mail: gradinquiry@alfred.edu.

Alliant International University–Fresno, Graduate School of Education, TeachersCHOICE Preparation Programs, Fresno, CA 93727. Offers MA. Part-time programs available. *Entrance requirements:* For master's, CBEST, CSET, interview; offer of employment as a teacher of record in a California school; minimum GPA of 3.0, 2 letters of recommendation.

See Close-Up on page 819.

Alliant International University–Irvine, Graduate School of Education, Teacher Education Programs, Irvine, CA 92612. Offers auditory oral education (Certificate); CLAD (Certificate); preliminary multiple subject (Credential); preliminary multiple subject with BCLAD (Credential); preliminary single subject (Credential); professional clear multiple subject (Credential); professional clear single subject (Credential); teaching (MA, Credential); technology and learning (MA). Part-time and evening/weekend programs available. *Students:* 4. In 2006, 6 degrees awarded. *Entrance requirements:* For degree, California Basic Educational Skills Test, minimum GPA of 2.5. Additional exam requirements/recommendations for international students: Required—TOEFL (minimum score 550 paper-based; 213 computer-based), TWE. *Application deadline:* For fall admission, 7/1 priority date for domestic and international students; for spring admission, 12/1 priority date for domestic and international students. Applications are processed on a rolling basis. Application fee: $55. Electronic applications accepted. *Financial support:* Career-related internships or fieldwork, Federal Work-Study, institutionally sponsored loans, and scholarships/grants available. Financial award applicants required to submit FAFSA. *Unit head:* Dr. Trudy Day, Assistant Dean, 866-825-5426, Fax: 949-833-3507, E-mail: admissions@alliant.edu. *Application contact:* Alliant International University Central Contact Center, 866-U-ALLIANT, Fax: 858-635-4555, E-mail: admissions@alliant.edu.

Alliant International University–Los Angeles, Graduate School of Education, TeachersCHOICE Preparation Programs, Alhambra, CA 91803-1360. Offers MA. Part-time programs available. *Entrance requirements:* For master's, CBEST, CSET, interview; offer of employment as a teacher of record in a California school; minimum GPA of 3.0, 2 letters of recommendation.

See Close-Up on page 819.

Alliant International University–México City, Graduate School of Education, Mexico City, Mexico. Offers teaching (MA). Part-time and evening/weekend programs available. Postbaccalaureate distance learning degree programs offered (no on-campus study). *Entrance requirements:* For master's, minimum GPA of 3.0, letters of recommendation, interview. Additional exam requirements/recommendations for international students: Required—TOEFL (minimum score 550 paper-based; 213 computer-based), TWE (minimum score 5). *Application deadline:* For fall admission, 8/1 priority date for domestic and international students; for spring admission, 12/1 priority date for domestic and international students. Application fee: $50. *Expenses:* Tuition: Full-time $5,640; part-time $235 per unit. Required fees: $300; $150 per semester. *Financial support:* Career-related internships or fieldwork, Federal Work-Study, institutionally sponsored loans, and scholarships/grants available. Financial award application deadline: 2/15; financial award applicants required to submit FAFSA. *Unit head:* Dr. Karen Schuster Webb, Systemwide Dean, 888-824-4421, E-mail: kwebb@alliant.edu. *Application contact:* Alliant International University Central Contact Center, 866-U-ALLIANT, Fax: 858-635-4555, E-mail: admissions@alliant.edu.

Alliant International University–Sacramento, Graduate School of Education, TeachersCHOICE Preparation Programs, Sacramento, CA 95825. Offers MA. *Entrance requirements:* For master's, CBEST, CSET, interview; offer of employment as a teacher of record in a California school; minimum GPA of 3.0; 2 letters of recommendation. *Expenses:* Tuition: Part-time $825 per unit. Tuition and fees vary according to degree level.

See Close-Up on page 819.

Alliant International University–San Diego, Graduate School of Education, Teacher Education Programs, San Diego, CA 92131-1799. Offers preliminary single subject (Credential); professional clear multiple subject (Credential); professional clear single subject (Credential); teacher education (MA). Part-time and evening/weekend programs available. *Students:* 57 full-time (44 women), 49 part-time (34 women); includes 28 minority (3 African Americans, 11 Asian Americans or Pacific Islanders, 14 Hispanic Americans), 28 international. In 2006, 25 degrees awarded. *Entrance requirements:* For degree, California Basic Educational Skills Test, minimum GPA of 2.5. Additional exam requirements/recommendations for international students: Required—TOEFL (minimum score 550 paper-based; 213 computer-based), TWE.

Application deadline: For fall admission, 7/1 priority date for domestic and international students; for spring admission, 12/1 priority date for domestic and international students. Applications are processed on a rolling basis. Application fee: $45. Electronic applications accepted. *Expenses:* Tuition: Part-time $825 per unit. Tuition and fees vary according to course load, degree level and program. *Financial support:* Career-related internships or fieldwork, Federal Work-Study, institutionally sponsored loans, and scholarships/grants available. Financial award application deadline: 2/15; financial award applicants required to submit FAFSA. *Faculty research:* Curriculum and instructional planning. *Unit head:* Dr. Trudy Day, Assistant Dean, 866-825-5426, Fax: 858-435-4739, E-mail: admissions@alliant.edu. *Application contact:* Alliant International University Central Contact Center, 866-U-ALLIANT, Fax: 858-635-4555, E-mail: admissions@alliant.edu.

See Close-Up on page 819.

Alliant International University–San Francisco, Graduate School of Education, Teacher Education Programs, San Francisco, CA 94133-1221. Offers auditory oral education (Certificate); CLAD (Certificate); preliminary multiple subject (Credential); preliminary multiple subject with BCLAD (Credential); preliminary single subject (Credential); professional clear multiple subject (Credential); professional clear single subject (Credential); teaching (MA). Part-time and evening/weekend programs available. *Faculty:* 2 full-time (1 woman), 7 part-time/adjunct (4 women). *Students:* 16 full-time (11 women), 73 part-time (45 women); includes 25 minority (8 African Americans, 10 Asian Americans or Pacific Islanders, 7 Hispanic Americans), 1 international. Average age 28. 91 applicants, 81% accepted, 65 enrolled. In 2006, 9 degrees awarded. *Entrance requirements:* For degree, California Basic Educational Skills Test, minimum GPA of 2.5. Additional exam requirements/recommendations for international students: Required—TOEFL (minimum score 550 paper-based; 213 computer-based), TWE. *Application deadline:* For fall admission, 7/1 priority date for domestic and international students; for spring admission, 12/1 priority date for domestic and international students. Application fee: $45. *Expenses:* Tuition: Part-time $825 per unit. Tuition and fees vary according to course load, degree level and program. *Financial support:* Career-related internships or fieldwork, Federal Work-Study, institutionally sponsored loans, and scholarships/grants available. Financial award application deadline: 2/15; financial award applicants required to submit FAFSA. *Unit head:* Dr. Trudy Day, Assistant Dean, 866-825-5426, Fax: 415-955-2179, E-mail: admissions@alliant.edu. *Application contact:* Alliant International University Central Contact Center, 866-U-ALLIANT, Fax: 858-635-4555, E-mail: admissions@alliant.edu.

See Close-Up on page 819.

Alvernia College, Graduate and Continuing Studies, Department of Education, Reading, PA 19607-1799. Offers M Ed. Part-time and evening/weekend programs available. *Degree requirements:* For master's, thesis optional. *Entrance requirements:* For master's, GRE or MAT (alumni excluded). Electronic applications accepted.

Alverno College, School of Education, Milwaukee, WI 53234-3922. Offers adaptive education (MA); administrative leadership (MA); adult education and organizational development (MA); adult educational and instructional design (MA); adult educational and instructional technology (MA); instructional leadership (MA); instructional technology for K-12 settings (MA); professional development (MA); reading education (MA); reading education with adaptive education (MA); science education (MA); teaching in alternative schools (MA). *Accreditation:* NCATE. Part-time and evening/weekend programs available. *Faculty:* 12 full-time (11 women), 12 part-time/adjunct (10 women). *Students:* 83 full-time (68 women), 74 part-time (60 women); includes 37 minority (32 African Americans, 2 American Indian/Alaska Native, 3 Hispanic Americans). Average age 35. 61 applicants, 82% accepted, 41 enrolled. In 2006, 46 degrees awarded. *Degree requirements:* For master's, presentation/defense of proposal, conference presentation of inquiry projects. *Entrance requirements:* For master's, bachelor's degree in related field, communication samples from work setting, 3 letters of recommendation. Additional exam requirements/recommendations for international students: Required—TOEFL. *Application deadline:* For fall admission, 8/1 priority date for domestic and international students; for spring admission, 12/15 priority date for domestic and international students. Applications are processed on a rolling basis. Application fee: $20. Electronic applications accepted. *Expenses:* Tuition: Full-time $9,288; part-time $516 per credit. Required fees: $250; $125 per semester. Tuition and fees vary according to program. *Financial support:* In 2006–07, 92 students received support. Federal Work-Study available. Support available to part-time students. Financial award application deadline: 4/15; financial award applicants required to submit FAFSA. *Faculty research:* Student self-assessment, self-reflection, integration of curriculum, identifying needs of students in strategic situations and designing appropriate classroom strategies, implementing guided. *Unit head:* Dr. Mary Diez, Graduate Dean, 414-382-6214, Fax: 414-382-6332, E-mail: mary.diez@alverno.edu. *Application contact:* Sarajane Kennedy, Associate Director, Admissions Graduate Programs, 414-382-6104, Fax: 414-382-6332, E-mail: sarajane.kennedy@alverno.edu.

American InterContinental University, Program in Education, Los Angeles, CA 90066. Offers instructional technology (M Ed). Part-time and evening/weekend programs available. *Faculty:* 2 full-time (1 woman). *Students:* 4 full-time (3 women); includes 1 minority (African American) Average age 33. In 2006, 4 degrees awarded. *Entrance requirements:* For master's, interview, proof of Baccalaureate. Additional exam requirements/recommendations for international students: Required—TOEFL (minimum score 550 paper-based; 79 iBT), IELTS (minimum score 7). *Application deadline:* Applications are processed on a rolling basis. Application fee: $50. Electronic applications accepted. *Expenses:* Tuition: Full-time $26,400. *Financial support:* Institutionally sponsored loans, scholarships/grants, and health care benefits available. Support available to part-time students. Financial award applicants required to submit FAFSA. *Faculty research:* Curriculum and instructional technology, educational psychology, computer and information technology. *Unit head:* Dr. Eleanore Miller, Associate Dean of Education, 310-302-2634, E-mail: emiller@la.aiuniv.edu. *Application contact:* Admissions Advisor, Fax: 310-302-2001.

American InterContinental University Online, Program in Education, Hoffman Estates, IL 60192. Offers curriculum and instruction (M Ed); educational assessment and evaluation (M Ed); instructional technology (M Ed); leadership of educational organizations (M Ed). Evening/weekend programs available. Postbaccalaureate distance learning degree programs offered (no on-campus study). *Entrance requirements:* Additional exam requirements/recommendations for international students: Required—TOEFL (minimum score 550 paper-based; 213 computer-based). *Application deadline:* Applications are processed on a rolling basis. Application fee: $50. Electronic applications accepted. *Financial support:* Institutionally sponsored loans and scholarships/grants available. Financial award applicants required to submit FAFSA. *Unit head:* Kerri J Holloway, Vice President of Academic Affairs, 847-851-5000 Ext. 15399, Fax: 847-586-6309, E-mail: kholloway@aivonline.edu. *Application contact:* 877-701-3800, E-mail: info@aiuonline.edu.

American International College, School of Psychology and Education, Department of Education, Springfield, MA 01109-3189. Offers administration (M Ed, CAGS); child development (MA, Ed D), including educational psychology; elementary education (M Ed, CAGS); reading (M Ed, CAGS); secondary education (M Ed, CAGS); special education (M Ed, CAGS); teaching (MAT). Part-time and evening/weekend programs available. *Faculty:* 5 full-time (3 women), 15 part-time/adjunct (9 women). *Students:* 31 full-time (27 women), 268 part-time (217 women); includes 25 minority (13 African Americans, 4 Asian Americans or Pacific Islanders, 8 Hispanic Americans), 2 international. Average age 39. In 2006, 38 master's, 2 doctorates, 5 other advanced degrees awarded. Terminal master's awarded for partial completion of doctoral program. *Degree requirements:* For master's, thesis (for some programs), practicum, comprehensive exam (for some programs), registration; for doctorate, thesis/dissertation, comprehensive exam (for some programs), registration; for CAGS, practicum. *Entrance requirements:* For master's, minimum B- average in undergraduate course work; for doctorate, GRE General Test, interview. Additional exam requirements/recommendations for international students: Required—TOEFL. *Application deadline:* For fall admission, 7/1 priority date for domestic and international students; for spring admission, 12/1 priority date for domestic and international students. Applications are processed on a rolling basis. Application fee: $50. *Expenses:* Tuition: Part-time $585 per semester hour. Required fees: $100 per year. Full-time tuition and fees vary according to program. *Financial support:* Career-related internships or fieldwork and institutionally sponsored loans available. Financial award applicants required to submit FAFSA. *Unit head:* Dr. Barbara Dautrich, Chair, 413-205-3407, Fax: 413-205-3943, E-mail: barbara.dautrich@aic.edu. *Application contact:* Keshawn Dodds, Associate Director of Graduate Admissions, 413-205-3549, Fax: 413-205-3911, E-mail: keshawn.dodds@aic.edu.

American Jewish University, Graduate School, Fingerhut School of Education, Program in Education, Bel Air, CA 90077-1599. Offers MA Ed. *Degree requirements:* For master's, one foreign language. *Entrance requirements:* For master's, GRE General Test, interview, minimum GPA of 3.0. Additional exam requirements/recommendations for international students: Required—TOEFL. *Faculty research:* Philosophy of education, curriculum development, teacher training.

American Jewish University, Graduate School, Fingerhut School of Education, Program in Education for Working Professionals, Bel Air, CA 90077-1599. Offers MA Ed. *Degree requirements:* For master's, internships. *Entrance requirements:* For master's, GRE General Test, interview. Additional exam requirements/recommendations for international students: Required—TOEFL.

American University, College of Arts and Sciences, School of Education, Teaching, and Health, Washington, DC 20016-8001. Offers MA, MAT, MS, PhD, Certificate. *Accreditation:* NCATE. Part-time and evening/weekend programs available. *Faculty:* 15 full-time (8 women), 41 part-time/adjunct (31 women). *Students:* 67 full-time (60 women), 402 part-time (295 women); includes 116 minority (81 African Americans, 13 Asian Americans or Pacific Islanders, 22 Hispanic Americans), 11 international. Average age 27. 265 applicants, 82% accepted, 149 enrolled. In 2006, 156 master's, 6 doctorates, 10 other advanced degrees awarded. *Degree requirements:* For master's, thesis or alternative. *Entrance requirements:* For master's and doctorate, GRE General Test or MAT, minimum GPA of 3.0. *Application deadline:* For fall admission, 2/1 priority date for domestic students; for spring admission, 10/1 priority date for domestic students. Applications are processed on a rolling basis. Application fee: $50. *Expenses:* Tuition: Full-time $18,864; part-time $1,048 per credit. Required fees: $380. Tuition and fees vary according to program. *Financial support:* Fellowships with full tuition reimbursements, research assistantships with partial tuition reimbursements, teaching assistantships, career-related internships or fieldwork, Federal Work-Study, and institutionally sponsored loans available. Support available to part-time students. Financial award application deadline: 2/1; financial award applicants required to submit FAFSA. *Faculty research:* Gender equity, socioeconomic technology, learning disabilities, gifted and talented education. *Unit head:* Dr. Sarah Irvine-Belson, Dean, 202-885-3714, Fax: 202-885-1187, E-mail: educate@american.edu.

American University of Beirut, Graduate Programs, Faculty of Arts and Sciences, Beirut, Lebanon. Offers anthropology (MA); Arabic language and literature (MA); archaeology (MA); biology (MS); chemistry (MS); computer science (MS); economics (MA); education (MA); English language (MA); English literature (MA); environmental policy planning (MSES); financial economics (MAFE); geology (MS); history (MA); mathematics (MA, MS); Middle Eastern studies (MA); philosophy (MA); physics (MS); political studies (MA); psychology (MA); public administration (MA); sociology (MA); statistics (MA, MS). Part-time programs available. *Faculty:* 101 full-time (28 women), 4 part-time/adjunct (1 woman). *Students:* 46 full-time (24 women), 368 part-time (269 women). Average age 25. 389 applicants, 71% accepted, 102 enrolled. In 2006, 131 degrees awarded. *Degree requirements:* For master's, one foreign language, thesis (for some programs), comprehensive exam, registration. *Entrance requirements:* For master's, GRE, letter of recommendation. Additional exam requirements/recommendations for international students: Required—TOEFL (minimum score 600 paper-based; 250 computer-based; 100 iBT), IELTS (minimum score 8). *Application deadline:* For fall admission, 4/30 for domestic and international students; for spring admission, 11/1 for domestic and international students. Application fee: $50. *Financial support:* In 2006–07, 23 students received support. Career-related internships or fieldwork, institutionally sponsored loans, scholarships/grants, health care benefits, and unspecified assistantships available. Financial award application deadline: 2/2; financial award applicants required to submit FAFSA. *Faculty research:* String theory, algebra and number theory, Hizbollahs Jihad concept, critical sociology, literature. Total annual research expenditures: $82,315. *Unit head:* Khalil Bitar, Dean, 961-1374374 Ext. 3800, Fax: 961-1744461, E-mail: kmb@aub.edu.lb. *Application contact:* Dr. Salim Kanaan, Director of Admissions Office, 961-1-374374 Ext. 2592, Fax: 961-1-750775, E-mail: admissions@aub.edu.lb.

American University of Puerto Rico, Program in Education, Bayamón, PR 00960-2037. Offers art history (M Ed); elementary education (4-6) (M Ed); elementary education (k-3) (M Ed); general science education (M Ed); physical education (k-12) (M Ed); special education at secondary level (transition) (M Ed). *Entrance requirements:* For master's, EXADEP or GRE or MAT, 2 letters of recommendation, minimum GPA of 2.5.

Anderson University, School of Education, Anderson, IN 46012-3495. Offers M Ed. *Accreditation:* NCATE.

Andrews University, School of Graduate Studies, School of Education, Berrien Springs, MI 49104. Offers MA, MAT, MS, Ed D, PhD, Ed S. *Accreditation:* NCATE. Part-time programs available. Terminal master's awarded for partial completion of doctoral program. *Degree requirements:* For doctorate, thesis/dissertation. *Entrance requirements:* For master's, GRE Subject Test.

Angelo State University, College of Graduate Studies, College of Education, Department of Teacher Education, San Angelo, TX 76909. Offers M Ed, MA. *Faculty:* 17 full-time (12 women). *Students:* 17 full-time (11 women), 129 part-time (87 women); includes 21 minority (2 African Americans, 1 American Indian/Alaska Native, 1 Asian American or Pacific Islander, 17 Hispanic Americans). Average age 39. In 2006, 48 degrees awarded. *Expenses:* Tuition, state resident: full-time $2,340; part-time $130 per hour. Tuition, nonresident: full-time $7,290; part-time $405 per hour. Required fees: $906; $56 per hour. *Financial support:* In 2006–07, 57 students received support. *Unit head:* Dr. Linda Lucksinger, Department Head, 325-942-2052 Ext. 266, E-mail: linda.lucksinger@angelo.edu. *Application contact:* Brenda Stewart, Assistant to the Dean, College of Graduate Studies, 325-942-2169, Fax: 325-942-2194, E-mail: brenda.stewart@angelo.edu.

Anna Maria College, Graduate Division, Program in Education, Paxton, MA 01612. Offers early childhood development (M Ed); education (CAGS); elementary education (M Ed); reading (M Ed). Part-time and evening/weekend programs available. *Faculty:* 6 full-time (5 women), 16 part-time/adjunct (15 women). *Students:* 13 full-time (all women), 84 part-time (82 women); includes 1 minority (Hispanic American) Average age 34. In 2006, 30 master's, 2 other advanced degrees awarded. *Degree requirements:* For master's, action research project. *Entrance requirements:* For master's, bachelor's degree in liberal arts or sciences, minimum GPA of 3.0. *Application deadline:* For fall admission, 3/1 priority date for domestic and international students; for spring admission, 11/1 priority date for domestic and international students. Applications are processed on a rolling basis. Application fee: $40. Electronic applications accepted. *Financial support:* Applicants required to submit FAFSA. *Unit head:* Christine Holmes, Director, 508-849-3418, Fax: 508-849-3343, E-mail: cholmes@annamaria.edu. *Application contact:* Janet LaPointe, Admissions Coordinator, Graduate and Continuing Education, 508-849-3234, Fax: 508-819-3362, E-mail: jlapointe@annamaria.edu.

Antioch University Los Angeles, Graduate Programs, Program in Education and Teacher Credentialing, Culver City, CA 90230. Offers education (MA). Evening/weekend programs available. *Entrance requirements:* Additional exam requirements/recommendations for international students: Required—TOEFL.

Education—General

Antioch University McGregor, Graduate Programs, Department of Teacher Education, Yellow Springs, OH 45387-1609. Offers M Ed. Evening/weekend programs available. *Faculty:* 11 full-time, 20 part-time/adjunct. *Students:* 244 full-time (185 women), 60 part-time (43 women); includes 102 minority (96 African Americans, 4 American Indian/Alaska Native, 1 Asian American or Pacific Islander, 1 Hispanic American). Average age 31. 210 applicants, 76% accepted, 152 enrolled. In 2006, 161 degrees awarded. *Degree requirements:* For master's, thesis or alternative, registration. *Entrance requirements:* For master's, resumé, 2 letters of reference. *Application deadline:* For fall admission, 9/7 for domestic students; for winter admission, 12/10 for domestic students; for spring admission, 3/8 for domestic students. Applications are processed on a rolling basis. Application fee: $50. Electronic applications accepted. *Expenses: Contact institution. Financial support:* Federal Work-Study available. Financial award applicants required to submit FAFSA. *Unit head:* Dr. Zak Shariff, Chair, 937-769-1880, Fax: 937-769-1805, E-mail: zsharif@mcgregor.edu. *Application contact:* Oscar Robinson, Enrollment Services Manager, 937-769-1823, Fax: 937-769-1804, E-mail: orobinson@mcgregor.edu.

Antioch University McGregor, Graduate Programs, Individualized Liberal and Professional Studies Program, Yellow Springs, OH 45387-1609. Offers liberal and professional studies (MA), including counseling, creative writing, education, film studies, liberal studies, management, modern literature, psychology, theatre, visual arts. Part-time and evening/weekend programs available. Postbaccalaureate distance learning degree programs offered (minimal on-campus study). *Faculty:* 4 full-time (2 women), 3 part-time/adjunct (all women). *Students:* Average age 41. 31 applicants, 74% accepted, 23 enrolled. In 2006, 54 degrees awarded. *Degree requirements:* For master's, thesis or alternative, registration. *Entrance requirements:* For master's, resumé, 2 letters of reference. *Application deadline:* For fall admission, 8/25 for domestic students; for winter admission, 12/5 for domestic students; for spring admission, 3/8 for domestic students. Applications are processed on a rolling basis. Application fee: $50. Electronic applications accepted. *Expenses: Contact institution. Financial support:* Federal Work-Study available. Financial award applicants required to submit FAFSA. *Application contact:* Seth Gordon, Enrollment Services Officer, 937-769-1800 Ext. 1825, Fax: 937-769-1804, E-mail: sgordon@mcgregor.edu.

Antioch University New England, Graduate School, Department of Education, Keene, NH 03431-3552. Offers experienced educators (M Ed); integrated learning (M Ed); Waldorf teacher training (M Ed). *Faculty:* 10 full-time (5 women), 11 part-time/adjunct (7 women). *Students:* 116 full-time (95 women), 37 part-time (26 women); includes 3 minority (all Hispanic Americans), 2 international. Average age 36. 148 applicants, 79% accepted, 105 enrolled. In 2006, 74 degrees awarded. *Degree requirements:* For master's, thesis (for some programs), internship. *Entrance requirements:* Additional exam requirements/recommendations for international students: Required—TOEFL (minimum score 600 paper-based; 250 computer-based). *Application deadline:* For fall admission, 8/1 for domestic and international students; for spring admission, 12/1 for domestic and international students. Applications are processed on a rolling basis. Application fee: $50. *Expenses: Contact institution.* Tuition and fees vary according to program and student level. *Financial support:* In 2006–07, 135 students received support, including 32 fellowships (averaging $900 per year); Federal Work-Study also available. Financial award applicants required to submit FAFSA. *Faculty research:* Classroom and school restructuring, problem-based learning, Waldorf collaborative leadership, ecological literacy. *Unit head:* Peter Eppig, Director, 603-283-2312, Fax: 603-357-0718, E-mail: peppig@antiochne.edu. *Application contact:* Leatrice A. Oram, Co-Director of Admissions, 800-490-3310, Fax: 603-357-0718, E-mail: admissions@antiochne.edu.

See Close-Up on page 821.

Antioch University Santa Barbara, Program in Education/Teacher Credentialing, Santa Barbara, CA 93101-1581. Offers MA. Part-time programs available. *Faculty:* 16 full-time (11 women), 55 part-time/adjunct (21 women). *Students:* 14 full-time (13 women), 17 part-time (14 women); includes 8 minority (3 African Americans, 5 Hispanic Americans). In 2006, 9 degrees awarded. Application fee: $60 ($100 for international students). *Expenses:* Tuition: Part-time $515 per unit. Part-time tuition and fees vary according to course load and program. *Financial support:* Federal Work-Study available. Support available to part-time students. Financial award application deadline: 8/8; financial award applicants required to submit FAFSA. *Unit head:* Dr. Michele Britton Bass, Chair, 805-962-8179 Ext. 114, Fax: 805-962-4786, E-mail: britbass@antiochsb.edu. *Application contact:* Director of Admissions, 805-962-8179 Ext. 330, Fax: 805-962-4786, E-mail: admissions@antiochsb.edu.

Antioch University Seattle, Graduate Programs, Program in Education, Seattle, WA 98121-1814. Offers MA. Part-time and evening/weekend programs available. Expenses: Contact institution. *Faculty research:* Transformative learning, intercultural studies, gay and lesbian studies.

See Close-Up on page 823.

Appalachian State University, Cratis D. Williams Graduate School, College of Education, Boone, NC 28608. Offers MA, MLS, MSA, Ed D, Ed S. *Accreditation:* NCATE. Part-time and evening/weekend programs available. Postbaccalaureate distance learning degree programs offered (minimal on-campus study). *Faculty:* 137 full-time (78 women), 14 part-time/adjunct (9 women). *Students:* 310 full-time (243 women), 827 part-time (634 women); includes 68 minority (65 African Americans, 1 American Indian/Alaska Native, 2 Hispanic Americans), 18 international. 622 applicants, 82% accepted, 436 enrolled. In 2006, 438 master's, 3 doctorates awarded. *Degree requirements:* For master's, internships, thesis optional; for doctorate, thesis/dissertation, comprehensive exam, registration. *Entrance requirements:* For master's, GRE General Test or MAT; for doctorate, GRE General Test. Additional exam requirements/recommendations for international students: Required—TOEFL (minimum score 570 paper-based; 230 computer-based). *Application deadline:* For fall admission, 7/1 for domestic students, 1/1 for international students; for spring admission, 11/1 for domestic students, 6/1 for international students. Application fee: $50. *Expenses:* Tuition, state resident: full-time $2,600; part-time $127 per hour. Tuition, nonresident: full-time $13,200; part-time $597 per hour. Required fees: $2,000; $546 per term. *Financial support:* In 2006–07, research assistantships (averaging $7,000 per year), teaching assistantships (averaging $7,000 per year) were awarded; fellowships, career-related internships or fieldwork, Federal Work-Study, scholarships/grants, and unspecified assistantships also available. Support available to part-time students. Financial award application deadline: 7/1; financial award applicants required to submit FAFSA. Total annual research expenditures: $2.6 million. *Unit head:* Dr. Charles Duke, Dean, 828-262-2232. *Application contact:* Dr. Holly Hirst, Associate Dean for Graduate Studies, 828-262-2130, Fax: 828-262-2709, E-mail: hirsthp@appstate.edu.

Aquinas College, School of Education, Grand Rapids, MI 49506-1799. Offers MAT, ME, MS. Part-time and evening/weekend programs available. *Faculty:* 24 full-time (16 women), 34 part-time/adjunct (28 women). *Students:* 65 full-time (46 women), 186 part-time (148 women); includes 25 minority (4 African Americans, 2 American Indian/Alaska Native, 2 Asian Americans or Pacific Islanders, 17 Hispanic Americans). Average age 35. 41 applicants, 80% accepted, 30 enrolled. In 2006, 117 degrees awarded. *Degree requirements:* For master's, teaching project. *Entrance requirements:* For master's, Michigan Basic Skills test, minimum undergraduate GPA of 3.0, teaching certificate. Additional exam requirements/recommendations for international students: Required—TOEFL (minimum score 550 paper-based; 213 computer-based). *Application deadline:* Applications are processed on a rolling basis. Application fee: $0. *Expenses: Contact institution. Financial support:* In 2006–07, 141 students received support. Scholarships/grants available. Support available to part-time students. Financial award application deadline: 3/15; financial award applicants required to submit FAFSA. *Unit head:* Nanette Clatterbuck, Dean, 616-632-2973, Fax: 616-732-4465, E-mail: clattnan@aquinas.edu. *Application contact:* Sandy Rademaker, Coordinator of Graduate Education Programs, 616-632-2443 Ext. 5400, E-mail: rademsan@aquinas.edu.

Arcadia University, Graduate Studies, Department of Education, Glenside, PA 19038-3295. Offers art education (M Ed, MA Ed); biology education (MA Ed); chemistry education (MA Ed); child development (CAS); computer education (M Ed, CAS); computer education 7–12 (MA Ed); early childhood education (M Ed, CAS), including individualized (M Ed), master teacher (M Ed), research in child development (M Ed); educational leadership (M Ed, CAS); educational psychology (CAS); elementary education (M Ed, CAS); English education (MA Ed); environmental education (MA Ed, CAS); history education (MA Ed); language arts (M Ed, CAS); mathematics education (M Ed, MA Ed, CAS); music education (MA Ed); psychology (MA Ed); pupil personnel services (CAS); reading (M Ed, CAS); school library science (M Ed); science education (M Ed, CAS); secondary education (M Ed, CAS); special education (M Ed, Ed D, CAS); theater arts (MA Ed); written communication (MA Ed). *Accreditation:* NASAD. Part-time and evening/weekend programs available. Postbaccalaureate distance learning degree programs offered (minimal on-campus study). *Faculty:* 12 full-time (8 women), 38 part-time/adjunct (26 women). *Students:* 60 full-time (56 women), 419 part-time (324 women); includes 70 minority (57 African Americans, 1 American Indian/Alaska Native, 6 Asian Americans or Pacific Islanders, 6 Hispanic Americans), 1 international. In 2006, 257 master's, 4 doctorates awarded. *Application deadline:* Applications are processed on a rolling basis. Application fee: $35. Electronic applications accepted. *Financial support:* Career-related internships or fieldwork, tuition waivers (partial), and unspecified assistantships available. *Unit head:* Dr. Steven P. Gulkus, Chair, 215-572-2120. *Application contact:* 215-572-2925, Fax: 215-572-2126, E-mail: grad@arcadia.edu.

Argosy University, Atlanta Campus, College of Education, Atlanta, GA 30328. Offers educational leadership (MAEd, Ed D, Ed S), including higher education administration (Ed D), k-12 administration (Ed D); instructional leadership (MAEd, Ed D, Ed S), including higher education (Ed D), K-12 education (Ed D). Evening/weekend programs available. *Students:* 459 full-time (377 women), 324 part-time (255 women); includes 388 minority (335 African Americans, 10 American Indian/Alaska Native, 14 Asian Americans or Pacific Islanders, 29 Hispanic Americans). *Entrance requirements:* For master's and doctorate, 3 letters of recommendation, minimum GPA of 3.0, resumé. Additional exam requirements/recommendations for international students: Required—TOEFL (minimum score 550 paper-based; 213 computer-based). *Application deadline:* For fall admission, 8/1 for domestic students; for spring admission, 10/1 for domestic students. Application fee: $50. *Financial support:* Teaching assistantships, Federal Work-Study available. *Unit head:* Jacqueline Jenkins, Department Chair, 770-407-1067, Fax: 770-671-0476, E-mail: jbeard@argosy.edu. *Application contact:* Christa Holton, Director of Admissions, 770-671-1200, Fax: 770-671-9050, E-mail: inquiry@argosy.edu.

See Close-Up on page 1101.

Argosy University, Chicago Campus, College of Education, Chicago, IL 60603. Offers community college executive leadership (Ed D); educational leadership (MA Ed, Ed D, Ed S), including administrative certification (MA Ed), district leadership (Ed D), higher education administration (Ed D), K-12 education (Ed D), principal/general (MA Ed), superintendent certification (Ed S); instructional leadership (MA Ed, Ed D, Ed S), including higher education (Ed D), K-12 education (Ed D). Part-time and evening/weekend programs available. *Faculty:* 3 full-time (1 woman), 7 part-time/adjunct (0 women). *Students:* 116 full-time (96 women), 42 part-time (32 women); includes 112 minority (108 African Americans, 1 Asian American or Pacific Islander, 3 Hispanic Americans). Average age 45. 56 applicants, 84% accepted, 45 enrolled. In 2006, 4 master's, 10 doctorates awarded. *Entrance requirements:* For master's and doctorate, minimum GPA of 3.0. Additional exam requirements/recommendations for international students: Required—TOEFL (minimum score 550 paper-based; 213 computer-based). *Application deadline:* For fall admission, 2/28 for domestic and international students; for spring admission, 10/30 for domestic and international students. Applications are processed on a rolling basis. Application fee: $50. Electronic applications accepted. *Financial support:* In 2006–07, 35 students received support. Scholarships/grants available. Financial award application deadline: 4/1. *Unit head:* Dr. Paul Busceni, Head, 800-626-4123, Fax: 312-777-7750, E-mail: pbusceni@argosy.edu. *Application contact:* Ashley Delaney, Director of Admissions, 800-626-4123, Fax: 312-777-7750, E-mail: argosyadmissions@argosy.edu.

See Close-Up on page 825.

Argosy University, Dallas Campus, College of Education, Dallas, TX 75231. Offers educational leadership (MA Ed); instructional leadership (MA Ed). Part-time and evening/weekend programs available. *Degree requirements:* For master's, capstone project. *Entrance requirements:* For master's, minimum GPA of 3.0, resumé, 3 letters of recommendation. Additional exam requirements/recommendations for international students: Required—TOEFL (minimum score 550 paper-based; 213 computer-based). *Application deadline:* For fall admission, 5/15 priority date for international students; for spring admission, 10/15 priority date for international students. Applications are processed on a rolling basis. Application fee: $50. Electronic applications accepted. *Financial support:* Federal Work-Study and scholarships/grants available. *Unit head:* Dr. Susan Bryza, Education Program Chair, E-mail: sbryza@argosy.edu. *Application contact:* Kara Smith, Director of Admissions, 214-459-2208, Fax: 214-378-8555, E-mail: dallas.admissions@argosyu.edu.

See Close-Up on page 827.

Argosy University, Denver Campus, College of Education, Denver, CO 80203. Offers educational leadership (MA Ed, Ed D), including higher education adminstration (Ed D), K-12 education (Ed D); instructional leadership (MA Ed, Ed D), including higher education (Ed D), K-12 education (Ed D).

See Close-Up on page 829.

Argosy University, Hawai'i Campus, College of Education, Honolulu, HI 96813. Offers educational leadership (MAEd, Ed D), including higher education administration (Ed D), K-12 education (Ed D); instructional leadership (MAEd, Ed D), including higher education (Ed D), K-12 education (Ed D). *Faculty:* 9 part-time/adjunct (4 women). *Students:* 26 full-time (18 women), 4 part-time (all women); includes 16 minority (13 Asian Americans or Pacific Islanders, 3 Hispanic Americans). 17 applicants, 94% accepted, 14 enrolled. *Degree requirements:* For doctorate, thesis/dissertation. *Entrance requirements:* Additional exam requirements/recommendations for international students: Required—TOEFL (minimum score 550 paper-based; 214 computer-based). *Application deadline:* For fall admission, 1/15 priority date for domestic students; for spring admission, 10/15 for domestic students. Applications are processed on a rolling basis. Application fee: $50. Electronic applications accepted. *Unit head:* Dr. Kristine Lesperance, Chair, 888-323-2777, Fax: 808-536-5505, E-mail: klesperance@argosy.edu. *Application contact:* Cherie Andrade, Director of Admissions, 888-323-2777, Fax: 808-536-5505, E-mail: candrade@argosy.edu.

See Close-Up on page 831.

Argosy University, Orange County Campus, College of Education, Santa Ana, CA 92704. Offers community college executive leadership (Ed D); educational leadership (MA Ed, Ed D), including higher education administration (Ed D), K-12 education (Ed D); instructional leadership (MA Ed, Ed D), including educational technology (Ed D), higher education (Ed D), K-12 education (Ed D), multiple subject teacher credential preparation (MA Ed), multiple subject teacher credential preparation with BCLAD (MA Ed), single subject teacher credential preparation (MA Ed), single subject teacher credential preparation with BCLAD (MA Ed). Part-time and evening/weekend programs available. *Faculty:* 3 full-time (2 women), 33 part-time/adjunct (15 women). *Students:* 185 full-time (112 women), 49 part-time (28 women). Average age 37. 91 applicants, 76 enrolled. In 2006, 58 master's, 17 doctorates awarded. Terminal master's awarded for partial completion of doctoral program. *Degree requirements:* For master's, comprehensive exam; for doctorate, thesis/dissertation, preliminary and final dissertation defense, comprehensive exam. *Entrance requirements:* For master's, minimum GPA of 3.0 in final 2 years of course work, 3 letters of recommendation, resumé; for doctorate, minimum GPA of 3.0 in graduate study, 3 letters of recommendation, resumé. Additional exam requirements/recommendations for international students: Required—TOEFL. *Application deadline:* Applications are processed on a rolling basis. Application fee: $50. Electronic applications accepted.

Financial support: Federal Work-Study and scholarships/grants available. Support available to part-time students. Financial award applicants required to submit FAFSA. *Faculty research:* Educational leadership, higher education, qualitative research, K-12 education, multicultural education. *Unit head:* Dr. Christine Zeppos, Dean, 800-7196-9598, Fax: 714-437-1287, E-mail: czeppos@argosy.edu. *Application contact:* Mark Betz, Director of Admissions, 800-716-9598, Fax: 714-437-1697, E-mail: mbetz@argosy.edu.

See Close-Up on page 833.

Argosy University, Phoenix Campus, College of Education, Phoenix, AZ 85021. Offers community college executive leadership (Ed D); educational leadership (MA Ed, Ed D, Ed S), including higher education administration (Ed D), K-12 education (Ed D); instructional leadership (MA Ed, Ed D, Ed S), including higher education (Ed D), K-12 education (Ed D). Part-time and evening/weekend programs available. *Faculty:* 13 part-time/adjunct (4 women). *Students:* 26 full-time (17 women), 2 part-time (1 woman); includes 3 minority (2 African Americans, 1 Hispanic American). Average age 44. 10 applicants, 100% accepted, 9 enrolled. *Entrance requirements:* For doctorate, minimum GPA of 3.0, master's degree. Additional exam requirements/recommendations for international students: Required—TOEFL (minimum score 550 paper-based; 213 computer-based). *Application deadline:* Applications are processed on a rolling basis. Application fee: $50. Electronic applications accepted. *Financial support:* Federal Work-Study available. Financial award applicants required to submit FAFSA. *Unit head:* Dr. Gayle Schou, Director, 866-216-2777, E-mail: argosyadmissions@argosy.edu. *Application contact:* Andy Hughes, Director of Admissions, 866-216-2777, Fax: 602-216-2601, E-mail: ahughes@argosy.edu.

See Close-Up on page 835.

Argosy University, San Diego Campus, College of Education, San Diego, CA 92108. Offers community college executive leadership (Ed D); educational leadership (MA Ed, Ed D), including higher education administration (Ed D), K-12 education (Ed D); instructional leadership (MA Ed, Ed D), including higher education (Ed D), K-12 education (Ed D), multiple subject teacher credential preparation (MA Ed), multiple subject teacher credential preparation with BCLAD (MA Ed), single subject teacher credential preparation (MA Ed), single subject teacher credential preparation with BCLAD (MA Ed).

See Close-Up on page 837.

Argosy University, San Francisco Bay Area Campus, College of Education, Point Richmond, CA 94804-3547. Offers community college executive leadership (Ed D); educational leadership (MA Ed, Ed D), including higher education administration (Ed D), K–12 education (Ed D); instructional leadership (MA Ed, Ed D), including higher education (Ed D), K–12 education (Ed D), multiple subject teacher credential preparation (MA Ed), multiple subject teacher credential preparation with BCLAD (MA Ed), single subject teacher credential preparation (MA Ed), single subject teacher credential preparation with BCLAD (MA Ed). Part-time and evening/weekend programs available. Postbaccalaureate distance learning degree programs offered (minimal on-campus study). *Faculty:* 1 (woman) full-time, 14 part-time/adjunct. *Students:* 59 full-time (41 women), 30 part-time (14 women); includes 26 minority (11 African Americans, 11 Asian Americans or Pacific Islanders, 4 Hispanic Americans), 1 international. 34 applicants, 82% accepted, 20 enrolled. In 2006, 7 degrees awarded. *Degree requirements:* For master's, capstone project; for doctorate, thesis/dissertation, comprehensive exam, registration. *Entrance requirements:* For master's and doctorate, minimum GPA of 3.0. Additional exam requirements/recommendations for international students: Required—TOEFL (minimum score 550 paper-based; 213 computer-based). *Application deadline:* For fall admission, 7/1 priority date for domestic students, 7/1 for international students; for winter admission, 11/1 priority date for domestic and international students; for spring admission, 4/1 priority date for domestic and international students. Applications are processed on a rolling basis. Application fee: $50. Electronic applications accepted. *Financial support:* Career-related internships or fieldwork, Federal Work-Study, and scholarships/grants available. Support available to part-time students. Financial award application deadline: 4/20; financial award applicants required to submit FAFSA. *Unit head:* Dr. Keyes Kelly, 510-837-3740, E-mail: kkelly@argosy.edu. *Application contact:* John Vincent Stofan, Director, Admissions, 510-215-0277, Fax: 510-215-0299, E-mail: jstofan@argosy.edu.

See Close-Up on page 839.

Argosy University, Santa Monica Campus, College of Education, Santa Monica, CA 90405. Offers community college executive leadership (Ed D); educational leadership (MA Ed, Ed D), including higher education administration (Ed D), K-12 education (Ed D); instructional leadership (MA Ed, Ed D), including higher education (Ed D), K-12 education (Ed D), multiple subject teacher credential preparation (MA Ed), multiple subject teacher credential preparation with BCLAD (MA Ed), single subject teacher credential preparation (MA Ed), single subject teacher credential preparation with BCLAD (MA Ed).

See Close-Up on page 841.

Argosy University, Sarasota Campus, College of Education, Sarasota, FL 34235-8246. Offers community college educational leadership (Ed D); educational leadership (MA Ed, Ed D, Ed S), including higher education administration (Ed D), K-12 education (Ed D); instructional leadership (MA Ed, Ed D, Ed S), including education technology (Ed D), higher education (Ed D), K-12 education (Ed D). Part-time and evening/weekend programs available. Postbaccalaureate distance learning degree programs offered (minimal on-campus study). *Faculty:* 15 full-time (8 women), 49 part-time/adjunct (21 women). *Students:* 149 applicants, 96% accepted, 121 enrolled. In 2006, 9 master's, 141 doctorates awarded. *Degree requirements:* For doctorate, thesis/dissertation, comprehensive exam. *Entrance requirements:* For doctorate, minimum undergraduate GPA of 3.0. Additional exam requirements/recommendations for international students: Required—TOEFL. *Application deadline:* Applications are processed on a rolling basis. Application fee: $50. Electronic applications accepted. *Expenses:* Contact institution. *Financial support:* Federal Work-Study available. Support available to part-time students. Financial award application deadline: 4/1; financial award applicants required to submit FAFSA. *Unit head:* Dr. Chuck Mlynarczyk, Dean, 800-331-5995, Fax: 941-371-9464, E-mail: cmlynarczyk@argosy.edu. *Application contact:* Admissions Representative, 800-331-5995 Ext. 221, Fax: 941-371-8910.

See Close-Up on page 843.

Argosy University, Schaumburg Campus, College of Education, Schaumburg, IL 60173-5403. Offers community college executive leadership (Ed D); educational leadership (MA Ed, Ed D, Ed S), including administrative certification (MA Ed), higher education administration (Ed D), K-12 education (Ed D), principal/general (MA Ed), superintendent certification (Ed S); instructional leadership (MA Ed, Ed D, Ed S), including higher education (Ed D), K-12 education (Ed D). Part-time and evening/weekend programs available. *Faculty:* 1 (woman) full-time, 7 part-time/adjunct (3 women). *Students:* 19 full-time, 19 part-time. 15 applicants, 80% accepted, 10 enrolled. In 2006, 1 master's, 3 doctorates, 2 other advanced degrees awarded. *Degree requirements:* For doctorate, thesis/dissertation, comprehensive exam. *Entrance requirements:* For master's and doctorate, minimum GPA of 3.0. Additional exam requirements/recommendations for international students: Required—TOEFL. *Application deadline:* For fall admission, 3/15 priority date for domestic and international students; for spring admission, 10/15 priority date for domestic and international students. Applications are processed on a rolling basis. Application fee: $50. Electronic applications accepted. *Expenses:* Contact institution. *Financial support:* Federal Work-Study and scholarships/grants available. *Unit head:* Dr. Narjis Hyder, Program Chair, 866-290-7400, Fax: 847-598-6158, E-mail: nhyder@argosy.edu. *Application contact:* Jamal Scott, Application Contact, 866-290-7400, Fax: 630-598-6191, E-mail: jscott@argosy.edu.

See Close-Up on page 845.

Argosy University, Seattle Campus, College of Education, Seattle, WA 98121. Offers community college executive leadership (Ed D); education (MA Ed); educational leadership (MA Ed, Ed D), including higher education administration (Ed D), K-12 education (Ed D); instructional leadership (MA Ed, Ed D), including education technology (Ed D), higher education (Ed D), K-12 education (Ed D). Part-time and evening/weekend programs available. *Students:* 29 full-time, 15 part-time. *Degree requirements:* For master's, thesis or alternative, capstone project; for doctorate, thesis/dissertation, comprehensive exam, registration. *Entrance requirements:* For master's, minimum GPA of 3.0 in last 60 hours of course work or minimum cumulative GPA of 2.7; for doctorate, minimum GPA of 3.0. Additional exam requirements/recommendations for international students: Required—TOEFL (minimum score 550 paper-based; 213 computer-based). *Application deadline:* For fall admission, 4/15 priority date for domestic students, 4/15 for international students. Application fee: $50. *Expenses:* Contact institution. *Financial support:* Teaching assistantships with partial tuition reimbursements, Federal Work-Study, scholarships/grants, and unspecified assistantships available. Support available to part-time students. Financial award application deadline: 4/19; financial award applicants required to submit FAFSA. *Unit head:* Dr. Leslie Aune Oja, Chair of Education, 206-393-3570, Fax: 206-283-5777, E-mail: ioja@argosy.edu. *Application contact:* Josh Pond, Director of Admissions, 206-283-4500, Fax: 206-283-5777, E-mail: jpond@argosyu.edu.

See Close-Up on page 847.

Argosy University, Tampa Campus, College of Education, Tampa, FL 33614. Offers community college executive leadership (Ed D); educational leadership (MA Ed, Ed D, Ed S), including higher education administration (Ed D), K-12 education (Ed D); instructional leadership (MA Ed, Ed D, Ed S), including higher education (Ed D), K-12 education (Ed D). *Faculty:* 1 (woman) full-time, 8 part-time/adjunct (3 women). *Degree requirements:* For master's, capstone project; for doctorate, thesis/dissertation. *Entrance requirements:* For master's, minimum GPA of 3.0 in last 2 years of undergraduate course work, resumé, 3 letters of recommendation; for doctorate, minimum GPA of 3.0, 3 letters of recommendation, resumé. Additional exam requirements/recommendations for international students: Required—TOEFL (minimum score 550 paper-based; 213 computer-based). *Application deadline:* Applications are processed on a rolling basis. Application fee: $50. Electronic applications accepted. *Faculty research:* Reading methods, elementary education, educational leadership, instructional design and instructional technology. *Unit head:* Dr. Patty O'Grady, Head, 813-246-4419, Fax: 813-246-4045, E-mail: pogrady@argosy.edu.

See Close-Up on page 849.

Argosy University, Twin Cities Campus, College of Education, Eagan, MN 55121. Offers educational leadership (MA Ed, Ed D, Ed S), including higher education administration (Ed D), K-12 education (Ed D); instructional leadership (MA Ed, Ed D, Ed S), including education technology (Ed D), higher education (Ed D), K-12 education (Ed D). Part-time and evening/weekend programs available. *Faculty:* 1 full-time (0 women), 10 part-time/adjunct (4 women). *Students:* 30 full-time (22 women), 12 part-time (9 women); includes 3 minority (1 African American, 1 American Indian/Alaska Native, 1 Asian American or Pacific Islander). Average age 45. 35 applicants, 86% accepted, 12 enrolled. In 2006, 1 master's, 6 doctorates awarded. *Degree requirements:* For doctorate, thesis/dissertation, comprehensive exam. *Entrance requirements:* For master's, 3 letters of recommendation, minimum undergraduate GPA of 3.0, resumé; for doctorate, 3 letters of recommendation, master's degree, minimum GPA of 3.0, resumé. Additional exam requirements/recommendations for international students: Required—TOEFL (minimum score 550 paper-based; 213 computer-based). *Application deadline:* For fall admission, 5/15 priority date for domestic students, 5/15 for international students; for spring admission, 10/15 priority date for domestic students, 10/15 for international students. Applications are processed on a rolling basis. Application fee: $50. Electronic applications accepted. *Financial support:* In 2006–07, 12 fellowships with partial tuition reimbursements, 3 teaching assistantships with partial tuition reimbursements were awarded; Federal Work-Study and scholarships/grants also available. Financial award applicants required to submit FAFSA. *Unit head:* Dr. David Lange, Program Chair, 888-844-2004. *Application contact:* Jennifer Radke, 2nd Director of Graduate Admissions, 651-846-3300, Fax: 651-994-7954, E-mail: tcadmissions@argosy.edu.

See Close-Up on page 851.

Argosy University, Washington DC Campus, College of Education, Arlington, VA 22209. Offers educational leadership (MA Ed, Ed D, Ed S), including higher education administration (Ed D), K-12 education (Ed D); instructional leadership (MA Ed, Ed D, Ed S), including higher education (Ed D), K-12 education (Ed D). Part-time and evening/weekend programs available. *Faculty:* 2 full-time (1 woman), 2 part-time/adjunct (0 women). *Students:* 22 full-time (16 women), 11 part-time (6 women); includes 24 minority (all African Americans) Average age 45. 16 applicants, 69% accepted, 9 enrolled. In 2006, 1 degree awarded. *Degree requirements:* For master's, thesis (for some programs), comprehensive exam (for some programs); for doctorate, thesis/dissertation, comprehensive exam. *Entrance requirements:* For master's and doctorate, minimum GPA of 3.0. Additional exam requirements/recommendations for international students: Required—TOEFL (minimum score 550 paper-based; 213 computer-based). *Application deadline:* For fall admission, 6/15 priority date for domestic and international students; for spring admission, 10/15 priority date for domestic and international students. Applications are processed on a rolling basis. Application fee: $50. Electronic applications accepted. *Financial support:* Federal Work-Study and scholarships/grants available. Financial award applicants required to submit FAFSA. *Unit head:* Dr. Colleen Logan, Academic Affairs Officer, 866-703-2777, Fax: 703-521-5850, E-mail: dcadmissions@argosy.edu. *Application contact:* Emily Peck, Director of Admissions, 866-703-2777 Ext. 5851, Fax: 703-526-5850, E-mail: dcadmissions@argosy.edu.

See Close-Up on page 853.

Arizona State University, Division of Graduate Studies, College of Education, Tempe, AZ 85287. Offers M Ed, MA, MC, Ed D, PhD. Part-time programs available. *Degree requirements:* For doctorate, thesis/dissertation. *Entrance requirements:* For master's and doctorate, GRE General Test or MAT.

Arizona State University at the Polytechnic Campus, The School of Educational Innovation and Teacher Preparation, Mesa, AZ 85212. Offers administration/supervision (M Ed); curriculum and instruction (M Ed); physical education (MPE, PhD). *Faculty:* 9 full-time (6 women), 1 part-time/adjunct (0 women). *Students:* 86 full-time (74 women), 119 part-time (92 women); includes 18 minority (1 African American, 1 American Indian/Alaska Native, 5 Asian Americans or Pacific Islanders, 11 Hispanic Americans), 1 international. Average age 33. 94 applicants, 84% accepted, 65 enrolled. In 2006, 19 degrees awarded. *Degree requirements:* For master's, written comprehensive exam or applied project; for doctorate, thesis/dissertation. *Entrance requirements:* For master's, 3 letters of recommendation, minimum GPA of 3.0. *Application deadline:* For fall admission, 4/15 priority date for domestic and international students; for spring admission, 10/15 priority date for domestic and international students. Applications are processed on a rolling basis. Application fee: $50. Electronic applications accepted. *Expenses:* Tuition, state resident: part-time $310 per credit hour. Tuition, nonresident: part-time $688 per credit hour. *Financial support:* In 2006–07, 4 teaching assistantships with full tuition reimbursements (averaging $12,978 per year) were awarded; fellowships, research assistantships with full tuition reimbursements also available. Financial award applicants required to submit FAFSA.

Arizona State University at the West campus, College of Teacher Education and Leadership, Phoenix, AZ 85069-7100. Offers educational administration and supervision (M Ed); elementary education (M Ed, Certificate); leadership/innovation (administration) (Ed D); leadership/innovation (teaching) (Ed D); secondary education (M Ed, Certificate); special education (M Ed). Part-time and evening/weekend programs available. *Faculty:* 25 full-time (18 women), 27 part-time/adjunct (21 women). *Students:* 169 full-time (133 women), 245 part-time (200 women); includes 76 minority (16 African Americans, 8 American Indian/Alaska Native, 7 Asian Americans or Pacific Islanders, 45 Hispanic Americans), 3 international.

Education—General

Arizona State University at the West campus (continued)

Average age 35. 308 applicants, 63% accepted, 171 enrolled. In 2006, 84 degrees awarded. *Degree requirements:* For master's, applied project or comprehensive exams; for doctorate, thesis/dissertation, comprehensive exam. *Entrance requirements:* For master's, 3 letters of recommendation; for doctorate, master's degree in education or related field, 3 professional references, resumé. Additional exam requirements/recommendations for international students: Required—TOEFL (minimum score 550 paper-based; 213 computer-based; 83 iBT), IELTS (minimum score 7). *Application deadline:* Applications are processed on a rolling basis. Application fee: $50. Electronic applications accepted. *Expenses:* Tuition, state resident: full-time $5,930. Tuition, nonresident: full-time $16,516. Tuition and fees vary according to course load. *Financial support:* In 2006–07, 2 research assistantships with partial tuition reimbursements (averaging $16,413 per year) were awarded; fellowships with tuition reimbursements, career-related internships or fieldwork, institutionally sponsored loans, scholarships/grants, tuition waivers (full and partial), and unspecified assistantships also available. Support available to part-time students. Financial award application deadline: 4/1; financial award applicants required to submit FAFSA. *Faculty research:* Self-regulated learning in students, collaboration and consultation skills for educators, school reform and restructuring, hands-on science and mathematics programs, educational technology. *Unit head:* Dr. Mari Koerner, Dean, 602-543-6352, Fax: 602-543-6350, E-mail: mari.koerner@asu.edu. *Application contact:* Marie Wright, Administrative Assistant, 602-543-3634, Fax: 602-543-6350, E-mail: marie.wright@asu.edu or ctelgrad@asu.edu.

Arkansas State University, Graduate School, College of Education, Jonesboro, State University, AR 72467. Offers MRC, MS, MSE, Ed D, Certificate, Ed S, SCCT. *Accreditation:* NCATE. Part-time programs available. *Faculty:* 37 full-time (17 women), 9 part-time/adjunct (3 women). *Students:* 96 full-time (67 women), 423 part-time (307 women); includes 94 minority (85 African Americans, 3 American Indian/Alaska Native, 2 Asian Americans or Pacific Islanders, 4 Hispanic Americans), 3 international. Average age 34. 289 applicants, 75% accepted, 128 enrolled. In 2006, 141 master's, 13 doctorates, 25 other advanced degrees awarded. *Degree requirements:* For master's and other advanced degree, thesis or alternative, comprehensive exam; for doctorate, thesis/dissertation, comprehensive exam. *Entrance requirements:* For master's, GRE General Test or MAT, appropriate bachelor's degree, interview, letters of reference; for doctorate, GRE General Test or MAT, interview, master's degree, letters of reference; for other advanced degree, GRE General Test, MAT, interview, master's degree, letters of reference. Additional exam requirements/recommendations for international students: Required—TOEFL (minimum score 213 computer-based). *Application deadline:* Applications are processed on a rolling basis. Application fee: $30 ($40 for international students). Electronic applications accepted. *Expenses:* Tuition, state resident: full-time $3,393; part-time $189 per hour. Tuition, nonresident: full-time $8,577; part-time $477 per hour. Required fees: $752; $39 per hour. $25 per semester. *Financial support:* Teaching assistantships, career-related internships or fieldwork, scholarships/grants, and unspecified assistantships available. Financial award application deadline: 7/1; financial award applicants required to submit FAFSA. *Unit head:* Dr. John Beineke, Dean, 870-972-3057, Fax: 870-972-3828, E-mail: jbeineke@astate.edu.

Arkansas Tech University, Graduate School, School of Education, Russellville, AR 72801. Offers college student personnel (MSE); educational leadership (M Ed, Ed S); English education (M Ed); gifted education (MSE); instructional improvement (M Ed); secondary education (M Ed); teaching, learning and leadership (M Ed). *Accreditation:* NCATE. Part-time programs available. *Students:* 44 full-time (33 women), 244 part-time (181 women); includes 20 minority (14 African Americans, 1 American Indian/Alaska Native, 3 Asian Americans or Pacific Islanders, 2 Hispanic Americans), 18 international. Average age 34. In 2006, 72 master's, 4 other advanced degrees awarded. *Degree requirements:* For master's, action research project, thesis optional. *Entrance requirements:* For master's, GRE General Test or MAT. Additional exam requirements/recommendations for international students: Required—TOEFL (minimum score 500 paper-based; 173 computer-based). *Application deadline:* For fall admission, 3/1 priority date for domestic students, 5/1 priority date for international students; for winter admission, 10/1 priority date for international students; for spring admission, 10/1 priority date for domestic and international students. Applications are processed on a rolling basis. Application fee: $0 ($30 for international students). Electronic applications accepted. *Expenses:* Tuition, state resident: full-time $3,060; part-time $170 per hour. Tuition, nonresident: full-time $6,120; part-time $340 per hour. Required fees: $312; $4 per hour. $84 per term. Part-time tuition and fees vary according to course load. *Financial support:* In 2006–07, teaching assistantships with full tuition reimbursements (averaging $4,000 per year); career-related internships or fieldwork, Federal Work-Study, scholarships/grants, health care benefits, and unspecified assistantships also available. Support available to part-time students. Financial award application deadline: 4/15; financial award applicants required to submit FAFSA. *Unit head:* Dr. C. Glenn Sheets, Dean, 479-968-0350, Fax: 479-968-0350, E-mail: glenn.sheets@atu.edu. *Application contact:* Dr. Eldon G. Clary, Dean of Graduate School, 479-968-0398, Fax: 479-964-0542, E-mail: graduate.school@atu.edu.

Arkansas Tech University, Graduate School, School of Liberal and Fine Arts, Russellville, AR 72801. Offers communication (MLA); English (M Ed, MA); fine arts (MLA); history (MA); multi-media journalism (MA); social science (MLA); social studies (M Ed); Spanish (MA, MLA); teaching English as a second language (MA, MLA). Part-time programs available. *Students:* 47 full-time (36 women), 102 part-time (82 women); includes 9 minority (2 African Americans, 1 American Indian/Alaska Native, 1 Asian American or Pacific Islander, 5 Hispanic Americans), 20 international. Average age 33. In 2006, 20 degrees awarded. *Degree requirements:* For master's, project. *Entrance requirements:* For master's, GRE General Test or MAT. Additional exam requirements/recommendations for international students: Required—TOEFL (minimum score 500 paper-based; 173 computer-based). *Application deadline:* For fall admission, 3/1 priority date for domestic students, 5/1 priority date for international students; for winter admission, 10/1 priority date for international students; for spring admission, 10/1 priority date for domestic and international students. Applications are processed on a rolling basis. Application fee: $0 ($30 for international students). Electronic applications accepted. *Expenses:* Tuition, state resident: full-time $3,060; part-time $170 per hour. Tuition, nonresident: full-time $6,120; part-time $340 per hour. Required fees: $312; $4 per hour. $84 per term. Part-time tuition and fees vary according to course load. *Financial support:* In 2006–07, teaching assistantships with full tuition reimbursements (averaging $4,000 per year); career-related internships or fieldwork, Federal Work-Study, scholarships/grants, health care benefits, and unspecified assistantships also available. Support available to part-time students. Financial award application deadline: 4/15; financial award applicants required to submit FAFSA. *Unit head:* Dr. Georgena Duncan, Dean, 479-968-0266, Fax: 479-968-0275, E-mail: georgena.duncan@atu.edu. *Application contact:* Dr. Eldon G. Clary, Dean of Graduate School, 479-968-0398, Fax: 479-964-0542, E-mail: graduate.school@atu.edu.

Armstrong Atlantic State University, School of Graduate Studies, Program in Education, Savannah, GA 31419-1997. Offers adult education (M Ed); early childhood education (M Ed); education (M Ed); elementary education (M Ed); middle grades education (M Ed); secondary education (M Ed), including business education, English education, mathematics education, science education, social science education; special education (M Ed), including behavioral disorders, curriculum and instruction, learning disabilities, speech-language pathology. *Accreditation:* NCATE. Part-time and evening/weekend programs available. Postbaccalaureate distance learning degree programs offered (minimal on-campus study). *Faculty:* 11 full-time (9 women), 13 part-time/adjunct (10 women). *Students:* 50 full-time (42 women), 219 part-time (175 women); includes 71 minority (67 African Americans, 3 Asian Americans or Pacific Islanders, 1 Hispanic American), 6 international. Average age 35. In 2006, 151 degrees awarded. *Degree requirements:* For master's, portfolio. *Entrance requirements:* For master's, GRE General Test or MAT, minimum GPA of 2.5, letters of recommendation. Additional exam requirements/recommendations for international students: Required—TOEFL (minimum score 523 paper-based; 193 computer-based). *Application deadline:* For fall admission, 7/1 priority date for domestic and international students; for spring admission, 11/15 priority date for domestic and international students. Applications are processed on a rolling basis. Application fee: $25. Electronic applications accepted. *Expenses:* Tuition, state resident: full-time $2,286; part-time $127 per credit. Tuition, nonresident: full-time $9,144; part-time $508 per credit. One-time fee: $257. *Financial support:* In 2006–07, research assistantships with partial tuition reimbursements (averaging $2,500 per year); career-related internships or fieldwork, Federal Work-Study, scholarships/grants, and unspecified assistantships also available. Support available to part-time students. Financial award applicants required to submit FAFSA. *Unit head:* Dr. Jane McHaney, College of Education Dean, 912-927-5398, Fax: 912-921-7425, E-mail: mchaneia@mail.armstrong.edu.

Ashland University, College of Education, Ashland, OH 44805-3702. Offers M Ed, Ed D. *Accreditation:* NCATE. Part-time and evening/weekend programs available. *Faculty:* 51 full-time (25 women), 176 part-time/adjunct (105 women). *Students:* 460 full-time (337 women), 856 part-time (646 women); includes 80 minority (63 African Americans, 2 American Indian/Alaska Native, 6 Asian Americans or Pacific Islanders, 9 Hispanic Americans), 11 international. Average age 33. In 2006, 624 master's, 5 doctorates awarded. *Median time to degree:* Of those who began their doctoral program in fall 1998, 100% received their degree in 8 years or less. *Degree requirements:* For master's, capstone project, thesis optional; for doctorate, thesis/dissertation, comprehensive exam, registration. *Entrance requirements:* For master's, GRE General Test or MAT, teaching certificate, minimum GPA of 2.75; for doctorate, GRE, master's degree, minimum GPA of 3.3, writing sample, letters of recommendation. Additional exam requirements/recommendations for international students: Required—TOEFL. *Application deadline:* For fall admission, 8/27 for domestic students; for spring admission, 1/14 for domestic students. Applications are processed on a rolling basis. Application fee: $30. *Expenses:* Tuition: Part-time $403 per credit. Tuition and fees vary according to degree level and program. *Financial support:* In 2006–07, 447 students received support; teaching assistantships with partial tuition reimbursements available, scholarships/grants available. Financial award application deadline: 4/15. *Faculty research:* Teacher performance, administrative performance, collaborative learning groups, talent development, environmental education. Total annual research expenditures: $180,000. *Unit head:* Dr. Frank E. Pettigrew, Dean, 419-289-5365, E-mail: fpettig@ashland.edu. *Application contact:* Dr. Ann C. Shelly, Director and Chair, Graduate Studies in Education and Associate Dean, 419-289-5388, Fax: 419-289-5331, E-mail: ashelly@ashland.edu.

Athabasca University, Centre for Distance Education, Athabasca, AB T9S 3A3, Canada. Offers distance education (MDE); distance education technology (Advanced Diploma). Part-time programs available. Postbaccalaureate distance learning degree programs offered (no on-campus study). *Faculty:* 10 full-time (3 women), 22 part-time/adjunct (8 women). *Students:* Average age 41. 88 applicants, 93% accepted. In 2006, 42 degrees awarded. *Degree requirements:* For master's, thesis optional. *Entrance requirements:* For master's, 3 or 4 year baccalaureate degree. *Application deadline:* For fall admission, 3/1 for domestic and international students. Application fee: $65. Electronic applications accepted. *Expenses:* Contact institution. *Faculty research:* Role development in distance education, interaction in distance education, educational technology in distance education, communities of practice in distance education, instructional design. *Unit head:* Dr. Bob Spencer, Head, 780-675-6238, Fax: 780-675-6170, E-mail: bobs@athabascau.ca. *Application contact:* Glenda Hawryluk, Administrative Assistant, 780-675-6179, Fax: 780-675-6170, E-mail: glendah@athabascau.ca.

Athabasca University, Centre for Integrated Studies, Athabasca, AB T9S 3A3, Canada. Offers adult education (MA); community studies (MA); cultural studies (MA); educational studies (MA); global change (MA); work, organization, and leadership (MA). Part-time and evening/weekend programs available. Postbaccalaureate distance learning degree programs offered (no on-campus study). *Faculty:* 4 full-time (0 women), 50 part-time/adjunct (27 women). *Students:* Average age 39. 150 applicants, 87% accepted, 112 enrolled. In 2006, 40 degrees awarded. *Degree requirements:* For master's, project. *Entrance requirements:* For master's, 3- or 4-year BA. Additional exam requirements/recommendations for international students: Required—TOEFL or ENG 255 class (75) or Michigan English Language Assessment Battery (85) or IELTS (6.5) or CAEL (65); Recommended—TOEFL (minimum score 560 paper-based; 220 computer-based). *Application deadline:* For fall admission, 3/1 for domestic and international students; for winter admission, 10/1 for domestic and international students. Application fee: $65. Electronic applications accepted. *Faculty research:* Women's history, literature and culture studies, sustainable development, labor and education. *Unit head:* Dr. Derek Briton, Program Director, 780-675-6218, Fax: 780-675-6921, E-mail: derekb@athabascau.ca. *Application contact:* Derek Stovin, Program Administrator, 780-675-6236, Fax: 780-675-6921, E-mail: mais@athabascau.ca.

Atlantic Union College, Graduate Education Program, South Lancaster, MA 01561-1000. Offers M Ed. Offered during summer only. Part-time programs available. Postbaccalaureate distance learning degree programs offered (minimal on-campus study). *Degree requirements:* For master's, thesis. *Entrance requirements:* For master's, GRE, minimum GPA of 3.0.

Auburn University, Graduate School, College of Education, Auburn University, AL 36849. Offers M Ed, MS, Ed D, PhD, Ed S. *Accreditation:* NCATE. Part-time programs available. *Faculty:* 85 full-time (48 women). *Students:* 292 full-time (202 women), 419 part-time (293 women); includes 162 minority (144 African Americans, 6 American Indian/Alaska Native, 4 Asian Americans or Pacific Islanders, 8 Hispanic Americans), 18 international. Average age 33. 558 applicants, 58% accepted, 200 enrolled. In 2006, 196 master's, 34 doctorates, 25 other advanced degrees awarded. *Degree requirements:* For master's, thesis (for some programs); for doctorate, thesis/dissertation. *Entrance requirements:* For master's, doctorate, and Ed S, GRE General Test. Application fee: $25 ($50 for international students). Electronic applications accepted. *Expenses:* Tuition, state resident: full-time $5,000. Tuition, nonresident: full-time $15,000. Required fees: $416. Tuition and fees vary according to program. *Financial support:* Fellowships, research assistantships, teaching assistantships, career-related internships or fieldwork and Federal Work-Study available. Support available to part-time students. Financial award application deadline: 3/15. *Faculty research:* Dropout phenomena, high school students and substance use and abuse. *Unit head:* Dr. Frances Kochan, Dean, 334-844-4446. *Application contact:* Dr. Joe Pittman, Interim Dean of the Graduate School, 334-844-4700.

See Close-Up on page 855.

Auburn University Montgomery, School of Education, Montgomery, AL 36124-4023. Offers M Ed, Ed S. *Accreditation:* NCATE. Part-time and evening/weekend programs available. *Faculty:* 23 full-time (15 women), 2 part-time/adjunct (1 woman). *Students:* 94 full-time (73 women), 238 part-time (199 women); includes 151 minority (142 African Americans, 2 American Indian/Alaska Native, 3 Asian Americans or Pacific Islanders, 4 Hispanic Americans), 1 international. Average age 34. In 2006, 78 master's, 18 other advanced degrees awarded. *Degree requirements:* For master's and Ed S, comprehensive exam. *Entrance requirements:* For master's, GRE General Test or MAT, BS in teaching, certification; for Ed S, GRE General Test or MAT, certification. *Application deadline:* Applications are processed on a rolling basis. Application fee: $25. Electronic applications accepted. *Financial support:* In 2006–07, 2 teaching assistantships were awarded; career-related internships or fieldwork and scholarships/grants also available. Support available to part-time students. Financial award application deadline: 3/1; financial award applicants required to submit FAFSA. *Unit head:* Dr. Jennifer A. Brown, Dean, 334-244-3413, Fax: 334-244-3835, E-mail: jbrown@mail.aum.edu. *Application contact:* Dr. Sam Flynt, Associate Graduate Coordinator, 334-244-3270, Fax: 334-244-3835, E-mail: sflynt@mail.aum.edu.

Augsburg College, Program in Education, Minneapolis, MN 55454-1351. Offers MAE. *Accreditation:* NCATE. Part-time and evening/weekend programs available. *Faculty:* 4 full-time (3 women), 3 part-time/adjunct (all women). *Students:* 97 full-time (59 women), 91 part-time (66 women); includes 17 minority (7 African Americans, 3 American Indian/Alaska Native, 6 Asian Americans or Pacific Islanders, 1 Hispanic American), 2 international. Average age 33. 405 applicants, 17% accepted, 43 enrolled. In 2006, 1 degree awarded. *Degree requirements:* For master's, final project. *Entrance requirements:* For master's, minimum GPA of 3.0. Additional exam requirements/recommendations for international students: Required—TOEFL (minimum score 600 paper-based; 250 computer-based). *Application deadline:* For fall admission, 8/15 for domestic and international students; for winter admission, 12/15 for domestic and international students; for spring admission, 3/26 for domestic and international students. Applications are processed on a rolling basis. Application fee: $35. Electronic applications accepted. *Expenses:* Tuition: Full-time $10,584; part-time $1,764 per course. Required fees: $300; $35 per course. Tuition and fees vary according to program. *Unit head:* Vicki Olson, Professor, 612-330-1131, E-mail: olsonv@augsburg.edu. *Application contact:* Karen Howell, Program Coordinator, 612-330-1354, E-mail: howell@augsburg.edu.

Augustana College, Department of Education, Program in Education, Sioux Falls, SD 57197. Offers elementary (MA); secondary (MA). *Accreditation:* NCATE. Part-time programs available. *Degree requirements:* For master's, oral exam, paper, synthesis portfolio. *Entrance requirements:* For master's, appropriate bachelor's degree, minimum GPA of 3.0, teaching certificate. Additional exam requirements/recommendations for international students: Required—TOEFL.

Augusta State University, Graduate Studies, College of Education, Augusta, GA 30904-2200. Offers M Ed, Ed S. *Accreditation:* NCATE. Part-time and evening/weekend programs available. *Faculty:* 21 full-time (12 women), 10 part-time/adjunct (9 women). *Students:* 128 full-time (98 women), 269 part-time (227 women); includes 95 minority (84 African Americans, 2 American Indian/Alaska Native, 4 Asian Americans or Pacific Islanders, 5 Hispanic Americans). Average age 36. 91 applicants, 100% accepted, 61 enrolled. In 2006, 56 master's, 49 other advanced degrees awarded. *Entrance requirements:* For master's, GRE, MAT, minimum GPA of 2.5. *Application deadline:* For fall admission, 7/16 priority date for domestic students. Applications are processed on a rolling basis. Application fee: $20. *Expenses:* Tuition, state resident: full-time $3,044; part-time $127 per credit hour. Tuition, nonresident: full-time $12,172; part-time $508 per credit hour. *Financial support:* Career-related internships or fieldwork, Federal Work-Study, institutionally sponsored loans, and unspecified assistantships available. Support available to part-time students. Financial award application deadline: 4/15; financial award applicants required to submit FAFSA. *Unit head:* Dr. Thomas E. Deering, Dean, 706-737-1499, Fax: 706-667-4706, E-mail: tdeering@aug.edu. *Application contact:* Andrea M. Scott, Secretary to the Dean, 706-737-1499, Fax: 706-667-4706, E-mail: ascott1@aug.edu.

Aurora University, College of Education, Aurora, IL 60506-4892. Offers curriculum and instruction (Ed D); education (MAT); education and administration (Ed D); educational leadership (MEL); reading instruction (MA). Part-time and evening/weekend programs available. *Faculty:* 20 full-time (10 women), 99 part-time/adjunct (55 women). *Students:* 144 full-time (102 women), 1,156 part-time (832 women); includes 169 minority (32 African Americans, 2 American Indian/Alaska Native, 10 Asian Americans or Pacific Islanders, 125 Hispanic Americans). Average age 36. 451 applicants, 99% accepted, 421 enrolled. In 2006, 439 master's, 9 doctorates awarded. *Degree requirements:* For doctorate, thesis/dissertation. *Entrance requirements:* For master's, 2 years of teaching experience, valid teaching certificate. Additional exam requirements/recommendations for international students: Required—TOEFL (minimum score 550 paper-based; 213 computer-based). *Application deadline:* For fall admission, 8/23 priority date for domestic students. Applications are processed on a rolling basis. Application fee: $25. Electronic applications accepted. *Expenses:* Contact institution. Tuition and fees vary according to campus/location and program. *Financial support:* In 2006–07, 355 students received support; fellowships, research assistantships, teaching assistantships, Federal Work-Study and scholarships/grants available. Support available to part-time students. Financial award application deadline: 4/15; financial award applicants required to submit FAFSA. *Unit head:* Dr. Donald C. Wold, Dean, 630-844-1542, Fax: 630-844-5530, E-mail: dwold@aurora.edu. *Application contact:* Donna DeSpain, Dean of Adult and Graduate Studies, 800-742-5281, Fax: 630-844-5535, E-mail: auadmission@aurora.edu.

Austin College, Program in Education, Sherman, TX 75090-4400. Offers art education (MA); elementary education (MA); middle school education (MA); music education (MA); physical education and coaching (MA); secondary education (MA). Applicants must meet Austin College's undergraduate curriculum requirements. Part-time programs available. *Faculty:* 5 full-time (3 women), 1 (woman) part-time/adjunct. *Students:* 33 full-time (26 women); includes 3 minority (2 Asian Americans or Pacific Islanders, 1 Hispanic American). Average age 25. In 2006, 24 degrees awarded. *Degree requirements:* For master's, one foreign language, thesis or alternative. *Entrance requirements:* For master's, Texas Academic Skills Program Test. *Application deadline:* For fall admission, 5/1 priority date for domestic students; for spring admission, 1/15 priority date for domestic students. Applications are processed on a rolling basis. Application fee: $35. Electronic applications accepted. *Expenses:* Tuition: Full-time $27,385. Required fees: $160. *Financial support:* In 2006–07, 27 students received support. Career-related internships or fieldwork, Federal Work-Study, scholarships/grants, and unspecified assistantships available. Support available to part-time students. Financial award application deadline: 4/1; financial award applicants required to submit FAFSA. *Unit head:* Dr. Barbara Sylvester, Director of Teaching Program, 903-813-2498, Fax: 903-813-2326, E-mail: bsylvester@austincollege.edu.

Austin Peay State University, College of Graduate Studies, College of Professional Programs and Social Sciences, School of Education, Clarksville, TN 37044. Offers curriculum and instruction (MA Ed); education (M Ed, Ed S); educational leadership studies (MA Ed); reading (MA Ed). *Accreditation:* NCATE. Part-time and evening/weekend programs available. Postbaccalaureate distance learning degree programs offered. *Faculty:* 24 full-time (14 women), 8 part-time/adjunct (4 women). *Students:* 81 full-time (65 women), 225 part-time (180 women); includes 48 minority (37 African Americans, 2 American Indian/Alaska Native, 1 Asian American or Pacific Islander, 8 Hispanic Americans). Average age 35. In 2006, 81 master's, 16 other advanced degrees awarded. *Degree requirements:* For master's, teaching license, thesis optional. *Entrance requirements:* For master's, GRE General Test, 3 letters of recommendation; for Ed S, GRE General Test, master's degree, minimum graduate GPA of 3.0, 3 letters of recommendation. Additional exam requirements/recommendations for international students: Required—TOEFL (minimum score 500 paper-based; 173 computer-based). *Application deadline:* For fall admission, 7/31 priority date for domestic students; for spring admission, 12/17 priority date for domestic students. Applications are processed on a rolling basis. Application fee: $25. Electronic applications accepted. *Expenses:* Tuition, state resident: full-time $5,138; part-time $272 per credit hour. Tuition, nonresident: full-time $14,832; part-time $693 per credit hour. Required fees: $1,009. *Financial support:* In 2006–07, research assistantships (averaging $10,270 per year); career-related internships or fieldwork, Federal Work-Study, institutionally sponsored loans, scholarships/grants, and unspecified assistantships also available. Support available to part-time students. Financial award application deadline: 3/1; financial award applicants required to submit FAFSA. *Unit head:* Dr. Carlette Hardin, Director, 931-221-7696, Fax: 931-221-1292, E-mail: forbusl@apsu.edu.

Averett University, Graduate Studies in Education, Danville, VA 24541-3692. Offers art education (M Ed); biology (M Ed); chemistry (M Ed); curriculum and instruction (M Ed); elementary education (M Ed); English (M Ed); health and physical education (M Ed); history and social studies (M Ed); mathematics education (M Ed); physical science (M Ed); reading (M Ed); special education (learning disabilities specialization PK-12) (M Ed). Part-time and evening/weekend programs available. *Faculty:* 10 full-time (4 women), 7 part-time/adjunct (6 women). *Students:* 14 full-time (10 women), 85 part-time (67 women); includes 20 minority (18 African Americans, 2 Asian Americans or Pacific Islanders). Average age 33. 52 applicants, 100% accepted, 40 enrolled. In 2006, 48 degrees awarded. *Degree requirements:* For master's, thesis optional. *Entrance requirements:* For master's, PRAXIS, GRE General Test, MAT or NTE, writing proficiency exam, 3 letters of recommendation, current teacher's licensure or eligibility for licensure, minimum undergraduate GPA of 3.0 in previous 2 years. Additional exam requirements/recommendations for international students: Required—TOEFL (minimum score 600 paper-based; 200 computer-based). *Application deadline:* Applications are processed on a rolling basis. Application fee: $20. *Expenses:* Contact institution. *Financial support:* In 2006–07, 23 students received support. Federal Work-Study and scholarships/grants available. Financial award application deadline: 4/1; financial award applicants required to submit FAFSA. *Faculty research:* Literary assessment-PreK-6, handwriting instruction and assessment-PreK-6, written language instruction and assessment-PreK-6 and special needs students learning styles, curriculum and instruction processes. *Unit head:* Dr. Lynn H. Wolf, Chair, 434-793-3995, Fax: 434-791-4392, E-mail: lynn.wolf@averett.edu.

Avila University, School of Education, Kansas City, MO 64145-1698. Offers education (MA); English for speakers of other languages (Advanced Certificate); special reading (Advanced Certificate). Part-time and evening/weekend programs available. *Faculty:* 7 full-time (5 women), 17 part-time/adjunct (13 women). *Students:* 144 full-time (112 women), 42 part-time (24 women); includes 17 minority (15 African Americans, 2 Hispanic Americans). Average age 37. 72 applicants, 42% accepted, 14 enrolled. In 2006, 34 degrees awarded. *Entrance requirements:* For master's, minimum GPA of 3.0. *Application deadline:* Applications are processed on a rolling basis. Application fee: $0. Electronic applications accepted. *Expenses:* Tuition: Full-time $7,470; part-time $415 per credit. *Financial support:* In 2006–07, 1 research assistantship was awarded; career-related internships or fieldwork also available. Support available to part-time students. Financial award applicants required to submit FAFSA. *Unit head:* Dr. Laura Sloan, Dean, 816-501-3663, Fax: 816-501-2455, E-mail: laura.sloan@avila.edu. *Application contact:* Deana Angotti, Director of Graduate Education, 816-501-2446, Fax: 816-501-2915, E-mail: deana.augotti@avila.edu.

Azusa Pacific University, School of Education, Department of Advanced Studies, Azusa, CA 91702-7000. Offers curriculum and instruction in a multicultural setting (MA); educational technology (M Ed); physical education (M Ed); school librarianship (MA); teaching (MA). *Faculty:* 18 full-time (13 women). *Students:* 14 full-time (12 women), 1,062 part-time (758 women); includes 344 minority (39 African Americans, 4 American Indian/Alaska Native, 51 Asian Americans or Pacific Islanders, 250 Hispanic Americans), 13 international. In 2006, 492 degrees awarded. *Expenses:* Tuition: Part-time $475 per credit. *Faculty research:* Social/cultural issues, literacy and technology in K–12 and higher education school settings, ethics and organizational leadership, teacher expectation/school reform, community education. *Unit head:* Dr. Maria Pacino, Chair, 626-815-5416, E-mail: mpacino@apu.edu.

Azusa Pacific University, School of Education, Department of Education, Azusa, CA 91702-7000. Offers educational leadership (Ed D); language development (MA); pupil personnel services (MA). *Accreditation:* NCATE. Part-time and evening/weekend programs available. *Students:* 3 full-time (2 women), 162 part-time (108 women); includes 58 minority (14 African Americans, 1 American Indian/Alaska Native, 10 Asian Americans or Pacific Islanders, 33 Hispanic Americans), 5 international. In 2006, 2 master's, 12 doctorates awarded. *Degree requirements:* For master's, core exams, oral presentation; for doctorate, oral defense of dissertation, qualifying exam. *Entrance requirements:* For master's, minimum GPA of 3.0; for doctorate, GRE General Test or MAT, 5 years of experience, writing sample. Additional exam requirements/recommendations for international students: Required—TOEFL. Application fee: $45 ($65 for international students). *Expenses:* Tuition: Part-time $475 per credit. *Financial support:* Career-related internships or fieldwork available. Support available to part-time students. Financial award applicants required to submit FAFSA. *Unit head:* Nancy Brashear, Director, 626-815-5376.

Baker University, School of Education, Baldwin City, KS 66006-0065. Offers MA Ed, MASL, Ed D. *Accreditation:* NCATE. Part-time and evening/weekend programs available. *Faculty:* 7 full-time (2 women), 89 part-time/adjunct (58 women). *Students:* 455 full-time (344 women), 284 part-time (194 women); includes 48 minority (30 African Americans, 3 American Indian/Alaska Native, 3 Asian Americans or Pacific Islanders, 12 Hispanic Americans). Average age 36. In 2006, 362 degrees awarded. *Degree requirements:* For master's, portfolio of learning. *Entrance requirements:* For master's, 1 year of teaching experience, teaching certificate. Additional exam requirements/recommendations for international students: Required—TOEFL (minimum score 600 paper-based; 250 computer-based). *Application deadline:* Applications are processed on a rolling basis. Application fee: $20. *Financial support:* Applicants required to submit FAFSA. *Unit head:* Dr. Peggy Harris, Interim Dean, School of Education, 785-594-8492, Fax: 785-594-8363, E-mail: peggy.harris@bakeru.edu.

Baldwin-Wallace College, Graduate Programs, Division of Education, Berea, OH 44017-2088. Offers educational technology (MA Ed); mild/moderate educational needs (MA Ed); pre-administration (MA Ed); reading (MA Ed). *Accreditation:* NCATE. Part-time and evening/weekend programs available. *Faculty:* 11 full-time (4 women), 5 part-time/adjunct (3 women). *Students:* 92 full-time (67 women), 202 part-time (161 women); includes 32 minority (18 African Americans, 8 Asian Americans or Pacific Islanders, 6 Hispanic Americans), 1 international. Average age 33. 138 applicants, 81% accepted, 72 enrolled. In 2006, 137 degrees awarded. *Degree requirements:* For master's, comprehensive exam. *Entrance requirements:* For master's, bachelor's degree in field, MAT or minimum GPA of 2.75. *Application deadline:* For fall admission, 8/15 priority date for domestic students; for spring admission, 12/15 priority date for domestic students. Applications are processed on a rolling basis. Application fee: $25. Electronic applications accepted. *Expenses:* Tuition: Part-time $760 per credit hour. Tuition and fees vary according to program. *Financial support:* Career-related internships or fieldwork available. Financial award applicants required to submit FAFSA. *Unit head:* Karen Kaye, Chair, 440-826-2168, Fax: 440-826-3779, E-mail: kkaye@bw.edu. *Application contact:* Winifred W. Gerhardt, Director of Admission for the Evening and Weekend College, 440-826-2222, Fax: 440-826-3830, E-mail: admission@bw.edu.

Ball State University, Graduate School, Teachers College, Muncie, IN 47306-1099. Offers MA, MAE, Ed D, PhD, Ed S. *Accreditation:* NCATE. Part-time and evening/weekend programs available. *Faculty:* 98. *Students:* 241 full-time (165 women), 800 part-time (557 women); includes 69 minority (44 African Americans, 6 American Indian/Alaska Native, 8 Asian Americans or Pacific Islanders, 11 Hispanic Americans), 41 international. Average age 28. 752 applicants, 51% accepted, 256 enrolled. In 2006, 296 master's, 36 doctorates, 17 other advanced degrees awarded. *Degree requirements:* For doctorate and Ed S, thesis/dissertation. *Entrance requirements:* For doctorate, GRE General Test, minimum graduate GPA of 3.2; for Ed S, GRE General Test. Application fee: $25 ($35 for international students). *Financial support:* In 2006–07, 4 fellowships with full tuition reimbursements (averaging $12,000 per year), 5 research assistantships with full tuition reimbursements (averaging $7,887 per year), 130 teaching assistantships with full tuition reimbursements (averaging $7,376 per year) were awarded; career-related internships or fieldwork and Federal Work-Study also available. Support available to part-time students. Financial award application deadline: 3/1. *Unit head:* Dr. Roy Weaver, Dean, 765-285-5251, Fax: 765-285-5455, E-mail: rweaver@bsu.edu.

Bank Street College of Education, Graduate School, New York, NY 10025. Offers Ed M, MS, MS Ed. *Accreditation:* NCATE. *Faculty:* 78 full-time (67 women), 56 part-time/adjunct (43 women). *Students:* 337 full-time (291 women), 593 part-time (526 women); includes 231 minority (85 African Americans, 1 American Indian/Alaska Native, 46 Asian Americans or Pacific Islanders, 99 Hispanic Americans), 9 international. Average age 30. 610 applicants, 80% accepted, 386 enrolled. In 2006, 357 degrees awarded. *Degree requirements:* For master's, thesis. *Entrance requirements:* For master's, interview. Additional exam requirements/recommendations for international students: Required—TOEFL (minimum score 600 paper-based; 250 computer-based). *Application deadline:* For fall admission, 3/1 priority date for domestic and international students; for spring admission, 11/1 priority date for domestic and international students. Applications are processed on a rolling basis. Application fee: $50. *Expenses:* Tuition: Part-time $940 per credit. Required fees: $100 per term. *Financial support:* In 2006–07, 579 students received support. Career-related internships or fieldwork, Federal Work-Study, scholarships/grants, and unspecified assistantships available. Support available to part-time students. Financial award application deadline: 4/15; financial award applicants required to submit FAFSA. *Faculty research:* Understanding developmental variations in inclusive classrooms, urban teacher education and technology, learner-centered education, improving teacher preparation. *Unit head:* Dr. Jon Snyder, Dean, 212-875-4466, Fax: 212-875-4753,

Education—General

Bank Street College of Education (continued)
E-mail: jsnyder@bankstreet.edu. *Application contact:* Ann Morgan, Director of Graduate Admissions, 212-875-4403, Fax: 212-875-4678, E-mail: amorgan@bankstreet.edu.

See Close-Up on page 857.

Bard College, Program in Teaching, Annandale-on-Hudson, NY 12504. Offers MAT. *Entrance requirements:* For master's, resumé, 3 letters of recommendation.

See Close-Up on page 859.

Barry University, School of Education, Miami Shores, FL 33161-6695. Offers MS, Ed D, PhD, Certificate, Ed S. Part-time and evening/weekend programs available. Postbaccalaureate distance learning degree programs offered. *Faculty:* 70. *Students:* 292 full-time (250 women), 717 part-time (546 women); includes 512 minority (269 African Americans, 1 American Indian/Alaska Native, 12 Asian Americans or Pacific Islanders, 230 Hispanic Americans), 35 international. Average age 39. In 2006, 284 master's, 29 doctorates, 30 other advanced degrees awarded. *Degree requirements:* For master's, comprehensive exam; for doctorate, thesis/dissertation. *Entrance requirements:* For master's, GRE General Test or MAT, minimum GPA of 3.0; for doctorate, GRE General Test, minimum GPA of 3.25; for other advanced degree, GRE General Test, minimum GPA of 3.0. Additional exam requirements/recommendations for international students: Required—TOEFL (minimum score 550 paper-based; 213 computer-based). *Application deadline:* For fall admission, 5/1 priority date for domestic students. Applications are processed on a rolling basis. Application fee: $30. Electronic applications accepted. *Financial support:* Career-related internships or fieldwork and scholarships/grants available. Support available to part-time students. Financial award applicants required to submit FAFSA. *Unit head:* Dr. Terry Piper, Dean, 305-899-3649, Fax: 305-899-3630, E-mail: tpiper@mail.barry.edu. *Application contact:* Dave Fletcher, Director of Graduate Admissions, 305-899-3113, Fax: 305-899-2971, E-mail: dfletcher@mail.barry.edu.

Bayamón Central University, Graduate Programs, Program in Education, Bayamón, PR 00960-1725. Offers administration and supervision (MA Ed); commercial education (MA Ed); education of the autistic (MA Ed); elementary education (K–3) (MA Ed); elementary education (K–6) (MA Ed); elementary physical education (MA Ed); guidance and counseling (MA Ed); pre-elementary teacher (MA Ed); special education (MA Ed), including attention deficit disorder, learning disabilities. Part-time and evening/weekend programs available. *Degree requirements:* For master's, comprehensive exam. *Entrance requirements:* For master's, EXADEP, bachelor's degree in education or related field.

Baylor University, Graduate School, School of Education, Waco, TX 76798. Offers MA, MS Ed, Ed D, PhD, Ed S. *Accreditation:* NCATE. Part-time programs available. Postbaccalaureate distance learning degree programs offered (minimal on-campus study). *Students:* 170 full-time (115 women), 77 part-time (50 women); includes 43 minority (27 African Americans, 5 American Indian/Alaska Native, 4 Asian Americans or Pacific Islanders, 7 Hispanic Americans), 13 international. In 2006, 81 master's, 18 doctorates, 1 other advanced degree awarded. *Degree requirements:* For doctorate, thesis/dissertation. *Application deadline:* Applications are processed on a rolling basis. Application fee: $25. Electronic applications accepted. *Financial support:* Research assistantships, teaching assistantships, career-related internships or fieldwork, Federal Work-Study, institutionally sponsored loans, scholarships/grants, and tuition waivers (partial) available. *Unit head:* Interim Dean, 254-710-3111, Fax: 254-710-3987. *Application contact:* Suzanne Keener, Administrative Assistant, 254-710-3588, Fax: 254-710-3870.

Belhaven College, School of Education, Jackson, MS 39202-1789. Offers elementary education (M Ed, MAT); secondary education (M Ed, MAT). *Degree requirements:* For master's, portfolio. *Entrance requirements:* For master's, PRAXIS I, PRAXIS II, minimum GPA of 2.8.

Bellarmine University, Annsley Frazier Thornton School of Education, Louisville, KY 40205-0671. Offers early elementary education (MA, MAT); instructional leadership and school administration/school principal (MA); learning and behavior disorders (MA); middle school education (MA, MAT); reading and writing endorsement (MA); secondary school education (MAT); Waldorf inspired curriculum (MA);). *Accreditation:* NCATE. Part-time and evening/weekend programs available. *Faculty:* 10 full-time (8 women), 5 part-time/adjunct (all women). *Students:* 92 full-time (68 women), 140 part-time (104 women); includes 16 minority (11 African Americans, 1 Asian American or Pacific Islander, 4 Hispanic Americans). Average age 32. In 2006, 98 degrees awarded. *Degree requirements:* For master's, thesis (for some programs), comprehensive exam. *Entrance requirements:* For master's, minimum overall GPA of 2.75, 3.0 in major; letters of recommendation; valid Kentucky provisional or professional certificate. Additional exam requirements/recommendations for international students: Required—TOEFL (minimum score 550 paper-based; 213 computer-based; 80 iBT), GRE. *Application deadline:* Applications are processed on a rolling basis. Application fee: $25. Electronic applications accepted. *Expenses: Contact institution.* Tuition and fees vary according to program. *Faculty research:* Social justice, service learning dispositions, educational technology, special education. *Unit head:* Dr. Milton Brown, Dean (Interim), 502-452-8486, Fax: 502-452-8189, E-mail: mbrown@bellarmine.edu. *Application contact:* Theresa Klapheke, Director of Graduate Programs, 502-452-8033, Fax: 502-452-8189, E-mail: tklapheke@bellarmine.edu.

Belmont University, College of Arts and Sciences, School of Education, Nashville, TN 37212-3757. Offers education (MAT); elementary education (M Ed), including early childhood education, elementary education, gifted education, language arts education; English (M Ed); history (M Ed); mathematics (M Ed); middle grade education (M Ed); science (M Ed); secondary education (M Ed), including gifted education; sports administration (MSA); technology (M Ed). *Accreditation:* NCATE. Part-time and evening/weekend programs available. *Faculty:* 9 full-time (7 women), 20 part-time/adjunct (15 women). *Students:* 50 full-time (36 women), 116 part-time (76 women); includes 23 minority (20 African Americans, 1 Asian American or Pacific Islander, 2 Hispanic Americans), 1 international. Average age 30. 55 applicants, 60% accepted, 30 enrolled. In 2006, 82 degrees awarded. *Degree requirements:* For master's, thesis, comprehensive exam. *Entrance requirements:* For master's, MAT or GRE, minimum GPA of 2.75. Additional exam requirements/recommendations for international students: Required—TOEFL. *Application deadline:* For fall admission, 8/1 priority date for domestic students, 5/1 for international students; for spring admission, 12/1 priority date for domestic students, 9/1 for international students. Applications are processed on a rolling basis. Application fee: $50. *Expenses: Contact institution. Financial support:* In 2006–07, 25 students received support; fellowships with partial tuition reimbursements available, institutionally sponsored loans and tuition waivers (partial) available. Financial award application deadline: 4/15; financial award applicants required to submit FAFSA. *Faculty research:* Technology grant, professional development schools. Total annual research expenditures: $6,500. *Unit head:* Dr. Trevor F. Hutchins, Associate Dean, 615-460-6232, Fax: 615-460-6414, E-mail: hutchinst@mail.belmont.edu. *Application contact:* Julie Hullett, Admission/Licensure Officer, 615-460-6879, Fax: 615-460-5556, E-mail: hullettj@email.belmont.edu.

Bemidji State University, School of Graduate Studies, College of Professional Studies, Program in Education, Bemidji, MN 56601-2699. Offers M Ed, MS. Part-time programs available. *Faculty:* 17 full-time (8 women). *Students:* 8 full-time (3 women), 47 part-time (31 women); includes 6 minority (2 African Americans, 4 American Indian/Alaska Native). Average age 41. 16 applicants, 94% accepted. In 2006, 16 degrees awarded. *Degree requirements:* For master's, thesis. *Entrance requirements:* Additional exam requirements/recommendations for international students: Required—TOEFL. *Application deadline:* For fall admission, 5/1 for domestic students. Applications are processed on a rolling basis. Application fee: $20. Electronic applications accepted. *Expenses:* Tuition, nonresident: part-time $284 per credit. Required fees: $86 per credit. *Financial support:* In 2006–07, 2 research assistantships with partial tuition reimbursements (averaging $8,250 per year), teaching assistantships with partial tuition reimbursements (averaging $8,250 per year) were awarded; career-related internships or fieldwork, Federal Work-Study, scholarships/grants, health care benefits, and unspecified assistantships also available. Support available to part-time students. Financial award application deadline: 5/1. *Unit head:* Dr. Jack Reynolds, Chair, 218-755-2931, Fax: 218-755-3787, E-mail: jreynolds@bemidjistate.edu.

Benedictine University, Graduate Programs, Program in Education, Lisle, IL 60532-0900. Offers curriculum and instruction and collaborative teaching (M Ed); elementary education (MA Ed); leadership and administration (M Ed); reading and literacy (M Ed); secondary education (MA Ed); special education (MA Ed). Part-time and evening/weekend programs available. *Faculty:* 4 full-time (2 women), 52 part-time/adjunct (30 women). *Students:* 257 (196 women); includes 22 minority (4 African Americans, 1 American Indian/Alaska Native, 3 Asian Americans or Pacific Islanders, 14 Hispanic Americans) 2 international. Average age 33. 130 applicants, 93% accepted, 13 enrolled. In 2006, 181 degrees awarded. *Degree requirements:* For master's, thesis (for some programs), comprehensive exam. *Entrance requirements:* For master's, GRE or MAT. Additional exam requirements/recommendations for international students: Required—TOEFL (minimum score 550 paper-based; 213 computer-based). *Application deadline:* For fall admission, 9/1 for domestic students; for winter admission, 12/1 for domestic students; for spring admission, 2/15 for domestic students. Applications are processed on a rolling basis. Application fee: $40. Electronic applications accepted. *Expenses: Contact institution. Financial support:* Career-related internships or fieldwork and health care benefits available. Support available to part-time students. *Unit head:* Dr. Richard Campbell, Director, 630-829-6242, Fax: 630-960-1126, E-mail: rcampbell@ben.edu. *Application contact:* Kari Gibbons, Director, Admissions, 630-829-6200, Fax: 630-829-6584, E-mail: kgibbons@ben.edu.

Bennington College, Graduate Programs, Program in Teaching, Bennington, VT 05201. Offers art education (MAT); early childhood (MAT); elementary education (MAT); English education (MAT); foreign language education (MAT); mathematics education (MAT); music education (MAT); science education (MAT); secondary education (MAT); social science education (MAT). *Faculty:* 4 part-time/adjunct (3 women). *Students:* 11 full-time (7 women), 1 (woman) part-time; includes 2 minority (both Hispanic Americans) Average age 31. 12 applicants, 75% accepted, 3 enrolled. In 2006, 13 degrees awarded. *Degree requirements:* For master's, 1 year teaching practicum, professional portfolio. *Entrance requirements:* For master's, interview. *Application deadline:* For fall admission, 3/1 for domestic students. Application fee: $60. *Expenses: Contact institution.* One-time fee: $75 full-time. Tuition and fees vary according to program. *Financial support:* In 2006–07, 10 students received support, including 4 fellowships (averaging $6,875 per year); scholarships/grants and unspecified assistantships also available. Financial award application deadline: 4/1; financial award applicants required to submit FAFSA. *Unit head:* George Kamberelis, Director of Center for Creative Teaching, 802-440-4863, E-mail: gkamberelis@bennington.edu. *Application contact:* Ken Himmelman, Dean of Admissions, 802-440-4312, Fax: 802-440-4320, E-mail: admissions@bennington.edu.

See Close-Up on page 861.

Bennington College, Graduate Programs, Program in Teaching a Second Language, Bennington, VT 05201. Offers education (MATSL); foreign language education (MATSL); French (MATSL); Spanish (MATSL). Part-time programs available. *Faculty:* 2 full-time (0 women), 5 part-time/adjunct (3 women). *Students:* Average age 40. 8 applicants, 75% accepted, 5 enrolled. In 2006, 5 degrees awarded. *Degree requirements:* For master's, one foreign language. *Entrance requirements:* For master's, oral proficiency interview (OPI). Additional exam requirements/recommendations for international students: Required—TOEFL (minimum score 577 paper-based; 233 computer-based). *Application deadline:* For spring admission, 4/1 priority date for domestic and international students. Applications are processed on a rolling basis. Application fee: $60. *Expenses: Contact institution.* One-time fee: $75 full-time. Tuition and fees vary according to program. *Financial support:* In 2006–07, 1 student received support. Scholarships/grants available. Financial award application deadline: 4/1; financial award applicants required to submit FAFSA. *Faculty research:* Acquisition, evaluation, assessment, conceptual teaching and learning content-driven communication, applied linguistics. *Unit head:* Carol Meyer, Director of Isabelle Kaplan Center for Languages and Cultures, 802-440-4710, Fax: 802-447-4269, E-mail: matsl@bennington.edu. *Application contact:* Nancy Pearlman, Assistant Director, 802-440-4710, Fax: 802-447-4269, E-mail: matsl@benington.edu.

Berry College, Graduate Programs, Graduate Programs in Education, Mount Berry, GA 30149-0159. Offers curriculum and instruction (Ed S); early childhood education (M Ed); middle-grades education and reading (M Ed); secondary education (M Ed). *Accreditation:* NCATE. Part-time programs available. *Faculty:* 11 part-time/adjunct (5 women). *Students:* 6 full-time (5 women), 92 part-time (75 women); includes 3 minority (1 African American, 2 Hispanic Americans), 1 international. Average age 34. In 2006, 38 degrees awarded. *Degree requirements:* For master's, oral exams, thesis optional; for Ed S, thesis, portfolio, oral exams. *Entrance requirements:* For master's, GRE General Test, MAT, or NTE, minimum GPA of 2.5; for Ed S, M Ed from NCATE accredited school, minimum GPA of 3.25. Additional exam requirements/recommendations for international students: Required—TOEFL (minimum score 550 paper-based; 213 computer-based). *Application deadline:* Applications are processed on a rolling basis. Application fee: $25 ($30 for international students). *Expenses:* Tuition: Full-time $6,174; part-time $343 per credit hour. *Financial support:* In 2006–07, 57 students received support, including 3 research assistantships with full tuition reimbursements available (averaging $3,500 per year); scholarships/grants and unspecified assistantships also available. Support available to part-time students. Financial award application deadline: 4/1; financial award applicants required to submit FAFSA. *Faculty research:* English as a second language, curriculum development, teaching strategies, teacher training. *Unit head:* Dr. Jacqueline McDowell, Dean, Charter School of Education and Human Sciences, 706-236-1717, Fax: 706-238-5827, E-mail: jmcdowell@berry.edu. *Application contact:* Richard D. Paul, Dean of Admissions and Financial Aid, 706-236-2215, Fax: 706-290-2178, E-mail: dpaul@berry.edu.

Bethany University, Program in Teacher Education, Scotts Valley, CA 95066-2820. Offers education (MA); educational leadership (MA). Part-time and evening/weekend programs available. *Degree requirements:* For master's, thesis. *Entrance requirements:* For master's, GRE General Test.

Bethel College, Division of Graduate Studies, Program in Education, Mishawaka, IN 46545-5591. Offers M Ed, MAT. *Accreditation:* NCATE. *Faculty:* 14 part-time/adjunct (9 women). *Students:* 16 full-time (10 women), 38 part-time (22 women); includes 6 minority (5 African Americans, 1 Asian American or Pacific Islander), 1 international. 73 applicants, 73% accepted, 47 enrolled. *Entrance requirements:* Additional exam requirements/recommendations for international students: Required—TOEFL (minimum score 540 paper-based; 207 computer-based). Application fee: $25. *Expenses:* Tuition: Full-time $5,940; part-time $330 per credit hour. *Unit head:* Dr. Ralph Stutzman, Director, 574-257-3493, E-mail: stutzmr@bethelcollege.edu.

Bethel College, Program in Education, McKenzie, TN 38201. Offers administration and supervision (MA Ed); biology education K8-12 (MAT); elementary education (MAT); English education K8-12 (MAT); history education K8-12 (MAT); physical education K8-12 (MAT); special education K8-12 (MAT). Part-time and evening/weekend programs available. *Degree requirements:* For master's, thesis (for some programs). *Entrance requirements:* For master's, GRE General Test or MAT, minimum undergraduate GPA of 2.5.

Bethel University, Graduate School, Department of Education, St. Paul, MN 55112-6999. Offers education K-12 (MA); educational administration (Ed D); literacy (Certificate); literacy education (MA); secondary education (MA); special education (M Ed). Evening/weekend programs available. *Faculty:* 20 full-time (10 women), 34 part-time/adjunct (18 women). *Students:* 192 full-time (119 women), 110 part-time (71 women); includes 16 minority (6 African Americans, 5 Asian Americans or Pacific Islanders, 5 Hispanic Americans). Average age 35. In 2006, 58 master's, 9 other advanced degrees awarded. *Degree requirements:* For master's, thesis, practicum; for doctorate, thesis/dissertation, registration. *Entrance requirements:* For master's, interview, current teaching license, minimum GPA of 3.0, teaching experience (if applicable), letters of reference; for doctorate, MAT or GRE, minimum GPA of 3.5, letters of reference, master's degree. Additional exam requirements/recommendations for international students: Required—TOEFL (minimum score 550 paper-based; 213 computer-based). *Application* *deadline:* For fall admission, 8/1 priority date for domestic students; for winter admission, 12/10 priority date for domestic students; for spring admission, 5/1 priority date for domestic students. Applications are processed on a rolling basis. Application fee: $25. Electronic applications accepted. *Expenses: Contact institution.* Tuition and fees vary according to program. *Financial support:* Institutionally sponsored loans and scholarships/grants available. Financial award applicants required to submit FAFSA. *Unit head:* Dr. Jay B. Rasmussen, Director, 651-638-6237, Fax: 651-638-8004, E-mail: jay-rasmussen@bethel.edu. *Application contact:* Michael Price, Director of Admissions, 651-635-8000 Ext. 8017, Fax: 651-635-8004, E-mail: m_price@bethel.edu.

Biola University, School of Arts and Sciences, La Mirada, CA 90639-0001. Offers MA Ed. Part-time and evening/weekend programs available. *Degree requirements:* For master's, thesis or alternative. *Entrance requirements:* For master's, California Basic Educational Skills Test, PRAXIS or MSAT, minimum GPA of 3.0. Additional exam requirements/recommendations for international students: Required—TOEFL (minimum score 550 paper-based; 213 computer-based).

Bishop's University, School of Education, Sherbrooke, QC J1M 0C8, Canada. Offers advanced studies in education (Diploma); education (M Ed, MA); teaching English as a second language (Certificate). Part-time programs available. Postbaccalaureate distance learning degree programs offered (minimal on-campus study). *Degree requirements:* For master's, thesis (for some programs). *Entrance requirements:* For master's, teaching license, 2 years of teaching experience. *Faculty research:* Integration of special needs students, multigrade classes/small schools, leadership in organizational development, second language acquisition.

Black Hills State University, College of Education, Spearfish, SD 57799. Offers curriculum and instruction (MS). *Accreditation:* NCATE. Part-time programs available. *Degree requirements:* For master's, thesis or portfolio. *Entrance requirements:* For master's, GRE General Test, bachelor's degree in education. *Faculty research:* Rural education, teacher/student self-concepts, teaching/learning styles, active learning technology in curriculum.

Announcement: The University offers a Master of Science in Curriculum and Instruction (MSCI) designed for the practicing teacher. The degree is offered either on campus or in an Internet-based delivery system. For additional information, visit the Web site at www.bhsu.edu or write to the Director of Graduate Studies.

Bloomsburg University of Pennsylvania, School of Graduate Studies, College of Professional Studies, School of Education, Bloomsburg, PA 17815-1301. Offers M Ed, MS. *Accreditation:* NCATE. *Faculty:* 29 full-time (14 women). *Students:* 133 full-time (93 women), 227 part-time (177 women); includes 2 minority (1 Asian American or Pacific Islander, 1 Hispanic American), 5 international. Average age 30. 158 applicants, 100% accepted, 99 enrolled. In 2006, 179 degrees awarded. *Entrance requirements:* For master's, minimum QPA of 3.0. Additional exam requirements/recommendations for international students: Required—TOEFL. Application fee: $30. Electronic applications accepted. *Expenses:* Tuition, state resident: full-time $6,048; part-time $336 per credit. Tuition, nonresident: full-time $9,678; part-time $538 per credit. Required fees: $1,415. *Financial support:* Unspecified assistantships available.

Bluffton University, Program in Education, Bluffton, OH 45817. Offers MA Ed. *Accreditation:* NCATE. Part-time programs available. *Faculty:* 6 full-time (3 women), 2 part-time/adjunct (1 woman). *Students:* 33 full-time (28 women), 21 part-time (19 women); includes 3 minority (2 African Americans, 1 Hispanic American). 32 applicants, 69% accepted, 20 enrolled. In 2006, 10 degrees awarded. *Degree requirements:* For master's, action research project, public presentation. *Entrance requirements:* Additional exam requirements/recommendations for international students: Required—TOEFL. *Application deadline:* For fall admission, 8/15 priority date for domestic students, 6/15 priority date for international students; for spring admission, 12/15 priority date for domestic students, 9/15 priority date for international students. Applications are processed on a rolling basis. Application fee: $20. Electronic applications accepted. *Financial support:* In 2006–07, 2 students received support. Health care benefits available. Support available to part-time students. Financial award application deadline: 9/15; financial award applicants required to submit FAFSA. *Faculty research:* Mentoring. *Unit head:* Dr. Gayle M. Trollinger, Director of Teacher Education, 419-358-3331, Fax: 419-358-3074, E-mail: trollingerg@bluffton.edu. *Application contact:* Susan White, Program Representative, 419-358-3560, Fax: 419-358-3399, E-mail: whites@bluffton.edu.

Boise State University, Graduate College, College of Education, Boise, ID 83725-0399. Offers M Ed, MA, MET, MPE, MS, MS Ed, Ed D. *Accreditation:* NCATE. Part-time programs available. *Faculty:* 84 full-time (39 women), 47 part-time/adjunct (29 women). *Students:* 97 full-time (62 women), 426 part-time (289 women); includes 37 minority (2 African Americans, 5 American Indian/Alaska Native, 4 Asian Americans or Pacific Islanders, 26 Hispanic Americans), 4 international. Average age 38. 178 applicants, 92% accepted, 57 enrolled. In 2006, 123 master's, 3 doctorates awarded. *Degree requirements:* For doctorate, thesis/dissertation. *Entrance requirements:* For master's, minimum GPA of 3.0; for doctorate, GRE General Test, minimum GPA of 3.0. *Application deadline:* For fall admission, 7/1 priority date for domestic students; for spring admission, 11/15 priority date for domestic students. Applications are processed on a rolling basis. Application fee: $0. Electronic applications accepted. *Financial support:* In 2006–07, 40 students received support, including 13 research assistantships with full tuition reimbursements available (averaging $12,268 per year); fellowships with full tuition reimbursements available, career-related internships or fieldwork, Federal Work-Study, institutionally sponsored loans, and unspecified assistantships also available. Support available to part-time students. Financial award application deadline: 3/1; financial award applicants required to submit FAFSA. *Unit head:* Diane Boothe, Dean, 208-426-1134, Fax: 208-426-4365. *Application contact:* Dr. Philip P. Kelly, Chair, 208-426-4977, Fax: 208-426-4365.

Boston College, Lynch Graduate School of Education, Chestnut Hill, MA 02467-3800. Offers M Ed, MA, MAT, MST, Ed D, PhD, CAES, JD/M Ed, JD/MA, M Ed/MA, MA/MA, MBA/MA. *Faculty:* 62 full-time (31 women), 33 part-time/adjunct (20 women). *Students:* 629 full-time (499 women), 248 part-time (168 women); includes 130 minority (50 African Americans, 2 American Indian/Alaska Native, 49 Asian Americans or Pacific Islanders, 29 Hispanic Americans), 89 international. 1,622 applicants, 54% accepted, 860 enrolled. In 2006, 385 master's, 35 doctorates, 4 other advanced degrees awarded. Terminal master's awarded for partial completion of doctoral program. *Degree requirements:* For master's and CAES, comprehensive exam; for doctorate, thesis/dissertation, comprehensive exam. *Entrance requirements:* For doctorate, GRE General Test; for CAES, GRE General Test or MAT. Additional exam requirements/recommendations for international students: Required—TOEFL. Application fee: $60. *Financial support:* In 2006–07, 940 fellowships with full and partial tuition reimbursements, 324 research assistantships with full and partial tuition reimbursements, 126 teaching assistantships with full and partial tuition reimbursements were awarded; career-related internships or fieldwork, Federal Work-Study, institutionally sponsored loans, scholarships/grants, traineeships, tuition waivers (full and partial), and unspecified assistantships also available. Support available to part-time students. Financial award applicants required to submit FAFSA. *Faculty research:* Assessment and public policy, human development, minority perspectives in education, full service schools, urban school leadership and organization, school inclusion. Total annual research expenditures: $12.5 million. *Unit head:* Rev. Joseph O'Keefe, SJ, Dean, 617-552-8426, Fax: 617-552-0812, E-mail: okeefejo@bc.edu. *Application contact:* Timothy P. Blackman, Director, Graduate Admission and Financial Aid, 617-552-4214, Fax: 617-552-0398, E-mail: timothy.blackman.1@bc.edu.

See Close-Up on page 863.

Boston University, School of Education, Boston, MA 02215. Offers Ed M, MAT, Ed D, CAGS, MSW/Ed D, MSW/Ed M. Part-time programs available. *Faculty:* 31 full-time, 57 part-time/adjunct. *Students:* 265 full-time (209 women), 256 part-time (196 women). Average age 31. In 2006, 298 master's, 23 doctorates, 5 other advanced degrees awarded. Terminal master's awarded for partial completion of doctoral program. *Degree requirements:* For master's, thesis optional; for doctorate, thesis/dissertation, comprehensive exam. *Entrance requirements:* For master's, doctorate, and CAGS, GRE General Test or MAT. Additional exam requirements/recommendations for international students: Required—TOEFL. *Application deadline:* For fall admission, 2/15 priority date for domestic and international students; for winter admission, 10/1 priority date for domestic and international students. Applications are processed on a rolling basis. Application fee: $65. Electronic applications accepted. *Expenses:* Tuition: Full-time $33,330; part-time $1,042 per credit. Required fees: $462; $40. *Financial support:* In 2006–07, 325 students received support, including 7 fellowships, 9 research assistantships, 32 teaching assistantships with partial tuition reimbursements available; career-related internships or fieldwork, Federal Work-Study, and scholarships/grants also available. Support available to part-time students. Financial award application deadline: 2/15; financial award applicants required to submit FAFSA. *Faculty research:* Moral development, language development in young children, mathematics curriculum development, educational reform and standards, science curriculum development. Total annual research expenditures: $2.1 million. *Unit head:* Dr. Charles L. Glenn, Dean ad interim, 617-353-3212, E-mail: glennsed@bu.edu. *Application contact:* Margaret Sullivan, Graduate Admissions Office, 617-353-4237, Fax: 617-353-8937, E-mail: sedgrad@bu.edu.

See Close-Up on page 865.

Bowie State University, Graduate Programs, Program in Teaching, Bowie, MD 20715-9465. Offers MAT. *Accreditation:* NCATE. Part-time and evening/weekend programs available. *Students:* 21 full-time (16 women), 42 part-time (30 women); includes 48 African Americans, 2 Asian Americans or Pacific Islanders, 1 Hispanic American. Average age 32. 34 applicants, 88% accepted, 18 enrolled. In 2006, 12 degrees awarded. *Entrance requirements:* For master's, PRAXIS I. *Application deadline:* For fall admission, 4/1 priority date for domestic and international students; for spring admission, 11/1 priority date for domestic and international students. Applications are processed on a rolling basis. Electronic applications accepted. *Expenses:* Tuition, state resident: full-time $7,344; part-time $306 per credit. Tuition, nonresident: full-time $14,304; part-time $396 per credit. Required fees: $1,078; $77 per credit. $539 per term. One-time fee: $40. *Unit head:* Dr. Constance Brooks, Program Coordinator, 301-860-3133, E-mail: cebrooks@bowiestate.edu. *Application contact:* Angela Issac, Information Contact.

Bowie State University, Graduate Programs, Programs in Education, Department of Learning and Professional Development, Bowie, MD 20715-9465. Offers MAT. *Degree requirements:* For master's, research paper, thesis optional. *Entrance requirements:* For master's, NTE, minimum GPA of 3.0 in major, teaching experience. *Expenses:* Tuition, state resident: full-time $7,344; part-time $306 per credit. Tuition, nonresident: full-time $14,304; part-time $396 per credit. Required fees: $1,078; $77 per credit. $539 per term. One-time fee: $40.

Bradley University, Graduate School, College of Education and Health Sciences, Peoria, IL 61625-0002. Offers MA, MSN, DPT. *Accreditation:* NCATE. Part-time and evening/weekend programs available. *Faculty:* 78. *Students:* 69 full-time (57 women), 173 part-time (122 women); includes 13 minority (1 African American, 1 American Indian/Alaska Native, 10 Asian Americans or Pacific Islanders, 1 Hispanic American), 1 international. 61 applicants, 61% accepted, 27 enrolled. In 2006, 84 degrees awarded. *Degree requirements:* For master's, thesis optional. *Entrance requirements:* For master's, GRE General Test or MAT, letters of recommendation; for doctorate, GRE, letters of recommendation. Additional exam requirements/recommendations for international students: Required—TOEFL (minimum score 550 paper-based; 213 computer-based; 79 iBT). *Application deadline:* For fall admission, 5/15 priority date for domestic students, 5/15 for international students; for spring admission, 10/15 priority date for domestic students, 10/15 for international students. Applications are processed on a rolling basis. Application fee: $40 ($50 for international students). *Financial support:* In 2006–07, 13 research assistantships with full and partial tuition reimbursements (averaging $5,060 per year) were awarded; teaching assistantships, career-related internships or fieldwork, institutionally sponsored loans, scholarships/grants, tuition waivers (partial), and unspecified assistantships also available. Support available to part-time students. Financial award application deadline: 4/1. *Faculty research:* Health care, professional nurse traineeship, gifted education. *Unit head:* Dr. Joan Sattler, Dean, 309-677-3180.

Brandon University, Faculty of Education, Brandon, MB R7A 6A9, Canada. Offers curriculum (Diploma); curriculum studies (M Ed); education administration (M Ed, Diploma); guidance and counseling (M Ed, Diploma); special education (M Ed, Diploma). *Degree requirements:* For master's, thesis. *Entrance requirements:* For master's, minimum GPA of 3.0, teaching certificate or equivalent. Additional exam requirements/recommendations for international students: Required—TOEFL. *Faculty research:* Comparative education, environmental studies, parent/school council.

Brenau University, Graduate Programs, School of Education, Gainesville, GA 30501. Offers early childhood education (M Ed, Ed S), including behavior disorders (M Ed); learning disabilities (M Ed), including special education; middle grades education (M Ed, Ed S). *Accreditation:* NCATE. Part-time and evening/weekend programs available. *Faculty:* 12 full-time (9 women), 17 part-time/adjunct (9 women). *Students:* 104 full-time (89 women), 160 part-time (140 women); includes 34 minority (28 African Americans, 3 Asian Americans or Pacific Islanders, 3 Hispanic Americans), 2 international. Average age 37. 187 applicants. In 2006, 92 master's, 24 other advanced degrees awarded. *Degree requirements:* For master's, comprehensive exam or applied research project, effective portfolio, thesis optional; for Ed S, applied research project. *Entrance requirements:* For master's, GRE, MAT, interview, minimum GPA of 3.0, teaching certificate, 3 references, writing samples; for Ed S, GRE, MAT, master's degree, minimum GPA of 3.0, writing sample, letters of reference. Additional exam requirements/recommendations for international students: Required—TOEFL (minimum score 550 paper-based). *Application deadline:* Applications are processed on a rolling basis. Application fee: $30. *Expenses: Contact institution. Financial support:* Career-related internships or fieldwork available. Financial award application deadline: 7/15; financial award applicants required to submit FAFSA. *Faculty research:* Environmental science literacy and awareness, curriculum integration for improved student success, teaching dispositions, impact of parent involvement on student success, grade inflation in higher education. *Unit head:* Dr. William B. Ware, Dean, 770-534-6220, Fax: 770-534-6221, E-mail: bware@brenau.edu. *Application contact:* Nathan Goss, Admissions Coordinator, 770-534-6162, Fax: 770-538-4701, E-mail: ngoss@brenau.edu.

Briar Cliff University, Program in Education, Sioux City, IA 51104-0100. Offers MA. Program offered during the summer only. Postbaccalaureate distance learning degree programs offered (minimal on-campus study). *Entrance requirements:* For master's, 2 letters of recommendation, writing sample. Electronic applications accepted.

Bridgewater State College, School of Graduate Studies, School of Education and Allied Science, Bridgewater, MA 02325-0001. Offers M Ed, MAT, MS, CAGS. *Accreditation:* NCATE. Part-time and evening/weekend programs available. *Students:* 1,575. *Degree requirements:* For CAGS, comprehensive exam. *Entrance requirements:* For master's, GRE General Test or Massachusetts Test for Educator Licensure; for CAGS, master's degree. Additional exam requirements/recommendations for international students: Required—TOEFL (minimum score 215 computer-based). *Application deadline:* For fall admission, 3/1 priority date for domestic students; for spring admission, 10/1 priority date for domestic students. Application fee: $50. *Financial support:* Career-related internships or fieldwork, health care benefits, and unspecified assistantships available. Support available to part-time students. *Unit head:* Dr. Anna Bradfield, Dean, 508-697-1347. *Application contact:* Dr. Raymond Charles Guillette, Assistant Dean School of Graduate Studies, 508-531-2919, Fax: 508-531-6162, E-mail: rguillette@bridgew.edu.

Brigham Young University, Graduate Studies, David O. McKay School of Education, Provo, UT 84602-1001. Offers M Ed, MA, MS, PhD, Ed S. *Accreditation:* NCATE. Part-time programs available. *Faculty:* 63 full-time (25 women), 28 part-time/adjunct (9 women). *Students:* 187 full-time (119 women), 112 part-time (64 women); includes 34 minority (2 African Americans,

Education—General

Brigham Young University (continued)

5 American Indian/Alaska Native, 22 Asian Americans or Pacific Islanders, 5 Hispanic Americans), 25 international. Average age 34. 250 applicants, 57% accepted, 105 enrolled. In 2006, 73 master's, 19 doctorates awarded. *Degree requirements:* For master's, comprehensive exam (for some programs), registration (for some programs); for doctorate, thesis/dissertation, comprehensive exam, registration (for some programs). *Entrance requirements:* For master's, GRE General Test, minimum GPA of 3.25, minimum 1 year of teaching experience, letters of recommendation; for doctorate, GRE General Test, minimum GPA of 3.0 in last 60 hours of coursework. Additional exam requirements/recommendations for international students: Required—TOEFL (minimum score 580 paper-based; 237 computer-based). *Application deadline:* For fall admission, 2/1 for domestic and international students; for winter admission, 2/1 for domestic and international students; for spring admission, 2/15 for domestic and international students. Application fee: $50. Electronic applications accepted. *Financial support:* In 2006–07, 108 students received support, including 58 research assistantships (averaging $25,120 per year), 34 teaching assistantships (averaging $18,000 per year); fellowships, career-related internships or fieldwork, institutionally sponsored loans, scholarships/grants, tuition waivers (partial), and unspecified assistantships also available. Support available to part-time students. Financial award applicants required to submit FAFSA. *Faculty research:* Reading, learning, teacher education, assessment and evaluation, speech-language pathology. Total annual research expenditures: $1.2 million. *Unit head:* Dr. K. Richard Young, Dean, 801-422-3695, Fax: 801-422-0200, E-mail: richard_young@byu.edu. *Application contact:* Linda Parker, Director, Education Advisement Center, 801-422-3428, Fax: 801-422-0195, E-mail: linda_parker@byu.edu.

Brock University, Faculty of Graduate Studies, Faculty of Education, St. Catharines, ON L2S 3A1, Canada. Offers M Ed, PhD. Part-time and evening/weekend programs available. *Faculty:* 40 full-time (24 women), 37 part-time/adjunct (18 women). *Students:* 73 full-time (62 women), 356 part-time (275 women). 277 applicants, 72% accepted, 141 enrolled. In 2006, 156 master's, 4 doctorates awarded. *Degree requirements:* For master's, thesis optional; for doctorate, thesis/dissertation. *Entrance requirements:* For master's, 1 year of teaching experience, honors degree; for doctorate, master's degree. Additional exam requirements/recommendations for international students: Required—TOEFL (minimum score 550 paper-based; 213 computer-based; 80 iBT), IELTS (minimum score 7), TWE (minimum score 4). *Application deadline:* For fall admission, 4/15 for domestic students. Application fee: $100. Electronic applications accepted. *Expenses:* Contact institution. *Financial support:* Fellowships, research assistantships, teaching assistantships, scholarships/grants available. *Faculty research:* International and comparative education, early childhood education, educational leadership, adult education. *Unit head:* Dr. James Heap, Dean, 905-688-5550 Ext. 3712, Fax: 905-685-4131, E-mail: jheap@brocku.ca. *Application contact:* Lynn Duhaime, Administrative Coordinator, 905-688-5550 Ext. 3340, Fax: 905-688-5091, E-mail: lynn.duhaime@brocku.ca.

Brooklyn College of the City University of New York, Division of Graduate Studies, School of Education, Brooklyn, NY 11210-2889. Offers MA, MS Ed, CAS. *Accreditation:* NCATE. Part-time and evening/weekend programs available. *Students:* 148 full-time (114 women), 1,688 part-time (1,233 women); includes 823 minority (546 African Americans, 2 American Indian/Alaska Native, 73 Asian Americans or Pacific Islanders, 202 Hispanic Americans), 66 international. 1,178 applicants, 73% accepted, 516 enrolled. In 2006, 731 master's, 170 other advanced degrees awarded. *Entrance requirements:* For master's, 2 letters of recommendation, essay, resumé; for CAS, master's degree. *Application deadline:* For fall admission, 3/1 priority date for domestic students, 2/1 priority date for international students; for spring admission, 11/1 priority date for domestic students, 10/1 priority date for international students. Applications are processed on a rolling basis. Application fee: $125. Electronic applications accepted. *Expenses:* Tuition, state resident: full-time $6,400; part-time $270 per credit. Tuition, nonresident: full-time $12,000; part-time $500 per credit. Required fees: $118 per semester. *Financial support:* Fellowships, career-related internships or fieldwork, Federal Work-Study, institutionally sponsored loans, scholarships/grants, and tuition waivers (full and partial) available. Support available to part-time students. Financial award application deadline: 5/1; financial award applicants required to submit FAFSA. *Unit head:* Dr. Deborah Shanley, Dean, 718-951-5214, Fax: 718-951-4816, E-mail: dshanley@brooklyn.cuny.edu. *Application contact:* Karen Alleyne-Pierre, Director of Admissions Services and Enrollment Communications, 718-951-5902, Fax: 718-951-4506, E-mail: grads@brooklyn.cuny.edu.

Brown University, Graduate School, Department of Education, Providence, RI 02912. Offers elementary education 1-6 (MAT); secondary biology (MAT); secondary English (MAT); secondary social studies/history (MAT). *Faculty:* 4 full-time (2 women), 7 part-time/adjunct (all women). *Students:* 28 full-time (23 women); includes 5 minority (2 African Americans, 1 Asian American or Pacific Islander, 2 Hispanic Americans). Average age 25. 89 applicants, 61% accepted, 28 enrolled. In 2006, 35 degrees awarded. *Degree requirements:* For master's, student teaching, portfolio. *Entrance requirements:* For master's, GRE General Test (secondary only), PRAXIS II (elementary), letters of recommendation, interview. *Application deadline:* For winter admission, 1/3 for domestic students. Application fee: $70. Electronic applications accepted. *Financial support:* In 2006–07, 23 students received support, including 2 fellowships (averaging $7,000 per year); Federal Work-Study, institutionally sponsored loans, scholarships/grants, tuition waivers (partial), and proctorships also available. Financial award application deadline: 2/1; financial award applicants required to submit FAFSA. *Faculty research:* Literacy, performance-based assessment, teaching English as a foreign language. *Unit head:* Lawrence Wakeford, Chairman, 401-863-3428, Fax: 401-863-1276, E-mail: lawrence_wakeford@brown.edu. *Application contact:* Carin Algava, Assistant Director, 401-863-3364, Fax: 401-863-1276, E-mail: carin_algava@brown.edu.

Bucknell University, Graduate Studies, College of Arts and Sciences, Department of Education, Lewisburg, PA 17837. Offers classroom teaching (MS Ed); educational research (MS Ed); elementary and secondary counseling (MA, MS Ed); elementary and secondary principalship (MA, MS Ed); reading (MA, MS Ed); school psychology (MS Ed); supervision of curriculum and instruction (MA, MS Ed). Part-time programs available. *Degree requirements:* For master's, thesis or alternative. *Entrance requirements:* For master's, GRE General Test, minimum GPA of 2.8. Additional exam requirements/recommendations for international students: Required—TOEFL.

Buena Vista University, School of Education, Storm Lake, IA 50588. Offers school guidance and counseling (MS Ed). Offered in summer only. Part-time and evening/weekend programs available. Postbaccalaureate distance learning degree programs offered (minimal on-campus study). *Faculty:* 3 full-time (2 women), 13 part-time/adjunct (10 women). *Students:* 105 full-time (95 women). Average age 36. 38 applicants, 58% accepted, 20 enrolled. In 2006, 24 degrees awarded. *Degree requirements:* For master's, thesis, fieldwork/practicum. *Entrance requirements:* For master's, GRE Writing Test, minimum undergraduate GPA of 2.75. *Application deadline:* For spring admission, 4/15 for domestic students. Application fee: $0. Electronic applications accepted. *Financial support:* In 2006–07, teaching assistantships with full tuition reimbursements (averaging $6,000 per year); career-related internships or fieldwork also available. Financial award application deadline: 5/15; financial award applicants required to submit FAFSA. *Faculty research:* Reading, curriculum, educational psychology, special education. *Unit head:* Dr. Kline Capps, Dean, 712-749-2275, Fax: 712-749-1408, E-mail: capps@bvu.edu. *Application contact:* Rita Mckenzie, Director of Graduate Studies, 712-749-2156, Fax: 712-749-1408, E-mail: mckenzie@bvu.edu.

Butler University, College of Education, Indianapolis, IN 46208-3485. Offers administration (MS); elementary education (MS); reading (MS); school counseling (MS); secondary education (MS); special education (MS). *Accreditation:* ACA; NCATE. Part-time and evening/weekend programs available. *Faculty:* 12 full-time (6 women), 11 part-time/adjunct (8 women). *Students:* 18 full-time (10 women), 156 part-time (125 women); includes 21 minority (16 African Americans, 2 Asian Americans or Pacific Islanders, 3 Hispanic Americans), 7 international. Average age 31. 56 applicants, 57% accepted, 29 enrolled. In 2006, 72 degrees awarded. *Entrance requirements:* For master's, GRE General Test, MAT, interview. *Application deadline:* For fall admission, 8/15 priority date for domestic students. Applications are processed on a rolling basis. Application fee: $35. Electronic applications accepted. *Expenses:* Tuition: Full-time $6,030; part-time $335 per credit. Tuition and fees vary according to program. *Financial support:* Institutionally sponsored loans available. Support available to part-time students. Financial award application deadline: 7/15; financial award applicants required to submit FAFSA. *Faculty research:* Ethics in cybercounseling, history of sports for disabled effect of fetal alcohol syndrome on perceptual learning, Reading Recovery's theoretical framework in teacher education. *Unit head:* Dr. Ena Shelley, Dean, 317-940-9752, Fax: 317-940-6481. *Application contact:* Karen Farrell, Department Secretary, 317-940-9220, E-mail: kfarrell@butler.edu.

Cabrini College, Graduate and Professional Studies, Radnor, PA 19087-3698. Offers biotechnology (Certificate); education (M Ed); educational leadership (Certificate); instructional systems technology (MS); organization leadership (MS); project management (Certificate). Part-time and evening/weekend programs available. *Faculty:* 11 full-time (7 women), 25 part-time/adjunct (11 women). *Students:* 91 full-time (63 women), 484 part-time (364 women); includes 43 minority (28 African Americans, 6 Asian Americans or Pacific Islanders, 9 Hispanic Americans), 6 international. Average age 32. In 2006, 143 degrees awarded. *Degree requirements:* For master's, thesis optional. *Entrance requirements:* For master's, GRE and/or MAT (in some cases), letter of recommendation, minimum GPA of 2.5. *Application deadline:* For fall admission, 7/29 priority date for domestic students; for spring admission, 12/9 for domestic students. Applications are processed on a rolling basis. Application fee: $50. Electronic applications accepted. *Expenses:* Tuition: Part-time $310 per credit. Required fees: $45 per term. Tuition and fees vary according to course load. *Financial support:* Career-related internships or fieldwork and unspecified assistantships available. Support available to part-time students. Financial award applicants required to submit FAFSA. *Faculty research:* Qualitative research in reading, ethnographic studies. *Unit head:* Dr. Michael W. Markowitz, Dean for Graduate and Professional Studies, 610-902-8501, Fax: 610-902-8522, E-mail: michael.w.markowitz@cabrini.edu. *Application contact:* Bruce D. Bryde, Director of Enrollment and Recruiting, 610-902-8291, Fax: 610-902-8522, E-mail: bruce.d.bryde@cabrini.edu.

California Baptist University, Program in Education, Riverside, CA 92504-3206. Offers cross-cultural language and academic development (MA Ed); educational leadership (MS Ed); educational technology (MS Ed); instructional computer applications (MS Ed); reading (MS Ed); special education (MS Ed); teaching (MS Ed). Part-time programs available. *Faculty:* 16 full-time (10 women), 16 part-time/adjunct (13 women). *Students:* 77 full-time (64 women), 408 part-time (342 women); includes 157 minority (41 African Americans, 12 American Indian/Alaska Native, 18 Asian Americans or Pacific Islanders, 86 Hispanic Americans), 2 international. 282 applicants, 70% accepted, 171 enrolled. In 2006, 63 degrees awarded. *Degree requirements:* For master's, thesis optional. *Entrance requirements:* For master's, minimum undergraduate GPA of 2.75, 12 semester hours of course work in education. Additional exam requirements/recommendations for international students: Required—TOEFL (minimum score 575 paper-based; 230 computer-based), IELTS (minimum score 7). *Application deadline:* For fall admission, 9/1 for domestic students, 7/15 priority date for international students; for spring admission, 1/3 for domestic students, 11/1 priority date for international students. Applications are processed on a rolling basis. Application fee: $45. Electronic applications accepted. *Expenses:* Tuition: Full-time $7,812; part-time $434 per unit. Required fees: $120 per semester. Tuition and fees vary according to program. *Financial support:* In 2006–07, 19 students received support. Career-related internships or fieldwork, Federal Work-Study, and scholarships/grants available. Support available to part-time students. Financial award applicants required to submit FAFSA. *Unit head:* Dr. Mary Crist, Dean, School of Education, 951-343-4313, Fax: 951-343-4516, E-mail: mcrist@calbaptist.edu. *Application contact:* Gail Ronveaux, Dean of Graduate Enrollment, 951-343-5045, Fax: 951-343-5095, E-mail: graduateadmissions@calbaptist.edu.

California Lutheran University, Graduate Studies, School of Education, Thousand Oaks, CA 91360-2787. Offers counseling and guidance (MS); curriculum and instruction (MA), including reading education; education (M Ed); educational administration (MA); special education (MS); teacher preparation (Certificate). *Accreditation:* NCATE. Part-time and evening/weekend programs available. *Entrance requirements:* For master's, GRE General Test, interview, minimum GPA of 3.0.

California Polytechnic State University, San Luis Obispo, College of Education, San Luis Obispo, CA 93407. Offers MA. Part-time and evening/weekend programs available. *Faculty:* 5 full-time (2 women), 8 part-time/adjunct (6 women). *Students:* 76 full-time (58 women), 25 part-time (22 women); includes 26 minority (1 African American, 6 Asian Americans or Pacific Islanders, 19 Hispanic Americans). 108 applicants, 62% accepted, 61 enrolled. In 2006, 66 degrees awarded. *Degree requirements:* For master's, thesis (for some programs), comprehensive exam (for some programs). *Entrance requirements:* For master's, minimum GPA of 3.0 in last 90 quarter units, letters of recommendation. Additional exam requirements/recommendations for international students: Required—TOEFL (minimum score 550 paper-based; 213 computer-based), TWE (minimum score 4.5). *Application deadline:* For fall admission, 4/1 priority date for domestic students, 11/30 for international students. Application fee: $55. *Financial support:* Research assistantships, career-related internships or fieldwork, Federal Work-Study, and institutionally sponsored loans available. Support available to part-time students. Financial award application deadline: 3/2; financial award applicants required to submit FAFSA. *Faculty research:* Rural school counseling, partner school effectiveness. *Unit head:* Dr. Bonnie Konopak, Dean, 805-756-2126, Fax: 805-756-5682, E-mail: bkonopak@calpoly.edu.

California State Polytechnic University, Pomona, Academic Affairs, College of Education and Integrative Studies, Pomona, CA 91768-2557. Offers MA. Part-time programs available. *Faculty:* 40 full-time (25 women), 44 part-time/adjunct (28 women). *Students:* 55 full-time (36 women), 48 part-time (36 women); includes 50 minority (3 African Americans, 14 Asian Americans or Pacific Islanders, 33 Hispanic Americans), 2 international. Average age 35. 56 applicants, 80% accepted, 25 enrolled. In 2006, 123 degrees awarded. *Degree requirements:* For master's, thesis or alternative. *Application deadline:* For fall admission, 5/1 priority date for domestic students; for winter admission, 10/15 priority date for domestic students; for spring admission, 1/20 priority date for domestic students. Applications are processed on a rolling basis. Application fee: $55. Electronic applications accepted. *Expenses:* Tuition, state resident: part-time $226 per unit. Tuition, nonresident: part-time $226 per unit. Required fees: $2,486 per year. *Financial support:* Career-related internships or fieldwork, Federal Work-Study, and institutionally sponsored loans available. Support available to part-time students. Financial award application deadline: 3/2; financial award applicants required to submit FAFSA. *Faculty research:* Cognitive style, human factors, learning-handicapped children, teaching and learning, severely handicapped children. *Unit head:* Dr. Barbara J. Way, Interim Dean, 909-869-2307, E-mail: bjway@csupomona.edu. *Application contact:* Dr. Gary Kinsey, Associate Dean, 909-869-2316, Fax: 909-869-4963, E-mail: gwkinsey@csupomona.edu.

California State University, Bakersfield, Division of Graduate Studies and Research, School of Education, Bakersfield, CA 93311-1022. Offers bilingual/bicultural education (MA); counseling (MS); curriculum and instruction (MA), including elementary curriculum and instruction, secondary curriculum and instruction; educational administration (MA); special education (MA). *Accreditation:* NCATE. *Degree requirements:* For master's, thesis or alternative, culminating projects.

California State University, Chico, Graduate School, College of Communication and Education, Department of Education, Program in Education, Chico, CA 95929-0722. Offers curriculum and instruction (MA); educational administration (MA); linguistically and culturally diverse learners (MA); reading/language arts (MA); special education (MA). *Students:* 23 full-time (14 women), 58 part-time (45 women); includes 10 minority (2 African Americans, 1 American Indian/Alaska Native, 1 Asian American or Pacific Islander, 6 Hispanic Americans), 1 international. Average age 37. 39 applicants, 100% accepted, 32 enrolled. In 2006, 37 degrees awarded. *Unit head:* Dr. Michael Kotar, Graduate Coordinator, 530-898-6610.

California State University, Dominguez Hills, College of Education, Division of Graduate Education, Carson, CA 90747-0001. Offers counseling (MA); curriculum and instruction (MA); educational administration (MA); individualized education (MA); multicultural education (MA); special education (MA), including early childhood, mild/moderate, moderate/severe; technology-based education (MA, Certificate). Part-time and evening/weekend programs available. *Faculty:* 16 full-time (10 women), 19 part-time/adjunct (14 women). *Students:* 313 full-time (216 women), 338 part-time (245 women); includes 414 minority (161 African Americans, 6 American Indian/Alaska Native, 50 Asian Americans or Pacific Islanders, 197 Hispanic Americans), 4 international. Average age 36. 305 applicants, 81% accepted, 116 enrolled. In 2006, 288 degrees awarded. *Entrance requirements:* For master's, minimum GPA of 2.75. *Application deadline:* For fall admission, 6/1 for domestic students. Application fee: $55. *Expenses:* Tuition, nonresident: part-time $339 per unit. Required fees: $1,148 per term. Tuition and fees vary according to program. *Unit head:* Dr. Farah Fisher, Chairperson, 310-243-3926, E-mail: ffisher@csudh.edu. *Application contact:* Admissions Office, 310-243-3530.

California State University, East Bay, Academic Programs and Graduate Studies, College of Education and Allied Studies, Department of Teacher Education, Hayward, CA 94542-3000. Offers education (MS), including curriculum, educational technology leadership, reading. *Faculty:* 8 full-time, 9 part-time/adjunct. *Students:* 58 full-time (41 women), 153 part-time (115 women); includes 67 minority (18 African Americans, 3 American Indian/Alaska Native, 21 Asian Americans or Pacific Islanders, 25 Hispanic Americans), 3 international. Average age 37. 98 applicants, 74% accepted, 54 enrolled. In 2006, 65 degrees awarded. *Degree requirements:* For master's, project or thesis. *Entrance requirements:* For master's, minimum GPA of 3.0 in field, 2.5 overall; teaching experience. Additional exam requirements/recommendations for international students: Required—TOEFL (minimum score 550 paper-based; 213 computer-based). *Application deadline:* For fall admission, 5/31 for domestic students, 4/30 for international students; for winter admission, 9/30 for domestic and international students; for spring admission, 12/31 for domestic students, 11/30 for international students. Application fee: $55. Electronic applications accepted. *Financial support:* Career-related internships or fieldwork, Federal Work-Study, and institutionally sponsored loans available. Support available to part-time students. Financial award application deadline: 3/2. *Unit head:* Dr. James Zarillo, Chair, 510-885-7439, E-mail: james.zarillo@csueastbay.edu. *Application contact:* My Huynh, Graduate Prospect Specialist, 510-885-2989, Fax: 510-885-4059, E-mail: my.huynh@csueastbay.edu.

California State University, Fresno, Division of Graduate Studies, School of Education and Human Development, Fresno, CA 93740-8027. Offers MA, MS, Ed D. *Accreditation:* NCATE. Part-time and evening/weekend programs available. *Degree requirements:* For master's, thesis or alternative; for doctorate, thesis/dissertation, registration. *Entrance requirements:* For master's, GRE General Test, MAT; for doctorate, GRE or MAT, minimum GPA of 3.2, master's degree. Additional exam requirements/recommendations for international students: Required—TOEFL. Electronic applications accepted. *Faculty research:* Adult community education, parenting, gifted and talented curriculum and instruction, peer mediation and conflict resolution.

California State University, Fullerton, Graduate Studies, College of Health and Human Development, Fullerton, CA 92834-9480. Offers MPH, MS. *Accreditation:* NCATE. Part-time programs available. *Students:* 293 full-time (209 women), 323 part-time (268 women); includes 255 minority (25 African Americans, 4 American Indian/Alaska Native, 111 Asian Americans or Pacific Islanders, 115 Hispanic Americans), 15 international. Average age 32. 689 applicants, 54% accepted, 269 enrolled. In 2006, 176 degrees awarded. Application fee: $55. *Expenses:* Tuition, nonresident: part-time $339 per unit. Required fees: $1,155 per semester. *Financial support:* Teaching assistantships, career-related internships or fieldwork, Federal Work-Study, institutionally sponsored loans, and scholarships/grants available. Support available to part-time students. Financial award application deadline: 3/1. *Faculty research:* Nursing and health, exercise and heart disease, time studies and counseling, sex bias and coaching, nutrition and self-image. *Unit head:* Dr. Roberta Rikli, Dean, 714-278-3311.

California State University, Long Beach, Graduate Studies, College of Education, Long Beach, CA 90840. Offers MA, MS, Ed D. *Accreditation:* NCATE. Part-time and evening/weekend programs available. *Faculty:* 70 full-time (54 women), 82 part-time/adjunct (59 women). *Students:* 202 full-time (144 women), 483 part-time (401 women); includes 360 minority (49 African Americans, 4 American Indian/Alaska Native, 101 Asian Americans or Pacific Islanders, 206 Hispanic Americans), 11 international. Average age 33. 718 applicants, 42% accepted, 216 enrolled. In 2006, 236 degrees awarded. *Entrance requirements:* For master's, GRE General Test, minimum GPA of 2.75. *Application deadline:* For fall admission, 7/1 for domestic students; for spring admission, 12/1 for domestic students. Applications are processed on a rolling basis. Application fee: $55. Electronic applications accepted. *Financial support:* Federal Work-Study, institutionally sponsored loans, and scholarships/grants available. Financial award application deadline: 3/2. *Faculty research:* K-16 educational reform and partnership, gender issues related to teaching and learning, urban education (poverty, diversity, language), assessment and standards-based education. *Unit head:* Dr. Jean Houck, Dean, 562-985-4513, Fax: 562-985-4951, E-mail: houck@csulb.edu. *Application contact:* Nancy L. McGlothin, Coordinator for Graduate Studies, 562-985-4547, Fax: 562-985-4951, E-mail: nmcgloth@csulb.edu.

California State University, Los Angeles, Graduate Studies, Charter College of Education, Los Angeles, CA 90032-8530. Offers MA, MS. *Accreditation:* NCATE. Part-time and evening/weekend programs available. *Faculty:* 63 full-time (41 women), 42 part-time/adjunct (25 women). *Students:* 591 full-time (423 women), 1,290 part-time (946 women); includes 1,161 minority (113 African Americans, 9 American Indian/Alaska Native, 274 Asian Americans or Pacific Islanders, 765 Hispanic Americans), 71 international. In 2006, 531 degrees awarded. *Entrance requirements:* For master's, minimum GPA of 2.75 in last 90 units of course work, teaching certificate. Additional exam requirements/recommendations for international students: Required—TOEFL. *Application deadline:* For fall admission, 6/30 for domestic students; for spring admission, 2/1 for domestic students. Applications are processed on a rolling basis. Application fee: $55. *Expenses:* Tuition, nonresident: part-time $226 per unit. *Financial support:* Career-related internships or fieldwork and Federal Work-Study available. Support available to part-time students. Financial award application deadline: 3/1. *Unit head:* Dr. Mary Falvey, Dean, 323-343-4300, Fax: 323-343-4318.

California State University, Monterey Bay, College of Professional Studies, Institute for Advanced Studies in Education, Seaside, CA 93955-8001. Offers MA. Part-time and evening/weekend programs available. *Degree requirements:* For master's, one foreign language, thesis, 2 years of teaching experience. *Entrance requirements:* Additional exam requirements/recommendations for international students: Required—TOEFL (minimum score 550 paper-based; 213 computer-based). Electronic applications accepted.

California State University, Northridge, Graduate Studies, College of Education, Northridge, CA 91330. Offers MA, MA Ed, MS. *Accreditation:* NCATE. Part-time and evening/weekend programs available. *Faculty:* 92 full-time (58 women), 279 part-time/adjunct (189 women). *Students:* 657 full-time (524 women), 1,393 part-time (1,011 women); includes 968 minority (154 African Americans, 10 American Indian/Alaska Native, 163 Asian Americans or Pacific Islanders, 641 Hispanic Americans), 31 international. Average age 36. 648 applicants, 74% accepted, 361 enrolled. In 2006, 586 degrees awarded. *Entrance requirements:* Additional exam requirements/recommendations for international students: Required—TOEFL. *Application deadline:* For fall admission, 11/30 for domestic students. Application fee: $55. *Expenses:* Tuition, nonresident: full-time $8,136; part-time $4,068 per year. Required fees: $3,624; $1,161 per term. *Financial support:* Fellowships, career-related internships or fieldwork, Federal Work-Study, institutionally sponsored loans, scholarships/grants, and tuition waivers (partial) available. Support available to part-time students. Financial award application deadline: 3/1. *Faculty research:* Federal teacher center support, bilingual teacher training. *Unit head:* Dr. Philip J. Rusche, Dean, 818-677-2590.

California State University, Sacramento, Graduate Studies, College of Education, Sacramento, CA 95819-6048. Offers MA, MS. Part-time programs available. *Students:* 542 full-time (435 women), 561 part-time (463 women); includes 384 minority (89 African Americans, 8 American Indian/Alaska Native, 92 Asian Americans or Pacific Islanders, 195 Hispanic Americans), 12 international. Average age 35. 1,254 applicants, 83% accepted, 764 enrolled. *Degree requirements:* For master's, thesis or alternative, writing proficiency exam. *Entrance requirements:* Additional exam requirements/recommendations for international students: Required—TOEFL. *Application deadline:* Applications are processed on a rolling basis. Application fee: $55. Electronic applications accepted. *Financial support:* Research assistantships, teaching assistantships, career-related internships or fieldwork and Federal Work-Study available. Support available to part-time students. Financial award application deadline: 3/1. *Unit head:* Dr. Vanessa Sheared, Dean, 916-278-6639, Fax: 916-278-5904.

California State University, San Bernardino, Graduate Studies, College of Education, San Bernardino, CA 92407-2397. Offers bilingual/cross-cultural education (MA); curriculum and instruction (MA); educational administration (MA); educational psychology and counseling (MA, MS), including counseling and guidance (MS), rehabilitation counseling (MA); elementary education (MA); English as a second language (MA); environmental education (MA); history and English for secondary teachers (MA); instructional technology (MA); reading (MA); secondary education (MA); special education and rehabilitation counseling (MA), including rehabilitation counseling, special education; teaching of science (MA); vocational and career education (MA). *Accreditation:* NCATE. Part-time and evening/weekend programs available. *Faculty:* 69 full-time, 145 part-time/adjunct. *Students:* 692 full-time (515 women), 345 part-time (245 women); includes 479 minority (145 African Americans, 12 American Indian/Alaska Native, 45 Asian Americans or Pacific Islanders, 277 Hispanic Americans), 17 international. Average age 33. 450 applicants, 82% accepted, 147 enrolled. In 2006, 349 degrees awarded. *Entrance requirements:* For master's, minimum GPA of 3.0 in education. *Application deadline:* For fall admission, 8/31 priority date for domestic students. Application fee: $55. *Financial support:* Career-related internships or fieldwork and Federal Work-Study available. Support available to part-time students. *Faculty research:* Multicultural education, brain-based learning, science education, social studies/global education. *Unit head:* Dr. Patricia Arlin, Dean, 909-537-5600, Fax: 909-537-7011, E-mail: parlin@csusb.edu.

California State University, San Marcos, College of Education, San Marcos, CA 92096-0001. Offers MA. *Accreditation:* NCATE. Part-time and evening/weekend programs available. *Faculty:* 30 full-time (24 women), 53 part-time/adjunct (36 women). *Students:* 36 full-time (34 women), 344 part-time (275 women); includes 87 minority (7 African Americans, 5 American Indian/Alaska Native, 18 Asian Americans or Pacific Islanders, 57 Hispanic Americans), 1 international. Average age 32. 156 applicants, 78% accepted, 43 enrolled. In 2006, 89 degrees awarded. *Degree requirements:* For master's, thesis. *Entrance requirements:* For master's, minimum GPA of 3.0, teaching credentials, 1 year of teaching experience. *Application deadline:* For fall admission, 2/1 priority date for domestic students. Applications are processed on a rolling basis. Application fee: $55. *Expenses:* Tuition, nonresident: part-time $339 per unit. Required fees: $1,186 per term. *Financial support:* Fellowships, teaching assistantships, career-related internships or fieldwork and Federal Work-Study available. Support available to part-time students. Financial award applicants required to submit FAFSA. *Faculty research:* Multicultural literature, art as knowledge, poetry and second language acquisition, restructuring K–12 education and improving the training of K–8 science teachers. *Unit head:* Dr. Mark Baldwin, Dean, 760-750-4306, Fax: 760-750-4323, E-mail: baldwin@csusm.edu. *Application contact:* Beverly Mahdavi, Graduate Admissions Coordinator, 760-750-4281, Fax: 760-750-3538, E-mail: bmahdavi@csusm.edu.

California State University, Stanislaus, Graduate School, College of Education, Turlock, CA 95382. Offers MA Ed. *Accreditation:* NCATE. Part-time and evening/weekend programs available. *Degree requirements:* For master's, thesis. *Entrance requirements:* For master's, MAT, minimum GPA of 3.0. Additional exam requirements/recommendations for international students: Required—TOEFL (minimum score 550 paper-based; 213 computer-based).

California University of Pennsylvania, School of Graduate Studies and Research, School of Education, California, PA 15419-1394. Offers M Ed, MAT, MS, MSW. *Accreditation:* NCATE. Part-time and evening/weekend programs available. Postbaccalaureate distance learning degree programs offered (minimal on-campus study). *Faculty:* 103 full-time (56 women), 12 part-time/adjunct (5 women). *Students:* 606 full-time (351 women), 471 part-time (313 women); includes 88 minority (50 African Americans, 3 American Indian/Alaska Native, 19 Asian Americans or Pacific Islanders, 16 Hispanic Americans). *Degree requirements:* For master's, thesis optional. *Entrance requirements:* For master's, PRAXIS, MAT, minimum QPA of 3.0. Additional exam requirements/recommendations for international students: Required—TOEFL (minimum score 550 paper-based; 213 computer-based; 80 iBT). *Application deadline:* For fall admission, 8/1 priority date for domestic and international students; for winter admission, 12/1 priority date for domestic and international students; for spring admission, 5/1 priority date for domestic and international students. Applications are processed on a rolling basis. Application fee: $25. Electronic applications accepted. *Expenses:* Tuition, state resident: full-time $6,048; part-time $336 per credit. Tuition, nonresident: full-time $9,678; part-time $538 per credit. Required fees: $1,854; $263 per credit. Full-time tuition and fees vary according to course load, campus/location and program. *Financial support:* Career-related internships or fieldwork, scholarships/grants, traineeships, and unspecified assistantships available. Financial award applicants required to submit FAFSA. *Faculty research:* Autism counseling, injury and education, early childhood education, National Board certification. Total annual research expenditures: $250,000. *Unit head:* Geraldine Jones, Dean, 724-938-4125, E-mail: jones_gm@cup.edu.

Calvin College, Graduate Programs in Education, Grand Rapids, MI 49546-4388. Offers curriculum and instruction (M Ed); educational leadership (M Ed); learning disabilities (M Ed); literacy (M Ed). *Accreditation:* NCATE. Part-time programs available. *Faculty:* 2 full-time (both women), 6 part-time/adjunct (2 women). *Students:* 6 full-time (5 women), 87 part-time (66 women); includes 9 minority (3 African Americans, 1 American Indian/Alaska Native, 4 Asian Americans or Pacific Islanders, 1 Hispanic American). Average age 29. 26 applicants, 100% accepted. In 2006, 14 degrees awarded. *Degree requirements:* For master's, thesis or seminar; for degree. *Entrance requirements:* For master's, teaching certificate. Additional exam requirements/recommendations for international students: Required—TOEFL (minimum score 550 paper-based; 213 computer-based). *Application deadline:* For fall admission, 8/1 priority date for domestic students, 5/1 priority date for international students; for spring admission, 1/1 priority date for domestic students, 11/1 priority date for international students. Applications are processed on a rolling basis. Application fee: $0. Electronic applications accepted. *Expenses:* Tuition: Part-time $420 per credit hour. *Financial support:* In 2006–07, 19 students received support. Federal Work-Study, scholarships/grants, and tuition waivers (full and partial) available. Support available to part-time students. Financial award application deadline: 4/3. *Faculty research:* Literacy, racialized gender and gendered identity, teacher learning, learning disabilities identification. *Unit head:* Dr. Susan S. Hasseler, Associate Dean for Teacher Education, 616-526-6597, Fax: 616-526-6505, E-mail: shassele@calvin.edu. *Application contact:* Deb Abbott, Administrative Assistant, 616-526-6105, Fax: 616-526-6505, E-mail: dka2@calvin.edu.

Cambridge College, Program in Education, Cambridge, MA 02138-5304. Offers education (CAGS); education leadership (Ed D); education/integrated studies (M Ed). Part-time and evening/weekend programs available. *Faculty:* 10 full-time (4 women), 309 part-time/adjunct (211 women). *Students:* 963 full-time (758 women), 1,500 part-time (1,182 women); includes 1,168 minority (780 African Americans, 8 American Indian/Alaska Native, 21 Asian Americans or Pacific Islanders, 359 Hispanic Americans), 8 international. Average age 36. 492 applicants, 91% accepted, 371 enrolled. In 2006, 1,063 master's, 287 other advanced degrees awarded. *Degree requirements:* For master's, thesis, internship/practicum. *Entrance requirements:* Additional exam requirements/recommendations for international students: Required—TOEFL. *Application deadline:* For fall admission, 10/3 priority date for domestic students; for spring admission, 2/13 priority date for domestic students. Applications are processed on a rolling basis. Application fee: $30. *Expenses:* Tuition: Full-time $10,935; part-time $405 per credit hour. One-time fee: $130 full-time. Tuition and fees vary according to degree level and program. *Financial support:* Teaching assistantships, career-related internships or fieldwork and Federal

Education—General

Cambridge College (continued)
Work-Study available. Financial award applicants required to submit FAFSA. *Faculty research:* Adult education, accelerated learning, mathematics education, brain compatible learning, special education and law. *Unit head:* Dr. Anthony DeMatteo, Dean, 617-873-0219, Fax: 617-349-3545. *Application contact:* Wendy D. Shattuck, Director of Graduate Admissions, 617-868-1000 Ext. 144, Fax: 617-349-3561, E-mail: admit@cambridgecollege.edu.

Cameron University, Office of Graduate Studies, Program in Education, Lawton, OK 73505-6377. Offers M Ed. *Accreditation:* NCATE. Part-time and evening/weekend programs available. *Faculty:* 13 full-time (9 women), 1 (woman) part-time/adjunct. *Students:* 13 full-time (11 women), 42 part-time (38 women); includes 11 minority (8 African Americans, 1 American Indian/Alaska Native, 1 Asian American or Pacific Islander, 1 Hispanic American). Average age 35. 35 applicants, 86% accepted. In 2006, 10 degrees awarded. *Degree requirements:* For master's, portfolio. *Entrance requirements:* Additional exam requirements/recommendations for international students: Required—TOEFL (minimum score 550 paper-based; 213 computer-based). *Application deadline:* Applications are processed on a rolling basis. Application fee: $15 ($35 for international students). Electronic applications accepted. *Expenses:* Tuition, state resident: full-time $2,479; part-time $138 per credit hour. Tuition, nonresident: full-time $5,976; part-time $332 per credit hour. Tuition and fees vary according to campus/location. *Financial support:* In 2006–07, 31 students received support. Federal Work-Study, scholarships/grants, and tuition waivers (partial) available. Support available to part-time students. Financial award application deadline: 4/15; financial award applicants required to submit FAFSA. *Faculty research:* Motivation, computer learning, special education mathematics, inquiry-based learning. *Unit head:* Claudia Edwards, MS Graduate Advisor, 580-581-7929, Fax: 580-581-2623, E-mail: cedwards@cameron.edu. *Application contact:* Teresa Enriquez, Graduate Admissions/Enrollment Coordinator, 580-581-2987, E-mail: teresae@cameron.edu.

Cameron University, Office of Graduate Studies, Program in Teaching, Lawton, OK 73505-6377. Offers MAT. *Accreditation:* NCATE. *Faculty:* 8 full-time (5 women), 2 part-time/adjunct (both women). *Students:* 29 full-time (17 women), 10 part-time (7 women); includes 5 minority (2 African Americans, 1 American Indian/Alaska Native, 2 Hispanic Americans). Average age 35. 21 applicants, 76% accepted. In 2006, 23 degrees awarded. *Degree requirements:* For master's, portfolio. *Entrance requirements:* Additional exam requirements/recommendations for international students: Required—TOEFL (minimum score 550 paper-based; 213 computer-based). *Application deadline:* Applications are processed on a rolling basis. Application fee: $15 ($35 for international students). Electronic applications accepted. *Expenses:* Tuition, state resident: full-time $2,479; part-time $138 per credit hour. Tuition, nonresident: full-time $5,976; part-time $332 per credit hour. Tuition and fees vary according to campus/location. *Financial support:* In 2006–07, 22 students received support. Federal Work-Study, scholarships/grants, and tuition waivers (partial) available. Support available to part-time students. Financial award application deadline: 4/15; financial award applicants required to submit FAFSA. *Faculty research:* Teacher retention/attrition, teacher education. Total annual research expenditures: $1,450. *Unit head:* Claudia Edwards, MS Graduate Advisor, 580-581-7929, Fax: 580-581-2623, E-mail: cedwards@cameron.edu. *Application contact:* Teresa Enriquez, Graduate Admissions/Enrollment Coordinator, 580-581-2987, E-mail: teresae@cameron.edu.

Campbellsville University, School of Education, Campbellsville, KY 42718-2799. Offers curriculum and instruction (MAE); special education (MASE). *Accreditation:* NCATE. Part-time and evening/weekend programs available. Postbaccalaureate distance learning degree programs offered (minimal on-campus study). *Faculty:* 5 full-time (2 women), 12 part-time/adjunct (7 women). *Students:* 365 full-time (230 women); includes 20 minority (14 African Americans, 1 Asian American or Pacific Islander, 5 Hispanic Americans), 1 international. Average age 31. 80 applicants, 99% accepted, 76 enrolled. In 2006, 110 degrees awarded. *Degree requirements:* For master's, thesis, research paper. *Entrance requirements:* For master's, GRE or PRAXIS, minimum undergraduate GPA of 2.75, teaching certificate, professional growth plan, letters of recommendation, disposition assessment, entrance interview. *Application deadline:* For fall admission, 6/1 priority date for domestic students, 5/1 priority date for international students; for spring admission, 11/1 priority date for domestic students, 10/1 priority date for international students. Applications are processed on a rolling basis. Application fee: $0. Electronic applications accepted. *Expenses:* Tuition: Full-time $6,570; part-time $365 per hour. Tuition and fees vary according to program. *Financial support:* In 2006–07, 250 students received support. Institutionally sponsored loans, scholarships/grants, and unspecified assistantships available. Support available to part-time students. Financial award application deadline: 6/1; financial award applicants required to submit FAFSA. *Faculty research:* Professional development, curriculum development, school governance, assessment, special education. *Unit head:* Dr. Brenda A. Priddy, Dean, 270-789-5344, Fax: 270-789-5206, E-mail: bapriddy@campbellsville.edu. *Application contact:* Karla Deaton, Assistant Director of Admissions, 270-789-5078, Fax: 270-789-5071, E-mail: redeaton@campbellsville.edu.

Campbell University, Graduate and Professional Programs, School of Education, Buies Creek, NC 27506. Offers administration (MSA); community counseling (MA); elementary education (M Ed); English education (M Ed); interdisciplinary studies (M Ed); mathematics education (M Ed); middle grades education (M Ed); physical education (M Ed); school counseling (M Ed); secondary education (M Ed); social science education (M Ed). *Accreditation:* NCATE. Part-time and evening/weekend programs available. *Faculty:* 14 full-time (9 women), 12 part-time/adjunct (7 women). *Students:* 27 full-time (25 women), 183 part-time (146 women); includes 30 minority (24 African Americans, 3 American Indian/Alaska Native, 3 Hispanic Americans), 1 international. Average age 31. 112 applicants, 74% accepted, 74 enrolled. In 2006, 65 degrees awarded. *Degree requirements:* For master's, comprehensive exam. *Entrance requirements:* For master's, GRE General Test, minimum GPA of 2.7. *Application deadline:* For fall admission, 8/1 priority date for domestic students; for spring admission, 1/2 priority date for domestic students. Applications are processed on a rolling basis. Application fee: $65. *Expenses:* Tuition: Part-time $380 per semester hour. *Financial support:* In 2006–07, 67 students received support. Career-related internships or fieldwork and Federal Work-Study available. Financial award application deadline: 4/15; financial award applicants required to submit FAFSA. *Faculty research:* Spiritual values and wellness issues in counseling, stress and professional burnout among counselors, thinking strategies, leadership, adaptive technology. *Unit head:* Dr. Karen P. Nery, Dean, 910-893-1630, Fax: 910-893-1999, E-mail: nery@campbell.edu. *Application contact:* James S. Farthing, Director of Graduate Admissions for Business and Education, 910-893-1200 Ext. 1318, Fax: 910-814-4718, E-mail: farthing@campbell.edu.

Canisius College, Graduate Division, School of Education and Human Services, Department of Graduate Education, Buffalo, NY 14208-1098. Offers business education (MS); childhood education (MS); college student personnel (MS); differentiated instruction (MS Ed); early childhood education (MS); education administration (MS); education of the deaf and hard of hearing (MS); general education (MS Ed); literacy education (MS Ed); reading education (MS Ed); secondary education (MS); special education (MS). *Accreditation:* NCATE. Part-time and evening/weekend programs available. *Faculty:* 13 full-time (12 women), 74 part-time/adjunct (44 women). *Students:* 377 full-time (267 women), 303 part-time (219 women); includes 43 minority (27 African Americans, 2 American Indian/Alaska Native, 6 Asian Americans or Pacific Islanders, 8 Hispanic Americans), 187 international. Average age 30. In 2006, 296 degrees awarded. Application fee: $25. *Expenses:* Tuition: Part-time $645 per credit hour. Required fees: $19 per credit hour. Tuition and fees vary according to program. *Financial support:* Research assistantships with full tuition reimbursements, career-related internships or fieldwork, institutionally sponsored loans, scholarships/grants, health care benefits, tuition waivers (full and partial), and unspecified assistantships available. *Faculty research:* Autism, Asperger's disease, private higher education, reading strategies. *Unit head:* Rev. Paul Nochelski, Chair of Graduate Education and Leadership, 716-888-3297, Fax: 716-888-3299. *Application contact:* James D. Bagwell, Director of Graduate Recruitment and Admissions, 716-888-2544, Fax: 716-888-3290, E-mail: bagwellj@canisius.edu.

Cape Breton University, School of Education, Health, and Wellness, Sydney, NS B1P 6L2, Canada. Offers educational counseling (Diploma); educational studies-arts education (Certificate); educational technology (Diploma). Part-time and evening/weekend programs available. Postbaccalaureate distance learning degree programs offered (no on-campus study). Electronic applications accepted.

Capella University, School of Education, Minneapolis, MN 55402. Offers college teaching (Certificate); curriculum and instruction (MS, PhD); education (MS); enrollment management (MS); instructional design for online learning (MS, PhD); k-12 studies in education (MS, PhD); leadership for higher education (MS, PhD); leadership in education administration (Certificate); leadership in educational administration (MS, PhD); postsecondary and adult education (MS, PhD); professional studies in education (MS, PhD); reading and literacy (MS); training and performance improvement (MS, PhD). Part-time and evening/weekend programs available. Postbaccalaureate distance learning degree programs offered (minimal on-campus study). Terminal master's awarded for partial completion of doctoral program. *Degree requirements:* For master's, integrative project, thesis optional; for doctorate, thesis/dissertation, comprehensive exam, registration. *Entrance requirements:* Additional exam requirements/recommendations for international students: Required—TOEFL (minimum score 550 paper-based; 213 computer-based), TWE (minimum score 4). Electronic applications accepted. *Faculty research:* Higher education administration, distance learning, adult education, training and curriculum design.

Cardinal Stritch University, College of Education, Milwaukee, WI 53217-3985. Offers MA, ME, MS, Ed D. *Accreditation:* NCATE. Part-time and evening/weekend programs available. *Degree requirements:* For master's, thesis (for some programs), comprehensive exam; for doctorate, thesis/dissertation, practica/field experience. *Entrance requirements:* For doctorate, minimum GPA of 3.5 in master's coursework, portfolio, interview, letters of recommendation (3).

Announcement: Cardinal Stritch University is known for innovative teacher education programs in initial teaching certification, reading, special education, instructional technology, professional development, and educational leadership. A doctoral program focuses on learning and service in the context of leadership, with an EdD or PhD strand. For more information, visit www.stritch.edu/education or call 800-347-8822, ext. 4042.

Caribbean University, Graduate School, Bayamón, PR 00960-0493. Offers accounting (MBA); administration and supervision (MA Ed); criminal justice (MA); curriculum and instruction (MA Ed); education (PhD); gerontology (MSN); human resources (MBA); museology, archiving and art history (MA Ed); neonatal pediatrics (MSN); physical education (MA Ed); special education (MA Ed). *Entrance requirements:* For master's, interview, minimum GPA of 2.5.

Carlow University, School of Education, Program in Educational Praxis, Pittsburgh, PA 15213-3165. Offers MA. Part-time and evening/weekend programs available. *Entrance requirements:* Additional exam requirements/recommendations for international students: Required—TOEFL. Electronic applications accepted.

Carnegie Mellon University, College of Humanities and Social Sciences, Center for Innovation in Learning, Pittsburgh, PA 15213-3891. Offers instructional science (PhD). *Faculty research:* Improvement of undergraduate education, teaching and learning at the college level.

Carroll College, Graduate Program in Education, Waukesha, WI 53186-5593. Offers education (M Ed); learning and teaching (M Ed). Part-time and evening/weekend programs available. *Faculty:* 7 full-time (4 women), 10 part-time/adjunct (8 women). *Students:* Average age 36. 80 applicants, 65% accepted, 20 enrolled. In 2006, 30 degrees awarded. *Degree requirements:* For master's, thesis. *Entrance requirements:* For master's, minimum undergraduate GPA of 2.5 in related field. Additional exam requirements/recommendations for international students: Required—TOEFL. *Application deadline:* For fall admission, 8/15 priority date for domestic students. Applications are processed on a rolling basis. Application fee: $0. Electronic applications accepted. *Expenses:* Tuition: Part-time $325 per credit. Part-time tuition and fees vary according to program. *Financial support:* In 2006–07, 18 students received support; fellowships available. Support available to part-time students. Financial award application deadline: 3/15; financial award applicants required to submit FAFSA. *Faculty research:* Qualitative research methods, whole language approaches to teaching, the writing process, multicultural education, gifted/talented learners. *Unit head:* Dr. Mary Ann Wisniewski, Director, 262-951-3944, Fax: 262-524-7139, E-mail: mwisniew@cc.edu. *Application contact:* Tina M. Wood, Non-Traditional Admission, 262-524-7518, Fax: 262-650-4851, E-mail: twood@cc.edu.

Carson-Newman College, Graduate Program in Education, Jefferson City, TN 37760. Offers curriculum and instruction (M Ed); elementary education (MAT); school counseling (M Ed); secondary education (MAT); teaching English as a second language (MATESL). *Accreditation:* NCATE. Part-time and evening/weekend programs available. *Faculty:* 5 full-time (2 women), 10 part-time/adjunct (3 women). *Students:* 77 full-time (60 women), 41 part-time (29 women); includes 2 minority (both African Americans), 27 international. Average age 32. 65 applicants, 97% accepted. In 2006, 64 degrees awarded. *Degree requirements:* For master's, thesis or alternative. *Entrance requirements:* For master's, NTE, minimum GPA of 3.0 in major, 2.5 overall. *Application deadline:* For fall admission, 7/15 priority date for domestic students. Applications are processed on a rolling basis. Application fee: $25 ($50 for international students). *Expenses:* Tuition: Part-time $270 per credit hour. *Financial support:* In 2006–07, 86 students received support. Federal Work-Study and unspecified assistantships available. Financial award application deadline: 4/1; financial award applicants required to submit FAFSA. *Unit head:* Dr. Jean Love, Chair, 865-471-3461. *Application contact:* Graduate Admissions and Services Adviser, 865-471-3460, Fax: 865-471-3875.

Carthage College, Division of Teacher Education, Kenosha, WI 53140. Offers classroom guidance and counseling (M Ed); creative arts (M Ed); gifted and talented children (M Ed); language arts (M Ed); modern language (M Ed); natural sciences (M Ed); reading (M Ed, Certificate); social sciences (M Ed); teacher leadership (M Ed). Part-time and evening/weekend programs available. *Degree requirements:* For master's, thesis optional. *Entrance requirements:* For master's, MAT, minimum B average, letters of reference.

Castleton State College, Division of Graduate Studies, Department of Education, Castleton, VT 05735. Offers curriculum and instruction (MA Ed); educational leadership (MA Ed, CAGS); language arts and reading (MA Ed, CAGS); special education (MA Ed, CAGS). Part-time and evening/weekend programs available. *Degree requirements:* For master's, thesis or alternative; for CAGS, publishable paper. *Entrance requirements:* For master's, GRE General Test, MAT, interview, minimum undergraduate GPA of 3.0; for CAGS, educational research, master's degree, minimum undergraduate GPA of 3.0. *Faculty research:* Assessment, narrative.

Catawba College, Program in Education, Salisbury, NC 28144-2488. Offers elementary education (M Ed). *Accreditation:* NCATE. Part-time and evening/weekend programs available. *Faculty:* 3 full-time (2 women), 2 part-time/adjunct (1 woman). In 2006, 3 degrees awarded. *Degree requirements:* For master's, project, practicum, and portfolio. *Entrance requirements:* For master's, NTE, PRAXIS, minimum undergraduate GPA of 3.0, valid teaching license. *Application deadline:* For fall admission, 8/1 priority date for domestic students; for winter admission, 12/1 priority date for domestic students; for spring admission, 5/1 priority date for domestic students. Applications are processed on a rolling basis. Application fee: $0. *Expenses:* Tuition: Part-time $130 per credit hour. *Financial support:* Scholarships/grants available. *Faculty research:* Integrated arts in elementary schools, professional development schools. *Unit head:* Dr. James K. Stringfield, Chair, Department of Teacher Education, 704-637-4461, Fax: 704-637-4732, E-mail: jstringf@catawba.edu. *Application contact:* Dr. Lou W. Kasias, Director, Graduate Program, 704-637-4462, Fax: 704-637-4732, E-mail: lakasias@catawba.edu.

The Catholic University of America, School of Arts and Sciences, Department of Education, Washington, DC 20064. Offers administration, curriculum, and policy studies (MA); Catholic school leadership (MA); counselor education (MA); educational administration (PhD); educational psychology (PhD); English as a second language (MA); learning and instruction (MA); policy studies (PhD); teacher education (MA). *Accreditation:* NCATE. Part-time programs available.

Faculty: 11 full-time (8 women), 3 part-time/adjunct (2 women). *Students:* 11 full-time (8 women), 52 part-time (34 women); includes 13 minority (9 African Americans, 1 Asian American or Pacific Islander, 3 Hispanic Americans), 2 international. Average age 35. 67 applicants, 55% accepted, 13 enrolled. In 2006, 19 master's, 2 doctorates awarded. *Degree requirements:* For master's, thesis or alternative, comprehensive exam; for doctorate, thesis/dissertation, comprehensive exam. *Entrance requirements:* For master's and doctorate, GRE General Test or MAT, 3 letters of recommendation. Additional exam requirements/recommendations for international students: Required—TOEFL (minimum score 580 paper-based; 237 computer-based). *Application deadline:* For fall admission, 2/1 priority date for domestic students; for spring admission, 11/15 priority date for domestic students. Applications are processed on a rolling basis. Application fee: $55. Electronic applications accepted. *Expenses:* Tuition: Full-time $27,700; part-time $1,045 per credit hour. Required fees: $1,290. Part-time tuition and fees vary according to campus/location and program. *Financial support:* Research assistantships, teaching assistantships, career-related internships or fieldwork, Federal Work-Study, scholarships/grants, tuition waivers (full and partial), and unspecified assistantships available. Support available to part-time students. Financial award application deadline: 2/1; financial award applicants required to submit FAFSA. *Faculty research:* Catholic school issues, reflective teaching, cognitive psychology, urban education. *Unit head:* Dr. Merylann Schuttloffel, Chair, 202-319-5805, Fax: 202-319-5815, E-mail: schuttloffel@cua.edu.

Cedar Crest College, Department of Education, Allentown, PA 18104-6196. Offers M Ed. *Entrance requirements:* For master's, GRE or MAT.

See Close-Up on page 867.

Cedarville University, Graduate Programs, Cedarville, OH 45314-0601. Offers M Ed. Part-time and evening/weekend programs available. *Faculty:* 13 part-time/adjunct (2 women). *Students:* Average age 33. 16 applicants, 94% accepted, 15 enrolled. In 2006, 3 degrees awarded. *Degree requirements:* For master's, thesis, registration. *Entrance requirements:* For master's, GRE, 2 professional recommendations. Additional exam requirements/recommendations for international students: Required—TOEFL (minimum score 550 paper-based; 213 computer-based). *Application deadline:* Applications are processed on a rolling basis. Application fee: $30. Electronic applications accepted. *Expenses:* Tuition: Part-time $298 per hour. *Financial support:* Scholarships/grants available. Support available to part-time students. Financial award applicants required to submit FAFSA. *Unit head:* Bruce Traeger, Director of Graduate Recruitment, 888-CEDARVILLE, Fax: 937-66-7575, E-mail: traegerb@cedarville.edu. *Application contact:* Roscoe Smith, Admissions Director, 937-766-7700, Fax: 937-766-7575, E-mail: smithr@cedarville.edu.

Centenary College, Program in Education, Hackettstown, NJ 07840-2100. Offers instructional leadership (MA); special education (MA). Part-time and evening/weekend programs available. Postbaccalaureate distance learning degree programs offered (minimal on-campus study). *Degree requirements:* For master's, thesis. *Entrance requirements:* For master's, interview, minimum undergraduate GPA of 2.8.

Centenary College of Louisiana, Graduate Programs, Department of Education, Shreveport, LA 71104. Offers administration (M Ed); elementary education (MAT); secondary education (MAT); supervision of instruction (M Ed). Part-time and evening/weekend programs available. *Degree requirements:* For master's, comprehensive exam. *Entrance requirements:* For master's, GRE General Test (M Ed), PRAXIS I and PRAXIS II (MAT), teacher certification (M Ed), minimum GPA of 2.5. Expenses: Contact institution. *Faculty research:* Teachers as advocates for teachers, portfolio assessment, disabled readers.

Central Connecticut State University, School of Graduate Studies, School of Education and Professional Studies, New Britain, CT 06050-4010. Offers MS, Ed D, Certificate, Sixth Year Certificate. *Accreditation:* NCATE. Part-time and evening/weekend programs available. *Faculty:* 63 full-time (38 women), 76 part-time/adjunct (53 women). *Students:* 212 full-time (163 women), 927 part-time (709 women); includes 106 minority (49 African Americans, 3 American Indian/Alaska Native, 6 Asian Americans or Pacific Islanders, 48 Hispanic Americans), 9 international. Average age 33. 635 applicants, 62% accepted, 283 enrolled. In 2006, 404 master's, 18 doctorates, 75 other advanced degrees awarded. *Degree requirements:* For master's, thesis or alternative; for other advanced degree, qualifying exam. *Entrance requirements:* For master's, minimum GPA of 2.7. Additional exam requirements/recommendations for international students: Required—TOEFL. *Application deadline:* For fall admission, 7/1 for domestic students; for spring admission, 12/1 for domestic students. Applications are processed on a rolling basis. Application fee: $50. Electronic applications accepted. *Expenses:* Tuition, area resident: Full-time $3,970; part-time $380 per credit. Tuition, state resident: full-time $5,955; part-time $380 per credit. Tuition, nonresident: full-time $11,061; part-time $380 per credit. Required fees: $3,189. One-time fee: $62 part-time. Tuition and fees vary according to degree level and program. *Financial support:* In 2006–07, 32 students received support, including 19 research assistantships (averaging $4,800 per year); career-related internships or fieldwork, Federal Work-Study, scholarships/grants, and unspecified assistantships also available. Support available to part-time students. Financial award application deadline: 3/1; financial award applicants required to submit FAFSA. *Unit head:* Dr. Mitchell Sakofs, Acting Dean, 860-832-2100.

Central Methodist University, College of Graduate and Extended Studies, Fayette, MO 65248-1198. Offers counseling (MS); education (M Ed). Part-time and evening/weekend programs available. Postbaccalaureate distance learning degree programs offered (no on-campus study). *Degree requirements:* For master's, thesis, registration. *Entrance requirements:* For master's, GRE General Test, minimum GPA of 2.75. Electronic applications accepted.

Central Michigan University, Central Michigan University Off-Campus Programs, Program in Education, Mount Pleasant, MI 48859. Offers education (MA); educational technology (MA); reading and literacy (MA). Part-time and evening/weekend programs available. *Entrance requirements:* For master's, minimum GPA of 2.7 in major. Additional exam requirements/recommendations for international students: Required—TOEFL. *Application deadline:* Applications are processed on a rolling basis. Application fee: $50. Electronic applications accepted. *Financial support:* Scholarships/grants available. Support available to part-time students. *Unit head:* Jennifer Cochran, Director, 989-774-2584, E-mail: jennifer.cochran@cmich.edu. *Application contact:* 877-268-4636, E-mail: cmuoffcampus@cmich.edu.

Central Michigan University, College of Graduate Studies, College of Education and Human Services, Mount Pleasant, MI 48859. Offers MA, MS, Ed D, Ed S. *Accreditation:* NCATE. *Degree requirements:* For master's, thesis or alternative, registration; for Ed S, thesis or alternative. *Entrance requirements:* For doctorate, GRE or MAT, master's degree in education, minimum GPA of 3.5, 3 years of full-time administrative experience; for Ed S, Michigan teaching certificate or equivalent.

Central State University, Program in Education, Wilberforce, OH 45384. Offers educational technology (M Ed); leadership (M Ed); literacy (M Ed). Part-time and evening/weekend programs available. *Degree requirements:* For master's, thesis or alternative. *Entrance requirements:* For master's, GRE.

Central Washington University, Graduate Studies, Research and Continuing Education, College of Education and Professional Studies, Department of Education, Ellensburg, WA 98926. Offers educational administration (M Ed); master teacher (M Ed); reading education (M Ed); special education (M Ed). *Application deadline:* Applications are processed on a rolling basis. Electronic applications accepted. *Expenses:* Tuition, state resident: full-time $6,312. Tuition, nonresident: full-time $14,112. Tuition and fees vary according to course load and degree level. *Unit head:* Dr. Steven Schmitz, Chair, 509-963-1461, Fax: 509-963-1162. *Application contact:* Justine Eason, Admissions Program Coordinator, 509-963-3103, Fax: 509-963-1799, E-mail: masters@cwu.edu.

Chadron State College, School of Professional and Graduate Studies, Department of Education, Chadron, NE 69337. Offers business (MA Ed); community counseling (MA Ed); educational administration (MS Ed, Sp Ed); elementary education (MS Ed); history (MA Ed); language and literature (MA Ed); secondary administration (MS Ed); secondary education (MS Ed). *Accreditation:* NCATE. Part-time and evening/weekend programs available. Postbaccalaureate distance learning degree programs offered. *Degree requirements:* For master's, thesis optional. *Entrance requirements:* For master's, GRE General Test, GRE Writing Test, minimum GPA of 2.75 or 12 graduate hours at CSC with minimum GPA of 3.25. Additional exam requirements/recommendations for international students: Required—TOEFL. Electronic applications accepted. *Faculty research:* Rural education, technology, mental health.

Chaminade University of Honolulu, Graduate Services, Program in Education, Honolulu, HI 96816-1578. Offers social science via peace education (M Ed). Part-time and evening/weekend programs available. Postbaccalaureate distance learning degree programs offered (minimal on-campus study). *Faculty:* 7 full-time (6 women), 19 part-time/adjunct (17 women). *Students:* 197 full-time (148 women), 127 part-time (97 women); includes 225 minority (19 African Americans, 1 American Indian/Alaska Native, 191 Asian Americans or Pacific Islanders, 14 Hispanic Americans), 2 international. Average age 35. 236 applicants, 81% accepted. In 2006, 102 degrees awarded. *Degree requirements:* For master's, thesis or alternative. *Entrance requirements:* For master's, minimum GPA of 2.75. Additional exam requirements/recommendations for international students: Required—TOEFL (minimum score 550 paper-based). *Application deadline:* For fall admission, 9/15 priority date for domestic students; for winter admission, 12/15 priority date for domestic students; for spring admission, 3/1 priority date for domestic students. Applications are processed on a rolling basis. Application fee: $50. *Expenses:* Tuition: Part-time $465 per credit. *Financial support:* In 2006–07, 172 students received support. Career-related internships or fieldwork, Federal Work-Study, institutionally sponsored loans, scholarships/grants, and tuition waivers (partial) available. Support available to part-time students. Financial award application deadline: 3/1; financial award applicants required to submit FAFSA. *Faculty research:* Peace and curriculum education. *Unit head:* Dr. David Jelinek, Dean, 808-440-4251, Fax: 808-739-4607. *Application contact:* Steve Wheeler, Graduate Services Representative, 808-739-4664, Fax: 808-739-8329, E-mail: swheeler@chaminade.edu.

Chapman University, Graduate Studies, School of Education, Orange, CA 92866. Offers MA, PhD, Ed S. Part-time and evening/weekend programs available. *Faculty:* 16 full-time (11 women), 25 part-time/adjunct (14 women). *Students:* 174 full-time (142 women), 194 part-time (151 women); includes 101 minority (6 African Americans, 2 American Indian/Alaska Native, 27 Asian Americans or Pacific Islanders, 66 Hispanic Americans), 2 international. Average age 29. 202 applicants, 55% accepted, 83 enrolled. In 2006, 150 degrees awarded. *Degree requirements:* For master's, thesis optional. *Entrance requirements:* For master's, GRE General Test, California Basic Educational Skills Test, minimum undergraduate GPA of 2.5. Additional exam requirements/recommendations for international students: Required—TOEFL (minimum score 550 paper-based). *Application deadline:* Applications are processed on a rolling basis. Application fee: $55. Electronic applications accepted. *Expenses:* Contact institution. *Financial support:* In 2006–07, 328 students received support, including 41 fellowships (averaging $1,927 per year); Federal Work-Study also available. Financial award application deadline: 6/30; financial award applicants required to submit FAFSA. *Unit head:* Dr. Donald Cardinal, Dean, 714-997-6781, E-mail: cardinal@chapman.edu. *Application contact:* Rika Judd, Graduate Admission Counselor, 714-997-6786, Fax: 714-997-6713, E-mail: rjudd@chapman.edu.

Charleston Southern University, Programs in Education, Charleston, SC 29423-8087. Offers administration and supervision (M Ed), including elementary, secondary; elementary education (M Ed); English (MAT); science (MAT); secondary education (M Ed); social studies (MAT). *Accreditation:* NCATE. Part-time and evening/weekend programs available. *Degree requirements:* For master's, thesis optional. *Entrance requirements:* For master's, GRE or MAT. Expenses: Contact institution. *Faculty research:* Economic education, multicultural education, restructuring teacher education, participation in mathematics and science by minorities and women, at-risk children.

Chatham University, Program in Education, Pittsburgh, PA 15232-2826. Offers early childhood education (MAT); elementary education (MAT); English—secondary (MAT); environmental education (K-12) (MAT); secondary art (MAT); secondary biology education (MAT); secondary chemistry education (MAT); secondary English education (MAT); secondary math education (MAT); secondary physics education (MAT); secondary social studies education (MAT); special education (MAT). *Students:* 60 full-time (43 women), 23 part-time (22 women). Average age 29. 48 applicants, 77% accepted, 32 enrolled. In 2006, 59 degrees awarded. *Degree requirements:* For master's, thesis, teaching experience. *Entrance requirements:* For master's, PRAXIS I, minimum GPA of 3.0, sample of written work, recommendation letters. Additional exam requirements/recommendations for international students: Required—TOEFL (minimum score 600 paper-based; 250 computer-based; 100 iBT); Recommended—IELTS (minimum score 7), TWE (minimum score 5). *Application deadline:* For fall admission, 5/1 priority date for domestic and international students; for winter admission, 10/1 priority date for domestic and international students. Applications are processed on a rolling basis. Application fee: $45. Electronic applications accepted. *Financial support:* Career-related internships or fieldwork available. Financial award applicants required to submit FAFSA. *Faculty research:* Gifted education, environmental education, technology in education, writing as learning, class size and achievement. *Unit head:* Dr. Wendy Weiner, Director, 412-365-1146, Fax: 412-365-1505, E-mail: wweiner@chatham.edu. *Application contact:* 412-365-1825, Fax: 412-365-1609, E-mail: admissions@chatham.edu.

Chestnut Hill College, School of Graduate Studies, Department of Education, Philadelphia, PA 19118-2693. Offers early childhood education (M Ed); educational leadership (M Ed); elementary education (M Ed); secondary education (M Ed). Part-time and evening/weekend programs available. *Faculty:* 33 part-time/adjunct (24 women). *Students:* 43 full-time (33 women), 186 part-time (159 women); includes 39 minority (26 African Americans, 10 Asian Americans or Pacific Islanders, 3 Hispanic Americans). Average age 30. In 2006, 52 degrees awarded. *Degree requirements:* For master's, thesis optional. *Entrance requirements:* For master's, writing sample. Additional exam requirements/recommendations for international students: Required—TOEFL (minimum score 500 paper-based). *Application deadline:* For fall admission, 7/15 priority date for domestic students, 7/15 for international students; for spring admission, 12/15 priority date for domestic students, 12/15 for international students. Applications are processed on a rolling basis. Application fee: $50. *Expenses:* Tuition: Part-time $470 per credit hour. Required fees: $30 per semester. Tuition and fees vary according to degree level. *Financial support:* Institutionally sponsored loans available. Financial award application deadline: 7/15; financial award applicants required to submit FAFSA. *Faculty research:* Effects of media on learning, use of online tests and virtual classrooms, emerging literacy, school reform, principal effectiveness. *Unit head:* Dr. Carol Pate, Chair, 215-248-7127, E-mail: cmpate@chc.edu. *Application contact:* Jayne Mashett, Director of Graduate Admissions, 215-248-7020, Fax: 215-248-7161, E-mail: mashettj@chc.edu.

Cheyney University of Pennsylvania, School of Education, Cheyney, PA 19319-0200. Offers M Ed, MAT, MS, Certificate. *Accreditation:* NCATE. Part-time and evening/weekend programs available. *Degree requirements:* For master's and Certificate, thesis or alternative. *Entrance requirements:* For master's and Certificate, GRE General Test, MAT, minimum GPA of 2.75. Electronic applications accepted. *Faculty research:* Teacher motivation, critical thinking.

Chicago State University, School of Graduate and Professional Studies, College of Education, Chicago, IL 60628. Offers M Ed, MA, MAT, MS Ed, Ed D. *Accreditation:* NCATE. Part-time programs available. *Degree requirements:* For master's, all theses are optional, thesis optional. *Entrance requirements:* For master's, minimum GPA of 2.75.

Christian Brothers University, Graduate Programs, School of Arts, Memphis, TN 38104-5581. Offers Catholic studies (MACS); curriculum and instruction (M Ed); educational leadership (MSEL); teacher-leadership (M Ed); teaching (MAT). Part-time and evening/weekend

Education—General

Christian Brothers University (continued)
programs available. *Faculty:* 6 full-time (4 women), 11 part-time/adjunct (5 women). *Students:* 47 full-time (38 women), 134 part-time (104 women); includes 70 minority (68 African Americans, 1 Asian American or Pacific Islander, 1 Hispanic American), 3 international. Average age 35. In 2006, 57 degrees awarded. *Entrance requirements:* For master's, GRE, MAT. *Application deadline:* Applications are processed on a rolling basis. Application fee: $25. *Expenses:* Contact institution. *Financial support:* Institutionally sponsored loans available. Support available to part-time students. *Unit head:* Dr. Marins Carriere, Dean, 901-321-3366, E-mail: mcarrier@cbu.edu. *Application contact:* Dr. Talana L. Vogel, Director, 901-321-4101, Fax: 901-321-3408, E-mail: tvogel@cbu.edu.

Christopher Newport University, Graduate Studies, Department of Teacher Preparation, Newport News, VA 23606-2998. Offers art (PK-12) (MAT); biology (6-12) (MAT); computer science (6-12) (MAT); elementary (PK-6) (MAT); English (6-12) (MAT); French (PK-12) (MAT); history (6-12) (MAT); history and social science (MAT); mathematics (6-12) (MAT); music (PK-12) (MAT), including choral, instrumental; physics (6-12) (MAT); Spanish (PK-12) (MAT); theater (PK-12) (MAT). Part-time and evening/weekend programs available. *Degree requirements:* For master's, thesis or alternative, comprehensive exam. *Entrance requirements:* For master's, PRAXIS I, minimum GPA of 3.0. Electronic applications accepted. *Faculty research:* Early literacy development, instructional innovations, professional teaching standards, multicultural issues, aesthetic education.

The Citadel, The Military College of South Carolina, College of Graduate and Professional Studies, School of Education, Charleston, SC 29409. Offers M Ed, MA, MAT, Ed S. *Accreditation:* NCATE. Part-time and evening/weekend programs available. *Students:* 89 full-time (70 women), 281 part-time (190 women); includes 75 minority (70 African Americans, 4 Asian Americans or Pacific Islanders, 1 Hispanic American), 2 international. Average age 30. In 2006, 119 master's, 18 other advanced degrees awarded. *Entrance requirements:* For master's, GRE General Test, MAT, or 12 hours of graduate course work with a minimum GPA of 3.0. Additional exam requirements/recommendations for international students: Required—TOEFL (minimum score 550 paper-based; 213 computer-based). *Application deadline:* For fall admission, 6/1 for domestic students; for spring admission, 3/1 for domestic students. Applications are processed on a rolling basis. Application fee: $30. *Expenses:* Tuition, state resident: part-time $259 per credit hour. Tuition, nonresident: part-time $482 per credit hour. *Financial support:* Fellowships available. Financial award application deadline: 7/1; financial award applicants required to submit FAFSA. *Unit head:* Dr. Tony Johnson, Head, 843-953-5097, Fax: 843-953-7258, E-mail: tony.johnson@citadel.edu. *Application contact:* Dr. Raymond S. Jones, Associate Dean, College of Graduate and Professional Studies, 843-953-5089, Fax: 843-953-7630, E-mail: ray.jones@citadel.edu.

City College of the City University of New York, Graduate School, School of Education, New York, NY 10031-9198. Offers MA, MS, AC. *Accreditation:* NCATE. Part-time and evening/weekend programs available. *Students:* 1,325. 576 applicants, 94% accepted, 460 enrolled. In 2006, 451 degrees awarded. *Entrance requirements:* For master's, Liberal Arts and Sciences Test (LAST), Content Specialty Test (CST). Additional exam requirements/recommendations for international students: Required—TOEFL. *Application deadline:* For fall admission, 3/15 for domestic students; for spring admission, 10/15 for domestic students. Application fee: $125. *Financial support:* Fellowships, research assistantships, teaching assistantships, career-related internships or fieldwork, Federal Work-Study, and tuition waivers (full and partial) available. Support available to part-time students. *Unit head:* Dr. Alfred Posamentier, Dean, 212-650-5354. *Application contact:* Stacia Pusey, Graduate Admissions Adviser-Education, 212-650-5345, E-mail: spusey@ccny.cuny.edu.

City University, Graduate Division, Gordon Albright School of Education, Bellevue, WA 98005. Offers curriculum and instruction (M Ed); educational leadership (M Ed); educational leadership: principal certification (M Ed, Certificate); educational leadership: principal/program administrator certification (Certificate); educational leadership: program administrator certification (M Ed, Certificate); guidance and counseling (M Ed, Certificate); integrated arts and performance learning (M Ed); professional certification-teachers (Certificate); reading (Certificate); reading and literacy (M Ed); reading. literacy, and ESL/ELL (M Ed); teacher certification (MIT); technology, curriculum and instruction (M Ed). Part-time and evening/weekend programs available. Postbaccalaureate distance learning degree programs offered (no on-campus study). *Entrance requirements:* Additional exam requirements/recommendations for international students: Required—TOEFL (minimum score 540 paper-based; 207 computer-based); Recommended—IELTS. Electronic applications accepted.

Claflin University, Graduate Programs, Orangeburg, SC 29115. Offers biotechnology (MS); business administration (MBA); educational studies (M Ed). *Entrance requirements:* For master's, GRE, minimum GPA of 3.0, 2 letters of recommendation. Application fee: $40 ($55 for international students).

Claremont Graduate University, Graduate Programs, School of Educational Studies, Claremont, CA 91711-6160. Offers Africana education (Certificate); education policy issues (MA, PhD); higher education (PhD); higher education administration (MA); human development (MA, PhD); public school administration (MA, PhD); teacher education (MA, PhD); teaching and learning (MA, PhD); urban education administration (MA, PhD); MBA/PhD. Part-time programs available. *Faculty:* 15 full-time (9 women), 11 part-time/adjunct (9 women). *Students:* 236 full-time (155 women), 168 part-time (117 women); includes 177 minority (34 African Americans, 2 American Indian/Alaska Native, 43 Asian Americans or Pacific Islanders, 98 Hispanic Americans), 7 international. Average age 38. In 2006, 90 master's, 20 doctorates awarded. Terminal master's awarded for partial completion of doctoral program. *Degree requirements:* For master's, thesis or alternative, comprehensive exam (for some programs); for doctorate, thesis/dissertation, comprehensive exam. *Entrance requirements:* For master's and doctorate, GRE General Test. *Application deadline:* For fall admission, 2/15 priority date for domestic students. Applications are processed on a rolling basis. Electronic applications accepted. *Financial support:* Fellowships, research assistantships, Federal Work-Study and institutionally sponsored loans available. Support available to part-time students. Financial award application deadline: 2/15; financial award applicants required to submit FAFSA. *Faculty research:* Education administration, K–12 and higher education, multicultural education, education policy, diversity in higher education, faculty issues. *Unit head:* Philip H. Dreyer, Dean, 909-621-8075, Fax: 909-621-8734, E-mail: philip.dreyer@cgu.edu. *Application contact:* Cece Gaddy, Administrative Director, 909-621-8317, Fax: 909-621-8734, E-mail: cece.gaddy@cgu.edu.

Clarion University of Pennsylvania, Office of Research and Graduate Studies, College of Education and Human Services, Clarion, PA 16214. Offers M Ed, MS, MSLS, CAS. *Accreditation:* NCATE. Part-time programs available. *Students:* 387. *Degree requirements:* For master's, thesis or alternative. *Entrance requirements:* For master's, minimum QPA of 3.0. *Application deadline:* Applications are processed on a rolling basis. *Expenses:* Tuition, state resident: part-time $336 per credit. Tuition, nonresident: part-time $538 per credit. *Financial support:* Research assistantships with full and partial tuition reimbursements, career-related internships or fieldwork available. Support available to part-time students. Financial award application deadline: 3/1. *Unit head:* Dr. Nancy Sayre, Interim Dean, 814-393-2146, Fax: 814-393-2446, E-mail: nsayre@clarion.edu.

Clark Atlanta University, School of Education, Atlanta, GA 30314. Offers MA, Ed D, PhD, Ed S. *Accreditation:* NCATE. Part-time and evening/weekend programs available. *Degree requirements:* For master's, one foreign language, thesis; for doctorate, thesis/dissertation. *Entrance requirements:* For master's, GRE General Test, minimum undergraduate GPA of 2.5; for doctorate, GRE General Test, minimum graduate GPA of 3.0.

Clarke College, Program in Education, Dubuque, IA 52001-3198. Offers early childhood/special education (MA); educational administration: elementary and secondary (MA); educational media: elementary and secondary (MA); multi-categorical resource K–12 (MA); multidisciplinary studies (MA); reading: elementary (MA); technology in education (MA). Part-time and evening/weekend programs available. Postbaccalaureate distance learning degree programs offered (minimal on-campus study). *Degree requirements:* For master's, thesis optional. *Entrance requirements:* For master's, GRE General Test or MAT, minimum GPA of 2.75. Electronic applications accepted.

Clark University, Graduate School, Department of Education, Worcester, MA 01610-1477. Offers MA Ed. *Faculty:* 11 full-time (7 women), 8 part-time/adjunct (5 women). *Students:* 33 full-time (25 women), 4 part-time (all women). Average age 25. 48 applicants, 77% accepted, 36 enrolled. In 2006, 40 degrees awarded. *Degree requirements:* For master's, thesis or alternative, oral exam. *Entrance requirements:* For master's, GRE General Test, minimum GPA of 3.0, professional experience. Additional exam requirements/recommendations for international students: Required—TOEFL. *Application deadline:* For fall admission, 2/15 priority date for domestic students. Applications are processed on a rolling basis. Application fee: $50. *Financial support:* Fellowships with full and partial tuition reimbursements, research assistantships with full and partial tuition reimbursements, teaching assistantships with full and partial tuition reimbursements, institutionally sponsored loans and tuition waivers (partial) available. Financial award application deadline: 5/1. *Faculty research:* Developmental learning, instructional theory, educational program management, special education, urban education. Total annual research expenditures: $418,000. *Unit head:* Dr. Thomas DelPrete, Chair, 508-793-7222. *Application contact:* Marlene Shepard, Program Coordinator, 508-793-7222, Fax: 508-793-8864, E-mail: education@clarku.edu.

Clemson University, Graduate School, College of Health, Education, and Human Development, School of Education, Clemson, SC 29634. Offers administration and supervision (M Ed, Ed S); counselor education (M Ed), including community counseling, school counseling, student affairs; curriculum and instruction (PhD); educational leadership (M Ed, PhD); elementary education (M Ed); human resource development (MHRD); middle grades education (MAT); reading (M Ed); secondary education (M Ed), including English, mathematics, natural sciences; special education (M Ed). Part-time programs available. *Faculty:* 50 full-time (34 women), 10 part-time/adjunct (6 women). *Students:* 230 full-time (165 women), 358 part-time (250 women); includes 67 minority (54 African Americans, 3 American Indian/Alaska Native, 2 Asian Americans or Pacific Islanders, 8 Hispanic Americans), 12 international. 280 applicants, 53% accepted, 108 enrolled. In 2006, 209 master's, 16 doctorates, 17 other advanced degrees awarded. *Degree requirements:* For doctorate, thesis/dissertation. *Entrance requirements:* For doctorate, GRE General Test; for Ed S, GRE General Test or MAT, 1 year of teaching experience. Additional exam requirements/recommendations for international students: Required—TOEFL. Application fee: $50. *Expenses:* Tuition, state resident: full-time $8,812; part-time $450 per hour. Tuition, nonresident: full-time $18,036; part-time $760 per hour. Required fees: $474; $5 per term. *Financial support:* Research assistantships, teaching assistantships, career-related internships or fieldwork, Federal Work-Study, tuition waivers (full), and stipends available. Support available to part-time students. Financial award application deadline: 6/1; financial award applicants required to submit FAFSA. *Unit head:* Dr. Nancy Dunlap, Head, 864-656-4444.

Cleveland State University, College of Graduate Studies, College of Education and Human Services, Cleveland, OH 44115. Offers M Ed, MSN, PhD, Ed S, MSN/MBA. *Accreditation:* NCATE. Part-time and evening/weekend programs available. Postbaccalaureate distance learning degree programs offered (minimal on-campus study). *Faculty:* 63 full-time (38 women), 16 part-time/adjunct (5 women). *Students:* 240 full-time (182 women), 1,742 part-time (1,365 women); includes 445 minority (390 African Americans, 1 American Indian/Alaska Native, 13 Asian Americans or Pacific Islanders, 41 Hispanic Americans), 16 international. Average age 34. 1,676 applicants, 40% accepted, 405 enrolled. In 2006, 497 master's, 9 doctorates, 27 other advanced degrees awarded. *Degree requirements:* For master's, thesis optional; for doctorate, one foreign language, thesis/dissertation, comprehensive exam, registration; for Ed S, internship, thesis optional. *Entrance requirements:* For master's, GRE General Test or MAT, minimum undergraduate GPA of 2.75; for doctorate, GRE General Test, minimum graduate GPA of 3.25; for Ed S, GRE General Test or MAT, master's degree, minimum graduate GPA of 3.0. Additional exam requirements/recommendations for international students: Required—TOEFL (minimum score 525 paper-based; 197 computer-based), IELTS (minimum score 6). *Application deadline:* For fall admission, 7/18 priority date for domestic students, 5/15 for international students; for spring admission, 12/5 priority date for domestic students, 11/1 for international students. Applications are processed on a rolling basis. Application fee: $30. Electronic applications accepted. *Financial support:* In 2006–07, 42 students received support, including 13 research assistantships with full tuition reimbursements available (averaging $6,960 per year), 2 teaching assistantships with full tuition reimbursements available (averaging $7,800 per year); career-related internships or fieldwork, Federal Work-Study, scholarships/grants, tuition waivers (partial), and unspecified assistantships also available. Support available to part-time students. Financial award application deadline: 8/1; financial award applicants required to submit FAFSA. *Faculty research:* Equity issues (race, ethnicity, gender, and socioeconomics), educational developmental consequences for special needs of urban populations, urban educational programming, adult learning and development, urban educational leadership. Total annual research expenditures: $12.3 million. *Unit head:* Dr. James A. McLoughlin, Dean, 216-687-3737, Fax: 216-687-5415, E-mail: j.mcloughlin@csuohio.edu.

Coastal Carolina University, College of Education, Conway, SC 29528-6054. Offers early childhood education (M Ed); education (MAT); elementary education (M Ed); secondary education (M Ed). *Accreditation:* NCATE. Part-time and evening/weekend programs available. *Faculty:* 8 full-time (4 women), 16 part-time/adjunct (10 women). *Students:* 48 full-time (31 women), 45 part-time (33 women); includes 8 minority (6 African Americans, 2 Asian Americans or Pacific Islanders). Average age 30. In 2006, 70 degrees awarded. *Degree requirements:* For master's, comprehensive exam. *Entrance requirements:* For master's, GRE General Test, MAT, 2 letters of recommendation, copy of teaching credential. Additional exam requirements/recommendations for international students: Required—TOEFL. *Application deadline:* For fall admission, 8/15 priority date for domestic students. Applications are processed on a rolling basis. Application fee: $45. Electronic applications accepted. *Expenses:* Tuition, state resident: full-time $7,920; part-time $330 per credit hour. Tuition, nonresident: full-time $9,600; part-time $400 per credit hour. Required fees: $80; $40 per term. *Financial support:* Fellowships, research assistantships, unspecified assistantships available. Support available to part-time students. Financial award application deadline: 4/1; financial award applicants required to submit FAFSA. *Unit head:* Dr. Gilbert H. Hunt, Dean, 843-349-2607, Fax: 843-349-2332, E-mail: hunt@coastal.edu. *Application contact:* Dr. Judy W. Vogt, Vice President, Enrollment Services, 843-349-2037, Fax: 843-349-2127, E-mail: jvogt@coastal.edu.

Coe College, Department of Education, Cedar Rapids, IA 52402-5092. Offers MAT. Part-time programs available. *Entrance requirements:* For master's, minimum undergraduate GPA of 2.75, letters of reference. *Faculty research:* Math education, international and multicultural education.

College Misericordia, College of Professional Studies and Social Sciences, Program in Education/Curriculum, Dallas, PA 18612-1098. Offers MS. Part-time and evening/weekend programs available. *Faculty:* 10 part-time/adjunct (4 women). *Students:* Average age 36. 8 applicants, 88% accepted, 7 enrolled. In 2006, 3 degrees awarded. *Degree requirements:* For master's, thesis or alternative. *Entrance requirements:* For master's, GRE General Test or MAT, minimum GPA of 3.0. *Application deadline:* For fall admission, 8/1 priority date for domestic students. Applications are processed on a rolling basis. Application fee: $25. Electronic applications accepted. *Expenses:* Tuition: Full-time $19,800; part-time $495 per credit. Required fees: $1,060. *Financial support:* Scholarships/grants available. Support available to part-time students. Financial award application deadline: 6/30; financial award applicants required to submit FAFSA. *Unit head:* Tom O'Neill, Dean of Adult and Continuing Education, 570-674-6331, E-mail: toneill@misericordia.edu. *Application contact:* Larree Brown, Coordinator of

Part-time Undergraduate and Graduate Programs, 570-674-6451, Fax: 570-674-6232, E-mail: lbrown@misericordia.edu.

College of Charleston, Graduate School, School of Education, Charleston, SC 29424-0001. Offers M Ed, MAT, Certificate. *Accreditation:* NCATE. Part-time and evening/weekend programs available. *Degree requirements:* For master's, thesis or alternative, written qualifying exam, student teaching experience (MAT). *Entrance requirements:* For master's, GRE, MAT, or NTE; South Carolina Education Entrance Exam (MAT), teaching certificate (M Ed). Additional exam requirements/recommendations for international students: Required—TOEFL. Electronic applications accepted. *Faculty research:* Computer-assisted instruction, higher education, faculty development, teaching study skills to college students.

College of Mount St. Joseph, Graduate Education Program, Cincinnati, OH 45233-1670. Offers adolescent young adult education (MA); art (MA); inclusive early childhood education (MA); instructional leadership (MA); middle childhood education (MA); multicultural special education (MA); music (MA); reading (MA). *Accreditation:* Teacher Education Accreditation Council. Part-time and evening/weekend programs available. Postbaccalaureate distance learning degree programs offered (minimal on-campus study). *Faculty:* 22 full-time (14 women), 11 part-time/adjunct (6 women). *Students:* 68 full-time (54 women), 115 part-time (96 women); includes 21 minority (16 African Americans, 2 American Indian/Alaska Native, 1 Asian American or Pacific Islander, 2 Hispanic Americans). Average age 34. 91 applicants, 98% accepted, 62 enrolled. In 2006, 61 degrees awarded. *Degree requirements:* For master's, research project. *Entrance requirements:* For master's, GRE, PRAXIS II in teaching content area (math or science), 2 letters of recommendation, interview, resumé, prerequisite courses in communications, behavioral sciences and mathematics. Additional exam requirements/recommendations for international students: Required—TOEFL (minimum score 560 paper-based; 220 computer-based). *Application deadline:* Applications are processed on a rolling basis. Application fee: $50. Electronic applications accepted. *Expenses: Contact institution. Financial support:* In 2006–07, 3 students received support. Career-related internships or fieldwork and scholarships/grants available. Support available to part-time students. Financial award application deadline: 6/1; financial award applicants required to submit FAFSA. *Faculty research:* Foreign and second language learning problems/reading disabilities/hyperlexia, multicultural/bilingual special education, alternative educator licensure, science education, pedagogical content knowledge. *Unit head:* Dr. Mifrando Obach, Chair, 513-244-3263, Fax: 513-244-4867, E-mail: mifrando_obach@mail.msj.edu. *Application contact:* Marilyn Hoskins, Assistant Director of Admissions for Graduate Recruitment, 513-244-4723, Fax: 513-244-4629, E-mail: marilyn_hoskins@mail.msg.edu.

College of Mount Saint Vincent, School of Professional and Continuing Studies, Department of Teacher Education, Riverdale, NY 10471-1093. Offers instructional technology and global perspectives (Certificate); middle level education (Certificate); multicultural studies (Certificate); urban and multicultural education (MS Ed). *Accreditation:* Teacher Education Accreditation Council. Part-time programs available. *Faculty:* 1 full-time (0 women), 18 part-time/adjunct (12 women). *Students:* 20 full-time (13 women), 239 part-time (172 women); includes 101 minority (50 African Americans, 11 Asian Americans or Pacific Islanders, 40 Hispanic Americans). Average age 38. 35 applicants, 57% accepted. In 2006, 124 degrees awarded. *Degree requirements:* For master's, comprehensive exam, registration. *Entrance requirements:* For master's, interview, New York teaching certificate. Additional exam requirements/recommendations for international students: Required—TOEFL. *Application deadline:* For fall admission, 9/1 priority date for domestic students, 7/1 priority date for international students; for winter admission, 11/1 priority date for domestic students, 10/1 priority date for international students; for spring admission, 12/1 priority date for domestic students, 11/1 priority date for international students. Applications are processed on a rolling basis. Application fee: $50. *Financial support:* Career-related internships or fieldwork available. Financial award applicants required to submit FAFSA. *Unit head:* Mary Ellen Sullivan, Chair, 718-405-3281, Fax: 718-601-6392. *Application contact:* Beigica Collado, Executive Assistant, 718-405-3322, Fax: 718-405-3764, E-mail: beigica.collado@mountsaintvincent.edu.

The College of New Jersey, Graduate Division, School of Education, Ewing, NJ 08628. Offers M Ed, MA, MAT, MS, Certificate, Ed S. *Accreditation:* NCATE. Part-time and evening/weekend programs available. *Students:* 93 full-time (68 women), 619 part-time (489 women); includes 95 minority (42 African Americans, 1 American Indian/Alaska Native, 31 Asian Americans or Pacific Islanders, 21 Hispanic Americans). 581 applicants, 74% accepted. In 2006, 353 master's, 24 other advanced degrees awarded. *Degree requirements:* For master's, comprehensive exam. *Entrance requirements:* For master's, GRE, minimum GPA of 3.0 in field or 2.75 overall; for other advanced degree, M Ed. Additional exam requirements/recommendations for international students: Required—TOEFL. *Application deadline:* For fall admission, 4/15 for domestic students; for spring admission, 10/15 for domestic students. Application fee: $60. Electronic applications accepted. *Financial support:* Unspecified assistantships available. Financial award application deadline: 5/1; financial award applicants required to submit FAFSA. *Unit head:* Dr. William Behre, Dean, 609-771-2100, Fax: 609-637-5117. *Application contact:* Susan L. Hydro, Office of Graduate Studies, Assistant Dean, 609-771-2300, Fax: 609-637-5105, E-mail: graduate@tcnj.edu.

The College of New Rochelle, Graduate School, Division of Education, New Rochelle, NY 10805-2308. Offers creative teaching and learning (MS Ed, Certificate); elementary education/early childhood education (MS Ed); literacy education (MS Ed); school administration and supervision (MS Ed, Certificate, PD); special education (MS Ed); speech-language pathology (MS); teaching English as a second language and multilingual/multicultural education (MS Ed, Certificate), including bilingual education (Certificate), teaching English as a second language (MS Ed). Part-time and evening/weekend programs available. *Faculty:* 11 full-time (8 women), 29 part-time/adjunct (20 women). *Students:* 70 full-time (64 women), 765 part-time (659 women); includes 119 minority (66 African Americans, 9 American Indian/Alaska Native, 5 Asian Americans or Pacific Islanders, 39 Hispanic Americans), 1 international. Average age 33. In 2006, 301 master's, 15 other advanced degrees awarded. *Degree requirements:* For master's, thesis (for some programs), comprehensive exam (for some programs), registration. *Entrance requirements:* For master's, interview, minimum GPA of 3.0 in field, 2.7 overall. *Application deadline:* For fall admission, 8/1 priority date for domestic students; for spring admission, 4/6 for domestic students. Applications are processed on a rolling basis. Application fee: $35. *Expenses:* Tuition: Part-time $575 per credit. Required fees: $90 per term. *Financial support:* In 2006–07, 4 research assistantships with tuition reimbursements were awarded; career-related internships or fieldwork, scholarships/grants, and unspecified assistantships also available. Support available to part-time students. *Unit head:* Dr. Marie Ribarich, Acting Division Head, 914-654-5333, Fax: 914-654-5593, E-mail: mribarich@cnr.edu.

College of Notre Dame of Maryland, Graduate Studies, Program in Teaching, Baltimore, MD 21210-2476. Offers MA. *Accreditation:* NCATE. *Students:* 24 full-time (23 women), 44 part-time (37 women). *Entrance requirements:* For master's, Watson-Glaser Critical Thinking Appraisal, writing test, grammar test, interview. Additional exam requirements/recommendations for international students: Required—TOEFL (minimum score 500 paper-based; 173 computer-based; 61 iBT). *Application deadline:* For fall admission, 7/5 for domestic students; for winter admission, 11/5 for domestic students; for spring admission, 12/5 for domestic students. Applications are processed on a rolling basis. Application fee: $40. Electronic applications accepted. *Financial support:* Application deadline: 6/30; *Unit head:* Sr. Sharon Slear, Head, 410-532-3169, Fax: 410-532-5333, E-mail: sslear@ndm.edu. *Application contact:* Kathy Benzinger, Education Office Manager, 410-532-5349, Fax: 410-532-5333, E-mail: kbenzinger@ndm.edu.

College of St. Catherine, Graduate Programs, Program in Education, St. Paul, MN 55105-1789. Offers MA. Part-time and evening/weekend programs available. Postbaccalaureate distance learning degree programs offered (no on-campus study). *Degree requirements:* For master's, thesis. *Entrance requirements:* For master's, current teaching license, classroom experience, minimum GPA of 3.0. Additional exam requirements/recommendations for international students: Required—Michigan English Language Assessment Battery or TOEFL. Expenses: Contact institution.

College of Saint Elizabeth, Department of Education, Morristown, NJ 07960-6989. Offers accelerated certification for teachers (Certificate); assistive technology (Certificate); education: human services leadership (MA); educational technology (MA). Part-time and evening/weekend programs available. *Faculty:* 8 full-time (3 women), 14 part-time/adjunct (8 women). *Students:* 69 full-time (58 women), 354 part-time (303 women); includes 21 minority (10 African Americans, 4 Asian Americans or Pacific Islanders, 7 Hispanic Americans). Average age 36. In 2006, 82 master's, 31 other advanced degrees awarded. *Degree requirements:* For master's, thesis or alternative, portfolio. *Entrance requirements:* For master's, interview, minimum undergraduate GPA of 3.0. *Application deadline:* For fall admission, 6/30 priority date for domestic students; for spring admission, 11/30 for domestic students. Applications are processed on a rolling basis. Application fee: $35. Electronic applications accepted. *Financial support:* Career-related internships or fieldwork, Federal Work-Study, tuition waivers (partial), and unspecified assistantships available. Support available to part-time students. Financial award application deadline: 3/15; financial award applicants required to submit FAFSA. *Faculty research:* Developmental stages for teaching and human services professionals, effectiveness of humanities core curriculum. *Unit head:* Dr. Alan H. Markowitz, Director of Graduate Education Programs, 973-290-4374, Fax: 973-290-4389, E-mail: amarkowitz@cse.edu. *Application contact:* Michael Szarek, Director of Enrollment Management, 973-290-4112, Fax: 973-290-4167, E-mail: mszarek@cse.edu.

College of St. Joseph, Graduate Program, Division of Education, Rutland, VT 05701-3899. Offers elementary education (M Ed); general education (M Ed); reading (M Ed); secondary education (M Ed), including English, mathematics, social studies; special education (M Ed). Part-time and evening/weekend programs available. *Faculty:* 3 full-time (2 women), 8 part-time/adjunct (5 women). *Students:* 32 full-time, 55 part-time. Average age 33. 47 applicants, 89% accepted, 39 enrolled. In 2006, 46 degrees awarded. *Degree requirements:* For master's, comprehensive exam, registration. *Entrance requirements:* For master's, 2 letters of reference, interview. *Application deadline:* Applications are processed on a rolling basis. Application fee: $35. *Expenses:* Tuition: Full-time $10,990; part-time $300 per credit. Part-time tuition and fees vary according to program. *Financial support:* Career-related internships or fieldwork, Federal Work-Study, and unspecified assistantships available. Support available to part-time students. Financial award application deadline: 3/1. *Unit head:* Dr. Kapi Reith, Chair, 802-773-5900 Ext. 3243, Fax: 802-773-5900, E-mail: kreith@csj.edu. *Application contact:* Tracy Gallipo, Director of Admissions, 802-773-5900 Ext. 3262, Fax: 802-773-5900, E-mail: tracygallipo@csj.edu.

The College of Saint Rose, Graduate Studies, School of Education, Albany, NY 12203-1419. Offers MS, MS Ed, Adv C, Certificate. *Accreditation:* NCATE. Part-time and evening/weekend programs available. *Degree requirements:* For master's, thesis or alternative. *Entrance requirements:* For master's, minimum undergraduate GPA of 3.0. Additional exam requirements/recommendations for international students: Required—TOEFL (minimum score 550 paper-based; 213 computer-based). Electronic applications accepted.

See Close-Up on page 869.

The College of St. Scholastica, Graduate Studies, Program in Curriculum and Instruction, Duluth, MN 55811-4199. Offers M Ed. Part-time and evening/weekend programs available. Postbaccalaureate distance learning degree programs offered (minimal on-campus study). *Faculty:* 5 full-time (4 women), 3 part-time/adjunct (all women). *Students:* 2 full-time (1 woman), 28 part-time (19 women); includes 1 minority (Hispanic American) Average age 40. 11 applicants, 82% accepted, 5 enrolled. In 2006, 20 degrees awarded. *Degree requirements:* For master's, thesis. *Entrance requirements:* For master's, interview, minimum GPA of 2.8, current teaching license. Additional exam requirements/recommendations for international students: Required—TOEFL (minimum score 550 paper-based; 213 computer-based; 79 iBT). *Application deadline:* For fall admission, 8/1 priority date for domestic students, 8/1 for international students; for spring admission, 11/1 priority date for domestic students, 11/1 for international students. Applications are processed on a rolling basis. Application fee: $50. Electronic applications accepted. *Expenses: Contact institution. Financial support:* In 2006–07, 11 students received support. Available to part-time students. Applicants required to submit FAFSA. *Faculty research:* Distance education, organizational change, feminist pedagogy, cognitive styles, science education. *Unit head:* Dr. Kay Lutz, Program Director, 218-723-5971, Fax: 218-733-2275, E-mail: klutz@css.edu. *Application contact:* Tonya J. Roth, Graduate Recruitment Counselor, 218-723-6285, Fax: 218-733-2275, E-mail: gradstudies@css.edu.

The College of St. Scholastica, Graduate Studies, Program in Teaching, Duluth, MN 55811-4199. Offers M Ed, Certificate. Part-time programs available. Postbaccalaureate distance learning degree programs offered (minimal on-campus study). *Faculty:* 2 full-time (1 woman), 10 part-time/adjunct (8 women). *Students:* 31 full-time (27 women), 44 part-time (30 women); includes 16 minority (1 African American, 11 American Indian/Alaska Native, 2 Asian Americans or Pacific Islanders, 2 Hispanic Americans), 1 international. Average age 34. 87 applicants, 95% accepted, 38 enrolled. *Entrance requirements:* Additional exam requirements/recommendations for international students: Required—TOEFL (minimum score 550 paper-based; 213 computer-based; 79 iBT). *Application deadline:* For fall admission, 8/1 priority date for domestic students, 8/1 for international students; for spring admission, 11/15 priority date for domestic students, 11/15 for international students. Applications are processed on a rolling basis. Application fee: $50. Electronic applications accepted. *Financial support:* In 2006–07, 70 students received support. Applicants required to submit FAFSA. *Unit head:* Dr. Chery Takkuneh, Program Director, 218-723-7052, Fax: 218-723-2275. *Application contact:* Tonya J. Roth, Graduate Recruitment Counselor, 218-723-6285, Fax: 218-733-2275, E-mail: troth@css.edu.

College of Santa Fe, Department of Education, Santa Fe, NM 87505-7634. Offers at-risk youth (MA), including bilingual/multicultural education, classroom teaching, community counseling, educational administration, leadership, school counseling, self-designed program, TESOL/Multicultural; curriculum and instruction (MA); multicultural special education (MA). Part-time and evening/weekend programs available. *Entrance requirements:* For master's, minimum GPA of 3.0. *Faculty research:* Integrated curriculum, child development, brain research, learning styles, systemic issues in education.

College of Staten Island of the City University of New York, Graduate Programs, Department of Education, Staten Island, NY 10314-6600. Offers adolescence education (MS Ed); childhood education (MS Ed); leadership in education (6th Year Certificate); special education (MS Ed). *Students:* 42 full-time (35 women), 609 part-time (510 women); includes 84 minority (24 African Americans, 2 American Indian/Alaska Native, 16 Asian Americans or Pacific Islanders, 42 Hispanic Americans), 5 international. Average age 31. 223 applicants, 85% accepted, 148 enrolled. In 2006, 235 master's, 27 other advanced degrees awarded. Application fee: $125. *Expenses:* Tuition, state resident: full-time $6,400; part-time $270 per credit. Tuition, nonresident: part-time $500 per credit. Required fees: $53 per semester. *Financial support:* In 2006–07, 2 students received support. Applicants required to submit FAFSA. *Faculty research:* Social capital and the structural transformation of New York City's Department of Education; pre-service teachers' knowledge and attention to reader, text and teacher in content area comprehension instruction; alternative routes to teaching: lessons from the National Teacher Corps; theory of political culture and school desegregation outcomes; teacher efficacy as it relates to teacher's behaviors in their classrooms. *Unit head:* Dr. Susan Sullivan, Chairperson, 718-982-3744, Fax: 718-982-3743, E-mail: sullivan@mail.csi.cuny.edu. *Application contact:* Emmanuel Esperance, Deputy Director of Office of Recruitment and Admissions, 718-982-2259, Fax: 718-982-2500, E-mail: admissions@csi.cuny.edu.

College of the Humanities and Sciences, Harrison Middleton University, Graduate Program, Tempe, AZ 85282. Offers education (MA, Ed D); humanities (MA); imaginative literature (MA); jurisprudence (MA); natural science (MA); philosophy and religion (MA); social science (MA).

Education—General

College of the Humanities and Sciences, Harrison Middleton University (continued)

Part-time and evening/weekend programs available. Postbaccalaureate distance learning degree programs offered (no on-campus study). *Faculty:* 17 full-time (7 women), 5 part-time/adjunct (2 women). *Students:* 38 full-time (9 women). In 2006, 10 degrees awarded. Application fee: $50. *Expenses:* Tuition: Part-time $275 per credit hour. *Application contact:* Kathleen Mirabile, Vice-President, Provost, 877-248-6724, Fax: 800-762-1622, E-mail: kmirabile@chumsci.edu.

College of the Southwest, School of Education, Hobbs, NM 88240-9129. Offers curriculum and instruction (MS); educational administration (MS); educational counseling (MS); educational diagnostician (MS). Part-time and evening/weekend programs available. Postbaccalaureate distance learning degree programs offered. *Faculty:* 2 full-time (both women), 6 part-time/adjunct (1 woman). *Students:* 41 full-time (28 women), 43 part-time (35 women); includes 24 minority (1 African American, 1 American Indian/Alaska Native, 1 Asian American or Pacific Islander, 21 Hispanic Americans), 1 international. Average age 38. 119 applicants, 29% accepted, 34 enrolled. In 2006, 26 degrees awarded. *Degree requirements:* For master's, comprehensive exam. *Entrance requirements:* For master's, GRE General Test. Additional exam requirements/recommendations for international students: Recommended—TOEFL (minimum score 550 paper-based; 213 computer-based). *Application deadline:* For fall admission, 3/1 priority date for domestic students; for spring admission, 10/1 for domestic students. Applications are processed on a rolling basis. Application fee: $50. *Expenses:* Tuition: Part-time $375 per credit hour. *Financial support:* In 2006–07, 58 students received support, including 1 research assistantship; Federal Work-Study, scholarships/grants, and tuition waivers (partial) also available. Support available to part-time students. Financial award application deadline: 4/1; financial award applicants required to submit FAFSA. *Unit head:* Dr. Dennis Atherton, Dean, 505-392-6561 Ext. 1069, Fax: 505-392-6006, E-mail: datherton@csw.edu. *Application contact:* Kerrie Mitchell, Coordinator of Financial Aid and Admissions Operations, 505-392-6563 Ext. 1048, Fax: 505-392-6006, E-mail: kmitchell@csw.edu.

The College of William and Mary, School of Education, Williamsburg, VA 23187-8795. Offers M Ed, MA Ed, Ed D, PhD, Ed S. *Accreditation:* NCATE. Part-time and evening/weekend programs available. *Faculty:* 36 full-time (17 women), 17 part-time/adjunct (15 women). *Students:* 245 full-time (205 women), 227 part-time (184 women); includes 55 minority (44 African Americans, 2 American Indian/Alaska Native, 6 Asian Americans or Pacific Islanders, 3 Hispanic Americans), 7 international. Average age 31. 480 applicants, 57% accepted, 155 enrolled. In 2006, 132 master's, 24 doctorates, 12 other advanced degrees awarded. *Degree requirements:* For master's, master's project; for doctorate, thesis/dissertation, comprehensive exam. *Entrance requirements:* For master's, GRE or MAT, minimum GPA of 2.5; for doctorate, GRE or MAT; for Ed S, GRE, minimum GPA of 3.0. Additional exam requirements/recommendations for international students: Required—TOEFL. *Application deadline:* For fall admission, 2/1 for domestic and international students; for spring admission, 10/1 for domestic and international students. Application fee: $30. *Expenses:* Tuition, state resident: full-time $6,100; part-time $260 per credit. Tuition, nonresident: full-time $18,790; part-time $725 per credit. Required fees: $3,314. Tuition and fees vary according to program. *Financial support:* In 2006–07, 206 students received support, including 1 fellowship with full tuition reimbursement available (averaging $20,000 per year), 124 research assistantships with full and partial tuition reimbursements available (averaging $10,800 per year); teaching assistantships, career-related internships or fieldwork, Federal Work-Study, institutionally sponsored loans, scholarships/grants, and unspecified assistantships also available. Financial award application deadline: 2/1; financial award applicants required to submit FAFSA. *Faculty research:* Writing, gifted education, curriculum and instruction, special education, leadership, faculty development, cultural diversity. Total annual research expenditures: $4.5 million. *Unit head:* Dr. Virginia McLaughlin, Dean, 757-221-2317, E-mail: vamcla@wm.edu. *Application contact:* Dorothy Osborne, Director of Admissions, 757-221-2317, E-mail: dsosbo@wm.edu.

Collège universitaire de Saint-Boniface, Department of Education, Saint-Boniface, MB R2H 0H7, Canada. Offers M Ed.

Colorado Christian University, Program in Curriculum and Instruction, Lakewood, CO 80226. Offers MA. Part-time and evening/weekend programs available. *Degree requirements:* For master's, practicum, thesis optional. *Entrance requirements:* For master's, interviews, letters of recommendation. Additional exam requirements/recommendations for international students: Required—TOEFL. Electronic applications accepted. Expenses: Contact institution.

The Colorado College, Department of Education, Colorado Springs, CO 80903-3294. Offers elementary education (MAT), including elementary school teaching; secondary education (MAT), including art teaching, English teaching, foreign language teaching, mathematics teaching, music teaching, science teaching, social studies teaching. *Faculty:* 4 full-time (2 women), 15 part-time/adjunct (10 women). *Students:* 27 full-time (19 women); includes 3 minority (1 African American, 1 Asian American or Pacific Islander, 1 Hispanic American). Average age 27. 49 applicants, 86% accepted, 27 enrolled. In 2006, 36 degrees awarded. *Degree requirements:* For master's, thesis, internship. *Entrance requirements:* For master's, PRAXIS II or PLACE. *Application deadline:* For fall admission, 2/1 for domestic and international students. Application fee: $50. *Expenses:* Tuition: Full-time $23,567. One-time fee: $1,485 full-time. *Financial support:* In 2006–07, 24 students received support, including 24 teaching assistantships (averaging $16,000 per year); career-related internships or fieldwork, institutionally sponsored loans, health care benefits, and tuition waivers (partial) also available. Financial award application deadline: 2/15; financial award applicants required to submit CSS PROFILE or FAFSA. *Unit head:* Charlotte Mendoza, Chair, 719-389-6474, Fax: 719-389-6473, E-mail: cmendoza@coloradocollege.edu. *Application contact:* Marsha E. Unruh, Director of Education Career Services, 719-389-6472, Fax: 719-389-6473, E-mail: munruh@coloradocollege.edu.

The Colorado College, Programs for Experienced Teachers, Colorado Springs, CO 80903-3294. Offers American Southwest studies for all teachers (MAT); arts and humanities for secondary school teachers and administrators (MAT); integrated natural science for all teachers (MAT); liberal arts for elementary school teachers and administrators (MAT). Programs offered during summer only. Part-time programs available. *Faculty:* 18 part-time/adjunct (8 women). *Students:* 78; includes 2 minority (both Hispanic Americans) Average age 31. In 2006, 28 degrees awarded. *Degree requirements:* For master's, thesis, oral exam, 50 page paper. *Application deadline:* Applications are processed on a rolling basis. Application fee: $50. *Expenses: Contact institution.* One-time fee: $1,485 full-time. *Financial support:* Institutionally sponsored loans and half-tuition waivers to teachers with a contract available. *Unit head:* Dr. Libby Rittenberg, Dean of Summer Programs, 719-389-6657, Fax: 719-389-6955. *Application contact:* Ann H. Van Horn, Assistant Dean of Summer Session, 719-389-6656, Fax: 719-389-6955, E-mail: avanhorn@coloradocollege.edu.

Columbia College, Graduate Programs, Department of Education, Columbia, SC 29203-5998. Offers divergent learning (M Ed). *Accreditation:* NCATE. Part-time and evening/weekend programs available. Postbaccalaureate distance learning degree programs offered (minimal on-campus study). *Faculty:* 4 full-time (2 women), 25 part-time/adjunct (15 women). *Students:* 234 full-time (219 women), 2 part-time (1 woman); includes 66 minority (64 African Americans, 2 Hispanic Americans). Average age 32. 144 applicants, 97% accepted, 122 enrolled. In 2006, 252 degrees awarded. *Degree requirements:* For master's, thesis. *Entrance requirements:* For master's, GRE General Test, MAT, 2 recommendations, current South Carolina teaching certificate, minimum GPA of 3.2. Additional exam requirements/recommendations for international students: Required—TOEFL. *Application deadline:* For fall admission, 7/15 for domestic and international students. Applications are processed on a rolling basis. Application fee: $50. Electronic applications accepted. *Expenses: Contact institution. Financial support:* Available to part-time students. Application deadline: 7/1; *Unit head:* Dr. Mary Steppling, Chair, 803-786-3782, Fax: 803-786-3034, E-mail: msteppling@colacoll.edu. *Application contact:* Carolyn Emeneker, Director of Graduate School and Evening College Admissions, 803-786-3766, Fax: 803-786-3674, E-mail: emeneker@colacoll.edu.

Columbia College, Program in Teaching, Columbia, MO 65216-0002. Offers MAT. Part-time and evening/weekend programs available. *Faculty:* 5 full-time (all women), 5 part-time/adjunct (2 women). *Students:* 77 full-time (61 women); includes 6 minority (4 African Americans, 1 Asian American or Pacific Islander, 1 Hispanic American), 1 international. Average age 33. 25 applicants, 80% accepted, 19 enrolled. In 2006, 20 degrees awarded. *Degree requirements:* For master's, final project. *Entrance requirements:* For master's, bachelor's degree in related area, minimum GPA of 3.0, 3 recommendations. Additional exam requirements/recommendations for international students: Required—TOEFL (minimum score 550 paper-based; 213 computer-based). *Application deadline:* For fall admission, 8/1 priority date for domestic and international students; for winter admission, 12/15 priority date for domestic and international students. Applications are processed on a rolling basis. Application fee: $55. *Expenses:* Tuition: Part-time $270 per credit hour. *Financial support:* Career-related internships or fieldwork, Federal Work-Study, and institutionally sponsored loans available. Support available to part-time students. Financial award application deadline: 3/15; financial award applicants required to submit FAFSA. *Unit head:* Dr. Judy Brown, Chair, 573-875-7590, Fax: 573-875-7209. *Application contact:* Regina Morin, Director of Admissions, 573-875-7354, Fax: 573-875-7506, E-mail: rmmorin@ccis.edu.

Columbia College Chicago, Graduate School, Department of Educational Studies, Chicago, IL 60605-1996. Offers elementary (MAT); English (MAT); interdisciplinary arts (MAT); multicultural education (MA); urban teaching (MA). Part-time and evening/weekend programs available. *Degree requirements:* For master's, thesis, student teaching experience, 100 pre-clinical hours. *Entrance requirements:* For master's, NTE, minimum GPA of 3.0, portfolio. Additional exam requirements/recommendations for international students: Required—TOEFL (minimum score 550 paper-based; 213 computer-based). Electronic applications accepted.

Columbia International University, Columbia Graduate School, Columbia, SC 29230-3122. Offers Bible teaching (MABT); Christian higher education leadership (Ed D); Christian school educational leadership (Ed D); counseling (MACN); curriculum and instruction (M Ed), including Christian school guidance, English as a second language, learning disabilities, school technology; early childhood and elementary education (MAT); educational administration (M Ed); teaching English as a foreign language (Certificate); teaching English as a foreign language and intercultural studies (MATF). Part-time and evening/weekend programs available. *Faculty:* 11 full-time (4 women), 7 part-time/adjunct (5 women). *Students:* 52 full-time (44 women), 93 part-time (59 women); includes 17 minority (11 African Americans, 2 Asian Americans or Pacific Islanders, 4 Hispanic Americans), 10 international. Average age 35. 107 applicants, 56% accepted, 41 enrolled. In 2006, 62 degrees awarded. *Degree requirements:* For master's, internships, professional project. *Entrance requirements:* For master's, Minnesota Multiphasic Personality Inventory, MAT, minimum GPA of 2.7. Additional exam requirements/recommendations for international students: Required—TOEFL. *Application deadline:* For fall admission, 8/1 priority date for domestic and international students; for winter admission, 12/15 priority date for domestic and international students; for spring admission, 1/15 priority date for domestic and international students. Applications are processed on a rolling basis. Application fee: $45. Electronic applications accepted. *Expenses:* Tuition: Part-time $400 per semester hour. Tuition and fees vary according to course load and program. *Financial support:* In 2006–07, 35 students received support. Career-related internships or fieldwork, Federal Work-Study, institutionally sponsored loans, and scholarships/grants available. Financial award application deadline: 3/17; financial award applicants required to submit FAFSA. *Unit head:* Dr. Milton Uecker, Dean, 803-807-5319, Fax: 803-786-4209, E-mail: muecker@ciu.edu. *Application contact:* Michelle MacGregor, Director of Admissions, 800-777-2227 Ext. 5335, Fax: 803-786-4209, E-mail: yescbs@ciu.edu.

Columbus State University, Graduate Studies, College of Education, Columbus, GA 31907-5645. Offers M Ed, MS, Ed S. *Accreditation:* ACA (one or more programs are accredited); NCATE. Part-time and evening/weekend programs available. Postbaccalaureate distance learning degree programs offered (minimal on-campus study). *Faculty:* 26 full-time (12 women), 10 part-time/adjunct (5 women). *Students:* 148 full-time (106 women), 175 part-time (127 women); includes 78 minority (69 African Americans, 4 Asian Americans or Pacific Islanders, 5 Hispanic Americans), 1 international. Average age 36. 117 applicants, 47% accepted, 39 enrolled. In 2006, 108 master's, 47 Ed Ss awarded. *Degree requirements:* For master's, thesis, exit exam; for Ed S, thesis or alternative. *Entrance requirements:* For master's, GRE General Test, minimum GPA of 2.75; for Ed S, GRE General Test. Additional exam requirements/recommendations for international students: Required—TOEFL (minimum score 550 paper-based; 213 computer-based). *Application deadline:* For fall admission, 5/1 priority date for domestic students, 5/1 for international students; for spring admission, 11/11 for domestic students, 11/1 for international students. Applications are processed on a rolling basis. Application fee: $25. Electronic applications accepted. *Expenses:* Tuition, state resident: part-time $127 per semester hour. Tuition, nonresident: part-time $508 per semester hour. Required fees: $264 per semester. Tuition and fees vary according to course load. *Financial support:* In 2006–07, 185 students received support, including 26 research assistantships with partial tuition reimbursements available (averaging $3,000 per year); career-related internships or fieldwork, Federal Work-Study, institutionally sponsored loans, scholarships/grants, tuition waivers (partial), and unspecified assistantships also available. Support available to part-time students. Financial award application deadline: 5/1; financial award applicants required to submit FAFSA. *Unit head:* Dr. David Rock, Dean, 706-568-2212, Fax: 706-569-3134, E-mail: rock_david@colstate.edu. *Application contact:* Katie Thornton, Graduate Admissions Specialist, 706-568-2035, Fax: 706-568-2462, E-mail: thornton_katie@colstate.edu.

Concordia University, College of Education, Portland, OR 97211-6099. Offers curriculum and instruction (elementary) (M Ed); educational administration (M Ed); elementary education (MAT); secondary education (MAT). Part-time programs available. Postbaccalaureate distance learning degree programs offered (no on-campus study). *Degree requirements:* For master's, work samples/portfolio. *Entrance requirements:* For master's, California Basic Educational Skills Test or PRAXIS I, minimum undergraduate GPA of 2.8, graduate 3.0; 2 letters of recommendation. Additional exam requirements/recommendations for international students: Required—TOEFL (minimum score 525 paper-based; 195 computer-based). Electronic applications accepted. *Faculty research:* Learner centered classroom, brain-based learning future of on-line learning.

Concordia University, College of Education, Program in Teaching, River Forest, IL 60305-1499. Offers MAT. *Degree requirements:* For master's, thesis or alternative. *Entrance requirements:* For master's, minimum GPA of 2.9. Additional exam requirements/recommendations for international students: Required—TOEFL (minimum score 550 paper-based; 195 computer-based). Electronic applications accepted.

Concordia University, Graduate Programs in Education, Seward, NE 68434-1599. Offers M Ed, MPE, MS. *Accreditation:* NCATE. Part-time and evening/weekend programs available. *Degree requirements:* For master's, thesis or alternative, comprehensive exam. *Entrance requirements:* For master's, GRE, MAT, or NTE, minimum GPA of 3.0, BS in education or equivalent. Additional exam requirements/recommendations for international students: Required—TOEFL. Electronic applications accepted.

Concordia University, School of Education, Irvine, CA 92612-3299. Offers curriculum and instruction (MA); education (M Ed); educational administration and administrative services credential (MA). Part-time and evening/weekend programs available. Postbaccalaureate distance learning degree programs offered (minimal on-campus study). *Faculty:* 13 full-time (6 women), 5 part-time/adjunct (3 women). *Students:* 228 full-time (185 women), 465 part-time (378 women); includes 145 minority (8 African Americans, 6 American Indian/Alaska Native, 38 Asian Americans or Pacific Islanders, 93 Hispanic Americans), 2 international. Average age 32. In 2006, 75 degrees awarded. *Degree requirements:* For master's, project or thesis. *Entrance requirements:* For master's, California Basic Educational Skills Test, California Subject Examinations for Teachers, minimum GPA of 3.0. Additional exam requirements/recommendations for international students: Required—TOEFL (minimum score 550 paper-based; 213 computer-based). *Application deadline:* For fall admission, 7/15 priority date for domestic students, 7/15 for international students; for spring admission, 11/30 priority date for domestic students, 11/30 for international students. Applications are processed on a rolling basis. Application fee: $50 ($300 for international students). *Financial support:* Application deadline: 3/2; *Unit head:* Dr. Joseph Bordeaux, Dean, 949-854-8002 Ext. 1345, Fax: 949-854-6878, E-mail: joseph.bordeaux@cui.edu. *Application contact:* Lindsay Anderson, Director of Graduate Enrollment, 949-854-8002 Ext. 1133, Fax: 949-854-6894, E-mail: lindsay.anderson@cui.edu.

Concordia University, School of Graduate Studies, Faculty of Arts and Science, Department of Education, Montréal, QC H3G 1M8, Canada. Offers adult education (Diploma); applied linguistics (MA); child study (MA); educational studies (MA); educational technology (MA, PhD); instructional technology (Diploma); teaching English as a second language (Certificate). *Students:* 138 full-time (97 women), 207 part-time (159 women). 285 applicants, 66% accepted, 99 enrolled. In 2006, 67 master's, 4 doctorates, 13 other advanced degrees awarded. *Degree requirements:* For master's, one foreign language, thesis optional; for doctorate, thesis/dissertation, comprehensive exam. *Entrance requirements:* For doctorate, MA in educational technology or equivalent. Application fee: $50. *Financial support:* Career-related internships or fieldwork available. *Unit head:* Dr. Ellen Jacobs, Chair, 514-848-2424 Ext. 2033, Fax: 514-848-4520. *Application contact:* Dr. Dennis Dicks, Director, 514-848-2424 Ext. 2030, Fax: 514-848-4250.

Concordia University at Austin, College of Education, Austin, TX 78705-2799. Offers M Ed. Part-time and evening/weekend programs available. *Degree requirements:* For master's, thesis (for some programs), portfolio presentation.

Concordia University, St. Paul, College of Education, St. Paul, MN 55104-5494. Offers differentiated instruction (MA Ed); early childhood (MA Ed); family life education (MAHS); special education (Certificate). *Accreditation:* NCATE. Evening/weekend programs available. Postbaccalaureate distance learning degree programs offered (minimal on-campus study). *Faculty:* 8 full-time (7 women), 12 part-time/adjunct (7 women). *Students:* 101 full-time (95 women), 10 part-time (9 women); includes 29 minority (21 African Americans, 1 American Indian/Alaska Native, 6 Asian Americans or Pacific Islanders, 1 Hispanic American). Average age 34. In 2006, 59 master's, 8 other advanced degrees awarded. *Entrance requirements:* Additional exam requirements/recommendations for international students: Required—TOEFL. *Application deadline:* Applications are processed on a rolling basis. Application fee: $50. Electronic applications accepted. *Unit head:* Prof. Lonn Maly, Dean, 651-641-8278, Fax: 651-641-8807, E-mail: maly@csp.edu. *Application contact:* Kimberly Craig, Director of Graduate and Cohort Admission, 651-603-6223, Fax: 651-603-6320, E-mail: craig@csp.edu.

Concordia University Wisconsin, Graduate Programs, Department of Education, Mequon, WI 53097-2402. Offers art education (MS Ed); curriculum and instruction (MS Ed); early childhood (MS Ed); educational administration (MS Ed); environmental education (MS Ed); family studies (MS Ed); reading (MS Ed); school counseling (MS Ed); special education (MS Ed). Part-time and evening/weekend programs available. Postbaccalaureate distance learning degree programs offered (minimal on-campus study). *Faculty:* 30. *Students:* 396 (284 women). In 2006, 51 degrees awarded. *Degree requirements:* For master's, thesis or alternative, comprehensive exam. *Entrance requirements:* For master's, minimum GPA of 3.0, teaching license. Additional exam requirements/recommendations for international students: Required—TOEFL. Application fee: $35. *Financial support:* Career-related internships or fieldwork and tuition waivers (partial) available. Financial award application deadline: 8/1. *Faculty research:* Motivation, developmental learning, learning styles. *Unit head:* Dr. James Juergensen, Director, 262-243-4214, E-mail: james.juergensen@cuw.edu. *Application contact:* Graduate Admissions, 262-243-4248, Fax: 262-243-4428.

Connecticut College, Graduate School, Programs in Education, New London, CT 06320-4196. Offers elementary education (MAT); secondary education (MAT). Part-time programs available. *Entrance requirements:* For master's, MAT.

Converse College, School of Education and Graduate Studies, Spartanburg, SC 29302-0006. Offers art education (M Ed); early childhood education (MAT); education (Ed S), including administration and supervision, curriculum and instruction, marriage and family therapy; elementary education (M Ed, MAT); gifted education (M Ed); leadership (M Ed); liberal arts (MLA), including English (M Ed, MAT, MLA), history, political science; secondary education (M Ed, MAT), including biology (MAT), chemistry (MAT), English (M Ed, MAT, MLA), mathematics, natural sciences (M Ed), social sciences; special education (M Ed, MAT), including learning disabilities (MAT), mental disabilities (MAT), special education (M Ed). Part-time and evening/weekend programs available. *Faculty:* 13 full-time (8 women), 23 part-time/adjunct (16 women). *Students:* 156 full-time (136 women), 1,069 part-time (847 women). Average age 35. 115 applicants, 88% accepted. In 2006, 186 master's, 26 other advanced degrees awarded. *Entrance requirements:* For master's, PRAXIS II (M Ed), minimum GPA of 2.75; for Ed S, GRE or MAT, minimum GPA of 3.0. *Application deadline:* For fall admission, 8/1 for domestic and international students; for winter admission, 11/15 for domestic and international students; for spring admission, 1/15 for domestic and international students. Applications are processed on a rolling basis. Application fee: $40. Electronic applications accepted. *Expenses:* Tuition: Part-time $305 per credit hour. Required fees: $20 per term. *Financial support:* In 2006–07, 500 students received support; research assistantships, career-related internships or fieldwork and scholarships/grants available. Support available to part-time students. Financial award applicants required to submit FAFSA. *Faculty research:* Motivation, classroom management, predictors of success in classroom teaching, sex equity in public education, gifted research. Total annual research expenditures: $50,000. *Unit head:* Thomas M. Faulkenberry, Dean of the School of Education and Graduate Studies, 864-596-9082, Fax: 864-596-9221, E-mail: tom.faulkenberry@converse.edu.

Coppin State University, Division of Graduate Studies, Division of Education, Department of Curriculum and Instruction, Program in Teaching, Baltimore, MD 21216-3698. Offers teacher education (MA). Part-time and evening/weekend programs available. Postbaccalaureate distance learning degree programs offered. *Faculty:* 2 full-time (both women), 2 part-time/adjunct (1 woman). *Students:* 5 full-time (3 women), 28 part-time (20 women); includes 29 minority (all African Americans), 1 international. Average age 35. 17 applicants, 53% accepted, 7 enrolled. In 2006, 3 degrees awarded. *Degree requirements:* For master's, thesis, exit portfolio. *Entrance requirements:* For master's, GRE, resumé, references. *Application deadline:* For fall admission, 8/15 for domestic students; for spring admission, 12/15 for domestic students. Application fee: $45. *Financial support:* Career-related internships or fieldwork available. Financial award application deadline: 6/30; financial award applicants required to submit FAFSA. *Unit head:* Dr. Richard Rembold, Acting Director/Associate Vice President for Academic Affairs, 410-951-3010, E-mail: rrembold@coppin.edu.

Cornell University, Graduate School, Graduate Fields of Agriculture and Life Sciences, Field of Education, Ithaca, NY 14853-0001. Offers agricultural education (MAT); biology (7-12) (MAT); chemistry (7-12) (MAT); curriculum and instruction (MPS, MS, PhD); earth science (7-12) (MAT); extension, and adult education (MPS, MS, PhD); mathematics (7-12) (MAT); physics (7-12) (MAT). *Faculty:* 26 full-time (9 women). *Students:* 56 full-time (33 women); includes 10 minority (1 African American, 5 Asian Americans or Pacific Islanders, 4 Hispanic Americans), 4 international. Average age 31. 96 applicants, 40% accepted, 18 enrolled. In 2006, 22 master's, 8 doctorates awarded. Terminal master's awarded for partial completion of doctoral program. *Degree requirements:* For master's, thesis (MS); for doctorate, thesis/dissertation, comprehensive exam. *Entrance requirements:* For master's and doctorate, GRE General Test, sample of written work (recommended), 2 letters of recommendation. Additional exam requirements/recommendations for international students: Required—TOEFL (minimum score 550 paper-based; 213 computer-based). *Application deadline:* For fall admission, 2/15 for domestic students. Application fee: $60. Electronic applications accepted. *Expenses:* Tuition: Full-time $32,800. Full-time tuition and fees vary according to program. *Financial support:* In 2006–07, 31 students received support, including 4 fellowships with full tuition reimbursements available, 7 research assistantships with full tuition reimbursements available, 20 teaching assistantships with full tuition reimbursements available; institutionally sponsored loans, scholarships/grants, health care benefits, tuition waivers (full and partial), and unspecified assistantships also available. Financial award applicants required to submit FAFSA. *Faculty research:* Moral development and professional ethics; public issues education and community development; socio/political issues in public education; teacher education and curriculum in agricultural science, and mathematics; extension research. *Unit head:* Director of Graduate Studies, 607-255-4278, Fax: 607-255-7905. *Application contact:* Graduate Field Assistant, 607-255-4278, Fax: 607-255-7905, E-mail: rh22@cornell.edu.

Covenant College, Program in Education, Lookout Mountain, GA 30750. Offers M Ed. Part-time programs available. *Faculty:* 4 full-time (1 woman), 9 part-time/adjunct (1 woman). *Students:* 46 full-time (29 women), 18 part-time (11 women); includes 4 minority (3 African Americans, 1 Hispanic American), 2 international. Average age 37. 30 applicants, 97% accepted, 20 enrolled. In 2006, 23 degrees awarded. *Median time to degree:* Master's–3.5 years full-time. *Degree requirements:* For master's, special project. *Entrance requirements:* For master's, GRE General Test, 2 professional recommendations, minimum GPA of 3.0, writing sample. *Application deadline:* For fall admission, 3/31 priority date for domestic students. Applications are processed on a rolling basis. Application fee: $35. *Expenses:* Tuition: Part-time $410 per credit. *Financial support:* In 2006–07, 33 students received support. Institutionally sponsored loans, scholarships/grants, and tuition waivers (partial) available. Support available to part-time students. Financial award application deadline: 3/1; financial award applicants required to submit FAFSA. *Unit head:* Dr. Jim Drexler, Director, 706-419-1408. *Application contact:* Rebecca Dodson, Associate Director, Program in Education, 706-419-1406, Fax: 706-820-0672, E-mail: rdodson@covenant.edu.

Creighton University, Graduate School, College of Arts and Sciences, Department of Education, Program in Education, Omaha, NE 68178-0001. Offers M Ed. Part-time and evening/weekend programs available. *Students:* 8 full-time (3 women), 18 part-time (6 women); includes 1 minority (Hispanic American) In 2006, 7 degrees awarded. *Entrance requirements:* For master's, GRE, 3 letters of recommendation. Additional exam requirements/recommendations for international students: Required—TOEFL (minimum score 550 paper-based; 213 computer-based; 80 iBT). *Application deadline:* For fall admission, 7/1 priority date for domestic and international students; for winter admission, 12/1 priority date for domestic and international students; for spring admission, 4/1 priority date for domestic and international students. Applications are processed on a rolling basis. Application fee: $40. Electronic applications accepted. *Expenses:* Tuition: Part-time $595 per credit hour. Required fees: $38 per semester. *Financial support:* Tuition waivers (partial) available. Financial award applicants required to submit FAFSA. *Unit head:* Dr. Timothy J. Cook, Director, 402-280-2561, E-mail: timothy.cook@creighton.edu. *Application contact:* LuAnn M. Schwery, Coordinator of Graduate Programs, 402-280-2870, Fax: 402-280-5762, E-mail: lschwery@creighton.edu.

Cumberland University, Program in Education, Lebanon, TN 37087-3408. Offers MAE. Part-time and evening/weekend programs available. Postbaccalaureate distance learning degree programs offered (no on-campus study). *Faculty:* 4 full-time (3 women), 8 part-time/adjunct (2 women). *Students:* 25 full-time (16 women), 154 part-time (114 women); includes 21 minority (18 African Americans, 1 American Indian/Alaska Native, 1 Asian American or Pacific Islander, 1 Hispanic American). Average age 33. 23 applicants, 100% accepted, 14 enrolled. In 2006, 195 degrees awarded. *Degree requirements:* For master's, comprehensive exam, registration. *Entrance requirements:* For master's, GRE General Test, MAT, or NTE, 3 letters of recommendation. Additional exam requirements/recommendations for international students: Required—TOEFL (minimum score 500 paper-based; 173 computer-based). Application fee: $50. *Expenses:* Tuition: Full-time $10,890; part-time $605 per credit. *Financial support:* Career-related internships or fieldwork, institutionally sponsored loans, and scholarships/grants available. Support available to part-time students. Financial award application deadline: 8/1; financial award applicants required to submit FAFSA. *Unit head:* Dr. Kenneth C. Collier, Dean, School of Education, 615-444-2562 Ext. 1170, Fax: 877-217-5284, E-mail: ccollier@cumberland.edu. *Application contact:* Debbie F. Whitaker, Coordinator, 615-444-2562 Ext. 1217, Fax: 615-444-2569, E-mail: dwhitaker@cumberland.edu.

Curry College, Division of Continuing Education and Graduate Studies, Program in Education, Milton, MA 02186-9984. Offers adult education (Certificate); educational administration (M Ed); educational therapy (Certificate); elementary education (M Ed); foundations (non-license) (M Ed); learning disabilities across the lifespan (Certificate); reading (M Ed, Certificate); special education (M Ed). Part-time and evening/weekend programs available. *Faculty:* 6 full-time (4 women), 11 part-time/adjunct (7 women). *Degree requirements:* For master's, research project. *Entrance requirements:* For master's, MAT, interview, recommendations, resumé. Additional exam requirements/recommendations for international students: Required—TOEFL (minimum score 550 paper-based). *Application deadline:* For fall admission, 8/1 priority date for domestic students; for spring admission, 1/1 for domestic students. Applications are processed on a rolling basis. Application fee: $50. *Expenses:* Contact institution. *Financial support:* Career-related internships or fieldwork and tuition waivers (partial) available. *Faculty research:* Classroom trauma, therapeutic writing, inclusionary practices. *Unit head:* Dr. Donald Gratz, Director and Associate Professor, 617-333-2243, E-mail: dgratz0703@curry.edu. *Application contact:* John Bresnahan, Director of Graduate Enrollment and Student Services, 617-333-2243, Fax: 617-333-2045, E-mail: jbresnah0104@curry.edu.

Daemen College, Education Department, Amherst, NY 14226-3592. Offers adolescence education (MS); childhood education (MS); childhood special education (MS). Part-time programs available. *Faculty:* 5 full-time (4 women), 53 part-time/adjunct (45 women). *Students:* 283 full-time (224 women), 238 part-time (202 women); includes 1 minority (African American), 192 international. Average age 33. 314 applicants, 71% accepted, 184 enrolled. In 2006, 284 degrees awarded. *Degree requirements:* For master's, thesis, registration. *Entrance requirements:* For master's, GRE, minimum GPA of 3.0, 3 letters of recommendation, proof of initial certification for licensure. Additional exam requirements/recommendations for international students: Required—TOEFL (minimum score 500 paper-based; 173 computer-based). *Application deadline:* For fall admission, 3/1 priority date for domestic and international students; for spring admission, 10/1 priority date for domestic and international students. Applications are processed on a rolling basis. Application fee: $25. Electronic applications accepted. *Expenses:* Tuition: Full-time $11,700; part-time $650 per credit hour. Required fees: $15 per credit hour. Tuition and fees vary according to course load. *Financial support:* In 2006–07, 48 students received support. Federal Work-Study, institutionally sponsored loans, traineeships, and tuition waivers (partial) available. Support available to part-time students. Financial award application deadline: 2/15; financial award applicants required to submit FAFSA. *Faculty research:* Transition for students with disabilities, early childhood special education, traumatic brain injury (TBI), reading assessment. *Unit head:* Dr. Mary H. Fox, Chair, 716-839-8530, Fax: 716-839-8516, E-mail: mfox@daemen.edu. *Application contact:* Karl Shallowhorn, Associate Director of Graduate Admissions, 716-839-8225, Fax: 716-839-8229, E-mail: kshallow@daemen.edu.

Dakota State University, College of Education, Madison, SD 57042-1799. Offers instructional technology (MSET). *Accreditation:* NCATE. Part-time programs available. Postbaccalaureate distance learning degree programs offered (minimal on-campus study). *Faculty:* 6 full-time (1 woman), 3 part-time/adjunct (1 woman). *Students:* Average age 36. 40 applicants, 95% accepted, 34 enrolled. In 2006, 9 degrees awarded. *Degree requirements:* For master's, thesis, electronic portfolio. *Entrance requirements:* For master's, GRE General Test, demonstration of technology skills, minimum GPA of 2.7. Additional exam requirements/recommendations for international students: Required—TOEFL. *Application deadline:* For fall admission, 8/1 for domestic students, 6/1 for international students. Applications are processed on a rolling basis. Application fee: $35 ($85 for international students). Electronic applications accepted. *Expenses:* Tuition, state resident: part-time $120 per credit hour. Tuition, nonresident: part-time $355 per credit hour. Required fees: $89 per credit hour. Tuition and fees vary according to course load, campus/location, program and reciprocity agreements. *Financial support:* In 2006–07, 17 students received support, including 1 research assistantship (averaging $4,812 per year);

Education—General

Dakota State University (continued)
teaching assistantships, Federal Work-Study, scholarships/grants, tuition waivers (partial), unspecified assistantships, and administrative assistantships also available. Support available to part-time students. Financial award applicants required to submit FAFSA. *Faculty research:* Educational technology evaluation, computer supported collaborative learning, cognitive theory and visual representation of the effects of ambiquitous wireless computing on student learning and productivity. *Unit head:* Dr. Judy Dittman, Dean (Interim), 605-256-5177, Fax: 605-256-7300, E-mail: judy.dittman@dsu.edu. *Application contact:* Jennifer Maher, Program Assistant II, Office of Studies and Research, 605-256-5799, Fax: 605-256-5093, E-mail: jennifer.maher@dsu.edu.

Dallas Baptist University, Dorothy M. Bush College of Education, Teaching Program, Dallas, TX 75211-9299. Offers MAT. Part-time and evening/weekend programs available. *Faculty:* 49 full-time (21 women), 112 part-time/adjunct (46 women). *Students:* 8 full-time (all women), 27 part-time (all women). 38 applicants, 18% accepted, 7 enrolled. In 2006, 8 degrees awarded. *Entrance requirements:* For master's, GRE General Test, minimum GPA of 3.0. Additional exam requirements/recommendations for international students: Required—TOEFL. *Application deadline:* Applications are processed on a rolling basis. Application fee: $25. Electronic applications accepted. *Expenses:* Tuition: Full-time $8,370; part-time $465 per credit hour. Required fees: $465 per credit hour. *Financial support:* Federal Work-Study, institutionally sponsored loans, scholarships/grants, and tuition waivers (full and partial) available. Support available to part-time students. *Unit head:* Dr. Bill Gilbert, Director, 214-333-5413, Fax: 214-333-5551, E-mail: graduate@dbu.edu. *Application contact:* Kit P. Montgomery, Director of Graduate Programs, 214-333-5242, Fax: 214-333-5579, E-mail: graduate@dbu.edu.

Defiance College, Program in Education, Defiance, OH 43512-1610. Offers MA. Part-time programs available. *Degree requirements:* For master's, thesis (for some programs). *Entrance requirements:* For master's, teaching certificate.

Delaware State University, Graduate Programs, Department of Education, Dover, DE 19901-2277. Offers curriculum and instruction (MA); education (MA); science education (MA); special education (MA). *Accreditation:* NCATE. Part-time and evening/weekend programs available. *Degree requirements:* For master's, thesis optional. *Entrance requirements:* For master's, GRE General Test, minimum GPA of 3.0 in major, 2.75 overall. Electronic applications accepted.

Delta State University, Graduate Programs, College of Education, Cleveland, MS 38733-0001. Offers M Ed, MAT, Ed D, Ed S. *Accreditation:* NCATE. Part-time and evening/weekend programs available. *Faculty:* 16 full-time (6 women), 23 part-time/adjunct (15 women). *Students:* 107 full-time (75 women), 334 part-time (280 women); includes 306 minority (302 African Americans, 2 Asian Americans or Pacific Islanders, 2 Hispanic Americans). Average age 32. In 2006, 97 master's, 3 doctorates, 18 other advanced degrees awarded. *Degree requirements:* For master's, thesis optional; for doctorate, thesis/dissertation. *Entrance requirements:* For doctorate, GRE General Test; for Ed S, master's degree, teaching certificate. *Application deadline:* For fall admission, 8/1 priority date for domestic students; for spring admission, 12/1 priority date for domestic students. Applications are processed on a rolling basis. Application fee: $0. *Financial support:* Research assistantships, career-related internships or fieldwork, Federal Work-Study, and institutionally sponsored loans available. Support available to part-time students. Financial award application deadline: 6/1. *Unit head:* Dr. Matthew Buckley, Dean, 662-846-4400, Fax: 662-846-4402.

DePaul University, School for New Learning, Chicago, IL 60604-2287. Offers applied technology (MS); educating adults (MA); integrated professional studies (MA). Part-time and evening/weekend programs available. *Faculty:* 8 full-time (2 women), 9 part-time/adjunct (5 women). *Students:* 16 full-time (9 women), 139 part-time (96 women); includes 75 minority (42 African Americans, 1 American Indian/Alaska Native, 25 Asian Americans or Pacific Islanders, 7 Hispanic Americans), 1 international. Average age 42. 30 applicants, 80% accepted. In 2006, 20 master's awarded. *Degree requirements:* For master's, thesis or alternative. *Entrance requirements:* For master's, 3 years of work experience, current related employment. *Application deadline:* For fall admission, 9/1 priority date for domestic students; for spring admission, 3/1 priority date for domestic students. Applications are processed on a rolling basis. Application fee: $25. Electronic applications accepted. *Financial support:* In 2006–07, 7 students received support. Scholarships/grants and tuition waivers (partial) available. Financial award applicants required to submit FAFSA. *Faculty research:* Interactive problem-based learning, liberal learning and professional competence, effective instructional practice. *Unit head:* Dr. Barbara Radner, Program Director, 312-362-5515, Fax: 312-362-8809, E-mail: bradner@depaul.edu. *Application contact:* Berni Thomas, Assistant Director, 312-362-5744, Fax: 312-362-8809, E-mail: bthoma10@depaul.edu.

DeSales University, Graduate Division, Program in Education, Center Valley, PA 18034-9568. Offers academic standards and information (Certificate); bilingual/ESL studies (Certificate); biology (M Ed); chemistry (M Ed); computers in education (K-12) (M Ed); computers in education (K-8) (M Ed); English (M Ed); instructional technology specialist (Certificate); mathematics (M Ed); special education (M Ed, Certificate); TESOL (M Ed). Part-time and evening/weekend programs available. Postbaccalaureate distance learning degree programs offered (minimal on-campus study). *Students:* 34 full-time, 190 part-time. In 2006, 30 degrees awarded. *Degree requirements:* For master's, thesis project. *Entrance requirements:* For master's, teaching certificate. *Application deadline:* Applications are processed on a rolling basis. Application fee: $35. Electronic applications accepted. *Expenses:* Contact institution. *Financial support:* Unspecified assistantships available. Support available to part-time students. Financial award application deadline: 5/1. *Faculty research:* Effective teaching, computer interfacing in chemistry labs, computer applications to teaching, history of philosophy, aesthetics multidrug-resistant cancer. *Unit head:* Dr. Lujean Baab, Director of M.Ed. Program, 610-282-1100 Ext. 1739, Fax: 610-282-3734, E-mail: lujean.baab@desales.edu. *Application contact:* Donna L. Cressman, Program Secretary, 610-282-1100 Ext. 1461, Fax: 610-282-3734, E-mail: med@desales.edu.

Doane College, Program in Education, Crete, NE 68333-2430. Offers curriculum and instruction (M Ed); educational leadership (M Ed). *Accreditation:* NCATE. Part-time and evening/weekend programs available. *Degree requirements:* For master's, thesis. *Entrance requirements:* For master's, minimum GPA of 2.5. Electronic applications accepted. Expenses: Contact institution.

Dominican College, Division of Teacher Education, Department of Teacher Education, Orangeburg, NY 10962-1210. Offers teacher of students with disabilities (MS Ed); teacher of visually impaired (MS Ed). Part-time and evening/weekend programs available. Postbaccalaureate distance learning degree programs offered (minimal on-campus study). *Faculty:* 2 full-time (both women), 6 part-time/adjunct (all women). *Students:* 1 (woman) full-time, 59 part-time (48 women); includes 10 minority (2 African Americans, 2 Asian Americans or Pacific Islanders, 6 Hispanic Americans). Average age 41. In 2006, 10 degrees awarded. *Degree requirements:* For master's, practicum, research project. *Entrance requirements:* For master's, interview, 3 letters of recommendation, minimum undergraduate GPA of 3.0. Additional exam requirements/recommendations for international students: Required—TOEFL (minimum score 550 paper-based; 213 computer-based). *Application deadline:* Applications are processed on a rolling basis. Application fee: $50. *Financial support:* Applicants required to submit FAFSA. *Unit head:* Dr. Rona Shaw, Program Director, 845-848-4081, Fax: 845-359-7802, E-mail: rona.shaw@dc.edu. *Application contact:* Director of Admissions, 845-848-7900, Fax: 845-365-3150, E-mail: admissions@dc.edu.

Dominican University, School of Education, River Forest, IL 60305-1099. Offers curriculum and instruction (MA Ed); early childhood education (MS); education (MAT); educational administration (MA); literacy (MS); special education (MS). Part-time and evening/weekend programs available. *Faculty:* 17 full-time (14 women), 37 part-time/adjunct (24 women). *Students:* 65 full-time (46 women), 514 part-time (425 women); includes 78 minority (23 African Americans, 16 Asian Americans or Pacific Islanders, 39 Hispanic Americans), 2 international. Average age 34. 130 applicants, 89% accepted, 100 enrolled. In 2006, 203 degrees awarded. *Entrance requirements:* For master's, Illinois certification test of basic skills. Additional exam requirements/recommendations for international students: Required—TOEFL (minimum score 550 paper-based; 213 computer-based). *Application deadline:* Applications are processed on a rolling basis. Application fee: $25. *Expenses:* Contact institution. Tuition and fees vary according to campus/location and program. *Financial support:* In 2006–07, 63 students received support. Career-related internships or fieldwork, scholarships/grants, and tuition waivers (partial) available. Support available to part-time students. Financial award application deadline: 8/15; financial award applicants required to submit FAFSA. *Faculty research:* Governance of private education institutions, reading and language arts, inclusion, organizational planning, leadership and vision. *Unit head:* Sr. Colleen McNicholas, Dean, 708-524-6830, Fax: 708-524-6665, E-mail: educate@dom.edu. *Application contact:* Keven Hansen, Coordinator of Admissions and Recruitment, 708-524-6921, Fax: 708-524-6665, E-mail: educate@dom.edu.

Dominican University of California, Graduate Programs, School of Business, Education and Leadership, Division of Education, Multiple Subject Credential Program, San Rafael, CA 94901-2298. Offers Credential. Program also offered in Ukiah, CA. *Entrance requirements:* For degree, California Basic Educational Skills Test, PRAXIS, 48 units of course work in education, bachelor's degree in area other than education, minimum GPA of 2.7. Additional exam requirements/recommendations for international students: Required—TOEFL (minimum score 550 paper-based; 213 computer-based). Electronic applications accepted.

Dominican University of California, Graduate Programs, School of Business, Education and Leadership, Division of Education, Program in Education, San Rafael, CA 94901-2298. Offers MS. *Entrance requirements:* For master's, minimum GPA of 3.0, research project. Additional exam requirements/recommendations for international students: Required—TOEFL (minimum score 550 paper-based; 213 computer-based). Electronic applications accepted.

Dominican University of California, Graduate Programs, School of Business, Education and Leadership, Division of Education, Single Subject Credential Program, San Rafael, CA 94901-2298. Offers Credential. *Entrance requirements:* For degree, California Basic Educational Skills Test, PRAXIS, minimum GPA of 2.7, bachelor's degree in area other than education, 48 units of course work in education. Additional exam requirements/recommendations for international students: Required—TOEFL (minimum score 550 paper-based; 213 computer-based). Electronic applications accepted.

Dordt College, Program in Education, Sioux Center, IA 51250-1697. Offers M Ed. Part-time programs available. Postbaccalaureate distance learning degree programs offered (minimal on-campus study). *Faculty:* 5 full-time (2 women), 3 part-time/adjunct (2 women). *Students:* 6 applicants, 100% accepted. In 2006, 7 degrees awarded. *Degree requirements:* For master's, thesis, comprehensive exam. *Entrance requirements:* For master's, GRE or MAT. Additional exam requirements/recommendations for international students: Required—TOEFL. *Application deadline:* For spring admission, 6/1 priority date for domestic and international students. Applications are processed on a rolling basis. Application fee: $25. Electronic applications accepted. *Unit head:* Dr. Pat Kornelis, Director of Graduate Education, 712-722-6235, Fax: 712-722-1198, E-mail: pkornelis@dordt.edu. *Application contact:* Kay DeBoom, Secretary of Graduate Education, 800-343-6738, Fax: 712-722-1198, E-mail: m_ed@dordt.edu.

Dowling College, Graduate Programs in Education, Oakdale, NY 11769-1999. Offers educational administration (Ed D, PD), including computers in education (PD), educational administration (Ed D), school administration and supervision (PD), school district administration (PD); human development and learning (MS Ed); literacy (MS Ed); literacy/special education (MS Ed); secondary education (MS Ed); special education (MS Ed). *Accreditation:* NCATE. Part-time and evening/weekend programs available. Postbaccalaureate distance learning degree programs offered. *Faculty:* 29 full-time (13 women), 91 part-time/adjunct (60 women). *Students:* 496 full-time (364 women), 1,083 part-time (827 women); includes 119 minority (37 African Americans, 20 Asian Americans or Pacific Islanders, 62 Hispanic Americans), 2 international. Average age 38. 618 applicants, 86% accepted, 300 enrolled. In 2006, 641 master's, 25 doctorates awarded. *Degree requirements:* For master's and PD, comprehensive exam; for doctorate, thesis/dissertation. *Entrance requirements:* For master's, minimum GPA of 3.0; for doctorate, GRE, master's degree; for PD, teaching certificate. Additional exam requirements/recommendations for international students: Required—TOEFL (minimum score 550 paper-based). *Application deadline:* For fall admission, 9/1 priority date for domestic students; for winter admission, 1/1 priority date for domestic students; for spring admission, 2/1 priority date for domestic students. Applications are processed on a rolling basis. Application fee: $25. Electronic applications accepted. *Expenses:* Tuition: Full-time $16,008; part-time $667 per credit. Tuition and fees vary according to course load. *Financial support:* In 2006–07, 358 students received support, including 20 research assistantships with tuition reimbursements available (averaging $3,150 per year); career-related internships or fieldwork, Federal Work-Study, scholarships/grants, tuition waivers (partial), and unspecified assistantships also available. Support available to part-time students. Financial award application deadline: 6/30; financial award applicants required to submit FAFSA. *Faculty research:* Natural readers, Korean styles and learning strategies, mothers of children with disabilities, computers in instruction, cultural background and organizational roadblocks to problem solving. *Unit head:* Dr. Clyde Payne, Associate Provost, 631-244-3404, Fax: 631-589-6644, E-mail: paynec@dowling.edu. *Application contact:* Franks S. Pizzardi, Director of Admissions Operations, 631-244-3227, Fax: 631-244-1059, E-mail: pizzardf@dowling.edu.

Drake University, School of Education, Des Moines, IA 50311-4516. Offers MAT, MS, MSE, MST, Ed D, Ed S. Part-time and evening/weekend programs available. *Faculty:* 10 full-time (3 women), 28 part-time/adjunct (16 women). *Students:* 29 full-time (18 women), 575 part-time (422 women); includes 16 African Americans, 5 Asian Americans or Pacific Islanders, 4 Hispanic Americans, 4 international. 498 applicants, 39% accepted, 175 enrolled. In 2006, 219 master's, 7 doctorates, 14 other advanced degrees awarded. *Degree requirements:* For master's and Ed S, internships (s); for doctorate, thesis/dissertation, internships (s), comprehensive exam, registration. *Entrance requirements:* For master's, GRE General Test, MAT, or Drake Writing Assessment, resumé, 2 letters of recommendation; for doctorate, GRE General Test or MAT, master's degree, 3 letters of recommendation; for Ed S, GRE General Test or MAT. Additional exam requirements/recommendations for international students: Required—TOEFL (minimum score 550 paper-based; 213 computer-based). *Application deadline:* For fall admission, 7/1 priority date for domestic students, 6/1 priority date for international students; for spring admission, 11/1 priority date for domestic students, 10/1 priority date for international students. Applications are processed on a rolling basis. Application fee: $25. Electronic applications accepted. *Expenses:* Contact institution. *Financial support:* In 2006–07, 14 research assistantships were awarded; career-related internships or fieldwork and unspecified assistantships also available. Support available to part-time students. *Faculty research:* Counseling and rehabilitation, behavioral supports, inquiry-based science methods, teacher quality enhancement. Total annual research expenditures: $1.5 million. *Unit head:* Dr. Janet McMahill, Dean, 515-271-3829, E-mail: janet.mcmahill@drake.edu. *Application contact:* Ann J. Martin, Graduate Coordinator, 515-271-2034, Fax: 515-271-2831, E-mail: ann.martin@drake.edu.

Drexel University, School of Education, Philadelphia, PA 19104-2875. Offers educational administration and collaborative learning (MS); educational leadership and learning technology (PhD); global and international education (MS); graduate intern teaching (Certificate); higher education (MS); instructional technology (Spt); post-bachelor's teaching (Certificate); school principal (Certificate); school superintendent (Certificate); science of instruction (MS); teaching English as a second language (Certificate); teaching, learning and curriculum (MS). Part-time and evening/weekend programs available. Postbaccalaureate distance learning degree programs offered. *Degree requirements:* For doctorate, thesis/dissertation. Electronic applications accepted. Expenses: Contact institution.

See Close-Up on page 871.

Drury University, Graduate Programs in Education, Springfield, MO 65802. Offers elementary education (M Ed); gifted education (M Ed); human services (M Ed); middle school teaching (M Ed); physical education (M Ed); secondary education (M Ed). *Accreditation:* NCATE. Part-time and evening/weekend programs available. *Degree requirements:* For master's, thesis. *Entrance requirements:* For master's, GRE or MAT, minimum GPA of 2.75. *Faculty research:* Cultural enrichment, research skills, parental involvement relating to reading skills, reading strategies for mainstreaming children.

Duke University, Graduate School, Program in Teaching, Durham, NC 27708. Offers MAT, MAT/MEM. *Accreditation:* NCATE. *Students:* 19 full-time (17 women); includes 4 minority (2 African Americans, 2 Asian Americans or Pacific Islanders), 1 international. 58 applicants, 47% accepted, 17 enrolled. In 2006, 13 degrees awarded. *Entrance requirements:* For master's, GRE General Test. Additional exam requirements/recommendations for international students: Required—TOEFL (minimum score 550 paper-based; 213 computer-based; 83 iBT), IELTS (minimum score 7). *Application deadline:* For fall admission, 12/15 priority date for domestic students; for spring admission, 11/1 for domestic students. Application fee: $75. Electronic applications accepted. *Financial support:* Application deadline: 12/31. *Unit head:* Rosemary Thorne, Director, 919-684-4353, Fax: 919-684-4483.

Duquesne University, School of Education, Pittsburgh, PA 15282-0001. Offers MS Ed, Ed D, PhD, CAGS. *Accreditation:* NCATE. Part-time and evening/weekend programs available. *Faculty:* 57 full-time (30 women), 40 part-time/adjunct (19 women). *Students:* 864; includes 52 minority (36 African Americans, 10 Asian Americans or Pacific Islanders, 6 Hispanic Americans), 8 international. Average age 30. 286 applicants, 80% accepted, 179 enrolled. In 2006, 282 master's, 30 doctorates, 8 other advanced degrees awarded. *Degree requirements:* For master's, thesis optional; for doctorate, thesis/dissertation. *Entrance requirements:* For master's, MAT, minimum GPA of 3.0; for doctorate, GRE General Test, MAT, minimum GPA of 3.25; for CAGS, MAT, GRE, interview. Additional exam requirements/recommendations for international students: Required—TOEFL. *Application deadline:* For fall admission, 8/1 for domestic and international students; for spring admission, 12/1 for domestic and international students. Applications are processed on a rolling basis. Application fee: $50. *Expenses:* Tuition: Part-time $723 per credit. Required fees: $71 per credit. Tuition and fees vary according to degree level and program. *Financial support:* In 2006–07, 458 students received support, including 12 research assistantships with full and partial tuition reimbursements available (averaging $5,200 per year), 7 teaching assistantships with full and partial tuition reimbursements available; career-related internships or fieldwork, Federal Work-Study, institutionally sponsored loans, and tuition waivers (partial) also available. Support available to part-time students. Total annual research expenditures: $40,000. *Unit head:* Dr. Olga Welch, Dean, 412-396-6102, Fax: 412-396-5585. *Application contact:* Scott Rhodes, Director of Student and Academic Services, 412-396-5193, E-mail: rhodesst@duq.edu.

D'Youville College, Department of Education, Buffalo, NY 14201-1084. Offers elementary education (MS Ed, Teaching Certificate); secondary education (MS Ed, Teaching Certificate); special education (MS Ed). Part-time and evening/weekend programs available. *Faculty:* 31 full-time (18 women), 38 part-time/adjunct (25 women). *Students:* 613 full-time (434 women), 303 part-time (223 women); includes 26 minority (14 African Americans, 1 American Indian/Alaska Native, 2 Asian Americans or Pacific Islanders, 9 Hispanic Americans), 727 international. Average age 28. 1,092 applicants. In 2006, 328 master's, 401 other advanced degrees awarded. *Degree requirements:* For master's, project or thesis. *Entrance requirements:* For master's, minimum GPA of 3.0. Additional exam requirements/recommendations for international students: Required—TOEFL (minimum score 500 paper-based; 173 computer-based). *Application deadline:* For fall admission, 5/1 priority date for international students; for spring admission, 9/1 priority date for international students. Applications are processed on a rolling basis. Application fee: $25. Electronic applications accepted. *Financial support:* In 2006–07, 1 research assistantship with partial tuition reimbursement (averaging $3,000 per year) was awarded; career-related internships or fieldwork and scholarships/grants also available. Support available to part-time students. Financial award application deadline: 3/1; financial award applicants required to submit FAFSA. *Faculty research:* Developmentally disabled, multiculturalism, early childhood education. *Unit head:* Dr. David Gorlewski, Chair, 716-829-8140, Fax: 716-829-7660. *Application contact:* Linda Fisher, Graduate Admissions Director, 716-829-8400, Fax: 716-829-7900, E-mail: graduateadmissions@dyc.edu.

Earlham College, Graduate Programs, Richmond, IN 47374-4095. Offers M Ed, MAT. *Degree requirements:* For master's, registration. *Entrance requirements:* For master's, GRE, PRAXIS I, PRAXIS II.

East Carolina University, Graduate School, College of Education, Greenville, NC 27858-4353. Offers MA, MA Ed, MLS, MS, MSA, Ed D, CAS, Ed S. *Accreditation:* NCATE. Part-time and evening/weekend programs available. Postbaccalaureate distance learning degree programs offered (no on-campus study). *Faculty:* 72 full-time (38 women), 9 part-time/adjunct (7 women). *Students:* 223 full-time (186 women), 999 part-time (831 women); includes 196 minority (172 African Americans, 7 American Indian/Alaska Native, 11 Asian Americans or Pacific Islanders, 6 Hispanic Americans), 3 international. Average age 35. 234 applicants, 30% accepted, 61 enrolled. In 2006, 444 master's, 24 doctorates, 9 other advanced degrees awarded. *Degree requirements:* For master's, thesis optional; for doctorate, thesis/dissertation. *Entrance requirements:* For master's, GRE or MAT, bachelor's degree in related field, minimum GPA of 2.5; for doctorate, GRE or MAT, interview, minimum GPA of 3.5. Additional exam requirements/recommendations for international students: Required—TOEFL. *Application deadline:* For fall admission, 6/1 priority date for domestic students. Applications are processed on a rolling basis. Application fee: $50. *Financial support:* Research assistantships with partial tuition reimbursements, teaching assistantships with partial tuition reimbursements, Federal Work-Study available. Support available to part-time students. Financial award application deadline: 6/1. *Unit head:* Dr. John Swope, Interim Dean, 252-328-1000, Fax: 252-328-4219, E-mail: swopej@ecu.edu. *Application contact:* Dean of Graduate School, 252-328-6012, Fax: 252-328-6071, E-mail: gradschool@ecu.edu.

East Central University, School of Graduate Studies, Department of Education, Ada, OK 74820-6899. Offers M Ed. *Accreditation:* NCATE. Evening/weekend programs available. *Faculty:* 34 part-time/adjunct (14 women). *Students:* 514 (398 women); includes 116 minority (19 African Americans, 89 American Indian/Alaska Native, 2 Asian Americans or Pacific Islanders, 6 Hispanic Americans). Average age 35. 145 applicants, 99% accepted. In 2006, 211 degrees awarded. *Entrance requirements:* For master's, minimum GPA of 2.5. Application fee: $0 ($50 for international students). *Financial support:* Fellowships, career-related internships or fieldwork and tuition waivers (partial) available. Support available to part-time students. *Unit head:* Dr. Bill Osborne, Dean, 580-332-8000 Ext. 350. *Application contact:* Juanita L. Pratt, Secretary, 580-310-5708, Fax: 580-282-8691, E-mail: jpratt@ecok.edu.

Eastern Connecticut State University, School of Education and Professional Studies/Graduate Division, Willimantic, CT 06226-2295. Offers MS. *Accreditation:* NCATE. Part-time and evening/weekend programs available. *Faculty:* 19 full-time (10 women), 16 part-time/adjunct (7 women). *Students:* 60 full-time (45 women), 239 part-time (174 women); includes 23 minority (11 African Americans, 4 Asian Americans or Pacific Islanders, 8 Hispanic Americans). Average age 35. 50 applicants, 80% accepted, 31 enrolled. In 2006, 102 degrees awarded. *Degree requirements:* For master's, thesis optional. *Entrance requirements:* For master's, minimum GPA of 2.7. Additional exam requirements/recommendations for international students: Required—TOEFL (minimum score 550 paper-based; 213 computer-based). *Application deadline:* For fall admission, 7/6 priority date for domestic and international students; for spring admission, 11/3 priority date for domestic and international students. Applications are processed on a rolling basis. Application fee: $50. *Expenses:* Tuition, state resident: full-time $3,970. Tuition, nonresident: full-time $11,061; part-time $336 per credit. Required fees: $35 per credit. *Financial support:* Teaching assistantships, career-related internships or fieldwork, scholarships/grants, and unspecified assistantships available. Support available to part-time students. Financial award application deadline: 3/15. *Unit head:* Dr. Patricia A. Kleine, Dean, 860-465-5293, Fax: 860-465-4538, E-mail: kleinep@easternct.edu. *Application contact:* Dr. Tuesday L. Cooper, Associate Dean, 860-465-4543, Fax: 860-465-4538, E-mail: coopert@easternct.edu.

Eastern Illinois University, Graduate School, College of Education and Professional Studies, Charleston, IL 61920-3099. Offers MS, MS Ed, Ed S. *Accreditation:* NCATE. Part-time and evening/weekend programs available. *Faculty:* 38 full-time (20 women). In 2006, 294 master's, 45 other advanced degrees awarded. *Degree requirements:* For Ed S, thesis. *Application deadline:* For fall admission, 7/31 priority date for domestic students. Applications are processed on a rolling basis. Application fee: $30. *Expenses:* Tuition, state resident: part-time $169 per semester hour. Tuition, nonresident: part-time $508 per semester hour. Required fees: $60 per semester hour. *Financial support:* In 2006–07, 12 research assistantships with tuition reimbursements (averaging $7,200 per year), 13 teaching assistantships with tuition reimbursements (averaging $7,200 per year) were awarded; career-related internships or fieldwork and Federal Work-Study also available. Support available to part-time students. *Unit head:* Dr. Diane Jackman, Dean, 217-581-2524, Fax: 217-581-2518, E-mail: dhjackman@eiu.edu.

Eastern Kentucky University, The Graduate School, College of Education, Richmond, KY 40475-3102. Offers MA, MA Ed. *Accreditation:* NCATE. Part-time programs available. Postbaccalaureate distance learning degree programs offered (minimal on-campus study). *Faculty:* 53 full-time (30 women), 32 part-time/adjunct (20 women). *Students:* 171 full-time (134 women), 969 part-time (751 women); includes 36 minority (26 African Americans, 3 American Indian/Alaska Native, 1 Asian American or Pacific Islander, 6 Hispanic Americans), 1 international. Average age 33. 1,186 applicants, 36% accepted, 346 enrolled. In 2006, 462 degrees awarded. *Entrance requirements:* For master's, GRE General Test, minimum GPA of 2.5. Application fee: $35. *Expenses:* Tuition, state resident: full-time $5,610. Tuition, nonresident: full-time $15,910. *Financial support:* In 2006–07, research assistantships (averaging $6,500 per year), teaching assistantships (averaging $6,500 per year) were awarded; fellowships, career-related internships or fieldwork, Federal Work-Study, and scholarships/grants also available. Support available to part-time students. *Faculty research:* Dispositions to teach, technology in education, distance learning. *Unit head:* Dr. William Phillips, Dean, 859-622-1175, Fax: 859-622-1831. *Application contact:* 859-622-1828, Fax: 859-622-1831.

Eastern Mennonite University, Program in Education, Harrisonburg, VA 22802-2462. Offers MA. *Accreditation:* NCATE. Part-time programs available. *Faculty:* 5 full-time (4 women), 27 part-time/adjunct (17 women). *Students:* Average age 34. 51 applicants, 100% accepted, 51 enrolled. In 2006, 22 degrees awarded. *Degree requirements:* For master's, portfolio, research projects. *Entrance requirements:* For master's, 1 year of teaching experience, interview, minimum undergraduate GPA of 2.75, state exam scores. Additional exam requirements/recommendations for international students: Required—TOEFL (minimum score 550 paper-based; 213 computer-based). *Application deadline:* Applications are processed on a rolling basis. Application fee: $25. *Expenses:* Contact institution. *Financial support:* Federal Work-Study and scholarships/grants available. Financial award application deadline: 6/30; financial award applicants required to submit FAFSA. *Faculty research:* Effective literacy instruction for middle school English language learners, beginning teacher's emotional experiences, constructivist learning environments, restorative discipline. *Unit head:* Dr. Donovan D. Steiner, Director, 540-432-4144, Fax: 540-432-4071, E-mail: steinerd@emu.edu. *Application contact:* Yvonne Martin, Education Secretary, 540-432-4350, Fax: 540-432-4071, E-mail: yvonne.martin@emu.edu.

Eastern Michigan University, Graduate School, College of Education, Ypsilanti, MI 48197. Offers MA, SPA, Ed D, Post Master's Certificate. *Accreditation:* NCATE. Part-time and evening/weekend programs available. Postbaccalaureate distance learning degree programs offered (minimal on-campus study). *Faculty:* 90 full-time (67 women). *Students:* 173 full-time (148 women), 1,140 part-time (866 women); includes 184 minority (144 African Americans, 5 American Indian/Alaska Native, 11 Asian Americans or Pacific Islanders, 24 Hispanic Americans), 19 international. Average age 34. In 2006, 317 master's, 11 doctorates, 14 other advanced degrees awarded. *Degree requirements:* For doctorate, thesis/dissertation. *Entrance requirements:* For master's, GRE; for doctorate, GRE General Test. Additional exam requirements/recommendations for international students: Required—TOEFL. *Application deadline:* For fall admission, 5/15 priority date for domestic students, 5/1 priority date for international students; for winter admission, 10/15 priority date for domestic students, 10/1 priority date for international students; for spring admission, 3/15 priority date for domestic students, 3/1 priority date for international students. Applications are processed on a rolling basis. Application fee: $35. *Expenses:* Tuition, state resident: part-time $341 per credit hour. Tuition, nonresident: full-time $16,104; part-time $671 per credit hour. Required fees: $816; $34 per credit hour. $40 per term. One-time fee: $82 full-time. Tuition and fees vary according to course level, course load, degree level and reciprocity agreements. *Financial support:* Fellowships, research assistantships with full tuition reimbursements, teaching assistantships with full tuition reimbursements, career-related internships or fieldwork, Federal Work-Study, institutionally sponsored loans, scholarships/grants, tuition waivers (partial), and unspecified assistantships available. Support available to part-time students. Financial award applicants required to submit FAFSA. *Unit head:* Dr. Vernon C. Polite, Dean, 734-487-1414, Fax: 734-484-6471, E-mail: vpolite@emich.edu.

Eastern Nazarene College, Adult and Graduate Studies, Division of Education, Quincy, MA 02170-2999. Offers early childhood education (M Ed, Certificate); elementary education (M Ed, Certificate); English as a second language (M Ed, Certificate); instructional enrichment and development (M Ed, Certificate); middle school education (M Ed, Certificate); moderate special needs education (M Ed, Certificate); principal (Certificate); program development and supervision (M Ed, Certificate); secondary education (M Ed, Certificate); special education administrator (Certificate); supervisor (Certificate); teacher of reading (M Ed, Certificate). M Ed and Certificate also available through weekend program for administration, special needs, and reading only. Part-time and evening/weekend programs available. *Faculty:* 9 full-time (5 women), 11 part-time/adjunct (5 women). *Students:* 135. Average age 35. 20 applicants, 100% accepted. In 2006, 2 degrees awarded. *Entrance requirements:* Additional exam requirements/recommendations for international students: Required—TOEFL (minimum score 550 paper-based). *Application deadline:* Applications are processed on a rolling basis. Application fee: $35. *Financial support:* Career-related internships or fieldwork available. Support available to part-time students. Financial award applicants required to submit FAFSA. *Unit head:* Dr. Lorne Ranstrom, Chair, 617-745-3528, E-mail: randstrol@enc.edu. *Application contact:* Christine Galbraith, Graduate Studies Recruiter, 617-774-6703, Fax: 617-984-4901, E-mail: christine.galbraith@enc.edu.

Eastern New Mexico University, Graduate School, College of Education and Technology, Department of Curriculum and Instruction, Portales, NM 88130. Offers M Ed. Part-time programs available. *Faculty:* 20 full-time (12 women), 5 part-time/adjunct (all women). *Students:* 10 full-time (4 women), 188 part-time (146 women); includes 52 minority (4 African Americans, 10 American Indian/Alaska Native, 38 Hispanic Americans), 1 international. Average age 38. 130 applicants, 53% accepted. In 2006, 52 degrees awarded. *Degree requirements:* For master's, thesis optional. *Entrance requirements:* For master's, minimum GPA of 2.5. *Application deadline:* For fall admission, 8/20 priority date for domestic students. Applications are processed on a rolling basis. Application fee: $0. Electronic applications accepted. *Expenses:* Tuition, state resident: full-time $2,478; part-time $103 per credit hour. Tuition, nonresident: full-time $8,034; part-time $335 per credit hour. Required fees: $35 per credit hour. *Financial support:* In 2006–07, 10 research assistantships (averaging $8,200 per year), teaching assistantships (averaging $8,200 per year) were awarded; fellowships, Federal Work-Study also available. Support available to part-time students. Financial award application deadline: 3/1. *Unit head:* Dr. Romelia Hurtado de Vivas, Graduate Coordinator, 505-562-2977, E-mail: romelia.hurtadodevivas@enmu.edu.

Eastern New Mexico University, Graduate School, College of Education and Technology, Department of Educational Studies, Portales, NM 88130. Offers counseling (MA); education (M Ed); school counseling (M Ed); special education (M Ed, M Sp Ed). *Accreditation:* NCATE.

Education—General

Eastern New Mexico University (continued)
Part-time and evening/weekend programs available. *Faculty:* 7 full-time (4 women). *Students:* 2 full-time (1 woman), 80 part-time (60 women); includes 26 minority (3 African Americans, 2 American Indian/Alaska Native, 21 Hispanic Americans). 29 applicants, 83% accepted. In 2006, 18 degrees awarded. *Degree requirements:* For master's, thesis optional. *Entrance requirements:* For master's, minimum GPA of 2.5. *Application deadline:* For fall admission, 8/20 priority date for domestic students. Applications are processed on a rolling basis. Application fee: $0. Electronic applications accepted. *Expenses:* Tuition, state resident: full-time $2,478; part-time $103 per credit hour. Tuition, nonresident: full-time $8,034; part-time $335 per credit hour. Required fees: $35 per credit hour. *Financial support:* In 2006–07, 5 research assistantships (averaging $8,200 per year) were awarded; fellowships, teaching assistantships, career-related internships or fieldwork and Federal Work-Study also available. Support available to part-time students. Financial award application deadline: 3/1. *Unit head:* Dr. Mark Isham, Graduate Coordinator, 505-562-2260, E-mail: mark.isham@enmu.edu.

Eastern Oregon University, School of Education and Business, Master of Science Degree Program, La Grande, OR 97850-2899. Offers education (MS). Part-time programs available. Postbaccalaureate distance learning degree programs offered (no on-campus study). *Degree requirements:* For master's, thesis. *Entrance requirements:* For master's, GRE General Test.

Eastern University, Graduate Education Programs, St. Davids, PA 19087-3696. Offers English as a second or foreign language (Certificate); multicultural education (M Ed); school health services (M Ed). Part-time programs available. *Entrance requirements:* For master's, minimum GPA of 2.5. Additional exam requirements/recommendations for international students: Required—TOEFL.

See Close-Up on page 873.

Eastern Washington University, Graduate Studies, College of Education and Human Development, Department of Education, Cheney, WA 99004-2431. Offers adult education (M Ed); college instruction (MA, MS); curriculum and instruction (M Ed); early childhood education (M Ed); educational leadership (M Ed); elementary teaching (M Ed); foundations of education (M Ed); instructional media and technology (M Ed); literacy specialist (M Ed); school library media administration (M Ed); science education (M Ed); social science education (M Ed); supervising (clinic) teaching (M Ed). *Accreditation:* NCATE. Part-time programs available. *Degree requirements:* For master's, comprehensive exam. *Entrance requirements:* For master's, minimum GPA of 3.0.

East Stroudsburg University of Pennsylvania, Graduate School, School of Professional Studies, East Stroudsburg, PA 18301-2999. Offers M Ed, MS. Part-time and evening/weekend programs available. *Faculty:* 34 full-time (18 women), 24 part-time/adjunct (14 women). *Students:* 107 full-time (77 women), 407 part-time (336 women); includes 32 minority (9 African Americans, 1 American Indian/Alaska Native, 3 Asian Americans or Pacific Islanders, 19 Hispanic Americans), 3 international. Average age 32. In 2006, 151 degrees awarded. *Degree requirements:* For master's, thesis (for some programs), comprehensive exam. *Entrance requirements:* Additional exam requirements/recommendations for international students: Required—TOEFL (minimum score 560 paper-based; 220 computer-based; 83 iBT). *Application deadline:* For fall admission, 7/31 priority date for domestic students, 5/1 priority date for international students; for spring admission, 11/30 for domestic students, 10/1 for international students. Applications are processed on a rolling basis. Application fee: $50. *Expenses:* Tuition, state resident: full-time $6,048; part-time $336 per credit. Tuition, nonresident: full-time $9,678; part-time $538 per credit. Required fees: $1,353; $67 per credit. One-time fee: $37 part-time. *Financial support:* In 2006–07, 33 research assistantships with full and partial tuition reimbursements were awarded; career-related internships or fieldwork, Federal Work-Study, and institutionally sponsored loans also available. Financial award application deadline: 3/1; financial award applicants required to submit FAFSA. *Unit head:* Dr. Pamela Kramer, Interim Dean, 570-422-3377, Fax: 570-422-3506, E-mail: pkramer@po-box.esu.edu.

East Tennessee State University, School of Graduate Studies, College of Education, Johnson City, TN 37614. Offers M Ed, MA, MAT, Ed D, Ed S. *Accreditation:* NCATE. Part-time and evening/weekend programs available. Terminal master's awarded for partial completion of doctoral program. *Degree requirements:* For doctorate, thesis/dissertation, oral and written exams; for Ed S, internship, practicum. *Entrance requirements:* For master's, GRE; for doctorate, GRE General Test, GRE Subject Test; for Ed S, GRE General Test, teacher certification. Additional exam requirements/recommendations for international students: Required—TOEFL (minimum score 550 paper-based; 213 computer-based).

Edgewood College, Program in Education, Madison, WI 53711-1997. Offers director of instruction (Certificate); director of special education and pupil services (Certificate); education (MA Ed); educational administration (MA); educational leadership (Ed D); emotional disturbances (MA, Certificate); learning disabilities (MA, Certificate); learning disabilities and emotional disturbances (MA, Certificate); school business administration (Certificate); school principalship K-12 (Certificate). *Accreditation:* NCATE (one or more programs are accredited). Part-time and evening/weekend programs available. *Students:* 30 full-time (21 women), 180 part-time (117 women); includes 7 minority (5 African Americans, 2 Asian Americans or Pacific Islanders), 2 international. Average age 38. In 2006, 25 master's, 20 doctorates awarded. *Degree requirements:* For master's, practicum, research project. *Entrance requirements:* For master's, minimum GPA of 2.75, 2 letters of recommendation. Additional exam requirements/recommendations for international students: Required—TOEFL. *Application deadline:* For fall admission, 8/24 for domestic students, 8/1 for international students; for spring admission, 1/10 for domestic students, 10/1 for international students. Applications are processed on a rolling basis. Application fee: $25. Electronic applications accepted. *Unit head:* Dr. Joseph Schmiedicke, Chair, 608-663-2293, Fax: 608-663-3291, E-mail: schmied@edgewood.edu. *Application contact:* Paula O'Malley, Graduate Student Admissions Counselor, 608-663-2282, Fax: 608-663-3291, E-mail: gradprograms@edgewood.edu.

Edinboro University of Pennsylvania, Graduate Studies and Research, School of Education, Edinboro, PA 16444. Offers M Ed, MA, Certificate. Certificates issued by a state agency. *Accreditation:* NCATE. Part-time and evening/weekend programs available. *Faculty:* 39 full-time (26 women). *Students:* 233 full-time (174 women), 398 part-time (308 women); includes 20 minority (14 African Americans, 1 American Indian/Alaska Native, 2 Asian Americans or Pacific Islanders, 3 Hispanic Americans). Average age 31. In 2006, 203 master's, 47 other advanced degrees awarded. *Degree requirements:* For master's and Certificate, competency exam. *Entrance requirements:* For master's and Certificate, GRE or MAT, minimum QPA of 2.5. *Application deadline:* Applications are processed on a rolling basis. Application fee: $30. Electronic applications accepted. *Expenses:* Tuition, state resident: full-time $6,048; part-time $336 per credit. Tuition, nonresident: full-time $9,678; part-time $538 per credit. Required fees: $1,849; $42 per credit. *Financial support:* In 2006–07, 66 research assistantships with full and partial tuition reimbursements (averaging $3,850 per year) were awarded; career-related internships or fieldwork, Federal Work-Study, institutionally sponsored loans, scholarships/grants, and unspecified assistantships also available. Support available to part-time students. Financial award application deadline: 2/15; financial award applicants required to submit FAFSA. *Unit head:* Dr. Kenneth Adams, Interim Dean, 814-732-2752, Fax: 814-732-2268, E-mail: kadams@edinboro.edu. *Application contact:* Dr. R. Scott Baldwin, Dean, 814-732-2752, Fax: 814-732-2268, E-mail: sbaldwin@edinboro.edu.

Elms College, Division of Education, Chicopee, MA 01013-2839. Offers early childhood education (MAT); education (M Ed, CAGS); elementary education (MAT); English as a second language (MAT); reading (MAT); secondary education (MAT), including biology education, English education, Spanish education; special education (MAT). Part-time and evening/weekend programs available. *Faculty:* 9 full-time (6 women), 4 part-time/adjunct (2 women). *Students:* 8 full-time (6 women), 97 part-time (89 women); includes 4 minority (2 Asian Americans or Pacific Islanders, 2 Hispanic Americans). Average age 36. 48 applicants, 90% accepted, 40 enrolled. In 2006, 37 master's, 8 other advanced degrees awarded. *Degree requirements:* For master's, thesis (for some programs). *Entrance requirements:* For master's, Massachusetts Educators Certification Test, minimum GPA of 3.0; for CAGS, master's degree in education. Additional exam requirements/recommendations for international students: Required—TOEFL. *Application deadline:* For fall admission, 7/1 priority date for domestic students; for spring admission, 11/1 priority date for domestic students. Applications are processed on a rolling basis. Application fee: $30. *Expenses:* Tuition: Full-time $9,180; part-time $510 per credit. Tuition and fees vary according to course load. *Financial support:* In 2006–07, 3 teaching assistantships with partial tuition reimbursements were awarded; tuition waivers (partial) also available. Support available to part-time students. Financial award application deadline: 4/15; financial award applicants required to submit FAFSA. *Unit head:* Dr. Mary Janeczek, Director, 413-594-2761, Fax: 413-592-4871, E-mail: janeczeke@elms.edu.

Elon University, Program in Education, Elon, NC 27244-2010. Offers elementary education (M Ed); gifted education (M Ed); special education (M Ed). *Accreditation:* NCATE. Part-time programs available. *Faculty:* 11 full-time (8 women), 5 part-time/adjunct (all women). *Students:* Average age 31. 62 applicants, 69% accepted, 30 enrolled. In 2006, 30 degrees awarded. *Entrance requirements:* For master's, GRE, MAT. Additional exam requirements/recommendations for international students: Required—TOEFL (minimum score 550 paper-based; 213 computer-based; 79 iBT). *Application deadline:* For winter admission, 6/1 priority date for domestic students. Applications are processed on a rolling basis. Application fee: $50. Electronic applications accepted. *Expenses:* Contact institution. *Financial support:* In 2006–07, 2 students received support, including 2 fellowships (averaging $2,635 per year); Federal Work-Study and scholarships/grants also available. Support available to part-time students. Financial award application deadline: 6/1; financial award applicants required to submit FAFSA. *Faculty research:* Teaching reading to low-achieving second and third graders; pre-and post-student teaching attitudes toward teaching; children's writing; whole language methodology; critical creative thinking. *Unit head:* Dr. Judith B. Howard, Director, 336-278-5885, Fax: 336-278-5919, E-mail: howardj@elon.edu. *Application contact:* Art Fadde, Director of Graduate Admissions, 800-334-8448 Ext. 3, Fax: 336-278-7699, E-mail: afadde@elon.edu.

Emmanuel College, Graduate Programs, Programs in Education, Boston, MA 02115. Offers educational leadership (CAGS); elementary education (MAT); school administration (M Ed); secondary education (MAT). Part-time and evening/weekend programs available. *Faculty:* 4 full-time (all women), 8 part-time/adjunct (4 women). *Students:* 5 full-time (all women), 34 part-time (24 women); includes 6 minority (3 African Americans, 1 Asian American or Pacific Islander, 2 Hispanic Americans). Average age 29. 44 applicants, 23% accepted, 10 enrolled. In 2006, 21 master's, 3 other advanced degrees awarded. *Entrance requirements:* For master's, interview, resumé, 2 letters of recommendation; for CAGS, interview, leadership statement, resumé, 2 letters of recommendation. Additional exam requirements/recommendations for international students: Required—TOEFL (minimum score 600 paper-based; 250 computer-based). *Application deadline:* For fall admission, 8/15 priority date for domestic students; for spring admission, 12/8 priority date for domestic students. Applications are processed on a rolling basis. Application fee: $50. Electronic applications accepted. *Expenses:* Tuition: Full-time $5,256. *Faculty research:* Literature/reading, history of education, multicultural education, special education. *Unit head:* Brian Minchello, Associate Director, Graduate and Professional Programs, 617-735-9928, Fax: 617-735-9708, E-mail: gpp@emmanuel.edu. *Application contact:* Kristin Balutis, Enrollment Counselor, 617-735-9859, Fax: 617-735-9708, E-mail: balutkr@emmanuel.edu.

Emory University, Graduate School of Arts and Sciences, Division of Educational Studies, Atlanta, GA 30322-1100. Offers educational studies (MA, PhD, DAST); middle grades teaching (M Ed, MAT); secondary teaching (M Ed, MAT). *Accreditation:* NCATE. Terminal master's awarded for partial completion of doctoral program. *Degree requirements:* For master's, thesis/dissertation, registration; for doctorate, thesis/dissertation, comprehensive exam, registration. *Entrance requirements:* For master's and doctorate, GRE General Test, minimum GPA of 3.0. Additional exam requirements/recommendations for international students: Required—TOEFL. Electronic applications accepted. *Expenses:* Tuition: Full-time $30,246. *Faculty research:* Educational policy, educational measurement, urban and multicultural education, mathematics and science education, comparative education.

Emporia State University, School of Graduate Studies, The Teachers College, Emporia, KS 66801-5087. Offers MS, Ed S. *Accreditation:* NCATE. Part-time programs available. Postbaccalaureate distance learning degree programs offered. *Faculty:* 74 full-time (38 women), 4 part-time/adjunct (3 women). *Students:* 143 full-time (98 women), 930 part-time (680 women); includes 49 minority (19 African Americans, 4 American Indian/Alaska Native, 6 Asian Americans or Pacific Islanders, 20 Hispanic Americans), 13 international. 252 applicants, 84% accepted, 164 enrolled. In 2006, 281 master's, 7 other advanced degrees awarded. *Degree requirements:* For master's, comprehensive exam or thesis; for Ed S, thesis or alternative, internship, comprehensive exam. *Entrance requirements:* For master's, appropriate bachelor's degree; for Ed S, GRE, graduate essay exam, letters of recommendation, teacher certification. *Application deadline:* Applications are processed on a rolling basis. Application fee: $30 ($75 for international students). Electronic applications accepted. *Expenses:* Tuition, state resident: full-time $3,438; part-time $143 per credit hour. Tuition, nonresident: full-time $10,398; part-time $433 per credit hour. Required fees: $724; $44 per credit hour. *Financial support:* In 2006–07, 3 research assistantships with full tuition reimbursements (averaging $6,752 per year), 29 teaching assistantships with full tuition reimbursements (averaging $6,752 per year) were awarded; fellowships, career-related internships or fieldwork, Federal Work-Study, institutionally sponsored loans, health care benefits, and unspecified assistantships also available. Financial award application deadline: 3/15; financial award applicants required to submit FAFSA. *Unit head:* Dr. Teresa Mehring, Dean, 620-341-5367, Fax: 620-341-5785, E-mail: tmehring@emporia.edu.

Evangel University, Department of Education, Springfield, MO 65802-2191. Offers educational leadership (M Ed); reading education (M Ed); secondary teaching (M Ed); teaching (MA). Part-time and evening/weekend programs available. *Faculty:* 4 full-time (2 women), 6 part-time/adjunct (5 women). *Students:* 2 full-time (both women), 17 part-time (14 women); includes 2 minority (1 Asian American or Pacific Islander, 1 Hispanic American). Average age 26. 10 applicants, 100% accepted, 10 enrolled. In 2006, 13 degrees awarded. *Degree requirements:* For master's, thesis optional. *Entrance requirements:* For master's, PRAXIS II (preferred), GRE (accepted). Additional exam requirements/recommendations for international students: Required—TOEFL (minimum score 550 paper-based; 213 computer-based). *Application deadline:* For fall admission, 7/15 priority date for domestic students; for spring admission, 11/15 priority date for domestic students. Applications are processed on a rolling basis. Application fee: $25. *Financial support:* In 2006–07, 6 students received support. Career-related internships or fieldwork, institutionally sponsored loans, and scholarships/grants available. Support available to part-time students. Financial award application deadline: 3/1; financial award applicants required to submit FAFSA. *Unit head:* Dr. Jeff Hittenberger, Chair, 417-865-2815 Ext. 8559, E-mail: hittenbergerj@evangel.edu. *Application contact:* Charity H. Fahlstrom, Director of Graduate and Professional Studies Admissions, 417-865-2811 Ext. 1227, Fax: 417-575-5484.

The Evergreen State College, Graduate Programs, Program in Teaching, Olympia, WA 98505. Offers MIT. *Faculty:* 6 full-time (3 women). *Students:* 77 full-time (53 women); includes 7 minority (2 African Americans, 1 American Indian/Alaska Native, 3 Asian Americans or Pacific Islanders, 1 Hispanic American). Average age 30. 60 applicants, 93% accepted, 41 enrolled. In 2006, 39 degrees awarded. *Degree requirements:* For master's, thesis, 20 week teaching internship. *Entrance requirements:* For master's, Washington Educator Skills TestùBasic, Washington Educator Skills TestûEndorsements/PRAXIS II, minimum undergraduate GPA of 3.0, related experience, resumé, endorsement area content worksheets, letters of recommendation. Additional exam requirements/recommendations for international students: Required—TOEFL (minimum score 600 paper-based; 250 computer-based). *Application deadline:* For fall admission, 4/15 priority date for domestic and international students. Applications are processed on a rolling basis. Application fee: $50. Electronic applications accepted.

Expenses: Tuition, state resident: full-time $6,546; part-time $218 per credit. Tuition, nonresident: full-time $19,982; part-time $666 per credit. Tuition and fees vary according to course load. *Financial support:* In 2006–07, 2 fellowships with partial tuition reimbursements were awarded; research assistantships with partial tuition reimbursements, career-related internships or fieldwork, Federal Work-Study, scholarships/grants, tuition waivers (full and partial), and unspecified assistantships also available. Financial award application deadline: 3/15; financial award applicants required to submit FAFSA. *Faculty research:* Assessment, multicultural education, curriculum development, math and science instruction, special education. *Unit head:* Dr. Sherry Walton, Director, 360-867-6753, Fax: 360-867-5430, E-mail: waltonsl@evergreen.edu. *Application contact:* Maggie Foran, Graduate Studies Office, 360-867-6559, Fax: 360-867-5430, E-mail: foranm@evergreen.edu.

Fairfield University, Graduate School of Education and Allied Professions, Fairfield, CT 06824-5195. Offers MA, CAS. Part-time and evening/weekend programs available. Postbaccalaureate distance learning degree programs offered. *Faculty:* 17 full-time (14 women), 25 part-time/adjunct (14 women). *Students:* 172 full-time (139 women), 416 part-time (342 women); includes 54 minority (16 African Americans, 2 American Indian/Alaska Native, 9 Asian Americans or Pacific Islanders, 27 Hispanic Americans), 7 international. Average age 30. 204 applicants, 46% accepted, 70 enrolled. In 2006, 144 master's, 26 other advanced degrees awarded. *Degree requirements:* For master's, comprehensive exam. *Entrance requirements:* For master's, minimum QPA of 2.67, 2 recommendations, resumè. Additional exam requirements/recommendations for international students: Required—TOEFL (minimum score 550 paper-based; 213 computer-based; 79 iBT). *Application deadline:* Applications are processed on a rolling basis. Application fee: $55. Electronic applications accepted. *Financial support:* In 2006–07, 10 research assistantships were awarded; career-related internships or fieldwork and tuition waivers (partial) also available. Financial award applicants required to submit FAFSA. Total annual research expenditures: $167,290. *Unit head:* Dr. Susan D. Franzosa, Dean, 203-254-4000 Ext. 4250, Fax: 203-254-4241, E-mail: sfranzosa@mail.fairfield.edu. *Application contact:* Marianne Gumpper, Director of Graduate and Continuing Studies Admissions, 203-254-4184, Fax: 203-254-4073, E-mail: gradadmis@mail.fairfield.edu.

See Close-Up on page 875.

Fairleigh Dickinson University, College at Florham, University College: Arts, Sciences, and Professional Studies, Peter Sammartino School of Education, Madison, NJ 07940-1099. Offers education for certified teachers (MA, Certificate); educational leadership (MA); instructional technology (Certificate); literacy/reading (Certificate); teaching (MAT). *Students:* 62 full-time (52 women), 58 part-time (41 women). Average age 29. 77 applicants, 83% accepted, 58 enrolled. In 2006, 86 degrees awarded. *Application deadline:* Applications are processed on a rolling basis. Application fee: $40.

See Close-Up on page 877.

Fairleigh Dickinson University, Metropolitan Campus, University College: Arts, Sciences, and Professional Studies, Peter Sammartino School of Education, Teaneck, NJ 07666-1914. Offers dyslexia specialist (Certificate); education for certified teachers (MA); educational leadership (MA); instructional technology (Certificate); learning disabilities (MA); literacy/reading (Certificate); multilingual education (MA); teacher of the handicapped (Certificate); teaching (MAT). Part-time programs available. *Students:* 70 full-time (54 women), 515 part-time (424 women), 14 international. Average age 36. 290 applicants, 92% accepted, 130 enrolled. In 2006, 106 degrees awarded. *Degree requirements:* For master's, research project (MAT). *Application deadline:* Applications are processed on a rolling basis. Application fee: $40. *Unit head:* Dr. Vicki Cohen, Director, 201-692-2525, Fax: 201-692-2603, E-mail: vicki_cohen@fdu.edu.

See Close-Up on page 877.

Felician College, Program in Education, Lodi, NJ 07644-2117. Offers elementary education (MA); supervisory (MA); teacher for students with disabilities (MA). Part-time and evening/weekend programs available. *Students:* 18 applicants, 50% accepted, 9 enrolled. *Degree requirements:* For master's, project. *Entrance requirements:* For master's, MAT, minimum GPA of 3.0, 3 letters of recommendation. Additional exam requirements/recommendations for international students: Recommended—TOEFL (minimum score 550 paper-based; 213 computer-based). *Application deadline:* Applications are processed on a rolling basis. Application fee: $40. *Expenses:* Tuition: Part-time $675 per credit. Tuition and fees vary according to program. *Financial support:* Federal Work-Study available. *Unit head:* Dr. Julie Goods, Associate Dean, 201-559-3529, E-mail: goodj@felician.edu. *Application contact:* Wendy Lin-Cook, Director of Adult and Graduate Admission, 201-559-6077, Fax: 201-559-6138, E-mail: adultandgraduate@felician.edu.

See Close-Up on page 879.

Ferris State University, College of Education and Human Services, School of Education, Big Rapids, MI 49307. Offers administration (MSCTE); curriculum and instruction (M Ed), including administration, elementary education, philanthropic education, reading, secondary education, special education, subject matter option; education technology (MSCTE); instructor (MSCTE); post-secondary administration (MSCTE); training and development (MSCTE). Part-time and evening/weekend programs available. Postbaccalaureate distance learning degree programs offered (no on-campus study). *Faculty:* 13 full-time (9 women), 26 part-time/adjunct (19 women). *Students:* 38 full-time (27 women), 254 part-time (164 women); includes 30 minority (22 African Americans, 1 American Indian/Alaska Native, 2 Asian Americans or Pacific Islanders, 5 Hispanic Americans), 1 international. Average age 37. 171 applicants, 99% accepted. In 2006, 92 degrees awarded. *Degree requirements:* For master's, thesis, research paper. *Entrance requirements:* For master's, 2 years of work experience, minimum GPA of 3.0. *Application deadline:* For fall admission, 6/1 priority date for domestic students; for winter admission, 12/10 priority date for domestic students. Applications are processed on a rolling basis. Application fee: $30. *Expenses:* Tuition, state resident: part-time $355 per credit hour. Tuition, nonresident: part-time $687 per credit hour. *Financial support:* Career-related internships or fieldwork and tuition waivers (full and partial) available. Support available to part-time students. Financial award applicants required to submit FAFSA. *Faculty research:* Suicide prevention, reading, women in education, special needs, administration. *Unit head:* Interim Director, 231-591-5362, Fax: 231-591-2041. *Application contact:* Sigrid Robertson, Secretary, 231-591-3511, Fax: 231-591-2041, E-mail: robertss@ferris.edu.

Florida Agricultural and Mechanical University, Division of Graduate Studies, Research, and Continuing Education, College of Education, Tallahassee, FL 32307-3200. Offers M Ed, MBE, MS Ed, PhD. *Accreditation:* NCATE. Part-time and evening/weekend programs available. *Degree requirements:* For master's, thesis (for some programs); for doctorate, thesis/dissertation. *Entrance requirements:* For master's, GRE General Test, minimum GPA of 3.0. Additional exam requirements/recommendations for international students: Required—TOEFL.

Florida Atlantic University, College of Education, Boca Raton, FL 33431-0991. Offers M Ed, MS, MSF, Ed D, PhD, Ed S. *Accreditation:* NCATE. Part-time and evening/weekend programs available. *Faculty:* 67 full-time (37 women), 36 part-time/adjunct (18 women). *Students:* 279 full-time (224 women), 532 part-time (418 women); includes 220 minority (109 African Americans, 2 American Indian/Alaska Native, 18 Asian Americans or Pacific Islanders, 91 Hispanic Americans), 14 international. Average age 35. 504 applicants, 54% accepted, 194 enrolled. In 2006, 264 master's, 22 doctorates, 20 other advanced degrees awarded. *Degree requirements:* For master's, registration; for doctorate, thesis/dissertation, comprehensive exam, registration; for Ed S, departmental qualifying exam. *Entrance requirements:* For master's, doctorate, and Ed S, GRE General Test. *Application deadline:* Applications are processed on a rolling basis. Application fee: $30. Electronic applications accepted. *Expenses:* Tuition, area resident: Full-time $4,394. Tuition, nonresident: full-time $16,441. *Financial support:* In 2006–07, 29 students received support, including 17 research assistantships with partial tuition reimbursements available (averaging $7,500 per year), 12 teaching assistantships with partial tuition reimbursements available (averaging $7,500 per year); fellowships with partial tuition reimbursements available, career-related internships or fieldwork, Federal Work-Study, and unspecified assistantships also available. *Faculty research:* Marriage and family counseling, multicultural education, self-directed learning, assessment, reading. Total annual research expenditures: $4.2 million. *Unit head:* Dr. Gregory Aloia, Dean, 561-297-3564, E-mail: galoia@fau.edu. *Application contact:* Dr. Eliah Watlington, Associate Dean, Office for Academic and Student Services, 561-297-3574, Fax: 261-297-2991, E-mail: ewatlinge@fau.edu.

Florida Atlantic University, Jupiter Campus, College of Education, Jupiter, FL 33458. Offers exceptional student education (M Ed); reading (M Ed).

Florida Gulf Coast University, College of Education, Fort Myers, FL 33965-6565. Offers M Ed, MA, MAT. Part-time and evening/weekend programs available. Postbaccalaureate distance learning degree programs offered (minimal on-campus study). *Faculty:* 31 full-time (21 women), 30 part-time/adjunct (24 women). *Students:* 229 full-time (179 women), 66 part-time (50 women); includes 31 minority (5 African Americans, 1 American Indian/Alaska Native, 2 Asian Americans or Pacific Islanders, 23 Hispanic Americans), 2 international. Average age 36. 143 applicants, 85% accepted, 95 enrolled. In 2006, 89 degrees awarded. *Entrance requirements:* For master's, GRE General Test, MAT, minimum GPA of 3.0. Additional exam requirements/recommendations for international students: Required—TOEFL (minimum score 550 paper-based; 213 computer-based). *Application deadline:* For fall admission, 7/1 priority date for domestic students; for spring admission, 10/15 for domestic students. Applications are processed on a rolling basis. Application fee: $30. Electronic applications accepted. *Expenses:* Tuition, state resident: full-time $4,326. Tuition, nonresident: full-time $18,523. Required fees: $1,211. One-time fee: $5 full-time. *Faculty research:* Inclusion, emergent literacy, preservice and inservice teacher education, education policy. Total annual research expenditures: $2.5 million. *Unit head:* Dr. Marci Greene, Dean, 239-590-7781, Fax: 239-590-7801, E-mail: mgreene@fgcu.edu. *Application contact:* Edward Beckett, Adviser/Counselor, 239-590-7759, Fax: 239-590-7801, E-mail: ebeckett@fgcu.edu.

Florida International University, College of Education, Miami, FL 33199. Offers MA, MAT, MS, Ed D, PhD, Certificate, Ed S. *Accreditation:* NCATE. Part-time and evening/weekend programs available. *Faculty:* 62 full-time (34 women), 41 part-time/adjunct (11 women). *Students:* 307 full-time (223 women), 613 part-time (493 women); includes 655 minority (202 African Americans, 21 Asian Americans or Pacific Islanders, 432 Hispanic Americans). Average age 33. 492 applicants, 53% accepted, 252 enrolled. In 2006, 272 master's, 17 doctorates, 25 other advanced degrees awarded. *Degree requirements:* For doctorate, thesis/dissertation, comprehensive exam, registration. *Entrance requirements:* For master's and other advanced degree, GRE General Test (some programs); for doctorate, GRE General Test. Additional exam requirements/recommendations for international students: Required—TOEFL (minimum score 550 paper-based; 213 computer-based; 80 iBT), IELTS (minimum score 6). *Application deadline:* For fall admission, 6/1 priority date for domestic students, 4/1 for international students; for winter admission, 10/1 priority date for domestic students, 9/1 for international students; for spring admission, 3/1 priority date for domestic students, 2/1 for international students. Applications are processed on a rolling basis. Application fee: $30. Electronic applications accepted. *Expenses:* Tuition, state resident: part-time $249 per credit hour. Tuition, nonresident: part-time $753 per credit hour. Tuition and fees vary according to program. *Financial support:* In 2006–07, 4 research assistantships, 25 teaching assistantships were awarded; fellowships, career-related internships or fieldwork, Federal Work-Study, institutionally sponsored loans, and tuition waivers (full and partial) also available. Support available to part-time students. *Faculty research:* School improvement, cognitive processes, international development, urban education, multicultural/multilingual education. *Unit head:* Dr. Luis Miron, Unit Head, 305-348-3202, Fax: 305-348-3205, E-mail: luis.miron@fiu.edu. *Application contact:* Marisa Salazar, Student Recruiter, 305-348-3002, Fax: 305-348-3227, E-mail: marisa.salazar@fiu.edu.

See Close-Up on page 881.

Florida Southern College, Programs in Teaching, Lakeland, FL 33801-5698. Offers teaching (MAT); teaching and learning (M Ed). Part-time and evening/weekend programs available. *Faculty:* 5 full-time (2 women), 6 part-time/adjunct (3 women). *Students:* Average age 32. 20 applicants, 80% accepted, 12 enrolled. In 2006, 25 degrees awarded. *Degree requirements:* For master's, FICE General Knowledge test and professional education exam (MAT), eligibility for the Florida Professional Teacher Certificate (M Ed). *Entrance requirements:* For master's, Florida Teacher Certification exam (MAT). Additional exam requirements/recommendations for international students: Required—TOEFL (minimum score 550 paper-based). *Application deadline:* For fall admission, 8/1 for domestic students; for spring admission, 12/1 for domestic students. Applications are processed on a rolling basis. Application fee: $30. *Expenses:* Tuition: Part-time $250 per credit hour. Required fees: $10 per term. Tuition and fees vary according to program. *Financial support:* In 2006–07, 24 students received support. Scholarships/grants available. Support available to part-time students. Financial award applicants required to submit FAFSA. *Unit head:* Dr. Charles B. Watts, Program Coordinator, 863-680-4958, Fax: 863-680-4102, E-mail: cwatts@flsouthern.edu. *Application contact:* Craig Story, Evening Program Director, 863-680-6276, Fax: 863-680-4205, E-mail: cstory@flsouthern.edu.

Florida State University, Graduate Studies, College of Education, Tallahassee, FL 32306. Offers MS, Ed D, PhD, Ed S. *Accreditation:* NCATE. Part-time and evening/weekend programs available. Postbaccalaureate distance learning degree programs offered. *Faculty:* 94 full-time (55 women), 34 part-time/adjunct (16 women). *Students:* 1,247; includes 355 minority (164 African Americans, 3 American Indian/Alaska Native, 125 Asian Americans or Pacific Islanders, 63 Hispanic Americans). 1,114 applicants, 52% accepted, 335 enrolled. In 2006, 330 master's, 58 doctorates, 37 other advanced degrees awarded. Terminal master's awarded for partial completion of doctoral program. *Degree requirements:* For master's and Ed S, thesis optional; for doctorate, thesis/dissertation, comprehensive exam. *Entrance requirements:* For master's, doctorate, and Ed S, GRE General Test, minimum GPA of 3.0. Additional exam requirements/recommendations for international students: Required—TOEFL. *Application deadline:* For fall admission, 7/1 priority date for domestic students; for spring admission, 11/1 for domestic students. Applications are processed on a rolling basis. Application fee: $30. Electronic applications accepted. *Expenses:* Tuition, state resident: full-time $5,822; part-time $243 per credit hour. Tuition, nonresident: full-time $20,976; part-time $874 per credit hour. Tuition and fees vary according to program. *Financial support:* In 2006–07, 13 fellowships, 207 research assistantships, 205 teaching assistantships were awarded; career-related internships or fieldwork and traineeships also available. Financial award applicants required to submit FAFSA. Total annual research expenditures: $12.5 million. *Unit head:* Dr. Marcy P Driscoll, Dean, 850-644-6885, Fax: 850-644-2725, E-mail: driscoll@coe.fsu.edu. *Application contact:* Gwendolyn Harris Johnson, Graduate Coordinator, Office of Academic Services, 850-644-3760, Fax: 850-644-6868, E-mail: johnson@coe.fsu.edu.

Fontbonne University, Graduate Programs, Department of Education, St. Louis, MO 63105-3098. Offers MA. *Accreditation:* NCATE. *Faculty:* 7 full-time (5 women), 24 part-time/adjunct (20 women). *Students:* 61 full-time (50 women), 169 part-time (143 women); includes 92 minority (all African Americans) Average age 35. 155 applicants, 90% accepted. In 2006, 69 degrees awarded. *Entrance requirements:* For master's, minimum GPA of 3.0. *Application deadline:* For fall admission, 8/1 priority date for domestic students. Applications are processed on a rolling basis. Application fee: $25. *Expenses:* Tuition: Full-time $4,890; part-time $489 per credit. Required fees: $160; $76 per credit. Full-time tuition and fees vary according to course load and program. *Financial support:* Teaching assistantships available. Support available to part-time students. Financial award application deadline: 4/1; financial award applicants required to submit FAFSA. *Unit head:* Dr. William Freeman, Dean, 314-719-3022, Fax: 314-889-1451, E-mail: wfreeman@fontbonne.edu. *Application contact:* Dr. James Muskopf, Director, 314-889-4536, Fax: 314-719-8002, E-mail: jmuskopf@fontbonne.edu.

Fordham University, Graduate School of Education, New York, NY 10023. Offers MAT, MS, MSE, MST, Ed D, PhD, Adv C. *Accreditation:* NCATE. Part-time and evening/weekend programs available. *Faculty:* 48 full-time (32 women), 81 part-time/adjunct (54 women). *Students:* 187 full-time (142 women), 1,164 part-time (883 women); includes 368 minority (136 African

Education—General

Fordham University (continued)

Americans, 1 American Indian/Alaska Native, 69 Asian Americans or Pacific Islanders, 162 Hispanic Americans), 5 international. Average age 34. 1,283 applicants, 73% accepted, 506 enrolled. In 2006, 573 master's, 45 doctorates, 6 other advanced degrees awarded. *Degree requirements:* For master's and Adv C, comprehensive exam (for some programs); for doctorate, thesis/dissertation. *Entrance requirements:* For master's and Adv C, minimum GPA of 3.0; for doctorate, GRE or MAT. Application fee: $65. *Expenses: Contact institution. Financial support:* In 2006–07, 557 students received support, including 131 fellowships with partial tuition reimbursements available (averaging $3,500 per year), 91 research assistantships with partial tuition reimbursements available (averaging $8,250 per year); career-related internships or fieldwork, Federal Work-Study, and scholarships/grants also available. Support available to part-time students. Financial award applicants required to submit FAFSA. *Unit head:* Dr. James Hennessy, Dean, 212-636-6400, E-mail: hennessy@fordham.edu. *Application contact:* Dr. Joseph Korevec, Director of Admissions and Financial Aid, 212-636-6400, Fax: 212-636-7826, E-mail: korevec@fordham.edu.

See Close-Up on page 883.

Fort Hays State University, Graduate School, College of Education and Technology, Hays, KS 67601-4099. Offers MS, MSE, Ed S. *Accreditation:* NCATE. Part-time programs available. *Faculty:* 23 full-time (9 women). *Students:* 25 full-time (17 women), 219 part-time (163 women); includes 16 minority (1 African American, 3 American Indian/Alaska Native, 6 Asian Americans or Pacific Islanders, 6 Hispanic Americans). Average age 36. 83 applicants, 76% accepted. In 2006, 87 degrees awarded. *Degree requirements:* For master's, thesis or alternative, comprehensive exam. *Entrance requirements:* Additional exam requirements/recommendations for international students: Required—TOEFL (minimum score 550 paper-based; 213 computer-based). *Application deadline:* For fall admission, 7/1 priority date for domestic students. Applications are processed on a rolling basis. Application fee: $35. Electronic applications accepted. *Financial support:* Research assistantships, teaching assistantships, career-related internships or fieldwork, institutionally sponsored loans, and tuition waivers (full) available. Support available to part-time students. *Unit head:* Dr. Deb Mercer, Dean, 785-628-5866, E-mail: dmercer@fhsu.edu.

Franciscan University of Steubenville, Graduate Programs, Department of Education, Steubenville, OH 43952-1763. Offers administration (MS Ed); teaching (MS Ed). Part-time and evening/weekend programs available. *Degree requirements:* For master's, project. *Entrance requirements:* For master's, minimum undergraduate GPA of 2.5 or written exam. Expenses: Contact institution.

Francis Marion University, Graduate Programs, School of Education, Florence, SC 29501-0547. Offers early childhood education (M Ed); elementary education (M Ed); learning disabilities (M Ed, MAT); remedial education (M Ed); secondary education (M Ed). *Accreditation:* NCATE. Part-time programs available. *Faculty:* 19 full-time (11 women), 1 part-time/adjunct (0 women). *Students:* 11 full-time (8 women), 158 part-time (141 women); includes 54 minority (all African Americans), 1 international. Average age 34. 248 applicants, 100% accepted. In 2006, 91 degrees awarded. *Degree requirements:* For master's, comprehensive exam. *Entrance requirements:* For master's, GRE General Test, MAT, NTE, or PRAXIS II. *Application deadline:* For fall admission, 4/15 priority date for domestic students; for spring admission, 10/15 priority date for domestic students. Applications are processed on a rolling basis. Application fee: $30. *Expenses:* Tuition, state resident: full-time $6,527; part-time $326 per credit hour. Tuition, nonresident: full-time $13,054; part-time $653 per credit hour. Required fees: $185; $5 per credit hour. $45 per term. *Financial support:* In 2006–07, 3 research assistantships (averaging $6,000 per year) were awarded; unspecified assistantships also available. Support available to part-time students. Financial award application deadline: 3/1; financial award applicants required to submit FAFSA. *Faculty research:* Identification and alternate assessment of at-risk students. *Unit head:* Dr. James R. Faulkenberry, Dean, 843-661-1460, Fax: 843-661-4647.

Freed-Hardeman University, Program in Education, Henderson, TN 38340-2399. Offers curriculum and instruction (M Ed); school counseling (M Ed); school leadership (Ed S). *Accreditation:* NCATE. Part-time and evening/weekend programs available. *Faculty:* 9 full-time (3 women), 6 part-time/adjunct (4 women). *Students:* 51 full-time (40 women), 286 part-time (235 women); includes 203 minority (202 African Americans, 1 Asian American or Pacific Islander), 2 international. Average age 34. In 2006, 78 master's, 24 other advanced degrees awarded. *Degree requirements:* For master's, thesis optional; for Ed S, thesis. *Entrance requirements:* For master's, GRE General Test or NTE; for Ed S, 3 years of teaching experience. Additional exam requirements/recommendations for international students: Required—TOEFL (minimum score 500 paper-based; 173 computer-based). *Application deadline:* For fall admission, 8/1 for domestic students; for spring admission, 12/1 for domestic students. Applications are processed on a rolling basis. Application fee: $32. *Expenses:* Tuition: Part-time $334 per credit hour. Required fees: $10 per credit hour. *Financial support:* Career-related internships or fieldwork, Federal Work-Study, tuition waivers (partial), and unspecified assistantships available. Support available to part-time students. Financial award application deadline: 8/1; financial award applicants required to submit FAFSA. *Unit head:* Dr. Elizabeth Saunders, Graduate Director, 731-989-6082, Fax: 731-989-6065, E-mail: esaunders@fhu.edu.

Fresno Pacific University, Graduate Programs, Programs in Education, Fresno, CA 93702-4709. Offers administration (MA Ed), including administrative services; foundations, curriculum and teaching (MA Ed), including curriculum and teaching, school library and information technology; language, literacy, and culture (MA Ed), including bilingual/cross-cultural education, language development, multilingual contexts, reading; mathematics/science/computer education (MA Ed), including educational technology, integrated mathematics/science education, mathematics education; pupil personnel services (MA Ed), including school counseling, school psychology; special education (MA Ed), including mild/moderate, moderate/severe, physical and health impairments. Part-time and evening/weekend programs available. *Faculty:* 12 full-time (5 women), 19 part-time/adjunct (9 women). *Students:* 73 full-time (59 women), 399 part-time (295 women); includes 136 minority (9 African Americans, 5 American Indian/Alaska Native, 12 Asian Americans or Pacific Islanders, 110 Hispanic Americans), 2 international. Average age 39. 124 applicants, 73% accepted, 10 enrolled. In 2006, 128 degrees awarded. *Degree requirements:* For master's, thesis (for some programs), registration. *Entrance requirements:* For master's, interview; GMAT, GRE, MAT, or 6 units of course work with a faculty recommendation. Additional exam requirements/recommendations for international students: Required—TOEFL (minimum score 550 paper-based; 213 computer-based). *Application deadline:* For fall admission, 7/15 for domestic and international students; for spring admission, 11/15 for domestic and international students. Applications are processed on a rolling basis. Application fee: $90. Electronic applications accepted. *Expenses:* Tuition: Full-time $7,470; part-time $415 per credit. *Financial support:* In 2006–07, 260 students received support. Career-related internships or fieldwork, scholarships/grants, and tuition waivers (full and partial) available. Support available to part-time students. Financial award applicants required to submit FAFSA.

Friends University, Graduate School, Division of Science, Arts, and Education, Program in Teaching, Wichita, KS 67213. Offers elementary education (MAT); secondary education (MAT). *Accreditation:* NCATE. Evening/weekend programs available. Postbaccalaureate distance learning degree programs offered (minimal on-campus study). *Faculty:* 1 (woman) full-time, 5 part-time/adjunct (2 women). *Students:* 79 full-time. In 2006, 32 degrees awarded. *Entrance requirements:* Additional exam requirements/recommendations for international students: Required—TOEFL (minimum score 560 paper-based; 220 computer-based). *Application deadline:* For fall admission, 3/15 priority date for domestic and international students; for spring admission, 12/15 priority date for domestic and international students. Applications are processed on a rolling basis. Application fee: $45 ($65 for international students). Electronic applications accepted. *Unit head:* Dr. Dona Gibson, Director, 800-794-6945 Ext. 5826. *Application contact:* Craig Davis, Executive Director of Recruitment-Adult and Graduate Studies, 800-794-6945 Ext. 5573, Fax: 316-295-5050, E-mail: cdavis@friends.edu.

Frostburg State University, Graduate School, College of Education, Frostburg, MD 21532-1099. Offers M Ed, MAT, MS. *Accreditation:* NCATE. Part-time and evening/weekend programs available. Electronic applications accepted.

Furman University, Graduate Division, Department of Education, Greenville, SC 29613. Offers early childhood education (MA); elementary education (MA); English as a second language (MA); middle school education (MA); reading (MA); school administration (MA); special education (MA). *Accreditation:* NCATE. Part-time and evening/weekend programs available. *Faculty:* 17 full-time (12 women), 19 part-time/adjunct (15 women). *Students:* 114 full-time (89 women), 72 part-time (59 women); includes 27 minority (23 African Americans, 4 Hispanic Americans). Average age 32. 36 applicants, 100% accepted, 36 enrolled. In 2006, 111 degrees awarded. *Degree requirements:* For master's, thesis (for some programs), comprehensive exam. *Entrance requirements:* For master's, GRE General Test or PRAXIS. *Application deadline:* For fall admission, 8/1 priority date for domestic and international students; for winter admission, 12/1 priority date for domestic and international students; for spring admission, 2/1 priority date for domestic and international students. Applications are processed on a rolling basis. Application fee: $50. *Expenses:* Tuition: Part-time $347 per credit. *Financial support:* In 2006–07, 97 students received support; fellowships, scholarships/grants and unspecified assistantships available. Financial award application deadline: 1/15; financial award applicants required to submit FAFSA. *Unit head:* Dr. Nelly Hecker, Head, 864-294-3385.

Gallaudet University, The Graduate School, School of Education and Human Services, Washington, DC 20002-3625. Offers MA, MS, PhD, Certificate, Ed S. *Accreditation:* NCATE. *Degree requirements:* For master's, thesis optional; for doctorate, thesis/dissertation. *Entrance requirements:* For master's, GRE General Test or MAT; for doctorate, GRE General Test or MAT, interview. *Faculty research:* Full inclusion and deaf education, use of American Sign Language in teaching, bilingual/bicultural education, training and licensure of deaf teachers.

Gannon University, School of Graduate Studies, College of Humanities, Business, and Education, School of Education, Erie, PA 16541-0001. Offers M Ed, MS, Certificate. Part-time and evening/weekend programs available. Postbaccalaureate distance learning degree programs offered (no on-campus study). *Faculty:* 8 full-time (6 women), 29 part-time/adjunct (10 women). *Students:* 15 full-time (11 women), 444 part-time (299 women); includes 8 minority (7 African Americans, 1 American Indian/Alaska Native), 1 international. Average age 31. 180 applicants, 93% accepted, 102 enrolled. In 2006, 219 master's, 2 other advanced degrees awarded. *Degree requirements:* For master's, thesis (for some programs), portfolio project. *Entrance requirements:* Additional exam requirements/recommendations for international students: Required—TOEFL (minimum score 550 paper-based; 173 computer-based). *Application deadline:* Applications are processed on a rolling basis. Application fee: $25. *Expenses:* Tuition: Full-time $12,240; part-time $680 per credit. Required fees: $496; $16 per credit. Tuition and fees vary according to course load, degree level, campus/location and program. *Financial support:* In 2006–07, 5 fellowships (averaging $3,813 per year) were awarded; teaching assistantships, career-related internships or fieldwork also available. Support available to part-time students. Financial award application deadline: 7/1; financial award applicants required to submit FAFSA. *Unit head:* Dr. Francis S. Grandinetti, Director, 814-871-7533, E-mail: grandine002@gannon.edu. *Application contact:* Debra Meszaros, Director of Graduate Recruitment, 814-871-5819, Fax: 814-871-5827, E-mail: cfal@gannon.edu.

Gardner-Webb University, Graduate School, Department of Education, Boiling Springs, NC 28017. Offers curriculum and instruction (Ed D); educational leadership (Ed D); elementary education (MA); middle grades education (MA); school administration (MA, Ed D), including educational leadership (Ed D), school administration (MA). *Accreditation:* NCATE. Part-time and evening/weekend programs available. *Faculty:* 7 full-time (3 women), 2 part-time/adjunct (both women). *Students:* 12 full-time (10 women), 422 part-time (288 women); includes 138 minority (133 African Americans, 1 American Indian/Alaska Native, 1 Asian American or Pacific Islander, 3 Hispanic Americans). Average age 29. In 2006, 178 master's, 8 doctorates awarded. *Degree requirements:* For master's, comprehensive exam. *Entrance requirements:* For master's, GRE General Test or NTE, PRAXIS, minimum GPA of 2.5. *Application deadline:* For fall admission, 8/1 priority date for domestic students. Applications are processed on a rolling basis. Application fee: $25. Electronic applications accepted. *Expenses:* Tuition: Full-time $3,144; part-time $262 per hour. *Financial support:* Unspecified assistantships available. *Unit head:* Dr. Donna Simmons, Chair, 704-406-4406, Fax: 704-406-3921, E-mail: dsimmons@gardner-webb.edu.

Geneva College, Program in Higher Education, Beaver Falls, PA 15010-3599. Offers campus ministry (MA); college teaching (MA); educational leadership (MA); student affairs administration (MA). Part-time and evening/weekend programs available. Postbaccalaureate distance learning degree programs offered (minimal on-campus study). *Degree requirements:* For master's, research seminar. *Entrance requirements:* For master's, minimum GPA of 2.8, writing sample, letters of recommendation (3). Additional exam requirements/recommendations for international students: Required—TOEFL. Electronic applications accepted. *Faculty research:* Student development, learning theories, church-related higher education, assessment, organizational culture.

George Fox University, School of Education, Newberg, OR 97132-2697. Offers counseling (MA, MS, Certificate), including counseling (MA), marriage and family therapy (MA, Certificate), school counseling (MA), school psychology (MS, Certificate), trauma (Certificate); educational foundations and leadership (M Ed, Ed D); teaching (MAT). Evening/weekend programs available. Postbaccalaureate distance learning degree programs offered (minimal on-campus study). *Faculty:* 34 full-time (18 women), 27 part-time/adjunct (19 women). *Students:* 157 full-time (125 women), 312 part-time (225 women); includes 15 minority (2 African Americans, 3 American Indian/Alaska Native, 3 Asian Americans or Pacific Islanders, 7 Hispanic Americans), 3 international. Average age 36. 165 applicants, 76% accepted, 106 enrolled. In 2006, 208 master's, 11 doctorates, 1 other advanced degree awarded. *Degree requirements:* For master's, thesis (for some programs). *Entrance requirements:* For master's, California Basic Educational Skills Test, PRAXIS II, minimum undergraduate GPA of 3.0 during previous 2 years. *Application deadline:* For fall admission, 2/1 for domestic students. Applications are processed on a rolling basis. Application fee: $40. Electronic applications accepted. *Expenses: Contact institution. Financial support:* Career-related internships or fieldwork available. Financial award applicants required to submit FAFSA. *Unit head:* Dr. James Worthington, Dean, 503-554-2871, E-mail: jworthington@georgefox.edu. *Application contact:* Beth Molzahn, Admissions Counselor, 800-631-0921, Fax: 503-554-3856, E-mail: bmolzahn@georgefox.edu.

George Mason University, Graduate School of Education, Fairfax, VA 22030. Offers M Ed, MA, MS, PhD. *Accreditation:* NCATE. Part-time and evening/weekend programs available. *Faculty:* 108 full-time (70 women), 193 part-time/adjunct (140 women). *Students:* 309 full-time (257 women), 2,160 part-time (1,735 women); includes 407 minority (209 African Americans, 3 American Indian/Alaska Native, 92 Asian Americans or Pacific Islanders, 103 Hispanic Americans), 52 international. Average age 35. 1,396 applicants, 68% accepted, 779 enrolled. In 2006, 904 master's, 26 doctorates awarded. *Degree requirements:* For doctorate, final project, internship. *Entrance requirements:* For master's, minimum GPA of 3.0 in last 60 hours of course work; for doctorate, GRE or MAT, appropriate master's degree, interview. *Application deadline:* For fall admission, 5/1 for domestic students; for spring admission, 11/1 for domestic students. Application fee: $60 ($75 for international students). Electronic applications accepted. *Expenses:* Tuition, state resident: full-time $5,724; part-time $238 per credit. Tuition, nonresident: full-time $16,896; part-time $704 per credit. Required fees: $1,656; $69 per credit. *Financial support:* Fellowships, research assistantships, teaching assistantships, career-related internships or fieldwork and Federal Work-Study available. Support available to part-time students. Financial award application deadline: 3/1; financial award applicants required to submit FAFSA. *Faculty research:* Special education/human disabilities, mathematics/science/technology education, education leadership, school/community/agency/higher education, counseling and administration. *Unit head:* Jeffrey Gorrell, Dean, 703-993-2004, E-mail: gseinfo@gmu.edu. *Application contact:* Dr. Mark Goor, Information Contact, 703-993-4648, E-mail: gseinfo@gmu.edu.

Georgetown College, Department of Education, Georgetown, KY 40324-1696. Offers MA Ed. Part-time programs available. *Degree requirements:* For master's, portfolio. *Entrance requirements:* For master's, teaching certificate, minimum GPA of 2.7 or GRE General Test.

The George Washington University, Graduate School of Education and Human Development, Washington, DC 20052. Offers M Ed, MA Ed, MAT, Ed D, PhD, Certificate, Ed S. *Accreditation:* NCATE. Part-time and evening/weekend programs available. Postbaccalaureate distance learning degree programs offered (no on-campus study). *Degree requirements:* For master's and other advanced degree, comprehensive exam; for doctorate, thesis/dissertation, comprehensive exam. *Entrance requirements:* For master's, GRE General Test or MAT, minimum GPA of 2.75; for doctorate, GRE General Test or MAT, interview, minimum GPA of 3.3; for other advanced degree, GRE General Test or MAT, minimum GPA of 3.3. Electronic applications accepted. *Faculty research:* Policy, special education, bilingual education, counseling, human resource development.

Georgia College & State University, Graduate School, School of Education, Milledgeville, GA 31061. Offers M Ed, MAT, Ed S. *Accreditation:* NCATE. Part-time programs available. *Faculty:* 44 full-time (30 women). *Students:* 219 full-time (166 women), 126 part-time (101 women); includes 79 minority (70 African Americans, 3 American Indian/Alaska Native, 1 Asian American or Pacific Islander, 5 Hispanic Americans), 3 international. Average age 35. 323 applicants, 52% accepted, 84 enrolled. In 2006, 152 master's, 46 other advanced degrees awarded. *Degree requirements:* For master's, comprehensive exam; for Ed S, residency requirement. *Entrance requirements:* For master's, GRE General Test or MAT, 2 professional recommendations; for Ed S, GRE General Test or MAT, master's degree, 2 years teaching experience, 2 professional recommendations. Additional exam requirements/recommendations for international students: Required—TOEFL. *Application deadline:* For fall admission, 7/1 priority date for domestic students. Applications are processed on a rolling basis. Application fee: $25. Electronic applications accepted. *Expenses:* Tuition, state resident: full-time $3,222; part-time $179 per credit hour. Tuition, nonresident: full-time $12,870; part-time $715 per credit hour. Required fees: $391 per semester. Tuition and fees vary according to course load. *Financial support:* In 2006–07, 11 research assistantships were awarded; career-related internships or fieldwork, Federal Work-Study, and unspecified assistantships also available. Support available to part-time students. Financial award application deadline: 3/1; financial award applicants required to submit FAFSA. *Unit head:* Dr. Linda Irwin-Devitis, Dean, 478-445-4546, E-mail: linda.irwin-devitis@gcsu.edu. *Application contact:* Dr. W. Bee Crews, Coordinator of Graduate Programs, 478-445-4056, E-mail: b.crews@gcsu.edu.

Georgian Court University, School of Education, Lakewood, NJ 08701-2697. Offers administration, supervision, and curriculum planning (MA); early intervention studies (Certificate); education (MA); instructional technology (MA, Certificate); special education (MA); substance awareness coordinator (Certificate). Part-time and evening/weekend programs available. *Faculty:* 25 full-time (14 women), 41 part-time/adjunct (23 women). *Students:* 128 full-time (110 women), 594 part-time (495 women); includes 56 minority (17 African Americans, 8 Asian Americans or Pacific Islanders, 31 Hispanic Americans), 1 international. Average age 34. 676 applicants, 80% accepted, 312 enrolled. In 2006, 130 master's, 4 other advanced degrees awarded. *Degree requirements:* For master's, thesis (for some programs), comprehensive exam (for some programs). *Entrance requirements:* For master's, GRE, MAT or NTE/PRAXIS, 3 letters of recommendation. Additional exam requirements/recommendations for international students: Required—TOEFL (minimum score 550 paper-based; 213 computer-based). *Application deadline:* For fall admission, 8/1 priority date for domestic students, 4/1 for international students; for spring admission, 1/1 priority date for domestic students, 7/1 for international students. Applications are processed on a rolling basis. Application fee: $40. Electronic applications accepted. *Financial support:* In 2006–07, 183 students received support. Scholarships/grants, health care benefits, and unspecified assistantships available. Financial award application deadline: 4/15; financial award applicants required to submit FAFSA. *Unit head:* Sr. Mary Gurley, OSF, Dean, 732-987-2525, E-mail: garleym@gergian.edu. *Application contact:* Eugene Soltys, Director of Graduate Admissions, 732-987-2760 Ext. 2760, Fax: 732-987-2000, E-mail: admissions@georgian.edu.

Georgia Southern University, Jack N. Averitt College of Graduate Studies, College of Education, Statesboro, GA 30460. Offers M Ed, MAT, Ed D, Ed S. *Accreditation:* NCATE. Part-time programs available. *Faculty:* 60 full-time (37 women), 19 part-time/adjunct (13 women). *Students:* 207 full-time (168 women), 907 part-time (734 women); includes 284 minority (269 African Americans, 3 American Indian/Alaska Native, 4 Asian Americans or Pacific Islanders, 8 Hispanic Americans), 2 international. Average age 36. 241 applicants, 85% accepted, 134 enrolled. In 2006, 172 master's, 27 doctorates, 66 Ed Ss awarded. *Degree requirements:* For master's, comprehensive exam (for some programs); for doctorate, thesis/dissertation, exams. *Entrance requirements:* For master's, GRE General Test or MAT, minimum GPA of 2.5; for doctorate, GRE General Test or MAT, minimum GPA of 3.5, letters reference, writing sample; for Ed S, GRE General Test or MAT, minimum graduate GPA of 3.25. Additional exam requirements/recommendations for international students: Required—TOEFL (minimum score 550 paper-based; 213 computer-based; 80 iBT). *Application deadline:* For fall admission, 3/1 priority date for domestic students, 3/1 for international students; for spring admission, 10/1 priority date for domestic students, 10/1 for international students. Applications are processed on a rolling basis. Application fee: $50. Electronic applications accepted. *Financial support:* In 2006–07, 483 students received support, including 26 research assistantships with partial tuition reimbursements available (averaging $5,500 per year), teaching assistantships with partial tuition reimbursements available (averaging $5,500 per year); career-related internships or fieldwork, Federal Work-Study, scholarships/grants, tuition waivers (partial), unspecified assistantships, and doctoral stipends also available. Support available to part-time students. Financial award application deadline: 4/15; financial award applicants required to submit FAFSA. *Faculty research:* Teacher preparation, curriculum improvement. Total annual research expenditures: $291,637. *Unit head:* Dr. Lucindia Chance, Dean, 912-681-5648, Fax: 912-681-5093, E-mail: lchance@georgiasouthern.edu. *Application contact:* 912-681-5384, Fax: 912-681-0740, E-mail: gradadmissions@georgiasouthern.edu.

Georgia Southwestern State University, Graduate Studies, School of Education, Americus, GA 31709-4693. Offers early childhood education (M Ed, Ed S); health and physical education (M Ed); middle grades education (M Ed, Ed S); reading (M Ed); secondary education (M Ed); special education (M Ed). *Accreditation:* NCATE. *Degree requirements:* For master's, comprehensive exam. *Entrance requirements:* For master's, GRE General Test or MAT, minimum GPA of 2.5; for Ed S, GRE General Test or MAT, minimum graduate GPA of 3.25, M Ed from accredited college or university, 3 years teaching experience. Electronic applications accepted.

Georgia State University, College of Education, Atlanta, GA 30303-3083. Offers M Ed, MLM, MS, PhD, Ed S. *Accreditation:* NCATE. Part-time and evening/weekend programs available. *Faculty:* 121 full-time (74 women), 74 part-time/adjunct (54 women). *Students:* 665 full-time (548 women), 904 part-time (707 women); includes 346 minority (286 African Americans, 14 American Indian/Alaska Native, 25 Asian Americans or Pacific Islanders, 21 Hispanic Americans), 47 international. Average age 33. 809 applicants, 67% accepted. In 2006, 421 master's, 49 doctorates, 100 other advanced degrees awarded. *Degree requirements:* For master's, comprehensive exam; for doctorate, thesis/dissertation, comprehensive exam. *Entrance requirements:* For master's, GRE General Test; for doctorate, GRE General Test, minimum GPA of 3.3; for Ed S, GRE General Test, minimum graduate GPA of 3.25. Application fee: $25. *Financial support:* In 2006–07, 194 research assistantships, 28 teaching assistantships were awarded; fellowships, career-related internships or fieldwork, Federal Work-Study, institutionally sponsored loans, and tuition waivers (partial) also available. Support available to part-time students. *Faculty research:* Evaluation and test development, teacher/school administration effectiveness, curriculum strategies and interventions. Total annual research expenditures: $5.2 million. *Unit head:* Dr. Ron P. Colarusso, Dean, 404-651-2310.

Goddard College, Graduate Program, Program in Teacher Education, Plainfield, VT 05667-9432. Offers MA. Postbaccalaureate distance learning degree programs offered (minimal on-campus study). *Faculty:* 1 full-time (0 women), 9 part-time/adjunct (5 women). *Students:* 35 full-time, 11 part-time. Average age 34. 32 applicants, 78% accepted, 21 enrolled. *Degree requirements:* For master's, thesis, registration. *Application deadline:* Applications are processed on a rolling basis. Application fee: $40. Electronic applications accepted. *Expenses:* Tuition: Full-time $12,506; part-time $10,392 per year. Required fees: $998; $499 per term. *Financial support:* In 2006–07, 46 students received support. Applicants required to submit FAFSA. *Faculty research:* Democratic curriculum leadership, service learning and academic achievement, middle grades curriculum. *Unit head:* Dr. Susan Fleming, Director, 802-454-8311 Ext. 270, Fax: 802-454-8017, E-mail: susan.fleming@goddard.edu. *Application contact:* Ryanne Putnam, Admissions Specialist, 800-906-8312 Ext. 262, Fax: 802-454-1029, E-mail: putnamr@goddard.edu.

Gonzaga University, School of Education, Spokane, WA 99258. Offers M Anesth Ed, MA Ed Ad, MAA, MAC, MAP, MASPAA, MES, MIT, MTA. *Accreditation:* NCATE. Part-time and evening/weekend programs available. *Students:* 68 full-time (48 women), 540 part-time (338 women); includes 42 minority (7 African Americans, 19 American Indian/Alaska Native, 6 Asian Americans or Pacific Islanders, 10 Hispanic Americans), 3 international. Average age 36. In 2006, 216 degrees awarded. *Degree requirements:* For master's, comprehensive exam. *Entrance requirements:* Additional exam requirements/recommendations for international students: Required—TOEFL. Application fee: $40. *Expenses:* Tuition: Full-time $10,620; part-time $590 per credit. *Financial support:* Teaching assistantships, Federal Work-Study and tuition waivers (full and partial) available. Support available to part-time students. Financial award application deadline: 3/1. *Unit head:* Dr. Shirley Williams, Dean, 509-328-4220 Ext. 3503, Fax: 509-324-5812.

Gordon College, Graduate Education, Wenham, MA 01984-1899. Offers education (M Ed, MAT); music education (MME). *Accreditation:* NASM. Part-time and evening/weekend programs available. *Faculty:* 5 full-time (4 women), 9 part-time/adjunct (5 women). *Students:* 2 full-time (both women), 131 part-time (107 women); includes 2 minority (both Asian Americans or Pacific Islanders) Average age 28. 133 applicants, 100% accepted, 133 enrolled. In 2006, 12 degrees awarded. *Entrance requirements:* For master's, GRE or MAT, references. Additional exam requirements/recommendations for international students: Required—TOEFL (minimum score 550 paper-based; 213 computer-based). *Application deadline:* Applications are processed on a rolling basis. Application fee: $50. *Faculty research:* Reading, early childhood development, ELL (English Language Learners). *Unit head:* Dr. Malcolm L. Patterson, Dean of Graduate Studies, 978-867-4355, Fax: 978-867-4663, E-mail: malcolm.patterson@gordon.edu. *Application contact:* E. Jean Bilsbury, Program Coordinator, 978-867-4322, Fax: 978-867-4663, E-mail: jean.bilsbury@gordon.edu.

Goucher College, Programs in Education, Baltimore, MD 21204-2794. Offers M Ed, MAT. Part-time and evening/weekend programs available. *Faculty:* 98 part-time/adjunct (75 women). *Students:* 40 full-time (33 women), 590 part-time (481 women); includes 86 minority (75 African Americans, 1 American Indian/Alaska Native, 5 Asian Americans or Pacific Islanders, 5 Hispanic Americans), 1 international. Average age 34. 40 applicants, 88% accepted, 25 enrolled. In 2006, 54 degrees awarded. *Degree requirements:* For master's, thesis (M Ed), final presentation (MAT). *Entrance requirements:* For master's, minimum GPA of 3.0. Additional exam requirements/recommendations for international students: Required—TOEFL (minimum score 560 paper-based). *Application deadline:* For fall admission, 9/1 priority date for domestic students; for spring admission, 1/15 for domestic students. Applications are processed on a rolling basis. Application fee: $25. *Financial support:* In 2006–07, 3 research assistantships with tuition reimbursements (averaging $4,500 per year) were awarded; career-related internships or fieldwork and need-based awards also available. Support available to part-time students. Financial award application deadline: 8/15; financial award applicants required to submit FAFSA. *Faculty research:* Urban education, middle school, school improvement, teacher education, at-risk student achievement. *Unit head:* Dr. Phyllis Sunshine, Director, 410-337-6047, Fax: 410-337-6394, E-mail: psunshin@goucher.edu. *Application contact:* Megan Cornett, Associate Director, Administrative Student Services, 410-337-6200, Fax: 410-337-6394, E-mail: mcornett@goucher.edu.

Governors State University, College of Education, Program in Education, University Park, IL 60466-0975. Offers MA. Part-time and evening/weekend programs available. *Students:* 1 full-time, 106 part-time. Average age 34. *Degree requirements:* For master's, thesis or alternative, practicum, comprehensive exam. *Entrance requirements:* For master's, minimum GPA of 2.75 in last 60 hours of undergraduate course work, minimum graduate GPA of 3.0. *Application deadline:* For fall admission, 7/15 priority date for domestic students; for spring admission, 11/10 for domestic students. Applications are processed on a rolling basis. Application fee: $25. *Expenses:* Tuition, state resident: full-time $4,104; part-time $171 per hour. Tuition, nonresident: part-time $513 per hour. *Financial support:* Career-related internships or fieldwork, Federal Work-Study, institutionally sponsored loans, tuition waivers (full and partial), and unspecified assistantships available. Support available to part-time students. Financial award application deadline: 5/1. *Faculty research:* Teaching problem-solving microcomputer use in special education, science, and mathematics. *Application contact:* Nick Battaglia, Adviser, 708-534-4393.

Graceland University, School of Education, Lamoni, IA 50140. Offers M Ed. *Accreditation:* NCATE. Part-time and evening/weekend programs available. Postbaccalaureate distance learning degree programs offered (minimal on-campus study). *Faculty:* 6 full-time (4 women), 20 part-time/adjunct (14 women). *Students:* 585 full-time (447 women). Average age 36. 240 applicants, 99% accepted, 213 enrolled. In 2006, 229 degrees awarded. *Median time to degree:* Master's–2 years full-time, 3 years part-time. *Degree requirements:* For master's, action research project. *Entrance requirements:* For master's, teaching certificate, minimum GPA of 3.0 or MAT. *Application deadline:* For spring admission, 1/15 priority date for domestic students. Application fee: $50. Electronic applications accepted. *Financial support:* In 2006–07, 451 students received support. Institutionally sponsored loans and scholarships/grants available. Financial award application deadline: 12/15; financial award applicants required to submit FAFSA. *Unit head:* Dr. William L. Armstrong, Dean, 641-784-5000 Ext. 5254, E-mail: billa@graceland.edu. *Application contact:* Tom Kotz, Associate Dean, 641-784-5313 Ext. 4520, E-mail: kotz@graceland.edu.

Grambling State University, School of Graduate Studies and Research, College of Education, Grambling, LA 71245. Offers M Ed, MS, Ed D. *Accreditation:* NCATE. Part-time and evening/weekend programs available. Postbaccalaureate distance learning degree programs offered (minimal on-campus study). *Faculty:* 21 full-time (10 women), 2 part-time/adjunct (0 women). *Students:* 64 full-time (33 women), 72 part-time (56 women); includes 112 minority (110 African Americans, 2 Asian Americans or Pacific Islanders), 2 international. Average age 36. In 2006, 32 master's, 4 doctorates awarded. *Degree requirements:* For doctorate, thesis/dissertation. *Entrance requirements:* For master's and doctorate, GRE. *Application deadline:* For fall admission, 7/1 for domestic students; for spring admission, 12/1 for domestic students. Applications are processed on a rolling basis. Application fee: $20 ($30 for international students). *Expenses:* Tuition, state resident: full-time $2,232; part-time $124 per credit hour. Tuition, nonresident: full-time $7,582; part-time $124 per credit hour. Required fees: $1,127. *Financial support:* In 2006–07, 100 students received support, including 12 research assistantships (averaging $5,333 per year); teaching assistantships, career-related internships or fieldwork, institutionally sponsored loans, and unspecified assistantships also available. Financial award application deadline: 5/31; financial award applicants required to submit FAFSA. *Faculty research:* Head Start services. *Unit head:* Dr. Sean Warner, Dean, 318-274-3235, Fax: 318-274-2799, E-mail: warners@gram.edu.

Education—General

Grand Canyon University, College of Education, Phoenix, AZ 85017-1097. Offers elementary education (M Ed, MA); reading education (MA); secondary education (M Ed); teaching (MAT); teaching English as a second language (MA). Part-time and evening/weekend programs available. Postbaccalaureate distance learning degree programs offered (no on-campus study). *Degree requirements:* For master's, publishable research paper (M Ed). *Entrance requirements:* For master's, MAT, GRE or minimum GPA of 3.0.

See Close-Up on page 885.

Grand Valley State University, College of Education, Programs in General Education, Allendale, MI 49401-9403. Offers adult and higher education (M Ed); early childhood education (M Ed); education of the gifted and talented (M Ed); educational leadership (M Ed); educational technology (M Ed); elementary education (M Ed); middle and high school education (M Ed); teaching English to speakers of other languages (M Ed). Part-time and evening/weekend programs available. Postbaccalaureate distance learning degree programs offered (minimal on-campus study). *Faculty:* 82 full-time (42 women), 43 part-time/adjunct (25 women). *Students:* 136 full-time (97 women), 828 part-time (565 women); includes 55 minority (26 African Americans, 7 American Indian/Alaska Native, 5 Asian Americans or Pacific Islanders, 17 Hispanic Americans). Average age 33. 280 applicants, 94% accepted, 188 enrolled. In 2006, 322 degrees awarded. *Degree requirements:* For master's, thesis. *Entrance requirements:* For master's, GRE General Test or minimum GPA of 3.0. Additional exam requirements/recommendations for international students: Required—TOEFL. *Application deadline:* Applications are processed on a rolling basis. Application fee: $30. Electronic applications accepted. *Expenses:* Tuition, state resident: full-time $5,850; part-time $325 per credit. Tuition, nonresident: full-time $10,800; part-time $600 per credit. Tuition and fees vary according to course load. *Financial support:* In 2006–07, 2 research assistantships with full and partial tuition reimbursements (averaging $8,000 per year) were awarded; career-related internships or fieldwork, Federal Work-Study, scholarships/grants, and unspecified assistantships also available. *Faculty research:* Effectiveness of technology in education, parental involvement, effective teaching, effective schools research. *Unit head:* Dr. Linda McCrea, Director, 616-331-2080, E-mail: mccreal@gvsu.edu. *Application contact:* Dr. Douglas Busman, Director, Student Information and Services, 616-331-6831, Fax: 616-331-6217, E-mail: busmando@gvsu.edu.

Gratz College, Graduate Programs, Program in Education, Melrose Park, PA 19027. Offers MA. Part-time programs available. *Degree requirements:* For master's, one foreign language. *Entrance requirements:* For master's, teaching certificate.

Greensboro College, Program in Education, Greensboro, NC 27401-1875. Offers elementary education (M Ed); special education (M Ed). Part-time and evening/weekend programs available. *Faculty:* 4 full-time (3 women). *Students:* 2 full-time (both women), 16 part-time (all women); includes 2 minority (1 African American, 1 Hispanic American). 5 applicants, 40% accepted, 2 enrolled. In 2006, 12 degrees awarded. *Degree requirements:* For master's, thesis. *Entrance requirements:* For master's, GRE, teacher license, 2 years of teaching experience, 2 letters of recommendation. Additional exam requirements/recommendations for international students: Required—TOEFL (minimum score 550 paper-based; 213 computer-based). *Application deadline:* For fall admission, 3/15 for domestic students. Applications are processed on a rolling basis. Application fee: $35. Electronic applications accepted. *Expenses:* Tuition: Part-time $275 per credit hour. Required fees: $30 per semester. *Financial support:* In 2006–07, 12 students received support. Scholarships/grants available. Support available to part-time students. *Unit head:* Dr. Rebecca Blomgren, Dean of Graduate and Professional Studies, 336-272-7102, Fax: 336-271-6634, E-mail: blomgrenr@gborocollege.edu.

Greenville College, Program in Education, Greenville, IL 62246-0159. Offers education (MAT); elementary education (MAE); secondary education (MAE). *Degree requirements:* For master's, thesis (for some programs). *Entrance requirements:* For master's, GRE, Illinois Basic Skills Test, teacher certification. Electronic applications accepted.

Gwynedd-Mercy College, School of Education, Gwynedd Valley, PA 19437-0901. Offers educational administration (MS); master teacher (MS); reading (MS); school counseling (MS); special education (MS). Part-time and evening/weekend programs available. *Faculty:* 9 full-time (5 women), 37 part-time/adjunct (17 women). *Students:* 92 full-time (66 women), 464 part-time (374 women); includes 52 minority (49 African Americans, 3 Hispanic Americans), 1 international. Average age 34. In 2006, 160 degrees awarded. *Degree requirements:* For master's, thesis, internship, practicum. *Entrance requirements:* For master's, GRE or MAT; PPST Praxis Test, minimum GPA of 3.0. *Application deadline:* Applications are processed on a rolling basis. Application fee: $25. *Expenses:* Tuition: Part-time $525 per credit hour. *Financial support:* In 2006–07, 2 research assistantships were awarded; career-related internships or fieldwork, Federal Work-Study, tuition waivers (full and partial), and unspecified assistantships also available. Financial award applicants required to submit FAFSA. *Faculty research:* Learning and the brain, reading literacy, ethics and moral judgment, leadership, teaching and multicultural education. *Unit head:* Dr. Lorraine Cavaliere, EdD, Dean, 215-641-5549, Fax: 215-542-4695, E-mail: cavaliere.l@gmc.edu. *Application contact:* Marian Watkins, Graduate Program Coordinator, 215-641-5561, Fax: 215-542-4695, E-mail: watkins.m@gmc.edu.

Hamline University, Graduate School of Education, St. Paul, MN 55104-1284. Offers MA Ed, MAESL, MAT, Ed D. *Accreditation:* NCATE (one or more programs are accredited). Part-time and evening/weekend programs available. *Faculty:* 22 full-time (15 women), 74 part-time/adjunct (55 women). *Students:* 224 full-time (165 women), 836 part-time (659 women); includes 60 minority (16 African Americans, 5 American Indian/Alaska Native, 30 Asian Americans or Pacific Islanders, 9 Hispanic Americans), 10 international. Average age 35. 332 applicants, 90% accepted, 254 enrolled. In 2006, 156 master's, 9 doctorates awarded. *Degree requirements:* For master's and doctorate, thesis/dissertation. *Entrance requirements:* For master's, letters of recommendation; for doctorate, master's degree, 3 years experience, letters of recommendation, writing sample, interview. Additional exam requirements/recommendations for international students: Required—TOEFL (minimum score 550 paper-based; 217 computer-based), TWE (minimum score 5). *Application deadline:* For fall admission, 6/15 priority date for domestic students; for spring admission, 6/1 priority date for domestic students. Applications are processed on a rolling basis. Application fee: $30. *Expenses:* Tuition: Full-time $5,104; part-time $319 per credit. One-time fee: $175. Tuition and fees vary according to course load, degree level and program. *Financial support:* Federal Work-Study available. Financial award applicants required to submit FAFSA. *Faculty research:* Teacher leadership, quantitative leadership. *Unit head:* Mary K. Boyd, Interim Dean, 651-523-2900, Fax: 651-523-2458, E-mail: mmurrayboyd01@hamline.edu. *Application contact:* Director, Graduate Admission, 651-523-2900, Fax: 651-523-2458, E-mail: gradprog@hamline.edu.

Hampton University, Graduate College, Department of Education, Hampton, VA 23668. Offers counseling (MA), including college student development, community agency counseling; elementary education (MA); special education (MA); teaching (MT). *Accreditation:* NCATE. Part-time and evening/weekend programs available. *Entrance requirements:* For master's, GRE General Test.

Harding University, College of Education, Searcy, AR 72149-0001. Offers advanced studies in teaching and learning (M Ed); art (MSE); behavioral science (MSE); Bible and religion (MSE); counseling (MS, Ed S); early childhood education (M Ed); early childhood special education (M Ed, MSE); education (MSE); educational leadership (M Ed, Ed S); elementary education (M Ed); English (MSE); family and consumer science (MSE); French (MSE); history/social science (MSE); kinesiology (MSE); math (MSE); physical science (MSE); reading (M Ed); secondary education (M Ed); Spanish (MSE); special education licensure (M Ed); teaching (MAT). *Accreditation:* NCATE. Part-time programs available. *Faculty:* 8 full-time (2 women), 45 part-time/adjunct (30 women). *Students:* 153 full-time (123 women), 469 part-time (341 women); includes 72 minority (63 African Americans, 4 American Indian/Alaska Native, 1 Asian American or Pacific Islander, 4 Hispanic Americans), 9 international. Average age 35. 175 applicants, 90% accepted, 147 enrolled. In 2006, 241 degrees awarded. *Degree requirements:* For master's, portfolio(s), thesis optional; for Ed S, portfolio, specialist project. *Entrance requirements:* For master's, GRE, MAT, PRAXIS; for Ed S, MAT or GRE. Additional exam requirements/recommendations for international students: Required—TOEFL (minimum score 550 paper-based). *Application deadline:* For fall admission, 8/1 for domestic and international students; for spring admission, 1/1 for domestic and international students. Applications are processed on a rolling basis. Application fee: $35. *Expenses:* Tuition: Part-time $455 per semester hour. Required fees: $20 per semester hour. Tuition and fees vary according to course load. *Financial support:* Scholarships/grants and unspecified assistantships available. Support available to part-time students. *Faculty research:* Reading, comprehension, school violence, educational technology, behavior, college choice, differentiated instruction, brain based teaching. *Unit head:* Pat Bashaw, Chair, 501-279-4183, Fax: 501-279-4051, E-mail: pbashaw@harding.edu.

Hardin-Simmons University, Graduate School, Irvin School of Education, Abilene, TX 79698-0001. Offers M Ed. Part-time programs available. *Faculty:* 9 full-time (4 women), 4 part-time/adjunct (1 woman). *Students:* 34 full-time (23 women), 74 part-time (56 women); includes 17 minority (5 African Americans, 2 Asian Americans or Pacific Islanders, 10 Hispanic Americans). Average age 32. 47 applicants, 100% accepted, 38 enrolled. In 2006, 55 degrees awarded. *Degree requirements:* For master's, comprehensive exam. *Entrance requirements:* For master's, minimum undergraduate GPA of 3.0 in major, 2.7 overall. Additional exam requirements/recommendations for international students: Required—TOEFL (minimum score 550 paper-based; 213 computer-based). *Application deadline:* For fall admission, 8/15 priority date for domestic students; for spring admission, 1/5 priority date for domestic students. Applications are processed on a rolling basis. Application fee: $50 ($100 for international students). *Expenses:* Tuition: Full-time $9,090; part-time $505 per hour. Required fees: $490; $66 per semester. One-time fee: $50. Tuition and fees vary according to course load and degree level. *Financial support:* In 2006–07, 101 students received support, including 29 fellowships (averaging $1,062 per year); career-related internships or fieldwork, scholarships/grants, unspecified assistantships, and coaching assistantships also available. Support available to part-time students. Financial award application deadline: 6/30; financial award applicants required to submit FAFSA. *Unit head:* Dr. Pam Williford, Dean, 325-670-1347, Fax: 325-670-5859, E-mail: pwilliford@hsutx.edu. *Application contact:* Dr. Gary Stanlake, Dean of Graduate Studies, 325-670-1298, Fax: 325-670-1564, E-mail: gradoff@hsutx.edu.

Harvard University, Graduate School of Education, Cambridge, MA 02138. Offers Ed M, Ed D. Part-time programs available. *Faculty:* 58 full-time (25 women), 40 part-time/adjunct (22 women). *Students:* 846 full-time (628 women), 125 part-time (96 women); includes 232 minority (87 African Americans, 6 American Indian/Alaska Native, 96 Asian Americans or Pacific Islanders, 43 Hispanic Americans), 116 international. Average age 31. 1,705 applicants, 47% accepted, 633 enrolled. In 2006, 591 master's, 70 doctorates awarded. Terminal master's awarded for partial completion of doctoral program. *Degree requirements:* For doctorate, thesis/dissertation. *Entrance requirements:* For master's and doctorate, GRE General Test, 3 letters of recommendation, official transcripts, statement of purpose. Additional exam requirements/recommendations for international students: Required—TOEFL (minimum score 600 paper-based; 250 computer-based; 100 iBT), TWE (minimum score 5). *Application deadline:* For fall admission, 1/2 for domestic and international students. Application fee: $85. Electronic applications accepted. *Expenses: Contact institution.* Full-time tuition and fees vary according to program and student level. *Financial support:* In 2006–07, 613 students received support, including 194 fellowships with full and partial tuition reimbursements available (averaging $12,008 per year), 47 research assistantships (averaging $9,340 per year), 153 teaching assistantships (averaging $7,710 per year); career-related internships or fieldwork, Federal Work-Study, institutionally sponsored loans, scholarships/grants, health care benefits, tuition waivers (full and partial), and unspecified assistantships also available. Support available to part-time students. Financial award application deadline: 2/2; financial award applicants required to submit FAFSA. *Faculty research:* Learning and development; educational leadership and organizations; education policy analysis. Total annual research expenditures: $14.8 million. *Unit head:* Dr. Kathleen McCartney, Dean, 617-495-3401. *Application contact:* Information Contact, 617-495-3414, Fax: 617-496-3577, E-mail: gseadmissions@harvard.edu.

See Close-Up on page 887.

Hastings College, Program in Teacher Education, Hastings, NE 68901-7696. Offers MAT. *Accreditation:* NCATE. Part-time programs available. *Degree requirements:* For master's, comprehensive exam, thesis, or teaching presentation. *Entrance requirements:* For master's, PRAXIS I. Additional exam requirements/recommendations for international students: Required—TOEFL. Electronic applications accepted. *Faculty research:* Assessments, performance competencies.

Hebrew College, Shoolman Graduate School of Education, Newton Centre, MA 02459. Offers early childhood Jewish education (Certificate); Jewish day school education (Certificate); Jewish education (MJ Ed); Jewish family education (Certificate); Jewish special education (Certificate); Jewish youth education, informal education and camping (Certificate). Part-time and evening/weekend programs available. Postbaccalaureate distance learning degree programs offered. *Faculty:* 6 full-time (1 woman), 19 part-time/adjunct (7 women). *Students:* 51 (42 women). Average age 37. 33 applicants, 79% accepted, 19 enrolled. In 2006, 5 degrees awarded. *Degree requirements:* For master's, one foreign language. *Entrance requirements:* For master's, GRE, interview. Additional exam requirements/recommendations for international students: Required—TOEFL. *Application deadline:* For fall admission, 12/15 priority date for domestic and international students; for winter admission, 2/15 priority date for domestic and international students; for spring admission, 5/30 priority date for domestic and international students. Application fee: $50. *Financial support:* Fellowships, career-related internships or fieldwork and tuition waivers (partial) available. Support available to part-time students. Financial award application deadline: 4/15; financial award applicants required to submit FAFSA. *Unit head:* Dr. Barry Mesch, Provost, 617-559-8600, Fax: 617-559-8601, E-mail: bmesch@hebrewcollege.edu. *Application contact:* Kate Nachman, Director of Admissions, 617-559-8610, Fax: 617-559-8601, E-mail: admissions@hebrewcollege.edu.

Hebrew Union College–Jewish Institute of Religion, Rhea Hirsch School of Education, Los Angeles, CA 90007-3796. Offers day school teaching (Certificate); Jewish education (MAJE, PhD); MAJCS/MAJE. *Faculty:* 3 full-time (2 women), 7 part-time/adjunct (5 women). *Students:* 21 full-time (15 women), 1 international. Average age 29. 11 applicants, 100% accepted, 11 enrolled. In 2006, 6 master's, 5 other advanced degrees awarded. Terminal master's awarded for partial completion of doctoral program. *Median time to degree:* Master's–3 years full-time. *Degree requirements:* For master's, one foreign language, thesis or alternative, Hebrew; for doctorate, one foreign language, thesis/dissertation, Hebrew. *Entrance requirements:* For master's, GRE General Test, Hebrew, interview, minimum undergraduate GPA of 3.0; for doctorate, GRE General Test, interview, knowledge of Hebrew, minimum GPA of 3.0. Additional exam requirements/recommendations for international students: Required—TOEFL (minimum score 550 paper-based). *Application deadline:* For fall admission, 2/1 for domestic and international students. Application fee: $50. *Expenses:* Tuition: Full-time $16,000; part-time $680 per unit. One-time fee: $100 full-time. *Financial support:* Career-related internships or fieldwork and scholarships/grants available. Support available to part-time students. Financial award application deadline: 3/2; financial award applicants required to submit FAFSA. *Unit head:* Dr. Michael Zeldin, Director, 213-749-3424 Ext. 4216, Fax: 213-747-6128, E-mail: mzeldin@huc.edu. *Application contact:* Director of Admissions and Recruitment, 213-749-3424 Ext. 4221, Fax: 213-7476128.

Hebrew Union College–Jewish Institute of Religion, School of Education, New York, NY 10012-1186. Offers MARE. Part-time programs available. *Faculty:* 21 full-time (9 women), 10 part-time/adjunct (4 women). *Students:* 8 full-time (6 women), 16 part-time (10 women), 3 international. Average age 32. In 2006, 5 degrees awarded. *Degree requirements:* For master's, one foreign language, thesis. *Entrance requirements:* For master's, GRE, minimum 2 years of college-level Hebrew. *Application deadline:* Applications are processed on a rolling basis. Application fee: $35. *Expenses:* Tuition: Full-time $16,000; part-time $680 per credit.

Required fees: $35. One-time fee: $75 full-time. *Financial support:* Career-related internships or fieldwork and scholarships/grants available. Financial award application deadline: 6/1; financial award applicants required to submit FAFSA. *Unit head:* Jo Kay, Director, 212-674-5300 Ext. 2213, Fax: 212-388-1720, E-mail: jkay@huc.edu. *Application contact:* Merline Denis, Administrative Assistant, 212-824-2252, Fax: 212-388-1720, E-mail: mdenis@huc.edu.

Heidelberg College, Program in Education, Tiffin, OH 44883-2462. Offers MA. Part-time and evening/weekend programs available. *Faculty:* 3 part-time/adjunct (2 women). *Students:* 9 full-time (4 women), 105 part-time (72 women); includes 10 minority (4 African Americans, 5 Asian Americans or Pacific Islanders, 1 Hispanic American). 24 applicants, 83% accepted, 19 enrolled. In 2006, 34 degrees awarded. *Degree requirements:* For master's, thesis or alternative, internship, practicum. *Entrance requirements:* For master's, minimum GPA of 2.5, 3 letters of reference. Additional exam requirements/recommendations for international students: Required—TOEFL (minimum score 550 paper-based). *Application deadline:* Applications are processed on a rolling basis. Application fee: $25. *Expenses:* Tuition: Part-time $345 per hour. Tuition and fees vary according to program. *Financial support:* In 2006–07, 20 students received support. Federal Work-Study available. Support available to part-time students. Financial award applicants required to submit FAFSA. *Unit head:* Dr. Jim Getz, Director of Graduate Studies in Education, 419-448-2068, Fax: 419-448-2072, E-mail: jgetz@heidelberg.edu. *Application contact:* Dr. G. Michael Pratt, Graduate Studies Office, 419-448-2288, Fax: 419-448-2072, E-mail: mpratt@heidelberg.edu.

Henderson State University, Graduate Studies, School of Education, Arkadelphia, AR 71999-0001. Offers MAT, MS, MSE, CP, Ed S. *Accreditation:* NCATE. Part-time programs available. *Faculty:* 37 full-time (12 women), 9 part-time/adjunct (4 women). *Students:* 89 full-time (60 women), 272 part-time (210 women); includes 37 minority (35 African Americans, 2 Hispanic Americans), 34 international. Average age 36. In 2006, 64 degrees awarded. *Entrance requirements:* For master's, GRE General Test or MAT, minimum GPA of 2.7, teacher certification. *Application deadline:* For fall admission, 5/1 priority date for domestic students, 5/1 for international students; for winter admission, 10/1 for international students; for spring admission, 12/1 priority date for domestic students, 4/1 for international students. Applications are processed on a rolling basis. Application fee: $0 ($30 for international students). *Expenses:* Tuition, state resident: full-time $3,294; part-time $183 per credit hour. Tuition, nonresident: full-time $6,588; part-time $366 per credit hour. Required fees: $176 per term. *Financial support:* In 2006–07, 7 teaching assistantships with full tuition reimbursements (averaging $4,000 per year) were awarded; research assistantships, Federal Work-Study and institutionally sponsored loans also available. Support available to part-time students. Financial award application deadline: 7/31. *Unit head:* Dr. Judy Harrison, Dean, 870-230-5358, Fax: 870-230-5455, E-mail: harrisj@hsu.edu. *Application contact:* Dr. Marck L. Beggs, Graduate Dean, 870-230-5126, Fax: 870-230-5479, E-mail: beggsm@hsu.edu.

Heritage University, Graduate Programs in Education, Toppenish, WA 98948-9599. Offers counseling (M Ed); educational administration (M Ed); professional studies (M Ed), including bilingual education/ESL, biology, English and literature, reading/literacy, special education; teaching (MIT). Part-time and evening/weekend programs available. *Faculty:* 21 full-time (13 women), 67 part-time/adjunct (35 women). *Students:* 328 full-time (232 women), 146 part-time (96 women); includes 135 minority (11 African Americans, 11 American Indian/Alaska Native, 12 Asian Americans or Pacific Islanders, 101 Hispanic Americans). Average age 38. 245 applicants, 76% accepted, 134 enrolled. In 2006, 254 degrees awarded. *Degree requirements:* For master's, thesis (for some programs), comprehensive exam, registration. *Entrance requirements:* For master's, interview, letters of recommendation, teaching certificate. Additional exam requirements/recommendations for international students: Recommended—TOEFL (minimum score 550 paper-based; 213 computer-based). *Application deadline:* For fall admission, 3/15 priority date for domestic and international students; for spring admission, 2/1 priority date for domestic and international students. Applications are processed on a rolling basis. Application fee: $50 ($100 for international students). *Financial support:* Career-related internships or fieldwork, Federal Work-Study, institutionally sponsored loans, and tuition waivers (partial) available. Support available to part-time students. Financial award application deadline: 2/10; financial award applicants required to submit FAFSA. *Unit head:* Jim Borst, Dean of the College of Education and Psychology, 509-865-8652, Fax: 509-865-8629, E-mail: borst_j@heritage.edu. *Application contact:* Kathy Otto, Coordinator of Administrative Services, 509-865-8635, Fax: 509-865-8629, E-mail: otto_k@heritage.edu.

Hodges University, Graduate Programs, Naples, FL 34119. Offers business administration (MBA); computer information technology (MS); criminal justice (MCJ); education (MPS); information systems management (MIS); interdisciplinary (MPS); law (MPS); management (MSM); professional studies (MPS); psychology (MPS); public administration (MPA). Part-time and evening/weekend programs available. Postbaccalaureate distance learning degree programs offered (no on-campus study). *Faculty:* 17 full-time (4 women). *Students:* 35 full-time (22 women), 156 part-time (100 women); includes 52 minority (24 African Americans, 1 American Indian/Alaska Native, 4 Asian Americans or Pacific Islanders, 23 Hispanic Americans). Average age 32. In 2006, 101 degrees awarded. *Median time to degree:* Master's–1.5 years full-time, 2.5 years part-time. *Degree requirements:* For master's, comprehensive exam (for some programs), registration. *Entrance requirements:* For master's, in-house entrance exam. Application fee: $50. Electronic applications accepted. *Financial support:* Federal Work-Study and scholarships/grants available. Financial award applicants required to submit FAFSA. *Unit head:* Terry McMahan, President, 239-513-1122, Fax: 239-598-6253, E-mail: tmcmahan@internationalcollege.edu. *Application contact:* Rita Lampus, Vice President of Student Enrollment Management, 239-513-1122, Fax: 239-598-6253, E-mail: rlampus@internationalcollege.edu.

Hofstra University, School of Education and Allied Human Services, Hempstead, NY 11549. Offers MA, MHA, MS, MS Ed, Ed D, PhD, Advanced Certificate, CAS, PD. *Accreditation:* NCATE. Part-time and evening/weekend programs available. Postbaccalaureate distance learning degree programs offered. *Faculty:* 62 full-time (45 women), 94 part-time/adjunct (60 women). *Students:* 702 full-time (551 women), 900 part-time (700 women); includes 131 minority (11 African Americans, 1 American Indian/Alaska Native, 35 Asian Americans or Pacific Islanders, 84 Hispanic Americans), 21 international. Average age 29. 1,094 applicants, 84% accepted, 545 enrolled. In 2006, 641 master's, 10 doctorates, 62 other advanced degrees awarded. Terminal master's awarded for partial completion of doctoral program. *Degree requirements:* For master's, one foreign language, thesis (for some programs), capstone, state exams, electronic portfolio, student teaching, comprehensive exam (for some programs), registration (for some programs); for doctorate and other advanced degree, one foreign language, thesis/dissertation, comprehensive exam, registration; for other advanced degree, one foreign language, thesis, electronic portfolio, fieldwork, internship, state exams, comprehensive exam, registration. *Entrance requirements:* For master's, GRE, letters of recommendation, interview, portfolio, resumé, essay, certification, minimum GPA, # hours in field of study; for doctorate, MAT, GMAT, GRE or LSAT, resumé, interview, letters of recommendation, essay; for other advanced degree, GRE, interview, essay, teaching certificate, letters of recommendation. Additional exam requirements/recommendations for international students: Required—TOEFL (minimum score 550 paper-based; 213 computer-based). *Application deadline:* Applications are processed on a rolling basis. Application fee: $60. Electronic applications accepted. *Expenses:* Tuition: Full-time $13,320; part-time $740 per credit. Required fees: $930; $155 per term. *Financial support:* In 2006–07, 593 students received support, including 104 fellowships with tuition reimbursements available (averaging $3,571 per year), 42 research assistantships with full and partial tuition reimbursements available (averaging $5,859 per year); career-related internships or fieldwork, Federal Work-Study, institutionally sponsored loans, scholarships/grants, traineeships, health care benefits, tuition waivers (full and partial), unspecified assistantships, and tuition vouchers for cooperating teachers also available. Support available to part-time students. Financial award applicants required to submit FAFSA. *Faculty research:* Curriculum development and institutional best practices, education technologies, assessment and data-driven decision making, autism spectrum disorders and the pre-school child, health care management. Total annual research expenditures: $2.1 mil-

lion. *Unit head:* Dr. Maureen O. Murphy, Interim Dean, 516-463-6775, E-mail: catmom@hofstra.edu. *Application contact:* Carol Drummer, Dean of Graduate Admissions, 516-463-4876, Fax: 516-463-4664, E-mail: gradstudent@hofstra.edu.

See Close-Up on page 889.

Hollins University, Graduate Programs, Program in Teaching, Roanoke, VA 24020-1603. Offers MAT. Part-time and evening/weekend programs available. *Faculty:* 3 full-time (all women), 3 part-time/adjunct (2 women). *Students:* 19 full-time (14 women), 33 part-time (28 women); includes 2 minority (both Hispanic Americans) Average age 30. 17 applicants, 88% accepted, 13 enrolled. In 2006, 16 degrees awarded. *Degree requirements:* For master's, thesis, registration. *Entrance requirements:* For master's, PRAXIS I, letters of recommendation, writing sample. Additional exam requirements/recommendations for international students: Required—TOEFL (minimum score 550 paper-based; 213 computer-based). *Application deadline:* For fall admission, 7/1 for domestic and international students; for spring admission, 12/1 for domestic and international students. Applications are processed on a rolling basis. Application fee: $40. Electronic applications accepted. *Financial support:* In 2006–07, 43 students received support, including 18 teaching assistantships (averaging $1,766 per year); Federal Work-Study and scholarships/grants also available. Support available to part-time students. Financial award application deadline: 7/15; financial award applicants required to submit FAFSA. *Faculty research:* TV violence and its effect on the developing brain, phonological/phonemic awareness, technology in the classroom. *Unit head:* Dr. Kristi Fowler, Director, 540-362-7460, Fax: 540-362-6288, E-mail: kfowler@hollins.edu. *Application contact:* Donna Martin, Secretary of Education, 540-362-7460, Fax: 540-362-6288, E-mail: dmartin@hollins.edu.

Holy Family University, Graduate School, School of Education, Philadelphia, PA 19114-2094. Offers education (M Ed); elementary education (M Ed); reading specialist (M Ed); secondary education (M Ed). Part-time and evening/weekend programs available. *Degree requirements:* For master's, thesis optional. *Entrance requirements:* For master's, GRE or MAT, interview. *Faculty research:* Cognition, developmental issues, sociological issues in education.

Holy Names University, Graduate Division, Department of Education, Oakland, CA 94619-1699. Offers advanced curriculum studies (M Ed); educational therapy (M Ed); mild/moderate disabilities (Ed S); multiple subject credential (M Ed); single subject credential (M Ed); special education (M Ed); teaching English as a second language (M Ed, Certificate); urban education (M Ed). Part-time programs available. *Faculty:* 6 full-time (all women), 9 part-time/adjunct (all women). *Students:* 17 full-time (14 women), 131 part-time (90 women); includes 58 minority (36 African Americans, 1 American Indian/Alaska Native, 11 Asian Americans or Pacific Islanders, 10 Hispanic Americans). Average age 40. 75 applicants, 80% accepted, 49 enrolled. In 2006, 11 master's, 29 Certificates awarded. *Degree requirements:* For master's, research paper, thesis or project. *Entrance requirements:* For master's, minimum undergraduate GPA of 2.6 overall, 3.0 in major. Additional exam requirements/recommendations for international students: Required—TOEFL. *Application deadline:* For fall admission, 8/1 priority date for domestic students; for spring admission, 12/1 priority date for domestic students. Applications are processed on a rolling basis. Application fee: $50. *Expenses:* Tuition: Full-time $10,800; part-time $600 per unit. Required fees: $240; $120 per term. *Financial support:* In 2006–07, 67 students received support. Scholarships/grants available. Support available to part-time students. Financial award application deadline: 3/2; financial award applicants required to submit FAFSA. *Faculty research:* Cognitive development, language development, learning handicaps. *Unit head:* Dr. Zaida McCall-Perez, Chairperson, 510-436-1288, E-mail: mccall-perez@hnu.edu. *Application contact:* 800-430-1351, Fax: 510-436-1325, E-mail: admissions@hnu.edu.

Hood College, Graduate School, Department of Education, Frederick, MD 21701-8575. Offers curriculum and instruction (MS), including early childhood education, elementary education, elementary school science and mathematics, secondary education, special education; educational leadership (MS); reading specialization (MS); teaching the struggling reader (Certificate). Part-time and evening/weekend programs available. *Faculty:* 4 full-time (3 women), 32 part-time/adjunct (16 women). *Students:* 5 full-time (3 women), 371 part-time (313 women); includes 30 minority (23 African Americans, 4 Asian Americans or Pacific Islanders, 3 Hispanic Americans). Average age 32. 71 applicants, 99% accepted, 59 enrolled. In 2006, 67 degrees awarded. *Degree requirements:* For master's, action research project, portfolio (reading). *Entrance requirements:* For master's, minimum GPA of 2.5, teaching certification. *Application deadline:* Applications are processed on a rolling basis. Application fee: $35. *Expenses:* Tuition: Part-time $350 per credit. Required fees: $20 per semester. *Financial support:* Applicants required to submit FAFSA. *Faculty research:* Leadership, action research, brain research, learning styles. *Unit head:* Dr. John George, Chairperson, 301-696-3471, Fax: 301-696-3597, E-mail: george@hood.edu. *Application contact:* Dr. Kathleen C. Bands, Associate Dean of Graduate School, 301-696-3811, Fax: 301-696-3597, E-mail: gofurther@hood.edu.

Hope International University, School of Graduate Studies, Program in Education, Fullerton, CA 92831-3138. Offers ME. Part-time and evening/weekend programs available. *Faculty:* 2 full-time (0 women), 10 part-time/adjunct (8 women). *Students:* 32 full-time (26 women), 46 part-time (35 women); includes 19 minority (4 African Americans, 7 Asian Americans or Pacific Islanders, 8 Hispanic Americans). Average age 27. 30 applicants, 67% accepted, 16 enrolled. In 2006, 27 degrees awarded. *Degree requirements:* For master's, project. *Entrance requirements:* For master's, minimum GPA of 3.0. Additional exam requirements/recommendations for international students: Required—TOEFL (minimum score 550 paper-based; 213 computer-based; 86 iBT). *Application deadline:* Applications are processed on a rolling basis. Application fee: $75. Electronic applications accepted. *Expenses:* Contact institution. *Financial support:* In 2006–07, 11 fellowships (averaging $1,349 per year) were awarded. Support available to part-time students. *Faculty research:* Distance education. *Unit head:* Dr. George West, Chair, 714-879-3901 Ext. 2409, Fax: 714-681-7450, E-mail: gewest@hiu.edu. *Application contact:* Jeremy Zweig, Assistant Director of Admissions, 800-762-1294 Ext. 2322, Fax: 714-681-7450.

Houston Baptist University, College of Education and Behavioral Sciences, Programs in Education, Houston, TX 77074-3298. Offers bilingual education (M Ed); counselor education (M Ed); curriculum and instruction (M Ed); educational administration (M Ed); educational diagnostician (M Ed); reading education (M Ed). Part-time programs available. *Degree requirements:* For master's, registration. *Entrance requirements:* For master's, GRE General Test or MAT. Additional exam requirements/recommendations for international students: Required—TOEFL (minimum score 550 paper-based; 213 computer-based).

Howard University, School of Education, Washington, DC 20059-0002. Offers M Ed, MA, MAT, MS, Ed D, PhD, CAGS. *Accreditation:* NCATE. Part-time and evening/weekend programs available. *Faculty:* 34 full-time (18 women), 5 part-time/adjunct (4 women). *Students:* 136 full-time (102 women), 132 part-time (94 women); includes 211 minority (206 African Americans, 4 Asian Americans or Pacific Islanders, 1 Hispanic American), 7 international. Average age 27. 297 applicants, 59% accepted, 114 enrolled. In 2006, 53 master's, 10 doctorates awarded. Terminal master's awarded for partial completion of doctoral program. *Median time to degree:* Of those who began their doctoral program in fall 1998, 60% received their degree in 8 years or less. *Degree requirements:* For master's, expository writing exam; for doctorate, one foreign language, thesis/dissertation, expository writing exam, internship, comprehensive exam. *Entrance requirements:* For master's, minimum GPA of 2.7; for doctorate, GRE General Test, minimum GPA of 3.4. Additional exam requirements/recommendations for international students: Required—TOEFL (minimum score 550 paper-based; 213 computer-based). *Application deadline:* For fall admission, 4/1 priority date for domestic students. Applications are processed on a rolling basis. Application fee: $45. *Financial support:* In 2006–07, 34 students received support, including 12 fellowships with full tuition reimbursements available (averaging $14,000 per year), 15 research assistantships (averaging $10,000 per year), 7 teaching assistantships with full tuition reimbursements available (averaging

Education—General

Howard University (continued)
$13,000 per year); career-related internships or fieldwork, Federal Work-Study, institutionally sponsored loans, scholarships/grants, tuition waivers (full and partial), and unspecified assistantships also available. Financial award application deadline: 4/1; financial award applicants required to submit FAFSA. *Faculty research:* Policy affecting education for African-Americans; information technology use in underserved school populations; increasing literacy skills for public school students; violence intervention and prevention; successes, problems, and needs of disabled African-Americans. Total annual research expenditures: $4.3 million. *Unit head:* Dr. Leslie T. Fenwick. *Application contact:* Dr. Marilyn M. Irving, Associate Dean, 202-806-7340, Fax: 202-806-5302, E-mail: mirving@howard.edu.

Humboldt State University, Graduate Studies, College of Professional Studies, School of Education, Arcata, CA 95521-8299. Offers MA. Part-time and evening/weekend programs available. *Students:* 5 full-time (all women), 20 part-time (17 women); includes 3 minority (1 African American, 1 Asian American or Pacific Islander, 1 Hispanic American). Average age 37. 19 applicants, 74% accepted, 11 enrolled. In 2006, 6 degrees awarded. *Degree requirements:* For master's, thesis or alternative. *Entrance requirements:* For master's, minimum GPA of 3.0. Additional exam requirements/recommendations for international students: Required—TOEFL (minimum score 500 paper-based; 173 computer-based). *Application deadline:* For fall admission, 2/1 for domestic and international students. Application fee: $55. *Financial support:* Application deadline: 3/1; *Unit head:* Dr. Cathleen Rafferty, Chair, 707-826-5873, Fax: 707-826-5868, E-mail: cdr11@humboldt.edu. *Application contact:* Dr. Eric VanDuzer, Information Contact, 707-826-3726, Fax: 707-826-5868, E-mail: evv1@humboldt.edu.

Hunter College of the City University of New York, Graduate School, School of Education, New York, NY 10021-5085. Offers MA, MS, MS Ed, AC. *Accreditation:* NCATE. *Faculty:* 112 full-time (64 women), 126 part-time/adjunct (77 women). *Students:* 204 full-time (183 women), 1,625 part-time (1,360 women); includes 333 minority (85 African Americans, 2 American Indian/Alaska Native, 86 Asian Americans or Pacific Islanders, 160 Hispanic Americans). Average age 31. 1,177 applicants, 52% accepted, 408 enrolled. In 2006, 439 master's, 55 other advanced degrees awarded. *Degree requirements:* For master's, thesis; for AC, portfolio review. *Entrance requirements:* For degree, minimum B average in graduate course work, teaching certificate, minimum 3 years of full-time teaching experience, interview, 2 letters of support. Additional exam requirements/recommendations for international students: Required—TOEFL. *Application deadline:* For fall admission, 4/1 for domestic students, 2/1 for international students; for spring admission, 11/1 for domestic students, 9/1 for international students. Applications are processed on a rolling basis. Application fee: $125. *Expenses:* Tuition, state resident: part-time $270 per credit. Tuition, nonresident: part-time $500 per credit. Required fees: $45 per semester. *Financial support:* Fellowships, career-related internships or fieldwork, Federal Work-Study, institutionally sponsored loans, and tuition waivers (full and partial) available. Support available to part-time students. *Faculty research:* Multicultural and multiracial urban education; mentoring new teachers; mathematics and science education; bilingual, bicultural, and special education. *Unit head:* Dr. David Steiner, Dean, 212-772-4622, E-mail: david.steiner@hunter.cuny.edu. *Application contact:* William Zlata, Director for Graduate Admissions, 212-772-4482, Fax: 212-650-3336, E-mail: admissions@hunter.cuny.edu.

Idaho State University, Office of Graduate Studies, College of Education, Pocatello, ID 83209. Offers M Ed, MPE, Ed D, PhD, 5th Year Certificate, 6th Year Certificate, Ed S. *Accreditation:* NCATE. Part-time and evening/weekend programs available. Postbaccalaureate distance learning degree programs offered (no on-campus study). *Faculty:* 23 full-time (11 women). *Students:* 76 full-time (40 women), 330 part-time (184 women); includes 18 minority (3 African Americans, 4 American Indian/Alaska Native, 6 Asian Americans or Pacific Islanders, 5 Hispanic Americans), 21 international. Average age 40. In 2006, 59 master's, 17 doctorates, 2 other advanced degrees awarded. *Degree requirements:* For master's, oral exam, written exam, thesis optional; for doctorate, thesis/dissertation, written exam, comprehensive exam, registration; for other advanced degree, oral exam, written exam. *Entrance requirements:* For master's, GRE General Test or MAT, minimum undergraduate GPA of 3.0, interview; for doctorate, GRE General Test or MAT, minimum undergraduate GPA of 3.0, 3.5 graduate; departmental interview; current curriculum vitae; for other advanced degree, GRE General Test, minimum graduate GPA of 3.0, master's degree. Additional exam requirements/recommendations for international students: Required—TOEFL (minimum score 550 paper-based; 213 computer-based; 80 iBT). *Application deadline:* For fall admission, 7/1 for domestic students, 6/1 for international students; for spring admission, 12/1 for domestic students, 11/1 for international students. Applications are processed on a rolling basis. Application fee: $55. *Expenses:* Tuition, state resident: part-time $251 per credit. Tuition, nonresident: part-time $366 per credit. Tuition and fees vary according to degree level, program and reciprocity agreements. *Financial support:* In 2006–07, 21 teaching assistantships with full and partial tuition reimbursements (averaging $8,694 per year) were awarded; career-related internships or fieldwork, Federal Work-Study, institutionally sponsored loans, scholarships/grants, tuition waivers (full and partial), and unspecified assistantships also available. Support available to part-time students. Financial award application deadline: 1/1. *Faculty research:* School reform, inclusion, students at risk, teacher education standards, teaching cases. Total annual research expenditures: $327,219. *Unit head:* Dr. Deborah Hedeen, Dean, 208-282-3259, Fax: 208-282-4697, E-mail: hededebo@isu.edu. *Application contact:* Dr. Peter Denner, Director, Office of Standards and Assessment, 208-282-2783, Fax: 208-282-4697, E-mail: dennpete@isu.edu.

Illinois State University, Graduate School, College of Education, Normal, IL 61790-2200. Offers MS, MS Ed, Ed D, PhD. *Accreditation:* NCATE. Part-time programs available. *Faculty:* 58 full-time (31 women), 3 part-time/adjunct (1 woman). *Students:* 71 full-time (49 women), 612 part-time (456 women); includes 69 minority (47 African Americans, 2 American Indian/Alaska Native, 11 Asian Americans or Pacific Islanders, 9 Hispanic Americans), 15 international. 119 applicants, 89% accepted. In 2006, 186 master's, 34 doctorates awarded. *Degree requirements:* For doctorate, thesis/dissertation, 2 terms of residency. *Entrance requirements:* For master's and doctorate, GRE General Test. *Application deadline:* Applications are processed on a rolling basis. Application fee: $40. *Expenses:* Tuition, state resident: full-time $3,330; part-time $185 per credit hour. Tuition, nonresident: full-time $6,948; part-time $438 per credit hour. Required fees: $1,259; $52 per credit hour. *Financial support:* In 2006–07, 52 research assistantships, 6 teaching assistantships were awarded; career-related internships or fieldwork, Federal Work-Study, institutionally sponsored loans, tuition waivers (full and partial), and unspecified assistantships also available. Support available to part-time students. Financial award application deadline: 4/1. *Unit head:* Dr. Deborah Curtis, Dean, 309-438-5415.

Indiana State University, School of Graduate Studies, College of Education, Terre Haute, IN 47809-1401. Offers M Ed, MA, MS, PhD, Ed S. *Accreditation:* NCATE. Part-time and evening/weekend programs available. *Faculty:* 38 full-time (16 women), 23 part-time/adjunct (16 women). *Students:* 229 full-time (157 women), 521 part-time (368 women); includes 74 minority (51 African Americans, 4 American Indian/Alaska Native, 7 Asian Americans or Pacific Islanders, 12 Hispanic Americans), 45 international. Average age 35. 385 applicants, 71% accepted, 140 enrolled. In 2006, 155 master's, 44 doctorates, 24 other advanced degrees awarded. *Degree requirements:* For doctorate, thesis/dissertation. *Entrance requirements:* For master's, minimum undergraduate GPA of 2.5; for doctorate, GRE General Test; for Ed S, GRE General Test, minimum graduate GPA of 3.25. *Application deadline:* Applications are processed on a rolling basis. Application fee: $35. Electronic applications accepted. *Expenses:* Tuition, state resident: part-time $278 per credit. Tuition, nonresident: part-time $552 per credit. *Financial support:* In 2006–07, 61 teaching assistantships with partial tuition reimbursements (averaging $5,793 per year) were awarded; fellowships with partial tuition reimbursements, research assistantships with partial tuition reimbursements, career-related internships or fieldwork, Federal Work-Study, institutionally sponsored loans, and tuition waivers (partial) also available. Support available to part-time students. Financial award application deadline: 3/1; financial award applicants required to submit FAFSA. *Unit head:* Dr. Bradley Balch, Dean, 812-237-2919.

Indiana University Bloomington, School of Education, Bloomington, IN 47405-7000. Offers MS, Ed D, PhD, Ed S. PhD offered through the University Graduate School. *Accreditation:* NCATE. Part-time programs available. Postbaccalaureate distance learning degree programs offered. *Faculty:* 102 full-time (43 women), 112 part-time/adjunct (45 women). *Students:* 471 full-time (322 women), 603 part-time (384 women); includes 120 minority (61 African Americans, 2 American Indian/Alaska Native, 24 Asian Americans or Pacific Islanders, 33 Hispanic Americans), 221 international. Average age 33. 1,837 applicants, 39% accepted, 354 enrolled. In 2006, 323 master's, 96 doctorates, 5 other advanced degrees awarded. Terminal master's awarded for partial completion of doctoral program. *Degree requirements:* For master's, thesis optional; for doctorate, thesis/dissertation, comprehensive exam, registration; for Ed S, thesis (for some programs), comprehensive exam or project, comprehensive exam (for some programs), registration (for some programs). *Entrance requirements:* For master's and Ed S, GRE General Test, minimum GPA of 3.0 (recommended), 3 letters of recommendation; for doctorate, GRE General Test, minimum GPA of 3.0, 3 letters of recommendation. Additional exam requirements/recommendations for international students: Required—TOEFL (minimum score 550 paper-based; 213 computer-based; 79 iBT). *Application deadline:* For fall admission, 1/15 priority date for domestic students, 12/1 priority date for international students; for spring admission, 11/1 priority date for domestic students, 9/1 priority date for international students. Applications are processed on a rolling basis. Application fee: $50 ($65 for international students). Electronic applications accepted. *Expenses:* Tuition, state resident: full-time $5,791; part-time $241 per credit hour. Tuition, nonresident: full-time $16,866; part-time $703 per credit hour. *Financial support:* In 2006–07, 122 fellowships with full and partial tuition reimbursements (averaging $18,000 per year), 91 research assistantships with tuition reimbursements (averaging $11,400 per year), 148 teaching assistantships with tuition reimbursements (averaging $13,600 per year) were awarded; Federal Work-Study, scholarships/grants, tuition waivers (full and partial), and unspecified assistantships also available. Financial award application deadline: 3/1. Total annual research expenditures: $5.6 million. *Unit head:* Dr. Gerardo Gonzalez, Dean, 812-856-8001, Fax: 812-856-8088, E-mail: gonzalez@indiana.edu. *Application contact:* Elizabeth Tilghman, Admissions Coordinator, 812-856-8552, Fax: 812-856-8505, E-mail: etilghma@indiana.edu.

See Close-Up on page 891.

Indiana University Kokomo, Division of Education, Kokomo, IN 46904-9003. Offers elementary education (MS); secondary education (MS). *Accreditation:* NCATE. Part-time and evening/weekend programs available. *Faculty:* 1 full-time (0 women). *Students:* Average age 32. In 2006, 3 degrees awarded. *Degree requirements:* For master's, research project, thesis optional. *Entrance requirements:* For master's, GRE General Test, minimum GPA of 2.5. *Application deadline:* For fall admission, 8/1 for domestic students; for spring admission, 12/1 for domestic students. Applications are processed on a rolling basis. Application fee: $40 ($50 for international students). *Expenses:* Tuition, state resident: full-time $4,391; part-time $183 per hour. Tuition, nonresident: full-time $10,043; part-time $418 per hour. Tuition and fees vary according to course load, campus/location and program. *Financial support:* Minority teacher scholarships available. *Faculty research:* Reading, teaching effectiveness, portfolio, curriculum development. *Unit head:* D. Antonio Cantu, Dean, 765-455-9287, Fax: 765-455-9503. *Application contact:* Charlotte Miller, Coordinator Educational/Student Resources, 765-455-9367, Fax: 765-455-9503, E-mail: cmiller@iuk.edu.

Indiana University Northwest, School of Education, Gary, IN 46408-1197. Offers elementary education (MS Ed); secondary education (MS Ed). *Accreditation:* NCATE. Part-time and evening/weekend programs available. *Faculty:* 5 full-time (2 women). *Students:* 3 full-time (all women), 64 part-time (49 women); includes 26 minority (23 African Americans, 3 Hispanic Americans). Average age 40. In 2006, 36 degrees awarded. *Degree requirements:* For master's, registration. *Entrance requirements:* For master's, GRE General Test or MAT, minimum GPA of 3.0. *Application deadline:* For fall admission, 7/15 priority date for domestic students; for spring admission, 11/15 for domestic students. Application fee: $25. *Expenses:* Tuition, state resident: full-time $4,332; part-time $181 per credit hour. Tuition, nonresident: full-time $10,081; part-time $420 per credit hour. Tuition and fees vary according to course load, campus/location and program. *Unit head:* Dr. Stanley E. Wigle, Dean, 219-980-6510, Fax: 219-981-4208, E-mail: amsanche@iun.edu.

Indiana University of Pennsylvania, School of Graduate Studies and Research, College of Education and Educational Technology, Indiana, PA 15705-1087. Offers M Ed, MA, MS, D Ed, Certificate. *Accreditation:* NCATE. Part-time and evening/weekend programs available. *Faculty:* 59 full-time (31 women), 9 part-time/adjunct (6 women). *Students:* 286 full-time (211 women), 604 part-time (438 women); includes 56 minority (48 African Americans, 4 Asian Americans or Pacific Islanders, 4 Hispanic Americans), 15 international. Average age 33. 1,114 applicants, 61% accepted. In 2006, 210 master's, 25 doctorates, 11 other advanced degrees awarded. Terminal master's awarded for partial completion of doctoral program. *Degree requirements:* For master's, thesis optional; for doctorate, thesis/dissertation, comprehensive exam. *Entrance requirements:* For master's and doctorate, 2 letters of recommendation. Additional exam requirements/recommendations for international students: Required—TOEFL. *Application deadline:* Applications are processed on a rolling basis. Application fee: $30. *Expenses:* Tuition, state resident: full-time $6,048; part-time $336 per credit. Tuition, nonresident: full-time $9,678; part-time $538 per credit. Required fees: $1,069; $148 per year. *Financial support:* In 2006–07, 14 fellowships (averaging $1,000 per year), 102 research assistantships (averaging $4,990 per year), 6 teaching assistantships with partial tuition reimbursements (averaging $17,001 per year) were awarded; career-related internships or fieldwork and Federal Work-Study also available. Support available to part-time students. Financial award application deadline: 3/15; financial award applicants required to submit FAFSA. *Unit head:* Dr. Mary Ann Rafoth, Dean, 724-357-2480, Fax: 724-357-5595. *Application contact:* Dr. Edward Nardi, Interim Associate Dean, 724-357-2480, Fax: 724-357-5595, E-mail: ewnardi@iup.edu.

Indiana University–Purdue University Fort Wayne, School of Education, Fort Wayne, IN 46805-1499. Offers MS Ed. *Accreditation:* NCATE. Part-time programs available. *Faculty:* 24 full-time (14 women). *Students:* 7 full-time (5 women), 268 part-time (193 women); includes 26 minority (16 African Americans, 1 Asian American or Pacific Islander, 9 Hispanic Americans), 1 international. Average age 37. 131 applicants, 87% accepted, 97 enrolled. In 2006, 104 degrees awarded. *Entrance requirements:* For master's, minimum GPA of 2.5. Additional exam requirements/recommendations for international students: Required—TOEFL (minimum score 600 paper-based; 260 computer-based). *Application deadline:* For fall admission, 7/1 priority date for domestic students; for spring admission, 12/1 for domestic students. Applications are processed on a rolling basis. Application fee: $30. *Expenses:* Tuition, state resident: full-time $4,039; part-time $224 per credit. Tuition, nonresident: full-time $9,220; part-time $512 per credit. Required fees: $429; $24 per credit. Tuition and fees vary according to course load. *Financial support:* In 2006–07, 1 teaching assistantship with partial tuition reimbursement (averaging $11,950 per year) was awarded; scholarships/grants also available. Support available to part-time students. Financial award application deadline: 3/1; financial award applicants required to submit FAFSA. *Faculty research:* Women in educational leadership, suspension and discipline data, principles of classroom design, Amish teacher dialogues, narratives of Southeast Asian refugees. Total annual research expenditures: $46,887. *Unit head:* Dr. Barry Kanpol, Dean, 260-481-4146, Fax: 260-481-5408, E-mail: kanpolb@ipfw.edu. *Application contact:* Vicky L. Schmidt, Graduate Recorder, 260-481-6450, Fax: 260-481-5408, E-mail: schmidt@ipfw.edu.

Indiana University–Purdue University Indianapolis, School of Education, Indianapolis, IN 46202-2896. Offers MS, Certificate. Part-time and evening/weekend programs available. *Faculty:* 13 full-time (7 women). *Students:* 77 full-time (66 women), 430 part-time (334 women); includes 46 minority (29 African Americans, 1 American Indian/Alaska Native, 7 Asian Americans or Pacific Islanders, 9 Hispanic Americans), 7 international. Average age 32. In 2006, 162 degrees awarded. *Degree requirements:* For master's, thesis optional. *Entrance requirements:* For master's, GRE General Test, minimum GPA of 3.0. Additional exam requirements/recommendations for international students: Required—TOEFL. *Application deadline:* For fall admission, 3/1 priority date for domestic students; for spring admission, 11/1 for domestic students. Application fee: $50 ($55 for international students). *Expenses:* Tuition, state resident: full-time $5,437; part-time $227 per credit hour. Tuition, nonresident: full-time $15,694; part-time $654 per credit hour. Required fees: $620. Tuition and fees vary according to course load, campus/location and program. *Financial support:* Fellowships, research assistantships with partial tuition reimbursements, teaching assistantships, Federal Work-Study, institutionally sponsored loans, scholarships/grants, and tuition waivers (partial) available. Support available to part-time students. *Faculty research:* Teachers in the process of change, learning cycles, children's concepts of science. Total annual research expenditures: $614,458. *Unit head:* Dr. Khaula Murtadha, Executive Associate Dean, 317-274-6801, Fax: 317-274-6864. *Application contact:* Marsha Schuler, Graduate Advisor, 317-274-6801, Fax: 317-274-6864, E-mail: edugrad@iupui.edu.

See Close-Up on page 891.

Indiana University South Bend, School of Education, South Bend, IN 46634-7111. Offers counseling and human services (MS Ed); elementary education (MS Ed); secondary education (MS Ed); special education (MS Ed). *Accreditation:* NCATE. Part-time and evening/weekend programs available. *Faculty:* 21 full-time (11 women), 9 part-time/adjunct (3 women). *Students:* 58 full-time (38 women), 237 part-time (186 women); includes 33 minority (22 African Americans, 1 American Indian/Alaska Native, 6 Asian Americans or Pacific Islanders, 4 Hispanic Americans), 5 international. Average age 35. 127 applicants, 100% accepted, 61 enrolled. In 2006, 141 degrees awarded. *Degree requirements:* For master's, thesis or alternative, exit project. *Entrance requirements:* For master's, letters of recommendation, GRE or minimum GPA of 3.0. Additional exam requirements/recommendations for international students: Required—TOEFL. *Application deadline:* For fall admission, 7/1 for domestic students; for spring admission, 11/1 for domestic students. Applications are processed on a rolling basis. Application fee: $45. Electronic applications accepted. *Expenses:* Tuition, state resident: full-time $4,450; part-time $185 per credit hour. Tuition, nonresident: full-time $10,954; part-time $456 per credit hour. Tuition and fees vary according to course load, campus/location and program. *Financial support:* Career-related internships or fieldwork available. Support available to part-time students. Financial award application deadline: 3/1; financial award applicants required to submit FAFSA. *Faculty research:* Professional dispositions, early childhood literacy, online learning, program assessments, problem-based learning. *Unit head:* Dr. Michael Horvath, Professor and Dean, School of Education, 574-520-4339, Fax: 574-520-4550. *Application contact:* Gil L. Martin, Graduate Admissions and Recruitment Officer, 574-520-4585, Fax: 574-520-5549, E-mail: marting@iusb.edu.

Indiana University Southeast, School of Education, New Albany, IN 47150-6405. Offers counselor education (MS Ed); elementary education (MS Ed); secondary education (MS Ed). *Accreditation:* NCATE. Part-time and evening/weekend programs available. *Students:* 5 full-time (4 women), 339 part-time (275 women); includes 19 minority (17 African Americans, 1 Asian American or Pacific Islander, 1 Hispanic American). Average age 32. In 2006, 176 degrees awarded. *Degree requirements:* For master's, registration. *Entrance requirements:* For master's, minimum undergraduate GPA of 2.5, graduate 3.0. *Application deadline:* Applications are processed on a rolling basis. Application fee: $30. *Expenses:* Tuition, state resident: full-time $4,458; part-time $186 per credit hour. Tuition, nonresident: full-time $10,196; part-time $425 per credit hour. Tuition and fees vary according to course load, campus/location and program. *Financial support:* In 2006–07, 29 students received support. Career-related internships or fieldwork, Federal Work-Study, and institutionally sponsored loans available. Support available to part-time students. Financial award applicants required to submit FAFSA. *Faculty research:* Learning styles, technology, constructivism, group process, innovative math strategies. *Unit head:* Dr. Gloria Murray, Dean, 812-941-2385, Fax: 812-941-2667, E-mail: soeinfo@ius.edu.

Indiana Wesleyan University, College of Adult and Professional Studies, Program in Graduate Teacher Education, Marion, IN 46953-4974. Offers curriculum and instruction (M Ed). *Accreditation:* NCATE. Evening/weekend programs available. *Faculty:* 8 full-time (5 women), 132 part-time/adjunct (54 women). *Students:* 999 full-time. Average age 33. 559 applicants, 99% accepted. *Entrance requirements:* For master's, GRE General Test, NTE, minimum GPA of 2.75, related experience, teaching license. Additional exam requirements/recommendations for international students: Required—TOEFL (minimum score 550 paper-based; 213 computer-based). *Application deadline:* Applications are processed on a rolling basis. Application fee: $25. Electronic applications accepted. *Expenses:* Tuition: Full-time $16,000; part-time $400 per credit. Required fees: $3,000. Tuition and fees vary according to degree level, campus/location and program. *Financial support:* Applicants required to submit FAFSA. *Unit head:* Dr. Jim Freemyer, Director of Graduate Education, 765-677-2278, Fax: 765-677-2023, E-mail: jfreemyer@indwes.edu. *Application contact:* Jerry Shepherd, Director of Marketing, 765-677-2856, E-mail: jerry.shepherd@indwes.edu.

Institute for Christian Studies, Graduate Programs, Toronto, ON M5T 1R4, Canada. Offers education (M Phil F, PhD); history of philosophy (M Phil F, PhD); philosophical aesthetics (M Phil F, PhD); philosophy of religion (M Phil F, PhD); political theory (M Phil F, PhD); systematic philosophy (M Phil F, PhD); theology (M Phil F, PhD); worldview studies (MWS). Part-time programs available. Postbaccalaureate distance learning degree programs offered (minimal on-campus study). *Degree requirements:* For master's, one foreign language, thesis; for doctorate, 2 foreign languages, thesis/dissertation. *Entrance requirements:* For master's and doctorate, philosophy background. Additional exam requirements/recommendations for international students: Required—TOEFL (minimum score 600 paper-based; 250 computer-based). *Faculty research:* Human rights, anthropology of self, medieval discourse, gender and body, post-modern thought; biblical hermeneutics, creational aesthetics, ecumenism, epistemology, political theory and public policy, relational psychotherapy.

Instituto Tecnologico de Santo Domingo, Graduate School, Santo Domingo, Dominican Republic. Offers corporate finance (M Mgmt); education (M Ed); engineering (M Eng), including data telecommunications, industrial engineering, sanitary and environmental engineering, structural engineering; environmental science (M En S); human resources administration (M Mgmt); management (M Mgmt); psychology (MA); social science (M Ed). *Entrance requirements:* For master's, birth certificate, minimum GPA of 2.0.

Instituto Tecnológico y de Estudios Superiores de Monterrey, Campus Central de Veracruz, Graduate Programs, Córdoba, Mexico. Offers administration (MA); administration of information technologies (MTI); computer sciences (MCC); education (MEE); educational institution administration (MAD); educational technology (MTE); electronic commerce (MCE); finance (MAF); humanistic studies (MEH); international business for Latin America (MNL); marketing (MMT); science (MCP); technology management (MTT). Part-time and evening/weekend programs available. Postbaccalaureate distance learning degree programs offered (minimal on-campus study). *Degree requirements:* For master's, thesis (for some programs). *Entrance requirements:* For master's, PAEP College Board. Electronic applications accepted.

Instituto Tecnológico y de Estudios Superiores de Monterrey, Campus Ciudad de México, Virtual University Division, Ciudad de Mexico, Mexico. Offers administration of information technologies (MA); computer sciences (MA); education (MA, PhD); educational technology (MA); environmental engineering (MA); environmental systems (MA); humanistic studies (MA); industrial engineering (MA); international business for Latin America (MA); quality systems (MA); quality systems and productivity (MA). Part-time and evening/weekend programs available. Postbaccalaureate distance learning degree programs offered (minimal on-campus study). *Entrance requirements:* For master's and doctorate, Instituto entrance exam. Additional exam requirements/recommendations for international students: Required—TOEFL.

Instituto Tecnológico y de Estudios Superiores de Monterrey, Campus Ciudad Juárez, Program in Education, Ciudad Juárez, Mexico. Offers M Ed.

Instituto Tecnológico y de Estudios Superiores de Monterrey, Campus Ciudad Obregón, Programs in Education, Ciudad Obregón, Mexico. Offers cognitive development (ME); communications (ME); mathematics (ME).

Instituto Tecnológico y de Estudios Superiores de Monterrey, Campus Estado de México, Professional and Graduate Division, Estado de Mexico, Mexico. Offers administration of information technologies (MITA); architecture (M Arch); business administration (GMBA, MBA); computer sciences (MCS, PhD); education (M Ed); educational institution administration (MAD); educational technology and innovation (PhD); electronic commerce (MEC); environmental systems (MS); finance (MAF); humanistic studies (MHS); information sciences and knowledge management (MISKM); information systems (MS); manufacturing systems (MS); marketing (MEM); quality systems and productivity (MS); science and materials engineering (PhD); telecommunications management (MTM). Part-time programs available. Postbaccalaureate distance learning degree programs offered (minimal on-campus study). *Degree requirements:* For master's, one foreign language, thesis (for some programs), registration; for doctorate, one foreign language, thesis/dissertation, registration (for some programs). *Entrance requirements:* For master's, E-PAEP 500, interview; for doctorate, E-PAEP 500, research proposal. Additional exam requirements/recommendations for international students: Required—TOEFL (minimum score 550 paper-based). *Faculty research:* Surface treatments by plasmas, mechanical properties, robotics, graphical computing, mechatronics security protocols.

Instituto Tecnológico y de Estudios Superiores de Monterrey, Campus Irapuato, Graduate Programs, Irapuato, Mexico. Offers administration (MBA); administration of information technology (MAIT); administration of telecommunications (MAT); architecture (M Arch); computer science (MCS); education (M Ed); educational administration (MEA); educational innovation and technology (DEIT); educational technology (MET); electronic commerce (MBA); environmental administration and planning (MEAP); environmental systems (MES); finances (MBA); humanistic studies (MHS); international management for Latin American executives (MIMLAE); library and information science (MLIS); manufacturing quality management (MMQM); marketing research (MBA).

Instituto Tecnológico y de Estudios Superiores de Monterrey, Campus Sonora Norte, Program in Education, Hermosillo, Mexico. Offers MA. *Entrance requirements:* For master's, MAT.

Inter American University of Puerto Rico, Arecibo Campus, Programs in Education, Arecibo, PR 00614-4050. Offers administration and educational supervision (MA Ed); counseling and guidance (MA Ed). *Degree requirements:* For master's, thesis optional. *Entrance requirements:* For master's, GRE, EXADEP, bachelor's degree in education or teaching license (administration and supervision) or courses in education and psychology (counseling and guidance), minimum GPA of 2.5 in last 60 credits.

Inter American University of Puerto Rico, Barranquitas Campus, Program in Education, Barranquitas, PR 00794. Offers educational administration and supervision (MA); elementary education (MA). *Degree requirements:* For master's, thesis optional. *Entrance requirements:* For master's, EXADEP, letter of recommendation. Electronic applications accepted.

Inter American University of Puerto Rico, Metropolitan Campus, Faculty of Education, San Juan, PR 00919-1293. Offers administration and supervision (MA); education (Ed D); elementary education (MA); guidance and counseling (MA); health and physical education (MA); higher education (MA Ed); occupational education (MA); special education (MA Ed); teaching of science (MA Ed); vocational evaluation (MA). Part-time and evening/weekend programs available. *Degree requirements:* For master's, comprehensive exam; for doctorate, thesis/dissertation, comprehensive exam. *Entrance requirements:* For master's, GRE or EXADEP, interview; for doctorate, GRE, MAT, or EXADEP. Electronic applications accepted.

Jackson State University, Graduate School, School of Education, Jackson, MS 39217. Offers MS, MS Ed, Ed D, PhD, Ed S. *Accreditation:* NCATE. Part-time and evening/weekend programs available. *Faculty:* 50 full-time (26 women), 11 part-time/adjunct (4 women). *Students:* 131 full-time (92 women), 187 part-time (130 women); includes 289 minority (all African Americans), 2 international. In 2006, 111 master's, 18 doctorates, 13 other advanced degrees awarded. Terminal master's awarded for partial completion of doctoral program. *Degree requirements:* For master's, comprehensive exam; for doctorate, thesis/dissertation, comprehensive exam. *Entrance requirements:* For master's, GRE General Test; for doctorate, MAT, teaching experience. Additional exam requirements/recommendations for international students: Required—TOEFL. *Application deadline:* For fall admission, 3/1 priority date for domestic students; for spring admission, 10/1 for domestic students. Applications are processed on a rolling basis. Application fee: $20. *Financial support:* Career-related internships or fieldwork, Federal Work-Study, scholarships/grants, and unspecified assistantships available. Support available to part-time students. Financial award application deadline: 3/1; financial award applicants required to submit FAFSA. *Unit head:* Dr. Daniel Watkins, Interim Dean, 601-979-2433, E-mail: daniel.watkins@jsums.edu. *Application contact:* Curtis Gore, Director of Graduate Admissions, 601-979-2455, Fax: 601-974-4325, E-mail: cgore@ccaix.jsums.edu.

Jacksonville State University, College of Graduate Studies and Continuing Education, College of Education and Professional Studies, Jacksonville, AL 36265-1602. Offers MS, MS Ed, Ed S. *Accreditation:* NCATE. Part-time and evening/weekend programs available. *Faculty:* 36 full-time (23 women), 18 part-time/adjunct (7 women). *Students:* 237 full-time (165 women), 782 part-time (574 women); includes 235 minority (222 African Americans, 8 American Indian/Alaska Native, 1 Asian American or Pacific Islander, 4 Hispanic Americans), 4 international. In 2006, 357 master's, 135 other advanced degrees awarded. *Entrance requirements:* For master's, GRE General Test or MAT. *Application deadline:* Applications are processed on a rolling basis. Application fee: $20. *Expenses:* Tuition, state resident: full-time $5,400; part-time $225 per credit hour. Tuition, nonresident: full-time $10,800; part-time $450 per credit hour. One-time fee: $20 full-time. *Financial support:* In 2006–07, 18 research assistantships were awarded. Support available to part-time students. Financial award application deadline: 4/1. *Unit head:* Dr. Cynthia Harper, Dean, 256-782-8213. *Application contact:* 256-782-5329.

Jacksonville University, College of Arts and Sciences, School of Education, Jacksonville, FL 32211-3394. Offers computer sciences (MAT); early childhood education (Certificate); elementary education (MAT); integrated learning with educational technology (MAT); mathematics education (MAT); music education (MAT); reading education (MAT); second careers as a teacher (Certificate). Part-time and evening/weekend programs available. *Degree requirements:* For master's, comprehensive exam. *Entrance requirements:* For master's, GRE General Test, minimum GPA of 3.0. Additional exam requirements/recommendations for international students: Required—TOEFL (minimum score 550 paper-based), TWE. Expenses: Contact institution.

John Carroll University, Graduate School, Department of Education and Allied Studies, University Heights, OH 44118-4581. Offers administration (M Ed, MA); educational and school psychology (M Ed, MA); professional teacher education (M Ed, MA); school based adolescent-young adult education (M Ed); school based early childhood education (M Ed); school based middle childhood education (M Ed); school based multi-age education (M Ed); school counseling (M Ed, MA). *Accreditation:* NCATE. Part-time and evening/weekend programs available. *Faculty:* 18 full-time (10 women), 18 part-time/adjunct (12 women). *Students:* 70 full-time (53 women), 131 part-time (114 women); includes 13 minority (12 African Americans, 1 Asian American or Pacific Islander). Average age 32. 149 applicants, 57% accepted, 72 enrolled. In 2006, 142 degrees awarded. *Degree requirements:* For master's, research essay or thesis (MA only). *Entrance requirements:* For master's, GRE General Test or MAT, minimum GPA of 2.75. *Application deadline:* Applications are processed on a rolling basis. Application fee: $25 ($35 for international students). *Expenses:* Tuition: Full-time $9,675; part-time $645 per credit hour. Tuition and fees vary according to program. *Financial support:* In 2006–07, 7 students received support, including 4 teaching assistantships with full tuition reimbursements available (averaging $8,000 per year); scholarships/grants, tuition waivers (partial), and unspecified assistantships also available. Financial award application deadline: 3/1; financial award applicants required to submit FAFSA. *Faculty research:* Children's literacy, diversity issues, teaching development, impact of technology. *Unit head:* Dr. Kathleen M. Manning, Chairperson, 216-397-3012, Fax: 216-397-3045, E-mail: manning@jcu.edu.

Education—General

John F. Kennedy University, School of Education and Liberal Arts, Department of Education, Pleasant Hill, CA 94523-4817. Offers MAT. Part-time and evening/weekend programs available. *Degree requirements:* For master's, thesis. *Entrance requirements:* For master's, California Basic Educational Skills Test, NTE, interview. Additional exam requirements/recommendations for international students: Required—TOEFL.

The Johns Hopkins University, School of Professional Studies in Business and Education, School of Education, Baltimore, MD 21218-2699. Offers MAT, MS, Ed D, CAGS, Certificate. *Accreditation:* NCATE. Part-time and evening/weekend programs available. Postbaccalaureate distance learning degree programs offered (minimal on-campus study). *Faculty:* 37 full-time (24 women), 174 part-time/adjunct (104 women). *Students:* 345 full-time (275 women), 1,397 part-time (1,125 women); includes 311 minority (229 African Americans, 6 American Indian/Alaska Native, 54 Asian Americans or Pacific Islanders, 22 Hispanic Americans), 11 international. Average age 31. 1,499 applicants, 77% accepted, 1046 enrolled. In 2006, 538 master's, 1 doctorate, 215 other advanced degrees awarded. *Degree requirements:* For master's, portfolio; for doctorate, thesis/dissertation, comprehensive exam, registration. *Entrance requirements:* For master's, PRAXIS I (MAT), minimum GPA of 3.0, interview, resumé, letters of recommendation; for doctorate, GRE, interview, minimum GPA of 3.0, letters of recommendation, professional experience, resumé; for other advanced degree, interview, minimum GPA of 3.0, resumé, letters of recommendation. Additional exam requirements/recommendations for international students: Required—TOEFL (minimum score 600 paper-based; 250 computer-based; 100 iBT). *Application deadline:* For fall admission, 5/1 for international students; for spring admission, 10/15 for international students. Applications are processed on a rolling basis. Application fee: $60. *Expenses:* Tuition: Full-time $32,976. Tuition and fees vary according to degree level and program. *Financial support:* In 2006–07, 667 students received support. Scholarships/grants available. Support available to part-time students. Financial award application deadline: 6/1; financial award applicants required to submit FAFSA. Total annual research expenditures: $8.2 million. *Unit head:* Dr. Ralph Fessler, Dean, 410-516-7820, Fax: 410-516-6697, E-mail: fess@jhu.edu. *Application contact:* Carol Herrman, Admissions Coordinator, 410-872-1234, Fax: 410-872-1251, E-mail: onestop.admissions@jhu.edu.

Johnson & Wales University, The Alan Shawn Feinstein Graduate School, Program in Teacher Education, Providence, RI 02903-3703. Offers business education and secondary special education (MAT); elementary education and special education (MAT); food service education and secondary special education (MAT). *Students:* 120 full-time (75 women), 15 part-time (10 women); includes 4 minority (3 African Americans, 1 Hispanic American), 19 international. Average age 31. In 2006, 55 degrees awarded. *Entrance requirements:* For master's, MAT, minimum GPA of 2.75. Additional exam requirements/recommendations for international students: Required—TOEFL (paper-based 550; computer-based 210) or IELTS recommended. *Application deadline:* For fall admission, 8/21 priority date for domestic students, 6/15 priority date for international students; for winter admission, 11/15 priority date for domestic students, 10/1 priority date for international students. Applications are processed on a rolling basis. Application fee: $0. *Financial support:* Unspecified assistantships available. Financial award application deadline: 5/1. *Faculty research:* Secondary education, student teaching, educational reform, evaluation procedures. *Unit head:* Dr. Robert Gable, Director, 401-598-4738, Fax: 401-598-1162, E-mail: rgable@jwu.edu. *Application contact:* Dr. Allan G. Freedman, Director of Graduate Admissions, 401-598-1015, Fax: 401-598-1286, E-mail: gradadm@jwu.edu.

Johnson Bible College, Teacher Education Program, Knoxville, TN 37998-1001. Offers Bible and educational technology (MA); holistic education (MA). Part-time programs available. *Faculty:* 1 (woman) full-time, 7 part-time/adjunct (3 women). *Students:* 12 full-time (all women), 13 part-time (10 women), 1 international. Average age 30. 18 applicants, 100% accepted, 18 enrolled. In 2006, 18 degrees awarded. *Degree requirements:* For master's, multimedia action research presentation. *Entrance requirements:* For master's, interview, minimum GPA of 3.0, portfolio, teaching license. Additional exam requirements/recommendations for international students: Required—TOEFL. *Application deadline:* For fall admission, 7/1 priority date for domestic and international students; for spring admission, 12/1 priority date for domestic and international students. Applications are processed on a rolling basis. Application fee: $50. *Expenses:* Tuition: Full-time $6,100. Required fees: $730. *Financial support:* Career-related internships or fieldwork available. Support available to part-time students. Financial award application deadline: 5/1; financial award applicants required to submit FAFSA. *Faculty research:* Instructional technology. *Unit head:* Dr. Chris Templar, Graduate Program Coordinator, 865-251-2348, Fax: 865-251-3438, E-mail: ctemplar@jbc.edu.

Johnson State College, Graduate Program in Education, Johnson, VT 05656-9405. Offers applied behavior analysis (MA Ed), including children's mental health, developmental disabilities; curriculum and instruction (MA Ed); education of the gifted (MA Ed); reading education (MA Ed); science education (MA Ed); secondary education (MA Ed, CAGS), including teaching all secondary students; special education (MA Ed). Part-time programs available. *Faculty:* 5 full-time (3 women), 6 part-time/adjunct (5 women). *Students:* 5 full-time (all women), 67 part-time (51 women). *Degree requirements:* For master's, thesis or alternative, comprehensive exam. *Entrance requirements:* For master's, interview. Additional exam requirements/recommendations for international students: Required—TOEFL. *Application deadline:* For fall admission, 7/15 priority date for domestic students, 4/15 priority date for international students; for spring admission, 11/1 priority date for domestic students, 8/15 priority date for international students. Applications are processed on a rolling basis. Application fee: $35. *Financial support:* Career-related internships or fieldwork, Federal Work-Study, institutionally sponsored loans, and unspecified assistantships available. Support available to part-time students. Financial award application deadline: 3/1; financial award applicants required to submit FAFSA. *Application contact:* Catherine H. Higley, Administrative Assistant for Graduate Programs, 800-635-2356 Ext. 1244, Fax: 802-635-1248, E-mail: higleyc@jsc.vsc.edu.

Jones International University, Graduate School of Education, Centennial, CO 80112. Offers adult education (M Ed); corporate training and knowledge management (M Ed); curriculum and instruction (M Ed), including elementary teacher licensure, secondary teacher licensure; e-learning technology and design (M Ed); educational leadership and administration (M Ed); educational leadership and administration: principal and administrator licensure (M Ed); elementary curriculum instruction and assessment (M Ed); higher education leadership and administration (M Ed); K-12 instructional technology (M Ed); K-12 instructional technology: teacher licensure (M Ed); secondary curriculum instruction and assessment (M Ed); technology and design (M Ed). Part-time and evening/weekend programs available. Postbaccalaureate distance learning degree programs offered (no on-campus study). *Entrance requirements:* For master's, minimum cumulative GPA of 2.5. Additional exam requirements/recommendations for international students: Recommended—TOEFL (minimum score 550 paper-based; 213 computer-based). Electronic applications accepted.

Kansas State University, Graduate School, College of Education, Manhattan, KS 66506. Offers MS, Ed D, PhD. *Accreditation:* NCATE. Part-time and evening/weekend programs available. Postbaccalaureate distance learning degree programs offered. *Faculty:* 58 full-time (26 women), 10 part-time/adjunct (2 women). *Students:* 278 full-time (189 women), 401 part-time (293 women); includes 70 minority (32 African Americans, 4 American Indian/Alaska Native, 11 Asian Americans or Pacific Islanders, 23 Hispanic Americans), 21 international. Average age 25. 155 applicants, 68% accepted, 82 enrolled. In 2006, 135 master's, 34 doctorates awarded. Terminal master's awarded for partial completion of doctoral program. *Degree requirements:* For master's, thesis or alternative, oral or comprehensive exam; for doctorate, thesis/dissertation, residency. *Entrance requirements:* For master's and doctorate, GRE or MAT. Additional exam requirements/recommendations for international students: Required—GRE General Test or TOEFL. *Application deadline:* For fall admission, 3/1 priority date for domestic students, 2/1 priority date for international students; for spring admission, 10/1 priority date for domestic students, 8/1 priority date for international students. Applications are processed on a rolling basis. Application fee: $30 ($55 for international students). Electronic applications accepted. *Expenses:* Tuition, state resident: full-time $6,352; part-time $240 per credit hour. Tuition, nonresident: full-time $14,296; part-time $571 per credit hour. Required fees: $585. *Financial support:* In 2006–07, 19 research assistantships (averaging $11,223 per year), 16 teaching assistantships with full tuition reimbursements (averaging $12,145 per year) were awarded; fellowships, career-related internships or fieldwork, Federal Work-Study, institutionally sponsored loans, and scholarships/grants also available. Support available to part-time students. Financial award application deadline: 3/1; financial award applicants required to submit FAFSA. *Faculty research:* Teacher preparation, program evaluation, science education, ESL-bilingual education, rural issues in education. Total annual research expenditures: $7 million. *Unit head:* Michael Holen, Dean, 785-532-5525, Fax: 785-532-7304, E-mail: mholen@ksu.edu. *Application contact:* Dr. Paul R. Burden, Head, 785-532-5595, Fax: 785-532-7304, E-mail: burden@ksu.edu.

Kean University, College of Education, Union, NJ 07083. Offers MA, MS, PMC. *Accreditation:* NCATE. Part-time programs available. *Faculty:* 84 full-time (55 women). *Students:* 203 full-time (170 women), 1,123 part-time (924 women); includes 330 minority (147 African Americans, 29 Asian Americans or Pacific Islanders, 154 Hispanic Americans), 7 international. Average age 33. 719 applicants, 80% accepted, 407 enrolled. In 2006, 390 degrees awarded. *Degree requirements:* For master's, thesis, practicum, portfolio, field experience, comprehensive exam. *Entrance requirements:* For master's, GRE General Test, MAT, PRAXIS, teaching certificate, letters of recommendation, interview. *Application deadline:* For fall admission, 5/1 for domestic students; for spring admission, 11/1 for domestic students. Application fee: $60 ($150 for international students). Electronic applications accepted. *Expenses:* Tuition, state resident: full-time $8,856; part-time $369 per credit. Tuition, nonresident: full-time $11,256; part-time $469 per credit. *Financial support:* In 2006–07, 34 research assistantships with full tuition reimbursements (averaging $3,217 per year) were awarded; career-related internships or fieldwork and unspecified assistantships also available. *Unit head:* Dr. Frank Esposito, Dean, 908-737-3750, Fax: 908-737-3760, E-mail: fesposito@kean.edu. *Application contact:* Joanne Morris, Director of Graduate Admissions, 908-737-3355, Fax: 908-737-3354, E-mail: gradadm@kean.edu.

Keene State College, Division of Graduate and Professional Studies, Keene, NH 03435. Offers M Ed, PMC. *Accreditation:* NCATE. Part-time and evening/weekend programs available. In 2006, 48 master's, 13 other advanced degrees awarded. *Entrance requirements:* For master's, resumé. Additional exam requirements/recommendations for international students: Required—TOEFL. *Expenses:* Tuition, area resident: Part-time $265 per credit. Tuition, state resident: full-time $5,780; part-time $290 per credit. Tuition, nonresident: full-time $13,050. Required fees: $80 per credit. Part-time tuition and fees vary according to course load. *Financial support:* Research assistantships, career-related internships or fieldwork, Federal Work-Study, institutionally sponsored loans, and unspecified assistantships available. Support available to part-time students. Financial award application deadline: 3/1; financial award applicants required to submit FAFSA. *Unit head:* Dr. John Couture, Dean, 603-358-2220, E-mail: jcouture@keene.edu. *Application contact:* Peggy Richmond, Director of Admissions, 603-358-2276, Fax: 603-358-2767, E-mail: admissions@keene.edu.

Kennesaw State University, Leland and Clarice C. Bagwell College of Education, Program in Graduate Education, Kennesaw, GA 30144-5591. Offers adolescent education (M Ed); early childhood education (M Ed); educational leadership (M Ed); special education (M Ed). *Accreditation:* NCATE. Part-time programs available. *Faculty:* 60 full-time (38 women), 12 part-time/adjunct (4 women). *Students:* 150 full-time (143 women), 489 part-time (371 women); includes 95 minority (85 African Americans, 1 American Indian/Alaska Native, 1 Asian American or Pacific Islander, 8 Hispanic Americans), 21 international. Average age 35. 165 applicants, 97% accepted, 142 enrolled. In 2006, 283 degrees awarded. *Degree requirements:* For master's, thesis or alternative. *Entrance requirements:* For master's, GRE General Test, T-4 state certification, minimum GPA of 2.75. Additional exam requirements/recommendations for international students: Required—TOEFL (minimum score 550 paper-based; 213 computer-based; 80 iBT), IELTS (minimum score 6). *Application deadline:* For fall admission, 7/15 priority date for domestic students; for spring admission, 10/15 priority date for domestic students. Application fee: $50. Electronic applications accepted. *Expenses:* Tuition, state resident: full-time $3,044; part-time $127 per semester hour. Tuition, nonresident: full-time $12,172; part-time $508 per semester hour. Required fees: $353 per semester. Full-time tuition and fees vary according to campus/location and program. *Financial support:* Federal Work-Study and unspecified assistantships available. Support available to part-time students. Financial award application deadline: 6/15; financial award applicants required to submit FAFSA. *Application contact:* Alisha O'Brien, Administrative Coordinator, 770-423-6043, Fax: 770-420-4435, E-mail: aobrien@kennesaw.edu.

Kennesaw State University, Leland and Clarice C. Bagwell College of Education, Program in Teaching, Kennesaw, GA 30144-5591. Offers MAT. Part-time and evening/weekend programs available. *Students:* 25 full-time (17 women), 16 part-time (12 women); includes 3 African Americans, 4 Asian Americans or Pacific Islanders, 2 Hispanic Americans, 1 international. Average age 36. 9 applicants, 100% accepted, 7 enrolled. *Entrance requirements:* For master's, GRE, GACE I (state certificate exam), minimum GPA of 2.75, 2 recommendations, resumé. Additional exam requirements/recommendations for international students: Required—TOEFL (minimum score 550 paper-based; 213 computer-based; 80 iBT), IELTS (minimum score 6). *Application deadline:* For spring admission, 4/1 for domestic students. Application fee: $50. Electronic applications accepted. *Expenses:* Tuition, state resident: full-time $3,044; part-time $127 per semester hour. Tuition, nonresident: full-time $12,172; part-time $508 per semester hour. Required fees: $353 per semester. Full-time tuition and fees vary according to campus/location and program. *Financial support:* Unspecified assistantships available. *Unit head:* Dr. Lynn Stallings, Director, 770-420-4477, E-mail: lstalling@kennesaw.edu. *Application contact:* Alisha O'Brien, Administrative Coordinator, 770-423-6043, Fax: 770-420-4435, E-mail: aobrien@kennesaw.edu.

Kent State University, Graduate School of Education, Health, and Human Services, Kent, OH 44242-0001. Offers M Ed, MA, MAT, MPH, MS, Au D, PhD, Ed S. *Accreditation:* NCATE. Part-time and evening/weekend programs available. Postbaccalaureate distance learning degree programs offered (no on-campus study). *Faculty:* 115 full-time (67 women), 87 part-time/adjunct (71 women). *Students:* 769 full-time (616 women), 964 part-time (757 women); includes 158 minority (125 African Americans, 5 American Indian/Alaska Native, 11 Asian Americans or Pacific Islanders, 17 Hispanic Americans), 76 international. 670 applicants, 63% accepted. In 2006, 422 master's, 31 doctorates, 25 other advanced degrees awarded. *Degree requirements:* For master's, thesis (for some programs), registration; for doctorate, thesis/dissertation, comprehensive exam, registration. *Entrance requirements:* For doctorate and Ed S, GRE General Test. Additional exam requirements/recommendations for international students: Required—TOEFL (minimum score 525 paper-based; 197 computer-based). *Application deadline:* Applications are processed on a rolling basis. Application fee: $30. Electronic applications accepted. *Financial support:* In 2006–07, 21 fellowships with full tuition reimbursements (averaging $8,497 per year), 124 research assistantships with full tuition reimbursements were awarded; teaching assistantships with full tuition reimbursements, career-related internships or fieldwork, Federal Work-Study, institutionally sponsored loans, scholarships/grants, health care benefits, and unspecified assistantships also available. Support available to part-time students. Financial award application deadline: 4/1; financial award applicants required to submit FAFSA. *Unit head:* Dr. David A. England, Dean, 330-672-2808, Fax: 330-672-3407, E-mail: denglan1@kent.edu. *Application contact:* Nancy Miller, Office of Student Services, Academic Program Coordinator, 330-672-2576, Fax: 330-672-9162, E-mail: nmiller1@kent.edu.

Kutztown University of Pennsylvania, College of Graduate Studies and Extended Learning, College of Education, Kutztown, PA 19530-0730. Offers M Ed, MLS, Certificate. *Accreditation:* NCATE. Part-time and evening/weekend programs available. *Faculty:* 20 full-time (12 women), 2 part-time/adjunct (both women). *Students:* 120 full-time (68 women), 297 part-time (230 women); includes 12 minority (3 African Americans, 1 American Indian/Alaska Native, 3 Asian Americans or Pacific Islanders, 5 Hispanic Americans), 3 international. Average age 32. 259

applicants, 84% accepted, 117 enrolled. In 2006, 70 degrees awarded. *Degree requirements:* For master's, comprehensive exam. *Entrance requirements:* For master's, GRE. Additional exam requirements/recommendations for international students: Required—TOEFL. *Application deadline:* Applications are processed on a rolling basis. Application fee: $35. Electronic applications accepted. *Expenses:* Tuition, state resident: full-time $6,048; part-time $336 per credit. Tuition, nonresident: full-time $9,678; part-time $538 per credit. *Financial support:* In 2006–07, research assistantships with full tuition reimbursements (averaging $5,000 per year); career-related internships or fieldwork, Federal Work-Study, and unspecified assistantships also available. Financial award application deadline: 3/15; financial award applicants required to submit FAFSA.

LaGrange College, Graduate Programs, Department of Education, LaGrange, GA 30240-2999. Offers art education (MAT); curriculum and instruction (M Ed); music education (MAT); secondary education (MAT). Part-time and evening/weekend programs available. *Degree requirements:* For master's, comprehensive exam. *Entrance requirements:* For master's, GRE, MAT, or NTE, minimum GPA of 2.5. Additional exam requirements/recommendations for international students: Required—TOEFL (minimum score 550 paper-based).

Lake Erie College, Division of Education, Painesville, OH 44077-3389. Offers curriculum and instruction (MS Ed); education (MS Ed); educational leadership (MS Ed); reading (MS Ed). Part-time and evening/weekend programs available. *Faculty:* 4 full-time (1 woman), 4 part-time/adjunct (1 woman). *Students:* Average age 37. 9 applicants, 89% accepted, 5 enrolled. In 2006, 20 degrees awarded. *Degree requirements:* For master's, thesis, applied research project, comprehensive exam. *Entrance requirements:* For master's, GRE General Test or minimum GPA of 3.0. Additional exam requirements/recommendations for international students: Required—TOEFL (minimum score 590 paper-based). *Application deadline:* For fall admission, 8/1 priority date for domestic students, 6/1 for international students; for spring admission, 12/15 for domestic students, 10/1 for international students. Applications are processed on a rolling basis. Application fee: $25 ($50 for international students). Electronic applications accepted. *Expenses: Contact institution. Financial support:* Applicants required to submit FAFSA. *Faculty research:* Cooperative learning, portfolio assessment, education systems in England, video case-based instruction. *Unit head:* Dr. Richard Bonde, Associate Dean, 440-375-7156, Fax: 440-375-7005, E-mail: rbonde@lec.edu. *Application contact:* 440-375-7050, Fax: 440-375-7005, E-mail: admissions@lec.edu.

Lakehead University, Graduate Studies, Faculty of Education, Thunder Bay, ON P7B 5E1, Canada. Offers curriculum development (M Ed); education administration (M Ed); educational studies (PhD). Part-time and evening/weekend programs available. *Degree requirements:* For master's, project or thesis. *Entrance requirements:* For master's, minimum B average. Additional exam requirements/recommendations for international students: Required—TOEFL. *Faculty research:* Art education, AIDS education, language arts education, gerontology, women's studies.

Lakeland College, Graduate Studies Division, Program in Education, Sheboygan, WI 53082-0359. Offers M Ed. *Degree requirements:* For master's, thesis. Expenses: Contact institution.

Lamar University, College of Graduate Studies, College of Education and Human Development, Beaumont, TX 77710. Offers M Ed, MS, DE, Ed D, Certificate. *Accreditation:* NCATE. Part-time and evening/weekend programs available. Postbaccalaureate distance learning degree programs offered. *Faculty:* 28 full-time (18 women), 14 part-time/adjunct (8 women). *Students:* 88 full-time (60 women), 149 part-time (113 women); includes 53 minority (41 African Americans, 1 American Indian/Alaska Native, 5 Asian Americans or Pacific Islanders, 6 Hispanic Americans), 4 international. Average age 36. 397 applicants, 36% accepted, 54 enrolled. In 2006, 80 degrees awarded. *Degree requirements:* For master's, thesis optional; for doctorate, thesis/dissertation, comprehensive exam. *Entrance requirements:* For master's, GRE General Test, minimum GPA of 2.5; for doctorate, GRE, interview. Additional exam requirements/recommendations for international students: Required—TOEFL. *Application deadline:* For fall admission, 8/1 for domestic students; for spring admission, 12/1 for domestic students. Applications are processed on a rolling basis. Application fee: $25 ($50 for international students). *Expenses:* Tuition, nonresident: part-time $33 per hour. Required fees: $43 per hour. $110 per semester. *Financial support:* Fellowships, research assistantships, teaching assistantships, career-related internships or fieldwork, Federal Work-Study, institutionally sponsored loans, and scholarships/grants available. Support available to part-time students. Financial award application deadline: 4/1. *Faculty research:* School dropouts, suicide prevention in public school students, school climate and gifted performance, teacher evaluation. Total annual research expenditures: $2.3 million. *Unit head:* Dr. H. Lowery-Moore, Dean, 409-880-8661. *Application contact:* Dr. Lula Henry, Director of Professional Service, 409-880-8218.

Lander University, School of Education, Greenwood, SC 29649-2099. Offers elementary education (M Ed); teaching (MAT). *Accreditation:* NCATE. Part-time programs available. *Faculty:* 6 full-time (3 women), 4 part-time/adjunct (all women). *Students:* 11 full-time (8 women), 29 part-time (25 women); includes 5 minority (all African Americans) Average age 34. In 2006, 41 degrees awarded. *Degree requirements:* For master's, thesis or alternative, comprehensive exam. *Entrance requirements:* For master's, GRE General Test. Additional exam requirements/recommendations for international students: Required—TOEFL (minimum score 550 paper-based; 213 computer-based). *Application deadline:* Applications are processed on a rolling basis. Application fee: $35. Electronic applications accepted. *Expenses:* Tuition, state resident: full-time $7,824; part-time $326 per credit hour. Tuition, nonresident: full-time $14,932; part-time $622 per credit hour. Required fees: $550. *Financial support:* Federal Work-Study available. Support available to part-time students. Financial award application deadline: 4/15; financial award applicants required to submit FAFSA. *Unit head:* Dr. Sandra Lemoine, Dean, 864-388-8225, Fax: 864-388-8890. *Application contact:* Dr. Linda Neely, Director of Graduate Studies, 864-388-8268, Fax: 864-388-8144, E-mail: lneely@lander.edu.

Langston University, School of Education and Behavioral Sciences, Langston, OK 73050-0907. Offers bilingual/multicultural (M Ed); elementary education (M Ed); English as a second language (M Ed); rehabilitation counseling (M Sc); urban education (M Ed). *Accreditation:* CORE; NCATE (one or more programs are accredited). Part-time programs available. *Degree requirements:* For master's, thesis optional. *Entrance requirements:* For master's, GRE, writing skills test, minimum GPA of 2.5, 3 letters of recommendation. Additional exam requirements/recommendations for international students: Required—TOEFL, TWE. *Faculty research:* Bilingual/multicultural education, financing post-secondary education.

La Salle University, School of Arts and Sciences, Program in Education, Philadelphia, PA 19141-1199. Offers MA. Part-time and evening/weekend programs available. *Degree requirements:* For master's, comprehensive exam. *Entrance requirements:* For master's, MAT. Expenses: Contact institution. *Faculty research:* Educational reform and social realities, adult development, curriculum design for special needs children, developmentally-based schooling.

La Sierra University, School of Education, Riverside, CA 92515. Offers MA, Ed D, Ed S. Part-time and evening/weekend programs available. Terminal master's awarded for partial completion of doctoral program. *Degree requirements:* For doctorate, thesis/dissertation; for Ed S, thesis optional. *Entrance requirements:* For master's, minimum GPA of 3.0; for doctorate, GRE General Test, GRE Subject Test, minimum GPA of 3.3; for Ed S, minimum GPA of 3.3.

Lee University, Program in Education, Cleveland, TN 37320-3450. Offers classroom teaching (M Ed); educational leadership (M Ed); elementary/secondary education (MAT); special education (elementary) (M Ed); special education (secondary) (M Ed, MAT); special education (severe disabilities) (M Ed). *Faculty:* 25 full-time (11 women). *Students:* 103 full-time (66 women), 22 part-time (15 women); includes 43 minority (5 African Americans, 36 American Indian/Alaska Native, 2 Hispanic Americans), 3 international. 49 applicants, 100% accepted, 28 enrolled. In 2006, 75 degrees awarded. *Degree requirements:* For master's, variable foreign language requirement, thesis, internship, comprehensive exam. *Entrance requirements:* For master's, MAT or GRE General Test, minimum GPA of 2.75, 3 letters of recommendation, interview, writing sample. Additional exam requirements/recommendations for international students: Required—TOEFL. *Application deadline:* For fall admission, 4/1 for domestic students; for spring admission, 10/1 for domestic students. Applications are processed on a rolling basis. Application fee: $25. *Expenses:* Tuition: Part-time $412 per credit. Required fees: $10 per semester. Tuition and fees vary according to course load. *Financial support:* Career-related internships or fieldwork, Federal Work-Study, and institutionally sponsored loans available. *Unit head:* Dr. Gary Riggins, Director, 423-614-8193. *Application contact:* Vicki Glasscock, Graduate Admissions Director, 423-614-8059, E-mail: vglasscock@leeuniversity.edu.

Lehigh University, College of Education, Department of Education and Human Services, Bethlehem, PA 18015-3094. Offers counseling psychology (M Ed, PhD, Certificate), including counseling and human services (M Ed), counseling psychology (PhD), international counseling (M Ed, Certificate), school counseling (M Ed); educational leadership (M Ed, Ed D, Certificate); educational technology (Ed D, PhD, Certificate), including educational technology (Ed D, PhD), learning sciences and technology (PhD), project management (Certificate), technology use in schools (Certificate); instructional technology (MS), including instructional technology; school psychology (PhD, Ed S); special education (M Ed, PhD, Certificate), including academic intervention (M Ed), special education; technology-based teacher education (M Ed, PhD), including elementary education (M Ed), learning sciences and technology (PhD), secondary education (M Ed, MA); technology-based teacher education (MA), including secondary education (M Ed, MA); MBA/M Ed. *Accreditation:* APA (one or more programs are accredited). Part-time and evening/weekend programs available. Postbaccalaureate distance learning degree programs offered (minimal on-campus study). *Faculty:* 29 full-time (16 women), 17 part-time/adjunct (9 women). *Students:* 164 full-time (137 women), 428 part-time (296 women); includes 40 minority (19 African Americans, 1 American Indian/Alaska Native, 11 Asian Americans or Pacific Islanders, 9 Hispanic Americans), 50 international. 389 applicants, 50% accepted, 89 enrolled. In 2006, 180 master's, 10 doctorates awarded. Terminal master's awarded for partial completion of doctoral program. *Degree requirements:* For doctorate, thesis/dissertation. *Entrance requirements:* For master's, minimum GPA of 2.75. Additional exam requirements/recommendations for international students: Required—TOEFL (minimum score 500 paper-based; 250 computer-based). Application fee: $60. Electronic applications accepted. *Financial support:* Fellowships with full and partial tuition reimbursements, research assistantships with full and partial tuition reimbursements, teaching assistantships with full and partial tuition reimbursements, career-related internships or fieldwork, Federal Work-Study, institutionally sponsored loans, scholarships/grants, tuition waivers (full and partial), and unspecified assistantships available. Financial award application deadline: 1/31. *Faculty research:* Severe disabilities curriculum-based assessment, behavioral assessment, career development, behavioral interventions. *Unit head:* Dr. Nicholas Ladany, Chairman, 610-758-3253, Fax: 610-758-6223, E-mail: nil3@lehigh.edu. *Application contact:* Donna M. Johnson, Admissions Coordinator, 610-758 Ext. 3231, Fax: 610-758-6223, E-mail: dmj4@lehigh.edu.

Lehman College of the City University of New York, Division of Education, Bronx, NY 10468-1589. Offers MA, MS Ed. *Accreditation:* NCATE. Part-time and evening/weekend programs available.

Le Moyne College, Department of Education, Syracuse, NY 13214. Offers MS Ed, MST. Part-time and evening/weekend programs available. *Faculty:* 12 full-time (6 women), 31 part-time/adjunct (18 women). *Students:* 63 full-time (55 women), 324 part-time (259 women); includes 21 minority (13 African Americans, 1 American Indian/Alaska Native, 3 Asian Americans or Pacific Islanders, 4 Hispanic Americans), 1 international. Average age 31. 105 applicants, 100% accepted, 105 enrolled. In 2006, 266 degrees awarded. *Degree requirements:* For master's, thesis. *Entrance requirements:* For master's, GRE General Test, Bachelors, 2 letters of recommendation, written statement, copy of teacher certification (if applicable). Additional exam requirements/recommendations for international students: Required—TOEFL (minimum score 550 paper-based; 213 computer-based). *Application deadline:* Applications are processed on a rolling basis. Application fee: $50. *Expenses: Contact institution.* Tuition and fees vary according to program. *Financial support:* In 2006–07, 247 students received support. Unspecified assistantships available. Support available to part-time students. Financial award applicants required to submit FAFSA. *Faculty research:* Recruitment/retention strategies minority teachers, special education advocacy, cultural cognition, multiculturalism, literacy, technology, video games learning. *Unit head:* Dr. Cathy Leogrande, Chair, Education Department and Director of Graduate Education, 315-445-4376, Fax: 315-445-4744, E-mail: leogracc@lemoyne.edu.

Lenoir-Rhyne College, Graduate Programs, School of Education, Hickory, NC 28603. Offers birth through kindergarten education (MA); elementary education (MA); literacy education K-12 (MA). *Accreditation:* NCATE. Part-time and evening/weekend programs available. *Degree requirements:* For master's, thesis optional. *Entrance requirements:* For master's, GRE General Test or MAT, minimum undergraduate GPA of 2.7, graduate 3.0. Additional exam requirements/recommendations for international students: Required—TOEFL (minimum score 600 paper-based). Electronic applications accepted.

Lesley University, School of Education, Cambridge, MA 02138-2790. Offers curriculum and instruction (M Ed, CAGS); early childhood education (M Ed); educational studies (PhD); elementary education (M Ed); individually designed (M Ed); middle school education (M Ed); moderate special needs (M Ed); reading (M Ed, CAGS); science in education (M Ed); severe special needs (M Ed); special needs (CAGS); technology in education (M Ed, CAGS). Part-time and evening/weekend programs available. Postbaccalaureate distance learning degree programs offered (no on-campus study). *Faculty:* 47 full-time (39 women), 208 part-time/adjunct (135 women). *Students:* 242 full-time (222 women), 2,903 part-time (2,495 women); includes 279 minority (179 African Americans, 7 American Indian/Alaska Native, 25 Asian Americans or Pacific Islanders, 68 Hispanic Americans), 10 international. Average age 36. 1,186 applicants, 96% accepted, 792 enrolled. In 2006, 1,724 master's, 6 doctorates, 17 other advanced degrees awarded. *Degree requirements:* For master's, practicum; for doctorate, thesis/dissertation. *Entrance requirements:* For doctorate, GRE General Test or MAT, interview, master's degree, resumé; for CAGS, interview, master's degree. Additional exam requirements/recommendations for international students: Required—TOEFL (minimum score 550 paper-based; 213 computer-based; 80 iBT). *Application deadline:* Applications are processed on a rolling basis. Application fee: $50. Electronic applications accepted. *Financial support:* In 2006–07, 26 students received support, including research assistantships (averaging $3,400 per year), teaching assistantships (averaging $3,400 per year); career-related internships or fieldwork, Federal Work-Study, scholarships/grants, and unspecified assistantships also available. Support available to part-time students. Financial award application deadline: 4/15; financial award applicants required to submit FAFSA. *Faculty research:* Assessment in literacy, mathematics and science; autism spectrum disorders; instructional technology and online learning; multicultural education and ELL. *Unit head:* Dr. Mario Borunda, Dean, 617-349-8375, Fax: 617-349-8607, E-mail: mborunda@lesley.edu. *Application contact:* Kristen Card, Associate Director of On-Campus Admissions, 617-349-8734, Fax: 617-349-8313, E-mail: kmcard@lesley.edu.

See Close-Up on page 893.

Lewis & Clark College, Graduate School of Education and Counseling, Portland, OR 97219-7899. Offers M Ed, MA, MAT, MS, Ed D, Ed S. *Accreditation:* NCATE. Part-time and evening/weekend programs available. *Faculty:* 39 full-time (27 women), 66 part-time/adjunct (40 women). *Students:* 234 full-time (182 women), 257 part-time (199 women); includes 52 minority (8 African Americans, 9 American Indian/Alaska Native, 16 Asian Americans or Pacific Islanders, 19 Hispanic Americans), 2 international. Average age 33. 429 applicants, 86% accepted, 237 enrolled. In 2006, 226 master's, 15 other advanced degrees awarded. *Entrance requirements:* For degree, GRE. Additional exam requirements/recommendations for international students: Required—TOEFL (minimum score 575 paper-based; 233 computer-based). Application fee: $50. Electronic applications accepted. *Expenses:* Tuition: Part-time $610 per semester hour. *Financial support:* In 2006–07, 353 students received support. Career-related internships or

Education—General

Lewis & Clark College (continued)
fieldwork, Federal Work-Study, institutionally sponsored loans, scholarships/grants, health care benefits, and tuition waivers (partial) available. Support available to part-time students. Financial award applicants required to submit FAFSA. *Unit head:* Dr. Peter W. Cookson, Dean, 503-768-6004, Fax: 503-768-6005, E-mail: graddean@lclark.edu. *Application contact:* Becky Haas, Director of Admissions, 503-768-6200, Fax: 503-768-6205, E-mail: gseadmit@lclark.edu.

Lewis & Clark College, Graduate School of Education and Counseling, Department of Education, Inservice Program, Portland, OR 97219-7899. Offers MAT. Part-time and evening/weekend programs available. *Faculty:* 4 full-time (all women), 7 part-time/adjunct (6 women). *Students:* Average age 38. 9 applicants, 100% accepted, 8 enrolled. In 2006, 15 degrees awarded. *Application deadline:* Applications are processed on a rolling basis. Application fee: $50. Electronic applications accepted. *Expenses:* Tuition: Part-time $610 per semester hour. *Financial support:* In 2006–07, 26 students received support. Tuition waivers (partial) available. *Application contact:* Becky Haas, Director of Admissions, 503-768-6200, Fax: 503-768-6205, E-mail: gseadmit@lclark.edu.

Lewis University, College of Arts and Sciences, Graduate Programs in Education, Romeoville, IL 60446. Offers administration/education (MA); curriculum and instruction (MA Ed), including educational leadership, instructional leadership; education (M Ed, MAE); general administrative program (CAS); school counseling and guidance (MA); special education (MA); superintendent endorsement program (CAS). *Accreditation:* NCATE. Part-time and evening/weekend programs available. *Degree requirements:* For master's, thesis optional. *Entrance requirements:* For master's, departmental qualifying exam, graduate entrance writing exam, minimum GPA of 2.75, 3 letters of recommendation, interview. Additional exam requirements/recommendations for international students: Required—TOEFL (minimum score 550 paper-based; 213 computer-based). Electronic applications accepted.

Liberty University, School of Education, Lynchburg, VA 24502. Offers administration and supervision (M Ed); curriculum and instruction (M Ed); early childhood education (M Ed); education specialist (Ed S); educational leadership (Ed D); elementary education (M Ed); gifted education (M Ed); reading specialist (M Ed); school counseling (M Ed); secondary education (M Ed); special education (M Ed). *Accreditation:* NCATE. Part-time programs available. Postbaccalaureate distance learning degree programs offered (minimal on-campus study). *Faculty:* 8 full-time (3 women), 7 part-time/adjunct (3 women). *Students:* 33 full-time (22 women), 308 part-time (180 women); includes 22 minority (12 African Americans, 2 American Indian/Alaska Native, 2 Asian Americans or Pacific Islanders, 6 Hispanic Americans), 5 international. Average age 39. 434 applicants, 77% accepted, 111 enrolled. In 2006, 39 master's, 12 doctorates, 16 other advanced degrees awarded. *Degree requirements:* For doctorate, thesis/dissertation, comprehensive exam. *Entrance requirements:* For master's, GRE General Test or MAT (if taken on or before 1999), 2 letters of recommendation, minimum undergraduate GPA of 3.0, curriculum vitae, graduate status record; for doctorate, GRE General Test or MAT (if taken before 1999), minimum master's GPA of 3.0, 3 years of teacher experience; for Ed S, GRE General Test or MAT (if taken before 1999), minimum master's GPA of 3.0, 3 years of teaching experience. Additional exam requirements/recommendations for international students: Required—TOEFL (minimum score 600 paper-based; 250 computer-based). *Application deadline:* For fall admission, 6/1 priority date for domestic students; for spring admission, 11/1 for domestic students. Applications are processed on a rolling basis. Application fee: $35. Electronic applications accepted. *Expenses:* Contact institution. *Financial support:* In 2006–07, 226 students received support. Federal Work-Study and tuition waivers (partial) available. *Faculty research:* Self-determination, character education, bibliotherapy, learning styles, distance education. *Unit head:* Dr. Karen L. Parker, Dean, 434-582-2195, Fax: 434-582-2468, E-mail: kparker@liberty.edu. *Application contact:* Kyle A Falce, Director of Graduate Admissions, 800-424-9596, Fax: 800-628-7977, E-mail: gradadmissions@liberty.edu.

Lincoln Memorial University, School of Education, Harrogate, TN 37752-1901. Offers administration and supervision (M Ed, Ed S); counseling and guidance (M Ed); curriculum and instruction (M Ed, Ed S). Part-time and evening/weekend programs available. *Faculty:* 25 full-time (13 women), 11 part-time/adjunct (6 women). *Students:* 207 full-time (159 women), 1,315 part-time (995 women); includes 106 minority (93 African Americans, 1 American Indian/Alaska Native, 1 Asian American or Pacific Islander, 11 Hispanic Americans), 2 international. 1,397 applicants, 98% accepted. In 2006, 194 master's, 778 other advanced degrees awarded. *Degree requirements:* For master's, thesis optional. *Entrance requirements:* For master's, GRE, MAT, or NTE. *Application deadline:* For fall admission, 8/10 priority date for domestic students. Application fee: $25. *Financial support:* Career-related internships or fieldwork and unspecified assistantships available. Support available to part-time students. Financial award application deadline: 4/1; financial award applicants required to submit FAFSA. *Unit head:* Dr. Fred Bedelle, Dean, School of Graduate Studies, 423-869-6223, Fax: 423-869-6261, E-mail: graduate@inetlmu.lmunet.edu. *Application contact:* Barbara McCune, Senior Assistant, Graduate Office, 423-869-6374, Fax: 423-869-6261, E-mail: graduate@lmunet.edu.

Lincoln University, School of Graduate Studies and Continuing Education, College of Liberal Arts, Education and Journalism, Department of Education, Jefferson City, MO 65102. Offers educational leadership (Ed S), including elementary leadership, secondary leadership, superintendency; guidance and counseling (M Ed), including community/agency counseling, elementary school, secondary school; school administration and supervision (M Ed), including elementary school administration, secondary school administration, special education administration; school teaching (M Ed), including elementary school teaching, secondary school teaching. *Accreditation:* NCATE. Part-time and evening/weekend programs available. *Faculty:* 1 (woman) full-time, 10 part-time/adjunct (5 women). *Students:* 24 full-time (21 women), 62 part-time (51 women); includes 10 minority (8 African Americans, 2 Asian Americans or Pacific Islanders), 4 international. Average age 35. 13 applicants, 100% accepted, 10 enrolled. In 2006, 25 master's, 3 other advanced degrees awarded. *Degree requirements:* For master's and Ed S, portfolio. *Entrance requirements:* For master's, GRE or MAT, teaching certificate (school administration and supervision); background check; interview (elementary and secondary school teaching); for Ed S, GRE or MAT, principal certificate. Additional exam requirements/recommendations for international students: Required—TOEFL (minimum score 500 paper-based; 173 computer-based; 61 iBT). *Application deadline:* For fall admission, 7/1 priority date for domestic and international students; for spring admission, 12/1 priority date for domestic and international students. Applications are processed on a rolling basis. Application fee: $17. *Expenses:* Tuition, state resident: part-time $189 per credit hour. Tuition, nonresident: part-time $351 per credit hour. Required fees: $15 per credit hour. $20 per semester. *Financial support:* Federal Work-Study and scholarships/grants available. Financial award application deadline: 4/1; financial award applicants required to submit FAFSA. *Unit head:* Dr. Cynthia Chapel, Department Head, 573-681-5250, Fax: 573-681-5257, E-mail: chapelc@lincolnu.edu.

Lindenwood University, Graduate Programs, Division of Education, St. Charles, MO 63301-1695. Offers education (MA); educational administration (MA, Ed D, Ed S); instructional leadership (Ed D, Ed S); library media (MA); professional and school counseling (MA); professional counseling (MA); school counseling (MA); teaching (MA). Part-time and evening/weekend programs available. *Faculty:* 15 full-time (6 women), 16 part-time/adjunct (11 women). *Students:* 569 full-time (446 women), 1,869 part-time (1,433 women); includes 526 minority (494 African Americans, 8 American Indian/Alaska Native, 9 Asian Americans or Pacific Islanders, 15 Hispanic Americans), 8 international. Average age 35. In 2006, 747 master's, 19 other advanced degrees awarded. *Degree requirements:* For master's, thesis (for some programs); for doctorate, thesis/dissertation; for Ed S, specialist project. *Entrance requirements:* For master's, interview, minimum GPA of 3.0, writing sample; for Ed S, master's degree in education, relevant work experience. Additional exam requirements/recommendations for international students: Required—TOEFL (minimum score 550 paper-based; 213 computer-based). *Application deadline:* For fall admission, 8/30 priority date for domestic and international students; for spring admission, 12/30 priority date for domestic and international students. Applications are processed on a rolling basis. Application fee: $30 ($100 for international students). Electronic applications accepted. *Expenses:* Tuition: Part-time $340 per credit hour. Tuition and fees vary according to course level, course load, degree level and program. *Financial support:* Career-related internships or fieldwork, institutionally sponsored loans, and tuition waivers (partial) available. Financial award application deadline: 6/30; financial award applicants required to submit FAFSA. *Unit head:* Dr. John Dougherty, Dean of Education, 636-949-4937, E-mail: jdougherty@lindenwood.edu. *Application contact:* Brett Barger, Dean, Adult, Corporate and Graduate Admissions, 636-949-4934, Fax: 636-949-4109, E-mail: adultadmissions@lindenwood.edu.

Lipscomb University, Program in Education, Nashville, TN 37204-3951. Offers instructional leadership (M Ed); learning and teaching (MALT); school administration and supervision (M Ed); special education instruction, K-12 (MASE). *Accreditation:* NCATE. Part-time and evening/weekend programs available. *Faculty:* 3 full-time (1 woman), 9 part-time/adjunct (6 women). *Students:* 95 full-time (59 women), 30 part-time (22 women); includes 14 minority (13 African Americans, 1 Asian American or Pacific Islander). Average age 32. In 2006, 25 degrees awarded. *Degree requirements:* For master's, registration. *Entrance requirements:* For master's, MAT or GRE General Test, 2 reference letters. Additional exam requirements/recommendations for international students: Required—TOEFL (minimum score 570 paper-based; 230 computer-based). *Application deadline:* For fall admission, 8/29 priority date for domestic students; for spring admission, 1/16 priority date for domestic students. Applications are processed on a rolling basis. Application fee: $60. *Expenses:* Tuition: Part-time $560 per semester hour. Tuition and fees vary according to program. *Financial support:* In 2006–07, 67 students received support. Federal Work-Study, tuition waivers (full), and unspecified assistantships available. Support available to part-time students. Financial award applicants required to submit FAFSA. *Faculty research:* Facilitative learning styles, leadership, student assessment, interactive multimedia inclusion. *Unit head:* Dr. Junior High, Director, 615-966-1000 Ext. 6067, Fax: 615-966-7628, E-mail: junior.high@lipscomb.edu. *Application contact:* Jackie Sanders, Administrative Assistant, 615-966-1000 Ext. 6081, Fax: 615-966-7628, E-mail: jackie.sanders@lipscomb.edu.

Lock Haven University of Pennsylvania, Office of Graduate Studies, Department of Education, Lock Haven, PA 17745-2390. Offers alternative education (M Ed); teaching and learning (M Ed). *Accreditation:* NCATE. Part-time and evening/weekend programs available. Postbaccalaureate distance learning degree programs offered. *Degree requirements:* For master's, thesis. *Entrance requirements:* For master's, minimum undergraduate GPA of 3.0. Additional exam requirements/recommendations for international students: Required—TOEFL. Electronic applications accepted.

Long Island University, Brentwood Campus, School of Education, Brentwood, NY 11717. Offers elementary education (MS); reading (MS); school counseling (MS); school district administration and supervision (MS); special education (MS). Part-time and evening/weekend programs available.

Long Island University, Brooklyn Campus, School of Education, Brooklyn, NY 11201-8423. Offers MS, MS Ed, Certificate. *Accreditation:* Teacher Education Accreditation Council. Part-time and evening/weekend programs available. *Degree requirements:* For master's, thesis optional. *Entrance requirements:* For master's, 2 letters of recommendation. Additional exam requirements/recommendations for international students: Required—TOEFL (minimum score 500 paper-based; 173 computer-based). Electronic applications accepted.

Long Island University, C.W. Post Campus, School of Education, Brookville, NY 11548-1300. Offers MA, MS, MS Ed, PD. Part-time and evening/weekend programs available. *Degree requirements:* For PD, internship. Electronic applications accepted.

Long Island University, Southampton Graduate Campus, Education Division, Southampton, NY 11968-4198. Offers MS Ed. Part-time and evening/weekend programs available. *Faculty:* 4 full-time (3 women), 9 part-time/adjunct (5 women). *Students:* 21 full-time (15 women), 79 part-time (59 women). Average age 31. 111 applicants. In 2006, 25 degrees awarded. *Degree requirements:* For master's, thesis. *Entrance requirements:* For master's, minimum GPA of 2.75, writing sample, 1 letter of reference. Additional exam requirements/recommendations for international students: Required—TOEFL (minimum score 550 paper-based; 250 computer-based). *Application deadline:* For fall admission, 6/21 priority date for domestic students, 4/15 priority date for international students; for winter admission, 12/1 priority date for domestic students, 10/1 priority date for international students; for spring admission, 12/30 priority date for domestic students, 10/30 priority date for international students. Applications are processed on a rolling basis. Application fee: $30. Electronic applications accepted. *Expenses:* Tuition: Part-time $790 per credit. Required fees: $220 per semester. *Financial support:* In 2006–07, 96 students received support. Scholarships/grants and tuition waivers (partial) available. Support available to part-time students. Financial award applicants required to submit FAFSA. *Unit head:* Dr. R. Lawrence McCann, Director, 631-287-8211, E-mail: admissions@southampton.liu.edu. *Application contact:* Joyce Tuttle, Director of Graduate Admissions and Program Administration, 631-287-8010, Fax: 631-287-8253, E-mail: joyce.tuttle@liu.edu.

Long Island University, Westchester Graduate Campus, Programs in Education-Teaching, Purchase, NY 10577. Offers early childhood education (MS Ed); elementary education (MS Ed); literacy education (MS Ed); second language, TESOL, bilingual education (MS Ed); special education and secondary education (MS Ed). Part-time and evening/weekend programs available. *Faculty:* 4 full-time, 32 part-time/adjunct. *Students:* 50 applicants, 92% accepted, 42 enrolled. In 2006, 72 degrees awarded. *Degree requirements:* For master's, comprehensive exam. *Application deadline:* Applications are processed on a rolling basis. Application fee: $30. *Expenses:* Tuition: Part-time $790 per credit. *Financial support:* In 2006–07, 38 students received support. Scholarships/grants, tuition waivers (partial), and unspecified assistantships available. *Unit head:* Dr. Sylvia Blake, Academic Dean, Associate Provost, 914-831-2704, Fax: 914-251-5959, E-mail: sylvia.blake@liu.edu. *Application contact:* Ellen Brief, Coordinator of Admissions, Marketing, Student Services and Public Relations, 914-831-2701, Fax: 914-251-5959, E-mail: ellen.brief@liu.edu.

Longwood University, Office of Graduate Studies, College of Education and Human Services, Farmville, VA 23909. Offers communication sciences and disorders (MS); community and college counseling (MS); curriculum and instruction specialist-elementary (MS), including mild disabilities, modern languages; curriculum and instruction specialist-secondary (MS), including English, mild disabilities, modern languages; educational leadership (MS); guidance and counseling (MS); literacy and culture (MS); school library media (MS). *Accreditation:* NCATE. Part-time and evening/weekend programs available. *Degree requirements:* For master's, thesis optional. *Entrance requirements:* For master's, GRE (communication sciences and disorders), minimum GPA of 2.75. Additional exam requirements/recommendations for international students: Required—TOEFL (minimum score 550 paper-based; 213 computer-based).

Louisiana State University and Agricultural and Mechanical College, Graduate School, College of Education, Baton Rouge, LA 70803. Offers M Ed, MA, MS, PhD, Ed S. *Accreditation:* NCATE. Part-time and evening/weekend programs available. *Faculty:* 53 full-time (29 women). *Students:* 194 full-time (135 women), 210 part-time (155 women); includes 75 minority (59 African Americans, 3 American Indian/Alaska Native, 6 Asian Americans or Pacific Islanders, 7 Hispanic Americans), 21 international. Average age 34. 159 applicants, 55% accepted, 18 enrolled. In 2006, 120 master's, 31 doctorates, 7 other advanced degrees awarded. Terminal master's awarded for partial completion of doctoral program. *Degree requirements:* For Ed S, thesis optional. *Entrance requirements:* For master's and doctorate, GRE General Test, minimum GPA of 3.0. Additional exam requirements/recommendations for international students: Required—TOEFL (minimum score 550 paper-based; 213 computer-based; 79 iBT). *Application deadline:* For fall admission, 1/25 priority date for domestic students, 5/15 for international students; for spring admission, 10/15 for international students. Applications are processed on a rolling basis. Application fee: $25. Electronic applications accepted. *Financial support:* In 2006–07, 117 students received support, including fellowships (averaging $24,345 per year), 26 research assistantships with partial tuition reimbursements available (averaging $9,904 per year), 50 teaching assistantships with partial tuition reimbursements available (averaging $12,622 per year); career-related internships or fieldwork, Federal Work-Study, institutionally sponsored loans, tuition waivers (partial), and unspecified assistantships also available. Support available to part-time students. Financial award applicants required to submit FAFSA. *Faculty research:* Instructional learning, educational administration, exercise physiology, sports psychology, literacy education curriculum and instruction. Total annual research expenditures: $513,977. *Unit head:* Dr. Jayne Fleener, Dean, 225-578-1258, Fax: 225-578-2267, E-mail: fleener@lsu.edu. *Application contact:* Dr. Patricia Exner, Associate Dean, 225-578-2208, Fax: 225-578-2267, E-mail: pexner@lsu.edu.

Louisiana State University in Shreveport, College of Education and Human Development, Program in Education, Shreveport, LA 71115-2399. Offers M Ed. *Faculty:* 5 full-time (4 women), 4 part-time/adjunct (3 women). *Students:* 1 (woman) full-time, 97 part-time (82 women); includes 31 minority (30 African Americans, 1 Asian American or Pacific Islander). Average age 33. 30 applicants, 93% accepted, 20 enrolled. In 2006, 39 degrees awarded. *Degree requirements:* For master's, thesis, prerequisite; undergraduate statistics. *Entrance requirements:* For master's, GRE. Additional exam requirements/recommendations for international students: Required—TOEFL. *Application deadline:* For fall admission, 8/5 for domestic students, 6/1 for international students; for spring admission, 12/15 for domestic students, 10/1 for international students. Applications are processed on a rolling basis. Application fee: $10. *Financial support:* In 2006–07, 2 research assistantships with full tuition reimbursements (averaging $2,000 per year) were awarded; scholarships/grants also available. Financial award application deadline: 3/1. *Unit head:* Dr. Ruth Ray, Coordinator of Graduate Programs in Education, 318-797-5036, Fax: 318-798-4144, E-mail: rray@pilot.lsus.edu. *Application contact:* Dr. John Jones, Director of Graduate Programs, 318-797-5032, E-mail: jjones2@isus.edu.

Louisiana Tech University, Graduate School, College of Education, Ruston, LA 71272. Offers M Ed, MA, MS, Ed D, PhD. *Accreditation:* NCATE. Part-time programs available. *Degree requirements:* For doctorate, thesis/dissertation. *Entrance requirements:* For master's and doctorate, GRE General Test.

Lourdes College, School of Graduate and Professional Studies, Program in Education, Sylvania, OH 43560-2898. Offers endorsement in computer technology (M Ed). Evening/weekend programs available. *Entrance requirements:* Additional exam requirements/recommendations for international students: Required—TOEFL.

Loyola College in Maryland, Graduate Programs, College of Arts and Sciences, Department of Education, Baltimore, MD 21210-2699. Offers administration and supervision (M Ed, MA, CAS); curriculum and instruction (M Ed, MA, CAS); educational technology (M Ed); guidance and counseling (M Ed, MA, CAS); Montessori education (M Ed, CAS); reading (M Ed, CAS); special education (M Ed, CAS). *Accreditation:* NCATE. Part-time and evening/weekend programs available. *Faculty:* 29 full-time (19 women), 28 part-time/adjunct (13 women). *Students:* 134 full-time (123 women), 493 part-time (423 women); includes 81 minority (61 African Americans, 1 American Indian/Alaska Native, 6 Asian Americans or Pacific Islanders, 13 Hispanic Americans), 12 international. Average age 31. In 2006, 319 master's, 4 other advanced degrees awarded. *Entrance requirements:* For master's and CAS, GRE General Test, GRE Subject Test (recommended). Additional exam requirements/recommendations for international students: Required—TOEFL (minimum score 550 paper-based; 213 computer-based). *Application deadline:* For fall admission, 7/1 priority date for domestic students; for spring admission, 10/1 priority date for domestic students. Applications are processed on a rolling basis. Application fee: $50. *Financial support:* Research assistantships, career-related internships or fieldwork available. Financial award applicants required to submit FAFSA. *Unit head:* Dr. Victor Delclos, Chair, 410-617-2000 Ext. 5379, E-mail: vdelclos@loyola.edu. *Application contact:* Scott Greatorex, Director, Graduate Admissions, 410-617-5020, Fax: 410-617-2002, E-mail: graduate@loyola.edu.

Loyola Marymount University, Graduate Division, School of Education, Los Angeles, CA 90045-2659. Offers M Ed, MA, Ed D. *Accreditation:* NCATE. Part-time and evening/weekend programs available. *Faculty:* 30 full-time (20 women), 138 part-time/adjunct (104 women). *Students:* 840 full-time (646 women), 269 part-time (201 women); includes 554 minority (94 African Americans, 6 American Indian/Alaska Native, 116 Asian Americans or Pacific Islanders, 338 Hispanic Americans), 16 international. Average age 29. 668 applicants, 69% accepted, 418 enrolled. In 2006, 340 degrees awarded. *Degree requirements:* For master's, comprehensive exam. *Application deadline:* For fall admission, 7/15 for domestic students; for spring admission, 11/15 for domestic students. Application fee: $50. Electronic applications accepted. *Financial support:* In 2006–07, 753 students received support, including 18 research assistantships (averaging $12,370 per year); Federal Work-Study and scholarships/grants also available. Support available to part-time students. Financial award application deadline: 6/1; financial award applicants required to submit FAFSA. *Unit head:* Dr. Shane Martin, Dean, 310-338-2863, Fax: 310-338-1976, E-mail: smartin@lmu.edu.

Loyola University Chicago, School of Education, Chicago, IL 60611-2196. Offers M Ed, MA, Ed D, PhD, Certificate, Ed S. *Accreditation:* NCATE. Part-time and evening/weekend programs available. *Faculty:* 41 full-time (29 women), 68 part-time/adjunct (44 women). *Students:* 366 full-time (300 women), 681 part-time (482 women). Average age 36. 717 applicants, 57% accepted, 217 enrolled. In 2006, 258 master's, 95 doctorates, 21 other advanced degrees awarded. *Degree requirements:* For master's, thesis (for some programs), comprehensive exam (for some programs); for doctorate, thesis/dissertation, comprehensive exam. *Entrance requirements:* For master's, minimum GPA of 3.0, 3 letters of recommendation, resumé; for doctorate, GRE, interview, minimum GPA of 3.0, 3 letters of recommendation, resumé; for other advanced degree, GRE, interview, minimum GPA of 3.0, letters of recommendation, resumé. Additional exam requirements/recommendations for international students: Required—TOEFL (minimum score 550 paper-based; 213 computer-based; 79 iBT). *Application deadline:* For fall admission, 7/1 for domestic and international students; for spring admission, 11/1 for domestic and international students. Applications are processed on a rolling basis. Application fee: $50. Electronic applications accepted. *Financial support:* In 2006–07, fellowships with full tuition reimbursements (averaging $11,000 per year), 15 research assistantships with full tuition reimbursements (averaging $8,500 per year), teaching assistantships with full tuition reimbursements (averaging $11,000 per year) were awarded; career-related internships or fieldwork, Federal Work-Study, institutionally sponsored loans, scholarships/grants, tuition waivers (partial), and unspecified assistantships also available. Support available to part-time students. Financial award application deadline: 2/15; financial award applicants required to submit FAFSA. *Faculty research:* Policy studies, historical foundations, teacher education, educational leadership, comparative education, positive behavior support. *Unit head:* Dr. David Prasse, Dean, 312-915-6992, Fax: 312-915-6630, E-mail: dprasse@luc.edu. *Application contact:* Marie Rosin-Dittmar, Information Contact, 312-915-6800, E-mail: schleduc@luc.edu.

Loyola University New Orleans, College of Arts and Sciences, Department of Education and Counseling, New Orleans, LA 70118-6195. Offers counseling (MS); elementary education (MS); reading education (MS); secondary education (MS). Part-time and evening/weekend programs available. *Degree requirements:* For master's, comprehensive exam. *Entrance requirements:* For master's, GRE or MAT (preferred), interview, letters of recommendation, writing sample. Additional exam requirements/recommendations for international students: Required—TOEFL (minimum score 550 paper-based; 213 computer-based). Electronic applications accepted. *Faculty research:* Counseling theory, spirituality issues, group counseling, multicultural application.

Lynchburg College, Graduate Studies, School of Education and Human Development, Lynchburg, VA 24501-3199. Offers counselor education (M Ed), including community counseling, school counseling; educational leadership (M Ed); English education (M Ed); science education (M Ed); special education (M Ed), including early childhood special education, mental retardation, severely/profoundly handicapped education, teaching children with learning disabilities, teaching the emotionally disturbed; teaching and learning (M Ed). Part-time and evening/weekend programs available. *Faculty:* 24 full-time (16 women), 8 part-time/adjunct (1 woman). *Students:* 78 full-time (67 women), 158 part-time (124 women); includes 25 minority (18 African Americans, 1 American Indian/Alaska Native, 1 Asian American or Pacific Islander, 5 Hispanic Americans), 27 international. Average age 34. 90 applicants, 60% accepted, 40 enrolled. In 2006, 83 degrees awarded. *Median time to degree:* Master's–3 years full-time, 4 years part-time. *Entrance requirements:* For master's, GRE, minimum undergraduate GPA of 3.0. Additional exam requirements/recommendations for international students: Required—TOEFL. *Application deadline:* For fall admission, 7/31 for domestic students, 6/1 for international students; for spring admission, 11/30 for domestic students, 10/1 for international students. Application fee: $30. *Expenses:* Tuition: Full-time $6,300; part-time $350 per credit. Required fees: $100. *Financial support:* Career-related internships or fieldwork, scholarships/grants, and unspecified assistantships available. Financial award applicants required to submit FAFSA. *Unit head:* Dr. Jan Stenette, Dean, 434-544-8662.

Lyndon State College, Graduate Programs in Education, Lyndonville, VT 05851-0919. Offers education (M Ed), including curriculum and instruction, reading specialist, special education, teaching and counseling; natural sciences (MST), including science education. Part-time and evening/weekend programs available. *Degree requirements:* For master's, exam or major field project. *Entrance requirements:* Additional exam requirements/recommendations for international students: Recommended—TOEFL (minimum score 500 paper-based; 173 computer-based). *Faculty research:* Impaired reading, cognitive style, counseling relationship.

Madonna University, Programs in Education, Livonia, MI 48150-1173. Offers Catholic school leadership (MSA); educational leadership (MSA); learning disabilities (MAT); literacy education (MAT); teaching and learning (MAT). *Accreditation:* NCATE. Part-time and evening/weekend programs available. *Faculty:* 11 full-time (7 women), 8 part-time/adjunct (2 women). *Students:* 2 full-time (both women), 154 part-time (134 women); includes 10 minority (6 African Americans, 1 Asian American or Pacific Islander, 3 Hispanic Americans), 2 international. Average age 36. 20 applicants, 85% accepted. In 2006, 133 degrees awarded. *Degree requirements:* For master's, thesis or alternative. *Application deadline:* For fall admission, 8/1 priority date for domestic students; for winter admission, 12/1 priority date for domestic students; for spring admission, 4/1 priority date for domestic students. Applications are processed on a rolling basis. Application fee: $25 ($200 for international students). Electronic applications accepted. *Financial support:* Career-related internships or fieldwork, Federal Work-Study, institutionally sponsored loans, and scholarships/grants available. Support available to part-time students. *Unit head:* Dr. Robert Kimball, Dean, 734-432-5652, E-mail: rkimball@madonna.edu. *Application contact:* Sandra Kellums, Coordinator of Graduate Admissions and Records, 734-432-5667, Fax: 734-432-5862, E-mail: skellum@madonna.edu.

Maharishi University of Management, Graduate Studies, Department of Education, Fairfield, IA 52557. Offers teaching elementary education (MA); teaching secondary education (MA). *Degree requirements:* For master's, thesis or alternative. *Entrance requirements:* For master's, GRE, minimum GPA of 3.0. Additional exam requirements/recommendations for international students: Required—TOEFL. *Faculty research:* Unified field-based approach to education, moral climate, scientific study of teaching.

Malone College, School of Education, Graduate Program in Education, Canton, OH 44709-3897. Offers curriculum and instruction (MA); curriculum, instruction, and professional development (MA); instructional technology (MA); intervention specialist (MA); reading (MA). Part-time and evening/weekend programs available. *Faculty:* 11 full-time (4 women), 12 part-time/adjunct (9 women). *Students:* 4 full-time (2 women), 96 part-time (78 women); includes 5 minority (1 African American, 2 Asian Americans or Pacific Islanders, 2 Hispanic Americans). Average age 33. In 2006, 26 degrees awarded. *Degree requirements:* For master's, research project. *Entrance requirements:* For master's, minimum GPA of 3.0, teaching license. *Application deadline:* Applications are processed on a rolling basis. Application fee: $25. *Expenses:* Tuition: Part-time $399 per credit hour. *Financial support:* Tuition waivers (partial) available. Support available to part-time students. Financial award application deadline: 6/30. *Faculty research:* The Bible as children's literature, special needs students and literacy development, middle level education, school/university partnerships and professional development, child/adolescent literature and popular culture. *Unit head:* Dr. Donald Williams, Director, 330-471-8509, Fax: 330-471-8563, E-mail: dwilliams@malone.edu. *Application contact:* Dr. David Kleffman, Recruiter, 330-471-8447, Fax: 330-471-8343, E-mail: dkleffman@malone.edu.

Manhattan College, Graduate Division, School of Education, Riverdale, NY 10471. Offers counseling (MA, Diploma); school building leadership (MS Ed, Diploma); special education (MS Ed), including 5 year dual childhood/special education, dual childhood/special education, special education. *Accreditation:* Teacher Education Accreditation Council. Part-time and evening/weekend programs available. *Faculty:* 14 full-time (8 women), 24 part-time/adjunct (17 women). *Students:* 44 full-time (38 women), 198 part-time (167 women). Average age 30. 172 applicants, 77% accepted, 118 enrolled. In 2006, 70 master's awarded. *Degree requirements:* For master's, thesis, internship. *Entrance requirements:* For master's, minimum GPA of 3.0. *Application deadline:* For fall admission, 8/10 priority date for domestic students; for spring admission, 1/7 priority date for domestic students. Applications are processed on a rolling basis. Application fee: $50. *Financial support:* Federal Work-Study, scholarships/grants, tuition waivers (partial), and unspecified assistantships available. Financial award application deadline: 2/1. *Faculty research:* Adapted physical education, cross-training of preschool regular and special education teachers. *Unit head:* Dr. William Merriman, Dean, 718-862-7373, Fax: 718-862-8011. *Application contact:* Weldon Jackson.

Manhattanville College, Graduate Programs, School of Education, Purchase, NY 10577-2132. Offers MAT, MPS. *Accreditation:* NCATE. Part-time and evening/weekend programs available. *Students:* 294 full-time (219 women), 474 part-time (337 women); includes 65 minority (20 African Americans, 6 Asian Americans or Pacific Islanders, 39 Hispanic Americans), 6 international. In 2006, 267 degrees awarded. *Entrance requirements:* For master's, minimum undergraduate GPA of 3.0, 2 letters of recommendation. Additional exam requirements/recommendations for international students: Required—TOEFL (minimum score 550 paper-based; 213 computer-based). *Application deadline:* Applications are processed on a rolling basis. Application fee: $55. Electronic applications accepted. *Financial support:* Career-related internships or fieldwork and institutionally sponsored loans available. Support available to part-time students. *Unit head:* Dr. Shelley Wepner, Dean, 914-323-5192, Fax: 914-694-2386, E-mail: wepners@mville.edu. *Application contact:* Alyce Ware Poli, Director of Admissions, 914-323-5142, Fax: 914-694-1732, E-mail: edschool@mville.edu.

See Close-Up on page 895.

Mansfield University of Pennsylvania, Graduate Studies, Department of Education and Special Education, Mansfield, PA 16933. Offers elementary education (M Ed); secondary education (MS). *Accreditation:* NCATE (one or more programs are accredited). Part-time and evening/weekend programs available. Postbaccalaureate distance learning degree programs offered (no on-campus study). *Faculty:* 13 full-time (9 women), 1 (woman) part-time/adjunct. *Students:* 50 full-time (44 women), 72 part-time (52 women); includes 8 minority (4 African Americans, 1 Asian American or Pacific Islander, 3 Hispanic Americans). Average age 31. 130 applicants, 80% accepted, 34 enrolled. In 2006, 47 degrees awarded. *Degree requirements:* For master's, thesis optional. *Entrance requirements:* For master's, minimum GPA of 3.0. Additional exam requirements/recommendations for international students: Required—TOEFL (minimum score 550 paper-based; 220 computer-based). *Application deadline:* For fall admission, 8/1 priority date for domestic students, 8/1 for international students; for spring admission, 11/1 priority date for domestic students, 9/1 for international students. Applications are processed on a rolling basis. Application fee: $25. Electronic applications accepted. *Expenses:* Tuition, state resident: part-time $336 per credit. Tuition, nonresident: part-time $538 per credit. Tuition and fees vary according to course load and reciprocity agreements. *Financial support:* Career-related internships or fieldwork and unspecified assistantships available. Sup-

Education—General

Mansfield University of Pennsylvania *(continued)*
port available to part-time students. Financial award application deadline: 5/1; financial award applicants required to submit FAFSA. *Unit head:* Dr. Celeste Burns, Chairperson, 570-662-4563, E-mail: cburns@mnsfld.edu. *Application contact:* Judi Brayer, Assistant Director of Enrollment Management/Graduate Admissions, 570-662-4818, Fax: 570-662-4121, E-mail: jbrayer@mansfield.edu.

Marian College, Department of Education, Indianapolis, IN 46222-1997. Offers MAT. *Accreditation:* NCATE.

Marian College of Fond du Lac, School of Education, Fond du Lac, WI 54935-4699. Offers educational leadership (MA, PhD); teacher development (MA). *Accreditation:* NCATE. Part-time programs available. *Faculty:* 15 full-time (5 women), 32 part-time/adjunct (20 women). *Students:* 30 full-time (16 women), 759 part-time (511 women); includes 37 minority (10 African Americans, 9 American Indian/Alaska Native, 6 Asian Americans or Pacific Islanders, 12 Hispanic Americans), 2 international. Average age 33. 96 applicants, 100% accepted, 96 enrolled. In 2006, 200 degrees awarded. *Degree requirements:* For master's, exam, field-based experience project, portfolio; for doctorate, thesis/dissertation, field-based experience, comprehensive exam. *Entrance requirements:* For master's, minimum GPA of 3.0, BA in education or related field, teaching license; for doctorate, GRE/MAT, resumé, 2 writing samples, interview. *Application deadline:* Applications are processed on a rolling basis. Application fee: $50. *Expenses:* Tuition: Part-time $310 per credit. Tuition and fees vary according to degree level and program. *Financial support:* In 2006–07, 197 students received support. Federal Work-Study and institutionally sponsored loans available. Support available to part-time students. Financial award application deadline: 3/1; financial award applicants required to submit FAFSA. *Faculty research:* At-risk youth, multicultural issues, values in education, teaching/learning strategies. *Unit head:* Dr. Kathryn Polmanteer, Dean, School of Education, 920-923-8099, Fax: 920-923-7663, E-mail: knpolmanteer94@mariancollege.edu. *Application contact:* Robert Bohnsack, Graduate Education Admissions, 920-923-8100, Fax: 920-923-7154, E-mail: bbohnsack@mariancollege.edu.

Marietta College, Program in Education, Marietta, OH 45750-4000. Offers MA. *Accreditation:* NCATE. Part-time and evening/weekend programs available. *Faculty:* 2 full-time (1 woman), 2 part-time/adjunct (1 woman). *Students:* 4 full-time (3 women), 31 part-time (23 women). Average age 35. *Degree requirements:* For master's, writing portfolio. *Entrance requirements:* For master's, MAT. *Application deadline:* For fall admission, 8/23 priority date for domestic students. Application fee: $25. *Financial support:* Available to part-time students. *Faculty research:* Teaching of reading. *Unit head:* Dr. Dorothy Erb, Chair, 740-376-4761.

Marist College, Graduate Programs, School of Social and Behavioral Sciences, Poughkeepsie, NY 12601-1387. Offers counseling psychology (MA); education (M Ed); education psychology (MA); school psychology (MA, Adv C). Part-time and evening/weekend programs available. *Faculty:* 21 full-time (9 women), 25 part-time/adjunct (14 women). *Students:* 98 full-time (81 women), 120 part-time (98 women); includes 21 minority (9 African Americans, 2 Asian Americans or Pacific Islanders, 10 Hispanic Americans), 4 international. Average age 30. 105 applicants, 72% accepted, 52 enrolled. In 2006, 105 master's, 4 other advanced degrees awarded. *Degree requirements:* For master's, thesis optional. *Entrance requirements:* For master's, GRE General Test, letters of recommendation, minimum undergraduate GPA of 3.0, interview, essay, official transcript. Additional exam requirements/recommendations for international students: Required—TOEFL (minimum score 550 paper-based; 213 computer-based; 80 iBT); Recommended—IELTS (minimum score 6). *Application deadline:* For fall admission, 8/1 for domestic students, 6/1 for international students; for spring admission, 12/1 for domestic students, 10/15 for international students. Applications are processed on a rolling basis. Application fee: $50. Electronic applications accepted. *Expenses:* Tuition: Full-time $11,340; part-time $630 per credit. Required fees: $60; $30 per semester. *Financial support:* In 2006–07, 146 students received support. Career-related internships or fieldwork, scholarships/grants, and unspecified assistantships available. Support available to part-time students. Financial award application deadline: 8/15; financial award applicants required to submit FAFSA. *Faculty research:* AIDS prevention, educational intervention, humanistic counseling research, aging and development, neuroimaging. *Unit head:* Margaret Calista, Dean, 845-575-3000 Ext. 2960, E-mail: margaret.calista@marist.edu. *Application contact:* Anu R. Ailawadhi, Director of Graduate Admissions, 845-575-3800, Fax: 845-575-3166, E-mail: graduate@marist.edu.

Marlboro College, Graduate Center, Program in Teaching with Internet Technologies, Marlboro, VT 05344. Offers MAT. Evening/weekend programs available. Postbaccalaureate distance learning degree programs offered (minimal on-campus study). *Faculty:* 7 part-time/adjunct (4 women). *Students:* 7 full-time (6 women), 8 part-time (4 women); includes 2 minority (both Hispanic Americans) In 2006, 7 degrees awarded. *Degree requirements:* For master's, capstone project. *Application deadline:* For fall admission, 3/1 priority date for domestic students. Applications are processed on a rolling basis. Application fee: $0. Electronic applications accepted. *Expenses:* Tuition: Full-time $18,900; part-time $630 per credit. Tuition and fees vary according to program. *Financial support:* Applicants required to submit FAFSA. *Unit head:* Kevin Bell, Academic Director, 802-258-9203, Fax: 802-258-9201, E-mail: kbell@gradcenter.marlboro.edu. *Application contact:* Bethany Catron, Director of Admissions, 802-258-9209, Fax: 802-258-9201, E-mail: bcatron@gradcenter.marlboro.edu.

Marquette University, Graduate School, School of Education, Milwaukee, WI 53201-1881. Offers MA, Ed D, PhD, Spec. *Accreditation:* NCATE. Part-time programs available. *Faculty:* 20 full-time (12 women), 27 part-time/adjunct (14 women). *Students:* 81 full-time (64 women), 142 part-time (104 women); includes 14 minority (7 African Americans, 2 Asian Americans or Pacific Islanders, 5 Hispanic Americans), 5 international. Average age 37. 310 applicants, 59% accepted, 152 enrolled. In 2006, 47 master's, 6 doctorates awarded. Terminal master's awarded for partial completion of doctoral program. *Degree requirements:* For master's, thesis, comprehensive exam; for doctorate, thesis/dissertation, qualifying exam. *Entrance requirements:* For master's, GRE General Test or MAT; for doctorate, GRE General Test, MAT, sample of written work; for Spec, GRE General Test or MAT, master's degree. Additional exam requirements/recommendations for international students: Required—TOEFL. Application fee: $40. *Expenses:* Contact institution. *Financial support:* In 2006–07, 5 research assistantships, 5 teaching assistantships were awarded; Federal Work-Study, institutionally sponsored loans, scholarships/grants, and tuition waivers (full and partial) also available. Support available to part-time students. Financial award application deadline: 2/15. *Faculty research:* Parenting, psychology of motivation, reading assessment, socialization of educational administrators, education philosophy of Cardinal Newman. Total annual research expenditures: $1.1 million. *Unit head:* Dr. Bill Henk, Dean, 414-288-7376. *Application contact:* Dr. Joan Whipp, Assistant Dean, 414-288-1421, Fax: 414-288-5333.

Marshall University, Academic Affairs Division, College of Education and Human Services, Huntington, WV 25755. Offers MA, MAT, MS, Ed D, Ed S. *Accreditation:* NCATE. Evening/weekend programs available. *Faculty:* 33 full-time (18 women), 7 part-time/adjunct (4 women). *Students:* 602 full-time (433 women), 1,304 part-time (1,038 women); includes 92 minority (69 African Americans, 6 American Indian/Alaska Native, 7 Asian Americans or Pacific Islanders, 10 Hispanic Americans), 66 international. Average age 35. In 2006, 462 master's, 9 doctorates, 29 other advanced degrees awarded. *Degree requirements:* For master's, comprehensive assessment, thesis optional. *Entrance requirements:* Additional exam requirements/recommendations for international students: Required—TOEFL (minimum score 550 paper-based). *Application deadline:* Applications are processed on a rolling basis. Application fee: $40 ($100 for international students). *Financial support:* Career-related internships or fieldwork, Federal Work-Study, tuition waivers (full and partial), and unspecified assistantships available. Support available to part-time students. *Unit head:* Dr. Rosalyn Anstine Templeton, Executive Dean, 304-696-3131, E-mail: templetonr@marshall.edu. *Application contact:* Information Contact, 304-746-1900, Fax: 304-746-1902, E-mail: services@marshall.edu.

Mary Baldwin College, Graduate Studies, Program in Teaching, Staunton, VA 24401-3610. Offers elementary education (MAT); middle grades education (MAT). *Faculty:* 5 full-time (3 women), 38 part-time/adjunct (20 women). *Students:* 104 full-time (76 women), 101 part-time (85 women). *Application deadline:* For fall admission, 7/15 priority date for domestic students; for spring admission, 11/15 priority date for domestic students. Application fee: $35. *Unit head:* Dr. Carole Grove, Program Director, 540-887-7134. *Application contact:* Lori Johnson, Administrative Assistant, 540-887-7333, E-mail: ljohnson@mbc.edu.

Marygrove College, Graduate Division, Education Unit, Program in the Art of Teaching, Detroit, MI 48221-2599. Offers MAT. Postbaccalaureate distance learning degree programs offered (no on-campus study). *Degree requirements:* For master's, portfolio. *Entrance requirements:* For master's, MAT, interview, minimum undergraduate GPA of 3.0, teaching certificate.

Marymount University, School of Education and Human Services, Program in Education, Arlington, VA 22207-4299. Offers alternative teacher licensure (Certificate); elementary education (M Ed); English as a second language (M Ed); learning disabilities (M Ed); professional studies (M Ed); secondary education (M Ed). *Accreditation:* NCATE. Part-time and evening/weekend programs available. Postbaccalaureate distance learning degree programs offered (minimal on-campus study). *Faculty:* 10 full-time (8 women), 5 part-time/adjunct (2 women). *Students:* 75 full-time (65 women), 95 part-time (82 women); includes 25 minority (13 African Americans, 2 American Indian/Alaska Native, 6 Asian Americans or Pacific Islanders, 4 Hispanic Americans), 6 international. Average age 32. 58 applicants, 100% accepted, 45 enrolled. In 2006, 113 degrees awarded. *Degree requirements:* For master's, thesis or alternative. *Entrance requirements:* For master's, GRE General Test or MAT, PRAXIS I or SAT/ACT, interview, 2 letters of recommendation. Additional exam requirements/recommendations for international students: Required—TOEFL (minimum score 600 paper-based; 250 computer-based). *Application deadline:* Applications are processed on a rolling basis. Application fee: $40. Electronic applications accepted. *Expenses:* Tuition: Full-time $11,160; part-time $620 per credit. Required fees: $113; $630 per credit. *Financial support:* Research assistantships with full tuition reimbursements, career-related internships or fieldwork, scholarships/grants, and unspecified assistantships available. Support available to part-time students. Financial award applicants required to submit FAFSA. *Unit head:* Dr. Shelly Haser, Chair, 703-284-6955, Fax: 703-284-1631, E-mail: shelly.haser@marymount.edu.

Maryville University of Saint Louis, School of Education, St. Louis, MO 63141-7299. Offers art education (MA Ed); early childhood education (MA Ed); education (Ed D); elementary education (MA Ed); elementary education/English (MA Ed); environmental education (MA Ed); gifted education (MA Ed); middle grades education (MA Ed); reading specialist (MA Ed); secondary education (MA Ed), including educational leadership, secondary teaching and inquiry. *Accreditation:* NASAD; NCATE. Part-time and evening/weekend programs available. *Students:* 17 full-time (14 women), 168 part-time (129 women); includes 20 African Americans, 2 Asian Americans or Pacific Islanders, 1 Hispanic American, 2 international. Average age 37. 39 applicants, 95% accepted, 24 enrolled. In 2006, 37 degrees awarded. *Degree requirements:* For master's, thesis, project. *Entrance requirements:* For master's and doctorate, minimum GPA of 3.0, 3 professional recommendations. Additional exam requirements/recommendations for international students: Required—TOEFL (minimum score 550 paper-based). *Application deadline:* Applications are processed on a rolling basis. Application fee: $35 ($50 for international students). Electronic applications accepted. *Expenses:* Tuition: Full-time $17,800; part-time $555 per credit. Required fees: $55 per semester. Tuition and fees vary according to degree level and program. *Financial support:* Career-related internships or fieldwork, Federal Work-Study, tuition waivers (partial), and professional educator discounts available. Financial award application deadline: 7/31; financial award applicants required to submit FAFSA. *Faculty research:* Collaboration with public schools, preservice program development, mathematics, diversity, literacy. *Unit head:* Dr. Sam Hausfather, Dean, 314-529-9466, Fax: 314-529-9921, E-mail: shausfather@maryville.edu. *Application contact:* Dr. Lillian Curtis, Graduate Admissions Coordinator, 314-529-9542, Fax: 314-529-9921, E-mail: teachered@maryville.edu.

Marywood University, Academic Affairs, College of Education and Human Development, Department of Education, Scranton, PA 18509-1598. Offers early childhood intervention (MS); education (M Ed); elementary education (MAT); higher education administration (MS); instructional leadership (M Ed); reading education (MS); school leadership (MS); secondary education (MAT). *Accreditation:* NCATE. Part-time and evening/weekend programs available. *Students:* 17 full-time (all women), 76 part-time (62 women). Average age 32. In 2006, 37 degrees awarded. *Degree requirements:* For master's, thesis or alternative. *Entrance requirements:* For master's, GRE or MAT. Additional exam requirements/recommendations for international students: Required—TOEFL (minimum score 550 paper-based; 213 computer-based). *Application deadline:* For fall admission, 4/15 priority date for domestic and international students; for spring admission, 11/15 priority date for domestic and international students. Applications are processed on a rolling basis. Application fee: $30. Electronic applications accepted. *Expenses:* Tuition: Part-time $672 per credit. Tuition and fees vary according to degree level, campus/location and program. *Financial support:* Research assistantships with tuition reimbursements, career-related internships or fieldwork, scholarships/grants, tuition waivers (partial), and unspecified assistantships available. Support available to part-time students. Financial award application deadline: 2/15; financial award applicants required to submit FAFSA. *Faculty research:* Catholic identity in higher education, school reading programs, teacher practice enhancement, cooperative learning, institutional and instructional leadership. *Unit head:* Dr. Kathy Ruthkosky, Administrator, 570-348-6211 Ext. 2492, E-mail: ruthkosky@marywood.edu. *Application contact:* Dr. Deborah M. Flynn, Coordinator of Graduate Advising (Enrollment Management), 570-348-6211, E-mail: flynn@ac.marywood.edu.

Massachusetts College of Liberal Arts, Program in Education, North Adams, MA 01247-4100. Offers curriculum and instruction (M Ed); educational administration (M Ed); reading (M Ed); special education (M Ed). Part-time and evening/weekend programs available. *Degree requirements:* For master's, thesis. *Entrance requirements:* For master's, writing sample. *Faculty research:* Anxiety, methodology, mainstreaming.

McGill University, Faculty of Graduate and Postdoctoral Studies, Faculty of Education, Department of Integrated Studies in Education, Montréal, QC H3A 2T5, Canada. Offers culture and values in education (MA, PhD); curriculum (MA); educational leadership (Certificate, Diploma); educational studies (PhD); integrated studies in education (M Ed); leadership (MA); second language education (MA, PhD). *Degree requirements:* For master's, thesis (for some programs), registration; for doctorate, thesis/dissertation, comprehensive exam, registration. *Entrance requirements:* For master's, 2 years of relevant experience, minimum GPA of 3.0; for doctorate, minimum GPA of 3.0, acquisition of prospective supervisor; for other advanced degree, minimum GPA of 3.0. Additional exam requirements/recommendations for international students: Required—TOEFL (minimum score 580 paper-based; 237 computer-based).

McKendree College, Graduate Programs, Lebanon, IL 62254-1299. Offers business administration (MBA); counseling (MA); education (M Ed); nursing (MSN).

McNeese State University, Graduate School, College of Education, Department of Teacher Education, Lake Charles, LA 70609. Offers curriculum and instruction (M Ed), including early childhood education, elementary education (M Ed, MAT), secondary education (M Ed, MAT); school counseling (M Ed); teaching (MAT), including elementary education (M Ed, MAT), secondary education (M Ed, MAT), special education (mild/moderate). *Accreditation:* NCATE. Evening/weekend programs available. *Faculty:* 14 full-time (10 women), 2 part-time/adjunct (1 woman). *Students:* 48 full-time (40 women), 216 part-time (191 women); includes 73 minority (66 African Americans, 1 American Indian/Alaska Native, 2 Asian Americans or Pacific Islanders, 4 Hispanic Americans), 2 international. In 2006, 50 degrees awarded. *Entrance requirements:* For master's, GRE, teaching certificate. *Application deadline:* For fall admission, 5/15 priority date for domestic students. Applications are processed on a rolling basis. Application fee: $20

($30 for international students). *Expenses:* Tuition, area resident: Full-time $2,226; part-time $193 per hour. Required fees: $919; $106 per hour. *Financial support:* Application deadline:5/1.

Medaille College, Program in Education, Buffalo, NY 14214-2695. Offers curriculum and instruction (MS Ed); education preparation (MS Ed); literacy (MS Ed); special education (MS). Part-time and evening/weekend programs available. *Faculty:* 30 full-time (20 women), 28 part-time/adjunct (18 women). *Students:* 516 full-time (417 women), 334 part-time (276 women); includes 16 minority (13 African Americans, 2 Asian Americans or Pacific Islanders, 1 Hispanic American), 654 international. Average age 27. 725 applicants, 97% accepted, 655 enrolled. In 2006, 229 degrees awarded. *Degree requirements:* For master's, thesis or alternative. *Entrance requirements:* For master's, minimum undergraduate GPA of 2.7. Additional exam requirements/recommendations for international students: Required—TOEFL (minimum score 550 paper-based; 213 computer-based). *Application deadline:* For fall admission, 8/15 priority date for domestic students; for spring admission, 1/15 priority date for domestic students. Applications are processed on a rolling basis. Application fee: $35. Electronic applications accepted. *Expenses:* Tuition: Part-time $580 per credit hour. Full-time tuition and fees vary according to program. *Financial support:* In 2006–07, 390 students received support. Federal Work-Study available. Financial award applicants required to submit FAFSA. *Faculty research:* Curriculum planning, truancy, tracking minority students, curriculum design, mentoring students. *Unit head:* Dr. Robert DiSibio, Director of Graduate Programs, 716-635-5033 Ext. 2017, Fax: 716-634-2232, E-mail: rdisibio@medaille.edu. *Application contact:* Susan Greenwald, Executive Director of Admissions, 716-635-5033 Ext. 2011, Fax: 716-631-1380, E-mail: sgreenwald@medaille.edu.

Memorial University of Newfoundland, School of Graduate Studies, Faculty of Education, St. John's, NL A1C 5S7, Canada. Offers counseling psychology (M Ed); curriculum, teaching, and learning studies (M Ed); education (PhD); educational leadership studies (M Ed); information technology (M Ed); post-secondary studies (M Ed, Diploma), including health professional education (Diploma). Part-time programs available. *Degree requirements:* For master's, internship, paper folio, project, thesis optional; for doctorate, thesis/dissertation, thesis seminar, oral defense of thesis, comprehensive exam. *Entrance requirements:* For master's, undergraduate degree with at least 2nd class standing, 1-2 years work experience; for doctorate, minimum A average in graduate course work, MA in education, 2 years professional experience; for Diploma, 2nd class degree, 2 years of work experience with adult learners, appropriate academic qualifications and work experience in a health-related field. Electronic applications accepted. *Faculty research:* Critical thinking, literacy, cognitive studies and counseling, educational change, technology in instruction.

Mercer University, Graduate Studies, Cecil B. Day Campus, Tift College of Education, Macon, GA 31207-0003. Offers early childhood education (M Ed, MAT); educational leadership (M Ed, PhD); middle grades education (M Ed, MAT); reading education (M Ed); secondary education (M Ed, MAT); teacher leadership (Ed S). Part-time and evening/weekend programs available. *Faculty:* 13 full-time (6 women), 7 part-time/adjunct (3 women). *Students:* 31 full-time (23 women), 211 part-time (174 women); includes 111 minority (101 African Americans, 2 American Indian/Alaska Native, 6 Asian Americans or Pacific Islanders, 2 Hispanic Americans), 2 international. Average age 33. In 2006, 57 master's, 4 other advanced degrees awarded. *Degree requirements:* For master's and Ed S, research project; for doctorate, thesis/dissertation. *Entrance requirements:* For master's, GRE or MAT, minimum undergraduate GPA of 2.75; for doctorate, GRE; for Ed S, GRE or MAT, minimum GPA of 3.25, 3 years of teaching experience. *Application deadline:* For fall admission, 8/1 for domestic and international students; for spring admission, 12/1 for domestic and international students. Applications are processed on a rolling basis. Application fee: $25. *Expenses: Contact institution. Financial support:* Federal Work-Study available. Support available to part-time students. Financial award application deadline: 5/1. *Faculty research:* Educational computing, content area reading, concept learning, importance of play for young children, multicultural literature. *Unit head:* Dr. Carl R. Martray, Dean, 478-301-5397, Fax: 478-301-2280, E-mail: martray_cr@mercer.edu. *Application contact:* Dr. Allison Gilmore, Associate Dean for Graduate Teacher Education, 678-547-6330, Fax: 678-547-6055, E-mail: gilmore_a@mercer.edu.

Mercer University, Graduate Studies, Macon Campus, Tift College of Education, Macon, GA 31207-0003. Offers collaborative education (M Ed); educational leadership (M Ed, PhD). Part-time and evening/weekend programs available. *Faculty:* 13 full-time (6 women), 4 part-time/adjunct (3 women). *Students:* 3 full-time (all women), 68 part-time (49 women); includes 23 minority (22 African Americans, 1 American Indian/Alaska Native). Average age 31. 25 applicants, 68% accepted, 11 enrolled. In 2006, 19 degrees awarded. *Degree requirements:* For master's, research project report. *Entrance requirements:* For master's, GRE or MAT, minimum GPA of 2.75; for doctorate, GRE. Additional exam requirements/recommendations for international students: Required—TOEFL. *Application deadline:* For fall admission, 8/1 for domestic students; for spring admission, 12/1 for domestic students. Applications are processed on a rolling basis. Application fee: $25. *Expenses: Contact institution. Financial support:* Federal Work-Study and institutionally sponsored loans available. Support available to part-time students. Financial award application deadline: 5/1. *Faculty research:* Teacher effectiveness, specific learning disabilities, inclusion. *Unit head:* Dr. Carl R. Martray, Dean, 478-301-5397, Fax: 478-301-2280, E-mail: martray_cr@mercer.edu. *Application contact:* Dr. Penny Elkins, Associate Dean, 678-547-6556, Fax: 678-547-6389, E-mail: elkins_pl@mercer.edu.

Mercy College, Division of Education, Dobbs Ferry, NY 10522-1189. Offers adolescence education: grades 7-12 (MS); applied behavior analysis (MS); bilingual education (MS); childhood education: grades 1-6 (MS); early childhood education: birth—grade 2 (MS); education (MS); elementary education (MS); learning technology (MS); middle childhood education: grades 5-9 (MS); reading (MS); school administration and supervision (MS); school building leadership (MS); school business administration (MS); secondary education (MS); special education (MS); students with disabilities: grades 5-9 (MS); students with disabilities: grades 7-12 (MS); teaching English to speakers of other languages (MS); teaching literacy: birth—grade 6 (MS); teaching literacy: grades 5-12 (MS); urban education (MS). *Students:* 572 full-time (467 women), 1,719 part-time (1,287 women); includes 943 minority (470 African Americans, 7 American Indian/Alaska Native, 48 Asian Americans or Pacific Islanders, 418 Hispanic Americans), 6 international. Average age 33. In 2006, 1090 degrees awarded. *Entrance requirements:* For master's, teaching certificate. *Application deadline:* For fall admission, 2/1 for domestic students. Applications are processed on a rolling basis. Application fee: $37. *Expenses: Contact institution.* Tuition and fees vary according to program. *Financial support:* Institutionally sponsored loans, scholarships/grants, and unspecified assistantships available. Support available to part-time students. *Faculty research:* Distance learning, literacy, assessment, community schools, impact of staff development. *Unit head:* Dr. William Prattella, Chairperson, 914-674-7555, Fax: 914-674-7352, E-mail: wprattella@mercy.edu. *Application contact:* Kathleen Jackson, Director of Admissions, 800-Mercy-NY, Fax: 914-674-7382, E-mail: admissions@mercy.edu.

Meredith College, John E. Weems Graduate School, School of Education, Raleigh, NC 27607-5298. Offers M Ed. *Accreditation:* NCATE. Part-time and evening/weekend programs available. *Faculty:* 4 full-time (all women), 1 (woman) part-time/adjunct. *Students:* 1 full-time (0 women), 23 part-time (all women); includes 1 minority (African American), 1 international. Average age 34. 12 applicants, 92% accepted, 7 enrolled. In 2006, 5 degrees awarded. *Degree requirements:* For master's, thesis optional. *Entrance requirements:* For master's, GRE General Test or MAT, minimum GPA of 2.5, teaching license, recommendations. Additional exam requirements/recommendations for international students: Required—TOEFL. *Application deadline:* For fall admission, 7/1 priority date for domestic students; for spring admission, 11/1 priority date for domestic students. Applications are processed on a rolling basis. Application fee: $50. Electronic applications accepted. *Expenses: Contact institution. Financial support:* Career-related internships or fieldwork, institutionally sponsored loans, and tuition waivers (partial) available. Support available to part-time students. Financial award application deadline: 2/15; financial award applicants required to submit FAFSA. *Unit head:* Erin Barrow, Graduate Program Manager, 919-760-8316, Fax: 919-760-2303, E-mail: barrower@meredith.edu. *Application contact:* Dr. Ellen Graden, Coordinator, 919-760-8077, Fax: 919-760-2303, E-mail: gradene@meredith.edu.

Merrimack College, Department of Education, North Andover, MA 01845-5800. Offers M Ed. Part-time and evening/weekend programs available. *Faculty:* 4 full-time (2 women), 5 part-time/adjunct (4 women). *Students:* Average age 30. 12 applicants, 100% accepted. In 2006, 8 degrees awarded. *Degree requirements:* For master's, research project, practicum or clinical experience. *Entrance requirements:* For master's, GRE General Test or MAT, Massachusetts Test for Educator License (communication and literacy), teaching license for professional options. *Application deadline:* For fall admission, 8/15 priority date for domestic students; for spring admission, 1/15 for domestic students. Applications are processed on a rolling basis. Application fee: $50. *Expenses:* Tuition: Part-time $400 per credit hour. Part-time tuition and fees vary according to course load. *Financial support:* Career-related internships or fieldwork and credit hour discount for teachers in local school districts available. *Faculty research:* Educational technology, teaching mathematics, leadership, teaching multi-cultural education, reading. *Unit head:* Dr. Claire M. Thornton, Chair, 978-837-5368, Fax: 978-837-5069, E-mail: claire.thornton@merrimack.edu.

Miami University, Graduate School, School of Education and Allied Professions, Oxford, OH 45056. Offers M Ed, MAT, MS, Ed D, PhD, Ed S. *Accreditation:* NCATE. Part-time programs available. *Entrance requirements:* For master's, minimum undergraduate GPA of 3.0 during previous 2 years or 2.75 overall; for doctorate, MAT, minimum undergraduate GPA of 2.75, graduate GPA of 3.0; for Ed S, GRE General Test or MAT.

Michigan State University, The Graduate School, College of Education, East Lansing, MI 48824. Offers MA, MS, PhD, Ed S. *Faculty:* 123 full-time (66 women), 1 (woman) part-time/adjunct. *Students:* 627 full-time (417 women), 580 part-time (433 women); includes 162 minority (101 African Americans, 5 American Indian/Alaska Native, 25 Asian Americans or Pacific Islanders, 31 Hispanic Americans), 167 international. Average age 32. 742 applicants, 55% accepted. In 2006, 575 master's, 101 doctorates awarded. *Entrance requirements:* Additional exam requirements/recommendations for international students: Required—TOEFL. Electronic applications accepted. *Expenses:* Tuition, state resident: part-time $346 per credit hour. Tuition, nonresident: part-time $730 per credit hour. Tuition and fees vary according to program. *Financial support:* In 2006–07, 234 fellowships with tuition reimbursements, 266 research assistantships with tuition reimbursements (averaging $13,686 per year), 176 teaching assistantships with tuition reimbursements (averaging $13,796 per year) were awarded. Total annual research expenditures: $10.7 million. *Unit head:* Dr. Carole Ames, Dean, 517-355-1734, Fax: 517-353-6393, E-mail: cames@msu.edu.

MidAmerica Nazarene University, Graduate Studies in Education, Olathe, KS 66062-1899. Offers curriculum and instruction (M Ed); educational technology (MET); special education (MA). *Accreditation:* NCATE. Evening/weekend programs available. *Degree requirements:* For master's, thesis or alternative, creative project, technology leadership practicum. *Entrance requirements:* For master's, minimum undergraduate GPA of 2.8, 2 years of teaching experience. Expenses: Contact institution.

Middle Tennessee State University, College of Graduate Studies, College of Education and Behavioral Science, Murfreesboro, TN 37132. Offers M Ed, MA, MCJ, MS, PhD, Ed S, Graduate Certificate. *Accreditation:* NCATE. Part-time and evening/weekend programs available. Postbaccalaureate distance learning degree programs offered. *Entrance requirements:* Additional exam requirements/recommendations for international students: Required—TOEFL (minimum score 525 paper-based; 195 computer-based). *Application deadline:* For fall admission, 8/1 priority date for domestic students. Applications are processed on a rolling basis. Application fee: $25. Electronic applications accepted. *Financial support:* In 2006–07, 57 students received support. Application deadline: 5/1; *Unit head:* Dr. Gloria Bonner, Dean, 615-898-2874, Fax: 615-898-2530, E-mail: gbonner@mtsu.edu.

Midwestern State University, Graduate Studies, College of Education, Wichita Falls, TX 76308. Offers M Ed, MA, ME. Part-time and evening/weekend programs available. *Faculty:* 14 full-time (9 women), 8 part-time/adjunct (6 women). *Students:* 18 full-time (15 women), 156 part-time (121 women); includes 14 minority (6 African Americans, 1 American Indian/Alaska Native, 1 Asian American or Pacific Islander, 6 Hispanic Americans), 5 international. Average age 36. 47 applicants, 77% accepted, 20 enrolled. In 2006, 68 degrees awarded. *Degree requirements:* For master's, thesis (for some programs), comprehensive exam. *Entrance requirements:* For master's, GRE General Test or MAT. Additional exam requirements/recommendations for international students: Required—TOEFL (minimum score 550 paper-based; 213 computer-based). *Application deadline:* For fall admission, 7/1 for domestic students, 4/1 for international students; for spring admission, 11/1 for domestic students, 8/1 for international students. Applications are processed on a rolling basis. Application fee: $35 ($50 for international students). Electronic applications accepted. *Financial support:* In 2006–07, 116 students received support, including 7 teaching assistantships with partial tuition reimbursements available (averaging $6,412 per year); career-related internships or fieldwork, Federal Work-Study, institutionally sponsored loans, tuition waivers (partial), and unspecified assistantships also available. Support available to part-time students. Financial award application deadline: 5/1; financial award applicants required to submit FAFSA. *Unit head:* Dr. Grant Simpson, Dean, 940-397-4564, Fax: 940-397-4694, E-mail: grant.simpson@mwsu.edu. *Application contact:* Dr. Ann Estrada, Chair, 940-397-4136, Fax: 940-397-4672, E-mail: ann.estrada@mwsu.edu.

Millersville University of Pennsylvania, Graduate School, School of Education, Millersville, PA 17551-0302. Offers M Ed, MS. *Accreditation:* NCATE. Part-time and evening/weekend programs available. *Faculty:* 90 full-time (52 women), 43 part-time/adjunct (17 women). *Students:* 83 full-time (64 women), 316 part-time (222 women); includes 17 minority (9 African Americans, 1 American Indian/Alaska Native, 1 Asian American or Pacific Islander, 6 Hispanic Americans), 3 international. Average age 29. 131 applicants, 65% accepted, 63 enrolled. In 2006, 177 degrees awarded. *Degree requirements:* For master's, thesis (for some programs), comprehensive exam (for some programs). *Entrance requirements:* For master's, MAT or GRE, minimum undergraduate GPA of 2.75. Additional exam requirements/recommendations for international students: Required—TOEFL (minimum score 500 paper-based; 183 computer-based). *Application deadline:* For fall admission, 3/1 priority date for domestic students; for spring admission, 10/1 priority date for domestic students. Applications are processed on a rolling basis. Application fee: $35. *Expenses:* Tuition, state resident: full-time $6,048; part-time $336 per credit. Tuition, nonresident: full-time $9,678; part-time $538 per credit. Required fees: $1,244. Tuition and fees vary according to course load. *Financial support:* In 2006–07, 63 students received support, including 63 research assistantships with full and partial tuition reimbursements available (averaging $4,250 per year); career-related internships or fieldwork, Federal Work-Study, institutionally sponsored loans, and unspecified assistantships also available. Support available to part-time students. Financial award application deadline: 3/15; financial award applicants required to submit FAFSA. *Unit head:* Dr. Jane S. Bray, Dean, 717-872-3379, Fax: 717-872-3856, E-mail: jane.bray@millersville.edu. *Application contact:* Dr. Victor S. DeSantis, Dean of Graduate Studies, 717-872-3099, Fax: 717-871-2022, E-mail: victor.desantis@millersville.edu.

Milligan College, Area of Teacher Education, Milligan College, TN 37682. Offers M Ed. *Accreditation:* NCATE. Part-time programs available. *Faculty:* 6 full-time (5 women), 6 part-time/adjunct (4 women). *Students:* 37 full-time (24 women), 50 part-time (38 women); includes 3 minority (all African Americans), 1 international. 52 applicants, 92% accepted, 41 enrolled. In 2006, 46 degrees awarded. *Degree requirements:* For master's, thesis, portfolio, research project. *Entrance requirements:* For master's, MAT or GRE General Test, interview. *Application deadline:* For fall admission, 8/1 priority date for domestic students; for winter admission, 11/15 priority date for domestic students; for spring admission, 4/1 priority date for domestic students. Applications are processed on a rolling basis. Application fee: $30. Electronic applications accepted. *Expenses: Contact institution. Financial support:* Career-related internships or

Education—General

Milligan College (continued)
fieldwork, institutionally sponsored loans, and scholarships/grants available. Financial award application deadline: 4/15; financial award applicants required to submit FAFSA. *Faculty research:* Teacher education evaluation, professional development centers, internship, early childhood, technology. *Unit head:* Dr. Lyn C. Howell, Director of Teacher Education, 423-461-8484, Fax: 423-461-3103, E-mail: lchowell@milligan.edu. *Application contact:* Carrie Davidson, Graduate Admissions Specialist, 423-461-8306, Fax: 423-461-8789, E-mail: cdavidson@milligan.edu.

Mills College, Graduate Studies, Education Department, Oakland, CA 94613-1000. Offers administration (Ed D); child life in health care settings (MA); early childhood education (MA); education (MA), including curriculum and instruction, elementary education, English education, mathematics education, science education, secondary education, social sciences education, teaching. Part-time and evening/weekend programs available. *Faculty:* 10 full-time (7 women), 15 part-time/adjunct (12 women). *Students:* 192 full-time (153 women), 41 part-time (36 women); includes 62 minority (28 African Americans, 13 Asian Americans or Pacific Islanders, 21 Hispanic Americans), 2 international. Average age 34. 160 applicants, 74% accepted, 73 enrolled. In 2006, 52 master's, 1 doctorate awarded. Terminal master's awarded for partial completion of doctoral program. *Degree requirements:* For master's, comprehensive exam. *Entrance requirements:* For doctorate, GRE General Test. Additional exam requirements/recommendations for international students: Required—TOEFL. *Application deadline:* For fall admission, 2/1 for domestic and international students; for spring admission, 11/1 for domestic and international students. Applications are processed on a rolling basis. Application fee: $50. Electronic applications accepted. *Financial support:* In 2006–07, 56 fellowships with tuition reimbursements (averaging $2,700 per year), 15 teaching assistantships (averaging $6,350 per year) were awarded; career-related internships or fieldwork, institutionally sponsored loans, scholarships/grants, and residence awards also available. Support available to part-time students. Financial award application deadline: 2/1; financial award applicants required to submit CSS PROFILE or FAFSA. *Faculty research:* Child development, gender and education, public policy, cross-cultural development, development of literacy. *Unit head:* Joseph Kahne, Chairperson, 510-430-3190, Fax: 510-430-3314, E-mail: grad-studies@mills.edu. *Application contact:* Randy McGlauthing, Director of Graduate Admissions, 510-430-2355, Fax: 510-430-2159, E-mail: rmglaut@mills.edu.

Minnesota State University Mankato, College of Graduate Studies, College of Education, Mankato, MN 56001. Offers MA, MAT, MS, MT, Certificate, SP. *Accreditation:* NCATE. Part-time and evening/weekend programs available. *Students:* 154 full-time (110 women), 429 part-time (304 women). Average age 35. In 2006, 162 master's, 46 other advanced degrees awarded. *Degree requirements:* For master's, thesis or alternative, comprehensive exam; for other advanced degree, thesis. *Entrance requirements:* For master's, GRE or MAT, minimum GPA of 3.0 during previous 2 years; for other advanced degree, minimum GPA of 3.0. Additional exam requirements/recommendations for international students: Required—TOEFL. *Application deadline:* Applications are processed on a rolling basis. Application fee: $40. Electronic applications accepted. *Financial support:* Fellowships with partial tuition reimbursements, research assistantships with full tuition reimbursements, teaching assistantships with full tuition reimbursements, career-related internships or fieldwork, Federal Work-Study, institutionally sponsored loans, and unspecified assistantships available. Support available to part-time students. Financial award application deadline: 3/15; financial award applicants required to submit FAFSA. *Faculty research:* Longitudinal studies of alternative education graduates, student achievement scores. *Unit head:* Dr. Michael Miller, Dean, 507-389-5445. *Application contact:* 507-389-2321, E-mail: grad@mnsu.edu.

Minnesota State University Moorhead, Graduate Studies, College of Education and Human Services, Moorhead, MN 56563-0002. Offers counseling and student affairs (MS); curriculum and instruction (MS); educational leadership (MS, Ed S); nursing (MS); reading (MS); special education (MS); speech-language pathology (MS). *Accreditation:* NCATE. Part-time and evening/weekend programs available. *Faculty:* 18 full-time (11 women), 25 part-time/adjunct (13 women). *Students:* 45 full-time (42 women), 167 part-time (130 women); includes 4 minority (2 American Indian/Alaska Native, 2 Hispanic Americans), 4 international. 154 applicants, 56% accepted. In 2006, 60 degrees awarded. *Degree requirements:* For master's, final oral exam, project or thesis. *Entrance requirements:* Additional exam requirements/recommendations for international students: Required—TOEFL. *Application deadline:* For fall admission, 4/15 priority date for domestic students; for spring admission, 11/1 priority date for domestic students. Applications are processed on a rolling basis. Application fee: $20. Electronic applications accepted. *Financial support:* Career-related internships or fieldwork, Federal Work-Study, and unspecified assistantships available. Financial award application deadline: 7/15; financial award applicants required to submit FAFSA. *Unit head:* Dr. Michael Parsons, Dean of Education and Human Services, 218-477-2096. *Application contact:* Karla Wenger, Graduate Studies Office, 218-477-2344, Fax: 218-477-2482, E-mail: wengerk@mnstate.edu.

Mississippi College, Graduate School, School of Education, Clinton, MS 39058. Offers M Ed, MS, Ed S. *Accreditation:* NCATE. Part-time and evening/weekend programs available. *Faculty:* 15 full-time (7 women), 16 part-time/adjunct (10 women). *Students:* 83 full-time (63 women), 345 part-time (300 women); includes 211 minority (207 African Americans, 3 American Indian/Alaska Native, 1 Hispanic American), 5 international. Average age 32. In 2006, 155 degrees awarded. *Degree requirements:* For master's, thesis optional. *Entrance requirements:* For master's, GRE or NTE, minimum GPA of 2.5, Class A Certificate (for some programs); for Ed S, NTE, minimum GPA of 3.0. Additional exam requirements/recommendations for international students: Recommended—IELTS. *Application deadline:* For fall admission, 8/15 priority date for domestic students. Applications are processed on a rolling basis. Application fee: $25. Electronic applications accepted. *Expenses:* Tuition: Full-time $7,290; part-time $405 per hour. Required fees: $150 per term. Tuition and fees vary according to campus/location and program. *Financial support:* Teaching assistantships, career-related internships or fieldwork, Federal Work-Study, scholarships/grants, and unspecified assistantships available. Support available to part-time students. Financial award application deadline: 4/1; financial award applicants required to submit FAFSA. *Unit head:* Dr. Don Locke, Dean, 601-925-3250, E-mail: locke@mc.edu.

Mississippi State University, College of Education, Mississippi State, MS 39762. Offers MS, MSIT, Ed D, PhD, Ed S. *Accreditation:* NCATE. Part-time and evening/weekend programs available. Postbaccalaureate distance learning degree programs offered (minimal on-campus study). *Faculty:* 107 full-time (57 women), 38 part-time/adjunct (34 women). *Students:* 327 full-time (230 women), 627 part-time (469 women); includes 389 minority (375 African Americans, 4 American Indian/Alaska Native, 4 Asian Americans or Pacific Islanders, 6 Hispanic Americans), 14 international. Average age 35. 245 applicants, 70% accepted, 122 enrolled. In 2006, 214 master's, 42 doctorates, 34 other advanced degrees awarded. Terminal master's awarded for partial completion of doctoral program. *Degree requirements:* For master's, comprehensive oral or written exam; for doctorate, thesis/dissertation; for Ed S, thesis or alternative, final written or oral exam. *Entrance requirements:* For master's, doctorate, and Ed S, GRE. Additional exam requirements/recommendations for international students: Required—TOEFL. *Application deadline:* For fall admission, 7/1 for domestic students; for spring admission, 11/1 for domestic students. Applications are processed on a rolling basis. Application fee: $30. *Expenses:* Tuition, state resident: full-time $4,550; part-time $253 per hour. Tuition, nonresident: full-time $10,552; part-time $584 per hour. International tuition: $10,882 full-time. Tuition and fees vary according to course load. *Financial support:* In 2006–07, 20 teaching assistantships (averaging $8,056 per year) were awarded; research assistantships, career-related internships or fieldwork, Federal Work-Study, institutionally sponsored loans, scholarships/grants, and unspecified assistantships also available. Financial award applicants required to submit FAFSA. *Faculty research:* Leadership behavior, creativity measures, early childhood education, employability of the blind, quality indicators of professional educators. *Unit head:* Dr. Richard Blackbourn, Dean, 662-325-3717, Fax: 662-325-8784, E-mail: rlb277@msstate.edu. *Application contact:* Dr. Phil Bonfanti, Director of Admissions, 662-325-4104, Fax: 662-325-8872, E-mail: admit@msstate.edu.

Mississippi University for Women, Graduate School, Division of Education and Human Sciences, Columbus, MS 39701-9998. Offers gifted studies (M Ed); instructional management (M Ed); speech/language pathology (MS). *Accreditation:* ASHA; NCATE. Part-time programs available. *Degree requirements:* For master's, thesis optional. *Entrance requirements:* For master's, GRE General Test or NTE (M Ed in gifted education or MS in speech/language pathology), MAT (M Ed in instructional management), minimum QPA of 3.0.

Mississippi Valley State University, Department of Education, Itta Bena, MS 38941-1400. Offers education (MAT); elementary education (MA). *Accreditation:* NCATE.

Missouri State University, Graduate College, College of Education, School of Teacher Education, Springfield, MO 65804-0094. Offers MAT, MS Ed. Part-time and evening/weekend programs available. Postbaccalaureate distance learning degree programs offered. *Faculty:* 24 full-time (14 women). *Students:* 87 full-time (64 women), 288 part-time (226 women); includes 17 minority (5 African Americans, 5 American Indian/Alaska Native, 3 Asian Americans or Pacific Islanders, 4 Hispanic Americans), 1 international. Average age 34. 50 applicants, 84% accepted, 34 enrolled. In 2006, 90 degrees awarded. *Degree requirements:* For master's, thesis or alternative, comprehensive exam. *Entrance requirements:* Additional exam requirements/recommendations for international students: Required—TOEFL (minimum score 550 paper-based; 213 computer-based; 79 iBT). Application fee: $35. *Expenses:* Tuition, state resident: full-time $3,582; part-time $199 per credit hour. Tuition, nonresident: full-time $6,984; part-time $199 per credit hour. Required fees: $548. Full-time tuition and fees vary according to course level, course load, program and reciprocity agreements. *Financial support:* Teaching assistantships available. Financial award application deadline: 3/31; financial award applicants required to submit FAFSA. *Unit head:* Dr. Fred Groves, Graduate Program Director, 417-836-6769, Fax: 417-836-6252, E-mail: fredgroves@missouristate.edu.

Monmouth University, Graduate School, School of Education, West Long Branch, NJ 07764-1898. Offers educational counseling (MS Ed); elementary education (MAT), including certified teachers, non-certified teachers; learning disabilities-teacher consultant (Certificate); principal studies (MS Ed); reading specialist (MS Ed, Certificate); special education (MS Ed); supervisor (Certificate); teacher of the handicapped (Certificate). Part-time and evening/weekend programs available. *Faculty:* 24 full-time (15 women), 25 part-time/adjunct (17 women). *Students:* 169 full-time (133 women), 426 part-time (374 women); includes 45 minority (21 African Americans, 2 American Indian/Alaska Native, 2 Asian Americans or Pacific Islanders, 20 Hispanic Americans). Average age 31. 355 applicants, 96% accepted, 138 enrolled. In 2006, 209 degrees awarded. *Entrance requirements:* For master's, minimum GPA of 3.0 in major, 2.75 overall. Additional exam requirements/recommendations for international students: Required—TOEFL (minimum score 550 paper-based; 213 computer-based; 79 iBT), IELTS (minimum score 5), MELAB 77, Cambridge A, B, C. *Application deadline:* For fall admission, 7/15 priority date for domestic students; for spring admission, 11/15 priority date for domestic students. Applications are processed on a rolling basis. Application fee: $50. Electronic applications accepted. *Expenses:* Tuition: Full-time $12,780; part-time $710 per credit. Required fees: $628; $314 per term. *Financial support:* In 2006–07, 221 fellowships (averaging $2,053 per year), 17 research assistantships (averaging $6,527 per year) were awarded; career-related internships or fieldwork, scholarships/grants, tuition waivers (partial), and unspecified assistantships also available. Support available to part-time students. Financial award application deadline: 3/1; financial award applicants required to submit FAFSA. *Faculty research:* Multicultural literacy, science and mathematics teaching strategies, teacher as reflective practitioner, children with disabilities, varied contexts of learning. *Unit head:* Dr. Lynn Romeo, Program Director, 732-571-4484, Fax: 732-263-5277, E-mail: lromeo@monmouth.edu. *Application contact:* Kevin Roane, Director, Office of Graduate Admission, 732-571-3452, Fax: 732-263-5123, E-mail: gradadm@monmouth.edu.

Montana State University, College of Graduate Studies, College of Education, Health, and Human Development, Department of Education, Bozeman, MT 59717. Offers M Ed, Ed D, Ed S. *Accreditation:* NCATE. Part-time programs available. Postbaccalaureate distance learning degree programs offered (no on-campus study). *Faculty:* 23 full-time (12 women), 13 part-time/adjunct (10 women). *Students:* 8 full-time (5 women), 131 part-time (51 women); includes 10 minority (3 African Americans, 4 American Indian/Alaska Native, 2 Asian Americans or Pacific Islanders, 1 Hispanic American). Average age 40. 47 applicants, 57% accepted, 27 enrolled. In 2006, 56 master's, 7 doctorates awarded. *Degree requirements:* For master's, comprehensive exam, registration; for doctorate, thesis/dissertation, comprehensive exam, registration. *Entrance requirements:* For master's and doctorate, GRE General Test. Additional exam requirements/recommendations for international students: Required—TOEFL (minimum score 550 paper-based; 213 computer-based). *Application deadline:* For fall admission, 7/15 priority date for domestic students, 5/15 priority date for international students; for spring admission, 12/1 priority date for domestic students, 10/1 priority date for international students. Applications are processed on a rolling basis. Application fee: $30. Electronic applications accepted. *Expenses:* Tuition, state resident: full-time $5,113. Tuition, nonresident: full-time $12,501. *Financial support:* In 2006–07, 12 students received support, including 4 teaching assistantships with full tuition reimbursements available (averaging $10,000 per year); career-related internships or fieldwork, health care benefits, and unspecified assistantships also available. Financial award application deadline: 3/1; financial award applicants required to submit FAFSA. Total annual research expenditures: $3.5 million. *Unit head:* Dr. Robert Carson, Head, 406-994-6670, Fax: 406-994-3261, E-mail: rcarson@montana.edu.

Montana State University–Billings, College of Education and Human Services, Billings, MT 59101-0298. Offers M Ed, MS Sp Ed, Certificate. *Accreditation:* NCATE. Part-time programs available. Postbaccalaureate distance learning degree programs offered (minimal on-campus study). *Faculty:* 28 full-time (17 women). *Students:* 216. 97 applicants, 100% accepted, 97 enrolled. In 2006, 41 degrees awarded. *Degree requirements:* For master's, thesis optional. *Entrance requirements:* For master's, GRE General Test. *Application deadline:* Applications are processed on a rolling basis. Application fee: $40. *Expenses:* Tuition, state resident: full-time $4,599. Tuition, nonresident: full-time $10,786. *Financial support:* Teaching assistantships with partial tuition reimbursements, career-related internships or fieldwork, Federal Work-Study, institutionally sponsored loans, scholarships/grants, tuition waivers (partial), and unspecified assistantships available. Support available to part-time students. Financial award application deadline: 5/1; financial award applicants required to submit FAFSA. *Faculty research:* Social studies education, science education. *Unit head:* Dr. Mary Susan Fishbaugh, Interim Dean, 406-657-2285, Fax: 406-657-2299, E-mail: mfishbaugh@msubillings.edu. *Application contact:* David M. Sullivan, Graduate Studies Counselor, 406-657-2053, Fax: 406-657-2299, E-mail: dsullivan@msubillings.edu.

Montana State University–Northern, College of Education and Graduate Programs, Havre, MT 59501-7751. Offers counselor education (M Ed); learning development (M Ed). *Accreditation:* NCATE. Part-time and evening/weekend programs available. Postbaccalaureate distance learning degree programs offered (minimal on-campus study). *Degree requirements:* For master's, oral exams or thesis. *Entrance requirements:* For master's, GRE General Test or MAT, minimum GPA of 3.0. Electronic applications accepted.

Montclair State University, The Graduate School, College of Education and Human Services, Department of Curriculum and Teaching, Montclair, NJ 07043-1624. Offers education (M Ed); educational technology (M Ed); school library media specialist (Certificate); teaching (MAT, Certificate), including art (MAT), biological science (MAT), early childhood education (P-3) (MAT), earth science (MAT), elementary education (K-8) (MAT), English (MAT), French (MAT), health and physical education (MAT), health education (MAT), home economics (MAT), mathematics (MAT), music (MAT), physical education (MAT), physical science (MAT), social studies (MAT), Spanish (MAT), teacher of ESL (MAT), teacher of students with disabilities (MAT). Part-time and evening/weekend programs available. *Faculty:* 16 full-time (12 women), 13 part-time/adjunct (8 women). *Students:* 147 full-time (113 women), 230 part-time (188 women);

includes 58 minority (33 African Americans, 1 American Indian/Alaska Native, 12 Asian Americans or Pacific Islanders, 12 Hispanic Americans), 4 international. Average age 33. 118 applicants, 38% accepted, 37 enrolled. In 2006, 166 master's, 11 other advanced degrees awarded. *Degree requirements:* For master's, field experience. *Entrance requirements:* For master's, PRAXIS II, minimum GPA of 2.67, 2 letters of recommendation. Additional exam requirements/recommendations for international students: Required—TOEFL (minimum score 83 computer-based). *Application deadline:* For fall admission, 2/15 for domestic and international students; for spring admission, 9/15 for domestic and international students. Applications are processed on a rolling basis. Application fee: $60. Electronic applications accepted. *Expenses:* Tuition, state resident: part-time $450 per credit. Tuition, nonresident: part-time $682 per credit. Tuition and fees vary according to degree level and program. *Financial support:* In 2006–07, 7 research assistantships with full tuition reimbursements (averaging $7,000 per year) were awarded; Federal Work-Study, scholarships/grants, and unspecified assistantships also available. Support available to part-time students. Financial award application deadline: 3/1; financial award applicants required to submit FAFSA. *Unit head:* Dr. Deborah Eldridge, Chairperson, 973-655-5187.

Montreat College, School of Professional and Adult Studies, Montreat, NC 28757-1267. Offers business administration (MBA); K-6 education (MA Ed). Evening/weekend programs available. Postbaccalaureate distance learning degree programs offered. *Entrance requirements:* Additional exam requirements/recommendations for international students: Required—TOEFL (minimum score 500 paper-based; 190 computer-based).

Moravian College, The Comenius Center for Continuing, Professional, and Graduate Studies, Program in Education, Bethlehem, PA 18018-6650. Offers curriculum and instruction (M Ed). Part-time programs available. *Faculty:* 7 full-time (4 women), 13 part-time/adjunct (9 women). In 2006, 26 degrees awarded. *Degree requirements:* For master's, thesis, action research. *Entrance requirements:* For master's, teaching certificate. Additional exam requirements/recommendations for international students: Required—TOEFL. *Application deadline:* Applications are processed on a rolling basis. Application fee: $30. *Expenses: Contact institution. Faculty research:* Action research for classroom teachers. *Unit head:* Dr. Joseph Shosh, Director, 610-861-1482, Fax: 610-861-1696, E-mail: mejms01@moravian.edu.

Morehead State University, Graduate Programs, College of Education, Morehead, KY 40351. Offers MA, MA Ed, MAT, Ed S. *Accreditation:* NCATE. Part-time and evening/weekend programs available. *Faculty:* 54 full-time (32 women), 37 part-time/adjunct (25 women). *Students:* 191 full-time (134 women), 535 part-time (395 women); includes 21 minority (12 African Americans, 5 American Indian/Alaska Native, 1 Asian American or Pacific Islander, 3 Hispanic Americans), 4 international. Average age 32. In 2006, 280 master's, 4 other advanced degrees awarded. *Degree requirements:* For master's, thesis optional; for Ed S, thesis. *Entrance requirements:* For master's, GRE General Test; for Ed S, GRE General Test, interview, master's degree, minimum GPA of 3.5, work experience. Additional exam requirements/recommendations for international students: Required—TOEFL (minimum score 500 paper-based; 173 computer-based). *Application deadline:* For fall admission, 8/1 priority date for domestic and international students; for spring admission, 12/1 priority date for domestic and international students. Applications are processed on a rolling basis. Application fee: $0 ($55 for international students). Electronic applications accepted. *Financial support:* In 2006–07, 1 research assistantship (averaging $6,000 per year), 8 teaching assistantships (averaging $6,000 per year) were awarded; career-related internships or fieldwork, Federal Work-Study, and unspecified assistantships also available. Financial award application deadline: 4/1; financial award applicants required to submit FAFSA. *Faculty research:* Regional economic development, computer applications for school administrators, effectiveness of teacher interns, perceptual processes, alcoholism. *Unit head:* Dr. Cathy Gunn, Dean, 606-783-2040, Fax: 606-783-5029, E-mail: c.gunn@moreheadstate.edu. *Application contact:* Michelle Barber, Graduate Admissions Counselor, 606-783-2039, Fax: 606-783-5061, E-mail: m.barber@moreheadstate.edu.

Morgan State University, School of Graduate Studies, School of Education and Urban Studies, Baltimore, MD 21251. Offers MAT, MS, MSW, Ed D, PhD. Part-time programs available. *Faculty:* 26. *Students:* 256. In 2006, 10 master's, 25 doctorates awarded. *Degree requirements:* For master's, comprehensive exam; for doctorate, thesis/dissertation, comprehensive exam. *Entrance requirements:* For doctorate, GRE General Test or MAT. Additional exam requirements/recommendations for international students: Required—TOEFL (minimum score 550 paper-based; 213 computer-based). *Application deadline:* For fall admission, 2/1 priority date for domestic students; for spring admission, 10/1 priority date for domestic students. Applications are processed on a rolling basis. Application fee: $0. *Expenses:* Tuition, state resident: part-time $272 per credit. Tuition, nonresident: part-time $478 per credit. Required fees: $38 per credit. *Financial support:* Fellowships, research assistantships, career-related internships or fieldwork, Federal Work-Study, institutionally sponsored loans, scholarships/grants, health care benefits, and unspecified assistantships available. Support available to part-time students. Financial award application deadline: 2/1. *Faculty research:* Multicultural education, cooperative learning, psychology of cognition. *Unit head:* Dr. Patricia L. Welch, Dean, 443-885-3385, Fax: 443-885-8240, E-mail: pmorris@moac.morgan.edu. *Application contact:* Dr. Maurice C. Taylor, Dean, 443-885-3185, Fax: 443-885-8226, E-mail: mctaylor@moac.morgan.edu.

Morningside College, Graduate Division, Department of Education, Sioux City, IA 51106. Offers elementary education (MAT); reading specialist (MAT); special education (MAT); technology based learning (MAT). Part-time and evening/weekend programs available. *Entrance requirements:* For master's, MAT, writing sample.

Mount Mary College, Graduate Programs, Programs in Education, Milwaukee, WI 53222-4597. Offers education (MA); professional development (MA). Part-time and evening/weekend programs available. *Faculty:* 2 full-time (both women), 5 part-time/adjunct (4 women). *Students:* 5 full-time (2 women), 73 part-time (63 women); includes 10 minority (4 African Americans, 1 Asian American or Pacific Islander, 5 Hispanic Americans). Average age 40. 66 applicants, 64% accepted, 38 enrolled. In 2006, 32 degrees awarded. *Degree requirements:* For master's, action research project. *Entrance requirements:* For master's, minimum GPA of 2.75, teaching license. Additional exam requirements/recommendations for international students: Required—TOEFL (minimum score 500 paper-based; 173 computer-based). *Application deadline:* For fall admission, 8/29 priority date for domestic and international students; for spring admission, 1/20 for domestic and international students. Applications are processed on a rolling basis. Application fee: $35 ($75 for international students). *Expenses:* Tuition: Part-time $490 per credit. Required fees: $48 per term. Tuition and fees vary according to course load and program. *Financial support:* In 2006–07, 7 students received support. Federal Work-Study available. Support available to part-time students. Financial award application deadline: 5/1; financial award applicants required to submit FAFSA. *Faculty research:* Staff development, writing across the curriculum, effective schools, critical thinking skills, mathematics education. *Unit head:* Dr. Deb Dosemagen, Director, 414-256-1214, E-mail: dosemagd@mtmary.edu.

Mount Saint Mary College, Division of Education, Newburgh, NY 12550-3494. Offers adolescence and special education (MS Ed); adolescence education (MS Ed); childhood and special education (MS Ed); childhood education (MS Ed); literacy and special education (MS Ed); literacy/childhood (MS Ed); middle school (5-6) (MS Ed); middle school (7-9) (MS Ed); special education (1-6) (MS Ed); special education (7-12) (MS Ed). *Accreditation:* NCATE. Part-time and evening/weekend programs available. *Faculty:* 11 full-time (8 women), 21 part-time/adjunct (18 women). *Students:* 87 full-time (74 women), 368 part-time (303 women); includes 38 minority (12 African Americans, 2 American Indian/Alaska Native, 5 Asian Americans or Pacific Islanders, 19 Hispanic Americans). Average age 31. 164 applicants, 45% accepted, 58 enrolled. In 2006, 131 degrees awarded. *Application deadline:* Applications are processed on a rolling basis. Application fee: $35. *Expenses:* Tuition: Full-time $11,880; part-time $660 per credit. *Financial support:* In 2006–07, 30 students received support. Unspecified assistantships available. Financial award application deadline: 3/15. *Faculty research:* Learning and teaching styles, computers in special education, language development. *Unit head:* Theresa Lewis, Coordinator, 845-569-3149, Fax: 845-569-3535, E-mail: tlewis@msmc.edu.

Mount St. Mary's College, Graduate Division, Department of Education, Los Angeles, CA 90049-1599. Offers administrative studies (MS); elementary education (MS); secondary education (MS); special education (MS). Part-time and evening/weekend programs available. *Faculty:* 4 full-time (all women), 10 part-time/adjunct (9 women). *Students:* 76 full-time (59 women), 88 part-time (70 women); includes 85 minority (20 African Americans, 12 Asian Americans or Pacific Islanders, 53 Hispanic Americans). Average age 33. In 2006, 26 degrees awarded. *Degree requirements:* For master's, thesis, research project. *Entrance requirements:* For master's, MAT, minimum GPA of 3.0. Application fee: $50 ($75 for international students). *Expenses:* Tuition: Part-time $630 per unit. *Financial support:* Institutionally sponsored loans and tuition waivers (full and partial) available. Support available to part-time students. Financial award application deadline: 3/15; financial award applicants required to submit FAFSA. *Unit head:* Dr. Anne Wilcoxen, Chair, 213-477-2622. *Application contact:* Tom Hoener, Director, Graduate Recruitment, 213-477-2800, Fax: 213-477-2519, E-mail: thoener@msmc.la.edu.

Mount St. Mary's University, Program in Education, Emmitsburg, MD 21727-7799. Offers M Ed, MAT. Part-time and evening/weekend programs available. *Faculty:* 2 full-time (both women), 7 part-time/adjunct (3 women). *Students:* 45 full-time (34 women), 70 part-time (55 women); includes 7 minority (4 African Americans, 1 American Indian/Alaska Native, 2 Hispanic Americans), 2 international. Average age 33. In 2006, 25 degrees awarded. *Median time to degree:* Master's–3 years part-time. *Degree requirements:* For master's, thesis (for some programs), exit portfolio/presentation. *Entrance requirements:* For master's, NTE, PRAXIS, minimum GPA of 2.7. Additional exam requirements/recommendations for international students: Required—TOEFL (minimum score 550 paper-based; 213 computer-based). *Application deadline:* For fall admission, 8/15 priority date for domestic students. Applications are processed on a rolling basis. Application fee: $35. *Expenses: Contact institution.* Tuition and fees vary according to program. *Financial support:* In 2006–07, 48 students received support. Career-related internships or fieldwork and unspecified assistantships available. Financial award applicants required to submit FAFSA. *Faculty research:* Reading comprehension, use of technology, autism/behavior change, language factors in math. *Unit head:* Laura Frazier, Director, 301-447-5371, Fax: 301-447-5250, E-mail: frazier@msmary.edu.

Mount Saint Vincent University, Graduate Programs, Faculty of Education, Halifax, NS B3M 2J6, Canada. Offers adult education (M Ed, MA Ed, MA-R); curriculum studies (M Ed, MA Ed, MA-R), including education of young adolescents, general studies, teaching English as a second language; educational foundations (M Ed, MA Ed, MA-R); educational psychology (M Ed, MA Ed, MA-R), including education of the blind or visually impaired (M Ed, MA Ed), education of the deaf or hard of hearing (M Ed, MA Ed), educational psychology (MA-R), human relations (M Ed, MA Ed); elementary education (M Ed, MA Ed, MA-R); literacy education (M Ed, MA Ed, MA-R); school psychology (MASP). Part-time and evening/weekend programs available. Postbaccalaureate distance learning degree programs offered (minimal on-campus study). *Degree requirements:* For master's, thesis (for some programs), practicum. *Entrance requirements:* For master's, bachelor's degree in related field. Electronic applications accepted.

Mount Vernon Nazarene University, Department of Education, Mount Vernon, OH 43050-9500. Offers education (MA Ed); professional educator's license (MA Ed). Part-time and evening/weekend programs available. *Degree requirements:* For master's, project.

Murray State University, College of Education, Murray, KY 42071. Offers MA Ed, MS, Ed D, PhD, Ed S. *Accreditation:* NCATE. Part-time programs available. *Faculty:* 41 full-time (15 women). *Students:* 67 full-time (50 women), 899 part-time (720 women); includes 63 minority (55 African Americans, 2 American Indian/Alaska Native, 2 Asian Americans or Pacific Islanders, 4 Hispanic Americans), 20 international. 196 applicants, 100% accepted. *Application deadline:* Applications are processed on a rolling basis. Application fee: $20. *Financial support:* Research assistantships, teaching assistantships, Federal Work-Study available. Financial award application deadline: 4/1. *Unit head:* Dr. Russ Wall, Dean, 270-809-3829, E-mail: russ.wall@coe.murraystate.edu. *Application contact:* Dr. Ken Purcell, Coordinator of Graduate Programs, 270-809-6123, Fax: 270-809-2540, E-mail: kp@coe.murraystate.edu.

Muskingum College, Graduate Program in Education, New Concord, OH 43762. Offers MAE. *Accreditation:* NCATE. Part-time programs available. *Entrance requirements:* For master's, minimum GPA of 2.7, teaching license. *Faculty research:* Brain behavior relationships, school partnerships, staff development, school law, proficiency testing, multi-age groupings.

Naropa University, Graduate Programs, Program in Contemplative Education, Boulder, CO 80302-6697. Offers MA. Part-time programs available. Postbaccalaureate distance learning degree programs offered (minimal on-campus study). *Faculty:* 1 full-time (0 women), 3 part-time/adjunct (all women). *Students:* Average age 36. 12 applicants, 100% accepted, 7 enrolled. In 2006, 3 degrees awarded. *Median time to degree:* Master's–2 years full-time. *Degree requirements:* For master's, thesis. *Entrance requirements:* For master's, interview (by phone or in person). Additional exam requirements/recommendations for international students: Required—TOEFL (minimum score 600 paper-based; 250 computer-based). *Application deadline:* For fall admission, 1/15 priority date for domestic and international students; for spring admission, 10/15 priority date for domestic students. Applications are processed on a rolling basis. Application fee: $60. Electronic applications accepted. *Expenses:* Tuition: Full-time $15,070; part-time $646 per credit. Tuition and fees vary according to course load. *Financial support:* In 2006–07, 2 students received support. Career-related internships or fieldwork, Federal Work-Study, scholarships/grants, and tuition waivers (partial) available. Support available to part-time students. Financial award application deadline: 3/1; financial award applicants required to submit FAFSA. *Unit head:* Richard Brown, Chair, 303-245-4765, E-mail: rbrown@naropa.edu. *Application contact:* Kate Levene, Assistant Director of Admissions, 303-245-4657, Fax: 303-546-3583, E-mail: klevene@naropa.edu.

National-Louis University, National College of Education, Chicago, IL 60603. Offers M Ed, MAT, MS Ed, Ed D, CAS, Ed S. *Accreditation:* NCATE. Part-time and evening/weekend programs available. *Faculty:* 163 full-time (118 women), 588 part-time/adjunct (416 women). *Students:* 1,127 full-time (855 women), 2,682 part-time (2,020 women); includes 731 minority (429 African Americans, 8 American Indian/Alaska Native, 77 Asian Americans or Pacific Islanders, 217 Hispanic Americans). Average age 35. 721 applicants, 99% accepted. In 2006, 1,503 master's, 13 doctorates, 70 other advanced degrees awarded. *Degree requirements:* For doctorate, thesis/dissertation, comprehensive exam. *Entrance requirements:* For master's, MAT or GRE, minimum GPA of 3.0; for doctorate, GRE General Test, minimum GPA of 3.25, interview, resumé, writing sample. *Application deadline:* Applications are processed on a rolling basis. Application fee: $25. *Expenses:* Tuition: Full-time $17,685. One-time fee: $40 full-time. *Financial support:* Fellowships, research assistantships, teaching assistantships, career-related internships or fieldwork, Federal Work-Study, institutionally sponsored loans, and scholarships/grants available. Support available to part-time students. Financial award applicants required to submit FAFSA. *Faculty research:* Methods of teaching behaviorally challenged, early childhood curriculum planning, individualized learning. *Unit head:* Dr. Alison Hilsobeck, Dean, 847-475-1100 Ext. 5336. *Application contact:* David McCulloch, Vice President for University Services, 800-443-5522 Ext. 5127, Fax: 847-465-0593, E-mail: dmcc@wheeling1.nl.edu.

National University, Academic Affairs, School of Education, La Jolla, CA 92037-1011. Offers M Ed, MA, MS. Part-time and evening/weekend programs available. Postbaccalaureate distance learning degree programs offered (no on-campus study). *Faculty:* 79 full-time (45 women), 1,560 part-time/adjunct (895 women). *Students:* 5,069 full-time (3,477 women), 9,206 part-time (5,886 women); includes 4,077 minority (1,132 African Americans, 91 American Indian/Alaska Native, 723 Asian Americans or Pacific Islanders, 2,131 Hispanic Americans), 39 international. Average age 36. 7,948 applicants, 7313 enrolled. In 2006, 2556 degrees awarded.

Education—General

National University (continued)

Degree requirements: For master's, thesis (for some programs). *Entrance requirements:* For master's, interview, minimum GPA of 2.5. Additional exam requirements/recommendations for international students: Required—TOEFL (minimum score 550 paper-based; 213 computer-based; 80 iBT), IELTS (minimum score 6). *Application deadline:* Applications are processed on a rolling basis. Application fee: $60 ($65 for international students). Electronic applications accepted. *Expenses:* Tuition: Full-time $7,722; part-time $286 per unit. One-time fee: $60. *Financial support:* Career-related internships or fieldwork, institutionally sponsored loans, scholarships/grants, and tuition waivers (partial) available. Support available to part-time students. Financial award application deadline: 6/30. *Unit head:* Dr. Gloria Johnston, Dean, 858-642-8320, E-mail: gjohnsto@nu.edu. *Application contact:* Dominick Giovanniello, Associate Regional Dean—San Diego, 800-NAT-UNIV, Fax: 858-642-8709, E-mail: dgiovann@nu.edu.

Nazareth College of Rochester, Graduate Studies, Department of Education, Rochester, NY 14618-3790. Offers educational technology/computer education (MS Ed); inclusive education-adolescence level (MS Ed); inclusive education-childhood level (MS Ed); inclusive education-early childhood level (MS Ed); literacy education (MS Ed); teaching English to speakers of other languages (MS Ed). *Accreditation:* Teacher Education Accreditation Council. Part-time and evening/weekend programs available. *Faculty:* 19 full-time (13 women), 50 part-time/adjunct (32 women). *Students:* 226 full-time (194 women), 332 part-time (283 women); includes 43 minority (15 African Americans, 5 American Indian/Alaska Native, 6 Asian Americans or Pacific Islanders, 17 Hispanic Americans). Average age 30. 262 applicants, 96% accepted, 159 enrolled. In 2006, 262 degrees awarded. *Entrance requirements:* For master's, minimum GPA of 3.0. *Application deadline:* For fall admission, 4/1 for domestic students; for spring admission, 10/1 for domestic students. Application fee: $40. *Financial support:* Research assistantships with partial tuition reimbursements available. Financial award application deadline: 3/1; financial award applicants required to submit FAFSA. *Unit head:* Dr. Timothy Glander, Dean, 585-389-2992, Fax: 585-389-2452, E-mail: tglande7@naz.edu. *Application contact:* Judith G. Baker, Director, Graduate Admissions, 585-389-2050, Fax: 585-389-2817, E-mail: gradstudies@naz.edu.

Neumann College, Program in Education, Aston, PA 19014-1298. Offers MS. Part-time programs available. *Faculty:* 5 full-time (1 woman), 2 part-time/adjunct (1 woman). *Students:* 21 full-time (16 women), 222 part-time (156 women); includes 20 minority (18 African Americans, 2 Hispanic Americans). Average age 34. 100 applicants, 100% accepted, 75 enrolled. In 2006, 78 degrees awarded. *Entrance requirements:* For master's, GRE, MAT, or PRAXIS. Additional exam requirements/recommendations for international students: Required—TOEFL. *Application deadline:* Applications are processed on a rolling basis. Application fee: $50. *Financial support:* Available to part-time students. Application deadline: 3/15; *Unit head:* Dr. Andrew DeSanto, Coordinator, Division of Education and Human Services, 610-558-5640, Fax: 610-459-1370, E-mail: desantoa@neumann.edu. *Application contact:* Louise Bank, Assistant Director of Admissions, Graduate and Evening Programs, 610-558-5604, Fax: 610-459-1370, E-mail: bankl@neumann.edu.

New College of California, School of Humanities, San Francisco, CA 94102-5206. Offers humanities and leadership (MA), including activism and social change, culture, ecology, and sustainable community; Irish studies (MA); media studies (MA); poetics (MA, MFA), including poetics (MA), poetics and writing (MFA); teaching (MAT); women's spirituality (MA); writing and consciousness (MA); MA/MFA. Part-time and evening/weekend programs available. *Degree requirements:* For master's, thesis.

New England College, Program in Education, Henniker, NH 03242-3293. Offers literacy and language arts (M Ed); meeting the needs of all learners/special education (M Ed); teacher leadership/school reform (M Ed). Part-time and evening/weekend programs available.

Newman University, School of Education, Wichita, KS 67213-2097. Offers building leadership (MS Ed); curriculum and instruction (MS Ed), including accountability, English as a second language. Part-time programs available. Postbaccalaureate distance learning degree programs offered (no on-campus study). *Faculty:* 3 full-time (0 women), 4 part-time/adjunct (all women). *Students:* 2 full-time (both women), 41 part-time (24 women); includes 3 minority (2 African Americans, 1 American Indian/Alaska Native), 3 international. Average age 35. 25 applicants, 92% accepted, 17 enrolled. In 2006, 35 degrees awarded. *Degree requirements:* For master's, thesis optional. *Entrance requirements:* For master's, GRE General Test or MAT, interview, minimum GPA of 3.0, writing sample, 3 letters of recommendation. Additional exam requirements/recommendations for international students: Required—TOEFL (minimum score 600 paper-based; 250 computer-based). *Application deadline:* For fall admission, 8/15 priority date for domestic students; for spring admission, 1/10 priority date for domestic students. Applications are processed on a rolling basis. Application fee: $25 ($40 for international students). Electronic applications accepted. *Financial support:* In 2006–07, 8 students received support. Federal Work-Study and tuition waivers (full) available. Financial award application deadline: 8/15; financial award applicants required to submit FAFSA. *Unit head:* Dr. Guy Glidden, Director, 316-942-4291 Ext. 2331, Fax: 316-942-4483, E-mail: gliddeng@newmanu.edu. *Application contact:* Linda Kay Sabala, Director of Graduate Admissions, 316-942-4291 Ext. 2230, Fax: 316-942-4483, E-mail: sabalal@newmanu.edu.

New Mexico Highlands University, Graduate Studies, School of Education, Las Vegas, NM 87701. Offers education (MA), including curriculum and instruction; educational leadership (MA); exercise and sport sciences (MA), including human performance and sport, sports administration, teacher education; guidance and counseling (MA), including professional counseling, rehabilitation counseling, school counseling; special education (MA), including). *Accreditation:* NCATE. Part-time programs available. *Faculty:* 14 full-time (6 women), 11 part-time/adjunct (9 women). *Students:* 171 full-time (117 women), 413 part-time (286 women); includes 305 minority (17 African Americans, 30 American Indian/Alaska Native, 4 Asian Americans or Pacific Islanders, 254 Hispanic Americans), 3 international. Average age 40. 111 applicants, 84% accepted, 63 enrolled. In 2006, 111 degrees awarded. *Degree requirements:* For master's, thesis or alternative, comprehensive exam, registration. *Entrance requirements:* For master's, minimum undergraduate GPA of 3.0. Additional exam requirements/recommendations for international students: Required—TOEFL (minimum score 540 paper-based; 190 computer-based). *Application deadline:* For fall admission, 8/1 priority date for domestic students. Applications are processed on a rolling basis. Application fee: $15. *Expenses:* Tuition, state resident: part-time $101 per credit hour. Tuition, nonresident: part-time $101 per credit hour. *Financial support:* In 2006–07, 205 students received support, including 16 teaching assistantships with full and partial tuition reimbursements available (averaging $6,500 per year); career-related internships or fieldwork, Federal Work-Study, institutionally sponsored loans, scholarships/grants, traineeships, tuition waivers (partial), and unspecified assistantships also available. Support available to part-time students. Financial award application deadline: 3/1; financial award applicants required to submit FAFSA. *Unit head:* Dr. Francisco Hidalgo, Dean, 505-454-3357, Fax: 505-454-3384, E-mail: fhidalgo@nmhu.edu. *Application contact:* Diane Trujillo, Administrative Assistant Graduate Studies, 505-454-3266, Fax: 505-454-3558, E-mail: dtrujillo@nmhu.edu.

New Mexico State University, Graduate School, College of Education, Las Cruces, NM 88003-8001. Offers MA, MAT, Ed D, PhD, Ed S. *Accreditation:* NCATE. Part-time and evening/weekend programs available. Postbaccalaureate distance learning degree programs offered (minimal on-campus study). *Faculty:* 58 full-time (30 women), 12 part-time/adjunct (4 women). *Students:* 358 full-time (276 women), 611 part-time (464 women); includes 434 minority (27 African Americans, 20 American Indian/Alaska Native, 10 Asian Americans or Pacific Islanders, 377 Hispanic Americans), 41 international. Average age 37. 403 applicants, 77% accepted. In 2006, 291 master's, 25 doctorates, 4 other advanced degrees awarded. *Degree requirements:* For doctorate, thesis/dissertation. *Application deadline:* Applications are processed on a rolling basis. Application fee: $30 ($50 for international students). Electronic applications accepted. *Financial support:* In 2006–07, 18 fellowships, 60 teaching assistantships were awarded; research assistantships, career-related internships or fieldwork, Federal Work-Study, and health care benefits also available. Support available to part-time students. Financial award application deadline: 3/1. *Faculty research:* Bilingual special education, early childhood education/Head Start, leadership in border settings, exercise physiology, school-based mental health. *Unit head:* Dr. Robert Moulton, Dean, 505-646-3404, Fax: 505-646-6032, E-mail: moulton@nmsu.edu.

New York Institute of Technology, Graduate Division, School of Education and Professional Services, Old Westbury, NY 11568-8000. Offers MS, Advanced Certificate, Professional Diploma. *Accreditation:* NCATE. Part-time and evening/weekend programs available. Postbaccalaureate distance learning degree programs offered. *Students:* 19 full-time (14 women), 339 part-time (223 women); includes 52 minority (28 African Americans, 1 American Indian/Alaska Native, 3 Asian Americans or Pacific Islanders, 20 Hispanic Americans), 8 international. Average age 34. 371 applicants, 81% accepted, 150 enrolled. In 2006, 123 master's, 3 other advanced degrees awarded. *Entrance requirements:* For master's, minimum QPA of 3.0. Additional exam requirements/recommendations for international students: Required—TOEFL (minimum score 550 paper-based; 213 computer-based). *Application deadline:* For fall admission, 7/1 priority date for domestic students; for spring admission, 12/1 priority date for domestic students. Applications are processed on a rolling basis. Application fee: $50. Electronic applications accepted. *Expenses:* Tuition: Full-time $16,800; part-time $700 per credit. *Financial support:* Research assistantships with partial tuition reimbursements, career-related internships or fieldwork, institutionally sponsored loans, and tuition waivers (full and partial) available. Support available to part-time students. Financial award applicants required to submit FAFSA. *Faculty research:* Distance learning, instructional uses of the World Wide Web, telecommunication technologies, emotional intelligence. *Unit head:* Dr. Jacqueline Kress, Dean, 516-686-7706, Fax: 516-686-7655. *Application contact:* Jacquelyn Nealon, Dean of Admissions and Financial Aid, 516-686-7925, Fax: 516-686-7613, E-mail: jnealon@nyit.edu.

New York University, Steinhardt School of Culture, Education and Human Development, New York, NY 10012-1019. Offers MA, MFA, MM, MPH, MS, DA, DPS, DPT, Ed D, PhD, Advanced Certificate, MA/MS. *Accreditation:* Teacher Education Accreditation Council. Part-time and evening/weekend programs available. *Faculty:* 241 full-time (141 women), 717 part-time/adjunct (399 women). *Students:* 2,065 full-time (1,661 women), 1,441 part-time (1,136 women); includes 758 minority (244 African Americans, 5 American Indian/Alaska Native, 278 Asian Americans or Pacific Islanders, 231 Hispanic Americans), 492 international. Average age 32. 4,826 applicants, 55% accepted, 1257 enrolled. In 2006, 1,271 master's, 97 doctorates, 11 other advanced degrees awarded. *Degree requirements:* For doctorate, thesis/dissertation, comprehensive exam (for some programs). *Entrance requirements:* For doctorate, GRE General Test, interview. Additional exam requirements/recommendations for international students: Required—TOEFL. *Application deadline:* For fall admission, 2/1 priority date for domestic students, 2/1 for international students; for spring admission, 12/1 for domestic and international students. Applications are processed on a rolling basis. Application fee: $50. *Expenses:* Contact institution. Tuition and fees vary according to program. *Financial support:* In 2006–07, fellowships with full and partial tuition reimbursements (averaging $15,000 per year); research assistantships with full and partial tuition reimbursements, teaching assistantships with full and partial tuition reimbursements, career-related internships or fieldwork, Federal Work-Study, institutionally sponsored loans, scholarships/grants, traineeships, tuition waivers (partial), and unspecified assistantships also available. Support available to part-time students. Financial award application deadline: 2/1; financial award applicants required to submit FAFSA. *Faculty research:* Equity, urban adolescents, arts in education, globalization, community and public health. Total annual research expenditures: $21.3 million. *Unit head:* Dr. Mary Brabeck, Dean, 212-998-5000. *Application contact:* 212-998-5030, Fax: 212-995-4328, E-mail: steinhardt.gradadmissions@nyu.edu.

See Close-Up on page 897.

Niagara University, Graduate Division of Education, Niagara Falls, Niagara University, NY 14109. Offers administration and supervision (MS Ed, Certificate); foundations of teaching (MA, MS Ed); inclusive education (MS Ed); literacy instruction (MS Ed); mental health counseling (MS Ed, Certificate); school counseling (MS Ed, Certificate), including school business administration; school psychology (MS); teacher education (MS Ed), including elementary education, secondary education. *Accreditation:* NCATE (one or more programs are accredited). Part-time and evening/weekend programs available. *Faculty:* 27 full-time (17 women), 29 part-time/adjunct (14 women). *Students:* 466 full-time (339 women), 272 part-time (207 women); includes 26 minority (15 African Americans, 7 American Indian/Alaska Native, 4 Hispanic Americans), 278 international. Average age 37. 382 applicants, 75% accepted. In 2006, 405 master's, 14 other advanced degrees awarded. *Entrance requirements:* For master's, GRE General Test or MAT. *Application deadline:* For fall admission, 8/1 for domestic students. Applications are processed on a rolling basis. Application fee: $30. *Expenses:* Contact institution. *Financial support:* In 2006–07, 2 fellowships, 3 research assistantships were awarded; career-related internships or fieldwork, Federal Work-Study, scholarships/grants, and unspecified assistantships also available. Support available to part-time students. Financial award application deadline: 3/15. *Faculty research:* Instructional supervision, appraisal and evaluation, career opportunities. *Unit head:* Dr. Debra A. Colley, Dean, 716-286-8560, Fax: 716-286-8561, E-mail: dcolley@niagara.edu.

Nicholls State University, Graduate Studies, College of Education, Department of Teacher Education, Thibodaux, LA 70310. Offers administration and supervision (M Ed); counselor education (M Ed); curriculum and instruction (M Ed). *Accreditation:* NCATE. Part-time and evening/weekend programs available. *Faculty:* 17 full-time (13 women), 6 part-time/adjunct (4 women). *Students:* 21 full-time (17 women), 174 part-time (155 women); includes 60 minority (52 African Americans, 5 American Indian/Alaska Native, 1 Asian American or Pacific Islander, 2 Hispanic Americans). Average age 33. In 2006, 77 degrees awarded. *Degree requirements:* For master's, portfolio. *Entrance requirements:* For master's, GRE General Test, teaching license. *Application deadline:* Applications are processed on a rolling basis. Application fee: $20 ($30 for international students). Electronic applications accepted. *Expenses:* Tuition, state resident: part-time $450 per hour. Tuition, nonresident: part-time $450 per hour. *Financial support:* In 2006–07, research assistantships with tuition reimbursements (averaging $4,000 per year). Financial award application deadline: 6/17. *Unit head:* Dr. J. Lavone Landry, Head, 985-448-4314, E-mail: lavone.landry@nicholls.edu.

Nipissing University, Faculty of Education, North Bay, ON P1B 8L7, Canada. Offers M Ed, Certificate. Part-time and evening/weekend programs available. *Faculty:* 50 full-time (25 women), 11 part-time/adjunct (5 women). *Students:* 844 full-time (611 women), 219 part-time (154 women). 5,007 applicants, 40% accepted, 842 enrolled. In 2006, 39 master's, 711 other advanced degrees awarded. *Degree requirements:* For master's, thesis (for some programs), professional experience, comprehensive exam (for some programs), registration. *Entrance requirements:* For master's, 1 year of experience, letters of recommendation, minimum undergraduate GPA of 3.0. Additional exam requirements/recommendations for international students: Required—TOEFL (minimum score 600 paper-based; 250 computer-based), IELTS (minimum score 7), TWE (minimum score 5). *Application deadline:* For fall admission, 6/15 for domestic students. Application fee: $140. *Expenses:* Tuition, area resident: Part-time $561 per course. Required fees: $37 per course. *Unit head:* Dr. Ronald Common, Dean of Education, 705-474-3461 Ext. 4268, Fax: 705-474-3264, E-mail: ronaldc@nipissingu.ca. *Application contact:* Rebecca Roome-Rancourt, Assistant Registrar, Admissions, 705-474-3461 Ext. 4292, Fax: 705-495-1772, E-mail: rebeccar@nipissingu.ca.

Norfolk State University, School of Graduate Studies, School of Education, Norfolk, VA 23504. Offers MA, MAT. *Accreditation:* NCATE. Part-time programs available. *Degree requirements:* For master's, comprehensive exam. *Entrance requirements:* For master's, PRAXIS, GRE/GMAT, interview, teacher license. *Faculty research:* Urban, pre-elementary, and special education.

North Carolina Agricultural and Technical State University, Graduate School, School of Education, Greensboro, NC 27411. Offers MS. *Accreditation:* NCATE. Part-time and evening/weekend programs available. *Degree requirements:* For master's, qualifying exam. *Entrance requirements:* For master's, GRE General Test.

North Carolina Central University, Division of Academic Affairs, School of Education, Durham, NC 27707-3129. Offers M Ed, MA. *Accreditation:* NCATE. Part-time and evening/weekend programs available. *Degree requirements:* For master's, thesis or alternative, comprehensive exam. *Entrance requirements:* For master's, minimum GPA of 3.0 in major, 2.5 overall. Additional exam requirements/recommendations for international students: Required—TOEFL.

North Carolina State University, Graduate School, College of Education, Raleigh, NC 27695. Offers M Ed, MS, MSA, Ed D, PhD, Certificate. *Accreditation:* NCATE. Part-time programs available. *Degree requirements:* For doctorate, thesis/dissertation. *Entrance requirements:* For master's, doctorate, and Certificate, GRE General Test or MAT, minimum GPA of 3.0 in major. Electronic applications accepted. *Faculty research:* Moral/ethical development, financial policy analysis, middle years education, adult education.

North Central College, Graduate Programs, Department of Education, Naperville, IL 60566-7063. Offers MA Ed. Part-time and evening/weekend programs available. *Degree requirements:* For master's, clinical practicum, project. *Entrance requirements:* For master's, interview. Expenses: Contact institution.

North Dakota State University, The Graduate School, College of Human Development and Education, School of Education, Fargo, ND 58105. Offers agricultural education (M Ed, MS), including agricultural education, agricultural extension education (MS); counseling (M Ed, MS, PhD); curriculum and instruction (M Ed, MS), including pedagogy, physical education and athletic administration; education (PhD); educational leadership (M Ed, MS, Ed S); family and consumer sciences education (M Ed, MS); history education (M Ed, MS); mathematics education (M Ed, MS); music education (M Ed, MS); science education (M Ed, MS). *Accreditation:* NCATE. Part-time and evening/weekend programs available. Postbaccalaureate distance learning degree programs offered (minimal on-campus study). *Faculty:* 25 full-time (9 women), 3 part-time/adjunct (1 woman). *Students:* 29 full-time (25 women), 207 part-time (132 women); includes 15 minority (4 African Americans, 6 American Indian/Alaska Native, 3 Asian Americans or Pacific Islanders, 2 Hispanic Americans), 4 international. 88 applicants, 67% accepted, 56 enrolled. In 2006, 44 master's, 5 doctorates awarded. *Degree requirements:* For master's, comprehensive exam; for doctorate and Ed S, thesis/dissertation. *Entrance requirements:* For degree, GRE General Test, master's degree, minimum GPA of 3.25. Additional exam requirements/recommendations for international students: Required—TOEFL. *Application deadline:* Applications are processed on a rolling basis. Application fee: $45 ($60 for international students). *Financial support:* Research assistantships, teaching assistantships, career-related internships or fieldwork, Federal Work-Study, institutionally sponsored loans, and tuition waivers (full) available. Financial award application deadline: 4/15. *Unit head:* Dr. William O. Martin, Chair, 701-231-7104, Fax: 701-231-7416, E-mail: william.martin@ndsu.edu.

Northeastern Illinois University, Graduate College, College of Education, Chicago, IL 60625-4699. Offers MA, MAT, MSI. Part-time and evening/weekend programs available. *Faculty:* 83 full-time (47 women), 64 part-time/adjunct (40 women). *Students:* 169 full-time (122 women), 976 part-time (751 women); includes 299 minority (125 African Americans, 1 American Indian/Alaska Native, 35 Asian Americans or Pacific Islanders, 138 Hispanic Americans), 11 international. Average age 35. 363 applicants, 86% accepted. In 2006, 145 degrees awarded. *Entrance requirements:* For master's, minimum GPA of 2.75. *Application deadline:* For fall admission, 4/1 priority date for domestic students; for spring admission, 8/15 for domestic students. Applications are processed on a rolling basis. Application fee: $25. *Financial support:* In 2006–07, 219 students received support, including 21 research assistantships with full tuition reimbursements available (averaging $6,600 per year); career-related internships or fieldwork, Federal Work-Study, institutionally sponsored loans, and tuition waivers (full and partial) also available. Support available to part-time students. Financial award applicants required to submit FAFSA. *Faculty research:* Leadership, problem-based learning strategies, school improvement, bilingual education, use of technology.

Northeastern State University, Graduate College, College of Education, Tahlequah, OK 74464-2399. Offers M Ed, MS, MS Ed. *Accreditation:* NCATE. Part-time and evening/weekend programs available. *Faculty:* 26 full-time (11 women). *Students:* 151 full-time (117 women), 422 part-time (319 women); includes 156 minority (28 African Americans, 103 American Indian/Alaska Native, 11 Asian Americans or Pacific Islanders, 14 Hispanic Americans), 2 international. In 2006, 187 degrees awarded. *Degree requirements:* For master's, thesis. *Entrance requirements:* For master's, GRE or MAT. Additional exam requirements/recommendations for international students: Required—TOEFL (minimum score 213 computer-based). *Application deadline:* For fall admission, 6/1 priority date for domestic students. Applications are processed on a rolling basis. Application fee: $0 ($25 for international students). Electronic applications accepted. *Financial support:* Teaching assistantships, career-related internships or fieldwork and Federal Work-Study available. Financial award application deadline: 3/1. *Unit head:* Dr. Kay Grant, Head, 918-456-5511 Ext. 3700.

Northern Arizona University, Graduate College, College of Education, Flagstaff, AZ 86011. Offers M Ed, MA, Ed D, Certificate. Part-time and evening/weekend programs available. *Degree requirements:* For doctorate, thesis/dissertation.

Northern Illinois University, Graduate School, College of Education, De Kalb, IL 60115-2854. Offers MS, MS Ed, Ed D, Ed S. *Accreditation:* NCATE. Part-time and evening/weekend programs available. Postbaccalaureate distance learning degree programs offered (minimal on-campus study). *Faculty:* 110 full-time (66 women), 5 part-time/adjunct (3 women). *Students:* 308 full-time (197 women), 1,745 part-time (1,227 women); includes 404 minority (184 African Americans, 4 American Indian/Alaska Native, 43 Asian Americans or Pacific Islanders, 173 Hispanic Americans), 46 international. Average age 37. 569 applicants, 77% accepted, 308 enrolled. In 2006, 635 master's, 57 doctorates, 56 other advanced degrees awarded. Terminal master's awarded for partial completion of doctoral program. *Degree requirements:* For master's and Ed S, thesis optional; for doctorate, thesis/dissertation, candidacy exam, dissertation defense. *Entrance requirements:* For master's, GRE General Test or MAT, minimum GPA of 2.75; for doctorate, GRE General Test or MAT, minimum GPA of 2.75 (undergraduate), 3.2 (graduate); for Ed S, GRE General Test, master's degree, minimum undergraduate GPA of 2.75, minimum graduate GPA of 3.2. Additional exam requirements/recommendations for international students: Required—TOEFL (minimum score 550 paper-based; 213 computer-based). *Application deadline:* For fall admission, 6/1 for domestic students, 5/1 for international students; for spring admission, 11/1 for domestic students, 10/1 for international students. Applications are processed on a rolling basis. Application fee: $30. Electronic applications accepted. *Financial support:* In 2006–07, 7 research assistantships with full tuition reimbursements, 5 teaching assistantships with full tuition reimbursements were awarded; fellowships with full tuition reimbursements, career-related internships or fieldwork, Federal Work-Study, scholarships/grants, tuition waivers (full), and unspecified assistantships also available. Support available to part-time students. Financial award applicants required to submit FAFSA. *Unit head:* Dr. Christine Sorensen, Dean, 815-753-9056, Fax: 815-753-2100, E-mail: csorensen@niu.edu.

Northern Kentucky University, Office of Graduate Programs, College of Education and Human Services, Highland Heights, KY 41099. Offers community counseling (MSCC); education (M Ed); instructional leadership (MA); school counseling (MASC); special education (Certificate); teaching (MAT). *Accreditation:* NCATE. Part-time and evening/weekend programs available. *Faculty:* 42 full-time (25 women), 8 part-time/adjunct (5 women). *Students:* 44 full-time (33 women), 432 part-time (345 women); includes 14 minority (6 African Americans, 2 American Indian/Alaska Native, 1 Asian American or Pacific Islander, 5 Hispanic Americans). Average age 35. 253 applicants, 62% accepted, 117 enrolled. In 2006, 193 degrees awarded. *Degree requirements:* For master's, portfolio, thesis optional. *Entrance requirements:* For master's,

GRE, teaching certificate, bachelor's degree in appropriate subject area (MAT). Additional exam requirements/recommendations for international students: Required—TOEFL (minimum score 550 paper-based; 213 computer-based; 79 iBT), Michigan (must be taken at NKU). *Application deadline:* For fall admission, 8/1 priority date for domestic students, 6/1 for international students; for spring admission, 12/1 priority date for domestic students, 10/1 for international students. Applications are processed on a rolling basis. Application fee: $30. Electronic applications accepted. *Expenses:* Tuition, state resident: full-time $5,274; part-time $293 per hour. Tuition, nonresident: full-time $10,314; part-time $573 per hour. Tuition and fees vary according to course load, program and reciprocity agreements. *Financial support:* In 2006–07, 253 students received support. Unspecified assistantships available. *Faculty research:* Teacher disposition, mathematic teacher strategies, middle school structure. *Unit head:* Dr. Elaine McNally Jarchow, Dean, 859-572-5229, Fax: 859-572-6623, E-mail: jarchowe1@nku.edu. *Application contact:* Dr. Peg Griffin, Director of Graduate Programs, 859-572-1555, Fax: 859-572-6670, E-mail: gradprog@nku.edu.

Northern Michigan University, College of Graduate Studies, College of Professional Studies, School of Education, Marquette, MI 49855-5301. Offers administration and supervision (MA Ed, Ed S); elementary education (MA Ed); secondary education (MA Ed); special education (MA Ed). *Accreditation:* NCATE. Part-time programs available. *Degree requirements:* For master's, thesis or alternative. *Entrance requirements:* For master's, minimum GPA of 3.0.

Northern State University, Division of Graduate Studies in Education, Aberdeen, SD 57401-7198. Offers MS, MS Ed. *Accreditation:* NCATE. Part-time and evening/weekend programs available. *Faculty:* 84 full-time (21 women). *Students:* 16 full-time (13 women), 137 part-time (93 women); includes 7 minority (1 African American, 1 American Indian/Alaska Native, 4 Asian Americans or Pacific Islanders, 1 Hispanic American). Average age 32. In 2006, 60 degrees awarded. *Degree requirements:* For master's, thesis optional. *Entrance requirements:* For master's, minimum GPA of 2.75. Additional exam requirements/recommendations for international students: Required—TOEFL (minimum score 550 paper-based; 213 computer-based). *Application deadline:* For fall admission, 8/15 priority date for domestic students; for spring admission, 12/15 for domestic students. Applications are processed on a rolling basis. Application fee: $35. Electronic applications accepted. *Expenses:* Tuition, state resident: full-time $3,373; part-time $120 per credit. Tuition, nonresident: full-time $9,943; part-time $355 per credit. International tuition: $13,000 full-time. Required fees: $86 per credit. One-time fee: $35 full-time. Tuition and fees vary according to course load, degree level and reciprocity agreements. *Financial support:* In 2006–07, 51 students received support, including 31 teaching assistantships with partial tuition reimbursements available (averaging $4,812 per year); career-related internships or fieldwork, Federal Work-Study, institutionally sponsored loans, scholarships/grants, and unspecified assistantships also available. Support available to part-time students. Financial award application deadline: 3/1; financial award applicants required to submit FAFSA. *Unit head:* Dr. Tom Hawley, Director of Graduate Studies, 605-626-2558, Fax: 605-626-2542, E-mail: thawley@northern.edu. *Application contact:* Tammy K. Griffith, Senior Secretary, 605-626-2558, Fax: 605-626-2542, E-mail: griffith@northern.edu.

North Georgia College & State University, Graduate Studies, Program in Teacher Education, Dahlonega, GA 30597. Offers early childhood education (M Ed); educational leadership (Ed S); middle grades education (M Ed); secondary education (M Ed), including art education, biology education, chemistry education, English education, history education, mathematics education, physical education, science education; special education (M Ed), including inter-related special education, learning disabilities. *Accreditation:* NCATE. Part-time and evening/weekend programs available. Postbaccalaureate distance learning degree programs offered (minimal on-campus study). *Faculty:* 35 full-time (18 women), 9 part-time/adjunct (6 women). *Students:* 260. Average age 32. 120 applicants, 63% accepted. In 2006, 134 degrees awarded. *Degree requirements:* For master's, thesis optional. *Entrance requirements:* For master's, GRE General Test or MAT, minimum GPA of 2.75; for Ed S, GRE General Test or MAT, 3 years of teaching experience, master's degree, minimum graduate GPA of 3.25. *Application deadline:* For fall admission, 7/1 priority date for domestic students; for spring admission, 12/10 priority date for domestic students. Applications are processed on a rolling basis. Application fee: $25. Electronic applications accepted. *Expenses:* Tuition, state resident: full-time $3,044; part-time $127 per credit hour. Tuition, nonresident: full-time $12,172; part-time $508 per credit hour. Required fees: $892; $458 per semester. *Financial support:* Teaching assistantships, career-related internships or fieldwork and scholarships/grants available. Support available to part-time students. Financial award application deadline: 5/1. *Faculty research:* Computers and teachers' attitudes, rural versus urban teacher attitudes, teacher leadership roles, minority recruitment in teaching force. *Unit head:* Dr. Bob Michael, Dean, School of Education, 706-864-1998, Fax: 706-867-2850, E-mail: bmichael@ngcsu.edu. *Application contact:* Dr. Donna A. Gessell, Director of Graduate Studies and External Programs, 706-864-1528, Fax: 706-867-2795, E-mail: dgessell@ngcsu.edu.

North Park University, School of Education, Chicago, IL 60625-4895. Offers MA. *Degree requirements:* For master's, thesis. *Entrance requirements:* For master's, GRE General Test. *Faculty research:* Teacher leadership, research design, teacher education.

Northwestern Oklahoma State University, School of Professional Studies, Alva, OK 73717-2799. Offers adult education management and administration (M Ed), including adult education management and administration, education: non-certificate option; counseling psychology (MCP); curriculum and instruction (M Ed); educational leadership (M Ed); elementary education (M Ed); guidance and counseling K–12 (M Ed); reading specialist (M Ed); secondary education (M Ed). *Accreditation:* NCATE (one or more programs are accredited). Part-time programs available. *Faculty:* 32 full-time (17 women), 12 part-time/adjunct (7 women). *Students:* 43 full-time (33 women), 111 part-time (88 women); includes 10 minority (1 African American, 6 American Indian/Alaska Native, 3 Hispanic Americans), 2 international. Average age 31. 75 applicants, 92% accepted, 57 enrolled. In 2006, 68 degrees awarded. *Degree requirements:* For master's, portfolio, thesis optional. *Entrance requirements:* For master's, GRE General Test or MAT, minimum GPA of 2.75. *Application deadline:* Applications are processed on a rolling basis. Application fee: $15. *Expenses:* Tuition, state resident: part-time $700 per year. Tuition, nonresident: part-time $1,715 per year. *Financial support:* Federal Work-Study available. Support available to part-time students. Financial award application deadline: 5/1. *Unit head:* Dr. James Bowen, Dean, 580-327-8455.

Northwestern State University of Louisiana, Graduate Studies and Research, College of Education, Natchitoches, LA 71497. Offers M Ed, MA, MAT, Ed S. *Accreditation:* ACA (one or more programs are accredited); NCATE. *Faculty:* 23 full-time (13 women), 20 part-time/adjunct (14 women). *Students:* 139 full-time (117 women), 532 part-time (438 women); includes 220 minority (200 African Americans, 8 American Indian/Alaska Native, 3 Asian Americans or Pacific Islanders, 9 Hispanic Americans). Average age 35. In 2006, 183 master's, 11 other advanced degrees awarded. *Degree requirements:* For master's, thesis (for some programs), comprehensive exam, registration; for Ed S, thesis, comprehensive exam, registration. *Entrance requirements:* For master's, GRE General Test, GRE Subject Test, minimum undergraduate GPA of 2.5; for Ed S, GRE General Test. *Application deadline:* For fall admission, 8/1 priority date for domestic students; for spring admission, 1/10 for domestic students. Applications are processed on a rolling basis. Application fee: $20 ($30 for international students). *Financial support:* Career-related internships or fieldwork and Federal Work-Study available. Financial award application deadline: 7/15. *Unit head:* Dr. Vickie Gentry, Chair, 318-357-6288, Fax: 318-357-6275, E-mail: education@nsula.edu. *Application contact:* Dr. Steven G. Horton, Associate Provost/Dean, Graduate Studies, Research, and Information Systems, 318-357-5851, Fax: 318-357-5019, E-mail: grad_school@nsula.edu.

Northwestern University, The Graduate School, School of Education and Social Policy, Evanston, IL 60208. Offers education (MS), including advanced teaching, elementary education and policy, higher education administration, secondary teaching; human development and social policy (PhD); learning and organizational change (MS); learning sciences (MA, PhD). MA and PhD admissions and degrees offered through The Graduate School. Part-time and

Education—General

Northwestern University (continued)

evening/weekend programs available. *Faculty:* 37 full-time (13 women), 64 part-time/adjunct (34 women). *Students:* 159 full-time (102 women), 138 part-time (104 women); includes 48 minority (18 African Americans, 1 American Indian/Alaska Native, 20 Asian Americans or Pacific Islanders, 9 Hispanic Americans), 13 international. Average age 30. 200 applicants, 39% accepted, 61 enrolled. In 2006, 88 master's, 11 doctorates awarded. *Degree requirements:* For doctorate, thesis/dissertation, comprehensive exam. *Entrance requirements:* For master's and doctorate, GRE General Test. Application fee: $60 ($75 for international students). Electronic applications accepted. *Expenses:* Contact institution. *Financial support:* In 2006–07, 42 fellowships with full tuition reimbursements (averaging $24,096 per year), 20 research assistantships with full tuition reimbursements, 15 teaching assistantships with full tuition reimbursements (averaging $19,740 per year) were awarded; career-related internships or fieldwork, Federal Work-Study, institutionally sponsored loans, scholarships/grants, and tuition waivers (partial) also available. Financial award application deadline: 1/15; financial award applicants required to submit FAFSA. *Faculty research:* Technology, curriculum design, welfare, education reform, learning. Total annual research expenditures: $9 million. *Unit head:* Mark P. Hoffman, Graduate Student Advisor, 847-491-3790, Fax: 847-491-4664, E-mail: markhoffman@northwestern.edu. *Application contact:* 847-491-3790, Fax: 847-491-4664, E-mail: sesp@northwestern.edu.

See Close-Ups on pages 899 and 901.

Northwest Missouri State University, Graduate School, College of Education and Human Services, Maryville, MO 64468-6001. Offers MS, MS Ed, Ed S. *Accreditation:* NCATE. Part-time programs available. *Faculty:* 44 full-time (27 women). *Students:* 67 full-time (40 women), 237 part-time (172 women); includes 9 minority (6 African Americans, 1 Asian American or Pacific Islander, 2 Hispanic Americans), 1 international. 136 applicants, 52% accepted, 70 enrolled. In 2006, 83 master's, 17 other advanced degrees awarded. *Degree requirements:* For master's, comprehensive exam; for Ed S, thesis, comprehensive exam. *Entrance requirements:* For master's, GRE General Test, writing sample; for Ed S, minimum graduate GPA of 3.25. Additional exam requirements/recommendations for international students: Required—TOEFL (minimum score 550 paper-based; 213 computer-based). *Application deadline:* For fall admission, 7/1 for domestic and international students; for spring admission, 11/15 for domestic and international students. Application fee: $0 ($50 for international students). Electronic applications accepted. *Financial support:* In 2006–07, 16 research assistantships with full tuition reimbursements (averaging $6,000 per year), 35 teaching assistantships with full tuition reimbursements (averaging $6,000 per year) were awarded; unspecified assistantships also available. Financial award application deadline: 3/1; financial award applicants required to submit FAFSA. *Faculty research:* Great books of educational administration. *Unit head:* Dr. Max Ruhl, Dean, 660-562-1778. *Application contact:* Dr. Frances Shipley, Dean of Graduate School, 660-562-1145, Fax: 660-562-1096, E-mail: gradsch@nwmissouri.edu.

Northwest Nazarene University, Graduate Studies, Program in Teacher Education, Nampa, ID 83686-5897. Offers curriculum and instruction (M Ed); educational leadership (M Ed); exceptional child (M Ed); reading education (M Ed); school counseling (M Ed). *Accreditation:* ACA; NCATE. Part-time programs available. *Faculty:* 11 full-time (4 women), 10 part-time/adjunct (6 women). *Students:* 113 full-time (79 women), 20 part-time (18 women); includes 4 minority (2 Asian Americans or Pacific Islanders, 2 Hispanic Americans). Average age 34. In 2006, 35 degrees awarded. *Degree requirements:* For master's, action research project. *Entrance requirements:* For master's, minimum undergraduate GPA of 2.8 overall or 3.0 during final 30 semester credits. *Application deadline:* For fall admission, 9/1 for domestic students. Applications are processed on a rolling basis. Application fee: $25. *Faculty research:* Action research, cooperative learning, accountability, institutional accreditation. *Unit head:* Dr. Karen Blacklock, Chair, 208-467-8399, Fax: 208-467-8562.

Northwest University, School of Education, Kirkland, WA 98033. Offers teaching (MIT). Part-time and evening/weekend programs available. *Faculty:* 6 full-time (4 women), 4 part-time/adjunct (1 woman). *Students:* 16 full-time (13 women), 1 (woman) part-time; includes 3 minority (1 American Indian/Alaska Native, 1 Asian American or Pacific Islander, 1 Hispanic American). 20 applicants, 95% accepted, 17 enrolled. *Degree requirements:* For master's, action research project. *Entrance requirements:* For master's, WEST-B, WEST-E, 3.3 GPA, coursework complete in endorsement. *Application deadline:* For fall admission, 5/1 priority date for domestic students. Applications are processed on a rolling basis. Application fee: $75. *Expenses:* Contact institution. *Financial support:* Federal Work-Study and health care benefits available. *Unit head:* Dr. Gary Newbill, Dean, School of Education, 425-889-5272, E-mail: gary.newbill@northwestu.edu. *Application contact:* Pam Skolrud, Coordinator and Certification Specialist, School of Education, 425-889-5299, Fax: 425-889-6332, E-mail: pam.skolrud@northwestu.edu.

Norwich University, School of Graduate Studies, Program in Education, Northfield, VT 05663. Offers M Ed. Postbaccalaureate distance learning degree programs offered. *Entrance requirements:* Additional exam requirements/recommendations for international students: Required—TOEFL (minimum score 550 paper-based). *Application deadline:* For fall admission, 7/1 for domestic and international students; for winter admission, 11/1 for domestic and international students; for spring admission, 3/1 for domestic and international students. Application fee: $50. Electronic applications accepted. *Financial support:* Scholarships/grants available. *Unit head:* Dr. Linda Lucas, Unit Head, 802-485-2730.

Notre Dame College, Graduate Studies, South Euclid, OH 44121-4293. Offers accounting (Certificate); creative critical thinking (M Ed); financial services management (Certificate); information systems (Certificate); learning disabilities (M Ed); management (Certificate); paralegal (Certificate); pastoral ministry (Certificate); reading (M Ed); teacher education (Certificate). Part-time and evening/weekend programs available. *Degree requirements:* For master's, thesis. *Entrance requirements:* For master's, GRE General Test, MAT, minimum GPA of 2.75, valid teaching certificate. *Faculty research:* Cognitive psychology, teaching critical thinking in the classroom.

Notre Dame de Namur University, Division of Academic Affairs, School of Education and Leadership, Program in Education, Belmont, CA 94002-1908. Offers education (MA); teaching (MAT). *Expenses:* Tuition: Part-time $655 per credit. *Unit head:* Dr. Kim Tolley, Director, 650-508-3464. *Application contact:* Helen Valine, Director of Graduate Admissions, 650-508-3534, Fax: 650-508-3426, E-mail: grad.admit@ndnu.edu.

Nova Southeastern University, Fischler School of Education and Human Services, Fort Lauderdale, FL 33314-7796. Offers MA, MS, Ed D, SLPD, Ed S. Part-time and evening/weekend programs available. *Faculty:* 131 full-time (78 women), 548 part-time/adjunct (342 women). *Students:* 2,474 full-time (1,926 women), 7,291 part-time (5,895 women); includes 5,034 minority (3,835 African Americans, 24 American Indian/Alaska Native, 93 Asian Americans or Pacific Islanders, 1,082 Hispanic Americans), 207 international. Average age 38. 2,813 applicants, 79% accepted. In 2006, 2,192 master's, 489 doctorates, 425 other advanced degrees awarded. *Degree requirements:* For master's, practicum, internship; for doctorate and Ed S, thesis/dissertation; for Ed S, thesis, practicum, internship. *Entrance requirements:* For master's, MAT or GRE (for some programs), CLAST, PRAXIS I, CBEST, GKT, teaching certification, minimum GPA of 2.5, verification of teaching, BS degree; for doctorate, MAT or GRE, master's degree, minimum cumulative GPA of 3.0; for Ed S, MAT or GRE, master's degree, teaching certificate, minimum GPA of 3.0. Additional exam requirements/recommendations for international students: Recommended—TOEFL (minimum score 550 paper-based; 213 computer-based), IELTS (minimum score 6). *Application deadline:* For fall admission, 8/11 priority date for domestic and international students; for winter admission, 12/28 priority date for domestic and international students; for spring admission, 4/22 priority date for domestic and international students. Applications are processed on a rolling basis. Application fee: $50. Electronic applications accepted. *Financial support:* In 2006–07, 5,072 students received support, including 2 fellowships (averaging $9,375 per year); career-related

internships or fieldwork, Federal Work-Study, and tuition waivers (full) also available. Support available to part-time students. Financial award application deadline: 1/7. *Unit head:* Dr. H. Wells Singleton, Provost/Dean, 954-262-8730, Fax: 954-262-3912, E-mail: singlew@nova.edu. *Application contact:* Jennifer Quiñones Nottingham, Dean of Student Affairs, 800-986-3223 Ext. 8624, Fax: 954-262-3911, E-mail: jlquinon@nova.edu.

See Close-Up on page 903.

Nyack College, Graduate and Professional Programs, School of Education, Nyack, NY 10960-3698. Offers inclusive education (MS). Part-time and evening/weekend programs available. *Degree requirements:* For master's, thesis, field experience, comprehensive exam. *Entrance requirements:* For master's, GRE, baccalaureate degree with minimum GPA of 3.0, evidence of initial/provisional teaching certification. Additional exam requirements/recommendations for international students: Required—TOEFL (minimum score 500 paper-based), TWE (minimum score 4). *Expenses:* Contact institution.

Oakland City University, School of Education and Technology, Oakland City, IN 47660-1099. Offers educational leadership (Ed D); teaching (MA). *Accreditation:* NCATE. Terminal master's awarded for partial completion of doctoral program. *Degree requirements:* For master's, thesis/dissertation; for doctorate, thesis/dissertation, comprehensive exam. *Entrance requirements:* For master's, MAT, minimum GPA of 3.0, interview, resumé, letters of recommendation; for doctorate, MAT, GRE, minimum GPA of 3.2, interview, resumé, letters of recommendation. *Expenses:* Contact institution. *Faculty research:* Assessment, cultural diversity, teacher education, education leadership.

Oakland University, Graduate Study and Lifelong Learning, School of Education and Human Services, Rochester, MI 48309-4401. Offers M Ed, MA, MAT, MTD, PhD, Certificate, Ed S. Part-time and evening/weekend programs available. *Faculty:* 56 full-time (32 women), 44 part-time/adjunct (31 women). *Students:* 624 full-time (540 women), 1,262 part-time (1,060 women); includes 174 minority (124 African Americans, 9 American Indian/Alaska Native, 21 Asian Americans or Pacific Islanders, 20 Hispanic Americans), 14 international. Average age 34. 634 applicants, 88% accepted, 468 enrolled. In 2006, 454 master's, 18 doctorates, 140 other advanced degrees awarded. *Degree requirements:* For doctorate, thesis/dissertation. *Entrance requirements:* For master's and doctorate, minimum GPA of 3.0 for unconditional admission. Additional exam requirements/recommendations for international students: Required—TOEFL (minimum score 550 paper-based; 213 computer-based). *Application deadline:* Applications are processed on a rolling basis. Application fee: $35. Electronic applications accepted. *Expenses:* Tuition, state resident: full-time $9,936; part-time $414 per credit. Tuition, nonresident: full-time $17,202; part-time $716 per credit. *Financial support:* Career-related internships or fieldwork, Federal Work-Study, institutionally sponsored loans, and tuition waivers (full) available. Financial award application deadline: 3/1; financial award applicants required to submit FAFSA. *Faculty research:* Earth science for middle and high school teachers. *Unit head:* Dr. Mary L. Otto, Dean, 248-370-3050, Fax: 248-370-4202, E-mail: otto@oakland.edu.

Occidental College, Graduate Studies, Department of Education, Los Angeles, CA 90041-3314. Offers elementary education (MAT), including liberal studies; secondary education (MAT), including English and comparative literary studies, history, life science, mathematics, physical science, social science, Spanish. Part-time programs available. *Faculty:* 3 full-time (2 women), 2 part-time/adjunct (both women). *Students:* 7 full-time (6 women), 5 part-time (3 women); includes 7 minority (2 Asian Americans or Pacific Islanders, 5 Hispanic Americans). Average age 25. 9 applicants, 100% accepted, 7 enrolled. In 2006, 9 degrees awarded. *Degree requirements:* For master's, final exam, graduate synthesis paper. *Entrance requirements:* For master's, GRE General Test, minimum GPA of 3.0. Additional exam requirements/recommendations for international students: Required—TOEFL (minimum score 625 paper-based; 263 computer-based). *Application deadline:* For fall admission, 3/1 for domestic and international students; for spring admission, 10/1 for domestic and international students. Applications are processed on a rolling basis. Application fee: $50. *Expenses:* Contact institution. *Financial support:* Fellowships, Federal Work-Study, institutionally sponsored loans, and scholarships/grants available. Support available to part-time students. Financial award application deadline: 3/1; financial award applicants required to submit FAFSA. *Faculty research:* Preparing teacher-leaders, curriculum development. *Unit head:* Chair, 323-259-2781, E-mail: edudept@oxy.edu. *Application contact:* Angela Allen, Credential Analyst/Department Services Coordinator, 323-259-2781, E-mail: edudept@oxy.edu.

Oglethorpe University, Division of Education, Atlanta, GA 30319-2797. Offers early childhood education (MAT). Part-time programs available. *Degree requirements:* For master's, comprehensive exam. *Entrance requirements:* For master's, GRE General Test, PRAXIS, minimum GPA of 2.5.

Ohio Dominican University, Graduate Programs, Division of Education, Columbus, OH 43219-2099. Offers M Ed. Part-time and evening/weekend programs available. *Students:* 18 full-time (14 women), 69 part-time (56 women); includes 6 minority (4 African Americans, 1 Asian American or Pacific Islander, 1 Hispanic American). Average age 35. In 2006, 9 degrees awarded. *Degree requirements:* For master's, thesis or alternative, registration. *Entrance requirements:* For master's, minimum undergraduate GPA of 3.0, teaching certificate, teaching experience, 3 letters of recommendation. Additional exam requirements/recommendations for international students: Required—TOEFL (minimum score 550 paper-based; 213 computer-based). *Application deadline:* For fall admission, 8/15 priority date for domestic and international students; for spring admission, 1/13 priority date for domestic and international students. Applications are processed on a rolling basis. Application fee: $25. *Expenses:* Tuition: Part-time $450 per credit. Required fees: $10 per semester. *Financial support:* Applicants required to submit FAFSA. *Unit head:* Dr. Mary Todd, Vice President for Academic Affairs, 614-251-4731, Fax: 614-251-4772, E-mail: toddm@ohiodominican.edu. *Application contact:* Jill M. Westerfeld, Graduate Admissions Recruiter, 614-251-4725, Fax: 614-251-4634, E-mail: westerfj@ohiodominican.edu.

The Ohio State University, Graduate School, College of Education and Human Ecology, Columbus, OH 43210. Offers M Ed, MA, MS, PhD. *Accreditation:* NCATE. *Faculty:* 178. *Students:* 829 full-time (612 women), 844 part-time (645 women); includes 222 minority (162 African Americans, 5 American Indian/Alaska Native, 32 Asian Americans or Pacific Islanders, 23 Hispanic Americans), 197 international. Average age 33. 868 applicants, 59% accepted, 187 enrolled. In 2006, 735 master's, 112 doctorates awarded. Terminal master's awarded for partial completion of doctoral program. *Degree requirements:* For master's, thesis optional; for doctorate, thesis/dissertation, comprehensive exam. *Entrance requirements:* For doctorate, GRE. Additional exam requirements/recommendations for international students: Required—TOEFL (minimum score 600 paper-based; 250 computer-based). *Application deadline:* For fall admission, 8/15 priority date for domestic students, 7/1 priority date for international students; for winter admission, 12/1 priority date for domestic students, 11/1 priority date for international students; for spring admission, 3/1 priority date for domestic students, 2/1 priority date for international students. Applications are processed on a rolling basis. Application fee: $40 ($50 for international students). Electronic applications accepted. *Expenses:* Tuition, state resident: full-time $9,438. Tuition, nonresident: full-time $22,791. Tuition and fees vary according to course load, campus/location and program. *Financial support:* Fellowships with tuition reimbursements, research assistantships with tuition reimbursements, teaching assistantships with tuition reimbursements, career-related internships or fieldwork, Federal Work-Study, institutionally sponsored loans, scholarships/grants, traineeships, health care benefits, and unspecified assistantships available. Support available to part-time students. *Faculty research:* Math and science education; teach professional development; issues related to urban education; health, well-being, and sports; literacy education. Total annual research expenditures: $19 million. *Unit head:* Dr. David Andrews, Dean, 614-292-2801, Fax: 614-292-2581, E-mail: andrews.128@osu.edu. *Application contact:* 614-292-9444, Fax: 614-292-3895, E-mail: domestic.grad@osu.edu.

See Close-Up on page 905.

The Ohio State University at Lima, Graduate Programs, Lima, OH 45804. Offers early childhood education (M Ed); education (MA); middle childhood education (M Ed); social work (MSW). *Students:* 46 full-time (37 women), 32 part-time (27 women), 1 international. Average age 30. *Degree requirements:* For master's, thesis (for some programs), comprehensive exam (for some programs). *Entrance requirements:* For master's, GRE, minimum GPA of 3.0. Additional exam requirements/recommendations for international students: Required—TOEFL, IELTS or Michigan English Language Assessment Battery. *Application deadline:* For fall admission, 8/15 priority date for domestic students, 7/1 priority date for international students; for winter admission, 12/1 priority date for domestic students, 11/1 priority date for international students; for spring admission, 3/1 priority date for domestic students, 2/1 priority date for international students. Applications are processed on a rolling basis. Application fee: $40 ($50 for international students). Electronic applications accepted. *Expenses:* Tuition, state resident: full-time $8,919. Tuition, nonresident: full-time $22,272. Tuition and fees vary according to course load, campus/location and program. *Unit head:* Dr. John Snyder, Dean/Director, 419-995-8481, E-mail: snyder.4@osu.edu. *Application contact:* Graduate Admissions, 614-292-9444, Fax: 614-292-3895, E-mail: domestic.grad@osu.edu.

The Ohio State University at Marion, Graduate Programs, Marion, OH 43302-5695. Offers early childhood education (pre-K to grade 3) (M Ed); integrated teaching and learning (MA); middle childhood education (grades 4-9) (M Ed); nursing (MS, PhD); social work (MSW); MS/PhD. *Students:* 63 full-time (56 women), 43 part-time (41 women); includes 2 minority (both African Americans), 1 international. Average age 32. *Degree requirements:* For master's, thesis (for some programs), comprehensive exam (for some programs). *Entrance requirements:* For master's and doctorate, GRE, minimum undergraduate GPA of 3.0. Additional exam requirements/recommendations for international students: Required—TOEFL, IELTS or Michigan English Language Assessment Battery. *Application deadline:* For fall admission, 8/15 priority date for domestic students, 7/1 priority date for international students; for winter admission, 12/1 priority date for domestic students, 11/1 priority date for international students; for spring admission, 3/1 priority date for domestic students, 2/1 priority date for international students. Applications are processed on a rolling basis. Application fee: $40 ($50 for international students). Electronic applications accepted. *Expenses:* Tuition, state resident: full-time $8,919. Tuition, nonresident: full-time $22,272. Tuition and fees vary according to course load, campus/location and program. *Unit head:* Gregory S. Rose, Dean/Director, 740-389-6786 Ext. 6218, E-mail: rose.9@osu.edu. *Application contact:* Graduate Admissions, 614-292-9444, Fax: 614-292-3895, E-mail: domestic.grad@osu.edu.

The Ohio State University–Newark Campus, Graduate Programs, Newark, OH 43055-1797. Offers early/middle childhood education (M Ed); integrated teaching and learning (MA); social work (MSW). *Students:* 31 full-time (25 women), 39 part-time (34 women); includes 3 minority (1 African American, 1 Asian American or Pacific Islander, 1 Hispanic American), 1 international. Average age 33. *Degree requirements:* For master's, thesis (for some programs), comprehensive exam (for some programs). *Entrance requirements:* For master's, GRE, minimum GPA of 3.0. Additional exam requirements/recommendations for international students: Required—TOEFL, IELTS or Michigan English Language Assessment Battery. *Application deadline:* For fall admission, 8/15 priority date for domestic students, 7/1 priority date for international students; for winter admission, 12/1 priority date for domestic students, 11/1 priority date for international students; for spring admission, 3/1 priority date for domestic students, 2/1 priority date for international students. Applications are processed on a rolling basis. Application fee: $40 ($50 for international students). Electronic applications accepted. *Expenses:* Tuition, state resident: full-time $8,919. Tuition, nonresident: full-time $22,272. Tuition and fees vary according to course level, campus/location and program. *Unit head:* Dr. William L. MacDonald, Dean/Director, 740-366-9333 Ext. 330, E-mail: macdonald.24@osu.edu. *Application contact:* Graduate Admissions, 614-292-9444, Fax: 614-292-3985, E-mail: domestic.grad@osu.edu.

Ohio University, Graduate Studies, College of Education, Athens, OH 45701-2979. Offers M Ed, Ed D, PhD. *Accreditation:* NCATE. Part-time and evening/weekend programs available. *Faculty:* 44 full-time (25 women), 21 part-time/adjunct (8 women). *Students:* 257 full-time (174 women), 218 part-time (147 women); includes 29 minority (23 African Americans, 2 Asian Americans or Pacific Islanders, 4 Hispanic Americans), 157 international. 423 applicants, 64% accepted, 192 enrolled. In 2006, 52 master's, 21 doctorates awarded. *Median time to degree:* Of those who began their doctoral program in fall 1998, 92% received their degree in 8 years or less. *Degree requirements:* For master's, thesis or alternative, registration; for doctorate, thesis/dissertation, comprehensive exam, registration. *Entrance requirements:* For master's, GRE General Test or MAT; for doctorate, GRE General Test, MAT, minimum GPA of 3.0, work experience. Additional exam requirements/recommendations for international students: Required—TOEFL (minimum score 550 paper-based; 213 computer-based). *Application deadline:* Applications are processed on a rolling basis. Application fee: $45. Electronic applications accepted. *Financial support:* In 2006–07, 164 students received support, including 100 research assistantships with full tuition reimbursements available (averaging $6,500 per year), 8 teaching assistantships with full tuition reimbursements available (averaging $7,200 per year); Federal Work-Study, institutionally sponsored loans, tuition waivers (full), and unspecified assistantships also available. Financial award application deadline: 3/15. *Faculty research:* School improvement, comprehensive partnerships, literacy. Total annual research expenditures: $1.3 million. *Unit head:* Dr. Ren'ee A. Middleton, Dean, 740-593-4403, E-mail: middletonr@ohio.edu. *Application contact:* Floyd J. Doney, Director of Student Affairs, 740-593-4400, Fax: 740-593-9310, E-mail: doney@ohio.edu.

Oklahoma City University, Petree College of Arts and Sciences, Division of Education and Kinesiology Exercise Studies, Oklahoma City, OK 73106-1402. Offers M Ed, MA. Part-time and evening/weekend programs available. *Faculty:* 5 full-time (3 women), 14 part-time/adjunct (9 women). *Students:* 66 full-time (53 women), 25 part-time (19 women); includes 8 minority (4 African Americans, 3 Asian Americans or Pacific Islanders, 1 Hispanic American), 54 international. Average age 33. 30 applicants, 77% accepted. In 2006, 41 degrees awarded. *Degree requirements:* For master's, thesis optional. *Entrance requirements:* For master's, minimum GPA of 3.0, two satisfactory letters of recommendation. Additional exam requirements/recommendations for international students: Required—TOEFL (minimum score 550 paper-based; 213 computer-based). *Application deadline:* For fall admission, 8/22 for domestic students; for spring admission, 1/15 for domestic students. Applications are processed on a rolling basis. Application fee: $35 ($70 for international students). *Expenses:* Tuition: Full-time $12,780; part-time $710 per hour. Required fees: $89 per hour. *Financial support:* Fellowships with partial tuition reimbursements, career-related internships or fieldwork, Federal Work-Study, institutionally sponsored loans, and tuition waivers (full and partial) available. Support available to part-time students. Financial award application deadline: 8/1; financial award applicants required to submit FAFSA. *Unit head:* Chair, 405-208-5368, Fax: 405-208-5447. *Application contact:* Leslie McKenzie, Director, Graduate Admissions, 800-633-7242, Fax: 405-208-5356, E-mail: gadmissions@okcu.edu.

Oklahoma State University, College of Education, Stillwater, OK 74078. Offers MS, Ed D, PhD, Ed S. *Accreditation:* NCATE. *Faculty:* 98 full-time (55 women), 63 part-time/adjunct (36 women). *Students:* 257 full-time (186 women), 551 part-time (369 women); includes 152 minority (52 African Americans, 63 American Indian/Alaska Native, 15 Asian Americans or Pacific Islanders, 22 Hispanic Americans), 47 international. Average age 37. 535 applicants, 33% accepted, 141 enrolled. In 2006, 137 master's, 63 doctorates awarded. *Degree requirements:* For master's, thesis or alternative; for doctorate, thesis/dissertation. *Entrance requirements:* For master's, GRE or MAT; for doctorate, GRE (PhD). Additional exam requirements/recommendations for international students: Required—TOEFL. *Application deadline:* For fall admission, 3/1 priority date for international students; for spring admission, 8/1 priority date for international students. Applications are processed on a rolling basis. Application fee: $40 ($75 for international students). Electronic applications accepted. *Expenses:* Tuition, state resident: part-time $146 per credit hour. Tuition, nonresident: part-time $516 per credit hour. Required fees: $44 per credit hour. Tuition and fees vary according to program. *Financial support:* In 2006–07, 52 research assistantships (averaging $7,658 per year), 90 teaching assistantships (averaging $8,353 per year) were awarded; career-related internships or fieldwork, Federal Work-Study, scholarships/grants, health care benefits, tuition waivers (partial), and unspecified assistantships also available. Support available to part-time students. Financial award application deadline: 3/1. *Unit head:* Dr. Pamela Fry, Dean, 405-744-3373.

Old Dominion University, Darden College of Education, Norfolk, VA 23529. Offers MS, MS Ed, PhD, Ed S. *Accreditation:* NCATE. Part-time and evening/weekend programs available. Postbaccalaureate distance learning degree programs offered (no on-campus study). *Faculty:* 93 full-time (50 women), 65 part-time/adjunct (44 women). *Students:* 453 full-time (359 women), 961 part-time (720 women); includes 207 minority (173 African Americans, 9 American Indian/Alaska Native, 17 Asian Americans or Pacific Islanders, 8 Hispanic Americans), 17 international. Average age 34. 1,125 applicants, 72% accepted. In 2006, 606 master's, 7 doctorates, 11 other advanced degrees awarded. *Degree requirements:* For master's, thesis (for some programs), exam, comprehensive exam (for some programs); for doctorate, thesis/dissertation, comprehensive exam. *Entrance requirements:* For doctorate, GRE General Test, master's degree, minimum GPA of 3.25; for Ed S, GRE General Test or MAT. Additional exam requirements/recommendations for international students: Required—TOEFL (minimum score 550 paper-based). *Application deadline:* For fall admission, 6/1 priority date for domestic students; for spring admission, 11/1 priority date for domestic students. Applications are processed on a rolling basis. Application fee: $40. Electronic applications accepted. *Expenses:* Tuition, area resident: Part-time $285 per credit hour. Tuition, nonresident: part-time $715 per credit hour. Required fees: $94 per semester. *Financial support:* In 2006–07, 4 fellowships with full and partial tuition reimbursements (averaging $15,000 per year), 60 research assistantships with full and partial tuition reimbursements (averaging $9,000 per year), 25 teaching assistantships with full and partial tuition reimbursements (averaging $9,000 per year) were awarded; career-related internships or fieldwork, Federal Work-Study, institutionally sponsored loans, scholarships/grants, tuition waivers (partial), and unspecified assistantships also available. Support available to part-time students. Financial award application deadline: 2/15; financial award applicants required to submit CSS PROFILE or FAFSA. *Faculty research:* Effective urban teaching practices, curriculum theory, clinical practices, special education, instructional technology. Total annual research expenditures: $8.1 million. *Unit head:* Dr. William H. Graves, Dean, 757-683-3938, Fax: 757-683-5083, E-mail: wgraves@odu.edu.

Olivet College, Program in Education, Olivet, MI 49076-9701. Offers MAT. *Degree requirements:* For master's, portfolio. *Entrance requirements:* For master's, current K-12 teacher certification. Electronic applications accepted.

Olivet Nazarene University, Graduate School, Division of Education, Bourbonnais, IL 60914-2271. Offers curriculum and instruction (MAE); elementary education (MAT); secondary education (MAT). *Accreditation:* NCATE. Evening/weekend programs available. *Degree requirements:* For master's, thesis or alternative.

Oral Roberts University, School of Education, Tulsa, OK 74171-0001. Offers Christian school administration (MA Ed, Ed D); Christian school administration (K-12) (MA Ed, Ed D); Christian school curriculum development (MA Ed); college and higher education administration (MA Ed, Ed D); public school administration (K-12) (MA Ed, Ed D); public school teaching (MA Ed); teaching English as a second language (MA Ed). *Accreditation:* NCATE. Part-time programs available. Postbaccalaureate distance learning degree programs offered (minimal on-campus study). *Faculty:* 9 full-time (2 women), 9 part-time/adjunct (4 women). *Students:* 331 full-time (217 women); includes 118 minority (96 African Americans, 7 American Indian/Alaska Native, 10 Asian Americans or Pacific Islanders, 5 Hispanic Americans). 125 applicants, 96% accepted, 116 enrolled. In 2006, 25 master's, 10 doctorates awarded. *Degree requirements:* For master's, thesis (for some programs), comprehensive exam; for doctorate, thesis/dissertation, comprehensive exam. *Entrance requirements:* For master's, GRE General Test or MAT, minimum GPA of 3.0; for doctorate, minimum GPA of 3.0. Additional exam requirements/recommendations for international students: Required—TOEFL (minimum score 500 paper-based; 173 computer-based). *Application deadline:* For fall admission, 7/1 priority date for domestic students, 5/1 priority date for international students; for spring admission, 12/1 priority date for domestic students, 10/1 priority date for international students. Applications are processed on a rolling basis. Application fee: $35. *Expenses:* Contact institution. *Financial support:* In 2006–07, 4 research assistantships (averaging $5,000 per year) were awarded; scholarships/grants and unspecified assistantships also available. Financial award application deadline: 6/1; financial award applicants required to submit FAFSA. *Faculty research:* Teacher effectiveness, college success in high achieving, African-Americans, professional development practices. *Unit head:* Dr. David Hand, Dean, 918-495-7084, Fax: 918-495-6050, E-mail: dhand@oru.edu. *Application contact:* Kim Schmeisser, Graduate Admissions, 918-495-6058, Fax: 918-495-6222, E-mail: gradeducation@oru.edu.

Oregon State University, Graduate School, College of Education, Program in General Education, Corvallis, OR 97331. Offers Ed M, MAIS, MS, Ed D, PhD. Part-time programs available. *Students:* 21 full-time (13 women), 117 part-time (78 women); includes 25 minority (8 African Americans, 2 American Indian/Alaska Native, 7 Asian Americans or Pacific Islanders, 8 Hispanic Americans), 4 international. Average age 46. In 2006, 12 master's, 12 doctorates awarded. Terminal master's awarded for partial completion of doctoral program. *Degree requirements:* For master's, variable foreign language requirement, thesis (for some programs); for doctorate, variable foreign language requirement, thesis/dissertation. *Entrance requirements:* For master's, California Basic Educational Skills Test, NTE, minimum GPA of 3.0 in last 90 hours of course work; for doctorate, GRE or MAT, master's degree, minimum GPA of 3.0 in last 90 hours of course work. Additional exam requirements/recommendations for international students: Required—TOEFL. *Application deadline:* For fall admission, 3/1 priority date for domestic students. Applications are processed on a rolling basis. Application fee: $50. *Financial support:* Fellowships, research assistantships, teaching assistantships, career-related internships or fieldwork, Federal Work-Study, and institutionally sponsored loans available. Support available to part-time students. Financial award application deadline: 2/1. *Faculty research:* School administration, educational foundations, research methodology, education policy development, higher education administration. *Unit head:* Dr. Kenneth J. Winograd, Chair, 541-737-4661.

Oregon State University–Cascades, Program in Education, Bend, OR 97701. Offers MAT.

Ottawa University, Graduate Studies-Arizona, Program in Education, Ottawa, KS 66067-3399. Offers community college counseling (MA); curriculum and instruction (MA); early childhood (MA); education intervention (MA); education leadership (MA); education technology (MA); Montessori early childhood education (MA); Montessori elementary education (MA); professional development (MA); school guidance counseling (MA); special education—cross categorical (MA). Programs offered in Mesa, Phoenix, Tempe and West Valley, AZ. *Accreditation:* NCATE. Part-time programs available. *Faculty:* 7 full-time (3 women), 24 part-time/adjunct (11 women). *Students:* 14 full-time (9 women), 162 part-time (128 women); includes 31 minority (13 African Americans, 2 American Indian/Alaska Native, 1 Asian American or Pacific Islander, 15 Hispanic Americans), 1 international. Average age 38. In 2006, 56 degrees awarded. *Degree requirements:* For master's, thesis or alternative, registration. *Entrance requirements:* For master's, minimum undergraduate GPA of 3.0, copy of current state certification or teaching license. Additional exam requirements/recommendations for international students: Required—TOEFL (minimum score 550 paper-based; 213 computer-based). *Application deadline:* For fall admission, 7/1 priority date for domestic students; for winter admission, 11/1 priority date for domestic students; for spring admission, 2/1 priority date for domestic students. Applications are processed on a rolling basis. Application fee: $50. Electronic applications accepted. *Expenses:* Contact institution. *Application contact:* Bunny Simpson, Secretary, 602-371-1188, Fax: 602-371-0035, E-mail: bunny.simpson@ottawa.edu.

Otterbein College, Department of Education, Westerville, OH 43081. Offers MAE, MAT. *Accreditation:* NCATE. *Students:* 24 full-time, 65 part-time. Average age 34. In 2006, 27 degrees awarded. *Degree requirements:* For master's, capstone project. *Entrance requirements:* For master's, official transcripts, 2 reference forms. Additional exam requirements/

Education—General

Otterbein College (continued)
recommendations for international students: Required—TOEFL (minimum score 550 paper-based; 213 computer-based; 79 iBT). *Application deadline:* Applications are processed on a rolling basis. Application fee: $0. *Expenses:* Tuition: Full-time $7,560; part-time $315 per credit. Tuition and fees vary according to program. *Financial support:* Unspecified assistantships available. Support available to part-time students. Financial award applicants required to submit FAFSA. *Faculty research:* Computer technology middle level education, assessment, teacher leadership, multicultural education. *Unit head:* Dr. Harriet Fayne, Chair, 614-823-1788, Fax: 614-823-3036, E-mail: hfayne@otterbein.edu. *Application contact:* Deb Williams, Administrative Assistant, Office of Graduate Programs, 614-823-3210, Fax: 614-823-3208, E-mail: grad@otterbein.edu.

Our Lady of Holy Cross College, Program in Education and Counseling, New Orleans, LA 70131-7399. Offers administration and supervision (M Ed); curriculum and instruction (M Ed); marriage and family counseling (MA); school counseling (M Ed, MA). *Accreditation:* ACA; NCATE. Part-time and evening/weekend programs available. *Degree requirements:* For master's, thesis. *Entrance requirements:* For master's, GRE General Test, minimum GPA of 2.7.

Our Lady of the Lake University of San Antonio, School of Education and Clinical Studies, San Antonio, TX 78207-4689. Offers communication and learning disorders (MA); counseling psychology (MS, Psy D), including counseling psychology, marriage and family therapy (MS), school psychology (MS); curriculum and instruction (M Ed); human sciences (MA); leadership studies (PhD); learning resources (M Ed); principal (M Ed); school counseling (M Ed); sociology (MA); special education (MA). Part-time and evening/weekend programs available. *Degree requirements:* For master's, comprehensive exam; for doctorate, thesis/dissertation, internship, qualifying exam. *Entrance requirements:* For master's, GRE General Test or MAT; for doctorate, GRE General Test or MAT, interview. Additional exam requirements/recommendations for international students: Required—TOEFL. Electronic applications accepted.

Pace University, School of Education, New York, NY 10038. Offers administration and supervision (MS Ed); curriculum and instruction (MS); education (MST); school business management (Certificate). *Accreditation:* NCATE. Part-time and evening/weekend programs available. *Faculty:* 9 full-time, 12 part-time/adjunct. *Students:* 130 full-time (106 women), 2,151 part-time (1,484 women); includes 96 minority (50 African Americans, 2 American Indian/Alaska Native, 21 Asian Americans or Pacific Islanders, 23 Hispanic Americans), 6 international. Average age 27. 229 applicants, 70% accepted, 70 enrolled. In 2006, 550 master's, 23 other advanced degrees awarded. *Degree requirements:* For master's, internship. *Entrance requirements:* For master's, interview, teaching certificate. *Application deadline:* For fall admission, 7/31 priority date for domestic students; for spring admission, 11/30 for domestic students. Applications are processed on a rolling basis. Application fee: $65. Electronic applications accepted. *Expenses: Contact institution. Financial support:* Research assistantships, career-related internships or fieldwork and Federal Work-Study available. Support available to part-time students. Financial award applicants required to submit FAFSA. *Unit head:* Dr. Harriet Feldman, Interim Dean, 212-346-1512. *Application contact:* Joanna Broda, Director of Admissions, 212-346-1652, Fax: 212-346-1585, E-mail: gradnyc@pace.edu.

See Close-Up on page 907.

Pacific Lutheran University, Division of Graduate Studies, School of Education, Tacoma, WA 98447. Offers MA. *Accreditation:* NCATE. Part-time and evening/weekend programs available. *Faculty:* 5 full-time (2 women), 3 part-time/adjunct (2 women). *Students:* 32 full-time (19 women), 19 part-time (15 women); includes 7 minority (2 African Americans, 4 Asian Americans or Pacific Islanders, 1 Hispanic American), 1 international. Average age 29. 65 applicants, 100% accepted, 46 enrolled. In 2006, 67 degrees awarded. *Degree requirements:* For master's, thesis optional. *Entrance requirements:* For master's, GRE General Test or MAT, interview. Additional exam requirements/recommendations for international students: Required—TOEFL (minimum score 550 paper-based; 213 computer-based). *Application deadline:* Applications are processed on a rolling basis. Application fee: $40. *Expenses:* Tuition: Full-time $17,544. Part-time tuition and fees vary according to program. *Financial support:* In 2006–07, 42 students received support, including 17 fellowships (averaging $47,500 per year); Federal Work-Study, scholarships/grants, and unspecified assistantships also available. Financial award application deadline: 3/1. *Unit head:* Dr. John Lee, Dean, 253-535-7272. *Application contact:* Linda DuBay, Senior Office Assistant, 253-535-7151, Fax: 253-536-5136, E-mail: admissions@plu.edu.

Pacific Union College, Department of Education, Angwin, CA 94508-9707. Offers teacher leadership (M Ed). Part-time programs available. *Faculty:* 4 full-time (2 women). *Students:* 4 full-time (all women), 14 part-time (10 women); includes 3 minority (all Asian Americans or Pacific Islanders) Average age 29. 5 applicants, 100% accepted. In 2006, 6 degrees awarded. *Median time to degree:* Master's–1 year full-time, 4 years part-time. *Degree requirements:* For master's, thesis, action research project. *Entrance requirements:* For master's, GRE, interview, teaching credential, letters of recommendation. *Application deadline:* For fall admission, 7/1 priority date for domestic students. Applications are processed on a rolling basis. Application fee: $0. *Expenses:* Tuition: Full-time $20,130; part-time $584 per quarter hour. Required fees: $135. Tuition and fees vary according to course load and student's religious affiliation. *Financial support:* In 2006–07, 2 students received support, including 2 teaching assistantships with full tuition reimbursements available (averaging $2,600 per year); Federal Work-Study, scholarships/grants, and unspecified assistantships also available. Support available to part-time students. Financial award application deadline: 3/1. *Faculty research:* Glasser biography and development of choice theory, reading instruction competence, teacher excellence, alternative assessments for high school teachers, educational psychology. *Unit head:* Dr. Jim Roy, Chair, 707-965-6644, Fax: 707-965-6645, E-mail: jroy@puc.edu. *Application contact:* Marsha Crow, Credential Analyst, 707-965-6643, Fax: 707-965-6645, E-mail: mcrow@puc.edu.

Pacific University, College of Education, Forest Grove, OR 97116-1797. Offers early childhood education (MAT); education (MAE); elementary education (MAT); high school education (MAT); middle school education (MAT); special education (MAT); visual function in learning (M Ed). Part-time and evening/weekend programs available. *Faculty:* 20 full-time (12 women), 40 part-time/adjunct (21 women). *Students:* 222 full-time (151 women), 115 part-time (90 women); includes 30 minority (3 African Americans, 5 American Indian/Alaska Native, 12 Asian Americans or Pacific Islanders, 10 Hispanic Americans). Average age 32. 92 applicants, 83% accepted, 69 enrolled. In 2006, 257 degrees awarded. *Degree requirements:* For master's, research project. *Entrance requirements:* For master's, California Basic Educational Skills Test, Praxis I, minimum undergraduate GPA of 2.75, 3.0 graduate. Additional exam requirements/recommendations for international students: Required—TOEFL. *Application deadline:* For fall admission, 6/15 priority date for domestic students; for spring admission, 10/15 for domestic students. Applications are processed on a rolling basis. Application fee: $35. Electronic applications accepted. *Expenses: Contact institution. Financial support:* In 2006–07, 287 students received support; fellowships, research assistantships, teaching assistantships, career-related internships or fieldwork, institutionally sponsored loans, and scholarships/grants available. Support available to part-time students. Financial award application deadline: 5/1; financial award applicants required to submit FAFSA. *Faculty research:* Defining a culturally competent classroom, technology in the k-12 classroom, Socratic seminars, social studies education. *Unit head:* Dr. Mark Ankeny, Acting Dean, 503-352-2102, E-mail: mankeny@pacificu.edu. *Application contact:* Diana Watkins, Assistant Director Graduate and Professional Admissions, 503-352-2958, Fax: 503-352-2907, E-mail: teach@pacificu.edu.

Palm Beach Atlantic University, School of Education and Behavioral Studies, West Palm Beach, FL 33416-4708. Offers counseling psychology (MSCP), including addictions/mental health, marriage and family therapy, mental health counseling, school guidance counseling; elementary education (M Ed). Part-time and evening/weekend programs available. *Faculty:* 13 full-time (3 women), 6 part-time/adjunct (5 women). *Students:* 211 full-time (169 women), 66 part-time (55 women); includes 103 minority (61 African Americans, 4 Asian Americans or Pacific Islanders, 38 Hispanic Americans), 7 international. Average age 36. 98 applicants, 71% accepted, 51 enrolled. In 2006, 49 degrees awarded. *Entrance requirements:* For master's, GRE General Test, minimum GPA of 3.0 in last 60 hours of course work. Additional exam requirements/recommendations for international students: Required—TOEFL (minimum score 550 paper-based; 213 computer-based). *Application deadline:* For fall admission, 7/15 priority date for domestic students; for spring admission, 11/15 priority date for domestic students. Applications are processed on a rolling basis. Application fee: $35. Electronic applications accepted. *Expenses:* Tuition: Full-time $10,665; part-time $395 per credit. Required fees: $90 per semester. *Financial support:* Unspecified assistantships available. Support available to part-time students. Financial award applicants required to submit FAFSA. *Unit head:* Dr. Melise Bunker, Dean, 561-803-2350, Fax: 561-803-2186, E-mail: melise_bunker@pba.edu. *Application contact:* Laura A. Leinweber, Director of Graduate and Evening Admissions, 888-468-6722, Fax: 561-803-2115, E-mail: grad@pba.edu.

Park University, College of Graduate and Professional Studies, Kansas City, MO 54105. Offers adult education (M Ed); at-risk students (M Ed); disaster and emergency management (MPA); educational administration (M Ed); entrepreneurship (MBA); general business (MBA); general education (M Ed); government/business relations (MPA); healthcare/services management (MBA, MPA); international business (MBA); K-12 certification (MAT); management information systems (MBA); management of information systems (MPA); middle school certification (MAT); multi-cultural education (M Ed); nonprofit management (MPA); public management (MPA); school law (M Ed); secondary school certification (MAT); special education (M Ed). Part-time and evening/weekend programs available. Postbaccalaureate distance learning degree programs offered (no on-campus study). *Degree requirements:* For master's, thesis (for some programs), comprehensive exam, registration. *Entrance requirements:* For master's, GRE, GMAT, teacher certification (M Ed). Additional exam requirements/recommendations for international students: Required—TOEFL (minimum score 550 paper-based). Electronic applications accepted. *Faculty research:* Literacy, leadership, brain based research, multicultural education, diversity.

Penn State Great Valley, Graduate Studies, Education Division, Malvern, PA 19355-1488. Offers curriculum and instruction (M Ed); instructional systems (M Ed, MS); special education (M Ed, MS). *Unit head:* Dr. Arlene Mitchell, Academic Division Head, 610-648-3355, E-mail: ahm13@psu.edu. *Application contact:* Dr. Arlene Mitchell, Academic Division Head, 610-648-3355, E-mail: ahm13@psu.edu.

Penn State Harrisburg, Graduate School, School of Behavioral Sciences and Education, Middletown, PA 17057-4898. Offers adult education (D Ed); applied behavior analysis (MA); applied clinical psychology (MA); applied psychological research (MA); community psychology and social change (MA); health education (M Ed); teaching and curriculum (M Ed); training and development (M Ed). Part-time and evening/weekend programs available. *Expenses:* Tuition, state resident: full-time $13,224; part-time $551 per credit. Tuition, nonresident: full-time $18,652; part-time $777 per credit. Required fees: $84 per semester. *Financial support:* Career-related internships or fieldwork available. *Unit head:* Dr. William D. Milheim, Director, 717-948-6205, Fax: 717-948-6209, E-mail: wdm2@psu.edu.

Penn State University Park, Graduate School, College of Education, State College, University Park, PA 16802-1503. Offers M Ed, MA, MS, D Ed, PhD. *Accreditation:* NCATE. *Students:* 509 full-time (333 women), 316 part-time (182 women); includes 127 minority (64 African Americans, 8 American Indian/Alaska Native, 28 Asian Americans or Pacific Islanders, 27 Hispanic Americans), 144 international. Average age 35. 746 applicants, 49% accepted, 207 enrolled. In 2006, 199 master's, 101 doctorates awarded. *Application deadline:* Applications are processed on a rolling basis. Electronic applications accepted. *Financial support:* In 2006–07, 38 fellowships, 36 research assistantships, 146 teaching assistantships were awarded. Financial award applicants required to submit FAFSA. *Unit head:* Dr. David H. Monk, Dean, 814-865-2526, Fax: 814-865-0555, E-mail: dhm6@psu.edu. *Application contact:* Cynthia E. Nicosia, Director Graduate Enrollment Services, 814-865-1834, Fax: 814-865-4627, E-mail: cey1@psu.edu.

Pepperdine University, Graduate School of Education and Psychology, Division of Education, Los Angeles, CA 90045. Offers MA, MS, Ed D. Part-time and evening/weekend programs available. Postbaccalaureate distance learning degree programs offered (minimal on-campus study). *Faculty:* 32 full-time (17 women), 32 part-time/adjunct (22 women). *Students:* 275 full-time (225 women), 502 part-time (284 women); includes 252 minority (93 African Americans, 3 American Indian/Alaska Native, 62 Asian Americans or Pacific Islanders, 94 Hispanic Americans), 26 international. 394 applicants, 86% accepted, 291 enrolled. In 2006, 413 master's, 52 doctorates awarded. *Degree requirements:* For doctorate, thesis/dissertation. *Entrance requirements:* For master's, GRE General Test; for doctorate, GRE General Test, MAT. Additional exam requirements/recommendations for international students: Required—TOEFL. *Application deadline:* Applications are processed on a rolling basis. Application fee: $45. *Expenses: Contact institution. Financial support:* Research assistantships, teaching assistantships, career-related internships or fieldwork, institutionally sponsored loans, and scholarships/grants available. Support available to part-time students. Financial award application deadline: 7/1; financial award applicants required to submit FAFSA. *Unit head:* Dr. Chester McCall, Associate Dean, 310-568-2323, E-mail: chester.mccall@pepperdine.edu. *Application contact:* Anne McLintock, Admissions Specialist, 310-258-2848, E-mail: anne.mclintock@pepperdine.edu.

See Close-Up on page 909.

Peru State College, Graduate Studies, Program in Education, Peru, NE 68421. Offers MS Ed. *Accreditation:* NCATE. Part-time programs available. *Degree requirements:* For master's, thesis optional. *Entrance requirements:* For master's, MAT.

Pfeiffer University, School of Education, Misenheimer, NC 28109-0960. Offers elementary education (MS); teaching (MAT). *Accreditation:* NCATE. *Faculty:* 4 full-time (3 women), 2 part-time/adjunct (1 woman). *Students:* 5 full-time (all women), 60 part-time (52 women); includes 22 minority (21 African Americans, 1 Hispanic American), 1 international. Average age 39. In 2006, 29 degrees awarded. *Entrance requirements:* For master's, GRE, MAT, minimum GPA of 2.75. *Application deadline:* Applications are processed on a rolling basis. Application fee: $75. *Expenses:* Tuition: Part-time $380 per semester hour. Tuition and fees vary according to campus/location. *Financial support:* Unspecified assistantships available. Support available to part-time students. Financial award applicants required to submit FAFSA. *Unit head:* Dr. Sandra Loehr, Director of Teacher Education, 704-521-9116 Ext. 239.

Philadelphia Biblical University, School of Education, Langhorne, PA 19047-2990. Offers educational leadership and administration (MS El); teacher education (MS Ed). Part-time and evening/weekend programs available. *Faculty:* 8 full-time (6 women), 3 part-time/adjunct (2 women). *Students:* 6 full-time (5 women), 70 part-time (42 women); includes 12 minority (4 African Americans, 7 Asian Americans or Pacific Islanders, 1 Hispanic American), 3 international. Average age 35. 29 applicants, 55% accepted, 12 enrolled. In 2006, 30 degrees awarded. *Entrance requirements:* Additional exam requirements/recommendations for international students: Required—TOEFL (minimum score 550 paper-based; 213 computer-based). *Application deadline:* Applications are processed on a rolling basis. Application fee: $25. Electronic applications accepted. *Expenses:* Tuition: Full-time $8,820; part-time $490 per credit. *Financial support:* In 2006–07, 27 students received support. Scholarships/grants available. Support available to part-time students. Financial award applicants required to submit FAFSA. *Unit head:* Dr. Martha MacCullough, Dean, 215-702-4387, E-mail: teacher.ed@pbu.edu. *Application contact:* Katerina Penkova, Enrollment Counselor, Graduate Education, 800-572-2472, Fax: 215-702-4248, E-mail: kpenkova@pbu.edu.

Piedmont College, School of Education, Demorest, GA 30535-0010. Offers early childhood education (MA, MAT); instruction (Ed S); secondary education (MA, MAT). Part-time and evening/weekend programs available. *Faculty:* 20 full-time (17 women), 22 part-time/adjunct (5 women). *Students:* 210 full-time (158 women), 846 part-time (734 women); includes 95 minority (72 African Americans, 2 American Indian/Alaska Native, 10 Asian Americans or Pacific Islanders, 11 Hispanic Americans), 7 international. 327 applicants, 92% accepted, 235 enrolled. In 2006, 422 master's, 203 other advanced degrees awarded. *Degree requirements:* For master's, thesis, field experience in the teaching classroom. *Entrance requirements:* For master's, GRE General Test, MAT, minimum undergraduate GPA of 2.5; for Ed S, minimum graduate GPA of 3.5, valid teaching certificate. Additional exam requirements/recommendations for international students: Required—TOEFL (minimum score 550 paper-based; 213 computer-based). *Application deadline:* For fall admission, 7/15 for domestic students; for spring admission, 12/1 for domestic students. Application fee: $30. *Expenses:* Tuition: Part-time $310 per credit hour. *Financial support:* Career-related internships or fieldwork, Federal Work-Study, institutionally sponsored loans, and unspecified assistantships available. Support available to part-time students. Financial award applicants required to submit FAFSA. *Unit head:* Dr. Jane McFerrin, Dean, 706-778-3000 Ext. 1201, Fax: 706-776-9608, E-mail: jmcferrin@piedmont.edu. *Application contact:* Carol E. Kokesh, Director of Graduate Studies, 706-778-8500 Ext. 1181, Fax: 706-776-6635, E-mail: ckokesh@piedmont.edu.

Pittsburg State University, Graduate School, College of Education, Pittsburg, KS 66762. Offers MAT, MS, Ed S. *Accreditation:* NCATE. *Students:* 474. *Degree requirements:* For master's, thesis or alternative. Application fee: $35 ($60 for international students). *Expenses:* Tuition, state resident: full-time $2,144; part-time $181 per credit hour. Tuition, nonresident: full-time $5,273; part-time $442 per credit hour. Tuition and fees vary according to course load and campus/location. *Financial support:* In 2006–07, teaching assistantships (averaging $5,000 per year); career-related internships or fieldwork, Federal Work-Study, and unspecified assistantships also available. *Unit head:* Dean, 620-235-4500. *Application contact:* Jamie Vanderbeck, Assistant Director, 620-235-4223, Fax: 620-235-4219, E-mail: jvanderb@pittstate.edu.

Plymouth State University, College of Graduate Studies, Graduate Studies in Education, Program in Certificate of Advanced Graduate Studies, Plymouth, NH 03264-1595. Offers CAGS. Part-time and evening/weekend programs available. *Students:* 3 full-time (all women), 185 part-time (141 women); includes 6 minority (3 African Americans, 3 Hispanic Americans). Average age 46. 40 applicants, 100% accepted, 40 enrolled. In 2006, 32 degrees awarded. Application fee: $100. *Expenses:* Tuition, state resident: part-time $369 per credit. Tuition, nonresident: part-time $407 per credit. Tuition and fees vary according to course level. *Unit head:* Dr. Michael Morgan, Interim program Coordinator.

Point Loma Nazarene University, Graduate Studies, Program in Education, San Diego, CA 92106-2899. Offers MA, Ed S. Part-time and evening/weekend programs available. *Faculty:* 17 full-time (9 women), 83 part-time/adjunct (50 women). *Students:* 355 full-time (253 women), 140 part-time (88 women); includes 193 minority (22 African Americans, 4 American Indian/Alaska Native, 35 Asian Americans or Pacific Islanders, 132 Hispanic Americans), 1 international. Average age 34. In 2006, 45 master's, 1 other advanced degree awarded. *Degree requirements:* For master's, thesis optional. *Entrance requirements:* For master's, GRE General Test or MAT, portfolio, letters of recommendation; for Ed S, GRE General Test or MAT, portfolio. *Application deadline:* For fall admission, 5/15 priority date for domestic students; for spring admission, 11/1 for domestic students. Applications are processed on a rolling basis. Application fee: $25. *Financial support:* Career-related internships or fieldwork available. Financial award application deadline: 4/10. *Unit head:* John Hawthorne, Interim Dean, 619-563-2820, Fax: 619-849-2579.

Point Park University, School of Arts and Sciences, Department of Education and Community Services, Pittsburgh, PA 15222-1984. Offers curriculum and instruction (MA); educational administration (MA). Part-time and evening/weekend programs available. *Faculty:* 3 full-time, 16 part-time/adjunct. *Students:* 20 full-time (15 women), 30 part-time (19 women); includes 8 minority (all African Americans), 2 international. Average age 33. 58 applicants, 62% accepted, 22 enrolled. In 2006, 15 degrees awarded. *Entrance requirements:* For master's, minimum GPA of 3.0, resumé, 2 letters of recommendation. Additional exam requirements/recommendations for international students: Required—TOEFL. *Application deadline:* Applications are processed on a rolling basis. Application fee: $30. Electronic applications accepted. *Expenses:* Tuition: Full-time $9,828; part-time $546 per credit. Required fees: $360; $20 per credit. *Financial support:* In 2006–07, 5 students received support, including 2 research assistantships with full tuition reimbursements available (averaging $5,400 per year); career-related internships or fieldwork, scholarships/grants, and unspecified assistantships also available. Support available to part-time students. Financial award application deadline: 5/1; financial award applicants required to submit FAFSA. *Unit head:* Dr. Karen McIntyre, Chair, 412-392-3972, Fax: 412-392-3927, E-mail: kmcintyre@pointpark.edu. *Application contact:* Marty Paonessa, Associate Director, Graduate and Adult Enrollment, 412-392-3915, Fax: 412-392-6164, E-mail: mpaonessa@pointpark.edu.

Pontifical Catholic University of Puerto Rico, College of Education, Ponce, PR 00717-0777. Offers commercial education (MRE); curriculum instruction (M Ed); education (PhD); education-general (MRE); English as a second language (MRE); religious education (MA Ed); scholar psychology (MRE). Part-time and evening/weekend programs available. *Degree requirements:* For master's, thesis (for some programs), comprehensive exam. *Entrance requirements:* For master's, GRE, 2 letters of recommendation, interview, minimum GPA of 2.75; for doctorate, EXADEP, GRE or MAT, 3 letters of recommendation. *Faculty research:* Teaching English as a second language, learning styles, leadership styles.

Portland State University, Graduate Studies, School of Education, Portland, OR 97207-0751. Offers M Ed, MA, MAT, MS, MST, Ed D. *Accreditation:* NCATE. Part-time and evening/weekend programs available. *Faculty:* 50 full-time (29 women), 50 part-time/adjunct (29 women). *Students:* 372 full-time (288 women), 634 part-time (452 women); includes 119 minority (21 African Americans, 16 American Indian/Alaska Native, 28 Asian Americans or Pacific Islanders, 54 Hispanic Americans), 25 international. Average age 36. 846 applicants, 85% accepted, 367 enrolled. In 2006, 532 master's, 8 doctorates awarded. *Degree requirements:* For doctorate, thesis/dissertation. *Entrance requirements:* For master's, minimum GPA of 3.0 in upper-division course work or 2.75 overall. Additional exam requirements/recommendations for international students: Required—TOEFL (minimum score 550 paper-based; 213 computer-based). *Application deadline:* For fall admission, 4/1 for domestic and international students; for winter admission, 9/1 for domestic and international students; for spring admission, 11/1 for domestic and international students. Application fee: $50. *Expenses:* Tuition, state resident: full-time $6,426; part-time $238 per credit. Tuition, nonresident: full-time $11,016; part-time $408 per credit. Tuition and fees vary according to course load. *Financial support:* In 2006–07, 21 research assistantships with full tuition reimbursements (averaging $5,742 per year) were awarded; teaching assistantships with full tuition reimbursements, career-related internships or fieldwork, Federal Work-Study, institutionally sponsored loans, scholarships/grants, and unspecified assistantships also available. Support available to part-time students. Financial award application deadline: 3/1; financial award applicants required to submit FAFSA. Total annual research expenditures: $1.8 million. *Unit head:* Dr. Randy Hitz, Dean, 503-725-4697, Fax: 503-725-5399. *Application contact:* Tasa Lehman, 503-725-4619, Fax: 503-725-5599, E-mail: lehmant@pdx.edu.

Prairie View A&M University, Graduate School, College of Education, Prairie View, TX 77446-0519. Offers M Ed, MA, MA Ed, MS, MS Ed, PhD. *Accreditation:* NCATE. Part-time and evening/weekend programs available. *Faculty:* 19 full-time (4 women), 36 part-time/adjunct (20 women). *Students:* 418 full-time (329 women), 1,145 part-time (881 women); includes 1,411 minority (1,368 African Americans, 2 American Indian/Alaska Native, 4 Asian Americans or Pacific Islanders, 37 Hispanic Americans), 9 international. Average age 36. 1,563 applicants, 100% accepted, 1563 enrolled. In 2006, 505 degrees awarded. *Degree requirements:* For master's, thesis optional; for doctorate, thesis/dissertation, comprehensive exam. *Entrance requirements:* For master's and doctorate, GRE General Test, 3 letters of reference, minimum undergraduate GPA of 2.5. Additional exam requirements/recommendations for international students: Required—TOEFL (minimum score 550 paper-based). *Application deadline:* For fall admission, 7/1 priority date for domestic students, 6/1 for international students; for spring admission, 11/1 priority date for domestic students, 10/1 for international students. Applications are processed on a rolling basis. Application fee: $50. *Financial support:* In 2006–07, 1,050 students received support, including 8 fellowships with tuition reimbursements available (averaging $12,000 per year), 10 research assistantships with tuition reimbursements available (averaging $15,000 per year); teaching assistantships, career-related internships or fieldwork, Federal Work-Study, and institutionally sponsored loans also available. Support available to part-time students. Financial award application deadline: 4/1; financial award applicants required to submit FAFSA. *Faculty research:* Mentoring, assessment, humanistic education, diversity, literacy education. *Unit head:* Dr. M. Paul Mehta, Dean, 936-857-3880, Fax: 936-857-2911. *Application contact:* Dr. Ben DeSpain, Head, 936-857-2312, Fax: 936-857-4127, E-mail: bcdespain@pvamu.edu.

Prescott College, Graduate Programs, Program in Education, Prescott, AZ 86301. Offers bilingual education (MA), including English as a second language, Native American bilingual teacher education; education (MA, PhD); multicultural education (MA). Part-time programs available. Postbaccalaureate distance learning degree programs offered (minimal on-campus study). *Faculty:* 1 (woman) full-time, 26 part-time/adjunct (18 women). *Students:* 44 full-time (24 women), 23 part-time (15 women); includes 8 minority (1 African American, 3 American Indian/Alaska Native, 1 Asian American or Pacific Islander, 3 Hispanic Americans), 2 international. Average age 40. In 2006, 17 degrees awarded. *Degree requirements:* For master's, thesis, fieldwork or internship, practicum; for doctorate, thesis/dissertation. *Entrance requirements:* For master's and doctorate, 2 letters of recommendation, resumé. *Application deadline:* For fall admission, 5/1 priority date for domestic students; for spring admission, 11/1 priority date for domestic students. Applications are processed on a rolling basis. Application fee: $40. Electronic applications accepted. *Expenses:* Tuition: Full-time $12,408; part-time $517 per credit. One-time fee: $130. *Financial support:* Career-related internships or fieldwork and Federal Work-Study available. Financial award applicants required to submit FAFSA. *Unit head:* Noël Caniglia, Head, 928-358-3201, Fax: 928-776-5151, E-mail: ncaniglia@prescott.edu. *Application contact:* Kerstin Alicki, Admissions Counselor, 877-350-2100 Ext. 2102, Fax: 928-776-5242, E-mail: admissions@prescott.edu.

Providence College, Graduate Studies, Department of Education, Providence, RI 02918. Offers administration (M Ed), including administration, elementary administration, secondary administration; education literacy (M Ed); guidance and counseling (M Ed); special education (M Ed). Part-time and evening/weekend programs available. *Faculty:* 6 full-time (5 women), 45 part-time/adjunct (25 women). *Students:* 62 full-time (50 women), 239 part-time (181 women); includes 10 minority (3 African Americans, 1 Asian American or Pacific Islander, 6 Hispanic Americans), 4 international. Average age 32. 86 applicants, 84% accepted. In 2006, 112 degrees awarded. *Degree requirements:* For master's, comprehensive exam. *Entrance requirements:* For master's, GRE General Test. Additional exam requirements/recommendations for international students: Required—TOEFL (minimum score 550 paper-based; 213 computer-based). *Application deadline:* For fall admission, 8/1 priority date for domestic students; for spring admission, 12/1 for domestic students. Applications are processed on a rolling basis. Application fee: $55. *Expenses:* Tuition: Full-time $6,573; part-time $939 per unit. *Financial support:* In 2006–07, 21 research assistantships with full tuition reimbursements (averaging $8,400 per year) were awarded; career-related internships or fieldwork, institutionally sponsored loans, and unspecified assistantships also available. Support available to part-time students. Financial award application deadline: 8/1; financial award applicants required to submit FAFSA. *Unit head:* Dr. Thomas Flaherty, Dean, Graduate Studies, 401-865-2247, E-mail: tflahert@providence.edu.

Purdue University, Graduate School, School of Education, West Lafayette, IN 47907. Offers MS, MS Ed, PhD, Ed S. *Accreditation:* NCATE. Part-time and evening/weekend programs available. *Faculty:* 58 full-time (32 women), 3 part-time/adjunct (all women). *Students:* 159 full-time (108 women), 238 part-time (147 women); includes 56 minority (32 African Americans, 5 American Indian/Alaska Native, 10 Asian Americans or Pacific Islanders, 9 Hispanic Americans), 71 international. Average age 35. 251 applicants, 65% accepted, 97 enrolled. In 2006, 103 master's, 40 doctorates, 5 other advanced degrees awarded. *Degree requirements:* For master's, thesis optional; for doctorate, thesis/dissertation, oral and written exams; for Ed S, oral presentation, project. *Entrance requirements:* For master's, minimum B average; for doctorate, GRE General Test; for Ed S, GRE, minimum B average. Additional exam requirements/recommendations for international students: Required—TOEFL. *Application deadline:* For fall admission, 1/15 for domestic students; for spring admission, 9/15 for domestic students. Application fee: $55. Electronic applications accepted. *Financial support:* Fellowships with full tuition reimbursements, research assistantships with full tuition reimbursements, teaching assistantships with full tuition reimbursements, career-related internships or fieldwork and tuition waivers (full) available. Support available to part-time students. Financial award application deadline: 3/1; financial award applicants required to submit FAFSA. *Unit head:* Dr. George W Hynd, Head, 765-494-2326, Fax: 765-496-1622. *Application contact:* Lauren Franks, Graduate Admissions Specialist, 765-494-2345, E-mail: lfranks@purdue.edu.

Purdue University Calumet, Graduate School, School of Education, Hammond, IN 46323-2094. Offers counseling and personnel services (MS Ed); educational administration (MS Ed); elementary education (MS Ed); instructional development (MS Ed); media sciences (MS Ed); secondary education (MS Ed). *Accreditation:* NCATE. *Entrance requirements:* Additional exam requirements/recommendations for international students: Required—TOEFL.

Purdue University North Central, Program in Education, Westville, IN 46391-9542. Offers elementary education (MS Ed). *Accreditation:* NCATE. Part-time and evening/weekend programs available. *Degree requirements:* For master's, one foreign language. *Entrance requirements:* For master's, GRE, minimum GPA of 3.0. *Faculty research:* Diversity, integration.

Queens College of the City University of New York, Division of Graduate Studies, Division of Education, Flushing, NY 11367-1597. Offers MA, MS Ed, AC. Part-time and evening/weekend programs available. *Faculty:* 73 full-time (50 women). *Students:* 211 full-time (168 women), 2,185 part-time (1,640 women). 1,518 applicants, 73% accepted, 893 enrolled. In 2006, 671 master's, 124 other advanced degrees awarded. *Degree requirements:* For master's, research project; for AC, thesis optional. *Entrance requirements:* For master's, minimum GPA of 3.0. Additional exam requirements/recommendations for international students: Required—TOEFL. *Application deadline:* For fall admission, 4/1 for domestic students; for spring admission, 11/1 for domestic students. Applications are processed on a rolling basis. Application fee: $125. *Financial support:* Career-related internships or fieldwork, Federal Work-Study, institutionally sponsored loans, and tuition waivers (partial) available. Support available to part-time students. Financial award application deadline: 4/1; financial award applicants required to submit FAFSA. *Unit head:* Dr. Penny Hammrich, Dean, 718-997-5220. *Application contact:* Mario Caruso, Director of Graduate Admissions, 718-997-5200, Fax: 718-997-5193, E-mail: graduate_admissions@qc.edu.

Queen's University at Kingston, School of Graduate Studies and Research, Faculty of Education, Kingston, ON K7L 3N6, Canada. Offers M Ed, PhD. Part-time programs available. *Degree requirements:* For master's, thesis optional; for doctorate, thesis/dissertation, comprehensive exam. *Entrance requirements:* Additional exam requirements/recommendations for international students: Required—TOEFL (minimum score 580 paper-based; 237 computer-based); Recommended—TWE (minimum score 4). *Faculty research:* Literacy, assessment and evaluation, special needs, mathematics, science and technology education.

Queens University of Charlotte, Hayworth College, Department of Education, Charlotte, NC 28274-0002. Offers elementary education (MAT). *Accreditation:* NCATE. Part-time and evening/weekend programs available. *Faculty:* 5 full-time (3 women). *Students:* 16 full-time (15 women), 74 part-time (69 women); includes 8 minority (4 African Americans, 1 American Indian/Alaska Native, 3 Hispanic Americans). Average age 27. 49 applicants, 80% accepted, 24 enrolled. In 2006, 42 degrees awarded. *Degree requirements:* For master's, comprehensive exam. *Entrance requirements:* For master's, GRE General Test. *Application*

Education—General

Queens University of Charlotte (continued)

deadline: Applications are processed on a rolling basis. Application fee: $40. *Expenses: Contact institution. Financial support:* Institutionally sponsored loans available. *Unit head:* Dr. Patrice D. Petroff, Chair, 704-337-2575, Fax: 704-337-2477. *Application contact:* Lori Morrow, Director of Admissions, 704-337-2580, Fax: 704-337-2415.

Quincy University, Division of Education, Quincy, IL 62301-2699. Offers MS Ed. Part-time programs available. *Faculty:* 4 full-time (3 women), 9 part-time/adjunct (5 women). *Students:* 25 full-time (15 women), 61 part-time (47 women); includes 4 minority (1 Asian American or Pacific Islander, 3 Hispanic Americans). Average age 34. In 2006, 22 degrees awarded. *Degree requirements:* For master's, thesis. *Entrance requirements:* For master's, MAT. *Application deadline:* Applications are processed on a rolling basis. Application fee: $25. *Financial support:* In 2006–07, 45 students received support. Available to part-time students. Applicants required to submit FAFSA. *Unit head:* Dr. Alice Mills, Director, 217-228-5420, E-mail: millsal@quincy.edu. *Application contact:* Syndi Peck, Director of Admissions, 217-228-5215, Fax: 217-228-5648, E-mail: admissions@quincy.edu.

Quinnipiac University, Division of Education, Hamden, CT 06518-1940. Offers MAT. Part-time programs available. *Faculty:* 7 full-time (5 women), 23 part-time/adjunct (14 women). *Students:* 147 full-time (116 women); includes 10 minority (2 African Americans, 8 Hispanic Americans), 1 international. Average age 26. 145 applicants, 91% accepted, 110 enrolled. In 2006, 101 degrees awarded. *Entrance requirements:* For master's, PRAXIS I, minimum GPA of 2.67, interview. Additional exam requirements/recommendations for international students: Required—TOEFL (minimum score 575 paper-based; 233 computer-based; 90 iBT), IELTS (minimum score 7). *Application deadline:* For fall admission, 7/30 priority date for domestic students; for spring admission, 12/15 priority date for domestic students. Applications are processed on a rolling basis. Application fee: $45. Electronic applications accepted. *Expenses:* Tuition: Part-time $675 per credit. Required fees: $30 per credit. *Financial support:* Career-related internships or fieldwork, tuition waivers (partial), and unspecified assistantships available. Financial award application deadline: 4/15; financial award applicants required to submit FAFSA. *Faculty research:* Equity and excellence in education. *Unit head:* Dr. Cynthia Dubea, Dean—Division of Education, College of Liberal Arts, 203-582-8730, Fax: 203-582-8709, E-mail: cynthia.dubea@quinnipiac.edu. *Application contact:* 800-462-1944, Fax: 203-582-3443, E-mail: graduate@quinnipiac.edu.

See Close-Up on page 911.

Radford University, Graduate College, College of Education and Human Development, Radford, VA 24142. Offers MS. *Accreditation:* NCATE. Part-time and evening/weekend programs available. Postbaccalaureate distance learning degree programs offered (minimal on-campus study). *Faculty:* 30 full-time (16 women), 17 part-time/adjunct (9 women). *Students:* 172 full-time (135 women), 324 part-time (276 women); includes 40 minority (29 African Americans, 7 Asian Americans or Pacific Islanders, 4 Hispanic Americans). Average age 32. 171 applicants, 95% accepted, 103 enrolled. In 2006, 121 degrees awarded. *Degree requirements:* For master's, thesis optional. *Entrance requirements:* For master's, GMAT, GRE or MAT. Additional exam requirements/recommendations for international students: Required—TOEFL. *Application deadline:* For fall admission, 3/1 priority date for domestic students, 4/1 for international students; for spring admission, 10/1 for domestic students, 8/1 for international students. Applications are processed on a rolling basis. Application fee: $40. Electronic applications accepted. *Expenses:* Tuition, state resident: full-time $4,680; part-time $260 per credit hour. Tuition, nonresident: full-time $8,604; part-time $478 per credit hour. *Financial support:* In 2006–07, 104 students received support, including 69 research assistantships with partial tuition reimbursements available (averaging $8,000 per year), teaching assistantships with partial tuition reimbursements available (averaging $8,700 per year); career-related internships or fieldwork, Federal Work-Study, institutionally sponsored loans, scholarships/grants, and unspecified assistantships also available. Financial award application deadline: 3/1; financial award applicants required to submit FAFSA. *Unit head:* Dr. Patricia Shoemaker, Acting Dean, 540-831-5277, Fax: 540-831-6053, E-mail: pshoemak@radford.edu.

Radford University, Graduate College, College of Education and Human Development, School of Teacher and Educational Leadership, Program in Education, Radford, VA 24142. Offers content area studies (MS); curriculum and instruction (MS); early childhood education (MS); educational technology (MS); library media (MS); teaching English as second language (MS). *Accreditation:* NCATE. Part-time and evening/weekend programs available. Postbaccalaureate distance learning degree programs offered (minimal on-campus study). *Faculty:* 8 full-time (3 women), 6 part-time/adjunct (4 women). *Students:* 42 full-time (32 women), 55 part-time (49 women); includes 6 minority (4 African Americans, 2 Asian Americans or Pacific Islanders). Average age 29. 37 applicants, 97% accepted, 24 enrolled. In 2006, 16 degrees awarded. *Degree requirements:* For master's, comprehensive exam. *Entrance requirements:* For master's, GRE or MAT. Additional exam requirements/recommendations for international students: Required—TOEFL. *Application deadline:* For fall admission, 3/1 priority date for domestic students, 4/1 for international students; for spring admission, 10/1 for domestic students, 8/1 for international students. Applications are processed on a rolling basis. Application fee: $40. Electronic applications accepted. *Expenses:* Tuition, state resident: full-time $4,680; part-time $260 per credit hour. Tuition, nonresident: full-time $8,604; part-time $478 per credit hour. *Financial support:* In 2006–07, 21 students received support, including 12 research assistantships with partial tuition reimbursements available (averaging $8,000 per year), teaching assistantships with partial tuition reimbursements available (averaging $8,700 per year); career-related internships or fieldwork, Federal Work-Study, institutionally sponsored loans, scholarships/grants, and unspecified assistantships also available. Financial award application deadline: 3/1; financial award applicants required to submit FAFSA. *Unit head:* Dr. Elizabeth Done, Coordinator, 540-831-5843.

Regent University, Graduate School, School of Education, Virginia Beach, VA 23464-9800. Offers Christian school program (M Ed); cross-categorical special education (M Ed); education (M Ed, Ed D); educational leadership (M Ed); elementary education (M Ed); individual degree plan (M Ed); master teacher (M Ed); special education leadership (Ed S); TESOL (M Ed). Part-time and evening/weekend programs available. Postbaccalaureate distance learning degree programs offered (minimal on-campus study). *Faculty:* 25 full-time (11 women), 132 part-time/adjunct (90 women). *Students:* 220 full-time (176 women), 501 part-time (374 women); includes 264 minority (229 African Americans, 9 Asian Americans or Pacific Islanders, 26 Hispanic Americans), 13 international. Average age 38. 472 applicants, 79% accepted, 256 enrolled. In 2006, 185 master's, 5 doctorates awarded. *Degree requirements:* For master's, thesis or alternative; for doctorate, thesis/dissertation, comprehensive exam. *Entrance requirements:* For master's, MAT, minimum undergraduate GPA of 2.75, writing sample, resumé; for doctorate, GRE, writing sample, 3 years of relevant professional experience, master's-level paper, copies of published work. Additional exam requirements/recommendations for international students: Required—TOEFL (minimum score 577 paper-based; 233 computer-based). *Application deadline:* For fall admission, 4/1 priority date for domestic students; for spring admission, 10/15 priority date for domestic students. Applications are processed on a rolling basis. Application fee: $50. Electronic applications accepted. *Expenses: Contact institution. Financial support:* In 2006–07, 721 students received support; fellowships, career-related internships or fieldwork, scholarships/grants, tuition waivers (full and partial), and unspecified assistantships available. Support available to part-time students. Financial award application deadline: 4/1; financial award applicants required to submit FAFSA. *Faculty research:* Character development and discipline for children, education leadership development, diversity in schools, classroom management, technology in education settings. *Unit head:* Dr. Alan A. Arroyo, Dean, 757-226-4261, Fax: 757-226-4318, E-mail: alanarr@regent.edu. *Application contact:* Althea Bishard, Registrar and Executive Director of Enrollment and Academic Services, 800-373-5504, Fax: 757-226-4381, E-mail: admissions@regent.edu.

Regis College, Department of Education, Weston, MA 02493. Offers MAT. Part-time and evening/weekend programs available. *Faculty:* 3 full-time (all women), 4 part-time/adjunct (all women). *Students:* 5 full-time (all women), 48 part-time (45 women); includes 4 minority (1 African American, 3 Asian Americans or Pacific Islanders), 1 international. Average age 35. 12 applicants, 100% accepted, 10 enrolled. In 2006, 13 degrees awarded. *Degree requirements:* For master's, thesis. *Entrance requirements:* For master's, GRE. *Application deadline:* Applications are processed on a rolling basis. Application fee: $40. Electronic applications accepted. *Expenses:* Tuition: Full-time $23,680; part-time $665 per credit hour. *Financial support:* In 2006–07, 7 students received support, including 1 fellowship with full tuition reimbursement available (averaging $11,970 per year); Federal Work-Study also available. Financial award applicants required to submit FAFSA. *Faculty research:* Reflective teaching, gender-based education, integrated teaching. *Unit head:* Dr. Leona McCaughey-Oreszak, Program Director, 781-768-7421, Fax: 781-768-7159, E-mail: leona.mccaughey-oreszak@regiscollege.edu.

Regis University, Regis College, Denver, CO 80221-1099. Offers education (MA). Offered at Northwest Denver Campus. Part-time and evening/weekend programs available. *Faculty:* 13. *Students:* 129. Average age 35. 5 applicants, 100% accepted. In 2006, 23 degrees awarded. *Degree requirements:* For master's, capstone presentation. *Entrance requirements:* For master's, 1 year of teaching experience, Colorado teaching certificate, videotape sample of teaching. *Application deadline:* Applications are processed on a rolling basis. Application fee: $75. *Expenses: Contact institution. Financial support:* Available to part-time students. Application deadline: 3/15; *Unit head:* Dr. Paul Ewald, Dean, 303-458-4040. *Application contact:* Kathleen Nutting, Director, 303-458-4349, Fax: 303-964-5421, E-mail: knutting@regis.edu.

Regis University, School for Professional Studies, Program in Teacher Education, Denver, CO 80221-1099. Offers adult learning, training, and development (M Ed); curriculum, instruction, and assessment (M Ed); early childhood (M Ed); educational technology (Certificate); elementary (M Ed); ESL (M Ed); fine arts (M Ed), including arts, music; instructional technology (M Ed); professional leadership (M Ed); reading (M Ed); secondary (M Ed); self-designed (M Ed); space studies (M Ed); special education (M Ed); teacher licensure (M Ed). Program also offered in Henderson and Las Vegas (Summerlin), NV. Postbaccalaureate distance learning degree programs offered. *Unit head:* Dr. Suzie Perry, Dean, 303-458-4302. *Application contact:* Partick Lowenthal, Assistant Director, 303-458-4300 Ext. 4314, E-mail: masters@regis.edu.

Rhode Island College, School of Graduate Studies, Feinstein School of Education and Human Development, Program in Education, Providence, RI 02908-1991. Offers PhD. *Accreditation:* NCATE. Part-time and evening/weekend programs available. *Faculty:* 6 part-time/adjunct (2 women). *Students:* Average age 42. In 2006, 1 degree awarded. *Application deadline:* For fall admission, 3/15 for domestic students; for spring admission, 11/1 for domestic students. Applications are processed on a rolling basis. Application fee: $50. *Expenses:* Tuition, state resident: part-time $244 per credit. Tuition, nonresident: part-time $512 per credit. Required fees: $12 per credit. $66 per term. Tuition and fees vary according to degree level, program and reciprocity agreements. *Financial support:* Health care benefits available. Support available to part-time students. Financial award application deadline: 5/15; financial award applicants required to submit FAFSA. *Unit head:* Dr. John J Gleason, Co-Director, 401-456-9703, E-mail: jgleason@ric.edu.

Rice University, Graduate Programs, Programs in Education Certification, Houston, TX 77251-1892. Offers MAT. *Faculty:* 2 full-time (both women), 4 part-time/adjunct (all women). *Students:* 11 full-time (4 women); includes 2 African Americans, 1 Asian American or Pacific Islander. Average age 31. 13 applicants, 77% accepted, 5 enrolled. In 2006, 6 degrees awarded. *Degree requirements:* For master's, registration. *Entrance requirements:* For master's, GRE General Test, minimum GPA of 3.0. Additional exam requirements/recommendations for international students: Required—TOEFL (minimum score 600 paper-based; 250 computer-based; 90 iBT). *Application deadline:* For fall admission, 2/1 priority date for domestic students; for spring admission, 11/1 for domestic students. Applications are processed on a rolling basis. Application fee: $35. Electronic applications accepted. *Expenses:* Tuition: Full-time $23,400; part-time $1,300 per hour. Required fees: $150; $75 per semester. Tuition and fees vary according to program. *Financial support:* In 2006–07, 3 students received support. Scholarships/grants and tuition waivers (full and partial) available. Financial award application deadline: 2/1. *Faculty research:* Assessment, integration of math and science. *Unit head:* Dr. Meredith Skura, Chair, 713-348-4826, Fax: 713-348-5459, E-mail: educ@rice.edu. *Application contact:* Olga C. Trejo, Education Programs Administrator, 713-348-4826, Fax: 713-348-5459, E-mail: educ@rice.edu.

The Richard Stockton College of New Jersey, Graduate Programs, Program in Education, Pomona, NJ 08240-0195. Offers MA. *Faculty:* 19 full-time (11 women), 2 part-time/adjunct (1 woman). *Students:* 3 full-time (2 women), 58 part-time (46 women); includes 4 minority (3 African Americans, 1 Asian American or Pacific Islander). Average age 37. *Entrance requirements:* For master's, GRE, minimum GPA of 2.75, teaching certificate. Additional exam requirements/recommendations for international students: Required—TOEFL. Application fee: $50. *Expenses:* Tuition, state resident: full-time $9,746. Tuition, nonresident: full-time $14,462. Required fees: $2,340. *Unit head:* Dr. Marion Hussong, Director, 609-652-4688, E-mail: marion.hussong@stockton.edu. *Application contact:* Alison Henry, Associate Director of Admissions, 609-652-4261, Fax: 609-626-5541, E-mail: admissions@stockston.edu.

Rider University, Department of Graduate Education, Leadership and Counseling, Lawrenceville, NJ 08648-3001. Offers counseling services (MA, Ed S); curriculum, instruction and supervision (MA); director of school counseling services (Certificate); educational administration (MA); organizational leadership (MA); principal (Certificate); reading/language arts (MA, Certificate), including reading specialist (Certificate), reading/language arts (MA); school business administrator (Certificate); school counseling services (Certificate); school psychology (Ed S); special education (MA); supervisor (Certificate); teacher certification (Certificate), including business education, elementary education, English as a second language, English education, mathematics education, preschool to grade 3, science education, social studies education, world languages; teaching (MA). *Accreditation:* NCATE. Part-time and evening/weekend programs available. *Faculty:* 24 full-time (12 women), 30 part-time/adjunct (15 women). *Students:* 90 full-time (75 women), 457 part-time (369 women); includes 73 minority (50 African Americans, 2 American Indian/Alaska Native, 6 Asian Americans or Pacific Islanders, 15 Hispanic Americans), 1 international. Average age 32. 314 applicants, 61% accepted, 138 enrolled. In 2006, 116 master's, 19 other advanced degrees awarded. *Degree requirements:* For master's, thesis or alternative, internship, portfolios, comprehensive exam (for some programs); for other advanced degree, internship, professional portfolio. *Entrance requirements:* For master's, GRE (counseling, school psychology), MAT, interview, resumé, letters of recommendation; for other advanced degree, PRAXIS. Additional exam requirements/recommendations for international students: Required—TOEFL (minimum score 550 paper-based; 213 computer-based). *Application deadline:* For fall admission, 5/1 priority date for domestic students, 6/1 priority date for international students; for spring admission, 11/1 priority date for domestic and international students. Applications are processed on a rolling basis. Application fee: $50. Electronic applications accepted. *Expenses:* Tuition: Part-time $525 per credit. Required fees: $35 per course. $30 per semester. *Financial support:* In 2006–07, 271 students received support. Career-related internships or fieldwork, Federal Work-Study, institutionally sponsored loans, and unspecified assistantships available. Support available to part-time students. Financial award applicants required to submit FAFSA. *Faculty research:* Gifted students, self-esteem, hope and mental health, conflicts in group work, cultural diversity and counseling assessment of special needs in children. *Unit head:* Dr. Dennis C. Buss, Chair, 609-895-5353, Fax: 609-896-5362, E-mail: dbuss@rider.edu. *Application contact:* Jamie L Mitchell, Director of Graduate Admissions, 609-896-5036, Fax: 609-895-5680, E-mail: jmitchell@rider.edu.

See Close-Up on page 913.

Rivier College, School of Graduate Studies, Department of Education, Nashua, NH 03060-5086. Offers curriculum and instruction (M Ed); early childhood education (M Ed); educational administration (M Ed); educational studies (M Ed); elementary education (M Ed); elementary education and general special education (M Ed); emotional and behavioral disorders (M Ed); general social education (M Ed); leadership and learning (CAGS); learning disabilities (M Ed); learning disabilities and reading (M Ed); mental health counseling (MA); reading (M Ed); school counseling (M Ed). Part-time and evening/weekend programs available. *Faculty:* 11 full-time (7 women), 40 part-time/adjunct (29 women). *Students:* 41 full-time (33 women), 221 part-time (192 women); includes 4 minority (2 African Americans, 2 Hispanic Americans). Average age 37. In 2006, 134 degrees awarded. *Degree requirements:* For master's, internships. *Entrance requirements:* For master's, GRE General Test or MAT. *Application deadline:* Applications are processed on a rolling basis. Application fee: $25. *Financial support:* Available to part-time students. Application deadline: 2/1; *Unit head:* Dr. Charles L. Mitsakos, Chairman, 603-888-1311 Ext. 8582. *Application contact:* Diane Monahan, Director of Graduate Admissions, 603-897-8129, Fax: 603-897-8810, E-mail: gradadm@rivier.edu.

Roberts Wesleyan College, Division of Teacher Education, Rochester, NY 14624-1997. Offers adolescence education (M Ed); childhood and special education (M Ed); literacy education (M Ed); urban education (M Ed). Part-time and evening/weekend programs available. *Faculty:* 17 part-time/adjunct (7 women). *Students:* 1 (woman) full-time, 66 part-time (47 women). Average age 33. 52 applicants, 63% accepted. In 2006, 20 degrees awarded. *Degree requirements:* For master's, thesis. *Application deadline:* For fall admission, 8/1 priority date for domestic students; for spring admission, 12/1 for domestic students. Applications are processed on a rolling basis. Application fee: $35. *Financial support:* In 2006–07, 7 students received support. Career-related internships or fieldwork available. Financial award application deadline: 9/1; financial award applicants required to submit FAFSA. *Unit head:* Dr. Richard Mace, Chair, 585-594-6934. *Application contact:* Paula Finch, Graduate Admissions Coordinator, 585-594-6683, E-mail: finch_paula@roberts.edu.

Rockford College, Graduate Studies, Department of Education, Rockford, IL 61108-2393. Offers elementary education (MAT); learning disabilities (MAT); reading (MAT); secondary education (MAT), including art education, English, history, political science, secondary education, social sciences. Part-time and evening/weekend programs available. *Degree requirements:* For master's, thesis optional. *Entrance requirements:* For master's, GRE General Test.

Rockhurst University, School of Graduate and Professional Studies, Program in Education, Kansas City, MO 64110-2561. Offers M Ed. *Accreditation:* Teacher Education Accreditation Council. *Faculty:* 10 full-time (8 women), 7 part-time/adjunct (4 women). *Students:* 56 full-time (40 women), 117 part-time (89 women); includes 13 minority (11 African Americans, 2 Hispanic Americans), 1 international. Average age 30. 75 applicants, 60% accepted, 41 enrolled. In 2006, 62 degrees awarded. *Entrance requirements:* For master's, minimum GPA of 2.5, 2 letters of recommendation. *Application deadline:* Applications are processed on a rolling basis. Application fee: $25. Electronic applications accepted. *Expenses:* Contact institution. *Faculty research:* English language learners: urban literacy, on-line discussions, character education, teaching k-12 students about math and literacy. *Unit head:* Dr. Debra Pellegrino, Chair of Education Department, 816-501-4140, E-mail: debra.pellegrino@rockhurst.edu. *Application contact:* Jyll Kafer, Director of Graduate Recruitment Admission, 816-501-4097, Fax: 816-501-4241, E-mail: jyll.kafer@rockhurst.edu.

Roger Williams University, School of Education, Bristol, RI 02809. Offers MA, MAT. Part-time and evening/weekend programs available. *Faculty:* 11 full-time (8 women), 3 part-time/adjunct (2 women). *Students:* 18 full-time (15 women), 84 part-time (78 women); includes 2 minority (1 Asian American or Pacific Islander, 1 Hispanic American). Average age 33. 20 applicants, 90% accepted, 13 enrolled. In 2006, 44 degrees awarded. *Entrance requirements:* For master's, GRE or MAT. *Application deadline:* Applications are processed on a rolling basis. Application fee: $50. Electronic applications accepted. *Expenses:* Tuition: Part-time $362 per credit. Tuition and fees vary according to program. *Financial support:* In 2006–07, 41 students received support. Career-related internships or fieldwork and health care benefits available. Financial award applicants required to submit FAFSA. *Unit head:* Dr. Bruce Marlowe, Dean, 401-254-3427, E-mail: bmarlowe@rwu.edu. *Application contact:* Suzanne Faubl, Director of Graduate Admissions, 401-254-3809, Fax: 401-254-3557, E-mail: sfaubl@rwu.edu.

Rollins College, Hamilton Holt School, Program in Education, Winter Park, FL 32789-4499. Offers elementary education (M Ed, MAT); secondary education (MAT), including English, mathematics, music. Part-time and evening/weekend programs available. *Students:* 14 full-time (12 women), 36 part-time (32 women); includes 5 minority (2 African Americans, 1 Asian American or Pacific Islander, 2 Hispanic Americans), 1 international. Average age 35. In 2006, 14 degrees awarded. *Degree requirements:* For master's, comprehensive exam. *Entrance requirements:* For master's, GRE or MAT, interview. Additional exam requirements/recommendations for international students: Required—TOEFL. *Application deadline:* For fall admission, 7/16 for domestic students; for winter admission, 12/3 for domestic students; for spring admission, 4/22 for domestic students. Applications are processed on a rolling basis. Application fee: $50. Electronic applications accepted. *Expenses:* Contact institution. *Financial support:* Teaching assistantships, scholarships/grants available. Support available to part-time students. *Unit head:* Dr. J. Scott Hewit, Director, 407-646-2300, E-mail: jhewit@rollins.edu. *Application contact:* Rebecca Cordray, Coordinator of Records and Registration, 407-646-1568, Fax: 407-975-6430, E-mail: rcordray@rollins.edu.

Roosevelt University, Graduate Division, College of Education, Chicago, IL 60605-1394. Offers MA, Ed D. *Accreditation:* ACA; NCATE. Part-time and evening/weekend programs available. *Faculty:* 35 full-time (26 women), 75 part-time/adjunct. *Students:* 219 full-time (176 women), 721 part-time (554 women); includes 261 minority (198 African Americans, 2 American Indian/Alaska Native, 21 Asian Americans or Pacific Islanders, 40 Hispanic Americans). Average age 37. 637 applicants, 64% accepted, 352 enrolled. In 2006, 315 master's, 7 doctorates awarded. *Degree requirements:* For doctorate, thesis/dissertation. *Entrance requirements:* For doctorate, GRE or MAT. *Application deadline:* For fall admission, 6/1 priority date for domestic students. Applications are processed on a rolling basis. Application fee: $25 ($35 for international students). *Financial support:* Federal Work-Study available. Support available to part-time students. Financial award application deadline: 2/15. *Unit head:* James Gandre, Interim Dean, 312-341-3700, E-mail: jgandre@roosevelt.edu. *Application contact:* Joanne Canyon-Heller, Coordinator of Graduate Admission, 877-APPLY RU, Fax: 312-281-3356, E-mail: applyru@roosevelt.edu.

Rowan University, Graduate School, College of Education, Glassboro, NJ 08028-1701. Offers M Ed, MA, MST, Ed D, CAGS, Ed S. *Accreditation:* NCATE. Part-time and evening/weekend programs available. *Students:* 131 full-time (111 women), 438 part-time (359 women); includes 77 minority (49 African Americans, 3 American Indian/Alaska Native, 11 Asian Americans or Pacific Islanders, 14 Hispanic Americans). Average age 34. 95 applicants, 52% accepted, 49 enrolled. In 2006, 234 master's, 5 doctorates awarded. *Degree requirements:* For master's, thesis/dissertation, comprehensive exam; for doctorate, thesis/dissertation. *Entrance requirements:* For master's, GRE General Test; for doctorate, GRE General Test, master's degree. Additional exam requirements/recommendations for international students: Required—TOEFL. *Application deadline:* Applications are processed on a rolling basis. Application fee: $50. Electronic applications accepted. *Expenses:* Tuition, state resident: full-time $9,882; part-time $549 per credit. Tuition, nonresident: full-time $9,882; part-time $549 per credit. Tuition and fees vary according to degree level. *Financial support:* Career-related internships or fieldwork, Federal Work-Study, and unspecified assistantships available. Support available to part-time students. *Unit head:* Dr. Carol Sharp, Dean, 856-256-4750.

Rutgers, The State University of New Jersey, New Brunswick, Graduate School of Education, New Brunswick, NJ 08901-1281. Offers Ed M, Ed D, PhD. Part-time and evening/weekend programs available. *Faculty:* 52 full-time (29 women), 54 part-time/adjunct (34 women). *Students:* 313 full-time (244 women), 462 part-time (333 women); includes 115 minority (39 African Americans, 45 Asian Americans or Pacific Islanders, 31 Hispanic Americans), 42 international. 946 applicants, 51% accepted, 337 enrolled. In 2006, 304 master's, 24 doctorates awarded. Terminal master's awarded for partial completion of doctoral program. *Degree requirements:* For master's, comprehensive exam (for some programs); for doctorate, thesis/dissertation. *Entrance requirements:* For master's and doctorate, GRE General Test. Additional exam requirements/recommendations for international students: Required—TOEFL (minimum score 575 paper-based; 233 computer-based). Application fee: $60. Electronic applications accepted. *Financial support:* In 2006–07, 142 students received support, including 7 fellowships with full and partial tuition reimbursements available, 8 research assistantships with full tuition reimbursements available (averaging $18,347 per year), 9 teaching assistantships with full tuition reimbursements available (averaging $18,347 per year); career-related internships or fieldwork, Federal Work-Study, institutionally sponsored loans, and scholarships/grants also available. Support available to part-time students. Financial award application deadline: 3/15; financial award applicants required to submit FAFSA. Total annual research expenditures: $6 million. *Unit head:* Dr. Richard DeLisi, Dean, 732-932-7496 Ext. 8117, Fax: 732-932-8206, E-mail: delisi@rci.rutgers.edu. *Application contact:* Dr. Warren Crown, Associate Dean for Academic Affairs, 732-932-7496 Ext. 8102, Fax: 732-932-8206, E-mail: wcrown@rci.rutgers.edu.

Sacred Heart University, Graduate Studies, College of Education and Health Professions, Department of Education, Fairfield, CT 06825-1000. Offers administration (CAS); educational technology (MAT); elementary education (MAT); reading (CAS); secondary education (MAT); teaching (CAS). Part-time and evening/weekend programs available. Postbaccalaureate distance learning degree programs offered (minimal on-campus study). *Faculty:* 23 full-time (10 women). *Students:* 360 full-time (285 women), 710 part-time (520 women); includes 39 minority (15 African Americans, 4 American Indian/Alaska Native, 5 Asian Americans or Pacific Islanders, 15 Hispanic Americans), 4 international. Average age 34. 335 applicants, 87% accepted, 270 enrolled. In 2006, 312 master's, 59 other advanced degrees awarded. *Degree requirements:* For master's, thesis or alternative. *Entrance requirements:* For master's, PRAXIS (teacher certification/MAT); for CAS, PRAXIS I. Additional exam requirements/recommendations for international students: Required—TOEFL (minimum score 550 paper-based; 213 computer-based). *Application deadline:* Applications are processed on a rolling basis. Application fee: $50 ($100 for international students). Electronic applications accepted. *Expenses:* Contact institution. Full-time tuition and fees vary according to degree level and program. *Financial support:* Teaching assistantships with partial tuition reimbursements, career-related internships or fieldwork, institutionally sponsored loans, traineeships, tuition waivers (partial), and unspecified assistantships available. Support available to part-time students. Financial award applicants required to submit FAFSA. *Faculty research:* Reading education, learning theory, teacher preparation, education of underachievers. *Unit head:* Dr. Edward Malin, Director, 203-371-7800, Fax: 203-365-7513. *Application contact:* Alexis Haakonsen, Dean of Graduate Admissions, 203-365-7619, Fax: 203-365-4732, E-mail: haakonsena@sacredheart.edu.

Sage Graduate School, Graduate School, Division of Education, Troy, NY 12180-4115. Offers childhood education (MS Ed); childhood education/literacy (MS); childhood special education (MS Ed); guidance and counseling (MS, Post Master's Certificate); literacy (MS Ed); literacy/childhood special education (MS Ed); school health education (MS); teaching (MAT), including art education, biology, English, mathematics, social studies. *Accreditation:* NCATE. Part-time and evening/weekend programs available. *Faculty:* 11 full-time (8 women), 20 part-time/adjunct (15 women). *Students:* 171 full-time (147 women), 230 part-time (194 women); includes 19 minority (7 African Americans, 1 American Indian/Alaska Native, 5 Asian Americans or Pacific Islanders, 6 Hispanic Americans). Average age 27. 267 applicants, 68% accepted, 107 enrolled. In 2006, 187 master's, 5 other advanced degrees awarded. *Entrance requirements:* Additional exam requirements/recommendations for international students: Required—TOEFL (minimum score 550 paper-based; 213 computer-based). *Application deadline:* Applications are processed on a rolling basis. Application fee: $40. *Expenses:* Tuition: Full-time $9,270; part-time $515 per credit hour. *Financial support:* Career-related internships or fieldwork, scholarships/grants, and unspecified assistantships available. Support available to part-time students. Financial award application deadline: 3/1; financial award applicants required to submit FAFSA. *Faculty research:* Literacy development in at-risk children, effective behavior strategies for class instruction. *Unit head:* Dr. Connell G. Frazer, Dean, 518-244-2326, Fax: 518-244-2334, E-mail: frazec@sage.edu. *Application contact:* Shannon K. Easton, Director of Graduate and Adult Admission, 518-244-2443, Fax: 518-244-6880, E-mail: sgsadm@sage.edu.

Saginaw Valley State University, College of Education, University Center, MI 48710. Offers M Ed, MAT, Ed S. *Accreditation:* NCATE. Part-time and evening/weekend programs available. *Faculty:* 40 full-time (29 women), 44 part-time/adjunct (33 women). *Students:* 74 full-time (58 women), 1,264 part-time (968 women); includes 48 minority (29 African Americans, 1 American Indian/Alaska Native, 7 Asian Americans or Pacific Islanders, 11 Hispanic Americans), 1 international. Average age 34. 280 applicants, 100% accepted, 211 enrolled. In 2006, 387 master's, 16 other advanced degrees awarded. *Entrance requirements:* For master's, minimum GPA of 3.0, teaching certificate. *Application deadline:* Applications are processed on a rolling basis. Application fee: $25. Electronic applications accepted. *Expenses:* Tuition, state resident: full-time $7,225; part-time $301 per credit hour. Tuition, nonresident: full-time $13,888; part-time $579 per credit hour. Required fees: $330; $14 per credit hour. Tuition and fees vary according to course load. *Financial support:* Federal Work-Study available. Support available to part-time students. Financial award applicants required to submit FAFSA. *Faculty research:* Effective schools, foundations of education, children's literature, English education, restructuring of schools. *Unit head:* Dr. Steve P. Barbus, Dean, 989-964-6067, Fax: 989-790-4385, E-mail: barbus@svsu.edu. *Application contact:* Jeanne Chipman, Certification Officer, 989-964-4083, Fax: 989-964-4385, E-mail: jdc@svsu.edu.

St. Ambrose University, College of Education and Health Sciences, Program in Education, Davenport, IA 52803-2898. Offers special education (M Ed); teaching (M Ed). Part-time and evening/weekend programs available. Postbaccalaureate distance learning degree programs offered (no on-campus study). *Faculty:* 3 full-time (0 women), 3 part-time/adjunct (2 women). *Students:* 5 full-time (all women), 67 part-time (61 women); includes 2 minority (both Hispanic Americans) Average age 39. 24 applicants, 92% accepted, 22 enrolled. In 2006, 5 degrees awarded. *Degree requirements:* For master's, comprehensive exam. *Entrance requirements:* For master's, GRE General Test or MAT, minimum GPA of 2.75. Additional exam requirements/recommendations for international students: Required—TOEFL. *Application deadline:* For fall admission, 8/15 priority date for domestic students; for spring admission, 11/1 for domestic students. Applications are processed on a rolling basis. Application fee: $25. Electronic applications accepted. *Financial support:* In 2006–07, 13 students received support, including 2 research assistantships with partial tuition reimbursements available (averaging $3,600 per year); career-related internships or fieldwork, tuition waivers (full and partial), and unspecified assistantships also available. Support available to part-time students. Financial award application deadline: 3/15; financial award applicants required to submit FAFSA. *Faculty research:* Disabilities and postsecondary career avenues, self-determination. *Unit head:* Dr. William Hitchings, Head, 563-333-6113, Fax: 563-333-6297. *Application contact:* Elizabeth Berridge, Director of Graduate Student Recruitment, 563-333-6271, Fax: 563-333-6268, E-mail: berridgeelizabethb@sau.edu.

St. Bonaventure University, School of Graduate Studies, School of Education, St. Bonaventure, NY 14778-2284. Offers MS, MS Ed, Adv C. *Accreditation:* NCATE. Part-time and evening/weekend programs available. *Faculty research:* Learning disabilities, self-concept, reading diagnosis, professional development schools.

St. Cloud State University, School of Graduate Studies, College of Education, St. Cloud, MN 56301-4498. Offers MS, Spt. *Accreditation:* NCATE. Part-time and evening/weekend programs available. *Faculty:* 96 full-time (52 women), 18 part-time/adjunct (14 women). *Students:* 207 full-time (145 women), 350 part-time (271 women); includes 25 minority (11 African Americans, 3 American Indian/Alaska Native, 5 Asian Americans or Pacific Islanders, 6 Hispanic Americans), 26 international. 390 applicants, 60% accepted. In 2006, 186 degrees awarded. *Degree requirements:* For master's, thesis or alternative, comprehensive exam (for some programs); for Spt, thesis, field study. *Entrance requirements:* For master's, GRE General Test, minimum GPA of 2.75; for Spt, GRE General Test, minimum GPA of 3.25. Additional

Education—General

St. Cloud State University (continued)
exam requirements/recommendations for international students: Required—MELAB; Recommended—TOEFL (minimum score 550 paper-based; 213 computer-based), IELTS (minimum score 7). *Application deadline:* Applications are processed on a rolling basis. Application fee: $35. *Financial support:* Career-related internships or fieldwork, Federal Work-Study, scholarships/grants, and unspecified assistantships available. Financial award application deadline: 3/1. *Unit head:* Dr. Kate Steffens, Interim Dean, 320-308-3023, Fax: 320-308-4237, E-mail: ksteffens@stcloudstate.edu. *Application contact:* Linda Lou Krueger, School of Graduate Studies, 320-308-2113, Fax: 320-308-5371, E-mail: lekrueger@stcloudstate.edu.

St. Edward's University, School of Education, Austin, TX 78704. Offers MA. Part-time and evening/weekend programs available. *Students:* Average age 35. 10 applicants, 70% accepted, 7 enrolled. *Degree requirements:* For master's, minimum 24 resident hours. *Entrance requirements:* For master's, GRE General Test, minimum GPA of 3.0 in last 60 hours or 2.75 overall.. Additional exam requirements/recommendations for international students: Required—TOEFL (minimum score 550 paper-based; 213 computer-based; 79 iBT). *Application deadline:* For fall admission, 8/1 for domestic students, 7/1 for international students; for spring admission, 12/1 for domestic students, 11/1 for international students. Applications are processed on a rolling basis. Application fee: $45 ($50 for international students). Electronic applications accepted. *Expenses:* Tuition: Full-time $11,682; part-time $649 per credit hour. Full-time tuition and fees vary according to course load and program. *Financial support:* Scholarships/grants available. *Unit head:* Dr. Karen Jenlink, Dean, 512-448-8655, Fax: 512-428-1372, E-mail: karenj@stedwards.edu. *Application contact:* Kay L. Arnold, Graduate Admissions Coordinator, 512-233-1636, Fax: 512-428-1032, E-mail: kayla@stedwards.edu.

Saint Francis University, Department of Education and Educational Leadership, Loretto, PA 15940-0600. Offers education (M Ed); educational leadership (MEDL); reading (M Ed). Part-time and evening/weekend programs available. *Faculty:* 24 part-time/adjunct (8 women). *Students:* Average age 30. 19 applicants, 100% accepted, 19 enrolled. In 2006, 35 degrees awarded. *Degree requirements:* For master's, thesis optional. *Entrance requirements:* For master's, GRE or MAT if undergraduate GPA is less than 2.8, minimum undergraduate QPA of 2.5. *Application deadline:* Applications are processed on a rolling basis. Application fee: $30. *Expenses: Contact institution.* Tuition and fees vary according to program. *Financial support:* Research assistantships with full and partial tuition reimbursements, teaching assistantships with full and partial tuition reimbursements, career-related internships or fieldwork and unspecified assistantships available. *Unit head:* Dr. Janette D. Kelly, Director, Graduate Education, 814-472-3058, Fax: 814-472-3864, E-mail: jkelly@francis.edu.

St. Francis Xavier University, Graduate Studies, Graduate Studies in Education, Antigonish, NS B2G 2W5, Canada. Offers curriculum and instruction (M Ed); educational administration and leadership (M Ed). Part-time programs available. Postbaccalaureate distance learning degree programs offered (minimal on-campus study). *Faculty:* 20 part-time/adjunct (10 women). *Students:* 2 full-time, 131 part-time. 55 applicants, 36% accepted. In 2006, 79 degrees awarded. *Degree requirements:* For master's, thesis, registration. *Entrance requirements:* For master's, minimum undergraduate B average, 2 years of teaching experience. *Application deadline:* For fall admission, 1/15 priority date for domestic students, 1/15 for international students. Application fee: $40. *Financial support:* In 2006–07, teaching assistantships (averaging $500 per year). *Faculty research:* Inclusive education, qualitative research. Total annual research expenditures: $70,000. *Unit head:* Dr. Jim Greenlaw, Chair, 902-867-5416, Fax: 902-867-3887, E-mail: jgreenla@stfx.ca. *Application contact:* Colleen Jones, Assistant, 902-867-3906, Fax: 902-867-5154, E-mail: med@stfx.ca.

St. John Fisher College, Office of the Provost, Ralph C. Wilson Jr. School of Education, Rochester, NY 14618-3597. Offers MS, MS Ed, Ed D, Certificate. *Accreditation:* NCATE. *Faculty:* 25 full-time (12 women), 30 part-time/adjunct (22 women). *Students:* 137 full-time (104 women), 377 part-time (289 women); includes 66 minority (46 African Americans, 3 American Indian/Alaska Native, 5 Asian Americans or Pacific Islanders, 12 Hispanic Americans). Average age 31. 319 applicants, 85% accepted, 189 enrolled. In 2006, 214 degrees awarded. *Entrance requirements:* For master's, minimum GPA of 3.0, letters of reference. Additional exam requirements/recommendations for international students: Required—TOEFL (minimum score 575 paper-based; 233 computer-based; 80 iBT). *Application deadline:* For spring admission, 10/30 for domestic students. Applications are processed on a rolling basis. Application fee: $30. *Expenses:* Tuition: Part-time $615 per credit. Tuition and fees vary according to program. *Financial support:* In 2006–07, 4 students received support. Federal Work-Study and scholarships/grants available. Financial award application deadline: 2/15; financial award applicants required to submit FAFSA. *Unit head:* Dr. Arthur Walton, Dean, 585-385-8387, E-mail: awalton@sjfc.edu. *Application contact:* Shannon Cleverley, Director of Graduate Admissions, 585-385-8161, Fax: 585-385-8344, E-mail: scleverley@sjfc.edu.

St. John's University, The School of Education, Queens, NY 11439. Offers MS Ed, Ed D, PD. *Accreditation:* Teacher Education Accreditation Council. Part-time and evening/weekend programs available. *Faculty:* 42 full-time (24 women), 111 part-time/adjunct (63 women). *Students:* 138 full-time (109 women), 1,512 part-time (1,160 women); includes 396 minority (179 African Americans, 4 American Indian/Alaska Native, 69 Asian Americans or Pacific Islanders, 144 Hispanic Americans), 43 international. Average age 33. 889 applicants, 74% accepted, 410 enrolled. In 2006, 403 master's, 21 doctorates, 37 other advanced degrees awarded. *Degree requirements:* For doctorate, one foreign language, thesis/dissertation, internship, comprehensive exam. *Entrance requirements:* For doctorate, GRE General Test, interview, writing sample, 2 years of teaching experience. Additional exam requirements/recommendations for international students: Required—TOEFL (minimum score 500 paper-based; 173 computer-based). *Application deadline:* For fall admission, 4/15 for domestic students, 5/1 priority date for international students; for spring admission, 11/1 priority date for international students. Applications are processed on a rolling basis. Application fee: $40. Electronic applications accepted. *Expenses:* Tuition: Full-time $18,480; part-time $770 per credit. Required fees: $125 per semester. Tuition and fees vary according to program. *Financial support:* In 2006–07, 1,576 students received support, including 156 fellowships with full and partial tuition reimbursements available (averaging $12,986 per year), 8 research assistantships with full and partial tuition reimbursements available (averaging $10,049 per year); teaching assistantships with full and partial tuition reimbursements available, career-related internships or fieldwork and scholarships/grants also available. Support available to part-time students. Financial award application deadline: 3/1; financial award applicants required to submit FAFSA. *Faculty research:* Bilingual education, learning disabilities, counseling special populations, organizational theory, school law. Total annual research expenditures: $6.8 million. *Unit head:* Dr. Jerrold Ross, Dean, 718-990-1305, Fax: 718-990-6096, E-mail: rossj@stjohns.edu. *Application contact:* Kelly Ronayne, Assistant Dean, 718-990-2303, Fax: 718-990-6069, E-mail: graded@stjohns.edu.

Saint Joseph College, Graduate Division, Department of Education, West Hartford, CT 06117-2700. Offers early childhood education (MA); education (MA), including self-designed specializations; special education (MA). Part-time and evening/weekend programs available. *Degree requirements:* For master's, thesis or alternative, comprehensive exam. *Entrance requirements:* For master's, 2 letters of recommendation. Electronic applications accepted.

St. Joseph's College, New York, Graduate Programs, Program in Education, Brooklyn, NY 11205-3688. Offers infant/toddler early childhood special education (MA); literacy and cognition (MA); special education (MA), including severe and multiple disabilities.

See Close-Up on page 915.

Saint Joseph's College of Maine, Program in Teacher Education, Standish, ME 04084-5263. Offers MS. Program available by correspondence. Part-time programs available. Postbaccalaureate distance learning degree programs offered (minimal on-campus study). *Faculty:* 19 part-time/adjunct (15 women). *Students:* 266 (195 women); includes 13 minority (3 African Americans, 1 American Indian/Alaska Native, 2 Asian Americans or Pacific Islanders, 7 Hispanic Americans). Average age 43. 164 applicants, 97% accepted, 154 enrolled. In 2006, 25 degrees awarded. *Degree requirements:* For master's, summer residency. *Application deadline:* Applications are processed on a rolling basis. Application fee: $50. Electronic applications accepted. *Expenses:* Tuition: Part-time $350 per credit. *Financial support:* Institutionally sponsored loans available. Support available to part-time students. *Unit head:* Dr. Richard Willis, Director, 207-893-7992, Fax: 207-892-7987, E-mail: rwillis@sjcme.edu. *Application contact:* 800-752-4723, Fax: 207-892-7480, E-mail: info@sjcme.edu.

Saint Joseph's University, College of Arts and Sciences, Department of Education, Philadelphia, PA 19131-1395. Offers educational leadership (Ed D); elementary education (MS); instructional technology (MS); professional education (MS); reading (MS); secondary education (MS); special education (MS); training and organizational development (MS, Certificate). Part-time and evening/weekend programs available. *Faculty:* 18 full-time (9 women), 67 part-time/adjunct (34 women). *Students:* 77 full-time (63 women), 551 part-time (417 women); includes 115 minority (94 African Americans, 2 American Indian/Alaska Native, 8 Asian Americans or Pacific Islanders, 11 Hispanic Americans), 12 international. In 2006, 286 master's, 5 doctorates awarded. *Entrance requirements:* For master's, 2 letters of recommendation, minimum GPA of 3.0; for doctorate, GRE/MAT, 2 letters of recommendation, resumé. Additional exam requirements/recommendations for international students: Required—TOEFL. *Application deadline:* For fall admission, 7/15 for domestic students. Application fee: $35. *Expenses: Contact institution. Financial support:* Fellowships, research assistantships, career-related internships or fieldwork and Federal Work-Study available. Support available to part-time students. *Unit head:* Dr. Encarnacion Rodriguez, Director of Graduate Education, 610-660-3348.

St. Lawrence University, Department of Education, Canton, NY 13617-1455. Offers counseling and human development (M Ed, CAS); education (Certificate); educational administration (M Ed, CAS); general studies (M Ed). *Accreditation:* Teacher Education Accreditation Council. Part-time and evening/weekend programs available. *Degree requirements:* For master's, thesis optional. *Entrance requirements:* For master's, GRE General Test. *Faculty research:* Defense mechanisms, conflict negotiations and mediation, teacher education policy.

Saint Leo University, Graduate Studies in Education, Saint Leo, FL 33574-6665. Offers education (MAT); educational leadership (M Ed); exceptional student education (M Ed); instructional leadership (M Ed); reading (M Ed). Part-time and evening/weekend programs available. Postbaccalaureate distance learning degree programs offered (minimal on-campus study). *Faculty:* 8 full-time (5 women), 10 part-time/adjunct (all women). *Students:* 96 full-time (77 women), 169 part-time (143 women); includes 22 minority (16 African Americans, 6 Hispanic Americans), 2 international. Average age 35. 365 applicants, 54% accepted, 116 enrolled. In 2006, 39 degrees awarded. *Degree requirements:* For master's, comprehensive exam or passing FELE scores. *Entrance requirements:* For master's, GRE General Test or MAT, 2 letters of recommendation, minimum undergraduate GPA of 3.0 or GRE or MAT, professional teaching certificate, resumé. Additional exam requirements/recommendations for international students: Required—TOEFL (minimum score 550 paper-based; 213 computer-based). *Application deadline:* For fall admission, 7/1 priority date for domestic students; for spring admission, 11/12 priority date for domestic students. Applications are processed on a rolling basis. Application fee: $45. Electronic applications accepted. *Financial support:* In 2006–07, 242 students received support. Career-related internships or fieldwork, Federal Work-Study, and scholarships/grants available. Support available to part-time students. Financial award application deadline: 3/1; financial award applicants required to submit FAFSA. *Faculty research:* The role of the school leader in (1) data analysis of student achievement (2) teacher recruitment (3) teacher effectiveness. *Unit head:* Dr. John Smith, Director, 352-588-8309, Fax: 352-588-8861, E-mail: med@saintleo.edu. *Application contact:* Scott Cathcart, Vice President of Enrollment, 800-707-8846, Fax: 352-588-7873, E-mail: grad.admission@saintleo.edu.

Saint Louis University, Graduate School, College of Public Service and Graduate School, Department of Educational Studies, St. Louis, MO 63103-2097. Offers curriculum and instruction (MA, Ed D, PhD); educational foundations (MA, Ed D, PhD); special education (MA); teaching (MAT). *Accreditation:* NCATE. Part-time programs available. *Faculty:* 12 full-time (8 women), 18 part-time/adjunct (12 women). *Students:* 15 full-time (10 women), 53 part-time (42 women); includes 3 minority (1 African American, 2 Asian Americans or Pacific Islanders), 4 international. Average age 36. 25 applicants, 80% accepted, 14 enrolled. In 2006, 2 master's, 5 doctorates awarded. *Degree requirements:* For master's, comprehensive exam, registration; for doctorate, thesis/dissertation, preliminary oral and written exams, comprehensive exam, registration. *Entrance requirements:* For master's, GRE General Test or MAT, letters of recommendation, resumé; for doctorate, GRE General Test, letters of recommendation, resumé. Additional exam requirements/recommendations for international students: Required—TOEFL (minimum score 525 paper-based; 194 computer-based). *Application deadline:* For fall admission, 7/1 for domestic and international students; for spring admission, 11/1 for domestic and international students. Applications are processed on a rolling basis. Application fee: $40. *Expenses:* Tuition: Part-time $800 per credit hour. Required fees: $105 per semester. *Financial support:* In 2006–07, 24 students received support, including 4 teaching assistantships with full tuition reimbursements available (averaging $11,000 per year); Federal Work-Study, scholarships/grants, traineeships, health care benefits, and unspecified assistantships also available. Support available to part-time students. Financial award application deadline: 6/1; financial award applicants required to submit FAFSA. *Faculty research:* Teacher preparation, multicultural issues, children with special needs, qualitative research in education, inclusion. *Unit head:* Dr. Mary Chittooran, Interim Chairperson, 314-977-4062, Fax: 314-977-3214, E-mail: chittomm@slu.edu. *Application contact:* Gary Behrman, Associate Dean of the Graduate School, 314-977-3827, E-mail: behrmang@slu.edu.

Saint Martin's University, Graduate Programs, Department of Education, Lacey, WA 98503-1297. Offers administration (M Ed); English as a second language (M Ed); guidance and counseling (M Ed); reading (M Ed); special education (M Ed); teaching (MIT); technology in education (M Ed). Part-time and evening/weekend programs available. *Degree requirements:* For master's, thesis or alternative, project or comprehensives, comprehensive exam (for some programs). *Entrance requirements:* For master's, GRE General Test or MAT, resumé. Additional exam requirements/recommendations for international students: Required—TOEFL (minimum score 560 paper-based). *Faculty research:* Reader's theatre and reader/writer workshops, curriculum and assessment integration, gender and equity, classroom evaluations, organizational leadership.

Saint Mary's College of California, School of Education, Moraga, CA 94575. Offers M Ed, MA, MAT, PhD. Part-time and evening/weekend programs available. *Faculty:* 28 full-time (22 women), 82 part-time/adjunct (63 women). *Students:* 230 full-time (188 women), 408 part-time (310 women); includes 133 minority (40 African Americans, 4 American Indian/Alaska Native, 32 Asian Americans or Pacific Islanders, 57 Hispanic Americans), 26 international. Average age 29. 409 applicants, 98% accepted. In 2006, 102 master's, 8 doctorates awarded. *Degree requirements:* For master's, thesis or alternative; for doctorate, thesis/dissertation. *Entrance requirements:* For master's, interview, minimum GPA of 3.0; for doctorate, GRE or MAT, interview, MA, minimum GPA of 3.0. *Application deadline:* Applications are processed on a rolling basis. Application fee: $50. *Expenses: Contact institution. Financial support:* In 2006–07, 44 students received support. Career-related internships or fieldwork and tuition waivers (partial) available. Support available to part-time students. Financial award application deadline: 2/15; financial award applicants required to submit FAFSA. *Faculty research:* Teacher effectiveness, school-based management, multicultural teaching, language and literacy development. Total annual research expenditures: $15,000. *Unit head:* Dr. Nancy L. Sorenson, Dean, 925-631-4309, Fax: 925-376-8379, E-mail: nsorenso@stmarys-ca.edu. *Application contact:* Jane Joyce, Coordinator Recruitment and Admissions, 925-631-4700, Fax: 925-376-8379, E-mail: soereq@stmarys-ca.edu.

Saint Mary's University of Minnesota, School of Graduate and Professional Programs, Program in Education, Winona, MN 55987-1399. Offers MA. *Unit head:* Claudia Risnes, Director, 612-728-5179, Fax: 612-728-5121, E-mail: crisnes@smumn.edu.

Saint Mary's University of Minnesota, School of Graduate and Professional Programs, Program in Teaching and Learning, Winona, MN 55987-1399. Offers M Ed. *Unit head:* Suzanne Peterson, Director, 952-891-3792, E-mail: speterso@smumn.edu.

St. Mary's University of San Antonio, Graduate School, Department of Teacher Education, San Antonio, TX 78228-8507. Offers Catholic principalship (Certificate); Catholic school leadership (MA, Certificate), including Catholic school administrators (Certificate), Catholic school leadership (MA), Catholic school teachers (Certificate); educational leadership (MA, Certificate), including educational leadership (MA), principalship (mid-management) (Certificate); reading (MA). Part-time and evening/weekend programs available. *Faculty:* 5 full-time (3 women), 1 part-time/adjunct (0 women). *Students:* 54; includes 21 minority (1 African American, 1 Asian American or Pacific Islander, 19 Hispanic Americans). Average age 34. In 2006, 23 degrees awarded. *Degree requirements:* For master's, comprehensive exam (for some programs), registration. *Entrance requirements:* For master's, GRE General Test. Additional exam requirements/recommendations for international students: Required—TOEFL (minimum score 550 paper-based; 213 computer-based). *Application deadline:* Applications are processed on a rolling basis. Application fee: $30. Electronic applications accepted. *Expenses:* Tuition: Full-time $10,890; part-time $605 per hour. Required fees: $500. Tuition and fees vary according to degree level. *Financial support:* Career-related internships or fieldwork, Federal Work-Study, institutionally sponsored loans, scholarships/grants, health care benefits, and unspecified assistantships available. Financial award application deadline: 3/31; financial award applicants required to submit FAFSA. *Unit head:* Dr. Dan Higgins, Chair, 210-436-3121.

Saint Michael's College, Graduate Programs, Program in Education, Colchester, VT 05439. Offers administration (M Ed, CAGS); arts in education (CAGS); curriculum and instruction (M Ed, CAGS); information technology (CAGS); reading (M Ed); special education (M Ed, CAGS); technology (M Ed). Part-time and evening/weekend programs available. *Faculty:* 5 full-time (3 women), 35 part-time/adjunct (29 women). *Students:* 26 full-time (18 women), 114 part-time (86 women), 2 international. Average age 34. 48 applicants, 81% accepted, 36 enrolled. In 2006, 46 degrees awarded. *Degree requirements:* For master's, thesis. *Entrance requirements:* For master's, minimum GPA of 3.0. *Application deadline:* Applications are processed on a rolling basis. Application fee: $35. Electronic applications accepted. *Financial support:* Fellowships, scholarships/grants available. Support available to part-time students. Financial award applicants required to submit FAFSA. *Faculty research:* Integrative curriculum, moral and spiritual dimensions of education, learning styles, multiple intelligences, integrating technology into the curriculum. *Unit head:* Dr. Anne P. Judson, Director, 802-654-2649, Fax: 802-654-2664, E-mail: ajudson@smcvt.edu.

St. Norbert College, Program in Education, De Pere, WI 54115-2099. Offers MS. Part-time and evening/weekend programs available. *Faculty:* 2 full-time (both women), 1 (woman) part-time/adjunct. *Students:* 30 applicants, 53% accepted, 15 enrolled. *Degree requirements:* For master's, advocacy project. *Entrance requirements:* For master's, minimum undergraduate GPA of 3.0 or graduate GPA of 3.25; 2 years of teaching experience, state teacher certification or proof of teaching experience. *Application deadline:* Applications are processed on a rolling basis. Application fee: $35. Electronic applications accepted. *Expenses:* Tuition: Part-time $335 per credit. *Financial support:* Scholarships/grants and tuition waivers (partial) available. Support available to part-time students. *Faculty research:* Literacy, portfolios, integrated curriculum, technology. *Unit head:* Dr. Susan Landt, Director/Professor, 920-403-1328, Fax: 920-403-4078, E-mail: susan.landt@snc.edu. *Application contact:* Karen L. Cleereman, Office Manager, Fax: 920-403-4078, E-mail: karen.cleereman@snc.edu.

Saint Peter's College, Graduate Programs in Education, Jersey City, NJ 07306-5997. Offers administration and supervision (MA); reading specialist (MA); teaching (MA, Certificate), including elementary teacher (Certificate), supervisor of instruction (Certificate), teaching (MA); urban education (MA). Part-time and evening/weekend programs available. *Degree requirements:* For master's, departmental qualifying exam. *Entrance requirements:* For master's, GRE or MAT.

St. Thomas Aquinas College, Division of Teacher Education, Sparkill, NY 10976. Offers adolescence education (MST); childhood and special education (MST); childhood education (MST); reading (MS Ed, PMC); special education (MS Ed, PMC); teaching (MS Ed), including elementary education, middle school education, secondary education. *Accreditation:* NCATE. Part-time and evening/weekend programs available. *Degree requirements:* For master's, comprehensive professional portfolio; for PMC, action research project. *Entrance requirements:* For master's, New York State Qualifying Exam, GRE General Test or minimum GPA of 3.0, teaching certificate; for PMC, GRE General Test or minimum GPA of 3.0. Electronic applications accepted. *Faculty research:* Computer applications in education, adolescent special education students, literacy development, inclusive practices for special education students.

See Close-Up on page 917.

St. Thomas University, School of Graduate Studies, Department of Education, Miami Gardens, FL 33054-6459. Offers educational administration (MS, Certificate); educational leadership (Ed D); elementary education (MS); reading (MS); special education (MS). Part-time and evening/weekend programs available. *Degree requirements:* For master's, comprehensive exam; for doctorate, thesis/dissertation, comprehensive exam. *Entrance requirements:* For master's, interview, minimum GPA of 3.0 or GRE; for doctorate, GRE or MAT. Additional exam requirements/recommendations for international students: Required—TOEFL. Electronic applications accepted.

Saint Vincent College, Program in Education, Latrobe, PA 15650-2690. Offers curriculum and instruction (MS); environmental education (MS); library media management (MS); school administration (MS); special education (MS). Part-time and evening/weekend programs available. *Degree requirements:* For master's, comprehensive exam. *Entrance requirements:* For master's, GRE (if undergraduate GPA is below 3.0). Additional exam requirements/recommendations for international students: Required—TOEFL (minimum score 550 paper-based; 213 computer-based). *Faculty research:* Assessment and instructional technology.

Saint Xavier University, Graduate Studies, School of Education, Chicago, IL 60655-3105. Offers counseling (MA); counselor education (MA); curriculum and instruction (MA); early childhood education (MA); education (CAS); educational administration (MA); elementary education (MA); field-based education (MA); general educational studies (MA); individualized program (MA); learning disabilities (MA); reading (MA); secondary education (MA). *Accreditation:* NCATE. Part-time and evening/weekend programs available. *Faculty:* 92. *Students:* 45 full-time (35 women), 1,529 part-time (1,309 women). In 2006, 474 degrees awarded. *Degree requirements:* For master's, thesis or project. *Entrance requirements:* For master's, minimum GPA of 3.0. *Application deadline:* For fall admission, 8/15 priority date for domestic students. Applications are processed on a rolling basis. Application fee: $35. *Expenses:* Contact institution. *Financial support:* Career-related internships or fieldwork available. Support available to part-time students. Financial award applicants required to submit FAFSA. *Unit head:* Dr. Beverly Gulley, Dean, 773-298-3221, Fax: 773-779-9061, E-mail: gulley@sxu.edu. *Application contact:* Beth Gierach, Managing Director of Admission, 773-298-3053, Fax: 773-298-3076, E-mail: gierach@sxu.edu.

Salem College, Department of Education, Winston-Salem, NC 27108-0548. Offers early education and leadership (MAT); elementary education (MAT); English as a second language (MAT); language and literacy (M Ed); middle school education (MAT); secondary education (MAT); special education (MAT). *Accreditation:* NCATE. Part-time and evening/weekend programs available. *Faculty:* 8 full-time (6 women), 5 part-time/adjunct (all women). *Students:* 8 full-time (all women), 250 part-time (238 women); includes 19 minority (16 African Americans, 1 Asian American or Pacific Islander, 2 Hispanic Americans). Average age 33. 110 applicants, 65% accepted, 68 enrolled. In 2006, 34 degrees awarded. *Degree requirements:* For master's, practicum (MAT), project (M Ed), oral and written comprehensive exams. *Entrance requirements:* For master's, GRE, minimum GPA of 2.5. *Application deadline:* Applications are processed on

a rolling basis. Application fee: $30. *Financial support:* In 2006–07, 152 students received support. Federal Work-Study and scholarships/grants available. Support available to part-time students. Financial award applicants required to submit FAFSA. *Faculty research:* Content area reading strategies, literacy development, brain compatible instruction. *Unit head:* Dr. Paula Grubbs, Director of Teacher Education, 336-721-2610, Fax: 336-721-2683, E-mail: grubbs@salem.edu.

Salem International University, School of Education, Salem, WV 26426-0500. Offers curriculum and instruction (M Ed), including curriculum and instruction, educational technology leadership, physical education/health, teaching English as a second language; educational administration (M Ed). Part-time and evening/weekend programs available. Postbaccalaureate distance learning degree programs offered. *Faculty:* 5 full-time (4 women), 17 part-time/adjunct (8 women). *Students:* 74 full-time (45 women), 154 part-time (75 women); includes 7 minority (2 African Americans, 5 Asian Americans or Pacific Islanders), 28 international. Average age 41. 200 applicants, 75% accepted, 130 enrolled. In 2006, 18 degrees awarded. *Degree requirements:* For master's, thesis (for some programs), comprehensive exam (for some programs), registration. *Entrance requirements:* For master's, GRE, MAT, NTE, 3 letters of recommendation. Additional exam requirements/recommendations for international students: Required—TOEFL (minimum score 550 paper-based; 213 computer-based). *Application deadline:* Applications are processed on a rolling basis. Application fee: $25. Electronic applications accepted. *Expenses:* Contact institution. One-time fee: $25 part-time. Tuition and fees vary according to program. *Financial support:* Application deadline: 4/15; *Faculty research:* Improved classroom effectiveness. *Unit head:* Dean, School of Education, 304-326-1253, Fax: 304-326-1246. *Application contact:* Thomas White, Director of Admissions, 304-326-1549, Fax: 304-326-1246, E-mail: admission@salemiu.edu.

Salem State College, Graduate School, Program in Field-Based Master's of Education, Salem, MA 01970-5353. Offers M Ed. Part-time and evening/weekend programs available. Postbaccalaureate distance learning degree programs offered. *Students:* 27 full-time (24 women), 9 part-time (8 women); includes 1 African American, 1 international. Average age 40. In 2006, 8 degrees awarded. *Application deadline:* Applications are processed on a rolling basis. Application fee: $35. *Unit head:* MaryLou Breitborde, Associate Dean of Education, 978-542-6262, E-mail: mbreitborde@salemstate.edu.

Salisbury University, Graduate Division, Department of Education, Salisbury, MD 21801-6837. Offers art (MAT); biology (MAT); business education (MAT); chemistry (MAT); early childhood education (M Ed); educational administration (M Ed); elementary education (M Ed); English (M Ed, MAT); French (MAT); geography (MAT); history (MAT); mathematics (MAT); media and technology (MAT); music (MAT); psychology (MAT); reading education (MAT); science (MAT); secondary education (MAT); social studies (MAT); Spanish (MAT). *Accreditation:* NCATE. Part-time and evening/weekend programs available. *Faculty:* 12 full-time (6 women), 10 part-time/adjunct (8 women). *Students:* 17 full-time (9 women), 84 part-time (72 women); includes 6 minority (5 African Americans, 1 Hispanic American). Average age 30. 15 applicants, 73% accepted, 11 enrolled. In 2006, 63 degrees awarded. *Degree requirements:* For master's, comprehensive exam (for some programs). *Entrance requirements:* For master's, PRAXIS, minimum GPA of 2.75. Additional exam requirements/recommendations for international students: Required—TOEFL (minimum score 550 paper-based; 213 computer-based). *Application deadline:* For fall admission, 8/1 priority date for domestic students; for spring admission, 1/1 for domestic students. Applications are processed on a rolling basis. Application fee: $45. *Expenses:* Tuition, state resident: part-time $260 per credit hour. Tuition, nonresident: part-time $546 per credit hour. Required fees: $52 per credit hour. *Financial support:* In 2006–07, 3 teaching assistantships with full tuition reimbursements were awarded; career-related internships or fieldwork and scholarships/grants also available. Support available to part-time students. Financial award applicants required to submit FAFSA. *Faculty research:* Middle-level education, student outcomes. *Unit head:* Dr. Edward C. Robeck, Program Coordinator, 410-543-6292, Fax: 410-548-2593, E-mail: ecrobeck@salisbury.edu. *Application contact:* Debra J. Clark, Administrative Assistant I, 410-543-6281, Fax: 410-548-2593, E-mail: djclark@salisbury.edu.

Samford University, School of Education, Birmingham, AL 35229-0002. Offers early childhood education (Ed S); early childhood/elementary education (MS Ed); educational administration (Ed S); educational leadership (Ed D); elementary education (Ed S); gifted education (MS Ed); M Div/MS Ed. *Accreditation:* NCATE. Part-time programs available. *Faculty:* 12 full-time (7 women), 8 part-time/adjunct (4 women). *Students:* 16 full-time (14 women), 160 part-time (124 women); includes 25 minority (all African Americans) Average age 38. 45 applicants, 100% accepted, 17 enrolled. In 2006, 15 master's, 20 doctorates, 20 other advanced degrees awarded. *Entrance requirements:* For master's, GRE or MAT, minimum GPA of 3.0; for doctorate, minimum GPA of 3.7; for Ed S, GRE, master's degree, teaching certificate, minimum GPA of 3.25. Additional exam requirements/recommendations for international students: Required—TOEFL (minimum score 550 paper-based; 213 computer-based). *Application deadline:* Applications are processed on a rolling basis. Application fee: $25. *Expenses:* Tuition: Part-time $500 per credit. One-time fee: $25 part-time. Full-time tuition and fees vary according to program and student level. *Financial support:* In 2006–07, 54 students received support; research assistantships, career-related internships or fieldwork, Federal Work-Study, scholarships/grants, and tuition waivers (partial) available. Support available to part-time students. Financial award applicants required to submit FAFSA. *Faculty research:* School law, the characteristics of beginning teachers, the nature of school reform, school culture, quality improvement in education, K-12 student achievement. *Unit head:* Dr. Jean Ann Box, Dean, 205-726-2559, E-mail: jabox@samford.edu. *Application contact:* Dr. Maurice Persall, Director, Graduate Office, 205-726-2019, E-mail: jmpersal@samford.edu.

San Diego State University, Graduate and Research Affairs, College of Education, San Diego, CA 92182. Offers MA, MS, Ed D, PhD. *Accreditation:* NCATE. Part-time and evening/weekend programs available. *Students:* 330 full-time (257 women), 374 part-time (304 women); includes 250 minority (39 African Americans, 10 American Indian/Alaska Native, 56 Asian Americans or Pacific Islanders, 145 Hispanic Americans), 20 international. Average age 31. 707 applicants, 53% accepted, 104 enrolled. In 2006, 395 master's, 10 doctorates awarded. *Degree requirements:* For master's, thesis optional; for doctorate, thesis/dissertation. *Entrance requirements:* For master's, GRE General Test, letters of reference; for doctorate, GRE General Test, 3 letters of reference, resumé. Additional exam requirements/recommendations for international students: Required—TOEFL. Application fee: $55. Electronic applications accepted. *Financial support:* In 2006–07, 28 teaching assistantships were awarded; fellowships, research assistantships, career-related internships or fieldwork also available. Support available to part-time students. Financial award applicants required to submit FAFSA. *Faculty research:* Special education, rehabilitation counseling, educational psychology. Total annual research expenditures: $10.1 million. *Unit head:* Lionel R. Meno, Dean, 619-594-1424, Fax: 619-594-7082, E-mail: lmeno@mail.sdsu.edu.

San Francisco State University, Division of Graduate Studies, College of Education, San Francisco, CA 94132-1722. Offers MA, MA Ed, MS, Ed D, PhD, AC. *Accreditation:* NCATE. Part-time and evening/weekend programs available. *Faculty:* 95 full-time, 121 part-time/adjunct. *Students:* 1,500. *Degree requirements:* For master's, thesis optional; for doctorate, thesis/dissertation. *Entrance requirements:* For master's, minimum GPA of 2.5 in last 60 units; for doctorate, GRE General Test. *Application deadline:* For fall admission, 11/30 priority date for domestic students. Applications are processed on a rolling basis. Application fee: $55. *Financial support:* Fellowships, career-related internships or fieldwork and Federal Work-Study available. Financial award application deadline: 3/1. *Unit head:* Dr. Jacob Perea, Dean, 415-338-2687, E-mail: pjoost@sfsu.edu. *Application contact:* Dr. David Hemphill, Associate Dean, 415-338-2684, E-mail: hemphill@sfsu.edu.

San Jose State University, Graduate Studies and Research, College of Education, San Jose, CA 95192-0001. Offers MA, Certificate. *Accreditation:* NCATE. Evening/weekend programs available. *Students:* 1,217 full-time (940 women), 667 part-time (519 women);

Education—General

San Jose State University (continued)
includes 629 minority (58 African Americans, 5 American Indian/Alaska Native, 260 Asian Americans or Pacific Islanders, 306 Hispanic Americans), 35 international. Average age 35. 1,308 applicants, 81% accepted, 773 enrolled. In 2006, 506 degrees awarded. *Application deadline:* For fall admission, 6/29 for domestic students; for spring admission, 11/30 for domestic students. Applications are processed on a rolling basis. Application fee: $59. Electronic applications accepted. *Financial support:* Career-related internships or fieldwork available. Financial award applicants required to submit FAFSA. *Unit head:* Dr. Susan Meyers, Dean, 408-924-3600, Fax: 408-924-3713.

Santa Clara University, School of Education, Counseling Psychology, and Pastoral Ministries, Department of Education, Santa Clara, CA 95053. Offers education (MA); educational administration (MA); special education (MA, Certificate); teacher education (Certificate), including multiple subject teaching, single subject teaching. Part-time and evening/weekend programs available. *Students:* 76 full-time (69 women), 225 part-time (178 women); includes 66 minority (9 African Americans, 1 American Indian/Alaska Native, 28 Asian Americans or Pacific Islanders, 28 Hispanic Americans), 2 international. Average age 34. 169 applicants, 76% accepted, 104 enrolled. In 2006, 110 master's, 33 other advanced degrees awarded. *Degree requirements:* For master's, thesis optional. *Entrance requirements:* For master's, GRE or MAT. Additional exam requirements/recommendations for international students: Required—TOEFL (minimum score 570 paper-based; 215 computer-based). *Application deadline:* For fall admission, 4/1 for domestic students; for winter admission, 10/1 for domestic students; for spring admission, 2/1 for domestic students. Application fee: $50. *Expenses:* Tuition: Part-time $627 per unit. Tuition and fees vary according to program. *Financial support:* Fellowships, teaching assistantships, career-related internships or fieldwork and Federal Work-Study available. Support available to part-time students. Financial award application deadline: 3/1; financial award applicants required to submit FAFSA. *Unit head:* Dr. Tom Savage, Chair, 408-551-1787.

Sarah Lawrence College, Graduate Studies, Program in Art of Teaching, Bronxville, NY 10708-5999. Offers MS Ed. Part-time programs available. *Faculty:* 8 part-time/adjunct (7 women). *Students:* 19 full-time (16 women), 11 part-time (all women); includes 5 minority (1 African American, 1 American Indian/Alaska Native, 3 Hispanic Americans), 2 international. Average age 32. 20 applicants, 85% accepted, 12 enrolled. In 2006, 13 degrees awarded. *Degree requirements:* For master's, thesis, fieldwork, oral presentation. *Entrance requirements:* For master's, minimum B average in undergraduate coursework. Additional exam requirements/recommendations for international students: Required—TOEFL (minimum score 600 paper-based). *Application deadline:* For fall admission, 3/31 priority date for domestic students, 3/21 priority date for international students. Applications are processed on a rolling basis. Application fee: $60. *Expenses: Contact institution.* Tuition and fees vary according to program and student level. *Financial support:* In 2006–07, 23 students received support, including 13 fellowships (averaging $7,744 per year); career-related internships or fieldwork, scholarships/grants, and unspecified assistantships also available. Support available to part-time students. Financial award application deadline: 3/1. *Unit head:* Sara Wilford, Director, 914-395-2353. *Application contact:* Susan Guma, Dean of Graduate Studies, 914-395-2373, E-mail: sguma@mail.slc.edu.

School for International Training, Graduate Programs, Programs in Language Teacher Education, Brattleboro, VT 05302-0676. Offers English for speakers of other languages (MAT); French (MAT); Spanish (MAT). *Students:* 55 full-time (45 women), 85 part-time (61 women); includes 15 minority (6 African Americans, 2 American Indian/Alaska Native, 1 Asian American or Pacific Islander, 6 Hispanic Americans), 33 international. Average age 32. 186 applicants, 81% accepted, 85 enrolled. In 2006, 61 degrees awarded. *Degree requirements:* For master's, one foreign language, thesis, practice teaching. *Entrance requirements:* For master's, 4 letters of reference. Additional exam requirements/recommendations for international students: Required—TOEFL. *Application deadline:* Applications are processed on a rolling basis. Application fee: $50. *Expenses:* Tuition: Full-time $27,355; part-time $638 per credit hour. Required fees: $1,092. *Financial support:* Career-related internships or fieldwork, Federal Work-Study, institutionally sponsored loans, and scholarships/grants available. Financial award application deadline: 3/1; financial award applicants required to submit FAFSA. *Unit head:* Marla Solomon, Graduate Dean, 802-258-3325, Fax: 802-258-3241, E-mail: marla.solomon@sit.edu. *Application contact:* Information Contact, 800-336-1616, Fax: 802-258-3500, E-mail: admissions@sit.edu.

Schreiner University, Program in Education, Kerrville, TX 78028-5697. Offers M Ed, MET. Evening/weekend programs available. *Degree requirements:* For master's, thesis, comprehensive exam. *Entrance requirements:* For master's, GRE General Test, minimum GPA of 3.0, interview. Electronic applications accepted. *Faculty research:* Gang behaviors, gifted and talented education, varied intelligences, reading, classroom management.

Seattle Pacific University, Graduate School, School of Education, Seattle, WA 98119-1997. Offers M Ed, MAT, Ed D. *Accreditation:* NCATE. Part-time and evening/weekend programs available. *Faculty:* 16 full-time (5 women). *Students:* 65 full-time (50 women), 263 part-time (190 women); includes 25 minority (7 African Americans, 3 American Indian/Alaska Native, 12 Asian Americans or Pacific Islanders, 3 Hispanic Americans), 3 international. 255 applicants, 73% accepted, 151 enrolled. In 2006, 89 master's, 7 doctorates awarded. *Degree requirements:* For doctorate, thesis/dissertation, comprehensive exam. *Entrance requirements:* For master's, GRE General Test or MAT, minimum GPA of 3.0; for doctorate, GRE, MAT. *Application deadline:* Applications are processed on a rolling basis. *Expenses: Contact institution. Financial support:* In 2006–07, 5 research assistantships (averaging $4,500 per year) were awarded; career-related internships or fieldwork also available. Financial award applicants required to submit FAFSA. *Unit head:* Dr. Rick Eigenbrood, Director of Graduate Programs, 206-281-2214. *Application contact:* Allan Blomquist, Graduate Programs Manager, 206-281-2378, Fax: 206-281-2756, E-mail: blomqa@spu.edu.

Seattle University, College of Education, Seattle, WA 98122-1090. Offers M Ed, MA, MIT, Ed D, Certificate, Ed S, Post-Master's Certificate. *Accreditation:* NCATE. Part-time and evening/weekend programs available. *Faculty:* 29 full-time (16 women), 13 part-time/adjunct (9 women). *Students:* 166 full-time (132 women), 323 part-time (252 women); includes 80 minority (17 African Americans, 3 American Indian/Alaska Native, 38 Asian Americans or Pacific Islanders, 22 Hispanic Americans), 11 international. Average age 33. 496 applicants, 38% accepted, 136 enrolled. In 2006, 215 master's, 16 doctorates, 29 other advanced degrees awarded. *Degree requirements:* For master's and other advanced degree, comprehensive exam; for doctorate, thesis/dissertation, comprehensive exam. *Entrance requirements:* For doctorate, GRE General Test, MAT, interview, MA, minimum GPA of 3.5, 3 years of related experience. Additional exam requirements/recommendations for international students: Required—TOEFL. Application fee: $55. *Expenses: Contact institution. Financial support:* Career-related internships or fieldwork, Federal Work-Study, and unspecified assistantships available. Support available to part-time students. Financial award applicants required to submit FAFSA. *Faculty research:* Service learning, learning and technology, assessment models of professional education, alternative delivery systems. *Unit head:* Dr. Sue Schmitt, Dean, 206-296-5760, E-mail: sschmitt@seattleu.edu. *Application contact:* Janet Shandley, Associate Dean of Graduate Admissions, 206-296-5900, Fax: 206-298-5656, E-mail: grad_admissions@seattleu.edu.

Seton Hall University, College of Education and Human Services, South Orange, NJ 07079-2697. Offers MA, MS, Ed D, Exec Ed D, PhD, Ed S. *Accreditation:* NCATE. Part-time and evening/weekend programs available. *Faculty:* 39 full-time (21 women), 116 part-time/adjunct (32 women). *Students:* 320 full-time (201 women), 746 part-time (469 women); includes 110 minority (71 African Americans, 2 American Indian/Alaska Native, 10 Asian Americans or Pacific Islanders, 27 Hispanic Americans), 11 international. Average age 35. 365 applicants, 86% accepted, 201 enrolled. In 2006, 286 master's, 53 doctorates, 47 other advanced degrees awarded. *Degree requirements:* For master's, comprehensive exam; for doctorate, thesis/dissertation, internship, comprehensive exam. *Entrance requirements:* For doctorate, interview. *Application deadline:* Applications are processed on a rolling basis. Application fee: $50. Electronic applications accepted. *Financial support:* In 2006–07, 13 students received support; fellowships, research assistantships, career-related internships or fieldwork, institutionally sponsored loans, and unspecified assistantships available. Financial award application deadline: 2/1. *Faculty research:* Information technology and classrooms, adult development including career family systems, therapy effectiveness, management systems, principal effectiveness. Total annual research expenditures: $30,000. *Unit head:* Dr. Joseph V. De Pierro, Dean, 973-761-9025. *Application contact:* Dr. Manina Urgolo Huckvale, Associate Dean, 973-761-9668, Fax: 973-275-2187, E-mail: huckvama@shu.edu.

Seton Hill University, Program in Inclusive Education, Greensburg, PA 15601. Offers MA. Part-time and evening/weekend programs available. Postbaccalaureate distance learning degree programs offered (no on-campus study). *Faculty:* 7 full-time (5 women). *Degree requirements:* For master's, thesis optional. *Entrance requirements:* For master's, minimum GPA of 3.0. *Expenses:* Tuition: Part-time $620 per credit. Required fees: $100 per semester. *Financial support:* Scholarships/grants, tuition waivers (partial), and unspecified assistantships available. Support available to part-time students. Financial award application deadline: 8/15; financial award applicants required to submit FAFSA. *Unit head:* Dr. Sondra Lettrich, Director, 724-830-1010, Fax: 724-830-1294, E-mail: lettrich@setonhill.edu. *Application contact:* Dane Zimmer, Advisor, 724-838-4209, Fax: 724-830-1891, E-mail: zimmer@setonhill.edu.

Shenandoah University, College of Arts and Sciences, Winchester, VA 22601-5195. Offers administrative leadership (D Ed); advanced professional teaching English to speakers of other languages (Certificate); education (MSE); elementary education (Certificate); middle school education (Certificate); professional studies (Certificate); professional teaching English to speakers of other languages (Certificate); public management (Certificate); secondary education (Certificate); women's studies (Certificate). Part-time and evening/weekend programs available. Postbaccalaureate distance learning degree programs offered (minimal on-campus study). *Faculty:* 14 full-time (9 women), 7 part-time/adjunct (4 women). *Students:* 28 full-time (16 women), 283 part-time (208 women); includes 8 minority (3 African Americans, 1 American Indian/Alaska Native, 3 Asian Americans or Pacific Islanders, 1 Hispanic American), 26 international. Average age 40. 182 applicants, 68% accepted, 98 enrolled. In 2006, 96 master's, 6 doctorates, 22 other advanced degrees awarded. *Degree requirements:* For master's, thesis (for some programs), internship, comprehensive exam (for some programs); for doctorate, thesis/dissertation, comprehensive exam. *Entrance requirements:* For master's, minimum GPA of 3.0 or satisfactory GRE, 3 letters of recommendation, valid teaching license; for doctorate, minimum GPA of 3.5 in master's, 3 years of teaching experience, 3 letters of recommendation, writing samples. Additional exam requirements/recommendations for international students: Required—TOEFL (minimum score 527 paper-based; 197 computer-based; 71 iBT). *Application deadline:* For fall admission, 7/15 for domestic students; for spring admission, 10/15 for domestic students. Applications are processed on a rolling basis. Application fee: $30. Electronic applications accepted. *Expenses:* Tuition: Full-time $12,200; part-time $610 per credit. Required fees: $150. Full-time tuition and fees vary according to course load and program. *Financial support:* In 2006–07, fellowships with partial tuition reimbursements (averaging $2,581 per year); career-related internships or fieldwork, institutionally sponsored loans, and unspecified assistantships also available. Support available to part-time students. Financial award application deadline: 3/15; financial award applicants required to submit FAFSA. *Faculty research:* Nanotechnology, writing pedagogy and writing centers, violence in schools, Virginia/Shenandoah Valley history and culture, stress in children. *Unit head:* Dr. Calvin Allen, Dean, 540-665-4587, Fax: 540-665-4644, E-mail: callen@su.edu. *Application contact:* David Anthony, Dean of Admissions, 540-665-4581, Fax: 540-665-4627, E-mail: admit@su.edu.

See Close-Up on page 919.

Shippensburg University of Pennsylvania, School of Graduate Studies, College of Education and Human Services, Shippensburg, PA 17257-2299. Offers M Ed, MS, MSW, Certificate. *Accreditation:* NCATE. Part-time and evening/weekend programs available. *Faculty:* 45 full-time (22 women), 8 part-time/adjunct (6 women). *Students:* 112 full-time (89 women), 438 part-time (340 women); includes 28 minority (20 African Americans, 3 Asian Americans or Pacific Islanders, 5 Hispanic Americans), 3 international. Average age 30. 303 applicants, 54% accepted, 122 enrolled. In 2006, 168 degrees awarded. *Entrance requirements:* Additional exam requirements/recommendations for international students: Required—TOEFL (minimum score 560 paper-based; 220 computer-based). *Application deadline:* For fall admission, 3/1 for international students; for spring admission, 7/1 for international students. Applications are processed on a rolling basis. Application fee: $30. Electronic applications accepted. *Expenses:* Tuition, state resident: part-time $336 per credit. Tuition, nonresident: part-time $538 per credit. *Financial support:* In 2006–07, 70 research assistantships with full tuition reimbursements (averaging $3,125 per year) were awarded; career-related internships or fieldwork, scholarships/grants, and unspecified assistantships also available. Support available to part-time students. Financial award application deadline: 3/1; financial award applicants required to submit FAFSA. *Unit head:* Dr. Robert B. Bartos, Dean, 717-477-1373, Fax: 717-477-4012, E-mail: rbbart@ship.edu. *Application contact:* Renee Payne, Associate Dean of Graduate Admissions, 717-477-1231, Fax: 717-477-4016, E-mail: rmpayn@ship.edu.

Siena Heights University, Graduate College, Program in Teacher Education, Adrian, MI 49221-1796. Offers curriculum and instruction (MA); early childhood education (MA), including Montessori education; elementary education (MA), including elementary education/reading; middle school education (MA); secondary education (MA), including secondary education/reading. Part-time programs available. *Degree requirements:* For master's, thesis, presentation. *Entrance requirements:* For master's, minimum GPA of 3.0, interview. *Faculty research:* Teaching/learning styles, outcomes-based teaching, multiple intelligences, assessment.

Sierra Nevada College, Teacher Education Program, Incline Village, NV 89451. Offers elementary education (MAT); secondary education (MAT). Part-time and evening/weekend programs available. *Faculty:* 2 full-time (both women), 26 part-time/adjunct (16 women). *Students:* 179 full-time (136 women), 85 part-time (58 women); includes 21 minority (6 African Americans, 1 American Indian/Alaska Native, 2 Asian Americans or Pacific Islanders, 12 Hispanic Americans). Average age 35. In 2006, 29 degrees awarded. *Median time to degree:* Master's–2.5 years full-time, 3.5 years part-time. *Degree requirements:* For master's, thesis, PRAXIS I and II, comprehensive exam, registration. *Entrance requirements:* For master's, 2 letters of recommendation, minimum GPA of 3.0. *Application deadline:* For fall admission, 8/16 priority date for domestic students; for winter admission, 1/10 priority date for domestic students; for spring admission, 5/25 priority date for domestic students. Applications are processed on a rolling basis. Application fee: $50. *Expenses:* Tuition: Full-time $3,590; part-time $350 per credit. *Financial support:* In 2006–07, 230 students received support. Federal Work-Study available. Support available to part-time students. Financial award application deadline: 8/16; financial award applicants required to submit FAFSA. *Unit head:* Dr. Francesca Bero, Statewide Director, 775-831-1314, Fax: 775-832-1686, E-mail: fbero@sierranevada.edu. *Application contact:* Katrina Midgley, Teacher Education Admissions Counselor, 775-831-1314 Ext. 7517, Fax: 775-832-1694, E-mail: kmidgley@sierranevada.edu.

Silver Lake College, Division of Graduate Studies, Program in Education, Manitowoc, WI 54220-9319. Offers administrative leadership (MA); teacher leadership (MA). *Accreditation:* NCATE. Part-time and evening/weekend programs available. Postbaccalaureate distance learning degree programs offered (no on-campus study). *Faculty:* 3 full-time (all women), 33 part-time/adjunct (23 women). *Students:* 1 (woman) full-time, 53 part-time (42 women); includes 6 minority (all Hispanic Americans) Average age 35. 30 applicants, 53% accepted, 6 enrolled. In 2006, 46 degrees awarded. *Degree requirements:* For master's, thesis or alternative, public presentation of culminating project, comprehensive exam, registration. *Entrance requirements:* For master's, interview, minimum undergraduate GPA of 3.0, writing sample, 3 letters of recommendation. *Application deadline:* Applications are processed on a rolling basis. Application fee: $35. Electronic applications accepted. *Expenses:* Tuition: Full-time $6,120; part-time $340 per credit. *Financial support:* Career-related internships or fieldwork, Federal Work-Study, and scholarships/grants available. Support available to part-time students. Financial award applicants required to submit FAFSA. *Unit head:* Julie A. Mayrose, Director, 800-236-4752 Ext. 370, Fax: 920-684-7082. *Application contact:* Jamie Grant, Associate Director-Admissions, 800-236-4752 Ext. 186, Fax: 920-684-7082, E-mail: jgrant@silver.sl.edu.

Simmons College, Graduate School, College of Arts and Sciences Graduate Studies, Department of Education, Boston, MA 02115. Offers special education (MS Ed, PhD, Ed S), including applied behavior analysis (PhD), assistive technology (MS Ed, Ed S), behavioral education (MS Ed, Ed S), health professions education (PhD), language and literacy (MS Ed, Ed S), moderate disabilities (Ed S), moderate special needs (MS Ed), severe disabilities (Ed S), severe special needs (MS Ed), special education administration; teacher preparation (MAT, MS, MS Ed, CAGS), including educational leadership (MS Ed, CAGS), elementary education (MAT, CAGS), general education (CAGS), general purposes (MS), middle school education (MAT, CAGS), professional license (CAGS), professional license: elementary (MS Ed), professional license: middle/high (MS Ed), secondary education (MAT, CAGS), urban education (MS Ed, CAGS); MAT/MA. *Faculty:* 15 full-time (11 women), 59 part-time/adjunct (39 women). *Students:* 116 full-time (103 women), 558 part-time (479 women); includes 65 minority (26 African Americans, 2 American Indian/Alaska Native, 17 Asian Americans or Pacific Islanders, 20 Hispanic Americans), 3 international. Average age 28. In 2006, 259 master's, 39 other advanced degrees awarded. *Entrance requirements:* For master's, interview. Additional exam requirements/recommendations for international students: Required—TOEFL (minimum score 550 paper-based; 213 computer-based). *Application deadline:* For fall admission, 8/1 priority date for domestic and international students; for spring admission, 12/15 priority date for domestic and international students. Applications are processed on a rolling basis. Application fee: $35. Electronic applications accepted. *Financial support:* Fellowships, teaching assistantships, career-related internships or fieldwork, Federal Work-Study, institutionally sponsored loans, scholarships/grants, and tuition waivers (partial) available. Support available to part-time students. Financial award application deadline: 3/1; financial award applicants required to submit FAFSA. *Faculty research:* Mentoring, clinical training of teachers, issues of race and adolescence. *Application contact:* Kristen Haack, Director, Graduate Studies Admission, 617-521-2915, Fax: 617-521-3058, E-mail: gsa@simmons.edu.

Simon Fraser University, Graduate Studies, Faculty of Education, Burnaby, BC V5A 1S6, Canada. Offers M Ed, M Sc, MA, PhD. *Degree requirements:* For master's, project or thesis; for doctorate, thesis/dissertation. *Entrance requirements:* For master's, minimum GPA of 3.0; for doctorate, GRE, master's degree or exceptional record in a bachelor's degree, minimum GPA of 3.5. Additional exam requirements/recommendations for international students: Required—TOEFL or IELTS. *Faculty research:* Drama education, gender equity, children's literature, theory and curriculum development, counseling psychology.

Simpson University, School of Education, Redding, CA 96003-8606. Offers education (MA); education and preliminary administrative services (MA); education and preliminary teaching (MA); teaching (MA). Part-time programs available. *Entrance requirements:* For master's, PRAXIS, California Basic Educational Skills Test, 2 letters of reference. Additional exam requirements/recommendations for international students: Required—TOEFL (minimum score 550 paper-based; 180 computer-based). Electronic applications accepted.

Sinte Gleska University, Graduate Education Program, Rosebud, SD 57555. Offers elementary education (M Ed). Part-time and evening/weekend programs available. *Degree requirements:* For master's, thesis. *Entrance requirements:* For master's, 2 years of experience in elementary education, minimum GPA of 2.5, South Dakota elementary education certification. *Faculty research:* American Indian graduate education, teaching of Native American students.

Slippery Rock University of Pennsylvania, Graduate Studies (Recruitment), College of Education, Slippery Rock, PA 16057-1383. Offers M Ed, MA, MS. *Accreditation:* NCATE. Part-time and evening/weekend programs available. *Degree requirements:* For master's, comprehensive exam. *Entrance requirements:* For master's, GRE General Test, MAT, minimum GPA of 2.75 (minimum GPA of 3.0 for initial certification programs). Additional exam requirements/recommendations for international students: Required—TOEFL (minimum score 550 paper-based; 213 computer-based). *Application deadline:* For fall admission, 7/1 priority date for domestic and international students; for spring admission, 11/1 priority date for domestic and international students. Applications are processed on a rolling basis. Application fee: $25. Electronic applications accepted. *Expenses:* Tuition, state resident: part-time $336 per credit. Tuition, nonresident: part-time $538 per credit. Required fees: $84 per credit. $37 per semester. *Financial support:* Career-related internships or fieldwork, Federal Work-Study, scholarships/grants, and unspecified assistantships available. Support available to part-time students. Financial award application deadline: 5/1; financial award applicants required to submit FAFSA. *Unit head:* Dr. Jay Hertzog, Interim Director of Graduate Studies, 724-738-2685, Fax: 724-738-2146, E-mail: graduate.studies@sru.edu. *Application contact:* Dr. Duncan M. Sargent, Director of Graduate Studies, 724-738-2051 Ext. 2116, Fax: 724-738-2146, E-mail: graduate.studies@sru.edu.

Smith College, Graduate Programs, Department of Education and Child Study, Northampton, MA 01063. Offers education of the deaf (MED); elementary education (Ed M), including middle school education; secondary education (MAT), including biological sciences education, chemistry education, English education, French education, geology education, government education, history education, mathematics education, physics education, Spanish education. Part-time programs available. *Faculty:* 6 full-time (4 women), 3 part-time/adjunct (2 women). *Students:* 26 full-time (20 women), 4 part-time (all women), 2 international. Average age 30. 54 applicants, 70% accepted, 30 enrolled. In 2006, 26 degrees awarded. *Entrance requirements:* For master's, GRE General Test, MAT (Ed M and MED). Additional exam requirements/recommendations for international students: Required—TOEFL. *Application deadline:* For fall admission, 4/1 for domestic students, 1/15 for international students. Application fee: $60. *Expenses:* Tuition: Full-time $32,320; part-time $1,010 per credit. Tuition and fees vary according to course load. *Financial support:* In 2006–07, 29 students received support, including 6 teaching assistantships with full tuition reimbursements available (averaging $11,150 per year); fellowships, research assistantships, career-related internships or fieldwork, institutionally sponsored loans, and scholarships/grants also available. Support available to part-time students. Financial award application deadline: 1/15; financial award applicants required to submit CSS PROFILE or FAFSA. *Unit head:* Alan Rudnitsky, Chair, 413-585-3261, Fax: 413-585-3268, E-mail: arudnits@smith.edu.

Sonoma State University, School of Education, Rohnert Park, CA 94928-3609. Offers MA. *Accreditation:* NCATE. Part-time and evening/weekend programs available. *Faculty:* 20 full-time (6 women), 1 (woman) part-time/adjunct. *Students:* 7 full-time (5 women), 148 part-time (108 women); includes 20 minority (1 African American, 2 American Indian/Alaska Native, 5 Asian Americans or Pacific Islanders, 12 Hispanic Americans). Average age 40. 77 applicants, 88% accepted, 51 enrolled. In 2006, 23 degrees awarded. *Degree requirements:* For master's, thesis or alternative. *Entrance requirements:* For master's, minimum GPA of 2.5. Application fee: $55. *Expenses:* Tuition, nonresident: part-time $339 per unit. Required fees: $1,464 per term. *Financial support:* Fellowships, career-related internships or fieldwork and Federal Work-Study available. Support available to part-time students. Financial award application deadline: 3/2. *Unit head:* Dr. Mary Gendernalik-Cooper, Dean, 707-664-2132, E-mail: gendernm@sonoma.edu.

South Dakota State University, Graduate School, College of Education and Counseling, Brookings, SD 57007. Offers M Ed, MS. *Accreditation:* ACA (one or more programs are accredited); NCATE. Part-time programs available. *Degree requirements:* For master's, thesis, oral exams, comprehensive exam. *Entrance requirements:* For master's, minimum GPA of 2.75. Additional exam requirements/recommendations for international students: Required—TOEFL. *Application deadline:* Applications are processed on a rolling basis. Application fee: $35. *Financial support:* Research assistantships, teaching assistantships, Federal Work-Study and unspecified assistantships available. *Unit head:* Dr. Dee Hopkins, Dean, 605-688-4321.

Southeastern Louisiana University, College of Education and Human Development, Hammond, LA 70402. Offers M Ed, MAT, Ed D. *Accreditation:* NCATE. Part-time programs available. *Faculty:* 41 full-time (27 women), 1 (woman) part-time/adjunct. *Students:* 86 full-time (74 women), 447 part-time (392 women); includes 74 minority (60 African Americans, 3 Asian Americans or Pacific Islanders, 11 Hispanic Americans), 4 international. Average age 33. 110 applicants, 99% accepted, 79 enrolled. In 2006, 184 degrees awarded. *Degree requirements:* For master's, comprehensive exam (for some programs). *Entrance requirements:* For master's, GRE General Test, bachelor's degree with minimum GPA of 2.5; for doctorate, GRE General Test, master's degree with minimum GPA of 3.25, minimum GPA of 3.0 on the last 60 undergraduate credits. Additional exam requirements/recommendations for international students: Required—TOEFL (minimum score 500 paper-based; 173 computer-based). *Application deadline:* For fall admission, 7/15 priority date for domestic students, 6/1 priority date for international students; for spring admission, 12/1 priority date for domestic students, 10/1 priority date for international students. Applications are processed on a rolling basis. Application fee: $20 ($30 for international students). Electronic applications accepted. *Expenses:* Tuition, state resident: full-time $2,216; part-time $123 per credit. Tuition, nonresident: full-time $6,212; part-time $345 per credit. Required fees: $986; $55 per credit. Part-time tuition and fees vary according to course load. *Financial support:* In 2006–07, 1 research assistantship with full tuition reimbursement (averaging $5,500 per year) was awarded; career-related internships or fieldwork, Federal Work-Study, institutionally sponsored loans, scholarships/grants, unspecified assistantships, and administrative assistantships also available. Support available to part-time students. Financial award application deadline: 5/1; financial award applicants required to submit FAFSA. *Unit head:* Dr. Diane Allen, Dean, 985-549-2217, Fax: 985-549-2070, E-mail: dallen@selu.edu. *Application contact:* Sandra Meyers, Graduate Admissions Analyst, 985-549-2066, Fax: 985-549-5632, E-mail: admissions@selu.edu.

Southeastern Oklahoma State University, Graduate School, School of Education, Durant, OK 74701-0609. Offers educational administration (M Ed); educational instruction and leadership (M Ed); educational technology (M Ed); elementary education (M Ed); school counseling (M Ed); secondary education (M Ed). *Accreditation:* NCATE. Part-time and evening/weekend programs available. *Degree requirements:* For master's, portfolio (M Ed), thesis optional. *Entrance requirements:* For master's, GRE General Test (MBS), minimum GPA of 3.0 in last 60 hours or 2.75 overall. Additional exam requirements/recommendations for international students: Required—TOEFL (minimum score 550 paper-based; 213 computer-based). Electronic applications accepted.

Southern Adventist University, School of Education and Psychology, Collegedale, TN 37315-0370. Offers curriculum and instruction (MS Ed); educational administration and supervision (MS Ed); inclusive education (MS Ed); literacy education (MS Ed); outdoor teacher education (MS Ed); professional counseling (MS); school counseling (MS). *Accreditation:* NCATE. Part-time and evening/weekend programs available. *Faculty:* 11 full-time (5 women), 1 (woman) part-time/adjunct. *Students:* 36 full-time (29 women), 7 part-time (6 women); includes 8 minority (6 African Americans, 2 Hispanic Americans). Average age 30. 15 applicants, 100% accepted, 15 enrolled. In 2006, 25 degrees awarded. *Degree requirements:* For master's, position paper (MS), portfolio (MS Ed in outdoor teacher education), thesis optional. *Entrance requirements:* For master's, GRE General Test, interview (MS); 9 semester hours of upper division course work in psychology or related field, including 1 course in psychology research or statistics; 9 semester hours of education (MS Ed). Additional exam requirements/recommendations for international students: Required—TOEFL (minimum score 600 paper-based; 250 computer-based; 100 iBT). *Application deadline:* For fall admission, 5/15 priority date for domestic and international students; for winter admission, 10/15 priority date for domestic and international students; for spring admission, 3/31 priority date for domestic and international students. Applications are processed on a rolling basis. Application fee: $25. Electronic applications accepted. *Financial support:* In 2006–07, 7 students received support, including 4 research assistantships with full tuition reimbursements available (averaging $10,000 per year); career-related internships or fieldwork, scholarships/grants, tuition waivers (partial), and unspecified assistantships also available. Support available to part-time students. Financial award application deadline: 4/1; financial award applicants required to submit FAFSA. *Unit head:* Dr. Denise Dunzweiler, Dean, 423-236-2776, Fax: 423-236-1765, E-mail: denise@southern.edu. *Application contact:* Mikhaile Spence, Information Contact, 423-236-2496, Fax: 423-236-1765, E-mail: maspence@southern.edu.

Southern Arkansas University–Magnolia, Graduate Programs, Magnolia, AR 71753. Offers computer and information sciences (MS); counseling (MS); education (M Ed), including counseling and development, educational administration and supervision, elementary education, secondary education; kinesiology (MS); library media and information specialist (M Ed); school counseling (M Ed); teaching (MAT). *Accreditation:* NCATE. Part-time and evening/weekend programs available. *Degree requirements:* For master's, thesis optional. *Entrance requirements:* For master's, GRE or MAT, minimum GPA of 2.75. *Faculty research:* Alternative certification for teachers, supervision of instruction, instructional leadership, counseling.

Southern Connecticut State University, School of Graduate Studies, School of Education, New Haven, CT 06515-1355. Offers MS, MS Ed, Ed D, Diploma. *Accreditation:* NCATE. Part-time programs available. *Faculty:* 52 full-time, 37 part-time/adjunct. *Students:* 1,507. 561 applicants, 71% accepted, 326 enrolled. In 2006, 363 master's, 151 other advanced degrees awarded. *Entrance requirements:* For degree, master's degree. Application fee: $50. Electronic applications accepted. *Financial support:* Research assistantships, teaching assistantships, career-related internships or fieldwork available. *Unit head:* Dr. James Granfield, Interim Dean, 203-392-5900.

Southern Illinois University Carbondale, Graduate School, College of Education, Carbondale, IL 62901-4701. Offers MPH, MS, MS Ed, MSW, PhD, Rh D, JD/MSW. *Accreditation:* NCATE. Part-time programs available. *Faculty:* 175 full-time (74 women), 25 part-time/adjunct (6 women). *Students:* 441 full-time (318 women), 886 part-time (592 women); includes 210 minority (167 African Americans, 4 American Indian/Alaska Native, 15 Asian Americans or Pacific Islanders, 24 Hispanic Americans), 144 international. Average age 34. 679 applicants, 47% accepted, 77 enrolled. In 2006, 301 master's, 43 doctorates awarded. Terminal master's awarded for partial completion of doctoral program. *Degree requirements:* For doctorate, thesis/dissertation. *Entrance requirements:* For master's, minimum GPA of 2.7. Additional exam requirements/recommendations for international students: Required—TOEFL. Application fee: $20. *Financial support:* In 2006–07, 306 students received support, including 8 fellowships, 115 research assistantships, 166 teaching assistantships; career-related internships or fieldwork, Federal Work-Study, institutionally sponsored loans, traineeships, tuition waivers (full), and unspecified assistantships also available. Support available to part-time students. *Faculty research:* Safety education, community health, curriculum development, gifted, effective schools. *Unit head:* Patricia Elmore, Interim Dean, 618-453-2415.

Southern Illinois University Edwardsville, Graduate Studies and Research, School of Education, Edwardsville, IL 62026-0001. Offers MA, MAT, MS, MS Ed, SD, Ed S, Postbaccalaureate Certificate. *Accreditation:* NCATE. Part-time programs available. *Faculty:* 74 full-time (39 women). *Students:* 145 full-time (117 women), 483 part-time (359 women); includes 35 minority (28 African Americans, 2 Asian Americans or Pacific Islanders, 5 Hispanic Americans), 4 international. Average age 33. 381 applicants, 44% accepted. In 2006, 252 master's, 13 other advanced degrees awarded. *Degree requirements:* For master's, thesis (for some programs), final exam, portfolio. *Entrance requirements:* For master's, MAT, GRE. Additional exam requirements/recommendations for international students: Required—TOEFL. *Application deadline:* For fall admission, 7/20 for domestic students, 6/1 for international students; for spring admission, 12/14 for domestic students, 10/1 for international students. Application fee: $30. Electronic applications accepted. *Financial support:* In 2006–07, 2 fellowships with full tuition reimbursements, 5 research assistantships with full tuition reimbursements, 2 teaching assistantships with full tuition reimbursements were awarded; career-related internships or fieldwork, Federal Work-Study, institutionally sponsored loans, traineeships, and unspecified assistantships also available. Support available to part-time students. Financial award applica-

Education—General

Southern Illinois University Edwardsville (continued)
tion deadline: 3/1; financial award applicants required to submit FAFSA. *Unit head:* Dr. Bill Searcy, Interim Dean, 618-650-3350. *Application contact:* Dr. Lela DeToye, Associate Dean, 618-650-3358, E-mail: ldetoye@siue.edu.

Southern Methodist University, School of Education and Human Development, Program in Teacher Education, Dallas, TX 75275. Offers M Ed. Part-time and evening/weekend programs available. *Faculty:* 8 full-time (6 women). *Students:* 1 (woman) full-time, 91 part-time (83 women); includes 10 minority (6 African Americans, 1 American Indian/Alaska Native, 2 Asian Americans or Pacific Islanders, 1 Hispanic American), 2 international. Average age 35. 20 applicants, 100% accepted, 19 enrolled. In 2006, 40 degrees awarded. *Entrance requirements:* For master's, GRE or minimum GPA of 3.0 (M Ed). Additional exam requirements/recommendations for international students: Required—TOEFL. *Application deadline:* For fall admission, 6/30 priority date for domestic and international students; for spring admission, 11/30 priority date for domestic and international students. Applications are processed on a rolling basis. Application fee: $50. *Expenses: Contact institution. Financial support:* In 2006–07, 39 students received support. Scholarships/grants available. Support available to part-time students. *Faculty research:* Bilingual education, gifted education, reading and literacy, bilingual education, Hispanic community. Total annual research expenditures: $40,462. *Unit head:* Dr. Katherine C. Hargrove, Associate Dean and Director, 214-768-1009, Fax: 214-768-3147, E-mail: khargrov@smu.edu. *Application contact:* Josie Acosta, Administrative Assistant, 214-768-2346, Fax: 214-768-2171, E-mail: jvacosta@smu.edu.

Southern Nazarene University, Graduate College, School of Education, Bethany, OK 73008. Offers curriculum and instruction (MA); educational leadership (MA). *Accreditation:* NCATE. Part-time and evening/weekend programs available. *Faculty:* 10. *Students:* 105. Average age 27. In 2006, 23 degrees awarded. *Degree requirements:* For master's, thesis optional. *Entrance requirements:* For master's, MAT, English proficiency exam, minimum GPA of 3.0 in last 60 hours/major, 2.7 overall. *Application deadline:* For fall admission, 8/1 priority date for domestic students. Applications are processed on a rolling basis. Application fee: $25 ($35 for international students). *Expenses:* Tuition: Part-time $507 per credit. *Financial support:* Teaching assistantships, career-related internships or fieldwork available. *Unit head:* Dr. Rex Tullis, Director, 405-491-6317, E-mail: rtullis@snu.edu.

Southern New Hampshire University, School of Education, Manchester, NH 03106-1045. Offers business education (MS); child development (M Ed); computer technology education (Certificate); curriculum and instruction (M Ed); education (M Ed, CAS); elementary education (M Ed); general special education (Certificate); school business administrator (Certificate); school counseling (M Ed); school psychology (M Ed); secondary education (M Ed); training and development (Certificate). Part-time and evening/weekend programs available. Post-baccalaureate distance learning degree programs offered. *Faculty:* 6 full-time (3 women), 9 part-time/adjunct (7 women). *Students:* Average age 35. In 2006, 52 degrees awarded. *Degree requirements:* For master's, thesis or alternative, comprehensive exam (for some programs). *Entrance requirements:* For master's, GRE General Test or MAT, minimum GPA of 3.0. Additional exam requirements/recommendations for international students: Required—TOEFL (minimum score 550 paper-based; 213 computer-based). *Application deadline:* Applications are processed on a rolling basis. Application fee: $25. Electronic applications accepted. *Expenses: Contact institution. Financial support:* Institutionally sponsored loans available. Financial award applicants required to submit FAFSA. *Unit head:* Dr. Patrick J. Hartwick, Dean, 603-668-2211 Ext. 4698, Fax: 603-629-4673, E-mail: p.hartwick@snhu.edu. *Application contact:* Scott Durand, Director of Graduate Enrollment Services, 603-644-3102 Ext. 3338, Fax: 603-644-3144, E-mail: s.durand@snhu.edu.

Southern Oregon University, Graduate Studies, School of Social Sciences, Department of Education, Ashland, OR 97520. Offers elementary education (MA Ed, MS Ed), including classroom teacher, early childhood, handicapped learner, reading, supervision; secondary education (MA Ed, MS Ed), including classroom teacher, handicapped learner, reading, supervision; teaching (MAT). *Degree requirements:* For master's, thesis optional. *Entrance requirements:* For master's, GRE General Test, minimum GPA of 3.0. Electronic applications accepted.

Southern University and Agricultural and Mechanical College, Graduate School, College of Education, Baton Rouge, LA 70813. Offers M Ed, MA, MS, PhD. *Accreditation:* NCATE. *Degree requirements:* For master's, thesis optional. *Entrance requirements:* For master's and doctorate, GRE General Test. Additional exam requirements/recommendations for international students: Required—TOEFL (minimum score 525 paper-based; 193 computer-based).

Southern Utah University, College of Education, Cedar City, UT 84720-2498. Offers M Ed. *Accreditation:* NCATE. Part-time programs available. *Faculty:* 7 full-time (3 women), 12 part-time/adjunct (4 women). *Students:* 18 full-time (9 women), 279 part-time (188 women); includes 9 minority (1 African American, 1 American Indian/Alaska Native, 2 Asian Americans or Pacific Islanders, 5 Hispanic Americans). Average age 39. 120 applicants, 75% accepted. In 2006, 126 degrees awarded. *Degree requirements:* For master's, thesis or alternative. *Entrance requirements:* For master's, GRE General Test, minimum GPA of 3.0, teaching certificate. *Application deadline:* Applications are processed on a rolling basis. Application fee: $50. *Expenses:* Tuition, state resident: full-time $3,888. Tuition, nonresident: full-time $12,830. Required fees: $505. Tuition and fees vary according to program. *Financial support:* In 2006–07, 16 teaching assistantships with full and partial tuition reimbursements (averaging $1,215 per year) were awarded; scholarships/grants also available. *Faculty research:* Reading, technology, educational administration, curriculum development. *Unit head:* Dr. Prent Klag, Associate Professor of Teacher Education, 435-586-7803, Fax: 435-865-8485, E-mail: klag@suu.edu.

Southern Wesleyan University, Program in Education, Central, SC 29630-1020. Offers M Ed. Evening/weekend programs available. *Entrance requirements:* For master's, 3 years teaching experience including current teacher status, minimum GPA of 2.7, teacher certification.

Southwest Baptist University, Graduate Studies, Program in Education, Bolivar, MO 65613-2597. Offers education (MS); educational administration (MS, Ed S). Part-time and evening/weekend programs available. *Degree requirements:* For master's, 6 hour residency, thesis optional; for Ed S, 5 hour residency. *Entrance requirements:* For master's, GRE or PRAXIS II, interviews, minimum GPA of 2.75; for Ed S, master's degree. Additional exam requirements/recommendations for international students: Required—TOEFL (minimum score 550 paper-based; 213 computer-based). *Faculty research:* At-risk programs, principal retention, mentoring beginning principals.

Southwestern Adventist University, Education Department, Graduate Program, Keene, TX 76059. Offers elementary education (M Ed). Part-time and evening/weekend programs available. *Degree requirements:* For master's, thesis or alternative, professional paper. *Entrance requirements:* For master's, GRE General Test.

Southwestern Assemblies of God University, Thomas F. Harrison School of Graduate Studies, Program in Education, Waxahachie, TX 75165-5735. Offers Christian school administration (MS); curriculum development (MS); MS/MA. *Degree requirements:* For master's, comprehensive written and oral exams. *Entrance requirements:* For master's, GRE General Test, minimum GPA of 2.5. Electronic applications accepted.

Southwestern College, Center for Teaching Excellence, Winfield, KS 67156-2499. Offers special education (M Ed). *Accreditation:* NCATE. Part-time and evening/weekend programs available. Postbaccalaureate distance learning degree programs offered (minimal on-campus study). *Degree requirements:* For master's, thesis, practicum, comprehensive exam, registration. Electronic applications accepted.

Southwestern Oklahoma State University, College of Professional and Graduate Studies, School of Behavioral Sciences and Education, Weatherford, OK 73096-3098. Offers community counseling (M Ed); early childhood education (M Ed); educational administration (M Ed); elementary education (M Ed); health sciences and microbiology (M Ed); kinesiology (M Ed); parks and recreation management (M Ed); school counseling (M Ed); school psychology (MS); school psychometry (M Ed); secondary education (M Ed); special education (M Ed). *Accreditation:* NCATE. Part-time and evening/weekend programs available. Postbaccalaureate distance learning degree programs offered (minimal on-campus study). *Degree requirements:* For master's, exam. *Entrance requirements:* For master's, GRE General Test or minimum undergraduate GPA of 3.0. Additional exam requirements/recommendations for international students: Required—TOEFL.

Southwest Minnesota State University, Department of Education, Marshall, MN 56258. Offers education (MS); education development and leadership (MS); special education (MS). *Faculty:* 8 full-time (4 women), 3 part-time/adjunct (2 women). *Students:* 119 full-time (89 women), 245 part-time (195 women); includes 5 minority (1 Asian American or Pacific Islander, 4 Hispanic Americans), 1 international. 148 applicants. In 2006, 172 degrees awarded. *Application deadline:* Applications are processed on a rolling basis. Application fee: $20. *Expenses:* Tuition, area resident: Full-time $4,835. Tuition, state resident: full-time $4,835; part-time $269 per credit. Tuition, nonresident: part-time $269 per credit. Required fees: $589; $33 per credit. Tuition and fees vary according to course load and reciprocity agreements. *Unit head:* Donna Burgraff, Dean, 507-537-6218, E-mail: burgraff@southwestmsu.edu. *Application contact:* Rich Shearer, Director of Enrollment Management, 507-537-6286, E-mail: shearerr@southwestmsu.edu.

Spalding University, Graduate Studies, College of Education, Louisville, KY 40203-2188. Offers MA, MAT, Ed D. *Accreditation:* NCATE. Part-time and evening/weekend programs available. *Degree requirements:* For master's, portfolio, final project, clinical experience; for doctorate, thesis/dissertation, comprehensive exam. *Entrance requirements:* For master's and doctorate, GRE General Test or MAT, interview, resumé, recommendations. Additional exam requirements/recommendations for international students: Required—TOEFL. Electronic applications accepted. *Faculty research:* School leadership, school law, assessment of student learning, classroom management.

Spring Arbor University, School of Education, Spring Arbor, MI 49283-9799. Offers MAE. *Accreditation:* NCATE. Part-time programs available. *Faculty:* 5 full-time (1 woman), 16 part-time/adjunct (9 women). *Students:* 15 full-time (12 women), 218 part-time (180 women); includes 13 minority (11 African Americans, 1 Asian American or Pacific Islander, 1 Hispanic American). In 2006, 69 degrees awarded. *Degree requirements:* For master's, thesis. *Entrance requirements:* For master's, GRE if GPA is below 2.5, writing sample, 2 professional letters of recommendation. Additional exam requirements/recommendations for international students: Required—TOEFL (minimum score 550 paper-based; 220 computer-based). *Application deadline:* For fall admission, 9/1 priority date for domestic students; for winter admission, 2/1 priority date for domestic students; for spring admission, 2/1 priority date for domestic students. Applications are processed on a rolling basis. Application fee: $30. Electronic applications accepted. *Expenses:* Tuition: Full-time $4,200; part-time $350 per credit. Required fees: $140; $48 per term. Tuition and fees vary according to course load and program. *Financial support:* Applicants required to submit FAFSA. *Unit head:* Carla Koontz, Interim Dean of Education, 517-750-6334, Fax: 517-750-6629, E-mail: ckoontz@arbor.edu. *Application contact:* Deb Scott, Graduate Coordinator, 517-750-6677, Fax: 517-750-6629, E-mail: debs@arbor.edu.

Springfield College, Graduate Programs, Program in Education, Springfield, MA 01109-3797. Offers counseling and secondary education (M Ed, MS); education (M Ed, MS). Part-time and evening/weekend programs available. *Faculty:* 9 full-time (6 women), 2 part-time/adjunct (both women). *Students:* 52; includes 4 minority (3 African Americans, 1 Hispanic American). Average age 30. 36 applicants, 78% accepted, 21 enrolled. In 2006, 10 master's awarded. *Degree requirements:* For master's, comprehensive exam. *Entrance requirements:* Additional exam requirements/recommendations for international students: Required—TOEFL (minimum score 550 paper-based; 213 computer-based). *Application deadline:* For fall admission, 1/15 for domestic students; for winter admission, 11/1 for domestic students; for spring admission, 12/1 for domestic students. Applications are processed on a rolling basis. Application fee: $50. Electronic applications accepted. *Expenses:* Tuition: Full-time $12,222; part-time $679 per credit. Required fees: $25; $25 per year. One-time fee: $25 full-time. *Financial support:* In 2006–07, 2 teaching assistantships with partial tuition reimbursements were awarded; fellowships with partial tuition reimbursements, career-related internships or fieldwork, Federal Work-Study, institutionally sponsored loans, and tuition waivers (full and partial) also available. Financial award application deadline: 3/1. *Faculty research:* Varied educational research. Total annual research expenditures: $50,000. *Unit head:* Dr. Gerard Thibodeau, Director, 413-748-3312, E-mail: gthibodeau@spfldcol.edu. *Application contact:* Donald James Shaw, Director of Graduate Admissions, 413-748-3060, Fax: 413-748-3069, E-mail: donald_shaw_jr@spfldcol.edu.

Spring Hill College, Graduate Programs, Program in Education, Mobile, AL 36608-1791. Offers early childhood education (MAT, MS Ed); elementary education (MAT, MS Ed); secondary education (MAT, MS Ed). Part-time and evening/weekend programs available. *Faculty:* 2 full-time (both women), 7 part-time/adjunct (5 women). *Students:* 11 full-time (10 women), 44 part-time (34 women); includes 19 minority (all African Americans) Average age 33. In 2006, 21 degrees awarded. *Degree requirements:* For master's, comprehensive exam. *Entrance requirements:* For master's, GRE, MAT, NTE, or PRAXIS, minimum undergraduate GPA of 3.0. Additional exam requirements/recommendations for international students: Required—TOEFL (minimum score 550 paper-based; 213 computer-based). *Application deadline:* For fall admission, 8/1 priority date for domestic students, 6/1 priority date for international students; for spring admission, 12/1 priority date for domestic students, 11/1 priority date for international students. Applications are processed on a rolling basis. Application fee: $25 ($35 for international students). Electronic applications accepted. *Expenses: Contact institution. Financial support:* In 2006–07, 49 students received support. Career-related internships or fieldwork and scholarships/grants available. Support available to part-time students. Financial award applicants required to submit FAFSA. *Unit head:* Dr. Ann A. Adams, Chair of Teacher Education, 251-380-3479, Fax: 251-460-2184, E-mail: aadams@shc.edu. *Application contact:* Joyce Genz, Dean of Life Long Learning and Director of Graduate Programs, 251-380-3094, Fax: 251-460-2190, E-mail: grad@shc.edu.

Stanford University, School of Education, Stanford, CA 94305-9991. Offers MA, Ed D, PhD. *Accreditation:* NCATE. *Degree requirements:* For doctorate, thesis/dissertation. *Entrance requirements:* For master's and doctorate, GRE General Test. Electronic applications accepted.

State University of New York at Binghamton, Graduate School, School of Education, Binghamton, NY 13902-6000. Offers MAT, MS Ed, MST, Ed D. *Accreditation:* Teacher Education Accreditation Council. Part-time and evening/weekend programs available. *Faculty:* 23 full-time (14 women), 18 part-time/adjunct (13 women). *Students:* 184 full-time (122 women), 204 part-time (163 women); includes 36 minority (16 African Americans, 1 American Indian/Alaska Native, 6 Asian Americans or Pacific Islanders, 13 Hispanic Americans), 5 international. Average age 32. 239 applicants, 70% accepted. In 2006, 132 master's, 5 doctorates awarded. *Degree requirements:* For doctorate, thesis/dissertation. *Entrance requirements:* For master's, GRE General Test; for doctorate, GRE General Test, writing sample. Additional exam requirements/recommendations for international students: Required—TOEFL. *Application deadline:* For fall admission, 4/15 priority date for domestic students, 1/15 priority date for international students; for spring admission, 11/1 for domestic students, 10/1 priority date for international students. Applications are processed on a rolling basis. Application fee: $60. Electronic applications accepted. *Financial support:* In 2006–07, 70 students received support, including 14 fellowships with full tuition reimbursements available (averaging $6,866 per year), 6 research assistantships with full tuition reimbursements available (averaging $5,775 per year), 44 teaching assistantships with full tuition reimbursements available (averaging $5,880 per year); career-related internships or fieldwork, Federal Work-Study, institutionally sponsored loans, tuition waivers (full and partial), and unspecified assistantships also available. Support available to part-time students. Financial award application deadline: 2/15. *Unit head:* Dr. Susan Strahle, Interim Dean, 607-777-7329, E-mail: sstrahle@binghamton.edu.

State University of New York at Fredonia, Graduate Studies, College of Education, Fredonia, NY 14063-1136. Offers educational administration (CAS); elementary education (MS Ed); literacy (MS Ed); secondary education (MS Ed); teaching English to speakers of other languages (MS Ed). *Accreditation:* NCATE. Part-time and evening/weekend programs available. *Faculty:* 19 full-time (12 women), 4 part-time/adjunct (0 women). *Students:* 77 full-time (31 women), 131 part-time (46 women); includes 5 minority (2 American Indian/Alaska Native, 3 Hispanic Americans). Average age 28. In 2006, 127 master's, 7 other advanced degrees awarded. *Degree requirements:* For master's, thesis optional; for CAS, thesis or alternative. *Application deadline:* For fall admission, 8/5 for domestic students; for spring admission, 12/1 for domestic students. Application fee: $50. *Expenses:* Tuition, state resident: full-time $6,900; part-time $288 per credit hour. Tuition, nonresident: full-time $10,920; part-time $455 per credit hour. Required fees: $1,132; $47 per credit hour. *Financial support:* In 2006–07, 10 teaching assistantships with partial tuition reimbursements (averaging $6,193 per year) were awarded; research assistantships, career-related internships or fieldwork and tuition waivers (full and partial) also available. Support available to part-time students. Financial award application deadline: 3/15. *Unit head:* Dr. Christine Givner, Dean, 716-673-3311, E-mail: christine.givner@fredonia.edu.

State University of New York at New Paltz, Graduate School, Faculty of Education, New Paltz, NY 12561. Offers MAT, MPS, MS Ed, MST, CAS. *Accreditation:* NCATE. Part-time and evening/weekend programs available. *Faculty:* 33 full-time (24 women), 97 part-time/adjunct (64 women). *Students:* 210 full-time (168 women), 492 part-time (368 women); includes 66 minority (21 African Americans, 2 American Indian/Alaska Native, 8 Asian Americans or Pacific Islanders, 35 Hispanic Americans), 7 international. Average age 32. 540 applicants. In 2006, 269 master's, 67 other advanced degrees awarded. *Degree requirements:* For master's, portfolio; for CAS, internship. *Entrance requirements:* For master's, GRE, MAT, minimum GPA of 3.0; for CAS, minimum GPA of 3.0. Additional exam requirements/recommendations for international students: Required—TOEFL (minimum score 550 paper-based; 213 computer-based; 80 iBT). *Application deadline:* For fall admission, 3/1 priority date for domestic and international students; for spring admission, 10/1 priority date for domestic and international students. Application fee: $50. Electronic applications accepted. *Expenses:* Tuition, state resident: full-time $6,900; part-time $288 per credit hour. Tuition, nonresident: full-time $10,920; part-time $455 per credit hour. *Financial support:* Career-related internships or fieldwork, Federal Work-Study, and institutionally sponsored loans available. *Unit head:* Dr. Robert Michael, Dean, 845-257-2800.

State University of New York at Oswego, Graduate Studies, School of Education, Oswego, NY 13126. Offers MAT, MS, MS Ed, CAS, MS Ed/CAS, MS/CAS. *Accreditation:* NCATE. Part-time programs available. *Faculty:* 38 full-time, 72 part-time/adjunct. *Students:* 292 full-time (216 women), 421 part-time (295 women); includes 25 minority (11 African Americans, 1 American Indian/Alaska Native, 1 Asian American or Pacific Islander, 12 Hispanic Americans), 2 international. Average age 33. 504 applicants, 85% accepted. In 2006, 356 master's, 46 other advanced degrees awarded. *Entrance requirements:* For degree, GRE General Test, interview, MA or MS, minimum GPA of 3.0. Additional exam requirements/recommendations for international students: Required—TOEFL (minimum score 560 paper-based; 220 computer-based). *Application deadline:* For fall admission, 2/1 for domestic students; for spring admission, 10/1 for domestic students. Application fee: $50. *Expenses:* Tuition, state resident: part-time $288 per credit. Tuition, nonresident: part-time $455 per credit. Tuition and fees vary according to program. *Financial support:* In 2006–07, 31 students received support, including 9 fellowships, 22 teaching assistantships with full and partial tuition reimbursements available; research assistantships, career-related internships or fieldwork, Federal Work-Study, institutionally sponsored loans, scholarships/grants, health care benefits, and unspecified assistantships also available. Support available to part-time students. Financial award application deadline: 4/1; financial award applicants required to submit FAFSA. *Unit head:* Dr. Linda Markert, Dean, 315-312-2102.

State University of New York College at Brockport, School of Professions, Department of Education and Human Development, Brockport, NY 14420-2997. Offers adolescence education (MS Ed), including biology education, chemistry education, earth science education, English education, mathematics education, physics education, social studies education; bilingual education (MS Ed); childhood curriculum specialist (MS Ed); childhood literacy (MS Ed). *Accreditation:* NCATE. *Students:* 87 full-time (67 women), 226 part-time (155 women); includes 17 minority (6 African Americans, 2 Asian Americans or Pacific Islanders, 9 Hispanic Americans). 140 applicants, 70% accepted, 85 enrolled. In 2006, 224 degrees awarded. *Degree requirements:* For master's, thesis or alternative. *Entrance requirements:* For master's, minimum GPA of 3.0, letters of recommendation, interview (for some programs). Additional exam requirements/recommendations for international students: Required—TOEFL (minimum score 550 paper-based; 213 computer-based; 80 iBT). *Application deadline:* For fall admission, 2/15 for domestic and international students; for spring admission, 9/15 for domestic and international students. Application fee: $50. *Expenses:* Tuition, state resident: full-time $6,900; part-time $288 per credit. Tuition, nonresident: full-time $10,920; part-time $455 per credit. *Financial support:* In 2006–07, 2 teaching assistantships with tuition reimbursements (averaging $6,000 per year) were awarded; career-related internships or fieldwork, Federal Work-Study, scholarships/grants, and unspecified assistantships also available. Support available to part-time students. Financial award application deadline: 3/15; financial award applicants required to submit FAFSA. *Faculty research:* Emerging literacy, educational assessment, classroom action research, democracy in classrooms, teacher identity development. *Unit head:* Dr. Sue Novinger, Chairperson, 585-395-2205, E-mail: snovinge@brockport.edu. *Application contact:* Coordinator of Certification and Graduate Advisement, 585-395-2344.

State University of New York College at Cortland, Graduate Studies, School of Education, Cortland, NY 13045. Offers childhood/early child education (MS Ed, MST); educational leadership (CAS); literacy (MS Ed); teaching students with disabilities (MS Ed). *Accreditation:* NCATE. Part-time and evening/weekend programs available. *Entrance requirements:* Additional exam requirements/recommendations for international students: Required—TOEFL.

State University of New York College at Geneseo, Graduate Studies, School of Education, Geneseo, NY 14454-1401. Offers early childhood education (MS Ed); elementary education (MS Ed); reading (MS Ed); secondary education (MS Ed). *Accreditation:* NCATE. Part-time and evening/weekend programs available. *Faculty:* 26 full-time (15 women). *Students:* 31 full-time (26 women), 71 part-time (56 women); includes 3 minority (2 Asian Americans or Pacific Islanders, 1 Hispanic American), 1 international. Average age 24. 50 applicants, 82% accepted, 29 enrolled. In 2006, 75 degrees awarded. *Degree requirements:* For master's, thesis optional. *Entrance requirements:* For master's, GRE General Test. Additional exam requirements/recommendations for international students: Required—TOEFL. *Application deadline:* For fall admission, 6/1 priority date for domestic students; for spring admission, 10/1 for domestic students. Application fee: $50. *Financial support:* In 2006–07, 5 students received support; fellowships, teaching assistantships with tuition reimbursements available, career-related internships or fieldwork, Federal Work-Study, and institutionally sponsored loans available. Financial award application deadline: 4/1; financial award applicants required to submit FAFSA. *Faculty research:* Whole language. Total annual research expenditures: $56,000. *Unit head:* Dr. Osman Alawiye, Chairperson, 585-245-5560, Fax: 585-245-5220.

State University of New York College at Oneonta, Graduate Studies, Division of Education, Oneonta, NY 13820-4015. Offers adolescence education (MS Ed), including adolescence education, family and consumer science education; educational psychology and counseling (MS Ed, CAS), including school counselor K-12; elementary and reading education (MS Ed), including childhood education, literacy education; family and consumer science education (MS Ed). *Accreditation:* NCATE. Part-time and evening/weekend programs available. *Entrance requirements:* For master's, GRE General Test.

State University of New York Empire State College, Graduate Studies, Program in Teaching, Saratoga Springs, NY 12866-4391. Offers MA.

Stephen F. Austin State University, Graduate School, College of Education, Nacogdoches, TX 75962. Offers M Ed, MA, MS, Ed D. *Accreditation:* NCATE. Part-time and evening/weekend programs available. *Degree requirements:* For master's, comprehensive exam; for doctorate, thesis/dissertation. *Entrance requirements:* For master's, GRE General Test; for doctorate, GRE General Test, interview, writing sample. Additional exam requirements/recommendations for international students: Required—TOEFL.

Stetson University, College of Arts and Sciences, Division of Education, DeLand, FL 32723. Offers M Ed, MS, Ed S. *Accreditation:* NCATE (one or more programs are accredited). Part-time and evening/weekend programs available. *Students:* 60 full-time (38 women), 110 part-time (98 women); includes 8 African Americans, 1 Asian American or Pacific Islander, 16 Hispanic Americans, 3 international. Average age 33. In 2006, 90 master's, 5 other advanced degrees awarded. *Entrance requirements:* For master's and Ed S, GRE General Test or MAT. *Application deadline:* For fall admission, 3/1 priority date for domestic students; for spring admission, 11/1 for domestic students. Applications are processed on a rolling basis. Application fee: $25. *Financial support:* Career-related internships or fieldwork, institutionally sponsored loans, scholarships/grants, and tuition waivers (partial) available. Support available to part-time students. *Faculty research:* Values, cultural diversity, cooperative learning, reading. *Application contact:* Midge McDaniel, Office of Graduate Studies, 386-822-7075, Fax: 386-822-7388, E-mail: mmcdanie@stetson.edu.

Suffolk University, College of Arts and Sciences, Department of Education and Human Services, Boston, MA 02108-2770. Offers adult and organizational learning (MS, CAGS), including adult and organizational learning (MS), human resources, instructional design (CAGS), organizational development (CAGS), organizational learning (CAGS); counseling and human relations (M Ed, MS, CAGS), including counseling and human relations (CAGS), mental health counseling (MS), school counseling (M Ed); foundations of education (M Ed, CAGS), including administration of higher education (M Ed), foundations of education (M Ed), leadership (CAGS); higher education administration (M Ed, CAGS), including educational administration (M Ed), leadership (CAGS); human resources (MS, CAGS); professional development in teaching programs (CAGS); secondary school teaching (MS); MPA/MS. Part-time and evening/weekend programs available. *Faculty:* 17 full-time (9 women), 8 part-time/adjunct (6 women). *Students:* 35 full-time (25 women), 171 part-time (139 women); includes 21 minority (11 African Americans, 3 American Indian/Alaska Native, 5 Asian Americans or Pacific Islanders, 2 Hispanic Americans), 5 international. Average age 30. 184 applicants, 88% accepted, 90 enrolled. In 2006, 34 master's, 6 other advanced degrees awarded. *Entrance requirements:* For master's, GRE General Test or MAT. Additional exam requirements/recommendations for international students: Required—TOEFL (minimum score 550 paper-based; 213 computer-based; 80 iBT). *Application deadline:* For fall admission, 6/15 priority date for domestic students, 6/15 for international students; for spring admission, 11/1 priority date for domestic students, 11/1 for international students. Applications are processed on a rolling basis. Application fee: $35. Electronic applications accepted. *Financial support:* In 2006–07, 60 fellowships with full and partial tuition reimbursements (averaging $8,996 per year) were awarded; career-related internships or fieldwork, Federal Work-Study, and institutionally sponsored loans also available. Support available to part-time students. Financial award application deadline: 4/1; financial award applicants required to submit FAFSA. *Faculty research:* Administration, personality disorders, assessment, psychological counseling development, diagnosis. *Unit head:* Dr. Glen Eskedal, Chairperson, 617-573-8264 Ext. 8261, Fax: 617-722-9440, E-mail: geskedal@suffolk.edu. *Application contact:* Judith Reynolds, Director of Graduate Admissions, 617-573-8302, Fax: 617-523-0116, E-mail: grad.admission@suffolk.edu.

Sul Ross State University, Rio Grande College of Sul Ross State University, Alpine, TX 79832. Offers business administration (MBA); teacher education (M Ed), including bilingual education, counseling, educational diagnostics, elementary education, general education, reading, school administration, secondary education. Part-time and evening/weekend programs available. *Degree requirements:* For master's, thesis optional. *Entrance requirements:* For master's, GMAT or GRE General Test, minimum GPA of 2.5 in last 60 hours of undergraduate work. *Faculty research:* Drug and substance abuse counseling, U.S.-Mexico border economic development.

Sul Ross State University, School of Professional Studies, Department of Teacher Education, Alpine, TX 79832. Offers bilingual education (M Ed); counseling (M Ed); educational diagnostics (M Ed); elementary education (M Ed); reading specialist (M Ed); school administration (M Ed); secondary education (M Ed); supervision (M Ed). Part-time and evening/weekend programs available. *Degree requirements:* For master's, thesis optional. *Entrance requirements:* For master's, GMAT or GRE General Test, minimum GPA of 2.5 in last 60 hours of undergraduate work. *Faculty research:* Critical thinking skills, adolescent eating disorders, reading-based study skills, cross-cultural adaptations, educational leadership.

Sunbridge College, Programs in Education, Spring Valley, NY 10977. Offers Waldorf early childhood education (MS Ed); Waldorf elementary school education (MS Ed). Part-time programs available. *Entrance requirements:* For master's, interview.

Sweet Briar College, Department of Education, Sweet Briar, VA 24595. Offers M Ed, MAT. Part-time and evening/weekend programs available. *Faculty:* 3 full-time (2 women), 4 part-time/adjunct (all women). *Students:* 8 full-time (7 women), 2 part-time (both women); includes 1 minority (Asian American or Pacific Islander) Average age 24. 15 applicants, 73% accepted, 10 enrolled. In 2006, 14 degrees awarded. *Median time to degree:* Master's–1 year full-time, 2 years part-time. *Degree requirements:* For master's, thesis, comprehensive exam (for some programs), registration. *Entrance requirements:* For master's, PRAXIS I and II, Virginia Communication and Literacy Assessment (MAT), GRE (M Ed), current teaching license (M Ed). *Application deadline:* For fall admission, 2/1 for domestic students. Application fee: $40. *Expenses:* Tuition: Full-time $13,500; part-time $300 per credit. Required fees: $300 per credit. Tuition and fees vary according to course load and program. *Financial support:* Available to part-time students. *Faculty research:* Differentiation K-12 student achievement, mentoring and teacher retention, teaching science by inquiry. *Unit head:* Dr. James L. Alouf, Education Department Chair, 434-381-6130, E-mail: alouf@sbc.edu. *Application contact:* Jill E. Gavitt, Assistant Director of Admissions, Special Programs Recruitment, 434-381-6240, Fax: 434-381-6152, E-mail: jgavitt@sbc.edu.

Syracuse University, Graduate School, School of Education, Syracuse, NY 13244. Offers M Mus, MS, Ed D, PhD, CAS, Ed D/PhD. *Accreditation:* NCATE. *Faculty:* 42 full-time (27 women), 33 part-time/adjunct (19 women). *Students:* 344 full-time (245 women), 321 part-time (233 women); includes 70 minority (37 African Americans, 7 American Indian/Alaska Native, 12 Asian Americans or Pacific Islanders, 14 Hispanic Americans), 62 international. 394 applicants, 71% accepted, 151 enrolled. In 2006, 178 master's, 23 doctorates, 17 other advanced degrees awarded. *Degree requirements:* For master's, thesis or alternative; for doctorate and CAS, thesis/dissertation. *Entrance requirements:* For master's, doctorate, and CAS, GRE. Additional exam requirements/recommendations for international students: Required—TOEFL. *Application deadline:* For fall admission, 2/1 priority date for domestic students; for spring admission, 10/15 for domestic students. Applications are processed on a rolling basis. Application fee: $65. Electronic applications accepted. *Expenses:* Tuition: Full-time $16,920; part-time $940 per credit hour. Required fees: $930; $930 per year. *Financial support:* Fellowships with full and partial tuition reimbursements, research assistantships with full and partial tuition reimbursements, teaching assistantships with full and partial tuition reimbursements, career-related internships or fieldwork, Federal Work-Study, institutionally sponsored loans, health care benefits, tuition waivers (full and partial), and unspecified assistantships available. Sup-

Education—General

Syracuse University (continued)
port available to part-time students. *Faculty research:* Teaching and curriculum, reading and language arts, literacy, inclusive education, communication sciences and disorders. *Unit head:* Dr. Douglas Biklen, Dean, 315-443-4751. *Application contact:* Liza Rochelson, Graduate Admission Recruiter, 315-443-2505, Fax: 315-443-2258, E-mail: gradcrt@gwmail.syr.edu.

See Close-Up on page 921.

Tarleton State University, College of Graduate Studies, College of Education, Stephenville, TX 76402. Offers M Ed, Ed D, Certificate. Part-time and evening/weekend programs available. Postbaccalaureate distance learning degree programs offered (minimal on-campus study). *Faculty:* 61 full-time (34 women), 55 part-time/adjunct (22 women). *Students:* 175 full-time (118 women), 833 part-time (646 women); includes 195 minority (112 African Americans, 5 American Indian/Alaska Native, 10 Asian Americans or Pacific Islanders, 68 Hispanic Americans), 2 international. Average age 39. In 2006, 280 degrees awarded. *Degree requirements:* For master's, thesis (for some programs), comprehensive exam. *Entrance requirements:* For master's, GRE General Test, minimum GPA of 3.0. Additional exam requirements/recommendations for international students: Required—TOEFL (minimum score 550 paper-based; 220 computer-based). *Application deadline:* For fall admission, 8/5 priority date for domestic students; for spring admission, 12/1 for domestic students. Applications are processed on a rolling basis. Application fee: $25 ($75 for international students). *Financial support:* In 2006–07, 3 research assistantships (averaging $12,000 per year), teaching assistantships with partial tuition reimbursements (averaging $12,000 per year) were awarded; career-related internships or fieldwork, Federal Work-Study, institutionally sponsored loans, and tuition waivers (partial) also available. Support available to part-time students. Financial award application deadline: 5/1; financial award applicants required to submit FAFSA. *Unit head:* Dr. Jill Burk, Dean, 254-968-9089.

Teachers College Columbia University, Graduate Faculty of Education, New York, NY 10027-6696. Offers Ed M, MA, MS, Ed D, Ed DCT, PhD, Certificate, MBA/Ed D. *Accreditation:* NCATE. Part-time and evening/weekend programs available. *Faculty:* 152 full-time (90 women). *Students:* 1,582 full-time (1,205 women), 3,290 part-time (2,427 women); includes 1,263 minority (453 African Americans, 8 American Indian/Alaska Native, 517 Asian Americans or Pacific Islanders, 285 Hispanic Americans), 529 international. Average age 32. 5,136 applicants, 58% accepted, 1408 enrolled. In 2006, 1,518 master's, 210 doctorates awarded. *Degree requirements:* For doctorate, thesis/dissertation, comprehensive exam. Application fee: $65. Electronic applications accepted. *Expenses:* Tuition: Full-time $23,400; part-time $975 per credit. Required fees: $320 per term. *Financial support:* Fellowships, research assistantships, teaching assistantships, career-related internships or fieldwork, Federal Work-Study, institutionally sponsored loans, traineeships, tuition waivers (full and partial), and unspecified assistantships available. Support available to part-time students. Financial award application deadline: 2/1. *Faculty research:* Education and the economy, postsecondary governance and finance, career success, dropout prevention evaluation, education across the lifespan. *Unit head:* Susan Furhman, President, 212-678-3050. *Application contact:* Thomas Rock, Director of Admissions, 212-678-3083, Fax: 212-678-4171, E-mail: rock@tc.edu.

See Close-Up on page 1127.

Temple University, Graduate School, College of Education, Philadelphia, PA 19122-6096. Offers Ed M, MS Ed, Ed D, PhD. Part-time and evening/weekend programs available. *Faculty:* 75 full-time (33 women). *Students:* 307 full-time (217 women), 930 part-time (630 women); includes 265 minority (185 African Americans, 5 American Indian/Alaska Native, 36 Asian Americans or Pacific Islanders, 39 Hispanic Americans), 48 international. 870 applicants, 49% accepted, 250 enrolled. In 2006, 352 master's, 75 doctorates awarded. Terminal master's awarded for partial completion of doctoral program. *Degree requirements:* For doctorate, thesis/dissertation. *Entrance requirements:* For master's, GRE General Test or MAT, minimum GPA of 3.0. Additional exam requirements/recommendations for international students: Required—TOEFL (minimum score 550 paper-based; 213 computer-based; 79 iBT). *Application deadline:* For fall admission, 12/15 for international students; for spring admission, 8/1 for international students. Applications are processed on a rolling basis. Application fee: $50. Electronic applications accepted. *Expenses:* Tuition, state resident: full-time $12,264; part-time $511 per credit. Tuition, nonresident: full-time $17,904; part-time $746 per credit. Required fees: $84 per course. Tuition and fees vary according to program. *Financial support:* Fellowships, research assistantships, teaching assistantships, career-related internships or fieldwork and Federal Work-Study available. Financial award application deadline: 1/15; financial award applicants required to submit FAFSA. *Faculty research:* School improvement in city schools, teaching strategies, student motivation, individual differences in learning, educational leadership and policy studies. *Unit head:* Dr. C. Kent McGuire, Dean, 215-204-8017, Fax: 215-204-5622, E-mail: kent.mcguire@temple.edu. *Application contact:* Dr. Jan Price Greenough, Associate Dean, 215-204-7962, E-mail: james.earl.davis@temple.edu.

Tennessee State University, The School of Graduate Studies and Research, College of Education, Nashville, TN 37209-1561. Offers M Ed, MA Ed, MS, Ed D, PhD, Ed S. *Accreditation:* NCATE. Part-time and evening/weekend programs available. *Degree requirements:* For doctorate, thesis/dissertation. *Entrance requirements:* For doctorate, minimum GPA of 3.25. *Application deadline:* Applications are processed on a rolling basis. *Financial support:* Fellowships, research assistantships, teaching assistantships, career-related internships or fieldwork and institutionally sponsored loans available. Support available to part-time students. Financial award application deadline: 5/1; financial award applicants required to submit FAFSA. *Faculty research:* Class size, biobehavioral research, equity, dropout rate, K–12 teachers: first 5 years of employment. *Unit head:* Dr. Leslie Drummonds, Dean, 615-963-5451. *Application contact:* Dr. Helen Barrett, Dean, 615-963-5139, Fax: 615-963-5963, E-mail: hbarrett@tnstate.edu.

Tennessee Technological University, Graduate School, College of Education, Cookeville, TN 38505. Offers MA, PhD, Ed S. *Accreditation:* NCATE. Part-time and evening/weekend programs available. *Faculty:* 58 full-time (16 women). *Students:* 443 full-time (322 women), 551 part-time (412 women); includes 76 minority (62 African Americans, 2 American Indian/Alaska Native, 8 Asian Americans or Pacific Islanders, 4 Hispanic Americans). Average age 27. 449 applicants, 86% accepted, 304 enrolled. In 2006, 379 master's, 6 doctorates, 291 other advanced degrees awarded. *Degree requirements:* For Ed S, thesis or alternative. *Entrance requirements:* For master's, MAT; for doctorate, GRE; for Ed S, MAT, NTE. Additional exam requirements/recommendations for international students: Required—TOEFL. *Application deadline:* For fall admission, 3/1 priority date for domestic students; for spring admission, 8/1 for domestic students. Application fee: $25 ($30 for international students). Electronic applications accepted. *Expenses:* Tuition, state resident: full-time $8,748; part-time $319 per hour. Tuition, nonresident: full-time $23,524; part-time $740 per hour. *Financial support:* In 2006–07, 42 fellowships (averaging $8,000 per year), 33 research assistantships (averaging $4,000 per year), 26 teaching assistantships (averaging $4,000 per year) were awarded; career-related internships or fieldwork also available. Support available to part-time students. Financial award application deadline: 4/1. *Faculty research:* Teacher evaluation. *Unit head:* Dr. Larry Peach, Interim Dean, 931-372-3124, Fax: 931-372-6319, E-mail: lpeach@tntech.edu. *Application contact:* Dr. Francis O. Otuonye, Associate Vice President for Research and Graduate Studies, 931-372-3233, Fax: 931-372-3497, E-mail: fotuonye@tntech.edu.

Tennessee Temple University, Graduate Studies Division, Chattanooga, TN 37404-3587. Offers MS. Part-time programs available. *Degree requirements:* For master's, thesis or alternative. *Entrance requirements:* For master's, GRE, minimum GPA of 3.0.

Texas A&M International University, Office of Graduate Studies and Research, College of Education, Laredo, TX 78041-1900. Offers MS, MS Ed, PhD. Part-time and evening/weekend programs available. *Faculty:* 17 full-time (7 women), 3 part-time/adjunct (0 women). *Students:* 19 full-time (14 women), 472 part-time (352 women); includes 464 minority (3 African Americans, 1 Asian American or Pacific Islander, 460 Hispanic Americans), 7 international. Average age 33. 372 applicants, 90% accepted, 203 enrolled. In 2006, 81 degrees awarded. *Degree requirements:* For master's, thesis (for some programs). *Entrance requirements:* For master's, GRE General Test. Additional exam requirements/recommendations for international students: Required—TOEFL (minimum score 550 paper-based; 213 computer-based). *Application deadline:* For fall admission, 7/15 priority date for domestic students; for spring admission, 11/12 for domestic students. Applications are processed on a rolling basis. Application fee: $25. *Expenses:* Tuition, state resident: full-time $1,580. Tuition, nonresident: full-time $5,432. Required fees: $3,808. *Financial support:* In 2006–07, 272 students received support; fellowships, Federal Work-Study and institutionally sponsored loans available. Support available to part-time students. Financial award application deadline: 11/1; financial award applicants required to submit FAFSA. *Unit head:* Dr. Humberto Gonzalez, Dean, 956-326-2420, E-mail: hgonzalez@tamiu.edu. *Application contact:* Rosie Espinoza-Dickinson, Director of Admissions, 956-326-2200, Fax: 956-326-2199, E-mail: enroll@tamiu.edu.

Texas A&M University, College of Education and Human Development, College Station, TX 77843. Offers M Ed, MS, Ed D, PhD. *Accreditation:* NCATE. Part-time and evening/weekend programs available. Postbaccalaureate distance learning degree programs offered (no on-campus study). *Faculty:* 94 full-time (37 women), 11 part-time/adjunct (6 women). *Students:* 597 full-time (399 women), 643 part-time (472 women); includes 317 minority (123 African Americans, 4 American Indian/Alaska Native, 22 Asian Americans or Pacific Islanders, 168 Hispanic Americans), 127 international. Average age 36. 509 applicants, 66% accepted, 223 enrolled. In 2006, 205 master's, 75 doctorates awarded. *Degree requirements:* For doctorate, thesis/dissertation. *Entrance requirements:* For master's and doctorate, GRE General Test. Additional exam requirements/recommendations for international students: Required—TOEFL. Application fee: $50 ($75 for international students). Electronic applications accepted. *Expenses:* Tuition, state resident: full-time $4,697. Tuition, nonresident: full-time $11,297. Required fees: $2,272. *Financial support:* In 2006–07, fellowships with partial tuition reimbursements (averaging $12,000 per year), research assistantships with partial tuition reimbursements (averaging $10,000 per year), teaching assistantships with partial tuition reimbursements (averaging $10,000 per year) were awarded; career-related internships or fieldwork, Federal Work-Study, institutionally sponsored loans, scholarships/grants, tuition waivers (partial), and unspecified assistantships also available. Financial award applicants required to submit FAFSA. *Unit head:* Doug Palmer, Interim Dean, 979-845-5311. *Application contact:* Becky Carr, Assistant Dean, 979-845-5311, Fax: 979-845-6129, E-mail: bcarr@tamu.edu.

Texas A&M University–Commerce, Graduate School, College of Education and Human Services, Commerce, TX 75429-3011. Offers M Ed, MA, MS, Ed D, PhD. Part-time programs available. Terminal master's awarded for partial completion of doctoral program. *Degree requirements:* For master's, comprehensive exam; for doctorate, thesis/dissertation, departmental qualifying exam. *Entrance requirements:* For master's and doctorate, GRE General Test. Electronic applications accepted. *Faculty research:* Reading, early childhood, deviance, migration, physical fitness.

Texas A&M University–Corpus Christi, Graduate Studies and Research, College of Education, Corpus Christi, TX 78412-5503. Offers counseling (MS, PhD), including counseling (MS), counselor education (PhD); curriculum and instruction (MS, Ed D); early childhood education (MS); educational administration (MS); educational leadership (Ed D); educational technology (MS); elementary education (MS); kinesiology (MS); occupational training and development (MS); reading (MS); secondary education (MS); special education (MS). Part-time and evening/weekend programs available. *Degree requirements:* For master's, thesis (for some programs), comprehensive exam, registration; for doctorate, thesis/dissertation, comprehensive exam, registration. *Entrance requirements:* For master's, GRE General Test. Additional exam requirements/recommendations for international students: Required—TOEFL. Electronic applications accepted.

Texas A&M University–Kingsville, College of Graduate Studies, College of Education, Kingsville, TX 78363. Offers M Ed, MA, MS, Ed D, PhD. Part-time and evening/weekend programs available. *Degree requirements:* For master's, comprehensive exam; for doctorate, one foreign language, thesis/dissertation, comprehensive exam. *Entrance requirements:* For master's, GRE General Test, minimum GPA of 3.0; for doctorate, GRE General Test, MAT, minimum GPA of 3.25. *Faculty research:* Rural schools, facilities planning, linguistics.

Texas A&M University–Texarkana, Graduate Studies and Research, College of Arts and Sciences and Education, Texarkana, TX 75505-5518. Offers adult education (MS); curriculum and instruction (MS); education (MS); educational administration (M Ed); English (MA); history (MS); instructional technology (MS); interdisciplinary studies (MA, MS); special education (M Ed, MS). Part-time and evening/weekend programs available. *Students:* 285. Average age 32. 41 applicants, 76% accepted. In 2006, 51 degrees awarded. *Degree requirements:* For master's, thesis optional. *Entrance requirements:* For master's, minimum GPA of 2.5 on last 60 hours of bachelor's degree. Additional exam requirements/recommendations for international students: Required—TOEFL. *Application deadline:* For fall admission, 7/15 priority date for domestic students; for spring admission, 12/1 priority date for domestic students. Applications are processed on a rolling basis. Application fee: $0 ($25 for international students). Electronic applications accepted. *Expenses:* Tuition, state resident: part-time $112 per credit hour. Tuition, nonresident: part-time $387 per credit hour. Required fees: $8 per credit hour. $8 per term. *Financial support:* Career-related internships or fieldwork and scholarships/grants available. Financial award applicants required to submit FAFSA. *Unit head:* Dr. Rosannce Stripling, Dean, 903-223-3073, E-mail: rosanne.stripling@tamut.edu. *Application contact:* Patricia E. Black, Director of Admissions and Registrar, 903-223-3068, Fax: 903-223-3140, E-mail: pat.black@tamut.edu.

Texas Christian University, School of Education, Fort Worth, TX 76129-0002. Offers M Ed, PhD, Certificate, MBA/Ed D. Part-time and evening/weekend programs available. *Faculty:* 21. *Entrance requirements:* Additional exam requirements/recommendations for international students: Required—TOEFL. *Application deadline:* For fall admission, 3/1 for domestic students; for spring admission, 12/1 for domestic students. Applications are processed on a rolling basis. Application fee: $50. *Expenses:* Tuition: Part-time $800 per credit hour. *Financial support:* Career-related internships or fieldwork and unspecified assistantships available. Financial award application deadline: 3/1. *Unit head:* Dr. Sam Deitz, Dean, 817-257-7663, E-mail: s.deitz@tcu.edu. *Application contact:* Director of Graduate Studies, 817-257-7664.

Texas Southern University, Graduate School, College of Education, Houston, TX 77004-4584. Offers M Ed, MS, Ed D. Part-time and evening/weekend programs available. *Faculty:* 26 full-time (13 women), 7 part-time/adjunct (2 women). *Students:* 149 full-time (118 women), 219 part-time (170 women); includes 337 minority (315 African Americans, 7 Asian Americans or Pacific Islanders, 15 Hispanic Americans), 3 international. Average age 29. 146 applicants, 81% accepted, 97 enrolled. In 2006, 75 master's, 18 doctorates awarded. *Degree requirements:* For master's, comprehensive exam; for doctorate, thesis/dissertation, comprehensive exam. *Entrance requirements:* For master's, GRE General Test, minimum GPA of 2.5; for doctorate, GRE General Test or MAT, master's degree, minimum B+ average. Additional exam requirements/recommendations for international students: Required—TOEFL. *Application deadline:* For fall admission, 7/15 priority date for domestic students. Applications are processed on a rolling basis. Application fee: $50 ($75 for international students). *Financial support:* Fellowships, research assistantships, teaching assistantships, career-related internships or fieldwork, Federal Work-Study, and institutionally sponsored loans available. Financial award application deadline: 5/1. *Unit head:* Dr. Jay Cummings, Dean, 713-313-7343.

Texas State University-San Marcos, Graduate School, College of Education, San Marcos, TX 78666. Offers M Ed, MA, MSRLS, PhD. Part-time and evening/weekend programs available. *Faculty:* 63 full-time (37 women), 33 part-time/adjunct (22 women). *Students:* 368 full-time (285 women), 768 part-time (607 women); includes 280 minority (55 African Americans, 1 American Indian/Alaska Native, 24 Asian Americans or Pacific Islanders, 200 Hispanic Americans), 24 international. Average age 32. 372 applicants, 84% accepted, 225 enrolled. In 2006, 355 master's, 7 doctorates awarded. *Degree requirements:* For master's, thesis optional. *Entrance requirements:* For master's, GRE General Test, minimum GPA of 2.75 in last 60 hours of undergraduate work. Additional exam requirements/recommendations for international students: Required—TOEFL. *Application deadline:* For fall admission, 6/15 priority date for domestic students; for spring admission, 10/15 priority date for domestic students. Applications are processed on a rolling basis. Application fee: $40 ($90 for international students). *Financial support:* In 2006–07, 735 students received support, including 58 research assistantships (averaging $6,801 per year), 45 teaching assistantships (averaging $5,735 per year); fellowships, career-related internships or fieldwork, Federal Work-Study, and institutionally sponsored loans also available. Support available to part-time students. Financial award application deadline: 4/1; financial award applicants required to submit FAFSA. *Unit head:* Dr. Rosalinda Barrera, Dean, 512-245-2150, Fax: 512-245-8345, E-mail: rb43@txstate.edu. *Application contact:* Dr. J. Michael Willoughby, Dean of Graduate School, 512-245-2581, Fax: 512-245-8365, E-mail: gradcollege@txstate.edu.

Texas Tech University, Graduate School, College of Education, Lubbock, TX 79409. Offers M Ed, Ed D, PhD, Certificate. *Accreditation:* NCATE. Part-time programs available. *Faculty:* 57 full-time (39 women), 3 part-time/adjunct (0 women). *Students:* 340 full-time (256 women), 564 part-time (409 women); includes 154 minority (43 African Americans, 1 American Indian/Alaska Native, 9 Asian Americans or Pacific Islanders, 101 Hispanic Americans), 33 international. Average age 35. 825 applicants, 67% accepted, 223 enrolled. In 2006, 171 master's, 23 doctorates awarded. *Degree requirements:* For master's, thesis optional; for doctorate, thesis/dissertation. *Entrance requirements:* For master's and doctorate, GRE General Test. Additional exam requirements/recommendations for international students: Required—TOEFL (minimum score 550 paper-based; 213 computer-based). *Application deadline:* For fall admission, 3/1 priority date for international students; for spring admission, 11/1 priority date for international students. Applications are processed on a rolling basis. Application fee: $50 ($60 for international students). Electronic applications accepted. *Expenses: Contact institution. Financial support:* In 2006–07, 575 students received support, including 2 research assistantships with partial tuition reimbursements available (averaging $10,800 per year), 13 teaching assistantships with partial tuition reimbursements available (averaging $10,835 per year); career-related internships or fieldwork, Federal Work-Study, and institutionally sponsored loans also available. Support available to part-time students. Financial award application deadline: 4/15; financial award applicants required to submit FAFSA. *Faculty research:* Multicultural foundations of education, teacher education, psychological processes of teaching and earning, teaching populations with special needs, instruction technology. Total annual research expenditures: $561,622. *Unit head:* Dr. Sheryl Santos, Dean, 806-742-1998 Ext. 450, Fax: 806-742-2179, E-mail: sheryl.santos@ttu.edu. *Application contact:* Patsy Ann Mountz, Administrative Assistant, 806-742-1988 Ext. 434, Fax: 806-742-2179, E-mail: patsy.mountz@ttu.edu.

Texas Wesleyan University, Graduate Programs, Programs in Education, Fort Worth, TX 76105-1536. Offers education (M Ed, MAT, MS Ed); professional counseling (MA); school counseling (MS). Part-time and evening/weekend programs available. Postbaccalaureate distance learning degree programs offered (no on-campus study). *Faculty:* 9 full-time (5 women), 6 part-time/adjunct (3 women). *Students:* 44 full-time (36 women), 167 part-time (146 women); includes 74 minority (46 African Americans, 2 American Indian/Alaska Native, 4 Asian Americans or Pacific Islanders, 22 Hispanic Americans). Average age 39. In 2006, 27 degrees awarded. *Degree requirements:* For master's, thesis optional. *Entrance requirements:* For master's, GRE General Test, minimum GPA of 3.0 in final 60 hours of undergraduate course work, interview. *Application deadline:* Applications are processed on a rolling basis. Application fee: $40 ($50 for international students). Electronic applications accepted. *Expenses:* Tuition: Full-time $4,230; part-time $470 per credit hour. Required fees: $53 per credit hour. Tuition and fees vary according to program. *Financial support:* Career-related internships or fieldwork, Federal Work-Study, institutionally sponsored loans, scholarships/grants, and tuition waivers (full and partial) available. Support available to part-time students. Financial award application deadline: 3/15; financial award applicants required to submit FAFSA. *Faculty research:* Teacher effectiveness, bilingual education, analytic teaching. *Unit head:* Dr. Carlos Martinez, Dean, School of Education, 817-531-4940, Fax: 817-531-4943.

Texas Woman's University, Graduate School, College of Professional Education, Denton, TX 76201. Offers M Ed, MA, MAT, MLS, MS, Ed D, PhD. Part-time and evening/weekend programs available. *Students:* 331 full-time (291 women), 1,322 part-time (1,219 women); includes 436 minority (227 African Americans, 10 American Indian/Alaska Native, 41 Asian Americans or Pacific Islanders, 158 Hispanic Americans), 46 international. Average age 37. In 2006, 488 master's, 28 doctorates awarded. *Degree requirements:* For doctorate, thesis/dissertation, comprehensive exam. *Entrance requirements:* Additional exam requirements/recommendations for international students: Required—TOEFL (minimum score 550 paper-based; 213 computer-based; 79 iBT). *Application deadline:* For fall admission, 4/1 for international students; for spring admission, 8/1 for international students. Applications are processed on a rolling basis. Application fee: $30 ($50 for international students). Electronic applications accepted. *Expenses:* Tuition, area resident: Part-time $168 per unit. Tuition, state resident: full-time $4,369. Tuition, nonresident: full-time $9,373; part-time $443 per unit. Required fees: $20 per unit. $177 per term. *Financial support:* In 2006–07, 34 research assistantships (averaging $10,764 per year), 14 teaching assistantships (averaging $10,764 per year) were awarded; career-related internships or fieldwork, Federal Work-Study, institutionally sponsored loans, scholarships/grants, traineeships, health care benefits, tuition waivers (partial), and unspecified assistantships also available. Support available to part-time students. Financial award application deadline: 3/1; financial award applicants required to submit FAFSA. *Faculty research:* Family therapy counseling, parenting/parent education, fathering, family life education, school counseling, distance education, home/school partnerships, classroom management, children's literature. *Unit head:* Dr. Nan L. Restine, Interim Dean, 940-898-2202, Fax: 940-898-2611, E-mail: lrestine@mail.twu.edu. *Application contact:* Samuel Wheeler, Coordinator of Graduate Admissions, 940-898-3188, Fax: 940-898-3081, E-mail: wheelersr@twu.edu.

Thomas University, Department of Education, Thomasville, GA 31792-7499. Offers M Ed. Part-time programs available. *Students:* 6 full-time (5 women), 7 part-time (all women); includes 2 minority (both African Americans), 1 international. *Entrance requirements:* For master's, resumé, 3 academic/professional references. Additional exam requirements/recommendations for international students: Required—TOEFL (minimum score 600 paper-based; 250 computer-based). *Application deadline:* For fall admission, 8/1 priority date for domestic students, 6/1 for international students; for spring admission, 12/1 priority date for domestic students, 10/1 for international students. Applications are processed on a rolling basis. Application fee: $50 ($125 for international students). Electronic applications accepted. *Expenses:* Tuition: Part-time $376 per credit. Required fees: $130 per semester. *Financial support:* Applicants required to submit FAFSA. *Unit head:* Dr. Melvin Gadson, Professor and Interim Chair of Education, 229-226-1621 Ext. 217, Fax: 229-226-1653, E-mail: mgadson@thomasu.edu. *Application contact:* Adrienne Diggs, Assistant Director of Admissions, 229-226-1621 Ext. 127, Fax: 229-227-6919, E-mail: adiggs@thomasu.edu.

Touro University College of Osteopathic Medicine, Professional Program, Vallejo, CA 94592. Offers education (MA); osteopathic medicine (DO); pharmacy (Pharm D); physician assistant studies (MS); public health (MPH). *Accreditation:* AOsA; ARC-PA. *Faculty:* 61 full-time (26 women), 30 part-time/adjunct (16 women). *Students:* 950 full-time (579 women); includes 354 minority (39 African Americans, 5 American Indian/Alaska Native, 258 Asian Americans or Pacific Islanders, 52 Hispanic Americans). Average age 26. 2,113 applicants, 13% accepted, 269 enrolled. In 2006, 109 first professional degrees, 43 master's awarded. *Median time to degree:* Of those who began their doctoral program in fall 1998, 98% received their degree in 8 years or less. *Entrance requirements:* For first professional degree and master's, BS/BA. *Application deadline:* For fall admission, 6/1 for domestic students. Applications are processed on a rolling basis. Application fee: $100. Electronic applications accepted. *Financial support:* In 2006–07, 3 fellowships (averaging $3,000 per year) were awarded. *Faculty research:* Diabetes, heart disease. *Application contact:* Steve Davis, Admissions Counselor, 707-638-5527, Fax: 707-638-5270, E-mail: sdavis@touro.edu.

Touro University International, College of Education, Cypress, CA 90630. Offers MA Ed, PhD, Certificate. Part-time and evening/weekend programs available. Postbaccalaureate distance learning degree programs offered (no on-campus study). In 2006, 19 master's, 13 doctorates awarded. *Degree requirements:* For doctorate, thesis/dissertation, defense of dissertation, comprehensive exam. *Entrance requirements:* For doctorate, minimum GPA of 3.4, curriculum vitae, course work in research methods or statistics. Additional exam requirements/recommendations for international students: Required—TOEFL (minimum score 550 paper-based). Application fee: $75. *Expenses:* Tuition: Part-time $300 per credit hour. Tuition and fees vary according to course level and program. *Unit head:* Dr. Edith Neumann, Vice President for Academic Affairs, 714-816-0366 Ext. 2030, Fax: 714-226-9844, E-mail: eneumann@tourou.edu.

Towson University, Graduate School, Program in Teaching, Towson, MD 21252-0001. Offers MAT. *Faculty:* 6 full-time (3 women). *Students:* 97 full-time (66 women), 87 part-time (65 women); includes 18 minority (8 African Americans, 1 American Indian/Alaska Native, 5 Asian Americans or Pacific Islanders, 4 Hispanic Americans), 2 international. 19 applicants, 79% accepted, 8 enrolled. In 2006, 112 degrees awarded. *Degree requirements:* For master's, portfolio. *Entrance requirements:* For master's, PRAXIS I, 2 letters of reference, resumé. Additional exam requirements/recommendations for international students: Required—TOEFL (minimum score 550 paper-based). *Application deadline:* For fall admission, 6/15 priority date for domestic and international students; for spring admission, 10/15 priority date for domestic and international students. Applications are processed on a rolling basis. Application fee: $50. Electronic applications accepted. *Expenses:* Tuition, state resident: part-time $275 per unit. Tuition, nonresident: part-time $577 per unit. Required fees: $72 per unit. *Financial support:* Unspecified assistantships available. Financial award application deadline: 4/1; financial award applicants required to submit FAFSA. *Faculty research:* Professional development. *Unit head:* Rachel Carter, Graduate Program Manager, 410-704-5388, Fax: 410-704-2733, E-mail: rcarter@towson.edu. *Application contact:* 410-704-2501, Fax: 410-704-4675, E-mail: grads@towson.edu.

Trevecca Nazarene University, Graduate Division, School of Education, Nashville, TN 37210-2877. Offers educational leadership (M Ed); English language learners (PreK-12) (M Ed); instructional effectiveness (M Ed); instructional technology (M Ed); leadership and professional practice (D Ed); library and information science (MLI Sc); reading PreK-12 (M Ed); teaching (MAT), including teaching 7-12, teaching K-6. Part-time and evening/weekend programs available. *Faculty:* 22 full-time (18 women), 42 part-time/adjunct (19 women). *Students:* 465 full-time (355 women), 78 part-time (53 women); includes 139 minority (126 African Americans, 3 American Indian/Alaska Native, 3 Asian Americans or Pacific Islanders, 7 Hispanic Americans), 3 international. Average age 36. In 2006, 240 master's, 24 doctorates awarded. *Degree requirements:* For master's, exit assessment; for doctorate, thesis/dissertation, proposal study, symposium presentation. *Entrance requirements:* For master's, GRE General Test, MAT, minimum GPA of 2.7, 2 reference forms; for doctorate, GMAT, GRE, MAT, or NTE, minimum GPA of 3.4, resumé, writing sample, interview, reference forms. Additional exam requirements/recommendations for international students: Required—TOEFL (minimum score 500 paper-based; 173 computer-based). *Application deadline:* Applications are processed on a rolling basis. Application fee: $50. *Expenses: Contact institution.* Tuition and fees vary according to degree level and program. *Financial support:* Applicants required to submit FAFSA. *Unit head:* Dr. Esther Swink, Dean, 615-248-1201, Fax: 615-248-1597, E-mail: eswink@trevecca.edu. *Application contact:* Admissions Office, 615-248-1201, Fax: 615-248-1597, E-mail: admissions_ged@trevecca.edu.

Trinity Baptist College, Graduate Programs, Jacksonville, FL 32221. Offers Bible (M Ed); Christian school administration (M Ed); classroom practices (M Ed); ministry (M Min); special education (M Ed). Postbaccalaureate distance learning degree programs offered. *Faculty:* 10. *Entrance requirements:* For master's, GRE (M Ed), 2 letters of recommendation; minimum GPA of 2.5 (M Min) or 3.0 (M Ed); computer proficiency.

Trinity International University, Trinity Graduate School, Deerfield, IL 60015-1284. Offers bioethics (MA); communication and culture (MA); counseling psychology (MA); instructional leadership (M Ed); teaching (MA). Part-time and evening/weekend programs available. Postbaccalaureate distance learning degree programs offered (minimal on-campus study). *Faculty:* 5 full-time (4 women), 39 part-time/adjunct (13 women). *Students:* 109 full-time (85 women), 130 part-time (81 women). In 2006, 29 degrees awarded. *Degree requirements:* For master's, comprehensive exam. *Entrance requirements:* For master's, GRE General Test or MAT, minimum undergraduate GPA of 3.0. Additional exam requirements/recommendations for international students: Required—TOEFL (minimum score 580 paper-based; 237 computer-based), TWE (minimum score 4). *Application deadline:* For fall admission, 7/15 priority date for domestic and international students. Applications are processed on a rolling basis. Application fee: $25. Electronic applications accepted. *Expenses:* Tuition: Full-time $13,200; part-time $630 per hour. Required fees: $43 per semester. *Financial support:* Career-related internships or fieldwork, Federal Work-Study, institutionally sponsored loans, and tuition waivers (partial) available. Support available to part-time students. Financial award application deadline: 4/1; financial award applicants required to submit FAFSA. *Unit head:* Dr. James Stamoolis, Academic Dean, 847-317-7001, Fax: 847-317-4786. *Application contact:* Ken Botton, Director of Enrollment Services for University Records and Graduate Admissions, 800-533-0975, Fax: 847-317-8097, E-mail: kbotton@tiu.edu.

Trinity University, Department of Education, San Antonio, TX 78212-7200. Offers school administration (M Ed); school psychology (MA); teacher education (MAT). *Accreditation:* NCATE. Part-time and evening/weekend programs available. *Faculty:* 6 full-time (4 women), 16 part-time/adjunct (11 women). *Students:* 48 full-time (39 women), 43 part-time (33 women); includes 26 minority (3 Asian Americans or Pacific Islanders, 23 Hispanic Americans). Average age 28. In 2006, 66 degrees awarded. *Entrance requirements:* For master's, GRE General Test, minimum GPA of 3.0, interview. *Application deadline:* For fall admission, 5/1 priority date for domestic students. Application fee: $30. *Financial support:* Fellowships, research assistantships, teaching assistantships, career-related internships or fieldwork, Federal Work-Study, institutionally sponsored loans, and scholarships/grants available. Support available to part-time students. Financial award application deadline: 4/1. *Unit head:* Dr. Paul Kelleher, Chair, 210-999-7501, Fax: 210-999-7592, E-mail: paul.kelleher@trinity.edu.

Trinity (Washington) University, School of Education, Washington, DC 20017-1094. Offers democracy, diversity, and social justice (M Ed); early childhood (MAT); educational administration (MSA); elementary education (MAT); English as a second language (M Ed, MAT); literacy and reading education (M Ed); school counseling (MA); secondary education (MAT), including English, math, science, social studies; special education (MAT). *Accreditation:* NCATE. Part-time and evening/weekend programs available. *Degree requirements:* For master's, thesis (for some programs), capstone project(s). *Entrance requirements:* For master's, PRAXIS I, minimum GPA of 2.8. Additional exam requirements/recommendations for international students: Required—TOEFL (minimum score 550 paper-based; 213 computer-based). *Faculty research:* Technology, literacy, special education, organizations, inclusion models.

Troy University, Graduate School, College of Education, Troy, AL 36082. Offers M Ed, ME, MS, MSE, Ed S. *Accreditation:* NCATE. Part-time and evening/weekend programs available. *Students:* 1,042 full-time (852 women), 1,548 part-time (1,189 women); includes 1,332 minority (1,149 African Americans, 116 American Indian/Alaska Native, 16 Asian Americans or Pacific Islanders, 51 Hispanic Americans). Average age 35. In 2006, 1,735 master's, 183 other advanced degrees awarded. *Degree requirements:* For master's, thesis, comprehensive exam, registration. *Entrance requirements:* For master's, GRE General Test, MAT or GMAT, minimum GPA of 2.5; for Ed S, GRE General Test, MAT or GMAT, Alabama Class A certificate or equivalent, minimum graduate GPA of 3.0. Additional exam requirements/recommendations for international students: Required—TOEFL (minimum score 523 paper-based; 200 computer-based). *Application deadline:* For fall admission, 6/1 for international students; for spring admission, 10/15 for international students. Applications are processed on a rolling basis.

Education—General

Troy University (continued)

Application fee: $50. Electronic applications accepted. *Expenses:* Tuition, state resident: full-time $4,368; part-time $182 per hour. Tuition, nonresident: full-time $8,736; part-time $364 per hour. Required fees: $50 per term. *Financial support:* Career-related internships or fieldwork available. Support available to part-time students. Financial award applicants required to submit FAFSA. *Unit head:* Dr. Lance Tatum, Interim Dean, 334-670-3365, Fax: 334-670-3474, E-mail: ltatum@troy.edu. *Application contact:* Brenda K. Campbell, Director of Graduate Admissions, 334-670-3178, Fax: 334-670-3733, E-mail: bcamp@troy.edu.

Truman State University, Graduate School, Division of Education, Program in Education, Kirksville, MO 63501-4221. Offers MAE. *Degree requirements:* For master's, thesis or alternative, comprehensive exam. *Entrance requirements:* For master's, GRE, minimum GPA of 2.75. Additional exam requirements/recommendations for international students: Required—TOEFL (minimum score 550 paper-based; 213 computer-based). Electronic applications accepted.

Tufts University, Graduate School of Arts and Sciences, Department of Education, Medford, MA 02155. Offers education (MA, MAT, MS, PhD), including education (MS, PhD), elementary education (MAT), middle and secondary education (MA, MAT), secondary education (MA); school psychology (MA, CAGS). *Faculty:* 13 full-time, 9 part-time/adjunct. *Students:* 158; includes 30 minority (12 African Americans, 8 Asian Americans or Pacific Islanders, 10 Hispanic Americans), 7 international. 299 applicants, 63% accepted, 91 enrolled. In 2006, 89 master's, 10 other advanced degrees awarded. *Degree requirements:* For doctorate, thesis/dissertation. *Entrance requirements:* For master's, GRE General Test. Additional exam requirements/recommendations for international students: Required—TOEFL (minimum score 550 paper-based; 213 computer-based; 80 iBT). *Application deadline:* For fall admission, 2/1 for domestic students, 12/30 for international students; for spring admission, 10/15 for domestic students, 9/15 for international students. Applications are processed on a rolling basis. Application fee: $70. Electronic applications accepted. *Expenses:* Tuition: Full-time $33,672. Tuition and fees vary according to degree level and program. *Financial support:* Teaching assistantships with full and partial tuition reimbursements, career-related internships or fieldwork, Federal Work-Study, scholarships/grants, and tuition waivers (full and partial) available. Support available to part-time students. Financial award application deadline: 2/1; financial award applicants required to submit FAFSA. *Unit head:* Analucia Schliemann, Chair, 617-627-3244, Fax: 617-627-3901.

Tusculum College, Graduate School, Program in Education, Greeneville, TN 37743-9997. Offers adult education (MA Ed); K–12 (MA Ed). Evening/weekend programs available. *Degree requirements:* For master's, thesis or alternative. *Entrance requirements:* For master's, GRE or MAT, NTE, 3 years of work experience, minimum GPA of 2.75.

Union College, Graduate Programs, Department of Education, Barbourville, KY 40906-1499. Offers elementary education (MA); health and physical education (MA); middle grades (MA); music education (MA); principalship (MA); reading specialist (MA); secondary education (MA); special education (MA). *Degree requirements:* For master's, thesis optional. *Entrance requirements:* For master's, GRE General Test, NTE.

Union Graduate College, School of Education, Schenectady, NY 12308-3107. Offers biology (MAT, MS); chemistry (MAT); earth science (MAT); English (MAT); French (MAT); general science (MAT); German (MAT); languages (MAT); Latin (MAT); mathematics (MAT); mathematics and technology (MS); physical science (MS); physics (MAT); social studies (MAT); Spanish (MAT). *Accreditation:* Teacher Education Accreditation Council. *Faculty:* 5 full-time (1 woman), 19 part-time/adjunct (10 women). *Students:* 57 full-time (36 women), 21 part-time (14 women); includes 2 African Americans, 2 Hispanic Americans, 2 international. Average age 31. 59 applicants, 83% accepted, 39 enrolled. In 2006, 56 degrees awarded. *Degree requirements:* For master's, thesis or project. *Entrance requirements:* For master's, minimum GPA of 3.0, letters of recommendation. Additional exam requirements/recommendations for international students: Required—TOEFL (minimum score 550 paper-based; 213 computer-based). Application fee: $60. *Expenses:* Contact institution. *Financial support:* In 2006–07, 12 research assistantships with tuition reimbursements (averaging $3,000 per year) were awarded; Federal Work-Study, scholarships/grants, health care benefits, and tuition waivers (partial) also available. Support available to part-time students. Financial award applicants required to submit FAFSA. *Unit head:* Dr. Patrick Allen, Dean, 518-388-6361, Fax: 518-388-6686, E-mail: mat@union.edu. *Application contact:* Rhonda Sheehan, Director of Graduate Admissions Registrar, 518-388-6238, Fax: 518-388-6686, E-mail: sheehanr@union.edu.

See Close-Up on page 923.

Union Institute & University, Program in Education (Florida Campus), Cincinnati, OH 45206-1925. Offers M Ed, Ed S. Postbaccalaureate distance learning degree programs offered (minimal on-campus study). *Degree requirements:* For master's, thesis. *Entrance requirements:* For master's, letters of recommendation. Expenses: Contact institution.

Union Institute & University, Program in Education (Vermont Campus), Montpelier, VT 45206-1925. Offers M Ed. *Degree requirements:* For master's, thesis, registration. *Entrance requirements:* For master's, 3 letters of reference. Expenses: Contact institution.

Union University, School of Education, Jackson, TN 38305-3697. Offers education (M Ed, MA Ed); education administration generalist (Ed S); educational leadership (Ed D); educational supervision (Ed S); higher education (Ed D). M Ed also available at Germantown campus. *Accreditation:* NCATE. Part-time and evening/weekend programs available. *Faculty:* 19 full-time (11 women), 18 part-time/adjunct (12 women). *Students:* 254 full-time (207 women), 161 part-time (120 women); includes 197 minority (193 African Americans, 1 American Indian/Alaska Native, 1 Asian American or Pacific Islander, 2 Hispanic Americans). Average age 32. In 2006, 184 master's, 22 doctorates, 77 other advanced degrees awarded. *Degree requirements:* For master's, thesis (for some programs), capstone research course; for doctorate, thesis/dissertation, comprehensive exam; for Ed S, thesis or alternative. *Entrance requirements:* For master's, MAT, PRAXIS II or GRE, minimum GPA of 3.0, teaching license, writing sample; for doctorate, GRE, minimum graduate GPA of 3.2, writing sample; for Ed S, PRAXIS II, minimum graduate GPA of 3.2, writing sample. *Application deadline:* Applications are processed on a rolling basis. Application fee: $25 ($50 for international students). *Financial support:* In 2006–07, 117 students received support. Application deadline: 2/15; *Faculty research:* Mathematics education, direct instruction, language disorders and special education, brain compatible learning, empathy and school leadership. *Unit head:* Dr. Tom R. Rosebrough, Dean, 731-661-5523, Fax: 731-661-5468, E-mail: trosebro@uu.edu. *Application contact:* Helen F. Fowler, Assistant to the Dean, 731-661-5374, Fax: 731-661-5468, E-mail: hfowler@uu.edu.

Universidad Adventista de las Antillas, Graduate School, Mayagüez, PR 00681-0118. Offers education (MA). *Degree requirements:* For master's, registration. *Entrance requirements:* For master's, EXADEP or GRE, recommendations. Electronic applications accepted.

Universidad Autonoma de Guadalajara, Graduate Programs, Guadalajara, Mexico. Offers architecture (M Arch); computational science (MCC); education (Ed M, Ed D); international business (MIB); manufacturing systems (MMS); quality systems (MQS);).

Universidad de las Americas, A.C., Program in Education, Mexico City, Mexico. Offers M Ed. *Entrance requirements:* For master's, 2 years of professional experience; undergraduate degree in early childhood education, human communication, psychology, science of education, special education or related fields.

Universidad de las Américas–Puebla, Division of Graduate Studies, School of Social Sciences, Program in Education, Puebla, Mexico. Offers MA. Part-time and evening/weekend programs available. *Degree requirements:* For master's, one foreign language, thesis. *Faculty research:* Curriculum development, curriculum evaluation, instructional technology, critical thinking.

Universidad del Este, Graduate School, Carolina, PR 00983. Offers accounting (MBA); administration (M Ed); criminal justice and criminology (MA); education (M Ed); elementary education (M Ed); human resources (MBA); management (MBA); social work (MA); teaching English (M Ed); teaching Spanish (M Ed).

Universidad del Turabo, Graduate Programs, Programs in Education, Gurabo, PR 00778-3030. Offers bilingual education (MA); education administration and supervision (MA); school libraries administration (MA); special education (MA); teaching English as a second language (MA). Part-time and evening/weekend programs available. *Entrance requirements:* For master's, GRE, EXADEP, interview.

Universidad Iberoamericana, Graduate School, Santo Domingo D.N., Dominican Republic. Offers dentistry (DMD); education (M Ed); international business (IMBA).

Universidad Metropolitana, Graduate Programs in Education, San Juan, PR 00928-1150. Offers curriculum and teaching (MA); educational administration and supervision (MA); environmental education (MA); fitness management (MA); managing leisure services (MA); preschool centers administration (MA); pre-school education (MA); special education (MA); teaching of physical education (MA). Part-time and evening/weekend programs available. *Degree requirements:* For master's, thesis or alternative. Electronic applications accepted.

Universidad Nacional Pedro Henriquez Urena, Graduate School, Santo Domingo, Dominican Republic. Offers accounting and auditing (M Acct); animal production (M Agr); business administration (MBA, PhD); Caribbean tropical architecture (M Arch); conservation of monuments and cultural goods (M Arch); economics (M Econ); education (PhD); environmental engineering (MEE); horticulture (M Agr); hospital administration (PhD); humanities (PhD); international relations (MPS); management of natural resources (MNRM); project management (M Man, MPM); public administration (MPS); sanitary engineering (ME); social science (PhD); veterinary medicine (DVM).

Université de Moncton, Faculty of Education, Graduate Studies in Education, Moncton, NB E1A 3E9, Canada. Offers educational psychology (M Ed, MA Ed); guidance (M Ed, MA Ed); school administration (M Ed, MA Ed); teaching (M Ed, MA Ed). Part-time programs available. *Degree requirements:* For master's, proficiency in English and French. *Entrance requirements:* For master's, minimum GPA of 3.0. *Faculty research:* Guidance, ethnolinguistic vitality, children's rights, ecological education, entrepreneurship.

Université de Montréal, Faculty of Graduate Studies, Faculty of Education, Montréal, QC H3C 3J7, Canada. Offers M Ed, MA, PhD, DESS. Part-time and evening/weekend programs available. *Faculty:* 72 full-time (41 women), 29 part-time/adjunct (14 women). *Students:* 2,074 full-time (1,636 women), 955 part-time (701 women). 947 applicants, 64% accepted, 496 enrolled. In 2006, 64 master's, 23 doctorates, 83 other advanced degrees awarded. *Degree requirements:* For doctorate, thesis/dissertation, general exam. *Application deadline:* For fall admission, 2/1 priority date for domestic students; for winter admission, 11/1 priority date for domestic students; for spring admission, 2/1 priority date for domestic students. Application fee: $30. Electronic applications accepted. *Financial support:* Fellowships, research assistantships, teaching assistantships available. *Unit head:* Michel D. Laurier, Dean, 514-343-6658, Fax: 514-343-7276. *Application contact:* François Bowen, Graduate Chairman and Vice Dean, 514-343-7491, Fax: 514-343-7276, E-mail: francois.bowen@umontreal.ca.

Université de Sherbrooke, Faculty of Education, Sherbrooke, QC J1K 2R1, Canada. Offers M Ed, MA, Diploma. Part-time and evening/weekend programs available. *Degree requirements:* For master's, thesis. *Faculty research:* Career education, teaching, professional instruction.

Université du Québec à Chicoutimi, Graduate Programs, Program in Education, Chicoutimi, QC G7H 2B1, Canada. Offers M Ed, MA, PhD. Part-time programs available. *Degree requirements:* For doctorate, thesis/dissertation. *Entrance requirements:* For master's, appropriate bachelor's degree, proficiency in French; for doctorate, appropriate master's degree, proficiency in French.

Université du Québec à Montréal, Graduate Programs, Program in Education, Montréal, QC H3C 3P8, Canada. Offers education (M Ed, MA, PhD); education of the environmental sciences (Diploma). Part-time programs available. *Degree requirements:* For master's, thesis (for some programs); for doctorate, thesis/dissertation. *Entrance requirements:* For master's and Diploma, appropriate bachelor's degree or equivalent, proficiency in French; for doctorate, appropriate master's degree or equivalent, proficiency in French.

Université du Québec à Rimouski, Graduate Programs, Program in Education, Rimouski, QC G5L 3A1, Canada. Offers M Ed, MA, PhD, Diploma. Part-time programs available. *Students:* 57 full-time, 80 part-time. In 2006, 22 degrees awarded. *Degree requirements:* For master's, thesis optional; for doctorate, thesis/dissertation. *Entrance requirements:* For master's, appropriate bachelor's degree, proficiency in French; for doctorate, appropriate master's degree, proficiency in French. *Application deadline:* For fall admission, 5/1 priority date for domestic students. Application fee: $50. *Financial support:* Fellowships, research assistantships, teaching assistantships available. *Unit head:* Abdellah Marzouk, Director, 418-833-8800 Ext. 3245, Fax: 418-833-1113, E-mail: abdellah_marzouk@uqar.ca. *Application contact:* Marc Berube, Office of Admissions, 418-724-1433, Fax: 418-724-1525, E-mail: marc_berube@uqar.ca.

Université du Québec à Trois-Rivières, Graduate Programs, Program in Education, Trois-Rivières, QC G9A 5H7, Canada. Offers M Ed, MA, DESS. Part-time programs available. *Degree requirements:* For master's, research report. *Entrance requirements:* For master's, appropriate bachelor's degree, proficiency in French.

Université du Québec en Abitibi-Témiscamingue, Graduate Programs, Program in Education, Rouyn-Noranda, QC J9X 5E4, Canada. Offers M Ed, MA, PhD. Part-time programs available. *Degree requirements:* For master's, thesis optional; for doctorate, thesis/dissertation. *Entrance requirements:* For master's, appropriate bachelor's degree, proficiency in French; for doctorate, appropriate master's degree, proficiency in French.

Université du Québec en Outaouais, Graduate Programs, Program in Education, Gatineau, QC J8X 3X7, Canada. Offers M Ed, MA, PhD, Diploma. Part-time programs available. *Students:* 6 full-time, 96 part-time. *Degree requirements:* For master's, thesis optional; for doctorate, thesis/dissertation. *Entrance requirements:* For master's, appropriate bachelor's degree, proficiency in French; for doctorate, appropriate master's degree, proficiency in French. *Application deadline:* For fall admission, 6/1 priority date for domestic students, 3/1 for international students; for winter admission, 11/1 priority date for domestic students, 10/1 for international students. Application fee: $30 Canadian dollars. *Financial support:* Fellowships, research assistantships, teaching assistantships available. *Unit head:* Sylvie Fontaine, Director, 819-595-4410, Fax: 819-595-4459, E-mail: sylvie.fontaine@uqo.ca. *Application contact:* Registrar's Office, 819-773-1850, Fax: 819-773-1835, E-mail: registraire@ugo.ca.

Université Laval, Faculty of Education, Québec, QC G1K 7P4, Canada. Offers MA, PhD, Diploma. Part-time programs available. *Degree requirements:* For doctorate, thesis/dissertation, comprehensive exam. Electronic applications accepted.

University at Albany, State University of New York, School of Education, Albany, NY 12222-0001. Offers MA, MS, Ed D, PhD, Psy D, CAS. *Accreditation:* Teacher Education Accreditation Council. Part-time and evening/weekend programs available. *Students:* 456 full-time (340 women), 669 part-time (520 women); includes 106 minority (45 African Americans, 2 American Indian/Alaska Native, 17 Asian Americans or Pacific Islanders, 42 Hispanic Americans), 63 international. Average age 34. In 2006, 455 master's, 30 doctorates, 50 other advanced degrees awarded. *Degree requirements:* For doctorate, thesis/dissertation. *Entrance requirements:* For doctorate, GRE General Test. Additional exam requirements/recommendations for international students: Required—TOEFL (minimum score 550 paper-based; 213 computer-based). Application fee: $75. Electronic applications accepted. *Expenses:* Tuition, state resident: full-time $6,900; part-time $288 per credit. Tuition, nonresident: full-time $10,920; part-time

$455 per credit. Required fees: $1,139. *Financial support:* Fellowships, career-related internships or fieldwork and Federal Work-Study available. *Unit head:* Susanne K. Phillips, Dean, 518-442-4988. *Application contact:* Christine Smith, Assistant to the Dean of Graduate Studies, E-mail: csmith2@albany.edu.

University at Buffalo, the State University of New York, Graduate School, Graduate School of Education, Buffalo, NY 14260. Offers Ed M, MA, MLS, MS, Ed D, PhD, Certificate. Part-time programs available. Postbaccalaureate distance learning degree programs offered (minimal on-campus study). *Faculty:* 80 full-time (48 women), 98 part-time/adjunct (68 women). *Students:* 835 full-time (620 women), 709 part-time (504 women); includes 145 minority (74 African Americans, 5 American Indian/Alaska Native, 29 Asian Americans or Pacific Islanders, 37 Hispanic Americans), 122 international. 1,248 applicants, 55% accepted, 459 enrolled. In 2006, 527 master's, 55 doctorates, 72 other advanced degrees awarded. Terminal master's awarded for partial completion of doctoral program. *Degree requirements:* For doctorate, thesis/dissertation. *Entrance requirements:* For master's, GRE General Test. Additional exam requirements/recommendations for international students: Required—TOEFL. *Application deadline:* Applications are processed on a rolling basis. Application fee: $50. Electronic applications accepted. *Financial support:* Fellowships with full tuition reimbursements, research assistantships with full tuition reimbursements, teaching assistantships with full tuition reimbursements, career-related internships or fieldwork, Federal Work-Study, institutionally sponsored loans, tuition waivers (full and partial), and unspecified assistantships available. Financial award applicants required to submit FAFSA. *Faculty research:* Early childhood mathematics education, finance and management of higher education, curricular policy, practice and reform, student behavior in small classes, psychological measurement and assessment. Total annual research expenditures: $4.7 million. *Unit head:* Dr. Mary H. Gresham, Dean, 716-645-6640, Fax: 716-645-2479, E-mail: gse-info@buffalo.edu. *Application contact:* Dr. Radhika Suresh, Director of Graduate Admissions and Student Services, 716-645-2110 Ext. 1209, Fax: 716-645-7937, E-mail: gse-info@buffalo.edu.

The University of Akron, Graduate School, College of Education, Akron, OH 44325. Offers MA, MS, Ed D, PhD. *Accreditation:* NCATE. Part-time programs available. *Faculty:* 53 full-time (34 women), 125 part-time/adjunct (82 women). *Students:* 342 full-time (245 women), 669 part-time (493 women); includes 120 minority (94 African Americans, 5 American Indian/Alaska Native, 10 Asian Americans or Pacific Islanders, 11 Hispanic Americans), 18 international. Average age 33. 357 applicants, 64% accepted, 175 enrolled. In 2006, 270 master's, 20 doctorates awarded. *Degree requirements:* For doctorate, one foreign language, thesis/dissertation, written and oral exams, comprehensive exam. *Entrance requirements:* For doctorate, GRE or MAT, minimum GPA of 2.75, writing sample, interview. Additional exam requirements/recommendations for international students: Required—TOEFL (minimum score 550 paper-based; 213 computer-based; 79 iBT). *Application deadline:* For fall admission, 8/15 for domestic students. Applications are processed on a rolling basis. Application fee: $30 ($40 for international students). Electronic applications accepted. *Expenses:* Tuition, state resident: full-time $6,164; part-time $342 per credit. Tuition, nonresident: full-time $10,575; part-time $588 per credit. Required fees: $806; $43 per credit. $12 per term. Tuition and fees vary according to course load, degree level and program. *Financial support:* In 2006–07, 78 research assistantships with full tuition reimbursements, 30 teaching assistantships with full tuition reimbursements were awarded; fellowships with full tuition reimbursements, career-related internships or fieldwork, Federal Work-Study, tuition waivers (full), and unspecified assistantships also available. *Faculty research:* History, philosophy of education, ethnographic research in education, case study methodology in education, multiple linear regression. Total annual research expenditures: $2.8 million. *Unit head:* Dr. Patricia Nelson, Dean, 330-972-7680.

The University of Alabama at Birmingham, School of Education, Birmingham, AL 35294. Offers MA, MA Ed, Ed D, PhD, Ed S. *Accreditation:* NCATE. Part-time and evening/weekend programs available. *Students:* 217 full-time (172 women), 535 part-time (426 women); includes 203 minority (189 African Americans, 4 American Indian/Alaska Native, 2 Asian Americans or Pacific Islanders, 8 Hispanic Americans), 15 international. Average age 34. 202 applicants, 83% accepted. In 2006, 356 master's, 13 doctorates, 59 other advanced degrees awarded. *Degree requirements:* For master's, thesis optional; for doctorate, thesis/dissertation; for Ed S, thesis optional. *Entrance requirements:* For master's, GRE General Test, MAT, or NTE, minimum GPA of 3.0; for doctorate, GRE General Test, MAT, minimum GPA of 3.25; for Ed S, GRE General Test, MAT, minimum GPA of 3.0, master's degree. *Application deadline:* Applications are processed on a rolling basis. Application fee: $35 ($60 for international students). Electronic applications accepted. *Expenses:* Tuition, state resident: part-time $170 per credit hour. Tuition, nonresident: part-time $425 per credit hour. Required fees: $15 per credit hour. $122 per term. Tuition and fees vary according to program. *Financial support:* Fellowships, career-related internships or fieldwork and Federal Work-Study available. Support available to part-time students. *Unit head:* Dr. Michael J. Froning, Dean, 205-934-5363, Fax: 205-934-4963.

University of Alaska Anchorage, College of Education, Anchorage, AK 99508-8060. Offers M Ed, MAT, Certificate. *Accreditation:* NCATE. Part-time programs available. *Students:* 29 full-time (24 women), 135 part-time (101 women); includes 19 minority (3 African Americans, 7 American Indian/Alaska Native, 5 Asian Americans or Pacific Islanders, 4 Hispanic Americans), 8 international. 78 applicants, 40% accepted. In 2006, 72 degrees awarded. *Degree requirements:* For master's, thesis or alternative, portfolio, comprehensive exam, registration. *Entrance requirements:* For master's, interview, minimum GPA of 3.0. Additional exam requirements/recommendations for international students: Required—TOEFL (minimum score 550 paper-based; 213 computer-based). *Application deadline:* For fall admission, 3/5 for domestic and international students; for spring admission, 10/15 for domestic and international students. Application fee: $45. *Expenses:* Tuition, state resident: part-time $268 per credit. Tuition, nonresident: part-time $547 per credit. Required fees: $124 per semester. Tuition and fees vary according to reciprocity agreements and student level. *Financial support:* Research assistantships, teaching assistantships, career-related internships or fieldwork, Federal Work-Study, scholarships/grants, traineeships, and unspecified assistantships available. Support available to part-time students. Financial award application deadline: 4/1; financial award applicants required to submit FAFSA. *Unit head:* Dr. Mary Snyder, Dean, 907-786-4484. *Application contact:* Jane Jordan, Graduate Programs Assistant, 907-786-4401, Fax: 907-786-4445, E-mail: anjmj@uaa.alaska.edu.

University of Alaska Fairbanks, School of Education, Fairbanks, AK 99775-7520. Offers cross cultural education (M Ed); curriculum instruction (M Ed); education (M Ed); guidance and counseling (M Ed); k-12 reading (M Ed); language and literacy (M Ed). *Accreditation:* NCATE. Part-time programs available. Postbaccalaureate distance learning degree programs offered. *Faculty:* 18 full-time (10 women), 3 part-time/adjunct (all women). *Students:* 56 full-time (40 women), 89 part-time (72 women); includes 31 minority (4 African Americans, 21 American Indian/Alaska Native, 2 Asian Americans or Pacific Islanders, 4 Hispanic Americans), 1 international. Average age 37. 69 applicants, 67% accepted, 42 enrolled. In 2006, 33 degrees awarded. *Degree requirements:* For master's, thesis or alternative, student teaching, comprehensive exam, registration. *Entrance requirements:* For master's, GRE General Test, PRAXIS I. Additional exam requirements/recommendations for international students: Required—TOEFL (minimum score 550 paper-based; 213 computer-based). *Application deadline:* For fall admission, 3/1 for domestic and international students; for spring admission, 10/1 for domestic students, 9/1 for international students. Application fee: $50. Electronic applications accepted. *Financial support:* In 2006–07, 2 research assistantships with tuition reimbursements (averaging $6,510 per year), 4 teaching assistantships with tuition reimbursements (averaging $10,441 per year) were awarded; fellowships with tuition reimbursements, career-related internships or fieldwork, Federal Work-Study, and scholarships/grants also available. Financial award applicants required to submit FAFSA. *Faculty research:* Native ways of knowing, classroom research in methods of literacy instruction, multiple intelligence theory, geometry concept development, mathematics and science curriculum development. *Unit head:* Dr. Eric C. Madsen, Dean, 907-474-7341, Fax: 907-474-5451, E-mail: fysoed@uaf.edu.

University of Alaska Southeast, Graduate Programs, Program in Education, Juneau, AK 99801. Offers early childhood education (M Ed, MAT); educational technology (M Ed); elementary education (MAT); reading (M Ed); secondary education (MAT). *Accreditation:* NCATE. Part-time and evening/weekend programs available. Postbaccalaureate distance learning degree programs offered (minimal on-campus study). *Faculty:* 12 full-time (7 women), 6 part-time/adjunct (5 women). *Students:* 81 full-time (49 women), 109 part-time (88 women); includes 24 minority (3 African Americans, 11 American Indian/Alaska Native, 5 Asian Americans or Pacific Islanders, 5 Hispanic Americans), 6 international. Average age 34. In 2006, 84 degrees awarded. *Degree requirements:* For master's, comprehensive exam or project, portfolio. *Entrance requirements:* For master's, PRAXIS, minimum GPA of 3.0, writing sample, letters of recommendation. *Application deadline:* For fall admission, 3/8 for domestic students. Applications are processed on a rolling basis. Application fee: $50. Electronic applications accepted. *Financial support:* Federal Work-Study, scholarships/grants, and tuition waivers (full and partial) available. Support available to part-time students. Financial award applicants required to submit FAFSA. *Faculty research:* Applied classroom research, culturally responsive practices, action research, teaching effectiveness. *Unit head:* Dr. Larry Harris, Dean, 907-796-6551, Fax: 907-796-6550, E-mail: larry.harris@uas.alaska.edu. *Application contact:* Susan A. Stuck, Administrative Assistant, 866-465-6424, Fax: 866-465-5159, E-mail: jnsas@uas.alaska.edu.

The University of Arizona, Graduate College, College of Education, Tucson, AZ 85721. Offers M Ed, MA, MS, Ed D, PhD, Ed S. Part-time programs available. Postbaccalaureate distance learning degree programs offered (no on-campus study). *Faculty:* 46 full-time (23 women), 14 part-time/adjunct (7 women). *Students:* 413 full-time (303 women), 410 part-time (292 women); includes 198 minority (29 African Americans, 35 American Indian/Alaska Native, 18 Asian Americans or Pacific Islanders, 116 Hispanic Americans), 67 international. Average age 38. 304 applicants, 56% accepted, 134 enrolled. In 2006, 212 master's, 44 doctorates, 14 other advanced degrees awarded. Terminal master's awarded for partial completion of doctoral program. *Degree requirements:* For master's, thesis (for some programs), comprehensive exam, registration; for doctorate, thesis/dissertation, comprehensive exam, registration. *Entrance requirements:* For doctorate, GRE. Additional exam requirements/recommendations for international students: Required—TOEFL. *Application deadline:* For fall admission, 2/1 priority date for domestic and international students; for spring admission, 10/1 priority date for domestic students, 9/1 priority date for international students. Applications are processed on a rolling basis. Application fee: $50. *Financial support:* In 2006–07, 297 fellowships with tuition reimbursements, 20 research assistantships with tuition reimbursements, 20 teaching assistantships with tuition reimbursements were awarded; career-related internships or fieldwork, Federal Work-Study, institutionally sponsored loans, scholarships/grants, tuition waivers (full and partial), and unspecified assistantships also available. Support available to part-time students. Financial award application deadline: 3/1. *Faculty research:* Teacher effectiveness, pupil achievement, learning skills, program evaluation, instructional method effects. Total annual research expenditures: $5 million. *Unit head:* Dr. Ronald Marx, Dean, 520-621-1081, Fax: 520-621-9271.

University of Arkansas, Graduate School, College of Education and Health Professions, Fayetteville, AR 72701-1201. Offers M Ed, MAT, MS, MSN, Ed D, PhD, Ed S. *Accreditation:* NCATE. *Students:* 372 full-time (246 women), 473 part-time (345 women); includes 126 minority (96 African Americans, 13 American Indian/Alaska Native, 5 Asian Americans or Pacific Islanders, 12 Hispanic Americans), 43 international. 461 applicants, 43% accepted. In 2006, 296 master's, 35 doctorates awarded. *Degree requirements:* For doctorate, thesis/dissertation. Application fee: $40 ($50 for international students). *Financial support:* In 2006–07, 39 fellowships with tuition reimbursements, 16 research assistantships, 37 teaching assistantships were awarded; career-related internships or fieldwork and Federal Work-Study also available. Support available to part-time students. Financial award application deadline: 4/1; financial award applicants required to submit FAFSA. *Unit head:* M. Reed Greenwood, Dean, 479-575-3208, Fax: 479-575-3119.

University of Arkansas at Little Rock, Graduate School, College of Education, Little Rock, AR 72204-1099. Offers M Ed, MA, Ed D, Ed S. *Accreditation:* CORE; NCATE (one or more programs are accredited). Part-time and evening/weekend programs available. *Degree requirements:* For doctorate and Ed S, oral defense of dissertation, residency. *Entrance requirements:* For master's, minimum GPA of 2.75; for doctorate, GRE General Test or MAT, minimum graduate GPA of 3.0, teaching certificate, work experience; for Ed S, GRE General Test or MAT, teaching certificate.

University of Arkansas at Monticello, School of Education, Monticello, AR 71656. Offers education (M Ed, MAT); educational leadership (M Ed). *Accreditation:* NCATE. Part-time and evening/weekend programs available. Postbaccalaureate distance learning degree programs offered (minimal on-campus study). *Faculty:* 33 full-time (13 women), 1 (woman) part-time/adjunct. *Students:* 21 full-time (14 women), 59 part-time (49 women); includes 10 minority (all African Americans) Average age 36. In 2006, 59 degrees awarded. *Degree requirements:* For master's, comprehensive exam. *Entrance requirements:* For master's, minimum GPA of 3.0. Additional exam requirements/recommendations for international students: Required—TOEFL (minimum score 550 paper-based; 213 computer-based). *Application deadline:* For fall admission, 8/16 priority date for domestic students, 8/1 priority date for international students; for spring admission, 1/3 priority date for domestic students, 12/1 priority date for international students. Applications are processed on a rolling basis. Application fee: $0 ($30 for international students). Electronic applications accepted. *Expenses:* Tuition, state resident: full-time $2,646; part-time $135 per hour. Tuition, nonresident: full-time $5,940; part-time $315 per hour. Required fees: $594; $30 per hour. Tuition and fees vary according to campus/location. *Financial support:* In 2006–07, 4 teaching assistantships with full tuition reimbursements were awarded; Federal Work-Study and tuition waivers (partial) also available. Support available to part-time students. *Unit head:* Dr. Peggy Doss, Dean, 870-460-1062, Fax: 870-460-1563, E-mail: dossp@uamont.edu.

University of Arkansas at Pine Bluff, Program in Education, Pine Bluff, AR 71601-2799. Offers elementary education (M Ed); secondary education (M Ed), including English, general science, mathematics, physical education, social studies. Part-time and evening/weekend programs available. *Degree requirements:* For master's, comprehensive exam. *Entrance requirements:* For master's, GRE, minimum GPA of 2.75, NTE or Standard Arkansas Teaching Certificate. *Faculty research:* Teacher certification, accreditation, assessment, standards, portfolio development, rehabilitation, technology.

University of Bridgeport, School of Education and Human Resources, Division of Education, Bridgeport, CT 06604. Offers education (MS); educational management (Ed D, Diploma), including intermediate administrator or supervisor (Diploma), leadership (Ed D); elementary education (MS, Diploma), including early childhood education, elementary education; secondary education (MS, Diploma), including computer specialist (Diploma), international education (Diploma), reading specialist, secondary education. Part-time and evening/weekend programs available. *Faculty:* 14 full-time (5 women), 74 part-time/adjunct (44 women). *Students:* 375 full-time (290 women), 308 part-time (204 women); includes 79 minority (31 African Americans, 1 American Indian/Alaska Native, 13 Asian Americans or Pacific Islanders, 34 Hispanic Americans), 22 international. Average age 33. 523 applicants, 62% accepted, 186 enrolled. In 2006, 272 master's, 4 doctorates, 25 other advanced degrees awarded. *Degree requirements:* For master's, final exam, final project, or thesis; for doctorate, thesis/dissertation; for Diploma, thesis or alternative, final project. *Entrance requirements:* For master's, GRE General Test, MAT, minimum undergraduate QPA of 2.5; for doctorate, GRE, MAT; for Diploma, GRE General Test or MAT, minimum graduate QPA of 3.0. *Application deadline:* For fall admission, 8/1 priority date for domestic students; for spring admission, 12/1 priority date for domestic students. Applications are processed on a rolling basis. Application fee: $25 ($35 for international students). Electronic applications accepted. *Financial support:* In 2006–07, 303 students received support; fellowships, research assistantships, teaching assistantships, career-related internships or fieldwork, Federal Work-Study, and institutionally sponsored loans available. Support available to part-time students. Financial award application deadline: 6/1; financial award applicants required to submit FAFSA. *Faculty research:* Self-concept, internship assess-

Education—General

University of Bridgeport (continued)

ment, stress and situational development, follow-up of graduation, trend analysis. *Unit head:* Dr. Allen P. Cook, Associate Dean, 203-576-4206, Fax: 203-576-4200, E-mail: acook@bridgeport.edu.

The University of British Columbia, Faculty of Graduate Studies, Faculty of Education, Vancouver, BC V6T 1Z1, Canada. Offers M Ed, M Sc, MA, MET, MHK, Ed D, PhD, Diploma. Part-time and evening/weekend programs available. Postbaccalaureate distance learning degree programs offered (no on-campus study). *Faculty:* 151 full-time (77 women). *Students:* 1,332 full-time (943 women), 199 part-time (141 women), 90 international. Average age 38. 1,035 applicants, 55% accepted. In 2006, 366 master's, 49 doctorates awarded. Terminal master's awarded for partial completion of doctoral program. *Degree requirements:* For master's, thesis (for some programs); for doctorate, thesis/dissertation, comprehensive exam. *Entrance requirements:* Additional exam requirements/recommendations for international students: Required—TOEFL. Application fee: $90 Canadian dollars ($150 Canadian dollars for international students). Electronic applications accepted. *Expenses:* Contact institution. *Financial support:* Fellowships with full and partial tuition reimbursements, research assistantships with full and partial tuition reimbursements, teaching assistantships with full and partial tuition reimbursements, career-related internships or fieldwork, Federal Work-Study, institutionally sponsored loans, and unspecified assistantships available. *Faculty research:* Schooling, collaborative research, counseling, continuing education, curriculum. *Unit head:* Dr. Robert J. Tierney, Dean, 604-822-5757, E-mail: dean.educ@ubc.ca. *Application contact:* Dr. Deborah Butler, Associate Dean, Graduate Programs and Research, 604-822-5513, Fax: 604-822-8971, E-mail: deborah.butler@ubc.ca.

University of California, Berkeley, Graduate Division, School of Education, Berkeley, CA 94720-1500. Offers MA, Ed D, PhD, MA/Credential, Ph D/Credential, PhD/MA. Terminal master's awarded for partial completion of doctoral program. *Degree requirements:* For master's, exam or thesis; for doctorate, thesis/dissertation, oral qualifying exam (PhD). *Entrance requirements:* For master's and doctorate, GRE General Test, minimum undergraduate GPA of 3.0 during last 2 years. *Application deadline:* For fall admission, 12/1 for domestic students. Application fee: $60 ($80 for international students). *Financial support:* Fellowships, research assistantships, teaching assistantships, career-related internships or fieldwork and unspecified assistantships available. *Faculty research:* Cognition and development; language, literacy and culture. *Unit head:* Dr. P. David Pearson, Dean, 510-643-6644, E-mail: ppearson@socrates.berkeley.edu. *Application contact:* Francisca Cazares, Admissions Assistant, 510-642-0841, Fax: 510-642-4808, E-mail: gse_info@berkeley.edu.

University of California, Davis, Graduate Studies, Graduate Group in Education, Davis, CA 95616. Offers education (MA, Ed D); instructional studies (PhD); psychological studies (PhD); sociocultural studies (PhD). Terminal master's awarded for partial completion of doctoral program. *Degree requirements:* For master's, thesis (for some programs), comprehensive exam (for some programs); for doctorate, thesis/dissertation. *Entrance requirements:* For master's and doctorate, GRE. Additional exam requirements/recommendations for international students: Required—TOEFL (minimum score 550 paper-based; 213 computer-based). Electronic applications accepted. *Faculty research:* Language and literacy, mathematics education, science education, teacher development, school psychology.

University of California, Irvine, Office of Graduate Studies, Department of Education, Irvine, CA 92697. Offers educational administration (Ed D); educational administration and leadership (Ed D); elementary and secondary education (MAT). Part-time and evening/weekend programs available. *Students:* 138 full-time (95 women), 3 part-time (all women); includes 61 minority (14 African Americans, 1 American Indian/Alaska Native, 26 Asian Americans or Pacific Islanders, 20 Hispanic Americans). Average age 34. In 2006, 67 master's, 8 doctorates awarded. *Degree requirements:* For doctorate, thesis/dissertation. *Entrance requirements:* For master's, GRE, minimum GPA of 3.0; for doctorate, GRE General Test, minimum GPA of 3.0. Additional exam requirements/recommendations for international students: Required—TOEFL (minimum score 550 paper-based; 213 computer-based). *Application deadline:* For fall admission, 4/1 priority date for domestic students. Application fee: $60. Electronic applications accepted. *Financial support:* Fellowships, research assistantships with full tuition reimbursements, institutionally sponsored loans, traineeships, health care benefits, and unspecified assistantships available. Financial award application deadline: 3/1; financial award applicants required to submit FAFSA. *Faculty research:* Education technology, learning theory, social theory, cultural diversity, postmodernism. *Unit head:* David Brant, Interim Chair, 949-824-7840, E-mail: dbrant@uci.edu. *Application contact:* Sarah K. Singh, Student Affairs Officer, 949-824-7832, Fax: 949-824-2965, E-mail: sksingh@uci.edu.

University of California, Los Angeles, Graduate Division, Graduate School of Education and Information Studies, Department of Education, Los Angeles, CA 90095. Offers M Ed, MA, Ed D, PhD, JD/MA, JD/PhD. *Degree requirements:* For master's, comprehensive exam; for doctorate, thesis/dissertation, oral and written qualifying exams. *Entrance requirements:* For master's, GRE General Test, minimum GPA of 3.0; for doctorate, GRE General Test, minimum undergraduate GPA of 3.0. Electronic applications accepted.

University of California, Riverside, Graduate Division, Graduate School of Education, Riverside, CA 92521-0102. Offers M Ed, MA, PhD. *Faculty:* 19 full-time (9 women), 36 part-time/adjunct (27 women). *Students:* 229 full-time (168 women), 2 part-time (1 woman); includes 65 minority (9 African Americans, 3 American Indian/Alaska Native, 25 Asian Americans or Pacific Islanders, 28 Hispanic Americans), 7 international. Average age 32. 214 applicants, 61% accepted, 111 enrolled. In 2006, 84 master's, 6 doctorates awarded. Terminal master's awarded for partial completion of doctoral program. *Degree requirements:* For master's, comprehensive exams or thesis, case portfolio; for doctorate, thesis/dissertation, qualifying exams, teaching experience. *Entrance requirements:* For master's, GRE General Test, GRE Subject Test, CBEST, CSET, minimum GPA of 3.2; for doctorate, GRE General Test, GRE Subject Test, master's degree, minimum GPA of 3.2. Additional exam requirements/recommendations for international students: Required—TOEFL (minimum score 550 paper-based; 213 computer-based; 80 iBT). *Application deadline:* For fall admission, 5/1 for domestic students, 2/1 for international students; for winter admission, 9/1 for domestic students, 7/1 for international students; for spring admission, 12/1 for domestic students, 10/1 for international students. Applications are processed on a rolling basis. Application fee: $60 ($75 for international students). Electronic applications accepted. *Financial support:* In 2006–07, 25 fellowships with full and partial tuition reimbursements, 39 research assistantships with full and partial tuition reimbursements (averaging $10,630 per year), 4 teaching assistantships with full and partial tuition reimbursements (averaging $8,952 per year) were awarded; career-related internships or fieldwork, Federal Work-Study, institutionally sponsored loans, and tuition waivers (full and partial) also available. Financial award application deadline: 2/15; financial award applicants required to submit FAFSA. *Faculty research:* Cognitive and affective development, school psychology, educational policy, special education, curriculum and instruction. Total annual research expenditures: $4.6 million. *Unit head:* Dr. Steven T. Bossert, Dean, 951-827-5802, Fax: 951-827-3942, E-mail: steven.bossert@ucr.edu. *Application contact:* Dr. Judith Sandholtz, Graduate Adviser, 951-827-6362, Fax: 951-827-3942, E-mail: edgrad@ucr.edu.

University of California, San Diego, Office of Graduate Studies, Program in Teacher Education, La Jolla, CA 92093. Offers bilingual education (MA); curriculum design (MA); teacher education (M Ed); teaching and learning (Ed D). *Entrance requirements:* For master's, GRE General Test. Electronic applications accepted.

University of California, Santa Barbara, Graduate Division, Gevirtz Graduate School of Education, Santa Barbara, CA 93106. Offers counseling, clinical and school psychology (PhD), including clinical psychology, counseling psychology; education (M Ed, MA, PhD), including child and adolescent development (MA, PhD), cultural perspectives and comparative education (MA, PhD), educational leadership and organizations (MA, PhD), research methodology (MA, PhD), special education disabilities and risk studies (MA), special education, dis-

abilities and risk studies (PhD), teaching and learning (MA, PhD); educational leadership (Ed D). *Accreditation:* APA (one or more programs are accredited). Postbaccalaureate distance learning degree programs offered (minimal on-campus study). *Faculty:* 39 full-time (18 women). *Students:* 375 full-time (285 women); includes 111 minority (13 African Americans, 2 American Indian/Alaska Native, 33 Asian Americans or Pacific Islanders, 63 Hispanic Americans), 14 international. Average age 29. 777 applicants, 36% accepted, 154 enrolled. In 2006, 151 master's, 31 doctorates awarded. Terminal master's awarded for partial completion of doctoral program. *Median time to degree:* Master's–1.5 years full-time; doctorate–5.5 years full-time. *Degree requirements:* For master's, thesis optional; for doctorate, thesis/dissertation, qualifying exam, comprehensive exam (for some programs), registration; for degree. *Entrance requirements:* For master's, GRE, MAT (M Ed); for doctorate, GRE. Additional exam requirements/recommendations for international students: Required—TOEFL (minimum score 550 paper-based; 213 computer-based; 80 iBT). *Application deadline:* For fall admission, 12/15 for domestic and international students. Application fee: $60. Electronic applications accepted. *Financial support:* In 2006–07, 181 fellowships with full and partial tuition reimbursements (averaging $4,200 per year), 64 research assistantships with full and partial tuition reimbursements (averaging $6,200 per year), 75 teaching assistantships with partial tuition reimbursements (averaging $7,500 per year) were awarded; career-related internships or fieldwork, Federal Work-Study, institutionally sponsored loans, scholarships/grants, traineeships, health care benefits, and unspecified assistantships also available. Support available to part-time students. Financial award application deadline: 12/15; financial award applicants required to submit FAFSA. Total annual research expenditures: $4 million. *Unit head:* Dr. Jane Conoley, Chair, 805-893-3917, E-mail: jane_conoley@education.ucsb.edu. *Application contact:* Student Affairs Office, 805-893-2137, E-mail: sao@education.ucsb.edu.

University of California, Santa Cruz, Division of Graduate Studies, Division of Social Sciences, Program in Education, Santa Cruz, CA 95064. Offers MA, Ed D, PhD. *Degree requirements:* For master's, thesis. *Faculty research:* Bilingual/multicultural education, special education, curriculum and instruction, child development.

University of Central Arkansas, Graduate School, College of Education, Conway, AR 72035-0001. Offers MAT, MS, MSE. *Accreditation:* NCATE. Part-time programs available. *Faculty:* 23 full-time (13 women), 1 (woman) part-time/adjunct. *Students:* 38 full-time (29 women), 470 part-time (422 women); includes 58 minority (42 African Americans, 1 American Indian/Alaska Native, 11 Asian Americans or Pacific Islanders, 4 Hispanic Americans), 1 international. 195 applicants, 99% accepted, 194 enrolled. In 2006, 54 degrees awarded. Terminal master's awarded for partial completion of doctoral program. *Degree requirements:* For master's, thesis optional. *Entrance requirements:* For master's, GRE General Test, minimum GPA of 2.7. Additional exam requirements/recommendations for international students: Required—TOEFL (minimum score 550 paper-based; 213 computer-based). *Application deadline:* For fall admission, 3/1 priority date for domestic and international students; for spring admission, 10/1 priority date for domestic and international students. Applications are processed on a rolling basis. Application fee: $25 ($40 for international students). *Expenses:* Tuition, state resident: full-time $4,194; part-time $233 per semester. Tuition, nonresident: full-time $5,963; part-time $429 per semester. International tuition: $6,162 full-time. Required fees: $65; $23 per semester. One-time fee: $65 part-time. *Financial support:* Career-related internships or fieldwork, Federal Work-Study, scholarships/grants, tuition waivers (partial), and unspecified assistantships available. Financial award application deadline: 2/15; financial award applicants required to submit FAFSA. *Unit head:* Dr. Larry Robinson, Dean, 501-450-5401, Fax: 501-450-5424, E-mail: lrobinson@uca.edu. *Application contact:* Brenda Herring, Admissions Assistant, 501-450-5065, Fax: 501-450-5678, E-mail: bherring@uca.edu.

University of Central Arkansas, Graduate School, College of Education, Department of Early Childhood and Special Education, Program in Master's of Arts in Teaching, Conway, AR 72035-0001. Offers MAT. Part-time programs available. Postbaccalaureate distance learning degree programs offered (minimal on-campus study). *Students:* 5 full-time (2 women), 68 part-time (57 women); includes 14 minority (13 African Americans, 1 Asian American or Pacific Islander). *Degree requirements:* For master's, thesis optional. *Entrance requirements:* For master's, GRE General Test, minimum GPA of 2.7. Additional exam requirements/recommendations for international students: Required—TOEFL (minimum score 550 paper-based; 213 computer-based). *Application deadline:* For fall admission, 3/1 priority date for domestic and international students; for spring admission, 10/1 priority date for domestic and international students. Applications are processed on a rolling basis. Application fee: $25 ($40 for international students). *Expenses:* Tuition, state resident: full-time $4,194; part-time $233 per semester. Tuition, nonresident: full-time $5,963; part-time $429 per semester. International tuition: $6,162 full-time. Required fees: $65; $23 per semester. One-time fee: $65 part-time. *Financial support:* Federal Work-Study, scholarships/grants, and unspecified assistantships available. Financial award application deadline: 2/15; financial award applicants required to submit FAFSA. *Unit head:* Tammy Benson, Unit Head, 501-450-5462. *Application contact:* Brenda Herring, Admissions Assistant, 501-450-5065, Fax: 501-450-5678, E-mail: bherring@uca.edu.

University of Central Arkansas, Graduate School, College of Education, Department of Middle/Secondary Education and Instructional Technologies, Program in Advanced Studies of Teaching and Learning, Conway, AR 72035-0001. Offers MSE. *Students:* 3 full-time (all women), 91 part-time (71 women); includes 10 minority (9 African Americans, 1 American Indian/Alaska Native). *Entrance requirements:* For master's, GRE General Test, Min. GPA of 2.7 . Additional exam requirements/recommendations for international students: Required—TOEFL (minimum score 550 paper-based; 213 computer-based). *Application deadline:* For fall admission, 3/1 priority date for domestic and international students; for spring admission, 10/1 priority date for domestic and international students. Applications are processed on a rolling basis. Application fee: $25 ($40 for international students). *Expenses:* Tuition, state resident: full-time $4,194; part-time $233 per semester. Tuition, nonresident: full-time $5,963; part-time $429 per semester. International tuition: $6,162 full-time. Required fees: $65; $23 per semester. One-time fee: $65 part-time. *Financial support:* Federal Work-Study, scholarships/grants, and unspecified assistantships available. Financial award application deadline: 2/15; financial award applicants required to submit FAFSA. *Unit head:* Ann Witcher, Unit Head, 501-450-5438, E-mail: awitcher@uca.edu.

University of Central Florida, College of Education, Department of Educational Studies, Orlando, FL 32816. Offers community college education (Certificate); educational studies (M Ed, MA, Ed D, Ed S). *Accreditation:* NCATE. Part-time and evening/weekend programs available. *Faculty:* 23 full-time (14 women), 11 part-time/adjunct (8 women). *Students:* 57 full-time (44 women), 155 part-time (121 women); includes 46 minority (22 African Americans, 1 American Indian/Alaska Native, 3 Asian Americans or Pacific Islanders, 20 Hispanic Americans), 6 international. 43 applicants, 91% accepted, 21 enrolled. In 2006, 7 master's, 18 doctorates, 39 Ed Ss awarded. *Degree requirements:* For other advanced degree, thesis or alternative, final exam. *Entrance requirements:* For degree, GRE General Test, minimum GPA of 3.0, resumé. Additional exam requirements/recommendations for international students: Required—TOEFL. *Application deadline:* For fall admission, 2/20 for domestic students; for spring admission, 9/20 for domestic students. Application fee: $30. Electronic applications accepted. *Expenses:* Tuition, state resident: full-time $6,167; part-time $257 per credit hour. Tuition, nonresident: full-time $22,790; part-time $950 per credit hour. *Financial support:* In 2006–07, 2 fellowships with partial tuition reimbursements (averaging $3,800 per year), 5 research assistantships with partial tuition reimbursements (averaging $7,600 per year), 1 teaching assistantship with partial tuition reimbursement (averaging $8,000 per year) were awarded; career-related internships or fieldwork, Federal Work-Study, institutionally sponsored loans, and unspecified assistantships also available. Financial award application deadline: 3/1; financial award applicants required to submit FAFSA. *Unit head:* Dr. Karen Biraimah, Chair, 407-823-2428, E-mail: biraimah@mail.ucf.edu.

University of Central Missouri, The Graduate School, College of Education, Warrensburg, MO 64093. Offers MS, MSE, Ed D, Ed S. *Faculty:* 96 full-time (53 women). *Students:* 97 full-time (73 women), 685 part-time (522 women); includes 62 minority (46 African Americans, 1

American Indian/Alaska Native, 3 Asian Americans or Pacific Islanders, 12 Hispanic Americans), 8 international. Average age 35. 301 applicants. In 2006, 191 master's, 19 other advanced degrees awarded. *Entrance requirements:* Additional exam requirements/recommendations for international students: Required—TOEFL (minimum score 500 paper-based; 173 computer-based). *Application deadline:* For fall admission, 6/1 priority date for domestic students, 5/1 priority date for international students; for spring admission, 10/1 priority date for domestic students, 10/1 for international students. Applications are processed on a rolling basis. *Expenses:* Tuition, state resident: full-time $5,448; part-time $227 per credit hour. Tuition, nonresident: full-time $10,896; part-time $454 per credit hour. Required fees: $336; $14 per credit hour. *Financial support:* In 2006–07, 10 students received support. Application deadline: 3/1. *Unit head:* Dr. Michael Wright, Interim Dean, 660-543-4272, Fax: 660-543-8753, E-mail: mwright@ucmo.edu.

University of Central Oklahoma, College of Graduate Studies and Research, College of Education, Edmond, OK 73034-5209. Offers M Ed, MA, MS. *Accreditation:* NCATE. Part-time programs available. *Entrance requirements:* For master's, GRE General Test. Additional exam requirements/recommendations for international students: Required—TOEFL (minimum score 550 paper-based; 213 computer-based). Electronic applications accepted.

University of Cincinnati, Division of Research and Advanced Studies, College of Education, Criminal Justice, and Human Services, Cincinnati, OH 45221. Offers M Ed, MA, MS, Ed D, PhD, CAGS, Certificate, Ed S. *Accreditation:* NCATE. Part-time programs available. Post-baccalaureate distance learning degree programs offered (no on-campus study). *Degree requirements:* For master's, thesis (for some programs), comprehensive exam (for some programs); for doctorate, thesis/dissertation, comprehensive exam. *Entrance requirements:* For master's and doctorate, GRE. Additional exam requirements/recommendations for international students: Required—TOEFL (minimum score 550 paper-based), OEPT 3. Electronic applications accepted. *Faculty research:* Alcohol and drug prevention, family-based prevention, criminal justice, literacy, urban education.

University of Colorado at Boulder, Graduate School, School of Education, Boulder, CO 80309. Offers MA, PhD. *Accreditation:* NCATE. Part-time programs available. *Faculty:* 28 full-time (13 women). *Students:* 165 full-time (123 women), 215 part-time (176 women); includes 57 minority (5 African Americans, 2 American Indian/Alaska Native, 12 Asian Americans or Pacific Islanders, 38 Hispanic Americans), 2 international. Average age 32. 156 applicants, 92% accepted. In 2006, 172 master's, 9 doctorates awarded. *Degree requirements:* For master's, thesis or alternative, comprehensive exam; for doctorate, one foreign language, thesis/dissertation, comprehensive exam. *Entrance requirements:* For master's, GRE General Test or MAT, minimum undergraduate GPA of 2.75; for doctorate, GRE General Test. *Application deadline:* For fall admission, 2/1 priority date for domestic students, 12/1 for international students; for spring admission, 9/1 for domestic students, 12/1 for international students. Application fee: $50 ($60 for international students). *Financial support:* In 2006–07, 42 fellowships (averaging $5,155 per year), 34 research assistantships (averaging $9,326 per year), 23 teaching assistantships (averaging $9,318 per year) were awarded; career-related internships or fieldwork, Federal Work-Study, scholarships/grants, and tuition waivers (full and partial) also available. Support available to part-time students. Financial award application deadline: 2/1. Total annual research expenditures: $960,416. *Unit head:* Lorrie Shepard, Dean, 303-492-6937, Fax: 303-492-7090, E-mail: lorrie.shepard@colorado.edu. *Application contact:* Graduate Program Assistant, 303-492-6555, Fax: 303-492-5839, E-mail: edadvise@colorado.edu.

University of Colorado at Colorado Springs, Graduate School, College of Education, Colorado Springs, CO 80933-7150. Offers counseling and human services (MA); curriculum and instruction (MA); educational administration (MA); educational leadership (MA, PhD); special education (MA). *Accreditation:* ACA; NCATE. Part-time and evening/weekend programs available. *Faculty:* 22 full-time (15 women), 29 part-time/adjunct (17 women). *Students:* 331 full-time (246 women), 173 part-time (135 women); includes 85 minority (26 African Americans, 4 American Indian/Alaska Native, 13 Asian Americans or Pacific Islanders, 42 Hispanic Americans). Average age 35. 107 applicants, 93% accepted, 49 enrolled. In 2006, 234 degrees awarded. *Degree requirements:* For master's, thesis or alternative, microcomputer proficiency, comprehensive exam; for doctorate, doctoral research lab requirement. *Entrance requirements:* For master's, GRE General Test, MAT. *Application deadline:* For fall admission, 6/15 for domestic students; for spring admission, 10/15 for domestic students. Applications are processed on a rolling basis. Application fee: $60 ($75 for international students). *Expenses:* Tuition, state resident: part-time $303 per credit hour. Tuition, nonresident: part-time $840 per credit hour. Tuition and fees vary according to course load, campus/location and program. *Financial support:* Fellowships, career-related internships or fieldwork and Federal Work-Study available. *Faculty research:* Job training for special populations, materials development for classroom. Total annual research expenditures: $961,803. *Unit head:* Dr. LaVonne Neal, Dean, 719-262-4111, Fax: 719-262-4110, E-mail: lneal@uccs.edu. *Application contact:* Connie Wroten, Professional Assistant, 719-262-4102, Fax: 719-262-4110, E-mail: cwroten@uccs.edu.

University of Colorado at Denver and Health Sciences Center, School of Education and Human Development, Denver, CO 80217-3364. Offers MA, PhD, Ed S. *Accreditation:* NCATE. Part-time and evening/weekend programs available. *Faculty:* 47 full-time (32 women). *Students:* 383 full-time (294 women), 798 part-time (663 women); includes 143 minority (29 African Americans, 10 American Indian/Alaska Native, 30 Asian Americans or Pacific Islanders, 74 Hispanic Americans), 6 international. Average age 34. 389 applicants, 70% accepted, 169 enrolled. In 2006, 562 master's, 9 doctorates, 25 other advanced degrees awarded. *Degree requirements:* For doctorate, one foreign language, thesis/dissertation, comprehensive exam, registration. *Entrance requirements:* For master's, minimum GPA of 2.75; for doctorate, GRE (LSAT, MCAT, or GMAT scores may be considered in place). Additional exam requirements/recommendations for international students: Required—TOEFL (minimum score 525 paper-based; 197 computer-based). *Application deadline:* For fall admission, 4/15 for domestic students; for spring admission, 9/15 for domestic students. Applications are processed on a rolling basis. Application fee: $50 ($75 for international students). Electronic applications accepted. *Expenses:* Contact institution. *Financial support:* Fellowships, research assistantships, teaching assistantships, Federal Work-Study, institutionally sponsored loans, and scholarships/grants available. Support available to part-time students. Financial award application deadline: 4/1; financial award applicants required to submit FAFSA. *Unit head:* Lynn K Rhodes, Dean, 303-556-2844, Fax: 303-556-4479, E-mail: lynn.rhodes@cudenver.edu. *Application contact:* Lori Sisneros, Student Services Coordinator, 303-556-8854, Fax: 303-556-4479, E-mail: bri.sisneros@cudenver.edu.

University of Connecticut, Graduate School, Neag School of Education, Storrs, CT 06269. Offers MA, Ed D, PhD. *Accreditation:* NCATE. *Faculty:* 81 full-time (36 women). *Students:* 431 full-time (316 women), 372 part-time (256 women); includes 89 minority (30 African Americans, 5 American Indian/Alaska Native, 18 Asian Americans or Pacific Islanders, 36 Hispanic Americans), 31 international. Average age 32. 917 applicants, 50% accepted, 463 enrolled. In 2006, 413 master's, 36 doctorates awarded. Terminal master's awarded for partial completion of doctoral program. *Degree requirements:* For master's, thesis or alternative, comprehensive exam; for doctorate, thesis/dissertation. *Entrance requirements:* For doctorate, GRE General Test. Additional exam requirements/recommendations for international students: Required—TOEFL (minimum score 550 paper-based; 213 computer-based). *Application deadline:* For fall admission, 2/1 priority date for domestic and international students; for spring admission, 11/1 for domestic students, 10/1 for international students. Applications are processed on a rolling basis. Application fee: $55. Electronic applications accepted. *Financial support:* In 2006–07, 183 research assistantships with full tuition reimbursements, 9 teaching assistantships with full tuition reimbursements were awarded; fellowships, Federal Work-Study, scholarships/grants, health care benefits, and unspecified assistantships also available. Financial award application deadline: 2/1; financial award applicants required to submit FAFSA. *Unit head:* Richard L. Schwab, Dean, 860-486-3813, Fax: 860-486-0210, E-mail: richard.schwab@uconn.edu. *Applica-*

tion contact: Thomas DeFranco, Chairperson, 860-486-3815, Fax: 860-486-0210, E-mail: thomas.defranco@uconn.edu.

University of Dayton, Graduate School, School of Education and Allied Professions, Dayton, OH 45469-1300. Offers MS Ed, DPT, PhD, Ed S. *Accreditation:* NCATE. Part-time and evening/weekend programs available. Postbaccalaureate distance learning degree programs offered (no on-campus study). *Faculty:* 65 full-time (30 women), 120 part-time/adjunct (59 women). *Students:* 629 full-time (484 women), 870 part-time (654 women); includes 162 minority (136 African Americans, 4 American Indian/Alaska Native, 6 Asian Americans or Pacific Islanders, 16 Hispanic Americans), 8 international. Average age 33. 619 applicants, 59% accepted, 253 enrolled. In 2006, 572 master's, 4 doctorates awarded. *Degree requirements:* For doctorate, thesis/dissertation, residency, comprehensive exam; for Ed S, thesis or alternative. *Entrance requirements:* For master's, GRE or MAT (if GPA is below 2.75); for doctorate, GRE General Test or MAT, administrative experience, master's degree, minimum GPA of 3.5. Additional exam requirements/recommendations for international students: Required—TOEFL (minimum score 550 paper-based; 213 computer-based). *Application deadline:* For fall admission, 3/15 priority date for domestic students, 3/1 priority date for international students. Applications are processed on a rolling basis. Application fee: $0. Electronic applications accepted. *Expenses:* Contact institution. Tuition and fees vary according to degree level and program. *Financial support:* In 2006–07, 29 research assistantships with full tuition reimbursements (averaging $7,620 per year), 13 teaching assistantships with full tuition reimbursements (averaging $8,000 per year) were awarded. Financial award applicants required to submit FAFSA. *Faculty research:* Charter schools. *Unit head:* Dr. Thomas J. Lasley, Dean, 937-229-3146, Fax: 937-229-3199, E-mail: thomas.lasley@notes.udayton.edu. *Application contact:* Erika Eavers, Graduate Admission Processor, 937-229-3065, Fax: 937-229-4729, E-mail: erika.eavers@notes.udayton.edu.

University of Delaware, College of Human Services, Education and Public Policy, School of Education, Newark, DE 19716. Offers curriculum and instruction (M Ed); education (PhD); educational leadership (M Ed, Ed D); exceptional children and youth (M Ed); instruction (MI); school counseling (M Ed); school psychology (MA); teaching English as a second language (TESL) (MA). *Accreditation:* NCATE. Part-time and evening/weekend programs available. Terminal master's awarded for partial completion of doctoral program. *Degree requirements:* For master's, thesis (for some programs), comprehensive exam (for some programs), registration; for doctorate, thesis/dissertation, comprehensive exam (for some programs), registration. *Entrance requirements:* For master's and doctorate, GRE, 3 letters of recommendation. Additional exam requirements/recommendations for international students: Required—TOEFL (minimum score 600 paper-based; 250 computer-based). Electronic applications accepted. *Faculty research:* Teacher education; education policy; educational assessment, measurement, and evaluation; curriculum theory and development; community based education models.

University of Denver, College of Education, Denver, CO 80208. Offers counseling psychology (MA, PhD); curriculum and instruction (MA, PhD, Certificate), including curriculum leadership (MA, PhD); educational administration and policy studies (Certificate); educational psychology (MA, PhD, Ed S), including child and family studies (MA, PhD), quantitative research methods (MA, PhD), school psychology (PhD, Ed S); higher education and adult studies (MA, PhD); library and information science (MLIS); library and information sciences (Certificate); school administration (PhD). *Accreditation:* ALA; APA (one or more programs are accredited). Part-time and evening/weekend programs available. Postbaccalaureate distance learning degree programs offered (no on-campus study). *Faculty:* 28 full-time (18 women). *Students:* 293 full-time (240 women), 439 part-time (357 women); includes 102 minority (28 African Americans, 7 American Indian/Alaska Native, 14 Asian Americans or Pacific Islanders, 53 Hispanic Americans), 11 international. Average age 34. 574 applicants, 72% accepted. In 2006, 168 master's, 28 doctorates, 67 other advanced degrees awarded. Terminal master's awarded for partial completion of doctoral program. *Degree requirements:* For master's, comprehensive exam; for doctorate, 2 foreign languages, thesis/dissertation, comprehensive exam. *Entrance requirements:* For master's, GRE General Test or MAT (for most programs); for doctorate, GRE General Test or MAT. *Application deadline:* Applications are processed on a rolling basis. Application fee: $50. Electronic applications accepted. *Expenses:* Tuition: Full-time $29,628; part-time $823 per credit. *Financial support:* In 2006–07, 51 teaching assistantships with full and partial tuition reimbursements (averaging $6,700 per year) were awarded; career-related internships or fieldwork, Federal Work-Study, institutionally sponsored loans, and scholarships/grants also available. Support available to part-time students. Financial award application deadline: 3/1; financial award applicants required to submit FAFSA. *Faculty research:* Parkinson's disease, personnel training, development and assessments, gifted education, service learning, transportation, public schools. Total annual research expenditures: $172,000. *Unit head:* Dr. Virginia Maloney, Dean, 303-871-2509. *Application contact:* Linda McCarthy, Contact, 303-871-2509, E-mail: edinfo@du.edu.

University of Detroit Mercy, College of Liberal Arts and Education, Department of Education, Detroit, MI 48221. Offers curriculum and instruction (MA); early childhood education (MA); educational administration (MA); special education (MA), including emotionally impaired, learning disabilities; teaching and learning (MA). Part-time and evening/weekend programs available. *Expenses:* Tuition: Full-time $15,750; part-time $875 per credit hour. Required fees: $570.

University of Evansville, College of Education and Health Sciences, Evansville, IN 47722. Offers MS. *Accreditation:* APTA; NCATE. Part-time and evening/weekend programs available. *Faculty:* 1 full-time (0 women), 4 part-time/adjunct (1 woman). *Students:* 1 full-time (0 women), 9 part-time (7 women), 1 international. Average age 42. 2 applicants, 100% accepted, 1 enrolled. In 2006, 11 degrees awarded. *Median time to degree:* Master's–1.5 years full-time, 2.75 years part-time. *Entrance requirements:* For master's, GRE or GMAT, 2 letters of reference, interview. Additional exam requirements/recommendations for international students: Required—TOEFL (minimum score 500 paper-based; 61 iBT). *Application deadline:* For fall admission, 7/1 priority date for domestic and international students; for spring admission, 10/1 priority date for domestic students. Applications are processed on a rolling basis. Application fee: $20 ($50 for international students). *Expenses:* Contact institution. Tuition and fees vary according to course load and program. *Financial support:* In 2006–07, 2 students received support. Career-related internships or fieldwork available. Support available to part-time students. Financial award application deadline: 7/1; financial award applicants required to submit FAFSA. *Faculty research:* Health services administration. *Unit head:* Dr. Lynn Penland, Director, 812-488-2981, Fax: 812-488-1146, E-mail: lp22@evansville.edu. *Application contact:* Dr. William Stroube, Director, Health Services Administration Program, 812-488-2343, Fax: 812-488-2717, E-mail: hsa@evansville.edu.

The University of Findlay, Graduate and Professional Studies, College of Education, Findlay, OH 45840-3653. Offers administration (MA Ed); early childhood (MA Ed); elementary education (MA Ed); human resource development (MA Ed); leadership (MA Ed); special education (MA Ed); technology (MA Ed); web instruction (MA Ed). *Accreditation:* NCATE. Part-time and evening/weekend programs available. *Faculty:* 12 full-time, 6 part-time/adjunct. *Students:* 84 full-time (65 women), 223 part-time (169 women); includes 11 minority (3 African Americans, 2 American Indian/Alaska Native, 1 Asian American or Pacific Islander, 5 Hispanic Americans), 13 international. Average age 35. 91 applicants, 97% accepted, 76 enrolled. In 2006, 146 degrees awarded. *Degree requirements:* For master's, thesis, cumulative project. *Entrance requirements:* For master's, minimum undergraduate GPA of 3.0 in last 60 hours of course work. Additional exam requirements/recommendations for international students: Required—TOEFL. *Application deadline:* Applications are processed on a rolling basis. Application fee: $25. Electronic applications accepted. *Expenses:* Contact institution. *Financial support:* In 2006–07, 6 students received support, including 6 teaching assistantships with full tuition reimbursements available (averaging $6,000 per year); unspecified assistantships also available. Financial award application deadline: 4/1; financial award applicants required to submit FAFSA. *Faculty research:* Children's literature, books and artwork, educational technology, professional development. *Unit head:* Dr. Melissa A. Cain, Dean, 419-434-4840, Fax: 419-434-4822.

Education—General

The University of Findlay (continued)

Application contact: Heather Riffle, Director, Graduate and Special Programs, 419-434-4642, Fax: 419-434-5517, E-mail: riffle@findlay.edu.

University of Florida, Graduate School, College of Education, Gainesville, FL 32611. Offers M Ed, MAE, Ed D, PhD, Ed S, PhD/JD. *Accreditation:* NCATE. Part-time programs available. *Faculty:* 91 full-time (57 women). Terminal master's awarded for partial completion of doctoral program. *Degree requirements:* For master's and Ed S, registration; for doctorate, thesis/dissertation, registration. *Entrance requirements:* For master's and doctorate, GRE General Test, minimum GPA of 3.0; for Ed S, GRE General Test. Additional exam requirements/recommendations for international students: Required—TOEFL (minimum score 550 paper-based; 213 computer-based). *Application deadline:* Applications are processed on a rolling basis. Application fee: $30. Electronic applications accepted. *Expenses:* Tuition, state resident: full-time $6,827. Tuition, nonresident: full-time $21,951. Required fees: $999. *Financial support:* Fellowships with tuition reimbursements, research assistantships with tuition reimbursements, teaching assistantships with tuition reimbursements, career-related internships or fieldwork, Federal Work-Study, and unspecified assistantships available. Support available to part-time students. Financial award application deadline: 1/4; financial award applicants required to submit FAFSA. Total annual research expenditures: $7.2 million. *Unit head:* Dr. Catherine Emihovich, Dean, 352-392-0728 Ext. 226, Fax: 352-392-6930, E-mail: cemihovich@coe.ufl.edu. *Application contact:* Dr. John H. Kranzler, Associate Dean, 352-392-0728 Ext. 234, Fax: 352-392-6930, E-mail: jkranzler@coe.ufl.edu.

University of Georgia, Graduate School, College of Education, Athens, GA 30602. Offers M Ed, MA, MAT, MM Ed, Ed D, PhD, Ed S. *Accreditation:* NCATE. *Faculty:* 170 full-time (84 women). *Students:* 903 full-time (628 women), 1,175 part-time (840 women); includes 301 minority (235 African Americans, 5 American Indian/Alaska Native, 28 Asian Americans or Pacific Islanders, 33 Hispanic Americans), 153 international. 1,715 applicants, 52% accepted, 549 enrolled. In 2006, 407 master's, 106 doctorates, 109 other advanced degrees awarded. *Degree requirements:* For doctorate, thesis/dissertation. *Entrance requirements:* For doctorate, GRE General Test. *Application deadline:* For fall admission, 7/1 priority date for domestic students; for spring admission, 11/15 for domestic students. Application fee: $50. Electronic applications accepted. *Financial support:* Fellowships, research assistantships, teaching assistantships, unspecified assistantships available. *Unit head:* Dr. Louis A. Castenell, Dean, 706-542-6446, Fax: 706-542-0360, E-mail: lcastene@coe.uga.edu.

University of Great Falls, Graduate Studies, Programs in Education, Great Falls, MT 59405. Offers M Ed. Part-time and evening/weekend programs available. *Faculty:* 5 full-time (1 woman), 4 part-time/adjunct (2 women). *Students:* Average age 35. In 2006, 4 degrees awarded. *Degree requirements:* For master's, thesis, extensive portfolio. *Entrance requirements:* For master's, GRE General Test or MAT, 3 letters of recommendation. Additional exam requirements/recommendations for international students: Required—TOEFL (minimum score 500 paper-based; 205 computer-based). *Application deadline:* For fall admission, 8/15 priority date for domestic students, 6/15 priority date for international students; for spring admission, 12/15 priority date for domestic students, 10/15 priority date for international students. Applications are processed on a rolling basis. Application fee: $50. Electronic applications accepted. *Financial support:* In 2006–07, 3 students received support. Career-related internships or fieldwork, Federal Work-Study, and institutionally sponsored loans available. Support available to part-time students. Financial award application deadline: 6/1; financial award applicants required to submit FAFSA. *Faculty research:* Native American attitudinal research. *Unit head:* Dr. Harold Jones, Director, 406-791-5346, Fax: 406-791-5993, E-mail: hjones@ugf.edu.

University of Great Falls, Graduate Studies, Secondary Teaching Program, Great Falls, MT 59405. Offers MAT. Part-time programs available. Postbaccalaureate distance learning degree programs offered (no on-campus study). *Faculty:* 5 full-time (1 woman), 3 part-time/adjunct (2 women). *Students:* 8 full-time (6 women), 6 part-time (4 women); includes 1 minority (Hispanic American) Average age 29. 12 applicants, 100% accepted, 2 enrolled. In 2006, 9 degrees awarded. *Degree requirements:* For master's, extensive portfolio, thesis optional. *Entrance requirements:* For master's, GRE General Test or MAT, bachelor's degree in teaching, teaching certificate, 3 years of teaching experience, interview, 3 letters of recommendation. Additional exam requirements/recommendations for international students: Required—TOEFL (minimum score 500 paper-based; 205 computer-based). *Application deadline:* For fall admission, 8/15 priority date for domestic students, 6/15 priority date for international students; for spring admission, 12/15 priority date for domestic students, 10/15 priority date for international students. Applications are processed on a rolling basis. Application fee: $50. Electronic applications accepted. *Financial support:* In 2006–07, 8 students received support. Career-related internships or fieldwork, Federal Work-Study, and institutionally sponsored loans available. Support available to part-time students. Financial award application deadline: 6/1. *Faculty research:* Gifted, curriculum design, administration. *Unit head:* Dr. Harold Jones, Director, 406-791-5346, Fax: 406-791-5993, E-mail: hjones@ugf.edu. *Application contact:* Howard Hahn, Application Contact, 406-791-5342, Fax: 406-791-5993, E-mail: hhahn01@ugf.edu.

University of Guam, Graduate School and Research, College of Education, Mangilao, GU 96923. Offers M Ed, MA. Part-time programs available. *Degree requirements:* For master's, comprehensive oral and written exams. *Entrance requirements:* For master's, GRE General Test. Additional exam requirements/recommendations for international students: Required—TOEFL. *Faculty research:* Multicultural issues, computerized student advising.

University of Hartford, College of Education, Nursing, and Health Professions, West Hartford, CT 06117-1599. Offers M Ed, MS, MSN, MSPT, DPT, Ed D, CAGS, Sixth Year Certificate. *Accreditation:* NCATE. Part-time and evening/weekend programs available. *Faculty:* 28 full-time (19 women), 13 part-time/adjunct (10 women). *Students:* 128 full-time (102 women), 339 part-time (293 women); includes 44 minority (24 African Americans, 1 American Indian/Alaska Native, 3 Asian Americans or Pacific Islanders, 16 Hispanic Americans), 5 international. Average age 38. 130 applicants, 87% accepted, 99 enrolled. In 2006, 112 master's, 21 doctorates, 21 other advanced degrees awarded. *Degree requirements:* For doctorate, thesis/dissertation; for other advanced degree, comprehensive exam or research project. *Entrance requirements:* For doctorate, MAT. Additional exam requirements/recommendations for international students: Required—TOEFL (minimum score 550 paper-based; 213 computer-based). *Application deadline:* Applications are processed on a rolling basis. Application fee: $40 ($55 for international students). Electronic applications accepted. *Expenses:* Contact institution. *Financial support:* In 2006–07, 3 research assistantships (averaging $4,333 per year) were awarded; teaching assistantships, institutionally sponsored loans and unspecified assistantships also available. Financial award application deadline: 6/1; financial award applicants required to submit FAFSA. *Unit head:* Dr. Dorothy A. Zeiser, Dean, 860-768-4649, Fax: 860-768-5043. *Application contact:* Susan Brown, Assistant Dean of Academic Services, 860-768-4692, Fax: 860-768-5043, E-mail: brown@hartford.edu.

University of Hawaii at Manoa, Graduate Division, College of Education, Honolulu, HI 96822. Offers M Ed, M Ed T, MS, PhD, Graduate Certificate. *Accreditation:* NCATE. Part-time and evening/weekend programs available. *Faculty:* 93 full-time (57 women), 9 part-time/adjunct (4 women). *Students:* 361 full-time (242 women), 573 part-time (410 women); includes 542 minority (19 African Americans, 3 American Indian/Alaska Native, 497 Asian Americans or Pacific Islanders, 23 Hispanic Americans), 52 international. 594 applicants, 62% accepted, 263 enrolled. In 2006, 233 master's, 19 doctorates, 3 other advanced degrees awarded. *Entrance requirements:* Additional exam requirements/recommendations for international students: Required—TOEFL or IELTS. Application fee: $50. *Financial support:* In 2006–07, 34 research assistantships (averaging $16,491 per year), 21 teaching assistantships (averaging $13,610 per year) were awarded; fellowships, career-related internships or fieldwork, Federal Work-Study, institutionally sponsored loans, and tuition waivers (full and partial) also available. Support available to part-time students. Total annual research expenditures: $8,579. *Application contact:* Donald Young, Information Contact, 808-956-7703.

University of Houston, College of Education, Houston, TX 77204. Offers M Ed, MS, Ed D, PhD. *Accreditation:* NCATE. Part-time and evening/weekend programs available. *Faculty:* 60 full-time (31 women), 39 part-time/adjunct (26 women). *Students:* 292 full-time (228 women), 648 part-time (490 women); includes 302 minority (124 African Americans, 2 American Indian/Alaska Native, 55 Asian Americans or Pacific Islanders, 121 Hispanic Americans), 27 international. Average age 35. 344 applicants, 57% accepted, 142 enrolled. In 2006, 208 master's, 52 doctorates awarded. *Degree requirements:* For master's, comprehensive exam or thesis; for doctorate, thesis/dissertation, comprehensive exam. *Entrance requirements:* For master's, GRE General Test or MAT; for doctorate, GRE General Test, interview. Application fee: $35 ($75 for international students). *Expenses:* Tuition, state resident: full-time $5,429; part-time $226 per credit. Tuition, nonresident: full-time $12,029; part-time $501 per credit. Required fees: $2,454. *Financial support:* In 2006–07, 9 fellowships with full tuition reimbursements (averaging $9,500 per year), 14 research assistantships with full tuition reimbursements (averaging $9,500 per year), 70 teaching assistantships with full tuition reimbursements (averaging $9,500 per year) were awarded; career-related internships or fieldwork, Federal Work-Study, institutionally sponsored loans, scholarships/grants, health care benefits, and unspecified assistantships also available. Support available to part-time students. Financial award application deadline: 3/10; financial award applicants required to submit FAFSA. Total annual research expenditures: $6.5 million. *Unit head:* Robert K. Wimpelberg, Dean, 713-743-5001, Fax: 713-743-5013, E-mail: rwimpelberg@uh.edu.

University of Houston–Clear Lake, School of Education, Houston, TX 77058-1098. Offers MS, Ed D. *Accreditation:* NCATE. Part-time and evening/weekend programs available. *Faculty:* 40 full-time (29 women), 42 part-time/adjunct (23 women). *Students:* 266 full-time (214 women), 1,067 part-time (858 women); includes 504 minority (236 African Americans, 7 American Indian/Alaska Native, 31 Asian Americans or Pacific Islanders, 230 Hispanic Americans), 30 international. Average age 36. In 2006, 331 degrees awarded. *Degree requirements:* For master's, thesis optional; for doctorate, thesis/dissertation, comprehensive exam. *Entrance requirements:* For master's, GRE or minimum GPA of 3.0 in last 60 hours; for doctorate, GRE, master's degree, letters of reference. Additional exam requirements/recommendations for international students: Required—TOEFL (minimum score 550 paper-based; 213 computer-based). *Application deadline:* For fall admission, 7/1 for domestic students, 6/1 for international students; for spring admission, 10/1 for domestic and international students. Applications are processed on a rolling basis. Application fee: $35 ($75 for international students). Electronic applications accepted. *Financial support:* Career-related internships or fieldwork, Federal Work-Study, institutionally sponsored loans, and scholarships/grants available. Support available to part-time students. Financial award application deadline: 5/1; financial award applicants required to submit FAFSA. *Unit head:* Dr. Dennis Spuck, Dean, 281-283-3501, Fax: 281-283-3599, E-mail: spuck@uhcl.edu. *Application contact:* Janis S. Bigelow, Assistant Director of Admissions, Recruitment and Communications, 281-283-2540, Fax: 281-283-2530, E-mail: bigelow@uhcl.edu.

University of Houston–Victoria, School of Education and Human Development, Victoria, TX 77901-4450. Offers M Ed. Part-time and evening/weekend programs available. Postbaccalaureate distance learning degree programs offered (no on-campus study). *Faculty:* 22 full-time (15 women). *Students:* 62 full-time (52 women), 439 part-time (353 women); includes 184 minority (112 African Americans, 1 American Indian/Alaska Native, 13 Asian Americans or Pacific Islanders, 58 Hispanic Americans), 2 international. Average age 38. In 2006, 125 degrees awarded. *Degree requirements:* For master's, project or thesis. *Entrance requirements:* For master's, GRE General Test. Additional exam requirements/recommendations for international students: Required—TOEFL. *Application deadline:* Applications are processed on a rolling basis. Application fee: $0. Electronic applications accepted. *Expenses:* Tuition, state resident: full-time $3,168; part-time $176 per semester hour. Tuition, nonresident: full-time $7,218; part-time $401 per semester hour. Required fees: $756; $42 per semester hour. Tuition and fees vary according to course load. *Financial support:* In 2006–07, research assistantships with partial tuition reimbursements (averaging $2,000 per year), teaching assistantships with partial tuition reimbursements (averaging $2,000 per year) were awarded; career-related internships or fieldwork, Federal Work-Study, scholarships/grants, and unspecified assistantships also available. Support available to part-time students. Financial award application deadline: 4/15. *Faculty research:* Reading and language arts education, evaluation and diagnosis of special children's abilities. *Unit head:* Dr. John Stansell, Dean, 361-570-4260, Fax: 361-570-4257, E-mail: stansell@uhv.edu.

University of Idaho, College of Graduate Studies, College of Education, Moscow, ID 83844-2282. Offers M Ed, MS, Ed D, PhD, Ed S, Ed Sp PTE. *Accreditation:* NCATE. *Students:* 168 full-time (92 women), 490 part-time (310 women). In 2006, 255 master's, 50 doctorates, 62 other advanced degrees awarded. *Degree requirements:* For doctorate, thesis/dissertation. *Entrance requirements:* For master's, minimum GPA of 2.8; for doctorate, minimum undergraduate GPA of 2.8, 3.0 graduate. *Application deadline:* For fall admission, 8/1 for domestic students; for spring admission, 12/15 for domestic students. Application fee: $55 ($60 for international students). *Expenses:* Tuition, nonresident: full-time $9,600; part-time $140 per credit. Required fees: $4,740; $227 per credit. *Financial support:* Teaching assistantships, Federal Work-Study available. Support available to part-time students. Financial award application deadline: 2/15. *Unit head:* Dr. Paul Rowland, Dean, 208-885-6773.

University of Illinois at Chicago, Graduate College, College of Education, Chicago, IL 60607-7128. Offers M Ed, PhD. Part-time and evening/weekend programs available. Terminal master's awarded for partial completion of doctoral program. *Degree requirements:* For doctorate, thesis/dissertation. *Entrance requirements:* For master's, minimum GPA of 2.75; for doctorate, GRE General Test, minimum GPA of 2.75. Additional exam requirements/recommendations for international students: Required—TOEFL. Electronic applications accepted. *Faculty research:* Teaching and learning, program design, school and classroom organization with emphasis on urban settings.

University of Illinois at Urbana–Champaign, Graduate College, College of Education, Champaign, IL 61820. Offers Ed M, MA, MS, Ed D, PhD, CAS, MBA/M Ed. Part-time programs available. *Faculty:* 95 full-time (56 women), 11 part-time/adjunct (6 women). *Students:* 439 full-time (314 women), 563 part-time (387 women); includes 213 minority (118 African Americans, 6 American Indian/Alaska Native, 52 Asian Americans or Pacific Islanders, 37 Hispanic Americans), 190 international. 676 applicants, 46% accepted, 182 enrolled. In 2006, 195 master's, 66 doctorates, 6 other advanced degrees awarded. *Degree requirements:* For doctorate, thesis/dissertation. *Application deadline:* Applications are processed on a rolling basis. Application fee: $50 ($60 for international students). Electronic applications accepted. *Financial support:* In 2006–07, 99 fellowships, 169 research assistantships, 194 teaching assistantships were awarded; career-related internships or fieldwork, Federal Work-Study, and tuition waivers (full and partial) also available. *Unit head:* Mary A. Kalantzis, Dean, 217-333-0960, Fax: 217-333-5847, E-mail: marykalantzis@uiuc.edu.

University of Illinois at Urbana–Champaign, Graduate College, College of Liberal Arts and Sciences, Second Language Acquisition and Teacher Education Program, Champaign, IL 61820. Offers CAS. *Unit head:* Dr. Sarah C. Mangelsdorf, Dean, College of Liberal Arts and Sciences, 217-333-1350, Fax: 217-333-9142, E-mail: smangels@uiuc.edu.

University of Indianapolis, Graduate Programs, School of Education, Indianapolis, IN 46227-3697. Offers art education (MAT); biology (MAT); chemistry (MAT); curriculum and instruction (MA); earth sciences (MAT); education (MA, MAT); educational leadership (MA); elementary education (MA); English (MAT); French (MAT); math (MAT); physical education (MAT); physics (MAT); secondary education (MA), including art education, education, English education, social studies education; social studies (MAT); Spanish (MAT). *Accreditation:* NCATE. Part-time and evening/weekend programs available. *Faculty:* 4 full-time (2 women), 6 part-time/adjunct (2 women). *Students:* 32 full-time (16 women), 70 part-time (42 women); includes 2 minority (1 African American, 1 Hispanic American). Average age 31. In 2006, 51 degrees awarded. *Entrance requirements:* For master's, GRE Subject Test, minimum GPA of 2.5, 3 letters of recommendation, interview, Praxis I, writing exercise, be within 9 hours of completing content requirements. Additional exam requirements/recommendations for international students: Required—TOEFL (minimum score 550 paper-based; 213 computer-based). *Application deadline:* Applications are processed on a rolling basis. Application fee: $50. *Financial support:* Federal Work-Study available. Financial award application deadline: 5/1; financial award applicants required to submit FAFSA. *Faculty research:* Assessment of teacher education, perceptions of prospective teachers by parents. *Unit head:* Dr. E. Lynne Weisenbach, Dean, 317-788-3446, Fax: 317-788-3300, E-mail: weisenbach@uindy.edu.

The University of Iowa, Graduate College, College of Education, Iowa City, IA 52242-1316. Offers MA, MAT, PhD, Ed S, JD/PhD. *Faculty:* 72 full-time, 15 part-time/adjunct. *Students:* 300 full-time (214 women), 278 part-time (196 women); includes 70 minority (33 African Americans, 3 American Indian/Alaska Native, 15 Asian Americans or Pacific Islanders, 19 Hispanic Americans), 95 international. 335 applicants, 50% accepted, 99 enrolled. In 2006, 103 master's, 40 doctorates, 5 other advanced degrees awarded. *Degree requirements:* For master's and Ed S, exam; for doctorate, thesis/dissertation, comprehensive exam, registration. *Entrance requirements:* For master's, doctorate, and Ed S, GRE General Test, minimum GPA of 3.0. Additional exam requirements/recommendations for international students: Required—TOEFL (minimum score 550 paper-based; 213 computer-based; 81 iBT). Application fee: $60 ($85 for international students). Electronic applications accepted. *Financial support:* In 2006–07, 13 fellowships, 147 research assistantships with partial tuition reimbursements, 117 teaching assistantships with partial tuition reimbursements were awarded; career-related internships or fieldwork, Federal Work-Study, institutionally sponsored loans, and unspecified assistantships also available. Financial award applicants required to submit FAFSA. *Faculty research:* Computer-assisted instrumentation, testing and measurement, instructional design. *Unit head:* Sandra Bowman Damico, Dean, 319-335-5380, Fax: 319-335-5386.

University of Kansas, Graduate Studies, School of Education, Lawrence, KS 66045. Offers MA, MS, MS Ed, Ed D, PhD, Ed S. *Accreditation:* NCATE. Part-time programs available. *Faculty:* 90. *Students:* 493 full-time (378 women), 622 part-time (460 women); includes 100 minority (38 African Americans, 9 American Indian/Alaska Native, 19 Asian Americans or Pacific Islanders, 34 Hispanic Americans), 121 international. Average age 33. 568 applicants, 61% accepted. In 2006, 348 master's, 69 doctorates, 11 other advanced degrees awarded. *Degree requirements:* For doctorate, thesis/dissertation. *Entrance requirements:* For master's and Ed S, minimum GPA of 3.0; for doctorate, GRE General Test. Additional exam requirements/recommendations for international students: Required—TOEFL. Application fee: $55 ($60 for international students). Electronic applications accepted. *Expenses:* Tuition, area resident: Part-time $227 per credit. Tuition, state resident: part-time $543 per credit. Tuition and fees vary according to course load, campus/location, program and reciprocity agreements. *Financial support:* Fellowships, research assistantships with partial tuition reimbursements, teaching assistantships with full and partial tuition reimbursements, career-related internships or fieldwork available. Financial award application deadline: 2/1. *Faculty research:* Effective schools, assessment, students with learning difficulties, learning in school situations, teacher preparation. *Unit head:* Dr. Rick Ginsberg, Dean, 785-864-4297. *Application contact:* Mary Ann Williams, Graduate Admissions Coordinator, 785-864-4510, Fax: 785-864-3566, E-mail: mwilliam@ku.edu.

University of Kentucky, Graduate School, College of Education, Lexington, KY 40506-0032. Offers M Ed, MA Ed, MRC, MS, MS Ed, Ed D, PhD, Ed S. *Accreditation:* NCATE. Part-time and evening/weekend programs available. *Faculty:* 77 full-time (44 women), 7 part-time/adjunct (6 women). *Students:* 496 full-time (349 women), 312 part-time (232 women); includes 104 minority (83 African Americans, 2 American Indian/Alaska Native, 13 Asian Americans or Pacific Islanders, 6 Hispanic Americans), 19 international. Average age 35. 184 applicants, 58% accepted, 78 enrolled. In 2006, 199 master's, 29 doctorates, 37 other advanced degrees awarded. Terminal master's awarded for partial completion of doctoral program. *Degree requirements:* For master's and Ed S, comprehensive exam; for doctorate, thesis/dissertation, comprehensive exam. *Entrance requirements:* For master's, GRE General Test, minimum undergraduate GPA of 2.75; for doctorate, GRE General Test, minimum graduate GPA of 3.0; for Ed S, GRE General Test. Additional exam requirements/recommendations for international students: Required—TOEFL (minimum score 550 paper-based; 213 computer-based). *Application deadline:* For fall admission, 7/17 priority date for domestic students, 2/1 priority date for international students; for spring admission, 12/13 priority date for domestic students, 6/15 priority date for international students. Application fee: $40 ($55 for international students). Electronic applications accepted. *Expenses:* Tuition, state resident: full-time $7,670; part-time $401 per credit hour. Tuition, nonresident: full-time $16,158; part-time $873 per credit hour. *Financial support:* In 2006–07, 26 fellowships with full tuition reimbursements (averaging $4,500 per year), 57 research assistantships with full tuition reimbursements (averaging $10,810 per year), 64 teaching assistantships with full tuition reimbursements (averaging $8,466 per year) were awarded; career-related internships or fieldwork, Federal Work-Study, institutionally sponsored loans, scholarships/grants, traineeships, health care benefits, tuition waivers (partial), and unspecified assistantships also available. Support available to part-time students. Financial award application deadline: 3/15. *Unit head:* Dr. James Cibulka, Dean, 859-257-6076, Fax: 859-323-1046, E-mail: cibulka@uky.edu. *Application contact:* Dr. Brian Jackson, Senior Associate Dean, 859-257-4667, Fax: 859-257-4676, E-mail: brian.jackson@uky.edu.

University of La Verne, College of Education and Organizational Leadership, Department of Education, Master's Program in Education, La Verne, CA 91750-4443. Offers advanced teaching skills (M Ed); education (special emphasis) (M Ed). Part-time programs available. *Faculty:* 18 full-time (13 women), 7 part-time/adjunct (all women). *Students:* 78 full-time (66 women), 212 part-time (157 women); includes 121 minority (17 African Americans, 8 Asian Americans or Pacific Islanders, 96 Hispanic Americans), 2 international. Average age 32. In 2006, 161 degrees awarded. *Degree requirements:* For master's, thesis optional. *Entrance requirements:* For master's, California Basic Educational Skills Test, interview, writing sample, minimum GPA of 3.0, 3 letters of recommendation. Additional exam requirements/recommendations for international students: Required—TOEFL (minimum score 550 paper-based; 213 computer-based). *Application deadline:* Applications are processed on a rolling basis. Application fee: $50. *Expenses: Contact institution. Financial support:* Institutionally sponsored loans and unspecified assistantships available. Financial award application deadline: 3/2; financial award applicants required to submit FAFSA. *Unit head:* Valerie Beltran, Chair, 909-593-3511 Ext. 4659, E-mail: beltranv@ulv.edu. *Application contact:* Jo Nell Baker, Director, Graduate Admissions and Academic Services, 909-593-3511 Ext. 4244, Fax: 909-392-2761, E-mail: gradadmt@ulv.edu.

University of La Verne, Regional Campus Administration, Graduate Credential Program in Education, California Statewide Campus, La Verne, CA 91750-4443. Offers cross cultural language and academic development (Credential); multiple subject (Credential); single subject (Credential). *Faculty:* 1 part-time/adjunct (0 women). *Students:* 113 full-time (95 women), 41 part-time (27 women); includes 49 minority (8 African Americans, 1 American Indian/Alaska Native, 40 Hispanic Americans). Average age 33. *Entrance requirements:* For degree, California Basic Educational Skills Test, minimum undergraduate GPA of 2.75, 3 letters of recommendation, interview. *Application deadline:* Applications are processed on a rolling basis. Application fee: $50. *Expenses: Contact institution. Financial support:* Institutionally sponsored loans available. Financial award application deadline: 3/2; financial award applicants required to submit FAFSA. *Unit head:* Juline Behrens, Director, 909-985-0944, Fax: 909-981-8695, E-mail: behrensj@ulv.edu.

University of La Verne, Regional Campus Administration, Master's Programs in Education, California Statewide Campus, La Verne, CA 91750-4443. Offers advanced teaching (M Ed); educational management (M Ed), including preliminary administrative services credential; reading (M Ed); school counseling (MS), including public personnel services credential. *Faculty:* 3 full-time (0 women), 60 part-time/adjunct (38 women). *Students:* 203 full-time (151 women), 268 part-time (210 women); includes 216 minority (42 African Americans, 5 American Indian/Alaska Native, 27 Asian Americans or Pacific Islanders, 142 Hispanic Americans). Average age 36. In 2006, 289 degrees awarded. *Entrance requirements:* For master's, California Basic Educational Skills Test, 3 letters of recommendation, teaching credential. *Application deadline:* Applications are processed on a rolling basis. Application fee: $50. *Expenses: Contact institution. Financial support:* Fellowships, institutionally sponsored loans available. Financial award application deadline: 3/2; financial award applicants required to submit FAFSA. *Unit head:* Juline Behrens, Director, 909-985-0944, Fax: 909-981-8695, E-mail: behrensj@ulv.edu.

University of Lethbridge, School of Graduate Studies, Lethbridge, AB T1K 3M4, Canada. Offers accounting (MScM); addictions counseling (M Sc); agricultural biotechnology (M Sc); agricultural studies (M Sc, MA); anthropology (MA); archaeology (MA); art (MA); biochemistry (M Sc); biological sciences (M Sc); biomolecular science (PhD); biosystems and biodiversity (PhD); Canadian studies (MA); chemistry (M Sc); computer science (M Sc); computer science and geographical information science (M Sc); counseling psychology (M Ed); dramatic arts (MA); earth, space, and physical science (PhD); economics (MA); educational leadership (M Ed); English (MA); environmental science (M Sc); evolution and behavior (PhD); exercise science (M Sc); finance (MScM); French (MA); French/German (MA); French/Spanish (MA); general education (M Ed); general management (MScM); geography (M Sc, MA); German (MA); health sciences (M Sc, MA); history (MA); human resource management and labour relations (MScM); individualized multidisciplinary (M Sc, MA); information systems (MScM); international management (MScM); kinesiology (M Sc, MA); management (M Sc, MA); marketing (MScM); mathematics (M Sc); music (MA); Native American studies (MA); neuroscience (M Sc, PhD); new media (MA); nursing (M Sc); philosophy (MA); physics (M Sc); policy and strategy (MScM); political science (MA); psychology (M Sc, MA); religious studies (MA); sociology (MA); theoretical and computational science (PhD); urban and regional studies (MA). Part-time and evening/weekend programs available. *Students:* 200 full-time, 90 part-time. In 2006, 105 master's, 3 doctorates awarded. *Degree requirements:* For doctorate, thesis/dissertation, comprehensive exam. *Entrance requirements:* For master's, GMAT (M Sc management), bachelor's degree in related field, minimum GPA of 3.0 during previous 20 graded semester courses, 2 years teaching or related experience (M Ed); for doctorate, master's degree, minimum graduate GPA of 3.5. Additional exam requirements/recommendations for international students: Required—TOEFL. Application fee: $60 Canadian dollars. *Financial support:* Fellowships, research assistantships, teaching assistantships, scholarships/grants, health care benefits, and unspecified assistantships available. *Faculty research:* Movement and brain plasticity, gibberellin physiology, photosynthesis, carbon cycling, molecular properties of main-group ring components. *Unit head:* Dr. Jo-Anne Fiske, Interim Dean, 403-329-2121, Fax: 403-329-2097. *Application contact:* Kathy Schrage, Administrative Assistant, Office of the Academic Vice President, 403-329-2121, Fax: 403-329-2097, E-mail: inquiries@uleth.ca.

University of Louisiana at Lafayette, Graduate School, College of Education, Lafayette, LA 70504. Offers M Ed, Ed D. *Accreditation:* NCATE. Part-time programs available. *Faculty:* 35 full-time (15 women), 1 part-time/adjunct (0 women). *Students:* 15 full-time (all women), 92 part-time (72 women); includes 20 minority (15 African Americans, 3 American Indian/Alaska Native, 2 Hispanic Americans), 1 international. Average age 36. 44 applicants, 39% accepted, 11 enrolled. In 2006, 46 degrees awarded. *Degree requirements:* For master's, thesis or alternative. *Entrance requirements:* For master's, GRE General Test, teaching certificate. Additional exam requirements/recommendations for international students: Required—TOEFL (minimum score 550 paper-based; 213 computer-based). *Application deadline:* For fall admission, 5/15 for domestic and international students; for spring admission, 10/1 for domestic and international students. Applications are processed on a rolling basis. Application fee: $25 ($30 for international students). Electronic applications accepted. *Expenses:* Tuition, state resident: full-time $3,247; part-time $93 per credit hour. Tuition, nonresident: full-time $9,427; part-time $350 per credit hour. *Financial support:* In 2006–07, 14 research assistantships with full tuition reimbursements (averaging $5,500 per year) were awarded; Federal Work-Study and unspecified assistantships also available. Financial award application deadline: 5/1. *Unit head:* Dr. Gerald B. Carlson, Dean, 337-482-6678, Fax: 337-482-5842, E-mail: gcarlson@louisiana.edu. *Application contact:* Dr. Nathan Roberts, Coordinator, 337-482-6747, Fax: 337-482-5842, E-mail: nmr0713@louisiana.edu.

University of Louisiana at Monroe, Graduate Studies and Research, College of Education and Human Development, Monroe, LA 71209-0001. Offers M Ed, MA, MAT, MS, Ed D, PhD, SSP. *Accreditation:* NCATE. Part-time and evening/weekend programs available. *Faculty:* 43 full-time (21 women), 7 part-time/adjunct (5 women). *Students:* 126 full-time (103 women), 232 part-time (188 women); includes 111 African Americans, 3 Asian Americans or Pacific Islanders, 2 Hispanic Americans, 8 international. Average age 34. In 2006, 144 master's, 5 doctorates awarded. *Degree requirements:* For doctorate, thesis/dissertation. *Entrance requirements:* For master's, GRE General Test. Application fee: $20 ($30 for international students). *Expenses:* Tuition, state resident: part-time $124 per credit hour. Tuition, nonresident: part-time $124 per credit hour. *Financial support:* Research assistantships, teaching assistantships, career-related internships or fieldwork, Federal Work-Study, institutionally sponsored loans, and unspecified assistantships available. Financial award application deadline: 7/1. *Unit head:* Dr. Luke Thomas, Dean, 318-342-1305, E-mail: lthomas@ulm.edu.

University of Louisville, Graduate School, College of Education and Human Development, Louisville, KY 40292-0001. Offers M Ed, MA, MAT, MS, Ed D, PhD, Ed S. *Accreditation:* NCATE. Part-time and evening/weekend programs available. *Faculty:* 93 full-time (60 women), 97 part-time/adjunct (62 women). *Students:* 514 full-time (354 women), 889 part-time (614 women); includes 173 minority (140 African Americans, 3 American Indian/Alaska Native, 21 Asian Americans or Pacific Islanders, 9 Hispanic Americans), 101 international. Average age 34. In 2006, 463 master's, 33 doctorates, 11 other advanced degrees awarded. Terminal master's awarded for partial completion of doctoral program. *Degree requirements:* For doctorate, thesis/dissertation. *Entrance requirements:* For master's, doctorate, and Ed S, GRE General Test. *Application deadline:* Applications are processed on a rolling basis. Application fee: $50. Electronic applications accepted. *Financial support:* In 2006–07, 9 fellowships with full tuition reimbursements (averaging $18,000 per year), 30 research assistantships with full tuition reimbursements, 6 teaching assistantships with full tuition reimbursements were awarded; career-related internships or fieldwork, Federal Work-Study, and scholarships/grants also available. *Faculty research:* Teacher education, professional development and classroom effectiveness; early childhood development; health promotions and exercise physiology; counseling psychology; educational leadership and reform; culturally responsive education. *Unit head:* Dr. Robert Felner, Dean, 502-852-6411, Fax: 502-852-0726, E-mail: rifelner@louisville.edu.

University of Maine, Graduate School, College of Education and Human Development, Orono, ME 04469. Offers counselor education (M Ed, MA, MS, Ed D, CAS); curriculum, assessment, and instruction (M Ed), including elementary and secondary education; educational leadership (M Ed, Ed D, CAS); elementary education (M Ed, MAT, MS, CAS); higher education (M Ed, MA, MS, Ed D, CAS); human development and family relations (MS), including human development; instructional technology (M Ed); kinesiology and physical education (M Ed, MS); literacy education (M Ed, MA, MS, Ed D, CAS); science education (M Ed, MS, CAS); secondary education (M Ed, MA, MAT, MS, CAS); social studies education (M Ed, MA, MS, CAS); special education (M Ed, CAS). *Accreditation:* NCATE. Part-time and evening/weekend programs available. *Faculty:* 34 full-time, 3 part-time/adjunct. *Students:* 232 full-time (177 women), 380 part-time (276 women); includes 16 minority (3 African Americans, 6 American Indian/Alaska Native, 4 Asian Americans or Pacific Islanders, 3 Hispanic Americans), 11 international. Average age 38. 213 applicants, 85% accepted, 154 enrolled. In 2006, 232 master's, 9 doctorates, 36 other advanced degrees awarded. *Degree requirements:* For doctorate, thesis/dissertation. *Entrance requirements:* For doctorate, GRE General Test; for CAS, MA, M Ed, or MS. Additional exam requirements/recommendations for international students: Required—TOEFL. *Application deadline:* For fall admission, 2/1 priority date for domestic students. Applications are processed on a rolling basis. Application fee: $50. Electronic applications accepted. *Financial support:* In 2006–07, 21 teaching assistantships with tuition reimbursements (averaging $9,010 per year) were awarded; research assistantships with tuition reimbursements, career-related internships or fieldwork, Federal Work-Study, institution-

Education—General

University of Maine (continued)
ally sponsored loans, and unspecified assistantships also available. Support available to part-time students. Financial award application deadline: 3/1. *Faculty research:* Development of training models for the severely handicapped, marine education, counselor training models. *Unit head:* Dr. Robert A. Cobb, Dean, 207-581-2441, Fax: 207-581-2423. *Application contact:* Scott G. Delcourt, Associate Dean of the Graduate School, 207-581-3219, Fax: 207-581-3232, E-mail: graduate@maine.edu.

Announcement: NCATE-accredited graduate study at the master's (MAT, MS, and M Ed), CAS, and doctoral levels offers the resources and collaboration essential to the development of influential educational leaders. Hallmarks include innovative technology, widely published faculty, supportive cohorts, national and statewide research centers, and strong partnerships with public schools. Program areas include educational leadership; literacy; higher education; elementary, secondary, (English, modern languages, mathematics, science, and social studies), middle level, and kinesiology and physical education; instructional technology; special education; and counselor education. The MS in human development offers advanced study in the development of individuals throughout the life span and of the family in its various forms. Flexibility allows comprehensive inquiry and concentration in specific interests.

See Close-Up on page 925.

University of Maine, Graduate School, Interdisciplinary Program in Teaching, Orono, ME 04469. Offers MST. *Students:* 21 full-time (6 women), 5 part-time (2 women), 1 international. Average age 30. 9 applicants, 100% accepted, 9 enrolled. In 2006, 2 degrees awarded. *Entrance requirements:* For master's, GRE General Test. *Financial support:* Teaching assistantships with tuition reimbursements available. *Unit head:* Dr. Susan McKay, Director, 207-581-1016. *Application contact:* Scott G. Delcourt, Associate Dean of the Graduate School, 207-581-3219, Fax: 207-581-3232, E-mail: graduate@maine.edu.

University of Manitoba, Faculty of Graduate Studies, College Universitaire de Saint Boniface, Education ProgramûSaint-Boniface, Winnipeg, MB R3T 2N2, Canada. Offers M Ed.

University of Manitoba, Faculty of Graduate Studies, Faculty of Education, Winnipeg, MB R3T 2N2, Canada. Offers M Ed, PhD. *Degree requirements:* For master's, thesis or alternative.

University of Mary, Program in Education, Bismarck, ND 58504-9652. Offers college teaching (MS Ed); curriculum and instruction (MS Ed); early childhood education (MS Ed); early childhood special education (MS Ed); elementary education administration (MS Ed); reading (MS Ed); secondary education administration (MS Ed); special education (MS Ed). Part-time programs available. *Faculty:* 8 full-time (4 women), 12 part-time/adjunct (7 women). *Students:* 2 full-time (1 woman), 34 part-time (25 women), 2 international. Average age 35. In 2006, 17 degrees awarded. *Degree requirements:* For master's, portfolio or thesis. *Entrance requirements:* For master's, interview, letters of reference. *Application deadline:* Applications are processed on a rolling basis. Application fee: $40. *Financial support:* In 2006–07, 1 teaching assistantship with full tuition reimbursement was awarded; career-related internships or fieldwork also available. Support available to part-time students. Financial award application deadline: 8/1; financial award applicants required to submit FAFSA. *Faculty research:* Innovative pedagogy in higher education, technology in education, content standards, children of poverty, children with diverse learning needs. *Unit head:* Dr. Rebecca Yunker Salveson, Director, 701-355-8186, E-mail: rysalves@umary.edu. *Application contact:* Leona Friedig, Administrative Secretary, 701-355-8058, E-mail: lfriedig@umary.edu.

University of Mary Hardin-Baylor, College of Education, Belton, TX 76513. Offers educational administration (M Ed, Ed D); educational psychology (M Ed); exercise and sport science (M Ed); general studies (M Ed); reading education (M Ed). Part-time and evening/weekend programs available. *Faculty:* 10 full-time (5 women), 1 part-time/adjunct (0 women). *Students:* 8 full-time (3 women), 36 part-time (26 women); includes 8 minority (3 African Americans, 5 Hispanic Americans). Average age 24. In 2006, 18 degrees awarded. *Degree requirements:* For master's, comprehensive exam, registration. *Entrance requirements:* For master's, GRE General Test, minimum GPA of 2.75, Texas teaching certificate. *Application deadline:* For fall admission, 6/1 priority date for domestic students; for spring admission, 11/1 for domestic students. Applications are processed on a rolling basis. Application fee: $35 ($135 for international students). Electronic applications accepted. *Expenses:* Tuition: Full-time $8,910; part-time $495 per hour. Required fees: $906; $47 per hour. $30 per term. Tuition and fees vary according to course load. *Financial support:* Federal Work-Study, scholarships/grants, and scholarships (for some active duty military personnel only) available. Support available to part-time students. Financial award application deadline: 6/1; financial award applicants required to submit FAFSA. *Unit head:* Dr. Marlene Zipperlen, Dean, 254-295-4572, Fax: 254-295-4480, E-mail: mzipperlen@umhb.edu. *Application contact:* Dr. Shirley Dahl, Director, Graduate Programs in Education, 254-295-4185, Fax: 254-295-4480, E-mail: sdahl@umhb.edu.

University of Maryland, Baltimore County, Graduate School, College of Arts, Humanities and Social Sciences, Department of Education, Baltimore, MD 21250. Offers computer/web-based instruction (Postbaccalaureate Certificate); distance education (Postbaccalaureate Certificate); early childhood education (MAT); education (MA); elementary education (MAT); instructional systems development (MA, Postbaccalaureate Certificate), including ESOL/bilingual education (Postbaccalaureate Certificate), ESOL/bilingual training systems (MA); secondary education (MA, MAT); teaching (MA). *Accreditation:* NCATE. Part-time and evening/weekend programs available. Postbaccalaureate distance learning degree programs offered (no on-campus study). *Faculty:* 17 full-time (15 women), 3 part-time/adjunct (all women). *Students:* 89 full-time (78 women), 422 part-time (340 women); includes 72 minority (41 African Americans, 19 Asian Americans or Pacific Islanders, 12 Hispanic Americans), 15 international. In 2006, 56 master's awarded. *Median time to degree:* Of those who began their doctoral program in fall 1998, 95% received their degree in 8 years or less. *Degree requirements:* For master's, thesis (for some programs), comprehensive exam, registration. *Entrance requirements:* For master's, GRE General Test, GRE Subject Test (MA), PRAXIS I (MAT), minimum GPA of 3.0. Additional exam requirements/recommendations for international students: Required—TOEFL. *Application deadline:* For fall admission, 7/1 for domestic students. Applications are processed on a rolling basis. Application fee: $50. Electronic applications accepted. *Expenses:* Tuition, state resident: part-time $412 per credit hour. Tuition, nonresident: part-time $681 per credit hour. Required fees: $91 per credit hour. One-time fee: $75 part-time. *Financial support:* In 2006–07, 75 students received support, including research assistantships with full tuition reimbursements available (averaging $12,000 per year); fellowships, teaching assistantships, career-related internships or fieldwork, Federal Work-Study, scholarships/grants, tuition waivers (partial), and unspecified assistantships also available. Financial award application deadline: 3/1. *Faculty research:* Teacher leadership; STEM education; ESOL/bilingual education; early childhood education; language, literacy and culture. Total annual research expenditures: $1.3 million. *Unit head:* Dr. Mary S. Rivkin, Department Chair, 410-455-2465, Fax: 410-455-3986, E-mail: rivkin@umbc.edu. *Application contact:* Dr. Susan M. Blunck, Director, 410-455-2869, Fax: 410-455-3986, E-mail: blunck@umbc.edu.

University of Maryland, College Park, Graduate Studies, College of Education, College Park, MD 20742. Offers M Ed, MA, Ed D, PhD, CAGS. *Accreditation:* NCATE. Part-time and evening/weekend programs available. Postbaccalaureate distance learning degree programs offered. *Faculty:* 180 full-time (125 women), 79 part-time/adjunct (70 women). *Students:* 732 full-time (567 women), 449 part-time (353 women); includes 336 minority (189 African Americans, 4 American Indian/Alaska Native, 75 Asian Americans or Pacific Islanders, 68 Hispanic Americans), 111 international. 1,141 applicants, 41% accepted, 278 enrolled. In 2006, 294 master's, 62 doctorates, 12 other advanced degrees awarded. *Degree requirements:* For doctorate, thesis/dissertation. *Entrance requirements:* For master's, GRE General Test or MAT, minimum GPA of 3.0. *Application deadline:* For fall admission, 5/1 for domestic students, 2/1 for international students; for spring admission, 10/1 for domestic students, 6/1 for international students. Applications are processed on a rolling basis. Application fee: $60. Electronic applications accepted. *Financial support:* In 2006–07, 151 fellowships with full tuition reimbursements (averaging $5,149 per year), 58 research assistantships with tuition reimbursements (averaging $15,131 per year), 293 teaching assistantships with tuition reimbursements (averaging $14,649 per year) were awarded; career-related internships or fieldwork, Federal Work-Study, and scholarships/grants also available. Support available to part-time students. Financial award applicants required to submit FAFSA. Total annual research expenditures: $14.1 million. *Unit head:* Dr. Dennis M. Kivlighan, Dean, 301-405-2334, Fax: 301-314-9890, E-mail: dennisk@umd.edu. *Application contact:* Dean of Graduate School, 301-405-4190, Fax: 301-314-9305.

See Close-Up on page 927.

University of Maryland Eastern Shore, Graduate Programs, Department of Education, Program in Teaching, Princess Anne, MD 21853-1299. Offers MAT. *Accreditation:* NCATE. *Faculty:* 1 (woman) full-time, 2 part-time/adjunct (both women). *Students:* 5 full-time (2 women), 3 part-time (1 woman); includes 2 minority (both African Americans), 2 international. Average age 30. 4 applicants, 75% accepted, 2 enrolled. In 2006, 16 degrees awarded. *Degree requirements:* For master's, internship, seminar paper, PRAXIS II. *Entrance requirements:* For master's, PRAXIS I, interview, minimum GPA of 3.0, writing sample. Additional exam requirements/recommendations for international students: Required—TOEFL (minimum score 213 computer-based). *Application deadline:* For winter admission, 10/1 for domestic and international students. Application fee: $30. Electronic applications accepted. *Financial support:* In 2006–07, 1 student received support, including 1 research assistantship with partial tuition reimbursement available (averaging $5,074 per year); career-related internships or fieldwork, scholarships/grants, and unspecified assistantships also available. Financial award application deadline: 3/1; financial award applicants required to submit FAFSA. *Unit head:* Dr. Mary Agnew, Coordinator, 410-651-6222, Fax: 410-651-7962, E-mail: mlagnew@umes.edu.

University of Maryland University College, Graduate School of Management and Technology, Program in Education, Adelphi, MD 20783. Offers M Ed. Part-time and evening/weekend programs available. Postbaccalaureate distance learning degree programs offered (no on-campus study). *Students:* 22 full-time (18 women), 187 part-time (140 women); includes 65 minority (52 African Americans, 1 American Indian/Alaska Native, 9 Asian Americans or Pacific Islanders, 3 Hispanic Americans). Average age 35. 41 applicants, 98% accepted, 20 enrolled. In 2006, 37 degrees awarded. *Degree requirements:* For master's, thesis or alternative. *Application deadline:* Applications are processed on a rolling basis. Application fee: $50. Electronic applications accepted. *Financial support:* Federal Work-Study and scholarships/grants available. Support available to part-time students. Financial award application deadline: 6/1; financial award applicants required to submit FAFSA. *Unit head:* Dr. Katherine Woodward, Chair, 301-985-7200, Fax: 301-985-4611, E-mail: kwoodward@umuc.edu. *Application contact:* Coordinator, Graduate Admissions, 301-985-7155, Fax: 301-985-7175, E-mail: gradinfo@umuc.edu.

University of Mary Washington, College of Graduate and Professional Studies, Fredericksburg, VA 22406-7239. Offers business administration (MBA); education (M Ed); management information systems (MSMIS). Part-time and evening/weekend programs available. *Faculty:* 25 full-time (17 women), 20 part-time/adjunct (10 women). *Students:* 121 full-time (92 women), 507 part-time (367 women); includes 95 minority (59 African Americans, 1 American Indian/Alaska Native, 10 Asian Americans or Pacific Islanders, 25 Hispanic Americans), 4 international. Average age 35. In 2006, 14 degrees awarded. *Entrance requirements:* For master's, GMAT (MBA), PRAXIS I (M Ed), minimum GPA of 3.0. Additional exam requirements/recommendations for international students: Required—TOEFL (minimum score 600 paper-based; 250 computer-based; 100 iBT). *Application deadline:* For fall admission, 6/1 priority date for domestic students, 6/1 for international students; for spring admission, 10/1 for domestic and international students. Application fee: $45. *Expenses:* Tuition, area resident: Part-time $275 per credit hour. Tuition, state resident: part-time $626 per credit. Required fees: $25 per term. One-time fee: $45 part-time. *Financial support:* In 2006–07, 46 students received support. Scholarships/grants available. Support available to part-time students. Financial award application deadline: 3/15; financial award applicants required to submit FAFSA. *Unit head:* Dr. Meta R. Braymer, Vice President for Graduate and Professional Studies and Dean of the Faculty, 540-286-8000, Fax: 540-286-8005, E-mail: mbraymer@umw.edu. *Application contact:* Matthew E. Mejia, Assistant Dean for Graduate and Professional Studies and Dean of the Faculty, 540-286-8017, Fax: 540-286-8085, E-mail: mmejia@umw.edu.

University of Massachusetts Amherst, Graduate School, School of Education, Amherst, MA 01003. Offers M Ed, Ed D, PhD, CAGS. *Accreditation:* NCATE. Part-time programs available. *Faculty:* 78 full-time (40 women). *Students:* 443 full-time (307 women), 452 part-time (324 women); includes 152 minority (72 African Americans, 4 American Indian/Alaska Native, 31 Asian Americans or Pacific Islanders, 45 Hispanic Americans), 82 international. Average age 34. 612 applicants. In 2006, 260 master's, 34 doctorates awarded. Terminal master's awarded for partial completion of doctoral program. *Degree requirements:* For doctorate, thesis/dissertation. *Entrance requirements:* For master's, GRE General Test. Additional exam requirements/recommendations for international students: Required—TOEFL (minimum score 530 paper-based; 197 computer-based). *Application deadline:* For fall admission, 1/15 for domestic and international students. Applications are processed on a rolling basis. Application fee: $40 ($65 for international students). Electronic applications accepted. *Expenses:* Tuition, state resident: full-time $2,640; part-time $110 per credit. Tuition, nonresident: full-time $9,936; part-time $414 per credit. Required fees: $8,969; $3,129 per term. One-time fee: $257 full-time. Tuition and fees vary according to class time, course load, campus/location and reciprocity agreements. *Financial support:* In 2006–07, 9 fellowships with full tuition reimbursements (averaging $2,523 per year), 112 research assistantships with full tuition reimbursements (averaging $7,847 per year), 91 teaching assistantships with full tuition reimbursements (averaging $5,106 per year) were awarded; career-related internships or fieldwork, Federal Work-Study, scholarships/grants, traineeships, and unspecified assistantships also available. Support available to part-time students. Financial award application deadline: 1/15. *Unit head:* Dr. Christine McCormick, Dean, 413-545-0233, Fax: 413-545-4240.

University of Massachusetts Boston, Office of Graduate Studies, Graduate College of Education, Boston, MA 02125-3393. Offers M Ed, MA, Ed D, CAGS, Certificate. *Accreditation:* NCATE. Part-time and evening/weekend programs available. *Students:* 272 full-time (209 women), 629 part-time (475 women); includes 129 minority (68 African Americans, 2 American Indian/Alaska Native, 24 Asian Americans or Pacific Islanders, 35 Hispanic Americans), 17 international. Average age 34. 622 applicants, 60% accepted. In 2006, 237 master's, 9 doctorates, 41 other advanced degrees awarded. *Degree requirements:* For master's, comprehensive exam; for doctorate, thesis/dissertation, comprehensive exam. *Entrance requirements:* For master's, GRE General Test or MAT; for doctorate, GRE General Test or MAT, minimum GPA of 2.75; for other advanced degree, minimum GPA of 2.75. *Application deadline:* For fall admission, 3/1 for domestic students. Application fee: $25 ($40 for international students). *Expenses:* Tuition, state resident: full-time $2,590; part-time $301 per credit. Tuition, nonresident: full-time $9,758; part-time $427 per credit. One-time fee: $40 full-time. *Financial support:* In 2006–07, 85 research assistantships with full tuition reimbursements (averaging $3,500 per year), 2 teaching assistantships with full tuition reimbursements (averaging $4,000 per year) were awarded; career-related internships or fieldwork, Federal Work-Study, and unspecified assistantships also available. Support available to part-time students. Financial award application deadline: 3/1; financial award applicants required to submit FAFSA. *Faculty research:* Effects of ethnicity on applied psychology and education, enhancing equity and excellence in public schools, diversity and change in higher education, improving the functioning of individuals with disabilities. *Unit head:* Dr. Peter Langer, Interim Dean, 617-287-7600. *Application contact:* Peggy Roldan, Graduate Admissions Coordinator, 617-287-6400, Fax: 617-287-6236, E-mail: bos.gadm@dpc.umassp.edu.

University of Massachusetts Dartmouth, Graduate School, College of Arts and Sciences, Program in Teaching, North Dartmouth, MA 02747-2300. Offers MAT, Certificate. *Faculty:* 6 full-time (5 women), 5 part-time/adjunct (3 women). *Students:* 4 full-time (3 women), 120 part-time (93 women); includes 4 minority (2 African Americans, 1 Asian American or Pacific Islander, 1 Hispanic American). Average age 25. 68 applicants, 99% accepted, 53 enrolled. In 2006, 19 master's, 1 other advanced degree awarded. *Degree requirements:* For master's, thesis or alternative. *Entrance requirements:* For master's, MAT or GRE, GMAT, minimum undergraduate GPA of 2.7, teacher certification. Additional exam requirements/recommendations for international students: Required—TOEFL (minimum score 500 paper-based). *Application deadline:* For fall admission, 4/20 priority date for domestic students, 2/20 for international students; for spring admission, 11/15 priority date for domestic students, 9/15 for international students. Applications are processed on a rolling basis. Application fee: $40 ($60 for international students). *Expenses:* Tuition, state resident: full-time $2,071; part-time $86 per credit. Tuition, nonresident: full-time $8,099; part-time $337 per credit. *Financial support:* Federal Work-Study available. Financial award application deadline: 3/1. Total annual research expenditures: $27,860. *Unit head:* Dr. Gerard Koot, Director, 508-999-8305, Fax: 508-999-9125, E-mail: gkoot@umassd.edu. *Application contact:* Carol Novo, Graduate Admissions Officer, 508-999-8604, Fax: 508-999-8183, E-mail: graduate@umassd.edu.

University of Massachusetts Lowell, Graduate School, Graduate School of Education, Lowell, MA 01854-2881. Offers administration, planning, and policy (CAGS); curriculum and instruction (M Ed, CAGS); educational administration (M Ed); language arts and literacy (Ed D); leadership in schooling (Ed D); math and science education (Ed D); reading and language (M Ed, CAGS). *Accreditation:* NCATE. Part-time and evening/weekend programs available. Postbaccalaureate distance learning degree programs offered (no on-campus study). Terminal master's awarded for partial completion of doctoral program. *Degree requirements:* For doctorate, thesis/dissertation. *Entrance requirements:* For master's and doctorate, GRE General Test. Additional exam requirements/recommendations for international students: Required—TOEFL. Electronic applications accepted.

University of Memphis, Graduate School, College of Education, Memphis, TN 38152. Offers MAT, MS, Ed D, PhD, Ed S. *Accreditation:* NCATE. Part-time and evening/weekend programs available. Terminal master's awarded for partial completion of doctoral program. *Degree requirements:* For master's, comprehensive exam; for doctorate, thesis/dissertation, comprehensive exam; for Ed S, thesis or alternative, comprehensive exam. *Entrance requirements:* For master's, GRE General Test or MAT; for doctorate, GRE General Test; for Ed S, GRE General Test, GRE Subject Test, 2 years of teaching experience. *Faculty research:* Urban school effectiveness, literacy development, teacher effectiveness, exercise physiology, crisis counseling.

University of Miami, Graduate School, School of Education, Coral Gables, FL 33124. Offers MS Ed, PhD, Certificate, Ed S. *Accreditation:* NCATE. Part-time and evening/weekend programs available. *Faculty:* 47 full-time (26 women), 43 part-time/adjunct (21 women). *Students:* 167 full-time (125 women), 212 part-time (181 women); includes 162 minority (44 African Americans, 3 Asian Americans or Pacific Islanders, 115 Hispanic Americans), 40 international. Average age 31. 331 applicants, 62% accepted, 106 enrolled. In 2006, 188 master's, 9 doctorates awarded. Terminal master's awarded for partial completion of doctoral program. *Median time to degree:* Of those who began their doctoral program in fall 1998, 75% received their degree in 8 years or less. *Degree requirements:* For master's, comprehensive exam (for some programs); for doctorate, thesis/dissertation. *Entrance requirements:* For master's and other advanced degree, GRE General Test; for doctorate, GRE General Test, GRE Subject Test. Additional exam requirements/recommendations for international students: Required—TOEFL (minimum score 550 paper-based; 213 computer-based). *Application deadline:* Applications are processed on a rolling basis. Application fee: $50. Electronic applications accepted. *Financial support:* In 2006–07, 3 fellowships with full tuition reimbursements (averaging $20,000 per year), 17 research assistantships with full and partial tuition reimbursements (averaging $18,000 per year), 12 teaching assistantships with full and partial tuition reimbursements (averaging $18,000 per year) were awarded; career-related internships or fieldwork, Federal Work-Study, institutionally sponsored loans, tuition waivers (full and partial), and unspecified assistantships also available. Support available to part-time students. Financial award application deadline: 3/1; financial award applicants required to submit FAFSA. *Faculty research:* Social skills and learning disabilities, planning for mainstreamed pupils, alcohol and drug abuse, restructuring education for all learners. Total annual research expenditures: $5.6 million. *Unit head:* Dr. Isaac Prilleltensky, Dean, 305-284-3505, Fax: 305-284-3003, E-mail: isaacp@miami.edu. *Application contact:* SOE Directory, 305-284-3711, Fax: 305-284-3003, E-mail: soe@miami.edu.

Announcement: The Department of Teaching and Learning offers master's degree programs in elementary education, exceptional student education/reading, exceptional student education/pre-K disabilities, and reading. Specialist and doctoral programs are also offered in specific areas. Educational and Psychological Studies Department offers master's programs in marriage & family therapy, mental health counseling, enrollment management, and research/evaluation. It offers doctoral programs in counseling psychology and research/evaluation. Exercise and Sport Sciences Department offers master's programs in sport administration, exercise physiology, and sports medicine and a doctoral program in exercise physiology. For more information, call 305-284-3711, visit www.education.miami.edu, or e-mail soe@miami.edu.

See Close-Up on page 929.

University of Michigan, Horace H. Rackham School of Graduate Studies and School of Education, Combined Program in Education and Psychology, Ann Arbor, MI 48109. Offers PhD. *Degree requirements:* For doctorate, thesis/dissertation, oral defense of dissertation, preliminary exam, independent research project. *Entrance requirements:* For doctorate, GRE General Test. Additional exam requirements/recommendations for international students: Required—TOEFL (minimum score 600 paper-based; 250 computer-based). Electronic applications accepted. *Faculty research:* Classroom research, instructional psychology.

University of Michigan, Horace H. Rackham School of Graduate Studies, School of Education, Ann Arbor, MI 48109-1259. Offers AM, MA, PhD, MA-Certification, MBA/MA, MPP/MA, PhD/MA. *Faculty:* 51 full-time (27 women). *Students:* 325 full-time (245 women), 67 part-time (56 women); includes 88 minority (42 African Americans, 2 American Indian/Alaska Native, 26 Asian Americans or Pacific Islanders, 18 Hispanic Americans), 37 international. 674 applicants, 41% accepted, 175 enrolled. In 2006, 134 master's, 43 doctorates awarded. Terminal master's awarded for partial completion of doctoral program. *Median time to degree:* Of those who began their doctoral program in fall 1998, 51% received their degree in 8 years or less. *Degree requirements:* For master's, thesis optional; for doctorate, thesis/dissertation, comprehensive exam. *Entrance requirements:* For master's and doctorate, GRE General Test. Additional exam requirements/recommendations for international students: Required—TOEFL (minimum score 600 paper-based; 250 computer-based). *Application deadline:* For fall admission, 12/1 priority date for domestic students, 12/1 for international students. Application fee: $60 ($75 for international students). Electronic applications accepted. *Financial support:* In 2006–07, 215 fellowships (averaging $5,852 per year), 109 research assistantships with full tuition reimbursements (averaging $14,695 per year), 32 teaching assistantships with full tuition reimbursements (averaging $14,756 per year) were awarded; career-related internships or fieldwork, Federal Work-Study, institutionally sponsored loans, scholarships/grants, health care benefits, tuition waivers, and unspecified assistantships also available. Support available to part-time students. Financial award applicants required to submit FAFSA. *Faculty research:* Teaching, learning, policy, leadership, technology. Total annual research expenditures: $15.6 million. *Unit head:* Deborah Loewenberg Ball, Dean, 734-764-9470, Fax: 734-763-1229, E-mail: dball@umich.edu. *Application contact:* Roberta Perry, Office of Student Services, 734-764-7563, Fax: 734-763-1495, E-mail: ed.grad.admit@umich.edu.

See Close-Up on page 931.

University of Michigan–Dearborn, School of Education, Program in Education, Dearborn, MI 48128-1491. Offers MA.

University of Michigan–Dearborn, School of Education, Program in Teaching, Dearborn, MI 48128-1491. Offers teaching (MA). *Entrance requirements:* Additional exam requirements/recommendations for international students: Required—TOEFL, TWE.

University of Michigan–Flint, School of Education and Human Services, Flint, MI 48502-1950. Offers early childhood education (MA, MA Ed); education (MA, MA Ed); elementary education with teacher certification (MA); elementary education with teaching certificate (MA Ed); literacy (K-12) (MA, MA Ed); special education (MA, MA Ed); technology in education (MA); urban and multicultural education (MA, MA Ed). Part-time programs available. *Faculty:* 19 full-time (15 women), 9 part-time/adjunct (6 women). *Students:* 42 full-time (36 women), 200 part-time (173 women); includes 20 minority (16 African Americans, 2 American Indian/Alaska Native, 2 Hispanic Americans), 2 international. Average age 35. 109 applicants, 80% accepted, 65 enrolled. In 2006, 54 degrees awarded. *Entrance requirements:* Additional exam requirements/recommendations for international students: Required—TOEFL (minimum score 560 paper-based; 220 computer-based), IELTS (minimum score 7). *Application deadline:* For fall admission, 8/1 priority date for domestic students, 3/1 priority date for international students; for winter admission, 11/15 priority date for domestic students, 7/15 priority date for international students; for spring admission, 3/15 priority date for domestic students, 11/15 priority date for international students. Applications are processed on a rolling basis. Application fee: $55. *Expenses:* Contact institution. Full-time tuition and fees vary according to degree level and program. Part-time tuition and fees vary according to course load and degree level. *Financial support:* In 2006–07, 101 students received support. Federal Work-Study and scholarships/grants available. Support available to part-time students. Financial award applicants required to submit FAFSA. *Unit head:* Dr. Susanne Chandler, Dean, 810-766-6878, Fax: 810-766-6891, E-mail: chandes@umflint.edu. *Application contact:* Beulah Alexander, Executive Secretary, 810-766-6879, Fax: 810-766-6891, E-mail: beulaha@umflint.edu.

University of Minnesota, Duluth, Graduate School, College of Education and Human Service Professions, Department of Education, Duluth, MN 55812-2496. Offers Ed D. *Unit head:* Dr. Joyce Strand, Director of Graduate Studies, 218-726-8482, Fax: 218-726-7008, E-mail: jstrand1@d.umn.edu.

University of Minnesota, Twin Cities Campus, Graduate School, College of Education and Human Development, Minneapolis, MN 55455-0213. Offers M Ed, MA, MSW, Ed D, PhD, Certificate, Ed S. *Accreditation:* NCATE. Part-time programs available. *Faculty:* 156 full-time (69 women). *Students:* 1,687 full-time (1,240 women), 1,194 part-time (810 women); includes 315 minority (120 African Americans, 35 American Indian/Alaska Native, 104 Asian Americans or Pacific Islanders, 56 Hispanic Americans), 256 international. Average age 28. 2,019 applicants, 63% accepted, 977 enrolled. In 2006, 1,147 master's, 185 doctorates, 94 other advanced degrees awarded. Application fee: $55. *Expenses:* Tuition, state resident: full-time $9,302; part-time $775 per credit. Tuition, nonresident: full-time $16,400; part-time $1,367 per credit. Full-time tuition and fees vary according to class time, course load, program, reciprocity agreements and student level. *Financial support:* In 2006–07, 59 fellowships, 278 research assistantships with full tuition reimbursements (averaging $24,775 per year), 238 teaching assistantships with full tuition reimbursements (averaging $24,775 per year) were awarded; scholarships/grants and tuition waivers (partial) also available. Financial award applicants required to submit FAFSA. *Faculty research:* Urban education, literacy, diversity in the teacher workforce, early childhood development, neurobehavioral research. Total annual research expenditures: $28 million. *Unit head:* Dr. Darlyne Bailey, Dean, 612-626-9252, Fax: 612-626-1580, E-mail: dbailey@umn.edu. *Application contact:* Dr. Mary Bents, Associate Dean, 612-625-6501, Fax: 612-626-1580, E-mail: mbents@tc.umn.edu.

University of Mississippi, Graduate School, School of Education, Oxford, University, MS 38677. Offers M Ed, MA, Ed D, PhD, Ed S, Specialist. *Accreditation:* NCATE. *Faculty:* 44 full-time (33 women), 10 part-time/adjunct (7 women). *Students:* 666 (509 women); includes 199 minority (182 African Americans, 12 Asian Americans or Pacific Islanders, 5 Hispanic Americans) 17 international. 702 applicants, 56% accepted, 306 enrolled. In 2006, 238 master's, 17 doctorates, 33 other advanced degrees awarded. *Degree requirements:* For doctorate, thesis/dissertation. *Entrance requirements:* For master's, GRE General Test, minimum GPA of 3.0; for doctorate, GRE General Test. Additional exam requirements/recommendations for international students: Required—TOEFL. *Application deadline:* For fall admission, 4/1 for domestic students; for spring admission, 10/1 for domestic students. Applications are processed on a rolling basis. Application fee: $25. Electronic applications accepted. *Expenses:* Tuition, state resident: full-time $4,602; part-time $256 per credit hour. Tuition, nonresident: full-time $10,566; part-time $587 per credit hour. *Financial support:* Scholarships/grants available. Financial award application deadline: 3/1; financial award applicants required to submit FAFSA. *Unit head:* Dr. Tom Burnham, Dean, 662-915-7063, Fax: 662-915-7249, E-mail: tburnham@olemiss.edu.

University of Missouri–Columbia, Graduate School, College of Education, Columbia, MO 65211. Offers M Ed, MA, Ed D, PhD, Ed S. *Accreditation:* NCATE. Part-time and evening/weekend programs available. *Faculty:* 96 full-time (47 women), 1 (woman) part-time/adjunct. *Students:* 728 full-time (520 women), 743 part-time (570 women); includes 118 minority (58 African Americans, 12 American Indian/Alaska Native, 24 Asian Americans or Pacific Islanders, 24 Hispanic Americans), 100 international. In 2006, 456 master's, 68 doctorates, 25 other advanced degrees awarded. Terminal master's awarded for partial completion of doctoral program. *Degree requirements:* For doctorate, thesis/dissertation. *Entrance requirements:* For master's, minimum GPA of 3.0; for doctorate, GRE General Test. *Application deadline:* Applications are processed on a rolling basis. Application fee: $45 ($60 for international students). *Financial support:* Fellowships, research assistantships, teaching assistantships, institutionally sponsored loans and scholarships/grants available. *Unit head:* Dr. Carolyn D. Herrington, Dean, 573-882-8311.

University of Missouri–Kansas City, School of Education, Kansas City, MO 64110-2499. Offers administration (Ed D); counseling and guidance (MA, Ed S); counseling psychology (PhD); curriculum and instruction (MA, Ed S); education (PhD); educational administration (Ed S); reading education (MA, Ed S); special education (MA). *Accreditation:* NCATE. Part-time and evening/weekend programs available. *Faculty:* 59 full-time (46 women), 39 part-time/adjunct (29 women). *Students:* 182 full-time (151 women), 470 part-time (344 women); includes 148 minority (117 African Americans, 5 American Indian/Alaska Native, 8 Asian Americans or Pacific Islanders, 18 Hispanic Americans), 9 international. Average age 34. 560 applicants, 79% accepted, 253 enrolled. In 2006, 196 master's, 4 doctorates, 41 other advanced degrees awarded. *Degree requirements:* For doctorate, thesis/dissertation, internship, practicum. *Entrance requirements:* For master's, GRE, minimum GPA of 2.75, 2 letters of reference, a written statement of purpose; for doctorate, GRE, minimum GPA of 3.0; for Ed S, minimum GPA of 3.0. Additional exam requirements/recommendations for international students: Required—TOEFL (minimum score 550 paper-based; 213 computer-based). *Application deadline:* For fall admission, 4/1 priority date for domestic students, 4/1 for international students; for winter admission, 10/1 priority date for domestic students, 10/1 for international students; for spring admission, 10/1 priority date for domestic students, 10/1 for international students. Applications are processed on a rolling basis. Application fee: $35 ($50 for international students). *Expenses:* Tuition, state resident: full-time $4,975; part-time $276 per credit. Tuition, nonresident: full-time $12,847; part-time $713 per credit. Required fees: $595; $595 per year. *Financial support:* In 2006–07, 361 students received support, including 13 research assistantships with partial tuition reimbursements available (averaging $10,560 per year); fellowships with full tuition reimbursements available, teaching assistantships, career-related internships or fieldwork, Federal Work-Study, institutionally sponsored loans, and tuition waivers (full and partial) also available. Support available to part-time students. Financial award application deadline: 3/1. *Faculty research:* Urban education, inquiry-based field study, theories of counseling and psychotherapy, school literacy, educational technology. Total annual research expenditures: $94,515. *Unit head:* Dr. Linda Edwards, Dean, 816-235-2236, Fax: 816-235-5270, E-mail: edwardsli@umkc.edu. *Application contact:* Dr. Lori Reesor, Assistant Dean, 816-235-1473, Fax: 816-235-5270, E-mail: reesorl@umkc.edu.

Education—General

University of Missouri–St. Louis, College of Education, St. Louis, MO 63121. Offers M Ed, Ed D, PhD, Certificate, Ed S. *Accreditation:* NCATE. Part-time and evening/weekend programs available. *Faculty:* 52 full-time (26 women), 9 part-time/adjunct (5 women). *Students:* 178 full-time (123 women), 927 part-time (685 women); includes 271 minority (233 African Americans, 2 American Indian/Alaska Native, 11 Asian Americans or Pacific Islanders, 25 Hispanic Americans), 15 international. Average age 37. In 2006, 247 master's, 16 doctorates, 40 other advanced degrees awarded. *Degree requirements:* For doctorate, thesis/dissertation. *Entrance requirements:* For doctorate, GRE General Test, 3 letters of recommendation. Additional exam requirements/recommendations for international students: Required—TOEFL (minimum score 550 paper-based; 213 computer-based). *Application deadline:* Applications are processed on a rolling basis. Application fee: $35 ($40 for international students). Electronic applications accepted. *Expenses:* Tuition, state resident: part-time $332 per credit hour. Tuition, nonresident: part-time $770 per credit hour. *Financial support:* In 2006–07, 24 research assistantships with full tuition reimbursements (averaging $11,161 per year), 9 teaching assistantships with full tuition reimbursements (averaging $14,200 per year) were awarded. Support available to part-time students. *Faculty research:* Remedial reading, literacy, educational policy and research, science education. *Unit head:* Dr. Kathleen Haywood, Director of Graduate Studies, 314-516-5483, Fax: 314-516-5227, E-mail: kathleen_haywood@umsl.edu. *Application contact:* 314-516-5458, Fax: 314-516-6996, E-mail: gradadm@umsl.edu.

University of Mobile, Graduate Programs, Program in Education, Mobile, AL 36613. Offers MA. Part-time programs available. *Faculty:* 7 full-time (4 women), 2 part-time/adjunct (0 women). *Students:* 30 full-time (29 women), 47 part-time (46 women); includes 45 minority (all African Americans) Average age 29. In 2006, 25 degrees awarded. *Degree requirements:* For master's, thesis optional. *Entrance requirements:* For master's, GRE, Alabama teaching certificate. Additional exam requirements/recommendations for international students: Required—TOEFL. *Application deadline:* For fall admission, 8/3 priority date for domestic students; for spring admission, 12/23 for domestic students. Applications are processed on a rolling basis. Application fee: $40 ($50 for international students). *Expenses:* Tuition: Part-time $340 per hour. Required fees: $121 per term. Tuition and fees vary according to course load. *Financial support:* Federal Work-Study available. Support available to part-time students. Financial award application deadline: 8/1. *Faculty research:* Retention, writing across the curriculum. *Unit head:* Dr. Peter Kingsford, Dean, School of Education, 251-442-2355, Fax: 251-442-2523, E-mail: pkingsford@mail.umobile.edu. *Application contact:* Dr. Kaye F. Brown, Associate Vice President for Academic Affairs, 251-442-2289, Fax: 251-442-2523, E-mail: kayeb@mail.umobile.edu.

The University of Montana, Graduate School, School of Education, Missoula, MT 59812-0002. Offers M Ed, MA, MS, Ed D, Ed S. *Accreditation:* NCATE. Part-time programs available. *Degree requirements:* For Ed S, thesis. *Entrance requirements:* For master's, GRE General Test, minimum GPA of 3.0; for Ed S, GRE General Test. Additional exam requirements/recommendations for international students: Required—TOEFL. *Faculty research:* Cooperative learning, administrative styles.

The University of Montana, Graduate School, School of Fine Arts, Department of Art, Missoula, MT 59812-0002. Offers fine arts (MA, MFA), including art (MA), art history (MA), ceramics (MFA), integrated arts and education (MA), media arts (MFA), painting and drawing (MFA), photography (MFA), printmaking (MFA), sculpture (MFA). *Accreditation:* NASAD (one or more programs are accredited). *Degree requirements:* For master's, thesis exhibit. *Entrance requirements:* For master's, GRE General Test, portfolio.

The University of Montana, Graduate School, School of Fine Arts, Department of Drama/Dance, Missoula, MT 59812-0002. Offers fine arts (MA, MFA), including acting (MFA), design/technology (MFA), directing (MFA), drama (MA), integrated arts and education (MA), media arts (MFA). *Accreditation:* NAST (one or more programs are accredited). *Degree requirements:* For master's, thesis or alternative. *Entrance requirements:* For master's, GRE General Test, audition, portfolio, production notebook.

University of Montevallo, College of Education, Montevallo, AL 35115. Offers M Ed, Ed S. *Accreditation:* NCATE. Part-time and evening/weekend programs available. *Degree requirements:* For master's, comprehensive exam. *Entrance requirements:* For master's, GRE General Test, MAT, minimum undergraduate GPA of 2.5. Additional exam requirements/recommendations for international students: Required—TOEFL (minimum score 550 paper-based).

University of Nebraska at Kearney, College of Graduate Study, College of Education, Kearney, NE 68849-0001. Offers MA Ed, MS Ed, Ed S. *Accreditation:* NCATE. Part-time and evening/weekend programs available. *Faculty:* 27 full-time (15 women). *Students:* 98 full-time (74 women), 471 part-time (311 women); includes 12 minority (2 African Americans, 1 Asian American or Pacific Islander, 9 Hispanic Americans), 16 international. 255 applicants, 69% accepted. In 2006, 210 master's, 18 other advanced degrees awarded. *Degree requirements:* For master's, thesis optional. *Entrance requirements:* For degree, GRE General Test. *Application deadline:* Applications are processed on a rolling basis. Application fee: $45. Electronic applications accepted. *Expenses:* Tuition, state resident: part-time $161 per hour. Tuition, nonresident: part-time $332 per hour. Required fees: $57 per hour. *Financial support:* In 2006–07, 22 research assistantships with full tuition reimbursements (averaging $8,200 per year), 11 teaching assistantships with full tuition reimbursements (averaging $8,200 per year) were awarded; career-related internships or fieldwork, scholarships/grants, and unspecified assistantships also available. Support available to part-time students. Financial award application deadline: 3/1; financial award applicants required to submit FAFSA. *Unit head:* Dr. Ed Scantling, Dean, 308-865-8502, E-mail: scantlinge@unk.edu.

University of Nebraska at Omaha, Graduate Studies and Research, College of Education, Omaha, NE 68182. Offers MA, MS, Ed D, Certificate, Ed S. *Accreditation:* NCATE. Part-time and evening/weekend programs available. *Faculty:* 56 full-time (28 women). *Students:* 148 full-time (109 women), 656 part-time (509 women); includes 54 minority (31 African Americans, 10 Asian Americans or Pacific Islanders, 13 Hispanic Americans), 9 international. Average age 32. 317 applicants, 66% accepted, 124 enrolled. In 2006, 273 master's, 6 doctorates, 5 other advanced degrees awarded. *Degree requirements:* For master's, thesis (for some programs), comprehensive exam; for doctorate, thesis/dissertation, comprehensive exam. *Entrance requirements:* For master's, minimum GPA of 3.0; for doctorate, GRE General Test, resumé, 3 samples of research/written work. Additional exam requirements/recommendations for international students: Required—TOEFL. *Application deadline:* For fall admission, 3/1 priority date for domestic students; for spring admission, 10/1 priority date for domestic students. Applications are processed on a rolling basis. Application fee: $45. *Financial support:* In 2006–07, 385 students received support; fellowships, research assistantships with tuition reimbursements available, teaching assistantships with tuition reimbursements available, career-related internships or fieldwork, Federal Work-Study, institutionally sponsored loans, scholarships/grants, tuition waivers (full), and unspecified assistantships available. Support available to part-time students. Financial award application deadline: 3/1; financial award applicants required to submit FAFSA. *Unit head:* Dr. John Langan, Chairperson, 402-554-2212.

University of Nebraska–Lincoln, Graduate College, College of Education and Human Services, Lincoln, NE 68588. Offers M Ed, MA, MPE, MS, MST, Ed D, PhD, Certificate, Ed S, JD/PhD. *Accreditation:* NCATE. *Degree requirements:* For doctorate, thesis/dissertation, comprehensive exam. *Entrance requirements:* Additional exam requirements/recommendations for international students: Required—TOEFL. Electronic applications accepted.

University of Nevada, Las Vegas, Graduate College, College of Education, Las Vegas, NV 89154-9900. Offers M Ed, MS, Ed D, PhD, Ed S. *Accreditation:* NCATE. Part-time and evening/weekend programs available. *Faculty:* 104 full-time (53 women), 66 part-time/adjunct (42 women). *Students:* 549 full-time (398 women), 888 part-time (642 women); includes 266 minority (97 African Americans, 8 American Indian/Alaska Native, 70 Asian Americans or Pacific Islanders, 91 Hispanic Americans), 31 international. 766 applicants, 67% accepted, 445 enrolled. In 2006, 492 master's, 30 doctorates, 17 other advanced degrees awarded. *Degree requirements:* For master's, comprehensive exam (for some programs); for doctorate, thesis/dissertation, oral exam. *Entrance requirements:* For doctorate, GRE General Test, minimum graduate GPA of 3.0. Additional exam requirements/recommendations for international students: Required—TOEFL (minimum score 550 paper-based; 213 computer-based; 80 iBT). Application fee: $60 ($75 for international students). Electronic applications accepted. *Financial support:* In 2006–07, 78 research assistantships with partial tuition reimbursements (averaging $10,400 per year), 25 teaching assistantships with partial tuition reimbursements (averaging $11,800 per year) were awarded; career-related internships or fieldwork, Federal Work-Study, institutionally sponsored loans, scholarships/grants, health care benefits, and unspecified assistantships also available. Support available to part-time students. Financial award application deadline: 3/1. *Unit head:* Dr. Jane McCarthy, Interim Dean, 702-895-9974. *Application contact:* Graduate College Admissions Evaluator, 702-895-3320, E-mail: gradcollege@unlv.edu.

University of Nevada, Reno, Graduate School, College of Education, Reno, NV 89557. Offers M Ed, MA, MS, Ed D, PhD, Ed S. *Accreditation:* NCATE. *Faculty:* 57. *Students:* 276 full-time (204 women), 434 part-time (337 women); includes 73 minority (9 African Americans, 9 American Indian/Alaska Native, 21 Asian Americans or Pacific Islanders, 34 Hispanic Americans), 31 international. Average age 36. 285 applicants, 84% accepted, 227 enrolled. In 2006, 117 master's, 19 doctorates, 5 other advanced degrees awarded. Terminal master's awarded for partial completion of doctoral program. *Degree requirements:* For master's, thesis optional; for doctorate, thesis/dissertation. *Entrance requirements:* For master's, GRE, minimum GPA of 2.75; for doctorate, GRE, minimum GPA of 3.0. Additional exam requirements/recommendations for international students: Required—TOEFL. Application fee: $60 ($95 for international students). *Financial support:* In 2006–07, 27 research assistantships with tuition reimbursements, 9 teaching assistantships with tuition reimbursements were awarded; Federal Work-Study, institutionally sponsored loans, and unspecified assistantships also available. Financial award application deadline: 3/1. *Unit head:* Dr. William E. Sparkman, Dean, 775-784-4345.

University of New Brunswick Fredericton, School of Graduate Studies, Faculty of Education, Fredericton, NB E3B 5A3, Canada. Offers M Ed, PhD. Part-time programs available. *Faculty:* 42 full-time (22 women). *Students:* 80 full-time (66 women), 190 part-time (161 women). In 2006, 101 master's, 4 doctorates awarded. *Entrance requirements:* For master's, minimum GPA of 3.0. Additional exam requirements/recommendations for international students: Required—TOEFL (minimum score 650 paper-based), TWE. *Application deadline:* 1/31 priority date for domestic and international students. Applications are processed on a rolling basis. Application fee: $50 Canadian dollars. *Financial support:* In 2006–07, 3 fellowships (averaging $4,500 per year), 27 research assistantships, 9 teaching assistantships were awarded; career-related internships or fieldwork also available. *Unit head:* Sharon Rich, Dean, 506-453-5018, Fax: 506-453-3569, E-mail: srich@unb.ca. *Application contact:* Carolyn King, Graduate Secretary, 506-458-7147, Fax: 506-453-3569, E-mail: kingc@unb.ca.

University of New England, College of Arts and Sciences, Program in Education, Biddeford, ME 04005-9526. Offers general studies (MS Ed); literacy (MS Ed); teaching methodologies (MS Ed). Part-time programs available. Postbaccalaureate distance learning degree programs offered (minimal on-campus study). *Faculty:* 4 full-time (2 women), 22 part-time/adjunct (13 women). *Students:* 12 full-time (9 women), 435 part-time (322 women); includes 11 minority (3 African Americans, 1 American Indian/Alaska Native, 3 Asian Americans or Pacific Islanders, 4 Hispanic Americans), 1 international. Average age 36. 148 applicants, 100% accepted, 116 enrolled. In 2006, 241 degrees awarded. *Degree requirements:* For master's, collaborative action research project, integrative seminar portfolio. *Entrance requirements:* For master's, teaching certificate, 2 years of teaching experience. Additional exam requirements/recommendations for international students: Required—TOEFL. *Application deadline:* For fall admission, 9/15 for domestic students; for spring admission, 1/15 for domestic students. Applications are processed on a rolling basis. Application fee: $40. Electronic applications accepted. *Expenses:* Contact institution. *Financial support:* Application deadline: 5/1; *Faculty research:* Distance learning, effective teaching, transition planning, adult learning. *Unit head:* Dr. Susan Hillman, Chair of Education Department, 207-283-0171 Ext. 2888, E-mail: shillman@une.edu. *Application contact:* Robert Pecchia, Associate Dean of Admissions, 207-283-0171 Ext. 2297, Fax: 207-602-5900, E-mail: admissions@une.edu.

University of New Hampshire, Graduate School, College of Liberal Arts, Department of Education, Durham, NH 03824. Offers counseling (M Ed, MA); early childhood education (M Ed), including early childhood education, special needs; education (PhD); educational administration (M Ed, CAGS); elementary education (M Ed, MAT); reading (M Ed); secondary education (M Ed, MAT); special education (M Ed); teacher leadership (M Ed). Part-time programs available. *Faculty:* 32 full-time. *Students:* 201 full-time (163 women), 293 part-time (217 women); includes 13 minority (3 African Americans, 1 American Indian/Alaska Native, 5 Asian Americans or Pacific Islanders, 4 Hispanic Americans), 2 international. Average age 31. 168 applicants, 82% accepted, 101 enrolled. In 2006, 232 master's, 2 doctorates, 4 other advanced degrees awarded. *Degree requirements:* For doctorate, thesis/dissertation. *Entrance requirements:* For master's, doctorate, and CAGS, GRE General Test. Additional exam requirements/recommendations for international students: Required—TOEFL (minimum score 550 paper-based; 213 computer-based). *Application deadline:* For fall admission, 4/1 priority date for domestic students, 4/1 for international students; for winter admission, 12/1 for domestic students; for spring admission, 4/1 priority date for domestic students. Applications are processed on a rolling basis. Application fee: $60. Electronic applications accepted. *Expenses:* Tuition, state resident: full-time $8,540; part-time $474 per credit hour. Tuition, nonresident: full-time $20,990; part-time $862 per credit hour. Required fees: $1,343; $356 per term. Tuition and fees vary according to course load, program and reciprocity agreements. *Financial support:* In 2006–07, 24 fellowships, 2 research assistantships, 20 teaching assistantships were awarded; career-related internships or fieldwork, Federal Work-Study, scholarships/grants, and tuition waivers (full and partial) also available. Support available to part-time students. Financial award application deadline: 2/15. *Unit head:* Dr. Scott Fletcher, Chairperson, 603-862-3445, E-mail: education.department@unh.edu. *Application contact:* Lisa Wilder, Graduate Coordinator, 603-862-2310, E-mail: education.department@unh.edu.

University of New Hampshire at Manchester, Center for Graduate and Professional Studies, Manchester, NH 03101-1113. Offers business administration (MBA); counseling (M Ed); education (M Ed, MAT); educational administration and supervision (M Ed, CAGS); industrial statistics (Certificate); public administration (MPA); public health (MPH, Certificate); social work (MSW).

University of New Haven, Graduate School, College of Arts and Sciences, Programs in Education, West Haven, CT 06516-1916. Offers MS.

University of New Mexico, Graduate School, College of Education, Department of Teacher Education, Albuquerque, NM 87131-2039. Offers MA, EDSPC. Part-time and evening/weekend programs available. *Faculty:* 19 full-time (12 women), 30 part-time/adjunct (29 women). *Students:* 85 full-time (44 women), 201 part-time (155 women); includes 89 minority (7 African Americans, 28 American Indian/Alaska Native, 4 Asian Americans or Pacific Islanders, 50 Hispanic Americans), 2 international. 120 applicants, 61% accepted, 60 enrolled. In 2006, 120 degrees awarded. *Degree requirements:* For master's, thesis optional. *Entrance requirements:* For master's, minimum overall GPA of 3.0, some experience working with students; for EDSPC, master's degree required, minimum overall GPA of 3.0, experience working with students. Additional exam requirements/recommendations for international students: Required—TOEFL (minimum score 550 paper-based; 213 computer-based). *Application deadline:* For fall admission, 3/1 for domestic students; for spring admission, 10/1 for domestic students. Applications are processed on a rolling basis. Application fee: $50. Electronic applications accepted. *Financial support:* In 2006–07, 4 teaching assistantships with partial tuition reimbursements (averaging $4,500 per year) were awarded; career-related internships or fieldwork, scholarships/grants, and unspecified assistantships also available. Financial award applicants required to submit FAFSA. Total annual research expenditures: $15,147. *Unit head:* Dr. Rosalita Mitchell, Chair, 505-277-9611, Fax: 505-277-0455, E-mail: rosalita@unm.edu. *Application contact:* Marianne OMeara, Application Contact, 505-277-0504, Fax: 505-277-0455, E-mail: momeara@unm.edu.

University of New Orleans, Graduate School, College of Education and Human Development, New Orleans, LA 70148. Offers M Ed, PhD, GCE. *Accreditation:* NCATE. Evening/weekend programs available. *Students:* 738 (592 women). Average age 39. In 2006, 163 master's, 18 doctorates awarded. Terminal master's awarded for partial completion of doctoral program. *Degree requirements:* For doctorate, thesis/dissertation. *Entrance requirements:* For master's and doctorate, GRE General Test. Additional exam requirements/recommendations for international students: Required—TOEFL (minimum score 550 paper-based; 213 computer-based). *Application deadline:* For fall admission, 7/1 priority date for domestic students, 6/1 for international students; for spring admission, 11/15 priority date for domestic students, 10/1 for international students. Applications are processed on a rolling basis. Application fee: $40. Electronic applications accepted. *Expenses:* Tuition, state resident: full-time $3,292. Tuition, nonresident: full-time $10,336. Required fees: $158. *Financial support:* Fellowships, research assistantships, teaching assistantships, career-related internships or fieldwork, institutionally sponsored loans, scholarships/grants, and tuition waivers (partial) available. Financial award application deadline: 3/15; financial award applicants required to submit FAFSA. *Faculty research:* Special education and habilitation, educational administration, exercise physiology, wellness, effective school instruction. Total annual research expenditures: $1.5 million. *Unit head:* Dr. James Meza, Dean, 504-280-6028, Fax: 504-280-6065, E-mail: jmeza@uno.edu. *Application contact:* Dr. William Sharpton, Associate Dean, 504-280-6253, Fax: 504-280-6065.

University of North Alabama, College of Education, Florence, AL 35632-0001. Offers MA, MA Ed, Ed S. *Accreditation:* NCATE. Part-time and evening/weekend programs available. *Faculty:* 6 full-time (3 women), 37 part-time/adjunct (19 women). *Students:* 100 full-time (69 women), 264 part-time (208 women); includes 34 minority (23 African Americans, 6 American Indian/Alaska Native, 3 Asian Americans or Pacific Islanders, 2 Hispanic Americans), 7 international. Average age 33. In 2006, 125 master's, 9 other advanced degrees awarded. *Degree requirements:* For master's, comprehensive exam. *Entrance requirements:* For master's, GRE, MAT, or NTE, minimum GPA of 2.5, Alabama Class B Certificate or equivalent, teaching experience. *Application deadline:* For fall admission, 7/1 priority date for domestic students; for spring admission, 12/1 for domestic students. Applications are processed on a rolling basis. Application fee: $25. Electronic applications accepted. *Expenses:* Tuition, state resident: full-time $4,080. Tuition, nonresident: full-time $8,160. Required fees: $764. *Financial support:* Federal Work-Study available. Support available to part-time students. Financial award application deadline: 4/1. *Unit head:* Dr. Donna Jacobs, Dean, 256-765-4252, Fax: 256-765-4664, E-mail: dpjacobs@una.edu. *Application contact:* Dr. Sue Wilson, Dean of Enrollment Management, 256-765-4316, Fax: 256-765-4349, E-mail: sjwilson@una.edu.

The University of North Carolina at Chapel Hill, Graduate School, School of Education, Chapel Hill, NC 27599. Offers M Ed, MA, MAT, MSA, Ed D, PhD. *Accreditation:* NCATE. Part-time programs available. *Faculty:* 59 full-time (32 women), 34 part-time/adjunct (17 women). In 2006, 118 master's, 30 doctorates awarded. *Median time to degree:* Of those who began their doctoral program in fall 1998, 69% received their degree in 8 years or less. *Degree requirements:* For master's, thesis (for some programs), comprehensive exam; for doctorate, thesis/dissertation, comprehensive exam, registration (for some programs). *Entrance requirements:* For master's and doctorate, GRE General Test, minimum GPA of 3.0 during last 2 years of undergraduate course work. Additional exam requirements/recommendations for international students: Required—TOEFL (minimum score 550 paper-based; 213 computer-based). *Application deadline:* For fall admission, 1/1 priority date for domestic and international students. Applications are processed on a rolling basis. Application fee: $60. Electronic applications accepted. *Financial support:* In 2006–07, 105 students received support, including 13 fellowships with full and partial tuition reimbursements available, 61 research assistantships with full and partial tuition reimbursements available, 26 teaching assistantships with full tuition reimbursements available; Federal Work-Study, traineeships, and unspecified assistantships also available. Support available to part-time students. Financial award application deadline: 3/1; financial award applicants required to submit FAFSA. *Faculty research:* Students with special needs, social and cultural studies, professional development/teacher education, policy studies, child and adolescent development, equity. Total annual research expenditures: $9.7 million. *Unit head:* Dr. Jill Fitzgerald, Interim Dean, 919-966-7000, Fax: 919-962-1533. *Application contact:* Janet Carroll, Registrar, 919-962-8690, Fax: 919-962-1533, E-mail: jscarrol@email.unc.edu.

The University of North Carolina at Charlotte, Graduate School, College of Education, Program in Teacher Education, Charlotte, NC 28223-0001. Offers art education (K-12) (MAT); dance education (K-12) (MAT); elementary education (K-6) (MAT); English as a second language (K-12) (MAT); foreign language education (K-12) (MAT); general teacher education (MAT); middle grades education (6-9) (MAT); music education (K-12) (MAT); secondary education (9-12) (MAT); special education (K-12) (MAT); theatre education (K-12) (MAT). *Students:* 16 full-time (12 women), 200 part-time (170 women); includes 30 minority (22 African Americans, 2 American Indian/Alaska Native, 2 Asian Americans or Pacific Islanders, 4 Hispanic Americans), 2 international. Average age 33. 74 applicants, 85% accepted, 49 enrolled. In 2006, 43 degrees awarded. *Entrance requirements:* For master's, GRE or MAT. Additional exam requirements/recommendations for international students: Required—TOEFL (minimum score 557 paper-based; 220 computer-based). *Application deadline:* For fall admission, 7/1 for domestic students, 5/1 for international students; for spring admission, 11/1 for domestic students, 10/1 for international students. Applications are processed on a rolling basis. Application fee: $55. Electronic applications accepted. *Expenses:* Tuition, state resident: full-time $2,719; part-time $170 per credit. Tuition, nonresident: full-time $12,926; part-time $808 per credit. Required fees: $1,555. *Financial support:* Fellowships, research assistantships, teaching assistantships, career-related internships or fieldwork, Federal Work-Study, institutionally sponsored loans, scholarships/grants, and unspecified assistantships available. Support available to part-time students. Financial award application deadline: 4/1; financial award applicants required to submit FAFSA. *Unit head:* Dr. Kimberly J. Hartman, Coordinator, 704-687-8883, Fax: 704-687-6430, E-mail: khartman@email.uncc.edu. *Application contact:* Kathy B. Giddings, Director of Graduate Admissions, 704-687-3366, Fax: 704-687-3279, E-mail: gradadm@email.uncc.edu.

The University of North Carolina at Greensboro, Graduate School, School of Education, Greensboro, NC 27412-5001. Offers M Ed, MLIS, MS, MSA, Ed D, PhD, Certificate, Ed S, PMC, MS/Ed S, MS/PhD. *Accreditation:* NCATE. Part-time and evening/weekend programs available. *Faculty:* 73 full-time (44 women), 33 part-time/adjunct (17 women). *Students:* 492 full-time (396 women), 551 part-time (453 women); includes 200 minority (163 African Americans, 4 American Indian/Alaska Native, 21 Asian Americans or Pacific Islanders, 12 Hispanic Americans). 780 applicants, 33% accepted. *Degree requirements:* For doctorate, thesis/dissertation. *Entrance requirements:* For master's, doctorate, and other advanced degree, GRE General Test. Additional exam requirements/recommendations for international students: Required—TOEFL. Application fee: $45. Electronic applications accepted. *Expenses:* Tuition, state resident: full-time $2,692. Tuition, nonresident: full-time $13,742. *Financial support:* Fellowships with full tuition reimbursements, research assistantships with full tuition reimbursements, teaching assistantships with full tuition reimbursements, career-related internships or fieldwork, institutionally sponsored loans, and unspecified assistantships available. *Faculty research:* Effects of homogeneous grouping, women in higher education, assessment of student achievement. *Unit head:* Dr. Dale Schunk, Dean, 336-334-3403, Fax: 336-334-4120, E-mail: dhschunk@uncg.edu. *Application contact:* Michelle Harkleroad, Director of Graduate Admissions, 336-334-4884, Fax: 336-334-4424, E-mail: mbharkle@uncg.edu.

The University of North Carolina at Pembroke, Graduate Studies, School of Education, Pembroke, NC 28372-1510. Offers elementary education (MA Ed); middle grades education (MA Ed, MAT); reading education (MA Ed); school administration (MSA). *Accreditation:* NCATE. Part-time and evening/weekend programs available. *Faculty:* 8 full-time (2 women), 1 part-time/adjunct (0 women). *Students:* 3 full-time (all women), 169 part-time (138 women); includes 42 minority (20 African Americans, 22 American Indian/Alaska Native). Average age 35. 172 applicants, 100% accepted, 172 enrolled. In 2006, 45 degrees awarded. *Degree requirements:* For master's, thesis optional. *Entrance requirements:* For master's, GRE General Test or MAT, minimum GPA of 3.0 in major, 2.5 overall. Additional exam requirements/recommendations for international students: Required—TOEFL. *Application deadline:* For fall admission, 7/15 priority date for domestic and international students; for spring admission, 12/1 priority date for domestic and international students. Applications are processed on a rolling basis. Application fee: $40. *Expenses:* Tuition, state resident: full-time $3,516; part-time $1,091 per semester. Tuition, nonresident: full-time $12,924; part-time $4,619 per semester. Tuition and fees vary according to class time, course load, degree level and campus/location. *Financial support:* In 2006–07, research assistantships with full tuition reimbursements (averaging $6,000 per year); career-related internships or fieldwork and unspecified assistantships also available. Support available to part-time students. Financial award application deadline: 4/15. *Unit head:* Dr. Zoe Locklear, Dean, 910-775-4041, Fax: 910-521-6165, E-mail: zoe.locklear@uncp.edu. *Application contact:* Dr. Kathleen C. Hilton, Dean of Graduate Studies, 910-521-6271, Fax: 910-521-6751, E-mail: grad@uncp.edu.

The University of North Carolina Wilmington, School of Education, Wilmington, NC 28403-3297. Offers M Ed, MAT, MS, MSA. *Accreditation:* NCATE. Part-time and evening/weekend programs available. *Faculty:* 34 full-time (18 women), 3 part-time/adjunct (2 women). *Students:* 69 full-time (51 women), 117 part-time (100 women); includes 14 minority (9 African Americans, 2 American Indian/Alaska Native, 3 Hispanic Americans), 1 international. Average age 37. 110 applicants, 69% accepted, 59 enrolled. In 2006, 84 degrees awarded. *Degree requirements:* For master's, comprehensive exam. *Entrance requirements:* For master's, GRE General Test, MAT, minimum B average in upper-division undergraduate course work. *Application deadline:* For fall admission, 6/1 for domestic students. Applications are processed on a rolling basis. Application fee: $45. *Financial support:* In 2006–07, 12 teaching assistantships were awarded; career-related internships or fieldwork, Federal Work-Study, and unspecified assistantships also available. Support available to part-time students. Financial award application deadline: 3/15. *Unit head:* Dr. Cathy L. Barlow, Dean, 910-962-3354, E-mail: barlowc@uncwil.edu. *Application contact:* Dr. Robert D. Roer, Dean, Graduate School, 910-962-4117, Fax: 910-962-3787, E-mail: roer@uncw.edu.

University of North Dakota, Graduate School, College of Education and Human Development, Grand Forks, ND 58202. Offers M Ed, MA, MS, MSW, Ed D, PhD, Specialist. *Accreditation:* NCATE. Part-time and evening/weekend programs available. Postbaccalaureate distance learning degree programs offered (minimal on-campus study). *Faculty:* 61 full-time (35 women), 7 part-time/adjunct (4 women). *Students:* 213 full-time (159 women), 488 part-time (364 women); includes 76 American Indian/Alaska Native, 4 Asian Americans or Pacific Islanders, 11 Hispanic Americans, 25 international. 254 applicants, 70% accepted, 123 enrolled. In 2006, 60 master's, 24 doctorates awarded. *Degree requirements:* For master's, thesis or alternative, comprehensive exam, registration; for doctorate, thesis/dissertation, comprehensive exam, registration. *Entrance requirements:* For master's, GRE General Test, MAT, GRE Subject Test, minimum GPA of 3.0; for doctorate, GRE Subject Test, minimum GPA of 3.5. Additional exam requirements/recommendations for international students: Required—TOEFL (minimum score 550 paper-based; 213 computer-based; 79 iBT), IELTS (minimum score 6). *Application deadline:* Applications are processed on a rolling basis. Application fee: $35. Electronic applications accepted. *Expenses:* Tuition, state resident: full-time $5,650; part-time $214 per credit. Tuition, nonresident: full-time $14,248; part-time $572 per credit. Required fees: $1,008; $42 per credit. Tuition and fees vary according to reciprocity agreements. *Financial support:* In 2006–07, 108 students received support, including 33 research assistantships with full tuition reimbursements available (averaging $7,232 per year), 60 teaching assistantships with full tuition reimbursements available (averaging $8,026 per year); fellowships, career-related internships or fieldwork, Federal Work-Study, institutionally sponsored loans, scholarships/grants, tuition waivers (full and partial), and unspecified assistantships also available. Support available to part-time students. Financial award application deadline: 3/15; financial award applicants required to submit FAFSA. Total annual research expenditures: $2.6 million. *Unit head:* Dr. Dan R. Rice, Dean, 701-777-4255, Fax: 701-777-4393, E-mail: dan.rice@mail.und.nodak.edu.

University of Northern British Columbia, Office of Graduate Studies, Prince George, BC V2N 4Z9, Canada. Offers business administration (Diploma); community health science (M Sc); disability management (MA); education (M Ed); first nations studies (MA); gender studies (MA); history (MA); interdisciplinary studies (MA); international studies (MA); mathematical, computer and physical sciences (M Sc); natural resources and environmental studies (M Sc, MA, MNRES, PhD); political science (MA); psychology (M Sc, PhD); social work (MSW). Part-time and evening/weekend programs available. Postbaccalaureate distance learning degree programs offered (no on-campus study). *Degree requirements:* For master's and doctorate, thesis/dissertation. *Entrance requirements:* For master's, GRE, minimum B average in undergraduate course work; for doctorate, candidacy exam, minimum A average in graduate course work.

University of Northern Colorado, Graduate School, College of Education and Behavioral Sciences, Greeley, CO 80639. Offers MA, MAT, MS, Ed D, PhD, Psy D, Ed S. *Accreditation:* NCATE. Part-time programs available. Postbaccalaureate distance learning degree programs offered. *Faculty:* 65 full-time (35 women). *Students:* 453 full-time (331 women), 272 part-time (200 women); includes 64 minority (11 African Americans, 5 American Indian/Alaska Native, 13 Asian Americans or Pacific Islanders, 35 Hispanic Americans), 24 international. Average age 35. 311 applicants, 79% accepted, 115 enrolled. In 2006, 387 master's, 27 doctorates, 34 other advanced degrees awarded. *Degree requirements:* For master's, thesis optional; for doctorate and Ed S, thesis/dissertation, comprehensive exam. *Entrance requirements:* For doctorate, GRE General Test. *Application deadline:* Applications are processed on a rolling basis. Application fee: $50 ($60 for international students). *Expenses:* Tuition, state resident: full-time $5,118; part-time $213 per credit hour. Tuition, nonresident: full-time $14,832; part-time $618 per credit hour. Required fees: $674; $34 per credit hour. *Financial support:* In 2006–07, 554 students received support, including 49 fellowships (averaging $1,789 per year), 76 research assistantships (averaging $11,856 per year), 42 teaching assistantships (averaging $10,310 per year); unspecified assistantships also available. Financial award application deadline: 3/1; financial award applicants required to submit FAFSA. *Unit head:* Dr. Eugene P. Sheehan, Dean, 970-351-2817, Fax: 970-351-2312, E-mail: coeinfo@unco.edu.

University of Northern Colorado, Graduate School, College of Education and Behavioral Sciences, School of Teacher Education, Interdisciplinary Studies Program, Greeley, CO 80639. Offers MA. Part-time programs available. *Faculty:* 1 (woman) full-time. *Students:* 3 full-time (2 women), 25 part-time (20 women); includes 4 minority (all Hispanic Americans) Average age 37. 5 applicants, 100% accepted, 2 enrolled. *Degree requirements:* For master's, comprehensive exam. *Application deadline:* Applications are processed on a rolling basis. Application fee: $50 ($60 for international students). *Expenses:* Tuition, state resident: full-time $5,118; part-time $213 per credit hour. Tuition, nonresident: full-time $14,832; part-time $618 per credit hour. Required fees: $674; $34 per credit hour. *Financial support:* In 2006–07, 28 students received support, including 1 research assistantship (averaging $15,541 per year); fellowships, teaching assistantships also available. Financial award application deadline: 3/1; financial award applicants required to submit FAFSA. *Application contact:* Dr. Madeline Milian, Program Coordinator, 970-351-2908.

University of Northern Iowa, Graduate College, College of Education, Cedar Falls, IA 50614. Offers MA, MAE, Ed D, Ed S. Part-time and evening/weekend programs available. *Students:* 211 full-time (140 women), 403 part-time (291 women); includes 56 minority (42 African Americans, 2 American Indian/Alaska Native, 4 Asian Americans or Pacific Islanders, 8 Hispanic Americans), 40 international. 327 applicants, 70% accepted, 175 enrolled. In 2006, 156 master's, 15 doctorates, 7 other advanced degrees awarded. *Degree requirements:* For Ed S, thesis or alternative. *Entrance requirements:* For master's, 3 years of educational experience,

Education—General

University of Northern Iowa (continued)
minimum GPA of 3.5; for doctorate, GRE, 3 years of educational experience, master's degree, minimum GPA of 3.2; for Ed S, GRE General Test, GRE Subject Test. Additional exam requirements/recommendations for international students: Required—TOEFL (minimum score 500 paper-based; 180 computer-based; 61 iBT). *Application deadline:* For fall admission, 8/1 priority date for domestic students. Applications are processed on a rolling basis. Application fee: $30 ($50 for international students). Electronic applications accepted. *Expenses:* Tuition, state resident: full-time $5,936. Tuition, nonresident: full-time $14,074. *Financial support:* Career-related internships or fieldwork, Federal Work-Study, institutionally sponsored loans, scholarships/grants, and tuition waivers (full and partial) available. Support available to part-time students. Financial award application deadline: 2/1. *Unit head:* Dr. Jeffrey Cornett, Dean, 319-273-2717, Fax: 319-273-2607, E-mail: jeffrey.cornett@uni.edu.

University of North Florida, College of Education and Human Services, Jacksonville, FL 32224-2645. Offers M Ed, Ed D. *Accreditation:* NCATE. Part-time and evening/weekend programs available. *Faculty:* 57 full-time (32 women). *Students:* 132 full-time (114 women), 357 part-time (270 women); includes 121 minority (92 African Americans, 2 American Indian/Alaska Native, 7 Asian Americans or Pacific Islanders, 20 Hispanic Americans), 7 international. Average age 36. 245 applicants, 49% accepted, 97 enrolled. In 2006, 174 master's, 13 doctorates awarded. Terminal master's awarded for partial completion of doctoral program. *Degree requirements:* For doctorate, thesis/dissertation. *Entrance requirements:* For master's, GRE General Test, minimum GPA of 3.0 in last 60 hours, interview, 3 letters of recommendation; for doctorate, GRE General Test, master's degree, interview, writing sample, 3 letters of recommendation. Additional exam requirements/recommendations for international students: Required—TOEFL (minimum score 500 paper-based; 173 computer-based). *Application deadline:* For fall admission, 7/1 priority date for domestic students, 5/1 for international students; for spring admission, 11/1 priority date for domestic students, 10/1 for international students. Applications are processed on a rolling basis. Application fee: $30. Electronic applications accepted. *Expenses:* Tuition, state resident: full-time $4,948; part-time $206 per semester hour. Tuition, nonresident: full-time $19,140; part-time $408 per semester hour. *Financial support:* In 2006–07, 170 students received support, including 3 teaching assistantships (averaging $3,004 per year); research assistantships, career-related internships or fieldwork, Federal Work-Study, scholarships/grants, and tuition waivers (partial) also available. Support available to part-time students. Financial award application deadline: 4/1; financial award applicants required to submit FAFSA. *Faculty research:* Effective instruction, technology education, exceptional student education, multiculturalism. Total annual research expenditures: $564,171. *Unit head:* Dr. Larry Daniel, Dean, 904-620-2520, E-mail: ldaniel@unf.edu. *Application contact:* Dr. John Kemppainen, Director, Office of Student Services, 904-620-2530, Fax: 904-620-1135, E-mail: jkemppai@unf.edu.

University of North Texas, Robert B. Toulouse School of Graduate Studies, College of Education, Denton, TX 76203. Offers M Ed, MS, Ed D, PhD, Certificate. *Accreditation:* NCATE. Part-time and evening/weekend programs available. *Faculty:* 124 full-time (68 women). *Students:* 358 full-time (271 women), 1,208 part-time (893 women); includes 347 minority (184 African Americans, 16 American Indian/Alaska Native, 32 Asian Americans or Pacific Islanders, 115 Hispanic Americans), 65 international. Average age 34. 615 applicants, 62% accepted, 233 enrolled. In 2006, 448 master's, 61 doctorates awarded. Terminal master's awarded for partial completion of doctoral program. *Degree requirements:* For doctorate, thesis/dissertation. *Entrance requirements:* For master's and doctorate, GRE General Test. Additional exam requirements/recommendations for international students: Recommended—TOEFL (minimum score 550 paper-based; 213 computer-based). *Application deadline:* For fall admission, 7/15 for domestic students; for spring admission, 11/15 for domestic students. Application fee: $50 ($75 for international students). *Expenses:* Tuition, state resident: full-time $3,573; part-time $198 per credit. Tuition, nonresident: full-time $8,577; part-time $476 per credit. Required fees: $1,258; $126 per credit. One-time fee: $150 full-time. Tuition and fees vary according to course load. *Financial support:* Fellowships, research assistantships, teaching assistantships, career-related internships or fieldwork, Federal Work-Study, institutionally sponsored loans, and tuition waivers (partial) available. Support available to part-time students. Financial award application deadline: 4/1. *Faculty research:* Teacher competency, educational measurement, higher education, biological and chemical bases of learning, technology in the classroom. *Unit head:* Dr. Jean Keller, Dean, 940-565-2233, Fax: 940-565-4415, E-mail: jkeller@unt.edu.

University of Notre Dame, Graduate School, College of Arts and Letters, Division of Social Science, Institute for Educational Initiatives, Notre Dame, IN 46556. Offers M Ed. Enrollment restricted to participants in the Alliance for Catholic Education (ACE) program. *Students:* 162 full-time (85 women); includes 22 minority (4 African Americans, 4 Asian Americans or Pacific Islanders, 14 Hispanic Americans), 5 international. In 2006, 88 degrees awarded. *Entrance requirements:* For master's, GRE General Test, acceptance into the Alliance for Catholic Education program. *Application deadline:* For fall admission, 1/23 for domestic students. Electronic applications accepted. *Financial support:* In 2006–07, 162 students received support; fellowships with full tuition reimbursements available, scholarships/grants available. *Faculty research:* Effective teaching, motivation, social and ethical development, literacy. *Unit head:* Dr. Joyce Johnstone, Academic Director, Alliance for Catholic Education, 574-631-3165, Fax: 574-631-3606, E-mail: nd.iei.1@nd.edu. *Application contact:* Dr. John J. Staud, Administrative Director of the Alliance for Catholic Education, 574-631-7052, E-mail: ace@nd.edu.

University of Oklahoma, Graduate College, College of Education, Department of Educational Leadership and Policy Studies, Norman, OK 73019-0390. Offers adult and higher education (M Ed, PhD); educational administration, curriculum and supervision (M Ed, Ed D, PhD); educational studies (M Ed, PhD); historical, philosophical, and social foundations of education (M Ed, PhD). *Accreditation:* NCATE. Part-time programs available. *Faculty:* 41 full-time (21 women), 29 part-time/adjunct (14 women). *Students:* 101 full-time (67 women), 208 part-time (133 women); includes 87 minority (44 African Americans, 31 American Indian/Alaska Native, 2 Asian Americans or Pacific Islanders, 10 Hispanic Americans), 4 international. 62 applicants, 89% accepted, 36 enrolled. In 2006, 84 master's, 16 doctorates awarded. Terminal master's awarded for partial completion of doctoral program. *Degree requirements:* For master's, comprehensive exam; for doctorate, thesis/dissertation, general exam. *Entrance requirements:* For master's, 12 hours of course work in education; for doctorate, GRE General Test, master's degree, minimum graduate GPA of 3.25. Additional exam requirements/recommendations for international students: Required—TOEFL (minimum score 550 paper-based; 213 computer-based). *Application deadline:* For fall admission, 6/1 for domestic students, 4/1 for international students; for spring admission, 10/1 for domestic students, 9/1 for international students. Application fee: $40 ($90 for international students). *Expenses:* Tuition, state resident: full-time $3,180; part-time $133 per credit hour. Tuition, nonresident: full-time $11,347; part-time $473 per credit hour. Required fees: $1,729; $62 per credit hour. $117 per semester. Tuition and fees vary according to course load and program. *Financial support:* In 2006–07, 150 students received support, including 31 research assistantships with partial tuition reimbursements available (averaging $9,581 per year), 1 teaching assistantship with partial tuition reimbursement available (averaging $9,900 per year); Federal Work-Study, institutionally sponsored loans, and tuition waivers (full) also available. Financial award applicants required to submit FAFSA. Total annual research expenditures: $869,594. *Unit head:* Dr. Grayson B. Noley, Chair, 405-325-4202, Fax: 405-325-2403, E-mail: gnoley@ou.edu. *Application contact:* Geri Evans, Programs Officer, 405-325-5978, Fax: 405-325-2403, E-mail: gevans@ou.edu.

University of Oregon, Graduate School, College of Education, Eugene, OR 97403. Offers M Ed, MA, MS, D Ed, PhD. Part-time programs available. *Faculty:* 107 full-time (70 women), 76 part-time/adjunct (55 women). *Students:* 465 full-time (350 women), 211 part-time (132 women); includes 84 minority (9 African Americans, 16 American Indian/Alaska Native, 22 Asian Americans or Pacific Islanders, 37 Hispanic Americans), 72 international. 390 applicants, 32% accepted. In 2006, 225 master's, 25 doctorates awarded. Terminal master's awarded for partial completion of doctoral program. *Degree requirements:* For master's, exam, paper, or project; for doctorate, thesis/dissertation, comprehensive exam. *Entrance requirements:* Additional exam requirements/recommendations for international students: Required—TOEFL. Application fee: $50. *Financial support:* In 2006–07, 86 teaching assistantships were awarded; fellowships, research assistantships, career-related internships or fieldwork, Federal Work-Study, institutionally sponsored loans, and tuition waivers (full) also available. *Faculty research:* Basic and applied research in teaching, learning and habilitation in all settings, schooling effectiveness. *Unit head:* Michael Bullis, Dean, 541-346-1396. *Application contact:* Ron Tuomi, Admissions Contact, 541-346-3528, Fax: 541-346-5818, E-mail: rtuomi@uoregon.edu.

University of Ottawa, Faculty of Graduate and Postdoctoral Studies, Faculty of Education, Ottawa, ON K1N 6N5, Canada. Offers M Ed, MA Ed, PhD, Certificate. Postbaccalaureate distance learning degree programs offered (minimal on-campus study). *Degree requirements:* For master's, thesis or alternative; for doctorate, thesis/dissertation, seminar, comprehensive exam. *Entrance requirements:* For master's, honors degree or equivalent, minimum B average; for doctorate, master's degree, minimum B+ average. Electronic applications accepted. *Faculty research:* Teaching, learning and evaluation; second language education; organizational studies in education; society, culture and literacies; educational counseling.

University of Pennsylvania, Graduate School of Education, Philadelphia, PA 19104. Offers MS Ed, Ed D, PhD, DMD/MS Ed. Part-time programs available. Terminal master's awarded for partial completion of doctoral program. *Degree requirements:* For master's, exam; for doctorate, thesis/dissertation, exam. *Entrance requirements:* For master's, GRE. Electronic applications accepted. Expenses: Contact institution.

See Close-Up on page 933.

University of Phoenix–Bay Area Campus, The Artemis School, College of Education, Pleasanton, CA 94588-3677. Offers curriculum instruction (MA Ed); curriculum instruction—adult education (MA Ed). Evening/weekend programs available. *Faculty:* 11 full-time (3 women), 100 part-time/adjunct (52 women). *Students:* 227 full-time (156 women); includes 50 minority (15 African Americans, 2 American Indian/Alaska Native, 19 Asian Americans or Pacific Islanders, 14 Hispanic Americans), 22 international. Average age 36. In 2006, 115 degrees awarded. *Degree requirements:* For master's, thesis (for some programs), registration. *Entrance requirements:* For master's, minimum undergraduate GPA of 2.5, 3 years of work experience. Additional exam requirements/recommendations for international students: Required—TOEFL (minimum score 550 paper-based; 213 computer-based; 79 iBT). *Application deadline:* Applications are processed on a rolling basis. Application fee: $45. Electronic applications accepted. *Expenses:* Tuition: Full-time $12,648. Required fees: $760. *Financial support:* Institutionally sponsored loans and scholarships/grants available. Financial award applicants required to submit FAFSA. *Unit head:* Dr. Marla LaRue, Dean/Executive Director, 480-557-1218, E-mail: marla.larue@phoenix.edu. *Application contact:* Chair, 408-435-8500, Fax: 408-435-8250.

University of Phoenix–Central Florida Campus, The Artemis School, College of Education, Maitland, FL 32751-7057. Offers administration and supervision (MA Ed); curriculum and instruction (MA Ed); elementary teacher education (MA Ed); secondary teacher education (MA Ed). Evening/weekend programs available. *Faculty:* 10 full-time (9 women), 16 part-time/adjunct (6 women). *Students:* 20 full-time (18 women); includes 5 minority (3 African Americans, 2 Hispanic Americans), 1 international. Average age 38. In 2006, 7 degrees awarded. *Degree requirements:* For master's, thesis (for some programs), registration. *Entrance requirements:* For master's, 3 years of work experience, minimum undergraduate GPA of 2.5. Additional exam requirements/recommendations for international students: Required—TOEFL (minimum score 550 paper-based; 213 computer-based; 79 iBT). *Application deadline:* Applications are processed on a rolling basis. Application fee: $45. Electronic applications accepted. *Expenses:* Tuition: Full-time $9,450. Required fees: $760. *Financial support:* Institutionally sponsored loans and scholarships/grants available. Financial award applicants required to submit FAFSA. *Unit head:* Dr. Marla LaRue, Dean/Executive Director, 480-557-1218. *Application contact:* Chair, 407-667-0555, Fax: 407-667-0560.

University of Phoenix–Central Massachusetts Campus, The Artemis School, College of Education, Westborough, MA 01581-3906. Offers MA Ed. Evening/weekend programs available. *Students:* Average age 24. *Degree requirements:* For master's, thesis (for some programs), registration. *Entrance requirements:* For master's, minimum undergraduate GPA of 2.5, 3 years of work experience. Additional exam requirements/recommendations for international students: Required—TOEFL (minimum score 550 paper-based; 213 computer-based; 79 iBT). *Application deadline:* Applications are processed on a rolling basis. Application fee: $45. Electronic applications accepted. *Expenses:* Tuition: Full-time $13,848. Required fees: $760. *Financial support:* Institutionally sponsored loans and scholarships/grants available. Financial award applicants required to submit FAFSA. *Unit head:* Dr. Marla LaRue, Dean/Executive Director, 480-557-1218, E-mail: marla.larue@phoenix.edu.

University of Phoenix–Central Valley Campus, College of Education, Fresno, CA 93720. Offers curriculum and instruction (MA Ed); elementary teacher education (MA Ed); secondary teacher education (MA Ed).

University of Phoenix–Denver Campus, The Artemis School, College of Education, Lone Tree, CO 80124-5453. Offers administration and supervision (MAEd); curriculum instruction (MAEd); elementary teacher education (MAEd); school counseling (MSC); secondary teacher education (MAEd). Evening/weekend programs available. *Faculty:* 19 full-time (14 women), 141 part-time/adjunct (84 women). *Students:* 738 full-time (513 women); includes 72 minority (27 African Americans, 4 American Indian/Alaska Native, 9 Asian Americans or Pacific Islanders, 32 Hispanic Americans), 66 international. Average age 37. In 2006, 435 master's awarded. *Degree requirements:* For master's, thesis (for some programs), registration. *Entrance requirements:* For master's, minimum undergraduate GPA of 2.5, 3 years work experience. Additional exam requirements/recommendations for international students: Required—TOEFL (minimum score 550 paper-based; 213 computer-based; 79 iBT). *Application deadline:* Applications are processed on a rolling basis. Application fee: $45. Electronic applications accepted. *Expenses:* Tuition: Full-time $10,032. Required fees: $760. *Financial support:* Institutionally sponsored loans and scholarships/grants available. Financial award applicants required to submit FAFSA. *Unit head:* Dr. Marla LaRue, Dean/Executive Director, 480-557-1218, E-mail: marla.larue@phoenix.edu. *Application contact:* Chair, 303-694-9093, Fax: 303-662-0911.

University of Phoenix–Fort Lauderdale Campus, The Artemis School, College of Education, Fort Lauderdale, FL 33309. Offers administration and supervision (MA Ed); computer education (MA Ed); curriculum and instruction (MA Ed); elementary teacher education (MA Ed); secondary teacher education (MA Ed). Evening/weekend programs available. *Faculty:* 10 full-time (5 women), 17 part-time/adjunct (7 women). *Students:* 132 full-time (114 women); includes 60 minority (52 African Americans, 1 Asian American or Pacific Islander, 7 Hispanic Americans), 5 international. Average age 39. In 2006, 25 degrees awarded. *Degree requirements:* For master's, thesis (for some programs), registration. *Entrance requirements:* For master's, 3 years of work experience, minimum undergraduate GPA of 2.5. Additional exam requirements/recommendations for international students: Required—TOEFL (minimum score 550 paper-based; 213 computer-based; 79 iBT). *Application deadline:* Applications are processed on a rolling basis. Application fee: $45. Electronic applications accepted. *Expenses:* Tuition: Full-time $9,450. Required fees: $760. *Financial support:* Institutionally sponsored loans and scholarships/grants available. Financial award applicants required to submit FAFSA. *Unit head:* Dr. Marla LaRue, Dean/Executive Director, 480-557-1218. *Application contact:* Chair, 954-382-5303, Fax: 954-382-5304.

University of Phoenix–Hawaii Campus, The Artemis School, College of Education, Honolulu, HI 96813-4317. Offers administration and supervision (MA Ed); curriculum and instruction (MA Ed); elementary education (MA Ed); secondary education (MA Ed); teacher education for elementary licensure (MA Ed). Evening/weekend programs available. *Faculty:* 10 full-time (7 women), 58 part-time/adjunct (34 women). *Students:* 261 full-time (176 women); includes 61 minority (1 African American, 1 American Indian/Alaska Native, 53 Asian Americans or Pacific

Islanders, 6 Hispanic Americans), 106 international. Average age 36. In 2006, 151 degrees awarded. *Degree requirements:* For master's, thesis (for some programs), registration. *Entrance requirements:* For master's, minimum undergraduate GPA of 2.5, 3 years of work experience. Additional exam requirements/recommendations for international students: Required—TOEFL (minimum score 550 paper-based; 213 computer-based; 79 iBT). *Application deadline:* Applications are processed on a rolling basis. Application fee: $45. Electronic applications accepted. *Expenses:* Tuition: Full-time $11,520. Required fees: $760. *Financial support:* Institutionally sponsored loans and scholarships/grants available. Financial award applicants required to submit FAFSA. *Unit head:* Dr. Marla LaRue, Dean/Executive Director, 480-557-1309, E-mail: marla.larue@phoenix.edu. *Application contact:* Chair, 580-536-2686, Fax: 808-536-3848.

University of Phoenix–Idaho Campus, The Artemis School, College of Education, Meridian, ID 83642-3014. Offers MA Ed. Evening/weekend programs available. *Faculty:* 7 part-time/adjunct (3 women). *Students:* 20 full-time (8 women); includes 1 Asian American or Pacific Islander. Average age 39. In 2006, 1 degree awarded. *Degree requirements:* For master's, thesis (for some programs), registration. *Entrance requirements:* For master's, minimum undergraduate GPA of 2.5, 3 years of work experience. Additional exam requirements/recommendations for international students: Required—TOEFL (minimum score 550 paper-based; 213 computer-based). *Application deadline:* Applications are processed on a rolling basis. Application fee: $45. Electronic applications accepted. *Expenses:* Tuition: Full-time $9,104. *Financial support:* Institutionally sponsored loans and scholarships/grants available. *Unit head:* Dr. Marla LaRue, Dean/Executive Director, 480-557-1218, E-mail: marla.larue@phoenix.edu. *Application contact:* College Chair, 208-888-1505, Fax: 208-888-4775.

University of Phoenix–Kansas City Campus, The Artemis School, College of Education, Kansas City, MO 64131-4517. Offers MA Ed. *Expenses:* Tuition: Full-time $11,064. Required fees: $760. *Unit head:* Dr. Marla LaRue, Dean/Executive Director, 480-557-1218.

University of Phoenix–Las Vegas Campus, The Artemis School, College of Education, Las Vegas, NV 89128. Offers administration and supervision (MA Ed); curriculum and instruction (MA Ed); school counseling (MSC); teacher education-elementary licensure (MA Ed). Evening/weekend programs available. *Faculty:* 9 full-time (8 women), 45 part-time/adjunct (27 women). *Students:* 494 full-time (388 women); includes 105 minority (51 African Americans, 2 American Indian/Alaska Native, 18 Asian Americans or Pacific Islanders, 34 Hispanic Americans), 9 international. Average age 35. In 2006, 227 degrees awarded. *Degree requirements:* For master's, thesis (for some programs), registration. *Entrance requirements:* For master's, minimum undergraduate GPA of 2.5, 3 years of work experience. Additional exam requirements/recommendations for international students: Required—TOEFL (minimum score 550 paper-based; 213 computer-based; 79 iBT). *Application deadline:* Applications are processed on a rolling basis. Application fee: $45. Electronic applications accepted. *Expenses:* Tuition: Full-time $9,576. Required fees: $760. *Financial support:* Institutionally sponsored loans and scholarships/grants available. Financial award applicants required to submit FAFSA. *Unit head:* Dr. Marla LaRue, Dean/Executive Director, 480-557-1218, E-mail: marla.larue@phoenix.edu. *Application contact:* Chair, 702-638-7249, Fax: 702-638-8085.

University of Phoenix–Louisiana Campus, The Artemis School, College of Education, Metairie, LA 70001-2082. Offers early childhood education (MA Ed). *Degree requirements:* For master's, thesis, registration (for some programs). *Entrance requirements:* For master's, minimum undergraduate GPA of 2.5, 3 years work experience. Additional exam requirements/recommendations for international students: Required—TOEFL (minimum score 550 paper-based; 213 computer-based; 79 iBT). Application fee: $45. *Expenses:* Tuition: Full-time $11,832. Required fees: $760. *Financial support:* Institutionally sponsored loans and scholarships/grants available. *Unit head:* Dr. Marla LaRue, Dean/Executive Director, 480-557-1218, E-mail: marla.larue@phoenix.edu. *Application contact:* Chair, 504-461-8852, Fax: 504-464-6373.

University of Phoenix–Memphis Campus, College of Education, Cordova, TN 38018. Offers curriculum and instruction (MA Ed).

University of Phoenix–Metro Detroit Campus, The Artemis School, College of Education, Troy, MI 48098-2623. Offers administration and supervision (MA Ed); adult education and distance learning (MA Ed); curriculum and development (MA Ed); special education (MA Ed); teacher education elementary (MA Ed). Evening/weekend programs available. *Faculty:* 8 full-time (3 women), 27 part-time/adjunct (21 women). *Students:* 102 full-time (75 women); includes 59 minority (57 African Americans, 1 American Indian/Alaska Native, 1 Asian American or Pacific Islander), 1 international. Average age 40. In 2006, 30 master's awarded. *Degree requirements:* For master's, thesis (for some programs), registration. *Entrance requirements:* For master's, 3 years of work experience, minimum undergraduate GPA of 2.5. Additional exam requirements/recommendations for international students: Required—TOEFL (minimum score 550 paper-based; 213 computer-based; 79 iBT). *Application deadline:* Applications are processed on a rolling basis. Application fee: $45. Electronic applications accepted. *Expenses:* Tuition: Full-time $12,168. Required fees: $760. *Financial support:* Institutionally sponsored loans and scholarships/grants available. Financial award applicants required to submit FAFSA. *Unit head:* Dr. Marla LaRue, Dean/Executive Director, 480-557-1218. *Application contact:* Chair, 800-834-2438, Fax: 248-267-0147.

University of Phoenix–Nashville Campus, The Artemis School, College of Education, Nashville, TN 37214-5048. Offers administration and supervision (MA Ed); curriculum and instruction (MA Ed); elementary teacher education (MA Ed); secondary teacher education (MA Ed). Evening/weekend programs available. *Degree requirements:* For master's, thesis (for some programs), registration. *Entrance requirements:* For master's, minimum undergraduate GPA of 2.5, 3 years work experience. Additional exam requirements/recommendations for international students: Required—TOEFL (minimum score 500 paper-based; 213 computer-based; 79 iBT). *Application deadline:* Applications are processed on a rolling basis. Application fee: $45. Electronic applications accepted. *Expenses:* Tuition: Full-time $10,104. Required fees: $760. *Financial support:* Institutionally sponsored loans and scholarships/grants available. Financial award applicants required to submit FAFSA. *Unit head:* Dr. Marla LaRue, Dean/Executive Director, 480-557-1218, E-mail: marla.larue@phoenix.edu. *Application contact:* Chair, 615-872-0188.

University of Phoenix–New Mexico Campus, The Artemis School, College of Education, Albuquerque, NM 87109-4645. Offers administration (MAEd); curriculum and instruction (MAEd); teacher education (MAEd), including elementary, secondary. Evening/weekend programs available. *Faculty:* 9 full-time (5 women), 62 part-time/adjunct (40 women). *Students:* 234 full-time (181 women); includes 116 minority (5 African Americans, 1 Asian American or Pacific Islander, 110 Hispanic Americans), 10 international. Average age 39. In 2006, 131 degrees awarded. *Degree requirements:* For master's, thesis (for some programs), registration. *Entrance requirements:* For master's, minimum undergraduate GPA of 2.5, 3 years of work experience. Additional exam requirements/recommendations for international students: Required—TOEFL (minimum score 550 paper-based; 213 computer-based; 79 iBT). *Application deadline:* Applications are processed on a rolling basis. Application fee: $45. Electronic applications accepted. *Expenses:* Tuition: Full-time $9,005. Required fees: $760. *Financial support:* Institutionally sponsored loans and scholarships/grants available. Financial award applicants required to submit FAFSA. *Unit head:* Dr. Marla LaRue, Dean/Executive Director, 480-557-1218, E-mail: marla.larue@phoenix.edu. *Application contact:* Chair, 505-821-4800, Fax: 505-821-5551.

University of Phoenix—Northern Nevada Campus, College of Education, Reno, NV 89511. Offers administration and supervision (MA Ed); elementary teacher educatino (MA Ed).

University of Phoenix–Northern Virginia Campus, College of Education, Reston, VA 20190. Offers administration and supervision (MA Ed).

University of Phoenix–North Florida Campus, The Artemis School, College of Education, Jacksonville, FL 32216-0959. Offers administration (MA Ed); curriculum and instruction (MA Ed); curriculum and instruction—computer education (MA Ed); elementary teacher education (MA Ed); secondary teacher education (MA Ed). Evening/weekend programs available. *Faculty:* 9 full-time (5 women), 10 part-time/adjunct (4 women). *Students:* 98 full-time (78 women); includes 41 minority (37 African Americans, 4 Hispanic Americans), 1 international. Average age 37. In 2006, 22 master's awarded. *Degree requirements:* For master's, thesis (for some programs), registration. *Entrance requirements:* For master's, 3 years of work experience, minimum undergraduate GPA of 2.5. Additional exam requirements/recommendations for international students: Required—TOEFL (minimum score 550 paper-based; 213 computer-based; 49 iBT). *Application deadline:* Applications are processed on a rolling basis. Application fee: $45. Electronic applications accepted. *Financial support:* Institutionally sponsored loans and scholarships/grants available. Financial award applicants required to submit FAFSA. *Unit head:* Dr. Marla LaRue, Dean, 480-557-1218, E-mail: marla.larue@phoenix.edu. *Application contact:* Chair, 904-636-6645, Fax: 904-636-0998.

University of Phoenix–Omaha Campus, College of Education, Omaha, NE 68154-5240. Offers administration and supervision (MA Ed); curriculum and instruction (MA Ed); curriculum and instruction—English and language arts education (MA Ed); curriculum and instruction—adult education (MA Ed); curriculum and instruction—computer education (MA Ed); curriculum and instruction—English as a second language (MA Ed); curriculum and instruction—mathematics education (MA Ed); elementary teacher education (MA Ed); secondary teacher education (MA Ed); special education (MA Ed).

University of Phoenix Online Campus, The Artemis School, College of Education, Phoenix, AZ 85034-7209. Offers administration and supervision (MAEd); adult education and training (MAEd); curriculum and instruction-adult education (MAEd); curriculum and instruction-English and language arts education (MAEd); curriculum and instruction-mathematics education (MAEd); curriculum education (MAEd); curriculum instruction (MAEd); early childhood (MAEd); English as a second language (MAEd); teacher education elementary (MAEd); teacher education secondary (MAEd). Evening/weekend programs available. Postbaccalaureate distance learning degree programs offered (no on-campus study). *Faculty:* 12 full-time (5 women), 8,196 part-time/adjunct (6,937 women). *Students:* 11,937 full-time (9,375 women); includes 2,972 minority (2,210 African Americans, 74 American Indian/Alaska Native, 205 Asian Americans or Pacific Islanders, 483 Hispanic Americans), 906 international. Average age 36. *Degree requirements:* For master's, thesis (for some programs), registration. *Entrance requirements:* For master's, 3 years of work experience, minimum GPA of 2.5. Additional exam requirements/recommendations for international students: Required—TOEFL (minimum score 550 paper-based; 213 computer-based; 79 iBT). *Application deadline:* Applications are processed on a rolling basis. Application fee: $45. Electronic applications accepted. *Expenses:* Tuition: Full-time $12,664. Required fees: $760. *Financial support:* Institutionally sponsored loans and scholarships/grants available. Financial award applicants required to submit FAFSA. *Unit head:* Dr. Marla LaRue, Dean/Executive Director, 480-557-1218, E-mail: marla.larue@phoenix.edu. *Application contact:* Dr. Marla LaRue, Dean/Executive Director, 480-557-1218, E-mail: marla.larue@phoenix.edu.

University of Phoenix Online Campus, School of Advanced Studies, Phoenix, AZ 85034-7209. Offers business administration (DBA); education (Ed D); health administration (DHA); organizational management (DM). Evening/weekend programs available. *Faculty:* 36 full-time (13 women), 551 part-time/adjunct (224 women). *Students:* 4,544 full-time (2,756 women); includes 1,550 minority (1,136 African Americans, 32 American Indian/Alaska Native, 152 Asian Americans or Pacific Islanders, 230 Hispanic Americans), 378 international. Average age 44. In 2006, 210 degrees awarded. *Degree requirements:* For doctorate, thesis/dissertation. *Entrance requirements:* For doctorate, 3 letters of recommendation, minimum master's GPA of 3.0, 3 years professional work experience. Additional exam requirements/recommendations for international students: Required—TOEFL (minimum score 550 paper-based; 213 computer-based; 79 iBT). *Application deadline:* Applications are processed on a rolling basis. Application fee: $45. Electronic applications accepted. *Expenses:* Tuition: Full-time $12,664. Required fees: $760. *Financial support:* Institutionally sponsored loans and scholarships/grants available. Financial award applicants required to submit FAFSA. *Unit head:* Dr. Dawn Iwamoto, Dean/Executive Director, 480-557-3228, E-mail: dawn.iwamoto@phoenix.edu. *Application contact:* Information Contact, 800-697-8223.

University of Phoenix–Oregon Campus, The Artemis School, College of Education, Tigard, OR 97223. Offers early childhood and elementary education (MA Ed); secondary education (MA Ed). Evening/weekend programs available. *Faculty:* 3 full-time (2 women), 33 part-time/adjunct (14 women). *Students:* 90 full-time (59 women); includes 7 minority (4 African Americans, 1 American Indian/Alaska Native, 2 Hispanic Americans), 14 international. Average age 36. In 2006, 12 degrees awarded. *Degree requirements:* For master's, thesis (for some programs), registration. *Entrance requirements:* For master's, minimum undergraduate GPA of 2.5, 3 years work experience. Additional exam requirements/recommendations for international students: Required—TOEFL (minimum score 550 paper-based; 213 computer-based; 79 iBT). *Application deadline:* Applications are processed on a rolling basis. Application fee: $45. Electronic applications accepted. *Expenses:* Tuition: Full-time $10,200. Required fees: $760. *Financial support:* Institutionally sponsored loans and scholarships/grants available. Financial award applicants required to submit FAFSA. *Unit head:* Dr. Marla LaRue, Dean/Executive Director, 480-557-1218, E-mail: marla.larue@phoenix.edu. *Application contact:* Chair, 503-403-2500, Fax: 503-670-0614.

University of Phoenix–Phoenix Campus, The Artemis School, College of Education, Phoenix, AZ 85040-1958. Offers administration and supervision (MA Ed); curriculum and instruction (MA Ed); elementary licensure (MA Ed); secondary licensure (MA Ed). Evening/weekend programs available. *Faculty:* 39 full-time (23 women), 422 part-time/adjunct (255 women). *Students:* 850 full-time (614 women); includes 135 minority (45 African Americans, 7 American Indian/Alaska Native, 20 Asian Americans or Pacific Islanders, 63 Hispanic Americans), 15 international. Average age 35. In 2006, 500 degrees awarded. *Degree requirements:* For master's, thesis (for some programs), registration. *Entrance requirements:* For master's, 3 years of work experience, minimum undergraduate GPA of 2.5. Additional exam requirements/recommendations for international students: Required—TOEFL (minimum score 550 paper-based; 213 computer-based; 79 iBT). *Application deadline:* Applications are processed on a rolling basis. Application fee: $45. Electronic applications accepted. *Financial support:* Institutionally sponsored loans and scholarships/grants available. Financial award applicants required to submit FAFSA. *Unit head:* Dr. Marla LaRue, Dean/Executive Director, 480-557-1218, E-mail: marla.larue@phoenix.edu. *Application contact:* College Chair, 480-804-7400, Fax: 480-557-2320.

University of Phoenix–Puerto Rico Campus, The Artemis School, College of Education, Guaynabo, PR 00968. Offers administration and supervision (MA Ed); early childhood education (MA Ed); school counselor (MSC). Evening/weekend programs available. *Faculty:* 8 full-time (all women), 28 part-time/adjunct (21 women). *Students:* 186 full-time (156 women); includes 91 minority (1 African American, 1 American Indian/Alaska Native, 89 Hispanic Americans), 4 international. Average age 37. In 2006, 39 degrees awarded. *Degree requirements:* For master's, thesis (for some programs), registration. *Entrance requirements:* For master's, minimum undergraduate GPA of 2.5, 3 years work experience. Additional exam requirements/recommendations for international students: Required—TOEFL (minimum score 550 paper-based; 213 computer-based; 79 iBT). *Application deadline:* Applications are processed on a rolling basis. Application fee: $45. Electronic applications accepted. *Expenses:* Tuition: Full-time $5,816. Required fees: $760. *Financial support:* Institutionally sponsored loans and scholarships/grants available. Financial award applicants required to submit FAFSA. *Unit head:* Dr. Marla LaRue, Dean/Executive Director, 480-557-1218, E-mail: marla.larue@phoenix.edu. *Application contact:* Chair, 787-731-5400, Fax: 787-731-1510.

University of Phoenix–Sacramento Valley Campus, The Artemis School, College of Education, Sacramento, CA 95833-3632. Offers adult education (MA Ed); curriculum instruction (MA Ed); elementary education (MA Ed); secondary education (MA Ed); teacher education (Certificate). Evening/weekend programs available. *Faculty:* 9 full-time (5 women), 95 part-

Education—General

University of Phoenix–Sacramento Valley Campus (continued)
time/adjunct (41 women). *Students:* 234 full-time (161 women); includes 51 minority (20 African Americans, 2 American Indian/Alaska Native, 9 Asian Americans or Pacific Islanders, 20 Hispanic Americans), 15 international. Average age 36. In 2006, 80 degrees awarded. *Degree requirements:* For master's, thesis (for some programs), registration. *Entrance requirements:* For master's, 3 years of work experience, minimum undergraduate GPA of 2.5. Additional exam requirements/recommendations for international students: Required—TOEFL (minimum score 550 paper-based; 213 computer-based; 79 iBT). *Application deadline:* Applications are processed on a rolling basis. Application fee: $45. Electronic applications accepted. *Expenses:* Tuition: Full-time $12,024. Required fees: $760. *Financial support:* Institutionally sponsored loans and scholarships/grants available. Financial award applicants required to submit FAFSA. *Unit head:* Dr. Marla LaRue, Dean, 480-557-1218, E-mail: marla.larue@phoenix.edu. *Application contact:* Campus College Chair, 916-923-2107, Fax: 916-923-3914.

University of Phoenix–San Diego Campus, The Artemis School, College of Education, San Diego, CA 92123. Offers curriculum and instruction (MA Ed); elementary education (MA Ed); secondary education (MA Ed). Evening/weekend programs available. *Faculty:* 6 full-time (3 women), 69 part-time/adjunct (36 women). *Students:* 165 full-time (110 women); includes 42 minority (9 African Americans, 8 Asian Americans or Pacific Islanders, 25 Hispanic Americans), 12 international. Average age 34. In 2006, 81 degrees awarded. *Degree requirements:* For master's, thesis (for some programs), registration. *Entrance requirements:* For master's, 3 years of work experience, minimum undergraduate GPA of 3.0. Additional exam requirements/recommendations for international students: Required—TOEFL (minimum score 550 paper-based; 213 computer-based; 79 iBT). *Application deadline:* Applications are processed on a rolling basis. Application fee: $45. Electronic applications accepted. *Expenses:* Tuition: Full-time $11,419. Required fees: $760. *Financial support:* Institutionally sponsored loans and scholarships/grants available. Financial award applicants required to submit FAFSA. *Unit head:* Dr. Marla LaRue, Dean/Executive Director, 480-557-1218, E-mail: marla.larue@phoenix.edu. *Application contact:* Campus College Chair, 888-UOP-INFO, Fax: 858-509-4399.

University of Phoenix–Southern Arizona Campus, The Artemis School, College of Education, Tucson, AZ 85712-2732. Offers curriculum instruction (MA Ed); educational counseling (MA Ed); elementary licensure (MA Ed); school counseling (MSC); secondary licensure (MA Ed); special education (Certificate). Evening/weekend programs available. *Faculty:* 101. *Students:* 75 full-time (55 women); includes 16 minority (2 African Americans, 1 American Indian/Alaska Native, 1 Asian American or Pacific Islander, 12 Hispanic Americans), 2 international. Average age 38. In 2006, 113 degrees awarded. *Degree requirements:* For master's, thesis (for some programs), registration. *Entrance requirements:* For master's, minimum undergraduate GPA of 2.5, 3 years of work experience. Additional exam requirements/recommendations for international students: Required—TOEFL (minimum score 550 paper-based; 213 computer-based; 79 iBT). *Application deadline:* Applications are processed on a rolling basis. Application fee: $45. Electronic applications accepted. *Expenses:* Tuition: Full-time $8,669. Required fees: $760. *Financial support:* Institutionally sponsored loans and scholarships/grants available. Financial award applicants required to submit FAFSA. *Unit head:* Dr. Marla LaRue, Dean/Executive Director, 480-557-1218, E-mail: marla.larue@phoenix.edu. *Application contact:* Campus College Chair, 520-881-6512, Fax: 520-795-6177.

University of Phoenix–Southern California Campus, The Artemis School, College of Education, Costa Mesa, CA 92626. Offers curriculum and instruction (MA Ed); elementary education (MA Ed); secondary education (MA Ed). Evening/weekend programs available. *Faculty:* 22 full-time (9 women), 195 part-time/adjunct (108 women). *Students:* 1,152 full-time (858 women); includes 420 minority (135 African Americans, 7 American Indian/Alaska Native, 59 Asian Americans or Pacific Islanders, 219 Hispanic Americans), 78 international. Average age 34. In 2006, 359 degrees awarded. *Degree requirements:* For master's, thesis (for some programs), registration. *Entrance requirements:* For master's, minimum undergraduate GPA of 2.5, 3 years work experience. Additional exam requirements/recommendations for international students: Required—TOEFL (minimum score 550 paper-based; 213 computer-based; 79 iBT). *Application deadline:* Applications are processed on a rolling basis. Application fee: $45. Electronic applications accepted. *Expenses:* Tuition: Full-time $13,512. Required fees: $760. *Financial support:* Institutionally sponsored loans and scholarships/grants available. Financial award applicants required to submit FAFSA. *Unit head:* Dr. Marla LaRue, Dean/Executive Director, 480-557-1218, E-mail: marla.larue@phoenix.edu. *Application contact:* Campus College Chair, 714-378-1878, Fax: 714-378-5875.

University of Phoenix–Southern Colorado Campus, The Artemis School, College of Education, Colorado Springs, CO 80919-2335. Offers administration and supervision (MA Ed); curriculum and instruction (MA Ed); elementary licensure (MA Ed); principal licensure certification (Certificate); school counseling (MSC); secondary licensure (MA Ed). Evening/weekend programs available. *Faculty:* 7 full-time (3 women), 90 part-time/adjunct (53 women). *Students:* 220 full-time (162 women); includes 22 minority (7 African Americans, 1 American Indian/Alaska Native, 4 Asian Americans or Pacific Islanders, 10 Hispanic Americans), 15 international. Average age 37. In 2006, 122 degrees awarded. *Degree requirements:* For master's, thesis (for some programs), registration. *Entrance requirements:* For master's, minimum undergraduate GPA of 2.5, 3 years of work experience. Additional exam requirements/recommendations for international students: Required—TOEFL (minimum score 550 paper-based; 213 computer-based; 79 iBT). *Application deadline:* Applications are processed on a rolling basis. Application fee: $45. Electronic applications accepted. *Expenses:* Tuition: Full-time $10,291. Required fees: $760. *Financial support:* Institutionally sponsored loans and scholarships/grants available. Financial award applicants required to submit FAFSA. *Unit head:* Dr. Marla LaRue, Dean/Executive Director, 480-557-1218, E-mail: marla.larue@phoenix.edu. *Application contact:* Chair, 719-599-5282, Fax: 719-599-7973.

University of Phoenix–Springfield Campus, College of Education, Springfield, MO 65804-7211. Offers administration and supervision (MA Ed); curriculum and instruction (MA Ed); curriculum and instruction/adult education (MA Ed); curriculum and instruction/computer education (MA Ed); curriculum and instruction/English as a second language (MA Ed); English and language arts education (MA Ed); mathematics education (MA Ed).

University of Phoenix–Utah Campus, The Artemis School, College of Education, Salt Lake City, UT 84123-4617. Offers administration and supervision (MA Ed); curriculum and instruction (MA Ed); elementary education (MA Ed); school counseling (MSC); secondary education (MA Ed). Evening/weekend programs available. *Faculty:* 14 full-time (8 women), 78 part-time/adjunct (39 women). *Students:* 395 full-time (246 women); includes 20 minority (2 African Americans, 1 American Indian/Alaska Native, 8 Asian Americans or Pacific Islanders, 9 Hispanic Americans), 4 international. Average age 37. In 2006, 233 degrees awarded. *Degree requirements:* For master's, thesis (for some programs), registration. *Entrance requirements:* For master's, minimum undergraduate GPA of 2.5, 3 years work experience. Additional exam requirements/recommendations for international students: Required—TOEFL (minimum score 550 paper-based; 213 computer-based; 79 iBT). *Application deadline:* Applications are processed on a rolling basis. Application fee: $45. Electronic applications accepted. *Expenses:* Tuition: Full-time $9,104. Required fees: $760. *Financial support:* Institutionally sponsored loans and scholarships/grants available. Financial award applicants required to submit FAFSA. *Unit head:* Dr. Marla LaRue, Dean/Executive Director, 480-557-1218, E-mail: marla.larue@phoenix.edu. *Application contact:* Chair, 801-263-1444, Fax: 801-269-9766.

University of Phoenix–Vancouver Campus, The Artemis School, College of Education, Burnaby, BC V5C 6G9, Canada. Offers administration and supervision (MA Ed); curriculum and instruction (MA Ed). Evening/weekend programs available. *Faculty:* 25. *Students:* 131 full-time (79 women); includes 6 minority (all Asian Americans or Pacific Islanders) Average age 40. In 2006, 49 degrees awarded. *Degree requirements:* For master's, thesis (for some programs), registration. *Entrance requirements:* For master's, minimum undergraduate GPA of 2.5, 3 years work experience. Additional exam requirements/recommendations for international students: Required—TOEFL (minimum score 550 paper-based; 213 computer-based; 79 iBT). *Application deadline:* Applications are processed on a rolling basis. Application fee: $45. Electronic applications accepted. *Expenses:* Tuition: Full-time $12,840. Required fees: $760. *Financial support:* Institutionally sponsored loans and scholarships/grants available. *Unit head:* Dr. Marla LaRue, Dean/Executive Director, 480-557-1218, E-mail: marla.larue@phoenix.edu. *Application contact:* Chair, 404-205-6999.

University of Phoenix–West Florida Campus, The Artemis School, College of Education, Temple Terrace, FL 33637. Offers administration and supervision (MA Ed); curriculum and instruction (MA Ed); curriculum and technology (MA Ed); elementary teacher education (MA Ed); secondary teacher education (MA Ed). Evening/weekend programs available. *Faculty:* 10 full-time (8 women), 15 part-time/adjunct (7 women). *Students:* 67 full-time (61 women); includes 24 minority (20 African Americans, 1 American Indian/Alaska Native, 3 Hispanic Americans), 3 international. Average age 40. In 2006, 8 degrees awarded. *Degree requirements:* For master's, thesis (for some programs), registration. *Entrance requirements:* For master's, 3 years of work experience, minimum undergraduate GPA of 2.5. Additional exam requirements/recommendations for international students: Required—TOEFL (minimum score 550 paper-based; 213 computer-based; 79 iBT). Application fee: $45. *Expenses:* Tuition: Full-time $9,450. Required fees: $760. *Financial support:* Institutionally sponsored loans and scholarships/grants available. Financial award applicants required to submit FAFSA. *Unit head:* Dr. Marla LaRue, Dean, 480-557-1218, E-mail: marla.larue@phoenix.edu. *Application contact:* Chair, 813-626-7911, Fax: 813-977-1449.

University of Phoenix–West Michigan Campus, The Artemis School, College of Education, Walker, MI 49544. Offers administration and supervision (MA Ed); curriculum and instruction (MA Ed). Evening/weekend programs available. *Faculty:* 5 full-time (1 woman), 15 part-time/adjunct (9 women). In 2006, 5 master's awarded. *Degree requirements:* For master's, thesis (for some programs), registration. *Entrance requirements:* For master's, 3 years of work experience, minimum undergraduate GPA of 2.5. Additional exam requirements/recommendations for international students: Required—TOEFL (minimum score 550 paper-based; 213 computer-based; 79 iBT). *Application deadline:* Applications are processed on a rolling basis. Application fee: $45. Electronic applications accepted. *Expenses:* Tuition: Full-time $12,043. Required fees: $760. *Financial support:* Institutionally sponsored loans and scholarships/grants available. Financial award applicants required to submit FAFSA. *Unit head:* Dr. Marla LaRue, Dean/Executive Director, 480-557-1218, E-mail: marla.larue@phoenix.edu. *Application contact:* Chair, 888-345-9699, Fax: 616-784-5300.

University of Pittsburgh, School of Education, Pittsburgh, PA 15260. Offers M Ed, MA, MAT, MS, Ed D, PhD. Part-time and evening/weekend programs available. Postbaccalaureate distance learning degree programs offered (minimal on-campus study). *Faculty:* 98 full-time (55 women), 115 part-time/adjunct (74 women). *Students:* 552 full-time (396 women), 665 part-time (499 women); includes 100 minority (70 African Americans, 1 American Indian/Alaska Native, 17 Asian Americans or Pacific Islanders, 12 Hispanic Americans), 77 international. 744 applicants, 78% accepted, 404 enrolled. In 2006, 331 master's, 54 doctorates awarded. *Degree requirements:* For doctorate, thesis/dissertation. *Entrance requirements:* For doctorate, GRE. Additional exam requirements/recommendations for international students: Required—TOEFL. *Application deadline:* For fall admission, 2/1 priority date for domestic students; for spring admission, 11/15 priority date for domestic students. Applications are processed on a rolling basis. Application fee: $50. Electronic applications accepted. *Financial support:* In 2006–07, 36 fellowships (averaging $6,464 per year), 40 research assistantships with full and partial tuition reimbursements (averaging $16,555 per year), 102 teaching assistantships with full and partial tuition reimbursements (averaging $14,301 per year) were awarded; career-related internships or fieldwork, Federal Work-Study, traineeships, tuition waivers (partial), and unspecified assistantships also available. Support available to part-time students. Financial award applicants required to submit FAFSA. *Unit head:* Dr. Alan Lesgold, Dean, 412-648-1773, Fax: 412-648-1825, E-mail: al@pitt.edu. *Application contact:* Joan M. Cutone, Director, School of Education Student Service Center, 412-648-2230, Fax: 412-648-1899, E-mail: soeinfo@pitt.edu.

University of Portland, Graduate School, School of Education, Portland, OR 97203-5798. Offers M Ed, MA, MAT. M Ed also available through the Graduate Outreach Program for teachers residing in the Oregon and Washington State areas. *Accreditation:* NCATE. Part-time and evening/weekend programs available. *Faculty:* 19 full-time (8 women), 10 part-time/adjunct (5 women). *Students:* 51 full-time, 192 part-time. *Entrance requirements:* For master's, minimum GPA of 3.0, teaching certificate, letters of recommendation, resumé. Additional exam requirements/recommendations for international students: Required—TOEFL (minimum score 550 paper-based; 80 iBT). *Application deadline:* For fall admission, 8/1 priority date for domestic students; for spring admission, 12/1 for domestic students. Applications are processed on a rolling basis. Application fee: $50. *Expenses:* Tuition: Part-time $728 per semester hour. Required fees: $5 per semester hour. Tuition and fees vary according to program. *Financial support:* Federal Work-Study and scholarships/grants available. Support available to part-time students. Financial award application deadline: 3/1; financial award applicants required to submit FAFSA. *Faculty research:* Multicultural education, supervision/leadership. *Unit head:* Dr. Maria Ciriello, OP, Dean, 503-943-7135, Fax: 503-943-8042, E-mail: ciriello@up.edu. *Application contact:* Dr. Thomas G. Greene, Associate Dean, 503-943-7135, Fax: 503-943-7315, E-mail: greene@up.edu.

University of Prince Edward Island, Faculty of Education, Charlottetown, PE C1A 4P3, Canada. Offers leadership and learning (M Ed). Part-time programs available. *Students:* 9 full-time (8 women), 110 part-time (85 women). 106 applicants, 55% accepted, 56 enrolled. In 2006, 72 degrees awarded. *Degree requirements:* For master's, thesis. *Entrance requirements:* For master's, 2 years of professional experience, bachelor of education, professional certificate. Additional exam requirements/recommendations for international students: Required—TOEFL (minimum score 550 paper-based; 213 computer-based; 80 iBT), Canadian Academic English Language Assessment, Michigan English Language Assessment Battery, Canadian Test of English for Scholars and Trainees. *Application deadline:* For fall admission, 1/15 for domestic and international students. Application fee: $75 ($100 for international students). *Faculty research:* Distance learning, aboriginal communities and education leadership development, international development, immersion language learning. *Unit head:* Dr. Graham Pike, Dean, 902-566-0731, Fax: 902-566-0416. *Application contact:* Dr. Gerald Hopkirk, Graduate Studies Coordinator, 902-566-0622, Fax: 902-566-0416, E-mail: ghopkirk@upei.ca.

University of Puerto Rico, Río Piedras, College of Education, San Juan, PR 00931-3300. Offers M Ed, MS, Ed D. *Accreditation:* NCATE. Part-time programs available. *Students:* 229 full-time (187 women), 290 part-time (224 women); all minorities (all Hispanic Americans) In 2006, 43 master's, 24 doctorates awarded. *Degree requirements:* For master's, thesis; for doctorate, thesis/dissertation, internship. *Entrance requirements:* For master's, GRE or PAEG, minimum GPA of 3.0, letter of recommendation; for doctorate, GRE or PAEG, master's degree, minimum GPA of 3.0, letter of recommendation (2), interview. *Application deadline:* For fall admission, 2/1 for domestic and international students. Application fee: $17. *Expenses:* Tuition, state resident: part-time $100 per credit. Tuition, nonresident: part-time $291 per credit. Required fees: $72 per semester. *Financial support:* Fellowships, research assistantships, teaching assistantships, career-related internships or fieldwork, Federal Work-Study, institutionally sponsored loans, and tuition waivers (partial) available. Financial award application deadline: 5/31. *Faculty research:* Bilingual education, education for the hearing impaired. *Unit head:* Dr. Angeles Molina Ilurrondo, Dean, 787-764-0000 Ext. 4344, Fax: 787-763-4130.

University of Puget Sound, Graduate Studies, School of Education, Tacoma, WA 98416. Offers M Ed, MAT. *Accreditation:* NCATE. *Faculty:* 12 full-time (8 women), 3 part-time/adjunct (all women). *Students:* 55 full-time (37 women), 28 part-time (22 women); includes 14 minority (7 African Americans, 2 American Indian/Alaska Native, 5 Asian Americans or Pacific Islanders), 2 international. Average age 27. 121 applicants, 82% accepted, 59 enrolled. In 2006, 60 degrees awarded. *Median time to degree:* Master's–1 year full-time, 2 years part-time. *Degree requirements:* For master's, capstone course. *Entrance requirements:* For master's, GRE

General Test, minimum GPA of 3.0. Additional exam requirements/recommendations for international students: Required—TOEFL (minimum score 550 paper-based; 213 computer-based; 80 iBT). *Application deadline:* For fall admission, 3/1 priority date for domestic and international students. Applications are processed on a rolling basis. Application fee: $65. Electronic applications accepted. *Expenses:* Tuition: Full-time $26,390. Tuition and fees vary according to course load. *Financial support:* In 2006–07, 24 students received support, including 16 fellowships (averaging $7,575 per year), 1 teaching assistantship with tuition reimbursement available (averaging $12,250 per year); career-related internships or fieldwork, scholarships/grants, and tuition waivers (full) also available. Support available to part-time students. Financial award application deadline: 3/31; financial award applicants required to submit FAFSA. *Unit head:* Dr. Christine Kline, Dean, 253-879-3377. *Application contact:* Dr. George H. Mills, Vice President for Enrollment, 253-879-3211, Fax: 253-879-3993, E-mail: admission@ups.edu.

University of Redlands, School of Education, Redlands, CA 92373-0999. Offers MA, Ed D, Certificate. Part-time and evening/weekend programs available. *Faculty:* 15 full-time, 47 part-time/adjunct. *Students:* 580 full-time (411 women), 4 part-time (3 women); includes 200 minority (45 African Americans, 7 American Indian/Alaska Native, 11 Asian Americans or Pacific Islanders, 137 Hispanic Americans), 7 international. Average age 32. In 2006, 79 master's, 209 other advanced degrees awarded. *Entrance requirements:* For master's, minimum undergraduate GPA of 3.0, 2 letters of recommendation. Additional exam requirements/recommendations for international students: Required—TOEFL (minimum score 550 paper-based; 213 computer-based). *Application deadline:* For fall admission, 8/6 for domestic students; for winter admission, 1/21 for domestic students. Applications are processed on a rolling basis. Application fee: $0. *Expenses:* *Contact institution.* Full-time tuition and fees vary according to program. *Financial support:* Research assistantships with partial tuition reimbursements, health care benefits available. Financial award application deadline: 3/2; financial award applicants required to submit FAFSA. *Unit head:* Dr. Hank Robin, Dean, 909-748-8064. *Application contact:* Information Contact, 909-748-8064, E-mail: education@redlands.edu.

University of Regina, Faculty of Graduate Studies and Research, Faculty of Education, Regina, SK S4S 0A2, Canada. Offers M Ad Ed, M Ed, MHRD, PhD. Part-time programs available. *Faculty:* 45 full-time (21 women), 6 part-time/adjunct (5 women). *Students:* 78 full-time (55 women), 241 part-time (168 women). 124 applicants, 81% accepted. In 2006, 72 master's, 4 doctorates awarded. *Degree requirements:* For master's, practicum, project, or thesis; for doctorate, thesis/dissertation, registration. *Entrance requirements:* Additional exam requirements/recommendations for international students: Required—TOEFL (minimum score 580 paper-based; 237 computer-based; 88 iBT). *Application deadline:* For fall admission, 2/15 for domestic students; for winter admission, 2/15 for domestic students; for spring admission, 2/15 for domestic students. Application fee: $60 ($100 for international students). *Expenses:* *Contact institution.* *Financial support:* In 2006–07, 23 students received support, including 11 fellowships (averaging $14,886 per year), 3 research assistantships (averaging $12,750 per year), 7 teaching assistantships (averaging $13,501 per year); career-related internships or fieldwork and scholarships/grants also available. Financial award application deadline: 6/15. *Faculty research:* Curriculum and instruction, administration. *Unit head:* Dr. Warren Wessel, Associate Dean, Graduate Program and Research, 306-585-4816, Fax: 306-585-5387, E-mail: warren.wessel@uregina.ca. *Application contact:* Vicki Minhinnick, Graduate Program Coordinator, 306-585-4506, Fax: 306-585-5387, E-mail: edgrad@uregina.ca.

University of Rhode Island, Graduate School, College of Human Science and Services, School of Education, Kingston, RI 02881. Offers adult education (MA); elementary education (MA); music education (MM); reading education (MA); secondary education (MA); MS/PhD. *Accreditation:* NCATE. Evening/weekend programs available. In 2006, 40 degrees awarded. *Entrance requirements:* For master's, GRE or MAT. Additional exam requirements/recommendations for international students: Required—TOEFL. *Application deadline:* For fall admission, 4/15 priority date for domestic students; for spring admission, 11/15 for domestic students. Applications are processed on a rolling basis. Application fee: $35. *Expenses:* Tuition, state resident: full-time $6,032; part-time $335 per credit. Tuition, nonresident: full-time $17,288; part-time $960 per credit. Required fees: $65 per credit. $30 per semester. One-time fee: $80 part-time. *Financial support:* Career-related internships or fieldwork available. *Unit head:* Dr. David Byrd, Director, 401-874-5484.

University of Rio Grande, Graduate School, Rio Grande, OH 45674. Offers classroom teaching (M Ed), including fine arts, learning disabilities, mathematics, reading education. Part-time and evening/weekend programs available. *Degree requirements:* For master's, final research project, portfolio. *Entrance requirements:* For master's, minimum GPA of 2.7 in major, 2.5 overall. *Faculty research:* Interagency collaboration, reading and mathematics, learning styles, college access, literacy.

University of Rochester, Margaret Warner Graduate School of Education and Human Development, Rochester, NY 14627-0250. Offers MAT, MS, Ed D, PhD, MS/PhD. *Accreditation:* ACA (one or more programs are accredited); NCATE. Part-time and evening/weekend programs available. Terminal master's awarded for partial completion of doctoral program. *Degree requirements:* For master's, thesis (for some programs); for doctorate, thesis/dissertation, qualifying exam.

University of St. Francis, College of Education, Joliet, IL 60435-6169. Offers curriculum and instruction (MS); educational leadership (MS), including reading, special education; elementary education certification (M Ed); secondary education certification (M Ed), including English education, math education, science education, social studies education; special education (M Ed); teaching and learning (MS). Part-time and evening/weekend programs available. *Faculty:* 11 full-time (10 women), 25 part-time/adjunct (12 women). *Students:* 52 full-time (38 women), 381 part-time (293 women); includes 38 minority (21 African Americans, 1 American Indian/Alaska Native, 4 Asian Americans or Pacific Islanders, 12 Hispanic Americans). Average age 33. 194 applicants, 80% accepted, 117 enrolled. In 2006, 165 degrees awarded. *Degree requirements:* For master's, comprehensive exam (for some programs), registration. *Entrance requirements:* For master's, minimum undergraduate GPA of 2.75, 2 letters of recommendation, computer competency. Additional exam requirements/recommendations for international students: Required—TOEFL (minimum score 550 paper-based; 213 computer-based). *Application deadline:* Applications are processed on a rolling basis. Application fee: $30. Electronic applications accepted. *Expenses:* *Contact institution.* Part-time tuition and fees vary according to campus/location and program. *Financial support:* In 2006–07, 272 students received support. Scholarships/grants, tuition waivers (partial), and unspecified assistantships available. Support available to part-time students. Financial award applicants required to submit FAFSA. *Unit head:* Dr. John Gambro, Dean, 815-740-3456, Fax: 815-740-2264, E-mail: jgambro@stfrancis.edu. *Application contact:* Sandra Sloka, Director of Admissions for Graduate and Degree Completion Programs, 800-735-7500, Fax: 815-740-5032, E-mail: ssloka@stfrancis.edu.

University of Saint Francis, Graduate School, Department of Education, Fort Wayne, IN 46808-3994. Offers special education (MS Ed). *Accreditation:* NCATE. Part-time and evening/weekend programs available. *Faculty:* 3 full-time (all women), 4 part-time/adjunct (all women). *Students:* 4 full-time (3 women), 17 part-time (13 women); includes 1 minority (African American) Average age 42. 2 applicants, 100% accepted. In 2006, 9 degrees awarded. *Entrance requirements:* For master's, MAT, minimum GPA of 2.5. *Application deadline:* For fall admission, 7/1 priority date for domestic students; for spring admission, 11/1 for domestic students. Applications are processed on a rolling basis. Application fee: $20. *Financial support:* In 2006–07, 21 students received support. Federal Work-Study and unspecified assistantships available. Support available to part-time students. Financial award applicants required to submit FAFSA. *Unit head:* Dr. Rolf Daniel, Dean, 260-399-7700 Ext. 8403, Fax: 260-399-8170, E-mail: rdaniel@sf.edu. *Application contact:* Michelle Kuhlhorst, Admissions Counselor, 260-434-7748, Fax: 260-434-7590, E-mail: mkuhlhorst@sf.edu.

University of Saint Mary, Graduate Programs, Program in Education, Leavenworth, KS 66048-5082. Offers curriculum and instruction (MAT). *Accreditation:* NCATE. Part-time and evening/weekend programs available. Postbaccalaureate distance learning degree programs offered (no on-campus study). *Degree requirements:* For master's, thesis, oral presentation. *Entrance requirements:* For master's, minimum undergraduate GPA of 2.75. *Faculty research:* Curriculum and instruction.

University of Saint Mary, Graduate Programs, Program in Teaching, Leavenworth, KS 66048-5082. Offers education (MA). Part-time and evening/weekend programs available. *Degree requirements:* For master's, thesis. *Entrance requirements:* For master's, minimum undergraduate GPA of 2.75.

University of St. Thomas, Graduate Studies, School of Education, Program in Teacher Education, St. Paul, MN 55105-1096. Offers MAT. *Accreditation:* NCATE. Part-time and evening/weekend programs available. *Students:* 30 full-time (21 women), 179 part-time (127 women); includes 19 minority (8 African Americans, 2 American Indian/Alaska Native, 3 Asian Americans or Pacific Islanders, 6 Hispanic Americans), 1 international. Average age 30. 124 applicants, 94% accepted, 105 enrolled. In 2006, 90 degrees awarded. *Entrance requirements:* For master's, minimum GPA of 2.75 or MAT. *Application deadline:* For fall admission, 6/1 for domestic students; for spring admission, 11/1 for domestic students. Applications are processed on a rolling basis. Application fee: $50. *Financial support:* In 2006–07, 186 students received support; fellowships, research assistantships, institutionally sponsored loans and scholarships/grants available. Support available to part-time students. Financial award applicants required to submit FAFSA. *Unit head:* Dr. Douglas F. Warring, Department Chair, 651-962-4877, Fax: 651-962-4169, E-mail: dfwarring@stthomas.edu. *Application contact:* Kathy J. Neary, Department Assistant, 651-962-4420, Fax: 651-962-4169, E-mail: kjneary@stthomas.edu.

University of St. Thomas, School of Education, Houston, TX 77006-4696. Offers M Ed. Part-time and evening/weekend programs available. *Faculty:* 13 full-time (7 women), 9 part-time/adjunct (6 women). *Students:* 3 full-time (all women), 280 part-time (222 women); includes 100 minority (37 African Americans, 2 American Indian/Alaska Native, 7 Asian Americans or Pacific Islanders, 54 Hispanic Americans), 10 international. Average age 36. 101 applicants, 100% accepted, 80 enrolled. In 2006, 69 degrees awarded. *Degree requirements:* For master's, comprehensive exam. *Entrance requirements:* For master's, GRE General Test, Texas teaching certificate or Texas Academic Skills Program Test, minimum GPA of 3.0 in last 60 hours of course work. Additional exam requirements/recommendations for international students: Required—TOEFL. *Application deadline:* Applications are processed on a rolling basis. Application fee: $35. *Expenses:* *Contact institution.* *Financial support:* In 2006–07, 36 students received support. Federal Work-Study and scholarships/grants available. Support available to part-time students. Financial award application deadline: 3/1; financial award applicants required to submit FAFSA. *Unit head:* Dr. Ruth M. Strudler, Dean, 713-525-3540, Fax: 713-525-3871, E-mail: strudler@stthom.edu. *Application contact:* Paula C. Hollis, Administrative Assistant, 713-525-3541, Fax: 713-525-3871, E-mail: hollisp@stthom.edu.

University of San Diego, School of Leadership and Education Sciences, San Diego, CA 92110-2492. Offers M Ed, MA, MAT, Ed D, PhD, Certificate. *Accreditation:* NCATE. Part-time and evening/weekend programs available. Postbaccalaureate distance learning degree programs offered. *Faculty:* 31 full-time (19 women), 42 part-time/adjunct (31 women). *Students:* 195 full-time (160 women), 252 part-time (193 women); includes 116 minority (15 African Americans, 4 American Indian/Alaska Native, 20 Asian Americans or Pacific Islanders, 77 Hispanic Americans), 8 international. Average age 31. 451 applicants, 65% accepted, 183 enrolled. In 2006, 196 master's, 11 doctorates awarded. *Degree requirements:* For doctorate, thesis/dissertation (for some programs), comprehensive exam (for some programs). *Entrance requirements:* For doctorate, GRE General Test or MAT, master's degree. Additional exam requirements/recommendations for international students: Required—TOEFL (minimum score 580 paper-based; 237 computer-based), TWE. *Application deadline:* For fall admission, 4/1 for domestic students. Application fee: $45. *Financial support:* In 2006–07, 50 fellowships were awarded; career-related internships or fieldwork, Federal Work-Study, institutionally sponsored loans, tuition waivers (partial), unspecified assistantships, and stipends also available. Support available to part-time students. Financial award application deadline: 5/1; financial award applicants required to submit FAFSA. *Unit head:* Dr. Paula A. Cordeiro, Dean, 619-260-4540, Fax: 619-260-6835, E-mail: cordeiro@sandiego.edu. *Application contact:* Stephen Pultz, Director of Admissions, 619-260-4524, Fax: 619-260-4158, E-mail: grads@sandiego.edu.

University of San Francisco, School of Education, San Francisco, CA 94117-1080. Offers MA, Ed D. Part-time and evening/weekend programs available. *Faculty:* 25 full-time (16 women), 68 part-time/adjunct (44 women). *Students:* 595 full-time (459 women), 308 part-time (221 women); includes 319 minority (76 African Americans, 6 American Indian/Alaska Native, 108 Asian Americans or Pacific Islanders, 129 Hispanic Americans), 52 international. Average age 35. 761 applicants, 83% accepted, 299 enrolled. In 2006, 287 master's, 46 doctorates awarded. *Degree requirements:* For doctorate, thesis/dissertation. Application fee: $55 ($65 for international students). *Expenses:* Tuition: Full-time $17,370; part-time $965 per unit. Tuition and fees vary according to degree level, campus/location and program. *Financial support:* In 2006–07, 561 students received support; fellowships, research assistantships, teaching assistantships available. Financial award application deadline: 3/2; financial award applicants required to submit FAFSA. *Unit head:* Dr. Walter Gmelch, Dean, 415-422-6525. *Application contact:* Jan Weiss, Associate Director of Graduate Outreach, 415-422-5467, E-mail: weissj@usfca.edu.

University of Saskatchewan, College of Graduate Studies and Research, College of Education, Saskatoon, SK S7N 5A2, Canada. Offers M Ed, MC Ed, PhD, Diploma. Part-time programs available. *Degree requirements:* For master's, thesis (for some programs), registration; for doctorate, thesis/dissertation, registration. *Entrance requirements:* Additional exam requirements/recommendations for international students: Required—TOEFL.

The University of Scranton, Graduate School, Department of Education, Scranton, PA 18510. Offers curriculum and instruction (MA, MS); early childhood education (MA, MS); educational administration (MS); elementary education (MS); English as a second language (MS); reading education (MS); secondary education (MS); special education (MS). *Accreditation:* NCATE. Part-time and evening/weekend programs available. Postbaccalaureate distance learning degree programs offered (no on-campus study). *Faculty:* 17 full-time (11 women), 47 part-time/adjunct (18 women). *Students:* 48 full-time (37 women), 617 part-time (429 women); includes 72 minority (45 African Americans, 2 American Indian/Alaska Native, 3 Asian Americans or Pacific Islanders, 22 Hispanic Americans), 6 international. Average age 34. 277 applicants, 96% accepted. In 2006, 54 degrees awarded. *Degree requirements:* For master's, thesis (for some programs), capstone experience, comprehensive exam, registration. *Entrance requirements:* For master's, minimum GPA of 2.75. Additional exam requirements/recommendations for international students: Required—TOEFL (minimum score 500 paper-based; 173 computer-based), IELTS (minimum score 6). *Application deadline:* Applications are processed on a rolling basis. Application fee: $50. *Expenses:* Tuition: Part-time $684 per credit. Required fees: $25 per term. *Financial support:* In 2006–07, 13 students received support, including 11 teaching assistantships with full and partial tuition reimbursements available (averaging $4,800 per year); fellowships, career-related internships or fieldwork, Federal Work-Study, and unspecified assistantships also available. Support available to part-time students. Financial award application deadline: 3/1. *Faculty research:* Meta-analysis as a research tool, family involvement in school activities, effect of curriculum integration on student learning and attitude, the effects of inclusion on students, development of emotional intelligence of young children. *Unit head:* Dr. Deborah E. Lo, Chair, 570-941-7579, Fax: 570-941-7401, E-mail: lodi@scranton.edu.

University of Sioux Falls, Program in Education, Sioux Falls, SD 57105-1699. Offers leadership (M Ed); reading (M Ed); superintendent (Ed S); teaching (M Ed); technology (M Ed). Summer admission only. *Accreditation:* NCATE. Part-time and evening/weekend programs available. Postbaccalaureate distance learning degree programs offered (minimal on-campus study). *Faculty:* 12 full-time (8 women), 13 part-time/adjunct (7 women). *Students:* 9 applicants, 100% accepted, 7 enrolled. In 2006, 46 master's, 26 other advanced degrees awarded. *Median time*

Education—General

University of Sioux Falls (continued)

to degree: Master's–2.5 years part-time; Ed S–2 years part-time. *Degree requirements:* For master's, research application project; for Ed S, portfolio. *Entrance requirements:* For master's, minimum GPA of 3.0, 1 year of teaching experience; for Ed S, administrative exam, minimum 3 years of teaching experience, minimum cumulative GPA of 3.5. Additional exam requirements/recommendations for international students: Required—TOEFL. *Application deadline:* Applications are processed on a rolling basis. Application fee: $25. *Expenses:* Tuition: Part-time $300 per semester hour. Required fees: $15 per term. Part-time tuition and fees vary according to program. *Financial support:* In 2006–07, 58 students received support. Scholarships/grants available. Support available to part-time students. *Unit head:* Dawn Olson, Director of Graduate Education, 605-575-2063, Fax: 605-575-2079, E-mail: dawn.olson@usiouxfalls.edu.

University of South Alabama, Graduate School, College of Education, Mobile, AL 36688-0002. Offers M Ed, MS, PhD, Ed S. *Accreditation:* NCATE. Part-time programs available. *Faculty:* 50 full-time (21 women). *Students:* 444 full-time (375 women), 436 part-time (361 women); includes 233 minority (210 African Americans, 13 American Indian/Alaska Native, 7 Asian Americans or Pacific Islanders, 3 Hispanic Americans), 16 international. 426 applicants, 81% accepted, 171 enrolled. In 2006, 245 master's, 2 doctorates, 12 other advanced degrees awarded. *Degree requirements:* For master's, comprehensive exam; for doctorate, thesis/dissertation, comprehensive exam. *Entrance requirements:* For master's, GRE General Test or MAT. *Application deadline:* For fall admission, 9/1 priority date for domestic students. Applications are processed on a rolling basis. Application fee: $25. *Financial support:* In 2006–07, 23 research assistantships, 10 teaching assistantships were awarded; career-related internships or fieldwork also available. Support available to part-time students. Financial award application deadline: 4/1. *Unit head:* Dr. Richard L Hayes, Dean, 251-380-2738.

University of South Carolina, The Graduate School, College of Education, Columbia, SC 29208. Offers IMA, M Ed, MA, MAT, MS, MT, Ed D, PhD, Certificate, Ed S. *Accreditation:* NCATE. Part-time and evening/weekend programs available. Postbaccalaureate distance learning degree programs offered (minimal on-campus study). *Degree requirements:* For master's, thesis (for some programs), foreign language (MA), comprehensive exam; for doctorate, one foreign language, thesis/dissertation, comprehensive exam. *Entrance requirements:* For master's, GRE General Test; for doctorate, GRE General Test, qualifying exam, interview. Electronic applications accepted. *Faculty research:* Inquiry learning, assessment of student learning, equity issues in education, multicultural education, cultural diversity.

University of South Carolina Aiken, School of Education, Aiken, SC 29801-6309. Offers M Ed. Part-time and evening/weekend programs available. *Faculty:* 6 full-time (3 women), 4 part-time/adjunct (2 women). *Students:* 1 (woman) full-time, 110 part-time (95 women); includes 17 minority (16 African Americans, 1 Asian American or Pacific Islander). In 2006, 10 degrees awarded. *Entrance requirements:* For master's, GRE or MAT. *Application deadline:* Applications are processed on a rolling basis. Application fee: $40. Electronic applications accepted. *Expenses:* Tuition, state resident: full-time $8,288; part-time $411 per hour. Tuition, nonresident: full-time $17,916; part-time $874 per hour. Required fees: $230; $8 per hour. $15 per hour. *Financial support:* Federal Work-Study and unspecified assistantships available. Support available to part-time students. Financial award application deadline: 3/15; financial award applicants required to submit FAFSA. *Unit head:* Dr. Jeff Priest, Head, 803-648-6851, Fax: 803-641-3698, E-mail: jeffp@usca.edu.

University of South Carolina Upstate, Graduate Programs, Spartanburg, SC 29303-4999. Offers early childhood education (M Ed); elementary education (M Ed); special education: visual impairment (M Ed). *Accreditation:* NCATE. Part-time and evening/weekend programs available. *Faculty:* 9 full-time (7 women). *Students:* 5 full-time (4 women), 29 part-time (26 women); includes 3 minority (all African Americans) Average age 34. 15 applicants, 100% accepted, 9 enrolled. In 2006, 9 degrees awarded. *Degree requirements:* For master's, graduate professional portfolio. *Entrance requirements:* For master's, GRE General Test, MAT, interview, minimum GPA of 2.5, teaching certificate. *Application deadline:* Applications are processed on a rolling basis. Application fee: $40. *Expenses:* Tuition, state resident: full-time $6,890; part-time $342 per semester hour. Tuition, nonresident: full-time $14,920; part-time $727 per semester hour. *Financial support:* Institutionally sponsored loans and institutional work-study available. Financial award application deadline: 7/15; financial award applicants required to submit FAFSA. *Faculty research:* Rough and tumble play, social justice education, American Indian literatures and cultures, diversity and multicultural education, science teaching strategy. *Unit head:* Dr. Rebecca L. Stevens, Director, 864-503-5521, Fax: 864-503-5574, E-mail: ystevens@uscupstate.edu. *Application contact:* Donette Stewart, Associate Vice Chancellor for Enrollment Services, 864-503-5280, E-mail: dstewart@uscupstate.edu.

The University of South Dakota, Graduate School, School of Education, Vermillion, SD 57069-2390. Offers MA, MS, Ed D, PhD, Ed S. *Accreditation:* NCATE. Part-time and evening/weekend programs available. Postbaccalaureate distance learning degree programs offered (no on-campus study). *Faculty:* 42 full-time (23 women), 1 (woman) part-time/adjunct. *Students:* 182 full-time (119 women), 379 part-time (241 women); includes 23 minority (5 African Americans, 11 American Indian/Alaska Native, 3 Asian Americans or Pacific Islanders, 4 Hispanic Americans), 11 international. In 2006, 120 master's, 41 doctorates, 24 other advanced degrees awarded. *Degree requirements:* For master's and Ed S, thesis or alternative, comprehensive exam; for doctorate, thesis/dissertation, comprehensive exam. *Entrance requirements:* For master's and doctorate, GRE General Test, minimum GPA of 2.7. Additional exam requirements/recommendations for international students: Required—TOEFL (minimum score 550 paper-based; 213 computer-based; 79 iBT). *Application deadline:* Applications are processed on a rolling basis. Application fee: $35. Electronic applications accepted. *Expenses:* Tuition, state resident: part-time $120 per credit hour. Tuition, nonresident: part-time $355 per credit hour. Required fees: $90 per credit hour. *Financial support:* In 2006–07, research assistantships with partial tuition reimbursements (averaging $4,626 per year), teaching assistantships with partial tuition reimbursements (averaging $4,626 per year) were awarded; career-related internships or fieldwork, Federal Work-Study, and unspecified assistantships also available. Support available to part-time students. Financial award applicants required to submit FAFSA. *Unit head:* Dr. Jeri Engelking, Campus Dean, 605-677-5437, Fax: 605-677-5438, E-mail: jengelki@usd.edu. *Application contact:* Kathy Peckham, Senior Secretary, 605-677-5051, E-mail: kathy.peckham@usd.edu.

University of Southern California, Graduate School, Rossier School of Education, Programs in Education, Los Angeles, CA 90089. Offers MS, Ed D, PhD. *Students:* 990 full-time (707 women), 97 part-time (69 women); includes 520 minority (128 African Americans, 10 American Indian/Alaska Native, 181 Asian Americans or Pacific Islanders, 201 Hispanic Americans), 120 international. In 2006, 212 master's, 134 doctorates awarded. *Application deadline:* For fall admission, 12/1 priority date for domestic students. Application fee: $85. *Expenses:* Tuition: Full-time $33,314; part-time $1,121 per credit. Required fees: $522. Full-time tuition and fees vary according to program. *Financial support:* In 2006–07, research assistantships (averaging $18,500 per year), teaching assistantships (averaging $18,500 per year) were awarded. *Unit head:* Dr. Karen Symms Gallagher, Dean, Rossier School of Education, 213-740-5756.

University of Southern Indiana, Graduate Studies, College of Education and Human Services, Department of Teacher Education, Evansville, IN 47712-3590. Offers elementary education (MS); secondary education (MS). *Accreditation:* NCATE. Part-time and evening/weekend programs available. *Faculty:* 13 full-time (5 women), 4 part-time/adjunct (1 woman). *Students:* 6 full-time (5 women), 116 part-time (88 women); includes 3 minority (1 American Indian/Alaska Native, 1 Asian American or Pacific Islander, 1 Hispanic American), 3 international. Average age 35. 61 applicants, 100% accepted, 33 enrolled. In 2006, 47 degrees awarded. *Entrance requirements:* For master's, GRE General Test, NTE or Praxis I, minimum GPA of 3.0, teaching license. Additional exam requirements/recommendations for international students: Required—TOEFL (minimum score 500 paper-based; 173 computer-based). *Application deadline:* For fall admission, 7/1 priority date for domestic students, 1/1 priority date for international students. Applications are processed on a rolling basis. Application fee: $25. *Expenses:* Tuition, state resident: full-time $3,888; part-time $216 per credit hour. Tuition, nonresident: full-time $7,688; part-time $426 per credit hour. Required fees: $220; $23 per term. Tuition and fees vary according to course load and reciprocity agreements. *Financial support:* In 2006–07, 30 students received support. Federal Work-Study, scholarships/grants, tuition waivers (full and partial), and unspecified assistantships available. Financial award application deadline: 3/1; financial award applicants required to submit FAFSA. *Unit head:* Robert Boostrom, Director, 812-465-7057, E-mail: rboostrom@usi.edu.

University of Southern Maine, College of Education and Human Development, Portland, ME 04104-9300. Offers MS, MS Ed, Psy D, CAS, Certificate. *Accreditation:* NCATE. Part-time and evening/weekend programs available. Postbaccalaureate distance learning degree programs offered (minimal on-campus study). *Faculty:* 39 full-time (21 women), 33 part-time/adjunct (17 women). *Students:* 195 full-time (151 women), 435 part-time (324 women); includes 9 minority (4 American Indian/Alaska Native, 2 Asian Americans or Pacific Islanders, 3 Hispanic Americans), 1 international. 430 applicants, 62% accepted, 195 enrolled. In 2006, 211 master's, 27 other advanced degrees awarded. Terminal master's awarded for partial completion of doctoral program. *Degree requirements:* For master's and other advanced degree, thesis or alternative. *Entrance requirements:* For master's, GRE General Test or MAT, PRAXIS (extended teacher education); for doctorate, GRE; for other advanced degree, master's degree. Additional exam requirements/recommendations for international students: Required—TOEFL. *Application deadline:* For fall admission, 2/1 for domestic students; for spring admission, 9/15 for domestic students. Application fee: $50. Electronic applications accepted. *Expenses:* Tuition, state resident: full-time $4,860; part-time $270 per credit hour. Tuition, nonresident: full-time $13,572; part-time $754 per credit hour. Required fees: $222 per semester. Tuition and fees vary according to course load. *Financial support:* In 2006–07, 81 students received support, including 20 research assistantships (averaging $4,500 per year), 2 teaching assistantships with tuition reimbursements available (averaging $5,000 per year); career-related internships or fieldwork, Federal Work-Study, institutionally sponsored loans, scholarships/grants, and unspecified assistantships also available. Support available to part-time students. Financial award application deadline: 3/1; financial award applicants required to submit FAFSA. *Faculty research:* Teacher development, library technology outreach, literacy through literature, college-bound, multicultural education. Total annual research expenditures: $3.3 million. *Unit head:* Betty Lou Whitford, Dean, 207-780-5371, Fax: 207-780-5315. *Application contact:* Robin Audesse, Associate Director of Graduate Admissions, 207-780-5306, Fax: 207-780-5193, E-mail: raudesse@usm.maine.edu.

University of Southern Mississippi, Graduate School, College of Education and Psychology, Hattiesburg, MS 39406-0001. Offers M Ed, MA, MAT, MLIS, MS, Ed D, PhD, Ed S, SLS. *Accreditation:* NCATE. Part-time programs available. *Faculty:* 89 full-time (40 women). *Students:* 287 full-time (234 women), 516 part-time (389 women); includes 163 minority (146 African Americans, 2 American Indian/Alaska Native, 6 Asian Americans or Pacific Islanders, 9 Hispanic Americans), 16 international. Average age 35. 533 applicants, 41% accepted, 183 enrolled. In 2006, 232 master's, 48 doctorates, 45 other advanced degrees awarded. Terminal master's awarded for partial completion of doctoral program. *Degree requirements:* For master's, thesis (for some programs), comprehensive exam, registration; for doctorate and other advanced degree, thesis/dissertation, comprehensive exam, registration. *Entrance requirements:* For master's, GRE General Test, MAT; for doctorate and other advanced degree, GRE General Test. Additional exam requirements/recommendations for international students: Required—TOEFL. *Application deadline:* For fall admission, 3/1 for domestic and international students; for spring admission, 11/1 for domestic and international students. Applications are processed on a rolling basis. Application fee: $25 ($30 for international students). Electronic applications accepted. *Financial support:* In 2006–07, 87 research assistantships with full tuition reimbursements (averaging $7,502 per year), 72 teaching assistantships with full tuition reimbursements (averaging $7,502 per year) were awarded; career-related internships or fieldwork, Federal Work-Study, and institutionally sponsored loans also available. Financial award application deadline: 3/15. *Faculty research:* Reading, sleep, animal cognition. *Unit head:* Dr. Wanda Maulding, Interim Chair, 601-266-4568, Fax: 601-266-4175.

University of South Florida, Graduate School, College of Education, Tampa, FL 33620-9951. Offers M Ed, MA, MAT, Ed D, PhD, Ed S. *Accreditation:* NCATE. Part-time and evening/weekend programs available. *Faculty:* 162 full-time (91 women), 69 part-time/adjunct (39 women). *Students:* 636 full-time (484 women), 1,342 part-time (1,034 women); includes 413 minority (191 African Americans, 7 American Indian/Alaska Native, 37 Asian Americans or Pacific Islanders, 178 Hispanic Americans), 63 international. Average age 30. 1,147 applicants, 68% accepted, 563 enrolled. In 2006, 538 master's, 54 doctorates awarded. *Degree requirements:* For doctorate, thesis/dissertation, 2 tools of research in foreign language, statistics, and/or computers. *Entrance requirements:* For master's, GRE General Test, minimum GPA of 3.5 in last 60 hours; for doctorate, GRE General Test, minimum undergraduate GPA of 3.5; for Ed S, GRE General Test. *Application deadline:* For fall admission, 6/1 for domestic students; for spring admission, 10/15 for domestic students. Application fee: $30. Electronic applications accepted. *Financial support:* Career-related internships or fieldwork, Federal Work-Study, institutionally sponsored loans, and scholarships/grants available. Support available to part-time students. Financial award applicants required to submit FAFSA. *Unit head:* Colleen S. Kennedy, Dean, 813-974-3400, Fax: 813-974-3826. *Application contact:* Diane Briscoe, 813-974-3406, Fax: 813-974-3391, E-mail: briscoe@tempest.coedu.usf.edu.

See Close-Up on page 935.

The University of Tampa, Program in Teaching, Tampa, FL 33606-1490. Offers education (MAT); math education (MAT); reading (M Ed); science education (MAT). *Students:* 66 applicants, 71% accepted, 40 enrolled.Application fee: $40. *Expenses:* Tuition: Part-time $426 per credit hour. Required fees: $35 per year. *Unit head:* Dr. Martine Harrison, Associate Professor of Education, 813-253-3333 Ext. 3373, E-mail: mharrison@ut.edu.

The University of Tennessee, Graduate School, College of Education, Health and Human Sciences, Knoxville, TN 37996. Offers MPH, MS, Ed D, PhD, Ed S, MS/MPH. *Accreditation:* NCATE. Part-time and evening/weekend programs available. Postbaccalaureate distance learning degree programs offered (no on-campus study). *Faculty:* 140 full-time (81 women). *Students:* 641 full-time (476 women), 397 part-time (270 women); includes 83 minority (59 African Americans, 3 American Indian/Alaska Native, 12 Asian Americans or Pacific Islanders, 9 Hispanic Americans), 69 international. 701 applicants, 52% accepted. In 2006, 499 master's, 52 doctorates awarded. Terminal master's awarded for partial completion of doctoral program. *Degree requirements:* For master's and Ed S, thesis optional; for doctorate, thesis/dissertation. *Entrance requirements:* For master's, minimum GPA of 2.7; for doctorate and Ed S, GRE General Test, minimum GPA of 2.7. Additional exam requirements/recommendations for international students: Required—TOEFL. *Application deadline:* For fall admission, 2/1 priority date for domestic students. Applications are processed on a rolling basis. Application fee: $35. Electronic applications accepted. *Expenses:* Tuition, state resident: full-time $5,574. Tuition, nonresident: full-time $16,840. Required fees: $792. *Financial support:* In 2006–07, 6 fellowships, 3 research assistantships, 46 teaching assistantships were awarded; career-related internships or fieldwork, Federal Work-Study, institutionally sponsored loans, and unspecified assistantships also available. Financial award application deadline: 2/1; financial award applicants required to submit FAFSA. *Unit head:* Dr. Robert Rider, Dean, 865-974-2201. *Application contact:* Dr. Tom George, Associate Dean, 865-974-0907, Fax: 865-974-8718, E-mail: tgeorge1@utk.edu.

The University of Tennessee at Chattanooga, Graduate School, College of Health, Education and Professional Studies, Graduate Studies Division of Education, Chattanooga, TN 37403-2598. Offers counseling (M Ed); educational leadership (Ed D); educational specialist (Ed S), including educational technology, school psychology; elementary education (M Ed); school leadership (M Ed); secondary education (M Ed); special education (M Ed). *Accreditation:* ACA; NCATE. Part-time and evening/weekend programs available. *Faculty:* 28 full-time (18 women), 7 part-time/adjunct (3 women). *Students:* 166 full-time (123 women), 309 part-time (238 women); includes 57 minority (46 African Americans, 2 American Indian/Alaska Native, 7

Asian Americans or Pacific Islanders, 2 Hispanic Americans). Average age 33. 138 applicants, 95% accepted, 66 enrolled. In 2006, 133 master's, 25 other advanced degrees awarded. *Degree requirements:* For master's, thesis optional; for doctorate, thesis, dissertation, comprehensive exam. *Entrance requirements:* For master's, GRE General Test or MAT, teaching certificate. *Application deadline:* For fall admission, 8/1 for domestic students; for spring admission, 12/1 for domestic students. Applications are processed on a rolling basis. Application fee: $30. *Expenses:* Tuition, state resident: full-time $5,434; part-time $339 per hour. Tuition, nonresident: full-time $14,830; part-time $861 per hour. Required fees: $940; $178 per hour. *Financial support:* Fellowships, research assistantships, Federal Work-Study and institutionally sponsored loans available. Support available to part-time students. Financial award application deadline: 4/1; financial award applicants required to submit FAFSA. *Faculty research:* School counseling, community counseling, elementary and secondary education, school leadership and administration. Total annual research expenditures: $258,901. *Unit head:* Dr. Anthony Lease, Head, 423-425-4211, Fax: 423-425-5380, E-mail: tony-lease@utc.edu. *Application contact:* Dr. Deborah E. Arfken, Dean of Graduate Studies, 423-425-4666, Fax: 423-425-5223, E-mail: deborah-arfken@utc.edu.

The University of Tennessee at Martin, Graduate Programs, College of Education and Behavioral Sciences, Martin, TN 38238-1000. Offers MS Ed. *Accreditation:* NCATE. Part-time programs available. Postbaccalaureate distance learning degree programs offered (minimal on-campus study). *Faculty:* 48. *Students:* 338 (259 women); includes 56 African Americans. 120 applicants, 60% accepted, 47 enrolled. In 2006, 101 degrees awarded. *Degree requirements:* For master's, comprehensive exam. *Entrance requirements:* For master's, GRE General Test, minimum GPA of 2.5. Additional exam requirements/recommendations for international students: Required—TOEFL (minimum score 525 paper-based; 197 computer-based). *Application deadline:* For fall admission, 8/1 priority date for domestic students, 8/1 for international students; for spring admission, 1/1 priority date for domestic students, 1/1 for international students. Applications are processed on a rolling basis. Application fee: $30 ($50 for international students). Electronic applications accepted. *Expenses:* Tuition, state resident: part-time $303 per credit hour. Tuition, nonresident: part-time $829 per credit hour. *Financial support:* In 2006–07, 30 students received support, including 6 teaching assistantships with full tuition reimbursements available (averaging $5,665 per year); career-related internships or fieldwork, scholarships/grants, tuition waivers (partial), and unspecified assistantships also available. Support available to part-time students. Financial award application deadline: 3/1. *Faculty research:* Environmental education, self-concept, science education, attention deficit disorder, special education. Total annual research expenditures: $1 million. *Unit head:* Dr. Mary Lee Hall, Dean, 731-881-7127, Fax: 731-881-7975, E-mail: mlhall@utm.edu. *Application contact:* Dr. Suzanne Maniss, Coordinator, 731-881-7163, Fax: 731-881-7975, E-mail: smaniss@utm.edu.

The University of Texas at Arlington, Graduate School, College of Education, Arlington, TX 76019. Offers curriculum and instruction (M Ed); educational leadership and policy studies (M Ed); physiology of exercise (MS); teaching (M Ed T). *Accreditation:* NCATE. Part-time and evening/weekend programs available. Postbaccalaureate distance learning degree programs offered (minimal on-campus study). *Faculty:* 19 full-time (11 women), 3 part-time/adjunct (2 women). *Students:* 171 full-time (107 women), 579 part-time (474 women); includes 278 minority (130 African Americans, 6 American Indian/Alaska Native, 20 Asian Americans or Pacific Islanders, 122 Hispanic Americans), 40 international. Average age 36. 579 applicants, 88% accepted, 368 enrolled. In 2006, 101 degrees awarded. *Degree requirements:* For master's, thesis (for some programs), comprehensive activity, research project, comprehensive exam (for some programs), registration. *Entrance requirements:* For master's, GRE General Test, minimum undergraduate GPA of 3.0 in last 60 hours of course work, writing sample, 3 letters of recommendation. Additional exam requirements/recommendations for international students: Required—TOEFL (minimum score 550 paper-based; 213 computer-based). *Application deadline:* For fall admission, 6/16 priority date for domestic students, 4/9 priority date for international students; for winter admission, 10/22 priority date for domestic students, 9/10 priority date for international students; for spring admission, 3/25 priority date for domestic and international students. Applications are processed on a rolling basis. Application fee: $35 ($50 for international students). Electronic applications accepted. *Expenses:* Tuition, state resident: full-time $5,528. Tuition, nonresident: full-time $10,478. International tuition: $10,608 full-time. *Financial support:* In 2006–07, 11 fellowships (averaging $1,000 per year), teaching assistantships with tuition reimbursements (averaging $9,000 per year) were awarded; career-related internships or fieldwork, Federal Work-Study, scholarships/grants, and unspecified assistantships also available. Financial award application deadline: 6/1; financial award applicants required to submit FAFSA. *Unit head:* Dr. Jeanne M. Gerlach, Dean, 817-272-2591, Fax: 817-272-2530, E-mail: soeadvising@uta.edu. *Application contact:* Brendan Hardy, Graduate Advisor, 817-272-2956, Fax: 817-272-7624, E-mail: coedadvising@uta.edu.

The University of Texas at Austin, Graduate School, College of Education, Austin, TX 78712-1111. Offers M Ed, MA, MHRDL, Ed D, PhD. Part-time programs available. *Entrance requirements:* For master's and doctorate, GRE General Test. Electronic applications accepted.

The University of Texas at Brownsville, Graduate Studies, School of Education, Brownsville, TX 78520-4991. Offers bilingual education (M Ed); counseling and guidance (M Ed); curriculum and instruction (M Ed); early childhood education (M Ed); educational administration (M Ed); educational technology (M Ed); English as a second language (M Ed); reading specialist (M Ed); special education/educational diagnostician (M Ed). Part-time and evening/weekend programs available. Postbaccalaureate distance learning degree programs offered (minimal on-campus study). *Degree requirements:* For master's, thesis optional. *Entrance requirements:* For master's, GRE General Test. Additional exam requirements/recommendations for international students: Required—TOEFL.

The University of Texas at El Paso, Graduate School, College of Education, El Paso, TX 79968-0001. Offers M Ed, MA, Ed D. Part-time and evening/weekend programs available. *Degree requirements:* For master's, thesis optional; for doctorate, thesis/dissertation. *Entrance requirements:* For doctorate, GRE General Test, minimum graduate GPA of 3.0. Additional exam requirements/recommendations for international students: Required—TOEFL. Electronic applications accepted.

The University of Texas at San Antonio, College of Education and Human Development, Department of Counseling, Educational Psychology, and Adult and Higher Education, San Antonio, TX 78249-0617. Offers counseling (MA); counselor education (PhD); education-adult and higher education (MA). Part-time programs available. *Faculty:* 17 full-time (9 women), 16 part-time/adjunct (4 women). *Students:* 154 full-time (125 women), 403 part-time (354 women); includes 299 minority (42 African Americans, 2 American Indian/Alaska Native, 7 Asian Americans or Pacific Islanders, 248 Hispanic Americans), 4 international. Average age 33. 210 applicants, 85% accepted, 172 enrolled. In 2006, 140 degrees awarded. *Degree requirements:* For master's, thesis optional. *Entrance requirements:* For master's, GRE General Test. Additional exam requirements/recommendations for international students: Required—TOEFL (minimum score 500 paper-based; 173 computer-based). *Application deadline:* For fall admission, 7/1 for domestic students, 4/1 for international students; for spring admission, 11/1 for domestic students, 9/1 for international students. Applications are processed on a rolling basis. Application fee: $45 ($80 for international students). Electronic applications accepted. *Expenses:* Tuition, state resident: full-time $1,730; part-time $192 per credit hour. Tuition, nonresident: full-time $6,680; part-time $742 per credit hour. Required fees: $733; $308,359 per credit hour. *Financial support:* In 2006–07, 1 research assistantship (averaging $18,720 per year) was awarded; career-related internships or fieldwork, Federal Work-Study, scholarships/grants, and unspecified assistantships also available. *Faculty research:* Early childhood, reading, special education, foundations, curriculum and instruction. *Unit head:* Dr. Marcheta P. Evans, Chair, 210-458-2600, Fax: 210-458-2605, E-mail: mevans@utsa.edu.

The University of Texas at Tyler, College of Education and Psychology, Tyler, TX 75799-0001. Offers M Ed, MA, MAT, MS, MSIS. Part-time and evening/weekend programs available.

Students: 87 applicants, 90% accepted, 65 enrolled. In 2006, 78 degrees awarded. Application fee: $0 ($50 for international students). *Expenses:* Tuition, state resident: part-time $50 per credit hour. Tuition, nonresident: part-time $328 per credit hour. Required fees: $107 per credit hour. $426 per term. *Financial support:* In 2006–07, 30 students received support; teaching assistantships, career-related internships or fieldwork, Federal Work-Study, institutionally sponsored loans, and scholarships/grants available. Support available to part-time students. Financial award application deadline: 4/1; financial award applicants required to submit FAFSA. *Faculty research:* Neuropsychology, bone density, muscle exercise, reading improvement. *Unit head:* Dr. William Geiger, Dean, 903-566-7081, Fax: 903-565-5648, E-mail: wgeiger@mail.uttyl.edu. *Application contact:* Bonnie Purser, Office of Graduate Studies, 903-566-7142, Fax: 903-566-7068, E-mail: bpurser@uttyler.edu.

The University of Texas of the Permian Basin, Office of Graduate Studies, School of Education, Odessa, TX 79762-0001. Offers MA. *Degree requirements:* For master's, registration. *Entrance requirements:* For master's, GRE General Test. Additional exam requirements/recommendations for international students: Required—TOEFL (minimum score 550 paper-based; 213 computer-based).

The University of Texas–Pan American, College of Education, Edinburg, TX 78541-2999. Offers M Ed, MA, MS, Ed D. Part-time and evening/weekend programs available. *Degree requirements:* For master's, thesis optional. *Entrance requirements:* For master's, GRE General Test. *Expenses:* Tuition, state resident: full-time $2,577; part-time $143 per credit hour. Tuition, nonresident: full-time $7,527; part-time $418 per credit hour. Required fees: $561. *Faculty research:* Literacy development, bilingual education, brain mapping.

University of the Cumberlands, Graduate Programs in Education, Williamsburg, KY 40769-1372. Offers early childhood education (MA Ed); elementary education (MA Ed, MAT), including elementary (P-5); middle school (5-9); elementary/secondary principalship (MA Ed, Certificate); elementary/secondary teaching (MA Ed, MAT, Certificate); middle school education (MA Ed, MAT); reading and writing specialist (MA Ed); secondary general education (MA Ed, MAT); special education (MA Ed, MAT). Part-time and evening/weekend programs available. *Degree requirements:* For master's, comprehensive exam. *Entrance requirements:* For master's, GRE or NTE, Kentucky teaching certificate; for Certificate, master's degree, 3 years of teaching experience.

University of the District of Columbia, College of Arts and Sciences, Department of Education, Washington, DC 20008-1175. Offers early childhood education (MA); special education (MA). *Accreditation:* NCATE. Part-time programs available. *Students:* 1 full-time (0 women), 5 part-time (4 women); includes 4 minority (all African Americans) Average age 35. 16 applicants. *Degree requirements:* For master's, research paper. *Entrance requirements:* For master's, GRE General Test, writing proficiency exam. *Application deadline:* For fall admission, 6/15 priority date for domestic students; for spring admission, 11/1 for domestic students. Applications are processed on a rolling basis. Application fee: $20. *Financial support:* Fellowships, research assistantships available. *Unit head:* Dr. Patricia Myers, Chair, 202-274-7401. *Application contact:* LaVerne Hill Flannigan, Director of Admission, 202-274-6069.

University of the Incarnate Word, School of Graduate Studies and Research, Dreeben School of Education, Program in Teaching, San Antonio, TX 78209-6397. Offers elementary teaching (MAT); secondary teaching (MAT). *Students:* 11 full-time (9 women), 90 part-time (64 women); includes 57 minority (8 African Americans, 2 Asian Americans or Pacific Islanders, 47 Hispanic Americans), 2 international. Average age 35. In 2006, 15 degrees awarded. Application fee: $20. *Expenses:* Tuition: Part-time $570 per credit hour. Required fees: $54 per credit hour. One-time fee: $195 part-time. Tuition and fees vary according to degree level. *Financial support:* Federal Work-Study and scholarships/grants available. *Unit head:* Dr. Elda Martinez, Director of Teacher Education, 210-832-3297, Fax: 210-829-3134, E-mail: eemartin@uiwtx.edu. *Application contact:* Andrea Cyterski-Acosta, Dean of Enrollment, 210-829-6005, Fax: 210-829-3921, E-mail: cyterski@uiwtx.edu.

University of the Incarnate Word, School of Graduate Studies and Research, Dreeben School of Education, Programs in Education, San Antonio, TX 78209-6397. Offers adult education (M Ed, MA); diversity education (M Ed, MA); early childhood education (M Ed, MA); instructional technology (M Ed, MA); international education and entrepreneurship (PhD); kinesiology (M Ed, MA); mathematics education (PhD); organizational leadership (PhD); organizational learning (M Ed, MA); reading (M Ed, MA); special education (M Ed, MA). *Students:* 15 full-time (8 women), 179 part-time (117 women); includes 70 minority (20 African Americans, 1 American Indian/Alaska Native, 1 Asian American or Pacific Islander, 48 Hispanic Americans), 54 international. Average age 39. In 2006, 15 degrees awarded. Application fee: $20. *Expenses:* Tuition: Part-time $570 per credit hour. Required fees: $54 per credit hour. One-time fee: $195 part-time. Tuition and fees vary according to degree level. *Financial support:* Federal Work-Study and scholarships/grants available. *Unit head:* Dr. Richard Gray, Director, 210-829-3138, Fax: 210-829-3134, E-mail: gray@uiwtx.edu. *Application contact:* Andrea Cyterski-Acosta, Dean of Enrollment, 210-829-6005, Fax: 210-829-3921, E-mail: cyterski@uiwtx.edu.

University of the Incarnate Word, School of Graduate Studies and Research, Dreeben School of Education, Programs in General Education, San Antonio, TX 78209-6397. Offers M Ed, MA. *Expenses:* Tuition: Part-time $570 per credit hour. Required fees: $54 per credit hour. One-time fee: $195 part-time. Tuition and fees vary according to degree level. *Application contact:* Andrea Cyterski-Acosta, Dean of Enrollment, 210-829-6005, Fax: 210-829-3921, E-mail: cyterski@uiwtx.edu.

University of the Pacific, School of Education, Stockton, CA 95211-0197. Offers M Ed, MA, Ed D, Ed S. *Accreditation:* NCATE. *Faculty:* 20 full-time (12 women), 9 part-time/adjunct (4 women). *Students:* 67 full-time (50 women), 105 part-time (66 women); includes 58 minority (11 African Americans, 1 American Indian/Alaska Native, 20 Asian Americans or Pacific Islanders, 26 Hispanic Americans), 5 international. Average age 33. 116 applicants, 62% accepted, 51 enrolled. In 2006, 57 master's, 9 doctorates awarded. *Degree requirements:* For doctorate, thesis/dissertation. *Entrance requirements:* For master's, GRE General Test; for doctorate, GRE General Test, GRE Subject Test. Additional exam requirements/recommendations for international students: Required—TOEFL (minimum score 475 paper-based; 150 computer-based). *Application deadline:* For fall admission, 3/1 priority date for domestic students; for spring admission, 10/15 for domestic students. Applications are processed on a rolling basis. Application fee: $75. *Expenses:* Tuition: Full-time $26,920. Required fees: $430. Tuition and fees vary according to course load. *Financial support:* In 2006–07, 13 teaching assistantships were awarded; institutionally sponsored loans also available. Support available to part-time students. Financial award application deadline: 3/1; financial award applicants required to submit FAFSA. *Unit head:* Dr. Lynn Beck, Dean, 209-946-2683, E-mail: lbeck@pacific.edu.

University of the Sacred Heart, Graduate Programs, Department of Education, San Juan, PR 00914-0383. Offers early childhood education (M Ed); instruction systems and education technology (M Ed). Part-time and evening/weekend programs available. *Degree requirements:* For master's, thesis. *Entrance requirements:* For master's, EXADEP, minimum undergraduate GPA of 2.75, interview.

University of the Virgin Islands, Graduate Programs, Division of Education, Saint Thomas, VI 00802-9990. Offers MAE. Part-time and evening/weekend programs available. *Faculty:* 9 full-time (5 women), 6 part-time/adjunct (4 women). *Students:* 22 full-time (14 women), 118 part-time (105 women); includes 105 minority (97 African Americans, 3 Asian Americans or Pacific Islanders, 5 Hispanic Americans), 21 international. Average age 36. 76 applicants, 66% accepted, 37 enrolled. In 2006, 29 degrees awarded. *Degree requirements:* For master's, thesis or alternative, comprehensive exam, registration. *Entrance requirements:* For master's, minimum GPA of 2.5. *Application deadline:* For fall admission, 4/30 for domestic and international students; for spring admission, 11/30 for domestic and international students. Application fee: $25. *Expenses:* Tuition, area resident: Full-time $4,950; part-time $275 per credit.

Education—General

University of the Virgin Islands *(continued)*

Tuition, nonresident: full-time $9,900; part-time $550 per credit. Required fees: $130 per term. Tuition and fees vary according to course load and degree level. *Financial support:* Scholarships/grants available. Financial award application deadline: 4/15. *Faculty research:* Student self-concept and sense of futility. *Unit head:* Dr. Cynthia L. Jackson, Chairperson, 340-692-4117, Fax: 340-692-4009, E-mail: cjackso2@uvi.edu. *Application contact:* Carolyn Cook-Roberts, Director of Admissions, 340-693-1224, Fax: 340-693-1155, E-mail: ccook@uvi.edu.

The University of Toledo, College of Graduate Studies, College of Education, Toledo, OH 43606-3390. Offers MAE, ME, MES, MME, DE, PhD, Ed S. *Accreditation:* NCATE. Part-time and evening/weekend programs available. *Faculty:* 38 full-time (19 women), 21 part-time/adjunct (11 women). *Students:* 244 full-time (176 women), 485 part-time (365 women); includes 115 minority (85 African Americans, 3 American Indian/Alaska Native, 5 Asian Americans or Pacific Islanders, 22 Hispanic Americans), 24 international. Average age 35. 240 applicants, 84% accepted, 148 enrolled. In 2006, 182 master's, 13 doctorates, 1 other advanced degree awarded. Terminal master's awarded for partial completion of doctoral program. *Degree requirements:* For doctorate, thesis/dissertation, comprehensive exam; for Ed S, thesis optional. *Entrance requirements:* For doctorate, GRE. *Application deadline:* Applications are processed on a rolling basis. Application fee: $45. Electronic applications accepted. *Financial support:* In 2006–07, 6 research assistantships with full tuition reimbursements (averaging $11,000 per year), 14 teaching assistantships with full tuition reimbursements (averaging $11,000 per year) were awarded; fellowships, career-related internships or fieldwork, Federal Work-Study, institutionally sponsored loans, scholarships/grants, tuition waivers (full), and administrative assistantships also available. Support available to part-time students. Financial award application deadline: 4/1; financial award applicants required to submit FAFSA. *Faculty research:* Cognitive studies, learning and memory, learning resources, whole language, administration of professional development schools. *Unit head:* Dr. Thomas J. Switzer, Dean, 419-530-2026, Fax: 419-530-7719, E-mail: thomas.switzer@utoledo.edu.

University of Toronto, School of Graduate Studies, Social Sciences Division, Faculty of Education, Toronto, ON M5S 1A1, Canada. Offers M Ed, MA, MT, Ed D, PhD. Part-time and evening/weekend programs available. *Degree requirements:* For master's, thesis (for some programs); for doctorate, thesis/dissertation. *Entrance requirements:* For master's, minimum B average in final year, 1 year of professional experience in field (MA, M Ed); for doctorate, minimum B+ average, professional experience in education or a relevant field (Ed D). *Expenses:* Contact institution.

University of Tulsa, Graduate School, College of Arts and Sciences, School of Education, Tulsa, OK 74104-3189. Offers education (MA); mathematics and science education (MSMSE); teaching arts (MTA). *Accreditation:* Teacher Education Accreditation Council. Part-time programs available. *Faculty:* 5 full-time (2 women), 3 part-time/adjunct (all women). *Students:* 11 full-time (all women), 5 part-time (2 women), 2 international. Average age 29. 15 applicants, 67% accepted, 6 enrolled. In 2006, 4 degrees awarded. *Median time to degree:* Master's–1.75 years full-time. *Degree requirements:* For master's, thesis optional. *Entrance requirements:* For master's, GRE General Test. Additional exam requirements/recommendations for international students: Required—TOEFL (minimum score 575 paper-based; 231 computer-based), IELTS (minimum score 7). *Application deadline:* For fall admission, 2/1 priority date for domestic students. Applications are processed on a rolling basis. Application fee: $40. Electronic applications accepted. *Expenses:* Tuition: Full-time $13,338; part-time $741 per credit hour. *Financial support:* In 2006–07, 1 research assistantship (averaging $10,300 per year), 7 teaching assistantships with full and partial tuition reimbursements (averaging $10,300 per year) were awarded; fellowships with full and partial tuition reimbursements, Federal Work-Study, scholarships/grants, tuition waivers (full and partial), and unspecified assistantships also available. Support available to part-time students. Financial award application deadline: 2/1; financial award applicants required to submit FAFSA. *Faculty research:* Math/science education, educational technology, curriculum and instruction, international comparative education, research and evaluation. Total annual research expenditures: $259,236. *Unit head:* Dr. Diane E. Beals, Chairperson, 918-631-2045, Fax: 918-631-2133, E-mail: diane-beals@utulsa. edu. *Application contact:* Dr. Alexander W. Wiseman, Head, 918-631-2371, Fax: 918-631-2133, E-mail: alexander-wiseman@utulsa.edu.

University of Utah, The Graduate School, College of Education, Salt Lake City, UT 84112-1107. Offers M Ed, M Phil, M Stat, MA, MAT, MS, Ed D, PhD, MPA/Ed D, MPA/PhD. Part-time and evening/weekend programs available. *Faculty:* 65 full-time (35 women), 13 part-time/adjunct (6 women). *Students:* 274 full-time (199 women), 336 part-time (237 women); includes 80 minority (12 African Americans, 18 American Indian/Alaska Native, 14 Asian Americans or Pacific Islanders, 36 Hispanic Americans), 12 international. Average age 35. 594 applicants, 61% accepted, 292 enrolled. In 2006, 215 master's, 34 doctorates awarded. *Median time to degree:* Of those who began their doctoral program in fall 1998, 56% received their degree in 8 years or less. *Entrance requirements:* For master's, minimum undergraduate GPA of 3.0. Additional exam requirements/recommendations for international students: Required—TOEFL (minimum score 500 paper-based; 173 computer-based). *Application deadline:* For fall admission, 4/1 for domestic and international students; for spring admission, 11/1 for domestic and international students. Applications are processed on a rolling basis. Application fee: $45 ($65 for international students). Electronic applications accepted. *Expenses:* Contact institution. Tuition and fees vary according to class time and program. *Financial support:* Fellowships with full tuition reimbursements, research assistantships with full tuition reimbursements, teaching assistantships with full and partial tuition reimbursements, career-related internships or fieldwork, Federal Work-Study, institutionally sponsored loans, scholarships/grants, tuition waivers (full and partial), and unspecified assistantships available. Support available to part-time students. Financial award application deadline: 2/1; financial award applicants required to submit FAFSA. *Faculty research:* Leadership, autism, reading instruction, mental retardation, diagnosis. Total annual research expenditures: $94,226. *Unit head:* David J. Sperry, Dean, 801-581-7411, Fax: 801-581-5223, E-mail: david.sperry@ed.utah.edu. *Application contact:* Kristin Anderson, Executive Secretary, 801-581-8221, Fax: 801-581-5223, E-mail: kristin.anderson@ed.utah.edu.

University of Vermont, Graduate College, College of Education and Social Services, Burlington, VT 05405. Offers M Ed, MS, MSW, Ed D. *Accreditation:* NCATE. Part-time programs available. *Students:* 435 (324 women); includes 25 minority (9 African Americans, 4 American Indian/Alaska Native, 8 Asian Americans or Pacific Islanders, 4 Hispanic Americans) 7 international. 479 applicants, 59% accepted, 175 enrolled. In 2006, 161 master's, 12 doctorates awarded. *Degree requirements:* For doctorate, thesis/dissertation. *Entrance requirements:* Additional exam requirements/recommendations for international students: Required—TOEFL (minimum score 550 paper-based; 213 computer-based). Application fee: $40. *Expenses:* Tuition, state resident: part-time $434 per credit. Tuition, nonresident: part-time $1,096 per credit. *Financial support:* Fellowships, research assistantships, teaching assistantships, career-related internships or fieldwork and Federal Work-Study available. *Unit head:* Dr. Fayneese Miller, Dean, 802-656-3424.

University of Vermont, Graduate College, College of Education and Social Services, Department of Education, Program in Educational Studies, Burlington, VT 05405. Offers M Ed. *Students:* 3 (all women) 7 applicants, 29% accepted, 1 enrolled. *Degree requirements:* For master's, thesis or alternative. *Entrance requirements:* Additional exam requirements/recommendations for international students: Required—TOEFL (minimum score 550 paper-based; 213 computer-based). *Application deadline:* For fall admission, 8/1 priority date for domestic students. Applications are processed on a rolling basis. Application fee: $40. *Expenses:* Tuition, state resident: part-time $434 per credit. Tuition, nonresident: part-time $1,096 per credit. *Financial support:* Fellowships, research assistantships, teaching assistantships available. Financial award application deadline: 3/1. *Unit head:* Dr. D. Shiman, Coordinator, 802-656-3356.

University of Victoria, Faculty of Graduate Studies, Faculty of Education, Victoria, BC V8W 2Y2, Canada. Offers M Ed, M Sc, MA, PhD.

University of Virginia, Curry School of Education, Charlottesville, VA 22903. Offers M Ed, MT, Ed D, PhD, Ed S. *Accreditation:* Teacher Education Accreditation Council. *Faculty:* 100 full-time (56 women), 7 part-time/adjunct (6 women). *Students:* 729 full-time (540 women), 156 part-time (102 women); includes 88 minority (48 African Americans, 1 American Indian/Alaska Native, 27 Asian Americans or Pacific Islanders, 12 Hispanic Americans), 34 international. Average age 30. 914 applicants, 52% accepted, 233 enrolled. In 2006, 551 master's, 86 doctorates, 48 other advanced degrees awarded. *Degree requirements:* For doctorate, thesis/dissertation. *Entrance requirements:* For master's, doctorate, and Ed S, GRE General Test. *Application deadline:* Applications are processed on a rolling basis. Application fee: $60. Electronic applications accepted. *Financial support:* Fellowships, Federal Work-Study available. Financial award applicants required to submit FAFSA. *Unit head:* David W. Breneman, Dean, 434-924-3332, Fax: 434-924-0888, E-mail: dbreneman@virginia.edu. *Application contact:* Linda Berry, Student Enrollment Coordinator, 434-924-0738, E-mail: curry-admissions@virginia.edu.

University of Washington, Graduate School, College of Education, Seattle, WA 98195. Offers curriculum and instruction (M Ed, Ed D, PhD), including educational technology, general curriculum (Ed D, PhD), language, literacy, and culture, mathematics education, multicultural education, reading and language arts education (Ed D), science education, social studies education, teaching and curriculum (M Ed); educational leadership and policy studies (M Ed, Ed D, PhD), including administration, educational organization and policy, higher education, school district leadership (Ed D), social/cultural foundations; educational psychology (M Ed, PhD), including human development and cognition, measurement and research, school counseling (M Ed), school psychology; special education (M Ed, Ed D, PhD), including early childhood education, elementary special education, emotional and behavioral disabilities (M Ed), general special education, severe disabilities; teacher education (MIT). *Accreditation:* APA. Part-time and evening/weekend programs available. *Degree requirements:* For master's, thesis optional; for doctorate, thesis/dissertation. *Entrance requirements:* For master's and doctorate, GRE General Test, minimum GPA of 3.0. Additional exam requirements/recommendations for international students: Required—TOEFL. Electronic applications accepted. *Faculty research:* School restructuring/effective schools, special education interventions, literacy and writing, technology, school partnerships, teacher preparation.

University of Washington, Graduate School, Education Programs, Bothell Campus, Seattle, WA 98195. Offers M Ed. Part-time and evening/weekend programs available. *Degree requirements:* For master's, thesis or alternative, registration. *Entrance requirements:* For master's, GRE, MAT. Electronic applications accepted.

University of Washington, Graduate School, Education Programs, Tacoma Campus, Seattle, WA 98195. Offers education (M Ed, Professional Certificate); K-8 education (Certificate); principalship (Certificate); school administration (Certificate). Part-time and evening/weekend programs available. *Degree requirements:* For master's, final project. *Entrance requirements:* For master's, GRE General Test; for other advanced degree, Washington Educator Skills Test - Basic. Electronic applications accepted. *Faculty research:* Special education, technology, literacy, children's literature, science.

University of Washington, Bothell, Program in Education, Bothell, WA 98011-8246. Offers MA. *Faculty:* 5 full-time (4 women). *Students:* 2 full-time (0 women), 63 part-time (52 women); includes 2 minority (1 African American, 1 American Indian/Alaska Native). Average age 34. 22 applicants, 50% accepted, 11 enrolled. In 2006, 22 degrees awarded. *Entrance requirements:* For master's, thesis. *Entrance requirements:* Additional exam requirements/recommendations for international students: Required—TOEFL. *Application deadline:* For fall admission, 8/31 priority date for domestic students; for spring admission, 2/26 priority date for domestic students. Applications are processed on a rolling basis. Application fee: $45. Electronic applications accepted. *Financial support:* Federal Work-Study and unspecified assistantships available. *Faculty research:* Leadership, multicultural education, literacy, science education, stratification. *Unit head:* Prof. Cherry Banks, Interim Director, 425-352-5336, Fax: 425-352-5234, E-mail: camb@uwb.edu. *Application contact:* Amelia Bowers, Education Program Advisor, 425-352-5274, Fax: 425-352-5455, E-mail: abowers@uwb.edu.

The University of West Alabama, School of Graduate Studies, College of Education, Livingston, AL 35470. Offers M Ed, MAT, MSCE. *Accreditation:* NCATE. Part-time and evening/weekend programs available. *Faculty:* 17 full-time (9 women), 42 part-time/adjunct (33 women). *Students:* 709 full-time (601 women), 888 part-time (772 women); includes 707 minority (673 African Americans, 8 American Indian/Alaska Native, 12 Asian Americans or Pacific Islanders, 14 Hispanic Americans), 2 international. In 2006, 344 degrees awarded. *Entrance requirements:* For master's, GRE General Test, MAT, minimum GPA of 2.75. *Application deadline:* For fall admission, 9/10 priority date for domestic students; for spring admission, 3/24 for domestic students. Applications are processed on a rolling basis. Application fee: $20 ($50 for international students). *Financial support:* In 2006–07, 13 students received support. Career-related internships or fieldwork, Federal Work-Study, scholarships/grants, and unspecified assistantships available. Support available to part-time students. Financial award applicants required to submit FAFSA. *Unit head:* Dr. Martha Hocutt, Dean, College of Education, 205-652-3421, Fax: 205-652-3706, E-mail: mhocutt@uwa.edu.

The University of Western Ontario, Faculty of Graduate Studies, Social Sciences Division, Faculty of Education, London, ON N6A 5B8, Canada. Offers M Ed. Part-time programs available. *Entrance requirements:* For master's, minimum B average. *Application deadline:* For fall admission, 2/1 for domestic students. Application fee: $50. *Financial support:* Research assistantships, teaching assistantships, career-related internships or fieldwork available. Financial award application deadline: 4/1. *Unit head:* Dr. Allan T. Pearson, Dean, 519-661-2111 Ext. 82080, E-mail: apearson@uwo.ca. *Application contact:* Allan Pitman, Graduate Supervisor, 519-661-2080 Ext. 88870, Fax: 519-661-3833, E-mail: pitman@uwo.ca.

University of West Georgia, Graduate School, College of Education, Carrollton, GA 30118. Offers M Ed, Ed D, Ed S. *Accreditation:* NCATE. Part-time and evening/weekend programs available. *Faculty:* 74 full-time (46 women), 12 part-time/adjunct (7 women). *Students:* 226 full-time (192 women), 1,166 part-time (948 women); includes 329 minority (309 African Americans, 1 American Indian/Alaska Native, 6 Asian Americans or Pacific Islanders, 13 Hispanic Americans), 1 international. Average age 29. In 2006, 372 master's, 2 doctorates, 123 other advanced degrees awarded. *Degree requirements:* For doctorate, thesis/dissertation, research paper; for Ed S, research paper. *Entrance requirements:* For master's, GRE, minimum GPA of 2.5; for doctorate, GRE, minimum GPA of 3.0; for Ed S, GRE, master's degree, minimum graduate GPA of 3.0. *Application deadline:* For fall admission, 8/1 for domestic students; for spring admission, 12/18 for domestic students. Applications are processed on a rolling basis. Application fee: $20. *Expenses:* Tuition, state resident: full-time $2,286; part-time $127 per credit. Tuition, nonresident: full-time $9,144; part-time $508 per credit. Required fees: $494; $27 per credit. $121 per semester. *Financial support:* In 2006–07, 46 research assistantships with partial tuition reimbursements (averaging $6,000 per year) were awarded; career-related internships or fieldwork and unspecified assistantships also available. Support available to part-time students. Financial award applicants required to submit FAFSA. *Faculty research:* Language and culture via distance education, speech pathology, staff development, mathematics/science instruction, alternative track: certification of noneducational degree. *Unit head:* Dr. Kent Layton, Dean, 678-839-6570, Fax: 678-839-6098, E-mail: klayton@westga.edu. *Application contact:* Dr. Charles W. Clark, Chair, 678-839-6508, E-mail: cclark@westga.edu.

University of Windsor, Faculty of Graduate Studies and Research, Faculty of Education, Windsor, ON N9B 3P4, Canada. Offers education (M Ed); educational studies (PhD). Part-time and evening/weekend programs available. *Degree requirements:* For master's, thesis or alternative; for doctorate, thesis/dissertation, comprehensive exam. *Entrance requirements:* For master's, minimum B average, teaching certificate; for doctorate, M Ed or MA in education, minimum A average, evidence of research competencies. Additional exam requirements/recommendations for international students: Required—TOEFL (minimum score 600 paper-based; 250 computer-based). Electronic applications accepted. *Faculty research:* School structures, teacher morale, cognitive deficits, new technologies in art education, internal and external factors that affect learning and teaching.

University of Wisconsin–Eau Claire, College of Education and Human Sciences, Eau Claire, WI 54702-4004. Offers MAT, MEPD, MS, MSE, MST. *Faculty:* 38 full-time (20 women). *Students:* 46 full-time (41 women), 56 part-time (47 women); includes 3 minority (1 American Indian/Alaska Native, 1 Asian American or Pacific Islander, 1 Hispanic American), 3 international. Average age 30. 161 applicants, 38% accepted, 31 enrolled. In 2006, 48 degrees awarded. *Degree requirements:* For master's, thesis optional. *Application deadline:* For fall admission, 7/1 for domestic students; for spring admission, 12/1 for domestic students. Applications are processed on a rolling basis. Application fee: $45. *Expenses:* Tuition, state resident: full-time $6,533; part-time $363 per credit. Tuition, nonresident: full-time $17,143; part-time $952 per credit. Tuition and fees vary according to program and reciprocity agreements. *Financial support:* In 2006–07, 54 students received support, including 6 teaching assistantships (averaging $5,800 per year); career-related internships or fieldwork and Federal Work-Study also available. Financial award application deadline: 3/1; financial award applicants required to submit FAFSA. *Unit head:* Dr. Katherine Rhoades, Dean, 715-836-3671, Fax: 715-836-3245, E-mail: rhoadeka@uwec.edu.

University of Wisconsin–Green Bay, Graduate Studies, Program in Applied Leadership for Teaching and Learning, Green Bay, WI 54311-7001. Offers MS Ed. Part-time and evening/weekend programs available. *Faculty:* 7 full-time (2 women), 2 part-time/adjunct (both women). *Students:* Average age 36. 13 applicants, 46% accepted, 3 enrolled. In 2006, 18 degrees awarded. *Degree requirements:* For master's, thesis or alternative. *Entrance requirements:* For master's, minimum GPA of 3.0. *Application deadline:* For fall admission, 8/1 for domestic students; for spring admission, 11/1 for domestic students. Applications are processed on a rolling basis. Application fee: $45. Electronic applications accepted. *Expenses:* Tuition, state resident: full-time $5,910; part-time $246 per credit. Tuition, nonresident: full-time $16,520; part-time $688 per credit. Required fees: $1,148; $48 per credit. *Financial support:* Application deadline: 7/15. *Faculty research:* Curriculum design, assessment. *Unit head:* Dr. Tim Kaufman, Director, 920-465-2964, E-mail: kaufman@uwgb.edu. *Application contact:* Pam Harvey-Jacobs, Director of Admissions, 920-465-2111, Fax: 920-465-5754, E-mail: uwgb@uwgb.edu.

University of Wisconsin–La Crosse, Office of University Graduate Studies, College of Liberal Studies, Department of Educational Studies, La Crosse, WI 54601-3742. Offers college student development and administration (MS Ed); professional development (MEPD), including elementary education, K–12, professional development, secondary education; reading (MS Ed); special education (MS Ed), including emotional disturbance, learning disabilities. Part-time programs available. *Faculty:* 18 full-time (6 women), 49 part-time/adjunct (35 women). *Students:* 34 full-time (24 women), 712 part-time (516 women); includes 20 minority (5 African Americans, 1 American Indian/Alaska Native, 10 Asian Americans or Pacific Islanders, 4 Hispanic Americans). Average age 35. 234 applicants, 91% accepted, 198 enrolled. In 2006, 236 degrees awarded. *Degree requirements:* For master's, thesis optional. *Entrance requirements:* For master's, minimum GPA of 2.85. Additional exam requirements/recommendations for international students: Required—TOEFL (minimum score 550 paper-based; 213 computer-based). *Application deadline:* Applications are processed on a rolling basis. Application fee: $45. Electronic applications accepted. *Financial support:* In 2006–07, 60 students received support; research assistantships, career-related internships or fieldwork, Federal Work-Study, institutionally sponsored loans, health care benefits, unspecified assistantships, and grant-funded positions available. Support available to part-time students. Financial award application deadline: 3/15; financial award applicants required to submit FAFSA. *Faculty research:* Reading techniques, diversity and social justice, special education services. Total annual research expenditures: $200,000. *Unit head:* Dr. Jon Davies, Chair, 608-785-5411, Fax: 608-785-8128, E-mail: davies.jon@uwlax.edu. *Application contact:* Kathryn Kiefer, Associate Director of Admissions, 608-785-8939, E-mail: admissions@uwlax.edu.

University of Wisconsin–Madison, Graduate School, School of Education, Madison, WI 53706-1380. Offers MA, MFA, MS, PhD, Certificate. *Faculty:* 156 full-time (71 women). *Students:* 648 full-time (434 women), 375 part-time (246 women). In 2006, 203 master's, 86 doctorates awarded. *Degree requirements:* For doctorate, thesis/dissertation. *Entrance requirements:* Additional exam requirements/recommendations for international students: Required—TOEFL (minimum score 550 paper-based; 213 computer-based; 80 iBT), IELTS (minimum score 6). Application fee: $45. *Financial support:* In 2006–07, 54 fellowships with full tuition reimbursements, 19 research assistantships with full tuition reimbursements, 166 teaching assistantships with full tuition reimbursements were awarded; traineeships and project assistantships also available. Total annual research expenditures: $24.8 million. *Unit head:* Dr. Julie K. Underwood, Dean, 608-262-1763.

University of Wisconsin–Milwaukee, Graduate School, School of Education, Milwaukee, WI 53201-0413. Offers MS, PhD, Certificate, Ed S. Part-time programs available. *Faculty:* 80 full-time (48 women). *Students:* 303 full-time (237 women), 366 part-time (270 women); includes 145 minority (90 African Americans, 10 American Indian/Alaska Native, 19 Asian Americans or Pacific Islanders, 26 Hispanic Americans), 14 international. Average age 35. 467 applicants, 44% accepted, 102 enrolled. In 2006, 154 master's, 24 doctorates awarded. *Degree requirements:* For doctorate, thesis/dissertation. *Entrance requirements:* For doctorate, GRE General Test. *Application deadline:* For fall admission, 1/1 priority date for domestic students; for spring admission, 9/1 for domestic students. Applications are processed on a rolling basis. Application fee: $45 ($75 for international students). *Expenses:* Tuition, state resident: part-time $510 per credit. Tuition, nonresident: part-time $1,408 per credit. Tuition and fees vary according to program. *Financial support:* In 2006–07, 6 teaching assistantships were awarded; fellowships, research assistantships, career-related internships or fieldwork, Federal Work-Study, and unspecified assistantships also available. Support available to part-time students. Financial award application deadline: 4/15. *Unit head:* Alfonzo Thurman, Dean, 414-229-4181, E-mail: athurman@uwm.edu.

University of Wisconsin–Oshkosh, The School of Graduate Studies, College of Education and Human Services, Oshkosh, WI 54901. Offers MS, MSE. *Accreditation:* NCATE. Part-time and evening/weekend programs available. *Degree requirements:* For master's, thesis or alternative, field report, comprehensive exam (for some programs), registration. *Entrance requirements:* For master's, teaching license, letters of recommendation, interview. Additional exam requirements/recommendations for international students: Required—TOEFL (minimum score 550 paper-based; 213 computer-based). Electronic applications accepted.

University of Wisconsin–Platteville, School of Graduate Studies, College of Liberal Arts and Education, School of Education, Platteville, WI 53818-3099. Offers adult education (MSE); elementary education (MSE); middle school education (MSE); secondary education (MSE); vocational and technical education (MSE). *Accreditation:* NCATE. Part-time programs available. *Faculty:* 8 part-time/adjunct (3 women). *Students:* 48 full-time (37 women), 103 part-time (72 women); includes 33 minority (27 African Americans, 1 Asian American or Pacific Islander, 5 Hispanic Americans), 39 international. 39 applicants, 72% accepted. In 2006, 55 degrees awarded. *Degree requirements:* For master's, thesis or alternative, comprehensive exam, registration. *Entrance requirements:* Additional exam requirements/recommendations for international students: Required—TOEFL (minimum score 500 paper-based; 173 computer-based). *Application deadline:* For fall admission, 7/1 priority date for domestic students; for spring admission, 11/1 for domestic students. Applications are processed on a rolling basis. Application fee: $45. Electronic applications accepted. *Expenses:* Tuition, state resident: part-time $365 per credit. Tuition, nonresident: part-time $955 per credit. *Financial support:* Research assistantships with partial tuition reimbursements, career-related internships or fieldwork, Federal Work-Study, institutionally sponsored loans, scholarships/grants, and unspecified assistantships available. Support available to part-time students. *Unit head:* Dr. Michael Anderson, Director, 608-342-1131, Fax: 608-342-1133, E-mail: andersonmi@uwplatt.edu. *Application contact:* Kristal Prohaska, Admissions and Enrollment Management, 608-342-1125, Fax: 608-342-1122, E-mail: admit@uwplatt.edu.

University of Wisconsin–River Falls, Outreach and Graduate Studies, College of Education and Professional Studies, Department of Teacher Education, River Falls, WI 54022-5001. Offers elementary education (MSE); reading (MSE). *Accreditation:* NCATE. Part-time programs available. *Degree requirements:* For master's, thesis or alternative, comprehensive exam, registration. *Entrance requirements:* For master's, minimum GPA of 2.75. Electronic applications accepted.

University of Wisconsin–Stevens Point, College of Professional Studies, School of Education, Stevens Point, WI 54481-3897. Offers education—general/reading (MSE); education—general/special (MSE); educational administration (MSE); elementary education (MSE); guidance and counseling (MSE). *Faculty:* 13 full-time (11 women). *Students:* 6 full-time (2 women), 66 part-time (54 women); includes 3 minority (2 Asian Americans or Pacific Islanders, 1 Hispanic American). Average age 26. In 2006, 76 degrees awarded. *Degree requirements:* For master's, thesis or alternative, comprehensive exam. *Entrance requirements:* For master's, teacher certification, minimum undergraduate GPA of 3.0, 2 years of teaching experience, letters of recommendation. Additional exam requirements/recommendations for international students: Required—TOEFL (minimum score 523 paper-based; 193 computer-based). *Application deadline:* For fall admission, 5/1 priority date for domestic students. Applications are processed on a rolling basis. Application fee: $45. *Expenses:* Tuition, state resident: full-time $5,910; part-time $328 per credit. Tuition, nonresident: full-time $16,520; part-time $918 per credit. Required fees: $756; $73 per credit. *Financial support:* In 2006–07, 4 research assistantships with partial tuition reimbursements (averaging $9,807 per year) were awarded; teaching assistantships, Federal Work-Study, tuition waivers (partial), and unspecified assistantships also available. Support available to part-time students. Financial award application deadline: 5/1; financial award applicants required to submit FAFSA. *Faculty research:* Gifted education early childhood, special education curriculum and instruction, standards-based education. *Unit head:* Dr. JoAnne Katzmarek, Associate Dean, 715-346-4430, Fax: 715-346-4846, E-mail: jkatzmar@uwsp.edu. *Application contact:* Dr. Patricia Caro, Director, 715-346-4403, Fax: 715-346-4846, E-mail: pcaro@uwsp.edu.

University of Wisconsin–Stout, Graduate School, School of Education, Menomonie, WI 54751. Offers MS, MS Ed, Ed S. Part-time programs available. Postbaccalaureate distance learning degree programs offered (no on-campus study). *Faculty:* 30 full-time (20 women). *Students:* 83 full-time (69 women), 160 part-time (114 women); includes 19 minority (6 African Americans, 2 American Indian/Alaska Native, 4 Asian Americans or Pacific Islanders, 7 Hispanic Americans), 2 international. Average age 32. 114 applicants, 59% accepted, 52 enrolled. In 2006, 67 master's, 12 other advanced degrees awarded. *Degree requirements:* For master's and Ed S, thesis. *Entrance requirements:* For master's, minimum GPA of 2.75, 3.0 for some programs; for Ed S, minimum GPA of 3.25. Additional exam requirements/recommendations for international students: Required—TOEFL (minimum score 500 paper-based; 173 computer-based; 61 iBT). Application fee: $45. Electronic applications accepted. *Expenses:* Tuition, state resident: part-time $317 per credit. Tuition, nonresident: part-time $543 per credit. Tuition and fees vary according to reciprocity agreements. *Financial support:* In 2006–07, 15 research assistantships with partial tuition reimbursements (averaging $5,855 per year), 5 teaching assistantships with partial tuition reimbursements (averaging $9,786 per year) were awarded; Federal Work-Study, scholarships/grants, health care benefits, tuition waivers (partial), and unspecified assistantships also available. Support available to part-time students. *Unit head:* Dr. Mary Hopkins-Best, Interim Dean, 715-232-1168, E-mail: hopkinsbestm@uwstout.edu. *Application contact:* Anne E. Johnson, Graduate Student Evaluator, 715-232-1322, Fax: 715-232-2413, E-mail: johnsona@wwstout.edu.

University of Wisconsin–Superior, Graduate Division, Department of Teacher Education, Superior, WI 54880-4500. Offers instruction (MSE); special education (MSE), including emotional/behavior disabilities, learning disabilities; teaching reading (MSE). Part-time and evening/weekend programs available. Postbaccalaureate distance learning degree programs offered (minimal on-campus study). *Degree requirements:* For master's, research project. *Entrance requirements:* For master's, minimum GPA of 2.75, teaching certificate. *Faculty research:* Science teaching.

University of Wisconsin–Whitewater, School of Graduate Studies, College of Education, Whitewater, WI 53190-1790. Offers MS, MS Ed. *Accreditation:* NCATE. Part-time and evening/weekend programs available. Postbaccalaureate distance learning degree programs offered (no on-campus study). *Students:* 99 full-time (77 women), 288 part-time (237 women); includes 38 minority (12 African Americans, 2 American Indian/Alaska Native, 3 Asian Americans or Pacific Islanders, 21 Hispanic Americans). Average age 30. 180 applicants, 42% accepted, 42 enrolled. In 2006, 142 degrees awarded. *Entrance requirements:* Additional exam requirements/recommendations for international students: Required—TOEFL (minimum score 550 paper-based; 213 computer-based). *Application deadline:* For fall admission, 7/15 priority date for domestic students; for spring admission, 12/1 priority date for domestic students. Applications are processed on a rolling basis. Application fee: $45. Electronic applications accepted. *Expenses:* Tuition, state resident: full-time $3,311. Tuition, nonresident: full-time $8,616. Required fees: $368 per credit. *Financial support:* In 2006–07, 1 research assistantship (averaging $9,875 per year) was awarded; career-related internships or fieldwork, Federal Work-Study, unspecified assistantships, and out of state fee waiver also available. Support available to part-time students. Financial award application deadline: 3/15; financial award applicants required to submit FAFSA. *Unit head:* Dr. Jeffrey Barnett, Dean, 262-472-1101, Fax: 262-472-5716, E-mail: barnettj@uww.edu. *Application contact:* Sally A. Lange, School of Graduate Studies, 262-472-1006, Fax: 262-472-5027, E-mail: gradschl@uww.edu.

Urbana University, Division of Education and Allied Professions, Urbana, OH 43078-2091. Offers classroom education (M Ed). Part-time and evening/weekend programs available. *Degree requirements:* For master's, comprehensive oral exam, capstone research project. *Entrance requirements:* For master's, minimum GPA of 2.7, teaching license. Additional exam requirements/recommendations for international students: Required—TOEFL (minimum score 550 paper-based; 213 computer-based). *Faculty research:* Best professional practices, reading, special education, classroom management, teaching models, school finance.

Ursuline College, School of Graduate Studies, Program in Education, Pepper Pike, OH 44124-4398. Offers MA. *Faculty:* 4 full-time (3 women), 5 part-time/adjunct (3 women). *Students:* 31 full-time (26 women), 122 part-time (109 women); includes 20 minority (17 African Americans, 3 Hispanic Americans). Average age 34. 103 applicants, 100% accepted, 103 enrolled. In 2006, 44 degrees awarded. *Degree requirements:* For master's, comprehensive exam. *Entrance requirements:* For master's, minimum undergraduate GPA of 3.0. Additional exam requirements/recommendations for international students: Required—TOEFL (minimum score 500 paper-based; 173 computer-based). *Application deadline:* For fall admission, 8/1 priority date for domestic students. Applications are processed on a rolling basis. Application fee: $25. *Expenses:* Contact institution. *Financial support:* In 2006–07, 89 students received support. Federal Work-Study available. Financial award application deadline: 3/1. *Unit head:* Dianne Runnestrand, Program Director, 440-684-6109, Fax: 440-684-6088, E-mail: drunnestrand@ursuline.edu. *Application contact:* Jo Mann, Secretary, 440-646-8119, Fax: 440-684-6088, E-mail: gradsch@ursuline.edu.

Utah State University, School of Graduate Studies, College of Education and Human Services, Logan, UT 84322. Offers M Ed, MA, MFHD, MRC, MS, AU D, Ed D, PhD, Ed S. *Accreditation:* NCATE. Part-time and evening/weekend programs available. Postbaccalaureate distance learning degree programs offered (no on-campus study). *Faculty:* 101 full-time (57 women), 20 part-time/adjunct (11 women). *Students:* 648 full-time (377 women), 264 part-time (180 women); includes 33 minority (9 African Americans, 4 American Indian/Alaska Native, 6 Asian Americans or Pacific Islanders, 14 Hispanic Americans), 100 international. Average age 32. 662 applicants, 51% accepted, 253 enrolled. In 2006, 261 master's, 32 doctorates awarded. *Degree requirements:* For doctorate, thesis/dissertation, comprehensive exam. *Entrance requirements:* For master's, GRE General Test, minimum GPA of 3.0; for doctorate, GRE General Test, master's degree; for Ed S, GRE General Test, GRE Subject Test. Additional exam requirements/

Education—General

Utah State University *(continued)*
recommendations for international students: Required—TOEFL (minimum score 550 paper-based; 213 computer-based). *Application deadline:* For fall admission, 6/15 for domestic students; for spring admission, 10/15 for domestic students. Applications are processed on a rolling basis. Application fee: $50 ($60 for international students). *Financial support:* In 2006–07, 7 fellowships with partial tuition reimbursements (averaging $8,163 per year), 58 research assistantships with partial tuition reimbursements (averaging $6,647 per year), 54 teaching assistantships with partial tuition reimbursements (averaging $7,050 per year) were awarded; career-related internships or fieldwork, Federal Work-Study, institutionally sponsored loans, tuition waivers (full and partial), unspecified assistantships, and stipends also available. Support available to part-time students. *Faculty research:* Literacy instruction, design and delivery of instruction, children at-risk and their families, hearing assessment and management, language and literacy development. Total annual research expenditures: $24.7 million. *Unit head:* Dr. Carol Strong, Dean, 435-797-1470, Fax: 435-797-3939. *Application contact:* Shannon Johnson, Staff Assistant, 435-797-1470, Fax: 435-797-3939, E-mail: shannon.johnson@usu.edu.

Utica College, Teacher Education Programs, Utica, NY 13502-4892. Offers MS, MS Ed, CAS. *Accreditation:* Teacher Education Accreditation Council. *Faculty:* 10 full-time (7 women). *Students:* 29 full-time (20 women), 96 part-time (64 women), 1 international. 40 applicants, 70% accepted, 20 enrolled. In 2006, 74 degrees awarded. *Degree requirements:* For master's, comprehensive exam or thesis. *Entrance requirements:* For master's, CST, LAST, minimum GPA of 3.0. Additional exam requirements/recommendations for international students: Required—TOEFL (minimum score 550 paper-based; 213 computer-based). *Application deadline:* Applications are processed on a rolling basis. Application fee: $50. Electronic applications accepted. *Expenses:* Contact institution. *Financial support:* In 2006–07, 90 students received support. Career-related internships or fieldwork, scholarships/grants, tuition waivers (partial), and unspecified assistantships available. Support available to part-time students. Financial award application deadline: 3/15; financial award applicants required to submit FAFSA. *Unit head:* Dr. Lois Fisch, Director, Institute for Excellence in Education, 315-792-3815, E-mail: lfisch@utica.edu. *Application contact:* John D. Rowe, Director of Graduate Admissions, 315-792-3824, Fax: 315-792-3003, E-mail: jrowe@utica.edu.

Valdosta State University, Graduate School, College of Education, Valdosta, GA 31698. Offers M Ed, MS, Ed D, Ed S. *Accreditation:* NCATE. Part-time and evening/weekend programs available. *Degree requirements:* For doctorate and Ed S, thesis/dissertation, comprehensive written and/or oral exams. *Entrance requirements:* For master's, GRE General Test; for doctorate, GRE General Test, minimum GPA of 3.5, 3 years of experience; for Ed S, GRE General Test or MAT. Additional exam requirements/recommendations for international students: Required—TOEFL (minimum score 523 paper-based; 193 computer-based). Electronic applications accepted.

Valparaiso University, Graduate Division, Department of Education, Valparaiso, IN 46383. Offers initial licensure (M Ed); teaching and learning (M Ed); M Ed/Ed S. *Accreditation:* NCATE. Part-time and evening/weekend programs available. *Faculty:* 11 part-time/adjunct (8 women). *Students:* 45 full-time (31 women), 16 part-time (15 women); includes 4 minority (1 African American, 1 Asian American or Pacific Islander, 2 Hispanic Americans). Average age 26. In 2006, 31 master's awarded. *Entrance requirements:* For master's, GRE General Test or MAT, minimum GPA of 3.0. Additional exam requirements/recommendations for international students: Required—TOEFL (minimum score 550 paper-based; 213 computer-based). *Application deadline:* Applications are processed on a rolling basis. Application fee: $30 ($50 for international students). Electronic applications accepted. *Expenses:* Tuition: Part-time $390 per credit hour. Required fees: $60 per term. Tuition and fees vary according to program. *Financial support:* Career-related internships or fieldwork, traineeships, and unspecified assistantships available. Support available to part-time students. Financial award applicants required to submit FAFSA. *Unit head:* Dr. Jan Westrick, Chair, 219-464-5074, Fax: 219-464-6720, E-mail: jan.westrick@valpo.edu. *Application contact:* Dr. Maryanne Dudzinski, Associate Professor of Education, 219-464-5473, Fax: 219-464-6720, E-mail: maryann.dudzinski@valpo.edu.

Vanderbilt University, Graduate School, Program in Learning, Teaching and Diversity, Nashville, TN 37240-1001. Offers MS, PhD. *Faculty:* 29 full-time (17 women). *Students:* 39 full-time (24 women); includes 4 minority (3 African Americans, 1 Asian American or Pacific Islander), 9 international. 68 applicants, 13% accepted, 7 enrolled. In 2006, 1 degree awarded. *Application deadline:* For fall admission, 1/15 for domestic and international students. Applications are processed on a rolling basis. Application fee: $0. Electronic applications accepted. *Expenses:* Tuition: Full-time $24,462. Required fees: $2,515. One-time fee: $30 full-time. Full-time tuition and fees vary according to course load, degree level and program. *Financial support:* Fellowships with tuition reimbursements, research assistantships with full tuition reimbursements, teaching assistantships with full tuition reimbursements, Federal Work-Study, institutionally sponsored loans, and traineeships available. Financial award application deadline: 1/15. *Unit head:* Leona Schauble, Chair, 615-322-8100, Fax: 615-322-8999, E-mail: leona.schauble@vanderbilt.edu. *Application contact:* Dr. Clifford A. Hofwolt, Director of Graduate Studies, 615-322-8100, Fax: 615-322-8999, E-mail: clifford.hofwolt@vanderbilt.edu.

Vanderbilt University, Peabody College, Nashville, TN 37240-1001. Offers M Ed, MPP, Ed D. *Accreditation:* APA (one or more programs are accredited); NCATE. Part-time programs available. *Faculty:* 114 full-time (55 women), 62 part-time/adjunct (38 women). *Students:* 347 full-time (284 women), 134 part-time (80 women); includes 64 minority (52 African Americans, 7 Asian Americans or Pacific Islanders, 5 Hispanic Americans), 21 international. Average age 29. 502 applicants, 62% accepted, 139 enrolled. In 2006, 181 master's, 16 doctorates awarded. *Median time to degree:* Of those who began their doctoral program in fall 1998, 62% received their degree in 8 years or less. *Degree requirements:* For master's, thesis optional; for doctorate, thesis/dissertation, qualifying examinations, residency. *Entrance requirements:* For master's, GRE General Test, MAT; for doctorate, GRE General Test. Additional exam requirements/recommendations for international students: Required—TOEFL (minimum score 550 paper-based; 213 computer-based). *Application deadline:* For fall admission, 12/31 priority date for domestic and international students; for spring admission, 11/1 priority date for domestic and international students. Applications are processed on a rolling basis. Application fee: $0. Electronic applications accepted. *Expenses:* Contact institution. One-time fee: $30 full-time. Full-time tuition and fees vary according to course load, degree level and program. *Financial support:* In 2006–07, 303 students received support, including 115 fellowships with full and partial tuition reimbursements available, 153 research assistantships with full and partial tuition reimbursements available, 35 teaching assistantships with full and partial tuition reimbursements available; career-related internships or fieldwork, Federal Work-Study, institutionally sponsored loans, scholarships/grants, traineeships, tuition waivers (partial), and unspecified assistantships also available. Support available to part-time students. Financial award application deadline: 2/1; financial award applicants required to submit FAFSA. Total annual research expenditures: $25.5 million. *Unit head:* Dr. Camilla P. Benbow, Dean, 615-322-8407, Fax: 615-322-8501, E-mail: camilla.benbow@vanderbilt.edu. *Application contact:* Kimberly Brazil-Tanner, Recruitment Coordinator, 615-332-8410, Fax: 615-322-8401, E-mail: kim.brazil@vanderbilt.edu.

See Close-Up on page 937.

Vanguard University of Southern California, School of Education, Costa Mesa, CA 92626-9601. Offers MA. Evening/weekend programs available. *Faculty:* 4 full-time (3 women), 9 part-time/adjunct (all women). *Students:* 46 full-time (32 women), 57 part-time (47 women); includes 22 minority (2 American Indian/Alaska Native, 8 Asian Americans or Pacific Islanders, 12 Hispanic Americans), 1 international. Average age 31. 77 applicants, 73% accepted, 42 enrolled. In 2006, 20 degrees awarded. *Entrance requirements:* For master's, California Basic Educational Skills Test, California Subject Examinations for Teachers, minimum GPA of 3.0. Additional exam requirements/recommendations for international students: Required—TOEFL (minimum score 550 paper-based; 213 computer-based; 79 iBT). *Application deadline:* For fall admission, 4/1 priority date for domestic students; for spring admission, 10/1

priority date for domestic and international students. Applications are processed on a rolling basis. Application fee: $45. Electronic applications accepted. *Financial support:* In 2006–07, 103 students received support, including 3 teaching assistantships (averaging $417 per year); scholarships/grants and unspecified assistantships also available. Financial award application deadline: 3/2; financial award applicants required to submit FAFSA. *Unit head:* Dr. Jerry Ternes, Dean, 714-556-3610 Ext. 3303, Fax: 714-966-5495, E-mail: jternes@vanguard.edu. *Application contact:* Michelle Romo, Graduate Education Coordinator, 714-556-3610 Ext. 3302, Fax: 714-966-5495, E-mail: mromo@vanguard.edu.

Villanova University, Graduate School of Liberal Arts and Sciences, Department of Education and Human Services, Villanova, PA 19085-1699. Offers community counseling (MS), including counseling and human relations; educational leadership (MA); elementary school counseling (MS), including counseling and human relations; elementary teacher education (MA); secondary school counseling (MS), including counseling and human relations; secondary teacher education (MA). Part-time and evening/weekend programs available. *Faculty:* 15 full-time (7 women), 15 part-time/adjunct (7 women). *Students:* 57 full-time (50 women), 142 part-time (107 women); includes 9 minority (5 African Americans, 1 American Indian/Alaska Native, 2 Asian Americans or Pacific Islanders, 1 Hispanic American), 1 international. Average age 29. 122 applicants. In 2006, 89 degrees awarded. *Degree requirements:* For master's, comprehensive exam. *Entrance requirements:* For master's, GRE or MAT, minimum GPA of 3.0. Additional exam requirements/recommendations for international students: Required—TOEFL. *Application deadline:* For fall admission, 8/1 priority date for domestic and international students; for spring admission, 12/1 for domestic and international students. Applications are processed on a rolling basis. Application fee: $50. Electronic applications accepted. *Expenses:* Tuition: Part-time $565 per credit. *Financial support:* Career-related internships or fieldwork and Federal Work-Study available. Financial award applicants required to submit FAFSA. *Unit head:* Dr. Connie Titone, Chairperson, 610-519-4620.

See Close-Up on page 939.

Virginia Commonwealth University, Graduate School, School of Education, Richmond, VA 23284-9005. Offers M Ed, MS, MT, PhD, Certificate. *Accreditation:* NCATE. Part-time programs available. *Students:* 324 full-time (252 women), 660 part-time (487 women); includes 195 minority (176 African Americans, 8 American Indian/Alaska Native, 5 Asian Americans or Pacific Islanders, 6 Hispanic Americans), 36 international. 551 applicants, 74% accepted, 326 enrolled. In 2006, 276 master's, 13 doctorates, 39 other advanced degrees awarded. *Degree requirements:* For doctorate, thesis/dissertation. *Entrance requirements:* For master's, GRE General Test or MAT; for doctorate, GRE, interview, master's degree. Application fee: $50. *Financial support:* Fellowships, research assistantships, teaching assistantships, career-related internships or fieldwork, Federal Work-Study, institutionally sponsored loans, and tuition waivers (full and partial) available. Support available to part-time students. Financial award application deadline: 3/1. *Unit head:* Dr. Beverly Warren, Chair, 804-828-3382, Fax: 804-828-1946, E-mail: bjwarren@vcu.edu. *Application contact:* Dr. Michael D. Davis, Director, Graduate Studies, 804-828-6530, Fax: 804-827-0676, E-mail: mddavis@vcu.edu.

See Close-Up on page 941.

Virginia State University, School of Graduate Studies, Research, and Outreach, School of Liberal Arts and Education, Petersburg, VA 23806-0001. Offers M Ed, MA, MS, CAGS. *Accreditation:* NCATE. Part-time and evening/weekend programs available.

Viterbo University, Graduate Program in Education, La Crosse, WI 54601-4797. Offers MA. Courses held on weekends and during summer. *Accreditation:* NCATE. Part-time and evening/weekend programs available. *Degree requirements:* For master's, thesis. *Entrance requirements:* For master's, MAT, teaching certificate, 2 years of teaching experience.

Wagner College, Division of Graduate Studies, Department of Education, Staten Island, NY 10301-4495. Offers adolescent education (MS Ed); childhood education (MS Ed); early childhood education (birth-grade 2) (MS Ed); educational leadership (Certificate), including school building leader, school district leader; literacy (B-6) (MS Ed); middle level education (5-9) (MS Ed). *Accreditation:* NCATE. Part-time and evening/weekend programs available. *Faculty:* 7 full-time (4 women), 16 part-time/adjunct (13 women). *Students:* 74 full-time (52 women), 20 part-time (15 women); includes 16 minority (4 African Americans, 2 Asian Americans or Pacific Islanders, 10 Hispanic Americans). 55 applicants, 93% accepted, 46 enrolled. In 2006, 44 degrees awarded. *Degree requirements:* For master's, thesis (for some programs), registration. *Entrance requirements:* For master's, Liberal Arts and Sciences Test (LAST), New York State Teacher Certification Examinations (NYSTCE), minimum GPA of 2.75. Additional exam requirements/recommendations for international students: Required—TOEFL (minimum score 550 paper-based; 217 computer-based). *Application deadline:* For fall admission, 8/1 priority date for domestic students, 6/30 priority date for international students; for spring admission, 12/10 for domestic students, 11/15 for international students. Applications are processed on a rolling basis. Application fee: $50 ($85 for international students). *Expenses:* Tuition: Full-time $15,120; part-time $840 per credit. *Financial support:* Fellowships, tuition waivers (partial) and unspecified assistantships available. *Unit head:* Dr. Jeffrey Glanz, Chair, 718-420-4070, Fax: 718-390-3456, E-mail: jglanz@wagner.edu. *Application contact:* Susan Rosenberg, Office of Graduate Studies, 718-390-3106, Fax: 718-390-3456, E-mail: graduate@wagner.edu.

Wake Forest University, Graduate School, Department of Education, Winston-Salem, NC 27109. Offers secondary education (MA Ed). *Accreditation:* ACA; NCATE. Part-time programs available. *Faculty:* 6 full-time (3 women), 5 part-time/adjunct (2 women). *Students:* 27 full-time (21 women), 15 part-time (12 women); includes 15 minority (7 African Americans, 1 Asian American or Pacific Islander, 7 Hispanic Americans). Average age 28. 76 applicants, 46% accepted, 35 enrolled. In 2006, 35 degrees awarded. *Degree requirements:* For master's, thesis optional. *Entrance requirements:* For master's, GRE General Test. Additional exam requirements/recommendations for international students: Required—TOEFL (minimum score 550 paper-based; 213 computer-based). *Application deadline:* For fall admission, 1/15 for domestic students, 1/15 priority date for international students. Application fee: $45 ($55 for international students). Electronic applications accepted. *Expenses:* Contact institution. *Financial support:* In 2006–07, 26 students received support, including 22 fellowships with full tuition reimbursements available (averaging $6,000 per year), 4 teaching assistantships with full tuition reimbursements available (averaging $7,000 per year); scholarships/grants and tuition waivers (full) also available. Support available to part-time students. Financial award application deadline: 2/15. *Faculty research:* Cognitive development, teacher performance appraisal, reading styles, teaching assessment and epistemology, reading achievement with heterogeneous classes. Total annual research expenditures: $37,603. *Unit head:* Dr. MaryLynn Redmond, Chairperson, 336-758-5341, Fax: 336-758-4591, E-mail: redmond@wfu.edu. *Application contact:* Linda Dunlap, Certification Officer, 336-758-5990, Fax: 336-758-4591, E-mail: dunlaplb@wfu.edu.

Walden University, Graduate Programs, School of Education, Minneapolis, MN 55401. Offers MS, Ed D, PhD. Part-time and evening/weekend programs available. Postbaccalaureate distance learning degree programs offered (minimal on-campus study). *Faculty:* 513. *Students:* 11,618 full-time (9,630 women), 2,152 part-time (1,745 women); includes 2,524 minority (1,744 African Americans, 61 American Indian/Alaska Native, 154 Asian Americans or Pacific Islanders, 565 Hispanic Americans), 29 international. Average age 35. 3,674 applicants, 95% accepted, 3230 enrolled. In 2006, 4,682 master's, 38 doctorates awarded. *Degree requirements:* For doctorate, thesis/dissertation, brief dispersed residency sessions. *Entrance requirements:* For master's, minimum 2 years of teaching experience or a teaching certificate; for doctorate, 3 years of professional experience, master's degree. Additional exam requirements/recommendations for international students: Required—TOEFL (minimum score 550 paper-based; 213 computer-based), IELTS (minimum score 7). *Application deadline:* For fall admission, 8/15 priority date for domestic and international students; for winter admission, 11/15 priority date for domestic and international students; for spring admission, 12/15 priority date for domestic and international students. Applications are processed on a rolling basis. Application fee: $50. Electronic applications accepted. *Financial support:* In 2006–07, 6 fellowships with partial tuition reimbursements were awarded; scholarships/grants and tuition waivers (partial) also available. Support available to part-time students. Financial award application deadline: 6/1; financial award applicants required to submit FAFSA. *Faculty research:* Early childhood, technology, adult education, special education, administration. *Unit head:* Dr. Manual Barrera, Dean, 800-925-3368, Fax: 612-338-5092. *Application contact:* Office of Admissions, 866-4-WALDEN, Fax: 410-843-8780, E-mail: request@waldenu.edu.

Walla Walla College, Graduate School, School of Education and Psychology, College Place, WA 99324-1198. Offers counseling psychology (MA); curriculum and instruction (M Ed, MA, MAT); educational leadership (M Ed, MA, MAT); literacy instruction (M Ed, MA, MAT); students at risk (M Ed, MA, MAT); teaching (MAT). Part-time programs available. *Faculty:* 7 full-time (3 women), 6 part-time/adjunct (4 women). *Students:* 18 full-time (9 women), 4 part-time (3 women); includes 1 minority (Asian American or Pacific Islander), 1 international. Average age 30. 46 applicants, 61% accepted, 13 enrolled. In 2006, 16 master's awarded. *Entrance requirements:* For master's, GRE General Test, minimum GPA of 2.75. *Application deadline:* For fall admission, 4/1 priority date for domestic students. Applications are processed on a rolling basis. Application fee: $50. Electronic applications accepted. *Expenses:* Tuition: Full-time $20,124; part-time $516 per quarter hour. *Financial support:* In 2006–07, 16 students received support; research assistantships, teaching assistantships, Federal Work-Study and tuition waivers (partial) available. Support available to part-time students. Financial award application deadline: 4/1; financial award applicants required to submit FAFSA. *Faculty research:* Admissions/retention, instructional psychology, moral development, teaching of reading. *Unit head:* Dr. Julian Melgosa, Dean, 509-527-2272, Fax: 509-527-2248, E-mail: melgju@wwc.edu. *Application contact:* Dr. Joe G. Galusha, Dean of Graduate Studies, 509-527-2421, Fax: 509-527-2237, E-mail: galujo@wwc.edu.

Walsh University, Graduate Programs, Program in Education, North Canton, OH 44720-3396. Offers MA. Part-time and evening/weekend programs available. *Faculty:* 6 full-time (5 women), 3 part-time/adjunct (1 woman). *Students:* 20 full-time (15 women), 57 part-time (48 women); includes 6 minority (4 African Americans, 2 Hispanic Americans), 1 international. Average age 34. 29 applicants, 76% accepted, 21 enrolled. In 2006, 26 degrees awarded. *Degree requirements:* For master's, teaching skills laboratory, thesis optional. *Entrance requirements:* For master's, MAT, interview, minimum GPA of 3.0, writing sample. Additional exam requirements/recommendations for international students: Required—TOEFL (minimum score 500 paper-based; 173 computer-based). *Application deadline:* For fall admission, 7/15 priority date for domestic students. Applications are processed on a rolling basis. Application fee: $25. Electronic applications accepted. *Expenses:* Tuition: Full-time $8,910; part-time $495 per credit. *Financial support:* In 2006–07, 24 students received support, including 7 research assistantships (averaging $7,803 per year); tuition waivers (partial), unspecified assistantships, and tuition discounts also available. Financial award application deadline: 12/31. *Faculty research:* Improving math/science instruction (grades 6-12). Total annual research expenditures: $148,800. *Unit head:* Dr. Gary Jacobs, Coordinator, 330-490-7336, Fax: 330-490-7165, E-mail: gjacobs@walsh.edu. *Application contact:* Brett D. Freshour, Vice President of Enrollment Management, 330-490-7286, Fax: 330-490-7165, E-mail: bfreshour@walsh.edu.

Washburn University, College of Arts and Sciences, Department of Education, Topeka, KS 66621. Offers curriculum and instruction (M Ed); educational leadership (M Ed); reading (M Ed); special education (M Ed). *Accreditation:* NCATE. Part-time programs available. *Faculty:* 12 full-time (6 women), 11 part-time/adjunct (8 women). *Students:* 1 full-time (0 women), 22 part-time (14 women). Average age 38. In 2006, 20 degrees awarded. *Degree requirements:* For master's, thesis or alternative, portfolio, comprehensive exam. *Entrance requirements:* For master's, GRE General Test, MAT, minimum GPA of 3.0 during previous 2 years. Additional exam requirements/recommendations for international students: Required—TOEFL (minimum score 523 paper-based; 193 computer-based). *Application deadline:* For fall admission, 3/1 for domestic and international students. Application fee: $0. Electronic applications accepted. *Expenses:* Tuition, state resident: full-time $4,338; part-time $241 per credit hour. Tuition, nonresident: full-time $8,820; part-time $490 per credit hour. Required fees: $62; $31 per semester. *Financial support:* Scholarships/grants available. Support available to part-time students. Financial award application deadline: 2/15; financial award applicants required to submit FAFSA. *Faculty research:* Teachers in math. Total annual research expenditures: $100,000. *Unit head:* Dr. Sandra Winn Tutwiler, Chairperson, 785-670-1435, Fax: 785-670-1046, E-mail: sandy.tutwiler@washburn.edu. *Application contact:* Tara Porter, Licensure Officer, 785-670-1434, Fax: 785-670-1046, E-mail: tara.porter@washburn.edu.

Washington State University, Graduate School, College of Education, Pullman, WA 99164. Offers Ed M, M Ed, MA, MIT, MS, Ed D, PhD. *Accreditation:* NCATE. *Faculty:* 88. *Students:* 158 full-time (105 women), 74 part-time (49 women); includes 56 minority (15 African Americans, 4 American Indian/Alaska Native, 14 Asian Americans or Pacific Islanders, 23 Hispanic Americans), 14 international. Average age 34. 313 applicants, 35% accepted, 42 enrolled. In 2006, 174 master's, 19 doctorates awarded. Terminal master's awarded for partial completion of doctoral program. *Degree requirements:* For master's, thesis (for some programs), oral and written exams, comprehensive exam (for some programs); for doctorate, thesis/dissertation, oral and written exams, comprehensive exam. *Entrance requirements:* For master's and doctorate, GRE General Test, minimum GPA of 3.0, 3 letters of recommendation. Additional exam requirements/recommendations for international students: Required—TOEFL (minimum score 550 paper-based; 213 computer-based). *Application deadline:* For fall admission, 3/1 for domestic and international students; for spring admission, 10/1 for domestic students, 7/1 for international students. Application fee: $50. Electronic applications accepted. *Expenses:* Tuition, state resident: full-time $7,066. Tuition, nonresident: full-time $17,204. *Financial support:* In 2006–07, 12 fellowships (averaging $2,844 per year), 58 research assistantships with partial tuition reimbursements (averaging $13,917 per year), 39 teaching assistantships with partial tuition reimbursements (averaging $13,056 per year) were awarded; career-related internships or fieldwork, Federal Work-Study, institutionally sponsored loans, scholarships/grants, tuition waivers (partial), and staff assistantships, teaching associateships also available. Financial award application deadline: 4/1; financial award applicants required to submit FAFSA. *Faculty research:* At-risk; bilingual/multicultural, mathematics, special, and cross-cultural education. Total annual research expenditures: $2 million. *Unit head:* Dr. Judy Mitchell, Dean, 509-335-4853. *Application contact:* Graduate School Admissions, 800-GRADWSU, Fax: 509-335-1949, E-mail: gradsch@wsu.edu.

Washington State University Spokane, Graduate Programs, Program in Education, Spokane, WA 99210-1495. Offers educational leadership (Ed M, MA); principal (Certificate); professional certification for teachers (Certificate); program administrator (Certificate); school psychologist (Certificate); superintendent (Certificate); teaching (MIT). *Faculty:* 9. *Students:* 24 full-time (15 women), 50 part-time (25 women); includes 8 minority (3 African Americans, 2 Asian Americans or Pacific Islanders, 3 Hispanic Americans). 22 applicants, 73% accepted, 8 enrolled. *Degree requirements:* For master's, thesis (for some programs), comprehensive exam (for some programs). *Entrance requirements:* For master's, GRE or GMAT, minimum GPA of 3.0, 3 letters of recommendation, resumé. Additional exam requirements/recommendations for international students: Required—TOEFL (minimum score 550 paper-based; 213 computer-based). *Application deadline:* For fall admission, 3/1 for international students; for spring admission, 10/1 for domestic students, 7/1 for international students. Application fee: $50. *Expenses:* Tuition, state resident: full-time $7,066. Tuition, nonresident: full-time $17,204. Tuition and fees vary according to program. *Financial support:* In 2006–07, 33 students received support, including 1 fellowship (averaging $4,296 per year), 1 teaching assistantship (averaging $13,056 per year). Total annual research expenditures: $16,557. *Unit head:* Dr. Joan Kingrey, Director, 509-358-7939, Fax: 509-358-7900, E-mail: kingrey@wsu.edu. *Application contact:* Graduate School Admissions, 800-GRADWSU, Fax: 509-335-1949, E-mail: gradsch@wsu.edu.

Washington State University Tri-Cities, Graduate Programs, Program in Education, Richland, WA 99352-1671. Offers counseling (Ed M); educational leadership (Ed M, Ed D); literacy (Ed M); secondary certification (Ed M); teaching (MIT). Part-time programs available. *Faculty:* 23. *Students:* 27 full-time (20 women), 87 part-time (68 women); includes 11 minority (all Hispanic Americans) Average age 36. 77 applicants, 71% accepted, 34 enrolled. *Degree requirements:* For master's, thesis or alternative, comprehensive exam, registration; for doctorate, thesis/dissertation, comprehensive exam. *Entrance requirements:* For master's, GRE, minimum GPA of 3.0, Working with Youth form, Character and Fitness form, 3 letters of recommendation. Additional exam requirements/recommendations for international students: Required—TOEFL. *Application deadline:* For fall admission, 2/1 priority date for domestic students, 3/1 for international students; for spring admission, 9/1 priority date for domestic students, 7/1 for international students. Applications are processed on a rolling basis. Application fee: $50. Electronic applications accepted. *Expenses:* Tuition, state resident: full-time $7,066. Tuition, nonresident: full-time $17,204. *Financial support:* In 2006–07, 59 students received support, including 1 fellowship (averaging $7,950 per year), teaching assistantships (averaging $13,056 per year); Federal Work-Study, scholarships/grants, and unspecified assistantships also available. *Faculty research:* Multicultural counseling, socio-cultural influences in schools, diverse learners, teacher education, K-12 educational leadership. *Unit head:* Dr. Nancy Kyle, Director, 509-372-7396.

Washington State University Vancouver, Graduate Programs, Program in Education, Vancouver, WA 98686. Offers Ed M, MIT, Ed D. Part-time programs available. *Faculty:* 20. *Students:* 64 full-time (51 women), 185 part-time (125 women); includes 18 minority (1 African American, 1 American Indian/Alaska Native, 10 Asian Americans or Pacific Islanders, 6 Hispanic Americans). Average age 35. 95 applicants, 76% accepted, 21 enrolled. *Degree requirements:* For master's, thesis (for some programs), comprehensive exam, registration; for doctorate, thesis/dissertation, comprehensive exam. *Entrance requirements:* For master's, WEST-B, PRAXIS II (MIT), minimum GPA of 3.0, 3 letters of recommendation. Additional exam requirements/recommendations for international students: Required—TOEFL (minimum score 550 paper-based; 213 computer-based). *Application deadline:* For fall admission, 5/15 for domestic students, 3/1 for international students; for spring admission, 10/1 for domestic students, 7/1 for international students. Application fee: $50. *Expenses:* Tuition, state resident: full-time $7,066. Tuition, nonresident: full-time $17,204. *Financial support:* In 2006–07, 109 students received support, including 4 fellowships with tuition reimbursements available (averaging $3,646 per year), research assistantships (averaging $13,917 per year), teaching assistantships (averaging $13,056 per year); Federal Work-Study, scholarships/grants, and unspecified assistantships also available. *Faculty research:* Language literacy and culture, developing learning community, developing teacher-mentors. Total annual research expenditures: $493,391. *Unit head:* Dr. June Canty, Academic Director, 360-546-9108, E-mail: canty@vancouver.wsu.edu. *Application contact:* Jennifer Gallagher, Graduate Secretary, 360-546-9763, Fax: 360-546-9040, E-mail: mcray@vancouver.wsu.edu.

Washington University in St. Louis, Graduate School of Arts and Sciences, Department of Education, St. Louis, MO 63130-4899. Offers educational research (PhD); elementary education (MA Ed); secondary education (MA Ed, MAT). *Degree requirements:* For master's, thesis or alternative; for doctorate, thesis/dissertation. *Entrance requirements:* For master's, GRE General Test or MAT; for doctorate, GRE General Test. Electronic applications accepted.

Announcement: Study toward the doctoral degree is available in education. Department faculty have expertise in urban education, science and mathematics education, discourse analysis, literacy, educational psychology, history of education, and policy studies. In addition, full-time master's degree programs are offered, leading to elementary or secondary teacher certification. A part-time evening master's degree program is available.

Wayland Baptist University, Graduate Programs, Program in Education, Plainview, TX 79072-6998. Offers M Ed. Part-time and evening/weekend programs available. *Faculty:* 5 full-time (4 women). *Students:* 3 full-time (2 women), 12 part-time (8 women); includes 3 minority (1 African American, 2 Hispanic Americans). Average age 27. 7 applicants, 100% accepted, 4 enrolled. In 2006, 7 degrees awarded. *Degree requirements:* For master's, comprehensive exam. *Entrance requirements:* For master's, GRE, GMAT or MAT. Additional exam requirements/recommendations for international students: Required—TOEFL (minimum score 500 paper-based; 173 computer-based). *Application deadline:* Applications are processed on a rolling basis. Application fee: $35. *Expenses:* Tuition: Full-time $6,120; part-time $340 per credit hour. Required fees: $50 per term. *Financial support:* Federal Work-Study, institutionally sponsored loans, and scholarships/grants available. Support available to part-time students. Financial award application deadline: 5/1; financial award applicants required to submit FAFSA. *Unit head:* Dr. Jim Todd, Chairman, 806-291-1045, Fax: 806-291-1951.

Wayne State College, School of Education and Counseling, Wayne, NE 68787. Offers MSE, Ed S. *Accreditation:* NCATE. Part-time and evening/weekend programs available. *Faculty:* 25 part-time/adjunct (15 women). *Students:* 29 full-time (18 women), 424 part-time (312 women); includes 13 minority (5 African Americans, 3 American Indian/Alaska Native, 2 Asian Americans or Pacific Islanders, 3 Hispanic Americans), 2 international. Average age 35. In 2006, 199 master's, 8 other advanced degrees awarded. *Degree requirements:* For master's, thesis (for some programs), comprehensive exam. *Entrance requirements:* For master's, GRE General Test, minimum cumulative GPA of 3.0; for Ed S, GRE General Test, minimum GPA of 3.2 in all program coursework. Additional exam requirements/recommendations for international students: Required—TOEFL (minimum score 550 paper-based; 213 computer-based). *Application deadline:* Applications are processed on a rolling basis. Application fee: $30. *Expenses:* Tuition, state resident: full-time $3,114; part-time $130 per credit hour. Tuition, nonresident: full-time $6,228; part-time $260 per credit hour. Required fees: $894; $37 per credit hour. Tuition and fees vary according to course load. *Financial support:* In 2006–07, 4 teaching assistantships with full tuition reimbursements (averaging $4,000 per year) were awarded; career-related internships or fieldwork also available. Financial award applicants required to submit FAFSA. *Unit head:* Dr. Anthony Koyzis, Dean, 402-375-7389, E-mail: ankoyzi1@wsc.edu.

Wayne State University, College of Education, Detroit, MI 48202. Offers M Ed, MA, MAT, Ed D, PhD, Certificate, Ed S. Evening/weekend programs available. *Faculty:* 116 full-time (53 women), 14 part-time/adjunct (10 women). *Students:* 766 full-time (551 women), 1,851 part-time (1,369 women); includes 1,008 minority (885 African Americans, 13 American Indian/Alaska Native, 49 Asian Americans or Pacific Islanders, 61 Hispanic Americans), 58 international. Average age 36. 619 applicants, 71% accepted, 325 enrolled. In 2006, 625 master's, 40 doctorates, 79 other advanced degrees awarded. Terminal master's awarded for partial completion of doctoral program. *Degree requirements:* For doctorate, thesis/dissertation. *Entrance requirements:* Additional exam requirements/recommendations for international students: Required—TOEFL (minimum score 550 paper-based; 213 computer-based); Recommended—TWE (minimum score 6). *Application deadline:* For fall admission, 7/1 for domestic students, 6/1 for international students; for winter admission, 10/1 for international students; for spring admission, 2/1 for international students. Applications are processed on a rolling basis. Application fee: $30 ($50 for international students). Electronic applications accepted. *Financial support:* In 2006–07, fellowships with tuition reimbursements (averaging $34,919 per year), 9 research assistantships (averaging $12,939 per year), 2 teaching assistantships (averaging $13,222 per year) were awarded; career-related internships or fieldwork, Federal Work-Study, and institutionally sponsored loans also available. Support available to part-time students. *Faculty research:* Alternative routes to teacher certification; innovations in science, mathematics and technology education; literacy; k-12 school reform, including special education and self-determination for special populations; adult workplace learning. Total annual research expenditures: $1.1 million. *Unit head:* Dr. Paula Wood, Dean, 313-577-1625, Fax: 313-577-3606, E-mail: ab2387@wayne.edu. *Application contact:* Janice Green, Assistant Dean, 313-577-1605, E-mail: jwgreen@wayne.edu.

See Close-Up on page 943.

Weber State University, Jerry and Vickie Moyes College of Education, Ogden, UT 84408-1001. Offers M Ed. *Accreditation:* NCATE. Part-time and evening/weekend programs avail-

Education—General

Weber State University (continued)
able. *Faculty:* 16 full-time (9 women), 7 part-time/adjunct (4 women). *Students:* 4 full-time (all women), 168 part-time (129 women); includes 6 minority (2 Asian Americans or Pacific Islanders, 4 Hispanic Americans), 1 international. Average age 40. 37 applicants, 84% accepted, 31 enrolled. In 2006, 48 degrees awarded. *Degree requirements:* For master's, project presentation and exam. *Entrance requirements:* For master's, minimum GPA of 3.0 in last 90 credits, 1 year full-time teaching experience. *Application deadline:* For fall admission, 5/1 priority date for domestic students; for spring admission, 11/1 priority date for domestic students. Applications are processed on a rolling basis. Application fee: $25. *Expenses:* Tuition, state resident: full-time $3,950; part-time $203 per semester. Tuition, nonresident: full-time $10,371; part-time $518 per semester. Required fees: $544; $24 per semester. Tuition and fees vary according to course load and program. *Financial support:* In 2006–07, 17 students received support. Institutionally sponsored loans, scholarships/grants, tuition waivers (full and partial), and unspecified assistantships available. Support available to part-time students. Financial award application deadline: 2/1. *Unit head:* Dr. Jack L. Rasmussen, Dean, 801-626-6273, Fax: 801-626-7427, E-mail: jrasmussen@weber.edu. *Application contact:* Dr. Claudia Eliason, Director, 801-626-7719, E-mail: eeliason@weber.edu.

Webster University, School of Education, St. Louis, MO 63119-3194. Offers MAT, Ed S. Part-time programs available. Postbaccalaureate distance learning degree programs offered. *Students:* 147 full-time (127 women), 970 part-time (824 women); includes 224 minority (188 African Americans, 3 American Indian/Alaska Native, 16 Asian Americans or Pacific Islanders, 17 Hispanic Americans), 11 international. Average age 34. 237 applicants, 99% accepted, 210 enrolled. In 2006, 330 master's, 28 other advanced degrees awarded. *Entrance requirements:* For master's, minimum GPA of 2.5. *Application deadline:* Applications are processed on a rolling basis. Application fee: $25 ($50 for international students). *Expenses:* Tuition: Full-time $8,820; part-time $490 per credit. Tuition and fees vary according to degree level, campus/location and program. *Financial support:* Career-related internships or fieldwork and Federal Work-Study available. Support available to part-time students. Financial award application deadline: 4/1; financial award applicants required to submit FAFSA. *Unit head:* Dr. Brenda Fyfe, Dean, 314-968-6913, Fax: 314-968-7118, E-mail: fyfebv@webster.edu. *Application contact:* Director of Graduate and Evening Student Admissions, Fax: 314-968-7116, E-mail: gadmit@webster.edu.

Wesleyan College, Department of Education, Macon, GA 31210-4462. Offers early childhood education (MA); middle-level mathematics and middle-level science education (MA). Part-time programs available. *Faculty:* 4 full-time (3 women), 4 part-time/adjunct (all women). *Students:* 13 full-time (12 women), 36 part-time (35 women); includes 19 minority (18 African Americans, 1 Asian American or Pacific Islander), 1 international. Average age 37. In 2006, 5 degrees awarded. *Degree requirements:* For master's, thesis or alternative, practicum, professional portfolio. *Entrance requirements:* For master's, GRE or MAT, interview, teaching certificate, 3 letters of recommendation. Additional exam requirements/recommendations for international students: Required—TOEFL. *Application deadline:* For fall admission, 7/1 priority date for domestic students; for spring admission, 12/1 priority date for domestic students. Applications are processed on a rolling basis. Application fee: $25. *Expenses:* Tuition: Full-time $14,500. Tuition and fees vary according to program. *Financial support:* Scholarships/grants available. Financial award application deadline: 4/1; financial award applicants required to submit FAFSA. *Faculty research:* Neuroscience, gender bias in science and mathematics. *Unit head:* Dr. Mae Sheftall, Chair, Education Department, 478-757-5198, Fax: 478-757-5148, E-mail: msheft@wesleyancollege.edu. *Application contact:* Amber E Poulson, MA Admissions Coordinator, 478-757-2480, E-mail: apoulson@wesleyancollege.edu.

Wesley College, Education Program, Dover, DE 19901-3875. Offers M Ed, MA Ed, MAT. *Accreditation:* NCATE. Part-time and evening/weekend programs available. *Faculty:* 4 full-time (3 women). *Students:* 9 full-time (6 women), 24 part-time (15 women), 3 international. Average age 30. 15 applicants, 67% accepted, 10 enrolled. In 2006, 12 degrees awarded. *Degree requirements:* For master's, thesis optional. *Entrance requirements:* For master's, GRE. *Application deadline:* Applications are processed on a rolling basis. Application fee: $25. *Expenses:* Tuition: Full-time $6,120; part-time $340 per credit. Required fees: $60; $60 per year. *Financial support:* In 2006–07, 7 students received support, including 7 teaching assistantships with full tuition reimbursements available (averaging $9,000 per year). *Faculty research:* Learning styles, community-higher education partnerships, curriculum models, science learning and teaching, literacy development in early elementary. *Unit head:* G. R. Myers, Director of Graduate Admissions, 302-736-2343, E-mail: myersgr@wesley.edu. *Application contact:* Marie Cusick, Coordinator of Graduate and Evening Programs, 302-736-2352, E-mail: cusickma@wesley.edu.

West Chester University of Pennsylvania, Graduate Studies, School of Education, West Chester, PA 19383. Offers counseling and educational psychology (M Ed, MS), including elementary school counseling (M Ed), higher education counseling (MS), secondary school counseling (M Ed); early childhood and special education (M Ed), including special education; elementary education (M Ed); literacy (M Ed), including reading; professional and secondary education (M Ed, MS), including educational research (MS), secondary education (M Ed); teaching and learning with technology (Certificate). *Accreditation:* NCATE. Part-time and evening/weekend programs available. *Students:* 189 full-time (159 women), 536 part-time (460 women); includes 31 African Americans, 3 Asian Americans or Pacific Islanders, 7 Hispanic Americans, 2 international. Average age 29. 309 applicants, 94% accepted, 157 enrolled. In 2006, 173 degrees awarded. *Degree requirements:* For master's, thesis (for some programs), comprehensive exam. *Entrance requirements:* For master's, MAT. *Application deadline:* For fall admission, 4/15 priority date for domestic students; for spring admission, 10/15 for domestic students. Applications are processed on a rolling basis. Application fee: $35. *Financial support:* In 2006–07, 25 research assistantships with full tuition reimbursements (averaging $5,000 per year) were awarded; unspecified assistantships also available. Support available to part-time students. Financial award application deadline: 2/15; financial award applicants required to submit FAFSA. *Unit head:* Dr. Joseph Malak, Dean, 610-436-2428, E-mail: jmalak@wcupa.edu.

Western Carolina University, Graduate School, College of Education and Allied Professions, Cullowhee, NC 28723. Offers M Ed, MA, MA Ed, MAT, MS, MSA, Ed D, Ed S. *Accreditation:* NCATE. Part-time and evening/weekend programs available. *Degree requirements:* For master's and Ed S, comprehensive exam; for doctorate, thesis/dissertation, comprehensive exam. *Entrance requirements:* For doctorate and Ed S, GRE General Test, minimum graduate GPA of 3.5. Additional exam requirements/recommendations for international students: Required—TOEFL (minimum score 550 paper-based; 213 computer-based).

Western Connecticut State University, Division of Graduate Studies, School of Professional Studies, Department of Education and Educational Psychology, Danbury, CT 06810-6885. Offers community counseling (MS); curriculum (MS); English education (MS); instructional technology (MS); mathematics education (MS); reading (MS); school counseling (MS); special education (MS). Part-time and evening/weekend programs available. *Students:* 17 full-time (16 women), 244 part-time (183 women); includes 15 minority (3 African Americans, 2 Asian Americans or Pacific Islanders, 10 Hispanic Americans), 2 international. Average age 31. In 2006, 119 degrees awarded. *Application deadline:* For fall admission, 8/1 priority date for domestic students. Applications are processed on a rolling basis. Application fee: $40. *Financial support:* Career-related internships or fieldwork available. Support available to part-time students. Financial award applicants required to submit FAFSA. *Unit head:* Dr. Darla Shaw, Professor, 203-837-8412. *Application contact:* Chris Shankle, Associate Director of Graduate Admissions, 203-837-8244, Fax: 203-837-8338, E-mail: shanklec@wcsu.edu.

Western Governors University, Teachers College, Salt Lake City, UT 84107. Offers English language learning (K-12) (MA); learning and technology (M Ed, MA); management and evaluation (M Ed); management and innovation (M Ed); mathematics education (5-12) (MA); mathematics education (5-9) (MA); mathematics education (K-6) (MA); science (5-12) (MA), including biology, geology; science education (509) (MA); technology (M Ed); technology for principals (Post-Graduate Certificate). *Accreditation:* NCATE. Part-time and evening/weekend programs available. Postbaccalaureate distance learning degree programs offered (no on-campus study). *Degree requirements:* For master's, comprehensive exam, registration. *Entrance requirements:* Additional exam requirements/recommendations for international students: Required—TOEFL (minimum score 450 paper-based). Electronic applications accepted. Expenses: Contact institution.

Western Illinois University, School of Graduate Studies, College of Education and Human Services, Macomb, IL 61455-1390. Offers MA, MAT, MS, MS Ed, Ed D, Certificate, Ed S. *Accreditation:* NCATE. Part-time and evening/weekend programs available. Postbaccalaureate distance learning degree programs offered (no on-campus study). *Students:* 275 full-time (154 women), 913 part-time (637 women); includes 74 minority (35 African Americans, 2 American Indian/Alaska Native, 8 Asian Americans or Pacific Islanders, 29 Hispanic Americans), 24 international. Average age 32. 433 applicants, 67% accepted. In 2006, 329 master's, 16 other advanced degrees awarded. *Degree requirements:* For master's, thesis or alternative, comprehensive exam (for some programs); for doctorate, thesis/dissertation, electronic portfolio, comprehensive exam. *Entrance requirements:* Additional exam requirements/recommendations for international students: Required—TOEFL. *Application deadline:* Applications are processed on a rolling basis. Application fee: $30. Electronic applications accepted. *Expenses:* Tuition, state resident: part-time $200 per credit hour. Tuition, nonresident: part-time $400 per credit hour. *Financial support:* In 2006–07, 163 students received support, including 151 research assistantships with full tuition reimbursements available (averaging $6,568 per year), 12 teaching assistantships (averaging $7,576 per year). Financial award applicants required to submit FAFSA. *Unit head:* Dr. Bonnie Smith, Dean, 309-298-1690. *Application contact:* Dr. Barbara Baily, Director of Graduate Studies/Associate Provost, 309-298-1806, Fax: 309-298-2345, E-mail: grad-office@wiu.edu.

Western Michigan University, Graduate College, College of Education, Kalamazoo, MI 49008-5202. Offers MA, Ed D, PhD, Ed S. *Accreditation:* NCATE. Part-time programs available. *Degree requirements:* For doctorate and Ed S, thesis/dissertation. *Entrance requirements:* For doctorate and Ed S, GRE General Test.

Western New Mexico University, Graduate Division, School of Education, Silver City, NM 88062-0680. Offers counselor education (MA); elementary education (MAT); reading education (MAT); school administration (MA); secondary education (MAT); special education (MAT). *Accreditation:* NCATE. *Degree requirements:* For master's, comprehensive exam. *Entrance requirements:* For master's, GRE General Test, GRE Subject Test, minimum GPA of 3.2 in last 64 hours of undergraduate study. Additional exam requirements/recommendations for international students: Required—TOEFL (minimum score 550 paper-based; 213 computer-based). Electronic applications accepted. *Expenses:* Tuition, state resident: full-time $1,329. Tuition, nonresident: full-time $4,779.

Western Oregon University, Graduate Programs, College of Education, Monmouth, OR 97361-1394. Offers MAT, MS, MS Ed. *Accreditation:* NCATE. Part-time and evening/weekend programs available. Postbaccalaureate distance learning degree programs offered (minimal on-campus study). *Faculty:* 20 full-time (14 women), 26 part-time/adjunct (18 women). *Students:* 120 full-time (69 women), 202 part-time (149 women). Average age 36. In 2006, 237 degrees awarded. *Degree requirements:* For master's, written exam. *Entrance requirements:* For master's, minimum GPA of 3.0. *Application deadline:* Applications are processed on a rolling basis. Application fee: $50. *Expenses:* Tuition, state resident: full-time $8,250; part-time $250 per credit. Tuition, nonresident: full-time $14,025; part-time $250 per credit. Required fees: $1,173. *Financial support:* In 2006–07, 6 research assistantships with full and partial tuition reimbursements (averaging $1,233 per year), 18 teaching assistantships with full and partial tuition reimbursements (averaging $870 per year) were awarded; career-related internships or fieldwork, Federal Work-Study, and tuition waivers (full and partial) also available. Support available to part-time students. Financial award application deadline: 3/1; financial award applicants required to submit FAFSA. *Faculty research:* Effectiveness of work, sample methodology, documentation of learning gains, appropriateness of advanced proficiency. *Unit head:* Dr. Hilda Rosselli, Dean, 503-838-8371, Fax: 503-838-8228, E-mail: rossellh@wou.edu. *Application contact:* Dr. David McDonald, Director of Admissions, 503-838-8919, Fax: 503-838-8067, E-mail: mcdonald@wou.edu.

Western Washington University, Graduate School, Woodring College of Education, Bellingham, WA 98225-5996. Offers M Ed, MA, MIT. *Accreditation:* NCATE. Part-time programs available. Postbaccalaureate distance learning degree programs offered (minimal on-campus study). *Degree requirements:* For master's, thesis optional. *Entrance requirements:* For master's, GRE General Test or MAT, minimum GPA of 3.0 in last 60 semester hours or last 90 quarter hours. Additional exam requirements/recommendations for international students: Required—TOEFL (minimum score 567 paper-based; 227 computer-based). *Application deadline:* For fall admission, 6/1 for domestic students; for winter admission, 10/1 for domestic students; for spring admission, 2/1 for domestic students. Applications are processed on a rolling basis. Application fee: $50. *Expenses:* Tuition, state resident: full-time $6,609; part-time $199 per credit. Tuition, nonresident: full-time $16,845; part-time $540 per credit. *Financial support:* In 2006–07, teaching assistantships with partial tuition reimbursements (averaging $9,339 per year); career-related internships or fieldwork, Federal Work-Study, institutionally sponsored loans, scholarships/grants, tuition waivers (partial), and unspecified assistantships also available. Support available to part-time students. Financial award application deadline: 2/15; financial award applicants required to submit FAFSA. *Unit head:* Dr. Stephanie Salzman, Dean, 360-650-3319.

Westfield State College, Division of Graduate and Continuing Education, Department of Education, Westfield, MA 01086. Offers early childhood education (M Ed); elementary education (M Ed); occupational education (M Ed, CAGS); reading (M Ed); school administration (M Ed, CAGS); secondary education (M Ed); special education (M Ed); technology for educators (M Ed). *Accreditation:* NCATE. Part-time and evening/weekend programs available. *Degree requirements:* For master's, comprehensive exam; for CAGS, research-based field internship. *Entrance requirements:* For master's, GRE General Test or MAT, minimum undergraduate GPA of 2.7; for CAGS, master's degree. *Faculty research:* Collaborative teacher education, developmental early childhood education.

Westminster College, Programs in Education, New Wilmington, PA 16172-0001. Offers administration (M Ed, Certificate); general education (M Ed); guidance and counseling (M Ed, Certificate); reading (M Ed, Certificate). Part-time and evening/weekend programs available. *Degree requirements:* For master's, portfolio. *Entrance requirements:* For master's, GRE or MAT, minimum GPA of 3.0.

Westminster College, School of Education, Salt Lake City, UT 84105-3697. Offers M Ed, MAT. *Accreditation:* Teacher Education Accreditation Council. Part-time and evening/weekend programs available. *Faculty:* 6 full-time (5 women), 4 part-time/adjunct (3 women). *Students:* 6 full-time (all women), 36 part-time (29 women); includes 2 minority (1 African American, 1 Hispanic American), 1 international. Average age 38. 27 applicants, 67% accepted, 12 enrolled. In 2006, 30 degrees awarded. *Degree requirements:* For master's, project or thesis. *Entrance requirements:* For master's, teaching certificate, resumé, minimum GPA of 3.0, 3 professional recommendations, baccalaureate degree information, official transcripts, completed graduate questionnaire. Additional exam requirements/recommendations for international students: Required—TOEFL (minimum score 600 paper-based; 213 computer-based). *Application deadline:* For fall admission, 8/1 priority date for domestic students. Applications are processed on a rolling basis. Application fee: $40. Electronic applications accepted. *Financial support:* In 2006–07, 32 students received support. Career-related internships or fieldwork and tuition remissions available. Support available to part-time students. Financial award applicants required to submit FAFSA. *Faculty research:* Early childhood literacy, technology for learning, special education, instructional delivery models. *Unit head:* David Stokes, Interim, 801-832-

2470, Fax: 801-832-3105. *Application contact:* Joel Bauman, Vice President of Enrollment Services, 801-832-2200, Fax: 801-832-3101, E-mail: admission@westminstercollege.edu.

West Texas A&M University, College of Education and Social Sciences, Division of Education, Canyon, TX 79016-0001. Offers administration (M Ed); counseling education (M Ed); curriculum and instruction (M Ed); educational diagnostician (M Ed); educational technology (M Ed); professional counseling (MA); reading (M Ed); special education (M Ed). Part-time and evening/weekend programs available. Postbaccalaureate distance learning degree programs offered (minimal on-campus study). *Degree requirements:* For master's, thesis optional. *Entrance requirements:* For master's, GRE General Test. Additional exam requirements/recommendations for international students: Required—TOEFL (minimum score 550 paper-based). Electronic applications accepted. *Faculty research:* Modified internship for novice teachers, effective instructional strategies, cognitive-relational group, community college, recruitment/retention.

West Virginia University, College of Human Resources and Education, Morgantown, WV 26506. Offers MA, MS, Au D, Ed D, PhD. *Accreditation:* NCATE. Part-time and evening/weekend programs available. Postbaccalaureate distance learning degree programs offered (no on-campus study). *Faculty:* 81 full-time (48 women), 13 part-time/adjunct (11 women). *Students:* 654 full-time (485 women), 715 part-time (551 women); includes 88 minority (51 African Americans, 5 American Indian/Alaska Native, 9 Asian Americans or Pacific Islanders, 23 Hispanic Americans), 57 international. Average age 34. 834 applicants, 71% accepted, 358 enrolled. In 2006, 481 master's, 32 doctorates awarded. *Degree requirements:* For master's, content exams; for doctorate, thesis/dissertation, comprehensive exam. *Entrance requirements:* Additional exam requirements/recommendations for international students: Required—TOEFL. *Application fee:* $50. Electronic applications accepted. *Expenses:* Tuition, state resident: full-time $4,926; part-time $276 per credit hour. Tuition, nonresident: full-time $14,278; part-time $796 per credit hour. Tuition and fees vary according to program. *Financial support:* In 2006–07, 780 students received support, including 2 fellowships with full tuition reimbursements available (averaging $15,000 per year), 20 research assistantships with full tuition reimbursements available (averaging $8,264 per year), 32 teaching assistantships with full tuition reimbursements available (averaging $8,265 per year); career-related internships or fieldwork, Federal Work-Study, institutionally sponsored loans, tuition waivers (full and partial), and graduate administrative assistantships also available. Financial award applicants required to submit FAFSA. *Faculty research:* Internet training and integration for teachers, rural education, teacher preparation, organization of schools, evaluation of personnel. Total annual research expenditures: $3 million. *Unit head:* Dr. Anne H. Nardi, Dean, 304-293-5703 Ext. 1811, Fax: 304-293-7565, E-mail: anne.nardi@mail.wvu.edu. *Application contact:* Dr. Jane Cardi, Director, Center for Student Advising and Records, 304-293-3441 Ext. 1323, Fax: 304-293-3802, E-mail: jane.cardi@mail.wvu.edu.

Wheaton College, Graduate School, Department of Education, Wheaton, IL 60187-5593. Offers elementary level (MAT); secondary level (MAT). *Accreditation:* NCATE. *Students:* 9. 10 applicants, 80% accepted, 4 enrolled. *Degree requirements:* For master's, thesis or alternative. *Entrance requirements:* For master's, GRE General Test. *Application deadline:* For fall admission, 3/1 priority date for domestic students; for spring admission, 11/1 for domestic students. Applications are processed on a rolling basis. *Application fee:* $30. *Financial support:* Career-related internships or fieldwork and Federal Work-Study available. Financial award application deadline: 3/1; financial award applicants required to submit FAFSA. *Unit head:* Dr. Andrew Brulle, Chair, 630-752-5763, E-mail: andrew.brulle@wheaton.edu. *Application contact:* Julie A. Huebner, Director of Graduate Admissions, 630-752-5195, Fax: 630-752-5935, E-mail: gradadm@wheaton.edu.

Wheelock College, Graduate Programs, Boston, MA 02215-4176. Offers MS, MSW. *Accreditation:* NCATE (one or more programs are accredited). Part-time and evening/weekend programs available. Postbaccalaureate distance learning degree programs offered (minimal on-campus study). *Entrance requirements:* For master's, interview. Additional exam requirements/recommendations for international students: Required—TOEFL (minimum score 550 paper-based; 260 computer-based). *Faculty research:* Teacher development and leadership, national standards science education, high academic achievement for students of color, cultural influences on development, media literacy.

Whittier College, Graduate Programs, Department of Education and Child Development, Whittier, CA 90608-0634. Offers educational administration (MA Ed); elementary education (MA Ed); secondary education (MA Ed). Part-time and evening/weekend programs available. *Degree requirements:* For master's, thesis, registration. *Entrance requirements:* For master's, GRE General Test, MAT, minimum GPA of 3.5, academic writing sample.

Whitworth University, School of Education, Graduate Studies in Education, Spokane, WA 99251-0001. Offers administration (M Ed); counseling (M Ed), including school counselors, social agency/church setting; elementary education (M Ed); gifted and talented (MAT); secondary education (M Ed); special education (MAT); teaching (MIT). *Accreditation:* NCATE. Part-time and evening/weekend programs available. *Faculty:* 2 full-time (both women), 25 part-time/adjunct (15 women). *Degree requirements:* For master's, thesis (for some programs), comprehensive exam. *Entrance requirements:* For master's, GRE General Test, MAT. Additional exam requirements/recommendations for international students: Required—TOEFL. *Application deadline:* For fall admission, 9/1 priority date for domestic students; for spring admission, 2/1 priority date for domestic students. Applications are processed on a rolling basis. *Application fee:* $35. *Financial support:* Fellowships with partial tuition reimbursements, career-related internships or fieldwork, institutionally sponsored loans, and scholarships/grants available. Financial award application deadline: 2/1. *Faculty research:* Rural program development, mainstreaming, special needs learners. *Unit head:* Dr. Sharon Mowry, Director, 509-777-4393, Fax: 509-777-3785, E-mail: smowry@whitworth.edu. *Application contact:* Pat Bailey, Program Assistant, 509-777-3228, Fax: 509-777-4753, E-mail: gse@whitworth.edu.

Wichita State University, Graduate School, College of Education, Wichita, KS 67260. Offers M Ed, MA, Ed D, PhD, Ed S. *Accreditation:* NCATE. Part-time and evening/weekend programs available. *Degree requirements:* For master's, comprehensive exam; for doctorate, one foreign language, thesis/dissertation; for Ed S, internship, practicum. *Entrance requirements:* For master's, minimum GPA of 2.75; for doctorate, GRE General Test. Additional exam requirements/recommendations for international students: Required—TOEFL. Electronic applications accepted. *Faculty research:* Language, hearing disabilities.

Widener University, School of Human Service Professions, Center for Education, Chester, PA 19013-5792. Offers adult education (M Ed); counseling in higher education (M Ed); counselor education (M Ed); early childhood education (M Ed); educational foundations (M Ed); educational leadership (M Ed); educational psychology (M Ed); elementary education (M Ed); English and language arts (M Ed); health education (M Ed); higher education leadership (Ed D); home and school visitor (M Ed); human sexuality (M Ed); mathematics education (M Ed); middle school education (M Ed); principalship (M Ed); reading and language arts (Ed D); reading education (M Ed); school administration (Ed D); science education (M Ed); social studies education (M Ed); special education (M Ed); technology education (M Ed). Part-time and evening/weekend programs available. Terminal master's awarded for partial completion of doctoral program. *Degree requirements:* For doctorate, thesis/dissertation. *Entrance requirements:* For master's, minimum GPA of 2.5; for doctorate, GRE or MAT, minimum GPA of 2.0 (undergraduate), 3.5 (graduate). Electronic applications accepted. Expenses: Contact institution. *Faculty research:* Reading and cognition, adult education, technology education, educational leadership, special education.

Wilkes University, Graduate Studies and Continued Learning, College of Arts, Humanities and Social Sciences, Program in Teacher Education, Wilkes-Barre, PA 18766-0002. Offers classroom technology (MS Ed); educational computing (MS Ed); educational development and strategies (MS Ed); educational leadership (MS Ed); elementary education (MS Ed); instructional technology (MS Ed); school business leadership (MS Ed); secondary education (MS Ed), including biology, chemistry, English, history; special education (MS Ed). Part-time and evening/

weekend programs available. Postbaccalaureate distance learning degree programs offered (minimal on-campus study). *Students:* 32 full-time (21 women), 1,588 part-time (1,106 women); includes 29 minority (6 African Americans, 2 American Indian/Alaska Native, 4 Asian Americans or Pacific Islanders, 17 Hispanic Americans). Average age 33. In 2006, 754 degrees awarded. *Entrance requirements:* Additional exam requirements/recommendations for international students: Required—TOEFL (minimum score 500 paper-based; 173 computer-based). *Application deadline:* Applications are processed on a rolling basis. Application fee: $40. *Expenses:* Contact institution. *Financial support:* Federal Work-Study and unspecified assistantships available. Financial award application deadline: 3/1; financial award applicants required to submit FAFSA. *Unit head:* Dr. Michael Speziale, Interim Dean, 570-408-4679, Fax: 570-408-4905, E-mail: michael.speziale@wilkes.edu. *Application contact:* Kathleen Houlihan, Director of Graduate Studies, 570-408-3235, Fax: 570-408-7846, E-mail: kathleen.houlihan@wilkes.edu.

Willamette University, School of Education, Salem, OR 97301-3931. Offers teaching (MAT). Evening/weekend programs available. *Faculty:* 12 full-time (9 women), 130 part-time/adjunct. *Students:* 66 full-time (44 women), 26 part-time (25 women); includes 5 minority (1 Asian American or Pacific Islander, 4 Hispanic Americans). Average age 28. 145 applicants, 72% accepted. In 2006, 78 degrees awarded. *Degree requirements:* For master's, leadership project (action research). *Entrance requirements:* For master's, California Basic Educational Skills Test, Multiple Subject Assessment for Teachers, PRAXIS, minimum GPA of 3.0, classroom experience, 2 letters of reference. *Application deadline:* For winter admission, 2/1 priority date for domestic students. Applications are processed on a rolling basis. Application fee: $50. Electronic applications accepted. *Expenses:* Contact institution. *Financial support:* In 2006–07, 75 students received support, including fellowships (averaging $4,000 per year); career-related internships or fieldwork, institutionally sponsored loans, scholarships/grants, and tuition waivers (partial) also available. Financial award application deadline: 2/1; financial award applicants required to submit FAFSA. *Faculty research:* Educational leadership, multicultural education, middle school education, clinical supervision, educational technology. *Unit head:* Dr. Maureen Musser, Fax: 503-375-5478, E-mail: mmusser@willamette.edu. *Application contact:* Debbie Harvey, Associate Director of Admissions, 503-375-5453, Fax: 503-375-5478, E-mail: dharvey@willamette.edu.

William Carey University, Graduate Studies, School of Education, Hattiesburg, MS 39401-5499. Offers art education (M Ed); art of teaching (M Ed); elementary education (M Ed, Ed S); English education (M Ed); gifted education (M Ed); history and social science (M Ed); mild/moderate disabilities (M Ed); secondary education (M Ed). Part-time programs available. *Faculty:* 19 full-time (12 women), 25 part-time/adjunct (17 women). *Students:* 142 full-time (111 women), 412 part-time (343 women); includes 123 minority (121 African Americans, 1 Asian American or Pacific Islander, 1 Hispanic American). In 2006, 305 master's, 2 other advanced degrees awarded. *Degree requirements:* For master's, comprehensive exam. *Entrance requirements:* For master's, GRE, MAT, minimum GPA of 2.5, Class A teacher's license. Additional exam requirements/recommendations for international students: Required—TOEFL (minimum score 550 paper-based; 213 computer-based). *Application deadline:* For fall admission, 8/7 for domestic and international students; for winter admission, 10/30 for domestic and international students; for spring admission, 2/12 for domestic and international students. Application fee: $25. *Expenses:* Tuition: Full-time $5,040; part-time $240 per credit hour. Tuition and fees vary according to course load. *Financial support:* In 2006–07, 371 students received support. Federal Work-Study and scholarships/grants available. Support available to part-time students. *Unit head:* Dr. Patty Ward, Dean, 601-318-6139, Fax: 601-318-6185, E-mail: patty.ward@wmcarey.edu. *Application contact:* Jason Douglas, Clerical Assistant, Graduate Admissions, 601-318-6774, Fax: 601-318-6765, E-mail: jason.douglas@wmcarey.edu.

William Howard Taft University, Graduate Programs, The Boyer Graduate School of Education, Santa Ana, CA 92704. Offers M Ed.

William Paterson University of New Jersey, College of Education, Wayne, NJ 07470-8420. Offers M Ed, MAT. *Accreditation:* NCATE. *Students:* 632. *Degree requirements:* For master's, comprehensive exam. *Entrance requirements:* For master's, GRE General Test, MAT, minimum GPA of 2.75, teaching certificate. *Application deadline:* Applications are processed on a rolling basis. Application fee: $50. Electronic applications accepted. *Financial support:* Research assistantships with full tuition reimbursements, career-related internships or fieldwork, Federal Work-Study, and unspecified assistantships available. Support available to part-time students. Financial award application deadline: 4/1; financial award applicants required to submit FAFSA. *Faculty research:* Urban community service. *Unit head:* Leslie Agard-Jones, Dean, 973-720-2413, Fax: 973-720-2955. *Application contact:* Danielle Liautaud, Director, 973-720-3579, Fax: 973-720-2035, E-mail: liautaudd@wpunj.edu.

Wilmington College, Department of Education, Wilmington, OH 45177. Offers reading (M Ed); special education (M Ed). Part-time programs available. *Degree requirements:* For master's, comprehensive exam. *Entrance requirements:* For master's, GRE or MAT, minimum GPA of 3.0, 2 letters of recommendation. Additional exam requirements/recommendations for international students: Required—TOEFL. *Faculty research:* Reading instruction, special education practices, conflict resolution in the schools, models of higher education for teachers.

Wilmington College, Division of Education, New Castle, DE 19720-6491. Offers applied education technology (M Ed); career and technical education (M Ed); elementary and secondary school counseling (M Ed); elementary special education (M Ed); elementary studies (M Ed); instruction: gifted and talented (M Ed); instruction: teaching and learning (M Ed); literacy (M Ed); reading (M Ed); school leadership (M Ed); secondary teaching (MAT). Part-time and evening/weekend programs available. *Faculty:* 7 full-time (4 women). *Students:* 609 full-time (447 women), 1,350 part-time (1,013 women); includes 144 minority (131 African Americans, 3 American Indian/Alaska Native, 1 Asian American or Pacific Islander, 9 Hispanic Americans). Average age 34. 818 applicants, 100% accepted, 599 enrolled. In 2006, 737 degrees awarded. *Entrance requirements:* For master's, 2 letters of recommendation, interview. Additional exam requirements/recommendations for international students: Required—TOEFL (minimum score 500 paper-based; 173 computer-based). *Application deadline:* For fall admission, 4/30 for domestic students. Applications are processed on a rolling basis. Application fee: $25. *Financial support:* Applicants required to submit FAFSA. *Unit head:* Dr. Richard Gochnauer, Chair, 302-328-6795 Ext. 163, Fax: 302-328-7081. *Application contact:* Chris Ferguson, Director of Admissions and Financial Aid, 302-328-9407 Ext. 256, Fax: 302-328-5164, E-mail: inquire@wilmcoll.edu.

Wingate University, Program in Education, Wingate, NC 28174-0159. Offers educational leadership (MA Ed); elementary education (MA Ed, MAT); physical education (MA Ed); sport administration (MA Ed). *Accreditation:* NCATE. Part-time and evening/weekend programs available. *Faculty:* 4 full-time (3 women), 4 part-time/adjunct (1 woman). *Students:* 1 (woman) full-time, 127 part-time (96 women); includes 2 minority (both African Americans) Average age 35. 19 applicants, 58% accepted, 11 enrolled. In 2006, 12 degrees awarded. *Degree requirements:* For master's, portfolio. *Entrance requirements:* For master's, GRE General Test or MAT, teaching certificate (MA Ed). *Application deadline:* For fall admission, 8/15 priority date for domestic students; for spring admission, 12/15 for domestic students. Applications are processed on a rolling basis. Application fee: $0. *Expenses:* Tuition: Full-time $3,330; part-time $185 per credit hour. *Financial support:* In 2006–07, 20 students received support. Scholarships/grants available. Support available to part-time students. Financial award applicants required to submit FAFSA. *Faculty research:* Teaching/learning styles, principles of teaching, homework, stress management, student's rights. *Unit head:* Dr. Robert Shaw, Dean, Thayer School of Education, 704-233-8128, Fax: 704-233-8273, E-mail: rshaw@wingate.edu. *Application contact:* Marsha Luke, Secretary, Thayer School of Education, 704-233-8127, Fax: 704-233-8273, E-mail: mluke@wingate.edu.

Winona State University, Graduate Studies, College of Education, Department of Education, Winona, MN 55987-5838. Offers MS. *Accreditation:* NCATE. Part-time and evening/weekend programs available. *Faculty:* 26 full-time (18 women). *Students:* 36 applicants, 97% accepted,

Education—General

Winona State University *(continued)*
31 enrolled. In 2006, 73 degrees awarded. *Application deadline:* For fall admission, 8/8 priority date for domestic students; for spring admission, 2/17 for domestic students. Applications are processed on a rolling basis. Application fee: $20. *Financial support:* In 2006–07, 5 teaching assistantships (averaging $6,000 per year) were awarded; unspecified assistantships also available. Financial award applicants required to submit FAFSA. *Unit head:* Dr. Celeste Miller, Chairperson, 507-457-5875, E-mail: cmiller@winona.edu.

Winthrop University, College of Education, Rock Hill, SC 29733. Offers M Ed, MAT, MS. *Accreditation:* NCATE. Part-time programs available. *Faculty:* 32 full-time (20 women), 30 part-time/adjunct (20 women). *Students:* 105 full-time (71 women), 203 part-time (160 women); includes 81 minority (78 African Americans, 1 American Indian/Alaska Native, 1 Asian American or Pacific Islander, 1 Hispanic American), 2 international. Average age 29. In 2006, 112 degrees awarded. *Application deadline:* For fall admission, 7/15 priority date for domestic students; for spring admission, 12/1 for domestic students. Applications are processed on a rolling basis. Application fee: $35 ($50 for international students). Electronic applications accepted. *Expenses:* Tuition, state resident: full-time $9,148; part-time $383 per hour. Tuition, nonresident: full-time $16,864; part-time $704 per hour. *Financial support:* Career-related internships or fieldwork, Federal Work-Study, scholarships/grants, and unspecified assistantships available. Support available to part-time students. Financial award application deadline: 2/1; financial award applicants required to submit FAFSA. *Unit head:* Dr. Patricia Graham, Dean, 803-323-2151, Fax: 803-323-4369, E-mail: grahamp@winthrop.edu. *Application contact:* 800-411-7041, Fax: 803-323-2292, E-mail: graduatestu@winthrop.edu.

Wittenberg University, Graduate Program, Springfield, OH 45501-0720. Offers education (MA).

Worcester State College, Graduate Studies, Department of Education, Worcester, MA 01602-2597. Offers early childhood education (M Ed); elementary education (M Ed); English (M Ed); health education (M Ed); history (M Ed); leadership and administration (M Ed); middle school education (M Ed); moderate special needs (M Ed); reading (M Ed); secondary education (M Ed); Spanish (M Ed). Part-time and evening/weekend programs available. *Students:* 3 full-time (all women), 155 part-time (116 women); includes 8 minority (2 African Americans, 1 Asian American or Pacific Islander, 5 Hispanic Americans), 2 international. Average age 35. 159 applicants, 67% accepted, 33 enrolled. *Degree requirements:* For master's, thesis optional. *Entrance requirements:* For master's, GRE General Test, MAT or GMAT, teaching certificate. Additional exam requirements/recommendations for international students: Required—TOEFL (minimum score 550 paper-based; 213 computer-based). *Application deadline:* Applications are processed on a rolling basis. Application fee: $30. *Expenses:* Tuition, state resident: full-time $4,518; part-time $251 per credit hour. Tuition, nonresident: full-time $4,518; part-time $251 per credit hour. *Financial support:* In 2006–07, 7 research assistantships with full tuition reimbursements (averaging $4,557 per year) were awarded; career-related internships or fieldwork, Federal Work-Study, institutionally sponsored loans, scholarships/grants, and unspecified assistantships also available. Support available to part-time students. Financial award application deadline: 3/1; financial award applicants required to submit FAFSA. *Unit head:* Dr. Elaine Tateronis, Coordinator, 508-929-8823. *Application contact:* Nicole Brown, Assistant Dean of Graduate and Continuing Education, 508-929-8787, Fax: 508-929-8100, E-mail: nbrown@worcester.edu.

Wright State University, School of Graduate Studies, College of Education and Human Services, Dayton, OH 45435. Offers M Ed, MA, MRC, MS, MST, Ed S. *Accreditation:* NCATE. Part-time and evening/weekend programs available. *Students:* 180 full-time (140 women), 627 part-time (509 women); includes 41 minority (36 African Americans, 1 American Indian/Alaska Native, 2 Asian Americans or Pacific Islanders, 2 Hispanic Americans), 2 international. Average age 34. 301 applicants, 95% accepted. In 2006, 394 master's, 1 other advanced degree awarded. *Degree requirements:* For Ed S, thesis. *Entrance requirements:* For master's, GRE General Test, MAT, PRAXIS II; for Ed S, GRE General Test, MAT. Additional exam requirements/recommendations for international students: Required—TOEFL. Application fee: $25. *Financial support:* In 2006–07, 40 fellowships with full tuition reimbursements were awarded; research assistantships, teaching assistantships, career-related internships or fieldwork, Federal Work-Study, institutionally sponsored loans, tuition waivers (full and partial),

and unspecified assistantships also available. Support available to part-time students. Financial award applicants required to submit FAFSA. *Unit head:* Dr. Gregory R. Bernhardt, Dean, 937-775-2822, Fax: 937-775-4855, E-mail: gregory.bernhardt@wright.edu. *Application contact:* John Kimble, Associate Director of Graduate Admissions and Records, 937-775-2957, Fax: 937-775-2453, E-mail: john.kimble@wright.edu.

Xavier University, College of Social Sciences, Health and Education, School of Education, Cincinnati, OH 45207. Offers M Ed, MA. Part-time and evening/weekend programs available. *Faculty:* 28 full-time (16 women), 69 part-time/adjunct (37 women). *Students:* 312 full-time (242 women), 668 part-time (513 women); includes 110 minority (97 African Americans, 1 American Indian/Alaska Native, 4 Asian Americans or Pacific Islanders, 8 Hispanic Americans), 7 international. Average age 33. 448 applicants, 60% accepted, 245 enrolled. In 2006, 395 degrees awarded. *Degree requirements:* For master's, comprehensive exam. *Entrance requirements:* For master's, GRE or MAT, minimum GPA of 2.7. Additional exam requirements/recommendations for international students: Required—TOEFL (minimum score 550 paper-based; 213 computer-based). *Application deadline:* Applications are processed on a rolling basis. Application fee: $35. Electronic applications accepted. *Expenses: Contact institution.* Part-time tuition and fees vary according to degree level, campus/location and program. *Financial support:* Career-related internships or fieldwork, scholarships/grants, and unspecified assistantships available. Support available to part-time students. Financial award applicants required to submit FAFSA. *Faculty research:* Reading achievement, student achievement in mathematics, science in elementary schools, instruction/curriculum ethics. *Unit head:* Dr. James Boothe, Acting Dean, 513-745-2951, Fax: 513-745-1052, E-mail: boothe@xavier.edu. *Application contact:* Roger Bosse, Interim Director of Graduate Studies, 513-745-3357, Fax: 513-745-1048, E-mail: bosse@xavier.edu.

Xavier University of Louisiana, Graduate School, Programs in Education, New Orleans, LA 70125-1098. Offers curriculum and instruction (MA); education administration and supervision (MA); guidance and counseling (MA). *Accreditation:* NCATE. Part-time and evening/weekend programs available. *Degree requirements:* For master's, thesis or alternative, comprehensive exam. *Entrance requirements:* For master's, GRE General Test, MAT, minimum GPA of 2.5. Additional exam requirements/recommendations for international students: Required—TOEFL.

York College of Pennsylvania, Department of Education, York, PA 17405-7199. Offers M Ed. Part-time and evening/weekend programs available. *Degree requirements:* For master's, portfolio, thesis optional. *Entrance requirements:* For master's, GRE, MAT or PRAXIS, letters of recommendation, portfolio. Additional exam requirements/recommendations for international students: Required—TOEFL. Electronic applications accepted. *Faculty research:* Mentoring, principal development, principal retention.

York University, Faculty of Graduate Studies, Faculty of Education, Toronto, ON M3J 1P3, Canada. Offers M Ed, PhD. Part-time programs available. *Faculty:* 63 full-time (39 women), 4 part-time/adjunct (2 women). *Students:* 78 full-time (65 women), 244 part-time (206 women). 306 applicants, 29% accepted, 90 enrolled. In 2006, 70 master's, 4 doctorates awarded. *Degree requirements:* For master's, thesis or alternative, registration; for doctorate, thesis/dissertation, comprehensive exam, registration. *Application deadline:* For fall admission, 2/1 for domestic students. Application fee: $80. Electronic applications accepted. *Financial support:* In 2006–07, 23 fellowships (averaging $13,369 per year), 40 research assistantships (averaging $4,273 per year), 37 teaching assistantships (averaging $9,307 per year) were awarded; fee bursaries also available. *Unit head:* Alison Griffith, Director, 416-736-5018.

Youngstown State University, Graduate School, College of Education, Youngstown, OH 44555-0001. Offers MS Ed, Ed D. *Accreditation:* NCATE. Part-time and evening/weekend programs available. *Degree requirements:* For master's, comprehensive exam; for doctorate, thesis/dissertation, comprehensive exam. *Entrance requirements:* For master's, minimum GPA of 2.7; for doctorate, GRE General Test, GRE Subject Test, interview, minimum GPA of 3.5. Additional exam requirements/recommendations for international students: Required—TOEFL. *Faculty research:* Euthanasia, psychometrics, ethical issues, community relations, educational law.

Cross-Discipline Announcement

Johnson & Wales University, The Alan Shawn Feinstein Graduate School, Program in Global Business, Providence, RI 02903-3703.

The Alan Shawn Feinstein Graduate School offers an MBA in Hospitality (with concentrations in marketing, financial management, and event leadership) and an MBA in Global Business (with concentrations in accounting, financial management, international trade, marketing, and organizational leadership). The School also offers an MAT in teacher education, an MEd in early childhood administration and leadership and an MEd in teaching and learning for certified teachers, and an EdD program in educational leadership.

ADELPHI UNIVERSITY

Ruth S. Ammon School of Education

Programs of Study

The Ruth S. Ammon School of Education at Adelphi University offers a comprehensive array of graduate programs in curriculum and instruction, communication disorders, and health and physical education. Dedicated faculty members, mentoring programs, a 16:1 student-faculty ratio, flexible scheduling, convenient off-campus centers in Hauppauge and Manhattan, extensive partnerships with community school districts and health-care institutions, and a Professional Development Initiative are designed to help candidates achieve their academic and professional goals.

The Department of Curriculum and Instruction offers in-service and precertification degree programs in the Master of Arts and advanced certificate in early childhood education; the Master of Science and advanced certificate in early childhood special education; the Master of Arts in childhood education; the Master of Science in childhood special education; the Master of Science in literacy; the Master of Arts in art education, English, mathematics, science, and social studies; the Master of Arts and advanced certificate in TESOL; the Master of Arts, advanced certificate, and certificate in educational leadership and technology; and bilingual education extensions to elementary, secondary, and special education; communication sciences and disorders; and school social work.

The Department of Health Studies, Physical Education, and Human Performance Sciences offers the Master of Arts in exercise science and sports management with specializations in adapted physical education, exercise physiology, and sports management; the Master of Arts in health education; the Master or Arts in physical education; and the Master of Arts and advanced certificate in community health education.

The Department of Communication Sciences and Disorders offers the Master of Science in communication disorders with concentrations in audiology or speech-language pathology; the Doctor of Arts in communication disorders; and the Doctor of Audiology.

The Ammon School of Education prepares teachers to make a difference. Many of the distinguished faculty members are leaders in their fields. They share their passion for teaching in an environment that fosters creativity and excellence. Students have the opportunity to collaborate on faculty research and presentations at national and international conferences. Adelphi students engage in meaningful partnerships with local schools and service organizations. Through established mentoring programs, students learn from master teachers and clinical experts who set the standards for best practices in teaching. Students get invaluable firsthand experience with mentors and clinicians in community-based service programs.

Research Facilities

The University's primary research holdings are at Swirbul Library and include 649,770 volumes (including bound periodicals and government publications), 803,998 microformats, 23,953 audiovisual items, and 1,904 periodical subscriptions.

Research, laboratory, and clinical programs and facilities are offered in all departments of the Ammon School of Education. The Hy Weinberg Center, dedicated to research in communication disorders and clinical and therapeutic services, is equipped with state-of-the-art clinical audiometric instrumentation as well as speech and hearing laboratories for the objective measurement of important parameters of speech and voice. Research conducted in the Human Performance Laboratory is showcased at the Annual Student Research Symposium. Its facilities include a multiple 12-lead ECG/exercise stress system, hydrostatic weighing, pulmonary-function testing, Cybex isokinetic muscle testing, an adult fitness and cardiopulmonary rehabilitation program, DEXA, and POLAR Heart Rate Training Center. The Center for Literacy and Learning offers a practicum in assessing and addressing literacy needs, and the Alice Brown Early Learning Center provides field experience in child development and early childhood curriculum.

Financial Aid

Adelphi University offers financial aid counseling, federal and state aid programs, and scholarship and fellowship programs that include a limited number of graduate assistantships. Programs include the Federal Stafford Student Loan; Federal Work-Study Program; Adelphi's Pathways to Teaching, scholarships for students seeking teacher certification in secondary mathematics and science that are funded by a grant from the U.S. Department of Education; the New York State Tuition Assistance Program (TAP); New York State Scholarship Programs; Vietnam and Persian Gulf Veterans Tuition Awards; and Regents Professional Opportunity Scholarships. Students with outstanding undergraduate or graduate records in education can apply for paid graduate internships in adolescent education.

Cost of Study

For the 2006–07 academic year, the tuition rate was $690 per credit. Full-time tuition for the communication disorders program was $11,850 per semester ($710 per credit). University fees ranged from $200 to $400 per semester.

Living and Housing Costs

Living and housing costs vary considerably depending on personal circumstances. Most graduate students in the Ammon School of Education attend on a part-time basis and live off campus in established households. Information on residence hall fees can be found on the University's Web site.

Student Group

In 2005, there were 1,571 graduate students in the Ammon School of Education. The majority are working adults from Long Island and New York City, attending part-time and enrolled in master's degree programs for career advancement in education and the allied professions. The student body is ethnically diverse; 79 percent are women, and the average age is 31. About 26 percent of the students have taken one or more of their classes at an off-campus location.

Student Outcomes

In the 2004–05 academic year, the University awarded 636 master's degrees in the Ammon School of Education, including 471 in curriculum and instruction, fifty-nine in communication disorders, and 106 in health and physical education. Graduates are respected teachers, administrators, coaches, and clinicians in schools, hospitals, sports facilities, and other settings throughout the region and the state.

Location

Located in historic Garden City, New York, 45 minutes from Manhattan and 20 minutes from Queens, Adelphi's 75-acre suburban campus is known for the beauty of its landscape and architecture. The campus is a short walk from the Long Island Railroad and is convenient to New York's major airports and several major highways. Off-campus centers are located in Manhattan, Hauppauge, and Poughkeepsie.

The University

Founded in 1896, Adelphi is a fully accredited, private university with 8,110 undergraduate, graduate, and returning-adult students in the arts and sciences, business, clinical psychology, education, nursing, and social work. The Ammon School of Education is responsible for having awarded 55 percent of all of the University's master's degrees in 2004–05. A visionary in the field of education, the School seeks to meet the personal needs and professional goals of its students through community partnerships and programs in education, communication disorders, and health sciences.

Applying

Candidates must possess a bachelor's degree from an accredited college or university and present evidence of their academic accomplishment. Admission is competitive, and requirements for specific programs in the Ammon School of Education vary considerably. Applications and admission requirements for specific programs can be found online at http://admissions.adelphi.edu/onlineapp.php.

Correspondence and Information

Ruth S. Ammon School of Education
Harvey Hall
Adelphi University
1 South Avenue
Garden City, New York 11530-4299
Phone: 516-877-4100
Fax: 516-877-4097
Web site: http://education.adelphi.edu/about/

Applications and inquiries:
Office of Admissions
Levermore Hall 114
Adelphi University
1 South Avenue
Garden City, New York 11530
Phone: 516-877-3050
        800-ADELPHI (toll-free)
Fax: 516-877-3039
E-mail: admissions@adelphi.edu
Web site: http://admissions.adelphi.edu/Grad/

Adelphi University

THE FACULTY

Full-time faculty members in the Ammon School of Education number more than 60 individuals in three departments. The following listing includes only administrators, department chairs, and general research activity. Prospective students should visit the Web site at http://academics.adelphi.edu/bulletins or http://www.adelphi.edu/faculty/profiles/ for complete faculty member information, including credentials and specific research projects.

The Department of Communication Science and Disorders

Susan Lederer, Associate Professor of Communication Sciences and Disorders and Chair; Ph.D., NYU.

Faculty members in this department specialize in research pertinent to assessing and developing intervention strategies for speech, language, and hearing disorders.

The Department of Curriculum and Instruction

Alan R. Cohen, Assistant Professor of Special Education and Director; Ph.D., Hofstra.

Faculty members in the Department of Curriculum and Instruction specialize in research pertaining to adolescent, childhood, and early childhood education; art education; bilingual/TESOL education; educational leadership; and special education.

The Department of Health Studies, Physical Education, and Human Performance Science

Stephen Virgilio, Professor of Health Studies, Physical Education, and Human Performance Science; Chair; and Interim Dean of the Ammon School of Education; Ph.D., Florida State.

Faculty members in this department specialize in research pertinent to human nutrition, stress reduction, and physical activity for a diverse population in school settings, the community, and the workplace.

ALLIANT INTERNATIONAL UNIVERSITY

Graduate School of Education
TeachersCHOICE Preparation Programs

Programs of Study
The Graduate School of Education (GSOE) at Alliant International University has developed a set of reality-based teacher education programs—Teachers*CHOICE*—with the understanding that students bring many different skills, experiences, and capacities to the teacher-preparation program. Programs focus on pragmatic skills development and professional practice. Teachers*CHOICE* programs include the following routes for the preliminary teaching credential: student teaching, standard intern teaching, and intern teaching (early completion option). The GSOE offers credential programs embedded in a master's program that lead to a Preliminary Multiple Subject or a Preliminary Single Subject (English, math, and science), English, and California teaching credential. The Master of Arts in Education (M.A.E.) with a teaching emphasis is offered at the Mexico City campus as well as 100 percent online.

The intern early completion option (ECO) is available on the Fresno, Los Angeles. Sacramento, San Diego, and San Francisco campuses. This nine-month accelerated, intern program makes it possible to waive most traditionally required teacher-education course work. Students are able to teach full-time while attending the program weekly. The program is for high achievers and those with some teaching or education knowledge who crave a hands-on experience and a high degree of support. The curriculum covers all state-mandated elements and is accredited by the California Commission on Teacher Credentialing (CCTC)..

The program's comprehensive design includes four major components. First, students complete the four California Teaching Performance Assessments. The tasks are interrelated yet separate and are sequenced throughout the program in response to the design of increasing complexity. Students participate in weekly seminars, peer/supervisor workshops, and identified Saturday seminars provided over two semesters; these give students an introduction to and complex preparation for the California Teaching Performance Assessments as well as highly advanced course work in strategies to advance student learning. Sixteen (eight in the fall and spring each) observations; mentoring, coaching, assessment sessions; intern reflection; and planning in collaboration with the candidate's university field supervisor are required. Finally, students must pass identified course work (3 units of online instruction) in instructional technology.

A unique feature of Teachers*CHOICE* is a two-year follow-up program that supports graduates as they enter their teaching careers. A combination of group support, structured mentoring, and access to experienced master teachers are offered to all program graduates as they solidify their skills and gain essential experience in the classroom.

Research Facilities
Alliant International offers excellent research facilities throughout the system. The Alliant libraries maintain a diverse available collection of more than 160,000 books, 1,150 current print journal subscriptions, 12 electronic database subscriptions, approximately 995 psychological test titles, 1,700 audiotapes, and more than 1,200 videotapes. Each campus library is a resource for a variety of research topics and works in cooperation with several other four-year institutions in the immediate area. Each academic school or college has research clusters, labs, and/or other resources to support original scholarly and applied research. The Computer Lab and Learning Center has a number of computers available for student use. The computers are loaded with current versions of word processing, statistical, and other software programs and are connected to laser printers. Further, Alliant maintains partnerships with area university libraries that allow students to access material.

Financial Aid
Most students interested in school-based financial aid pursue college work-study. Students work as teaching or research assistants to core faculty members. In addition, students can work on campus in a number of departments, including admissions and field placement. Stipends generally average about $1000 per assistantship per semester. For complete information, students should contact the Financial Aid Office.

Cost of Study
Master's programs are $500 per semester unit; doctoral programs cost $900 per semester unit. Application fees apply but may be waived in cases of documented financial hardship.

Living and Housing Costs
On-campus housing is not available on the Fresno, Los Angeles, Sacramento, and San Francisco campuses. Most Alliant students live in communities adjacent to the campuses. The estimated cost of living for a graduate student (including housing and food, transportation, and personal expenses) for the nine-month academic year is $17,262. Room and board on the San Diego campus cost $9820 for the academic year for a private room and $7430 for double occupancy. Students can expect to pay between $700 and $1000 per month plus utilities (gas and electricity) for an off-campus unfurnished, one-bedroom apartment. The estimated cost for books and supplies is $1500 per year.

Student Group
Alliant ranked first in international students in *U.S. News & World Report*'s 2007 nationwide survey. *Diverse* magazine ranked Alliant sixth for awarding doctorates to minority women and fourteenth for doctorates to minorities (all disciplines combined). Alliant International University has students from almost every state plus 407 international students from sixty-nine countries, including Botswana, Cameroon, Greece, Iceland, Portugal, and Turkey.

Location
The ambience on the Fresno campus is friendly and warm, a reflection of its Central Valley location. Blessed with abundant sunshine and mild temperatures, the region brims with orchards and blossoms. Conveniently located adjacent to Fresno's Yosemite International Airport, Alliant's Fresno campus serves one of the fastest growing cities in California. The Los Angeles–area campus is in Alhambra, conveniently located 6 miles east of downtown Los Angeles and Hollywood and easily accessible from the San Bernardino and Long Beach freeways. The Alhambra complex features 24-hour gated security and plenty of parking spaces for students and faculty and staff members. Famous Venice Beach, Malibu, and Santa Monica are 20 minutes away. Alliant Sacramento is easily accessible from all major thoroughfares in the metropolitan Sacramento area. The small class sizes at the Sacramento site offer an opportunity for students to have greater individual interaction with the professors and each other. While geographically distant from the parent campus in Fresno, students at the Sacramento site have access to all Alliant student benefits, including library services. The San Diego campus is located in what is often called "America's Finest City." San Diego is a dynamic, multicultural location in which to study. A vibrant, metropolitan city with a laid-back, small-town feel, the area is filled with an incredible selection of activities and attractions. There are many cultural and historic attractions, shopping centers, fine dining establishments, and places to relax and reenergize. From the beautiful beaches to the inland mountains, the views are spectacular, and San Diego has a climate unmatched for mildness nationwide. Alliant's San Francisco's campus is located on the waterfront, with the restaurants and amusements of Pier 39 just across the street. The music, food, art, and politics of this city provide a dynamic backdrop to graduate studies.

The University and The School
Alliant International University focuses on preparing students for professional careers. Alliant International University was officially formed in 2001 by the combination of the California School of Professional Psychology (CSPP), founded in 1969, and United States International University (USIU), founded in 1967. But their history goes back more than the forty plus years since USIU's founding. USIU was the successor to two other institutions: California Western University, founded in 1952, and Balboa College, founded in 1924.

The Graduate School of Education trains professionals who make a difference in the lives of others through teaching, counseling, leadership, advocacy, administration, management, and community work. GSOE infuses its curricula with multicultural content and emphasizes student achievement, instructional technology, assessment, neuropsychology, mentoring of diverse populations, and comprehensive community service. At the core of its professional practitioner model is the cohort structure, which supports learning while students are enrolled in advanced studies and provides a professional support system of colleagues throughout their career.

Applying
Applicants must possess a bachelor's degree from a regionally accredited institution of higher education, with a minimum overall GPA of 2.5. In general, applicants should submit the completed application, the $60 application fee, all official transcripts, a personal essay, and two letters of recommendation. For the Early Completion Option Credential Program, students must present proof of passing the California Subject Examination for Teachers (CSET) and the Teaching Foundations Exam (TFE). They must also have an offer of employment as a teacher of record in a California public school or a California accredited private school. A CCTC Certificate of Clearance is necessary. For additional details, students should see http://teacherschoice.alliant.edu. International students must also submit TOEFL scores. An interview is required.

Correspondence and Information
Alliant Admissions
Alliant International University
10455 Pomerado Road
San Diego, California 92131

Phone: 866-U-ALLIANT (toll-free)
E-mail: admissions@alliant.edu
Web site: http://alliant.edu/gsoe

Alliant International University

THE FACULTY AND THEIR RESEARCH

Core and Noncore Faculty

Joseph Adwere-Boamah, Assistant Professor and Program Coordinator, Educational Leadership (San Diego); Ph.D., Berkeley, 1970.

Hassana Alidou, Professor and Program Coordinator, TESOL (San Diego and Irvine); Ph.D., Illinois at Urbana–Champaign, 1997. Sociolinguistics, teacher training in TESOL.

Frederick Ansoff, Assistant Professor, Educational Leadership and Management (San Diego); Ph.D., Georgetown, 1998. Statistical analyses.

Shirley Baker, Instructor, TESOL (Fresno) and Director, International Language and Cultural Center; M.A., Kentucky, 1987; M.A., US International, 1999. TESOL program description, TESOL teacher preparation.

Suzanne Borman, Professor (San Diego); Ed.D., Columbia Teachers College, 1983. Curriculum and instructional planning.

Mary Ellen Butler-Pascoe, Professor and Systemwide Program Director, TESOL (San Diego); Ph.D., US International, 1990. ESL/EFL teacher training, integration of technology and second-language instruction, program and curriculum design.

Ana Guisela Chupina, Assistant Professor, Teacher Education, Higher Education (San Francisco); Ph.D., Iowa State, 2004. Immigrant women as adult learners, first-generation and culturally diverse students in higher education, methodological issues in cross-cultural research.

Geoffrey M. Cox, Professor of Higher Education (San Francisco) and President, Alliant International University; Ph.D., Chicago, 1987. Social and political philosophy, leadership in higher education.

Trudy Day, Assistant Professor, Teacher Education, Higher Education (San Francisco); Systemwide Assistant Dean, Graduate School of Education; and Systemwide Director, TeachersCHOICE; Ed.D., Louisville, 1996. Leadership and crisis, first-year teachers, shared governance, instructional strategies for the university professor.

Steven Fisher, Assistant Professor and Program Director, School and Educational Psychology (San Diego); Ph.D., US International, 1998. Clinical psychology.

Xuanning Fu, Assistant Professor and Program Coordinator, Educational Leadership and Management (Fresno); Ph.D., Brigham Young, 1993. Program analysis and evaluation.

James F. Hiramoto, Principal Lecturer and Program Coordinator, School and Educational Psychology (San Francisco); Ph.D., Berkeley, 2004. Effects of sightedness on areas of knowledge, social skills, and perceptions of self; ADHD.

Kenneth Kelch, Assistant Professor of TESOL and Director, International Languages and Cultural Center (San Diego); Ed.D., Alliant International, 2005. TESOL pedagogy.

Jerry Kill, Assistant Professor and Coordinator, Educational Leadership and Management (Irvine); Ed.D., California Coast, 2005. Educational leadership, school administration.

Yury Kostin, Assistant Professor (Fresno); Ed.D., California State, Fresno, 2003. Technological applications.

Robert D. Kreger, Associate Professor (San Francisco); Ph.D., Michigan, 1980. Teacher preparation, child development and disorder issues in education, special education.

Irving Leung, Assistant Professor and Field Services Coordinator, Teacher Education–Early Completion Option (San Francisco); Ed.D., San Francisco, 1998. Bilingual education, special education.

Estela C. Matriano, Professor and Secretary, World Council for Curriculum and Instruction (San Diego); Ed.D., Indiana, 1968. Global education.

Jerold D. Miller, Professor; Program Director, Teacher Education; and Director, Partners for Success Tech and Media Center (San Diego); Ed.D., US International, 1985. Technology planning and curriculum development.

Beverly J. Palley, Field Services Coordinator, Teacher Education; Ed.D., Fielding Graduate University, 2003. Teacher-training programs, improving alternative certification approaches in teacher internship programs.

Carlton Parks, Professor and Campus Program Director, Educational Psychology (Los Angeles); Ph.D., Minnesota, 1986. Interpersonal relations, interpersonal violence, sexual and ethnic minorities, psychosocial aspects of HIV infection/AIDS, feminist studies, spirituality and mental health.

Connell Persico, University Professor and Systemwide Program Director, Educational Leadership, Educational Administration; Ph.D., Stanford, 1974. Education leadership, higher education organization, politics of education.

Debra Reeves-Gutierrez, Assistant Professor, Teacher Education–Early Completion Option (San Francisco); Ed.D., University of the Pacific, 2005. Pedagogy.

Robert Reyes, Assistant Professor and Program Coordinator, Educational Leadership and Management (Los Angeles); Ph.D., Berne, 2001. English language development, educational leadership, global education.

Karen Schuster Webb, Professor of Higher Education and TESOL and Systemwide Dean, Graduate School of Education (San Francisco); Ph.D., Indiana–Bloomington, 1980. Language and cognition, discourse pragmatics, inclusive pedagogy.

Ed Shenk, Associate Professor and Program Director, Educational Leadership and Management, Higher Education (San Francisco); Ed.D., Oregon, 1981. Student services, student discipline, leadership, organizational structures.

George Stamos, Associate Professor; Ed.D., Northern Arizona, 1996. Teacher education reform.

Barbara Stein-Stover, Assistant Professor and Program Director, Teacher Education–Early Completion Option (Los Angeles and San Diego); Ed.D., Alliant International, 2006. Adolescent mental health issues, pedagogy.

Holly Wilson, Associate Professor (San Diego); Ph.D., New Mexico, 1999. Second-language-learner errors, grammar instruction, proposed use of covert grammar.

Donald Wofford, Assistant Professor and Interim Systemwide Director, Educational and School Psychology (Irvine); Psy.D., California School of Professional Psychology, 2002. School-based mental health.

Adjunct Faculty

Christine Alexander (San Diego); Ed.D., US International, 2001.

Remijio Alvarez, Lecturer (Irvine); M.A., Pepperdine, 1976.

Robert Appenzeller (San Diego); M.A., US International, 1987.

Theresa M. Ashby (Los Angeles); Ph.D., Alliant International, 2002.

Tomiko Lynn Bobo (Los Angeles), PPS Credential in School Counseling, National.

Celeste Cusumano, Senior Lecturer (Fresno); Ed.D., University of the Pacific, 1984.

Diane DeBoer (Los Angeles); Ph.D., US International, 1997.

Greg Dhuyvettor, Lecturer (Irvine); M.A., US International, 2002.

Diane di Bari (San Francisco); M.S., California State, Fresno, 1976.

Richard G. Duke (Fresno); Ed.D., Brigham Young, 1981.

Krystel Edmonds-Biglow (Los Angeles); Psy.D., Alliant International, 2001.

Joe Fox (Irvine); M.A., Northern Colorado, 1966.

La Faune Yvette Gordon (Los Angeles); Ph.D., California School of Professional Psychology, 1993.

Michelyn Gould (Los Angeles); Psy.D., California School of Professional Psychology, 1999.

Mary Lou Hamaker, Lecturer (Irvine), Ph.D., USC, 1986.

Leanne Harmon-Doyle (Los Angeles); Psy.D., Alliant International, 2003.

Christine A. Hoffman (Irvine); Ed.D., Northern Arizona, 1997.

Erica L. Holmes (Los Angeles); Psy.D., US International, 2001.

Elena M. Ingrao (San Diego); M.S., National, 1993.

Adi´na Janzen (Fresno); J.D., San Joaquin College of Law, 1985.

Vallarie Johnson (Los Angeles); Psy.D., Alliant International, 2004.

Dan Kettlehake (San Diego); Ph.D., Bowling Green State, 1997.

Lori Lambertson, Lecturer (San Francisco); M.A., San Francisco State, 1993.

Susan Lees (Los Angeles); Psy.D., Alliant International, 2003.

Bill Madigan (San Diego); M.A., San Diego State, 1990.

Sally Madruga (San Diego); M.A., San Diego State, 1981.

N. Bert McIntosh Jr. (San Diego); M.A., San Diego State, 1969.

Erv Metzgar (San Diego); M.A., San Diego State.

Susan Moore (San Diego); Ed.D., Alliant International, 2005.

Emil Nolte, Lecturer (Irvine).

Romelia Orozco (San Diego); Ed.D., Alliant International, 2002.

Cyndi Paik, Lecturer (Irvine); M.A., US International, 2002.

Walter T. Parry (San Diego); M.A., Stanford, 1964.

Ernest Proud (Los Angeles); Ph.D., California School of Professional Psychology.

Thomas Ryerson (Los Angeles); Psy.D., Alliant International, 2004.

Jerry Salazar, Lecturer (Irvine); M.A., California State, Long Beach, 1972.

Marilyn Shepherd (Fresno); Ed.D., California, Davis, 1996.

Erlinda Teisinger (Fresno); Ed.D., USC, 2000.

Marvin Warner (San Diego); M.A., Azusa Pacific, 1978.

Gary E. Warren (Los Angeles); Ed.D., US International, 1987.

Lori Williams (Los Angeles); Psy.D., Alliant International, 2004.

ANTIOCH UNIVERSITY NEW ENGLAND

Department of Education

Programs of Study	Antioch University New England (ANE) is deeply rooted in the heritage of progressive education and social responsibility. Its education programs apply the Antioch philosophy to current and future educators. From workshops to certificates to graduate degree programs, the University educates in ways that open graduates' minds to the many dimensions of the students they teach. Its student-centered, activity-based learning approach is blended with a sense of community responsibility that underscores each program.
	The Department's broad range of options meets students' specific needs—whether as a future teacher or a seasoned educator—with a wide variety of degree programs, concentrations, and advanced learning opportunities.
	Antioch students are part of a community that promotes personal reflection and professional growth. They explore ways to strike a balance as an educator between cultivating rational, logical thought and artistic intuition. As a result, it empowers teachers to build bridges between the dreams of childhood and the integrity of adulthood. Students share and learn from life diversity and bring the richness of their life experiences to class. Students from a broad range of backgrounds explore the art of teaching together, which enhances the learning experience and promotes a more stimulating and enlightening course of study.
	Teacher preparation programs include the Integrated Learning Program, which offers the Master of Education (M.Ed.) degree in elementary/ early childhood education (with concentrations in arts and humanities and science and environmental education), and the Waldorf Teacher Training Programs (M.Ed. and certificate), offered in both a year-round program (with or without New Hampshire state certification) and a summer sequence program.
	The Experienced Educators Program offers the Master of Education degree in foundations of education. It is offered as both a year-round program and a summer program.
	The Antioch Center for School Renewal (ACSR) is the service division of the Department of Education. The staff of highly skilled, experienced K–12 teacher-leaders and core University faculty members are part of an educational institution that embodies the values of progressive, student-centered education. Over the last twenty years, ACSR faculty have worked with thousands of educators from more than 500 schools throughout New England and around the world to support the development of classrooms and schools into strong, dynamic learning communities.
Research Facilities	The librarians at Antioch New England offer professional and personalized reference service for graduate research. Extensive class and research support is available via the library's Web site. Access to the library catalog is available through Horace, the library's automated catalog system. Also available are specialized online reference pages for classes and key topics, access to many online bibliographic databases, reserve reading, and links to scholarly Internet resources with full Internet access. In addition, detailed reference instruction, specific research information, an electronic book collection, and specific class support resources are also available on the library's Web site. All library services, such as book requests, renewals, reference help, and interlibrary loan requests are available online.
	Antioch New England's focused library collection includes print and electronic books and journals, dissertations and theses, audiovisual materials, and government documents. This collection is enhanced by the large collection of more than 300,000 books and 13,000 journal titles at Antioch College, the Graduate School's partner in the larger Antioch University Library system. Recent additions include OhioLINK, which offers more than 100 electronic research databases, including a variety of full-text resources and RefWORKS, a bibliographic management program. The Antioch New England Library also participates in local, regional, and national interlibrary loan services.
Financial Aid	Approximately 70 percent of students receive some type of aid, usually in the form of federal loans and work-study. The Jonathan Daniels Scholarship, established in 2003, strives to increase the diversity of the student body in its racial, ethnic, cultural, international, and socioeconomic makeup and to encourage service to underserved groups. All full-time Antioch New England students are eligible, although funding is limited. The completed scholarship form, along with relevant information from the Office of Financial Aid, is forwarded to each academic department for decisions. Awards range from $500 to 50 percent of tuition for a given year.
Cost of Study	In 2007–08, the cost for the M.Ed. Experienced Educators Program is $3000 per semester ($3600 if adding in the Certificate in Autism Spectrum Disorders, $4250 if pursuing principal certification) with a $250 comprehensive fee. The M.Ed. Integrated Learning Program is $6550 per semester, with a $250 comprehensive fee. The Waldorf certificate program cost is $4925 per semester; the Waldorf 3+2 certificate (summer sequence), $4175; the Waldorf M.Ed. (year-round), $5525; and the Waldorf M.Ed. (summer sequence), $4125. Each semester, Waldorf students must pay a comprehensive fee of $375.
Living and Housing Costs	ANE's location enables a large portion of students to commute to classes from their established homes in various parts of New England. Other students move close to Antioch New England, where they have a varied selection of settings—urban, rural, semirural, coast, mountains, or valley—in which to live. The Office of Admissions provides information resources for those relocating to the Monadnock region, the greater Brattleboro area, or northern Massachusetts.
Student Group	About 1,200 students attend Antioch New England. The average age ranges between 25 and 55; women make up 69 percent of the population. Students have an average of three to six years of professional experience upon entering their program, and most continue employment while pursuing their studies.
Location	Located in Keene, New Hampshire, Antioch New England is in the heart of the Monadnock region, a picturesque area that has been described as the "Currier & Ives" corner of New Hampshire. The School is geographically situated so that students also have easy access to several popular metropolitan areas, including Boston and Montreal. With a population of nearly 23,000, Keene has been named by the National Trust for Historic Preservation as one of "America's Dozen Distinctive Destinations."
The University and The Department	Antioch New England offers a rich array of master's and doctoral-level academic programming and institutional activities. The School's values-driven mission and focus on experiential learning, peer interaction, and reflective practice make the Antioch experience unique for each individual who is part of this learning community.
	The tradition of progressive education is maintained and cultivated in the Department of Education. Firmly committed to child-centered and activity-based learning, the faculty members encourage teachers to develop a deep respect for the processes of child development. This respect is wedded to a sense of responsibility to the social community, and the result is teachers who can build bridges between the dreams of childhood and the integrity of adulthood.
Applying	Students must submit the completed application form, including a resume and an essay; a nonrefundable application fee of $50; one official transcript from each accredited college or university attended, indicating courses taken and degree(s) earned; and three letters of recommendation (four letters for Alternative Admissions Process applicants), preferably from persons who are, or have been, in a position to evaluate the applicant's work. An interview with a department faculty member is required. Antioch New England does not require master's-level applicants to take the Graduate Record Examinations (GRE) or similar written examinations.
	The Experienced Educators program accepts applications on a rolling basis. Applications for the Integrated Learning program are reviewed after November 1, February 1, April 1, and June 1. Waldorf Teacher Training program applications are reviewed after November 1, February 1, and May 1.
Correspondence and Information	Office of Admissions Antioch University New England 40 Avon Street Keene, New Hampshire 03431-3516 Phone: 800-490-3310 (toll-free) Fax: 603-357-0718 E-mail: petersons@antiochne.edu Web site: http://www.antiochne.edu

Antioch University New England

THE FACULTY AND THEIR RESEARCH

Arthur Auer, Core Faculty; M.Ed., Antioch New England.

Judy Coven, Core Faculty; M.S., Bank Street College of Education.

Peter Eppig, Chair; M.Ed., New Hampshire. Innovative teaching practices, specifically in the areas of problem-based learning; curriculum development as defined in areas of integrated learning and multidisciplinary curricula; alternative assessment models, including holistic grading and reporting schemes; evolving roles of teachers as reflective practitioners, action researchers, student and peer coaches, curriculum builders, collaborative problem solvers and decision makers, and school leaders contributing to policy making and school governance.

Torin M. Finser, Director of Waldorf Teacher Training; Ph.D., Union (Ohio). Chairman of New England Waldorf Teacher Training.

Tom Julius, Director of the Experienced Educators Program; Ed.D., Massachusetts Amherst. Perceptions of an elementary teacher who is newly involved in portfolios, history of integrated day philosophy.

Ron LaBrusciano, Core Faculty; M.S., Southern Connecticut State. How the arts relate to teaching and learning, thematic curriculum, multiage grouping.

Susan Dreyer Leon, Core Faculty; Ed.D., Columbia. Alternative and second-chance education, democratic schooling, student voice, teacher leadership.

Jane Miller, Core Faculty; Ed.D., Massachusetts Amherst.

Talu Robertson, Faculty Emerita; Ed.D. Gifted and/or talented students; students defined as being at risk, as dropouts, as unmotivated; issues of oppression that inhibit optimum development for children and adults.

David Sobel, Director of the Integrated Learning Program; M.Ed., Antioch New England. Developmental psychology and ecoliteracy.

Laura Thomas, Director, Antioch Center for School Renewal; M.Ed., Antioch New England. School change, particularly resistance to change; student involvement in and perspective on the school experience; arts education; service learning.

ANTIOCH UNIVERSITY SEATTLE

Graduate Programs

Programs of Study

Antioch University Seattle offers graduate degree programs in art therapy, counselor therapist, education, environment and community, management, organizational psychology, psychology, strategic communication, and whole systems design. A Doctor of Psychology (Psy.D.) in clinical psychology and several graduate certificates are also offered.

The graduate programs in education provide a collaborative and challenging academic environment that continues Antioch's long tradition of progressive education. The graduate programs in education emphasize current research and its implications for student learning, the integration of theory and practice, and leadership for educational change.

The M.A. in education for experienced educators program offers options for K–12 and adult educators. Beyond the Seattle campus, several programs are offered in Tacoma, the Muckleshoot Tribal College, and other off-campus locations.

The graduate teacher preparation program is a full-time postbaccalaureate program to prepare elementary and middle school teachers. Students may prepare for the Washington State Teaching Certificate in five to six quarters, or students may build certification into a master's in education program. Students come to the program with backgrounds in many fields, including art, business, social service, law, and engineering.

The Psy.D. in clinical psychology program provides doctoral-level study and training in the theory and application of clinical psychology. This doctoral program integrates supervised practical experiences throughout, including practical experiences at an on-campus clinic and dozens of community agencies. There are several concentrations from which to choose: advanced art therapy, art therapy, forensic psychology, cognitive behavior approach, and existential-humanistic psychology. With classes offered on Fridays and Saturdays, licensed counselors and therapists may maintain their private practice while enrolling either full- or part-time in this doctoral program.

The M.A. in psychology programs offer clinical and individualized options. Clinical options include mental health counseling; child, couple, and family therapy; and art therapy. Graduates are able to meet the educational requirements for Washington State licensure as a mental health counselor or a marriage and family therapist. The art therapy program is approved by the American Art Therapy Association and prepares students to become registered art therapists. The individualized option includes a self-directed, self-designed program for those who wish to pursue interdisciplinary studies in psychology (e.g., applying psychology as teachers, consultants, mediators, personal coaches, or trainers) or for those who wish to interweave psychology with another discipline for social action and community development. A postgraduate certificate is also offered in art therapy.

The M.A. in organizational psychology program prepares students to transform and revitalize organizations and communities. Students gain a practical understanding of organizations, systems, and strategic intervention. Graduates work as project managers, trainers, and human resource managers in corporations, government and nonprofit groups, and start ups; others are self-employed professionals.

The M.S. in management program is designed to prepare leaders of progressive change in their organizations and businesses. The program integrates leadership skills with course work in economics, finance strategy, ethics, and marketing. Teamwork, collaborative learning, and personal mastery are major emphases throughout the program.

The M.A. in environment and community program is for practitioners and educators who want to be leaders and problem solvers in fostering environmental stewardship and accountability. Students represent many professions and vocations and arrive from all over the United States and other countries. The program accommodates those students with a Pacific Northwest focus and those with a national/international focus.

The M.A. in strategic communication program brings together the evolution of communication and the dynamics between ideas and people in political and cultural environments. Graduates lead grassroots organizations, nonprofit start-ups, and businesses of all sizes. With electives, students may choose related courses in legal and ethical issues, effective communications strategies, and communicating across cultures.

The M.A. in whole systems design program brings together science, the humanities, and design to prepare students to go beyond the narrow problem definitions and thinking of the status quo. Students learn to understand a situation in terms of its context, interrelationships, and dynamics and to imagine and create new possibilities for organizations to create systemic and sustainable change.

Research Facilities

In addition to Antioch's library, online resources, and computer labs, Antioch students have complete access to the University of Washington's extensive research library and its eighteen branch libraries.

Financial Aid

Antioch participates in the Federal Stafford Loan, the Federal Perkins Loan, Federal Work-Study Programs, Pell Grants, and Supplemental Educational Opportunity Grants. Other state aid and payment options are available. In addition, several graduate assistantships, fellowships, and scholarships are available; students with financial need are given priority. Approximately 71 percent of students receive financial aid.

Cost of Study

Each degree program differs in cost depending on the number of credits needed to graduate. Antioch is a moderately priced private, liberal arts university. Annual tuition costs, by program, are available at http://www.antiochseattle.edu.

Living Costs

The University offers residential housing in conjunction with a neighboring college. More details about these housing options are available at the University Web site (http://www.antiochseattle.edu). Most students commute and work full- or part-time.

Student Group

Student activities focus on events organized within the academic programs.

Location

Antioch University Seattle is located in downtown Seattle, Washington. The location is close to the thriving downtown Seattle shopping district and the world famous Seattle Space Needle. The location allows for easy access to community service and student teaching opportunities.

The University

Founded in 1852, Antioch University has had a proud history of progressive education with excellence for more than 150 years. Under the guidance of Horace Mann, the father of public education, Antioch was the first college to offer equal opportunities to women as students and faculty members. As part of the underground railroad during the Civil War, Antioch was one of the first colleges to admit African American students and celebrates Coretta Scott King as one of its distinguished alumni. The commitment continues today, as community participation and service is an integral part of the higher education curriculum. In 1996, Antioch received the prestigious John D. and Catherine T. MacArthur Foundation Award for creative genius in recognition of its history of innovative education. Today, Antioch University has six campuses across the United States: Antioch University Seattle; Antioch College and Antioch University McGregor in Yellow Springs, Ohio; Antioch New England University in New Hampshire; and Antioch University Los Angeles and Antioch University Santa Barbara in California.

Applying

Applications are accepted throughout the year. Application deadlines vary by program; application procedures and deadlines are outlined at http://www.antiochseattle.edu/admit/. Applicants must take part in a personal interview before acceptance to a program. GRE or GMAT scores are not required for admission. Financial aid applications should be submitted six to ten weeks before the quarter starts to ensure timely receipt of aid, loans, and grants.

Correspondence and Information

Admissions
Antioch University Seattle
2326 Sixth Avenue
Seattle, Washington 98121
Phone: 206-268-4202
　　　　888-268-4477 (toll-free)
Fax: 206-268-4242
E-mail: admissions@antiochseattle.edu
Web site: http://www.antiochseattle.edu

Antioch University Seattle

PROGRAM DIRECTORS/CHAIRS

Graduate Teacher Preparation Program: Robert Delilse, Chair; Ed.D., Boston University. Student achievement, curriculum reform.

Master of Arts in Education Program: Edward Mikel, Chair; Ph.D., Washington (St. Louis). Application of participatory democratic principles to curriculum and instruction, school governance, role of schools in progressive social change.

Master of Arts in Psychology Programs: Bill Forisha, Chair; Ph.D., Maryland. Human development and family studies, marriage and family therapy.

Doctor of Psychology Program: Andy Benjamin, Chair; Ph.D., Arizona. Couples, families, people who have endured trauma.

Management Program: Sadruddin Boga, Chair; Ph.D., Fielding Graduate Institute. Engineering, organizational development, and training; organizational transformation through individual and collective learning.

Environment and Community Programs: Katherine Davies, Chair; D.Phil., Oxford. Environmental health, especially the effects of toxic chemicals and children's environmental health.

Whole Systems Design Program: Betsy Geist, Chair; Ph.D., Union (Ohio). Essayist, comparative study of Chinese and American approaches to law and dispute resolution.

Strategic Communication Program: B. J. Bullert, Chair; Ph.D., Washington (Seattle). Visual media, political communication and documentary filmmaking, civic engagement.

Organizational Psychology Program: Shana Hormann, Chair; M.S.W., Washington (Seattle). Training and consultation in conflict resolution, group dynamics, and child abuse and family violence intervention.

EDUCATION FACULTY

Stevie Bravmann, Ph.D., Washington (Seattle). Teacher, educational consultant.

Bruce Campbell, Ph.D., Antioch Seattle. Teacher, curriculum specialist, author, school consultant.

Robert Delisle, Ed.D., Boston University. Student achievement, curriculum reform.

Geraldine Douglass, M.Ed., Seattle. Educational paradigm shift from Eurocentric to culturally inclusive pedagogy, cultural competence of educators in the use of curriculum, effective teaching.

Jacque Ensign, Ph.D., Virginia. Culturally relevant teaching, environmental education.

Lila J. Henderson-Leonard, Ed.S, Seattle Pacific. Reading programs, special education inclusion.

Kamuela Ka'ahanui, Ed.D., Simon Fraser (Canada). Demystification of indigenous people's histories and cultural stories, investigation of multiple intelligences and indigenous epistemologies, ethnic and cultural identity development.

Christie E. Kaaland, Ed.D., Washington (Seattle). Literacy development, children's literature, curriculum integration.

Anne Maxham, Ph.D., Idaho. Adult learning and writing apprehension, writing communities, qualitative research methodology.

Edward Mikel, Ph.D., Washington (St. Louis). Application of participatory democratic principles to curriculum and instruction, school governance, role of schools in progressive social change.

Melissa J. Rickey, Ed.D., Washington (Seattle). Reading and language arts, children's and young-adult literature, language acquisition and development, inquiry/teacher research.

Wendy J. Rosen, Ph.D., Michigan State. Power, diversity and equity issues, multicultural education, Native American women in higher education and leadership positions, social and cultural foundation of education.

Ophelia Taylor-Walker, M.A. Iowa. Speech-language pathology.

Ted Wright, Ph.D., Penn State. Educational leadership and change, place-based and community-based education, critical theory/pedagogy, American Indian and Alaska Native education transformation.

PSYCHOLOGY FACULTY

Andy Benjamin, Ph.D., Arizona. Couples, families, trauma.

Ann B. Blake, Ph.D., Washington (Seattle). Application of Jungian analytical psychology to specific populations.

Rebecca Bloom, M.P.S., Pratt. Anxiety, depression, life transitions, GLBT issues.

Larry D'Arienzo, M.A., Antioch Seattle. Adolescent and adult psychotherapy.

Paul David, Ph.D., Saybrook Institute. Marriage and family therapy, couples therapy.

Gail Dubin, M.A., Drake. Organizational systems, child-family work, developmental disabilities.

Ned Farley, Ph.D., Union (Ohio). Existential psychology, phenomenology, adult development, gay/lesbian/bi/transgendered issues in therapy, domestic violence.

Bill E. Forisha, Ph.D., Maryland. Human development and family studies, marriage and family therapy.

Jayashree George, D.A., NYU; ATR-BC. Multiculturalism, contemporary art, art therapy.

Janice Hoshino, Ph.D., U.S. International. Family art therapy, multicultural issues in art therapy.

Jane Harmon Jacobs, Ph.D., Washington (Seattle). Child, adolescent, and adult psychology.

Gwendolyn Jones, Ph.D., Washington (Seattle). Racial and gender stereotypes, psychological impacts of sexual coercion and racial discrimination, cultural understanding in the counseling process.

Ann Lazaroff, M.A., Antioch Seattle. Therapy for individuals, groups, couples, and families, with an emphasis on family-of-origin issues, mood disorders, and post-traumatic stress disorder.

Pat Linn, Ph.D., Kansas. Science of learning in cooperative education, infant behavior and development, effects of U.S. social policy on immigrant children.

Benny Ray Martin, Ph.D., California, Santa Barbara. Training, dialectical behavioral therapy, group skills therapy.

Alex Suarez, Ph.D., Washington (Seattle). Experimental psychology.

Liang Tien, Psy.D., Denver. Couples, families with adolescent children, women with history of trauma.

Mary Wieneke, Ph.D., California School of Professional Psychology/Alliant International University. Mind-body-culture integration, trauma, health and the long-term effects of chemotherapy on neurocognitive functioning.

Haiwen Yang, Ph.D., Nevada, Reno. Cross-cultural counseling, cultural identity development model for international students.

ORGANIZATION, MANAGEMENT, ENVIRONMENT, COMMUNICATIONS, AND WHOLE SYSTEMS FACULTY

Sadruddin Boga, Ph.D., Fielding Graduate Institute. Innovation and creativity, strategic planning, workplace diversity, empowerment and participative democracy.

B. J. Bullert, Ph.D., Washington (Seattle), 1995. Visual media, political communication, documentary filmmaking, civic engagement.

Steve Cato, Ph.D., Case Western Reserve. Appreciative inquiry, cocreating wholeness in people and organizations.

Donald E. Comstock, Ph.D., Stanford. Adult learning and social change, political economy, participatory action research, globalization.

Katherine S. Davies, D.Phil., Oxford. Environmental health, especially the effects of toxic chemicals and children's environmental health.

Betsy W. Geist, Ph.D., Union (Ohio). Essayist, comparative study of Chinese and American approaches to law and dispute resolution.

Shana Hormann, M.S.W., Washington (Seattle). Training and consultation in conflict resolution, group dynamics, and child abuse and family violence intervention.

Karyn Lazarus, M.A., Antioch Seattle. Organizational development, human resources, management of change and training for both profit and nonprofit organizations.

Jonathan M. Scherch, Ph.D., Tennessee. Social work, permaculture, local and international community organizing, sustainable development initiatives.

Farouk Y. Seif, Ph.D., Washington (Seattle). Metaphysics of design, wholeness, and design communication.

Barbara Spraker, M.B.A., City (Seattle). Organizational design and effective managerial practices, effective organizational behavior.

Pat Vivian, M.A., Antioch (Ohio). Multiorganizational strategies for systems change for nonprofit organizations.

Britt Yamamoto, Ph.D., Washington (Seattle). Civil society initiatives focused on human and community development.

Antioch University Seattle offers the only Master of Arts degree in environment and community in the world.

Challenging classes are designed to complement the schedules of working adults.

ARGOSY UNIVERSITY

ARGOSY UNIVERSITY, CHICAGO CAMPUS

College of Education

Programs of Study

Argosy University, Chicago Campus, offers the Master of Arts in Education (M.A.Ed.) and the Education Specialist (Ed.S.) degrees in educational leadership and instructional leadership and the Doctor of Education (Ed.D.) degree in educational leadership, instructional leadership, and community college executive leadership.

The M.A.Ed. in Educational Leadership program is designed to instill key philosophies, theories, and values that impact education. It prepares students to improve policies and practices within organizations through the motivation and supervision of others. Students develop skills needed to design, implement, and evaluate educational programs and curricula. Courses include educational law, educational finance, organizational communication, human resource management, instruction supervision, and organizational management. The program now offers Principal/General Administrative Certification, also known as Type 75 Certification.

The M.A.Ed. in Instructional Leadership program examines the challenges and problems encountered in today's educational environment. Course work encompasses the historical, philosophical, psychological, social, technical, and theoretical aspects of education. Students develop skills in analysis, oral and written communication, problem solving, critical thinking, team building, and computer technology. The program is designed for those who wish to develop or enhance classroom skills, become curriculum supervisors, or become educational leaders with a focus on instruction.

The Ed.S. in Educational Leadership program concentrates on applied organizational theory within the context of educational organizations. This specialized program develops the competencies required to secure educational administrator positions at the elementary or secondary school level. The program now offers Superintendent Certification.

The Ed.S. in Instructional Leadership program enables experienced teachers to become more effective practitioners and educational leaders with a focus on instruction. Course work is designed to satisfy the requirements of students seeking career advancement and those who are working toward a doctoral degree.

The Ed.D. in Community College Executive Leadership program offers an accelerated course of study intended to meet the needs of community college administrators who are looking to move into senior administrative positions (such as president, vice president, dean, and director) in community colleges.

The Ed.D. in Educational Leadership program is designed to enhance educational leadership strengths. Students learn innovative and collaborative techniques used to manage and govern educational institutions. The program prepares students for administrative leadership positions at the district, regional, state, or national level. Students must choose a concentration in district leadership, higher education administration, or K–12 education.

The Ed.D. in Instructional Leadership program draws upon educational theories and practices to help students discover new learning techniques for diverse audiences. Students enrolled in this program master teaching methodologies, hone classroom skills, and gain the knowledge required to become curriculum administrators or educational leaders with a focus on instruction. Students must choose a concentration in higher education or K–12 education.

Research Facilities

Argosy University libraries provide curriculum support and educational resources, including current text materials, diagnostic training documents, reference materials and databases, journals and dissertations, and major and current titles in program areas. They provide an online public-access catalog of library resources throughout the Argosy University system. Students enjoy full remote access to their campus library database, enabling them to study and conduct research at home. Academic databases offer dissertation abstracts, academic journals, and professional periodicals. All library computers are Internet accessible. Software applications include Word, Excel, PowerPoint, SPSS, and various test-scoring programs.

Financial Aid

A wide range of financial aid options is available to students who qualify. Argosy University's Chicago Campus offers access to federal and state aid programs, merit-based awards, grants, loans, and a work-study program. As a first step, students should complete the Free Application for Federal Student Aid (FAFSA). Prospective students can apply electronically at http://www.fafsa.ed.gov or at the campus. To receive consideration for the maximum amount of aid and ensure timely receipt of funds, it is best to submit an application promptly.

Cost of Study

Tuition varies by program. Students should contact Argosy University's Chicago Campus for tuition information.

Living and Housing Costs

Students typically live in apartments in the metropolitan Chicago area. Living expenses vary according to each student's preferred standard of living, housing, and transportation. The University does not offer or operate student housing. Most of the students are full-time working professionals who live within driving distance of the campus. Several nearby hotels offer special rates for those who commute from long distances. The Admissions Department also maintains a list of housing options, including contact information for University students who wish to share housing. For more information, students should contact the Admissions Department.

Student Group

Admission to Argosy University's Chicago Campus is selective to ensure a highly qualified student body. It encourages diversity in academic and employment backgrounds and promotes integration of the student body into professional life through established connections with local and national professional associations. Argosy University offers a professionally oriented education with rich opportunities to gain practical experience in class, field placements, and internships. Full-time students and working professionals gain the extensive knowledge and range of skills necessary for effective performance in their chosen fields.

Student Outcomes

Students can register with the University's online career-services system and use select services from a distance, such as degree-specific career e-mail lists, national job posts, and virtual job fairs. Students should contact the University for more information.

Location

Chicago is a city of world-class status and beauty, drawing visitors from around the globe. Argosy University's Chicago Campus sits in the heart of The Loop, the city's business and entertainment center. Located on the shores of Lake Michigan, Chicago is home to world-champion sports teams, an internationally acclaimed symphony orchestra, renowned architecture, and a variety of history and art museums. Recreational opportunities include hiking and cycling on miles of lakefront trails, golfing, and shopping.

Many educational institutions and agencies in the area provide excellent opportunities for student training. Chicago's thriving business environment includes a broad array of companies, including Boeing and Pepsi America. The commercial banking headquarters of JPMorgan Chase is also located in Chicago.

The University

Argosy University is a private institution with eighteen locations across the nation. Argosy University's Chicago Campus provides a career resources office, an academic resources center, and extensive information access for research. It offers the resources of a large university, plus the friendliness and personal attention of a small campus. Argosy University's Chicago Campus is closely associated with the University's Schaumburg, Illinois, campus located 45 minutes from downtown Chicago.

The innovative programs feature dynamic, relevant, and practical curricula delivered in flexible class formats. Students enjoy scheduling options that make it easier to fit school into their busy lives, choosing from day and evening courses, on campus or online. Many students find a combination of class formats to be an ideal way of continuing their education while meeting family and professional demands.

Argosy University is accredited by the Higher Learning Commission and is a member of the North Central Association (NCA, 30 North LaSalle Street, Suite 2400, Chicago, Illinois 60602; 800-621-7440 (toll-free); http://www.ncahlc.org).

Applying

Argosy University, Chicago Campus, accepts students year-round on a rolling admissions basis, depending on availability of required courses. Applications for admission are available online or by contacting the campus.

Correspondence and Information

Argosy University, Chicago Campus
350 North Orleans Street
Chicago, Illinois 60654
Phone: 312-777-7600
         800-626-4123 (toll-free)
Fax: 312-777-7748
E-mail: auadmissions@argosy.edu
Web site: http://www.argosy.edu/chicago

Argosy University, Chicago Campus

THE FACULTY

The Argosy University faculty comprises working professionals who are eager to help students succeed. Members bring real-world experience and the latest practice innovations to the academic setting. The diverse faculty members of the College of Education are widely recognized for contributions to the field. Most hold doctoral degrees. They provide a substantive education that combines comprehensive knowledge with critical skills and practical workplace relevance. Above all, faculty members are committed to their students' personal and professional development.

ARGOSY UNIVERSITY, DALLAS CAMPUS

College of Education

Programs of Study

Argosy University, Dallas Campus, offers the Master of Arts in Education (M.A.Ed.) and the Doctor of Education (Ed.D.) degrees in educational leadership and instructional leadership.

The M.A.Ed. in Educational Leadership program is designed to instill key philosophies, theories, and values that impact education. It prepares students to improve policies and practices within organizations through the motivation and supervision of others. Students develop skills needed to design, implement, and evaluate educational programs and curricula. Courses include educational law, educational finance, organizational communication, human resource management, instruction supervision, and organizational management.

The M.A.Ed. in Instructional Leadership program examines the challenges and problems encountered in today's educational environment. Course work encompasses the historical, philosophical, psychological, social, technical, and theoretical aspects of education. Students develop skills in analysis, oral and written communication, problem solving, critical thinking, team building, and computer technology. The program is designed for those who wish to develop or enhance classroom skills, become curriculum supervisors, or become educational leaders with a focus on instruction.

The Ed.D. in Educational Leadership program is designed to enhance educational leadership strengths. Students learn innovative and collaborative techniques used to manage and govern educational institutions. The program prepares students for administrative leadership positions at the district, regional, state, or national level. Students must choose a concentration in higher education administration or K–12 education.

The Ed.D. in Instructional Leadership program draws upon educational theories and practices to help students discover new learning techniques for diverse audiences. Students enrolled in this program master teaching methodologies, hone classroom skills, and gain the knowledge required to become curriculum administrators or educational leaders with a focus on instruction. Students must choose a concentration in higher education or K–12 education.

Research Facilities

Argosy University libraries provide curriculum support and educational resources, including current text materials, diagnostic training documents, reference materials and databases, journals and dissertations, and major and current titles in program areas. They provide an online public-access catalog of library resources throughout the Argosy University system. Students enjoy full remote access to their campus library database, enabling them to study and conduct research at home. Academic databases offer dissertation abstracts, academic journals, and professional periodicals. All library computers are Internet accessible. Software applications include Word, Excel, PowerPoint, SPSS, and various test-scoring programs.

Financial Aid

A wide range of financial aid options is available to students who qualify. Argosy University's Dallas Campus offers access to federal and state aid programs, merit-based awards, grants, loans, and a work-study program. As a first step, students should complete the Free Application for Federal Student Aid (FAFSA). Prospective students can apply electronically at http://www.fafsa.ed.gov or at the campus. To receive consideration for the maximum amount of aid and ensure timely receipt of funds, it is best to submit an application promptly.

Cost of Study

Tuition varies by program. Students should contact Argosy University's Dallas Campus for tuition information.

Living and Housing Costs

Students typically live in apartments in the metropolitan Dallas area. Living expenses vary according to each student's preferred standard of living, housing, and transportation. The University does not offer or operate student housing. Most of the students are full-time working professionals who live within driving distance of the campus. Several nearby hotels offer special rates for those who commute from long distances. The Admissions Department also maintains a list of housing options, including contact information for University students who wish to share housing. For more information, students should contact the Admissions Department.

Student Group

Admission to Argosy University's Dallas Campus is selective to ensure a highly qualified student body. It encourages diversity in academic and employment backgrounds and promotes integration of the student body into professional life through established connections with local and national professional associations. Argosy University offers a professionally oriented education with rich opportunities to gain practical experience in class, field placements, and internships. Full-time students and working professionals gain the extensive knowledge and range of skills necessary for effective performance in their chosen fields.

Student Outcomes

Students can register with the University's online career-services system and use select services from a distance, such as degree-specific career e-mail lists, national job posts, and virtual job fairs. Students should contact the University for more information.

Location

Argosy University's Dallas Campus offers a north-central location in Dallas, with easy access to freeways, libraries, shops, restaurants, theaters, art museums, and other tourist attractions. Many educational institutions and agencies in the area provide excellent opportunities for student training. The thriving business environment in the Dallas/Ft. Worth metropolitan area includes a broad array of companies, including Lockheed Martin Corporation, Baylor University Medical System, and Southwest Airlines.

The University

Argosy University is a private institution with eighteen locations across the nation. Argosy University's Dallas Campus provides students with a network of resources found at larger universities and the friendliness and personal attention of a small campus.

The innovative programs feature dynamic, relevant, and practical curricula delivered in flexible class formats. Students enjoy scheduling options that make it easier to fit school into their busy lives, choosing from day and evening courses, on campus or online. Many students find a combination of class formats to be an ideal way of continuing their education while meeting family and professional demands.

Argosy University is accredited by the Higher Learning Commission and is a member of the North Central Association (NCA, 30 North LaSalle Street, Suite 2400, Chicago, Illinois 60602; 800-621-7440 (toll-free); http://www.ncahlc.org).

Applying

Argosy University, Dallas Campus, accepts students year-round on a rolling admissions basis, depending on availability of required courses. Applications for admission are available online or by contacting the campus.

Correspondence and Information

Argosy University, Dallas Campus
8080 Park Lane, Suite 500
Dallas, Texas 75231
Phone: 214-890-9900
        866-954-9900 (toll-free)
Fax: 214-696-3900
E-mail: auadmissions@argosy.edu
Web site: http://www.argosy.edu/dallas

Argosy University, Dallas Campus

THE FACULTY

The Argosy University faculty comprises working professionals who are eager to help students succeed. Members bring real-world experience and the latest practice innovations to the academic setting. The diverse faculty members of the College of Education are widely recognized for contributions to the field. Most hold doctoral degrees. They provide a substantive education that combines comprehensive knowledge with critical skills and practical workplace relevance. Above all, faculty members are committed to their students' personal and professional development.

ARGOSY UNIVERSITY.

ARGOSY UNIVERSITY, DENVER CAMPUS

College of Education

Program of Study	Argosy University, Denver Campus, offers the Master of Arts in Education (M.A.Ed.) and the Doctor of Education (Ed.D.) degrees in educational leadership and instructional leadership.
	The M.A.Ed. in Educational Leadership program is designed to instill key philosophies, theories, and values that impact education. It prepares students to improve policies and practices within organizations through the motivation and supervision of others. Students develop skills needed to design, implement, and evaluate educational programs and curricula. Courses include educational law, educational finance, organizational communication, human resource management, instruction supervision, and organizational management.
	The M.A.Ed. in Instructional Leadership program examines the challenges and problems encountered in today's educational environment. Course work encompasses the historical, philosophical, psychological, social, technical, and theoretical aspects of education. Students develop skills in analysis, oral and written communication, problem solving, critical thinking, team building, and computer technology. The program is designed for those who wish to develop or enhance classroom skills, become curriculum supervisors, or become educational leaders with a focus on instruction.
	The Ed.D. in Educational Leadership program is designed to enhance educational leadership strengths. Students learn innovative and collaborative techniques used to manage and govern educational institutions. The program prepares students for administrative leadership positions at the district, regional, state, or national level. Students must choose a concentration in higher education administration or K–12 education.
	The Ed.D. in Instructional Leadership program draws upon educational theories and practices to help students discover new learning techniques for diverse audiences. Students enrolled in this program master teaching methodologies, hone classroom skills, and gain the knowledge required to become curriculum administrators or educational leaders with a focus on instruction. Students must choose a concentration in higher education or K–12 education.
Research Facilities	Argosy University libraries provide curriculum support and educational resources, including current text materials, diagnostic training documents, reference materials and databases, journals and dissertations, and major and current titles in program areas. They provide an online public-access catalog of library resources throughout the Argosy University system. Students enjoy full remote access to their campus library database, enabling them to study and conduct research at home. Academic databases offer dissertation abstracts, academic journals, and professional periodicals. All library computers are Internet accessible. Software applications include Word, Excel, PowerPoint, SPSS, and various test-scoring programs.
Financial Aid	A wide range of financial aid options is available to students who qualify. Argosy University's Denver Campus offers access to federal and state aid programs, merit-based awards, grants, loans, and a work-study program. As a first step, students should complete the Free Application for Federal Student Aid (FAFSA). Prospective students can apply electronically at http://www.fafsa.ed.gov or at the campus. To receive consideration for the maximum amount of aid and ensure timely receipt of funds, it is best to submit an application promptly.
Cost of Study	Tuition varies by program. Students should contact Argosy University's Denver Campus for tuition information.
Living and Housing Costs	Students typically live in apartments in the metropolitan Denver area. Living expenses vary according to each student's preferred standard of living, housing, and transportation. The University does not offer or operate student housing. Most of the students are full-time working professionals who live within driving distance of the campus. Several nearby hotels offer special rates for those who commute from long distances. The Admissions Department also maintains a list of housing options, including contact information for University students who wish to share housing. For more information, students should contact the Admissions Department.
Student Group	Admission to Argosy University's Denver Campus is selective to ensure a highly qualified student body. The University encourages diversity in academic and employment backgrounds and promotes integration of the student body into professional life through established connections with local and national professional associations. Argosy University offers a professionally oriented education with rich opportunities to gain practical experience in class, field placements, and internships. Full-time students and working professionals gain the extensive knowledge and range of skills necessary for effective performance in their chosen fields.
Student Outcomes	Students can register with the University's online career-services system and use select services from a distance, such as degree-specific career e-mail lists, national job posts, and virtual job fairs. Students should contact the University for more information.
Location	Argosy University, Denver Campus, is located at 1200 Lincoln Street in Denver, Colorado. The ten-story downtown facility includes classrooms, computer labs, a resource center with Internet access, a student lounge, staff and faculty offices, and other amenities. The campus is close to a variety of local libraries, shops, restaurants, theaters, and art museums. Denver's thriving professional organizations, major corporations, high-tech companies, hospitals, schools, clinics, and social service agencies can also provide outstanding training opportunities for students.
The University	Argosy University is a private institution with eighteen locations across the nation. Argosy University's Denver Campus provides students with a network of resources found at larger universities and the friendliness and personal attention of a small campus.
	The innovative programs feature dynamic, relevant, and practical curricula delivered in flexible class formats. Students enjoy scheduling options that make it easier to fit school into their busy lives, choosing from day and evening courses, on campus or online. Many students find a combination of class formats to be an ideal way of continuing their education while meeting family and professional demands.
	Argosy University is accredited by the Higher Learning Commission and is a member of the North Central Association (NCA, 30 North LaSalle Street, Suite 2400, Chicago, Illinois 60602; 800-621-7440 (toll-free); http://www.ncahlc.org).
Applying	Argosy University, Denver Campus, accepts students year-round on a rolling admissions basis, depending on availability of required courses. Applications for admission are available online or by contacting the campus.
Correspondence and Information	Argosy University, Denver Campus 1200 Lincoln Street Denver, Colorado 80203 Phone: 303-248-2700 866-431-5981 (toll-free) Fax: 303-248-2800 E-mail: auadmissions@argosy.edu Web site: http://www.argosy.edu/denver

Argosy University, Denver Campus

THE FACULTY

The Argosy University faculty comprises working professionals who are eager to help students succeed. Members bring real-world experience and the latest practice innovations to the academic setting. The diverse faculty members of the College of Education are widely recognized for contributions to the field. Most hold doctoral degrees. They provide a substantive education that combines comprehensive knowledge with critical skills and practical workplace relevance. Above all, faculty members are committed to their students' personal and professional development.

ARGOSY UNIVERSITY, HAWAI'I CAMPUS

College of Education

ARGOSY UNIVERSITY.

Program of Study	Argosy University, Hawai'i Campus, offers the Master of Arts in Education (M.A.Ed.) and the Doctor of Education (Ed.D.) degrees in educational leadership and instructional leadership. The M.A.Ed. in Educational Leadership program is designed to instill key philosophies, theories, and values that impact education. It prepares students to improve policies and practices within organizations through the motivation and supervision of others. Students develop skills needed to design, implement, and evaluate educational programs and curricula. Courses include educational law, educational finance, organizational communication, human resource management, instruction supervision, and organizational management. The M.A.Ed. in Instructional Leadership program examines the challenges and problems encountered in today's educational environment. Course work encompasses the historical, philosophical, psychological, social, technical, and theoretical aspects of education. Students develop skills in analysis, oral and written communication, problem solving, critical thinking, team building, and computer technology. The program is designed for those who wish to develop or enhance classroom skills, become curriculum supervisors, or become educational leaders with a focus on instruction. The Ed.D. in Educational Leadership program is designed to enhance educational leadership strengths. Students learn innovative and collaborative techniques used to manage and govern educational institutions. The program prepares students for administrative leadership positions at the district, regional, state, or national level. Students must choose a concentration in higher education administration or K–12 education. The Ed.D. in Instructional Leadership program draws upon educational theories and practices to help students discover new learning techniques for diverse audiences. Students enrolled in this program master teaching methodologies, hone classroom skills, and gain the knowledge required to become curriculum administrators or educational leaders with a focus on instruction. Students must choose a concentration in higher education or K–12 education.
Research Facilities	Argosy University libraries provide curriculum support and educational resources, including current text materials, diagnostic training documents, reference materials and databases, journals and dissertations, and major and current titles in program areas. They provide an online public-access catalog of library resources throughout the Argosy University system. Students enjoy full remote access to their campus library database, enabling them to study and conduct research at home. Academic databases offer dissertation abstracts, academic journals, and professional periodicals. All library computers are Internet accessible. Software applications include Word, Excel, PowerPoint, SPSS, and various test-scoring programs.
Financial Aid	A wide range of financial aid options is available to students who qualify. Argosy University's Hawai'i Campus offers access to federal and state aid programs, merit-based awards, grants, loans, and a work-study program. As a first step, students should complete the Free Application for Federal Student Aid (FAFSA). Prospective students can apply electronically at http://www.fafsa.ed.gov or at the campus. To receive consideration for the maximum amount of aid and ensure timely receipt of funds, it is best to submit an application promptly.
Cost of Study	Tuition varies by program. Students should contact Argosy University's Hawai'i Campus for tuition information.
Living and Housing Costs	Students typically live in apartments in the metropolitan Honolulu area. Living expenses vary according to each student's preferred standard of living, housing, and transportation. The University does not offer or operate student housing. Most of the students are full-time working professionals who live within driving distance of the campus. Several nearby hotels offer special rates for those who commute from long distances. The Admissions Department also maintains a list of housing options, including contact information for University students who wish to share housing. For more information, students should contact the Admissions Department.
Student Group	Admission to Argosy University's Hawai'i Campus is selective to ensure a highly qualified student body. The University encourages diversity in academic and employment backgrounds and promotes integration of the student body into professional life through established connections with local and national professional associations. Argosy University offers a professionally oriented education with rich opportunities to gain practical experience in class, field placements, and internships. Full-time students and working professionals gain the extensive knowledge and range of skills necessary for effective performance in their chosen fields.
Student Outcomes	Students can register with the University's online career-services system and use select services from a distance, such as degree-specific career e-mail lists, national job posts, and virtual job fairs. Students should contact the University for more information.
Location	Argosy University's Hawai'i Campus is located in downtown Honolulu on Oahu. Additional satellite locations on Maui and in Hilo on the island of Hawaii offer programs to communities on the neighbor islands. These locations connect the campus to Hawaii and to the local and native communities of the Pacific Islands and the Pacific Rim. Students enjoy the cultural and recreational opportunities that these locations provide. University faculty and staff members often work in cooperation with the Hawaiian community to create an educational focus on social issues, human diversity, and programs that make a difference to underserved populations. Many educational institutions and agencies in the area provide excellent opportunities for student training. Honolulu's thriving business environment includes a broad array of companies. The area's largest employers include Bank of Hawaii, Queens Medical Center, and the U.S. government.
The University	Argosy University is a private institution with eighteen locations across the nation. Argosy University's Hawai'i Campus provides students with a career resources office, an academic resources center, and extensive information access for research. It offers the resources of a large university, plus the friendliness and personal attention of a small campus. The innovative programs feature dynamic, relevant, and practical curricula delivered in flexible class formats. Students enjoy scheduling options that make it easier to fit school into their busy lives, choosing from day and evening courses, on campus or online. Many students find a combination of class formats to be an ideal way of continuing their education while meeting family and professional demands. Argosy University is accredited by the Higher Learning Commission and is a member of the North Central Association (NCA, 30 North LaSalle Street, Suite 2400, Chicago, Illinois 60602; 800-621-7440 (toll-free); http://www.ncahlc.org).
Applying	Argosy University, Hawai'i Campus, accepts students year-round on a rolling admissions basis, depending on availability of required courses. Applications for admission are available online or by contacting the campus.
Correspondence and Information	Argosy University, Hawai'i Campus 400 ASB Tower 1001 Bishop Street Honolulu, Hawaii 96813 Phone: 808-536-5555 888-323-2777 (toll-free) Fax: 808-536-5505 E-mail: auadmissions@argosy.edu Web site: http://www.argosy.edu/honolulu

Argosy University, Hawai'i Campus

THE FACULTY

The Argosy University faculty comprises working professionals who are eager to help students succeed. Members bring real-world experience and the latest practice innovations to the academic setting. The diverse faculty members of the College of Education are widely recognized for contributions to the field. Most hold doctoral degrees. They provide a substantive education that combines comprehensive knowledge with critical skills and practical workplace relevance. Above all, faculty members are committed to their students' personal and professional development.

ARGOSY UNIVERSITY, ORANGE COUNTY CAMPUS

ARGOSY UNIVERSITY.

College of Education

Programs of Study
Argosy University, Orange County Campus, offers the Master of Arts in Education (M.A.Ed.) degree in educational leadership and instructional leadership and the Doctor of Education (Ed.D.) degree in community college executive leadership, educational leadership, and instructional leadership.

The M.A.Ed. in Educational Leadership program is designed to instill key philosophies, theories, and values that impact education. It prepares students to improve policies and practices within organizations through the motivation and supervision of others. Students develop skills needed to design, implement, and evaluate educational programs and curricula. Courses include educational law, educational finance, organizational communication, human resource management, instruction supervision, and organizational management.

The M.A.Ed. in Instructional Leadership program examines the challenges and problems encountered in today's educational environment. Course work encompasses the historical, philosophical, psychological, social, technical, and theoretical aspects of education. Students develop skills in analysis, oral and written communication, problem solving, critical thinking, team building, and computer technology. The program is designed for those who wish to develop or enhance classroom skills, become curriculum supervisors, or become educational leaders with a focus on instruction. Students may choose one of four optional concentrations: single or multiple subject teacher credential preparation or single or multiple subject teacher credential preparation with bilingual cross-cultural language and academic development (BCLAD).

The Ed.D. in Community College Executive Leadership program offers an accelerated course of study intended to meet the needs of community college administrators who are looking to move into senior administrative positions (such as president, vice president, dean, and director) in community colleges.

The Ed.D. in Educational Leadership program is designed to enhance educational leadership strengths. Students learn innovative and collaborative techniques used to manage and govern educational institutions. The program prepares students for administrative leadership positions at the district, regional, state, or national level. Students must choose a concentration in higher education administration or K–12 education.

The Ed.D. in Instructional Leadership program draws upon educational theories and practices to help students discover new learning techniques for diverse audiences. Students enrolled in this program master teaching methodologies, hone classroom skills, and gain the knowledge required to become curriculum administrators or educational leaders with a focus on instruction. Students must choose a concentration in education technology, higher education, or K–12 education.

Research Facilities
Argosy University libraries provide curriculum support and educational resources, including current text materials, diagnostic training documents, reference materials and databases, journals and dissertations, and major and current titles in program areas. They provide an online public-access catalog of library resources throughout the Argosy University system. Students enjoy full remote access to their campus library database, enabling them to study and conduct research at home. Academic databases offer dissertation abstracts, academic journals, and professional periodicals. All library computers are Internet accessible. Software applications include Word, Excel, PowerPoint, SPSS, and various test-scoring programs.

Financial Aid
A wide range of financial aid options is available to students who qualify. Argosy University's Orange County Campus offers access to federal and state aid programs, merit-based awards, grants, loans, and a work-study program. As a first step, students should complete the Free Application for Federal Student Aid (FAFSA). Prospective students can apply electronically at http://www.fafsa.ed.gov or at the campus. To receive consideration for the maximum amount of aid and ensure timely receipt of funds, it is best to submit an application promptly.

Cost of Study
Tuition varies by program. Students should contact Argosy University's Orange County Campus for tuition information.

Living and Housing Costs
Students typically live in apartments in the metropolitan area. Living expenses vary according to each student's preferred standard of living, housing, and transportation. The University does not offer or operate student housing. Most of the students are full-time working professionals who live within driving distance of the campus. Several nearby hotels offer special rates for those who commute from long distances. The Admissions Department also maintains a list of housing options, including contact information for University students who wish to share housing. For more information, students should contact the Admissions Department.

Student Group
Admission to Argosy University's Orange County Campus is selective to ensure a highly qualified student body. It encourages diversity in academic and employment backgrounds and promotes integration of the student body into professional life through established connections with local and national professional associations. Argosy University offers a professionally oriented education with rich opportunities to gain practical experience in class, field placements, and internships. Full-time students and working professionals gain the extensive knowledge and range of skills necessary for effective performance in their chosen fields.

Student Outcomes
Students can register with the University's online career-services system and use select services from a distance, such as degree-specific career e-mail lists, national job posts, and virtual job fairs. Students should contact the University for more information.

Location
Argosy University's Orange County Campus attracts students from Southern California, as well as from around the country and the world. Orange County features a temperate climate, sunny beaches, and a host of cultural and entertainment options. The campus is located approximately 30 miles south of downtown Los Angeles, 90 miles north of San Diego, and just minutes from one of the many freeways that connect the Southern California basin. Regional parks and preserved lands provide opportunities for hiking, biking, riding, and other recreational activities. Whether it's ultrachic Newport Beach, artsy Laguna Beach, or unspoiled Catalina Island, Orange County's ocean-side personalities are as varied as the people who visit the area.

Many educational institutions and agencies in the area provide excellent opportunities for student training. Orange County's thriving business environment includes a broad array of companies. The area's largest employers include Ingram Micro Inc., Orange County Register, ITT Industries, and OneSource.

The University
Argosy University is a private institution with eighteen locations across the nation. Argosy University's Orange County Campus provides students with a career resources office, an academic resources center, and extensive information access for research. It offers the resources of a large university, plus the friendliness and personal attention of a small campus.

The innovative programs feature dynamic, relevant, and practical curricula delivered in flexible class formats. Students enjoy scheduling options that make it easier to fit school into their busy lives, choosing from day and evening courses, on campus or online. Many students find a combination of class formats to be an ideal way of continuing their education while meeting family and professional demands.

Argosy University is accredited by the Higher Learning Commission and is a member of the North Central Association (NCA, 30 North LaSalle Street, Suite 2400, Chicago, Illinois 60602; 800-621-7440 (toll-free); http://www.ncahlc.org).

Applying
Argosy University, Orange County Campus, accepts students year-round on a rolling admissions basis, depending on availability of required courses. Applications for admission are available online or by contacting the campus.

Correspondence and Information
Argosy University, Orange County Campus
3501 West Sunflower Avenue, Suite 110
Santa Ana, California 92704

Phone: 714-338-6200
    800-716-9598 (toll-free)
Fax: 714-437-1697
E-mail: auadmissions@argosy.edu
Web site: http://www.argosy.edu/orangecounty

Argosy University, Orange County Campus

THE FACULTY

The Argosy University faculty comprises working professionals who are eager to help students succeed. Members bring real-world experience and the latest practice innovations to the academic setting. The diverse faculty members of the College of Education are widely recognized for contributions to the field. Most hold doctoral degrees. They provide a substantive education that combines comprehensive knowledge with critical skills and practical workplace relevance. Above all, faculty members are committed to their students' personal and professional development.

ARGOSY UNIVERSITY

ARGOSY UNIVERSITY, PHOENIX CAMPUS

College of Education

Programs of Study

Argosy University, Phoenix Campus, offers the Master of Arts in Education (M.A.Ed.) and the Education Specialist (Ed.S.) degrees in educational leadership and instructional leadership and the Doctor of Education (Ed.D.) degree in community college executive leadership, educational leadership, and instructional leadership.

The M.A.Ed. in Educational Leadership program is designed to instill key philosophies, theories, and values that impact education. It prepares students to improve policies and practices within organizations through the motivation and supervision of others. Students develop skills needed to design, implement, and evaluate educational programs and curricula. Courses include educational law, educational finance, organizational communication, human resource management, instruction supervision, and organizational management.

The M.A.Ed. in Instructional Leadership program examines the challenges and problems encountered in today's educational environment. Course work encompasses the historical, philosophical, psychological, social, technical, and theoretical aspects of education. Students develop skills in analysis, oral and written communication, problem solving, critical thinking, team building, and computer technology. The program is designed for those who wish to develop or enhance classroom skills, become curriculum supervisors, or become educational leaders with a focus on instruction.

The Ed.S. in Educational Leadership program concentrates on applied organizational theory within the context of educational organizations. This specialized program develops the competencies required to secure educational administrator positions at the elementary or secondary school level.

The Ed.S. in Instructional Leadership program enables experienced teachers to become more effective practitioners and educational leaders with a focus on instruction. Course work is designed to satisfy the requirements of students seeking career advancement and those who are working toward a doctoral degree.

The Ed.D. in Community College Executive Leadership program offers an accelerated course of study intended to meet the needs of community college administrators who are looking to move into senior administrative positions (such as president, vice president, dean, and director) in community colleges.

The Ed.D. in Educational Leadership program is designed to enhance educational leadership strengths. Students learn innovative and collaborative techniques used to manage and govern educational institutions. The program prepares students for administrative leadership positions at the district, regional, state, or national level. Students must choose a concentration in higher education administration or K–12 education.

The Ed.D. in Instructional Leadership program draws upon educational theories and practices to help students discover new learning techniques for diverse audiences. Students enrolled in this program master teaching methodologies, hone classroom skills, and gain the knowledge required to become curriculum administrators or educational leaders with a focus on instruction. Students must choose a concentration in higher education or K–12 education.

Research Facilities

Argosy University libraries provide curriculum support and educational resources, including current text materials, diagnostic training documents, reference materials and databases, journals and dissertations, and major and current titles in program areas. They provide an online public-access catalog of library resources throughout the Argosy University system. Students enjoy full remote access to their campus library database, enabling them to study and conduct research at home. Academic databases offer dissertation abstracts, academic journals, and professional periodicals. All library computers are Internet accessible. Software applications include Word, Excel, PowerPoint, SPSS, and various test-scoring programs.

Financial Aid

A wide range of financial aid options is available to students who qualify. Argosy University's Phoenix Campus offers access to federal and state aid programs, merit-based awards, grants, loans, and a work-study program. As a first step, students should complete the Free Application for Federal Student Aid (FAFSA). Prospective students can apply electronically at http://www.fafsa.ed.gov or at the campus. To receive consideration for the maximum amount of aid and ensure timely receipt of funds, it is best to submit an application promptly.

Cost of Study

Tuition varies by program. Students should contact Argosy University's Phoenix Campus for tuition information.

Living and Housing Costs

Students typically live in apartments in the metropolitan Phoenix area. Living expenses vary according to each student's preferred standard of living, housing, and transportation. The University does not offer or operate student housing. Most of the students are full-time working professionals who live within driving distance of the campus. Several nearby hotels offer special rates for those who commute from long distances. The Admissions Department also maintains a list of housing options, including contact information for University students who wish to share housing. For more information, students should contact the Admissions Department.

Student Group

Admission to Argosy University's Phoenix Campus is selective to ensure a highly qualified student body. It encourages diversity in academic and employment backgrounds and promotes integration of the student body into professional life through established connections with local and national professional associations. Argosy University offers a professionally oriented education with rich opportunities to gain practical experience in class, field placements, and internships. Full-time students and working professionals gain the extensive knowledge and range of skills necessary for effective performance in their chosen fields.

Student Outcomes

Students can register with the University's online career-services system and use select services from a distance, such as degree-specific career e-mail lists, national job posts, and virtual job fairs. Students should contact the University for more information.

Location

Argosy University's Phoenix Campus offers a high-quality education in an intimate, small-group setting. The campus is located near I-17, close to shops, restaurants, and recreational areas. Phoenix is home to several major-league sports teams, and the city offers an array of cultural activities ranging from opera and theater to science museums. The multicultural environment of Arizona, coupled with Argosy University's professional training affiliations throughout the state, creates an exciting opportunity for students to work with urban, rural, and culturally diverse populations.

The thriving business environment in Phoenix includes a wide variety of companies, such as Intel and Go Daddy Group, an Internet company. Wells Fargo, Home Depot, Lowe's, and Wal-Mart also represent some of the area's largest employers.

The University

Argosy University is a private institution with eighteen locations across the nation. Argosy University's Phoenix Campus provides students with a career resources office, an academic resources center, and extensive information access for research. It offers the resources of a large university, plus the friendliness and personal attention of a small campus.

The innovative programs feature dynamic, relevant, and practical curricula delivered in flexible class formats. Students enjoy scheduling options that make it easier to fit school into their busy lives, choosing from day and evening courses, on campus or online. Many students find a combination of class formats to be an ideal way of continuing their education while meeting family and professional demands.

Argosy University is accredited by the Higher Learning Commission and is a member of the North Central Association (NCA, 30 North LaSalle Street, Suite 2400, Chicago, Illinois 60602; 800-621-7440 (toll-free); http://www.ncahlc.org).

Applying

Argosy University, Phoenix Campus, accepts students year-round on a rolling admissions basis, depending on availability of required courses. Applications for admission are available online or by contacting the campus.

Correspondence and Information

Argosy University, Phoenix Campus
2233 West Dunlap Avenue
Phoenix, Arizona 85021
Phone: 602-216-2600
　　　 866-216-2777 (toll-free)
Fax: 602-216-2601
E-mail: auadmissions@argosy.edu
Web site: http://argosy.edu/phoenix

Argosy University, Phoenix Campus

THE FACULTY

The Argosy University faculty comprises working professionals who are eager to help students succeed. Members bring real-world experience and the latest practice innovations to the academic setting. The diverse faculty members of the College of Education are widely recognized for contributions to the field. Most hold doctoral degrees. They provide a substantive education that combines comprehensive knowledge with critical skills and practical workplace relevance. Above all, faculty members are committed to their students' personal and professional development.

Peterson's Graduate Programs in Business, Education, Health, Information Studies, Law & Social Work 2008

ARGOSY UNIVERSITY.

ARGOSY UNIVERSITY, SAN DIEGO CAMPUS

College of Education

Programs of Study

Argosy University, San Diego Campus offers the Master of Arts in Education (M.A.Ed.) degree in educational leadership and instructional leadership and the Doctor of Education (Ed.D.) degree in community college executive leadership, educational leadership, and instructional leadership.

The M.A.Ed. in educational leadership program is designed to instill key philosophies, theories, and values that impact education. It prepares students to improve policies and practices within organizations through the motivation and supervision of others. Students develop skills needed to design, implement, and evaluate educational programs and curricula. Courses include educational law, educational finance, organizational communication, human resource management, instruction supervision, and organizational management.

The M.A.Ed. in instructional leadership program examines the challenges and problems encountered in today's educational environment. Course work encompasses the historical, philosophical, psychological, social, technical, and theoretical aspects of education. Students develop skills in analysis, oral and written communication, problem solving, critical thinking, team building, and computer technology. The program is designed for those who wish to develop or enhance classroom skills, become curriculum supervisors, or become educational leaders with a focus on instruction. Students may choose one of four optional concentrations: single- or multiple-subject teacher credential preparation or single- or multiple-subject teacher credential preparation with bilingual cross-cultural language and academic development (BCLAD).

The Ed.D. in community college executive leadership program offers an accelerated course of study intended to meet the needs of community college administrators who are looking to move into senior administrative positions (such as president, vice president, dean, and director) in community colleges.

The Ed.D. in educational leadership program is designed to enhance educational leadership strengths. Students learn innovative and collaborative techniques used to manage and govern educational institutions. The program prepares students for administrative leadership positions at the district, regional, state, or national level. Students must choose a concentration in higher education administration or K–12 education.

The Ed.D. in instructional leadership program draws upon educational theories and practices to help students discover new learning techniques for diverse audiences. Students enrolled in this program master teaching methodologies, hone classroom skills, and gain the knowledge required to become curriculum administrators or educational leaders with a focus on instruction. Students must choose a concentration in higher education or K–12 education.

Research Facilities

Argosy University libraries provide curriculum support and educational resources, including current text materials, diagnostic training documents, reference materials and databases, journals and dissertations, and major and current titles in program areas. They provide an online public-access catalog of library resources throughout the Argosy University system. Students enjoy full remote access to their campus library database, enabling them to study and conduct research at home. Academic databases offer dissertation abstracts, academic journals, and professional periodicals. All library computers are Internet accessible. Software applications include Word, Excel, PowerPoint, SPSS, and various test-scoring programs.

Financial Aid

A wide range of financial aid options is available to students who qualify. Argosy University's San Diego Campus offers access to federal and state aid programs, merit-based awards, grants, loans, and a work-study program. As a first step, students should complete the Free Application for Federal Student Aid (FAFSA). Prospective students can apply electronically at http://www.fafsa.ed.gov or at the campus. To receive consideration for the maximum amount of aid and ensure timely receipt of funds, students should submit an application promptly.

Cost of Study

Tuition varies by program. Students should contact Argosy University's San Diego Campus for tuition information.

Living and Housing Costs

Students typically live in apartments in the metropolitan San Diego area. Living expenses vary according to each student's preferred standard of living, housing, and transportation. The University does not offer or operate student housing. Most of the students are full-time working professionals who live within driving distance of the campus. Several nearby hotels offer special rates for those who commute from long distances. The Admissions Department also maintains a list of housing options, including contact information for University students who wish to share housing. For more information, students should contact the Admissions Department.

Student Group

Admission to Argosy University's San Diego Campus is selective to ensure a highly qualified student body. It encourages diversity in academic and employment backgrounds and promotes integration of the student body into professional life through established connections with local and national professional associations. Argosy University offers a professionally oriented education with rich opportunities to gain practical experience in class, field placements, and internships. Full-time students and working professionals gain the extensive knowledge and range of skills necessary for effective performance in their chosen fields.

Student Outcomes

Students can register with the University's online career-services system and use select services from a distance, such as degree-specific career e-mail lists, national job posts, and virtual job fairs. Students should contact the University for more information.

Location

San Diego, southern California's second-largest city, offers an ideal climate year-round, 70 miles of beautiful beaches, colorful neighborhoods, and a dynamic downtown district. Argosy University's San Diego Campus offers classrooms, a library resource center, student lounge, staff and faculty offices, and other amenities. The area offers numerous attractions, including Sea World and the famous San Diego Zoo and Wild Animal Park.

San Diego's thriving business environment includes several Fortune 500 companies such as QUALCOMM and Pfizer, Inc., and a concentration of high-tech companies. Many educational institutions and agencies in the area provide excellent opportunities for student training.

The University

Argosy University is a private institution with eighteen locations across the nation. Argosy University's San Diego Campus provides a career resources office, an academic resources center, and extensive information access for research. It offers the resources of a large university plus the friendliness and personal attention of a small campus.

The innovative programs feature dynamic, relevant, and practical curricula delivered in flexible class formats. Students enjoy scheduling options that make it easier to fit school into their busy lives, choosing from day and evening courses, on campus or online. Many students find a combination of class formats to be an ideal way of continuing their education while meeting family and professional demands.

Argosy University is accredited by the Higher Learning Commission and is a member of the North Central Association (NCA, 30 North LaSalle Street, Suite 2400, Chicago, Illinois 60602; 800-621-7440 (toll-free); http://www.ncahlc.org).

Applying

Argosy University, San Diego Campus accepts students year-round on a rolling admissions basis, depending on availability of required courses. Applications for admission are available online or by contacting the campus.

Correspondence and Information

Argosy University, San Diego Campus
7650 Mission Valley Road
San Diego, California 92108
Phone: 858-598-1900
  866-505-0333 (toll-free)
Fax: 619-291-0553
E-mail: auadmissions@argosy.edu
Web site: http://argosy.edu/sandiego

Argosy University, San Diego Campus

THE FACULTY

The Argosy University faculty comprises working professionals who are eager to help students succeed. Members bring real-world experience and the latest practice innovations to the academic setting. The diverse faculty members of the College of Education are widely recognized for contributions to their field. Many are published scholars, and most hold doctoral degrees. They provide a substantive education that combines comprehensive knowledge with critical skills and practical workplace relevance. Above all, faculty members are committed to their students' personal and professional development.

ARGOSY UNIVERSITY

ARGOSY UNIVERSITY, SAN FRANCISCO BAY AREA CAMPUS

College of Education

Programs of Study

Argosy University, San Francisco Bay Area Campus, offers the Master of Arts in Education (M.A.Ed.) degree in educational leadership and instructional leadership and the Doctor of Education (Ed.D.) degree in community college executive leadership, educational leadership, and instructional leadership.

The M.A.Ed. in Educational Leadership program is designed to instill key philosophies, theories, and values that impact education. It prepares students to improve policies and practices within organizations through the motivation and supervision of others. Students develop skills needed to design, implement, and evaluate educational programs and curricula. Courses include educational law, educational finance, organizational communication, human resource management, instruction supervision, and organizational management.

The M.A.Ed. in Instructional Leadership program examines the challenges and problems encountered in today's educational environment. Course work encompasses the historical, philosophical, psychological, social, technical, and theoretical aspects of education. Students develop skills in analysis, oral and written communication, problem solving, critical thinking, team building, and computer technology. The program is designed for those who wish to develop or enhance classroom skills, become curriculum supervisors, or become educational leaders with a focus on instruction. Students may choose one of four optional concentrations: single- or multiple-subject teacher credential preparation or single- or multiple-subject teacher credential preparation with bilingual cross-cultural language and academic development (BCLAD).

The Ed.D. in Community College Executive Leadership program offers an accelerated course of study intended to meet the needs of community college administrators who are looking to move into senior administrative positions (such as president, vice president, dean, and director) in community colleges.

The Ed.D. in Educational Leadership program is designed to enhance educational leadership strengths. Students learn innovative and collaborative techniques used to manage and govern educational institutions. The program prepares students for administrative leadership positions at the district, regional, state, or national level. Students must choose a concentration in higher education administration or K–12 education.

The Ed.D. in Instructional Leadership program draws on educational theories and practices to help students discover new learning techniques for diverse audiences. Students enrolled in this program master teaching methodologies, hone classroom skills, and gain the knowledge required to become curriculum administrators or educational leaders with a focus on instruction. Students must choose a concentration in higher education or K–12 education.

Research Facilities

Argosy University libraries provide curriculum support and educational resources, including current text materials, diagnostic training documents, reference materials and databases, journals and dissertations, and major and current titles in program areas. They provide an online public-access catalog of library resources throughout the Argosy University system. Students enjoy full remote access to their campus library database, enabling them to study and conduct research at home. Academic databases offer dissertation abstracts, academic journals, and professional periodicals. All library computers are Internet accessible. Software applications include Word, Excel, PowerPoint, SPSS, and various test-scoring programs.

Financial Aid

A wide range of financial aid options is available to students who qualify. Argosy University's San Francisco Bay Area Campus offers access to federal and state aid programs, merit-based awards, grants, loans, and a work-study program. As a first step, students should complete the Free Application for Federal Student Aid (FAFSA). Prospective students can apply electronically at http://www.fafsa.ed.gov or at the campus. To receive consideration for the maximum amount of aid and ensure timely receipt of funds, it is best to submit an application promptly.

Cost of Study

Tuition varies by program. Students should contact Argosy University's San Francisco Bay Area Campus for tuition information.

Living and Housing Costs

Students typically live in apartments in the metropolitan area. Living expenses vary according to each student's preferred standard of living, housing, and transportation. The University does not offer or operate student housing. Most of the students are full-time working professionals who live within driving distance of the campus. Several nearby hotels offer special rates for those who commute from long distances. The Admissions Department also maintains a list of housing options, including contact information for University students who wish to share housing. For more information, students should contact the Admissions Department.

Student Group

Admission to Argosy University's San Francisco Bay Area Campus is selective to ensure a highly qualified student body. It encourages diversity in academic and employment backgrounds and promotes integration of the student body into professional life through established connections with local and national professional associations. Argosy University offers a professionally oriented education with rich opportunities to gain practical experience in class, field placements, and internships. Full-time students and working professionals gain the extensive knowledge and range of skills necessary for effective performance in their chosen fields.

Student Outcomes

Students can register with the University's online career-services system and use select services from a distance, such as degree-specific career e-mail lists, national job posts, and virtual job fairs. Students should contact the University for more information.

Location

Located in northern California, Argosy University's San Francisco Bay Area Campus attracts students from the immediate area as well as from around the country and the world. The energy in San Francisco is contagious. Numerous surveys rank San Francisco as the most wired city in the world, thanks to its high concentration of computer-savvy citizens and businesses.

Many educational institutions and agencies in the area provide excellent opportunities for student training. The Bay Area and nearby Silicon Valley are home to leading new media companies such as Pixar, ILM, and Sega. A who's who of technology companies call the Bay Area home, including Apple, Cisco, Hewlett-Packard, Intel, Oracle, and Sun Microsystems. The Bay Area also is the home of traditional companies such as BankAmerica, Chevron, Levi-Strauss, Safeway, and Wells Fargo.

The University

Argosy University is a private institution with eighteen locations across the nation. Argosy University's San Francisco Bay Area Campus provides students with a career resources office, an academic resources center, and extensive information access for research. It offers the resources of a large university plus the friendliness and personal attention of a small campus. The innovative programs feature dynamic, relevant, and practical curricula delivered in flexible class formats. Students enjoy scheduling options that make it easier to fit school into their busy lives, choosing from day and evening courses, on campus or online. Many students find a combination of class formats to be an ideal way of continuing their education while meeting family and professional demands.

Argosy University is accredited by the Higher Learning Commission and is a member of the North Central Association (NCA, 30 North LaSalle Street, Suite 2400, Chicago, Illinois 60602; 800-621-7440 (toll-free); http://www.ncahlc.org).

Applying

Argosy University, San Francisco Bay Area Campus, accepts students year-round on a rolling admissions basis, depending on availability of required courses. Applications for admission are available online or by contacting the campus.

Correspondence and Information

Argosy University, San Francisco Bay Area
1005 Atlantic Avenue
Alameda, California 94501
Phone: 510-215-0277
        866-215-2777 (toll free)
Fax: 510-215-0299
E-mail: auadmissions@argosy.edu
Web site: http://www.argosy.edu/sanfrancisco

Argosy University, San Francisco Bay Area Campus

THE FACULTY

The Argosy University faculty comprises working professionals who are eager to help students succeed. Members bring real-world experience and the latest practice innovations to the academic setting. The diverse faculty members of the College of Education are widely recognized for contributions to the field. Most hold doctoral degrees. They provide a substantive education that combines comprehensive knowledge with critical skills and practical workplace relevance. Above all, faculty members are committed to their students' personal and professional development.

ARGOSY UNIVERSITY.

ARGOSY UNIVERSITY, SANTA MONICA CAMPUS
College of Education

Programs of Study	Argosy University, Santa Monica Campus offers the Master of Arts in Education (M.A.Ed.) degree in educational leadership and instructional leadership and the Doctor of Education (Ed.D.) degree in community college executive leadership, educational leadership, and instructional leadership.
	The M.A.Ed. in Educational Leadership program is designed to instill key philosophies, theories, and values that impact education. It prepares students to improve policies and practices within organizations through the motivation and supervision of others. Students develop skills needed to design, implement, and evaluate educational programs and curricula. Courses include educational law, educational finance, organizational communication, human resource management, instruction supervision, and organizational management.
	The M.A.Ed. in Instructional Leadership program examines the challenges and problems encountered in today's educational environment. Course work encompasses the historical, philosophical, psychological, social, technical, and theoretical aspects of education. Students develop skills in analysis, oral and written communication, problem solving, critical thinking, team building, and computer technology. The program is designed for those who wish to develop or enhance classroom skills, become curriculum supervisors, or become educational leaders with a focus on instruction. Students may choose one of four optional concentrations: single- or multiple-subject teacher credential preparation or single- or multiple-subject teacher credential preparation with bilingual cross-cultural language and academic development (BCLAD).
	The Ed.D. in Community College Executive Leadership program offers an accelerated course of study intended to meet the needs of community college administrators who are looking to move into senior administrative positions (such as president, vice president, dean, and director) in community colleges.
	The Ed.D. in Educational Leadership program is designed to enhance educational leadership strengths. Students learn innovative and collaborative techniques used to manage and govern educational institutions. The program prepares students for administrative leadership positions at the district, regional, state, or national level. Students must choose a concentration in higher education administration or K–12 education.
	The Ed.D. in Instructional Leadership program draws on educational theories and practices to help students discover new learning techniques for diverse audiences. Students enrolled in this program master teaching methodologies, hone classroom skills, and gain the knowledge required to become curriculum administrators or educational leaders with a focus on instruction. Students must choose a concentration in higher education or K–12 education.
Research Facilities	Argosy University libraries provide curriculum support and educational resources, including current text materials, diagnostic training documents, reference materials and databases, journals and dissertations, and major and current titles in program areas. They provide an online public-access catalog of library resources throughout the Argosy University system. Students enjoy full remote access to their campus library database, enabling them to study and conduct research at home. Academic databases offer dissertation abstracts, academic journals, and professional periodicals. All library computers are Internet accessible. Software applications include Word, Excel, PowerPoint, SPSS, and various test-scoring programs.
Financial Aid	A wide range of financial aid options is available to students who qualify. Argosy University's Santa Monica Campus offers access to federal and state aid programs, merit-based awards, grants, loans, and a work-study program. As a first step, students should complete the Free Application for Federal Student Aid (FAFSA). Prospective students can apply electronically at http://www.fafsa.ed.gov or at the campus. To receive consideration for the maximum amount of aid and ensure timely receipt of funds, it is best to submit an application promptly.
Cost of Study	Tuition varies by program. Students should contact Argosy University's Santa Monica Campus for tuition information.
Living and Housing Costs	Students typically live in apartments in the metropolitan Santa Monica area. Living expenses vary according to each student's preferred standard of living, housing, and transportation. The University does not offer or operate student housing. Most of the students are full-time working professionals who live within driving distance of the campus. Several nearby hotels offer special rates for those who commute from long distances. The Admissions Department also maintains a list of housing options, including contact information for University students who wish to share housing. For more information, students should contact the Admissions Department.
Student Group	Admission to Argosy University's Santa Monica Campus is selective to ensure a highly qualified student body. It encourages diversity in academic and employment backgrounds and promotes integration of the student body into professional life through established connections with local and national professional associations. Argosy University offers a professionally oriented education with rich opportunities to gain practical experience in class, field placements, and internships. Full-time students and working professionals gain the extensive knowledge and range of skills necessary for effective performance in their chosen fields.
Student Outcomes	Students can register with the University's online career-services system and use select services from a distance, such as degree-specific career e-mail lists, national job posts, and virtual job fairs. Students should contact the University for more information.
Location	Argosy University's Santa Monica Campus is located in the beach community of Santa Monica, California. This undeniably sophisticated urban environment is coupled with the charm of the famous Santa Monica Pier, beautiful beaches, and farmer's markets. On campus, the main facility covers approximately 107,000 square feet and houses classrooms, laboratories, offices, a student lounge, and a library. Many educational institutions and agencies in the area provide excellent opportunities for student training. The thriving business environment in Santa Monica includes a broad array of companies, including a proliferation of entertainment, high-tech, and software firms. Principal employers in the area include Yahoo, MTV Networks, RAND Corporation, and Symantec Corporation.
The University	Argosy University is a private institution with eighteen locations across the nation. Argosy University's Santa Monica Campus provides students with a career resources office, an academic resources center, and extensive information access for research. It offers the resources of a large university plus the friendliness and personal attention of a small campus.
	The innovative programs feature dynamic, relevant, and practical curricula delivered in flexible class formats. Students enjoy scheduling options that make it easier to fit school into their busy lives, choosing from day and evening courses, on campus or online. Many students find a combination of class formats to be an ideal way of continuing their education while meeting family and professional demands.
	Argosy University is accredited by the Higher Learning Commission and is a member of the North Central Association (NCA, 30 North LaSalle Street, Suite 2400, Chicago, Illinois 60602; 800-621-7440 (toll-free); http://www.ncahlc.org).
Applying	Argosy University's Santa Monica Campus accepts students year-round on a rolling admissions basis, depending on availability of required courses. Applications for admission are available online or by contacting the campus.
Correspondence and Information	Argosy University, Santa Monica Campus 2950 31st Street Santa Monica, California 90405 Phone: 310-866-4000 866-505-0332 (toll-free) Fax: 310-399-1804 E-mail: auadmissions@argosy.edu Web site: http://www.argosy.edu/santamonica

Argosy University, Santa Monica Campus

THE FACULTY

The Argosy University faculty comprises working professionals who are eager to help students succeed. Members bring real-world experience and the latest-practice innovations to the academic setting. The diverse faculty members of the College of Education are widely recognized for contributions to the field. Most hold doctoral degrees. They provide a substantive education that combines comprehensive knowledge with critical skills and practical workplace relevance. Above all, faculty members are committed to their students' personal and professional development.

ARGOSY UNIVERSITY

ARGOSY UNIVERSITY, SARASOTA CAMPUS

College of Education

Programs of Study

Argosy University, Sarasota Campus offers the Master of Arts in Education (M.A.Ed.) degree and the Education Specialist (Ed.S.) degree in educational leadership and instructional leadership and the Doctor of Education (Ed.D.) degree in community college executive leadership, educational leadership, and instructional leadership.

The M.A.Ed. in educational leadership program is designed to instill key philosophies, theories, and values that impact education. It prepares students to improve policies and practices within organizations through the motivation and supervision of others. Students develop skills needed to design, implement, and evaluate educational programs and curricula. Courses include educational law, educational finance, organizational communication, human resource management, instruction supervision, and organizational management.

The M.A.Ed. in instructional leadership program examines the challenges and problems encountered in today's educational environment. Course work encompasses the historical, philosophical, psychological, social, technical, and theoretical aspects of education. Students develop skills in analysis, oral and written communication, problem solving, critical thinking, team building, and computer technology. The program is designed for those who wish to develop or enhance classroom skills, become curriculum supervisors, or become educational leaders with a focus on instruction.

The Ed.S. in educational leadership program concentrates on applied organizational theory within the context of educational organizations. This specialized program develops the competencies required to secure educational administrator positions at the elementary or secondary school level.

The Ed.S. in instructional leadership program enables experienced teachers to become more effective practitioners and educational leaders with a focus on instruction. Course work is designed to satisfy the requirements of students seeking career advancement and those who are working toward a doctoral degree.

The Ed.D. in community college executive leadership program offers an accelerated course of study intended to meet the needs of community college administrators who are looking to move into senior administrative positions (such as president, vice president, dean, and director) in community colleges.

The Ed.D. in educational leadership program is designed to enhance educational leadership strengths. Students learn innovative and collaborative techniques used to manage and govern educational institutions. The program prepares students for administrative leadership positions at the district, regional, state, or national level. Students must choose a concentration in higher education administration or K–12 education.

The Ed.D. in instructional leadership program draws upon educational theories and practices to help students discover new learning techniques for diverse audiences. Students enrolled in this program master teaching methodologies, hone classroom skills, and gain the knowledge required to become curriculum administrators or educational leaders with a focus on instruction. Students must choose a concentration in education technology, higher education, or K–12 education.

Research Facilities

Argosy University libraries provide curriculum support and educational resources, including current text materials, diagnostic training documents, reference materials and databases, journals and dissertations, and major and current titles in program areas. They provide an online public-access catalog of library resources throughout the Argosy University system. Students enjoy full remote access to their campus library database, enabling them to study and conduct research at home. Academic databases offer dissertation abstracts, academic journals, and professional periodicals. All library computers are Internet accessible. Software applications include Word, Excel, PowerPoint, SPSS, and various test-scoring programs.

Financial Aid

A wide range of financial aid options is available to students who qualify. Argosy University's Sarasota Campus offers access to federal and state aid programs, merit-based awards, grants, loans, and a work-study program. As a first step, students should complete the Free Application for Federal Student Aid (FAFSA). Prospective students can apply electronically at http://www.fafsa.ed.gov or at the campus. To receive consideration for the maximum amount of aid and ensure timely receipt of funds, students should submit an application promptly.

Cost of Study

Tuition varies by program. Students should contact Argosy University's Sarasota Campus for tuition information.

Living and Housing Costs

Students typically live in apartments in the metropolitan Sarasota area. Living expenses vary according to each student's preferred standard of living, housing, and transportation. The University does not offer or operate student housing. Most of the students are full-time working professionals who live within driving distance of the campus. Several nearby hotels offer special rates for students when they attend one-week in-residence intersessions. The Admissions Department also maintains a list of housing options, including contact information for University students who wish to share housing. For more information, students should contact the Admissions Department.

Student Group

Admission to Argosy University's Sarasota Campus is selective to ensure a highly qualified student body. It encourages diversity in academic and employment backgrounds and promotes integration of the student body into professional life through established connections with local and national professional associations. Argosy University offers a professionally oriented education with rich opportunities to gain practical experience in class, field placements, and internships. Full-time students and working professionals gain the extensive knowledge and range of skills necessary for effective performance in their chosen fields.

Student Outcomes

Students can register with the University's online career-services system and use select services from a distance, such as degree-specific career e-mail lists, national job posts, and virtual job fairs. Students should contact the University for more information.

Location

Located in northeast Sarasota, the campus is specifically designed for postsecondary and graduate-level instruction through a unique combination of in-residence course work, tutorials, and online study courses. Several of the programs are off-site tutorials and intensive one-week classroom sessions. Students may also complete up to 49 percent of the work of some degree programs via online courses that allow interaction with faculty members and classmates from any Internet connection.

Sarasota is recognized as Florida's cultural center and is home to a professional symphony, ballet, and opera as well as dozens of theaters and art galleries. Well-known vacation attractions such as Disney World, Busch Gardens-Tampa, and the city of Miami are within a few hours' drive. The area enjoys mild winters and endless summer beauty.

The growing business sector in the Gulf Coast community helps make it one of the top 20 places to live and work. ASO Corporation, Nelson Publishing, and Select Technology Group are among the numerous companies headquartered in Sarasota County. The area's top employers include Sarasota Memorial Hospital and Publix Supermarkets. Many educational institutions and agencies in the area provide excellent opportunities for student training.

The University

Argosy University is a private institution with eighteen locations across the nation. Argosy University's Sarasota Campus provides students with a career resources office, an academic resources center, and extensive information access for research. It offers the resources of a large university plus the friendliness and personal attention of a small campus.

The innovative programs feature dynamic, relevant, and practical curricula delivered in flexible class formats. Students enjoy scheduling options that make it easier to fit school into their busy lives, choosing from day and evening courses, on campus or online. Many students find a combination of class formats to be an ideal way of continuing their education while meeting family and professional demands.

Argosy University is accredited by the Higher Learning Commission and is a member of the North Central Association (NCA, 30 North LaSalle Street, Suite 2400, Chicago, Illinois 60602; 800-621-7440 (toll-free); http://www.ncahlc.org).

Applying

Argosy University, Sarasota Campus accepts students year-round on a rolling admissions basis, depending on availability of required courses. Applications for admission are available online or by contacting the campus.

Correspondence and Information

Argosy University, Sarasota Campus
5250 17th Street
Sarasota, Florida 34235
Phone: 941-379-0404
          800-331-5995 (toll-free)
Fax: 941-371-8910
E-mail: auadmissions@argosy.edu
Web site: http://argosy.edu/sarasota

Argosy University, Sarasota Campus

THE FACULTY

The Argosy University faculty comprises working professionals who are eager to help students succeed. Members bring real-world experience and the latest practice innovations to the academic setting. The diverse faculty members of the College of Education are widely recognized for contributions to their field. Most hold doctoral degrees. They provide a substantive education that combines comprehensive knowledge with critical skills and practical workplace relevance. Above all, faculty members are committed to their students' personal and professional development.

ARGOSY UNIVERSITY.

ARGOSY UNIVERSITY, SCHAUMBURG CAMPUS

College of Education

Programs of Study

Argosy University, Schaumburg Campus, offers the Master of Arts in Education (M.A.Ed.) and the Education Specialist (Ed.S.) degrees in educational leadership and instructional leadership and the Doctor of Education (Ed.D.) degree in community college executive leadership, educational leadership, and instructional leadership.

The M.A.Ed. in Educational Leadership program is designed to instill key philosophies, theories, and values that impact education. It prepares students to improve policies and practices within organizations through the motivation and supervision of others. Students develop skills needed to design, implement, and evaluate educational programs and curricula. Courses include educational law, educational finance, organizational communication, human resource management, instruction supervision, and organizational management. The program now offers Principal/General Administrative Certification, also known as Type 75 Certification.

The M.A.Ed. in Instructional Leadership program examines the challenges and problems encountered in today's educational environment. Course work encompasses the historical, philosophical, psychological, social, technical, and theoretical aspects of education. Students develop skills in analysis, oral and written communication, problem solving, critical thinking, team building, and computer technology. The program is designed for those who wish to develop or enhance classroom skills, become curriculum supervisors, or become educational leaders with a focus on instruction.

The Ed.S. in Educational Leadership program concentrates on applied organizational theory within the context of educational organizations. This specialized program develops the competencies required to secure educational administrator positions at the elementary or secondary school level. The program now offers Superintendent Certification.

The Ed.S. in Instructional Leadership program enables experienced teachers to become more effective practitioners and educational leaders with a focus on instruction. Course work is designed to satisfy the requirements of students seeking career advancement and those who are working toward a doctoral degree.

The Ed.D. in Community College Executive Leadership program offers an accelerated course of study intended to meet the needs of community college administrators who are looking to move into senior administrative positions (such as president, vice president, dean, and director) in community colleges.

The Ed.D. in Educational Leadership program is designed to enhance educational leadership strengths. Students learn innovative and collaborative techniques used to manage and govern educational institutions. The program prepares students for administrative leadership positions at the district, regional, state, or national level. Students must choose a concentration in higher education administration or K–12 education. The program now offers an optional concentration in district leadership.

The Ed.D. in Instructional Leadership program draws upon educational theories and practices to help students discover new learning techniques for diverse audiences. Students enrolled in this program master teaching methodologies, hone classroom skills, and gain the knowledge required to become curriculum administrators or educational leaders with a focus on instruction. Students must choose a concentration in education technology, higher education, or K–12 education.

Research Facilities

Argosy University libraries provide curriculum support and educational resources, including current text materials, diagnostic training documents, reference materials and databases, journals and dissertations, and major and current titles in program areas. They provide an online public-access catalog of library resources throughout the Argosy University system. Students enjoy full remote access to their campus library database, enabling them to study and conduct research at home. Academic databases offer dissertation abstracts, academic journals, and professional periodicals. All library computers are Internet accessible. Software applications include Word, Excel, PowerPoint, SPSS, and various test-scoring programs.

Financial Aid

A wide range of financial aid options is available to students who qualify. Argosy University's Schaumburg Campus offers access to federal and state aid programs, merit-based awards, grants, loans, and a work-study program. As a first step, students should complete the Free Application for Federal Student Aid (FAFSA). Prospective students can apply electronically at http://www.fafsa.ed.gov or at the campus. To receive consideration for the maximum amount of aid and ensure timely receipt of funds, it is best to submit an application promptly.

Cost of Study

Tuition varies by program. Students should contact Argosy University's Schaumburg Campus for tuition information.

Living and Housing Costs

Students typically live in apartments in the metropolitan Schaumburg area. Living expenses vary according to each student's preferred standard of living, housing, and transportation. The University does not offer or operate student housing. Most of the students are full-time working professionals who live within driving distance of the campus. Several nearby hotels offer special rates for those who commute from long distances. The Admissions Department also maintains a list of housing options, including contact information for University students who wish to share housing. For more information, students should contact the Admissions Department.

Student Group

Admission to Argosy University's Schaumburg Campus is selective to ensure a highly qualified student body. It encourages diversity in academic and employment backgrounds and promotes integration of the student body into professional life through established connections with local and national professional associations. Argosy University offers a professionally oriented education with rich opportunities to gain practical experience in class, field placements, and internships. Full-time students and working professionals gain the extensive knowledge and range of skills necessary for effective performance in their chosen fields.

Student Outcomes

Students can register with the University's online career-services system and use select services from a distance, such as degree-specific career e-mail lists, national job posts, and virtual job fairs. Students should contact the University for more information.

Location

Argosy University's Schaumburg Campus is conveniently located in the northwest suburban area, approximately 45 minutes from downtown Chicago. The University's small size offers a highly personal atmosphere and flexible programs tailored to students' needs. Visitors to Chicago experience a range of attractions to stimulate both intellectual and recreational pursuits. Located on the shores of Lake Michigan in the Midwest, Chicago is home to world-champion sports teams, an internationally acclaimed symphony orchestra, renowned architecture, and nearly 3 million residents. Among the variety of history and art museums in the city, the Chicago Cultural Center offers more than 600 art programs and exhibits each year. Recreational opportunities include hiking and cycling on miles of lakefront trails, golfing, and shopping. Many educational institutions and agencies in the area provide excellent opportunities for student training. Schaumburg's thriving business environment includes 5,000 businesses that employ 80,000 people. The area's largest employers are Motorola, Experian, Cingular, and IBM.

The University

Argosy University is a private institution with eighteen locations across the nation. Argosy University's Schaumburg Campus provides students with a career resources office, an academic resources center, and extensive information access for research. It offers the resources of a large university, plus the friendliness and personal attention of a small campus. Argosy University's Schaumburg Campus is an approved degree site that is closely associated with the University's Chicago campus.

The innovative programs feature dynamic, relevant, and practical curricula delivered in flexible class formats. Students enjoy scheduling options that make it easier to fit school into their busy lives, choosing from day and evening courses, on campus or online. Many students find a combination of class formats to be an ideal way of continuing their education while meeting family and professional demands.

Argosy University is accredited by the Higher Learning Commission and is a member of the North Central Association (NCA, 30 North LaSalle Street, Suite 2400, Chicago, Illinois 60602; 800-621-7440 (toll-free); http://www.ncahlc.org).

Applying

Argosy University, Schaumburg Campus, accepts students year-round on a rolling admissions basis, depending on availability of required courses. Applications for admission are available online or by contacting the campus.

Correspondence and Information

Argosy University, Schaumburg Campus
999 North Plaza Drive, Suite 111
Schaumburg, Illinois 60173-5403
Phone: 847-969-4900
          866-290-2777 (toll-free)
Fax: 847-969-4998
E-mail: auadmissions@argosy.edu
Web site: http://www.argosy.edu/schaumburg

Argosy University, Schaumburg Campus

THE FACULTY

The Argosy University faculty comprises working professionals who are eager to help students succeed. Members bring real-world experience and the latest practice innovations to the academic setting. The diverse faculty members of the College of Education are widely recognized for contributions to the field. Most hold doctoral degrees. They provide a substantive education that combines comprehensive knowledge with critical skills and practical workplace relevance. Above all, faculty members are committed to their students' personal and professional development.

ARGOSY UNIVERSITY, SEATTLE CAMPUS

College of Education

Programs of Study

Argosy University, Seattle Campus, offers the Master of Arts in Education (M.A.Ed.) degree in educational leadership and instructional leadership and the Doctor of Education (Ed.D.) degree in community college executive leadership, educational leadership, and instructional leadership.

The M.A.Ed. in Educational Leadership program is designed to instill key philosophies, theories, and values that impact education. It prepares students to improve policies and practices within organizations through the motivation and supervision of others. Students develop skills needed to design, implement, and evaluate educational programs and curricula. Courses include educational law, educational finance, organizational communication, human resource management, instruction supervision, and organizational management.

The M.A.Ed. in Instructional Leadership program examines the challenges and problems encountered in today's educational environment. Course work encompasses the historical, philosophical, psychological, social, technical, and theoretical aspects of education. Students develop skills in analysis, oral and written communication, problem solving, critical thinking, team building, and computer technology. The program is designed for those who wish to develop or enhance classroom skills, become curriculum supervisors, or become educational leaders with a focus on instruction.

The Ed.D. in Community College Executive Leadership program offers an accelerated course of study intended to meet the needs of community college administrators who are looking to move into senior administrative positions (such as president, vice president, dean, and director) in community colleges.

The Ed.D. in Educational Leadership program is designed to enhance educational leadership strengths. Students learn innovative and collaborative techniques used to manage and govern educational institutions. The program prepares students for administrative leadership positions at the district, regional, state, or national level. Students must choose a concentration in district leadership, higher education administration, or K–12 education.

The Ed.D. in Instructional Leadership program draws on educational theories and practices to help students discover new learning techniques for diverse audiences. Students enrolled in this program master teaching methodologies, hone classroom skills, and gain the knowledge required to become curriculum administrators or educational leaders with a focus on instruction. Students must choose a concentration in education technology, higher education, or K–12 education.

Research Facilities

Argosy University libraries provide curriculum support and educational resources, including current text materials, diagnostic training documents, reference materials and databases, journals and dissertations, and major and current titles in program areas. They provide an online public-access catalog of library resources throughout the Argosy University system. Students enjoy full remote access to their campus library database, enabling them to study and conduct research at home. Academic databases offer dissertation abstracts, academic journals, and professional periodicals. All library computers are Internet accessible. Software applications include Word, Excel, PowerPoint, SPSS, and various test-scoring programs.

Financial Aid

A wide range of financial aid options is available to students who qualify. Argosy University's Seattle Campus offers access to federal and state aid programs, merit-based awards, grants, loans, and a work-study program. As a first step, students should complete the Free Application for Federal Student Aid (FAFSA). Prospective students can apply electronically at http://www.fafsa.ed.gov or at the campus. To receive consideration for the maximum amount of aid and ensure timely receipt of funds, it is best to submit an application promptly.

Cost of Study

Tuition varies by program. Students should contact Argosy University's Seattle Campus for tuition information.

Living and Housing Costs

Students typically live in apartments in the Seattle metropolitan area. Living expenses vary according to each student's preferred standard of living, housing, and transportation. The University does not offer or operate student housing. Most of the students are full-time working professionals who live within driving distance of the campus. Several nearby hotels offer special rates for those who commute from long distances. The Admissions Department also maintains a list of housing options, including contact information for University students who wish to share housing. For more information, students should contact the Admissions Department.

Student Group

Admission to Argosy University's Seattle Campus is selective to ensure a highly qualified student body. It encourages diversity in academic and employment backgrounds and promotes integration of the student body into professional life through established connections with local and national professional associations. Argosy University offers a professionally oriented education with rich opportunities to gain practical experience in class, field placements, and internships. Full-time students and working professionals gain the extensive knowledge and range of skills necessary for effective performance in their chosen fields.

Student Outcomes

Students can register with the University's online career-services system and use select services from a distance, such as degree-specific career e-mail lists, national job posts, and virtual job fairs. Students should contact the University for more information.

Location

Argosy University's Seattle Campus aspires to provide a supportive, collaborative, engaging, yet challenging learning environment. Easily reached through the King County Public Transportation System, the campus offers convenient access to local libraries, shops, restaurants, theaters, and art museums. Seattle offers numerous historical and multicultural museums, a symphony, the ballet, and many theater companies. The city is home to several major-league sports teams and offers myriad outdoor recreational opportunities, such as camping, hiking, fishing, skiing, and rock-climbing.

Many educational institutions and agencies in the area provide excellent opportunities for student training. Seattle's thriving business environment encompasses a wide range of industries and features such giants as Microsoft, Boeing, and Alaska Air Group. The Port of Seattle and the University of Washington are also among the area's largest employers.

The University

Argosy University is a private institution with eighteen locations across the nation. Argosy University's Seattle Campus provides students with a career resources office, an academic resources center, and extensive information access for research. It offers the resources of a large university plus the friendliness and personal attention of a small campus. The innovative programs feature dynamic, relevant, and practical curricula delivered in flexible class formats. Students enjoy scheduling options that make it easier to fit school into their busy lives, choosing from day and evening courses, on campus or online. Many students find a combination of class formats to be an ideal way of continuing their education while meeting family and professional demands.

Argosy University is accredited by the Higher Learning Commission and is a member of the North Central Association (NCA, 30 North LaSalle Street, Suite 2400, Chicago, Illinois 60602; 800-621-7440 (toll-free); http://www.ncahlc.org).

Applying

Argosy University, Seattle Campus, accepts students year-round on a rolling admissions basis, depending on availability of required courses. Applications for admission are available online or by contacting the campus.

Correspondence and Information

Argosy University, Seattle Campus
2601-A Elliott Avenue
Seattle, Washington 98121
Phone: 206-283-4500
        866-283-2777 (toll-free)
Fax: 206-283-5777
E-mail: auadmissions@argosy.edu
Web site: http://www.argosy.edu/seattle

Argosy University, Seattle Campus

THE FACULTY

The Argosy University faculty comprises working professionals who are eager to help students succeed. Members bring real-world experience and the latest practice innovations to the academic setting. The diverse faculty members of the College of Education are widely recognized for contributions to the field. Most hold doctoral degrees. They provide a substantive education that combines comprehensive knowledge with critical skills and practical workplace relevance. Above all, faculty members of the College of Education are committed to their students' personal and professional development.

ARGOSY UNIVERSITY, TAMPA CAMPUS

ARGOSY UNIVERSITY.

College of Education

Programs of Study	Argosy University, Tampa Campus, offers the Master of Arts in Education (M.A.Ed.), the Education Specialist (Ed.S.) degree in educational leadership and instructional leadership, and the Doctor of Education (Ed.D.) degree in community college executive leadership, educational leadership, and instructional leadership.
	The M.A.Ed. in Educational Leadership program is designed to instill key philosophies, theories, and values that impact education. It prepares students to improve policies and practices within organizations through the motivation and supervision of others. Students develop skills needed to design, implement, and evaluate educational programs and curricula. Courses include educational law, educational finance, organizational communication, human resource management, instruction supervision, and organizational management.
	The M.A.Ed. in Instructional Leadership program examines the challenges and problems encountered in today's educational environment. Course work encompasses the historical, philosophical, psychological, social, technical, and theoretical aspects of education. Students develop skills in analysis, oral and written communication, problem solving, critical thinking, team building, and computer technology. The program is designed for those who wish to develop or enhance classroom skills, become curriculum supervisors, or become educational leaders with a focus on instruction.
	The Ed.S. in Educational Leadership program concentrates on applied organizational theory within the context of educational organizations. This specialized program develops the competencies required to secure educational administrator positions at the elementary or secondary school level.
	The Ed.S. in Instructional Leadership program enables experienced teachers to become more effective practitioners and educational leaders with a focus on instruction. Course work is designed to satisfy the requirements of students seeking career advancement and those who are working toward a doctoral degree.
	The Ed.D. in Community College Executive Leadership program offers an accelerated course of study intended to meet the needs of community college administrators who are looking to move into senior administrative positions (such as president, vice president, dean, and director) in community colleges.
	The Ed.D. in Educational Leadership program is designed to enhance educational leadership strengths. Students learn innovative and collaborative techniques used to manage and govern educational institutions. The program prepares students for administrative leadership positions at the district, regional, state, or national level. Students must choose a concentration in higher education administration or K–12 education.
	The Ed.D. in Instructional Leadership program draws upon educational theories and practices to help students discover new learning techniques for diverse audiences. Students enrolled in this program master teaching methodologies, hone classroom skills, and gain the knowledge required to become curriculum administrators or educational leaders with a focus on instruction. Students must choose a concentration in higher education or K–12 education.
Research Facilities	Argosy University libraries provide curriculum support and educational resources, including current text materials, diagnostic training documents, reference materials and databases, journals and dissertations, and major and current titles in program areas. They provide an online public-access catalog of library resources throughout the Argosy University system. Students enjoy full remote access to their campus library database, enabling them to study and conduct research at home. Academic databases offer dissertation abstracts, academic journals, and professional periodicals. All library computers are Internet accessible. Software applications include Word, Excel, PowerPoint, SPSS, and various test-scoring programs.
Financial Aid	A wide range of financial aid options is available to students who qualify. Argosy University's Tampa Campus offers access to federal and state aid programs, merit-based awards, grants, loans, and a work-study program. As a first step, students should complete the Free Application for Federal Student Aid (FAFSA). Prospective students can apply electronically at http://www.fafsa.ed.gov or at the campus. To receive consideration for the maximum amount of aid and ensure timely receipt of funds, it is best to submit an application promptly.
Cost of Study	Tuition varies by program. Students should contact Argosy University's Tampa Campus for tuition information.
Living and Housing Costs	Students typically live in apartments in the metropolitan Tampa area. Living expenses vary according to each student's preferred standard of living, housing, and transportation. The University does not offer or operate student housing. Most of the students are full-time working professionals who live within driving distance of the campus. Several nearby hotels offer special rates for those who commute from long distances. The Admissions Department also maintains a list of housing options, including contact information, for University students who wish to share housing. For more information, students should contact the Admissions Department.
Student Group	Admission to Argosy University's Tampa Campus is selective to ensure a highly qualified student body. It encourages diversity in academic and employment backgrounds and promotes integration of the student body into professional life through established connections with local and national professional associations. Argosy University offers a professionally oriented education with rich opportunities to gain practical experience in class, field placements, and internships. Full-time students and working professionals gain the extensive knowledge and range of skills necessary for effective performance in their chosen fields.
Student Outcomes	Students can register with the University's online career-services system and use select services from a distance, such as degree-specific career e-mail lists, national job posts, and virtual job fairs. Students should contact the University for more information.
Location	Located in sunny Florida, Argosy University's Tampa Campus attracts a diverse student population from throughout the United States, the Caribbean, Europe, Africa, and Asia. The school offers rigorous programs of study in a supportive, collaborative environment. The campus sits within an hour's drive of some of the most popular tourist destinations in the world, including the Disney theme parks, Busch Gardens, and the Florida Gulf Coast beaches. Major-league sporting events, concerts, theaters, world-renowned restaurants, recreational facilities, and a cosmopolitan social scene are all within easy reach. The University's location provides easy access to I-4 and I-75. Tampa combines the opportunities of a large city with the friendliness of a small town with a strong sense of community.
	Many educational institutions and agencies in the area provide excellent opportunities for student training. The Tampa-St. Petersburg-Clearwater metropolitan area offers a diversified economic base fueled by a broad array of companies, including Verizon Communications and JP Morgan Chase.
The University	Argosy University is a private institution with eighteen locations across the nation. Argosy University's Tampa Campus provides students with a career resources office, an academic resources center, and extensive information access for research. It offers the resources of a large university, plus the friendliness and personal attention of a small campus. The innovative programs feature dynamic, relevant, and practical curricula delivered in flexible class formats. Students enjoy scheduling options that make it easier to fit school into their busy lives, choosing from day and evening courses, on campus or online. Many students find a combination of class formats to be an ideal way of continuing their education while meeting family and professional demands.
	Argosy University is accredited by the Higher Learning Commission and is a member of the North Central Association (NCA, 30 North LaSalle Street, Suite 2400, Chicago, Illinois 60602; 800-621-7440 (toll-free); http://www.ncahlc.org).
Applying	Argosy University, Tampa Campus, accepts students year-round on a rolling admissions basis, depending on availability of required courses. Applications for admission are available online or by contacting the campus.
Correspondence and Information	Argosy University, Tampa Campus Parkside at Tampa Bay Park 4401 North Himes Avenue, Suite 150 Tampa, Florida 33614 Phone: 813-393-5290 800-850-6488 (toll-free) Fax: 813-874-1989 E-mail: auadmissions@argosy.edu Web site: http://www.argosy.edu/tampa

Argosy University, Tampa Campus

THE FACULTY

The Argosy University faculty comprises working professionals who are eager to help students succeed. Members bring real-world experience and the latest practice innovations to the academic setting. The diverse faculty members of the College of Education are widely recognized for contributions to the field. Most hold doctoral degrees. They provide a substantive education that combines comprehensive knowledge with critical skills and practical workplace relevance. Above all, faculty members are committed to their students' personal and professional development.

ARGOSY UNIVERSITY.

ARGOSY UNIVERSITY, TWIN CITIES CAMPUS

College of Education

Programs of Study

Argosy University, Twin Cities Campus, offers the Master of Arts in Education (M.A.Ed.), the Education Specialist (Ed.S.), and the Doctor of Education (Ed.D.) degrees in educational leadership and instructional leadership.

The M.A.Ed. in Educational Leadership program is designed to instill key philosophies, theories, and values that impact education. It prepares students to improve policies and practices within organizations through the motivation and supervision of others. Students develop skills needed to design, implement, and evaluate educational programs and curricula. Courses include educational law, educational finance, organizational communication, human resource management, instruction supervision, and organizational management.

The M.A.Ed. in Instructional Leadership program examines the challenges and problems encountered in today's educational environment. Course work encompasses the historical, philosophical, psychological, social, technical, and theoretical aspects of education. Students develop skills in analysis, oral and written communication, problem solving, critical thinking, team building, and computer technology. The program is designed for those who wish to develop or enhance classroom skills, become curriculum supervisors, or become educational leaders with a focus on instruction.

The Ed.S. in Educational Leadership program concentrates on applied organizational theory within the context of educational organizations. This specialized program develops the competencies required to secure educational administrator positions at the elementary or secondary school level.

The Ed.S. in Instructional Leadership program enables experienced teachers to become more effective practitioners and educational leaders with a focus on instruction. Course work is designed to satisfy the requirements of students seeking career advancement and those who are working toward a doctoral degree.

The Ed.D. in Educational Leadership program is designed to enhance educational leadership strengths. Students learn innovative and collaborative techniques used to manage and govern educational institutions. The program prepares students for administrative leadership positions at the district, regional, state, or national level. Students must choose a concentration in higher education administration or K–12 education.

The Ed.D. in Instructional Leadership program draws upon educational theories and practices to help students discover new learning techniques for diverse audiences. Students enrolled in this program master teaching methodologies, hone classroom skills, and gain the knowledge required to become curriculum administrators or educational leaders with a focus on instruction. Students must choose a concentration in educational technology, higher education, or K–12 education.

Research Facilities

Argosy University libraries provide curriculum support and educational resources including current text materials, diagnostic training documents, reference materials and databases, journals and dissertations, and major and current titles in program areas. They provide an online public-access catalog of library resources throughout the Argosy University system. Students enjoy full remote access to their campus library database, enabling them to study and conduct research at home. Academic databases offer dissertation abstracts, academic journals, and professional periodicals. All library computers are Internet accessible. Software applications include Word, Excel, PowerPoint, SPSS, and various test-scoring programs.

Financial Aid

A wide range of financial aid options is available to students who qualify. Argosy University's Twin Cities Campus offers access to federal and state aid programs, merit-based awards, grants, loans, and a work-study program. As a first step, students should complete the Free Application for Federal Student Aid (FAFSA). Prospective students can apply electronically at http://www.fafsa.ed.gov or at the campus. To receive consideration for the maximum amount of aid and ensure timely receipt of funds, it is best to submit an application promptly.

Cost of Study

Tuition varies by program. Students should contact Argosy University's Twin Cities Campus for tuition information.

Living and Housing Costs

Students typically live in apartments in the metropolitan area. Living expenses vary according to each student's preferred standard of living, housing, and transportation. The University does not offer or operate student housing. Most of the students are full-time working professionals who live within driving distance of the campus. Several nearby hotels offer special rates for those who commute from long distances. The Admissions Department also maintains a list of housing options, including contact information for University students who wish to share housing. For more information, students should contact the Admissions Department.

Student Group

Admission to Argosy University's Twin Cities Campus is selective to ensure a highly qualified student body. The University encourages diversity in academic and employment backgrounds and promotes integration of the student body into professional life through established connections with local and national professional associations. Argosy University offers a professionally oriented education with rich opportunities to gain practical experience in class, field placements, and internships. Full-time students and working professionals gain the extensive knowledge and range of skills necessary for effective performance in their chosen fields.

Student Outcomes

Students can register with the University's online career-services system and use select services from a distance, such as degree-specific career e-mail lists, national job posts, and virtual job fairs. Students should contact the University for more information.

Location

Argosy University's Twin Cities Campus offers rigorous academics in a supportive environment. The campus is nestled in a parklike suburban setting within 10 miles of the airport and the Mall of America. Students enjoy the convenience of nearby shops, restaurants, and housing and easy freeway access. The neighboring Eagan Community Center offers many amenities, including walking paths, a fitness center, meeting rooms, and an outdoor amphitheater. The Twin Cities of Minneapolis and St. Paul have been rated by popular magazines as one of the most livable metropolitan areas in the country. With a population of 2.5 million, the area offers an abundance of recreational activities. Year-round outdoor activities, nationally acclaimed venues for theater art and music, and professional sports teams attract residents and visitors alike.

Many educational institutions and agencies in the area provide excellent opportunities for student training. The Minneapolis-St. Paul metropolitan area offers a diversified economic base fueled by a broad array of companies. Among the numerous publicly traded companies headquartered in the area are Target, UnitedHealth Group, 3M, General Mills, and U.S. Bancorp.

The University

Argosy University is a private institution with eighteen locations across the nation. Argosy University's Twin Cities Campus provides students with a career resources office, an academic resources center and extensive information access for research. It offers the resources of a large university plus the friendliness and personal attention of a small campus. The innovative programs feature dynamic, relevant, and practical curricula delivered in flexible class formats. Students enjoy scheduling options that make it easier to fit school into their busy lives, choosing from day and evening courses, on campus or online. Many students find a combination of class formats to be an ideal way of continuing their education while meeting family and professional demands.

Argosy University is accredited by the Higher Learning Commission and is a member of the North Central Association (NCA, 30 North LaSalle Street, Suite 2400, Chicago, Illinois 60602; 800-621-7440 (toll-free); http://www.ncahlc.org).

Applying

Argosy University, Twin Cities Campus, accepts students year-round on a rolling admissions basis, depending on the availability of required courses. Applications for admission are available online or by contacting the campus.

Correspondence and Information

Argosy University, Twin Cities Campus
1515 Central Parkway
Eagan, Minnesota 55121
Phone: 651-846-2882
          888-844-2004 (toll-free)
Fax: 651-994-7956
E-mail: auadmissions@argosy.edu
Web site: http://www.argosy.edu/twincities

Argosy University, Twin Cities Campus

THE FACULTY

The Argosy University faculty comprises working professionals who are eager to help students succeed. Members bring real-world experience and the latest practice innovations to the academic setting. The diverse faculty members of the College of Education are widely recognized for contributions to the field. Most hold doctoral degrees. They provide a substantive education that combines comprehensive knowledge with critical skills and practical workplace relevance. Above all, faculty members are committed to their students' personal and professional development.

ARGOSY UNIVERSITY, WASHINGTON DC CAMPUS

ARGOSY UNIVERSITY

College of Education

Programs of Study

Argosy University, Washington DC Campus, offers the Master of Arts in Education (M.A.Ed.), the Education Specialist (Ed.S.), and the Doctor of Education (Ed.D.) degrees in educational leadership and instructional leadership.

The M.A.Ed. in Educational Leadership program is designed to instill key philosophies, theories, and values that impact education. It prepares students to improve policies and practices within organizations through the motivation and supervision of others. Students develop skills needed to design, implement, and evaluate educational programs and curricula. Courses include educational law, educational finance, organizational communication, human resource management, instruction supervision, and organizational management.

The M.A.Ed. in Instructional Leadership program examines the challenges and problems encountered in today's educational environment. Course work encompasses the historical, philosophical, psychological, social, technical, and theoretical aspects of education. Students develop skills in analysis, oral and written communication, problem solving, critical thinking, team building, and computer technology. The program is designed for those who wish to develop or enhance classroom skills, become curriculum supervisors, or become educational leaders with a focus on instruction.

The Ed.S. in Educational Leadership program concentrates on applied organizational theory within the context of educational organizations. This specialized program develops the competencies required to secure educational administrator positions at the elementary or secondary school level.

The Ed.S. in Instructional Leadership program enables experienced teachers to become more effective practitioners and educational leaders with a focus on instruction. Course work was designed by faculty members to satisfy the requirements of students seeking career advancement and those working toward a doctoral degree.

The Ed.D. in Educational Leadership program is designed to enhance educational leadership strengths. Students learn innovative and collaborative techniques used to manage and govern educational institutions. The program prepares students for administrative leadership positions at the district, regional, state, or national level. Students must choose a concentration in higher education administration or K–12 education.

The Ed.D. in Instructional Leadership program draws upon educational theories and practices to help students discover new learning techniques for diverse audiences. Students enrolled in this program master teaching methodologies, hone classroom skills, and gain the knowledge required to become curriculum administrators or educational leaders with a focus on instruction. Students must choose a concentration in higher education or K–12 education.

Research Facilities

Argosy University libraries provide curriculum support and educational resources, including current text materials, diagnostic training documents, reference materials and databases, journals and dissertations, and major and current titles in program areas. They provide an online public-access catalog of library resources throughout the Argosy University system. Students enjoy full remote access to their campus library database, enabling them to study and conduct research at home. Academic databases offer dissertation abstracts, academic journals, and professional periodicals. All library computers are Internet accessible. Software applications include Word, Excel, PowerPoint, SPSS, and various test-scoring programs.

Financial Aid

A wide range of financial aid options is available to students who qualify. Argosy University's Washington DC Campus offers access to federal and state aid programs, merit-based awards, grants, loans, and a work-study program. As a first step, students should complete the Free Application for Federal Student Aid (FAFSA). Prospective students can apply electronically at http://www.fafsa.ed.gov or at the campus. To receive consideration for the maximum amount of aid and ensure timely receipt of funds, it is best to submit an application promptly.

Cost of Study

Tuition varies by program. Students should contact Argosy University's Washington DC Campus for tuition information.

Living and Housing Costs

Students typically live in apartments in the metropolitan Washington, D.C., area. Living expenses vary according to each student's preferred standard of living, housing, and transportation. The University does not offer or operate student housing. Most of the students are full-time working professionals who live within driving distance of the campus. Several nearby hotels offer special rates for those who commute from long distances. The Admissions Department also maintains a list of housing options, including contact information for university students who wish to share housing. For more information, students should contact the Admissions Department.

Student Group

Admission to Argosy University's Washington DC Campus is selective to ensure a highly qualified student body. It encourages diversity in academic and employment backgrounds and promotes integration of the student body into professional life through established connections with local and national professional associations. Argosy University offers a professionally oriented education with rich opportunities to gain practical experience in class, field placements, and internships. Full-time students and working professionals gain the extensive knowledge and range of skills necessary for effective performance in their chosen fields.

Student Outcomes

Students can register with the University's online career-services system and use select services from a distance, such as degree-specific career e-mail lists, national job posts, and virtual job fairs. Students should contact the University for more information.

Location

Argosy University's Washington DC Campus is located in suburban Arlington, Virginia. The University is conveniently situated to provide access to most major highways in the area and is easily accessible by public transportation. In proximity to Georgetown, students enjoy access to the many diverse attractions of the D.C. area. Additional campus space is located at The Art Institute of Washington Building (1820 Fort Myer Drive). The University houses administrative offices and seven classrooms at this location. Perhaps best known as the home of the Pentagon and Arlington National Cemetery, Arlington, Virginia, is one of the most highly educated areas in the nation. It is also one of the most diverse.

Many educational institutions and agencies in the area provide excellent opportunities for student training. Major employers in the region include MCI Telecommunications Corporation, Bell Atlantic Network Services, and Gannett/USA Today Company, Inc.

The University

Argosy University is a private institution with eighteen locations across the nation. Argosy University's Washington DC Campus provides students with a career resources office, an academic resources center, and extensive information access for research. It offers the resources of a large university, plus the friendliness and personal attention of a small campus. The innovative programs feature dynamic, relevant, and practical curricula delivered in flexible class formats. Students enjoy scheduling options that make it easier to fit school into their busy lives, choosing from day and evening courses, on campus or online. Many students find a combination of class formats to be an ideal way of continuing their education while meeting family and professional demands.

Argosy University is accredited by the Higher Learning Commission and is a member of the North Central Association (NCA, 30 North LaSalle Street, Suite 2400, Chicago, Illinois 60602; 800-621-7440 (toll-free); http://www.ncahlc.org).

Applying

Argosy University, Washington DC Campus, accepts students year-round on a rolling admissions basis, depending on availability of required courses. Applications for admission are available online or by contacting the campus.

Correspondence and Information

Argosy University, Washington DC Campus
1550 Wilson Boulevard, Suite 600
Arlington, Virginia 22209
Phone: 703-526-5800
    866-703-2777 (toll-free)
Fax: 703-243-8973
E-mail: auadmissions@argosy.edu
Web site: http://www.argosy.edu/washingtondc

Argosy University, Washington DC Campus

THE FACULTY

The Argosy University faculty comprises working professionals who are eager to help students succeed. Members bring real-world experience and the latest practice innovations to the academic setting. The diverse faculty members of the College of Education are widely recognized for contributions to the field. Most hold doctoral degrees. They provide a substantive education that combines comprehensive knowledge with critical skills and practical workplace relevance. Above all, faculty members are committed to their students' personal and professional development.

AUBURN
UNIVERSITY

COLLEGE OF EDUCATION

AUBURN UNIVERSITY

College of Education

Programs of Study	The College of Education prepares competent, committed, and reflective professionals for schools and other settings through innovative programs built on a strong research foundation. The College has a strong tradition of graduate study, evidenced by the University's largest enrollment of graduate students being found in the College of Education. Graduate programs in education provide advanced study for teachers, curriculum directors, media specialists (school library and audiovisual personnel), K–12 and higher education administrators, supervisors, counseling and student personnel specialists, and rehabilitation services personnel.
	Graduate degrees are offered in thirty-six program areas at Auburn University (AU) and include the Master of Education (nonthesis), Master of Science (thesis), Specialist in Education, Doctor of Education, and Doctor of Philosophy. Graduate program areas include nineteen offering advanced continuing teacher-preparation degrees and six offering advanced degrees for other professional school personnel. Research opportunities in each area connect basic research with professional practice and give students a chance to engage in projects that have potential impact on improvement of education.
	All programs preparing teachers and other professional school personnel hold accreditation through the National Council for Accreditation of Teacher Education (NCATE) and are approved by the Alabama State Board of Education. In addition, the state of Alabama signs the National Association of State Directors of Teacher Education and Certification (NASDTEC) Interstate Agreement, which facilitates the applications of AU's graduates when they apply for certification in other states. Other professional organizations accrediting, endorsing, or reviewing programs within the College include the Council for Accreditation of Counseling and Related Educational Programs (CACREP), the American Psychological Association (APA), the National Association of Schools of Music (NASM), the Council on Rehabilitation Education (CORE), and the University Council for Educational Administration (UCEA). The College was ranked sixty-second, and the rehabilitation counseling program was ranked seventeenth, in the 2008 "Best Graduate Schools" edition published by *U.S. News & World Report*. In addition, the College's graduate kinesiology programs were ranked twenty-eighth by the American Academy of Kinesiology and Physical Education in 2006. For more information, students should visit http://education.auburn.edu/aboutus/accreditations.htm.
	Alternative master's certification programs offer qualified students who hold nonteaching baccalaureate degrees a route to initial teacher certification while simultaneously earning a master's degree.
	Additional information about graduate studies and programs can be found online at http://education.auburn.edu/edustudents or by e-mailing eduinfo@auburn.edu.
Research Facilities	Program-specific research and outreach efforts occur within each of the College's five academic departments. This research and outreach is supported by the College's Truman Pierce Institute and Learning Resources Center (LRC) in addition to University computing centers and Auburn University Libraries. The Truman Pierce Institute serves as a research and outreach center devoted to the study and improvement of teaching and learning. The institute's roles include fostering collaboration between higher education and public schools, developing professional development schools, assisting with leadership and management training for schools, and improving the conditions within schools and communities that influence the effectiveness of leadership.
	The Learning Resources Center serves as an information, resource, and technology center for the College. The center assists students and faculty members by providing computer and Internet access as well as instructional technology for classroom learning, circulating materials, preparing project and presentation materials, and offering other College support services such as word processing, graphic design, and room scheduling. In addition to services related to information technology and assessment noted above, the LRC maintains and updates library and circulation materials for faculty members and students.
	The University library system features one of the most technologically advanced and frequently awarded library systems in the United States. The Auburn University Libraries include the Ralph Brown Draughon Library (the main library, known as RBD); the Library of Architecture, Design, and Construction; and the Charles Allen Cary Veterinary Medical Library. The combined collections of the libraries contain more than 2.7 million volumes as well as 2.6 million government documents, 2.5 million microforms, and more than 148,000 maps. The libraries receive more than 35,000 current periodicals, many of which are available online. The library also provides access to more than 227 electronic databases. Books are classified by the Library of Congress (LC) system and are arranged in open stacks by subject. Due to ease of accessibility and electronic connection with multiple data sources, AU libraries were ranked third among more than 300 of the nation's top colleges and universities, according to students polled by The Princeton Review for its annual guide to the best universities.
Financial Aid	A number of graduate assistantships and fellowships are available to qualified applicants in the College of Education. Additional assistantships are provided through grants and contracts from external sources. Those receiving assistantships are eligible for Alabama resident fees.
Cost of Study	Full-time (10–15 hours) tuition and fees for 2007–08 are $2625 per semester for Alabama residents and $7875 per semester for nonresidents. Nonresident fees do not apply to any out-of-state student receiving a one-fourth-time or greater appointment as a graduate assistant. Detailed information about additional course fees and other financial obligations can be found online at http://www.auburn.edu/bulletin.
Living and Housing Costs	Both on-campus and off-campus housing are available to graduate students. The University maintains dormitories for men and women, as well as apartments for married students. Additional information about on-campus student housing is available online at http://www.auburn.edu/housing. Off-campus housing includes a wide selection of apartments, private dormitories, and mobile-home facilities.
Student Group	Of the 2,245 students enrolled in the College of Education in spring 2007, 685 were graduate students. The College's most popular graduate programs, in order of enrollment, are higher education administration, exercise science, adult education, rehabilitation services, and collaborative teacher special education. There is nearly an equal distribution of master's and doctoral students within the College's graduate enrollment. There is a 2:1 ratio of women to men. Graduate students represent a wide geographical area, including a number of students from other countries, mostly those in Asia.
Student Outcomes	Recent doctoral graduates have found positions at major research universities, colleges of education, research centers, and public and private educational settings. Graduates from the master's programs generally are employed in public schools and other community service settings (e.g., community counseling centers, recreation departments, and rehabilitation centers).
Location	Auburn University is the largest land-grant institution in Alabama. The University's 1,840-acre campus and 375-building complex is located in Auburn, a city of approximately 48,000 located in the east-central part of the state. The campus is conveniently located off Interstate 85 and is easily accessible to many major metropolitan areas: Montgomery, Alabama (60 miles southwest); Birmingham, Alabama (120 miles northwest); and Atlanta, Georgia (110 miles northeast). The Alabama and Florida Gulf Coasts are each about a 4-hour drive from the campus.
The University and The College	Auburn University traces its beginnings to the East Alabama Male College, a private liberal arts school that was chartered on February 1, 1856, and opened with 5 faculty members and 80 students. From 1861 to 1866, the college was closed because of the Civil War. The college established an affiliation with the Methodist Church before the war, but, due to financial straits, the church transferred the institution to the state of Alabama in 1872 for use as a land-grant university under the Morrill Act, which was signed by President Lincoln in 1862. The Agricultural and Mechanical College of Alabama, as it was named, was the first land-grant college in the South established separately from the state university. Women were admitted in 1892, making Auburn the oldest four-year coeducational school in Alabama and the second-oldest in the Southeast. In 1899, the state legislature renamed the school Alabama Polytechnic Institute. In 1960, the institution was renamed Auburn University, a title more appropriate for its location, size, and complexity.
	Auburn University's mission is defined by its land-grant traditions of service and access. The University serves the citizens of the state through its instructional, research, and outreach programs and prepares Alabamians to respond successfully to the challenges of a global economy. The University provides traditional and nontraditional students broad access to the institution's educational resources. In the delivery of educational programs on campus and beyond, the University draws heavily upon the new instructional and outreach technologies available in the emerging information age.
	The College of Education, established in 1915, housed Auburn's largest graduate enrollment and fifth-largest undergraduate enrollment during the 2006–07 academic year. Among the University's twelve academic schools and colleges, the College of Education is its sixth-oldest unit.
Applying	Minimum admission requirements include a baccalaureate degree from an accredited four-year college or university and satisfactory GRE General Test scores that are no more than five years old. For admission to all programs, international students are required to submit TOEFL scores unless they have completed a degree at a U.S. institution. Application forms and a copy of the catalog of graduate programs may be obtained from the Graduate School, Hargis Hall. Admission to most programs occurs year-round.
	The College of Education has long recognized that cultural and ethnic diversity greatly enhance the quality of its programs. Members of minority groups are strongly encouraged to apply.
	Additional information about the application process can be found online at http://www.grad.auburn.edu or in the Auburn University Bulletin at http://www.auburn.edu/bulletin.
Correspondence and Information	Dr. Frances Kochan, Dean, and Wayne T. Smith, Distinguished Professor College of Education 3084 Haley Center Auburn University Auburn, Alabama 36849-5218 Phone: 334-844-4446 Fax: 334-844-5785 E-mail: edudean@auburn.edu Web site: http://education.auburn.edu

Auburn University

THE DEPARTMENTS AND THEIR FACULTY

Frances Kochan, Dean of the College of Education; Ph.D., Florida State.

Counselor Education, Counseling Psychology, and School Psychology: 334-844-5160.
Holly A. Stadler, Head; Ph.D., Purdue.
Joseph Buckhalt, Ph.D., George Peabody.
Jamie Carney, Ph.D., Ohio.
Debra C. Cobia, Ed.D., Alabama.
John Dagley, Ph.D., Missouri.
Gregory S. Ern, Ph.D., South Florida.
Annette Kluck, Ph.D., Texas Tech.
Randolph Pipes, Ph.D., Texas at Austin.
Suhyan Park Suh, Ed.D., Alabama.
Chippewa M. Thomas, Ph.D., Auburn.

Curriculum and Teaching: 334-844-4434.
Nancy Berry, Head; Florida State.
Barbara H. Ash, Ph.D., Florida State.
Lora Batte Bailey, Ph.D., Auburn.
Mary Sue Barry, Ph.D., Purdue.
Pamela C. Boyd, Ed.D., Mississippi State.
Edna Greene Brabham, Ph.D., Florida State.
Sarah H. Carrier, Ph.D., Florida.
Janna Dresden, Ph.D., Georgia.
Charles Eick, Ph.D., Auburn.
Jennifer Good, Ph.D., Auburn.
Jada Kohlmeier, Ph.D., Kansas.
Jane M. Kuehn, Ph.D., Florida State.
Gary Martin, Ed.D., Georgia.
Theresa M. McMormick, Ph.D., Alabama.
Bruce Murray, Ph.D., Georgia.
Gordon Patterson, Ph.D., Maryland.
Melody L. Russell, Ph.D., Georgia.
John W. Saye Jr., Ed.D., Georgia.
Elizabeth Senger, Ph.D., Arizona.
Steven Silvern, Ph.D., Wisconsin–Madison.
Leane B. Skinner, Ed.D., Auburn.
Marilyn Strutchens, Ph.D., Georgia.
Kathleen J. Tate, Ph.D., Florida State.
Octavia L. Tripp, Ed.D., Oklahoma State.
Susan Villaume, Ph.D., Ohio State.
Kimberly C. Walls, Ph.D., Florida State.
Bonnie White, Ed.D., Tennessee.
Alyson Whyte, Ph.D., Stanford.

Educational Foundations, Leadership, and Technology: 334-844-4460.
Jose Llanes, Head; Ph.D., Havana.
Olin Adams, Ph.D., Ohio.
Susan Bannon, Ed.D., LSU.
David DiRamio, Ph.D., Nevada.
Sean Forbes, Ph.D., Florida.
James Groccia, Ed.D., Tennessee.

Anthony Guarino, Ph.D., USC.
Gerald Halpin, Ed.D., Georgia.
Glennelle Halpin, Ph.D., Georgia.
James S. Kaminsky, Ph.D., Michigan State.
Kimberly King-Jupiter, Ph.D., Indiana.
Frances Kochan, Ph.D., Florida State.
Marie Kraska-Miller, Ph.D., Missouri.
Judith Lechner, Ed.D., UCLA.
Cynthia J. Reed, Ed.D., Pittsburgh.
Margaret E. Ross, Ph.D., Kansas.
Jill D. Salisbury-Glennon, Ph.D., Penn State.
David Shannon, Ph.D., Virginia.
William Spencer, Ph.D., Illinois.
Paris Strom, Ph.D., Arizona State.
Ivan Watts, Ph.D., Cincinnati.
James Witte, Ph.D., South Florida.
Maria Witte, Ed.D., South Florida.
Sarah Wolf, Ph.D., Arizona State.

Kinesiology: 334-844-4483.
Mary Rudisell, Acting Head; Ph.D., Florida State.
Daniel Blessing, Ph.D., LSU.
Sheri Brock, Ph.D., Alabama.
Alice Buchanan, Ph.D., Texas A&M.
Mark Fischman, Ph.D., Penn State.
Bruce Gladden, Ph.D., Tennessee.
Peter W. Grandjean, Ph.D., Texas A&M.
Peter Hastie, Ph.D., Queensland (Australia).
David Pascoe, Ph.D., Ball State.
Mary Rudisill, Ph.D., Florida State.
Jared Russell, Ph.D., Georgia.
Danielle Wadsworth, Ph.D., Mississippi.
Wendi Weimar, Ph.D., Auburn.
Dennis Wilson, Ed.D., Tennessee.

Rehabilitation and Special Education: 334-844-5943.
Philip Browning, Head; Ph.D., Wisconsin–Madison.
Rebecca Curtis, Ph.D., Auburn.
Craig Darch, Ph.D., Oregon.
Caroline Dunn, Ph.D., Texas at Austin.
Ronald Eaves, Ph.D., Georgia.
Vivian Larkin, Ph.D., Auburn.
Everett Martin, Ed.D., Virginia.
Randall McDaniel, Ed.D., Auburn.
Karen Rabren, Ph.D., Auburn.
AmySue Reilly, Ph.D., New Mexico.
Peggy Shippen, Ph.D., Auburn.
Robert Simpson, Ph.D., Florida.
Suzanne Tew-Washburn, Ph.D., Auburn.

DEPARTMENTAL RESEARCH AREAS

Counselor Education, Counseling Psychology, and School Psychology
Research centers upon school- and community-based action studies related to problems of children and their families: school achievement, disability, substance abuse, violence, suicide, identity development, counseling supervision, and professional ethics.

Curriculum and Teaching
Most research in the department involves issues associated with the improvement of teaching and school reform. Some examples are professional development of teachers, children's learning science, portfolio use and evaluation in the classroom, minorities and mathematics success, language and learning in early childhood, and effectiveness of university and public school collaborations.

Educational Foundations, Leadership, and Technology
Research focuses upon numerous topics, such as measurement and evaluation, school climate and health, student life in higher education settings, applying networked interactive computing in the classroom, improving efficiency and effectiveness of digital technologies in the classroom, improvement of reasoning and problem solving, children's self-regulation and motivation, international studies in cognitive development, and informational children's literature.

Kinesiology
Research areas include physical education (teaching and learning in school-based programs), biomechanics (analysis of human movement using mechanical principles of motion), exercise physiology (physiological bases of exercise in preventing disease and improving performance), motor behavior (psychological bases of development, learning, and control of skillful movement), and health promotion (risk factors and interventions for healthy lifestyles).

Rehabilitation and Special Education
Departmental research focuses on social, educational, behavioral, and vocational factors that contribute to the successful academic and community integration of infants, toddlers, children, youth, and adults with disabilities.

Bank Street

BANK STREET COLLEGE OF EDUCATION

Graduate School

Programs of Study	Grounded in progressive education and in learner-centered humanistic traditions, Bank Street College Graduate School of Education is committed to providing outstanding master's degree programs for graduate students through small classes combined with extensive supervised fieldwork and advisement. The programs integrate direct experience with children, teachers, and families with theoretical material and with observation and reflection. Bank Street's creative approach to teaching and learning recognizes that children learn best when they are actively engaged with materials, ideas, and people. The Graduate School prepares individuals to be educators who facilitate learning, aim for clear educational objectives, and encourage learners to engage fully in the process of discovery and of creating understanding.

The Graduate School prepares adults for professional work in schools and in other settings where graduates focus on teaching, leading, and child advocacy. Recognized for its innovative leadership in the field of education, Bank Street College grants the degree of Master of Science in Education, with specializations in bilingual education, infant and parent development and early intervention, early childhood education, elementary education, middle school education, special and general education, educational leadership, leadership in mathematics education, leadership in museum education, leadership in early childhood, supervision and administration in the visual arts, museum education, reading and literacy, and studies in education. The College also grants the degree of Master of Science, with a specialization in child life. The College offers an advanced Master of Education (M.Ed.) degree in teaching literacy, special education, or educational leadership for qualified students who already hold a master's degree in education.

Both the National Commission on Teaching and America's Future and the foundations supporting the Teachers for a New Era initiative recently hailed Bank Street's Graduate School for demonstrating exemplary teacher preparation.

All programs include extensive fieldwork during which students put into practice what they are learning in their courses. Faculty advisers at Bank Street work closely with graduate students to promote and support each student's professional growth and development. |
Research Facilities	The Bank Street library is a resource for research, graduate study, and professional development. It contains a wide range of books, journals, online databases, Graduate School theses and portfolios, and an extraordinary children's book collection. Bank Street also houses a nationally known demonstration school for children ages 3 to 13. Graduate students have opportunities for study, research, and observation with children, experienced teachers, and parents both in this setting and in the many public and independent schools with which Bank Street College is associated.
Financial Aid	Bank Street's financial aid program makes it possible for full- and part-time students to receive partial support to finance their graduate study. Financial aid may be in the form of tuition scholarships and low-interest loans. Scholarships and grants are awarded based on financial need. Work-study opportunities are available. Students apply for aid using the Free Application for Federal Student Aid. Students should contact the Office of Financial Aid at 212-875-4408.
Cost of Study	Tuition for each credit was $940 for 2006–07.
Living and Housing Costs	Applicants may contact the Office of Financial Aid for information on estimating the cost of living. Students may contact the Office of Graduate Admissions to gain information about housing at International House, a private graduate residence, or in local apartments.
Student Group	The College enrolls about 950 graduate students. These students usually have undergraduate degrees in the liberal arts and sciences or in education. Often students come to Bank Street to pursue education as a career change. Others may be recent college graduates or they may be seasoned teachers seeking their master's degree while continuing to work in the classroom. Approximately 30 percent of the student body are members of minority groups.
Location	Located on Manhattan's Upper West Side and close to the parks along the Hudson River, Bank Street College is in a residential and academic community convenient to New York City's museums, restaurants, parks, theaters, and public transportation.
The College	Founded in 1916, Bank Street College of Education is an independent graduate institution committed to finding better ways to help all children learn; to developing improved teaching methods, curricula, and materials; and to preparing new and seasoned educators to work effectively with young people, parents, and community groups. The faculty's primary commitment is to the professional growth and development of the graduate students. The Graduate School is accredited by the National Council for the Accreditation of Teacher Education (NCATE) and by the Middle States Association of Colleges and Schools.
Applying	Applicants may apply at any time throughout the year. The priority deadline for the fall semester is March 1. The priority deadline for the spring semester is November 1. Applications are available by mail or online at http://www.bankstreet.edu. Applicants must submit transcripts, three letters of reference, and a reflective autobiography. The College seeks students who have an undergraduate average of B or better, strong motivation for professional development, and a commitment to learner-centered education. Applicants to the middle school programs need to have completed an undergraduate major in a subject that is taught at the middle school level.
Correspondence and Information	Ann Morgan, Director of Admissions Graduate School Bank Street College of Education 610 West 112th Street New York, New York 10025 Phone: 212-875-4404 Fax: 212-875-4678 E-mail: gradcourses@bankstreet.edu Web site: http://www.bankstreet.edu

Bank Street College of Education

THE FACULTY AND THEIR RESEARCH

Bilingual Education:
Director: Olga Romero, Ph.D., CUNY Graduate Center. Practitioner background: elementary and middle school teacher in bilingual and monolingual classrooms, bilingual speech and language pathologist, and bilingual speech and language evaluator. Academic interests: language development and disorders, bilingualism, dual language and bilingual education, the preparation of teachers of color. (212-875-4468; olgar@bankstreet.edu)

The bilingual education programs prepare teachers to provide effective bilingual education and dual-language immersion experiences for children. The programs integrate courses for the bilingual extension with the core programs in general education or in special and general education. Applicants must be fluent in English and in Spanish.

Child Life
Director: Troy Pinkney-Ragsdale, M.A., Ohio State. Practitioner background: director of therapeutic recreation for skilled and assisted living facilities, director of child life for pediatric facilities within various major hospitals. Academic interests: diversity issues as they relate to health care and education, literacy initiatives, the preparation of child life professionals, health care, especially in pediatrics. (212-875-4473; tpinkney-ragsdale@bankstreet.edu)

The master's degree program in child life is for those who wish to work with and advocate for ill children in child life departments in hospital and clinical settings. Graduates earn certification as child life specialists through the Child Life Council.

Early Childhood Education
Chair: Michele Morales, M.S.Ed., Bank Street College of Education. Practitioner background: New York City public school teacher, mathematics staff developer in public schools. Academic interests: early childhood mathematics, early childhood literacy issues, quality education in urban classrooms. (212-875-4588; mmorales@bankstreet.edu)

All of the early childhood education master's degree programs lead to certification to work with children ages birth through grade 2. The programs include early childhood general education, early childhood and childhood general education dual certification in general education birth through grade 6 (Michele Morales, 212-875-4588), and early childhood special and general education (Judy Lesch, 212-875-4548).

Elementary Education
Chair: Michele Morales, M.S.Ed., Bank Street College of Education. Practitioner background: New York City public school teacher, mathematics staff developer in public schools. Academic interests: early childhood mathematics, early childhood literacy issues, quality education in urban classrooms. (212-875-4588; mmorales@bankstreet.edu)

These programs in elementary education prepare individuals to work with children in grades 1 through 6. Included are programs in elementary general education; early childhood and elementary education dual certification in general education leading to certification to work with children birth through grade 6 (Michele Morales, 212-875-4588); elementary special and general education dual certification (Penny Spencer, 212-875-4602); museum education (Nina Jensen, 212-875-4491), and elementary education and reading dual certification (Peggy McNamara, 212-875-4568).

Infant and Parent Development and Early Intervention
Director: Carla Poole, M.S.Ed., Ed.M., Bank Street College of Education. Practitioner background: child development specialist in hospital child life departments, teacher of toddlers. Academic interests: child development with a focus on birth to age 3, parent support and parent education, best practices in infant and toddler child-care settings. (212-875-4523; cpoole@bankstreet.edu)

These master's degree programs emphasize early childhood development and early intervention and include both certification and noncertification versions. The programs are for those who wish to focus on working with children ages birth through age three and with their families. Graduate students may choose dual certification in early childhood special and general education with an emphasis on early intervention with infants and toddlers.

Leadership in the Arts
Director: Cathleen Wiggins, M.S.Ed., Bank Street College of Education. Practitioner background: public school teacher, community garden and arts program worker, facilitator of SEED (Seeking Educational Equity and Diversity). Academic interests: cultural diversity and the arts, diversity training, school leadership preparation. (212-875-4529; cathleenh@bankstreet.edu)

This is a collaborative master's degree program between Bank Street College and Parsons School of Design in leadership for art educators. The program leads to certification as a school building leader for those who have been teaching for at least three years. In this two-year program, courses are taken during July for three summers.

Leadership in Early Childhood
Director: Denise Prince, M.S.Ed., Bank Street College of Education. Practitioner background: teacher and director of early childhood programs, program planner in New York City early intervention program. Academic interests: early childhood education, professional development of teachers, school reform, parent involvement, inclusive education. (212-875-4585; dprince@bankstreet.edu)

The master's degree program in early childhood leadership is for early childhood professionals who wish to move into management and supervisory positions. The program leads to certification as a school building leader. In this two-year program, courses are taken during July for three summers.

Leadership for Educational Change
Director: Gil Schmerler, Ed.D., Columbia Teachers College. Practitioner background: high school English teacher, director of an alternative public high school, principal of independent middle school and independent high school. Academic interests: small schools, middle schools, teacher leadership, service learning, team building in schools. (212-875-4709; ace@bankstreet.edu)

The leadership for educational change program is open to teachers who wish to prepare for positions of leadership and staff development, leading to certification as a school building leader.

Leadership in Mathematics Education
Director: Barbara Dubitsky, Ed.D., Columbia Teachers College. Practitioner background: middle school math teacher and math coordinator, mathematics consultant to schools and school districts, public school teacher (grades 4–6). Academic interests: mathematics education in elementary and middle schools, preparing teachers to engage children in mathematical thinking and problem solving. (212-875-4712; dubitsky@bankstreet.edu)

This program is for teachers in elementary education or in middle schools who wish to enhance their curriculum in mathematics or to become staff developers in their schools. The master's degree program in leadership in mathematics education leads to certification as a school building leader. Courses are taken during July for three summers.

Leadership in Museum Education
Director: Leslie Bedford, M.A.T., Harvard. Practitioner background: high school teacher, museum educator, exhibit developer, senior museum administrator and consultant, professional development for arts organizations. Academic interests: museum studies with a focus on museum exhibitions and the creative power of imagination. (212-875-4704; Lbedford@bankstreet.edu)

This program is for professionals working in museum settings or other cultural and community organizations who wish to move into management and supervisory positions. It is a two-year program, with courses given one weekend each month.

Middle School Education
Director: Sue Ruskin-Mayher, Ph.D., NYU. Practitioner background: junior high language arts teacher. Academic interests: middle school education, reading and literacy, urban education, social studies education in the middle school. (212-875-4780; sruskin-mayher@bankstreet.edu)

The master's degree programs in middle school education are for individuals preparing to teach all subjects across the curriculum as well as specialize in a subject area in grades 5 through 9. Students may apply to a program in middle school general education or in middle school special and general education dual certification. Those seeking information about programs in middle school special education should see Special Education, below. Students should also see Museum Education, below.

Museum Education
Director: Nina Jensen, M.Ph., CUNY Graduate Center. Practitioner background: museum educator. Academic interests: visitor experiences and learning in museums, community access to museums. (212-875-4491; ninajensen@bankstreet.edu)

This master's degree program is for individuals preparing to work in museum education and/or in schools. The program focuses on the educational role and mission of museums in a pluralistic society. Graduate students may choose programs combining museum education with certification in elementary education or in middle school education.

Reading and Literacy
Director: Peggy McNamara, M.Ph., CUNY Graduate Center. Practitioner background: classroom teacher (grades N–8, general and special education), professional developer (K–12) in school change and literacy. Academic interests: reading and literacy, assessment, second language learners, special education. (212-875-4586; mam@bankstreet.edu)

The master's degree programs in teaching literacy view reading, writing, and language development as integrated processes. Graduate students may choose a dual certification program in teaching literacy and elementary education leading to certification as a reading and literacy specialist and as a classroom teacher, first grade through sixth grade.

Special Education
Co-Chairs: Penny Spencer, Ph.D., Connecticut and K. K. Zutter, M.S.Ed., Ed.M., Bank Street College of Education.
Spencer: Practitioner background: program director in private special education settings, administrator in a regional education service center. Academic interests: special and alternative education for children with emotional, learning and behavioral problems. (212-875-4602; aspencer@bankstreet.edu).
Zutter: Practitioner background: staff developer; facilitator/national instructor of School Attuned, museum educator/curator, and classroom teacher (grades preK–6). Academic interests: special education, neurodevelopmental constructs, social studies. (212-875-4474; kzutter@bankstreet.edu)

These single and dual certification programs in special education are for individuals preparing to work with children who have learning disabilities, behavioral problems, and emotional disturbances. Applicants with prior certification in general education may apply to single-certification programs for teaching children with disabilities. The programs in special education are at three age levels: early childhood (Judy Lesch, 212-875-4548), elementary education (Penny Spencer, 212-875-4602), and middle school, grades 5 through 9 (K. K. Zutter, 212-875-4474). Applicants may also choose programs leading to dual certification in general education and special education and in social work with Columbia University School of Social Work. Applicants to the dual degree in special education and social work program with Columbia University School of Social Work need to apply to each institution.

Studies in Education
Director: Lia Gelb, M.S.Ed., Bank Street College of Education. Practitioner background: early childhood classroom teacher. Academic interests: early childhood curriculum, professional development, educational development and practice in nontraditional settings. (212-875-4489; liag@bankstreet.edu)

This program is an individually structured, noncertification master's degree program in education.

BARD COLLEGE

Master of Arts in Teaching Program

Program of Study	The Master of Arts in Teaching (M.A.T.) Program at Bard College responds to an urgent need for change in public education. This transformation requires teachers who can help high school students develop the thoughtful self-determination that builds from a genuine enthusiasm for learning. In its commitment to fostering change, the M.A.T. Program engages students, faculty members, and public school teachers in advancing the best ideas about teacher preparation and the improvement of secondary and postsecondary education. The core of Bard's yearlong M.A.T. Program is an integrated curriculum that leads to a Master of Arts in Teaching degree and a teaching certificate in adolescent education in one of four areas: biology, English, history, or mathematics. In future years, the program will be expanded to include certification in other fields, including art, chemistry, foreign languages, and music. The program is unique in its approach, requiring advanced study in the academic disciplines as well as complementary field-based study of issues in teaching and learning. Concurrently, M.A.T. students take education courses that challenge them to apply the results of research and pedagogical analysis to the actual work of teaching. Linked to advanced study in the field, the education curriculum helps students consider how they learn and how alternative approaches to teaching and learning provide broader access to academic competence. Combined with student-teaching experiences spread over the full academic year and the active participation of mentor teachers and M.A.T. faculty advisers, the program's instructionally innovative courses provide the basis for critical reflection about educational practice. The M.A.T. Program focuses on teaching as a clinical profession and on the teacher as a professional. Research indicates that teachers tend to teach in the same way they were taught. In the M.A.T. Program, students participate firsthand in a different educational model and are challenged to rethink their assumptions about teaching and learning. They are immersed in an approach to learning that recognizes the role of language in the development of thinking. In teaching M.A.T. students to treat writing as an educational technology that facilitates individual learning in the classroom, the program benefits from its close association with Bard's Institute for Writing and Thinking, a nationally recognized program of workshops for teachers at all levels. M.A.T. students take six graduate-level courses in their elected discipline. Concurrently, M.A.T. students take six graduate-level courses in education, covering a wide range of issues, ideas, and practices. These courses, which concentrate on adolescent education, are thematically designed to answer essential questions about teaching and learning. Courses are framed by practice-based research. This process culminates in a final research project that must demonstrate a high level of understanding within the field. As teaching interns, M.A.T. students work closely with mentor teachers in public school classrooms from September through June. They design and teach lessons and units, assess student understanding, and modify practices to adapt to their students' needs in the context of educational priorities. Throughout each phase of their teaching experience, M.A.T. students pursue a research question that engages them in the kind of reflective practice that is essential to teaching effectively and growing professionally. New York State requires fingerprinting of all teachers prior to certification. In addition, all graduating students must successfully complete two NYSED-approved workshops in child abuse notification and violence prevention. Students must also successfully complete a sequence of three tests required by New York State. It is the responsibility of the student to fulfill the mandated fingerprinting, workshops, and test requirements in a timely manner, and the student must supply the results to the M.A.T. Program in order to graduate.
Research Facilities	The Charles P. Stevenson Jr. Library complex consists of the Stevenson, Hoffman, and Kellogg Libraries. Together, these resources provide a total of more than 54,000 square feet of space, including reading rooms, music listening rooms, and facilities for group study and for viewing videos, slides, videodiscs, and microforms. The resources of the Stevenson Library and the College's satellite libraries in the Levy Economics Institute, the Center for Curatorial Studies, and Bard Graduate Center for Studies in the Decorative Arts, Design, and Culture include 280,000 volumes and more than 4,000 journals, which are available in print or online via the library's Web site. In addition, online databases central to all the disciplines in Bard's curriculum provide access to indexes and abstracts. A writing and instruction lab funded by the Andrew W. Mellon Foundation makes available both PC and Macintosh computers equipped with Microsoft Office Suite and other applications. ReserveWeb, an online service, makes the full text of many course reserve readings available 24 hours a day, seven days a week, from any location. The Henderson Computer Resources Center houses approximately ninety computers of different types and capabilities, including Macintoshes and Windows-based PCs; specialized multimedia workstations; IBM RS/600, Sun, and Linux workstations; and X-station equipment, in addition to an extensive software library. The Henderson Technology Laboratories building features a large, mixed Macintosh and Windows-based PC public computing lab, which is open 24 hours a day, seven days a week, and a PC-based computer classroom. A fiber-optic backbone network and 100-Mb switched Ethernet link the College's various facilities and provide students and faculty members with unlimited access to the Internet, e-mail, and the World Wide Web.
Financial Aid	The M.A.T. Program is committed to assisting qualified students whose personal financial resources are insufficient to meet the expenses of graduate study. Fellowships are available. Financial aid is awarded on the basis of achievement and promise as well as financial need, according to criteria determined annually by the Office of Financial Aid. Awards are made without regard to sex, sexual orientation, race, color, age, marital status, religion, ethnic or national origin, or handicapping conditions.
Cost of Study	The tuition for the 2007–08 academic year is $29,970. A nonrefundable $500 enrollment deposit is required to hold a student's place in the M.A.T. Program. An annual fee of $250 covers registration and use of facilities. Health insurance coverage is required of all students, but fees may vary depending on existing policies and student elective options. Graduating students are charged a fee of $110 for preparations prior to commencement. A fee of $50 is required at the end of the academic year for submission of certification materials to the New York State Education Department. Total costs for the required New York State fingerprinting, workshops, tests, and certification filing may vary depending on the provider and current registration fees, but they should not exceed $500. Students are fully responsible for all fees associated with these requirements. More details about these costs, dates, and other test information are available online at http://www.nystce.nesinc.com.
Living and Housing Costs	Limited on-campus dorm housing is available for graduate students on a first come, first served basis. The cost varies per year, but it is generally under $900 per month. Houses and apartments at reasonable rents can be found near the Bard College campus. More information on accommodations can be found on the M.A.T. Program's Web site under accommodations.
Student Group	The 2006–07 academic year was the third year for the M.A.T. Program, with 46 students enrolled, including 28 women. The program expects to enroll about 65 students for the 2007–08 academic year.
Student Outcomes	About 90 percent of the graduates from the classes of 2004–05 and 2005–06 obtained full-time teaching jobs in their disciplines after graduation. Many have taken jobs in New York City and the surrounding areas, and others have accepted jobs in states such as California, New Jersey, Vermont, and Massachusetts.
Location	Situated on the eastern shore of the Hudson River, with majestic views of the Catskill Mountains, Bard College is an ideal location from which to explore the abundant natural and cultural offerings of the Hudson Valley. The Bard campus borders Tivoli Bays, a 1,700-acre tidal marsh that is part of the Hudson River National Estuarine Research Reserve, a New York State Wildlife Management Area. Scenic trails furnish further opportunities for outdoor exploration by boat or on foot in the adjacent near-shore shallows. Area parks and trails provide cross-country skiing and biking opportunities. Rock climbing, downhill skiing, and snowboarding in the Catskill or Berkshire Mountains are within an hour's drive.
The College and The Program	In forming partnerships with public schools, the M.A.T. Program at Bard College has been inspired by the concept of a Professional Development School (PDS). The PDS concept, which has a long history in the field of education reform, was revitalized in the 1980s. It is based on the idea of forging an alliance between a college, several public schools, and student teachers. Bard College and the M.A.T. Program have modified the concept to support change in the public schools by improving teaching and learning relative to public secondary school students, student teachers, and educators at the public schools as well as Bard College. The M.A.T. Program is ideally situated to further three interdependent goals: preparing teachers, improving secondary and postsecondary education, and supporting the revision of public school programs.
Applying	Program applicants must have received a bachelor's degree from an accredited institution, with a major in the discipline (or the equivalent) they intend to study at Bard. Students are accepted into the M.A.T. Program on the basis of an assessment of their record of academic achievement, showing a minimum cumulative average of B (3.0); evaluations in the letters of reference; and professional goals. The application deadline for admission to the program for the 2007–08 academic year beginning in June is March 31, 2007. Application forms can be downloaded from the program's Web site (http://www.bard.edu/mat) or requested by e-mailing mat@bard.edu or calling 845-758-7145. They can also be found on the back of the program's catalog.
Correspondence and Information	Master of Arts in Teaching Program Bard College P.O. Box 5000 Annandale-on-Hudson, New York 12504-5000 Phone: 845-758-7145 Fax: 845-758-7149 E-mail: mat@bard.edu Web site: http://www.bard.edu/mat

Bard College

THE FACULTY

The M.A.T. Program faculty consists of a distinguished full-time core group supplemented by affiliated instructors who also have appointments in Bard College's undergraduate program. They have all been intimately involved in creating the M.A.T. Program and are committed to teaching courses in their disciplines at the graduate level. To access faculty biographies, students should go to http://www.bard.edu/mat/faculty/.

Jaime Osterman Alves, Professor of English; Ph.D., Maryland, College Park. Nineteenth-century American literature and culture, with an emphasis on representations of adolescent schoolgirls and female education.

Myra Young Armstead, Professor of History; Codirector, American Studies Program; and Director, Historical Studies Program; Ph.D., Chicago. U.S. social history, with emphasis on urban and African-American history.

Ethan Bloch, Professor of Mathematics and Chair, Division of Natural Sciences, Mathematics and Computing; Ph.D., Cornell. Geometric topology.

Ric Campbell, Director, Bard Master of Arts in Teaching Program; Ph.D. candidate, Harvard. Curriculum design and writing instruction for teachers.

Elizabeth Craig, Professor of Education; Ed.D., Columbia Teachers College. Demographics and quality of the public school teaching force, student resistance and school failure, development of pedagogical content knowledge in social studies teachers.

Deirdre d'Albertis, Associate Professor of English; Codirector, Gender Studies and Victorian Studies Programs; and Codirector, First-Year Seminar; Ph.D., Harvard. Victorian literature and culture, gender studies, narrative theory.

Matthew Deady, Professor of Physics and Director, Physics Program; Ph.D., MIT. Nuclear physics, mathematical physics, musical acoustics.

Julia Emig, Professor of Literacy Education; M.A.T., Columbia Teachers College; Ed.D. candidate, Boston University. Adolescent literacy, with emphasis on urban education reform and teacher education.

Derek Furr, Professor of English; Ph.D., Virginia. Romantic and Victorian period literature, writing pedagogy and practice, adolescent literacy, reading disabilities.

Kelly Gaddis, Professor of Mathematics Education; Ph.D., Cornell. Mathematics education.

Mark D. Halsey, Associate Professor of Mathematics and Associate Dean of Academic Affairs; Ph.D., Dartmouth. Pure and applied discrete math, advanced computing environment for the sciences.

Felicia Keesing, Associate Professor of Biology; Ph.D., Berkeley. Biodiversity, ecology, ecology of African savannas, sex and gender.

Mary Krembs, Professor of Mathematics; Ph.D., Rensselaer. Computational geometry (Voronoi nets), computer graphics, software development methodology, human-computer interaction, mathematical methods to compose and represent music.

Nancy Leonard, Professor of English; Ph.D., Indiana. Shakespeare, poetry, aesthetics.

Mark Lytle, Professor of History and American Studies; Ph.D., Yale. American, environmental, global, and historical studies.

Stephen Mucher, Professor of Education, Master of Arts in Teaching Program; Ph.D., Michigan. History education, history of American education, development of historical thinking processes in adolescents, historiography and disciplined inquiry in secondary classrooms, museum education, history of teacher preparation, progressivism, Americanization.

Caroline Ramaley, Academic Support Associate; Ph.D., Virginia. Basic and advanced composition, Shakespeare, eighteenth- and nineteenth-century British literature.

Lauren Rose, Associate Professor of Mathematics and Director, Mathematics Program; Ph.D., Cornell. Algebraic combinatorics, commutative algebra, discrete geometry.

Michael Sadowski, Professor of Education; Ed.D., Harvard. How factors such as ability/disability, ethnicity, gender, race, sexual orientation, and socioeconomic status affect adolescents' identity formation and school experiences.

Wendy Urban-Mead, Professor of History; Ph.D., Columbia. History of southern Africa, European imperialism, religion and gender.

Laura Elizabeth Wellman, Professor of Educational Psychology; Ed.D., UCLA. Learning environments, technology, discourse and literacy, teacher scholarship.

Japheth Wood, Professor of Mathematics; Ph.D., Berkeley. Universal algebra, tame congruence theory, semigroups, voting theory.

BENNINGTON COLLEGE

Program in Teaching

Programs of Study	The Master of Arts in Teaching program at Bennington College offers small classes, one-on-one working relationships with faculty members, and the opportunity for a self-directed, interdisciplinary education. Working closely with the program's director and faculty, students develop an individualized program of study that enables them to better their practice as teachers.
	Candidates who already hold teaching certification must complete a total of 32 credits; candidates seeking teaching certification must complete 64 credits. Certification is available in the fields of early childhood education, elementary education, and secondary education (in the areas of art, English, French, mathematics, music, science, social studies, Spanish, and theater arts). K–12 certification is available in music, French, and Spanish.
	In their first year, candidates take a combination of required Teaching Seminars and elective course work in the liberal arts. Teaching Seminars do not aim to show students the best way to teach a certain subject at a particular level. Instead, these courses give candidates the chance to think about what they really hope to accomplish as teachers and to develop their ability to invent the methods they need. In their second year, students spend two full terms student teaching with cooperating teachers in local schools, under the supervision of faculty supervisors. During each term, candidates take Reflective Seminars and liberal arts courses.
	Students complete two teaching portfolios during the course of the program, one before they begin their year of student teaching and one during the student teaching year. While demonstrating the professional and subject-matter competencies that are required for teacher certification, these portfolios give shape to each student's distinctive philosophy of teaching and learning. The portfolios primarily consist of written work and often include materials in other media.
	Candidates must also fulfill the requirements of the Center for Creative Teaching, the Vermont State Board of Education, and the Vermont Standards Board of Professional Educators, including the attainment of passing scores on both the PRAXIS I and PRAXIS II exams.
Research Facilities	The Early Childhood Center is a licensed preschool and kindergarten serving community children aged 2–6. The Edward Clark Crossett Library contains books, periodicals, and audiovisual media and provides access to a number of electronic databases. In addition to its own collections, interlibrary loan privileges enable students to borrow from more than 13,000 libraries across the country. The Computer Center is equipped with a number of Macintosh and PC stations and software supporting student research and projects; it also provides training and support.
Financial Aid	For 2007–08, master's candidates may borrow up to $20,500 under the Federal Stafford Student Loan Program. The interest rate is fixed at 6.8 percent. Assistantships are available for qualified students teaching at the Early Childhood Center or working with at-risk youth in the Quantum Leap Program. Applicants who require financial assistance must submit a Free Application for Federal Student Aid (FAFSA), a signed tax return and W-2s, and a Bennington financial aid application by April 1.
Cost of Study	During the 2006–07 academic year, tuition was $20,000 per year. Other costs included an enrollment deposit of $500, a parking permit of $50 per term, a graduation fee of $75, and an optional health services charge of $640.
Living and Housing Costs	Most students live off campus while in the program, but they can purchase a full-board plan for $4050 or a lunch plan for $1210. Other estimated costs include $8400 for living expenses; $3800 for books, supplies, and personal expenses; and $100 to $800 for transportation.
Student Group	The program is for teachers who are either seeking certification or already have certification and want to continue their education. There are approximately 30 students enrolled in the program.
Student Outcomes	Graduates of this program are certified in early childhood, elementary, or secondary education and earn a license to teach in the state of Vermont. Vermont participates in the Interstate Agreement with forty-eight other states, plus the District of Columbia. This agreement provides for the recognition of current teacher licensure or, for recent graduates, recommendation for licensure by all member states. Certification is available in early childhood education, elementary education, or secondary education.
Location	The College is located in Bennington, Vermont, nestled between the Taconic and Green Mountains. It is just minutes from the Berkshires and within 45 minutes of Albany. Bennington is rich in the arts, history, and outdoor recreation. The town includes museums, theaters, wineries, and craft shops. The Appalachian Trail is nearby.
The College	Bennington was founded in 1932 on the belief that a student should create his or her own education. The College challenges its 820 undergraduate and graduate students to discover their own intellectual identity and to design an education that will help them achieve their personal and educational goals. Students learn from faculty members who are actively engaged in their fields. Past faculty members include Martha Graham, Mary Oliver, Peter Drucker, and Erich Fromm.
Applying	Admission to the program requires a completed application, including a current resume, three application essays, two letters of recommendation, official transcripts from each college or university attended, and a $60 nonrefundable application fee. The deadline to apply is March 1 for fall admission and November 15 for spring admission.
Correspondence and Information	Ken Himmelman, Dean of Admissions and Financial Aid Bennington College One College Drive Bennington, Vermont 05201-6003 Phone: 802-440-4312 Fax: 802-440-4320 E-mail: admissions@bennington.edu Web site: http://www.bennington.edu/main.htm

Bennington College

THE FACULTY AND THEIR RESEARCH

Carol Meyer, Director, Programs in Languages and Teacher Education; Ph.D., SUNY at Albany. Intersection of content, conceptual, and linguistic development in language classrooms; conceptual teaching and learning.

Jonathan Pitcher, Ph.D., University College (London). Latin American literature and philosophy; structured, content-driven communication in language teaching.

BOSTON COLLEGE

Lynch School of Education

Programs of Study

Programs leading to master's and doctoral degrees are available in a number of areas. NCATE-accredited programs in teacher preparation include early childhood, elementary, and secondary levels in both regular and special education, as well as a reading specialist program. Special education programs include both moderate and severe special needs. Programs in curriculum and instruction offer specialties in reading/literacy, math, science, and technology. A special ELL concentration, preparing students for multilingual classroom teaching, can be added to all teacher education programs. Administration programs are available in higher education/student personnel and educational administration for both public and Catholic school settings. Psychology programs are available in counseling psychology (APA accredited), mental health counseling, and guidance counseling (all leading to licensure), and developmental and educational psychology. A program in educational research, measurement, and evaluation provides students with expertise in research methodologies and educational assessment. Many of the programs prepare practitioners who are able to apply scholarship to the practical problems encountered in school or clinic activities and who engage in research and evaluation. Other programs focus on the development of research skills that are appropriate for more scholarly activity, leading to university positions. Applicants can obtain additional information by calling the Graduate Admissions Office. Dual-degree programs with other graduate departments in arts and sciences, the Law School, the Institute for Religious Education and Pastoral Ministry, and the School of Management are offered, and students are allowed to take some of their courses through a consortium of major universities in the Boston area. Both full-time and part-time studies are offered in many programs. Typical master's programs require from 30 to 39 credits. A 60-credit master's program in mental health counseling leads to licensure. Doctoral programs typically require a minimum of 54 credits beyond the master's degree, as well as comprehensive examinations and a dissertation. In selected cases, the educational research, measurement, and evaluation program, the applied developmental psychology program, and the counseling psychology program admit students without the usual requirement of a master's degree. Credit requirements for these direct admit programs vary.

Research Facilities

There are several research groups operating within the School, and students often participate in collaborative projects. Major research projects are conducted under the auspices of the five major centers and institutes located in the Lynch School, and most faculty members employ graduate research assistants. Excellent practicum sites are located in schools, clinics, and hospitals throughout greater Boston and especially in the Boston public schools, and students have opportunities to participate in research projects in these sites. The Boston College Campus School, which serves about 50 multiply disabled children, can be used as a research and practicum site for students in teacher education programs. There are nine international practice teaching sites in American schools abroad. The *Journal of Teacher Education, Teaching Exceptional Children*, the *Journal for Educational Change*, and the *Journal of Technology, Learning, and Assessment* are housed at the Lynch School. The Lynch School, in collaboration with the College of Arts and Sciences, is working with a $5-million grant from the Carnegie Corporation of New York as part of its "Teachers for New Era" initiative. The Center for International Higher Education serves as a center of dialogue and communication among academic institutions in the industrialized nations and in the developing countries of the Third World and is home to the journals *Journal of Higher Education in Africa, Educational Policy, and International Higher Education.* The Center for Child, Family, and Community Partnerships engages in outreach scholarship in areas affecting the life chances of youth and their families. The Institute for the Study and Promotion of Race and Culture works to promote understanding of race and culture through psychological study and related psychoeducational interventions. The Center for Human Rights and International Justice offers a certificate in human rights/justice.

Boston College has an extensive network infrastructure that offers Web-based access to student services and scholarly research. A large microcomputer laboratory with an extensive collection of educationally oriented software is housed in the Educational Resource Center in the School of Education. The O'Neill Library houses the university's major collections, including extensive collections in the areas of education and psychology. The online catalog provides access to more than 2 million volumes and periodicals in the social sciences, humanities, and sciences. An electronic network provides access to numerous Web and CD-ROM scholarly indexes. Boston College's membership in the Boston Library Consortium provides access to nineteen major research libraries in the Boston area.

Financial Aid

Financial support is available for many graduate students. Teaching and research assistantships are offered to most doctoral students. Research and training grants also provide support for a large number of students. The amount awarded depends on the source of funds and the amount of work required. Five University-wide Doctoral Minority Fellowships provided tuition remission of 18 credits for the academic year 2006–07 and a stipend of approximately $17,000, which is renewable. A number of doctoral programs extend a limited number of four-year fellowships to students with career interests in university research and teaching. The Charles F. Donovan Teaching Scholars program offers an award covering one half of tuition costs to academically talented applicants to teacher education programs who have a desire to teach in an urban setting. The Peter Jay Sharp Teaching Scholars award offers $10,000 to 10 students pursuing careers in urban teaching who are underrepresented in the profession. A Bank of America Award offers $15,000 and a $5000 tuition scholarship to 10 students each year who are underrepresented in the profession and/or in the high-need areas of mathematics, science, and languages. A Catholic Educator award provides varying amounts of support to students who are pursuing careers in Catholic schools. A special award sponsored by Lynch School alumni is offered to an incoming master's degree student with outstanding academic credentials and promise for leadership in his or her chosen field. The William and Mary Lam Graduate Student Scholarship is awarded to a Chinese student committed to enhancing the educational experiences of poor rural students in China. It is comprised of a stipend and a generous tuition scholarship. Dean's awards are tuition scholarships offered to a select number of students based upon demonstrated financial need and evidence of commitment to the values of social equality and justice. Financial aid applications should be submitted as early as possible.

Cost of Study

Tuition was $922 per credit in 2006–07. Full-time students are also charged a $30 activity fee each semester.

Living and Housing Costs

Most graduate students live off campus in nearby apartments, and costs vary widely. The University Off-Campus Housing Office maintains lists of available housing and lists of students looking for roommates, and hosts a housing fair each June. Local realtors are quite helpful. A limited number of on-campus resident assistant positions are available for qualified applicants. New university-leased housing residences are now available to graduate students in three newly renovated buildings very close to campus (http://bc.edu/gradhousing). Rents include all utilities plus cable and broadband.

Student Group

There are more than 1,000 graduate students in the Lynch School of Education, representing a wide variety of national and cultural backgrounds. Since the specific program that the student enters has much to do with employment prospects after graduation, it is difficult to generalize about placement, but Lynch School programs have a very high placement rate. Students participate in the Graduate Education Association, which is involved in both academic and social activities.

Location

Metropolitan Boston offers a fine setting for graduate study. The numerous local colleges make the city a mecca for students seeking academic, social, and cultural enrichment. The Boston College campus, located in beautiful Chestnut Hill, a short distance from downtown Boston, offers many fine programs and facilities for cultural and athletic pursuits.

The College

Founded in 1863, Boston College is now the largest Jesuit university in the United States. The total graduate student enrollment of approximately 5,000 is distributed among seven schools: the Lynch School of Education, the Law School, the Graduate School of Arts and Sciences, the Graduate School of Social Work, the Wallace E. Carroll Graduate School of Management, the Connell School of Nursing, and the Woods College of Advancing Studies. Located on two campuses in Boston and suburban Newton, the university enjoys a rich academic and social milieu. The Lynch School of Education at Boston College is consistently ranked in the top twenty education schools in the nation by *U.S. News & World Report*'s annual survey.

Applying

Applicants are encouraged to contact the Graduate Admissions Office to obtain application information. Doctoral programs require the Graduate Record Examinations (GRE), but many master's programs accept either the GRE or the Miller Analogy Test (MAT).

Correspondence and Information

Tim Blackman, Assistant Dean
Office of Graduate Admissions
Lynch School of Education
Campion Hall, Room 103
Boston College
Chestnut Hill, Massachusetts 02467-3813

Phone: 617-552-4214
E-mail: lsadmissions@bc.edu
Web site: http://www.bc.edu/lynchschool

Boston College

THE FACULTY AND THEIR RESEARCH

Department of Educational Research, Measurement, and Evaluation

Larry H. Ludlow, Chair; Ph.D., Chicago. Psychometrics, course evaluations, Rasch measurement models, teaching statistics, teacher testing.

Peter W. Airasian, Emeritus; Ph.D., Chicago. Testing and educational policy, classroom assessment.

Damian Betebenner, Ph.D., Colorado; Ph.D., Wyoming. Multilevel modeling.

Harry Braun, Ph.D., Stanford. Mathematical statistics and stochastic modeling, analysis of large-scale assessment data, test design, expert systems, assessment technology.

Walter M. Haney, Ed.D., Harvard. Testing and public policy, exploratory data analysis, cheating on tests.

Ina V. S. Mullis, Ph.D., Colorado. Design, development, and implementation of large-scale national and international assessments; policy analysis and reporting.

Laura M. O'Dwyer, Ph.D., Boston College. International comparative studies and the effects of organizational characteristics on individualized outcomes, recently focusing on impacts of school organizational characteristics on adoption of technology as a teaching and learning tool.

Joseph J. Pedulla, Ph.D., Boston College. Impact of testing on public policy, alternative assessment, program evaluation.

Michael Russell, Ph.D., Boston College. Technology and assessment, computer-based testing, impact of computers on teaching and learning.

Department of Counseling, Developmental, and Educational Psychology

Elizabeth Sparks, Chair; Ph.D., Boston College. Children and community violence; multicultural issues; intersection of culture, race, and feminist psychology.

David Blustein, Ph.D., Columbia. School to work transition, career development, socioeconomic class issues, group psychotherapy.

M. Beth Casey, Ph.D., Brown. Biological/environmental interactions on gender differences in spatial/mathematical skills, planning and problem solving, ADHD, handedness.

Rebekah Levine Coley, Ph.D., Michigan. Urban families, father-child relationships, poverty, child care, federal welfare policy.

Eric Dearing, Ph.D., New Hampshire. Child development within impoverished and dangerous contexts, parenting and parent-child relationships, self-regulatory processes.

Anderson J. Franklin, Honorable David S. Nelson Professional Chair in Education; Ph.D., Oregon. Resilience and psychological well-being of African Americans, especially African American men.

Lisa Goodman, Ph.D., Boston University. Domestic violence and institutional responses, psychological trauma among homeless and seriously mentally ill women.

Penny Hauser-Cram, Ed.D., Harvard. Development of children with disabilities and of children living in poverty, program evaluation.

Janet E. Helms, Augustus Long Chair; Ph.D., Iowa State. Racial identity, psychological testing, racial/cultural counseling and psychotherapy.

Maureen E. Kenny; Ph.D., Pennsylvania. Adolescent-family relationships, psychosocial factors and adolescent depression, preventive interventions for promoting positive youth development.

Jacqueline V. Lerner, Ph.D., Penn State. Contexts of child development, temperament, maternal employment, early adolescent transitions, life span development.

Belle Liang, Ph.D., Michigan State. Community intervention and prevention from cross-cultural and developmental perspectives (social support and mentoring in adolescence and young adulthood), trauma recovery and resiliency.

Joan Lucariello, Ph.D., CUNY Graduate Center. Cognitive development, language development, cultural psychology, sociocultural effects on cognition.

M. Brinton Lykes, Associate Dean; M.Div., Harvard, Ph.D., Boston College. Gender, culture, and theories of self; effects of state-sponsored terror and organized violence; human rights; participatory action research; community-based strategies for change.

James R. Mahalik, Ph.D., Maryland. Gender role strain, effects of gender role socialization on men's experiences with counseling and psychotherapy.

Guerda Nicolas, Ph.D., Boston University. Role of social support networks for black families and psychopathology treatment.

Marina Vasilyeva, Ph.D., Chicago. Cognitive development with a particular interest in the relationship between environmental factors and intellectual growth.

Mary E. Walsh, Daniel E. Kearns Chair; Ph.D., Clark. Developmental conceptions of illness (including AIDS) across the life span, homeless mothers and children, interprofessional collaboration in urban schools and agencies.

Department of Teacher Education/Special Education and Curriculum and Instruction

Audrey A. Friedman, Chair; Ph.D., Boston College. Developing reflective judgment in adolescents and adults, alternative assessment.

Lillie R. Albert, Ph.D., Illinois at Urbana-Champaign. Writing to learn, application of Vygotskian psychology to mathematical problem solving, social justice education.

Michael Barnett, Ed.D., Indiana. Science and technology education.

Maria Estela Brisk, Ph.D., New Mexico. Bilingualism, bilingual education, literacy development.

Marilyn Cochran-Smith, John E. Cawthorne Professor of Education; Ph.D., Pennsylvania. Teacher education across the professional life span; race, class, culture, and gender; teacher research/practical inquiry; children's early language and literacy learning.

Philip A. DiMattia, Ph.D., Boston College. Special education leadership and legal issues, learning and behavior disorders, classroom management, Eagle Eyes technology.

Curt Dudley-Marling, Ph.D., Wisconsin–Madison. Reading problems, needs of diverse learners, teaching as a moral enterprise, impact of school failure on families.

Andrew Hargreaves, Ph.D., Leeds (England). Teacher development, culture of the school, education reform, sustainable leadership.

Richard M. Jackson, Ed.D., Columbia. Assistive technology, low vision, delivery of services for children with disabilities.

George T. Ladd, Emeritus; Ed.D., Indiana. Science education, curriculum reconstructing, authentic assessment, school/college partnerships in education, in-service education.

Katherine McNeil, Ph.D., Michigan. Science education; supporting students in scientific inquiry, explanation, and argumentation; design and enactment of science curriculum materials.

Patrick J. McQuillan, Ph.D., Brown. School reform, impact of concentrated poverty on educational achievement, student empowerment, anthropology and education.

Mariela Paez, Ed.D., Harvard. Early childhood education and second language learning.

Alec F. Peck, Ph.D., Pennsylvania. Attention-deficit disorder, technology for people with disabilities, educational technology.

Gerald J. Pine, Ed.D., Boston University. Action research; adult and professional development; educational change.

C. Patrick Procter, Ed.D., Harvard. Bilingualism, literacy development, reading comprehension, special education and English learners, literacy and technology, immigration, autism and developmental delays.

Claudia Rinaldi, Ph.D., Miami (Florida). Language competence and social behavior of children with emotional and behavioral disorders, relationship between children's pragmatic language abilities and cultural background, oral reading fluency.

David J. Scanlon, Ph.D., Arizona. Learning disabilities, inclusion, literacy, social implications of special education.

Michael Schiro, Ed.D., Harvard. Mathematics education, curriculum theory, children's literature.

Dennis L. Shirley, Ed.D., Harvard. Models of community organizing for school reform, history of education.

Lisa Patel Stevens, Ph.D., Nevada. Critical literacy with a focus on analysis of adolescent discourses, content area literacy, and high-stakes assessment; educational policy in literacy.

Department of Educational Administration and Higher Education

Irwin Blumer, Chair; Ed.D., Boston College. Educational leadership, relationship between systems and schools, racism, improving instruction, unionism.

Philip G. Altbach, J. Donald Monan Chair in Education; Ph.D., Chicago. Comparative education, higher education, international education, student political activism, the academic profession, knowledge networks.

Karen Arnold, Ph.D., Illinois at Urbana-Champaign. Women in higher education, student development, academic talent development, American elites.

Kevin Duffy, Ph.D., Boston College. Student affairs administration, current issues in student life, personal formation in Jesuit education, space and facilities planning.

Ana M. Martínez-Alemán, Ed.D., Massachusetts Amherst. Higher education; race, culture, and gender; feminist theory and pedagogy; cross-cultural studies.

Joseph O'Keefe, S.J., Dean; M.Div., Weston Jesuit School of Theology; Ed.D., Harvard. Urban Catholic schools, international comparative education, ethics.

Diana C. Pullin, Ph.D., J.D., Iowa. Testing and the law, equity issues in testing, education law and policy, rights of students with disabilities, teacher performance assessment.

Robert J. Starratt, Ed.D., Illinois. Renewal in Catholic school systems, leadership, learning environments, building ethical schools.

Elizabeth M. Twomey, Ed.D., Boston College. Education administration, relationships of boards/administration, roles of principal and superintendent, leadership in school reform.

Ted I. K. Youn, Ph.D., Yale. Qualitative methods, sociology and politics of education, organizational theory, the academic profession, the American elite.

BOSTON UNIVERSITY

School of Education

Programs of Study
The School of Education offers graduate degrees in more than twenty areas through the Master of Education degree, the Master of Arts in Teaching degree, the Certificate of Advanced Graduate Study, and the Doctor of Education degree. Although programs are grouped within academic departments that reflect the chief teaching and research interests of the faculty, course work and projects often extend across departmental lines into other areas of the School and University.

Programs in the Department of Administration, Training, and Policy prepare students for a variety of responsibilities in administration, training, and policy-centered development work. Graduates can be found in elementary, secondary, and postsecondary school administration, student and alumni affairs, corporate training and development, international educational development, and directing international schools.

Programs in the Department of Curriculum and Teaching prepare professionals for teaching and other leadership responsibilities in education. Students prepare for educational work in schools, media centers, school libraries, community agencies, and educational research projects, as well as state and national educational organizations. Most programs include courses leading to classroom teaching certification. Boston University's special education program offers a dual-degree program with the School of Social Work that enables qualified students to earn either the M.S.W./Ed.M. or the M.S.W./Ed.D.

The Department of Literacy and Language, Counseling and Development includes programs in counseling, health education, and human development and education that focus on applying theory to policy and practice. Other programs emphasize educational interventions intended to improve effectiveness in literacy and language. Specialty areas include literacy and language study, bilingual education, teaching English to speakers of other languages (TESOL), modern foreign language education, and education of the deaf.

Master's degree and C.A.G.S. programs usually require the equivalent of one year of full-time study. Doctoral programs generally require the equivalent of two or more years of full-time study.

Research Facilities
The Educational Resources Library houses materials on curriculum and instruction, including textbooks, tests, and a special K–12 collection. The library's Web page includes electronic indexes and journals, Web-linked research guides, bibliographies, and a large collection of Web sites to support the School's curriculum. Students in the School have access to all libraries within the University system, as well as the Boston Library Consortium. The University collection contains about 2.1 million volumes, with the equivalent of an additional 3.9 million volumes stored on microform, and a growing collection of Web-based resources. University media services include video services and photographic facilities. The School's Instructional Materials Center supports a wide range of instructional and communications aids: computing and printing resources, telecommunications, photography, audio-visual materials, video technology, and overhead transparencies and graphics. School-based clinics and learning laboratories offer opportunities for research and firsthand learning experiences.

Financial Aid
Each year, Boston University School of Education awards more than $3 million in scholarships to graduate students. Research and teaching assistantships, grants, Federal Work-Study awards, Federal Perkins Loans, Direct Stafford/Ford Loans, MassPlan Loan, resident assistant positions, tuition payment plans, and special University fellowships are also available. Career-related internships may be available, depending on the student's field of study. The School's Office of Graduate Financial Assistance provides information on eligibility requirements and application procedures.

Cost of Study
For the 2006–07 academic year, tuition for full-time study was $33,330 ($1042 per credit) for the academic year. Part-time students paid $493 per credit.

Living and Housing Costs
Limited dormitory facilities are available for graduate students, most of whom must acquire privately owned apartments or rooms. Living expenses for the 2006–07 academic year are estimated to be $11,008 for rent and food; $1136, books and supplies; $2646, personal expenses; $942, transportation; and $1228, medical.

Student Group
There were 582 graduate students in the School during semester I of the 2006–07 year. Seventy-five percent were women and 10 percent were international students from twenty-three countries. The majority of these students had professional experience before enrolling.

Location
Boston, the largest city in New England, is a seaport whose character reveals a rich blend of historical heritage, an active cultural life, and much contemporary growth in high technology, medicine, and business. Within the city are the Boston Common and the Public Garden, Faneuil Hall Marketplace, the Museum of Fine Arts, a host of art galleries, Chinatown, and the Freedom Trail.

The University
Boston University is independent, coeducational, and nonsectarian, with an enrollment of approximately 22,729 full-time students, 5,038 part-time students, and a faculty of 3,318. Its academic and cultural diversity meets the needs of one of the world's largest bodies of scholars. Incorporated in 1869, it provides today's students with the advantages of a large, contemporary educational complex while maintaining many traditional priorities. The main campus occupies 100 acres on the south bank of the Charles River.

Applying
Most programs offer the option of rolling admissions, that is, applications are reviewed as they are received. Master's degree applicants seeking financial assistance are advised to submit a completed application no later than February 15; doctoral applicants who wish to apply for funding should apply by January 15.

Completed admission applications include official transcripts from all universities or colleges attended, two or more letters of reference, a statement of qualifications and objectives, an analytical essay (doctoral applicants only), a $70 application fee, and an official score report for either the Miller Analogies Test (MAT) or Graduate Record Examinations (GRE). International master's applicants whose bachelor's degree is from an institution where English was not the language of instruction must submit a score report for the Test of English as a Foreign Language (TOEFL) instead of the MAT or GRE.

Correspondence and Information
Office of Graduate Admissions
School of Education
Boston University
Two Sherborn Street
Boston, Massachusetts 02215
Phone: 617-353-4237
E-mail: sedgrad@bu.edu
Web site: http://www.bu.edu/education

Boston University

THE FACULTY AND THEIR RESEARCH

The departments of the School of Education are listed below. Each departmental section includes a description of faculty research and teaching interests and lists the academic programs and faculty contacts for each program.

Administration, Training, and Policy

Kathleen Vaughan, Acting Chair; Ed.D., Boston University.

Faculty research and teaching interests: policy analysis from a comparative perspective; planning, group problem solving, and organizational change in corporate, higher education, and school settings; urban and community education, including parent empowerment; international educational development; school choice and educational reform; immigrant and language-minority pupils; desegregation; religion in public and nonpublic schools; leadership in charter, independent, and international schools.

Community Agency Education: Marylee Rambaud, Ed.D., Harvard.
Higher Education Administration: Kathleen Vaughan, Ed.D., Boston University.
Human Resource Education: Alan K. Gaynor, Ph.D., NYU.
Independent and International Schools: Michael Aeschliman, Ph.D., Columbia.
International Educational Development: Karen Boatman, B.A., Michigan.
Policy, Planning, and Administration: Charles Glenn, Ed.D., Harvard; Ph.D., Boston University.

Curriculum and Teaching

Stephan Ellenwood, Chair; Ph.D., Northwestern.

Faculty research and teaching interests: curriculum development, design, and evaluation; learning theory; diagnosis and correction of difficulties in reading and mathematical problem solving; preschool literacy development; law-focused and intercultural education; character education; ethnographic methodologies for research; interdisciplinary social science, humanities, and science curricula; elementary education; sport theory; equity and access in physical education; media facilities planning and environmental design; and special education.

Early Childhood Education: Jane Lannak, Ph.D., USC.
Educational Media and Technology: David Whittier, Ed.D., Boston University.
Elementary Education: Carol Jenkins, Ph.D., Boston College.
English Education/English and Language Arts Education: Jean Goddard, M.A., Middlebury.
Physical Education: Eileen C. Sullivan, Ed.D., Boston University.
Master of Arts in Teaching (biology, chemistry, English, French, history, Italian, Latin and classical humanities, mathematics, physics, political science, psychology, sociology): Stephan Ellenwood, Ph.D., Northwestern.
Mathematics Education: Carol Findell, Ed.D., Boston University.
Science Education: Douglas Zook, Ph.D., Clark.
Special Education: Donna Lehr, Ph.D., Kansas.
Social Studies Education: Stephan Ellenwood, Ph.D., Northwestern.

Literacy and Language, Counseling and Development

Stanley Allen, Chair; Ph.D., McGill.

Faculty research and teaching interests: human development, counseling, sports psychology, literacy development across the life span, bilingual education and second language teaching, theoretical and applied linguistics, modern foreign language, education of the deaf, health education and leisure studies.

Applied Linguistics (joint program with the Graduate School): Mary Catherine O'Connor, Ph.D., California, Berkeley.
Bilingual Education: Julie Coppola, Ed.D., Boston University.
Counseling and Counseling Psychology: Deborah Youngman, Ed.D., Boston University; Amy Baltzell, Ed.D., Boston University.
Developmental Studies: Deborah Youngman, Ed.D., Boston University.
Education of the Deaf: Robert Hoffmeister, Ph.D., Minnesota.
Human Development and Education: Deborah Youngman, Ed.D., Boston University.
Modern Foreign Language Education: Julie Coppola, Ed.D., Boston University.
Reading Education: Jeanne Paratore, Ed.D., Boston University.
Second Language Education (TESOL): Marnie Reed, Ed.D., Boston University.

Boston University, Charles River Campus.

CEDAR CREST COLLEGE

Master of Education Program

Program of Study

Cedar Crest College's Master of Education degree in learning and teaching in a democratic society is designed to prepare master's-level elementary and secondary teachers to meet the challenges of the twenty-first century. Students in the program learn the skills needed to provide high-quality learning experiences for all students and influence educational policy development and reform through leadership in political engagement and advocacy for children, families, and the profession. The program is accredited by the Middle States Commission on Higher Education.

Prospective students select one of three concentrations within the master's degree program: elementary education, secondary education, or the art of teaching (for those already certified at the elementary or secondary level). Concentrations are designed to meet the needs of both certified education professionals and candidates seeking initial teaching certification. The elementary certification concentration requires 44 credits and is designed for prospective teachers who seek initial certification as a K–6 teacher. The secondary certification concentration requires 40 credits and is designed for prospective teachers who seek initial certification to teach one of the following subjects in grades 7–12: biology, chemistry, English, general science, mathematics, social studies, or Spanish. The art of teaching concentration requires 30 credits and is designed for teachers already holding state certification who want to gain master's-level competence in all aspects of learning and teaching. Add-on special education certification is also available.

All students begin the program by taking 12 credits in core courses, including law and politics in American education, research design and methodology, and educational philosophy and ethics. Core courses are followed by courses in the chosen concentration, and the program culminates in a final project, either in the form of a thesis, which is recommended for those students planning to enroll in a doctoral program, or an integrated capstone application project.

Research Facilities

The Education Department has a state-of-the-art demonstration classroom, which is fitted with the latest in educational materials and equipment. The College's Cressman Library houses a curriculum library that includes an extensive collection of children's literature. The library's collections include more than 133,000 volumes, 561 periodical subscriptions, more than 12,000 microform units, nearly 1,500 films and videos, and more than 4,000 records and CDs. The library system is affiliated with the LVAIC consortium and daily document delivery services, which provide links to more than 2 million volumes for study and research. It has network affiliation with PALINET, OCLC, and the Internet to extend access to collections in libraries in the Lehigh Valley, the United States, and worldwide.

Financial Aid

Students formally accepted to the Master of Education program and enrolled for a minimum of 6 credits per semester may apply for a graduate-level Federal Stafford Loan.

Students who are provisionally accepted who are required to complete 9 credits and have a minimum GPA of 3.6 in order to be formally accepted and are enrolled for a minimum of 6 credits per semester may apply for a graduate-level Federal Stafford Loan.

Students who are provisionally accepted who are required to complete undergraduate prerequisite courses in order to be formally accepted and are enrolled for a minimum of 6 credits per semester may apply for an undergraduate-level Federal Stafford Loan for up to twelve months of study.

Cost of Study

In 2007–08, tuition is $374 per credit. Other fees include a $50 full-time ($10 part-time) student activity fee per semester and a $25 application fee. There is also a $300 honorarium fee for student teaching.

Living and Housing Costs

Students living off campus typically spend $600–$1000 per month for a one-bedroom apartment or $800–$1200 for two bedrooms.

Student Group

Students in the program are either currently working as teachers or seeking certification to pursue teaching careers.

Student Outcomes

Graduates of the program are certified to teach in the state of Pennsylvania and hold positions at elementary and secondary schools throughout the United States.

Location

Allentown is the third-largest city in Pennsylvania and one of three that make up Lehigh Valley. The city offers a wide variety of shops, restaurants, museums, nightlife, and sports and leisure. The Pocono Mountains, with their many recreational opportunities, and the Pocono Raceway are nearby, as is Dorney Park and Wildwater Kingdom. Allentown is also within an hour of Philadelphia, less than 2 hours from New York City, and 3 hours from Washington, D.C. There are more than 24,000 college students at eight private and public colleges and universities within 30 minutes of the campus.

The University and The Department

Since its founding in 1867, Cedar Crest College, an independent woman's college, has provided students with an education that is grounded in the liberal arts and informed by humanistic values. The campus is in a parklike setting on 84-acres, with a nationally registered arboretum of more than 130 species of trees. It enrolls more than 1,400 students each year from a wide variety of backgrounds from almost thirty states and more than twenty countries. The curriculum is designed to enhance the development of critical thinking and leadership skills, creative abilities, social awareness, and technological literacy, which empower students to be ethical, engaged, and responsible members of society.

Applying

Applicants must submit a completed application form, a $25 application fee, official transcripts of all prior college-level course work, and two letters of recommendation; three letters of recommendation are required for the art of teaching concentration. Students seeking certification must submit child abuse, police, and tuberculosis clearances that are less than one year old. Admissions occur on a rolling basis throughout the year.

Correspondence and Information

The Center for Lifelong Learning
Blaney Hall, Room 105
Cedar Crest College
100 College Drive
Allentown, Pennsylvania 18104
Phone: 610-740-3770
E-mail: lifelong@cedarcrest.edu
Web site: http://www.cedarcrest.edu

Cedar Crest College

THE FACULTY AND THEIR RESEARCH

James Ealy Jr., Assistant Professor; M.Ed., Lehigh.
James Mauch, Assistant Professor and Department Co-Chair; Ph.D., Penn State.
Mary Beth O'Connell, Assistant Professor and Department Co-Chair; M.Ed., Lehigh.
Jill Purdy, Assistant Professor and Program Director; Ed.D., Widener.
Kim E. Spiezio, Professor of Political Science and Dean of Graduate Studies; Ph.D., SUNY at Binghamton.

THE COLLEGE OF SAINT ROSE

Graduate School of Education

Programs of Study

The School of Education graduate programs are committed to developing leaders in the field of education by serving a variety of populations: students who want to pursue careers as teachers, counselors, or school psychologists; teachers revitalizing their professional skills; educators interested in becoming school administrators or superintendents; and individuals who want to pursue education-related professions such as speech-language pathology.

The School of Education offers curricula leading to a Master of Science in Education degree (M.S.Ed.) in adolescence education, childhood education, college student services administration, communication sciences and disorders, counseling, early childhood education, education leadership and administration, educational psychology, literacy, professional teacher education, school psychology, special education, teacher education, and technology education. The School of Education also offers programs leading to a Certificate of Advanced Studies (CAS) in educational computing, school building administrator studies, school district administrator studies, and school psychology.

Students who are provisionally certified to teach in New York state can earn permanent certification through one of the graduate education degree programs, while students who do not have provisional certification may earn it through related degree programs. All programs are accredited by the National Council for Accreditation of Teacher Education (NCATE) and approved by the New York State Department of Education.

Since most programs include a required field-experience component such as student teaching, an internship, or a clinical practicum, Saint Rose works cooperatively with public and private schools and agencies in the Capital Region to provide students with opportunities for professional experiences in education.

Courses are scheduled in the late afternoon and evening to accommodate students whose days are filled with professional and/or personal commitments. Part-time students usually finish in two to three years, while full-time students usually finish in 1½ years.

Research Facilities

The new 56,000-square-foot Thelma P. Lally School of Education advances Saint Rose as one of the premier teacher education institutions in the Northeast. Education graduate students benefit from the building's state-of-the-art facilities, including the Carl E. Touhey Forum, the Education and Clinical Services Center, and the Carondelet Symposium Center. The Touhey Forum serves as the venue for educators to gather together to address matters of policy and practice through panel discussions and lectures. The School of Education as a whole promotes community engagement in perhaps the most important commitment any community makes—the education of its youth and its future. The building also includes classrooms and faculty offices, providing a central location for students to interact and form mentoring relationships with education faculty members.

The Neil Hellman library houses approximately 211,000 volumes, 715 periodical subscriptions, 282,400 titles on microform, and a collection of rare books. In addition, the College's membership in a nationwide interlibrary loan cooperative enables student access to virtually any printed piece in the world. Students have access to computer labs featuring IBM and Macintosh computers, with Internet access on a recently installed $3-million T3 computer network.

Financial Aid

Saint Rose serves graduate students through a variety of federal, state, and institutional programs that include loans, grants, and employment opportunities. Graduate assistantships and merit, multicultural, international, and second-chance scholarships are available. Graduate students may apply for campus-based assistance (college assistantships and Federal Perkins Loans) by completing the Free Application for Federal Student Aid (FAFSA). The College deadline for receipt of these documents is March 1 for the fall semester and November 15 for the spring semester.

Cost of Study

The cost of graduate tuition for 2007–08 is $560 per credit hour. There are a $20-per-credit technology fee and a $45-per-year student record fee.

Living and Housing Costs

The College's Office of Residence Life assists graduate students in locating suitable off-campus housing.

Student Group

Saint Rose has a total enrollment of 5,000 students, nearly half of whom are enrolled in the School of Education. Of the College's 2,000 graduate students, approximately 60 percent attend part-time. Students come from colleges and universities throughout the United States and other countries, with the largest number from New York and neighboring states. Saint Rose welcomes graduate education students interested in pursuing graduate education degree programs, as well as individuals interested in taking courses toward teaching or administrative certification.

Location

Located in the residential Pine Hills neighborhood of New York's capital city, the College enjoys all the advantages of a major metropolitan area. In addition to the many extracurricular activities offered by the College, students enjoy the Albany Symphony Orchestra, entertainment and athletic events at the Times Union Center, and various theater groups, museums, and historic sites as well as the forever wild Adirondack Park. New York City, Boston, and Montreal are all less than a 4-hour drive from Saint Rose.

The College

Founded in 1920, the College of Saint Rose is a private, coeducational liberal arts and sciences college with a strong tradition of academic excellence and service to the community. The College's 25-acre campus, with its combination of modern buildings and traditional Victorian homes, creates an informal environment that is conducive to professional, as well as personal, growth and enrichment.

Applying

Applicants must file an application form, official transcripts of all postsecondary work, a statement of purpose, two letters of recommendation for graduate study, and any other forms of evidence to support their credentials by the application deadline before the beginning of the semester in which they wish to begin study. The preferred application deadline for the fall semester is June 1; for the spring semester, it is October 15; and for the summer, it is March 15. Candidates applying to the M.S.Ed. program in communication sciences and disorders must submit their applications by February 1 for fall admission and by October 1 for spring admission. The nonrefundable application fee is $35.

Candidates applying to the M.S.Ed. program in school psychology must submit their applications by March 1 for consideration for the fall semester. Applicants to the M.S.Ed. program in counseling or in college student services administration must submit their applications by April 1 for the fall semester or by October 15 for the spring semester.

Correspondence and Information

Graduate and Continuing Education Admissions
The College of Saint Rose
432 Western Avenue
Albany, New York 12203-1490
Phone: 518-454-5143
      800-637-8556 Ext. 3 (toll-free)
Fax: 518-458-5479
E-mail: grad@strose.edu
Web site: http://www.strose.edu/grad

The College of Saint Rose

THE FACULTY AND THEIR RESEARCH

James Allen, Ph.D., California, Santa Barbara. Educational psychology, motivation and learning, classroom management, case-study pedagogy.

Penny Axelrod, Ed.D., Columbia. Special education, learning disabilities, psychoeducational assessment, literacy instruction.

Patricia Baldwin, M.S., SUNY at New Paltz. Childhood education.

Perry Berkowitz, Ed.D., Massachusetts. Organizational development; educational leadership; education leadership and administration; power, change, and conflict resolution.

Steven Birchak, Ed.D., Northern Colorado. Counselor education, character education.

Sr. Charleen Bloom, C.S.J., Ph.D., Illinois. Speech-language pathology and audiology, fluency, counseling.

Huey Bogan, Ph.D., Miami (Ohio). Educational leadership, reading, curriculum and instruction.

Michael Bologna, Ph.D., SUNY at Albany. Social welfare, relationship violence in homosexual couples, postmodern theory and treatment with battered women.

Martha Boose, Ph.D., Wichita State. Communication disorders AAC, emergent literacy, phonology.

Aviva Bower, Ph.D., SUNY at Buffalo. Educational psychology.

Richard Brody, Ph.D., SUNY at Albany. Educational psychology, identity development, critical thinking.

Donna Burns, Ph.D., SUNY at Albany. Educational psychology, developmental psychology, thanatology, human sexuality, humor.

James Burns, Ph.D., Minnesota. Educational psychology, learning disabilities, behavior disorders, behavior management.

Tonya Chacon, Psy.D. candidate, SUNY at Albany. Curriculum and instruction, learning, school psychology, educational interventions.

Sarah Coons, M.S., Northeastern. Preschool speech and language development, speech-language pathology.

Donna Cooperman, D.A., Adelphi. Communication disorders, fluency disorders, differential diagnosis of communication disorders.

David DeBonis, Ph.D., SUNY at Albany. Educational psychology, ADHD, pediatric audiology, auditory processing disorders.

Susan DeLuke, Ph.D., Syracuse. Special education, severe disabilities, autism, social skills and behavior.

Ronald F. Dugan, Ph.D. candidate, SUNY at Albany. Educational psychology, self-regulation, measurement and statistics, educational technology evaluation.

Maria Fast, Ph.D., SUNY at Albany. School psychology, child development, child psychopathology, clinical and milieu interventions.

James Feeney, M.S., Saint Rose. Communication disorders, adults with developmental disabilities, clinical supervision, adolescents and adults with traumatic brain injury, child and adolescent language, written language and literacy, augmentative and alternative communication systems.

Sheila Flihan, Ph.D. candidate, SUNY at Albany. Curriculum and instruction, adolescent literacy, sociocognitive theory.

Kristi Fragnoli, Ed.D., SUNY at Binghamton. Curriculum and instruction, adolescent social studies, elementary education, high-stakes testing.

Steven Hoff, Psy.D., NYU; NCSP. Child/school psychology, child and teen trauma and resiliency, crisis intervention.

Robert Judge, Ed.D., SUNY at Albany. K–6 literacy development, reading in the content areas.

Kathleen Kelleher-Assael, M.S., Saint Rose. Speech and language pathology.

Deborah Kelsh, Ph.D., SUNY at Albany. English literacy, cultural studies, critical theory, writing theory and practice, critical thinking, classical Marxism, pedagogy.

Jelane Kennedy, Ed.D., William and Mary. Homophobia, diversity, women's issues.

Margaret Kirwin, Ed.D., SUNY at Albany. Curriculum and instruction, high-stakes testing, sociology of education, the writing process, elementary education.

Kimberly Lamparelli, M.S., North Carolina at Chapel Hill. Speech pathology, communication disorders, child speech and language, supervision.

Claudia Lingertat, Psy.D., Philadelphia College of Osteopathic Medicine. Clinical psychology, adolescence, grief and loss, trauma.

Marguerite Lodico, Ed.D., Houston. Educational psychology, child development, educational research.

Kathleen Lyon, Ph.D., SUNY at Albany. Reading, diagnosis and remediation of reading disabilities, psychophysiological factors related to reading disabilities.

Marcia Margolin, Ph.D., SUNY at Albany. Educational psychology, methodology/statistics, instructional practice, teacher evaluation, foreign language instruction.

Robert McClure, Ed.D., SUNY at Buffalo. Educational leadership.

Margaret McLane, Ph.D., SUNY at Albany. Educational psychology, with a concentration in special education; social skills of students with disabilities, especially in general education settings; inclusive educational practices; collaboration and co-teaching; action research.

Richard Medved, Ed.D., SUNY at Albany. Educational administration, learning disabilities, dyslexia, behavior management, multisensory teaching of reading and written language, special education administration.

Heta-Maria Miller, Ph.D., SUNY at Albany. Classroom management, classroom assessment.

John Pickering Jr., Ph.D., Ohio. Speech and hearing science, voice disorders, speech science, issues in higher education.

Edward Pieper, Ed.D., Kansas. Learning disabilities, math and learning disabilities, inclusion in elementary through middle school.

Travis Plowman, Ed.D., George Washington. Higher education administration, educational technology, systems approach to curriculum development, self-directed learning, academic integrity.

Christine Preisinger, M.S., Southern Illinois. Special education, learning disabilities, literacy.

Patricia Price, Ph.D., Syracuse. Science education/administration, science education.

Ismael Ramos, Ph.D., SUNY at Albany. Educational psychology, assessment, testing, lifespan development.

Carol Rasowsky, Ph.D. candidate, SUNY at Albany. Educational psychology, early childhood special education, collaboration in inclusive early childhood settings.

Irene Rosenthal, Ph.D., SUNY at Albany. Reading, response to literature, children/young adult literature.

Anne Toolan Rowley, M.A., Catholic University. Speech pathology, literacy, language development, language disorders, written language.

Joseph Schaefer, M.S., Saint Rose. Childhood education, curriculum and instruction, school administration and leadership.

Kathleen Scott, Ph.D., SUNY at Albany. Reading, literacy, reading and writing.

Andrew Shanock, Ph.D., Temple. School psychology, educational assessment.

Dean Spaulding, Ph.D., SUNY at Albany. Educational psychology, statistics.

Lori Strong, Ph.D., SUNY at Albany. Educational theory and practice, reading, teaching students with learning disabilities, developmental and remedial reading.

Katherine Verbeck, Ed.D., Nova; Ph.D. candidate, SUNY at Albany. Educational leadership, reading, language arts curriculum.

Katherine Voegtle, Ph.D., Cincinnati. Cognitive psychology, child development, gay/lesbian allies, life-span development.

Theresa Ward, Ed.D., Central Florida. Curriculum and instruction, whole-school reform, co-teaching and collaboration as it relates to inclusive education and diverse learners.

Willard Washburn, Ed.D., Boston University. Instruction and leadership, urban education.

Mark Ylvisaker, Ph.D., Pittsburgh. Communication sciences and disorders, brain injury in children and adults, outcome and intervention.

DREXEL UNIVERSITY

School of Education

Programs of Study

The Drexel School of Education offers the Master of Science (M.S.) in higher education; the M.S. in the science of instruction; the M.S. in teaching, learning, and curriculum; the M.S. in global and international education; the M.S. in learning technologies; the M.S. in educational administration; the M.S. in human resource development; the M.S. in mathematics, learning, and teaching; and the Doctor of Philosophy (Ph.D.) degree in educational leadership development and learning technologies. In addition, the School offers the following certification programs: Instructional Technology Specialist, Post-Bachelor's Teaching Certificate, School Principal, School Superintendent, and Teaching English as a Second Language.

The mission of the School of Education is to enrich knowledge and practice related to lifespan learning, based on the most current and appropriate research and practice. The goal of the School is to improve human understanding through programs and activities that emphasize creative uses of human effort, technology, and problem solving.

Graduate students in the School of Education have the benefit of the resources of Drexel, Philadelphia, and the School's multiple partnerships with the School District of Philadelphia and surrounding school districts.

The School of Education offers its programs through a variety of formats: on-campus, entirely online (no residency requirements or classroom attendance), and an executive format blending on-campus and online (students meet on campus twice per quarter). The School of Education also offers a bachelor's and master's dual-degree program. Undergraduate students take both undergraduate and graduate courses (master's degree in the science of instruction or higher education) simultaneously until both degrees are completed.

Research Facilities

The Drexel School of Education is home to the Math Forum @ Drexel, a leading center for mathematics and mathematics education on the Internet. The mission of the Math Forum is to provide resources, materials, activities, person-to-person interactions, and educational products and services that enrich and support teaching and learning in an increasingly technological world. The Math Forum's online community includes teachers, students, researchers, parents, educators, and citizens at all levels who have an interest in math and math education. In addition, the Drexel Center for the Prevention of School Violence operates under the School of Education. The center conducts research and provides technical support to teachers, administrators, parents, University faculty members, students, and other stakeholders in structuring activities and programs within a framework that appreciates exploiting creative strengths and problem solving to prevent violence and improve the academic performance of disadvantaged and minority youth.

Financial Aid

Research assistantships are available to Ph.D. candidates on a limited basis. In addition, the Teacher's Incentive Grant is available to current teachers interested in pursuing an advanced degree from Drexel's School of Education. Eligible students may receive a discount of 25 percent on graduate work. Students taking graduate courses through Drexel eLearning, the University's online education subsidiary, receive a 25 percent discount on regular tuition.

The Drexel Dean's Fellowship is an academic-achievement, non-need-based award. The Drexel Dean's Fellowship provides a percentage of a student's tuition each quarter, and students are not assigned duties as part of the fellowship so that they can concentrate on their studies. The fellowship is renewable, on a quarter-by-quarter basis, provided the recipient maintains a minimum 3.5 cumulative GPA and full-time status (9 credits per quarter).

Cost of Study

For 2007–08, tuition for graduate study in the School of Education is $835 per credit. Tuition for the online programs is $627 per credit. This special tuition rate is available to students enrolling in a fully online School of Education graduate program and cannot be combined with any other discounts.

Living and Housing Costs

Graduate students can apply for housing in upper-class housing locations. Bedrooms are located in 4- or 6-person suites in North or East Halls or in two-bedroom, 4-person apartments at University Crossings. All housing is double occupancy. The University also provides a comprehensive resource for graduate students seeking housing in the city of Philadelphia. For more information, students should visit the Off-Campus Housing page of the University's Web site.

Student Group

The student body of the Drexel School of Education graduate programs consists of a diverse group of teachers, K–12 administrators, higher education professionals, and students with a wide variety of skills and backgrounds in other fields who are seeking to become education professionals.

Student Outcomes

Graduates of the Drexel School of Education are known for their technological savvy and assume positions of leadership in the areas of instructional technology and implementation. In addition, the School of Education's nationally ranked graduate programs have produced teachers, principals, superintendents, curriculum specialists, higher education administrators, and college and university professors.

Location

Drexel University and its neighbor, the University of Pennsylvania, compose the University City section of historic Philadelphia. With more than fifty colleges and universities, Philadelphia is one of the nation's major education hubs. Drexel University is close to the city's major transportation hubs, which include the 30th Street Rail Station and Philadelphia International Airport. In addition to its many college and universities, the region boasts world-class museums, fine dining, a wide variety of arts and entertainment, and major- and minor-league sports teams in football, baseball, basketball, hockey, soccer, and lacrosse.

The University and The School

As part of Drexel University, the Drexel School of Education has the benefits and resources of one of the nation's top technological universities. The School's graduate programs' offerings play to the strengths of the University and the vast resources of the greater Philadelphia region. The School ranks among America's best graduate schools and is home to one of the nation's top online mathematics resources, the Math Forum @ Drexel, and the Drexel Center for the Prevention of School Violence. Many of the School's graduate programs can be completed online through Drexel eLearning, the University's online education subsidiary.

Applying

Prospective applicants for on-campus programs should apply through the Office of Graduate Admissions. Prospective applicants for online programs offered through Drexel eLearning should apply directly through the University's online education subsidiary. Information on all of the Drexel School of Education graduate programs can be found on the School's Web site.

Correspondence and Information

Office of Graduate Admissions
Drexel University
3141 Chestnut Street
Philadelphia, Pennsylvania 19104
Phone: 215-895-6700
E-mail: education@drexel.edu
Web site: http://www.drexel.edu/soe

Drexel University

THE FACULTY AND THEIR RESEARCH

Prospective students should directly contact the Program Director listed for more information about individual programs.

Kristen S. Betts, Ed.D., Assistant Professor. Higher education, governance and administration, strategic planning, distance education.

W. Edward Bureau, Ph.D., Associate Professor.

Rebecca Clothey, Ph.D., Assistant Professor and Director, Higher Education Program. Higher education, comparative and international education.

Joan May Timtiman Cordova, Ed.D., Assistant Professor. Multicultural education.

Marion Dugan, Ed.D., Associate Professor and Director, Educational Administration Program. Language arts, student teaching.

Mary Jo Grdina, Ph.D., Assistant Professor. Undergraduate studies, curriculum design, science education.

Francis Harvey, Ed.D., Associate Professor. Enhanced learning, sociocultural learning, distance education.

Elizabeth Haslam, Ph.D., Associate Professor and Director, Learning Technologies Program. Educational field coordinator, instructional design, qualitative evaluation, writing across the curriculum.

Kristine Lewis, Ph.D., Assistant Professor of Urban and Multicultural Education.

William Lynch, Ph.D., Professor and Director, School of Education. Curriculum and educational leadership, educational technology, distance learning policy development, higher and adult education.

Sonya Martin, Ph.D., Assistant Professor of Science Education.

Michel Miller, Ph.D., Assistant Professor. Special education.

Ellen B. Scales, Ph.D., Assistant Professor and Director, B.S. Online Completion Program. Literacy.

Jason Silverman, Ph.D., Assistant Professor and Director, Mathematics Learning and Teaching Program. Mathematics education.

David Alexander Urias, Ph.D., Assistant Professor and Director, Global and International Education Program. International education, comparative education.

Sheila Rao Vaidya, Ph.D., Associate Professor, Associate Director for Research, and Ph.D Program Director. Educational psychology, school psychology, research design.

EASTERN UNIVERSITY

Graduate Programs in Education

Programs of Study

Eastern University offers graduate programs that speak to the multicultural nature of professional education today. The University offers graduate and professional development programs and courses in supervision, teaching, and training that are designed to develop education professionals for the twenty-first century.

The Master of Education (M.Ed.) in multicultural education requires 30 semester credits and provides educators with the skills needed to work with multicultural populations as well as diversify their teaching to include materials and resources from many cultures. The program may be combined with the following certifications at Instructional I or II levels: early childhood, elementary education, K–12 foreign language (French and Spanish), reading, secondary education (biology, chemistry, citizenship communications, English, mathematics, and social studies), K–12 music education, and K–12 special education. General Supervisor I or II certification is also available in the teaching fields listed.

The Master of Education in school health services is a 30-credit program designed for those health majors or nurses who hold or wish to earn either Instructional I or II–level certification in K–12 health or Education Specialist I or II as a school nurse. The program is designed to broaden and enhance the professional skills that are appropriate for those who provide health services to children in schools.

The Master of Arts (M.A.) in educational counseling is designed for those who seek Education Specialist I or II certification as an elementary and/or secondary counselor. The program is structured to meet all categories of study required by the Pennsylvania Department of Education (PDE) for certification as a school counselor. The distinction of the program is the integration of a Christian worldview into the curriculum while maintaining a high standard for academic rigor, multicultural awareness, and practical application of counseling skills that meet all PDE requirements for certification in the field of school counseling at either the elementary or secondary level. A clinical emphasis undergirds this program, and the program was noted for this strength in a recent PDE review. With more complex and challenging situations occurring in schools, a thorough clinical understanding of student behavior is in demand. This program trains students to meet these demands.

The Master of Science (M.S.) in school psychology is designed for those who seek Education Specialist I or II certification as a school psychologist. Students who are interested in the school psychology or school counseling master's degree programs must apply specifically for those programs. Educational leadership certification is offered as well.

The Ph.D. in organizational leadership is designed to equip leaders in business, education, and nonprofit sectors through interdisciplinary studies and original research to effectively engage in the transformation of their organizations, communities, and society as practitioners and scholars.

The distinctives of the Ph.D program are that it is interdisciplinary, is a hybrid of classroom and online instruction, and incorporates the Eastern tradition. The interdisciplinary aspect allows students from business, education, and nonprofits to study together through the core curriculum, followed by focused studies and research in their respective disciplines. The combination of classroom and online instruction requires four to seven days of residency at the beginning of each term, followed by 60 hours of online work and individual instruction. The Eastern tradition is the University's core identity, which affirms the centrality of Christ through its concern for the poor, a global view, a collaborative learning style, critical thought, and entrepreneurial thinking. The program requires a total of 60 credits. Students take 18 credits per year—three terms per year, two courses per term. The first cohort begins September 2007. Information and application materials can be found at http://www.eastern.edu/academic/ccgps/oip/OLPhD. For further questions, students should contact Dr. David Greenhalgh at greenha@eastern.edu.

Research Facilities

The Frank Warner Memorial Library houses a wide collection of bound volumes, periodicals, and microfilms. The computer center operates a minicomputer system with more than fifty terminals and IBM-compatible personal computers.

Financial Aid

Financial assistance is available through federally sponsored loan programs and graduate assistantships. Assistantships are limited and awarded competitively to full-time students (enrolled in a minimum of 9 credit hours per semester) for work performed as researchers, grading assistants, and office administrators. Assistantships can provide a waiver for as much as half the cost of tuition in exchange for work hours. The hours worked are determined by the amount of the stipend. Financial aid in the form of assistantships is usually not provided during Winterim or summer sessions and is not available if courses are being repeated.

Cost of Study

Tuition is $510 per credit. Fall 2007 tuition is $530 per credit. Deferred payment and monthly payments are available. Additional fees apply.

Living and Housing Costs

Eastern University does not provide on-campus housing for graduate students.

Student Group

Nearly half of the graduate student population is enrolled in education programs. Students exhibit diverse undergraduate educational backgrounds, and some hold earned graduate degrees. Full-time students come from across the United States, and part-time students commute from throughout the Philadelphia metropolitan area.

Location

Eastern University is located in St. Davids, one of the western Main Line suburbs of Philadelphia. Center City is 20 minutes away. St. Davids, primarily residential in nature, is complemented by Philadelphia, which provides a variety of cultural, social, spiritual, and athletic activities. Eastern University also offers graduate course work at its 10th and Spring Garden Street location in the city of Philadelphia. This location is only a 7-minute ride from Center City Philadelphia.

The University

Eastern University is known for its innovative academic programs, caring community, commitment to social action, and exceptionally beautiful campus. Class sizes are small, and professors are both role models to their students and highly accomplished experts in their fields. In addition to integrating faith and learning, Eastern's creative academic programs encourage students to learn from many disciplines. The campus community is highly diverse, with a multiethnic student body that includes representatives from more than thirty countries.

Applying

To apply, interested students should contact the graduate admissions office for an application. Eastern requests that two letters of recommendation, an essay, and official transcripts from all schools attended accompany all applications. Applications are accepted as received. The nonrefundable application fee is $35. Prospective students may also apply online at http://www.eastern.edu by scrolling down to "Graduate" under the "Admissions" button and then, at the admissions page, clicking on "Apply Online Now!" next to the appropriate program or school. Students submit online applications free of charge.

For more information, students should contact Mike Perpiglia at the Campolo College for Graduate and Professional Studies at Eastern University.

Correspondence and Information

Graduate Admissions Office
Eastern University
1300 Eagle Road
St. Davids, Pennsylvania 19087
Phone: 610-341-5972
          800-732-7669 (toll-free)
Fax: 610-341-1468
E-mail: mperpigl@eastern.edu
Web site: http://www.eastern.edu

Eastern University

THE FACULTY

Helen W. Loeb, Ph.D., Chair, Education Department.
Heewon Chang, Ph.D.
Kathy-Ann Hernandez, Ph.D.
Dorothy Hurley, Ed.D.
Jean Landis, Ed.D.
William Yerger, Ed.D.
Susan Seltzer, M.S.N., Coordinator of School Nursing and School Health Supervisor Certification Programs.

FAIRFIELD UNIVERSITY

Graduate School of Education and Allied Professions

Programs of Study

The Graduate School's programs prepare students for professional positions in schools, agencies, and corporate settings as well as for entrance into doctoral studies.

Programs lead to the Master of Arts (M.A.), the Certificate of Advanced Study (C.A.S.), and/or state certification. Courses are offered within the following majors: applied psychology, including foundations of advanced psychology, human services, and industrial/organizational/personnel psychology; bilingual/multicultural education; counselor education, including community counseling and school counseling; elementary teaching; marriage and family therapy; media/educational technology; professional development for teachers; school psychology; secondary teaching; special education, including bilingual special education; teaching and foundations; and TESOL. Teaching internships (paid) are available to matriculated students.

Master of Arts candidates must complete a minimum of 33 credits (depending on their program) and pass a comprehensive examination or project or write a master's thesis.

Certificate of Advanced Study (sixth-year) candidates must complete a minimum of 30 credits, including 15 credits in the major field and other courses required by the program, and an internship or practicum at the end of most programs. Students should note that the CAS programs in all departments, except school psychology, are being reviewed and are not admitting students during this academic year.

Research Facilities

The DiMenna-Nyselius Library is a state-of-the-art facility containing more than 300,000 carefully selected bound volumes, 1,800 journals and newspapers, more than 10,000 audiovisual items, and the equivalent of 95,000 volumes in microform. It also offers an automated information and inventory system; impressive media, computing, and Internet resources; and extensive single and group meeting spaces.

Financial Aid

A limited number of graduate assistantships providing tuition remission of 6 to 12 credits are available from the Graduate School. Assistantships are also available from other departments such as Residence Life, and some of these provide free tuition plus a stipend. Periodically, funds are available through federal and other grants. The Financial Aid Office assists those applying for loans and other forms of financial aid.

Cost of Study

For 2007–08, tuition is $500 per credit. Most courses are 3 credits. The registration fee is $25 per semester. Laboratory and/or material fees of $15 per credit ($45 per 3-credit course) are charged for selected courses in psychology, computers, and media.

Living and Housing Costs

No housing is available on campus for graduate students. Rents for off-campus housing within reasonable commuting distance begin at $450 per month for a room in a private home and $700 per month for an efficiency apartment. Often students share apartments. The Dean's Office (telephone: 203-254-4000 Ext. 2413) has off-campus housing information.

Student Group

The majority of students are employed by boards of education in the area and attend classes part-time in the late afternoon and evening. An increasing number of students are seeking state certification as part of a career change. Many others anticipate working outside of school settings in areas such as community counseling, marriage and family therapy, media production, and applied psychology. There are approximately 800 students; 150 are full-time.

Location

Fairfield is a suburban Connecticut town bordering Long Island Sound. It is 1 hour from New York City, 3 hours from Boston, and about 30 minutes from Yale University. Fairfield University occupies a 225-acre landscaped and wooded campus. The town has numerous beaches; a marina; a launching and storage area for small boats; and public athletic facilities, including tennis courts, golf courses, and softball and baseball fields. A public library, town-sponsored concerts, churches of various denominations, a historical society, a train station, an art-film movie house, and two multiplex cinemas are near the campus.

The University and The School

Fairfield University offers Jesuit education at its best. Its long-standing tradition of preparing professionals in education and human services dates back to 1950 when the first classes in graduate education were offered. *U.S. News & World Report* rates Fairfield University among the top three comprehensive universities in the North.

Applying

The formal application fee for all programs is $55. An application/information packet is sent upon request. The TESOL/ bilingual education program admits on a rolling basis. The application deadlines for other programs are as follows: curriculum and teaching and secondary education, May 1 for fall, October 1 for spring, February 1 for summer admission; elementary education, February 1 for summer and fall, October 1 for spring; marriage and family therapy, March 15 for summer and fall, October 15 for spring; school psychology, January 15 for fall; counselor education, March 1 for summer and fall, November 1 for spring; applied psychology and special education, February 1 for summer and fall, October 1 for spring; and educational technology, March 1 for summer and fall, and November 1 for spring. Applicants for the master's programs must hold a bachelor's degree from a regionally accredited college and it is recommended that they have a minimum cumulative GPA of 2.67. Applicants for the C.A.S. program must hold a master's degree from a regionally accredited institution, with a recommended minimum GPA of 3.0. Individual programs may set specific requirements regarding admission.

Students may apply informally as nonmatriculated status students and take a maximum of 6 credits in a certification program and 9 credits in a non-certification program. A transcript review and interview are necessary for advisement before registration in course work as a nonmatriculated student.

The Teaching Internship Program has a strict application deadline of June 15, with internships starting in August or September. Formal admission to a degree program is required. Internships start in the fall term; however, internships starting in the spring term may also be available.

Correspondence and Information

For applications:
Office of Graduate and Continuing Studies Admission
Kelly Administrative Center
Fairfield University
1073 North Benson Road
Fairfield, Connecticut 06824-5195

Phone: 203-254-4184
E-mail: gradadmis@mail.fairfield.edu
Web site: http://www.fairfield.edu

For questions regarding degree programs or certification:
Karen L. Creecy
Associate Dean/Certification Officer
Canisius Hall, Room 102
Fairfield University
Fairfield, Connecticut 06824-5195

Phone: 203-254-4000 Ext. 4250
E-mail: graded@mail.fairfield.edu

Fairfield University

THE FACULTY AND THEIR RESEARCH

Marsha Alibrandi, Assistant Professor; Ed.D., Massachusetts. Geographic education and spatial cognition, learning and teaching with geographic information systems (GIS) and teacher education, integrating instructional technologies, collaborative research.

Sandra Billings, Assistant Professor; Ph.D., Connecticut. Teacher education, Connecticut's Beginning Educator Support Training (BEST) program, professional development, diversity issues, at-risk youth.

Patricia E. Calderwood, Associate Professor; Ph.D., Pennsylvania. Social construction of community, teacher education, ethnographic research.

Yvel C. Crevecoeur, Visiting Instructor; Ph.D. candidate, Connecticut. Learning disabilities, second language acquisition and literacy, educational policy, educational administration/leadership.

Faith-Anne Dohm, Associate Professor; Ph.D., Maryland, Baltimore County. Risk factors for psychological disorders, research mentoring, judgment of food amounts, the process of research.

Daniel Geller, Professor; Ph.D., Yeshiva. Disabilities, families with disabled members, parent/child relationships, parent/school collaboration, clinical and diagnostic interviewing, premarital and divorce relationships.

Jennifer Goldberg, Assistant Professor; Ph.D., UCLA. Research design and methods, classroom discourse, sociocultural views of learning and development.

Ingeborg Haug, Associate Professor; D.Min., Andover Newton Theological School. Couple therapy, professional ethics, parenting issues.

Diana Hulse-Killacky, Professor; Ed.D., Indiana. Role of corrective feedback in success of groups in a variety of settings, enhancement of classroom instruction in group work and counselor education, conceptual models that promote group work practice, collaborative teaching teams.

William Kaplan, Visiting Instructor; SYC, Southern Connecticut State. Educational leadership, mentoring in professional development of educators, teacher preparation.

Virginia A. Kelly, Associate Professor; Ph.D., North Carolina at Greensboro. Spirituality and counseling, assessment and treatment of chemically dependent women, domestic violence, psychological abuse, familial alcoholism.

Hyun Uk Kim, Assistant Professor; Ph.D., UCLA. Autism spectrum disorders, special education and atypical development, brain and language development, language development in children with developmental disabilities.

Wendy R. Kohli, Professor; Ph.D., Syracuse. Philosophy of education, feminist theory, urban school reform, clinical pedagogy, curriculum theory.

Elizabeth Langran, Assistant Professor; Ph.D., Virginia. K–12 technology integration, technology leadership, copyright in the classroom, international education, digital storytelling.

Paula Gill Lopez, Associate Professor; Ph.D., Berkeley. Dropout prevention, clinical supervision of pre- and in-service school psychologists, violence prevention, cultural competence, emotional intelligence, bullying intervention.

Bogusia Molina, Associate Professor; Ph.D., Southern Illinois at Carbondale. Group processes, life-span human development, clinical supervision.

Julianna Poole, S.S.N.D., Assistant Professor; Ed.D., Rochester. English as a second language, bilingual and multicultural education, teacher education.

Rona Preli, Associate Professor; Ph.D., Virginia Tech. Addictions and family therapy, supervision, accreditation, diversity.

Tracey Robert, Assistant Professor; Ph.D., Mississippi State. Work and spirituality, career development, clinical supervision.

Christine Siegel, Assistant Professor; Ph.D., SUNY at Albany. Implementation and treatment acceptability of evidence-based interventions in schools, application of qualitative methods to school-based intervention research, early elementary prevention programs.

Emily Smith, Assistant Professor; Ph.D., Michigan State. Teacher education, teacher learning, mentoring, English education.

Anibal Torres Bernal, Assistant Professor; Ph.D., Syracuse. Meta-theoretical and normative analysis of couple and family therapy theories, self-conceptualization of underrepresented populations, study and utilization of democratic and social justice principles in family/couple therapeutic intervention.

David Aloyzy Zera, Associate Professor; Ph.D., Connecticut. Learning disabilities, attention, self-organizing systems, bilingual special education.

THE LEADER IN GLOBAL EDUCATION

FAIRLEIGH DICKINSON
U N I V E R S I T Y

FAIRLEIGH DICKINSON UNIVERSITY

Sammartino School of Education

Programs of Study	While diverse, the graduate education programs of Fairleigh Dickinson's Sammartino School of Education in northern New Jersey share three common themes: a commitment to excellence in education, integrating current research and technologies in teaching practices; a collegial approach that fosters a spirit of teamwork among the education and arts and sciences faculties to produce well-prepared educators; and close and ongoing collaborative partnerships with P–12 school districts and educational/business organizations.
	The School of Education is based on Fairleigh Dickinson's Metropolitan Campus (Teaneck). However, graduate programs are also offered at the University's College at Florham (Madison) and at select locations statewide, at school districts, and at other delivery sites. All graduate education programs for teacher certification are approved by the New Jersey Department of Education.
	Graduate education program offerings include the Master of Arts (M.A.) in education for certified teachers (with certificate programs in New Jersey certification as a reading specialist, instructional technology specialist, teacher of students with disabilities, teacher of English as a second language plus bilingual education endorsement, mathematics education specialist, and a professional studies concentration for alternate route teachers), educational leadership (with New Jersey certification for principal and supervisor available), and learning disabilities (with New Jersey certification as teacher of students with disabilities and learning disabilities teacher consultant available). An FDU certificate is also available for dyslexia specialist and instructional technology programs. International students can enroll in the multilingual Master of Arts program for teaching English as a second language (TESL).
	Programs leading to the Master of Arts in Teaching (M.A.T.) are also offered for initial certification, with programs in elementary education (with certification in grades K–5), middle school endorsement (with certification in grades 5–8), English as a second language (with certification in grades K–12), and subject area certification, grades K–12, in biological science, chemistry, English language and literacy, mathematics, physical sciences, social studies, or world languages.
Research Facilities	On each campus, the University provides extensive facilities to support education, research, and training, including strong library resources, research laboratories, and computer facilities.
Financial Aid	A limited number of graduate scholarships may be available to qualified students. Applications are available through the Office of Admissions. An international scholarship program is offered for non-U.S., full-time graduate students. The University's application, available through the Office of International Admissions, evaluates the student on both academic merit and financial need.
	Eligible domestic graduate students enrolled at least half-time may borrow up to a maximum of $20,500 annually in subsidized and unsubsidized loans under the Federal Stafford Student Loan program. In addition, the University offers a number of attractive flexible financing programs to its students.
Cost of Study	Tuition for master's-level studies in 2007–08 is $869 per credit for either full- or part-time students. An annual technology fee of $244 for part-time students or $304 for full-time students is also assessed. As part of its commitment to ongoing professional development for teachers and administrators, the University offers its M.A. degrees for certified teachers and educational leadership at a special 38 percent reduced tuition rate for all programs offered at an off-site location.
Living and Housing Costs	The University currently offers limited on-campus housing for graduate students, offered on a first-come, first-served basis. The annual costs at the Metropolitan Campus are $6420 for a standard double room and $3508 for the standard eleven-meal plan, which includes $300 in flex dollars. International students should contact the University's international student organizations for assistance in locating housing.
Student Group	The School of Education focuses on the needs of today's professional educators as they face the challenges of preparing tomorrow's citizens. In partnership with urban, suburban, and rural public, and nonpublic, school districts, significant educational and business organizations, and state agencies, the School supports programs and special initiatives to continually improve professional development and performance of preservice, novice, and veteran teachers. The University's graduate education programs attract a broad range of both aspiring and professional educators. Most classes are under 20 students in size, and students are afforded individual attention from assigned faculty advisers.
Location	The University has two locations in northern New Jersey. The Metropolitan Campus is located less than 10 miles from New York City on a modern, 88-acre site in Teaneck. The College at Florham is situated in the heart of New Jersey's growing corporate center. The campus's stately, Georgian-style buildings span 166 acres of wooded ground on what once was a private estate.
	The strategic location of each campus offers graduate education majors access to a wide range of educational settings. The faculty members are actively involved as leaders in their fields and maintain close networking relationships in the educational community on a local, state, and national level that lead to invaluable opportunities for students.
The University	Founded in 1942, Fairleigh Dickinson is one of New Jersey's largest private universities, with more than 10,500 students. In addition to its two major New Jersey campuses, the University offers many programs throughout the state and operates its own overseas campuses in Wroxton, England, and Vancouver, British Columbia, Canada.
Applying	The Sammartino School of Education seeks a highly qualified and diverse student body. Applicants of varied educational and professional backgrounds are welcome.
	Applicants for the state certification and the Master of Arts in Teaching degree must have a bachelor's or a master's degree from an accredited college or university, with a minimum overall 2.75 grade point average (GPA) out of possible 4.0 in their undergraduate program. Applicants with GPA lower than 2.75 may take additional undergraduate courses to raise their GPA to the required minimum. Continuation in the M.A.T. program is contingent upon maintaining at least a 3.0 academic average.
	Students must pass the PRAXIS test and submit two letters of recommendation to matriculate and be eligible for state certification. A valid New Jersey teaching certificate is required of candidates seeking a second certification for English as a second language or teacher of the handicapped, and those who seek admission to the Master of Arts in learning disabilities program, Master of Arts in education for certified teachers, and Master of Arts in educational leadership. Applicants must also submit a graduate studies application, a one-time nonrefundable application fee, two letters of recommendation, and official transcripts for all postsecondary school academic work.
Correspondence and Information	Susan Neihart Graduate Admissions Fairleigh Dickinson University 1000 River Road, T-KB1-01 Teaneck, New Jersey 07666 Phone: 201-692-2554 E-mail: grad@fdu.edu Web site: http://www.fdu.edu

Fairleigh Dickinson University

THE FACULTY

Members of the School of Education faculty represent a wide range of trained educational specialists. Their professional backgrounds include experience as school administrators, practicing teachers, specialists, technologists, and clinicians. They are deeply involved in advancing the teaching profession through their work in research, publications in professional journals, consulting activities, and presentations at local, state, national, and international educational conferences. The School's faculty members are also actively engaged in national and state professional educational organizations. The faculty members are encouraged to think critically and creatively to develop solutions that respond to the real-world problems faced by today's teachers and scholars.

Daniel Aronoff, Lecturer; M.A., Seton Hall. Educational leadership, mathematics education.

Ellen Campbell, Assistant Professor and Director, Master of Arts for Certified Teachers Program; Ed.D., Kutztown. Visual studies, technology.

Vicki Cohen, Professor and Director, School of Education; Ed.D., Columbia. Literacy, instructional technology.

John Cowen, Associate Professor; Ed.D., Columbia. Literacy and poetry.

Mary L. Farrell, Professor, Director, Institute for Dyslexic Studies, and Director, Center for Clinical Teaching; Ph.D., Columbia. Learning disabilities and dyslexia.

Khyati Joshi, Assistant Professor; Ed.D., Massachusetts Amherst. Social justice education.

Carol Karpinski, Assistant Professor and Director, Master of Arts in Teaching (M.A.T.) Program; Ed.D., Rutgers. Educational administration, history of education.

Teresa Montani, Associate Professor and Associate Director, School of Education; Ed.D., Rutgers. Mathematics for students with learning disabilities.

Louis Ray, Assistant Professor; Ph.D., NYU. Multicultural education, history of education.

Marlene Rosenbaum, Associate Professor and Associate Dean, University College; Ed.D., Rutgers. Curriculum development, educational transformation.

Carl Schavio, Assistant Professor and Director, Educational Leadership Program; Ed.D., Rutgers. Educational leadership, assessment.

Marie Simone, Lecturer; Ed.D., Rutgers. Administration and supervision.

Miriam Singer, Assistant Professor; Ed.D., Seton Hall, Outcomes of whole school reforms in Abbott School Districts.

FELICIAN COLLEGE

Programs in Education

Programs of Study
The "Teacher as Leader" Master of Arts (M.A.) program in education at Felician College is designed to prepare certified teachers seeking endorsements in elementary education, special education, or supervisor to become instructional leaders in their schools or districts. The program integrates the philosophies of curriculum development with an awareness of current national, state, and local trends. Students are exposed to effective instruction and a variety of teaching models for individuals as well as small and large groups. The program is offered at the Felician College campus in Rutherford, New Jersey. Courses can be taken during evenings and on weekends, and students can complete the program at their own pace, based on advisement and availability of courses.

The program begins with 21 credits (seven courses) in the core curriculum and then branches into elementary, special education, and supervisory components. Thirty-three credits are required for the elementary track, 39 credits for the special education track, and 33 credits for the supervisory track. Within the program, students may work toward fulfilling their licensing requirements as an elementary teacher, special education teacher, or as a supervisor.

Students who pursue the supervisory track can focus on either special education or on public, private, or parochial education. The program encourages reflection and personal growth and helps students develop ethical leadership skills to promote a strong, professional, values-based learning environment.

The elementary education and the teacher of students with disabilities tracks prepare students for advancement in or entry into the field with a solid foundation, balancing skills and knowledge with compassion and an emphasis on learner-centered education. The programs cover issues of importance and relevance for today's educators, such as changes in trends, practices, research, legislation, and policies, thereby giving students the knowledge and ability to lead and excel with an informed mind and an understanding heart.

Noncertified teachers who are enrolled in the master's program may obtain teacher certification by completing an additional 4 credits in their chosen track. Students may work toward fulfilling the requirements for licensure as an elementary or special education teacher, or they may fulfill the requirements for supervisor licensure.

Research Facilities
The College Library is a two-story building that serves the needs of students, faculty and staff members, and alumni with more than 110,000 books and over 800 periodical subscriptions. This collection is enhanced by large holdings of materials in microform, which can be used on the library's reader/printer equipment. With its computers linked to information services such as DIALOG and OCLC, and as a member of the New Jersey Library Network and VALE, the library locates and obtains information, journal articles, and books not available in its collection from sources all over the country. Computerized databases can also be accessed directly by users through the online First Search workstation, where up-to-date information on 40 million books and an index of 15,000 periodicals is available. The library is also connected to the Internet and has several CD-ROM workstations. Through EBSCOhost, Bell & Howell's Proquest, CINAHL, and other services, students and faculty and staff members have access to numerous online journal indexes—as well as articles from thousands of periodicals—from anywhere on the campus computer network or from their home computers. An experienced staff of professional librarians is available to assist users.

The College's computer facilities include an academic and administrative network, four computerized labs, a computerized learning center, and two computer centers that are available for students, with a total of about 200 computers available for student/faculty member use. All classrooms, offices, and facilities are wired for Internet and e-mail.

Financial Aid
Scholarships, fellowships, work-study programs, and loans are available. To qualify for financial aid, a student must complete the Free Application for Federal Student Aid (FAFSA).

Cost of Study
In 2006–07, graduate tuition was $675 per credit. Fees are additional.

Living and Housing Costs
Students are housed in two dormitories on the Rutherford campus, Milton and Elliott Halls. Both buildings have housing organized around student suites containing semiprivate baths. On-campus room and board ranges between $3200 and $5500 per semester. On-campus housing is not available to married students.

Student Group
In total, there are about 1,800 students. In fall 2005, there were 69 students (5 percent) enrolled in the graduate education programs.

Location
Felician College's Lodi campus is located on the banks of the Saddle River on a beautifully landscaped campus of 27 acres and offers a collegiate setting in suburban Bergen County, within easy driving distance of New York City. The Felician College Rutherford Campus is set on 10.5 beautifully landscaped acres in the heart of the historic community of Rutherford, New Jersey. Only 15 minutes from the Lodi campus, the Rutherford complex contains student residences, classroom buildings, a student center, and a gymnasium. The campus is a short distance from downtown Rutherford, where there are many shops and businesses of interest to students.

The College
Felician College, a coeducational liberal arts college, is a Catholic, private, independent institution for students representing diverse religious, racial, and ethnic backgrounds. The College operates on two campuses in Lodi and Rutherford, New Jersey. The College is one of the institutions of higher learning conducted by the Felician Sisters in the United States. Its mission is to provide a values-oriented education based in the liberal arts while it prepares students for meaningful lives and careers in contemporary society. To meet the needs of students and to provide personal enrichment courses to matriculated and nonmatriculated students, Felician College offers day, evening, and weekend programs. The College is accredited by the Middle States Association of Colleges and Schools and carries program accreditation from the National League for Nursing Accrediting Commission, the National Accrediting Agency for Clinical Laboratory Sciences, and the International Assembly for Collegiate Business Education.

Applying
Applicants must have a bachelor's and/or a master's degree awarded by an accredited college or university and a minimum 3.0 undergraduate cumulative grade point average. Students must submit the completed application, the $40 nonrefundable application fee, official transcripts from all colleges/universities previously attended, scores from the Miller Analogies Test, and three letters of recommendation.

Correspondence and Information
Programs in Education
Felician College
262 South Main Street
Lodi, New Jersey 07644-2117
Phone: 201-559-6077
Fax: 201-559-6138
E-mail: adultandgraduate@felician.edu
Web site: http://www.felician.edu/

Felician College

THE FACULTY

Donna Barron, Associate Professor and Dean of Teacher Education; Ph.D., Dayton.

Robert Brown, Instructor of Teacher Education; M.A., William Paterson; M.B.A., Fairleigh Dickinson.

Rosemarie Crownover, Instructor of Teacher Education; M.S., Fordham.

Anne DeGroot, Instructor of Teacher Education; M.Ed., William Paterson.

Kathleen DeNoble, Assistant Professor of Teacher Education; Ed.D., Nova Southeastern.

Lillian Garcia, Assistant Professor of Special Education; Psy.D., Yeshiva.

Deborah Herman, Instructor of Teacher Education; M.S., Fordham.

M. Robert Hillenbrand, Instructor of Teacher Education; M.A., Montclair State.

Willard Kobuskie, Instructor of Teacher Education; M.A., Columbia.

Rosemarie Liebmann, Assistant Professor of Teacher Education; Ed.D., Seton Hall.

Julie Norflus-Good, Assistant Professor of Teacher Education; Ed.D., Columbia.

Annette Rycharski, Instructor of Teacher Education and Director, Placement and Certification; M.S., St. John's (New York).

Mary Anne Witowski, Assistant Professor of Teacher Education and Chair of Elementary Education; M.A., St. John's (New York).

FLORIDA INTERNATIONAL UNIVERSITY

College of Education

Programs of Study	The College of Education at Florida International University (FIU) exists in an urban, multicultural setting and has a three-part mission: to prepare professionals to facilitate and enhance learning and development within diverse settings; to discover and disseminate knowledge related to learning, teaching, and development; and to develop professional partnerships to promote meaningful educational, social, economic, and political change.

The College has received one of the highest endorsements available to colleges of education with approval by the National Council for Accreditation of Teacher Education NCATE. It offers more than forty programs at the graduate level in four departments: Curriculum and Instruction; Educational and Psychological Studies; Educational Leadership and Policy Studies; and Health, Physical Education and Recreation. Programs of advanced study include the Master of Science (M.S.), Education Specialist (Ed.S.), Doctor of Education (Ed.D.), and Doctor of Philosophy (Ph.D.) degrees.

Master's degrees provide specialization in a variety of fields and include courses, seminars, field experiences, and research projects selected to meet the student's level and area of emphasis. The Ed.S. degree is available for professionals seeking an advanced degree for professional development and/or career advancement. Some of the programs lead to state certification. Ed.D. programs are offered in curriculum and instruction, educational leadership, adult education and human resource development, higher education, and special education. A Ph.D. is offered in curriculum and instruction. The Ph.D. program is uniquely geared to applicants whose career goals are expected to include research or other careers where demands are made for expertise in specialized areas.

The Department of Curriculum and Instruction offers a Master in the Art of Teaching (M.A.T.) degree for persons without a background in teaching and the M.S. degree for those individuals already certified as teachers. Ed.S., Ed.D., and Ph.D. degrees are also offered. Programs of study include early childhood education (age 3 to grade 3), elementary education (grades 1–6), middle school education, secondary level education, and an advanced master's program in reading and in teaching English to speakers of other languages (TESOL). For more information, students should visit the Web site at http://www.fiu.edu/graduate.htm.

The Department of Educational and Psychological Studies offers programs that provide the knowledge and skills necessary for the practice of special education, counselor education, and school psychology professions. The department offers M.A.T., M.S., and Ed.D. degrees in special education. The M.S. in counselor education is offered, with specialization tracks in school, community mental health, and rehabilitation counseling. A specialist degree in school psychology is also available. In addition, the department offers graduate level courses in educational psychology, research, methodology, program evaluation, and measurement. For more information, students should visit the Web site at http://www.fiu.edu/ graduate.htm.

The Department of Educational Leadership and Policy Studies offers preparation for leadership at the highest levels in colleges, universities, educational settings, and in business and nonprofit settings. The department empowers professional educators and leaders through the acquisition of knowledge, skills, and attitudes to promote individual and organizational change. The department offers the M.S., Ed.S., and Ed.D. degrees in a number of specialties, including adult education and human resource development, educational administration, higher education, and international education. For more information, students should visit the Web site at http://www.fiu.edu/ graduate.htm.

The Department of Health, Physical Education and Recreation offers M.S. degrees in exercise and sports sciences, parks and recreation management, and physical education, with specializations in athletic training, exercise physiology, leisure service management, sports management, strength and conditioning, and therapeutic recreation. Students should visit the Web site at http://www.fiu.edu/ graduate.htm for additional information. |
Research Facilities	The College of Education is home to four important research centers. The Center for Urban Education and Innovation is a leading force in addressing critical issues facing urban schools. Programs and activities focus on improving student achievement, enhancing the quality and responsiveness of schools as learning organizations, and contributing to the development of theory and practice in areas addressing the needs of students and families from diverse racial, cultural, socioeconomic, and linguistic backgrounds. The Center for Labor Research and Studies promotes research, curriculum development, teaching, and community service in labor-management relations across the state. A variety of programs and projects are undertaken, including credit and noncredit classes, conferences, research, and a publication series. The Intercultural Institute for Education Initiatives conducts and promotes activities that support global awareness and strengthen communities to link diverse groups across cultural, geographic, sectoral, and racial divides. The Institute for Workforce Competitiveness provides services and resources in research, evaluation, and technical assistance for workforce development and education reform initiatives, such as Tech Prep and School-to-Work.
Financial Aid	Financial aid in the form of grants, scholarships, assistantships, fellowships, loans, and work-study is awarded on the basis of academic achievement and/or financial need. More information can be obtained online at http://www.fiu.edu/orgs/finaid/. Prospective students should contact their department about assistantships. For scholarship information, students should visit the Web site at http://www.fiu.edu/gradadm/scholarships.html.
Cost of Study	For the 2006–07 academic year, tuition cost $249.16 per credit hour for Florida residents and $753.22 per credit hour for nonresidents. Tuition and fees are established by the State University System Board of Regents and are subject to change without notice.
Living and Housing Costs	Housing and Residential Life provides housing for students at both the University Park and Biscayne Bay campuses. For more information regarding services and accommodations, students should visit the Web site at http://www.fiu.edu/~housing.
Student Group	In fall 2006, Florida International University enrollment was approximately 38,000 and included students from almost all fifty states and more than 130 other countries. The student body is a microcosm of the diverse Miami community, with nearly 70 percent of the student enrollment from minority groups: 51 percent Hispanic, 14 percent black, and 3.5 percent Asian. International students comprise approximately 10 percent of the student population.
Student Outcomes	The College of Education's alumni play an influential role in the local community, the state, and throughout the U.S. Sixty percent of the graduates are teachers, principals, superintendents, and other administrators in the Miami–Dade County Public Schools. More than 25 percent of the new teachers hired each year by Miami–Dade County Public Schools are FIU graduates. FIU graduates are leaders in school systems and agencies throughout Florida and around the nation.
Location	FIU has two major campuses, University Park in western Miami-Dade County and the Biscayne Bay Campus in north Miami. The urban metropolis of Miami is a place of great contrast and cultural exchange. Students at FIU can take advantage of a breathtaking array of real-life opportunities both inside and outside the classroom.
The University	Florida International University—Miami's public research university—is one of America's most dynamic institutions of higher learning. The University has a nationally renowned faculty, known for their outstanding teaching and cutting-edge research; students from throughout the U.S. and more than 130 foreign countries; and alumni who have risen to prominence in every field and are a testament to the University's academic excellence. FIU has the highest research university ranking conferred by the Carnegie Foundation as well as a chapter of Phi Beta Kappa, the most prestigious academic honor society. The University offers more than 190 baccalaureate, master's, and doctoral degree programs in nineteen colleges and schools. FIU has approximately 34,000 students, 1,000 full-time faculty members, and 100,000 alumni, making it the largest public university in South Florida.
Applying	Graduate applications are processed within a department of Florida International University known as the University Graduate School (UGS). Applications may be completed online; there is no hard copy or downloadable version of the graduate application. Complete admission and application requirements can be found on the COE and UGS Web sites, and students are encouraged to review them before proceeding with the application. In addition, students should check with the department or program director of their program of interest to determine if there are special admission requirements. Special admission requirements may include interviews, portfolios, or other materials that are not included in the UGS online process. Program specific admission requirements can be found at http://education.fiu.edu/graduate.htm. The online application for graduate admission can be found at the UGS Web site at http://gradschool.fiu.edu.
Correspondence and Information	College of Education
Sanford and Dolores Ziff and Family Education Building (ZEB)
Florida International University–University Park
11200 S.W. 8th Street
Miami, Florida 33199
Phone: 305-348-3002
Web site: http://education.fiu.edu/

Florida International University

THE FACULTY

Judith A. Blucker, Interim Dean; Ph.D., Florida State.
Adriana McEachern, Associate Dean of Academic Affairs; Ph.D., Florida State.
Robert M. Wolff, Associate Dean; Ph.D., Ohio State.
Carmen Mendez, Assistant Dean of Budget; M.P.A., Florida International.

Dawn Addy, Director; Ph.D., Minnesota.
Cengiz Alacaci, Associate Professor; Ph.D., Pittsburgh.
Carlos M. Alvarez, Associate Professor; Ph.D., Florida.
Benjamin Baez, Associate Professor; Ph.D., Syracuse.
Kingsley Banya, Professor; Ph.D., Toronto.
Patricia Barbetta, Associate Professor; Ph.D., Ohio State.
Nicholas Benson, Associate Professor; Ph.D., Florida.
Linda P. Blanton, Professor; Ed.D., Indiana.
Charles Bleiker, Associate Professor; Ph.D., Stanford.
Leonard Bliss, Professor; Ph.D., Syracuse.
Laura Blitzer, Associate Professor; Ph.D., Georgia.
Judith A. Blucker, Professor; Ph.D., Florida State.
David Y. Chang, Professor; M.F.A., M.S., Florida International.
Peter J. Cistone, Professor; Ph.D., Penn State.
Michelle A. Cleary, Assistant Professor; Ph.D., Temple.
Judith Cohen, Director; Ed.D., Florida International.
Elizabeth D. Cramer, Assistant Professor; Ph.D., Miami (Florida).
Charmaine DeFrancesco, Associate Professor; Ph.D., Florida State.
Lisa Delpit, Professor; Ed.D., Harvard.
Frank DiVesta, Coordinator; Ph.D., Cornell.
Erskine S. Dottin, Professor; Ph.D., Miami (Ohio).
Eric Dwyer, Associate Professor; Ph.D., Texas.
Mohammed K. Farouk, Associate Professor; Ed.D., West Virginia.
Joyce C. Fine, Associate Professor; Ed.D., Florida International.
Paul D. Gallagher, Associate Professor; Ph.D., Florida State.
Delia C. Garcia, Associate Professor; Ed.D., Florida International.
Roger Geertz Gonzalez, Assistant Professor; Ph.D., Penn State.
Gail P. Gregg, Associate Professor; Ph.D., Florida State.
Thomas Humphries, Associate Director; M.S., Florida International.
Lynn Ilon, Associate Professor; Ph.D., Florida State.
Gaetane Jean-Marie, Assistant Professor; Ph.D., North Carolina.
Maureen Kenny, Assistant Professor; Ph.D., Nova-Southeastern.
Sharon W. Kossack, Professor; Ph.D., Georgia.
Lisbeth Dixon Krauss, Associate Professor; Ph.D., Florida.
Hilary Landorf, Assistant Professor; Ph.D., NYU.
Philip J. Lazarus, Associate Professor; Ph.D., Florida.
Richard Lopez, Associate Professor; Ed.D., Florida Atlantic.
Luretha Lucky, Associate Professor; Ed.D., Arizona State.
Louis Manfra, Assistant Professor; Ph.D., George Mason.
Nancy Marshall, Associate Professor; Ph.D., Cornell.
Adriana McEachern, Associate Professor; Ph.D., Florida.
Alexis McKenney, Assistant Professor; Ph.D., Georgia.
Carmen Mendez, Instructor; M.P.A., Florida International.
Alicia Mendoza, Associate Professor; Ed.D., Miami (Florida).
Lynne D. Miller, Associate Professor; Ph.D., Arizona.
Dominic A. Mohamed, Professor; Ph.D., Minnesota.
Bryan Moseley, Assistant Professor; Ph.D., California, Santa Barbara.
Glenda Droogsma Musoba, Assistant Professor; Ph.D., Indiana.
Bruce Nissen, Director; Ph.D., Columbia.
Anthony H. Normore, Assistant Professor; Ph.D., Toronto.
George E. O'Brien, Associate Professor; Ph.D., Iowa.
Martha Pelaez, Professor; Ph.D., Florida International.
Aixa Perez-Prado, Assistant Professor; Ph.D., Florida State.
William M. Ritzi, Instructor; M.S., Florida International.
Tonette S. Rocco, Assistant Professor; Ph.D., Ohio State.
Louie Rodriguez, Assistant Professor; Ph.D., Harvard.
Howard Rosenberg, Associate Professor; Ed.D., Columbia Teachers College.
Janice R. Sandiford, Professor; Ph.D., Ohio State.
Monica Shealey, Assistant Professor; Ph.D., Central Florida.
Linda Spears-Bunton, Associate Professor; Ed.D., Kentucky.
Abbas Tashakkori, Professor; Ph.D., North Carolina at Chapel Hill.
M. O. Thirunarayanan, Associate Professor; Ph.D., Arizona State.
Jethro W. Toomer, Professor; Ph.D., Temple.
Brady Tripp, Assistant Professor; Ph.D., Kentucky.
Robert Vos, Associate Professor; Ed.D., Rutgers.
Joan Wynne, Associate Director; Ph.D., Georgia State.
Robert M. Wolff, Associate Professor; Ph.D., Ohio State.

FORDHAM UNIVERSITY

Graduate School of Education

Programs of Study

The Fordham University Graduate School of Education is a leader in the development of the knowledge and skills needed by teachers, counselors, psychologists, administrators, and other educators to prepare a diverse population for satisfying and productive lives in the twenty-first century. Its faculty members are committed to providing the skills necessary for practitioner-researchers to apply and expand theory to meet the changing demand of the multilingual, multicultural, urban environment. Fordham offers the following master's degree programs: early childhood education B–2, early childhood special education, bilingual childhood education, childhood education 1–6, childhood special education, literacy education B–6, literacy education 5–12, adolescence biology 7–12, adolescence chemistry 7–12, adolescence English 7–12, adolescence mathematics 7–12, adolescence physics 7–12, adolescence social studies 7–12, adult education and human resource development, counseling and personnel services, educational psychology, therapeutic interventions, and educational administration and supervision. Programs leading to the professional diploma, an advanced certificate degree, are offered in the fields of bilingual school psychology, school psychology, and teacher leadership. Doctor of Education programs are available in educational administration and supervision. Programs leading to the Doctor of Philosophy are offered in language, literacy, and learning; counseling psychology; educational psychology; school psychology; and educational administration and supervision. Programs in Catholic educational leadership and administration are offered at the master's and doctoral levels. In addition, the University offers middle childhood and bilingual extension certificates for all of its adolescence 7–12 programs. All graduate programs provide for participation in a core of urban multicultural studies and include ample opportunity for interrelating theory and practice through appropriate field activities. Students in the Graduate School of Education may also enroll in suitable courses in the Graduate School of Arts and Sciences, the Graduate School of Social Service, the Graduate School of Business Administration, and the Graduate School of Religion and Religious Education. The Graduate School of Education is accredited by the National Council for Accreditation of Teacher Education. In addition, the programs in early childhood are approved by the National Association for the Education of Young Children (NAEYC), the elementary education program by the Association of Childhood Education International (ACEI), and the reading and literacy programs by the Council for Exceptional Children (CEC). The doctoral programs in school psychology and counseling psychology are accredited by the American Psychological Association (APA). The school psychology program is approved by the National Association of School Psychologists (NASP). The School holds membership in the University Council of Educational Administration, the American Association of Colleges for Teacher Education, and the Council of Graduate Departments of Psychology.

Research Facilities

Fordham has library facilities at the Lincoln Center–Manhattan, Rose Hill–Bronx, and Westchester campuses. The Walsh Library (Rose Hill–Bronx) is the home of the Regional Educational Technology Center, which works with area educators to advance computer and information technology use in the classroom. The Graduate School of Education has the Psychological Services Institute, a Center for Technology in Education, and a computer center that is integrated with the University computer facilities. The School Consultation and the Early Childhood Centers provide psychoeducational services to children in the public and nonpublic schools. The Center for Catholic School Leadership offers programs with a special focus on skilled leadership in nonpublic education in several off-campus sites convenient to teachers and administrators in Catholic and other nonpublic schools. The National Center for Schools and Communities fosters service integration in public schools through collaboration among social work and education professionals in university training programs. The Center for Educational Partnerships provides services to teachers, administrators, students, and parents, as well as education and government agencies in an effort to enable all children to succeed. The Fordham University/New York City Leadership Network is a model of professional development experience for school leaders that reflects a vision of a learning community and engages school leaders in their own programs.

Financial Aid

Scholarships are available for most programs of study, and are merit- and need-based. The average award for full-time study (12 credits per semester) is approximately $2900 per semester. Assistantships are available in all divisions of the Graduate School of Education and provide tuition remission and/or stipends in return for service to the Graduate School of Education. The average assistantship covers the cost of two courses per year.

Cost of Study

Tuition for graduate courses is $875 per credit hour in 2007–08. Fees for other services are listed in the catalog.

Living and Housing Costs

A limited number of Fordham-subsidized studio and one-bedroom apartments are available near the campus.

Student Group

Enrollment in the Graduate School of Education is approximately 1,400 students. Minority candidates compose approximately 25 to 30 percent of the student population. A majority of students attend full-time and most are preparing for teaching or administrative positions in metropolitan elementary and secondary schools or for practitioner leadership positions in service-delivery systems. In addition, other students are preparing to work in a psychological context with diverse populations in a variety of settings.

Location

The Lincoln Center Campus is located in the heart of New York City, convenient to centers of finance, industry, community arts, and theater. The School is adjacent to the Lincoln Center for the Performing Arts, one of the world's most renowned cultural centers. The Westchester facility is located in Tarrytown, New York. Courses are also offered at the University's Rose Hill–Bronx campus and at a number of off-campus sites in Queens, Staten Island, the Bronx, and other locations.

The School

The Graduate School of Education is dedicated to broadening opportunities and meeting the challenges of urban education for children, ranging from the most academically talented to those struggling with basic education. The Graduate School of Education engages in cooperative programs and partnerships with schools in the area and with other professional schools and academic divisions of the University.

Applying

Admissions decisions for master's (except counseling and personnel services) and most professional diploma programs (except school psychology) are made throughout the year. The deadline for applying to the doctoral program in counseling psychology is December 15; the doctoral programs in educational psychology and school psychology and the professional diploma in school psychology, January 15; the master's program in counseling and personnel services, March 1; and the doctoral program in administration and supervision, March 15.

Applications for assistantships are due by February 1 (January 15 if admissions application is due January 15 or earlier); applications for scholarships are due by March 1 for fall and by October 15 for spring start dates. Application fees are $50 online and $100 hard copy.

Correspondence and Information

Office of Admissions
Graduate School of Education
Fordham University
113 West 60th Street, Room 1115
New York, New York 10023

Phone: 212-636-6400
E-mail: gse_admiss@fordham.edu
Web site: http://www.fordham.edu/gse

Fordham University

THE FACULTY

Graduate School of Education Administration
James J. Hennessy, Ph.D., NYU. Professor and Dean.
Vincent C. Alfonso, Ph.D., Hofstra. Professor and Associate Dean for Academic Affairs.
Anita Batisti, Ph.D., Fordham. Associate Dean for Educational Partnerships.
Michael McGrath, Ed.D., Fordham. Associate Dean for Administration and Westchester Campus.
Tamara Masson, M.S.W., Fordham. Assistant Dean for Administrative Services.
Linda Horisk, M.S.E., SUNY at New Paltz. Director of Admissions and Financial Aid.

Division of Educational Leadership, Administration, and Policy
Matt Bromme, M.S.E., Fordham. Instructional leadership, data-based instructional decision making.
Gerald Cattaro, Ph.D., Columbia. Administration, Catholic school leadership, nonpublic school policy.
Bruce S. Cooper, Ph.D., Chicago. School finance, restructuring, shared decision making, school choice, change processes.
Rita Guare, Ph.D., Fordham. Administration and supervision, leadership, religious education, aesthetics.
Barbara Jackson, Ed.D., Harvard. School/community/family partners, urban schools, women administrators, race and culture.
John Lee, Ed.D., NYU. Administration and supervision, superintendency, high school reform, educational leadership.
Sheldon Marcus, Ed.D., Yeshiva. Administration and supervision, college administration, multiculturalism.
Toby Tetenbaum, Ph.D., NYU. Human resource education, workplace issues and trends.

Division of Curriculum and Teaching
Anthony Baratta, Ed.D., Penn State. Curriculum and teaching, adult education, teacher education, multicultural education.
Jane Bolgatz, Ph.D., Iowa. Social studies education, multicultural education.
Rita Brause, Ed.D., NYU. Reading, literature and literacy education, teaching/learning, teacher research.
Diana Caballero, Ed.D., Columbia. Bilingual/multicultural education, equity and social justice, teacher education.
Angela Carrasquillo, Ph.D., NYU. ESL, language, literacy and learning, bilingual/second language education, multicultural education.
Su-Je Cho, Ph.D., California, Santa Barbara. Families with exceptional children, social and academic performance of Asian-American students.
Theresa Cicchelli, Ph.D., Syracuse. Professional development, teaching strategies: K–8, teaching/learning styles and processes.
Marshall George, Ed.D., Tennessee. Secondary English education, adolescent literature, secondary school curriculum.
Barbara P. Heuer, Ed.D., Georgia. Adult education, information literacy, adult development.
Roland Hughes, Ph.D., Fordham. Math education, curriculum and teaching, cognitive skills teaching, mathematics education K–12.
Kathleen P. King, Ed.D., Widener. Adult education, transformational learning, educational technology.
Usha Kotelawala, Ph.D., Columbia Teachers College. Math education, teacher attitudes and beliefs, reliability theory, professional development.
Kelley A. Lassman, Ph.D., Vanderbilt. Special education, adolescent language development, emotional and behavior disorders in children and youth, special education law.
Carolyn McGown, M.S., CUNY. Elementary and special education, new teacher training and retention.
Arlene Moliterno, Ph.D., Fordham. Language, literacy and learning, instructional technology, field supervision.
Molly Ness, Ph.D., Virginia. Reading comprehension, secondary literacy, effective instructional practices, achievement gap.
Aida Nevarez-La Torre, Ed.D., Harvard. Linguistic diversity in teacher preparation, practitioner research, literacy development in English language learners.
Terry Osborn, Ph.D., Connecticut. Critical pedagogy, world language education, educational linguistics.
Valerie Rowe, Ph.D., Fordham. Teacher preparation, reflective practitioner.
Patricia Shea-Bischoff, Ph.D., Fordham. Literacy, professional development, secondary teacher education.
Kristin Turner, Ph.D., Rutgers. Writing, connection between talk and writing, argumentative genres, transfer of knowledge.
Joanna Uhry, Ed.D., Columbia. Reading, initial teacher preparation, at-risk students, early literacy, reading.
Chun Zhang, Ph.D., Illinois at Urbana-Champaign. Early intervention, inclusion, family-centered practice, cultural and linguistic diversity, HS and EHS children, families and programs.

Division of Psychological and Educational Services
Francine Blumberg, Ph.D., Purdue. Educational psychology, attention and learning strategies.
Karen Brobst, Ph.D., Columbia. School psychology, learning strategies, parent education.
Anthony Cancelli, Ed.D., Oklahoma State. School psychology, behavioral intervention, consultation.
Eric C. Chen, Ph.D., Arizona State. Counseling psychology, career development, counseling supervision, cultural diversity.
Amelio D'Onofrio, Ph.D., Fordham. Psychodiagnostic assessment and evaluation, solution focused therapy, family therapy, couples therapy.
Giselle Esquivel, Psy.D., Yeshiva. School psychology, bilingual school psychology, gifted/talented/creative students, personality.
Elizabeth Finn, Ph.D., Fordham. Family involvement in early childhood literacy, adolescent intervention/substance use and abuse, neuropsychology/individual differences.
Jairo Fuertes, Ph.D., Maryland. Counseling, noncognitive variables in school success, Hispanic students.
Abigail Harris, Ph.D., Berkeley. School psychology, curriculum assessment, multicultural assessment, gender.
John Houtz, Ph.D., Purdue. Problem solving and creativity, gifted/talented teacher education, assessment and evaluation, statistical methods.
Margo Jackson, Ph.D., Stanford. Counseling psychology, career assessment and intervention, cultural diversity, attribution bias.
Merle Keitel, Ph.D., SUNY at Buffalo. Counseling psychology, grief and loss counseling, stress management, health psychology.
Sangwon Kim, Ph.D., Georgia. Cognitive assessment, measurement, and multicultural evaluation.
Zsuzsanna Kiraly, Ph.D., Fordham. School consultation and early childhood centers.
Jennie Park-Taylor, Ph.D., Boston College. Counseling psychology, acculturation, immigrant children, multicultural counseling, University-community collaboration.
Joseph Ponterotto, Ph.D., California, Santa Barbara. Counseling psychology, multicultural counseling.
Mitchell Rabinowitz, Ph.D., California, San Diego. Educational psychology, cognition, educational technology, metacognition.
Patricio Romero, Ph.D., St. John's. School psychology, aggression, victimization, role of ethnicity of the child, adolescent peer relations.
Akane Zusho, Ph.D., Michigan. Educational psychology, motivation, self-regulation, cultural diversity.

GRAND CANYON UNIVERSITY

College of Education

Programs of Study

The College of Education at Grand Canyon University offers the following on-campus graduate degree programs: Master of Education (M.Ed.) in elementary education, M.Ed. in secondary education, M.Ed. in education administration, M.Ed. in elementary school counseling, M.Ed. in secondary school counseling, and Master of Arts in Teaching (M.A.T.) (noncredentialed).

The M.Ed. in elementary education and M.Ed. in secondary education programs are designed for adult learners who have bachelor's degrees in areas other than teacher education and are interested in obtaining initial teacher certification. However, individuals who must postpone student teaching or who do not seek certification may also participate in these programs. The programs are arranged in accelerated, nontraditional formats, so the adult learner can complete either program in four or fewer semesters. Classes are offered in the evening using multiple methods of instruction that encourage mutual interaction with other working adults.

The M.Ed. in elementary education requires 45 credits: eleven required 3-credit courses and a 12-credit student teaching internship. The M.Ed. in secondary education degree program requires 30 total credits: six required 3-credit courses and a 12-credit student teaching internship.

The Master of Education in education administration is an Arizona state–approved program designed for educators seeking licensure as school principals. It is based upon the Arizona Professional Administrative Standards and the Interstate School Leaders Licensure Consortium Standards. The program requires 36 credits and internship hours under a practicing licensed school principal.

The Master of Arts in Teaching program (30 credits) is designed for certified elementary and secondary school teachers interested in advanced studies in education. The format and courses of the regionally accredited program are tailored to meet the needs of the adult learner and to maximize strengths that the student already possesses. Courses are taught by experts in their respective fields who share knowledge and experience in areas of instructional leadership, technology-enhanced instruction design, curriculum, and assessment for school improvement and legal issues. Opportunities are provided to apply concepts, theories, and research throughout the program. Assignments within each course guide students through observational and practice-based experiences. Students must have access to a K–12 classroom to complete the program assignments.

Research Facilities

Grand Canyon University consists of thirty-six buildings on a 90-acre campus. The campus features the Grand Canyon University Library, which houses a collection of more than 132,852 volumes, 58,895 periodicals, newspapers, microfilm, and audiovisual materials. Grand Canyon University Library is a member of the CCLC network and as a designated depository receives a variety of government documents. Library holdings are expanded by CD-ROM databases, computerized database searches, and interlibrary loans. Computers housed in the library have Internet access to assist students. Grand Canyon University also offers all students access to the Online Library.

There are two computer labs on campus, both outfitted with Dell OptiPlex computers and 17-inch monitors. The computer labs offer Internet access and a host of applications for use outside of the classroom. Each student has an individual login, which includes secured space on a server to store personal files. In addition to the lab computers, wireless access is available for students with laptops.

Financial Aid

Scholarships and grants are offered, and federal loan and work-study programs are also available. In addition, many companies and school districts offer assistance through Direct Bill, whereby GCU bills the student's employer directly.

Cost of Study

Tuition is $390 per credit.

Living and Housing Costs

In 2006–07, University apartments rented for $3160 to $4352 per semester. Individual costs depend on the size of the apartment and the number of roommates.

Student Outcomes

College of Education graduates are quick to be hired, sharing the best of reputations among principals and other administrators throughout Arizona.

Location

Grand Canyon University is located just minutes from Phoenix, Arizona's state capital and the sixth-largest city in the United States. Phoenix is the nerve center of the Southwest, one of the fastest-growing regions in the nation. The greater Phoenix metropolitan area, known as the "Valley of the Sun" for its more than 300 days of sunshine each year, offers numerous educational, social, cultural, and recreational activities that enhance University life.

The University

Grand Canyon University has a fifty-five-year tradition of excellence in education and is Arizona's only private, accredited Christian university. Based in Phoenix, the University offers four-year liberal arts, sciences, business, Christian studies, and nursing undergraduate degrees as well as master's degree programs in business, education, Christian studies, and nursing. Thousands of students from around the nation and the world come to Grand Canyon University each year—creating a diverse student life and intriguing classroom experiences.

Applying

Master of Education degree candidates must submit to the College of Education a completed graduate application, official transcripts from all regionally accredited colleges or universities attended, and a $100 application fee. A cumulative undergraduate GPA of at least 2.8 is required.

Correspondence and Information

Grand Canyon University
3300 West Camelback Road
Phoenix, Arizona 85017
Phone: 800-800-9776 (toll-free)
E-mail: admissionsground@gcu.edu
Web site: http://www.gcu.net/petersons

Grand Canyon University

THE FACULTY

The faculty members are highly qualified in their respective fields, having garnered many awards as authors, presenters, and teachers. They all have significant experience in the K–12 school system, and many adjunct faculty members hold concurrent employment in classrooms and in administrative positions. They give individual attention to students, stress mutual interaction with others, and use cutting-edge, research-based pedagogy to convey the most current information. Multiple methods of instruction are utilized to meet the needs of all students. Course content is rigorous, purposeful, and focused on the adult learner.

HARVARD UNIVERSITY

Graduate School of Education

Programs of Study

The Harvard Graduate School of Education (HGSE) offers programs of study leading to the Doctor of Education (Ed.D.) and the Master of Education (Ed.M.). The Ed.D. prepares leaders to understand research, policy, and practice, as well as the relationships among them. Graduates are prepared to assume roles as faculty members, senior-level educational leaders, policy makers, and researchers. Within the doctoral program, students are able to enroll in one of six possible concentrations: culture, communities, and education; education policy, leadership, and instructional practice; higher education; human development and education; quantitative policy analysis in education; and urban superintendents program. The Ed.D. generally requires two years of full-time course work, followed by the completion of a qualifying paper and a dissertation.

The Ed.M. is designed to be a yearlong intensive program for students who wish to study a particular field in education, obtain licensure, acquire a general theoretical background for understanding past and future experiences, and/or develop skills as a professional educator. Ed.M. program offerings include: arts in education; education policy and management; higher education; human development and psychology; international education policy; language and literacy; learning and teaching; mind, brain, and education; risk and prevention; school leadership; special studies; technology, innovation, and education; and teacher education.

Research Facilities

The Monroe C. Gutman Library is one of more than 90 libraries in the Harvard library system and holds nearly 200,000 volumes relating directly to education. With more than 15 million volumes, the Harvard library system constitutes one of the largest university library systems in the world. Much of the research conducted by the faculty takes place in schools and organizations throughout Boston and around the world. Examples of research projects at HGSE include the Center on the Developing Child, the Dynamic Development Laboratory, the Harvard Family Research Project, the Jeanne Chall Reading Lab, the National Center for the Study of Adult Learning and Literacy, the Project on the Next Generation of Teachers, Project Zero, the Project for Policy Innovation in Education, the Public Education Leadership Project, the Collaborative on Academic Careers in Higher Education, and Understanding the Roots of Tolerance and Prejudice.

Financial Aid

HGSE offers a number of financial aid programs to assist students in financing the cost of education. Financial support at the doctoral level may include: tuition and health fee funding for the first three years of study, merit-based Presidential Fellowships, dissertation support grants, low-interest federal loans, and employment opportunities including the Teaching Fellowship Program, the Teacher Education Advisors Program, and Research Assistantships. Master's students may be eligible for merit-based fellowships, need-based grants, low-interest federal loans, and employment opportunities, including the Federal Work-Study Program and Field Experience Program (i.e., academic internships).

Cost of Study

Tuition for the 2007–08 academic year is $31,696. The cost of books and supplies averages $1886, and health insurance costs $2788 annually.

Living and Housing Costs

Students can choose to live in graduate student residence halls or dorms, Harvard-affiliated housing (studios to three-bedroom apartments), or off-campus housing in the Cambridge and Boston areas. Room and board for the 2007–08 academic year is estimated at $13,905.

Student Group

Students come to HGSE from all walks of professional life, bringing with them a variety of perspectives and experiences that enable them to engage deeply in dialogues about critical issues in education both in and out of the classroom. The class admitted for the 2006–07 academic year came from forty states and thirty-two countries and included 11 percent international students and 24 percent students of color. Students come to HGSE after serving as teachers, school and district administrators, policymakers, counselors, researchers, program directors, and college and university administrators. Others have experience in educational media, government, community social service agencies, health organizations, and the corporate sector. Master's degree recipients go on to work in public and private schools, educational service agencies, government, media and technology firms, international organizations, research and consulting firms, museums, foundations and corporations; some elect to go on for further graduate study. Doctoral students bring a combination of proven leadership experience and research experience, and recipients of the Ed.D. often seek positions as university faculty members, senior-level educational leaders, policy makers, and researchers.

Location

HGSE's location in Cambridge and near Boston makes it an ideal setting for graduate study in education. Faculty members and students are able to take advantage of the many schools (e.g., public, private, and charter), colleges and universities, and organizations as sites for internships and research. Harvard University's setting permits a variety of seasonal outdoor activities, and its proximity to Boston adds symphonies, ballet, opera, museums, live theater, music, and restaurants to the wealth of cultural opportunities already available in Cambridge.

The University and The School

Founded in 1636, Harvard University is a private institution named in honor of John Harvard, a young minister who left his library and half his estate to the new institution. Harvard comprises ten graduate and professional schools. It has a teaching faculty of about 2,500 and an enrollment of approximately 20,000 undergraduate and graduate degree candidates.

Since its founding in 1920, the Graduate School of Education has been training leaders to transform education in the United States and around the globe. Today, HGSE faculty members, students, and alumni are studying and solving the most critical challenges facing education: student assessment, the achievement gap, urban education, and teacher shortages, to name just a few. Their work is shaping how people lead, learn, and teach in schools and colleges as well as in after-school programs, high-tech companies, and international organizations. In addition to degree study, HGSE offers countless opportunities for professional development. Programs in professional education, the Principals' Center, and a variety of institutes and partnerships integrate the larger community in a shared commitment to lifelong learning. These programs make a difference in the lives of students, in the work of institutions, and in the practice of educators. The HGSE community is pushing the frontiers of education, and the effects of its entrepreneurship are improving the world.

Applying

Information and applications for admission and financial aid can be found on the HGSE Web site. Applicants are evaluated on the basis of their statement of purpose, work experience, fit with a program, letters of recommendation, academic record, and GRE scores, which must be from a test administered on or after February 1, 2003. Applicants whose native language is not English and whose baccalaureate degree is from an institution where English is not the language of instruction must also submit TOEFL scores from a test administered no earlier than February 1, 2006. The online submission and transcript receipt deadline for Ed.D. application materials is December 14, 2007, while the deadline for Ed.M. application materials is January 4, 2008. Decisions will be made available electronically in March. The deadline for all financial aid applications is February 1, 2008.

Correspondence and Information

Harvard Graduate School of Education
Admissions Office
111 Longfellow Hall
13 Appian Way
Cambridge, Massachusetts 02138
Phone: 617-495-3414
Fax: 617-496-3577
E-mail: gseadmissions@harvard.edu
Web site: http://www.gse.harvard.edu

Harvard University

THE FACULTY AND THEIR RESEARCH

Joseph Blatt, Lecturer; Ed.M., Harvard. Educational media, technology, schools.

Christopher Dede, Professor; Ed.D., Massachusetts Amherst. Technology in education.

John Diamond, Assistant Professor; Ph.D., Northwestern. Sociology of education, educational equity, family issues, urban schooling.

Eleanor Duckworth, Professor; Docteur en sciences de l'éducation, Geneva. Experience of teachers and learners of all ages both in and out of schools.

Catherine Z. Elgin, Professor; Ph.D., Brandeis. Philosophy of education, philosophy of language, philosophy of science, philosophy of art.

Richard Elmore, Professor; Ed.D., Harvard. Effects of educational policy on schools and classrooms.

Kurt Fischer, Professor; Ph.D., Harvard. Development and change, relations between cognitive development and brain change.

Vanessa Fong, Assistant Professor; Ph.D., Harvard. China's one-child policy, cultural studies, immigrant issues.

Howard Gardner, Professor; Ph.D., Harvard. Development of human symbol-using capacities, nature and assessment of human intelligences, growth and nurturance of creativity, good work.

Paul L. Harris, Professor; D.Phil., Oxford. Children's understanding of reality versus fantasy, theory of mind, children's emotional development and understanding of emotions.

Thomas Hehir, Professor of Practice; Ed.D., Harvard. School leadership, learning disorders, reform issues, special education.

Monica Higgins, Associate Professor; Ph.D., Harvard. Leadership development, organizational change.

Susan Moore Johnson, Professor; Ed.D., Harvard. Effects of educational policies on schools.

Matthew Jukes, Assistant Professor; Ph.D., Oxford. Health and education, international education, poverty and children.

Thomas Kane, Professor; Ph.D., Harvard. Education policy, program evaluation, economics.

Robert Kegan, Professor; Ph.D., Harvard. Adult education and the development of mental capacities throughout the life span.

Daniel Koretz, Professor; Ph.D., Cornell. Educational assessment, particularly as a tool of educational policy.

Ellen Condliffe Lagemann, Professor; Ph.D., Columbia. History of education.

Sara Lawrence-Lightfoot, Professor; Ed.D., Harvard. Sociology of education, relationships between culture and schools, family issues.

Nonie Lesaux, Assistant Professor; Ph.D., British Columbia. Reading development, bilingual education, learning disorders.

Richard Light, Professor; Ph.D., Harvard. Using statistical information to improve quality of services (e.g., education), testing, higher education curriculum.

Bridget Terry Long, Associate Professor; Ph.D., Harvard. Economics of higher education.

Vivian Shuh Ming Louie, Assistant Professor; Ph.D., Yale. Immigrant issues, cultural studies, achievement issues, racial discrimination.

Wendy Luttrell, Associate Professor; Ph.D., California, Santa Cruz. School ethnography; gender, race, class, and sexual identities and schooling process; teenage sexuality, pregnancy, self, and schooling.

Pamela A. Mason, Lecturer; Ed.D., Harvard. Reading comprehension, issues of literacy learning for diverse student populations, process of developing effective schoolwide literacy programs.

Kathleen McCartney, Professor and Dean; Ph.D., Yale. Children's development, poverty and children, policy analysis and evaluation, early childhood development, parenting issues, day care, family issues, psychology.

Judith Block McLaughlin, Senior Lecturer; Ed.D., Harvard. Higher education administration, leadership transitions, presidential assessment, politics of school structure and governance.

Katherine K. Merseth, Senior Lecturer; Ed.D., Harvard. Teacher education and certification, professional development for educators, politics of school structure and governance, reform issues, mathematics education.

Richard Murnane, Professor; Ph.D., Yale. Teacher labor markets, education and the economy, quantitative research methods.

Jerome T. Murphy, Professor; Ed.D., Harvard. Administrative practice and organizational leadership, government policy, politics of education.

Thomas W. Payzant, Professor of Practice; Ed.D., Harvard. Urban education, achievement gap, systemic reform.

David N. Perkins, Professor; Ph.D., MIT. Cognitive psychology and education, emphasizing learning for understanding and the active, thoughtful use of knowledge; research and development translating cognitive science into educational practice, emphasizing psychologically informed instruction that also takes into account classroom realities.

Robert S. Peterkin, Professor; Ed.D., Massachusetts Amherst. Urban superintendents program, school choice, school governance, impact of school reform on achievement of African-American children, educational equity issues.

Mica Pollock, Associate Professor; Ph.D., Stanford. Race, ethnicity, national origin, inequality, discrimination, diversity, civil rights, theory and method in the anthropological study of difference.

Fernando Reimers, Professor of Practice; Ed.D., Harvard. Education policy reform and implementation of educational change in developing countries, focusing on improvement of equity; education and poverty in Latin America.

Julie Reuben, Professor; Ph.D., Stanford. History of American education.

S. Paul Reville, Lecturer; Ed.M., Stanford. School reform, education policy analysis and evaluation, educational equity and standards.

Melinda Savitz-Romer, Lecturer; Ph.D., Boston College. College access and retention for urban students, early college planning and awareness, school counselor development, K-16 policies and reform, school-university partnerships.

Sally Schwager, Lecturer; Ed.D., Harvard. History of education, women's studies, teacher education and certification.

Steven Seidel, Lecturer; Ed.D., Harvard. Arts in education, assessment, curriculum development, professional development for teachers.

Robert Selman, Professor; Ph.D., Boston University. Growth of interpersonal understanding and behavior, particularly of both normal and emotionally troubled preadolescents and early adolescents.

Jack P. Shonkoff, Professor; M.D., New York. Intersection of science, policy, and practice; the developing child; child care policy.

Judith Singer, Professor; Ph.D., Harvard. Developing better quantitative methods for addressing questions of educational relevance.

Catherine Snow, Professor; Ph.D., McGill. Infant development and language acquisition, cross-cultural differences in parent-child interaction, role of children's experiences in contributing to school achievement, acquisition of reading skills.

Terrence Tivnan, Lecturer; Ed.D., Harvard. Quantitative research methods and data analysis, child development, educational psychology.

John Willett, Professor; Ph.D., Stanford. Improving statistical methodology in use in education, psychological and social research.

Hirokazu Yoshikawa, Professor; Ph.D., New York. Development of young children in immigrant families, effects of public policies (particularly antipoverty policies and early childhood intervention) on children's development.

HOFSTRA UNIVERSITY

School of Education and Allied Human Services

Programs of Study

Hofstra University offers 155 graduate degree programs—each designed to give students the edge they need to succeed.

The School of Education and Allied Human Services offers a wide range of professional diploma, certificate, and graduate degree programs in the areas of education, health, and human services. The following degrees are offered: Master of Arts (M.A.), Master of Science (M.S.), Master of Health Administration (M.H.A.), Master of Science in Education (M.S.Ed.), Doctor of Education (Ed.D.), and Doctor of Philosophy (Ph.D.).

Building on the strength of its existing programs, the School recently announced the following new programs, which are planned to launch in fall 2007: Ed.D. in learning and teaching; M.S. in educational leadership and policy studies, concentration in higher education; and Certificate of Advanced Studies in educational leadership: school district business leadership (SDBL), which qualifies students for New York State school district business leader (SDBL) certification. The School also recently added two programs leading to a New York state licensure qualifying degree: an M.A. in mental health counseling and an M.S.Ed. in rehabilitation counseling in mental health. In addition, the School revised its Master of Arts in creative arts therapy and Master of Arts in marriage and family therapy programs to also qualify for licensure.

The School of Education and Allied Human Services' programs are accredited by the National Council for Accreditation of Teacher Education (NCATE). In addition, individual programs are approved by professional organizations such as the American Art Therapy Association and the Council on Rehabilitation Education.

Research Facilities

Hofstra's graduate programs are supported by extensive academic resources and state-of-the-art facilities.

The Hofstra libraries contain 1.4 million print volumes and provide 24/7 electronic access to more than 50,000 journals and electronic books. Hagedorn Hall, home of the School of Education and Allied Human Services, is a new building that provides a technology-rich learning environment, complete with interactive whiteboards, computer-driven instructor stations, and wireless communication.

Students have the opportunity to participate in programs conducted by the Institute for the Development of Education in the Advanced Sciences (IDEAS) and to work at the Joan and Arnold Saltzman Community Services Center, which comprises an accredited child care institute, marriage and family clinic, psychological evaluation clinic, reading/writing clinic, and speech-language-hearing clinic. Internships and student teaching offer additional research and experience.

Financial Aid

Financial aid is available in the form of fellowships, scholarships, grants, loans, and graduate assistantship positions. All applicants for financial assistance must file the Free Application for Federal Student Aid (FAFSA). Information about financial aid for graduate students may be obtained from the Office of Financial Aid or the graduate academic departments.

Cost of Study

Tuition is $790 per credit hour in 2007–08. University fees range from $78 to $300 each semester, depending on the number of credits taken.

Living and Housing Costs

The cost of housing in University residence halls for 2007–08 ranges from $2775 to $6000 per semester, depending on the type of accommodation. Board prices range from $495 to $1700 per semester, depending on the plan chosen. The Office of Residential Life maintains listings of available off-campus accommodations.

Student Group

The 2,900 students enrolled in Hofstra's graduate programs form a dynamic group that is ethnically, culturally and geographically diverse. These students represent twenty-six states and nineteen countries. About 15 percent are members of minority groups, 3 percent are international students, and 69 percent are women. Many students in these graduate programs have previous work experience.

Student Outcomes

The School of Education and Allied Human Services is committed to attracting strong candidates and to assisting them in locating employment after graduation. The Hofstra Career Center offers a wide range of services, including career counseling, assistance with resume writing, mock interviews, a job referral service, and extensive electronic links to education career information.

Location

Hofstra's distinctive 240-acre campus, a registered arboretum, is located in suburban Long Island, just 25 miles from New York City.

With New York City just a short ride away, students take advantage of the museums, concerts and professional sports as well as internships the city offers. Students can also explore Long Island, which offers spectacular beaches, museums, and internship opportunities.

The University

Hofstra University is a dynamic private institution where students find their edge to succeed in 140 undergraduate and 155 graduate programs in the liberal arts and sciences, business, communication, education and allied human services, and law.

With an outstanding faculty, advanced technological resources, and state-of-the-art facilities, Hofstra has a growing national reputation. Yet the average graduate class size is just 13, ensuring that students receive the personal attention they deserve.

Applying

Candidates generally are required to complete the graduate application and all supporting forms and to submit two letters of recommendation, a statement of professional objectives, official transcripts from every college or university attended, and scores obtained on the Graduate Record Examination (GRE). International students must also submit scores obtained on the TOEFL. Application requirements vary depending on the program. For further information, candidates should contact the Office of Graduate Admissions or individual departments. Applicants may file online or by mail.

Correspondence and Information

Office of Graduate Admissions
126 Hofstra University
105 Memorial Hall
Hofstra University
Hempstead, New York 11549-1260
Phone: 516-463-4723
      800-HOFSTRA Ext. 624 (toll-free)
Fax: 516-463-4664
E-mail: graddean@hofstra.edu
Web site: http://www.hofstra.edu/graduate

Hofstra University

DEPARTMENT CHAIRPERSONS

Counseling, Research, Special Education, and Rehabilitation
Darra Pace, Associate Professor and Chairperson; Ed.D., Hofstra, 2000.

Curriculum and Teaching
Judith Kaufman, Associate Professor and Chairperson; Ph.D., SUNY, Albany, 1989.
Alan Singer, Professor and Assistant Chairperson; Ph.D., Rutgers, 1982.

Foundations, Leadership, and Policy Studies
Karen Osterman, Professor and Chairperson; Ph.D., Washington, 1984.

Health Professions and Family Studies
Michael Ludwig, Associate Professor and Chairperson; Ph.D., Penn State, 1994.

Literacy Studies
Debra Goodman, Associate Professor and Chairperson; Ph.D., Michigan State, 1999.

Physical Education and Sports Sciences
Nancy Halliday, Associate Professor and Chairperson; Ph.D., Temple, 1992.

INDIANA UNIVERSITY

School of Education

Programs of Study

The School of Education core campus at Indiana University Bloomington and Indiana University–Purdue University Indianapolis (IUPUI) offers nationally recognized programs leading to the degrees of Master of Science in Education, Specialist in Education, Doctor of Education (Ed.D.), and Doctor of Philosophy (Ph.D.).

Most graduate programs are offered on the Bloomington residential campus. The Master of Science in Education degree is offered in art education; counseling and counselor education; educational psychology; elementary and early childhood education; higher education; history and philosophy of education; instructional systems technology; international and comparative education; language education; educational leadership; secondary education, with tracks in mathematics education and science education; social studies education; special education; and students affairs administration. The Specialist in Education degree is offered in counseling and counselor education, elementary and early childhood education, instructional systems technology, language education, educational leadership, school psychology, secondary education, and special education. The Ph.D. is offered in counseling psychology; curriculum and instruction, with tracks in art education, curriculum studies, mathematics education and science education; learning and developmental sciences; school psychology; higher education; history, philosophy, and policy studies; instructional systems technology; language education; and special education.

On the Indianapolis campus, master's degrees are offered in the school track in counseling and counselor education, elementary education, language education, secondary education, and special education. Doctoral-level course work is available in educational leadership and higher education.

All programs in teacher preparation and educational leadership have full accreditation from the National Council for Accreditation of Teacher Education (NCATE). In addition, the Indiana Professional Standards Board has accepted all teacher education programs. The American Psychological Association has approved the school psychology and counseling psychology programs.

Research Facilities

The Bloomington campus is a major research center where leading scholars investigate national and international educational issues. The Indianapolis campus provides the opportunity to study in a major urban and policy center and to work in diverse school settings. Research facilities in Bloomington include the Wright Education Building, featuring a distance education studio/classroom, multimedia laboratories, and many other specialized educational settings; the Education Library, containing an extensive collection of 70,000 monographs and journals; and access to the ERIC Clearinghouse for Social Studies/Social Science Education and the ERIC Clearinghouse on Reading, English, and Communication, as well as educational research centers. A highlight of the Indianapolis campus is the state-of-the-art electronic library that allows researchers access to information worldwide. The campus has been a leader in the application of computer and video technology, including a distance education studio/classroom located in the School of Education.

Financial Aid

Graduate students may qualify for financial assistance, including teaching and research assistantships, fellowships, fee remission scholarships, hourly appointments, and loans. Most doctoral students are able to secure graduate research or teaching assistantships. Fellowships and scholarships may be granted to doctoral students with superior academic credentials. Students from underrepresented groups may receive financial assistance through the School of Education and the University Graduate School fellowship office. Additional student support opportunities are available through financial aid offices on each campus.

Cost of Study

In 2007–08, tuition for Indiana residents is $269 per graduate credit hour. For nonresidents, tuition is $784 per graduate credit hour.

Living and Housing Costs

The cost of living in Bloomington and Indianapolis is comparable to other Midwestern college campuses. In 2006–07, students paid $6375 per semester for room and board in a residence hall or $700 a month to rent a furnished efficiency apartment, including utilities, on the Bloomington campus. A furnished, two-bedroom apartment, suitable for married students, ranges from $850 to $900 a month, including utilities. Students also live nearby in off-campus housing. Campus housing is very limited in Indianapolis.

Student Group

About 2,300 graduate students attend the School of Education. These students come from all the states and from many other countries. More than 625 doctoral students, 465 master's degree students, and 250 graduate licensure students are enrolled in course work in Bloomington. Graduate students enrolled in Indianapolis include 450 working toward degrees and 475 preparing for teacher licensure.

Location

Bloomington is an exciting college town featuring top-notch athletic and cultural events. The rolling hills of southern Indiana offer excellent recreational facilities within an hour of campus. City life is nearby with Indianapolis only 50 miles away. The modern Indianapolis campus is located close to cultural attractions, including a symphony orchestra, repertory theater, and museums as well as many amateur and professional athletic activities.

The School

Established in 1852, the School of Education has a long and distinguished history of service to the state and nation, preparing educators for a broad spectrum of professional responsibilities in classrooms, laboratories, and administrative offices. In national rankings of research productivity and quality of academic programs, the School is acclaimed as one of the leading educational institutions in the world. Its full-time faculty is composed of 115 professors in Bloomington and 38 professors in Indianapolis.

Applying

Applications for master's degrees must be submitted to the campus where the degree is offered. Applications to all Ph.D., Ed.D., and specialist degree programs must be submitted to the Bloomington office. Applicants are encouraged to apply online (http://www.indiana.edu/educate/~appadvice.html), although paper applications are available upon request. An application must include completed application forms, two or three letters of recommendation (depending on the program), a personal goal statement explaining academic and career objectives, transcripts from all colleges and universities attended, GRE test scores, an application fee, and other materials as required by the degree program. Admission application fees for U.S. citizens and permanent residents are $55 at Bloomington and $45 at IUPUI; for international students, the fees are $65 at both campuses.

Correspondence and Information

Office of Graduate Studies
Wright Education Building, Room 4214
Indiana University
201 North Rose Avenue
Bloomington, Indiana 47405-1006
Phone: 812-856-8504
Fax: 812-856-8505
E-mail: educate@indiana.edu
Web site: http://www.indiana.edu/~educate

Office of Student Services
Education/Social Work Building, Room 3122
Indiana University–Purdue University Indianapolis
902 West New York Street
Indianapolis, Indiana 46202-5155
Phone: 317-274-6812
Fax: 317-274-6864
Web site: http://www.iupui.edu

Indiana University

THE DEPARTMENTS AND AREAS OF RESEARCH

BLOOMINGTON CAMPUS

Department of Counseling and Educational Psychology. Chair: Joyce Alexander, Education 4008, 812-856-8301/8322. Programs offered include counseling and counselor education, educational psychology, counseling psychology, and school psychology. Students gain valuable insights through interactive video applications for behavioral observation and analysis of classroom environments. Faculty members and students in these programs investigate questions about personal, social, and cognitive development; learning and instructional psychology; qualitative and quantitative research methodology; and interventions for academic and emotional problems in school, family, and social settings. The counseling and school psychology programs are accredited by APA and CACREP.

Department of Curriculum and Instruction. Chair: Cary Buzzelli, Education 3140, 812-856-8100. Programs include art education, curriculum studies, early childhood education, elementary education, mathematics education, multicultural education, science education, secondary education, social studies education, and special education. The department's diverse and internationally known faculty conducts many large-scale research and service projects funded by state, federal, and corporate sources.

Department of Educational Leadership and Policy Studies. Chair: Martha McCarthy, Education 4228, 812-856-8360. Programs include college student affairs administration, comparative education, educational leadership, higher education, history of education, philosophy of education, policy studies, and school administration. Several of the department's programs are ranked among the best in the United States. Faculty members are internationally recognized for research and publication record in their respective fields.

Department of Instructional Systems Technology. Chair: Elizabeth Boling, Education 2276, 812-856-8450. The department has one of the best programs in the nation, preparing students in educational technology using the newest multimedia tools and facilities. Specializations in instructional systems technology are offered in instructional development, product development, or management. The department also develops national and international corporate training projects. Faculty members demonstrate outstanding expertise and research in multimedia instructional design and production.

Department of Language Education. Chair: Mary Beth Hines, Education 3044, 812-856-8260. Programs include English education, English as a second language/bilingual education, foreign language education, and reading education. Bridge courses integrate language study across program areas. Faculty members are known internationally for their excellent teaching, research, and service records.

INDIANAPOLIS CAMPUS

Graduate Programs and Continuing Professional Development. Chair: Robert Osgood, Education/Social Work 3128, 317-274-6812. The division offers exemplary master's degree programs in elementary education (educational technology, early childhood, or elementary curriculum), secondary education (educational technology or secondary curriculum), language education (English, English as a new language, foreign language, or reading), special education, school counseling education, and educational leadership (school administration). Graduate certification is offered in special education and English as a new language, along with a new certificate in community building and urban education. Extensive professional development opportunities are offered via Summer in the City, online courses and nontraditional workshops, and individualized partnerships with schools and other community entities.

A magnificent limestone structure on the Bloomington campus, the Wendell W. Wright Education Building is a national demonstration site for the application of technology to teaching and learning.

The School of Education on the Indianapolis campus is located in the modern Education/Social Work Building near the heart of downtown.

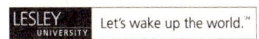

LESLEY UNIVERSITY

School of Education

Programs of Study

The School of Education at Lesley University offers programs of study in early childhood, elementary, middle school, and special education as well as art education, curriculum and instruction, educational leadership, math, reading, science, and technology in education. Degrees offered include the Master of Education (M.Ed.), the Certificate of Advanced Graduate Study (CAGS), and the doctorate (Ph.D.) in educational studies. Lesley offers degree programs that lead to both initial teacher licensure as well as professional licensure.

Lesley's education programs offer entry-level and advanced teacher preparation and unique career alternative options. For those who want to begin a career in teaching, Lesley offers a variety of master's degree programs in art education; early childhood, elementary, middle school, high school, and special education; school counseling; and technology in education. Field experience is a major component of an education at Lesley, particularly for those who wish to teach. Lesley's relationship with local schools provides an excellent opportunity for students to gain practical teaching experience. The Collaborative Internship Program, for example, combines theory and practice in a field-based master's program. Collaborative programs are currently offered at Belmont Day School, Brookline Public Schools, Brookwood School, Buckingham Browne & Nichols School, Carroll School, Hillside School, Pike School, and Shady Hill School.

For certified or experienced teachers, advanced master's degrees and CAGS programs are offered in numerous education programs. For the educator with an undergraduate degree and an initial license, approved master's degree programs leading to professional licensure are offered in art education, early childhood and elementary education, specialist teacher studies in reading, and technology in education. For the educator with a master's degree and an initial license, Lesley offers 12-credit post-master's degree programs to advance his or her career, strengthen subject knowledge, and further enhance the academic performance of his or her students. These programs are offered in early childhood, elementary, middle school, and high school education and technology in education.

A Certificate of Advanced Graduate Study (CAGS) from Lesley offers students flexibility in their roles as educators. These highly regarded certificates provide learning that is geared to the educator's professional goals and offer the opportunity to expand and develop skills, acquire additional research techniques, and enhance career and salary opportunities. CAGS are offered in art education, curriculum and instruction, and specialist teacher and reading. CAGS candidates must hold a master's degree in a related field of study.

Not only do the educational programs at Lesley fulfill the Massachusetts teacher licensure regulations instituted by the Massachusetts Department of Education, they are also approved by the National Association of State Directors of Teacher Education and Certification (NASDTEC), which enables graduates approved for licensure in Massachusetts to apply for comparable positions in forty-five states.

Lesley's School of Education offers its students a superior education through challenging course work, classroom-based reflection, research and clinical experiences that model a strong commitment, and belief in cultural pluralism, technology, and inclusive communities. These experiences, in turn, inspire graduates to take leadership roles in helping to initiate reform in their schools and to contribute to the restructuring of education for future generations. The education faculty members, in their various roles as teacher-mentors, facilitators, researchers, consultants, writers, conference speakers, and members of educational boards, commissions, and focus groups, are the primary force in setting the high academic standards and the visionary goals of the School of Education.

In addition to the Cambridge-based programs, Lesley offers master's degree programs at more than 250 learning sites in twenty-three states. Three online programs, in science, mathematics, and technology, are also available to educators seeking a high-quality, convenient M.Ed. program. Courses are delivered one weekend a month to cohorts of teachers pursuing their graduate degrees.

Most courses are 3 credits. The total number of credit hours needed to complete graduate degrees varies from 30 to 56, depending upon the student's program and past experience. Most programs are 33 or 36 credits.

Research Facilities

The Ludcke Library maintains a working collection of books, periodicals, microfilm and microfiches, curriculum materials, nonprint materials, and software resources. The library provides Internet resources and database access to general and subject-specific resources appropriate to the subject focuses of the University. The Kresge Center for Teaching Resources provides instructional resources for individual and group instruction, and the Microcomputer Center houses the Instructional Computing activities of the University, including a collection of educational software. Through the Fenway Consortium, students can access thirteen other libraries in Boston-Cambridge area.

Financial Aid

The Lesley University Financial Aid Office administers all federal financial aid programs. There are opportunities in college teaching, advising, and research activities, as well as field placements in public and private schools. A limited number of assistantships are awarded by semester or academic year. Most positions require about 10 to 15 hours of work per week.

Cost of Study

Tuition for on-campus graduate students was $650 per credit in 2006. Tuition for off-campus graduate students ranges from $430 to $450 per credit, depending on location. Online graduate courses are $450. The cost of books and supplies averages $500 per year.

Living and Housing Costs

Lesley University does not have on-campus housing for its graduate students. Information on housing in the surrounding area and assistance in obtaining information is available from the Residence Life Office of Student Affairs.

Student Group

The graduate on- and off-campus enrollment at Lesley University consists of more than 6,000 students: men and women ranging in age from their mid-20s to early 70s, in all stages of professional development. Students come from fifty states and thirty-two countries; most have worked in the professional field of their choice and returned to graduate school to upgrade their training, learn new skills, or change careers.

Location

Lesley University occupies a campus near Harvard Square in Cambridge, Massachusetts, an area that benefits from the many advantages of the cities of Boston and Cambridge. The University is connected to downtown Boston by public transportation. Numerous historical sites and cultural attractions are within a 6-mile radius, including theaters, museums, and concerts. Graduate programs are also available in classrooms and online formats across the United States.

The University

Lesley University, founded in 1909 offers graduate and Ph.D. programs in the fields of education, environmental studies, human services, counseling and psychology, and the arts. With today's student in mind, Lesley University has successfully pioneered a wide variety of flexible programs for adult learners that share a commitment to quality, innovation, and the integration of theory with practice.

Lesley offers degree for learners at all levels. The University also supports several centers and hosts a variety of academic and professional conferences and institutes. Lesley programs operate throughout Massachusetts and in twenty-three other states, as well as at an affiliated international site in Israel.

Applying

Applications are reviewed and acted upon as they are completed. Applications from international students not residing in the United States should be completed by April 1 for the fall semester and October 1 for the spring semester. Requirements for admission to graduate degree programs are a bachelor's degree (for the M.Ed. program) or a master's degree (for the CAGS and Ph.D. programs) from a nationally accredited college or university as well as a satisfactory grade average, official transcripts of undergraduate and graduate work, letters of recommendation, a written personal statement, and a nonrefundable $50 application fee. Application materials should be requested from the Office of Admissions for Graduate and Adult Bachelor's Programs.

Correspondence and Information

Office of Graduate and Adult Bachelor's Admissions
Lesley University
29 Everett Street
Cambridge, Massachusetts 02138-2790
Phone: 617-349-8300
      888-LESLEY-U (toll-free)
Fax: 617-349-8313
E-mail: info@lesley.edu
Web site: http://www.lesley.edu

Lesley University

THE FACULTY

Abraham Abadi, Assistant Professor; Ed.D., Boston University.
Karen Kuelthau Allan, Professor; Ph.D., Wisconsin–Madison.
Polly Attwood, Assistant Professor; M.Div., Harvard.
William Barowy, Associate Professor; Ph.D., Massachusetts Amherst.
George Blakeslee, Professor and Co-Director of Technology in Educational Division; Ed.D., Boston University.
Alice Pierce Bonifaz, Assistant Professor; Ph.D., Texas.
Sharyn Boornazian, Assistant Professor and Certification Officer; Ph.D., Union (Ohio).
Mario R. Borunda, Dean, School of Education; Ed.D., Harvard.
Carole Brandon, Instructor and Coordinator of Field Placement Office for Undergraduate Education Programs; M.S., Wheelock.
Linda Brion-Meisels, Professor; Ph.D., Boston College.
Marcia Bromfield, Professor, Director of Field Placement and Professional Partnerships; Ph.D., Syracuse.
Cynthia Farr Brown, Associate Professor and Senior Associate Dean; Ph.D., Brandeis.
Phyllis C. Brown, Assistant Professor; Ed.D., Massachusetts Amherst.
Joseph Cambone, Associate Dean; Ed.D., Harvard.
Mary Ann Cappiello, Assistant Professor; Ed.D., Columbia.
Vivian Dalila Carlo, Associate Professor; Ed.D., Boston University.
Nancy Carlsson-Paige, Professor; Ed.D., Massachusetts Amherst.
Gail M. Carney, Assistant Professor and Director of Undergraduate Education Programs; Ed.D., Boston University.
Richard Carter, Assistant Professor; Ph.D., MIT.
Stephan Cohen, Associate Professor; Ed.D., Harvard.
Anne Collins, Assistant Professor and Director of Mathematics Programs; Ph.D., Boston College.
Constantina Comnenou, Associate Professor; Ed.D., Massachusetts Amherst.
Mary E. Curtis, Professor and Director of Center for Special Education; Ph.D., Pittsburgh.
Linda Dacey, Professor; Ed.D., Boston University.
William L. Dandridge, Associate Professor; Ed.D., Massachusetts Amherst.
Erika Thulin Dawes, Assistant Professor; Ed.D., Columbia Teachers College.
Harriet Deane, Assistant Professor and Assistant Dean; M.Ed., Boston University; M.B.A., Simmons.
Susan J. Doubler, Associate Professor and Director of Science Education Online Program; Ph.D., Liverpool (England).
Edna May Duffy, Associate Professor; Ph.D., Boston College.
Lisa B. Fiore, Assistant Professor; Ph.D., Boston College.
Irene Fountas, Professor and Director of Center for Reading Recovery and Literacy Collaborative; Ed.D., Boston University.
June Fox, Professor Emerita; Ph.D., Ohio State.
Barbara Francis, Associate Professor and Program Director, Middle/High School; Ed.D., Rochester.
Barbara P. Gibson, Assistant Professor and Director of Special Education Program; M.Ed., Temple; CAGS, Lesley.
Barbara L. Govendo, Associate Professor; Ph.D., Boston College.
Lorraine J. Greenfield, Assistant Professor and Director of the Curriculum and Instruction Division; Ed.D., Boston University.
Linda Grisham, Associate Professor and Director of Science in Education Program; Ph.D., Stanford.
Jo-Anne Hart, Associate Professor; Ph.D., NYU.
Caroline Heller, Associate Professor; Ed.D., Berkeley.
Paul Jablon, Associate Professor and Director of Middle School Program; Ph.D., NYU.
Roberta Jackson, Assistant Professor; M.Ed., Massachusetts Boston.
Judith Mathis Johnson, Assistant Professor; Ph.D., Oregon.
Sondra Langer, Professor Emerita; M.A., Simmons.
Anne Larkin, Professor and Director of Project Promise; Ph.D., Boston College.
Mary Beth Lawton, Assistant Professor; Ed.D., Massachusetts Amherst.
Solange de Azambuja Lira, Associate Professor; Ph.D., Pennsylvania.
Ben Mardell, Associate Professor; Ph.D., Tufts.
Brenda Matthis, Assistant Professor; Ed.D., Harvard.
Mary C. McMackin, Professor; Ed.D., Massachusetts Lowell.
Linda Mensing-Triplett, Assistant Professor; Ed.D. candidate, Massachusetts.
Susan Merrifield, Professor; Ed.D., Harvard.
Margery Staman Miller, Professor, Director of Literacy and Language Division, and Director of the Consultant Teacher of Reading Programs; Ed.D., Pennsylvania.
Mary Mindess, Professor; Ed.M., Boston University.
Michael Pabian, Instructor; M.Ed., Boston State College.
Bart Pisha, Associate Professor; Ed.D., Harvard.
Diane J. Powell, Assistant Professor; M.A., Ohio State.
Susan I. Rauchwerk, Assistant Professor; Ed.D., Harvard.
Marianne Reiff, Assistant Professor; Ph.D., California, Santa Barbara.
Maureen Riley, Associate Professor; M.Ed., Harvard.
Nancy Roberts, Professor; Ed.D., Boston University.
Arlyn Roffman, Professor; Ph.D., Boston College.
Sheryl Saunders, Assistant Professor; M.A., Simmons.
Maria de Lourdes B. Serpa, Professor; Ed.D., Boston University.
Stephanie A. Spadorcia, Associate Professor; Ph.D., North Carolina at Chapel Hill.
William Stokes, Professor and Dean of Faculty; Ed.D., Boston University.
Elizabeth Stringer, Assistant Professor; M.Ed., Lesley.
Joanne M. Szamreta, Professor; Ph.D., Boston College.
Robert J. Thomas, Director of Teaching, Learning and Leadership Division; Ed.D., Harvard.
Joan Thormann, Professor; Ph.D., Oregon.
Nancy Wolf, Assistant Professor and Director of Oregon Program; Ph.D., Nebraska.
Maureen Brown Yoder, Professor and Director of Technology in Education Online Degree Program; Ed.D., Boston University.

MANHATTANVILLE COLLEGE

School of Education

Programs of Study

The School of Education at Manhattanville College offers programs to prepare graduates for careers in education at all levels, from teaching to leadership and administration. Undergraduate s often earn a double major in education and another liberal arts concentration, while the Graduate Program is geared to students interested in becoming teachers, often after having had other careers, and to classroom teachers who want to extend their teaching certifications or update their knowledge base. All programs are registered with and approved by the New York State Education Department. Education programs at Manhattanville are accredited by the National Council for Accreditation of Teacher Education (NCATE).

Manhattanville offers a graduate-level accelerated teacher certification program, Jump Start, which is especially popular with adults who are changing careers. Jump Start classes begin in February, and its students are in their own classrooms by September as well-prepared, fully paid teachers with full benefits while they finish the additional requirements for the master's degree.

Manhattanville offers two master's programs, the Master of Arts in Teaching (M.A.T.) and the Master of Professional Studies (M.P.S.). In addition, Manhattanville offers classes in more than 60 areas of concentration leading to 18 different New York State certifications. Manhattanville also offers post-master's certifications and a professional diploma in educational leadership.

The Master of Arts in Teaching degree program is intended for strong liberal arts graduates with few or no prior courses in education. Upon completion of the program, the candidate is eligible for New York State certification as a teacher of childhood (grades 1–6), early childhood (birth–grade 2), early childhood and childhood (birth–grade 6), biology (grades 5–12),chemistry (grades 5–12), English (grades 5–12), French (grades 7–12), Italian (grades 7–12), Latin (grades 7–12), mathematics (grades 5–12), music (all grades), physical education and sports pedagogy (all grades), physics (grades 7–12), social studies (grades 5–12), Spanish (grades 7–12), or visual arts (all grades). Most M.A.T. programs range from 36 to 39 credits. The program in childhood/early childhood is 46 credits. All M.A.T. programs include one semester of full-time student teaching or supervised fieldwork. The College also offers the accelerated teaching program (JumpStart) that leads to an M.A.T. degree and certification in eighteen months.

The Master of Professional Studies degree includes programs in educational leadership (SBL), literacy (specialization in reading and writing), special education, or teaching English to speakers of another language (all grades or adult and international settings). There are also dual-certification programs in childhood, secondary, or middle child/adolescence literacy and special education. Upon completion of the program, the candidate is eligible for either initial or professional certification. The classification is determined by the credentials presented at the time of matriculation into the selected program. M.P.S. programs range from 36 to 47 credits, depending upon the program and the area in which certification is sought.

The certification programs offer students who already hold a functionally related master's degree an opportunity to complete a program of 27 to 30 credits that makes them eligible for certification in a specific field and level of education. Manhattanville also offers a 15-credit Teacher Leader program for those interested in serving as leaders in their schools.

Research Facilities

Manhattanville's teaching library ranks among the foremost undergraduate teaching libraries in the country. The Manhattanville Library capitalizes on the power of the Internet to connect students with information and analysis found in powerful subscription databases, electronic journals, and electronic books. Manhattanville is one of the first colleges in the U.S. to outsource a service that enables students to interact online with experienced reference librarians at any time of the day or night from anywhere in the world. The virtual research service, "Ask a Librarian 24/7," uses co-browsing to connect students with professional librarians who can answer questions about research and help students navigate the College's extensive array of subscription databases and other library resources. An Educational Resource Center has curriculum materials to assist new teachers. It also houses the Homework Bytes program in cooperation with Westchester County middle schools and the Gannett newspapers. The Music Listening and Reference Room provides the material and the technology for accessing one of the richest collections at Manhattanville.

The Menendez Language Laboratory includes tapes and record libraries that provide materials for class instruction and individual practice in French, Spanish, Russian, Italian, German, Chinese, Japanese, Hindi, Marathi, modern Hebrew, and English as a second language. The College provides a writing clinic, a reading clinic, audiovisual facilities, and a bibliographic instruction program. The library building is open 24 hours, 7 days a week through most of the fall and spring semesters, and it has computer labs, quiet study areas, group-study rooms and a café, where students and faculty can meet informally.

Manhattanville, which was named one of the "Top 100 Wired Colleges in the U.S.," has state-of-the-art computers, computer labs, and campus networking for student use and instruction.

Financial Aid

Family Educational Loans are available to graduate students. A Deferred Payment Plan is also available. There are a limited number of graduate assistantships, for which matriculated students work 200 hours to earn the cost of 6 credit hours. A maximum of three assistantships per student are possible, and courses must be taken concurrently with the assistantship. For further information, prospective students should contact the Office of Financial Aid, Reid Hall, Purchase, New York 10577 (telephone: 914-323-5357).

Cost of Study

Tuition was $725 per credit for 2006–07. There was a semester registration fee of $40, and there were some course fees.

Living and Housing Costs

Most School of Education graduate students live and work in their own homes and communities throughout Westchester and the surrounding counties. For campus housing information, students should call Residence Life at 914-323-5217.

Student Group

There are approximately 850 students in the School of Education at Manhattanville College. Sixty percent are career changers. Their average age is 32.

Location

Manhattanville's campus, 100 acres of suburban countryside, is located in New York's Westchester County, just minutes from White Plains to the west and Greenwich, Connecticut, to the east. It is 30 miles from Manhattan. The campus is accessible via public transportation.

The College

Manhattanville College is a coeducational, independent liberal arts college whose mission is to educate ethically and socially responsible leaders for the global community. Founded in 1841, the College has 1,600 undergraduate students and 1,000 graduate students. Of the graduate students, 850 are enrolled in the School of Education. Manhattanville offers bachelor's and master's degrees in more than fifty academic concentrations in the arts and sciences. Its curriculum nurtures intellectual curiosity and independent thinking.

Applying

Applications are reviewed on a continuing basis. Applicants are encouraged to apply at least sixty days in advance of the semester for which matriculation is sought (fall, spring, summer I, summer II). Application requirements are the submission of a completed application form, a fee of $40, two recommendations, a two- to three-page typewritten essay on the applicant's background and philosophy of education, and official transcripts of all previous college work (both undergraduate and graduate). Under certain circumstances, limited study as a nonmatriculated student is permitted.

Correspondence and Information

Alyce Poli
Director of Admissions
School of Education
Manhattanville College
2900 Purchase Street
Purchase, New York 10577
Phone: 914-323-5142 (Admissions)
Fax: 914-694-1732
E-mail: edschool@mville.edu
Web site: http://www.manhattanville.edu/education

Manhattanville College

THE FACULTY

School of Education Administration
Shelley B. Wepner, Professor and Dean; Ed.D., Pennsylvania.
Susan Jacobs, Associate Dean of Accreditation and Technology; Ed.D., Columbia Teachers College.
Laurence Krute, Associate Professor of ESL/Foreign Language and Associate Dean of Graduate Advising; Ph.D., Columbia.
Joan Rudel Weinreich, Associate Professor and Associate Dean of Undergraduate Advising; Ph.D., Fordham.
Laura Bigaouette, Assistant Dean; M.B.A., Pace.
Stephanie Coxen, Assistant Dean; B.A., Maryland.
William DiBartolo, Coordinator of Certification, Testing and Partnership Agreements; M.S., Iona.
James Finger, Director of Jump Start and Special Initiatives; M.B.A., North Carolina.
Susan Harper, Coordinator of Accelerated Programs; M.S., NYU; M.A., New Rochelle.
Alyce Poli, Director of Admissions; M.S., Pace.
Gail Robinson, Director of Field Placement, Certification, and Community Outreach; M.S., CUNY, Hunter.

Curriculum and Instruction
JoAnne Ferrara, Assistant Professor and Department Chair of Curriculum and Instruction; Ed.D., Nova Southeastern.
Frederick Heckendorn III, Assistant Professor of Secondary/Social Studies Education; Ed.D., Hofstra.
Victor Mazmanian, Assistant Professor of Math and Science and Program Coordinator for Secondary Programs; Ed.D., Columbia Teachers College.
Christina Siry, Instructor of Childhood Education; M.S., CUNY, Hunter.
Donna Tropsa, Assistant Professor of Secondary English; J.D., Suffolk.

Early Childhood
Patricia Vardin, Associate Professor and Department Chair of Early Childhood Education; Ed.D., Columbia Teachers College.
Diane Lang, Instructor of Early Childhood/Childhood Education; Ph.D., Cornell.

Educational Leadership and Special Subjects
Kathleen Rockwood, Associate Professor and Department Chair of Educational Leadership and Special Subjects; Ed.D., Fordham.
Rhonda Clements, Professor and Program Director of Physical Education and Sports Pedagogy; Ed.D., Columbia Teachers College.

Literacy
Jane Gangi, Associate Professor; Ph.D., NYU.
Mary Ellen Levin, Associate Professor; Ed.D., Columbia Teachers College.
Mary Ann Reilly, Associate Professor; Ed.D., Columbia Teachers College.

Special Education
Ellis I. Barowsky, Assistant Professor and Department Chair; Ph.D., CUNY Graduate Center.
Andrew Dowling, Assistant Professor and Department Chair; Ed.D., Fordham.
Michael S. Malow-Iroff, Assistant Professor; Ph.D., CUNY Graduate Center.

NEW YORK UNIVERSITY

NEW YORK UNIVERSITY

Steinhardt School of Culture, Education, and Human Development

Programs of Study

The Steinhardt School of Culture, Education, and Human Development, the largest graduate school at New York University, offers a diverse range of graduate programs in applied psychology, art, communication, education, health, and music.

The School has a long history of connecting theory to applied learning experiences through dozens of affiliations and partnerships with urban institutions, building communities within and beyond its classrooms and nurturing the human spirit. The faculty members are intellectually adventurous and socially conscious. The School's master's and doctoral students study in the expansive environment of a great research university and use the urban neighborhoods of New York City and countries around the world as their laboratories. Now in its 117th year of educating professionals, scholars, and researchers, Steinhardt's faculty members continue to apply their creativity and knowledge where they are needed most.

Degrees and certificates offered include Postbaccalaureate Advanced Certificates, Master of Arts, Master of Fine Arts, Master of Science, Master of Public Health, Master of Music, Sixth-Year Certificates, Doctor of Education, Doctor of Philosophy, Doctor of Physical Therapy, and Doctor of Professional Studies.

More than fifteen summer and six January intersession graduate study-abroad programs, with locations throughout Europe, Asia, Africa, and South America, are offered every year and provide superb opportunities to gain global experience.

Over 225 full-time faculty members in eleven separate academic departments and divisions form the academic core of the School—teaching, undertaking research, leading curricular reform, developing and implementing innovative field-based projects, providing leadership in professional organizations throughout the country, and engaging in global partnerships. They are examining some of the most important and fascinating questions facing society today, including childhood obesity, school discipline, charter schools, Internet communication, poverty and schooling, and HIV/AIDS. They receive millions of dollars annually from a wide array of funders—such as the National Science Foundation, the National Institutes of Health, the Ford Foundation, and the Carnegie Corporation—to support their research and field projects. Faculty members serve on the editorial boards of dozens of leading academic journals and are leaders in their professional associations.

Research Facilities

Members of the School's faculty direct or participate in several unique research and service centers. These enterprises engage in work that spans the arts, communications, education, health, and policy arenas serving scholars, students, teachers, and leaders in education, government, and industry. The Steinhardt School of Culture, Education, and Human Development receives nearly $25 million annually from government agencies, private foundations, and individual donors to fund research, field projects, scholarships and fellowships, and faculty positions. The centers include the Institute for Education and Social Policy; the Center for Research on Culture, Development, and Education; the Center for Research on Teaching and Learning; the Ruth Horowitz Center for Teacher Development; the Consortium for Research and Evaluation of Advanced Technologies in Education; the Child and Family Policy Center; the Institute for Globalization and Education in Metropolitan Settings, which houses the Metropolitan Center for Urban Education and Immigration Studies at NYU; the Reading Recovery Program Northeast Regional Site; the Steinhardt Institute for Higher Education Policy Studies; the Center for Health, Identity, Behavior, and Prevention Studies; the Institute for Human Development and Contextual Change; and the Nordoff-Robbins Center for Music Therapy. Eight distinct libraries at the University contain 4.9 million volumes.

Financial Aid

The School annually awards more than $7 million in financial assistance to new and continuing graduate students. Assistance is based on merit and need and is offered to both full-time and part-time students. Special merit- and need-based scholarships include the Deans' Opportunity Scholarship, the Peace Corps Scholarship, the Historically Black Colleges and Universities Scholarship, the Health Professions Opportunity Scholarship, the Centennial Scholarship (for part-time students), the New York University Opportunity Fellowships, the Jonathan Levin Urban Education Scholarship, the Teach New York: NYC Partnership for Teacher Excellence Scholarship, the Steinhardt Fellowships for Doctoral Study, the Phyllis and Gerald LeBoff Fellowship in Media Ecology, the NYU Reynolds Fellowship Program in Social Entrepreneurship, and the Steinhardt Fellowship in Education and Jewish Studies. Graduate assistantships, teaching assistantships, research assistantships, resident assistantships, federally insured loans, and student employment are also available.

Cost of Study

Tuition for New York State residents is $3622.50 per semester or $302 per credit. Out-of-state residents' tuition is $5733 per semester or $478 per credit. Tuition and fees are subject to change at the discretion of FIT's Board of Trustees. Additional expenses for class materials, textbooks, and travel may apply and vary per program.

Living and Housing Costs

Residence facilities are available to graduate students. For fall 2007, per-semester housing rates are $3051–$3190 for traditional (meal plan required) accommodations and $3819–$7250 for apartment-style. A $325 annual fee for technology services and the Student Resident Association is required of all residence hall students. Meal plans range from $2790 to $3590. All costs are subject to change.

Student Group

The School has a diverse graduate student body of 3,700 (and 2,300 undergraduate students), which includes students from nearly every state. International students represent 10 percent, and students who are members of minorities represent 23 percent of the graduate student population.

Student Outcomes

Graduates hold leadership roles in schools, hospitals, communities, government and international agencies, colleges and universities, and industry. Graduates are teachers, health-care professionals, administrators, professors, psychologists, counselors, artists, and performers. In addition, they are policy makers; private consultants; producers of children's media; publishers; program directors for museums and science centers; record and video producers; concert promoters; art dealers; executives in public relations, advertising, television, and corporate relations; registered dietitians; food industry specialists; and researchers.

Location

Located in the historic Greenwich Village neighborhood of New York City, the School provides easy access to the nation's premier educational, cultural, artistic, research, and health institutions.

The University

Founded in 1831, New York University is one of the world's great universities, dedicated to research, scholarship, and the education of leaders for the twenty-first century. From its location in historic Greenwich Village in Manhattan, the University's commitment reaches from the local urban setting to a global involvement with the world community.

Applying

Applicants for degree programs must meet Schoolwide admissions criteria. Graduate Record Examinations (GRE) scores are required for doctoral and Master of Public Health applicants only (M.P.H. applicants may substitute scores from the MCAT exam). The fall deadline is February 1 for most master's applications and December 15 for most doctoral applications. The deadline for the Fast-Track M.A. programs in teacher education is January 5, and for the Three-Summer M.A. in Studio Art program, it is March 1. Several programs also accept master's students for the spring term; the application deadline is November 1. The Doctor of Physical Therapy has a December 1 application deadline for summer matriculation. Additional departmental application materials may also be required. The TOEFL is required for all nonnative speakers of English.

Correspondence and Information

Office of Graduate Admissions
Steinhardt School of Culture, Education, and Human Development
New York University
82 Washington Square East, 3rd Floor
New York, New York 10003-6680
Phone: 212-998-5030
Fax: 212-995-4328
E-mail: steinhardt.gradadmissions@nyu.edu
Web site: http://www.steinhardt.nyu.edu/graduate.admissions

New York University

DEPARTMENTS AND PROGRAMS

Administration

Mary M. Brabeck, Dean.
Patricia M. Carey, Associate Dean for Student Affairs.
Joseph Giovannelli, Associate Dean for Administration and Finance.
Perry N. Halkitis, Associate Dean for Research and Doctoral Studies.
Ron Robin, Associate Dean for Academic Affairs.
Dawn Duncan, Assistant Dean for Development and Alumni Relations.
Lindsay Wright, Assistant Dean for Planning and Communications.

Department of Administration, Leadership, and Technology

Richard Richardson, Professor and Chair (212-998-5520).
Business Education (M.A., Sixth-Year Certificate).
Educational Administration (Ed.D., Ph.D.).
Educational Leadership (M.A., Sixth-Year Certificate).
Educational Communication and Technology (M.A., Sixth-Year Certificate, Ed.D., Ph.D.).
Higher Education (M.A., Ph.D.).

Department of Applied Psychology

Carola Suarez-Orozco, Associate Professor and Chair (212-998-5555).
Counseling and Guidance (M.A.).
Counseling for Mental Health and Wellness (M.A.).
Counseling Psychology (Ph.D.).
Educational Psychology (M.A.).
Psychological Development (Ph.D.).
Psychology and Social Intervention (Ph.D.).
School Psychology (Ph.D.).

Department of Art and Art Professions

Nancy Barton, Clinical Associate Professor and Chair (212-998-5700).
Art Education (M.A.).
Art Therapy (M.A.).
Studio Art (M.A., M.F.A.).
Visual Arts Administration (M.A.).
Visual Culture–Costume Studies (M.A.).
Visual Culture–Theory (M.A.).
Visual Culture and Education (Ph.D.).

Department of Culture and Communication

Ted Magder, Associate Professor and Chair (212-998-5191).
Media, Culture, and Communication (M.A.).
Media Ecology (Ph.D.).

Department of Humanities and Social Sciences

Rene Arcilla, Associate Professor and Chair (212-992-9475).
Education and Jewish Studies (Ph.D.).
Environmental Conservation Education (M.A.).
History of Education (M.A., Ph.D.).
International Education (M.A., Ph.D.).
Philosophy of Education (M.A., Ph.D.).
Sociology of Education (M.A., Ph.D.).
Studies in Arts and Humanities Education (M.A., Ph.D.).

Department of Music and Performing Arts Professions

Lawrence Ferrara, Professor and Chair (212-998-5424).
Dance Education (M.A., Ed.D., Ph.D.).
Drama Therapy (M.A.).
Educational Theatre (M.A., Ed.D., Ph.D.).
Music Business (M.A.).
Music Education (M.A., Sixth-Year Certificate, Ed.D., Ph.D.).
Music Performance and Composition (M.A., Ph.D.).
Music Technology (M.M.).
Music Therapy (M.A.).
Performing Arts Administration (M.A.).

Department of Nutrition, Food Studies, and Public Health

Judith Gilbride, Professor and Chair (212-998-5580).
Community Public Health (M.P.H.).
Food Studies and Food Management (M.A., Ph.D.).
Nutrition and Dietetics (M.S., Ph.D.).
Public Health (Ph.D.).

Department of Occupational Therapy

Jim Hinojosa, Professor and Chair (212-998-5825).
Occupational Therapy (M.S., D.P.S.).
Postprofessional Advanced Occupational Therapy (M.A.).
Research in Occupational Therapy (Ph.D.).

Department of Physical Therapy

Wen K. Ling, Associate Professor and Chair (212-998-9400).
Physical Therapy: Pathokinesiology (M.A.).
Physical Therapy (D.P.T.).
Physical Therapy for Practicing Physical Therapists (D.P.T.).
Research in Physical Therapy (Ph.D.).

Department of Speech-Language Pathology and Audiology

Celia Stewart, Associate Professor and Chair (212-998-5230).
Speech-Language Pathology (M.A., Ph.D.).

Department of Teaching and Learning

Robert Cohen, Professor and Chair (212-998-5470).
Bilingual Education (M.A., Sixth-Year Certificate, Ph.D.).
Childhood Education (M.A.).
Childhood Education/Special Education (M.A.).
Early Childhood Education (M.A.).
Early Childhood Education/Special Education (M.A.).
English Education (M.A., Ph.D.).
Foreign Language Education, Dual Foreign Language Education and TESOL (M.A., Sixth-Year Certificate).
Literacy Education (M.A.).
Mathematics Education (M.A., Ph.D.).
Positions of Leadership: Early Childhood and Elementary Education (Sixth-Year Certificate).
Science Education (M.A.).
Social Studies Education (M.A.).
Special Education (M.A.).
Teaching and Learning (Ed.D., Ph.D.).
TESOL (M.A., Sixth-Year Certificate, Ph.D.).

Pursue your goals. Be the future. Be NYU Steinhardt.

NORTHWESTERN UNIVERSITY

School of Education and Social Policy

Programs of Study

The School of Education and Social Policy offers programs leading to the M.S., M.A., and Ph.D. degrees. Programming is provided in four areas—the M.S. in education, M.S. in learning and organizational change, the M.A. and Ph.D. in the learning sciences, and the Ph.D. in human development and social policy.

The learning sciences M.A. and Ph.D. programs are dedicated to the preparation of researchers, developers, and practitioners qualified to advance the scientific understanding and practice of teaching and learning. Both programs in the learning sciences are interdisciplinary, offering a synthesis of computational, educational, and social science research; linguistics; computer science; anthropology; and cognitive science.

The Ph.D. program in human development and social policy prepares students to bridge human development, social science, and social policy. Graduates of this program assume positions as teachers, researchers, and policy makers who can bring multidisciplinary knowledge about human development directly to bear upon policy.

Concentrations in the M.S. program in education include public and private school teaching, advanced teaching, and higher education administration. Students enrolled full-time typically complete the program in twelve months, provided they matriculate with no course deficiencies; opportunities for part-time study toward a master's degree are also available.

Research Facilities

Research libraries contain more than 4.6 million volumes, 4.3 million microfilm units, and nearly 42,000 current periodical and serial publications. Research and teaching activities are supported by a state-of-the-art multimedia computing network with full Internet access. The School is actively involved with the Institute for Policy Research, a University-wide research center that promotes interdisciplinary urban policy research and training. Specialized research and service resources within the School include the Center for Talent Development, a nationally prominent center that identifies and provides programming for academically talented youth, their parents, and the professionals who work with them. The Tarry Center for Collaborative Teaching and Learning provides state-of-the-art facilities for innovative teaching with technology.

Financial Aid

Several forms of aid are available, including fellowships and scholarships. In addition, there are teaching assistantships awarded to doctoral students who work with the School's undergraduate programs. Special opportunities for research assistantships and other employment also exist within the School's and the University's many research centers. Arrangements for loans are also possible.

Cost of Study

Tuition for full-time study in the M.S. programs in 2006–07 was $45,000 for the fifteen-course program; part-time enrollment is possible at $3000 per course. Tuition for full-time study (three courses per quarter) in pursuit of the M.A. or Ph.D. in 2006–07 was $33,400 for the academic year, or $11,136 per quarter; part-time enrollment was assessed at $3712 per course.

Living and Housing Costs

The University operates a residence in Evanston for the use of graduate students. For those Northwestern students interested in securing off-campus housing near the University, information and assistance are also available.

Student Group

Graduate study occurs within the context of individualized instruction, and enrollments are selective. Currently, 190 students are enrolled in the M.S. programs and 74 in the M.A. and Ph.D. programs. Since an interdisciplinary perspective is valued, students with preparation in a wide range of disciplinary areas are encouraged to apply.

Student Outcomes

Graduates teach and conduct research in academic and nonacademic settings; occupy strategic policy positions in government, corporations, and institutions; and assume positions of responsibility in a wide range of service organizations. Potential professional settings for learning sciences graduates include University research and teaching as well as business, industry, or school system-based careers studying, designing, and/or implementing learning environments. Graduates of the Ph.D. program in human development and social policy assume positions as teachers, researchers, or policy makers who can bring multidisciplinary knowledge about human development directly to bear upon policy. Graduates of the learning sciences M.A. program are practitioners in the vanguard of teaching and learning systems development and instructional resource development. Most students in the M.S. program in education gain on-site experience through supervised internships for future careers as professional educators.

Location

The campus is located on Lake Michigan, 12 miles north of Chicago. The beautiful lakefront campus offers a rich cultural environment through a wealth of theatrical, musical, and athletic events. The extensive cultural resources of Chicago are readily accessible via public transportation.

The University and The School

Established in 1851, Northwestern has grown to become one of the most distinguished private universities in the country. The School of Education and Social Policy has developed from its origins as a department of pedagogy by continually broadening its scope to encompass those educative, learning, and socializing experiences that take place throughout the life span in families, schools, communities, and the workplace.

Applying

Applications for admission are reviewed and acted upon as they are received. Students should consult program brochures for specific application deadlines. Applicants planning to seek financial aid must meet early submission deadlines.

Correspondence and Information

School of Education and Social Policy
(Please specify program)
Northwestern University
2120 Campus Drive
Evanston, Illinois 60208-2610
Phone: 847-491-3790 (Office of Student Affairs)
   847-467-1458 (M.S. in education)
   847-491-7494 (Ph.D. in learning sciences)
   847-491-4329 (Ph.D. in human development and social policy)
   847-491-7376 (M.A. in learning sciences and M.S. in learning and organizational change)
Web site: http://www.sesp.northwestern.edu

Northwestern University

THE FACULTY AND THEIR RESEARCH

Emma Adam, Ph.D., Minnesota. Parent, child, and adolescent stress and emotion; attachment; health policy.

Lawrence A. Birnbaum, Ph.D., Yale. Natural language understanding, opportunistic planning systems, machine learning.

Justine Cassell, Ph.D., Chicago. Designing technological tools to understand and enhance human communication, embodied conversational agents.

Lindsay Chase-Lansdale, Ph.D., Michigan. Child and adolescent development, family functioning, public policy, multidisciplinary research, poverty and welfare reform, family structure, risk and resilience.

Fay L. Cook, Ph.D., Chicago. Social welfare policy, public attitudes, policy issues in aging, family support systems.

Thomas D. Cook, Ph.D., Stanford. Social-psychological processes, measurement of attitudes, evaluation of social programs.

Solomon Cytrynbaum, Ph.D., Michigan. Developmental and psychodynamic processes, group and organization dynamics, gender and group relations, adult development.

Gregory Duncan, Ph.D., Michigan. Poverty and public policy, longitudinal research methods.

Daniel C. Edelson, Ph.D., Northwestern. Artificial intelligence, case-based teaching systems, collaborative learning environments.

Kenneth D. Forbus, Ph.D., MIT. Qualitative physics, cognitive simulation of analogy, intelligence tutoring systems and learning environments for science and engineering.

Dedre Gentner, Ph.D., California, San Diego. Learning, reasoning, and conceptual change in adults and children; mental models; acquisition of meaning.

Louis M. Gomez, Ph.D., Berkeley. Applied cognitive science, application of computing and networking technology to learning and instruction, human-computer interaction, computer-supported cooperative work.

Kristian Hammond, Ph.D., Yale. Building computer systems designed around human needs and abilities.

Sophie Haroutunian-Gordon, Ph.D., Chicago. Philosophy of education, philosophy of psychology, inquiry, interpretive discussion, teacher preparation.

Larry Hedges, Ph.D., Stanford. Statistical methods for research in education, social sciences, and policy studies; social distribution of test scores.

Phillip Herman, Ph.D., North Carolina. Science education reform, teacher and student efficacy.

Barton J. Hirsch, Ph.D., Oregon. Community psychology, social networks, ecology of adolescent development, after-school programs.

Kemi Jona, Ph.D., Northwestern. Design and development of innovative learning environments, online learning.

David Kanter, Ph.D., Johns Hopkins. Learning technologies in urban schools.

Spyros Konstantopoulos, Ph.D., Chicago. Education measurement, evaluation, and statistical analysis.

John Kretzmann, Ph.D., Northwestern. Sociology, community development.

Eva Lam, Ph.D., Berkeley. Education in language, literacy, and culture.

Carol D. Lee, Ph.D., Chicago. Sociocultural foundations of literacy, literacy expertise within specific ethnic speech communities and their implications for learning and teaching processes, cultural models for knowledge representations in literacy-related tasks.

Dan A. Lewis, Ph.D., California, Santa Cruz. Policy analysis, urban social problems, community organization, urban school reform.

Gregory Light, Ph.D., London. Learning and teaching higher education.

Jelani Mandara, Ph.D., California, Riverside. Families and communities.

Dan P. McAdams, Ph.D., Harvard. Personality development, identity and life stories, intimacy, adult development.

Ann McKenna, Ph.D., Berkeley. Examining effective teaching and learning methods in biomedical engineering education.

Douglas L. Medin, Ph.D., South Dakota. Theories of learning, memory and induction, computational models of cognition, concepts and classification of learning, models of similarity.

Paula M. Olszewski-Kubilius, Ph.D., Northwestern. Gifted education, child development, minority gifted child development.

Andrew Ortony, Ph.D., London. Knowledge representation and figurative language comprehension; models of cognition, motivation, and emotion.

Jennifer Pals, Ph.D., Berkeley. Personality/social psychology.

Penelope L. Peterson, Ph.D., Stanford. Learning and teaching in schools and classrooms, particularly in mathematics and literacy; teacher learning in reform contexts; relations among educational research, policy, and practice.

Carla Pugh, Ph.D., Stanford; M.D., Howard. Technology and medical education.

David Rapp, Ph.D., SUNY at Stony Brook. Experimental psychology, comprehension of texts, psychology of learning.

Michelle Reininger, Ph.D., Stanford. Economics of education, teacher labor markets; teacher quality; educational policy.

Brian J. Reiser, Ph.D., Yale. Intelligent tutoring systems, interactive learning environments for science and technology, scientific inquiry skills.

Christopher K. Riesbeck, Ph.D., Stanford. Natural language and analyzers, case-based reasoners, intelligent computational media.

James E. Rosenbaum, Ph.D., Harvard. Adolescent and adult development, organizational careers.

Kimberly Scott, Ph.D., Ohio State. Organizational effectiveness and change, organizational learning, job satisfaction.

Bruce Sherin, Ph.D., Berkeley. Science education, instructional technology, external representations in science and mathematical learning.

Miriam Sherin, Ph.D., Berkeley. Mathematics teaching and learning, teacher cognition, teacher education.

Bruce D. Spencer, Ph.D., Yale. Social and educational measurement, statistics for policy analysis, demography, decision theory.

James P. Spillane, Ph.D., Michigan State. Educational policy, intergovernmental relations, school reform, relations between policy and local practice.

Lois Trautvetter, Ph.D., Michigan. Higher education, gender issues and females in science.

David H. Uttal, Ph.D., Michigan. Mental representation, cognitive development, spatial cognition, early symbolization.

Sandra R. Waxman, Ph.D., Pennsylvania. Language and conceptual development, early cognitive development, language and thought.

Whitney Whitt, Ph.D., Johns Hopkins. Health care for school-aged children and their families, health policy.

Uri Wilensky, Ph.D., MIT. Science and mathematics learning and technology.

NORTHWESTERN UNIVERSITY

School of Education and Social Policy
Learning Sciences Programs

Programs of Study	The M.A. and Ph.D. programs in the learning sciences are dedicated to the preparation of researchers, developers, and practitioners qualified to advance the scientific understanding and the practice of teaching and learning. The programs are interdisciplinary, drawing on theories and approaches from education, cognitive psychology, developmental psychology, artificial intelligence, computer science, anthropology, and communications. The programs focus on understanding and improving learning environments, not only in schools and classrooms but also in homes, neighborhoods, and work environments. Research projects focus on developing and studying pedagogical, technological, and social policy innovations aimed at improving education. The design of technology plays a special role in the program, exploring ways that technological innovations can facilitate new cognitive and social roles for students and teachers. Through course work and research apprenticeships, students become engaged in the three major themes that permeate research and theory in the learning sciences: (1) social context: the social, organizational, and cultural dynamics of learning and teaching in classrooms, museums, corporations and homes; (2) cognition: scientific models of the structure and processes of learning and teaching by which knowledge skills are structured; and (3) design: building environments for learning and teaching incorporating multimedia, artificial intelligence, network technologies, and innovative curricular and classroom activity structures.
Research Facilities	Research facilities for the Learning Sciences Program in the School of Education and Social Policy are housed in the Tarry Center for Collaborative Teaching and Learning. The Tarry Center opened in December 1999 and occupies the entire third floor of Walter Annenberg Hall. The Tarry Center contains two state-of-the-art Learning Studios with thirty laptop computers connected to large video screens so students can display their work, a Multimedia Lab with fifteen computer workstations with video capabilities for creating multimedia software applications, and a Digital Video Production Suite for recording, editing, compiling, and producing high resolution video records for educational training and research purposes. Special learning dynamics conference rooms allow research groups to work together to study learning interactions. The center contains a high-speed network for digital video, which enables researchers to access and study digital video archives of videotape collected in studies of learning interactions. Walter Annenberg Hall is served by a state-of-the-art, standards-compliant, wireless network system. The School is also involved with the Center for Urban Affairs and Policy Research, which promotes interdisciplinary urban policy and research and training. Northwestern's research libraries contain holdings totaling 4 million volumes, 3.4 million microfilm units, and 40,100 serial publications.
Financial Aid	Several forms of aid are available, including fellowships and teaching and research assistantships for Ph.D. students. A twelve-month stipend of $24,096 and full tuition support are provided to each Ph.D. student accepted to the program. Special opportunities exist within the School's and the University's many research centers. Learning sciences Ph.D. students are eligible for multiyear funding, including summer support, which is competitively awarded.
Cost of Study	Tuition for both the Ph.D. program and the twelve-month M.A. program from September 2007 through August 2008 is $11,688, which is defined as 3 or 4 course units (each term). Health insurance is available.
Living and Housing Costs	The University operates two residences in Evanston for graduate students. Information and assistance in securing off-campus housing are also available for students who wish to inquire.
Student Group	Graduate study occurs within the context of individualized personalized instruction, and, accordingly, enrollments are selective. The combined enrollment for 2005–06 for the Learning Sciences Program was 47 students. Enrollment in all other programs at the School of Education and Social Policy was 260 students.
Student Outcomes	Recent Ph.D. graduates have joined university faculties in leading departments of education and media arts. M.A. graduates work as educational designers, human factors engineers, and school technologists, employed by schools, universities, large and small software companies, international consulting firms, financial institutions, and training providers.
Location	The campus is located on Lake Michigan, 12 miles north of Chicago, which is easily accessible by public transportation. The beautiful lakefront campus offers a rich cultural environment through a wealth of theatrical, musical, and athletic events. Its proximity to a major metropolitan complex further enriches Northwestern's student life.
The University and The School	Established in 1851, Northwestern has grown to become one of the most distinguished private universities in the country. The School of Education and Social Policy has developed from its origins as a department of pedagogy by continually broadening its scope to encompass those educative, learning, and socializing experiences that take place throughout the life span in families, schools, communities, and the workplace. The Learning Sciences Ph.D. Program was established in 1991.
Applying	Applications for admissions are reviewed and acted upon as they are received. Applications are accepted for fall quarter only. Applicants planning to seek financial aid must meet early submission deadlines. Admission to the Learning Sciences Ph.D. Program is highly selective. Students with preparation in a range of disciplinary areas are encouraged to apply, since an interdisciplinary perspective is valued. No part-time students are accepted at this time.
Correspondence and Information	Learning Sciences Ph.D. Program or Learning Sciences M.A. Program School of Education and Social Policy Northwestern University 2120 Campus Drive Evanston, Illinois 60208-2610 Phone: 847-491-7494 E-mail: ls-programs@mail.sesp.northwestern.edu Web site: http://www.sesp.northwestern.edu/ls/

Northwestern University

THE FACULTY AND THEIR RESEARCH

Professors

Solomon Cytrynbaum, Professor of Undergraduate, SESP, and of Psychiatry and Behavioral Sciences and Coordinator, Counseling, Psychology Graduate Program; Ph.D. (psychology), Michigan, 1971. Evaluation of school reform, gender and authority in groups and organizations, organizational consultation, application of group and systems theory and research to school change.

Louis Gomez, Aon Professor of Learning Sciences, Professor of Computer Science, and Coordinator of Learning Sciences Ph.D. Program; Ph.D. (cognitive psychology), Berkeley, 1979. Curriculum design and systemic school reform, school and classroom organization support through technology, application of computing and networking technology to teaching and learning, applied cognitive science, human-computer interaction.

Carol Lee, Professor of Learning Sciences and of African-American Studies and Co-Coordinator, SESP Spencer Research Training Program; Ph.D. (education, curriculum and instruction), Chicago, 1991. Cultural contexts affecting learning broadly and literacy specifically, teacher preparation and development, classroom discourse, urban education.

Andrew Ortony, Professor of Learning Sciences; of Psychology, Weinberg College of Arts and Sciences; of Computer Science, McCormick School of Engineering and Applied Science; and Coordinator, Master's Program, Learning Sciences; Ph.D. (computer science), London, 1972. Emotion and cognition, knowledge representation and figurative language comprehension, human-computer interaction and interface design.

Penelope Peterson, Eleanor R. Baldwin Professor of Education and Dean, School of Education and Social Policy; Ph.D. (psychological studies in education), Stanford, 1976. Learning and teaching in schools and classrooms, particularly in literacy and mathematics; student and teacher learning in reform contexts; relations among educational research, policy, and practice.

Brian Reiser, Professor of Learning Sciences; Ph.D. (cognitive science), Yale, 1983. Design of learning environments and curriculum materials for science that supports authentic practices including explanation, argumentation, and designing investigations; cognitive and social interaction aspects of scientific inquiry; principles for scaffolding practices in software and curriculum materials; teaching practices; curriculum design frameworks.

James Spillane, Professor of Learning Sciences and of Human Development and Social Policy and Faculty Fellow, Institute for Policy Research; Ph.D. (curriculum, teaching, and education policy), Michigan State, 1993. Policy implementation, educational policy, organizational change, school leadership, relations between policy and teachers' and administrators' practice.

Associate Professors

Daniel Edelson, Associate Professor of Learning Sciences and of Computer Science; Ph.D. (computer sciences), Northwestern, 1993. Computer support for authentic learning activities, design and implementation of inquiry-based science curricula, earth and environmental science education, teacher professional development, motivation and learning.

Bruce Sherin, Associate Professor of Learning Sciences; Ph.D., (science and mathematics education), Berkeley, 1996. Conceptual change in science, programming environments for learning, external representations in science and mathematics.

Miriam Sherin, Associate Professor of Learning Sciences; Ph.D., (science and mathematics education), Berkeley, 1996. Mathematics teaching and learning, teacher cognition and teacher education.

David Uttal, Associate Professor of Psychology and of Education; Ph.D., Michigan, 1989. Mental representation, cognitive development, spatial cognition, early symbolization.

Uri Wilensky, Associate Professor of Learning Sciences and of Computer Science and Director, Center for Connected Learning and Computer-Based Modeling; Ph.D. (media arts and sciences), MIT, 1993. Mathematics and science education in the context of computation, connected learning, constructionism, computer-based modeling, agent-based modeling, and complex systems and education.

Assistant Professors

Spyros Konstantopoulos, Assistant Professor of Human Development and Social Policy and of Learning Sciences; Ph.D. (research methodology), Chicago, 2003.

Mixed effects models, meta-analysis, teacher and school effects, class size effects, group differences in achievement.

Eva Lam, Assistant Professor of Learning Sciences and of Asian-American Studies; Ph.D. (education in language, literacy, and culture), Berkeley, 2003. Second language literacy development, literacy and technology, language and identity, language socialization, globalization and English learning, critical discourse analysis, postcolonial study of second language education.

David Rapp, Assistant Professor of Learning Sciences; Ph.D. (experimental psychology), SUNY at Stony Brook, 2000. Reader preferences and the application of temporal situation models, reading comprehension, updating and revising memory/prior knowledge, cognitive processes and consequences of narrative and expository experiences, learning from text and multimedia, automatic and strategic components of text comprehension, spatial language and map comprehension.

Michelle Reininger, Assistant Professor of Learning Sciences and of Human Development and Social Policy and Faculty Fellow, Institute for Policy Research; Ph.D. (social sciences, policy and educational practice), Stanford, 2006. Dynamics of teacher labor markets, including preparation, recruitment, and retention: importance of geography in the occupational decision making of teachers as well as the role of community colleges in the supply of teachers in areas with hard-to-staff schools.

Edd V. Taylor, Assistant Professor of Learning Sciences; Ph.D. (cognition and development in education), Berkeley, 2005. Issues of equity in mathematics education as they relate to understanding the relationship between culture and mathematical cognition; religious practices related to mathematical thinking, specifically tithing.

Faculty Affiliates

Lawrence Birnbaum, Associate Professor of Computer Science and Director, Intellectual Property Management; Ph.D., Yale, 1986. Natural language understanding, opportunistic planning, machine learning.

Kenneth Forbus, Professor of Computer Science and of Education; Ph.D., MIT, 1984. Artificial intelligence: specifically qualitative reasoning, spatial reasoning, analogical reasoning and learning, and inference engine design; cognitive science: understanding how analogy and similarity work, including the roles they play in cognitive and perceptual processes; education: using AI techniques to create new types of educational software and activities; human-computer interaction: the use of sketching as an interface modality to knowledge-rich systems; computer game design: the roles AI, and especially articulate software, can play in creating better game engines and synthetic characters.

Dedre Gentner, Professor of Psychology and of Education; Ph.D., Berkeley, 1974. Learning, reasoning, and conceptual change in adults and children, especially processes of similarity, metaphor, and analogy; mental models; acquisition of meaning.

Sophie Haroutunian-Gordon, Professor of Education and Social Policy and Director, Master of Science in Education Program; Ph.D. (philosophy of education), Chicago, 1976. Philosophy of education, teacher education, interpretive discussion, philosophy of psychology.

Ann McKenna, Research Assistant Professor of Learning Sciences and of the Department of Mechanical Engineering; Ph.D. (science and mathematics education), Berkeley, 2001. Learning through design and complex problem solving; mechanical reasoning; design and implementation of innovative learning environments; assessment of engineering design competency.

Douglas Medin, Professor of Psychology and of Education; Co-Director, Program in Cognitive Studies of the Environment; and Director, Program in Culture, Language, and Cognition; Ph.D., South Dakota, 1968. Learning, reasoning, and conceptual change in adults and children; mental models; acquisition of meaning, culture, and education.

Christopher Riesbeck, Associate Professor of Computer Science and of Education; Ph.D., Stanford, 1983. Natural-language understanding, case-based reasoning, authorable learning-by-doing environments, critiquing tools for education.

Sandra Waxman, Professor of Psychology and of Education; Ph.D., Pennsylvania, 1985. Language and conceptual development, early cognitive development, language and thought.

High school students discuss the progress of their investigation of an evolution scenario developed by students in Professor Reiser's research group.

NOVA SOUTHEASTERN UNIVERSITY

Fischler School of Education and Human Services

Programs of Study

The Fischler School of Education and Human Services of Nova Southeastern University (NSU) offers programs in education and human services leading to the associate (A.A.), bachelor's (B.S.), master's (M.S. and M.A.), educational specialist (Ed.S.), and doctoral (Ed.D. and SLP.D.) degrees. Areas of study include educational leadership, health-care education, higher education, human services administration, instructional leadership, instructional technology and distance education, organizational leadership, special education, speech-language pathology, TESOL, and thirty-three specializations within teacher education. The master's and doctoral programs in speech-language pathology are clinically based. Ed.D. programs, which are offered in more than sixty clusters throughout the U.S. and Latin American and Caribbean countries, provide working professionals with the advanced training and knowledge that they need to benefit their schools and organizations. Research underpins two- to three-year doctoral programs that include periodic on-campus institutes and culminate in a practicum (dissertation) that is applicable to the student's work environment. Virtually all programs are field based, site based, or offered via distance technology to locations throughout the U.S. and the world at times and locations that are convenient to the student. International study and placement opportunities exist as well. Many courses and several degrees are available in an entirely online format. Certificate programs, which are also offered online, are available in several fields. Term lengths vary according to the program of study; most master's degrees can be completed in fifteen months or less.

Research Facilities

Ever-developing community-based interactions and partnerships provide students in most disciplines ample opportunity to design and conduct research that is appropriate to their own program of study. Most Fischler School students are employed in the field in which they are studying, which enables students to use their own workplaces and real needs as the basis for applied research projects (practicums). Students in the speech-language pathology programs have access to one of the largest clinical populations anywhere and support research programs in equipment design, augmentative communication, and other fields that are unique to speech and hearing professionals, in addition to collaborative programs with NSU's medical, dental, and pharmacy schools. All students, regardless of location, have access to hundreds of databases and online resources through NSU's Electronic Library.

Financial Aid

Nova Southeastern University's Office of Student Financial Assistance administers comprehensive federal, state, institutional, and private financial aid programs. Students who are interested in receiving a financial aid packet should contact the office at 800-806-3680 (toll-free) or 954-262-3380 or visit the Web site at http://www.nova.edu/cwis/finaid. Some programs in the Fischler School offer a limited number of graduate student assistantships, fellowships, and/or scholarships. Prospective students should also inquire whether their states offer some form of support for advanced study in particular areas (such as special education or substance abuse).

Cost of Study

Tuition for programs in 2006–07 ranged from $225 per credit to $718 per credit.

Living and Housing Costs

Virtually all Fischler School students live and work in their own homes and communities throughout Florida, the U.S., and other countries.

Student Group

There are more than 15,000 students in the Fischler School of Education and Human Services, representing a diverse range of cultures and backgrounds, from more than thirty states and nearly a dozen countries. Virtually all work in their fields of study. NSU leads all colleges and universities in doctoral degrees granted to African Americans and is a leader in degrees awarded to Hispanics. The average age of doctoral students is 44.

Location

The Fischler School of Education and Human Services' home campus is a 250,000-square-foot complex in North Miami Beach, Florida, amid one of the most diverse and fastest-growing metropolitan areas in the country, with nearly 5 million residents. The School also has permanent classroom and administrative facilities in Orlando, Miami, Fort Lauderdale, Tampa, West Palm Beach, and Jacksonville, Florida, and in Las Vegas, Nevada, and part-time classroom facilities in nearly a dozen other cities.

The University

Nova Southeastern University, with its home campus in Fort Lauderdale, Florida, is the sixth-largest independent not-for-profit university in the country, based on enrollment. Since its founding in 1964, NSU has been a pioneer of nontraditional approaches to high-quality higher education. Today, the University has more than 2,800 employees, 25,000 students, and 86,000 graduates in fields ranging from law and medicine to psychology, business, and education. The University is accredited through 2008 by the Southern Association of Colleges and Schools.

Applying

Applicants are encouraged to contact the individual programs of study for admissions requirements, packets, and timetables. Admission to the programs requires the appropriate prerequisite degree from an accredited school and a minimum grade point average. The MAT or GRE is required for admission to doctoral programs.

Correspondence and Information

Associate Dean of Student Services
Fischler School of Education and Human Services
Nova Southeastern University
1750 Northeast 167th Street
North Miami Beach, Florida 33162-3017
Phone: 954-262-8500
      800-986-3223 (toll-free)
E-mail: eduinfo@nova.edu
Web site: http://www.FischlerSchool.nova.edu

Nova Southeastern University

ACADEMIC PROGRAMS

To request program information and application materials, students should contact the School via telephone (800-986-3223 or 954-262-8500) or e-mail (eduinfo@nova.edu).

DOCTORAL DEGREE PROGRAMS
Ed.D. (Doctor of Education), with nine concentrations in:
- educational leadership
- health-care education
- higher education
- human services administration
- instructional leadership
- instructional technology and distance education
- organizational leadership
- special education
- speech-language pathology

SLP.D. (Doctor of Speech-Language Pathology)

EDUCATIONAL SPECIALIST PROGRAM
Ed.S., with fifteen specializations in:
- brain research (BrainSMART Program)
- computer science education
- curriculum and teaching
- curriculum/instruction management and administration
- early literacy and reading education
- educational leadership
- educational media
- elementary education
- English education
- gifted education
- mathematics education
- reading education
- science education
- teaching English to speakers of other languages (TESOL)
- technology management and administration

MASTER'S DEGREE PROGRAMS
M.A. in Teaching and Learning, with four concentrations in:
- curriculum and instruction
- elementary mathematics
- elementary reading
- K–12 instructional technology

M.S. in Human Services, with three specializations in:
- child- and youth-care administration
- early childhood education administration
- family support studies

M.S. in Child Protection, with four specializations in:
- administration for child, youth, and family support programs
- advocating for the special needs child's education
- child protection and juvenile justice
- child, youth, and family support

M.S. in Criminal Justice, with two specializations in:
- child protection and juvenile justice
- substance abuse

M.S. in Health Professions Education, with nine concentrations in:
- dental education
- medical education
- medical science education
- occupational therapy education
- optometry education
- pharmacy education
- physical therapy education
- physician assistance education
- public health education

M.S. in Instructional Technology and Distance Education

M.S. in Leadership

M.S. in Speech-Language Pathology

M.S. in Education, with thirty-three specializations in:
- athletic administration
- brain research (BrainSMART Program)
- charter school education/leadership
- cognitive and behavioral disabilities
- computer science education
- curriculum, instruction, and technology
- early childhood special education
- early literacy education
- educational leadership
- educational media
- educational technology
- elementary education
- English education
- environmental education
- exceptional student education
- gifted child education
- high/scope early childhood education
- interdisciplinary arts
- literacy education (scholastic)
- management and administration of educational programs
- mathematics education
- multicultural early intervention
- prekindergarten and primary education
- preschool education
- reading education
- science education
- secondary education
- social studies education
- Spanish language education
- teaching and learning
- teaching English as a foreign language (TEFL)
- teaching English to speakers of other languages (TESOL)
- urban studies education

THE OHIO STATE UNIVERSITY

College of Education and Human Ecology

Programs of Study

The Ohio State University (OSU) College of Education and Human Ecology awards the M.A., M.S., M.Ed., and Ph.D. degrees from six academic units.

The School of Educational Policy and Leadership includes programs in curriculum studies; diversity studies; educational administration; educational psychology; higher education; historical, philosophical, and comparative studies; policy studies; quantitative research, evaluation, and measurement in education; teacher education; and technology of instruction and media.

The School of Physical Activity and Educational Services has programs in counselor education, school psychology, special education, sport and exercise education, sport and exercise humanities, sport and exercise management, sport and exercise science, sport and exercise studies, and workforce development and education (adult education, business education, and vocational-technical education).

The School of Teaching and Learning offers programs in early and middle childhood education, physical and sensory disabilities, English education, foreign language and second language education, social studies and global education, drama, language arts, children's literature, reading education, and mathematics, science, and technology education.

The Department of Consumer Sciences offers programs in family resource management, hospitality management, and textiles and clothing.

The Department of Human Development and Family Science offers early child development and education, family science, human development, family life education, and the AAMFT-accredited couples and family therapy Ph.D. program.

The interdisciplinary Family and Consumer Sciences postbaccalaureate program prepares students for licensure to teach in middle and high schools.

The Department of Human Nutrition offers the M.S. in human nutrition and a dietetic internship accredited by the American Dietetic Association. The department also participates in the Interdisciplinary Ph.D. Program in Nutrition.

Other OSU colleges offer agriculture, art, dance, and music education programs. The M.Ed. in early and middle childhood education is also offered at Ohio State's regional campuses at Lima, Mansfield, Marion, and Newark. Information on all degree programs is located on the College's Web site.

Research Facilities

The Ohio State University, ranked in the top twenty-five U.S. public universities, is a comprehensive research university with a wide range of facilities for study. Its 5.7-million-volume library system includes an education and human sciences library with more than 500,000 volumes. The University's $550 million per year in research expenditures places it ninth among public research universities in the U.S. by the National Science Foundation. The College received $27 million in federal and nonfederal research grants in 2004–05.

Financial Aid

The College has an $850,000 scholarship program for top applicants. Grants are varied. There are 170 awards from the College and its academic units. In addition, Ohio State offers thousands of graduate associateships and fellowships. All financial aid is competitive, and stipends vary. Information is available on the Web site at http://gradadmissions.osu.edu/.

Cost of Study

The cost of graduate tuition for three quarters is $8250 for a U.S. citizen, permanent resident, aslyee, or refugee and a legal resident of the state of Ohio; and $20,133 for a U.S. citizen, permanent resident, aslyee, or refugee whose legal residence is outside of Ohio. Part-time students are assessed a fee per quarter hour.

Living and Housing Costs

An Ohio resident pays an estimated $12,048 per year for health insurance and lodging.

Student Group

Enrollment is 58,000 at the Columbus and five regional campuses. The College of Education and Human Ecology graduate enrollment totals approximately 1,700, with a minority enrollment of 15 percent. In addition, there are 200 international students enrolled in the College's graduate programs. They come from thirty-six countries. Ohio State is listed among the top twenty institutions for granting doctoral degrees to American Indians and Alaskan Natives and is ranked as one of the country's fifty best colleges for African Americans by *Black Enterprise* magazine. For more information, students from minority and international groups should contact the College's Office of Diversity, Urban, and International/Global Affairs at 614-292-1936.

Location

The main campus is located in Columbus, Ohio, the state capital and one of the fastest-growing urban areas in the United States. The city is a global center for high technology.

The College

The new College of Education and Human Ecology was formed in July 2006. The College has more resources, scholarly talent, and academic strength than ever before. It has a true multidisciplinary program that takes a comprehensive, holistic approach to complex educational, human, and consumer issues. The graduate education program has been ranked in the top tier of graduate programs for the past ten years, and the human ecology programs have a strong professional reputation nationwide. The College has 172 full-time faculty members, 15 percent of whom are members of minority groups, and approximately 1,700 graduate students, including 200 international students. A total of 15 percent of the students are members of minority groups.

Applying

Applicants may apply online or download application materials from the Graduate Admissions Web site at http://gradadmissions.osu.edu/. Applicants with disabilities can learn about services at http://www.ods.ohio-state.edu or by calling 614-292-3307 (voice) or 614-292-0901 (TDD).

Correspondence and Information

General information about the College of Education and Human Ecology can be found at http://ehe.osu.edu or by contacting the individual school or department.

School of Physical Activity and
 Educational Services
100 PAES Building
The Ohio State University
305 West 17th Avenue
Columbus, Ohio 43210
Phone: 614-292-6787

Department of Consumer Sciences
231 Campbell Hall
The Ohio State University
1787 Neil Avenue
Columbus, Ohio 43210
Phone: 614-292-4389

School of Educational Policy and
 Leadership
122 Ramseyer Hall
The Ohio State University
29 West Woodruff Avenue
Columbus, Ohio 43210
Phone: 614-292-5181

Department of Human Development and
 Family Science
135 Campbell Hall
The Ohio State University
1787 Neil Avenue
Columbus, Ohio 43210
Phone: 614-292-7705

School of Teaching and Learning
227 Arps Hall
The Ohio State University
1945 North High Street
Columbus, Ohio 43210
Phone: 614-292-2332

Department of Human Nutrition
325 Campbell Hall
The Ohio State University
1787 Neil Avenue
Columbus, Ohio 43210
Phone: 614-292-4485

The Ohio State University

THE FACULTY

School of Educational Policy and Leadership
Ann Allen, Assistant Professor; Ph.D., Michigan State.
Leonard Baird, Professor; Ed.D., UCLA.
Sebnam Cilesiz, Assistant Professor; Ph.D., Florida.
Suzanne Damarin, Professor; Ph.D., Ohio State.
Philip T. K. Daniel, Flesher Professor; Ph.D., Illinois at Urbana-Champaign.
Heather Davis, Assistant Professor; Ph.D., Georgia.
Ayres D'Costa, Associate Professor; Ph.D., Ohio.
Ada Demb, Associate Professor; Ph.D., Harvard.
Peter Demerath, Associate Professor; Ed.D., Massachusetts.
Antoinette Errante, Associate Professor; Ph.D., Minnesota.
Dorinda Gallant, Assistant Professor; Ph.D., South Carolina.
Belinda Gimbert, Assistant Professor; Ph.D., Penn State.
Beverly Gordon, Associate Professor; Ph.D., Wisconsin–Madison.
D. Ted Hall, Assistant Professor; Ph.D., Michigan State.
Robert Hite, Associate Professor; Ph.D., Ohio State.
Anita Woolfolk Hoy, Professor; Ph.D., Texas at Austin.
Wayne Hoy, Professor and Fawcett Chair; Ed.D., Penn State.
Patricia Lather, Professor; Ph.D., Indiana.
Robert Lawson, Professor; Ph.D., Michigan.
Xiaodong Liu, Assistant Professor; Ed.D., Harvard.
William Loadman, Professor; Ph.D., Michigan State.
Richard Lomax, Professor; Ph.D., Pittsburgh.
Douglas Macbeth, Associate Professor; Ph.D., Berkeley.
Helen Marks, Associate Professor; Ph.D., Michigan.
Philip Smith, Associate Professor; Ph.D., Michigan.
Tatiana Suspitsyna, Assistant Professor; Ph.D., Michigan.
Scott Sweetland, Associate Professor; Ph.D., SUNY at Buffalo.
William Taylor, Associate Professor; Ph.D., Indiana.
Bruce Tuckman, Professor; Ph.D., Princeton.
Richard Voithofer, Assistant Professor; Ph.D., Wisconsin–Madison.
Bryan Warnick, Assistant Professor; Ph.D., Illinois at Urbana-Champaign.
Michele Welkener, Assistant Professor; Ph.D., Miami (Ohio).

School of Physical Activity and Educational Services
Melvin Adelman, Associate Professor; Ph.D., Illinois at Chicago.
Janet Buckworth, Associate Professor; Ph.D., Georgia.
Gwendolyn Cartledge, Professor; Ph.D., Ohio State.
R. Michael Casto, Associate Professor; Ph.D., Duke.
P. Chelladurai, Professor; Ph.D., Waterloo.
Steven Devor, Associate Professor; Ph.D., Berkeley.
Sarah Fields, Assistant Professor; Ph.D., J.D., Iowa.
Janet Fink, Associate Professor; Ph.D., Ohio State.
Ralph Gardner III, Associate Professor; Ph.D., Ohio State.
Jacqueline Goodway-Shiebler, Associate Professor; Ph.D., Michigan State.
Darcy Haag Granello, Associate Professor; Ph.D., Ohio.
Paul Granello, Associate Professor; Ph.D., Ohio.
Bruce Growick, Associate Professor; Ph.D., Wisconsin–Madison.
Joshua Hawley, Assistant Professor; Ph.D., Harvard.
Leah Herner, Assistant Professor; Ed.D., Nevada, Las Vegas.
Terri Hessler, Assistant Professor; Ph.D., Ohio State.
Lisa Hinkleman, Assistant Professor; Ph.D., Ohio State.
Samuel Hodge, Associate Professor; Ph.D., Ohio State.
Ronald Jacobs, Professor; Ph.D., Indiana Bloomington.
Laurice Joseph, Associate Professor; Ph.D., Ohio State.
Timothy Kirby, Associate Professor; Ph.D., Texas A&M.
Michael Klein, Associate Professor; Ph.D., Penn State.
Moira Konrad, Assistant Professor; Ph.D., North Carolina at Charlotte.
Larry Magliocca, Associate Professor; Ph.D., Ohio State.
Helen Malone, Assistant Professor; Ph.D., Texas at Austin.
Antoinette Miranda, Associate Professor; Ph.D., Cincinnati.
James Moore III, Assistant Professor; Ph.D., Virginia Tech.
Sheila Morgan, Associate Professor; Ph.D., Ohio State.
William Morgan, Professor; Ph.D., Minnesota.
Nancy Neef, Professor; Ph.D., Western Michigan.
Donna Pastore, Professor and Director; Ph.D., Ohio State.
Richard Petosa, Associate Professor; Ph.D., Southern Illinois.
David Porretta, Professor; Ph.D., Temple.
Diane Sainato, Associate Professor; Ph.D., Pittsburgh.
W. Michael Sherman, Professor; Ph.D., Texas at Austin.
David Stein, Associate Professor; Ph.D., Ohio State.
Sandra Stroot, Professor; Ph.D., Northern Colorado.
Brian Turner, Assistant Professor; Ph.D., Ohio State.
Phillip Ward, Professor; Ph.D., Ohio State.

Joseph Wheaton, Associate Professor; Ph.D., Wisconsin.
Christopher Wood, Assistant Professor; Ph.D., Oregon State.
Christopher Zirkle, Assistant Professor; Ph.D., Ohio State.

School of Teaching and Learning
Rhoda Becher, Associate Professor; Ph.D., Ohio State.
Mary Bendixen-Noe, Associate Professor; Ph.D., Ohio State.
Donna G. Berlin, Professor; Ph.D., Ohio State.
Mollie Blackburn, Assistant Professor; Ph.D., Pennsylvania.
David Bloome, Professor; Ph.D., Kent State.
Patricia Brosnan, Associate Professor; Ph.D., SUNY at Buffalo.
Terri Teal Bucci, Assistant Professor; Ph.D., Ohio State.
Mary Christenson, Assistant Professor; Ph.D., Ohio State.
Caroline Clark, Associate Professor; Ph.D., Michigan.
Jeane Copenhaver-Johnson, Assistant Professor; Ph.D., South Florida.
Dean Cristol, Associate Professor; Ph.D., Old Dominion.
Scot Danforth, Associate Professor; Ph.D., South Florida.
Cynthia Dillard, Associate Professor; Ph.D., Washington State.
Adrienne D. Dixson, Assistant Professor; Ph.D., Wisconsin–Madison.
Brian Edmiston, Associate Professor; Ph.D., Ohio State.
Patricia Enciso, Associate Professor; Ph.D., Ohio State.
Diana Erchick, Associate Professor; Ph.D., Ohio State.
Donna Farland, Assistant Professor; Ph.D., Massachusetts.
Marcia Farr, Professor; Ph.D., Georgetown.
Lucia Flevares, Assistant Professor; Ph.D., Illinois at Urbana-Champaign.
Evelyn B. Freeman, Professor; Ph.D., Ohio State.
Mary Jo Fresch, Associate Professor; Ph.D., Ohio State.
Charles Hancock, Professor; Ph.D., Ohio State.
Mariko Haneda, Assistant Professor; Ph.D., Toronto.
David Haury, Associate Professor; Ph.D., Washington (Seattle).
Alan Hirvela, Assistant Professor; Ph.D., Stirling (Scotland).
Karen Irving, Assistant Professor; Ph.D., Virginia.
Lynn Johnson, Associate Professor; Ph.D., Indiana State.
Rebecca Kantor-Martin, Professor and Director; Ed.D., Boston University.
Laurie Katz, Associate Professor; Ed.D., Massachusetts.
Barbara Kiefer, Charlotte Huck Professor of Language, Literacy, and Culture; Ph.D., Ohio State.
Hea-Jin Lee, Assistant Professor; Ph.D., Ohio State.
Barbara Lehman, Professor; Ed.D., Virginia.
Guarav Mathur, Assistant Professor; Ph.D., MIT.
Lea McGee, Marie Clay Professor of Reading Recovery and Early Literacy; Ed.D., Virginia Tech.
Merry Merryfield, Professor; Ed.D., Indiana.
Maia Pank Mertz, Professor; Ph.D., Minnesota.
Steven L. Miller, Associate Professor; Ph.D., Ohio State.
Leslie Moore, Assistant Professor; Ph.D., UCLA.
George Newell, Professor; Ph.D., Stanford.
Karen Newman, Assistant Professor; Ph.D., Indiana.
Thomas O'Brien, Associate Professor; Ph.D., Emory.
Douglas Owens, Professor; Ed.D., Georgia.
Peter Paul, Professor; Ph.D., Illinois at Urbana-Champaign.
Paul Post, Assistant Professor; Ph.D., Purdue.
Adrian Rodgers, Assistant Professor; Ph.D., Ohio State.
Emily Rodgers, Associate Professor; Ph.D., Ohio State.
Anita Roychoudhury, Associate Professor; Ph.D., Indiana.
Keiko Samimy, Associate Professor; Ph.D., Illinois at Urbana-Champaign.
Patricia Scharer, Professor; Ph.D., Ohio State.
Barbara Seidl, Associate Professor; Ph.D., Wisconsin–Milwaukee.
Anna Soter, Associate Professor; Ph.D., Illinois at Urbana-Champaign.
Binaya Subedi, Assistant Professor; Ph.D., Ohio State.
Barbara Thomson, Associate Professor; Ph.D., Ohio State.
Kathy Cabe Trundle, Assistant Professor; Ph.D., Tennessee.
Cynthia Tyson, Associate Professor; Ph.D., Ohio State.
Sigrid Wagner, Professor; Ph.D., NYU.
Christine Warner, Assistant Professor; Ph.D., Ohio State.
Arthur L. White, Professor; Ph.D., Colorado.
Ian A. G. Wilkinson, Associate Professor; Ph.D., Illinois at Urbana-Champaign.
Karen Zuga, Professor; Ph.D., Ohio State.

Department of Consumer Sciences
Patricia Cunningham, Associate Professor; Ph.D., Florida State.
Jonathan Fox, Associate Professor; Ph.D., Maryland.
Loren Geistfeld, Professor; Ph.D., Minnesota.
Tom George, Associate Professor; Ed.D., Cincinnati.
Sherman Hanna, Professor; Ph.D., Cornell.
Gong-Soog Hong, Professor and Chair; Ph.D., Cornell.

Golden Jackson, Associate Professor; Ph.D., Ohio State.
Kathryn Jakes, Professor; Ph.D., Clemson.
Wayne Johnson, Associate Professor; Ph.D., North Dakota.
Jay Kandampully, Professor; Ph.D., Exeter (England).
Jinkook Lee, Professor; Ph.D., Ohio State.
Cäzilia Loibl, Assistant Professor; Ph.D., Technical University of Munich.
Catherine Montalto, Associate Professor; Ph.D., Cornell.
H. G. Parsa, Associate Professor; Ph.D., Virginia Tech.
Nancy A. Rudd, Associate Professor; Ph.D., Ohio State.
Robert L. Scharff, Assistant Professor; Ph.D., Duke; J.D., George Mason.
Sharon Seiling, Associate Professor; Ph.D., Cornell.
Kathryn Stafford, Associate Professor; Ph.D., Cornell.
Leslie Stoel, Associate Professor; Ph.D., Michigan State.
Michael J. Tews, Assistant Professor; Ph.D., Cornell.
Susan Zavotka, Associate Professor; Ph.D., Ohio State.

Department of Human Development and Family Science
David W. Andrews, Dean; Ph.D., Florida State.
Suzanne Bartle-Haring, Professor; Ph.D., Connecticut.
Amy Bonomi, Associate Professor; M.P.H., Ph.D., Washington (Seattle).
Stephen M. Gavazzi, Professor; Ph.D., Connecticut.
Michael Glassman, Associate Professor; Ph.D., CUNY Graduate Center.
Stephen Petrill, Professor; Ph.D., Case Western Reserve.
Sarah Schoppe-Sullivan, Assistant Professor; Ph.D., Illinois at Urbana-Champaign.
Jerelyn B. Schultz, Professor; Ph.D., Iowa State.
Julianne Serovich, Professor and Chair; Ph.D., Georgia.
Natasha Slesnick, Associate Professor; Ph.D., New Mexico.
Vladimir Sloutsky, Professor and Associate Dean; Ph.D., USSR Academy of Pedagogical Sciences.
Deanna Wilkinson, Associate Professor; Ph.D., Rutgers.

Department of Human Nutrition
Martha A. Belury, Associate Professor; Ph.D., Texas at Austin; RD.
Joshua Bomser, Assistant Professor; Ph.D., Illinois at Urbana-Champaign.
Tony Buffington, Professor; Ph.D., D.V.M., California, Davis.
Steven K. Clinton, Associate Professor; M.D., Ph.D., Illinois at Chicago.
Konrad Dabrowski, Professor; D.Sc., Ph.D., Agricultural University (Poland).
Burk Dehority, Professor; Ph.D., Ohio State.
Steven T. Devor, Associate Professor; Ph.D., California, Berkeley.
Robert A. DiSilvestro, Professor; Ph.D., Texas A&M.
Maurice Eastridge, Professor; Ph.D., Purdue.
Mark Failla, Professor and Chair; Ph.D., Indiana.
Jeffrey Firkins, Professor; Ph.D., Illinois at Urbana-Champaign.
Earl Harrison, Duhamel Professor; Ph.D., Columbia.
Rebecca Jackson, Professor; M.D., Ohio State.
Douglas Kniss, Professor; Ph.D., Ohio State.
Laura Kresty, Assistant Professor; Ph.D., Ohio State.
David Latshaw, Professor; Ph.D., Washington State.
Ken Lee, Professor; Ph.D., Massachusetts Amherst.
Kichoon Lee, Assistant Professor; Ph.D., Georgia.
Michael Lilburn, Professor; Ph.D., Penn State.
Young C. Lin, Professor; Ph.D., Tokyo; D.V.M., National Taiwan.
Steven Loerch, Professor; Ph.D., Illinois.
Donald Mahan, Professor; Ph.D., Illinois.
Velimir Matkovic, Professor; M.D., Ph.D., Zagreb (Croatia).
Lydia Medeiros, Associate Professor; Ph.D., Wyoming; RD.
Kamal D. Mehta, Professor; Ph.D., McMaster.
Hugo Melgár-Quiñonez, Assistant Professor; M.D., Ph.D., Friedrich Schiller (Germany).
Mark Morrison, Professor; Ph.D., Illinois.
Robert Murray, Professor; M.D., Indiana.
Kwame Osei, Professor; M.D., Ghana Medical School.
Sampath Parthasarathy, Klassen Professor; Ph.D., Indian Institute of Science.
Electra Paskett, Rowley Professor; Ph.D., Washington (Seattle).
Chris K. Reynolds, Associate Professor; Ph.D., Tennessee.
Steven Schwartz, Haas Professor; Ph.D., Wisconsin.
Chandan Sen, Professor; Ph.D., Kuopio (Finland).
Normand St-Pierre, Professor; Ph.D., Purdue.
Anne M. Smith, Associate Professor; Ph.D., Illinois at Urbana-Champaign; RD.
Gary Stoner, Professor; Ph.D., Michigan.
Helen Wang, Assistant Professor; Ph.D., Minnesota.
William Weiss, Professor; Ph.D., Ohio State.
Lisa Yee, Associate Professor; M.D., Yale.

PACE UNIVERSITY

School of Education

Programs of Study

The School of Education offers distinguished programs resulting in the Master of Science for Teachers (M.S.T.); the Master of Science in Education (M.S.Ed.), with specializations in educational leadership, educational technology, literacy, and special education; a Certificate of Advanced Graduate Study (C.A.G.S.) in educational leadership; and Advanced Certificates in early childhood administration, educational technology, and teaching/adolescent track.

The M.S.Ed. in educational leadership is a 33-credit program designed to provide future administrators with a sound foundation of knowledge and experience for making thoughtful decisions for schools and other educational institutions. Experienced teachers who complete the program are eligible for the New York State School Based Leader (SBL) certification.

Three additional 36-credit M.S.Ed. programs are offered in educational technology, literacy, and special education. These programs are designed for individuals holding a baccalaureate degree in education and/or those holding provisional, initial, or permanent certification as elementary or secondary school teachers. The educational technology program offers a hands-on format where teachers learn to use technology tools to enhance instruction. The program prepares candidates to teach with and about technology and to support colleagues in their use of technologies. Program candidates are not required to hold a teaching certificate upon entry into the program and may come with or without a background in technology or education. Candidates gain competencies stipulated by the International Society for Technology in Education (ISTE) and qualify for New York State's Educational Technology Specialist certificate. The literacy program offers innovative collaboration for classroom and reading teachers to serve the varying needs, interests, and skills of students at the elementary and secondary level. The special education program focuses on inclusionary practices and techniques, studying assessment, support, and education of students with disabilities.

The M.S.T. program is an intensive 36-credit program for career changers and college graduates who want to teach but do not have an undergraduate degree in education. The program prepares educators who are reflective professionals who promote justice, create caring classroom and school communities, and enable all students to be successful learners. Candidates are challenged to reflect on their images of schools, classrooms, teaching, and learning. These reflections are grounded in the context of the socially just and caring classroom. Student teaching, an action research project, and a teaching portfolio are required capstone experiences in the program. The program emphasizes an integrated theory and practice model of pedagogy and is available with concentrations in childhood education (grades 1–6) and adolescent education (grades 7–12). Adolescent education specializations are offered in biology, business education, chemistry, earth science, English, mathematics, modern languages other than English, physics, social studies, and visual arts. Degree completion, satisfactory completion of the New York State certification examinations, and full-time teaching result in eligibility for the New York State initial and professional teaching certification.

The School also provides the opportunity for students to extend their teaching certificates in several areas. Individuals who meet the requirements may extend their certificates to teach in middle schools (grades 5–8), bilingual and early childhood environments, and gifted students.

Research Facilities

The Pace University Library is a comprehensive teaching library and student-learning center, a virtual library that combines strong core collections with ubiquitous access to global Internet resources to support broad and diversified curricula. Reciprocal borrowing and access accords, traditional interlibrary loan services, and commercial document delivery options supplement the aggregate library. Pace offers Instructional Services Librarians, a state-of-the-art electronic classroom, digital reference services, and multimedia applications.

Pace's computer resource centers are linked to high-speed data networks and feature sophisticated hardware and software to facilitate active learning. Recognized as one of America's most wired universities, Pace supports high-speed Internet and Internet2 access on every campus; resident facilities are wired, and most public areas are enabled for wireless connectivity. Full-motion videoconference facilities enable remote delivery of instruction between campus sites for synchronous learning applications. Many courses are Web-assisted with state-of-the-art software, and some courses and programs are completely Web-based.

Financial Aid

Pace's comprehensive student financial aid assistance program includes scholarships, graduate assistantships, student loans, and tuition payment plans. Scholarships are awarded to students in recognition of academic achievement and are available for full- and part-time study. Highly qualified students may be eligible for assistantships awarded by departments, which paid up to $5100 in stipends and up to 24 credits in tuition remission during the 2006–07 academic year. Pace participates in all major federal and state financial aid programs, such as federal loans, New York State Tuition Assistance Program (TAP), Perkins Loans, and Federal Work-Study. All students are encouraged to apply for these programs by filing the Free Application for Federal Student Aid (FAFSA).

Cost of Study

Tuition for graduate courses is $734 per credit in 2007–08.

Living and Housing Costs

Residence facilities are available in both New York City and Westchester. Double-occupancy rooms range from approximately $8500 to $12,000 for the 2007–08 academic year. University-operated, off-campus housing is available within proximity of the New York City campus.

Student Group

Pace students represent diversified personal, cultural, and educational backgrounds. Many students are employed and pursue graduate study for personal growth and career advancement. Eighty-nine percent are enrolled part-time in evening classes. Current enrollment in the education programs is approximately 1,175 students.

Location

Pace University is a multicampus institution with campuses in both New York City and Westchester County, New York. All locations are within reach of cultural, business, and social resources and opportunities. The downtown Manhattan campus is adjacent to Wall Street and City Hall. Pace's Midtown Center is a short distance from Times Square, theaters, and Grand Central Station. The Pleasantville/Briarcliff campus is a suburban setting, surrounded by towns offering various forms of recreation. The Graduate Center and the School of Law are located in White Plains, among major retail districts and many corporate headquarters. All locations are accessible by public transportation. Graduate education programs are available at both the New York City and Westchester campuses.

The University

Founded in 1906, Pace University is a private, nonsectarian, coeducational institution. Originally founded as a school of accounting, Pace Institute was designated Pace College in 1948. Through growth and various successes, it was renamed Pace University in 1973 as approved by the New York State Board of Regents. Today, Pace offers comprehensive undergraduate, graduate, doctoral, and professional programs at several campus locations through six schools and colleges.

Applying

Admission to Pace University requires successful completion of a U.S. baccalaureate degree or its equivalent from an accredited institution. Students must submit a completed application, the application fee, official transcripts from all postsecondary institutions, a personal statement, a resume, and two letters of recommendation. International students must also submit official TOEFL scores and official transcripts in their native language with a professional English translation. Applications should be submitted by August 1, December 1, and May 1 for fall, spring, and summer semesters, respectively. International applications should be submitted one month prior to these dates.

Correspondence and Information

Office of Graduate Admission
Pace University
1 Pace Plaza
New York, New York 10038
Phone: 212-346-1531
Fax: 212-346-1585
E-mail: gradnyc@pace.edu
Web site: http://www.pace.edu

Office of Graduate Admission
Pace University
1 Martine Avenue
White Plains, New York 10606
Phone: 914-422-4283
Fax: 914-422-4287
E-mail: gradwp@pace.edu
Web site: http://www.pace.edu

Pace University

THE FACULTY

Ainsley Adams, Lecturer; M.P.S., Manhattanville.
Kathryn Ahern, Assistant Professor; Ph.D., Nebraska–Lincoln.
Anthony Alfonso, Lecturer; M.S., Fordham.
David D. Avdul, Professor; Ed.D., Columbia Teachers College.
Vincent Baldari, Instructor; M.S., CUNY, Hunter.
Sam Blank, Instructor; Ed.M., Columbia Teachers College.
Roy Jules Blash, Adjunct Associate Professor; J.D., New York Law.
Charles Bonnici, Adjunct Instructor; M.A., NYU; Professional Diploma, Fordham.
Patricia Brock, Adjunct Assistant Professor; Ed.D., Rutgers.
Nadine Bryce, Assistant Professor; Ed.D., Columbia Teachers College.
Linda Carlson, Adjunct Instructor; M.A., Ohio State.
Joel Chabon, Adjunct Instructor; M.S.Ed., Hofstra.
Christine Clayton, Assistant Professor; Ed.D., Columbia Teachers College.
Carol Corbin, Adjunct Instructor; M.S., Pace.
Robert Dancik, Adjunct Instructor; M.A., Northern Illinois.
Sonja de Groot Kim, Assistant Professor; Ph.D., NYU.
Sr. St. John Delany, Associate Professor; Ph.D., Fordham.
Kathryn De Lawter, Assistant Professor; Ed.D., Columbia Teachers College.
Andrew DeSimone, Adjunct Associate Professor; M.S., Pace.
Suzanne Dohm, Adjunct Lecturer; M.A., Pace.
Gail Epstein, Adjunct Assistant Professor; M.S.Ed., Pace.
Joanne Falinski, Assistant Professor; Ph.D., Syracuse.
Susan Fine, Adjunct Assistant Professor; Ph.D., Columbia.
Sandra Flank, Professor; Ph.D., Fordham.
Rochelle Frei, Assistant Professor; Ed.D., Hofstra.
Richard Freyman, Adjunct Assistant Professor; M.B.A., Columbia.
Marina Gair, Assistant Professor; Ph.D., Arizona State.
Judith Kaplan, Adjunct Assistant Professor; M.A., Columbia Teachers College.
Beth Kava, Lecturer; M.A.T., Brown; M.S.Ed., Pace.
Carol Keyes, Professor; Ph.D., Union (Ohio).
Michael Kirsch, Adjunct Associate Professor; Ed.D., Pennsylvania.
Mona Lener, Adjunct Assistant Professor; M.S., CUNY, Brooklyn.
Alan Lentin, Adjunct Assistant Professor; Ph.D., Fordham.
Eleanore Livesey, Adjunct Assistant Professor; M.S., CUNY, Lehman; Professional Diploma, Pace.
Alfred Lodovico, Adjunct Assistant Professor; Ed.D., Bridgeport.
Arthur Maloney, Assistant Professor; Ed.D., Columbia Teachers College.
Janet Matthews, Adjunct Instructor; M.A., Manhattanville.
Mary Rose McCarthy, Assistant Professor; Ph.D., Buffalo, SUNY.
Janet McDonald, Professor and Dean; Ph.D., SUNY at Albany.
Sharon Medow, Lecturer; M.S., CUNY, Brooklyn.
Michael Mehmet, Instructor; M.A., CUNY, Brooklyn.
Erik Morales, Assistant Professor; Ph.D., NYU.
W. Daniel Morgan, Adjunct Associate Professor; Ed.D., SUNY at Albany.
Kathleen Murphy, Adjunct Instructor; M.A., Columbia Teachers College.
Joan Myers, Assistant Professor; Ph.D., Yeshiva.
Laksmi Nor, Adjunct Instructor; M.S.Ed., Bank Street College of Education.
Elaine Pasternack, Adjunct Assistant Professor; Ed.D., Columbia Teachers College.
Fedora Cozy Perullo, Adjunct Assistant Professor; M.A., Florence.
James Reed, Lecturer; M.A., Columbia Teachers College.
Carol Rhoder, Associate Professor; Ph.D., Columbia.
Rita Silverman, Professor; Ph.D., Pittsburgh.
Leslie Soodak, Associate Professor; Ph.D., NYU.
Mary Sweet-Darter, Assistant Professor; Ph.D., Oklahoma.
Mary Versteck, Associate Professor; Ed.D., Columbia Teachers College.
Xiao-Lei Wang, Assistant Professor; Ph.D., Chicago.
Eric Ward, Adjunct Instructor; M.A., CUNY, City College.
Michael Weinraub, Lecturer; M.A., CUNY, Hunter.
Roberta Wiener, Assistant Professor; Ed.D., Columbia Teachers College.
Frederick Wilhelm, Adjunct Professor; Ed.D., SUNY at Albany.
Jan Yablow, Adjunct Instructor; M.S., CUNY, Hunter.
Dianne Zager, Professor; Ph.D., Hofstra.

PEPPERDINE UNIVERSITY

Graduate School of Education and Psychology
Education Programs

Programs of Study

The demand for dedicated, well-trained leaders, teachers, and school administrators has never been greater in California and across the nation. Students should consider the great advantages of Pepperdine University's Graduate School of Education and Psychology as they plan to strengthen their contacts, credentials, knowledge, and earning power in education. The Graduate School of Education and Psychology offers degree and credential programs designed to prepare teachers and educational administrators, consultants, change agents, and technology specialists.

Pepperdine offers a variety of graduate degrees in education, including a Master of Science in Administration, a Master of Arts in Education, a Master of Arts in Educational Technology, and a Doctor of Education (Ed.D.), which is offered with four different emphases. Several teaching credentials and Tier I and II administrative credentials are also offered.

The Doctor of Education program has four unique concentrations: educational leadership, administration, and policy; educational technology; organization change; and organizational leadership. Each doctoral concentration has its own format that has been designed for working professionals. The educational leadership, administration, and policy program is 60 percent face-to-face and 40 percent online. The educational technology program is a combination of three face-to-face sessions and 85 percent online course work. The organization change program has a sequence-oriented, seminar-style curriculum. The program in organizational leadership is a mix of traditional and virtual learning environments.

Research Facilities

A computer network links each of the University's libraries, which collectively contain more than 800,000 books, bound journals, and microforms. Each facility is fully supported with library services, wireless networking, and a computer center. The West Los Angeles Graduate Campus houses the Multimedia Center.

Financial Aid

Scholarships, grants, loans, assistantships, and payment plans are available to qualified students. More than 80 percent of students qualify for federal loans, and more than 40 percent are eligible for Pepperdine-funded assistance. Current information and all forms that are necessary to apply for financial aid are available online at http://gsep.pepperdine.edu/financialaid. Veterans should follow regular admission procedures and secure the certificate of eligibility from the Veterans Administration or the state of California. For additional information, students should contact the Financial Aid Office (phone: 310-258-2848; e-mail: gsepfinaid@pepperdine.edu).

Cost of Study

Charges for one semester unit of instruction in 2007–08 vary from $840 to $1055, depending on the program.

Living and Housing Costs

The Pepperdine University graduate campuses are in proximity to apartment buildings and residential areas. Pepperdine staff members can assist students in locating housing near their specific campus, whether the housing is an apartment, a town house, a condominium, or a guest room.

Student Group

Total University enrollment is approximately 7,500, and enrollment at the Graduate School of Education and Psychology is 1,800. Students cover a wide range of age and experience, with many returning to the workforce or changing careers and others entering the programs upon completion of their undergraduate degree.

Location

The headquarters for the Graduate School of Education and Psychology is the West Los Angeles Graduate Campus, which is located 30 minutes west of downtown Los Angeles. The Drescher Graduate Campus in Malibu overlooks the Pacific Ocean from the Santa Monica Mountains. The Encino Graduate Campus is located in the San Fernando Valley. The Irvine Graduate Campus is in Orange County near the John Wayne Airport. The Westlake Village Graduate Campus is in Ventura County. Program offerings vary by location.

The University

Pepperdine is an independent, medium-sized Christian university with two major campuses, four graduate schools, and one undergraduate college. The headquarters for the Graduate School of Education and Psychology and the Graziadio School of Business and Management is in West Los Angeles. Pepperdine's undergraduate residential college, Seaver College, as well as the School of Public Policy and the School of Law are located at the 830-acre campus in Malibu.

Applying

Admission requirements vary by program. For more information, prospective students should contact the Office of Admissions.

Correspondence and Information

Office of Admissions
Graduate School of Education and Psychology
6100 Center Drive, Suite 500
Los Angeles, California 90045
Phone: 800-347-4849 (toll-free)
Web site: http://gsep.pepperdine.edu

Pepperdine University

THE FACULTY

Education

Jeanmarie Boone, Assistant Professor; Ph.D., Claremont.
Vance Caesar, Visiting Faculty; Ph.D., Walden.
Kathy Church, Assistant Professor; Ed.D., Ball State.
Anthony Collatos, Assistant Professor; Ph.D., UCLA.
Margot Condon, Assistant Director of Student Teaching; Ed.D., Pepperdine.
Kay Davis, Lecturer; Ed.D., Pepperdine.
Cynthia Dollins, Visiting Faculty; Ed.D., Pepperdine.
John Fitzpatrick, Superintendent in Residence; Ed.D., USC.
J. L. Fortson, Lecturer; Ed.D., San Francisco.
Cara Garcia, Professor; Ph.D., Arizona.
Nancy Harding, Associate Professor and Director of Student Teaching; Ph.D., UCLA.
Diana Hiatt-Michael, Professor; Ed.D., UCLA.
Martine Jago, Associate Professor; Ph.D., Kent (England).
Ed Kur, Visiting Faculty; Ph.D., UCLA.
Doug Leigh, Associate Professor; Ph.D., Florida State.
Farzin Madjidi, Professor of Leadership; Ed.D., Pepperdine.
John McManus, Professor; Ph.D., Connecticut.
Ken Murrell, Visiting Faculty; D.B.A., George Washington.
Susan Nero, Visiting Faculty; Ph.D., UCLA.
Linda Polin, Professor and Davidson Endowed Professor; Ph.D., UCLA.
Linda Purrington, Lecturer; Ed.D., Pepperdine.
Reyna Garcia Ramos, Associate Professor; Ph.D., California, Santa Barbara.
Elizabeth Reilly, Associate Professor; Ed.D., San Francisco.
Kent Rhodes, Visiting Faculty; Ed.D., Pepperdine.
Margaret Riel, Visiting Faculty; Ph.D., California, Irvine.
June Schmieder-Ramirez, Professor; Ph.D., Stanford.
Jack Scott, Distinguished Professor of Higher Education; Ph.D., Claremont.
Thomas Skewes-Cox, Visiting Faculty; Ph.D., UCLA.
Paul Sparks, Associate Professor; Ph.D., USC.
Ronald Stephens, Professor; Ed.D., USC.
Sue Talley, Visiting Faculty; Ed.D., Pepperdine.
Margaret Weber, Professor and Dean; Ph.D., Missouri.

The Pepperdine University Malibu Campus.

The headquarters of the Graduate School of Education and Psychology in West Los Angeles.

QUINNIPIAC UNIVERSITY

Division of Education
Master of Arts in Teaching Program

Program of Study

Quinnipiac University's Master of Arts in Teaching (M.A.T.) program is a challenging course of study that prepares teacher candidates for certification to teach at the elementary, middle grades, or secondary level. Students receive extensive classroom experience and a solid integration of educational theory and pedagogy through an intensive sequence of course work, internship, and student teaching. The internship experiences provide students with a working knowledge of school protocols and actual teaching practices, and students are quickly involved with area schools beginning in the first semester. Research opportunities are also available through the program's partnerships with area school districts. Through a combined emphasis on research-based pedagogy, subject-area mastery, and multicultural education, students develop the skills, understanding, and dispositions needed to create classroom environments that are conducive to learning for all students. They become professionals who are advocates for their students' learning needs and committed to the highest professional and ethical standards.

The 51–57 credit M.A.T. program is a five-semester course of study. Candidates begin in the fall semester and can complete the program, including student teaching, at the end of the second spring semester. Graduates are eligible for both initial certification in the state of Connecticut (which has reciprocity with nearly forty other states) and the M.A.T. degree. Middle grades and secondary certification programs are offered in biology, chemistry, English, history/social studies, mathematics, and Spanish. The program is open to individuals who have earned their undergraduate degrees and wish to move directly on to graduate school, as well as individuals who are career changers.

Connecticut participates in the National Association of State Directors of Teacher Education and Certification (NASDTEC) Interstate Compact. Participating states agree to accept the planned program of study of graduates from an accredited teacher preparation program in any state in the compact. More information is available at http://www.state.ct.us/sde/dtl/cert.

Research Facilities

The growing base of technology at Quinnipiac includes instructional labs, student computer labs, and a state-of-the-art library technology center. The new Arnold Bernhard Library is one of the most technologically advanced libraries and centers for electronic information and learning resources anywhere in the country. The library provides students with access to print, Web-based, and microform resources. Education students can utilize the ERIC (Educational Resources Information Center) database, PsychInfo, the Wilson Full-Text Educational Service, and more than 500 journals in education. The library also houses a children's and young adults' literature collection, K–12 textbooks and curriculum materials, and more than 100 educational software titles. All the classrooms are wired, so the faculty members can utilize the Internet and the library databases and resources in their classes.

Financial Aid

Several avenues are available to help students fund their education. Students may be eligible for Federal Stafford Student Loans. M.A.T. students receive a full or partial tuition waiver during their internship semesters.

Cost of Study

Tuition in 2006–07 was $625 per credit hour. In addition, student fees were $275 per semester for full-time students and $30 per credit for part-time students.

Living and Housing Costs

On-campus housing is available during the summer. Privately owned housing is available near the campus. For more information concerning off-campus housing, students should contact the Office of Residential Life or visit the University Web site.

Student Group

Approximately 50 students begin the program each fall. Each class contains a mixture of recent college graduates and professionals seeking a career change.

Location

Quinnipiac's location in Hamden, Connecticut, is easily accessible and close to opportunities for internships and fieldwork. A suburb of New Haven, Hamden is approximately 30 minutes from Hartford, 90 minutes from New York City, and 2 hours from Boston.

The University

Quinnipiac University is nationally recognized as one of the leading centers for higher learning in the Northeast and is consistently ranked among the best master's-level universities in the north in *U.S. News & World Report's* Guide to America's Best Colleges. All programs have integrated computer technology into academic and campus life, and Quinnipiac has been recognized in *Yahoo! Internet Life* for its achievements in technology. In 2006, Quinnipiac was ranked ninth in *PC Magazine*'s 2007 Top Wired Colleges.

The University enrolls about 5,000 undergraduate and 1,800 graduate students and offers a full range of undergraduate and graduate programs through the School of Health Sciences, the School of Communications, the School of Business, the College of Liberal Arts, and the School of Law.

Applying

Admission to the graduate programs at Quinnipiac University is competitive. Applications are considered on a rolling basis. However, students should apply before March 31 to ensure an internship placement. In addition to a completed application, the applicant must furnish an essay describing the reasons an education career is being pursued, official postsecondary transcripts, two letters of reference, and the Connecticut PRAXIS I exam or waiver. An interview is required. Students are admitted for the fall semester only.

Correspondence and Information

Office of Graduate Admissions
Quinnipiac University
275 Mount Carmel Avenue
Hamden, Connecticut 06518
Phone: 203-582-8672
        800-462-1944 (toll-free)
Fax: 203-582-3443
E-mail: graduate@quinnipiac.edu
Web site: http://www.quinnipiac.edu

Quinnipiac University

THE FACULTY AND THEIR RESEARCH

The faculty comprises experienced educators from all levels of education. Faculty members as well as field personnel become mentors who guide and direct each student.

Luis Arata, Assistant Professor of Modern Languages; Ph.D., Cornell. Fine arts.
Daryll Borst, Professor of Biology; Ph.D., Illinois. Biology.
Pearl LeBlanc Brown, Professor of English; Ph.D., Arkansas. English.
Susan Clarke, Assistant Professor of Education; Ed.D., Massachusetts. Secondary teacher education.
Anne Dichele, Assistant Professor of Education; Ph.D., Connecticut. English.
Cynthia Dubea, Dean of Division of Education; Ed.D., Columbia. Curriculum and instruction.
Len Engel, Professor of English; Ph.D., Fordham. English.
Steve Gottlieb, Professor and Chair, English Department; M.A., NYU. English.
Kim Hartmann, Assistant Professor and Chair; M.H.S., Quinnipiac. Occupational therapy.
Ronald Heiferman, Professor of History; Ph.D., NYU. History.
Gloria Holmes, Assistant Professor of Education; Ph.D., SUNY at Stony Brook. English.
Mark Johnston Jr., Professor of English; Ph.D., Yale. English.
Bernardine Krawczyk, Assistant Dean of the Division of Education; M.S., Western Connecticut State. Education.
Kenneth McGeary, Associate Professor of Biology; Ph.D., New Hampshire. Biology.
Neil Nelan, Assistant Professor of Mathematics; Ph.D., Johns Hopkins. Mathematics.
Lakshmi Nigam, Professor of Mathematics; Ph.D., Indian Institute of Technology. Mathematics.
Dennis Opheim, Professor of Biology; Ph.D., Minnesota. Biology.
Rachel Ranis, Professor of Sociology; M.S., Yale. Sociology.
Stanley Rothman, Professor of Mathematics; Ph.D., Wisconsin. Mathematics.
George Schiro, Professor of History; Ph.D., NYU. History.
Alex Welleck, Associate Professor of History and Political Science; Ph.D., Connecticut. History and political science.
David Zucker, Professor of English; Ph.D., Syracuse. English.

RIDER

U N I V E R S I T Y

RIDER UNIVERSITY

College of Liberal Arts, Education, and Science
Department of Graduate Education and Human Services

Programs of Study

The Department of Graduate Education and Human Services offers several programs of study. The M.A. in counseling services program prepares students to work as elementary or secondary school counselors or to work in community counseling settings. The M.A. in curriculum, instruction, and supervision program prepares teachers and other education specialists as curricular and instructional change agents in their work settings. The M.A. in educational administration program serves both teachers and non-teachers by helping them develop administrative leadership skills applicable to elementary and secondary schools, colleges, and related educational organizations. The M.A. in organizational leadership is designed to enhance students' leadership capabilities and understanding of the world in which today's leaders must function. The M.A. in reading/language arts program prepares students to become reading specialists and teachers of reading in schools and other settings. The M.A. in special education program prepares teachers to meet the needs of students with special needs. The Ed.S. in counseling services program is an advanced terminal degree program beyond the master's level that provides students with in-depth training in a specialized area and meets the New Jersey Licensed Professional Counselor requirements. The Ed.S. in school psychology program prepares students to become certified school psychologists at the state and national levels. The Master of Arts in Teaching (M.A.T.) is a professional development degree that enables students to tailor an individual program blending training in pedagogy with courses in chosen content disciplines. The Graduate Level Teacher Certification program and other certification programs are also available.

All courses are offered in the evenings, Monday through Thursday. While most students attend part time, full-time enrollment is possible with enrollment in up to four courses per semester, depending on the program.

Research Facilities

Wireless connectivity is available on campus free of charge. Several computer labs are also available and offer up-to-date hardware and software and a wide range of programming languages, utilities, and statistical packages that support instruction and research. The campus also houses video conferencing facilities. A central library contains extensive hard copy, database, and media collections to support research. The library's collection contains 378,000 volumes, approximately 874,000 microforms, 114 online databases, and approximately 27,500 audiovisual holdings.

Financial Aid

Financial aid is available to qualified graduate students under several state and federal loan programs, including the Federal Stafford Student Loan program. A limited number of graduate assistantship positions are also available.

Cost of Study

Tuition for 2007–08 is $540 per credit hour plus any applicable fees. Tuition for the graduate counseling program is $550 per credit.

Living and Housing Costs

On-campus graduate student housing is available in Ridge House. Students must be enrolled in two or more graduate courses each semester. The cost is approximately $3640 per semester. The optional University meal plan is approximately $2070 per semester and is optional. A community kitchen facility is also available.

Student Group

Approximately 18 percent of the graduate education students are men. Eighty-three percent are pursuing their program of study on a part-time basis. Students enrolled in the Graduate Education and Human Services programs come from all areas of industry; teaching, health care, military and law enforcement, and state government, to name a few. Some students are pursuing their programs of study immediately after completing their undergraduate degrees.

Student Outcomes

Students who complete Department of Graduate Education and Human Services programs find employment soon after graduation in areas that are relevant to the programs of study. These areas include school administration, teaching, counseling, school psychology, hospitals, social services organizations, and public and private mental health agencies.

Location

Rider University maintains campuses in Lawrenceville and Princeton, New Jersey—locations rich in tradition, culture, and beauty. The Department of Graduate Education and Human Services is located in Memorial Hall on the Lawrenceville campus. The campus location is in the heart of the New York and Philadelphia corridor, a major center of corporate, financial, and cultural vitality.

The University and The Department

Rider University has historically been recognized for its ability to educate professionals. Department faculty members view themselves as teachers-scholars, dedicated to effective teaching and to adding value to a student's academic pursuits.

The professional education graduate programs are accredited by the National Council for Accreditation of Teacher Education (NCATE) and meet the standards of the National Association of State Directors of Teacher Education (NASDTEC) as required by the State of New Jersey. The Master of Arts programs in counseling services are accredited by the Council for Accreditation of Counseling and Related Educational Programs (CACREP). All education curricula are approved by the Department of Education of the State of New Jersey.

Applying

Applicants should submit a completed graduate application, $50 application fee, two recommendation letters, personal statement, resume, official Praxis scores (for teacher certification), official GRE or MAT scores (for counseling services and school psychology), and official transcripts from each college or university attended. Some programs require an interview. For applicants whose native language is not English, satisfactory scores on the TOEFL are required. International applicants must provide transcripts evaluated by a recognized credential evaluation service. The application for admission should be submitted by May 1 for the fall semester, November 1 for spring, and April 1 for summer. Admission to the Ed.S. in school psychology program occurs for the summer and fall semesters only. Applications must be received by March 1 or May 1, respectively; however, March 1 is the recommended date for optimal consideration.

Correspondence and Information

Office of Graduate Admissions
Rider University
2083 Lawrenceville Road
Lawrenceville, New Jersey 08648
Phone: 609-896-5036
Fax: 609-895-5680
E-mail: gradadm@rider.edu
Web site: http://www.rider.edu

Rider University

THE FACULTY

C. Emmanuel Ahia, Associate Professor of Education; J.D., Arkansas; Ph.D., Southern Illinois.
Don Ambrose, Associate Professor of Education; Ph.D., Oregon.
Lisa Marie Angello, Assistant Professor of Education; Ph.D., Lehigh.
Carol Brown, Associate Dean of Education; Ph.D., Pennsylvania.
Dennis C. Buss, Associate Professor of Education; Ed.D., Rutgers.
Jesse B. DeEsch, Associate Professor of Education; Ph.D., Indiana State.
Stefan Dombrowski, Professor of Education; Ph.D., Georgia.
Phyllis Fantauzzo, Assistant Director of the Center for Reading and Writing; M.A., Rider; Certified School Psychologist, Rider.
Judith L. Fraivillig, Associate Professor of Education; Ph.D., Northwestern.
Susan M. Glazer, Professor of Education and Director, Center for Reading and Writing; Ed.D., Pennsylvania.
Leonard Goduto, Assistant Professor of Education; Ed.D., Columbia, Teachers College.
William D. Guthrie, Professor of Education; Ph.D., NYU.
Michelle W. Kamens, Professor of Education; Ed.D., Temple.
James Murphy, Associate Professor of Education; D.Ed., Penn State.
Kathleen M. Pierce, Associate Professor of Education; Ph.D., Pennsylvania.
JoAnn Susko, Assistant Professor of Education; Ed.D., Rutgers.
Timothy R. Wade, Assistant Professor of Education; Ed.D., Delaware.
Elizabeth Watson, Associate Professor of Education; Ed.D., Columbia Teachers College.
Nancy G. Westburg, Professor of Education; Ph.D., Indiana State.
Austin A. Winther, Assistant Professor of Education; Ph.D., Southern Illinois Carbondale.

ST. JOSEPH'S COLLEGE, NEW YORK

Programs in Education

Programs of Study

St. Joseph's College (SJC) offers graduate education that balances in-depth research and theoretical study with hands-on professional training. This unique educational experience enables students to enter the workplace extremely well-prepared and able to apply their knowledge with confidence born from experience.

The Master of Arts program in special education with annotation in severe and multiple disabilities provides students with basic core classes (12 credits) and courses that link special education to the New York State Learning Standards in the area of special education as well as severe and multiple disabilities. The 36-credit program includes a strong research component, which is characteristic of the integration of theory and practice.

The Master of Arts in literacy and cognition responds to the No Child Left Behind Act, providing students with basic core classes that link literacy instruction to the New York State Learning Standards. The program addresses the challenges teachers face in the area of literacy as they work with students and families of diverse cultures. The M.A. in literacy and cognition program grants certifications in literacy and cognition from birth through grade 6.

The Master of Arts in infant/toddler early childhood special education was introduced in 1995 as the Master of Arts in Therapeutic Education and underwent a name change in 2003. The courses offered are appropriate for teachers who wish to augment their expertise in teaching by acquiring the knowledge and developing competencies working with infants, toddlers, and young children and their families. The M.A. in infant/toddler early childhood special education program grants certifications in early childhood and early childhood special education, from birth to grade 2.

Research Facilities

The Dillon Child Study Center offers toddler, preschool, and kindergarten programs based on the child development approach to the education of young children. Located on SJC's Brooklyn campus, the center is historically one of the first college preschools on the East Coast.

The Callahan Library at the Long Island Campus is a modern, 25,000-square-foot, freestanding facility with seating for more than 300 readers. A curriculum library, seminar rooms, administrative offices, and two classrooms are housed in this building. Holdings include more than 105,000 volumes and 307 periodical titles, and they are supplemented by videos and other instructional aids. Patrons have access to the Internet and to several online academic databases. A fully automated library system, Endeavor, ensures the efficient retrieval and management of all library resources. Other resources include the library at St. Joseph's Brooklyn Campus, with more than 109,000 volumes, and membership in the Long Island Library Resources Council, which facilitates cooperative associations with the academic and special libraries on Long Island. Internet access, subscriptions to several online full-text databases, and membership in the international bibliographic utility, OCLC, allow almost limitless access to available information.

McEntegart Hall is a fully air-conditioned five-level structure. Three spacious reading areas with a capacity for 300 readers, including individual study carrels and shelf space for 200,000 volumes, provide an excellent environment for research. In addition, McEntegart Hall houses the college archives, a curriculum library, three computer laboratories, a nursing education laboratory, and a videoconference room. There are eight classrooms, a chapel, cafeteria, and faculty and student lounges.

A high-speed fiber-optic intracampus network connects all offices, instructional facilities, computer laboratories, and libraries on both the Brooklyn and Patchogue campuses. The network provides Internet access to all students and faculty and staff members. An integrated online library system enables students to search for and check out books at either campus. Online databases and other electronic resources are available to students from either campus or from their home computers. Two wireless laptop classrooms with "smart classroom" features provide flexible instruction spaces with the latest technologies. Videoconferencing facilities connect the two campuses, allowing for real-time distance learning in a small-group setting.

Financial Aid

Financial aid is available in the form of federal and private loans, scholarships, and work-study programs. Students should contact the Financial Aid Office for more information (Brooklyn Campus, telephone: 718-636-6808; Long Island Campus, telephone: 631-447-3214).

Cost of Study

In 2006–07, tuition was $530 per credit. Per semester, the college and technology fees for 12 or more credits totaled $200.

Living and Housing Costs

On-campus housing is not available. The St. George Hotel, New York's number-one resource for student housing, and St. Joseph's College have partnered to offer off-campus housing. In 2006–07, the cost was $5450 per semester, or $10,900 for the year. Accommodations include a double room, cable TV, high-speed access, a completely furnished bedroom, a full bath, a closet, a kitchen on each floor, and 24-hour security. Housing applications are available online.

Student Group

The total enrollment for all graduate programs on both campuses is 508.

Location

St. Joseph's College has two campuses—the main campus in the residential Clinton Hill section of Brooklyn and the campus in Patchogue, Long Island. The main campus offers easy access to all transit lines; to the Long Island Expressway; to all bridges in Brooklyn, Manhattan, and Queens; and to the Verrazano-Narrows Bridge to Staten Island. Within the space of half an hour, students leaving St. Joseph's College may find themselves in the Metropolitan Museum of Art, the 42nd Street Library, Carnegie Hall and Lincoln Center, the Broadway theater district, Madison Square Garden, or Shea Stadium. The College itself stands in the center of one of the nation's most diversified academic communities, consisting of six colleges and universities within a 2-mile radius of each other. The 27-acre Long Island campus, adjacent to Great Patchogue Lake, is an ideal setting for studying, socializing, and partaking in extracurricular activities. Just off Sunrise Highway, the College is easily accessible from all parts of Long Island.

The University and The Programs

St. Joseph's College is a fully accredited institution that has been dedicated to providing a diverse population of students in the New York metropolitan area with an affordable education rooted in the liberal arts tradition since 1916. Independent and coeducational, the College provides a strong academic and value-oriented education at the undergraduate and graduate levels. For the fifth year in a row, the 2007 ranking of America's Best Colleges by *U.S. News & World Report* named St. Joseph's College to the top tier of the Northern Comprehensive Colleges–Bachelor's category.

Building on the strength of the St. Joseph's College long-renowned teacher education program, the master's programs in infant/toddler early childhood special education and in literacy/cognition are designed to produce innovative teachers in the fields of early childhood, childhood, and special education and in literacy and English language arts.

Applying

Students should have a bachelor's degree from an accredited institution, with a minimum GPA of 3.0. Applicants must submit the completed application, the application fee, official transcripts, a current resume, copies of all teaching certificates, and two letters of recommendation. An interview is required.

Correspondence and Information

Brooklyn Campus
St. Joseph's College
245 Clinton Avenue
Brooklyn, New York 11205
Phone: 718-399-0068
E-mail: msmbab@sjcny.edu
Web site: http://www.sjcny.edu/page.php?prmID/185

Long Island Campus
St. Joseph's College
155 West Roe Boulevard
Patchogue, New York 11772
Phone: 631-447-3250
E-mail: msmbab@sjcny.edu

St. Joseph's College, New York

THE FACULTY

Esther Berkowitz, Assistant Professor of Child Study and Director of the M.A. in Literacy and Cognition; Ph.D., Fordham.
S. Elizabeth Calfapietra, Associate Professor of Child Study; Ed.D., Columbia.
S. Frances Carmody, Professor of Child Study Development; Ph.D., Syracuse.
Susan Straut Collard, Professor of Child Study, Co-Director of Child Study Department, and Director of Dillon Child Study Center; Ph.D., Columbia.
S. Miriam Honora Corr, Chairperson of the Child Study Department; Ed.D., Columbia.
Barry Friedman, Assistant Professor of Child Study; Ph.D., Hofstra.
Wendy P. Hope, Associate Professor of Child Study; Ph.D., NYU.
S. Helen Kearney, Assistant Professor of Child Study; Ph.D., NYU.
Claire Lenz, Assistant Professor of Child Study and Director of the Master of Arts in Literacy and Cognition, Suffolk Program; Ed.D., St. John's (New York).
Karen Russo, Assistant Professor of Child Study; St. John's (New York).

ST. THOMAS AQUINAS COLLEGE

Teacher Education

Programs of Study

In collaboration with the broader St. Thomas Aquinas College community and the professional community in schools surrounding the College, the teacher education program seeks to prepare educators who are able to meet the challenges of teaching in the twenty-first century. It is the vision of the teacher education program to prepare knowledgeable, caring educators who are dedicated to their students' intellectual growth and overall well-being.

The mission of the St. Thomas Aquinas College teacher education program is to prepare educators as informed decision makers who create effective learning opportunities for all students. They are knowledgeable, caring professionals who have a passion for learning and can develop that passion in their students. They possess a level of content-area knowledge and skills that allow them to continue to learn and to apply their knowledge in their vocation as educators. They effectively promote learning through a socially mediated process that supports the learner's personal construction of knowledge. They are effective communicators and collaborators and create supportive, inclusive environments for learning. They are thoughtful educators who critically reflect on practice and are committed to lifelong learning in order to help all students achieve to their fullest potential.

To achieve its mission, the St. Thomas Aquinas College teacher education program creates a caring, challenging environment for learning that supports each candidate's development as an educator. In this environment, learning is a collaborative endeavor in which candidates speak and write about what they are discovering and question, analyze, and discuss ideas with others who are at varying levels of expertise.

The College is scheduled to begin a new Master of Science in Education (M.S.Ed.) in Educational Leadership Program in July 2007. Applications are being accepted now for this 30-credit program, which can be completed in fourteen months of part-time study. The program leads to eligibility for New York State School Building Leader (SBL) certification.

The Division of Teacher Education offers the following programs: a Master of Science in Teaching (M.S.T.) in childhood education (grades 1–6), childhood and special education (grades 1–6), or adolescence education (grades 7–12); a Master of Science (M.S.Ed.) with concentrations in literacy or special education; and a post-master's professional certificate in either literacy or special education

Research Facilities

The Lougheed Library, named for Sister M. Alfred Lougheed, the College's founding librarian, is a two-story structure forming the western-most wing of Spellman Hall. The library was renovated in 2003, at which time it added wireless connectivity, new public-access computers, new furnishings, and improved facilities for reading, study, and teaching. It has seating for more than 200 in open study areas, individual carrels, and enclosed study rooms. The library develops and maintains a collection of print, audiovisual, compact disc, Web resources, and government documents. Off-campus access to all of the library's online resources is available to members of the College community. As teaching partners in the academic life of the College, the librarians provide information literacy instruction, wherein students learn to find, select, evaluate, use, and cite information from a wealth of print, audiovisual, and online information resources. In collaboration with faculty members, librarians design information literacy presentations and hands-on workshops to support and complement course assignments.

Financial Aid

Assistantships are available to full-time graduate students during the academic year and/or the summer. A student receiving an assistantship for the academic year receives 24 credits of tuition free of charge and is awarded a stipend of $2000. The student works an average of 15 hours per week. Summer assistants work a total of 60 hours during the summer semester when the assistantship is effective and take one 3-credit course free of tuition. Tutorial assistantships are available for graduate students whose writing proficiency is such that they can assist other students in the writing lab of the academic skills center. Tutors are eligible for the same benefits and hourly requirements as all other graduate assistants.

Cost of Study

For 2006–07, tuition was $590 per credit. Most courses are 3 credits.

Living and Housing Costs

There is no on-campus housing for graduate students.

Student Group

Most students in the M.S.Ed. programs are employed by a school district and attend classes part-time in the late afternoon and evening as well as during the summer sessions. The M.S.T. program is for career shifters, and many of those students are employed in other areas and are seeking certification as a teacher.

Location

The St. Thomas Aquinas College campus is a short distance from the breathtaking panorama that is New York City. Located on Route 340 in Sparkill, St. Thomas Aquinas College's main campus is approximately 15 miles from the George Washington Bridge and about 6 miles from the Tappan Zee Bridge. The village of Sparkill may be easily reached by car via the Palisades Parkway (Exit 5, Sparkill) or the New York State Thruway (Exits 10 or 12). The sprawling 48-acre campus provides students with free, ample parking and an easy walk to any class location on its connected campus.

The College

St. Thomas Aquinas College is incorporated by the Legislature of the State of New York. The College has an absolute charter from the Board of Regents of the University of the State of New York. It is fully accredited by the Middle States Association of Colleges and Schools and most recently received accreditation from the National Council for Accreditation of Teacher Education (NCATE).

Applying

Matriculated students are those who have been accepted as candidates for the M.S.T. or M.S.Ed. and who have successfully completed 12 credits of graduate study at St. Thomas Aquinas College. Admission requirements include a baccalaureate degree from an accredited undergraduate institution (the Division of Teacher Education reserves the right to require applicants to complete prerequisites prior to acceptance according to program and/or New York State requirements); a teaching certificate (required only for M.S.Ed. candidates); a cumulative grade point average of 3.0 or above on a 4.0 scale (the Division of Teacher Education reserves the right to require GRE scores from promising candidates whose GPA falls below this standard); evidence of potential to complete a graduate degree in education (provided through letters of professional references and a statement of professional goals); and an interview with the Director of Graduate Education. All admission inquiries may be made to the Director of Admissions via telephone or e-mail.

To be eligible for a graduate assistantship, students must meet entrance requirements for the Master of Science in education, plan to study full-time, and apply to the Director. The Admissions Committee of the Graduate Faculty considers the student's past academic performance, recommendations, professional experience or promise, and, where appropriate, need. Applications are available in the Graduate Education Office.

Correspondence and Information

Graduate Admissions Office
Spellman Hall
St. Thomas Aquinas College
125 Route 340
Sparkill, New York 10976
Phone: 845-398-4100
        800-999-STAC (toll-free)
E-mail: admissions@stac.edu
Web site: http://www.stac.edu

SHENANDOAH UNIVERSITY

Graduate Programs in Education

Programs of Study	The School of Education and Human Development at Shenandoah University offers programs of study leading to the Doctor of Education (Ed.D.) in leadership and administration and the Master of Science in Education (M.S.Ed.) in administration, teaching, reading specialist, individualized option, and TESOL. Certificate programs include professional and advanced professional certificates in TESOL and teacher licensure. Study in these programs is formed by students' life-shaped and knowledge-prepared experiences and is applied to the concentrated examination of public education's foundations, current situations, and future possibilities through course requirements, internships, and field research. All programs seek to produce knowledge-based, competent decision makers who are prepared to be capable teachers and administrators and effective classroom and institutional managers—practitioners who are prepared to engage in educational improvement through an action-research orientation.
	The 9-credit Professional Certificate in TESOL provides an entry-level credential for students who want academic training in the essential elements of the TESOL profession. The three courses provide an overview of the field, a basic grasp of English linguistics, and a survey of important language teaching methods. The courses can be applied toward the requirements for the Advanced Professional Certificate in TESOL and the M.S.Ed. in TESOL.
	The 18-credit Advanced Professional Certificate in TESOL builds on the professional certificate, adding course work on language and culture, second-language acquisition, and language teaching materials and assessments. All of the Advanced Professional Certificate courses can be applied toward the M.S.Ed. with TOEFL concentration.
	The M.S.Ed. with TESOL concentration builds on the Advanced Professional Certificate, adding course work in program and curriculum design, research and statistics, and current issues in the field, along with a practicum and a culminating experience (internship or portfolio). This program results in the highest academic credential that is normally held by professionals in this field.
	All M.S.Ed. degrees require 33 credits, including a thesis. The M.S.Ed. in education administrative leadership degree is designed to meet the current and changing administrative needs of school systems in the region. Each option meets the requirements for a master's degree and for licensure by the Virginia Department of Education. The M.S.Ed. reading specialist program is designed for applicants possessing an undergraduate degree and a teaching license prior to admission to the program.
	The Ed.D. in leadership and administration centers on an interdisciplinary leadership and research core, with opportunities for students to concentrate in an area of their particular interest. For professional school personnel, there are established tracks in K–12 education administration and in curricular leadership.
	More information about each program and its requirements is available online at http://www.su.edu/sas/programs.cfm?program= GraduateEducation.
Research Facilities	The library collections of Shenandoah University are housed in two facilities. The Alson H. Smith Jr. Library, located in the center of the Winchester campus, is the main library facility for the University. The branch Health Sciences Library is located in the Health Professions Building on the grounds of the Winchester Medical Center. Current total holdings number more than 275,000 items, including 123,000 books and bound journals, 13,000 recordings, 16,000 scores, 1,500 videotapes, and 115,000 ERIC documents. The University subscribes to more than 1,100 print periodicals and has access to more than 10,000 electronic journals. More than 60 Internet-accessible databases are available through the library's Web site. Subject disciplines represented in the Smith Library are biology, business, chemistry, computer science, education, history, literature, mathematics, music, philosophy, physics, psychology, religion, and sociology. Most materials in occupational therapy and physical therapy are located in the Smith Library. The Smith Library also houses the media center, the Macintosh computer lab, and the Children's Literature Center.
Financial Aid	A limited number of assistantships, which cover up to 9 credits and provide a stipend, and scholarships may be available for full-time students. Loans through commercial and governmental sources are available. Information regarding financial aid may be obtained from the Office of Financial Aid.
Cost of Study	In 2005–06, tuition was $610 per credit. Fees are additional.
Living and Housing Costs	Room and board costs range from $2656 to $3795 per term, depending on the meal plan chosen. Off-campus housing is also available.
Student Group	The University attracts students from throughout the region and around the globe. Total enrollment is approximately 3,000 students. Of these, 57 percent are from Virginia; the remaining students represent forty-five states and forty-one countries. Forty percent of the students are men. The Graduate Education Division has 422 students. Of these, 275 are women and 386 are part-time students. There are 26 minority students enrolled in education programs.
Location	The Shenandoah campus is located 72 miles west of Washington, D.C., in the historic Shenandoah Valley of Virginia. The University is on the southeast edge of the city of Winchester, Virginia. Winchester–Frederick County, rich in history, is a vigorous community of approximately 70,000 people. Shenandoah's students have the distinct advantage of being on a small campus near large metropolitan cultural centers.
The University	Shenandoah University, established in 1875, is a comprehensive Level V private university. The University offers more than sixty programs of study at the undergraduate, master's, doctoral, and professional levels at the main campus in Winchester, the Health Professions Building on the campus of the Winchester Medical Center, and the Northern Virginia Campus in Leesburg. With a 10:1 student-faculty ratio, small classes, and individualized learning opportunities, the School of Education and Human Development puts students at the center of all its decisions and events. Faculty members are dynamic and innovative, and 96 percent of them hold a doctoral degree.
Applying	In general, students should have a bachelor's degree from an accredited institution and a minimum GPA of 2.8 for the most recent 48 hours of undergraduate or graduate course work. Applicants should submit the completed application, the $30 application fee, official college transcripts, Praxis I scores (or satisfactory scores on SAT or ACT tests), three letters of recommendation, and a typed, one-page essay that describes professional goals, objectives, and rationale for entering the teaching profession. Specific requirements vary by program, so prospective students should contact the School. Applications are processed on a rolling basis.
Correspondence and Information	John Goss School of Education and Human Development Shenandoah University Winchester, Virginia 22601-5195 Phone: 540-678-4447 Fax: 540-665-4627 E-mail: jgoss@su.edu Web site: http://www.su.edu/sas/programs.cfm?program=GraduateEducation

Shenandoah University

THE FACULTY

John Goss, Chair; Ph.D., American.
Mary Bowser, Professor of Secondary Education; Ed.D., Virginia.
Larry Brooks, Assistant Professor of Education; Ed.D., Nova Southeastern.
Robert Carter, Adjunct Associate Professor of Education; Ed.D., Virginia.
Carol Cohen, Adjunct Assistant Professor of Education; M.Ed., George Mason.
Jurgen Combs, Associate Professor of Education; Ed.D., Nova Southeastern.
Diana Crites, Adjunct Instructor of Education; M.S., Shenandoah.
Donald Dyer, Adjunct Associate Professor of Education; Ed.D., Virginia Tech.
Dale Foreman, Associate Professor of Education; Ph.D., Minnesota.
James Gowdy, Adjunct Assistant Professor of Education; M.S.Ed., Shenandoah.
Ashley Hastings, Professor of Teaching English to Speakers of Other Languages; Ph.D., Indiana.
Terrence W. Hill, Adjunct Instructor of Education; M.Ed., Virginia.
Lynda Hollidge, Adjunct Assistant Professor of Education; Ed.D., Virginia Tech.
Brenda Murphy, Associate Professor of Teaching English to Speakers of Other Languages; Ph.D., NYU.
W. Jack Newhouse, Adjunct Associate Professor of Education; Ph.D., Ohio.
Melanie Oates, Adjunct Assistant Professor of Education; M.A., West Virginia.
Shirley Place, Adjunct Assistant Professor of Education; M.A., James Madison.
Linda Sittig, Adjunct Assistant Professor of Education; M.Ed., Bowie State.
Karen Huff Stewart, Professor of Education; Ed.D., Virginia.
Thomas Woodall, Adjunct Professor of Education; Ed.D., Vanderbilt.
Kelly Wright, Adjunct Instructor of Education; M.S.Ed., Shenandoah.
Xiaobo Yang, Assistant Professor of Education; Ph.D., Beijing Normal; Ph.D., Texas A&M.

SYRACUSE UNIVERSITY

School of Education

Programs of Study

Graduate study in the School of Education offers a variety of instructional and research opportunities leading to the Master of Science (M.S.), Doctor of Education (Ed.D.), or Doctor of Philosophy (Ph.D.) degree or a Certificate of Advanced Study (C.A.S.). Available degrees vary by program area. Programs are available for educational practitioners as well as for those aspiring to research careers. Programs include art education; childhood education 1–6; community counseling; cultural foundations of education; disability studies; early childhood education/early childhood special education; educational leadership; English education; exercise science; higher education; inclusive special education: 1–6 or 7–12; instructional design, development, and evaluation; literacy education; mathematics education; music education; reading education; rehabilitation counseling; school counseling; science education; social studies education; special education; student affairs counseling; and teaching and curriculum.

To receive an M.S. degree, students must earn a minimum of 30 credits and take comprehensive exams or write a thesis. Requirements for the C.A.S. programs vary by program area. Requirements for the doctorate include at least 90 credits of course work beyond the bachelor's degree, examinations, development of research competence, and the dissertation (details of these requirements are specified by the program areas). For more information on individual program requirements, prospective students should contact the appropriate program chair and/or graduate recruiter.

Graduate programs in education at Syracuse University are varied in scope and purpose. The School has found that the number of students who receive their doctorates and subsequently pursue academic careers (teachers and researchers in institutions of higher education) is about equal to the number of those who enter or continue in administrative, supervisory, or other field positions (school superintendents, deans, and other administrative, supervising, and coordinating positions) in schools and colleges.

Research Facilities

Syracuse University's extensive computer facilities and library collections totaling almost 5 million volumes provide extensive support for learning and research. Other centers that support and enrich the work of the students and faculty of the School of Education include computer classrooms; the Facilitated Communication Institute; the Center on Disability Studies, Law, and Human Policy; the Psychoeducational Teaching Laboratory; the Reading and Language Arts Center; five exercise science laboratories; and teaching centers located in area school districts.

Financial Aid

Scholarships, fellowships, and graduate assistantships are available from the University and from the School. Assistantships require approximately 20 hours of service per week and provide both a tuition scholarship and a stipend. Federal and state aid is also available in the form of scholarships, fellowships, loans, and work-study programs. Detailed financial aid information can be found on the Web at http://soe.syr.edu and http://financialaid.syr.edu.

Cost of Study

Graduate tuition charges for 2006–07 were $940 per credit hour. Additional expenses include a health services fee for full-time students and graduate student activity fees.

Living and Housing Costs

Living expenses for a single graduate student are approximately $12,200 per academic year. The campus and surrounding areas offer excellent housing facilities for single and married graduate students. The University has on-campus residence halls for graduate students at the Skytop Apartment Complex, which overlooks the city. Further information can be obtained from the South Campus Housing Office, 206 Goldstein Student Center, Syracuse University, 401 Skytop Road, Syracuse, New York 13244; telephone: 315-443-2567; e-mail: schousng@syr.edu.

Student Group

Syracuse University has a total enrollment of more than 18,000. Approximately 600 are undergraduate students in education, and 750 are registered for graduate study in the School of Education.

Location

Located in a major metropolitan area in central New York, with a population of more than 500,000 and in a city of almost 200,000, Syracuse University is surrounded by many cultural, recreational, and research opportunities. The Finger Lakes, the Thousand Islands, and the Adirondacks are nearby.

The University and The School

Syracuse University, established in 1870, is a private, chartered institution offering coeducational programs through its twelve schools and colleges. Main Campus comprises more than 200 acres surrounding a central quadrangle known as the Quad, on a hill overlooking the city of Syracuse in the heart of New York State. Less than a mile from Main Campus is South Campus, where additional student housing and facilities are located. The University also operates facilities in the downtown area.

The School of Education has more than 90 full-time, part-time, and adjunct faculty members. Virtually all full-time faculty members have attained the highest professional degrees in their specializations, and some hold dual appointments with SU's College of Arts and Sciences, Maxwell School of Citizenship and Public Affairs, and the College of Visual and Performing Arts. This broad range of backgrounds provides variety and depth in the academic and research fields available for study. Many of the faculty members are nationally and internationally known in their areas of expertise.

Applying

Students may apply online at https://apply.embark.com/grad/syracuse. To receive application materials, students should e-mail the Graduate Enrollment Management Center at grad@gwmail.syr.edu or visit the Web site at http://gradsch.syr.edu/. There is a nonrefundable application fee of $65.

Correspondence and Information

Graduate Admissions Recruiter
School of Education
270 Huntington Hall
Syracuse University
Syracuse, New York 13244-2340

Phone: 315-443-2505
E-mail: gradrcrt@gwmail.syr.edu
Web site: http://soe.syr.edu/

Syracuse University

THE FACULTY AND THEIR RESEARCH

Counseling and Human Services (315-443-2266)
Through study in community counseling, rehabilitation counseling, school counseling, or student affairs counseling, students are encouraged to view counseling as a range of interventions that help individuals respond effectively to crucial issues in their lives. The program prepares students for counseling careers in such settings as mental health agencies, universities, career placement centers, schools, hospitals, and rehabilitation agencies.

Janine Bernard, Chair; Ph.D., Purdue. Clinical supervision, life-span human development, professional credentialing. James Bellini, Ph.D., Arkansas. Rehabilitation policy research, assessment. Dennis Gilbride, Ph.D., USC. Transition to work for persons with disabilities, use of the Internet for instruction and practice. Harold Hackney, Ed.D., Massachusetts. Counseling theory, research methodology, professional identity development and counseling process analysis. Richard Shin, Ph.D., Loyola Chicago. Community and mental health counseling, multicultural counseling skills, resiliency factors of urban youth.

Cultural Foundations of Education (315-443-3343)
Cultural Foundations of Education (CFE) is a highly demanding interdisciplinary graduate program created to support fundamental inquiry into the nature of education. Graduate students draw on the disciplines of history, philosophy, and sociology to analyze such issues as inequality, disability, the relationship of popular culture and mass media to education, the philosophy of multiculturalism, gender studies, and racism and education. Alumni have a high rate of success in finding jobs in higher education, foundations, policy research institutes, school systems, international schools and agencies, and government agencies. The department offers unusually strong resources for training in qualitative methods. Many graduates find that their sophisticated training in this research approach enhances their competitiveness for university positions.

Sari Knopp Biklen, Chair, Ed.D., Massachusetts. Sociology of education, qualitative research methods, popular culture, gender and race, adolescence. Cecil Abrahams, Ph.D., Alberta. Comparative higher education and diversity. Kal Alston Ph.D., Chicago. Philosophy in education, gender and race, popular culture. Barbara Applebaum, Ph.D., Toronto. Philosophy of education, critical race studies, critical whiteness studies. Douglas Biklen, Ph.D., Syracuse. Public policy on disability, child advocacy. John Briggs, Ph.D., Minnesota. History of education. Gretchen Lopez, Ph.D., Michigan. Intergroup relations, multicultural education, social identities. Emily Robertson, Ph.D., Syracuse. Philosophy of education. Dalia Rodriguez, Ph.D., Illinois at Urbana-Champaign. Racial inequality, qualitative research methods, policy studies. Kenneth Strike, Ph.D., Northwestern. Philosophy of education and educational policy. Steven Taylor, Ph.D., Syracuse. Disability studies, public policy, sociology of education.

Exercise Science (315-443-2114)
The program's emphasis is on pursuing cutting-edge research. Students can explore their interests in exercise and sport sciences and utilize the department's state-of-the-art laboratory facilities. Students specialize in applied physiology and pursue careers in educational, corporate, clinical, and research settings.

Lori Ploutz-Snyder, Chair; Ph.D., Ohio. Exercise physiology, skeletal muscle, and aging. Keith DeRuisseau, Ph.D., Florida State. Role of oxidative stress in the development of skeletal muscle atrophy during disuse and aging. Timothy Fairchild, Ph.D., Western Australia. Glycogen resynthesis following exercise. Jill Kanaley, Ph.D., Illinois. Exercise physiology/endocrinology, exercise in aging. Dali Xu, Ph.D., Illinois at Urbana-Champaign. Neuromechanics, exploring motor control, biomechanical mechanisms of human motion.

Higher Education (315-443-4763)
This program prepares students to participate in the ever-changing, increasingly diverse collegiate environment by enhancing their understanding of the history and structure of higher education, theories and practices of student development, student learning and attainment, and higher education/student affairs administration. Areas of study include learning communities and innovative pedagogies to promote student learning, diversity, student affairs and higher education administration, student success and attainment, legal issues, and advising in higher education.

Catherine Engstrom, Chair; Ph.D., Maryland. Student learning, diversity and educational reform. Kalena Cortes, Ph.D., Berkeley. Economics of education, labor economics, economic demography. Dawn Johnson, Ph.D. candidate, Maryland. Multiculturalism, student affairs administration. Vincent Tinto, Ph.D., Chicago. Attrition, learning communities. Stephanie Waterman, Ph.D., Syracuse. Native American postsecondary education, race and gender in higher education.

Instructional Design, Development, and Evaluation (315-443-3703)
This program prepares students to identify and evaluate learning problems and to design and develop appropriate instructional solutions to these problems. Students apply instructional analysis, prepare materials, evaluate programs, and assess learning. Through the curriculum, students learn a variety of soft (process and communication) and hard technologies. Through practical projects, students acquire competencies for creation and use of technology-supported solutions in educational and professional settings.

Gerald Mager, Chair; Ph.D., Ohio State. Teacher education, supervision and curriculum. Tiffany Koszalka, Ph.D., Penn State. Instructional systems. Jing Lei, Ph.D., Michigan State. Educational technology. Nick Smith, Ph.D., Illinois. Evaluation research. Adjunct faculty: Gerald Edmonds, Ph.D., Syracuse. Jerry Klein, Ph.D., Florida State. Alexander Romiszowski, Ph.D., Loughborough (England). Charles Spuches, Ed.D. Syracuse. Barbara Yonai, Ph.D., Syracuse.

Reading and Language Arts (315-443-4755)
With opportunities to earn advanced degrees in literacy education and English education, students are prepared as teachers in K–12 settings. Students gain valuable research experiences in public and private schools, where they work to upgrade literacy, English, and language arts instruction, as well as have an impact on broader program assessment and instructional issues.

Kathleen Hinchman, Chair; Ph.D., Syracuse. Adolescent literacy, social perspectives, teacher education. Benita Blachman, Ph.D., Connecticut. Educational psychology, learning disabilities. Marlene Blumin, Ph.D., Cornell. College learning strategies. Rachel Brown, Ph.D., Maryland. Comprehension strategies, technologies. Kelly Chandler-Olcott, Ed.D., Maine. Teacher research, adolescent literacy. Kristiina Montero, Ph.D., Georgia. Multiculturalism and inclusion, English language and heritage language learners. Zaline Roy-Campbell, Ph.D., Wisconsin–Madison. Social perspectives, African American and English-language learners. Louise Wilkinson, Ed.D., Harvard. Psychology and communication sciences, children's language and literacy learning.

Teaching and Leadership (315-443-2685)
With an emphasis on addressing student diversity and inclusion, students may pursue programs in art, mathematics, music, science, or social studies education, as well as programs in elementary education, special education, educational administration, and teaching and curriculum. Programs provide for initial teacher preparation, continued professional support of in-service teachers, and the education of those who will provide leadership through school administration, policy development, research on teaching, and the practice of teacher education.

Corinne Smith, Chair; Ph.D., Syracuse. School psychology, learning disabilities. Francis Albino, M.S., Boston College. Curriculum and instruction. Frank Ambrosie, Ed.D., SUNY at Buffalo. Educational administration. Douglas Biklen, Ph.D., Syracuse. Disability studies, autism, inclusion, public policy in special education. John Briggs, Ph.D., Minnesota. History of education. Diane Canino-Rispoli, C.A.S., Syracuse. Educational leadership. Julie Causton-Theoharis, Ph.D., Wisconsin–Madison. Special education and inclusion. Jill Christian-Lynch, C.A.S., SUNY at Cortland. Staff and curriculum development, elementary education. John Coggiola, Ph.D., Florida State. Music education. Elisa Macedo Dekaney, Ph.D., Florida State. Music education. Helen Doerr, Ph.D., Cornell. Mathematics education, mathematical modeling, functions, and problem solving using computing technology. Benjamin Dotger, Ph.D., North Carolina State. Curriculum and instruction. Sharon Dotger, Ph.D., North Carolina State. Science education. Marvin Druger, Ph.D., Columbia. Science education. Gail Ensher, Ed.D., Boston University. Educating infants and young children with special needs. Beth Ferri, Ph.D., Georgia. Inclusive education, disability studies. Emma Rodriguez-Suarez, Ph.D., Toronto. Music education. Hope Irvine, Ph.D., NYU. Art education. Gerald Mager, Ph.D., Ohio State. Teacher education, supervision, and curriculum. Jeffrey Mangram, Ph.D., Syracuse. Social studies education, popular culture and media literacy. Joanna Masingila, Ph.D., Indiana. Mathematics education. Gloria Quadrini, Ed.D., Syracuse. Teaching and leadership. Jerry Rispoli, C.A.S., Syracuse. Technology integration and elementary education. Mara Sapon-Shevin, Ph.D., Rochester. Teacher education, inclusive schools. Joseph Shedd, Ph.D., Cornell. Educational leadership, collective bargaining, labor law and history. George Theoharis, Ph.D., Wisconsin–Madison. Educational leadership, policy analysis. John Tillotson, Ph.D., Iowa. Science teaching, preparation, constructive teaching. Patricia Tinto, Ph.D., Syracuse. Mathematics education, teaching and curriculum. Harry Tuttle, Ed.D., SUNY at Buffalo. Content in action.

UNION GRADUATE COLLEGE

School of Education

Programs of Study

The Union Graduate College School of Education focuses exclusively on the art of teaching at the secondary level. Its programs were designed by teachers and, without exception, are taught by proven practitioners who excel in their subject matter and in the classroom. Renowned for their rigor and high quality, these programs are aligned with National Board Certification standards and principles and serve as a model for certification programs in New York State.

Students learn a broad range of effective research-based teaching methods. Every lesson is conducted using multiple approaches, giving students the opportunity to reflect on and assess their own teaching methods with an eye toward improvement. In addition, the School of Education offers yearlong mentored internships that fully prepare graduates to take the lead in the classroom, and students may choose a concentration in a wide variety of academic subjects.

For students with no prior teaching experience, the Master of Arts in Teaching (M.A.T.) program provides initial certification and the master's degree necessary for professional certification. Students are required to earn 42 units in their areas of concentration. Full-time students generally complete the program in one calendar year, and part-time students complete it in two to three calendar years.

The Combined M.A.T. program is designed for Union College undergraduates who wish to pursue a career in teaching. This program is usually completed in one calendar year after the bachelor's degree is attained. The CORE M.A.T. program is available for career changers who already hold at least a master's degree, and most students typically take one year to complete this program.

The Master of Science (M.S.) for Teachers of Mathematics and Science program allows practicing teachers in math, science, and technology who have initial certification to earn a master's degree for professional certification or a second certification in science. Students must earn 50 units in their area of certification, and most complete the program in two to three calendar years. Academic concentrations include biology, chemistry, English, French, geology (Earth science), German, Greek, history (social studies), Latin, mathematics, physics, political science (social studies), Spanish, and technology.

Research Facilities

The School of Education's Curriculum Library is a noncirculating collection of books, magazines, articles, textbooks, and other professional materials that have been purchased and/or donated to the education program. The School of Education has accumulated substantial holdings on current and historical material on topics central to teachers, schools, and teaching in each of the disciplines. The Schaffer Library's collection consists of more than 550,000 volumes and 1,500 current journal subscriptions as well as a wide range of CDs, DVDs, and other media and a number of special collections, such as the Union Collection, the Schenectady, and the Union College Archives.

Financial Aid

The M.A.T. program offers a limited number of program fellowships or fee-remission scholarships. Other students who qualify based on financial need may receive some assistance in the form of tuition reduction through the graduate program. The Harriet and Roscoe L. Williams '30 Endowed Scholarship is awarded to graduate students preparing for careers in classroom teaching and educational administration in New York. The New York State Tuition Assistance Program awards up to $550 per year to New York State residents who are enrolled as full-time graduate students. Federal Stafford loans are available to full- and part-time students.

Cost of Study

For the 2006–07 academic year, tuition was $1750 per course. Other charges included a one-time resource fee of $250 and an annual paring fee of $15. Full-time students are also required to enroll in Union Graduate College's health insurance program.

Living and Housing Costs

There is limited graduate housing one block from the campus; rent is approximately $300 per month. Other apartments are available within walking distance of the campus. Housing and board for graduate students cost approximately $8800 per year, depending on the students' individual needs. Books and supplies typically cost about $1200 per year for full-time students.

Student Group

In the School of Education in 2005–06, there were 68 full-time and 27 part-time students; there were 54 women, 4 students who are members of minority groups, and 2 international students. Some students are practicing teachers who want to earn additional certification. Others with no prior teaching experience are either seeking their training and certification or are changing careers but already hold a masters degree.

Student Outcomes

Graduates of the program have begun or are continuing their careers in education throughout New York State and other regions—not only as teachers but also as curriculum coordinators and in other administrative roles.

Location

Union Graduate College is located in Schenectady, in the Capital District of New York State—in the heart of upstate New York. Centrally located, the College is within a 3-hour drive of New York City, Boston, Rochester, and Montreal. Schenectady's rich history includes the founding of General Electric and the invention of the rotary engine and air brakes, but its present-day appeal is just as impressive. Art lovers can visit the Schenectady Museum and Empire State Plaza or enjoy shows at Proctor Theater and Capital Repertory. Nearby parks and hiking trails are also available for outdoor recreation.

The College

Union Graduate College provides outstanding master's-level professional degree programs that meet the needs of New York's Capital Region and beyond. The College dates back to the early twentieth century when the first advanced degrees were being awarded in electrical engineering. Today, its rich and varied connection to the liberal arts and sciences provides the foundation for cutting-edge programs that prepare students to enter, or re-enter, their professional fields as team-oriented leaders.

Applying

Prospective students are required to submit an application, official transcripts from all colleges/universities attended, three letters of recommendation, an essay describing the applicant's reasons and qualifications for becoming a teacher, and a $60 application fee. The deadline to apply is March 1. Applications can be submitted online or sent to the Union Graduate College admission coordinator.

Correspondence and Information

Patrick F. Allen, Ph.D.
Dean of the School of Education
Union Graduate College
807 Union Street, Lamont House
Schenectady, New York 12308

Phone: 518-388-6361
Fax: 518-388-6686
E-mail: mat@union.edu
Web site: http://www.gcuu.edu/

Union Graduate College

THE FACULTY AND THEIR RESEARCH

Patrick F. Allen, Professor and Dean, School of Education; Ph.D. (English and American studies), Indiana, 1974. National board certification, mentoring, quality instruction, assessment, nineteenth- and twentieth-century American fiction.

Ken Blom, Clinical Assistant Professor of Education; Ph.D., SUNY at Albany, 1988. Assessment in teacher education, teaching science, science curriculum.

William Garcia, Professor of Spanish and Chair of Department of Modern Languages. Ph.D., Rutgers, 1995. Latin American and Spanish theater, Latin American cinema, Caribbean literature.

Beatrice A. Hall, Clinical Assistant Professor of Education; Ph.D. (curriculum and instruction), North Adams State, 1983. Writing to learn, teacher responses to student writing, curriculum design, interdisciplinary teaching, authentic assessment, the role of speaking in learning, reading and writing literacy, teacher professional initiatives.

Carol Hobday, Adjunct Clinical Associate Professor of Education; M.S., SUNY at Albany, 1974.

Les Hull, Professor of Chemistry. Ph.D., Harvard, 1971.

Anupama Jain, Assistant Professor of English; Ph.D., Wisconsin–Madison, 2001.

Tim Keeley, Adjunct Clinical Associate Professor of Education. M.S., Saint Rose, 1980.

Karen Kelley, Adjunct Clinical Associate Professor of Education; Ed.D., SUNY at Albany, 1991.

Patricia Kennedy, Adjunct Clinical Associate Professor of Education; Ph.D. candidate, SUNY at Albany.

Kim Lanaro, Adjunct Professor of Education.

Marna Lehnert, Adjunct Clinical Associate Professor of Education; M.A.T., Union (New York), 2005.

Victoria Martinez, Associate Professor of Spanish; Ph.D., Arizona State, 1992. Contemporary Latin-American narrative, border studies, literature of the Southern Cone.

Lori Maloney, Adjunct Clinical Associate Professor of Education; M.S., Saint Rose, 2002.

Catey Merriman, Adjunct Clinical Associate Professor of Education; M.A.T., Union (New York), 1991.

Kelly Moore, Adjunct Clinical Associate Professor of Education; Ph.D. candidate, SUNY at Albany.

Alan Remaley, Adjunct Clinical Professor of Education; Ph.D., SUNY at Albany, 1990.

Rebecca Remis, Adjunct Clinical Associate Professor of Education; M.A.T., Union (New York), 1994.

Carol Reynolds, Adjunct Clinical Associate Professor of Education; M.A., Rochester, 1968.

Richard Reynolds, Adjunct Clinical Associate Professor of Education; M.S., SUNY at Oneonta, 1975.

Randy Roeser, Adjunct Clinical Associate Professor of Education; M.A., Tufts, 1979.

Steve Sargent, Professor of History; Ph.D., Pennsylvania, 1982.

Catherine Snyder, Adjunct Clinical Associate Professor of Education; M.A.T., Union (New York), 1996.

Ruth M. Stevenson, Professor of English; Ph.D., Duke, 1972.

Tom Venezio, Adjunct Clinical Associate Professor of Education; M.S., SUNY at Albany, 1979.

Kate Vrtiak, Adjunct Clinical Associate Professor of Education; M.A., SUNY at Albany, 1970.

Diane Wilkinson, Adjunct Clinical Associate Professor of Education; M.S., SUNY at Cortland, 1993.

Dave Williams, Adjunct Associate Professor of Education; Ph.D. (educational administration), SUNY at Albany.

Karen Williams, Adjunct Clinical Associate Professor of Education; Ph.D., Union (New York), 1979.

Bill Wojcik, Adjunct Clinical Associate Professor of Education; M.A.T., Union (New York), 1993.

UNIVERSITY OF MAINE

College of Education and Human Development

Programs of Study

The University of Maine College of Education and Human Development offers NCATE-accredited graduate study at the master's levels: Master of Arts in Teaching, Master of Education, Master of Science); Certificate of Advanced Study; and doctoral levels (Ed.D.). Program areas include teacher education (M.A.T., M.Ed., C.A.S.) in elementary, middle level, secondary, science, and social studies education; human development (M.S.); literacy (M.A., M.S., M.Ed., C.A.S., Ed.D.); counselor education (M.A., M.S., M.Ed., C.A.S., Ed.D.); educational leadership PreK–12 (M.Ed., C.A.S., Ed.D.); higher education (M.Ed., C.A.S., Ed.D.); kinesiology and physical education (M.S., M.Ed.); instructional technology (M.Ed.); special education (M.Ed., C.A.S.); and an individually designed Ed.D. Secondary education concentrations include English, modern languages, mathematics, science, and social studies.

Research-based programs and extensive field experiences and internships are designed to further the scholarship and advance the preparation and continuing development of leaders and specialists in a variety of educational and other professional fields. Innovative technology, faculty mentoring, creative inquiry, action research, and strong partnerships with public schools are among the graduate program hallmarks.

Research Facilities

The College encourages, supports, and conducts research to help meet the needs and challenges of education and society. For example, it is home to the Institute for the Study of Students at Risk, the Maine Center for Sport and Coaching, and the broad-based Center for Research and Evaluation, which publishes the *Journal of Research in Rural Education*. The College is also the site of rich literacy area programs, including the University Training Center for Reading Recovery, the Maine Literacy Partnership, and the Maine Writing Project.

Financial Aid

A number of graduate assistantships are available for qualified students at the master's and doctoral levels. Funding to assist doctoral students with professional development pursuits, such as presenting at a conference, is awarded through the Linda N. Lancaster Professional Development Fund.

Cost of Study

In 2006–07, graduate tuition was $296 per credit hour for Maine residents and $845 for nonresident students. The unified fee for those taking 6 to 11 credit hours was $322.

Living and Housing Costs

Campus room and meal plans are approximately $3545 per semester. The University operates a family housing complex, as well as a graduate dorm, and there are a variety of apartments, rooms, and other housing options available in nearby communities.

Student Group

The College enrolls approximately 920 graduate students. The majority are practicing professionals who bring a variety of valuable life and work experience to their courses and colleagues.

Location

The University of Maine is the flagship campus of the University of Maine System. It is located on a 1,100-acre campus adjoining the town of Orono and city of Old Town, and it is located 9 miles from Bangor, Maine's third-largest city. Access is convenient to both urban and rural areas and many outdoor activities in the mountains or on the coast. A variety of year-round cultural and athletic events take place both on and off campus.

The University and The College

Founded in 1865, the University of Maine is the state's land-grant university and sea-grant college. The College of Education and Human Development, one of five colleges at the University, provides leadership, professional development, research, and resources to advance education at all levels, address concerns that affect children and families, and help people of all ages and abilities pursue lifelong learning and achievement. The College centers its teaching, research, and service on broad developmental, educational, and social issues to generate insights that shape perception, policy, and practice.

The College is a statewide and regional force for stronger ties between schools and universities. Its research and faculty inform and influence the policy and practice essential to schools and society in transition. As a founding member of the Penobscot River Educational Partnership—a model university/public school collaboration—the College works with regional schools to address issues and initiate timely, innovative programs and projects. The College's ongoing externally funded projects and relevant work in schools and communities provide extensive experience and information about the continuum of learners and their changing needs.

Applying

Specific program information, requirements, and application forms are available from the College of Education and Human Development. Applications for admission should be sent to the Graduate School, 2 Winslow Hall, University of Maine, Orono, Maine 04469. Applicants seeking awards or graduate assistantships should have their applications on file at the Graduate School by January 15 for the following academic year.

Correspondence and Information

College of Education and Human Development
University of Maine
5766 Shibles Hall
Orono, Maine 04469-5766
Phone: 207-581-2444
E-mail: becky.libby@umit.maine.edu
Web site: http://www.umaine.edu/edhd/ (College)
          http://www.umaine.edu/graduate (Graduate School)

University of Maine

THE FACULTY AND THEIR RESEARCH

Robert A. Cobb, Professor and Dean; Ed.D., Springfield, 1969. Aspirations of youths and adults, school policy development, teacher preparation, educational leadership.

Anne E. Pooler, Associate Professor and Associate Dean for Instruction; Ed.D., Maine, 1975. Curriculum development/social studies, economic education, teacher preparation.

O. J. Logue, Associate Dean for Academic Services; Ed.D., Vanderbilt, 1992. Recruitment and retention factors impacting educators, predictors of success among deaf higher education leaders.

Richard Ackerman, Associate Professor, Educational Leadership; Ed.D., Harvard, 1989. Leadership formation, school organization, professional development.

Elizabeth J. Allen, Associate Professor, Educational Leadership; Ph.D., Ohio State, 1999. Higher education, equity policy, gender and education, policy discourse analysis.

A. James Artesani, Associate Professor, Special Education; Ed.D., West Virginia, 1992. Transition programs, positive behavioral practices, severe disabilities.

V. Susan Bennett-Armistead, Assistant Professor, Literacy; Ph.D., Michigan State, 2006. Curriculum and teacher education, with an emphasis in literacy.

Mary Bird, Instructor, Science and Environmental Education; Ed.D., Harvard, 2006. Learning/teaching science in informal settings.

Edward N. Brazee, Professor, Middle Level Education; Ed.D., Northern Colorado, 1975. Curriculum development, school restructuring/reform, parent involvement.

Phyllis E. Brazee, Associate Professor, Education; Ed.D., Northern Colorado, 1976. Reading and writing processes, integrated curriculum, assessment.

Dorothy Tysse Breen, Associate Professor, Counselor Education; Ph.D., Wisconsin–Madison, 1987. Play theories and techniques, developmental guidance, changing families.

Stephen A. Butterfield, Professor, Kinesiology and Physical Education; Ph.D., Ohio State, 1984. Adaptive physical education, motor skills development, special education.

Sandra Caron, Professor, Human Development and Family Relations; Ph.D., Syracuse, 1986. Human sexuality, AIDS and families, sexuality education and curriculum development.

Julie Cheville, Assistant Professor, Literacy Education; Ph.D., Iowa, 1997. Language, literacy, and culture.

James Chiavacci, Instructional Technologist; Ph.D., Colorado at Denver, 1987. Instructional technology.

Theodore Coladarci, Professor, Educational Psychology; Ph.D., Stanford, 1980. Learning and cognition, research methodology, educational assessment.

Nellie Orr Cyr, Associate Professor, Kinesiology and Physical Education; Ph.D., Pittsburgh, 1997. Exercise physiology, cardiovascular conditioning, wellness programming.

William E. Davis, Professor, Special Education; Ph.D., Connecticut, 1968. Children and youth at risk, interagency collaboration, school role in mental health.

Marcia Davidson, Assistant Professor, Special Education; Ph.D., Washington (Seattle), 1991. Early childhood reading acquisition, reading fluency, intervention and assessment.

Julie DellaMattera, Assistant Professor, Early Childhood Education; Ed.D., Maine, 2006. Early childhood development and education, with a focus on early education policy.

Gordon A. Donaldson Jr., Professor, Educational Leadership; Ed.D., Harvard, 1976. School administration/effectiveness, the principalship.

John Donovan, Assistant Professor, Mathematics Education; Ph.D., Buffalo, 2002. Cross-tier professional development, students' understanding of mathematical concepts, curriculum development integrating different content areas of mathematics.

Suzanne Estler, Associate Professor, Higher Education; Ph.D., Stanford, 1978. Dynamics of change; social context of higher education; gender, race, and sexual orientation in higher education.

Janet Fairman, Assistant Research Professor; Ph.D., Rutgers, 1999. Public policy, school reform, assessment, qualitative research.

Abigail Garthwait, Associate Professor, Instructional Technology; Ed.D., Maine, 2000. Best practice involving appropriate integration of technology in K–12 classrooms and higher education.

Walter J. Harris, Professor, Special Education; Ph.D., Syracuse, 1973. Behavior disorders in children and adolescents, issues in special education.

Dianne L. Hoff, Assistant Professor, Educational Leadership; Ed.D., Louisville, 1998. School legal issues, special populations, the superintendency and the principalship.

Diane Jackson, Clinical Instructor, Education; Ed.D., Maine, 2000. Adapting instruction for students with special needs, math methods in special education, graduate field supervision.

Edward Jadallah, Associate Professor, Social Studies Education; Ph.D., Ohio State, 1984. Curriculum and instructional design/evaluation, reflective practices.

Richard Kent, Assistant Professor, Literacy; Ph.D., Claremont, 2002. Portfolio pedagogy, adolescent male underachievement in literacy, innovative middle and high school classrooms, secondary school independent study projects.

Janice V. Kristo, Professor, Literacy; Ph.D., Connecticut, 1979. Children's literature, reading and language arts, elementary school curriculum design.

Robert A. Lehnhard, Associate Professor, Kinesiology and Physical Education; Ph.D., Ohio State, 1984. Exercise physiology.

Mary Ellin Logue, Assistant Professor, Early Childhood Education; Ed.D., Massachusetts Amherst, 1984. Social development, special education.

Sarah V. Mackenzie, Assistant Professor, Educational Leadership; Ed.D., Maine, 2002. Collective efficacy and collaborative climate in Maine high schools.

John Maddaus, Associate Professor, Education; Ph.D., Syracuse, 1987. Sociology of education, school to work transitions, professional development schools.

Mary Madden, Assistant Research Professor; Ph.D., Maine, 2001. Development and education of adolescent girls.

George F. Marnik, Clinical Instructor, Educational Leadership; Ed.D., Maine, 1997. Change process in high schools, the principalship.

Craig Mason, Associate Professor, Research and Evaluation; Ph.D., Washington, 1993. Child clinical psychology, quantitative and developmental psychology.

Robert M. Milardo, Professor, Human Development; Ph.D., Penn State, 1982. Family/domestic violence, social networks, friendship/kin relationships.

Sidney Mitchell, Assistant Professor, Educational Psychology; Ph.D., McGill, 2001. Student motivation and low achievement, teacher as researcher.

Gert Nesin, Clinical Instructor; Ph.D., Georgia, 2000. Middle-level education, curriculum integration, students at risk.

Eric A. Pandiscio, Associate Professor, Math Education; Ph.D., Texas at Austin, 1994. Secondary math education, geometric construction software.

Constance M. Perry, Professor, Education; Ed.D., Maine, 1976. Values education, moral development, instructional strategies, supervision.

Glenn Reif, Associate Professor, Kinesiology and Physical Education; Ed.D., Virginia Tech, 1990. Physical fitness of children, pedagogy, psychomotor domain activities.

James A. Rog, Associate Professor, Education; Ed.D., Massachusetts, 1979. Staff development, creating successful working conditions, instruction/assessment.

Gary L. Schilmoeller, Associate Professor, Child Development and Family Relations; Ph.D., Kansas, 1977. Support for families with members with a disability.

Janet E. Spector, Associate Professor, Special Education; Ph.D., Stanford, 1983. Measurement and evaluation research methodology, dyslexia/learning disabilities.

Sydney Carroll Thomas, Associate Professor, Counselor Education; Ph.D., Rochester, 1993. Peer rejection in schools; humane education and humane school climate/curriculum; poetry therapy and school counseling.

Shihfen Tu, Assistant Professor, Research and Evaluation; Ph.D., Washington, 1994. Cognition and perception.

Herman G. Weller, Associate Professor; Ed.D., Virginia Tech, 1990. Science education, computer-based science learning students' misconceptions of science.

Jane Wellman-Little, Instructor; C.A.S., Maine, 1997. Developmental reading, Reading Recovery.

UNIVERSITY OF MARYLAND,
COLLEGE PARK
College of Education

Programs of Study

The University of Maryland, College Park is the flagship campus of the University System of Maryland. The College of Education offers an array of graduate concentrations leading to the degrees of the Doctor of Philosophy (Ph.D.), the Doctor of Education (Ed.D.), the Master of Arts (M.A.), and the Master of Education (M.Ed.), and is home to the Maryland Institute for Minority Achievement and Urban Education. Some departments offer the advanced graduate specialist (AGS) certificate.

The Department of Counseling and Personnel Services offers master's degree programs in college student personnel, rehabilitation counseling, and school counseling. An AGS certificate is offered in school psychology. Doctoral programs are offered in college student personnel administration, counselor education, counseling psychology, and school psychology.

The Department of Curriculum and Instruction offers a rich and diverse academic experience grounded in rigorous scholarship through its undergraduate, graduate certification, master's, and doctoral degree programs. The department is composed of ten interrelated program areas that span the following educational disciplines and are available across most degree options: art education, elementary education, English/speech/theater education, mathematics education, minority and urban education, reading education, science education, second language/TESOL, social studies education, and teacher education/professional development.

The Department of Education Policy and Leadership offers graduate degree programs to prepare educational leaders for a wide variety of leadership roles to institutions, organizations, or agencies; prepares graduate students for positions in research, teaching, and international education development; and assists in the preparation of elementary and secondary school teachers. Master's and doctoral programs are offered in curriculum theory and development (Ph.D., Ed.D., and M.A., with concentrations available in African American studies and Jewish studies), higher education (Ph.D. and M.A.), international education policy (Ph.D. and M.A.), organizational leadership and policy studies (Ph.D. and Ed.D.), and educational policy and social foundations (Ph.D. and M.A.).

The Department of Human Development/Institute for Child Study offers graduate degrees to develop competencies in the scientific knowledge of human development. Programs prepare students for careers in research, teaching, and the application of knowledge in human development and learning. Master's degrees are offered in human development and a concentration in early childhood. The Ed.D. and Ph.D. degrees offered are in human development, with areas of concentration in social development, cognitive development, and physiological development. At the doctoral level, the educational psychology specialty focuses on research-based training in the application of psychological theory and research; the early childhood concentration offers comprehensive training in the study of development and education of young children; and the developmental sciences specialty (jointly administered with the psychology department) focuses on research training linking the psychophysiological, social, emotional, and cognitive aspects of development. The department operates the Center for Young Children in support of graduate studies and research, and houses the Center for Children, Relationships, and Culture, a research center devoted to these topics.

The Department of Measurement, Statistics, and Evaluation offers programs at the master's (M.A.) and doctoral (Ph.D.) levels in the areas of program evaluation, measurement, and statistics. Ample opportunity exists to engage in research with faculty members and to present research results in areas such as computer-based testing, design of experiments, construction and evaluation of measuring instruments, generalizability theory, measurement theory, multidimensional scaling, multivariate analysis, program evaluation, latent class analysis, structured equations modeling, and research methodology.

The Department of Special Education offers graduate programs at the master's (including a teacher certification program) and doctoral levels with areas of concentration in policy studies, behavior disorders, infancy and early childhood special education, learning disabilities, secondary and transition special education, and severe disabilities. Graduate degrees emphasize research, instruction, and policy studies.

Research Facilities

The College of Education is home to thirteen research-based centers and institutions. The campus libraries contain more than 2.3 million volumes and subscribe to some 26,000 periodicals and newspapers. Additional collections of research materials are available on microfilm, microfiche, phonograph records, tapes, and films and in electronic formats. Maryland's libraries system has six branches and houses an extensive collection of books, periodicals, reserves, and other materials. More information on library resources and services is available by calling 301-405-0800 or visiting the Web at http://www.lib.umd.edu.

Financial Aid

A limited number of teaching and research assistantships are available through the departments within the College of Education. Other types of financial assistance are offered through the Graduate School. Financial aid applications should be submitted with the application for graduate study. For more information, students should call 301-314-9000. Graduate assistantships are listed by employment services (301-405-5679).

Cost of Study

Tuition for the 2006–07 academic year was as follows: Maryland residents paid $393 per credit hour; nonresidents paid $820 per credit hour. All students admitted to the Graduate School must pay graduate tuition, whether or not the credit will be used to satisfy program requirements. Graduate students are charged for tuition at the graduate rate, regardless of the level of courses for which they register. Mandatory fees, such as registration, shuttle bus, and health, are assessed each semester.

Living and Housing Costs

Housing costs vary on and off campus. Current information on housing for graduate students is available from the Office of Commuter Services (telephone: 301-314-3645; Web site: http://www.cacs.umd.edu/och).

Student Group

The College enrolls 2,002 students, of whom 1,181 are graduate students. Of the total graduate enrollment, 920 are women; 336 are members of minority groups (189 African Americans, 75 Asian Americans or Pacific Islanders, 68 Hispanic Americans, and 4 Native Americans); and 111 are international students.

Location

Nestled on 1,300 acres in suburban College Park, the University is located in the thriving Baltimore-Washington corridor. The University's location—just 9 miles from downtown Washington, D.C., and approximately 30 miles from both Baltimore and Annapolis—enhances the research opportunities of its faculty members and students by providing access to some of the finest libraries and research centers in the country.

The University and The College

With more than 3,000 faculty members, the University of Maryland is an internationally recognized premier research institution offering master's degrees in eighty areas and doctoral degrees in sixty-eight. Programs within each of the College's six departments rank in the top fifteen nationwide; *U.S. News & World Report 2007* ranks Counseling and Personnel Services first in the nation and Special Education seventh.

Applying

Information and application forms can be obtained from Graduate School Admissions, University of Maryland, 2123 Lee Building, College Park, Maryland 20742-5121, or by calling 301-405-0376. Application can also be made online through the College of Education Web site at http://www.education.umd.edu. Students can also visit http://www.vprgs.umd.edu for an application and the latest electronic edition of the Graduate Catalog. Application deadlines are as follows: September 1 (domestic students) or June 1 (international students) for spring semester and February 1 (international students) or March 1 (domestic students) for fall semester. Some programs have earlier admission deadlines. International applicants should apply at least six months before department program deadlines.

Correspondence and Information

College of Education, Student Services Office
1204 Benjamin Building
University of Maryland
College Park, Maryland 20742-1121
Phone: 301-405-0006
Fax: 301-314-5887
Web site: http://www.education.umd.edu

University of Maryland, College Park

THE FACULTY AND THEIR RESEARCH

Department of Counseling and Personnel Services

Alfred J. Amado, Ph.D. Effects of psychosocial risk and resiliency factors on development of ethnic minority students, school mental health policies. Vivian S. Boyd, Ph.D. Delivery of counseling services in colleges and universities. Ellen S. Fabian, Ph.D. Support systems for adults with disabilities, school-to-work transition for special needs young adults. Ruth E. Fassinger, Ph.D., Chair. Psychology of women and gender, sexuality, feminist therapy, vocational psychology. Gary D. Gottfredson, Ph.D. Organization and program development, multicultural education. Mary Ann Hoffman, Ph.D. Psychosocial aspects of health and wellness, counselor training and supervision. Cheryl Holcomb-McCoy, Ph.D. Multicultural counseling competence, impact of racial identity in school counseling programs. Karen Kurotsuchi Inkelas, Ph.D. Living-learning programs, Asian American students. Susan Robb Jones, Ph.D. Service-learning and community partnerships in higher education, psychosocial identity development, qualitative research, student affairs leadership. Dennis M. Kivlighan Jr., Ph.D., Interim Dean. Process and outcome of group and individual counseling and psychotherapy, counseling interventions in influencing achievement goal. Susan Komives, Ed.D. Student leadership, leadership identity development, generational cohorts. Courtland C. Lee, Ph.D. Psychosocial development of African American males, evaluation of culturally specific counseling interventions in schools. Robert W. Lent, Ph.D. Social cognitive career theory, psychological adjustment processes. Margaretha Lucas, Ph.D. Career and identity development, evaluation of clinical services. Kim MacDonald-Wilson, Ph.D. Rehabilitation counseling, psychiatric rehabilitation. Marylu K. McEwen, Ph.D. Development of college students, psychosocial development for students of color. Natasha A. Mitchell, Ph.D. Acculturation among immigrant students, counselor education, urban school counseling. Pepper Phillips, Ph.D. Homophobia in schools, gay-, lesbian-, bisexual-headed family coping strategies. Sylvia A. Rosenfield, Ph.D. School consultation services, instructional consultation, urban education. William E. Sedlacek, Ph.D. Student and faculty research, multicultural issues. William O. Strein, Ed.D. Children's self-perceptions of competence, affective correlations of learning/schooling. Hedwig Teglasi-Golubcow, Ph.D. Temperament and personality assessment, integration of cognitive processes in personality development.

Department of Curriculum and Instruction

Peter P. Afflerbach, Ph.D. Reading assessment, development of reading strategies, think-aloud protocol. Tara Brown, Ed.D. Urban education, critical literacies in media and technology, race, class, gender and culture in education, youth culture. Patricia F. Campbell, Ph.D. Enhancing instructional practice, increasing mathematics achievement in urban schools. Marilyn J. Chambliss, Ph.D. Literacy development in science and social studies among elementary school children. Daniel Chazan, Ed.D. Teaching with technology, student-centered mathematics teaching. Joseph Cirrincione, Ph.D. Social studies and geography education. Janet E. Coffey, Ph.D. Assessment in science education, science education reform. Mariam J. Dreher, Ph.D. Effective reading instruction, reading motivation in elementary school. James T. Fey, Ph.D. Professional development of middle and high school and mathematics teachers. Anna O. Graeber, Ed.D. Teaching and learning mathematics in middle schools. David M. Hammer, Ph.D. Teacher thinking and physics education. William G. Holliday, Ph.D. Science education, motivation and literacy in science. Martin L. Johnson, Ed.D., Associate Dean. Mathematics learning in young and minority children. Stephen M. Koziol, Ph.D., Chair. Teacher education program design, English teaching methodology, secondary literacy. Millicent Kushner, Ed.D. Applied psycholinguistics, bilingual education. Marvin Lynn, Ph.D. Urban teacher education. Elizabeth Marshall, Ph.D. Sociocultural perspectives in literacy, children's literature. Melinda Martin-Beltran, Ph.D. Second-language learning, bilingualism and classroom interaction, cultural and linguistic diversity. Joseph L. McCaleb, Ph.D. Literacy education, storytelling, literacy and community. James R. McGinnis, Ph.D. Science teacher education, equity in science teaching and learning. Chauncey Monte-Sano, Ph.D. Learning to write and reason with evidence in history classrooms, effective history/social studies teaching. John F. O'Flahavan, Ph.D. Early literacy, teacher professional development. Rebecca L. Oxford, Ph.D. Language learning styles, strategies and motivation. Megan Madigan Peercy, Ph.D. Second-language learning, bilingualism and classroom interaction, cultural and linguistic diversity. Olivia N. Saracho, Ph.D. Emergent literacy, teacher preparation, cognitive style. Wayne H. Slater, Ph.D. Written communication, reading comprehension, teacher education. Mike Stieff, Ph.D. Visuospatial reasoning, diagrammatic reasoning, computer-based learning environments in science. Denis F. Sullivan, Ph.D. Computers in education, history of technical education. Jennifer Danridge Turner, Ph.D. Cultural diversity issues in early literacy teaching and learning, urban education. Linda R. Valli, Ph.D. Teacher learning, cultural diversity, school improvement. Bruce A. VanSledright, Ph.D. American history in diverse classrooms, citizenship education. Thomas D. Weible, Ph.D., Senior Associate Dean and Interim Chair, EDPL. Certification standards in social studies, history instruction. Donna L. Wiseman, Ph.D., Associate Dean. Teacher education program development, school-university partnerships.

Department of Education Policy and Leadership

Alberto Cabrera, Ph.D. Research methodologies, college choice, minorities in higher education, economics of education. Jacqueline M. Cossentino, Ed.D. Cultural dimensions of school reform, conceptual challenges of school leadership. Robert G. Croninger, Ph.D. Policy analysis, sociology, equity, quantitative research. Barbara J. Finkelstein, Ed.D. History, transcultural educational policy and practice, biographical studies. Sharon Fries-Britt, Ph.D. Experiences of high-achieving black collegians, recruitment and retention of minority faculty. Dennis Herschbach, Ph.D. Vocational and technical education, education in developing countries. Francine H. Hultgren, Ph.D. Hermeneutic phenomenological inquiry, curriculum theory and development. Steven J. Klees, Ph.D. Comparative and international education, political economy and education. Jing Lin, Ed.D. Comparative education, gender and peace education. Betty Malen, Ph.D. Education policy and politics, theories of political behavior, politics of education reforms. Hanne B. Mawhinney, Ph.D. Institutional dynamics of leadership and policy change, accountability, critical feminist theory. Carol S. Parham, Ed.D. Personnel administration, educational leadership, labor negotiations. Jennifer King Rice, Ph.D. Education policy, education reform for at-risk students. Patricia K. Richardson, Ph.D. Public school administration, school improvement. Steven Selden, Ed.D. Critical curriculum theory, eugenics, comparative curriculum. Carol A. Spreen, Ph.D. Comparative and international education, school reform, restructuring. John B. Williams III, Ed.D. Higher education management, federal and state higher education policy.

Department of Human Development

Patricia A. Alexander, Ph.D. Cognition, strategic processing, domain knowledge development. Natasha J. Cabrera, Ph.D. Paternal involvement, low-income families. Charles H. Flatter, Ed.D. Parent education, grandparenting, drug prevention education. Nathan A. Fox, Ph.D. Attachment, emotion regulation, developmental psychophysiology. John T. Guthrie, Ph.D. Cognitive and motivational processes of reading, literacy learning, and instruction. Brenda Jones-Harden, Ph.D. Development and mental health of foster and at-risk children. Melanie A. Killen, Ph.D. Social and moral development in children and adolescents, conflict resolution. Elisa L. Klein, Ph.D. Early childhood education, social policy and children. Robert F. Marcus, Ph.D. Family relationships, social skills, delinquency and violence. Susan J. Parault, Ph.D. Semantic processing, language development, literacy. Elizabeth Robertson-Tchabo, Ph.D. Cognitive development and aging. Kenneth H. Rubin, Ph.D. Socioemotional and personality development, parent-child relationships. Judith Torney-Purta, Ph.D. Social/political cognition, worldwide civic education. Min Wang, Ph.D. Language and reading acquisition, second-language/bilingual literacy development. Kathryn R. Wentzel, Ph.D. Motivation, social relationships, academic achievement. Allan L. Wigfield, Ph.D., Chair. Motivation and self-concept in children and adolescents.

Department of Measurement, Statistics and Evaluation

Chan Mitchell Dayton, Ph.D., Chair. Latent class analysis, information criteria for model selection. Gregory R. Hancock, Ph.D. Structural equation modeling, multiple comparisons procedures. Jeffrey R. Harring, Ph.D. Modeling of longitudinal data. Robert W. Lissitz, Ph.D. Psychometrics, educational assessment, program evaluation. George B. Macready, Ph.D. Latent class models, assessment of model fit, adaptive testing. Robert J. Mislevy, Ph.D. Educational assessment, statistical methods.

Department of Special Education

Paula J. Beckman, Ph.D. Infancy and early childhood special education, working with families. Philip J. Burke, Ph.D., Chair. Policy studies, teacher education. David H. Cooper, Ph.D. Preschool and primary school children with behavioral and learning disabilities. William Drakeford, Ph.D. Behavioral and emotional disorders, literacy, adolescent education. Andrew L. Egel, Ph.D. Autism and other severe disabilities. Frances L. Kohl, Ph.D. Severe and multiple disabilities, inclusion in school and community. Peter E. Leone, Ph.D. Emotional and behavioral disorders of children and adolescents, juvenile justice. Joan A. Lieber, Ph.D. Early childhood social interaction, inclusion of preschoolers with disabilities. Paula Maccini, Ph.D. Mathematics intervention for secondary students with learning disabilities. Margaret J. McLaughlin, Ph.D. Policy studies and inclusion. M. Sherril Moon, Ed.D. School-to-work transition and community integration of students with severe disabilities. Debra Ann Neubert, Ph.D. School-to-adult-life transition, transition assessment. Rebecca Silverman, Ed.D. Early prevention and intervention for children at risk for experiencing reading difficulties. Deborah L. Speece, Ph.D. Educational handicaps, learning disabilities, identifying learning disabilities. Jeanine M. Staples, Ph.D. Adolescent literacies and learning, media/cultural studies, urban education.

UNIVERSITY OF MIAMI

School of Education

Programs of Study
The School of Education of the University of Miami offers curricula leading to the degrees of Master of Science in Education, Specialist in Education, and Doctor of Philosophy in education.

At the master's level, programs are available in elementary education/ESOL; exceptional student education/prekindergarten disabilities/ESOL (ESE/pre-K disabilities/ESOL); exceptional student education/reading/ESOL (ESE/reading/ESOL); exercise physiology; higher education/administration; marriage and family therapy; mental health counseling; reading/ESOL; research, measurement, and evaluation; sport administration; and sports medicine.

Specialist degrees are offered in elementary education, exceptional student education/reading, exceptional student education/prekindergarten disabilities, and reading.

Doctoral degrees are offered in counseling psychology, exceptional student education, exercise physiology, language and literacy learning in multilingual settings, math and science, and research, measurement, and evaluation.

All programs in teacher preparation are approved by the state of Florida. The counseling psychology doctoral program is accredited by the American Psychological Association (APA).

Research Facilities
All students may use the University library. In addition, a special computer laboratory, administered by the School of Education, is available. The School also operates an exercise physiology laboratory and a training clinic for counseling students.

Financial Aid
Graduate assistantships are available to doctoral program applicants. Full-time teachers under contract and teachers on official leave or sabbatical may be eligible for the teacher tuition discount scholarships. Other tuition assistance may be available through grants.

Cost of Study
Tuition was $1350 per credit for graduate course work in fall 2007.

Living and Housing Costs
Residential colleges are not open to graduate students; however, University Village, an apartment-style residential community is available on a limited basis to graduate students.

Student Group
Approximately 500 students are enrolled in the School of Education for study in programs leading to graduate degrees. These include students from all the states and from many countries.

Location
The suburb of Coral Gables is one of the municipalities that make up metropolitan Miami. This subtropical area, which stretches from Fort Lauderdale to the Florida Keys, is an exciting, multicultural cosmopolitan community that offers substantial cultural and recreational attractions. For those interested in outdoor recreation, the Florida Keys, Biscayne Bay, and Everglades National Park are nearby.

The University
The University, founded in Coral Gables in 1925, is an independent, nonprofit, nonsectarian institution open to all qualified men and women. Its schools, colleges, and research institutes now occupy four campuses. The main campus is in Coral Gables, the medical campus is in Miami, the marine sciences campus is on Virginia Key, and the south campus—primarily a research campus—is in south Dade County. The University supports a full calendar of significant events during the year. Almost all departments and schools sponsor weekly seminars open to graduate students.

The University is a member of a number of consortia established for teaching or research purposes with other universities in the United States and with universities in Latin America and the Caribbean.

Applying
All applications for admission to graduate study must be sent to Marissa Stevenson if the student is applying to the Department of Educational and Psychological Studies (EPS) or the Department of Exercise and Sport Sciences (ESS), and to Christopher Gardner if the student is applying to the Department of Teaching and Learning (TAL). All applicants must submit an application with fee, a statement of goals, a current resume, transcripts from all institutions attended, three recommendations, and scores on the Graduate Record Examinations General Test. Teachers with at least three years of full-time teaching experience may be eligible to apply for a GRE waiver when applying to master's and specialist programs offered by the Department of Teaching and Learning. Doctoral applications for counseling psychology are reviewed once each year and must be received by January 2. The deadline for applications to the Ph.D. programs in teaching and learning is February 15 for fall semester admission and October 15 for the spring semester. Admission to most other graduate programs is on a rolling basis.

Correspondence and Information
Marissa Stevenson (EPS or ESS programs)
or Christopher Gardner (TAL program)
Graduate Admissions Office
School of Education
University of Miami
P.O. Box 248065
Coral Gables, Florida 33124-2040

Phone: 305-284-3711
E-mail: soe@miami.edu
Web site: http://www.education.miami.edu

University of Miami

THE FACULTY AND THEIR RESEARCH

Etiony Aldarondo, Associate Professor and Dean of Research; Ph.D., Massachusetts Amherst, 1992. Family violence, multicultural counseling.

Mary Avalos, Research Assistant Professor; Ph.D., California, Riverside, 1999. Curriculum and instruction, TESOL and reading.

Ann Bessell, Research Assistant Professor; Miami (Florida), 1999. Special education, classroom and behavior management.

William Blanton, Professor; Ed.D., Georgia, 1970. Reading education.

Kent Burnett, Associate Professor; Ph.D., Stanford, 1984. Health psychology, behavioral medicine, assessment, computer applications in psychology.

Cory A. Buxton, Assistant Professor; Ph.D., Colorado, 2000. Instruction and curriculum, science education.

Maria Carlo, Assistant Professor; Ph.D., Massachusetts, 1994. Bilingual education, literacy.

Wendy Cavendish, Assistant Professor; Ph.D., Miami (Florida), 2006. Special education.

Arlene Clachar, Associate Professor; Ph.D., Columbia, 1987. Sociolinguistics, applied linguistics.

Galen Clavio, Visiting Assistant Professor; M.S.Ed., Indiana, 2005. Sport management.

Margaret Crosbie-Burnett, Visiting Associate Professor; Ph.D., Stanford, 1983. Stepfamilies, gay and lesbian families, children and adolescents at risk, the interface between schools and families.

Joshua Diem, Instructor; Ph.D., North Carolina at Chapel Hill, 2004. Culture, curriculum, and change.

Batya Elbaum, Associate Professor; Ph.D., Utah, 1994. Special education research and policy.

Blaine Fowers, Professor and Department Chair; Ph.D., Texas at Austin, 1987. Marriage and family therapy, research with couples, philosophy of psychology.

Andrew Gillentine, Associate Dean of Graduate Studies and Faculty and Staff Administration; Ph.D., Southern Mississippi, 1995. Education administration and teaching, sport management, sport marketing.

Mileidis Gort, Assistant Professor; Ed.D., Boston University, 2001. Literacy, language, and culture.

Kysha Harriell, Director of Clinical Education; M.S.Ed., Miami (Florida), 1999, 2001. Sports medicine, sport administration, athletic training.

Beth Harry, Professor; Ph.D., Syracuse, 1989. Family and multicultural issues.

Anne Hocutt, Assistant Research Professor; Ph.D., North Carolina at Chapel Hill, 1980. Qualitative and descriptive research methods, special education, program evaluation, enrollment management.

Kevin A. Jacobs, Assistant Professor; Ph.D., Ohio State, 2000. Exercise biochemistry, metabolism, cardiovascular physiology.

Jeremy Jordan, Assistant Professor; Ph.D., Ohio State, 2001. Sport management, organizational behavior.

Okhee Lee-Salwen, Professor; Ph.D., Michigan State, 1989. Science education, educational psychology.

Brian Lewis, Lecturer; Ph.D., Florida, 1984. Health psychology, stress and wellness, clinical training, therapy, outcomes assessment.

Kay Lopate, Associate Professor; Ph.D., Miami (Florida), 1985. Reading.

Eveleen Lorton, Professor; Ph.D., LSU, 1966. Secondary education.

James D. McKinney, Professor; Ph.D., North Carolina State, 1969. Research design and methodology, learning disabilities.

Robert McMahon, Professor; Ph.D., Wisconsin–Madison, 1973. Substance abuse disorders; HIV/AIDS; psychological assessment; stress, coping, and social support.

Anita Meinbach, Visiting Assistant Professor; Ed.D., Miami (Florida), 1982. Elementary education.

Marjorie Montague, Professor; Ph.D., Arizona, 1984. Learning disabilities and behavior disorders.

Robert Moore, Associate Professor; Ed.D., Indiana, 1969. Learning and behavior problems.

Susan Mullane, Associate Professor; Ph.D., Miami (Florida), 1995. Leadership, ethics, sport administration.

Nicholas D. Myers, Assistant Professor; Ph.D., Michigan State, 2005. Measurement and quantitative methods.

Prathiba Natesan, Visiting Assistant Professor; Ph.D., Texas A&M, 2007. Educational curriculum and instruction.

Marilyn Neff, Research Assistant Professor and Assistant Dean; Ed.D., Miami (Florida), 1986. Educational leadership.

Ana Pazos-Rego, Research Assistant Professor; Ph.D., Kent State, 2002. Special education, reading.

Randall D. Penfield, Associate Professor; Ph.D., Toronto, 2000. Statistics, measurement, and psychometrics.

Arlette Perry, Professor and Department Chair; Ph.D., NYU, 1981. Cardiovascular physiology, obesity, women's health, pediatric physiology.

Carol-Anne Phekoo, Lecturer; Ph.D., Miami (Florida), 1999. Higher education/enrollment management.

Shawn Post-Klauber, Associate Dean of Undergraduate Studies; Ph.D., Miami (Florida), 1977. Reading and learning disabilities.

Ora Prilleltensky, Lecturer; Ed.D., Toronto, 1998. Counseling psychology, disability studies.

Eugene Provenzo Jr., Professor; Ph.D., Washington (St. Louis), 1976. Foundations of education.

Bobby Robertson, Professor; Ed.D., Oregon, 1972. Anatomy and kinesiology, athletic sports injury, gross anatomy.

Stephanie Schmitz, Lecturer; Ph.D., North Carolina at Chapel Hill, 1987. Clinical psychology, family and human services.

Jeanne Schumm, Professor; Ph.D., Miami (Florida), 1984. Reading.

Walter G. Secada, Professor and Department Chair; Ph.D., Northwestern, 1985. Mathematics education.

Joseph Signorile, Professor; Ph.D., Texas A&M, 1990. Exercise physiology, muscle physiology, power training, aging.

Yosuke Tsuji, Visiting Assistant Professor; Ph.D., Texas A&M, 2007. Sport administration.

UNIVERSITY OF MICHIGAN
SCHOOL OF EDUCATION

UNIVERSITY OF MICHIGAN

School of Education

Programs of Study

Graduate studies at the School of Education at the University of Michigan (U-M) are organized into two programs: Educational Studies (ES) and the Center for the Study of Higher and Postsecondary Education (CSHPE).

The ES program offers Master of Arts and Doctor of Philosophy degrees. Specializations and degree opportunities are available in curriculum development; early childhood education; educational administration and policy; educational foundations, administration, policy, and research methods; educational foundations and policy; educational studies and M.B.A. (dual degree); English education; learning technologies; literacy, language, and culture; mathematics education; quantitative methods in education and statistics (dual degree); science education; social studies education; special education; and teaching and teacher education, and students may individually design a cross-specialization. In addition, graduate students may enroll in the Master of Arts in education with the teaching certification (MAC) program, a one-year intensive course of study available for prospective elementary or secondary school teachers.

The CSHPE offers the Doctor of Philosophy degree in higher education with concentrations in academic affairs and student development; organizational behavior and management; public policy; research, evaluation, and assessment; and an opportunity for an individually designed concentration. The Master of Arts degree is offered with a concentration in higher education, and a dual degree is offered by the CSHPE and the University of Michigan School of Public Policy. The interdisciplinary Combined Program in Education and Psychology and the Joint Program in English and Education also offer courses of study leading to the Ph.D.

Research Facilities

As part of one of the nation's primary research universities, the School of Education has access to superior research facilities and resources, including more than 24,000 computer workstations throughout the campus and a library system with 7.1 million volumes and nearly 70,000 periodical and newspaper subscriptions. The School itself provides research centers, traditional library resources, computer workstations with software for statistical analysis, multimedia materials, a multimedia laboratory, and interactive multimedia classrooms.

Financial Aid

Sources of financial aid for School of Education graduate students include teaching, research, and staff assistantships, which offer a stipend/salary and some University benefits and may offer tuition assistance. A complete listing of current financial aid resources is available from the School of Education Office of Student Services and on the Web.

Cost of Study

In 2006–07, graduate student tuition per semester was $7546 for Michigan residents and $15,276 for nonresidents. Tuition for doctoral candidates was $4893 for one semester for both residents and nonresidents. Tuition charges are subject to change by the Board of Regents.

Living and Housing Costs

The School of Education estimated that living expenses for a single graduate student were approximately $16,000 for the 2006–07 academic year.

Student Group

In fall 2006, the School of Education enrolled 802 students, 533 of whom were graduate students. Members of minority groups made up approximately 21 percent of the School's graduate students. Overall, approximately 40,000 students, including almost 15,000 graduate students, attend the University of Michigan in Ann Arbor.

Student Outcomes

ES graduates become K–12 administrators, professors and researchers, education and government agency leaders, and teachers. Graduates of the CSHPE serve as presidents and executive officers at public and private universities, liberal arts colleges, and community colleges; as policy makers and administrators in government; and as leaders in faculty and research roles. Graduates of the Joint Program in English and Education become university English and education teachers and leaders in writing programs. Combined Program in Education and Psychology graduates become researchers and teachers in colleges and universities and researchers at federal and state agencies and foundations.

Location

Ann Arbor and the University of Michigan are located 50 miles west of Detroit and 40 minutes from Detroit Metropolitan Airport. Ann Arbor has a permanent population of nearly 114,000. The community offers a wide range of easily accessible, year-round cultural and recreational opportunities.

The School

As one of the U-M's smaller units, the School of Education provides an environment that fosters close interaction and collaboration between graduate students and faculty members, together with all the resources of a large, internationally renowned university. In the 2008 *U.S. News & World Report* graduate school rankings, the School's graduate programs rank sixth in the nation.

Applying

All applicants for admission to graduate studies in the School of Education must apply through the School of Education Office of Student Services. Students also must be accepted into the Horace H. Rackham School of Graduate Studies with a specialization in education. Applications must include the results of the GRE General Test.

The deadline for non–winter term applications with financial aid consideration to the ES program is December 1 for international and domestic applicants. Domestic master's applicants not applying for financial aid may apply through May 1. All winter term master's program applications for ES are due October 1. The CSHPE accepts applications for fall term only for both the doctoral and master's programs. The deadline for applications with financial aid consideration is December 1 for all international applicants and domestic doctoral applicants and January 1 for domestic master's applicants. Domestic applicants not applying for financial aid may apply to the CSHPE through May 1.

Correspondence and Information

Office of Student Services
School of Education
1033 School of Education Building
University of Michigan
610 East University Avenue
Ann Arbor, Michigan 48109-1259
Phone: 734-764-7563
E-mail: ed.grad.admit@umich.edu
Web site: http://www.soe.umich.edu

University of Michigan

THE FACULTY AND THEIR RESEARCH

PROGRAM IN EDUCATIONAL STUDIES

Professors

Paula Allen-Meares, Ph.D. Tasks and functions of social workers employed in educational settings; psychopathology in children, adolescents, and families; adolescent sexuality; premature parenthood.

Deborah Loewenberg Ball, Ph.D., Dean. Mathematics education, mathematics and teaching through hypermedia, teacher preparation, educational policy and practice.

Hyman Bass, Ph.D. Algebraic K-theory, number theory, group theory (geometric methods, algebraic geometry), mathematics education.

Percy Bates, Ph.D. Special education of the mentally impaired, educational and psychological assessment.

Phyllis C. Blumenfeld, Ph.D. Cognitive and social development and school practices, classroom processes, motivation.

Phillip J. Bowman, Ph.D. Diversity issues in research methodology, higher education, and public policy; social psychological issues in racial/ethnic disparities; African American studies.

Joanne Carlisle, Ph.D. Language and literacy acquisition of typical and atypical learners.

David K. Cohen, Ph.D. Educational policy, relationships between policy and instruction, the nature of teaching practice.

Holly K. Craig, Ph.D. Speech and language behaviors in normal and communicatively disordered children, assessment and intervention procedures for child and adult language disorders.

Jacquelynne S. Eccles, Ph.D. Developmental psychology.

Anne R. Gere, Ph.D. English and education, writing, teaching writing.

Deborah Keller-Cohen, Ph.D. Linguistics and literacy.

Joseph S. Krajcik, Ph.D., Associate Dean. Theory and research in science education, microcomputer-based laboratories, how students learn science concepts using instructional software.

Magdalene Lampert, Ed.D. Teacher education, mathematics education.

Diane Larsen-Freeman, Ph.D. Second-language acquisition, language teacher education, English linguistics and language methodology.

Valerie Lee, Ed.D. Statistics, data analysis, and quantitative methods of educational and social science research in the substantive field of sociology of education.

Jay Lemke, Ph.D. Science education, language in education, social semiotics and discourse linguistics.

Kevin Miller, Ph.D. Nature and sources of early mathematical and literacy development, cross-cultural similarities and differences in academic learning and performance.

Jeff Mirel, Ph.D. History of American education.

Frederick Morrison, Ph.D. Nature and sources of literacy acquisition in children during the transition to school.

Pamela A. Moss, Ph.D. Assessment of writing skills, measurement of critical-thinking skills, measurement of levels of student discussion.

Susan B. Neuman, Ed.D. Early childhood and literacy.

Annemarie Sullivan Palincsar, Ph.D. Acquisition of study skills by junior high students, acquisition and instruction of literacy with primary students at risk for academic difficulty.

Scott G. Paris, Ph.D. Cognitive development, reading, memory and learning.

Brian Rowan, Ph.D. Organizational theory and school effectiveness research.

Mary Schleppegrell, Ph.D. Relationship between language and learning in various disciplines, with focus on students for whom English is a second language.

Edward A. Silver, Ed.D., Associate Dean. Mathematics education.

Elliot Soloway, Ph.D. Technology.

Nancy Butler Songer, Ph.D. Science and mathematics education, instructional technology.

Addison Stone, Ph.D., Chair. Learning disabilities.

Elizabeth Sulzby, Ph.D. Elementary education, reading education, psycholinguistics.

Karen K. Wixson, Ph.D. Literacy and learning disabilities; curriculum, instruction, and assessment.

Associate Professors

Robert B. Bain, Ph.D. Social studies education, history of education, social policy history, curriculum/foundations.

Tabbye Chavous, Ph.D. Adolescent development, racial/ethnic relationships and identities, gender differences and factors affecting the participation and success of African Americans in higher education.

Anne Curzan, Ph.D. History of the English language, language and gender, historical sociolinguistics, lexicography, composition and rhetoric, pedagogy.

Elizabeth A. Davis, Ph.D. Science, technology, and mathematics.

Barry J. Fishman, Ph.D. Education and social policy, learning sciences.

Roger D. Goddard, Ph.D. Educational policy, organizational behavior, school finance and economics, hierarchical linear modeling.

Patricio G. Herbst, Ph.D. Mathematics education, mathematical reasoning in classroom discourse.

Robert Jogers, Ph.D. African American youth development in the context of community and school-based interventions in urban settings.

Elizabeth B. Moje, Ph.D. Literacy and language, research methodology.

Carla O'Connor, Ph.D. Urban education, social psychology of education, sociology of education, qualitative methods, school leadership and reform.

Lesley A. Rex, Ph.D. Language, culture, literacy.

Assistant Professors

Elisabeth DeGroot, Ph.D. Motivation and cognition.

Yvonne Goddard, Ph.D. Special education (K–12, birth–adult), literacy, effective teaching and learning strategies.

Lori Diane Hill, Ph.D. Sociology education, inequality and stratification, organizations, research methodology for social organizations, South Africa.

Vilma Mesa, Ph.D. Undergraduate mathematics education and international comparisons of curriculum.

Chris Quintana, Ph.D. Software and user interface design, educational software development, social applications of computer technology.

Clinical/Practice Faculty

Teresa McMahon, Ph.D. Collegiality and reflection in the practice of teachers and teacher developers.

Charles W. Peters, Ph.D. Curriculum and instruction, reading.

Catherine H. Reischl, Ph.D. Teacher education in multilingual contexts, elementary literacy instruction, literacy and language development for multilingual students.

Shari Saunders, Ph.D. Social justice education, multicultural education and teacher education.

Instructor

Henry O. Meares, Ed.D., Assistant Dean. Elementary/middle school curriculum and school administration.

CENTER FOR THE STUDY OF HIGHER AND POSTSECONDARY EDUCATION

Professors

Kim Cameron, Ph.D. Organizational behavior and human resource management.

Patricia King, Ph.D. Cognitive development from adolescence to adulthood, moral and identity development, educational experiences that enhance college student learning and development.

Brian P. McCall, Ph.D. Applied econometrics, economics of education and education policy, research design and quasi experimental research, econometric theory, labor economics, social insurance, health economics.

Marvin Peterson, Ph.D. Nature and role of environment in promoting or improving undergraduate teaching and learning, factors influencing support for diversity.

Edward St. John, Ed.D. Impact of public finance and educational policies on education opportunity in both K–12 and higher education.

Associate Professors

Richard Alfred, Ed.D. Community college governance and administration, financial management and public policy of postsecondary education.

Deborah Carter, Ph.D., Director. Access and equity issues in higher education, particularly as they relate to race and socioeconomic status.

Constance Cook, Ph.D. Public policy and politics of postsecondary education, faculty and instructional development, improvement of teaching and learning in higher education.

Steve DesJardins, Ph.D. Public and higher education policy analysis, economics of education, strategic enrollment management.

Eric Dey, Ph.D. Statistics and research design, education at the undergraduate level.

Janet Lawrence, Ph.D. College and university faculty, curriculum, instruction, international and comparative higher education.

Assistant Professors

Michael Bastedo, Ph.D. Public policy, governance, and organization of higher public higher education.

Larry Rowley, Ph.D. Social theoretical frameworks and empirical analyses of higher education issues, developments, and institutions.

Clinical/Practice Faculty

John Burkhardt, Ph.D. Leadership theory and development.

UNIVERSITY OF PENNSYLVANIA

Graduate School of Education

Programs of Study

The Penn Graduate School of Education (Penn GSE) offers programs leading to the Master of Science in Education (M.S.Ed.), the Master of Science (M.S.), the Master of Philosophy in Education (M.Phil.Ed.), the Doctor of Education (Ed.D.), and the Doctor of Philosophy (Ph.D.) degrees. The degree programs offer a range of professional preparation for those seeking to begin or advance a career in education. The School's twenty-one programs are organized in four academic divisions—Applied Psychology–Human Development, Foundations and Practices in Education, Language and Literacy in Education, and Policy, Management and Evaluation.

GSE seeks students who are interested in promoting a deeper understanding of educational issues and contributing to societal change. The curriculum places a strong emphasis on the interactive relationship of theory, research, and practice, often focusing on urban education. Students engage in extensive fieldwork throughout their studies and are both learners and agents of change within the University and the surrounding Philadelphia neighborhoods.

For the working professional, Penn GSE offers executive programs in educational leadership, higher education management, and school counseling. In addition, many master's and Ed.D. programs may be completed part-time.

Research Facilities

Research centers at Penn GSE bring faculty members and students together to study the various intersections of education and society. This research includes international studies of cross-cultural and comparative education. The centers include the Campbell Collaboration; the Center for Health, Achievement, Neighborhood Growth, and Ethnic Studies; the Center for Research and Evaluation in Social Policy; the Center for Urban Ethnography; the Consortium for Policy Research in Education; the National Center on Fathers and Families; and the W. E. B. Du Bois Collective Institute.

Financial Aid

Financial aid for Penn GSE students is available through the School, the University, and private sources as well as from the state and federal governments. Aid is awarded on the basis of both demonstrated financial need and academic merit and is available in the form of loans, assistantships, scholarships, fellowships, research assistantships, and work-study jobs. Awards in the 2006–07 academic year ranged from $2000 scholarships to fellowships that provided full tuition and a stipend.

Cost of Study

In 2007–08, the total tuition per semester for full-time students is $17,820, which includes the general fee.

Living and Housing Costs

University graduate housing is available on campus for single students as well as married students and their families. On-campus housing ranges from $652 per month for a single room to $1138 per month for an apartment. Off-campus apartment rents range upward from $475 per month.

Student Group

Penn GSE students range from recent college graduates to career changers and experienced practitioners. The approximately 500 students beginning course work in 2006 represented a broad demographic spectrum: 15 percent were international students from eleven countries and 34 percent were students of color. The average age of the master's students was 26, and the average age of the doctoral students was 34.

Student Outcomes

Penn GSE graduates pursue careers in a variety of fields, including schools, government agencies, universities, think tanks, foundations, and corporations. In these fields, they work in positions that include superintendents, principals, teachers, counselors, university professors, policy analysts, researchers, foundation officers, psychologists, and higher education administrators.

Location

Penn GSE's location in a major metropolitan area enhances the quality of its programs, research, and student life. Philadelphia is a thriving mix of ethnic neighborhoods, historic colonial streets, and contemporary architecture. With close to 100 institutions of higher learning, the city is a magnet for students from around the world. The city's cultural and recreational life has a world-class orchestra and opera, dozens of museums, four professional sports teams, art galleries, secondhand bookstores, jazz clubs, an Italian market, and a renowned international film festival. The city is conveniently located in the cradle of the metropolitan northeastern United States, within 2 hours of Baltimore, New York, and Washington, D.C.

The School

Penn GSE, one of the best graduate schools of education in the United States, is one of only three Ivy League schools of education. The School is noted for excellence in educational research in the areas of policy, evaluation, sociocultural foundations, and urban education. The student experience at Penn GSE is shaped by the small size of the School. Students find both the flexibility to pursue their own research interests and the support they need to do so. The interdisciplinary nature of educational programs means that Penn GSE students take courses across the University. Penn GSE also maintains community connections, which are an important resource for students, faculty members, and neighboring schools.

Applying

Applicants should contact the office of admissions for a CD-ROM. Application deadlines and information on the Penn Graduate School of Education can also be found at the School's Web site.

Correspondence and Information

Admissions Office
Graduate School of Education
University of Pennsylvania
3700 Walnut Street
Philadelphia, Pennsylvania 19104-6216
Phone: 215-898-6415
E-mail: admissions@gse.upenn.edu
Web site: http://www.gse.upenn.edu

University of Pennsylvania

THE FACULTY

For a full list of all Penn GSE faculty members, including associated faculty members, students should visit http://www.gse.upenn.edu/faculty_research/.

UNIVERSITY OF SOUTH FLORIDA

College of Education

Programs of Study

The USF College of Education is committed to excellence in teaching, research, and service. It offers a variety of graduate programs that lead to the Doctor of Philosophy (Ph.D.), Doctor of Education (Ed.D.), Education Specialist (Ed.S.), Master of Education (M.Ed.), Master of Arts (M.A.), and Master of Arts in Teaching (M.A.T.) degrees. Doctoral degrees are designed to prepare graduates to conduct research, teach in a college or university setting, and hold administrative or leadership positions in educational institutions, school systems, and other public or private agencies. The master's and education specialist programs are designed to prepare educational practitioners in advanced studies in their field.

The Ph.D. degree is offered in school psychology, second language acquisition/instructional technology, and curriculum and instruction, with specializations in the areas of adult education, career and workforce education, counselor education, elementary education, English education, higher education, instructional technology, interdisciplinary education, mathematics education, measurement and evaluation, reading education, science education, secondary education (social science), special education, and teaching and learning in the content area (general education). The Ed.D is offered in educational leadership (K–12), community college leadership, and educational program development with concentrations in adult education and elementary education. The Ed.S., M.Ed., and M.A. degrees are offered in most of the areas listed above. M.A. degrees are offered in the areas noted as well as in career and technical education, college teaching, counselor education, early childhood education, exercise science, foreign language education/ESOL, physical education, and social science education. The M.A.T. degree is offered in elementary education/ESOL, English education/ESOL, exceptional student education varying exceptionalities/ESOL, foreign language education/ESOL, mathematics education, science education, and social science education. The doctoral programs require completion of core courses and courses in the specialization area, satisfactory performance on a qualifying examination, and completion of a dissertation. The Ph.D. program requires two semesters of full-time residency on the Tampa campus. The Ed.S. programs require a minimum of 36 credit hours, including completion of a thesis and a written comprehensive examination. The master's programs require a minimum of 30 to 33 credit hours and a comprehensive examination.

Research Facilities

The University of South Florida (USF) library system is among the finest in the Florida State University System. It houses more than 2 million volumes, 20,000 journals and periodicals, and an extensive collection of electronic resources, including 6,500 e-journal subscriptions, 500 aggregator databases containing another 13,000 unique e-journal titles, 48,000 e-books, and 150,000 digital images. In addition, it boasts a Special Collections Department with more than 1 million items and a Government Documents Collection. College of Education students have access to a number of research centers and institutes that are housed within the College and in the broader USF community. The College's state-of-the-art technology system serves to enhance teaching and research and link faculty members and graduate students to national and international networks. Laboratories for exercise physiology and biomechanics provide students with opportunities for research.

Financial Aid

Financial aid is available to qualified graduate students in the form of graduate assistantships, fellowships, scholarships, and loan programs. For the 2006–07 academic year, graduate assistantship stipends ranged from $7800 (master's students) to $15,000 (doctoral students) for 20 hours of work per week for two semesters (fall and spring); additional summer employment is available. Students on graduate assistantships and some fellowships are granted tuition waivers. Inquiries about fellowships, grants, and scholarships should be directed to the USF Graduate School or the College of Education's Office of Graduate Studies.

Cost of Study

For the 2006–07 academic year, graduate tuition was $251.98 per credit hour for Florida residents and $897.05 per credit hour for nonresidents.

Living and Housing Costs

On-campus and off-campus housing is available to graduate students, although on-campus housing is limited. The University operates an apartment village that provides housing for graduate students at a monthly rate of about $700 (single occupancy, including utilities, local phone service, Internet access, and cable). Most graduate students live off campus, selecting from a variety of housing options available in the area. The average cost of apartment rentals in the USF area is $520–$590 per month for a one-bedroom and $490–$520 per person per month if 2 people share a two-bedroom unit.

Student Group

The University's total enrollment for fall 2006 was more than 40,000, with a graduate enrollment of approximately 7,395 students. Graduate enrollment (including full-time and part-time students) in the College of Education was approximately 1,975 for fall 2006—accounting for 27 percent of USF's graduate enrollment. Full-time graduate students account for 32.2 percent of the College's graduate enrollment. Approximately 77 percent of the graduate students are women, 25 percent are members of minority groups, and 3.2 percent are international students.

Student Outcomes

Graduates of the College of Education are employed in a variety of settings, including universities, four- and two-year colleges, K–12 schools and school systems, central offices of school systems, business, and industry. A number of alumni of the College are recipients of outstanding teaching and leadership awards.

Location

The USF College of Education offers programs at its Tampa, Lakeland, and Sarasota/Manatee campuses. Located in the vibrant Tampa Bay area on the west coast of Florida, it is in one of the fastest-growing metropolitan areas of the nation. It is easily accessible to the waters of the Gulf of Mexico and Tampa Bay and within a 90-minute drive of the Orlando area. The region thrives with its variety of cultural and sports activities.

The University and The College

The University of South Florida, founded in 1956, is a multicampus, comprehensive research university and is strongly committed to the balanced pursuit of teaching, research, and service. The ninth-largest university in the nation, it comprises ten colleges on three campuses and is home to a medical school, a major mental health research institute, and three public broadcasting stations. The College of Education is one of the largest urban colleges of education in the country, with a student enrollment of approximately 4,800 (declared majors only), and is accredited by the National Council for Accreditation of Teacher Education (NCATE).

Applying

A completed graduate application form, GRE General Test scores, and official transcripts from all institutions of higher education attended are required. Individual departments may have additional requirements. The GRE may be waived at the discretion of individual graduate programs. Applicants whose native language is not English are required to submit scores from the Test of English as a Foreign Language (TOEFL). Application forms may be obtained from the Office of Graduate Admissions. Completed applications are due no later than June 1 (for the fall semester), October 15 (for the spring semester), and March 2 (for the summer semester). Some programs may have earlier application deadlines and may admit only for the fall semester. Applications for graduate assistantships should be made directly to the department in which the student's program is housed.

Correspondence and Information

Coordinator of Graduate Studies
Office of Student Academic Services, EDU 106
University of South Florida
Tampa, Florida 33620-5650
Phone: 813-974-3406
Fax: 813-974-3391
E-mail: briscoe@tempest.coedu.usf.edu
Web site: http://www.coedu.usf.edu

Office of Graduate Admissions
University of South Florida
4202 Fowler Avenue—FAO 100 N
Tampa, Florida 33620United States

University of South Florida

THE FACULTY

Adult, Career, and Higher Education

William E. Blank, Professor; Ph.D., Florida State, 1976.
Rosemary Closson, Assistant Professor; Ph.D., Florida State, 1994.
Donald A. Dellow, Associate Professor; Ed.D., Florida, 1971.
James Eison, Professor; Ph.D., Tennessee, 1979.
Victor Hernandez-Gantes, Associate Professor; Ph.D., Virginia Tech, 1993.
Jan Ignash, Associate Professor; Ph.D., UCLA, 1994.
Waynne B. James, Professor; Ed.D., Tennessee, 1976.
Derek Mulenga, Instructor; Ed.D., Northern Illinois, 1999.
Janet Scaglione, Associate Professor; Ph.D., South Florida, 1990.
W. Robert Sullins, Professor; Ed.D., Florida, 1968.
William Young, Professor; Ed.D., Penn State, 1976.

Childhood Education

Nancy Anderson, Associate Professor; Ed.D., Southern Mississippi, 1982..
Ilene Berson, Associate Professor; Ph.D., Toledo, 1997.
Jolyn Blank, Assistant Professor; Ph.D., Illinois at Urbana-Champaign, 2006.
Roger Brindley, Associate Professor; Ed.D., Georgia, 1996.
Danielle Dennis, Assistant Professor; Ph.D., Tennessee, Knoxville, 2007.
Stephen Graves, Professor; Ph.D., South Carolina, 1986.
Ann Hall, Instructor; Ph.D., Georgia, 1979.
Susan P. Homan, Professor; Ph.D., Florida, 1978.
James R. King, Professor; Ed.D., West Virginia, 1980.
Sherry Kragler, Associate Professor; Ph.D., Florida, 1986.
Kathryn Laframboise, Associate Professor; Ph.D., South Florida, 1989.
Elizabeth Larkin, Associate Professor; Ed.D., Harvard, 1992.
Charlie Lippincott, Instructor; Ed.D., Arkansas, 1980.
Marcia Mann, Professor; Ph.D., Nebraska, 1970.
John Manning, Assistant Professor; Ed.D., Massachusetts Amherst, 1998.
Weiman Mo, Associate Professor; Ed.D., Indiana of Pennsylvania, 1993.
Mary Lou Morton, Associate Professor; Ph.D., Indiana, 1999.
Audra Parker, Assistant Professor; Ph.D., Georgia, 2005.
Suzanne Quinn, Assistant Professor; Ph.D., Syracuse, 2003.
Janet Richards, Professor; Ph.D., New Orleans, 1985.
Stephen P. Rushton, Associate Professor; Ph.D., Tennessee, 1997.
Jenifer J. Schneider, Associate Professor; Ph.D., Ohio State, 1996.
Donna Stewart, Instructor; M.A., California State Polytechnic, 1970, Ohio State, 1973.
Nancy Lynn Williams, Associate Professor; Ph.D., LSU, 1989.
G. Pat Wilson, Assistant Professor; Ph.D., Toledo, 1999.

Educational Leadership and Policy Studies

William F. Benjamin, Professor; Ph.D., George Peabody, 1961.
William R. Black, Assistant Professor; Ph.D., Texas at Austin, 2004.
Darlene Bruner, Associate Professor; Ed.D., South Florida, 1997.
Judy Carr, Associate Professor; Ed.D., Vermont, 1989.
Philip Rodney Evans, Associate Professor; Ph.D., Alberta, 1989.
Janice Fauske, Professor; Ph.D., Utah, 1985.
Bobbie Greenlee, Assistant Professor; Ed.D., South Florida, 1997.
Marie Somers Hill, Professor; Ed.D. Mississippi State, 1980.
Valerie Janesick, Professor; Ph.D., Michigan State, 1977.
Zorka Karanxha, Assistant Professor; Ed.D., Lehigh, 2004.
Richard King, Professor; Ph.D., SUNY at Buffalo, 1976.
Donald E. Orlosky, Professor Emeritus; Ed.D., Indiana, 1959.
Judith A. Ponticell, Professor; Ph.D., Illinois at Chicago, 1991.
Len Sutton, Assistant Professor; Ph.D., Florida, 1998.

Educational Measurement Research

Yi-Hsin Chen, Assistant Professor; Ph.D., Arizona State, 2006.
Robert F. Dedrick, Associate Professor; Ph.D., Michigan, 1988.
John M. Ferron, Professor; Ph.D., North Carolina at Chapel Hill, 1993.
Constance V. Hines, Professor; Ph.D., Ohio State, 1981.
Jeffrey D. Kromrey, Professor; Ph.D., South Florida, 1989.
Liliana Rodriguez-Campos, Assistant Professor; Ph.D., Western Michigan, 2002.

School of Physical Education & Exercise Science

Candi D. Ashley, Associate Professor; Ph.D., Alabama, 1995.
Bonnie Bie, Assistant Professor; Ph.D., Florida State, 1994.
Bill Campbell, Assistant Professor; Ph.D., Baylor, 2007.
Joann Eickhoff-Shemek, Professor; Ph.D., Nebraska, 1995.
Nell Faucette, Professor; Ed.D., Georgia, 1984.
Marcus Kilpatrick, Assistant Professor; Ph.D., Texas at Austin, 1999.
Amber Phillips, Assistant Professor; Ed.D., South Carolina, 2007.
Stephen Sanders, Professor; Ed.D., Virginia Tech, 1993.
Michael Stewart, Professor; Ph.D., Ohio State, 1977.
Haichun Sun, Assistant Professor; Ph.D., Maryland, 2007.
Ralph C. Wilcox, Professor; Ph.D., Alberta, 1982.

Psychological and Social Foundations

Jennifer Baggerly, Associate Professor; Ph.D., North Texas, 1999.
George M. Batsche Jr., Professor; Ed.D., Ball State, 1978.
Kathy L. Bradley-Klug, Associate Professor; Ph.D., Lehigh, 1996.
Deirdre L. Cobb-Roberts, Associate Professor; Ph.D., Illinois at Urbana-Champaign, 1998.
Michael J. Curtis, Professor; Ph.D., Texas at Austin, 1974.
Darlene DeMarie, Associate Professor; Ph.D., Florida, 1988.
Sherman J. Dorn, Associate Professor; Ph.D., Pennsylvania, 1992.
Herbert A. Exum, Professor; Ph.D., Minnesota, 1978.
Wendy Greenidge, Assistant Professor; Ph.D., Central Florida, 2007.
Wilma Henry, Associate Professor; Ed.D., East Texas State, 1980.
Erwin V. Johanningmeier, Professor; Ph.D., Illinois, 1967.
Harold Keller, Professor; Ph.D., Florida State, 1968.
Sarah Kiefer, Assistant Professor; Ph.D., Illinois at Urbana-Champaign, 2007.
Lisa Lopez, Assistant Professor; Ph.D., Miami (Florida), 2001.
Kofi Marfo, Professor; Ph.D., Alberta, 1985..
Jennifer Mariano, Assistant Professor; Ph.D., Stanford, 2007.
Richard Marshall, Associate Professor; Ph.D., Georgia, 1992.
Smita Mathur, Assistant Professor; Ph.D., Syracuse, 2000.
J. Lynn McBrien, Assistant Professor; Ph.D., Emory, 2005.
Thomas E. Miller, Associate Professor; Ed.D., Indiana, 1979.
Michelle Mitcham-Smith, Assistant Professor; Ph.D., Central Florida, 2005.
Debra Osborn, Associate Professor; Ph.D., Florida State, 1998.
Linda M. Raffaele-Mendez, Associate Professor; Ph.D., Texas at Austin, 1993.
Tomas D. Rodriguez, Assistant Professor; Ph.D., Johns Hopkins, 1999.
Barbara Shircliffe, Associate Professor; Ph.D., SUNY at Buffalo, 1997.
Marian S. Street, Associate Professor; Ph.D., Florida, 1980.
Shannon Suldo, Assistant Professor; Ph.D., South Carolina, 2004.
Tony X. Tan, Assistant Professor; Ed.D., Harvard, 2004.
Carlos Zalaquett, Associate Professor; Ph.D., Texas, 1993.

Secondary Education

Jane Applegate, Professor; Ph.D., Ohio State, 1978.
Richard A. Austin, Associate Professor; Ph.D., Florida, 1983.
Ann Barron, Professor; Ed.D., Central Florida, 1991.
Michael J. Berson, Professor; Ph.D., Toledo, 1993.
Frank D. Breit, Associate Professor; Ph.D., Texas at Austin, 1968.
Barbara C. Cruz, Professor; Ed.D., Florida International, 1990.
Patricia L. Daniel, Associate Professor; Ph.D., Oklahoma, 1991.
Steven E. Downey, Assistant Professor; Ph.D., Illinois at Urbana-Champaign, 2000.
James A. Duplass, Professor; Ph.D., Saint Louis, 1974.
Linda Evans, Assistant Professor; Ph.D., South Florida, 1997.
Helen Gerretson, Assistant Professor; Ph.D., Florida, 1998.
Elaine V. Howes, Assistant Professor; Ph.D., Michigan State, 1997.
J. Howard Johnston, Professor; Ph.D., Wyoming, 1974.
Joan F. Kaywell, Professor; Ph.D., Florida, 1987.
Colleen S. Kennedy, Professor; Ph.D., Washington, 1976.
Gladis Kersaint, Associate Professor; Ph.D., Illinois State, 1998.
Deoksoon Kim, Assistant Professor; Ph.D., New Mexico, 2005.
Dick J. Puglisi, Professor; Ph.D., Georgia State, 1973.
Glenn G. Smith, Assistant Professor; Ph.D., Arizona State, 1998.
Philip Smith, Instructor; Ph.D., South Florida, 2005.
Barbara Spector, Professor; Ph.D., Syracuse, 1977.
H. Edwin Steiner, Professor Emeritus; Ph.D., Texas at Austin, 1970.
Denisse R. Thompson, Professor; Ph.D., Chicago, 1992.
Stephen J. Thornton, Professor; Ph.D., Stanford 1985.
Marcela van Olphen, Assistant Professor; Ph.D., Purdue, 2002.
Anete Vasquez, Instructor; Ph.D. candidate, South Florida.
James A. White, Associate Professor; Ph.D., South Florida, 1989.
Dana L. Zeidler, Professor; Ph.D., Syracuse, 1982.

Special Education

David Allsopp, Associate Professor; Ph.D., Florida, 1995.
Michael Churton, Professor; Ed.D., Southern Mississippi, 1979.
Karen L. Colucci, Instructor; Ph.D., South Florida, 1994.
Ann M. Cranston-Gingras, Professor; Ph.D., South Florida, 1987.
Elizabeth M. Doone, Instructor; Ph.D., South Florida, 1998.
Albert J. Duchnowski, Professor; Ph.D., Vanderbilt, 1969.
Phyllis Jones, Associate Professor; Ph.D., Northumbria, 2002.
Patricia Jeannie Kleinhammer-Tramill, Professor; Ph.D., Kansas, 1981.
Barbara Loeding, Associate Professor; Ph.D., Purdue, 1989.
Michael Stuart Matthews, Assistant Professor; Ph.D., Georgia, 2002.
Patricia Alvarez McHatton, Assistant Professor; Ph.D., South Florida, 2004.
James L. Paul, Professor; Ed.D., Syracuse, 1967.
Elizabeth Shaunessy, Assistant Professor; Ph.D., Southern Mississippi, 2003.
Surrendra P. Singh, Emeritus Professor; Ed.D., UCLA, 1967.
Daphne D. Thomas, Associate Professor; Ph.D., North Carolina at Chapel Hill, 1989.
Brenda L. Townsend, Professor; Ph.D., Kansas, 1991.
Julia M. White, Assistant Professor; Ph.D., Syracuse, 2007.

VANDERBILT UNIVERSITY

Peabody College

Programs of Study

Peabody College, the school of education and human development of Vanderbilt University, offers programs leading to the Master of Education, Master of Public Policy, and Doctor of Education degrees. The Vanderbilt Graduate School, through Peabody departments, offers the Doctor of Philosophy (Ph.D.) degree. Peabody is committed to preparing students to become research scholars or innovative practitioners in the field of education and human development. Students may attend full- or part-time. Weekend courses are offered in several programs for working professionals who want to earn an advanced degree.

Students may major in child studies; community development action; community research and action; counseling; curriculum and instructional leadership; early childhood education; education policy; elementary education; English education; English language learners; higher education administration (including specializations in administration, college student personnel services, institutional advancement, and service-learning); human resource development; international education policy and management; language and literacy education; learning, teaching, and diversity; mathematics education; organizational leadership; psychology (including specializations in clinical psychology, cognitive studies, developmental psychology, and quantitative methods and evaluation); reading education, school administration; science education; secondary education, and special education (including specializations in behavior analysis, comprehensive, early childhood, high-incidence disabilities, low-incidence disabilities, and visual impairment).

Teacher education and advanced certification programs of Peabody College are approved by the National Council for Accreditation of Teacher Education (NCATE). The programs in psychology and counseling are accredited by the American Psychological Association and the Council on Accreditation of Counseling and Related Educational Programs (CACREP), respectively.

Research Facilities

In addition to the Vanderbilt University Library System, which has more than 2.6 million volumes, excellent research facilities are available through the Center for Educational Policy, the John F. Kennedy Center for Research on Human Development, the Learning Sciences Institute, and the Vanderbilt Institute for Public Policy Studies. The many field sites available for research include hospitals, the Metropolitan Nashville Public Schools, rehabilitation centers, schools for the handicapped, government agencies, corporations, and day-care centers.

Financial Aid

More than 60 percent of new students at Peabody College receive financial aid. The College sponsors several substantial scholarship programs with offerings that range from partial to full tuition, including several scholarships designated for outstanding students from minority groups. In addition, assistantships, traineeships, loans, and part-time employment are available. Awards are made annually, and every attempt is made to meet a student's financial need. Application for financial aid does not affect the admission decision.

Cost of Study

Tuition for study at Peabody College for the 2006–07 academic year was $967 per semester credit hour for the M.Ed. and Ed.D. programs and $1359 per semester credit hour for the M.A.T., M.S., and Ph.D. programs.

Living and Housing Costs

Vanderbilt's location in Nashville offers students the advantage of a wide range of living choices. Costs for housing, food, and other living expenses are moderate when compared with other metropolitan areas nationwide. Information about on-campus housing costs may be found online at http://www.vanderbilt.edu/stuaccts/g_estimate.html.

Student Group

Vanderbilt University has a diverse student body of about 10,500. Peabody College has an enrollment of approximately 1,660 students, of whom about 560 are graduate students. Women make up about 74 percent of Peabody's graduate students, while students from minority groups make up about 20 percent. Students have a broad range of academic backgrounds and include recent graduates of baccalaureate programs as well as men and women who have many years of professional experience. The median age of current students is 29.

Student Outcomes

Graduates who earn a master's or doctoral degree from Vanderbilt's Peabody College are prepared to work for educational, corporate, government, and service organizations in a variety of roles. More than 10,000 alumni are practicing teachers, more than 175 are school superintendents, and more than 30 are college or university presidents.

Location

Nashville, the capital of Tennessee and the educational and cultural center of its region, is a cosmopolitan city with a population of more than 1 million. Vanderbilt University is one of more than a dozen institutions of higher learning located in Nashville and the surrounding area, leading Nashville to be called the "Athens of the South."

Internationally known as home to the American music and entertainment industries, Nashville offers residents and visitors much in the way of music, art, and recreation. More than 100 local venues provide a wide variety of music from blues to pop performed by well-known artists, while classical and contemporary music is performed by the Nashville Symphony Orchestra and the Nashville Chamber Orchestra. In addition, the Tennessee Performing Arts Center (TPAC) is home to two theater companies, a ballet company, and an opera company. TPAC also offers traveling productions of Broadway shows. The Great Performances series at Vanderbilt frequently brings the best in chamber music, new music, theater, and all forms of dance to the Vanderbilt campus. Outstanding exhibitions of fine art can be seen at the Frist Center for the Visual Arts, located downtown in a beautifully restored art deco post office, and at Cheekwood Botanical Garden and Museum of Art. There are more than 6,000 acres of public parks in the city, and the surrounding region of rolling hills and lakes is dotted with state parks and recreation areas.

The University and The College

Vanderbilt University, founded in 1873, is a private nondenominational institution with a strong tradition of graduate and professional education. Peabody College, recognized for more than a century as one of the nation's foremost independent colleges of education, merged with Vanderbilt in 1979. Peabody, which is routinely ranked among the best colleges of education in the nation, focuses on creating knowledge in the fields of education, psychology, and human development and applying that knowledge to societal problems.

Applying

Admission to professional degree programs is based on an evaluation of the applicant's potential for academic success and professional service, with consideration given to transcripts of previous course work, GRE General Test or MAT scores, letters of reference, and a letter outlining personal goals. Additional supporting credentials, such as a sample of the applicant's scholarly writing or a personal interview, may also be required. A nonrefundable $40 fee must accompany each application. Applying online at http://peabody.vanderbilt.edu is strongly recommended. Applicants who apply after the December 31 deadline should know that admission and financial assistance depend upon the availability of space and funds in the department in which they seek to study.

Correspondence and Information

Graduate Admissions
Peabody College of Vanderbilt University
Peabody Station, Box 327
Nashville, Tennessee 37203
Phone: 615-322-8410
Fax: 615-343-3474
E-mail: peabody.admissions@vanderbilt.edu
Web site: http://peabody.vanderbilt.edu

Vanderbilt University

THE FACULTY

Department of Human and Organizational Development
Vera Chatman, Professor of the Practice; Ph.D., George Peabody.
Victoria J. Davis, Clinical Assistant Professor; Ed.D., Vanderbilt.
Paul R. Dokecki, Professor; Ph.D., George Peabody.
Gina Frieden, Assistant Professor of the Practice; Ph.D., Memphis State.
Brian Griffith, Assistant Clinical Professor; Ph.D., South Carolina.
Craig Anne Heflinger, Associate Professor; Ph.D., Vanderbilt.
Robert B. Innes, Associate Professor; Ph.D., Michigan.
Maury Nation, Assistant Professor; Ph.D., South Carolina.
William Partridge, Professor; Ph.D., Florida.
Douglas Perkins, Associate Professor; Ph.D., NYU.
Sharon Shields, Professor of the Practice; Ph.D., George Peabody.
Paul Speer, Associate Professor; Ph.D., Missouri–Kansas City.

Department of Leadership, Policy, and Organizations
Robert Dale Ballou, Associate Professor; Ph.D., Yale.
Mark Berends, Associate Professor; Ph.D., Wisconsin.
Leonard Bradley, Lecturer; M.A., Tennessee.
John Braxton, Professor; D.Ed., Penn State.
Timothy Caboni, Lecturer; Ph.D., Vanderbilt.
Bruce T. Caine, Assistant Professor of the Practice; Ph.D., Florida.
Mark D. Cannon, Assistant Professor; Ph.D., Harvard.
R. Wilburn Clouse, Associate Professor; Ph.D., George Peabody.
Robert L. Crowson, Professor; Ph.D., Chicago.
Laura M. Desimone, Assistant Professor; Ph.D., North Carolina.
William R. Doyle, Assistant Professor; Ph.D., Stanford.
Janet Eyler, Associate Professor of the Practice; Ph.D., Indiana.
Michael Gavlick, Lecturer; Ph.D., Vanderbilt.
Constance Bumgarner Gee, Associate Professor; Ph.D., Penn State.
Ellen Goldring, Professor; Ph.D., Chicago.
James W. Guthrie, Professor; Ph.D., Stanford.
Stephen P. Heyneman, Professor; Ph.D., Chicago.
Trish Kelly, Senior Lecturer; Ph.D., Massachusetts.
Michael McLendon, Associate Professor; Ph.D., Florida State.
Joseph Murphy, Professor; Ph.D., Ohio State.
Andrew Calvin Porter, Professor; Ph.D., Wisconsin.
R. Anthony Rolle, Assistant Professor; Ph.D., Indiana.
Pearl Sims, Lecturer; Ed.D., Vanderbilt.
Steven H. Smartt, Assistant Professor of the Practice; Ph.D., Florida State.
Thomas M. Smith, Assistant Professor; Ph.D., Penn State.
Claire Smrekar, Associate Professor; Ph.D., Stanford.

Department of Psychology and Human Development
Camilla P. Benbow, Professor; Ed.D., Johns Hopkins.
Leonard Bickman, Professor; Ph.D., CUNY.
David A. Cole, Professor; Ph.D., Houston.
Bruce E. Compas, Professor; Ph.D., UCLA.
David Cordray, Professor; Ph.D., Claremont.
Elizabeth May Dykens, Professor; Ph.D., Kansas.
Judy Garber, Associate Professor; Ph.D., Minnesota.
Jessica W. Giles, Assistant Professor; Ph.D., California, San Diego.
James H. Hogge, Professor; Ph.D., Texas.
Kathleen Hoover-Dempsey, Associate Professor; Ph.D., Michigan State.
Daniel T. Levin, Associate Professor; Ph.D., Cornell.

David Lubinski, Professor; Ph.D., Minnesota.
Laura R. Novick, Associate Professor; Ph.D., Stanford.
John R. Rieser, Professor; Ph.D., Minnesota.
Bethany Rittle-Johnson, Assistant Professor; Ph.D., Carnegie Mellon.
Howard M. Sandler, Professor; Ph.D., Northwestern.
Megan M. Saylor, Assistant Professor; Ph.D., Oregon.
Craig A. Smith, Associate Professor; Ph.D., Stanford.
James Steiger, Professor; Ph.D., Purdue.
Georgene Troseth, Assistant Professor; Ph.D., Illinois.
Patti Van Eys, Assistant Clinical Professor; Ph.D., Bowling Green State.
Tedra Ann Walden, Professor; Ph.D., Florida.
Bahr Weiss, Associate Professor; Ph.D., North Carolina.

Department of Special Education
Donald Compton, Associate Professor; Ph.D., Northwestern.
Anne L. Corn, Professor; Ed.D., Columbia.
Joseph Cunningham, Associate Professor; Ed.D., Illinois.
Stephen N. Elliott, Professor; Ph.D., Arizona State.
Donna Y. Ford, Professor; Ph.D., Cleveland State.
Douglas Fuchs, Professor; Ph.D., Minnesota.
Lynn S. Fuchs, Professor; Ph.D., Minnesota.
Robert Hodapp, Professor; Ph.D., Boston University.
Carolyn Hughes, Professor; Ph.D., Illinois.
Ann Kaiser, Professor; Ph.D., Kansas.
Craig Kennedy, Professor; Ph.D., California, Santa Barbara.
Kathleen L. Lane, Assistant Professor; Ph.D., California, Riverside.
Kim Paulsen, Associate Professor of the Practice; Ed.D., Nevada, Las Vegas.
Dan Reschly, Professor; Ph.D., Oregon.
Joseph H. Wehby, Associate Professor; Ph.D., Vanderbilt.
Mark Wolery, Professor; Ph.D., Washington (Seattle).
Ruth Wolery, Assistant Professor of the Practice; Ph.D., Pittsburgh.
Paul J. Yoder, Professor; Ph.D., North Carolina.

Department of Teaching and Learning
Tisha L. Bennett, Assistant Clinical Professor; Ed.D., North Texas.
Kefyn Catley, Assistant Professor; Ph.D., Cornell.
Paul A. Cobb, Professor; Ph.D., Georgia.
Dale C. Farran, Professor; Ph.D., Bryn Mawr.
Marie Hardenbrook, Assistant Professor of the Practice; Ph.D., Arizona State.
Clifford A. Hofwolt, Associate Professor; Ed.D., Northern Colorado.
Robert T. Jimenez, Professor; Ph.D., Illinois at Urbana-Champaign.
Kevin Leander, Associate Professor; Ph.D., Illinois.
Richard Lehrer, Professor; Ph.D., Chicago.
Kay J. McClain, Assistant Professor; Ed.D., Vanderbilt.
Henry Richard Milner, Assistant Professor; M.A., Ohio State.
Ann M. Neely, Associate Professor of the Practice; Ed.D., Georgia.
Caron Neitzel, Assistant Professor; B.A., Indiana.
Karon Jean Nicol-LeCompte, Assistant Clinical Professor; M.S., Sam Houston State.
Amy Palmeri, Assistant Professor of the Practice; Ph.D., Indiana Bloomington.
Victoria J. Risko, Professor; Ed.D., West Virginia.
Deborah W. Rowe, Associate Professor; Ph.D., Indiana.
Leona Schauble, Professor; Ph.D., Columbia.

VILLANOVA UNIVERSITY

Graduate Programs in Education

Programs of Study

The Department of Education and Human Services at Villanova University offers a Master of Arts degree (M.A.) in three areas: graduate teacher education (GTE), educational leadership, and a master's degree with Pennsylvania Instructional I certification. The curriculum of each program explores educational theory and pedagogy through a historical perspective, providing instruction in assessment and educational research. The programs prepare graduates for successful positions in educational settings.

To satisfy the requirements for a master's degree in GTE, students move through a 30-credit program, with a core curriculum of statistics, research, philosophy, and curriculum and instruction courses. In addition, students may enroll in courses in their specific content area and must attend three workshops. Following the completion of mandated courses, students have the freedom to select from a number of electives pertaining to various educational areas. Students must also pass a comprehensive examination (administered three times a year) before a degree is awarded.

Those enrolled in the Educational Leadership Program take a 33-credit curriculum, with the option of submitting a research thesis. This option is recommended for students who are likely to pursue a doctoral degree at another institution. This program also offers principal certification or supervisory certification to those who have five years of professional experience in the schools. The core curriculum and mandated comprehensive examination mirror that of the GTE program. For more details, prospective students should contact the Department of Education and Human Services.

The Master of Arts in Education plus Teacher Certification Program is a twelve-month course of study that requires the completion of 36 credits, which includes student teaching. The curriculum explores educational theory and pedagogy through a historical perspective, providing instruction in assessment and educational research. Upon completion, those enrolled receive an M.A. in education plus their Pennsylvania Instructional I certification.

Research Facilities

The Falvey Memorial Library at Villanova University houses about 600,000 volumes and an excellent collection of more than 3,000 periodicals. An interlibrary loan system operates with the efficiency of e-mail. The library is located in the middle of the campus and includes numerous public-use computer stations that are equipped with sophisticated search engines and data retrieval mechanisms.

Financial Aid

Applicants may compete for full financial awards, including tuition remission and a yearly stipend, which are renewable for a second year. Tuition scholarships (tuition remission without a stipend) are also offered and are renewable for the second year. The work these awards require ranges from assisting individual faculty members with research materials to aiding with instruction and related activities. Tuition reduction is also available for current teachers.

Cost of Study

Fees and expenses for graduate students in 2006–07 were $50 for the application fee, $565 per credit for tuition, and $60 per semester for general University fees. Currently, a tuition-relief agenda is offered, granting a 20 percent tuition reduction for educators in nonparochial schools and a 40 percent tuition reduction for parochial school educators. Prospective students should contact the Department of Education and Human Services for details at 610-519-4620.

Living and Housing Costs

A variety of affordable housing possibilities are available near the Villanova University campus. Housing costs vary in accordance with the option chosen. Room and board for a single graduate student may average about $8000 for a twelve-month period. Villanova does not provide on-campus housing for graduate students; however, some serve as resident heads and assistants in the dormitories.

Student Group

Many students enter the program as a career-changing opportunity, while others wish to take on administrative roles or simply continue their education. Therefore, the majority of the student body is employed full-time.

Student Outcomes

Students find that the degrees offer a multitude of opportunities to further their career and publish academic material, and many have continued on to doctoral studies in highly regarded universities throughout the world.

Location

Villanova University is situated on the historic Main Line, in a safe, western suburb of Philadelphia. The campus is on Lancaster Avenue (Route 30), 2 minutes from the Blue Route (Route 476) and 15 minutes from the Pennsylvania Turnpike, the Schuylkill Expressway, and Route 202. With ample parking and mass transit stops right on campus grounds, students can travel easily to and from the campus by car, bus, train, or light rail.

The University and The Department

Villanova University is an institution that is rich in history and tradition. From its modest beginnings on the country estate of a Revolutionary War officer, the University has seen significant growth in its student population and in its position as a leading coeducational institution of higher learning. Among the highly respected graduate programs that the College of Liberal Arts and Sciences features, the Ph.D. program in Continental philosophy and the M.A. programs in history, psychology, and political science offer special resources of collateral interest for the education programs.

Applying

Applications are welcome from all students who are interested in advanced educational study, and Villanova's graduates are increasingly earning both admission to and financial aid from distinguished Ph.D. programs. Applications for admission must include complete undergraduate transcripts (from all institutions attended), three letters of recommendation, and a one-page, typed statement outlining the applicant's objectives.

Correspondence and Information

Director of Graduate Studies or
Department of Education and Human Services
Villanova University
Villanova, Pennsylvania 19085

Phone: 610-519-4620
Fax: 610-519-4623
E-mail: eduhs@villanova.edu
Web site: http://education.villanova.edu

Villanova University

THE FACULTY

Department of Education and Human Services

Connie Titone, Professor and Chairperson; Ed.D., Harvard, 1995.
Victor D. Brooks, Professor; Ed.D., Pennsylvania, 1974.
John H. Durnin, Associate Professor; Ph.D., Pennsylvania, 1971.
Edward Garcia Fierros, Assistant Professor; Ph.D., Boston College, 1999.
Wm. Ray Heitzmann, Professor; Ph.D., Delaware, 1974.
Catherine M. Hill, Assistant Professor and Associate Dean (Arts and Sciences); Ed.D., Harvard, 1996.
Richard M. Jacobs, O.S.A., Professor; M.Div., Ph.D., Tulsa, 1990.
Robert J. Murray, O.S.A., Assistant Professor; Ph.D., Temple, 1995.
Ernest E. Ramirez, Assistant Professor; Ph.D., Oklahoma, 1981.
Deborah L. Schussler, Assistant Professor; Ed.D., Vanderbilt, 2002.

VIRGINIA COMMONWEALTH UNIVERSITY

School of Education

Programs of Study

Virginia Commonwealth University (VCU), through the School of Education, offers several graduate programs. Graduates are reflective practitioners across a broad array of disciplines, including P–12 teaching, educational leadership, counselor education, special education, health and physical education, exercise science, and research and evaluation. The faculty members—representing six departments and ten centers—are nationally and internationally recognized for their professional accomplishments and offer a rich learning experience for all students. They pursue active research agendas that focus on theoretical frameworks as well as applied action-based research. The School is a member of the American Association of Colleges of Teacher Education, the Holmes Partnership, and the Urban Serving Universities.

Several master's programs are available—the M.Ed. in adult learning, counselor education, educational leadership (with concentrations in administration and supervision and in leadership studies), health and human performance, reading, and special education (with concentrations in early childhood special education, emotional disturbance, learning disabilities, mental retardation, and severe disabilities); the M.S. in health and movement sciences; the M.S. in athletic training (MSAT); and the Master of Teaching (with concentrations in early and elementary education and in secondary education).

Postbaccalaureate certificates are offered in autism spectrum disorders, instructional technology, and teaching (secondary only).

Post-master's certificates are available in college student development and counseling, educational leadership, and reading specialist.

Doctoral programs available are the Ph.D. in education (with concentrations in educational leadership, instructional leadership, research and evaluation, special education and disability leadership, and urban services leadership) and the Ph.D. in rehabilitation and movement science. All academic programs are accredited by the National Council for Accreditation of Teacher Education and the Commission on Accreditation of Allied Health Education Programs.

Research Facilities

VCU libraries provide a combined capacity of more than 1.7 million volumes, 10,200 periodical titles, and an online bibliographic search service accessing hundreds of databases. In addition, the Virginia state and Richmond public libraries are within walking distance of both VCU campuses. Academic Computing provides a variety of microcomputer, minicomputer, and mainframe computing services to support the research and instructional endeavors of its faculty and students, including consultation, instruction, and computer acquisition.

The School of Education sponsors a variety of centers and institutes that connect students and faculty to the field of practice, including the Center for School Community Collaboration, the Center for Teacher Leadership, the Child Development Center, the Commonwealth Educational Policy Institute (CEPI), the Metropolitan Educational Research Consortium (MERC), the Partnership for People with Disabilities, the Virginia Department of Education's (VDOE) Training & Technical Assistance Center (T/TAC), the Rehabilitation Research and Training Center, the Virginia Adult Learning Resource Center, the Virginia Center for Teaching International Studies, and the Metropolitan Educational Training Alliance (META).

Financial Aid

Students may apply for need-based assistance through the University's Financial Aid Office. Current information on financial aid programs, policies, and procedures is available at http://www.vcu.edu/enroll/finaid.

Cost of Study

For full-time study (9–15 credits) in 2007–08, Virginia residents pay tuition and fees of $4452 per semester; nonresidents, $8876 per semester. For part-time study, Virginia residents pay tuition and fees of $465 per hour; nonresidents, $954 per hour. Some programs require additional fees. On the Medical College of Virginia (MCV) campus, tuition, fees, and other expenses vary in the medicine, pharmacy, nurse anesthesia, dentistry, and School of Allied Health programs.

Living and Housing Costs

Graduate student housing is available on both the MCV campus and the academic campus of Virginia Commonwealth University. Many graduate students live in off-campus housing, which is reasonably priced and readily available in a variety of styles and settings in nearby residential areas or within easy commuting distance. On- and off-campus housing information is available on the Web at http://www.housing.vcu.edu/.

Student Group

VCU enrolls 30,452 students, 7,611 of whom are graduate students. More than 200 clubs and organizations reflect the diverse social, recreational, educational, political, and religious interests of the student body.

Location

Richmond is Virginia's capital and a major East Coast financial and manufacturing center that offers students a wide range of cultural, educational, and recreational activities. Richmond is located in central Virginia at the intersection of Interstates 95 and 64, 2 hours south of Washington, D.C., and nestled between the Blue Ridge Mountains and the Atlantic coast. The Richmond region is easily accessible by plane, car, and train. With nearly 1 million residents, the historic city of Richmond combines big-city offerings with small-town hospitality. Applicants are encouraged to explore http://www.visit.richmond.com/ for more information on the city.

The University

VCU is a state-supported coeducational university with a graduate school, a major teaching hospital, and twelve academic and professional units that offer fifty-two undergraduate, twenty-two postbaccalaureate certificate, sixty-five master's, six post-master's certificate, and twenty-nine Ph.D. programs. VCU also offers M.D., D.D.S., D.P.T., and Pharm.D. programs as well as cooperative degree programs with other major Virginia colleges and universities. VCU has one of the largest evening colleges in the United States. The academic campus is located in Richmond's historic Fan District. The health sciences campus and hospital are located 2 miles east in the downtown business district. A University bus service provides free intercampus transportation for faculty members and students.

With more than $211 million in annual research funding, Virginia Commonwealth University is classified as one of the nation's top research universities by the Carnegie Foundation for the Advancement of Teaching. More than 29,000 undergraduate, certificate, graduate, post-master's, professional, and doctoral students are enrolled in 162 academic programs, forty of which are unique in the commonwealth of Virginia. The faculty members represent the finest American and international graduate institutions and enhance the University's position among the important institutions of higher learning in the United States and the world via their work in the classroom, laboratory, studio, and clinic and in their scholarly publications.

Applying

Admission procedures and program requirements are detailed in the *Graduate Bulletin*. Application deadlines and materials, including the application and the *Graduate Bulletin*, are available online at the Graduate School Web site at http://www.graduate.vcu.edu. Virginia Commonwealth University is an equal opportunity/affirmative action institution providing access to education and employment without regard to age, race, color, national origin, gender, religion, sexual orientation, veteran's status, political affiliation, or disability.

Correspondence and Information

School of Education
1015 West Main Street
Virginia Commonwealth University
Richmond, Virginia 23284-2020

Phone: 804-828-3382
Fax: 804-828-1323
E-mail: soessc@vcu.edu
Web site: http://www.soe.vcu.edu/

Virginia Commonwealth University

THE FACULTY AND THEIR RESEARCH

Counselor Education

Donna J. Dockery, Assistant Professor; Ph.D., Virginia. Effective counseling for at-risk and nontraditional students, psychosocial needs of gifted youth, multicultural populations and counseling.

Mary Hermann, Assistant Professor; J.D., Loyola New Orleans, 1995; Ph.D., New Orleans, 2001. School counseling, legal and ethical issues in counseling, gender issues in counseling.

Susan Leone, Associate Professor and Chair; Ed.D., Virginia, 1994. Counseling ethics, group work, counseling history and professionalism.

Educational Leadership

Jonathan Becker, Assistant Professor; J.D., Boston College, 1997; Ph.D., Columbia Teachers College, 2003. Digital equity in education, educational equity as a multilevel organizational phenomenon, the use of technology in data-driven decision making.

William C. Bosher Jr., Distinguished Professor; Ed.D., Virginia, 1974. Federal, state, and local policy development; school finance; educational accountability and leadership for reform.

Cheryl Magill, Assistant Professor; Ph.D., Virginia, 1999. Development of federal and state education law and policy, particularly by the development and implementation of the accountability components of the No Child Left Behind Act of 2001.

John Marshak, Associate Professor; Ph.D., Michigan, 1985. School finance policy development, court-ordered state educational finance reform, best practices in school leadership.

Martin Reardon, Assistant Professor; Ph.D., William and Mary, 2000. Improving the quality of supervision of instruction and personnel development in schools and school districts.

Charol Shakeshaft, Professor and Chair; Ph.D., Texas A&M. Gender patterns in educational delivery and classroom interactions.

Whitney Sherman, Assistant Professor, Ph.D. Women in leadership, leadership preparation and mentoring, social justice and equity issues in leadership.

Foundations of Education

Lisa Abrams, Assistant Professor; Ph.D., Boston College, 2003. Impact of test-based accountability policies on teachers, students, and classroom practice in general and special education settings; impact of high-stakes testing policies on student progress through the K–12 public school system, with particular emphasis on the grade 9 transition, dropout and retention rates, and graduation rates; intersection of test-based accountability programs and federal special education policies, with a focus on graduation rates and diploma earning patterns of students with disabilities.

Kathleen Cauley, Associate Professor; Ph.D., Delaware, 1985. Transition of students into middle school and high school, impact of high-stakes tests on student motivation, academic engagement, and other measures of student learning.

Henry Clark, Professor and Associate Dean; Ph.D., Columbia, 1982. Quantitative methods, human learning and cognition, cognitive and metacognative aspects of text processing.

Paul Gerber, Professor; Ph.D., Michigan, 1978. Adults with learning disabilities, post-school, and lifespan issues.

James McMillan, Professor and Chair; Ph.D., Northwestern, 1976. Classroom assessment, grading, student motivation, research methods.

Gina Pannozzo, Assistant Professor; Ph.D., SUNY at Buffalo, 2005. Student encouragement in school; classroom and school climate, culture, and sense of community; impact of small class size on students and teachers.

Maike Philipsen, Associate Professor; Ph.D., North Carolina at Chapel Hill, 1993. Sociology, anthropology, history, and philosophy of education; service learning; qualitative research methods; oral history; educational equality (issues on race, class, and gender in education); faculty roles in higher education; reform debates in education.

Kurt Stemhagen, Assistant Professor; Ph.D., Virginia, 2004. The intersections of philosophy of education, mathematics education, and ethics; the school-society relationship and the role of social foundations of education in teacher preparation; social justice.

Health and Human Performance

Edmund Acevedo, Professor and Chair; Ph.D., North Carolina at Greensboro, 1989. Impact of stress and fitness level on an individual's health.

Brent Arnold, Associate Professor; Ph.D., Virginia, 1994. Proprioceptive loss in functional ankle instability, ability to perceive force and its relationship to joint stability, impairments in balance and movement following lower extremity injury.

Ted Conway, Professor, Ph.D. Optimization of an accurate elastic and time-dependent load-deformation relationship for biological tissues to develop a more robust human joint mechanics model; inclusion of underrepresented groups in science, technology, engineering, and math education.

Robert Davis, Professor; Ph.D., Maryland, 1973. Children's fitness.

Ronald Evans, Assistant Professor; Ph.D., Auburn, 2000. Skeletal and myocardial alterations associated with myocardial volume overload and chronic heart failure, lactate transport and metabolism, physical activity and obesity in children and adolescents, the role of physical activity in successful weight loss following gastric bypass surgery.

Alan Freedman, Instructor; M.Ed., Virginia, 1991. Educational standards in athletic training; clinical education in athletic training; hip-joint pathology, proprioception, and kinesthesia.

Richard Gayle, Associate Professor; Ed.D., Tennessee, 1979. Measurement of habitual physical activity, relationship of habitual physical activity to risks for chronic degenerative diseases.

Deborah Getty, Assistant Professor; Ph.D., Berkeley, 1996. Gender issues in sport and physical activity, character development and healthy competition in sport, team-building and positive coaching in physical activity.

Joann Richardson, Associate Professor; Ph.D., Virginia Commonwealth, 1993. Women's health, minority health (i.e., African American), rural health, international health, secondary prevention of chronic disease (i.e., breast and prostate cancer, cardiovascular disease), accessibility for underserved populations.

Scott Ross, Assistant Professor; Ph.D., North Carolina at Chapel Hill, 2003. Effects of functional ankle instability on postural stability, effects of functional ankle instability on time to stabilization measures following single-leg jump landings, improving postural stability with balance training exercises and stochastic resonance.

Beverly Warren, Dean and Professor; Ed.D., Alabama, 1985; Ph.D., Auburn, 1990; FACSM. Impact of physical activity on weight loss and weight maintenance in weight-challenged populations, environmental influences on obesity, treatment and prevention strategies for decreasing childhood obesity.

Special Education and Disability Policy

Maureen Conroy, Professor; Ph.D., Vanderbilt, 1986. Functional assessment and analysis of behavioral problems, assessment and intervention of social skills, antecedent intervention.

Paul Gerber, Professor; Ph.D., Michigan, 1978. Adults with learning disabilities, post-school, and lifespan issues.

John Kregel, Professor and Chair; Ed.D., Georgia, 1983. Identifying and eliminating barriers to employment and economic self-sufficiency for people with disabilities.

Fred Orelove, Professor; Ph.D., Illinois, 1978. Learners with severe disabilities.

Evelyn Reed-Victor, Associate Professor; Ph.D., William and Mary, 1998. Infants and young children with developmental delays or disabilities and their families, children and families living in poverty, particularly those experiencing homelessness.

Diane Simon, Associate Professor; Ph.D., NYU, 1981. Recruitment and retention in higher education, engaging at-risk middle school students.

Kevin Sutherland, Assistant Professor; Ph.D., Vanderbilt, 2000. Effective practices for students with emotional and behavioral disorders (EBD), teacher/student interactions in classrooms for students with EBD, the teacher's role in systems of care.

Colleen Thoma, Associate Professor; Ph.D., Indiana, 1997. Self-determination in transition planning, transition assessment, transition from school to post-secondary education, universal design for instruction, positive behavior supports, preparing special educators to facilitate self-determined transition planning for students with disabilities.

Paul Wehman, Professor; Ph.D., Wisconsin, 1976. Transition from school to adulthood, special education as it relates for young adulthood.

Yaoying Xu, Assistant Professor; Ph.D., Nevada, Las Vegas. Culturally appropriate learning contexts for young English-language learners, impact of social interactions of young children on their school performance, empowering culturally diverse families of young children with disabilities, linking assessment and intervention for infants and young children who are at risk for disabilities/delays.

Teaching and Learning

Nora Alder, Associate Professor; Ed.D., Nevada, 1996. Caring student/teacher relationships and urban schooling and teacher education.

Terry Carter, Assistant Professor; Ph.D., George Washington, 2001. Transformative learning among professionals in the workplace, learning through developmental relationships, including mentoring.

Seonhee Cho, Assistant Professor; Ph.D., Tennessee, 2005. ESL/international students' academic socialization issues that include relationships with peers and teachers, group work, institutional support, and access to academic resources.

Leila Christenbury, Professor; Ed.D., Virginia Tech, 1980. Classroom interaction strategies, specifically questioning; all aspects of young adult literature; the teaching of writing to secondary school students; approaches to teaching and learning in the secondary English classroom.

Michael Davis, Professor and Chair; Ph.D., Illinois, 1975. School change, teacher preparation.

Terry Dozier, Associate Professor and Director of the Center for Teacher Leadership; Ed.D., South Carolina. Promoting and supporting teacher leadership that enhances the quality of teaching and the teaching profession.

Ena Gross, Associate Professor; Ph.D., Georgia State, 1980. Math education.

Jacqueline McDonnough, Assistant Professor; Ph.D., Virginia, 2002. Assessing how pre-service teachers' K-12 science experiences interact with their self-efficacy as future teachers of science.

Tammy Milby, Instructor; M.Ed., Radford, 1995. Struggling readers and writers, teacher quality/professional development practices, low-performing schools.

William Muth, Assistant Professor; Ph.D., George Mason, 2004. Thirdspace and reading components theories, especially as these apply to prison-based family literacy programs and children of incarcerated parents.

Gabriel Reich, Assistant Professor, Ph.D. Social studies teaching and learning, assessment, curriculum.

Joan Rhodes, Assistant Professor; Ph.D., Virginia Commonwealth, 1998. Early literacy development, using hypertext for increasing comprehension, instant messaging and social networking, electronic study skills, emerging and new literacies, assessment and instructional strategies for remediating reading difficulties.

Valerie Robnolt, Assistant Professor; Ph.D., Virginia, 2004. Assessment and instruction of reading comprehension, vocabulary, and fluency; the most effective methods of providing professional development to elementary teachers.

Gary Sarkozi, Assistant Professor; Ph.D., Virginia Commonwealth, 2001. Collecting, analyzing, and evaluating data on activities related to technological integration in the many facets of today's global environment.

Loraine Stewart, Associate Professor; Ed.D., North Carolina at Greensboro, 1991. Examining strategies used by classroom teachers to integrate African American children's literature into the elementary curriculum and the impact this literature has on student achievement.

Doris White, Associate Professor; Ed.D., Illinois, 1971. Multicultural education, urban education, testing and achievement outcomes.

WAYNE STATE UNIVERSITY

College of Education

Programs of Study

Programs of study lead to the following degrees: M.A., M.A.T., M.Ed., Ed.D., and Ph.D. and the Education Specialist Certificate. Programs are offered in elementary, secondary, and K–12 education. Initial certification specializations include English education, foreign language education, mathematics education, science education, social studies education, and career and technical education. K–12 areas include special education, reading language and literacy, art education, and kinesiology.

In addition to the above-mentioned areas, graduate degrees are also offered in bilingual-bicultural education, early childhood education, educational leadership and policy studies, instructional technology, administration and supervision, counseling, marriage and family therapy, art therapy, educational psychology, school and community psychology, evaluation and research, rehabilitation and community inclusion, health education, and sports administration.

Graduate programs are designed to prepare leaders in teaching, administration, curriculum, and research at all levels, extending beyond schools and universities to corporations seeking to expand education and training programs. College faculty members are making significant contributions toward infusing instructional technology into the full range of instructional programs.

Research Facilities

Students have access not only to the vast library collections at Wayne State but also to the collections of Michigan's two other research institutions through the interlibrary loan system that utilizes a state-of-the-art online cataloging system.

The College has three classrooms equipped with more than 100 networked Macintosh and IBM computers for instructional purposes. In addition, the College maintains an instructional technology laboratory, a video production studio, a distance education room, an adolescent research laboratory, and a counseling laboratory and houses a research support laboratory, all of which contain some of the most advanced hardware and software available.

The College also operates a full-day early childhood center (toddlers to 4-year-olds) as part of the teacher education program, which offers a wide range of training and research opportunities.

Financial Aid

The University provides a range of graduate scholarships and fellowships to outstanding students. Some of these, such as the Rumble Fellowship, cover tuition, books, and housing, with an additional stipend for living expenses. The College also provides several graduate tuition scholarships annually.

Cost of Study

The in-state tuition for the 2005–06 academic year ranged from $1270.70 for 3 hours to $4712.30 for a full 12-hour course load. Comparable expenses for a nonresident were $2565.50 and $9891.50, respectively.

Living and Housing Costs

The cost of living in metropolitan Detroit is moderate in comparison to the living expenses in metropolitan areas of the eastern or western parts of the nation. The University Housing Office can provide housing information and assist students in locating housing on campus.

Student Group

The College of Education has the largest number of graduate students of any college in the University. The majority of students work as faculty members and administrators in schools and colleges throughout southeast Michigan. Graduates of the College have assumed leadership positions both inside and outside education throughout the country.

Location

The main campus is located in the center of Detroit's expanding cultural center. In addition to its own Hilberry and Bonstelle theaters, the University is in proximity to the Fisher Theater, the Detroit Institute of Arts, the Charles H. Wright Museum of African-American History, the Detroit Historical Museum, the Detroit Main Library, and the Detroit Medical Center.

The University

As one of the fifty-six public universities classified as a major research university by the Carnegie Commission on Higher Education, Wayne State has schools and colleges of medicine, law, engineering, education, liberal arts and science, business administration, nursing, social work, fine performing and communication arts, and pharmacy and health sciences.

The College of Education is located in the heart of the main campus and within walking distance of the central offices of the Detroit Public Schools. The College has a long history of working cooperatively with Detroit and suburban teachers and administrators in joint research and teaching initiatives.

Applying

Students who have not been formally admitted to the Graduate School should file their initial applications with the University Admissions Office, Welcome Center. Students may apply online at http://gradadmissions.wayne.edu.

Correspondence and Information

Dr. Janice W. Green
Assistant Dean, Academic Services
489 Education Building
Wayne State University
Detroit, Michigan 48202-3489
Phone: 313-577-1605
E-mail: askcoe@wayne.edu
Web site: http://www.wayne.edu/

Wayne State University

THE FACULTY

Administrative and Organizational Studies (AOS)
JoAnne Holbert, Interim Assistant Dean; Ed.D., Indiana, 341 Education.

Michael Addonizio, Ph.D., Michigan State. Roger A. DeMont, Ed.D., Tennessee. Marytza Gawlik, Ph.D., Berkeley. Joella Gipson, Ph.D., Illinois. Ingrid Guerra, Ph.D., Florida State. William Hill, Ph.D., Wayne State. Frances LaPlante-Sosnowsky, Ed.D., Wayne State. Thomas McLennan, Ed.D., Wayne State. James Moseley, Ed.D., Wayne State. Monte Piliawsky, Ph.D., Tulane. Lee Randall, Ed.D., Nova. Rita C. Richey, Ph.D., Wayne State. Timothy Spannaus, Ph.D., Wayne State. Karen Tonso, Ph.D., Colorado at Boulder. Ke Zhang, Ph.D., Penn State.

Kinesiology, Health, and Sports Studies (KHSS)
Sarah J. Erbaugh, Assistant Dean, Ph.D., Wisconsin–Madison, 261 Matthaei.

Judith S. Anderson, M.A., Wayne State. Yun-Seok Choi, Ph.D., New Mexico. Joseph Dake, M.P.H., Bowling Green State. Suzanna Dillon, Ph.D., Texas Woman's. Hermann-Josef Engels, Ph.D., Florida State. Mariane Fahlman, Ph.D., Toledo. Randall Gretebeck, Ph.D., Wisconsin–Madison. Avanelle Kidwell, M.A., Ohio State. Jenny Lee, Ph.D., South Carolina. Jeffrey J. Martin, Ph.D., North Carolina at Greensboro. Nathan McCaughtry, Ph.D., Wisconsin. Peter A. Roberts, M.A., Michigan State. Bo Shen, Ph.D., Maryland. Steven Singleton, Ph.D., Michigan. William W. Sloan, M.A., Maryland. Delano Tucker, Ed.D., Wayne State. John C. Wirth, Ph.D., Illinois.

Teacher Education (TED)
Gerald Oglan, Assistant Dean, Ph.D., Windsor, 241 Education.

Poonam Arya, Ph.D., NYU. Elsie Babcock, M.A., Wayne State. Navaz Bhavnagri, Ph.D., Illinois. Carmen Bosch, B.A., Detroit. Mary Brady, Ph.D., Wayne State. James F. G. Brown, Ph.D., Union University. John S. Camp, Ph.D., Columbia. Kathleen Crawford-McKinney, Ph.D., Arizona. Gina DeBlase, Ph.D., SUNY at Buffalo. Hal Dittenber, M.A., Eastern Michigan. Jazlin Ebenezer, Ph.D., British Columbia. Thomas Edwards, Ph.D., Ohio State. Sharon L. Elliott, Ed.D., Wayne State. Karen Feathers, Ed.D., Indiana. Holly Feen-Calligan, Ph.D., Wright State. Maria Ferreira, Ph.D., Indiana. Janice E. Hale, Ph.D., Georgia State. Steven Ilmer, Ph.D., Michigan. Leonard Kaplan, Ed.D., Rochester. Mark Larson, Ed.D., Washington. Anna Miller, M.A., Wayne State. S. Asli Ozgun-Koca, Ph.D., Ohio. J. Michael Peterson, Ph.D., North Texas State. Robert Pettapiece, Ed.D., Wayne State. Kariann Reno, M.S., Northern Michigan. Sally Roberts, Ed.D., Wayne State. R. Craig Roney, Ph.D., Colorado. Marc Rosa, Ed.D., Wayne State. Sharon Sellers-Clark, Ph.D., Wayne State. Gary R. Smith, Ph.D., Northwestern. Jo-Ann Snyder, Ed.D., Wayne State. Geralyn Stephens, Ed.D., Wayne State. Jacqueline Tilles, Ph.D., Michigan. David Whitin, Ed.D., Indiana. Phyllis Whitin, Ph.D., South Carolina. Anne W. Williamson, M.S.L.S., Wayne State. Paula C. Wood, Ph.D., Michigan State. Marshall F. Zumberg, Ph.D., Michigan State. Gregory Zyric, Ph.D., South Carolina.

Theoretical and Behavioral Foundations (TBF)
JoAnne Holbert, Assistant Dean, Ed.D., Indiana, 341 Education.

Ann Cavallo, Ph.D., Syracuse. Arnold B. Coven, Ed.D., Arizona. Daisy Ellington, Ph.D., Wayne State. Gail Fahoome, Ph.D., Wayne State. Stephen B. Hillman, Ph.D., Indiana. Alan M. Hoffman, Ed.D., Penn State. Stuart Itzkowitz, Ph.D., Wayne State. Donald R. Marcotte, Ph.D., Connecticut. Barry S. Markman, Ph.D., Emory. Delila Owens, Ph.D., Michigan State. George Parris, Ph.D., Michigan State. Francesca Pernice-Duca, Ph.D., Michigan State. John J. Pietrofesa, Ed.D., Miami (Florida). Shlomo Sawilowsky, Ph.D., South Florida. Cheryl Somers, Ph.D., Ball State. Jina Yoon, Ph.D., Texas A&M.

Section 23
Administration, Instruction, and Theory

This section contains a directory of institutions offering graduate work in administration, instruction, and theory, followed by in-depth entries submitted by institutions that chose to prepare detailed program descriptions. Additional information about programs listed in the directory but not augmented by an in-depth entry may be obtained by writing directly to the dean of a graduate school or chair of a department at the address given in the directory.

For programs offering related work, see also in this book Education, Health-Related Professions, Instructional Levels, Leisure Studies and Recreation, Physical Education and Kinesiology, Special Focus, and Subject Areas; and in Book 2, Psychology and Counseling (School Psychology).

CONTENTS

Curriculum and Instruction

Acadia University, Faculty of Professional Studies, School of Education, Program in Curriculum Studies, Wolfville, NS B4P 2R6, Canada. Offers cultural and media studies (M Ed); inclusive education (M Ed); learning and technology (M Ed); science, math and technology (M Ed). Evening/weekend programs available. *Faculty:* 12 full-time (5 women). *Students:* 2 full-time (both women), 27 part-time (19 women). In 2006, 25 degrees awarded. *Degree requirements:* For master's, thesis optional. *Entrance requirements:* For master's, B Ed or the equivalent, minimum B average in undergraduate course work, 2 years of teaching experience. Additional exam requirements/recommendations for international students: Required—TOEFL (minimum score 580 paper-based; 237 computer-based). *Application deadline:* For fall admission, 3/15 priority date for domestic and international students. Application fee: $50. Electronic applications accepted. *Financial support:* Teaching assistantships available. Financial award application deadline: 2/1. *Faculty research:* Literacy development, postmodern philosophy and curriculum theory, historiography, philosophy of education, learning and technology. *Application contact:* Sheila Langille, Secretary, 902-585-1229, Fax: 902-585-1071, E-mail: sheila.langille@acadiau.ca.

American InterContinental University Online, Program in Education, Hoffman Estates, IL 60192. Offers curriculum and instruction (M Ed); educational assessment and evaluation (M Ed); instructional technology (M Ed); leadership of educational organizations (M Ed). Evening/weekend programs available. Postbaccalaureate distance learning degree programs offered (no on-campus study). *Entrance requirements:* Additional exam requirements/recommendations for international students: Required—TOEFL (minimum score 550 paper-based; 213 computer-based). *Application deadline:* Applications are processed on a rolling basis. Application fee: $50. Electronic applications accepted. *Financial support:* Institutionally sponsored loans and scholarships/grants available. Financial award applicants required to submit FAFSA. *Unit head:* Kerri J Holloway, Vice President of Academic Affairs, 847-851-5000 Ext. 15399, Fax: 847-586-6309, E-mail: kholloway@aivonline.edu. *Application contact:* 877-701-3800, E-mail: info@aiuonline.edu.

Andrews University, School of Graduate Studies, School of Education, Department of Teaching, Learning, and Curriculum, Program in Curriculum and Instruction, Berrien Springs, MI 49104. Offers MA, Ed D, PhD, Ed S. *Degree requirements:* For master's, thesis optional; for doctorate, thesis/dissertation. *Entrance requirements:* For master's, GRE Subject Test.

Angelo State University, College of Graduate Studies, College of Education, Department of Teacher Education, Program in Curriculum and Instruction, San Angelo, TX 76909. Offers MA. Part-time and evening/weekend programs available. *Faculty:* 17 full-time (12 women). *Students:* Average age 38. 10 applicants, 90% accepted, 7 enrolled. In 2006, 6 degrees awarded. *Degree requirements:* For master's, comprehensive exam. *Entrance requirements:* For master's, GRE General Test. Additional exam requirements/recommendations for international students: Required—TOEFL or IELTS. *Application deadline:* For fall admission, 7/15 priority date for domestic students, 6/15 for international students; for spring admission, 12/8 for domestic students, 11/1 for international students. Applications are processed on a rolling basis. Application fee: $40 ($50 for international students). Electronic applications accepted. *Expenses:* Tuition, state resident: full-time $2,340; part-time $130 per hour. Tuition, nonresident: full-time $7,290; part-time $405 per hour. Required fees: $906; $56 per hour. *Financial support:* In 2006–07, 6 students received support. Career-related internships or fieldwork, Federal Work-Study, scholarships/grants, and unspecified assistantships available. Support available to part-time students. Financial award application deadline: 3/1; financial award applicants required to submit FAFSA. *Application contact:* Dr. Nancy J. Hadley, Information Contact, 325-942-2052 Ext. 252, E-mail: nancy.hadley@angelo.edu.

Appalachian State University, Cratis D. Williams Graduate School, College of Education, Department of Curriculum and Instruction, Boone, NC 28608. Offers curriculum specialist (MA); educational media (MA); elementary education (MA); secondary education (MA). *Accreditation:* NCATE. Part-time and evening/weekend programs available. Postbaccalaureate distance learning degree programs offered (minimal on-campus study). *Faculty:* 32 full-time (21 women). *Students:* 7 full-time (5 women), 206 part-time (172 women); includes 2 minority (both African Americans), 2 international. 100 applicants, 97% accepted, 95 enrolled. In 2006, 96 degrees awarded. *Degree requirements:* For master's, thesis or alternative, comprehensive exam, registration. *Entrance requirements:* For master's, GRE General Test or MAT. Additional exam requirements/recommendations for international students: Required—TOEFL (minimum score 570 paper-based; 230 computer-based). *Application deadline:* For fall admission, 7/1 priority date for domestic students, 1/1 for international students; for spring admission, 11/1 for domestic students, 6/1 for international students. Application fee: $50. *Expenses:* Tuition, state resident: full-time $2,600; part-time $127 per hour. Tuition, nonresident: full-time $13,200; part-time $597 per hour. Required fees: $2,000; $546 per term. *Financial support:* In 2006–07, 6 teaching assistantships (averaging $7,000 per year) were awarded; fellowships, research assistantships, career-related internships or fieldwork, Federal Work-Study, scholarships/grants, and unspecified assistantships also available. Support available to part-time students. Financial award application deadline: 7/1; financial award applicants required to submit FAFSA. Total annual research expenditures: $366,043. *Unit head:* Dr. Michael Jacobson, Chairperson, 828-262-2224.

Arizona State University, Division of Graduate Studies, College of Education, Division of Curriculum and Instruction, Academic Program in Curriculum and Instruction, Tempe, AZ 85287. Offers M Ed, MA, Ed D. *Degree requirements:* For doctorate, thesis/dissertation. *Entrance requirements:* For master's and doctorate, GRE General Test or MAT. *Faculty research:* Early childhood, media and computers, elementary education, English education, exercise and wellness education.

Arizona State University, Division of Graduate Studies, College of Education, Interdisciplinary Program in Curriculum and Instruction, Tempe, AZ 85287. Offers PhD. *Degree requirements:* For doctorate, thesis/dissertation.

Arizona State University at the Polytechnic Campus, The School of Educational Innovation and Teacher Preparation, Mesa, AZ 85212. Offers administration/supervision (M Ed); curriculum and instruction (M Ed); physical education (MPE, PhD). *Faculty:* 9 full-time (6 women), 1 part-time/adjunct (0 women). *Students:* 86 full-time (74 women), 119 part-time (92 women); includes 18 minority (1 African American, 1 American Indian/Alaska Native, 5 Asian Americans or Pacific Islanders, 11 Hispanic Americans), 1 international. Average age 33. 94 applicants, 84% accepted, 65 enrolled. In 2006, 19 degrees awarded. *Degree requirements:* For master's, written comprehensive exam or applied project; for doctorate, thesis/dissertation. *Entrance requirements:* For master's, 3 letters of recommendation, minimum GPA of 3.0. *Application deadline:* For fall admission, 4/15 priority date for domestic and international students; for spring admission, 10/15 priority date for domestic and international students. Applications are processed on a rolling basis. Application fee: $50. Electronic applications accepted. *Expenses:* Tuition, state resident: part-time $310 per credit hour. Tuition, nonresident: part-time $688 per credit hour. *Financial support:* In 2006–07, 4 teaching assistantships with full tuition reimbursements (averaging $12,978 per year) were awarded; fellowships, research assistantships with full tuition reimbursements also available. Financial award applicants required to submit FAFSA.

Arkansas State University, Graduate School, College of Education, Department of Educational Leadership, Curriculum, and Special Education, Jonesboro, State University, AR 72467. Offers community college administration education (SCCT); education theory and practice (MSE); educational leadership (MSE, Ed D, Ed S), including curriculum and instruction (Ed S), elementary curriculum and instruction (MSE), elementary principalship (Ed S), secondary principalship (Ed S), superintendency (Ed S); special education (MSE), including emotionally disturbed, gifted, talented and creative, instructional specialist 4-12, instructional specialist P-4; special education program administration (Ed S). *Accreditation:* NCATE. Part-time programs available. *Faculty:* 14 full-time (7 women), 5 part-time/adjunct (2 women). *Students:* 28 full-time (21 women), 328 part-time (233 women); includes 63 minority (58 African Americans, 3 American Indian/Alaska Native, 1 Asian American or Pacific Islander, 1 Hispanic American), 2 international. Average age 36. 181 applicants, 78% accepted, 70 enrolled. In 2006, 70 master's, 13 doctorates, 14 other advanced degrees awarded. *Degree requirements:* For master's, thesis or alternative, comprehensive exam; for doctorate, thesis/dissertation, comprehensive exam. *Entrance requirements:* For master's, GRE General Test or MAT, appropriate bachelor's degree, letters of reference, interview, official transcript; for doctorate and other advanced degree, GRE General Test or MAT, interview, master's degree, letters of reference, official transcript. Additional exam requirements/recommendations for international students: Required—TOEFL (minimum score 213 computer-based). *Application deadline:* Applications are processed on a rolling basis. Application fee: $30 ($40 for international students). Electronic applications accepted. *Expenses:* Tuition, state resident: full-time $3,393; part-time $189 per hour. Tuition, nonresident: full-time $8,577; part-time $477 per hour. Required fees: $752; $39 per hour. $25 per semester. *Financial support:* Teaching assistantships, career-related internships or fieldwork, scholarships/grants, and unspecified assistantships available. Financial award application deadline: 7/1; financial award applicants required to submit FAFSA. *Unit head:* Dr. Mitchell Holifield, Chair, 870-972-3062, Fax: 870-680-8130, E-mail: hfield@astate.edu.

Arkansas Tech University, Graduate School, School of Education, Russellville, AR 72801. Offers college student personnel (MSE); educational leadership (M Ed, Ed S); English education (M Ed); gifted education (MSE); instructional improvement (M Ed); secondary education (M Ed); teaching, learning and leadership (M Ed). *Accreditation:* NCATE. Part-time programs available. *Students:* 44 full-time (33 women), 244 part-time (181 women); includes 20 minority (14 African Americans, 1 American Indian/Alaska Native, 3 Asian Americans or Pacific Islanders, 2 Hispanic Americans), 18 international. Average age 34. In 2006, 72 master's, 4 other advanced degrees awarded. *Degree requirements:* For master's, action research project, thesis optional. *Entrance requirements:* For master's, GRE General Test or MAT. Additional exam requirements/recommendations for international students: Required—TOEFL (minimum score 500 paper-based; 173 computer-based). *Application deadline:* For fall admission, 3/1 priority date for domestic students, 5/1 priority date for international students; for winter admission, 10/1 priority date for international students; for spring admission, 10/1 priority date for domestic and international students. Applications are processed on a rolling basis. Application fee: $0 ($30 for international students). Electronic applications accepted. *Expenses:* Tuition, state resident: full-time $3,060; part-time $170 per hour. Tuition, nonresident: full-time $6,120; part-time $340 per hour. Required fees: $312; $4 per hour. $84 per term. Part-time tuition and fees vary according to course load. *Financial support:* In 2006–07, teaching assistantships with full tuition reimbursements (averaging $4,000 per year); career-related internships or fieldwork, Federal Work-Study, scholarships/grants, health care benefits, and unspecified assistantships also available. Support available to part-time students. Financial award application deadline: 4/15; financial award applicants required to submit FAFSA. *Unit head:* Dr. C. Glenn Sheets, Dean, 479-968-0350, Fax: 479-968-0350, E-mail: glenn.sheets@atu.edu. *Application contact:* Dr. Eldon G. Clary, Dean of Graduate School, 479-968-0398, Fax: 479-964-0542, E-mail: graduate.school@atu.edu.

Armstrong Atlantic State University, School of Graduate Studies, Program in Education, Savannah, GA 31419-1997. Offers adult education (M Ed); early childhood education (M Ed); education (M Ed); elementary education (M Ed); middle grades education (M Ed); secondary education (M Ed), including business education, English education, mathematics education, science education, social science education; special education (M Ed), including behavioral disorders, curriculum and instruction, learning disabilities, speech-language pathology. *Accreditation:* NCATE. Part-time and evening/weekend programs available. Postbaccalaureate distance learning degree programs offered (minimal on-campus study). *Faculty:* 11 full-time (9 women), 13 part-time/adjunct (10 women). *Students:* 50 full-time (42 women), 219 part-time (175 women); includes 71 minority (67 African Americans, 3 Asian Americans or Pacific Islanders, 1 Hispanic American), 6 international. Average age 35. In 2006, 151 degrees awarded. *Degree requirements:* For master's, portfolio. *Entrance requirements:* For master's, GRE General Test or MAT, minimum GPA of 2.5, letters of recommendation. Additional exam requirements/recommendations for international students: Required—TOEFL (minimum score 523 paper-based; 193 computer-based). *Application deadline:* For fall admission, 7/1 priority date for domestic and international students; for spring admission, 11/15 priority date for domestic and international students. Applications are processed on a rolling basis. Application fee: $25. Electronic applications accepted. *Expenses:* Tuition, state resident: full-time $2,286; part-time $127 per credit. Tuition, nonresident: full-time $9,144; part-time $508 per credit. One-time fee: $257. *Financial support:* In 2006–07, research assistantships with partial tuition reimbursements (averaging $2,500 per year); career-related internships or fieldwork, Federal Work-Study, scholarships/grants, and unspecified assistantships also available. Support available to part-time students. Financial award applicants required to submit FAFSA. *Unit head:* Dr. Jane McHaney, College of Education Dean, 912-927-5398, Fax: 912-921-7425, E-mail: mchaneja@mail.armstrong.edu.

Ashland University, College of Education, Graduate Studies in Education, Department of Educational Foundations, Ashland, OH 44805-3702. Offers classroom instruction (M Ed). Part-time and evening/weekend programs available. *Faculty:* 15 full-time (9 women), 67 part-time/adjunct (36 women). *Students:* 88 full-time (72 women), 216 part-time (171 women); includes 18 minority (13 African Americans, 1 American Indian/Alaska Native, 2 Asian Americans or Pacific Islanders, 2 Hispanic Americans), 8 international. Average age 34. In 2006, 217 degrees awarded. *Degree requirements:* For master's, thesis or alternative. *Entrance requirements:* For master's, GRE General Test or MAT, teaching certificate, minimum GPA of 2.75. Additional exam requirements/recommendations for international students: Required—TOEFL. Application fee: $30. *Expenses:* Tuition: Part-time $403 per credit. Tuition and fees vary according to degree level and program. *Financial support:* In 2006–07, 103 students received support. Application deadline: 4/15. *Faculty research:* Character education, teacher reflection, religion and education, professional education, environmental education. *Unit head:* Dr. Kathleen Flanagan Hudson, Chair, 419-289-5356, E-mail: kflanag@ashland.edu.

Ashland University, College of Education, Graduate Studies in Education, Program in Educational Administration, Ashland, OH 44805-3702. Offers administration (M Ed); business manager (M Ed); curriculum specialist (M Ed); principalship (M Ed); pupil services (M Ed); school treasurer (M Ed); superintendency (M Ed). Part-time programs available. *Faculty:* 10 full-time (3 women), 23 part-time/adjunct (6 women). *Students:* 134 full-time (76 women), 220 part-time (121 women); includes 27 minority (23 African Americans, 1 Asian American or Pacific Islander, 3 Hispanic Americans), 2 international. Average age 33. 68 applicants, 100% accepted, 68 enrolled. In 2006, 144 degrees awarded. *Degree requirements:* For master's, thesis or alternative, internship. *Entrance requirements:* For master's, teaching certificate, minimum GPA of 2.75. Additional exam requirements/recommendations for international students: Required—TOEFL. *Application deadline:* Applications are processed on a rolling basis. Application fee: $30. *Expenses:* Tuition: Part-time $403 per credit. Tuition and fees vary according to degree level and program. *Financial support:* In 2006–07, 116 students received support. Institutionally sponsored loans and scholarships/grants available. Financial award application deadline: 4/15. *Faculty research:* Gender and religious considerations in employment, ISLLC standards, adjunct faculty training, politics of school finance, ethnicity and employment. *Unit head:* Dr. John Bailey, Chair, 419-289-5396, Fax: 419-207-6702, E-mail: jbailey@ashland.edu. *Application contact:* Fred Slater, Director, Graduate Education, 419-289-5367, Fax: 419-207-4942, E-mail: fslater@ashland.edu.

Auburn University, Graduate School, College of Education, Department of Educational Foundations, Leadership, and Technology, Auburn University, AL 36849. Offers adult education (M Ed, MS, Ed D); curriculum and instruction (M Ed, MS, Ed D, Ed S); curriculum supervision (M Ed, MS, Ed D, Ed S); educational psychology (PhD); higher education administration (M Ed, MS,

Ed D, Ed S); media instructional design (MS); media specialist (M Ed); school administration (M Ed, MS, Ed D, Ed S). *Accreditation:* NCATE. Part-time programs available. *Faculty:* 23 full-time (11 women). *Students:* 40 full-time (26 women), 148 part-time (93 women); includes 64 minority (60 African Americans, 3 American Indian/Alaska Native, 1 Asian American or Pacific Islander), 6 international. Average age 38. 99 applicants, 57% accepted, 37 enrolled. In 2006, 32 master's, 10 doctorates, 7 other advanced degrees awarded. *Degree requirements:* For master's, thesis (for some programs); for doctorate, thesis/dissertation; for Ed S, field project. *Entrance requirements:* For master's, doctorate, and Ed S, GRE General Test. *Application deadline:* For fall admission, 7/7 for domestic students; for spring admission, 11/24 for domestic students. Applications are processed on a rolling basis. Application fee: $25 ($50 for international students). Electronic applications accepted. *Expenses:* Tuition, state resident: full-time $5,000. Tuition, nonresident: full-time $15,000. Required fees: $416. Tuition and fees vary according to program. *Financial support:* Teaching assistantships, Federal Work-Study available. Support available to part-time students. Financial award application deadline: 3/15. *Unit head:* Dr. William A. Spencer, Head, 334-844-4460. *Application contact:* Dr. Joe Pittman, Interim Dean of the Graduate School, 334-844-4700.

Aurora University, College of Education, Aurora, IL 60506-4892. Offers curriculum and instruction (Ed D); education (MAT); education and administration (Ed D); educational leadership (MEL); reading instruction (MA). Part-time and evening/weekend programs available. *Faculty:* 20 full-time (10 women), 99 part-time/adjunct (55 women). *Students:* 144 full-time (102 women), 1,156 part-time (832 women); includes 169 minority (32 African Americans, 2 American Indian/Alaska Native, 10 Asian Americans or Pacific Islanders, 125 Hispanic Americans). Average age 36. 451 applicants, 99% accepted, 421 enrolled. In 2006, 439 master's, 9 doctorates awarded. *Degree requirements:* For doctorate, thesis/dissertation. *Entrance requirements:* For master's, 2 years of teaching experience, valid teaching certificate. Additional exam requirements/recommendations for international students: Required—TOEFL (minimum score 550 paper-based; 213 computer-based). *Application deadline:* For fall admission, 8/23 priority date for domestic students. Applications are processed on a rolling basis. Application fee: $25. Electronic applications accepted. *Expenses:* Contact institution. Tuition and fees vary according to campus/location and program. *Financial support:* In 2006–07, 355 students received support; fellowships, research assistantships, teaching assistantships, Federal Work-Study and scholarships/grants available. Support available to part-time students. Financial award application deadline: 4/15; financial award applicants required to submit FAFSA. *Unit head:* Dr. Donald C. Wold, Dean, 630-844-1542, Fax: 630-844-5530, E-mail: dwold@aurora.edu. *Application contact:* Donna DeSpain, Dean of Adult and Graduate Studies, 800-742-5281, Fax: 630-844-5535, E-mail: auadmission@aurora.edu.

Austin Peay State University, College of Graduate Studies, College of Professional Programs and Social Sciences, School of Education, Clarksville, TN 37044. Offers curriculum and instruction (MA Ed); education (M Ed, Ed S); educational leadership studies (MA Ed); reading (MA Ed). *Accreditation:* NCATE. Part-time and evening/weekend programs available. Postbaccalaureate distance learning degree programs offered. *Faculty:* 24 full-time (14 women), 8 part-time/adjunct (4 women). *Students:* 81 full-time (65 women), 225 part-time (180 women); includes 48 minority (37 African Americans, 2 American Indian/Alaska Native, 1 Asian American or Pacific Islander, 8 Hispanic Americans). Average age 35. In 2006, 81 master's, 16 other advanced degrees awarded. *Degree requirements:* For master's, teaching license, thesis optional. *Entrance requirements:* For master's, GRE General Test, 3 letters of recommendation; for Ed S, GRE General Test, master's degree, minimum graduate GPA of 3.0, 3 letters of recommendation. Additional exam requirements/recommendations for international students: Required—TOEFL (minimum score 500 paper-based; 173 computer-based). *Application deadline:* For fall admission, 7/31 priority date for domestic students; for spring admission, 12/17 priority date for domestic students. Applications are processed on a rolling basis. Application fee: $25. Electronic applications accepted. *Expenses:* Tuition, state resident: full-time $5,138; part-time $272 per credit hour. Tuition, nonresident: full-time $14,832; part-time $693 per credit hour. Required fees: $1,009. *Financial support:* In 2006–07, research assistantships (averaging $10,270 per year); career-related internships or fieldwork, Federal Work-Study, institutionally sponsored loans, scholarships/grants, and unspecified assistantships also available. Support available to part-time students. Financial award application deadline: 3/1; financial award applicants required to submit FAFSA. *Unit head:* Dr. Carlette Hardin, Director, 931-221-7696, Fax: 931-221-1292, E-mail: forbusl@apsu.edu.

Averett University, Graduate Studies in Education, Danville, VA 24541-3692. Offers art education (M Ed); biology (M Ed); chemistry (M Ed); curriculum and instruction (M Ed); elementary education (M Ed); English (M Ed); health and physical education (M Ed); history and social studies (M Ed); mathematics education (M Ed); physical science (M Ed); reading (M Ed); special education (learning disabilities specialization PK-12) (M Ed). Part-time and evening/weekend programs available. *Faculty:* 10 full-time (4 women), 7 part-time/adjunct (6 women). *Students:* 14 full-time (10 women), 85 part-time (67 women); includes 20 minority (18 African Americans, 2 Asian Americans or Pacific Islanders). Average age 33. 52 applicants, 100% accepted, 40 enrolled. In 2006, 48 degrees awarded. *Degree requirements:* For master's, thesis optional. *Entrance requirements:* For master's, PRAXIS, GRE General Test, MAT or NTE, writing proficiency exam, 3 letters of recommendation, current teacher's licensure or eligibility for licensure, minimum undergraduate GPA of 3.0 in previous 2 years. Additional exam requirements/recommendations for international students: Required—TOEFL (minimum score 600 paper-based; 200 computer-based). *Application deadline:* Applications are processed on a rolling basis. Application fee: $20. *Expenses:* Contact institution. *Financial support:* In 2006–07, 23 students received support. Federal Work-Study and scholarships/grants available. Financial award application deadline: 4/1; financial award applicants required to submit FAFSA. *Faculty research:* Literary assessment-PreK-6, handwriting instruction and assessment-PreK-6, written language instruction and assessment-PreK-6 and special needs students learning styles, curriculum and instruction processes. *Unit head:* Dr. Lynn H. Wolf, Chair, 434-793-3995, Fax: 434-791-4392, E-mail: lynn.wolf@averett.edu.

Azusa Pacific University, School of Education, Department of Advanced Studies, Program in Curriculum and Instruction in a Multicultural Setting, Azusa, CA 91702-7000. Offers MA. *Accreditation:* NCATE. Part-time and evening/weekend programs available. In 2006, 42 degrees awarded. *Degree requirements:* For master's, core exams, oral presentation. *Entrance requirements:* For master's, 12 units of course work in education, minimum GPA of 3.0. Application fee: $45 ($65 for international students). *Expenses:* Tuition: Part-time $475 per credit. *Faculty research:* Diversity in teacher education programs, teacher morale, student perception of school, case study instruction. *Unit head:* Dr. Susan Warren, Director, 626-815-5416, E-mail: swarren@apu.edu.

Azusa Pacific University, School of Education, Department of Advanced Studies, Program in Teaching, Azusa, CA 91702-7000. Offers MA. *Students:* 12 full-time (11 women), 800 part-time (601 women); includes 269 minority (29 African Americans, 2 American Indian/Alaska Native, 35 Asian Americans or Pacific Islanders, 203 Hispanic Americans), 10 international. In 2006, 319 degrees awarded. *Expenses:* Tuition: Part-time $475 per credit. *Unit head:* Dr. Susan Warren, Director, 626-815-5416, E-mail: swarren@apu.edu.

Ball State University, Graduate School, Teachers College, Department of Educational Studies, Program in Curriculum and Instruction, Muncie, IN 47306-1099. Offers curriculum (MAE, Ed S). *Accreditation:* NCATE. *Students:* Average age 36. 5 applicants, 40% accepted, 1 enrolled. *Degree requirements:* For Ed S, thesis. *Entrance requirements:* For degree, GRE General Test, interview. Application fee: $25 ($35 for international students). *Financial support:* Application deadline: 3/1. *Unit head:* Barbara Graham, Head, 785-285-5460, Fax: 785-285-5489.

Bank Street College of Education, Graduate School, Department of Curriculum and Instruction, New York, NY 10025. Offers bilingual education (Ed M, MS Ed), including bilingual childhood special education, bilingual early childhood education (MS Ed), bilingual early childhood special and general education (MS Ed), bilingual early childhood special education, bilingual elementary/childhood general education (MS Ed), bilingual elementary/childhood special and general education (MS Ed), bilingual middle school general education (MS Ed), bilingual middle school special and general education, bilingual middle school special education (MS Ed); early childhood education (MS Ed); elementary/childhood education (MS Ed), including early childhood and elementary/childhood education, elementary/childhood education; infant and parent development and early intervention (Ed M, MS Ed), including infant and parent development and early intervention (MS Ed), infant and parent development and early intervention/early childhood special and general education (MS Ed), infant and parent development and early intervention/early childhood special education (Ed M); middle school education (MS Ed); museum education (MS Ed), including museum education, museum education: elementary education certification, museum education: middle school certification, museum studies; reading and literacy (Ed M, MS Ed), including advanced literacy specialization (Ed M), reading and literacy (MS Ed), teaching literacy (MS Ed), teaching literacy and elementary education (MS Ed); special education (Ed M, MS Ed), including early childhood special and general education (MS Ed), early childhood special education, elementary/childhood special and general education (MS Ed), elementary/childhood special education (MS Ed), elementary/childhood special education certification (Ed M), middle school special and general education (MS Ed), middle school special education. *Students:* 258 full-time (236 women), 451 part-time (421 women); includes 151 minority (52 African Americans, 34 Asian Americans or Pacific Islanders, 65 Hispanic Americans), 4 international. Average age 29. 474 applicants, 78% accepted, 278 enrolled. In 2006, 265 degrees awarded. *Degree requirements:* For master's, thesis. *Entrance requirements:* For master's, interview. Additional exam requirements/recommendations for international students: Required—TOEFL (minimum score 600 paper-based; 250 computer-based). *Application deadline:* For fall admission, 3/1 priority date for domestic students; for spring admission, 11/1 priority date for domestic students. Applications are processed on a rolling basis. Application fee: $50. *Expenses:* Tuition: Part-time $940 per credit. Required fees: $100 per term. *Financial support:* Career-related internships or fieldwork, Federal Work-Study, scholarships/grants, and unspecified assistantships available. Support available to part-time students. Financial award application deadline: 4/15; financial award applicants required to submit FAFSA. *Faculty research:* Conditions that support teacher learning, urban education, child centered learning experiences, experiential learning. *Unit head:* Dr. Virginia Casper, Academic Dean, 212-875-4703, Fax: 212-875-4753, E-mail: vcasper@bankstreet.edu. *Application contact:* Ann Morgan, Director of Graduate Admissions, 212-875-4403, Fax: 212-875-4678, E-mail: gradcourses@bankstreet.edu.

Barry University, School of Education, Program in Curriculum and Instruction, Miami Shores, FL 33161-6695. Offers accomplished teacher (Ed S); culture, language and literacy (TESOL) (PhD); curriculum evaluation and research (PhD); early childhood (Ed S); early childhood education (PhD); elementary (Ed S); elementary education (PhD); ESOL (Ed S); gifted (Ed S); Montessori (Ed S); PKP/elementary (Ed S); reading (Ed S); reading, language and cognition (PhD). *Students:* 2 full-time (both women), 36 part-time (27 women); includes 21 minority (12 African Americans, 9 Hispanic Americans), 6 international. 45 applicants, 33% accepted, 4 enrolled. In 2006, 4 degrees awarded. *Entrance requirements:* For doctorate, GRE, minimum GPA of 3.25. Application fee: $30. *Unit head:* Dr. Jill Farrell, Director, 305-899-3198, Fax: 305-899-4708, E-mail: jfarrell@mail.barry.edu. *Application contact:* Dave Fletcher, Director of Graduate Admissions, 305-899-3113, Fax: 305-899-2971, E-mail: dfletcher@mail.barry.edu.

Baylor University, Graduate School, School of Education, Department of Curriculum and Instruction, Waco, TX 76798. Offers MA, MS Ed, Ed D, Ed S. *Accreditation:* NCATE. Postbaccalaureate distance learning degree programs offered (minimal on-campus study). *Faculty:* 11 full-time (5 women), 2 part-time/adjunct (1 woman). *Students:* 37 full-time (27 women), 17 part-time (12 women); includes 5 minority (3 African Americans, 1 Asian American or Pacific Islander, 1 Hispanic American), 4 international. Average age 30. 19 applicants, 79% accepted. In 2006, 14 master's, 3 doctorates awarded. *Degree requirements:* For doctorate, thesis/dissertation. *Entrance requirements:* For master's and doctorate, GRE General Test or GMAT. *Application deadline:* For fall admission, 7/30 priority date for domestic students; for spring admission, 12/1 for domestic students. Applications are processed on a rolling basis. Application fee: $25. *Financial support:* Research assistantships, teaching assistantships, Federal Work-Study and institutionally sponsored loans available. *Faculty research:* Teacher education, language and literacy. *Unit head:* Dr. Betty Conaway, Graduate Program Director, 254-710-3113, Fax: 254-710-3987, E-mail: betty_conaway@baylor.edu. *Application contact:* Suzanne Keener, Administrative Assistant, 254-710-3588, Fax: 254-710-3870.

Benedictine University, Graduate Programs, Program in Education, Lisle, IL 60532-0900. Offers curriculum and instruction and collaborative teaching (M Ed); elementary education (MA Ed); leadership and administration (M Ed); reading and literacy (M Ed); secondary education (MA Ed); special education (MA Ed). Part-time and evening/weekend programs available. *Faculty:* 4 full-time (2 women), 52 part-time/adjunct (30 women). *Students:* 257 (196 women); includes 22 minority (4 African Americans, 1 American Indian/Alaska Native, 3 Asian Americans or Pacific Islanders, 14 Hispanic Americans) 2 international. Average age 33. 130 applicants, 93% accepted, 13 enrolled. In 2006, 181 degrees awarded. *Degree requirements:* For master's, thesis (for some programs), comprehensive exam. *Entrance requirements:* For master's, GRE or MAT. Additional exam requirements/recommendations for international students: Required—TOEFL (minimum score 550 paper-based; 213 computer-based). *Application deadline:* For fall admission, 9/1 for domestic students; for winter admission, 12/1 for domestic students; for spring admission, 2/15 for domestic students. Applications are processed on a rolling basis. Application fee: $40. Electronic applications accepted. *Expenses:* Contact institution. *Financial support:* Career-related internships or fieldwork and health care benefits available. Support available to part-time students. *Unit head:* Dr. Richard Campbell, Director, 630-829-6242, Fax: 630-960-1126, E-mail: rcampbell@ben.edu. *Application contact:* Kari Gibbons, Director, Admissions, 630-829-6200, Fax: 630-829-6584, E-mail: kgibbons@ben.edu.

Berry College, Graduate Programs, Graduate Programs in Education, Program in Curriculum and Instruction, Mount Berry, GA 30149-0159. Offers Ed S. *Accreditation:* NCATE. *Faculty:* 1 part-time/adjunct (0 women). *Students:* Average age 41. *Degree requirements:* For Ed S, thesis, portfolio, oral exams. *Entrance requirements:* For degree, M Ed from NCATE accredited school, minimum GPA of 3.25. Additional exam requirements/recommendations for international students: Required—TOEFL (minimum score 550 paper-based; 213 computer-based). *Application deadline:* For fall admission, 5/1 for domestic students; for spring admission, 10/1 for domestic students. Applications are processed on a rolling basis. Application fee: $25 ($30 for international students). *Expenses:* Tuition: Full-time $6,174; part-time $343 per credit hour. *Financial support:* Scholarships/grants available. Support available to part-time students. Financial award application deadline: 4/1; financial award applicants required to submit FAFSA. *Faculty research:* Curriculum development, teacher training, pedagogy. *Application contact:* Richard D. Paul, Dean of Admissions and Financial Aid, 706-236-2215, Fax: 706-290-2178, E-mail: dpaul@berry.edu.

Black Hills State University, College of Education, Spearfish, SD 57799. Offers curriculum and instruction (MS). *Accreditation:* NCATE. Part-time programs available. *Degree requirements:* For master's, thesis or portfolio. *Entrance requirements:* For master's, GRE General Test, bachelor's degree in education. *Faculty research:* Rural education, teacher/student self-concepts, teaching/learning styles, active learning technology in curriculum.

Bloomsburg University of Pennsylvania, School of Graduate Studies, College of Professional Studies, School of Education, Department of Educational Studies and Secondary Education, Program in Curriculum and Instruction, Bloomsburg, PA 17815-1301. Offers M Ed. *Accreditation:* NCATE. *Faculty:* 8 full-time (3 women). *Students:* 50 full-time (25 women), 98 part-time (60 women); includes 1 minority (Hispanic American), 3 international. Average age 31. 74 applicants, 100% accepted, 43 enrolled. In 2006, 56 degrees awarded. *Degree requirements:* For master's, thesis. *Entrance requirements:* For master's, MAT or PRAXIS, minimum QPA of 3.0. Additional exam requirements/recommendations for international students: Required—TOEFL (minimum score 550 paper-based; 213 computer-based; 79 iBT). *Application deadline:* Applications are processed on a rolling basis. Application fee: $30. Electronic

Curriculum and Instruction

Bloomsburg University of Pennsylvania (continued)
applications accepted. *Expenses:* Tuition, state resident: full-time $6,048; part-time $336 per credit. Tuition, nonresident: full-time $9,678; part-time $538 per credit. Required fees: $1,415. *Financial support:* Unspecified assistantships available. *Faculty research:* Administration.

Bob Jones University, Graduate Programs, Greenville, SC 29614. Offers accountancy (MS); Bible (MA); Bible translation (MA); Biblical studies (Certificate); broadcast management (MS); business administration (MBA); church history (MA, PhD); church ministries (MA); church music (MM); cinema and video production (MA); counseling (MS); curriculum and instruction (Ed D); divinity (M Div); dramatic production (MA); educational leadership (MS, Ed D, Ed S); elementary education (M Ed, MAT); English (M Ed, MA, MAT); fine arts (MA); graphic design (MA); history (M Ed, MA); illustration (MA); interpretative speech (MA); mathematics (M Ed, MAT); medical missions (Certificate); ministry (MM, D Min); multi-categorical special education (M Ed, MAT); music (M Ed); New Testament interpretation (PhD); Old Testament interpretation (PhD); orchestral instrument performance (MM); organ performance (MM); pastoral studies (MA); personnel services (MS, Ed S); piano pedagogy (MM); piano performance (MM); platform arts (MA); radio and television broadcasting (MS); rhetoric and public address (MA); secondary education (M Ed); studio art (MA); teaching Bible (MA); theology (MA, PhD); voice performance (MM); youth ministries (MA); M Div/MM.

Boise State University, Graduate College, College of Education, Department of Curriculum, Instruction and Foundational Studies, Doctoral Program in Curriculum and Instruction, Boise, ID 83725-0399. Offers Ed D. *Accreditation:* NCATE. Part-time programs available. *Students:* 1 (woman) full-time, 38 part-time (33 women); includes 2 minority (1 American Indian/Alaska Native, 1 Hispanic American). Average age 44. 10 applicants, 80% accepted, 1 enrolled. In 2006, 3 degrees awarded. *Degree requirements:* For doctorate, thesis/dissertation. *Entrance requirements:* For doctorate, GRE General Test, minimum GPA of 3.0. *Application deadline:* For fall admission, 7/1 priority date for domestic students; for spring admission, 11/15 priority date for domestic students. Applications are processed on a rolling basis. Application fee: $0. Electronic applications accepted. *Financial support:* In 2006–07, 4 students received support; fellowships with full tuition reimbursements available, career-related internships or fieldwork, Federal Work-Study, institutionally sponsored loans, and unspecified assistantships available. Support available to part-time students. Financial award application deadline: 3/1. *Unit head:* Dr. Keith Thiede, Coordinator, 208-426-1278, Fax: 208-426-4365, E-mail: keiththiede@boisestate.edu.

Boston College, Lynch Graduate School of Education, Department of Teacher Education/Special Education and Curriculum and Instruction, Curriculum and Instruction Specialization, Chestnut Hill, MA 02467-3800. Offers M Ed, PhD, CAES, JD/M Ed. *Students:* 87 full-time (67 women), 30 part-time (21 women); includes 17 minority (6 African Americans, 6 Asian Americans or Pacific Islanders, 5 Hispanic Americans), 12 international. 149 applicants, 45% accepted, 42 enrolled. In 2006, 37 master's, 13 doctorates, 2 other advanced degrees awarded. Terminal master's awarded for partial completion of doctoral program. *Degree requirements:* For master's and CAES, comprehensive exam; for doctorate, thesis/dissertation, comprehensive exam. *Entrance requirements:* For master's and CAES, GRE General Test or MAT; for doctorate, GRE General Test. Additional exam requirements/recommendations for international students: Required—TOEFL. Application fee: $60. *Financial support:* Fellowships with full and partial tuition reimbursements, research assistantships with full and partial tuition reimbursements, teaching assistantships with full and partial tuition reimbursements, career-related internships or fieldwork, Federal Work-Study, scholarships/grants, traineeships, tuition waivers (full and partial), and unspecified assistantships available. Support available to part-time students. Financial award applicants required to submit FAFSA. *Faculty research:* In-service education, language, bilingualism, urban education. *Application contact:* Timothy P. Blackman, Director, Graduate Admission and Financial Aid, 617-552-4214, Fax: 617-552-0398, E-mail: timothy.blackman.1@bc.edu.

Boston University, School of Education, Department of Curriculum and Teaching, Program in Curriculum and Teaching, Boston, MA 02215. Offers Ed M, MAT, Ed D, CAGS. *Students:* 16 full-time (10 women), 33 part-time (25 women). Average age 37. 68 applicants, 54% accepted. In 2006, 5 master's, 15 doctorates, 2 other advanced degrees awarded. *Degree requirements:* For master's, thesis optional; for doctorate, thesis/dissertation, comprehensive exam. *Entrance requirements:* For doctorate, GRE General Test or MAT. Additional exam requirements/recommendations for international students: Required—TOEFL. *Application deadline:* For fall admission, 2/15 priority date for domestic students; for winter admission, 11/1 priority date for domestic students. Applications are processed on a rolling basis. Application fee: $70. Electronic applications accepted. *Expenses:* Tuition: Full-time $33,330; part-time $1,042 per credit. Required fees: $462; $40. *Financial support:* Application deadline: 2/15. *Application contact:* 617-353-4237, Fax: 617-353-8937, E-mail: sedgrad@bu.edu.

Bowling Green State University, Graduate College, College of Education and Human Development, School of Education and Intervention Services, Teacher and Learning Division, Program in Curriculum and Teaching, Bowling Green, OH 43403. Offers curriculum (M Ed); master teaching (M Ed). Part-time and evening/weekend programs available. *Students:* 23 full-time (11 women), 283 part-time (242 women); includes 12 minority (2 African Americans, 1 American Indian/Alaska Native, 1 Asian American or Pacific Islander, 8 Hispanic Americans), 3 international. Average age 32. 156 applicants, 97% accepted, 101 enrolled. In 2006, 176 degrees awarded. *Degree requirements:* For master's, thesis or alternative. *Entrance requirements:* For master's, GRE General Test or PRAXIS. Additional exam requirements/recommendations for international students: Required—TOEFL. *Application deadline:* For fall admission, 3/15 priority date for domestic students. Applications are processed on a rolling basis. Application fee: $30. Electronic applications accepted. *Expenses:* Tuition, state resident: part-time $535 per hour. Tuition, nonresident: part-time $884 per hour. *Financial support:* In 2006–07, 15 research assistantships with full tuition reimbursements (averaging $6,566 per year), 8 teaching assistantships with full tuition reimbursements (averaging $18,000 per year) were awarded; career-related internships or fieldwork, Federal Work-Study, and unspecified assistantships also available. Financial award applicants required to submit FAFSA. *Faculty research:* Cognitive development in cultural context, sociocultural and activity theory, philosophy in education, performance assessment. *Unit head:* Dr. Leigh Chiarelott, Director, 419-372-7352.

Bradley University, Graduate School, College of Education and Health Sciences, Department of Curriculum and Instruction, Peoria, IL 61625-0002. Offers MA. *Accreditation:* NCATE. Part-time and evening/weekend programs available. *Students:* 1 (woman) full-time, 26 part-time (23 women). 5 applicants, 60% accepted, 3 enrolled. In 2006, 5 degrees awarded. *Degree requirements:* For master's, thesis optional. *Entrance requirements:* For master's, GRE General Test or MAT, 2 letters of recommendation. Additional exam requirements/recommendations for international students: Required—TOEFL (minimum score 550 paper-based; 213 computer-based; 79 iBT). *Application deadline:* For fall admission, 5/15 priority date for domestic and international students; for spring admission, 10/15 priority date for domestic and international students. Applications are processed on a rolling basis. Application fee: $40 ($50 for international students). *Financial support:* Research assistantships with full and partial tuition reimbursements, career-related internships or fieldwork, scholarships/grants, tuition waivers (partial), and unspecified assistantships available. Financial award application deadline: 4/1. *Unit head:* Dr. Rex Morrow, Chairperson, 309-677-3190, E-mail: rmorrow@bradley.edu. *Application contact:* Dr. Kevin Finson, Graduate Coordinator, 309-677-3196, E-mail: finson@bradley.edu.

Brandon University, Faculty of Education, Brandon, MB R7A 6A9, Canada. Offers curriculum (Diploma); curriculum studies (M Ed); education administration (M Ed, Diploma); guidance and counseling (M Ed, Diploma); special education (M Ed, Diploma). *Degree requirements:* For master's, thesis. *Entrance requirements:* For master's, minimum GPA of 3.0, teaching certificate or equivalent. Additional exam requirements/recommendations for international students: Required—TOEFL. *Faculty research:* Comparative education, environmental studies, parent/school council.

Brescia University, Program in Curriculum and Instruction, Owensboro, KY 42301-3023. Offers MSCI. Part-time and evening/weekend programs available. *Degree requirements:* For master's, action research project, portfolio. *Entrance requirements:* For master's, PRAXIS II, interview, minimum GPA of 2.5. Electronic applications accepted.

Bucknell University, Graduate Studies, College of Arts and Sciences, Department of Education, Specialization in Supervision of Curriculum and Instruction, Lewisburg, PA 17837. Offers MA, MS Ed. *Degree requirements:* For master's, thesis or alternative. *Entrance requirements:* For master's, GRE General Test, minimum GPA of 2.8. Additional exam requirements/recommendations for international students: Required—TOEFL.

Caldwell College, Graduate Studies, Program in Curriculum and Instruction, Caldwell, NJ 07006-6195. Offers MA. Part-time and evening/weekend programs available. *Degree requirements:* For master's, thesis, research paper. *Entrance requirements:* For master's, GRE General Test, MAT, interview, minimum GPA of 2.75, teaching certificate, writing sample. Additional exam requirements/recommendations for international students: Required—TOEFL (minimum score 580 paper-based; 237 computer-based). Electronic applications accepted. *Faculty research:* Early childhood, information technology, educational leadership.

California Baptist University, Program in Education, Riverside, CA 92504-3206. Offers cross-cultural language and academic development (MA Ed); educational leadership (MS Ed); educational technology (MS Ed); instructional computer applications (MS Ed); reading (MS Ed); special education (MS Ed); teaching (MS Ed). Part-time programs available. *Faculty:* 16 full-time (10 women), 16 part-time/adjunct (13 women). *Students:* 77 full-time (64 women), 408 part-time (342 women); includes 157 minority (41 African Americans, 12 American Indian/Alaska Native, 18 Asian Americans or Pacific Islanders, 86 Hispanic Americans), 2 international. 282 applicants, 70% accepted, 171 enrolled. In 2006, 63 degrees awarded. *Degree requirements:* For master's, thesis optional. *Entrance requirements:* For master's, minimum undergraduate GPA of 2.75, 12 semester hours of course work in education. Additional exam requirements/recommendations for international students: Required—TOEFL (minimum score 575 paper-based; 230 computer-based), IELTS (minimum score 7). *Application deadline:* For fall admission, 9/1 for domestic students, 7/15 priority date for international students; for spring admission, 1/3 for domestic students, 11/1 priority date for international students. Applications are processed on a rolling basis. Application fee: $45. Electronic applications accepted. *Expenses:* Tuition: Full-time $7,812; part-time $434 per unit. Required fees: $120 per semester. Tuition and fees vary according to program. *Financial support:* In 2006–07, 19 students received support. Career-related internships or fieldwork, Federal Work-Study, and scholarships/grants available. Support available to part-time students. Financial award applicants required to submit FAFSA. *Unit head:* Dr. Mary Crist, Dean, School of Education, 951-343-4313, Fax: 951-343-4516, E-mail: mcrist@calbaptist.edu. *Application contact:* Gail Ronveaux, Dean of Graduate Enrollment, 951-343-5045, Fax: 951-343-5095, E-mail: graduateadmissions@calbaptist.edu.

California State University, Bakersfield, Division of Graduate Studies and Research, School of Education, Program in Curriculum and Instruction, Bakersfield, CA 93311-1022. Offers elementary curriculum and instruction (MA); secondary curriculum and instruction (MA). *Accreditation:* NCATE. *Degree requirements:* For master's, thesis or alternative, culminating projects.

California State University, Chico, Graduate School, College of Communication and Education, Department of Education, Program in Education, Chico, CA 95929-0722. Offers curriculum and instruction (MA); educational administration (MA); linguistically and culturally diverse learners (MA); reading/language arts (MA); special education (MA). *Students:* 23 full-time (14 women), 58 part-time (45 women); includes 10 minority (2 African Americans, 1 American Indian/Alaska Native, 1 Asian American or Pacific Islander, 6 Hispanic Americans), 1 international. Average age 37. 39 applicants, 100% accepted, 32 enrolled. In 2006, 37 degrees awarded. *Unit head:* Dr. Michael Kotar, Graduate Coordinator, 530-898-6610.

California State University, Dominguez Hills, College of Education, Division of Graduate Education, Program in Curriculum and Instruction, Carson, CA 90747-0001. Offers MA. Part-time and evening/weekend programs available. *Faculty:* 2 full-time (1 woman), 4 part-time/adjunct (all women). *Students:* 3 full-time (all women), 13 part-time (9 women); includes 9 minority (5 African Americans, 1 Asian American or Pacific Islander, 3 Hispanic Americans). Average age 36. 14 applicants, 93% accepted, 6 enrolled. *Degree requirements:* For master's, comprehensive exam, registration. *Entrance requirements:* For master's, minimum GPA of 2.75. *Application deadline:* For fall admission, 6/1 for domestic students. Applications are processed on a rolling basis. Application fee: $55. *Expenses:* Tuition, nonresident: part-time $339 per unit. Required fees: $1,148 per term. Tuition and fees vary according to program. *Faculty research:* Cooperative learning, student engagement. *Unit head:* Dr. James L. Cooper, Professor, 310-243-3961, E-mail: jcooper@csudh.edu. *Application contact:* Admissions Office, 310-243-3530.

California State University, East Bay, Academic Programs and Graduate Studies, College of Education and Allied Studies, Department of Teacher Education, Hayward, CA 94542-3000. Offers education (MS), including curriculum, educational technology leadership, reading. *Faculty:* 8 full-time, 9 part-time/adjunct. *Students:* 58 full-time (41 women), 153 part-time (115 women); includes 67 minority (18 African Americans, 3 American Indian/Alaska Native, 21 Asian Americans or Pacific Islanders, 25 Hispanic Americans), 3 international. Average age 37. 98 applicants, 74% accepted, 54 enrolled. In 2006, 65 degrees awarded. *Degree requirements:* For master's, project or thesis. *Entrance requirements:* For master's, minimum GPA of 3.0 in field, 2.5 overall; teaching experience. Additional exam requirements/recommendations for international students: Required—TOEFL (minimum score 550 paper-based; 213 computer-based). *Application deadline:* For fall admission, 5/31 for domestic students, 4/30 for international students; for winter admission, 9/30 for domestic and international students; for spring admission, 12/31 for domestic students, 11/30 for international students. Application fee: $55. Electronic applications accepted. *Financial support:* Career-related internships or fieldwork, Federal Work-Study, and institutionally sponsored loans available. Support available to part-time students. Financial award application deadline: 3/2. *Unit head:* Dr. James Zarillo, Chair, 510-885-7439, E-mail: james.zarillo@csueastbay.edu. *Application contact:* My Huynh, Graduate Prospect Specialist, 510-885-2989, Fax: 510-885-4059, E-mail: my.huynh@csueastbay.edu.

California State University, Fresno, Division of Graduate Studies, School of Education and Human Development, Department of Curriculum, Teaching, and Educational Technology, Fresno, CA 93740-8027. Offers education (MA), including curriculum and instruction. *Accreditation:* NCATE. Part-time and evening/weekend programs available. *Degree requirements:* For master's, thesis or alternative. *Entrance requirements:* For master's, GRE General Test, MAT, minimum GPA of 2.75. Additional exam requirements/recommendations for international students: Required—TOEFL. Electronic applications accepted. *Faculty research:* Teacher excellence, teacher quality improvement, online assessment.

California State University, Sacramento, Graduate Studies, College of Education, Department of Teacher Education, Program in Curriculum and Instruction, Sacramento, CA 95819-6048. Offers MA. Part-time programs available. *Degree requirements:* For master's, thesis or alternative, writing proficiency exam. *Entrance requirements:* For master's, minimum GPA of 3.0, teaching credentials. Additional exam requirements/recommendations for international students: Required—TOEFL. *Application deadline:* Applications are processed on a rolling basis. Application fee: $55. Electronic applications accepted. *Financial support:* Career-related internships or fieldwork and Federal Work-Study available. Support available to part-time students. Financial award application deadline: 3/1.

California State University, San Bernardino, Graduate Studies, College of Education, Program in Curriculum and Instruction, San Bernardino, CA 92407-2397. Offers MA. *Students:* 24 full-time (17 women), 47 part-time (37 women); includes 20 minority (7 African Americans, 2 Asian Americans or Pacific Islanders, 11 Hispanic Americans). Average age 33. 42 applicants,

86% accepted, 8 enrolled. In 2006, 42 degrees awarded. Application fee: $55. *Unit head:* Dr. Angela Louque, Chair, 909-537-7621, Fax: 909-537-7510, E-mail: alouque@csusb.edu.

California State University, Stanislaus, Graduate School, College of Education, Department of Teacher Education, Turlock, CA 95382. Offers curriculum and instruction (MA Ed), including elementary education, multilingual education, reading education, secondary education. Part-time and evening/weekend programs available. *Degree requirements:* For master's, thesis. *Entrance requirements:* For master's, MAT or GRE, minimum GPA of 3.0. Additional exam requirements/recommendations for international students: Required—TOEFL (minimum score 550 paper-based; 213 computer-based).

Calvin College, Graduate Programs in Education, Grand Rapids, MI 49546-4388. Offers curriculum and instruction (M Ed); educational leadership (M Ed); learning disabilities (M Ed); literacy (M Ed). *Accreditation:* NCATE. Part-time programs available. *Faculty:* 2 full-time (both women), 6 part-time/adjunct (2 women). *Students:* 6 full-time (5 women), 87 part-time (66 women); includes 9 minority (3 African Americans, 1 American Indian/Alaska Native, 4 Asian Americans or Pacific Islanders, 1 Hispanic American). Average age 29. 26 applicants, 100% accepted. In 2006, 14 degrees awarded. *Degree requirements:* For master's, thesis or seminar; for degree. *Entrance requirements:* For master's, teaching certificate. Additional exam requirements/recommendations for international students: Required—TOEFL (minimum score 550 paper-based; 213 computer-based). *Application deadline:* For fall admission, 8/1 priority date for domestic students, 5/1 priority date for international students; for spring admission, 1/1 priority date for domestic students, 11/1 priority date for international students. Applications are processed on a rolling basis. Application fee: $0. Electronic applications accepted. *Expenses:* Tuition: Part-time $420 per credit hour. *Financial support:* In 2006–07, 19 students received support. Federal Work-Study, scholarships/grants, and tuition waivers (full and partial) available. Support available to part-time students. Financial award application deadline: 4/3. *Faculty research:* Literacy, racialized gender and gendered identity, teacher learning, learning disabilities identification. *Unit head:* Dr. Susan S. Hasseler, Associate Dean for Teacher Education, 616-526-6597, Fax: 616-526-6505, E-mail: shassele@calvin.edu. *Application contact:* Deb Abbott, Administrative Assistant, 616-526-6105, Fax: 616-526-6505, E-mail: dka2@calvin.edu.

Campbellsville University, School of Education, Campbellsville, KY 42718-2799. Offers curriculum and instruction (MAE); special education (MASE). *Accreditation:* NCATE. Part-time and evening/weekend programs available. Postbaccalaureate distance learning degree programs offered (minimal on-campus study). *Faculty:* 5 full-time (2 women), 12 part-time/adjunct (7 women). *Students:* 365 full-time (230 women); includes 20 minority (14 African Americans, 1 Asian American or Pacific Islander, 5 Hispanic Americans), 1 international. Average age 31. 80 applicants, 99% accepted, 76 enrolled. In 2006, 110 degrees awarded. *Degree requirements:* For master's, thesis, research paper. *Entrance requirements:* For master's, GRE or PRAXIS, minimum undergraduate GPA of 2.75, teaching certificate, professional growth plan, letters of recommendation, disposition assessment, entrance interview. *Application deadline:* For fall admission, 6/1 priority date for domestic students, 5/1 priority date for international students; for spring admission, 11/1 priority date for domestic students, 10/1 priority date for international students. Applications are processed on a rolling basis. Application fee: $0. Electronic applications accepted. *Expenses:* Tuition: Full-time $6,570; part-time $365 per hour. Tuition and fees vary according to program. *Financial support:* In 2006–07, 250 students received support. Institutionally sponsored loans, scholarships/grants, and unspecified assistantships available. Support available to part-time students. Financial award application deadline: 6/1; financial award applicants required to submit FAFSA. *Faculty research:* Professional development, curriculum development, school governance, assessment, special education. *Unit head:* Dr. Brenda A. Priddy, Dean, 270-789-5344, Fax: 270-789-5206, E-mail: bapriddy@campbellsville.edu. *Application contact:* Karla Deaton, Assistant Director of Admissions, 270-789-5078, Fax: 270-789-5071, E-mail: redeaton@campbellsville.edu.

Capella University, School of Education, Minneapolis, MN 55402. Offers college teaching (Certificate); curriculum and instruction (MS, PhD); education (MS); enrollment management (MS); instructional design for online learning (MS, PhD); k-12 studies in education (MS, PhD); leadership for higher education (MS, PhD); leadership in education administration (Certificate); leadership in educational administration (MS, PhD); postsecondary and adult education (MS, PhD); professional studies in education (MS, PhD); reading and literacy (MS); training and performance improvement (MS, PhD). Part-time and evening/weekend programs available. Postbaccalaureate distance learning degree programs offered (minimal on-campus study). Terminal master's awarded for partial completion of doctoral program. *Degree requirements:* For master's, integrative project, thesis optional; for doctorate, thesis/dissertation, comprehensive exam, registration. *Entrance requirements:* Additional exam requirements/recommendations for international students: Required—TOEFL (minimum score 550 paper-based; 213 computer-based), TWE (minimum score 4). Electronic applications accepted. *Faculty research:* Higher education administration, distance learning, adult education, training and curriculum design.

Caribbean University, Graduate School, Bayamón, PR 00960-0493. Offers accounting (MBA); administration and supervision (MA Ed); criminal justice (MA); curriculum and instruction (MA Ed); education (PhD); gerontology (MSN); human resources (MBA); museology, archiving and art history (MA Ed); neonatal pediatrics (MSN); physical education (MA Ed); special education (MA Ed). *Entrance requirements:* For master's, interview, minimum GPA of 2.5.

Carson-Newman College, Graduate Program in Education, Jefferson City, TN 37760. Offers curriculum and instruction (M Ed); elementary education (MAT); school counseling (M Ed); secondary education (MAT); teaching English as a second language (MATESL). *Accreditation:* NCATE. Part-time and evening/weekend programs available. *Faculty:* 5 full-time (2 women), 10 part-time/adjunct (3 women). *Students:* 77 full-time (60 women), 41 part-time (29 women); includes 2 minority (both African Americans), 27 international. Average age 32. 65 applicants, 97% accepted. In 2006, 64 degrees awarded. *Degree requirements:* For master's, thesis or alternative. *Entrance requirements:* For master's, NTE, minimum GPA of 3.0 in major, 2.5 overall. *Application deadline:* For fall admission, 7/15 priority date for domestic students. Applications are processed on a rolling basis. Application fee: $25 ($50 for international students). *Expenses:* Tuition: Part-time $270 per credit hour. *Financial support:* In 2006–07, 86 students received support. Federal Work-Study and unspecified assistantships available. Financial award application deadline: 4/1; financial award applicants required to submit FAFSA. *Unit head:* Dr. Jean Love, Chair, 865-471-3461. *Application contact:* Graduate Admissions and Services Adviser, 865-471-3460, Fax: 865-471-3875.

Castleton State College, Division of Graduate Studies, Department of Education, Program in Curriculum and Instruction, Castleton, VT 05735. Offers MA Ed. Part-time and evening/weekend programs available. *Degree requirements:* For master's, thesis or alternative. *Entrance requirements:* For master's, GRE General Test, MAT, interview, minimum undergraduate GPA of 3.0.

The Catholic University of America, School of Arts and Sciences, Department of Education, Washington, DC 20064. Offers administration, curriculum, and policy studies (MA); Catholic school leadership (MA); counselor education (MA); educational administration (PhD); educational psychology (PhD); English as a second language (MA); learning and instruction (MA); policy studies (PhD); teacher education (MA). *Accreditation:* NCATE. Part-time programs available. *Faculty:* 11 full-time (8 women), 3 part-time/adjunct (2 women). *Students:* 11 full-time (8 women), 52 part-time (34 women); includes 13 minority (9 African Americans, 1 Asian American or Pacific Islander, 3 Hispanic Americans), 2 international. Average age 35. 67 applicants, 55% accepted, 13 enrolled. In 2006, 19 master's, 2 doctorates awarded. *Degree requirements:* For master's, thesis or alternative, comprehensive exam; for doctorate, thesis/dissertation, comprehensive exam. *Entrance requirements:* For master's and doctorate, GRE General Test or MAT, 3 letters of recommendation. Additional exam requirements/recommendations for international students: Required—TOEFL (minimum score 580 paper-based; 237 computer-based). *Application deadline:* For fall admission, 2/1 priority date for domestic students; for spring admission, 11/15 priority date for domestic students. Applications are processed on a

rolling basis. Application fee: $55. Electronic applications accepted. *Expenses:* Tuition: Full-time $27,700; part-time $1,045 per credit hour. Required fees: $1,290. Part-time tuition and fees vary according to campus/location and program. *Financial support:* Research assistantships, teaching assistantships, career-related internships or fieldwork, Federal Work-Study, scholarships/grants, tuition waivers (full and partial), and unspecified assistantships available. Support available to part-time students. Financial award application deadline: 2/1; financial award applicants required to submit FAFSA. *Faculty research:* Catholic school issues, reflective teaching, cognitive psychology, urban education. *Unit head:* Dr. Merylann Schuttloffel, Chair, 202-319-5805, Fax: 202-319-5815, E-mail: schuttloffel@cua.edu.

Centenary College of Louisiana, Graduate Programs, Department of Education, Shreveport, LA 71104. Offers administration (M Ed); elementary education (MAT); secondary education (MAT); supervision of instruction (M Ed). Part-time and evening/weekend programs available. *Degree requirements:* For master's, comprehensive exam. *Entrance requirements:* For master's, GRE General Test (M Ed), PRAXIS I and PRAXIS II (MAT), teacher certification (M Ed), minimum GPA of 2.5. *Expenses:* Contact institution. *Faculty research:* Teachers as advocates for teachers, portfolio assessment, disabled readers.

Chapman University, Graduate Studies, School of Education, Concentration in Curriculum and Instruction, Orange, CA 92866. Offers MA. Part-time and evening/weekend programs available. *Faculty:* 16 full-time (11 women), 25 part-time/adjunct (14 women). *Students:* 2 full-time (both women), 38 part-time (32 women); includes 11 minority (1 African American, 1 American Indian/Alaska Native, 4 Asian Americans or Pacific Islanders, 5 Hispanic Americans). Average age 29. 17 applicants, 53% accepted, 7 enrolled. In 2006, 29 degrees awarded. *Degree requirements:* For master's, thesis optional. *Entrance requirements:* For master's, GRE General Test, MAT, or California Subject Examinations for Teachers, minimum undergraduate GPA of 2.5. Additional exam requirements/recommendations for international students: Required—TOEFL (minimum score 550 paper-based). *Application deadline:* Applications are processed on a rolling basis. Application fee: $55. Electronic applications accepted. *Expenses:* Contact institution. *Financial support:* In 2006–07, 25 students received support; fellowships, Federal Work-Study available. Financial award application deadline: 6/30; financial award applicants required to submit FAFSA. *Unit head:* Dr. Barbara Tye, Coordinator, 714-997-6781. *Application contact:* Rika Judd, Information Contact, 714-997-6786, Fax: 714-997-6713, E-mail: rjudd@chapman.edu.

Chapman University, Graduate Studies, School of Education, Program in Cultural and Curricular Studies, Orange, CA 92866. Offers PhD. *Unit head:* Dr. Joel Colbert, Director, 714-744-7076.

Christian Brothers University, Graduate Programs, School of Arts, Memphis, TN 38104-5581. Offers Catholic studies (MACS); curriculum and instruction (M Ed); educational leadership (MSEL); teacher-leadership (M Ed); teaching (MAT). Part-time and evening/weekend programs available. *Faculty:* 6 full-time (4 women), 11 part-time/adjunct (5 women). *Students:* 47 full-time (38 women), 134 part-time (104 women); includes 70 minority (68 African Americans, 1 Asian American or Pacific Islander, 1 Hispanic American), 3 international. Average age 35. In 2006, 57 degrees awarded. *Entrance requirements:* For master's, GRE, MAT. *Application deadline:* Applications are processed on a rolling basis. Application fee: $25. *Expenses:* Contact institution. *Financial support:* Institutionally sponsored loans available. Support available to part-time students. *Unit head:* Dr. Marins Carriere, Dean, 901-321-3366, E-mail: mcarrier@cbu.edu. *Application contact:* Dr. Talana L. Vogel, Director, 901-321-4101, Fax: 901-321-3408, E-mail: tvogel@cbu.edu.

City University, Graduate Division, Gordon Albright School of Education, Bellevue, WA 98005. Offers curriculum and instruction (M Ed); educational leadership (M Ed); educational leadership: principal certification (M Ed, Certificate); educational leadership: principal/program administrator certification (Certificate); educational leadership: program administrator certification (M Ed, Certificate); guidance and counseling (M Ed, Certificate); integrated arts and performance learning (M Ed); professional certification-teachers (Certificate); reading (Certificate); reading and literacy (M Ed); reading. literacy, and ESL/ELL (M Ed); teacher certification (MIT); technology, curriculum and instruction (M Ed). Part-time and evening/weekend programs available. Postbaccalaureate distance learning degree programs offered (no on-campus study). *Entrance requirements:* Additional exam requirements/recommendations for international students: Required—TOEFL (minimum score 540 paper-based; 207 computer-based); Recommended—IELTS. Electronic applications accepted.

Clarion University of Pennsylvania, Office of Research and Graduate Studies, College of Education and Human Services, Department of Education, Program in Education, Clarion, PA 16214. Offers curriculum and instruction (M Ed); early childhood (M Ed); English (M Ed); history (M Ed); literacy (M Ed); science (M Ed); technology (M Ed). *Accreditation:* NCATE. Part-time programs available. *Faculty:* 18 full-time (13 women). *Students:* 11 full-time (4 women), 54 part-time (37 women); includes 4 minority (3 African Americans, 1 Asian American or Pacific Islander). 50 applicants, 90% accepted. In 2006, 7 degrees awarded. *Degree requirements:* For master's, thesis or alternative, comprehensive exam. *Entrance requirements:* For master's, minimum QPA of 3.0, teacher certification. Additional exam requirements/recommendations for international students: Required—TOEFL (minimum score 550 paper-based; 213 computer-based; 80 iBT). *Application deadline:* For fall admission, 8/1 priority date for domestic students, 4/15 priority date for international students; for spring admission, 12/1 priority date for domestic students, 9/15 priority date for international students. Applications are processed on a rolling basis. Application fee: $30. Electronic applications accepted. *Expenses:* Tuition, state resident: part-time $336 per credit. Tuition, nonresident: part-time $538 per credit. *Financial support:* In 2006–07, 2 research assistantships with full tuition reimbursements (averaging $4,002 per year) were awarded. Support available to part-time students. Financial award application deadline: 3/1. *Application contact:* Dr. Brian Maguire, Coordinator, 814-393-2058, Fax: 814-393-2558, E-mail: bmaguire@clarion.edu.

Clark Atlanta University, School of Education, Department of Curriculum, Atlanta, GA 30314. Offers MA, Ed S. *Degree requirements:* For master's, one foreign language, thesis. *Entrance requirements:* For master's, GRE General Test, minimum undergraduate GPA of 2.5.

Clemson University, Graduate School, College of Health, Education, and Human Development, School of Education, Program in Curriculum and Instruction, Clemson, SC 29634. Offers PhD. *Accreditation:* NCATE. *Students:* 12 full-time (10 women), 18 part-time (16 women); includes 1 minority (Hispanic American), 1 international. 12 applicants, 50% accepted, 6 enrolled. In 2006, 4 degrees awarded. *Degree requirements:* For doctorate, thesis/dissertation. *Entrance requirements:* For doctorate, GRE General Test, teaching certificate. Additional exam requirements/recommendations for international students: Required—TOEFL. *Application deadline:* For fall admission, 6/1 for domestic students. Application fee: $50. *Expenses:* Tuition, state resident: full-time $8,812; part-time $450 per hour. Tuition, nonresident: full-time $18,036; part-time $760 per hour. Required fees: $474; $5 per term. *Financial support:* Application deadline: 6/1; *Unit head:* Dr. William Fisk, Graduate Coordinator, 864-656-5119, Fax: 864-656-1322, E-mail: bill252@clemson.edu.

See Close-Up on page 1109.

College Misericordia, College of Professional Studies and Social Sciences, Program in Education/Curriculum, Dallas, PA 18612-1098. Offers MS. Part-time and evening/weekend programs available. *Faculty:* 10 part-time/adjunct (4 women). *Students:* Average age 36. 8 applicants, 88% accepted, 7 enrolled. In 2006, 3 degrees awarded. *Degree requirements:* For master's, thesis or alternative. *Entrance requirements:* For master's, GRE General Test or MAT, minimum GPA of 3.0. *Application deadline:* For fall admission, 8/1 priority date for domestic students. Applications are processed on a rolling basis. Application fee: $25. Electronic applications accepted. *Expenses:* Tuition: Full-time $19,800; part-time $495 per credit. Required fees: $1,060. *Financial support:* Scholarships/grants available. Support available to part-time students. Financial award application deadline: 6/30; financial award applicants required to

Curriculum and Instruction

College Misericordia (continued)
submit FAFSA. *Unit head:* Tom O'Neill, Dean of Adult and Continuing Education, 570-674-6331, E-mail: toneill@misericordia.edu. *Application contact:* Larree Brown, Coordinator of Part-time Undergraduate and Graduate Programs, 570-674-6451, Fax: 570-674-6232, E-mail: lbrown@misericordia.edu.

The College of St. Scholastica, Graduate Studies, Program in Curriculum and Instruction, Duluth, MN 55811-4199. Offers M Ed. Part-time and evening/weekend programs available. Postbaccalaureate distance learning degree programs offered (minimal on-campus study). *Faculty:* 5 full-time (4 women), 3 part-time/adjunct (all women). *Students:* 2 full-time (1 woman), 28 part-time (19 women); includes 1 minority (Hispanic American) Average age 40. 11 applicants, 82% accepted, 5 enrolled. In 2006, 20 degrees awarded. *Degree requirements:* For master's, thesis. *Entrance requirements:* For master's, interview, minimum GPA of 2.8, current teaching license. Additional exam requirements/recommendations for international students: Required—TOEFL (minimum score 550 paper-based; 213 computer-based; 79 iBT). *Application deadline:* For fall admission, 8/1 priority date for domestic students, 8/1 for international students; for spring admission, 11/1 priority date for domestic students, 11/1 for international students. Applications are processed on a rolling basis. Application fee: $50. Electronic applications accepted. *Expenses: Contact institution. Financial support:* In 2006–07, 11 students received support. Available to part-time students. Applicants required to submit FAFSA. *Faculty research:* Distance education, organizational change, feminist pedagogy, cognitive styles, science education. *Unit head:* Dr. Kay Lutz, Program Director, 218-723-5971, Fax: 218-733-2275, E-mail: klutz@css.edu. *Application contact:* Tonya J. Roth, Graduate Recruitment Counselor, 218-723-6285, Fax: 218-733-2275, E-mail: gradstudies@css.edu.

College of Santa Fe, Department of Education, Santa Fe, NM 87505-7634. Offers at-risk youth (MA), including bilingual/multicultural education, classroom teaching, community counseling, educational administration, leadership, school counseling, self-designed program, TESOL/Multicultural; curriculum and instruction (MA); multicultural special education (MA). Part-time and evening/weekend programs available. *Entrance requirements:* For master's, minimum GPA of 3.0. *Faculty research:* Integrated curriculum, child development, brain research, learning styles, systemic issues in education.

College of the Southwest, School of Education, Hobbs, NM 88240-9129. Offers curriculum and instruction (MS); educational administration (MS); educational counseling (MS); educational diagnostician (MS). Part-time and evening/weekend programs available. Postbaccalaureate distance learning degree programs offered. *Faculty:* 2 full-time (both women), 6 part-time/adjunct (1 woman). *Students:* 41 full-time (28 women), 43 part-time (35 women); includes 24 minority (1 African American, 1 American Indian/Alaska Native, 1 Asian American or Pacific Islander, 21 Hispanic Americans), 1 international. Average age 38. 119 applicants, 29% accepted, 34 enrolled. In 2006, 26 degrees awarded. *Degree requirements:* For master's, comprehensive exam. *Entrance requirements:* For master's, GRE General Test. Additional exam requirements/recommendations for international students: Recommended—TOEFL (minimum score 550 paper-based; 213 computer-based). *Application deadline:* For fall admission, 3/1 priority date for domestic students; for spring admission, 10/1 for domestic students. Applications are processed on a rolling basis. Application fee: $50. *Expenses:* Tuition: Part-time $375 per credit hour. *Financial support:* In 2006–07, 58 students received support, including 1 research assistantship; Federal Work-Study, scholarships/grants, and tuition waivers (partial) also available. Support available to part-time students. Financial award application deadline: 4/1; financial award applicants required to submit FAFSA. *Unit head:* Dr. Dennis Atherton, Dean, 505-392-6561 Ext. 1069, Fax: 505-392-6006, E-mail: datherton@csw.edu. *Application contact:* Kerrie Mitchell, Coordinator of Financial Aid and Admissions Operations, 505-392-6563 Ext. 1048, Fax: 505-392-6006, E-mail: kmitchell@csw.edu.

The College of William and Mary, School of Education, Program in Curriculum and Instruction, Williamsburg, VA 23187-8795. Offers elementary education (MA Ed); gifted education (MA Ed); reading education (MA Ed); secondary education (MA Ed), including English education, mathematics education, modern foreign languages education, science education, social studies education; special education (MA Ed), including emotionally disturbed, learning disabled, mental retardation, resource collaborating teaching. *Accreditation:* NCATE. Part-time programs available. *Faculty:* 15 full-time (6 women), 13 part-time/adjunct (10 women). *Students:* 51 full-time (39 women), 51 part-time (45 women); includes 6 minority (all African Americans) Average age 29. 161 applicants, 68% accepted, 61 enrolled. In 2006, 68 degrees awarded. *Degree requirements:* For master's, master's project. *Entrance requirements:* For master's, GRE or MAT, minimum GPA of 2.5. Additional exam requirements/recommendations for international students: Required—TOEFL. *Application deadline:* For fall admission, 2/1 for domestic and international students; for spring admission, 10/1 for domestic and international students. Application fee: $30. *Expenses:* Tuition, state resident: full-time $6,100; part-time $260 per credit. Tuition, nonresident: full-time $18,790; part-time $725 per credit. Required fees: $3,314. Tuition and fees vary according to program. *Financial support:* In 2006–07, 10 research assistantships with full and partial tuition reimbursements (averaging $5,000 per year) were awarded; career-related internships or fieldwork, Federal Work-Study, institutionally sponsored loans, scholarships/grants, and unspecified assistantships also available. Financial award application deadline: 2/1; financial award applicants required to submit FAFSA. *Faculty research:* National Council of Teachers of Mathematics Standards, counseling, self-concept and self-esteem, special education, curriculum development. *Unit head:* Dr. John Moore, Area Coordinator, 757-221-2333, E-mail: jnmoor@wm.edu. *Application contact:* Dorothy Osborne, Director of Admissions, 757-221-2317, E-mail: dsosbo@wm.edu.

The College of William and Mary, School of Education, Program in Education Policy, Planning, and Leadership, Williamsburg, VA 23187-8795. Offers curriculum and educational technology (Ed D, PhD); curriculum leadership (Ed D, PhD); educational leadership (M Ed), including higher education administration (M Ed, Ed D, PhD), K-12 administration and supervision; educational policy, planning, and leadership (Ed D, PhD), including general education administration, gifted education administration, higher education administration (M Ed, Ed D, PhD), special education administration; gifted education administration (M Ed). *Accreditation:* NCATE. Part-time and evening/weekend programs available. *Faculty:* 10 full-time (5 women), 4 part-time/adjunct (2 women). *Students:* 51 full-time (44 women), 101 part-time (64 women); includes 28 minority (27 African Americans, 1 Hispanic American), 7 international. Average age 28. 114 applicants, 55% accepted, 42 enrolled. In 2006, 38 master's, 12 doctorates awarded. *Degree requirements:* For doctorate, thesis/dissertation, comprehensive exam. *Entrance requirements:* For master's, GRE or MAT, minimum GPA of 2.5; for doctorate, GRE or MAT, minimum GPA of 3.0. Additional exam requirements/recommendations for international students: Required—TOEFL. *Application deadline:* For fall admission, 2/1 for domestic and international students; for spring admission, 10/1 for domestic and international students. Application fee: $30. *Expenses:* Tuition, state resident: full-time $6,100; part-time $260 per credit. Tuition, nonresident: full-time $18,790; part-time $725 per credit. Required fees: $3,314. Tuition and fees vary according to program. *Financial support:* In 2006–07, 41 research assistantships with full and partial tuition reimbursements (averaging $13,300 per year) were awarded; career-related internships or fieldwork, Federal Work-Study, institutionally sponsored loans, scholarships/grants, and unspecified assistantships also available. Support available to part-time students. Financial award application deadline: 2/1; financial award applicants required to submit FAFSA. *Faculty research:* Higher education policy, faculty incentives, history of adversity, resilience, leadership. *Unit head:* Dr. Megan Tschannen-Moran, Area Coordinator, 757-221-2187, E-mail: mxtsch@wm.edu. *Application contact:* Patricia Burleson, Director of Admissions, 757-221-2317, E-mail: paburl@wm.edu.

Colorado Christian University, Program in Curriculum and Instruction, Lakewood, CO 80226. Offers MA. Part-time and evening/weekend programs available. *Degree requirements:* For master's, practicum, thesis optional. *Entrance requirements:* For master's, interviews, letters of recommendation. Additional exam requirements/recommendations for international students: Required—TOEFL. Electronic applications accepted. Expenses: Contact institution.

Columbia International University, Columbia Graduate School, Columbia, SC 29230-3122. Offers Bible teaching (MABT); Christian higher education leadership (Ed D); Christian school educational leadership (Ed D); counseling (MACN); curriculum and instruction (M Ed), including Christian school guidance, English as a second language, learning disabilities, school technology; early childhood and elementary education (MAT); educational administration (M Ed); teaching English as a foreign language (Certificate); teaching English as a foreign language and intercultural studies (MATF). Part-time and evening/weekend programs available. *Faculty:* 11 full-time (4 women), 7 part-time/adjunct (5 women). *Students:* 52 full-time (44 women), 93 part-time (59 women); includes 17 minority (11 African Americans, 2 Asian Americans or Pacific Islanders, 4 Hispanic Americans), 10 international. Average age 35. 107 applicants, 56% accepted, 41 enrolled. In 2006, 62 degrees awarded. *Degree requirements:* For master's, internships, professional project. *Entrance requirements:* For master's, Minnesota Multiphasic Personality Inventory, MAT, minimum GPA of 2.7. Additional exam requirements/recommendations for international students: Required—TOEFL. *Application deadline:* For fall admission, 8/1 priority date for domestic and international students; for winter admission, 12/15 priority date for domestic and international students; for spring admission, 1/15 priority date for domestic and international students. Applications are processed on a rolling basis. Application fee: $45. Electronic applications accepted. *Expenses:* Tuition: Part-time $400 per semester hour. Tuition and fees vary according to course load and program. *Financial support:* In 2006–07, 35 students received support. Career-related internships or fieldwork, Federal Work-Study, institutionally sponsored loans, and scholarships/grants available. Financial award application deadline: 3/17; financial award applicants required to submit FAFSA. *Unit head:* Dr. Milton Uecker, Dean, 803-807-5319, Fax: 803-786-4209, E-mail: muecker@ciu.edu. *Application contact:* Michelle MacGregor, Director of Admissions, 800-777-2227 Ext. 5335, Fax: 803-786-4209, E-mail: yescbs@ciu.edu.

Concordia University, College of Education, Portland, OR 97211-6099. Offers curriculum and instruction (elementary) (M Ed); educational administration (M Ed); elementary education (MAT); secondary education (MAT). Part-time programs available. Postbaccalaureate distance learning degree programs offered (no on-campus study). *Degree requirements:* For master's, work samples/portfolio. *Entrance requirements:* For master's, California Basic Educational Skills Test or PRAXIS I, minimum undergraduate GPA of 2.8, graduate 3.0; 2 letters of recommendation. Additional exam requirements/recommendations for international students: Required—TOEFL (minimum score 525 paper-based; 195 computer-based). Electronic applications accepted. *Faculty research:* Learner centered classroom, brain-based learning future of on-line learning.

Concordia University, College of Education, Program in Curriculum and Instruction, River Forest, IL 60305-1499. Offers MA. MA offered jointly with the Chicago Consortium of Colleges and Universities. *Accreditation:* NCATE. Part-time and evening/weekend programs available. *Degree requirements:* For master's, thesis, comprehensive exam. *Entrance requirements:* For master's, minimum GPA of 2.9. Additional exam requirements/recommendations for international students: Required—TOEFL (minimum score 550 paper-based; 195 computer-based). Electronic applications accepted. *Faculty research:* School discipline, school improvement, leadership.

Concordia University, Graduate Programs in Education, Program in Curriculum and Instruction, Seward, NE 68434-1599. Offers M Ed. *Accreditation:* NCATE. Part-time programs available. *Degree requirements:* For master's, thesis or alternative, comprehensive exam. *Entrance requirements:* For master's, GRE, MAT, or NTE, minimum GPA of 3.0, BS in education or equivalent.

Concordia University, School of Education, Irvine, CA 92612-3299. Offers curriculum and instruction (MA); education (M Ed); educational administration and administrative services credential (MA). Part-time and evening/weekend programs available. Postbaccalaureate distance learning degree programs offered (minimal on-campus study). *Faculty:* 13 full-time (6 women), 5 part-time/adjunct (3 women). *Students:* 228 full-time (185 women), 465 part-time (378 women); includes 145 minority (8 African Americans, 6 American Indian/Alaska Native, 38 Asian Americans or Pacific Islanders, 93 Hispanic Americans), 2 international. Average age 32. In 2006, 75 degrees awarded. *Degree requirements:* For master's, project or thesis. *Entrance requirements:* For master's, California Basic Educational Skills Test, California Subject Examinations for Teachers, minimum GPA of 3.0. Additional exam requirements/recommendations for international students: Required—TOEFL (minimum score 550 paper-based; 213 computer-based). *Application deadline:* For fall admission, 7/15 priority date for domestic students, 7/15 for international students; for spring admission, 11/30 priority date for domestic students, 11/30 for international students. Applications are processed on a rolling basis. Application fee: $50 ($300 for international students). *Financial support:* Application deadline: 3/2; *Unit head:* Dr. Joseph Bordeaux, Dean, 949-854-8002 Ext. 1345, Fax: 949-854-6878, E-mail: joseph.bordeaux@cui.edu. *Application contact:* Lindsay Anderson, Director of Graduate Enrollment, 949-854-8002 Ext. 1133, Fax: 949-854-6894, E-mail: lindsay.anderson@cui.edu.

Concordia University Wisconsin, Graduate Programs, Department of Education, Program in Curriculum and Instruction, Mequon, WI 53097-2402. Offers MS Ed. Postbaccalaureate distance learning degree programs offered (minimal on-campus study). *Students:* 40 (27 women). In 2006, 30 degrees awarded. *Degree requirements:* For master's, thesis or alternative, comprehensive exam. *Entrance requirements:* For master's, minimum GPA of 3.0, teaching license. Additional exam requirements/recommendations for international students: Required—TOEFL. Application fee: $35. *Financial support:* Application deadline: 8/1. *Unit head:* Dr. Ross Stueber, Head, 262-243-4285, Fax: 262-243-4428, E-mail: ross.stueber@cuw.edu. *Application contact:* Graduate Admissions, 262-243-4248, Fax: 262-243-4428, E-mail: ross.steuber@cuw.edu.

Converse College, School of Education and Graduate Studies, Education Specialist Program, Spartanburg, SC 29302-0006. Offers administration and supervision (Ed S); curriculum and instruction (Ed S); marriage and family therapy (Ed S). *Accreditation:* AAMFT/COAMFTE. Part-time programs available. *Faculty:* 7 full-time, 15 part-time/adjunct. *Students:* Average age 35. In 2006, 26 degrees awarded. *Entrance requirements:* For degree, GRE or MAT (marriage and family therapy), minimum GPA of 3.0. *Application deadline:* For fall admission, 8/1 for domestic and international students; for winter admission, 11/15 for domestic and international students; for spring admission, 1/15 for domestic students. Applications are processed on a rolling basis. Application fee: $40. Electronic applications accepted. *Expenses:* Tuition: Part-time $305 per credit hour. Required fees: $20 per term.

Coppin State University, Division of Graduate Studies, Division of Education, Baltimore, MD 21216-3698. Offers adult and general education (MS); curriculum and instruction (M Ed, MA, MS), including curriculum and instruction (M Ed), reading education (MS), teaching (MA); special education (M Ed). *Accreditation:* NCATE. Part-time and evening/weekend programs available. Postbaccalaureate distance learning degree programs offered. *Faculty:* 18 full-time (13 women), 8 part-time/adjunct (4 women). *Students:* 34 full-time (25 women), 126 part-time (91 women); includes 131 minority (all African Americans), 4 international. Average age 37. 97 applicants, 76% accepted, 66 enrolled. In 2006, 21 degrees awarded. *Degree requirements:* For master's, thesis (for some programs), comprehensive exam (for some programs), registration. *Application deadline:* For fall admission, 8/15 priority date for domestic students; for spring admission, 12/15 priority date for domestic students. Applications are processed on a rolling basis. Application fee: $45. *Financial support:* Career-related internships or fieldwork, Federal Work-Study, institutionally sponsored loans, and scholarships/grants available. Support available to part-time students. Financial award application deadline: 6/30; financial award applicants required to submit FAFSA. *Unit head:* Dr. Julius Chapman, Chair, 410-951-3082, Fax: 410-951-3089, E-mail: jchapman@coppin.edu.

Coppin State University, Division of Graduate Studies, Division of Education, Department of Curriculum and Instruction, Program in Curriculum and Instruction, Baltimore, MD 21216-3698. Offers M Ed. Part-time and evening/weekend programs available. Postbaccalaureate distance learning degree programs offered. *Faculty:* 2 full-time (both women), 1 (woman) part-time/adjunct. *Students:* 5 full-time (all women), 13 part-time (10 women); includes 13 minority (all African Americans), 1 international. Average age 41. 13 applicants, 85% accepted, 10 enrolled. In 2006, 1 degree awarded. *Degree requirements:* For master's, thesis. *Entrance requirements:* For master's, GRE or MAT, minimum GPA of 3.0, teacher certification. *Application deadline:* For fall admission, 8/15 priority date for domestic students; for spring admission, 12/15 priority date for domestic students. Applications are processed on a rolling basis. Application fee: $45. *Financial support:* Application deadline: 6/30; *Unit head:* Dr. Leontye Lewis, Chairperson, Department of Curriculum and Instruction, 410-951-3069, Fax: 410-951-3067, E-mail: llewis@coppin.edu.

Cornell University, Graduate School, Graduate Fields of Agriculture and Life Sciences, Field of Education, Ithaca, NY 14853-0001. Offers agricultural education (MAT); biology (7-12) (MAT); chemistry (7-12) (MAT); curriculum and instruction (MPS, MS, PhD); earth science (7-12) (MAT); extension, and adult education (MPS, MS, PhD); mathematics (7-12) (MAT); physics (7-12) (MAT). *Faculty:* 26 full-time (9 women). *Students:* 56 full-time (33 women); includes 10 minority (1 African American, 5 Asian Americans or Pacific Islanders, 4 Hispanic Americans), 4 international. Average age 31. 96 applicants, 40% accepted, 18 enrolled. In 2006, 22 master's, 8 doctorates awarded. Terminal master's awarded for partial completion of doctoral program. *Degree requirements:* For master's, thesis (MS); for doctorate, thesis/dissertation, comprehensive exam. *Entrance requirements:* For master's and doctorate, GRE General Test, sample of written work (recommended), 2 letters of recommendation. Additional exam requirements/recommendations for international students: Required—TOEFL (minimum score 550 paper-based; 213 computer-based). *Application deadline:* For fall admission, 2/15 for domestic students. Application fee: $60. Electronic applications accepted. *Expenses:* Tuition: Full-time $32,800. Full-time tuition and fees vary according to program. *Financial support:* In 2006–07, 31 students received support, including 4 fellowships with full tuition reimbursements available, 7 research assistantships with full tuition reimbursements available, 20 teaching assistantships with full tuition reimbursements available; institutionally sponsored loans, scholarships/grants, health care benefits, tuition waivers (full and partial), and unspecified assistantships also available. Financial award applicants required to submit FAFSA. *Faculty research:* Moral development and professional ethics; public issues education and community development; socio/political issues in public education; teacher education and curriculum in agricultural science, and mathematics; extension research. *Unit head:* Director of Graduate Studies, 607-255-4278, Fax: 607-255-7905. *Application contact:* Graduate Field Assistant, 607-255-4278, Fax: 607-255-7905, E-mail: rh22@cornell.edu.

Dallas Baptist University, Dorothy M. Bush College of Education, Program in Education in Curriculum and Instruction, Dallas, TX 75211-9299. Offers M Ed. *Faculty:* 49 full-time (21 women), 112 part-time/adjunct (46 women). Application fee: $25. *Expenses:* Tuition: Full-time $8,370; part-time $465 per credit hour. Required fees: $465 per credit hour. *Unit head:* Judy Abercrombie, Director, 214-333-5200, Fax: 214-333-5551, E-mail: graduate@dbu.edu. *Application contact:* Kit P. Montgomery, Director of Graduate Programs, 214-333-5242, Fax: 214-333-5579, E-mail: graduate@dbu.edu.

Delaware State University, Graduate Programs, Department of Education, Program in Curriculum and Instruction, Dover, DE 19901-2277. Offers MA. Part-time and evening/weekend programs available. *Degree requirements:* For master's, thesis optional. *Entrance requirements:* For master's, GRE General Test, minimum GPA of 3.0 in major, 2.75 overall. Electronic applications accepted.

DePaul University, School of Education, Doctoral Program in Education, Chicago, IL 60604-2287. Offers curriculum studies (Ed D); educational leadership (Ed D). Part-time and evening/weekend programs available. *Faculty:* 11 full-time (5 women), 1 (woman) part-time/adjunct. *Students:* 88 full-time (62 women), 131 part-time (94 women); includes 66 minority (44 African Americans, 6 Asian Americans or Pacific Islanders, 16 Hispanic Americans), 5 international. 25 applicants, 48% accepted, 10 enrolled. *Degree requirements:* For doctorate, thesis/dissertation, candidacy paper before dissertation, defense of dissertation. *Entrance requirements:* For doctorate, interview, master's degree, 3 years of work experience (recommended), writing sample, 3 letters of recommendation. Additional exam requirements/recommendations for international students: Required—TOEFL (minimum score 550 paper-based; 221 computer-based). *Application deadline:* For fall admission, 2/15 for domestic and international students. Application fee: $40. Electronic applications accepted. *Financial support:* In 2006–07, 2 research assistantships with full tuition reimbursements (averaging $6,000 per year), 1 teaching assistantship with full tuition reimbursement (averaging $6,000 per year) were awarded. Financial award applicants required to submit FAFSA. *Faculty research:* Philosophy and sociology of education, education and social justice, curriculum theory, use of technology in schools, youth and community development, education law. *Unit head:* Dr. Clara Jennings, Dean, 773-325-7581, Fax: 773-325-7728, E-mail: cjennings@depaul.edu. *Application contact:* Dr. John Bollwark, Data Projects Manager, 773-325-7582, Fax: 773-325-7748, E-mail: jbollwar@depaul.edu.

Doane College, Program in Education, Crete, NE 68333-2430. Offers curriculum and instruction (M Ed); educational leadership (M Ed). *Accreditation:* NCATE. Part-time and evening/weekend programs available. *Degree requirements:* For master's, thesis. *Entrance requirements:* For master's, minimum GPA of 2.5. Electronic applications accepted. Expenses: Contact institution.

Dominican University, School of Education, River Forest, IL 60305-1099. Offers curriculum and instruction (MA Ed); early childhood education (MS); education (MAT); educational administration (MA); literacy (MS); special education (MS). Part-time and evening/weekend programs available. *Faculty:* 17 full-time (14 women), 37 part-time/adjunct (24 women). *Students:* 65 full-time (46 women), 514 part-time (425 women); includes 78 minority (23 African Americans, 16 Asian Americans or Pacific Islanders, 39 Hispanic Americans), 2 international. Average age 34. 130 applicants, 89% accepted, 100 enrolled. In 2006, 203 degrees awarded. *Entrance requirements:* For master's, Illinois certification test of basic skills. Additional exam requirements/recommendations for international students: Required—TOEFL (minimum score 550 paper-based; 213 computer-based). *Application deadline:* Applications are processed on a rolling basis. Application fee: $25. *Expenses: Contact institution.* Tuition and fees vary according to campus/location and program. *Financial support:* In 2006–07, 63 students received support. Career-related internships or fieldwork, scholarships/grants, and tuition waivers (partial) available. Support available to part-time students. Financial award application deadline: 8/15; financial award applicants required to submit FAFSA. *Faculty research:* Governance of private education institutions, reading and language arts, inclusion, organizational planning, leadership and vision. *Unit head:* Sr. Colleen McNicholas, Dean, 708-524-6830, Fax: 708-524-6665, E-mail: educate@dom.edu. *Application contact:* Keven Hansen, Coordinator of Admissions and Recruitment, 708-524-6921, Fax: 708-524-6665, E-mail: educate@dom.edu.

Dominican University of California, Graduate Programs, School of Business, Education and Leadership, Division of Education, Program in Curriculum and Instruction, San Rafael, CA 94901-2298. Offers MS. Program also offered in Ukiah, CA. Part-time programs available. Postbaccalaureate distance learning degree programs offered. *Degree requirements:* For master's, research project. *Entrance requirements:* For master's, Dominican credential program, minimum GPA of 3.0. Additional exam requirements/recommendations for international students: Required—TOEFL (minimum score 550 paper-based; 213 computer-based). Electronic applications accepted. *Faculty research:* Parent education.

Drexel University, School of Education, Program in Science of Instruction, Philadelphia, PA 19104-2875. Offers MS. Part-time and evening/weekend programs available. *Entrance requirements:* For master's, GRE, bachelor's degree in related field. Additional exam requirements/recommendations for international students: Required—TOEFL. Electronic applications accepted.

Drexel University, School of Education, Program in Teaching, Learning and Curriculum, Philadelphia, PA 19104-2875. Offers MS.

Duquesne University, School of Education, Department of Instruction and Leadership, Pittsburgh, PA 15282-0001. Offers early childhood education (MS Ed); elementary education (MS Ed); English as a second language (MS Ed); instructional leadership excellence (Ed D); instructional technology (MS Ed, Ed D); reading and language arts (MS Ed); secondary education (MS Ed). Part-time and evening/weekend programs available. *Faculty:* 21 full-time (11 women), 17 part-time/adjunct (8 women). *Students:* 369. 128 applicants, 92% accepted, 102 enrolled. In 2006, 142 master's, 7 doctorates awarded. *Degree requirements:* For doctorate, thesis/dissertation. *Entrance requirements:* For master's, MAT, minimum GPA of 3.0; for doctorate, GRE General Test, MAT, interview, minimum GPA of 3.25. *Application deadline:* For fall admission, 8/1 priority date for domestic students; for spring admission, 12/1 priority date for domestic students. Applications are processed on a rolling basis. *Expenses:* Tuition: Part-time $723 per credit. Required fees: $71 per credit. Tuition and fees vary according to degree level and program. *Financial support:* In 2006–07, 3 research assistantships with full and partial tuition reimbursements (averaging $5,200 per year), 6 teaching assistantships with full and partial tuition reimbursements were awarded; career-related internships or fieldwork, Federal Work-Study, and institutionally sponsored loans also available. Support available to part-time students. Total annual research expenditures: $10,000. *Unit head:* Dr. Barbara Manner, Chair, 412-396-6106, Fax: 412-396-5388, E-mail: manner@duq.edu.

East Carolina University, Graduate School, College of Education, Department of Curriculum and Instruction, Greenville, NC 27858-4353. Offers behavior/emotional disabilities (MA Ed); elementary education (MA Ed); English education (MA Ed); learning disabilities (MA Ed); low incidence disabilities (MA Ed); mental retardation (MA Ed); middle grade education (MA Ed); reading education (MA Ed); social studies education (MA Ed). Part-time programs available. Postbaccalaureate distance learning degree programs offered. *Students:* 92 full-time (85 women), 233 part-time (211 women); includes 42 minority (39 African Americans, 1 American Indian/Alaska Native, 1 Asian American or Pacific Islander, 1 Hispanic American). Average age 30. 25 applicants, 100% accepted, 25 enrolled. In 2006, 195 degrees awarded. *Degree requirements:* For master's, thesis optional. *Entrance requirements:* For master's, GRE General Test or MAT, interview, bachelor's degree in related field, minimum GPA of 2.5, teaching license. Additional exam requirements/recommendations for international students: Required—TOEFL. *Application deadline:* For fall admission, 6/1 priority date for domestic students. Applications are processed on a rolling basis. Application fee: $50. *Financial support:* Research assistantships, teaching assistantships, Federal Work-Study available. Support available to part-time students. Financial award application deadline: 6/1; financial award applicants required to submit FAFSA. *Unit head:* Dr. Sandra H. Warren, Interim Chair, 252-328-2699, E-mail: warrens@ecu.edu. *Application contact:* Dean of Graduate School, 252-328-6012, Fax: 252-328-6071, E-mail: gradschool@ecu.edu.

Eastern Kentucky University, The Graduate School, College of Education, Department of Curriculum and Instruction, Richmond, KY 40475-3102. Offers elementary education general (MA Ed), including early elementary education, elementary education general, reading; music education (MA Ed); secondary and higher education (MA Ed), including agricultural education, allied health sciences education, art education, biological sciences education, business education, chemistry education, earth science education, English education, general science education, geography education, history education, home economics education, industrial education, mathematical sciences education, physical education, physics education, political science education, psychology education, reading, school health education, sociology education. *Accreditation:* NCATE. Part-time programs available. *Faculty:* 22 full-time (13 women), 18 part-time/adjunct (14 women). *Students:* 62 full-time (51 women), 300 part-time (257 women); includes 9 minority (5 African Americans, 2 American Indian/Alaska Native, 1 Asian American or Pacific Islander, 1 Hispanic American), 1 international. Average age 32. 437 applicants, 22% accepted. In 2006, 166 degrees awarded. *Entrance requirements:* For master's, GRE General Test, minimum GPA of 2.5. Application fee: $35. *Expenses:* Tuition, state resident: full-time $5,610. Tuition, nonresident: full-time $15,910. *Financial support:* In 2006–07, research assistantships (averaging $6,500 per year), teaching assistantships (averaging $6,500 per year) were awarded; career-related internships or fieldwork and Federal Work-Study also available. Support available to part-time students. *Faculty research:* Technology in education, reading instruction, e-portfolios, induction to teacher education, dispositions of teachers. *Unit head:* Dr. Michael Martin, Chair, 859-622-2154, Fax: 859-622-2004.

Eastern Michigan University, Graduate School, College of Education, Department of Teacher Education, Program in K–12 Curriculum, Ypsilanti, MI 48197. Offers MA. *Accreditation:* NCATE. Part-time and evening/weekend programs available. Postbaccalaureate distance learning degree programs offered (minimal on-campus study). *Students:* Average age 32. In 2006, 15 degrees awarded. *Entrance requirements:* For master's, GRE. Additional exam requirements/recommendations for international students: Required—TOEFL. *Application deadline:* For fall admission, 5/15 priority date for domestic students, 5/1 priority date for international students; for winter admission, 10/15 priority date for domestic students, 10/1 priority date for international students; for spring admission, 3/15 priority date for domestic students, 3/1 priority date for international students. Applications are processed on a rolling basis. Application fee: $35. *Expenses:* Tuition, state resident: part-time $341 per credit hour. Tuition, nonresident: full-time $16,104; part-time $671 per credit hour. Required fees: $816; $34 per credit hour. $40 per term. One-time fee: $82 full-time. Tuition and fees vary according to course level, course load, degree level and reciprocity agreements. *Financial support:* Fellowships, research assistantships with full tuition reimbursements, teaching assistantships with full tuition reimbursements, career-related internships or fieldwork, Federal Work-Study, institutionally sponsored loans, scholarships/grants, tuition waivers (partial), and unspecified assistantships available. Support available to part-time students. Financial award applicants required to submit FAFSA.

Eastern Washington University, Graduate Studies, College of Education and Human Development, Department of Education, Program in Curriculum and Instruction, Cheney, WA 99004-2431. Offers M Ed. *Accreditation:* NCATE. *Degree requirements:* For master's, comprehensive exam. *Entrance requirements:* For master's, minimum GPA of 3.0.

East Tennessee State University, School of Graduate Studies, College of Education, Department of Curriculum and Instruction, Johnson City, TN 37614. Offers 7-12 (MAT); classroom technology (M Ed); educational communication (M Ed); educational media/educational technology (M Ed); elementary education (M Ed, MAT); K-12 (MAT); reading and storytelling (M Ed, MA); reading education (M Ed, MA); school library media (M Ed); secondary education (M Ed, MAT). *Accreditation:* NCATE. Part-time and evening/weekend programs available. *Degree requirements:* For master's, thesis (for some programs). *Entrance requirements:* For master's, GRE, minimum GPA of 3.0. Additional exam requirements/recommendations for international students: Required—TOEFL (minimum score 550 paper-based; 213 computer-based). *Faculty research:* Critical thinking, curriculum development, cultural diversity, cognitive processes, effective teaching strategies.

Emporia State University, School of Graduate Studies, The Teachers College, Department of School Leadership/Middle and Secondary Teacher Education, Program in Curriculum and Instruction, Emporia, KS 66801-5087. Offers curriculum and instruction (MS), including curriculum leadership, effective practitioner, national board certification. *Accreditation:* NCATE. Part-time programs available. *Students:* 1 (woman) full-time, 156 part-time (140 women); includes 4 minority (1 African American, 2 American Indian/Alaska Native, 1 Hispanic American). 52 applicants, 88% accepted, 45 enrolled. In 2006, 28 degrees awarded. *Degree requirements:* For master's, comprehensive exam or thesis, practicum. *Entrance requirements:* For master's, GRE or MAT, appropriate bachelor's degree, teacher certification, 1 year of teaching experience, letters of recommendation. *Application deadline:* For fall admission, 8/15 priority date for domestic students. Applications are processed on a rolling basis. Application fee: $30 ($75 for international students). Electronic applications accepted. *Expenses:* Tuition, state resident: full-time $3,438; part-time $143 per credit hour. Tuition, nonresident: full-time $10,398; part-time $433 per credit hour. Required fees: $724; $44 per credit hour. *Financial support:* Career-related internships or fieldwork, Federal Work-Study, institutionally sponsored loans, health care benefits, and unspecified assistantships available. Financial award application

Curriculum and Instruction

Emporia State University (continued)
deadline: 3/15; financial award applicants required to submit FAFSA. *Unit head:* Dr. Jerry Will, Chair, Department of School Leadership/Middle and Secondary Teacher Education, 620-341-5777, E-mail: jwill@emporia.edu.

Fairleigh Dickinson University, Metropolitan Campus, University College: Arts, Sciences, and Professional Studies, Peter Sammartino School of Education, Program in Teaching, Teaneck, NJ 07666-1914. Offers MAT. *Students:* 44 full-time (36 women), 104 part-time (87 women). Average age 32. 75 applicants, 83% accepted, 58 enrolled. In 2006, 63 degrees awarded. *Degree requirements:* For master's, research project. *Application deadline:* Applications are processed on a rolling basis. Application fee: $40. *Unit head:* Dr. Vicki Cohen, Director, Peter Sammartino School of Education, 201-692-2525, Fax: 201-692-2603, E-mail: vicki_cohen@fdu.edu.

See Close-Up on page 877.

Ferris State University, College of Education and Human Services, School of Education, Big Rapids, MI 49307. Offers administration (MSCTE); curriculum and instruction (M Ed), including administration, elementary education, philanthropic education, reading, secondary education, special education, subject matter option; education technology (MSCTE); instructor (MSCTE); post-secondary administration (MSCTE); training and development (MSCTE). Part-time and evening/weekend programs available. Postbaccalaureate distance learning degree programs offered (no on-campus study). *Faculty:* 13 full-time (9 women), 26 part-time/adjunct (19 women). *Students:* 38 full-time (27 women), 254 part-time (164 women); includes 30 minority (22 African Americans, 1 American Indian/Alaska Native, 2 Asian Americans or Pacific Islanders, 5 Hispanic Americans), 1 international. Average age 37. 171 applicants, 99% accepted. In 2006, 92 degrees awarded. *Degree requirements:* For master's, thesis, research paper. *Entrance requirements:* For master's, 2 years of work experience, minimum GPA of 3.0. *Application deadline:* For fall admission, 6/1 priority date for domestic students; for winter admission, 12/10 priority date for domestic students. Applications are processed on a rolling basis. Application fee: $30. *Expenses:* Tuition, state resident: part-time $355 per credit hour. Tuition, nonresident: part-time $687 per credit hour. *Financial support:* Career-related internships or fieldwork and tuition waivers (full and partial) available. Support available to part-time students. Financial award applicants required to submit FAFSA. *Faculty research:* Suicide prevention, reading, women in education, special needs, administration. *Unit head:* Interim Director, 231-591-5362, Fax: 231-591-2041. *Application contact:* Sigrid Robertson, Secretary, 231-591-3511, Fax: 231-591-2041, E-mail: robertss@ferris.edu.

Florida Atlantic University, College of Education, Department of Teacher Education, Boca Raton, FL 33431-0991. Offers art teacher education (M Ed); curriculum and instruction (M Ed, Ed D, Ed S); educational psychology (MSF); elementary education (M Ed); foundations of education (M Ed); multicultural education (MSF); reading teacher education (M Ed). *Accreditation:* NCATE. Part-time and evening/weekend programs available. *Faculty:* 29 full-time (23 women), 75 part-time/adjunct (50 women). *Students:* 78 full-time (65 women), 176 part-time (159 women); includes 50 minority (20 African Americans, 1 American Indian/Alaska Native, 6 Asian Americans or Pacific Islanders, 23 Hispanic Americans), 1 international. Average age 35. 132 applicants, 64% accepted, 62 enrolled. In 2006, 95 master's, 2 doctorates awarded. *Degree requirements:* For master's, registration; for doctorate, thesis/dissertation, departmental qualifying exam, comprehensive exam, registration; for Ed S, departmental qualifying exam. *Entrance requirements:* For master's, GRE General Test, minimum GPA of 3.0 in last 2 years of undergraduate course work; for doctorate, GRE General Test, GRE Subject Test, minimum graduate GPA of 3.2, 3.0 in last 2 years of undergraduate course work; for Ed S, GRE General Test. Additional exam requirements/recommendations for international students: Required—TOEFL. *Application deadline:* Applications are processed on a rolling basis. Application fee: $30. *Expenses:* Tuition, area resident: Full-time $4,394. Tuition, nonresident: full-time $16,441. *Financial support:* In 2006–07, 4 research assistantships with partial tuition reimbursements (averaging $8,000 per year), 3 teaching assistantships with partial tuition reimbursements (averaging $8,000 per year) were awarded; fellowships with partial tuition reimbursements, career-related internships or fieldwork, scholarships/grants, and unspecified assistantships also available. *Faculty research:* Technology, teaching English to speakers of other languages, math teaching, electronic portfolio assessment, global perspectives through social studies. *Unit head:* Dr. Penelope Fritzer, Chairperson, 561-297-3584.

Florida Gulf Coast University, College of Education, Program in Curriculum and Instruction, Fort Myers, FL 33965-6565. Offers educational technology (M Ed, MA). Part-time and evening/weekend programs available. Postbaccalaureate distance learning degree programs offered (minimal on-campus study). *Faculty:* 31 full-time (21 women), 30 part-time/adjunct (24 women). *Students:* 41 full-time (23 women), 7 part-time (3 women); includes 7 minority (2 African Americans, 5 Hispanic Americans). Average age 39. 16 applicants, 81% accepted, 8 enrolled. In 2006, 11 degrees awarded. *Degree requirements:* For master's, final project or portfolio. *Entrance requirements:* For master's, GRE General Test, MAT, minimum undergraduate GPA of 3.0 in last 2 years. Additional exam requirements/recommendations for international students: Required—TOEFL (minimum score 550 paper-based; 213 computer-based). *Application deadline:* For fall admission, 7/1 priority date for domestic students; for spring admission, 10/15 for domestic students. Applications are processed on a rolling basis. Application fee: $30. Electronic applications accepted. *Expenses:* Tuition, state resident: full-time $4,326. Tuition, nonresident: full-time $18,523. Required fees: $1,211. One-time fee: $5 full-time. *Faculty research:* Internet in schools, technology in pre-service and in-service teacher training. *Unit head:* Dr. Pat Wachholz, Associate Dean, 239-590-7808, Fax: 239-590-7801, E-mail: wachhol@fgcu.edu.

Florida International University, College of Education, Department of Curriculum and Instruction, Miami, FL 33199. Offers art education (MAT, MS, Ed D); curriculum and instruction (Ed S); curriculum development (MS); curriculum studies (PhD); early childhood education (MS, Ed D); elementary education (MS, Ed D); English education (MAT, MS, Ed D); foreign language education—teaching English to speakers of other languages (TESOL) (Certificate), including foreign language education; foreign language education—teaching English to speakers of other languages (TESOL) (MS), including teaching English; French education—initial teacher preparation (MAT); international and intercultural development education (Ed D); international and intercultural developmental education (MS); language, literacy and culture (PhD); learning technologies (MS, Ed D, PhD); mathematics education (MAT, MS, Ed D, PhD); modern language education/bilingual education (MS, Ed D); physical education (MS); reading education (MS, Ed D); science education (MAT, MS, Ed D, PhD); social studies education (MAT, MS, Ed D); Spanish education—initial teacher preparation (MAT); special education (MS). Part-time and evening/weekend programs available. *Faculty:* 19 full-time (11 women). *Students:* 89 full-time (66 women), 258 part-time (221 women); includes 99 minority (72 African Americans, 10 Asian Americans or Pacific Islanders, 17 Hispanic Americans). Average age 35. 167 applicants, 50% accepted, 81 enrolled. In 2006, 141 master's, 8 doctorates, 1 other advanced degree awarded. *Degree requirements:* For doctorate, thesis/dissertation, comprehensive exam, registration. *Entrance requirements:* For master's, GRE General Test, Florida General Knowledge Test or Florida College Level Academic Skills Test; for doctorate and other advanced degree, GRE General Test. Additional exam requirements/recommendations for international students: Required—TOEFL (minimum score 550 paper-based; 213 computer-based; 80 iBT), IELTS (minimum score 6). *Application deadline:* For fall admission, 6/1 priority date for domestic students, 4/1 for international students; for winter admission, 10/1 priority date for domestic students, 9/1 for international students; for spring admission, 3/1 priority date for domestic students, 2/1 for international students. Applications are processed on a rolling basis. Application fee: $30. Electronic applications accepted. *Expenses:* Tuition, state resident: part-time $249 per credit hour. Tuition, nonresident: part-time $753 per credit hour. Tuition and fees vary according to program. *Financial support:* Research assistantships with full and partial tuition reimbursements, teaching assistantships with full and partial tuition reimbursements available. *Unit head:* Dr. Lisbeth Dixon-Krauss, Interim Chairperson, 305-348-3609,

Fax: 305-348-2086, E-mail: kraussl@fiu.edu. *Application contact:* Marisa Salazar, Student Recruiter, 305-348-3002, Fax: 305-348-3227, E-mail: marisa.salazar@fiu.edu.

Fordham University, Graduate School of Education, Division of Curriculum and Teaching, New York, NY 10023. Offers adult education (MS, MSE); bilingual teacher education (MSE); curriculum and teaching (MSE); early childhood education (MSE); elementary education (MST); language, literacy, and learning (PhD); reading education (MSE, Adv C); secondary education (MAT, MSE); special education (MSE, Adv C); teaching English as a second language (MSE). *Accreditation:* NCATE. *Faculty:* 22 full-time (18 women), 38 part-time/adjunct (28 women). *Students:* 68 full-time (51 women), 663 part-time (612 women); includes 200 minority (74 African Americans, 1 American Indian/Alaska Native, 37 Asian Americans or Pacific Islanders, 88 Hispanic Americans), 3 international. Average age 32. 636 applicants, 86% accepted, 322 enrolled. In 2006, 351 master's, 8 doctorates awarded. *Degree requirements:* For doctorate and Adv C, thesis/dissertation. *Entrance requirements:* For doctorate, MAT, GRE General Test. Application fee: $65. *Financial support:* Applicants required to submit FAFSA. *Unit head:* Dr. Terry Osborn, Chairperson, 212-636-6450.

Framingham State College, Division of Graduate and Continuing Education, Program in Curriculum and Instructional Technology, Framingham, MA 01701-9101. Offers M Ed. *Students:* 60. In 2006, 30 degrees awarded. *Unit head:* Dr. Claire Graham, Coordinator, 508-224-1550, Fax: 508-626-4030, E-mail: czgraham@hotmail.com. *Application contact:* 508-626-4550, Fax: 508-626-4030, E-mail: dgce@frc.mass.edu.

Franciscan University of Steubenville, Graduate Programs, Department of Education, Steubenville, OH 43952-1763. Offers administration (MS Ed); teaching (MS Ed). Part-time and evening/weekend programs available. *Degree requirements:* For master's, project. *Entrance requirements:* For master's, minimum undergraduate GPA of 2.5 or written exam. Expenses: Contact institution.

Freed-Hardeman University, Program in Education, Henderson, TN 38340-2399. Offers curriculum and instruction (M Ed); school counseling (M Ed); school leadership (Ed S). *Accreditation:* NCATE. Part-time and evening/weekend programs available. *Faculty:* 9 full-time (3 women), 6 part-time/adjunct (4 women). *Students:* 51 full-time (40 women), 286 part-time (235 women); includes 203 minority (202 African Americans, 1 Asian American or Pacific Islander), 2 international. Average age 34. In 2006, 78 master's, 24 other advanced degrees awarded. *Degree requirements:* For master's, thesis optional; for Ed S, thesis. *Entrance requirements:* For master's, GRE General Test or NTE; for Ed S, 3 years of teaching experience. Additional exam requirements/recommendations for international students: Required—TOEFL (minimum score 500 paper-based; 173 computer-based). *Application deadline:* For fall admission, 8/1 for domestic students; for spring admission, 12/1 for domestic students. Applications are processed on a rolling basis. Application fee: $32. *Expenses:* Tuition: Part-time $334 per credit hour. Required fees: $10 per credit hour. *Financial support:* Career-related internships or fieldwork, Federal Work-Study, tuition waivers (partial), and unspecified assistantships available. Support available to part-time students. Financial award application deadline: 8/1; financial award applicants required to submit FAFSA. *Unit head:* Dr. Elizabeth Saunders, Graduate Director, 731-989-6082, Fax: 731-989-6065, E-mail: esaunders@fhu.edu.

Fresno Pacific University, Graduate Programs, Programs in Education, Fresno, CA 93702-4709. Offers administration (MA Ed), including administrative services; foundations, curriculum and teaching (MA Ed), including curriculum and teaching, school library and information technology; language, literacy, and culture (MA Ed), including bilingual/cross-cultural education, language development, multilingual contexts, reading; mathematics/science/computer education (MA Ed), including educational technology, integrated mathematics/science education, mathematics education; pupil personnel services (MA Ed), including school counseling, school psychology; special education (MA Ed), including mild/moderate, moderate/severe, physical and health impairments. Part-time and evening/weekend programs available. *Faculty:* 12 full-time (5 women), 19 part-time/adjunct (9 women). *Students:* 73 full-time (59 women), 399 part-time (295 women); includes 136 minority (9 African Americans, 5 American Indian/Alaska Native, 12 Asian Americans or Pacific Islanders, 110 Hispanic Americans), 2 international. Average age 39. 124 applicants, 73% accepted, 10 enrolled. In 2006, 128 degrees awarded. *Degree requirements:* For master's, thesis (for some programs), registration. *Entrance requirements:* For master's, interview; GMAT, GRE, MAT, or 6 units of course work with a faculty recommendation. Additional exam requirements/recommendations for international students: Required—TOEFL (minimum score 550 paper-based; 213 computer-based). *Application deadline:* For fall admission, 7/15 for domestic and international students; for spring admission, 11/15 for domestic and international students. Applications are processed on a rolling basis. Application fee: $90. Electronic applications accepted. *Expenses:* Tuition: Full-time $7,470; part-time $415 per credit. *Financial support:* In 2006–07, 260 students received support. Career-related internships or fieldwork, scholarships/grants, and tuition waivers (full and partial) available. Support available to part-time students. Financial award applicants required to submit FAFSA.

Fresno Pacific University, Graduate Programs, Programs in Education, Division of Foundations, Curriculum and Teaching, Program in Curriculum and Teaching, Fresno, CA 93702-4709. Offers MA Ed. Part-time and evening/weekend programs available. *Students:* 3 full-time (all women), 35 part-time (33 women); includes 12 minority (1 American Indian/Alaska Native, 1 Asian American or Pacific Islander, 10 Hispanic Americans). Average age 38. 23 applicants, 78% accepted, 3 enrolled. In 2006, 3 degrees awarded. *Degree requirements:* For master's, thesis or alternative, registration. *Entrance requirements:* Additional exam requirements/recommendations for international students: Required—TOEFL (minimum score 550 paper-based; 213 computer-based). *Application deadline:* For fall admission, 7/15 for domestic and international students; for spring admission, 11/15 for domestic and international students. Applications are processed on a rolling basis. Application fee: $90. Electronic applications accepted. *Expenses:* Tuition: Full-time $7,470; part-time $415 per credit. *Financial support:* In 2006–07, 18 students received support. Scholarships/grants and tuition waivers (full and partial) available. Support available to part-time students. Financial award applicants required to submit FAFSA. *Unit head:* Dr. Jeanne Janzen, Director, 559-453-5550, Fax: 559-453-2001, E-mail: jjanzen@fresno.edu.

Frostburg State University, Graduate School, College of Education, Department of Educational Professions, Program in Curriculum and Instruction, Frostburg, MD 21532-1099. Offers educational technology (M Ed); elementary education (M Ed); secondary education (M Ed). Part-time and evening/weekend programs available. *Degree requirements:* For master's, thesis or alternative. *Entrance requirements:* For master's, teaching certificate. Electronic applications accepted.

Gannon University, School of Graduate Studies, College of Humanities, Business, and Education, School of Education, Program in Curriculum and Instruction, Erie, PA 16541-0001. Offers M Ed. Part-time and evening/weekend programs available. Postbaccalaureate distance learning degree programs offered (no on-campus study). *Students:* 6 full-time (all women), 347 part-time (245 women); includes 6 minority (5 African Americans, 1 American Indian/Alaska Native). Average age 30. 84 applicants, 95% accepted, 38 enrolled. In 2006, 202 degrees awarded. *Degree requirements:* For master's, research project. *Entrance requirements:* For master's, interview, teaching certificate. Additional exam requirements/recommendations for international students: Required—TOEFL (minimum score 500 paper-based; 173 computer-based). *Application deadline:* Applications are processed on a rolling basis. Application fee: $25. *Expenses:* Tuition: Full-time $12,240; part-time $680 per credit. Required fees: $496; $16 per credit. Tuition and fees vary according to course load, degree level, campus/location and program. *Financial support:* Available to part-time students. Application deadline: 7/1; *Application contact:* Debra Meszaros, Director of Graduate Recruitment, 814-871-5819, Fax: 814-871-5827, E-mail: cfal@gannon.edu.

Gardner-Webb University, Graduate School, Department of Education, Program in Curriculum and Instruction, Boiling Springs, NC 28017. Offers Ed D. In 2006, 8 degrees awarded. *Expenses:* Tuition: Full-time $3,144; part-time $262 per hour. *Unit head:* Dr. Donna Simmons, Chair, Department of Education, 704-406-4406, Fax: 704-406-3921, E-mail: dsimmons@gardner-webb.edu.

The George Washington University, Graduate School of Education and Human Development, Department of Teacher Preparation and Special Education, Program in Curriculum and Instruction, Washington, DC 20052. Offers MA Ed, Ed D, Ed S. *Accreditation:* NCATE. Evening/weekend programs available. *Degree requirements:* For master's and Ed S, comprehensive exam; for doctorate, thesis/dissertation, comprehensive exam. *Entrance requirements:* For master's, GRE General Test or MAT, minimum GPA of 2.75, resumé; for doctorate and Ed S, GRE General Test or MAT, interview, minimum GPA of 3.3. *Faculty research:* Cognitive skills-teaching, metacognitive strategies, adult basic literacy.

Georgia Southern University, Jack N. Averitt College of Graduate Studies, College of Education, Department of Curriculum, Foundations, and Reading, Program in Curriculum Studies, Statesboro, GA 30460. Offers Ed D. Part-time and evening/weekend programs available. *Students:* 44 full-time (36 women), 193 part-time (159 women); includes 51 minority (46 African Americans, 2 Asian Americans or Pacific Islanders, 3 Hispanic Americans), 1 international. Average age 40. 32 applicants, 69% accepted, 13 enrolled. In 2006, 14 degrees awarded. *Degree requirements:* For doctorate, thesis/dissertation, exams. *Entrance requirements:* For doctorate, GRE or MAT, letters of reference, minimum GPA 3.5, writing sample. Additional exam requirements/recommendations for international students: Required—TOEFL (minimum score 550 paper-based; 213 computer-based; 80 iBT). *Application deadline:* For fall admission, 3/1 priority date for domestic students, 3/1 for international students; for spring admission, 10/1 priority date for domestic students, 10/1 for international students. Application fee: $50. *Financial support:* In 2006–07, 85 students received support, including research assistantships with partial tuition reimbursements available (averaging $9,500 per year), teaching assistantships with partial tuition reimbursements available (averaging $9,500 per year); career-related internships or fieldwork, Federal Work-Study, scholarships/grants, and unspecified assistantships also available. Support available to part-time students. Financial award application deadline: 4/15; financial award applicants required to submit FAFSA. *Unit head:* Dr. Gregory Dmitriyev, Coordinator, 912-681-5545, E-mail: gregodmi@georgiasouthern.edu. *Application contact:* 912-681-5384, Fax: 912-681-0740, E-mail: gradadmissions@georgiasouthern.edu.

Grambling State University, School of Graduate Studies and Research, College of Education, Department of Educational Leadership, Grambling, LA 71245. Offers curriculum and instruction (Ed D); developmental education (Ed D); educational leadership (M Ed, Ed D); special education (M Ed). Part-time and evening/weekend programs available. Postbaccalaureate distance learning degree programs offered (minimal on-campus study). *Faculty:* 8 full-time (1 woman), 2 part-time/adjunct (0 women). *Students:* 19 full-time (17 women), 63 part-time (49 women); includes 59 minority (58 African Americans, 1 Asian American or Pacific Islander), 2 international. Average age 41. In 2006, 5 master's, 4 doctorates awarded. *Degree requirements:* For master's, thesis (for some programs), comprehensive exam; for doctorate, thesis/dissertation, comprehensive exam. *Entrance requirements:* For master's, GRE, TOEFL, minimum GPA of 2.5 on last degree; for doctorate, GRE, master's degree, minimum 1000 on GRE, minimum GPA of 3.0 on last degree, minimum 500 on GRE Verbal. *Application deadline:* For fall admission, 7/1 for domestic students; for spring admission, 12/1 for domestic students. Application fee: $20 ($30 for international students). *Expenses:* Tuition, state resident: full-time $2,232; part-time $124 per credit hour. Tuition, nonresident: full-time $7,582; part-time $124 per credit hour. Required fees: $1,127. *Financial support:* In 2006–07, 59 students received support, including 7 research assistantships (averaging $5,786 per year); institutionally sponsored loans and unspecified assistantships also available. Financial award application deadline: 5/31; financial award applicants required to submit FAFSA. *Unit head:* Dr. Olatunde Ogunyemi, Director, 318-274-6105, Fax: 318-274-2799, E-mail: ogunymio@gram.edu.

Harvard University, Graduate School of Education, Master's Programs in Education, Cambridge, MA 02138. Offers arts in education (Ed M); education policy and management (Ed M); higher education (Ed M); human development and psychology (Ed M); international education policy (Ed M); language and literacy (Ed M); learning and teaching (Ed M); mid-career mathematics and science (teaching certificate) (Ed M); mind brain and education (Ed M); risk and prevention (Ed M); school leadership (Ed M); special studies (Ed M); teaching and curriculum (teaching certificate) (Ed M); technology innovation and education (Ed M). Part-time programs available. *Faculty:* 58 full-time (25 women), 40 part-time/adjunct (22 women). *Students:* 540 full-time (412 women), 90 part-time (70 women); includes 137 minority (49 African Americans, 2 American Indian/Alaska Native, 61 Asian Americans or Pacific Islanders, 25 Hispanic Americans), 70 international. Average age 29. 1,211 applicants, 61% accepted, 585 enrolled. In 2006, 591 degrees awarded. *Entrance requirements:* For master's, GRE General Test, 3 letters of recommendation, official transcripts, statement of purpose. Additional exam requirements/recommendations for international students: Required—TOEFL (minimum score 600 paper-based; 250 computer-based; 100 iBT), TWE (minimum score 5). *Application deadline:* For fall admission, 1/2 for domestic and international students. Application fee: $85. Electronic applications accepted. *Expenses: Contact institution. Financial support:* In 2006–07, 392 students received support, including 23 fellowships (averaging $15,870 per year); career-related internships or fieldwork, Federal Work-Study, institutionally sponsored loans, scholarships/grants, health care benefits, tuition waivers (full and partial), and unspecified assistantships also available. Support available to part-time students. Financial award application deadline: 2/2; financial award applicants required to submit FAFSA. *Faculty research:* Learning and development; educational leadership and organizations; educational policy analysis. Total annual research expenditures: $14.8 million. *Unit head:* Dr. James Stiles, Associate Dean for Degree Programs. *Application contact:* Information Contact, 617-495-3414, Fax: 617-496-3577, E-mail: gseadmissions@harvard.edu.

Henderson State University, Graduate Studies, School of Education, Department of Curriculum, Instruction and Leadership, Arkadelphia, AR 71999-0001. Offers early childhood (P-4) (MSE); English (MSE); English as a second language (MSE, CP); math (MSE); middle school (MSE); reading (MSE); social science (MSE). *Accreditation:* NCATE. Part-time programs available. *Faculty:* 19 full-time (6 women), 4 part-time/adjunct (2 women). *Students:* 38 full-time (36 women), 49 part-time (47 women); includes 6 minority (5 African Americans, 1 Hispanic American), 16 international. Average age 37. In 2006, 31 degrees awarded. *Entrance requirements:* For master's, GRE General Test or MAT, minimum GPA of 2.7, teacher certification. *Application deadline:* For fall admission, 5/1 priority date for domestic students, 5/1 for international students; for winter admission, 10/1 for international students; for spring admission, 12/1 priority date for domestic students, 4/1 for international students. Applications are processed on a rolling basis. Application fee: $0 ($30 for international students). *Expenses:* Tuition, state resident: full-time $3,294; part-time $183 per credit hour. Tuition, nonresident: full-time $6,588; part-time $366 per credit hour. Required fees: $176 per term. *Financial support:* In 2006–07, 1 teaching assistantship with full tuition reimbursement (averaging $4,000 per year) was awarded; research assistantships, Federal Work-Study and institutionally sponsored loans also available. Support available to part-time students. Financial award application deadline: 7/31. *Unit head:* Dr. Kenneth Harris, Chairperson, 870-230-5203, Fax: 870-230-5455, E-mail: harris@hsu.edu. *Application contact:* Dr. Marck L. Beggs, Graduate Dean, 870-230-5126, Fax: 870-230-5479, E-mail: beggsm@hsu.edu.

Henderson State University, Graduate Studies, School of Education, Department of Educational Leadership and Special Education, Arkadelphia, AR 71999-0001. Offers early childhood special education (MSE); education (MAT); educational leadership (Ed S); instructional specialist (MSE); school administration (MSE). *Faculty:* 7 full-time (4 women), 3 part-time/adjunct (2 women). *Students:* 6 full-time (3 women), 144 part-time (113 women); includes 14 minority (all African Americans) Average age 35. In 2006, 18 degrees awarded. *Expenses:* Tuition, state resident: full-time $3,294; part-time $183 per credit hour. Tuition, nonresident: full-time $6,588; part-time $366 per credit hour. Required fees: $176 per term. *Unit head:* Dr. Bruce Smith, Chairperson, 870-230-5282. *Application contact:* Dr. Marck L. Beggs, Graduate Dean, 870-230-5126, Fax: 870-230-5479, E-mail: beggsm@hsu.edu.

Holy Names University, Graduate Division, Department of Education, Oakland, CA 94619-1699. Offers advanced curriculum studies (M Ed); educational therapy (M Ed); mild/moderate disabilities (Ed S); multiple subject credential (M Ed); single subject credential (M Ed); special education (M Ed); teaching English as a second language (M Ed, Certificate); urban education (M Ed). Part-time programs available. *Faculty:* 6 full-time (all women), 9 part-time/adjunct (all women). *Students:* 17 full-time (14 women), 131 part-time (90 women); includes 58 minority (36 African Americans, 1 American Indian/Alaska Native, 11 Asian Americans or Pacific Islanders, 10 Hispanic Americans). Average age 40. 75 applicants, 80% accepted, 49 enrolled. In 2006, 11 master's, 29 Certificates awarded. *Degree requirements:* For master's, research paper, thesis or project. *Entrance requirements:* For master's, minimum undergraduate GPA of 2.6 overall, 3.0 in major. Additional exam requirements/recommendations for international students: Required—TOEFL. *Application deadline:* For fall admission, 8/1 priority date for domestic students; for spring admission, 12/1 priority date for domestic students. Applications are processed on a rolling basis. Application fee: $50. *Expenses:* Tuition: Full-time $10,800; part-time $600 per unit. Required fees: $240; $120 per term. *Financial support:* In 2006–07, 67 students received support. Scholarships/grants available. Support available to part-time students. Financial award application deadline: 3/2; financial award applicants required to submit FAFSA. *Faculty research:* Cognitive development, language development, learning handicaps. *Unit head:* Dr. Zaida McCall-Perez, Chairperson, 510-436-1288, E-mail: mccall-perez@hnu.edu. *Application contact:* 800-430-1351, Fax: 510-436-1325, E-mail: admissions@hnu.edu.

Hood College, Graduate School, Department of Education, Frederick, MD 21701-8575. Offers curriculum and instruction (MS), including early childhood education, elementary education, elementary school science and mathematics, secondary education, special education; educational leadership (MS); reading specialization (MS); teaching the struggling reader (Certificate). Part-time and evening/weekend programs available. *Faculty:* 4 full-time (3 women), 32 part-time/adjunct (16 women). *Students:* 5 full-time (3 women), 371 part-time (313 women); includes 30 minority (23 African Americans, 4 Asian Americans or Pacific Islanders, 3 Hispanic Americans). Average age 32. 71 applicants, 99% accepted, 59 enrolled. In 2006, 67 degrees awarded. *Degree requirements:* For master's, action research project, portfolio (reading). *Entrance requirements:* For master's, minimum GPA of 2.5, teaching certification. *Application deadline:* Applications are processed on a rolling basis. Application fee: $35. *Expenses:* Tuition: Part-time $350 per credit. Required fees: $20 per semester. *Financial support:* Applicants required to submit FAFSA. *Faculty research:* Leadership, action research, brain research, learning styles. *Unit head:* Dr. John George, Chairperson, 301-696-3471, Fax: 301-696-3597, E-mail: george@hood.edu. *Application contact:* Dr. Kathleen C. Bands, Associate Dean of Graduate School, 301-696-3811, Fax: 301-696-3597, E-mail: gofurther@hood.edu.

Houston Baptist University, College of Education and Behavioral Sciences, Programs in Education, Houston, TX 77074-3298. Offers bilingual education (M Ed); counselor education (M Ed); curriculum and instruction (M Ed); educational administration (M Ed); educational diagnostician (M Ed); reading education (M Ed). Part-time programs available. *Degree requirements:* For master's, registration. *Entrance requirements:* For master's, GRE General Test or MAT. Additional exam requirements/recommendations for international students: Required—TOEFL (minimum score 550 paper-based; 213 computer-based).

Idaho State University, Office of Graduate Studies, College of Education, Department of Educational Foundations, Pocatello, ID 83209. Offers child and family studies (M Ed); curriculum leadership (M Ed); education (M Ed); educational administration (M Ed); educational foundations (5th Year Certificate); elementary education (M Ed), including K-12 education, literacy, secondary education. Part-time and evening/weekend programs available. Postbaccalaureate distance learning degree programs offered (no on-campus study). *Faculty:* 12 full-time (8 women). *Students:* 16 full-time (11 women), 161 part-time (102 women); includes 2 minority (1 Asian American or Pacific Islander, 1 Hispanic American), 2 international. Average age 40. In 2006, 15 degrees awarded. *Degree requirements:* For master's, oral exam, written exam, thesis optional; for 5th Year Certificate, thesis (for some programs), oral exam, written exam, comprehensive exam, registration (for some programs). *Entrance requirements:* For master's, GRE General Test or MAT, minimum undergraduate GPA of 3.0; for 5th Year Certificate, GRE General Test, minimum undergraduate GPA of 3.0, master's degree. Additional exam requirements/recommendations for international students: Required—TOEFL (minimum score 550 paper-based; 213 computer-based; 80 iBT). *Application deadline:* For fall admission, 7/1 for domestic students, 6/1 for international students; for spring admission, 12/1 for domestic students, 11/1 for international students. Applications are processed on a rolling basis. Application fee: $55. *Expenses:* Tuition, state resident: part-time $251 per credit. Tuition, nonresident: part-time $366 per credit. Tuition and fees vary according to degree level, program and reciprocity agreements. *Financial support:* Career-related internships or fieldwork, Federal Work-Study, institutionally sponsored loans, scholarships/grants, tuition waivers, and unspecified assistantships available. Support available to part-time students. Financial award application deadline: 1/1. *Faculty research:* Child and families studies; business education; special education; math, science, and technology education. *Unit head:* Dr. Jack Newsome, Chair, 208-282-4838, E-mail: newsjack@isu.edu. *Application contact:* Dr. Peter Denner, Assistant Dean, 208-282-3807, Fax: 208-282-4697, E-mail: dennpete@isu.edu.

Illinois State University, Graduate School, College of Education, Department of Curriculum and Instruction, Normal, IL 61790-2200. Offers curriculum and instruction (MS, MS Ed, Ed D); educational policies (Ed D); postsecondary education (Ed D); reading (MS Ed); supervision (Ed D). *Accreditation:* NCATE. *Faculty:* 28 full-time (13 women). *Students:* 21 full-time (16 women), 157 part-time (123 women); includes 20 minority (11 African Americans, 5 Asian Americans or Pacific Islanders, 4 Hispanic Americans), 11 international. 26 applicants, 73% accepted. In 2006, 60 master's, 14 doctorates awarded. *Degree requirements:* For master's, variable foreign language requirement, thesis or alternative; for doctorate, variable foreign language requirement, thesis/dissertation, 2 terms of residency, internship. *Entrance requirements:* For master's, GRE General Test, minimum GPA of 3.0 in last 60 hours of course work; for doctorate, GRE General Test. *Application deadline:* Applications are processed on a rolling basis. Application fee: $40. *Expenses:* Tuition, state resident: full-time $3,330; part-time $185 per credit hour. Tuition, nonresident: full-time $6,948; part-time $438 per credit hour. Required fees: $1,259; $52 per credit hour. *Financial support:* In 2006–07, 15 research assistantships (averaging $7,056 per year), 5 teaching assistantships (averaging $9,675 per year) were awarded; tuition waivers (full) and unspecified assistantships also available. Financial award application deadline: 4/1. *Faculty research:* In-service and pre-service teacher education for teachers of English language learners; teachers for all children: developing a model for alternative, bilingual elementary certification for paraprofessionals in Illinois; Illinois Geographic Alliance. Total annual research expenditures: $1 million. *Unit head:* Dr. Barbara Nourie, Acting Chairperson, 309-438-5425.

Indiana State University, School of Graduate Studies, College of Education, Department of Curriculum and Instruction and Media Technology, Terre Haute, IN 47809-1401. Offers curriculum and instruction (M Ed, PhD); educational technology (MS). *Accreditation:* NCATE. *Faculty:* 7 full-time (3 women). *Students:* 45 full-time (22 women), 131 part-time (96 women); includes 13 minority (7 African Americans, 3 Asian Americans or Pacific Islanders, 3 Hispanic Americans), 37 international. Average age 37. 54 applicants, 96% accepted, 17 enrolled. In 2006, 25 master's, 11 doctorates awarded. *Degree requirements:* For doctorate, thesis/dissertation. *Entrance requirements:* For doctorate, GRE General Test. *Application deadline:* For fall admission, 7/1 priority date for domestic students; for spring admission, 11/1 priority date for domestic students. Applications are processed on a rolling basis. Application fee: $20. Electronic applications accepted. *Expenses:* Tuition, state resident: part-time $278 per credit. Tuition, nonresident: part-time $552 per credit. *Financial support:* In 2006–07, 7 research assistantships with partial tuition reimbursements (averaging $7,000 per year) were awarded;

Curriculum and Instruction

Indiana State University (continued)
fellowships with partial tuition reimbursements, teaching assistantships with partial tuition reimbursements, tuition waivers (partial) also available. Financial award application deadline: 3/1; financial award applicants required to submit FAFSA. *Faculty research:* Discipline FERPA reading, teacher strengths and needs. *Unit head:* Dr. Susan Kiger, Interim Chairperson, 812-237-2960.

Indiana University Bloomington, School of Education, Department of Curriculum and Instruction, Bloomington, IN 47405-7000. Offers art education (MS, Ed D, PhD); curriculum studies (Ed D, PhD); elementary education (MS, Ed D, PhD, Ed S); mathematics education (MS, Ed D, PhD); science education (MS, Ed D, PhD); secondary education (MS, Ed D, PhD); social studies education (MS, PhD); special education (MS, Ed D, PhD, Ed S). PhD offered through the University Graduate School. *Accreditation:* NCATE. Part-time and evening/weekend programs available. *Students:* 39 full-time (28 women), 82 part-time (54 women); includes 15 minority (5 African Americans, 1 American Indian/Alaska Native, 6 Asian Americans or Pacific Islanders, 3 Hispanic Americans), 33 international. Average age 37. In 2006, 1 degree awarded. Terminal master's awarded for partial completion of doctoral program. *Degree requirements:* For doctorate, thesis/dissertation; for Ed S, comprehensive exam or project. *Entrance requirements:* For master's, doctorate, and Ed S, GRE General Test. *Application deadline:* For fall admission, 6/1 priority date for domestic students, 3/1 for international students; for winter admission, 11/1 priority date for domestic students; for spring admission, 9/1 for international students. Applications are processed on a rolling basis. Application fee: $50 ($60 for international students). Electronic applications accepted. *Expenses:* Tuition, state resident: full-time $5,791; part-time $241 per credit hour. Tuition, nonresident: full-time $16,866; part-time $703 per credit hour. *Financial support:* Fellowships with full and partial tuition reimbursements, research assistantships with full and partial tuition reimbursements, teaching assistantships with full and partial tuition reimbursements, career-related internships or fieldwork, Federal Work-Study, institutionally sponsored loans, and tuition waivers (partial) available. Support available to part-time students. *Unit head:* Cary Buzzelli, Chairperson, 812-856-8100. *Application contact:* Bobbie Partenheimer, Admissions Services Coordinator, 812-856-8127, Fax: 812-856-8333, E-mail: partenhe@indiana.edu.

Indiana University of Pennsylvania, School of Graduate Studies and Research, College of Education and Educational Technology, Department of Professional Studies in Education, Program in Curriculum and Instruction, Indiana, PA 15705-1087. Offers M Ed, D Ed. *Accreditation:* NCATE. *Faculty:* 4 full-time (3 women), 1 (woman) part-time/adjunct. *Students:* 17 full-time (15 women), 51 part-time (37 women); includes 3 minority (2 African Americans, 1 Hispanic American), 5 international. Average age 42. 36 applicants, 56% accepted. In 2006, 8 degrees awarded. *Degree requirements:* For doctorate, one foreign language, thesis/dissertation, comprehensive exam. *Entrance requirements:* For doctorate, 2 letters of recommendation. Additional exam requirements/recommendations for international students: Required—TOEFL. *Application deadline:* For fall admission, 7/1 priority date for domestic students; for spring admission, 11/1 for domestic students. Applications are processed on a rolling basis. Application fee: $30. *Expenses:* Tuition, state resident: full-time $6,048; part-time $336 per credit. Tuition, nonresident: full-time $9,678; part-time $538 per credit. Required fees: $1,069; $148 per year. *Financial support:* In 2006–07, 6 fellowships (averaging $1,000 per year), 15 research assistantships with full and partial tuition reimbursements (averaging $3,090 per year), 3 teaching assistantships (averaging $17,001 per year) were awarded; career-related internships or fieldwork and Federal Work-Study also available. Support available to part-time students. Financial award application deadline: 3/15; financial award applicants required to submit FAFSA. *Unit head:* Dr. Mary R. Jalongo, Graduate Coordinator, 724-357-2417, E-mail: mjalongo@iup.edu.

Indiana Wesleyan University, College of Adult and Professional Studies, Program in Graduate Teacher Education, Marion, IN 46953-4974. Offers curriculum and instruction (M Ed). *Accreditation:* NCATE. Evening/weekend programs available. *Faculty:* 8 full-time (5 women), 132 part-time/adjunct (54 women). *Students:* 999 full-time. Average age 33. 559 applicants, 99% accepted. *Entrance requirements:* For master's, GRE General Test, NTE, minimum GPA of 2.75, related experience, teaching license. Additional exam requirements/recommendations for international students: Required—TOEFL (minimum score 550 paper-based; 213 computer-based). *Application deadline:* Applications are processed on a rolling basis. Application fee: $25. Electronic applications accepted. *Expenses:* Tuition: Full-time $16,000; part-time $400 per credit. Required fees: $3,000. Tuition and fees vary according to degree level, campus/location and program. *Financial support:* Applicants required to submit FAFSA. *Unit head:* Dr. Jim Freemyer, Director of Graduate Education, 765-677-2278, Fax: 765-677-2023, E-mail: jfreemyer@indwes.edu. *Application contact:* Jerry Shepherd, Director of Marketing, 765-677-2856, E-mail: jerry.shepherd@indwes.edu.

Iowa State University of Science and Technology, Graduate College, College of Human Sciences, Department of Curriculum and Instruction, Ames, IA 50011. Offers curriculum and instructional technology (M Ed, MS, PhD); elementary education (M Ed, MS); historical, philosophical, and comparative studies in education (M Ed, MS); special education (M Ed, MS). *Faculty:* 28 full-time, 3 part-time/adjunct. *Students:* 54 full-time (40 women), 78 part-time (54 women); includes 11 minority (3 African Americans, 4 Asian Americans or Pacific Islanders, 4 Hispanic Americans), 26 international. 64 applicants, 69% accepted, 32 enrolled. In 2006, 31 master's, 10 doctorates awarded. *Degree requirements:* For master's, thesis or alternative; for doctorate, thesis/dissertation. *Entrance requirements:* For doctorate, GRE General Test. Additional exam requirements/recommendations for international students: Required—TOEFL (paper-based 560; computer-based 220; iBT 83) or IELTS (6.5). *Application deadline:* For fall admission, 1/1 priority date for domestic and international students; for spring admission, 9/1 for domestic and international students. Application fee: $30 ($70 for international students). Electronic applications accepted. *Expenses:* Tuition, state resident: full-time $5,936; part-time $330 per credit. Tuition, nonresident: full-time $16,350; part-time $330 per credit. *Financial support:* In 2006–07, 22 research assistantships with full and partial tuition reimbursements (averaging $17,457 per year), 17 teaching assistantships with full and partial tuition reimbursements (averaging $17,788 per year) were awarded; fellowships, scholarships/grants, health care benefits, and unspecified assistantships also available. *Unit head:* Dr. Carl Smith, Chair, 515-294-7021, E-mail: cigrad@iastate.edu. *Application contact:* Dr. Patricia Leigh, Director of Graduate Education, 515-294-7021, E-mail: cigrad@iastate.edu.

The Johns Hopkins University, School of Professional Studies in Business and Education, School of Education, Department of Teacher Preparation, Baltimore, MD 21218-2699. Offers elementary education (MAT); English for speakers of other languages (MAT); secondary education (MAT). Part-time and evening/weekend programs available. *Students:* 234 full-time (173 women), 240 part-time (172 women); includes 87 minority (61 African Americans, 19 Asian Americans or Pacific Islanders, 7 Hispanic Americans), 4 international. Average age 27. 360 applicants, 71% accepted, 243 enrolled. In 2006, 218 degrees awarded. *Degree requirements:* For master's, portfolio. *Entrance requirements:* For master's, PRAXIS I, minimum GPA of 3.0, interview, resumé, letter of recommendation. Additional exam requirements/recommendations for international students: Required—TOEFL (minimum score 600 paper-based; 250 computer-based; 100 iBT). *Application deadline:* For fall admission, 4/1 priority date for domestic students, 4/1 for international students; for winter admission, 10/1 priority date for domestic students; for spring admission, 10/1 priority date for domestic students, 10/1 for international students. Applications are processed on a rolling basis. Application fee: $60. *Expenses:* Tuition: Full-time $32,976. Tuition and fees vary according to degree level and program. *Financial support:* Scholarships/grants available. Support available to part-time students. Financial award application deadline: 6/1; financial award applicants required to submit FAFSA. *Faculty research:* Professional development schools, data-informed instruction, alternative certification, dispositions. *Unit head:* Dr. Elaine Stotko, Chair, 410-309-1289, Fax: 410-290-0467, E-mail: matjhu@jhu.edu. *Application contact:* Carol Herrman, Admissions Coordinator, 410-872-1234, Fax: 410-872-1251, E-mail: onestop.admissions@jhu.edu.

Johnson State College, Graduate Program in Education, Program in Curriculum and Instruction, Johnson, VT 05656-9405. Offers MA Ed. Part-time programs available. *Students:* 1 (woman) full-time, 11 part-time (6 women). *Degree requirements:* For master's, thesis or alternative, comprehensive exam. *Entrance requirements:* For master's, interview. Additional exam requirements/recommendations for international students: Required—TOEFL. *Application deadline:* For fall admission, 7/15 priority date for domestic students, 4/15 priority date for international students; for spring admission, 11/1 priority date for domestic students, 8/15 priority date for international students. Applications are processed on a rolling basis. Application fee: $35. *Financial support:* Career-related internships or fieldwork, Federal Work-Study, and institutionally sponsored loans available. Support available to part-time students. Financial award application deadline: 3/1; financial award applicants required to submit FAFSA. *Application contact:* Catherine H. Higley, Administrative Assistant for Graduate Programs, 800-635-2356 Ext. 1244, Fax: 802-635-1248, E-mail: higleyc@jsc.vsc.edu.

Jones International University, Graduate School of Education, Centennial, CO 80112. Offers adult education (M Ed); corporate training and knowledge management (M Ed); curriculum and instruction (M Ed), including elementary teacher licensure, secondary teacher licensure; e-learning technology and design (M Ed); educational leadership and administration (M Ed); educational leadership and administration: principal and administrator licensure (M Ed); elementary curriculum instruction and assessment (M Ed); higher education leadership and administration (M Ed); K-12 instructional technology (M Ed); K-12 instructional technology: teacher licensure (M Ed); secondary curriculum instruction and assessment (M Ed); technology and design (M Ed). Part-time and evening/weekend programs available. Postbaccalaureate distance learning degree programs offered (no on-campus study). *Entrance requirements:* For master's, minimum cumulative GPA of 2.5. Additional exam requirements/recommendations for international students: Recommended—TOEFL (minimum score 550 paper-based; 213 computer-based). Electronic applications accepted.

Kansas State University, Graduate School, College of Education, Department of Elementary Education, Manhattan, KS 66506. Offers curriculum and instruction (MS, Ed D, PhD). *Faculty:* 8 full-time (6 women). *Application deadline:* For fall admission, 3/1 priority date for domestic students, 2/1 priority date for international students; for spring admission, 10/1 priority date for domestic students, 8/1 priority date for international students. Application fee: $30 ($55 for international students). *Expenses:* Tuition, state resident: full-time $6,352; part-time $240 per credit hour. Tuition, nonresident: full-time $14,296; part-time $571 per credit hour. Required fees: $585. *Financial support:* In 2006–07, 2 research assistantships (averaging $12,095 per year), 2 teaching assistantships (averaging $15,745 per year) were awarded. Total annual research expenditures: $297,757. *Unit head:* Dr. Paul R. Burden, Head, 785-532-5595, Fax: 785-532-7304, E-mail: burden@ksu.edu. *Application contact:* Linda Thurston, Director, 785-532-5595, Fax: 785-532-7304, E-mail: coegrads@ksu.edu.

Kansas State University, Graduate School, College of Education, Department of Secondary Education, Manhattan, KS 66506. Offers curriculum and instruction (MS, Ed D, PhD). *Faculty:* 15 full-time (6 women), 1 part-time/adjunct (0 women). *Application deadline:* For fall admission, 3/1 priority date for domestic students, 2/1 priority date for international students; for spring admission, 10/1 priority date for domestic students, 8/1 priority date for international students. Application fee: $30 ($55 for international students). *Expenses:* Tuition, state resident: full-time $6,352; part-time $240 per credit hour. Tuition, nonresident: full-time $14,296; part-time $571 per credit hour. Required fees: $585. *Financial support:* In 2006–07, 2 research assistantships (averaging $12,227 per year), 5 teaching assistantships (averaging $11,411 per year) were awarded. *Faculty research:* Curriculum development, gender issues in teaching and learning, instructional improvement, nature of science and instructional role of scientific theories, discourse communities. Total annual research expenditures: $450,541. *Unit head:* Lawrence Scharmann, Head, 785-532-5904, Fax: 785-532-7304, E-mail: lscharm@ksu.edu. *Application contact:* Linda Thurston, Director, 785-532-5595, Fax: 785-532-7304, E-mail: coegrads@ksu.edu.

Kansas State University, Graduate School, College of Education, Program in Curriculum and Instruction, Manhattan, KS 66506. Offers MS, Ed D, PhD. *Accreditation:* NCATE. *Students:* 46 full-time (37 women), 79 part-time (50 women); includes 23 minority (7 African Americans, 5 American Indian/Alaska Native, 5 Asian Americans or Pacific Islanders, 6 Hispanic Americans), 12 international. Average age 34. 60 applicants, 87% accepted, 28 enrolled. In 2006, 72 master's, 18 doctorates awarded. *Degree requirements:* For doctorate, thesis/dissertation, preliminary exam, comprehensive exam. *Entrance requirements:* For doctorate, GRE or MAT. Additional exam requirements/recommendations for international students: Required—TOEFL. *Application deadline:* For fall admission, 3/1 priority date for domestic students, 2/1 priority date for international students; for spring admission, 10/1 priority date for domestic students, 8/1 priority date for international students. Applications are processed on a rolling basis. Application fee: $30 ($55 for international students). Electronic applications accepted. *Expenses:* Tuition, state resident: full-time $6,352; part-time $240 per credit hour. Tuition, nonresident: full-time $14,296; part-time $571 per credit hour. Required fees: $585. *Financial support:* Teaching assistantships with tuition reimbursements, career-related internships or fieldwork, institutionally sponsored loans, and scholarships/grants available. Support available to part-time students. Financial award application deadline: 3/1; financial award applicants required to submit FAFSA. *Faculty research:* Teaching subject fields (reading, language arts, social studies, science, mathematics); professional development; culturally and linguistically diverse populations; foundations of education; assessment. *Unit head:* Dr. Marjorie Hancock, Head, 785-532-5917, Fax: 785-532-7304, E-mail: mrhanc@ksu.edu. *Application contact:* Linda Thurston, Director, 785-532-5595, Fax: 785-532-7304, E-mail: coegrads@ksu.edu.

Kean University, College of Education, Program in Classroom Instruction and Curriculum, Union, NJ 07083. Offers bilingual/bicultural education (MA); classroom instruction (MA); earth science (MA); educational technology (MA); elementary education (MA); mathematics/science/computer education (MA); teaching (MA); teaching English as a second language (MA). *Accreditation:* NCATE. Part-time and evening/weekend programs available. *Faculty:* 19 full-time (10 women). *Students:* 34 full-time (29 women), 174 part-time (139 women); includes 73 minority (9 African Americans, 7 Asian Americans or Pacific Islanders, 57 Hispanic Americans), 4 international. Average age 34. 103 applicants, 93% accepted, 67 enrolled. In 2006, 82 degrees awarded. *Degree requirements:* For master's, 2 foreign languages, thesis, comprehensive exam. *Entrance requirements:* For master's, GRE General Test or MAT, PRAXIS, minimum GPA of 2.75, 2 letters of recommendation, interview. *Application deadline:* For fall admission, 5/1 for domestic students; for spring admission, 11/1 for domestic students. Application fee: $60 ($150 for international students). Electronic applications accepted. *Expenses:* Tuition, state resident: full-time $8,856; part-time $369 per credit. Tuition, nonresident: full-time $11,256; part-time $469 per credit. *Financial support:* In 2006–07, 2 research assistantships with full tuition reimbursements (averaging $3,217 per year) were awarded; unspecified assistantships also available. *Unit head:* Dr. Frank H. Osborn, Program Coordinator, 908-737-4289, E-mail: fosborne@kean.edu. *Application contact:* Joanne Morris, Director of Graduate Admissions, 908-737-3355, Fax: 908-737-3354, E-mail: grad-adm@kean.edu.

Kean University, College of Education, Program in Early Childhood Education, Union, NJ 07083. Offers administration in early childhood and family studies (MA); advanced curriculum and teaching (MA); classroom instruction (MA), including preschool-third grade; early childhood education (MA); education for family living (MA). *Accreditation:* NCATE. Part-time and evening/weekend programs available. *Faculty:* 11 full-time (10 women). *Students:* 12 full-time (11 women), 90 part-time (88 women); includes 22 minority (11 African Americans, 1 Asian American or Pacific Islander, 10 Hispanic Americans), 2 international. Average age 31. 51 applicants, 82% accepted, 28 enrolled. In 2006, 27 degrees awarded. *Degree requirements:* For master's, thesis, portfolio, comprehensive exam. *Entrance requirements:* For master's, GRE General Test, 2 letters of recommendation, interview, writing sample, minimum GPA of 2.5. *Application deadline:* For fall admission, 5/1 for domestic students; for spring admission, 11/1 for domestic students. Application fee: $60 ($150 for international students). Electronic applications accepted. *Expenses:* Tuition, state resident: full-time $8,856; part-time $369 per credit. Tuition, nonresident: full-time $11,256; part-time $469 per credit. *Financial support:* Research assistantships with full tuition reimbursements, unspecified assistantships available. *Unit head:* Dr. Marjorie Kelly, Program Coordinator, 908-737-3789, E-mail: mkelly@kean.edu. *Application contact:* Joanne Morris, Director of Graduate Admissions, 908-737-3355, Fax: 908-737-3354, E-mail: grad-adm@kean.edu.

Keene State College, Division of Graduate and Professional Studies, Program in Curriculum and Instruction, Keene, NH 03435. Offers M Ed. Part-time and evening/weekend programs available. *Degree requirements:* For master's, project or thesis. *Entrance requirements:* For master's, PRAXIS I, MAT or GRE, resumé, teaching certificate, teaching experience. *Application deadline:* For fall admission, 6/15 for domestic students; for spring admission, 10/15 for domestic students. Applications are processed on a rolling basis. Application fee: $25 ($35 for international students). *Expenses:* Tuition, area resident: Part-time $265 per credit. Tuition, state resident: full-time $5,780; part-time $290 per credit. Tuition, nonresident: full-time $13,050. Required fees: $80 per credit. Part-time tuition and fees vary according to course load. *Financial support:* Research assistantships, career-related internships or fieldwork, Federal Work-Study, and institutionally sponsored loans available. Financial award application deadline: 3/1; financial award applicants required to submit FAFSA. *Application contact:* Peggy Richmond, Director of Admissions, 603-358-2276, Fax: 603-358-2767, E-mail: admissions@keene.edu.

Kent State University, Graduate School of Education, Health, and Human Services, Department of Teaching, Leadership, and Curriculum Studies, Program in Curriculum and Instruction, Kent, OH 44242-0001. Offers M Ed, MA, PhD, Ed S. *Accreditation:* NCATE. Part-time and evening/weekend programs available. *Faculty:* 32 full-time (23 women), 4 part-time/adjunct (all women). *Students:* 80 full-time (69 women), 118 part-time (103 women); includes 16 minority (15 African Americans, 1 Asian American or Pacific Islander), 21 international. 30 applicants, 93% accepted. In 2006, 32 master's, 6 doctorates, 1 other advanced degree awarded. *Degree requirements:* For master's, thesis (for some programs), registration; for doctorate, thesis/dissertation, comprehensive exam, registration. *Entrance requirements:* For doctorate and Ed S, GRE General Test. Additional exam requirements/recommendations for international students: Required—TOEFL. *Application deadline:* Applications are processed on a rolling basis. Application fee: $30. Electronic applications accepted. *Financial support:* In 2006–07, fellowships with full tuition reimbursements (averaging $8,497 per year); research assistantships with full tuition reimbursements, teaching assistantships with full tuition reimbursements, career-related internships or fieldwork, Federal Work-Study, institutionally sponsored loans, scholarships/grants, health care benefits, and unspecified assistantships also available. Support available to part-time students. Financial award application deadline: 4/1; financial award applicants required to submit FAFSA. *Faculty research:* Gender equity issues in teaching, learning math and science, teaching as inquiry artistry, curriculum studies for democratic humanism. *Unit head:* Dr. James Henderson, Coordinator, 330-672-2580, E-mail: jhenders@kent.edu. *Application contact:* Nancy Miller, Academic Program Coordinator, Office of Graduate Student Services, 330-672-2576, Fax: 330-672-9162, E-mail: ogs@kent.edu.

Kutztown University of Pennsylvania, College of Graduate Studies and Extended Learning, College of Education, Program in Secondary Education, Kutztown, PA 19530-0730. Offers biology (M Ed); curriculum and instruction (M Ed); English (M Ed); mathematics (M Ed); secondary education (Certificate); social studies (M Ed). *Accreditation:* NCATE. Part-time and evening/weekend programs available. *Faculty:* 5 full-time (2 women). *Students:* 69 full-time (32 women), 80 part-time (44 women); includes 5 minority (1 African American, 1 American Indian/Alaska Native, 2 Asian Americans or Pacific Islanders, 1 Hispanic American), 3 international. Average age 32. 80 applicants, 88% accepted, 34 enrolled. In 2006, 26 degrees awarded. *Degree requirements:* For master's, thesis optional. *Entrance requirements:* For master's, GRE General Test. Additional exam requirements/recommendations for international students: Required—TOEFL. *Application deadline:* Applications are processed on a rolling basis. Application fee: $35. Electronic applications accepted. *Expenses:* Tuition, state resident: full-time $6,048; part-time $336 per credit. Tuition, nonresident: full-time $9,678; part-time $538 per credit. *Financial support:* In 2006–07, research assistantships with full tuition reimbursements (averaging $5,000 per year); career-related internships or fieldwork, Federal Work-Study, and unspecified assistantships also available. Financial award application deadline: 3/15; financial award applicants required to submit FAFSA. *Unit head:* Dr. Kathleen Dolgos, Chairperson, 610-683-4279, Fax: 610-683-1338, E-mail: dolgos@kutztown.edu.

LaGrange College, Graduate Programs, Department of Education, LaGrange, GA 30240-2999. Offers art education (MAT); curriculum and instruction (M Ed); music education (MAT); secondary education (MAT). Part-time and evening/weekend programs available. *Degree requirements:* For master's, comprehensive exam. *Entrance requirements:* For master's, GRE, MAT, or NTE, minimum GPA of 2.5. Additional exam requirements/recommendations for international students: Required—TOEFL (minimum score 550 paper-based).

Lake Erie College, Division of Education, Painesville, OH 44077-3389. Offers curriculum and instruction (MS Ed); education (MS Ed); educational leadership (MS Ed); reading (MS Ed). Part-time and evening/weekend programs available. *Faculty:* 4 full-time (1 woman), 4 part-time/adjunct (1 woman). *Students:* Average age 37. 9 applicants, 89% accepted, 5 enrolled. In 2006, 20 degrees awarded. *Degree requirements:* For master's, thesis, applied research project, comprehensive exam. *Entrance requirements:* For master's, GRE General Test or minimum GPA of 3.0. Additional exam requirements/recommendations for international students: Required—TOEFL (minimum score 590 paper-based). *Application deadline:* For fall admission, 8/1 priority date for domestic students, 6/1 for international students; for spring admission, 12/15 for domestic students, 10/1 for international students. Applications are processed on a rolling basis. Application fee: $25 ($50 for international students). Electronic applications accepted. *Expenses:* Contact institution. *Financial support:* Applicants required to submit FAFSA. *Faculty research:* Cooperative learning, portfolio assessment, education systems in England, video case-based instruction. *Unit head:* Dr. Richard Bonde, Associate Dean, 440-375-7156, Fax: 440-375-7005, E-mail: rbonde@lec.edu. *Application contact:* 440-375-7050, Fax: 440-375-7005, E-mail: admissions@lec.edu.

Lakehead University, Graduate Studies, Faculty of Education, Thunder Bay, ON P7B 5E1, Canada. Offers curriculum development (M Ed); education administration (M Ed); educational studies (PhD). Part-time and evening/weekend programs available. *Degree requirements:* For master's, project or thesis. *Entrance requirements:* For master's, minimum B average. Additional exam requirements/recommendations for international students: Required—TOEFL. *Faculty research:* Art education, AIDS education, language arts education, gerontology, women's studies.

Lander University, School of Education, Greenwood, SC 29649-2099. Offers elementary education (M Ed); teaching (MAT). *Accreditation:* NCATE. Part-time programs available. *Faculty:* 6 full-time (3 women), 4 part-time/adjunct (all women). *Students:* 11 full-time (8 women), 29 part-time (25 women); includes 5 minority (all African Americans) Average age 34. In 2006, 41 degrees awarded. *Degree requirements:* For master's, thesis or alternative, comprehensive exam. *Entrance requirements:* For master's, GRE General Test. Additional exam requirements/recommendations for international students: Required—TOEFL (minimum score 550 paper-based; 213 computer-based). *Application deadline:* Applications are processed on a rolling basis. Application fee: $35. Electronic applications accepted. *Expenses:* Tuition, state resident: full-time $7,824; part-time $326 per credit hour. Tuition, nonresident: full-time $14,932; part-time $622 per credit hour. Required fees: $550. *Financial support:* Federal Work-Study available. Support available to part-time students. Financial award application deadline: 4/15; financial award applicants required to submit FAFSA. *Unit head:* Dr. Sandra Lemoine, Dean, 864-388-8225, Fax: 864-388-8890. *Application contact:* Dr. Linda Neely, Director of Graduate Studies, 864-388-8268, Fax: 864-388-8144, E-mail: lneely@lander.edu.

La Sierra University, School of Education, Department of Curriculum and Instruction, Riverside, CA 92515. Offers curriculum and instruction (MA, Ed D, Ed S); special education (MA). Part-time and evening/weekend programs available. *Degree requirements:* For doctorate, thesis/dissertation; for Ed S, thesis optional. *Entrance requirements:* For master's, minimum GPA of 3.0; for doctorate, GRE General Test, GRE Subject Test, minimum GPA of 3.3; for Ed S, minimum GPA of 3.3. *Faculty research:* New teacher success, politics of knowledge, computer-assisted instruction, diversity issues.

Lesley University, School of Education, Cambridge, MA 02138-2790. Offers curriculum and instruction (M Ed, CAGS); early childhood education (M Ed); educational studies (PhD); elementary education (M Ed); individually designed (M Ed); middle school education (M Ed); moderate special needs (M Ed); reading (M Ed, CAGS); science in education (M Ed); severe special needs (M Ed); special needs (CAGS); technology in education (M Ed, CAGS). Part-time and evening/weekend programs available. Postbaccalaureate distance learning degree programs offered (no on-campus study). *Faculty:* 47 full-time (39 women), 208 part-time/adjunct (135 women). *Students:* 242 full-time (222 women), 2,903 part-time (2,495 women); includes 279 minority (179 African Americans, 7 American Indian/Alaska Native, 25 Asian Americans or Pacific Islanders, 68 Hispanic Americans), 10 international. Average age 36. 1,186 applicants, 96% accepted, 792 enrolled. In 2006, 1,724 master's, 6 doctorates, 17 other advanced degrees awarded. *Degree requirements:* For master's, practicum; for doctorate, thesis/dissertation. *Entrance requirements:* For doctorate, GRE General Test or MAT, interview, master's degree, resumé; for CAGS, interview, master's degree. Additional exam requirements/recommendations for international students: Required—TOEFL (minimum score 550 paper-based; 213 computer-based; 80 iBT). *Application deadline:* Applications are processed on a rolling basis. Application fee: $50. Electronic applications accepted. *Financial support:* In 2006–07, 26 students received support, including research assistantships (averaging $3,400 per year), teaching assistantships (averaging $3,400 per year); career-related internships or fieldwork, Federal Work-Study, scholarships/grants, and unspecified assistantships also available. Support available to part-time students. Financial award application deadline: 4/15; financial award applicants required to submit FAFSA. *Faculty research:* Assessment in literacy, mathematics and science; autism spectrum disorders; instructional technology and online learning; multicultural education and ELL. *Unit head:* Dr. Mario Borunda, Dean, 617-349-8375, Fax: 617-349-8607, E-mail: mborunda@lesley.edu. *Application contact:* Kristen Card, Associate Director of On-Campus Admissions, 617-349-8734, Fax: 617-349-8313, E-mail: kmcard@lesley.edu.

See Close-Up on page 893.

Lewis University, College of Arts and Sciences, Graduate Programs in Education, Program in Curriculum and Instruction, Romeoville, IL 60446. Offers educational leadership (MA Ed); instructional leadership (MA Ed). Part-time and evening/weekend programs available. *Entrance requirements:* For master's, entrance writing exam, minimum GPA of 2.75, 3 letters of recommendation, interview. Additional exam requirements/recommendations for international students: Required—TOEFL (minimum score 550 paper-based; 213 computer-based). Electronic applications accepted.

Liberty University, School of Education, Lynchburg, VA 24502. Offers administration and supervision (M Ed); curriculum and instruction (M Ed); early childhood education (M Ed); education specialist (Ed S); educational leadership (Ed D); elementary education (M Ed); gifted education (M Ed); reading specialist (M Ed); school counseling (M Ed); secondary education (M Ed); special education (M Ed). *Accreditation:* NCATE. Part-time programs available. Postbaccalaureate distance learning degree programs offered (minimal on-campus study). *Faculty:* 8 full-time (3 women), 7 part-time/adjunct (3 women). *Students:* 33 full-time (22 women), 308 part-time (180 women); includes 22 minority (12 African Americans, 2 American Indian/Alaska Native, 2 Asian Americans or Pacific Islanders, 6 Hispanic Americans), 5 international. Average age 39. 434 applicants, 77% accepted, 111 enrolled. In 2006, 39 master's, 12 doctorates, 16 other advanced degrees awarded. *Degree requirements:* For doctorate, thesis/dissertation, comprehensive exam. *Entrance requirements:* For master's, GRE General Test or MAT (if taken on or before 1999), 2 letters of recommendation, minimum undergraduate GPA of 3.0, curriculum vitae, graduate status record; for doctorate, GRE General Test or MAT (if taken before 1999), minimum master's GPA of 3.0, 3 years of teacher experience; for Ed S, GRE General Test or MAT (if taken before 1999), minimum master's GPA of 3.0, 3 years of teaching experience. Additional exam requirements/recommendations for international students: Required—TOEFL (minimum score 600 paper-based; 250 computer-based). *Application deadline:* For fall admission, 6/1 priority date for domestic students; for spring admission, 11/1 for domestic students. Applications are processed on a rolling basis. Application fee: $35. Electronic applications accepted. *Expenses:* Contact institution. *Financial support:* In 2006–07, 226 students received support. Federal Work-Study and tuition waivers (partial) available. *Faculty research:* Self-determination, character education, bibliotherapy, learning styles, distance education. *Unit head:* Dr. Karen L. Parker, Dean, 434-582-2195, Fax: 434-582-2468, E-mail: kparker@liberty.edu. *Application contact:* Kyle A Falce, Director of Graduate Admissions, 800-424-9596, Fax: 800-628-7977, E-mail: gradadmissions@liberty.edu.

Lincoln Memorial University, School of Education, Harrogate, TN 37752-1901. Offers administration and supervision (M Ed, Ed S); counseling and guidance (M Ed); curriculum and instruction (M Ed, Ed S). Part-time and evening/weekend programs available. *Faculty:* 25 full-time (13 women), 11 part-time/adjunct (6 women). *Students:* 207 full-time (159 women), 1,315 part-time (995 women); includes 106 minority (93 African Americans, 1 American Indian/Alaska Native, 1 Asian American or Pacific Islander, 11 Hispanic Americans), 2 international. 1,397 applicants, 98% accepted. In 2006, 194 master's, 778 other advanced degrees awarded. *Degree requirements:* For master's, thesis optional. *Entrance requirements:* For master's, GRE, MAT, or NTE. *Application deadline:* For fall admission, 8/10 priority date for domestic students. Application fee: $25. *Financial support:* Career-related internships or fieldwork and unspecified assistantships available. Support available to part-time students. Financial award application deadline: 4/1; financial award applicants required to submit FAFSA. *Unit head:* Dr. Fred Bedelle, Dean, School of Graduate Studies, 423-869-6223, Fax: 423-869-6261, E-mail: graduate@inetlmu.lmunet.edu. *Application contact:* Barbara McCune, Senior Assistant, Graduate Office, 423-869-6374, Fax: 423-869-6261, E-mail: graduate@lmunet.edu.

Lipscomb University, Program in Education, Nashville, TN 37204-3951. Offers instructional leadership (M Ed); learning and teaching (MALT); school administration and supervision (M Ed); special education instruction, K-12 (MASE). *Accreditation:* NCATE. Part-time and evening/weekend programs available. *Faculty:* 3 full-time (1 woman), 9 part-time/adjunct (6 women). *Students:* 95 full-time (59 women), 30 part-time (22 women); includes 14 minority (13 African Americans, 1 Asian American or Pacific Islander). Average age 32. In 2006, 25 degrees awarded. *Degree requirements:* For master's, registration. *Entrance requirements:* For master's, MAT or GRE General Test, 2 reference letters. Additional exam requirements/recommendations for international students: Required—TOEFL (minimum score 570 paper-based; 230 computer-based). *Application deadline:* For fall admission, 8/29 priority date for domestic students; for spring admission, 1/16 priority date for domestic students. Applications are processed on a rolling basis. Application fee: $60. *Expenses:* Tuition: Part-time $560 per semester hour. Tuition and fees vary according to program. *Financial support:* In 2006–07, 67 students received support. Federal Work-Study, tuition waivers (full), and unspecified assistantships available. Support available to part-time students. Financial award applicants required to submit FAFSA. *Faculty research:* Facilitative learning styles, leadership, student assessment, interactive multimedia inclusion. *Unit head:* Dr. Junior High, Director, 615-966-1000 Ext. 6067, Fax: 615-966-7628, E-mail: junior.high@lipscomb.edu. *Application contact:* Jackie Sanders, Administrative Assistant, 615-966-1000 Ext. 6081, Fax: 615-966-7628, E-mail: jackie.sanders@lipscomb.edu.

Louisiana Tech University, Graduate School, College of Education, Department of Curriculum, Instruction and Leadership, Ruston, LA 71272. Offers curriculum and instruction (MS, Ed D); educational leadership (Ed D); secondary education (M Ed), including business education, English education, foreign language education, health and physical education, mathematics education, science education, social studies education, speech education. *Accreditation:*

Curriculum and Instruction

Louisiana Tech University (continued)
NCATE. Part-time programs available. *Degree requirements:* For doctorate, thesis/dissertation. *Entrance requirements:* For master's and doctorate, GRE General Test.

Loyola College in Maryland, Graduate Programs, College of Arts and Sciences, Department of Education, Program in Curriculum and Instruction, Baltimore, MD 21210-2699. Offers M Ed, MA, CAS. Part-time and evening/weekend programs available. *Students:* 13 full-time (11 women), 141 part-time (117 women); includes 24 minority (21 African Americans, 1 American Indian/Alaska Native, 2 Asian Americans or Pacific Islanders), 5 international. Average age 31. 134 applicants, 76% accepted, 59 enrolled. In 2006, 44 degrees awarded. *Entrance requirements:* For master's and CAS, GRE General Test, GRE Subject Test (recommended). Additional exam requirements/recommendations for international students: Required—TOEFL (minimum score 550 paper-based; 213 computer-based). *Application deadline:* For fall admission, 7/1 priority date for domestic students; for spring admission, 10/1 priority date for domestic students. Applications are processed on a rolling basis. Application fee: $50. *Financial support:* Career-related internships or fieldwork available. Financial award applicants required to submit FAFSA. *Unit head:* Michael O'Neal, Director, 410-617-2000 Ext. 5379, E-mail: moneal@loyola.edu.

Loyola University Chicago, School of Education, Program in Curriculum and Instruction, Chicago, IL 60611-2196. Offers M Ed, Ed D. Part-time and evening/weekend programs available. *Faculty:* 5 full-time (3 women), 9 part-time/adjunct (5 women). *Students:* 169. 52 applicants, 81% accepted, 28 enrolled. In 2006, 23 master's, 37 doctorates awarded. Terminal master's awarded for partial completion of doctoral program. *Degree requirements:* For master's, comprehensive exam; for doctorate, thesis/dissertation, comprehensive exam. *Entrance requirements:* For master's, 3 references, minimum GPA of 3.0, resumé; for doctorate, GRE, 3 references, interview, minimum GPA of 3.0, resumé. Additional exam requirements/recommendations for international students: Required—TOEFL (minimum score 550 paper-based; 213 computer-based; 79 iBT). *Application deadline:* For fall admission, 3/1 for domestic and international students; for spring admission, 11/1 for domestic and international students. Applications are processed on a rolling basis. Application fee: $50. Electronic applications accepted. *Financial support:* In 2006–07, 1 research assistantship with tuition reimbursement (averaging $8,500 per year) was awarded; Federal Work-Study and institutionally sponsored loans also available. Financial award application deadline: 2/15. *Faculty research:* School improvement, technology, change, reading. *Unit head:* Dr. Dorothy Giroux, Director, 312-915-7027, E-mail: dgiroux@luc.edu. *Application contact:* Marie Rosin-Dittmar, Information Contact, 312-915-6800, E-mail: schleduc@luc.edu.

Lyndon State College, Graduate Programs in Education, Department of Education, Lyndonville, VT 05851-0919. Offers curriculum and instruction (M Ed); reading specialist (M Ed); special education (M Ed); teaching and counseling (M Ed). Part-time and evening/weekend programs available. *Degree requirements:* For master's, exam or major field project. *Entrance requirements:* Additional exam requirements/recommendations for international students: Recommended—TOEFL (minimum score 500 paper-based; 173 computer-based).

Malone College, School of Education, Graduate Program in Education, Canton, OH 44709-3897. Offers curriculum and instruction (MA); curriculum, instruction, and professional development (MA); instructional technology (MA); intervention specialist (MA); reading (MA). Part-time and evening/weekend programs available. *Faculty:* 11 full-time (4 women), 12 part-time/adjunct (9 women). *Students:* 4 full-time (2 women), 96 part-time (78 women); includes 5 minority (1 African American, 2 Asian Americans or Pacific Islanders, 2 Hispanic Americans). Average age 33. In 2006, 26 degrees awarded. *Degree requirements:* For master's, research project. *Entrance requirements:* For master's, minimum GPA of 3.0, teaching license. *Application deadline:* Applications are processed on a rolling basis. Application fee: $25. *Expenses:* Tuition: Part-time $399 per credit hour. *Financial support:* Tuition waivers (partial) available. Support available to part-time students. Financial award application deadline: 6/30. *Faculty research:* The Bible as children's literature, special needs students and literacy development, middle level education, school/university partnerships and professional development, child/adolescent literature and popular culture. *Unit head:* Dr. Donald Williams, Director, 330-471-8509, Fax: 330-471-8563, E-mail: dwilliams@malone.edu. *Application contact:* Dr. David Kleffman, Recruiter, 330-471-8447, Fax: 330-471-8343, E-mail: dkleffman@malone.edu.

Massachusetts College of Liberal Arts, Program in Education, North Adams, MA 01247-4100. Offers curriculum and instruction (M Ed); educational administration (M Ed); reading (M Ed); special education (M Ed). Part-time and evening/weekend programs available. *Degree requirements:* For master's, thesis. *Entrance requirements:* For master's, writing sample. *Faculty research:* Anxiety, methodology, mainstreaming.

McDaniel College, Graduate and Professional Studies, Program in Curriculum and Instruction, Westminster, MD 21157-4390. Offers MS. *Degree requirements:* For master's, thesis optional. *Entrance requirements:* For master's, letter of reference. Additional exam requirements/recommendations for international students: Required—TOEFL (minimum score 213 computer-based).

McGill University, Faculty of Graduate and Postdoctoral Studies, Faculty of Education, Department of Integrated Studies in Education, Montréal, QC H3A 2T5, Canada. Offers culture and values in education (MA, PhD); curriculum (MA); educational leadership (Certificate, Diploma); educational studies (PhD); integrated studies in education (M Ed); leadership (MA); second language education (MA, PhD). *Degree requirements:* For master's, thesis (for some programs), registration; for doctorate, thesis/dissertation, comprehensive exam, registration. *Entrance requirements:* For master's, 2 years of relevant experience, minimum GPA of 3.0; for doctorate, minimum GPA of 3.0, acquisition of prospective supervisor; for other advanced degree, minimum GPA of 3.0. Additional exam requirements/recommendations for international students: Required—TOEFL (minimum score 580 paper-based; 237 computer-based).

McNeese State University, Graduate School, College of Education, Department of Teacher Education, Program in Curriculum and Instruction, Lake Charles, LA 70609. Offers early childhood education (M Ed); elementary education (M Ed); secondary education (M Ed). Evening/weekend programs available. *Faculty:* 12 full-time (8 women), 2 part-time/adjunct (1 woman). *Students:* 7 full-time (6 women), 40 part-time (37 women); includes 20 minority (19 African Americans, 1 American Indian/Alaska Native). In 2006, 22 degrees awarded. *Entrance requirements:* For master's, GRE, teaching certificate. *Application deadline:* For fall admission, 5/15 priority date for domestic students. Applications are processed on a rolling basis. Application fee: $20 ($30 for international students). *Expenses:* Tuition: area resident: Full-time $2,226; part-time $193 per hour. Required fees: $919; $106 per hour. *Financial support:* Application deadline: 5/1. *Unit head:* Dr. Wayne R Fetter, Dean, College of Education, 337-475-5432, Fax: 337-475-5467, E-mail: wfetter@mcneese.edu.

Medaille College, Program in Education, Buffalo, NY 14214-2695. Offers curriculum and instruction (MS Ed); education preparation (MS Ed); literacy (MS Ed); special education (MS). Part-time and evening/weekend programs available. *Faculty:* 30 full-time (20 women), 28 part-time/adjunct (18 women). *Students:* 516 full-time (417 women), 334 part-time (276 women); includes 16 minority (13 African Americans, 2 Asian Americans or Pacific Islanders, 1 Hispanic American), 654 international. Average age 27. 725 applicants, 97% accepted, 655 enrolled. In 2006, 229 degrees awarded. *Degree requirements:* For master's, thesis or alternative. *Entrance requirements:* For master's, minimum undergraduate GPA of 2.7. Additional exam requirements/recommendations for international students: Required—TOEFL (minimum score 550 paper-based; 213 computer-based). *Application deadline:* For fall admission, 8/15 priority date for domestic students; for spring admission, 1/15 priority date for domestic students. Applications are processed on a rolling basis. Application fee: $35. Electronic applications accepted. *Expenses:* Tuition: Part-time $580 per credit hour. Full-time tuition and fees vary according to program. *Financial support:* In 2006–07, 390 students received support. Federal Work-Study

available. Financial award applicants required to submit FAFSA. *Faculty research:* Curriculum planning, truancy, tracking minority students, curriculum design, mentoring students. *Unit head:* Dr. Robert DiSibio, Director of Graduate Programs, 716-635-5033 Ext. 2017, Fax: 716-634-2232, E-mail: rdisibio@medaille.edu. *Application contact:* Susan Greenwald, Executive Director of Admissions, 716-635-5033 Ext. 2011, Fax: 716-631-1380, E-mail: sgreenwald@medaille.edu.

Memorial University of Newfoundland, School of Graduate Studies, Faculty of Education, St. John's, NL A1C 5S7, Canada. Offers counseling psychology (M Ed); curriculum, teaching, and learning studies (M Ed); education (PhD); educational leadership studies (M Ed); information technology (M Ed); post-secondary studies (M Ed, Diploma), including health professional education (Diploma). Part-time programs available. *Degree requirements:* For master's, internship, paper folio, project, thesis optional; for doctorate, thesis/dissertation, thesis seminar, oral defense of thesis, comprehensive exam. *Entrance requirements:* For master's, undergraduate degree with at least 2nd class standing, 1-2 years work experience; for doctorate, minimum A average in graduate course work, MA in education, 2 years professional experience; for Diploma, 2nd class degree, 2 years of work experience with adult learners, appropriate academic qualifications and work experience in a health-related field. Electronic applications accepted. *Faculty research:* Critical thinking, literacy, cognitive studies and counseling, educational change, technology in instruction.

Miami University, Graduate School, School of Education and Allied Professions, Department of Educational Leadership, Program in Curriculum and Teacher Leadership, Oxford, OH 45056. Offers M Ed. *Accreditation:* NCATE. Part-time programs available. *Degree requirements:* For master's, thesis or alternative, oral or written exam. *Entrance requirements:* For master's, MAT, minimum undergraduate GPA of 3.0 during previous 2 years or 2.75 overall. *Faculty research:* Curriculum theory.

Michigan State University, The Graduate School, College of Education, Department of Teacher Education, East Lansing, MI 48824. Offers curriculum and teaching (MA); curriculum, teaching and education policy (PhD, Ed S). Part-time programs available. *Faculty:* 47 full-time (29 women), 1 (woman) part-time/adjunct. *Students:* 154 full-time (117 women), 140 part-time (127 women); includes 27 minority (14 African Americans, 1 American Indian/Alaska Native, 6 Asian Americans or Pacific Islanders, 6 Hispanic Americans), 45 international. Average age 31. 112 applicants, 71% accepted. In 2006, 218 master's, 24 doctorates awarded. *Entrance requirements:* Additional exam requirements/recommendations for international students: Required—TOEFL. *Application deadline:* Applications are processed on a rolling basis. Electronic applications accepted. *Expenses:* Tuition, state resident: part-time $346 per credit hour. Tuition, nonresident: part-time $730 per credit hour. Tuition and fees vary according to program. *Financial support:* In 2006–07, 36 fellowships with tuition reimbursements, 79 research assistantships with tuition reimbursements (averaging $13,685 per year), 68 teaching assistantships with tuition reimbursements (averaging $13,916 per year) were awarded; scholarships/grants and unspecified assistantships also available. Total annual research expenditures: $3.7 million. *Unit head:* Dr. Mary A. Lundeberg, Chairperson, 517-353-5091, Fax: 517-432-5092, E-mail: mlunde@msu.edu. *Application contact:* Department Information, 517-355-5091, Fax: 517-432-5092.

MidAmerica Nazarene University, Graduate Studies in Education, Olathe, KS 66062-1899. Offers curriculum and instruction (M Ed); educational technology (MET); special education (MA). *Accreditation:* NCATE. Evening/weekend programs available. *Degree requirements:* For master's, thesis or alternative, creative project, technology leadership practicum. *Entrance requirements:* For master's, minimum undergraduate GPA of 2.8, 2 years of teaching experience. Expenses: Contact institution.

Middle Tennessee State University, College of Graduate Studies, College of Education and Behavioral Science, Department of Educational Leadership, Major in Curriculum and Instruction, Murfreesboro, TN 37132. Offers curriculum and instruction (M Ed, Ed S); English as a second language (M Ed). *Accreditation:* NCATE. Part-time and evening/weekend programs available. Postbaccalaureate distance learning degree programs offered. *Students:* 9 full-time (8 women), 140 part-time (118 women); includes 11 minority (4 African Americans, 1 American Indian/Alaska Native, 1 Asian American or Pacific Islander, 5 Hispanic Americans). 42 applicants, 100% accepted. In 2006, 66 degrees awarded. *Degree requirements:* For master's, comprehensive exam. *Entrance requirements:* For master's and Ed S, GRE or MAT. Additional exam requirements/recommendations for international students: Required—TOEFL (minimum score 525 paper-based; 195 computer-based). *Application deadline:* For fall admission, 8/1 priority date for domestic students. Applications are processed on a rolling basis. Application fee: $25. Electronic applications accepted. *Financial support:* Application deadline: 5/1. *Unit head:* Dr. James Huffman, Chair, Department of Educational Leadership, 615-898-2855, Fax: 615-898-2859.

Midwestern State University, Graduate Studies, College of Education, Program in Curriculum and Instruction, Wichita Falls, TX 76308. Offers ME. Part-time and evening/weekend programs available. *Faculty:* 8 full-time (5 women), 3 part-time/adjunct (all women). *Students:* 2 full-time (both women), 16 part-time (12 women); includes 4 minority (2 African Americans, 2 Asian Americans or Pacific Islanders), 2 international. Average age 38. 9 applicants, 89% accepted, 2 enrolled. In 2006, 5 degrees awarded. *Degree requirements:* For master's, comprehensive exam. *Entrance requirements:* For master's, GRE General Test, MAT, or GMAT. Additional exam requirements/recommendations for international students: Required—TOEFL (minimum score 550 paper-based; 213 computer-based). *Application deadline:* For fall admission, 7/1 for domestic students, 4/1 for international students; for spring admission, 11/1 for domestic students, 8/1 for international students. Applications are processed on a rolling basis. Application fee: $35 ($50 for international students). Electronic applications accepted. *Financial support:* In 2006–07, 9 students received support, including 1 teaching assistantship with partial tuition reimbursement available (averaging $7,500 per year); career-related internships or fieldwork, Federal Work-Study, institutionally sponsored loans, scholarships/grants, tuition waivers (partial), and unspecified assistantships also available. Support available to part-time students. Financial award application deadline: 5/1; financial award applicants required to submit FAFSA. *Unit head:* Dr. Ann Estrada, Chair, 940-397-4136, Fax: 940-397-4672, E-mail: ann.estrada@mwsu.edu. *Application contact:* Dr. Robert Redmon, Program Coordinator, 940-397-6264, Fax: 940-397-4694, E-mail: bob.redmon@mwsu.edu.

Mills College, Graduate Studies, Education Department, Oakland, CA 94613-1000. Offers administration (Ed D); child life in health care settings (MA); early childhood education (MA); education (MA), including curriculum and instruction, elementary education, English education, mathematics education, science education, secondary education, social sciences education, teaching. Part-time and evening/weekend programs available. *Faculty:* 10 full-time (7 women), 15 part-time/adjunct (12 women). *Students:* 192 full-time (153 women), 41 part-time (36 women); includes 62 minority (28 African Americans, 13 Asian Americans or Pacific Islanders, 21 Hispanic Americans), 2 international. Average age 34. 160 applicants, 74% accepted, 73 enrolled. In 2006, 52 master's, 1 doctorate awarded. Terminal master's awarded for partial completion of doctoral program. *Degree requirements:* For master's, comprehensive exam. *Entrance requirements:* For doctorate, GRE General Test. Additional exam requirements/recommendations for international students: Required—TOEFL. *Application deadline:* For fall admission, 2/1 for domestic and international students; for spring admission, 11/1 for domestic and international students. Applications are processed on a rolling basis. Application fee: $50. Electronic applications accepted. *Financial support:* In 2006–07, 56 fellowships with tuition reimbursements (averaging $2,700 per year), 15 teaching assistantships (averaging $6,350 per year) were awarded; career-related internships or fieldwork, institutionally sponsored loans, scholarships/grants, and residence awards also available. Support available to part-time students. Financial award application deadline: 2/1; financial award applicants required to submit CSS PROFILE or FAFSA. *Faculty research:* Child development, gender and education, public policy, cross-cultural development, development of literacy. *Unit head:* Joseph Kahne, Chairperson, 510-430-3190, Fax: 510-430-3314, E-mail: grad-studies@mills.edu. *Application* *contact:* Randy McGlauthing, Director of Graduate Admissions, 510-430-2355, Fax: 510-430-2159, E-mail: rmglaut@mills.edu.

Minnesota State University Mankato, College of Graduate Studies, College of Education, Educational Studies: K–12 and Secondary Programs, Mankato, MN 56001. Offers curriculum and instruction (SP); library media education (MS, Certificate, SP); teaching and learning (MS, Certificate). *Accreditation:* NCATE. *Students:* 26 full-time (16 women), 80 part-time (57 women). In 2006, 27 degrees awarded. *Degree requirements:* For master's, thesis or alternative, comprehensive exam; for other advanced degree, thesis, comprehensive exam. *Entrance requirements:* For master's, GRE General Test or MAT, minimum GPA of 3.0 during previous 2 years; for other advanced degree, GRE, minimum GPA of 3.0. Additional exam requirements/recommendations for international students: Required—TOEFL. *Application deadline:* For fall admission, 7/1 priority date for domestic students; for spring admission, 10/1 for domestic students. Applications are processed on a rolling basis. Application fee: $40. Electronic applications accepted. *Financial support:* Application deadline: 3/15. *Unit head:* Dr. Patricia Hoffman, Chairperson, 507-389-1965. *Application contact:* 507-389-2321, E-mail: grad@mnsu.edu.

Minnesota State University Moorhead, Graduate Studies, College of Education and Human Services, Program in Curriculum and Instruction, Moorhead, MN 56563-0002. Offers MS. *Accreditation:* NCATE. Part-time programs available. *Faculty:* 6 part-time/adjunct (2 women). *Students:* 33 applicants, 100% accepted. In 2006, 3 degrees awarded. *Degree requirements:* For master's, final oral exam, project or thesis. *Entrance requirements:* For master's, MAT, bachelor's degree in education, minimum GPA of 2.75, one year teaching experience. Additional exam requirements/recommendations for international students: Required—TOEFL (minimum score 550 paper-based; 213 computer-based). *Application deadline:* For fall admission, 4/15 priority date for domestic students, 3/15 for international students; for spring admission, 11/1 priority date for domestic students. Applications are processed on a rolling basis. Application fee: $20. Electronic applications accepted. *Financial support:* In 2006–07, 1 research assistantship (averaging $1,000 per year) was awarded; Federal Work-Study and unspecified assistantships also available. Financial award application deadline: 7/15; financial award applicants required to submit FAFSA. *Unit head:* Dr. Steven Grineski, Coordinator, 218-477-2017, E-mail: grineski@mnstate.edu.

Mississippi College, Graduate School, School of Education, Department of Teacher Education and Leadership, Clinton, MS 39058. Offers art (M Ed); biological science (M Ed); business education (M Ed); computer science (M Ed); dyslexia therapy (M Ed); educational leadership (M Ed, Ed S); elementary education (M Ed, Ed S); English (M Ed); higher education administration (MS); mathematics (M Ed); secondary education (M Ed); social studies (history) (M Ed); teaching arts (M Ed). Part-time programs available. *Faculty:* 9 full-time (5 women), 14 part-time/adjunct (10 women). *Students:* 52 full-time (36 women), 286 part-time (247 women); includes 173 minority (171 African Americans, 1 American Indian/Alaska Native, 1 Hispanic American), 1 international. Average age 32. In 2006, 131 degrees awarded. *Degree requirements:* For master's, thesis optional. *Entrance requirements:* For master's, NTE. Additional exam requirements/recommendations for international students: Recommended—IELTS. *Application deadline:* Applications are processed on a rolling basis. Application fee: $25. Electronic applications accepted. *Expenses:* Tuition: Full-time $7,290; part-time $405 per hour. Required fees: $150 per term. Tuition and fees vary according to campus/location and program. *Financial support:* Teaching assistantships, career-related internships or fieldwork, Federal Work-Study, scholarships/grants, and unspecified assistantships available. Support available to part-time students. Financial award applicants required to submit FAFSA. *Unit head:* Dr. Tom Williams, Chair, 601-925-3844, E-mail: twilliams@mc.edu.

Mississippi State University, College of Education, Department of Curriculum and Instruction, Mississippi State, MS 39762. Offers curriculum and instruction (PhD); elementary education (MS, Ed D, PhD, Ed S); secondary education (MS, Ed D, PhD, Ed S). *Accreditation:* NCATE. Part-time and evening/weekend programs available. *Faculty:* 23 full-time (20 women), 13 part-time/adjunct (9 women). *Students:* 15 full-time (8 women), 85 part-time (67 women); includes 23 minority (22 African Americans, 1 American Indian/Alaska Native). Average age 31. 10 applicants, 60% accepted, 4 enrolled. In 2006, 48 master's, 14 doctorates awarded. *Degree requirements:* For master's, comprehensive exam; for doctorate, thesis/dissertation; for Ed S, thesis or alternative, comprehensive exam. *Entrance requirements:* For master's, GRE, minimum GPA of 2.75 in junior and senior year, eligibility for initial teacher certification; for doctorate, GRE, minimum graduate GPA of 3.4; for Ed S, GRE, minimum graduate GPA of 3.2. *Application deadline:* For fall admission, 3/1 priority date for domestic students; for spring admission, 9/1 priority date for domestic students. Applications are processed on a rolling basis. Application fee: $30. Electronic applications accepted. *Expenses:* Tuition, state resident: full-time $4,550; part-time $253 per hour. Tuition, nonresident: full-time $10,552; part-time $584 per hour. International tuition: $10,882 full-time. Tuition and fees vary according to course load. *Financial support:* In 2006–07, 30 students received support; research assistantships with tuition reimbursements available, teaching assistantships with tuition reimbursements available, Federal Work-Study, institutionally sponsored loans, scholarships/grants, unspecified assistantships, and work on faculty secured grants available. Financial award applicants required to submit FAFSA. *Faculty research:* Early childhood education, reading, rural schools, multicultural education, use of technology in instruction. *Unit head:* Dr. Unda T. Coats, Interim Head, 662-325-3747, Fax: 662-325-7857, E-mail: ltc1@ra.msstate.edu. *Application contact:* Dr. Phil Bonfanti, Director of Admissions, 662-325-4104, Fax: 662-325-8872, E-mail: admit@msstate.edu.

Missouri State University, Graduate College, College of Education, School of Teacher Education, Program in Teaching, Springfield, MO 65804-0094. Offers MAT. *Students:* 52 full-time (32 women), 69 part-time (38 women); includes 6 minority (1 African American, 1 American Indian/Alaska Native, 2 Asian Americans or Pacific Islanders, 2 Hispanic Americans), 1 international. Average age 32. 9 applicants, 67% accepted, 4 enrolled. In 2006, 25 degrees awarded. *Degree requirements:* For master's, project. *Entrance requirements:* For master's, PRAXIS II. Additional exam requirements/recommendations for international students: Required—TOEFL (minimum score 550 paper-based; 213 computer-based; 79 iBT). *Application deadline:* For fall admission, 2/15 priority date for domestic and international students. Application fee: $35. Electronic applications accepted. *Expenses:* Tuition, state resident: full-time $3,582; part-time $199 per credit hour. Tuition, nonresident: full-time $6,984; part-time $199 per credit hour. Required fees: $548. Full-time tuition and fees vary according to course level, course load, program and reciprocity agreements. *Financial support:* Teaching assistantships with tuition reimbursements, Federal Work-Study, scholarships/grants, tuition waivers (full), and unspecified assistantships available. Financial award application deadline: 3/31; financial award applicants required to submit FAFSA. *Unit head:* Dr. Emmett Sawyer, Coordinator, 417-836-3170, E-mail: emmettsawyer@missouristate.edu.

Montana State University–Billings, College of Education and Human Services, Department of Educational Theory and Practice, Option in General Curriculum, Billings, MT 59101-0298. Offers M Ed. *Accreditation:* NCATE. Part-time programs available. *Students:* 1. In 2006, 2 degrees awarded. *Degree requirements:* For master's, thesis or professional paper and/or field experience, thesis optional. *Entrance requirements:* For master's, GRE General Test or MAT, minimum GPA of 3.0 (undergraduate), 3.25 (graduate). *Application deadline:* Applications are processed on a rolling basis. Application fee: $40. *Expenses:* Tuition, state resident: full-time $4,599. Tuition, nonresident: full-time $10,786. *Financial support:* Teaching assistantships, career-related internships or fieldwork, Federal Work-Study, institutionally sponsored loans, scholarships/grants, tuition waivers (partial), and unspecified assistantships available. Support available to part-time students. Financial award application deadline: 5/1. *Faculty research:* Social studies education, science education. *Application contact:* David M. Sullivan, Graduate Studies Counselor, 406-657-2053, Fax: 406-657-2299, E-mail: dsullivan@msubillings.edu.

Montclair State University, The Graduate School, College of Education and Human Services, Center of Pedagogy, Montclair, NJ 07043-1624. Offers mathematics education (Ed D); philosophy for children (Ed D). Part-time programs available. *Faculty:* 18. *Degree requirements:* For doctorate, thesis/dissertation. *Entrance requirements:* For doctorate, GRE, 3 letters of recommendation. Additional exam requirements/recommendations for international students: Required—TOEFL (minimum score 117 computer-based). *Application deadline:* For fall admission, 2/1 for domestic students, 11/15 for international students. Application fee: $60. Electronic applications accepted. *Expenses:* Tuition, state resident: part-time $450 per credit. Tuition, nonresident: part-time $682 per credit. Tuition and fees vary according to degree level and program. *Financial support:* Research assistantships with full tuition reimbursements, institutionally sponsored loans and scholarships/grants available. Financial award application deadline: 3/1; financial award applicants required to submit FAFSA. *Unit head:* Jennifer Robinson, Director, 973-655-4262.

See Close-Up on page 1115.

Montclair State University, The Graduate School, College of Education and Human Services, Department of Curriculum and Teaching, Montclair, NJ 07043-1624. Offers education (M Ed); educational technology (M Ed); school library media specialist (Certificate); teaching (MAT, Certificate), including art (MAT), biological science (MAT), early childhood education (P-3) (MAT), earth science (MAT), elementary education (K-8) (MAT), English (MAT), French (MAT), health and physical education (MAT), health education (MAT), home economics (MAT), mathematics (MAT), music (MAT), physical education (MAT), physical science (MAT), social studies (MAT), Spanish (MAT), teacher of ESL (MAT), teacher of students with disabilities (MAT). Part-time and evening/weekend programs available. *Faculty:* 16 full-time (12 women), 13 part-time/adjunct (8 women). *Students:* 147 full-time (113 women), 230 part-time (188 women); includes 58 minority (33 African Americans, 1 American Indian/Alaska Native, 12 Asian Americans or Pacific Islanders, 12 Hispanic Americans), 4 international. Average age 33. 118 applicants, 38% accepted, 37 enrolled. In 2006, 166 master's, 11 other advanced degrees awarded. *Degree requirements:* For master's, field experience. *Entrance requirements:* For master's, PRAXIS II, minimum GPA of 2.67, 2 letters of recommendation. Additional exam requirements/recommendations for international students: Required—TOEFL (minimum score 83 computer-based). *Application deadline:* For fall admission, 2/15 for domestic and international students; for spring admission, 9/15 for domestic and international students. Applications are processed on a rolling basis. Application fee: $60. Electronic applications accepted. *Expenses:* Tuition, state resident: part-time $450 per credit. Tuition, nonresident: part-time $682 per credit. Tuition and fees vary according to degree level and program. *Financial support:* In 2006–07, 7 research assistantships with full tuition reimbursements (averaging $7,000 per year) were awarded; Federal Work-Study, scholarships/grants, and unspecified assistantships also available. Support available to part-time students. Financial award application deadline: 3/1; financial award applicants required to submit FAFSA. *Unit head:* Dr. Deborah Eldridge, Chairperson, 973-655-5187.

Moravian College, The Comenius Center for Continuing, Professional, and Graduate Studies, Program in Education, Bethlehem, PA 18018-6650. Offers curriculum and instruction (M Ed). Part-time programs available. *Faculty:* 7 full-time (4 women), 13 part-time/adjunct (9 women). In 2006, 26 degrees awarded. *Degree requirements:* For master's, thesis, action research. *Entrance requirements:* For master's, teaching certificate. Additional exam requirements/recommendations for international students: Required—TOEFL. *Application deadline:* Applications are processed on a rolling basis. Application fee: $30. *Expenses:* Contact institution. *Faculty research:* Action research for classroom teachers. *Unit head:* Dr. Joseph Shosh, Director, 610-861-1482, Fax: 610-861-1696, E-mail: mejms01@moravian.edu.

Morehead State University, Graduate Programs, College of Education, Department of Curriculum and Instruction, Program in Curriculum and Instruction, Morehead, KY 40351. Offers Ed S. *Accreditation:* NCATE. Part-time and evening/weekend programs available. In 2006, 3 degrees awarded. *Degree requirements:* For Ed S, thesis, oral exam. *Entrance requirements:* For degree, GRE General Test, interview, master's degree, minimum GPA of 3.5, work experience. Additional exam requirements/recommendations for international students: Required—TOEFL (minimum score 525 paper-based; 197 computer-based). *Application deadline:* For fall admission, 8/1 priority date for domestic and international students; for spring admission, 12/1 priority date for domestic and international students. Applications are processed on a rolling basis. Application fee: $0 ($55 for international students). Electronic applications accepted. *Financial support:* Career-related internships or fieldwork, Federal Work-Study, and unspecified assistantships available. Financial award application deadline: 4/1; financial award applicants required to submit FAFSA. *Faculty research:* Ungraded primary school organization. *Application contact:* Michelle Barber, Graduate Admissions Counselor, 606-783-2039, Fax: 606-783-5061, E-mail: m.barber@moreheadstate.edu.

Mount Saint Vincent University, Graduate Programs, Faculty of Education, Program in Curriculum Studies, Halifax, NS B3M 2J6, Canada. Offers education of young adolescents (M Ed, MA Ed, MA-R); general studies (M Ed, MA Ed, MA-R); teaching English as a second language (M Ed, MA Ed, MA-R). Part-time and evening/weekend programs available. Postbaccalaureate distance learning degree programs offered (minimal on-campus study). *Degree requirements:* For master's, thesis (for some programs). *Entrance requirements:* For master's, bachelor's degree in related field, minimum B average, 1 year of teaching experience. Electronic applications accepted. *Faculty research:* Science education, cultural studies, international education, curriculum development.

National-Louis University, National College of Education, Doctoral Programs in Education, Program in Curriculum and Social Inquiry, Chicago, IL 60603. Offers Ed D. Part-time and evening/weekend programs available. *Students:* 1 (woman) full-time, 23 part-time (12 women); includes 9 minority (7 African Americans, 2 Hispanic Americans). Average age 44. 1 applicant, 100% accepted. In 2006, 4 degrees awarded. *Degree requirements:* For doctorate, thesis/dissertation, comprehensive exam. *Entrance requirements:* For doctorate, GRE General Test, interview, minimum GPA of 3.25, resumé, writing sample. *Application deadline:* For fall admission, 5/1 for domestic students; for spring admission, 1/15 for domestic students. Application fee: $25. *Expenses:* Tuition: Full-time $17,685. One-time fee: $40 full-time. *Financial support:* Fellowships, research assistantships, teaching assistantships, career-related internships or fieldwork, Federal Work-Study, institutionally sponsored loans, and scholarships/grants available. Support available to part-time students. Financial award application deadline: 4/15; financial award applicants required to submit FAFSA. *Unit head:* Patrick Roberts, Assistant Professor, 847-905-2767, E-mail: proberts@nl.edu. *Application contact:* David McCulloch, Vice President for University Services, 800-443-5522 Ext. 5127, Fax: 847-465-0593, E-mail: dmcc@wheeling1.nl.edu.

National-Louis University, National College of Education, Program in Curriculum and Instruction, Chicago, IL 60603. Offers M Ed, MS Ed, CAS. Part-time and evening/weekend programs available. *Students:* 6 full-time (5 women), 233 part-time (206 women); includes 62 minority (12 African Americans, 12 Asian Americans or Pacific Islanders, 38 Hispanic Americans). Average age 36. 37 applicants, 100% accepted. In 2006, 82 master's, 1 other advanced degree awarded. *Entrance requirements:* For master's, GRE or MAT, minimum GPA of 3.0, teaching certificate; for CAS, master's degree, teaching certificate. *Application deadline:* Applications are processed on a rolling basis. Application fee: $25. *Expenses:* Tuition: Full-time $17,685. One-time fee: $40 full-time. *Financial support:* Fellowships, career-related internships or fieldwork, Federal Work-Study, institutionally sponsored loans, and scholarships/grants available. Support available to part-time students. Financial award applicants required to submit FAFSA. *Unit head:* Dr. Darrell Bloom, Coordinator, 847-475-1100 Ext. 5622. *Application contact:* David McCulloch, Vice President for University Services, 800-443-5522 Ext. 5127, Fax: 847-465-0593, E-mail: dmcc@wheeling1.nl.edu.

National-Louis University, National College of Education, Program in Interdisciplinary Studies in Curriculum and Instruction, Chicago, IL 60603. Offers M Ed. Part-time and evening/weekend programs available. *Students:* 505 full-time (416 women), 35 part-time (33 women); includes 76 minority (46 African Americans, 2 American Indian/Alaska Native, 4 Asian Americans or Pacific Islanders, 24 Hispanic Americans). Average age 36. 338 applicants, 100% accepted.

Curriculum and Instruction

National-Louis University (continued)

Entrance requirements: For master's, GRE or MAT, minimum GPA of 3.0, teaching certificate. *Application deadline:* Applications are processed on a rolling basis. Application fee: $25. *Expenses:* Tuition: Full-time $17,685. One-time fee: $40 full-time. *Financial support:* Fellowships, career-related internships or fieldwork, Federal Work-Study, institutionally sponsored loans, and scholarships/grants available. Support available to part-time students. Financial award applicants required to submit FAFSA. *Unit head:* Dr. Jerry Ligon, Coordinator, 847-475-1100 Ext. 6840. *Application contact:* David McCulloch, Vice President for University Services, 800-443-5522 Ext. 5127, Fax: 847-465-0593, E-mail: dmcc@wheeling1.nl.edu.

Newman University, School of Education, Wichita, KS 67213-2097. Offers building leadership (MS Ed); curriculum and instruction (MS Ed), including accountability, English as a second language. Part-time programs available. Postbaccalaureate distance learning degree programs offered (no on-campus study). *Faculty:* 3 full-time (0 women), 4 part-time/adjunct (all women). *Students:* 2 full-time (both women), 41 part-time (24 women); includes 3 minority (2 African Americans, 1 American Indian/Alaska Native), 3 international. Average age 35. 25 applicants, 92% accepted, 17 enrolled. In 2006, 35 degrees awarded. *Degree requirements:* For master's, thesis optional. *Entrance requirements:* For master's, GRE General Test or MAT, interview, minimum GPA of 3.0, writing sample, 3 letters of recommendation. Additional exam requirements/recommendations for international students: Required—TOEFL (minimum score 600 paper-based; 250 computer-based). *Application deadline:* For fall admission, 8/15 priority date for domestic students; for spring admission, 1/10 priority date for domestic students. Applications are processed on a rolling basis. Application fee: $25 ($40 for international students). Electronic applications accepted. *Financial support:* In 2006–07, 8 students received support. Federal Work-Study and tuition waivers (full) available. Financial award application deadline: 8/15; financial award applicants required to submit FAFSA. *Unit head:* Dr. Guy Glidden, Director, 316-942-4291 Ext. 2331, Fax: 316-942-4483, E-mail: gliddeng@newmanu.edu. *Application contact:* Linda Kay Sabala, Director of Graduate Admissions, 316-942-4291 Ext. 2230, Fax: 316-942-4483, E-mail: sabalal@newmanu.edu.

New Mexico Highlands University, Graduate Studies, School of Education, Las Vegas, NM 87701. Offers education (MA), including curriculum and instruction; educational leadership (MA); exercise and sport sciences (MA), including human performance and sport, sports administration, teacher education; guidance and counseling (MA), including professional counseling, rehabilitation counseling, school counseling; special education (MA), including). *Accreditation:* NCATE. Part-time programs available. *Faculty:* 14 full-time (6 women), 11 part-time/adjunct (9 women). *Students:* 171 full-time (117 women), 413 part-time (286 women); includes 305 minority (17 African Americans, 30 American Indian/Alaska Native, 4 Asian Americans or Pacific Islanders, 254 Hispanic Americans), 3 international. Average age 40. 111 applicants, 84% accepted, 63 enrolled. In 2006, 111 degrees awarded. *Degree requirements:* For master's, thesis or alternative, comprehensive exam, registration. *Entrance requirements:* For master's, minimum undergraduate GPA of 3.0. Additional exam requirements/recommendations for international students: Required—TOEFL (minimum score 540 paper-based; 190 computer-based). *Application deadline:* For fall admission, 8/1 priority date for domestic students. Applications are processed on a rolling basis. Application fee: $15. *Expenses:* Tuition, state resident: part-time $101 per credit hour. Tuition, nonresident: part-time $101 per credit hour. *Financial support:* In 2006–07, 205 students received support, including 16 teaching assistantships with full and partial tuition reimbursements available (averaging $6,500 per year); career-related internships or fieldwork, Federal Work-Study, institutionally sponsored loans, scholarships/grants, traineeships, tuition waivers (partial), and unspecified assistantships also available. Support available to part-time students. Financial award application deadline: 3/1; financial award applicants required to submit FAFSA. *Unit head:* Dr. Francisco Hidalgo, Dean, 505-454-3357, Fax: 505-454-3384, E-mail: fhidalgo@nmhu.edu. *Application contact:* Diane Trujillo, Administrative Assistant Graduate Studies, 505-454-3266, Fax: 505-454-3558, E-mail: dtrujillo@nmhu.edu.

New Mexico State University, Graduate School, College of Education, Department of Curriculum and Instruction, Las Cruces, NM 88003-8001. Offers curriculum and instruction (MAT, Ed D, PhD, Ed S); general education (MA); reading (Ed S). *Accreditation:* NCATE. Part-time programs available. Postbaccalaureate distance learning degree programs offered (minimal on-campus study). *Faculty:* 22 full-time (10 women), 11 part-time/adjunct (3 women). *Students:* 200 full-time (155 women), 399 part-time (312 women); includes 267 minority (16 African Americans, 12 American Indian/Alaska Native, 7 Asian Americans or Pacific Islanders, 232 Hispanic Americans), 33 international. Average age 37. 233 applicants, 82% accepted. In 2006, 213 master's, 17 doctorates awarded. *Degree requirements:* For master's, thesis optional; for doctorate, thesis/dissertation, comprehensive exam. *Entrance requirements:* For master's, minimum GPA of 2.5 in last 12 hours of course work; for doctorate, portfolio. *Application deadline:* For fall admission, 7/1 priority date for domestic students; for spring admission, 11/1 for domestic students. Applications are processed on a rolling basis. Application fee: $30 ($50 for international students). *Financial support:* In 2006–07, 1 fellowship, 20 teaching assistantships were awarded; research assistantships, career-related internships or fieldwork, Federal Work-Study, scholarships/grants, health care benefits, and unspecified assistantships also available. Support available to part-time students. Financial award application deadline: 3/1. *Faculty research:* Multicultural education, literacy/biliteracy education, bilingual and English as a second language education, critical pedagogy, education for democratic society. *Unit head:* Dr. James O'Donnell, Head, 505-646-2990, Fax: 505-646-5436, E-mail: jodonnel@nmsu.edu.

Nicholls State University, Graduate Studies, College of Education, Department of Teacher Education, Thibodaux, LA 70310. Offers administration and supervision (M Ed); counselor education (M Ed); curriculum and instruction (M Ed). *Accreditation:* NCATE. Part-time and evening/weekend programs available. *Faculty:* 17 full-time (13 women), 6 part-time/adjunct (4 women). *Students:* 21 full-time (17 women), 174 part-time (155 women); includes 60 minority (52 African Americans, 5 American Indian/Alaska Native, 1 Asian American or Pacific Islander, 2 Hispanic Americans). Average age 33. In 2006, 77 degrees awarded. *Degree requirements:* For master's, portfolio. *Entrance requirements:* For master's, GRE General Test, teaching license. *Application deadline:* Applications are processed on a rolling basis. Application fee: $20 ($30 for international students). Electronic applications accepted. *Expenses:* Tuition, state resident: part-time $450 per hour. Tuition, nonresident: part-time $450 per hour. *Financial support:* In 2006–07, research assistantships with tuition reimbursements (averaging $4,000 per year). Financial award application deadline: 6/17. *Unit head:* Dr. J. Lavone Landry, Head, 985-448-4314, E-mail: lavone.landry@nicholls.edu.

North Carolina State University, Graduate School, College of Education, Department of Curriculum and Instruction, Program in Curriculum and Instruction, Raleigh, NC 27695. Offers M Ed, MS, PhD. *Accreditation:* NCATE. *Degree requirements:* For master's, thesis (for some programs); for doctorate, thesis/dissertation. *Entrance requirements:* For master's, GRE General Test or MAT, minimum GPA of 3.0 in major; for doctorate, GRE General Test, minimum GPA of 3.0 in major. Electronic applications accepted. *Faculty research:* Curriculum development, teacher development, intervention for exceptional children, literacy development.

Northern Arizona University, Graduate College, College of Education, Program in Curriculum and Instruction, Flagstaff, AZ 86011. Offers Ed D. *Degree requirements:* For doctorate, thesis/dissertation. *Faculty research:* Leadership issues, evaluation of education, personnel evaluation, international education, multicultural education.

Northern Illinois University, Graduate School, College of Education, Department of Teaching and Learning, De Kalb, IL 60115-2854. Offers curriculum and instruction (MS Ed, Ed D), including curriculum leadership (Ed D), elementary education (Ed D), secondary education (Ed D); early childhood education (MS Ed); elementary education (MS Ed); special education (MS Ed). Part-time and evening/weekend programs available. *Faculty:* 22 full-time (14 women), 2 part-time/adjunct (both women). *Students:* 81 full-time (64 women), 534 part-time (417 women); includes 122 minority (21 African Americans, 12 Asian Americans or Pacific Islanders, 89 Hispanic Americans), 11 international. Average age 36. 92 applicants, 57% accepted, 43 enrolled. In 2006, 256 master's, 12 doctorates awarded. *Degree requirements:* For master's, thesis optional; for doctorate, thesis/dissertation, candidacy exam, dissertation defense. *Entrance requirements:* For master's, GRE General Test or MAT, minimum undergraduate GPA of 2.75; for doctorate, GRE General Test or MAT, minimum undergraduate GPA of 2.75, graduate 3.2. Additional exam requirements/recommendations for international students: Required—TOEFL (minimum score 550 paper-based; 213 computer-based). *Application deadline:* For fall admission, 6/1 for domestic students, 5/1 for international students; for spring admission, 11/1 for domestic students, 10/1 for international students. Applications are processed on a rolling basis. Application fee: $30. Electronic applications accepted. *Financial support:* In 2006–07, 27 research assistantships with full tuition reimbursements, 1 teaching assistantship with full tuition reimbursement were awarded; fellowships with full tuition reimbursements, career-related internships or fieldwork, Federal Work-Study, scholarships/grants, tuition waivers (full), and unspecified assistantships also available. Support available to part-time students. Financial award applicants required to submit FAFSA. *Faculty research:* Teacher certification, stress reduction during student teaching, teaching history, portfolios in student teaching. *Unit head:* Dr. Pamela Jackson, Acting Chair, 815-753-8452, E-mail: p30ngd1@wpo.cso.niu.edu.

Northwestern Oklahoma State University, School of Professional Studies, Alva, OK 73717-2799. Offers adult education management and administration (M Ed), including adult education management and administration, education: non-certificate option; counseling psychology (MCP); curriculum and instruction (M Ed); educational leadership (M Ed); elementary education (M Ed); guidance and counseling K–12 (M Ed); reading specialist (M Ed); secondary education (M Ed). *Accreditation:* NCATE (one or more programs are accredited). Part-time programs available. *Faculty:* 32 full-time (17 women), 12 part-time/adjunct (7 women). *Students:* 43 full-time (33 women), 111 part-time (88 women); includes 10 minority (1 African American, 6 American Indian/Alaska Native, 3 Hispanic Americans), 2 international. Average age 31. 75 applicants, 92% accepted, 57 enrolled. In 2006, 68 degrees awarded. *Degree requirements:* For master's, portfolio, thesis optional. *Entrance requirements:* For master's, GRE General Test or MAT, minimum GPA of 2.75. *Application deadline:* Applications are processed on a rolling basis. Application fee: $15. *Expenses:* Tuition, state resident: part-time $700 per year. Tuition, nonresident: part-time $1,715 per year. *Financial support:* Federal Work-Study available. Support available to part-time students. Financial award application deadline: 5/1. *Unit head:* Dr. James Bowen, Dean, 580-327-8455.

Northwestern State University of Louisiana, Graduate Studies and Research, College of Education, Program in Curriculum and Instruction, Natchitoches, LA 71497. Offers M Ed. *Students:* 7 full-time (6 women), 30 part-time (28 women); includes 13 minority (12 African Americans, 1 Hispanic American). Average age 36. *Unit head:* Dr. Steven G. Horton, Associate Provost/Dean, Graduate Studies, Research, and Information Systems, 318-357-5851, Fax: 318-357-5019, E-mail: grad_school@nsula.edu.

Northwest Nazarene University, Graduate Studies, Program in Teacher Education, Nampa, ID 83686-5897. Offers curriculum and instruction (M Ed); educational leadership (M Ed); exceptional child (M Ed); reading education (M Ed); school counseling (M Ed). *Accreditation:* ACA; NCATE. Part-time programs available. *Faculty:* 11 full-time (4 women), 10 part-time/adjunct (6 women). *Students:* 113 full-time (79 women), 20 part-time (18 women); includes 4 minority (2 Asian Americans or Pacific Islanders, 2 Hispanic Americans). Average age 34. In 2006, 35 degrees awarded. *Degree requirements:* For master's, action research project. *Entrance requirements:* For master's, minimum undergraduate GPA of 2.8 overall or 3.0 during final 30 semester credits. *Application deadline:* For fall admission, 9/1 for domestic students. Applications are processed on a rolling basis. Application fee: $25. *Faculty research:* Action research, cooperative learning, accountability, institutional accreditation. *Unit head:* Dr. Karen Blacklock, Chair, 208-467-8399, Fax: 208-467-8562.

Nova Southeastern University, Fischler School of Education and Human Services, Graduate Teacher Education Program, Fort Lauderdale, FL 33314-7796. Offers athletic administration (MS); cognitive and behavioral disabilities (MS); computer science education (Ed S); computer science education (K-12) (MS); curriculum and teaching (Ed S); curriculum, instruction and technology (MS); curriculum, instruction, management and administration (Ed S); early childhood special education (MS); early literacy and reading (Ed S); early literacy education (MS); education technology (MS); educational leadership (administration K–12) (MS, Ed S); educational media (Ed S); educational media (K-12) (MS); elementary education (MS, Ed S), including ESOL endorsement (MS); English (MS, Ed S); exceptional student education (MS), including ESOL endorsement; gifted education (MS, Ed S); interdisciplinary arts education (MS); management and administration of educational programs (MS); mathematics (MS, Ed S); multicultural early intervention (MS); pre-kindergarten/primary (MS); preschool education (MS); reading (MS, Ed S); science (MS, Ed S); secondary education (MS); social studies (MS, Ed S); Spanish language (MS); teaching and learning (MA, MS), including curriculum and instruction (MA), elementary mathematics (MA), elementary reading (MA), K-12 technology integration (MA); teaching English to speakers of other languages (MS, Ed S); technology management and administration (Ed S); urban studies education (MS); varying exceptionalities (Ed S). Part-time and evening/weekend programs available. Postbaccalaureate distance learning degree programs offered. *Faculty:* 131 full-time (78 women), 548 part-time/adjunct (342 women). *Students:* 1,418 full-time (1,139 women), 3,464 part-time (2,877 women); includes 2,462 minority (1,732 African Americans, 13 American Indian/Alaska Native, 44 Asian Americans or Pacific Islanders, 673 Hispanic Americans), 77 international. Average age 38. 1,771 applicants, 80% accepted, 1419 enrolled. In 2006, 2,078 master's, 425 other advanced degrees awarded. *Degree requirements:* For master's and Ed S, thesis, practicum, internship. *Entrance requirements:* For master's, MAT, GRE, CLAST, CBEST, PRAXIS I, GKT, minimum GPA of 2.5; for Ed S, MAT or GRE, master's degree, teaching certificate, minimum GPA of 3.0. Additional exam requirements/recommendations for international students: Recommended—TOEFL (minimum score 550 paper-based; 213 computer-based), IELTS (minimum score 6). *Application deadline:* For fall admission, 8/11 priority date for domestic and international students; for winter admission, 12/28 priority date for domestic and international students; for spring admission, 4/22 priority date for domestic and international students. Applications are processed on a rolling basis. Application fee: $50. Electronic applications accepted. *Financial support:* Federal Work-Study available. Support available to part-time students. Financial award application deadline: 1/7. *Faculty research:* School effectiveness, critical thinking, leadership skills acquisition, child education, multicultural education. *Unit head:* Dr. Meline Kevorkian, Associate Dean of Master's and Educational Programs, 954-262-8500, Fax: 954-262-3606, E-mail: melinek@nova.edu. *Application contact:* Jennifer Quiñones Nottingham, Dean of Student Affairs, 800-986-3223 Ext. 8624, Fax: 954-262-3911, E-mail: jlquinon@nova.edu.

Ohio University, Graduate Studies, College of Education, Department of Teacher Education, Athens, OH 45701-2979. Offers adolescent to young adult education (M Ed); curriculum and instruction (M Ed, PhD); mathematics education (PhD); middle child education (M Ed); reading and language arts (PhD); reading education (M Ed); social studies education (PhD); special education (M Ed, PhD). Part-time and evening/weekend programs available. *Faculty:* 21 full-time (13 women), 7 part-time/adjunct (all women). *Students:* 57 full-time (44 women), 61 part-time (46 women); includes 4 minority (2 African Americans, 1 Asian American or Pacific Islander, 1 Hispanic American), 36 international. 93 applicants, 61% accepted, 37 enrolled. *Median time to degree:* Of those who began their doctoral program in fall 1998, 92% received their degree in 8 years or less. *Degree requirements:* For master's, thesis or alternative, registration; for doctorate, thesis/dissertation, comprehensive exam, registration. *Entrance requirements:* For master's, GRE General Test or MAT if GPA is less than 2.9; for doctorate, GRE General Test, minimum GPA of 3.4, work experience. Additional exam requirements/recommendations for international students: Required—TOEFL (minimum score 550 paper-based; 213 computer-based). *Application deadline:* For fall admission, 4/1 priority date for domestic and international students. Applications are processed on a rolling basis. Application fee: $45. Electronic applications accepted. *Financial support:* In 2006–07, 52 students received support, including 31 research assistantships with full tuition reimbursements available (averaging $6,500 per year), teaching assistantships with full tuition reimbursements available (averaging $7,200 per year); Federal Work-Study, institutionally sponsored loans, tuition waivers (full), and unspecified assistantships also available. Financial award application deadline: 3/15. *Faculty research:* Cognition literacy, character education, teacher's education reform, disabilities. Total annual research expenditures: $605,070. *Unit head:* Dr. William Earl Smith, Chair, 740-593-4483, Fax: 740-593-0477, E-mail: smithw@ohio.edu. *Application contact:* Floyd J. Doney, Director of Student Affairs, 740-593-4400, Fax: 740-593-9310, E-mail: doney@ohio.edu.

Oklahoma State University, College of Education, School of Teaching and Curriculum Leadership, Stillwater, OK 74078. Offers MS, PhD. *Faculty:* 32 full-time (27 women), 26 part-time/adjunct (22 women). *Students:* 28 full-time (21 women), 211 part-time (163 women); includes 43 minority (13 African Americans, 18 American Indian/Alaska Native, 5 Asian Americans or Pacific Islanders, 7 Hispanic Americans), 12 international. Average age 40. 136 applicants, 34% accepted, 40 enrolled. In 2006, 58 master's, 13 doctorates awarded. *Degree requirements:* For master's, thesis or alternative; for doctorate, thesis/dissertation. *Entrance requirements:* For master's, GRE or MAT; for doctorate, GRE. Additional exam requirements/recommendations for international students: Required—TOEFL. *Application deadline:* For fall admission, 7/1 priority date for domestic students, 3/1 priority date for international students; for spring admission, 8/1 priority date for international students. Applications are processed on a rolling basis. Application fee: $40 ($75 for international students). Electronic applications accepted. *Expenses:* Tuition, state resident: part-time $146 per credit hour. Tuition, nonresident: part-time $516 per credit hour. Required fees: $44 per credit hour. Tuition and fees vary according to program. *Financial support:* In 2006–07, 10 research assistantships (averaging $9,621 per year), 19 teaching assistantships (averaging $8,939 per year) were awarded; career-related internships or fieldwork, Federal Work-Study, scholarships/grants, health care benefits, tuition waivers (partial), and unspecified assistantships also available. Support available to part-time students. Financial award application deadline: 3/1. *Unit head:* Dr. Christine Ormsbee, Head, 405-744-7125.

Old Dominion University, Darden College of Education, Doctoral Program in Curriculum and Instruction, Norfolk, VA 23529. Offers PhD. Part-time and evening/weekend programs available. *Faculty:* 12 full-time (8 women). *Students:* 2 full-time (both women), 6 part-time (4 women). Average age 38. 10 applicants, 80% accepted, 8 enrolled. *Degree requirements:* For doctorate, thesis/dissertation, comprehensive exam, registration. *Entrance requirements:* For doctorate, GRE, letters of recommendation, minimum undergraduate GPA of 2.8, minimum graduate GPA of 3.2. Additional exam requirements/recommendations for international students: Required—TOEFL (minimum score 600 paper-based; 250 computer-based). *Application deadline:* For fall admission, 3/15 priority date for domestic and international students. Applications are processed on a rolling basis. Application fee: $40. Electronic applications accepted. *Expenses:* Tuition, area resident: Part-time $285 per credit hour. Tuition, nonresident: part-time $715 per credit hour. Required fees: $94 per semester. *Financial support:* In 2006–07, 3 students received support, including 1 fellowship with tuition reimbursement available (averaging $15,000 per year), 1 research assistantship (averaging $15,000 per year), 1 teaching assistantship (averaging $15,000 per year); scholarships/grants and unspecified assistantships also available. Financial award application deadline: 4/15. *Faculty research:* Curriculum change, language arts, library science, multicultural education, foundations in education. *Unit head:* Dr. Linda Bol, Graduate Program Director, 757-683-4584, E-mail: lbol@odu.edu.

Old Dominion University, Darden College of Education, Program in Physical Education, Curriculum and Instruction Emphasis, Norfolk, VA 23529. Offers MS Ed. Part-time and evening/weekend programs available. *Faculty:* 2 full-time (both women), 1 (woman) part-time/adjunct. *Students:* 2 full-time (1 woman), 9 part-time (6 women); includes 1 minority (African American) Average age 29. 6 applicants, 83% accepted, 1 enrolled. In 2006, 2 degrees awarded. *Degree requirements:* For master's, thesis or alternative, internship, research project, comprehensive exam. *Entrance requirements:* For master's, GRE, PRAXIS I (for licensure only), minimum GPA of 2.8 overall, minimum of 3.0 in major. Additional exam requirements/recommendations for international students: Required—TOEFL (minimum score 500 paper-based; 200 computer-based). *Application deadline:* For fall admission, 7/1 for domestic students; for spring admission, 11/1 for domestic students. Applications are processed on a rolling basis. Application fee: $40. *Expenses:* Tuition, area resident: Part-time $285 per credit hour. Tuition, nonresident: part-time $715 per credit hour. Required fees: $94 per semester. *Financial support:* In 2006–07, 1 teaching assistantship with partial tuition reimbursement (averaging $9,000 per year) was awarded; career-related internships or fieldwork and scholarships/grants also available. Financial award application deadline: 4/15. *Faculty research:* Motor development dynamical systems, motor learning attentional focus, adapted physical education. *Unit head:* Linda Gagen, Graduate Program Director, 757-683-3545, E-mail: lgagen@odu.edu. *Application contact:* Linda Gagen, Graduate Program Director, 757-683-3545, E-mail: lgagen@odu.edu.

Olivet Nazarene University, Graduate School, Division of Education, Program in Curriculum and Instruction, Bourbonnais, IL 60914-2271. Offers MAE. Evening/weekend programs available. *Degree requirements:* For master's, thesis or alternative.

Oral Roberts University, School of Education, Tulsa, OK 74171-0001. Offers Christian school administration (MA Ed, Ed D); Christian school administration (K-12) (MA Ed, Ed D); Christian school curriculum development (MA Ed); college and higher education administration (MA Ed, Ed D); public school administration (K-12) (MA Ed, Ed D); public school teaching (MA Ed); teaching English as a second language (MA Ed). *Accreditation:* NCATE. Part-time programs available. Postbaccalaureate distance learning degree programs offered (minimal on-campus study). *Faculty:* 9 full-time (2 women), 9 part-time/adjunct (4 women). *Students:* 331 full-time (217 women); includes 118 minority (96 African Americans, 7 American Indian/Alaska Native, 10 Asian Americans or Pacific Islanders, 5 Hispanic Americans). 125 applicants, 96% accepted, 116 enrolled. In 2006, 25 master's, 10 doctorates awarded. *Degree requirements:* For master's, thesis (for some programs), comprehensive exam; for doctorate, thesis/dissertation, comprehensive exam. *Entrance requirements:* For master's, GRE General Test or MAT, minimum GPA of 3.0; for doctorate, minimum GPA of 3.0. Additional exam requirements/recommendations for international students: Required—TOEFL (minimum score 500 paper-based; 173 computer-based). *Application deadline:* For fall admission, 7/1 priority date for domestic students, 5/1 priority date for international students; for spring admission, 12/1 priority date for domestic students, 10/1 priority date for international students. Applications are processed on a rolling basis. Application fee: $35. *Expenses:* Contact institution. *Financial support:* In 2006–07, 4 research assistantships (averaging $5,000 per year) were awarded; scholarships/grants and unspecified assistantships also available. Financial award application deadline: 6/1; financial award applicants required to submit FAFSA. *Faculty research:* Teacher effectiveness, college success in high achieving, African-Americans, professional development practices. *Unit head:* Dr. David Hand, Dean, 918-495-7084, Fax: 918-495-6050, E-mail: dhand@oru.edu. *Application contact:* Kim Schmeisser, Graduate Admissions, 918-495-6058, Fax: 918-495-6222, E-mail: gradeducation@oru.edu.

Ottawa University, Graduate Studies-Arizona, Program in Education, Ottawa, KS 66067-3399. Offers community college counseling (MA); curriculum and instruction (MA); early childhood (MA); education intervention (MA); education leadership (MA); education technology (MA); Montessori early childhood education (MA); Montessori elementary education (MA); professional development (MA); school guidance counseling (MA); special education—cross categorical (MA). Programs offered in Mesa, Phoenix, Tempe and West Valley, AZ. *Accreditation:* NCATE. Part-time programs available. *Faculty:* 7 full-time (3 women), 24 part-time/adjunct (11 women). *Students:* 14 full-time (9 women), 162 part-time (128 women); includes 31 minority (13 African Americans, 2 American Indian/Alaska Native, 1 Asian American or Pacific Islander, 15 Hispanic Americans), 1 international. Average age 38. In 2006, 56 degrees awarded. *Degree requirements:* For master's, thesis or alternative, registration. *Entrance requirements:* For master's, minimum undergraduate GPA of 3.0, copy of current state certification or teaching license. Additional exam requirements/recommendations for international students: Required—TOEFL (minimum score 550 paper-based; 213 computer-based). *Application deadline:* For fall admission, 7/1 priority date for domestic students; for winter admission, 11/1 priority date for domestic students; for spring admission, 2/1 priority date for domestic students. Applications are processed on a rolling basis. Application fee: $50. Electronic applications accepted. *Expenses:* Contact institution. *Application contact:* Bunny Simpson, Secretary, 602-371-1188, Fax: 602-371-0035, E-mail: bunny.simpson@ottawa.edu.

Our Lady of Holy Cross College, Program in Education and Counseling, New Orleans, LA 70131-7399. Offers administration and supervision (M Ed); curriculum and instruction (M Ed); marriage and family counseling (MA); school counseling (M Ed, MA). *Accreditation:* ACA; NCATE. Part-time and evening/weekend programs available. *Degree requirements:* For master's, thesis. *Entrance requirements:* For master's, GRE General Test, minimum GPA of 2.7.

Our Lady of the Lake University of San Antonio, School of Education and Clinical Studies, San Antonio, TX 78207-4689. Offers communication and learning disorders (MA); counseling psychology (MS, Psy D), including counseling psychology, marriage and family therapy (MS), school psychology (MS); curriculum and instruction (M Ed); human sciences (MA); leadership studies (PhD); learning resources (M Ed); principal (M Ed); school counseling (M Ed); sociology (MA); special education (MA). Part-time and evening/weekend programs available. *Degree requirements:* For master's, comprehensive exam; for doctorate, thesis/dissertation, internship, qualifying exam. *Entrance requirements:* For master's, GRE General Test or MAT; for doctorate, GRE General Test or MAT, interview. Additional exam requirements/recommendations for international students: Required—TOEFL. Electronic applications accepted.

Pace University, School of Education, New York, NY 10038. Offers administration and supervision (MS Ed); curriculum and instruction (MS); education (MST); school business management (Certificate). *Accreditation:* NCATE. Part-time and evening/weekend programs available. *Faculty:* 9 full-time, 12 part-time/adjunct. *Students:* 130 full-time (106 women), 2,151 part-time (1,484 women); includes 96 minority (50 African Americans, 2 American Indian/Alaska Native, 21 Asian Americans or Pacific Islanders, 23 Hispanic Americans), 6 international. Average age 27. 229 applicants, 70% accepted, 70 enrolled. In 2006, 550 master's, 23 other advanced degrees awarded. *Degree requirements:* For master's, internship. *Entrance requirements:* For master's, interview, teaching certificate. *Application deadline:* For fall admission, 7/31 priority date for domestic students; for spring admission, 11/30 for domestic students. Applications are processed on a rolling basis. Application fee: $65. Electronic applications accepted. *Expenses:* Contact institution. *Financial support:* Research assistantships, career-related internships or fieldwork and Federal Work-Study available. Support available to part-time students. Financial award applicants required to submit FAFSA. *Unit head:* Dr. Harriet Feldman, Interim Dean, 212-346-1512. *Application contact:* Joanna Broda, Director of Admissions, 212-346-1652, Fax: 212-346-1585, E-mail: gradnyc@pace.edu.

See Close-Up on page 907.

Pacific Lutheran University, Division of Graduate Studies, School of Education, Residency Program in Teaching, Tacoma, WA 98447. Offers MA. *Accreditation:* NCATE. *Faculty:* 5 full-time (2 women), 3 part-time/adjunct (2 women). *Students:* 30 full-time (18 women), 5 part-time (4 women); includes 4 minority (1 African American, 2 Asian Americans or Pacific Islanders, 1 Hispanic American). Average age 29. 47 applicants, 100% accepted, 30 enrolled. In 2006, 45 degrees awarded. *Degree requirements:* For master's, thesis, comprehensive exam, registration. *Entrance requirements:* For master's, GRE General Test or MAT, interview. Additional exam requirements/recommendations for international students: Required—TOEFL (minimum score 550 paper-based; 213 computer-based). *Application deadline:* For fall admission, 1/31 priority date for domestic students. Application fee: $40. *Expenses:* Contact institution. Part-time tuition and fees vary according to program. *Financial support:* In 2006–07, 32 students received support. Federal Work-Study, scholarships/grants, and unspecified assistantships available. Financial award application deadline: 3/1. *Unit head:* Dr. Michael Hillis, Graduate Director, 253-535-7272, Fax: 253-535-7184, E-mail: hillis@plu.edu. *Application contact:* Linda DuBay, Senior Office Assistant, 253-535-7151, Fax: 253-536-5136, E-mail: admissions@plu.edu.

Penn State Great Valley, Graduate Studies, Education Division, Malvern, PA 19355-1488. Offers curriculum and instruction (M Ed); instructional systems (M Ed, MS); special education (M Ed, MS). *Unit head:* Dr. Arlene Mitchell, Academic Division Head, 610-648-3355, E-mail: ahm13@psu.edu. *Application contact:* Dr. Arlene Mitchell, Academic Division Head, 610-648-3355, E-mail: ahm13@psu.edu.

Penn State Harrisburg, Graduate School, School of Behavioral Sciences and Education, Middletown, PA 17057-4898. Offers adult education (D Ed); applied behavior analysis (MA); applied clinical psychology (MA); applied psychological research (MA); community psychology and social change (MA); health education (M Ed); teaching and curriculum (M Ed); training and development (M Ed). Part-time and evening/weekend programs available. *Expenses:* Tuition, state resident: full-time $13,224; part-time $551 per credit. Tuition, nonresident: full-time $18,652; part-time $777 per credit. Required fees: $84 per semester. *Financial support:* Career-related internships or fieldwork available. *Unit head:* Dr. William D. Milheim, Director, 717-948-6205, Fax: 717-948-6209, E-mail: wdm2@psu.edu.

Penn State University Park, Graduate School, College of Education, Department of Curriculum and Instruction, State College, University Park, PA 16802-1503. Offers bilingual education (M Ed, MS, PhD); early childhood education (M Ed, MS, PhD); elementary education (M Ed, MS, PhD); instructional systems (M Ed, MS, PhD); language arts and reading (M Ed, MS, PhD); science education (M Ed, MS, PhD); social studies education (MS, PhD); supervisor and curriculum development (M Ed, MS, PhD). *Accreditation:* NCATE. *Unit head:* Dr. Murry R. Nelson, Head, 814-865-6321, Fax: 814-863-7602, E-mail: mrn2@psu.edu. *Application contact:* Judy Nastase, Graduate Staff Assistant, 814-865-2168, E-mail: jcn3@psu.edu.

Philadelphia Biblical University, School of Education, Langhorne, PA 19047-2990. Offers educational leadership and administration (MS El); teacher education (MS Ed). Part-time and evening/weekend programs available. *Faculty:* 8 full-time (6 women), 3 part-time/adjunct (2 women). *Students:* 6 full-time (5 women), 70 part-time (42 women); includes 12 minority (4 African Americans, 7 Asian Americans or Pacific Islanders, 1 Hispanic American), 3 international. Average age 35. 29 applicants, 55% accepted, 12 enrolled. In 2006, 30 degrees awarded. *Entrance requirements:* Additional exam requirements/recommendations for international students: Required—TOEFL (minimum score 550 paper-based; 213 computer-based). *Application deadline:* Applications are processed on a rolling basis. Application fee: $25. Electronic applications accepted. *Expenses:* Tuition: Full-time $8,820; part-time $490 per credit. *Financial support:* In 2006–07, 27 students received support. Scholarships/grants available. Support available to part-time students. Financial award applicants required to submit FAFSA. *Unit head:* Dr. Martha MacCullough, Dean, 215-702-4387, E-mail: teacher.ed@pbu.edu. *Application contact:* Katerina Penkova, Enrollment Counselor, Graduate Education, 800-572-2472, Fax: 215-702-4248, E-mail: kpenkova@pbu.edu.

Piedmont College, School of Education, Demorest, GA 30535-0010. Offers early childhood education (MA, MAT); instruction (Ed S); secondary education (MA, MAT). Part-time and evening/weekend programs available. *Faculty:* 20 full-time (17 women), 22 part-time/adjunct (5 women). *Students:* 210 full-time (158 women), 846 part-time (734 women); includes 95 minority (72 African Americans, 2 American Indian/Alaska Native, 10 Asian Americans or Pacific Islanders, 11 Hispanic Americans), 7 international. 327 applicants, 92% accepted, 235 enrolled. In 2006, 422 master's, 203 other advanced degrees awarded. *Degree requirements:* For master's, thesis, field experience in the teaching classroom. *Entrance requirements:* For master's, GRE General Test, MAT, minimum undergraduate GPA of 2.5; for Ed S, minimum graduate GPA of 3.5, valid teaching certificate. Additional exam requirements/recommendations for international students: Required—TOEFL (minimum score 550 paper-based; 213 computer-based). *Application deadline:* For fall admission, 7/15 for domestic students; for spring admission, 12/1 for domestic students. Application fee: $30. *Expenses:* Tuition: Part-time $310 per credit hour. *Financial support:* Career-related internships or fieldwork, Federal Work-Study,

Curriculum and Instruction

Piedmont College (continued)
institutionally sponsored loans, and unspecified assistantships available. Support available to part-time students. Financial award applicants required to submit FAFSA. *Unit head:* Dr. Jane McFerrin, Dean, 706-778-3000 Ext. 1201, Fax: 706-776-9608, E-mail: jmcferrin@piedmont.edu. *Application contact:* Carol E. Kokesh, Director of Graduate Studies, 706-778-8500 Ext. 1181, Fax: 706-776-6635, E-mail: ckokesh@piedmont.edu.

Point Park University, School of Arts and Sciences, Department of Education and Community Services, Pittsburgh, PA 15222-1984. Offers curriculum and instruction (MA); educational administration (MA). Part-time and evening/weekend programs available. *Faculty:* 3 full-time, 16 part-time/adjunct. *Students:* 20 full-time (15 women), 30 part-time (19 women); includes 8 minority (all African Americans), 2 international. Average age 33. 58 applicants, 62% accepted, 22 enrolled. In 2006, 15 degrees awarded. *Entrance requirements:* For master's, minimum GPA of 3.0, resumé, 2 letters of recommendation. Additional exam requirements/recommendations for international students: Required—TOEFL. *Application deadline:* Applications are processed on a rolling basis. Application fee: $30. Electronic applications accepted. *Expenses:* Tuition: Full-time $9,828; part-time $546 per credit. Required fees: $360; $20 per credit. *Financial support:* In 2006–07, 5 students received support, including 2 research assistantships with full tuition reimbursements available (averaging $5,400 per year); career-related internships or fieldwork, scholarships/grants, and unspecified assistantships also available. Support available to part-time students. Financial award application deadline: 5/1; financial award applicants required to submit FAFSA. *Unit head:* Dr. Karen McIntyre, Chair, 412-392-3972, Fax: 412-392-3927, E-mail: kmcintyre@pointpark.edu. *Application contact:* Marty Paonessa, Associate Director, Graduate and Adult Enrollment, 412-392-3915, Fax: 412-392-6164, E-mail: mpaonessa@pointpark.edu.

Pontifical Catholic University of Puerto Rico, College of Education, Ponce, PR 00717-0777. Offers commercial education (MRE); curriculum instruction (M Ed); education (PhD); education-general (MRE); English as a second language (MRE); religious education (MA Ed); scholar psychology (MRE). Part-time and evening/weekend programs available. *Degree requirements:* For master's, thesis (for some programs), comprehensive exam. *Entrance requirements:* For master's, GRE, 2 letters of recommendation, interview, minimum GPA of 2.75; for doctorate, EXADEP, GRE or MAT, 3 letters of recommendation. *Faculty research:* Teaching English as a second language, learning styles, leadership styles.

Portland State University, Graduate Studies, School of Education, Department of Curriculum and Instruction, Portland, OR 97207-0751. Offers early childhood education (MA, MS); education (M Ed, MA, MS); educational leadership: curriculum and instruction (Ed D); educational media/school librarianship (MA, MS); elementary education (M Ed, MAT, MST); reading (MA, MS); secondary education (M Ed, MAT, MST). *Accreditation:* NCATE. Part-time programs available. *Faculty:* 20 full-time (14 women), 18 part-time/adjunct (9 women). *Students:* 185 full-time (135 women), 209 part-time (160 women); includes 53 minority (7 African Americans, 4 American Indian/Alaska Native, 13 Asian Americans or Pacific Islanders, 29 Hispanic Americans), 13 international. Average age 32. 372 applicants, 87% accepted, 171 enrolled. In 2006, 352 master's, 4 doctorates awarded. *Degree requirements:* For master's, special project or thesis, written exam; for doctorate, thesis/dissertation. *Entrance requirements:* For master's, California Basic Educational Skills Test, minimum GPA of 3.0 in upper-division course work or 2.75 overall. Additional exam requirements/recommendations for international students: Required—TOEFL (minimum score 550 paper-based; 213 computer-based). *Application deadline:* For fall admission, 4/1 for domestic and international students; for winter admission, 9/1 for domestic and international students; for spring admission, 11/1 for domestic and international students. Applications are processed on a rolling basis. Application fee: $50. *Expenses:* Tuition, state resident: full-time $6,426; part-time $238 per credit. Tuition, nonresident: full-time $11,016; part-time $408 per credit. Tuition and fees vary according to course load. *Financial support:* In 2006–07, 5 research assistantships with full tuition reimbursements (averaging $5,508 per year) were awarded; teaching assistantships with full tuition reimbursements, career-related internships or fieldwork, Federal Work-Study, and institutionally sponsored loans also available. Support available to part-time students. Financial award application deadline: 3/1; financial award applicants required to submit FAFSA. *Faculty research:* Early literacy, characteristics of successful teachers of at-risk students, participation of women/minorities in technology courses, selection of cooperating teachers. Total annual research expenditures: $308,420. *Unit head:* Steven Lee, Head, 503-725-4689, Fax: 503-725-8475. *Application contact:* Majken Elek, Department Secretary, 503-725-4756, Fax: 503-725-8475, E-mail: majkene@pdx.edu.

Prairie View A&M University, Graduate School, College of Education, Department of Curriculum and Instruction, Prairie View, TX 77446-0519. Offers curriculum and instruction (M Ed, MA Ed, MS Ed); special education (M Ed, MS Ed). *Accreditation:* NCATE. Part-time and evening/weekend programs available. *Faculty:* 10 full-time (5 women), 7 part-time/adjunct (all women). *Students:* 11 full-time (7 women), 162 part-time (128 women); includes 156 minority (155 African Americans, 1 Hispanic American), 5 international. Average age 37. 173 applicants, 98% accepted, 167 enrolled. In 2006, 57 degrees awarded. *Median time to degree:* Master's–1.5 years full-time, 2 years part-time. *Entrance requirements:* For master's, GRE General Test. *Application deadline:* For fall admission, 10/2 priority date for domestic students; for spring admission, 2/19 priority date for domestic students. Applications are processed on a rolling basis. Application fee: $50. *Financial support:* In 2006–07, 160 students received support, including 1 research assistantship with tuition reimbursement available (averaging $15,000 per year); fellowships with tuition reimbursements available, teaching assistantships, career-related internships or fieldwork, Federal Work-Study, institutionally sponsored loans, and tuition waivers (full and partial) also available. Support available to part-time students. Financial award application deadline: 4/1. *Faculty research:* Metacognitive strategies, emotionally disturbed, language arts, teachers recruit, diversity. Total annual research expenditures: $25,000. *Unit head:* Dr. Edward Mason, Head, 936-261-3403, Fax: 936-857-4414, E-mail: elmason@pvamu.edu.

Purdue University, Graduate School, School of Education, Department of Curriculum and Instruction, West Lafayette, IN 47907. Offers agricultural and extension education (PhD, Ed S); agriculture and extension education (MS, MS Ed); art education (PhD); consumer and family sciences and extension education (MS Ed, PhD, Ed S); curriculum studies (MS Ed, PhD, Ed S); educational technology (MS Ed, PhD, Ed S); elementary education (MS Ed); foreign language education (MS Ed, PhD, Ed S); industrial technology (PhD, Ed S); language arts (MS Ed, PhD, Ed S); literacy (MS Ed, PhD, Ed S); mathematics/science education (MS, MS Ed, PhD, Ed S); social studies (MS Ed, PhD); social studies education (Ed S); vocational/industrial education (MS Ed, PhD, Ed S); vocational/technical education (MS Ed, PhD, Ed S). *Accreditation:* NCATE. Part-time and evening/weekend programs available. *Faculty:* 26 full-time (13 women), 3 part-time/adjunct (all women). *Students:* 59 full-time (37 women), 112 part-time (70 women); includes 24 minority (13 African Americans, 3 American Indian/Alaska Native, 4 Asian Americans or Pacific Islanders, 4 Hispanic Americans), 38 international. Average age 35. 92 applicants, 68% accepted, 38 enrolled. In 2006, 52 master's, 23 doctorates awarded. *Degree requirements:* For master's, thesis optional; for doctorate, thesis/dissertation, oral and written exams; for Ed S, oral presentation, project. *Entrance requirements:* For master's, GRE General Test, minimum B average; for doctorate, GRE General Test; for Ed S, GRE, minimum B average. Additional exam requirements/recommendations for international students: Required—TOEFL. *Application deadline:* For fall admission, 1/15 priority date for domestic students, 1/15 for international students; for spring admission, 9/15 for domestic and international students. Applications are processed on a rolling basis. Application fee: $55. Electronic applications accepted. *Financial support:* In 2006–07, 3 fellowships with full tuition reimbursements (averaging $10,500 per year), 11 research assistantships with full tuition reimbursements (averaging $11,500 per year), 43 teaching assistantships with full tuition reimbursements (averaging $10,800 per year) were awarded; career-related internships or fieldwork and tuition waivers (full) also available. Support available to part-time students. Financial award application deadline: 3/1; financial award applicants required to submit FAFSA. *Faculty research:* Literacy acquisition and development, teacher beliefs and knowledge, recruitment and retention of underrepresented students, economic education, literacy discourse. *Unit head:* Dr. James D Lehman, Head, 765-494-7935, Fax: 765-496-1622. *Application contact:* Patricia Mason, Coordinator of Graduate Studies, 765-494-2345, Fax: 765-494-5832, E-mail: gradoffice@soe.purdue.edu.

Purdue University Calumet, Graduate School, School of Education, Program in Instructional Development, Hammond, IN 46323-2094. Offers MS Ed. *Entrance requirements:* Additional exam requirements/recommendations for international students: Required—TOEFL.

Regis University, School for Professional Studies, Program in Teacher Education, Denver, CO 80221-1099. Offers adult learning, training, and development (M Ed); curriculum, instruction, and assessment (M Ed); early childhood (M Ed); educational technology (Certificate); elementary (M Ed); ESL (M Ed); fine arts (M Ed), including arts, music; instructional technology (M Ed); professional leadership (M Ed); reading (M Ed); secondary (M Ed); self-designed (M Ed); space studies (M Ed); special education (M Ed); teacher licensure (M Ed). Program also offered in Henderson and Las Vegas (Summerlin), NV. Postbaccalaureate distance learning degree programs offered. *Unit head:* Dr. Suzie Perry, Dean, 303-458-4302. *Application contact:* Partick Lowenthal, Assistant Director, 303-458-4300 Ext. 4314, E-mail: masters@regis.edu.

Rider University, Department of Graduate Education, Leadership and Counseling, Lawrenceville, NJ 08648-3001. Offers counseling services (MA, Ed S); curriculum, instruction and supervision (MA); director of school counseling services (Certificate); educational administration (MA); organizational leadership (MA); principal (Certificate); reading/language arts (MA, Certificate), including reading specialist (Certificate), reading/language arts (MA); school business administrator (Certificate); school counseling services (Certificate); school psychology (Ed S); special education (MA); supervisor (Certificate); teacher certification (Certificate), including business education, elementary education, English as a second language, English education, mathematics education, preschool to grade 3, science education, social studies education, world languages; teaching (MA). *Accreditation:* NCATE. Part-time and evening/weekend programs available. *Faculty:* 24 full-time (12 women), 30 part-time/adjunct (15 women). *Students:* 90 full-time (75 women), 457 part-time (369 women); includes 73 minority (50 African Americans, 2 American Indian/Alaska Native, 6 Asian Americans or Pacific Islanders, 15 Hispanic Americans), 1 international. Average age 32. 314 applicants, 61% accepted, 138 enrolled. In 2006, 116 master's, 19 other advanced degrees awarded. *Degree requirements:* For master's, thesis or alternative, internship, portfolios, comprehensive exam (for some programs); for other advanced degree, internship, professional portfolio. *Entrance requirements:* For master's, GRE (counseling, school psychology), MAT, interview, resumé, letters of recommendation; for other advanced degree, PRAXIS. Additional exam requirements/recommendations for international students: Required—TOEFL (minimum score 550 paper-based; 213 computer-based). *Application deadline:* For fall admission, 5/1 priority date for domestic students, 6/1 priority date for international students; for spring admission, 11/1 priority date for domestic and international students. Applications are processed on a rolling basis. Application fee: $50. Electronic applications accepted. *Expenses:* Tuition: Part-time $525 per credit. Required fees: $35 per course. $30 per semester. *Financial support:* In 2006–07, 271 students received support. Career-related internships or fieldwork, Federal Work-Study, institutionally sponsored loans, and unspecified assistantships available. Support available to part-time students. Financial award applicants required to submit FAFSA. *Faculty research:* Gifted students, self-esteem, hope and mental health, conflicts in group work, cultural diversity and counseling assessment of special needs in children. *Unit head:* Dr. Dennis C. Buss, Chair, 609-895-5353, Fax: 609-896-5362, E-mail: dbuss@rider.edu. *Application contact:* Jamie L Mitchell, Director of Graduate Admissions, 609-896-5036, Fax: 609-895-5680, E-mail: jmitchell@rider.edu.

See Close-Up on page 913.

Rivier College, School of Graduate Studies, Department of Education, Nashua, NH 03060-5086. Offers curriculum and instruction (M Ed); early childhood education (M Ed); educational administration (M Ed); educational studies (M Ed); elementary education (M Ed); elementary education and general special education (M Ed); emotional and behavioral disorders (M Ed); general social education (M Ed); leadership and learning (CAGS); learning disabilities (M Ed); learning disabilities and reading (M Ed); mental health counseling (MA); reading (M Ed); school counseling (M Ed). Part-time and evening/weekend programs available. *Faculty:* 11 full-time (7 women), 40 part-time/adjunct (29 women). *Students:* 41 full-time (33 women), 221 part-time (192 women); includes 4 minority (2 African Americans, 2 Hispanic Americans). Average age 37. In 2006, 134 degrees awarded. *Degree requirements:* For master's, internships. *Entrance requirements:* For master's, GRE General Test or MAT. *Application deadline:* Applications are processed on a rolling basis. Application fee: $25. *Financial support:* Available to part-time students. Application deadline: 2/1; *Unit head:* Dr. Charles L. Mitsakos, Chairman, 603-888-1311 Ext. 8582. *Application contact:* Diane Monahan, Director of Graduate Admissions, 603-897-8129, Fax: 603-897-8810, E-mail: gradadm@rivier.edu.

Rosemont College, Graduate School, Program in Curriculum and Instruction, Rosemont, PA 19010-1699. Offers elementary certification (MA). Part-time and evening/weekend programs available. *Entrance requirements:* Additional exam requirements/recommendations for international students: Required—TOEFL. Electronic applications accepted.

Rowan University, Graduate School, College of Education, Department of Educational Leadership, Program in Supervision and Curriculum Development, Glassboro, NJ 08028-1701. Offers MA. *Accreditation:* NCATE. Part-time and evening/weekend programs available. *Students:* Average age 38. 2 applicants, 0% accepted. In 2006, 5 degrees awarded. *Degree requirements:* For master's, thesis, internship, comprehensive exam. *Entrance requirements:* For master's, GRE General Test, minimum GPA of 2.8, 2 years of teaching experience. Additional exam requirements/recommendations for international students: Required—TOEFL. *Application deadline:* Applications are processed on a rolling basis. Application fee: $50. Electronic applications accepted. *Expenses:* Tuition, state resident: full-time $9,882; part-time $549 per credit. Tuition, nonresident: full-time $9,882; part-time $549 per credit. Tuition and fees vary according to degree level. *Financial support:* Career-related internships or fieldwork and unspecified assistantships available. Support available to part-time students. *Unit head:* Dr. Thomas Monahan, Advisor, 856-256-4748, E-mail: monahan@rowan.edu.

St. Cloud State University, School of Graduate Studies, College of Education, Program in Curriculum and Instruction, St. Cloud, MN 56301-4498. Offers MS. *Faculty:* 17 full-time (9 women). *Students:* 17 applicants, 100% accepted. In 2006, 20 degrees awarded. *Degree requirements:* For master's, thesis or alternative. *Entrance requirements:* For master's, GRE General Test, minimum GPA of 2.75. Additional exam requirements/recommendations for international students: Required—MELAB; Recommended—TOEFL (minimum score 550 paper-based; 213 computer-based), IELTS (minimum score 7). *Application deadline:* For fall admission, 6/1 for domestic students, 4/1 for international students; for spring admission, 10/1 for domestic students, 8/1 for international students. Applications are processed on a rolling basis. Application fee: $35. Electronic applications accepted. *Financial support:* Federal Work-Study, scholarships/grants, and unspecified assistantships available. Financial award application deadline: 3/1. *Unit head:* Dr. Ramon Serrano, Chairperson, 320-308-3007, E-mail: raserrano@stcloudstate.edu. *Application contact:* Linda Lou Krueger, School of Graduate Studies, 320-308-2113, Fax: 320-308-5371, E-mail: lekrueger@stcloudstate.edu.

St. Francis Xavier University, Graduate Studies, Graduate Studies in Education, Antigonish, NS B2G 2W5, Canada. Offers curriculum and instruction (M Ed); educational administration and leadership (M Ed). Part-time programs available. Postbaccalaureate distance learning degree programs offered (minimal on-campus study). *Faculty:* 20 part-time/adjunct (10 women). *Students:* 2 full-time, 131 part-time. 55 applicants, 36% accepted. In 2006, 79 degrees awarded. *Degree requirements:* For master's, thesis, registration. *Entrance requirements:* For master's, minimum undergraduate B average, 2 years of teaching experience. *Application deadline:* For fall admission, 1/15 priority date for domestic students, 1/15 for international students. Application fee: $40. *Financial support:* In 2006–07, teaching assistantships (averaging $500 per year). *Faculty research:* Inclusive education, qualitative research. Total annual research expenditures: $70,000. *Unit head:* Dr. Jim Greenlaw, Chair, 902-867-5416, Fax: 902-867-3887, E-mail: jgreenla@stfx.ca. *Application contact:* Colleen Jones, Assistant, 902-867-3906, Fax: 902-867-5154, E-mail: med@stfx.ca.

Saint Leo University, Graduate Studies in Education, Saint Leo, FL 33574-6665. Offers education (MAT); educational leadership (M Ed); exceptional student education (M Ed); instructional leadership (M Ed); reading (M Ed). Part-time and evening/weekend programs available. Postbaccalaureate distance learning degree programs offered (minimal on-campus study). *Faculty:* 8 full-time (5 women), 10 part-time/adjunct (all women). *Students:* 96 full-time (77 women), 169 part-time (143 women); includes 22 minority (16 African Americans, 6 Hispanic Americans), 2 international. Average age 35. 365 applicants, 54% accepted, 116 enrolled. In 2006, 39 degrees awarded. *Degree requirements:* For master's, comprehensive exam or passing FELE scores. *Entrance requirements:* For master's, GRE General Test or MAT, 2 letters of recommendation, minimum undergraduate GPA of 3.0 or GRE or MAT, professional teaching certificate, resumé. Additional exam requirements/recommendations for international students: Required—TOEFL (minimum score 550 paper-based; 213 computer-based). *Application deadline:* For fall admission, 7/1 priority date for domestic students; for spring admission, 11/12 priority date for domestic students. Applications are processed on a rolling basis. Application fee: $45. Electronic applications accepted. *Financial support:* In 2006–07, 242 students received support. Career-related internships or fieldwork, Federal Work-Study, and scholarships/grants available. Support available to part-time students. Financial award application deadline: 3/1; financial award applicants required to submit FAFSA. *Faculty research:* The role of the school leader in (1) data analysis of student achievement (2) teacher recruitment (3) teacher effectiveness. *Unit head:* Dr. John Smith, Director, 352-588-8309, Fax: 352-588-8861, E-mail: med@saintleo.edu. *Application contact:* Scott Cathcart, Vice President of Enrollment, 800-707-8846, Fax: 352-588-7873, E-mail: grad.admission@saintleo.edu.

Saint Louis University, Graduate School, College of Public Service and Graduate School, Department of Educational Studies, St. Louis, MO 63103-2097. Offers curriculum and instruction (MA, Ed D, PhD); educational foundations (MA, Ed D, PhD); special education (MA); teaching (MAT). *Accreditation:* NCATE. Part-time programs available. *Faculty:* 12 full-time (8 women), 18 part-time/adjunct (12 women). *Students:* 15 full-time (10 women), 53 part-time (42 women); includes 3 minority (1 African American, 2 Asian Americans or Pacific Islanders), 4 international. Average age 36. 25 applicants, 80% accepted, 14 enrolled. In 2006, 2 master's, 5 doctorates awarded. *Degree requirements:* For master's, comprehensive exam, registration; for doctorate, thesis/dissertation, preliminary oral and written exams, comprehensive exam, registration. *Entrance requirements:* For master's, GRE General Test or MAT, letters of recommendation, resumé; for doctorate, GRE General Test, letters of recommendation, resumé. Additional exam requirements/recommendations for international students: Required—TOEFL (minimum score 525 paper-based; 194 computer-based). *Application deadline:* For fall admission, 7/1 for domestic and international students; for spring admission, 11/1 for domestic and international students. Applications are processed on a rolling basis. Application fee: $40. *Expenses:* Tuition: Part-time $800 per credit hour. Required fees: $105 per semester. *Financial support:* In 2006–07, 24 students received support, including 4 teaching assistantships with full tuition reimbursements available (averaging $11,000 per year); Federal Work-Study, scholarships/grants, traineeships, health care benefits, and unspecified assistantships also available. Support available to part-time students. Financial award application deadline: 6/1; financial award applicants required to submit FAFSA. *Faculty research:* Teacher preparation, multicultural issues, children with special needs, qualitative research in education, inclusion. *Unit head:* Dr. Mary Chittooran, Interim Chairperson, 314-977-4062, Fax: 314-977-3214, E-mail: chittomm@slu.edu. *Application contact:* Gary Behrman, Associate Dean of the Graduate School, 314-977-3827, E-mail: behrmang@slu.edu.

Saint Mary's College of California, School of Education, Program in Instruction, Moraga, CA 94575. Offers M Ed. *Faculty:* 1 full-time (0 women), 4 part-time/adjunct (all women). In 2006, 10 degrees awarded. *Median time to degree:* Master's–1.5 years part-time. *Unit head:* Mary Parish, Director, 925-631-4249, E-mail: mparish@stmarys-ca.edu.

Saint Michael's College, Graduate Programs, Program in Education, Colchester, VT 05439. Offers administration (M Ed, CAGS); arts in education (CAGS); curriculum and instruction (M Ed, CAGS); information technology (CAGS); reading (M Ed); special education (M Ed, CAGS); technology (M Ed). Part-time and evening/weekend programs available. *Faculty:* 5 full-time (3 women), 35 part-time/adjunct (29 women). *Students:* 26 full-time (18 women), 114 part-time (86 women), 2 international. Average age 34. 48 applicants, 81% accepted, 36 enrolled. In 2006, 46 degrees awarded. *Degree requirements:* For master's, thesis. *Entrance requirements:* For master's, minimum GPA of 3.0. *Application deadline:* Applications are processed on a rolling basis. Application fee: $35. Electronic applications accepted. *Financial support:* Fellowships, scholarships/grants available. Support available to part-time students. Financial award applicants required to submit FAFSA. *Faculty research:* Integrative curriculum, moral and spiritual dimensions of education, learning styles, multiple intelligences, integrating technology into the curriculum. *Unit head:* Dr. Anne P. Judson, Director, 802-654-2649, Fax: 802-654-2664, E-mail: ajudson@smcvt.edu.

Saint Peter's College, Graduate Programs in Education, Program in Teaching, Jersey City, NJ 07306-5997. Offers elementary teacher (Certificate); supervisor of instruction (Certificate); teaching (MA). Part-time and evening/weekend programs available. *Degree requirements:* For master's, departmental qualifying exam. *Entrance requirements:* For master's, GRE General Test or MAT.

Saint Vincent College, Program in Education, Latrobe, PA 15650-2690. Offers curriculum and instruction (MS); environmental education (MS); library media management (MS); school administration (MS); special education (MS). Part-time and evening/weekend programs available. *Degree requirements:* For master's, comprehensive exam. *Entrance requirements:* For master's, GRE (if undergraduate GPA is below 3.0). Additional exam requirements/recommendations for international students: Required—TOEFL (minimum score 550 paper-based; 213 computer-based). *Faculty research:* Assessment and instructional technology.

Saint Xavier University, Graduate Studies, School of Education, Chicago, IL 60655-3105. Offers counseling (MA); counselor education (MA); curriculum and instruction (MA); early childhood education (MA); education (CAS); educational administration (MA); elementary education (MA); field-based education (MA); general educational studies (MA); individualized program (MA); learning disabilities (MA); reading (MA); secondary education (MA). *Accreditation:* NCATE. Part-time and evening/weekend programs available. *Faculty:* 92. *Students:* 45 full-time (35 women), 1,529 part-time (1,309 women). In 2006, 474 degrees awarded. *Degree requirements:* For master's, thesis or project. *Entrance requirements:* For master's, minimum GPA of 3.0. *Application deadline:* For fall admission, 8/15 priority date for domestic students. Applications are processed on a rolling basis. Application fee: $35. *Expenses:* Contact institution. *Financial support:* Career-related internships or fieldwork available. Support available to part-time students. Financial award applicants required to submit FAFSA. *Unit head:* Dr. Beverly Gulley, Dean, 773-298-3221, Fax: 773-779-9061, E-mail: gulley@sxu.edu. *Application contact:* Beth Gierach, Managing Director of Admission, 773-298-3053, Fax: 773-298-3076, E-mail: gierach@sxu.edu.

Salem International University, School of Education, Salem, WV 26426-0500. Offers curriculum and instruction (M Ed), including curriculum and instruction, educational technology leadership, physical education/health, teaching English as a second language; educational administration (M Ed). Part-time and evening/weekend programs available. Postbaccalaureate distance learning degree programs offered. *Faculty:* 5 full-time (4 women), 17 part-time/adjunct (8 women). *Students:* 74 full-time (45 women), 154 part-time (75 women); includes 7 minority (2 African Americans, 5 Asian Americans or Pacific Islanders), 28 international. Average age 41. 200 applicants, 75% accepted, 130 enrolled. In 2006, 18 degrees awarded. *Degree requirements:* For master's, thesis (for some programs), comprehensive exam (for

some programs), registration. *Entrance requirements:* For master's, GRE, MAT, NTE, 3 letters of recommendation. Additional exam requirements/recommendations for international students: Required—TOEFL (minimum score 550 paper-based; 213 computer-based). *Application deadline:* Applications are processed on a rolling basis. Application fee: $25. Electronic applications accepted. *Expenses:* Contact institution. One-time fee: $25 part-time. Tuition and fees vary according to program. *Financial support:* Application deadline: 4/15; *Faculty research:* Improved classroom effectiveness. *Unit head:* Dean, School of Education, 304-326-1253, Fax: 304-326-1246. *Application contact:* Thomas White, Director of Admissions, 304-326-1549, Fax: 304-326-1246, E-mail: admission@salemiu.edu.

San Diego State University, Graduate and Research Affairs, College of Education, School of Teacher Education, Program in Elementary Curriculum and Instruction, San Diego, CA 92182. Offers MA. *Accreditation:* NCATE. Evening/weekend programs available. *Students:* 16 full-time (12 women), 38 part-time (36 women); includes 14 minority (1 African American, 2 American Indian/Alaska Native, 6 Asian Americans or Pacific Islanders, 5 Hispanic Americans). Average age 29. 34 applicants, 71% accepted, 2 enrolled. In 2006, 68 degrees awarded. *Entrance requirements:* For master's, GRE General Test, letters of reference. Additional exam requirements/recommendations for international students: Required—TOEFL. *Application deadline:* For fall admission, 5/1 for domestic and international students; for spring admission, 11/1 for domestic students, 10/1 for international students. Applications are processed on a rolling basis. Application fee: $55. Electronic applications accepted. *Financial support:* Applicants required to submit FAFSA. *Unit head:* Dr. Valerie Pang, Graduate Advisor, 619-594-6286, Fax: 619-594-7828.

San Diego State University, Graduate and Research Affairs, College of Education, School of Teacher Education, Program in Secondary Curriculum and Instruction, San Diego, CA 92182. Offers MA. *Accreditation:* NCATE. *Students:* 3 full-time (all women), 27 part-time (17 women); includes 8 minority (1 African American, 4 Asian Americans or Pacific Islanders, 3 Hispanic Americans). Average age 29. 26 applicants, 62% accepted, 0 enrolled. In 2006, 47 degrees awarded. *Entrance requirements:* For master's, GRE General Test, letters of reference. Additional exam requirements/recommendations for international students: Required—TOEFL. *Application deadline:* For fall admission, 5/1 for domestic and international students; for spring admission, 11/1 for domestic students, 10/1 for international students. Applications are processed on a rolling basis. Application fee: $55. Electronic applications accepted. *Financial support:* Applicants required to submit FAFSA. *Unit head:* Dr. Valerie Pang, Graduate Advisor, 619-594-6286, Fax: 619-594-7828.

Seattle University, College of Education, Program in Curriculum and Instruction, Seattle, WA 98122-1090. Offers M Ed, MA, Certificate. *Accreditation:* NCATE. Part-time and evening/weekend programs available. *Students:* 4 full-time (3 women), 28 part-time (25 women); includes 4 minority (3 Asian Americans or Pacific Islanders, 1 Hispanic American). Average age 33. 17 applicants, 59% accepted, 10 enrolled. In 2006, 25 master's, 1 other advanced degree awarded. *Degree requirements:* For master's, comprehensive exam. *Entrance requirements:* For master's, GRE, MAT, or minimum GPA of 3.0; 1 year of related experience. Additional exam requirements/recommendations for international students: Required—TOEFL. *Application deadline:* For fall admission, 8/20 for domestic students; for winter admission, 11/20 for domestic students; for spring admission, 2/20 for domestic students. Applications are processed on a rolling basis. Application fee: $55. *Financial support:* Career-related internships or fieldwork and Federal Work-Study available. Support available to part-time students. Financial award applicants required to submit FAFSA. *Unit head:* Dr. Katherine Schlick Noe, Director, 206-296-5768, E-mail: kschlnoe@seattleu.edu. *Application contact:* Janet Shandley, Associate Dean of Graduate Admissions, 206-296-5900, Fax: 206-298-5656, E-mail: grad_admissions@seattleu.edu.

Shaw University, Department of Education, Raleigh, NC 27601-2399. Offers curriculum and instruction (MS). Part-time and evening/weekend programs available. *Degree requirements:* For master's, thesis, practicum/internship, PRAXIS II, comprehensive exam. *Entrance requirements:* For master's, GRE General Test, letters of recommendation. Additional exam requirements/recommendations for international students: Required—TOEFL (minimum score 500 paper-based). Electronic applications accepted. *Faculty research:* Multicultural education, instructional technology.

Shepherd University, Program in Curriculum and Instruction, Shepherdstown, WV 25443-3210. Offers MA. *Accreditation:* NCATE.

Shippensburg University of Pennsylvania, School of Graduate Studies, College of Education and Human Services, Department of Teacher Education, Shippensburg, PA 17257-2299. Offers curriculum and instruction (M Ed); reading (M Ed); special education (M Ed). *Accreditation:* NCATE. Part-time and evening/weekend programs available. *Faculty:* 16 full-time (11 women), 3 part-time/adjunct (all women). *Students:* 14 full-time (9 women), 201 part-time (181 women); includes 4 minority (3 African Americans, 1 Hispanic American). Average age 30. 66 applicants, 52% accepted, 28 enrolled. In 2006, 75 degrees awarded. *Degree requirements:* For master's, practicum or internship required for some programs. *Entrance requirements:* For master's, MAT (if GPA is below 2.75), interview, letters of recommendation, writing sample, resumé. Additional exam requirements/recommendations for international students: Required—TOEFL (minimum score 560 paper-based; 220 computer-based). *Application deadline:* For fall admission, 6/1 priority date for domestic students, 3/1 for international students; for spring admission, 9/1 priority date for domestic students, 7/1 for international students. Applications are processed on a rolling basis. Application fee: $30. Electronic applications accepted. *Expenses:* Tuition, state resident: part-time $336 per credit. Tuition, nonresident: part-time $538 per credit. *Financial support:* In 2006–07, 10 research assistantships with full tuition reimbursements (averaging $3,125 per year) were awarded; career-related internships or fieldwork, scholarships/grants, and unspecified assistantships also available. Support available to part-time students. Financial award application deadline: 3/1; financial award applicants required to submit FAFSA. *Unit head:* Dr. Elizabeth Vaughan, Chairperson, 717-477-1688, Fax: 717-477-4046, E-mail: ejvaug@ship.edu. *Application contact:* Renee Payne, Associate Dean of Graduate Admissions, 717-477-1231, Fax: 717-477-4016, E-mail: rmpayn@ship.edu.

Siena Heights University, Graduate College, Program in Teacher Education, Adrian, MI 49221-1796. Offers curriculum and instruction (MA); early childhood education (MA), including Montessori education; elementary education (MA), including elementary education/reading; middle school education (MA); secondary education (MA), including secondary education/reading. Part-time programs available. *Degree requirements:* For master's, thesis, presentation. *Entrance requirements:* For master's, minimum GPA of 3.0, interview. *Faculty research:* Teaching/learning styles, outcomes-based teaching, multiple intelligences, assessment.

Simon Fraser University, Graduate Studies, Faculty of Education, Programs in Curriculum and Instruction, Burnaby, BC V5A 1S6, Canada. Offers M Ed, M Sc, MA, PhD. *Degree requirements:* For master's, project or thesis; for doctorate, thesis/dissertation. *Entrance requirements:* For master's, minimum GPA of 3.0; for doctorate, GRE, master's degree or exceptional record in a bachelor's degree, minimum GPA of 3.5. Additional exam requirements/recommendations for international students: Required—TOEFL or IELTS. *Faculty research:* Theory and implementation.

Sonoma State University, School of Education, Department of Curriculum and Secondary Education, Rohnert Park, CA 94928-3609. Offers MA. Part-time and evening/weekend programs available. *Faculty:* 4 full-time (2 women). *Degree requirements:* For master's, thesis or alternative. *Entrance requirements:* For master's, minimum GPA of 2.5. Application fee: $55. *Expenses:* Tuition, nonresident: part-time $339 per unit. Required fees: $1,464 per term. *Financial support:* Application deadline: 3/2. *Unit head:* Dr. Perry Marker, Chair, 707-664-3115.

South Dakota State University, Graduate School, College of Education and Counseling, Department of Educational Leadership, Brookings, SD 57007. Offers curriculum and instruction (M Ed); educational administration (M Ed). Part-time and evening/weekend programs avail-

Curriculum and Instruction

South Dakota State University (continued)
able. Postbaccalaureate distance learning degree programs offered (minimal on-campus study). *Faculty:* 12 full-time (4 women), 6 part-time/adjunct (1 woman). *Students:* 17 full-time (12 women), 132 part-time (67 women); includes 10 minority (3 African Americans, 4 American Indian/Alaska Native, 2 Asian Americans or Pacific Islanders, 1 Hispanic American). 61 applicants, 72% accepted, 44 enrolled. In 2006, 37 degrees awarded. *Degree requirements:* For master's, portfolio and oral exam. *Entrance requirements:* For master's, minimum GPA of 2.75. Additional exam requirements/recommendations for international students: Required—TOEFL (minimum score 550 paper-based). *Application deadline:* For fall admission, 4/30 priority date for international students; for spring admission, 8/30 priority date for international students. Applications are processed on a rolling basis. Application fee: $35. *Financial support:* In 2006–07, 2 research assistantships with partial tuition reimbursements were awarded. *Faculty research:* Inclusion school climate, K–12 reform and restructuring, rural development, ESL, leadership. *Unit head:* Dr. Kenneth Rasmussen, Head, 605-688-6365, Fax: 605-688-5784, E-mail: kenneth.rasmussen@sdstate.edu.

Southeastern Louisiana University, College of Education and Human Development, Department of Teaching and Learning, Hammond, LA 70402. Offers curriculum and instruction (M Ed); elementary education (MAT); secondary education (MAT); special education (M Ed, MAT). *Accreditation:* NCATE. Part-time programs available. *Faculty:* 23 full-time (18 women), 1 (woman) part-time/adjunct. *Students:* 31 full-time (27 women), 300 part-time (269 women); includes 50 minority (39 African Americans, 2 Asian Americans or Pacific Islanders, 9 Hispanic Americans), 3 international. Average age 33. 47 applicants, 100% accepted, 31 enrolled. In 2006, 101 degrees awarded. *Degree requirements:* For master's, comprehensive exam (for some programs). *Entrance requirements:* For master's, GRE, PRAXIS (MAT), minimum GPA of 2.5. Additional exam requirements/recommendations for international students: Required—TOEFL (minimum score 500 paper-based; 173 computer-based). *Application deadline:* For fall admission, 7/15 priority date for domestic students, 6/1 priority date for international students; for spring admission, 12/1 priority date for domestic students, 10/1 priority date for international students. Applications are processed on a rolling basis. Application fee: $20 ($30 for international students). Electronic applications accepted. *Expenses:* Tuition, state resident: full-time $2,216; part-time $123 per credit. Tuition, nonresident: full-time $6,212; part-time $345 per credit. Required fees: $986; $55 per credit. Part-time tuition and fees vary according to course load. *Financial support:* Federal Work-Study, institutionally sponsored loans, unspecified assistantships, and administrative assistantship available. Support available to part-time students. Financial award application deadline: 5/1; financial award applicants required to submit FAFSA. *Faculty research:* Reading, instructional methodology, science education, math education, early childhood. *Unit head:* Dr. Shirley Jacob, Department Head, 985-549-2221, Fax: 985-549-5009, E-mail: sjacob@selu.edu. *Application contact:* Sandra Meyers, Graduate Admissions Analyst, 985-549-2066, Fax: 985-549-5632, E-mail: admissions@selu.edu.

Southern Adventist University, School of Education and Psychology, Collegedale, TN 37315-0370. Offers curriculum and instruction (MS Ed); educational administration and supervision (MS Ed); inclusive education (MS Ed); literacy education (MS Ed); outdoor teacher education (MS Ed); professional counseling (MS); school counseling (MS). *Accreditation:* NCATE. Part-time and evening/weekend programs available. *Faculty:* 11 full-time (5 women), 1 (woman) part-time/adjunct. *Students:* 36 full-time (29 women), 7 part-time (6 women); includes 8 minority (6 African Americans, 2 Hispanic Americans). Average age 30. 15 applicants, 100% accepted, 15 enrolled. In 2006, 25 degrees awarded. *Degree requirements:* For master's, position paper (MS), portfolio (MS Ed in outdoor teacher education), thesis optional. *Entrance requirements:* For master's, GRE General Test, interview (MS); 9 semester hours of upper division course work in psychology or related field, including 1 course in psychology research or statistics; 9 semester hours of education (MS Ed). Additional exam requirements/recommendations for international students: Required—TOEFL (minimum score 600 paper-based; 250 computer-based; 100 iBT). *Application deadline:* For fall admission, 5/15 priority date for domestic and international students; for winter admission, 10/15 priority date for domestic and international students; for spring admission, 3/31 priority date for domestic and international students. Applications are processed on a rolling basis. Application fee: $25. Electronic applications accepted. *Financial support:* In 2006–07, 7 students received support, including 4 research assistantships with full tuition reimbursements available (averaging $10,000 per year); career-related internships or fieldwork, scholarships/grants, tuition waivers (partial), and unspecified assistantships also available. Support available to part-time students. Financial award application deadline: 4/1; financial award applicants required to submit FAFSA. *Unit head:* Dr. Denise Dunzweiler, Dean, 423-236-2776, Fax: 423-236-1765, E-mail: denise@southern.edu. *Application contact:* Mikhaile Spence, Information Contact, 423-236-2496, Fax: 423-236-1765, E-mail: maspence@southern.edu.

Southern Illinois University Carbondale, Graduate School, College of Education, Department of Curriculum and Instruction, Carbondale, IL 62901-4701. Offers MS Ed, PhD. *Accreditation:* NCATE. Part-time programs available. *Faculty:* 30 full-time (12 women), 2 part-time/adjunct (0 women). *Students:* 58 full-time (40 women), 191 part-time (161 women); includes 31 minority (21 African Americans, 3 Asian Americans or Pacific Islanders, 7 Hispanic Americans), 28 international. 108 applicants, 67% accepted, 9 enrolled. In 2006, 56 master's, 6 doctorates awarded. *Degree requirements:* For doctorate, variable foreign language requirement, thesis/dissertation. *Entrance requirements:* For master's, minimum GPA of 2.7; for doctorate, GRE or MAT, minimum GPA of 3.25. Additional exam requirements/recommendations for international students: Required—TOEFL. *Application deadline:* Applications are processed on a rolling basis. Application fee: $20. *Financial support:* In 2006–07, 4 fellowships with full tuition reimbursements, 10 research assistantships with full tuition reimbursements, 45 teaching assistantships with full tuition reimbursements were awarded; career-related internships or fieldwork, Federal Work-Study, institutionally sponsored loans, and tuition waivers (full) also available. Support available to part-time students. *Faculty research:* Early childhood, science/environmental education, teacher education, instructional development/technology, reading. Total annual research expenditures: $3 million. *Unit head:* Dr. Lynn C. Smith, Interim Chair, 618-536-2441, E-mail: lcsmith@siu.edu. *Application contact:* Lois Cornett, Administrative Clerk, 618-453-4267, Fax: 618-453-4244, E-mail: lcorn@siu.edu.

Announcement: The Department of Curriculum and Instruction offers degree programs leading to the Master of Science in Education and the Doctor of Philosophy. The program provides advanced study in one of 12 specialty areas, each of which is intended to enhance students' instructional skills and to prepare them to be knowledgeable consumers of educational research.

See Close-Up on page 1121.

Southern Nazarene University, Graduate College, School of Education, Bethany, OK 73008. Offers curriculum and instruction (MA); educational leadership (MA). *Accreditation:* NCATE. Part-time and evening/weekend programs available. *Faculty:* 10. *Students:* 105. Average age 27. In 2006, 23 degrees awarded. *Degree requirements:* For master's, thesis optional. *Entrance requirements:* For master's, MAT, English proficiency exam, minimum GPA of 3.0 in last 60 hours/major, 2.7 overall. *Application deadline:* For fall admission, 8/1 priority date for domestic students. Applications are processed on a rolling basis. Application fee: $25 ($35 for international students). *Expenses:* Tuition: Part-time $507 per credit. *Financial support:* Teaching assistantships, career-related internships or fieldwork available. *Unit head:* Dr. Rex Tullis, Director, 405-491-6317, E-mail: rtullis@snu.edu.

Southern New Hampshire University, School of Education, Manchester, NH 03106-1045. Offers business education (MS); child development (M Ed); computer technology education (Certificate); curriculum and instruction (M Ed); education (M Ed, CAS); elementary education (M Ed); general special education (Certificate); school business administrator (Certificate); school counseling (M Ed); school psychology (M Ed); secondary education (M Ed); training and development (Certificate). Part-time and evening/weekend programs available. Postbaccalaureate distance learning degree programs offered. *Faculty:* 6 full-time (3 women), 9 part-time/adjunct (7 women). *Students:* Average age 35. In 2006, 52 degrees awarded. *Degree requirements:* For master's, thesis or alternative, comprehensive exam (for some programs). *Entrance requirements:* For master's, GRE General Test or MAT, minimum GPA of 3.0. Additional exam requirements/recommendations for international students: Required—TOEFL (minimum score 550 paper-based; 213 computer-based). *Application deadline:* Applications are processed on a rolling basis. Application fee: $25. Electronic applications accepted. *Expenses:* Contact institution. *Financial support:* Institutionally sponsored loans available. Financial award applicants required to submit FAFSA. *Unit head:* Dr. Patrick J. Hartwick, Dean, 603-668-2211 Ext. 4698, Fax: 603-629-4673, E-mail: p.hartwick@snhu.edu. *Application contact:* Scott Durand, Director of Graduate Enrollment Services, 603-644-3102 Ext. 3338, Fax: 603-644-3144, E-mail: s.durand@snhu.edu.

Southwestern Assemblies of God University, Thomas F. Harrison School of Graduate Studies, Program in Education, Waxahachie, TX 75165-5735. Offers Christian school administration (MS); curriculum development (MS); MS/MA. *Degree requirements:* For master's, comprehensive written and oral exams. *Entrance requirements:* For master's, GRE General Test, minimum GPA of 2.5. Electronic applications accepted.

Stanford University, School of Education, Program in Curriculum Studies and Teacher Education, Stanford, CA 94305-9991. Offers art education (MA, PhD); dance education (MA); English education (MA, PhD); general curriculum studies (MA, PhD); mathematics education (MA, PhD); science education (MA, PhD); social studies education (PhD); teacher education (MA, PhD). *Degree requirements:* For master's, thesis (for some programs); for doctorate, thesis/dissertation. *Entrance requirements:* For master's and doctorate, GRE General Test. Electronic applications accepted.

State University of New York at Plattsburgh, Division of Education, Health, and Human Services, Program in Curriculum and Instruction, Plattsburgh, NY 12901-2681. Offers MS Ed. *Faculty:* 1 (woman) full-time, 8 part-time/adjunct (2 women). *Students:* 32 full-time (20 women), 115 part-time (74 women); includes 2 minority (1 Asian American or Pacific Islander, 1 Hispanic American), 1 international. Average age 30. 44 applicants, 95% accepted, 20 enrolled. In 2006, 103 degrees awarded. *Degree requirements:* For master's, comprehensive exam or research project. *Entrance requirements:* For master's, GRE General Test or MAT, minimum GPA of 2.5. *Application deadline:* For fall admission, 2/15 priority date for domestic students; for spring admission, 10/15 priority date for domestic students. Applications are processed on a rolling basis. Application fee: $50. *Expenses:* Tuition, state resident: full-time $6,900; part-time $288 per credit hour. Tuition, nonresident: full-time $10,920; part-time $455 per credit hour. *Financial support:* Application deadline: 4/15; *Unit head:* Dr. Lawrence Glandomenico, Coordinator, 518-564-5133, E-mail: glandoll@plattsburgh.edu.

State University of New York College at Brockport, School of Professions, Department of Education and Human Development, Program in Childhood Curriculum Specialist, Brockport, NY 14420-2997. Offers MS Ed. *Accreditation:* NCATE. Part-time programs available. *Students:* 13 full-time (all women), 101 part-time (81 women); includes 8 minority (3 African Americans, 1 Asian American or Pacific Islander, 4 Hispanic Americans). 22 applicants, 73% accepted, 14 enrolled. In 2006, 105 degrees awarded. *Degree requirements:* For master's, thesis or alternative. *Entrance requirements:* For master's, minimum GPA of 3.0, letters of recommendation. Additional exam requirements/recommendations for international students: Required—TOEFL (minimum score 550 paper-based; 213 computer-based; 80 iBT). *Application deadline:* For fall admission, 2/15 for domestic and international students; for spring admission, 9/15 for domestic and international students. Application fee: $50. *Expenses:* Tuition, state resident: full-time $6,900; part-time $288 per credit. Tuition, nonresident: full-time $10,920; part-time $455 per credit. *Financial support:* Career-related internships or fieldwork, Federal Work-Study, scholarships/grants, and unspecified assistantships available. Support available to part-time students. Financial award application deadline: 3/15; financial award applicants required to submit FAFSA. *Application contact:* Coordinator of Certification and Graduate Advisement, 585-395-2344.

State University of New York College at Potsdam, School of Education, Program in Curriculum and Instruction, Potsdam, NY 13676. Offers MS Ed. *Accreditation:* NCATE. Evening/weekend programs available. Postbaccalaureate distance learning degree programs offered (minimal on-campus study). *Faculty:* 1 (woman) full-time, 3 part-time/adjunct (1 woman). *Students:* 28 full-time (20 women), 23 part-time (19 women), 22 international. In 2006, 45 degrees awarded. *Degree requirements:* For master's, thesis. *Entrance requirements:* For master's, minimum GPA of 2.75 in last 60 credit hours of undergraduate study. Additional exam requirements/recommendations for international students: Required—TOEFL (minimum score 550 paper-based; 213 computer-based). *Application deadline:* Applications are processed on a rolling basis. Application fee: $50. *Financial support:* Federal Work-Study and scholarships/grants available. Support available to part-time students. *Unit head:* Kathleen Valentine, Chairperson, Curriculum and Instruction, 315-267-3314, Fax: 315-267-4802, E-mail: valentkm@potsdam.edu. *Application contact:* Peter Cutler, Graduate Admissions Counselor, 315-267-3154, Fax: 315-267-4802, E-mail: cutlerpj@potsdam.edu.

Stephens College, Division of Graduate and Continuing Studies, Program in Curriculum and Instruction, Columbia, MO 65215-0002. Offers M Ed. Part-time programs available. Postbaccalaureate distance learning degree programs offered (minimal on-campus study). *Entrance requirements:* Additional exam requirements/recommendations for international students: Required—TOEFL (minimum score 213 computer-based). *Application deadline:* Applications are processed on a rolling basis. *Unit head:* Dr. Leslie Willey, Program Chair, 800-388-7579, E-mail: lwilley@stephens.edu. *Application contact:* Dr. Kate Getty, Associate Director, 800-388-7579, E-mail: online@stephens.edu.

Stetson University, College of Arts and Sciences, Division of Education, Department of Teacher Education, Program in Curriculum and Instruction, DeLand, FL 32723. Offers Ed S. *Students:* Average age 52. In 2006, 2 degrees awarded. *Unit head:* Dr. Elizabeth Heins, Coordinator, 386-822-7075. *Application contact:* Midge McDaniel, Office of Graduate Studies, 386-822-7075, Fax: 386-822-7388, E-mail: mmcdanie@stetson.edu.

Suffolk University, College of Arts and Sciences, Department of Education and Human Services, Program in Adult and Organizational Learning, Boston, MA 02108-2770. Offers adult and organizational learning (MS); human resources (MS, CAGS); instructional design (CAGS); organizational development (CAGS); organizational learning (CAGS). Part-time and evening/weekend programs available. *Entrance requirements:* For master's, GRE General Test or MAT. *Application deadline:* For fall admission, 6/15 priority date for domestic students, 6/15 for international students; for spring admission, 11/15 priority date for domestic students, 11/15 for international students. Applications are processed on a rolling basis. Application fee: $35. *Financial support:* Fellowships available. Financial award application deadline: 4/1. *Faculty research:* Adult training methods, adult learning theory, instructional design, learning and teaching styles, systems thinking. *Unit head:* Dr. Christine M. Westphal, Graduate Program Director, 617-994-6455, Fax: 617-722-9440, E-mail: cwestphal@suffolk.edu. *Application contact:* Judith Reynolds, Director of Graduate Admissions, 617-573-8302, Fax: 617-523-0116, E-mail: grad.admission@suffolk.edu.

Syracuse University, Graduate School, School of Education, Department of Teaching and Leadership, Program in Teaching and Curriculum, Syracuse, NY 13244. Offers MS, PhD. Part-time and evening/weekend programs available. *Students:* 16 full-time (14 women), 22 part-time (11 women); includes 2 minority (both African Americans), 7 international. 18 applicants, 44% accepted, 7 enrolled. *Degree requirements:* For master's, thesis or alternative; for doctorate, thesis/dissertation. *Entrance requirements:* For doctorate, GRE. Additional exam requirements/recommendations for international students: Required—TOEFL. *Application deadline:* For fall admission, 2/1 priority date for domestic students. Applications are processed on a rolling basis. Application fee: $65. Electronic applications accepted. *Expenses:* Tuition: Full-time $16,920; part-time $940 per credit hour. Required fees: $930; $930 per year. *Financial support:* Fellowships with tuition reimbursements, teaching assistantships with full tuition reimbursements available. *Unit head:* Dr. Gerald Mager, Program Coordinator, 315-443-2685, E-mail: gmmager@syr.edu. *Application contact:* Liza Rochelson, Graduate Admission Recruiter, 315-443-2505, Fax: 315-443-2258, E-mail: gradcrt@gwmail.syr.edu.

Syracuse University, Graduate School, School of Education, Instructional Design, Development, and Evaluation Program, Syracuse, NY 13244. Offers MS, PhD, CAS. Part-time programs available. *Students:* 44 full-time (21 women), 36 part-time (23 women); includes 8 minority (4 African Americans, 1 American Indian/Alaska Native, 2 Asian Americans or Pacific Islanders, 1 Hispanic American), 20 international. 35 applicants, 57% accepted, 11 enrolled. *Degree requirements:* For master's, thesis or alternative; for doctorate, thesis/dissertation. *Entrance requirements:* For master's, GRE; for doctorate and CAS, GRE, interview. *Application deadline:* For fall admission, 2/1 for domestic students. Applications are processed on a rolling basis. Application fee: $65. Electronic applications accepted. *Expenses:* Tuition: Full-time $16,920; part-time $940 per credit hour. Required fees: $930; $930 per year. *Financial support:* Fellowships with full tuition reimbursements, research assistantships with full and partial tuition reimbursements, teaching assistantships with full tuition reimbursements available. *Faculty research:* Cultural pluralism and instructional design, corrections training, aging and learning, the University and social change, investigative evaluation. *Unit head:* Dr. Gerald Mager, Chair, 315-443-2685, E-mail: gmmager@syr.edu. *Application contact:* Liza Rochelson, Graduate Admission Recruiter, 315-443-2505, Fax: 315-443-2258, E-mail: gradcrt@gwmail.syr.edu.

Tarleton State University, College of Graduate Studies, College of Education, Department of Curriculum and Instruction, Stephenville, TX 76402. Offers M Ed. Part-time and evening/weekend programs available. *Faculty:* 15 full-time (11 women), 15 part-time/adjunct (12 women). *Students:* 7 full-time (all women), 206 part-time (171 women); includes 49 minority (26 African Americans, 1 American Indian/Alaska Native, 1 Asian American or Pacific Islander, 21 Hispanic Americans), 2 international. Average age 38. In 2006, 30 degrees awarded. *Degree requirements:* For master's, comprehensive exam. *Entrance requirements:* For master's, GRE General Test, minimum GPA of 3.0. Additional exam requirements/recommendations for international students: Required—TOEFL (minimum score 550 paper-based; 220 computer-based). *Application deadline:* For fall admission, 8/5 priority date for domestic students; for spring admission, 12/1 for domestic students. Applications are processed on a rolling basis. Application fee: $25 ($75 for international students). *Financial support:* Teaching assistantships, career-related internships or fieldwork, Federal Work-Study, and institutionally sponsored loans available. Support available to part-time students. Financial award application deadline: 5/1; financial award applicants required to submit FAFSA. *Unit head:* Dr. Ann Calahan, Head, 254-968-9933, Fax: 254-968-9947, E-mail: acalahan@tarleton.edu.

Teachers College Columbia University, Graduate Faculty of Education, Department of Curriculum and Teaching, Program in Curriculum and Teaching, New York, NY 10027-6696. Offers Ed M, MA, Ed D. *Faculty:* 9 full-time (all women), 13 part-time/adjunct. *Students:* 61 full-time (48 women), 161 part-time (133 women); includes 63 minority (23 African Americans, 30 Asian Americans or Pacific Islanders, 10 Hispanic Americans), 16 international. Average age 33. 174 applicants, 54% accepted, 45 enrolled. In 2006, 46 master's, 16 doctorates awarded. *Degree requirements:* For doctorate, thesis/dissertation. *Entrance requirements:* For doctorate, GRE General Test or MAT. *Application deadline:* For fall admission, 5/15 for domestic students; for spring admission, 12/1 for domestic students. Application fee: $65. *Expenses:* Tuition: Full-time $23,400; part-time $975 per credit. Required fees: $320 per term. *Financial support:* Career-related internships or fieldwork, Federal Work-Study, institutionally sponsored loans, and tuition waivers (full and partial) available. Support available to part-time students. Financial award application deadline: 2/1. *Faculty research:* Teacher education, reading education, curriculum development. *Application contact:* Peter Shon, Assistant Director of Admission, 212-678-3305, Fax: 212-678-4171, E-mail: shon@exchange.tc.columbia.edu.

See Close-Up on page 1127.

Tennessee State University, The School of Graduate Studies and Research, College of Education, Department of Teaching and Learning, Program in Curriculum and Instruction, Nashville, TN 37209-1561. Offers M Ed, Ed D. *Accreditation:* NCATE. *Faculty:* 13 full-time (8 women). *Students:* 112 full-time (90 women), 295 part-time (230 women); includes 197 minority (188 African Americans, 1 American Indian/Alaska Native, 6 Asian Americans or Pacific Islanders, 2 Hispanic Americans), 5 international. Average age 36. 176 applicants, 68% accepted, 97 enrolled. In 2006, 130 master's, 12 doctorates awarded. *Degree requirements:* For master's, thesis optional; for doctorate, thesis/dissertation. *Entrance requirements:* For master's, GRE General Test, GRE Subject Test, or MAT, minimum GPA of 2.5; for doctorate, GRE General Test, GRE Subject Test, or MAT. *Unit head:* Dr. James Ronald Groseclose, Head, 615-963-5620, E-mail: jrgroseclose@tnstate.edu. *Application contact:* Dr. Helen Barrett, Dean, 615-963-5139, Fax: 615-963-5963, E-mail: hbarrett@tnstate.edu.

Tennessee Technological University, Graduate School, College of Education, Department of Curriculum and Instruction, Program in Curriculum, Cookeville, TN 38505. Offers MA, Ed S. *Accreditation:* NCATE. Part-time and evening/weekend programs available. *Faculty:* 2 full-time (1 woman). *Students:* 20 full-time (15 women), 37 part-time (34 women); includes 2 minority (1 African American, 1 Asian American or Pacific Islander). Average age 27. 22 applicants, 91% accepted, 18 enrolled. In 2006, 20 master's, 2 other advanced degrees awarded. *Degree requirements:* For Ed S, thesis or alternative. *Entrance requirements:* For master's, MAT; for Ed S, MAT, NTE. Additional exam requirements/recommendations for international students: Required—TOEFL. *Application deadline:* For fall admission, 3/1 priority date for domestic students; for spring admission, 8/1 for domestic students. Application fee: $25 ($30 for international students). *Expenses:* Tuition, state resident: full-time $8,748; part-time $319 per hour. Tuition, nonresident: full-time $23,524; part-time $740 per hour. *Financial support:* In 2006–07, 2 fellowships (averaging $8,000 per year), research assistantships (averaging $4,000 per year), 1 teaching assistantship (averaging $4,000 per year) were awarded. Financial award application deadline: 4/1. *Application contact:* Dr. Francis O. Otuonye, Associate Vice President for Research and Graduate Studies, 931-372-3233, Fax: 931-372-3497, E-mail: fotuonye@tntech.edu.

Tennessee Temple University, Graduate Studies Division, Program in Curriculum and Instruction, Chattanooga, TN 37404-3587. Offers MS. *Degree requirements:* For master's, thesis or alternative.

Texas A&M International University, Office of Graduate Studies and Research, College of Education, Department of Curriculum and Instruction, Laredo, TX 78041-1900. Offers bilingual education (PhD); curriculum and instruction (MS, PhD); early childhood education (PhD); reading (MS). *Expenses:* Tuition, state resident: full-time $1,580. Tuition, nonresident: full-time $5,432. Required fees: $3,808. *Unit head:* Dr. Barbara Greybeck, Interim Chair, 956-326-2678, E-mail: bgreybeck@tamiu.edu. *Application contact:* Rosie Dickinson, Director of Admissions, 956-326-2200.

Texas A&M University, College of Education and Human Development, Department of Teaching, Learning, and Culture, College Station, TX 77843. Offers curriculum and instruction (M Ed, MS, PhD); mathematics education (M Ed, MS, PhD); multicultural/urban/ESL/international education (M Ed, MS, PhD); reading/language arts (M Ed, MS, PhD); science education (M Ed, MS, PhD); social studies education (M Ed, MS, PhD). *Accreditation:* NCATE. Part-time programs available. *Faculty:* 25 full-time (9 women), 2 part-time/adjunct (both women). *Students:* 156 full-time (115 women), 226 part-time (191 women); includes 95 minority (43 African Americans, 1 American Indian/Alaska Native, 9 Asian Americans or Pacific Islanders, 42 Hispanic Americans), 36 international. Average age 36. 137 applicants, 83% accepted, 80 enrolled. In 2006, 69 master's, 15 doctorates awarded. *Median time to degree:* Of those who began their doctoral program in fall 1998, 77% received their degree in 8 years or less. *Degree requirements:* For master's, thesis (for some programs), comprehensive exam; for doctorate, thesis/dissertation, comprehensive exam. *Entrance requirements:* For master's, GRE General Test, minimum GPA of 3.0; for doctorate, GRE General Test, 3 years of teaching experience. Additional exam requirements/recommendations for international students: Required—TOEFL (minimum score 550 paper-based; 213 computer-based). *Application deadline:* For fall admission, 1/15 priority date for domestic and international students; for spring admission, 9/15 priority date for domestic and international students. Applications are processed on a rolling basis. Application fee: $50 ($75 for international students). Electronic applications accepted. *Expenses:* Tuition, state resident: full-time $4,697. Tuition, nonresident: full-time $11,297. Required fees: $2,272. *Financial support:* In 2006–07, fellowships with partial tuition reimbursements (averaging $3,000 per year), teaching assistantships with partial tuition reimbursements (averaging $7,200 per year) were awarded; research assistantships with partial tuition reimbursements, career-related internships or fieldwork, Federal Work-Study, institutionally sponsored loans, scholarships/grants, tuition waivers (partial), and unspecified assistantships also available. Support available to part-time students. Financial award application deadline: 4/1; financial award applicants required to submit FAFSA. *Unit head:* Dr. Dennie Smith, Head, 979-845-8384, Fax: 979-845-9663. *Application contact:* Graduate Admissions Supervisor, 979-845-8382, Fax: 979-845-9663.

Texas A&M University–Commerce, Graduate School, College of Education and Human Services, Department of Secondary and Higher Education, Commerce, TX 75429-3011. Offers higher education (MS), including administration, teaching; learning technology and information systems (M Ed, MS), including educational computing, library and information science, media and technology; secondary education (M Ed, MS); supervision, curriculum, and instruction (Ed D); training and development (MS). Part-time programs available. Terminal master's awarded for partial completion of doctoral program. *Degree requirements:* For master's, thesis (for some programs), comprehensive exam; for doctorate, thesis/dissertation, departmental qualifying exam. *Entrance requirements:* For master's and doctorate, GRE General Test. Electronic applications accepted. *Faculty research:* Deviance, migration.

Texas A&M University–Corpus Christi, Graduate Studies and Research, College of Education, Program in Curriculum and Instruction, Corpus Christi, TX 78412-5503. Offers MS, Ed D. Part-time and evening/weekend programs available. *Degree requirements:* For master's, thesis (for some programs), comprehensive exam, registration. *Entrance requirements:* For master's, GRE General Test. Additional exam requirements/recommendations for international students: Required—TOEFL. Electronic applications accepted.

Texas A&M University–Texarkana, Graduate Studies and Research, College of Arts and Sciences and Education, Texarkana, TX 75505-5518. Offers adult education (MS); curriculum and instruction (MS); education (MS); educational administration (M Ed); English (MA); history (MS); instructional technology (MS); interdisciplinary studies (MA, MS); special education (M Ed, MS). Part-time and evening/weekend programs available. *Students:* 285. Average age 32. 41 applicants, 76% accepted. In 2006, 51 degrees awarded. *Degree requirements:* For master's, thesis optional. *Entrance requirements:* For master's, minimum GPA of 2.5 on last 60 hours of bachelor's degree. Additional exam requirements/recommendations for international students: Required—TOEFL. *Application deadline:* For fall admission, 7/15 priority date for domestic students; for spring admission, 12/1 priority date for domestic students. Applications are processed on a rolling basis. Application fee: $0 ($25 for international students). Electronic applications accepted. *Expenses:* Tuition, state resident: part-time $112 per credit hour. Tuition, nonresident: part-time $387 per credit hour. Required fees: $8 per credit hour. $8 per term. *Financial support:* Career-related internships or fieldwork and scholarships/grants available. Financial award applicants required to submit FAFSA. *Unit head:* Dr. Rosannce Stripling, Dean, 903-223-3073, E-mail: rosanne.stripling@tamut.edu. *Application contact:* Patricia E. Black, Director of Admissions and Registrar, 903-223-3068, Fax: 903-223-3140, E-mail: pat.black@tamut.edu.

Texas Southern University, Graduate School, College of Education, Area of Curriculum and Instruction, Houston, TX 77004-4584. Offers bilingual education (M Ed); curriculum, instruction, and urban education (Ed D); early childhood education (M Ed); elementary education (M Ed); reading education (M Ed); secondary education (M Ed); special education (M Ed). Part-time and evening/weekend programs available. *Faculty:* 8 full-time (6 women), 1 part-time/adjunct (0 women). *Students:* 41 full-time (36 women), 43 part-time (38 women); includes 82 minority (77 African Americans, 2 Asian Americans or Pacific Islanders, 3 Hispanic Americans). Average age 36. 34 applicants, 82% accepted, 24 enrolled. In 2006, 6 master's, 13 doctorates awarded. *Degree requirements:* For master's, comprehensive exam; for doctorate, thesis/dissertation, comprehensive exam. *Entrance requirements:* For master's, GRE General Test, minimum GPA of 2.5; for doctorate, GRE General Test or MAT, master's degree, minimum B+ average. Additional exam requirements/recommendations for international students: Required—TOEFL. *Application deadline:* For fall admission, 7/15 priority date for domestic students. Applications are processed on a rolling basis. Application fee: $50 ($75 for international students). *Financial support:* Federal Work-Study and institutionally sponsored loans available. Financial award application deadline: 5/1. *Unit head:* Dr. Cherry Gooden, Chair, 713-313-7496, Fax: 713-313-7496, E-mail: gooden_cr@tsu.edu.

Texas Tech University, Graduate School, College of Education, Division of Curriculum and Instruction, Lubbock, TX 79409. Offers bilingual education (M Ed); curriculum and instruction (M Ed, PhD); elementary education (M Ed); language and literacy education (M Ed); secondary education (M Ed). *Accreditation:* NCATE. Part-time programs available. *Students:* 68 full-time (48 women), 99 part-time (82 women); includes 35 minority (6 African Americans, 1 Asian American or Pacific Islander, 28 Hispanic Americans), 10 international. Average age 34. 165 applicants, 59% accepted, 10 enrolled. In 2006, 61 master's, 7 doctorates awarded. *Degree requirements:* For master's, thesis optional; for doctorate, thesis/dissertation. *Entrance requirements:* For master's and doctorate, GRE General Test. Additional exam requirements/recommendations for international students: Required—TOEFL (minimum score 550 paper-based; 213 computer-based). *Application deadline:* For fall admission, 3/1 priority date for international students; for spring admission, 11/1 priority date for international students. Applications are processed on a rolling basis. Application fee: $50 ($60 for international students). Electronic applications accepted. *Expenses:* Tuition, state resident: full-time $4,440. Tuition, nonresident: full-time $11,040. Required fees: $2,136. *Financial support:* In 2006–07, 100 students received support; research assistantships with partial tuition reimbursements available, teaching assistantships with partial tuition reimbursements available, career-related internships or fieldwork, Federal Work-Study, and institutionally sponsored loans available. Support available to part-time students. Financial award application deadline: 4/15; financial award applicants required to submit FAFSA. *Faculty research:* Multicultural foundations of education, teacher education, instruction and pedagogy in subject areas, curriculum theory, language and literary. *Unit head:* Dr. Peggy Johnson, Associate Dean, 806-742-1988 Ext. 437, Fax: 806-742-2179, E-mail: peggy.johnson@ttu.edu.

Trevecca Nazarene University, Graduate Division, School of Education, Major in Instructional Effectiveness, Nashville, TN 37210-2877. Offers M Ed. Part-time and evening/weekend programs available. *Students:* 20 full-time (17 women), 1 (woman) part-time; includes 7 minority (6 African Americans, 1 Hispanic American). In 2006, 10 degrees awarded. *Degree requirements:* For master's, exit assessment. *Entrance requirements:* For master's, GRE General Test, MAT, minimum GPA of 2.7, 2 reference forms. Additional exam requirements/recommendations for international students: Required—TOEFL (minimum score 500 paper-based; 173 computer-based). *Application deadline:* Applications are processed on a rolling basis. Application fee: $25. *Expenses:* Contact institution. Tuition and fees vary according to degree level and program. *Financial support:* Applicants required to submit FAFSA. *Application contact:* Admissions Office, 615-248-1201, Fax: 615-248-1597, E-mail: admissions_ged@trevecca.edu.

Universidad Metropolitana, Graduate Programs in Education, Program in Curriculum and Teaching, San Juan, PR 00928-1150. Offers MA. Part-time and evening/weekend programs available. *Degree requirements:* For master's, thesis or alternative. *Entrance requirements:* For master's, EXADEP, interview.

Curriculum and Instruction

Université de Montréal, Faculty of Graduate Studies, Faculty of Education, Department of Didactics, Montréal, QC H3C 3J7, Canada. Offers M Ed, MA, PhD, DESS. *Faculty:* 25 full-time (17 women), 6 part-time/adjunct (3 women). *Students:* 109 full-time (76 women), 142 part-time (119 women). 131 applicants, 66% accepted, 75 enrolled. In 2006, 25 master's, 6 doctorates awarded. Terminal master's awarded for partial completion of doctoral program. *Degree requirements:* For master's, thesis (for some programs); for doctorate, thesis/dissertation, general exam. *Application deadline:* For fall admission, 2/1 priority date for domestic students; for winter admission, 11/1 priority date for domestic students; for spring admission, 2/1 priority date for domestic students. Application fee: $30. Electronic applications accepted. *Financial support:* Fellowships, teaching assistantships available. *Faculty research:* Teaching of French as a first or second language, teaching of science and technology, teaching of mathematics, teaching of arts. *Unit head:* Louise Poirier, Director, 514-343-7247, Fax: 514-343-7286. *Application contact:* Graduate Chairman, 514-343-7028, Fax: 514-343-7286.

Université Laval, Faculty of Education, Department of Teaching and Learning Studies, Programs in Didactics, Québec, QC G1K 7P4, Canada. Offers MA, PhD. Terminal master's awarded for partial completion of doctoral program. *Degree requirements:* For master's, thesis (for some programs); for doctorate, thesis/dissertation, comprehensive exam. *Entrance requirements:* For master's and doctorate, English exam (comprehension of written English), knowledge of French. Electronic applications accepted.

University at Albany, State University of New York, School of Education, Department of Educational Theory and Practice, Albany, NY 12222-0001. Offers curriculum and instruction (MS, Ed D, CAS); curriculum planning and development (MA); educational communications (MS, CAS). Evening/weekend programs available. *Students:* 169 full-time (114 women), 213 part-time (147 women). Average age 33. 144 applicants, 53% accepted, 41 enrolled. In 2006, 151 master's, 8 doctorates awarded. *Degree requirements:* For doctorate, one foreign language, thesis/dissertation. *Entrance requirements:* For doctorate, GRE General Test. Additional exam requirements/recommendations for international students: Required—TOEFL (minimum score 550 paper-based; 213 computer-based). *Application deadline:* For fall admission, 2/1 for domestic students, 1/31 for international students. Application fee: $75. Electronic applications accepted. *Expenses:* Tuition, state resident: full-time $6,900; part-time $288 per credit. Tuition, nonresident: full-time $10,920; part-time $455 per credit. Required fees: $1,139. *Financial support:* Fellowships available. *Unit head:* Arthur Appleby, Chair, 518-442-5020.

University of Alaska Fairbanks, School of Education, Fairbanks, AK 99775-7520. Offers cross cultural education (M Ed); curriculum instruction (M Ed); education (M Ed); guidance and counseling (M Ed); k-12 reading (M Ed); language and literacy (M Ed). *Accreditation:* NCATE. Part-time programs available. Postbaccalaureate distance learning degree programs offered. *Faculty:* 18 full-time (10 women), 3 part-time/adjunct (all women). *Students:* 56 full-time (40 women), 89 part-time (72 women); includes 31 minority (4 African Americans, 21 American Indian/Alaska Native, 2 Asian Americans or Pacific Islanders, 4 Hispanic Americans), 1 international. Average age 37. 69 applicants, 67% accepted, 42 enrolled. In 2006, 33 degrees awarded. *Degree requirements:* For master's, thesis or alternative, student teaching, comprehensive exam, registration. *Entrance requirements:* For master's, GRE General Test, PRAXIS I. Additional exam requirements/recommendations for international students: Required—TOEFL (minimum score 550 paper-based; 213 computer-based). *Application deadline:* For fall admission, 3/1 for domestic and international students; for spring admission, 10/1 for domestic students, 9/1 for international students. Application fee: $50. Electronic applications accepted. *Financial support:* In 2006–07, 2 research assistantships with tuition reimbursements (averaging $6,510 per year), 4 teaching assistantships with tuition reimbursements (averaging $10,441 per year) were awarded; fellowships with tuition reimbursements, career-related internships or fieldwork, Federal Work-Study, and scholarships/grants also available. Financial award applicants required to submit FAFSA. *Faculty research:* Native ways of knowing, classroom research in methods of literacy instruction, multiple intelligence theory, geometry concept development, mathematics and science curriculum development. *Unit head:* Dr. Eric C. Madsen, Dean, 907-474-7341, Fax: 907-474-5451, E-mail: fysoed@uaf.edu.

University of Arkansas, Graduate School, College of Education and Health Professions, Department of Curriculum and Instruction, Program in Curriculum and Instruction, Fayetteville, AR 72701-1201. Offers PhD. Part-time programs available. *Students:* 19 full-time (14 women), 27 part-time (22 women); includes 7 minority (5 African Americans, 2 Hispanic Americans), 11 international. 28 applicants, 39% accepted. In 2006, 2 degrees awarded. *Degree requirements:* For doctorate, thesis/dissertation. *Entrance requirements:* For doctorate, GRE General Test. Application fee: $40 ($50 for international students). *Financial support:* In 2006–07, 4 fellowships with tuition reimbursements, 1 research assistantship, 9 teaching assistantships were awarded. Financial award application deadline: 4/1. *Unit head:* Unit Head, 479-575-4209.

The University of British Columbia, Faculty of Graduate Studies, Faculty of Education, Centre for Cross-Faculty Inquiry in Education, Vancouver, BC V6T 1Z1, Canada. Offers curriculum and instruction (M Ed, MA, PhD); early childhood education (M Ed, MA). Part-time and evening/weekend programs available. *Faculty:* 50 full-time (22 women). *Students:* 88 full-time, 36 part-time. 41 applicants, 46% accepted, 18 enrolled. In 2006, 28 master's, 8 doctorates awarded. Terminal master's awarded for partial completion of doctoral program. *Degree requirements:* For master's, thesis (for some programs), thesis (MA); for doctorate, thesis/dissertation, registration. *Entrance requirements:* Additional exam requirements/recommendations for international students: Required—TOEFL (minimum score 567 paper-based; 227 computer-based). *Application deadline:* For fall admission, 1/1 for domestic and international students. Application fee: $90 Canadian dollars ($150 Canadian dollars for international students). Electronic applications accepted. *Financial support:* In 2006–07, 20 students received support; fellowships with tuition reimbursements available, research assistantships with tuition reimbursements available, teaching assistantships with tuition reimbursements available, institutionally sponsored loans, scholarships/grants, and tuition waivers (full and partial) available. *Unit head:* Dr. Graeme Chalmers, Director, 604-822-6502, Fax: 604-822-8234, E-mail: f.graeme.chalmers@ubc.ca. *Application contact:* Oliva dela-Cruz Cordero, Graduate Secretary, 604-822-6502, Fax: 604-822-8234, E-mail: oliva.dela.cruz-cordero@ubc.ca.

The University of British Columbia, Faculty of Graduate Studies, Faculty of Education, Department of Curriculum Studies, Vancouver, BC V6T 1Z1, Canada. Offers art education (M Ed, MA); curriculum studies (M Ed, MA, PhD); home economics education (M Ed, MA); math education (M Ed, MA); music education (M Ed, MA); physical education (M Ed, MA); science education (M Ed, MA); social studies education (M Ed, MA); technical studies education (M Ed, MA). Part-time programs available. *Faculty:* 31 full-time (17 women), 1 (woman) part-time/adjunct. *Students:* 153 full-time (102 women), 101 part-time (67 women), 25 international. Average age 40. 118 applicants, 64% accepted, 62 enrolled. In 2006, 46 master's, 4 doctorates awarded. *Degree requirements:* For master's, thesis (MA); for doctorate, thesis/dissertation, comprehensive exam, registration. *Entrance requirements:* Additional exam requirements/recommendations for international students: Required—TOEFL (minimum score 580 paper-based; 237 computer-based). *Application deadline:* For fall admission, 2/1 for domestic students, 1/1 for international students; for spring admission, 10/1 for domestic students, 9/1 for international students. Application fee: $90 ($150 for international students). Electronic applications accepted. *Expenses:* Contact institution. *Financial support:* In 2006–07, 10 fellowships with partial tuition reimbursements (averaging $16,000 per year), 11 research assistantships with partial tuition reimbursements (averaging $14,000 per year), 27 teaching assistantships with partial tuition reimbursements (averaging $14,000 per year) were awarded; tuition waivers (partial) also available. *Faculty research:* School subjects, teaching and learning. *Unit head:* Dr. Linda Peterat, Interim Head, 604-822-5422, Fax: 604-822-4714. *Application contact:* Basia Zurek, Graduate Secretary, 604-822-5367, Fax: 604-822-4714, E-mail: cust.grad@ubc.ca.

University of Calgary, Faculty of Graduate Studies, Faculty of Education, Graduate Division of Educational Research, Calgary, AB T2N 1N4, Canada. Offers community rehabilitation and disability studies (M Ed, M Sc, Ed D, PhD, Graduate Certificate, Graduate Diploma); curriculum, teaching and learning (M Ed, M Sc, MA, Ed D, PhD, Graduate Certificate, Graduate Diploma); educational contexts (M Ed, MA, Ed D, PhD, Graduate Certificate, Graduate Diploma); educational leadership (M Ed, MA, Ed D, PhD, Graduate Certificate, Graduate Diploma); educational technology (M Ed, M Sc, MA, Ed D, PhD, Graduate Certificate, Graduate Diploma); gifted education (M Sc, MA, Ed D, PhD, Graduate Certificate, Graduate Diploma); higher education administration (Ed D); interpretive studies in education (M Ed, M Sc, MA, Ed D, PhD, Graduate Certificate, Graduate Diploma); second language teaching (M Ed, Ed D, PhD, Graduate Certificate, Graduate Diploma); teaching English as a second language (M Ed, M Sc, MA, Ed D, PhD, Graduate Certificate, Graduate Diploma); workplace and adult learning (M Ed, MA, Ed D, PhD, Graduate Certificate, Graduate Diploma). Ed D in both higher education administration and educational leadership offered via distance delivery. Part-time and evening/weekend programs available. Postbaccalaureate distance learning degree programs offered (minimal on-campus study). *Faculty:* 44 full-time, 52 part-time/adjunct. *Students:* 488 full-time, 550 part-time. 400 applicants, 50% accepted. In 2006, 102 master's, 18 doctorates awarded. *Degree requirements:* For master's, thesis (for some programs); for doctorate, thesis/dissertation, candidacy exam. *Entrance requirements:* For master's, minimum GPA of 3.0, 3 letters of reference; for doctorate, minimum GPA of 3.5, 3 letters of reference; for other advanced degree, minimum GPA of 3.0. Additional exam requirements/recommendations for international students: Required—TOEFL, IELTS. *Application deadline:* For fall admission, 2/15 for domestic students, 2/5 for international students; for winter admission, 6/15 for domestic and international students. Application fee: $100. Electronic applications accepted. *Financial support:* In 2006–07, research assistantships (averaging $3,920 per year); teaching assistantships, career-related internships or fieldwork, scholarships/grants, and unspecified assistantships also available. Financial award application deadline: 2/1. *Faculty research:* Curriculum, leadership, technology, contexts, gifted, second language teaching, work place and adult learning. *Unit head:* Dr. Charles F. Webber, Associate Dean, 403-220-5675, Fax: 403-282-3005, E-mail: cwebber@ucalgary.ca. *Application contact:* Patricia A. Brown, Program Officer, Graduate Division of Educational Research, 403-220-3178, Fax: 403-282-3005, E-mail: brownp@ucalgary.ca.

University of California, Davis, Graduate Studies, Graduate Group in Education, Davis, CA 95616. Offers education (MA, Ed D); instructional studies (PhD); psychological studies (PhD); sociocultural studies (PhD). Terminal master's awarded for partial completion of doctoral program. *Degree requirements:* For master's, thesis (for some programs), comprehensive exam (for some programs); for doctorate, thesis/dissertation. *Entrance requirements:* For master's and doctorate, GRE. Additional exam requirements/recommendations for international students: Required—TOEFL (minimum score 550 paper-based; 213 computer-based). Electronic applications accepted. *Faculty research:* Language and literacy, mathematics education, science education, teacher development, school psychology.

University of Central Florida, College of Education, Doctoral Program in Education, Orlando, FL 32816. Offers communication sciences and disorders (PhD); counselor education (PhD); curriculum and instruction (PhD); elementary education (PhD); exceptional education (PhD); hospitality education (PhD); instructional technology (PhD); mathematics education (PhD). *Students:* 86 full-time (63 women), 9 part-time (4 women); includes 21 minority (15 African Americans, 2 Asian Americans or Pacific Islanders, 4 Hispanic Americans), 19 international. Average age 39. In 2006, 16 degrees awarded. Application fee: $30. Electronic applications accepted. *Expenses:* Tuition, state resident: full-time $6,167; part-time $257 per credit hour. Tuition, nonresident: full-time $22,790; part-time $950 per credit hour. *Financial support:* In 2006–07, 44 fellowships with partial tuition reimbursements (averaging $3,700 per year), 54 research assistantships with partial tuition reimbursements (averaging $7,000 per year), 9 teaching assistantships with partial tuition reimbursements (averaging $7,000 per year) were awarded.

University of Central Missouri, The Graduate School, College of Education, Department of Curriculum and Instruction, Warrensburg, MO 64093. Offers curriculum and instruction (Ed S); elementary education (MSE); K–12 education (MSE); literacy education (MSE); secondary education (MSE). *Accreditation:* NCATE. Part-time programs available. *Faculty:* 22 full-time (14 women). *Students:* 43 full-time (33 women), 309 part-time (237 women); includes 27 minority (23 African Americans, 1 Asian American or Pacific Islander, 3 Hispanic Americans), 3 international. Average age 33. 81 applicants, 81% accepted, 65 enrolled. In 2006, 70 master's, 1 other advanced degree awarded. *Degree requirements:* For master's, comprehensive exam or thesis; for Ed S, thesis, comprehensive exam. *Entrance requirements:* For master's, GRE General Test, minimum GPA of 2.75, teaching certificate; for Ed S, GRE General Test, minimum GPA of 3.25, teaching certificate. Additional exam requirements/recommendations for international students: Required—TOEFL (minimum score 500 paper-based; 173 computer-based). *Application deadline:* For fall admission, 6/1 priority date for domestic students, 5/1 priority date for international students; for spring admission, 10/1 priority date for domestic students, 10/1 for international students. Applications are processed on a rolling basis. Application fee: $30 ($50 for international students). *Expenses:* Tuition, state resident: full-time $5,448; part-time $227 per credit hour. Tuition, nonresident: full-time $10,896; part-time $454 per credit hour. Required fees: $336; $14 per credit hour. *Financial support:* In 2006–07, 4 students received support. Federal Work-Study, scholarships/grants, unspecified assistantships, and administrative and laboratory assistantships available. Support available to part-time students. Financial award application deadline: 3/1; financial award applicants required to submit FAFSA. *Faculty research:* Reading maturity, student and faculty evaluation, online teaching and learning, video documentation, teacher candidates' assessment of student thinking and learning. *Unit head:* Dr. Sharon Lamson, Chair, 660-543-4235, Fax: 660-543-4167, E-mail: lamson@ucmo.edu.

University of Cincinnati, Division of Research and Advanced Studies, College of Education, Criminal Justice, and Human Services, Division of Teacher Education, Program in Curriculum and Instruction, Cincinnati, OH 45221. Offers M Ed, Ed D. *Accreditation:* NCATE. Part-time programs available. *Students:* 117. *Degree requirements:* For master's and doctorate, thesis/dissertation. *Entrance requirements:* For master's, GRE General Test; for doctorate, GRE General Test, GRE Subject Test. Additional exam requirements/recommendations for international students: Required—TOEFL (minimum score 550 paper-based; 213 computer-based), TWE (minimum score 4.5), OEPT. *Application deadline:* For fall admission, 2/1 for domestic students. Application fee: $40. Electronic applications accepted. *Financial support:* Fellowships, tuition waivers (partial) available. *Application contact:* Keith Barton, Chair, 513-556-3384, Fax: 513-556-3384, E-mail: keith.barton@uc.edu.

University of Colorado at Boulder, Graduate School, School of Education, Division of Instruction and Curriculum, Boulder, CO 80309. Offers MA, PhD. *Accreditation:* NCATE. Part-time programs available. *Students:* 90 full-time (66 women), 111 part-time (89 women); includes 21 minority (1 African American, 1 American Indian/Alaska Native, 7 Asian Americans or Pacific Islanders, 12 Hispanic Americans), 1 international. Average age 31. 95 applicants, 98% accepted. In 2006, 96 master's, 6 doctorates awarded. *Degree requirements:* For master's, thesis or alternative, comprehensive exam; for doctorate, one foreign language, thesis/dissertation, comprehensive exam. *Entrance requirements:* For master's, GRE General Test or MAT, minimum undergraduate GPA of 2.75; for doctorate, GRE General Test. *Application deadline:* For fall admission, 2/1 priority date for domestic students, 12/1 for international students; for spring admission, 9/1 for domestic students, 12/1 for international students. Application fee: $50 ($60 for international students). *Financial support:* In 2006–07, 23 fellowships (averaging $3,230 per year), 12 research assistantships (averaging $9,521 per year), 10 teaching assistantships (averaging $7,948 per year) were awarded; career-related internships or fieldwork, Federal Work-Study, and scholarships/grants also available. Support available to part-time students. Financial award application deadline: 2/1. *Unit head:* Kenneth Howe, Director of Graduate Studies, 303-492-7229, Fax: 303-492-7090, E-mail: ken.howe@colorado.edu. *Application contact:* 303-492-6555, Fax: 303-492-5839, E-mail: edadvise@colorado.edu.

University of Colorado at Colorado Springs, Graduate School, College of Education, Colorado Springs, CO 80933-7150. Offers counseling and human services (MA); curriculum and instruction (MA); educational administration (MA); educational leadership (MA, PhD); special education (MA). *Accreditation:* ACA; NCATE. Part-time and evening/weekend programs available. *Faculty:* 22 full-time (15 women), 29 part-time/adjunct (17 women). *Students:* 331 full-time (246 women), 173 part-time (135 women); includes 85 minority (26 African Americans, 4 American Indian/Alaska Native, 13 Asian Americans or Pacific Islanders, 42 Hispanic Americans). Average age 35. 107 applicants, 93% accepted, 49 enrolled. In 2006, 234 degrees awarded. *Degree requirements:* For master's, thesis or alternative, microcomputer proficiency, comprehensive exam; for doctorate, doctoral research lab requirement. *Entrance requirements:* For master's, GRE General Test, MAT. *Application deadline:* For fall admission, 6/15 for domestic students; for spring admission, 10/15 for domestic students. Applications are processed on a rolling basis. Application fee: $60 ($75 for international students). *Expenses:* Tuition, state resident: part-time $303 per credit hour. Tuition, nonresident: part-time $840 per credit hour. Tuition and fees vary according to course load, campus/location and program. *Financial support:* Fellowships, career-related internships or fieldwork and Federal Work-Study available. *Faculty research:* Job training for special populations, materials development for classroom. Total annual research expenditures: $961,803. *Unit head:* Dr. LaVonne Neal, Dean, 719-262-4111, Fax: 719-262-4110, E-mail: lneal@uccs.edu. *Application contact:* Connie Wroten, Professional Assistant, 719-262-4102, Fax: 719-262-4110, E-mail: cwroten@uccs.edu.

University of Connecticut, Graduate School, Neag School of Education, Department of Curriculum and Instruction, Field of Curriculum and Instruction, Storrs, CT 06269. Offers agriculture education (MA, PhD); bilingual and bicultural education (MA, PhD); elementary education (MA, PhD); English education (MA, PhD); history and social sciences education (MA, PhD); mathematics education (MA, PhD); reading education (MA, PhD); science education (MA, PhD); secondary education (MA, PhD); world languages education (MA, PhD). *Faculty:* 25 full-time (12 women). *Students:* 158 full-time (120 women), 54 part-time (44 women); includes 24 minority (3 African Americans, 1 American Indian/Alaska Native, 3 Asian Americans or Pacific Islanders, 17 Hispanic Americans), 2 international. Average age 27. 268 applicants, 76% accepted, 203 enrolled. In 2006, 181 master's, 4 doctorates awarded. *Degree requirements:* For master's, comprehensive exam; for doctorate, thesis/dissertation. *Entrance requirements:* For doctorate, GRE General Test. Additional exam requirements/recommendations for international students: Required—TOEFL (minimum score 550 paper-based; 213 computer-based). *Application deadline:* For fall admission, 2/1 priority date for domestic and international students; for spring admission, 11/1 for domestic students, 10/1 for international students. Applications are processed on a rolling basis. Application fee: $55. Electronic applications accepted. *Financial support:* In 2006–07, 14 research assistantships with full tuition reimbursements, 4 teaching assistantships with full tuition reimbursements were awarded; fellowships, Federal Work-Study, scholarships/grants, health care benefits, and unspecified assistantships also available. Financial award application deadline: 2/1; financial award applicants required to submit FAFSA. *Application contact:* Lisa Rasicot, Graduate Coordinator, 860-486-3065, Fax: 860-486-0210, E-mail: soeadm02@uconnvm.uconn.edu.

University of Delaware, College of Human Services, Education and Public Policy, School of Education, Newark, DE 19716. Offers curriculum and instruction (M Ed); education (PhD); educational leadership (M Ed, Ed D); exceptional children and youth (M Ed); instruction (MI); school counseling (M Ed); school psychology (MA); teaching English as a second language (TESL) (MA). *Accreditation:* NCATE. Part-time and evening/weekend programs available. Terminal master's awarded for partial completion of doctoral program. *Degree requirements:* For master's, thesis (for some programs), comprehensive exam (for some programs), registration; for doctorate, thesis/dissertation, comprehensive exam (for some programs), registration. *Entrance requirements:* For master's and doctorate, GRE, 3 letters of recommendation. Additional exam requirements/recommendations for international students: Required—TOEFL (minimum score 600 paper-based; 250 computer-based). Electronic applications accepted. *Faculty research:* Teacher education; education policy; educational assessment, measurement, and evaluation; curriculum theory and development; community based education models.

University of Denver, College of Education, Denver, CO 80208. Offers counseling psychology (MA, PhD); curriculum and instruction (MA, PhD, Certificate), including curriculum leadership (MA, PhD); educational administration and policy studies (Certificate); educational psychology (MA, PhD, Ed S), including child and family studies (MA, PhD), quantitative research methods (MA, PhD), school psychology (PhD, Ed S); higher education and adult studies (MA, PhD); library and information science (MLIS); library and information sciences (Certificate); school administration (PhD). *Accreditation:* ALA; APA (one or more programs are accredited). Part-time and evening/weekend programs available. Postbaccalaureate distance learning degree programs offered (no on-campus study). *Faculty:* 28 full-time (18 women). *Students:* 293 full-time (240 women), 439 part-time (357 women); includes 102 minority (28 African Americans, 7 American Indian/Alaska Native, 14 Asian Americans or Pacific Islanders, 53 Hispanic Americans), 11 international. Average age 34. 574 applicants, 72% accepted. In 2006, 168 master's, 28 doctorates, 67 other advanced degrees awarded. Terminal master's awarded for partial completion of doctoral program. *Degree requirements:* For master's, comprehensive exam; for doctorate, 2 foreign languages, thesis/dissertation, comprehensive exam. *Entrance requirements:* For master's, GRE General Test or MAT (for most programs); for doctorate, GRE General Test or MAT. *Application deadline:* Applications are processed on a rolling basis. Application fee: $50. Electronic applications accepted. *Expenses:* Tuition: Full-time $29,628; part-time $823 per credit. *Financial support:* In 2006–07, 51 teaching assistantships with full and partial tuition reimbursements (averaging $6,700 per year) were awarded; career-related internships or fieldwork, Federal Work-Study, institutionally sponsored loans, and scholarships/grants also available. Support available to part-time students. Financial award application deadline: 3/1; financial award applicants required to submit FAFSA. *Faculty research:* Parkinson's disease, personnel training, development and assessments, gifted education, service learning, transportation, public schools. Total annual research expenditures: $172,000. *Unit head:* Dr. Virginia Maloney, Dean, 303-871-2509. *Application contact:* Linda McCarthy, Contact, 303-871-2509, E-mail: edinfo@du.edu.

University of Detroit Mercy, College of Liberal Arts and Education, Department of Education, Program in Curriculum and Instruction, Detroit, MI 48221. Offers MA. Part-time and evening/weekend programs available. *Degree requirements:* For master's, thesis or alternative. *Entrance requirements:* For master's, minimum GPA of 2.75. *Expenses:* Tuition: Full-time $15,750; part-time $875 per credit hour. Required fees: $570. *Faculty research:* Integrative curriculum planning, curriculum planning for ethical and character education.

University of Florida, Graduate School, College of Education, Department of Educational Administration and Policy, Gainesville, FL 32611. Offers curriculum and instruction (Ed D, PhD); educational leadership (M Ed, MAE, Ed D, PhD, Ed S); higher education administration (Ed D, PhD, Ed S); student personnel in higher education (M Ed, MAE); PhD/JD. *Accreditation:* NCATE. *Faculty:* 10 full-time (3 women). *Degree requirements:* For master's, thesis optional; for doctorate, variable foreign language requirement, thesis/dissertation. *Entrance requirements:* For master's, GRE General Test, minimum GPA of 3.0, teaching experience; for doctorate and Ed S, GRE General Test, minimum GPA of 3.0. Additional exam requirements/recommendations for international students: Required—TOEFL (minimum score 550 paper-based; 213 computer-based). *Application deadline:* For fall admission, 6/1 priority date for domestic students. Applications are processed on a rolling basis. Application fee: $30. Electronic applications accepted. *Expenses:* Tuition, state resident: full-time $6,827. Tuition, nonresident: full-time $21,951. Required fees: $999. *Financial support:* In 2006–07, 2 research assistantships (averaging $9,424 per year) were awarded; fellowships, teaching assistantships, career-related internships or fieldwork and unspecified assistantships also available. *Faculty research:* Educational finance, community education, middle school curriculum, community college administration. *Unit head:* Linda Hagedorn, Chair, 352-392-2391 Ext. 275. *Application contact:* Dr. Katherine Gratto, Coordinator, 352-392-2391 Ext. 274, Fax: 352-392-0038, E-mail: kgratto@coe.ufl.edu.

University of Florida, Graduate School, College of Education, School of Teaching and Learning, Gainesville, FL 32611. Offers bilingual/ESOL education (M Ed, MAE, Ed D, PhD, Ed S); curriculum and instruction (M Ed, MAE, Ed D, PhD, Ed S); early childhood education (Ed D, PhD, Ed S); elementary education (M Ed, MAE); English education (M Ed, MAE); mathematics education (M Ed, MAE); reading education (M Ed, MAE); science education (M Ed, MAE); social foundations (M Ed, MAE, Ed D, PhD); social studies education (M Ed, MAE). *Accreditation:* NCATE. *Faculty:* 29 full-time (20 women). *Students:* 506 (406 women); includes 87 minority (20 African Americans, 3 American Indian/Alaska Native, 13 Asian Americans or Pacific Islanders, 51 Hispanic Americans) 34 international. In 2006, 278 master's, 8 doctorates awarded. *Degree requirements:* For master's, thesis optional; for doctorate, variable foreign language requirement, thesis/dissertation. *Entrance requirements:* For master's and doctorate, GRE General Test, minimum GPA of 3.0; for Ed S, GRE General Test. Additional exam requirements/recommendations for international students: Required—TOEFL (minimum score 550 paper-based; 213 computer-based). *Application deadline:* For fall admission, 6/1 for domestic students. Applications are processed on a rolling basis. Application fee: $30. Electronic applications accepted. *Expenses:* Tuition, state resident: full-time $6,827. Tuition, nonresident: full-time $21,951. Required fees: $999. *Financial support:* In 2006–07, 5 research assistantships (averaging $11,947 per year), 22 teaching assistantships (averaging $9,709 per year) were awarded; fellowships, career-related internships or fieldwork and unspecified assistantships also available. *Faculty research:* Teacher education, inclusive education, classroom processes, curriculum and technology. *Unit head:* Dr. Tom Dana, Director, 352-392-9191 Ext. 200, Fax: 352-392-9193, E-mail: tdana@coe.ufl.edu. *Application contact:* Dr. Linda C. Jones, Coordinator, 352-392-0761 Ext. 267, Fax: 352-392-9193, E-mail: lcjones@coe.ufl.edu.

University of Hawaii at Manoa, Graduate Division, College of Education, Department of Curriculum Studies, Program in Curriculum Studies, Honolulu, HI 96822. Offers M Ed. *Faculty:* 46 full-time (31 women). *Students:* 29 full-time (14 women), 210 part-time (170 women); includes 33 minority (2 African Americans, 1 American Indian/Alaska Native, 26 Asian Americans or Pacific Islanders, 4 Hispanic Americans), 8 international. 107 applicants, 84% accepted, 76 enrolled. In 2006, 76 degrees awarded. *Degree requirements:* For master's, thesis optional. *Entrance requirements:* Additional exam requirements/recommendations for international students: Required—TOEFL (minimum score 500 paper-based; 173 computer-based; 61 iBT). *Financial support:* In 2006–07, 1 research assistantship (averaging $16,176 per year), 1 teaching assistantship (averaging $14,382 per year) were awarded. *Application contact:* Neil Pateman, 808-956-4401, Fax: 808-956-9905.

University of Hawaii at Manoa, Graduate Division, College of Education, Education Program, Honolulu, HI 96822. Offers curriculum and instruction (PhD); educational administration (PhD); educational foundations (PhD); educational policy studies (PhD); exceptionalities (PhD). Evening/weekend programs available. *Faculty:* 78 full-time (44 women), 1 part-time/adjunct (0 women). *Students:* 54 full-time (37 women), 97 part-time (66 women); includes 28 minority (6 African Americans, 1 American Indian/Alaska Native, 19 Asian Americans or Pacific Islanders, 2 Hispanic Americans), 3 international. Average age 45. 63 applicants, 52% accepted, 24 enrolled. In 2006, 17 degrees awarded. *Median time to degree:* Of those who began their doctoral program in fall 1998, 35% received their degree in 8 years or less. *Degree requirements:* For doctorate, thesis/dissertation. *Entrance requirements:* For doctorate, GRE General Test, sample of written work. Additional exam requirements/recommendations for international students: Required—TOEFL (minimum score 600 paper-based; 250 computer-based; 100 iBT). *Application deadline:* For fall admission, 2/1 for domestic students, 1/15 for international students. Application fee: $50. *Financial support:* In 2006–07, 12 research assistantships (averaging $16,565 per year), 5 teaching assistantships (averaging $13,964 per year) were awarded; career-related internships or fieldwork, Federal Work-Study, and tuition waivers (full and partial) also available. *Application contact:* Dr. Helen Slaughter, Chairperson, 808-956-7913, Fax: 808-956-9100, E-mail: slaughte@hawaii.edu.

University of Houston, College of Education, Department of Curriculum and Instruction, Houston, TX 77204. Offers art education (M Ed); bilingual education (M Ed); curriculum and instruction (Ed D); early childhood education (M Ed); education of the gifted (M Ed); elementary education (M Ed); mathematics education (M Ed); reading and language arts education (M Ed); science education (M Ed); second language education (M Ed); secondary education (M Ed); social studies education (M Ed); teaching (M Ed). *Accreditation:* NCATE. Part-time and evening/weekend programs available. *Faculty:* 24 full-time (11 women), 16 part-time/adjunct (14 women). *Students:* 134 full-time (102 women), 327 part-time (256 women); includes 142 minority (49 African Americans, 1 American Indian/Alaska Native, 29 Asian Americans or Pacific Islanders, 63 Hispanic Americans), 19 international. Average age 37. 113 applicants, 72% accepted, 61 enrolled. In 2006, 106 master's, 32 doctorates awarded. *Degree requirements:* For master's, comprehensive exam or thesis; for doctorate, thesis/dissertation, comprehensive exam. *Entrance requirements:* For master's, GRE General Test or MAT; for doctorate, GRE General Test, interview. *Application deadline:* For fall admission, 7/3 priority date for domestic students. Applications are processed on a rolling basis. Application fee: $35 ($75 for international students). *Expenses:* Tuition, state resident: full-time $5,429; part-time $226 per credit. Tuition, nonresident: full-time $12,029; part-time $501 per credit. Required fees: $2,454. *Financial support:* In 2006–07, 2 fellowships with full tuition reimbursements (averaging $9,500 per year), 6 research assistantships with full tuition reimbursements (averaging $8,800 per year), 25 teaching assistantships with full tuition reimbursements (averaging $8,800 per year) were awarded; career-related internships or fieldwork, Federal Work-Study, institutionally sponsored loans, scholarships/grants, health care benefits, and unspecified assistantships also available. Support available to part-time students. Financial award application deadline: 3/10. *Faculty research:* Teaching-learning process, instructional technology in schools, teacher education, classroom management, at-risk students. *Unit head:* Dr. Juanita Copley, Chairperson, 713-743-4950, Fax: 713-743-4990, E-mail: ncopley@aol.com.

University of Houston–Clear Lake, School of Education, Program in Curriculum and Instruction, Houston, TX 77058-1098. Offers curriculum and instruction (MS); early childhood education (MS); reading (MS); school library and information science (MS). Part-time and evening/weekend programs available. *Faculty:* 17 full-time (15 women), 9 part-time/adjunct (7 women). *Students:* 40 full-time (39 women), 185 part-time (176 women); includes 66 minority (32 African Americans, 7 Asian Americans or Pacific Islanders, 27 Hispanic Americans), 6 international. Average age 34. In 2006, 80 degrees awarded. *Degree requirements:* For master's, thesis (for some programs). *Entrance requirements:* For master's, GRE or minimum GPA of 3.0 in last 60 hours. Additional exam requirements/recommendations for international students: Required—TOEFL (minimum score 550 paper-based; 213 computer-based). *Application deadline:* For fall admission, 7/1 for domestic students, 6/1 for international students; for spring admission, 10/1 for domestic and international students. Applications are processed on a rolling basis. Application fee: $35 ($75 for international students). Electronic applications accepted. *Financial support:* Career-related internships or fieldwork, Federal Work-Study, institutionally sponsored loans, and scholarships/grants available. Support available to part-time students. Financial award application deadline: 5/1; financial award applicants required to submit FAFSA. *Unit head:* Dr. Suzanne Brown, Chair, 281-283-3540, E-mail: brownsue@uhcl.edu. *Application contact:* Janis S. Bigelow, Assistant Director of Admissions, Recruitment and Communications, 281-283-2540, Fax: 281-283-2530, E-mail: bigelow@uhcl.edu.

University of Idaho, College of Graduate Studies, College of Education, Department of Curriculum and Instruction, Moscow, ID 83844-2282. Offers M Ed, MS. *Students:* 28 full-time, 65 part-time. In 2006, 64 master's awarded. *Entrance requirements:* For master's, minimum GPA of 2.8. *Application deadline:* For fall admission, 8/1 for domestic students; for spring admission, 12/15 for domestic students. Application fee: $55 ($60 for international students). *Expenses:* Tuition, nonresident: full-time $9,600; part-time $140 per credit. Required fees: $4,740; $227 per credit. *Financial support:* Research assistantships, teaching assistantships available. Financial award application deadline: 2/15. *Unit head:* John Darrs, Interim Department Chair, 208-885-6587.

University of Idaho, College of Graduate Studies, College of Education, Doctoral Programs in Education, Moscow, ID 83844-2282. Offers adult and organizational learning (Ed D, PhD); counseliing and human services (PhD); counseling and human services (Ed D); curriculum and

Curriculum and Instruction

University of Idaho (continued)
intstruction (Ed D); curriculum and instruction (PhD); educational leadership (Ed D, PhD); physical education (PhD); professional-technical and technology education (PhD); professional-technical and tecnology education (Ed D). *Students:* 208 (118 women). In 2006, 50 degrees awarded. *Expenses:* Tuition, nonresident: full-time $9,600; part-time $140 per credit. Required fees: $4,740; $227 per credit. *Application contact:* Shirley Green, Information Contact, 208-885-6773.

University of Illinois at Chicago, Graduate College, College of Education, Department of Curriculum and Instruction, Chicago, IL 60607-7128. Offers curriculum and instruction (PhD); educational psychology (PhD); instructional leadership (M Ed), including elementary education, reading, secondary education; leadership and administration (M Ed); policy and administration (PhD); policy studies in urban education (PhD). Part-time and evening/weekend programs available. *Degree requirements:* For doctorate, thesis/dissertation. *Entrance requirements:* For master's, minimum GPA of 2.75; for doctorate, GRE General Test, minimum GPA of 2.75. Additional exam requirements/recommendations for international students: Required—TOEFL. Electronic applications accepted. *Faculty research:* Curriculum theory, curriculum development, research on teaching, curriculum and context, reading/literacy.

University of Illinois at Urbana–Champaign, Graduate College, College of Education, Department of Curriculum and Instruction, Champaign, IL 61820. Offers Ed M, MA, MS, Ed D, PhD, CAS. Part-time programs available. *Faculty:* 29 full-time (21 women). *Students:* 118 full-time (85 women), 110 part-time (92 women); includes 33 minority (17 African Americans, 10 Asian Americans or Pacific Islanders, 6 Hispanic Americans), 72 international. 173 applicants, 50% accepted, 38 enrolled. In 2006, 59 master's, 12 doctorates awarded. *Degree requirements:* For doctorate, thesis/dissertation. *Entrance requirements:* For master's, GRE General Test; for doctorate, GRE General Test, writing sample. *Application deadline:* Applications are processed on a rolling basis. Application fee: $50 ($60 for international students). Electronic applications accepted. *Financial support:* In 2006–07, 6 fellowships, 37 research assistantships, 59 teaching assistantships were awarded; Federal Work-Study and tuition waivers (full and partial) also available. Financial award application deadline: 2/15. *Unit head:* Raymond Price, Head, 217-333-5794, Fax: 217-244-4572, E-mail: pricel@uiuc.edu. *Application contact:* Kathy Stalter, Secretary, 217-244-3391, Fax: 217-244-4572, E-mail: kstalter@uiuc.edu.

University of Indianapolis, Graduate Programs, School of Education, Indianapolis, IN 46227-3697. Offers art education (MAT); biology (MAT); chemistry (MAT); curriculum and instruction (MA); earth sciences (MAT); education (MA, MAT); educational leadership (MA); elementary education (MA); English (MAT); French (MAT); math (MAT); physical education (MAT); physics (MAT); secondary education (MA), including art education, education, English education, social studies education; social studies (MAT); Spanish (MAT). *Accreditation:* NCATE. Part-time and evening/weekend programs available. *Faculty:* 4 full-time (2 women), 6 part-time/adjunct (2 women). *Students:* 32 full-time (16 women), 70 part-time (42 women); includes 2 minority (1 African American, 1 Hispanic American). Average age 31. In 2006, 51 degrees awarded. *Entrance requirements:* For master's, GRE Subject Test, minimum GPA of 2.5, 3 letters of recommendation, interview, Praxis I, writing exercise, be within 9 hours of completing content requirements. Additional exam requirements/recommendations for international students: Required—TOEFL (minimum score 550 paper-based; 213 computer-based). *Application deadline:* Applications are processed on a rolling basis. Application fee: $50. *Financial support:* Federal Work-Study available. Financial award application deadline: 5/1; financial award applicants required to submit FAFSA. *Faculty research:* Assessment of teacher education, perceptions of prospective teachers by parents. *Unit head:* Dr. E. Lynne Weisenbach, Dean, 317-788-3446, Fax: 317-788-3300, E-mail: weisenbach@uindy.edu.

The University of Iowa, Graduate College, College of Education, Department of Teaching and Learning, Program in Early Childhood and Elementary Education, Iowa City, IA 52242-1316. Offers curriculum and supervision (MA, PhD); developmental reading (MA); early childhood education and care (MA); elementary education (MA, PhD); language, literature and culture (PhD). *Faculty:* 7 full-time, 4 part-time/adjunct. *Students:* 8 full-time (7 women), 23 part-time (all women); includes 2 minority (both African Americans), 5 international. 6 applicants, 67% accepted, 4 enrolled. In 2006, 11 master's, 1 doctorate awarded. *Degree requirements:* For master's, exam, thesis optional; for doctorate, thesis/dissertation, comprehensive exam, registration. *Entrance requirements:* For master's and doctorate, GRE General Test, minimum GPA of 3.0. Additional exam requirements/recommendations for international students: Required—TOEFL (minimum score 550 paper-based; 213 computer-based; 81 iBT). Application fee: $60 ($85 for international students). Electronic applications accepted. *Financial support:* In 2006–07, 1 fellowship, 2 research assistantships with partial tuition reimbursements, 8 teaching assistantships with partial tuition reimbursements were awarded. Financial award applicants required to submit FAFSA. *Unit head:* Gary Sasso, Chair, 319-335-5324, Fax: 319-335-5608.

The University of Iowa, Graduate College, College of Education, Department of Teaching and Learning, Program in Secondary Education, Iowa City, IA 52242-1316. Offers art education (MA, PhD); curriculum and supervision (PhD); curriculum supervision (MA); developmental reading (MA); English education (MA, MAT, PhD); foreign language education (MA, MAT); foreign language/ESL education (PhD); language, literature and culture (PhD); math education (PhD); mathematics education (MA); music education (MA, PhD); social studies (MA, PhD). *Faculty:* 11 full-time. *Students:* 53 full-time (33 women), 53 part-time (41 women); includes 5 minority (1 African American, 1 American Indian/Alaska Native, 2 Asian Americans or Pacific Islanders, 1 Hispanic American), 19 international. 66 applicants, 47% accepted, 17 enrolled. In 2006, 22 master's, 14 doctorates awarded. *Degree requirements:* For master's, exam, thesis optional; for doctorate, thesis/dissertation, comprehensive exam, registration. *Entrance requirements:* For master's and doctorate, GRE General Test, minimum GPA of 3.0. Additional exam requirements/recommendations for international students: Required—TOEFL (minimum score 550 paper-based; 213 computer-based; 81 iBT). Application fee: $60 ($85 for international students). Electronic applications accepted. *Financial support:* In 2006–07, 1 fellowship, 12 research assistantships with partial tuition reimbursements, 31 teaching assistantships with partial tuition reimbursements were awarded. Financial award applicants required to submit FAFSA. *Unit head:* Gary Sasso, Chair, 319-335-5324, Fax: 319-335-5608.

University of Kansas, Graduate Studies, School of Education, Department of Curriculum and Teaching, Lawrence, KS 66045. Offers curriculum and instruction (MA, MS Ed, Ed D, PhD). Part-time and evening/weekend programs available. *Faculty:* 23 full-time (15 women), 1 part-time/adjunct (0 women). *Students:* 197 full-time (155 women), 240 part-time (192 women); includes 41 minority (10 African Americans, 3 American Indian/Alaska Native, 11 Asian Americans or Pacific Islanders, 17 Hispanic Americans), 64 international. Average age 33. 192 applicants, 77% accepted, 2 enrolled. In 2006, 130 master's, 19 doctorates awarded. *Degree requirements:* For master's, thesis optional; for doctorate, thesis/dissertation, comprehensive exam. *Entrance requirements:* For master's, minimum GPA of 3.0; for doctorate, GRE General Test, minimum graduate GPA of 3.5. Additional exam requirements/recommendations for international students: Required—TOEFL (minimum score 590 paper-based; 243 computer-based). *Application deadline:* For fall admission, 2/1 priority date for domestic and international students; for spring admission, 10/15 priority date for domestic and international students. Applications are processed on a rolling basis. Application fee: $55 ($60 for international students). Electronic applications accepted. *Expenses:* Tuition, area resident: Part-time $227 per credit. Tuition, state resident: part-time $543 per credit. Tuition and fees vary according to course load, campus/location, program and reciprocity agreements. *Financial support:* In 2006–07, 2 students received support; fellowships, research assistantships with full and partial tuition reimbursements available, teaching assistantships with full and partial tuition reimbursements available, Federal Work-Study, scholarships/grants, and unspecified assistantships available. Financial award application deadline: 3/15. *Faculty research:* Reading, teacher preparation, math education, science education, geographic literacy. *Unit head:* Marc Mahlios, Professor and Chair, 785-864-9666, Fax: 785-864-5207, E-mail: mahlios@ku.edu. *Application contact:* Jan Kazar, Graduate Admissions Coordinator, 785-864-4437, Fax: 785-864-5207, E-mail: jkazar@ku.edu.

University of Kentucky, Graduate School, College of Education, Program in Curriculum and Instruction, Lexington, KY 40506-0032. Offers curriculum and instruction (MA Ed, Ed D); instruction and administration (Ed D); instruction system design (MS Ed); middle school education (MS Ed). *Accreditation:* NCATE. *Faculty:* 22 full-time (13 women), 2 part-time/adjunct (both women). *Students:* 116 full-time (85 women), 84 part-time (70 women); includes 26 minority (19 African Americans, 6 Asian Americans or Pacific Islanders, 1 Hispanic American), 6 international. Average age 34. 179 applicants, 51% accepted, 36 enrolled. In 2006, 72 master's, 4 doctorates awarded. *Degree requirements:* For master's, thesis optional; for doctorate, thesis/dissertation, comprehensive exam. *Entrance requirements:* For master's, GRE General Test, minimum undergraduate GPA of 2.75; for doctorate, GRE General Test, minimum graduate GPA of 3.0. Additional exam requirements/recommendations for international students: Required—TOEFL (minimum score 550 paper-based; 213 computer-based). *Application deadline:* For fall admission, 7/18 for domestic students, 2/1 priority date for international students; for spring admission, 12/15 for domestic students, 6/16 priority date for international students. Application fee: $35 ($45 for international students). Electronic applications accepted. *Expenses:* Tuition, state resident: full-time $7,670; part-time $401 per credit hour. Tuition, nonresident: full-time $16,158; part-time $873 per credit hour. *Financial support:* In 2006–07, 4 fellowships (averaging $8,018 per year), 13 research assistantships (averaging $15,000 per year), 11 teaching assistantships (averaging $9,384 per year) were awarded; career-related internships or fieldwork, Federal Work-Study, and institutionally sponsored loans also available. Support available to part-time students. *Faculty research:* Educational reform, multicultural education, classroom instructional practices, performance based assessment, primary school programs. *Unit head:* Dr. Mary Shake, Director of Graduate Studies, 859-257-5676, Fax: 859-257-1602. *Application contact:* Dr. Brian Jackson, Senior Associate Dean, 859-257-4667, Fax: 859-257-4676, E-mail: brian.jackson@uky.edu.

University of Louisiana at Lafayette, Graduate School, College of Education, Graduate Studies and Research in Education, Program in Curriculum and Instruction, Lafayette, LA 70504. Offers M Ed. *Accreditation:* NCATE. *Faculty:* 16 full-time (9 women). *Students:* 5 full-time (all women), 25 part-time (22 women); includes 8 minority (5 African Americans, 2 American Indian/Alaska Native, 1 Hispanic American). Average age 31. 18 applicants, 28% accepted, 2 enrolled. In 2006, 15 degrees awarded. *Degree requirements:* For master's, thesis or alternative. *Entrance requirements:* For master's, GRE General Test, teaching certificate. Additional exam requirements/recommendations for international students: Required—TOEFL (minimum score 550 paper-based; 213 computer-based). *Application deadline:* For fall admission, 5/15 for domestic and international students; for spring admission, 10/1 for domestic and international students. Applications are processed on a rolling basis. Application fee: $25 ($30 for international students). Electronic applications accepted. *Expenses:* Tuition, state resident: full-time $3,247; part-time $93 per credit hour. Tuition, nonresident: full-time $9,427; part-time $350 per credit hour. *Financial support:* Federal Work-Study available. Financial award application deadline: 5/1. *Unit head:* Dr. Mary Jane Ford, Head, 337-482-5733, Fax: 337-482-5904, E-mail: mjford@louisiana.edu. *Application contact:* Dr. Nathan Roberts, Coordinator, 337-482-6747, Fax: 337-482-5842, E-mail: nmr0713@louisiana.edu.

University of Louisiana at Monroe, Graduate Studies and Research, College of Education and Human Development, Department of Curriculum and Instruction, Program in Curriculum and Instruction, Monroe, LA 71209-0001. Offers M Ed, Ed D. *Accreditation:* NCATE. *Students:* Average age 38. *Degree requirements:* For doctorate, thesis/dissertation. *Entrance requirements:* For doctorate, GRE General Test, minimum undergraduate GPA of 2.75, graduate GPA of 3.25. *Application deadline:* For spring admission, 11/1 for domestic students. Application fee: $20 ($30 for international students). *Expenses:* Tuition, state resident: part-time $124 per credit hour. Tuition, nonresident: part-time $124 per credit hour. *Financial support:* Application deadline: 7/1. *Unit head:* Dr. Gary Stringer, Head, Department of Curriculum and Instruction, 318-342-1266, Fax: 318-342-1240, E-mail: stringer@ulm.edu.

University of Louisville, Graduate School, College of Education and Human Development, Department of Teaching and Learning, Program In Curriculum and Instruction, Louisville, KY 40292-0001. Offers Ed D. *Students:* 19 full-time (17 women), 40 part-time (27 women); includes 5 minority (3 African Americans, 1 American Indian/Alaska Native, 1 Asian American or Pacific Islander), 3 international. Average age 45. In 2006, 6 degrees awarded. Application fee: $50. *Unit head:* Dr. Tom Tretter, Program Head, 502-852-0595, Fax: 502-852-1497, E-mail: tom.tretter@louisville.edu.

University of Maine, Graduate School, College of Education and Human Development, Program in Curriculum, Assessment, and Instruction, Orono, ME 04469. Offers elementary and secondary education (M Ed). *Students:* 1 (woman) full-time, 7 part-time (all women); includes 1 minority (American Indian/Alaska Native). Average age 31. 13 applicants, 92% accepted. *Application contact:* Scott G. Delcourt, Associate Dean of the Graduate School, 207-581-3219, Fax: 207-581-3232, E-mail: graduate@maine.edu.

University of Manitoba, Faculty of Graduate Studies, Faculty of Education, Department of Curriculum, Teaching and Learning, Winnipeg, MB R3T 2N2, Canada. Offers general curriculum (M Ed); language and literacy (M Ed); post-secondary studies (M Ed); teaching English as a second language (M Ed). *Degree requirements:* For master's, thesis or alternative.

University of Mary, Program in Education, Bismarck, ND 58504-9652. Offers college teaching (MS Ed); curriculum and instruction (MS Ed); early childhood education (MS Ed); early childhood special education (MS Ed); elementary education administration (MS Ed); reading (MS Ed); secondary education administration (MS Ed); special education (MS Ed). Part-time programs available. *Faculty:* 8 full-time (4 women), 12 part-time/adjunct (7 women). *Students:* 2 full-time (1 woman), 34 part-time (25 women), 2 international. Average age 35. In 2006, 17 degrees awarded. *Degree requirements:* For master's, portfolio or thesis. *Entrance requirements:* For master's, interview, letters of reference. *Application deadline:* Applications are processed on a rolling basis. Application fee: $40. *Financial support:* In 2006–07, 1 teaching assistantship with full tuition reimbursement was awarded; career-related internships or fieldwork also available. Support available to part-time students. Financial award application deadline: 8/1; financial award applicants required to submit FAFSA. *Faculty research:* Innovative pedagogy in higher education, technology in education, content standards, children of poverty, children with diverse learning needs. *Unit head:* Dr. Rebecca Yunker Salveson, Director, 701-355-8186, E-mail: rysalves@umary.edu. *Application contact:* Leona Friedig, Administrative Secretary, 701-355-8058, E-mail: lfriedig@umary.edu.

University of Maryland, Baltimore County, Graduate School, College of Arts, Humanities and Social Sciences, Department of Education, Baltimore, MD 21250. Offers computer/web-based instruction (Postbaccalaureate Certificate); distance education (Postbaccalaureate Certificate); early childhood education (MAT); education (MA); elementary education (MAT); instructional systems development (MA, Postbaccalaureate Certificate), including ESOL/bilingual education (Postbaccalaureate Certificate), ESOL/bilingual training systems (MA); secondary education (MA, MAT); teaching (MA). *Accreditation:* NCATE. Part-time and evening/weekend programs available. Postbaccalaureate distance learning degree programs offered (no on-campus study). *Faculty:* 17 full-time (15 women), 3 part-time/adjunct (all women). *Students:* 89 full-time (78 women), 422 part-time (340 women); includes 72 minority (41 African Americans, 19 Asian Americans or Pacific Islanders, 12 Hispanic Americans), 15 international. In 2006, 56 master's awarded. *Median time to degree:* Of those who began their doctoral program in fall 1998, 95% received their degree in 8 years or less. *Degree requirements:* For master's, thesis (for some programs), comprehensive exam, registration. *Entrance requirements:* For master's, GRE General Test, GRE Subject Test (MA), PRAXIS I (MAT), minimum GPA of 3.0. Additional exam requirements/recommendations for international students: Required—TOEFL. *Application deadline:* For fall admission, 7/1 for domestic students. Applications are processed on a rolling basis. Application fee: $50. Electronic applications accepted. *Expenses:* Tuition, state resident: part-time $412 per credit hour. Tuition, nonresident: part-time $681 per credit hour. Required fees: $91 per credit hour. One-time fee: $75 part-time. *Financial support:* In 2006–07, 75 students received support, including research assistantships with full tuition reimbursements available (averaging $12,000 per year); fellowships, teaching assistantships, career-related internships or fieldwork, Federal Work-Study, scholarships/grants, tuition waivers (partial), and unspecified assistantships also available. Financial award application deadline: 3/1. *Faculty research:* Teacher leadership; STEM education; ESOL/bilingual education; early childhood education; language, literacy and culture. Total annual research expenditures: $1.3 million. *Unit head:* Dr. Mary S. Rivkin, Department Chair, 410-455-2465, Fax: 410-455-3986, E-mail: rivkin@umbc.edu. *Application contact:* Dr. Susan M. Blunck, Director, 410-455-2869, Fax: 410-455-3986, E-mail: blunck@umbc.edu.

University of Maryland, College Park, Graduate Studies, College of Education, Department of Curriculum and Instruction, College Park, MD 20742. Offers reading (M Ed, MA, PhD, CAGS); secondary education (M Ed, MA, Ed D, PhD, CAGS); teaching English to speakers of other languages (M Ed). *Accreditation:* NCATE. Part-time and evening/weekend programs available. Postbaccalaureate distance learning degree programs offered (no on-campus study). *Faculty:* 52 full-time (32 women), 33 part-time/adjunct (30 women). *Students:* 200 full-time (159 women), 189 part-time (155 women); includes 101 minority (48 African Americans, 30 Asian Americans or Pacific Islanders, 23 Hispanic Americans), 33 international. 258 applicants, 62% accepted, 101 enrolled. In 2006, 118 master's, 14 doctorates awarded. *Median time to degree:* Of those who began their doctoral program in fall 1998, 38% received their degree in 8 years or less. *Degree requirements:* For master's, seminar paper; for doctorate, thesis/dissertation, published paper, oral exam, comprehensive exam. *Entrance requirements:* For master's, GRE General Test or MAT, minimum GPA of 3.0, 3 letters of recommendation; for doctorate, GRE General Test or MAT, minimum undergraduate GPA of 3.0, graduate 3.5; 3 letters of recommendation. *Application deadline:* For fall admission, 1/15 for domestic students, 2/1 for international students; for spring admission, 9/1 for domestic students, 6/1 for international students. Applications are processed on a rolling basis. Application fee: $60. Electronic applications accepted. *Financial support:* In 2006–07, 3 fellowships with full tuition reimbursements (averaging $5,677 per year), 25 research assistantships with tuition reimbursements (averaging $16,943 per year), 53 teaching assistantships with tuition reimbursements (averaging $14,810 per year) were awarded; Federal Work-Study and scholarships/grants also available. Support available to part-time students. Financial award applicants required to submit FAFSA. *Faculty research:* Teacher preparation, curriculum study, in-service education. Total annual research expenditures: $3.3 million. *Unit head:* Dr. Stephen M. Koziol, Chairman, 301-405-3117, Fax: 301-314-9055, E-mail: skoziol@umd.edu. *Application contact:* Dean of Graduate School, 301-405-0358, Fax: 301-314-9305.

University of Massachusetts Amherst, Graduate School, School of Education, Program in Education, Amherst, MA 01003. Offers cultural diversity and curriculum reform (M Ed, Ed D, CAGS); early childhood education and development (M Ed, Ed D, CAGS); educational administration (M Ed, Ed D, CAGS); elementary teacher education (M Ed, Ed D, CAGS); higher education (M Ed, Ed D, CAGS); international education (M Ed, Ed D, CAGS); mathematics, science, and instructional technology (M Ed, Ed D, CAGS); physical education teacher education (M Ed, Ed D, CAGS); reading and writing (M Ed, Ed D, CAGS); research and evaluation methods (M Ed, Ed D, CAGS); school psychology and school counseling (M Ed, Ed D, CAGS); secondary teacher education (M Ed, Ed D, CAGS); social justice education (M Ed, Ed D, CAGS); special education (M Ed, Ed D, CAGS). *Accreditation:* NCATE. *Students:* 418 full-time (286 women), 447 part-time (319 women); includes 147 minority (70 African Americans, 4 American Indian/Alaska Native, 28 Asian Americans or Pacific Islanders, 45 Hispanic Americans), 81 international. Average age 36. In 2006, 260 master's, 30 doctorates awarded. *Degree requirements:* For doctorate, thesis/dissertation. *Entrance requirements:* For master's and doctorate, GRE General Test. Additional exam requirements/recommendations for international students: Required—TOEFL (minimum score 530 paper-based; 197 computer-based). *Application deadline:* For fall admission, 1/15 for domestic and international students; for spring admission, 10/1 for domestic and international students. Applications are processed on a rolling basis. Application fee: $40 ($65 for international students). Electronic applications accepted. *Expenses:* Tuition, state resident: full-time $2,640; part-time $110 per credit. Tuition, nonresident: full-time $9,936; part-time $414 per credit. Required fees: $8,969; $3,129 per term. One-time fee: $257 full-time. Tuition and fees vary according to class time, course load, campus/location and reciprocity agreements. *Financial support:* Fellowships with full tuition reimbursements, research assistantships with full tuition reimbursements, teaching assistantships with full tuition reimbursements, career-related internships or fieldwork, Federal Work-Study, scholarships/grants, traineeships, and unspecified assistantships available. Support available to part-time students. Financial award application deadline: 1/15. *Unit head:* Linda L. Griffin, Professor, 413-545-6984.

University of Massachusetts Boston, Office of Graduate Studies, Graduate College of Education, Program in Instructional Design, Boston, MA 02125-3393. Offers M Ed. Part-time and evening/weekend programs available. *Students:* 10 full-time (7 women), 70 part-time (43 women); includes 12 minority (6 African Americans, 3 Asian Americans or Pacific Islanders, 3 Hispanic Americans), 1 international. Average age 44. 29 applicants, 52% accepted. In 2006, 2 degrees awarded. *Median time to degree:* Master's–4 years full-time. *Degree requirements:* For master's, practicum, thesis optional. *Entrance requirements:* For master's, MAT, minimum GPA of 2.75. *Application deadline:* For fall admission, 3/1 priority date for domestic students; for spring admission, 11/1 for domestic students. Application fee: $25 ($40 for international students). *Expenses:* Tuition, state resident: full-time $2,590; part-time $301 per credit. Tuition, nonresident: full-time $9,758; part-time $427 per credit. One-time fee: $495 full-time. *Financial support:* In 2006–07, 3 research assistantships with full tuition reimbursements (averaging $13,000 per year), teaching assistantships with full tuition reimbursements (averaging $2,000 per year) were awarded; career-related internships or fieldwork, Federal Work-Study, and unspecified assistantships also available. Support available to part-time students. Financial award application deadline: 3/1; financial award applicants required to submit FAFSA. *Faculty research:* Distance education, adult education. *Unit head:* Dr. Canice McGarry, Director, 617-287-7622, E-mail: canice.mcgarry@umb.edu. *Application contact:* Peggy Roldan, Graduate Admissions Coordinator, 617-287-6400, Fax: 617-287-6236, E-mail: bos.gadm@dpc.umassp.edu.

University of Massachusetts Lowell, Graduate School, Graduate School of Education, Lowell, MA 01854-2881. Offers administration, planning, and policy (CAGS); curriculum and instruction (M Ed, CAGS); educational administration (M Ed); language arts and literacy (Ed D); leadership in schooling (Ed D); math and science education (Ed D); reading and language (M Ed, CAGS). *Accreditation:* NCATE. Part-time and evening/weekend programs available. Postbaccalaureate distance learning degree programs offered (no on-campus study). Terminal master's awarded for partial completion of doctoral program. *Degree requirements:* For doctorate, thesis/dissertation. *Entrance requirements:* For master's and doctorate, GRE General Test. Additional exam requirements/recommendations for international students: Required—TOEFL. Electronic applications accepted.

University of Memphis, Graduate School, College of Education, Department of Instruction and Curriculum Leadership, Memphis, TN 38152. Offers early childhood education (MAT, MS, Ed D); elementary education (MAT); instruction and curriculum (MS, Ed D); instruction design and technology (MS, Ed D); reading (MS, Ed D); secondary education (MAT); special education (MAT, MS, Ed D). *Accreditation:* NCATE (one or more programs are accredited). Part-time programs available. Terminal master's awarded for partial completion of doctoral program. *Degree requirements:* For master's, thesis or alternative, comprehensive exam; for doctorate, thesis/dissertation, comprehensive exam. *Entrance requirements:* For master's, GRE General Test, minimum GPA of 2.5; for doctorate, GRE General Test, GRE Subject Test, 2 years of teaching experience. Electronic applications accepted. *Faculty research:* Effective urban teachers, preparation and retention of urban teachers, technology utilization in schools, field-based preparation teacher preparation programs, effective use of online instruction.

University of Michigan, Horace H. Rackham School of Graduate Studies, School of Education, Programs in Educational Studies, Ann Arbor, MI 48109. Offers curriculum development (MA); early childhood education (MA, PhD); educational administration and policy (MA, PhD); educational foundation, administration, policy, and research methods (MA); educational foundations and policy (MA, PhD); elementary education (MA-Certification); English education (MA); English language learning in school settings (MA); learning technologies (MA, PhD); literacy, language, and culture (MA, PhD); mathematics education (MA, PhD); research methods (MA); science education (MA, PhD); secondary education (MA-Certification); social studies education (MA); special education (PhD); teaching and teacher education (PhD); MA-Certification; MBA/MA; PhD/MA. Terminal master's awarded for partial completion of doctoral program. *Degree requirements:* For master's, thesis (for some programs); for doctorate, thesis/dissertation, comprehensive exam. *Entrance requirements:* For master's and doctorate, GRE General Test. Additional exam requirements/recommendations for international students: Required—TOEFL (minimum score 600 paper-based; 250 computer-based). *Application deadline:* For fall admission, 12/1 priority date for domestic students, 12/1 for international students. Application fee: $60 ($75 for international students). Electronic applications accepted. *Financial support:* Applicants required to submit FAFSA. *Unit head:* Dr. Addison Stone, Chairperson, 734-763-7500, Fax: 734-615-1290, E-mail: addison@umich.edu. *Application contact:* Roberta Perry, Office of Student Services, 734-764-7563, Fax: 734-763-1495, E-mail: ed.grad.admit@umich.edu.

University of Minnesota, Twin Cities Campus, Graduate School, College of Education and Human Development, Department of Curriculum and Instruction, Minneapolis, MN 55455-0213. Offers art education (M Ed, MA, PhD); children's literature (M Ed, MA, PhD); curriculum and instruction (MA, PhD); early childhood education (M Ed, PhD); elementary education (M Ed, MA, PhD); English education (MA, PhD); environmental education (M Ed); family education (M Ed, MA, Ed D, PhD); instructional systems and technology (M Ed, MA, PhD); language arts (MA, PhD); language immersion education (Certificate); literacy education (MA); mathematics education (MA, PhD); reading education (MA, PhD); science education (MA, PhD); second languages and cultures education (MA, PhD); social studies education (MA, PhD); teaching (M Ed), including Chinese, earth science, elementary special education, English, English as a second language, French, German, Hebrew, Japanese, life sciences, mathematics, middle school science, science, second languages and cultures, social studies, Spanish; technology enhanced learning (Certificate); writing education (M Ed, MA, PhD). *Faculty:* 30 full-time (18 women). *Students:* 496 full-time (363 women), 338 part-time (235 women); includes 89 minority (26 African Americans, 4 American Indian/Alaska Native, 42 Asian Americans or Pacific Islanders, 17 Hispanic Americans), 33 international. Average age 29. 734 applicants, 66% accepted, 425 enrolled. In 2006, 644 master's, 18 doctorates, 11 other advanced degrees awarded. *Expenses:* Tuition, state resident: full-time $9,302; part-time $775 per credit. Tuition, nonresident: full-time $16,400; part-time $1,367 per credit. Full-time tuition and fees vary according to class time, course load, program, reciprocity agreements and student level. *Financial support:* In 2006–07, 7 fellowships (averaging $24,775 per year), 22 research assistantships with full tuition reimbursements (averaging $24,775 per year), 52 teaching assistantships with full tuition reimbursements (averaging $24,775 per year) were awarded. *Faculty research:* Educational practice for a democratic and just society; curriculum history and development/assessment; teacher preparation/induction/mentoring/development; cultural, linguistic, social, political, technological, and economic factors that influence teaching and learning. Total annual research expenditures: $1.2 million. *Unit head:* Dr. Ruth Thomas, Chair, 612-624-4772, Fax: 612-624-8277, E-mail: thoma006@umn.edu. *Application contact:* Dr. Mary Bents, Associate Dean, 612-625-6501, Fax: 612-626-1580, E-mail: mbents@tc.umn.edu.

University of Mississippi, Graduate School, School of Education, Department of Curriculum and Instruction, Oxford, University, MS 38677. Offers curriculum and instruction (M Ed, Ed D, Ed S); education (PhD); secondary education (MA). *Accreditation:* NCATE. *Faculty:* 30 full-time (24 women), 6 part-time/adjunct (5 women). *Students:* 69 full-time (59 women), 268 part-time (227 women); includes 106 minority (94 African Americans, 10 Asian Americans or Pacific Islanders, 2 Hispanic Americans), 6 international. In 2006, 162 master's, 8 doctorates, 11 other advanced degrees awarded. *Degree requirements:* For master's, thesis (for some programs); for doctorate, one foreign language, thesis/dissertation. *Entrance requirements:* For master's, GRE General Test, minimum GPA of 3.0; for doctorate, GRE General Test. Additional exam requirements/recommendations for international students: Required—TOEFL. *Application deadline:* For fall admission, 7/1 for domestic students; for spring admission, 10/1 for domestic students. Applications are processed on a rolling basis. Application fee: $25. *Expenses:* Tuition, state resident: full-time $4,602; part-time $256 per credit hour. Tuition, nonresident: full-time $10,566; part-time $587 per credit hour. *Financial support:* Scholarships/grants available. Financial award application deadline: 3/1; financial award applicants required to submit FAFSA. *Unit head:* Dr. Fannye Love, Chair, 662-915-7530, E-mail: flove@olemiss.edu.

University of Missouri–Columbia, Graduate School, College of Education, Department of Curriculum and Instruction, Columbia, MO 65211. Offers agricultural education (M Ed, PhD, Ed S); art education (M Ed, PhD, Ed S); business and office education (M Ed, PhD, Ed S); early childhood education (M Ed, PhD, Ed S); elementary education (M Ed, PhD, Ed S); English education (M Ed, PhD, Ed S); foreign language education (M Ed, PhD, Ed S); health education and promotion (M Ed, PhD); learning and instruction (M Ed); marketing education (M Ed, PhD, Ed S); mathematics education (M Ed, PhD, Ed S); music education (M Ed, PhD, Ed S); reading education (M Ed, PhD, Ed S); science education (M Ed, PhD, Ed S); social studies education (M Ed, PhD, Ed S); vocational education (M Ed, PhD, Ed S). Part-time programs available. *Faculty:* 24 full-time (12 women). *Students:* 195 full-time (148 women), 260 part-time (214 women); includes 27 minority (8 African Americans, 1 American Indian/Alaska Native, 10 Asian Americans or Pacific Islanders, 8 Hispanic Americans), 19 international. In 2006, 186 master's, 12 doctorates awarded. Terminal master's awarded for partial completion of doctoral program. *Degree requirements:* For doctorate, thesis/dissertation. *Entrance requirements:* For master's and Ed S, GRE General Test or MAT, minimum GPA of 3.0; for doctorate, GRE General Test, minimum GPA of 3.0. *Application deadline:* Applications are processed on a rolling basis. Application fee: $45 ($60 for international students). *Financial support:* Fellowships, research assistantships, teaching assistantships, institutionally sponsored loans available. *Unit head:* Dr. Lloyd H. Barrow, Director of Graduate Studies, 573-882-8247, E-mail: robinsonr@missouri.edu.

University of Missouri–Columbia, Graduate School, College of Education, Department of Educational, School, and Counseling Psychology, Columbia, MO 65211. Offers counseling psychology (M Ed, MA, PhD, Ed S); educational psychology (M Ed, MA, PhD, Ed S); learning and instruction (M Ed); school psychology (M Ed, MA, PhD, Ed S). *Accreditation:* APA (one or more programs are accredited); CORE. Part-time programs available. *Faculty:* 31 full-time (10 women), 1 (woman) part-time/adjunct. *Students:* 134 full-time (99 women), 59 part-time (45 women); includes 33 minority (20 African Americans, 2 American Indian/Alaska Native, 6 Asian Americans or Pacific Islanders, 5 Hispanic Americans), 23 international. In 2006, 56 master's, 13 doctorates, 13 other advanced degrees awarded. *Degree requirements:* For doctorate, thesis/dissertation. *Entrance requirements:* For master's, doctorate, and Ed S, GRE General Test, minimum GPA of 3.0. *Application deadline:* For fall admission, 1/8 priority date for domestic students. Applications are processed on a rolling basis. Application fee: $45 ($60 for international students). *Financial support:* Fellowships, research assistantships, teaching assistantships, institutionally sponsored loans available. *Unit head:* Dr. David Bergin, Director of Graduate Studies, 573-882-1303, E-mail: bergind@missouri.edu.

University of Missouri–Columbia, Graduate School, College of Education, Department of Special Education, Columbia, MO 65211. Offers administration and supervision of special education (PhD); behavior disorders (M Ed, PhD); curriculum development of exceptional students (M Ed, PhD); early childhood special education (M Ed, PhD); general special education (M Ed, MA, PhD); learning and instruction (M Ed); learning disabilities (M Ed, PhD); mental retardation (M Ed, PhD). *Accreditation:* NCATE. Part-time and evening/weekend programs available. Postbaccalaureate distance learning degree programs offered (no on-campus study). *Faculty:* 8 full-time (6 women). *Students:* 27 full-time (26 women), 28

Curriculum and Instruction

University of Missouri–Columbia (continued)
part-time (24 women); includes 2 minority (both Asian Americans or Pacific Islanders), 5 international. 22 applicants, 77% accepted, 14 enrolled. In 2006, 12 master's, 3 doctorates awarded. *Degree requirements:* For master's, thesis or alternative, comprehensive exam; for doctorate, thesis/dissertation, comprehensive exam. *Entrance requirements:* For master's and doctorate, GRE General Test, letters of recommendation. Additional exam requirements/recommendations for international students: Required—TOEFL (minimum score 500 paper-based; 173 computer-based). *Application deadline:* For fall admission, 7/1 priority date for domestic and international students; for winter admission, 11/1 priority date for domestic and international students; for spring admission, 4/1 priority date for domestic and international students. Application fee: $45 ($60 for international students). Electronic applications accepted. *Financial support:* Fellowships with full and partial tuition reimbursements, research assistantships with full and partial tuition reimbursements, teaching assistantships with full and partial tuition reimbursements, career-related internships or fieldwork, scholarships/grants, health care benefits, and unspecified assistantships available. *Faculty research:* Positive behavior support, applied behavior analysis, attention deficit disorder, pre-linguistic development, school discipline. Total annual research expenditures: $1.4 million. *Unit head:* Dr. Melissa Stormont, Director of Graduate Studies, 573-882-7383, E-mail: stormontm@missouri.edu. *Application contact:* Fran Colley, Office Support Staff III, 573-882-6462, Fax: 573-884-2917, E-mail: cigrad@coe.missouri.edu.

University of Missouri–Kansas City, School of Education, Kansas City, MO 64110-2499. Offers administration (Ed D); counseling and guidance (MA, Ed S); counseling psychology (PhD); curriculum and instruction (MA, Ed S); education (PhD); educational administration (Ed S); reading education (MA, Ed S); special education (MA). *Accreditation:* NCATE. Part-time and evening/weekend programs available. *Faculty:* 59 full-time (46 women), 39 part-time/adjunct (29 women). *Students:* 182 full-time (151 women), 470 part-time (344 women); includes 148 minority (117 African Americans, 5 American Indian/Alaska Native, 8 Asian Americans or Pacific Islanders, 18 Hispanic Americans), 9 international. Average age 34. 560 applicants, 79% accepted, 253 enrolled. In 2006, 196 master's, 4 doctorates, 41 other advanced degrees awarded. *Degree requirements:* For doctorate, thesis/dissertation, internship, practicum. *Entrance requirements:* For master's, GRE, minimum GPA of 2.75, 2 letters of references, a written statement of purpose; for doctorate, GRE, minimum GPA of 3.0; for Ed S, minimum GPA of 3.0. Additional exam requirements/recommendations for international students: Required—TOEFL (minimum score 550 paper-based; 213 computer-based). *Application deadline:* For fall admission, 4/1 priority date for domestic students, 4/1 for international students; for winter admission, 10/1 priority date for domestic students, 10/1 for international students; for spring admission, 10/1 priority date for domestic students, 10/1 for international students. Applications are processed on a rolling basis. Application fee: $35 ($50 for international students). *Expenses:* Tuition, state resident: full-time $4,975; part-time $276 per credit. Tuition, nonresident: full-time $12,847; part-time $713 per credit. Required fees: $595; $595 per year. *Financial support:* In 2006–07, 361 students received support, including 13 research assistantships with partial tuition reimbursements available (averaging $10,560 per year); fellowships with full tuition reimbursements available, teaching assistantships, career-related internships or fieldwork, Federal Work-Study, institutionally sponsored loans, and tuition waivers (full and partial) also available. Support available to part-time students. Financial award application deadline: 3/1. *Faculty research:* Urban education, inquiry-based field study, theories of counseling and psychotherapy, school literacy, educational technology. Total annual research expenditures: $94,515. *Unit head:* Dr. Linda Edwards, Dean, 816-235-2236, Fax: 816-235-5270, E-mail: edwardsli@umkc.edu. *Application contact:* Dr. Lori Reesor, Assistant Dean, 816-235-1473, Fax: 816-235-5270, E-mail: reesorl@umkc.edu.

University of Missouri–St. Louis, College of Education, Division of Teaching and Learning, St. Louis, MO 63121. Offers elementary education (M Ed), including reading; secondary education (M Ed), including curriculum and instruction, middle school, reading; special education (M Ed), including behavioral disorders, early childhood special education, learning disabilities, mentally retardation; teaching-learning processes (Ed D, PhD). *Faculty:* 20 full-time (13 women), 5 part-time/adjunct (4 women). *Students:* 118 full-time (84 women), 353 part-time (311 women); includes 90 minority (75 African Americans, 1 American Indian/Alaska Native, 3 Asian Americans or Pacific Islanders, 11 Hispanic Americans), 4 international. Average age 36. In 2006, 136 master's, 3 doctorates awarded. *Entrance requirements:* For doctorate, GRE General Test, 3 letters of recommendation. *Application deadline:* For fall admission, 7/15 for domestic students; for spring admission, 12/15 for domestic students. *Expenses:* Tuition, state resident: part-time $332 per credit hour. Tuition, nonresident: part-time $770 per credit hour. *Financial support:* In 2006–07, 9 teaching assistantships (averaging $14,250 per year) were awarded; research assistantships. *Unit head:* Dr. Gayle Wilkinson, Chair, 314-516-5791. *Application contact:* 314-516-5458, Fax: 314-516-6996, E-mail: gadadm@umsl.edu.

The University of Montana, Graduate School, School of Education, Department of Curriculum and Instruction, Missoula, MT 59812-0002. Offers M Ed, Ed D. Part-time programs available. *Degree requirements:* For doctorate, thesis/dissertation. *Entrance requirements:* For master's, GRE General Test. Additional exam requirements/recommendations for international students: Required—TOEFL.

University of Nebraska at Kearney, College of Graduate Study, College of Education, Department of Teacher Education, Kearney, NE 68849-0001. Offers curriculum and instruction (MS Ed); instructional technology (MS Ed); reading education (MA Ed); special education (MA Ed). Part-time and evening/weekend programs available. *Faculty:* 9 full-time (5 women). *Students:* 15 full-time (10 women), 226 part-time (173 women); includes 5 minority (1 African American, 1 Asian American or Pacific Islander, 3 Hispanic Americans), 4 international. 46 applicants, 78% accepted. In 2006, 66 degrees awarded. *Degree requirements:* For master's, thesis optional. *Entrance requirements:* For master's, portfolio or GRE. Additional exam requirements/recommendations for international students: Required—TOEFL (minimum score 550 paper-based; 213 computer-based). *Application deadline:* For fall admission, 5/1 for domestic and international students; for spring admission, 8/15 for domestic students, 8/1 for international students. Applications are processed on a rolling basis. Application fee: $45. Electronic applications accepted. *Expenses:* Tuition, state resident: part-time $161 per hour. Tuition, nonresident: part-time $332 per hour. Required fees: $57 per hour. *Financial support:* In 2006–07, 8 research assistantships with full tuition reimbursements (averaging $8,200 per year) were awarded; career-related internships or fieldwork, scholarships/grants, and unspecified assistantships also available. Support available to part-time students. *Unit head:* Dr. Dennis Pottnoff, Chair, 308-865-8513, E-mail: pottnoffd@unk.edu.

University of Nebraska–Lincoln, Graduate College, College of Education and Human Services, Department of Teaching, Learning and Teacher Education, Lincoln, NE 68588. Offers M Ed, MA, MST, Ed S. *Accreditation:* NCATE. *Degree requirements:* For master's, thesis optional. *Entrance requirements:* Additional exam requirements/recommendations for international students: Required—TOEFL (minimum score 550 paper-based; 213 computer-based). Electronic applications accepted. *Faculty research:* Teacher education, instructional leadership, literacy education, technology, improvement of school curriculum.

University of Nebraska–Lincoln, Graduate College, College of Education and Human Services, Interdepartmental Area of Administration, Curriculum and Instruction, Lincoln, NE 68588. Offers Ed D, PhD, JD/PhD. *Accreditation:* NCATE. Postbaccalaureate distance learning degree programs offered. *Degree requirements:* For doctorate, thesis/dissertation, comprehensive exam. *Entrance requirements:* For doctorate, GRE, writing samples, curriculum vitae. Additional exam requirements/recommendations for international students: Required—TOEFL (minimum score 550 paper-based; 213 computer-based). Electronic applications accepted.

University of Nevada, Las Vegas, Graduate College, College of Education, Department of Curriculum and Instruction, Las Vegas, NV 89154-9900. Offers curriculum and instruction (Ed D, PhD, Ed S); elementary education (M Ed, MS); English education (M Ed, MS); library science (M Ed, MS); literacy education (M Ed, MS); mathematics education (M Ed, MS); multicultural education (M Ed, MS); reading specialist (M Ed, MS); secondary education (M Ed, MS); teacher leadership (M Ed, MS); teaching English as a second language (M Ed, MS); technology integration and leadership (M Ed, MS). *Accreditation:* NCATE. Part-time and evening/weekend programs available. *Faculty:* 40 full-time (19 women), 21 part-time/adjunct (14 women). *Students:* 257 full-time (189 women), 387 part-time (296 women); includes 114 minority (28 African Americans, 5 American Indian/Alaska Native, 34 Asian Americans or Pacific Islanders, 47 Hispanic Americans), 7 international. 261 applicants, 70% accepted, 168 enrolled. In 2006, 231 master's, 5 doctorates awarded. *Degree requirements:* For master's, thesis (for some programs), comprehensive exam (for some programs); for doctorate, thesis/dissertation, oral exam. *Entrance requirements:* For master's, minimum GPA of 3.0; for doctorate, GRE General Test, minimum graduate GPA of 3.0. Additional exam requirements/recommendations for international students: Required—TOEFL (minimum score 550 paper-based; 213 computer-based; 80 iBT). *Application deadline:* For fall admission, 2/15 for domestic and international students; for spring admission, 9/30 for domestic and international students. Application fee: $60 ($75 for international students). Electronic applications accepted. *Financial support:* In 2006–07, 30 research assistantships with partial tuition reimbursements (averaging $10,000 per year), 7 teaching assistantships with partial tuition reimbursements (averaging $12,000 per year) were awarded; career-related internships or fieldwork, Federal Work-Study, institutionally sponsored loans, scholarships/grants, health care benefits, and unspecified assistantships also available. Support available to part-time students. Financial award application deadline: 3/1. *Unit head:* Dr. Greg Levitt, Chair, 702-895-3241. *Application contact:* Graduate College Admissions Evaluator, 702-895-3320, E-mail: gradcollege@unlv.edu.

University of Nevada, Reno, Graduate School, College of Education, Department of Curriculum, Teaching and Learning, Reno, NV 89557. Offers curriculum, teaching and learning (Ed D, PhD); elementary education (M Ed, MA, Ed S); secondary education (M Ed, MA, MS, Ed S); special education and disability studies (PhD). *Students:* 82 full-time (65 women), 74 part-time (58 women); includes 12 minority (1 African American, 3 American Indian/Alaska Native, 5 Asian Americans or Pacific Islanders, 3 Hispanic Americans), 2 international. Average age 35. 66 applicants, 85% accepted, 0 enrolled. In 2006, 51 degrees awarded. *Degree requirements:* For master's, thesis optional. *Entrance requirements:* For master's, GRE General Test, minimum GPA of 2.75. Additional exam requirements/recommendations for international students: Required—TOEFL (minimum score 500 paper-based; 173 computer-based). *Application deadline:* For fall admission, 3/1 priority date for domestic students; for spring admission, 10/1 for domestic students. Applications are processed on a rolling basis. Application fee: $60 ($95 for international students). Electronic applications accepted. *Unit head:* Dr. Margaret Ferrara, Program Director, 775-682-7530, E-mail: ferrara@unr.edu.

University of New Orleans, Graduate School, College of Education and Human Development, Department of Curriculum and Instruction, New Orleans, LA 70148. Offers M Ed, PhD, GCE. *Accreditation:* NCATE. Evening/weekend programs available. *Students:* 105 (88 women). Average age 40. In 2006, 37 master's, 7 doctorates awarded. *Degree requirements:* For doctorate, variable foreign language requirement, thesis/dissertation. *Entrance requirements:* For master's, GRE General Test; for doctorate, GRE General Test, GRE Subject Test. Additional exam requirements/recommendations for international students: Required—TOEFL (minimum score 550 paper-based; 213 computer-based). *Application deadline:* For fall admission, 7/1 priority date for domestic students, 6/1 for international students; for spring admission, 11/15 priority date for domestic students, 10/1 for international students. Applications are processed on a rolling basis. Application fee: $40. Electronic applications accepted. *Expenses:* Tuition, state resident: full-time $3,292. Tuition, nonresident: full-time $10,336. Required fees: $158. *Financial support:* Teaching assistantships, career-related internships or fieldwork, institutionally sponsored loans, and tuition waivers (partial) available. Financial award application deadline: 3/15; financial award applicants required to submit FAFSA. *Unit head:* Dr. April Bedford-Whatley, Chairperson, 504-280-6607, Fax: 504-280-1120, E-mail: awhatley@uno.edu. *Application contact:* Dr. Judith Kieff, Graduate Coordinator, 504-280-6527, Fax: 504-280-1120, E-mail: jkieff@uno.edu.

The University of North Carolina at Chapel Hill, Graduate School, School of Education, Program in Curriculum and Instruction, Chapel Hill, NC 27599. Offers Ed D. *Accreditation:* NCATE. In 2006, 3 degrees awarded. *Degree requirements:* For doctorate, thesis/dissertation, comprehensive exam. *Entrance requirements:* For doctorate, GRE General Test, minimum GPA of 3.0 during last 2 years of undergraduate course work. Additional exam requirements/recommendations for international students: Required—TOEFL (minimum score 550 paper-based; 213 computer-based). *Application deadline:* For fall admission, 1/1 priority date for domestic and international students. Applications are processed on a rolling basis. Application fee: $60. *Financial support:* Federal Work-Study available. Support available to part-time students. Financial award application deadline: 1/1. *Faculty research:* Professional development. *Unit head:* Dr. Barbara Day, Coordinator, 919-962-7739, Fax: 919-962-1533. *Application contact:* Janet Carroll, Registrar, 919-962-8690, Fax: 919-962-1533, E-mail: jscarrol@email.unc.edu.

The University of North Carolina at Chapel Hill, Graduate School, School of Education, Program in Education, Chapel Hill, NC 27599. Offers culture, curriculum and change (PhD); culture, curriculum, and change (MA); early childhood, families, and literacy studies (MA, PhD); educational psychology measurements, and evaluation (PhD); educational psychology, measurement, and evaluation (MA). *Accreditation:* NCATE. In 2006, 11 master's, 10 doctorates awarded. *Degree requirements:* For master's, thesis/dissertation; for doctorate, thesis/dissertation, comprehensive exam, registration. *Entrance requirements:* For master's, GRE General Test, minimum GPA of 3.0 during last 2 years of undergraduates course work; for doctorate, GRE General Test, minimum GPA of 3.0 during last 2 years of undergraduate course work. Additional exam requirements/recommendations for international students: Required—TOEFL (minimum score 550 paper-based; 213 computer-based). *Application deadline:* For fall admission, 1/1 priority date for domestic and international students. Applications are processed on a rolling basis. Application fee: $60. Electronic applications accepted. *Financial support:* Federal Work-Study available. Support available to part-time students. Financial award application deadline: 3/1; financial award applicants required to submit FAFSA. *Application contact:* Janet Carroll, Registrar, 919-962-8690, Fax: 919-962-1533, E-mail: jscarrol@email.unc.edu.

The University of North Carolina at Charlotte, Graduate School, College of Education, Department of Educational Leadership, Charlotte, NC 28223-0001. Offers curriculum and supervision (M Ed); educational administration (CAS); educational leadership (Ed D); instructional systems technology (M Ed); school administration (MSA). Part-time and evening/weekend programs available. *Faculty:* 17 full-time (4 women), 10 part-time/adjunct (5 women). *Students:* 67 full-time (55 women), 158 part-time (112 women); includes 68 minority (63 African Americans, 1 American Indian/Alaska Native, 1 Asian American or Pacific Islander, 3 Hispanic Americans), 1 international. Average age 38. 149 applicants, 71% accepted, 90 enrolled. In 2006, 61 degrees awarded. *Entrance requirements:* For master's and doctorate, GRE or MAT. Additional exam requirements/recommendations for international students: Required—TOEFL (minimum score 550 paper-based; 220 computer-based). *Application deadline:* For fall admission, 7/1 for domestic students, 5/1 for international students; for spring admission, 11/1 for domestic students, 10/1 for international students. Applications are processed on a rolling basis. Application fee: $55. Electronic applications accepted. *Expenses:* Tuition, state resident: full-time $2,719; part-time $170 per credit. Tuition, nonresident: full-time $12,926; part-time $808 per credit. Required fees: $1,555. *Financial support:* In 2006–07, 3 teaching assistantships (averaging $8,027 per year) were awarded; fellowships, research assistantships, career-related internships or fieldwork, Federal Work-Study, institutionally sponsored loans, scholarships/grants, and unspecified assistantships also available. Support available to part-time students. Financial award application deadline: 4/1; financial award applicants required to submit FAFSA. *Faculty research:* Educational leadership theory and practice, instructional systems technology, educational research methodology, curriculum and supervision in the schools, school law and finance. Total annual research expenditures: $800,000. *Unit head:* Dr. Dawson R. Hancock, Interim Chair, 704-687-8730, Fax: 704-687-3493. *Application contact:* Kathy B. Giddings,

Director of Graduate Admissions, 704-687-3366, Fax: 704-687-3279, E-mail: gradadm@email.uncc.edu.

The University of North Carolina at Charlotte, Graduate School, College of Education, Program in Curriculum and Instruction, Charlotte, NC 28223-0001. Offers urban education (PhD); urban literacy (PhD); urban math (PhD). *Students:* 16 full-time (14 women), 46 part-time (33 women); includes 14 minority (11 African Americans, 1 Asian American or Pacific Islander, 2 Hispanic Americans), 2 international. Average age 41. 39 applicants, 38% accepted, 14 enrolled. *Entrance requirements:* For doctorate, GRE or MAT. Additional exam requirements/recommendations for international students: Required—TOEFL (minimum score 557 paper-based; 220 computer-based). *Application deadline:* For fall admission, 7/15 for domestic students, 5/1 for international students; for spring admission, 11/15 for domestic students, 10/1 for international students. Application fee: $55. *Expenses:* Tuition, state resident: full-time $2,719; part-time $170 per credit. Tuition, nonresident: full-time $12,926; part-time $808 per credit. Required fees: $1,555. *Financial support:* Fellowships, research assistantships, teaching assistantships available. Financial award application deadline: 4/1; financial award applicants required to submit FAFSA. *Unit head:* Dr. Jeanneine P. Jones, Chair, Department of Middle Secondary and K-12 Education, 704-687-8875, Fax: 704-687-6430, E-mail: jpjones@email.uncc.edu. *Application contact:* Kathy B. Giddings, Director of Graduate Admissions, 704-687-3366, Fax: 704-687-3279, E-mail: gradadm@email.uncc.edu.

The University of North Carolina at Greensboro, Graduate School, School of Education, Department of Curriculum and Instruction, Greensboro, NC 27412-5001. Offers college teaching and adult learning (Certificate); curriculum and instruction (M Ed), including chemistry education, elementary education, English as a second language, French education, instructional technology, mathematics education, middle grades education, reading education, science education, social studies education, Spanish education; curriculum and teaching (PhD), including higher education, teacher education and development; English as a second language (Certificate); higher education (M Ed); supervision (M Ed). *Accreditation:* NCATE. Part-time programs available. *Faculty:* 27 full-time (18 women), 8 part-time/adjunct (3 women). *Students:* 137 full-time (114 women), 231 part-time (195 women); includes 63 minority (52 African Americans, 2 American Indian/Alaska Native, 5 Asian Americans or Pacific Islanders, 4 Hispanic Americans). 146 applicants, 32% accepted. *Degree requirements:* For doctorate, thesis/dissertation. *Entrance requirements:* For master's and doctorate, GRE General Test. Additional exam requirements/recommendations for international students: Required—TOEFL. Application fee: $45. Electronic applications accepted. *Expenses:* Tuition, state resident: full-time $2,692. Tuition, nonresident: full-time $13,742. *Financial support:* Fellowships, research assistantships with full tuition reimbursements, teaching assistantships with full tuition reimbursements, career-related internships or fieldwork, Federal Work-Study, scholarships/grants, traineeships, and unspecified assistantships available. Support available to part-time students. *Faculty research:* Community college literacy program, middle school mathematics/computer mathematics. *Unit head:* Dr. Sam Miller, Chair, 336-334-3445, Fax: 336-334-4120, E-mail: sdmille2@uncg.edu. *Application contact:* Michelle Harkleroad, Director of Graduate Admissions, 336-334-4884, Fax: 336-334-4424, E-mail: mbharkle@uncg.edu.

The University of North Carolina at Greensboro, Graduate School, School of Education, Department of Educational Leadership and Cultural Foundations, Greensboro, NC 27412-5001. Offers curriculum and teaching (PhD), including cultural studies; educational leadership (Ed D, Ed S); school administration (MSA). *Accreditation:* NCATE. *Faculty:* 12 full-time (7 women), 1 part-time/adjunct (0 women). *Students:* 100 full-time (71 women), 113 part-time (79 women); includes 74 minority (70 African Americans, 1 American Indian/Alaska Native, 1 Asian American or Pacific Islander, 2 Hispanic Americans). 124 applicants, 35% accepted. *Degree requirements:* For doctorate, thesis/dissertation. *Entrance requirements:* For master's, doctorate, and Ed S, GRE General Test. Additional exam requirements/recommendations for international students: Required—TOEFL. *Application deadline:* For fall admission, 1/1 priority date for domestic students; for spring admission, 11/1 for domestic students. Applications are processed on a rolling basis. Application fee: $45. Electronic applications accepted. *Expenses:* Tuition, state resident: full-time $2,692. Tuition, nonresident: full-time $13,742. *Financial support:* Fellowships with full tuition reimbursements, research assistantships with full tuition reimbursements, teaching assistantships with full tuition reimbursements, career-related internships or fieldwork, Federal Work-Study, scholarships/grants, and traineeships available. Support available to part-time students. *Unit head:* Dr. Ulrich Reitzug, Chair, 336-334-3490, Fax: 336-334-4120, E-mail: ucreitzu@uncg.edu. *Application contact:* Michelle Harkleroad, Director of Graduate Admissions, 336-334-4884, Fax: 336-334-4424, E-mail: mbharkle@uncg.edu.

The University of North Carolina Wilmington, School of Education, Department of Educational Leadership, Program in Curriculum, Instruction and Supervision, Wilmington, NC 28403-3297. Offers M Ed. *Students:* 1 full-time (0 women), 19 part-time (all women). 10 applicants, 70% accepted, 6 enrolled. In 2006, 4 degrees awarded. *Degree requirements:* For master's, comprehensive exam. Application fee: $45. *Unit head:* Dr. Kenneth Anderson, Coordinator, 910-962-3175. *Application contact:* Dr. Robert D. Roer, Dean, Graduate School, 910-962-4117, Fax: 910-962-3787, E-mail: roer@uncw.edu.

University of Northern Iowa, Graduate College, College of Education, Department of Curriculum and Instruction, Program in Curriculum and Instruction, Cedar Falls, IA 50614. Offers MAE, Ed D. Part-time and evening/weekend programs available. *Students:* 5 full-time (4 women), 26 part-time (21 women); includes 5 minority (3 African Americans, 1 American Indian/Alaska Native, 1 Asian American or Pacific Islander), 9 international. 1 applicant, 100% accepted, 1 enrolled. In 2006, 6 degrees awarded. *Degree requirements:* For master's, thesis or alternative, comprehensive exam (for some programs); for doctorate, thesis/dissertation. *Entrance requirements:* For master's, minimum GPA of 3.5, 3 years of educational experience; for doctorate, GRE, minimum GPA of 3.2, 3 years of educational experience, master's degree. Additional exam requirements/recommendations for international students: Required—TOEFL (minimum score 500 paper-based; 180 computer-based; 61 iBT). *Application deadline:* For fall admission, 8/1 priority date for domestic students. Applications are processed on a rolling basis. Application fee: $30 ($50 for international students). *Expenses:* Tuition, state resident: full-time $5,936. Tuition, nonresident: full-time $14,074. *Financial support:* Career-related internships or fieldwork, Federal Work-Study, and tuition waivers (full and partial) available. Support available to part-time students. Financial award application deadline: 2/1. *Unit head:* Dr. Rebecca Edmiaston, Coordinator, 319-273-3250, Fax: 319-273-5886, E-mail: rebecca.edmiaston@uni.edu.

University of North Texas, Robert B. Toulouse School of Graduate Studies, College of Education, Department of Teacher Education and Administration, Program in Curriculum and Instruction, Denton, TX 76203. Offers Ed D, PhD. *Accreditation:* NCATE. *Students:* 23 full-time (22 women), 153 part-time (133 women); includes 32 minority (13 African Americans, 2 American Indian/Alaska Native, 1 Asian American or Pacific Islander, 16 Hispanic Americans), 3 international. Average age 34. 56 applicants, 77% accepted, 24 enrolled. In 2006, 11 doctorates awarded. *Degree requirements:* For doctorate, thesis/dissertation. *Entrance requirements:* For doctorate, GRE General Test. Additional exam requirements/recommendations for international students: Recommended—TOEFL (minimum score 550 paper-based; 213 computer-based). *Application deadline:* For fall admission, 7/15 for domestic students. Application fee: $50 ($75 for international students). *Expenses:* Tuition, state resident: full-time $3,573; part-time $198 per credit. Tuition, nonresident: full-time $8,577; part-time $476 per credit. Required fees: $1,258; $126 per credit. One-time fee: $150 full-time. Tuition and fees vary according to course load. *Financial support:* Fellowships, research assistantships, teaching assistantships, career-related internships or fieldwork, Federal Work-Study, and institutionally sponsored loans available. Financial award application deadline: 4/1. *Application contact:* Dr. Jim Laney, Graduate Adviser, 940-565-2602, Fax: 940-565-4952, E-mail: laney@unt.edu.

University of Oklahoma, Graduate College, College of Education, Department of Instructional Leadership and Academic Curriculum, Norman, OK 73019-0390. Offers education (Certificate); instructional leadership and academic curriculum (M Ed, PhD), including bilingual education, early childhood education, elementary education, English education, math education, reading education, science education, secondary education, social studies education. *Accreditation:* NCATE. Part-time and evening/weekend programs available. *Faculty:* 20 full-time (11 women), 6 part-time/adjunct (all women). *Students:* 76 full-time (63 women), 115 part-time (89 women); includes 25 minority (8 African Americans, 12 American Indian/Alaska Native, 4 Asian Americans or Pacific Islanders, 1 Hispanic American), 12 international. 72 applicants, 96% accepted, 56 enrolled. In 2006, 11 master's, 10 doctorates awarded. *Degree requirements:* For doctorate, thesis/dissertation. *Entrance requirements:* For master's, 12 hours of course work in education; for doctorate, GRE General Test, master's degree, minimum graduate GPA of 3.0. Additional exam requirements/recommendations for international students: Required—TOEFL (minimum score 550 paper-based; 213 computer-based). *Application deadline:* For fall admission, 6/1 priority date for domestic students, 4/1 for international students; for spring admission, 11/1 for domestic students, 9/1 for international students. Applications are processed on a rolling basis. Application fee: $40 ($90 for international students). *Expenses:* Tuition, state resident: full-time $3,180; part-time $133 per credit hour. Tuition, nonresident: full-time $11,347; part-time $473 per credit hour. Required fees: $1,729; $62 per credit hour. $117 per semester. Tuition and fees vary according to course load and program. *Financial support:* In 2006–07, 76 students received support, including 5 research assistantships with partial tuition reimbursements available (averaging $9,773 per year), 7 teaching assistantships with partial tuition reimbursements available (averaging $10,403 per year); scholarships/grants and unspecified assistantships also available. Financial award applicants required to submit FAFSA. *Faculty research:* Early literacy, learning cycle, social justice, teacher education. Total annual research expenditures: $119,917. *Unit head:* Dr. Priscilla Griffith, Chair and Graduate Liaison, 405-325-1498, Fax: 405-325-4061, E-mail: pgriffith@ou.edu.

University of Phoenix–Bay Area Campus, The Artemis School, College of Education, Pleasanton, CA 94588-3677. Offers curriculum instruction (MA Ed); curriculum instruction—adult education (MA Ed). Evening/weekend programs available. *Faculty:* 11 full-time (3 women), 100 part-time/adjunct (52 women). *Students:* 227 full-time (156 women); includes 50 minority (15 African Americans, 2 American Indian/Alaska Native, 19 Asian Americans or Pacific Islanders, 14 Hispanic Americans), 22 international. Average age 36. In 2006, 115 degrees awarded. *Degree requirements:* For master's, thesis (for some programs), registration. *Entrance requirements:* For master's, minimum undergraduate GPA of 2.5, 3 years of work experience. Additional exam requirements/recommendations for international students: Required—TOEFL (minimum score 550 paper-based; 213 computer-based; 79 iBT). *Application deadline:* Applications are processed on a rolling basis. Application fee: $45. Electronic applications accepted. *Expenses:* Tuition: Full-time $12,648. Required fees: $760. *Financial support:* Institutionally sponsored loans and scholarships/grants available. Financial award applicants required to submit FAFSA. *Unit head:* Dr. Marla LaRue, Dean/Executive Director, 480-557-1218, E-mail: marla.larue@phoenix.edu. *Application contact:* Chair, 408-435-8500, Fax: 408-435-8250.

University of Phoenix–Central Florida Campus, The Artemis School, College of Education, Maitland, FL 32751-7057. Offers administration and supervision (MA Ed); curriculum and instruction (MA Ed); elementary teacher education (MA Ed); secondary teacher education (MA Ed). Evening/weekend programs available. *Faculty:* 10 full-time (9 women), 16 part-time/adjunct (6 women). *Students:* 20 full-time (18 women); includes 5 minority (3 African Americans, 2 Hispanic Americans), 1 international. Average age 38. In 2006, 7 degrees awarded. *Degree requirements:* For master's, thesis (for some programs), registration. *Entrance requirements:* For master's, 3 years of work experience, minimum undergraduate GPA of 2.5. Additional exam requirements/recommendations for international students: Required—TOEFL (minimum score 550 paper-based; 213 computer-based; 79 iBT). *Application deadline:* Applications are processed on a rolling basis. Application fee: $45. Electronic applications accepted. *Expenses:* Tuition: Full-time $9,450. Required fees: $760. *Financial support:* Institutionally sponsored loans and scholarships/grants available. Financial award applicants required to submit FAFSA. *Unit head:* Dr. Marla LaRue, Dean/Executive Director, 480-557-1218. *Application contact:* Chair, 407-667-0555, Fax: 407-667-0560.

University of Phoenix–Central Valley Campus, College of Education, Fresno, CA 93720. Offers curriculum and instruction (MA Ed); elementary teacher education (MA Ed); secondary teacher education (MA Ed).

University of Phoenix–Denver Campus, The Artemis School, College of Education, Lone Tree, CO 80124-5453. Offers administration and supervision (MAEd); curriculum instruction (MAEd); elementary teacher education (MAEd); school counseling (MSC); secondary teacher education (MAEd). Evening/weekend programs available. *Faculty:* 19 full-time (14 women), 141 part-time/adjunct (84 women). *Students:* 738 full-time (513 women); includes 72 minority (27 African Americans, 4 American Indian/Alaska Native, 9 Asian Americans or Pacific Islanders, 32 Hispanic Americans), 66 international. Average age 37. In 2006, 435 master's awarded. *Degree requirements:* For master's, thesis (for some programs), registration. *Entrance requirements:* For master's, minimum undergraduate GPA of 2.5, 3 years work experience. Additional exam requirements/recommendations for international students: Required—TOEFL (minimum score 550 paper-based; 213 computer-based; 79 iBT). *Application deadline:* Applications are processed on a rolling basis. Application fee: $45. Electronic applications accepted. *Expenses:* Tuition: Full-time $10,032. Required fees: $760. *Financial support:* Institutionally sponsored loans and scholarships/grants available. Financial award applicants required to submit FAFSA. *Unit head:* Dr. Marla LaRue, Dean/Executive Director, 480-557-1218, E-mail: marla.larue@phoenix.edu. *Application contact:* Chair, 303-694-9093, Fax: 303-662-0911.

University of Phoenix–Fort Lauderdale Campus, The Artemis School, College of Education, Fort Lauderdale, FL 33309. Offers administration and supervision (MA Ed); computer education (MA Ed); curriculum and instruction (MA Ed); elementary teacher education (MA Ed); secondary teacher education (MA Ed). Evening/weekend programs available. *Faculty:* 10 full-time (5 women), 17 part-time/adjunct (7 women). *Students:* 132 full-time (114 women); includes 60 minority (52 African Americans, 1 Asian American or Pacific Islander, 7 Hispanic Americans), 5 international. Average age 39. In 2006, 25 degrees awarded. *Degree requirements:* For master's, thesis (for some programs), registration. *Entrance requirements:* For master's, 3 years of work experience, minimum undergraduate GPA of 2.5. Additional exam requirements/recommendations for international students: Required—TOEFL (minimum score 550 paper-based; 213 computer-based; 79 iBT). *Application deadline:* Applications are processed on a rolling basis. Application fee: $45. Electronic applications accepted. *Expenses:* Tuition: Full-time $9,450. Required fees: $760. *Financial support:* Institutionally sponsored loans and scholarships/grants available. Financial award applicants required to submit FAFSA. *Unit head:* Dr. Marla LaRue, Dean/Executive Director, 480-557-1218. *Application contact:* Chair, 954-382-5303, Fax: 954-382-5304.

University of Phoenix–Hawaii Campus, The Artemis School, College of Education, Honolulu, HI 96813-4317. Offers administration and supervision (MA Ed); curriculum and instruction (MA Ed); elementary education (MA Ed); secondary education (MA Ed); teacher education for elementary licensure (MA Ed). Evening/weekend programs available. *Faculty:* 10 full-time (7 women), 58 part-time/adjunct (34 women). *Students:* 261 full-time (176 women); includes 61 minority (1 African American, 1 American Indian/Alaska Native, 53 Asian Americans or Pacific Islanders, 6 Hispanic Americans), 106 international. Average age 36. In 2006, 151 degrees awarded. *Degree requirements:* For master's, thesis (for some programs), registration. *Entrance requirements:* For master's, minimum undergraduate GPA of 2.5, 3 years of work experience. Additional exam requirements/recommendations for international students: Required—TOEFL (minimum score 550 paper-based; 213 computer-based; 79 iBT). *Application deadline:* Applications are processed on a rolling basis. Application fee: $45. Electronic applications accepted. *Expenses:* Tuition: Full-time $11,520. Required fees: $760. *Financial support:* Institutionally sponsored loans and scholarships/grants available. Financial award applicants required to submit FAFSA. *Unit head:* Dr. Marla LaRue, Dean/Executive Director, 480-557-1309, E-mail: marla.larue@phoenix.edu. *Application contact:* Chair, 580-536-2686, Fax: 808-536-3848.

Curriculum and Instruction

University of Phoenix–Las Vegas Campus, The Artemis School, College of Education, Las Vegas, NV 89128. Offers administration and supervision (MA Ed); curriculum and instruction (MA Ed); school counseling (MSC); teacher education-elementary licensure (MA Ed). Evening/weekend programs available. *Faculty:* 9 full-time (8 women), 45 part-time/adjunct (27 women). *Students:* 494 full-time (388 women); includes 105 minority (51 African Americans, 2 American Indian/Alaska Native, 18 Asian Americans or Pacific Islanders, 34 Hispanic Americans), 9 international. Average age 35. In 2006, 227 degrees awarded. *Degree requirements:* For master's, thesis (for some programs), registration. *Entrance requirements:* For master's, minimum undergraduate GPA of 2.5, 3 years of work experience. Additional exam requirements/recommendations for international students: Required—TOEFL (minimum score 550 paper-based; 213 computer-based; 79 iBT). *Application deadline:* Applications are processed on a rolling basis. Application fee: $45. Electronic applications accepted. *Expenses:* Tuition: Full-time $9,576. Required fees: $760. *Financial support:* Institutionally sponsored loans and scholarships/grants available. Financial award applicants required to submit FAFSA. *Unit head:* Dr. Marla LaRue, Dean/Executive Director, 480-557-1218, E-mail: marla.larue@phoenix.edu. *Application contact:* Chair, 702-638-7249, Fax: 702-638-8085.

University of Phoenix–Memphis Campus, College of Education, Cordova, TN 38018. Offers curriculum and instruction (MA Ed).

University of Phoenix–Metro Detroit Campus, The Artemis School, College of Education, Troy, MI 48098-2623. Offers administration and supervision (MA Ed); adult education and distance learning (MA Ed); curriculum and development (MA Ed); special education (MA Ed); teacher education elementary (MA Ed). Evening/weekend programs available. *Faculty:* 8 full-time (3 women), 27 part-time/adjunct (21 women). *Students:* 102 full-time (75 women); includes 59 minority (57 African Americans, 1 American Indian/Alaska Native, 1 Asian American or Pacific Islander), 1 international. Average age 40. In 2006, 30 master's awarded. *Degree requirements:* For master's, thesis (for some programs), registration. *Entrance requirements:* For master's, 3 years of work experience, minimum undergraduate GPA of 2.5. Additional exam requirements/recommendations for international students: Required—TOEFL (minimum score 550 paper-based; 213 computer-based; 79 iBT). *Application deadline:* Applications are processed on a rolling basis. Application fee: $45. Electronic applications accepted. *Expenses:* Tuition: Full-time $12,168. Required fees: $760. *Financial support:* Institutionally sponsored loans and scholarships/grants available. Financial award applicants required to submit FAFSA. *Unit head:* Dr. Marla LaRue, Dean/Executive Director, 480-557-1218. *Application contact:* Chair, 800-834-2438, Fax: 248-267-0147.

University of Phoenix–Nashville Campus, The Artemis School, College of Education, Nashville, TN 37214-5048. Offers administration and supervision (MA Ed); curriculum and instruction (MA Ed); elementary teacher education (MA Ed); secondary teacher education (MA Ed). Evening/weekend programs available. *Degree requirements:* For master's, thesis (for some programs), registration. *Entrance requirements:* For master's, minimum undergraduate GPA of 2.5, 3 years work experience. Additional exam requirements/recommendations for international students: Required—TOEFL (minimum score 500 paper-based; 213 computer-based; 79 iBT). *Application deadline:* Applications are processed on a rolling basis. Application fee: $45. Electronic applications accepted. *Expenses:* Tuition: Full-time $10,104. Required fees: $760. *Financial support:* Institutionally sponsored loans and scholarships/grants available. Financial award applicants required to submit FAFSA. *Unit head:* Dr. Marla LaRue, Dean/Executive Director, 480-557-1218, E-mail: marla.larue@phoenix.edu. *Application contact:* Chair, 615-872-0188.

University of Phoenix–New Mexico Campus, The Artemis School, College of Education, Albuquerque, NM 87109-4645. Offers administration (MAEd); curriculum and instruction (MAEd); teacher education (MAEd), including elementary, secondary. Evening/weekend programs available. *Faculty:* 9 full-time (5 women), 62 part-time/adjunct (40 women). *Students:* 234 full-time (181 women); includes 116 minority (5 African Americans, 1 Asian American or Pacific Islander, 110 Hispanic Americans), 10 international. Average age 39. In 2006, 131 degrees awarded. *Degree requirements:* For master's, thesis (for some programs), registration. *Entrance requirements:* For master's, minimum undergraduate GPA of 2.5, 3 years of work experience. Additional exam requirements/recommendations for international students: Required—TOEFL (minimum score 550 paper-based; 213 computer-based; 79 iBT). *Application deadline:* Applications are processed on a rolling basis. Application fee: $45. Electronic applications accepted. *Expenses:* Tuition: Full-time $9,005. Required fees: $760. *Financial support:* Institutionally sponsored loans and scholarships/grants available. Financial award applicants required to submit FAFSA. *Unit head:* Dr. Marla LaRue, Dean/Executive Director, 480-557-1218, E-mail: marla.larue@phoenix.edu. *Application contact:* Chair, 505-821-4800, Fax: 505-821-5551.

University of Phoenix–North Florida Campus, The Artemis School, College of Education, Jacksonville, FL 32216-0959. Offers administration (MA Ed); curriculum and instruction (MA Ed); curriculum and instruction—computer education (MA Ed); elementary teacher education (MA Ed); secondary teacher education (MA Ed). Evening/weekend programs available. *Faculty:* 9 full-time (5 women), 10 part-time/adjunct (4 women). *Students:* 98 full-time (78 women); includes 41 minority (37 African Americans, 4 Hispanic Americans), 1 international. Average age 37. In 2006, 22 master's awarded. *Degree requirements:* For master's, thesis (for some programs), registration. *Entrance requirements:* For master's, 3 years of work experience, minimum undergraduate GPA of 2.5. Additional exam requirements/recommendations for international students: Required—TOEFL (minimum score 550 paper-based; 213 computer-based; 49 iBT). *Application deadline:* Applications are processed on a rolling basis. Application fee: $45. Electronic applications accepted. *Financial support:* Institutionally sponsored loans and scholarships/grants available. Financial award applicants required to submit FAFSA. *Unit head:* Dr. Marla LaRue, Dean, 480-557-1218, E-mail: marla.larue@phoenix.edu. *Application contact:* Chair, 904-636-6645, Fax: 904-636-0998.

University of Phoenix–Omaha Campus, College of Education, Omaha, NE 68154-5240. Offers administration and supervision (MA Ed); curriculum and instruction (MA Ed); curriculum and instruction—English and language arts education (MA Ed); curriculum and instruction—adult education (MA Ed); curriculum and instruction—computer education (MA Ed); curriculum and instruction—English as a second language (MA Ed); curriculum and instruction—mathematics education (MA Ed); elementary teacher education (MA Ed); secondary teacher education (MA Ed); special education (MA Ed).

University of Phoenix Online Campus, The Artemis School, College of Education, Phoenix, AZ 85034-7209. Offers administration and supervision (MAEd); adult education and training (MAEd); curriculum and instruction-adult education (MAEd); curriculum and instruction-English and language arts education (MAEd); curriculum and instruction-mathematics education (MAEd); curriculum education (MAEd); curriculum instruction (MAEd); early childhood (MAEd); English as a second language (MAEd); teacher education elementary (MAEd); teacher education secondary (MAEd). Evening/weekend programs available. Postbaccalaureate distance learning degree programs offered (no on-campus study). *Faculty:* 12 full-time (5 women), 8,196 part-time/adjunct (6,937 women). *Students:* 11,937 full-time (9,375 women); includes 2,972 minority (2,210 African Americans, 74 American Indian/Alaska Native, 205 Asian Americans or Pacific Islanders, 483 Hispanic Americans), 906 international. Average age 36. *Degree requirements:* For master's, thesis (for some programs), registration. *Entrance requirements:* For master's, 3 years of work experience, minimum GPA of 2.5. Additional exam requirements/recommendations for international students: Required—TOEFL (minimum score 550 paper-based; 213 computer-based; 79 iBT). *Application deadline:* Applications are processed on a rolling basis. Application fee: $45. Electronic applications accepted. *Expenses:* Tuition: Full-time $12,664. Required fees: $760. *Financial support:* Institutionally sponsored loans and scholarships/grants available. Financial award applicants required to submit FAFSA. *Unit head:* Dr. Marla LaRue, Dean/Executive Director, 480-557-1218, E-mail: marla.larue@phoenix.edu. *Application contact:* Dr. Marla LaRue, Dean/Executive Director, 480-557-1218, E-mail: marla.larue@phoenix.edu.

University of Phoenix–Phoenix Campus, The Artemis School, College of Education, Phoenix, AZ 85040-1958. Offers administration and supervision (MA Ed); curriculum and instruction (MA Ed); elementary licensure (MA Ed); secondary licensure (MA Ed). Evening/weekend programs available. *Faculty:* 39 full-time (23 women), 422 part-time/adjunct (255 women). *Students:* 850 full-time (614 women); includes 135 minority (45 African Americans, 7 American Indian/Alaska Native, 20 Asian Americans or Pacific Islanders, 63 Hispanic Americans), 15 international. Average age 35. In 2006, 500 degrees awarded. *Degree requirements:* For master's, thesis (for some programs), registration. *Entrance requirements:* For master's, 3 years of work experience, minimum undergraduate GPA of 2.5. Additional exam requirements/recommendations for international students: Required—TOEFL (minimum score 550 paper-based; 213 computer-based; 79 iBT). *Application deadline:* Applications are processed on a rolling basis. Application fee: $45. Electronic applications accepted. *Financial support:* Institutionally sponsored loans and scholarships/grants available. Financial award applicants required to submit FAFSA. *Unit head:* Dr. Marla LaRue, Dean/Executive Director, 480-557-1218, E-mail: marla.larue@phoenix.edu. *Application contact:* College Chair, 480-804-7400, Fax: 480-557-2320.

University of Phoenix–Sacramento Valley Campus, The Artemis School, College of Education, Sacramento, CA 95833-3632. Offers adult education (MA Ed); curriculum instruction (MA Ed); elementary education (MA Ed); secondary education (MA Ed); teacher education (Certificate). Evening/weekend programs available. *Faculty:* 9 full-time (5 women), 95 part-time/adjunct (41 women). *Students:* 234 full-time (161 women); includes 51 minority (20 African Americans, 2 American Indian/Alaska Native, 9 Asian Americans or Pacific Islanders, 20 Hispanic Americans), 15 international. Average age 36. In 2006, 80 degrees awarded. *Degree requirements:* For master's, thesis (for some programs), registration. *Entrance requirements:* For master's, 3 years of work experience, minimum undergraduate GPA of 2.5. Additional exam requirements/recommendations for international students: Required—TOEFL (minimum score 550 paper-based; 213 computer-based; 79 iBT). *Application deadline:* Applications are processed on a rolling basis. Application fee: $45. Electronic applications accepted. *Expenses:* Tuition: Full-time $12,024. Required fees: $760. *Financial support:* Institutionally sponsored loans and scholarships/grants available. Financial award applicants required to submit FAFSA. *Unit head:* Dr. Marla LaRue, Dean, 480-557-1218, E-mail: marla.larue@phoenix.edu. *Application contact:* Campus College Chair, 916-923-2107, Fax: 916-923-3914.

University of Phoenix–San Diego Campus, The Artemis School, College of Education, San Diego, CA 92123. Offers curriculum and instruction (MA Ed); elementary education (MA Ed); secondary education (MA Ed). Evening/weekend programs available. *Faculty:* 6 full-time (3 women), 69 part-time/adjunct (36 women). *Students:* 165 full-time (110 women); includes 42 minority (9 African Americans, 8 Asian Americans or Pacific Islanders, 25 Hispanic Americans), 12 international. Average age 34. In 2006, 81 degrees awarded. *Degree requirements:* For master's, thesis (for some programs), registration. *Entrance requirements:* For master's, 3 years of work experience, minimum undergraduate GPA of 3.0. Additional exam requirements/recommendations for international students: Required—TOEFL (minimum score 550 paper-based; 213 computer-based; 79 iBT). *Application deadline:* Applications are processed on a rolling basis. Application fee: $45. Electronic applications accepted. *Expenses:* Tuition: Full-time $11,419. Required fees: $760. *Financial support:* Institutionally sponsored loans and scholarships/grants available. Financial award applicants required to submit FAFSA. *Unit head:* Dr. Marla LaRue, Dean/Executive Director, 480-557-1218, E-mail: marla.larue@phoenix.edu. *Application contact:* Campus College Chair, 888-UOP-INFO, Fax: 858-509-4399.

University of Phoenix–Southern Arizona Campus, The Artemis School, College of Education, Tucson, AZ 85712-2732. Offers curriculum instruction (MA Ed); educational counseling (MA Ed); elementary licensure (MA Ed); school counseling (MSC); secondary licensure (MA Ed); special education (Certificate). Evening/weekend programs available. *Faculty:* 101. *Students:* 75 full-time (55 women); includes 16 minority (2 African Americans, 1 American Indian/Alaska Native, 1 Asian American or Pacific Islander, 12 Hispanic Americans), 2 international. Average age 38. In 2006, 113 degrees awarded. *Degree requirements:* For master's, thesis (for some programs), registration. *Entrance requirements:* For master's, minimum undergraduate GPA of 2.5, 3 years of work experience. Additional exam requirements/recommendations for international students: Required—TOEFL (minimum score 550 paper-based; 213 computer-based; 79 iBT). *Application deadline:* Applications are processed on a rolling basis. Application fee: $45. Electronic applications accepted. *Expenses:* Tuition: Full-time $8,669. Required fees: $760. *Financial support:* Institutionally sponsored loans and scholarships/grants available. Financial award applicants required to submit FAFSA. *Unit head:* Dr. Marla LaRue, Dean/Executive Director, 480-557-1218, E-mail: marla.larue@phoenix.edu. *Application contact:* Campus College Chair, 520-881-6512, Fax: 520-795-6177.

University of Phoenix–Southern California Campus, The Artemis School, College of Education, Costa Mesa, CA 92626. Offers curriculum and instruction (MA Ed); elementary education (MA Ed); secondary education (MA Ed). Evening/weekend programs available. *Faculty:* 22 full-time (9 women), 195 part-time/adjunct (108 women). *Students:* 1,152 full-time (858 women); includes 420 minority (135 African Americans, 7 American Indian/Alaska Native, 59 Asian Americans or Pacific Islanders, 219 Hispanic Americans), 78 international. Average age 34. In 2006, 359 degrees awarded. *Degree requirements:* For master's, thesis (for some programs), registration. *Entrance requirements:* For master's, minimum undergraduate GPA of 2.5, 3 years work experience. Additional exam requirements/recommendations for international students: Required—TOEFL (minimum score 550 paper-based; 213 computer-based; 79 iBT). *Application deadline:* Applications are processed on a rolling basis. Application fee: $45. Electronic applications accepted. *Expenses:* Tuition: Full-time $13,512. Required fees: $760. *Financial support:* Institutionally sponsored loans and scholarships/grants available. Financial award applicants required to submit FAFSA. *Unit head:* Dr. Marla LaRue, Dean/Executive Director, 480-557-1218, E-mail: marla.larue@phoenix.edu. *Application contact:* Campus College Chair, 714-378-1878, Fax: 714-378-5875.

University of Phoenix–Southern Colorado Campus, The Artemis School, College of Education, Colorado Springs, CO 80919-2335. Offers administration and supervision (MA Ed); curriculum and instruction (MA Ed); elementary licensure (MA Ed); principal licensure certification (Certificate); school counseling (MSC); secondary licensure (MA Ed). Evening/weekend programs available. *Faculty:* 7 full-time (3 women), 90 part-time/adjunct (53 women). *Students:* 220 full-time (162 women); includes 22 minority (7 African Americans, 1 American Indian/Alaska Native, 4 Asian Americans or Pacific Islanders, 10 Hispanic Americans), 15 international. Average age 37. In 2006, 122 degrees awarded. *Degree requirements:* For master's, thesis (for some programs), registration. *Entrance requirements:* For master's, minimum undergraduate GPA of 2.5, 3 years of work experience. Additional exam requirements/recommendations for international students: Required—TOEFL (minimum score 550 paper-based; 213 computer-based; 79 iBT). *Application deadline:* Applications are processed on a rolling basis. Application fee: $45. Electronic applications accepted. *Expenses:* Tuition: Full-time $10,291. Required fees: $760. *Financial support:* Institutionally sponsored loans and scholarships/grants available. Financial award applicants required to submit FAFSA. *Unit head:* Dr. Marla LaRue, Dean/Executive Director, 480-557-1218, E-mail: marla.larue@phoenix.edu. *Application contact:* Chair, 719-599-5282, Fax: 719-599-7973.

University of Phoenix–Springfield Campus, College of Education, Springfield, MO 65804-7211. Offers administration and supervision (MA Ed); curriculum and instruction (MA Ed); curriculum and instruction/adult education (MA Ed); curriculum and instruction/computer education (MA Ed); curriculum and instruction/English as a second language (MA Ed); English and language arts education (MA Ed); mathematics education (MA Ed).

University of Phoenix–Utah Campus, The Artemis School, College of Education, Salt Lake City, UT 84123-4617. Offers administration and supervision (MA Ed); curriculum and instruction (MA Ed); elementary education (MA Ed); school counseling (MSC); secondary education (MA Ed). Evening/weekend programs available. *Faculty:* 14 full-time (8 women), 78 part-time/adjunct (39 women). *Students:* 395 full-time (246 women); includes 20 minority (2

African Americans, 1 American Indian/Alaska Native, 8 Asian Americans or Pacific Islanders, 9 Hispanic Americans), 4 international. Average age 37. In 2006, 233 degrees awarded. *Degree requirements:* For master's, thesis (for some programs), registration. *Entrance requirements:* For master's, minimum undergraduate GPA of 2.5, 3 years work experience. Additional exam requirements/recommendations for international students: Required—TOEFL (minimum score 550 paper-based; 213 computer-based; 79 iBT). *Application deadline:* Applications are processed on a rolling basis. Application fee: $45. Electronic applications accepted. *Expenses:* Tuition: Full-time $9,104. Required fees: $760. *Financial support:* Institutionally sponsored loans and scholarships/grants available. Financial award applicants required to submit FAFSA. *Unit head:* Dr. Marla LaRue, Dean/Executive Director, 480-557-1218, E-mail: marla.larue@phoenix.edu. *Application contact:* Chair, 801-263-1444, Fax: 801-269-9766.

University of Phoenix–Vancouver Campus, The Artemis School, College of Education, Burnaby, BC V5C 6G9, Canada. Offers administration and supervision (MA Ed); curriculum and instruction (MA Ed). Evening/weekend programs available. *Faculty:* 25. *Students:* 131 full-time (79 women); includes 6 minority (all Asian Americans or Pacific Islanders) Average age 40. In 2006, 49 degrees awarded. *Degree requirements:* For master's, thesis (for some programs), registration. *Entrance requirements:* For master's, minimum undergraduate GPA of 2.5, 3 years work experience. Additional exam requirements/recommendations for international students: Required—TOEFL (minimum score 550 paper-based; 213 computer-based; 79 iBT). *Application deadline:* Applications are processed on a rolling basis. Application fee: $45. Electronic applications accepted. *Expenses:* Tuition: Full-time $12,840. Required fees: $760. *Financial support:* Institutionally sponsored loans and scholarships/grants available. *Unit head:* Dr. Marla LaRue, Dean/Executive Director, 480-557-1218, E-mail: marla.larue@phoenix.edu. *Application contact:* Chair, 404-205-6999.

University of Phoenix–West Florida Campus, The Artemis School, College of Education, Temple Terrace, FL 33637. Offers administration and supervision (MA Ed); curriculum and instruction (MA Ed); curriculum and technology (MA Ed); elementary teacher education (MA Ed); secondary teacher education (MA Ed). Evening/weekend programs available. *Faculty:* 10 full-time (8 women), 15 part-time/adjunct (7 women). *Students:* 67 full-time (61 women); includes 24 minority (20 African Americans, 1 American Indian/Alaska Native, 3 Hispanic Americans), 3 international. Average age 40. In 2006, 8 degrees awarded. *Degree requirements:* For master's, thesis (for some programs), registration. *Entrance requirements:* For master's, 3 years of work experience, minimum undergraduate GPA of 2.5. Additional exam requirements/recommendations for international students: Required—TOEFL (minimum score 550 paper-based; 213 computer-based; 79 iBT). Application fee: $45. *Expenses:* Tuition: Full-time $9,450. Required fees: $760. *Financial support:* Institutionally sponsored loans and scholarships/grants available. Financial award applicants required to submit FAFSA. *Unit head:* Dr. Marla LaRue, Dean, 480-557-1218, E-mail: marla.larue@phoenix.edu. *Application contact:* Chair, 813-626-7911, Fax: 813-977-1449.

University of Phoenix–West Michigan Campus, The Artemis School, College of Education, Walker, MI 49544. Offers administration and supervision (MA Ed); curriculum and instruction (MA Ed). Evening/weekend programs available. *Faculty:* 5 full-time (1 woman), 15 part-time/adjunct (9 women). In 2006, 5 master's awarded. *Degree requirements:* For master's, thesis (for some programs), registration. *Entrance requirements:* For master's, 3 years of work experience, minimum undergraduate GPA of 2.5. Additional exam requirements/recommendations for international students: Required—TOEFL (minimum score 550 paper-based; 213 computer-based; 79 iBT). *Application deadline:* Applications are processed on a rolling basis. Application fee: $45. Electronic applications accepted. *Expenses:* Tuition: Full-time $12,043. Required fees: $760. *Financial support:* Institutionally sponsored loans and scholarships/grants available. Financial award applicants required to submit FAFSA. *Unit head:* Dr. Marla LaRue, Dean/Executive Director, 480-557-1218, E-mail: marla.larue@phoenix.edu. *Application contact:* Chair, 888-345-9699, Fax: 616-784-5300.

University of Puerto Rico, Río Piedras, College of Education, Program in Curriculum and Teaching, San Juan, PR 00931-3300. Offers biology education (M Ed); chemistry education (M Ed); curriculum and teaching (Ed D); English education (M Ed); history education (M Ed); mathematics education (M Ed); physics education (M Ed); secondary education (M Ed); Spanish education (M Ed). Part-time programs available. *Students:* 64 full-time (42 women), 123 part-time (91 women); all minorities (all Hispanic Americans) In 2006, 8 master's, 19 doctorates awarded. *Degree requirements:* For master's, thesis; for doctorate, thesis/dissertation, internship. *Entrance requirements:* For master's, PAEG or GRE, minimum GPA of 3.0, letter of recommendation; for doctorate, GRE or PAEG, master's degree, minimum GPA of 3.0, letter of recommendation (2), interview. *Application deadline:* For fall admission, 2/1 for domestic and international students. Application fee: $17. *Expenses:* Tuition, state resident: part-time $100 per credit. Tuition, nonresident: part-time $291 per credit. Required fees: $72 per semester. *Financial support:* Fellowships, research assistantships, teaching assistantships, career-related internships or fieldwork, Federal Work-Study, institutionally sponsored loans, and tuition waivers (partial) available. Financial award application deadline: 5/31. *Faculty research:* Science curriculum, administration management. *Unit head:* Dr. Loyda Martinez, Coordinator, 787-764-0000 Ext. 4361, Fax: 787-763-4130. *Application contact:* Information Contact, 787-764-0000 Ext. 4368, Fax: 787-763-4130.

University of Regina, Faculty of Graduate Studies and Research, Faculty of Education, Department of Curriculum and Instruction, Regina, SK S4S 0A2, Canada. Offers M Ed. Part-time programs available. *Faculty:* 28 full-time (13 women), 2 part-time/adjunct (both women). *Students:* 17 full-time (13 women), 92 part-time (72 women). 22 applicants, 100% accepted. In 2006, 18 degrees awarded. *Degree requirements:* For master's, practicum, project, or thesis. *Entrance requirements:* For master's, bachelor's degree in education, 2 years of teaching experience. Additional exam requirements/recommendations for international students: Required—TOEFL (minimum score 580 paper-based; 237 computer-based; 88 iBT). *Application deadline:* For fall admission, 2/15 for domestic students; for spring admission, 2/15 for domestic students. Application fee: $60 ($100 for international students). *Financial support:* Fellowships, research assistantships, teaching assistantships available. Financial award application deadline: 6/15. *Application contact:* Vicki Minhinnick, Graduate Program Coordinator, 306-585-4506, Fax: 306-585-5387, E-mail: edgrad@uregina.ca.

University of St. Francis, College of Education, Joliet, IL 60435-6169. Offers curriculum and instruction (MS); educational leadership (MS), including reading, special education; elementary education certification (M Ed); secondary education certification (M Ed), including English education, math education, science education, social studies education; special education (M Ed); teaching and learning (MS). Part-time and evening/weekend programs available. *Faculty:* 11 full-time (10 women), 25 part-time/adjunct (12 women). *Students:* 52 full-time (38 women), 381 part-time (293 women); includes 38 minority (21 African Americans, 1 American Indian/Alaska Native, 4 Asian Americans or Pacific Islanders, 12 Hispanic Americans). Average age 33. 194 applicants, 80% accepted, 117 enrolled. In 2006, 165 degrees awarded. *Degree requirements:* For master's, comprehensive exam (for some programs), registration. *Entrance requirements:* For master's, minimum undergraduate GPA of 2.75, 2 letters of recommendation, computer competency. Additional exam requirements/recommendations for international students: Required—TOEFL (minimum score 550 paper-based; 213 computer-based). *Application deadline:* Applications are processed on a rolling basis. Application fee: $30. Electronic applications accepted. *Expenses:* Contact institution. Part-time tuition and fees vary according to campus/location and program. *Financial support:* In 2006–07, 272 students received support. Scholarships/grants, tuition waivers (partial), and unspecified assistantships available. Support available to part-time students. Financial award applicants required to submit FAFSA. *Unit head:* Dr. John Gambro, Dean, 815-740-3456, Fax: 815-740-2264, E-mail: jgambro@stfrancis.edu. *Application contact:* Sandra Sloka, Director of Admissions for Graduate and Degree Completion Programs, 800-735-7500, Fax: 815-740-5032, E-mail: ssloka@stfrancis.edu.

University of Saint Mary, Graduate Programs, Program in Education, Leavenworth, KS 66048-5082. Offers curriculum and instruction (MAT). *Accreditation:* NCATE. Part-time and evening/weekend programs available. Postbaccalaureate distance learning degree programs offered (no on-campus study). *Degree requirements:* For master's, thesis, oral presentation. *Entrance requirements:* For master's, minimum undergraduate GPA of 2.75. *Faculty research:* Curriculum and instruction.

University of St. Thomas, Graduate Studies, School of Education, Department of Curriculum and Instruction, St. Paul, MN 55105-1096. Offers critical pedagogy (Ed D); curriculum and instruction (MA, Ed S), including elementary (MA), K-12 (MA), secondary (MA); gifted, creative, and talented education (MA, Certificate); learning technology (MA, Certificate); reading (MA). Part-time and evening/weekend programs available. Postbaccalaureate distance learning degree programs offered (minimal on-campus study). *Students:* 5 full-time (all women), 109 part-time (91 women); includes 12 minority (7 African Americans, 1 American Indian/Alaska Native, 2 Asian Americans or Pacific Islanders, 2 Hispanic Americans), 2 international. Average age 35. 103 applicants, 91% accepted, 89 enrolled. In 2006, 13 master's, 7 doctorates, 11 other advanced degrees awarded. *Degree requirements:* For master's, thesis (for some programs), registration; for doctorate and other advanced degree, thesis/dissertation, registration. *Entrance requirements:* For master's, minimum GPA of 2.75 or MAT; for doctorate, minimum 3 years of experience as an educator; master's degree; minimum graduate GPA of 2.75, interview, writing sample; for other advanced degree, MAT, minimum graduate GPA of 2.75. Additional exam requirements/recommendations for international students: Required—TOEFL (minimum score 550 paper-based; 213 computer-based). *Application deadline:* For fall admission, 6/1 priority date for domestic students; for spring admission, 11/1 priority date for domestic students. Applications are processed on a rolling basis. Application fee: $50. *Financial support:* In 2006–07, 59 students received support; fellowships, research assistantships, institutionally sponsored loans and scholarships/grants available. Support available to part-time students. *Faculty research:* Multicultural education for gifted children, education plans for gifted children, globalization and adult learning, best gifted practices in Minnesota, exploring cultural tools. *Unit head:* Dr. Karen L. Westberg, Department Chair, 651-962-4985, Fax: 651-962-4169, E-mail: klwestberg@stthomas.edu. *Application contact:* Daniel Vevang, Department Assistant, 651-962-4460, Fax: 651-962-4169, E-mail: dvevang@stthomas.edu.

University of San Diego, School of Leadership and Education Sciences, Program in Learning and Teaching, San Diego, CA 92110-2492. Offers learning and teaching (M Ed); teaching (MAT); teaching and learning (Ed D). Part-time and evening/weekend programs available. *Faculty:* 16 full-time (11 women), 19 part-time/adjunct (16 women). *Students:* 58 full-time (47 women), 126 part-time (109 women); includes 42 minority (5 African Americans, 2 American Indian/Alaska Native, 10 Asian Americans or Pacific Islanders, 25 Hispanic Americans). Average age 31. 133 applicants, 78% accepted, 62 enrolled. In 2006, 104 master's, 3 doctorates awarded. *Degree requirements:* For master's, thesis (for some programs). *Entrance requirements:* For master's, minimum GPA of 3.0. Additional exam requirements/recommendations for international students: Required—TOEFL (minimum score 580 paper-based; 237 computer-based), TWE. *Application deadline:* For fall admission, 7/1 priority date for domestic students; for spring admission, 11/15 priority date for domestic students. Applications are processed on a rolling basis. Application fee: $45. Electronic applications accepted. *Financial support:* Career-related internships or fieldwork, Federal Work-Study, institutionally sponsored loans, tuition waivers (partial), and stipends available. Support available to part-time students. Financial award application deadline: 5/1; financial award applicants required to submit FAFSA. *Unit head:* Dr. Jerry Ammer, Director, 619-260-4893, Fax: 619-260-6835. *Application contact:* Stephen Pultz, Director of Admissions, 619-260-4524, Fax: 619-260-4158, E-mail: grads@sandiego.edu.

University of San Francisco, School of Education, Department of Learning and Instruction, San Francisco, CA 94117-1080. Offers MA, Ed D. *Faculty:* 6 full-time (4 women), 7 part-time/adjunct (4 women). *Students:* 92 full-time (73 women), 46 part-time (32 women); includes 41 minority (15 African Americans, 3 American Indian/Alaska Native, 10 Asian Americans or Pacific Islanders, 13 Hispanic Americans), 2 international. Average age 40. 87 applicants, 82% accepted, 41 enrolled. In 2006, 30 master's, 7 doctorates awarded. *Degree requirements:* For doctorate, thesis/dissertation. Application fee: $55 ($65 for international students). *Expenses:* Tuition: Full-time $17,370; part-time $965 per unit. Tuition and fees vary according to degree level, campus/location and program. *Financial support:* In 2006–07, 76 students received support; fellowships, research assistantships, teaching assistantships available. Financial award application deadline: 3/2; financial award applicants required to submit FAFSA. *Unit head:* Dr. Robert Burns, Chair, 415-422-6289.

University of Saskatchewan, College of Graduate Studies and Research, College of Education, Department of Curriculum Studies, Saskatoon, SK S7N 5A2, Canada. Offers M Ed, PhD, Diploma. Part-time programs available. *Degree requirements:* For master's, thesis (for some programs), registration; for doctorate, thesis/dissertation, registration. *Entrance requirements:* For master's, MAT. Additional exam requirements/recommendations for international students: Required—TOEFL.

The University of Scranton, Graduate School, Department of Education, Program in Curriculum and Instruction, Scranton, PA 18510. Offers MA, MS. Part-time and evening/weekend programs available. Postbaccalaureate distance learning degree programs offered (no on-campus study). *Students:* Average age 35. 87 applicants, 92% accepted. In 2006, 11 degrees awarded. *Degree requirements:* For master's, thesis (for some programs), capstone experience, comprehensive exam, registration. *Entrance requirements:* For master's, minimum GPA of 2.75. Additional exam requirements/recommendations for international students: Required—TOEFL (minimum score 500 paper-based; 173 computer-based), IELTS (minimum score 5). *Application deadline:* Applications are processed on a rolling basis. Application fee: $50. *Expenses:* Tuition: Part-time $684 per credit. Required fees: $25 per term. *Financial support:* Federal Work-Study and unspecified assistantships available. Financial award application deadline: 3/1. *Unit head:* Dr. Derry Stufft, Director, 570-941-7421, Fax: 570-941-7401, E-mail: stufftd@scranton.edu.

University of South Carolina, The Graduate School, College of Education, Department of Educational Leadership and Policies and Department of Instruction and Teacher Education, Program in Curriculum and Instruction, Columbia, SC 29208. Offers Ed D. This degree cuts across two departments and represents 6 different concentrations. *Accreditation:* NCATE. Part-time and evening/weekend programs available. *Degree requirements:* For doctorate, thesis/dissertation, comprehensive exam. *Entrance requirements:* For doctorate, GRE General Test or MAT, interview. Electronic applications accepted. *Faculty research:* Teacher education, historian recording project, curriculum development in international areas, human sexuality.

University of South Carolina, The Graduate School, College of Education, Department of Instruction and Teacher Education, Columbia, SC 29208. Offers curriculum and instruction (Ed D); early childhood education (M Ed, MAT, PhD); elementary education (M Ed, MAT, PhD); health education administration (Ed D); language and literacy (M Ed, PhD); secondary education (IMA, M Ed, MA, MAT, MT, PhD), including art education (IMA, MAT), business education (IMA, MAT), English (MAT), foreign language (MAT), health education (MAT), mathematics (MAT), science (IMA, MAT), secondary education (M Ed, MA, MT, PhD), social studies (IMA, MAT), theatre and speech (IMA, MAT); teaching (Ed S). Part-time and evening/weekend programs available. *Degree requirements:* For master's, foreign language (MA); for doctorate, one foreign language, thesis/dissertation, comprehensive exam. *Entrance requirements:* For master's, MAT, GRE, teaching certificate (M Ed); for doctorate, GRE General Test, MAT, qualifying exam, resumé; for Ed S, GRE General Test or MAT, resumé.

The University of South Dakota, Graduate School, School of Education, Division of Curriculum and Instruction, Vermillion, SD 57069-2390. Offers curriculum and instruction (Ed D, Ed S); elementary education (MA); secondary education (MA); special education (MA). *Accreditation:* NCATE. Part-time programs available. Postbaccalaureate distance learning degree programs offered. *Students:* 99 (77 women). In 2006, 53 master's, 6 doctorates awarded. *Degree requirements:* For master's and Ed S, thesis or alternative, comprehensive exam; for doctorate, thesis/dissertation, comprehensive exam. *Entrance requirements:* For master's,

Curriculum and Instruction

The University of South Dakota (continued)
doctorate, and Ed S, GRE General Test, MAT, minimum GPA of 2.7. Additional exam requirements/recommendations for international students: Required—TOEFL (minimum score 550 paper-based; 213 computer-based; 79 iBT). *Application deadline:* Applications are processed on a rolling basis. Application fee: $35. Electronic applications accepted. *Expenses:* Tuition, state resident: part-time $120 per credit hour. Tuition, nonresident: part-time $355 per credit hour. Required fees: $90 per credit hour. *Financial support:* In 2006–07, research assistantships with partial tuition reimbursements (averaging $4,626 per year), teaching assistantships with partial tuition reimbursements (averaging $4,626 per year) were awarded; career-related internships or fieldwork, Federal Work-Study, and unspecified assistantships also available. Financial award applicants required to submit FAFSA. *Unit head:* Dr. Garreth Zalud, Chair, 605-677-5210, Fax: 605-677-3102, E-mail: ci@usd.edu.

University of Southern Mississippi, Graduate School, College of Education and Psychology, Department of Curriculum, Instruction, and Special Education, Hattiesburg, MS 39406-0001. Offers alternative secondary teacher education (MAT); early childhood education (M Ed, Ed S); education of the gifted (M Ed, Ed D, PhD, Ed S); elementary education (M Ed, Ed D, PhD, Ed S); reading (M Ed, MS, Ed S); secondary education (M Ed, MS, Ed D, PhD, Ed S); special education (M Ed, Ed D, PhD, Ed S). *Faculty:* 16 full-time (11 women). *Students:* 31 full-time (28 women), 54 part-time (51 women); includes 5 minority (4 African Americans, 1 Hispanic American), 1 international. Average age 35. 59 applicants, 27% accepted, 11 enrolled. In 2006, 43 master's, 3 doctorates, 4 other advanced degrees awarded. *Degree requirements:* For master's, thesis (for some programs), comprehensive exam, registration; for doctorate and Ed S, thesis/dissertation, comprehensive exam, registration. *Entrance requirements:* For master's, GRE General Test, MAT, minimum GPA of 3.0; for doctorate, GRE General Test, minimum GPA of 3.5; for Ed S, GRE General Test, MAT, minimum GPA of 3.25. Additional exam requirements/recommendations for international students: Required—TOEFL. *Application deadline:* For fall admission, 3/1 priority date for domestic students, 3/1 for international students. Applications are processed on a rolling basis. Application fee: $25 ($30 for international students). *Financial support:* In 2006–07, 10 research assistantships with tuition reimbursements (averaging $22,333 per year), 2 teaching assistantships with full tuition reimbursements (averaging $22,333 per year) were awarded; Federal Work-Study, institutionally sponsored loans, and tuition waivers (partial) also available. Financial award application deadline: 3/15. *Faculty research:* Mathematical problem solving, integrative curriculum, writing process, teacher education models. Total annual research expenditures: $100,000. *Unit head:* Dr. Dana Thames, Chair, 601-266-4547, Fax: 601-266-4175. *Application contact:* B.J. Davis, Administrative Assistant, 601-266-6987, Fax: 601-266-4548.

The University of Tennessee, Graduate School, College of Education, Health and Human Sciences, Program in Education, Knoxville, TN 37996. Offers art education (MS); counseling education (PhD); cultural studies in education (PhD); curriculum (MS, Ed S); curriculum, educational research and evaluation (Ed D, PhD); early childhood education (PhD); early childhood special education (MS); education of deaf and hard of hearing (MS); educational administration and policy studies (Ed D, PhD); educational administration and supervision (Ed S); educational psychology (Ed D, PhD); elementary education (MS, Ed S); elementary teaching (MS); English education (MS, Ed S); exercise science (PhD); foreign language/ESL education (MS, Ed S); instructional technology (MS, Ed D, PhD, Ed S); literacy, language and ESL education (PhD); literacy, language education, and ESL education (Ed D); mathematics education (MS, Ed S); modified and comprehensive special education (MS); reading education (MS, Ed S); school counseling (Ed S); school psychology (PhD, Ed S); science education (MS, Ed S); secondary teaching (MS); social foundations (MS); social science education (MS, Ed S); socio-cultural foundations of sports and education (PhD); special education (Ed S); teacher education (Ed D, PhD). *Accreditation:* NCATE. Part-time and evening/weekend programs available. *Students:* 529 (401 women); includes 39 minority (23 African Americans, 2 American Indian/Alaska Native, 9 Asian Americans or Pacific Islanders, 5 Hispanic Americans) 34 international. 420 applicants, 50% accepted. In 2006, 258 master's, 28 doctorates awarded. *Degree requirements:* For master's and Ed S, thesis optional; for doctorate, variable foreign language requirement, thesis/dissertation. *Entrance requirements:* For master's, minimum GPA of 2.7; for doctorate and Ed S, GRE General Test, minimum GPA of 2.7. Additional exam requirements/recommendations for international students: Required—TOEFL. *Application deadline:* For fall admission, 2/1 priority date for domestic students. Applications are processed on a rolling basis. Application fee: $35. Electronic applications accepted. *Expenses:* Tuition, state resident: full-time $5,574. Tuition, nonresident: full-time $16,840. Required fees: $792. *Financial support:* In 2006–07, 4 fellowships, 9 teaching assistantships were awarded; career-related internships or fieldwork, Federal Work-Study, institutionally sponsored loans, and unspecified assistantships also available. Financial award application deadline: 2/1; financial award applicants required to submit FAFSA. *Unit head:* Dr. Lester Knight, Head, 865-974-0907, Fax: 865-974-8718, E-mail: lknight@utk.edu.

The University of Texas at Arlington, Graduate School, College of Education, Arlington, TX 76019. Offers curriculum and instruction (M Ed); educational leadership and policy studies (M Ed); physiology of exercise (MS); teaching (M Ed T). *Accreditation:* NCATE. Part-time and evening/weekend programs available. Postbaccalaureate distance learning degree programs offered (minimal on-campus study). *Faculty:* 19 full-time (11 women), 3 part-time/adjunct (2 women). *Students:* 171 full-time (107 women), 579 part-time (474 women); includes 278 minority (130 African Americans, 6 American Indian/Alaska Native, 20 Asian Americans or Pacific Islanders, 122 Hispanic Americans), 40 international. Average age 36. 579 applicants, 88% accepted, 368 enrolled. In 2006, 101 degrees awarded. *Degree requirements:* For master's, thesis (for some programs), comprehensive activity, research project, comprehensive exam (for some programs), registration. *Entrance requirements:* For master's, GRE General Test, minimum undergraduate GPA of 3.0 in last 60 hours of course work, writing sample, 3 letters of recommendation. Additional exam requirements/recommendations for international students: Required—TOEFL (minimum score 550 paper-based; 213 computer-based). *Application deadline:* For fall admission, 6/16 priority date for domestic students, 4/9 priority date for international students; for winter admission, 10/22 priority date for domestic students, 9/10 priority date for international students; for spring admission, 3/25 priority date for domestic and international students. Applications are processed on a rolling basis. Application fee: $35 ($50 for international students). Electronic applications accepted. *Expenses:* Tuition, state resident: full-time $5,528. Tuition, nonresident: full-time $10,478. International tuition: $10,608 full-time. *Financial support:* In 2006–07, 11 fellowships (averaging $1,000 per year), teaching assistantships with tuition reimbursements (averaging $9,000 per year) were awarded; career-related internships or fieldwork, Federal Work-Study, scholarships/grants, and unspecified assistantships also available. Financial award application deadline: 6/1; financial award applicants required to submit FAFSA. *Unit head:* Dr. Jeanne M. Gerlach, Dean, 817-272-2591, Fax: 817-272-2530, E-mail: soeadvising@uta.edu. *Application contact:* Brendan Hardy, Graduate Advisor, 817-272-2956, Fax: 817-272-7624, E-mail: coedadvising@uta.edu.

The University of Texas at Austin, Graduate School, College of Education, Department of Curriculum and Instruction, Austin, TX 78712-1111. Offers M Ed, MA, Ed D, PhD. Terminal master's awarded for partial completion of doctoral program. *Degree requirements:* For doctorate, thesis/dissertation. *Entrance requirements:* For master's and doctorate, GRE General Test. Electronic applications accepted.

The University of Texas at Brownsville, Graduate Studies, School of Education, Brownsville, TX 78520-4991. Offers bilingual education (M Ed); counseling and guidance (M Ed); curriculum and instruction (M Ed); early childhood education (M Ed); educational administration (M Ed); educational technology (M Ed); English as a second language (M Ed); reading specialist (M Ed); special education/educational diagnostician (M Ed). Part-time and evening/weekend programs available. Postbaccalaureate distance learning degree programs offered (minimal on-campus study). *Degree requirements:* For master's, thesis optional. *Entrance requirements:* For master's, GRE General Test. Additional exam requirements/recommendations for international students: Required—TOEFL.

The University of Texas at El Paso, Graduate School, College of Education, Department of Educational Curriculum and Instruction, El Paso, TX 79968-0001. Offers M Ed, MA. Part-time and evening/weekend programs available. *Degree requirements:* For master's, thesis optional. *Entrance requirements:* For master's, minimum graduate GPA of 3.0. Additional exam requirements/recommendations for international students: Required—TOEFL. Electronic applications accepted.

The University of Texas at San Antonio, College of Education and Human Development, Department of Interdisciplinary Learning and Teaching, San Antonio, TX 78249-0617. Offers curriculum and instruction (MA); early childhood and elementary education (MA); educational psychology/special education (MA); instructional technology (MA); reading and literacy (MA). Part-time and evening/weekend programs available. *Faculty:* 26 full-time (all women), 1 part-time/adjunct (0 women). *Students:* 40 full-time (32 women), 240 part-time (207 women); includes 155 minority (20 African Americans, 1 American Indian/Alaska Native, 6 Asian Americans or Pacific Islanders, 128 Hispanic Americans), 3 international. Average age 35. 94 applicants, 100% accepted, 94 enrolled. In 2006, 61 degrees awarded. *Degree requirements:* For master's, thesis optional. *Entrance requirements:* For master's, GRE General Test. Additional exam requirements/recommendations for international students: Required—TOEFL (minimum score 500 paper-based; 173 computer-based). *Application deadline:* For fall admission, 7/1 for domestic students, 4/1 for international students; for spring admission, 11/1 for domestic students, 9/1 for international students. Applications are processed on a rolling basis. Application fee: $45 ($80 for international students). Electronic applications accepted. *Expenses:* Tuition, state resident: full-time $1,730; part-time $192 per credit hour. Tuition, nonresident: full-time $6,680; part-time $742 per credit hour. Required fees: $733; $308,359 per credit hour. *Financial support:* In 2006–07, 3 research assistantships (averaging $28,891 per year) were awarded; career-related internships or fieldwork, Federal Work-Study, scholarships/grants, and unspecified assistantships also available. *Faculty research:* Early childhood, reading, special education, foundations, curriculum and instruction. Total annual research expenditures: $570,791. *Unit head:* Dr. Belinda B. Flores, Chair, 210-458-5969, Fax: 210-458-7281, E-mail: belinda.flores@utsa.edu.

The University of Texas at Tyler, College of Education and Psychology, Department of Curriculum and Instruction, Tyler, TX 75799-0001. Offers curriculum and instruction (M Ed); secondary teaching (MAT), including art, biology, computer science, English, history, journalism, mathematics, music, political science, sociology, speech, theatre. Part-time programs available. *Faculty:* 10 full-time (6 women), 2 part-time/adjunct (1 woman). *Students:* 3 full-time (2 women), 7 part-time (6 women); includes 1 minority (African American) Average age 32. 1 applicant, 100% accepted, 1 enrolled. In 2006, 6 degrees awarded. *Degree requirements:* For master's, research project (M Ed). *Entrance requirements:* For master's, GRE or MAT. Application fee: $0 ($50 for international students). Electronic applications accepted. *Expenses:* Tuition, state resident: part-time $50 per credit hour. Tuition, nonresident: part-time $328 per credit hour. Required fees: $107 per credit hour. $426 per term. *Financial support:* Scholarships/grants available. *Unit head:* Dr. Robert Stevens, Chair/Professor of Education, 903-566-7315, E-mail: rstevens@uttyler.edu. *Application contact:* Bonnie Purser, Office of Graduate Studies, 903-566-7142, Fax: 903-566-7068, E-mail: bpurser@uttyler.edu.

University of the Pacific, School of Education, Department of Curriculum and Instruction, Stockton, CA 95211-0197. Offers curriculum and instruction (M Ed, MA, Ed D); education (M Ed); special education (MA). *Accreditation:* NCATE. *Faculty:* 11 full-time (7 women), 5 part-time/adjunct (2 women). *Students:* 20 full-time (19 women), 21 part-time (16 women); includes 15 minority (2 African Americans, 5 Asian Americans or Pacific Islanders, 8 Hispanic Americans), 1 international. Average age 33. 42 applicants, 69% accepted, 24 enrolled. In 2006, 34 master's, 4 doctorates awarded. *Degree requirements:* For master's, thesis (for some programs). *Entrance requirements:* For master's, GRE General Test. Additional exam requirements/recommendations for international students: Required—TOEFL (minimum score 475 paper-based; 150 computer-based). *Application deadline:* For fall admission, 3/1 priority date for domestic students; for spring admission, 10/1 priority date for domestic students. Applications are processed on a rolling basis. Application fee: $75. *Expenses:* Tuition: Full-time $26,920. Required fees: $430. Tuition and fees vary according to course load. *Financial support:* In 2006–07, 7 teaching assistantships were awarded. Financial award application deadline: 3/1; financial award applicants required to submit FAFSA. *Unit head:* Dr. Marilyn Draheim, Chairperson, 209-946-2685, E-mail: mdraheim@pacific.edu.

The University of Toledo, College of Graduate Studies, College of Education, Department of Curriculum and Instruction, Program in Curriculum and Instruction, Toledo, OH 43606-3390. Offers ME, DE, PhD, Ed S. *Students:* 19 full-time (17 women), 43 part-time (37 women); includes 10 minority (5 African Americans, 1 American Indian/Alaska Native, 4 Hispanic Americans), 1 international. 15 applicants, 80% accepted, 6 enrolled. In 2006, 15 degrees awarded. *Entrance requirements:* For master's, minimum GPA of 2.7; for doctorate, GRE, minimum undergraduate GPA of 2.7.

University of Vermont, Graduate College, College of Education and Social Services, Department of Education, Program in Curriculum and Instruction, Burlington, VT 05405. Offers M Ed. *Accreditation:* NCATE. *Students:* 109 (81 women); includes 2 minority (1 African American, 1 Asian American or Pacific Islander) 2 international. 89 applicants, 82% accepted, 50 enrolled. In 2006, 56 degrees awarded. *Entrance requirements:* Additional exam requirements/recommendations for international students: Required—TOEFL (minimum score 550 paper-based; 213 computer-based). *Application deadline:* For fall admission, 8/1 priority date for domestic students. Applications are processed on a rolling basis. Application fee: $40. *Expenses:* Tuition, state resident: part-time $434 per credit. Tuition, nonresident: part-time $1,096 per credit. *Financial support:* Fellowships, teaching assistantships, career-related internships or fieldwork available. Financial award application deadline: 3/1. *Unit head:* Dr. Russell M. Agne, Chairperson, 802-656-3356.

University of Victoria, Faculty of Graduate Studies, Faculty of Education, Department of Curriculum and Instruction, Victoria, BC V8W 2Y2, Canada. Offers art (M Ed, MA, PhD); curriculum studies (M Ed, MA, PhD); early childhood (M Ed, MA, PhD); language and literacy (M Ed, MA, PhD); mathematics (M Ed, MA, PhD); music (M Ed, MA); music education (PhD); science (M Ed, MA, PhD); social studies (M Ed, MA); social, cultural and foundational studies (PhD); technology and environmental education (PhD). Part-time programs available. *Degree requirements:* For master's, thesis, project (M Ed); for doctorate, thesis/dissertation, comprehensive exam, registration. *Entrance requirements:* For master's, minimum B average. Additional exam requirements/recommendations for international students: Required—TOEFL (minimum score 575 paper-based; 233 computer-based), IELTS (minimum score 7). Electronic applications accepted. *Faculty research:* Elementary and secondary English, language arts, curriculum theory and practice, educational media and technology, educational administration and leadership, history and philosophy of education.

University of Virginia, Curry School of Education, Department of Curriculum, Instruction, and Special Education, Program in Curriculum and Instruction, Charlottesville, VA 22903. Offers M Ed, Ed D, Ed S. *Students:* 25 full-time (21 women), 41 part-time (33 women); includes 2 minority (both African Americans), 3 international. Average age 33. 61 applicants, 82% accepted, 26 enrolled. In 2006, 172 master's, 1 doctorate, 22 other advanced degrees awarded. *Degree requirements:* For master's, thesis (for some programs), comprehensive exam (for some programs); for doctorate, thesis/dissertation, comprehensive exam (for some programs). *Entrance requirements:* For master's, doctorate, and Ed S, GRE General Test. Additional exam requirements/recommendations for international students: Required—TOEFL (minimum score 600 paper-based; 250 computer-based). *Application deadline:* For fall admission, 3/1 priority date for domestic students. Applications are processed on a rolling basis. Application fee: $60. *Financial support:* Fellowships with tuition reimbursements, research assistantships with tuition reimbursements, teaching assistantships with tuition reimbursements available. Financial award applicants required to submit FAFSA. *Application contact:* Joanne McNergney, Student Enrollment Coordinator, 434-924-0757.

University of Washington, Graduate School, College of Education, Seattle, WA 98195. Offers curriculum and instruction (M Ed, Ed D, PhD), including educational technology, general curriculum (Ed D, PhD), language, literacy, and culture, mathematics education, multicultural education, reading and language arts education (Ed D), science education, social studies education, teaching and curriculum (M Ed); educational leadership and policy studies (M Ed, Ed D, PhD), including administration, educational organization and policy, higher education, school district leadership (Ed D), social/cultural foundations; educational psychology (M Ed, PhD), including human development and cognition, measurement and research, school counseling (M Ed), school psychology; special education (M Ed, Ed D, PhD), including early childhood education, elementary special education, emotional and behavioral disabilities (M Ed), general special education, severe disabilities; teacher education (MIT). *Accreditation:* APA. Part-time and evening/weekend programs available. *Degree requirements:* For master's, thesis optional; for doctorate, thesis/dissertation. *Entrance requirements:* For master's and doctorate, GRE General Test, minimum GPA of 3.0. Additional exam requirements/recommendations for international students: Required—TOEFL. Electronic applications accepted. *Faculty research:* School restructuring/effective schools, special education interventions, literacy and writing, technology, school partnerships, teacher preparation.

The University of Western Ontario, Faculty of Graduate Studies, Social Sciences Division, Faculty of Education, Program in Educational Studies, London, ON N6A 5B8, Canada. Offers curriculum studies (M Ed); educational policy studies (M Ed); educational psychology/special education (M Ed). Part-time programs available. *Application deadline:* For fall admission, 2/1 for domestic students. Application fee: $50. *Financial support:* Research assistantships, teaching assistantships available. Financial award application deadline: 4/1. *Faculty research:* Reflective practice, gender and schooling, feminist pedagogy, narrative inquiry, second language, multiculturalism in Canada, education and law. *Unit head:* Allan Pitman, Graduate Chair, 519-661-2111 Ext. 88870, Fax: 519-661-3833, E-mail: pitman@uwo.ca. *Application contact:* L. Kulak, Graduate Supervisor, 519-661-2099, Fax: 519-661-3833, E-mail: kulak@edu.uwo.ca.

University of West Florida, College of Professional Studies, Division of Graduate Education, Program in Curriculum and Instruction, Pensacola, FL 32514-5750. Offers Ed D, Ed S. *Accreditation:* NCATE. Evening/weekend programs available. *Students:* 23 full-time (16 women), 213 part-time (139 women); includes 63 minority (48 African Americans, 3 American Indian/Alaska Native, 9 Asian Americans or Pacific Islanders, 3 Hispanic Americans), 4 international. Average age 43. 58 applicants, 66% accepted, 34 enrolled. In 2006, 21 doctorates, 13 Ed Ss awarded. *Degree requirements:* For doctorate, thesis/dissertation. *Entrance requirements:* Additional exam requirements/recommendations for international students: Required—TOEFL (minimum score 550 paper-based; 213 computer-based). *Application deadline:* For fall admission, 6/1 for domestic students, 5/15 for international students; for spring admission, 11/1 for domestic students, 10/1 for international students. Applications are processed on a rolling basis. Application fee: $30. *Expenses:* Tuition, state resident: full-time $5,871; part-time $245 per credit hour. Tuition, nonresident: full-time $21,241; part-time $885 per credit hour. *Financial support:* Fellowships, career-related internships or fieldwork, Federal Work-Study, institutionally sponsored loans, scholarships/grants, and unspecified assistantships available. Support available to part-time students. Financial award application deadline: 4/15; financial award applicants required to submit FAFSA. *Unit head:* Dr. Thomas J. Kramer, Chairperson, Division of Graduate Education, 850-474-2768.

University of West Florida, College of Professional Studies, Division of Teacher Education, Master's Program in Curriculum and Instruction, Specialization in Curriculum and Instruction, Pensacola, FL 32514-5750. Offers M Ed. *Entrance requirements:* Additional exam requirements/recommendations for international students: Required—TOEFL (minimum score 550 paper-based; 213 computer-based). *Application deadline:* For fall admission, 6/1 for domestic students, 5/15 for international students; for spring admission, 11/1 for domestic students, 10/1 for international students. Application fee: $30. *Expenses:* Tuition, state resident: full-time $5,871; part-time $245 per credit hour. Tuition, nonresident: full-time $21,241; part-time $885 per credit hour. *Financial support:* Application deadline: 4/15;

University of Wisconsin–Madison, Graduate School, School of Education, Department of Curriculum and Instruction, Madison, WI 53706-1380. Offers art education (MA); curriculum and instruction (MS, PhD); education and mathematics (MA); French education (MA); German education (MA); music education (MS); science education (MS); Spanish education (MA). *Accreditation:* NASM (one or more programs are accredited). *Degree requirements:* For doctorate, thesis/dissertation. Application fee: $45. *Financial support:* Project assistantships available. *Unit head:* Dr. Alan Lockwood, Chair, 608-262-4000.

University of Wisconsin–Milwaukee, Graduate School, School of Education, Department of Curriculum and Instruction, Milwaukee, WI 53201-0413. Offers curriculum planning and instruction improvement (MS); early childhood education (MS); elementary education (MS); junior high/middle school education (MS); reading education (MS); secondary education (MS); teaching in an urban setting (MS). Part-time programs available. *Faculty:* 27 full-time (17 women). *Students:* 21 full-time (17 women), 67 part-time (54 women); includes 15 minority (8 African Americans, 3 Asian Americans or Pacific Islanders, 4 Hispanic Americans), 3 international. 44 applicants, 43% accepted, 19 enrolled. In 2006, 38 degrees awarded. *Degree requirements:* For master's, thesis or alternative. *Application deadline:* For fall admission, 1/1 priority date for domestic students; for spring admission, 9/1 for domestic students. Applications are processed on a rolling basis. Application fee: $45 ($75 for international students). *Expenses:* Tuition, state resident: part-time $510 per credit. Tuition, nonresident: part-time $1,408 per credit. Tuition and fees vary according to program. *Financial support:* Fellowships, research assistantships, teaching assistantships, career-related internships or fieldwork and unspecified assistantships available. Support available to part-time students. Financial award application deadline: 4/15. *Unit head:* Linda Post, Chair, 414-229-4884, Fax: 414-229-5571, E-mail: lpost@uwm.edu.

University of Wisconsin–Oshkosh, The School of Graduate Studies, College of Education and Human Services, Department of Curriculum and Instruction, Oshkosh, WI 54901. Offers MSE. *Accreditation:* NCATE. Part-time and evening/weekend programs available. *Degree requirements:* For master's, thesis or alternative, seminar paper. *Entrance requirements:* For master's, teaching license, letters of recommendation. Additional exam requirements/recommendations for international students: Required—TOEFL (minimum score 550 paper-based; 213 computer-based). Electronic applications accepted. *Faculty research:* Early childhood, middle school teaching, literacy, elementary teaching, bilingual education.

University of Wisconsin–Superior, Graduate Division, Department of Teacher Education, Program in Instruction, Superior, WI 54880-4500. Offers MSE. Part-time and evening/weekend programs available. *Degree requirements:* For master's, thesis or alternative, research project, comprehensive exam. *Entrance requirements:* For master's, minimum GPA of 2.75, teaching certificate.

University of Wisconsin–Whitewater, School of Graduate Studies, College of Education, Department of Curriculum and Instruction, Whitewater, WI 53190-1790. Offers MS. *Accreditation:* NCATE. Part-time and evening/weekend programs available. Postbaccalaureate distance learning degree programs offered. *Students:* 9 full-time (3 women), 100 part-time (79 women); includes 19 minority (2 African Americans, 1 American Indian/Alaska Native, 1 Asian American or Pacific Islander, 15 Hispanic Americans). Average age 29. 24 applicants, 50% accepted, 10 enrolled. In 2006, 40 degrees awarded. *Degree requirements:* For master's, thesis or integrated project. *Entrance requirements:* Additional exam requirements/recommendations for international students: Required—TOEFL (minimum score 550 paper-based; 213 computer-based). *Application deadline:* For fall admission, 7/15 priority date for domestic and international students; for spring admission, 12/1 priority date for domestic and international students. Applications are processed on a rolling basis. Application fee: $45. Electronic applications accepted. *Expenses:* Tuition, state resident: full-time $3,311. Tuition, nonresident: full-time $8,616. Required fees: $368 per credit. *Financial support:* Research assistantships, Federal Work-Study, unspecified assistantships, and out-of-state fee waivers available. Support available to part-time students. Financial award application deadline: 3/15; financial award applicants required to submit FAFSA. *Faculty research:* Hybrid of exercise physiology and psychology; gender equity; education, pedagogy, and technology; comprehensive school health education. *Unit head:* Dr. John Zbikowski, Coordinator, 262-472-4860, Fax: 262-472-1988, E-mail: zbikowskij@uww.edu. *Application contact:* Sally A. Lange, School of Graduate Studies, 262-472-1006, Fax: 262-472-5027, E-mail: gradschl@uww.edu.

University of Wyoming, Graduate School, College of Education, Programs in Curriculum and Instruction, Laramie, WY 82070. Offers MA, Ed D, PhD. Part-time programs available. Postbaccalaureate distance learning degree programs offered. *Faculty:* 23 full-time (14 women). *Students:* 6 full-time (all women), 72 part-time (58 women); includes 7 minority (1 African American, 2 American Indian/Alaska Native, 1 Asian American or Pacific Islander, 3 Hispanic Americans). Average age 42. 10 applicants, 100% accepted. In 2006, 11 master's, 8 doctorates awarded. Terminal master's awarded for partial completion of doctoral program. *Degree requirements:* For master's and doctorate, thesis/dissertation, comprehensive exam, registration. *Entrance requirements:* For master's, minimum GPA of 3.0, 3 letters of reference, writing samples; for doctorate, accredited master's degree, 3 letters of reference, 3 years of teaching experience, writing sample. Additional exam requirements/recommendations for international students: Required—TOEFL (minimum score 525 paper-based). *Application deadline:* For fall admission, 4/1 priority date for domestic students, 4/1 for international students; for spring admission, 10/1 for domestic and international students. Applications are processed on a rolling basis. Application fee: $50. *Financial support:* In 2006–07, teaching assistantships with tuition reimbursements (averaging $10,062 per year). Financial award application deadline: 3/1. *Faculty research:* Teaching and learning teacher education, multi-cultural education, early childhood, discipline-specific pedagogy. Total annual research expenditures: $510,000. *Unit head:* Dr. Linda Hutchison, Head, 307-766-3275, Fax: 307-766-2018, E-mail: lhutch@uwyo.edu. *Application contact:* Jennifer Martin, Office Associate, 307-766-3275, Fax: 307-766-2018, E-mail: jmartin@uwyo.edu.

Utah State University, School of Graduate Studies, College of Education and Human Services, Doctoral Program in Education, Logan, UT 84322. Offers business information systems (Ed D, PhD); curriculum and instruction (Ed D, PhD); research and evaluation (PhD). *Accreditation:* NCATE. *Faculty:* 61 full-time (19 women). *Students:* 107 full-time (75 women), 100 part-time (60 women); includes 6 minority (3 African Americans, 3 Hispanic Americans), 18 international. Average age 36. 43 applicants, 49% accepted, 12 enrolled. In 2006, 14 degrees awarded. *Degree requirements:* For doctorate, thesis/dissertation, comprehensive exam, registration. *Entrance requirements:* For doctorate, GRE General Test, minimum GPA of 3.0, master's degree. Additional exam requirements/recommendations for international students: Required—TOEFL. *Application deadline:* For fall admission, 6/15 priority date for domestic and international students; for spring admission, 10/15 priority date for domestic and international students. Applications are processed on a rolling basis. Application fee: $50 ($60 for international students). Electronic applications accepted. *Financial support:* In 2006–07, 7 fellowships were awarded; research assistantships with partial tuition reimbursements, teaching assistantships with partial tuition reimbursements, career-related internships or fieldwork, Federal Work-Study, and institutionally sponsored loans also available. Financial award application deadline: 2/1. *Faculty research:* Language and literacy development, math and science education, instructional technology, hearing problems/deafness, domestic violence and animal abuse. Total annual research expenditures: $30.6 million. *Application contact:* Shannon Johnson, Staff Assistant, 435-797-1470, Fax: 435-797-3939, E-mail: shannon.johnson@usu.edu.

Valdosta State University, Graduate School, College of Education, Department of Curriculum and Instructional Technology, Valdosta, GA 31698. Offers curriculum and instruction (Ed D); instructional technology (M Ed, Ed S), including library/media technology (M Ed), technology application (M Ed).

Vanderbilt University, Peabody College, Department of Teaching and Learning, Nashville, TN 37240-1001. Offers curriculum and instructional leadership (M Ed); early childhood education (M Ed); early childhood leadership (Ed D); elementary education (M Ed); English education (M Ed); English language learners (M Ed); mathematics education (M Ed); reading education (M Ed); science education (M Ed); secondary education (M Ed). *Accreditation:* NCATE. *Faculty:* 23 full-time (13 women), 28 part-time/adjunct (19 women). *Students:* 71 full-time (62 women), 21 part-time (15 women); includes 9 minority (8 African Americans, 1 Hispanic American), 2 international. Average age 27. 102 applicants, 60% accepted, 27 enrolled. In 2006, 53 master's, 3 doctorates awarded. *Degree requirements:* For master's, thesis optional. *Entrance requirements:* For master's, GRE General Test, MAT. Additional exam requirements/recommendations for international students: Required—TOEFL (minimum score 550 paper-based; 213 computer-based). *Application deadline:* For fall admission, 12/31 priority date for domestic and international students; for spring admission, 11/1 priority date for domestic and international students. Applications are processed on a rolling basis. Application fee: $0. Electronic applications accepted. *Expenses:* Tuition: Full-time $24,462. Required fees: $2,515. One-time fee: $30 full-time. Full-time tuition and fees vary according to course load, degree level and program. *Financial support:* In 2006–07, 62 students received support, including 36 fellowships with full and partial tuition reimbursements available, 13 research assistantships with full and partial tuition reimbursements available, 13 teaching assistantships with full and partial tuition reimbursements available; Federal Work-Study, institutionally sponsored loans, scholarships/grants, tuition waivers (partial), and unspecified assistantships also available. Support available to part-time students. Financial award application deadline: 2/1; financial award applicants required to submit FAFSA. *Faculty research:* Teaching and learning; development of subject matter knowledge; learning and policy; development students' mathematical and scientific knowledge, development of literacy. *Unit head:* Leona Schauble, Chair, 615-322-8100, Fax: 615-322-8999, E-mail: leona.schauble@vanderbilt.edu. *Application contact:* Angela Saylor, Educational Coordinator, 615-322-8092, Fax: 615-322-8999.

Virginia Commonwealth University, Graduate School, School of Education, Program in Curriculum and Instruction, Richmond, VA 23284-9005. Offers M Ed. *Accreditation:* NCATE. Part-time programs available. *Students:* 3 full-time (all women), 42 part-time (38 women); includes 5 minority (all African Americans), 1 international. 5 applicants, 100% accepted. In 2006, 21 degrees awarded. *Degree requirements:* For master's, comprehensive exam. *Entrance requirements:* For master's, GRE General Test or MAT. *Application deadline:* For fall admission, 5/15 for domestic students; for spring admission, 11/15 for domestic students. Applications are processed on a rolling basis. Application fee: $50. *Financial support:* Tuition waivers (partial) available. Financial award application deadline: 3/1. *Unit head:* Dr. Michael D. Davis, Director, Graduate Studies, 804-828-6530, Fax: 804-827-0676, E-mail: mddavis@vcu.edu. *Application contact:* Dr. Michael D. Davis, Director, Graduate Studies, 804-828-6530, Fax: 804-827-0676, E-mail: mddavis@vcu.edu.

Virginia Commonwealth University, Graduate School, School of Education, Program in Teaching and Learning, Richmond, VA 23284-9005. Offers early education (MT); middle education (MT); secondary education (MT, Certificate); special education (MT). *Accreditation:* NCATE. Part-time programs available. *Faculty:* 22 full-time (12 women). *Students:* 152 full-time (130 women), 126 part-time (111 women); includes 42 minority (35 African Americans, 2 American Indian/Alaska Native, 4 Asian Americans or Pacific Islanders, 1 Hispanic American), 4 international. 551 applicants, 74% accepted. In 2006, 77 degrees awarded. *Entrance requirements:* For master's, GRE General Test or MAT. *Application deadline:* For fall admission, 5/15 for domestic students; for spring admission, 11/15 for domestic students. Applications are processed on a rolling basis. Application fee: $50. *Financial support:* Application deadline: 3/1. *Unit head:* Dr. Michael D. Davis, Director, Graduate Studies, 804-828-6530, Fax: 804-827-0676, E-mail: mddavis@vcu.edu. *Application contact:* Dr. Michael D. Davis, Director, Graduate Studies, 804-828-6530, Fax: 804-827-0676, E-mail: mddavis@vcu.edu.

See Close-Up on page 1137.

Virginia Polytechnic Institute and State University, Graduate School, College of Liberal Arts and Human Sciences, School of Education, Department of Teaching and Learning,

Curriculum and Instruction

Virginia Polytechnic Institute and State University *(continued)*
Blacksburg, VA 24061. Offers curriculum and instruction (MA Ed, Ed D, PhD, Ed S); health and physical education (MS Ed); instructional technology (ITMA). *Accreditation:* NCATE. Post-baccalaureate distance learning degree programs offered (no on-campus study). *Students:* 274 full-time (184 women), 400 part-time (271 women); includes 83 minority (55 African Americans, 2 American Indian/Alaska Native, 18 Asian Americans or Pacific Islanders, 8 Hispanic Americans), 36 international. Average age 34. 374 applicants, 71% accepted, 237 enrolled. In 2006, 245 master's, 21 doctorates, 4 other advanced degrees awarded. *Entrance requirements:* Additional exam requirements/recommendations for international students: Required—TOEFL (minimum score 550 paper-based; 213 computer-based). *Application deadline:* For fall admission, 5/15 for international students; for spring admission, 10/15 for international students. Applications are processed on a rolling basis. Application fee: $45. Electronic applications accepted. *Expenses:* Tuition, state resident: full-time $7,017; part-time $390 per credit hour. Tuition, nonresident: full-time $12,414; part-time $690 per credit hour. International tuition: $11,296 full-time. Required fees: $1,523; $256 per term. *Financial support:* Career-related internships or fieldwork, Federal Work-Study, scholarships/grants, and unspecified assistantships available. Financial award application deadline: 4/1. *Faculty research:* Instructional technology, teacher evaluation, school change, literacy, teaching strategies. *Unit head:* Dr. Daisy L. Stewart, Head, 540-231-8327, Fax: 540-231-3717. *Application contact:* Nancy Nolen, Information Contact, 540-231-5348, Fax: 540-231-3717, E-mail: nanolen@vt.edu.

Walla Walla College, Graduate School, School of Education and Psychology, Specialization in Curriculum and Instruction, College Place, WA 99324-1198. Offers M Ed, MA, MAT. *Faculty:* 8 full-time (3 women), 3 part-time/adjunct (1 woman). *Degree requirements:* For master's, thesis (for some programs), 9 months of work experience in education. *Entrance requirements:* For master's, GRE General Test, minimum GPA of 2.75, 30 hours in professional education. *Application deadline:* For fall admission, 4/1 priority date for domestic students. Applications are processed on a rolling basis. Application fee: $50. Electronic applications accepted. *Expenses:* Tuition: Full-time $20,124; part-time $516 per quarter hour. *Financial support:* Teaching assistantships with partial tuition reimbursements available. Financial award application deadline: 4/1; financial award applicants required to submit FAFSA. *Faculty research:* Instructional psychology. *Application contact:* Dr. Joe G. Galusha, Dean of Graduate Studies, 509-527-2421, Fax: 509-527-2237, E-mail: galujo@wwc.edu.

Washburn University, College of Arts and Sciences, Department of Education, Program in Curriculum and Instruction, Topeka, KS 66621. Offers M Ed. *Accreditation:* NCATE. *Expenses:* Tuition, state resident: full-time $4,338; part-time $241 per credit hour. Tuition, nonresident: full-time $8,820; part-time $490 per credit hour. Required fees: $62; $31 per semester. *Application contact:* Tara Porter, Licensure Officer, 785-670-1434, Fax: 785-670-1046, E-mail: tara.porter@washburn.edu.

Washington State University, Graduate School, College of Education, Department of Teaching and Learning, Pullman, WA 99164. Offers curriculum and instruction (Ed D, PhD); diverse languages (M Ed, MA); elementary education (M Ed, MA, MIT); exercise science (MS); literacy education (M Ed, MA, PhD); math education (PhD); secondary education (M Ed, MA). *Accreditation:* NCATE. *Faculty:* 27. *Students:* 54 full-time (43 women), 20 part-time (14 women); includes 13 minority (4 African Americans, 2 American Indian/Alaska Native, 2 Asian Americans or Pacific Islanders, 5 Hispanic Americans), 5 international. Average age 34. 244 applicants, 16% accepted, 11 enrolled. In 2006, 20 master's, 3 doctorates awarded. *Degree requirements:* For master's, thesis (for some programs), oral or written exam, comprehensive exam (for some programs); for doctorate, thesis/dissertation, oral, written exam, comprehensive exam. *Entrance requirements:* For master's and doctorate, GRE General Test, minimum GPA of 3.0, 3 letters of recommendation. Additional exam requirements/recommendations for international students: Required—TOEFL. *Application deadline:* For fall admission, 2/1 for domestic students, 3/1 for international students; for spring admission, 9/1 for domestic students, 7/1 for international students. Applications are processed on a rolling basis. Application fee: $50. *Expenses:* Tuition, state resident: full-time $7,066. Tuition, nonresident: full-time $17,204. *Financial support:* In 2006–07, 13 research assistantships with partial tuition reimbursements (averaging $13,917 per year), 22 teaching assistantships with partial tuition reimbursements (averaging $13,056 per year) were awarded; career-related internships or fieldwork, Federal Work-Study, institutionally sponsored loans, tuition waivers (partial), unspecified assistantships, and staff assistantships, teaching associateships also available. Financial award application deadline: 4/1. *Faculty research:* Evolution of middle school education issues in special education, computer-assisted language learning. Total annual research expenditures: $1.1 million. *Unit head:* Dr. Corinne Mantle-Bromley, Chair, 509-335-5027. *Application contact:* Graduate School Admissions, 800-GRADWSU, Fax: 509-335-1949, E-mail: gradsch@wsu.edu.

Wayne State University, College of Education, Division of Administrative and Organizational Studies, Detroit, MI 48202. Offers administration and supervision-secondary (Ed S); college and university teaching (Certificate); curriculum and instruction (PhD); educational leadership (M Ed, Ed S); educational leadership and policy studies (Ed D, PhD); elementary education curriculum and instruction (MA, Ed S); general administration and supervision (Ed D, PhD, Ed S); higher education (Ed D, PhD); instructional technology (M Ed, Ed D, PhD, Ed S); secondary curriculum and instruction (M Ed, Ed S). *Faculty:* 24 full-time (13 women), 1 (woman) part-time/adjunct. *Students:* 153 full-time (103 women), 389 part-time (266 women); includes 252 minority (223 African Americans, 6 American Indian/Alaska Native, 8 Asian Americans or Pacific Islanders, 15 Hispanic Americans), 19 international. Average age 38. 138 applicants, 79% accepted, 74 enrolled. In 2006, 116 master's, 30 doctorates, 64 other advanced degrees awarded. *Degree requirements:* For doctorate, thesis/dissertation. *Entrance requirements:* For doctorate, interview, minimum GPA of 3.0. Additional exam requirements/recommendations for international students: Required—TOEFL (minimum score 550 paper-based; 213 computer-based), TWE (minimum score 6). *Application deadline:* For fall admission, 7/1 for domestic students, 6/1 for international students; for winter admission, 10/1 for international students; for spring admission, 2/1 for international students. Application fee: $30 ($50 for international students). Electronic applications accepted. *Financial support:* In 2006–07, 4 research assistantships (averaging $12,797 per year) were awarded; career-related internships or fieldwork, Federal Work-Study, and institutionally sponsored loans also available. Support available to part-time students. *Faculty research:* Total quality management, participatory management, administering educational technology, school improvement, principalship. Total annual research expenditures: $344,504. *Unit head:* Dr. JoAnne Holbert, Assistant Dean, 313-577-1721, E-mail: jholbert@wayne.edu.

Wayne State University, College of Education, Division of Teacher Education, Detroit, MI 48202. Offers adult and continuing education (M Ed); art education (M Ed); bilingual/bicultural education (M Ed, MAT); business education (M Ed, MAT); career and technical education (M Ed, Ed D, PhD, Ed S); curriculum and instruction (Ed D, PhD, Ed S); distributive education (M Ed, MAT); early childhood education (M Ed); elementary education (M Ed, MAT, Ed D, PhD, Ed S); elementary education curriculum and instruction (M Ed); English education (M Ed); English education-secondary (M Ed, Ed S); foreign language education (M Ed); general education (Ed D, Ed S); health occupations education (M Ed); industrial education (M Ed); mathematics education (M Ed, Ed S); pre-school and parent education (M Ed); reading (M Ed, Ed D, Ed S); reading, languages and literature (Ed D); school music-vocal (M Ed); science education (M Ed, MAT, Ed S); secondary education (MAT); secondary school reading (M Ed); social studies education (M Ed, Ed S), including education-secondary (M Ed); special education (M Ed, Ed D, PhD, Ed S); teacher education (MAT, Ed D, PhD). *Faculty:* 41 full-time (22 women), 2 part-time/adjunct (both women). *Students:* 401 full-time (295 women), 1,021 part-time (784 women); includes 527 minority (452 African Americans, 6 American Indian/Alaska Native, 32 Asian Americans or Pacific Islanders, 37 Hispanic Americans), 18 international. Average age 36. 296 applicants, 81% accepted, 132 enrolled. In 2006, 386 master's, 1 doctorate awarded. *Degree requirements:* For doctorate, thesis/dissertation. *Entrance*

requirements: For master's, minimum GPA of 2.6; for doctorate, minimum undergraduate GPA of 3.0, graduate 3.5; interview. Additional exam requirements/recommendations for international students: Required—TOEFL (minimum score 550 paper-based; 213 computer-based), TWE (minimum score 6). *Application deadline:* For fall admission, 7/1 for domestic students, 6/1 for international students; for winter admission, 10/1 for international students; for spring admission, 2/1 for international students. Application fee: $30 ($50 for international students). Electronic applications accepted. *Financial support:* In 2006–07, 1 fellowship (averaging $34,919 per year) was awarded; research assistantships. *Faculty research:* Reading and writing literacy and literature. Total annual research expenditures: $209,400. *Unit head:* Dr. Joann Snyder, Academic Director, 313-577-1644, E-mail: joanne.snyder@wayne.edu. *Application contact:* Sharon Elliott, Assistant Dean, 313-577-0902, E-mail: sharon.elliott@wayne.edu.

Weber State University, Jerry and Vickie Moyes College of Education, Program in Curriculum and Instruction, Ogden, UT 84408-1001. Offers M Ed. *Accreditation:* NCATE. Part-time and evening/weekend programs available. *Faculty:* 22 full-time (14 women), 2 part-time/adjunct (both women). *Students:* 4 full-time (all women), 168 part-time (129 women); includes 6 minority (2 Asian Americans or Pacific Islanders, 4 Hispanic Americans), 1 international. Average age 40. 37 applicants, 84% accepted, 31 enrolled. In 2006, 48 degrees awarded. *Degree requirements:* For master's, thesis or alternative, project presentation and exam. *Entrance requirements:* For master's, minimum GPA of 3.0 in last 90 credits, 1 year full-time teaching experience. *Application deadline:* For fall admission, 5/1 priority date for domestic students; for spring admission, 11/1 priority date for domestic students. Applications are processed on a rolling basis. Application fee: $25. *Expenses:* Tuition, state resident: full-time $3,950; part-time $203 per semester. Tuition, nonresident: full-time $10,371; part-time $518 per semester. Required fees: $544; $24 per semester. Tuition and fees vary according to course load and program. *Financial support:* In 2006–07, 17 students received support. Institutionally sponsored loans, scholarships/grants, tuition waivers (partial), and unspecified assistantships available. Support available to part-time students. Financial award application deadline: 2/1. *Unit head:* Dr. Claudia Eliason, Director, 801-626-7719, E-mail: eeliason@weber.edu.

Western Connecticut State University, Division of Graduate Studies, School of Professional Studies, Department of Education and Educational Psychology, Curriculum Option, Danbury, CT 06810-6885. Offers MS. Part-time and evening/weekend programs available. *Students:* 1 (woman) full-time, 41 part-time (25 women); includes 2 minority (both Hispanic Americans) Average age 29. In 2006, 28 degrees awarded. *Degree requirements:* For master's, thesis or research project. *Entrance requirements:* For master's, minimum GPA of 2.8, teaching certificate in elementary or secondary education. *Application deadline:* For fall admission, 8/1 priority date for domestic students. Applications are processed on a rolling basis. Application fee: $40. *Financial support:* Fellowships, career-related internships or fieldwork available. Support available to part-time students. Financial award application deadline: 5/1; financial award applicants required to submit FAFSA. *Application contact:* Chris Shankle, Associate Director of Graduate Admissions, 203-837-8244, Fax: 203-837-8338, E-mail: shanklec@wcsu.edu.

West Texas A&M University, College of Education and Social Sciences, Division of Education, Program in Curriculum and Instruction, Canyon, TX 79016-0001. Offers M Ed. Part-time and evening/weekend programs available. Postbaccalaureate distance learning degree programs offered. *Degree requirements:* For master's, thesis optional. *Entrance requirements:* For master's, GRE General Test, 18 semester hours of education coursework. Additional exam requirements/recommendations for international students: Required—TOEFL (minimum score 550 paper-based). Electronic applications accepted.

West Virginia University, College of Human Resources and Education, Department of Curriculum and Instruction-Literacy, Morgantown, WV 26506. Offers curriculum and instruction (Ed D); elementary education (MA); reading (MA); secondary education (MA), including higher education curriculum and teaching, secondary education; special education (Ed D), including special education. *Accreditation:* NCATE. Part-time and evening/weekend programs available. *Faculty:* 18 full-time (13 women), 4 part-time/adjunct (3 women). *Students:* 314 full-time (238 women), 187 part-time (163 women); includes 27 minority (15 African Americans, 1 American Indian/Alaska Native, 2 Asian Americans or Pacific Islanders, 9 Hispanic Americans), 26 international. Average age 31. 239 applicants, 86% accepted, 135 enrolled. In 2006, 242 master's, 8 doctorates awarded. *Degree requirements:* For doctorate, thesis/dissertation, comprehensive exam. *Entrance requirements:* For master's, minimum GPA of 2.75; for doctorate, GRE General Test or MAT, 3 letters of recommendation, curriculum vitae. Additional exam requirements/recommendations for international students: Required—TOEFL. *Application deadline:* Applications are processed on a rolling basis. Application fee: $50. *Expenses:* Tuition, state resident: full-time $4,926; part-time $276 per credit hour. Tuition, nonresident: full-time $14,278; part-time $796 per credit hour. Tuition and fees vary according to program. *Financial support:* In 2006–07, 313 students received support, including 1 research assistantship with full tuition reimbursement available (averaging $8,264 per year), 5 teaching assistantships with full tuition reimbursements available (averaging $8,264 per year); fellowships, career-related internships or fieldwork, Federal Work-Study, institutionally sponsored loans, tuition waivers (full and partial), and graduate administrative assistantships also available. Financial award application deadline: 2/1; financial award applicants required to submit FAFSA. *Faculty research:* Teacher education, curriculum development, educational technology, curriculum assessment. Total annual research expenditures: $440,189. *Unit head:* Dr. Elizabeth A. Dooley, Chair, 304-293-3441, Fax: 304-293-3802, E-mail: elizabeth.dooley@mail.wvu.edu.

Wichita State University, Graduate School, College of Education, Department of Curriculum and Instruction, Wichita, KS 67260. Offers curriculum and instruction (M Ed); special education (M Ed). *Accreditation:* NCATE. Part-time and evening/weekend programs available. *Degree requirements:* For master's, portfolio, thesis optional. *Entrance requirements:* For master's, MAT, minimum GPA of 2.75. Additional exam requirements/recommendations for international students: Required—TOEFL. Electronic applications accepted.

William Woods University, Graduate and Adult Studies, Fulton, MO 65251-1098. Offers administration (M Ed, Ed S); agribusiness (MBA); curriculum/instruction (M Ed); health management (MBA); human services (MBA); instructional leadership (Ed S). Evening/weekend programs available. *Faculty:* 38 full-time (14 women), 174 part-time/adjunct (50 women). *Students:* 1,944 full-time (1,230 women); includes 71 minority (43 African Americans, 16 American Indian/Alaska Native, 7 Asian Americans or Pacific Islanders, 5 Hispanic Americans), 41 international. 824 applicants, 86% accepted, 631 enrolled. In 2006, 919 master's, 112 other advanced degrees awarded. *Median time to degree:* Master's–1.5 years full-time; Ed S–1.5 years full-time. *Degree requirements:* For master's, capstone course (MBA), action research (M Ed); for Ed S, field experience. *Entrance requirements:* For master's, 2 recommendations, resumé, BA/BS; teaching certification (M Ed); course work in economics and accounting (MBA); for Ed S, M Ed, 2 letters of recommendation, resumé, teaching certification. Additional exam requirements/recommendations for international students: Required—TOEFL (minimum score 550 paper-based). *Application deadline:* Applications are processed on a rolling basis. Application fee: $25. Electronic applications accepted. *Expenses:* Tuition: Part-time $255 per credit hour. Tuition and fees vary according to program. *Financial support:* Institutionally sponsored loans available. Financial award applicants required to submit FAFSA. *Unit head:* Sean Siebert, Dean of Graduate and Adult Studies Enrollment Services, 573-592-4383, Fax: 573-592-1164. *Application contact:* Linda Rembish, Administrative Assistant, 800-995-3199, Fax: 573-592-1164, E-mail: cgas@williamwoods.edu.

Wright State University, School of Graduate Studies, College of Education and Human Services, Department of Educational Leadership, Program in Advanced Educational Leadership, Dayton, OH 45435. Offers advanced curriculum and instruction (Ed S); higher education-adult education (Ed S); superintendent (Ed S). *Accreditation:* NCATE. *Students:* 6 full-time (4 women), 10 part-time (6 women); includes 3 minority (all African Americans) Average age 35. 3 applicants, 100% accepted. In 2006, 1 degree awarded. *Degree requirements:* For Ed S, thesis.

Entrance requirements: For degree, GRE General Test, MAT. Additional exam requirements/recommendations for international students: Required—TOEFL. Application fee: $25. *Financial support:* Available to part-time students. Applicants required to submit FAFSA. *Unit head:* Dr. Thomas Diamantes, Director, 937-775-3008, Fax: 937-775-2405, E-mail: thomas.diamantes@wright.edu. *Application contact:* John Kimble, Associate Director of Graduate Admissions and Records, 937-775-2957, Fax: 937-775-2453, E-mail: john.kimble@wright.edu.

Wright State University, School of Graduate Studies, College of Education and Human Services, Department of Educational Leadership, Programs in Educational Leadership, Dayton, OH 45435. Offers curriculum and instruction: teacher leader (MA); educational administrative specialist: teacher leader (M Ed); educational administrative specialist: vocational education administration (M Ed, MA); student affairs in higher education-administration (M Ed, MA). *Accreditation:* NCATE. *Students:* 26 full-time (22 women), 430 part-time (344 women); includes 10 minority (8 African Americans, 1 American Indian/Alaska Native, 1 Hispanic American), 1 international. Average age 33. 179 applicants, 97% accepted. In 2006, 211 degrees awarded. *Degree requirements:* For master's, thesis (for some programs). *Entrance requirements:* For master's, GRE General Test, MAT. Additional exam requirements/recommendations for international students: Required—TOEFL. Application fee: $25. *Financial support:* Available to part-time students. Applicants required to submit FAFSA. *Unit head:* Dr. Charles W. Ryan, Director and Director of Graduate Programs in Education, 937-775-3286, Fax: 937-775-2405, E-mail: charles.ryan@wright.edu. *Application contact:* John Kimble, Associate Director of Graduate Admissions and Records, 937-775-2957, Fax: 937-775-2453, E-mail: john.kimble@wright.edu.

Xavier University of Louisiana, Graduate School, Programs in Education, New Orleans, LA 70125-1098. Offers curriculum and instruction (MA); education administration and supervision (MA); guidance and counseling (MA). *Accreditation:* NCATE. Part-time and evening/weekend programs available. *Degree requirements:* For master's, thesis or alternative, comprehensive exam. *Entrance requirements:* For master's, GRE General Test, MAT, minimum GPA of 2.5. Additional exam requirements/recommendations for international students: Required—TOEFL.

Distance Education Development

Athabasca University, Centre for Distance Education, Athabasca, AB T9S 3A3, Canada. Offers distance education (MDE); distance education technology (Advanced Diploma). Part-time programs available. Postbaccalaureate distance learning degree programs offered (no on-campus study). *Faculty:* 10 full-time (3 women), 22 part-time/adjunct (8 women). *Students:* Average age 41. 88 applicants, 93% accepted. In 2006, 42 degrees awarded. *Degree requirements:* For master's, thesis optional. *Entrance requirements:* For master's, 3 or 4 year baccalaureate degree. *Application deadline:* For fall admission, 3/1 for domestic and international students. Application fee: $65. Electronic applications accepted. *Expenses:* Contact institution. *Faculty research:* Role development in distance education, interaction in distance education, educational technology in distance education, communities of practice in distance education, instructional design. *Unit head:* Dr. Bob Spencer, Head, 780-675-6238, Fax: 780-675-6170, E-mail: bobs@athabascau.ca. *Application contact:* Glenda Hawryluk, Administrative Assistant, 780-675-6179, Fax: 780-675-6170, E-mail: glendah@athabascau.ca.

Barry University, School of Education, Graduate Certificate Programs, Miami Shores, FL 33161-6695. Offers advanced teaching and learning with technology (Certificate); distance education (Certificate); higher education technology integration (Certificate); human resources: not for profit and religious organizations (Certificate); K-12 technology integration (Certificate). *Application contact:* Dave Fletcher, Director of Graduate Admissions, 305-899-3113, Fax: 305-899-2971, E-mail: dfletcher@mail.barry.edu.

Endicott College, Van Loan School of Graduate and Professional Studies, Program in Integrative Learning, Beverly, MA 01915-2096. Offers M Ed. Evening/weekend programs available. Postbaccalaureate distance learning degree programs offered. *Faculty:* 3 full-time (2 women), 4 part-time/adjunct (3 women). *Students:* 34 full-time (29 women); includes 3 minority (2 African Americans, 1 American Indian/Alaska Native), 6 international. Average age 37. 65 applicants, 82% accepted. In 2006, 22 degrees awarded. *Degree requirements:* For master's, thesis. *Application deadline:* Applications are processed on a rolling basis. Application fee: $50. *Expenses:* Tuition: Part-time $279 per credit. Tuition and fees vary according to program. *Financial support:* Tuition waivers (partial) available. *Unit head:* Enid E. Larsen, Assistant Dean of Academic Programs, 978-232-2198, Fax: 978-232-3000, E-mail: elarsen@endicott.edu. *Application contact:* Dr. Phil Snow Gang, Dean, 406-387-5107, Fax: 413-778-9644, E-mail: ties@endicott.edu.

Florida State University, Graduate Studies, College of Education, Department of Educational Psychology and Learning Systems, Program in Instructional Systems, Tallahassee, FL 32306. Offers instructional systems (MS, PhD, Ed S); open and distance learning (MS). *Faculty:* 6 full-time (2 women), 4 part-time/adjunct (1 woman). *Students:* 51 full-time (30 women), 78 part-time (46 women); includes 41 minority (10 African Americans, 22 Asian Americans or Pacific Islanders, 9 Hispanic Americans). Average age 20. 106 applicants, 41% accepted, 41 enrolled. In 2006, 35 master's, 6 doctorates awarded. *Degree requirements:* For master's and Ed S, thesis optional; for doctorate, thesis/dissertation, comprehensive exam. *Entrance requirements:* For master's, doctorate, and Ed S, GRE General Test, minimum GPA of 3.0. *Application deadline:* For fall admission, 7/1 priority date for domestic students; for spring admission, 11/1 for domestic students. Applications are processed on a rolling basis. Application fee: $30. *Expenses:* Tuition, state resident: full-time $5,822; part-time $243 per credit hour. Tuition, nonresident: full-time $20,976; part-time $874 per credit hour. Tuition and fees vary according to program. *Financial support:* In 2006–07, fellowships with partial tuition reimbursements (averaging $5,000 per year), research assistantships with partial tuition reimbursements (averaging $18,000 per year), teaching assistantships with partial tuition reimbursements (averaging $18,000 per year) were awarded; career-related internships or fieldwork also available. Financial award applicants required to submit FAFSA. *Unit head:* Dr. Robert Reiser, Program Leader, 850-644-4592, Fax: 850-644-8776, E-mail: rreiser@mailer.fsu.edu. *Application contact:* Mary Kate McKee, Program Coordinator, 850-644-8792, Fax: 850-644-8776, E-mail: mmckee@oddl.fsu.edu.

Jones International University, Graduate School of Education, Centennial, CO 80112. Offers adult education (M Ed); corporate training and knowledge management (M Ed); curriculum and instruction (M Ed), including elementary teacher licensure, secondary teacher licensure; e-learning technology and design (M Ed); educational leadership and administration (M Ed); educational leadership and administration: principal and administrator licensure (M Ed); elementary curriculum instruction and assessment (M Ed); higher education leadership and administration (M Ed); K-12 instructional technology (M Ed); K-12 instructional technology: teacher licensure (M Ed); secondary curriculum instruction and assessment (M Ed); technology and design (M Ed). Part-time and evening/weekend programs available. Postbaccalaureate distance learning degree programs offered (no on-campus study). *Entrance requirements:* For master's, minimum cumulative GPA of 2.5. Additional exam requirements/recommendations for international students: Recommended—TOEFL (minimum score 550 paper-based; 213 computer-based). Electronic applications accepted.

New York Institute of Technology, Graduate Division, School of Education and Professional Services, Program in Elementary Education, Old Westbury, NY 11568-8000. Offers distance learning (Advanced Certificate); elementary education (MS). Part-time and evening/weekend programs available. Postbaccalaureate distance learning degree programs offered. *Students:* 2 full-time (both women), 14 part-time (12 women); includes 1 minority (Hispanic American) Average age 38. 10 applicants, 10% accepted, 1 enrolled. In 2006, 1 master's, 1 other advanced degree awarded. *Degree requirements:* For master's, thesis. *Entrance requirements:* For master's, minimum QPA of 3.0. Additional exam requirements/recommendations for international students: Required—TOEFL. *Application deadline:* For fall admission, 7/1 priority date for domestic students; for spring admission, 12/1 priority date for domestic students. Applications are processed on a rolling basis. Application fee: $50. Electronic applications accepted. *Expenses:* Tuition: Full-time $16,800; part-time $700 per credit. *Financial support:* Research assistantships with partial tuition reimbursements available. Financial award applicants required to submit FAFSA. *Faculty research:* Course development. *Unit head:* Dr. David Arneson, Chair, 516-686-7852, Fax: 516-686-7655, E-mail: darneson@nyit.edu. *Application contact:* Jacquelyn Nealon, Dean of Admissions and Financial Aid, 516-686-7925, Fax: 516-686-7613, E-mail: jnealon@nyit.edu.

New York Institute of Technology, Graduate Division, School of Education and Professional Services, Program in Instructional Technology, Old Westbury, NY 11568-8000. Offers distance learning (Advanced Certificate); instructional technology (MS); multimedia (Advanced Certificate). Part-time and evening/weekend programs available. Postbaccalaureate distance learning degree programs offered. *Students:* 13 full-time (8 women), 240 part-time (132 women); includes 33 minority (17 African Americans, 1 American Indian/Alaska Native, 2 Asian Americans or Pacific Islanders, 13 Hispanic Americans), 5 international. Average age 33. 79 applicants, 73% accepted, 47 enrolled. In 2006, 98 degrees awarded. *Degree requirements:* For master's, thesis. *Entrance requirements:* For master's, minimum QPA of 3.0; for Advanced Certificate, master's degree, minimum GPA of 3.0, 3 years of teaching experience, New York teaching certificate, 2 letters of recommendation. Additional exam requirements/recommendations for international students: Required—TOEFL. *Application deadline:* For fall admission, 7/1 priority date for domestic students; for spring admission, 12/1 priority date for domestic students. Applications are processed on a rolling basis. Application fee: $50. Electronic applications accepted. *Expenses:* Tuition: Full-time $16,800; part-time $700 per credit. *Financial support:* Research assistantships with partial tuition reimbursements, career-related internships or fieldwork, institutionally sponsored loans, and tuition waivers (full and partial) available. Support available to part-time students. Financial award applicants required to submit FAFSA. *Faculty research:* Distance learning, teacher training resources and strategies. *Unit head:* Dr. Joanne Clemente, Coordinator, 516-686-7494, Fax: 516-686-7655, E-mail: jclement@nyit.edu. *Application contact:* Jacquelyn Nealon, Dean of Admissions and Financial Aid, 516-686-7925, Fax: 516-686-7613, E-mail: jnealon@nyit.edu.

Nova Southeastern University, Fischler School of Education and Human Services, Programs in Instructional Technology and Distance Education, Fort Lauderdale, FL 33314-7796. Offers MS, Ed D. Part-time and evening/weekend programs available. Postbaccalaureate distance learning degree programs offered. *Faculty:* 6 full-time (2 women), 22 part-time/adjunct (14 women). *Students:* 6 full-time (5 women), 234 part-time (150 women); includes 87 minority (17 African Americans, 1 American Indian/Alaska Native, 2 Asian Americans or Pacific Islanders, 67 Hispanic Americans), 68 international. In 2006, 4 master's, 21 doctorates awarded. *Degree requirements:* For master's, practicum; for doctorate, thesis/dissertation, practicum. *Entrance requirements:* For master's, interview, current employment in a position using technology; for doctorate, MAT, minimum GPA of 3.0, interview, current employment in a position using technology. *Application deadline:* Applications are processed on a rolling basis. Application fee: $50. *Financial support:* Fellowships available. *Unit head:* Dr. Maryellen Maher, Executive Dean, 954-262-8554, Fax: 954-262-3905, E-mail: maherm@nova.edu. *Application contact:* Dr. Marsha Burmeister, Head, 800-986-3223 Ext. 8572, Fax: 954-262-3905, E-mail: burmeist@nova.edu.

Télé-université, Graduate Programs, Québec, QC G1K 9H5, Canada. Offers computer science (PhD); corporate finance (MS); distance learning (MS). Part-time programs available.

University of Maryland, Baltimore County, Graduate School, College of Arts, Humanities and Social Sciences, Department of Education, Baltimore, MD 21250. Offers computer/web-based instruction (Postbaccalaureate Certificate); distance education (Postbaccalaureate Certificate); early childhood education (MAT); education (MA); elementary education (MAT); instructional systems development (MA, Postbaccalaureate Certificate), including ESOL/bilingual education (Postbaccalaureate Certificate), ESOL/bilingual training systems (MA); secondary education (MA, MAT); teaching (MA). *Accreditation:* NCATE. Part-time and evening/weekend programs available. Postbaccalaureate distance learning degree programs offered (no on-campus study). *Faculty:* 17 full-time (15 women), 3 part-time/adjunct (all women). *Students:* 89 full-time (78 women), 422 part-time (340 women); includes 72 minority (41 African Americans, 19 Asian Americans or Pacific Islanders, 12 Hispanic Americans), 15 international. In 2006, 56 master's awarded. *Median time to degree:* Of those who began their doctoral program in fall 1998, 95% received their degree in 8 years or less. *Degree requirements:* For master's, thesis (for some programs), comprehensive exam, registration. *Entrance requirements:* For master's, GRE General Test, GRE Subject Test (MA), PRAXIS I (MAT), minimum GPA of 3.0. Additional exam requirements/recommendations for international students: Required—TOEFL. *Application deadline:* For fall admission, 7/1 for domestic students. Applications are processed on a rolling basis. Application fee: $50. Electronic applications accepted. *Expenses:* Tuition, state resident: part-time $412 per credit hour. Tuition, nonresident: part-time $681 per credit hour. Required fees: $91 per credit hour. One-time fee: $75 part-time. *Financial support:* In 2006–07, 75 students received support, including research assistantships with full tuition reimbursements available (averaging $12,000 per year); fellowships, teaching assistantships, career-related internships or fieldwork, Federal Work-Study, scholarships/grants, tuition waivers (partial), and unspecified assistantships also available. Financial award application deadline: 3/1. *Faculty research:* Teacher leadership; STEM education; ESOL/bilingual education; early childhood education; language, literacy and culture. Total annual research expenditures: $1.3 million. *Unit head:* Dr. Mary S. Rivkin, Department Chair, 410-455-2465, Fax: 410-455-3986, E-mail: rivkin@umbc.edu. *Application contact:* Dr. Susan M. Blunck, Director, 410-455-2869, Fax: 410-455-3986, E-mail: blunck@umbc.edu.

University of Maryland University College, Graduate School of Management and Technology, Program in Distance Education, Adelphi, MD 20783. Offers MDE, Certificate. Part-time and evening/weekend programs available. Postbaccalaureate distance learning degree programs offered (no on-campus study). *Students:* Average age 42. 46 applicants, 100% accepted, 39 enrolled. In 2006, 19 master's, 39 other advanced degrees awarded. *Degree requirements:* For master's, thesis or alternative. *Application deadline:* Applications are processed on a rolling basis. Application fee: $50. Electronic applications accepted. *Financial support:* Federal Work-Study and scholarships/grants available. Support available to part-time students. Financial award application deadline: 6/1; financial award applicants required to submit FAFSA. *Unit head:* Dr. Stella Porto, 301-985-7200, E-mail: sporto@umuc.edu. *Application contact:* Coordinator, Graduate Admissions, 301-985-7155, Fax: 301-985-7175, E-mail: gradinfo@umuc.edu.

University of Phoenix–Metro Detroit Campus, The Artemis School, College of Education, Troy, MI 48098-2623. Offers administration and supervision (MA Ed); adult education and distance learning (MA Ed); curriculum and development (MA Ed); special education (MA Ed);

Distance Education Development

University of Phoenix–Metro Detroit Campus (continued)
teacher education elementary (MA Ed). Evening/weekend programs available. *Faculty:* 8 full-time (3 women), 27 part-time/adjunct (21 women). *Students:* 102 full-time (75 women); includes 59 minority (57 African Americans, 1 American Indian/Alaska Native, 1 Asian American or Pacific Islander), 1 international. Average age 40. In 2006, 30 master's awarded. *Degree requirements:* For master's, thesis (for some programs), registration. *Entrance requirements:* For master's, 3 years of work experience, minimum undergraduate GPA of 2.5. Additional exam requirements/recommendations for international students: Required—TOEFL (minimum score 550 paper-based; 213 computer-based; 79 iBT). *Application deadline:* Applications are processed on a rolling basis. Application fee: $45. Electronic applications accepted. *Expenses:* Tuition: Full-time $12,168. Required fees: $760. *Financial support:* Institutionally sponsored loans and scholarships/grants available. Financial award applicants required to submit FAFSA. *Unit head:* Dr. Marla LaRue, Dean/Executive Director, 480-557-1218. *Application contact:* Chair, 800-834-2438, Fax: 248-267-0147.

University of Wyoming, Graduate School, College of Education, Department of Adult Learning and Technology, Laramie, WY 82070. Offers adult and post secondary education (Ed S); adult and postsecondary education (MA, Ed D, PhD); distance education (Ed D, PhD); instructional technology (MS, Ed D, PhD). Part-time programs available. Postbaccalaureate distance learning degree programs offered (no on-campus study). *Faculty:* 6 full-time (3 women), 11 part-time/adjunct (5 women). *Students:* 14 full-time (10 women), 91 part-time (52 women); includes 10 minority (2 African Americans, 1 American Indian/Alaska Native, 2 Asian Americans or Pacific Islanders, 5 Hispanic Americans), 4 international. Average age 44. 26 applicants, 85% accepted, 20 enrolled. In 2006, 24 master's, 5 doctorates awarded. *Degree requirements:* For master's, thesis or alternative; for doctorate, thesis/dissertation, comprehensive exam. *Entrance requirements:* For master's, GRE, minimum GPA of 3.0; for doctorate, MS or MA, minimum GPA of 3.0. Additional exam requirements/recommendations for international students: Required—TOEFL. *Application deadline:* For fall admission, 2/1 for domestic and international students; for spring admission, 10/1 for domestic and international students. Application fee: $50. Electronic applications accepted. *Financial support:* In 2006–07, 1 student received support, including 1 teaching assistantship with tuition reimbursement available (averaging $14,400 per year); scholarships/grants also available. Financial award application deadline: 2/1. *Faculty research:* Web based instruction, instructional decision, adult education history, literacy in adults, international distance education. *Unit head:* Dr. John J. Cochenour, Head, 307-766-3608, Fax: 307-766-3237, E-mail: johncoc@uwyo.edu. *Application contact:* Jeannete A. Skinner, Office Associate, 307-766-3247, Fax: 307-766-3237, E-mail: ask-alt@uwyo.edu.

Western Illinois University, School of Graduate Studies, College of Education and Human Services, Department of Instructional Design and Technology, Macomb, IL 61455-1390. Offers distance learning (Certificate); graphic applications (Certificate); instructional technology and telecommunications (MS); multimedia (Certificate); technology integration in education (Certificate); training development (Certificate). Part-time programs available. Postbaccalaureate distance learning degree programs offered (no on-campus study). *Students:* 17 full-time (7 women), 68 part-time (42 women); includes 8 minority (4 African Americans, 4 Asian Americans or Pacific Islanders), 6 international. Average age 36. 18 applicants, 61% accepted. In 2006, 17 master's, 1 other advanced degree awarded. *Degree requirements:* For master's, thesis or alternative. *Entrance requirements:* For master's, minimum GPA of 2.75. Additional exam requirements/recommendations for international students: Required—TOEFL (minimum score 550 paper-based; 213 computer-based; 80 iBT). *Application deadline:* Applications are processed on a rolling basis. Application fee: $30. Electronic applications accepted. *Expenses:* Tuition, state resident: part-time $200 per credit hour. Tuition, nonresident: part-time $400 per credit hour. *Financial support:* In 2006–07, 13 students received support, including 11 research assistantships with full tuition reimbursements available (averaging $6,568 per year), 2 teaching assistantships with full tuition reimbursements available (averaging $7,576 per year). Financial award applicants required to submit FAFSA. *Unit head:* Dr. Hoyet Hemphill, Chairperson, 309-298-1952. *Application contact:* Dr. Barbara Baily, Director of Graduate Studies/Associate Provost, 309-298-1806, Fax: 309-298-2345, E-mail: grad-office@wiu.edu.

Educational Administration

Abilene Christian University, Graduate School, College of Education and Human Services, Graduate Studies in Education, Leadership of Learning Program, Abilene, TX 79699-9100. Offers M Ed, Certificate. Part-time programs available. *Faculty:* 9 part-time/adjunct (6 women). *Students:* 3 full-time (1 woman), 58 part-time (34 women); includes 7 minority (2 African Americans, 5 Hispanic Americans). 88 applicants, 69% accepted, 51 enrolled. In 2006, 10 degrees awarded. *Degree requirements:* For master's, comprehensive exam. *Entrance requirements:* For master's, GRE General Test or MAT. *Application deadline:* For fall admission, 4/1 priority date for domestic students; for spring admission, 11/1 for domestic students. Applications are processed on a rolling basis. Application fee: $40 ($45 for international students). Electronic applications accepted. *Expenses:* Tuition: Full-time $12,504; part-time $521 per hour. Required fees: $700; $34 per hour. *Financial support:* Career-related internships or fieldwork and Federal Work-Study available. Support available to part-time students. Financial award application deadline: 4/1. *Application contact:* William Horn, Graduate Admissions Counselor, 325-674-2656, Fax: 325-674-6717, E-mail: gradinfo@acu.edu.

Acadia University, Faculty of Professional Studies, School of Education, Program in Organizational Leadership, Wolfville, NS B4P 2R6, Canada. Offers M Ed. Part-time and evening/weekend programs available. *Faculty:* 2 full-time (1 woman). *Students:* 1 (woman) full-time, 44 part-time (31 women). In 2006, 23 degrees awarded. *Degree requirements:* For master's, thesis optional. *Entrance requirements:* For master's, B Ed or the equivalent, minimum B average, 2 years teaching or related experience. Additional exam requirements/recommendations for international students: Required—TOEFL (minimum score 580 paper-based; 237 computer-based). *Application deadline:* For fall admission, 3/15 priority date for domestic and international students. Application fee: $50. Electronic applications accepted. *Financial support:* In 2006–07, teaching assistantships (averaging $4,000 per year). Financial award application deadline: 2/1. *Faculty research:* Organizational theory and structural change, professionalism, sexuality education. *Application contact:* Sheila Langille, Secretary, 902-585-1229, Fax: 902-585-1071, E-mail: sheila.langille@acadiau.ca.

Adelphi University, School of Education, Program in Educational Leadership and Technology, Garden City, NY 11530-0701. Offers MA, Certificate. *Students:* 7 full-time (6 women), 50 part-time (40 women); includes 25 minority (16 African Americans, 3 Asian Americans or Pacific Islanders, 6 Hispanic Americans). Average age 40. In 2006, 25 master's, 2 other advanced degrees awarded. *Entrance requirements:* For master's, 2 letters of recommendation, resumé, letter attesting to teaching experience (3 years full-time K-12). Additional exam requirements/recommendations for international students: Required—TOEFL (minimum score 550 paper-based; 213 computer-based). *Application deadline:* For fall admission, 8/15 priority date for domestic students; for spring admission, 1/15 priority date for domestic students. Applications are processed on a rolling basis. Application fee: $50. Electronic applications accepted. *Financial support:* Research assistantships with partial tuition reimbursements, institutionally sponsored loans available. Financial award application deadline: 2/15; financial award applicants required to submit FAFSA. *Faculty research:* Technology methodology focusing on in-service and pre-service curriculum. *Unit head:* Dr. Devin Thornburg, Director, 516-877-4026, E-mail: thornburg@adelphi.edu. *Application contact:* Christine Murphy, Director of Admissions, 516-877-3050, Fax: 516-877-3039, E-mail: graduateadmissions@adelphi.edu.

Alabama Agricultural and Mechanical University, School of Graduate Studies, School of Education, Department of Curriculum and Instruction, Area in Secondary Education, Huntsville, AL 35811. Offers education (M Ed, Ed S); higher administration (MS). *Accreditation:* NCATE. Evening/weekend programs available. *Faculty:* 8 full-time (3 women), 2 part-time/adjunct (0 women). *Students:* 50 full-time (36 women), 124 part-time (82 women); includes 128 minority (122 African Americans, 3 Asian Americans or Pacific Islanders, 3 Hispanic Americans), 4 international. In 2006, 47 degrees awarded. *Degree requirements:* For master's, comprehensive exam; for Ed S, thesis. *Entrance requirements:* For master's, GRE General Test. *Application deadline:* For fall admission, 5/1 for domestic students. Applications are processed on a rolling basis. Application fee: $25. Electronic applications accepted. *Financial support:* In 2006–07, 2 research assistantships (averaging $5,300 per year) were awarded; career-related internships or fieldwork, Federal Work-Study, institutionally sponsored loans, and traineeships also available. Financial award application deadline: 4/1. *Faculty research:* World peace through education, computer-assisted instruction. *Unit head:* Dr. Bruce Crawford, Chairperson, 256-372-5520, Fax: 256-372-5526.

Alabama State University, School of Graduate Studies, College of Education, Department of Instructional Support, Program in Educational Administration, Montgomery, AL 36101-0271. Offers educational administration (M Ed, Ed S); educational leadership, policy and law (Ed D). Part-time programs available. *Students:* 16 full-time (11 women), 128 part-time (84 women); includes 108 minority (all African Americans) Average age 45. In 2006, 31 master's, 4 other advanced degrees awarded. *Degree requirements:* For master's, thesis optional; for Ed S, thesis. *Entrance requirements:* For master's, GRE General Test, MAT, graduate writing competency test; for Ed S, graduate writing competency test, GRE, MAT. Additional exam requirements/recommendations for international students: Required—TOEFL (minimum score 500 paper-based; 173 computer-based). *Application deadline:* For fall admission, 7/15 for domestic students; for spring admission, 12/15 for domestic students. Applications are processed on a rolling basis. Application fee: $10. *Expenses:* Tuition, state resident: full-time $1,728; part-time $192 per hour. Tuition, nonresident: full-time $3,456; part-time $334 per hour. *Financial support:* In 2006–07, research assistantships (averaging $9,450 per year). *Faculty research:* Nontraditional roles, computer applications for principals, women in educational administration. *Unit head:* Dr. Hyacinth Findlay, Coordinator, 334-229-4417, E-mail: hfindlay@alasu.edu.

Albany State University, College of Education, Program in Educational Administration and Supervision, Albany, GA 31705-2717. Offers M Ed, Certificate, Ed S. *Accreditation:* NCATE. Part-time programs available. *Degree requirements:* For master's, comprehensive exam; for other advanced degree, PRAXIS II. *Entrance requirements:* For master's, GRE General Test, MAT or NTE, minimum GPA of 2.5; for other advanced degree, GRE General Test, MAT. Electronic applications accepted. *Faculty research:* Student achievement, student motivation, preparing teachers for technology, student attitude toward science, education e-courses.

Alliant International University–Fresno, Graduate School of Education, Program in Educational Leadership, Fresno, CA 93727. Offers educational leadership and management (Ed D). Part-time programs available. *Students:* 1 (woman) full-time, 33 part-time (27 women); includes 19 minority (6 African Americans, 1 American Indian/Alaska Native, 2 Asian Americans or Pacific Islanders, 10 Hispanic Americans), 1 international. Average age 50. In 2006, 2 degrees awarded. *Entrance requirements:* For doctorate, minimum GPA of 3.0, letters of recommendation. Additional exam requirements/recommendations for international students: Required—TOEFL (minimum score 550 paper-based; 213 computer-based), TWE (minimum score 5). *Application deadline:* For fall admission, 7/1 priority date for domestic and international students; for spring admission, 12/1 priority date for domestic and international students. Applications are processed on a rolling basis. Application fee: $55. Electronic applications accepted. *Financial support:* Federal Work-Study, institutionally sponsored loans, and scholarships/grants available. Financial award application deadline: 2/15; financial award applicants required to submit FAFSA. *Faculty research:* School administration, cross cultural leadership. *Unit head:* Dr. Xuanning Fu, Program Coordinator, 866-825-8426, Fax: 559-253-2267, E-mail: admissions@alliant.edu. *Application contact:* Alliant International University Central Contact Center, 866-U-ALLIANT, Fax: 858-635-4555, E-mail: admissions@alliant.edu.

See Close-Up on page 1097.

Alliant International University–Irvine, Graduate School of Education, Educational Leadership Programs, Irvine, CA 92612. Offers educational administration (MA, Credential); educational leadership and management (K-12) (Ed D); higher education (Ed D); preliminary administrative services (Credential). Part-time programs available. *Students:* 11. In 2006, 8 master's, 4 doctorates awarded. *Entrance requirements:* For master's and doctorate, minimum GPA of 3.0, letters of recommendation. Additional exam requirements/recommendations for international students: Required—TOEFL (minimum score 550 paper-based; 213 computer-based), TWE (minimum score 5). *Application deadline:* For fall admission, 7/1 priority date for domestic and international students; for spring admission, 12/1 priority date for domestic and international students. Applications are processed on a rolling basis. Application fee: $55. Electronic applications accepted. *Financial support:* Federal Work-Study, institutionally sponsored loans, and scholarships/grants available. Financial award application deadline: 2/15. *Unit head:* Dr. Suzanne Power, Acting Director, 866-825-5426, Fax: 949-833-3507, E-mail: admissions@alliant.edu. *Application contact:* Alliant International University Central Contact Center, 866-U-ALLIANT, Fax: 858-635-4555, E-mail: admissions@alliant.edu.

See Close-Up on page 1097.

Alliant International University–Los Angeles, Graduate School of Education, Educational Leadership Programs, Alhambra, CA 91803-1360. Offers educational administration (MA); educational leadership and management (K-12) (Ed D); higher education (Ed D); preliminary administrative services (Credential). Part-time programs available. *Students:* 14 (9 women). In 2006, 13 degrees awarded. *Entrance requirements:* For master's and doctorate, minimum GPA of 3.0, letters of recommendation. Additional exam requirements/recommendations for international students: Required—TOEFL (minimum score 550 paper-based; 213 computer-based), TWE (minimum score 5). *Application deadline:* For fall admission, 7/1 priority date for domestic students, 7/1 for international students; for spring admission, 12/1 priority date for domestic students, 12/1 for international students. Application fee: $55. *Financial support:* Federal Work-Study, institutionally sponsored loans, and scholarships/grants available. Financial award application deadline: 2/15; financial award applicants required to submit FAFSA. *Unit head:* Dr. Suzanne Power, Acting Director, 866-825-5426, Fax: 620-284-0550, E-mail: admissions@alliant.edu. *Application contact:* Alliant International University Central Contact Center, 866-U-ALLIANT, Fax: 858-635-4555, E-mail: admissions@alliant.edu.

See Close-Up on page 1097.

Alliant International University–San Diego, Graduate School of Education, Educational Leadership Programs, San Diego, CA 92131-1799. Offers educational administration (MA);

educational leadership and management (K-12) (Ed D); higher education (Ed D, Certificate); preliminary administrative services (Credential). Part-time programs available. *Faculty:* 2 full-time (0 women), 15 part-time/adjunct (6 women). *Students:* 39 full-time (30 women), 44 part-time (33 women); includes 28 minority (14 African Americans, 2 American Indian/Alaska Native, 4 Asian Americans or Pacific Islanders, 8 Hispanic Americans), 4 international. In 2006, 4 master's, 10 doctorates awarded. *Entrance requirements:* For master's and doctorate, minimum GPA of 3.0, letters of recommendation. Additional exam requirements/recommendations for international students: Required—TOEFL (minimum score 550 paper-based; 213 computer-based), TWE (minimum score 5). *Application deadline:* For fall admission, 7/1 priority date for domestic and international students; for spring admission, 12/1 priority date for domestic and international students. Applications are processed on a rolling basis. Application fee: $55. Electronic applications accepted. *Expenses:* Tuition: Part-time $825 per unit. Tuition and fees vary according to course load, degree level and program. *Financial support:* In 2006–07, 75 students received support. Federal Work-Study, institutionally sponsored loans, and scholarships/grants available. Financial award application deadline: 2/15; financial award applicants required to submit FAFSA. *Unit head:* Dr. Suzanne Borman, Acting Director, 866-825-5426, Fax: 858-635-4739, E-mail: admissions@alliant.edu. *Application contact:* Alliant International University Central Contact Center, 866-U-ALLIANT, Fax: 858-635-4555, E-mail: admissions@alliant.edu.

See Close-Up on page 1097.

Alliant International University–San Francisco, Graduate School of Education, Educational Leadership Programs, San Francisco, CA 94133-1221. Offers community college administration (Ed D); educational administration (MA); educational leadership and management (K-12) (Ed D); higher education (Ed D); preliminary administrative services (Credential); university administration (Ed D). Part-time programs available. *Faculty:* 2 full-time (0 women), 4 part-time/adjunct. *Students:* 1 (woman) full-time, 21 part-time (11 women); includes 9 minority (3 African Americans, 1 American Indian/Alaska Native, 1 Asian American or Pacific Islander, 4 Hispanic Americans), 2 international. Average age 45. 5 applicants, 60% accepted, 3 enrolled. In 2006, 2 degrees awarded. *Entrance requirements:* For master's and doctorate, minimum GPA of 3.0, letters of recommendation. Additional exam requirements/recommendations for international students: Required—TOEFL (minimum score 550 paper-based; 213 computer-based), TWE (minimum score 5). *Application deadline:* For fall admission, 7/1 priority date for domestic and international students; for spring admission, 12/1 priority date for domestic and international students. Applications are processed on a rolling basis. Application fee: $70. Electronic applications accepted. *Expenses:* Tuition: Part-time $825 per unit. Tuition and fees vary according to course load, degree level and program. *Financial support:* Federal Work-Study, institutionally sponsored loans, and scholarships/grants available. Financial award application deadline: 2/15; financial award applicants required to submit FAFSA. *Faculty research:* Leadership in higher education, community colleges. *Unit head:* Dr. Joseph Adwere-Boamah, Program Coordinator, 415-955-2103, Fax: 415-955-2179, E-mail: admissions@alliant.edu. *Application contact:* Jen Kulbeck, Alliant International University Central Contact Center, 866-U-ALLIANT, Fax: 858-635-4555, E-mail: admissions@alliant.edu.

See Close-Up on page 1097.

Alverno College, School of Education, Milwaukee, WI 53234-3922. Offers adaptive education (MA); administrative leadership (MA); adult education and organizational development (MA); adult educational and instructional design (MA); adult educational and instructional technology (MA); instructional leadership (MA); instructional technology for K-12 settings (MA); professional development (MA); reading education (MA); reading education with adaptive education (MA); science education (MA); teaching in alternative schools (MA). *Accreditation:* NCATE. Part-time and evening/weekend programs available. *Faculty:* 12 full-time (11 women), 12 part-time/adjunct (10 women). *Students:* 83 full-time (68 women), 74 part-time (60 women); includes 37 minority (32 African Americans, 2 American Indian/Alaska Native, 3 Hispanic Americans). Average age 35. 61 applicants, 82% accepted, 41 enrolled. In 2006, 46 degrees awarded. *Degree requirements:* For master's, presentation/defense of proposal, conference presentation of inquiry projects. *Entrance requirements:* For master's, bachelor's degree in related field, communication samples from work setting, 3 letters of recommendation. Additional exam requirements/recommendations for international students: Required—TOEFL. *Application deadline:* For fall admission, 8/1 priority date for domestic and international students; for spring admission, 12/15 priority date for domestic and international students. Applications are processed on a rolling basis. Application fee: $20. Electronic applications accepted. *Expenses:* Tuition: Full-time $9,288; part-time $516 per credit. Required fees: $250; $125 per semester. Tuition and fees vary according to program. *Financial support:* In 2006–07, 92 students received support. Federal Work-Study available. Support available to part-time students. Financial award application deadline: 4/15; financial award applicants required to submit FAFSA. *Faculty research:* Student self-assessment, self-reflection, integration of curriculum, identifying needs of students in strategic situations and designing appropriate classroom strategies, implementing guided. *Unit head:* Dr. Mary Diez, Graduate Dean, 414-382-6214, Fax: 414-382-6332, E-mail: mary.diez@alverno.edu. *Application contact:* Sarajane Kennedy, Associate Director, Admissions Graduate Programs, 414-382-6104, Fax: 414-382-6332, E-mail: sarajane.kennedy@alverno.edu.

American InterContinental University Online, Program in Education, Hoffman Estates, IL 60192. Offers curriculum and instruction (M Ed); educational assessment and evaluation (M Ed); instructional technology (M Ed); leadership of educational organizations (M Ed). Evening/weekend programs available. Postbaccalaureate distance learning degree programs offered (no on-campus study). *Entrance requirements:* Additional exam requirements/recommendations for international students: Required—TOEFL (minimum score 550 paper-based; 213 computer-based). *Application deadline:* Applications are processed on a rolling basis. Application fee: $50. Electronic applications accepted. *Financial support:* Institutionally sponsored loans and scholarships/grants available. Financial award applicants required to submit FAFSA. *Unit head:* Kerri J Holloway, Vice President of Academic Affairs, 847-851-5000 Ext. 15399, Fax: 847-586-6309, E-mail: kholloway@aivonline.edu. *Application contact:* 877-701-3800, E-mail: info@aiuonline.edu.

American International College, School of Psychology and Education, Department of Education, Springfield, MA 01109-3189. Offers administration (M Ed, CAGS); child development (MA, Ed D), including educational psychology; elementary education (M Ed, CAGS); reading (M Ed, CAGS); secondary education (M Ed, CAGS); special education (M Ed, CAGS); teaching (MAT). Part-time and evening/weekend programs available. *Faculty:* 5 full-time (3 women), 15 part-time/adjunct (9 women). *Students:* 31 full-time (27 women), 268 part-time (217 women); includes 25 minority (13 African Americans, 4 Asian Americans or Pacific Islanders, 8 Hispanic Americans), 2 international. Average age 39. In 2006, 38 master's, 2 doctorates, 5 other advanced degrees awarded. Terminal master's awarded for partial completion of doctoral program. *Degree requirements:* For master's, thesis (for some programs), practicum, comprehensive exam (for some programs), registration; for doctorate, thesis/dissertation, comprehensive exam (for some programs), registration; for CAGS, practicum. *Entrance requirements:* For master's, minimum B- average in undergraduate course work; for doctorate, GRE General Test, interview. Additional exam requirements/recommendations for international students: Required—TOEFL. *Application deadline:* For fall admission, 7/1 priority date for domestic and international students; for spring admission, 12/1 priority date for domestic and international students. Applications are processed on a rolling basis. Application fee: $50. *Expenses:* Tuition: Part-time $585 per semester hour. Required fees: $100 per year. Full-time tuition and fees vary according to program. *Financial support:* Career-related internships or fieldwork and institutionally sponsored loans available. Financial award applicants required to submit FAFSA. *Unit head:* Dr. Barbara Dautrich, Chair, 413-205-3407, Fax: 413-205-3943, E-mail: barbara.dautrich@aic.edu. *Application contact:* Keshawn Dodds, Associate Director of Graduate Admissions, 413-205-3549, Fax: 413-205-3911, E-mail: keshawn.dodds@aic.edu.

American University, College of Arts and Sciences, School of Education, Teaching, and Health, Program in Education, Washington, DC 20016-8001. Offers education (PhD); educational leadership (MA); educational technology (MA). Part-time and evening/weekend programs available. In 2006, 6 degrees awarded. *Entrance requirements:* For doctorate, GRE General Test or MAT, minimum GPA of 3.0. *Application deadline:* For fall admission, 2/1 priority date for domestic students; for spring admission, 10/1 priority date for domestic students. Applications are processed on a rolling basis. Application fee: $50. *Expenses:* Tuition: Full-time $18,864; part-time $1,048 per credit. Required fees: $380. Tuition and fees vary according to program. *Financial support:* Fellowships with full tuition reimbursements, research assistantships with partial tuition reimbursements, teaching assistantships, career-related internships or fieldwork, Federal Work-Study, and institutionally sponsored loans available. Support available to part-time students. Financial award application deadline: 2/1; financial award applicants required to submit FAFSA.

Andrews University, School of Graduate Studies, School of Education, Department of Leadership, Program in Educational Administration and Leadership, Berrien Springs, MI 49104. Offers MA, Ed D, PhD, Ed S. *Degree requirements:* For master's, thesis or alternative; for doctorate, thesis/dissertation. *Entrance requirements:* For master's and doctorate, GRE Subject Test.

Andrews University, School of Graduate Studies, School of Education, Department of Leadership, Program in Leadership, Berrien Springs, MI 49104. Offers MA, Ed D, PhD.

Angelo State University, College of Graduate Studies, College of Education, Department of Teacher Education, Program in School Administration, San Angelo, TX 76909. Offers M Ed. Part-time and evening/weekend programs available. *Faculty:* 17 full-time (12 women). *Students:* 5 full-time (1 woman), 82 part-time (46 women); includes 15 minority (2 African Americans, 1 American Indian/Alaska Native, 12 Hispanic Americans). Average age 40. 31 applicants, 94% accepted, 26 enrolled. In 2006, 13 degrees awarded. *Degree requirements:* For master's, comprehensive exam. *Entrance requirements:* For master's, GRE General Test, minimum GPA of 2.5. Additional exam requirements/recommendations for international students: Required—TOEFL or IELTS. *Application deadline:* For fall admission, 7/15 priority date for domestic students, 6/15 for international students; for spring admission, 12/8 for domestic students, 11/1 for international students. Applications are processed on a rolling basis. Application fee: $40 ($50 for international students). Electronic applications accepted. *Expenses:* Tuition, state resident: full-time $2,340; part-time $130 per hour. Tuition, nonresident: full-time $7,290; part-time $405 per hour. Required fees: $906; $56 per hour. *Financial support:* In 2006–07, 19 students received support. Career-related internships or fieldwork, Federal Work-Study, scholarships/grants, and unspecified assistantships available. Support available to part-time students. Financial award application deadline: 3/1; financial award applicants required to submit FAFSA. *Application contact:* Dr. K. Fritz Leifeste, Head, 325-942-2052 Ext. 266, E-mail: fritz.leifeste@angelo.edu.

Antioch University McGregor, Graduate Programs, Community College Management Program, Yellow Springs, OH 45387-1609. Offers MA. Postbaccalaureate distance learning degree programs offered. *Faculty:* 1 (woman) full-time, 5 part-time/adjunct (1 woman). *Students:* 21 full-time (14 women); includes 7 minority (6 African Americans, 1 Asian American or Pacific Islander). Average age 44. In 2006, 14 degrees awarded. *Degree requirements:* For master's, registration. *Entrance requirements:* For master's, 2 letters of reference, resumé. *Application deadline:* For fall admission, 9/1 for domestic students; for winter admission, 12/1 for domestic students; for spring admission, 3/10 for domestic students. Applications are processed on a rolling basis. Application fee: $50. Electronic applications accepted. *Expenses: Contact institution. Financial support:* Federal Work-Study available. Financial award applicants required to submit FAFSA. *Unit head:* Michael Robinson, Director, 937-769-1877, Fax: 937-769-1805, E-mail: rrobinson@mcgregor.edu. *Application contact:* Seth Gordon, Enrollment Services Officer, 937-769-1800 Ext. 1825, Fax: 937-769-1804, E-mail: sgordon@mcgregor.edu.

Antioch University New England, Graduate School, Department of Organization and Management, Program in Educational Administration and Supervision, Keene, NH 03431-3552. Offers M Ed. *Faculty:* 3 full-time (1 woman), 5 part-time/adjunct (3 women). *Students:* 10 full-time (8 women), 1 (woman) part-time. Average age 40. 12 applicants, 100% accepted, 10 enrolled. In 2006, 9 degrees awarded. *Degree requirements:* For master's, practicum. *Entrance requirements:* For master's, previous course work and work experience in organization and management. Additional exam requirements/recommendations for international students: Required—TOEFL (minimum score 600 paper-based; 250 computer-based). *Application deadline:* For fall admission, 8/1 for domestic and international students; for spring admission, 12/1 for domestic and international students. Applications are processed on a rolling basis. Application fee: $50. Electronic applications accepted. *Expenses: Contact institution.* Tuition and fees vary according to program and student level. *Financial support:* Career-related internships or fieldwork and Federal Work-Study available. Financial award applicants required to submit FAFSA. *Faculty research:* Collaborative research programs in Waldorf schools and communities, shared decision making in schools, rational to creative problem solving, competency to shift paradigms of thinking. *Unit head:* Dr. Steven P. Guerriero, Director, 603-283-2410, Fax: 603-357-0718, E-mail: sguerriero@antiochne.edu. *Application contact:* Leatrice A. Oram, Co-Director of Admissions, 800-490-3310, Fax: 603-357-0718, E-mail: admissions@antiochne.edu.

See Close-Up on page 205.

Appalachian State University, Cratis D. Williams Graduate School, College of Education, Department of Leadership and Educational Studies, Program in School Administration, Boone, NC 28608. Offers educational administration (Ed S); school administration (MSA). *Accreditation:* NCATE. *Students:* 53 full-time (33 women), 108 part-time (62 women); includes 17 minority (all African Americans) 50 applicants, 78% accepted, 38 enrolled. In 2006, 63 degrees awarded. *Degree requirements:* For master's, thesis or alternative, comprehensive exam. *Entrance requirements:* For master's, GRE General Test. *Application deadline:* For fall admission, 4/1 for domestic students; for spring admission, 11/1 for domestic students. Application fee: $45. *Expenses:* Tuition, state resident: full-time $2,600; part-time $127 per hour. Tuition, nonresident: full-time $13,200; part-time $597 per hour. Required fees: $2,000; $546 per term. *Financial support:* Research assistantships, Federal Work-Study, scholarships/grants, and unspecified assistantships available. Financial award application deadline: 7/1. *Faculty research:* Educational policy, leadership praxis, classroom assessment, leadership of teaching and learning, organizational theory.

Appalachian State University, Cratis D. Williams Graduate School, College of Education, Program in Educational Leadership, Boone, NC 28608. Offers Ed D. *Accreditation:* NCATE. Part-time programs available. *Students:* 11 full-time (8 women), 45 part-time (27 women); includes 4 minority (all African Americans), 1 international. 31 applicants, 48% accepted, 15 enrolled. In 2006, 3 degrees awarded. *Degree requirements:* For doctorate, thesis/dissertation, comprehensive exam. *Entrance requirements:* For doctorate, GRE General Test. Additional exam requirements/recommendations for international students: Required—TOEFL (minimum score 570 paper-based; 230 computer-based). *Application deadline:* For fall admission, 7/1 for domestic students, 1/1 for international students; for spring admission, 6/1 for international students. Application fee: $50. *Expenses:* Tuition, state resident: full-time $2,600; part-time $127 per hour. Tuition, nonresident: full-time $13,200; part-time $597 per hour. Required fees: $2,000; $546 per term. *Financial support:* In 2006–07, 8 research assistantships (averaging $16,000 per year) were awarded; Federal Work-Study, scholarships/grants, and unspecified assistantships also available. Financial award application deadline: 7/1. *Faculty research:* Sustainability of organizations, cultural pedagogy. *Unit head:* Dr. Alice Naylor, Director, 828-262-3168, E-mail: naylorap@appstate.edu.

Arcadia University, Graduate Studies, Department of Education, Glenside, PA 19038-3295. Offers art education (M Ed, MA Ed); biology education (MA Ed); chemistry education (MA Ed); child development (CAS); computer education (M Ed, CAS); computer education 7–12 (MA Ed); early childhood education (M Ed, CAS), including individualized (M Ed), master teacher

Educational Administration

Arcadia University (continued)
(M Ed), research in child development (M Ed); educational leadership (M Ed, CAS); educational psychology (CAS); elementary education (M Ed, CAS); English education (MA Ed); environmental education (MA Ed, CAS); history education (MA Ed); language arts (M Ed, CAS); mathematics education (M Ed, MA Ed, CAS); music education (MA Ed); psychology (MA Ed); pupil personnel services (CAS); reading (M Ed, CAS); school library science (M Ed); science education (M Ed, CAS); secondary education (M Ed, CAS); special education (M Ed, Ed D, CAS); theater arts (MA Ed); written communication (MA Ed). *Accreditation:* NASAD. Part-time and evening/weekend programs available. Postbaccalaureate distance learning degree programs offered (minimal on-campus study). *Faculty:* 12 full-time (8 women), 38 part-time/adjunct (26 women). *Students:* 60 full-time (56 women), 419 part-time (324 women); includes 70 minority (57 African Americans, 1 American Indian/Alaska Native, 6 Asian Americans or Pacific Islanders, 6 Hispanic Americans), 1 international. In 2006, 257 master's, 4 doctorates awarded. *Application deadline:* Applications are processed on a rolling basis. Application fee: $35. Electronic applications accepted. *Financial support:* Career-related internships or fieldwork, tuition waivers (partial), and unspecified assistantships available. *Unit head:* Dr. Steven P. Gulkus, Chair, 215-572-2120. *Application contact:* 215-572-2925, Fax: 215-572-2126, E-mail: grad@arcadia.edu.

Argosy University, Atlanta Campus, College of Education, Atlanta, GA 30328. Offers educational leadership (MAEd, Ed D, Ed S), including higher education administration (Ed D), k-12 administration (Ed D); instructional leadership (MAEd, Ed D, Ed S), including higher education (Ed D), K-12 education (Ed D). Evening/weekend programs available. *Students:* 459 full-time (377 women), 324 part-time (255 women); includes 388 minority (335 African Americans, 10 American Indian/Alaska Native, 14 Asian Americans or Pacific Islanders, 29 Hispanic Americans). *Entrance requirements:* For master's and doctorate, 3 letters of recommendation, minimum GPA of 3.0, resumé. Additional exam requirements/recommendations for international students: Required—TOEFL (minimum score 550 paper-based; 213 computer-based). *Application deadline:* For fall admission, 8/1 for domestic students; for spring admission, 10/1 for domestic students. Application fee: $50. *Financial support:* Teaching assistantships, Federal Work-Study available. *Unit head:* Jacqueline Jenkins, Department Chair, 770-407-1067, Fax: 770-671-0476, E-mail: jbeard@argosy.edu. *Application contact:* Christa Holton, Director of Admissions, 770-671-1200, Fax: 770-671-9050, E-mail: inquiry@argosy.edu.

See Close-Up on page 1101.

Argosy University, Chicago Campus, College of Education, Chicago, IL 60603. Offers community college executive leadership (Ed D); educational leadership (MA Ed, Ed D, Ed S), including administrative certification (MA Ed), district leadership (Ed D), higher education administration (Ed D), K-12 education (Ed D), principal/general (MA Ed), superintendent certification (Ed S); instructional leadership (MA Ed, Ed D, Ed S), including higher education (Ed D), K-12 education (Ed D). Part-time and evening/weekend programs available. *Faculty:* 3 full-time (1 woman), 7 part-time/adjunct (0 women). *Students:* 116 full-time (96 women), 42 part-time (32 women); includes 112 minority (108 African Americans, 1 Asian American or Pacific Islander, 3 Hispanic Americans). Average age 45. 56 applicants, 84% accepted, 45 enrolled. In 2006, 4 master's, 10 doctorates awarded. *Entrance requirements:* For master's and doctorate, minimum GPA of 3.0. Additional exam requirements/recommendations for international students: Required—TOEFL (minimum score 550 paper-based; 213 computer-based). *Application deadline:* For fall admission, 2/28 for domestic and international students; for spring admission, 10/30 for domestic and international students. Applications are processed on a rolling basis. Application fee: $50. Electronic applications accepted. *Financial support:* In 2006–07, 35 students received support. Scholarships/grants available. Financial award application deadline: 4/1. *Unit head:* Dr. Paul Busceni, Head, 800-626-4123, Fax: 312-777-7750, E-mail: pbusceni@argosy.edu. *Application contact:* Ashley Delaney, Director of Admissions, 800-626-4123, Fax: 312-777-7750, E-mail: argosyadmissions@argosy.edu.

See Close-Up on page 825.

Argosy University, Dallas Campus, College of Education, Dallas, TX 75231. Offers educational leadership (MA Ed); instructional leadership (MA Ed). Part-time and evening/weekend programs available. *Degree requirements:* For master's, capstone project. *Entrance requirements:* For master's, minimum GPA of 3.0, resumé, 3 letters of recommendation. Additional exam requirements/recommendations for international students: Required—TOEFL (minimum score 550 paper-based; 213 computer-based). *Application deadline:* For fall admission, 5/15 priority date for international students; for spring admission, 10/15 priority date for international students. Applications are processed on a rolling basis. Application fee: $50. Electronic applications accepted. *Financial support:* Federal Work-Study and scholarships/grants available. *Unit head:* Dr. Susan Bryza, Education Program Chair, E-mail: sbryza@argosy.edu. *Application contact:* Kara Smith, Director of Admissions, 214-459-2208, Fax: 214-378-8555, E-mail: dallas.admissions@argosyu.edu.

See Close-Up on page 827.

Argosy University, Denver Campus, College of Education, Denver, CO 80203. Offers educational leadership (MA Ed, Ed D), including higher education adminstration (Ed D), K-12 education (Ed D); instructional leadership (MA Ed, Ed D), including higher education (Ed D), K-12 education (Ed D).

See Close-Up on page 829.

Argosy University, Hawai'i Campus, College of Education, Honolulu, HI 96813. Offers educational leadership (MAEd, Ed D), including higher education administration (Ed D), K-12 education (Ed D); instructional leadership (MAEd, Ed D), including higher education (Ed D), K-12 education (Ed D). *Faculty:* 9 part-time/adjunct (4 women). *Students:* 26 full-time (18 women), 4 part-time (all women); includes 16 minority (13 Asian Americans or Pacific Islanders, 3 Hispanic Americans). 17 applicants, 94% accepted, 14 enrolled. *Degree requirements:* For doctorate, thesis/dissertation. *Entrance requirements:* Additional exam requirements/recommendations for international students: Required—TOEFL (minimum score 550 paper-based; 214 computer-based). *Application deadline:* For fall admission, 1/15 priority date for domestic students; for spring admission, 10/15 for domestic students. Applications are processed on a rolling basis. Application fee: $50. Electronic applications accepted. *Unit head:* Dr. Kristine Lesperance, Chair, 888-323-2777, Fax: 808-536-5505, E-mail: klesperance@argosy.edu. *Application contact:* Cherie Andrade, Director of Admissions, 888-323-2777, Fax: 808-536-5505, E-mail: candrade@argosy.edu.

See Close-Up on page 831.

Argosy University, Inland Empire Campus, College of Education, San Bernardino, CA 92408. Offers community college executive leadership (Ed D); educational leadership (MA Ed, Ed D), including higher education administration (Ed D), K-12 education (Ed D); instructional leadership (MA Ed, Ed D), including higher education (Ed D), K-12 education (Ed D), multiple subject teacher credential preparation (MA Ed), multiple subject teacher credntial preparation with BCLAD (MA Ed), single subject teacher credential preparation (MA Ed), single subject teacher credential preparation with BCLAD (MA Ed).

See Close-Up on page 1103.

Argosy University, Nashville Campus, College of Education, Program in Educational Leadership, Franklin, TN 37067-7226. Offers educational leadership (MA Ed); higher education administration (Ed D); K-12 education (Ed D).

See Close-Up on page 1105.

Argosy University, Nashville Campus, College of Education, Program in Instructional Leadership, Franklin, TN 37067-7226. Offers higher education administration (Ed D); instructional leadership (MA Ed); K-12 education (Ed D).

Argosy University, Orange County Campus, College of Education, Santa Ana, CA 92704. Offers community college executive leadership (Ed D); educational leadership (MA Ed, Ed D), including higher education administration (Ed D), K-12 education (Ed D); instructional leadership (MA Ed, Ed D), including educational technology (Ed D), higher education (Ed D), K-12 education (Ed D), multiple subject teacher credential preparation (MA Ed), multiple subject teacher credential preparation with BCLAD (MA Ed), single subject teacher credential preparation (MA Ed), single subject teacher credential preparation with BCLAD (MA Ed). Part-time and evening/weekend programs available. *Faculty:* 3 full-time (2 women), 33 part-time/adjunct (15 women). *Students:* 185 full-time (112 women), 49 part-time (28 women). Average age 37. 91 applicants, 76 enrolled. In 2006, 58 master's, 17 doctorates awarded. Terminal master's awarded for partial completion of doctoral program. *Degree requirements:* For master's, comprehensive exam; for doctorate, thesis/dissertation, preliminary and final dissertation defense, comprehensive exam. *Entrance requirements:* For master's, minimum GPA of 3.0 in final 2 years of course work, 3 letters of recommendation, resumé; for doctorate, minimum GPA of 3.0 in graduate study, 3 letters of recommendation, resumé. Additional exam requirements/recommendations for international students: Required—TOEFL. *Application deadline:* Applications are processed on a rolling basis. Application fee: $50. Electronic applications accepted. *Financial support:* Federal Work-Study and scholarships/grants available. Support available to part-time students. Financial award applicants required to submit FAFSA. *Faculty research:* Educational leadership, higher education, qualitative research, K-12 education, multicultural education. *Unit head:* Dr. Christine Zeppos, Dean, 800-7196-9598, Fax: 714-437-1287, E-mail: czeppos@argosy.edu. *Application contact:* Mark Betz, Director of Admissions, 800-716-9598, Fax: 714-437-1697, E-mail: mbetz@argosy.edu.

See Close-Up on page 833.

Argosy University, Phoenix Campus, College of Education, Phoenix, AZ 85021. Offers community college executive leadership (Ed D); educational leadership (MA Ed, Ed D, Ed S), including higher education administration (Ed D), K-12 education (Ed D); instructional leadership (MA Ed, Ed D, Ed S), including higher education (Ed D), K-12 education (Ed D). Part-time and evening/weekend programs available. *Faculty:* 13 part-time/adjunct (4 women). *Students:* 26 full-time (17 women), 2 part-time (1 woman); includes 3 minority (2 African Americans, 1 Hispanic American). Average age 44. 10 applicants, 100% accepted, 9 enrolled. *Entrance requirements:* For doctorate, minimum GPA of 3.0, master's degree. Additional exam requirements/recommendations for international students: Required—TOEFL (minimum score 550 paper-based; 213 computer-based). *Application deadline:* Applications are processed on a rolling basis. Application fee: $50. Electronic applications accepted. *Financial support:* Federal Work-Study available. Financial award applicants required to submit FAFSA. *Unit head:* Dr. Gayle Schou, Director, 866-216-2777, E-mail: argosyadmissions@argosy.edu. *Application contact:* Andy Hughes, Director of Admissions, 866-216-2777, Fax: 602-216-2601, E-mail: ahughes@argosy.edu.

See Close-Up on page 835.

Argosy University, San Diego Campus, College of Education, San Diego, CA 92108. Offers community college executive leadership (Ed D); educational leadership (MA Ed, Ed D), including higher education administration (Ed D), K-12 education (Ed D); instructional leadership (MA Ed, Ed D), including higher education (Ed D), K-12 education (Ed D), multiple subject teacher credential preparation (MA Ed), multiple subject teacher credential preparation with BCLAD (MA Ed), single subject teacher credential preparation (MA Ed), single subject teacher credential preparation with BCLAD (MA Ed).

See Close-Up on page 837.

Argosy University, San Francisco Bay Area Campus, College of Education, Point Richmond, CA 94804-3547. Offers community college executive leadership (Ed D); educational leadership (MA Ed, Ed D), including higher education administration (Ed D), K–12 education (Ed D); instructional leadership (MA Ed, Ed D), including higher education (Ed D), K–12 education (Ed D), multiple subject teacher credential preparation (MA Ed), multiple subject teacher credential preparation with BCLAD (MA Ed), single subject teacher credential preparation (MA Ed), single subject teacher credential preparation with BCLAD (MA Ed). Part-time and evening/weekend programs available. Postbaccalaureate distance learning degree programs offered (minimal on-campus study). *Faculty:* 1 (woman) full-time, 14 part-time/adjunct. *Students:* 59 full-time (41 women), 30 part-time (14 women); includes 26 minority (11 African Americans, 11 Asian Americans or Pacific Islanders, 4 Hispanic Americans), 1 international. 34 applicants, 82% accepted, 20 enrolled. In 2006, 7 degrees awarded. *Degree requirements:* For master's, capstone project; for doctorate, thesis/dissertation, comprehensive exam, registration. *Entrance requirements:* For master's and doctorate, minimum GPA of 3.0. Additional exam requirements/recommendations for international students: Required—TOEFL (minimum score 550 paper-based; 213 computer-based). *Application deadline:* For fall admission, 7/1 priority date for domestic students, 7/1 for international students; for winter admission, 11/1 priority date for domestic and international students; for spring admission, 4/1 priority date for domestic and international students. Applications are processed on a rolling basis. Application fee: $50. Electronic applications accepted. *Financial support:* Career-related internships or fieldwork, Federal Work-Study, and scholarships/grants available. Support available to part-time students. Financial award application deadline: 4/20; financial award applicants required to submit FAFSA. *Unit head:* Dr. Keyes Kelly, 510-837-3740, E-mail: kkelly@argosy.edu. *Application contact:* John Vincent Stofan, Director, Admissions, 510-215-0277, Fax: 510-215-0299, E-mail: jstofan@argosy.edu.

See Close-Up on page 839.

Argosy University, Santa Monica Campus, College of Education, Santa Monica, CA 90405. Offers community college executive leadership (Ed D); educational leadership (MA Ed, Ed D), including higher education administration (Ed D), K-12 education (Ed D); instructional leadership (MA Ed, Ed D), including higher education (Ed D), K-12 education (Ed D), multiple subject teacher credential preparation (MA Ed), multiple subject teacher credential preparation with BCLAD (MA Ed), single subject teacher credential preparation (MA Ed), single subject teacher credential preparation with BCLAD (MA Ed).

See Close-Up on page 841.

Argosy University, Sarasota Campus, College of Education, Sarasota, FL 34235-8246. Offers community college educational leadership (Ed D); educational leadership (MA Ed, Ed D, Ed S), including higher education administration (Ed D), K-12 education (Ed D); instructional leadership (MA Ed, Ed D, Ed S), including education technology (Ed D), higher education (Ed D), K-12 education (Ed D). Part-time and evening/weekend programs available. Postbaccalaureate distance learning degree programs offered (minimal on-campus study). *Faculty:* 15 full-time (8 women), 49 part-time/adjunct (21 women). *Students:* 149 applicants, 96% accepted, 121 enrolled. In 2006, 9 master's, 141 doctorates awarded. *Degree requirements:* For doctorate, thesis/dissertation, comprehensive exam. *Entrance requirements:* For doctorate, minimum undergraduate GPA of 3.0. Additional exam requirements/recommendations for international students: Required—TOEFL. *Application deadline:* Applications are processed on a rolling basis. Application fee: $50. Electronic applications accepted. *Expenses:* Contact institution. *Financial support:* Federal Work-Study available. Support available to part-time students. Financial award application deadline: 4/1; financial award applicants required to submit FAFSA. *Unit head:* Dr. Chuck Mlynarczyk, Dean, 800-331-5995, Fax: 941-371-9464, E-mail: cmlynarczyk@argosy.edu. *Application contact:* Admissions Representative, 800-331-5995 Ext. 221, Fax: 941-371-8910.

See Close-Up on page 843.

Argosy University, Schaumburg Campus, College of Education, Schaumburg, IL 60173-5403. Offers community college executive leadership (Ed D); educational leadership (MA Ed, Ed D, Ed S), including administrative certification (MA Ed), higher education administration (Ed D), K-12 education (Ed D), principal/general (MA Ed), superintendent certification (Ed S);

instructional leadership (MA Ed, Ed D, Ed S), including higher education (Ed D), K-12 education (Ed D). Part-time and evening/weekend programs available. *Faculty:* 1 (woman) full-time, 7 part-time/adjunct (3 women). *Students:* 19 full-time, 19 part-time. 15 applicants, 80% accepted, 10 enrolled. In 2006, 1 master's, 3 doctorates, 2 other advanced degrees awarded. *Degree requirements:* For doctorate, thesis/dissertation, comprehensive exam. *Entrance requirements:* For master's and doctorate, minimum GPA of 3.0. Additional exam requirements/recommendations for international students: Required—TOEFL. *Application deadline:* For fall admission, 3/15 priority date for domestic and international students; for spring admission, 10/15 priority date for domestic and international students. Applications are processed on a rolling basis. Application fee: $50. Electronic applications accepted. *Expenses: Contact institution. Financial support:* Federal Work-Study and scholarships/grants available. *Unit head:* Dr. Narjis Hyder, Program Chair, 866-290-7400, Fax: 847-598-6158, E-mail: nhyder@argosy.edu. *Application contact:* Jamal Scott, Application Contact, 866-290-7400, Fax: 630-598-6191, E-mail: jscott@argosy.edu.

See Close-Up on page 845.

Argosy University, Seattle Campus, College of Education, Seattle, WA 98121. Offers community college executive leadership (Ed D); education (MA Ed); educational leadership (MA Ed, Ed D), including higher education administration (Ed D), K-12 education (Ed D); instructional leadership (MA Ed, Ed D), including education technology (Ed D), higher education (Ed D), K-12 education (Ed D). Part-time and evening/weekend programs available. *Students:* 29 full-time, 15 part-time. *Degree requirements:* For master's, thesis or alternative, capstone project; for doctorate, thesis/dissertation, comprehensive exam, registration. *Entrance requirements:* For master's, minimum GPA of 3.0 in last 60 hours of course work or minimum cumulative GPA of 2.7; for doctorate, minimum GPA of 3.0. Additional exam requirements/recommendations for international students: Required—TOEFL (minimum score 550 paper-based; 213 computer-based). *Application deadline:* For fall admission, 4/15 priority date for domestic students, 4/15 for international students. Application fee: $50. *Expenses: Contact institution. Financial support:* Teaching assistantships with partial tuition reimbursements, Federal Work-Study, scholarships/grants, and unspecified assistantships available. Support available to part-time students. Financial award application deadline: 4/19; financial award applicants required to submit FAFSA. *Unit head:* Dr. Leslie Aune Oja, Chair of Education, 206-393-3570, Fax: 206-283-5777, E-mail: ioja@argosy.edu. *Application contact:* Josh Pond, Director of Admissions, 206-283-4500, Fax: 206-283-5777, E-mail: jpond@argosyu.edu.

See Close-Up on page 847.

Argosy University, Tampa Campus, College of Education, Tampa, FL 33614. Offers community college executive leadership (Ed D); educational leadership (MA Ed, Ed D, Ed S), including higher education administration (Ed D), K-12 education (Ed D); instructional leadership (MA Ed, Ed D, Ed S), including higher education (Ed D), K-12 education (Ed D). *Faculty:* 1 (woman) full-time, 8 part-time/adjunct (3 women). *Degree requirements:* For master's, capstone project; for doctorate, thesis/dissertation. *Entrance requirements:* For master's, minimum GPA of 3.0 in last 2 years of undergraduate course work, resumé, 3 letters of recommendation; for doctorate, minimum GPA of 3.0, 3 letters of recommendation, resumé. Additional exam requirements/recommendations for international students: Required—TOEFL (minimum score 550 paper-based; 213 computer-based). *Application deadline:* Applications are processed on a rolling basis. Application fee: $50. Electronic applications accepted. *Faculty research:* Reading methods, elementary education, educational leadership, instructional design and instructional technology. *Unit head:* Dr. Patty O'Grady, Head, 813-246-4419, Fax: 813-246-4045, E-mail: pogrady@argosy.edu.

See Close-Up on page 849.

Argosy University, Twin Cities Campus, College of Education, Eagan, MN 55121. Offers educational leadership (MA Ed, Ed D, Ed S), including higher education administration (Ed D), K-12 education (Ed D); instructional leadership (MA Ed, Ed D, Ed S), including education technology (Ed D), higher education (Ed D), K-12 education (Ed D). Part-time and evening/weekend programs available. *Faculty:* 1 full-time (0 women), 10 part-time/adjunct (4 women). *Students:* 30 full-time (22 women), 12 part-time (9 women); includes 3 minority (1 African American, 1 American Indian/Alaska Native, 1 Asian American or Pacific Islander). Average age 45. 35 applicants, 86% accepted, 12 enrolled. In 2006, 1 master's, 6 doctorates awarded. *Degree requirements:* For doctorate, thesis/dissertation, comprehensive exam. *Entrance requirements:* For master's, 3 letters of recommendation, minimum undergraduate GPA of 3.0, resumé; for doctorate, 3 letters of recommendation, master's degree, minimum GPA of 3.0, resumé. Additional exam requirements/recommendations for international students: Required—TOEFL (minimum score 550 paper-based; 213 computer-based). *Application deadline:* For fall admission, 5/15 priority date for domestic students, 5/15 for international students; for spring admission, 10/15 priority date for domestic students, 10/15 for international students. Applications are processed on a rolling basis. Application fee: $50. Electronic applications accepted. *Financial support:* In 2006–07, 12 fellowships with partial tuition reimbursements, 3 teaching assistantships with partial tuition reimbursements were awarded; Federal Work-Study and scholarships/grants also available. Financial award applicants required to submit FAFSA. *Unit head:* Dr. David Lange, Program Chair, 888-844-2004. *Application contact:* Jennifer Radke, 2nd Director of Graduate Admissions, 651-846-3300, Fax: 651-994-7954, E-mail: tcadmissions@argosy.edu.

See Close-Up on page 851.

Argosy University, Washington DC Campus, College of Education, Arlington, VA 22209. Offers educational leadership (MA Ed, Ed D, Ed S), including higher education administration (Ed D), K-12 education (Ed D); instructional leadership (MA Ed, Ed D, Ed S), including higher education (Ed D), K-12 education (Ed D). Part-time and evening/weekend programs available. *Faculty:* 2 full-time (1 woman), 2 part-time/adjunct (0 women). *Students:* 22 full-time (16 women), 11 part-time (6 women); includes 24 minority (all African Americans) Average age 45. 16 applicants, 69% accepted, 9 enrolled. In 2006, 1 degree awarded. *Degree requirements:* For master's, thesis (for some programs), comprehensive exam (for some programs); for doctorate, thesis/dissertation, comprehensive exam. *Entrance requirements:* For master's and doctorate, minimum GPA of 3.0. Additional exam requirements/recommendations for international students: Required—TOEFL (minimum score 550 paper-based; 213 computer-based). *Application deadline:* For fall admission, 6/15 priority date for domestic and international students; for spring admission, 10/15 priority date for domestic and international students. Applications are processed on a rolling basis. Application fee: $50. Electronic applications accepted. *Financial support:* Federal Work-Study and scholarships/grants available. Financial award applicants required to submit FAFSA. *Unit head:* Dr. Colleen Logan, Academic Affairs Officer, 866-703-2777, Fax: 703-521-5850, E-mail: dcadmissions@argosy.edu. *Application contact:* Emily Peck, Director of Admissions, 866-703-2777 Ext. 5851, Fax: 703-526-5850, E-mail: dcadmissions@argosy.edu.

See Close-Up on page 853.

Arizona State University, Division of Graduate Studies, College of Education, Division of Educational Leadership and Policy Studies, Academic Program in Educational Leadership and Policy Studies, Tempe, AZ 85287. Offers PhD. *Degree requirements:* For doctorate, thesis/dissertation. *Entrance requirements:* For doctorate, GRE General Test or MAT.

Arizona State University, Division of Graduate Studies, College of Education, Division of Educational Leadership and Policy Studies, Academic Program of Educational Administration and Supervision, Tempe, AZ 85287. Offers M Ed, Ed D. *Degree requirements:* For master's, thesis or alternative; for doctorate, thesis/dissertation. *Entrance requirements:* For master's and doctorate, GRE General Test or MAT.

Arizona State University at the Polytechnic Campus, The School of Educational Innovation and Teacher Preparation, Mesa, AZ 85212. Offers administration/supervision (M Ed); curriculum and instruction (M Ed); physical education (MPE, PhD). *Faculty:* 9 full-time (6 women), 1 part-time/adjunct (0 women). *Students:* 86 full-time (74 women), 119 part-time (92 women); includes 18 minority (1 African American, 1 American Indian/Alaska Native, 5 Asian Americans or Pacific Islanders, 11 Hispanic Americans), 1 international. Average age 33. 94 applicants, 84% accepted, 65 enrolled. In 2006, 19 degrees awarded. *Degree requirements:* For master's, written comprehensive exam or applied project; for doctorate, thesis/dissertation. *Entrance requirements:* For master's, 3 letters of recommendation, minimum GPA of 3.0. *Application deadline:* For fall admission, 4/15 priority date for domestic and international students; for spring admission, 10/15 priority date for domestic and international students. Applications are processed on a rolling basis. Application fee: $50. Electronic applications accepted. *Expenses:* Tuition, state resident: part-time $310 per credit hour. Tuition, nonresident: part-time $688 per credit hour. *Financial support:* In 2006–07, 4 teaching assistantships with full tuition reimbursements (averaging $12,978 per year) were awarded; fellowships, research assistantships with full tuition reimbursements also available. Financial award applicants required to submit FAFSA.

Arizona State University at the West campus, College of Teacher Education and Leadership, Phoenix, AZ 85069-7100. Offers educational administration and supervision (M Ed); elementary education (M Ed, Certificate); leadership/innovation (administration) (Ed D); leadership/innovation (teaching) (Ed D); secondary education (M Ed, Certificate); special education (M Ed). Part-time and evening/weekend programs available. *Faculty:* 25 full-time (18 women), 27 part-time/adjunct (21 women). *Students:* 169 full-time (133 women), 245 part-time (200 women); includes 76 minority (16 African Americans, 8 American Indian/Alaska Native, 7 Asian Americans or Pacific Islanders, 45 Hispanic Americans), 3 international. Average age 35. 308 applicants, 63% accepted, 171 enrolled. In 2006, 84 degrees awarded. *Degree requirements:* For master's, applied project or comprehensive exams; for doctorate, thesis/dissertation, comprehensive exam. *Entrance requirements:* For master's, 3 letters of recommendation; for doctorate, master's degree in education or related field, 3 professional references, resumé. Additional exam requirements/recommendations for international students: Required—TOEFL (minimum score 550 paper-based; 213 computer-based; 83 iBT), IELTS (minimum score 7). *Application deadline:* Applications are processed on a rolling basis. Application fee: $50. Electronic applications accepted. *Expenses:* Tuition, state resident: full-time $5,930. Tuition, nonresident: full-time $16,516. Tuition and fees vary according to course load. *Financial support:* In 2006–07, 2 research assistantships with partial tuition reimbursements (averaging $16,413 per year) were awarded; fellowships with tuition reimbursements, career-related internships or fieldwork, institutionally sponsored loans, scholarships/grants, tuition waivers (full and partial), and unspecified assistantships also available. Support available to part-time students. Financial award application deadline: 4/1; financial award applicants required to submit FAFSA. *Faculty research:* Self-regulated learning in students, collaboration and consultation skills for educators, school reform and restructuring, hands-on science and mathematics programs, educational technology. *Unit head:* Dr. Mari Koerner, Dean, 602-543-6352, Fax: 602-543-6350, E-mail: mari.koerner@asu.edu. *Application contact:* Marie Wright, Administrative Assistant, 602-543-3634, Fax: 602-543-6350, E-mail: marie.wright@asu.edu or ctelgrad@asu.edu.

Arkansas State University, Graduate School, College of Education, Department of Educational Leadership, Curriculum, and Special Education, Jonesboro, State University, AR 72467. Offers community college administration education (SCCT); education theory and practice (MSE); educational leadership (MSE, Ed D, Ed S), including curriculum and instruction (Ed S), elementary curriculum and instruction (MSE), elementary principalship (Ed S), secondary principalship (Ed S), superintendency (Ed S); special education (MSE), including emotionally disturbed, gifted, talented and creative, instructional specialist 4-12, instructional specialist P-4; special education program administration (Ed S). *Accreditation:* NCATE. Part-time programs available. *Faculty:* 14 full-time (7 women), 5 part-time/adjunct (2 women). *Students:* 28 full-time (21 women), 328 part-time (233 women); includes 63 minority (58 African Americans, 3 American Indian/Alaska Native, 1 Asian American or Pacific Islander, 1 Hispanic American), 2 international. Average age 36. 181 applicants, 78% accepted, 70 enrolled. In 2006, 70 master's, 13 doctorates, 14 other advanced degrees awarded. *Degree requirements:* For master's, thesis or alternative, comprehensive exam; for doctorate, thesis/dissertation, comprehensive exam. *Entrance requirements:* For master's, GRE General Test or MAT, appropriate bachelor's degree, letters of reference, interview, official transcript; for doctorate and other advanced degree, GRE General Test or MAT, interview, master's degree, letters of reference, official transcript. Additional exam requirements/recommendations for international students: Required—TOEFL (minimum score 213 computer-based). *Application deadline:* Applications are processed on a rolling basis. Application fee: $30 ($40 for international students). Electronic applications accepted. *Expenses:* Tuition, state resident: full-time $3,393; part-time $189 per hour. Tuition, nonresident: full-time $8,577; part-time $477 per hour. Required fees: $752; $39 per hour. $25 per semester. *Financial support:* Teaching assistantships, career-related internships or fieldwork, scholarships/grants, and unspecified assistantships available. Financial award application deadline: 7/1; financial award applicants required to submit FAFSA. *Unit head:* Dr. Mitchell Holifield, Chair, 870-972-3062, Fax: 870-680-8130, E-mail: hfield@astate.edu.

Arkansas Tech University, Graduate School, School of Education, Russellville, AR 72801. Offers college student personnel (MSE); educational leadership (M Ed, Ed S); English education (M Ed); gifted education (MSE); instructional improvement (M Ed); secondary education (M Ed); teaching, learning and leadership (M Ed). *Accreditation:* NCATE. Part-time programs available. *Students:* 44 full-time (33 women), 244 part-time (181 women); includes 20 minority (14 African Americans, 1 American Indian/Alaska Native, 3 Asian Americans or Pacific Islanders, 2 Hispanic Americans), 18 international. Average age 34. In 2006, 72 master's, 4 other advanced degrees awarded. *Degree requirements:* For master's, action research project, thesis optional. *Entrance requirements:* For master's, GRE General Test or MAT. Additional exam requirements/recommendations for international students: Required—TOEFL (minimum score 500 paper-based; 173 computer-based). *Application deadline:* For fall admission, 3/1 priority date for domestic students, 5/1 priority date for international students; for winter admission, 10/1 priority date for international students; for spring admission, 10/1 priority date for domestic and international students. Applications are processed on a rolling basis. Application fee: $0 ($30 for international students). Electronic applications accepted. *Expenses:* Tuition, state resident: full-time $3,060; part-time $170 per hour. Tuition, nonresident: full-time $6,120; part-time $340 per hour. Required fees: $312; $4 per hour. $84 per term. Part-time tuition and fees vary according to course load. *Financial support:* In 2006–07, teaching assistantships with full tuition reimbursements (averaging $4,000 per year); career-related internships or fieldwork, Federal Work-Study, scholarships/grants, health care benefits, and unspecified assistantships also available. Support available to part-time students. Financial award application deadline: 4/15; financial award applicants required to submit FAFSA. *Unit head:* Dr. C. Glenn Sheets, Dean, 479-968-0350, Fax: 479-968-0350, E-mail: glenn.sheets@atu.edu. *Application contact:* Dr. Eldon G. Clary, Dean of Graduate School, 479-968-0398, Fax: 479-964-0542, E-mail: graduate.school@atu.edu.

Ashland University, College of Education, Doctoral Program in Educational Leadership Studies, Ashland, OH 44805-3702. Offers Ed D. Evening/weekend programs available. *Faculty:* 8 full-time (4 women), 1 (woman) part-time/adjunct. *Students:* 18 full-time (10 women), 21 part-time (12 women); includes 4 minority (2 African Americans, 1 American Indian/Alaska Native, 1 Hispanic American). Average age 42. 21 applicants, 71% accepted, 14 enrolled. In 2006, 5 degrees awarded. *Degree requirements:* For doctorate, thesis/dissertation, comprehensive exam, registration. *Entrance requirements:* For doctorate, GRE, master's degree, minimum GPA of 3.3, writing sample, letters of recommendation. Additional exam requirements/recommendations for international students: Required—TOEFL. *Application deadline:* For spring admission, 3/1 for domestic students. Applications are processed on a rolling basis. Application fee: $30. *Expenses: Contact institution.* Tuition and fees vary according to degree level and program. *Financial support:* In 2006–07, 12 students received support, including 8 teaching assistantships (averaging $2,800 per year). Financial award application deadline: 4/15. *Faculty research:* School funding, charter schools, administrative jobs, continuous improvement, marginalized groups. *Unit head:* Dr. W. Gregory Gerrick, Director, 419-289-5343, Fax: 419-289-5097, E-mail: ggerrick@ashland.edu.

Educational Administration

Ashland University, College of Education, Graduate Studies in Education, Program in Educational Administration, Ashland, OH 44805-3702. Offers administration (M Ed); business manager (M Ed); curriculum specialist (M Ed); principalship (M Ed); pupil services (M Ed); school treasurer (M Ed); superintendency (M Ed). Part-time programs available. *Faculty:* 10 full-time (3 women), 23 part-time/adjunct (6 women). *Students:* 134 full-time (76 women), 220 part-time (121 women); includes 27 minority (23 African Americans, 1 Asian American or Pacific Islander, 3 Hispanic Americans), 2 international. Average age 33. 68 applicants, 100% accepted, 68 enrolled. In 2006, 144 degrees awarded. *Degree requirements:* For master's, thesis or alternative, internship. *Entrance requirements:* For master's, teaching certificate, minimum GPA of 2.75. Additional exam requirements/recommendations for international students: Required—TOEFL. *Application deadline:* Applications are processed on a rolling basis. Application fee: $30. *Expenses:* Tuition: Part-time $403 per credit. Tuition and fees vary according to degree level and program. *Financial support:* In 2006–07, 116 students received support. Institutionally sponsored loans and scholarships/grants available. Financial award application deadline: 4/15. *Faculty research:* Gender and religious considerations in employment, ISLLC standards, adjunct faculty training, politics of school finance, ethnicity and employment. *Unit head:* Dr. John Bailey, Chair, 419-289-5396, Fax: 419-207-6702, E-mail: jbailey@ashland.edu. *Application contact:* Fred Slater, Director, Graduate Education, 419-289-5367, Fax: 419-207-4942, E-mail: fslater@ashland.edu.

Auburn University, Graduate School, College of Education, Department of Educational Foundations, Leadership, and Technology, Auburn University, AL 36849. Offers adult education (M Ed, MS, Ed D); curriculum and instruction (M Ed, MS, Ed D, Ed S); curriculum supervision (M Ed, MS, Ed D, Ed S); educational psychology (PhD); higher education administration (M Ed, MS, Ed D, Ed S); media instructional design (MS); media specialist (M Ed); school administration (M Ed, MS, Ed D, Ed S). *Accreditation:* NCATE. Part-time programs available. *Faculty:* 23 full-time (11 women). *Students:* 40 full-time (26 women), 148 part-time (93 women); includes 64 minority (60 African Americans, 3 American Indian/Alaska Native, 1 Asian American or Pacific Islander), 6 international. Average age 38. 99 applicants, 57% accepted, 37 enrolled. In 2006, 32 master's, 10 doctorates, 7 other advanced degrees awarded. *Degree requirements:* For master's, thesis (for some programs); for doctorate, thesis/dissertation; for Ed S, field project. *Entrance requirements:* For master's, doctorate, and Ed S, GRE General Test. *Application deadline:* For fall admission, 7/7 for domestic students; for spring admission, 11/24 for domestic students. Applications are processed on a rolling basis. Application fee: $25 ($50 for international students). Electronic applications accepted. *Expenses:* Tuition, state resident: full-time $5,000. Tuition, nonresident: full-time $15,000. Required fees: $416. Tuition and fees vary according to program. *Financial support:* Teaching assistantships, Federal Work-Study available. Support available to part-time students. Financial award application deadline: 3/15. *Unit head:* Dr. William A. Spencer, Head, 334-844-4460. *Application contact:* Dr. Joe Pittman, Interim Dean of the Graduate School, 334-844-4700.

Auburn University Montgomery, School of Education, Department of Counselor Leadership and Special Education, Montgomery, AL 36124-4023. Offers counseling (M Ed, Ed S); education administration (M Ed, Ed S); special education (M Ed, Ed S). *Accreditation:* NCATE. Part-time and evening/weekend programs available. *Faculty:* 8 full-time (4 women), 1 part-time/adjunct (0 women). *Students:* 34 full-time (28 women), 91 part-time (66 women); includes 75 minority (72 African Americans, 1 American Indian/Alaska Native, 1 Asian American or Pacific Islander, 1 Hispanic American). Average age 35. In 2006, 12 master's, 3 other advanced degrees awarded. *Degree requirements:* For master's and Ed S, comprehensive exam. *Entrance requirements:* For master's, GRE General Test or MAT, certification, BS in teaching; for Ed S, GRE General Test or MAT, certification. *Application deadline:* Applications are processed on a rolling basis. Application fee: $25. Electronic applications accepted. *Financial support:* In 2006–07, 1 teaching assistantship was awarded; career-related internships or fieldwork and scholarships/grants also available. Support available to part-time students. Financial award application deadline: 3/1; financial award applicants required to submit FAFSA. *Unit head:* Dr. James V. Wright, Head, 334-244-3457, Fax: 334-344-3102, E-mail: jwright@mail.aum.edu.

Augusta State University, Graduate Studies, College of Education, Program in Educational Leadership, Augusta, GA 30904-2200. Offers M Ed, Ed S. *Accreditation:* NCATE. Part-time and evening/weekend programs available. *Faculty:* 5 full-time (2 women), 1 part-time/adjunct (0 women). *Students:* 63 full-time (44 women), 63 part-time (44 women); includes 37 minority (34 African Americans, 1 Asian American or Pacific Islander, 2 Hispanic Americans). Average age 37. 42 applicants, 100% accepted, 21 enrolled. In 2006, 26 master's, 41 other advanced degrees awarded. *Degree requirements:* For master's, comprehensive exam; for Ed S, thesis, comprehensive exam. *Entrance requirements:* For master's, GRE, MAT, minimum GPA of 2.5; for Ed S, GRE, MAT. *Application deadline:* For fall admission, 8/1 priority date for domestic students. Applications are processed on a rolling basis. Application fee: $20. *Expenses:* Tuition, state resident: full-time $3,044; part-time $127 per credit hour. Tuition, nonresident: full-time $12,172; part-time $508 per credit hour. *Financial support:* In 2006–07, 2 students received support. Career-related internships or fieldwork, Federal Work-Study, institutionally sponsored loans, and unspecified assistantships available. Support available to part-time students. Financial award application deadline: 4/15; financial award applicants required to submit FAFSA. *Faculty research:* Restructuring schools, financing education, student transition. *Unit head:* Dr. Samuel B Hardy, Acting Chair, 706-737-1497, Fax: 706-667-4706, E-mail: shardy@aug.edu. *Application contact:* Andrea M. Scott, Secretary to the Dean, 706-737-1499, Fax: 706-667-4706, E-mail: ascott1@aug.edu.

Aurora University, College of Education, Aurora, IL 60506-4892. Offers curriculum and instruction (Ed D); education (MAT); education and administration (Ed D); educational leadership (MEL); reading instruction (MA). Part-time and evening/weekend programs available. *Faculty:* 20 full-time (10 women), 99 part-time/adjunct (55 women). *Students:* 144 full-time (102 women), 1,156 part-time (832 women); includes 169 minority (32 African Americans, 2 American Indian/Alaska Native, 10 Asian Americans or Pacific Islanders, 125 Hispanic Americans). Average age 36. 451 applicants, 99% accepted, 421 enrolled. In 2006, 439 master's, 9 doctorates awarded. *Degree requirements:* For doctorate, thesis/dissertation. *Entrance requirements:* For master's, 2 years of teaching experience, valid teaching certificate. Additional exam requirements/recommendations for international students: Required—TOEFL (minimum score 550 paper-based; 213 computer-based). *Application deadline:* For fall admission, 8/23 priority date for domestic students. Applications are processed on a rolling basis. Application fee: $25. Electronic applications accepted. *Expenses: Contact institution.* Tuition and fees vary according to campus/location and program. *Financial support:* In 2006–07, 355 students received support; fellowships, research assistantships, teaching assistantships, Federal Work-Study and scholarships/grants available. Support available to part-time students. Financial award application deadline: 4/15; financial award applicants required to submit FAFSA. *Unit head:* Dr. Donald C. Wold, Dean, 630-844-1542, Fax: 630-844-5530, E-mail: dwold@aurora.edu. *Application contact:* Donna DeSpain, Dean of Adult and Graduate Studies, 800-742-5281, Fax: 630-844-5535, E-mail: auadmission@aurora.edu.

Austin Peay State University, College of Graduate Studies, College of Professional Programs and Social Sciences, School of Education, Clarksville, TN 37044. Offers curriculum and instruction (MA Ed); education (M Ed, Ed S); educational leadership studies (MA Ed); reading (MA Ed). *Accreditation:* NCATE. Part-time and evening/weekend programs available. Postbaccalaureate distance learning degree programs offered. *Faculty:* 24 full-time (14 women), 8 part-time/adjunct (4 women). *Students:* 81 full-time (65 women), 225 part-time (180 women); includes 48 minority (37 African Americans, 2 American Indian/Alaska Native, 1 Asian American or Pacific Islander, 8 Hispanic Americans). Average age 35. In 2006, 81 master's, 16 other advanced degrees awarded. *Degree requirements:* For master's, teaching license, thesis optional. *Entrance requirements:* For master's, GRE General Test, 3 letters of recommendation; for Ed S, GRE General Test, master's degree, minimum graduate GPA of 3.0, 3 letters of recommendation. Additional exam requirements/recommendations for international students: Required—TOEFL (minimum score 500 paper-based; 173 computer-based). *Application deadline:* For fall admission, 7/31 priority date for domestic students; for spring admission, 12/17 priority date for domestic students. Applications are processed on a rolling basis. Application fee: $25. Electronic applications accepted. *Expenses:* Tuition, state resident: full-time $5,138; part-time $272 per credit hour. Tuition, nonresident: full-time $14,832; part-time $693 per credit hour. Required fees: $1,009. *Financial support:* In 2006–07, research assistantships (averaging $10,270 per year); career-related internships or fieldwork, Federal Work-Study, institutionally sponsored loans, scholarships/grants, and unspecified assistantships also available. Support available to part-time students. Financial award application deadline: 3/1; financial award applicants required to submit FAFSA. *Unit head:* Dr. Carlette Hardin, Director, 931-221-7696, Fax: 931-221-1292, E-mail: forbusl@apsu.edu.

Azusa Pacific University, School of Behavioral and Applied Sciences, Department of Higher Education and Organizational Leadership, Program in Higher Education Leadership, Azusa, CA 91702-7000. Offers Ed D. *Students:* 15 full-time (7 women), 30 part-time (10 women); includes 3 minority (2 African Americans, 1 Asian American or Pacific Islander), 4 international. In 2006, 3 degrees awarded. *Expenses:* Tuition: Part-time $475 per credit. *Unit head:* Dr. Dennis A. Sheridan, Director, Department of Higher Education and Organizational Leadership, 626-815-5485, Fax: 626-815-3868.

Azusa Pacific University, School of Education, Department of Education, Program in Educational Leadership, Azusa, CA 91702-7000. Offers Ed D. Part-time and evening/weekend programs available. *Faculty:* 6 full-time (1 woman). *Students:* 2 full-time (1 woman), 159 part-time (107 women); includes 56 minority (14 African Americans, 1 American Indian/Alaska Native, 10 Asian Americans or Pacific Islanders, 31 Hispanic Americans), 4 international. Average age 45. In 2006, 12 degrees awarded. *Degree requirements:* For doctorate, oral defense of dissertation, qualifying exam. *Entrance requirements:* For doctorate, GRE General Test or MAT, 5 years of experience, writing sample. Additional exam requirements/recommendations for international students: Required—TOEFL. *Application deadline:* For fall admission, 6/16 priority date for domestic students; for spring admission, 11/18 for domestic students. Applications are processed on a rolling basis. Application fee: $45 ($65 for international students). *Expenses: Contact institution. Financial support:* Career-related internships or fieldwork available. Support available to part-time students. Financial award applicants required to submit FAFSA. *Faculty research:* Ethics in educational administration. Total annual research expenditures: $2,750. *Unit head:* Dr. Laurie Schriener, Chair, 626-815-5322, Fax: 626-815-5416, E-mail: lschriener@apu.edu.

Azusa Pacific University, School of Education, Program in School Administration, Azusa, CA 91702-7000. Offers MA. Part-time and evening/weekend programs available. In 2006, 94 degrees awarded. *Degree requirements:* For master's, comprehensive exam or thesis, core exams, oral presentation. *Entrance requirements:* For master's, 12 units of course work in education, minimum GPA of 3.0. *Application deadline:* For fall admission, 9/15 priority date for domestic students; for spring admission, 2/5 for domestic students. Applications are processed on a rolling basis. Application fee: $45 ($65 for international students). *Expenses:* Tuition: Part-time $475 per credit. *Faculty research:* Instructional supervision, outcome-based education, technology and online searching, teacher preparation. *Unit head:* Dr. Gail Houghton, Chair, 626-815-5459, Fax: 626-815-5416, E-mail: ghoughton@apu.edu.

Baldwin-Wallace College, Graduate Programs, Division of Education, Specialization in Pre-Administration, Berea, OH 44017-2088. Offers MA Ed. Part-time and evening/weekend programs available. *Students:* Average age 28. In 2006, 12 degrees awarded. *Degree requirements:* For master's, comprehensive exam. *Entrance requirements:* For master's, bachelor's degree in field, MAT or minimum GPA of 2.75. *Application deadline:* For fall admission, 8/15 priority date for domestic students; for spring admission, 12/15 priority date for domestic students. Applications are processed on a rolling basis. Application fee: $25. Electronic applications accepted. *Expenses:* Tuition: Part-time $760 per credit hour. Tuition and fees vary according to program. *Financial support:* Career-related internships or fieldwork available. Financial award applicants required to submit FAFSA. *Application contact:* Winifred W. Gerhardt, Director of Admission for the Evening and Weekend College, 440-826-2222, Fax: 440-826-3830, E-mail: admission@bw.edu.

Ball State University, Graduate School, Teachers College, Department of Educational Leadership, Program in Educational Administration, Muncie, IN 47306-1099. Offers MAE, Ed D. *Accreditation:* NCATE. *Faculty:* 5. *Students:* 10 full-time (8 women), 258 part-time (134 women); includes 18 minority (14 African Americans, 1 Asian American or Pacific Islander, 3 Hispanic Americans), 2 international. Average age 29. 57 applicants, 84% accepted, 41 enrolled. In 2006, 59 master's, 3 doctorates awarded. *Degree requirements:* For doctorate, thesis/dissertation. *Entrance requirements:* For doctorate, GRE General Test, interview, minimum graduate GPA of 3.2. Application fee: $25 ($35 for international students). *Financial support:* In 2006–07, 5 teaching assistantships with full tuition reimbursements (averaging $7,774 per year) were awarded. Financial award application deadline: 3/1. *Unit head:* Dr. John Hill, Head, 765-285-2762.

Ball State University, Graduate School, Teachers College, Department of Educational Leadership, Program in School Superintendency, Muncie, IN 47306-1099. Offers Ed S. *Accreditation:* NCATE. *Faculty:* 5. *Students:* Average age 38. 8 applicants, 63% accepted, 3 enrolled. In 2006, 4 degrees awarded. *Degree requirements:* For Ed S, thesis. *Entrance requirements:* For degree, GRE General Test, interview. Application fee: $25 ($35 for international students). *Financial support:* Application deadline: 3/1. *Unit head:* Dr. William Sharp, Director of Doctoral and Specialist Programs, 765-285-8488, Fax: 765-285-2166, E-mail: bsharp@bsu.edu.

Ball State University, Graduate School, Teachers College, Department of Educational Studies, Program in Executive Development, Muncie, IN 47306-1099. Offers MA. *Students:* 11 full-time (5 women), 31 part-time (23 women); includes 7 minority (6 African Americans, 1 Asian American or Pacific Islander), 2 international. Average age 31. 20 applicants, 85% accepted, 13 enrolled. In 2006, 17 degrees awarded. Application fee: $25 ($35 for international students). *Financial support:* Application deadline: 3/1. *Unit head:* Michelle Dudka, Director, 765-285-5460, Fax: 765-285-5489.

Ball State University, Graduate School, Teachers College, Department of Educational Studies, Program in Student Affairs Administration in Higher Education, Muncie, IN 47306-1099. Offers MA. *Accreditation:* NCATE. *Students:* 28 full-time (13 women), 7 part-time (all women); includes 6 minority (4 African Americans, 1 Asian American or Pacific Islander, 1 Hispanic American), 2 international. Average age 22. 105 applicants, 41% accepted, 25 enrolled. In 2006, 27 degrees awarded. *Entrance requirements:* For master's, GRE General Test, interview. Application fee: $25 ($35 for international students). *Financial support:* In 2006–07, 24 research assistantships with full tuition reimbursements (averaging $6,150 per year) were awarded. Financial award application deadline: 3/1. *Unit head:* Dr. Randy Hyman, Director, 765-285-5343, Fax: 765-285-2464.

Bank Street College of Education, Graduate School, Department of Educational Leadership, New York, NY 10025. Offers early childhood leadership (MS Ed); educational leadership (MS Ed); leadership for educational change (Ed M, MS Ed); leadership in mathematics education (MS Ed); leadership in museum education (MS Ed); leadership in the arts (MS Ed). *Students:* 59 full-time (35 women), 137 part-time (100 women); includes 75 minority (31 African Americans, 1 American Indian/Alaska Native, 10 Asian Americans or Pacific Islanders, 33 Hispanic Americans), 5 international. Average age 36. 107 applicants, 89% accepted, 89 enrolled. In 2006, 88 degrees awarded. *Degree requirements:* For master's, thesis, registration. *Entrance requirements:* For master's, interview, minimum of 2 years experience in the classroom. Additional exam requirements/recommendations for international students: Required—TOEFL (minimum score 600 paper-based; 250 computer-based). *Application deadline:* For fall admission, 3/1 priority date for domestic students; for spring admission, 11/1 priority date for domestic students. Applications are processed on a rolling basis. Application fee: $50. *Expenses:* Tuition: Part-time $940 per credit. Required fees: $100 per term. *Financial support:* Career-related internships or fieldwork, Federal Work-Study, scholarships/grants, and unspecified assistantships available. Support available to part-time students. Financial award application deadline: 4/15; financial award applicants required to submit FAFSA. *Faculty research:* Leadership in small schools, mathematics education in elementary schools, professional development in early childhood, leadership in arts education, leadership in special education. *Unit head:* Dr. Rima Shore, Chairperson, 212-875-4478, Fax: 212-875-8753, E-mail: rshore@bankstreet.edu. *Application contact:* Ann Morgan, Director of Graduate Admissions, 212-875-4403, Fax: 212-875-4678, E-mail: amorgan@bankstreet.edu.

Barry University, School of Education, Program in Educational Leadership, Miami Shores, FL 33161-6695. Offers MS, Ed D, Certificate, Ed S. Part-time and evening/weekend programs available. *Students:* 12 full-time (9 women), 64 part-time (47 women); includes 55 minority (37 African Americans, 18 Hispanic Americans). 53 applicants, 60% accepted, 18 enrolled. In 2006, 27 master's, 3 doctorates, 11 other advanced degrees awarded. *Degree requirements:* For master's and other advanced degree, comprehensive exam. *Entrance requirements:* For master's, GRE General Test or MAT, minimum GPA of 3.0; for other advanced degree, GRE General Test, minimum GPA of 3.0. *Application deadline:* For fall admission, 5/1 priority date for domestic students. Applications are processed on a rolling basis. Application fee: $30. Electronic applications accepted. *Unit head:* Dr. Carmen McCrink, Director, 305-899-3702, Fax: 305-899-4708, E-mail: cmccrink@mail.barry.edu. *Application contact:* Dave Fletcher, Director of Graduate Admissions, 305-899-3113, Fax: 305-899-2971, E-mail: dfletcher@mail.barry.edu.

Barry University, School of Education, Program in Higher Education Administration, Miami Shores, FL 33161-6695. Offers higher education administration (MS). Part-time and evening/weekend programs available. *Students:* 4 full-time (3 women), 6 part-time (5 women); includes 4 minority (3 African Americans, 1 Hispanic American), 1 international. 7 applicants, 29% accepted, 1 enrolled. In 2006, 2 degrees awarded. *Degree requirements:* For master's, comprehensive exam. *Entrance requirements:* For master's, GRE General Test or MAT, minimum GPA of 3.0. *Application deadline:* For fall admission, 5/1 priority date for domestic students. Applications are processed on a rolling basis. Application fee: $30. Electronic applications accepted. *Unit head:* Dr. Carmen McCrink, Director, 305-899-3702, Fax: 305-899-4708, E-mail: cmccrink@mail.barry.edu. *Application contact:* Dave Fletcher, Director of Graduate Admissions, 305-899-3113, Fax: 305-899-2971, E-mail: dfletcher@mail.barry.edu.

Barry University, School of Education, Program in Leadership and Education, Miami Shores, FL 33161-6695. Offers educational technology (PhD); exceptional student education (PhD); higher education administration (PhD); human resource development (PhD); leadership (PhD). Part-time and evening/weekend programs available. *Students:* 15 full-time (7 women), 233 part-time (147 women); includes 97 minority (52 African Americans, 45 Hispanic Americans), 7 international. 58 applicants, 34% accepted, 18 enrolled. In 2006, 23 degrees awarded. *Degree requirements:* For doctorate, thesis/dissertation. *Entrance requirements:* For doctorate, GRE General Test, minimum GPA of 3.25. *Application deadline:* For fall admission, 5/1 priority date for domestic students. Applications are processed on a rolling basis. Application fee: $30. Electronic applications accepted. *Unit head:* Dr. Carmen McCrink, Director, 305-899-3702, Fax: 305-899-4708, E-mail: cmccrink@mail.barry.edu. *Application contact:* Dave Fletcher, Director of Graduate Admissions, 305-899-3113, Fax: 305-899-2971, E-mail: dfletcher@mail.barry.edu.

Bayamón Central University, Graduate Programs, Program in Education, Bayamón, PR 00960-1725. Offers administration and supervision (MA Ed); commercial education (MA Ed); education of the autistic (MA Ed); elementary education (K–3) (MA Ed); elementary education (K–6) (MA Ed); elementary physical education (MA Ed); guidance and counseling (MA Ed); pre-elementary teacher (MA Ed); special education (MA Ed), including attention deficit disorder, learning disabilities. Part-time and evening/weekend programs available. *Degree requirements:* For master's, comprehensive exam. *Entrance requirements:* For master's, EXADEP, bachelor's degree in education or related field.

Baylor University, Graduate School, School of Education, Department of Educational Administration, Waco, TX 76798. Offers MS Ed, Ed S. *Accreditation:* NCATE. *Students:* 49 full-time (32 women), 7 part-time (4 women); includes 16 minority (10 African Americans, 1 American Indian/Alaska Native, 1 Asian American or Pacific Islander, 4 Hispanic Americans), 1 international. 90 applicants, 44% accepted. In 2006, 14 master's awarded. *Entrance requirements:* For master's, GRE General Test. *Application deadline:* Applications are processed on a rolling basis. Application fee: $25. *Financial support:* In 2006–07, 20 students received support, including 2 research assistantships; teaching assistantships, Federal Work-Study, institutionally sponsored loans, and scholarships/grants also available. *Unit head:* Dr. Al Smith, Graduate Program Director, 254-710-3117, Fax: 254-710-3265, E-mail: al_smith@baylor.edu. *Application contact:* Suzanne Keener, Administrative Assistant, 254-710-3588, Fax: 254-710-3870.

Bellarmine University, Annsley Frazier Thornton School of Education, Louisville, KY 40205-0671. Offers early elementary education (MA, MAT); instructional leadership and school administration/school principal (MA); learning and behavior disorders (MA); middle school education (MA, MAT); reading and writing endorsement (MA); secondary school education (MAT); Waldorf inspired curriculum (MA);). *Accreditation:* NCATE. Part-time and evening/weekend programs available. *Faculty:* 10 full-time (8 women), 5 part-time/adjunct (all women). *Students:* 92 full-time (68 women), 140 part-time (104 women); includes 16 minority (11 African Americans, 1 Asian American or Pacific Islander, 4 Hispanic Americans). Average age 32. In 2006, 98 degrees awarded. *Degree requirements:* For master's, thesis (for some programs), comprehensive exam. *Entrance requirements:* For master's, minimum overall GPA of 2.75, 3.0 in major; letters of recommendation; valid Kentucky provisional or professional certificate. Additional exam requirements/recommendations for international students: Required—TOEFL (minimum score 550 paper-based; 213 computer-based; 80 iBT), GRE. *Application deadline:* Applications are processed on a rolling basis. Application fee: $25. Electronic applications accepted. *Expenses: Contact institution.* Tuition and fees vary according to program. *Faculty research:* Social justice, service learning dispositions, educational technology, special education. *Unit head:* Dr. Milton Brown, Dean (Interim), 502-452-8486, Fax: 502-452-8189, E-mail: mbrown@bellarmine.edu. *Application contact:* Theresa Klapheke, Director of Graduate Programs, 502-452-8033, Fax: 502-452-8189, E-mail: tklapheke@bellarmine.edu.

Benedictine College, Program in Educational Administration, Atchison, KS 66002-1499. Offers MA. *Accreditation:* NCATE. Part-time and evening/weekend programs available. *Degree requirements:* For master's, thesis or alternative, practicum. *Entrance requirements:* For master's, GRE General Test or MAT, minimum GPA of 3.0. Expenses: Contact institution. *Faculty research:* Collaborative learning, career mobility, multicultural education.

Benedictine University, Graduate Programs, Program in Education, Lisle, IL 60532-0900. Offers curriculum and instruction and collaborative teaching (M Ed); elementary education (MA Ed); leadership and administration (M Ed); reading and literacy (M Ed); secondary education (MA Ed); special education (MA Ed). Part-time and evening/weekend programs available. *Faculty:* 4 full-time (2 women), 52 part-time/adjunct (30 women). *Students:* 257 (196 women); includes 22 minority (4 African Americans, 1 American Indian/Alaska Native, 3 Asian Americans or Pacific Islanders, 14 Hispanic Americans) 2 international. Average age 33. 130 applicants, 93% accepted, 13 enrolled. In 2006, 181 degrees awarded. *Degree requirements:* For master's, thesis (for some programs), comprehensive exam. *Entrance requirements:* For master's, GRE or MAT. Additional exam requirements/recommendations for international students: Required—TOEFL (minimum score 550 paper-based; 213 computer-based). *Application deadline:* For fall admission, 9/1 for domestic students; for winter admission, 12/1 for domestic students; for spring admission, 2/15 for domestic students. Applications are processed on a rolling basis. Application fee: $40. Electronic applications accepted. *Expenses: Contact institution. Financial support:* Career-related internships or fieldwork and health care benefits available. Support available to part-time students. *Unit head:* Dr. Richard Campbell, Director, 630-829-6242, Fax: 630-960-1126, E-mail: rcampbell@ben.edu. *Application contact:* Kari Gibbons, Director, Admissions, 630-829-6200, Fax: 630-829-6584, E-mail: kgibbons@ben.edu.

Benedictine University, Graduate Programs, Program in Higher Education and Organizational Change, Lisle, IL 60532-0900. Offers Ed D. *Expenses:* Tuition: Full-time $12,150; part-time $450 per credit hour. *Unit head:* Dr. Donald Fouts, Director, 630-829-6343.

Bernard M. Baruch College of the City University of New York, School of Public Affairs, Program in Educational Administration and Supervision, New York, NY 10010-5585. Offers MS Ed. Part-time and evening/weekend programs available. *Students:* 29 full-time (14 women), 165 part-time (107 women); includes 73 minority (35 African Americans, 11 Asian Americans or Pacific Islanders, 27 Hispanic Americans). Average age 36. 109 applicants, 81% accepted, 81 enrolled. In 2006, 59 master's awarded. *Degree requirements:* For master's, internship. *Entrance requirements:* For master's, GRE or master's degree, minimum GPA of 3.0. Additional exam requirements/recommendations for international students: Required—TOEFL (minimum score 650 paper-based; 257 computer-based). *Application deadline:* For fall admission, 4/1 priority date for domestic and international students. Applications are processed on a rolling basis. Application fee: $125. Electronic applications accepted. *Expenses: Contact institution. Financial support:* In 2006–07, 2 students received support. Career-related internships or fieldwork, Federal Work-Study, and scholarships/grants available. Support available to part-time students. Financial award application deadline: 5/30; financial award applicants required to submit FAFSA. *Faculty research:* School administration, program development, school leadership, violence in schools, school leadership development, school reform, school discipline policy, program development. Total annual research expenditures: $429,000. *Application contact:* Michael J. Lovaglio, Director of Graduate Admissions and Student Services, 646-660-6750, Fax: 646-660-6751, E-mail: michael_lovaglio@baruch.cuny.edu.

Bernard M. Baruch College of the City University of New York, School of Public Affairs, Program in Higher Education Administration, New York, NY 10010-5585. Offers MS Ed. Part-time and evening/weekend programs available. *Students:* 3 full-time (2 women), 68 part-time (44 women); includes 38 minority (17 African Americans, 4 Asian Americans or Pacific Islanders, 17 Hispanic Americans). Average age 34. 51 applicants, 57% accepted, 22 enrolled. In 2006, 31 degrees awarded. *Degree requirements:* For master's, internship. *Entrance requirements:* For master's, GRE General Test, minimum GPA of 3.0. Additional exam requirements/recommendations for international students: Required—TOEFL (minimum score 650 paper-based; 257 computer-based). *Application deadline:* For fall admission, 4/1 priority date for domestic and international students; for spring admission, 11/1 priority date for domestic and international students. Applications are processed on a rolling basis. Application fee: $125. Electronic applications accepted. *Expenses: Contact institution. Financial support:* In 2006–07, 8 students received support, including 7 fellowships (averaging $3,000 per year), 1 research assistantship (averaging $9,800 per year); teaching assistantships, career-related internships or fieldwork, Federal Work-Study, scholarships/grants, tuition waivers (partial), and unspecified assistantships also available. Support available to part-time students. Financial award application deadline: 5/30; financial award applicants required to submit FAFSA. *Application contact:* Michael J. Lovaglio, Director of Graduate Admissions and Student Services, 646-660-6750, Fax: 646-660-6751, E-mail: michael_lovaglio@baruch.cuny.edu.

Bethany University, Program in Teacher Education, Scotts Valley, CA 95066-2820. Offers education (MA); educational leadership (MA). Part-time and evening/weekend programs available. *Degree requirements:* For master's, thesis. *Entrance requirements:* For master's, GRE General Test.

Bethel College, Program in Education, McKenzie, TN 38201. Offers administration and supervision (MA Ed); biology education K8-12 (MAT); elementary education (MAT); English education K8-12 (MAT); history education K8-12 (MAT); physical education K8-12 (MAT); special education K8-12 (MAT). Part-time and evening/weekend programs available. *Degree requirements:* For master's, thesis (for some programs). *Entrance requirements:* For master's, GRE General Test or MAT, minimum undergraduate GPA of 2.5.

Bethel University, Graduate School, Department of Education, St. Paul, MN 55112-6999. Offers education K-12 (MA); educational administration (Ed D); literacy (Certificate); literacy education (MA); secondary education (MA); special education (M Ed). Evening/weekend programs available. *Faculty:* 20 full-time (10 women), 34 part-time/adjunct (18 women). *Students:* 192 full-time (119 women), 110 part-time (71 women); includes 16 minority (6 African Americans, 5 Asian Americans or Pacific Islanders, 5 Hispanic Americans). Average age 35. In 2006, 58 master's, 9 other advanced degrees awarded. *Degree requirements:* For master's, thesis, practicum; for doctorate, thesis/dissertation, registration. *Entrance requirements:* For master's, interview, current teaching license, minimum GPA of 3.0, teaching experience (if applicable), letters of reference; for doctorate, MAT or GRE, minimum GPA of 3.5, letters of reference, master's degree. Additional exam requirements/recommendations for international students: Required—TOEFL (minimum score 550 paper-based; 213 computer-based). *Application deadline:* For fall admission, 8/1 priority date for domestic students; for winter admission, 12/10 priority date for domestic students; for spring admission, 5/1 priority date for domestic students. Applications are processed on a rolling basis. Application fee: $25. Electronic applications accepted. *Expenses: Contact institution.* Tuition and fees vary according to program. *Financial support:* Institutionally sponsored loans and scholarships/grants available. Financial award applicants required to submit FAFSA. *Unit head:* Dr. Jay B. Rasmussen, Director, 651-638-6237, Fax: 651-638-8004, E-mail: jay-rasmussen@bethel.edu. *Application contact:* Michael Price, Director of Admissions, 651-635-8000 Ext. 8017, Fax: 651-635-8004, E-mail: m_price@bethel.edu.

Bob Jones University, Graduate Programs, Greenville, SC 29614. Offers accountancy (MS); Bible (MA); Bible translation (MA); Biblical studies (Certificate); broadcast management (MS); business administration (MBA); church history (MA, PhD); church ministries (MA); church music (MM); cinema and video production (MA); counseling (MS); curriculum and instruction (Ed D); divinity (M Div); dramatic production (MA); educational leadership (MS, Ed D, Ed S); elementary education (M Ed, MAT); English (M Ed, MA, MAT); fine arts (MA); graphic design (MA); history (M Ed, MA); illustration (MA); interpretative speech (MA); mathematics (M Ed, MAT); medical missions (Certificate); ministry (MM, D Min); multi-categorical special education (M Ed, MAT); music (M Ed); New Testament interpretation (PhD); Old Testament interpretation (PhD); orchestral instrument performance (MM); organ performance (MM); pastoral studies (MA); personnel services (MS, Ed S); piano pedagogy (MM); piano performance (MM); platform arts (MA); radio and television broadcasting (MS); rhetoric and public address (MA); secondary education (M Ed); studio art (MA); teaching Bible (MA); theology (MA, PhD); voice performance (MM); youth ministries (MA); M Div/MM.

Boise State University, Graduate College, College of Education, Department of Curriculum, Instruction and Foundational Studies, Boise, ID 83725-0399. Offers curriculum and instruction (Ed D); curriculum instruction (MA); educational leadership (M Ed). *Accreditation:* NCATE. Part-time programs available. *Faculty:* 18 full-time (7 women), 21 part-time/adjunct (14 women). *Students:* 56 full-time (34 women), 122 part-time (83 women); includes 19 minority (1 American Indian/Alaska Native, 1 Asian American or Pacific Islander, 17 Hispanic Americans). Average age 36. 48 applicants, 98% accepted, 10 enrolled. In 2006, 48 degrees awarded. *Degree requirements:* For master's, thesis optional. *Entrance requirements:* For master's, minimum GPA of 3.0. *Application deadline:* For fall admission, 7/1 priority date for domestic students; for spring admission, 11/15 priority date for domestic students. Applications are processed on a rolling basis. Application fee: $30. Electronic applications accepted. *Financial support:* Career-related internships or fieldwork, Federal Work-Study, institutionally sponsored loans, and unspecified assistantships available. Support available to part-time students. Financial award application deadline: 3/1. *Unit head:* Dr. Philip P. Kelly, Chair, 208-426-4977, Fax: 208-426-4365. *Application contact:* Crystal Calais, Graduate Coordinator, 208-426-1672, Fax: 208-426-4006.

Boston College, Lynch Graduate School of Education, Department of Educational Administration and Higher Education, Educational Administration Specialization, Chestnut Hill, MA 02467-3800. Offers M Ed, PhD, CAES, JD/M Ed, M Ed/MA. *Students:* 31 full-time (23 women), 20 part-time (8 women); includes 7 minority (4 African Americans, 2 Asian Americans or Pacific

Educational Administration

Boston College (continued)

Islanders, 1 Hispanic American), 6 international. 68 applicants, 68% accepted, 13 enrolled. In 2006, 24 master's, 4 doctorates, 1 other advanced degree awarded. Terminal master's awarded for partial completion of doctoral program. *Degree requirements:* For master's and CAES, comprehensive exam; for doctorate, thesis/dissertation, comprehensive exam. *Entrance requirements:* For master's and CAES, GRE General Test or MAT; for doctorate, GRE General Test. Additional exam requirements/recommendations for international students: Required—TOEFL. Application fee: $60. *Financial support:* Fellowships with full and partial tuition reimbursements, research assistantships with full and partial tuition reimbursements, teaching assistantships with full and partial tuition reimbursements, career-related internships or fieldwork, Federal Work-Study, scholarships/grants, traineeships, tuition waivers (full and partial), and unspecified assistantships available. Support available to part-time students. Financial award applicants required to submit FAFSA. *Faculty research:* Politics of urban education, principalship, cultural aspects of teaching, urban school leadership, experience of low-income minority students in private schools. *Application contact:* Timothy P. Blackman, Director, Graduate Admission and Financial Aid, 617-552-4214, Fax: 617-552-0398, E-mail: timothy.blackman.1@bc.edu.

Boston College, Lynch Graduate School of Education, Department of Educational Administration and Higher Education, Higher Education Specialization, Chestnut Hill, MA 02467-3800. Offers MA, PhD, JD/MA, MBA/MA. *Students:* 63 full-time (38 women), 43 part-time (30 women); includes 16 minority (6 African Americans, 7 Asian Americans or Pacific Islanders, 3 Hispanic Americans), 12 international. 198 applicants, 47% accepted, 33 enrolled. In 2006, 43 master's, 6 doctorates awarded. Terminal master's awarded for partial completion of doctoral program. *Degree requirements:* For master's, comprehensive exam; for doctorate, thesis/dissertation, comprehensive exam. *Entrance requirements:* For master's, GRE General Test or MAT; for doctorate, GRE General Test. Additional exam requirements/recommendations for international students: Required—TOEFL. Application fee: $60. *Financial support:* Fellowships with full and partial tuition reimbursements, research assistantships with full and partial tuition reimbursements, teaching assistantships with full and partial tuition reimbursements, career-related internships or fieldwork, Federal Work-Study, scholarships/grants, traineeships, tuition waivers (full and partial), and unspecified assistantships available. Support available to part-time students. Financial award applicants required to submit FAFSA. *Faculty research:* Administration and leadership theory, change process in policy making, organizational analysis, comparative education, higher education in developing countries. *Application contact:* Timothy P. Blackman, Director, Graduate Admission and Financial Aid, 617-552-4214, Fax: 617-552-0398, E-mail: timothy.blackman.1@bc.edu.

Boston College, Lynch Graduate School of Education, Department of Educational Administration and Higher Education, Massachusetts Elementary School Principal Association/Professional School Administrator Program, Chestnut Hill, MA 02467-3800. Offers Ed D. Part-time and evening/weekend programs available. *Students:* 5 full-time (2 women), 37 part-time (18 women); includes 5 minority (4 African Americans, 1 Hispanic American). 44 applicants, 50% accepted, 20 enrolled. In 2006, 1 degree awarded. *Degree requirements:* For doctorate, thesis/dissertation, comprehensive exam. *Entrance requirements:* For doctorate, GRE General Test. Additional exam requirements/recommendations for international students: Required—TOEFL. *Application deadline:* For fall admission, 2/1 for domestic students. Application fee: $60. *Financial support:* Fellowships with full and partial tuition reimbursements, research assistantships with full and partial tuition reimbursements, teaching assistantships with full and partial tuition reimbursements, career-related internships or fieldwork, Federal Work-Study, scholarships/grants, traineeships, tuition waivers (full and partial), and unspecified assistantships available. Support available to part-time students. Financial award applicants required to submit FAFSA. *Faculty research:* Educational leadership, high stakes testing, diversity. *Application contact:* Timothy P. Blackman, Director, Graduate Admission and Financial Aid, 617-552-4214, Fax: 617-552-0398, E-mail: timothy.blackman.1@bc.edu.

Boston University, School of Education, Department of Administration, Training, and Policy Studies, Program in Human Resource Education, Boston, MA 02215. Offers Ed M, CAGS. Part-time programs available. *Students:* 10 full-time (8 women), 8 part-time (6 women); includes 1 minority (Hispanic American), 1 international. Average age 36. 21 applicants, 67% accepted, 12 enrolled. *Degree requirements:* For master's, thesis optional. *Entrance requirements:* For master's and CAGS, GRE General Test or MAT. Additional exam requirements/recommendations for international students: Required—TOEFL. *Application deadline:* For fall admission, 2/15 priority date for domestic students; for winter admission, 11/1 priority date for domestic students. Applications are processed on a rolling basis. Application fee: $70. Electronic applications accepted. *Expenses:* Tuition: Full-time $33,330; part-time $1,042 per credit. Required fees: $462; $40. *Financial support:* Application deadline: 2/15; *Unit head:* Dr. Alan Gaynor, Coordinator, 617-353-3307, E-mail: agaynor@bu.edu. *Application contact:* 617-353-4237, Fax: 617-353-8937, E-mail: sedgrad@bu.edu.

Boston University, School of Education, Department of Administration, Training, and Policy Studies, Program in Policy, Planning, and Administration, Boston, MA 02215. Offers educational administration (Ed M); policy, planning, and administration (Ed M, CAGS); MSW/Ed M. Part-time programs available. *Students:* 5 full-time (4 women), 40 part-time (30 women); includes 2 minority (1 African American, 1 Asian American or Pacific Islander), 5 international. Average age 31. 96 applicants, 90% accepted, 30 enrolled. *Degree requirements:* For master's, thesis optional. *Entrance requirements:* For master's and CAGS, GRE General Test or MAT. Additional exam requirements/recommendations for international students: Required—TOEFL. *Application deadline:* For fall admission, 2/15 priority date for domestic students; for winter admission, 10/1 priority date for domestic students. Applications are processed on a rolling basis. Application fee: $70. Electronic applications accepted. *Expenses:* Tuition: Full-time $33,330; part-time $1,042 per credit. Required fees: $462; $40. *Financial support:* Application deadline: 2/15. *Faculty research:* School effectiveness, creative problem solving, parent involvement, community education, curriculum theory and evaluation. *Application contact:* 617-353-4237, Fax: 617-353-8937, E-mail: sedgrad@bu.edu.

Bowie State University, Graduate Programs, Program in Educational Leadership/Executive Fellows, Bowie, MD 20715-9465. Offers Ed D. Part-time and evening/weekend programs available. *Students:* 1 (woman) full-time, 90 part-time (64 women); includes 82 minority (81 African Americans, 1 Hispanic American). Average age 44. *Degree requirements:* For doctorate, thesis/dissertation, comprehensive exam. *Application deadline:* For fall admission, 4/1 priority date for domestic and international students; for spring admission, 11/1 priority date for domestic and international students. Applications are processed on a rolling basis. Electronic applications accepted. *Expenses:* Tuition, state resident: full-time $7,344; part-time $306 per credit. Tuition, nonresident: full-time $14,304; part-time $396 per credit. Required fees: $1,078; $77 per credit. $539 per term. One-time fee: $40. *Unit head:* Dr. Barbara Jackson, Chairperson, 301-860-3125, E-mail: bjackson@bowiestate.edu. *Application contact:* Angela Issac, Information Contact.

Bowie State University, Graduate Programs, Program in Elementary and Secondary School Administration, Bowie, MD 20715-9465. Offers M Ed. Part-time and evening/weekend programs available. *Students:* 4 full-time (2 women), 38 part-time (25 women). Average age 38. 14 applicants, 100% accepted, 14 enrolled. In 2006, 22 degrees awarded. *Degree requirements:* For master's, comprehensive exam. *Entrance requirements:* For master's, copy of Advance Teaching Certificate, 3 years teaching experience, letter of recommendation from current supervisor. *Application deadline:* For fall admission, 4/11 priority date for domestic students, 4/1 priority date for international students; for spring admission, 11/1 priority date for domestic and international students. Applications are processed on a rolling basis. Application fee: $40. Electronic applications accepted. *Expenses:* Tuition, state resident: full-time $7,344; part-time $306 per credit. Tuition, nonresident: full-time $14,304; part-time $396 per credit. Required fees: $1,078; $77 per credit. $539 per term. One-time fee: $40. *Unit head:* Dr. Barbara Jackson, Program Coordinator, 301-860, E-mail: bjackson@bowiestate.edu.

Bowie State University, Graduate Programs, Programs in Education, Program in School Administration and Supervision, Bowie, MD 20715-9465. Offers M Ed. Part-time and evening/weekend programs available. *Degree requirements:* For master's, research paper, thesis optional. *Entrance requirements:* For master's, minimum undergraduate GPA of 3.0, 3 years of teaching experience, teaching certificate. *Expenses:* Tuition, state resident: full-time $7,344; part-time $306 per credit. Tuition, nonresident: full-time $14,304; part-time $396 per credit. Required fees: $1,078; $77 per credit. $539 per term. One-time fee: $40.

Bowling Green State University, Graduate College, College of Education and Human Development, School of Leadership and Policy Studies, Program in Educational Administration and Supervision, Bowling Green, OH 43403. Offers educational administration and supervision (M Ed, Ed S); leadership studies (Ed D). *Accreditation:* NCATE. Part-time and evening/weekend programs available. *Faculty:* 6 full-time (3 women), 76 part-time/adjunct (28 women). *Students:* 21 full-time (17 women), 121 part-time (61 women); includes 21 minority (16 African Americans, 1 Asian American or Pacific Islander, 4 Hispanic Americans), 1 international. Average age 35. 57 applicants, 75% accepted, 28 enrolled. In 2006, 67 master's, 10 doctorates awarded. *Degree requirements:* For master's, thesis or alternative; for doctorate, thesis/dissertation, comprehensive exam; for Ed S, thesis or alternative, field experience or internship. *Entrance requirements:* For master's, doctorate, and Ed S, GRE General Test. Additional exam requirements/recommendations for international students: Required—TOEFL. *Application deadline:* Applications are processed on a rolling basis. Application fee: $30. Electronic applications accepted. *Expenses:* Tuition, state resident: part-time $535 per hour. Tuition, nonresident: part-time $884 per hour. *Financial support:* In 2006–07, 6 research assistantships with full tuition reimbursements (averaging $10,285 per year), 2 teaching assistantships with full tuition reimbursements (averaging $11,367 per year) were awarded; career-related internships or fieldwork, Federal Work-Study, institutionally sponsored loans, tuition waivers (partial), and unspecified assistantships also available. Support available to part-time students. Financial award applicants required to submit FAFSA. *Faculty research:* Professional development for school leaders, organizational development, school finance, legal challenges to school decision making, administering urban schools. *Application contact:* Dr. Patrick Pauken, Graduate Coordinator, 419-372-7313.

Bowling Green State University, Graduate College, College of Education and Human Development, School of Leadership and Policy Studies, Program in Higher Education Administration, Bowling Green, OH 43403. Offers PhD. *Accreditation:* NCATE. Part-time programs available. *Students:* 20 full-time (16 women), 19 part-time (17 women); includes 7 minority (4 African Americans, 2 Asian Americans or Pacific Islanders, 1 Hispanic American), 1 international. Average age 38. 17 applicants, 71% accepted, 8 enrolled. In 2006, 4 degrees awarded. *Degree requirements:* For doctorate, thesis/dissertation, comprehensive exam. *Entrance requirements:* For doctorate, GRE General Test. Additional exam requirements/recommendations for international students: Required—TOEFL. *Application deadline:* For fall admission, 1/15 for domestic students. Application fee: $30. Electronic applications accepted. *Expenses:* Tuition, state resident: part-time $535 per hour. Tuition, nonresident: part-time $884 per hour. *Financial support:* In 2006–07, 17 research assistantships with full tuition reimbursements (averaging $11,207 per year) were awarded; teaching assistantships, career-related internships or fieldwork, Federal Work-Study, institutionally sponsored loans, and unspecified assistantships also available. Support available to part-time students. Financial award applicants required to submit FAFSA. *Faculty research:* Adult learners, legal issues, intellectual development. *Application contact:* Dr. Michael Coomes, Graduate Coordinator, 419-372-7157.

Bradley University, Graduate School, College of Education and Health Sciences, Department of Educational Leadership and Human Development, Peoria, IL 61625-0002. Offers human development counseling (MA), including community and agency counseling, school counseling; leadership in educational administration (MA); leadership in human service administration (MA). *Accreditation:* ACA; NCATE. Part-time and evening/weekend programs available. *Students:* 25 full-time (23 women), 100 part-time (70 women); includes 7 minority (6 Asian Americans or Pacific Islanders, 1 Hispanic American), 1 international. 36 applicants, 78% accepted, 18 enrolled. In 2006, 41 degrees awarded. *Degree requirements:* For master's, thesis optional. *Entrance requirements:* For master's, GRE General Test or MAT, interview, 3 letters of recommendation. Additional exam requirements/recommendations for international students: Required—TOEFL (minimum score 550 paper-based; 213 computer-based; 79 iBT). *Application deadline:* For fall admission, 5/15 priority date for domestic and international students; for spring admission, 10/15 priority date for domestic and international students. Applications are processed on a rolling basis. Application fee: $40 ($50 for international students). *Financial support:* Research assistantships, scholarships/grants, tuition waivers (partial), and unspecified assistantships available. Financial award application deadline: 4/1. *Unit head:* Dr. Christopher Rybak, Chairperson, 309-677-3171, E-mail: cjr@bradley.edu.

Brandon University, Faculty of Education, Brandon, MB R7A 6A9, Canada. Offers curriculum (Diploma); curriculum studies (M Ed); education administration (M Ed, Diploma); guidance and counseling (M Ed, Diploma); special education (M Ed, Diploma). *Degree requirements:* For master's, thesis. *Entrance requirements:* For master's, minimum GPA of 3.0, teaching certificate or equivalent. Additional exam requirements/recommendations for international students: Required—TOEFL. *Faculty research:* Comparative education, environmental studies, parent/school council.

Bridgewater State College, School of Graduate Studies, School of Education and Allied Science, Department of Secondary Education and Professional Programs, Program in Educational Leadership, Bridgewater, MA 02325-0001. Offers M Ed, CAGS. *Accreditation:* NCATE. Part-time and evening/weekend programs available. *Degree requirements:* For master's and CAGS, comprehensive exam. *Entrance requirements:* For master's, GRE General Test or Massachusetts Test for Educator Licensure, work experience; for CAGS, master's degree. *Application deadline:* For fall admission, 3/1 priority date for domestic students; for spring admission, 10/1 priority date for domestic students. Application fee: $50. *Financial support:* Career-related internships or fieldwork, health care benefits, and unspecified assistantships available. Support available to part-time students.

Brigham Young University, Graduate Studies, David O. McKay School of Education, Department of Educational Leadership and Foundations, Provo, UT 84602-1001. Offers M Ed, PhD. *Accreditation:* NCATE. Part-time and evening/weekend programs available. *Faculty:* 12 full-time (4 women), 3 part-time/adjunct (1 woman). *Students:* 37 full-time (18 women), 56 part-time (28 women); includes 15 minority (1 African American, 12 Asian Americans or Pacific Islanders, 2 Hispanic Americans), 8 international. Average age 38. 73 applicants, 81% accepted, 44 enrolled. In 2006, 28 master's, 6 doctorates awarded. *Median time to degree:* Of those who began their doctoral program in fall 1998, 50% received their degree in 8 years or less. *Degree requirements:* For master's, thesis or alternative, comprehensive exam, registration; for doctorate, thesis/dissertation, comprehensive exam, registration. *Entrance requirements:* For master's and doctorate, GRE. Additional exam requirements/recommendations for international students: Required—TOEFL (minimum score 580 paper-based; 237 computer-based). *Application deadline:* For fall admission, 2/15 for domestic and international students; for spring admission, 2/1 for domestic and international students. Application fee: $50. Electronic applications accepted. *Financial support:* In 2006–07, 11 students received support, including 9 research assistantships (averaging $5,000 per year), 2 teaching assistantships (averaging $2,500 per year); career-related internships or fieldwork, scholarships/grants, and unspecified assistantships also available. *Faculty research:* Mentoring, pre-service training of administrators, policy development, cross cultural studies of educational leadership. *Unit head:* Dr. A. LeGrand Richards, Chair, 801-422-5073, Fax: 801-422-0196, E-mail: buddy_richards@byu.edu. *Application contact:* Bonnie Bennett, Department Secretary, 801-422-4291, Fax: 801-422-0196, E-mail: bonnie_bennett@byu.edu.

Brooklyn College of the City University of New York, Division of Graduate Studies, School of Education, Program in Educational Leadership, Brooklyn, NY 11210-2889. Offers CAS. Part-time and evening/weekend programs available. *Students:* 54 applicants, 94% accepted,

38 enrolled. In 2006, 105 degrees awarded. *Degree requirements:* For CAS, internship. *Entrance requirements:* For degree, master's degree, minimum GPA of 3.0, teaching certificate, 3 years of teaching experience, 2 letters of recommendation. Additional exam requirements/recommendations for international students: Required—TOEFL. *Application deadline:* For fall admission, 3/1 priority date for domestic students, 2/1 priority date for international students; for spring admission, 11/1 priority date for domestic students, 10/1 priority date for international students. Applications are processed on a rolling basis. Application fee: $125. Electronic applications accepted. *Expenses:* Tuition, state resident: full-time $6,400; part-time $270 per credit. Tuition, nonresident: full-time $12,000; part-time $500 per credit. Required fees: $118 per semester. *Financial support:* Career-related internships or fieldwork, Federal Work-Study, institutionally sponsored loans, and scholarships/grants available. Support available to part-time students. Financial award application deadline: 5/1; financial award applicants required to submit FAFSA. *Unit head:* Dr. David Bloomfield, Program Head, 718-951-5214, E-mail: brumberg@brooklyn.cuny.edu. *Application contact:* Karen Alleyne-Pierre, Director of Admissions Services and Enrollment Communications, 718-951-5902, Fax: 718-951-4506, E-mail: grads@brooklyn.cuny.edu.

Bucknell University, Graduate Studies, College of Arts and Sciences, Department of Education, Specialization in Elementary and Secondary Principalship, Lewisburg, PA 17837. Offers MA, MS Ed. *Degree requirements:* For master's, thesis or alternative. *Entrance requirements:* For master's, GRE General Test, minimum GPA of 2.8. Additional exam requirements/recommendations for international students: Required—TOEFL.

Buffalo State College, State University of New York, Graduate Studies and Research, Faculty of Applied Science and Education, Department of Elementary Education and Reading, Program in Educational Leadership and Facilitation, Buffalo, NY 14222-1095. Offers CAS. *Accreditation:* NCATE. Part-time and evening/weekend programs available. *Degree requirements:* For CAS, internship. *Entrance requirements:* For degree, master's degree, New York teaching certificate, 3 years of teaching experience. Additional exam requirements/recommendations for international students: Required—TOEFL (minimum score 550 paper-based; 213 computer-based).

Butler University, College of Education, Indianapolis, IN 46208-3485. Offers administration (MS); elementary education (MS); reading (MS); school counseling (MS); secondary education (MS); special education (MS). *Accreditation:* ACA; NCATE. Part-time and evening/weekend programs available. *Faculty:* 12 full-time (6 women), 11 part-time/adjunct (8 women). *Students:* 18 full-time (10 women), 156 part-time (125 women); includes 21 minority (16 African Americans, 2 Asian Americans or Pacific Islanders, 3 Hispanic Americans), 7 international. Average age 31. 56 applicants, 57% accepted, 29 enrolled. In 2006, 72 degrees awarded. *Entrance requirements:* For master's, GRE General Test, MAT, interview. *Application deadline:* For fall admission, 8/15 priority date for domestic students. Applications are processed on a rolling basis. Application fee: $35. Electronic applications accepted. *Expenses:* Tuition: Full-time $6,030; part-time $335 per credit. Tuition and fees vary according to program. *Financial support:* Institutionally sponsored loans available. Support available to part-time students. Financial award application deadline: 7/15; financial award applicants required to submit FAFSA. *Faculty research:* Ethics in cybercounseling, history of sports for disabled effect of fetal alcohol syndrome on perceptual learning, Reading Recovery's theoretical framework in teacher education. *Unit head:* Dr. Ena Shelley, Dean, 317-940-9752, Fax: 317-940-6481. *Application contact:* Karen Farrell, Department Secretary, 317-940-9220, E-mail: kfarrell@butler.edu.

Cabrini College, Graduate and Professional Studies, Radnor, PA 19087-3698. Offers biotechnology (Certificate); education (M Ed); educational leadership (Certificate); instructional systems technology (MS); organization leadership (MS); project management (Certificate). Part-time and evening/weekend programs available. *Faculty:* 11 full-time (7 women), 25 part-time/adjunct (11 women). *Students:* 91 full-time (63 women), 484 part-time (364 women); includes 43 minority (28 African Americans, 6 Asian Americans or Pacific Islanders, 9 Hispanic Americans), 6 international. Average age 32. In 2006, 143 degrees awarded. *Degree requirements:* For master's, thesis optional. *Entrance requirements:* For master's, GRE and/or MAT (in some cases), letter of recommendation, minimum GPA of 2.5. *Application deadline:* For fall admission, 7/29 priority date for domestic students; for spring admission, 12/9 for domestic students. Applications are processed on a rolling basis. Application fee: $50. Electronic applications accepted. *Expenses:* Tuition: Part-time $310 per credit. Required fees: $45 per term. Tuition and fees vary according to course load. *Financial support:* Career-related internships or fieldwork and unspecified assistantships available. Support available to part-time students. Financial award applicants required to submit FAFSA. *Faculty research:* Qualitative research in reading, ethnographic studies. *Unit head:* Dr. Michael W. Markowitz, Dean for Graduate and Professional Studies, 610-902-8501, Fax: 610-902-8522, E-mail: michael.w.markowitz@cabrini.edu. *Application contact:* Bruce D. Bryde, Director of Enrollment and Recruiting, 610-902-8291, Fax: 610-902-8522, E-mail: bruce.d.bryde@cabrini.edu.

Caldwell College, Graduate Studies, Program in Educational Administration, Caldwell, NJ 07006-6195. Offers MA. Part-time and evening/weekend programs available. *Degree requirements:* For master's, thesis, research paper. *Entrance requirements:* For master's, GRE General Test or MAT, interview, minimum GPA of 2.75, teaching certificate, 3 years of teaching experience, writing sample. Additional exam requirements/recommendations for international students: Required—TOEFL (minimum score 580 paper-based; 237 computer-based). Electronic applications accepted.

California Baptist University, Program in Education, Riverside, CA 92504-3206. Offers cross-cultural language and academic development (MA Ed); educational leadership (MS Ed); educational technology (MS Ed); instructional computer applications (MS Ed); reading (MS Ed); special education (MS Ed); teaching (MS Ed). Part-time programs available. *Faculty:* 16 full-time (10 women), 16 part-time/adjunct (13 women). *Students:* 77 full-time (64 women), 408 part-time (342 women); includes 157 minority (41 African Americans, 12 American Indian/Alaska Native, 18 Asian Americans or Pacific Islanders, 86 Hispanic Americans), 2 international. 282 applicants, 70% accepted, 171 enrolled. In 2006, 63 degrees awarded. *Degree requirements:* For master's, thesis optional. *Entrance requirements:* For master's, minimum undergraduate GPA of 2.75, 12 semester hours of course work in education. Additional exam requirements/recommendations for international students: Required—TOEFL (minimum score 575 paper-based; 230 computer-based), IELTS (minimum score 7). *Application deadline:* For fall admission, 9/1 for domestic students, 7/15 priority date for international students; for spring admission, 1/3 for domestic students, 11/1 priority date for international students. Applications are processed on a rolling basis. Application fee: $45. Electronic applications accepted. *Expenses:* Tuition: Full-time $7,812; part-time $434 per unit. Required fees: $120 per semester. Tuition and fees vary according to program. *Financial support:* In 2006–07, 19 students received support. Career-related internships or fieldwork, Federal Work-Study, and scholarships/grants available. Support available to part-time students. Financial award applicants required to submit FAFSA. *Unit head:* Dr. Mary Crist, Dean, School of Education, 951-343-4313, Fax: 951-343-4516, E-mail: mcrist@calbaptist.edu. *Application contact:* Gail Ronveaux, Dean of Graduate Enrollment, 951-343-5045, Fax: 951-343-5095, E-mail: graduateadmissions@calbaptist.edu.

California Lutheran University, Graduate Studies, School of Education, Emphasis in Educational Administration, Thousand Oaks, CA 91360-2787. Offers MA. Part-time and evening/weekend programs available. *Degree requirements:* For master's, thesis or comprehensive exam. *Entrance requirements:* For master's, GRE General Test, interview, minimum GPA of 3.0.

California State University, Bakersfield, Division of Graduate Studies and Research, School of Education, Program in Educational Administration, Bakersfield, CA 93311-1022. Offers MA. *Degree requirements:* For master's, thesis or alternative, culminating projects .

California State University Channel Islands, Extended Education, Program in Educational Leadership, Camarillo, CA 93012. Offers MAEd. *Students:* 31. *Unit head:* Dr. Tim Rummel, Coordinator, 805-437-2748.

California State University, Chico, Graduate School, College of Communication and Education, Department of Education, Program in Education, Chico, CA 95929-0722. Offers curriculum and instruction (MA); educational administration (MA); linguistically and culturally diverse learners (MA); reading/language arts (MA); special education (MA). *Students:* 23 full-time (14 women), 58 part-time (45 women); includes 10 minority (2 African Americans, 1 American Indian/Alaska Native, 1 Asian American or Pacific Islander, 6 Hispanic Americans), 1 international. Average age 37. 39 applicants, 100% accepted, 32 enrolled. In 2006, 37 degrees awarded. *Unit head:* Dr. Michael Kotar, Graduate Coordinator, 530-898-6610.

California State University, Dominguez Hills, College of Education, Division of Graduate Education, Program in Educational Administration, Carson, CA 90747-0001. Offers MA. Evening/weekend programs available. *Faculty:* 4 full-time (2 women), 8 part-time/adjunct (3 women). *Students:* 136 full-time (86 women), 66 part-time (45 women); includes 129 minority (67 African Americans, 2 American Indian/Alaska Native, 11 Asian Americans or Pacific Islanders, 49 Hispanic Americans), 1 international. Average age 38. 122 applicants, 88% accepted, 57 enrolled. In 2006, 174 degrees awarded. *Degree requirements:* For master's, comprehensive exam, registration. *Entrance requirements:* For master's, minimum GPA of 2.75. *Application deadline:* For fall admission, 6/1 for domestic students. Applications are processed on a rolling basis. Application fee: $55. *Expenses:* Tuition, nonresident: part-time $339 per unit. Required fees: $1,148 per term. Tuition and fees vary according to program. *Faculty research:* Educational leadership, teacher retention, accountability, decision making. *Unit head:* Dr. Ann Chlebicki, Chairperson, 310-243-2517, E-mail: achlebicki@csudh.edu. *Application contact:* Admissions Office, 310-243-3530.

California State University, East Bay, Academic Programs and Graduate Studies, College of Education and Allied Studies, Department of Educational Leadership, Hayward, CA 94542-3000. Offers educational leadership (MS); specializing in urban teaching leadership (MS). *Accreditation:* NCATE. Part-time and evening/weekend programs available. *Students:* 73 full-time (52 women), 93 part-time (64 women); includes 69 minority (29 African Americans, 2 American Indian/Alaska Native, 8 Asian Americans or Pacific Islanders, 30 Hispanic Americans), 1 international. Average age 38. 128 applicants, 89% accepted, 106 enrolled. In 2006, 30 degrees awarded. *Degree requirements:* For master's, project or thesis. *Entrance requirements:* For master's, teaching or services credential and experience. Additional exam requirements/recommendations for international students: Required—TOEFL (minimum score 550 paper-based; 213 computer-based). *Application deadline:* For fall admission, 5/31 for domestic students, 4/30 for international students; for winter admission, 9/30 for domestic and international students; for spring admission, 12/31 for domestic students, 11/30 for international students. Application fee: $55. Electronic applications accepted. *Financial support:* Career-related internships or fieldwork, Federal Work-Study, and institutionally sponsored loans available. Support available to part-time students. Financial award application deadline: 3/2. *Unit head:* Dr. Jose Lopez, Interim Chair, 510-885-4145, Fax: 510-885-4642, E-mail: jose.lopez@csueastbay.edu. *Application contact:* My Huynh, Graduate Prospect Specialist, 510-885-2989, Fax: 510-885-4059, E-mail: my.huynh@csueastbay.edu.

California State University, Fresno, Division of Graduate Studies, School of Education and Human Development, Department of Educational Research, Administration and Foundations, Fresno, CA 93740-8027. Offers education (MA), including administration and supervision. *Accreditation:* NCATE. Part-time and evening/weekend programs available. *Degree requirements:* For master's, thesis or alternative. *Entrance requirements:* For master's, GRE General Test, MAT, minimum GPA of 2.75. Additional exam requirements/recommendations for international students: Required—TOEFL. Electronic applications accepted. *Faculty research:* Substance abuse on youth education.

California State University, Fresno, Division of Graduate Studies, School of Education and Human Development, Joint Doctoral Program in Educational Leadership, Fresno, CA 93740-8027. Offers Ed D. Part-time programs available. *Degree requirements:* For doctorate, thesis/dissertation. *Entrance requirements:* For doctorate, GRE or MAT, minimum GPA of 3.2, master's degree. Additional exam requirements/recommendations for international students: Required—TOEFL. Electronic applications accepted. *Faculty research:* Minority special education leadership, literacy, ethics of leadership, organizational planning, language development.

California State University, Fullerton, Graduate Studies, College of Education, Department of Educational Leadership, Fullerton, CA 92834-9480. Offers MS. *Accreditation:* NCATE. Part-time programs available. *Students:* 6 full-time (2 women), 184 part-time (129 women); includes 71 minority (4 African Americans, 2 American Indian/Alaska Native, 25 Asian Americans or Pacific Islanders, 40 Hispanic Americans), 1 international. Average age 36. 146 applicants, 85% accepted, 106 enrolled. In 2006, 84 degrees awarded. *Degree requirements:* For master's, thesis or alternative, project. *Entrance requirements:* For master's, minimum GPA of 2.5. Application fee: $55. *Expenses:* Tuition, nonresident: part-time $339 per unit. Required fees: $1,155 per semester. *Financial support:* Career-related internships or fieldwork, Federal Work-Study, institutionally sponsored loans, and scholarships/grants available. Support available to part-time students. Financial award application deadline: 3/1. *Faculty research:* Creation of a substance abuse training and demonstration program. *Unit head:* Dr. Louise Adler, Head, 714-278-3911.

California State University, Northridge, Graduate Studies, College of Education, Department of Educational Leadership and Policy Studies, Northridge, CA 91330. Offers education (MA); educational administration (MA). *Accreditation:* NCATE. Part-time and evening/weekend programs available. *Faculty:* 17 full-time (8 women), 63 part-time/adjunct (36 women). *Students:* 184 full-time (65 women), 755 part-time (258 women); includes 546 minority (94 African Americans, 2 American Indian/Alaska Native, 64 Asian Americans or Pacific Islanders, 386 Hispanic Americans), 9 international. Average age 37. 234 applicants, 93% accepted, 159 enrolled. In 2006, 276 degrees awarded. *Entrance requirements:* For master's, 2 letters of recommendation. Additional exam requirements/recommendations for international students: Required—TOEFL. *Application deadline:* For fall admission, 11/30 for domestic students. Application fee: $55. *Expenses:* Tuition, nonresident: full-time $8,136; part-time $4,068 per year. Required fees: $3,624; $1,161 per term. *Financial support:* Fellowships available. Financial award application deadline: 3/1. *Faculty research:* Bilingual educational training. *Unit head:* Dr. Richard Castallo, Chair, 818-677-2591.

California State University, Sacramento, Graduate Studies, College of Education, Department of Educational Administration, Sacramento, CA 95819-6048. Offers MA. Part-time programs available. *Students:* 160 full-time (107 women), 128 part-time (88 women); includes 126 minority (34 African Americans, 24 Asian Americans or Pacific Islanders, 68 Hispanic Americans), 1 international. Average age 37. 73 applicants, 78% accepted, 47 enrolled. *Degree requirements:* For master's, thesis or alternative, writing proficiency exam. *Entrance requirements:* For master's, minimum GPA of 2.5. Additional exam requirements/recommendations for international students: Required—TOEFL. *Application deadline:* Applications are processed on a rolling basis. Application fee: $55. Electronic applications accepted. *Financial support:* Career-related internships or fieldwork and Federal Work-Study available. Support available to part-time students. Financial award application deadline: 3/1. *Unit head:* Dr. Edmund W. Lee, Chair, 916-278-5388, Fax: 916-278-4608. *Application contact:* Coordinator, 916-278-7023.

California State University, San Bernardino, Graduate Studies, College of Education, Program in Educational Administration, San Bernardino, CA 92407-2397. Offers MA. Part-time and evening/weekend programs available. *Faculty:* 8 full-time (2 women), 4 part-time/adjunct (2 women). *Students:* 129 full-time (83 women), 61 part-time (39 women); includes 82 minority (30 African Americans, 2 American Indian/Alaska Native, 7 Asian Americans or Pacific Islanders, 43 Hispanic Americans). Average age 34. 100 applicants, 84% accepted, 29 enrolled. In 2006, 133 degrees awarded. *Degree requirements:* For master's, thesis or alternative. *Entrance requirements:* For master's, minimum GPA of 3.0 in education. *Application deadline:* For fall admission, 8/31 priority date for domestic students. Application fee: $55. *Financial support:*

Educational Administration

California State University, San Bernardino (continued)
Career-related internships or fieldwork available. Support available to part-time students. *Unit head:* Dr. Angela Louque, Chair, 909-537-7621, Fax: 909-537-7510, E-mail: alouque@csusb.edu.

California University of Pennsylvania, School of Graduate Studies and Research, School of Education, Program in School Administration, California, PA 15419-1394. Offers M Ed. *Accreditation:* NCATE. Part-time and evening/weekend programs available. *Faculty:* 6 full-time (3 women). *Students:* 4 full-time (2 women), 167 part-time (84 women); includes 6 minority (5 African Americans, 1 Asian American or Pacific Islander). Average age 40. In 2006, 52 degrees awarded. *Degree requirements:* For master's, thesis optional. *Entrance requirements:* For master's, MAT, interview, minimum GPA of 3.0, teaching certificate, 2 years of teaching experience. Additional exam requirements/recommendations for international students: Required—TOEFL (minimum score 550 paper-based; 213 computer-based; 80 iBT). *Application deadline:* For fall admission, 8/1 priority date for domestic and international students; for winter admission, 12/1 priority date for domestic and international students; for spring admission, 5/1 priority date for domestic and international students. Applications are processed on a rolling basis. Application fee: $25. Electronic applications accepted. *Expenses:* Tuition, state resident: full-time $6,048; part-time $336 per credit. Tuition, nonresident: full-time $9,678; part-time $538 per credit. Required fees: $1,854; $263 per credit. Full-time tuition and fees vary according to course load, campus/location and program. *Financial support:* Career-related internships or fieldwork, scholarships/grants, traineeships, and unspecified assistantships available. Financial award applicants required to submit FAFSA. *Faculty research:* Educational leadership, peer coaching, online education-effective teaching strategies, instruction strategies, school law. *Unit head:* Dr. Lizbeth Gillette, Coordinator, 412-467-1348, Fax: 412-467-1380, E-mail: gillette@cup.edu.

Calvin College, Graduate Programs in Education, Grand Rapids, MI 49546-4388. Offers curriculum and instruction (M Ed); educational leadership (M Ed); learning disabilities (M Ed); literacy (M Ed). *Accreditation:* NCATE. Part-time programs available. *Faculty:* 2 full-time (both women), 6 part-time/adjunct (2 women). *Students:* 6 full-time (5 women), 87 part-time (66 women); includes 9 minority (3 African Americans, 1 American Indian/Alaska Native, 4 Asian Americans or Pacific Islanders, 1 Hispanic American). Average age 29. 26 applicants, 100% accepted. In 2006, 14 degrees awarded. *Degree requirements:* For master's, thesis or seminar; for degree. *Entrance requirements:* For master's, teaching certificate. Additional exam requirements/recommendations for international students: Required—TOEFL (minimum score 550 paper-based; 213 computer-based). *Application deadline:* For fall admission, 8/1 priority date for domestic students, 5/1 priority date for international students; for spring admission, 1/1 priority date for domestic students, 11/1 priority date for international students. Applications are processed on a rolling basis. Application fee: $0. Electronic applications accepted. *Expenses:* Tuition: Part-time $420 per credit hour. *Financial support:* In 2006–07, 19 students received support. Federal Work-Study, scholarships/grants, and tuition waivers (full and partial) available. Support available to part-time students. Financial award application deadline: 4/3. *Faculty research:* Literacy, racialized gender and gendered identity, teacher learning, learning disabilities identification. *Unit head:* Dr. Susan S. Hasseler, Associate Dean for Teacher Education, 616-526-6597, Fax: 616-526-6505, E-mail: shassele@calvin.edu. *Application contact:* Deb Abbott, Administrative Assistant, 616-526-6105, Fax: 616-526-6505, E-mail: dka2@calvin.edu.

Cambridge College, Program in Education, Cambridge, MA 02138-5304. Offers education (CAGS); education leadership (Ed D); education/integrated studies (M Ed). Part-time and evening/weekend programs available. *Faculty:* 10 full-time (4 women), 309 part-time/adjunct (211 women). *Students:* 963 full-time (758 women), 1,500 part-time (1,182 women); includes 1,168 minority (780 African Americans, 8 American Indian/Alaska Native, 21 Asian Americans or Pacific Islanders, 359 Hispanic Americans), 8 international. Average age 36. 492 applicants, 91% accepted, 371 enrolled. In 2006, 1,063 master's, 287 other advanced degrees awarded. *Degree requirements:* For master's, thesis, internship/practicum. *Entrance requirements:* Additional exam requirements/recommendations for international students: Required—TOEFL. *Application deadline:* For fall admission, 10/3 priority date for domestic students; for spring admission, 2/13 priority date for domestic students. Applications are processed on a rolling basis. Application fee: $30. *Expenses:* Tuition: Full-time $10,935; part-time $405 per credit hour. One-time fee: $130 full-time. Tuition and fees vary according to degree level and program. *Financial support:* Teaching assistantships, career-related internships or fieldwork and Federal Work-Study available. Financial award applicants required to submit FAFSA. *Faculty research:* Adult education, accelerated learning, mathematics education, brain compatible learning, special education and law. *Unit head:* Dr. Anthony DeMatteo, Dean, 617-873-0219, Fax: 617-349-3545. *Application contact:* Wendy D. Shattuck, Director of Graduate Admissions, 617-868-1000 Ext. 144, Fax: 617-349-3561, E-mail: admit@cambridgecollege.edu.

Cameron University, Office of Graduate Studies, Program in Educational Leadership, Lawton, OK 73505-6377. Offers MS. Part-time and evening/weekend programs available. *Students:* 3 full-time (all women), 30 part-time (21 women); includes 7 minority (5 African Americans, 1 American Indian/Alaska Native, 1 Hispanic American). Average age 35. In 2006, 9 degrees awarded. *Degree requirements:* For master's, portfolio. Application fee: $15 ($35 for international students). *Expenses:* Tuition, state resident: full-time $2,479; part-time $138 per credit hour. Tuition, nonresident: full-time $5,976; part-time $332 per credit hour. Tuition and fees vary according to campus/location. *Financial support:* Application deadline: 4/15. *Unit head:* Claudia Edwards, MS Graduate Advisor, 580-581-7929, Fax: 580-581-2623, E-mail: cedwards@cameron.edu. *Application contact:* Teresa Enriquez, Graduate Admissions/Enrollment Coordinator, 580-581-2987, E-mail: teresae@cameron.edu.

Campbell University, Graduate and Professional Programs, School of Education, Buies Creek, NC 27506. Offers administration (MSA); community counseling (MA); elementary education (M Ed); English education (M Ed); interdisciplinary studies (M Ed); mathematics education (M Ed); middle grades education (M Ed); physical education (M Ed); school counseling (M Ed); secondary education (M Ed); social science education (M Ed). *Accreditation:* NCATE. Part-time and evening/weekend programs available. *Faculty:* 14 full-time (9 women), 12 part-time/adjunct (7 women). *Students:* 27 full-time (25 women), 183 part-time (146 women); includes 30 minority (24 African Americans, 3 American Indian/Alaska Native, 3 Hispanic Americans), 1 international. Average age 31. 112 applicants, 74% accepted, 74 enrolled. In 2006, 65 degrees awarded. *Degree requirements:* For master's, comprehensive exam. *Entrance requirements:* For master's, GRE General Test, minimum GPA of 2.7. *Application deadline:* For fall admission, 8/1 priority date for domestic students; for spring admission, 1/2 priority date for domestic students. Applications are processed on a rolling basis. Application fee: $65. *Expenses:* Tuition: Part-time $380 per semester hour. *Financial support:* In 2006–07, 67 students received support. Career-related internships or fieldwork and Federal Work-Study available. Financial award application deadline: 4/15; financial award applicants required to submit FAFSA. *Faculty research:* Spiritual values and wellness issues in counseling, stress and professional burnout among counselors, thinking strategies, leadership, adaptive technology. *Unit head:* Dr. Karen P. Nery, Dean, 910-893-1630, Fax: 910-893-1999, E-mail: nery@campbell.edu. *Application contact:* James S. Farthing, Director of Graduate Admissions for Business and Education, 910-893-1200 Ext. 1318, Fax: 910-814-4718, E-mail: farthing@campbell.edu.

Canisius College, Graduate Division, School of Education and Human Services, Department of Graduate Education, Buffalo, NY 14208-1098. Offers business education (MS); childhood education (MS); college student personnel (MS); differentiated instruction (MS Ed); early childhood education (MS); education administration (MS); education of the deaf and hard of hearing (MS); general education (MS Ed); literacy education (MS Ed); reading education (MS Ed); secondary education (MS); special education (MS). *Accreditation:* NCATE. Part-time and evening/weekend programs available. *Faculty:* 13 full-time (12 women), 74 part-time/adjunct (44 women). *Students:* 377 full-time (267 women), 303 part-time (219 women); includes 43 minority (27 African Americans, 2 American Indian/Alaska Native, 6 Asian Americans or Pacific Islanders, 8 Hispanic Americans), 187 international. Average age 30. In 2006, 296 degrees awarded. Application fee: $25. *Expenses:* Tuition: Part-time $645 per credit hour. Required fees: $19 per credit hour. Tuition and fees vary according to program. *Financial support:* Research assistantships with full tuition reimbursements, career-related internships or fieldwork, institutionally sponsored loans, scholarships/grants, health care benefits, tuition waivers (full and partial), and unspecified assistantships available. *Faculty research:* Autism, Asperger's disease, private higher education, reading strategies. *Unit head:* Rev. Paul Nochelski, Chair of Graduate Education and Leadership, 716-888-3297, Fax: 716-888-3299. *Application contact:* James D. Bagwell, Director of Graduate Recruitment and Admissions, 716-888-2544, Fax: 716-888-3290, E-mail: bagwellj@canisius.edu.

Capella University, School of Education, Minneapolis, MN 55402. Offers college teaching (Certificate); curriculum and instruction (MS, PhD); education (MS); enrollment management (MS); instructional design for online learning (MS, PhD); k-12 studies in education (MS, PhD); leadership for higher education (MS, PhD); leadership in education administration (Certificate); leadership in educational administration (MS, PhD); postsecondary and adult education (MS, PhD); professional studies in education (MS, PhD); reading and literacy (MS); training and performance improvement (MS, PhD). Part-time and evening/weekend programs available. Postbaccalaureate distance learning degree programs offered (minimal on-campus study). Terminal master's awarded for partial completion of doctoral program. *Degree requirements:* For master's, integrative project, thesis optional; for doctorate, thesis/dissertation, comprehensive exam, registration. *Entrance requirements:* Additional exam requirements/recommendations for international students: Required—TOEFL (minimum score 550 paper-based; 213 computer-based), TWE (minimum score 4). Electronic applications accepted. *Faculty research:* Higher education administration, distance learning, adult education, training and curriculum design.

Cardinal Stritch University, College of Education, Department of Education, Milwaukee, WI 53217-3985. Offers educational leadership (MS); leadership (Ed D); professional development (ME). ME (Catholic urban educator) offered in collaboration with the Archdiocese of Milwaukee. *Accreditation:* NCATE. Evening/weekend programs available. *Degree requirements:* For master's, thesis (for some programs), research project, faculty recommendation, comprehensive exam; for doctorate, thesis/dissertation, practica, field experience. *Entrance requirements:* For master's, letters of recommendation (3), minimum GPA of 3.0; for doctorate, minimum GPA of 3.5 in master's coursework, letters of recommendation (3).

Caribbean University, Graduate School, Bayamón, PR 00960-0493. Offers accounting (MBA); administration and supervision (MA Ed); criminal justice (MA); curriculum and instruction (MA Ed); education (PhD); gerontology (MSN); human resources (MBA); museology, archiving and art history (MA Ed); neonatal pediatrics (MSN); physical education (MA Ed); special education (MA Ed). *Entrance requirements:* For master's, interview, minimum GPA of 2.5.

Carlow University, School of Education, Program in Educational Leadership, Pittsburgh, PA 15213-3165. Offers M Ed. Part-time and evening/weekend programs available. *Degree requirements:* For master's, thesis or alternative. *Entrance requirements:* For master's, interview, minimum GPA of 3.0, resumé, 3 years professional experience, 3 letters of recommendation, teacher certification. Additional exam requirements/recommendations for international students: Required—TOEFL. Electronic applications accepted.

Carthage College, Division of Teacher Education, Kenosha, WI 53140. Offers classroom guidance and counseling (M Ed); creative arts (M Ed); gifted and talented children (M Ed); language arts (M Ed); modern language (M Ed); natural sciences (M Ed); reading (M Ed, Certificate); social sciences (M Ed); teacher leadership (M Ed). Part-time and evening/weekend programs available. *Degree requirements:* For master's, thesis optional. *Entrance requirements:* For master's, MAT, minimum B average, letters of reference.

Castleton State College, Division of Graduate Studies, Department of Education, Program in Educational Leadership, Castleton, VT 05735. Offers MA Ed, CAGS. Part-time and evening/weekend programs available. *Degree requirements:* For master's, thesis or alternative; for CAGS, publishable paper. *Entrance requirements:* For master's, GRE General Test, MAT, interview, minimum undergraduate GPA of 3.0; for CAGS, educational research, master's degree, minimum undergraduate GPA of 3.0.

The Catholic University of America, School of Arts and Sciences, Department of Education, Washington, DC 20064. Offers administration, curriculum, and policy studies (MA); Catholic school leadership (MA); counselor education (MA); educational administration (PhD); educational psychology (PhD); English as a second language (MA); learning and instruction (MA); policy studies (PhD); teacher education (MA). *Accreditation:* NCATE. Part-time programs available. *Faculty:* 11 full-time (8 women), 3 part-time/adjunct (2 women). *Students:* 11 full-time (8 women), 52 part-time (34 women); includes 13 minority (9 African Americans, 1 Asian American or Pacific Islander, 3 Hispanic Americans), 2 international. Average age 35. 67 applicants, 55% accepted, 13 enrolled. In 2006, 19 master's, 2 doctorates awarded. *Degree requirements:* For master's, thesis or alternative, comprehensive exam; for doctorate, thesis/dissertation, comprehensive exam. *Entrance requirements:* For master's and doctorate, GRE General Test or MAT, 3 letters of recommendation. Additional exam requirements/recommendations for international students: Required—TOEFL (minimum score 580 paper-based; 237 computer-based). *Application deadline:* For fall admission, 2/1 priority date for domestic students; for spring admission, 11/15 priority date for domestic students. Applications are processed on a rolling basis. Application fee: $55. Electronic applications accepted. *Expenses:* Tuition: Full-time $27,700; part-time $1,045 per credit hour. Required fees: $1,290. Part-time tuition and fees vary according to campus/location and program. *Financial support:* Research assistantships, teaching assistantships, career-related internships or fieldwork, Federal Work-Study, scholarships/grants, tuition waivers (full and partial), and unspecified assistantships available. Support available to part-time students. Financial award application deadline: 2/1; financial award applicants required to submit FAFSA. *Faculty research:* Catholic school issues, reflective teaching, cognitive psychology, urban education. *Unit head:* Dr. Merylann Schuttloffel, Chair, 202-319-5805, Fax: 202-319-5815, E-mail: schuttloffel@cua.edu.

Centenary College, Program in Education, Hackettstown, NJ 07840-2100. Offers instructional leadership (MA); special education (MA). Part-time and evening/weekend programs available. Postbaccalaureate distance learning degree programs offered (minimal on-campus study). *Degree requirements:* For master's, thesis. *Entrance requirements:* For master's, interview, minimum undergraduate GPA of 2.8.

Centenary College of Louisiana, Graduate Programs, Department of Education, Shreveport, LA 71104. Offers administration (M Ed); elementary education (MAT); secondary education (MAT); supervision of instruction (M Ed). Part-time and evening/weekend programs available. *Degree requirements:* For master's, comprehensive exam. *Entrance requirements:* For master's, GRE General Test (M Ed), PRAXIS I and PRAXIS II (MAT), teacher certification (M Ed), minimum GPA of 2.5. Expenses: Contact institution. *Faculty research:* Teachers as advocates for teachers, portfolio assessment, disabled readers.

Central Connecticut State University, School of Graduate Studies, School of Education and Professional Studies, Department of Educational Leadership, Program in Educational Leadership, New Britain, CT 06050-4010. Offers MS, Ed D, Sixth Year Certificate. *Students:* 7 full-time (5 women), 247 part-time (155 women); includes 35 minority (19 African Americans, 2 Asian Americans or Pacific Islanders, 14 Hispanic Americans), 1 international. 90 applicants, 70% accepted, 49 enrolled. In 2006, 83 master's, 18 doctorates, 38 Sixth Year Certificates awarded. *Degree requirements:* For Sixth Year Certificate, thesis or alternative, qualifying exam. *Entrance requirements:* Additional exam requirements/recommendations for international students: Required—TOEFL. *Application deadline:* For fall admission, 7/1 for domestic students; for spring admission, 12/1 for domestic students. Applications are processed on a rolling basis. Application fee: $50. Electronic applications accepted. *Expenses:* Tuition, area resident: Full-time $3,970; part-time $380 per credit. Tuition, state resident: full-time $5,955; part-time

$380 per credit. Tuition, nonresident: full-time $11,061; part-time $380 per credit. Required fees: $3,189. One-time fee: $62 part-time. Tuition and fees vary according to degree level and program.

Central Michigan University, Central Michigan University Off-Campus Programs, Program in Educational Administration and Community Leadership, Mount Pleasant, MI 48859. Offers educational administration (Ed S); educational administration and community leadership (Ed D); school principalship (MA). Part-time and evening/weekend programs available. *Entrance requirements:* For master's, minimum GPA of 2.7 in major. Additional exam requirements/recommendations for international students: Required—TOEFL. *Application deadline:* Applications are processed on a rolling basis. Application fee: $50. Electronic applications accepted. *Financial support:* Scholarships/grants available. Support available to part-time students. *Unit head:* Dr. Stephen Lawton, Chair, 989-774-1534, Fax: 989-774-4374, E-mail: lawto1sb@cmich.edu. *Application contact:* 877-268-4636, E-mail: cmuoffcampus@cmich.edu.

Central Michigan University, College of Graduate Studies, College of Education and Human Services, Department of Educational Administration and Community Leadership, Mount Pleasant, MI 48859. Offers community leadership (MA); educational administration (MA, Ed S); educational leadership (Ed D); school principalship (MA). *Accreditation:* NCATE. *Degree requirements:* For master's and Ed S, thesis or alternative, registration. *Entrance requirements:* For master's and Ed S, Michigan teaching certificate or equivalent; for doctorate, GRE or MAT, 3 years of full-time administrative experience, master's degree in education, minimum GPA of 3.5. *Faculty research:* Elementary administration, secondary administration, student achievement, in-service training, internships in administration.

Central State University, Program in Education, Wilberforce, OH 45384. Offers educational technology (M Ed); leadership (M Ed); literacy (M Ed). Part-time and evening/weekend programs available. *Degree requirements:* For master's, thesis or alternative. *Entrance requirements:* For master's, GRE.

Central Washington University, Graduate Studies, Research and Continuing Education, College of Education and Professional Studies, Department of Education, Program in Educational Administration, Ellensburg, WA 98926. Offers M Ed. Part-time programs available. *Faculty:* 21 full-time (10 women). *Students:* 5 full-time (2 women), 19 part-time (7 women); includes 3 minority (1 African American, 1 American Indian/Alaska Native, 1 Hispanic American). 10 applicants, 80% accepted, 8 enrolled. In 2006, 7 degrees awarded. *Degree requirements:* For master's, thesis or alternative. *Entrance requirements:* For master's, minimum GPA of 3.0. Additional exam requirements/recommendations for international students: Required—TOEFL (minimum score 550 paper-based; 213 computer-based; 79 iBT). *Application deadline:* For fall admission, 4/1 priority date for domestic students; for winter admission, 10/1 for domestic students; for spring admission, 1/1 for domestic students. Applications are processed on a rolling basis. Application fee: $50. *Expenses:* Tuition, state resident: full-time $6,312. Tuition, nonresident: full-time $14,112. Tuition and fees vary according to course load and degree level. *Financial support:* Research assistantships with partial tuition reimbursements, teaching assistantships with partial tuition reimbursements, Federal Work-Study, health care benefits, and unspecified assistantships available. Financial award application deadline: 3/1; financial award applicants required to submit FAFSA. *Application contact:* Justine Eason, Admissions Program Coordinator, 509-963-3103, Fax: 509-963-1799, E-mail: masters@cwu.edu.

Chadron State College, School of Professional and Graduate Studies, Department of Education, Chadron, NE 69337. Offers business (MA Ed); community counseling (MA Ed); educational administration (MS Ed, Sp Ed); elementary education (MS Ed); history (MA Ed); language and literature (MA Ed); secondary administration (MS Ed); secondary education (MS Ed). *Accreditation:* NCATE. Part-time and evening/weekend programs available. Postbaccalaureate distance learning degree programs offered. *Degree requirements:* For master's, thesis optional. *Entrance requirements:* For master's, GRE General Test, GRE Writing Test, minimum GPA of 2.75 or 12 graduate hours at CSC with minimum GPA of 3.25. Additional exam requirements/recommendations for international students: Required—TOEFL. Electronic applications accepted. *Faculty research:* Rural education, technology, mental health.

Chapman University, Graduate Studies, School of Education, Concentration in Educational Leadership and Administration, Orange, CA 92866. Offers MA. Part-time and evening/weekend programs available. *Faculty:* 16 full-time (11 women), 25 part-time/adjunct (14 women). *Students:* 4 full-time (2 women), 24 part-time (15 women); includes 7 minority (1 African American, 6 Hispanic Americans). Average age 34. 20 applicants, 65% accepted, 11 enrolled. In 2006, 10 degrees awarded. *Degree requirements:* For master's, thesis optional. *Entrance requirements:* For master's, GRE General Test, MAT, or California Subject Examinations for Teachers, minimum undergraduate GPA of 2.5. Additional exam requirements/recommendations for international students: Required—TOEFL (minimum score 550 paper-based). *Application deadline:* Applications are processed on a rolling basis. Application fee: $55. Electronic applications accepted. *Expenses:* Contact institution. *Financial support:* In 2006–07, 12 students received support; fellowships, Federal Work-Study available. Financial award application deadline: 6/30; financial award applicants required to submit FAFSA. *Unit head:* Dr. Penny Bryan, Coordinator, 714-997-6781. *Application contact:* Rika Judd, Information Contact, 714-997-6786, Fax: 714-997-6713, E-mail: rjudd@chapman.edu.

Charleston Southern University, Programs in Education, Charleston, SC 29423-8087. Offers administration and supervision (M Ed), including elementary, secondary; elementary education (M Ed); English (MAT); science (MAT); secondary education (M Ed); social studies (MAT). *Accreditation:* NCATE. Part-time and evening/weekend programs available. *Degree requirements:* For master's, thesis optional. *Entrance requirements:* For master's, GRE or MAT. Expenses: Contact institution. *Faculty research:* Economic education, multicultural education, restructuring teacher education, participation in mathematics and science by minorities and women, at-risk children.

Chestnut Hill College, School of Graduate Studies, Department of Education, Program in Educational Leadership, Philadelphia, PA 19118-2693. Offers M Ed. Part-time and evening/weekend programs available. *Faculty:* 33 part-time/adjunct (24 women). *Students:* 1 (woman) full-time, 5 part-time (4 women); includes 1 minority (African American) Average age 29. *Degree requirements:* For master's, thesis optional. *Entrance requirements:* For master's, GRE General Test, writing sample. Additional exam requirements/recommendations for international students: Required—TOEFL (minimum score 500 paper-based). *Application deadline:* For fall admission, 7/15 priority date for domestic students, 7/15 for international students; for spring admission, 12/15 priority date for domestic students, 12/15 for international students. Applications are processed on a rolling basis. Application fee: $50. *Expenses:* Tuition: Part-time $470 per credit hour. Required fees: $30 per semester. Tuition and fees vary according to degree level. *Financial support:* Institutionally sponsored loans available. Financial award application deadline: 7/15; financial award applicants required to submit FAFSA. *Faculty research:* Principal effectiveness, school reform, urban education, personnel preparation, instructional leadership. *Application contact:* Jayne Mashett, Director of Graduate Admissions, 215-248-7020, Fax: 215-248-7161, E-mail: mashettj@chc.edu.

Cheyney University of Pennsylvania, School of Education, Program in Educational Administration and Supervision, Cheyney, PA 19319-0200. Offers M Ed, Certificate. *Accreditation:* NCATE. Part-time and evening/weekend programs available. *Degree requirements:* For master's, thesis or alternative. *Entrance requirements:* For master's, GRE General Test, MAT, minimum GPA of 2.75. Electronic applications accepted. *Faculty research:* Teacher motivation, critical thinking.

Cheyney University of Pennsylvania, School of Education, Program in Educational Administration of Adult and Continuing Education, Cheyney, PA 19319-0200. Offers M Ed, MS. Part-time and evening/weekend programs available. *Degree requirements:* For master's, thesis or alternative. Electronic applications accepted.

Cheyney University of Pennsylvania, School of Education, Program in Elementary and Secondary Principalship, Cheyney, PA 19319-0200. Offers Certificate.

Chicago State University, School of Graduate and Professional Studies, College of Education, Department of Educational Leadership, Curriculum and Foundations, Program in Educational Leadership, Chicago, IL 60628. Offers educational leadership (Ed D); general administration (MA); higher education administration (MA). *Accreditation:* NCATE. *Degree requirements:* For master's, thesis optional. *Entrance requirements:* For master's, minimum GPA of 2.75.

Christian Brothers University, Graduate Programs, School of Arts, Memphis, TN 38104-5581. Offers Catholic studies (MACS); curriculum and instruction (M Ed); educational leadership (MSEL); teacher-leadership (M Ed); teaching (MAT). Part-time and evening/weekend programs available. *Faculty:* 6 full-time (4 women), 11 part-time/adjunct (5 women). *Students:* 47 full-time (38 women), 134 part-time (104 women); includes 70 minority (68 African Americans, 1 Asian American or Pacific Islander, 1 Hispanic American), 3 international. Average age 35. In 2006, 57 degrees awarded. *Entrance requirements:* For master's, GRE, MAT. *Application deadline:* Applications are processed on a rolling basis. Application fee: $25. *Expenses:* Contact institution. *Financial support:* Institutionally sponsored loans available. Support available to part-time students. *Unit head:* Dr. Marins Carriere, Dean, 901-321-3366, E-mail: mcarrier@cbu.edu. *Application contact:* Dr. Talana L. Vogel, Director, 901-321-4101, Fax: 901-321-3408, E-mail: tvogel@cbu.edu.

The Citadel, The Military College of South Carolina, College of Graduate and Professional Studies, School of Education, Program in Educational Administration, Charleston, SC 29409. Offers M Ed, Ed S. *Accreditation:* NCATE. Part-time and evening/weekend programs available. *Students:* 6 full-time (4 women), 87 part-time (51 women); includes 35 minority (33 African Americans, 1 Asian American or Pacific Islander, 1 Hispanic American). Average age 34. In 2006, 38 master's, 4 other advanced degrees awarded. *Entrance requirements:* For master's, GRE General Test, MAT, or 12 hours of graduate course work with a minimum GPA of 3.0. Additional exam requirements/recommendations for international students: Required—TOEFL (minimum score 550 paper-based; 213 computer-based). *Application deadline:* Applications are processed on a rolling basis. Application fee: $30. *Expenses:* Tuition, state resident: part-time $259 per credit hour. Tuition, nonresident: part-time $482 per credit hour. *Financial support:* Application deadline: 7/1; *Unit head:* Dr. Kathy Brown, Head, 843-953-2064, E-mail: kathy.brown@citadel.edu. *Application contact:* Dr. Raymond S. Jones, Associate Dean, College of Graduate and Professional Studies, 843-953-5089, Fax: 843-953-7630, E-mail: ray.jones@citadel.edu.

City College of the City University of New York, Graduate School, School of Education, Department of Administration and Supervision, New York, NY 10031-9198. Offers MS, AC. *Students:* 33 applicants, 4 enrolled. In 2006, 24 degrees awarded. *Degree requirements:* For master's, thesis, research paper. *Entrance requirements:* For master's, Liberal Arts and Sciences Test (LAST), Content Specialty Test (CST), interview; minimum GPA of 3.0 in major, 2.5 overall. Additional exam requirements/recommendations for international students: Required—TOEFL. *Application deadline:* For fall admission, 3/15 for domestic students; for spring admission, 10/15 for domestic students. Application fee: $125. *Financial support:* Career-related internships or fieldwork available. Financial award application deadline: 5/1. *Faculty research:* Dynamics of organizational change, impact of laws on educational policy, leadership development in schools. *Unit head:* Sylvia Roberts, Head, 212-650-5187, Fax: 212-650-5191, E-mail: profesrob@aol.com. *Application contact:* Stacia Pusey, Graduate Admissions Adviser-Education, 212-650-5345, E-mail: spusey@ccny.cuny.edu.

City University, Graduate Division, Gordon Albright School of Education, Bellevue, WA 98005. Offers curriculum and instruction (M Ed); educational leadership (M Ed); educational leadership: principal certification (M Ed, Certificate); educational leadership: principal/program administrator certification (Certificate); educational leadership: program administrator certification (M Ed, Certificate); guidance and counseling (M Ed, Certificate); integrated arts and performance learning (M Ed); professional certification-teachers (Certificate); reading (Certificate); reading and literacy (M Ed); reading. literacy, and ESL/ELL (M Ed); teacher certification (MIT); technology, curriculum and instruction (M Ed). Part-time and evening/weekend programs available. Postbaccalaureate distance learning degree programs offered (no on-campus study). *Entrance requirements:* Additional exam requirements/recommendations for international students: Required—TOEFL (minimum score 540 paper-based; 207 computer-based); Recommended—IELTS. Electronic applications accepted.

Claremont Graduate University, Graduate Programs, School of Educational Studies, Claremont, CA 91711-6160. Offers Africana education (Certificate); education policy issues (MA, PhD); higher education (PhD); higher education administration (MA); human development (MA, PhD); public school administration (MA, PhD); teacher education (MA, PhD); teaching and learning (MA, PhD); urban education administration (MA, PhD); MBA/PhD. Part-time programs available. *Faculty:* 15 full-time (9 women), 11 part-time/adjunct (9 women). *Students:* 236 full-time (155 women), 168 part-time (117 women); includes 177 minority (34 African Americans, 2 American Indian/Alaska Native, 43 Asian Americans or Pacific Islanders, 98 Hispanic Americans), 7 international. Average age 38. In 2006, 90 master's, 20 doctorates awarded. Terminal master's awarded for partial completion of doctoral program. *Degree requirements:* For master's, thesis or alternative, comprehensive exam (for some programs); for doctorate, thesis/dissertation, comprehensive exam. *Entrance requirements:* For master's and doctorate, GRE General Test. *Application deadline:* For fall admission, 2/15 priority date for domestic students. Applications are processed on a rolling basis. Electronic applications accepted. *Financial support:* Fellowships, research assistantships, Federal Work-Study and institutionally sponsored loans available. Support available to part-time students. Financial award application deadline: 2/15; financial award applicants required to submit FAFSA. *Faculty research:* Education administration, K–12 and higher education, multicultural education, education policy, diversity in higher education, faculty issues. *Unit head:* Philip H. Dreyer, Dean, 909-621-8075, Fax: 909-621-8734, E-mail: philip.dreyer@cgu.edu. *Application contact:* Cece Gaddy, Administrative Director, 909-621-8317, Fax: 909-621-8734, E-mail: cece.gaddy@cgu.edu.

Clark Atlanta University, School of Education, Department of Educational Leadership, Atlanta, GA 30314. Offers MA, Ed D, Ed S. *Degree requirements:* For master's and doctorate, one foreign language, thesis/dissertation; for Ed S, thesis. *Entrance requirements:* For master's, GRE General Test, minimum undergraduate GPA of 2.5; for doctorate and Ed S, GRE General Test, minimum graduate GPA of 3.0.

Clarke College, Program in Education, Dubuque, IA 52001-3198. Offers early childhood/special education (MA); educational administration: elementary and secondary (MA); educational media: elementary and secondary (MA); multi-categorical resource K–12 (MA); multidisciplinary studies (MA); reading: elementary (MA); technology in education (MA). Part-time and evening/weekend programs available. Postbaccalaureate distance learning degree programs offered (minimal on-campus study). *Degree requirements:* For master's, thesis optional. *Entrance requirements:* For master's, GRE General Test or MAT, minimum GPA of 2.75. Electronic applications accepted.

Clemson University, Graduate School, College of Health, Education, and Human Development, School of Education, Program in Administration and Supervision, Clemson, SC 29634. Offers M Ed, Ed S. *Students:* 7 full-time (4 women), 96 part-time (62 women); includes 8 minority (6 African Americans, 1 American Indian/Alaska Native, 1 Asian American or Pacific Islander). 23 applicants, 78% accepted, 17 enrolled. In 2006, 20 master's, 17 other advanced degrees awarded. *Entrance requirements:* For master's and Ed S, GRE General Test or MAT, 1 year of teaching experience. Additional exam requirements/recommendations for international students: Required—TOEFL. *Application deadline:* For fall admission, 6/1 for domestic students. Application fee: $50. *Expenses:* Tuition, state resident: full-time $8,812; part-time $450 per hour. Tuition, nonresident: full-time $18,036; part-time $760 per hour. Required fees: $474; $5 per term. *Financial support:* Application deadline: 6/1; *Unit head:* Dr. Diane Ricciardi, Coordinator, 864-656-4506, Fax: 864-656-0311, E-mail: pdr@clemson.edu.

See Close-Up on page 1107.

Educational Administration

Clemson University, Graduate School, College of Health, Education, and Human Development, School of Education, Program in Educational Leadership, Clemson, SC 29634. Offers M Ed, PhD. *Accreditation:* NCATE. *Students:* 13 full-time (8 women), 57 part-time (29 women); includes 11 minority (10 African Americans, 1 Asian American or Pacific Islander). 33 applicants, 42% accepted, 8 enrolled. In 2006, 8 degrees awarded. *Degree requirements:* For doctorate, thesis/dissertation. *Entrance requirements:* For master's, GRE General Test; for doctorate, GRE General Test, master's degree in related field. Additional exam requirements/recommendations for international students: Required—TOEFL. Application fee: $50. *Expenses:* Tuition, state resident: full-time $8,812; part-time $450 per hour. Tuition, nonresident: full-time $18,036; part-time $760 per hour. Required fees: $474; $5 per term. *Financial support:* Application deadline: 6/1; *Unit head:* Dr. Frankie K. Williams, Coordinator, 864-656-5105.

See Close-Up on page 1111.

Cleveland State University, College of Graduate Studies, College of Education and Human Services, Department of Counseling, Administration, Supervision and Adult Learning, Cleveland, OH 44115. Offers adult learning and development (M Ed); community agency counseling (M Ed); counseling and pupil personnel administration (Ed S); educational administration (Ed S); educational administration and supervision (M Ed); school counseling (M Ed). *Accreditation:* ACA (one or more programs are accredited). Part-time programs available. *Faculty:* 15 full-time (9 women), 8 part-time/adjunct (5 women). *Students:* 43 full-time (33 women), 304 part-time (236 women); includes 91 minority (78 African Americans, 2 Asian Americans or Pacific Islanders, 11 Hispanic Americans). Average age 35. 205 applicants, 36% accepted, 54 enrolled. In 2006, 136 master's, 6 other advanced degrees awarded. *Degree requirements:* For master's, thesis optional; for Ed S, internship, thesis optional. *Entrance requirements:* For master's, GRE General Test or MAT, letter of recommendation, minimum GPA of 2.75. Additional exam requirements/recommendations for international students: Required—TOEFL (minimum score 525 paper-based; 197 computer-based), IELTS (minimum score 6). *Application deadline:* For fall admission, 6/21 for domestic students; for spring admission, 8/31 for domestic students. Application fee: $30. *Financial support:* In 2006–07, 8 students received support, including research assistantships with full and partial tuition reimbursements available (averaging $3,287 per year), teaching assistantships with full and partial tuition reimbursements available (averaging $3,480 per year); career-related internships or fieldwork, scholarships/grants, tuition waivers (full), and unspecified assistantships also available. Support available to part-time students. *Faculty research:* Education law, career development, women in school administration, psychopharmacology, counseling and spirituality. Total annual research expenditures: $478,265. *Unit head:* Dr. Rollin D. Nordgren, Interim Chairperson, 216-523-7499, Fax: 216-687-5378, E-mail: r.nordgren@csuohio.edu.

Cleveland State University, College of Graduate Studies, College of Education and Human Services, Program in Urban Education, Cleveland, OH 44115. Offers counseling (PhD); counseling psychology (PhD); leadership and lifelong learning (PhD); learning and development (PhD); policy studies (PhD); school administration (PhD). Part-time programs available. *Faculty:* 14 full-time (9 women), 4 part-time/adjunct (2 women). *Students:* 16 full-time (11 women), 78 part-time (47 women); includes 22 minority (20 African Americans, 2 Asian Americans or Pacific Islanders), 5 international. Average age 43. 29 applicants, 24% accepted, 4 enrolled. In 2006, 9 degrees awarded. *Degree requirements:* For doctorate, one foreign language, thesis/dissertation, comprehensive exam, registration. *Entrance requirements:* For doctorate, GRE General Test, minimum graduate GPA of 3.25. Additional exam requirements/recommendations for international students: Required—TOEFL (minimum score 525 paper-based; 197 computer-based), IELTS (minimum score 6). *Application deadline:* For fall admission, 2/5 for domestic students. Application fee: $30. *Financial support:* In 2006–07, 7 students received support, including 4 research assistantships with full and partial tuition reimbursements available (averaging $7,800 per year), 3 teaching assistantships with full and partial tuition reimbursements available (averaging $7,800 per year); tuition waivers (full) and unspecified assistantships also available. Financial award applicants required to submit FAFSA. *Faculty research:* Equity issues (race, ethnicity, and gender), education development consequences for special needs of urban populations, urban education programming, counseling the violent or aggressive adolescent. Total annual research expenditures: $5,662. *Unit head:* Dr. Joshua Bagakas, Director, 216-687-4591, Fax: 216-875-9697, E-mail: j.bagakas@csuohio.edu. *Application contact:* Wanda Butler, Administrative Assistant, 216-687-4697, Fax: 216-875-9697, E-mail: w.pruett-butler@csuohio.edu.

College of Mount St. Joseph, Graduate Education Program, Cincinnati, OH 45233-1670. Offers adolescent young adult education (MA); art (MA); inclusive early childhood education (MA); instructional leadership (MA); middle childhood education (MA); multicultural special education (MA); music (MA); reading (MA). *Accreditation:* Teacher Education Accreditation Council. Part-time and evening/weekend programs available. Postbaccalaureate distance learning degree programs offered (minimal on-campus study). *Faculty:* 22 full-time (14 women), 11 part-time/adjunct (6 women). *Students:* 68 full-time (54 women), 115 part-time (96 women); includes 21 minority (16 African Americans, 2 American Indian/Alaska Native, 1 Asian American or Pacific Islander, 2 Hispanic Americans). Average age 34. 91 applicants, 98% accepted, 62 enrolled. In 2006, 61 degrees awarded. *Degree requirements:* For master's, research project. *Entrance requirements:* For master's, GRE, PRAXIS II in teaching content area (math or science), 2 letters of recommendation, interview, resumé, prerequisite courses in communications, behavioral sciences and mathematics. Additional exam requirements/recommendations for international students: Required—TOEFL (minimum score 560 paper-based; 220 computer-based). *Application deadline:* Applications are processed on a rolling basis. Application fee: $50. Electronic applications accepted. *Expenses: Contact institution. Financial support:* In 2006–07, 3 students received support. Career-related internships or fieldwork and scholarships/grants available. Support available to part-time students. Financial award application deadline: 6/1; financial award applicants required to submit FAFSA. *Faculty research:* Foreign and second language learning problems/reading disabilities/hyperlexia, multicultural/bilingual special education, alternative educator licensure, science education, pedagogical content knowledge. *Unit head:* Dr. Mifrando Obach, Chair, 513-244-3263, Fax: 513-244-4867, E-mail: mifrando_obach@mail.msj.edu. *Application contact:* Marilyn Hoskins, Assistant Director of Admissions for Graduate Recruitment, 513-244-4723, Fax: 513-244-4629, E-mail: marilyn_hoskins@mail.msg.edu.

The College of New Jersey, Graduate Division, School of Education, Department of Educational Administration and Secondary Education, Program in Educational Leadership, Ewing, NJ 08628. Offers M Ed, Certificate. *Students:* 1 (woman) full-time, 144 part-time (83 women); includes 25 minority (16 African Americans, 3 Asian Americans or Pacific Islanders, 6 Hispanic Americans). 132 applicants, 95% accepted. In 2006, 51 degrees awarded. *Degree requirements:* For master's, comprehensive exam. *Entrance requirements:* For master's, GRE, minimum GPA of 3.0 in field or 2.75 overall. Additional exam requirements/recommendations for international students: Required—TOEFL. *Application deadline:* For fall admission, 4/15 for domestic students; for spring admission, 10/15 for domestic students. Application fee: $60. Electronic applications accepted. *Financial support:* Unspecified assistantships available. *Unit head:* Dr. Donald Leake, Coordinator, 609-771-2229, E-mail: leake@tcnj.edu. *Application contact:* Susan L. Hydro, Office of Graduate Studies, Assistant Dean, 609-771-2300, Fax: 609-637-5105, E-mail: graduate@tcnj.edu.

The College of New Rochelle, Graduate School, Division of Education, Program in School Administration and Supervision, New Rochelle, NY 10805-2308. Offers MS Ed, Certificate, PD. *Faculty:* 2 full-time (1 woman), 4 part-time/adjunct (2 women). *Students:* 6 full-time (5 women), 105 part-time (71 women); includes 26 minority (15 African Americans, 4 American Indian/Alaska Native, 7 Hispanic Americans). Average age 37. In 2006, 133 master's, 15 other advanced degrees awarded. *Degree requirements:* For master's, internship. *Entrance requirements:* For master's, interview, minimum GPA of 3.0 in field, 2.7 overall, minimum 3 years teaching or education administration experience. *Application deadline:* For fall admission, 8/1 priority date for domestic students; for spring admission, 4/6 for domestic students. Applications are processed on a rolling basis. Application fee: $35. *Expenses:* Tuition: Part-time $575 per credit. Required fees: $90 per term. *Financial support:* Scholarships/grants available. *Faculty research:* Training administrators in Eastern Europe, leadership.

College of Notre Dame of Maryland, Graduate Studies, Leadership in Teaching Program, Baltimore, MD 21210-2476. Offers MA. *Students:* 18 full-time (14 women), 505 part-time (397 women). *Entrance requirements:* For master's, interview, 1 year of teaching experience, minimum GPA of 3.0. Additional exam requirements/recommendations for international students: Required—TOEFL (minimum score 500 paper-based; 173 computer-based; 61 iBT). *Application deadline:* For fall admission, 7/5 for domestic students; for winter admission, 11/5 for domestic students; for spring admission, 12/5 for domestic students. Applications are processed on a rolling basis. Application fee: $40. Electronic applications accepted. *Financial support:* Institutionally sponsored loans available. Financial award application deadline: 6/30. *Unit head:* Sr. Sharon Slear, Head, 410-532-3169, Fax: 410-532-5333, E-mail: sslear@ndm.edu. *Application contact:* Erica D. Jones, Graduate Admissions Coordinator, 410-532-5317, Fax: 410-532-5333, E-mail: gradadm@ndm.edu.

College of Notre Dame of Maryland, Graduate Studies, Program in Instructional Leadership for Changing Populations, Baltimore, MD 21210-2476. Offers PhD. *Entrance requirements:* Additional exam requirements/recommendations for international students: Required—TOEFL (minimum score 500 paper-based; 173 computer-based; 61 iBT). *Application deadline:* For fall admission, 2/15 for domestic students. Applications are processed on a rolling basis. Application fee: $60. *Unit head:* Sr. Sharon Slear, Head, 410-532-3169, Fax: 410-532-5333, E-mail: sslear@ndm.edu. *Application contact:* Kathy Nikolaidis, Education Program Administrator, 410-532-5305, Fax: 410-532-5333, E-mail: knikolaidis@ndm.edu.

College of Saint Elizabeth, Department of Education, Morristown, NJ 07960-6989. Offers accelerated certification for teachers (Certificate); assistive technology (Certificate); education: human services leadership (MA); educational technology (MA). Part-time and evening/weekend programs available. *Faculty:* 8 full-time (3 women), 14 part-time/adjunct (8 women). *Students:* 69 full-time (58 women), 354 part-time (303 women); includes 21 minority (10 African Americans, 4 Asian Americans or Pacific Islanders, 7 Hispanic Americans). Average age 36. In 2006, 82 master's, 31 other advanced degrees awarded. *Degree requirements:* For master's, thesis or alternative, portfolio. *Entrance requirements:* For master's, interview, minimum undergraduate GPA of 3.0. *Application deadline:* For fall admission, 6/30 priority date for domestic students; for spring admission, 11/30 for domestic students. Applications are processed on a rolling basis. Application fee: $35. Electronic applications accepted. *Financial support:* Career-related internships or fieldwork, Federal Work-Study, tuition waivers (partial), and unspecified assistantships available. Support available to part-time students. Financial award application deadline: 3/15; financial award applicants required to submit FAFSA. *Faculty research:* Developmental stages for teaching and human services professionals, effectiveness of humanities core curriculum. *Unit head:* Dr. Alan H. Markowitz, Director of Graduate Education Programs, 973-290-4374, Fax: 973-290-4389, E-mail: amarkowitz@cse.edu. *Application contact:* Michael Szarek, Director of Enrollment Management, 973-290-4112, Fax: 973-290-4167, E-mail: mszarek@cse.edu.

The College of Saint Rose, Graduate Studies, School of Education, Department of Counseling and Educational Administration, Program in Educational Administration and Supervision, Albany, NY 12203-1419. Offers college student services administration (MS Ed); educational administration and supervision (MS Ed, Certificate); school administrator and supervisor (Certificate). Part-time and evening/weekend programs available. *Degree requirements:* For master's, comprehensive exam or thesis. *Entrance requirements:* For master's, minimum undergraduate GPA of 3.0, timed writing sample, interview, permanent certification or 3 years teaching experience. Additional exam requirements/recommendations for international students: Required—TOEFL (minimum score 550 paper-based; 213 computer-based). Electronic applications accepted.

College of Santa Fe, Department of Education, Santa Fe, NM 87505-7634. Offers at-risk youth (MA), including bilingual/multicultural education, classroom teaching, community counseling, educational administration, leadership, school counseling, self-designed program, TESOL/Multicultural; curriculum and instruction (MA); multicultural special education (MA). Part-time and evening/weekend programs available. *Entrance requirements:* For master's, minimum GPA of 3.0. *Faculty research:* Integrated curriculum, child development, brain research, learning styles, systemic issues in education.

College of Staten Island of the City University of New York, Graduate Programs, Department of Education, Program in Leadership in Education, Staten Island, NY 10314-6600. Offers 6th Year Certificate. New students enter during summer. Part-time and evening/weekend programs available. *Faculty:* 1 (woman) full-time, 1 part-time/adjunct (0 women). *Students:* Average age 36. 40 applicants, 75% accepted, 25 enrolled. In 2006, 24 degrees awarded. *Entrance requirements:* For degree, master's degree, minimum GPA of 3.0, 4 years of teaching experience, 3 professional recommendations, interview. Additional exam requirements/recommendations for international students: Required—TOEFL (minimum score 550 paper-based; 213 computer-based; 79 iBT). *Application deadline:* For fall admission, 4/15 for domestic students. Applications are processed on a rolling basis. Application fee: $125. *Expenses:* Tuition, state resident: full-time $6,400; part-time $270 per credit. Tuition, nonresident: part-time $500 per credit. Required fees: $53 per semester. *Financial support:* Applicants required to submit FAFSA. *Unit head:* Dr. Ruth Silverberg, Coordinator, 718-982-3726, Fax: 718-982-3743, E-mail: silverberg@mailbox.csi.cuny.edu. *Application contact:* Emmanuel Esperance, Deputy Director of Office of Recruitment and Admissions, 718-982-2190, Fax: 718-982-2500, E-mail: admissions@mail.csi.cuny.edu.

College of the Southwest, School of Education, Hobbs, NM 88240-9129. Offers curriculum and instruction (MS); educational administration (MS); educational counseling (MS); educational diagnostician (MS). Part-time and evening/weekend programs available. Postbaccalaureate distance learning degree programs offered. *Faculty:* 2 full-time (both women), 6 part-time/adjunct (1 woman). *Students:* 41 full-time (28 women), 43 part-time (35 women); includes 24 minority (1 African American, 1 American Indian/Alaska Native, 1 Asian American or Pacific Islander, 21 Hispanic Americans), 1 international. Average age 38. 119 applicants, 29% accepted, 34 enrolled. In 2006, 26 degrees awarded. *Degree requirements:* For master's, comprehensive exam. *Entrance requirements:* For master's, GRE General Test. Additional exam requirements/recommendations for international students: Recommended—TOEFL (minimum score 550 paper-based; 213 computer-based). *Application deadline:* For fall admission, 3/1 priority date for domestic students; for spring admission, 10/1 for domestic students. Applications are processed on a rolling basis. Application fee: $50. *Expenses:* Tuition: Part-time $375 per credit hour. *Financial support:* In 2006–07, 58 students received support, including 1 research assistantship; Federal Work-Study, scholarships/grants, and tuition waivers (partial) also available. Support available to part-time students. Financial award application deadline: 4/1; financial award applicants required to submit FAFSA. *Unit head:* Dr. Dennis Atherton, Dean, 505-392-6561 Ext. 1069, Fax: 505-392-6006, E-mail: datherton@csw.edu. *Application contact:* Kerrie Mitchell, Coordinator of Financial Aid and Admissions Operations, 505-392-6563 Ext. 1048, Fax: 505-392-6006, E-mail: kmitchell@csw.edu.

The College of William and Mary, School of Education, Program in Education Policy, Planning, and Leadership, Williamsburg, VA 23187-8795. Offers curriculum and educational technology (Ed D, PhD); curriculum leadership (Ed D, PhD); educational leadership (M Ed), including higher education administration (M Ed, Ed D, PhD), K-12 administration and supervision; educational policy, planning, and leadership (Ed D, PhD), including general education administration, gifted education administration, higher education administration (M Ed, Ed D, PhD), special education administration; gifted education administration (M Ed). *Accreditation:* NCATE. Part-time and evening/weekend programs available. *Faculty:* 10 full-time (5 women), 4 part-time/adjunct (2 women). *Students:* 51 full-time (44 women), 101 part-time (64 women); includes 28 minority (27 African Americans, 1 Hispanic American), 7 international. Average age 28. 114 applicants, 55% accepted, 42 enrolled. In 2006, 38 master's, 12 doctorates awarded. *Degree requirements:* For doctorate, thesis/dissertation, comprehensive exam.

Entrance requirements: For master's, GRE or MAT, minimum GPA of 2.5; for doctorate, GRE or MAT, minimum GPA of 3.0. Additional exam requirements/recommendations for international students: Required—TOEFL. *Application deadline:* For fall admission, 2/1 for domestic and international students; for spring admission, 10/1 for domestic and international students. Application fee: $30. *Expenses:* Tuition, state resident: full-time $6,100; part-time $260 per credit. Tuition, nonresident: full-time $18,790; part-time $725 per credit. Required fees: $3,314. Tuition and fees vary according to program. *Financial support:* In 2006–07, 41 research assistantships with full and partial tuition reimbursements (averaging $13,300 per year) were awarded; career-related internships or fieldwork, Federal Work-Study, institutionally sponsored loans, scholarships/grants, and unspecified assistantships also available. Support available to part-time students. Financial award application deadline: 2/1; financial award applicants required to submit FAFSA. *Faculty research:* Higher education policy, faculty incentives, history of adversity, resilience, leadership. *Unit head:* Dr. Megan Tschannen-Moran, Area Coordinator, 757-221-2187, E-mail: mxtsch@wm.edu. *Application contact:* Patricia Burleson, Director of Admissions, 757-221-2317, E-mail: paburl@wm.edu.

Columbia International University, Columbia Graduate School, Columbia, SC 29230-3122. Offers Bible teaching (MABT); Christian higher education leadership (Ed D); Christian school educational leadership (Ed D); counseling (MACN); curriculum and instruction (M Ed), including Christian school guidance, English as a second language, learning disabilities, school technology; early childhood and elementary education (MAT); educational administration (M Ed); teaching English as a foreign language (Certificate); teaching English as a foreign language and intercultural studies (MATF). Part-time and evening/weekend programs available. *Faculty:* 11 full-time (4 women), 7 part-time/adjunct (5 women). *Students:* 52 full-time (44 women), 93 part-time (59 women); includes 17 minority (11 African Americans, 2 Asian Americans or Pacific Islanders, 4 Hispanic Americans), 10 international. Average age 35. 107 applicants, 56% accepted, 41 enrolled. In 2006, 62 degrees awarded. *Degree requirements:* For master's, internships, professional project. *Entrance requirements:* For master's, Minnesota Multiphasic Personality Inventory, MAT, minimum GPA of 2.7. Additional exam requirements/recommendations for international students: Required—TOEFL. *Application deadline:* For fall admission, 8/1 priority date for domestic and international students; for winter admission, 12/15 priority date for domestic and international students; for spring admission, 1/15 priority date for domestic and international students. Applications are processed on a rolling basis. Application fee: $45. Electronic applications accepted. *Expenses:* Tuition: Part-time $400 per semester hour. Tuition and fees vary according to course load and program. *Financial support:* In 2006–07, 35 students received support. Career-related internships or fieldwork, Federal Work-Study, institutionally sponsored loans, and scholarships/grants available. Financial award application deadline: 3/17; financial award applicants required to submit FAFSA. *Unit head:* Dr. Milton Uecker, Dean, 803-807-5319, Fax: 803-786-4209, E-mail: muecker@ciu.edu. *Application contact:* Michelle MacGregor, Director of Admissions, 800-777-2227 Ext. 5335, Fax: 803-786-4209, E-mail: yescbs@ciu.edu.

Columbus State University, Graduate Studies, College of Education, Department of Counseling, Educational Leadership and Professional Studies, Columbus, GA 31907-5645. Offers community counseling (MS); educational leadership (M Ed, Ed S); school counseling (M Ed, Ed S). *Accreditation:* ACA; NCATE. Part-time and evening/weekend programs available. Postbaccalaureate distance learning degree programs offered (minimal on-campus study). *Faculty:* 10 full-time (4 women), 8 part-time/adjunct (4 women). *Students:* 87 full-time (61 women), 47 part-time (38 women); includes 34 minority (33 African Americans, 1 Asian American or Pacific Islander). Average age 36. 40 applicants, 43% accepted, 13 enrolled. In 2006, 42 master's, 34 other advanced degrees awarded. *Degree requirements:* For master's, thesis, exit exam; for Ed S, thesis or alternative. *Entrance requirements:* For master's, GRE General Test, minimum GPA of 2.75; for Ed S, GRE General Test. Additional exam requirements/recommendations for international students: Required—TOEFL (minimum score 550 paper-based; 213 computer-based). *Application deadline:* For fall admission, 5/1 priority date for domestic students, 5/1 for international students; for spring admission, 11/1 for domestic and international students. Applications are processed on a rolling basis. Application fee: $25. Electronic applications accepted. *Expenses:* Tuition, state resident: part-time $127 per semester hour. Tuition, nonresident: part-time $508 per semester hour. Required fees: $264 per semester. Tuition and fees vary according to course load. *Financial support:* In 2006–07, 67 students received support, including 5 research assistantships with partial tuition reimbursements available (averaging $3,000 per year); career-related internships or fieldwork, Federal Work-Study, institutionally sponsored loans, scholarships/grants, tuition waivers (partial), and unspecified assistantships also available. Support available to part-time students. Financial award application deadline: 5/1; financial award applicants required to submit FAFSA. *Unit head:* Dr. Paul Tom Hackett, Chair, 706-568-5061, Fax: 706-569-3134, E-mail: hackett_paul@colstate.edu. *Application contact:* Katie Thornton, Graduate Admissions Specialist, 706-568-2035, Fax: 706-568-2462, E-mail: thornton_katie@colstate.edu.

Concordia University, College of Education, Portland, OR 97211-6099. Offers curriculum and instruction (elementary) (M Ed); educational administration (M Ed); elementary education (MAT); secondary education (MAT). Part-time programs available. Postbaccalaureate distance learning degree programs offered (no on-campus study). *Degree requirements:* For master's, work samples/portfolio. *Entrance requirements:* For master's, California Basic Educational Skills Test or PRAXIS I, minimum undergraduate GPA of 2.8, graduate 3.0; 2 letters of recommendation. Additional exam requirements/recommendations for international students: Required—TOEFL (minimum score 525 paper-based; 195 computer-based). Electronic applications accepted. *Faculty research:* Learner centered classroom, brain-based learning future of on-line learning.

Concordia University, College of Education, Program in Educational Leadership, River Forest, IL 60305-1499. Offers Ed D. *Entrance requirements:* For doctorate, MAT or GRE, minimum graduate GPA of 3.5, interview. Additional exam requirements/recommendations for international students: Required—TOEFL (minimum score 550 paper-based; 195 computer-based). Electronic applications accepted.

Concordia University, College of Education, Program in School Leadership, River Forest, IL 60305-1499. Offers school administration (MA, CAS). MA offered jointly with the Chicago Consortium of Colleges and Universities. *Accreditation:* NCATE. Part-time and evening/weekend programs available. *Degree requirements:* For master's, thesis optional; for CAS, thesis, final project. *Entrance requirements:* For master's, minimum GPA of 2.9; for CAS, master's degree. Additional exam requirements/recommendations for international students: Required—TOEFL (minimum score 550 paper-based; 195 computer-based). Electronic applications accepted. *Faculty research:* Effectiveness of urban Lutheran schools in impacting children's faith development, effectiveness of centers for urban ministries in supporting urban ministry and teaching science.

Concordia University, Graduate Programs, Ann Arbor, MI 48105-2797. Offers educational leadership (MS); organizational leadership and administration (MS). Part-time and evening/weekend programs available. *Faculty:* 6 full-time (3 women), 56 part-time/adjunct (27 women). *Students:* 399 full-time (290 women), 8 part-time (4 women); includes 112 minority (97 African Americans, 3 American Indian/Alaska Native, 8 Asian Americans or Pacific Islanders, 4 Hispanic Americans). Average age 39. 542 applicants, 69% accepted, 349 enrolled. *Degree requirements:* For master's, thesis. *Entrance requirements:* Additional exam requirements/recommendations for international students: Required—TOEFL (minimum score 520 paper-based; 190 computer-based; 68 iBT); Recommended—IELTS, TWE. *Application deadline:* For fall admission, 9/7 priority date for domestic students, 8/15 priority date for international students; for winter admission, 1/18 priority date for domestic students, 12/15 priority date for international students; for spring admission, 5/10 priority date for domestic students, 4/15 priority date for international students. Applications are processed on a rolling basis. Application fee: $100. *Expenses:* Tuition: Full-time $7,020; part-time $390 per credit. Tuition and fees vary according to program. *Financial support:* In 2006–07, 263 students received support. Applicants required to submit FAFSA.

Concordia University, Graduate Programs in Education, Program in Educational Administration, Seward, NE 68434-1599. Offers M Ed. *Accreditation:* NCATE. Part-time programs available. *Degree requirements:* For master's, thesis or alternative. *Entrance requirements:* For master's, GRE, MAT, or NTE, BS in education or equivalent, minimum GPA of 3.0.

Concordia University, School of Education, Irvine, CA 92612-3299. Offers curriculum and instruction (MA); education (M Ed); educational administration and administrative services credential (MA). Part-time and evening/weekend programs available. Postbaccalaureate distance learning degree programs offered (minimal on-campus study). *Faculty:* 13 full-time (6 women), 5 part-time/adjunct (3 women). *Students:* 228 full-time (185 women), 465 part-time (378 women); includes 145 minority (8 African Americans, 6 American Indian/Alaska Native, 38 Asian Americans or Pacific Islanders, 93 Hispanic Americans), 2 international. Average age 32. In 2006, 75 degrees awarded. *Degree requirements:* For master's, project or thesis. *Entrance requirements:* For master's, California Basic Educational Skills Test, California Subject Examinations for Teachers, minimum GPA of 3.0. Additional exam requirements/recommendations for international students: Required—TOEFL (minimum score 550 paper-based; 213 computer-based). *Application deadline:* For fall admission, 7/15 priority date for domestic students, 7/15 for international students; for spring admission, 11/30 priority date for domestic students, 11/30 for international students. Applications are processed on a rolling basis. Application fee: $50 ($300 for international students). *Financial support:* Application deadline: 3/2; *Unit head:* Dr. Joseph Bordeaux, Dean, 949-854-8002 Ext. 1345, Fax: 949-854-6878, E-mail: joseph.bordeaux@cui.edu. *Application contact:* Lindsay Anderson, Director of Graduate Enrollment, 949-854-8002 Ext. 1133, Fax: 949-854-6894, E-mail: lindsay.anderson@cui.edu.

Concordia University Wisconsin, Graduate Programs, Department of Education, Program in Educational Administration, Mequon, WI 53097-2402. Offers MS Ed. Part-time and evening/weekend programs available. Postbaccalaureate distance learning degree programs offered (minimal on-campus study). *Students:* 79 (26 women). In 2006, 8 degrees awarded. *Degree requirements:* For master's, thesis or alternative, comprehensive exam. *Entrance requirements:* For master's, minimum GPA of 3.0. Additional exam requirements/recommendations for international students: Required—TOEFL. Application fee: $35. *Financial support:* Application deadline: 8/1. *Unit head:* Dr. Ross Stueber, Head, 262-243-4285, Fax: 262-243-4428, E-mail: ross.stueber@cuw.edu. *Application contact:* Graduate Admissions, 262-243-4248, Fax: 262-243-4428.

Converse College, School of Education and Graduate Studies, Education Specialist Program, Spartanburg, SC 29302-0006. Offers administration and supervision (Ed S); curriculum and instruction (Ed S); marriage and family therapy (Ed S). *Accreditation:* AAMFT/COAMFTE. Part-time programs available. *Faculty:* 7 full-time, 15 part-time/adjunct. *Students:* Average age 35. In 2006, 26 degrees awarded. *Entrance requirements:* For degree, GRE or MAT (marriage and family therapy), minimum GPA of 3.0. *Application deadline:* For fall admission, 8/1 for domestic and international students; for winter admission, 11/15 for domestic and international students; for spring admission, 1/15 for domestic and international students. Applications are processed on a rolling basis. Application fee: $40. Electronic applications accepted. *Expenses:* Tuition: Part-time $305 per credit hour. Required fees: $20 per term.

Converse College, School of Education and Graduate Studies, Program in Leadership, Spartanburg, SC 29302-0006. Offers M Ed. *Faculty:* 4 full-time (2 women), 8 part-time/adjunct (2 women). In 2006, 25 degrees awarded. *Degree requirements:* For master's, capstone paper. *Entrance requirements:* For master's, NTE, minimum GPA of 2.75, nomination by school district, 3 recommendations. *Application deadline:* For fall admission, 8/1 for domestic and international students; for winter admission, 11/15 for domestic and international students; for spring admission, 1/15 for domestic and international students. Application fee: $40. Electronic applications accepted. *Expenses:* Tuition: Part-time $305 per credit hour. Required fees: $20 per term.

Creighton University, Graduate School, College of Arts and Sciences, Department of Education, Program in Educational Leadership, Omaha, NE 68178-0001. Offers MS. Part-time and evening/weekend programs available. *Faculty:* 3 full-time. *Students:* 1 applicant, 100% accepted, 1 enrolled. In 2006, 2 degrees awarded. *Entrance requirements:* For master's, GRE General Test, 2 writing samples, 3 letters of recommendation. Additional exam requirements/recommendations for international students: Required—TOEFL (minimum score 550 paper-based; 213 computer-based; 80 iBT). *Application deadline:* For fall admission, 3/1 for domestic and international students. Applications are processed on a rolling basis. Application fee: $40. Electronic applications accepted. *Expenses:* Tuition: Part-time $595 per credit hour. Required fees: $38 per semester. *Financial support:* Tuition waivers (partial) available. *Application contact:* Dr. Gail M. Jenson, Dean, 402-280-2870, Fax: 402-280-5762, E-mail: gjenson@creighton.edu.

Curry College, Division of Continuing Education and Graduate Studies, Program in Education, Milton, MA 02186-9984. Offers adult education (Certificate); educational administration (M Ed); educational therapy (Certificate); elementary education (M Ed); foundations (non-license) (M Ed); learning disabilities across the lifespan (Certificate); reading (M Ed, Certificate); special education (M Ed). Part-time and evening/weekend programs available. *Faculty:* 6 full-time (4 women), 11 part-time/adjunct (7 women). *Degree requirements:* For master's, research project. *Entrance requirements:* For master's, MAT, interview, recommendations, resumé. Additional exam requirements/recommendations for international students: Required—TOEFL (minimum score 550 paper-based). *Application deadline:* For fall admission, 8/1 priority date for domestic students; for spring admission, 1/1 for domestic students. Applications are processed on a rolling basis. Application fee: $50. *Expenses:* Contact institution. *Financial support:* Career-related internships or fieldwork and tuition waivers (partial) available. *Faculty research:* Classroom trauma, therapeutic writing, inclusionary practices. *Unit head:* Dr. Donald Gratz, Director and Associate Professor, 617-333-2243, E-mail: dgratz0703@curry.edu. *Application contact:* John Bresnahan, Director of Graduate Enrollment and Student Services, 617-333-2243, Fax: 617-333-2045, E-mail: jbresnah0104@curry.edu.

Dallas Baptist University, Dorothy M. Bush College of Education, Education Program, Dallas, TX 75211-9299. Offers early childhood education (M Ed); educational leadership (M Ed); elementary reading education (M Ed); general elementary education (M Ed); reading specialist (M Ed). Part-time and evening/weekend programs available. *Faculty:* 49 full-time (21 women), 112 part-time/adjunct (46 women). *Students:* 47 full-time, 149 part-time. 65 applicants, 58% accepted, 36 enrolled. In 2006, 67 degrees awarded. *Entrance requirements:* For master's, GRE General Test, minimum GPA of 3.0. Additional exam requirements/recommendations for international students: Required—TOEFL. *Application deadline:* Applications are processed on a rolling basis. Application fee: $25. Electronic applications accepted. *Expenses:* Tuition: Full-time $8,370; part-time $465 per credit hour. Required fees: $465 per credit hour. *Financial support:* Federal Work-Study, institutionally sponsored loans, scholarships/grants, and tuition waivers (full and partial) available. Support available to part-time students. *Faculty research:* Emerging literacy, self-directed schools. *Unit head:* Dr. Elaine Wilmore, Interim Director, 214-333-5413, Fax: 214-333-5551, E-mail: graduate@dbu.edu. *Application contact:* Kit P. Montgomery, Director of Graduate Programs, 214-333-5242, Fax: 214-333-5579, E-mail: graduate@dbu.edu.

Delaware Valley College, Program in Educational Leadership, Doylestown, PA 18901-2697. Offers MS. Part-time and evening/weekend programs available. *Faculty:* 15 part-time/adjunct (5 women). *Students:* Average age 36. 5 applicants, 80% accepted, 4 enrolled. In 2006, 20 degrees awarded. *Degree requirements:* For master's, comprehensive exam. *Entrance requirements:* For master's, GRE or MAT, minimum undergraduate GPA of 3.0. *Application deadline:* For fall admission, 9/7 for domestic students; for spring admission, 1/24 for domestic students. Applications are processed on a rolling basis. Application fee: $50. *Unit head:* Dr. Robert W. Valente, Director of Educational Leadership, 215-489-4833, Fax: 215-489-4832, E-mail: robert.valente@devalcol.edu.

Educational Administration

Delta State University, Graduate Programs, College of Education, Thad Cochran Center for Rural School Leadership and Research, Program in Administration and Supervision, Cleveland, MS 38733-0001. Offers educational administration and supervision (Ed S); educational leadership (M Ed); elementary education (Ed S); secondary education (Ed S). *Accreditation:* NCATE. Part-time and evening/weekend programs available. *Degree requirements:* For master's, thesis optional. *Entrance requirements:* For master's, GRE General Test or MAT; for Ed S, master's degree, teaching certificate. *Application deadline:* For fall admission, 8/1 priority date for domestic students; for spring admission, 12/1 priority date for domestic students. Applications are processed on a rolling basis. Application fee: $0. *Financial support:* Research assistantships, career-related internships or fieldwork, Federal Work-Study, and institutionally sponsored loans available. Support available to part-time students. Financial award application deadline: 6/1.

Delta State University, Graduate Programs, College of Education, Thad Cochran Center for Rural School Leadership and Research, Program in Professional Studies, Cleveland, MS 38733-0001. Offers Ed D. Part-time and evening/weekend programs available. *Degree requirements:* For doctorate, thesis/dissertation. *Entrance requirements:* For doctorate, GRE General Test. *Application deadline:* For fall admission, 8/1 priority date for domestic students; for spring admission, 12/1 priority date for domestic students. Applications are processed on a rolling basis. Application fee: $0. *Financial support:* Research assistantships, career-related internships or fieldwork, Federal Work-Study, and institutionally sponsored loans available. Support available to part-time students. Financial award application deadline: 6/1.

DePaul University, School of Education, Doctoral Program in Education, Chicago, IL 60604-2287. Offers curriculum studies (Ed D); educational leadership (Ed D). Part-time and evening/weekend programs available. *Faculty:* 11 full-time (5 women), 1 (woman) part-time/adjunct. *Students:* 88 full-time (62 women), 131 part-time (94 women); includes 66 minority (44 African Americans, 6 Asian Americans or Pacific Islanders, 16 Hispanic Americans), 5 international. 25 applicants, 48% accepted, 10 enrolled. *Degree requirements:* For doctorate, thesis/dissertation, candidacy paper before dissertation, defense of dissertation. *Entrance requirements:* For doctorate, interview, master's degree, 3 years of work experience (recommended), writing sample, 3 letters of recommendation. Additional exam requirements/recommendations for international students: Required—TOEFL (minimum score 550 paper-based; 221 computer-based). *Application deadline:* For fall admission, 2/15 for domestic and international students. Application fee: $40. Electronic applications accepted. *Financial support:* In 2006–07, 2 research assistantships with full tuition reimbursements (averaging $6,000 per year), 1 teaching assistantship with full tuition reimbursement (averaging $6,000 per year) were awarded. Financial award applicants required to submit FAFSA. *Faculty research:* Philosophy and sociology of education, education and social justice, curriculum theory, use of technology in schools, youth and community development, education law. *Unit head:* Dr. Clara Jennings, Dean, 773-325-7581, Fax: 773-325-7728, E-mail: cjennings@depaul.edu. *Application contact:* Dr. John Bollwark, Data Projects Manager, 773-325-7582, Fax: 773-325-7748, E-mail: jbollwar@depaul.edu.

Doane College, Program in Education, Crete, NE 68333-2430. Offers curriculum and instruction (M Ed); educational leadership (M Ed). *Accreditation:* NCATE. Part-time and evening/weekend programs available. *Degree requirements:* For master's, thesis. *Entrance requirements:* For master's, minimum GPA of 2.5. Electronic applications accepted. Expenses: Contact institution.

Dominican University, School of Education, River Forest, IL 60305-1099. Offers curriculum and instruction (MA Ed); early childhood education (MS); education (MAT); educational administration (MA); literacy (MS); special education (MS). Part-time and evening/weekend programs available. *Faculty:* 17 full-time (14 women), 37 part-time/adjunct (24 women). *Students:* 65 full-time (46 women), 514 part-time (425 women); includes 78 minority (23 African Americans, 16 Asian Americans or Pacific Islanders, 39 Hispanic Americans), 2 international. Average age 34. 130 applicants, 89% accepted, 100 enrolled. In 2006, 203 degrees awarded. *Entrance requirements:* For master's, Illinois certification test of basic skills. Additional exam requirements/recommendations for international students: Required—TOEFL (minimum score 550 paper-based; 213 computer-based). *Application deadline:* Applications are processed on a rolling basis. Application fee: $25. *Expenses: Contact institution.* Tuition and fees vary according to campus/location and program. *Financial support:* In 2006–07, 63 students received support. Career-related internships or fieldwork, scholarships/grants, and tuition waivers (partial) available. Support available to part-time students. Financial award application deadline: 8/15; financial award applicants required to submit FAFSA. *Faculty research:* Governance of private education institutions, reading and language arts, inclusion, organizational planning, leadership and vision. *Unit head:* Sr. Colleen McNicholas, Dean, 708-524-6830, Fax: 708-524-6665, E-mail: educate@dom.edu. *Application contact:* Keven Hansen, Coordinator of Admissions and Recruitment, 708-524-6921, Fax: 708-524-6665, E-mail: educate@dom.edu.

Dowling College, Graduate Programs in Education, Oakdale, NY 11769-1999. Offers educational administration (Ed D, PD), including computers in education (PD), educational administration (Ed D), school administration and supervision (PD), school district administration (PD); human development and learning (MS Ed); literacy (MS Ed); literacy/special education (MS Ed); secondary education (MS Ed); special education (MS Ed). *Accreditation:* NCATE. Part-time and evening/weekend programs available. Postbaccalaureate distance learning degree programs offered. *Faculty:* 29 full-time (13 women), 91 part-time/adjunct (60 women). *Students:* 496 full-time (364 women), 1,083 part-time (827 women); includes 119 minority (37 African Americans, 20 Asian Americans or Pacific Islanders, 62 Hispanic Americans), 2 international. Average age 38. 618 applicants, 86% accepted, 300 enrolled. In 2006, 641 master's, 25 doctorates awarded. *Degree requirements:* For master's and PD, comprehensive exam; for doctorate, thesis/dissertation. *Entrance requirements:* For master's, minimum GPA of 3.0; for doctorate, GRE, master's degree; for PD, teaching certificate. Additional exam requirements/recommendations for international students: Required—TOEFL (minimum score 550 paper-based). *Application deadline:* For fall admission, 9/1 priority date for domestic students; for winter admission, 1/1 priority date for domestic students; for spring admission, 2/1 priority date for domestic students. Applications are processed on a rolling basis. Application fee: $25. Electronic applications accepted. *Expenses:* Tuition: Full-time $16,008; part-time $667 per credit. Tuition and fees vary according to course load. *Financial support:* In 2006–07, 358 students received support, including 20 research assistantships with tuition reimbursements available (averaging $3,150 per year); career-related internships or fieldwork, Federal Work-Study, scholarships/grants, tuition waivers (partial), and unspecified assistantships also available. Support available to part-time students. Financial award application deadline: 6/30; financial award applicants required to submit FAFSA. *Faculty research:* Natural readers, Korean styles and learning strategies, mothers of children with disabilities, computers in instruction, cultural background and organizational roadblocks to problem solving. *Unit head:* Dr. Clyde Payne, Associate Provost, 631-244-3404, Fax: 631-589-6644, E-mail: paynec@dowling.edu. *Application contact:* Franks S. Pizzardi, Director of Admissions Operations, 631-244-3227, Fax: 631-244-1059, E-mail: pizzardf@dowling.edu.

Drake University, School of Education, Department of Leadership, Counseling and Adult Development, Program in Education Leadership, Des Moines, IA 50311-4516. Offers MSE, Ed D, Ed S. Part-time and evening/weekend programs available. *Faculty:* 10 full-time (3 women), 28 part-time/adjunct (16 women). *Students:* 120 applicants, 74% accepted. In 2006, 105 master's, 12 other advanced degrees awarded. *Degree requirements:* For master's, comprehensive exam; for doctorate, thesis/dissertation, comprehensive exam, registration; for Ed S, thesis or alternative, comprehensive exam. *Entrance requirements:* For master's, GRE General Test, MAT, or Drake Writing Assessment, resumé, 2 letters of recommendation; for doctorate, GRE General Test or MAT, master's degree, 3 letters of recommendation; for Ed S, GRE General Test or MAT, master's degree, minimum GPA of 3.0. Additional exam requirements/recommendations for international students: Required—TOEFL (minimum score 550 paper-based; 213 computer-based). *Application deadline:* For fall admission, 7/1 priority date for domestic students, 6/1 priority date for international students; for spring admission, 11/1 priority date for domestic students, 10/1 priority date for international students. Applications are processed on a rolling basis. Application fee: $25. Electronic applications accepted. *Financial support:* Career-related internships or fieldwork and unspecified assistantships available. Support available to part-time students. *Faculty research:* Counseling and rehabilitation, behavioral supports, inquiry-based science methods, teacher quality enhancement. Total annual research expenditures: $1.5 million. *Application contact:* Ann J. Martin, Graduate Coordinator, 515-271-2034, Fax: 515-271-2831, E-mail: ann.martin@drake.edu.

Drake University, School of Education, Department of Teaching and Learning, Des Moines, IA 50311-4516. Offers effective teaching, learning and leadership (MSE); elementary education (MST); secondary education (MAT), including art, biology, business, chemistry, English, general science, history-American, history-world, journalism, mathematics, physical science, physics, sociology, speech, speech communication, theatre; special education (MSE); teacher education (MSE). Part-time programs available. *Faculty:* 10 full-time (3 women), 28 part-time/adjunct (16 women). *Students:* 29 full-time (18 women), 154 part-time (127 women); includes 6 minority (4 African Americans, 1 Asian American or Pacific Islander, 1 Hispanic American), 1 international. 124 applicants, 61% accepted, 36 enrolled. In 2006, 77 degrees awarded. *Degree requirements:* For master's, thesis (for some programs), internships (s), comprehensive exam, registration. *Entrance requirements:* For master's, GRE General Test, MAT, or Drake Writing Assessment, resumé, 2 letters of recommendation. Additional exam requirements/recommendations for international students: Required—TOEFL (minimum score 550 paper-based; 213 computer-based). *Application deadline:* For fall admission, 7/1 priority date for domestic students, 6/1 priority date for international students; for spring admission, 11/1 priority date for domestic students, 10/1 priority date for international students. Applications are processed on a rolling basis. Application fee: $25. Electronic applications accepted. *Financial support:* Career-related internships or fieldwork and unspecified assistantships available. Support available to part-time students. *Faculty research:* Counseling and rehabilitation, behavioral supports, inquiry-based science methods, teacher quality enhancement. Total annual research expenditures: $1.5 million. *Unit head:* Dr. Catherine Gillespie, Chair, 515-271-4602, E-mail: catherine.gillespie@drake.edu. *Application contact:* Ann J. Martin, Graduate Coordinator, 515-271-2034, Fax: 515-271-2831, E-mail: ann.martin@drake.edu.

Drexel University, School of Education, Program in Educational Administration, Philadelphia, PA 19104-2875. Offers MS.

Drexel University, School of Education, Program in Educational Leadership and Learning Technology, Philadelphia, PA 19104-2875. Offers PhD. *Degree requirements:* For doctorate, thesis/dissertation. Electronic applications accepted.

Duquesne University, School of Education, Department of Foundations and Leadership, Interdisciplinary Doctoral Program for Educational Leaders, Pittsburgh, PA 15282-0001. Offers Ed D. Part-time and evening/weekend programs available. *Faculty:* 2 full-time (1 woman), 4 part-time/adjunct (3 women). *Students:* 90. In 2006, 19 degrees awarded. *Degree requirements:* For doctorate, thesis/dissertation. *Entrance requirements:* For doctorate, GRE General Test, MAT, interview, minimum GPA of 3.25, writing sample. *Application deadline:* For fall admission, 8/1 for domestic students; for spring admission, 12/1 for domestic students. Application fee: $100. *Expenses:* Tuition: Part-time $723 per credit. Required fees: $71 per credit. Tuition and fees vary according to degree level and program. *Financial support:* In 2006–07, 1 research assistantship with full and partial tuition reimbursement (averaging $5,200 per year) was awarded; career-related internships or fieldwork, institutionally sponsored loans, and tuition waivers (partial) also available. Support available to part-time students. Financial award application deadline: 5/31. *Faculty research:* Leader effectiveness, shared decision making, organizational climate and health, leader authenticity. *Unit head:* Dr. James Henderson, Director, 412-396-4038, Fax: 412-396-5585, E-mail: henderson@duq.edu.

Duquesne University, School of Education, Department of Foundations and Leadership, Program in School Administration and Supervision, Pittsburgh, PA 15282-0001. Offers school administration (MS Ed), including elementary administration, secondary administration; school supervision (MS Ed). Part-time and evening/weekend programs available. *Faculty:* 3 full-time (1 woman), 3 part-time/adjunct (1 woman). *Students:* 94; includes 6 minority (all African Americans), 2 international. 20 applicants, 35% accepted, 7 enrolled. In 2006, 42 degrees awarded. *Degree requirements:* For master's, thesis. *Entrance requirements:* For master's, MAT, minimum GPA of 3.0. Additional exam requirements/recommendations for international students: Required—TOEFL. *Application deadline:* For fall admission, 8/1 for domestic students; for spring admission, 12/1 for domestic students. Applications are processed on a rolling basis. Application fee: $50. *Expenses:* Tuition: Part-time $723 per credit. Required fees: $71 per credit. Tuition and fees vary according to degree level and program. *Financial support:* In 2006–07, 1 research assistantship with full and partial tuition reimbursement (averaging $5,200 per year) was awarded. Support available to part-time students. *Unit head:* Dr. Robert Furman, Coordinator, 412-396-5274, Fax: 412-396-5585, E-mail: furman@duq.edu.

Duquesne University, School of Education, Department of Instruction and Leadership, Instructional Leadership Excellence Doctoral Program (ILEAD), Pittsburgh, PA 15282-0001. Offers Ed D. Part-time and evening/weekend programs available. *Faculty:* 6 full-time (3 women), 4 part-time/adjunct (2 women). *Students:* 45. Average age 41. In 2006, 7 degrees awarded. *Degree requirements:* For doctorate, thesis/dissertation. *Entrance requirements:* For doctorate, GRE General Test, MAT, interview, minimum GPA of 3.25. Additional exam requirements/recommendations for international students: Required—TOEFL. *Application deadline:* For spring admission, 12/1 for domestic students. Application fee: $100. *Expenses:* Tuition: Part-time $723 per credit. Required fees: $71 per credit. Tuition and fees vary according to degree level and program. *Financial support:* In 2006–07, 6 research assistantships with full and partial tuition reimbursements were awarded; teaching assistantships with partial tuition reimbursements, career-related internships or fieldwork, Federal Work-Study, institutionally sponsored loans, and scholarships/grants also available. Support available to part-time students. Financial award applicants required to submit FAFSA. *Unit head:* Dr. Robert Agostino, Director, 412-396-6104, Fax: 412-396-5388, E-mail: agostino@duq.edu.

East Carolina University, Graduate School, College of Education, Department of Educational Leadership, Greenville, NC 27858-4353. Offers educational administration and supervision (Ed S); educational leadership (Ed D); higher education administration (Ed D); school administration (MSA); supervision (MA Ed). *Accreditation:* NCATE. Part-time and evening/weekend programs available. Postbaccalaureate distance learning degree programs offered (minimal on-campus study). *Students:* 54 full-time (37 women), 279 part-time (193 women); includes 75 minority (68 African Americans, 3 American Indian/Alaska Native, 4 Asian Americans or Pacific Islanders), 2 international. Average age 39. 53 applicants, 34% accepted, 13 enrolled. In 2006, 54 master's, 24 doctorates, 4 Ed Ss awarded. *Degree requirements:* For master's, thesis optional; for doctorate, thesis/dissertation. *Entrance requirements:* For master's, GRE General Test or MAT, interview, minimum GPA of 2.5, bachelor's degree in related field, teaching license (MA Ed); for doctorate, GRE or MAT, interview, minimum GPA of 3.5. Additional exam requirements/recommendations for international students: Required—TOEFL. *Application deadline:* For fall admission, 6/1 priority date for domestic students. Applications are processed on a rolling basis. Application fee: $50. *Financial support:* Research assistantships with partial tuition reimbursements, teaching assistantships with partial tuition reimbursements, Federal Work-Study available. Support available to part-time students. Financial award application deadline: 6/1. *Unit head:* Dr. Lynn Bradshaw, Chair, 252-328-6444, Fax: 252-328-4219, E-mail: bradshawl@ecu.edu. *Application contact:* Dean of Graduate School, 252-328-6012, Fax: 252-328-6071, E-mail: gradschool@ecu.edu.

Eastern Illinois University, Graduate School, College of Education and Professional Studies, Department of Educational Administration, Charleston, IL 61920-3099. Offers MS Ed, Ed S. *Accreditation:* NCATE. Part-time and evening/weekend programs available. *Faculty:* 5 full-time (1 woman). In 2006, 157 master's, 45 other advanced degrees awarded. *Degree requirements:* For master's, fieldwork; for Ed S, thesis. *Application deadline:* For fall admission, 7/31 priority date for domestic students. Applications are processed on a rolling basis. Application fee: $30. *Expenses:* Tuition, state resident: part-time $169 per semester hour.

Tuition, nonresident: part-time $508 per semester hour. Required fees: $60 per semester hour. *Financial support:* In 2006–07, research assistantships with tuition reimbursements (averaging $7,200 per year), teaching assistantships with tuition reimbursements (averaging $7,200 per year) were awarded; career-related internships or fieldwork also available. *Unit head:* Dr. Linda Morford, Chairperson, 217-581-2919, Fax: 217-581-7147, E-mail: lmmorford@eiu.edu.

Eastern Kentucky University, The Graduate School, College of Education, Department of Counseling and Educational Leadership, Richmond, KY 40475-3102. Offers human services (MA); instructional leadership (MA Ed); mental health counseling (MA); school counseling (MA Ed). *Accreditation:* ACA (one or more programs are accredited); NCATE. Part-time programs available. Postbaccalaureate distance learning degree programs offered. *Students:* 73 full-time (48 women), 581 part-time (421 women); includes 22 minority (18 African Americans, 1 American Indian/Alaska Native, 3 Hispanic Americans). Average age 24. 614 applicants, 46% accepted, 199 enrolled. In 2006, 245 degrees awarded. *Entrance requirements:* For master's, GRE General Test, minimum GPA of 2.5. Application fee: $35. *Expenses:* Tuition, state resident: full-time $5,610. Tuition, nonresident: full-time $15,910. *Financial support:* In 2006–07, 2 research assistantships (averaging $6,500 per year), teaching assistantships (averaging $6,500 per year) were awarded; career-related internships or fieldwork, Federal Work-Study, and scholarships/grants also available. Support available to part-time students. *Unit head:* Dr. Kim Naugle, Chair, 859-622-1863, Fax: 859-622-1126.

Eastern Michigan University, Graduate School, College of Education, Department of Leadership and Counseling, Programs in Leadership, Ypsilanti, MI 48197. Offers educational leadership (Ed D); higher education general administration (MA); higher education student affairs (MA); K-12 administration (MA); leadership (SPA). Part-time and evening/weekend programs available. Postbaccalaureate distance learning degree programs offered (minimal on-campus study). *Students:* 27 full-time (18 women), 338 part-time (193 women); includes 73 minority (67 African Americans, 1 American Indian/Alaska Native, 1 Asian American or Pacific Islander, 4 Hispanic Americans), 6 international. Average age 37. In 2006, 91 master's, 11 doctorates awarded. *Entrance requirements:* Additional exam requirements/recommendations for international students: Required—TOEFL. *Application deadline:* For fall admission, 5/15 priority date for domestic students, 5/1 priority date for international students; for winter admission, 10/15 priority date for domestic students, 10/1 priority date for international students; for spring admission, 3/15 priority date for domestic students, 3/1 priority date for international students. Applications are processed on a rolling basis. Application fee: $35. *Expenses:* Tuition, state resident: part-time $341 per credit hour. Tuition, nonresident: full-time $16,104; part-time $671 per credit hour. Required fees: $816; $34 per credit hour. $40 per term. One-time fee: $82 full-time. Tuition and fees vary according to course level, course load, degree level and reciprocity agreements. *Financial support:* Fellowships, research assistantships with full tuition reimbursements, teaching assistantships with full tuition reimbursements, career-related internships or fieldwork, Federal Work-Study, institutionally sponsored loans, scholarships/grants, tuition waivers (partial), and unspecified assistantships available. Support available to part-time students. *Unit head:* Dr. Jaclynn Tracy, Head, Department of Leadership and Counseling, 734-487-0255, Fax: 734-487-4608, E-mail: jackie.tracy@emich.edu.

Eastern Nazarene College, Adult and Graduate Studies, Division of Education, Quincy, MA 02170-2999. Offers early childhood education (M Ed, Certificate); elementary education (M Ed, Certificate); English as a second language (M Ed, Certificate); instructional enrichment and development (M Ed, Certificate); middle school education (M Ed, Certificate); moderate special needs education (M Ed, Certificate); principal (Certificate); program development and supervision (M Ed, Certificate); secondary education (M Ed, Certificate); special education administrator (Certificate); supervisor (Certificate); teacher of reading (M Ed, Certificate). M Ed and Certificate also available through weekend program for administration, special needs, and reading only. Part-time and evening/weekend programs available. *Faculty:* 9 full-time (5 women), 11 part-time/adjunct (5 women). *Students:* 135. Average age 35. 20 applicants, 100% accepted. In 2006, 2 degrees awarded. *Entrance requirements:* Additional exam requirements/recommendations for international students: Required—TOEFL (minimum score 550 paper-based). *Application deadline:* Applications are processed on a rolling basis. Application fee: $35. *Financial support:* Career-related internships or fieldwork available. Support available to part-time students. Financial award applicants required to submit FAFSA. *Unit head:* Dr. Lorne Ranstrom, Chair, 617-745-3528, E-mail: randstrol@enc.edu. *Application contact:* Christine Galbraith, Graduate Studies Recruiter, 617-774-6703, Fax: 617-984-4901, E-mail: christine. galbraith@enc.edu.

Eastern Washington University, Graduate Studies, College of Education and Human Development, Department of Education, Program in Educational Leadership, Cheney, WA 99004-2431. Offers M Ed. *Accreditation:* NCATE. *Degree requirements:* For master's, thesis or alternative, comprehensive exam. *Entrance requirements:* For master's, minimum GPA of 3.0.

East Tennessee State University, School of Graduate Studies, College of Education, Department of Educational Leadership and Policy Analysis, Johnson City, TN 37614. Offers administrative endorsement (M Ed, Ed D, Ed S); classroom leadership (Ed D); educational leadership (M Ed, Ed D, Ed S); post secondary and private sector leadership (Ed D); school leadership (Ed D); school system leadership (Ed S); teacher leadership (Ed S). *Accreditation:* NCATE. Terminal master's awarded for partial completion of doctoral program. *Degree requirements:* For master's, oral exam or thesis; for doctorate, thesis/dissertation, oral and written exams; for Ed S, internship, practicum. *Entrance requirements:* For master's, GRE, interview, minimum GPA of 2.75, teaching certificate; for doctorate, GRE General Test, GRE Subject Test; for Ed S, GRE General Test, teaching certificate. Additional exam requirements/recommendations for international students: Required—TOEFL (minimum score 550 paper-based; 213 computer-based). *Faculty research:* Needs of principals in the new century, funding accountability and policy formulation for US community college systems, use of technology in principal preparation programs, multiple intelligence and the adult learner, leadership development in youth and young adults.

Edgewood College, Program in Education, Madison, WI 53711-1997. Offers director of instruction (Certificate); director of special education and pupil services (Certificate); education (MA Ed); educational administration (MA); educational leadership (Ed D); emotional disturbances (MA, Certificate); learning disabilities (MA, Certificate); learning disabilities and emotional disturbances (MA, Certificate); school business administration (Certificate); school principalship K-12 (Certificate). *Accreditation:* NCATE (one or more programs are accredited). Part-time and evening/weekend programs available. *Students:* 30 full-time (21 women), 180 part-time (117 women); includes 7 minority (5 African Americans, 2 Asian Americans or Pacific Islanders), 2 international. Average age 38. In 2006, 25 master's, 20 doctorates awarded. *Degree requirements:* For master's, practicum, research project. *Entrance requirements:* For master's, minimum GPA of 2.75, 2 letters of recommendation. Additional exam requirements/recommendations for international students: Required—TOEFL. *Application deadline:* For fall admission, 8/24 for domestic students, 8/1 for international students; for spring admission, 1/10 for domestic students, 10/1 for international students. Applications are processed on a rolling basis. Application fee: $25. Electronic applications accepted. *Unit head:* Dr. Joseph Schmiedicke, Chair, 608-663-2293, Fax: 608-663-3291, E-mail: schmied@edgewood.edu. *Application contact:* Paula O'Malley, Graduate Student Admissions Counselor, 608-663-2282, Fax: 608-663-3291, E-mail: gradprograms@edgewood.edu.

Edinboro University of Pennsylvania, Graduate Studies and Research, School of Education, Department of Professional Studies, Program in Educational Leadership, Edinboro, PA 16444. Offers elementary school administration (M Ed); secondary school administration (M Ed). Part-time programs available. Postbaccalaureate distance learning degree programs offered. *Students:* 2 full-time (0 women), 75 part-time (40 women); includes 2 minority (both African Americans) Average age 31. In 2006, 16 degrees awarded. Application fee: $30. *Expenses:* Tuition, state resident: full-time $6,048; part-time $336 per credit. Tuition, nonresident: full-time $9,678; part-time $538 per credit. Required fees: $1,849; $42 per credit. *Financial support:* In 2006–07, 2 research assistantships with full and partial tuition

reimbursements (averaging $3,850 per year) were awarded; career-related internships or fieldwork, Federal Work-Study, scholarships/grants, and unspecified assistantships also available. Support available to part-time students. Financial award application deadline: 2/15. *Unit head:* Dr. Andrew Pushchack, Head, 814-732-1548, E-mail: apushchak@edinboro.edu.

Edinboro University of Pennsylvania, Graduate Studies and Research, School of Education, Department of Professional Studies, Program in Letter of Eligibility, Edinboro, PA 16444. Offers Certificate. Part-time and evening/weekend programs available. *Students:* 1 full-time (0 women), 13 part-time (5 women). Average age 42. In 2006, 9 degrees awarded. *Degree requirements:* For Certificate, thesis or alternative. *Entrance requirements:* For degree, GRE or MAT, master's degree in school administration or related field, minimum QPA of 2.5. *Application deadline:* Applications are processed on a rolling basis. Application fee: $30. Electronic applications accepted. *Expenses:* Tuition, state resident: full-time $6,048; part-time $336 per credit. Tuition, nonresident: full-time $9,678; part-time $538 per credit. Required fees: $1,849; $42 per credit. *Financial support:* Research assistantships, career-related internships or fieldwork, Federal Work-Study, and scholarships/grants available. Support available to part-time students. Financial award application deadline: 2/15; financial award applicants required to submit FAFSA. *Unit head:* Dr. James Bolton, Head, 814-732-1734. *Application contact:* Dr. R. Scott Baldwin, Dean, 814-732-2752, Fax: 814-732-2268, E-mail: sbaldwin@edinboro.edu.

Elmhurst College, Graduate Programs, Program in Teacher Leadership, Elmhurst, IL 60126-3296. Offers M Ed. Part-time and evening/weekend programs available. *Faculty:* 4 full-time (3 women). *Students:* Average age 27. 8 applicants, 100% accepted, 8 enrolled. *Entrance requirements:* For master's, 3 recommendations. Additional exam requirements/recommendations for international students: Required—TOEFL (minimum score 550 paper-based; 213 computer-based). *Application deadline:* Applications are processed on a rolling basis. Application fee: $25. Electronic applications accepted. *Expenses:* Tuition: Part-time $781 per hour. Required fees: $75 per hour. Part-time tuition and fees vary according to course load and student level. *Financial support:* In 2006–07, 15 students received support. Federal Work-Study and scholarships/grants available. Support available to part-time students. Financial award application deadline: 6/1; financial award applicants required to submit FAFSA. *Application contact:* Elizabeth D. Kuebler, Director of Adult and Graduate Admission, 630-617-3069, Fax: 630-617-5501, E-mail: betsyk@elmhurst.edu.

Emmanuel College, Graduate Programs, Programs in Education, Boston, MA 02115. Offers educational leadership (CAGS); elementary education (MAT); school administration (M Ed); secondary education (MAT). Part-time and evening/weekend programs available. *Faculty:* 4 full-time (all women), 8 part-time/adjunct (4 women). *Students:* 5 full-time (all women), 34 part-time (24 women); includes 6 minority (3 African Americans, 1 Asian American or Pacific Islander, 2 Hispanic Americans). Average age 29. 44 applicants, 23% accepted, 10 enrolled. In 2006, 21 master's, 3 other advanced degrees awarded. *Entrance requirements:* For master's, interview, resumé, 2 letters of recommendation; for CAGS, interview, leadership statement, resumé, 2 letters of recommendation. Additional exam requirements/recommendations for international students: Required—TOEFL (minimum score 600 paper-based; 250 computer-based). *Application deadline:* For fall admission, 8/15 priority date for domestic students; for spring admission, 12/8 priority date for domestic students. Applications are processed on a rolling basis. Application fee: $50. Electronic applications accepted. *Expenses:* Tuition: Full-time $5,256. *Faculty research:* Literature/reading, history of education, multicultural education, special education. *Unit head:* Brian Minchello, Associate Director, Graduate and Professional Programs, 617-735-9928, Fax: 617-735-9708, E-mail: gpp@emmanuel.edu. *Application contact:* Kristin Balutis, Enrollment Counselor, 617-735-9859, Fax: 617-735-9708, E-mail: balutkr@emmanuel.edu.

Emporia State University, School of Graduate Studies, The Teachers College, Department of School Leadership/Middle and Secondary Teacher Education, Program in Curriculum and Instruction, Emporia, KS 66801-5087. Offers curriculum and instruction (MS), including curriculum leadership, effective practitioner, national board certification. *Accreditation:* NCATE. Part-time programs available. *Students:* 1 (woman) full-time, 156 part-time (140 women); includes 4 minority (1 African American, 2 American Indian/Alaska Native, 1 Hispanic American). 52 applicants, 88% accepted, 45 enrolled. In 2006, 28 degrees awarded. *Degree requirements:* For master's, comprehensive exam or thesis, practicum. *Entrance requirements:* For master's, GRE or MAT, appropriate bachelor's degree, teacher certification, 1 year of teaching experience, letters of recommendation. *Application deadline:* For fall admission, 8/15 priority date for domestic students. Applications are processed on a rolling basis. Application fee: $30 ($75 for international students). Electronic applications accepted. *Expenses:* Tuition, state resident: full-time $3,438; part-time $143 per credit hour. Tuition, nonresident: full-time $10,398; part-time $433 per credit hour. Required fees: $724; $44 per credit hour. *Financial support:* Career-related internships or fieldwork, Federal Work-Study, institutionally sponsored loans, health care benefits, and unspecified assistantships available. Financial award application deadline: 3/15; financial award applicants required to submit FAFSA. *Unit head:* Dr. Jerry Will, Chair, Department of School Leadership/Middle and Secondary Teacher Education, 620-341-5777, E-mail: jwill@emporia.edu.

Emporia State University, School of Graduate Studies, The Teachers College, Department of School Leadership/Middle and Secondary Teacher Education, Program in Educational Administration, Emporia, KS 66801-5087. Offers educational administration (MS), including elementary administration, elementary/secondary administration, secondary administration. *Accreditation:* NCATE. Part-time programs available. *Students:* 3 full-time (0 women), 108 part-time (45 women); includes 3 minority (all Hispanic Americans) 17 applicants, 88% accepted, 13 enrolled. In 2006, 32 degrees awarded. *Degree requirements:* For master's, comprehensive exam or thesis, practicum. *Entrance requirements:* For master's, GRE or MAT, appropriate bachelor's degree, letters of recommendation, teacher certification, 1 year teaching experience. *Application deadline:* For fall admission, 8/15 priority date for domestic students. Applications are processed on a rolling basis. Application fee: $30 ($75 for international students). Electronic applications accepted. *Expenses:* Tuition, state resident: full-time $3,438; part-time $143 per credit hour. Tuition, nonresident: full-time $10,398; part-time $433 per credit hour. Required fees: $724; $44 per credit hour. *Financial support:* Career-related internships or fieldwork, Federal Work-Study, institutionally sponsored loans, health care benefits, and unspecified assistantships available. Financial award application deadline: 3/15; financial award applicants required to submit FAFSA. *Unit head:* Dr. Jerry Will, Chair, Department of School Leadership/Middle and Secondary Teacher Education, 620-341-5777, E-mail: jwill@emporia.edu.

Evangel University, Department of Education, Springfield, MO 65802-2191. Offers educational leadership (M Ed); reading education (M Ed); secondary teaching (M Ed); teaching (MA). Part-time and evening/weekend programs available. *Faculty:* 4 full-time (2 women), 6 part-time/adjunct (5 women). *Students:* 2 full-time (both women), 17 part-time (14 women); includes 2 minority (1 Asian American or Pacific Islander, 1 Hispanic American). Average age 26. 10 applicants, 100% accepted, 10 enrolled. In 2006, 13 degrees awarded. *Degree requirements:* For master's, thesis optional. *Entrance requirements:* For master's, PRAXIS II (preferred), GRE (accepted). Additional exam requirements/recommendations for international students: Required—TOEFL (minimum score 550 paper-based; 213 computer-based). *Application deadline:* For fall admission, 7/15 priority date for domestic students; for spring admission, 11/15 priority date for domestic students. Applications are processed on a rolling basis. Application fee: $25. *Financial support:* In 2006–07, 6 students received support. Career-related internships or fieldwork, institutionally sponsored loans, and scholarships/grants available. Support available to part-time students. Financial award application deadline: 3/1; financial award applicants required to submit FAFSA. *Unit head:* Dr. Jeff Hittenberger, Chair, 417-865-2815 Ext. 8559, E-mail: hittenbergerj@evangel.edu. *Application contact:* Charity H. Fahlstrom, Director of Graduate and Professional Studies Admissions, 417-865-2811 Ext. 1227, Fax: 417-575-5484.

Educational Administration

Fairleigh Dickinson University, College at Florham, University College: Arts, Sciences, and Professional Studies, Peter Sammartino School of Education, Program in Educational Leadership, Madison, NJ 07940-1099. Offers MA. *Students:* 1 applicant, 100% accepted, 1 enrolled.

Fairleigh Dickinson University, Metropolitan Campus, University College: Arts, Sciences, and Professional Studies, Peter Sammartino School of Education, Program in Educational Leadership, Teaneck, NJ 07666-1914. Offers MA. *Students:* 4 full-time (1 woman), 95 part-time (58 women). Average age 36. 39 applicants, 97% accepted, 24 enrolled. In 2006, 14 degrees awarded. *Application deadline:* Applications are processed on a rolling basis. Application fee: $40. *Unit head:* Dr. Vicki Cohen, Director, Peter Sammartino School of Education, 201-692-2525, Fax: 201-692-2603, E-mail: vicki_cohen@fdu.edu.

Fayetteville State University, Graduate School, Programs in Educational Leadership and School Administration, Fayetteville, NC 28301-4298. Offers educational leadership (Ed D); school administration (MSA). *Accreditation:* NCATE (one or more programs are accredited). Part-time and evening/weekend programs available. *Faculty:* 18 full-time (6 women). *Students:* 34 full-time (23 women), 74 part-time (55 women); includes 79 minority (74 African Americans, 4 American Indian/Alaska Native, 1 Hispanic American). Average age 41. 27 applicants, 100% accepted, 27 enrolled. In 2006, 21 master's, 3 doctorates awarded. *Degree requirements:* For master's, internship, written and oral exams. *Entrance requirements:* For master's, GRE or MAT, minimum GPA of 2.5. *Application deadline:* For fall admission, 7/1 for domestic students; for spring admission, 12/1 for domestic students. Applications are processed on a rolling basis. Application fee: $25. Electronic applications accepted. *Expenses:* Tuition, state resident: full-time $2,118. Tuition, nonresident: full-time $11,708. Required fees: $1,099. Tuition and fees vary according to course load. *Faculty research:* School choice and school reform, college student issues, Brown Board of Education Fifty Years Later, African American males and achievement, web-enhanced instructional strategies. *Unit head:* Dr. Genniver Bell, Acting Director, 910-672-1731, E-mail: gbell@uncfsu.edu.

Felician College, Program in Education, Lodi, NJ 07644-2117. Offers elementary education (MA); supervisory (MA); teacher for students with disabilities (MA). Part-time and evening/weekend programs available. *Students:* 18 applicants, 50% accepted, 9 enrolled. *Degree requirements:* For master's, project. *Entrance requirements:* For master's, MAT, minimum GPA of 3.0, 3 letters of recommendation. Additional exam requirements/recommendations for international students: Recommended—TOEFL (minimum score 550 paper-based; 213 computer-based). *Application deadline:* Applications are processed on a rolling basis. Application fee: $40. *Expenses:* Tuition: Part-time $675 per credit. Tuition and fees vary according to program. *Financial support:* Federal Work-Study available. *Unit head:* Dr. Julie Goods, Associate Dean, 201-559-3529, E-mail: goodj@felician.edu. *Application contact:* Wendy Lin-Cook, Director of Adult and Graduate Admission, 201-559-6077, Fax: 201-559-6138, E-mail: adultandgraduate@felician.edu.

See Close-Up on page 879.

Ferris State University, College of Education and Human Services, School of Education, Big Rapids, MI 49307. Offers administration (MSCTE); curriculum and instruction (M Ed), including administration, elementary education, philanthropic education, reading, secondary education, special education, subject matter option; education technology (MSCTE); instructor (MSCTE); post-secondary administration (MSCTE); training and development (MSCTE). Part-time and evening/weekend programs available. Postbaccalaureate distance learning degree programs offered (no on-campus study). *Faculty:* 13 full-time (9 women), 26 part-time/adjunct (19 women). *Students:* 38 full-time (27 women), 254 part-time (164 women); includes 30 minority (22 African Americans, 1 American Indian/Alaska Native, 2 Asian Americans or Pacific Islanders, 5 Hispanic Americans), 1 international. Average age 37. 171 applicants, 99% accepted. In 2006, 92 degrees awarded. *Degree requirements:* For master's, thesis, research paper. *Entrance requirements:* For master's, 2 years of work experience, minimum GPA of 3.0. *Application deadline:* For fall admission, 6/1 priority date for domestic students; for winter admission, 12/10 priority date for domestic students. Applications are processed on a rolling basis. Application fee: $30. *Expenses:* Tuition, state resident: part-time $355 per credit hour. Tuition, nonresident: part-time $687 per credit hour. *Financial support:* Career-related internships or fieldwork and tuition waivers (full and partial) available. Support available to part-time students. Financial award applicants required to submit FAFSA. *Faculty research:* Suicide prevention, reading, women in education, special needs, administration. *Unit head:* Interim Director, 231-591-5362, Fax: 231-591-2041. *Application contact:* Sigrid Robertson, Secretary, 231-591-3511, Fax: 231-591-2041, E-mail: robertss@ferris.edu.

Fielding Graduate University, Graduate Programs, School of Educational Leadership and Change, Santa Barbara, CA 93105-3538. Offers collaborative educational leadership (MA); educational leadership (Ed D). *Faculty:* 18 full-time (10 women), 30 part-time/adjunct (14 women). *Students:* 383 full-time (276 women); includes 162 minority (105 African Americans, 13 American Indian/Alaska Native, 21 Asian Americans or Pacific Islanders, 23 Hispanic Americans). Average age 48. 104 applicants, 96% accepted, 70 enrolled. In 2006, 39 master's, 29 doctorates awarded. *Median time to degree:* Master's–1.8 years full-time; doctorate–4.1 years full-time. Of those who began their doctoral program in fall 1998, 37% received their degree in 8 years or less. *Degree requirements:* For doctorate, thesis/dissertation, comprehensive exam, registration. *Entrance requirements:* For master's, minimum GPA of 2.5; for doctorate, resumé, 2 letters of recommendation, writing sample. *Application deadline:* For fall admission, 7/1 priority date for domestic students; for spring admission, 12/31 priority date for domestic students. Applications are processed on a rolling basis. Application fee: $75. Electronic applications accepted. *Expenses: Contact institution. Financial support:* In 2006–07, 330 students received support. Institutionally sponsored loans, scholarships/grants, and tuition waivers (partial) available. Financial award application deadline: 3/1; financial award applicants required to submit FAFSA. *Unit head:* Dr. Judy Witt, Dean, 805-898-2940, E-mail: jwitt@fielding.edu. *Application contact:* David Brule, Admission Counselor, 800-340-1099, Fax: 805-687-9793, E-mail: dbrule@fielding.edu.

See Close-Up on page 1113.

Fitchburg State College, Division of Graduate and Continuing Education, Program in Educational Leadership and Management, Fitchburg, MA 01420-2697. Offers educational technology (Certificate); higher education administration (CAGS); non-licensure (M Ed, CAGS); professional mentoring for teachers (Certificate); school principal (M Ed, CAGS); supervisor director (M Ed, CAGS); technology leader (M Ed, CAGS). *Accreditation:* NCATE. Part-time and evening/weekend programs available. *Students:* 19 full-time (14 women), 44 part-time (30 women); includes 2 minority (both African Americans), 1 international. Average age 39. 33 applicants, 97% accepted, 15 enrolled. In 2006, 24 master's, 20 other advanced degrees awarded. *Degree requirements:* For master's, thesis or alternative, comprehensive exam. *Entrance requirements:* For master's, GRE General Test or MAT, 3 years of teaching experience, teaching certificate, letters of recommendation, resumé; for other advanced degree, master's degree, letters of recommendation, resumé. Additional exam requirements/recommendations for international students: Required—TOEFL (minimum score 550 paper-based; 213 computer-based; 79 iBT). *Application deadline:* Applications are processed on a rolling basis. Application fee: $25 ($50 for international students). *Expenses:* Tuition, state resident: part-time $150 per credit. Tuition, nonresident: part-time $150 per credit. Required fees: $90 per credit. *Financial support:* In 2006–07, research assistantships with partial tuition reimbursements (averaging $5,500 per year); Federal Work-Study, scholarships/grants, and unspecified assistantships also available. Support available to part-time students. Financial award application deadline: 3/1; financial award applicants required to submit FAFSA. *Unit head:* Dr. Randy Howe, Chair, 978-665-3544, Fax: 978-665-3658, E-mail: gce@fsc.edu. *Application contact:* Director of Admissions, 978-665-3144, Fax: 978-665-4540, E-mail: admissions@fsc.edu.

Florida Agricultural and Mechanical University, Division of Graduate Studies, Research, and Continuing Education, College of Education, Department of Educational Leadership and Human Services, Tallahassee, FL 32307-3200. Offers administration and supervision (M Ed, MS Ed, PhD); adult education (M Ed, MS Ed); educational leadership (PhD); guidance and counseling (M Ed, MS Ed). *Accreditation:* NCATE. *Degree requirements:* For master's, thesis (for some programs); for doctorate, thesis/dissertation. *Entrance requirements:* For master's, GRE General Test, minimum GPA of 3.0. Additional exam requirements/recommendations for international students: Required—TOEFL.

Florida Atlantic University, College of Education, Department of Educational Leadership, Boca Raton, FL 33431-0991. Offers adult/community education (M Ed, PhD, Ed S); educational leadership (M Ed, PhD, Ed S); higher education management (M Ed, PhD). *Accreditation:* NCATE. Part-time and evening/weekend programs available. Postbaccalaureate distance learning degree programs offered (minimal on-campus study). *Faculty:* 19 full-time (8 women), 18 part-time/adjunct (11 women). *Students:* 65 full-time (43 women), 187 part-time (119 women); includes 81 minority (52 African Americans, 1 American Indian/Alaska Native, 4 Asian Americans or Pacific Islanders, 24 Hispanic Americans), 3 international. Average age 37. 114 applicants, 51% accepted, 50 enrolled. In 2006, 63 master's, 19 doctorates, 13 other advanced degrees awarded. *Degree requirements:* For master's, registration; for doctorate, thesis/dissertation, departmental qualifying exam, comprehensive exam, registration; for Ed S, departmental qualifying exam. *Entrance requirements:* For master's, GRE General Test, minimum GPA of 3.0 during previous 2 years; for doctorate, GRE General Test, minimum GPA of 3.5; for Ed S, GRE General Test. *Application deadline:* Applications are processed on a rolling basis. Application fee: $30. Electronic applications accepted. *Expenses:* Tuition, area resident: Full-time $4,394. Tuition, nonresident: full-time $16,441. *Financial support:* In 2006–07, 6 students received support, including 1 fellowship, 2 research assistantships, 2 teaching assistantships; career-related internships or fieldwork and tuition waivers (partial) also available. *Faculty research:* Self-directed learning, school reform issues, legal issues, mentoring, school leadership. *Unit head:* Dr. Anthony C. Townsend, Chairperson, 561-297-3550, Fax: 561-297-3618, E-mail: townsend@fau.edu. *Application contact:* Catherine Politi, Senior Secretary, 561-297-3550, Fax: 561-297-3618, E-mail: cpoliti@fau.edu.

Florida Gulf Coast University, College of Education, Program in Educational Leadership, Fort Myers, FL 33965-6565. Offers M Ed. Part-time and evening/weekend programs available. *Faculty:* 31 full-time (21 women), 30 part-time/adjunct (24 women). *Students:* 54 full-time (38 women), 20 part-time (14 women); includes 7 minority (3 African Americans, 4 Hispanic Americans). Average age 35. 38 applicants, 87% accepted, 28 enrolled. In 2006, 10 degrees awarded. *Degree requirements:* For master's, thesis or alternative, learning and professional portfolios. *Entrance requirements:* For master's, GRE General Test, MAT, minimum GPA of 3.0. Additional exam requirements/recommendations for international students: Required—TOEFL (minimum score 550 paper-based; 213 computer-based). *Application deadline:* For fall admission, 7/1 priority date for domestic students; for spring admission, 10/15 for domestic students. Applications are processed on a rolling basis. Application fee: $30. Electronic applications accepted. *Expenses:* Tuition, state resident: full-time $4,326. Tuition, nonresident: full-time $18,523. Required fees: $1,211. One-time fee: $5 full-time. *Faculty research:* Inclusion, technology in teaching, curriculum development in educational leadership, education policy and law. *Unit head:* Dr. Pat Wachholz, Associate Dean, 239-590-7808, Fax: 239-590-7801, E-mail: wachhol@fgcu.edu.

Florida International University, College of Education, Department of Educational Leadership and Policy Studies, Program in Educational Administration and Supervision, Miami, FL 33199. Offers Ed D. *Accreditation:* NCATE. Part-time and evening/weekend programs available. *Faculty:* 3 full-time (1 woman). *Students:* Average age 41. 7 applicants, 14% accepted, 1 enrolled. In 2006, 3 degrees awarded. *Degree requirements:* For doctorate, thesis/dissertation. *Entrance requirements:* For doctorate, GRE General Test, teaching certificate, 3 years full-time teaching. Additional exam requirements/recommendations for international students: Required—TOEFL (minimum score 550 paper-based; 213 computer-based; 80 iBT), IELTS (minimum score 6). *Application deadline:* For fall admission, 6/1 priority date for domestic students, 4/1 for international students; for winter admission, 10/1 priority date for domestic students, 9/1 for international students; for spring admission, 3/1 priority date for domestic students, 2/1 for international students. Applications are processed on a rolling basis. Application fee: $30. Electronic applications accepted. *Expenses:* Tuition, state resident: part-time $249 per credit hour. Tuition, nonresident: part-time $753 per credit hour. Tuition and fees vary according to program. *Financial support:* Research assistantships, teaching assistantships available. *Unit head:* Dr. Peter Cistone, Program Leader, 301-348-2665. *Application contact:* Marisa Salazar, Student Recruiter, 305-348-3002, Fax: 305-348-3227, E-mail: marisa.salazar@fiu.edu.

Florida International University, College of Education, Department of Educational Leadership and Policy Studies, Program in Educational Leadership, Miami, FL 33199. Offers MS, Certificate, Ed S. *Accreditation:* NCATE. Part-time and evening/weekend programs available. *Faculty:* 3 full-time (1 woman). *Students:* 5 full-time (all women), 46 part-time (30 women); includes 39 minority (8 African Americans, 31 Hispanic Americans). 43 applicants, 44% accepted, 18 enrolled. In 2006, 14 degrees awarded. *Entrance requirements:* For master's, 3 years full-time teaching; for other advanced degree, GRE General Test, 3 years full-time teaching. Additional exam requirements/recommendations for international students: Required—TOEFL (minimum score 550 paper-based; 213 computer-based; 80 iBT), IELTS (minimum score 6). *Application deadline:* For fall admission, 6/1 priority date for domestic students, 4/1 for international students; for winter admission, 10/1 priority date for domestic students, 9/1 for international students; for spring admission, 3/1 priority date for domestic students, 2/1 for international students. Applications are processed on a rolling basis. Application fee: $30. *Expenses:* Tuition, state resident: part-time $249 per credit hour. Tuition, nonresident: part-time $753 per credit hour. Tuition and fees vary according to program. *Financial support:* Fellowships, research assistantships, teaching assistantships, Federal Work-Study and tuition waivers (full and partial) available. Support available to part-time students. *Unit head:* Dr. Peter Cistone, Program Leader, 301-348-2665. *Application contact:* Marisa Salazar, Student Recruiter, 305-348-3002, Fax: 305-348-3227, E-mail: marisa.salazar@fiu.edu.

Florida International University, College of Education, Department of Educational Leadership and Policy Studies, Program in Higher Education Administration, Miami, FL 33199. Offers MS. Part-time and evening/weekend programs available. *Faculty:* 4 full-time (2 women), 5 part-time/adjunct (3 women). *Students:* 35 full-time (22 women), 18 part-time (all women); includes 38 minority (18 African Americans, 20 Hispanic Americans). Average age 30. 34 applicants, 88% accepted, 30 enrolled. In 2006, 5 degrees awarded. *Degree requirements:* For master's, comprehensive exam. *Entrance requirements:* For master's, minimum GPA of 3.0. Additional exam requirements/recommendations for international students: Required—TOEFL (minimum score 550 paper-based; 213 computer-based; 80 iBT), IELTS (minimum score 6). *Application deadline:* For fall admission, 6/1 priority date for domestic students, 4/1 for international students; for winter admission, 10/1 priority date for domestic students, 9/1 for international students; for spring admission, 3/1 priority date for domestic students, 2/1 for international students. Applications are processed on a rolling basis. Application fee: $30. Electronic applications accepted. *Expenses:* Tuition, state resident: part-time $249 per credit hour. Tuition, nonresident: part-time $753 per credit hour. Tuition and fees vary according to program. *Financial support:* Fellowships, research assistantships with full and partial tuition reimbursements, teaching assistantships with full and partial tuition reimbursements, Federal Work-Study and tuition waivers (full and partial) available. Support available to part-time students. *Faculty research:* Access and equity in college admission, social justice, higher education law, faculty and tenure for individuals of color, affirmative action. *Unit head:* Dr. Benjamin Baez, Associate Professor, 305-348-5214, E-mail: baezb@fiu.edu. *Application contact:* Marisa Salazar, Student Recruiter, 305-348-3002, Fax: 305-348-3227, E-mail: marisa.salazar@fiu.edu.

Florida State University, Graduate Studies, College of Education, Department of Educational Leadership and Policy Studies, Program in Educational Leadership/Administration, Tallahassee, FL 32306. Offers educational administration/leadership (MS, Ed D, PhD, Ed S); policy planning and analysis (MS, Ed D, PhD, Ed S). Part-time and evening/weekend programs available. *Faculty:* 7 full-time (4 women), 6 part-time/adjunct (3 women). *Students:* 24 full-time (13 women), 61 part-time (41 women); includes 28 minority (20 African Americans, 3 Asian

Americans or Pacific Islanders, 5 Hispanic Americans). 86 applicants, 33% accepted, 16 enrolled. In 2006, 42 master's, 3 doctorates, 1 other advanced degree awarded. Terminal master's awarded for partial completion of doctoral program. *Degree requirements:* For master's and Ed S, thesis optional; for doctorate, thesis/dissertation, comprehensive exam. *Entrance requirements:* For master's, GRE General Test, minimum GPA of 3.0; for doctorate and Ed S, GRE General Test, minimum graduate GPA of 3.0. *Application deadline:* For fall admission, 7/1 priority date for domestic students; for spring admission, 11/1 for domestic students. Applications are processed on a rolling basis. Application fee: $30. *Expenses:* Tuition, state resident: full-time $5,822; part-time $243 per credit hour. Tuition, nonresident: full-time $20,976; part-time $874 per credit hour. Tuition and fees vary according to program. *Financial support:* Fellowships with partial tuition reimbursements, research assistantships with partial tuition reimbursements, teaching assistantships with partial tuition reimbursements, career-related internships or fieldwork, scholarships/grants, and unspecified assistantships available. Financial award applicants required to submit FAFSA. *Unit head:* Dr. Lynn A Wicker, Associate Dean for Academic Affairs and Coordinator, 850-644-6885, Fax: 850-644-2725, E-mail: wicker@coe.fsu.edu. *Application contact:* Jimmy Pastrano, Program Assistant, 850-644-6777, Fax: 850-644-1258, E-mail: pastrano@coe.fsu.edu.

Fordham University, Graduate School of Education, Division of Educational Leadership, Administration and Policy, New York, NY 10023. Offers administration and supervision (MSE, Adv C); administration and supervision for church leaders (PhD); educational administration and supervision (Ed D, PhD); human resource program administration (MS). *Accreditation:* NCATE. *Faculty:* 8 full-time (3 women), 20 part-time/adjunct (12 women). *Students:* 1 full-time (0 women), 229 part-time (174 women); includes 62 minority (23 African Americans, 12 Asian Americans or Pacific Islanders, 27 Hispanic Americans), 1 international. Average age 39. 144 applicants, 73% accepted, 82 enrolled. In 2006, 105 master's, 19 doctorates awarded. *Degree requirements:* For doctorate, thesis/dissertation. *Entrance requirements:* For doctorate, MAT, GRE General Test. Application fee: $65. *Financial support:* Career-related internships or fieldwork available. Financial award applicants required to submit FAFSA. *Unit head:* Dr. Gerald Cattaro, Chairperson, 212-636-6441.

Fort Hays State University, Graduate School, College of Education and Technology, Department of Educational Administration and Counseling, Program in Educational Administration, Hays, KS 67601-4099. Offers MS, Ed S. *Accreditation:* NCATE. *Faculty:* 9 full-time (2 women). *Students:* 5 full-time (2 women), 44 part-time (24 women); includes 10 minority (1 American Indian/Alaska Native, 5 Asian Americans or Pacific Islanders, 4 Hispanic Americans). Average age 37. 7 applicants, 100% accepted. In 2006, 33 degrees awarded. *Degree requirements:* For master's and Ed S, thesis or alternative, comprehensive exam. *Entrance requirements:* For master's, GRE General Test or MAT, minimum undergraduate GPA in last 60 hours. Additional exam requirements/recommendations for international students: Required—TOEFL (minimum score 550 paper-based; 213 computer-based). *Application deadline:* For fall admission, 7/1 priority date for domestic students. Applications are processed on a rolling basis. Application fee: $35. Electronic applications accepted. *Financial support:* In 2006–07, 2 teaching assistantships (averaging $5,000 per year) were awarded; research assistantships, institutionally sponsored loans and tuition waivers (full) also available. *Faculty research:* Guide to negotiations, nutrition program for disadvantaged, accountability, student insurance practices, student liability. *Unit head:* Dr. Michael Slattery, Coordinator, 785-628-4546, E-mail: mslattery@fhsu.edu.

Framingham State College, Division of Graduate and Continuing Education, Program in Educational Leadership, Framingham, MA 01701-9101. Offers MA. Part-time and evening/weekend programs available. *Faculty:* 1 full-time, 2 part-time/adjunct. *Students:* 56. In 2006, 25 degrees awarded. *Entrance requirements:* For master's, MAT. *Unit head:* Dr. James O'Connell, Coordinator, 508-626-4550, Fax: 508-626-4030, E-mail: ocon@verizon.com. *Application contact:* 508-626-4550, Fax: 508-626-4030, E-mail: dgce@frc.mass.edu.

Franciscan University of Steubenville, Graduate Programs, Department of Education, Steubenville, OH 43952-1763. Offers administration (MS Ed); teaching (MS Ed). Part-time and evening/weekend programs available. *Degree requirements:* For master's, project. *Entrance requirements:* For master's, minimum undergraduate GPA of 2.5 or written exam. Expenses: Contact institution.

Freed-Hardeman University, Program in Education, Henderson, TN 38340-2399. Offers curriculum and instruction (M Ed); school counseling (M Ed); school leadership (Ed S). *Accreditation:* NCATE. Part-time and evening/weekend programs available. *Faculty:* 9 full-time (3 women), 6 part-time/adjunct (4 women). *Students:* 51 full-time (40 women), 286 part-time (235 women); includes 203 minority (202 African Americans, 1 Asian American or Pacific Islander), 2 international. Average age 34. In 2006, 78 master's, 24 other advanced degrees awarded. *Degree requirements:* For master's, thesis optional; for Ed S, thesis. *Entrance requirements:* For master's, GRE General Test or NTE; for Ed S, 3 years of teaching experience. Additional exam requirements/recommendations for international students: Required—TOEFL (minimum score 500 paper-based; 173 computer-based). *Application deadline:* For fall admission, 8/1 for domestic students; for spring admission, 12/1 for domestic students. Applications are processed on a rolling basis. Application fee: $32. *Expenses:* Tuition: Part-time $334 per credit hour. Required fees: $10 per credit hour. *Financial support:* Career-related internships or fieldwork, Federal Work-Study, tuition waivers (partial), and unspecified assistantships available. Support available to part-time students. Financial award application deadline: 8/1; financial award applicants required to submit FAFSA. *Unit head:* Dr. Elizabeth Saunders, Graduate Director, 731-989-6082, Fax: 731-989-6065, E-mail: esaunders@fhu.edu.

Fresno Pacific University, Graduate Programs, Programs in Education, Division of Administration, Fresno, CA 93702-4709. Offers administrative services (MA Ed). Part-time and evening/weekend programs available. *Faculty:* 2 full-time (1 woman), 3 part-time/adjunct (0 women). *Students:* 5 full-time (4 women), 95 part-time (59 women); includes 32 minority (1 African American, 1 Asian American or Pacific Islander, 30 Hispanic Americans). Average age 39. 43 applicants, 81% accepted, 2 enrolled. In 2006, 19 degrees awarded. *Degree requirements:* For master's, thesis or alternative, 4 practica. *Entrance requirements:* Additional exam requirements/recommendations for international students: Required—TOEFL (minimum score 550 paper-based; 213 computer-based). *Application deadline:* For fall admission, 7/15 for domestic and international students; for spring admission, 11/15 for domestic students, 1/15 for international students. Applications are processed on a rolling basis. Application fee: $90. Electronic applications accepted. *Expenses:* Tuition: Full-time $7,470; part-time $415 per credit. *Financial support:* In 2006–07, 37 students received support. Career-related internships or fieldwork, scholarships/grants, and tuition waivers (full and partial) available. Support available to part-time students. Financial award applicants required to submit FAFSA. *Unit head:* Dr. Larry Wilder, Head, 559-453-2203, Fax: 559-453-2001, E-mail: larry.wilder@fresno.edu.

Friends University, Graduate School, Division of Science, Arts, and Education, Program in School Leadership, Wichita, KS 67213. Offers MSL. Evening/weekend programs available. *Faculty:* 1 (woman) full-time, 6 part-time/adjunct (1 woman). *Students:* 18 full-time. In 2006, 10 degrees awarded. *Entrance requirements:* Additional exam requirements/recommendations for international students: Required—TOEFL (minimum score 560 paper-based; 220 computer-based). *Application deadline:* For fall admission, 3/15 priority date for domestic and international students. Applications are processed on a rolling basis. Application fee: $45 ($65 for international students). Electronic applications accepted. *Unit head:* Dr. Brenda L. Cain, Director, 800-794-6945 Ext. 5592, E-mail: brendac@friends.edu. *Application contact:* Craig Davis, Executive Director of Recruitment-Adult and Graduate Studies, 800-794-6945 Ext. 5573, Fax: 316-295-5050, E-mail: cdavis@friends.edu.

Frostburg State University, Graduate School, College of Education, Department of Educational Professions, Program in Educational Administration and Supervision, Frostburg, MD 21532-1099. Offers elementary (M Ed); secondary (M Ed). Part-time and evening/weekend programs available. *Degree requirements:* For master's, thesis or alternative. *Entrance requirements:* For master's, teaching certificate. Electronic applications accepted. *Faculty research:* Practicum experience in schools.

Furman University, Graduate Division, Department of Education, Greenville, SC 29613. Offers early childhood education (MA); elementary education (MA); English as a second language (MA); middle school education (MA); reading (MA); school administration (MA); special education (MA). *Accreditation:* NCATE. Part-time and evening/weekend programs available. *Faculty:* 17 full-time (12 women), 19 part-time/adjunct (15 women). *Students:* 114 full-time (89 women), 72 part-time (59 women); includes 27 minority (23 African Americans, 4 Hispanic Americans). Average age 32. 36 applicants, 100% accepted, 36 enrolled. In 2006, 111 degrees awarded. *Degree requirements:* For master's, thesis (for some programs), comprehensive exam. *Entrance requirements:* For master's, GRE General Test or PRAXIS. *Application deadline:* For fall admission, 8/1 priority date for domestic and international students; for winter admission, 12/1 priority date for domestic and international students; for spring admission, 2/1 priority date for domestic and international students. Applications are processed on a rolling basis. Application fee: $50. *Expenses:* Tuition: Part-time $347 per credit. *Financial support:* In 2006–07, 97 students received support; fellowships, scholarships/grants and unspecified assistantships available. Financial award application deadline: 1/15; financial award applicants required to submit FAFSA. *Unit head:* Dr. Nelly Hecker, Head, 864-294-3385.

Gallaudet University, The Graduate School, School of Education and Human Services, Department of Administration and Supervision, Washington, DC 20002-3625. Offers administration (MS); administration and supervision (PhD, Ed S); instructional supervision (Ed S); leadership training (MS); special education administration (PhD). *Degree requirements:* For master's, thesis optional; for doctorate, 2 foreign languages, thesis/dissertation; for Ed S, 2 foreign languages, thesis (for some programs). *Entrance requirements:* For master's, GRE General Test or MAT; for doctorate, GRE General Test or MAT, interview.

Gannon University, School of Graduate Studies, College of Humanities, Business, and Education, School of Education, Program in Educational Leadership, Erie, PA 16541-0001. Offers M Ed. Part-time and evening/weekend programs available. *Students:* 5 full-time (3 women), 11 part-time (5 women), 1 international. Average age 31. 6 applicants, 83% accepted. In 2006, 8 degrees awarded. *Degree requirements:* For master's, thesis, comprehensive exam. *Entrance requirements:* For master's, GRE or MAT, interview, teaching certificate. Additional exam requirements/recommendations for international students: Required—TOEFL (minimum score 500 paper-based; 173 computer-based). *Application deadline:* Applications are processed on a rolling basis. Application fee: $25. *Expenses:* Tuition: Full-time $12,240; part-time $680 per credit. Required fees: $496; $16 per credit. Tuition and fees vary according to course load, degree level, campus/location and program. *Financial support:* Available to part-time students. Application deadline: 7/1; *Faculty research:* English, natural sciences, environmental education. *Application contact:* Debra Meszaros, Director of Graduate Recruitment, 814-871-5819, Fax: 814-871-5827, E-mail: cfal@gannon.edu.

Gannon University, School of Graduate Studies, College of Humanities, Business, and Education, School of Education, Program in Principal Certification, Erie, PA 16541-0001. Offers Certificate. Part-time and evening/weekend programs available. Postbaccalaureate distance learning degree programs offered (no on-campus study). *Students:* 2 full-time (0 women), 47 part-time (27 women); includes 1 minority (African American) Average age 36. 54 applicants, 96% accepted, 34 enrolled. *Entrance requirements:* Additional exam requirements/recommendations for international students: Required—TOEFL (minimum score 500 paper-based; 173 computer-based). *Application deadline:* Applications are processed on a rolling basis. Application fee: $25. *Expenses:* Tuition: Full-time $12,240; part-time $680 per credit. Required fees: $496; $16 per credit. Tuition and fees vary according to course load, degree level, campus/location and program. *Financial support:* Application deadline: 7/1; *Application contact:* Debra Meszaros, Director of Graduate Recruitment, 814-871-5819, Fax: 814-871-5827, E-mail: cfal@gannon.edu.

Gannon University, School of Graduate Studies, College of Humanities, Business, and Education, School of Education, Program in Superintendent Letter of Eligibility Certification, Erie, PA 16541-0001. Offers Certificate. Part-time and evening/weekend programs available. Postbaccalaureate distance learning degree programs offered (no on-campus study). *Students:* Average age 42. 27 applicants, 85% accepted, 18 enrolled. *Entrance requirements:* Additional exam requirements/recommendations for international students: Required—TOEFL (minimum score 500 paper-based; 173 computer-based). *Application deadline:* Applications are processed on a rolling basis. Application fee: $25. *Expenses:* Tuition: Full-time $12,240; part-time $680 per credit. Required fees: $496; $16 per credit. Tuition and fees vary according to course load, degree level, campus/location and program. *Financial support:* Application deadline: 7/1; *Application contact:* Debra Meszaros, Director of Graduate Recruitment, 814-871-5819, Fax: 814-871-5827, E-mail: cfal@gannon.edu.

Gardner-Webb University, Graduate School, Department of Education, Program in Educational Leadership, Boiling Springs, NC 28017. Offers Ed D. *Expenses:* Tuition: Full-time $3,144; part-time $262 per hour. *Unit head:* Dr. Donna Simmons, Chair, Department of Education, 704-406-4406, Fax: 704-406-3921, E-mail: dsimmons@gardner-webb.edu.

Gardner-Webb University, Graduate School, Department of Education, Program in School Administration, Boiling Springs, NC 28017. Offers educational leadership (Ed D); school administration (MA). *Accreditation:* NCATE. Part-time and evening/weekend programs available. *Faculty:* 7 full-time (3 women), 2 part-time/adjunct (both women). *Students:* 11 full-time (9 women), 315 part-time (209 women); includes 109 minority (107 African Americans, 1 Asian American or Pacific Islander, 1 Hispanic American). Average age 36. 80 applicants, 98% accepted, 78 enrolled. In 2006, 132 degrees awarded. *Degree requirements:* For master's, comprehensive exam. *Entrance requirements:* For master's, GRE General Test or NTE, PRAXIS, minimum GPA of 2.5. *Application deadline:* For fall admission, 8/1 priority date for domestic students. Applications are processed on a rolling basis. Application fee: $25. Electronic applications accepted. *Expenses:* Tuition: Full-time $3,144; part-time $262 per hour. *Financial support:* Unspecified assistantships available.

Geneva College, Program in Higher Education, Beaver Falls, PA 15010-3599. Offers campus ministry (MA); college teaching (MA); educational leadership (MA); student affairs administration (MA). Part-time and evening/weekend programs available. Postbaccalaureate distance learning degree programs offered (minimal on-campus study). *Degree requirements:* For master's, research seminar. *Entrance requirements:* For master's, minimum GPA of 2.8, writing sample, letters of recommendation (3). Additional exam requirements/recommendations for international students: Required—TOEFL. Electronic applications accepted. *Faculty research:* Student development, learning theories, church-related higher education, assessment, organizational culture.

George Fox University, School of Education, Newberg, OR 97132-2697. Offers counseling (MA, MS, Certificate), including counseling (MA), marriage and family therapy (MA, Certificate), school counseling (MA), school psychology (MS, Certificate), trauma (Certificate); educational foundations and leadership (M Ed, Ed D); teaching (MAT). Evening/weekend programs available. Postbaccalaureate distance learning degree programs offered (minimal on-campus study). *Faculty:* 34 full-time (18 women), 27 part-time/adjunct (19 women). *Students:* 157 full-time (125 women), 312 part-time (225 women); includes 15 minority (2 African Americans, 3 American Indian/Alaska Native, 3 Asian Americans or Pacific Islanders, 7 Hispanic Americans), 3 international. Average age 36. 165 applicants, 76% accepted, 106 enrolled. In 2006, 208 master's, 11 doctorates, 1 other advanced degree awarded. *Degree requirements:* For master's, thesis (for some programs). *Entrance requirements:* For master's, California Basic Educational Skills Test, PRAXIS II, minimum undergraduate GPA of 3.0 during previous 2 years. *Application deadline:* For fall admission, 2/1 for domestic students. Applications are processed on a rolling basis. Application fee: $40. Electronic applications accepted. *Expenses:* Contact institution. *Financial support:* Career-related internships or fieldwork available. Financial award applicants required to submit FAFSA. *Unit head:* Dr. James Worthington, Dean, 503-554-2871, E-mail:

Educational Administration

George Fox University (continued)
jworthington@georgefox.edu. *Application contact:* Beth Molzahn, Admissions Counselor, 800-631-0921, Fax: 503-554-3856, E-mail: bmolzahn@georgefox.edu.

George Mason University, Graduate School of Education, Program in Education Leadership, Fairfax, VA 22030. Offers M Ed. *Accreditation:* NCATE. Part-time and evening/weekend programs available. *Faculty:* 108 full-time (70 women), 193 part-time/adjunct (140 women). *Students:* 7 full-time (5 women), 293 part-time (176 women); includes 61 minority (49 African Americans, 5 Asian Americans or Pacific Islanders, 7 Hispanic Americans), 3 international. Average age 36. 190 applicants, 67% accepted, 117 enrolled. In 2006, 93 degrees awarded. *Entrance requirements:* For master's, minimum GPA of 3.0 in last 60 hours, 2 years of teaching experience. *Application deadline:* For fall admission, 5/1 for domestic students; for spring admission, 11/1 for domestic students. Application fee: $60 ($75 for international students). Electronic applications accepted. *Expenses:* Tuition, state resident: full-time $5,724; part-time $238 per credit. Tuition, nonresident: full-time $16,896; part-time $704 per credit. Required fees: $1,656; $69 per credit. *Financial support:* Career-related internships or fieldwork available. Support available to part-time students. Financial award application deadline: 3/1; financial award applicants required to submit FAFSA. *Unit head:* Scott Bauer, Acting Coordinator, 703-993-3775, Fax: 703-993-3643.

The George Washington University, Graduate School of Education and Human Development, Department of Educational Leadership, Program in Educational Administration and Policy Studies, Washington, DC 20052. Offers Ed D. *Accreditation:* NCATE. *Degree requirements:* For doctorate, thesis/dissertation, comprehensive exam. *Entrance requirements:* For doctorate, GRE General Test or MAT, interview, minimum GPA of 3.3.

The George Washington University, Graduate School of Education and Human Development, Department of Educational Leadership, Program in Educational Leadership and Administration, Washington, DC 20052. Offers MA Ed, Ed S. *Accreditation:* NCATE. Evening/weekend programs available. *Degree requirements:* For master's, comprehensive exam. *Entrance requirements:* For master's, GRE General Test or MAT, interview, minimum GPA of 2.75. *Faculty research:* Organizational learning.

The George Washington University, Graduate School of Education and Human Development, Department of Educational Leadership, Program in Higher Education Administration, Washington, DC 20052. Offers MA Ed, Ed D, Ed S. *Accreditation:* NCATE. *Degree requirements:* For master's and Ed S, comprehensive exam; for doctorate, thesis/dissertation, comprehensive exam. *Entrance requirements:* For master's, GRE General Test or MAT, minimum GPA of 2.75; for doctorate, GRE General Test or MAT, interview, minimum GPA of 3.3; for Ed S, GRE General Test or MAT, minimum GPA of 3.3. *Faculty research:* Technology in higher education administration.

Georgia College & State University, Graduate School, School of Education, Department of Special Education and Administration, Program in Administration and Supervision, Milledgeville, GA 31061. Offers M Ed, Ed S. *Accreditation:* NCATE. *Students:* 141 full-time (107 women), 2 part-time (both women); includes 43 minority (38 African Americans, 3 American Indian/Alaska Native, 2 Hispanic Americans). 149 applicants, 62% accepted, 63 enrolled. In 2006, 24 master's, 39 other advanced degrees awarded. *Degree requirements:* For master's, comprehensive exam; for Ed S, oral exam, research project, thesis optional. *Entrance requirements:* For master's, GRE General Test or MAT; for Ed S, GRE General Test, master's degree. Additional exam requirements/recommendations for international students: Required—TOEFL. *Application deadline:* For fall admission, 7/15 priority date for domestic students. Applications are processed on a rolling basis. Application fee: $25. Electronic applications accepted. *Expenses:* Tuition, state resident: full-time $3,222; part-time $179 per credit hour. Tuition, nonresident: full-time $12,870; part-time $715 per credit hour. Required fees: $391 per semester. Tuition and fees vary according to course load. *Financial support:* In 2006–07, 1 research assistantship (averaging $3,800 per year) was awarded; career-related internships or fieldwork and Federal Work-Study also available. Support available to part-time students. Financial award application deadline: 3/1; financial award applicants required to submit FAFSA. *Unit head:* Dr. Craig Smith, Chair, Department of Special Education and Administration, 478-445-4577, E-mail: craig.smith@gcsu.edu.

Georgian Court University, School of Education, Lakewood, NJ 08701-2697. Offers administration, supervision, and curriculum planning (MA); early intervention studies (Certificate); education (MA); instructional technology (MA, Certificate); special education (MA); substance awareness coordinator (Certificate). Part-time and evening/weekend programs available. *Faculty:* 25 full-time (14 women), 41 part-time/adjunct (23 women). *Students:* 128 full-time (110 women), 594 part-time (495 women); includes 56 minority (17 African Americans, 8 Asian Americans or Pacific Islanders, 31 Hispanic Americans), 1 international. Average age 34. 676 applicants, 80% accepted, 312 enrolled. In 2006, 130 master's, 4 other advanced degrees awarded. *Degree requirements:* For master's, thesis (for some programs), comprehensive exam (for some programs). *Entrance requirements:* For master's, GRE, MAT or NTE/PRAXIS, 3 letters of recommendation. Additional exam requirements/recommendations for international students: Required—TOEFL (minimum score 550 paper-based; 213 computer-based). *Application deadline:* For fall admission, 8/1 priority date for domestic students, 4/1 for international students; for spring admission, 1/1 priority date for domestic students, 7/1 for international students. Applications are processed on a rolling basis. Application fee: $40. Electronic applications accepted. *Financial support:* In 2006–07, 183 students received support. Scholarships/grants, health care benefits, and unspecified assistantships available. Financial award application deadline: 4/15; financial award applicants required to submit FAFSA. *Unit head:* Sr. Mary Gurley, OSF, Dean, 732-987-2525, E-mail: garleym@gergian.edu. *Application contact:* Eugene Soltys, Director of Graduate Admissions, 732-987-2760 Ext. 2760, Fax: 732-987-2000, E-mail: admissions@georgian.edu.

Georgia Southern University, Jack N. Averitt College of Graduate Studies, College of Education, Department of Leadership, Technology, and Human Development, Program in Educational Administration, Statesboro, GA 30460. Offers Ed D. Part-time and evening/weekend programs available. *Students:* 5 full-time (3 women), 234 part-time (169 women); includes 97 minority (95 African Americans, 1 American Indian/Alaska Native, 1 Hispanic American). Average age 42. 26 applicants, 92% accepted, 20 enrolled. In 2006, 13 degrees awarded. *Degree requirements:* For doctorate, thesis/dissertation, exams. *Entrance requirements:* For doctorate, GRE General Test or MAT, minimum GPA of 3.5, letters of reference, resumé. Additional exam requirements/recommendations for international students: Required—TOEFL (minimum score 550 paper-based; 213 computer-based; 80 iBT). *Application deadline:* For fall admission, 3/1 priority date for domestic students, 3/1 for international students; for spring admission, 10/1 priority date for domestic students, 10/1 for international students. Applications are processed on a rolling basis. Application fee: $50. Electronic applications accepted. *Financial support:* In 2006–07, 77 students received support, including fellowships with partial tuition reimbursements available (averaging $9,500 per year), research assistantships with partial tuition reimbursements available (averaging $5,500 per year), teaching assistantships with partial tuition reimbursements available (averaging $5,500 per year); Federal Work-Study, scholarships/grants, tuition waivers (partial), and unspecified assistantships also available. Support available to part-time students. Financial award applicants required to submit FAFSA. *Unit head:* Dr. Walter Polka, Associate Professor, 912-681-5600, Fax: 912-486-7104, E-mail: wpolka@georgiasouthern.edu. *Application contact:* 912-681-5384, Fax: 912-681-0740, E-mail: gradadmissions@georgiasouthern.edu.

Georgia Southern University, Jack N. Averitt College of Graduate Studies, College of Education, Department of Leadership, Technology, and Human Development, Program in Educational Leadership, Statesboro, GA 30460. Offers M Ed, Ed S. *Accreditation:* NCATE. Evening/weekend programs available. *Students:* 7 full-time (4 women), 75 part-time (51 women); includes 14 minority (11 African Americans, 1 American Indian/Alaska Native, 1 Asian American or Pacific Islander, 1 Hispanic American). Average age 38. 18 applicants, 83% accepted, 9 enrolled. In 2006, 25 master's, 20 other advanced degrees awarded. *Degree requirements:* For master's and Ed S, exams. *Entrance requirements:* For master's, GRE General Test or MAT, minimum GPA of 2.5, 3 years teaching experience; for Ed S, GRE General Test or MAT, minimum graduate GPA of 3.25. Additional exam requirements/recommendations for international students: Required—TOEFL (minimum score 550 paper-based; 213 computer-based; 80 iBT). *Application deadline:* For fall admission, 3/1 priority date for domestic students, 3/1 for international students; for spring admission, 10/1 priority date for domestic students, 10/1 for international students. Applications are processed on a rolling basis. Application fee: $50. Electronic applications accepted. *Financial support:* In 2006–07, 26 students received support, including research assistantships with partial tuition reimbursements available (averaging $5,500 per year), teaching assistantships with partial tuition reimbursements available (averaging $5,500 per year); career-related internships or fieldwork, Federal Work-Study, scholarships/grants, tuition waivers (partial), and unspecified assistantships also available. Support available to part-time students. Financial award application deadline: 4/15; financial award applicants required to submit FAFSA. *Faculty research:* Principalship, school finance, supervision. *Unit head:* Dr. Barbara Mallory, Associate Professor, 912-681-5307, Fax: 912-486-7104, E-mail: bmallory@georgiasouthern.edu. *Application contact:* 912-681-5384, Fax: 912-681-0740, E-mail: gradadmissions@georgiasouthern.edu.

Georgia State University, College of Education, Department of Educational Policy Studies, Program in Educational Leadership, Atlanta, GA 30303-3083. Offers M Ed, PhD, Ed S. *Accreditation:* NCATE. Part-time and evening/weekend programs available. *Students:* 41 full-time (32 women), 43 part-time (24 women); includes 23 minority (20 African Americans, 1 American Indian/Alaska Native, 1 Asian American or Pacific Islander, 1 Hispanic American), 1 international. Average age 39. 38 applicants, 71% accepted. In 2006, 25 master's, 3 doctorates, 13 other advanced degrees awarded. *Degree requirements:* For master's, comprehensive exam; for doctorate, thesis/dissertation, comprehensive exam. *Entrance requirements:* For master's, GRE General Test, minimum GPA of 2.5; for doctorate, GRE General Test or MAT, minimum GPA of 3.3; for Ed S, GRE General Test or MAT, minimum graduate GPA of 3.25. Application fee: $25. *Financial support:* Research assistantships, Federal Work-Study available. Support available to part-time students. *Faculty research:* Principal effectiveness, teacher empowerment, restructuring of schools. *Unit head:* Dr. Asa G. Hilliard, Chair, Department of Educational Policy Studies, 404-651-1269, Fax: 404-651-1009, E-mail: ahilliard@gsu.edu.

Golden Gate Baptist Theological Seminary, Graduate and Professional Programs, Mill Valley, CA 94941-3197. Offers divinity (M Div); early childhood education (Certificate); education leadership (MAEL, Diploma); ministry (D Min); theological studies (MTS); theology (Th M); youth ministry (Certificate). *Accreditation:* ACIPE; ATS (one or more programs are accredited). Part-time and evening/weekend programs available. *Degree requirements:* For M Div, 2 foreign languages; for master's, thesis (for some programs); for doctorate, 2 foreign languages, thesis/dissertation. *Entrance requirements:* For doctorate, MAT. Additional exam requirements/recommendations for international students: Required—TOEFL (minimum score 550 paper-based; 213 computer-based). Electronic applications accepted.

Gonzaga University, School of Education, Program in Administration and Curriculum, Spokane, WA 99258. Offers MAA. *Accreditation:* NCATE. *Faculty:* 18 full-time (5 women), 20 part-time/adjunct (9 women). *Students:* Average age 39. In 2006, 112 degrees awarded. *Degree requirements:* For master's, comprehensive exam. *Entrance requirements:* For master's, GRE General Test or MAT, minimum B average in undergraduate course work. Additional exam requirements/recommendations for international students: Required—TOEFL. *Application deadline:* For fall admission, 7/20 priority date for domestic students; for spring admission, 11/1 for domestic students. Applications are processed on a rolling basis. Application fee: $40. *Expenses:* Tuition: Full-time $10,620; part-time $590 per credit. *Financial support:* Teaching assistantships available. Support available to part-time students. Financial award application deadline: 3/1. *Unit head:* Dr. Robert Bialozer, Director, 509-328-4220 Ext. 3491.

Gonzaga University, School of Education, Program in Educational Administration, Spokane, WA 99258. Offers MA Ed Ad. *Students:* Average age 37. In 2006, 3 degrees awarded. *Expenses:* Tuition: Full-time $10,620; part-time $590 per credit. *Unit head:* Dr. Dennis Conners, Chair.

Gonzaga University, School of Professional Studies, Program in Leadership Studies, Spokane, WA 99258. Offers PhD. *Students:* 106 full-time (62 women), 14 part-time (7 women); includes 16 minority (3 African Americans, 2 American Indian/Alaska Native, 6 Asian Americans or Pacific Islanders, 5 Hispanic Americans), 4 international. Average age 45. In 2006, 16 degrees awarded. *Entrance requirements:* For doctorate, MAT and/or GRE. *Expenses:* Tuition: Full-time $10,620; part-time $590 per credit. *Unit head:* Dr. Sandra Wilson, Chairperson, 509-328-4220 Ext. 3517.

Governors State University, College of Education, Program in Educational Administration and Supervision, University Park, IL 60466-0975. Offers MA. Part-time and evening/weekend programs available. *Students:* 16 full-time, 370 part-time. Average age 36. *Degree requirements:* For master's, practicum. *Entrance requirements:* For master's, minimum GPA of 2.75 in last 60 hours of undergraduate course work, minimum graduate GPA of 3.0. *Application deadline:* For fall admission, 7/15 priority date for domestic students; for spring admission, 11/10 for domestic students. Applications are processed on a rolling basis. Application fee: $25. *Expenses:* Tuition, state resident: full-time $4,104; part-time $171 per hour. Tuition, nonresident: part-time $513 per hour. *Financial support:* Career-related internships or fieldwork, Federal Work-Study, institutionally sponsored loans, and tuition waivers (full and partial) available. Support available to part-time students. Financial award application deadline: 5/1.

Grambling State University, School of Graduate Studies and Research, College of Education, Department of Educational Leadership, Grambling, LA 71245. Offers curriculum and instruction (Ed D); developmental education (Ed D); educational leadership (M Ed, Ed D); special education (M Ed). Part-time and evening/weekend programs available. Postbaccalaureate distance learning degree programs offered (minimal on-campus study). *Faculty:* 8 full-time (1 woman), 2 part-time/adjunct (0 women). *Students:* 19 full-time (17 women), 63 part-time (49 women); includes 59 minority (58 African Americans, 1 Asian American or Pacific Islander), 2 international. Average age 41. In 2006, 5 master's, 4 doctorates awarded. *Degree requirements:* For master's, thesis (for some programs), comprehensive exam; for doctorate, thesis/dissertation, comprehensive exam. *Entrance requirements:* For master's, GRE, TOEFL, minimum GPA of 2.5 on last degree; for doctorate, GRE, master's degree, minimum 1000 on GRE, minimum GPA of 3.0 on last degree, minimum 500 on GRE Verbal. *Application deadline:* For fall admission, 7/1 for domestic students; for spring admission, 12/1 for domestic students. Application fee: $20 ($30 for international students). *Expenses:* Tuition, state resident: full-time $2,232; part-time $124 per credit hour. Tuition, nonresident: full-time $7,582; part-time $124 per credit hour. Required fees: $1,127. *Financial support:* In 2006–07, 59 students received support, including 7 research assistantships (averaging $5,786 per year); institutionally sponsored loans and unspecified assistantships also available. Financial award application deadline: 5/31; financial award applicants required to submit FAFSA. *Unit head:* Dr. Olatunde Ogunyemi, Director, 318-274-6105, Fax: 318-274-2799, E-mail: ogunymio@gram.edu.

Grand Valley State University, College of Education, Programs in General Education, Allendale, MI 49401-9403. Offers adult and higher education (M Ed); early childhood education (M Ed); education of the gifted and talented (M Ed); educational leadership (M Ed); educational technology (M Ed); elementary education (M Ed); middle and high school education (M Ed); teaching English to speakers of other languages (M Ed). Part-time and evening/weekend programs available. Postbaccalaureate distance learning degree programs offered (minimal on-campus study). *Faculty:* 82 full-time (42 women), 43 part-time/adjunct (25 women). *Students:* 136 full-time (97 women), 828 part-time (565 women); includes 55 minority (26 African Americans, 7 American Indian/Alaska Native, 5 Asian Americans or Pacific Islanders, 17 Hispanic Americans). Average age 33. 280 applicants, 94% accepted, 188 enrolled. In 2006, 322 degrees awarded. *Degree requirements:* For master's, thesis. *Entrance requirements:* For master's, GRE General Test or minimum GPA of 3.0. Additional exam requirements/recommendations for international students: Required—TOEFL. *Application deadline:* Applications are processed on a rolling basis. Application fee: $30. Electronic applications accepted. *Expenses:* Tuition, state resident: full-time $5,850; part-time $325 per credit. Tuition, nonresident: full-time $10,800; part-time $600 per credit. Tuition and fees vary according to course load. *Financial support:* In 2006–07, 2 research assistantships with full and partial tuition reimbursements (averaging $8,000 per year) were awarded; career-related internships or fieldwork, Federal Work-Study, scholarships/grants, and unspecified assistantships also available. *Faculty research:* Effectiveness of technology in education, parental involvement, effective teaching, effective schools research. *Unit head:* Dr. Linda McCrea, Director, 616-331-2080, E-mail: mccreal@gvsu.edu. *Application contact:* Dr. Douglas Busman, Director, Student Information and Services, 616-331-6831, Fax: 616-331-6217, E-mail: busmando@gvsu.edu.

Gwynedd-Mercy College, School of Education, Gwynedd Valley, PA 19437-0901. Offers educational administration (MS); master teacher (MS); reading (MS); school counseling (MS); special education (MS). Part-time and evening/weekend programs available. *Faculty:* 9 full-time (5 women), 37 part-time/adjunct (17 women). *Students:* 92 full-time (66 women), 464 part-time (374 women); includes 52 minority (49 African Americans, 3 Hispanic Americans), 1 international. Average age 34. In 2006, 160 degrees awarded. *Degree requirements:* For master's, thesis, internship, practicum. *Entrance requirements:* For master's, GRE or MAT; PPST Praxis Test, minimum GPA of 3.0. *Application deadline:* Applications are processed on a rolling basis. Application fee: $25. *Expenses:* Tuition: Part-time $525 per credit hour. *Financial support:* In 2006–07, 2 research assistantships were awarded; career-related internships or fieldwork, Federal Work-Study, tuition waivers (full and partial), and unspecified assistantships also available. Financial award applicants required to submit FAFSA. *Faculty research:* Learning and the brain, reading literacy, ethics and moral judgment, leadership, teaching and multicultural education. *Unit head:* Dr. Lorraine Cavaliere, EdD, Dean, 215-641-5549, Fax: 215-542-4695, E-mail: cavaliere.l@gmc.edu. *Application contact:* Marian Watkins, Graduate Program Coordinator, 215-641-5561, Fax: 215-542-4695, E-mail: watkins.m@gmc.edu.

Harding University, College of Education, Searcy, AR 72149-0001. Offers advanced studies in teaching and learning (M Ed); art (MSE); behavioral science (MSE); Bible and religion (MSE); counseling (MS, Ed S); early childhood education (M Ed); early childhood special education (M Ed, MSE); education (MSE); educational leadership (M Ed, Ed S); elementary education (M Ed); English (MSE); family and consumer science (MSE); French (MSE); history/social science (MSE); kinesiology (MSE); math (MSE); physical science (MSE); reading (M Ed); secondary education (M Ed); Spanish (MSE); special education licensure (M Ed); teaching (MAT). *Accreditation:* NCATE. Part-time programs available. *Faculty:* 8 full-time (2 women), 45 part-time/adjunct (30 women). *Students:* 153 full-time (123 women), 469 part-time (341 women); includes 72 minority (63 African Americans, 4 American Indian/Alaska Native, 1 Asian American or Pacific Islander, 4 Hispanic Americans), 9 international. Average age 35. 175 applicants, 90% accepted, 147 enrolled. In 2006, 241 degrees awarded. *Degree requirements:* For master's, portfolio(s), thesis optional; for Ed S, portfolio, specialist project. *Entrance requirements:* For master's, GRE, MAT, PRAXIS; for Ed S, MAT or GRE. Additional exam requirements/recommendations for international students: Required—TOEFL (minimum score 550 paper-based). *Application deadline:* For fall admission, 8/1 for domestic and international students; for spring admission, 1/1 for domestic and international students. Applications are processed on a rolling basis. Application fee: $35. *Expenses:* Tuition: Part-time $455 per semester hour. Required fees: $20 per semester hour. Tuition and fees vary according to course load. *Financial support:* Scholarships/grants and unspecified assistantships available. Support available to part-time students. *Faculty research:* Reading, comprehension, school violence, educational technology, behavior, college choice, differentiated instruction, brain based teaching. *Unit head:* Pat Bashaw, Chair, 501-279-4183, Fax: 501-279-4051, E-mail: pbashaw@harding.edu.

Harvard University, Graduate School of Education, Doctoral Program in Education, Cambridge, MA 02138. Offers culture, communities and education (Ed D); education policy (Ed D); education policy, leadership and instructional practice (Ed D); higher education (Ed D); human development and education (Ed D); quantitative policy analysis in education (Ed D); urban superintendency (Ed D). Part-time programs available. *Faculty:* 58 full-time (25 women), 40 part-time/adjunct (22 women). *Students:* 306 full-time (216 women), 35 part-time (26 women); includes 95 minority (38 African Americans, 4 American Indian/Alaska Native, 35 Asian Americans or Pacific Islanders, 18 Hispanic Americans), 46 international. Average age 35. 494 applicants, 12% accepted, 48 enrolled. In 2006, 70 degrees awarded. Terminal master's awarded for partial completion of doctoral program. *Degree requirements:* For doctorate, thesis/dissertation. *Entrance requirements:* For doctorate, GRE General Test, 3 letters of recommendation, official transcripts, statement of purpose. Additional exam requirements/recommendations for international students: Required—TOEFL (minimum score 600 paper-based; 250 computer-based; 100 iBT), TWE (minimum score 5). *Application deadline:* For fall admission, 12/14 for domestic and international students. Application fee: $85. Electronic applications accepted. *Expenses:* Contact institution. *Financial support:* In 2006–07, 171 fellowships with full and partial tuition reimbursements (averaging $11,489 per year), 47 research assistantships (averaging $9,340 per year), 153 teaching assistantships (averaging $7,710 per year) were awarded; career-related internships or fieldwork, Federal Work-Study, institutionally sponsored loans, scholarships/grants, health care benefits, tuition waivers (full and partial), and unspecified assistantships also available. Support available to part-time students. Financial award application deadline: 2/2; financial award applicants required to submit FAFSA. *Faculty research:* Learning and development; educational leadership and organizations; education policy analysis. Total annual research expenditures: $4.8 million. *Unit head:* Dr. James Stiles, Associate Dean for Degree Programs. *Application contact:* Information Contact, 617-495-3414, Fax: 617-496-3577, E-mail: gseadmissions@harvard.edu.

Harvard University, Graduate School of Education, Master's Programs in Education, Cambridge, MA 02138. Offers arts in education (Ed M); education policy and management (Ed M); higher education (Ed M); human development and psychology (Ed M); international education policy (Ed M); language and literacy (Ed M); learning and teaching (Ed M); mid-career mathematics and science (teaching certificate) (Ed M); mind brain and education (Ed M); risk and prevention (Ed M); school leadership (Ed M); special studies (Ed M); teaching and curriculum (teaching certificate) (Ed M); technology innovation and education (Ed M). Part-time programs available. *Faculty:* 58 full-time (25 women), 40 part-time/adjunct (22 women). *Students:* 540 full-time (412 women), 90 part-time (70 women); includes 137 minority (49 African Americans, 2 American Indian/Alaska Native, 61 Asian Americans or Pacific Islanders, 25 Hispanic Americans), 70 international. Average age 29. 1,211 applicants, 61% accepted, 585 enrolled. In 2006, 591 degrees awarded. *Entrance requirements:* For master's, GRE General Test, 3 letters of recommendation, official transcripts, statement of purpose. Additional exam requirements/recommendations for international students: Required—TOEFL (minimum score 600 paper-based; 250 computer-based; 100 iBT), TWE (minimum score 5). *Application deadline:* For fall admission, 1/2 for domestic and international students. Application fee: $85. Electronic applications accepted. *Expenses:* Contact institution. *Financial support:* In 2006–07, 392 students received support, including 23 fellowships (averaging $15,870 per year); career-related internships or fieldwork, Federal Work-Study, institutionally sponsored loans, scholarships/grants, health care benefits, tuition waivers (full and partial), and unspecified assistantships also available. Support available to part-time students. Financial award application deadline: 2/2; financial award applicants required to submit FAFSA. *Faculty research:* Learning and development; educational leadership and organizations; educational policy analysis. Total annual research expenditures: $14.8 million. *Unit head:* Dr. James Stiles, Associate Dean for Degree Programs. *Application contact:* Information Contact, 617-495-3414, Fax: 617-496-3577, E-mail: gseadmissions@harvard.edu.

Henderson State University, Graduate Studies, School of Education, Department of Educational Leadership and Special Education, Arkadelphia, AR 71999-0001. Offers early childhood special education (MSE); education (MAT); educational leadership (Ed S); instructional specialist (MSE); school administration (MSE). *Faculty:* 7 full-time (4 women), 3 part-time/adjunct (2 women). *Students:* 6 full-time (3 women), 144 part-time (113 women); includes 14 minority (all African Americans) Average age 35. In 2006, 18 degrees awarded. *Expenses:* Tuition, state resident: full-time $3,294; part-time $183 per credit hour. Tuition, nonresident: full-time $6,588; part-time $366 per credit hour. Required fees: $176 per term. *Unit head:* Dr. Bruce Smith, Chairperson, 870-230-5282. *Application contact:* Dr. Marck L. Beggs, Graduate Dean, 870-230-5126, Fax: 870-230-5479, E-mail: beggsm@hsu.edu.

Heritage University, Graduate Programs in Education, Program in Educational Administration, Toppenish, WA 98948-9599. Offers M Ed. Part-time and evening/weekend programs available. *Students:* 81 (37 women); includes 11 minority (2 American Indian/Alaska Native, 9 Hispanic Americans). Average age 40. In 2006, 11 degrees awarded. *Degree requirements:* For master's, special project, thesis optional. *Entrance requirements:* For master's, valid teaching certificate, 3 years of teaching experience, interview, letters of recommendation. *Application deadline:* Applications are processed on a rolling basis. Application fee: $50 ($100 for international students). *Financial support:* Career-related internships or fieldwork, Federal Work-Study, institutionally sponsored loans, and tuition waivers (partial) available. Support available to part-time students. *Unit head:* Karen Campbell, Head, 509-865-8591, E-mail: campbell_k@heritage.edu. *Application contact:* Kathy Otto, Coordinator of Administrative Services, 509-865-8635, Fax: 509-865-8629, E-mail: otto_k@heritage.edu.

High Point University, Norcross Graduate School, High Point, NC 27262-3598. Offers business administration (MBA); educational leadership (M Ed); elementary education (M Ed); history (MA); nonprofit organizations (MPA); special education (M Ed); sport studies (MS). *Accreditation:* ACBSP; NCATE. Part-time and evening/weekend programs available. *Faculty:* 31 full-time (11 women), 1 part-time/adjunct (0 women). *Students:* 49 full-time (29 women), 202 part-time (130 women); includes 72 minority (66 African Americans, 1 American Indian/Alaska Native, 2 Asian Americans or Pacific Islanders, 3 Hispanic Americans), 11 international. Average age 33. 171 applicants, 71% accepted, 94 enrolled. In 2006, 95 degrees awarded. *Degree requirements:* For master's, thesis (for some programs), comprehensive exam (for some programs), registration. *Entrance requirements:* For master's, GMAT (MBA), GRE, MAT, minimum GPA of 3.0. Additional exam requirements/recommendations for international students: Required—TOEFL (minimum score 550 paper-based). *Application deadline:* For fall admission, 4/15 priority date for domestic and international students; for spring admission, 10/15 priority date for domestic and international students. Applications are processed on a rolling basis. Application fee: $50. Electronic applications accepted. *Expenses:* Tuition: Full-time $9,270; part-time $1,545 per course. *Financial support:* In 2006–07, 190 students received support. Federal Work-Study, scholarships/grants, and unspecified assistantships available. Support available to part-time students. Financial award application deadline: 3/1; financial award applicants required to submit FAFSA. *Application contact:* Dr. Alberta Haynes Herron, Dean of Norcross Graduate School, 336-841-9198, Fax: 336-888-6378, E-mail: aherron@highpoint.edu.

Hofstra University, School of Education and Allied Human Services, Department of Foundations, Leadership, and Policy Studies, Program in Educational Administration, Hempstead, NY 11549. Offers educational administration and policy studies (MS Ed); educational leadership (CAS); school district business leader (CAS). *Accreditation:* NCATE. Part-time programs available. *Students:* 8 full-time (7 women), 72 part-time (50 women); includes 10 minority (7 African Americans, 1 American Indian/Alaska Native, 2 Hispanic Americans), 3 international. Average age 39. 47 applicants, 70% accepted, 28 enrolled. In 2006, 32 CASs awarded. *Degree requirements:* For master's, thesis or alternative, registration; for CAS, state exam, earned masters degree. *Entrance requirements:* For master's, 3 letters of recommendation, resumé, essay; for CAS, interview, 3 letters of recommendation, resumé, essay. Additional exam requirements/recommendations for international students: Required—TOEFL (minimum score 550 paper-based; 213 computer-based). *Application deadline:* Applications are processed on a rolling basis. Application fee: $60. Electronic applications accepted. *Expenses:* Tuition: Full-time $13,320; part-time $740 per credit. Required fees: $930; $155 per term. *Financial support:* In 2006–07, 36 students received support, including 19 fellowships with tuition reimbursements available (averaging $4,960 per year); research assistantships with full and partial tuition reimbursements available, scholarships/grants and tuition waivers (full and partial) also available. Financial award applicants required to submit FAFSA. *Faculty research:* Reconceptualizing NCLB in African American schools, African American representation at the superintendency level, education administration program design effectiveness, data use for administration decision-making, student artifacts as a supervisory model. *Unit head:* Dr. Eustace G. Thompson, Director, 516-463-5749, Fax: 516-463-5949, E-mail: edaegt@hofstra.edu. *Application contact:* Carol Drummer, Dean of Graduate Admissions, 516-463-4876, Fax: 516-463-4664, E-mail: gradstudent@hofstra.edu.

Hofstra University, School of Education and Allied Human Services, Department of Foundations, Leadership, and Policy Studies, Program in Educational and Policy Leadership, Hempstead, NY 11549. Offers Ed D. Part-time and evening/weekend programs available. *Students:* Average age 36. 24 applicants, 83% accepted, 13 enrolled. *Degree requirements:* For doctorate, thesis/dissertation, comprehensive exam, registration. *Entrance requirements:* For doctorate, GMAT, GRE, LSAT, or MAT, 3 letters of recommendation, resumé, interview, essay. Additional exam requirements/recommendations for international students: Required—TOEFL (minimum score 550 paper-based; 213 computer-based). *Application deadline:* Applications are processed on a rolling basis. Application fee: $60. Electronic applications accepted. *Expenses:* Tuition: Full-time $13,320; part-time $740 per credit. Required fees: $930; $155 per term. *Financial support:* In 2006–07, 10 students received support, including 5 fellowships with tuition reimbursements available (averaging $4,394 per year); research assistantships with full and partial tuition reimbursements available, scholarships/grants, tuition waivers (full and partial), and unspecified assistantships also available. Support available to part-time students. *Faculty research:* Educational equity, educational technologies, efficacy of educational leadership preparation programs, professional development of educational leaders, data-driven decision making. *Unit head:* Dr. Jonathan D. Becker, Program Director, 516-463-5760, E-mail: soejob@hofstra.edu. *Application contact:* Carol Drummer, Dean of Graduate Admissions, 516-463-4876, Fax: 516-463-4664, E-mail: gradstudent@hofstra.edu.

Hood College, Graduate School, Department of Education, Frederick, MD 21701-8575. Offers curriculum and instruction (MS), including early childhood education, elementary education, elementary school science and mathematics, secondary education, special education; educational leadership (MS); reading specialization (MS); teaching the struggling reader (Certificate). Part-time and evening/weekend programs available. *Faculty:* 4 full-time (3 women), 32 part-time/adjunct (16 women). *Students:* 5 full-time (3 women), 371 part-time (313 women); includes 30 minority (23 African Americans, 4 Asian Americans or Pacific Islanders, 3 Hispanic Americans). Average age 32. 71 applicants, 99% accepted, 59 enrolled. In 2006, 67 degrees awarded. *Degree requirements:* For master's, action research project, portfolio (reading). *Entrance requirements:* For master's, minimum GPA of 2.5, teaching certification. *Application deadline:* Applications are processed on a rolling basis. Application fee: $35. *Expenses:* Tuition: Part-time $350 per credit. Required fees: $20 per semester. *Financial support:* Applicants required to submit FAFSA. *Faculty research:* Leadership, action research, brain research, learning styles. *Unit head:* Dr. John George, Chairperson, 301-696-3471, Fax: 301-696-3597, E-mail: george@hood.edu. *Application contact:* Dr. Kathleen C. Bands, Associate Dean of Graduate School, 301-696-3811, Fax: 301-696-3597, E-mail: gofurther@hood.edu.

Houston Baptist University, College of Education and Behavioral Sciences, Programs in Education, Houston, TX 77074-3298. Offers bilingual education (M Ed); counselor education (M Ed); curriculum and instruction (M Ed); educational administration (M Ed); educational diagnostician (M Ed); reading education (M Ed). Part-time programs available. *Degree requirements:* For master's, registration. *Entrance requirements:* For master's, GRE General Test or MAT. Additional exam requirements/recommendations for international students: Required—TOEFL (minimum score 550 paper-based; 213 computer-based).

Howard University, School of Education, Department of Educational Administration and Policy, Program in Educational Administration, Washington, DC 20059-0002. Offers educational administration (M Ed, MA, CAGS); educational administration and policy (Ed D). MA offered

Educational Administration

Howard University (continued)

through the Graduate School of Arts and Sciences. *Accreditation:* NCATE. Part-time programs available. *Faculty:* 7 full-time (2 women). *Students:* 20 full-time (10 women), 11 part-time (10 women); includes 26 minority (all African Americans), 1 international. Average age 37. 16 applicants, 75% accepted, 10 enrolled. In 2006, 5 degrees awarded. Terminal master's awarded for partial completion of doctoral program. *Degree requirements:* For master's, thesis (for some programs), comprehensive exam; for doctorate, thesis/dissertation, internship, comprehensive exam; for CAGS, thesis. *Entrance requirements:* For master's, GRE General Test (MA), minimum GPA of 3.0; for doctorate, minimum GPA of 3.0. *Application deadline:* For fall admission, 4/1 priority date for domestic students; for spring admission, 10/1 for domestic students. Applications are processed on a rolling basis. Application fee: $45. *Financial support:* Fellowships, research assistantships, teaching assistantships, career-related internships or fieldwork, Federal Work-Study, institutionally sponsored loans, scholarships/grants, and unspecified assistantships available. Financial award application deadline: 4/1. *Faculty research:* Educational policy, reform, achievement gap, disability reform policy, school governance delivery of social services to students. *Unit head:* Dr. Jerome Jones, Professor/Coordinator, Doctoral Program, 202-806-6013, E-mail: jerjones@howard.edu. *Application contact:* Dr. Dawn G. Williams, Coordinator, 202-806-7060, E-mail: dgwilliams@howard.edu.

Hunter College of the City University of New York, Graduate School, School of Education, Department of Curriculum and Teaching, Program in Educational Supervision and Administration, New York, NY 10021-5085. Offers AC. *Faculty:* 13 full-time (11 women). *Students:* Average age 39. 40 applicants, 78% accepted, 27 enrolled. In 2006, 55 degrees awarded. *Degree requirements:* For AC, portfolio review. *Entrance requirements:* For degree, minimum B average in graduate course work, teaching certificate, minimum 3 years of full-time teaching experience, interview, 2 letters of support. Additional exam requirements/recommendations for international students: Required—TOEFL. *Application deadline:* For fall admission, 4/1 for domestic students, 2/1 for international students; for spring admission, 11/1 for domestic students, 9/1 for international students. Applications are processed on a rolling basis. Application fee: $125. *Expenses:* Tuition, state resident: part-time $270 per credit. Tuition, nonresident: part-time $500 per credit. Required fees: $45 per semester. *Financial support:* Federal Work-Study and tuition waivers (partial) available. Support available to part-time students. *Faculty research:* Supervision of instruction, theory in action, human relations and leadership. *Unit head:* Dr. Sherry Graves, Coordinator, 212-772-4710, E-mail: sgraves@hunter.cuny.edu. *Application contact:* William Zlata, Director for Graduate Admissions, 212-772-4482, Fax: 212-650-3336, E-mail: admissions@hunter.cuny.edu.

Idaho State University, Office of Graduate Studies, College of Education, Department of Educational Foundations, Pocatello, ID 83209. Offers child and family studies (M Ed); curriculum leadership (M Ed); education (M Ed); educational administration (M Ed); educational foundations (5th Year Certificate); elementary education (M Ed), including K-12 education, literacy, secondary education. Part-time and evening/weekend programs available. Postbaccalaureate distance learning degree programs offered (no on-campus study). *Faculty:* 12 full-time (8 women). *Students:* 16 full-time (11 women), 161 part-time (102 women); includes 2 minority (1 Asian American or Pacific Islander, 1 Hispanic American), 2 international. Average age 40. In 2006, 15 degrees awarded. *Degree requirements:* For master's, oral exam, written exam, thesis optional; for 5th Year Certificate, thesis (for some programs), oral exam, written exam, comprehensive exam, registration (for some programs). *Entrance requirements:* For master's, GRE General Test or MAT, minimum undergraduate GPA of 3.0; for 5th Year Certificate, GRE General Test, minimum undergraduate GPA of 3.0, master's degree. Additional exam requirements/recommendations for international students: Required—TOEFL (minimum score 550 paper-based; 213 computer-based; 80 iBT). *Application deadline:* For fall admission, 7/1 for domestic students, 6/1 for international students; for spring admission, 12/1 for domestic students, 11/1 for international students. Applications are processed on a rolling basis. Application fee: $55. *Expenses:* Tuition, state resident: part-time $251 per credit. Tuition, nonresident: part-time $366 per credit. Tuition and fees vary according to degree level, program and reciprocity agreements. *Financial support:* Career-related internships or fieldwork, Federal Work-Study, institutionally sponsored loans, scholarships/grants, tuition waivers, and unspecified assistantships available. Support available to part-time students. Financial award application deadline: 1/1. *Faculty research:* Child and families studies; business education; special education; math, science, and technology education. *Unit head:* Dr. Jack Newsome, Chair, 208-282-4838, E-mail: newsjack@isu.edu. *Application contact:* Dr. Peter Denner, Assistant Dean, 208-282-3807, Fax: 208-282-4697, E-mail: dennpete@isu.edu.

Idaho State University, Office of Graduate Studies, College of Education, Department of Educational Leadership, Pocatello, ID 83209. Offers educational administration (6th Year Certificate, Ed S); educational leadership (Ed D), including education training and development, educational administration, educational technology, higher education administration. Part-time and evening/weekend programs available. Postbaccalaureate distance learning degree programs offered (no on-campus study). *Faculty:* 5 full-time (2 women). *Students:* 12 full-time (5 women), 93 part-time (39 women); includes 8 minority (2 African Americans, 3 American Indian/Alaska Native, 1 Asian American or Pacific Islander, 2 Hispanic Americans), 13 international. Average age 44. In 2006, 17 doctorates, 1 other advanced degree awarded. *Degree requirements:* For doctorate, thesis/dissertation, written exam, comprehensive exam, registration; for other advanced degree, thesis (for some programs), written and oral exam, comprehensive exam, registration (for some programs). *Entrance requirements:* For doctorate, GRE General Test or MAT, minimum GPA of 3.0 (undergraduate), 3.5 (graduate), departmental interview; for other advanced degree, GRE General Test, minimum GPA of 3.0, master's degree. Additional exam requirements/recommendations for international students: Required—TOEFL (minimum score 550 paper-based; 213 computer-based; 80 iBT). *Application deadline:* For fall admission, 7/1 for domestic students, 6/1 for international students; for spring admission, 12/1 for domestic students, 11/1 for international students. Applications are processed on a rolling basis. Application fee: $55. *Expenses:* Tuition, state resident: part-time $251 per credit. Tuition, nonresident: part-time $366 per credit. Tuition and fees vary according to degree level, program and reciprocity agreements. *Financial support:* In 2006–07, teaching assistantships with full and partial tuition reimbursements (averaging $8,694 per year); career-related internships or fieldwork, Federal Work-Study, institutionally sponsored loans, scholarships/grants, tuition waivers, and unspecified assistantships also available. Support available to part-time students. Financial award application deadline: 1/1. *Faculty research:* Educational leadership, gender issues in education and sport, staff development. *Unit head:* Dr. E.E. 'Gene" Davis, Chair, 208-282-3202, Fax: 208-282-4697.

Illinois State University, Graduate School, College of Education, Department of Educational Administration and Foundations, Normal, IL 61790-2200. Offers MS, MS Ed, Ed D, PhD. *Accreditation:* NCATE. *Faculty:* 21 full-time (11 women), 3 part-time/adjunct (1 woman). *Students:* 40 full-time (23 women), 252 part-time (140 women); includes 41 minority (31 African Americans, 2 American Indian/Alaska Native, 4 Asian Americans or Pacific Islanders, 4 Hispanic Americans), 3 international. 56 applicants, 98% accepted. In 2006, 50 master's, 19 doctorates awarded. *Degree requirements:* For doctorate, variable foreign language requirement, thesis/dissertation, 2 terms of residency. *Entrance requirements:* For master's, GRE General Test, minimum GPA of 2.6 in last 60 hours of course work; for doctorate, GRE General Test, master's degree or equivalent, minimum GPA of 3.5. *Application deadline:* Applications are processed on a rolling basis. Application fee: $40. *Expenses:* Tuition, state resident: full-time $3,330; part-time $185 per credit hour. Tuition, nonresident: full-time $6,948; part-time $438 per credit hour. Required fees: $1,259; $52 per credit hour. *Financial support:* In 2006–07, 31 research assistantships (averaging $7,264 per year), 1 teaching assistantship (averaging $9,900 per year) were awarded; tuition waivers (full) and unspecified assistantships also available. Financial award application deadline: 4/1. *Faculty research:* Illinois Association of School Administrators, Illinois Principals Association, Illinois State Action for Education leadership project, special populations professional development and technical assistance project. Total annual research expenditures: $2.8 million. *Unit head:* Dr. Patricia Klass, Chairperson, 309-438-5422.

Immaculata University, College of Graduate Studies, Program in Educational Leadership and Administration, Immaculata, PA 19345. Offers educational leadership and administration (MA, Ed D); elementary education (Certificate); intermediate unit director (Certificate); school principal (Certificate); school superintendent (Certificate); secondary education (Certificate); special education (Certificate). Part-time and evening/weekend programs available. *Students:* 27 full-time (15 women), 510 part-time (353 women). Average age 33. 86 applicants, 74% accepted, 53 enrolled. In 2006, 47 master's, 27 doctorates awarded. *Degree requirements:* For master's, thesis optional; for doctorate, thesis/dissertation, comprehensive exam. *Entrance requirements:* For master's, GRE or MAT, minimum GPA of 3.0; for doctorate, GRE General Test, minimum GPA of 3.5. Additional exam requirements/recommendations for international students: Required—TOEFL. Application fee: $35. *Financial support:* Application deadline:5/1. *Faculty research:* Cooperative learning, school-based management, whole language, performance assessment. *Unit head:* Sr. Carol Anne Couchara, Chair, 610-647-4400 Ext. 3280, E-mail: ccouchara@immaculata.edu. *Application contact:* 610-647-4400 Ext. 3211, Fax: 610-993-8550, E-mail: graduate@immaculata.edu.

Indiana State University, School of Graduate Studies, College of Education, Department of Counseling, Terre Haute, IN 47809-1401. Offers counseling psychology (MS, PhD); counselor education (PhD); marriage and family counseling (MS); school counseling (M Ed); student affairs administration (PhD); student affairs and higher education (MS). *Accreditation:* ACA; NCATE. Part-time and evening/weekend programs available. *Faculty:* 4 full-time (1 woman), 5 part-time/adjunct (4 women). *Students:* 67 full-time (50 women), 87 part-time (65 women); includes 24 minority (16 African Americans, 2 American Indian/Alaska Native, 2 Asian Americans or Pacific Islanders, 4 Hispanic Americans), 3 international. Average age 30. 56 applicants, 45% accepted, 19 enrolled. In 2006, 43 master's, 7 doctorates awarded. *Degree requirements:* For master's, thesis optional; for doctorate, thesis/dissertation, research tools proficiency tests. *Entrance requirements:* For master's, GRE General Test or MAT, minimum undergraduate GPA of 2.75; for doctorate, GRE General Test, master's degree, minimum undergraduate GPA of 3.5. *Application deadline:* For fall admission, 2/15 for domestic students. Applications are processed on a rolling basis. Application fee: $35. Electronic applications accepted. *Expenses:* Tuition, state resident: part-time $278 per credit. Tuition, nonresident: part-time $552 per credit. *Financial support:* In 2006–07, 25 research assistantships with partial tuition reimbursements (averaging $5,500 per year) were awarded; teaching assistantships, career-related internships or fieldwork and tuition waivers (partial) also available. Financial award application deadline: 3/1; financial award applicants required to submit FAFSA. *Faculty research:* Vocational development supervision. *Unit head:* Dr. Michele Boyer, Chairperson, 812-237-2832.

Indiana State University, School of Graduate Studies, College of Education, Department of Educational Leadership, Administration, and Foundations, Terre Haute, IN 47809-1401. Offers educational administration (PhD, Ed S); school administration and supervision (M Ed). *Accreditation:* NCATE. Part-time and evening/weekend programs available. *Faculty:* 11 full-time (2 women), 5 part-time/adjunct (3 women). *Students:* 60 full-time (34 women), 157 part-time (80 women); includes 27 minority (22 African Americans, 2 American Indian/Alaska Native, 3 Hispanic Americans), 2 international. Average age 38. 121 applicants, 77% accepted, 56 enrolled. In 2006, 27 master's, 24 doctorates, 18 other advanced degrees awarded. Terminal master's awarded for partial completion of doctoral program. *Degree requirements:* For master's and doctorate, thesis/dissertation. *Entrance requirements:* For master's, GRE General Test, minimum undergraduate GPA of 2.5; for doctorate, GRE General Test, minimum undergraduate GPA of 3.5; for Ed S, GRE General Test, minimum graduate GPA of 3.25. *Application deadline:* For fall admission, 7/1 priority date for domestic students; for spring admission, 11/1 priority date for domestic students. Applications are processed on a rolling basis. Application fee: $35. Electronic applications accepted. *Expenses:* Tuition, state resident: part-time $278 per credit. Tuition, nonresident: part-time $552 per credit. *Financial support:* In 2006–07, 3 research assistantships with partial tuition reimbursements (averaging $6,300 per year) were awarded; teaching assistantships with partial tuition reimbursements, career-related internships or fieldwork and tuition waivers (partial) also available. Financial award application deadline: 3/1; financial award applicants required to submit FAFSA. *Unit head:* Dr. Joshua Powers, Chairperson, 812-237-2900.

Indiana University Bloomington, School of Education, Department of Educational Leadership and Policy Studies, Bloomington, IN 47405-7000. Offers education policy studies (PhD); educational leadership (MS, Ed D, PhD, Ed S); higher education (MS, Ed D, PhD); history and philosophy of education (MS); history of education (PhD); international and comparative education (MS, PhD); philosophy of education (PhD); student affairs administration (MS). PhD offered through the University Graduate School. *Accreditation:* NCATE. Part-time and evening/weekend programs available. *Students:* 12 full-time (5 women), 28 part-time (14 women). Average age 35. In 2006, 32 master's, 4 doctorates awarded. *Degree requirements:* For master's, thesis optional; for doctorate, thesis/dissertation; for Ed S, comprehensive exam or project. *Entrance requirements:* For master's, doctorate, and Ed S, GRE General Test. *Application deadline:* For fall admission, 6/1 for domestic students, 3/1 for international students; for spring admission, 9/1 for international students. Application fee: $45 ($55 for international students). *Expenses:* Tuition, state resident: full-time $5,791; part-time $241 per credit hour. Tuition, nonresident: full-time $16,866; part-time $703 per credit hour. *Financial support:* Fellowships, research assistantships, teaching assistantships, career-related internships or fieldwork, Federal Work-Study, institutionally sponsored loans, and tuition waivers (full and partial) available. Support available to part-time students. *Unit head:* Martha McCarthy, Chair, 812-856-8377. *Application contact:* Sandy Strain, Department Secretary, 812-856-8360, Fax: 812-856-8394, E-mail: strain@indiana.edu.

Indiana University of Pennsylvania, School of Graduate Studies and Research, College of Education and Educational Technology, Department of Professional Studies in Education, Certification Program for Principal, Indiana, PA 15705-1087. Offers Certificate. *Faculty:* 2 full-time (1 woman). *Students:* Average age 40. 41 applicants, 90% accepted. *Entrance requirements:* For degree, GRE General Test, GRE Subject Test, 2 letters of recommendation. Additional exam requirements/recommendations for international students: Required—TOEFL. *Application deadline:* For fall admission, 7/1 priority date for domestic students; for spring admission, 11/1 for domestic students. Applications are processed on a rolling basis. Application fee: $30. *Expenses:* Tuition, state resident: full-time $6,048; part-time $336 per credit. Tuition, nonresident: full-time $9,678; part-time $538 per credit. Required fees: $1,069; $148 per year. *Financial support:* Application deadline: 3/15; *Unit head:* Dr. Cathy Kauffman, Graduate Coordinator, 724-357-3928, E-mail: ckaufman@iup.edu.

Indiana University of Pennsylvania, School of Graduate Studies and Research, College of Education and Educational Technology, Department of Professional Studies in Education, Doctoral Program in Administration and Leadership Studies, Indiana, PA 15705-1087. Offers D Ed. Part-time and evening/weekend programs available. *Faculty:* 5 full-time (2 women). *Students:* 16 full-time (9 women), 76 part-time (27 women); includes 10 minority (9 African Americans, 1 Asian American or Pacific Islander). Average age 45. 69 applicants, 71% accepted. In 2006, 15 degrees awarded. *Degree requirements:* For doctorate, one foreign language, thesis/dissertation, comprehensive exam. *Entrance requirements:* For doctorate, written exam, 2 letters of recommendation, interview. Additional exam requirements/recommendations for international students: Required—TOEFL. *Application deadline:* For fall admission, 7/1 priority date for domestic students; for spring admission, 11/1 for domestic students. Applications are processed on a rolling basis. Application fee: $30. *Expenses:* Tuition, state resident: full-time $6,048; part-time $336 per credit. Tuition, nonresident: full-time $9,678; part-time $538 per credit. Required fees: $1,069; $148 per year. *Financial support:* In 2006–07, 2 fellowships (averaging $1,000 per year), 2 research assistantships with full and partial tuition reimbursements (averaging $4,990 per year) were awarded. Financial award application deadline: 3/15; financial award applicants required to submit FAFSA. *Unit head:* Dr. Robert Millward, Graduate Coordinator, 724-357-5593, E-mail: millward@iup.edu.

Indiana University of Pennsylvania, School of Graduate Studies and Research, College of Education and Educational Technology, Department of Student Affairs in Higher Education,

Indiana, PA 15705-1087. Offers MA. *Accreditation:* NCATE. Part-time programs available. *Faculty:* 4 full-time (2 women). *Students:* 55 full-time (33 women), 10 part-time (7 women); includes 6 minority (3 African Americans, 2 Asian Americans or Pacific Islanders, 1 Hispanic American), 1 international. Average age 24. 110 applicants, 38% accepted. In 2006, 34 degrees awarded. *Degree requirements:* For master's, thesis optional. *Entrance requirements:* For master's, resumé, interview, 2 letters of recommendation, writing sample. Additional exam requirements/recommendations for international students: Required—TOEFL. *Application deadline:* For fall admission, 7/1 priority date for domestic students; for spring admission, 11/1 for domestic students. Applications are processed on a rolling basis. Application fee: $30. *Expenses:* Tuition, state resident: full-time $6,048; part-time $336 per credit. Tuition, nonresident: full-time $9,678; part-time $538 per credit. Required fees: $1,069; $148 per year. *Financial support:* In 2006–07, 1 fellowship (averaging $500 per year), 21 research assistantships with full and partial tuition reimbursements (averaging $4,900 per year) were awarded; career-related internships or fieldwork and Federal Work-Study also available. Support available to part-time students. Financial award application deadline: 3/15; financial award applicants required to submit FAFSA. *Unit head:* Dr. Ronald W. Lunardini, Chairperson and Graduate Coordinator, 724-357-4535, E-mail: lunar@iup.edu.

Indiana University of Pennsylvania, School of Graduate Studies and Research, College of Humanities and Social Sciences, Department of Sociology, Program in Administration and Leadership Studies, Indiana, PA 15705-1087. Offers PhD. Part-time and evening/weekend programs available. *Students:* 41 full-time (23 women), 46 part-time (25 women); includes 17 minority (13 African Americans, 2 Asian Americans or Pacific Islanders, 2 Hispanic Americans), 4 international. Average age 44. 39 applicants, 54% accepted. In 2006, 6 degrees awarded. *Degree requirements:* For doctorate, thesis/dissertation, comprehensive exam. *Entrance requirements:* For doctorate, GRE, resumé, writing sample, 3 letters of recommendation. Additional exam requirements/recommendations for international students: Required—TOEFL. *Application deadline:* For fall admission, 7/1 priority date for domestic students; for spring admission, 11/1 for domestic students. Applications are processed on a rolling basis. Application fee: $30. *Expenses:* Tuition, state resident: full-time $6,048; part-time $336 per credit. Tuition, nonresident: full-time $9,678; part-time $538 per credit. Required fees: $1,069; $148 per year. *Financial support:* In 2006–07, fellowships (averaging $5,000 per year), 3 research assistantships with full and partial tuition reimbursements (averaging $6,180 per year) were awarded. Financial award applicants required to submit FAFSA. *Unit head:* Dr. Susan Boser, Graduate Coordinator, 724-357-1291, E-mail: sboser@iup.edu.

Indiana University–Purdue University Fort Wayne, School of Education, Department of Professional Studies, Fort Wayne, IN 46805-1499. Offers counselor education (MS Ed); educational administration (MS Ed). Part-time programs available. *Faculty:* 10 full-time (4 women). *Students:* 2 full-time (1 woman), 151 part-time (100 women); includes 18 minority (11 African Americans, 1 Asian American or Pacific Islander, 6 Hispanic Americans). Average age 34. 65 applicants, 74% accepted, 38 enrolled. In 2006, 67 degrees awarded. *Degree requirements:* For master's, practicum, internship, portfolio. *Entrance requirements:* For master's, minimum GPA of 2.5. Additional exam requirements/recommendations for international students: Required—TOEFL (minimum score 600 paper-based; 260 computer-based). *Application deadline:* For fall admission, 7/1 priority date for domestic students; for spring admission, 12/1 for domestic students. Applications are processed on a rolling basis. Application fee: $30. *Expenses:* Tuition, state resident: full-time $4,039; part-time $224 per credit. Tuition, nonresident: full-time $9,220; part-time $512 per credit. Required fees: $429; $24 per credit. Tuition and fees vary according to course load. *Financial support:* In 2006–07, 1 teaching assistantship with partial tuition reimbursement (averaging $11,950 per year) was awarded; research assistantships with partial tuition reimbursements, scholarships/grants also available. Support available to part-time students. Financial award application deadline: 3/1; financial award applicants required to submit FAFSA. *Unit head:* Dr. James Burg, Interim Chair of Professional Studies, 260-481-4146, Fax: 260-481-5408, E-mail: burgj@ipfw.edu. *Application contact:* Vicky L. Schmidt, Graduate Recorder, 260-481-6450, Fax: 260-481-5408, E-mail: schmidt@ipfw.edu.

Instituto Tecnológico y de Estudios Superiores de Monterrey, Campus Central de Veracruz, Graduate Programs, Córdoba, Mexico. Offers administration (MA); administration of information technologies (MTI); computer sciences (MCC); education (MEE); educational institution administration (MAD); educational technology (MTE); electronic commerce (MCE); finance (MAF); humanistic studies (MEH); international business for Latin America (MNL); marketing (MMT); science (MCP); technology management (MTT). Part-time and evening/weekend programs available. Postbaccalaureate distance learning degree programs offered (minimal on-campus study). *Degree requirements:* For master's, thesis (for some programs). *Entrance requirements:* For master's, PAEP College Board. Electronic applications accepted.

Instituto Tecnológico y de Estudios Superiores de Monterrey, Campus Estado de México, Professional and Graduate Division, Estado de Mexico, Mexico. Offers administration of information technologies (MITA); architecture (M Arch); business administration (GMBA, MBA); computer sciences (MCS, PhD); education (M Ed); educational institution administration (MAD); educational technology and innovation (PhD); electronic commerce (MEC); environmental systems (MS); finance (MAF); humanistic studies (MHS); information sciences and knowledge management (MISKM); information systems (MS); manufacturing systems (MS); marketing (MEM); quality systems and productivity (MS); science and materials engineering (PhD); telecommunications management (MTM). Part-time programs available. Postbaccalaureate distance learning degree programs offered (minimal on-campus study). *Degree requirements:* For master's, one foreign language, thesis (for some programs), registration; for doctorate, one foreign language, thesis/dissertation, registration (for some programs). *Entrance requirements:* For master's, E-PAEP 500, interview; for doctorate, E-PAEP 500, research proposal. Additional exam requirements/recommendations for international students: Required—TOEFL (minimum score 550 paper-based). *Faculty research:* Surface treatments by plasmas, mechanical properties, robotics, graphical computing, mechatronics security protocols.

Instituto Tecnológico y de Estudios Superiores de Monterrey, Campus Irapuato, Graduate Programs, Irapuato, Mexico. Offers administration (MBA); administration of information technology (MAIT); administration of telecommunications (MAT); architecture (M Arch); computer science (MCS); education (M Ed); educational administration (MEA); educational innovation and technology (DEIT); educational technology (MET); electronic commerce (MBA); environmental administration and planning (MEAP); environmental systems (MES); finances (MBA); humanistic studies (MHS); international management for Latin American executives (MIMLAE); library and information science (MLIS); manufacturing quality management (MMQM); marketing research (MBA).

Inter American University of Puerto Rico, Aguadilla Campus, Graduate School, Aguadilla, PR 00605. Offers administration and supervision (MA); criminal justice (MA); elementary education (MA). Part-time and evening/weekend programs available. *Degree requirements:* For master's, comprehensive exam. *Entrance requirements:* For master's, EXADEP, 2 letters of recommendation, minimum GPA of 2.5. Electronic applications accepted.

Inter American University of Puerto Rico, Arecibo Campus, Programs in Education, Arecibo, PR 00614-4050. Offers administration and educational supervision (MA Ed); counseling and guidance (MA Ed). *Degree requirements:* For master's, thesis optional. *Entrance requirements:* For master's, GRE, EXADEP, bachelor's degree in education or teaching license (administration and supervision) or courses in education and psychology (counseling and guidance), minimum GPA of 2.5 in last 60 credits.

Inter American University of Puerto Rico, Barranquitas Campus, Program in Education, Barranquitas, PR 00794. Offers educational administration and supervision (MA); elementary education (MA). *Degree requirements:* For master's, thesis optional. *Entrance requirements:* For master's, EXADEP, letter of recommendation. Electronic applications accepted.

Inter American University of Puerto Rico, Metropolitan Campus, Faculty of Education, Program in Administration and Supervision, San Juan, PR 00919-1293. Offers MA. *Degree requirements:* For master's, comprehensive exam. *Entrance requirements:* For master's, GRE or EXADEP, interview. Electronic applications accepted.

Inter American University of Puerto Rico, San Germán Campus, Graduate Studies Center, Graduate Program in Administration and Supervision, San Germán, PR 00683-5008. Offers MA. Part-time and evening/weekend programs available. *Faculty:* 8 full-time, 11 part-time/adjunct. *Students:* 13. In 2006, 1 degree awarded. *Degree requirements:* For master's, comprehensive exam. *Entrance requirements:* For master's, GRE General Test or EXADEP, minimum GPA of 3.0. *Application deadline:* For fall admission, 4/30 priority date for domestic students; for spring admission, 11/15 for domestic students. Applications are processed on a rolling basis. Application fee: $31. *Expenses:* Tuition: Part-time $175 per credit. Required fees: $238 per semester. Tuition and fees vary according to degree level. *Financial support:* Teaching assistantships, Federal Work-Study and unspecified assistantships available. *Application contact:* Dr. Aurora Graniela, Graduate Coordinator, 787-264-1912 Ext. 7355, Fax: 787-892-7510, E-mail: aurora@sg.inter.edu.

Iona College, School of Arts and Science, Program in Educational Leadership, New Rochelle, NY 10801-1890. Offers MS Ed. Part-time and evening/weekend programs available. *Faculty:* 11 full-time (6 women), 21 part-time/adjunct (13 women). *Students:* 1 full-time (0 women), 5 part-time (3 women). Average age 40. 5 applicants, 60% accepted, 2 enrolled. In 2006, 2 degrees awarded. *Degree requirements:* For master's, internships. *Entrance requirements:* For master's, New York teaching certificate, 3 years of teaching or supervisory experience, minimum GPA of 2.75. *Application deadline:* Applications are processed on a rolling basis. Application fee: $50. Electronic applications accepted. *Expenses:* Contact institution. *Financial support:* Career-related internships or fieldwork, tuition waivers (partial), and unspecified assistantships available. Support available to part-time students. *Faculty research:* Educational technology, staff development, multicultural education, reading and writing, early literacy assessment. *Unit head:* Dr. Patricia Antonacci, Chair, 914-633-2080, Fax: 914-633-2608, E-mail: pantonacci@iona.edu. *Application contact:* Veronica Jarek-Prinz, Graduate Admissions, 914-633-2289, Fax: 914-633-2012, E-mail: vjarekprinz@iona.edu.

Iowa State University of Science and Technology, Graduate College, College of Human Sciences, Department of Educational Leadership and Policy Studies, Ames, IA 50011. Offers counselor education (M Ed, MS); educational administration (M Ed, MS); educational leadership (PhD); higher education (M Ed, MS); organizational learning and human resource development (M Ed, MS); research and evaluation (MS). *Faculty:* 19 full-time, 9 part-time/adjunct. *Students:* 82 full-time (53 women), 191 part-time (109 women); includes 40 minority (23 African Americans, 4 American Indian/Alaska Native, 5 Asian Americans or Pacific Islanders, 8 Hispanic Americans), 5 international. 156 applicants, 70% accepted, 76 enrolled. In 2006, 95 master's, 13 doctorates awarded. *Degree requirements:* For master's, thesis or alternative; for doctorate, thesis/dissertation. *Entrance requirements:* For doctorate, GRE General Test. Additional exam requirements/recommendations for international students: Required—TOEFL (paper-based 560; computer-based 220; iBT 79) or IELTS (6.0). *Application deadline:* For fall admission, 1/1 priority date for domestic and international students. Applications are processed on a rolling basis. Application fee: $30 ($70 for international students). Electronic applications accepted. *Expenses:* Tuition, state resident: full-time $5,936; part-time $330 per credit. Tuition, nonresident: full-time $16,350; part-time $330 per credit. *Financial support:* In 2006–07, 17 research assistantships with full and partial tuition reimbursements (averaging $16,419 per year) were awarded; fellowships, teaching assistantships with full and partial tuition reimbursements, scholarships/grants, health care benefits, and unspecified assistantships also available. *Unit head:* Dr. Laura Rendon, Chair, 515-294-7093, E-mail: lrendon@iastate.edu. *Application contact:* Dr. Daniel Robinson, Information Contact, 515-294-1241, E-mail: eldrshp@iastate.edu.

Jackson State University, Graduate School, School of Education, Department of Educational Foundations and Leadership, Jackson, MS 39217. Offers education administration (Ed S); educational administration (MS Ed, PhD); secondary education (MS Ed, Ed S), including educational technology (MS Ed). *Accreditation:* NCATE. Part-time and evening/weekend programs available. *Faculty:* 21 full-time (10 women), 5 part-time/adjunct (1 woman). *Students:* 43 full-time (24 women), 58 part-time (34 women); includes 82 minority (all African Americans), 2 international. In 2006, 38 master's, 5 doctorates, 5 other advanced degrees awarded. *Degree requirements:* For master's, thesis or alternative, comprehensive exam; for doctorate and Ed S, thesis/dissertation, comprehensive exam. *Entrance requirements:* For master's, GRE General Test; for doctorate, MAT, GRE, teaching experience. Additional exam requirements/recommendations for international students: Required—TOEFL. *Application deadline:* For fall admission, 3/1 priority date for domestic students; for spring admission, 10/1 for domestic students. Applications are processed on a rolling basis. Application fee: $20. *Financial support:* In 2006–07, 33 students received support. Career-related internships or fieldwork, Federal Work-Study, scholarships/grants, and unspecified assistantships available. Support available to part-time students. Financial award application deadline: 3/1; financial award applicants required to submit FAFSA. *Unit head:* Dr. Carrine Bishop, Interim Chair, 601-968-2351, Fax: 601-968-2213, E-mail: carrine.h.bishop@jsums.edu. *Application contact:* Curtis Gore, Director of Graduate Admissions, 601-979-2455, Fax: 601-974-4325, E-mail: cgore@ccaix.jsums.edu.

Jacksonville State University, College of Graduate Studies and Continuing Education, College of Education and Professional Studies, Program in Educational Administration, Jacksonville, AL 36265-1602. Offers MS Ed, Ed S. *Accreditation:* NCATE. *Faculty:* 5 full-time (2 women), 4 part-time/adjunct (0 women). *Students:* 59 full-time (31 women), 309 part-time (211 women); includes 98 minority (97 African Americans, 1 American Indian/Alaska Native), 3 international. In 2006, 134 master's, 135 other advanced degrees awarded. *Entrance requirements:* For master's, GRE General Test or MAT. *Application deadline:* Applications are processed on a rolling basis. Application fee: $20. *Expenses:* Tuition, state resident: full-time $5,400; part-time $225 per credit hour. Tuition, nonresident: full-time $10,800; part-time $450 per credit hour. One-time fee: $20 full-time. *Financial support:* In 2006–07, 1 research assistantship was awarded. Support available to part-time students. Financial award application deadline: 4/1. *Unit head:* Dr. Mary Montgomery, Head, 256-782-5837. *Application contact:* 256-782-5329.

James Madison University, College of Graduate and Outreach Programs, College of Education, Learning, Technology, and Leadership Department, Program in Educational Leadership, Harrisonburg, VA 22807. Offers M Ed. *Accreditation:* NCATE. Part-time and evening/weekend programs available. *Students:* Average age 27. *Entrance requirements:* For master's, GRE General Test. Additional exam requirements/recommendations for international students: Required—TOEFL. *Application deadline:* For fall admission, 5/1 priority date for domestic students; for spring admission, 9/1 priority date for domestic students. Applications are processed on a rolling basis. Application fee: $55. Electronic applications accepted. *Expenses:* Tuition, state resident: full-time $6,336; part-time $264 per credit hour. Tuition, nonresident: full-time $17,832; part-time $743 per credit hour. *Financial support:* Federal Work-Study available. Financial award application deadline: 3/1; financial award applicants required to submit FAFSA. *Unit head:* Dr. Diane Foucar-Szocki, Academic Unit Head, 540-568-6794.

John Carroll University, Graduate School, Department of Education and Allied Studies, Program in Administration, University Heights, OH 44118-4581. Offers M Ed, MA. *Accreditation:* NCATE. Part-time and evening/weekend programs available. *Faculty:* 4 full-time (1 woman). *Students:* Average age 33. 6 applicants, 100% accepted, 4 enrolled. In 2006, 8 degrees awarded. *Degree requirements:* For master's, research essay or thesis (MA only). *Entrance requirements:* For master's, GRE General Test or MAT, minimum GPA of 2.75. *Application deadline:* For fall admission, 8/15 priority date for domestic students; for spring admission, 1/3 for domestic students. Applications are processed on a rolling basis. Application fee: $25 ($35 for international students). *Expenses:* Tuition: Full-time $9,675; part-time $645 per credit hour. Tuition and fees vary according to program. *Financial support:* Scholarships/grants, tuition waivers (partial), and unspecified assistantships available. Financial award application deadline: 3/1; financial award applicants required to submit FAFSA. *Unit head:* Dr. Lisa Shoaf, Coordinator of Educational Administration, 216-397-4331, Fax: 216-397-4331, E-mail: lshoaf@jcu.edu.

Educational Administration

The Johns Hopkins University, School of Professional Studies in Business and Education, School of Education, Department of Teacher Development and Leadership, Baltimore, MD 21218-2699. Offers adult learning (Certificate); business leadership for independent schools (Certificate); earth/space science (Certificate); educational leadership for independent schools (Certificate); educational studies (MS); effective teaching of reading (Certificate); ESL instruction (Certificate); gifted education (Certificate); leadership for school, family and community collaboration (Certificate); reading (MS); school administration and supervision (MS, Certificate); teacher development and leadership (Ed D); teacher leadership (Certificate); technology for educators (MS); urban education (Certificate). Part-time and evening/weekend programs available. Postbaccalaureate distance learning degree programs offered (minimal on-campus study). *Students:* 19 full-time (18 women), 535 part-time (413 women); includes 98 minority (76 African Americans, 1 American Indian/Alaska Native, 18 Asian Americans or Pacific Islanders, 3 Hispanic Americans), 2 international. Average age 31. 544 applicants, 79% accepted, 374 enrolled. In 2006, 151 master's, 180 other advanced degrees awarded. *Degree requirements:* For master's and Certificate, portfolio; for doctorate, thesis/dissertation, comprehensive exam, registration. *Entrance requirements:* For master's and Certificate, minimum GPA of 3.0; for doctorate, GRE, interview, master's degree, minimum GPA of 3.0, resumé, letters of recommendation. Additional exam requirements/recommendations for international students: Required—TOEFL (minimum score 600 paper-based; 250 computer-based; 100 iBT). *Application deadline:* For fall admission, 5/1 for international students; for spring admission, 10/15 for international students. Applications are processed on a rolling basis. Application fee: $60. *Expenses:* Tuition: Full-time $32,976. Tuition and fees vary according to degree level and program. *Financial support:* Scholarships/grants available. Support available to part-time students. Financial award application deadline: 6/1; financial award applicants required to submit FAFSA. *Unit head:* Dr. Edward Pajak, Chair, 410-309-1265, Fax: 410-290-0467. *Application contact:* Carol Herrman, Admissions Coordinator, 410-872-1234, Fax: 410-872-1251, E-mail: onestop.admissions@jhu.edu.

Johnson & Wales University, The Alan Shawn Feinstein Graduate School, Program in Educational Leadership, Providence, RI 02903-3703. Offers Ed D. *Faculty:* 5 full-time (2 women), 3 part-time/adjunct (1 woman). *Students:* 89 full-time (41 women); includes 4 African Americans, 1 Asian American or Pacific Islander. Average age 42. In 2006, 17 degrees awarded. *Degree requirements:* For doctorate, thesis/dissertation. *Entrance requirements:* For doctorate, MAT, minimum GPA of 3.25. Additional exam requirements/recommendations for international students: Required—TOEFL (paper-based 550; computer-based 210) or IELTS recommended; Recommended—TWE. *Application deadline:* Applications are processed on a rolling basis. Application fee: $0. *Financial support:* Application deadline: 5/1. *Faculty research:* Site-based management, collaborative learning, technology and education, K–16 education. *Unit head:* Dr. Robert Gable, Director, 401-598-4738, Fax: 401-598-1162, E-mail: rgable@jwu.edu. *Application contact:* Dr. Allan G. Freedman, Director of Graduate Admissions, 401-598-1015, Fax: 401-598-1286, E-mail: gradadm@jwu.edu.

Jones International University, Graduate School of Education, Centennial, CO 80112. Offers adult education (M Ed); corporate training and knowledge management (M Ed); curriculum and instruction (M Ed), including elementary teacher licensure, secondary teacher licensure; e-learning technology and design (M Ed); educational leadership and administration (M Ed); educational leadership and administration: principal and administrator licensure (M Ed); elementary curriculum instruction and assessment (M Ed); higher education leadership and administration (M Ed); K-12 instructional technology (M Ed); K-12 instructional technology: teacher licensure (M Ed); secondary curriculum instruction and assessment (M Ed); technology and design (M Ed). Part-time and evening/weekend programs available. Postbaccalaureate distance learning degree programs offered (no on-campus study). *Entrance requirements:* For master's, minimum cumulative GPA of 2.5. Additional exam requirements/recommendations for international students: Recommended—TOEFL (minimum score 550 paper-based; 213 computer-based). Electronic applications accepted.

Kansas State University, Graduate School, College of Education, Department of Educational Administration and Leadership, Manhattan, KS 66506. Offers adult and continuing education (MS, Ed D); educational administration (MS, Ed D). *Accreditation:* NCATE. *Faculty:* 10 full-time (5 women), 3 part-time/adjunct (0 women). *Students:* 36 full-time (23 women), 35 part-time (17 women); includes 8 minority (1 African American, 2 American Indian/Alaska Native, 2 Asian Americans or Pacific Islanders, 3 Hispanic Americans), 1 international. Average age 32. 64 applicants, 58% accepted, 29 enrolled. In 2006, 15 master's, 10 doctorates awarded. *Degree requirements:* For master's, thesis or alternative, final written exam; for doctorate, thesis/dissertation, preliminary exam, residency, comprehensive exam. *Entrance requirements:* For master's, GRE General Test, MAT, minimum undergraduate GPA of 3.0; for doctorate, GRE General Test, MAT, minimum GPA of 3.0. Additional exam requirements/recommendations for international students: Required—TOEFL. *Application deadline:* For fall admission, 3/1 priority date for domestic students, 2/1 priority date for international students; for spring admission, 10/1 priority date for domestic students, 8/1 priority date for international students. Applications are processed on a rolling basis. Application fee: $30 ($55 for international students). Electronic applications accepted. *Expenses:* Tuition, state resident: full-time $6,352; part-time $240 per credit hour. Tuition, nonresident: full-time $14,296; part-time $571 per credit hour. Required fees: $585. *Financial support:* In 2006–07, 5 research assistantships (averaging $8,552 per year), 2 teaching assistantships with full tuition reimbursements (averaging $12,172 per year) were awarded; career-related internships or fieldwork, institutionally sponsored loans, and scholarships/grants also available. Support available to part-time students. Financial award application deadline: 3/1; financial award applicants required to submit FAFSA. *Faculty research:* Educational law, finance, technology ethics, application, and leadership in education; distance learning/education; program evaluation. Total annual research expenditures: $42,204. *Unit head:* Dr. David C. Thompson, Head, 785-532-5543, Fax: 785-532-7304, E-mail: thomsond@ksu.edu. *Application contact:* Linda Thurston, Director, 785-532-5595, Fax: 785-532-7304, E-mail: coegrads@ksu.edu.

Kean University, College of Education, Program in Educational Administration, Union, NJ 07083. Offers principals and supervisors (MA); school business administration (MA); supervisors (MA). *Accreditation:* NCATE. Part-time and evening/weekend programs available. *Faculty:* 5 full-time (1 woman). *Students:* 13 full-time (9 women), 247 part-time (153 women); includes 68 minority (34 African Americans, 5 Asian Americans or Pacific Islanders, 29 Hispanic Americans), 1 international. Average age 34. 111 applicants, 95% accepted, 86 enrolled. In 2006, 107 degrees awarded. *Degree requirements:* For master's, portfolio, field experience, research component. *Entrance requirements:* For master's, GRE General Test or MAT, interview, 2 letters of recommendation, 1 year of teaching experience, teaching certificate. *Application deadline:* For fall admission, 5/1 for domestic students; for spring admission, 11/1 for domestic students. Application fee: $60 ($150 for international students). Electronic applications accepted. *Expenses:* Tuition, state resident: full-time $8,856; part-time $369 per credit. Tuition, nonresident: full-time $11,256; part-time $469 per credit. *Financial support:* Research assistantships with full tuition reimbursements, unspecified assistantships available. *Unit head:* Dr. Leonard Elovitz, Program Coordinator, 908-737-4276, E-mail: lelovitz@kean.edu. *Application contact:* Joanne Morris, Director of Graduate Admissions, 908-737-3355, Fax: 908-737-3354, E-mail: gradadm@kean.edu.

Keene State College, Division of Graduate and Professional Studies, Program in Educational Administration, Keene, NH 03435. Offers educational administration (M Ed); educational leadership (PMC). Part-time and evening/weekend programs available. *Entrance requirements:* For master's, PRAXIS I, MAT or GRE, teaching certificate, 2 years teaching experience, resumé. *Application deadline:* For fall admission, 6/15 for domestic students; for spring admission, 10/15 for domestic students. Applications are processed on a rolling basis. Application fee: $25 ($35 for international students). *Expenses:* Tuition, area resident: Part-time $265 per credit. Tuition, state resident: full-time $5,780; part-time $290 per credit. Tuition, nonresident: full-time $13,050. Required fees: $80 per credit. Part-time tuition and fees vary according to course load. *Financial support:* Research assistantships available. Financial award application deadline: 3/1; financial award applicants required to submit FAFSA. *Application contact:* Peggy Richmond, Director of Admissions, 603-358-2276, Fax: 603-358-2767, E-mail: admissions@keene.edu.

Kennesaw State University, Leland and Clarice C. Bagwell College of Education, Program in Graduate Education, Kennesaw, GA 30144-5591. Offers adolescent education (M Ed); early childhood education (M Ed); educational leadership (M Ed); special education (M Ed). *Accreditation:* NCATE. Part-time programs available. *Faculty:* 60 full-time (38 women), 12 part-time/adjunct (4 women). *Students:* 150 full-time (143 women), 489 part-time (371 women); includes 95 minority (85 African Americans, 1 American Indian/Alaska Native, 1 Asian American or Pacific Islander, 8 Hispanic Americans), 21 international. Average age 35. 165 applicants, 97% accepted, 142 enrolled. In 2006, 283 degrees awarded. *Degree requirements:* For master's, thesis or alternative. *Entrance requirements:* For master's, GRE General Test, T-4 state certification, minimum GPA of 2.75. Additional exam requirements/recommendations for international students: Required—TOEFL (minimum score 550 paper-based; 213 computer-based; 80 iBT), IELTS (minimum score 6). *Application deadline:* For fall admission, 7/15 priority date for domestic students; for spring admission, 10/15 priority date for domestic students. Application fee: $50. Electronic applications accepted. *Expenses:* Tuition, state resident: full-time $3,044; part-time $127 per semester hour. Tuition, nonresident: full-time $12,172; part-time $508 per semester hour. Required fees: $353 per semester. Full-time tuition and fees vary according to campus/location and program. *Financial support:* Federal Work-Study and unspecified assistantships available. Support available to part-time students. Financial award application deadline: 6/15; financial award applicants required to submit FAFSA. *Application contact:* Alisha O'Brien, Administrative Coordinator, 770-423-6043, Fax: 770-420-4435, E-mail: aobrien@kennesaw.edu.

Kennesaw State University, Leland and Clarice C. Bagwell College of Education, Program in Leadership for Learning, Kennesaw, GA 30144-5591. Offers Ed D, Ed S. *Expenses:* Tuition, state resident: full-time $3,044; part-time $127 per semester hour. Tuition, nonresident: full-time $12,172; part-time $508 per semester hour. Required fees: $353 per semester. Full-time tuition and fees vary according to campus/location and program. *Unit head:* Dr. Nita Paris, Director, 770-423-6636, E-mail: nparis@kennesaw.edu. *Application contact:* Alisha O'Brien, Administrative Coordinator, 770-423-6043, Fax: 770-420-4435, E-mail: aobrien@kennesaw.edu.

Kent State University, Graduate School of Education, Health, and Human Services, Department of Teaching, Leadership, and Curriculum Studies, Program in Educational Administration, Kent, OH 44242-0001. Offers PhD, Ed S. *Accreditation:* NCATE. Part-time and evening/weekend programs available. *Faculty:* 9 full-time (5 women), 2 part-time/adjunct (1 woman). *Students:* 19 full-time (15 women), 17 part-time (11 women); includes 8 minority (5 African Americans, 1 Asian American or Pacific Islander, 2 Hispanic Americans), 1 international. 7 applicants, 14% accepted. In 2006, 2 doctorates, 2 Ed Ss awarded. *Degree requirements:* For doctorate, thesis/dissertation, comprehensive exam, registration. *Entrance requirements:* For doctorate and Ed S, GRE General Test. Additional exam requirements/recommendations for international students: Required—TOEFL. *Application deadline:* Applications are processed on a rolling basis. Application fee: $30. Electronic applications accepted. *Financial support:* In 2006–07, fellowships with full tuition reimbursements (averaging $8,497 per year); research assistantships with full tuition reimbursements, teaching assistantships with full tuition reimbursements, career-related internships or fieldwork, Federal Work-Study, institutionally sponsored loans, scholarships/grants, health care benefits, and unspecified assistantships also available. Support available to part-time students. Financial award application deadline: 4/1; financial award applicants required to submit FAFSA. *Faculty research:* Leadership, the superintendency. *Unit head:* Dr. Eunsook Hyun, Coordinator, 330-672-5839, E-mail: ehyun@kent.edu. *Application contact:* Nancy Miller, Academic Program Coordinator, Office of Graduate Student Services, 330-672-2576, Fax: 330-672-9162, E-mail: ogs@kent.edu.

Kent State University, Graduate School of Education, Health, and Human Services, Department of Teaching, Leadership, and Curriculum Studies, Program in Higher Education Administration and Student Personnel, Kent, OH 44242-0001. Offers M Ed, MA. *Accreditation:* NCATE. *Faculty:* 6 full-time (2 women), 2 part-time/adjunct (both women). *Students:* 52 full-time (41 women), 30 part-time (21 women); includes 8 minority (7 African Americans, 1 Asian American or Pacific Islander), 1 international. 65 applicants, 55% accepted. In 2006, 31 degrees awarded. *Degree requirements:* For master's, thesis (for some programs), registration. *Entrance requirements:* Additional exam requirements/recommendations for international students: Required—TOEFL. *Application deadline:* Applications are processed on a rolling basis. Application fee: $30. Electronic applications accepted. *Financial support:* In 2006–07, fellowships with full tuition reimbursements (averaging $7,210 per year); research assistantships with full tuition reimbursements, teaching assistantships with full tuition reimbursements, career-related internships or fieldwork, Federal Work-Study, institutionally sponsored loans, scholarships/grants, health care benefits, and unspecified assistantships also available. Support available to part-time students. Financial award application deadline: 4/1; financial award applicants required to submit FAFSA. *Faculty research:* History/sociology of higher education, organization and administration in higher education. *Unit head:* Dr. Mark Kretovics, Coordinator, 330-672-2477, E-mail: mkretov1@kent.edu. *Application contact:* Nancy Miller, Academic Program Coordinator, Office of Graduate Student Services, 330-672-2576, Fax: 330-672-9162, E-mail: ogs@kent.edu.

Kent State University, Graduate School of Education, Health, and Human Services, Department of Teaching, Leadership, and Curriculum Studies, Program in K-12 Leadership, Kent, OH 44242-0001. Offers M Ed, MA, PhD, Ed S. *Faculty:* 5 full-time (3 women). *Students:* 10 full-time (6 women), 62 part-time (32 women); includes 4 minority (all African Americans), 1 international. 21 applicants, 52% accepted. In 2006, 40 master's, 2 doctorates, 3 other advanced degrees awarded. *Entrance requirements:* For doctorate and Ed S, GRE. Additional exam requirements/recommendations for international students: Required—TOEFL. *Application deadline:* Applications are processed on a rolling basis. Application fee: $30. Electronic applications accepted. *Financial support:* In 2006–07, fellowships (averaging $8,497 per year); research assistantships, teaching assistantships, career-related internships or fieldwork, Federal Work-Study, institutionally sponsored loans, scholarships/grants, health care benefits, and unspecified assistantships also available. Support available to part-time students. *Unit head:* Dr. Autumn Tooms, Coordinator, 330-672-2580, E-mail: atooms@kent.edu. *Application contact:* Nancy Miller, Academic Program Coordinator, Office of Graduate Student Services, 330-672-2576, Fax: 330-672-9162, E-mail: ogs@kent.edu.

Kutztown University of Pennsylvania, College of Graduate Studies and Extended Learning, Program in Student Affairs in Higher Education, Kutztown, PA 19530-0730. Offers M Ed. *Accreditation:* NCATE. Part-time and evening/weekend programs available. *Faculty:* 10 full-time (5 women), 2 part-time/adjunct (0 women). *Students:* 9 full-time (5 women), 16 part-time (12 women); includes 1 minority (Hispanic American) Average age 27. 22 applicants, 64% accepted, 3 enrolled. In 2006, 6 degrees awarded. *Degree requirements:* For master's, comprehensive exam. *Entrance requirements:* For master's, GRE General Test, interview. Additional exam requirements/recommendations for international students: Required—TOEFL. *Application deadline:* For fall admission, 3/1 for domestic students; for spring admission, 9/1 for domestic students. Application fee: $35. Electronic applications accepted. *Expenses:* Tuition, state resident: full-time $6,048; part-time $336 per credit. Tuition, nonresident: full-time $9,678; part-time $538 per credit. *Financial support:* In 2006–07, research assistantships with full tuition reimbursements (averaging $5,000 per year); career-related internships or fieldwork, Federal Work-Study, and unspecified assistantships also available. Financial award application deadline: 3/15; financial award applicants required to submit FAFSA. *Unit head:* Dr. Kelley R. Kenney, Graduate Coordinator, 610-683-4223, E-mail: kenney@kutztown.edu.

Lake Erie College, Division of Education, Painesville, OH 44077-3389. Offers curriculum and instruction (MS Ed); education (MS Ed); educational leadership (MS Ed); reading (MS Ed). Part-time and evening/weekend programs available. *Faculty:* 4 full-time (1 woman), 4 part-time/adjunct (1 woman). *Students:* Average age 37. 9 applicants, 89% accepted, 5 enrolled. In 2006, 20 degrees awarded. *Degree requirements:* For master's, thesis, applied research project, comprehensive exam. *Entrance requirements:* For master's, GRE General Test or minimum GPA of 3.0. Additional exam requirements/recommendations for international students: Required—TOEFL (minimum score 590 paper-based). *Application deadline:* For fall admission, 8/1 priority date for domestic students, 6/1 for international students; for spring admission, 12/15 for domestic students, 10/1 for international students. Applications are processed on a rolling basis. Application fee: $25 ($50 for international students). Electronic applications accepted. *Expenses:* Contact institution. *Financial support:* Applicants required to submit FAFSA. *Faculty research:* Cooperative learning, portfolio assessment, education systems in England, video case-based instruction. *Unit head:* Dr. Richard Bonde, Associate Dean, 440-375-7156, Fax: 440-375-7005, E-mail: rbonde@lec.edu. *Application contact:* 440-375-7050, Fax: 440-375-7005, E-mail: admissions@lec.edu.

Lakehead University, Graduate Studies, Faculty of Education, Thunder Bay, ON P7B 5E1, Canada. Offers curriculum development (M Ed); education administration (M Ed); educational studies (PhD). Part-time and evening/weekend programs available. *Degree requirements:* For master's, project or thesis. *Entrance requirements:* For master's, minimum B average. Additional exam requirements/recommendations for international students: Required—TOEFL. *Faculty research:* Art education, AIDS education, language arts education, gerontology, women's studies.

Lamar University, College of Graduate Studies, College of Education and Human Development, Department of Educational Leadership, Beaumont, TX 77710. Offers counseling and development (M Ed, Certificate); education administration (M Ed); educational leadership (DE); principal (Certificate); school superintendent (Certificate); supervision (M Ed); technology application (Certificate). Part-time and evening/weekend programs available. *Faculty:* 11 full-time (5 women), 4 part-time/adjunct (1 woman). *Students:* 44 full-time (34 women), 113 part-time (86 women); includes 34 minority (27 African Americans, 2 Asian Americans or Pacific Islanders, 5 Hispanic Americans), 2 international. Average age 35. 301 applicants, 33% accepted, 32 enrolled. In 2006, 68 degrees awarded. Terminal master's awarded for partial completion of doctoral program. *Degree requirements:* For master's, thesis optional; for doctorate, thesis/dissertation, registration. *Entrance requirements:* For master's, GRE General Test, minimum GPA of 2.5; for doctorate, GRE. Additional exam requirements/recommendations for international students: Required—TOEFL. *Application deadline:* For fall admission, 8/1 priority date for domestic students; for spring admission, 12/1 priority date for domestic students. Applications are processed on a rolling basis. Application fee: $25 ($50 for international students). *Expenses:* Tuition, nonresident: part-time $33 per hour. Required fees: $43 per hour. $110 per semester. *Financial support:* In 2006–07, 3 fellowships (averaging $20,000 per year), 1 research assistantship with tuition reimbursement (averaging $6,500 per year) were awarded; teaching assistantships with tuition reimbursements, career-related internships or fieldwork and scholarships/grants also available. Support available to part-time students. Financial award application deadline: 4/1. *Faculty research:* School dropouts, suicide prevention in public school students, school climate and gifted performance, teacher evaluation. *Unit head:* Dr. Carolyn Crawford, Chair, 409-880-8689, Fax: 409-880-8685.

La Sierra University, School of Education, Department of Administration and Leadership, Riverside, CA 92515. Offers MA, Ed D, Ed S. Part-time and evening/weekend programs available. Terminal master's awarded for partial completion of doctoral program. *Degree requirements:* For master's, thesis optional; for doctorate, thesis/dissertation, fieldwork, qualifying exam; for Ed S, fieldwork, thesis optional. *Entrance requirements:* For master's, minimum GPA of 3.0; for doctorate, GRE General Test, GRE Subject Test, minimum GPA of 3.3, Ed S; for Ed S, master's degree, minimum GPA of 3.3.

Lee University, Program in Education, Cleveland, TN 37320-3450. Offers classroom teaching (M Ed); educational leadership (M Ed); elementary/secondary education (MAT); special education (elementary) (M Ed); special education (secondary) (M Ed, MAT); special education (severe disabilities) (M Ed). *Faculty:* 25 full-time (11 women). *Students:* 103 full-time (66 women), 22 part-time (15 women); includes 43 minority (5 African Americans, 36 American Indian/Alaska Native, 2 Hispanic Americans), 3 international. 49 applicants, 100% accepted, 28 enrolled. In 2006, 75 degrees awarded. *Degree requirements:* For master's, variable foreign language requirement, thesis, internship, comprehensive exam. *Entrance requirements:* For master's, MAT or GRE General Test, minimum GPA of 2.75, 3 letters of recommendation, interview, writing sample. Additional exam requirements/recommendations for international students: Required—TOEFL. *Application deadline:* For fall admission, 4/1 for domestic students; for spring admission, 10/1 for domestic students. Applications are processed on a rolling basis. Application fee: $25. *Expenses:* Tuition: Part-time $412 per credit. Required fees: $10 per semester. Tuition and fees vary according to course load. *Financial support:* Career-related internships or fieldwork, Federal Work-Study, and institutionally sponsored loans available. *Unit head:* Dr. Gary Riggins, Director, 423-614-8193. *Application contact:* Vicki Glasscock, Graduate Admissions Director, 423-614-8059, E-mail: vglasscock@leeuniversity.edu.

Lehigh University, College of Education, Department of Education and Human Services, Program in Educational Leadership, Bethlehem, PA 18015-3094. Offers M Ed, Ed D, Certificate, MBA/M Ed. Part-time and evening/weekend programs available. Postbaccalaureate distance learning degree programs offered (minimal on-campus study). *Faculty:* 29 full-time (16 women), 17 part-time/adjunct (9 women). *Students:* 14 full-time (11 women), 222 part-time (139 women); includes 7 minority (1 African American, 2 Asian Americans or Pacific Islanders, 4 Hispanic Americans), 21 international. 40 applicants, 75% accepted, 12 enrolled. In 2006, 51 master's, 5 doctorates awarded. *Degree requirements:* For doctorate, thesis/dissertation. *Entrance requirements:* For master's, GRE General Test or MAT, minimum GPA of 3.0; for doctorate, GRE General Test or MAT, minimum graduate GPA of 3.6. Additional exam requirements/recommendations for international students: Required—TOEFL (minimum score 600 paper-based; 250 computer-based). *Application deadline:* Applications are processed on a rolling basis. Application fee: $60. Electronic applications accepted. *Financial support:* Career-related internships or fieldwork, Federal Work-Study, institutionally sponsored loans, scholarships/grants, and tuition waivers (full and partial) available. Financial award application deadline: 1/31. *Faculty research:* School finance and law, supervision of instruction, curriculum development, middle-level education, organizational change. *Unit head:* Dr. George P. White, Coordinator, 610-758-3262, Fax: 610-758-3227, E-mail: gpw1@lehigh.edu.

LeTourneau University, Graduate and Professional Studies, Longview, TX 75607-7001. Offers business administration (MBA); educational leadership (MBA). Part-time and evening/weekend programs available. Postbaccalaureate distance learning degree programs offered (no on-campus study). *Faculty:* 7 full-time (0 women), 29 part-time/adjunct (7 women). *Students:* 217 full-time (135 women), 123 part-time (71 women); includes 165 minority (124 African Americans, 8 American Indian/Alaska Native, 7 Asian Americans or Pacific Islanders, 26 Hispanic Americans), 2 international. Average age 37. 394 applicants, 90% accepted, 337 enrolled. In 2006, 182 degrees awarded. *Entrance requirements:* For master's, minimum GPA of 2.8, 3 years of full-time work experience. Additional exam requirements/recommendations for international students: Required—TOEFL. *Application deadline:* Applications are processed on a rolling basis. Application fee: $50. Electronic applications accepted. *Expenses:* Tuition: Full-time $10,043; part-time $510 per credit hour. Required fees: $975; $50 per credit hour. One-time fee: $75 full-time. *Financial support:* Applicants required to submit FAFSA. *Unit head:* Dr. Scott Ray, Associate Vice President for the school of Graduate and Professional Studies, 903-233-3250, Fax: 903-233-3227, E-mail: scottray@letu.edu. *Application contact:* Chris Fontaine, Assistant VP for Enrollment Management and Market Research, 903-233-3250, Fax: 903-233-3227, E-mail: chrisfontaine@letu.edu.

Lewis & Clark College, Graduate School of Education and Counseling, Department of Education, Program in Educational Leadership, Portland, OR 97219-7899. Offers M Ed, Ed D. Part-time and evening/weekend programs available. *Faculty:* 4 full-time (2 women), 20 part-time/adjunct (11 women). *Students:* 6 full-time (3 women), 47 part-time (29 women); includes 10 minority (4 African Americans, 4 American Indian/Alaska Native, 2 Asian Americans or Pacific Islanders). Average age 45. 44 applicants, 86% accepted, 28 enrolled. In 2006, 3 degrees awarded. *Degree requirements:* For doctorate, thesis/dissertation. *Entrance requirements:* For master's, minimum undergraduate GPA of 2.75; for doctorate, minimum undergraduate GPA of 3.0. Additional exam requirements/recommendations for international students: Required—TOEFL (minimum score 575 paper-based; 233 computer-based). *Application deadline:* For fall admission, 3/12 for domestic and international students; for spring admission, 11/6 for international students. Applications are processed on a rolling basis. Application fee: $50. *Expenses:* Tuition: Part-time $610 per semester hour. *Financial support:* In 2006–07, 18 students received support. Career-related internships or fieldwork, Federal Work-Study, institutionally sponsored loans, health care benefits, and tuition waivers (partial) available. Support available to part-time students. Financial award applicants required to submit FAFSA. *Faculty research:* Socialization of administrators, teacher evaluation effectiveness, instructional leadership, gender and leadership. *Unit head:* Dr. Dick Sagor, Coordinator, 503-768-6080, Fax: 503-768-6085, E-mail: eda@lclark.edu. *Application contact:* Becky Haas, Director of Admissions, 503-768-6200, Fax: 503-768-6205, E-mail: gseadmit@lclark.edu.

Lewis University, College of Arts and Sciences, Graduate Programs in Education, Program in Administration/Education, Romeoville, IL 60446. Offers MA.

Lewis University, College of Arts and Sciences, Graduate Programs in Education, Program in Curriculum and Instruction, Romeoville, IL 60446. Offers educational leadership (MA Ed); instructional leadership (MA Ed). Part-time and evening/weekend programs available. *Entrance requirements:* For master's, entrance writing exam, minimum GPA of 2.75, 3 letters of recommendation, interview. Additional exam requirements/recommendations for international students: Required—TOEFL (minimum score 550 paper-based; 213 computer-based). Electronic applications accepted.

Lewis University, College of Arts and Sciences, Program in Organizational Leadership, Romeoville, IL 60446. Offers higher education/student services (MA); organizational management (MA); public administration (MA); training and development (MA). Part-time and evening/weekend programs available. *Entrance requirements:* For master's, bachelor's degree, at least 25 years of age, minimum of 3 years of work experience, minimum GPA of 3.0 (provisional admission possible), letter of recommendation, interview. Additional exam requirements/recommendations for international students: Required—TOEFL (minimum score 550 paper-based; 213 computer-based). Electronic applications accepted.

Liberty University, School of Education, Lynchburg, VA 24502. Offers administration and supervision (M Ed); curriculum and instruction (M Ed); early childhood education (M Ed); education specialist (Ed S); educational leadership (Ed D); elementary education (M Ed); gifted education (M Ed); reading specialist (M Ed); school counseling (M Ed); secondary education (M Ed); special education (M Ed). *Accreditation:* NCATE. Part-time programs available. Postbaccalaureate distance learning degree programs offered (minimal on-campus study). *Faculty:* 8 full-time (3 women), 7 part-time/adjunct (3 women). *Students:* 33 full-time (22 women), 308 part-time (180 women); includes 22 minority (12 African Americans, 2 American Indian/Alaska Native, 2 Asian Americans or Pacific Islanders, 6 Hispanic Americans), 5 international. Average age 39. 434 applicants, 77% accepted, 111 enrolled. In 2006, 39 master's, 12 doctorates, 16 other advanced degrees awarded. *Degree requirements:* For doctorate, thesis/dissertation, comprehensive exam. *Entrance requirements:* For master's, GRE General Test or MAT (if taken on or before 1999), 2 letters of recommendation, minimum undergraduate GPA of 3.0, curriculum vitae, graduate status record; for doctorate, GRE General Test or MAT (if taken before 1999), minimum master's GPA of 3.0, 3 years of teacher experience; for Ed S, GRE General Test or MAT (if taken before 1999), minimum master's GPA of 3.0, 3 years of teaching experience. Additional exam requirements/recommendations for international students: Required—TOEFL (minimum score 600 paper-based; 250 computer-based). *Application deadline:* For fall admission, 6/1 priority date for domestic students; for spring admission, 11/1 for domestic students. Applications are processed on a rolling basis. Application fee: $35. Electronic applications accepted. *Expenses:* Contact institution. *Financial support:* In 2006–07, 226 students received support. Federal Work-Study and tuition waivers (partial) available. *Faculty research:* Self-determination, character education, bibliotherapy, learning styles, distance education. *Unit head:* Dr. Karen L. Parker, Dean, 434-582-2195, Fax: 434-582-2468, E-mail: kparker@liberty.edu. *Application contact:* Kyle A Falce, Director of Graduate Admissions, 800-424-9596, Fax: 800-628-7977, E-mail: gradadmissions@liberty.edu.

Lincoln Memorial University, School of Education, Harrogate, TN 37752-1901. Offers administration and supervision (M Ed, Ed S); counseling and guidance (M Ed); curriculum and instruction (M Ed, Ed S). Part-time and evening/weekend programs available. *Faculty:* 25 full-time (13 women), 11 part-time/adjunct (6 women). *Students:* 207 full-time (159 women), 1,315 part-time (995 women); includes 106 minority (93 African Americans, 1 American Indian/Alaska Native, 1 Asian American or Pacific Islander, 11 Hispanic Americans), 2 international. 1,397 applicants, 98% accepted. In 2006, 194 master's, 778 other advanced degrees awarded. *Degree requirements:* For master's, thesis optional. *Entrance requirements:* For master's, GRE, MAT, or NTE. *Application deadline:* For fall admission, 8/10 priority date for domestic students. Application fee: $25. *Financial support:* Career-related internships or fieldwork and unspecified assistantships available. Support available to part-time students. Financial award application deadline: 4/1; financial award applicants required to submit FAFSA. *Unit head:* Dr. Fred Bedelle, Dean, School of Graduate Studies, 423-869-6223, Fax: 423-869-6261, E-mail: graduate@inetlmu.lmunet.edu. *Application contact:* Barbara McCune, Senior Assistant, Graduate Office, 423-869-6374, Fax: 423-869-6261, E-mail: graduate@lmunet.edu.

Lincoln University, School of Graduate Studies and Continuing Education, College of Liberal Arts, Education and Journalism, Department of Education, Jefferson City, MO 65102. Offers educational leadership (Ed S), including elementary leadership, secondary leadership, superintendency; guidance and counseling (M Ed), including community/agency counseling, elementary school, secondary school; school administration and supervision (M Ed), including elementary school administration, secondary school administration, special education administration; school teaching (M Ed), including elementary school teaching, secondary school teaching. *Accreditation:* NCATE. Part-time and evening/weekend programs available. *Faculty:* 1 (woman) full-time, 10 part-time/adjunct (5 women). *Students:* 24 full-time (21 women), 62 part-time (51 women); includes 10 minority (8 African Americans, 2 Asian Americans or Pacific Islanders), 4 international. Average age 35. 13 applicants, 100% accepted, 10 enrolled. In 2006, 25 master's, 3 other advanced degrees awarded. *Degree requirements:* For master's and Ed S, portfolio. *Entrance requirements:* For master's, GRE or MAT, teaching certificate (school administration and supervision); background check; interview (elementary and secondary school teaching); for Ed S, GRE or MAT, principal certificate. Additional exam requirements/recommendations for international students: Required—TOEFL (minimum score 500 paper-based; 173 computer-based; 61 iBT). *Application deadline:* For fall admission, 7/1 priority date for domestic and international students; for spring admission, 12/1 priority date for domestic and international students. Applications are processed on a rolling basis. Application fee: $17. *Expenses:* Tuition, state resident: part-time $189 per credit hour. Tuition, nonresident: part-time $351 per credit hour. Required fees: $15 per credit hour. $20 per semester. *Financial support:* Federal Work-Study and scholarships/grants available. Financial award application deadline: 4/1; financial award applicants required to submit FAFSA. *Unit head:* Dr. Cynthia Chapel, Department Head, 573-681-5250, Fax: 573-681-5257, E-mail: chapelc@lincolnu.edu.

Lindenwood University, Graduate Programs, Division of Education, St. Charles, MO 63301-1695. Offers education (MA); educational administration (MA, Ed D, Ed S); instructional leadership (Ed D, Ed S); library media (MA); professional and school counseling (MA); professional counseling (MA); school counseling (MA); teaching (MA). Part-time and evening/weekend programs available. *Faculty:* 15 full-time (6 women), 16 part-time/adjunct (11 women). *Students:* 569 full-time (446 women), 1,869 part-time (1,433 women); includes 526 minority (494 African Americans, 8 American Indian/Alaska Native, 9 Asian Americans or Pacific

Educational Administration

Lindenwood University (continued)
Islanders, 15 Hispanic Americans), 8 international. Average age 35. In 2006, 747 master's, 19 other advanced degrees awarded. *Degree requirements:* For master's, thesis (for some programs); for doctorate, thesis/dissertation; for Ed S, specialist project. *Entrance requirements:* For master's, interview, minimum GPA of 3.0, writing sample; for Ed S, master's degree in education, relevant work experience. Additional exam requirements/recommendations for international students: Required—TOEFL (minimum score 550 paper-based; 213 computer-based). *Application deadline:* For fall admission, 8/30 priority date for domestic and international students; for spring admission, 12/30 priority date for domestic and international students. Applications are processed on a rolling basis. Application fee: $30 ($100 for international students). Electronic applications accepted. *Expenses:* Tuition: Part-time $340 per credit hour. Tuition and fees vary according to course level, course load, degree level and program. *Financial support:* Career-related internships or fieldwork, institutionally sponsored loans, and tuition waivers (partial) available. Financial award application deadline: 6/30; financial award applicants required to submit FAFSA. *Unit head:* Dr. John Dougherty, Dean of Education, 636-949-4937, E-mail: jdougherty@lindenwood.edu. *Application contact:* Brett Barger, Dean, Adult, Corporate and Graduate Admissions, 636-949-4934, Fax: 636-949-4109, E-mail: adultadmissions@lindenwood.edu.

Lipscomb University, Program in Education, Nashville, TN 37204-3951. Offers instructional leadership (M Ed); learning and teaching (MALT); school administration and supervision (M Ed); special education instruction, K-12 (MASE). *Accreditation:* NCATE. Part-time and evening/weekend programs available. *Faculty:* 3 full-time (1 woman), 9 part-time/adjunct (6 women). *Students:* 95 full-time (59 women), 30 part-time (22 women); includes 14 minority (13 African Americans, 1 Asian American or Pacific Islander). Average age 32. In 2006, 25 degrees awarded. *Degree requirements:* For master's, registration. *Entrance requirements:* For master's, MAT or GRE General Test, 2 reference letters. Additional exam requirements/recommendations for international students: Required—TOEFL (minimum score 570 paper-based; 230 computer-based). *Application deadline:* For fall admission, 8/29 priority date for domestic students; for spring admission, 1/16 priority date for domestic students. Applications are processed on a rolling basis. Application fee: $60. *Expenses:* Tuition: Part-time $560 per semester hour. Tuition and fees vary according to program. *Financial support:* In 2006–07, 67 students received support. Federal Work-Study, tuition waivers (full), and unspecified assistantships available. Support available to part-time students. Financial award applicants required to submit FAFSA. *Faculty research:* Facilitative learning styles, leadership, student assessment, interactive multimedia inclusion. *Unit head:* Dr. Junior High, Director, 615-966-1000 Ext. 6067, Fax: 615-966-7628, E-mail: junior.high@lipscomb.edu. *Application contact:* Jackie Sanders, Administrative Assistant, 615-966-1000 Ext. 6081, Fax: 615-966-7628, E-mail: jackie.sanders@lipscomb.edu.

Long Island University, Brentwood Campus, School of Education, Brentwood, NY 11717. Offers elementary education (MS); reading (MS); school counseling (MS); school district administration and supervision (MS); special education (MS). Part-time and evening/weekend programs available.

Long Island University, Brooklyn Campus, School of Education, Department of Human Development and Leadership, Program in Leadership and Policy, Brooklyn, NY 11201-8423. Offers MS. *Degree requirements:* For master's, thesis optional. *Entrance requirements:* For master's, 2 letters of recommendation. Additional exam requirements/recommendations for international students: Required—TOEFL (minimum score 500 paper-based; 173 computer-based).

Long Island University, C.W. Post Campus, School of Education, Department of Educational Leadership and Administration, Brookville, NY 11548-1300. Offers school administration and supervision (MS Ed); school business administration (PD); school district administration (PD). Part-time and evening/weekend programs available. *Degree requirements:* For master's, comprehensive exam or research project, internship; for PD, internship. *Entrance requirements:* For master's, minimum GPA of 3.0, 3 years of teaching experience. Electronic applications accepted. *Faculty research:* Leadership administration, computers in decision making, curricular innovation and school business administration.

Long Island University, Rockland Graduate Campus, Graduate School, Program in Educational Administration, Orangeburg, NY 10962. Offers school building leader (MS Ed, Advanced Certificate); school district business leader (Advanced Certificate); school district leader (Advanced Certificate).

Longwood University, Office of Graduate Studies, College of Education and Human Services, Farmville, VA 23909. Offers communication sciences and disorders (MS); community and college counseling (MS); curriculum and instruction specialist-elementary (MS), including mild disabilities, modern languages; curriculum and instruction specialist-secondary (MS), including English, mild disabilities, modern languages; educational leadership (MS); guidance and counseling (MS); literacy and culture (MS); school library media (MS). *Accreditation:* NCATE. Part-time and evening/weekend programs available. *Degree requirements:* For master's, thesis optional. *Entrance requirements:* For master's, GRE (communication sciences and disorders), minimum GPA of 2.75. Additional exam requirements/recommendations for international students: Required—TOEFL (minimum score 550 paper-based; 213 computer-based).

Loras College, Graduate Division, Program in Educational Leadership, Dubuque, IA 52004-0178. Offers MA. Part-time and evening/weekend programs available. *Faculty:* 1 full-time (0 women), 1 part-time/adjunct (0 women). *Students:* Average age 33. In 2006, 16 degrees awarded. *Degree requirements:* For master's, thesis optional. *Entrance requirements:* For master's, minimum cumulative undergraduate GPA of 3.0. *Application deadline:* Applications are processed on a rolling basis. Application fee: $25. *Expenses:* Tuition: Full-time $7,650; part-time $425 per credit. *Financial support:* Applicants required to submit FAFSA. *Unit head:* Dr. David Salyer, Graduate Coordinator, 563-588-7836, E-mail: david.salyer@loras.edu. *Application contact:* Michelle Rice, Graduate Admissions Counselor, 563-588-7166, E-mail: michelle.rice@loras.edu.

Louisiana State University and Agricultural and Mechanical College, Graduate School, College of Education, Department of Educational Theory, Policy and Practice, Baton Rouge, LA 70803. Offers counseling (M Ed, MA, Ed S); educational administration (M Ed, MA, PhD, Ed S); educational technology (MA); elementary education (M Ed); higher education (PhD); research methodology (PhD); secondary education (M Ed). *Accreditation:* ACA (one or more programs are accredited); NCATE. Part-time and evening/weekend programs available. *Faculty:* 39 full-time (24 women). *Students:* 147 full-time (115 women), 183 part-time (143 women); includes 63 minority (51 African Americans, 3 American Indian/Alaska Native, 3 Asian Americans or Pacific Islanders, 6 Hispanic Americans), 14 international. Average age 35. 110 applicants, 58% accepted, 15 enrolled. In 2006, 93 master's, 24 doctorates awarded. Terminal master's awarded for partial completion of doctoral program. *Degree requirements:* For doctorate, thesis/dissertation; for Ed S, thesis optional. *Entrance requirements:* For master's and doctorate, GRE General Test, minimum GPA of 3.0. Additional exam requirements/recommendations for international students: Required—TOEFL (minimum score 550 paper-based; 213 computer-based; 79 iBT). *Application deadline:* For fall admission, 1/25 priority date for domestic students, 5/15 for international students; for spring admission, 10/15 for international students. Applications are processed on a rolling basis. Application fee: $25. Electronic applications accepted. *Financial support:* In 2006–07, 82 students received support, including 6 fellowships with full tuition reimbursements available (averaging $26,273 per year), 24 research assistantships with full and partial tuition reimbursements available (averaging $9,812 per year), teaching assistantships with full and partial tuition reimbursements available (averaging $11,693 per year); career-related internships or fieldwork, Federal Work-Study, institutionally sponsored loans, and unspecified assistantships also available. Support available to part-time students. Financial award applicants required to submit FAFSA. *Faculty research:* Literary,

curriculum studies, science education, K-12 leadership, higher education. Total annual research expenditures: $335,618. *Unit head:* Dr. Earl Cheek, Chair, 225-578-6897, Fax: 225-578-1045, E-mail: echeek@lsu.edu.

Louisiana Tech University, Graduate School, College of Education, Department of Curriculum, Instruction and Leadership, Ruston, LA 71272. Offers curriculum and instruction (MS, Ed D); educational leadership (Ed D); secondary education (M Ed), including business education, English education, foreign language education, health and physical education, mathematics education, science education, social studies education, speech education. *Accreditation:* NCATE. Part-time programs available. *Degree requirements:* For doctorate, thesis/dissertation. *Entrance requirements:* For master's and doctorate, GRE General Test.

Loyola College in Maryland, Graduate Programs, College of Arts and Sciences, Department of Education, Program in Administration and Supervision, Baltimore, MD 21210-2699. Offers M Ed, MA, CAS. Part-time and evening/weekend programs available. *Students:* 4 full-time (all women), 62 part-time (42 women); includes 14 minority (11 African Americans, 1 Asian American or Pacific Islander, 2 Hispanic Americans). Average age 32. 49 applicants, 90% accepted, 29 enrolled. In 2006, 30 degrees awarded. *Entrance requirements:* For master's and CAS, GRE General Test, GRE Subject Test (recommended). Additional exam requirements/recommendations for international students: Required—TOEFL (minimum score 550 paper-based; 213 computer-based). *Application deadline:* For fall admission, 7/1 priority date for domestic students; for spring admission, 10/1 priority date for domestic students. Applications are processed on a rolling basis. Application fee: $50. *Financial support:* Career-related internships or fieldwork available. Financial award applicants required to submit FAFSA. *Unit head:* Peggy Golden, Director, 410-617-1656, E-mail: pgolden@loyola.edu.

Loyola Marymount University, Graduate Division, School of Education, Doctorate in Educational Leadership in Social Justice Program, Los Angeles, CA 90045-2659. Offers Ed D. Part-time and evening/weekend programs available. *Students:* 19 full-time (12 women), 20 part-time (12 women); includes 14 minority (2 African Americans, 4 Asian Americans or Pacific Islanders, 8 Hispanic Americans), 1 international. Average age 37. *Application deadline:* For fall admission, 1/9 for domestic students. Application fee: $50. *Financial support:* In 2006–07, 19 students received support. *Application deadline:* 2/8; *Unit head:* Dr. Shane Martin, Dean, 310-338-2863, Fax: 310-338-1976, E-mail: smartin@lmu.edu. *Application contact:* Information Contact, 310-338-2863.

Loyola Marymount University, Graduate Division, School of Education, Program in Catholic School Administration, Los Angeles, CA 90045-2659. Offers MA. In 2006, 2 degrees awarded. *Degree requirements:* For master's, comprehensive exam. *Application deadline:* For fall admission, 7/15 for domestic students; for spring admission, 11/15 for domestic students. Application fee: $50. Electronic applications accepted. *Financial support:* Application deadline: 6/1; *Unit head:* Dr. Mary McCullough, Head, 310-338-7312, E-mail: mmccullo@lmu.edu.

Loyola Marymount University, Graduate Division, School of Education, Program in School Administration, Los Angeles, CA 90045-2659. Offers M Ed. Part-time and evening/weekend programs available. *Students:* 14 full-time (10 women), 17 part-time (11 women); includes 21 minority (6 African Americans, 1 American Indian/Alaska Native, 2 Asian Americans or Pacific Islanders, 12 Hispanic Americans), 2 international. In 2006, 7 degrees awarded. *Degree requirements:* For master's, comprehensive exam. *Entrance requirements:* For master's, GRE General Test, interview. Additional exam requirements/recommendations for international students: Required—TOEFL. *Application deadline:* For fall admission, 7/15 for domestic students; for spring admission, 11/15 for domestic students. Application fee: $50. Electronic applications accepted. *Financial support:* In 2006–07, 8 students received support. Scholarships/grants available. Support available to part-time students. Financial award application deadline: 6/1; financial award applicants required to submit FAFSA. *Unit head:* Dr. Mary McCullough, Head, 310-338-7312, E-mail: mmccullo@lmu.edu.

Loyola University Chicago, School of Education, Program in Administration and Supervision, Chicago, IL 60611-2196. Offers M Ed, Ed D, Certificate. MA and PhD offered through the Graduate School. Part-time programs available. *Faculty:* 4 full-time (all women), 12 part-time/adjunct (4 women). *Students:* 183. Average age 35. 52 applicants, 37% accepted, 12 enrolled. In 2006, 48 master's, 20 doctorates awarded. *Degree requirements:* For master's, comprehensive exam (M Ed), thesis (MA); for doctorate, thesis/dissertation, comprehensive exam. *Entrance requirements:* For master's, minimum GPA of 3.0, letters of recommendation, resumé, transcripts; for doctorate, GRE General Test, MAT, interview, minimum GPA of 3.0, letters of recommendation, resumé. Additional exam requirements/recommendations for international students: Required—TOEFL (minimum score 550 paper-based; 213 computer-based; 79 iBT). *Application deadline:* For fall admission, 7/1 for domestic and international students; for winter admission, 4/1 for domestic students; for spring admission, 11/1 for domestic and international students. Applications are processed on a rolling basis. Application fee: $50. Electronic applications accepted. *Financial support:* In 2006–07, 2 research assistantships with full tuition reimbursements (averaging $11,000 per year) were awarded; career-related internships or fieldwork and institutionally sponsored loans also available. Financial award application deadline: 2/15; financial award applicants required to submit FAFSA. *Faculty research:* Policy, leadership, staff development, school law, school administration, supervision, ethics. *Unit head:* Dr. Janis Fine, Director, 312-915-7022, Fax: 312-915-6980, E-mail: jfine@luc.edu. *Application contact:* Marie Rosin-Dittmar, Information Contact, 312-915-6800, E-mail: schleduc@luc.edu.

Loyola University Chicago, School of Education, Program in Instructional Leadership, Chicago, IL 60611-2196. Offers M Ed. Part-time and evening/weekend programs available. *Faculty:* 4 full-time (all women), 1 (woman) part-time/adjunct. *Students:* 14. Average age 38. 19 applicants, 74% accepted. In 2006, 1 degree awarded. *Degree requirements:* For master's, comprehensive exam. *Entrance requirements:* For master's, minimum GPA of 3.0, transcripts, letters of recommendation, resumé. Additional exam requirements/recommendations for international students: Required—TOEFL (minimum score 550 paper-based; 213 computer-based; 79 iBT). *Application deadline:* For fall admission, 7/1 for domestic students; for spring admission, 11/1 for domestic students. Applications are processed on a rolling basis. Application fee: $50. Electronic applications accepted. *Financial support:* Application deadline: 5/1. *Faculty research:* Staff development, school leadership, school change. *Unit head:* Dr. Janis Fine, Director, 312-915-7022, Fax: 312-915-6980, E-mail: jfine@luc.edu. *Application contact:* Marie Rosin-Dittmar, Information Contact, 312-915-6800, E-mail: schleduc@luc.edu.

Lynchburg College, Graduate Studies, School of Education and Human Development, Program in Educational Leadership, Lynchburg, VA 24501-3199. Offers M Ed. *Faculty:* 1 full-time (0 women), 3 part-time/adjunct (0 women). *Students:* 9 full-time (4 women), 93 part-time (73 women); includes 11 minority (10 African Americans, 1 Hispanic American), 26 international. In 2006, 37 degrees awarded. *Median time to degree:* Master's–2 years full-time, 4 years part-time. *Expenses:* Tuition: Full-time $6,300; part-time $350 per credit. Required fees: $100. *Financial support:* Fellowships, teaching assistantships, career-related internships or fieldwork, scholarships/grants, and unspecified assistantships available. *Unit head:* Dr. Roger Jones, Program Coordinator, 434-544-8444.

Lynn University, College of Business and Management, Boca Raton, FL 33431-5598. Offers aviation management (MBA); financial valuation and investment management (MBA); global leadership (PhD); hospitality management (MBA); international business (MBA); marketing (MBA); mass communication and media management (MBA); sports and athletics administration (MBA). Part-time and evening/weekend programs available. Postbaccalaureate distance learning degree programs offered. *Faculty:* 13 full-time (5 women), 7 part-time/adjunct (3 women). *Students:* 71 full-time (37 women), 113 part-time (47 women); includes 35 minority (13 African Americans, 6 Asian Americans or Pacific Islanders, 16 Hispanic Americans), 55 international. Average age 32. 114 applicants, 88% accepted, 71 enrolled. In 2006, 83 master's, 9 doctorates awarded. *Degree requirements:* For master's, project; for doctorate, thesis/dissertation, qualifying paper. *Entrance requirements:* For master's, GMAT or GRE, minimum undergraduate GPA of 3.0, resumé, 2 letters of recommendation; for doctorate, GRE or GMAT, minimum graduate GPA of 3.25, resumé, 2 letters of recommendation. Additional exam requirements/recommendations for international students: Required—TOEFL (minimum score 550 paper-based; 213 computer-based). *Application deadline:* Applications are processed on a rolling basis. Application fee: $50. Electronic applications accepted. *Expenses:* Tuition: Full-time $26,200. Required fees: $1,500. Tuition and fees vary according to class time, course load and degree level. *Financial support:* In 2006–07, 160 students received support. Career-related internships or fieldwork, Federal Work-Study, institutionally sponsored loans, scholarships/grants, tuition waivers (full and partial), and unspecified assistantships available. Support available to part-time students. Financial award application deadline: 8/1; financial award applicants required to submit FAFSA. *Faculty research:* Labor relations, dynamic balance in leisure-time skills, ethics in athletics, hotel development. *Unit head:* Dr. Russell Boisjoly, Dean, 561-237-7458, Fax: 561-237-7014, E-mail: rboisjoly@lynn.edu. *Application contact:* Dr. Larissa Baia, Assistant Director of Graduate Admissions, 561-237-7916, Fax: 561-237-7100, E-mail: admissionpm@lynn.edu.

Lynn University, Donald and Helen Ross College of Education, Boca Raton, FL 33431-5598. Offers exceptional student education (M Ed); global leadership (PhD). Part-time and evening/weekend programs available. *Faculty:* 5 full-time (3 women), 8 part-time/adjunct (4 women). *Students:* 29 full-time (22 women), 88 part-time (61 women); includes 30 minority (18 African Americans, 1 Asian American or Pacific Islander, 11 Hispanic Americans), 10 international. Average age 36. 48 applicants, 79% accepted, 33 enrolled. In 2006, 69 master's, 6 doctorates awarded. *Degree requirements:* For master's, thesis (for some programs); for doctorate, thesis/dissertation, qualifying paper. *Entrance requirements:* For master's, GRE, minimum undergraduate GPA of 3.0, resumé, 2 letters of recommendation; for doctorate, GRE or GMAT, minimum GPA of 3.25, resumé, 2 letters of recommendation. Additional exam requirements/recommendations for international students: Required—TOEFL (minimum score 550 paper-based; 213 computer-based). *Application deadline:* Applications are processed on a rolling basis. Application fee: $50. Electronic applications accepted. *Expenses:* Tuition: Full-time $26,200. Required fees: $1,500. Tuition and fees vary according to class time, course load and degree level. *Financial support:* Career-related internships or fieldwork, Federal Work-Study, institutionally sponsored loans, scholarships/grants, tuition waivers (partial), and unspecified assistantships available. Support available to part-time students. Financial award application deadline: 8/1; financial award applicants required to submit FAFSA. *Faculty research:* Non-traditional education, innovative curricula, multicultural education, simulation games. *Unit head:* Dr. Patrick Hartwick, Dean, 561-237-7441, Fax: 561-237-7792, E-mail: phartwick@lynn.edu. *Application contact:* Dr. Larissa Baia, Assistant Director of Graduate Admissions, 561-237-7916, Fax: 561-237-7100, E-mail: lbaia@lynn.edu.

Madonna University, Programs in Education, Livonia, MI 48150-1173. Offers Catholic school leadership (MSA); educational leadership (MSA); learning disabilities (MAT); literacy education (MAT); teaching and learning (MAT). *Accreditation:* NCATE. Part-time and evening/weekend programs available. *Faculty:* 11 full-time (7 women), 8 part-time/adjunct (2 women). *Students:* 2 full-time (both women), 154 part-time (134 women); includes 10 minority (6 African Americans, 1 Asian American or Pacific Islander, 3 Hispanic Americans), 2 international. Average age 36. 20 applicants, 85% accepted. In 2006, 133 degrees awarded. *Degree requirements:* For master's, thesis or alternative. *Application deadline:* For fall admission, 8/1 priority date for domestic students; for winter admission, 12/1 priority date for domestic students; for spring admission, 4/1 priority date for domestic students. Applications are processed on a rolling basis. Application fee: $25 ($200 for international students). Electronic applications accepted. *Financial support:* Career-related internships or fieldwork, Federal Work-Study, institutionally sponsored loans, and scholarships/grants available. Support available to part-time students. *Unit head:* Dr. Robert Kimball, Dean, 734-432-5652, E-mail: rkimball@madonna.edu. *Application contact:* Sandra Kellums, Coordinator of Graduate Admissions and Records, 734-432-5667, Fax: 734-432-5862, E-mail: skellum@madonna.edu.

Manhattan College, Graduate Division, School of Education, Program in School Building Leadership, Riverdale, NY 10471. Offers MS Ed, Diploma. Part-time and evening/weekend programs available. *Faculty:* 1 (woman) full-time, 3 part-time/adjunct (2 women). *Students:* 2 full-time (1 woman), 55 part-time (44 women). Average age 39. 40 applicants, 88% accepted, 30 enrolled. In 2006, 7 master's awarded. *Degree requirements:* For master's, thesis, internship. *Entrance requirements:* For master's, minimum GPA of 3.0, 3 years teaching, professional recommendation; for Diploma, minimum GPA of 3.0. Additional exam requirements/recommendations for international students: Required—TOEFL. *Application deadline:* For fall admission, 8/10 priority date for domestic students, 5/1 for international students; for spring admission, 1/7 priority date for domestic students, 9/1 for international students. Applications are processed on a rolling basis. Application fee: $50. *Financial support:* Scholarships/grants, tuition waivers (partial), and unspecified assistantships available. Financial award application deadline: 2/1. *Faculty research:* Distance learning and teacher efficacy, leadership and student achievement, professional development and student achievement, leadership development, professional development for teachers. *Unit head:* Sr. Remigia Kushner, Program Director, 718-862-7473, Fax: 718-862-7816, E-mail: sr.remigia.kushner@manhattan.edu. *Application contact:* Weldon Jackson.

Manhattanville College, Graduate Programs, School of Education, Program in Educational Leadership, Purchase, NY 10577-2132. Offers MPS. Part-time and evening/weekend programs available. In 2006, 4 degrees awarded. *Entrance requirements:* For master's, minimum undergraduate GPA of 3.0, 2 letters of recommendation. *Application deadline:* Applications are processed on a rolling basis. Application fee: $55. *Financial support:* Career-related internships or fieldwork and institutionally sponsored loans available. Support available to part-time students. *Application contact:* Alyce Ware Poli, Director of Admissions, 914-323-5142, Fax: 914-694-1732, E-mail: edschool@mville.edu.

Marian College of Fond du Lac, School of Education, Fond du Lac, WI 54935-4699. Offers educational leadership (MA, PhD); teacher development (MA). *Accreditation:* NCATE. Part-time programs available. *Faculty:* 15 full-time (5 women), 32 part-time/adjunct (20 women). *Students:* 30 full-time (16 women), 759 part-time (511 women); includes 37 minority (10 African Americans, 9 American Indian/Alaska Native, 6 Asian Americans or Pacific Islanders, 12 Hispanic Americans), 2 international. Average age 33. 96 applicants, 100% accepted, 96 enrolled. In 2006, 200 degrees awarded. *Degree requirements:* For master's, exam, field-based experience project, portfolio; for doctorate, thesis/dissertation, field-based experience, comprehensive exam. *Entrance requirements:* For master's, minimum GPA of 3.0, BA in education or related field, teaching license; for doctorate, GRE/MAT, resumé, 2 writing samples, interview. *Application deadline:* Applications are processed on a rolling basis. Application fee: $50. *Expenses:* Tuition: Part-time $310 per credit. Tuition and fees vary according to degree level and program. *Financial support:* In 2006–07, 197 students received support. Federal Work-Study and institutionally sponsored loans available. Support available to part-time students. Financial award application deadline: 3/1; financial award applicants required to submit FAFSA. *Faculty research:* At-risk youth, multicultural issues, values in education, teaching/learning strategies. *Unit head:* Dr. Kathryn Polmanteer, Dean, School of Education, 920-923-8099, Fax: 920-923-7663, E-mail: knpolmanteer94@mariancollege.edu. *Application contact:* Robert Bohnsack, Graduate Education Admissions, 920-923-8100, Fax: 920-923-7154, E-mail: bbohnsack@mariancollege.edu.

Marshall University, Academic Affairs Division, College of Education and Human Services, Graduate School of Education and Professional Development, Program in Leadership Studies, Huntington, WV 25755. Offers MA, Ed D, Ed S. Part-time and evening/weekend programs available. *Faculty:* 8 full-time (4 women), 6 part-time/adjunct (5 women). *Students:* 37 full-time (25 women), 206 part-time (134 women); includes 11 minority (7 African Americans, 2 American Indian/Alaska Native, 1 Asian American or Pacific Islander, 1 Hispanic American), 4 international. Average age 40. In 2006, 29 master's, 9 doctorates, 12 other advanced degrees awarded. *Degree requirements:* For master's, comprehensive or oral assessment, thesis optional. *Entrance requirements:* For master's, GRE General Test or MAT. Application fee: $40. *Financial support:* Career-related internships or fieldwork, Federal Work-Study,

tuition waivers (full), and unspecified assistantships available. Support available to part-time students. Financial award applicants required to submit FAFSA. *Unit head:* Dr. Michael Cunningham, Director, 800-642-9842 Ext. 61912, E-mail: mcunningham@marshall.edu. *Application contact:* Information Contact, 304-746-1900, Fax: 304-746-1902, E-mail: services@marshall.edu.

Marygrove College, Graduate Division, Department of Educational Leadership, Detroit, MI 48221-2599. Offers MA. Part-time and evening/weekend programs available. *Degree requirements:* For master's, research project. *Entrance requirements:* For master's, MAT, interview, minimum undergraduate GPA of 3.0.

Marymount University, School of Education and Human Services, Program in Catholic School Leadership, Arlington, VA 22207-4299. Offers M Ed, Certificate. Part-time and evening/weekend programs available. Postbaccalaureate distance learning degree programs offered (minimal on-campus study). *Students:* Average age 42. In 2006, 10 master's, 2 other advanced degrees awarded. *Degree requirements:* For master's, thesis or alternative. *Entrance requirements:* For master's, GRE General Test or MAT, 3 letters of recommendation, resumé, interview. Additional exam requirements/recommendations for international students: Required—TOEFL (minimum score 600 paper-based; 250 computer-based). Application fee: $40. Electronic applications accepted. *Expenses:* Tuition: Full-time $11,160; part-time $620 per credit. Required fees: $113; $630 per credit. *Financial support:* Research assistantships with full tuition reimbursements, career-related internships or fieldwork, scholarships/grants, and unspecified assistantships available. Support available to part-time students. Financial award applicants required to submit FAFSA. *Unit head:* Sr. Patricia Earl, Coordinator, 703-284-1517, E-mail: patricia.earl@marymount.edu.

Maryville University of Saint Louis, School of Education, St. Louis, MO 63141-7299. Offers art education (MA Ed); early childhood education (MA Ed); education (Ed D); elementary education (MA Ed); elementary education/English (MA Ed); environmental education (MA Ed); gifted education (MA Ed); middle grades education (MA Ed); reading specialist (MA Ed); secondary education (MA Ed), including educational leadership, secondary teaching and inquiry. *Accreditation:* NASAD; NCATE. Part-time and evening/weekend programs available. *Students:* 17 full-time (14 women), 168 part-time (129 women); includes 20 African Americans, 2 Asian Americans or Pacific Islanders, 1 Hispanic American, 2 international. Average age 37. 39 applicants, 95% accepted, 24 enrolled. In 2006, 37 degrees awarded. *Degree requirements:* For master's, thesis, project. *Entrance requirements:* For master's and doctorate, minimum GPA of 3.0, 3 professional recommendations. Additional exam requirements/recommendations for international students: Required—TOEFL (minimum score 550 paper-based). *Application deadline:* Applications are processed on a rolling basis. Application fee: $35 ($50 for international students). Electronic applications accepted. *Expenses:* Tuition: Full-time $17,800; part-time $555 per credit. Required fees: $55 per semester. Tuition and fees vary according to degree level and program. *Financial support:* Career-related internships or fieldwork, Federal Work-Study, tuition waivers (partial), and professional educator discounts available. Financial award application deadline: 7/31; financial award applicants required to submit FAFSA. *Faculty research:* Collaboration with public schools, preservice program development, mathematics, diversity, literacy. *Unit head:* Dr. Sam Hausfather, Dean, 314-529-9466, Fax: 314-529-9921, E-mail: shausfather@maryville.edu. *Application contact:* Dr. Lillian Curtis, Graduate Admissions Coordinator, 314-529-9542, Fax: 314-529-9921, E-mail: teachered@maryville.edu.

Marywood University, Academic Affairs, College of Education and Human Development, Department of Education, Program in Higher Education Administration, Scranton, PA 18509-1598. Offers MS. Part-time and evening/weekend programs available. *Students:* 2 full-time (both women), 8 part-time (4 women). Average age 30. 6 applicants, 100% accepted. In 2006, 4 degrees awarded. *Degree requirements:* For master's, thesis or alternative, internship/practicum. *Entrance requirements:* For master's, GRE or MAT. Additional exam requirements/recommendations for international students: Required—TOEFL (minimum score 550 paper-based; 213 computer-based). *Application deadline:* For fall admission, 4/15 priority date for domestic and international students; for spring admission, 11/15 priority date for domestic and international students. Applications are processed on a rolling basis. Application fee: $30. Electronic applications accepted. *Expenses:* Tuition: Part-time $672 per credit. Tuition and fees vary according to degree level, campus/location and program. *Financial support:* Research assistantships with tuition reimbursements, career-related internships or fieldwork, scholarships/grants, tuition waivers (partial), and unspecified assistantships available. Support available to part-time students. Financial award application deadline: 2/15; financial award applicants required to submit FAFSA. *Faculty research:* Integrated thematic instruction. *Application contact:* Dr. Deborah M. Flynn, Coordinator of Graduate Advising (Enrollment Management), 570-348-6211, E-mail: flynn@ac.marywood.edu.

Marywood University, Academic Affairs, College of Education and Human Development, Department of Education, Program in Instructional Leadership, Scranton, PA 18509-1598. Offers M Ed. *Students:* Average age 32. *Expenses:* Tuition: Part-time $672 per credit. Tuition and fees vary according to degree level, campus/location and program. *Application contact:* Dr. Deborah M. Flynn, Coordinator of Graduate Advising (Enrollment Management), 570-348-6211, E-mail: flynn@ac.marywood.edu.

Marywood University, Academic Affairs, College of Education and Human Development, Department of Education, Program in School Leadership, Scranton, PA 18509-1598. Offers MS. *Accreditation:* NCATE. Part-time and evening/weekend programs available. *Students:* Average age 35. In 2006, 3 degrees awarded. *Degree requirements:* For master's, thesis or alternative, internship. *Entrance requirements:* For master's, GRE or MAT, interview. Additional exam requirements/recommendations for international students: Required—TOEFL (minimum score 550 paper-based; 213 computer-based). *Application deadline:* For fall admission, 4/15 priority date for domestic and international students; for spring admission, 11/15 priority date for domestic and international students. Applications are processed on a rolling basis. Application fee: $30. Electronic applications accepted. *Expenses:* Tuition: Part-time $672 per credit. Tuition and fees vary according to degree level, campus/location and program. *Financial support:* Research assistantships with tuition reimbursements, career-related internships or fieldwork, scholarships/grants, tuition waivers (partial), and unspecified assistantships available. Support available to part-time students. Financial award application deadline: 2/15; financial award applicants required to submit FAFSA. *Faculty research:* School board leadership and development, site-based decision making, educational administration. *Application contact:* Dr. Deborah M. Flynn, Coordinator of Graduate Advising (Enrollment Management), 570-348-6211, E-mail: flynn@ac.marywood.edu.

Marywood University, Academic Affairs, College of Education and Human Development, Department of Human Development, Emphasis in Educational Administration, Scranton, PA 18509-1598. Offers PhD. *Students:* Average age 41. *Expenses:* Tuition: Part-time $672 per credit. Tuition and fees vary according to degree level, campus/location and program. *Unit head:* Dr. Marie Loftus, Director, Department of Human Development, 570-348-6292, E-mail: loftus@es.marywood.edu.

Marywood University, Academic Affairs, College of Education and Human Development, Department of Human Development, Emphasis in Higher Education Administration, Scranton, PA 18509-1598. Offers PhD. *Students:* 2 full-time (1 woman), 20 part-time (14 women); includes 1 minority (Hispanic American), 2 international. Average age 37. *Expenses:* Tuition: Part-time $672 per credit. Tuition and fees vary according to degree level, campus/location and program. *Unit head:* Dr. Marie Loftus, Director, Department of Human Development, 570-348-6292, E-mail: loftus@es.marywood.edu.

Marywood University, Academic Affairs, College of Education and Human Development, Department of Human Development, Emphasis in Instructional Leadership, Scranton, PA 18509-1598. Offers PhD. *Students:* 2 full-time (both women), 23 part-time (18 women); includes 2 minority (1 African American, 1 Asian American or Pacific Islander), 1 international. Average age 43. *Expenses:* Tuition: Part-time $672 per credit. Tuition and fees vary according to

Educational Administration

Marywood University (continued)
degree level, campus/location and program. *Unit head:* Dr. Marie Loftus, Director, Department of Human Development, 570-348-6292, E-mail: loftus@es.marywood.edu.

Massachusetts College of Liberal Arts, Program in Education, North Adams, MA 01247-4100. Offers curriculum and instruction (M Ed); educational administration (M Ed); reading (M Ed); special education (M Ed). Part-time and evening/weekend programs available. *Degree requirements:* For master's, thesis. *Entrance requirements:* For master's, writing sample. *Faculty research:* Anxiety, methodology, mainstreaming.

McDaniel College, Graduate and Professional Studies, Program in Educational Administration, Westminster, MD 21157-4390. Offers MS. Part-time and evening/weekend programs available. *Degree requirements:* For master's, portfolio, thesis optional. *Entrance requirements:* For master's, GRE General Test, MAT, or NTE/PRAXIS I. Additional exam requirements/recommendations for international students: Required—TOEFL (minimum score 213 computer-based).

McGill University, Faculty of Graduate and Postdoctoral Studies, Faculty of Education, Department of Integrated Studies in Education, Montréal, QC H3A 2T5, Canada. Offers culture and values in education (MA, PhD); curriculum (MA); educational leadership (Certificate, Diploma); educational studies (PhD); integrated studies in education (M Ed); leadership (MA); second language education (MA, PhD). *Degree requirements:* For master's, thesis (for some programs), registration; for doctorate, thesis/dissertation, comprehensive exam, registration. *Entrance requirements:* For master's, 2 years of relevant experience, minimum GPA of 3.0; for doctorate, minimum GPA of 3.0, acquisition of prospective supervisor; for other advanced degree, minimum GPA of 3.0. Additional exam requirements/recommendations for international students: Required—TOEFL (minimum score 580 paper-based; 237 computer-based).

McNeese State University, Graduate School, College of Education, Department of Educational Leadership and Instructional Technology, Program in Educational Leadership, Lake Charles, LA 70609. Offers M Ed, Ed S. Evening/weekend programs available. *Faculty:* 5 full-time (0 women). *Students:* 10 full-time (8 women), 69 part-time (48 women); includes 13 minority (11 African Americans, 2 Hispanic Americans). In 2006, 64 master's, 2 other advanced degrees awarded. *Degree requirements:* For Ed S, comprehensive exam. *Entrance requirements:* For master's, GRE, teaching certificate, 3 years full-time teaching experience; for Ed S, teaching certificate, 3 years of teaching experience, 1 year of administration or supervision experience. *Application deadline:* For fall admission, 5/15 priority date for domestic students. Applications are processed on a rolling basis. Application fee: $20 ($30 for international students). *Expenses:* Tuition, area resident: Full-time $2,226; part-time $193 per hour. Required fees: $919; $106 per hour. *Financial support:* Fellowships available. Financial award application deadline: 5/1. *Unit head:* Dr. Sharon Van Metre, Head, Department of Educational Leadership and Instructional Technology, 337-475-5423, Fax: 337-475-5402, E-mail: svanmetr@mcneese.edu.

Memorial University of Newfoundland, School of Graduate Studies, Faculty of Education, St. John's, NL A1C 5S7, Canada. Offers counseling psychology (M Ed); curriculum, teaching, and learning studies (M Ed); education (PhD); educational leadership studies (M Ed); information technology (M Ed); post-secondary studies (M Ed, Diploma), including health professional education (Diploma). Part-time programs available. *Degree requirements:* For master's, internship, paper folio, project, thesis optional; for doctorate, thesis/dissertation, thesis seminar, oral defense of thesis, comprehensive exam. *Entrance requirements:* For master's, undergraduate degree with at least 2nd class standing, 1-2 years work experience; for doctorate, minimum A average in graduate course work, MA in education, 2 years professional experience; for Diploma, 2nd class degree, 2 years of work experience with adult learners, appropriate academic qualifications and work experience in a health-related field. Electronic applications accepted. *Faculty research:* Critical thinking, literacy, cognitive studies and counseling, educational change, technology in instruction.

Mercer University, Graduate Studies, Cecil B. Day Campus, Tift College of Education, Macon, GA 31207-0003. Offers early childhood education (M Ed, MAT); educational leadership (M Ed, PhD); middle grades education (M Ed, MAT); reading education (M Ed); secondary education (M Ed, MAT); teacher leadership (Ed S). Part-time and evening/weekend programs available. *Faculty:* 13 full-time (6 women), 7 part-time/adjunct (3 women). *Students:* 31 full-time (23 women), 211 part-time (174 women); includes 111 minority (101 African Americans, 2 American Indian/Alaska Native, 6 Asian Americans or Pacific Islanders, 2 Hispanic Americans), 2 international. Average age 33. In 2006, 57 master's, 4 other advanced degrees awarded. *Degree requirements:* For master's and Ed S, research project; for doctorate, thesis/dissertation. *Entrance requirements:* For master's, GRE or MAT, minimum undergraduate GPA of 2.75; for doctorate, GRE; for Ed S, GRE or MAT, minimum GPA of 3.25, 3 years of teaching experience. *Application deadline:* For fall admission, 8/1 for domestic and international students; for spring admission, 12/1 for domestic and international students. Applications are processed on a rolling basis. Application fee: $25. *Expenses: Contact institution. Financial support:* Federal Work-Study available. Support available to part-time students. Financial award application deadline: 5/1. *Faculty research:* Educational computing, content area reading, concept learning, importance of play for young children, multicultural literature. *Unit head:* Dr. Carl R. Martray, Dean, 478-301-5397, Fax: 478-301-2280, E-mail: martray_cr@mercer.edu. *Application contact:* Dr. Allison Gilmore, Associate Dean for Graduate Teacher Education, 678-547-6330, Fax: 678-547-6055, E-mail: gilmore_a@mercer.edu.

Mercer University, Graduate Studies, Macon Campus, Tift College of Education, Macon, GA 31207-0003. Offers collaborative education (M Ed); educational leadership (M Ed, PhD). Part-time and evening/weekend programs available. *Faculty:* 13 full-time (6 women), 4 part-time/adjunct (3 women). *Students:* 3 full-time (all women), 68 part-time (49 women); includes 23 minority (22 African Americans, 1 American Indian/Alaska Native). Average age 31. 25 applicants, 68% accepted, 11 enrolled. In 2006, 19 degrees awarded. *Degree requirements:* For master's, research project report. *Entrance requirements:* For master's, GRE or MAT, minimum GPA of 2.75; for doctorate, GRE. Additional exam requirements/recommendations for international students: Required—TOEFL. *Application deadline:* For fall admission, 8/1 for domestic students; for spring admission, 12/1 for domestic students. Applications are processed on a rolling basis. Application fee: $25. *Expenses: Contact institution. Financial support:* Federal Work-Study and institutionally sponsored loans available. Support available to part-time students. Financial award application deadline: 5/1. *Faculty research:* Teacher effectiveness, specific learning disabilities, inclusion. *Unit head:* Dr. Carl R. Martray, Dean, 478-301-5397, Fax: 478-301-2280, E-mail: martray_cr@mercer.edu. *Application contact:* Dr. Penny Elkins, Associate Dean, 678-547-6556, Fax: 678-547-6389, E-mail: elkins_pl@mercer.edu.

Mercy College, Division of Education, Dobbs Ferry, NY 10522-1189. Offers adolescence education: grades 7-12 (MS); applied behavior analysis (MS); bilingual education (MS); childhood education: grades 1-6 (MS); early childhood education: birth—grade 2 (MS); education (MS); elementary education (MS); learning technology (MS); middle childhood education: grades 5-9 (MS); reading (MS); school administration and supervision (MS); school building leadership (MS); school business administration (MS); secondary education (MS); special education (MS); students with disabilities: grades 5-9 (MS); students with disabilities: grades 7-12 (MS); teaching English to speakers of other languages (MS); teaching literacy: birth—grade 6 (MS); teaching literacy: grades 5-12 (MS); urban education (MS). *Students:* 572 full-time (467 women), 1,719 part-time (1,287 women); includes 943 minority (470 African Americans, 7 American Indian/Alaska Native, 48 Asian Americans or Pacific Islanders, 418 Hispanic Americans), 6 international. Average age 33. In 2006, 1090 degrees awarded. *Entrance requirements:* For master's, teaching certificate. *Application deadline:* For fall admission, 2/1 for domestic students. Applications are processed on a rolling basis. Application fee: $37. *Expenses: Contact institution.* Tuition and fees vary according to program. *Financial support:* Institutionally sponsored loans, scholarships/grants, and unspecified assistantships available. Support available to part-time students. *Faculty research:* Distance learning, literacy, assessment, community schools, impact of staff development. *Unit head:* Dr. William Prattella, Chairperson, 914-674-7555, Fax: 914-674-7352, E-mail: wprattella@mercy.edu. *Application contact:* Kathleen Jackson, Director of Admissions, 800-Mercy-NY, Fax: 914-674-7382, E-mail: admissions@mercy.edu.

Mercyhurst College, Graduate Program, Program in Special Education, Erie, PA 16546. Offers bilingual/bicultural special education (MS); educational leadership (Certificate); special education (MS). Part-time and evening/weekend programs available. *Degree requirements:* For master's, thesis optional. *Entrance requirements:* For master's, GRE General Test, MAT, or minimum GPA of 3.0, interview. Additional exam requirements/recommendations for international students: Required—TOEFL. Electronic applications accepted. *Faculty research:* College age learning disabled program, teacher preparation/collaboration, applied behavior analysis, special education policy issues.

Miami University, Graduate School, School of Education and Allied Professions, Department of Educational Leadership, Program in Educational Administration, Oxford, OH 45056. Offers Ed D, PhD. *Accreditation:* NCATE. *Degree requirements:* For doctorate, thesis/dissertation, final exams, comprehensive exam. *Entrance requirements:* For doctorate, MAT, minimum undergraduate GPA of 2.75, graduate GPA of 3.0.

Miami University, Graduate School, School of Education and Allied Professions, Department of Educational Leadership, Program in Educational Leadership, Oxford, OH 45056. Offers M Ed. *Degree requirements:* For master's, oral or written exam.

Michigan State University, The Graduate School, College of Education, Department of Educational Administration, East Lansing, MI 48824. Offers higher, adult and lifelong education (MA, PhD); K–12 educational administration (MA, PhD, Ed S); student affairs administration (MA). Part-time programs available. *Faculty:* 20 full-time (9 women). *Students:* 158 full-time (103 women), 181 part-time (95 women); includes 70 minority (42 African Americans, 4 American Indian/Alaska Native, 10 Asian Americans or Pacific Islanders, 14 Hispanic Americans), 44 international. Average age 35. 190 applicants, 54% accepted. In 2006, 109 master's, 29 doctorates awarded. *Entrance requirements:* Additional exam requirements/recommendations for international students: Required—TOEFL. Electronic applications accepted. *Expenses:* Tuition, state resident: part-time $346 per credit hour. Tuition, nonresident: part-time $730 per credit hour. Tuition and fees vary according to program. *Financial support:* In 2006–07, 40 fellowships with tuition reimbursements, 50 research assistantships with tuition reimbursements (averaging $13,143 per year), 6 teaching assistantships with tuition reimbursements (averaging $13,228 per year) were awarded. Total annual research expenditures: $1.5 million. *Unit head:* Dr. Marilyn J. Amey, Chairperson, 517-355-4538, Fax: 517-353-6393, E-mail: amey@msu.edu. *Application contact:* Graduate Admissions Assistant, E-mail: haleadm@msu.edu.

Middle Tennessee State University, College of Graduate Studies, College of Education and Behavioral Science, Department of Educational Leadership, Major in Administration and Supervision, Murfreesboro, TN 37132. Offers M Ed, Ed S. Part-time and evening/weekend programs available. Postbaccalaureate distance learning degree programs offered. *Students:* 17 full-time (11 women), 194 part-time (136 women); includes 33 minority (31 African Americans, 2 American Indian/Alaska Native). 40 applicants, 98% accepted. In 2006, 65 master's, 30 other advanced degrees awarded. *Degree requirements:* For master's, comprehensive exam. *Entrance requirements:* For master's and Ed S, GRE or MAT. Additional exam requirements/recommendations for international students: Required—TOEFL (minimum score 525 paper-based; 195 computer-based). *Application deadline:* For fall admission, 8/1 priority date for domestic students. Applications are processed on a rolling basis. Application fee: $25. Electronic applications accepted. *Financial support:* Application deadline: 5/1. *Unit head:* Dr. James Huffman, Chair, Department of Educational Leadership, 615-898-2855, Fax: 615-898-2859.

Midwestern State University, Graduate Studies, College of Education, Program in Educational Leadership and Technology, Wichita Falls, TX 76308. Offers ME. Part-time and evening/weekend programs available. *Faculty:* 11 full-time (7 women), 3 part-time/adjunct (2 women). *Students:* 1 full-time (0 women), 28 part-time (15 women); includes 3 minority (1 African American, 2 Hispanic Americans). Average age 38. 5 applicants, 80% accepted, 1 enrolled. In 2006, 23 degrees awarded. *Degree requirements:* For master's, comprehensive exam. *Entrance requirements:* For master's, GRE General Test or MAT. Additional exam requirements/recommendations for international students: Required—TOEFL (minimum score 550 paper-based; 213 computer-based). *Application deadline:* For fall admission, 7/1 for domestic students, 4/1 for international students; for spring admission, 11/1 for domestic students, 8/1 for international students. Applications are processed on a rolling basis. Application fee: $35 ($50 for international students). Electronic applications accepted. *Financial support:* In 2006–07, 17 students received support. Career-related internships or fieldwork, Federal Work-Study, institutionally sponsored loans, scholarships/grants, tuition waivers (partial), and unspecified assistantships available. Support available to part-time students. Financial award application deadline: 5/1; financial award applicants required to submit FAFSA. *Unit head:* Dr. Michael Land, Chair, 940-397-4139, Fax: 940-397-4694, E-mail: michael.land@mwsu.edu. *Application contact:* Dr. Martha Burger, Admissions Office, 940-397-6220, Fax: 940-397-4694, E-mail: martha.burger@mwsu.edu.

Mills College, Graduate Studies, Education Department, Oakland, CA 94613-1000. Offers administration (Ed D); child life in health care settings (MA); early childhood education (MA); education (MA), including curriculum and instruction, elementary education, English education, mathematics education, science education, secondary education, social sciences education, teaching. Part-time and evening/weekend programs available. *Faculty:* 10 full-time (7 women), 15 part-time/adjunct (12 women). *Students:* 192 full-time (153 women), 41 part-time (36 women); includes 62 minority (28 African Americans, 13 Asian Americans or Pacific Islanders, 21 Hispanic Americans), 2 international. Average age 34. 160 applicants, 74% accepted, 73 enrolled. In 2006, 52 master's, 1 doctorate awarded. Terminal master's awarded for partial completion of doctoral program. *Degree requirements:* For master's, comprehensive exam. *Entrance requirements:* For doctorate, GRE General Test. Additional exam requirements/recommendations for international students: Required—TOEFL. *Application deadline:* For fall admission, 2/1 for domestic and international students; for spring admission, 11/1 for domestic and international students. Applications are processed on a rolling basis. Application fee: $50. Electronic applications accepted. *Financial support:* In 2006–07, 56 fellowships with tuition reimbursements (averaging $2,700 per year), 15 teaching assistantships (averaging $6,350 per year) were awarded; career-related internships or fieldwork, institutionally sponsored loans, scholarships/grants, and residence awards also available. Support available to part-time students. Financial award application deadline: 2/1; financial award applicants required to submit CSS PROFILE or FAFSA. *Faculty research:* Child development, gender and education, public policy, cross-cultural development, development of literacy. *Unit head:* Joseph Kahne, Chairperson, 510-430-3190, Fax: 510-430-3314, E-mail: grad-studies@mills.edu. *Application contact:* Randy McGlauthing, Director of Graduate Admissions, 510-430-2355, Fax: 510-430-2159, E-mail: rmglaut@mills.edu.

Minnesota State University Mankato, College of Graduate Studies, College of Education, Department of Educational Leadership, Program in Experiential Education, Mankato, MN 56001. Offers educational administration (Certificate); elementary school administration (SP); experiential education (MS); secondary administration (SP). *Accreditation:* NCATE. Part-time and evening/weekend programs available. *Students:* 29 full-time (17 women), 22 part-time (10 women). Average age 37. In 2006, 24 degrees awarded. *Degree requirements:* For master's, thesis or alternative; for other advanced degree, thesis. *Entrance requirements:* For master's, minimum GPA of 3.0 during previous 2 years; for other advanced degree, minimum GPA of 3.0. Additional exam requirements/recommendations for international students: Required—TOEFL. *Application deadline:* For fall admission, 7/1 priority date for domestic students; for spring admission, 11/1 for domestic students. Applications are processed on a rolling basis. Application fee: $40. Electronic applications accepted. *Financial support:* Research assistantships with full tuition reimbursements, teaching assistantships with full tuition reimbursements, career-related internships or fieldwork, Federal Work-Study, and unspecified assistantships available. Support available to part-time students. Financial award application deadline: 3/15; financial award applicants required to submit FAFSA. *Unit head:* Dr. Scott Wurdinger, Chairperson, 507-389-1116. *Application contact:* 507-389-2321, E-mail: grad@mnsu.edu.

Minnesota State University Moorhead, Graduate Studies, College of Education and Human Services, Program in Educational Leadership, Moorhead, MN 56563-0002. Offers MS, Ed S. *Accreditation:* NCATE. Part-time programs available. *Faculty:* 1 full-time (0 women), 6 part-time/adjunct (1 woman). *Students:* 7 full-time (5 women), 38 part-time (18 women), 1 international. 16 applicants, 100% accepted. In 2006, 4 degrees awarded. *Degree requirements:* For master's, final oral exam, project or thesis. *Entrance requirements:* For master's, 2 letters of recommendation, minimum GPA of 3.0. Additional exam requirements/recommendations for international students: Required—TOEFL (minimum score 550 paper-based; 213 computer-based). *Application deadline:* For fall admission, 4/15 priority date for domestic students, 3/15 for international students; for spring admission, 11/1 priority date for domestic students. Applications are processed on a rolling basis. Application fee: $20. Electronic applications accepted. *Financial support:* In 2006–07, 1 research assistantship (averaging $2,000 per year) was awarded; Federal Work-Study and unspecified assistantships also available. Financial award application deadline: 7/15; financial award applicants required to submit FAFSA. *Unit head:* Dr. Dorothy Suomala, 218-477-2530, E-mail: suomalad@mnstate.edu.

Mississippi College, Graduate School, School of Education, Department of Teacher Education and Leadership, Clinton, MS 39058. Offers art (M Ed); biological science (M Ed); business education (M Ed); computer science (M Ed); dyslexia therapy (M Ed); educational leadership (M Ed, Ed S); elementary education (M Ed, Ed S); English (M Ed); higher education administration (MS); mathematics (M Ed); secondary education (M Ed); social studies (history) (M Ed); teaching arts (M Ed). Part-time programs available. *Faculty:* 9 full-time (5 women), 14 part-time/adjunct (10 women). *Students:* 52 full-time (36 women), 286 part-time (247 women); includes 173 minority (171 African Americans, 1 American Indian/Alaska Native, 1 Hispanic American), 1 international. Average age 32. In 2006, 131 degrees awarded. *Degree requirements:* For master's, thesis optional. *Entrance requirements:* For master's, NTE. Additional exam requirements/recommendations for international students: Recommended—IELTS. *Application deadline:* Applications are processed on a rolling basis. Application fee: $25. Electronic applications accepted. *Expenses:* Tuition: Full-time $7,290; part-time $405 per hour. Required fees: $150 per term. Tuition and fees vary according to campus/location and program. *Financial support:* Teaching assistantships, career-related internships or fieldwork, Federal Work-Study, scholarships/grants, and unspecified assistantships available. Support available to part-time students. Financial award applicants required to submit FAFSA. *Unit head:* Dr. Tom Williams, Chair, 601-925-3844, E-mail: twilliams@mc.edu.

Mississippi State University, College of Education, Department of Instructional Systems, Leadership, and Workforce Development, Mississippi State, MS 39762. Offers instructional technology (MSIT); technology (MS, Ed D, PhD, Ed S); workforce education leadership (MS). *Faculty:* 20 full-time (7 women), 1 (woman) part-time/adjunct. *Students:* 48 full-time (30 women), 62 part-time (48 women); includes 54 minority (53 African Americans, 1 Hispanic American). Average age 34. 28 applicants, 75% accepted, 17 enrolled. In 2006, 65 master's, 8 doctorates awarded. *Degree requirements:* For master's, comprehensive oral or written exam, thesis optional; for doctorate, thesis/dissertation, comprehensive oral and written exam. *Entrance requirements:* For master's, GRE, minimum GPA of 2.75 in junior and senior courses; for doctorate, GRE. Additional exam requirements/recommendations for international students: Required—TOEFL. *Application deadline:* For fall admission, 7/1 for domestic students; for spring admission, 11/1 for domestic students. Applications are processed on a rolling basis. Application fee: $30. *Expenses:* Tuition, state resident: full-time $4,550; part-time $253 per hour. Tuition, nonresident: full-time $10,552; part-time $584 per hour. International tuition: $10,882 full-time. Tuition and fees vary according to course load. *Financial support:* In 2006–07, 6 teaching assistantships with full tuition reimbursements (averaging $8,923 per year) were awarded; Federal Work-Study, institutionally sponsored loans, and unspecified assistantships also available. Financial award applicants required to submit FAFSA. *Faculty research:* Computer technology, nontraditional students, interactive video, instructional technology, educational leadership. *Unit head:* Dr. Linda Cornelius, Interim Head, 662-325-2281, Fax: 662-325-7599, E-mail: lcornelius@colled.msstate.edu. *Application contact:* Dr. Phil Bonfanti, Director of Admissions, 662-325-4104, Fax: 662-325-8872, E-mail: admit@msstate.edu.

Missouri State University, Graduate College, College of Education, Department of Educational Administration, Springfield, MO 65804-0094. Offers director of special education (Ed S); educational administration (MS Ed, Ed S); elementary education (MS Ed); elementary principal (Ed S); secondary education (MS Ed); secondary principal (Ed S); special education (MS Ed); superintendent (Ed S). Part-time and evening/weekend programs available. *Faculty:* 6 full-time (1 woman), 3 part-time/adjunct (0 women). *Students:* 10 full-time (8 women), 143 part-time (94 women); includes 1 minority (African American), 1 international. Average age 37. 13 applicants, 92% accepted, 10 enrolled. In 2006, 33 master's, 17 other advanced degrees awarded. *Degree requirements:* For master's and Ed S, thesis or alternative, comprehensive exam. *Entrance requirements:* For master's, minimum GPA of 2.75; for Ed S, GRE General Test, MAT, minimum GPA of 2.75. Additional exam requirements/recommendations for international students: Required—TOEFL (minimum score 550 paper-based; 213 computer-based; 79 iBT). *Application deadline:* For fall admission, 7/20 priority date for domestic students; for spring admission, 12/20 priority date for domestic students. Applications are processed on a rolling basis. Application fee: $35. Electronic applications accepted. *Expenses:* Tuition, state resident: full-time $3,582; part-time $199 per credit hour. Tuition, nonresident: full-time $6,984; part-time $199 per credit hour. Required fees: $548. Full-time tuition and fees vary according to course level, course load, program and reciprocity agreements. *Financial support:* In 2006–07, 1 teaching assistantship with full tuition reimbursement (averaging $6,780 per year) was awarded; career-related internships or fieldwork, Federal Work-Study, scholarships/grants, and unspecified assistantships also available. Financial award application deadline: 3/31; financial award applicants required to submit FAFSA. *Unit head:* Dr. Charles Barke, Acting Head, 417-836-5392, Fax: 417-836-6905, E-mail: edadmin@missouristate.edu.

Monmouth University, Graduate School, School of Education, West Long Branch, NJ 07764-1898. Offers educational counseling (MS Ed); elementary education (MAT), including certified teachers, non-certified teachers; learning disabilities-teacher consultant (Certificate); principal studies (MS Ed); reading specialist (MS Ed, Certificate); special education (MS Ed); supervisor (Certificate); teacher of the handicapped (Certificate). Part-time and evening/weekend programs available. *Faculty:* 24 full-time (15 women), 25 part-time/adjunct (17 women). *Students:* 169 full-time (133 women), 426 part-time (374 women); includes 45 minority (21 African Americans, 2 American Indian/Alaska Native, 2 Asian Americans or Pacific Islanders, 20 Hispanic Americans). Average age 31. 355 applicants, 96% accepted, 138 enrolled. In 2006, 209 degrees awarded. *Entrance requirements:* For master's, minimum GPA of 3.0 in major, 2.75 overall. Additional exam requirements/recommendations for international students: Required—TOEFL (minimum score 550 paper-based; 213 computer-based; 79 iBT), IELTS (minimum score 5), MELAB 77, Cambridge A, B, C. *Application deadline:* For fall admission, 7/15 priority date for domestic students; for spring admission, 11/15 priority date for domestic students. Applications are processed on a rolling basis. Application fee: $50. Electronic applications accepted. *Expenses:* Tuition: Full-time $12,780; part-time $710 per credit. Required fees: $628; $314 per term. *Financial support:* In 2006–07, 221 fellowships (averaging $2,053 per year), 17 research assistantships (averaging $6,527 per year) were awarded; career-related internships or fieldwork, scholarships/grants, tuition waivers (partial), and unspecified assistantships also available. Support available to part-time students. Financial award application deadline: 3/1; financial award applicants required to submit FAFSA. *Faculty research:* Multicultural literacy, science and mathematics teaching strategies, teacher as reflective practitioner, children with disabilities, varied contexts of learning. *Unit head:* Dr. Lynn Romeo, Program Director, 732-571-4484, Fax: 732-263-5277, E-mail: lromeo@monmouth.edu. *Application contact:* Kevin Roane, Director, Office of Graduate Admission, 732-571-3452, Fax: 732-263-5123, E-mail: gradadm@monmouth.edu.

Montclair State University, The Graduate School, College of Education and Human Services, Department of Counseling, Human Development, and Educational Leadership, Montclair, NJ 07043-1624. Offers administration and supervision (MA), including administration and supervision, educator/trainer; advanced counseling (Certificate); counseling and guidance (MA), including addictions counseling, community counseling, student affairs; school administrator (Certificate); school business administrator (Certificate); school counselor (Certificate); substance awareness coordinator (Certificate). *Accreditation:* NCATE. Part-time and evening/weekend programs available. *Faculty:* 14 full-time (10 women), 18 part-time/adjunct (7 women). *Students:* 144 full-time (122 women), 551 part-time (406 women); includes 142 minority (66 African Americans, 18 Asian Americans or Pacific Islanders, 58 Hispanic Americans), 5 international. Average age 33. 217 applicants, 56% accepted, 90 enrolled. In 2006, 65 master's, 10 other advanced degrees awarded. *Degree requirements:* For master's, thesis or alternative, comprehensive exam. *Entrance requirements:* For master's, GRE General Test, interview, 2 letters of recommendation. Additional exam requirements/recommendations for international students: Required—TOEFL (minimum score 83 computer-based). *Application deadline:* For fall admission, 6/1 for international students; for spring admission, 10/1 for international students. Applications are processed on a rolling basis. Application fee: $60. Electronic applications accepted. *Expenses:* Tuition, state resident: part-time $450 per credit. Tuition, nonresident: part-time $682 per credit. Tuition and fees vary according to degree level and program. *Financial support:* In 2006–07, 14 research assistantships with full tuition reimbursements (averaging $7,000 per year) were awarded; Federal Work-Study, scholarships/grants, and unspecified assistantships also available. Support available to part-time students. Financial award application deadline: 3/1; financial award applicants required to submit FAFSA. *Faculty research:* K-12 education, data collection. Total annual research expenditures: $24,000. *Unit head:* Dr. Catherine Roland, Chairperson, 973-655-7216, E-mail: rolandc@mail.montclair.edu.

Morehead State University, Graduate Programs, College of Education, Department of Professional Programs in Education, Program in School Administration, Morehead, KY 40351. Offers MA, Ed S. Part-time and evening/weekend programs available. *Students:* 4 full-time (all women), 84 part-time (44 women); includes 1 minority (African American) Average age 32. In 2006, 57 degrees awarded. *Degree requirements:* For master's, national and state exam. *Entrance requirements:* For master's, GRE General Test, minimum GPA of 3.2, 3 years of teaching experience. Additional exam requirements/recommendations for international students: Required—TOEFL (minimum score 500 paper-based; 173 computer-based). *Application deadline:* For fall admission, 8/1 priority date for domestic and international students; for spring admission, 12/1 priority date for domestic and international students. Applications are processed on a rolling basis. Application fee: $0. Electronic applications accepted. *Financial support:* In 2006–07, teaching assistantships (averaging $6,000 per year); career-related internships or fieldwork and Federal Work-Study also available. Financial award application deadline: 4/1. *Application contact:* Michelle Barber, Graduate Admissions Counselor, 606-783-2039, Fax: 606-783-5061, E-mail: m.barber@moreheadstate.edu.

Morgan State University, School of Graduate Studies, School of Education and Urban Studies, Department of Teacher Education and Administration, Program in Educational Administration and Supervision, Baltimore, MD 21251. Offers MS. *Accreditation:* NCATE. Part-time and evening/weekend programs available. *Students:* 8. Average age 35. In 2006, 1 degree awarded. *Degree requirements:* For master's, thesis optional. *Entrance requirements:* For master's, GRE General Test or MAT. *Application deadline:* For fall admission, 2/1 priority date for domestic students; for spring admission, 10/1 priority date for domestic students. Applications are processed on a rolling basis. Application fee: $0. *Expenses:* Tuition, state resident: part-time $272 per credit. Tuition, nonresident: part-time $478 per credit. Required fees: $38 per credit. *Financial support:* Fellowships available. Financial award application deadline: 4/1. *Faculty research:* Multicultural education, cooperative learning, psychology of cognition. *Unit head:* Dr. Flossie Windley, Graduate Coordinator, 443-885-2982, E-mail: fwindley@moac.morgan.edu. *Application contact:* Dr. Maurice C. Taylor, Dean, 443-885-3185, Fax: 443-885-8226, E-mail: mctaylor@moac.morgan.edu.

Morgan State University, School of Graduate Studies, School of Education and Urban Studies, Program in Higher Education Administration, Baltimore, MD 21251. Offers PhD. *Students:* 23. In 2006, 2 degrees awarded. *Degree requirements:* For doctorate, thesis/dissertation, comprehensive exam. *Entrance requirements:* For doctorate, GRE General Test or MAT, minimum GPA of 3.0. *Application deadline:* For fall admission, 2/1 priority date for domestic students; for spring admission, 10/1 priority date for domestic students. Applications are processed on a rolling basis. Application fee: $0. *Expenses:* Tuition, state resident: part-time $272 per credit. Tuition, nonresident: part-time $478 per credit. Required fees: $38 per credit. *Financial support:* Fellowships, research assistantships, teaching assistantships, career-related internships or fieldwork, Federal Work-Study, institutionally sponsored loans, scholarships/grants, health care benefits, tuition waivers (full and partial), and unspecified assistantships available. Support available to part-time students. Financial award application deadline: 2/1. *Unit head:* Dr. Howard Simmons, Chairperson, Advanced Studies Leadership and Policy, 443-885-1969, E-mail: hsimmons@moac.morgan.edu. *Application contact:* Dr. Maurice C. Taylor, Dean, 443-885-3185, Fax: 443-885-8226, E-mail: mctaylor@moac.morgan.edu.

Morgan State University, School of Graduate Studies, School of Education and Urban Studies, Program in Higher Education-Community College Leadership, Baltimore, MD 21251. Offers Ed D. *Accreditation:* NCATE. Part-time and evening/weekend programs available. *Faculty:* 5 full-time (1 woman), 4 part-time/adjunct (1 woman). *Students:* 45. Average age 40. 29 applicants, 28% accepted. In 2006, 6 degrees awarded. *Degree requirements:* For doctorate, thesis/dissertation, comprehensive exam. *Entrance requirements:* For doctorate, GRE General Test or MAT. Additional exam requirements/recommendations for international students: Required—TOEFL (minimum score 550 paper-based; 213 computer-based). *Application deadline:* For fall admission, 2/1 priority date for domestic students; for spring admission, 10/1 priority date for domestic students. Applications are processed on a rolling basis. Application fee: $0. *Expenses:* Tuition, state resident: part-time $272 per credit. Tuition, nonresident: part-time $478 per credit. Required fees: $38 per credit. *Financial support:* Fellowships, research assistantships, teaching assistantships, career-related internships or fieldwork, Federal Work-Study, institutionally sponsored loans, scholarships/grants, health care benefits, and unspecified assistantships available. Support available to part-time students. Financial award application deadline: 2/1. *Faculty research:* Multicultural education, cooperative learning, psychology of cognition. *Unit head:* Dr. Christine Johnson McPhail, Coordinator, 443-885-1983. *Application contact:* Dr. Maurice C. Taylor, Dean, 443-885-3185, Fax: 443-885-8226, E-mail: mctaylor@moac.morgan.edu.

Mount St. Mary's College, Graduate Division, Department of Education, Specialization in Administrative Studies, Los Angeles, CA 90049-1599. Offers MS. Part-time and evening/weekend programs available. *Students:* Average age 36. In 2006, 8 degrees awarded. *Degree requirements:* For master's, thesis, research project. *Entrance requirements:* For master's, MAT, minimum GPA of 3.0. Application fee: $50 ($75 for international students). *Expenses:* Tuition: Part-time $630 per unit. *Financial support:* Institutionally sponsored loans and tuition waivers (full and partial) available. Support available to part-time students. Financial award application deadline: 3/15; financial award applicants required to submit FAFSA. *Application contact:* Tom Hoener, Director, Graduate Recruitment, 213-477-2800, Fax: 213-477-2519, E-mail: thoener@msmc.la.edu.

Murray State University, College of Education, Department of Educational Studies, Leadership and Counseling, Program in School Administration, Murray, KY 42071. Offers MA Ed, Ed S. *Accreditation:* NCATE. Part-time programs available. *Students:* 203. *Degree requirements:* For master's and Ed S, comprehensive exam. *Entrance requirements:* For degree, GRE General Test. Additional exam requirements/recommendations for international students:

Educational Administration

Murray State University (continued)

Required—TOEFL. *Application deadline:* Applications are processed on a rolling basis. Application fee: $25. *Financial support:* Research assistantships, teaching assistantships, Federal Work-Study available. Financial award application deadline: 4/1. *Unit head:* Dr. Robert Lyons, Graduate Coordinator, 270-809-6471, Fax: 270-809-3799, E-mail: robert.lyons@coe.murraystate.edu.

National-Louis University, National College of Education, Doctoral Programs in Education, Program in Educational Leadership, Chicago, IL 60603. Offers educational leadership/superintendent endorsement (Ed D). Part-time and evening/weekend programs available. *Students:* Average age 42. 3 applicants, 67% accepted. In 2006, 4 degrees awarded. *Degree requirements:* For doctorate, thesis/dissertation, internship, comprehensive exam. *Entrance requirements:* For doctorate, GRE General Test, minimum GPA of 3.25, interview, resumé, writing sample. *Application deadline:* For fall admission, 5/1 for domestic students; for spring admission, 1/15 for domestic students. Application fee: $25. *Expenses:* Tuition: Full-time $17,685. One-time fee: $40 full-time. *Financial support:* Fellowships, research assistantships, teaching assistantships, career-related internships or fieldwork, Federal Work-Study, institutionally sponsored loans, and scholarships/grants available. Support available to part-time students. Financial award application deadline: 4/15; financial award applicants required to submit FAFSA. *Unit head:* Norman Weston, Associate Professor, 847-947-5255, E-mail: nweston@nl.edu. *Application contact:* David McCulloch, Vice President for University Services, 800-443-5522 Ext. 5127, Fax: 847-465-0593, E-mail: dmcc@wheeling1.nl.edu.

National-Louis University, National College of Education, Program in Early Childhood Administration, Chicago, IL 60603. Offers M Ed, CAS. *Students:* Average age 40. 4 applicants, 100% accepted. In 2006, 10 degrees awarded. *Entrance requirements:* For master's, GRE or MAT, minimum GPA of 3.0, teaching certificate; for CAS, master's degree, teaching certificate. *Application deadline:* Applications are processed on a rolling basis. Application fee: $25. *Expenses:* Tuition: Full-time $17,685. One-time fee: $40 full-time. *Financial support:* Fellowships, career-related internships or fieldwork, Federal Work-Study, institutionally sponsored loans, and scholarships/grants available. Support available to part-time students. *Unit head:* Dr. Paula Jorde-Bloom, Coordinator, 847-475-1100 Ext. 5551. *Application contact:* David McCulloch, Vice President for University Services, 800-443-5522 Ext. 5127, Fax: 847-465-0593, E-mail: dmcc@wheeling1.nl.edu.

National-Louis University, National College of Education, Program in Educational Leadership, Chicago, IL 60603. Offers administration and supervision (M Ed, CAS, Ed S), including superintendent endorsement (Ed S). Part-time and evening/weekend programs available. *Students:* 42 full-time (23 women), 514 part-time (313 women); includes 184 minority (145 African Americans, 1 American Indian/Alaska Native, 6 Asian Americans or Pacific Islanders, 32 Hispanic Americans). Average age 38. 75 applicants, 100% accepted. In 2006, 77 master's, 35 other advanced degrees awarded. *Degree requirements:* For other advanced degree, internship (Ed S). *Entrance requirements:* For master's, GRE or MAT, minimum GPA of 3.0, teaching certificate; for other advanced degree, GRE or MAT, master's degree, teaching certificate (CAS), writing sample, interview (Ed S). *Application deadline:* Applications are processed on a rolling basis. Application fee: $25. *Expenses:* Tuition: Full-time $17,685. One-time fee: $40 full-time. *Financial support:* Fellowships, career-related internships or fieldwork, Federal Work-Study, institutionally sponsored loans, and scholarships/grants available. Support available to part-time students. Financial award applicants required to submit FAFSA. *Unit head:* Dr. Paul Jung, Coordinator, 847-475-1100 Ext. 5108. *Application contact:* David McCulloch, Vice President for University Services, 800-443-5522 Ext. 5127, Fax: 847-465-0593, E-mail: dmcc@wheeling1.nl.edu.

National University, Academic Affairs, School of Education, Department of Educational Administration, La Jolla, CA 92037-1011. Offers MS. Part-time and evening/weekend programs available. Postbaccalaureate distance learning degree programs offered (no on-campus study). *Faculty:* 11 full-time (2 women), 121 part-time/adjunct (43 women). *Students:* 455 full-time (252 women), 1,056 part-time (616 women); includes 522 minority (220 African Americans, 11 American Indian/Alaska Native, 62 Asian Americans or Pacific Islanders, 229 Hispanic Americans), 2 international. Average age 40. 983 applicants, 942 enrolled. In 2006, 187 degrees awarded. *Degree requirements:* For master's, thesis. *Entrance requirements:* For master's, interview, minimum GPA of 2.5. Additional exam requirements/recommendations for international students: Required—TOEFL (minimum score 550 paper-based; 213 computer-based; 80 iBT), IELTS (minimum score 6). *Application deadline:* Applications are processed on a rolling basis. Application fee: $60 ($65 for international students). Electronic applications accepted. *Expenses:* Tuition: Full-time $7,722; part-time $286 per unit. One-time fee: $60. *Financial support:* Career-related internships or fieldwork, institutionally sponsored loans, scholarships/grants, and tuition waivers (partial) available. Support available to part-time students. Financial award application deadline: 6/30; financial award applicants required to submit FAFSA. *Unit head:* Dr. Gary Hoban, Chair, 858-642-8320, Fax: 858-642-8724, E-mail: ghoban@nu.edu. *Application contact:* Dominick Giovanniello, Associate Regional Dean—San Diego, 800-NAT-UNIV, Fax: 858-642-8709, E-mail: dgiovann@nu.edu.

New England College, Program in Education, Henniker, NH 03242-3293. Offers literacy and language arts (M Ed); meeting the needs of all learners/special education (M Ed); teacher leadership/school reform (M Ed). Part-time and evening/weekend programs available.

New Jersey City University, Graduate and Continuing Education, College of Education, Department of Educational Leadership, Jersey City, NJ 07305-1597. Offers basics and urban studies (MA); bilingual/bicultural education and English as a second language (MA); educational administration and supervision (MA). Evening/weekend programs available. *Students:* 4 full-time (3 women), 237 part-time (149 women); includes 52 minority (11 African Americans, 4 Asian Americans or Pacific Islanders, 37 Hispanic Americans), 26 international. Average age 35. In 2006, 162 degrees awarded. *Entrance requirements:* For master's, GRE General Test or MAT. Additional exam requirements/recommendations for international students: Required—TOEFL. *Application deadline:* For fall admission, 8/1 priority date for domestic students; for spring admission, 12/1 for domestic students. Applications are processed on a rolling basis. Application fee: $0. *Expenses:* Tuition, state resident: full-time $7,038; part-time $391 per credit. Tuition, nonresident: full-time $12,510; part-time $695 per credit. Required fees: $65 per credit. *Financial support:* Fellowships, teaching assistantships, career-related internships or fieldwork and unspecified assistantships available. *Unit head:* Dr. Carrie Robinson, Chairperson, 201-200-3400, E-mail: crobinson@njcu.edu.

Newman Theological College, Religious Education Program, Edmonton, AB T6V 1H3, Canada. Offers Catholic school administration (CCSA); religious education (MRE, GDRE). Part-time programs available. Postbaccalaureate distance learning degree programs offered (no on-campus study). *Faculty:* 1 full-time (0 women), 5 part-time/adjunct (3 women). *Students:* Average age 44. 50 applicants, 80% accepted, 32 enrolled. In 2006, 4 master's, 8 other advanced degrees awarded. *Degree requirements:* For master's, thesis or alternative. *Entrance requirements:* For master's, 2 years of successful teaching experience; graduate diploma in religious education; for other advanced degree, bachelor's degree in education, teaching certificate. Additional exam requirements/recommendations for international students: Required—TOEFL (minimum score 560 paper-based; 220 computer-based). *Application deadline:* For fall admission, 8/30 priority date for domestic students; for winter admission, 12/21 for domestic students; for spring admission, 4/30 for domestic students. Application fee: $25. *Expenses:* Tuition: Full-time $9,000; part-time $900 per term. Required fees: $50; $20 per term. One-time fee: $40 full-time. *Financial support:* Tuition bursaries available. Support available to part-time students. Financial award application deadline: 5/30. *Unit head:* Dr. Dan Kingdon, Director, 780-447-2993 Ext. 224, Fax: 780-447-2685, E-mail: dan.kingdon@newman.edu. *Application contact:* Carol Anne Seed, Registrar, 780-447-2993 Ext. 227, Fax: 780-447-2685.

Newman University, School of Education, Wichita, KS 67213-2097. Offers building leadership (MS Ed); curriculum and instruction (MS Ed), including accountability, English as a second language. Part-time programs available. Postbaccalaureate distance learning degree programs offered (no on-campus study). *Faculty:* 3 full-time (0 women), 4 part-time/adjunct (all women). *Students:* 2 full-time (both women), 41 part-time (24 women); includes 3 minority (2 African Americans, 1 American Indian/Alaska Native), 3 international. Average age 35. 25 applicants, 92% accepted, 17 enrolled. In 2006, 35 degrees awarded. *Degree requirements:* For master's, thesis optional. *Entrance requirements:* For master's, GRE General Test or MAT, interview, minimum GPA of 3.0, writing sample, 3 letters of recommendation. Additional exam requirements/recommendations for international students: Required—TOEFL (minimum score 600 paper-based; 250 computer-based). *Application deadline:* For fall admission, 8/15 priority date for domestic students; for spring admission, 1/10 priority date for domestic students. Applications are processed on a rolling basis. Application fee: $25 ($40 for international students). Electronic applications accepted. *Financial support:* In 2006–07, 8 students received support. Federal Work-Study and tuition waivers (full) available. Financial award application deadline: 8/15; financial award applicants required to submit FAFSA. *Unit head:* Dr. Guy Glidden, Director, 316-942-4291 Ext. 2331, Fax: 316-942-4483, E-mail: gliddeng@newmanu.edu. *Application contact:* Linda Kay Sabala, Director of Graduate Admissions, 316-942-4291 Ext. 2230, Fax: 316-942-4483, E-mail: sabalal@newmanu.edu.

New Mexico Highlands University, Graduate Studies, School of Education, Las Vegas, NM 87701. Offers education (MA), including curriculum and instruction; educational leadership (MA); exercise and sport sciences (MA), including human performance and sport, sports administration, teacher education; guidance and counseling (MA), including professional counseling, rehabilitation counseling, school counseling; special education (MA), including). *Accreditation:* NCATE. Part-time programs available. *Faculty:* 14 full-time (6 women), 11 part-time/adjunct (9 women). *Students:* 171 full-time (117 women), 413 part-time (286 women); includes 305 minority (17 African Americans, 30 American Indian/Alaska Native, 4 Asian Americans or Pacific Islanders, 254 Hispanic Americans), 3 international. Average age 40. 111 applicants, 84% accepted, 63 enrolled. In 2006, 111 degrees awarded. *Degree requirements:* For master's, thesis or alternative, comprehensive exam, registration. *Entrance requirements:* For master's, minimum undergraduate GPA of 3.0. Additional exam requirements/recommendations for international students: Required—TOEFL (minimum score 540 paper-based; 190 computer-based). *Application deadline:* For fall admission, 8/1 priority date for domestic students. Applications are processed on a rolling basis. Application fee: $15. *Expenses:* Tuition, state resident: part-time $101 per credit hour. Tuition, nonresident: part-time $101 per credit hour. *Financial support:* In 2006–07, 205 students received support, including 16 teaching assistantships with full and partial tuition reimbursements available (averaging $6,500 per year); career-related internships or fieldwork, Federal Work-Study, institutionally sponsored loans, scholarships/grants, traineeships, tuition waivers (partial), and unspecified assistantships also available. Support available to part-time students. Financial award application deadline: 3/1; financial award applicants required to submit FAFSA. *Unit head:* Dr. Francisco Hidalgo, Dean, 505-454-3357, Fax: 505-454-3384, E-mail: fhidalgo@nmhu.edu. *Application contact:* Diane Trujillo, Administrative Assistant Graduate Studies, 505-454-3266, Fax: 505-454-3558, E-mail: dtrujillo@nmhu.edu.

New Mexico State University, Graduate School, College of Education, Department of Educational Management and Development, Las Cruces, NM 88003-8001. Offers educational administration (MA, PhD); educational management and development (Ed D). *Accreditation:* NCATE. Part-time and evening/weekend programs available. Postbaccalaureate distance learning degree programs offered (minimal on-campus study). *Faculty:* 13 full-time (7 women). *Students:* 35 full-time (21 women), 91 part-time (61 women); includes 55 minority (1 African American, 4 American Indian/Alaska Native, 1 Asian American or Pacific Islander, 49 Hispanic Americans), 4 international. Average age 42. 91 applicants, 86% accepted. In 2006, 69 master's, 8 doctorates awarded. *Degree requirements:* For master's, internship; for doctorate, thesis/dissertation, internship. *Entrance requirements:* For master's and doctorate, minimum GPA of 3.0. *Application deadline:* Applications are processed on a rolling basis. Application fee: $30 ($50 for international students). Electronic applications accepted. *Financial support:* In 2006–07, 15 fellowships with tuition reimbursements, 13 teaching assistantships were awarded; research assistantships, career-related internships or fieldwork, Federal Work-Study, and health care benefits also available. Support available to part-time students. Financial award application deadline: 7/2. *Faculty research:* Leadership in K–12 and postsecondary education, management technology, community college administration, diversity in educational administration, program evaluation. *Unit head:* Marivel Oropeza, Program Coordinator, 505-646-4050, Fax: 505-646-4767, E-mail: oropeza@nmsu.edu. *Application contact:* Herb Torres, College Instructor, 505-646-3495, Fax: 505-646-4767, E-mail: htorres@nmsu.edu.

New York Institute of Technology, Graduate Division, School of Education and Professional Services, Program in Leadership and Technology, Old Westbury, NY 11568-8000. Offers district leadership and technology (Professional Diploma); school leadership and technology (Professional Diploma). Part-time and evening/weekend programs available. *Students:* 2 applicants, 50% accepted, 0 enrolled. In 2006, 2 degrees awarded. *Degree requirements:* For Professional Diploma, internship. *Entrance requirements:* For degree, must be full-time teacher with 3 years experience, permanent teacher certification in New York state. *Application deadline:* For fall admission, 7/1 for domestic students; for spring admission, 12/1 for domestic students. Application fee: $50. *Expenses:* Tuition: Full-time $16,800; part-time $700 per credit. *Financial support:* Career-related internships or fieldwork available. Financial award applicants required to submit FAFSA. *Application contact:* Jacquelyn Nealon, Dean of Admissions and Financial Aid, 516-686-7925, Fax: 516-686-7613, E-mail: jnealon@nyit.edu.

New York University, Steinhardt School of Culture, Education and Human Development, Department of Administration, Leadership, and Technology, Program in Educational Leadership, New York, NY 10012-1019. Offers MA, Ed D, PhD, Advanced Certificate. Part-time and evening/weekend programs available. *Faculty:* 5 full-time (4 women). *Students:* 10 full-time (8 women), 71 part-time (50 women); includes 35 minority (17 African Americans, 3 Asian Americans or Pacific Islanders, 15 Hispanic Americans), 1 international. 81 applicants, 52% accepted, 19 enrolled. In 2006, 17 master's, 2 doctorates, 1 other advanced degree awarded. Terminal master's awarded for partial completion of doctoral program. *Degree requirements:* For master's, thesis (for some programs); for doctorate, thesis/dissertation. *Entrance requirements:* For doctorate, GRE General Test, interview; for Advanced Certificate, master's degree. Additional exam requirements/recommendations for international students: Required—TOEFL. *Application deadline:* For fall admission, 12/15 priority date for domestic and international students; for spring admission, 11/1 for domestic and international students. Applications are processed on a rolling basis. Application fee: $50. *Expenses:* Tuition: Part-time $1,080 per unit. Required fees: $56 per unit. $329 per term. Tuition and fees vary according to program. *Financial support:* Fellowships with full and partial tuition reimbursements, teaching assistantships with partial tuition reimbursements, career-related internships or fieldwork, Federal Work-Study, institutionally sponsored loans, scholarships/grants, tuition waivers (partial), and unspecified assistantships available. Support available to part-time students. Financial award application deadline: 2/1; financial award applicants required to submit FAFSA. *Faculty research:* Schools and communities; critical theories of race, class and gender; school restructuring; educational reform; social organization of schools. *Unit head:* Dr. Mary E. Driscoll, Director, 212-998-5520, Fax: 212-995-4041. *Application contact:* 212-998-5030, Fax: 212-995-4328, E-mail: steinhardt.gradadmissions@nyu.edu.

New York University, Steinhardt School of Culture, Education and Human Development, Department of Administration, Leadership, and Technology, Program in Higher Education, New York, NY 10012-1019. Offers higher education administration (PhD); student personnel administration higher education (MA). *Accreditation:* Teacher Education Accreditation Council. Part-time and evening/weekend programs available. *Faculty:* 7 full-time (3 women). *Students:* 42 full-time (31 women), 67 part-time (49 women); includes 32 minority (14 African Americans, 9 Asian Americans or Pacific Islanders, 9 Hispanic Americans), 3 international. 148 applicants, 25% accepted, 31 enrolled. In 2006, 27 master's, 7 doctorates awarded. Terminal master's awarded for partial completion of doctoral program. *Degree requirements:* For master's, thesis (for some programs); for doctorate, thesis/dissertation. *Entrance requirements:* For master's, interview, 2 letters of recommendation; for doctorate, GRE General Test, interview. Additional exam requirements/recommendations for international students: Required—TOEFL. *Application deadline:* For fall admission, 12/15 priority date for domestic and international students; for spring admission, 11/1 for domestic and international students. Applications are processed on a rolling basis. Application fee: $50. *Expenses:* Tuition: Part-time $1,080 per unit. Required fees: $56 per unit. $329 per term. Tuition and fees vary according to program. *Financial support:* Fellowships with full and partial tuition reimbursements, career-related internships or fieldwork, Federal Work-Study, institutionally sponsored loans, scholarships/grants, tuition waivers (partial), and unspecified assistantships available. Support available to part-time students. Financial award application deadline: 2/1; financial award applicants required to submit FAFSA. *Faculty research:* Organizational theory and culture, systemic change, leadership development, access, equity and diversity. *Unit head:* Dr. Ann Marcus, Head, 212-998-4041, Fax: 212-995-4041. *Application contact:* 212-998-5030, Fax: 212-995-4328, E-mail: steinhardt.gradadmissions@nyu.edu.

Niagara University, Graduate Division of Education, Concentration in Administration and Supervision, Niagara Falls, Niagara University, NY 14109. Offers MS Ed, Certificate. Part-time and evening/weekend programs available. *Faculty:* 2 full-time (0 women), 7 part-time/adjunct (1 woman). *Students:* 9 full-time (4 women), 57 part-time (32 women); includes 2 minority (both African Americans), 10 international. In 2006, 25 master's, 2 other advanced degrees awarded. *Entrance requirements:* For master's, GRE General Test or MAT; for Certificate, GRE General Test and GRE Subject Test or MAT. *Application deadline:* For fall admission, 8/1 for domestic students. Applications are processed on a rolling basis. Application fee: $30. *Expenses: Contact institution. Financial support:* In 2006–07, 1 research assistantship was awarded; career-related internships or fieldwork, Federal Work-Study, and unspecified assistantships also available. Support available to part-time students. Financial award application deadline: 3/15. *Unit head:* Dr. Barbara Iannarelli, Chair, 716-286-8547. *Application contact:* Dr. Debra A. Colley, Dean of Education, 716-286-8560, Fax: 716-286-8561, E-mail: dcolley@niagara.edu.

Niagara University, Graduate Division of Education, Concentration in School Counseling, Niagara Falls, Niagara University, NY 14109. Offers school business administration (MS Ed, Certificate). *Accreditation:* NCATE. Part-time and evening/weekend programs available. *Faculty:* 2 full-time (1 woman), 3 part-time/adjunct (all women). *Students:* 26 full-time (18 women), 20 part-time (16 women); includes 5 minority (1 African American, 3 American Indian/Alaska Native, 1 Hispanic American), 1 international. In 2006, 17 master's, 9 other advanced degrees awarded. *Entrance requirements:* For master's, GRE General Test or MAT; for Certificate, GRE General Test, GRE Subject Test or MAT. *Application deadline:* For fall admission, 8/1 for domestic students. Applications are processed on a rolling basis. Application fee: $30. *Expenses: Contact institution. Financial support:* Career-related internships or fieldwork and Federal Work-Study available. Financial award application deadline: 3/15. *Unit head:* Dr. Barbara Iannarelli, Chair, 716-286-8547. *Application contact:* Dr. Debra A. Colley, Dean of Education, 716-286-8560, Fax: 716-286-8561, E-mail: dcolley@niagara.edu.

Nicholls State University, Graduate Studies, College of Education, Department of Teacher Education, Thibodaux, LA 70310. Offers administration and supervision (M Ed); counselor education (M Ed); curriculum and instruction (M Ed). *Accreditation:* NCATE. Part-time and evening/weekend programs available. *Faculty:* 17 full-time (13 women), 6 part-time/adjunct (4 women). *Students:* 21 full-time (17 women), 174 part-time (155 women); includes 60 minority (52 African Americans, 5 American Indian/Alaska Native, 1 Asian American or Pacific Islander, 2 Hispanic Americans). Average age 33. In 2006, 77 degrees awarded. *Degree requirements:* For master's, portfolio. *Entrance requirements:* For master's, GRE General Test, teaching license. *Application deadline:* Applications are processed on a rolling basis. Application fee: $20 ($30 for international students). Electronic applications accepted. *Expenses:* Tuition, state resident: part-time $450 per hour. Tuition, nonresident: part-time $450 per hour. *Financial support:* In 2006–07, research assistantships with tuition reimbursements (averaging $4,000 per year). Financial award application deadline: 6/17. *Unit head:* Dr. J. Lavone Landry, Head, 985-448-4314, E-mail: lavone.landry@nicholls.edu.

Norfolk State University, School of Graduate Studies, School of Education, Department of Secondary Education and School Leadership, Norfolk, VA 23504. Offers principal preparation (MA); secondary education (MAT); urban education/administration (MA), including teaching. *Accreditation:* NCATE. Part-time programs available. *Entrance requirements:* For master's, GRE General Test, PRAXIS I, minimum GPA of 3.0 in major, 2.5 overall. Additional exam requirements/recommendations for international students: Required—TOEFL (minimum score 500 paper-based).

North Carolina Agricultural and Technical State University, Graduate School, School of Education, Department of Educational Leadership and Policy, Greensboro, NC 27411. Offers adult education (MS); educational administration (MS), including educational administration, educational supervision. *Accreditation:* NCATE. Part-time and evening/weekend programs available. *Degree requirements:* For master's, thesis or alternative, qualifying exam, comprehensive exam. *Entrance requirements:* For master's, GRE General Test, minimum GPA of 2.6.

North Carolina Central University, Division of Academic Affairs, School of Education, Program in Development Leadership and Professional Studies, Durham, NC 27707-3129. Offers MA. *Accreditation:* NCATE. Part-time and evening/weekend programs available. *Degree requirements:* For master's, thesis or alternative, comprehensive exam. *Entrance requirements:* For master's, minimum GPA of 3.0 in major, 2.5 overall. Additional exam requirements/recommendations for international students: Required—TOEFL. *Faculty research:* Simulation of decision-making behavior of school boards.

North Carolina State University, Graduate School, College of Education, Department of Adult and Community College Education, Program in Higher Education Administration, Raleigh, NC 27695. Offers M Ed, MS, Ed D. *Degree requirements:* For master's, thesis (for some programs); for doctorate, thesis/dissertation. *Entrance requirements:* For master's and doctorate, GRE General Test or MAT, minimum GPA of 3.0 in major. Electronic applications accepted.

North Carolina State University, Graduate School, College of Education, Department of Educational Research, Leadership and Counselor Education, Program in Educational Administration and Supervision, Raleigh, NC 27695. Offers Ed D. *Degree requirements:* For doctorate, thesis/dissertation. *Entrance requirements:* For doctorate, GRE General Test or MAT, minimum GPA of 3.0, interview, sample of work. Electronic applications accepted.

North Carolina State University, Graduate School, College of Education, Department of Educational Research, Leadership and Counselor Education, Program in School Administration, Raleigh, NC 27695. Offers MSA. *Degree requirements:* For master's, thesis optional. *Entrance requirements:* For master's, GRE General Test or MAT, minimum GPA of 3.0 in major. Electronic applications accepted. *Faculty research:* State and national policy, educational evaluation, cohort preparation programs.

North Central College, Graduate Programs, Department of Leadership Studies, Naperville, IL 60566-7063. Offers MLD. Part-time and evening/weekend programs available. *Degree requirements:* For master's, project. *Entrance requirements:* For master's, interview.

North Dakota State University, The Graduate School, College of Human Development and Education, School of Education, Program in Educational Leadership, Fargo, ND 58105. Offers M Ed, MS, Ed S. *Accreditation:* NCATE. Part-time and evening/weekend programs available. Postbaccalaureate distance learning degree programs offered (minimal on-campus study). *Faculty:* 9. *Students:* 4 full-time (2 women), 92 part-time (39 women); includes 4 minority (3 American Indian/Alaska Native, 1 Hispanic American). Average age 32. 17 applicants, 94% accepted. In 2006, 30 master's, 1 other advanced degree awarded. *Entrance requirements:* For degree, GRE General Test, master's degree, minimum GPA of 3.25. Additional exam

requirements/recommendations for international students: Required—TOEFL. *Application deadline:* Applications are processed on a rolling basis. Application fee: $45 ($60 for international students). *Financial support:* In 2006–07, 1 teaching assistantship with full tuition reimbursement (averaging $800 per year) was awarded; career-related internships or fieldwork, Federal Work-Study, institutionally sponsored loans, and tuition waivers (full) also available. Financial award application deadline: 4/15. *Faculty research:* Organizational change and development, goal setting and systematic planning, beginning teacher assistance. *Unit head:* Dr. Richard Warner, Chair, TCU Educational Administration, 701-231-5778, Fax: 701-231-7205, E-mail: richard.b.warner@ndsu.edu. *Application contact:* Vicki Ihry, Administrative Assistant, 701-231-9732, Fax: 701-231-7205, E-mail: vicki.ihry@ndsu.edu.

Northeastern Illinois University, Graduate College, College of Education, Department of Educational Leadership and Development, Program in Educational Leadership, Chicago, IL 60625-4699. Offers educational administration and supervision (MA), including chief school business official, community college administration. Part-time and evening/weekend programs available. *Faculty:* 25 full-time (11 women), 22 part-time/adjunct (8 women). *Students:* Average age 41. 1 applicant, 0% accepted. *Degree requirements:* For master's, practicum. *Entrance requirements:* For master's, 2 years of teaching experience, minimum GPA of 2.75. *Application deadline:* For fall admission, 4/1 priority date for domestic students; for spring admission, 8/15 for domestic students. Applications are processed on a rolling basis. Application fee: $25. *Financial support:* In 2006–07, 3 research assistantships with full tuition reimbursements (averaging $6,600 per year) were awarded; career-related internships or fieldwork, Federal Work-Study, institutionally sponsored loans, and tuition waivers (full and partial) also available. Support available to part-time students. *Faculty research:* Student motivation, leadership, teacher expectation, educational partnerships, community/school relations.

Northeastern State University, Graduate College, College of Education, Department of Educational Foundation and Leadership, Program in School Administration, Tahlequah, OK 74464-2399. Offers M Ed. Part-time and evening/weekend programs available. *Students:* 14 full-time (12 women), 132 part-time (72 women); includes 40 minority (8 African Americans, 32 American Indian/Alaska Native). In 2006, 70 degrees awarded. *Degree requirements:* For master's, thesis. *Entrance requirements:* For master's, MAT or GRE, minimum GPA of 3.0. Additional exam requirements/recommendations for international students: Required—TOEFL (minimum score 213 computer-based). *Application deadline:* For fall admission, 6/1 priority date for domestic students. Applications are processed on a rolling basis. Application fee: $0 ($25 for international students). Electronic applications accepted. *Financial support:* Teaching assistantships, Federal Work-Study available. Financial award application deadline: 3/1. *Unit head:* Dr. Ken Hancock, Coordinator, 918-449-6000 Ext. 6563, Fax: 918-458-2351, E-mail: hancockl@nsuok.edu.

Northern Arizona University, Graduate College, College of Education, Program in Career and Technical Education, Flagstaff, AZ 86011. Offers administration (M Ed); educational technology (M Ed); teaching (M Ed). *Degree requirements:* For master's, final oral exam, project, thesis optional.

Northern Arizona University, Graduate College, College of Education, Program in Educational Leadership, Flagstaff, AZ 86011. Offers community college (M Ed); educational leadership (Ed D); school leadership (M Ed). Part-time programs available. *Degree requirements:* For master's, thesis optional; for doctorate, thesis/dissertation, comprehensive exam. *Faculty research:* Change processes, African education, law and education, program evaluation.

Northern Illinois University, Graduate School, College of Education, Department of Leadership, Educational Psychology and Foundations, De Kalb, IL 60115-2854. Offers educational administration (MS Ed, Ed D, Ed S); educational psychology (MS Ed, Ed D); foundations of education (MS Ed); school business management (MS Ed). Part-time and evening/weekend programs available. Postbaccalaureate distance learning degree programs offered (minimal on-campus study). *Faculty:* 23 full-time (12 women). *Students:* 15 full-time (7 women), 499 part-time (289 women); includes 75 minority (53 African Americans, 2 American Indian/Alaska Native, 6 Asian Americans or Pacific Islanders, 14 Hispanic Americans), 2 international. Average age 37. 186 applicants, 62% accepted, 92 enrolled. In 2006, 171 master's, 10 doctorates, 50 other advanced degrees awarded. *Degree requirements:* For master's, thesis optional; for doctorate, thesis/dissertation, candidacy exam, dissertation defense. *Entrance requirements:* For master's, minimum undergraduate GPA of 2.75; for doctorate, GRE General Test, minimum undergraduate GPA of 2.75, 3.2 graduate; for Ed S, GRE General Test, minimum GPA of 2.75 (undergraduate), 3.2 (graduate). Additional exam requirements/recommendations for international students: Required—TOEFL (minimum score 550 paper-based; 213 computer-based). *Application deadline:* For fall admission, 6/1 for domestic students, 5/1 for international students; for spring admission, 11/1 for domestic students, 10/1 for international students. Applications are processed on a rolling basis. Application fee: $30. Electronic applications accepted. *Financial support:* In 2006–07, 3 research assistantships with full tuition reimbursements, 8 teaching assistantships with full tuition reimbursements were awarded; fellowships with full tuition reimbursements, career-related internships or fieldwork, Federal Work-Study, scholarships/grants, tuition waivers (full), and unspecified assistantships also available. Support available to part-time students. Financial award applicants required to submit FAFSA. *Faculty research:* Interpersonal forgiveness, learner-centered education, psychedelic studies, senior theory, professional growth. *Unit head:* Dr. Wilma Miranda, Chair, 815-753-1562, E-mail: wmiranda@niu.edu.

Northern Illinois University, Graduate School, College of Education, Department of Teaching and Learning, De Kalb, IL 60115-2854. Offers curriculum and instruction (MS Ed, Ed D), including curriculum leadership (Ed D), elementary education (Ed D), secondary education (Ed D); early childhood education (MS Ed); elementary education (MS Ed); special education (MS Ed). Part-time and evening/weekend programs available. *Faculty:* 22 full-time (14 women), 2 part-time/adjunct (both women). *Students:* 81 full-time (64 women), 534 part-time (417 women); includes 122 minority (21 African Americans, 12 Asian Americans or Pacific Islanders, 89 Hispanic Americans), 11 international. Average age 36. 92 applicants, 57% accepted, 43 enrolled. In 2006, 256 master's, 12 doctorates awarded. *Degree requirements:* For master's, thesis optional; for doctorate, thesis/dissertation, candidacy exam, dissertation defense. *Entrance requirements:* For master's, GRE General Test or MAT, minimum undergraduate GPA of 2.75; for doctorate, GRE General Test or MAT, minimum undergraduate GPA of 2.75, graduate 3.2. Additional exam requirements/recommendations for international students: Required—TOEFL (minimum score 550 paper-based; 213 computer-based). *Application deadline:* For fall admission, 6/1 for domestic students, 5/1 for international students; for spring admission, 11/1 for domestic students, 10/1 for international students. Applications are processed on a rolling basis. Application fee: $30. Electronic applications accepted. *Financial support:* In 2006–07, 27 research assistantships with full tuition reimbursements, 1 teaching assistantship with full tuition reimbursement were awarded; fellowships with full tuition reimbursements, career-related internships or fieldwork, Federal Work-Study, scholarships/grants, tuition waivers (full), and unspecified assistantships also available. Support available to part-time students. Financial award applicants required to submit FAFSA. *Faculty research:* Teacher certification, stress reduction during student teaching, teaching history, portfolios in student teaching. *Unit head:* Dr. Pamela Jackson, Acting Chair, 815-753-8452, E-mail: p30ngd1@wpo.cso.niu.edu.

Northern Kentucky University, Office of Graduate Programs, College of Education and Human Services, Program in Instructional Leadership, Highland Heights, KY 41099. Offers MA. Part-time and evening/weekend programs available. *Faculty:* 1 (woman) full-time, 5 part-time/adjunct (3 women). *Students:* 8 full-time (7 women), 36 part-time (19 women). Average age 31. 17 applicants, 76% accepted, 13 enrolled. In 2006, 28 degrees awarded. *Degree requirements:* For master's, comprehensive exam. *Entrance requirements:* For master's, GRE, 1 year of teaching, minimum GPA of 2.5, teaching certificate. Additional exam requirements/recommendations for international students: Required—TOEFL (minimum score 550 paper-based; 213 computer-based; 79 iBT), Michigan (must be taken at NKU). *Application deadline:*

Educational Administration

Northern Kentucky University (continued)
For fall admission, 8/1 priority date for domestic students, 6/1 for international students; for spring admission, 12/1 priority date for domestic students, 10/1 for international students. Applications are processed on a rolling basis. Application fee: $30. Electronic applications accepted. *Expenses:* Tuition, state resident: full-time $5,274; part-time $293 per hour. Tuition, nonresident: full-time $10,314; part-time $573 per hour. Tuition and fees vary according to course load, program and reciprocity agreements. *Financial support:* In 2006–07, 28 students received support. *Faculty research:* Leadership, principalship, legal issues, ethics. *Unit head:* Dr. Rosa Weaver, Director, 859-572-5536, Fax: 859-572-6096, E-mail: weaverro@nku.edu. *Application contact:* Dr. Peg Griffin, Director of Graduate Programs, 859-572-1555, Fax: 859-572-6670, E-mail: gradprog@nku.edu.

Northern Michigan University, College of Graduate Studies, College of Professional Studies, School of Education, Program in Administration and Supervision, Marquette, MI 49855-5301. Offers MA Ed, Ed S. Part-time programs available. *Degree requirements:* For master's, thesis or alternative. *Entrance requirements:* For master's, GRE General Test, minimum GPA of 3.0. *Faculty research:* Supervision and improvement of instruction, the principal as educational leader, women in K–12 educational administration.

Northern State University, Division of Graduate Studies in Education, Program in Elementary and Secondary School Administration, Aberdeen, SD 57401-7198. Offers elementary school administration (MS Ed); secondary school administration (MS Ed). *Accreditation:* NCATE. Part-time and evening/weekend programs available. *Faculty:* 7 full-time (3 women). *Students:* 1 (woman) full-time, 20 part-time (9 women); includes 1 minority (American Indian/Alaska Native). Average age 32. In 2006, 16 degrees awarded. *Degree requirements:* For master's, thesis optional. *Entrance requirements:* For master's, minimum GPA of 2.75. Additional exam requirements/recommendations for international students: Required—TOEFL (minimum score 550 paper-based; 213 computer-based). *Application deadline:* For fall admission, 8/15 priority date for domestic students; for spring admission, 12/15 for domestic students. Applications are processed on a rolling basis. Application fee: $35. Electronic applications accepted. *Expenses:* Tuition, state resident: full-time $3,373; part-time $120 per credit. Tuition, nonresident: full-time $9,943; part-time $355 per credit. International tuition: $13,000 full-time. Required fees: $86 per credit. One-time fee: $35 full-time. Tuition and fees vary according to course load, degree level and reciprocity agreements. *Financial support:* In 2006–07, 5 students received support, including 2 teaching assistantships with partial tuition reimbursements available (averaging $4,812 per year); career-related internships or fieldwork, Federal Work-Study, institutionally sponsored loans, scholarships/grants, and unspecified assistantships also available. Support available to part-time students. Financial award application deadline: 3/1; financial award applicants required to submit FAFSA. *Unit head:* Dr. Craig D. Kono, Head, 605-626-2448, E-mail: konoc@northern.edu. *Application contact:* Tammy K. Griffith, Senior Secretary, 605-626-2558, Fax: 605-626-2542, E-mail: griffith@northern.edu.

North Georgia College & State University, Graduate Studies, Program in Teacher Education, Dahlonega, GA 30597. Offers early childhood education (M Ed); educational leadership (Ed S); middle grades education (M Ed); secondary education (M Ed), including art education, biology education, chemistry education, English education, history education, mathematics education, physical education, science education; special education (M Ed), including interrelated special education, learning disabilities. *Accreditation:* NCATE. Part-time and evening/weekend programs available. Postbaccalaureate distance learning degree programs offered (minimal on-campus study). *Faculty:* 35 full-time (18 women), 9 part-time/adjunct (6 women). *Students:* 260. Average age 32. 120 applicants, 63% accepted. In 2006, 134 degrees awarded. *Degree requirements:* For master's, thesis optional. *Entrance requirements:* For master's, GRE General Test or MAT, minimum GPA of 2.75; for Ed S, GRE General Test or MAT, 3 years of teaching experience, master's degree, minimum graduate GPA of 3.25. *Application deadline:* For fall admission, 7/1 priority date for domestic students; for spring admission, 12/10 priority date for domestic students. Applications are processed on a rolling basis. Application fee: $25. Electronic applications accepted. *Expenses:* Tuition, state resident: full-time $3,044; part-time $127 per credit hour. Tuition, nonresident: full-time $12,172; part-time $508 per credit hour. Required fees: $892; $458 per semester. *Financial support:* Teaching assistantships, career-related internships or fieldwork and scholarships/grants available. Support available to part-time students. Financial award application deadline: 5/1. *Faculty research:* Computers and teachers' attitudes, rural versus urban teacher attitudes, teacher leadership roles, minority recruitment in teaching force. *Unit head:* Dr. Bob Michael, Dean, School of Education, 706-864-1998, Fax: 706-867-2850, E-mail: bmichael@ngcsu.edu. *Application contact:* Dr. Donna A. Gessell, Director of Graduate Studies and External Programs, 706-864-1528, Fax: 706-867-2795, E-mail: dgessell@ngcsu.edu.

Northwestern Oklahoma State University, School of Professional Studies, Alva, OK 73717-2799. Offers adult education management and administration (M Ed), including adult education management and administration, education: non-certificate option; counseling psychology (MCP); curriculum and instruction (M Ed); educational leadership (M Ed); elementary education (M Ed); guidance and counseling K–12 (M Ed); reading specialist (M Ed); secondary education (M Ed). *Accreditation:* NCATE (one or more programs are accredited). Part-time programs available. *Faculty:* 32 full-time (17 women), 12 part-time/adjunct (7 women). *Students:* 43 full-time (33 women), 111 part-time (88 women); includes 10 minority (1 African American, 6 American Indian/Alaska Native, 3 Hispanic Americans), 2 international. Average age 31. 75 applicants, 92% accepted, 57 enrolled. In 2006, 68 degrees awarded. *Degree requirements:* For master's, portfolio, thesis optional. *Entrance requirements:* For master's, GRE General Test or MAT, minimum GPA of 2.75. *Application deadline:* Applications are processed on a rolling basis. Application fee: $15. *Expenses:* Tuition, state resident: part-time $700 per year. Tuition, nonresident: part-time $1,715 per year. *Financial support:* Federal Work-Study available. Support available to part-time students. Financial award application deadline: 5/1. *Unit head:* Dr. James Bowen, Dean, 580-327-8455.

Northwestern State University of Louisiana, Graduate Studies and Research, College of Education, Programs in Education, Natchitoches, LA 71497. Offers business and distributive education (M Ed); counseling (M Ed); early childhood education (M Ed); education (M Ed); education leadership (M Ed); educational technology (M Ed); elementary teaching (M Ed); English education (M Ed); home economics education (M Ed); mathematics education (M Ed); reading (M Ed); science education (M Ed); secondary teaching (M Ed); social sciences education (M Ed). *Students:* 49 full-time (41 women), 245 part-time (206 women); includes 78 minority (70 African Americans, 5 American Indian/Alaska Native, 2 Asian Americans or Pacific Islanders, 1 Hispanic American). Average age 35. In 2006, 158 degrees awarded. *Degree requirements:* For master's, thesis or alternative, comprehensive exam, registration. *Entrance requirements:* For master's, GRE General Test, minimum undergraduate GPA of 2.5. *Application contact:* Dr. Steven G. Horton, Associate Provost/Dean, Graduate Studies, Research, and Information Systems, 318-357-5851, Fax: 318-357-5019, E-mail: grad_school@nsula.edu.

Northwestern State University of Louisiana, Graduate Studies and Research, College of Education, Programs in Educational Leadership and Instruction, Natchitoches, LA 71497. Offers counseling (Ed S); educational leadership (Ed S); educational technology (Ed S); elementary teaching (Ed S); reading (Ed S); secondary teaching (Ed S); special education (Ed S). *Students:* 17 full-time (15 women), 114 part-time (87 women); includes 55 minority (51 African Americans, 1 Asian American or Pacific Islander, 3 Hispanic Americans). Average age 39. In 2006, 11 degrees awarded. *Entrance requirements:* For degree, GRE General Test. *Application contact:* Dr. Steven G. Horton, Associate Provost/Dean, Graduate Studies, Research, and Information Systems, 318-357-5851, Fax: 318-357-5019, E-mail: grad_school@nsula.edu.

Northwest Missouri State University, Graduate School, College of Education and Human Services, Department of Educational Leadership, Program in Educational Leadership, Maryville, MO 64468-6001. Offers educational leadership: elementary (MS Ed); educational leadership: secondary (MS Ed); elementary principalship (Ed S); secondary principalship (Ed S); superintendency (Ed S). *Accreditation:* NCATE. Part-time programs available. *Faculty:* 12 full-time (4 women). *Students:* 13 full-time (7 women), 87 part-time (56 women); includes 5 minority (4 African Americans, 1 Asian American or Pacific Islander). 29 applicants, 93% accepted, 20 enrolled. In 2006, 42 master's, 17 other advanced degrees awarded. *Degree requirements:* For master's, comprehensive exam; for Ed S, thesis, comprehensive exam. *Entrance requirements:* For master's, GRE General Test, minimum undergraduate GPA of 2.75, teaching certificate, writing sample; for Ed S, minimum graduate GPA of 3.25. Additional exam requirements/recommendations for international students: Required—TOEFL (minimum score 550 paper-based; 213 computer-based). *Application deadline:* For fall admission, 7/1 for domestic and international students; for spring admission, 11/15 for domestic and international students. Application fee: $0 ($50 for international students). *Financial support:* In 2006–07, 3 research assistantships with full tuition reimbursements (averaging $6,000 per year), 2 teaching assistantships with full tuition reimbursements (averaging $6,000 per year) were awarded; unspecified assistantships also available. Financial award application deadline: 3/1; financial award applicants required to submit FAFSA. *Application contact:* Dr. Frances Shipley, Dean of Graduate School, 660-562-1145, Fax: 660-562-1096, E-mail: gradsch@nwmissouri.edu.

Northwest Nazarene University, Graduate Studies, Program in Teacher Education, Nampa, ID 83686-5897. Offers curriculum and instruction (M Ed); educational leadership (M Ed); exceptional child (M Ed); reading education (M Ed); school counseling (M Ed). *Accreditation:* ACA; NCATE. Part-time programs available. *Faculty:* 11 full-time (4 women), 10 part-time/adjunct (6 women). *Students:* 113 full-time (79 women), 20 part-time (18 women); includes 4 minority (2 Asian Americans or Pacific Islanders, 2 Hispanic Americans). Average age 34. In 2006, 35 degrees awarded. *Degree requirements:* For master's, action research project. *Entrance requirements:* For master's, minimum undergraduate GPA of 2.8 overall or 3.0 during final 30 semester credits. *Application deadline:* For fall admission, 9/1 for domestic students. Applications are processed on a rolling basis. Application fee: $25. *Faculty research:* Action research, cooperative learning, accountability, institutional accreditation. *Unit head:* Dr. Karen Blacklock, Chair, 208-467-8399, Fax: 208-467-8562.

Notre Dame de Namur University, Division of Academic Affairs, School of Education and Leadership, Program in Education in Technology Leadership, Belmont, CA 94002-1908. Offers MA, Certificate. *Degree requirements:* For master's, thesis. *Application deadline:* For fall admission, 8/1 priority date for domestic students; for spring admission, 12/1 priority date for domestic students. Applications are processed on a rolling basis. Application fee: $50. Electronic applications accepted. *Expenses:* Tuition: Part-time $655 per credit. *Financial support:* Applicants required to submit FAFSA. *Unit head:* Dr. Diane Guay, Director, 650-508-3702. *Application contact:* Helen Valine, Director of Graduate Admissions, 650-508-3534, Fax: 650-508-3426, E-mail: grad.admit@ndnu.edu.

Nova Southeastern University, Fischler School of Education and Human Services, Graduate Teacher Education Program, Fort Lauderdale, FL 33314-7796. Offers athletic administration (MS); cognitive and behavioral disabilities (MS); computer science education (Ed S); computer science education (K-12) (MS); curriculum and teaching (Ed S); curriculum, instruction and technology (MS); curriculum, instruction, management and administration (Ed S); early childhood special education (MS); early literacy and reading (Ed S); early literacy education (MS); education technology (MS); educational leadership (administration K–12) (MS, Ed S); educational media (Ed S); educational media (K-12) (MS); elementary education (MS, Ed S), including ESOL endorsement (MS); English (MS, Ed S); exceptional student education (MS), including ESOL endorsement; gifted education (MS, Ed S); interdisciplinary arts education (MS); management and administration of educational programs (MS); mathematics (MS, Ed S); multicultural early intervention (MS); pre-kindergarten/primary (MS); preschool education (MS); reading (MS, Ed S); science (MS, Ed S); secondary education (MS); social studies (MS, Ed S); Spanish language (MS); teaching and learning (MA, MS), including curriculum and instruction (MA), elementary mathematics (MA), elementary reading (MA), K-12 technology integration (MA); teaching English to speakers of other languages (MS, Ed S); technology management and administration (Ed S); urban studies education (MS); varying exceptionalities (Ed S). Part-time and evening/weekend programs available. Postbaccalaureate distance learning degree programs offered. *Faculty:* 131 full-time (78 women), 548 part-time/adjunct (342 women). *Students:* 1,418 full-time (1,139 women), 3,464 part-time (2,877 women); includes 2,462 minority (1,732 African Americans, 13 American Indian/Alaska Native, 44 Asian Americans or Pacific Islanders, 673 Hispanic Americans), 77 international. Average age 38. 1,771 applicants, 80% accepted, 1419 enrolled. In 2006, 2,078 master's, 425 other advanced degrees awarded. *Degree requirements:* For master's and Ed S, thesis, practicum, internship. *Entrance requirements:* For master's, MAT, GRE, CLAST, CBEST, PRAXIS I, GKT, minimum GPA of 2.5; for Ed S, MAT or GRE, master's degree, teaching certificate, minimum GPA of 3.0. Additional exam requirements/recommendations for international students: Recommended—TOEFL (minimum score 550 paper-based; 213 computer-based), IELTS (minimum score 6). *Application deadline:* For fall admission, 8/11 priority date for domestic and international students; for winter admission, 12/28 priority date for domestic and international students; for spring admission, 4/22 priority date for domestic and international students. Applications are processed on a rolling basis. Application fee: $50. Electronic applications accepted. *Financial support:* Federal Work-Study available. Support available to part-time students. Financial award application deadline: 1/7. *Faculty research:* School effectiveness, critical thinking, leadership skills acquisition, child education, multicultural education. *Unit head:* Dr. Meline Kevorkian, Associate Dean of Master's and Educational Programs, 954-262-8500, Fax: 954-262-3606, E-mail: melinek@nova.edu. *Application contact:* Jennifer Quiñones Nottingham, Dean of Student Affairs, 800-986-3223 Ext. 8624, Fax: 954-262-3911, E-mail: jlquinon@nova.edu.

Nova Southeastern University, Fischler School of Education and Human Services, National Program for Educational Leaders, Fort Lauderdale, FL 33314-7796. Offers Ed D. Part-time and evening/weekend programs available. *Students:* 213 full-time (164 women), 1,037 part-time (786 women); includes 796 minority (733 African Americans, 4 American Indian/Alaska Native, 9 Asian Americans or Pacific Islanders, 50 Hispanic Americans), 3 international. Average age 38. 3 applicants, 67% accepted, 2 enrolled. In 2006, 274 degrees awarded. *Degree requirements:* For doctorate, thesis/dissertation, research project. *Entrance requirements:* For doctorate, MAT or GRE, master's degree, professional certification, current position as a practicing school administrator, letter of recommendation, resumé. Additional exam requirements/recommendations for international students: Recommended—TOEFL (minimum score 550 paper-based; 213 computer-based), IELTS (minimum score 6). *Application deadline:* For fall admission, 8/11 priority date for domestic and international students; for winter admission, 12/28 priority date for domestic and international students; for spring admission, 4/22 priority date for domestic and international students. Applications are processed on a rolling basis. Application fee: $50. Electronic applications accepted. *Expenses:* Contact institution. *Financial support:* In 2006–07, 2 fellowships were awarded; tuition waivers (full) also available. Financial award application deadline: 1/7. *Unit head:* Dr. Karen D. Bowser, Associate Dean of Doctoral Programs, 954-262-8500, Fax: 954-262-3912, E-mail: bowserk@nova.edu. *Application contact:* Jennifer Quiñones Nottingham, Dean of Student Affairs, 800-986-3223 Ext. 8624, Fax: 954-262-3911, E-mail: jlquinon@nova.edu.

Nova Southeastern University, Fischler School of Education and Human Services, Program in Education, Fort Lauderdale, FL 33314-7796. Offers educational leadership (Ed D); health care education (Ed D); higher education (Ed D); human serviced administration (Ed D); instructional leadership (Ed D); instructional technology distance education (Ed D); organizational leadership (Ed D); special education (Ed D); speech language pathology (Ed D). *Students:* 619 full-time (452 women), 615 part-time (473 women); includes 737 minority (616 African Americans, 2 American Indian/Alaska Native, 14 Asian Americans or Pacific Islanders, 105 Hispanic Americans), 8 international. Average age 38. 480 applicants, 83% accepted, 398 enrolled. *Degree requirements:* For doctorate, thesis/dissertation. *Entrance requirements:* For doctorate, MAT or GRE, master's degree, 2 letters of recommendation, work experience. Additional exam requirements/recommendations for international students: Required—TSE (recommended) with a minimum score of 50; Recommended—TOEFL (minimum score 550 paper-based; 213 computer-based), IELTS (minimum score 6). *Application deadline:* For fall admission, 8/11 priority date for domestic and international students; for winter admission, 12/28 priority date for domestic and international students; for spring admission, 4/22 priority date for domestic and international students. Applications are processed on a rolling basis. Application fee: $50. Electronic applications accepted. *Financial support:* In 2006–07, 2 fellowships (averaging $9,375 per year) were awarded; scholarships/grants and tuition waivers (full) also available. Support available to part-time students. Financial award application deadline: 1/7; financial award applicants required to submit FAFSA. *Unit head:* Dr. Karen D. Bowser, Associate Dean of Doctoral Programs, 954-262-8500, Fax: 954-262-3912, E-mail: bowserk@nova.edu. *Application contact:* Jennifer Quiñones Nottingham, Dean of Student Affairs, 800-986-3223 Ext. 8624, Fax: 954-262-3911, E-mail: jlquinon@nova.edu.

Nova Southeastern University, Fischler School of Education and Human Services, Programs in Child, Youth and Family Studies, Fort Lauderdale, FL 33314-7796. Offers child and youth care administration (MS); child and youth studies (Ed D); early childhood education administration (MS); family support studies (MS); substance abuse counseling and education (MS). Part-time and evening/weekend programs available. *Students:* 50 full-time (42 women), 251 part-time (219 women); includes 166 minority (135 African Americans, 3 Asian Americans or Pacific Islanders, 28 Hispanic Americans), 5 international. Average age 38. 26 applicants, 77% accepted, 20 enrolled. In 2006, 14 master's, 49 doctorates awarded. *Degree requirements:* For master's and doctorate, thesis/dissertation, practicum. *Entrance requirements:* For master's, GRE or MAT, work experience in field, minimum GPA of 2.5; for doctorate, GRE or MAT, master's degree, minimum GPA of 3.0, work experience. Additional exam requirements/recommendations for international students: Recommended—TOEFL (minimum score 550 paper-based; 213 computer-based), IELTS (minimum score 6). *Application deadline:* For fall admission, 8/11 priority date for domestic and international students; for winter admission, 12/28 priority date for domestic and international students; for spring admission, 4/22 priority date for domestic and international students. Applications are processed on a rolling basis. Application fee: $50. Electronic applications accepted. *Expenses: Contact institution. Financial support:* Career-related internships or fieldwork and Federal Work-Study available. Support available to part-time students. Financial award application deadline: 1/7. *Unit head:* Dr. Michael Gaffley, Director, 954-262-8629, Fax: 954-262-3911, E-mail: gaffleym@nova.edu. *Application contact:* Jennifer Quiñones Nottingham, Dean of Student Affairs, 800-986-3223 Ext. 8624, Fax: 954-262-3911, E-mail: jlquinon@nova.edu.

Oakland City University, School of Education and Technology, Oakland City, IN 47660-1099. Offers educational leadership (Ed D); teaching (MA). *Accreditation:* NCATE. Terminal master's awarded for partial completion of doctoral program. *Degree requirements:* For master's, thesis/dissertation; for doctorate, thesis/dissertation, comprehensive exam. *Entrance requirements:* For master's, MAT, minimum GPA of 3.0, interview, resumé, letters of recommendation; for doctorate, MAT, GRE, minimum GPA of 3.2, interview, resumé, letters of recommendation. Expenses: Contact institution. *Faculty research:* Assessment, cultural diversity, teacher education, education leadership.

Oakland University, Graduate Study and Lifelong Learning, School of Education and Human Services, Department of Educational Leadership, Rochester, MI 48309-4401. Offers educational leadership (M Ed, PhD); higher education (Certificate); higher education administration (Certificate); school administration (Ed S). *Faculty:* 10 full-time (6 women), 2 part-time/adjunct (0 women). *Students:* 13 full-time (9 women), 287 part-time (200 women); includes 37 minority (31 African Americans, 1 American Indian/Alaska Native, 2 Asian Americans or Pacific Islanders, 3 Hispanic Americans), 2 international. Average age 38. 125 applicants, 89% accepted, 96 enrolled. In 2006, 29 master's, 6 doctorates, 139 Certificates awarded. *Entrance requirements:* Additional exam requirements/recommendations for international students: Required—TOEFL (minimum score 550 paper-based; 213 computer-based). *Application deadline:* For fall admission, 7/15 for domestic students, 5/1 priority date for international students; for winter admission, 9/1 priority date for international students. Application fee: $35. *Expenses:* Tuition, state resident: full-time $9,936; part-time $414 per credit. Tuition, nonresident: full-time $17,202; part-time $716 per credit. *Financial support:* Federal Work-Study, institutionally sponsored loans, and tuition waivers (full) available. Financial award application deadline: 3/1; financial award applicants required to submit FAFSA. *Unit head:* Dr. William G. Keane, Chair, 248-370-3070, Fax: 248-370-4605. *Application contact:* Information Contact, 248-370-3070.

See Close-Up on page 1117.

Oakland University, Graduate Study and Lifelong Learning, School of Education and Human Services, Department of Teacher Development and Educational Studies, Rochester, MI 48309-4401. Offers education studies (M Ed); secondary education (MAT). *Accreditation:* NCATE. *Faculty:* 6 full-time (5 women), 2 part-time/adjunct (both women). *Students:* 190 full-time (158 women), 170 part-time (130 women); includes 24 minority (13 African Americans, 1 American Indian/Alaska Native, 8 Asian Americans or Pacific Islanders, 2 Hispanic Americans). Average age 32. 146 applicants, 97% accepted, 125 enrolled. In 2006, 57 degrees awarded. *Entrance requirements:* For master's, minimum GPA of 3.0 for unconditional admission. *Application deadline:* For fall admission, 3/1 for domestic students. Application fee: $35. Electronic applications accepted. *Expenses:* Tuition, state resident: full-time $9,936; part-time $414 per credit. Tuition, nonresident: full-time $17,202; part-time $716 per credit. *Financial support:* Federal Work-Study, institutionally sponsored loans, and tuition waivers (full) available. Financial award application deadline: 3/1; financial award applicants required to submit FAFSA. *Faculty research:* Earth science for middle and high school teachers through real world connections, learning communities, content enrichment. *Unit head:* Dr. Dyanne M Tracy, Chair, 248-370-3064, Fax: 248-370-4605, E-mail: dtracy@oakland.edu.

Oglala Lakota College, Graduate Studies, Program in Educational Administration, Kyle, SD 57752-0490. Offers MA. Part-time and evening/weekend programs available. *Entrance requirements:* For master's, minimum GPA of 2.5.

The Ohio State University, Graduate School, College of Education and Human Ecology, School of Educational Policy and Leadership, Columbus, OH 43210. Offers M Ed, MA, PhD. *Accreditation:* NCATE. *Faculty:* 41. *Students:* 137 full-time (98 women), 206 part-time (133 women); includes 70 minority (58 African Americans, 1 American Indian/Alaska Native, 8 Asian Americans or Pacific Islanders, 3 Hispanic Americans), 30 international. Average age 33. 401 applicants, 51% accepted, 77 enrolled. In 2006, 76 master's, 19 doctorates awarded. *Degree requirements:* For master's, thesis optional; for doctorate, thesis/dissertation. *Entrance requirements:* For master's, GRE (for some MA applicants); for doctorate, GRE General Test. Additional exam requirements/recommendations for international students: Required—TOEFL (minimum score 600 paper-based; 250 computer-based). *Application deadline:* For fall admission, 8/15 priority date for domestic students, 7/1 priority date for international students; for winter admission, 12/1 priority date for domestic students, 11/1 priority date for international students; for spring admission, 3/1 priority date for domestic students, 2/1 priority date for international students. Applications are processed on a rolling basis. Application fee: $40 ($50 for international students). Electronic applications accepted. *Expenses:* Tuition, state resident: full-time $9,438. Tuition, nonresident: full-time $22,791. Tuition and fees vary according to course load, campus/location and program. *Financial support:* Fellowships, research assistantships, teaching assistantships, Federal Work-Study, institutionally sponsored loans, and unspecified assistantships available. Support available to part-time students. *Unit head:* Philip L. Smith, Graduate Studies Committee Chair, 614-688-4791, Fax: 614-292-2581, E-mail: smith.133@osu.edu. *Application contact:* 614-292-9444, Fax: 614-292-3895, E-mail: domestic.grad@osu.edu.

Ohio University, Graduate Studies, College of Education, Department of Educational Studies, Athens, OH 45701-2979. Offers computer education and technology (M Ed); educational administration (M Ed, Ed D); educational research and evaluation (M Ed, PhD); instructional technology (PhD). Part-time and evening/weekend programs available. Postbaccalaureate distance learning degree programs offered (minimal on-campus study). *Faculty:* 13 full-time (7 women), 1 (woman) part-time/adjunct. *Students:* 77 full-time (41 women), 120 part-time (55 women); includes 5 minority (3 African Americans, 1 Asian American or Pacific Islander, 1 Hispanic American), 79 international. 121 applicants, 69% accepted, 49 enrolled. In 2006, 12 master's, 14 doctorates awarded. *Median time to degree:* Of those who began their doctoral program in fall 1998, 92% received their degree in 8 years or less. *Degree requirements:* For master's, thesis or alternative, registration; for doctorate, thesis/dissertation, comprehensive exam, registration. *Entrance requirements:* For master's, GRE General Test if GPA is less than 2.8; for doctorate, GRE General Test, minimum GPA of 3.4, work experience, 3 letters of reference, autobiography. Additional exam requirements/recommendations for international students: Required—TOEFL (minimum score 550 paper-based; 213 computer-based). *Application deadline:* For fall admission, 4/1 priority date for domestic and international students. Applications are processed on a rolling basis. Application fee: $45. Electronic applications accepted. *Financial support:* In 2006–07, 26 research assistantships with full tuition reimbursements (averaging $6,500 per year), 2 teaching assistantships with full tuition reimbursements (averaging $7,200 per year) were awarded; Federal Work-Study, institutionally sponsored loans, tuition waivers (full), and unspecified assistantships also available. Financial award application deadline: 3/15. *Faculty research:* Race, class and gender; computer programs; development and organization theory; evaluation/development of instruments, leadership. Total annual research expenditures: $158,037. *Unit head:* Dr. Catherine H. Glascock, Chair, 740-593-4464, Fax: 740-593-0477, E-mail: glascock@ohio.edu. *Application contact:* Floyd J. Doney, Director of Student Affairs, 740-593-4400, Fax: 740-593-9310, E-mail: doney@ohio.edu.

Oklahoma State University, College of Education, School of Educational Studies, Stillwater, OK 74078. Offers educational administration (MS); higher education (MS, Ed D); technical education (MS, Ed D); trade and industrial education (MS, Ed D). *Faculty:* 28 full-time (10 women), 25 part-time/adjunct (6 women). *Students:* 40 full-time (28 women), 160 part-time (93 women); includes 34 minority (14 African Americans, 11 American Indian/Alaska Native, 5 Asian Americans or Pacific Islanders, 4 Hispanic Americans), 8 international. Average age 40. 124 applicants, 43% accepted, 37 enrolled. In 2006, 34 master's, 29 doctorates awarded. *Degree requirements:* For master's, thesis or alternative; for doctorate, thesis/dissertation. *Entrance requirements:* For master's and doctorate, GRE or MAT. Additional exam requirements/recommendations for international students: Required—TOEFL. *Application deadline:* For fall admission, 7/1 priority date for domestic students, 3/1 priority date for international students; for spring admission, 8/1 priority date for international students. Applications are processed on a rolling basis. Application fee: $40 ($75 for international students). Electronic applications accepted. *Expenses:* Tuition, state resident: part-time $146 per credit hour. Tuition, nonresident: part-time $516 per credit hour. Required fees: $44 per credit hour. Tuition and fees vary according to program. *Financial support:* In 2006–07, 13 research assistantships (averaging $8,838 per year), 7 teaching assistantships (averaging $7,586 per year) were awarded; career-related internships or fieldwork, Federal Work-Study, and tuition waivers (partial) also available. Support available to part-time students. Financial award application deadline: 3/1. *Unit head:* Dr. Bert Jacobson, Head, 405-744-6275.

Oklahoma State University, College of Education, School of Teaching and Curriculum Leadership, Stillwater, OK 74078. Offers MS, PhD. *Faculty:* 32 full-time (27 women), 26 part-time/adjunct (22 women). *Students:* 28 full-time (21 women), 211 part-time (163 women); includes 43 minority (13 African Americans, 18 American Indian/Alaska Native, 5 Asian Americans or Pacific Islanders, 7 Hispanic Americans), 12 international. Average age 40. 136 applicants, 34% accepted, 40 enrolled. In 2006, 58 master's, 13 doctorates awarded. *Degree requirements:* For master's, thesis or alternative; for doctorate, thesis/dissertation. *Entrance requirements:* For master's, GRE or MAT; for doctorate, GRE. Additional exam requirements/recommendations for international students: Required—TOEFL. *Application deadline:* For fall admission, 7/1 priority date for domestic students, 3/1 priority date for international students; for spring admission, 8/1 priority date for international students. Applications are processed on a rolling basis. Application fee: $40 ($75 for international students). Electronic applications accepted. *Expenses:* Tuition, state resident: part-time $146 per credit hour. Tuition, nonresident: part-time $516 per credit hour. Required fees: $44 per credit hour. Tuition and fees vary according to program. *Financial support:* In 2006–07, 10 research assistantships (averaging $9,621 per year), 19 teaching assistantships (averaging $8,939 per year) were awarded; career-related internships or fieldwork, Federal Work-Study, scholarships/grants, health care benefits, tuition waivers (partial), and unspecified assistantships also available. Support available to part-time students. Financial award application deadline: 3/1. *Unit head:* Dr. Christine Ormsbee, Head, 405-744-7125.

Old Dominion University, Darden College of Education, Programs in Educational Leadership and Administration, Norfolk, VA 23529. Offers educational leadership (PhD, Ed S); educational training (MS Ed); principal preparation (MS Ed). *Accreditation:* NCATE. Part-time and evening/weekend programs available. Postbaccalaureate distance learning degree programs offered (minimal on-campus study). *Faculty:* 7 full-time (4 women), 6 part-time/adjunct (4 women). *Students:* 15 full-time (8 women), 93 part-time (60 women); includes 42 minority (41 African Americans, 1 Hispanic American). Average age 37. 29 applicants, 90% accepted, 18 enrolled. In 2006, 14 master's, 2 other advanced degrees awarded. *Degree requirements:* For master's, practicum, research project, thesis optional; for doctorate, thesis/dissertation, comprehensive exam; for Ed S, field research, thesis optional. *Entrance requirements:* For master's, GRE General Test or MAT, minimum GPA of 3.0 in major, letter of recommendation; for doctorate, GRE, minimum graduate GPA of 3.5, 3 letters of recommendation; for Ed S, GRE General Test or MAT, minimum GPA of 3.0 in major, 2 letters of recommendation. Additional exam requirements/recommendations for international students: Required—TOEFL (minimum score 550 paper-based). *Application deadline:* For fall admission, 6/1 priority date for domestic students, 2/15 priority date for international students; for winter admission, 10/1 priority date for international students; for spring admission, 11/1 priority date for domestic students, 2/1 priority date for international students. Applications are processed on a rolling basis. Application fee: $40. Electronic applications accepted. *Expenses:* Tuition, area resident: Part-time $285 per credit hour. Tuition, nonresident: part-time $715 per credit hour. Required fees: $94 per semester. *Financial support:* In 2006–07, 48 students received support, including 3 fellowships (averaging $4,545 per year), 1 research assistantship with partial tuition reimbursement available (averaging $9,000 per year); career-related internships or fieldwork, scholarships/grants, and tuition waivers (partial) also available. Support available to part-time students. Financial award application deadline: 2/15; financial award applicants required to submit FAFSA. *Faculty research:* Principal and leadership preparation, supervision, policy studies, finance, teacher quality. Total annual research expenditures: $225,000. *Unit head:* Dr. Dana D. Burnett, Interim Graduate Program Director, 757-683-3221, Fax: 757-683-5756, E-mail: elceagpd@odu.edu.

Old Dominion University, Darden College of Education, Programs in Higher Education, Norfolk, VA 23529. Offers educational leadership (MS Ed, Ed S), including higher education. Part-time programs available. *Faculty:* 3 full-time (1 woman), 10 part-time/adjunct (5 women). *Students:* 37 full-time (22 women), 13 part-time (12 women); includes 10 minority (9 African Americans, 1 American Indian/Alaska Native), 1 international. Average age 25. 50 applicants, 70% accepted, 27 enrolled. In 2006, 10 degrees awarded. *Degree requirements:* For master's, comprehensive exam, registration. *Entrance requirements:* For master's, GRE or MAT, minimum undergraduate GPA of 2.8; for Ed S, GRE or MAT, 2 letters of reference, minimum GPA of 3.5, master's degree. Additional exam requirements/recommendations for international students: Required—TOEFL. *Application deadline:* For fall admission, 5/1 for domestic and international students; for winter admission, 10/1 for domestic and international students; for spring admission, 3/1 for domestic and international students. Applications are processed on a rolling basis. Application fee: $40. Electronic applications accepted. *Expenses:* Tuition, area resident: Part-time $285 per credit hour. Tuition, nonresident: part-time $715 per credit hour. Required fees: $94 per semester. *Financial support:* Research assistantships with partial tuition reimbursements, career-related internships or fieldwork, scholarships/grants, and unspecified assistantships available. *Faculty research:* Law leadership, student development, research administration, international higher education administration. *Unit head:* Dr. Dennis Edward Gregory, Graduate Program Director, 757-683-3702, Fax: 757-683-5756, E-mail: dgregory@odu.edu.

Educational Administration

Oral Roberts University, School of Education, Tulsa, OK 74171-0001. Offers Christian school administration (MA Ed, Ed D); Christian school administration (K-12) (MA Ed, Ed D); Christian school curriculum development (MA Ed); college and higher education administration (MA Ed, Ed D); public school administration (K-12) (MA Ed, Ed D); public school teaching (MA Ed); teaching English as a second language (MA Ed). *Accreditation:* NCATE. Part-time programs available. Postbaccalaureate distance learning degree programs offered (minimal on-campus study). *Faculty:* 9 full-time (2 women), 9 part-time/adjunct (4 women). *Students:* 331 full-time (217 women); includes 118 minority (96 African Americans, 7 American Indian/Alaska Native, 10 Asian Americans or Pacific Islanders, 5 Hispanic Americans). 125 applicants, 96% accepted, 116 enrolled. In 2006, 25 master's, 10 doctorates awarded. *Degree requirements:* For master's, thesis (for some programs), comprehensive exam; for doctorate, thesis/dissertation, comprehensive exam. *Entrance requirements:* For master's, GRE General Test or MAT, minimum GPA of 3.0; for doctorate, minimum GPA of 3.0. Additional exam requirements/recommendations for international students: Required—TOEFL (minimum score 500 paper-based; 173 computer-based). *Application deadline:* For fall admission, 7/1 priority date for domestic students, 5/1 priority date for international students; for spring admission, 12/1 priority date for domestic students, 10/1 priority date for international students. Applications are processed on a rolling basis. Application fee: $35. *Expenses: Contact institution. Financial support:* In 2006–07, 4 research assistantships (averaging $5,000 per year) were awarded; scholarships/grants and unspecified assistantships also available. Financial award application deadline: 6/1; financial award applicants required to submit FAFSA. *Faculty research:* Teacher effectiveness, college success in high achieving, African-Americans, professional development practices. *Unit head:* Dr. David Hand, Dean, 918-495-7084, Fax: 918-495-6050, E-mail: dhand@oru.edu. *Application contact:* Kim Schmeisser, Graduate Admissions, 918-495-6058, Fax: 918-495-6222, E-mail: gradeducation@oru.edu.

Oregon State University, Graduate School, College of Education, Program in Adult Education and Higher Education Leadership, Corvallis, OR 97331. Offers Ed M, MAIS. *Accreditation:* NCATE. Part-time programs available. *Students:* 2 full-time (both women), 50 part-time (38 women); includes 4 minority (2 African Americans, 1 Asian American or Pacific Islander, 1 Hispanic American). Average age 45. In 2006, 19 degrees awarded. *Degree requirements:* For master's, thesis or alternative. *Entrance requirements:* For master's, minimum GPA of 3.0 in last 90 hours. Additional exam requirements/recommendations for international students: Required—TOEFL. *Application deadline:* For fall admission, 3/1 for domestic students. Applications are processed on a rolling basis. Application fee: $50. *Financial support:* Research assistantships, teaching assistantships, career-related internships or fieldwork, Federal Work-Study, and institutionally sponsored loans available. Support available to part-time students. Financial award application deadline: 2/1. *Faculty research:* Adult training and developmental psychology, cross-cultural communication, leadership development and human relations, adult literacy. *Unit head:* Dr. Richard Shintaku, Head, 541-737-9324.

Ottawa University, Graduate Studies-Arizona, Program in Education, Ottawa, KS 66067-3399. Offers community college counseling (MA); curriculum and instruction (MA); early childhood (MA); education intervention (MA); education leadership (MA); education technology (MA); Montessori early childhood education (MA); Montessori elementary education (MA); professional development (MA); school guidance counseling (MA); special education—cross categorical (MA). Programs offered in Mesa, Phoenix, Tempe and West Valley, AZ. *Accreditation:* NCATE. Part-time programs available. *Faculty:* 7 full-time (3 women), 24 part-time/adjunct (11 women). *Students:* 14 full-time (9 women), 162 part-time (128 women); includes 31 minority (13 African Americans, 2 American Indian/Alaska Native, 1 Asian American or Pacific Islander, 15 Hispanic Americans), 1 international. Average age 38. In 2006, 56 degrees awarded. *Degree requirements:* For master's, thesis or alternative, registration. *Entrance requirements:* For master's, minimum undergraduate GPA of 3.0, copy of current state certification or teaching license. Additional exam requirements/recommendations for international students: Required—TOEFL (minimum score 550 paper-based; 213 computer-based). *Application deadline:* For fall admission, 7/1 priority date for domestic students; for winter admission, 11/1 priority date for domestic students; for spring admission, 2/1 priority date for domestic students. Applications are processed on a rolling basis. Application fee: $50. Electronic applications accepted. *Expenses: Contact institution. Application contact:* Bunny Simpson, Secretary, 602-371-1188, Fax: 602-371-0035, E-mail: bunny.simpson@ottawa.edu.

Our Lady of Holy Cross College, Program in Education and Counseling, New Orleans, LA 70131-7399. Offers administration and supervision (M Ed); curriculum and instruction (M Ed); marriage and family counseling (MA); school counseling (M Ed, MA). *Accreditation:* ACA; NCATE. Part-time and evening/weekend programs available. *Degree requirements:* For master's, thesis. *Entrance requirements:* For master's, GRE General Test, minimum GPA of 2.7.

Our Lady of the Lake University of San Antonio, School of Education and Clinical Studies, Program in Leadership Studies, San Antonio, TX 78207-4689. Offers PhD. *Degree requirements:* For doctorate, thesis/dissertation, internship, qualifying exam. *Entrance requirements:* For doctorate, GRE General Test or MAT, interview.

Our Lady of the Lake University of San Antonio, School of Education and Clinical Studies, Program in Principal, San Antonio, TX 78207-4689. Offers M Ed. Part-time and evening/weekend programs available. *Degree requirements:* For master's, exam, internship. *Entrance requirements:* For master's, GRE General Test or MAT. Additional exam requirements/recommendations for international students: Required—TOEFL. Electronic applications accepted. *Faculty research:* Leadership, organizational behavior.

Pace University, School of Education, New York, NY 10038. Offers administration and supervision (MS Ed); curriculum and instruction (MS); education (MST); school business management (Certificate). *Accreditation:* NCATE. Part-time and evening/weekend programs available. *Faculty:* 9 full-time, 12 part-time/adjunct. *Students:* 130 full-time (106 women), 2,151 part-time (1,484 women); includes 96 minority (50 African Americans, 2 American Indian/Alaska Native, 21 Asian Americans or Pacific Islanders, 23 Hispanic Americans), 6 international. Average age 27. 229 applicants, 70% accepted, 70 enrolled. In 2006, 550 master's, 23 other advanced degrees awarded. *Degree requirements:* For master's, internship. *Entrance requirements:* For master's, interview, teaching certificate. *Application deadline:* For fall admission, 7/31 priority date for domestic students; for spring admission, 11/30 for domestic students. Applications are processed on a rolling basis. Application fee: $65. Electronic applications accepted. *Expenses: Contact institution. Financial support:* Research assistantships, career-related internships or fieldwork and Federal Work-Study available. Support available to part-time students. Financial award applicants required to submit FAFSA. *Unit head:* Dr. Harriet Feldman, Interim Dean, 212-346-1512. *Application contact:* Joanna Broda, Director of Admissions, 212-346-1652, Fax: 212-346-1585, E-mail: gradnyc@pace.edu.

See Close-Up on page 907.

Pacific Lutheran University, Division of Graduate Studies, School of Education, Program in Educational Leadership, Tacoma, WA 98447. Offers MA. *Accreditation:* NCATE. Part-time and evening/weekend programs available. *Faculty:* 5 full-time (2 women), 3 part-time/adjunct (2 women). *Students:* 2 full-time (1 woman), 14 part-time (11 women); includes 3 minority (1 African American, 2 Asian Americans or Pacific Islanders), 1 international. Average age 29. 18 applicants, 100% accepted, 16 enrolled. In 2006, 22 degrees awarded. *Degree requirements:* For master's, thesis or alternative, comprehensive exam. *Entrance requirements:* For master's, GRE General Test or MAT, interview. Additional exam requirements/recommendations for international students: Required—TOEFL (minimum score 550 paper-based; 213 computer-based). *Application deadline:* For fall admission, 5/1 priority date for domestic students. Application fee: $40. *Expenses:* Tuition: Full-time $17,544. Part-time tuition and fees vary according to program. *Financial support:* In 2006–07, 10 students received support; fellowships, research assistantships, Federal Work-Study, scholarships/grants, and unspecified assistantships available. Financial award application deadline: 3/1. *Unit head:* Dr. Michael Hillis, Graduate Director, 253-535-7272, Fax: 253-535-7184, E-mail: hillis@plu.edu. *Application contact:* Linda DuBay, Senior Office Assistant, 253-535-7151, Fax: 253-536-5136, E-mail: admissions@plu.edu.

Pacific Union College, Department of Education, Angwin, CA 94508-9707. Offers teacher leadership (M Ed). Part-time programs available. *Faculty:* 4 full-time (2 women). *Students:* 4 full-time (all women), 14 part-time (10 women); includes 3 minority (all Asian Americans or Pacific Islanders) Average age 29. 5 applicants, 100% accepted. In 2006, 6 degrees awarded. *Median time to degree:* Master's–1 year full-time, 4 years part-time. *Degree requirements:* For master's, thesis, action research project. *Entrance requirements:* For master's, GRE, interview, teaching credential, letters of recommendation. *Application deadline:* For fall admission, 7/1 priority date for domestic students. Applications are processed on a rolling basis. Application fee: $0. *Expenses:* Tuition: Full-time $20,130; part-time $584 per quarter hour. Required fees: $135. Tuition and fees vary according to course load and student's religious affiliation. *Financial support:* In 2006–07, 2 students received support, including 2 teaching assistantships with full tuition reimbursements available (averaging $2,600 per year); Federal Work-Study, scholarships/grants, and unspecified assistantships also available. Support available to part-time students. Financial award application deadline: 3/1. *Faculty research:* Glasser biography and development of choice theory, reading instruction competence, teacher excellence, alternative assessments for high school teachers, educational psychology. *Unit head:* Dr. Jim Roy, Chair, 707-965-6644, Fax: 707-965-6645, E-mail: jroy@puc.edu. *Application contact:* Marsha Crow, Credential Analyst, 707-965-6643, Fax: 707-965-6645, E-mail: mcrow@puc.edu.

Park University, College of Graduate and Professional Studies, Kansas City, MO 54105. Offers adult education (M Ed); at-risk students (M Ed); disaster and emergency management (MPA); educational administration (M Ed); entrepreneurship (MBA); general business (MBA); general education (M Ed); government/business relations (MPA); healthcare/services management (MBA, MPA); international business (MBA); K-12 certification (MAT); management information systems (MBA); management of information systems (MPA); middle school certification (MAT); multi-cultural education (M Ed); nonprofit management (MPA); public management (MPA); school law (M Ed); secondary school certification (MAT); special education (M Ed). Part-time and evening/weekend programs available. Postbaccalaureate distance learning degree programs offered (no on-campus study). *Degree requirements:* For master's, thesis (for some programs), comprehensive exam, registration. *Entrance requirements:* For master's, GRE, GMAT, teacher certification (M Ed). Additional exam requirements/recommendations for international students: Required—TOEFL (minimum score 550 paper-based). Electronic applications accepted. *Faculty research:* Literacy, leadership, brain based research, multicultural education, diversity.

Penn State University Park, Graduate School, College of Education, Department of Education Policy Studies, State College, University Park, PA 16802-1503. Offers college student affairs (M Ed); educational leadership (M Ed, MS, D Ed, PhD); educational theory and policy (MA, PhD); higher education (M Ed, D Ed, PhD). *Accreditation:* NCATE. *Unit head:* Dr. Jacqueline A. Stefkovich, Head, 814-863-0619, E-mail: jas71@psu.edu.

Pepperdine University, Graduate School of Education and Psychology, Division of Education, Program in Administration, Los Angeles, CA 90045. Offers education (MS). *Students:* 39 full-time (29 women), 26 part-time (15 women); includes 24 minority (9 African Americans, 2 Asian Americans or Pacific Islanders, 13 Hispanic Americans). Average age 39. 70 applicants, 91% accepted, 64 enrolled. In 2006, 63 degrees awarded. *Entrance requirements:* For master's, GRE General Test. Additional exam requirements/recommendations for international students: Required—TOEFL. *Application deadline:* For fall admission, 7/1 for domestic students. Applications are processed on a rolling basis. Application fee: $45. *Financial support:* Research assistantships, teaching assistantships available. Financial award application deadline: 7/1. *Unit head:* Dr. Linda Purrington, Director, 310-258-2568, E-mail: linda.purrington@pepperdine.edu. *Application contact:* Henry P. Price, IV, Program Administrator, 310-568-5622, E-mail: henry.price.iv@pepperdine.edu.

Pepperdine University, Graduate School of Education and Psychology, Division of Education, Program in Educational Leadership, Administration, and Policy, Los Angeles, CA 90045. Offers Ed D. *Students:* 1 applicant, 0% accepted. In 2006, 28 degrees awarded. *Degree requirements:* For doctorate, thesis/dissertation. *Entrance requirements:* For doctorate, GRE General Test, MAT. Additional exam requirements/recommendations for international students: Required—TOEFL. *Application deadline:* For fall admission, 3/30 priority date for domestic students. Applications are processed on a rolling basis. Application fee: $50. *Expenses: Contact institution. Financial support:* Application deadline: 7/1. *Unit head:* Dr. Susan Parks, Director, 310-568-5640, E-mail: susan.parks@pepperdine.edu. *Application contact:* Henry P. Price, IV, Program Administrator, 310-568-5622, E-mail: henry.price.iv@pepperdine.edu.

Pepperdine University, Graduate School of Education and Psychology, Division of Education, Program in Organizational Leadership, Los Angeles, CA 90045. Offers Ed D. Part-time and evening/weekend programs available. *Students:* 2 full-time (both women), 224 part-time (122 women); includes 83 minority (38 African Americans, 22 Asian Americans or Pacific Islanders, 23 Hispanic Americans), 4 international. 61 applicants, 85% accepted, 44 enrolled. In 2006, 5 degrees awarded. *Degree requirements:* For doctorate, thesis/dissertation. *Entrance requirements:* For doctorate, GMAT or GRE General Test, MAT. Additional exam requirements/recommendations for international students: Required—TOEFL. *Application deadline:* For fall admission, 7/1 for domestic students. Applications are processed on a rolling basis. Application fee: $55. *Expenses: Contact institution. Financial support:* Research assistantships, teaching assistantships, institutionally sponsored loans and scholarships/grants available. Support available to part-time students. Financial award application deadline: 7/1. *Unit head:* Dr. Farzin Madjidi, Director, 310-568-5726, E-mail: farzin.madjidi@pepperdine.edu. *Application contact:* Christie Dailo, Program Administrator, 310-568-5612, E-mail: christie.dailo@pepperdine.edu.

Pepperdine University, Graduate School of Education and Psychology, Division of Education, Program in Organization Change, Los Angeles, CA 90045. Offers Ed D. Part-time and evening/weekend programs available. *Students:* Average age 45. 31 applicants, 81% accepted, 19 enrolled. In 2006, 3 degrees awarded. *Degree requirements:* For doctorate, thesis/dissertation. *Entrance requirements:* For doctorate, GMAT, GRE General Test, MAT. Additional exam requirements/recommendations for international students: Required—TOEFL. *Application deadline:* Applications are processed on a rolling basis. Application fee: $55. *Expenses: Contact institution. Financial support:* Research assistantships, teaching assistantships, institutionally sponsored loans and scholarships/grants available. Support available to part-time students. Financial award application deadline: 7/1; financial award applicants required to submit FAFSA. *Unit head:* Dr. Kay Davis, Director, 310-568-5660, E-mail: kay.davis@pepperdine.edu. *Application contact:* Gabriella Miramontes, Program Administrator, 310-568-2835, E-mail: gabriella.miramontes@pepperdine.edu.

Philadelphia Biblical University, School of Education, Langhorne, PA 19047-2990. Offers educational leadership and administration (MS El); teacher education (MS Ed). Part-time and evening/weekend programs available. *Faculty:* 8 full-time (6 women), 3 part-time/adjunct (2 women). *Students:* 6 full-time (5 women), 70 part-time (42 women); includes 12 minority (4 African Americans, 7 Asian Americans or Pacific Islanders, 1 Hispanic American), 3 international. Average age 35. 29 applicants, 55% accepted, 12 enrolled. In 2006, 30 degrees awarded. *Entrance requirements:* Additional exam requirements/recommendations for international students: Required—TOEFL (minimum score 550 paper-based; 213 computer-based). *Application deadline:* Applications are processed on a rolling basis. Application fee: $25. Electronic applications accepted. *Expenses:* Tuition: Full-time $8,820; part-time $490 per credit. *Financial support:* In 2006–07, 27 students received support. Scholarships/grants available. Support available to part-time students. Financial award applicants required to submit FAFSA. *Unit head:* Dr. Martha MacCullough, Dean, 215-702-4387, E-mail: teacher.ed@pbu.edu. *Application contact:* Katerina Penkova, Enrollment Counselor, Graduate Education, 800-572-2472, Fax: 215-702-4248, E-mail: kpenkova@pbu.edu.

Pittsburg State University, Graduate School, College of Education, Department of Special Services and Leadership Studies, Program in Educational Leadership, Pittsburg, KS 66762. Offers educational technology (MS). *Accreditation:* NCATE. *Students:* 109. *Degree requirements:* For master's, thesis or alternative. *Entrance requirements:* For master's, GRE General Test or MAT. Application fee: $35 ($60 for international students). *Expenses:* Tuition, state resident: full-time $2,144; part-time $181 per credit hour. Tuition, nonresident: full-time $5,273; part-time $442 per credit hour. Tuition and fees vary according to course load and campus/location. *Financial support:* In 2006–07, teaching assistantships (averaging $5,000 per year); career-related internships or fieldwork, Federal Work-Study, and unspecified assistantships also available. *Application contact:* Marvene Darraugh, Administrative Officer, 620-235-4220, Fax: 620-235-4219, E-mail: mdarraug@pittstate.edu.

Plymouth State University, College of Graduate Studies, Graduate Studies in Education, Program in Educational Leadership, Plymouth, NH 03264-1595. Offers M Ed. *Accreditation:* NCATE. Part-time and evening/weekend programs available. *Students:* 1 full-time (0 women), 84 part-time (49 women); includes 1 minority (American Indian/Alaska Native). Average age 38. 21 applicants, 100% accepted, 21 enrolled. In 2006, 30 degrees awarded. *Degree requirements:* For master's, PRAXIS. *Entrance requirements:* For master's, MAT, minimum GPA of 3.0. *Application deadline:* Applications are processed on a rolling basis. Application fee: $75. *Expenses:* Tuition, state resident: part-time $369 per credit. Tuition, nonresident: part-time $407 per credit. Tuition and fees vary according to course level. *Financial support:* Career-related internships or fieldwork, scholarships/grants, and unspecified assistantships available. Support available to part-time students. Financial award applicants required to submit FAFSA. *Unit head:* Dr. Marianne True, Program Coordinator, 603-535-2660, E-mail: mtrue@plymouth.edu.

Point Park University, School of Arts and Sciences, Department of Education and Community Services, Pittsburgh, PA 15222-1984. Offers curriculum and instruction (MA); educational administration (MA). Part-time and evening/weekend programs available. *Faculty:* 3 full-time, 16 part-time/adjunct. *Students:* 20 full-time (15 women), 30 part-time (19 women); includes 8 minority (all African Americans), 2 international. Average age 33. 58 applicants, 62% accepted, 22 enrolled. In 2006, 15 degrees awarded. *Entrance requirements:* For master's, minimum GPA of 3.0, resumé, 2 letters of recommendation. Additional exam requirements/recommendations for international students: Required—TOEFL. *Application deadline:* Applications are processed on a rolling basis. Application fee: $30. Electronic applications accepted. *Expenses:* Tuition: Full-time $9,828; part-time $546 per credit. Required fees: $360; $20 per credit. *Financial support:* In 2006–07, 5 students received support, including 2 research assistantships with full tuition reimbursements available (averaging $5,400 per year); career-related internships or fieldwork, scholarships/grants, and unspecified assistantships also available. Support available to part-time students. Financial award application deadline: 5/1; financial award applicants required to submit FAFSA. *Unit head:* Dr. Karen McIntyre, Chair, 412-392-3972, Fax: 412-392-3927, E-mail: kmcintyre@pointpark.edu. *Application contact:* Marty Paonessa, Associate Director, Graduate and Adult Enrollment, 412-392-3915, Fax: 412-392-6164, E-mail: mpaonessa@pointpark.edu.

Pontificia Universidad Catolica Madre y Maestra, Graduate School, Santiago, Dominican Republic. Offers administration (M Adm, M Ed); architecture of interiors (M Arch); architecture of tourist lodgings (M Arch); construction administration (ME); convergent networks (ME); earthquake-resistant engineering (ME); environmental engineering (MEE); financial (M Mgmt); human resources (EMBA); international (M Mgmt); labor law and Social Security (M Mgmt); logistics management (ME); urban planning (M Urb). *Entrance requirements:* For master's, curriculum vitae, interview.

Portland State University, Graduate Studies, School of Education, Department of Educational Policy, Foundations, and Administrative Studies, Portland, OR 97207-0751. Offers educational leadership (MA, MS, Ed D); postsecondary, adult and continuing education (Ed D). *Accreditation:* NCATE. Part-time and evening/weekend programs available. *Faculty:* 11 full-time (5 women), 10 part-time/adjunct (4 women). *Students:* 62 full-time (51 women), 227 part-time (149 women); includes 41 minority (7 African Americans, 10 American Indian/Alaska Native, 8 Asian Americans or Pacific Islanders, 16 Hispanic Americans), 10 international. Average age 40. 234 applicants, 91% accepted, 67 enrolled. In 2006, 69 master's, 4 doctorates awarded. *Degree requirements:* For master's, thesis or alternative, written exam; for doctorate, thesis/dissertation, comprehensive exam. *Entrance requirements:* For master's, California Basic Educational Skills Test, minimum GPA of 3.0 in upper-division course work or 2.75 overall; for doctorate, GRE General Test or MAT. Additional exam requirements/recommendations for international students: Required—TOEFL (minimum score 550 paper-based; 213 computer-based). *Application deadline:* For fall admission, 4/1 for domestic and international students; for winter admission, 9/1 for domestic and international students; for spring admission, 11/1 for domestic and international students. Applications are processed on a rolling basis. Application fee: $50. *Expenses:* Tuition, state resident: full-time $6,426; part-time $238 per credit. Tuition, nonresident: full-time $11,016; part-time $408 per credit. Tuition and fees vary according to course load. *Financial support:* In 2006–07, 10 research assistantships with full tuition reimbursements (averaging $5,453 per year) were awarded; teaching assistantships with full tuition reimbursements, career-related internships or fieldwork, Federal Work-Study, and institutionally sponsored loans also available. Support available to part-time students. Financial award application deadline: 3/1; financial award applicants required to submit FAFSA. *Faculty research:* Leadership development and research, principals and urban schools, accelerated schools, cooperative learning, family involvement in schools. Total annual research expenditures: $322,962. *Unit head:* Dilafroz Williams, Head, 503-725-4676, Fax: 503-725-8475. *Application contact:* Kellie Walker, Admission Secretary, 503-725-4716, Fax: 503-725-8475.

Prairie View A&M University, Graduate School, College of Education, Department of Educational Leadership and Counseling, Prairie View, TX 77446-0519. Offers counseling (MA, MS Ed); educational leadership (PhD); school administration (M Ed, MS Ed); school supervision (M Ed, MS Ed). *Accreditation:* NCATE. Part-time and evening/weekend programs available. *Degree requirements:* For master's, thesis optional; for doctorate, thesis/dissertation, comprehensive exam. *Entrance requirements:* For master's, GRE General Test, 3 letters of reference, minimum undergraduate GPA of 2.5; for doctorate, GRE General Test, 3 letters of reference. Additional exam requirements/recommendations for international students: Required—TOEFL (minimum score 550 paper-based). Electronic applications accepted. *Faculty research:* Mentoring, personality assessment, holistic/humanistic education.

Providence College, Graduate Studies, Department of Education, Programs in Administration, Providence, RI 02918. Offers administration (M Ed); elementary administration (M Ed); secondary administration (M Ed). Part-time and evening/weekend programs available. *Faculty:* 6 full-time (5 women), 45 part-time/adjunct (25 women). *Students:* 3 full-time (1 woman), 68 part-time (38 women); includes 3 minority (1 Asian American or Pacific Islander, 2 Hispanic Americans). Average age 35. 13 applicants, 85% accepted. In 2006, 24 degrees awarded. *Degree requirements:* For master's, comprehensive exam. *Entrance requirements:* For master's, GRE General Test. Additional exam requirements/recommendations for international students: Required—TOEFL (minimum score 550 paper-based; 213 computer-based). *Application deadline:* For fall admission, 8/1 for domestic students; for spring admission, 12/1 for domestic students. Applications are processed on a rolling basis. Application fee: $55. *Expenses:* Tuition: Full-time $6,573; part-time $939 per unit. *Financial support:* In 2006–07, 1 research assistantship with full tuition reimbursement (averaging $8,400 per year) was awarded; career-related internships or fieldwork, institutionally sponsored loans, and unspecified assistantships also available. Support available to part-time students. Financial award application deadline: 8/1; financial award applicants required to submit FAFSA. *Unit head:* Francis J. Leary, Head, 401-865-2247, Fax: 401-865-1147.

Purdue University, Graduate School, School of Education, Department of Educational Studies, West Lafayette, IN 47907. Offers administration (MS Ed, PhD, Ed S); counseling and development (MS Ed, PhD); education of the gifted (MS Ed); educational psychology (MS Ed, PhD); foundations of education (MS Ed, PhD); higher education administration (MS Ed, PhD); special education (MS Ed, PhD). *Accreditation:* ACA (one or more programs are accredited); NCATE (one or more programs are accredited). Part-time and evening/weekend programs available. *Faculty:* 28 full-time (18 women). *Students:* 100 full-time (71 women), 126 part-time (77 women); includes 32 minority (19 African Americans, 2 American Indian/Alaska Native, 6 Asian Americans or Pacific Islanders, 5 Hispanic Americans), 33 international. Average age 36. 152 applicants, 62% accepted, 56 enrolled. In 2006, 51 master's, 17 doctorates awarded. *Degree requirements:* For master's, thesis optional; for doctorate, thesis/dissertation, oral and written exams; for Ed S, oral presentation, project. *Entrance requirements:* For master's, GRE General Test, minimum undergraduate GPA of 3.0; for doctorate, GRE General Test; for Ed S, GRE, minimum B average. Additional exam requirements/recommendations for international students: Required—TOEFL. *Application deadline:* For fall admission, 1/15 for domestic students; for spring admission, 9/15 for domestic students. Applications are processed on a rolling basis. Application fee: $55. Electronic applications accepted. *Financial support:* In 2006–07, 6 fellowships with full tuition reimbursements (averaging $13,300 per year), 23 research assistantships with full tuition reimbursements (averaging $11,500 per year), 33 teaching assistantships with full tuition reimbursements (averaging $10,800 per year) were awarded; career-related internships or fieldwork and tuition waivers (full) also available. Support available to part-time students. Financial award application deadline: 3/1; financial award applicants required to submit FAFSA. *Faculty research:* Motivation, learning disabilities, school learning, group processes, cognitive development. *Unit head:* Dr. Kevin R Kelly, Head, 765-494-9170, Fax: 765-496-1228. *Application contact:* Patricia Mason, Coordinator of Graduate Studies, 765-494-2346, Fax: 765-494-5832, E-mail: gradoffice@soe.purdue.edu.

Purdue University Calumet, Graduate School, School of Education, Program in Educational Administration, Hammond, IN 46323-2094. Offers MS Ed. *Entrance requirements:* Additional exam requirements/recommendations for international students: Required—TOEFL.

Queens College of the City University of New York, Division of Graduate Studies, Division of Education, Department of Educational and Community Programs, Program in Educational Leadership, Flushing, NY 11367-1597. Offers AC. Part-time programs available. *Faculty:* 4 full-time (0 women). *Students:* 2 full-time (1 woman), 139 part-time (94 women). 112 applicants, 96% accepted, 90 enrolled. In 2006, 124 degrees awarded. *Degree requirements:* For AC, internship, thesis optional. *Entrance requirements:* For degree, master's degree or equivalent. Additional exam requirements/recommendations for international students: Required—TOEFL. *Application deadline:* For fall admission, 4/1 for domestic students; for spring admission, 11/1 for domestic students. Applications are processed on a rolling basis. Application fee: $125. *Financial support:* Career-related internships or fieldwork, Federal Work-Study, institutionally sponsored loans, and tuition waivers (partial) available. Support available to part-time students. Financial award application deadline: 4/1; financial award applicants required to submit FAFSA. *Unit head:* Dr. Kenneth Dunn, Coordinator, 718-997-5240. *Application contact:* Mario Caruso, Director of Graduate Admissions, 718-997-5200, Fax: 718-997-5193, E-mail: graduate_admissions@qc.edu.

Radford University, Graduate College, College of Education and Human Development, School of Teacher and Educational Leadership, Program in Educational Leadership, Radford, VA 24142. Offers MS. *Accreditation:* NCATE. Part-time and evening/weekend programs available. Postbaccalaureate distance learning degree programs offered (minimal on-campus study). *Faculty:* 1 full-time (0 women), 1 part-time/adjunct (0 women). *Students:* 3 full-time (2 women), 55 part-time (37 women); includes 2 minority (both African Americans) Average age 35. 24 applicants, 100% accepted, 15 enrolled. In 2006, 22 degrees awarded. *Degree requirements:* For master's, comprehensive exam. *Entrance requirements:* For master's, GRE or MAT. Additional exam requirements/recommendations for international students: Required—TOEFL. *Application deadline:* For fall admission, 3/1 priority date for domestic students, 4/1 for international students; for spring admission, 10/1 for domestic students, 8/1 for international students. Applications are processed on a rolling basis. Application fee: $40. Electronic applications accepted. *Expenses:* Tuition, state resident: full-time $4,680; part-time $260 per credit hour. Tuition, nonresident: full-time $8,604; part-time $478 per credit hour. *Financial support:* In 2006–07, research assistantships with partial tuition reimbursements (averaging $8,000 per year); teaching assistantships, career-related internships or fieldwork, Federal Work-Study, institutionally sponsored loans, scholarships/grants, and unspecified assistantships also available. Financial award application deadline: 3/1; financial award applicants required to submit FAFSA. *Unit head:* Dr. William F. Flora, Coordinator, 540-831-5302, Fax: 540-831-5059, E-mail: wfflora@radford.edu.

Regent University, Graduate School, School of Education, Virginia Beach, VA 23464-9800. Offers Christian school program (M Ed); cross-categorical special education (M Ed); education (M Ed, Ed D); educational leadership (M Ed); elementary education (M Ed); individual degree plan (M Ed); master teacher (M Ed); special education leadership (Ed S); TESOL (M Ed). Part-time and evening/weekend programs available. Postbaccalaureate distance learning degree programs offered (minimal on-campus study). *Faculty:* 25 full-time (11 women), 132 part-time/adjunct (90 women). *Students:* 220 full-time (176 women), 501 part-time (374 women); includes 264 minority (229 African Americans, 9 Asian Americans or Pacific Islanders, 26 Hispanic Americans), 13 international. Average age 38. 472 applicants, 79% accepted, 256 enrolled. In 2006, 185 master's, 5 doctorates awarded. *Degree requirements:* For master's, thesis or alternative; for doctorate, thesis/dissertation, comprehensive exam. *Entrance requirements:* For master's, MAT, minimum undergraduate GPA of 2.75, writing sample, resumé; for doctorate, GRE, writing sample, 3 years of relevant professional experience, master's-level paper, copies of published work. Additional exam requirements/recommendations for international students: Required—TOEFL (minimum score 577 paper-based; 233 computer-based). *Application deadline:* For fall admission, 4/1 priority date for domestic students; for spring admission, 10/15 priority date for domestic students. Applications are processed on a rolling basis. Application fee: $50. Electronic applications accepted. *Expenses:* Contact institution. *Financial support:* In 2006–07, 721 students received support; fellowships, career-related internships or fieldwork, scholarships/grants, tuition waivers (full and partial), and unspecified assistantships available. Support available to part-time students. Financial award application deadline: 4/1; financial award applicants required to submit FAFSA. *Faculty research:* Character development and discipline for children, education leadership development, diversity in schools, classroom management, technology in education settings. *Unit head:* Dr. Alan A. Arroyo, Dean, 757-226-4261, Fax: 757-226-4318, E-mail: alanarr@regent.edu. *Application contact:* Althea Bishard, Registrar and Executive Director of Enrollment and Academic Services, 800-373-5504, Fax: 757-226-4381, E-mail: admissions@regent.edu.

Regis University, School for Professional Studies, Program in Teacher Education, Denver, CO 80221-1099. Offers adult learning, training, and development (M Ed); curriculum, instruction, and assessment (M Ed); early childhood (M Ed); educational technology (Certificate); elementary (M Ed); ESL (M Ed); fine arts (M Ed), including arts, music; instructional technology (M Ed); professional leadership (M Ed); reading (M Ed); secondary (M Ed); self-designed (M Ed); space studies (M Ed); special education (M Ed); teacher licensure (M Ed). Program also offered in Henderson and Las Vegas (Summerlin), NV. Postbaccalaureate distance learning degree programs offered. *Unit head:* Dr. Suzie Perry, Dean, 303-458-4302. *Application contact:* Partick Lowenthal, Assistant Director, 303-458-4300 Ext. 4314, E-mail: masters@regis.edu.

Rhode Island College, School of Graduate Studies, Feinstein School of Education and Human Development, Department of Counseling, Educational Leadership, and School Psychology, Providence, RI 02908-1991. Offers counseling (MA); educational leadership (M Ed); school administration (M Ed); school counseling (CAGS). *Accreditation:* NCATE. Part-time and evening/weekend programs available. *Faculty:* 3 full-time (1 woman), 12 part-time/adjunct (5 women). *Students:* 42 full-time (39 women), 102 part-time (83 women); includes 4 minority (3 African Americans, 1 Hispanic American). Average age 33. In 2006, 52 master's, 12 other advanced degrees awarded. *Entrance requirements:* For master's, GRE General Test or MAT, 3 letters of recommendation. *Application deadline:* For fall admission, 3/15 for domestic

Educational Administration

Rhode Island College (continued)

students; for spring admission, 11/1 for domestic students. Applications are processed on a rolling basis. Application fee: $50. *Expenses:* Tuition, state resident: part-time $244 per credit. Tuition, nonresident: part-time $512 per credit. Required fees: $12 per credit. $66 per term. Tuition and fees vary according to degree level, program and reciprocity agreements. *Financial support:* Teaching assistantships with full tuition reimbursements, career-related internships or fieldwork, Federal Work-Study, scholarships/grants, health care benefits, and unspecified assistantships available. Support available to part-time students. Financial award application deadline: 5/15; financial award applicants required to submit FAFSA. *Unit head:* Dr. Monica Darcy, Chair, 401-456-8023, E-mail: mdarcy@ric.edu.

Rhode Island College, School of Graduate Studies, Feinstein School of Education and Human Development, Department of Educational Studies, Providence, RI 02908-1991. Offers bilingual/bicultural education (M Ed); educational administration (CAGS); English (MAT); French (MAT); history (MAT); math (MAT); secondary education (M Ed); Spanish (MAT); teaching English as a second language (M Ed, MAT); technology education (M Ed). *Accreditation:* NCATE. Part-time and evening/weekend programs available. *Faculty:* 12 full-time (5 women), 4 part-time/adjunct (all women). *Students:* 10 full-time (7 women), 27 part-time (23 women); includes 1 minority (Hispanic American) Average age 32. In 2006, 22 degrees awarded. *Entrance requirements:* For master's, BA in English, French, history, math or Spanish; evaluation of content area knowledge; 3 letters of recommendation; interview. *Application deadline:* For fall admission, 3/15 for domestic students; for spring admission, 11/1 for domestic students. Applications are processed on a rolling basis. Application fee: $50. *Expenses:* Tuition, state resident: part-time $244 per credit. Tuition, nonresident: part-time $512 per credit. Required fees: $12 per credit. $66 per term. Tuition and fees vary according to degree level, program and reciprocity agreements. *Financial support:* Teaching assistantships with full tuition reimbursements, career-related internships or fieldwork, Federal Work-Study, scholarships/grants, health care benefits, and unspecified assistantships available. Support available to part-time students. Financial award application deadline: 5/15; financial award applicants required to submit FAFSA. *Faculty research:* School administration, school/college articulation. *Unit head:* Dr. Charles McLaughlin, Chair, 401-456-8170.

Rider University, Department of Graduate Education, Leadership and Counseling, Lawrenceville, NJ 08648-3001. Offers counseling services (MA, Ed S); curriculum, instruction and supervision (MA); director of school counseling services (Certificate); educational administration (MA); organizational leadership (MA); principal (Certificate); reading/language arts (MA, Certificate), including reading specialist (Certificate), reading/language arts (MA); school business administrator (Certificate); school counseling services (Certificate); school psychology (Ed S); special education (MA); supervisor (Certificate); teacher certification (Certificate), including business education, elementary education, English as a second language, English education, mathematics education, preschool to grade 3, science education, social studies education, world languages; teaching (MA). *Accreditation:* NCATE. Part-time and evening/weekend programs available. *Faculty:* 24 full-time (12 women), 30 part-time/adjunct (15 women). *Students:* 90 full-time (75 women), 457 part-time (369 women); includes 73 minority (50 African Americans, 2 American Indian/Alaska Native, 6 Asian Americans or Pacific Islanders, 15 Hispanic Americans), 1 international. Average age 32. 314 applicants, 61% accepted, 138 enrolled. In 2006, 116 master's, 19 other advanced degrees awarded. *Degree requirements:* For master's, thesis or alternative, internship, portfolios, comprehensive exam (for some programs); for other advanced degree, internship, professional portfolio. *Entrance requirements:* For master's, GRE (counseling, school psychology), MAT, interview, resumé, letters of recommendation; for other advanced degree, PRAXIS. Additional exam requirements/recommendations for international students: Required—TOEFL (minimum score 550 paper-based; 213 computer-based). *Application deadline:* For fall admission, 5/1 priority date for domestic students, 6/1 priority date for international students; for spring admission, 11/1 priority date for domestic and international students. Applications are processed on a rolling basis. Application fee: $50. Electronic applications accepted. *Expenses:* Tuition: Part-time $525 per credit. Required fees: $35 per course. $30 per semester. *Financial support:* In 2006–07, 271 students received support. Career-related internships or fieldwork, Federal Work-Study, institutionally sponsored loans, and unspecified assistantships available. Support available to part-time students. Financial award applicants required to submit FAFSA. *Faculty research:* Gifted students, self-esteem, hope and mental health, conflicts in group work, cultural diversity and counseling assessment of special needs in children. *Unit head:* Dr. Dennis C. Buss, Chair, 609-895-5353, Fax: 609-896-5362, E-mail: dbuss@rider.edu. *Application contact:* Jamie L Mitchell, Director of Graduate Admissions, 609-896-5036, Fax: 609-895-5680, E-mail: jmitchell@rider.edu.

See Close-Up on page 913.

Rivier College, School of Graduate Studies, Department of Education, Nashua, NH 03060-5086. Offers curriculum and instruction (M Ed); early childhood education (M Ed); educational administration (M Ed); educational studies (M Ed); elementary education (M Ed); elementary education and general special education (M Ed); emotional and behavioral disorders (M Ed); general social education (M Ed); leadership and learning (CAGS); learning disabilities (M Ed); learning disabilities and reading (M Ed); mental health counseling (MA); reading (M Ed); school counseling (M Ed). Part-time and evening/weekend programs available. *Faculty:* 11 full-time (7 women), 40 part-time/adjunct (29 women). *Students:* 41 full-time (33 women), 221 part-time (192 women); includes 4 minority (2 African Americans, 2 Hispanic Americans). Average age 37. In 2006, 134 degrees awarded. *Degree requirements:* For master's, internships. *Entrance requirements:* For master's, GRE General Test or MAT. *Application deadline:* Applications are processed on a rolling basis. Application fee: $25. *Financial support:* Available to part-time students. Application deadline: 2/1; *Unit head:* Dr. Charles L. Mitsakos, Chairman, 603-888-1311 Ext. 8582. *Application contact:* Diane Monahan, Director of Graduate Admissions, 603-897-8129, Fax: 603-897-8810, E-mail: gradadm@rivier.edu.

Roosevelt University, Graduate Division, College of Education, Program in Educational Leadership and Organizational Change, Chicago, IL 60605-1394. Offers MA, Ed D. *Students:* 28 full-time (19 women), 97 part-time (58 women); includes 24 minority (21 African Americans, 2 Asian Americans or Pacific Islanders, 1 Hispanic American). Average age 38. 74 applicants, 59% accepted, 42 enrolled. In 2006, 23 master's, 7 doctorates awarded. *Unit head:* Dr. Susan Katz, Chair, 312-341-6498. *Application contact:* Joanne Canyon-Heller, Coordinator of Graduate Admission, 877-APPLY RU, Fax: 312-281-3356, E-mail: applyru@roosevelt.edu.

Roosevelt University, Graduate Division, College of Education, Program in Teacher Leadership (LEAD), Chicago, IL 60605-1394. Offers MA. *Students:* 1 (woman) full-time, 71 part-time (56 women). Average age 32. 21 applicants, 76% accepted, 13 enrolled. In 2006, 40 degrees awarded. *Unit head:* Daniel White, Director, 847-619-7969. *Application contact:* Joanne Canyon-Heller, Coordinator of Graduate Admission, 877-APPLY RU, Fax: 312-281-3356, E-mail: applyru@roosevelt.edu.

Rowan University, Graduate School, College of Education, Department of Educational Leadership, Program in Educational Leadership, Glassboro, NJ 08028-1701. Offers Ed D. *Accreditation:* NCATE. Part-time and evening/weekend programs available. *Students:* 12 full-time (9 women), 48 part-time (33 women); includes 25 minority (19 African Americans, 2 Asian Americans or Pacific Islanders, 4 Hispanic Americans). Average age 41. 10 applicants, 40% accepted, 4 enrolled. In 2006, 5 degrees awarded. *Degree requirements:* For doctorate, thesis/dissertation. *Entrance requirements:* For doctorate, GRE General Test, master's degree. Additional exam requirements/recommendations for international students: Required—TOEFL. Application fee: $50. Electronic applications accepted. *Expenses:* Tuition, state resident: full-time $9,882; part-time $549 per credit. Tuition, nonresident: full-time $9,882; part-time $549 per credit. Tuition and fees vary according to degree level. *Financial support:* Career-related internships or fieldwork and unspecified assistantships available. Support available to part-time students. *Unit head:* Dr. Mary Beth Walpole, Head, 856-256-4744.

Rowan University, Graduate School, College of Education, Department of Educational Leadership, Program in Higher Education Administration, Glassboro, NJ 08028-1701. Offers MA. *Accreditation:* NCATE. Part-time and evening/weekend programs available. *Students:* 12 full-time (7 women), 20 part-time (17 women); includes 28 minority (4 African Americans, 1 Asian American or Pacific Islander, 23 Hispanic Americans). Average age 31. 11 applicants, 45% accepted, 5 enrolled. In 2006, 15 degrees awarded. *Degree requirements:* For master's, thesis, comprehensive exam. *Entrance requirements:* For master's, GRE General Test, minimum GPA of 2.8, 2 years of teaching experience. Additional exam requirements/recommendations for international students: Required—TOEFL. *Application deadline:* Applications are processed on a rolling basis. Application fee: $50. Electronic applications accepted. *Expenses:* Tuition, state resident: full-time $9,882; part-time $549 per credit. Tuition, nonresident: full-time $9,882; part-time $549 per credit. Tuition and fees vary according to degree level. *Financial support:* Career-related internships or fieldwork and unspecified assistantships available. Support available to part-time students. *Unit head:* Dr. Burton Sisko, Advisor, 856-256-4500 Ext. 3717.

Rowan University, Graduate School, College of Education, Department of Educational Leadership, Program in School Administration, Glassboro, NJ 08028-1701. Offers business administration (MA); principal preparation (MA); school administration (CAGS). *Accreditation:* NCATE. Part-time and evening/weekend programs available. *Students:* 1 full-time (0 women), 75 part-time (43 women); includes 8 minority (all African Americans) Average age 34. 10 applicants, 40% accepted, 4 enrolled. In 2006, 29 degrees awarded. *Degree requirements:* For master's, thesis, internship, comprehensive exam. *Entrance requirements:* For master's, GRE General Test, NTE, minimum GPA of 2.8, 2 years of teaching experience. Additional exam requirements/recommendations for international students: Required—TOEFL. *Application deadline:* Applications are processed on a rolling basis. Application fee: $50. Electronic applications accepted. *Expenses:* Tuition, state resident: full-time $9,882; part-time $549 per credit. Tuition, nonresident: full-time $9,882; part-time $549 per credit. Tuition and fees vary according to degree level. *Financial support:* Career-related internships or fieldwork and unspecified assistantships available. Support available to part-time students. *Unit head:* Dr. Ronald Herpe, Chairperson, 856-256-4702, E-mail: herpe@rowan.edu.

Rowan University, Graduate School, College of Education, Department of Teacher Education, Program in Standards-Based Practice, Glassboro, NJ 08028-1701. Offers M Ed. *Students:* Average age 34. 5 applicants, 60% accepted, 3 enrolled. *Expenses:* Tuition, state resident: full-time $9,882; part-time $549 per credit. Tuition, nonresident: full-time $9,882; part-time $549 per credit. Tuition and fees vary according to degree level.

Royal Roads University, Graduate Studies, Organizational Leadership and Training Program, Victoria, BC V9B 5Y2, Canada. Offers distributed learning (MA); leadership and training (MA). Postbaccalaureate distance learning degree programs offered (minimal on-campus study). *Degree requirements:* For master's, thesis. *Entrance requirements:* For master's, 5-7 years of related work experience. Additional exam requirements/recommendations for international students: Required—TOEFL (paper-based 570; computer-based 233) or IELTS (paper-based 7) (recommended). Electronic applications accepted. Expenses: Contact institution. *Faculty research:* Approaches to leadership development, professional learning, problem-based learning, effective leadership styles, use of self-knowledge instruments in leadership development.

Rutgers, The State University of New Jersey, Camden, Graduate School of Arts and Sciences, Department of Public Policy and Administration, Camden, NJ 08102-1401. Offers education policy and leadeship (MPA); international public service and development (MPA); public management (MPA); JD/MPA. *Accreditation:* NASPAA. Part-time and evening/weekend programs available. *Faculty:* 14 full-time (6 women). *Students:* 50 full-time (33 women), 32 part-time (26 women); includes 30 minority (19 African Americans, 1 Asian American or Pacific Islander, 10 Hispanic Americans), 2 international. Average age 27. 79 applicants, 70% accepted, 31 enrolled. In 2006, 39 degrees awarded. *Degree requirements:* For master's, directed study, research workshop. *Entrance requirements:* For master's, GRE General Test, GMAT or LSAT. Additional exam requirements/recommendations for international students: Required—TOEFL (minimum score 550 paper-based; 213 computer-based). *Application deadline:* For fall admission, 5/1 priority date for domestic students; for spring admission, 12/1 priority date for domestic students. Applications are processed on a rolling basis. Application fee: $50. Electronic applications accepted. *Financial support:* In 2006–07, 14 students received support, including 5 fellowships (averaging $1,000 per year), 2 research assistantships with full tuition reimbursements available (averaging $6,000 per year), 1 teaching assistantship with full tuition reimbursement available (averaging $12,186 per year); career-related internships or fieldwork, Federal Work-Study, and scholarships/grants also available. Financial award application deadline: 3/15; financial award applicants required to submit FAFSA. *Faculty research:* Nonprofit management, county and municipal administration, health and human services, government communication, administrative law, educational finance. *Unit head:* Dr. Richard Harris, Chair, 856-225-6339, Fax: 856-225-6559, E-mail: raharris@camden.rutgers.edu. *Application contact:* Sandra J. Cheesman, Department Administrator, 856-225-6860, Fax: 856-225-6559, E-mail: scheesma@camden.rutgers.edu.

Rutgers, The State University of New Jersey, New Brunswick, Graduate School of Education, Department of Educational Theory, Policy and Administration, Programs in Educational Administration and Supervision, New Brunswick, NJ 08901-1281. Offers Ed M, Ed D. Part-time and evening/weekend programs available. *Faculty:* 5 full-time (1 woman). *Students:* 2 full-time (both women), 96 part-time (40 women). Average age 30. 87 applicants, 38% accepted, 25 enrolled. In 2006, 29 master's, 4 doctorates awarded. *Degree requirements:* For doctorate, thesis/dissertation, qualifying exam. *Entrance requirements:* For master's, GRE General Test, minimum GPA of 3.0; for doctorate, GRE General Test, minimum GPA of 3.0, master's degree in educational administration. Additional exam requirements/recommendations for international students: Required—TOEFL. *Application deadline:* For fall admission, 2/1 for domestic and international students; for spring admission, 11/1 for domestic and international students. Application fee: $60. Electronic applications accepted. *Financial support:* Application deadline: 3/15; *Faculty research:* 5. *Unit head:* Dr. James Bliss, Coordinator, 732-932-7496 Ext. 8239, Fax: 732-932-6803, E-mail: bliss@rci.rutgers.edu. *Application contact:* Sandy Chubrick, Administrative Assistant, 732-932-7496 Ext. 8239, Fax: 732-932-6803, E-mail: chubrick@rci.rutgers.edu.

Sacred Heart University, Graduate Studies, College of Education and Health Professions, Department of Education, Fairfield, CT 06825-1000. Offers administration (CAS); educational technology (MAT); elementary education (MAT); reading (CAS); secondary education (MAT); teaching (CAS). Part-time and evening/weekend programs available. Postbaccalaureate distance learning degree programs offered (minimal on-campus study). *Faculty:* 23 full-time (10 women). *Students:* 360 full-time (285 women), 710 part-time (520 women); includes 39 minority (15 African Americans, 4 American Indian/Alaska Native, 5 Asian Americans or Pacific Islanders, 15 Hispanic Americans), 4 international. Average age 34. 335 applicants, 87% accepted, 270 enrolled. In 2006, 312 master's, 59 other advanced degrees awarded. *Degree requirements:* For master's, thesis or alternative. *Entrance requirements:* For master's, PRAXIS (teacher certification/MAT); for CAS, PRAXIS I. Additional exam requirements/recommendations for international students: Required—TOEFL (minimum score 550 paper-based; 213 computer-based). *Application deadline:* Applications are processed on a rolling basis. Application fee: $50 ($100 for international students). Electronic applications accepted. *Expenses: Contact institution.* Full-time tuition and fees vary according to degree level and program. *Financial support:* Teaching assistantships with partial tuition reimbursements, career-related internships or fieldwork, institutionally sponsored loans, traineeships, tuition waivers (partial), and unspecified assistantships available. Support available to part-time students. Financial award applicants required to submit FAFSA. *Faculty research:* Reading education, learning theory, teacher preparation, education of underachievers. *Unit head:* Dr. Edward Malin, Director, 203-371-7800, Fax: 203-365-7513. *Application contact:* Alexis Haakonsen, Dean of Graduate Admissions, 203-365-7619, Fax: 203-365-4732, E-mail: haakonsena@sacredheart.edu.

Saginaw Valley State University, College of Education, Program in Educational Leadership, University Center, MI 48710. Offers chief business officers (M Ed); education leadership

(Ed S); educational administration and supervision (M Ed); principalship (M Ed); superintendency (M Ed). *Accreditation:* NCATE. Part-time and evening/weekend programs available. *Students:* 32 full-time (23 women), 401 part-time (236 women); includes 29 minority (22 African Americans, 2 Asian Americans or Pacific Islanders, 5 Hispanic Americans), 1 international. Average age 34. 102 applicants, 100% accepted, 74 enrolled. In 2006, 144 master's, 16 other advanced degrees awarded. *Degree requirements:* For master's, practicum. *Entrance requirements:* For master's, minimum GPA of 3.0, teaching certificate. *Application deadline:* Applications are processed on a rolling basis. Application fee: $25. Electronic applications accepted. *Expenses:* Tuition, state resident: full-time $7,225; part-time $301 per credit hour. Tuition, nonresident: full-time $13,888; part-time $579 per credit hour. Required fees: $330; $14 per credit hour. Tuition and fees vary according to course load. *Financial support:* Applicants required to submit FAFSA. *Application contact:* Jeanne Chipman, Certification Officer, 989-964-4083, Fax: 989-964-4385, E-mail: jdc@svsu.edu.

St. Ambrose University, College of Education and Health Sciences, Program in Educational Leadership, Davenport, IA 52803-2898. Offers MEA. Part-time and evening/weekend programs available. *Faculty:* 1 (woman) full-time, 1 part-time/adjunct (0 women). *Students:* Average age 36. 5 applicants, 100% accepted, 5 enrolled. In 2006, 6 degrees awarded. *Entrance requirements:* Additional exam requirements/recommendations for international students: Required—TOEFL. *Application deadline:* Applications are processed on a rolling basis. Application fee: $25. Electronic applications accepted. *Financial support:* In 2006–07, 9 students received support. *Unit head:* Dr. Charles Mangus, Director, 563-333-6081, Fax: 563-333-6028, E-mail: manguscharles@sau.edu. *Application contact:* Elizabeth Berridge, Director of Graduate Student Recruitment, 563-333-6271, Fax: 563-333-6268, E-mail: berridgeelizabethb@sau.edu.

St. Bonaventure University, School of Graduate Studies, School of Education, Program in Educational Leadership, St. Bonaventure, NY 14778-2284. Offers MS Ed, Adv C. Part-time and evening/weekend programs available. *Degree requirements:* For master's, thesis optional. *Entrance requirements:* Additional exam requirements/recommendations for international students: Required—TOEFL. *Faculty research:* Collective bargaining, curriculum development, self-esteem, rural schools program, leadership issues.

St. Cloud State University, School of Graduate Studies, College of Education, Department of Educational Leadership and Community Psychology, Program in Educational Administration and Leadership, St. Cloud, MN 56301-4498. Offers MS. Part-time programs available. *Faculty:* 5 full-time (4 women), 3 part-time/adjunct (all women). *Students:* 15 full-time (12 women), 38 part-time (18 women); includes 3 minority (1 African American, 1 American Indian/Alaska Native, 1 Hispanic American). 17 applicants, 100% accepted. In 2006, 6 degrees awarded. *Degree requirements:* For master's, thesis or alternative, comprehensive exam (for some programs). *Entrance requirements:* For master's, GRE General Test, minimum GPA of 2.75. Additional exam requirements/recommendations for international students: Required—MELAB; Recommended—TOEFL (minimum score 550 paper-based; 213 computer-based), IELTS (minimum score 7). *Application deadline:* For fall admission, 6/1 priority date for domestic students, 4/1 for international students; for spring admission, 10/1 priority date for domestic students, 8/1 for international students. Applications are processed on a rolling basis. Application fee: $35. Electronic applications accepted. *Financial support:* Federal Work-Study, scholarships/grants, and unspecified assistantships available. *Unit head:* Dr. Janine Dahigs-Walker, Coordinator, 320-308-2946, E-mail: jdwalker@stcloudstate.edu. *Application contact:* Linda Lou Krueger, School of Graduate Studies, 320-308-2113, Fax: 320-308-5371, E-mail: lekrueger@stcloudstate.edu.

St. Cloud State University, School of Graduate Studies, College of Education, Department of Educational Leadership and Community Psychology, Program in Higher Education Administration, St. Cloud, MN 56301-4498. Offers MS. *Students:* 11 full-time (6 women), 4 part-time (all women), 1 international. In 2006, 6 degrees awarded. Application fee: $35. *Unit head:* Dr. Christine Imbra, Head, 320-308-4909, E-mail: cmimbra@stcloudstate.edu.

Saint Francis University, Department of Education and Educational Leadership, Loretto, PA 15940-0600. Offers education (M Ed); educational leadership (MEDL); reading (M Ed). Part-time and evening/weekend programs available. *Faculty:* 24 part-time/adjunct (8 women). *Students:* Average age 30. 19 applicants, 100% accepted, 19 enrolled. In 2006, 35 degrees awarded. *Degree requirements:* For master's, thesis optional. *Entrance requirements:* For master's, GRE or MAT if undergraduate GPA is less than 2.8, minimum undergraduate QPA of 2.5. *Application deadline:* Applications are processed on a rolling basis. Application fee: $30. *Expenses:* Contact institution. Tuition and fees vary according to program. *Financial support:* Research assistantships with full and partial tuition reimbursements, teaching assistantships with full and partial tuition reimbursements, career-related internships or fieldwork and unspecified assistantships available. *Unit head:* Dr. Janette D. Kelly, Director, Graduate Education, 814-472-3058, Fax: 814-472-3864, E-mail: jkelly@francis.edu.

St. Francis Xavier University, Graduate Studies, Graduate Studies in Education, Antigonish, NS B2G 2W5, Canada. Offers curriculum and instruction (M Ed); educational administration and leadership (M Ed). Part-time programs available. Postbaccalaureate distance learning degree programs offered (minimal on-campus study). *Faculty:* 20 part-time/adjunct (10 women). *Students:* 2 full-time, 131 part-time. 55 applicants, 36% accepted. In 2006, 79 degrees awarded. *Degree requirements:* For master's, thesis, registration. *Entrance requirements:* For master's, minimum undergraduate B average, 2 years of teaching experience. *Application deadline:* For fall admission, 1/15 priority date for domestic students, 1/15 for international students. Application fee: $40. *Financial support:* In 2006–07, teaching assistantships (averaging $500 per year). *Faculty research:* Inclusive education, qualitative research. Total annual research expenditures: $70,000. *Unit head:* Dr. Jim Greenlaw, Chair, 902-867-5416, Fax: 902-867-3887, E-mail: jgreenla@stfx.ca. *Application contact:* Colleen Jones, Assistant, 902-867-3906, Fax: 902-867-5154, E-mail: med@stfx.ca.

St. John Fisher College, Office of the Provost, Ralph C. Wilson Jr. School of Education, Educational Leadership Program, Rochester, NY 14618-3597. Offers MS Ed. Part-time programs available. *Faculty:* 3 full-time (1 woman), 1 (woman) part-time/adjunct. *Students:* Average age 34. 43 applicants, 88% accepted, 30 enrolled. In 2006, 51 degrees awarded. *Degree requirements:* For master's, project, internships. *Entrance requirements:* For master's, GRE (if GPA is below 3.0), minimum GPA of 3.0, teacher certification, minimum 2 years of teaching experience, 2 letters of reference. Additional exam requirements/recommendations for international students: Required—TOEFL (minimum score 575 paper-based; 233 computer-based; 80 iBT). *Application deadline:* For fall admission, 8/15 for domestic students; for spring admission, 10/30 for domestic students. Applications are processed on a rolling basis. Application fee: $30. *Expenses:* Tuition: Part-time $615 per credit. Tuition and fees vary according to program. *Financial support:* Federal Work-Study and scholarships/grants available. Financial award application deadline: 2/15; financial award applicants required to submit FAFSA. *Faculty research:* Urban school leadership, assessment, effective school leadership. *Unit head:* Dr. William Stroud, Director, 585-385-7258, E-mail: wstroud@sjfc.edu. *Application contact:* Shannon Cleverley, Director of Graduate Admissions, 585-385-8161, Fax: 585-385-8344, E-mail: scleverley@sjfc.edu.

St. John Fisher College, Office of the Provost, Ralph C. Wilson Jr. School of Education, Executive Leadership Program, Rochester, NY 14618-3597. Offers Ed D. Evening/weekend programs available. *Faculty:* 2 full-time (0 women), 1 part-time/adjunct (0 women). *Students:* 27 full-time (18 women); includes 12 minority (all African Americans) Average age 43. 41 applicants, 73% accepted, 27 enrolled. *Degree requirements:* For doctorate, thesis/dissertation, field experiences, comprehensive exam. *Entrance requirements:* For doctorate, writing sample, references, interview, recommendations. Additional exam requirements/recommendations for international students: Required—TOEFL (minimum score 575 paper-based; 233 computer-based; 80 iBT). *Application deadline:* For fall admission, 3/15 for domestic and international students. Applications are processed on a rolling basis. *Expenses:* Tuition: Part-time $615 per credit. Tuition and fees vary according to program. *Faculty research:* Leadership, organizational development. *Application contact:* Shannon Cleverley, Director of Graduate Admissions, 585-385-8161, Fax: 585-385-8344, E-mail: scleverley@sjfc.edu.

St. John's University, The School of Education, Division of Administration and Instructional Leadership, Instructional Leadership Program, Queens, NY 11439. Offers Ed D, PD. Part-time and evening/weekend programs available. *Students:* 8 full-time (7 women), 87 part-time (66 women); includes 13 minority (10 African Americans, 1 Asian American or Pacific Islander, 2 Hispanic Americans), 4 international. Average age 41. 61 applicants, 59% accepted, 22 enrolled. In 2006, 8 doctorates, 6 other advanced degrees awarded. *Degree requirements:* For doctorate, one foreign language, thesis/dissertation, internship, comprehensive exam; for PD, internship. *Entrance requirements:* For doctorate, GRE General Test, interview, New York teaching certificate, writing sample, 2 years of teaching experience; for PD, interview, New York teaching certificate, writing sample, 2 years of teaching experience. Additional exam requirements/recommendations for international students: Required—TOEFL (minimum score 500 paper-based; 173 computer-based). *Application deadline:* For fall admission, 4/15 for domestic students, 5/1 priority date for international students; for spring admission, 11/1 priority date for international students. Applications are processed on a rolling basis. Application fee: $40. Electronic applications accepted. *Expenses:* Tuition: Full-time $18,480; part-time $770 per credit. Required fees: $125 per semester. Tuition and fees vary according to program. *Financial support:* Fellowships, research assistantships, career-related internships or fieldwork and scholarships/grants available. Support available to part-time students. Financial award application deadline: 3/1; financial award applicants required to submit FAFSA. *Faculty research:* Learning styles, gifted and talented. *Application contact:* Kelly Ronayne, Assistant Dean, 718-990-2303, Fax: 718-990-6069, E-mail: graded@stjohns.edu.

St. John's University, The School of Education, Division of Administration and Instructional Leadership, Program in School Building Leadership, Queens, NY 11439. Offers MS Ed, PD. Part-time and evening/weekend programs available. Postbaccalaureate distance learning degree programs offered. *Students:* 9 full-time (4 women), 498 part-time (363 women); includes 119 minority (68 African Americans, 3 American Indian/Alaska Native, 6 Asian Americans or Pacific Islanders, 42 Hispanic Americans), 15 international. Average age 40. 174 applicants, 83% accepted, 85 enrolled. In 2006, 23 master's, 28 other advanced degrees awarded. *Degree requirements:* For master's, thesis optional. *Entrance requirements:* For master's, GRE General Test. Additional exam requirements/recommendations for international students: Required—TOEFL (minimum score 500 paper-based; 173 computer-based). *Application deadline:* For fall admission, 4/15 for domestic students, 5/1 priority date for international students; for spring admission, 11/1 priority date for international students. Applications are processed on a rolling basis. Application fee: $40. Electronic applications accepted. *Expenses:* Contact institution. Tuition and fees vary according to program. *Financial support:* Research assistantships, career-related internships or fieldwork and scholarships/grants available. Support available to part-time students. Financial award application deadline: 3/1; financial award applicants required to submit FAFSA. *Application contact:* Kelly Ronayne, Assistant Dean, 718-990-2303, Fax: 718-990-6069, E-mail: graded@stjohns.edu.

Saint Joseph's University, College of Arts and Sciences, Department of Education, Philadelphia, PA 19131-1395. Offers educational leadership (Ed D); elementary education (MS); instructional technology (MS); professional education (MS); reading (MS); secondary education (MS); special education (MS); training and organizational development (MS, Certificate). Part-time and evening/weekend programs available. *Faculty:* 18 full-time (9 women), 67 part-time/adjunct (34 women). *Students:* 77 full-time (63 women), 551 part-time (417 women); includes 115 minority (94 African Americans, 2 American Indian/Alaska Native, 8 Asian Americans or Pacific Islanders, 11 Hispanic Americans), 12 international. In 2006, 286 master's, 5 doctorates awarded. *Entrance requirements:* For master's, 2 letters of recommendation, minimum GPA of 3.0; for doctorate, GRE/MAT, 2 letters of recommendation, resumé. Additional exam requirements/recommendations for international students: Required—TOEFL. *Application deadline:* For fall admission, 7/15 for domestic students. Application fee: $35. *Expenses:* Contact institution. *Financial support:* Fellowships, research assistantships, career-related internships or fieldwork and Federal Work-Study available. Support available to part-time students. *Unit head:* Dr. Encarnacion Rodriguez, Director of Graduate Education, 610-660-3348.

St. Lawrence University, Department of Education, Program in Educational Administration, Canton, NY 13617-1455. Offers M Ed, CAS. Part-time and evening/weekend programs available. *Entrance requirements:* For master's, GRE General Test. *Faculty research:* Leadership.

Saint Leo University, Graduate Studies in Education, Saint Leo, FL 33574-6665. Offers education (MAT); educational leadership (M Ed); exceptional student education (M Ed); instructional leadership (M Ed); reading (M Ed). Part-time and evening/weekend programs available. Postbaccalaureate distance learning degree programs offered (minimal on-campus study). *Faculty:* 8 full-time (5 women), 10 part-time/adjunct (all women). *Students:* 96 full-time (77 women), 169 part-time (143 women); includes 22 minority (16 African Americans, 6 Hispanic Americans), 2 international. Average age 35. 365 applicants, 54% accepted, 116 enrolled. In 2006, 39 degrees awarded. *Degree requirements:* For master's, comprehensive exam or passing FELE scores. *Entrance requirements:* For master's, GRE General Test or MAT, 2 letters of recommendation, minimum undergraduate GPA of 3.0 or GRE or MAT, professional teaching certificate, resumé. Additional exam requirements/recommendations for international students: Required—TOEFL (minimum score 550 paper-based; 213 computer-based). *Application deadline:* For fall admission, 7/1 priority date for domestic students; for spring admission, 11/12 priority date for domestic students. Applications are processed on a rolling basis. Application fee: $45. Electronic applications accepted. *Financial support:* In 2006–07, 242 students received support. Career-related internships or fieldwork, Federal Work-Study, and scholarships/grants available. Support available to part-time students. Financial award application deadline: 3/1; financial award applicants required to submit FAFSA. *Faculty research:* The role of the school leader in (1) data analysis of student achievement (2) teacher recruitment (3) teacher effectiveness. *Unit head:* Dr. John Smith, Director, 352-588-8309, Fax: 352-588-8861, E-mail: med@saintleo.edu. *Application contact:* Scott Cathcart, Vice President of Enrollment, 800-707-8846, Fax: 352-588-7873, E-mail: grad.admission@saintleo.edu.

Saint Louis University, Graduate School, College of Public Service and Graduate School, Department of Educational Leadership and Higher Education, St. Louis, MO 63103-2097. Offers Catholic school leadership (MA); educational administration (MA, Ed D, PhD, Ed S); higher education (MA, Ed D, PhD); student personnel administration (MA). *Accreditation:* NCATE. *Faculty:* 11 full-time (4 women), 13 part-time/adjunct (4 women). *Students:* 43 full-time (26 women), 280 part-time (148 women); includes 38 minority (33 African Americans, 1 American Indian/Alaska Native, 3 Asian Americans or Pacific Islanders, 1 Hispanic American). Average age 38. 157 applicants, 79% accepted, 88 enrolled. In 2006, 18 master's, 55 doctorates, 16 other advanced degrees awarded. *Degree requirements:* For master's, comprehensive written and oral exam; for doctorate, thesis/dissertation, preliminary oral and written exams, comprehensive exam, registration. *Entrance requirements:* For master's, GRE General Test, MAT, LSAT, GMAT, MCAT, letters of recommendation, resumé; for doctorate and Ed S, GRE General Test, LSAT, GMAT, MCAT, letters of recommendation, resumé. Additional exam requirements/recommendations for international students: Required—TOEFL (minimum score 525 paper-based; 194 computer-based). *Application deadline:* For fall admission, 7/1 for domestic and international students; for spring admission, 11/1 for domestic and international students. Applications are processed on a rolling basis. Application fee: $40. *Expenses:* Tuition: Part-time $800 per credit hour. Required fees: $105 per semester. *Financial support:* In 2006–07, 84 students received support, including 6 teaching assistantships with full tuition reimbursements available (averaging $11,000 per year); Federal Work-Study, scholarships/grants, traineeships, health care benefits, tuition waivers (partial), and unspecified assistantships also available. Support available to part-time students. Financial award application deadline: 6/1; financial award applicants required to submit FAFSA. *Faculty research:* Superintendent of schools, school finance, school facilities, student personal administration, building leadership. Total annual research expenditures: $100,000. *Unit head:* Dr. William T.

Educational Administration

Saint Louis University (continued)

Rebore, Chairperson, 314-977-2508, E-mail: reborewt@slu.edu. *Application contact:* Gary Behrman, Associate Dean of the Graduate School, 314-977-3827, E-mail: behrmang@slu.edu.

Saint Martin's University, Graduate Programs, Department of Education, Lacey, WA 98503-1297. Offers administration (M Ed); English as a second language (M Ed); guidance and counseling (M Ed); reading (M Ed); special education (M Ed); teaching (MIT); technology in education (M Ed). Part-time and evening/weekend programs available. *Degree requirements:* For master's, thesis or alternative, project or comprehensives, comprehensive exam (for some programs). *Entrance requirements:* For master's, GRE General Test or MAT, resumé. Additional exam requirements/recommendations for international students: Required—TOEFL (minimum score 560 paper-based). *Faculty research:* Reader's theatre and reader/writer workshops, curriculum and assessment integration, gender and equity, classroom evaluations, organizational leadership.

Saint Mary's College of California, School of Education, Program in Educational Leadership, Moraga, CA 94575. Offers MA, PhD. Part-time and evening/weekend programs available. *Faculty:* 3 full-time (1 woman), 23 part-time/adjunct (7 women). *Students:* 41 full-time (22 women), 83 part-time (42 women); includes 29 minority (13 African Americans, 2 American Indian/Alaska Native, 5 Asian Americans or Pacific Islanders, 9 Hispanic Americans), 5 international. Average age 35. 111 applicants. In 2006, 10 master's, 8 doctorates awarded. *Median time to degree:* Master's–1.6 years full-time; doctorate–4 years full-time. *Degree requirements:* For master's, thesis or alternative, comprehensive exam. *Entrance requirements:* For master's, interview, minimum GPA of 3.0, teaching credential; for doctorate, GRE or MAT, interview, MA, minimum GPA of 3.0. *Application deadline:* For fall admission, 12/15 priority date for domestic students; for spring admission, 4/15 priority date for domestic students. Applications are processed on a rolling basis. Application fee: $50. *Financial support:* Career-related internships or fieldwork available. Support available to part-time students. Financial award application deadline: 2/15. *Faculty research:* Building communities, programs in educational leadership, alignment of curriculum to standards. *Unit head:* Dr. Nancy L. Sorenson, Director, 925-631-4309, Fax: 925-376-8379, E-mail: nsorenso@stmarys-ca.edu.

Saint Mary's College of California, School of Education, Teaching Leadership Program, Moraga, CA 94575. Offers MA. *Faculty:* 1 (woman) full-time, 16 part-time/adjunct (10 women). In 2006, 38 degrees awarded. *Median time to degree:* Master's–3 years part-time. *Unit head:* Katherine D. Perez, Unit Head, 925-631-4350, Fax: 925-376-8379, E-mail: kperez@stmarys-ca.edu.

Saint Mary's University of Minnesota, School of Graduate and Professional Programs, Program in Educational Administration, Winona, MN 55987-1399. Offers MA, Certificate, Ed S. *Unit head:* Dr. William Bjorum, Director, 612-728-5192, Fax: 612-728-5121, E-mail: wbjorum@smumn.edu.

Saint Mary's University of Minnesota, School of Graduate and Professional Programs, Program in Educational Leadership, Winona, MN 55987-1399. Offers Ed D. *Unit head:* Dr. William Kelly, Director, 612-728-5183, Fax: 612-728-5121, E-mail: wkelly@snumn.edu.

St. Mary's University of San Antonio, Graduate School, Department of Teacher Education, Program in Catholic School Leadership, San Antonio, TX 78228-8507. Offers Catholic school administrators (Certificate); Catholic school leadership (MA); Catholic school teachers (Certificate). Part-time and evening/weekend programs available. Postbaccalaureate distance learning degree programs offered (minimal on-campus study). *Faculty:* 5 full-time (3 women), 1 part-time/adjunct (0 women). *Students:* 4. Average age 38. In 2006, 6 degrees awarded. *Degree requirements:* For master's, registration. *Entrance requirements:* For master's, GRE General Test. Additional exam requirements/recommendations for international students: Required—TOEFL (minimum score 550 paper-based; 213 computer-based). *Application deadline:* Applications are processed on a rolling basis. Application fee: $30. Electronic applications accepted. *Expenses:* Tuition: Full-time $10,890; part-time $605 per hour. Required fees: $500. Tuition and fees vary according to degree level. *Financial support:* Career-related internships or fieldwork, Federal Work-Study, institutionally sponsored loans, scholarships/grants, health care benefits, and unspecified assistantships available. Financial award application deadline: 3/31; financial award applicants required to submit FAFSA. *Unit head:* Fr. Richard Wosman, Director, 210-436-3121, Fax: 210-431-2246.

St. Mary's University of San Antonio, Graduate School, Department of Teacher Education, Program in Educational Leadership, San Antonio, TX 78228-8507. Offers educational leadership (MA); principalship (mid-management) (Certificate). *Faculty:* 5 full-time (3 women), 1 part-time/adjunct (0 women). *Students:* 27; includes 4 minority (1 African American, 1 Asian American or Pacific Islander, 2 Hispanic Americans). Average age 30. In 2006, 6 degrees awarded. *Degree requirements:* For master's, registration. *Entrance requirements:* For master's, GRE. Additional exam requirements/recommendations for international students: Required—TOEFL (minimum score 550 paper-based; 213 computer-based). *Application deadline:* Applications are processed on a rolling basis. Application fee: $30. Electronic applications accepted. *Expenses:* Tuition: Full-time $10,890; part-time $605 per hour. Required fees: $500. Tuition and fees vary according to degree level. *Financial support:* Career-related internships or fieldwork, Federal Work-Study, institutionally sponsored loans, scholarships/grants, health care benefits, and unspecified assistantships available. Financial award application deadline: 3/31; financial award applicants required to submit FAFSA.

Saint Michael's College, Graduate Programs, Program in Education, Colchester, VT 05439. Offers administration (M Ed, CAGS); arts in education (CAGS); curriculum and instruction (M Ed, CAGS); information technology (CAGS); reading (M Ed); special education (M Ed, CAGS); technology (M Ed). Part-time and evening/weekend programs available. *Faculty:* 5 full-time (3 women), 35 part-time/adjunct (29 women). *Students:* 26 full-time (18 women), 114 part-time (86 women), 2 international. Average age 34. 48 applicants, 81% accepted, 36 enrolled. In 2006, 46 degrees awarded. *Degree requirements:* For master's, thesis. *Entrance requirements:* For master's, minimum GPA of 3.0. *Application deadline:* Applications are processed on a rolling basis. Application fee: $35. Electronic applications accepted. *Financial support:* Fellowships, scholarships/grants available. Support available to part-time students. Financial award applicants required to submit FAFSA. *Faculty research:* Integrative curriculum, moral and spiritual dimensions of education, learning styles, multiple intelligences, integrating technology into the curriculum. *Unit head:* Dr. Anne P. Judson, Director, 802-654-2649, Fax: 802-654-2664, E-mail: ajudson@smcvt.edu.

Saint Peter's College, Graduate Programs in Education, Program in Administration and Supervision, Jersey City, NJ 07306-5997. Offers MA. Part-time and evening/weekend programs available. *Degree requirements:* For master's, departmental qualifying exam. *Entrance requirements:* For master's, GRE or MAT, matriculation exam.

Saint Peter's College, Graduate Programs in Education, Program in Teaching, Jersey City, NJ 07306-5997. Offers elementary teacher (Certificate); supervisor of instruction (Certificate); teaching (MA). Part-time and evening/weekend programs available. *Degree requirements:* For master's, departmental qualifying exam. *Entrance requirements:* For master's, GRE General Test or MAT.

St. Thomas University, School of Graduate Studies, Department of Education, Miami Gardens, FL 33054-6459. Offers educational administration (MS, Certificate); educational leadership (Ed D); elementary education (MS); reading (MS); special education (MS). Part-time and evening/weekend programs available. *Degree requirements:* For master's, comprehensive exam; for doctorate, thesis/dissertation, comprehensive exam. *Entrance requirements:* For master's, interview, minimum GPA of 3.0 or GRE; for doctorate, GRE or MAT. Additional exam requirements/recommendations for international students: Required—TOEFL. Electronic applications accepted.

Saint Vincent College, Program in Education, Latrobe, PA 15650-2690. Offers curriculum and instruction (MS); environmental education (MS); library media management (MS); school administration (MS); special education (MS). Part-time and evening/weekend programs available. *Degree requirements:* For master's, comprehensive exam. *Entrance requirements:* For master's, GRE (if undergraduate GPA is below 3.0). Additional exam requirements/recommendations for international students: Required—TOEFL (minimum score 550 paper-based; 213 computer-based). *Faculty research:* Assessment and instructional technology.

Saint Xavier University, Graduate Studies, School of Education, Chicago, IL 60655-3105. Offers counseling (MA); counselor education (MA); curriculum and instruction (MA); early childhood education (MA); education (CAS); educational administration (MA); elementary education (MA); field-based education (MA); general educational studies (MA); individualized program (MA); learning disabilities (MA); reading (MA); secondary education (MA). *Accreditation:* NCATE. Part-time and evening/weekend programs available. *Faculty:* 92. *Students:* 45 full-time (35 women), 1,529 part-time (1,309 women). In 2006, 474 degrees awarded. *Degree requirements:* For master's, thesis or project. *Entrance requirements:* For master's, minimum GPA of 3.0. *Application deadline:* For fall admission, 8/15 priority date for domestic students. Applications are processed on a rolling basis. Application fee: $35. *Expenses: Contact institution. Financial support:* Career-related internships or fieldwork available. Support available to part-time students. Financial award applicants required to submit FAFSA. *Unit head:* Dr. Beverly Gulley, Dean, 773-298-3221, Fax: 773-779-9061, E-mail: gulley@sxu.edu. *Application contact:* Beth Gierach, Managing Director of Admission, 773-298-3053, Fax: 773-298-3076, E-mail: gierach@sxu.edu.

Salem International University, School of Education, Salem, WV 26426-0500. Offers curriculum and instruction (M Ed), including curriculum and instruction, educational technology leadership, physical education/health, teaching English as a second language; educational administration (M Ed). Part-time and evening/weekend programs available. Postbaccalaureate distance learning degree programs offered. *Faculty:* 5 full-time (4 women), 17 part-time/adjunct (8 women). *Students:* 74 full-time (45 women), 154 part-time (75 women); includes 7 minority (2 African Americans, 5 Asian Americans or Pacific Islanders), 28 international. Average age 41. 200 applicants, 75% accepted, 130 enrolled. In 2006, 18 degrees awarded. *Degree requirements:* For master's, thesis (for some programs), comprehensive exam (for some programs), registration. *Entrance requirements:* For master's, GRE, MAT, NTE, 3 letters of recommendation. Additional exam requirements/recommendations for international students: Required—TOEFL (minimum score 550 paper-based; 213 computer-based). *Application deadline:* Applications are processed on a rolling basis. Application fee: $25. Electronic applications accepted. *Expenses: Contact institution.* One-time fee: $25 part-time. Tuition and fees vary according to program. *Financial support:* Application deadline: 4/15; *Faculty research:* Improved classroom effectiveness. *Unit head:* Dean, School of Education, 304-326-1253, Fax: 304-326-1246. *Application contact:* Thomas White, Director of Admissions, 304-326-1549, Fax: 304-326-1246, E-mail: admission@salemiu.edu.

Salem State College, Graduate School, Program in Educational Leadership, Salem, MA 01970-5353. Offers M Ed. *Students:* 1 (woman) full-time, 15 part-time (6 women); includes 1 minority (Asian American or Pacific Islander) Average age 36. In 2006, 6 degrees awarded. Application fee: $35. *Unit head:* Kevin Fahey, Chairperson, 978-542-6321, Fax: 978-542-7215.

Salem State College, Graduate School, Program in Higher Education in Student Affairs, Salem, MA 01970-5353. Offers M Ed. Part-time and evening/weekend programs available. *Students:* 7 full-time (6 women), 21 part-time (17 women); includes 1 African American, 1 Hispanic American, 1 international. Average age 32. In 2006, 15 degrees awarded. Application fee: $35. *Unit head:* Lee Brossoit, 978-542-6401, E-mail: lbrossoit@salemstate.edu.

Salem State College, Graduate School, Program in School Business Officer, Salem, MA 01970-5353. Offers M Ed. *Accreditation:* NCATE. Part-time and evening/weekend programs available. *Students:* Average age 38. *Entrance requirements:* For master's, GRE General Test, MAT. *Application deadline:* Applications are processed on a rolling basis. Application fee: $35. *Unit head:* James Picone, Coordinator, 978-542-6321, Fax: 978-542-7023, E-mail: jpicone@salemstate.edu.

Salisbury University, Graduate Division, Department of Education, Salisbury, MD 21801-6837. Offers art (MAT); biology (MAT); business education (MAT); chemistry (MAT); early childhood education (M Ed); educational administration (M Ed); elementary education (M Ed); English (M Ed, MAT); French (MAT); geography (MAT); history (MAT); mathematics (MAT); media and technology (MAT); music (MAT); psychology (MAT); reading education (MAT); science (MAT); secondary education (MAT); social studies (MAT); Spanish (MAT). *Accreditation:* NCATE. Part-time and evening/weekend programs available. *Faculty:* 12 full-time (6 women), 10 part-time/adjunct (8 women). *Students:* 17 full-time (9 women), 84 part-time (72 women); includes 6 minority (5 African Americans, 1 Hispanic American). Average age 30. 15 applicants, 73% accepted, 11 enrolled. In 2006, 63 degrees awarded. *Degree requirements:* For master's, comprehensive exam (for some programs). *Entrance requirements:* For master's, PRAXIS, minimum GPA of 2.75. Additional exam requirements/recommendations for international students: Required—TOEFL (minimum score 550 paper-based; 213 computer-based). *Application deadline:* For fall admission, 8/1 priority date for domestic students; for spring admission, 1/1 for domestic students. Applications are processed on a rolling basis. Application fee: $45. *Expenses:* Tuition, state resident: part-time $260 per credit hour. Tuition, nonresident: part-time $546 per credit hour. Required fees: $52 per credit hour. *Financial support:* In 2006–07, 3 teaching assistantships with full tuition reimbursements were awarded; career-related internships or fieldwork and scholarships/grants also available. Support available to part-time students. Financial award applicants required to submit FAFSA. *Faculty research:* Middle-level education, student outcomes. *Unit head:* Dr. Edward C. Robeck, Program Coordinator, 410-543-6292, Fax: 410-548-2593, E-mail: ecrobeck@salisbury.edu. *Application contact:* Debra J. Clark, Administrative Assistant I, 410-543-6281, Fax: 410-548-2593, E-mail: djclark@salisbury.edu.

Salisbury University, Graduate Division, Program in Public School Administration, Salisbury, MD 21801-6837. Offers MS Ed. Part-time and evening/weekend programs available. *Faculty:* 2 full-time (0 women), 2 part-time/adjunct (1 woman). *Students:* Average age 34. 3 applicants, 100% accepted, 3 enrolled. In 2006, 6 degrees awarded. *Entrance requirements:* For master's, minimum GPA of 2.75, 2 letters of recommendation, 2 years teaching experience. Additional exam requirements/recommendations for international students: Required—TOEFL (minimum score 550 paper-based; 213 computer-based). *Application deadline:* For fall admission, 8/1 for domestic students; for spring admission, 1/1 for domestic students. Applications are processed on a rolling basis. Application fee: $45. Electronic applications accepted. *Expenses:* Tuition, state resident: part-time $260 per credit hour. Tuition, nonresident: part-time $546 per credit hour. Required fees: $52 per credit hour. *Financial support:* Applicants required to submit FAFSA. *Unit head:* Dr. Edward C. Robeck, Program Coordinator, 410-543-6292, Fax: 410-548-2593, E-mail: ecrobeck@salisbury.edu. *Application contact:* Stephanie Staab, Administrative Assistant II, 410-543-6509, E-mail: skstaab@salisbury.edu.

Samford University, School of Education, Birmingham, AL 35229-0002. Offers early childhood education (Ed S); early childhood/elementary education (MS Ed); educational administration (Ed S); educational leadership (Ed D); elementary education (Ed S); gifted education (MS Ed); M Div/MS Ed. *Accreditation:* NCATE. Part-time programs available. *Faculty:* 12 full-time (7 women), 8 part-time/adjunct (4 women). *Students:* 16 full-time (14 women), 160 part-time (124 women); includes 25 minority (all African Americans) Average age 38. 45 applicants, 100% accepted, 17 enrolled. In 2006, 15 master's, 20 doctorates, 20 other advanced degrees awarded. *Entrance requirements:* For master's, GRE or MAT, minimum GPA of 3.0; for doctorate, minimum GPA of 3.7; for Ed S, GRE, master's degree, teaching certificate, minimum GPA of 3.25. Additional exam requirements/recommendations for international students: Required—TOEFL (minimum score 550 paper-based; 213 computer-based). *Application deadline:* Applications are processed on a rolling basis. Application fee: $25. *Expenses:* Tuition: Part-time $500 per credit. One-time fee: $25 part-time. Full-time tuition and fees vary according to program and student level. *Financial support:* In 2006–07, 54 students received support; research assistantships, career-related internships or fieldwork, Federal Work-Study, scholarships/grants, and tuition waivers (partial) available. Support available to part-time students. Financial award applicants required to submit FAFSA. *Faculty research:* School law, the characteristics of beginning teachers, the nature of school reform, school culture, quality improvement in education, K-12 student achievement. *Unit head:* Dr. Jean Ann Box, Dean, 205-726-2559, E-mail: jabox@samford.edu. *Application contact:* Dr. Maurice Persall, Director, Graduate Office, 205-726-2019, E-mail: jmpersal@samford.edu.

Sam Houston State University, College of Education and Applied Science, Department of Educational Leadership and Counseling, Huntsville, TX 77341. Offers administration (M Ed, MA); counseling (M Ed, MA); counselor education (MA, PhD); educational leadership (Ed D); instructional leadership (M Ed, MA). Part-time programs available. *Faculty:* 15 full-time (10 women). *Students:* 74 full-time (59 women), 598 part-time (458 women); includes 181 minority (74 African Americans, 3 American Indian/Alaska Native, 4 Asian Americans or Pacific Islanders, 100 Hispanic Americans), 7 international. Average age 37. In 2006, 233 master's, 20 doctorates awarded. *Entrance requirements:* For master's, GRE General Test. *Application deadline:* For fall admission, 8/1 for domestic students; for spring admission, 12/1 for domestic students. Application fee: $20. *Expenses:* Tuition, state resident: full-time $5,904; part-time $164 per semester hour. Tuition, nonresident: full-time $15,804; part-time $439 per semester hour. Required fees: $1,374; $462 per semester. *Financial support:* Career-related internships or fieldwork, Federal Work-Study, and institutionally sponsored loans available. Support available to part-time students. Financial award application deadline: 5/31; financial award applicants required to submit FAFSA. *Unit head:* Dr. Beverly Irby, Chair, 936-294-1134, Fax: 936-294-3886, E-mail: edu_bid@shsu.edu. *Application contact:* Dr. Stacey Edmondson, Advisor, 936-294-1752, E-mail: sedmonson@shsu.edu.

San Diego State University, Graduate and Research Affairs, College of Education, Department of Administration, Rehabilitation and Post-Secondary Education, San Diego, CA 92182. Offers educational leadership in post-secondary education (MA); rehabilitation counseling (MS), including deafness. Evening/weekend programs available. Postbaccalaureate distance learning degree programs offered. *Students:* 56 full-time (41 women), 4 part-time (1 woman); includes 21 minority (7 African Americans, 1 American Indian/Alaska Native, 4 Asian Americans or Pacific Islanders, 9 Hispanic Americans), 1 international. 50 applicants, 72% accepted, 11 enrolled. In 2006, 41 degrees awarded. *Degree requirements:* For master's, thesis (for some programs), comprehensive exam (for some programs). *Entrance requirements:* For master's, GRE General Test, letters of reference. Additional exam requirements/recommendations for international students: Required—TOEFL. *Application deadline:* For fall admission, 5/1 for domestic and international students; for spring admission, 11/1 for domestic students, 10/1 for international students. Applications are processed on a rolling basis. Application fee: $55. Electronic applications accepted. *Financial support:* Career-related internships or fieldwork available. Financial award applicants required to submit FAFSA. *Faculty research:* Rehabilitation in cultural diversity, distance learning technology. Total annual research expenditures: $3.3 million. *Unit head:* Fred McFarlane, Chair, 619-594-6115, Fax: 619-594-4208, E-mail: fmcfarla@mail.sdsu.edu.

San Diego State University, Graduate and Research Affairs, College of Education, Department of Educational Leadership, San Diego, CA 92182. Offers MA. *Accreditation:* NCATE. Evening/weekend programs available. *Students:* 48 full-time (33 women), 58 part-time (40 women); includes 36 minority (8 African Americans, 9 Asian Americans or Pacific Islanders, 19 Hispanic Americans). Average age 28. 127 applicants, 74% accepted, 14 enrolled. In 2006, 74 degrees awarded. *Entrance requirements:* For master's, GRE General Test, letters of reference. Additional exam requirements/recommendations for international students: Required—TOEFL. *Application deadline:* For fall admission, 5/1 for domestic and international students; for spring admission, 11/1 for domestic students, 10/1 for international students. Applications are processed on a rolling basis. Application fee: $55. Electronic applications accepted. *Financial support:* Career-related internships or fieldwork available. Financial award applicants required to submit FAFSA. *Unit head:* Kathy Cohn, Chair, 619-594-8395.

San Francisco State University, Division of Graduate Studies, College of Education, Department of Administration and Interdisciplinary Studies, Program in Educational Administration, San Francisco, CA 94132-1722. Offers MA, AC. *Accreditation:* NCATE. Part-time programs available. *Faculty:* 3 full-time (1 woman), 12 part-time/adjunct (5 women). *Students:* 54 (41 women). *Entrance requirements:* For master's, minimum GPA of 2.5 in last 60 units. *Application deadline:* For fall admission, 11/30 priority date for domestic students. Applications are processed on a rolling basis. Application fee: $55. *Financial support:* Application deadline: 3/1. *Application contact:* Dr. Reynaldo Contreras, Graduate Coordinator, 415-338-7626, E-mail: arc@sfsu.edu.

San Jose State University, Graduate Studies and Research, College of Education, Department of Educational Leadership, San Jose, CA 95192-0001. Offers educational administration (MA); higher education administration (MA); school business management (Certificate). *Accreditation:* NCATE. *Students:* 286 full-time (201 women), 69 part-time (54 women); includes 110 minority (9 African Americans, 25 Asian Americans or Pacific Islanders, 76 Hispanic Americans), 2 international. Average age 38. 330 applicants, 88% accepted, 169 enrolled. In 2006, 263 degrees awarded. *Degree requirements:* For master's, thesis or alternative. *Application deadline:* For fall admission, 6/29 for domestic students; for spring admission, 11/30 for domestic students. Applications are processed on a rolling basis. Application fee: $59. Electronic applications accepted. *Financial support:* Career-related internships or fieldwork available. Financial award applicants required to submit FAFSA. *Unit head:* Dr. Noni Reis, Chair, 408-924-3622, Fax: 408-924-3713.

Santa Clara University, School of Education, Counseling Psychology, and Pastoral Ministries, Department of Education, Program in Educational Administration, Santa Clara, CA 95053. Offers MA. Part-time and evening/weekend programs available. *Students:* 5 full-time (all women), 36 part-time (26 women); includes 9 minority (3 African Americans, 2 Asian Americans or Pacific Islanders, 4 Hispanic Americans). Average age 36. 12 applicants, 75% accepted, 5 enrolled. In 2006, 63 degrees awarded. *Degree requirements:* For master's, comprehensive exam. *Entrance requirements:* For master's, GRE or MAT, minimum GPA of 3.0. Additional exam requirements/recommendations for international students: Required—TOEFL. *Application deadline:* Applications are processed on a rolling basis. *Expenses:* Tuition: Part-time $627 per unit. Tuition and fees vary according to program. *Financial support:* Fellowships, teaching assistantships, career-related internships or fieldwork and Federal Work-Study available. Support available to part-time students. Financial award application deadline: 3/1; financial award applicants required to submit FAFSA. *Unit head:* Patricia DeMarlo, Director, 408-554-4696.

Seattle Pacific University, Graduate School, School of Education, Program in Educational Leadership, Seattle, WA 98119-1997. Offers M Ed, Ed D. *Accreditation:* NCATE. Part-time and evening/weekend programs available. *Students:* 4 full-time (2 women), 54 part-time (36 women); includes 5 minority (2 African Americans, 1 American Indian/Alaska Native, 2 Asian Americans or Pacific Islanders), 2 international. 31 applicants, 84% accepted, 21 enrolled. In 2006, 7 master's, 7 doctorates awarded. *Entrance requirements:* For master's, GRE General Test or MAT, minimum GPA of 3.0. *Application deadline:* For fall admission, 7/1 priority date for domestic students; for spring admission, 3/1 priority date for domestic students. Applications are processed on a rolling basis. Application fee: $50. *Expenses:* Contact institution. *Financial support:* Career-related internships or fieldwork available. Financial award applicants required to submit FAFSA. *Unit head:* Dr. Richard Smith, Chair, 206-281-2214, Fax: 206-281-2756, E-mail: rsmith@spu.edu. *Application contact:* Allan Blomquist, Graduate Programs Manager, 206-281-2378, Fax: 206-281-2756, E-mail: blomqa@spu.edu.

Seattle University, College of Education, Program in Educational Administration, Seattle, WA 98122-1090. Offers M Ed, MA, Certificate, Ed S. *Accreditation:* NCATE. Part-time and evening/weekend programs available. *Students:* Average age 40. 12 applicants, 58% accepted, 7 enrolled. In 2006, 5 master's, 1 other advanced degree awarded. *Degree requirements:* For master's and other advanced degree, comprehensive exam. *Entrance requirements:* For master's, GRE, MAT, or minimum GPA of 3.0; interview; 1 year of related experience. Additional exam requirements/recommendations for international students: Required—TOEFL. *Application deadline:* For fall admission, 8/20 priority date for domestic students; for winter admission, 11/20 for domestic students; for spring admission, 2/20 for domestic students. Applications are processed on a rolling basis. Application fee: $55. *Financial support:* Career-related internships or fieldwork and Federal Work-Study available. Support available to part-time students. Financial award applicants required to submit FAFSA. *Unit head:* Dr. Michael Silver, Director, 206-296-5798, E-mail: silverm@seattleu.edu. *Application contact:* Janet Shandley, Associate Dean of Graduate Admissions, 206-296-5900, Fax: 206-298-5656, E-mail: grad_admissions@seattleu.edu.

Seattle University, College of Education, Program in Educational Leadership, Seattle, WA 98122-1090. Offers Ed D. *Accreditation:* NCATE. Part-time and evening/weekend programs available. *Students:* 18 full-time (14 women), 47 part-time (33 women); includes 8 minority (4 African Americans, 1 American Indian/Alaska Native, 2 Asian Americans or Pacific Islanders, 1 Hispanic American), 2 international. Average age 43. In 2006, 9 degrees awarded. *Degree requirements:* For doctorate, thesis/dissertation, comprehensive exam. *Entrance requirements:* For doctorate, GRE General Test, MAT, interview, MA, minimum GPA of 3.5, 3 years of related experience. Additional exam requirements/recommendations for international students: Required—TOEFL. *Application deadline:* For fall admission, 4/1 for domestic students. Application fee: $55. *Expenses:* Contact institution. *Financial support:* Career-related internships or fieldwork and Federal Work-Study available. Support available to part-time students. Financial award applicants required to submit FAFSA. *Unit head:* Dr. Robert Pena, Chair, 206-296-6170, E-mail: penar@seattleu.edu.

Seattle University, College of Education, Program in Student Development Administration, Seattle, WA 98122-1090. Offers M Ed, MA. Part-time and evening/weekend programs available. *Students:* 21 full-time (19 women), 27 part-time (24 women); includes 12 minority (3 African Americans, 6 Asian Americans or Pacific Islanders, 3 Hispanic Americans). Average age 27. 16 applicants, 81% accepted, 8 enrolled. In 2006, 14 degrees awarded. *Degree requirements:* For master's, comprehensive exam. *Entrance requirements:* For master's, GRE, MAT, or minimum GPA of 3.0. Additional exam requirements/recommendations for international students: Required—TOEFL. *Application deadline:* For fall admission, 8/20 priority date for domestic students; for winter admission, 11/20 for domestic students; for spring admission, 2/20 for domestic students. Applications are processed on a rolling basis. Application fee: $55. *Financial support:* Career-related internships or fieldwork, Federal Work-Study, and unspecified assistantships available. Support available to part-time students. Financial award applicants required to submit FAFSA. *Unit head:* Dr. Jeremy Stringer, Coordinator, 206-296-6170, E-mail: stringer@seattleu.edu. *Application contact:* Janet Shandley, Associate Dean of Graduate Admissions, 206-296-5900, Fax: 206-298-5656, E-mail: grad_admissions@seattleu.edu.

Seton Hall University, College of Education and Human Services, Department of Education Leadership, Management and Policy, Program in Catholic School Leadership, South Orange, NJ 07079-2697. Offers MA. Evening/weekend programs available. *Faculty:* 7 full-time (2 women), 4 part-time/adjunct (2 women). *Students:* 25 full-time (15 women). Average age 40. 25 applicants, 100% accepted, 15 enrolled. In 2006, 13 degrees awarded. *Degree requirements:* For master's, comprehensive exam. *Entrance requirements:* For master's, MAT. *Application deadline:* For fall admission, 4/1 for domestic students. Application fee: $50. *Unit head:* Rev. Kevin M. Hanbury, Program Director, 973-761-9668, Fax: 973-275-2187, E-mail: hanburke@shu.edu. *Application contact:* Rev. Kevin M. Hanbury, Program Director, 973-761-9668, Fax: 973-275-2187, E-mail: hanburke@shu.edu.

Seton Hall University, College of Education and Human Services, Department of Education Leadership, Management and Policy, Program in Higher Education Administration, South Orange, NJ 07079-2697. Offers PhD. *Accreditation:* NCATE. Part-time and evening/weekend programs available. *Faculty:* 12 full-time (4 women), 1 part-time/adjunct (0 women). *Students:* 5 full-time (1 woman), 52 part-time (29 women); includes 7 minority (3 African Americans, 3 Asian Americans or Pacific Islanders, 1 Hispanic American), 1 international. Average age 41. 12 applicants, 50% accepted, 5 enrolled. In 2006, 4 degrees awarded. *Degree requirements:* For doctorate, thesis/dissertation, internship, comprehensive exam. *Entrance requirements:* For doctorate, GRE or MAT, interview, minimum GPA of 3.5. *Application deadline:* For fall admission, 2/1 priority date for domestic students; for spring admission, 10/1 for domestic students. Applications are processed on a rolling basis. Application fee: $50. *Financial support:* Application deadline: 2/1. *Unit head:* Charles Mitchell, Chair, 973-275-2056.

Seton Hall University, College of Education and Human Services, Department of Education Leadership, Management and Policy, Program in K–12 Leadership, Management and Policy, South Orange, NJ 07079-2697. Offers Ed D, Exec Ed D, Ed S. Part-time and evening/weekend programs available. *Faculty:* 12 full-time (4 women), 1 part-time/adjunct (0 women). *Students:* 142 full-time (75 women), 90 part-time (34 women); includes 21 minority (15 African Americans, 1 Asian American or Pacific Islander, 5 Hispanic Americans), 1 international. Average age 43. 39 applicants, 72% accepted, 17 enrolled. In 2006, 42 doctorates, 21 other advanced degrees awarded. *Degree requirements:* For doctorate, thesis/dissertation, internship, comprehensive exam. *Entrance requirements:* For doctorate, MAT, interview. *Application deadline:* For fall admission, 2/1 for domestic students; for spring admission, 12/1 for domestic students. Applications are processed on a rolling basis. Application fee: $50. *Financial support:* In 2006–07, 2 research assistantships with full tuition reimbursements (averaging $4,500 per year) were awarded; unspecified assistantships also available. Financial award application deadline: 2/1. *Application contact:* 973-761-9397.

Shasta Bible College, Program in School/Church Administration, Redding, CA 96002. Offers MS. Part-time and evening/weekend programs available. *Degree requirements:* For master's, thesis or alternative, comprehensive exam (for some programs), registration. *Entrance requirements:* For master's, cumulative GPA of 3.0, 9 semester hours of education or psychology courses. Additional exam requirements/recommendations for international students: Required—TOEFL (minimum score 550 paper-based; 213 computer-based).

Shenandoah University, College of Arts and Sciences, Winchester, VA 22601-5195. Offers administrative leadership (D Ed); advanced professional teaching English to speakers of other languages (Certificate); education (MSE); elementary education (Certificate); middle school education (Certificate); professional studies (Certificate); professional teaching English to speakers of other languages (Certificate); public management (Certificate); secondary education (Certificate); women's studies (Certificate). Part-time and evening/weekend programs available. Postbaccalaureate distance learning degree programs offered (minimal on-campus study). *Faculty:* 14 full-time (9 women), 7 part-time/adjunct (4 women). *Students:* 28 full-time (16 women), 283 part-time (208 women); includes 8 minority (3 African Americans, 1 American Indian/Alaska Native, 3 Asian Americans or Pacific Islanders, 1 Hispanic American), 26 international. Average age 40. 182 applicants, 68% accepted, 98 enrolled. In 2006, 96 master's, 6 doctorates, 22 other advanced degrees awarded. *Degree requirements:* For master's, thesis (for some programs), internship, comprehensive exam (for some programs); for doctorate, thesis/dissertation, comprehensive exam. *Entrance requirements:* For master's, minimum GPA of 3.0 or satisfactory GRE, 3 letters of recommendation, valid teaching license; for doctorate, minimum GPA of 3.5 in master's, 3 years of teaching experience, 3 letters of recommendation, writing samples. Additional exam requirements/recommendations for international students: Required—TOEFL (minimum score 527 paper-based; 197 computer-based; 71 iBT). *Application deadline:* For fall admission, 7/15 for domestic students; for spring admission, 10/15 for domestic students. Applications are processed on a rolling basis. Application fee: $30. Electronic applications accepted. *Expenses:* Tuition: Full-time $12,200; part-time $610 per credit. Required fees: $150. Full-time tuition and fees vary according to course load and program. *Financial support:* In 2006–07, fellowships with partial tuition reimbursements (averaging $2,581 per year); career-related internships or fieldwork, institutionally sponsored loans, and unspecified assistantships also available. Support available to part-time students. Financial

Educational Administration

Shenandoah University (continued)
award application deadline: 3/15; financial award applicants required to submit FAFSA. *Faculty research:* Nanotechnology, writing pedagogy and writing centers, violence in schools, Virginia/Shenandoah Valley history and culture, stress in children. *Unit head:* Dr. Calvin Allen, Dean, 540-665-4587, Fax: 540-665-4644, E-mail: callen@su.edu. *Application contact:* David Anthony, Dean of Admissions, 540-665-4581, Fax: 540-665-4627, E-mail: admit@su.edu.

See Close-Up on page 919.

Shippensburg University of Pennsylvania, School of Graduate Studies, College of Education and Human Services, Department of Educational Leadership and Policy, Shippensburg, PA 17257-2299. Offers school administration (M Ed). *Accreditation:* NCATE. Part-time and evening/weekend programs available. *Faculty:* 4 full-time (1 woman), 2 part-time/adjunct (1 woman). *Students:* Average age 32. 30 applicants, 77% accepted, 16 enrolled. In 2006, 14 degrees awarded. *Degree requirements:* For master's, 2 years of teaching or related experience, candidacy, thesis optional. *Entrance requirements:* For master's, instructional or educational specialist certificate, 2 letters of reference, interview required if GPA < 2.75. Additional exam requirements/recommendations for international students: Required—TOEFL (minimum score 560 paper-based; 220 computer-based). *Application deadline:* For fall admission, 3/1 for international students; for spring admission, 7/1 for international students. Applications are processed on a rolling basis. Application fee: $30. Electronic applications accepted. *Expenses:* Tuition, state resident: part-time $336 per credit. Tuition, nonresident: part-time $538 per credit. *Financial support:* In 2006–07, research assistantships with full tuition reimbursements (averaging $3,125 per year); career-related internships or fieldwork, scholarships/grants, and unspecified assistantships also available. Support available to part-time students. Financial award application deadline: 3/1; financial award applicants required to submit FAFSA. *Unit head:* Dr. Nancy H. Stankus, Chairperson, 717-477-1591, Fax: 717-477-4036, E-mail: nhstan@ship.edu. *Application contact:* Renee Payne, Associate Dean of Graduate Admissions, 717-477-1231, Fax: 717-477-4016, E-mail: rmpayn@ship.edu.

Silver Lake College, Division of Graduate Studies, Program in Education, Manitowoc, WI 54220-9319. Offers administrative leadership (MA); teacher leadership (MA). *Accreditation:* NCATE. Part-time and evening/weekend programs available. Postbaccalaureate distance learning degree programs offered (no on-campus study). *Faculty:* 3 full-time (all women), 33 part-time/adjunct (23 women). *Students:* 1 (woman) full-time, 53 part-time (42 women); includes 6 minority (all Hispanic Americans) Average age 35. 30 applicants, 53% accepted, 6 enrolled. In 2006, 46 degrees awarded. *Degree requirements:* For master's, thesis or alternative, public presentation of culminating project, comprehensive exam, registration. *Entrance requirements:* For master's, interview, minimum undergraduate GPA of 3.0, writing sample, 3 letters of recommendation. *Application deadline:* Applications are processed on a rolling basis. Application fee: $35. Electronic applications accepted. *Expenses:* Tuition: Full-time $6,120; part-time $340 per credit. *Financial support:* Career-related internships or fieldwork, Federal Work-Study, and scholarships/grants available. Support available to part-time students. Financial award applicants required to submit FAFSA. *Unit head:* Julie A. Mayrose, Director, 800-236-4752 Ext. 370, Fax: 920-684-7082. *Application contact:* Jamie Grant, Associate Director-Admissions, 800-236-4752 Ext. 186, Fax: 920-684-7082, E-mail: jgrant@silver.sl.edu.

Simmons College, Graduate School, College of Arts and Sciences Graduate Studies, Department of Education, Program in Teacher Preparation, Boston, MA 02115. Offers educational leadership (MS Ed, CAGS); elementary education (MAT, CAGS); general education (CAGS); general purposes (MS); middle school education (MAT, CAGS); professional license (CAGS); professional license: elementary (MS Ed); professional license: middle/high (MS Ed); secondary education (MAT, CAGS); urban education (MS Ed, CAGS). *Faculty:* 4 full-time (3 women), 22 part-time/adjunct (13 women). *Students:* 61 full-time (53 women), 141 part-time (128 women); includes 33 minority (13 African Americans, 10 Asian Americans or Pacific Islanders, 10 Hispanic Americans), 1 international. Average age 24. 86 applicants, 77% accepted, 39 enrolled. In 2006, 128 master's, 12 other advanced degrees awarded. *Degree requirements:* For master's, student teaching experience or internship. *Entrance requirements:* For master's, GRE General Test, MAT or Massachusetts Tests for Educator Licensure (MTEL). Additional exam requirements/recommendations for international students: Required—TOEFL (minimum score 600 paper-based; 250 computer-based; 100 iBT). *Application deadline:* For fall admission, 8/1 priority date for domestic and international students; for spring admission, 12/15 priority date for domestic and international students. Applications are processed on a rolling basis. Application fee: $35. Electronic applications accepted. *Expenses: Contact institution. Financial support:* Teaching assistantships, career-related internships or fieldwork, Federal Work-Study, institutionally sponsored loans, scholarships/grants, and tuition waivers (partial) available. Support available to part-time students. Financial award application deadline: 3/1; financial award applicants required to submit FAFSA. *Faculty research:* Putting standards/frameworks into practice, restructuring middle and high schools, interactive teaching and learning developing curriculum for Third World countries. Total annual research expenditures: $110,000. *Unit head:* Lynda Johnson, Assistant Dean, 617-521-2576, Fax: 617-521-3133, E-mail: gsa@simmons.edu. *Application contact:* Kristen Haack, Director, Graduate Studies Admission, 617-521-2915, Fax: 617-521-3058, E-mail: gsa@simmons.edu.

Simon Fraser University, Graduate Studies, Faculty of Education, Program in Administrative Leadership, Burnaby, BC V5A 1S6, Canada. Offers M Ed, MA. *Degree requirements:* For master's, project or thesis. *Entrance requirements:* For master's, minimum GPA of 3.0. Additional exam requirements/recommendations for international students: Required—TOEFL or IELTS.

Simpson University, School of Education, Redding, CA 96003-8606. Offers education (MA); education and preliminary administrative services (MA); education and preliminary teaching (MA); teaching (MA). Part-time programs available. *Entrance requirements:* For master's, PRAXIS, California Basic Educational Skills Test, 2 letters of reference. Additional exam requirements/recommendations for international students: Required—TOEFL (minimum score 550 paper-based; 180 computer-based). Electronic applications accepted.

Slippery Rock University of Pennsylvania, Graduate Studies (Recruitment), College of Education, Department of Special Education, Slippery Rock, PA 16057-1383. Offers master teacher (M Ed); supervision (M Ed). *Accreditation:* NCATE. Part-time and evening/weekend programs available. *Degree requirements:* For master's, thesis (for some programs), portfolio presentation, comprehensive exam (for some programs). *Entrance requirements:* For master's, GRE General Test, MAT, minimum GPA of 2.75 (minimum GPA of 3.0 for initial certification). Additional exam requirements/recommendations for international students: Required—TOEFL (minimum score 550 paper-based; 213 computer-based). *Application deadline:* For fall admission, 7/1 priority date for domestic and international students; for spring admission, 11/1 priority date for domestic and international students. Applications are processed on a rolling basis. Application fee: $25. Electronic applications accepted. *Expenses:* Tuition, state resident: part-time $336 per credit. Tuition, nonresident: part-time $538 per credit. Required fees: $84 per credit. $37 per semester. *Financial support:* Career-related internships or fieldwork, Federal Work-Study, scholarships/grants, and unspecified assistantships available. Support available to part-time students. Financial award application deadline: 5/1. *Faculty research:* In-service teacher education, contemporary issues in special education, education for developmentally disabled, educational assessment. *Unit head:* Dr. Dennis Fair, Graduate Coordinator, 724-738-2085, Fax: 724-738-4395, E-mail: dennis.fair@sru.edu. *Application contact:* April Longwell, Interim Director of Graduate Studies, 724-738-2051 Ext. 2116, Fax: 724-738-2146, E-mail: graduate.studies@sru.edu.

Sonoma State University, School of Education, Department of Educational Leadership and Special Education, Rohnert Park, CA 94928-3609. Offers educational leadership (MA); special education (MA). Part-time and evening/weekend programs available. *Faculty:* 7 full-time (0 women). *Degree requirements:* For master's, thesis or alternative. *Entrance requirements:* For master's, GRE General Test, minimum GPA of 2.5. Application fee: $55. *Expenses:* Tuition, nonresident: part-time $339 per unit. Required fees: $1,464 per term. *Financial support:* Application deadline: 3/2.

South Carolina State University, School of Graduate Studies, Department of Educational Leadership, Orangeburg, SC 29117-0001. Offers educational leadership (Ed D, Ed S). *Accreditation:* ACA; NCATE. Part-time and evening/weekend programs available. *Faculty:* 10 full-time (3 women), 3 part-time/adjunct (2 women). *Students:* 25 full-time (12 women), 134 part-time (93 women); includes 127 minority (124 African Americans, 1 American Indian/Alaska Native, 2 Asian Americans or Pacific Islanders). Average age 41. 65 applicants, 69% accepted, 19 enrolled. In 2006, 27 doctorates, 28 other advanced degrees awarded. *Degree requirements:* For doctorate, thesis/dissertation, preliminary exams, internship, practicum, comprehensive exam; for Ed S, thesis. *Entrance requirements:* For doctorate, GRE General Test or MAT, teaching certificate, teaching experience; for Ed S, GRE General Test or MAT, interview, teaching certificate, teaching experience. *Application deadline:* For fall admission, 6/15 priority date for domestic students, 6/15 for international students; for spring admission, 11/1 for domestic and international students. Applications are processed on a rolling basis. Application fee: $25. Electronic applications accepted. *Expenses:* Tuition, state resident: full-time $7,278. Tuition, nonresident: full-time $14,322. *Financial support:* Fellowships, research assistantships, career-related internships or fieldwork and institutionally sponsored loans available. Financial award application deadline: 6/1. *Faculty research:* Decision making, relaxation theory, learning styles, student recruitment, academic achievement. *Unit head:* Dr. Thomas Thompson, Dean of the School of Graduate Studies, 803-516-4734, Fax: 803-536-8812, E-mail: tthompson@scsu.edu. *Application contact:* Annette Hazzard-Jones, Program Coordinator II, 803-536-8809, Fax: 803-536-8812, E-mail: zs_ahazzard@scsu.edu.

South Dakota State University, Graduate School, College of Education and Counseling, Department of Educational Leadership, Brookings, SD 57007. Offers curriculum and instruction (M Ed); educational administration (M Ed). Part-time and evening/weekend programs available. Postbaccalaureate distance learning degree programs offered (minimal on-campus study). *Faculty:* 12 full-time (4 women), 6 part-time/adjunct (1 woman). *Students:* 17 full-time (12 women), 132 part-time (67 women); includes 10 minority (3 African Americans, 4 American Indian/Alaska Native, 2 Asian Americans or Pacific Islanders, 1 Hispanic American). 61 applicants, 72% accepted, 44 enrolled. In 2006, 37 degrees awarded. *Degree requirements:* For master's, portfolio and oral exam. *Entrance requirements:* For master's, minimum GPA of 2.75. Additional exam requirements/recommendations for international students: Required—TOEFL (minimum score 550 paper-based). *Application deadline:* For fall admission, 4/30 priority date for international students; for spring admission, 8/30 priority date for international students. Applications are processed on a rolling basis. Application fee: $35. *Financial support:* In 2006–07, 2 research assistantships with partial tuition reimbursements were awarded. *Faculty research:* Inclusion school climate, K–12 reform and restructuring, rural development, ESL, leadership. *Unit head:* Dr. Kenneth Rasmussen, Head, 605-688-6365, Fax: 605-688-5784, E-mail: kenneth.rasmussen@sdstate.edu.

Southeastern Louisiana University, College of Education and Human Development, Department of Educational Leadership and Technology, Hammond, LA 70402. Offers educational leadership (M Ed, Ed D). Part-time and evening/weekend programs available. *Faculty:* 11 full-time (4 women). *Students:* 5 full-time (all women), 122 part-time (102 women); includes 10 minority (9 African Americans, 1 Hispanic American). Average age 37. 24 applicants, 100% accepted, 19 enrolled. In 2006, 62 degrees awarded. *Degree requirements:* For master's, comprehensive exam (for some programs). *Entrance requirements:* For master's, GRE General Test, 18 hours of course work in professional education or an undergraduate degree in education, standard teaching certificate; for doctorate, GRE General Test, master's degree with minimum GPA of 3.25, minimum GPA of 3.0 on the last 60 undergraduate hours. Additional exam requirements/recommendations for international students: Required—TOEFL (minimum score 500 paper-based; 173 computer-based). *Application deadline:* For fall admission, 7/15 priority date for domestic students, 6/1 priority date for international students; for spring admission, 12/1 priority date for domestic students, 10/1 priority date for international students. Applications are processed on a rolling basis. Application fee: $20 ($30 for international students). Electronic applications accepted. *Expenses:* Tuition, state resident: full-time $2,216; part-time $123 per credit. Tuition, nonresident: full-time $6,212; part-time $345 per credit. Required fees: $986; $55 per credit. Part-time tuition and fees vary according to course load. *Financial support:* Federal Work-Study, institutionally sponsored loans, unspecified assistantships, and administrative assistantships available. Support available to part-time students. Financial award application deadline: 5/1; financial award applicants required to submit FAFSA. *Faculty research:* Legal and ethical issues in education, school culture and gender perceptions, cognitive development in young children, using the Web and professional development in technology integration, basic training needs to prepare school board members and superintendents. *Unit head:* Dr. Frederick Dembowski, Department Head, 985-549-5713, Fax: 985-549-5712, E-mail: fdembowski@selu.edu. *Application contact:* Sandra Meyers, Graduate Admissions Analyst, 985-549-2066, Fax: 985-549-5632, E-mail: admissions@selu.edu.

Southeastern Oklahoma State University, Graduate School, School of Education, Durant, OK 74701-0609. Offers educational administration (M Ed); educational instruction and leadership (M Ed); educational technology (M Ed); elementary education (M Ed); school counseling (M Ed); secondary education (M Ed). *Accreditation:* NCATE. Part-time and evening/weekend programs available. *Degree requirements:* For master's, portfolio (M Ed), thesis optional. *Entrance requirements:* For master's, GRE General Test (MBS), minimum GPA of 3.0 in last 60 hours or 2.75 overall. Additional exam requirements/recommendations for international students: Required—TOEFL (minimum score 550 paper-based; 213 computer-based). Electronic applications accepted.

Southeast Missouri State University, School of Graduate Studies, Department of Educational Leadership and Counseling, Program in Educational Administration, Cape Girardeau, MO 63701-4799. Offers MA, Ed S. *Accreditation:* NCATE. Part-time and evening/weekend programs available. *Faculty:* 9 full-time (5 women). *Students:* 33 full-time (22 women), 180 part-time (128 women); includes 4 minority (2 African Americans, 2 Asian Americans or Pacific Islanders). Average age 36. 71 applicants, 89% accepted. In 2006, 26 master's, 8 other advanced degrees awarded. *Degree requirements:* For master's, thesis or alternative. *Entrance requirements:* For master's, GRE General Test, PRAXIS or MAT, minimum GPA of 2.75, teacher certification; for Ed S, GRE General Test, PRAXIS or MAT, minimum graduate GPA of 3.5. Additional exam requirements/recommendations for international students: Required—TOEFL (minimum score 550 paper-based; 213 computer-based). *Application deadline:* For fall admission, 8/1 for domestic students, 4/1 for international students; for spring admission, 11/21 for domestic students, 10/1 for international students. Applications are processed on a rolling basis. Application fee: $20 ($100 for international students). Electronic applications accepted. *Financial support:* In 2006–07, 53 students received support, including 10 research assistantships with full tuition reimbursements available (averaging $7,100 per year); career-related internships or fieldwork and unspecified assistantships also available. Financial award applicants required to submit FAFSA. *Application contact:* Marsha L. Arant, Senior Administrative Assistant, Office of Graduate Studies, 573-651-2192, Fax: 573-651-2001, E-mail: marant@semo.edu.

Southern Adventist University, School of Education and Psychology, Collegedale, TN 37315-0370. Offers curriculum and instruction (MS Ed); educational administration and supervision (MS Ed); inclusive education (MS Ed); literacy education (MS Ed); outdoor teacher education (MS Ed); professional counseling (MS); school counseling (MS). *Accreditation:* NCATE. Part-time and evening/weekend programs available. *Faculty:* 11 full-time (5 women), 1 (woman) part-time/adjunct. *Students:* 36 full-time (29 women), 7 part-time (6 women); includes 8 minority (6 African Americans, 2 Hispanic Americans). Average age 30. 15 applicants, 100% accepted, 15 enrolled. In 2006, 25 degrees awarded. *Degree requirements:* For master's, position paper (MS), portfolio (MS Ed in outdoor teacher education), thesis optional. *Entrance requirements:* For master's, GRE General Test, interview (MS); 9 semester hours of upper division course work in psychology or related field, including 1 course in psychology research or statistics; 9 semester hours of education (MS Ed). Additional exam requirements/recommendations for international students: Required—TOEFL (minimum score 600 paper-based; 250 computer-based; 100 iBT). *Application deadline:* For fall admission, 5/15 priority date for domestic and international students; for winter admission, 10/15 priority date for domestic and international students; for spring admission, 3/31 priority date for domestic and international students. Applications are processed on a rolling basis. Application fee: $25. Electronic applications accepted. *Financial support:* In 2006–07, 7 students received support, including 4 research assistantships with full tuition reimbursements available (averaging $10,000 per year); career-related internships or fieldwork, scholarships/grants, tuition waivers (partial), and unspecified assistantships also available. Support available to part-time students. Financial award application deadline: 4/1; financial award applicants required to submit FAFSA. *Unit head:* Dr. Denise Dunzweiler, Dean, 423-236-2776, Fax: 423-236-1765, E-mail: denise@southern.edu. *Application contact:* Mikhaile Spence, Information Contact, 423-236-2496, Fax: 423-236-1765, E-mail: maspence@southern.edu.

Southern Arkansas University–Magnolia, Graduate Programs, Magnolia, AR 71753. Offers computer and information sciences (MS); counseling (MS); education (M Ed), including counseling and development, educational administration and supervision, elementary education, secondary education; kinesiology (MS); library media and information specialist (M Ed); school counseling (M Ed); teaching (MAT). *Accreditation:* NCATE. Part-time and evening/weekend programs available. *Degree requirements:* For master's, thesis optional. *Entrance requirements:* For master's, GRE or MAT, minimum GPA of 2.75. *Faculty research:* Alternative certification for teachers, supervision of instruction, instructional leadership, counseling.

Southern Connecticut State University, School of Graduate Studies, School of Education, Department of Educational Leadership, New Haven, CT 06515-1355. Offers Ed D, Diploma. Part-time and evening/weekend programs available. *Faculty:* 6 full-time, 6 part-time/adjunct. *Students:* 7 full-time (5 women), 240 part-time (164 women); includes 33 minority (26 African Americans, 1 American Indian/Alaska Native, 6 Hispanic Americans), 1 international. 142 applicants, 77% accepted, 93 enrolled. In 2006, 98 degrees awarded. *Entrance requirements:* For degree, master's degree, minimum GPA of 3.0, writing sample. *Application deadline:* For fall admission, 7/15 priority date for domestic students. Applications are processed on a rolling basis. Application fee: $50. Electronic applications accepted. *Financial support:* Application deadline: 4/15; *Unit head:* Dr. Brian Perkins, Chairperson, 203-392-5345, E-mail: perkinsb1@southernct.edu. *Application contact:* Dr. Lystra Richardson, Graduate Coordinator, 203-392-5346, Fax: 203-392-5347, E-mail: richardsonl1@southernct.edu.

Southern Illinois University Carbondale, Graduate School, College of Education, Department of Educational Administration and Higher Education, Program in Educational Administration, Carbondale, IL 62901-4701. Offers MS Ed, PhD. *Accreditation:* NCATE. Part-time programs available. *Faculty:* 9 full-time (3 women). *Students:* 11 full-time (8 women), 143 part-time (73 women); includes 21 minority (18 African Americans, 1 American Indian/Alaska Native, 2 Hispanic Americans), 12 international. 35 applicants, 23% accepted, 1 enrolled. In 2006, 9 master's, 10 doctorates awarded. *Degree requirements:* For master's, thesis or alternative; for doctorate, thesis/dissertation. *Entrance requirements:* For master's, GRE General Test, MAT, minimum GPA of 2.7; for doctorate, GRE General Test, MAT, minimum GPA of 3.5. Additional exam requirements/recommendations for international students: Required—TOEFL. *Application deadline:* For fall admission, 5/15 for domestic students; for spring admission, 9/15 for domestic students. Applications are processed on a rolling basis. Application fee: $20. *Financial support:* In 2006–07, 7 students received support, including 1 research assistantship with full tuition reimbursement available, 3 teaching assistantships with full tuition reimbursements available; fellowships with full tuition reimbursements available, career-related internships or fieldwork, Federal Work-Study, institutionally sponsored loans, and tuition waivers (full) also available. Support available to part-time students. Financial award application deadline: 4/1. *Faculty research:* School principalship, history and philosophy of education, supervision. *Application contact:* Debra Mibb, Admissions Secretary, 618-536-4434, Fax: 618-453-4338, E-mail: dmibb@siu.edu.

Announcement: The master's program in educational administration is creating a joint MS Ed/JD program with the SIUC School of Law. This initiative will allow a student to earn the General Administrative Certificate along with the law degree.

See Close-Up on page 1123.

Southern Illinois University Edwardsville, Graduate Studies and Research, School of Education, Department of Educational Leadership, Program in Educational Administration, Edwardsville, IL 62026-0001. Offers MS Ed, Ed S. *Accreditation:* NCATE. Part-time and evening/weekend programs available. *Students:* 1 full-time (0 women), 179 part-time (123 women); includes 16 minority (14 African Americans, 1 Asian American or Pacific Islander, 1 Hispanic American). Average age 33. 29 applicants, 69% accepted. In 2006, 51 master's, 5 Ed Ss awarded. *Degree requirements:* For master's, thesis or alternative, portfolio. *Entrance requirements:* For master's, MAT, ISBE. Additional exam requirements/recommendations for international students: Required—TOEFL. *Application deadline:* For fall admission, 7/20 for domestic students, 6/1 for international students; for spring admission, 12/14 for domestic students, 10/1 for international students. Application fee: $30. Electronic applications accepted. *Financial support:* Fellowships, research assistantships with full tuition reimbursements, teaching assistantships, Federal Work-Study, institutionally sponsored loans, and unspecified assistantships available. Support available to part-time students. Financial award application deadline: 3/1; financial award applicants required to submit FAFSA. *Unit head:* Dr. Linda Morice, Director, 618-650-3277, E-mail: lmorice@siue.edu.

Southern Nazarene University, Graduate College, School of Education, Bethany, OK 73008. Offers curriculum and instruction (MA); educational leadership (MA). *Accreditation:* NCATE. Part-time and evening/weekend programs available. *Faculty:* 10. *Students:* 105. Average age 27. In 2006, 23 degrees awarded. *Degree requirements:* For master's, thesis optional. *Entrance requirements:* For master's, MAT, English proficiency exam, minimum GPA of 3.0 in last 60 hours/major, 2.7 overall. *Application deadline:* For fall admission, 8/1 priority date for domestic students. Applications are processed on a rolling basis. Application fee: $25 ($35 for international students). *Expenses:* Tuition: Part-time $507 per credit. *Financial support:* Teaching assistantships, career-related internships or fieldwork available. *Unit head:* Dr. Rex Tullis, Director, 405-491-6317, E-mail: rtullis@snu.edu.

Southern New Hampshire University, School of Education, Manchester, NH 03106-1045. Offers business education (MS); child development (M Ed); computer technology education (Certificate); curriculum and instruction (M Ed); education (M Ed, CAS); elementary education (M Ed); general special education (Certificate); school business administrator (Certificate); school counseling (M Ed); school psychology (M Ed); secondary education (M Ed); training and development (Certificate). Part-time and evening/weekend programs available. Postbaccalaureate distance learning degree programs offered. *Faculty:* 6 full-time (3 women), 9 part-time/adjunct (7 women). *Students:* Average age 35. In 2006, 52 degrees awarded. *Degree requirements:* For master's, thesis or alternative, comprehensive exam (for some programs). *Entrance requirements:* For master's, GRE General Test or MAT, minimum GPA of 3.0. Additional exam requirements/recommendations for international students: Required—TOEFL (minimum score 550 paper-based; 213 computer-based). *Application deadline:* Applications are processed on a rolling basis. Application fee: $25. Electronic applications accepted. *Expenses:* Contact institution. *Financial support:* Institutionally sponsored loans available. Financial award applicants required to submit FAFSA. *Unit head:* Dr. Patrick J. Hartwick, Dean, 603-668-2211 Ext. 4698, Fax: 603-629-4673, E-mail: p.hartwick@snhu.edu. *Application contact:* Scott Durand, Director of Graduate Enrollment Services, 603-644-3102 Ext. 3338, Fax: 603-644-3144, E-mail: s.durand@snhu.edu.

Southern Oregon University, Graduate Studies, School of Social Sciences, Department of Education, Ashland, OR 97520. Offers elementary education (MA Ed, MS Ed), including classroom teacher, early childhood, handicapped learner, reading, supervision; secondary education (MA Ed, MS Ed), including classroom teacher, handicapped learner, reading, supervision; teaching (MAT). *Degree requirements:* For master's, thesis optional. *Entrance requirements:* For master's, GRE General Test, minimum GPA of 3.0. Electronic applications accepted.

Southern University and Agricultural and Mechanical College, Graduate School, College of Education, Department of Behavioral Studies and Educational Leadership, Baton Rouge, LA 70813. Offers administration and supervision (M Ed); counselor education (MA); mental health counseling (MA). *Accreditation:* ACA; NCATE. *Degree requirements:* For master's, thesis optional. *Entrance requirements:* For master's, GRE General Test. Additional exam requirements/recommendations for international students: Required—TOEFL (minimum score 525 paper-based; 193 computer-based). *Faculty research:* Mental health, computer assisted programs, families relations, head start improvements, careers.

Southwest Baptist University, Graduate Studies, Program in Education, Bolivar, MO 65613-2597. Offers education (MS); educational administration (MS, Ed S). Part-time and evening/weekend programs available. *Degree requirements:* For master's, 6 hour residency, thesis optional; for Ed S, 5 hour residency. *Entrance requirements:* For master's, GRE or PRAXIS II, interviews, minimum GPA of 2.75; for Ed S, master's degree. Additional exam requirements/recommendations for international students: Required—TOEFL (minimum score 550 paper-based; 213 computer-based). *Faculty research:* At-risk programs, principal retention, mentoring beginning principals.

Southwestern Assemblies of God University, Thomas F. Harrison School of Graduate Studies, Program in Education, Waxahachie, TX 75165-5735. Offers Christian school administration (MS); curriculum development (MS); MS/MA. *Degree requirements:* For master's, comprehensive written and oral exams. *Entrance requirements:* For master's, GRE General Test, minimum GPA of 2.5. Electronic applications accepted.

Southwestern Oklahoma State University, College of Professional and Graduate Studies, School of Behavioral Sciences and Education, Specialization in Educational Administration, Weatherford, OK 73096-3098. Offers M Ed. M Ed distance learning degree program offered to Oklahoma residents only. *Accreditation:* NCATE. Part-time and evening/weekend programs available. Postbaccalaureate distance learning degree programs offered (minimal on-campus study). *Degree requirements:* For master's, exam. *Entrance requirements:* For master's, GRE General Test or minimum undergraduate GPA of 3.0, portfolio. Additional exam requirements/recommendations for international students: Required—TOEFL.

Southwest Minnesota State University, Department of Education, Marshall, MN 56258. Offers education (MS); education development and leadership (MS); special education (MS). *Faculty:* 8 full-time (4 women), 3 part-time/adjunct (2 women). *Students:* 119 full-time (89 women), 245 part-time (195 women); includes 5 minority (1 Asian American or Pacific Islander, 4 Hispanic Americans), 1 international. 148 applicants. In 2006, 172 degrees awarded. *Application deadline:* Applications are processed on a rolling basis. Application fee: $20. *Expenses:* Tuition, area resident: Full-time $4,835. Tuition, state resident: full-time $4,835; part-time $269 per credit. Tuition, nonresident: part-time $269 per credit. Required fees: $589; $33 per credit. Tuition and fees vary according to course load and reciprocity agreements. *Unit head:* Donna Burgraff, Dean, 507-537-6218, E-mail: burgraff@southwestmsu.edu. *Application contact:* Rich Shearer, Director of Enrollment Management, 507-537-6286, E-mail: shearerr@southwestmsu.edu.

Spalding University, Graduate Studies, College of Education, Program in Leadership Education, Louisville, KY 40203-2188. Offers Ed D. *Accreditation:* NCATE. Part-time and evening/weekend programs available. *Degree requirements:* For doctorate, thesis/dissertation, comprehensive exam. *Entrance requirements:* For doctorate, GRE General Test or MAT, interview, recommendations, resumé. Electronic applications accepted. *Faculty research:* School law, leadership of schools, achievement gap, women in leadership.

Spalding University, Graduate Studies, College of Education, Programs in Education, Louisville, KY 40203-2188. Offers elementary school education (MAT); general education (MA); high school education (MAT); middle school education (MAT); school administration (MA); special education (learning and behavioral disorders) (MAT). MAT degree programs offered for first teaching certificate/license students. *Accreditation:* NCATE. Part-time and evening/weekend programs available. *Degree requirements:* For master's, portfolio, final project, clinical experience. *Entrance requirements:* For master's, GRE General Test or MAT, interview, recommendations, resumé. Additional exam requirements/recommendations for international students: Required—TOEFL. Electronic applications accepted. *Faculty research:* Instructional technology, achievement gap, classroom management, assessment.

Stanford University, School of Education, Program in Social Sciences, Policy, and Educational Practice, Stanford, CA 94305-9991. Offers administration and policy analysis (Ed D, PhD); anthropology of education (PhD); economics of education (PhD); educational linguistics (PhD); evaluation (MA), including interdisciplinary studies; higher education (PhD); history of education (PhD); interdisciplinary studies (PhD); international comparative education (MA, PhD); international education administration and policy analysis (MA); philosophy of education (PhD); policy analysis (MA); prospective principal's program (MA); sociology of education (PhD). *Degree requirements:* For master's, thesis (for some programs); for doctorate, thesis/dissertation. *Entrance requirements:* For master's and doctorate, GRE General Test. Electronic applications accepted.

State University of New York at Fredonia, Graduate Studies, College of Education, Program in Educational Administration, Fredonia, NY 14063-1136. Offers CAS. Part-time and evening/weekend programs available. *Faculty:* 2 full-time (1 woman). *Students:* 15 full-time (8 women), 14 part-time (9 women). Average age 38. In 2006, 7 degrees awarded. *Degree requirements:* For CAS, thesis or alternative. *Application deadline:* For fall admission, 8/5 for domestic students; for spring admission, 12/1 for domestic students. Application fee: $50. *Expenses:* Tuition, state resident: full-time $6,900; part-time $288 per credit hour. Tuition, nonresident: full-time $10,920; part-time $455 per credit hour. Required fees: $1,132; $47 per credit hour. *Financial support:* Research assistantships, teaching assistantships, career-related internships or fieldwork and tuition waivers (full and partial) available. Support available to part-time students. Financial award application deadline: 3/15. *Unit head:* Dr. Christine Givner, Dean, College of Education, 716-673-3311, E-mail: christine.givner@fredonia.edu.

State University of New York at New Paltz, Graduate School, Faculty of Education, Department of Educational Administration, New Paltz, NY 12561. Offers MS Ed, CAS. Part-time and evening/weekend programs available. *Faculty:* 4 full-time (2 women), 4 part-time/adjunct (1 woman). *Students:* 23 full-time (14 women), 107 part-time (66 women); includes 13 minority (7 African Americans, 6 Hispanic Americans). Average age 38. 73 applicants. In 2006, 7 master's, 67 other advanced degrees awarded. *Degree requirements:* For CAS, internship. *Entrance requirements:* For master's, GRE General Test or MAT, minimum GPA of 3.0, teaching certificate; for CAS, minimum GPA of 3.0, proof of 3 years teaching experience. Additional exam requirements/recommendations for international students: Required—TOEFL (minimum score 550 paper-based; 213 computer-based; 80 iBT). *Application deadline:* For fall admission, 5/15 priority date for domestic and international students; for spring admission, 11/15 priority date for domestic and international students. Applications are processed on a rolling basis. Application fee: $50. Electronic applications accepted. *Expenses:* Tuition, state resident: full-time $6,900; part-time $288 per credit hour. Tuition, nonresident: full-time $10,920; part-time $455 per credit hour. *Financial support:* Career-related internships or fieldwork, Federal Work-Study, and institutionally sponsored loans available. *Unit head:* Dr. Michael Muffs, Chair, 845-257-2814.

State University of New York at Oswego, Graduate Studies, School of Education, Department of Educational Administration, Oswego, NY 13126. Offers educational administration and supervision (CAS); school building leadership (CAS); MS Ed/CAS. Part-time programs available. *Faculty:* 3 full-time, 7 part-time/adjunct. *Students:* 6 full-time (5 women), 86 part-time (55 women); includes 1 minority (Hispanic American) Average age 40. 68 applicants, 100%

Educational Administration

State University of New York at Oswego (continued)
accepted. In 2006, 44 degrees awarded. *Degree requirements:* For CAS, internship. *Entrance requirements:* For degree, interview, MA or MS, minimum GPA of 3.0, teaching certificate. Additional exam requirements/recommendations for international students: Required—TOEFL (minimum score 560 paper-based; 220 computer-based). *Application deadline:* For fall admission, 4/1 for domestic students; for spring admission, 10/1 for domestic students. Applications are processed on a rolling basis. *Application fee:* $50. *Expenses:* Tuition, state resident: part-time $288 per credit. Tuition, nonresident: part-time $455 per credit. Tuition and fees vary according to program. *Financial support:* Teaching assistantships, career-related internships or fieldwork, institutionally sponsored loans, and health care benefits available. Support available to part-time students. Financial award application deadline: 4/1; financial award applicants required to submit FAFSA. *Faculty research:* Professional growth and development, leadership, governance, strategic planning, shared decision making. *Unit head:* Dr. Suzanne Gilmour, Chair, 315-312-2264.

State University of New York at Plattsburgh, Division of Education, Health, and Human Services, Program in Educational Leadership, Plattsburgh, NY 12901-2681. Offers CAS. *Faculty:* 1 full-time (0 women), 3 part-time/adjunct (0 women). *Students:* 3 full-time (1 woman), 35 part-time (18 women), 1 international. Average age 38. 5 applicants, 80% accepted, 4 enrolled. In 2006, 3 degrees awarded. *Degree requirements:* For CAS, comprehensive exam. *Application deadline:* For fall admission, 2/15 priority date for domestic students; for spring admission, 10/15 priority date for domestic students. Applications are processed on a rolling basis. *Application fee:* $50. *Expenses:* Tuition, state resident: full-time $6,900; part-time $288 per credit hour. Tuition, nonresident: full-time $10,920; part-time $455 per credit hour. *Financial support:* In 2006–07, 3 students received support. Federal Work-Study available. Support available to part-time students. Financial award application deadline: 4/15; financial award applicants required to submit FAFSA. *Unit head:* Dr. Steven Black, Coordinator, 518-564-2125, E-mail: blacksn@plattsburgh.edu. *Application contact:* Sharon Derr, Assistant Director, Graduate Admission, 518-564-4723, Fax: 518-564-4722, E-mail: derrsl@plattsburgh.edu.

State University of New York College at Brockport, School of Professions, Department of Educational Administration, Brockport, NY 14420-2997. Offers school administration and supervision (MS Ed, CAS); school business administration (CAS); school district administration (CAS). Part-time programs available. *Students:* 14 full-time (10 women), 152 part-time (86 women); includes 10 minority (7 African Americans, 1 American Indian/Alaska Native, 1 Asian American or Pacific Islander, 1 Hispanic American). 59 applicants, 100% accepted, 58 enrolled. In 2006, 4 master's, 110 other advanced degrees awarded. *Degree requirements:* For CAS, thesis or alternative, 6 hour internship. *Entrance requirements:* For master's, minimum GPA of 3.0, letter of recommendation; for CAS, minimum GPA of 3.0 (undergraduate), 3.5 (graduate); MS. Additional exam requirements/recommendations for international students: Required—TOEFL (minimum score 550 paper-based; 213 computer-based; 80 iBT). *Application deadline:* For fall admission, 7/15 for domestic and international students; for spring admission, 11/15 for domestic and international students. *Application fee:* $50. *Expenses:* Tuition, state resident: full-time $6,900; part-time $288 per credit. Tuition, nonresident: full-time $10,920; part-time $455 per credit. *Financial support:* Career-related internships or fieldwork, Federal Work-Study, scholarships/grants, and unspecified assistantships available. Financial award application deadline: 3/15; financial award applicants required to submit FAFSA. *Faculty research:* Superintendency, budgeting, school business administration, leadership, special education administration. *Unit head:* Dr. Sandra Graczyk, Chairperson, 585-395-2661, Fax: 585-395-2172, E-mail: slgraczyk@aol.com.

State University of New York College at Cortland, Graduate Studies, School of Education, Program in Educational Leadership, Cortland, NY 13045. Offers CAS. Part-time and evening/weekend programs available. *Degree requirements:* For CAS, one foreign language. *Entrance requirements:* For degree, MS in education, permanent New York teaching certificate. Additional exam requirements/recommendations for international students: Required—TOEFL.

Stephen F. Austin State University, Graduate School, College of Education, Department of Secondary Education and Educational Leadership, Nacogdoches, TX 75962. Offers educational leadership (Ed D); secondary education (M Ed). *Accreditation:* NCATE. *Degree requirements:* For master's, comprehensive exam; for doctorate, thesis/dissertation. *Entrance requirements:* For master's, GRE General Test; for doctorate, GRE General Test, interview, writing sample. Additional exam requirements/recommendations for international students: Required—TOEFL. Electronic applications accepted.

Stetson University, College of Arts and Sciences, Division of Education, Department of Teacher Education, Program in Educational Leadership, DeLand, FL 32723. Offers M Ed, Ed S. *Accreditation:* NCATE. Evening/weekend programs available. *Students:* 43 full-time (24 women), 6 part-time (5 women); includes 7 minority (2 African Americans, 5 Hispanic Americans). Average age 34. In 2006, 37 master's, 3 other advanced degrees awarded. *Degree requirements:* For master's, comprehensive exam. *Entrance requirements:* For master's and Ed S, GRE General Test or MAT. *Application deadline:* For fall admission, 3/1 priority date for domestic students; for spring admission, 11/1 for domestic students. Applications are processed on a rolling basis. *Application fee:* $25. *Financial support:* Career-related internships or fieldwork available. *Unit head:* Dr. Debra Touchton, Coordinator, 386-822-7075. *Application contact:* Midge McDaniel, Office of Graduate Studies, 386-822-7075, Fax: 386-822-7388, E-mail: mmcdanie@stetson.edu.

Stony Brook University, State University of New York, School of Professional Development, Stony Brook, NY 11794. Offers adolescence education: mathematics (Certificate); biology 7-12 (MAT); chemistry-grade 7-12 (MAT); coaching (Certificate); computer integrated engineering (Certificate); cultural studies (Certificate); earth science-grade 7-12 (MAT); educational computing (Advanced Certificate, Certificate); English-grade 7-12 (MAT); environmental and waste management (MS, Advanced Certificate); environmental systems management (Certificate); environmental/occupational health and safety (Certificate); French-grade 7-12 (MAT); German-grade 7-12 (MAT); human resource management (Certificate); industrial management (Certificate); information systems management (Certificate); Italian-grade 7-12 (MAT); liberal studies (MA); liberal studies online (MA); Long Island regional studies (Certificate); operation research (Certificate); physics-grade 7-12 (MAT); Russian-grade 7-12 (MAT); school administration and supervision (Certificate); school district administration (Certificate); social science and the professions (MPS), including human resources management, labor management, public affairs, waste management; social studies 7-12 (MAT); waste management (Certificate); women's studies (Certificate). Part-time and evening/weekend programs available. Postbaccalaureate distance learning degree programs offered. *Faculty:* 1 full-time (0 women), 118 part-time/adjunct (45 women). *Students:* 322 full-time (202 women), 1,188 part-time (728 women); includes 164 minority (69 African Americans, 2 American Indian/Alaska Native, 29 Asian Americans or Pacific Islanders, 64 Hispanic Americans), 11 international. Average age 28. In 2006, 738 master's, 405 other advanced degrees awarded. *Degree requirements:* For master's, one foreign language, thesis or alternative. *Application deadline:* Applications are processed on a rolling basis. *Application fee:* $62. *Expenses:* Tuition, state resident: full-time $6,900; part-time $288 per credit. Tuition, nonresident: full-time $10,920; part-time $455 per credit. *Financial support:* In 2006–07, 5 teaching assistantships were awarded; fellowships, research assistantships, career-related internships or fieldwork also available. Support available to part-time students. *Unit head:* Dr. Paul J. Edelson, Dean, 631-632-7052, Fax: 631-632-9046, E-mail: paul.edelson@sunysb.edu. *Application contact:* Sandra Romansky, Director of Admissions and Advisement, 631-632-7050, Fax: 631-632-9046, E-mail: sandra.romansky@sunysb.edu.

Suffolk University, College of Arts and Sciences, Department of Education and Human Services, Program in Foundations of Education, Boston, MA 02108-2770. Offers administration of higher education (M Ed); foundations of education (M Ed), including administration of higher education; leadership (CAGS). Part-time and evening/weekend programs available. *Entrance requirements:* For master's, GRE General Test or MAT. *Application deadline:* For fall

admission, 6/15 priority date for domestic students, 6/15 for international students; for spring admission, 11/15 priority date for domestic students, 11/15 for international students. Applications are processed on a rolling basis. *Application fee:* $35. *Financial support:* Fellowships, career-related internships or fieldwork, Federal Work-Study, and institutionally sponsored loans available. Support available to part-time students. Financial award application deadline: 4/1; financial award applicants required to submit FAFSA. *Faculty research:* History of medieval education, history of universities, philosophy of education. *Unit head:* Dr. Sarah M. Carroll, Program Director, 617-573-8262, Fax: 617-722-9440, E-mail: scaroll@suffolk.edu. *Application contact:* Judith Reynolds, Director of Graduate Admissions, 617-573-8302, Fax: 617-523-0116, E-mail: grad.admission@suffolk.edu.

Suffolk University, College of Arts and Sciences, Department of Education and Human Services, Program in Higher Education Administration, Boston, MA 02108-2770. Offers educational administration (M Ed), including administration of higher education; leadership (CAGS). Part-time and evening/weekend programs available. *Entrance requirements:* For master's, GRE General Test or MAT. *Application deadline:* For fall admission, 6/15 priority date for domestic students, 6/15 for international students; for spring admission, 11/15 priority date for domestic students, 11/15 for international students. Applications are processed on a rolling basis. *Application fee:* $35. *Financial support:* Fellowships, career-related internships or fieldwork, Federal Work-Study, and institutionally sponsored loans available. Support available to part-time students. Financial award application deadline: 4/1; financial award applicants required to submit FAFSA. *Faculty research:* History of universities, student financial aid, leadership. *Unit head:* Dr. Michael Siegel, Graduate Program Director, 617-994-6456, Fax: 617-722-9440, E-mail: msiegel@suffolk.edu. *Application contact:* Judith Reynolds, Director of Graduate Admissions, 617-573-8302, Fax: 617-523-0116, E-mail: grad.admission@suffolk.edu.

Sul Ross State University, Rio Grande College of Sul Ross State University, Alpine, TX 79832. Offers business administration (MBA); teacher education (M Ed), including bilingual education, counseling, educational diagnostics, elementary education, general education, reading, school administration, secondary education. Part-time and evening/weekend programs available. *Degree requirements:* For master's, thesis optional. *Entrance requirements:* For master's, GMAT or GRE General Test, minimum GPA of 2.5 in last 60 hours of undergraduate work. *Faculty research:* Drug and substance abuse counseling, U.S.-Mexico border economic development.

Sul Ross State University, School of Professional Studies, Department of Teacher Education, Program in School Administration, Alpine, TX 79832. Offers M Ed. Part-time and evening/weekend programs available. *Degree requirements:* For master's, thesis optional. *Entrance requirements:* For master's, GMAT or GRE General Test, minimum GPA of 2.5 in last 60 hours of undergraduate work.

Sul Ross State University, School of Professional Studies, Department of Teacher Education, Program in Supervision, Alpine, TX 79832. Offers M Ed. Part-time and evening/weekend programs available. *Degree requirements:* For master's, thesis optional. *Entrance requirements:* For master's, GMAT or GRE General Test, minimum GPA of 2.5 in last 60 hours of undergraduate work.

Syracuse University, Graduate School, School of Education, Department of Teaching and Leadership, Program in Educational Leadership, Syracuse, NY 13244. Offers MS, Ed D, CAS. Part-time and evening/weekend programs available. *Students:* 13 applicants, 69% accepted, 4 enrolled. *Degree requirements:* For master's, thesis or alternative; for doctorate and CAS, thesis/dissertation. *Entrance requirements:* For doctorate, GRE. Additional exam requirements/recommendations for international students: Required—TOEFL. *Application deadline:* For fall admission, 2/1 priority date for domestic students. Applications are processed on a rolling basis. *Application fee:* $65. Electronic applications accepted. *Expenses:* Tuition: Full-time $16,920; part-time $940 per credit hour. Required fees: $930; $930 per year. *Financial support:* Fellowships with tuition reimbursements, teaching assistantships with tuition reimbursements available. *Unit head:* Dr. Diane Conio-Rispoli, Program Director, 315-443-1721. *Application contact:* Liza Rochelson, Graduate Admission Recruiter, 315-443-2505, Fax: 315-443-2258, E-mail: gradcrt@gwmail.syr.edu.

Tarleton State University, College of Graduate Studies, College of Education, Department of Educational Administration, Counseling, and Psychology, Program in Educational Administration, Stephenville, TX 76402. Offers M Ed, Certificate. Part-time and evening/weekend programs available. Postbaccalaureate distance learning degree programs offered (minimal on-campus study). *Faculty:* 45 full-time (23 women), 37 part-time/adjunct (9 women). *Students:* 60 full-time (38 women), 336 part-time (212 women); includes 68 minority (42 African Americans, 2 American Indian/Alaska Native, 4 Asian Americans or Pacific Islanders, 20 Hispanic Americans), 1 international. Average age 34. 55 applicants, 93% accepted. In 2006, 125 degrees awarded. *Degree requirements:* For master's, thesis optional. *Entrance requirements:* For master's, GRE General Test, minimum GPA of 3.0. Additional exam requirements/recommendations for international students: Required—TOEFL (minimum score 550 paper-based; 220 computer-based). *Application deadline:* For fall admission, 8/5 priority date for domestic students; for spring admission, 12/1 for domestic students. Applications are processed on a rolling basis. *Application fee:* $25 ($75 for international students). *Financial support:* Teaching assistantships, career-related internships or fieldwork, Federal Work-Study, and institutionally sponsored loans available. Support available to part-time students. Financial award application deadline: 5/1; financial award applicants required to submit FAFSA. *Unit head:* Dr. Mark Littleton, Coordinator, 254-968-9804.

Tarleton State University, College of Graduate Studies, College of Education, Department of Educational Administration, Counseling, and Psychology, Program in Educational Leadership, Stephenville, TX 76402. Offers Ed D. *Faculty:* 18 full-time (9 women), 2 part-time/adjunct (1 woman). *Entrance requirements:* For doctorate, GRE, 4 letters of reference, leadership portfolio. *Unit head:* Dr. Betty Jo Monk, Unit Head, 254-968-9090.

Teachers College Columbia University, Graduate Faculty of Education, Department of Organization and Leadership, Program in Education Leadership, New York, NY 10027-6696. Offers education leadership (PhD); education leadership studies (Ed M, MA, Ed D); leadership, policy and politics (Ed M, MA, Ed D, PhD); private school leadership (Ed M, MA, Ed D); public school and school district leadership (Ed M, MA, Ed D); MBA/Ed D. *Students:* 82 full-time (48 women), 137 part-time (71 women); includes 53 minority (26 African Americans, 16 Asian Americans or Pacific Islanders, 11 Hispanic Americans), 8 international. 292 applicants, 53% accepted, 72 enrolled. In 2006, 8 master's, 61 doctorates awarded. *Application fee:* $65. *Expenses:* Tuition: Full-time $23,400; part-time $975 per credit. Required fees: $320 per term. *Application contact:* Debbie Lesperance, Assistant Director of Admission, 212-678-3710, Fax: 212-678-4171.

See Close-Up on page 1131.

Teachers College Columbia University, Graduate Faculty of Education, Program in Administration and Supervision in Special Education, New York, NY 10027-6696. Offers Ed M, MA, Ed D, PhD. *Accreditation:* NCATE. *Students:* 3 full-time (2 women), 20 part-time (13 women); includes 6 minority (4 African Americans, 1 Asian American or Pacific Islander, 1 Hispanic American), 2 international. Average age 35. In 2006, 1 degree awarded. *Degree requirements:* For doctorate, thesis/dissertation. *Application deadline:* For fall admission, 5/15 for domestic students. *Application fee:* $65. *Expenses:* Tuition: Full-time $23,400; part-time $975 per credit. Required fees: $320 per term. *Financial support:* Career-related internships or fieldwork, Federal Work-Study, institutionally sponsored loans, and tuition waivers (full and partial) available. Support available to part-time students. Financial award application deadline: 2/1. *Faculty research:* Cognition and comprehension, disability studies, self-determination, literacy development. *Application contact:* Ursula Felton, Office of Admissions, 212-678-3710, Fax: 212-678-4171.

See Close-Up on page 1127.

Temple University, Graduate School, College of Education, Department of Educational Leadership and Policy Studies, Philadelphia, PA 19122-6096. Offers educational administration (Ed M, Ed D); urban education (Ed M, Ed D). Part-time and evening/weekend programs available. *Faculty:* 12 full-time (6 women). *Students:* 40 full-time (28 women), 128 part-time (79 women); includes 41 minority (34 African Americans, 2 American Indian/Alaska Native, 1 Asian American or Pacific Islander, 4 Hispanic Americans), 3 international. 134 applicants, 46% accepted, 31 enrolled. In 2006, 48 master's, 14 doctorates awarded. Terminal master's awarded for partial completion of doctoral program. *Degree requirements:* For master's, thesis or alternative, comprehensive exam; for doctorate, thesis/dissertation, preliminary exam. *Entrance requirements:* For master's and doctorate, GRE General Test or MAT, minimum GPA of 3.0. Additional exam requirements/recommendations for international students: Required—TOEFL (minimum score 550 paper-based; 213 computer-based; 79 iBT). *Application deadline:* For fall admission, 12/15 for international students; for spring admission, 8/1 for international students. Application fee: $50. Electronic applications accepted. *Expenses:* Tuition, state resident: full-time $12,264; part-time $511 per credit. Tuition, nonresident: full-time $17,904; part-time $746 per credit. Required fees: $84 per course. Tuition and fees vary according to program. *Financial support:* Fellowships, research assistantships with full tuition reimbursements, teaching assistantships with full tuition reimbursements, career-related internships or fieldwork and Federal Work-Study available. Financial award application deadline: 1/15; financial award applicants required to submit FAFSA. *Faculty research:* Women in education, school effectiveness, financial policy, school improvement in city schools, nongraded schools. *Unit head:* Dr. Erin McNamara Horvat, Chair, 215-204-8061, E-mail: horvat@temple.edu.

Tennessee State University, The School of Graduate Studies and Research, College of Education, Department of Educational Administration, Nashville, TN 37209-1561. Offers administration and supervision (M Ed, Ed D, Ed S). *Accreditation:* NCATE. *Faculty:* 10 full-time (4 women). *Students:* 52 full-time (33 women), 269 part-time (170 women); includes 210 minority (202 African Americans, 3 Asian Americans or Pacific Islanders, 5 Hispanic Americans), 4 international. Average age 36. 190 applicants, 57% accepted, 104 enrolled. In 2006, 65 master's, 25 doctorates, 51 other advanced degrees awarded. *Entrance requirements:* For master's, GRE General Test, GRE Subject Test, minimum GPA of 2.5; for doctorate, GRE General Test, MAT, interview, minimum GPA of 3.25, work experience. Application fee: $25. *Unit head:* Dr. Janet Finch, Head, 615-963-5452.

Tennessee Technological University, Graduate School, College of Education, Department of Curriculum and Instruction, Program in Instructional Leadership, Cookeville, TN 38505. Offers MA, Ed S. *Accreditation:* NCATE. Part-time and evening/weekend programs available. *Faculty:* 9 full-time (3 women). *Students:* 280 full-time (203 women), 310 part-time (227 women); includes 41 minority (37 African Americans, 1 American Indian/Alaska Native, 1 Asian American or Pacific Islander, 2 Hispanic Americans). Average age 27. 254 applicants, 91% accepted, 199 enrolled. In 2006, 269 master's, 269 other advanced degrees awarded. *Degree requirements:* For Ed S, thesis or alternative. *Entrance requirements:* For master's, MAT; for Ed S, MAT, NTE. Additional exam requirements/recommendations for international students: Required—TOEFL. *Application deadline:* For fall admission, 3/1 priority date for domestic students; for spring admission, 8/1 for domestic students. Application fee: $25 ($30 for international students). *Expenses:* Tuition, state resident: full-time $8,748; part-time $319 per hour. Tuition, nonresident: full-time $23,524; part-time $740 per hour. *Financial support:* In 2006–07, 33 fellowships (averaging $8,000 per year), 11 research assistantships (averaging $4,000 per year), 7 teaching assistantships (averaging $4,000 per year) were awarded; career-related internships or fieldwork also available. Financial award application deadline: 4/1. *Faculty research:* School board member training, community school education. *Application contact:* Dr. Francis O. Otuonye, Associate Vice President for Research and Graduate Studies, 931-372-3233, Fax: 931-372-3497, E-mail: fotuonye@tntech.edu.

Tennessee Temple University, Graduate Studies Division, Program in Educational Administration and Supervision, Chattanooga, TN 37404-3587. Offers MS. *Degree requirements:* For master's, thesis or alternative.

Texas A&M International University, Office of Graduate Studies and Research, Department of Professional Programs, Laredo, TX 78041-1900. Offers educational administration (MS Ed); generic special education (MS Ed); school counseling (MS). *Expenses:* Tuition, state resident: full-time $1,580. Tuition, nonresident: full-time $5,432. Required fees: $3,808. *Application contact:* Rosie Dickinson, Director of Admissions, 956-326-2200.

Texas A&M University, College of Education and Human Development, Department of Educational Administration and Human Resource Development, College Station, TX 77843. Offers M Ed, MS, Ed D, PhD. *Accreditation:* NCATE. Part-time programs available. *Faculty:* 19 full-time (10 women), 4 part-time/adjunct (2 women). *Students:* 164 full-time (111 women), 289 part-time (185 women); includes 133 minority (50 African Americans, 2 American Indian/Alaska Native, 4 Asian Americans or Pacific Islanders, 77 Hispanic Americans), 31 international. Average age 37. 103 applicants, 68% accepted, 40 enrolled. In 2006, 47 master's, 26 doctorates awarded. *Degree requirements:* For master's, thesis optional; for doctorate, thesis/dissertation. *Entrance requirements:* For master's, GRE General Test, writing exam, interview, professional experience; for doctorate, GRE General Test, writing exam, interview/presentation, professional experience. Additional exam requirements/recommendations for international students: Required—TOEFL. *Application deadline:* For fall admission, 12/1 for domestic and international students; for spring admission, 8/15 for domestic and international students. Application fee: $50 ($75 for international students). Electronic applications accepted. *Expenses:* Tuition, state resident: full-time $4,697. Tuition, nonresident: full-time $11,297. Required fees: $2,272. *Financial support:* In 2006–07, fellowships (averaging $20,000 per year), research assistantships (averaging $12,000 per year) were awarded; career-related internships or fieldwork and institutionally sponsored loans also available. Support available to part-time students. Financial award application deadline: 3/1; financial award applicants required to submit FAFSA. *Faculty research:* Higher education administration, public school administration, student affairs. *Unit head:* Dr. Yvonna Lincoln, Head, 979-845-2716, Fax: 979-862-4347. *Application contact:* Joyce Nelson, Senior Academic Advisor, 979-847-9098, Fax: 979-862-4347, E-mail: jnelson@tamu.edu.

Texas A&M University–Commerce, Graduate School, College of Education and Human Services, Department of Educational Administration, Commerce, TX 75429-3011. Offers M Ed, MS, Ed D. Part-time programs available. Terminal master's awarded for partial completion of doctoral program. *Degree requirements:* For master's, thesis (for some programs), comprehensive exam; for doctorate, thesis/dissertation, departmental qualifying exam. *Entrance requirements:* For master's, GRE General Test; for doctorate, GRE General Test, writing skills exam, interview. Electronic applications accepted. *Faculty research:* Property tax reform, politics of education, administrative stress.

Texas A&M University–Corpus Christi, Graduate Studies and Research, College of Education, Program in Educational Administration, Corpus Christi, TX 78412-5503. Offers MS. Part-time and evening/weekend programs available. *Degree requirements:* For master's, thesis (for some programs), comprehensive exam, registration. *Entrance requirements:* For master's, GRE General Test. Additional exam requirements/recommendations for international students: Required—TOEFL. Electronic applications accepted.

Texas A&M University–Corpus Christi, Graduate Studies and Research, College of Education, Program in Educational Leadership, Corpus Christi, TX 78412-5503. Offers Ed D. Part-time and evening/weekend programs available. *Degree requirements:* For doctorate, thesis/dissertation, comprehensive exam, registration. *Entrance requirements:* Additional exam requirements/recommendations for international students: Required—TOEFL. Electronic applications accepted.

Texas A&M University–Kingsville, College of Graduate Studies, College of Education, Department of Education, Program in Higher Education Administration Leadership, Kingsville, TX 78363. Offers PhD. *Degree requirements:* For doctorate, one foreign language, thesis/dissertation, comprehensive exam. *Entrance requirements:* For doctorate, GRE General Test, MAT, minimum GPA of 3.25.

Texas A&M University–Kingsville, College of Graduate Studies, College of Education, Department of Education, Program in School Administration, Kingsville, TX 78363. Offers MA, MS, Ed D. Part-time and evening/weekend programs available. *Degree requirements:* For master's, mini-thesis; for doctorate, one foreign language, thesis/dissertation, comprehensive exam. *Entrance requirements:* For master's, GRE General Test, MAT, minimum GPA of 3.0; for doctorate, GRE General Test, MAT, minimum GPA of 3.25. *Faculty research:* Funding sources in public education.

Texas A&M University–Kingsville, College of Graduate Studies, College of Education, Department of Education, Program in Supervision, Kingsville, TX 78363. Offers MA, MS. Part-time programs available. *Degree requirements:* For master's, mini-thesis. *Entrance requirements:* For master's, GRE General Test, MAT, minimum GPA of 3.0.

Texas A&M University–Texarkana, Graduate Studies and Research, College of Arts and Sciences and Education, Texarkana, TX 75505-5518. Offers adult education (MS); curriculum and instruction (MS); education (MS); educational administration (M Ed); English (MA); history (MS); instructional technology (MS); interdisciplinary studies (MA, MS); special education (M Ed, MS). Part-time and evening/weekend programs available. *Students:* 285. Average age 32. 41 applicants, 76% accepted. In 2006, 51 degrees awarded. *Degree requirements:* For master's, thesis optional. *Entrance requirements:* For master's, minimum GPA of 2.5 on last 60 hours of bachelor's degree. Additional exam requirements/recommendations for international students: Required—TOEFL. *Application deadline:* For fall admission, 7/15 priority date for domestic students; for spring admission, 12/1 priority date for domestic students. Applications are processed on a rolling basis. Application fee: $0 ($25 for international students). Electronic applications accepted. *Expenses:* Tuition, state resident: part-time $112 per credit hour. Tuition, nonresident: part-time $387 per credit hour. Required fees: $8 per credit hour. $8 per term. *Financial support:* Career-related internships or fieldwork and scholarships/grants available. Financial award applicants required to submit FAFSA. *Unit head:* Dr. Rosannce Stripling, Dean, 903-223-3073, E-mail: rosanne.stripling@tamut.edu. *Application contact:* Patricia E. Black, Director of Admissions and Registrar, 903-223-3068, Fax: 903-223-3140, E-mail: pat.black@tamut.edu.

Texas Christian University, M. J. Neeley School of Business, Program in Educational Leadership, Fort Worth, TX 76129-0002. Offers MBA/Ed D. Part-time and evening/weekend programs available. *Application deadline:* For fall admission, 3/1 for domestic students; for spring admission, 12/1 for domestic students. Applications are processed on a rolling basis. Application fee: $0. *Expenses:* Tuition: Part-time $800 per credit hour. *Financial support:* Application deadline: 3/1. *Unit head:* Dr. Bill Cron, Associate Dean, Graduate Programs, 817-257-7531. *Application contact:* Dr. Sherrie Reynolds, Director of Graduate Studies, 817-257-7664, E-mail: s.reynolds@tcu.edu.

Texas Christian University, School of Education, Program in Educational Administration, Fort Worth, TX 76129-0002. Offers M Ed. Part-time and evening/weekend programs available. *Entrance requirements:* For master's, interview. Additional exam requirements/recommendations for international students: Required—TOEFL. *Application deadline:* For fall admission, 3/1 for domestic students; for spring admission, 12/1 for domestic students. Applications are processed on a rolling basis. Application fee: $0. *Expenses:* Tuition: Part-time $800 per credit hour. *Financial support:* Unspecified assistantships available. Financial award application deadline: 3/1. *Application contact:* Director of Graduate Studies, 817-257-7664.

Texas Christian University, School of Education, Program in Educational Leadership, Fort Worth, TX 76129-0002. Offers MBA/Ed D. *Expenses:* Tuition: Part-time $800 per credit hour. *Application contact:* Director of Graduate Studies, 817-257-7664.

Texas Southern University, Graduate School, College of Education, Department of Educational Administration and Foundation, Houston, TX 77004-4584. Offers educational administration (M Ed, Ed D); higher education administration (Ed D); mid-management superintending (Ed D); research education and certification (Ed D); research education and education (Ed D). Part-time and evening/weekend programs available. *Faculty:* 7 full-time (3 women), 5 part-time/adjunct (1 woman). *Students:* 40 full-time (29 women), 72 part-time (53 women); includes 109 minority (105 African Americans, 1 Asian American or Pacific Islander, 3 Hispanic Americans). Average age 37. 45 applicants, 80% accepted, 30 enrolled. In 2006, 32 degrees awarded. *Degree requirements:* For master's, comprehensive exam; for doctorate, thesis/dissertation, comprehensive exam. *Entrance requirements:* For master's, GRE General Test, minimum GPA of 2.5; for doctorate, GRE General Test or MAT, master's degree, minimum B+ average. Additional exam requirements/recommendations for international students: Required—TOEFL. *Application deadline:* For fall admission, 7/15 priority date for domestic students. Applications are processed on a rolling basis. Application fee: $50 ($75 for international students). *Financial support:* In 2006–07, 2 fellowships (averaging $1,750 per year) were awarded; Federal Work-Study and institutionally sponsored loans also available. Financial award application deadline: 5/1. *Unit head:* Dr. Emmanuel Nwagwu, Chairperson, 713-313-1055, E-mail: nwagwu_ec@tsu.edu.

Texas State University-San Marcos, Graduate School, College of Education, Department of Educational Administration and Psychological Services, Program in Educational Administration, San Marcos, TX 78666. Offers M Ed, MA. Part-time and evening/weekend programs available. *Faculty:* 5 full-time (3 women), 8 part-time/adjunct (3 women). *Students:* 11 full-time (8 women), 164 part-time (119 women); includes 44 minority (10 African Americans, 2 Asian Americans or Pacific Islanders, 32 Hispanic Americans), 2 international. Average age 34. 36 applicants, 97% accepted, 25 enrolled. In 2006, 44 degrees awarded. *Degree requirements:* For master's, thesis (for some programs), comprehensive exam. *Entrance requirements:* For master's, GRE General Test, minimum GPA of 2.75 in last 60 hours of course work. Additional exam requirements/recommendations for international students: Required—TOEFL. *Application deadline:* For fall admission, 6/15 for domestic students, 6/1 for international students. Applications are processed on a rolling basis. Application fee: $40 ($90 for international students). *Financial support:* In 2006–07, 72 students received support, including 2 teaching assistantships (averaging $5,076 per year); research assistantships, career-related internships or fieldwork, Federal Work-Study, and institutionally sponsored loans also available. Support available to part-time students. Financial award application deadline: 4/1; financial award applicants required to submit FAFSA. *Faculty research:* Superintendency, middle management, supervision, junior college. *Unit head:* Dr. Michael Boone, Graduate Advisor, 512-245-3759, E-mail: mb01@txstate.edu.

Texas State University-San Marcos, Graduate School, Interdisciplinary Studies Program in Educational Administration and Psychological Services, San Marcos, TX 78666. Offers MAIS. *Students:* Average age 33. *Degree requirements:* For master's, comprehensive exam. *Application deadline:* For fall admission, 6/15 priority date for domestic students; for spring admission, 10/15 priority date for domestic students. Applications are processed on a rolling basis. Application fee: $40 ($90 for international students). *Financial support:* Application deadline: 4/1; *Unit head:* Dr. Rosalinda Barrera, Dean, 512-245-2150, Fax: 512-245-8345, E-mail: rb43@txstate.edu.

Texas Tech University, Graduate School, College of Education, Department of Educational Psychology and Leadership, Lubbock, TX 79409. Offers counselor (Certificate); counselor education (M Ed, PhD); education diagnostician (Certificate); educational leadership (M Ed, Ed D); educational psychology (M Ed, PhD); gifted and talented (Certificate); higher education (M Ed, Ed D, PhD); information processing technologist (Certificate); instructional technology (M Ed, Ed D); principal (Certificate); special education (M Ed, Ed D); special education counselor (Certificate); superintendent (Certificate); visually handicapped (Certificate). *Accreditation:* ACA; NCATE. Part-time programs available. *Students:* 128 full-time (88 women), 321 part-time (233 women); includes 67 minority (23 African Americans, 1 American Indian/

Educational Administration

Texas Tech University (continued)
Alaska Native, 5 Asian Americans or Pacific Islanders, 38 Hispanic Americans), 22 international. Average age 38. 347 applicants, 49% accepted, 61 enrolled. In 2006, 110 master's, 16 doctorates awarded. *Degree requirements:* For master's, thesis optional; for doctorate, thesis/dissertation. *Entrance requirements:* For master's and doctorate, GRE General Test. Additional exam requirements/recommendations for international students: Required—TOEFL (minimum score 550 paper-based; 213 computer-based). *Application deadline:* For fall admission, 3/1 priority date for international students; for spring admission, 11/1 priority date for international students. Applications are processed on a rolling basis. Application fee: $50 ($60 for international students). Electronic applications accepted. *Expenses:* Tuition, state resident: full-time $4,440. Tuition, nonresident: full-time $11,040. Required fees: $2,136. *Financial support:* In 2006–07, 242 students received support; research assistantships with partial tuition reimbursements available, teaching assistantships with partial tuition reimbursements available, career-related internships or fieldwork, Federal Work-Study, and institutionally sponsored loans available. Support available to part-time students. Financial award application deadline: 4/15; financial award applicants required to submit FAFSA. *Faculty research:* Psychological processes of teaching and learning, teaching populations with special needs, instructional technology, educational administration in education, theories and practice in counseling and counselor education K-12 and higher. *Unit head:* Dr. Fred Hartmeister, Chair, 806-742-1998 Ext. 436, Fax: 806-742-2179, E-mail: fred.hartmeister@ttu.edu. *Application contact:* Graduate Adviser, 806-742-1998, Fax: 806-742-2179.

Texas Woman's University, Graduate School, College of Professional Education, Department of Teacher Education, Denton, TX 76201. Offers education administration (M Ed, MA); elementary education (M Ed, MA); special education (M Ed, MA, PhD), including educational diagnostician (M Ed, MA), mental retardation (M Ed, MA), physically handicapped (M Ed, MA); teaching (MAT). Part-time programs available. *Students:* 45 full-time (30 women), 226 part-time (194 women); includes 95 minority (53 African Americans, 1 American Indian/Alaska Native, 5 Asian Americans or Pacific Islanders, 36 Hispanic Americans), 11 international. Average age 37. In 2006, 106 master's, 6 doctorates awarded. Terminal master's awarded for partial completion of doctoral program. *Degree requirements:* For master's, professional paper (M Ed); for doctorate, thesis/dissertation, comprehensive exam. *Entrance requirements:* For master's, 3 letters of reference, curriculum vitae, copy of certifications, Teacher Service Record; for doctorate, minimum graduate GPA of 3.5, 3 reference letters, resumé, copy of certifications, Teacher Service Record. Additional exam requirements/recommendations for international students: Required—TOEFL (minimum score 550 paper-based; 213 computer-based; 79 iBT). *Application deadline:* For fall admission, 4/1 for international students; for spring admission, 8/1 for international students. Applications are processed on a rolling basis. Application fee: $30 ($50 for international students). Electronic applications accepted. *Expenses:* Tuition, area resident: Part-time $168 per unit. Tuition, state resident: full-time $4,369. Tuition, nonresident: full-time $9,373; part-time $443 per unit. Required fees: $20 per unit. $177 per term. *Financial support:* In 2006–07, 3 research assistantships (averaging $10,206 per year), teaching assistantships (averaging $10,206 per year) were awarded; career-related internships or fieldwork, Federal Work-Study, institutionally sponsored loans, scholarships/grants, traineeships, health care benefits, tuition waivers (partial), and unspecified assistantships also available. Support available to part-time students. Financial award application deadline: 3/1; financial award applicants required to submit FAFSA. *Faculty research:* Classroom management, learning disabilities, staff and professional development, leadership assessment. *Application contact:* Samuel Wheeler, Coordinator of Graduate Admissions, 940-898-3188, Fax: 940-898-3081, E-mail: wheelersr@twu.edu.

Touro University International, College of Education, Program in Educational Leadership, Cypress, CA 90630. Offers e-learning leadership (MA Ed, PhD); educational leadership (MA Ed); higher education leadership (PhD); K-12 leadership (PhD). Part-time and evening/weekend programs available. Postbaccalaureate distance learning degree programs offered (no on-campus study). In 2006, 13 degrees awarded. *Degree requirements:* For doctorate, thesis/dissertation, defense of dissertation, comprehensive exam. *Entrance requirements:* For doctorate, minimum GPA of 3.4, course work in research methods or statistics. Additional exam requirements/recommendations for international students: Required—TOEFL (minimum score 550 paper-based). Application fee: $75. *Expenses:* Tuition: Part-time $300 per credit hour. Tuition and fees vary according to course level and program. *Unit head:* Dr. Edith Neumann, Vice President for Academic Affairs, College of Education, 714-816-0366 Ext. 2030, Fax: 714-226-9844, E-mail: eneumann@tourou.edu.

Towson University, Graduate School, Program in Educational Leadership, Towson, MD 21252-0001. Offers Certificate. Application fee: $50. *Expenses:* Tuition, state resident: part-time $275 per unit. Tuition, nonresident: part-time $577 per unit. Required fees: $72 per unit. *Financial support:* Application deadline: 4/1; *Unit head:* Dr. Roxana Marie Della Vecchia, Assistant Dean, 410-704-2422, Fax: 410-704-2733, E-mail: rdellavecchia@towson.edu. *Application contact:* 410-704-2501, Fax: 410-704-4675, E-mail: grads@towson.edu.

Towson University, Graduate School, Program in Human Resource Development, Towson, MD 21252-0001. Offers educational leadership (administrator I certification) (CAS); human resource development (MS). Part-time and evening/weekend programs available. *Faculty:* 10 full-time (5 women). *Students:* 45 full-time (37 women), 139 part-time (103 women); includes 45 minority (40 African Americans, 3 Asian Americans or Pacific Islanders, 2 Hispanic Americans), 10 international. 105 applicants, 74% accepted, 44 enrolled. In 2006, 51 degrees awarded. *Degree requirements:* For master's, comprehensive exam; for CAS, exam, internship. *Entrance requirements:* For master's, 2 letters of recommendation, minimum GPA of 3.0. Additional exam requirements/recommendations for international students: Required—TOEFL. *Application deadline:* Applications are processed on a rolling basis. Application fee: $50. Electronic applications accepted. *Expenses:* Tuition, state resident: part-time $275 per unit. Tuition, nonresident: part-time $577 per unit. Required fees: $72 per unit. *Financial support:* In 2006–07, 1 research assistantship with full and partial tuition reimbursement was awarded; career-related internships or fieldwork, Federal Work-Study, and unspecified assistantships also available. Financial award application deadline: 4/1; financial award applicants required to submit FAFSA. *Faculty research:* Workforce training and development. *Unit head:* Dr. Mark Arvisais, Graduate Program Director, 410-704-4661. *Application contact:* 410-704-2501, Fax: 410-704-4675, E-mail: grads@towson.edu.

Trevecca Nazarene University, Graduate Division, School of Education, Major in Educational Leadership, Nashville, TN 37210-2877. Offers M Ed. Part-time and evening/weekend programs available. *Students:* 133 full-time (93 women), 4 part-time (2 women); includes 34 minority (33 African Americans, 1 Asian American or Pacific Islander). In 2006, 136 degrees awarded. *Degree requirements:* For master's, exit assessment. *Entrance requirements:* For master's, GRE General Test, MAT, interview, minimum GPA of 2.7, 2 references. Additional exam requirements/recommendations for international students: Required—TOEFL (minimum score 500 paper-based; 173 computer-based). *Application deadline:* Applications are processed on a rolling basis. Application fee: $25. *Expenses: Contact institution.* Tuition and fees vary according to degree level and program. *Financial support:* Applicants required to submit FAFSA. *Application contact:* Admissions Office, 615-248-1201, Fax: 615-248-1597, E-mail: admissions_ged@trevecca.edu.

Trevecca Nazarene University, Graduate Division, School of Education, Major in Leadership and Professional Practice, Nashville, TN 37210-2877. Offers D Ed. *Students:* 68 full-time (42 women), 26 part-time (17 women); includes 17 minority (14 African Americans, 1 American Indian/Alaska Native, 2 Hispanic Americans), 1 international. Average age 42. In 2006, 24 degrees awarded. *Degree requirements:* For doctorate, thesis/dissertation, proposal study, symposium presentation. *Entrance requirements:* For doctorate, GMAT, GRE, MAT, or NTE, minimum GPA of 3.4, resumé, writing sample, interview. Additional exam requirements/recommendations for international students: Required—TOEFL (minimum score 500 paper-based; 173 computer-based). *Application deadline:* Applications are processed on a rolling basis. Application fee: $50. *Expenses: Contact institution.* Tuition and fees vary according to degree level and program. *Financial support:* Applicants required to submit FAFSA. *Application contact:* Admissions Office, 615-248-1201, Fax: 615-248-1597, E-mail: admissions_ged@trevecca.edu.

Trinity Baptist College, Graduate Programs, Jacksonville, FL 32221. Offers Bible (M Ed); Christian school administration (M Ed); classroom practices (M Ed); ministry (M Min); special education (M Ed). Postbaccalaureate distance learning degree programs offered. *Faculty:* 10. *Entrance requirements:* For master's, GRE (M Ed), 2 letters of recommendation; minimum GPA of 2.5 (M Min) or 3.0 (M Ed); computer proficiency.

Trinity International University, Trinity Graduate School, Deerfield, IL 60015-1284. Offers bioethics (MA); communication and culture (MA); counseling psychology (MA); instructional leadership (M Ed); teaching (MA). Part-time and evening/weekend programs available. Postbaccalaureate distance learning degree programs offered (minimal on-campus study). *Faculty:* 5 full-time (4 women), 39 part-time/adjunct (13 women). *Students:* 109 full-time (85 women), 130 part-time (81 women). In 2006, 29 degrees awarded. *Degree requirements:* For master's, comprehensive exam. *Entrance requirements:* For master's, GRE General Test or MAT, minimum undergraduate GPA of 3.0. Additional exam requirements/recommendations for international students: Required—TOEFL (minimum score 580 paper-based; 237 computer-based), TWE (minimum score 4). *Application deadline:* For fall admission, 7/15 priority date for domestic and international students. Applications are processed on a rolling basis. Application fee: $25. Electronic applications accepted. *Expenses:* Tuition: Full-time $13,200; part-time $630 per hour. Required fees: $43 per semester. *Financial support:* Career-related internships or fieldwork, Federal Work-Study, institutionally sponsored loans, and tuition waivers (partial) available. Support available to part-time students. Financial award application deadline: 4/1; financial award applicants required to submit FAFSA. *Unit head:* Dr. James Stamoolis, Academic Dean, 847-317-7001, Fax: 847-317-4786. *Application contact:* Ken Botton, Director of Enrollment Services for University Records and Graduate Admissions, 800-533-0975, Fax: 847-317-8097, E-mail: kbotton@tiu.edu.

Trinity University, Department of Education, Program in School Administration, San Antonio, TX 78212-7200. Offers M Ed. *Accreditation:* NCATE. Part-time and evening/weekend programs available. *Faculty:* 6 full-time (4 women), 16 part-time/adjunct (11 women). *Students:* Average age 28. In 2006, 15 degrees awarded. *Entrance requirements:* For master's, GRE General Test, interview, minimum GPA of 3.0. *Application deadline:* For fall admission, 5/1 priority date for domestic students. Application fee: $30. *Financial support:* Fellowships, research assistantships, career-related internships or fieldwork, Federal Work-Study, institutionally sponsored loans, and scholarships/grants available. Support available to part-time students. Financial award application deadline: 4/1. *Unit head:* Dr. Thomas Sergiovanni, Director, 210-999-7501, Fax: 210-999-7592, E-mail: tsergiov@trinity.edu.

Trinity (Washington) University, School of Education, Washington, DC 20017-1094. Offers democracy, diversity, and social justice (M Ed); early childhood (MAT); educational administration (MSA); elementary education (MAT); English as a second language (M Ed, MAT); literacy and reading education (M Ed); school counseling (MA); secondary education (MAT), including English, math, science, social studies; special education (MAT). *Accreditation:* NCATE. Part-time and evening/weekend programs available. *Degree requirements:* For master's, thesis (for some programs), capstone project(s). *Entrance requirements:* For master's, PRAXIS I, minimum GPA of 2.8. Additional exam requirements/recommendations for international students: Required—TOEFL (minimum score 550 paper-based; 213 computer-based). *Faculty research:* Technology, literacy, special education, organizations, inclusion models.

Trinity Western University, Program in Leadership, Langley, BC V2Y 1Y1, Canada. Offers MA. Postbaccalaureate distance learning degree programs offered (minimal on-campus study). *Degree requirements:* For master's, major project. *Entrance requirements:* For master's, minimum GPA of 2.7. Additional exam requirements/recommendations for international students: Required—TOEFL (minimum score 600 paper-based; 250 computer-based). Expenses: Contact institution. *Faculty research:* Servant leadership.

Troy University, Graduate School, College of Education, Program in Educational Administration/Leadership, Troy, AL 36082. Offers MS, Ed S. *Accreditation:* NCATE. Part-time and evening/weekend programs available. *Students:* 63 full-time (45 women), 136 part-time (82 women); includes 94 minority (92 African Americans, 1 American Indian/Alaska Native, 1 Hispanic American). Average age 38. In 2006, 45 master's, 46 other advanced degrees awarded. *Degree requirements:* For master's, thesis, comprehensive exam, registration. *Entrance requirements:* For master's, minimum GPA of 2.5; for Ed S, MS. Additional exam requirements/recommendations for international students: Required—TOEFL (minimum score 523 paper-based; 200 computer-based). *Application deadline:* Applications are processed on a rolling basis. Application fee: $50. Electronic applications accepted. *Expenses:* Tuition, state resident: full-time $4,368; part-time $182 per hour. Tuition, nonresident: full-time $8,736; part-time $364 per hour. Required fees: $50 per term. *Financial support:* Available to part-time students. Applicants required to submit FAFSA. *Unit head:* Larry Thacker, Chair, 334-448-5140, Fax: 334-448-5205, E-mail: lthacker@troy.edu. *Application contact:* Jessida McConnell, Graduate Admissions, 334-448-5106, Fax: 334-448-5299, E-mail: jcmcconnell@troy.edu.

Union College, Graduate Programs, Department of Education, Barbourville, KY 40906-1499. Offers elementary education (MA); health and physical education (MA); middle grades (MA); music education (MA); principalship (MA); reading specialist (MA); secondary education (MA); special education (MA). *Degree requirements:* For master's, thesis optional. *Entrance requirements:* For master's, GRE General Test, NTE.

Union College, Graduate Programs, Educational Leadership Program, Barbourville, KY 40906-1499. Offers elementary principalship (Certificate); middle grades principalship (Certificate); secondary school principalship (Certificate); supervisor of instruction (Certificate).

Union University, School of Education, Jackson, TN 38305-3697. Offers education (M Ed, MA Ed); education administration generalist (Ed S); educational leadership (Ed D); educational supervision (Ed S); higher education (Ed D). M Ed also available at Germantown campus. *Accreditation:* NCATE. Part-time and evening/weekend programs available. *Faculty:* 19 full-time (11 women), 18 part-time/adjunct (12 women). *Students:* 254 full-time (207 women), 161 part-time (120 women); includes 197 minority (193 African Americans, 1 American Indian/Alaska Native, 1 Asian American or Pacific Islander, 2 Hispanic Americans). Average age 32. In 2006, 184 master's, 22 doctorates, 77 other advanced degrees awarded. *Degree requirements:* For master's, thesis (for some programs), capstone research course; for doctorate, thesis/dissertation, comprehensive exam; for Ed S, thesis or alternative. *Entrance requirements:* For master's, MAT, PRAXIS II or GRE, minimum GPA of 3.0, teaching license, writing sample; for doctorate, GRE, minimum graduate GPA of 3.2, writing sample; for Ed S, PRAXIS II, minimum graduate GPA of 3.2, writing sample. *Application deadline:* Applications are processed on a rolling basis. Application fee: $25 ($50 for international students). *Financial support:* In 2006–07, 117 students received support. Application deadline: 2/15; *Faculty research:* Mathematics education, direct instruction, language disorders and special education, brain compatible learning, empathy and school leadership. *Unit head:* Dr. Tom R. Rosebrough, Dean, 731-661-5523, Fax: 731-661-5468, E-mail: trosebro@uu.edu. *Application contact:* Helen F. Fowler, Assistant to the Dean, 731-661-5374, Fax: 731-661-5468, E-mail: hfowler@uu.edu.

Universidad del Este, Graduate School, Carolina, PR 00983. Offers accounting (MBA); administration (M Ed); criminal justice and criminology (MA); education (M Ed); elementary education (M Ed); human resources (MBA); management (MBA); social work (MA); teaching English (M Ed); teaching Spanish (M Ed).

Universidad del Turabo, Graduate Programs, Programs in Education, Gurabo, PR 00778-3030. Offers bilingual education (MA); education administration and supervision (MA); school libraries administration (MA); special education (MA); teaching English as a second language (MA). Part-time and evening/weekend programs available. *Entrance requirements:* For master's, GRE, EXADEP, interview.

Universidad Metropolitana, Graduate Programs in Education, Program in Educational Administration and Supervision, San Juan, PR 00928-1150. Offers MA. Part-time programs available. *Degree requirements:* For master's, thesis or alternative. *Entrance requirements:* For master's, EXADEP, interview. Electronic applications accepted.

Universidad Metropolitana, Graduate Programs in Education, Program in Fitness Management, San Juan, PR 00928-1150. Offers MA. Part-time programs available. *Degree requirements:* For master's, thesis or alternative. *Entrance requirements:* For master's, EXADEP, interview. Electronic applications accepted.

Universidad Metropolitana, Graduate Programs in Education, Program in Pre-School Centers Administration, San Juan, PR 00928-1150. Offers MA. Part-time programs available. *Degree requirements:* For master's, thesis or alternative. *Entrance requirements:* For master's, EXADEP, interview. Electronic applications accepted.

Université de Moncton, Faculty of Education, Graduate Studies in Education, Moncton, NB E1A 3E9, Canada. Offers educational psychology (M Ed, MA Ed); guidance (M Ed, MA Ed); school administration (M Ed, MA Ed); teaching (M Ed, MA Ed). Part-time programs available. *Degree requirements:* For master's, proficiency in English and French. *Entrance requirements:* For master's, minimum GPA of 3.0. *Faculty research:* Guidance, ethnolinguistic vitality, children's rights, ecological education, entrepreneurship.

Université de Montréal, Faculty of Graduate Studies, Faculty of Education, Department of Administration and Foundations of Education, Montréal, QC H3C 3J7, Canada. Offers M Ed, MA, PhD, DESS. Part-time programs available. *Faculty:* 20 full-time (5 women), 14 part-time/adjunct (5 women). *Students:* 72 full-time (41 women), 610 part-time (438 women). 331 applicants, 72% accepted, 208 enrolled. In 2006, 10 master's, 4 doctorates, 35 other advanced degrees awarded. *Degree requirements:* For master's, thesis; for doctorate, thesis/dissertation, general exam. *Entrance requirements:* For master's and DESS, bachelor's degree in related field with minimum B average; for doctorate, master's degree in related field with minimum B average. *Application deadline:* For fall admission, 2/1 priority date for domestic students; for winter admission, 11/1 priority date for domestic students; for spring admission, 2/1 priority date for domestic students. Application fee: $30. Electronic applications accepted. *Financial support:* Teaching assistantships available. *Faculty research:* Pluriethnicity, formative education, comparative education, diagnostic evaluation. *Unit head:* Jean-Marie Van der Maren, Director, 514-343-6659, Fax: 514-343-2497. *Application contact:* Diane Moreau-Dagenais, Information Contact, 514-343-6649, Fax: 514-343-2497.

Université de Sherbrooke, Faculty of Education, Program in School Administration, Sherbrooke, QC J1K 2R1, Canada. Offers M Ed. Part-time and evening/weekend programs available. *Degree requirements:* For master's, thesis.

Université du Québec à Trois-Rivières, Graduate Programs, Program in Educational Administration, Trois-Rivières, QC G9A 5H7, Canada. Offers PhD. *Degree requirements:* For doctorate, thesis/dissertation.

Université Laval, Faculty of Education, Department of Foundations and Interventions in Education, Programs in Educational Administration and Evaluation, Québec, QC G1K 7P4, Canada. Offers MA, PhD. Terminal master's awarded for partial completion of doctoral program. *Degree requirements:* For master's, thesis (for some programs); for doctorate, thesis/dissertation, comprehensive exam. *Entrance requirements:* For master's and doctorate, English exam (comprehension of written English), knowledge of French and English. Electronic applications accepted.

Université Laval, Faculty of Education, Department of Foundations and Interventions in Education, Programs in Educational Practice, Québec, QC G1K 7P4, Canada. Offers educational pedagogy (Diploma); pedagogy management and development (Diploma); school adaptation (Diploma). Part-time programs available. *Entrance requirements:* For degree, English exam (comprehension of written English), knowledge of French and English. Electronic applications accepted.

University at Albany, State University of New York, School of Education, Department of Educational Administration and Policy Studies, Albany, NY 12222-0001. Offers MS, PhD, CAS. Evening/weekend programs available. *Students:* 39 full-time (24 women), 129 part-time (81 women). Average age 35. In 2006, 69 master's, 4 doctorates, 29 other advanced degrees awarded. *Degree requirements:* For doctorate, one foreign language, thesis/dissertation. *Entrance requirements:* For doctorate, GRE General Test, GRE Subject Test. Additional exam requirements/recommendations for international students: Required—TOEFL (minimum score 550 paper-based; 213 computer-based). *Application deadline:* For fall admission, 2/1 for domestic students, 5/1 for international students; for spring admission, 9/1 for domestic students, 11/1 for international students. Applications are processed on a rolling basis. Application fee: $75. Electronic applications accepted. *Expenses:* Tuition, state resident: full-time $6,900; part-time $288 per credit. Tuition, nonresident: full-time $10,920; part-time $455 per credit. Required fees: $1,139. *Financial support:* Fellowships, career-related internships or fieldwork available. Financial award application deadline: 3/15. *Unit head:* Dr. Alan Wagner, Chair, 518-442-5080.

University at Buffalo, the State University of New York, Graduate School, Graduate School of Education, Department of Educational Leadership and Policy, Buffalo, NY 14260. Offers educational administration (Ed M, Ed D, PhD); general education (Ed M); higher education (PhD); higher education administration (Ed M); school business and human resource administration (Certificate); social foundations (PhD); specialist in education administration (Certificate). Part-time and evening/weekend programs available. *Faculty:* 12 full-time (7 women), 6 part-time/adjunct (3 women). *Students:* 107 full-time (73 women), 141 part-time (89 women); includes 50 minority (35 African Americans, 1 American Indian/Alaska Native, 7 Asian Americans or Pacific Islanders, 7 Hispanic Americans), 25 international. Average age 37. 262 applicants, 36% accepted, 58 enrolled. In 2006, 28 master's, 17 doctorates, 12 other advanced degrees awarded. Terminal master's awarded for partial completion of doctoral program. *Median time to degree:* Master's–2 years full-time, 4 years part-time; doctorate–4 years full-time, 6 years part-time; Certificate–2 years part-time. *Degree requirements:* For master's, thesis optional; for doctorate, thesis/dissertation, comprehensive exam, registration. *Entrance requirements:* For doctorate, GRE General Test or MAT, writing sample. Additional exam requirements/recommendations for international students: Required—TOEFL (minimum score 550 paper-based; 213 computer-based). *Application deadline:* For fall admission, 3/1 priority date for domestic students, 3/1 for international students; for spring admission, 11/15 priority date for domestic students, 10/1 for international students. Applications are processed on a rolling basis. Application fee: $50. Electronic applications accepted. *Financial support:* In 2006–07, 50 students received support, including 1 fellowship with full tuition reimbursement available (averaging $10,000 per year), 10 research assistantships with full tuition reimbursements available (averaging $9,000 per year); career-related internships or fieldwork, Federal Work-Study, institutionally sponsored loans, health care benefits, tuition waivers (full and partial), and unspecified assistantships also available. Financial award application deadline: 3/15; financial award applicants required to submit FAFSA. *Faculty research:* Academic collective bargaining, faculty governance, educational technology, educational policy studies, multicultural issues. Total annual research expenditures: $326,191. *Unit head:* Dr. William C. Barba, Chairman, 716-645-2471 Ext. 1097, Fax: 716-645-2481, E-mail: barba@buffalo.edu. *Application contact:* Bonnie Fisher, Secretary, 716-645-2110 Ext. 1255, Fax: 716-645-2481, E-mail: brfisher@buffalo.edu.

University at Buffalo, the State University of New York, Graduate School, Graduate School of Education, Department of Learning and Instruction, Buffalo, NY 14260. Offers adolescence education (Certificate); biology (Ed M); chemistry (Ed M); childhood education (Ed M); early

childhood and childhood education with bilingual extension (Ed M); early childhood education (Ed M); earth science (Ed M); elementary education (Ed D, PhD); English (Ed M); English education (PhD); English for speakers of other languages (Ed M); foreign and second language education (PhD); French (Ed M); general education (Ed M); German (Ed M); Italian (Ed M); Japanese (Ed M); Latin (Ed M); literary specialist (Ed M); mathematics (Ed M); mathematics education (PhD); mentoring teachers (Certificate); music education (Ed M, Certificate); physics (Ed M); reading education (PhD); Russian (Ed M); school administrator and supervisor (Certificate); science education (PhD); social studies (Ed M); Spanish (Ed M); special education (PhD); teaching and leading for diversity (Certificate); teaching English to speakers of other languages (Ed M). Part-time and evening/weekend programs available. Postbaccalaureate distance learning degree programs offered (no on-campus study). *Faculty:* 30 full-time (20 women), 53 part-time/adjunct (38 women). *Students:* 368 full-time (269 women), 297 part-time (226 women); includes 50 minority (15 African Americans, 2 American Indian/Alaska Native, 14 Asian Americans or Pacific Islanders, 19 Hispanic Americans), 66 international. Average age 31. 638 applicants, 75% accepted, 298 enrolled. In 2006, 248 master's, 18 doctorates, 48 other advanced degrees awarded. Terminal master's awarded for partial completion of doctoral program. *Degree requirements:* For master's, comprehensive exam, registration; for doctorate, thesis/dissertation, research analysis exam, research experience component. *Entrance requirements:* For doctorate, GRE General Test or MAT, interview, writing sample, letters of recommendation. Additional exam requirements/recommendations for international students: Required—TOEFL (minimum score 600 paper-based; 250 computer-based). *Application deadline:* For fall admission, 2/1 priority date for domestic and international students; for spring admission, 11/15 priority date for domestic students, 10/1 for international students. Applications are processed on a rolling basis. Application fee: $50. Electronic applications accepted. *Financial support:* In 2006–07, 70 students received support, including 6 fellowships with full tuition reimbursements available (averaging $10,000 per year), 16 research assistantships with full tuition reimbursements available (averaging $9,000 per year), teaching assistantships with full tuition reimbursements available (averaging $9,000 per year); career-related internships or fieldwork, Federal Work-Study, institutionally sponsored loans, scholarships/grants, tuition waivers (partial), and unspecified assistantships also available. Financial award application deadline: 2/28; financial award applicants required to submit FAFSA. *Faculty research:* Science assessment, state-level testing, early learning, literacy, second language acquisition. Total annual research expenditures: $432,366. *Unit head:* Dr. Maria E. Runfola, Chair, 716-645-2455, Fax: 716-645-3161. *Application contact:* Barbara Belz, Admissions Secretary, 716-645-2110 Ext. 1159, Fax: 716-645-3161, E-mail: belz@buffalo.edu.

The University of Akron, Graduate School, College of Education, Department of Educational Foundations and Leadership, Program in Administrative Specialist, Akron, OH 44325. Offers MA, MS. *Students:* Average age 32. *Degree requirements:* For master's, written comprehensive exam or portfolio assessment. *Entrance requirements:* For master's, minimum GPA of 2.75. Additional exam requirements/recommendations for international students: Required—TOEFL (minimum score 550 paper-based; 213 computer-based; 79 iBT). *Application deadline:* For fall admission, 8/15 for domestic students. Applications are processed on a rolling basis. Application fee: $30 ($40 for international students). Electronic applications accepted. *Expenses:* Tuition, state resident: full-time $6,164; part-time $342 per credit. Tuition, nonresident: full-time $10,575; part-time $588 per credit. Required fees: $806; $43 per credit. $12 per term. Tuition and fees vary according to course load, degree level and program. *Unit head:* Dr. Sharon Kruse, Coordinator, 330-972-8177, E-mail: skruse@uakron.edu.

The University of Akron, Graduate School, College of Education, Department of Educational Foundations and Leadership, Program in Educational Administration, Akron, OH 44325. Offers MA, MS, Ed D. *Accreditation:* NCATE. *Students:* 8 full-time (7 women), 23 part-time (9 women); includes 4 minority (all African Americans), 3 international. Average age 38. 6 applicants, 17% accepted, 1 enrolled. In 2006, 13 master's, 4 doctorates awarded. Terminal master's awarded for partial completion of doctoral program. *Degree requirements:* For master's, written comprehensive exam or portfolio assessment; for doctorate, one foreign language, thesis/dissertation, written and oral exams, comprehensive exam. *Entrance requirements:* For master's, minimum GPA of 2.75; for doctorate, GRE, interview, minimum GPA of 2.75, writing sample, letters of reference. Additional exam requirements/recommendations for international students: Required—TOEFL (minimum score 550 paper-based; 213 computer-based; 79 iBT). *Application deadline:* For fall admission, 3/15 for domestic students. Applications are processed on a rolling basis. Application fee: $30 ($40 for international students). Electronic applications accepted. *Expenses:* Tuition, state resident: full-time $6,164; part-time $342 per credit. Tuition, nonresident: full-time $10,575; part-time $588 per credit. Required fees: $806; $43 per credit. $12 per term. Tuition and fees vary according to course load, degree level and program. *Unit head:* Dr. Sharon Kruse, Coordinator, 330-972-8177, E-mail: skruse@uakron.edu.

The University of Akron, Graduate School, College of Education, Department of Educational Foundations and Leadership, Program in Higher Education Administration, Akron, OH 44325. Offers MA, MS. *Accreditation:* NCATE. *Students:* 42 full-time (28 women), 34 part-time (20 women); includes 20 minority (19 African Americans, 1 Hispanic American), 3 international. Average age 30. 47 applicants, 83% accepted, 26 enrolled. In 2006, 35 degrees awarded. *Degree requirements:* For master's, written comprehensive exam or portfolio assessment. *Entrance requirements:* For master's, minimum GPA of 2.75. Additional exam requirements/recommendations for international students: Required—TOEFL (minimum score 550 paper-based; 213 computer-based; 79 iBT). *Application deadline:* For fall admission, 8/15 for domestic students. Applications are processed on a rolling basis. Application fee: $30 ($40 for international students). Electronic applications accepted. *Expenses:* Tuition, state resident: full-time $6,164; part-time $342 per credit. Tuition, nonresident: full-time $10,575; part-time $588 per credit. Required fees: $806; $43 per credit. $12 per term. Tuition and fees vary according to course load, degree level and program. *Financial support:* Fellowships with full tuition reimbursements, research assistantships with full tuition reimbursements, teaching assistantships with full tuition reimbursements, career-related internships or fieldwork and unspecified assistantships available. *Unit head:* Dr. Sandra Coyner, Coordinator, 330-972-5822, E-mail: scoyner@uakron.edu.

The University of Akron, Graduate School, College of Education, Department of Educational Foundations and Leadership, Program in Principalship, Akron, OH 44325. Offers MA, MS. *Students:* 5 full-time (2 women), 93 part-time (55 women); includes 16 minority (12 African Americans, 1 American Indian/Alaska Native, 3 Hispanic Americans). Average age 33. 29 applicants, 86% accepted, 21 enrolled. In 2006, 17 degrees awarded. *Degree requirements:* For master's, written comprehensive exam or portfolio assessment. *Entrance requirements:* For master's, minimum GPA of 2.75. Additional exam requirements/recommendations for international students: Required—TOEFL (minimum score 550 paper-based; 213 computer-based; 79 iBT). *Application deadline:* For fall admission, 8/15 for domestic students. Applications are processed on a rolling basis. Application fee: $30 ($40 for international students). Electronic applications accepted. *Expenses:* Tuition, state resident: full-time $6,164; part-time $342 per credit. Tuition, nonresident: full-time $10,575; part-time $588 per credit. Required fees: $806; $43 per credit. $12 per term. Tuition and fees vary according to course load, degree level and program. *Unit head:* Dr. Sharon Kruse, Coordinator, 330-972-8177, E-mail: skruse@uakron.edu.

The University of Akron, Graduate School, College of Education, Department of Educational Foundations and Leadership, Program in Superintendent, Akron, OH 44325. Offers MA, MS. *Students:* Average age 39. *Degree requirements:* For master's, written comprehensive exam or portfolio assessment. *Entrance requirements:* For master's, minimum GPA of 2.75. Additional exam requirements/recommendations for international students: Required—TOEFL (minimum score 550 paper-based; 213 computer-based; 79 iBT). *Application deadline:* For fall admission, 8/15 for domestic students. Applications are processed on a rolling basis. Application fee: $30 ($40 for international students). Electronic applications accepted. *Expenses:* Tuition, state resident: full-time $6,164; part-time $342 per credit. Tuition, nonresident: full-time $10,575; part-time $588 per credit. Required fees: $806; $43 per credit. $12 per term. Tuition and fees

Educational Administration

The University of Akron (continued)
vary according to course load, degree level and program. *Unit head:* Dr. Sharon Kruse, Coordinator, 330-972-8177, E-mail: skruse@uakron.edu.

The University of Alabama, Graduate School, College of Education, Department of Educational Leadership, Policy, and Technology Studies, Educational Administration Program, Tuscaloosa, AL 35487. Offers Ed D, PhD. Evening/weekend programs available. *Median time to degree:* Doctorate–3.8 years full-time, 4.6 years part-time. Of those who began their doctoral program in fall 1998, 80% received their degree in 8 years or less. *Degree requirements:* For doctorate, thesis/dissertation, comprehensive exam, registration. *Entrance requirements:* For doctorate, MAT, GRE, Masters in field. *Application deadline:* For fall admission, 9/1 priority date for domestic and international students; for winter admission, 2/1 priority date for domestic and international students; for spring admission, 4/1 priority date for domestic and international students. Applications are processed on a rolling basis. Application fee: $25. Electronic applications accepted. *Financial support:* In 2006–07, 3 research assistantships with tuition reimbursements (averaging $14,000 per year), teaching assistantships with tuition reimbursements (averaging $14,000 per year) were awarded; unspecified assistantships also available. Financial award application deadline: 4/1. *Unit head:* Dr. David R. Dagley, Professor of Educational Leadership, 205-348-5159, Fax: 205-348-2161, E-mail: ddagley@bamaed.ua.edu.

The University of Alabama, Graduate School, College of Education, Department of Educational Leadership, Policy, and Technology Studies, Educational Leadership Program, Tuscaloosa, AL 35487. Offers MA, Ed S. Part-time and evening/weekend programs available. Postbaccalaureate distance learning degree programs offered (minimal on-campus study). *Students:* 27 full-time (10 women), 81 part-time (42 women); includes 13 minority (11 African Americans, 2 American Indian/Alaska Native). *Median time to degree:* Master's–2.4 years part-time. Of those who began their doctoral program in fall 1998, 98% received their degree in 8 years or less. *Degree requirements:* For master's, internship. *Entrance requirements:* For master's, MAT, GRE, 3 years of teaching experience, teaching certification. *Application deadline:* For fall admission, 9/1 priority date for domestic and international students; for winter admission, 2/1 priority date for domestic and international students; for spring admission, 4/1 priority date for domestic and international students. Applications are processed on a rolling basis. Application fee: $25. Electronic applications accepted. *Unit head:* Dr. David R. Dagley, Professor of Educational Leadership, 205-348-5159, Fax: 205-348-2161, E-mail: ddagley@bamaed.ua.edu.

The University of Alabama, Graduate School, College of Education, Department of Educational Leadership, Policy, and Technology Studies, Higher Education Administration Program, Tuscaloosa, AL 35487. Offers MA, Ed D, PhD. Evening/weekend programs available. *Students:* 4 full-time (3 women), 15 part-time (3 women); includes 4 minority (3 African Americans, 1 Hispanic American). Terminal master's awarded for partial completion of doctoral program. *Degree requirements:* For master's, comprehensive exam, registration; for doctorate, thesis/dissertation, comprehensive exam, registration. *Entrance requirements:* For master's, GRE, MAT or GMAT; for doctorate, GRE or MAT. Application fee: $25. Electronic applications accepted. *Financial support:* In 2006–07, 5 students received support. Career-related internships or fieldwork, scholarships/grants, and unspecified assistantships available. *Unit head:* Dr. Claire H. Major, Coordinator and Associate Professor, 205-348-6871, Fax: 205-348-2161, E-mail: bea@bamaed.ua.edu. *Application contact:* Donna Smith, Administration Assistant, 205-348-6871, Fax: 205-348-2161, E-mail: dbsmith@bamaed.ua.edu.

The University of Alabama, Graduate School, College of Education, Department of Educational Leadership, Policy, and Technology Studies, Instructional Leadership Program, Tuscaloosa, AL 35487. Offers Ed D, PhD. Evening/weekend programs available. *Degree requirements:* For doctorate, thesis/dissertation, comprehensive exam, registration. *Entrance requirements:* For doctorate, GRE, MAT, Masters. *Application deadline:* For fall admission, 9/1 priority date for domestic and international students; for winter admission, 2/1 priority date for domestic and international students; for spring admission, 4/1 priority date for domestic and international students. Applications are processed on a rolling basis. Application fee: $25. Electronic applications accepted. *Financial support:* In 2006–07, 2 research assistantships (averaging $14,000 per year), 2 teaching assistantships (averaging $14,000 per year) were awarded; health care benefits and unspecified assistantships also available. *Unit head:* Dr. John Petroric, Professor in Foundations of Education, 205-348-0465, Fax: 205-348-2161, E-mail: petroric@bamaed.ua.edu.

The University of Alabama at Birmingham, School of Education, Department of Leadership, Special Education and Foundations, Program in Educational Leadership, Birmingham, AL 35294. Offers MA Ed, Ed D, PhD, Ed S. *Accreditation:* NCATE. *Students:* 14 full-time (11 women), 80 part-time (54 women); includes 51 minority (49 African Americans, 2 American Indian/Alaska Native). 24 applicants, 63% accepted. In 2006, 19 master's, 7 doctorates, 42 other advanced degrees awarded. *Degree requirements:* For master's, thesis optional; for doctorate, thesis/dissertation; for Ed S, thesis optional. *Entrance requirements:* For master's, GRE General Test, MAT, or NTE, minimum GPA of 3.0; for doctorate, GRE General Test, MAT, minimum GPA of 3.25; for Ed S, GRE General Test, MAT, minimum GPA of 3.0, master's degree. *Application deadline:* Applications are processed on a rolling basis. Application fee: $35 ($60 for international students). Electronic applications accepted. *Expenses:* Tuition, state resident: part-time $170 per credit hour. Tuition, nonresident: part-time $425 per credit hour. Required fees: $15 per credit hour. $122 per term. Tuition and fees vary according to program. *Unit head:* Dr. William Boyd Rogan, Chair, Department of Leadership, Special Education and Foundations, 205-934-4892, Fax: 205-934-2317, E-mail: nrogan@uab.edu.

University of Alaska Anchorage, College of Education, Program in Educational Leadership, Anchorage, AK 99508-8060. Offers educational leadership (M Ed); principal licensure (Certificate); superintendent (Certificate). Part-time programs available. *Students:* 6 full-time (4 women), 42 part-time (21 women); includes 5 minority (1 African American, 2 American Indian/Alaska Native, 1 Asian American or Pacific Islander, 1 Hispanic American), 2 international. 25 applicants, 52% accepted. In 2006, 31 degrees awarded. *Entrance requirements:* For master's, GRE or MAT, interview, minimum GPA of 3.0. Additional exam requirements/recommendations for international students: Required—TOEFL (minimum score 550 paper-based; 213 computer-based). *Application deadline:* For fall admission, 5/1 for domestic students; for spring admission, 11/1 for domestic students. Application fee: $45. *Expenses:* Tuition, state resident: part-time $268 per credit. Tuition, nonresident: part-time $547 per credit. Required fees: $124 per semester. Tuition and fees vary according to reciprocity agreements and student level. *Financial support:* Career-related internships or fieldwork and Federal Work-Study available. Support available to part-time students. Financial award application deadline: 4/1; financial award applicants required to submit FAFSA. *Unit head:* Dr. Carolyn Coe, Chair, 907-786-1654, Fax: 907-786-4445, E-mail: afcmc@uaa.alaska.edu. *Application contact:* Jane Jordan, Graduate Programs Assistant, 907-786-4401, Fax: 907-786-4445, E-mail: anjmj@uaa.alaska.edu.

University of Alberta, Faculty of Graduate Studies and Research, Department of Educational Policy Studies, Edmonton, AB T6G 2E1, Canada. Offers adult education (M Ed, Ed D, PhD); educational administration and leadership (M Ed, Ed D, PhD, Postgraduate Diploma); First Nations education (M Ed, Ed D, PhD); theoretical, cultural and international studies in education (M Ed, Ed D, PhD). *Faculty:* 19 full-time (10 women), 5 part-time/adjunct (1 woman). *Students:* 73 full-time (47 women), 144 part-time (86 women). 141 applicants, 44% accepted. In 2006, 52 master's, 20 doctorates awarded. *Degree requirements:* For master's, thesis (for some programs); for doctorate, thesis/dissertation. *Entrance requirements:* For master's, minimum GPA of 6.5 on a 9.0 scale; for doctorate, minimum GPA of 7.5 on a 9.0 scale. Additional exam requirements/recommendations for international students: Required—TOEFL (minimum score 580 paper-based; 237 computer-based). *Application deadline:* For spring admission, 2/1 for domestic and international students. Electronic applications accepted. *Financial support:* In 2006–07, 7 fellowships with partial tuition reimbursements, 10 research assistantships with partial tuition reimbursements (averaging $6,936 per year), 30 teaching assistantships with partial tuition reimbursements (averaging $11,130 per year) were awarded; scholarships/grants and unspecified assistantships also available. *Unit head:* Dr. Frank Peters, Graduate Coordinator, 780-492-3679, Fax: 780-492-2024, E-mail: epscoord@ualberta.ca. *Application contact:* Joan A. White, Secretary, 780-492-3679, Fax: 780-492-2024, E-mail: joan.white@ualberta.ca.

The University of Arizona, Graduate College, College of Education, Program in Educational Leadership, Tucson, AZ 85721. Offers M Ed, Ed D, Ed S. Part-time programs available. *Faculty:* 6 full-time (3 women), 3 part-time/adjunct (0 women). *Students:* 18 full-time (10 women), 50 part-time (31 women); includes 15 minority (1 African American, 2 American Indian/Alaska Native, 1 Asian American or Pacific Islander, 11 Hispanic Americans). Average age 41. 28 applicants, 54% accepted, 13 enrolled. In 2006, 4 master's, 4 doctorates, 1 other advanced degree awarded. *Degree requirements:* For master's and Ed S, Capstone experience; for doctorate, thesis/dissertation, comprehensive exam, registration. *Entrance requirements:* For doctorate, GRE General Test or MAT, master's degree. Additional exam requirements/recommendations for international students: Required—TOEFL. *Application deadline:* For fall admission, 3/24 for domestic students. Applications are processed on a rolling basis. Application fee: $50. *Financial support:* In 2006–07, 3 students received support, including 1 research assistantship with full tuition reimbursement available (averaging $23,787 per year), 1 teaching assistantship with full tuition reimbursement available (averaging $21,795 per year); fellowships, career-related internships or fieldwork, scholarships/grants, and unspecified assistantships also available. *Faculty research:* School governance, higher order thinking, restructuring schools, bilingual education policy, authority in education. Total annual research expenditures: $500,000. *Unit head:* Dr. Kris Bosworth, Professor/Program Head, 520-621-6658, Fax: 520-626-6005, E-mail: boswortk@u.arizona.edu. *Application contact:* Kathy Bayham, Administrative Assistant, 520-621-6658, Fax: 520-626-6005, E-mail: bayhams@email.arizona.edu.

University of Arkansas, Graduate School, College of Education and Health Professions, Department of Educational Leadership, Counseling and Foundations, Program in Educational Administration, Fayetteville, AR 72701-1201. Offers M Ed, Ed D, Ed S. *Accreditation:* NCATE. Part-time and evening/weekend programs available. *Students:* 1 full-time (0 women), 59 part-time (39 women); includes 3 minority (2 African Americans, 1 American Indian/Alaska Native). 39 applicants, 38% accepted. In 2006, 18 master's, 5 doctorates awarded. *Degree requirements:* For doctorate, thesis/dissertation. *Entrance requirements:* For master's, GRE General Test, MAT or minimum GPA of 3.0; for doctorate, GRE General Test or MAT. Application fee: $40 ($50 for international students). *Financial support:* In 2006–07, 2 research assistantships were awarded; fellowships with tuition reimbursements, teaching assistantships, career-related internships or fieldwork and Federal Work-Study also available. Support available to part-time students. Financial award application deadline: 4/1; financial award applicants required to submit FAFSA. *Application contact:* Dr. Carl Holt, Graduate Coordinator, 479-575-2207, E-mail: cholt@uark.edu.

University of Arkansas at Little Rock, Graduate School, College of Education, Department of Educational Leadership, Program in Educational Administration, Little Rock, AR 72204-1099. Offers educational administration and supervision (M Ed, Ed D, Ed S). Part-time and evening/weekend programs available. *Degree requirements:* For master's, comprehensive exam; for doctorate and Ed S, oral defense of dissertation, residency; for Ed S, professional project. *Entrance requirements:* For master's, GRE General Test or MAT, 4 years of work experience (minimum 3 in teaching), interview, minimum GPA of 2.75, teaching certificate; for doctorate, GRE General Test or MAT, 4 years of work experience, minimum graduate GPA of 3.0, teaching certificate; for Ed S, GRE General Test or MAT, 4 years of work experience, minimum GPA of 2.75, teaching certificate.

University of Arkansas at Little Rock, Graduate School, College of Education, Department of Educational Leadership, Program in Higher Education Administration, Little Rock, AR 72204-1099. Offers Ed D. *Degree requirements:* For doctorate, oral defense of dissertation, residency. *Entrance requirements:* For doctorate, GRE General Test or MAT, interview, minimum graduate GPA of 3.0, teaching certificate, work experience.

University of Arkansas at Monticello, School of Education, Monticello, AR 71656. Offers education (M Ed, MAT); educational leadership (M Ed). *Accreditation:* NCATE. Part-time and evening/weekend programs available. Postbaccalaureate distance learning degree programs offered (minimal on-campus study). *Faculty:* 33 full-time (13 women), 1 (woman) part-time/adjunct. *Students:* 21 full-time (14 women), 59 part-time (49 women); includes 10 minority (all African Americans) Average age 36. In 2006, 59 degrees awarded. *Degree requirements:* For master's, comprehensive exam. *Entrance requirements:* For master's, minimum GPA of 3.0. Additional exam requirements/recommendations for international students: Required—TOEFL (minimum score 550 paper-based; 213 computer-based). *Application deadline:* For fall admission, 8/16 priority date for domestic students, 8/1 priority date for international students; for spring admission, 1/3 priority date for domestic students, 12/1 priority date for international students. Applications are processed on a rolling basis. Application fee: $0 ($30 for international students). Electronic applications accepted. *Expenses:* Tuition, state resident: full-time $2,646; part-time $135 per hour. Tuition, nonresident: full-time $5,940; part-time $315 per hour. Required fees: $594; $30 per hour. Tuition and fees vary according to campus/location. *Financial support:* In 2006–07, 4 teaching assistantships with full tuition reimbursements were awarded; Federal Work-Study and tuition waivers (partial) also available. Support available to part-time students. *Unit head:* Dr. Peggy Doss, Dean, 870-460-1062, Fax: 870-460-1563, E-mail: dossp@uamont.edu.

University of Bridgeport, School of Education and Human Resources, Division of Education, Program in Educational Management, Bridgeport, CT 06604. Offers intermediate administrator or supervisor (Diploma); leadership (Ed D). *Faculty:* 2 full-time (0 women), 2 part-time/adjunct (0 women). *Students:* 4 full-time (all women), 100 part-time (58 women); includes 19 minority (12 African Americans, 1 American Indian/Alaska Native, 2 Asian Americans or Pacific Islanders, 4 Hispanic Americans), 1 international. Average age 40. 74 applicants, 61% accepted, 22 enrolled. In 2006, 4 doctorates, 11 other advanced degrees awarded. *Degree requirements:* For doctorate, thesis/dissertation; for Diploma, thesis or alternative, final project. *Entrance requirements:* For doctorate, GRE, MAT; for Diploma, GRE General Test or MAT, minimum graduate QPA of 3.0. *Application deadline:* For fall admission, 8/1 priority date for domestic students; for spring admission, 12/1 priority date for domestic students. Applications are processed on a rolling basis. Application fee: $25 ($35 for international students). Electronic applications accepted. *Expenses:* Contact institution. *Financial support:* In 2006–07, 17 students received support; fellowships, research assistantships, teaching assistantships, career-related internships or fieldwork, Federal Work-Study, and institutionally sponsored loans available. Support available to part-time students. Financial award application deadline: 6/1; financial award applicants required to submit FAFSA. *Unit head:* Dr. John W. Mulcahy, Coordinator, 203-576-4028, Fax: 203-576-4102, E-mail: jmulcahy@bridgeport.edu.

The University of British Columbia, Faculty of Graduate Studies, Faculty of Education, Department of Educational Studies, Vancouver, BC V6T 1Z1, Canada. Offers adult education (M Ed, MA); adult learning and global change (M Ed); educational administration (M Ed, MA); educational leadership and policy (Ed D); educational studies (M Ed, PhD), including history of education (M Ed), philosophy of education (M Ed), sociology of education (M Ed); higher education (M Ed, MA); society, culture and politics in education (M Ed, MA). Part-time and evening/weekend programs available. *Faculty:* 30 full-time (15 women), 9 part-time/adjunct (6 women). *Students:* 308 full-time (217 women), 45 part-time (31 women). Average age 35. 211 applicants, 60% accepted. In 2006, 128 master's, 15 doctorates awarded. Terminal master's awarded for partial completion of doctoral program. *Degree requirements:* For master's, thesis (MA); for doctorate, thesis/dissertation. *Entrance requirements:* Additional exam requirements/recommendations for international students: Required—TOEFL, TOEFL or IELTS. Electronic applications accepted. *Financial support:* Fellowships, research assistantships, teaching assistantships available. *Faculty research:* Educational leadership educational administration adult education politics in education, global change and adult learning. Total annual research expenditures: $547,440. *Unit head:* Dr. Tara Fenwick, Head, 604-822-5359, Fax: 604-82-4244.

Application contact: Christine Adams, Graduate Secretary, 604-822-6647, Fax: 604-822-4244, E-mail: grad.edst@ubc.ca.

University of Calgary, Faculty of Graduate Studies, Faculty of Education, Graduate Division of Educational Research, Calgary, AB T2N 1N4, Canada. Offers community rehabilitation and disability studies (M Ed, M Sc, Ed D, PhD, Graduate Certificate, Graduate Diploma); curriculum, teaching and learning (M Ed, M Sc, MA, Ed D, PhD, Graduate Certificate, Graduate Diploma); educational contexts (M Ed, MA, Ed D, PhD, Graduate Certificate, Graduate Diploma); educational leadership (M Ed, MA, Ed D, PhD, Graduate Certificate, Graduate Diploma); educational technology (M Ed, M Sc, MA, Ed D, PhD, Graduate Certificate, Graduate Diploma); gifted education (M Sc, MA, Ed D, PhD, Graduate Certificate, Graduate Diploma); higher education administration (Ed D); interpretive studies in education (M Ed, M Sc, MA, Ed D, PhD, Graduate Certificate, Graduate Diploma); second language teaching (M Ed, Ed D, PhD, Graduate Certificate, Graduate Diploma); teaching English as a second language (M Ed, M Sc, MA, Ed D, PhD, Graduate Certificate, Graduate Diploma); workplace and adult learning (M Ed, MA, Ed D, PhD, Graduate Certificate, Graduate Diploma). Ed D in both higher education administration and educational leadership offered via distance delivery. Part-time and evening/weekend programs available. Postbaccalaureate distance learning degree programs offered (minimal on-campus study). *Faculty:* 44 full-time, 52 part-time/adjunct. *Students:* 488 full-time, 550 part-time. 400 applicants, 50% accepted. In 2006, 102 master's, 18 doctorates awarded. *Degree requirements:* For master's, thesis (for some programs); for doctorate, thesis/dissertation, candidacy exam. *Entrance requirements:* For master's, minimum GPA of 3.0, 3 letters of reference; for doctorate, minimum GPA of 3.5, 3 letters of reference; for other advanced degree, minimum GPA of 3.0. Additional exam requirements/recommendations for international students: Required—TOEFL, IELTS. *Application deadline:* For fall admission, 2/15 for domestic students, 2/5 for international students; for winter admission, 6/15 for domestic and international students. Application fee: $100. Electronic applications accepted. *Financial support:* In 2006–07, research assistantships (averaging $3,920 per year); teaching assistantships, career-related internships or fieldwork, scholarships/grants, and unspecified assistantships also available. Financial award application deadline: 2/1. *Faculty research:* Curriculum, leadership, technology, contexts, gifted, second language teaching, work place and adult learning. *Unit head:* Dr. Charles F. Webber, Associate Dean, 403-220-5675, Fax: 403-282-3005, E-mail: cwebber@ucalgary.ca. *Application contact:* Patricia A. Brown, Program Officer, Graduate Division of Educational Research, 403-220-3178, Fax: 403-282-3005, E-mail: brownp@ucalgary.ca.

University of California, Berkeley, Graduate Division, School of Education, Division of Policy, Organization, Measurement and Evaluation, Berkeley, CA 94720-1500. Offers educational leadership (Ed D); policy and organizational research (MA, PhD); principal leadership (MA); program evaluation and assessment (Ed D); quantitative methods and evaluation (MA, PhD); PhD/MA. Terminal master's awarded for partial completion of doctoral program. *Degree requirements:* For master's, exam or thesis; for doctorate, thesis/dissertation, oral qualifying exam (PhD). *Entrance requirements:* For master's and doctorate, GRE General Test, minimum undergraduate GPA of 3.0 during last 2 years. *Application deadline:* For fall admission, 12/15 for domestic and international students. Application fee: $60 ($80 for international students). Electronic applications accepted. *Financial support:* Fellowships, research assistantships, teaching assistantships, unspecified assistantships available. *Application contact:* Admissions Office, 510-642-0841, Fax: 510-642-4808, E-mail: gse_info@uclink.berkeley.edu.

University of California, Irvine, Office of Graduate Studies, Department of Education, Irvine, CA 92697. Offers educational administration (Ed D); educational administration and leadership (Ed D); elementary and secondary education (MAT). Part-time and evening/weekend programs available. *Students:* 138 full-time (95 women), 3 part-time (all women); includes 61 minority (14 African Americans, 1 American Indian/Alaska Native, 26 Asian Americans or Pacific Islanders, 20 Hispanic Americans). Average age 34. In 2006, 67 master's, 8 doctorates awarded. *Degree requirements:* For doctorate, thesis/dissertation. *Entrance requirements:* For master's, GRE, minimum GPA of 3.0; for doctorate, GRE General Test, minimum GPA of 3.0. Additional exam requirements/recommendations for international students: Required—TOEFL (minimum score 550 paper-based; 213 computer-based). *Application deadline:* For fall admission, 4/1 priority date for domestic students. Application fee: $60. Electronic applications accepted. *Financial support:* Fellowships, research assistantships with full tuition reimbursements, institutionally sponsored loans, traineeships, health care benefits, and unspecified assistantships available. Financial award application deadline: 3/1; financial award applicants required to submit FAFSA. *Faculty research:* Education technology, learning theory, social theory, cultural diversity, postmodernism. *Unit head:* David Brant, Interim Chair, 949-824-7840, E-mail: dbrant@uci.edu. *Application contact:* Sarah K. Singh, Student Affairs Officer, 949-824-7832, Fax: 949-824-2965, E-mail: sksingh@uci.edu.

University of California, Santa Barbara, Graduate Division, Gevirtz Graduate School of Education, Santa Barbara, CA 93106. Offers counseling, clinical and school psychology (PhD), including clinical psychology, counseling psychology; education (M Ed, MA, PhD), including child and adolescent development (MA, PhD), cultural perspectives and comparative education (MA, PhD), educational leadership and organizations (MA, PhD), research methodology (MA, PhD), special education disabilities and risk studies (MA), special education, disabilities and risk studies (PhD), teaching and learning (MA, PhD); educational leadership (Ed D). *Accreditation:* APA (one or more programs are accredited). Postbaccalaureate distance learning degree programs offered (minimal on-campus study). *Faculty:* 39 full-time (18 women). *Students:* 375 full-time (285 women); includes 111 minority (13 African Americans, 2 American Indian/Alaska Native, 33 Asian Americans or Pacific Islanders, 63 Hispanic Americans), 14 international. Average age 29. 777 applicants, 36% accepted, 154 enrolled. In 2006, 151 master's, 31 doctorates awarded. Terminal master's awarded for partial completion of doctoral program. *Median time to degree:* Master's–1.5 years full-time; doctorate–5.5 years full-time. *Degree requirements:* For master's, thesis optional; for doctorate, thesis/dissertation, qualifying exam, comprehensive exam (for some programs), registration; for degree. *Entrance requirements:* For master's, GRE, MAT (M Ed); for doctorate, GRE. Additional exam requirements/recommendations for international students: Required—TOEFL (minimum score 550 paper-based; 213 computer-based; 80 iBT). *Application deadline:* For fall admission, 12/15 for domestic and international students. Application fee: $60. Electronic applications accepted. *Financial support:* In 2006–07, 181 fellowships with full and partial tuition reimbursements (averaging $4,200 per year), 64 research assistantships with full and partial tuition reimbursements (averaging $6,200 per year), 75 teaching assistantships with partial tuition reimbursements (averaging $7,500 per year) were awarded; career-related internships or fieldwork, Federal Work-Study, institutionally sponsored loans, scholarships/grants, traineeships, health care benefits, and unspecified assistantships also available. Support available to part-time students. Financial award application deadline: 12/15; financial award applicants required to submit FAFSA. Total annual research expenditures: $4 million. *Unit head:* Dr. Jane Conoley, Chair, 805-893-3917, E-mail: jane_conoley@education.ucsb.edu. *Application contact:* Student Affairs Office, 805-893-2137, E-mail: sao@education.ucsb.edu.

University of Central Arkansas, Graduate School, Graduate School of Management, Leadership, and Administration, Programs in School Leadership, Conway, AR 72035-0001. Offers educational leadership—district level (Ed S). *Accreditation:* NCATE. Part-time programs available. *Students:* 2 applicants, 100% accepted, 2 enrolled. *Degree requirements:* For Ed S, comprehensive exam. *Application deadline:* For fall admission, 3/1 priority date for domestic students; for spring admission, 10/1 priority date for domestic students. Applications are processed on a rolling basis. Application fee: $25 ($40 for international students). *Expenses:* Contact institution. One-time fee: $65 part-time. *Financial support:* Federal Work-Study, scholarships/grants, and tuition waivers (partial) available. Financial award application deadline: 2/15; financial award applicants required to submit FAFSA. *Unit head:* Dr. Jack Klotz, Coordinator, 501-450-5209, Fax: 501-450-5302, E-mail: jackk@uca.edu. *Application contact:* Nanette Fitzhugh, Administrative Assistant, 501-450-5063, Fax: 501-450-5678, E-mail: fitzhugh@uca.edu.

University of Central Florida, College of Education, Department of Educational Research, Technology and Leadership, Program in Educational Leadership, Orlando, FL 32816. Offers M Ed, MA, Ed D, Ed S. Part-time and evening/weekend programs available. *Students:* 100 full-time (70 women), 146 part-time (90 women); includes 39 minority (20 African Americans, 2 Asian Americans or Pacific Islanders, 17 Hispanic Americans), 1 international. In 2006, 65 master's, 26 doctorates awarded. *Degree requirements:* For master's, thesis or alternative; for doctorate, thesis/dissertation, candidacy exam; for Ed S, thesis or alternative, final exam. *Entrance requirements:* For master's, GRE General Test; for doctorate, GRE General Test, GRE Subject Test, minimum GPA of 3.0, resumé; for Ed S, GRE General Test, minimum GPA of 3.0, resumé. Additional exam requirements/recommendations for international students: Required—TOEFL. *Application deadline:* For fall admission, 2/20 priority date for domestic students; for spring admission, 9/20 priority date for domestic students. Application fee: $30. Electronic applications accepted. *Expenses:* Tuition, state resident: full-time $6,167; part-time $257 per credit hour. Tuition, nonresident: full-time $22,790; part-time $950 per credit hour. *Financial support:* In 2006–07, 16 research assistantships with partial tuition reimbursements (averaging $8,000 per year) were awarded; fellowships with partial tuition reimbursements, teaching assistantships with partial tuition reimbursements, career-related internships or fieldwork, Federal Work-Study, institutionally sponsored loans, tuition waivers (partial), and unspecified assistantships also available. Financial award application deadline: 3/1; financial award applicants required to submit FAFSA. *Unit head:* Dr. Kenneth Murray, Coordinator, 407-823-1468, Fax: 407-823-4880, E-mail: murray@mail.ucf.edu.

University of Central Missouri, The Graduate School, College of Education, Department of Educational Leadership and Human Development, Program in School Administration, Warrensburg, MO 64093. Offers school administration (MSE, Ed S), including elementary education (MSE), school principalship (Ed S), secondary education (MSE), superintendency (Ed S). *Expenses:* Tuition, state resident: full-time $5,448; part-time $227 per credit hour. Tuition, nonresident: full-time $10,896; part-time $454 per credit hour. Required fees: $336; $14 per credit hour. *Unit head:* Dr. Patricia Antrim, Chair, Department of Educational Leadership and Human Development, 660-543-4341, Fax: 660-543-4164, E-mail: antrim@ucmo.edu.

University of Central Oklahoma, College of Graduate Studies and Research, College of Education, Department of Advanced Professional Services, Program in Educational Administration, Edmond, OK 73034-5209. Offers M Ed. *Accreditation:* NCATE. Part-time programs available. *Entrance requirements:* For master's, GRE General Test. Additional exam requirements/recommendations for international students: Required—TOEFL (minimum score 550 paper-based; 213 computer-based). Electronic applications accepted.

University of Cincinnati, Division of Research and Advanced Studies, College of Education, Criminal Justice, and Human Services, Division of Educational Studies, Program in Educational Administration, Cincinnati, OH 45221. Offers M Ed, Ed S. *Accreditation:* NCATE. Part-time programs available. *Degree requirements:* For master's, thesis or alternative. *Entrance requirements:* For master's, GRE General Test, references, interview; for Ed S, references, interview. Additional exam requirements/recommendations for international students: Required—TOEFL (minimum score 550 paper-based), OEPT 3. Electronic applications accepted. *Faculty research:* Educational leadership.

University of Cincinnati, Division of Research and Advanced Studies, College of Education, Criminal Justice, and Human Services, Division of Educational Studies, Program in Urban Educational Leadership, Cincinnati, OH 45221. Offers Ed D. *Students:* 20. *Degree requirements:* For doctorate, thesis/dissertation, registration. *Entrance requirements:* For doctorate, GRE General Test, GRE Subject Test. Additional exam requirements/recommendations for international students: Required—TOEFL (minimum score 550 paper-based), OEPT. *Application deadline:* For fall admission, 2/15 for domestic students. Application fee: $40. *Financial support:* In 2006–07, 16 students received support; fellowships with full tuition reimbursements available, research assistantships with full tuition reimbursements available, teaching assistantships with full tuition reimbursements available, unspecified assistantships available. Total annual research expenditures: $63,090. *Unit head:* Mary Brydon-Miller, Graduate Coordinator, 513-556-5108, Fax: 513-556-2483, E-mail: mary.brydon-miller@uc.edu. *Application contact:* Cheryl Deardorff, Program Coordinator, 513-556-3238, Fax: 513-556-3535, E-mail: cheryl.deardorff@uc.edu.

University of Colorado at Colorado Springs, Graduate School, College of Education, Colorado Springs, CO 80933-7150. Offers counseling and human services (MA); curriculum and instruction (MA); educational administration (MA); educational leadership (MA, PhD); special education (MA). *Accreditation:* ACA; NCATE. Part-time and evening/weekend programs available. *Faculty:* 22 full-time (15 women), 29 part-time/adjunct (17 women). *Students:* 331 full-time (246 women), 173 part-time (135 women); includes 85 minority (26 African Americans, 4 American Indian/Alaska Native, 13 Asian Americans or Pacific Islanders, 42 Hispanic Americans). Average age 35. 107 applicants, 93% accepted, 49 enrolled. In 2006, 234 degrees awarded. *Degree requirements:* For master's, thesis or alternative, microcomputer proficiency, comprehensive exam; for doctorate, doctoral research lab requirement. *Entrance requirements:* For master's, GRE General Test, MAT. *Application deadline:* For fall admission, 6/15 for domestic students; for spring admission, 10/15 for domestic students. Applications are processed on a rolling basis. Application fee: $60 ($75 for international students). *Expenses:* Tuition, state resident: part-time $303 per credit hour. Tuition, nonresident: part-time $840 per credit hour. Tuition and fees vary according to course load, campus/location and program. *Financial support:* Fellowships, career-related internships or fieldwork and Federal Work-Study available. *Faculty research:* Job training for special populations, materials development for classroom. Total annual research expenditures: $961,803. *Unit head:* Dr. LaVonne Neal, Dean, 719-262-4111, Fax: 719-262-4110, E-mail: lneal@uccs.edu. *Application contact:* Connie Wroten, Professional Assistant, 719-262-4102, Fax: 719-262-4110, E-mail: cwroten@uccs.edu.

University of Colorado at Denver and Health Sciences Center, School of Education and Human Development, Program in Administration Leadership and Policy Studies, Denver, CO 80217-3364. Offers MA, Ed S. *Accreditation:* NCATE. Part-time and evening/weekend programs available. *Faculty:* 4 full-time (2 women). *Students:* 100 full-time (62 women), 25 part-time (20 women); includes 19 minority (3 African Americans, 1 American Indian/Alaska Native, 2 Asian Americans or Pacific Islanders, 13 Hispanic Americans), 1 international. Average age 38. 31 applicants, 81% accepted, 21 enrolled. In 2006, 33 master's, 9 other advanced degrees awarded. *Degree requirements:* For master's, thesis or alternative, portfolio, final paper. *Entrance requirements:* For master's, GRE, MAT, minimum GPA of 2.75, interview, 3 letters of recommendation, resumé. Additional exam requirements/recommendations for international students: Required—TOEFL (minimum score 525 paper-based; 197 computer-based). *Application deadline:* For fall admission, 5/15 for domestic students; for spring admission, 10/15 for domestic students. Applications are processed on a rolling basis. Application fee: $50 ($75 for international students). Electronic applications accepted. *Financial support:* Research assistantships, teaching assistantships, Federal Work-Study available. Financial award application deadline: 4/1; financial award applicants required to submit FAFSA. *Faculty research:* Learning cultures, teaching and learning in educational administration. *Unit head:* Connie Fulmer, Area Coordinator, 303-556-6286, Fax: 303-556-4479, E-mail: connie_fulmer@ceo.cudenver.edu. *Application contact:* Lori Sisneros, Student Services Coordinator, 303-556-8854, Fax: 303-556-4479, E-mail: bri.sisneros@cudenver.edu.

University of Colorado at Denver and Health Sciences Center, School of Education and Human Development, Program in Educational Leadership and Innovation, Denver, CO 80217-3364. Offers PhD. Part-time and evening/weekend programs available. *Students:* 14 full-time (11 women), 68 part-time (45 women); includes 19 minority (7 African Americans, 2 American Indian/Alaska Native, 4 Asian Americans or Pacific Islanders, 6 Hispanic Americans). Average age 45. 10 applicants, 20% accepted, 1 enrolled. In 2006, 9 degrees awarded. *Degree requirements:* For doctorate, one foreign language, thesis/dissertation, comprehensive exam, registration. *Entrance requirements:* For doctorate, GRE (LSAT, MCAT, or GMAT scores may

Educational Administration

University of Colorado at Denver and Health Sciences Center (continued)

be considered in place), writing sample, resumé. Additional exam requirements/recommendations for international students: Required—TOEFL (minimum score 525 paper-based; 197 computer-based). *Application deadline:* For fall admission, 1/15 for domestic students. Application fee: $50 ($75 for international students). *Financial support:* Application deadline: 4/1; *Faculty research:* Administrative leadership and policy studies, early childhood education, research in diversity, paraprofessionals in education, urban schools lab. *Unit head:* Elizabeth Kozleski, Associate Dean, 303-556-2844, Fax: 303-556-4479, E-mail: elizabeth_kozleski@ceo.cudenver.edu. *Application contact:* Lori Sisneros, Student Services Coordinator, 303-556-8854, Fax: 303-556-4479, E-mail: bri.sisneros@cudenver.edu.

University of Connecticut, Graduate School, Neag School of Education, Department of Educational Leadership, Field of Educational Administration, Storrs, CT 06269. Offers Ed D, PhD. *Accreditation:* NCATE. *Faculty:* 12 full-time (4 women). *Students:* 34 full-time (23 women), 116 part-time (65 women); includes 12 minority (5 African Americans, 1 American Indian/Alaska Native, 1 Asian American or Pacific Islander, 5 Hispanic Americans). Average age 34. 184 applicants, 35% accepted, 65 enrolled. In 2006, 4 doctorates awarded. *Degree requirements:* For doctorate, thesis/dissertation. *Entrance requirements:* For doctorate, GRE General Test. Additional exam requirements/recommendations for international students: Required—TOEFL (minimum score 550 paper-based; 213 computer-based). *Application deadline:* For fall admission, 2/1 priority date for domestic and international students; for spring admission, 11/1 for domestic students, 10/1 for international students. Applications are processed on a rolling basis. Electronic applications accepted. *Financial support:* In 2006–07, 2 research assistantships with full tuition reimbursements were awarded; fellowships, teaching assistantships with full tuition reimbursements, Federal Work-Study, scholarships/grants, health care benefits, and unspecified assistantships also available. Financial award application deadline: 2/1; financial award applicants required to submit FAFSA. *Application contact:* Lisa Rasicot, Graduate Coordinator, 860-486-3065, Fax: 860-486-0210, E-mail: soeadm02@uconnvm.uconn.edu.

University of Dayton, Graduate School, School of Education and Allied Professions, Department of Counselor Education and Human Services, Dayton, OH 45469-1300. Offers college student personnel (MS Ed); community counseling (MS Ed); higher education administration (MS Ed); human development services (MS Ed); school counseling (MS Ed); school psychology (MS Ed, Ed S); teacher as child/youth development specialist (MS Ed). *Accreditation:* NCATE. Part-time and evening/weekend programs available. *Faculty:* 11 full-time (7 women), 32 part-time/adjunct (17 women). *Students:* 271 full-time (234 women), 316 part-time (263 women); includes 85 minority (69 African Americans, 3 American Indian/Alaska Native, 13 Hispanic Americans), 1 international. Average age 32. 363 applicants, 47% accepted, 121 enrolled. In 2006, 267 degrees awarded. *Degree requirements:* For master's, exit exam, thesis optional. *Entrance requirements:* For master's, MAT or GRE (if GPA is below 2.75), interview. Additional exam requirements/recommendations for international students: Required—TOEFL (minimum score 550 paper-based; 213 computer-based). *Application deadline:* For fall admission, 2/15 priority date for domestic students, 4/10 priority date for international students; for winter admission, 9/10 priority date for international students; for spring admission, 1/10 priority date for international students. Applications are processed on a rolling basis. Application fee: $0. Electronic applications accepted. *Expenses:* Tuition: Part-time $601 per semester hour. Tuition and fees vary according to degree level and program. *Financial support:* In 2006–07, 1 research assistantship with partial tuition reimbursement (averaging $7,400 per year), 4 teaching assistantships with partial tuition reimbursements (averaging $7,600 per year) were awarded; career-related internships or fieldwork, institutionally sponsored loans, health care benefits, and unspecified assistantships also available. Financial award applicants required to submit FAFSA. *Faculty research:* Anger as part of the grief process, inclusion of children with severe disabilities, comparisons of school counselors in Bosnia and the U. S., graduate and professional student socialization, use of cohort groups in doctoral programs. *Unit head:* Dr. Thomas W. Rueth, Chairperson, 937-229-3644, Fax: 937-229-1055, E-mail: thomas.rueth@notes.udayton.edu. *Application contact:* Erika Eavers, Graduate Admission Processor, 937-229-3065, Fax: 937-229-4729, E-mail: erika.eavers@notes.udayton.edu.

University of Dayton, Graduate School, School of Education and Allied Professions, Department of Educational Leadership, Doctoral Program in Educational Leadership, Dayton, OH 45469-1300. Offers PhD. Evening/weekend programs available. *Faculty:* 13 full-time (4 women). *Students:* 22 full-time (12 women); includes 4 minority (all African Americans) 39 applicants, 36% accepted, 5 enrolled. In 2006, 4 degrees awarded. *Degree requirements:* For doctorate, thesis/dissertation, comprehensive exam. *Entrance requirements:* For doctorate, GRE or MAT, administration experience, minimum GPA of 3.25. Additional exam requirements/recommendations for international students: Required—TOEFL (minimum score 550 paper-based; 213 computer-based). *Application deadline:* For fall admission, 8/1 for domestic students, 3/1 priority date for international students. Applications are processed on a rolling basis. Application fee: $0. Electronic applications accepted. *Expenses:* Tuition: Part-time $601 per semester hour. Tuition and fees vary according to degree level and program. *Financial support:* In 2006–07, 6 research assistantships with full tuition reimbursements (averaging $10,750 per year) were awarded. Financial award applicants required to submit FAFSA. *Faculty research:* School choice, superintendency, critical theory, ethics, policy. *Unit head:* Dr. A. William Place, Director, Doctoral Studies, 937-229-4003, Fax: 937-229-4003, E-mail: andrew.place@notes.udayton.edu. *Application contact:* Nancy Crouchley, Administrative Assistant, 937-229-4003, E-mail: nancy.crouchley@notes.udayton.edu.

University of Dayton, Graduate School, School of Education and Allied Professions, Department of Educational Leadership, Program in Educational Leadership, Dayton, OH 45469-1300. Offers MS Ed, Ed S. Part-time and evening/weekend programs available. Postbaccalaureate distance learning degree programs offered (no on-campus study). *Faculty:* 12 full-time (5 women), 18 part-time/adjunct (8 women). *Students:* 157 full-time (97 women), 263 part-time (145 women); includes 32 minority (29 African Americans, 3 Asian Americans or Pacific Islanders), 2 international. 256 applicants, 76% accepted, 132 enrolled. In 2006, 154 degrees awarded. *Entrance requirements:* For master's, MAT or GRE (if GPA is below 2.75), minimum GPA of 2.75. Additional exam requirements/recommendations for international students: Required—TOEFL (minimum score 550 paper-based; 213 computer-based). *Application deadline:* For fall admission, 3/15 priority date for domestic students, 3/1 priority date for international students. Applications are processed on a rolling basis. Application fee: $0. Electronic applications accepted. *Expenses:* Tuition: Part-time $601 per semester hour. Tuition and fees vary according to degree level and program. *Financial support:* In 2006–07, 3 teaching assistantships with partial tuition reimbursements (averaging $5,066 per year) were awarded; career-related internships or fieldwork, institutionally sponsored loans, health care benefits, and unspecified assistantships also available. Financial award applicants required to submit FAFSA. *Faculty research:* Preparation for school superintendents, issues in diversity, legal issues in special education, online education, Catholic school leadership. *Unit head:* Rev. Joseph Massucci, Chairperson, 937-229-3737. *Application contact:* Erika Eavers, Graduate Admission Processor, 937-229-3065, Fax: 937-229-4729, E-mail: erika.eavers@notes.udayton.edu.

University of Dayton, Graduate School, School of Education and Allied Professions, Department of Teacher Education, Dayton, OH 45469-1300. Offers adolescent/young adult (MS Ed); art education (MS Ed); early childhood education (MS Ed); inclusive early childhood (MS Ed); interdisciplinary education (MS Ed); intervention specialist education, mild/moderate (MS Ed); literacy (MS Ed); middle childhood (MS Ed); multi-age education (MS Ed); music education (MS Ed); teacher as leader (MS Ed); technology in education (MS Ed). Part-time and evening/weekend programs available. *Faculty:* 13 full-time (9 women), 33 part-time/adjunct (25 women). *Students:* 149 full-time (120 women), 284 part-time (241 women); includes 37 minority (31 African Americans, 3 Asian Americans or Pacific Islanders, 3 Hispanic Americans), 3 international. Average age 33. 201 applicants, 58% accepted, 31 enrolled. In 2006, 150 degrees awarded. *Degree requirements:* For master's, thesis, capstone research project. *Entrance requirements:* For master's, GRE General Test, minimum GPA of 2.75. Additional exam requirements/recommendations for international students: Required—TOEFL (minimum score 550 paper-based; 213 computer-based). *Application deadline:* For fall admission, 3/15 priority date for domestic students, 3/1 priority date for international students. Applications are processed on a rolling basis. Application fee: $0. Electronic applications accepted. *Expenses: Contact institution. Financial support:* In 2006–07, 8 teaching assistantships with partial tuition reimbursements (averaging $7,600 per year) were awarded; career-related internships or fieldwork, institutionally sponsored loans, health care benefits, and unspecified assistantships also available. Financial award applicants required to submit FAFSA. *Faculty research:* Diversity, literacy, art representation by young children, preservice teacher preparation. Total annual research expenditures: $330,000. *Unit head:* Dr. Katie A. Kinnucan-Welsch, Chair, 937-229-3346. *Application contact:* Erika Eavers, Graduate Admission Processor, 937-229-3065, Fax: 937-229-4729, E-mail: erika.eavers@notes.udayton.edu.

University of Delaware, College of Human Services, Education and Public Policy, School of Education, Newark, DE 19716. Offers curriculum and instruction (M Ed); education (PhD); educational leadership (M Ed, Ed D); exceptional children and youth (M Ed); instruction (MI); school counseling (M Ed); school psychology (MA); teaching English as a second language (TESL) (MA). *Accreditation:* NCATE. Part-time and evening/weekend programs available. Terminal master's awarded for partial completion of doctoral program. *Degree requirements:* For master's, thesis (for some programs), comprehensive exam (for some programs), registration; for doctorate, thesis/dissertation, comprehensive exam (for some programs), registration. *Entrance requirements:* For master's and doctorate, GRE, 3 letters of recommendation. Additional exam requirements/recommendations for international students: Required—TOEFL (minimum score 600 paper-based; 250 computer-based). Electronic applications accepted. *Faculty research:* Teacher education; education policy; educational assessment, measurement, and evaluation; curriculum theory and development; community based education models.

University of Denver, College of Education, Denver, CO 80208. Offers counseling psychology (MA, PhD); curriculum and instruction (MA, PhD, Certificate), including curriculum leadership (MA, PhD); educational administration and policy studies (Certificate); educational psychology (MA, PhD, Ed S), including child and family studies (MA, PhD), quantitative research methods (MA, PhD), school psychology (PhD, Ed S); higher education and adult studies (MA, PhD); library and information science (MLIS); library and information sciences (Certificate); school administration (PhD). *Accreditation:* ALA; APA (one or more programs are accredited). Part-time and evening/weekend programs available. Postbaccalaureate distance learning degree programs offered (no on-campus study). *Faculty:* 28 full-time (18 women). *Students:* 293 full-time (240 women), 439 part-time (357 women); includes 102 minority (28 African Americans, 7 American Indian/Alaska Native, 14 Asian Americans or Pacific Islanders, 53 Hispanic Americans), 11 international. Average age 34. 574 applicants, 72% accepted. In 2006, 168 master's, 28 doctorates, 67 other advanced degrees awarded. Terminal master's awarded for partial completion of doctoral program. *Degree requirements:* For master's, comprehensive exam; for doctorate, 2 foreign languages, thesis/dissertation, comprehensive exam. *Entrance requirements:* For master's, GRE General Test or MAT (for most programs); for doctorate, GRE General Test or MAT. *Application deadline:* Applications are processed on a rolling basis. Application fee: $50. Electronic applications accepted. *Expenses:* Tuition: Full-time $29,628; part-time $823 per credit. *Financial support:* In 2006–07, 51 teaching assistantships with full and partial tuition reimbursements (averaging $6,700 per year) were awarded; career-related internships or fieldwork, Federal Work-Study, institutionally sponsored loans, and scholarships/grants also available. Support available to part-time students. Financial award application deadline: 3/1; financial award applicants required to submit FAFSA. *Faculty research:* Parkinson's disease, personnel training, development and assessments, gifted education, service learning, transportation, public schools. Total annual research expenditures: $172,000. *Unit head:* Dr. Virginia Maloney, Dean, 303-871-2509. *Application contact:* Linda McCarthy, Contact, 303-871-2509, E-mail: edinfo@du.edu.

University of Detroit Mercy, College of Liberal Arts and Education, Department of Education, Program in Educational Administration, Detroit, MI 48221. Offers MA. *Degree requirements:* For master's, thesis or alternative. *Entrance requirements:* For master's, minimum GPA of 2.75. *Expenses:* Tuition: Full-time $15,750; part-time $875 per credit hour. Required fees: $570.

The University of Findlay, Graduate and Professional Studies, College of Education, Findlay, OH 45840-3653. Offers administration (MA Ed); early childhood (MA Ed); elementary education (MA Ed); human resource development (MA Ed); leadership (MA Ed); special education (MA Ed); technology (MA Ed); web instruction (MA Ed). *Accreditation:* NCATE. Part-time and evening/weekend programs available. *Faculty:* 12 full-time, 6 part-time/adjunct. *Students:* 84 full-time (65 women), 223 part-time (169 women); includes 11 minority (3 African Americans, 2 American Indian/Alaska Native, 1 Asian American or Pacific Islander, 5 Hispanic Americans), 13 international. Average age 35. 91 applicants, 97% accepted, 76 enrolled. In 2006, 146 degrees awarded. *Degree requirements:* For master's, thesis, cumulative project. *Entrance requirements:* For master's, minimum undergraduate GPA of 3.0 in last 60 hours of course work. Additional exam requirements/recommendations for international students: Required—TOEFL. *Application deadline:* Applications are processed on a rolling basis. Application fee: $25. Electronic applications accepted. *Expenses: Contact institution. Financial support:* In 2006–07, 6 students received support, including 6 teaching assistantships with full tuition reimbursements available (averaging $6,000 per year); unspecified assistantships also available. Financial award application deadline: 4/1; financial award applicants required to submit FAFSA. *Faculty research:* Children's literature, books and artwork, educational technology, professional development. *Unit head:* Dr. Melissa A. Cain, Dean, 419-434-4840, Fax: 419-434-4822. *Application contact:* Heather Riffle, Director, Graduate and Special Programs, 419-434-4642, Fax: 419-434-5517, E-mail: riffle@findlay.edu.

University of Florida, Graduate School, College of Education, Department of Educational Administration and Policy, Gainesville, FL 32611. Offers curriculum and instruction (Ed D, PhD); educational leadership (M Ed, MAE, Ed D, PhD, Ed S); higher education administration (Ed D, PhD, Ed S); student personnel in higher education (M Ed, MAE); PhD/JD. *Accreditation:* NCATE. *Faculty:* 10 full-time (3 women). *Degree requirements:* For master's, thesis optional; for doctorate, variable foreign language requirement, thesis/dissertation. *Entrance requirements:* For master's, GRE General Test, minimum GPA of 3.0, teaching experience; for doctorate and Ed S, GRE General Test, minimum GPA of 3.0. Additional exam requirements/recommendations for international students: Required—TOEFL (minimum score 550 paper-based; 213 computer-based). *Application deadline:* For fall admission, 6/1 priority date for domestic students. Applications are processed on a rolling basis. Application fee: $30. Electronic applications accepted. *Expenses:* Tuition, state resident: full-time $6,827. Tuition, nonresident: full-time $21,951. Required fees: $999. *Financial support:* In 2006–07, 2 research assistantships (averaging $9,424 per year) were awarded; fellowships, teaching assistantships, career-related internships or fieldwork and unspecified assistantships also available. *Faculty research:* Educational finance, community education, middle school curriculum, community college administration. *Unit head:* Linda Hagedorn, Chair, 352-392-2391 Ext. 275. *Application contact:* Dr. Katherine Gratto, Coordinator, 352-392-2391 Ext. 274, Fax: 352-392-0038, E-mail: kgratto@coe.ufl.edu.

University of Georgia, Graduate School, College of Education, Department of Lifelong Education, Administration and Policy, Athens, GA 30602. Offers M Ed, MA, Ed D, PhD, Ed S. *Accreditation:* NCATE. *Faculty:* 21 full-time (13 women). *Students:* 68 full-time (45 women), 248 part-time (159 women); includes 62 minority (54 African Americans, 1 American Indian/Alaska Native, 5 Asian Americans or Pacific Islanders, 2 Hispanic Americans), 21 international. 205 applicants, 63% accepted, 97 enrolled. In 2006, 61 master's, 12 doctorates, 15 other advanced degrees awarded. *Entrance requirements:* For master's and Ed S, GRE General Test or MAT; for doctorate, GRE General Test. *Application deadline:* For fall admission, 7/1 priority date for domestic students; for spring admission, 11/15 for domestic students. Application fee: $50. Electronic applications accepted. *Unit head:* Dr. Ronald M. Cervero, Head, 706-542-2221, Fax: 706-542-4024, E-mail: rcervero@coe.uga.edu.

University of Guam, Graduate School and Research, College of Education, Program in Administration and Supervision, Mangilao, GU 96923. Offers M Ed. *Degree requirements:* For master's, comprehensive oral and written exams, special project or thesis. *Entrance requirements:* For master's, GRE General Test. Additional exam requirements/recommendations for international students: Required—TOEFL.

University of Guam, Graduate School and Research, College of Education, Program in Instructional Leadership, Mangilao, GU 96923. Offers MA. Part-time programs available. *Degree requirements:* For master's, thesis, comprehensive oral and written exams. *Entrance requirements:* For master's, GRE General Test. Additional exam requirements/recommendations for international students: Required—TOEFL.

University of Hartford, College of Education, Nursing, and Health Professions, Program in Educational Leadership, West Hartford, CT 06117-1599. Offers administration and supervision (CAGS). *Accreditation:* NCATE. Part-time and evening/weekend programs available. *Faculty:* 2 full-time (both women), 3 part-time/adjunct (1 woman). *Students:* 4 full-time (3 women), 4 part-time (2 women). Average age 45. 3 applicants, 100% accepted, 3 enrolled. In 2006, 10 degrees awarded. *Degree requirements:* For CAGS, comprehensive exam or research project. *Entrance requirements:* For degree, GRE General Test or MAT, interview. Additional exam requirements/recommendations for international students: Required—TOEFL (minimum score 550 paper-based; 213 computer-based). *Application deadline:* For fall admission, 4/15 for domestic students. Applications are processed on a rolling basis. Application fee: $40 ($55 for international students). Electronic applications accepted. *Expenses:* Tuition: Part-time $515 per credit. Required fees: $200 per term. *Financial support:* Teaching assistantships, institutionally sponsored loans and unspecified assistantships available. Financial award application deadline: 6/1; financial award applicants required to submit FAFSA. *Unit head:* Dr. Barbara Intriligator, Director, 860-768-4772, E-mail: intriliga@hartford.edu. *Application contact:* Suzanne Cohen, Coordinator, 860-768-5263.

University of Hartford, College of Education, Nursing, and Health Professions, Program in Educational Leadership (Doctoral), West Hartford, CT 06117-1599. Offers Ed D. *Accreditation:* NCATE. Part-time and evening/weekend programs available. *Faculty:* 5 full-time (4 women). *Students:* 61 full-time (40 women), 36 part-time (22 women); includes 10 minority (7 African Americans, 3 Hispanic Americans), 1 international. Average age 45. 2 applicants, 100% accepted, 2 enrolled. In 2006, 21 degrees awarded. *Degree requirements:* For doctorate, thesis/dissertation. *Entrance requirements:* For doctorate, MAT, 3 letters of recommendation, writing samples, interview, resumé, letter of support from employer. *Application deadline:* For fall admission, 4/15 for domestic students. Applications are processed on a rolling basis. Application fee: $40 ($55 for international students). *Expenses:* Contact institution. *Financial support:* Teaching assistantships, institutionally sponsored loans and unspecified assistantships available. Financial award application deadline: 6/1; financial award applicants required to submit FAFSA. *Unit head:* Dr. Barbara Intriligator, Director, 860-768-4772, E-mail: intriliga@hartford.edu. *Application contact:* Suzanne Cohen, Coordinator, 860-768-5263.

University of Hawaii at Manoa, Graduate Division, College of Education, Department of Educational Administration, Honolulu, HI 96822. Offers M Ed. Part-time programs available. *Faculty:* 7 full-time (4 women), 1 (woman) part-time/adjunct. *Students:* 20 full-time (13 women), 74 part-time (41 women); includes 36 minority (4 African Americans, 27 Asian Americans or Pacific Islanders, 5 Hispanic Americans), 2 international. Average age 39. 52 applicants, 67% accepted, 25 enrolled. In 2006, 24 degrees awarded. *Degree requirements:* For master's, thesis optional. *Entrance requirements:* Additional exam requirements/recommendations for international students: Required—TOEFL (minimum score 600 paper-based; 250 computer-based; 100 iBT). *Application deadline:* For fall admission, 3/1 for domestic students, 1/15 for international students; for spring admission, 9/1 for domestic students, 8/1 for international students. Application fee: $50. *Financial support:* In 2006–07, 8 students received support, including 2 research assistantships (averaging $16,176 per year), 6 teaching assistantships (averaging $14,382 per year); career-related internships or fieldwork, Federal Work-Study, institutionally sponsored loans, and tuition waivers (full and partial) also available. *Faculty research:* Leadership, educational policy, organizational processes, finance. *Application contact:* Ron Heck, Information Contact, 808-956-7843, Fax: 808-956-4120.

University of Hawaii at Manoa, Graduate Division, College of Education, Education Program, Honolulu, HI 96822. Offers curriculum and instruction (PhD); educational administration (PhD); educational foundations (PhD); educational policy studies (PhD); exceptionalities (PhD). Evening/weekend programs available. *Faculty:* 78 full-time (44 women), 1 part-time/adjunct (0 women). *Students:* 54 full-time (37 women), 97 part-time (66 women); includes 28 minority (6 African Americans, 1 American Indian/Alaska Native, 19 Asian Americans or Pacific Islanders, 2 Hispanic Americans), 3 international. Average age 45. 63 applicants, 52% accepted, 24 enrolled. In 2006, 17 degrees awarded. *Median time to degree:* Of those who began their doctoral program in fall 1998, 35% received their degree in 8 years or less. *Degree requirements:* For doctorate, thesis/dissertation. *Entrance requirements:* For doctorate, GRE General Test, sample of written work. Additional exam requirements/recommendations for international students: Required—TOEFL (minimum score 600 paper-based; 250 computer-based; 100 iBT). *Application deadline:* For fall admission, 2/1 for domestic students, 1/15 for international students. Application fee: $50. *Financial support:* In 2006–07, 12 research assistantships (averaging $16,565 per year), 5 teaching assistantships (averaging $13,964 per year) were awarded; career-related internships or fieldwork, Federal Work-Study, and tuition waivers (full and partial) also available. *Application contact:* Dr. Helen Slaughter, Chairperson, 808-956-7913, Fax: 808-956-9100, E-mail: slaughte@hawaii.edu.

University of Houston, College of Education, Department of Educational Leadership and Cultural Studies, Houston, TX 77204. Offers educational administration (M Ed, Ed D); higher education (M Ed); historical, social, and cultural foundations of education (M Ed, Ed D). *Accreditation:* NCATE. Part-time and evening/weekend programs available. *Faculty:* 8 full-time (6 women), 8 part-time/adjunct (3 women). *Students:* 19 full-time (12 women), 169 part-time (110 women); includes 72 minority (39 African Americans, 10 Asian Americans or Pacific Islanders, 23 Hispanic Americans), 3 international. Average age 36. 89 applicants, 60% accepted, 43 enrolled. In 2006, 31 master's, 5 doctorates awarded. *Degree requirements:* For master's, comprehensive exam or thesis; for doctorate, thesis/dissertation, comprehensive exam. *Entrance requirements:* For master's, GRE General Test or MAT, minimum GPA of 3.0 in last 60 hours of course work; for doctorate, GRE General Test, interview, minimum GPA of 3.0 in last 60 hours. *Application deadline:* For fall admission, 7/18 priority date for domestic students; for spring admission, 12/18 for domestic students. Applications are processed on a rolling basis. Application fee: $35 ($75 for international students). *Expenses:* Tuition, state resident: full-time $5,429; part-time $226 per credit. Tuition, nonresident: full-time $12,029; part-time $501 per credit. Required fees: $2,454. *Financial support:* In 2006–07, 1 fellowship with full tuition reimbursement (averaging $9,500 per year), 1 research assistantship with full tuition reimbursement (averaging $9,500 per year), 1 teaching assistantship with full tuition reimbursement (averaging $9,500 per year) were awarded; career-related internships or fieldwork, Federal Work-Study, institutionally sponsored loans, scholarships/grants, health care benefits, and unspecified assistantships also available. Support available to part-time students. Financial award application deadline: 3/10; financial award applicants required to submit FAFSA. *Faculty research:* Change, supervision, multiculturalism, evaluation, policy. *Unit head:* Robert McPherson, Interim Dean, 713-743-5003, Fax: 713-743-8650, E-mail: bmcph@uh.edu. *Application contact:* Rose L. Hernandez, Office Assistant, 713-743-5044, Fax: 713-743-4979.

University of Houston–Clear Lake, School of Education, Program in Educational Leadership, Houston, TX 77058-1098. Offers educational leadership (Ed D); educational management (MS). *Faculty:* 6 full-time (1 woman), 22 part-time/adjunct (11 women). *Students:* 78 full-time (57 women), 472 part-time (349 women); includes 251 minority (111 African Americans, 4 American Indian/Alaska Native, 10 Asian Americans or Pacific Islanders, 126 Hispanic Americans), 12 international. In 2006, 165 degrees awarded. *Degree requirements:* For master's, thesis optional; for doctorate, thesis/dissertation, comprehensive exam. Application fee: $95. *Unit head:* Dr. Lawrence Kajs, Chair, 281-283-3555, E-mail: kajs@uhcl.edu. *Application contact:* Janis S. Bigelow, Assistant Director of Admissions, Recruitment and Communications, 281-283-2540, Fax: 281-283-2530, E-mail: bigelow@uhcl.edu.

University of Idaho, College of Graduate Studies, College of Education, Department of Counseling and School Psychology, Special Education, and Educational Leadership, Program in Educational Leadership, Moscow, ID 83844-2282. Offers M Ed, MS, Ed S. *Accreditation:* NCATE. *Students:* 150 (82 women). Average age 37. In 2006, 50 master's awarded. *Entrance requirements:* For master's, minimum GPA of 2.8. *Application deadline:* For fall admission, 8/1 for domestic students; for spring admission, 12/15 for domestic students. Application fee: $55 ($60 for international students). *Expenses:* Tuition, nonresident: full-time $9,600; part-time $140 per credit. Required fees: $4,740; $227 per credit. *Financial support:* Application deadline: 2/15. *Unit head:* Dr. Russell A. Joki, Chair, Department of Counseling and School Psychology, Special Education, and Educational Leadership, 208-364-4099, E-mail: rjoki@uidaho.edu.

University of Idaho, College of Graduate Studies, College of Education, Doctoral Programs in Education, Moscow, ID 83844-2282. Offers adult and organizational learning (Ed D, PhD); counseliing and human services (PhD); counseling and human services (Ed D); curriculm and intstruction (Ed D); curriculm and instruction (PhD); educational leadership (Ed D, PhD); physical education (PhD); professional-technical and technology education (PhD); professional-technical and tecnology education (Ed D). *Students:* 208 (118 women). In 2006, 50 degrees awarded. *Expenses:* Tuition, nonresident: full-time $9,600; part-time $140 per credit. Required fees: $4,740; $227 per credit. *Application contact:* Shirley Green, Information Contact, 208-885-6773.

University of Illinois at Chicago, Graduate College, College of Education, Department of Curriculum and Instruction, Chicago, IL 60607-7128. Offers curriculum and instruction (PhD); educational psychology (PhD); instructional leadership (M Ed), including elementary education, reading, secondary education; leadership and administration (M Ed); policy and administration (PhD); policy studies in urban education (PhD). Part-time and evening/weekend programs available. *Degree requirements:* For doctorate, thesis/dissertation. *Entrance requirements:* For master's, minimum GPA of 2.75; for doctorate, GRE General Test, minimum GPA of 2.75. Additional exam requirements/recommendations for international students: Required—TOEFL. Electronic applications accepted. *Faculty research:* Curriculum theory, curriculum development, research on teaching, curriculum and context, reading/literacy.

University of Illinois at Springfield, Graduate Programs, College of Education and Human Services, Program in Educational Leadership, Springfield, IL 62703-5407. Offers educational leadership (MA); teacher leadership (MA). Part-time and evening/weekend programs available. Postbaccalaureate distance learning degree programs offered (no on-campus study). *Faculty:* 14 full-time (6 women), 23 part-time/adjunct (10 women). *Students:* 15 full-time (10 women), 392 part-time (281 women); includes 23 minority (18 African Americans, 1 American Indian/Alaska Native, 3 Asian Americans or Pacific Islanders, 1 Hispanic American), 1 international. Average age 35. 99 applicants, 67% accepted, 59 enrolled. In 2006, 115 degrees awarded. *Degree requirements:* For master's, project or thesis, thesis optional. *Entrance requirements:* For master's, minimum undergraduate GPA of 3.0. Additional exam requirements/recommendations for international students: Required—TOEFL (minimum score 550 paper-based; 213 computer-based). *Application deadline:* For fall admission, 6/15 for domestic and international students; for spring admission, 11/15 for domestic and international students. Applications are processed on a rolling basis. Application fee: $50 ($60 for international students). Electronic applications accepted. *Expenses:* Tuition, state resident: full-time $4,722; part-time $197 per credit hour. Tuition, nonresident: full-time $12,558; part-time $523 per credit hour. Required fees: $1,614; $8 per credit hour. $597 per term. *Financial support:* In 2006–07, research assistantships with full tuition reimbursements (averaging $7,425 per year), teaching assistantships with full tuition reimbursements (averaging $7,425 per year) were awarded; career-related internships or fieldwork, Federal Work-Study, scholarships/grants, health care benefits, tuition waivers (full and partial), and unspecified assistantships also available. Support available to part-time students. Financial award application deadline: 11/15; financial award applicants required to submit FAFSA. *Unit head:* Dr. Scott Day, Program Administrator, 217-206-7520, Fax: 217-206-6775, E-mail: day.scott@uis.edu.

University of Illinois at Urbana–Champaign, Graduate College, College of Education, Department of Education, Organization and Leadership, Champaign, IL 61820. Offers Ed M, MA, MS, Ed D, PhD, CAS. Part-time programs available. *Faculty:* 8 full-time (2 women), 1 part-time/adjunct (0 women). *Students:* 32 full-time (17 women), 172 part-time (116 women); includes 29 minority (22 African Americans, 3 Asian Americans or Pacific Islanders, 4 Hispanic Americans), 1 international. 100 applicants, 68% accepted, 31 enrolled. In 2006, 18 master's, 15 doctorates, 4 other advanced degrees awarded. *Degree requirements:* For doctorate, thesis/dissertation. *Entrance requirements:* For master's, GRE or MAT, interview, minimum GPA of 3.0; for doctorate, GRE General Test or MAT, interview, minimum GPA of 3.0. *Application deadline:* For fall admission, 1/15 for domestic students; for spring admission, 4/15 for domestic students. Applications are processed on a rolling basis. Application fee: $50 ($60 for international students). Electronic applications accepted. *Financial support:* In 2006–07, 4 fellowships, 8 research assistantships, 2 teaching assistantships were awarded; tuition waivers (full and partial) also available. Financial award application deadline: 1/15. *Unit head:* Carolyn M. Shields, Head, 217-333-2155, Fax: 217-244-3378, E-mail: cshields@uiuc.edu. *Application contact:* Jean Bettridge, Assistant to the Head, 217-333-2155, Fax: 217-244-3378, E-mail: jeanb@uiuc.edu.

University of Indianapolis, Graduate Programs, School of Education, Indianapolis, IN 46227-3697. Offers art education (MAT); biology (MAT); chemistry (MAT); curriculum and instruction (MA); earth sciences (MAT); education (MA, MAT); educational leadership (MA); elementary education (MA); English (MAT); French (MAT); math (MAT); physical education (MAT); physics (MAT); secondary education (MA), including art education, education, English education, social studies education; social studies (MAT); Spanish (MAT). *Accreditation:* NCATE. Part-time and evening/weekend programs available. *Faculty:* 4 full-time (2 women), 6 part-time/adjunct (2 women). *Students:* 32 full-time (16 women), 70 part-time (42 women); includes 2 minority (1 African American, 1 Hispanic American). Average age 31. In 2006, 51 degrees awarded. *Entrance requirements:* For master's, GRE Subject Test, minimum GPA of 2.5, 3 letters of recommendation, interview, Praxis I, writing exercise, be within 9 hours of completing content requirements. Additional exam requirements/recommendations for international students: Required—TOEFL (minimum score 550 paper-based; 213 computer-based). *Application deadline:* Applications are processed on a rolling basis. Application fee: $50. *Financial support:* Federal Work-Study available. Financial award application deadline: 5/1; financial award applicants required to submit FAFSA. *Faculty research:* Assessment of teacher education, perceptions of prospective teachers by parents. *Unit head:* Dr. E. Lynne Weisenbach, Dean, 317-788-3446, Fax: 317-788-3300, E-mail: weisenbach@uindy.edu.

The University of Iowa, Graduate College, College of Education, Department of Counseling, Rehabilitation, and Student Development, Iowa City, IA 52242-1316. Offers administration and research (PhD); counselor education and supervision (PhD); rehabilitation counseling (MA); rehabilitation counselor education (PhD); school counseling (MA); student development (MA, PhD). *Accreditation:* ACA (one or more programs are accredited); CORE (one or more programs are accredited). *Faculty:* 14 full-time, 3 part-time/adjunct. *Students:* 86 full-time (67 women), 31 part-time (21 women); includes 20 minority (15 African Americans, 2 Asian Americans or Pacific Islanders, 3 Hispanic Americans), 7 international. 63 applicants, 60% accepted, 25 enrolled. In 2006, 34 master's, 4 doctorates awarded. *Degree requirements:* For master's, exam, thesis optional; for doctorate, thesis/dissertation, comprehensive exam, registration. *Entrance requirements:* For master's and doctorate, GRE General Test, minimum GPA of 3.0. Additional exam requirements/recommendations for international students: Required—TOEFL (minimum score 550 paper-based; 213 computer-based; 81 iBT). Applica-

Educational Administration

The University of Iowa (continued)

tion fee: $60 ($85 for international students). Electronic applications accepted. *Financial support:* In 2006–07, 1 fellowship, 21 research assistantships with partial tuition reimbursements, 37 teaching assistantships with partial tuition reimbursements were awarded. Financial award applicants required to submit FAFSA. *Unit head:* Dr. Dennis R. Maki, Chair, 319-335-5275, Fax: 319-335-5291.

The University of Iowa, Graduate College, College of Education, Department of Educational Policy and Leadership Studies, Program in Educational Administration, Iowa City, IA 52242-1316. Offers MA, PhD, Ed S. *Faculty:* 4 full-time. *Students:* 8 full-time (4 women), 28 part-time (8 women); includes 3 minority (2 African Americans, 1 Hispanic American), 3 international. 17 applicants, 53% accepted, 6 enrolled. In 2006, 6 master's, 1 doctorate, 1 other advanced degree awarded. *Degree requirements:* For master's and Ed S, exam; for doctorate, thesis/dissertation, comprehensive exam, registration. *Entrance requirements:* For master's, doctorate, and Ed S, GRE General Test, minimum GPA of 3.0. Additional exam requirements/recommendations for international students: Required—TOEFL (minimum score 550 paper-based; 213 computer-based; 81 iBT). *Application deadline:* For fall admission, 12/1 priority date for domestic and international students. Applications are processed on a rolling basis. Application fee: $60 ($85 for international students). Electronic applications accepted. *Financial support:* In 2006–07, 1 research assistantship with partial tuition reimbursement was awarded; fellowships, teaching assistantships with partial tuition reimbursements also available. Financial award applicants required to submit FAFSA. *Unit head:* Dr. Marcus Haack, Coordinator, 319-335-5320, Fax: 319-384-0587.

University of Kansas, Graduate Studies, School of Education, Department of Educational Leadership and Policy Studies, Program in Education Administration, Lawrence, KS 66045. Offers MS Ed, Ed S. Part-time and evening/weekend programs available. *Faculty:* 19. *Students:* 4 full-time (3 women), 19 part-time (12 women); includes 2 minority (1 African American, 1 Hispanic American), 3 international. Average age 35. 4 applicants. In 2006, 14 degrees awarded. *Degree requirements:* For master's, comprehensive exam. *Entrance requirements:* For master's, MAT or GRE, minimum GPA of 3.0. Additional exam requirements/recommendations for international students: Required—TOEFL. *Application deadline:* For fall admission, 3/1 for domestic students. Application fee: $55 ($60 for international students). Electronic applications accepted. *Expenses:* Tuition, area resident: Part-time $227 per credit. Tuition, state resident: part-time $543 per credit. Tuition and fees vary according to course load, campus/location, program and reciprocity agreements. *Financial support:* Fellowships available. *Faculty research:* Policy studies, law, personnel, leadership, organizational studies. *Application contact:* Denise Brubaker, Admissions Coordinator, 785-864-4458, Fax: 785-864-4697, E-mail: elps@ku.edu.

University of Kansas, Graduate Studies, School of Education, Department of Educational Leadership and Policy Studies, Program in Policy Studies, Lawrence, KS 66045. Offers foundations (Ed D, PhD); higher education (Ed D, PhD); school administration (Ed D, PhD). Part-time and evening/weekend programs available. *Faculty:* 19. *Students:* 18 full-time (10 women), 133 part-time (69 women); includes 17 minority (7 African Americans, 4 American Indian/Alaska Native, 2 Asian Americans or Pacific Islanders, 4 Hispanic Americans), 5 international. Average age 40. 17 applicants, 59% accepted. In 2006, 21 degrees awarded. *Degree requirements:* For doctorate, thesis/dissertation, comprehensive exam. *Entrance requirements:* For doctorate, GRE General Test, minimum graduate GPA of 3.5. Additional exam requirements/recommendations for international students: Required—TOEFL. *Application deadline:* For fall admission, 7/1 priority date for domestic and international students; for spring admission, 11/1 priority date for domestic and international students. Applications are processed on a rolling basis. Application fee: $55 ($60 for international students). Electronic applications accepted. *Expenses:* Tuition, area resident: Part-time $227 per credit. Tuition, state resident: part-time $543 per credit. Tuition and fees vary according to course load, campus/location, program and reciprocity agreements. *Financial support:* Fellowships, research assistantships with full and partial tuition reimbursements, teaching assistantships with full and partial tuition reimbursements available. Financial award application deadline: 3/15. *Faculty research:* Policy studies in higher education, policy studies in foundations, policy studies in educational leaderships. *Application contact:* Denise Brubaker, Admissions Coordinator, 785-864-4458, Fax: 785-864-4697, E-mail: elps@ku.edu.

University of Kentucky, Graduate School, College of Education, Program in Educational Leadership Studies, Lexington, KY 40506-0032. Offers administration and supervision (Ed S); instruction and administration (Ed D); school administration (M Ed). *Faculty:* 8 full-time (3 women). *Students:* 29 full-time (16 women), 71 part-time (46 women); includes 10 minority (8 African Americans, 1 American Indian/Alaska Native, 1 Hispanic American), 2 international. Average age 40. In 2006, 9 master's, 2 doctorates awarded. *Median time to degree:* Of those who began their doctoral program in fall 1998, 47% received their degree in 8 years or less. *Degree requirements:* For master's and Ed S, comprehensive exam; for doctorate, thesis/dissertation, comprehensive exam. *Entrance requirements:* For master's, GRE General Test, minimum undergraduate GPA of 2.75; for doctorate, GRE General Test, minimum graduate GPA of 3.0. Additional exam requirements/recommendations for international students: Required—TOEFL (minimum score 550 paper-based; 213 computer-based). *Application deadline:* For fall admission, 7/17 priority date for domestic students, 2/1 priority date for international students; for spring admission, 12/13 priority date for domestic students, 6/15 priority date for international students. Application fee: $40 ($55 for international students). Electronic applications accepted. *Expenses:* Tuition, state resident: full-time $7,670; part-time $401 per credit hour. Tuition, nonresident: full-time $16,158; part-time $873 per credit hour. *Financial support:* In 2006–07, 1 student received support, including 1 research assistantship with full tuition reimbursement available (averaging $8,000 per year); fellowships, teaching assistantships, Federal Work-Study, scholarships/grants, traineeships, health care benefits, tuition waivers (partial), and unspecified assistantships also available. Support available to part-time students. Financial award application deadline: 3/15. *Faculty research:* School governance, teacher empowerment, planned change, systemic reform, issues of equity and fairness. *Unit head:* Dr. James S. Rinehart, Director of Graduate Studies, 859-257-8921, Fax: 859-257-1015, E-mail: james.rinehart@uky.edu. *Application contact:* Dr. Brian Jackson, Senior Associate Dean, 859-257-4667, Fax: 859-257-4676, E-mail: brian.jackson@uky.edu.

University of La Verne, College of Education and Organizational Leadership, Department of Organizational Leadership, Doctoral Program in Organizational Leadership, La Verne, CA 91750-4443. Offers Ed D. Part-time programs available. *Faculty:* 14 full-time (8 women), 9 part-time/adjunct (8 women). *Students:* 155 full-time (108 women), 146 part-time (91 women); includes 90 minority (38 African Americans, 2 American Indian/Alaska Native, 9 Asian Americans or Pacific Islanders, 41 Hispanic Americans). Average age 45. In 2006, 46 degrees awarded. *Degree requirements:* For doctorate, thesis/dissertation. *Entrance requirements:* For doctorate, GRE or MAT, minimum graduate GPA of 3.0, resumé, 2 endorsement forms. Additional exam requirements/recommendations for international students: Required—TOEFL (minimum score 550 paper-based; 213 computer-based). *Application deadline:* Applications are processed on a rolling basis. Application fee: $75. *Expenses:* Contact institution. *Financial support:* Institutionally sponsored loans available. Financial award application deadline: 3/2; financial award applicants required to submit FAFSA. *Application contact:* Jo Nell Baker, Director, Graduate Admissions and Academic Services, 909-593-3511 Ext. 4244, Fax: 909-392-2761, E-mail: gradadmt@ulv.edu.

University of La Verne, College of Education and Organizational Leadership, Department of Organizational Leadership, Program in Educational Management, La Verne, CA 91750-4443. Offers educational management (M Ed); preliminary administrative services (Credential); professional administrative services (Credential). *Faculty:* 14 full-time (8 women), 9 part-time/adjunct (8 women). *Students:* 3 full-time (2 women), 32 part-time (18 women); includes 13 minority (1 African American, 3 Asian Americans or Pacific Islanders, 9 Hispanic Americans), 1 international. Average age 40. In 2006, 12 degrees awarded. *Entrance requirements:* For master's, California Basic Educational Skills Test, 2 years experience in teaching, pupil personnel services, health, or librarian services; California teaching credential. Additional exam requirements/recommendations for international students: Required—TOEFL (minimum score 550 paper-based; 213 computer-based). *Application deadline:* Applications are processed on a rolling basis. Application fee: $50. *Expenses:* Contact institution. *Financial support:* Institutionally sponsored loans available. Financial award application deadline: 3/2; financial award applicants required to submit FAFSA. *Application contact:* Jo Nell Baker, Director, Graduate Admissions and Academic Services, 909-593-3511 Ext. 4244, Fax: 909-392-2761, E-mail: gradadmt@ulv.edu.

University of La Verne, Regional Campus Administration, Master's Programs in Education, California Statewide Campus, La Verne, CA 91750-4443. Offers advanced teaching (M Ed); educational management (M Ed), including preliminary administrative services credential; reading (M Ed); school counseling (MS), including public personnel services credential. *Faculty:* 3 full-time (0 women), 60 part-time/adjunct (38 women). *Students:* 203 full-time (151 women), 268 part-time (210 women); includes 216 minority (42 African Americans, 5 American Indian/Alaska Native, 27 Asian Americans or Pacific Islanders, 142 Hispanic Americans). Average age 36. In 2006, 289 degrees awarded. *Entrance requirements:* For master's, California Basic Educational Skills Test, 3 letters of recommendation, teaching credential. *Application deadline:* Applications are processed on a rolling basis. Application fee: $50. *Expenses:* Contact institution. *Financial support:* Fellowships, institutionally sponsored loans available. Financial award application deadline: 3/2; financial award applicants required to submit FAFSA. *Unit head:* Juline Behrens, Director, 909-985-0944, Fax: 909-981-8695, E-mail: behrensj@ulv.edu.

University of Lethbridge, School of Graduate Studies, Lethbridge, AB T1K 3M4, Canada. Offers accounting (MScM); addictions counseling (M Sc); agricultural biotechnology (M Sc); agricultural studies (M Sc, MA); anthropology (MA); archaeology (MA); art (MA); biochemistry (M Sc); biological sciences (M Sc); biomolecular science (PhD); biosystems and biodiversity (PhD); Canadian studies (MA); chemistry (M Sc); computer science (M Sc); computer science and geographical information science (M Sc); counseling psychology (M Ed); dramatic arts (MA); earth, space, and physical science (PhD); economics (MA); educational leadership (M Ed); English (MA); environmental science (M Sc); evolution and behavior (PhD); exercise science (M Sc); finance (MScM); French (MA); French/German (MA); French/Spanish (MA); general education (M Ed); general management (MScM); geography (M Sc, MA); German (MA); health sciences (M Sc, MA); history (MA); human resource management and labour relations (MScM); individualized multidisciplinary (M Sc, MA); information systems (MScM); international management (MScM); kinesiology (M Sc, MA); management (M Sc, MA); marketing (MScM); mathematics (M Sc); music (MA); Native American studies (MA); neuroscience (M Sc, PhD); new media (MA); nursing (M Sc); philosophy (MA); physics (M Sc); policy and strategy (MScM); political science (MA); psychology (M Sc, MA); religious studies (MA); sociology (MA); theoretical and computational science (PhD); urban and regional studies (MA). Part-time and evening/weekend programs available. *Students:* 200 full-time, 90 part-time. In 2006, 105 master's, 3 doctorates awarded. *Degree requirements:* For doctorate, thesis/dissertation, comprehensive exam. *Entrance requirements:* For master's, GMAT (M Sc management), bachelor's degree in related field, minimum GPA of 3.0 during previous 20 graded semester courses, 2 years teaching or related experience (M Ed); for doctorate, master's degree, minimum graduate GPA of 3.5. Additional exam requirements/recommendations for international students: Required—TOEFL. Application fee: $60 Canadian dollars. *Financial support:* Fellowships, research assistantships, teaching assistantships, scholarships/grants, health care benefits, and unspecified assistantships available. *Faculty research:* Movement and brain plasticity, gibberellin physiology, photosynthesis, carbon cycling, molecular properties of main-group ring components. *Unit head:* Dr. Jo-Anne Fiske, Interim Dean, 403-329-2121, Fax: 403-329-2097. *Application contact:* Kathy Schrage, Administrative Assistant, Office of the Academic Vice President, 403-329-2121, Fax: 403-329-2097, E-mail: inquiries@uleth.ca.

University of Louisiana at Lafayette, Graduate School, College of Education, Graduate Studies and Research in Education, Program in Administration and Supervision, Lafayette, LA 70504. Offers M Ed. *Faculty:* 9 full-time (3 women). *Students:* 6 full-time (all women), 19 part-time (14 women); includes 3 minority (all African Americans) Average age 36. 2 applicants, 50% accepted, 1 enrolled. In 2006, 27 degrees awarded. *Degree requirements:* For master's, thesis or alternative. *Entrance requirements:* For master's, GRE General Test, teaching certificate. Additional exam requirements/recommendations for international students: Required—TOEFL (minimum score 550 paper-based; 213 computer-based). *Application deadline:* For fall admission, 5/15 for domestic and international students; for spring admission, 10/1 for domestic and international students. Applications are processed on a rolling basis. Application fee: $25 ($30 for international students). Electronic applications accepted. *Expenses:* Tuition, state resident: full-time $3,247; part-time $93 per credit hour. Tuition, nonresident: full-time $9,427; part-time $350 per credit hour. *Financial support:* Federal Work-Study available. Financial award application deadline: 5/1. *Unit head:* Dr. Paula Montgomery, Head, 337-482-6680, Fax: 337-482-5262, E-mail: pmontgomery@louisiana.edu. *Application contact:* Dr. Nathan Roberts, Coordinator, 337-482-6747, Fax: 337-482-5842, E-mail: nmr0713@louisiana.edu.

University of Louisiana at Lafayette, Graduate School, College of Education, Graduate Studies and Research in Education, Program in Educational Leadership, Lafayette, LA 70504. Offers M Ed, Ed D. *Faculty:* 9 full-time (3 women). *Students:* 1 (woman) full-time, 35 part-time (24 women); includes 6 African Americans, 1 American Indian/Alaska Native, 1 Hispanic American. Average age 40. 18 applicants, 56% accepted, 8 enrolled. *Entrance requirements:* Additional exam requirements/recommendations for international students: Required—TOEFL (minimum score 550 paper-based; 213 computer-based). *Application deadline:* For fall admission, 5/15 for domestic and international students; for spring admission, 10/1 for domestic and international students. Application fee: $25 ($30 for international students). *Expenses:* Tuition, state resident: full-time $3,247; part-time $93 per credit hour. Tuition, nonresident: full-time $9,427; part-time $350 per credit hour. *Unit head:* Dr. Paula Montgomery, Head, 337-482-6680, Fax: 337-482-5262, E-mail: pmontgomery@louisiana.edu. *Application contact:* Dr. Nathan Roberts, Coordinator, 337-482-6747, Fax: 337-482-5842, E-mail: nmr0713@louisiana.edu.

University of Louisiana at Monroe, Graduate Studies and Research, College of Education and Human Development, Department of Educational Leadership and Counseling, Program in Administration and Supervision, Monroe, LA 71209-0001. Offers M Ed. *Accreditation:* NCATE. Part-time and evening/weekend programs available. *Students:* 6 full-time (5 women), 30 part-time (22 women); includes 11 minority (10 African Americans, 1 Hispanic American), 1 international. Average age 37. In 2006, 15 degrees awarded. *Degree requirements:* For master's, comprehensive exam. *Entrance requirements:* For master's, GRE General Test, minimum undergraduate GPA of 2.5. *Application deadline:* For fall admission, 6/1 priority date for domestic students; for spring admission, 11/1 for domestic students. Applications are processed on a rolling basis. Application fee: $20 ($30 for international students). *Expenses:* Tuition, state resident: part-time $124 per credit hour. Tuition, nonresident: part-time $124 per credit hour. *Financial support:* Research assistantships, teaching assistantships, career-related internships or fieldwork and unspecified assistantships available. Financial award application deadline: 7/1. *Faculty research:* School facilities utilization.

University of Louisiana at Monroe, Graduate Studies and Research, College of Education and Human Development, Department of Educational Leadership and Counseling, Program in Educational Leadership, Monroe, LA 71209-0001. Offers Ed D. *Accreditation:* NCATE. *Students:* Average age 40. *Degree requirements:* For doctorate, thesis/dissertation. *Entrance requirements:* For doctorate, GRE General Test. *Application deadline:* For fall admission, 6/1 priority date for domestic students; for spring admission, 11/1 for domestic students. Applications are processed on a rolling basis. Application fee: $20 ($30 for international students). *Expenses:* Tuition, state resident: part-time $124 per credit hour. Tuition, nonresident: part-time $124 per credit hour. *Financial support:* Research assistantships, teaching assistantships, career-related internships or fieldwork available. Financial award application deadline: 7/1. *Unit head:* Dr. Bob Cage, Director, 318-342-1288, Fax: 318-342-3131, E-mail: cage@ulm.edu.

University of Louisville, Graduate School, College of Education and Human Development, Department of Leadership, Foundations and Human Resource Education, Program in Educational Leadership and Organizational Development, Louisville, KY 40292-0001. Offers PhD. *Students:* 33 full-time (14 women), 97 part-time (55 women); includes 19 minority (13 African Americans, 3 Asian Americans or Pacific Islanders, 3 Hispanic Americans), 10 international. Average age 41. In 2006, 17 degrees awarded. *Unit head:* Dr. Paul Winter, Program Head, 502-852-0617, Fax: 502-852-4563, E-mail: winter@louisville.edu.

University of Louisville, Graduate School, College of Education and Human Development, Department of Leadership, Foundations and Human Resource Education, Program in P-12 Educational Administration, Louisville, KY 40292-0001. Offers M Ed, PhD, Ed S. *Students:* 5 full-time (all women), 46 part-time (26 women); includes 5 minority (4 African Americans, 1 Asian American or Pacific Islander), 5 international. Average age 39. In 2006, 4 master's, 1 doctorate, 8 other advanced degrees awarded. Application fee: $50. *Unit head:* Dr. Freda Merriweather, Director, 502-852-0635, Fax: 502-852-4563, E-mail: f.merriweather@louisville.edu.

University of Maine, Graduate School, College of Education and Human Development, Program in Educational Leadership, Orono, ME 04469. Offers M Ed, Ed D, CAS. *Accreditation:* NCATE. Part-time and evening/weekend programs available. *Students:* 22 full-time (12 women), 117 part-time (59 women); includes 2 minority (1 American Indian/Alaska Native, 1 Hispanic American). Average age 41. 58 applicants, 91% accepted, 48 enrolled. In 2006, 18 master's, 4 doctorates, 14 other advanced degrees awarded. *Degree requirements:* For master's, thesis or alternative; for doctorate, thesis/dissertation. *Entrance requirements:* For master's, MAT; for doctorate, GRE General Test, MA, M Ed, or MS; for CAS, MA, M Ed, or MS. Additional exam requirements/recommendations for international students: Required—TOEFL. *Application deadline:* For fall admission, 2/1 priority date for domestic students. Applications are processed on a rolling basis. Application fee: $50. Electronic applications accepted. *Financial support:* In 2006–07, teaching assistantships with tuition reimbursements (averaging $9,010 per year); research assistantships with tuition reimbursements, career-related internships or fieldwork, Federal Work-Study, institutionally sponsored loans, tuition waivers (full and partial), and unspecified assistantships also available. Support available to part-time students. Financial award application deadline: 3/1. *Unit head:* Dr. Dorothy Breen, Coordinator, 207-581-2444, Fax: 207-581-2423. *Application contact:* Scott G. Delcourt, Associate Dean of the Graduate School, 207-581-3219, Fax: 207-581-3232, E-mail: graduate@maine.edu.

University of Manitoba, Faculty of Graduate Studies, Faculty of Education, Department of Educational Administration, Foundations and Psychology, Winnipeg, MB R3T 2N2, Canada. Offers adult education (M Ed); educational administration (M Ed); guidance and counseling (M Ed); inclusive special education (M Ed); special foundations education (M Ed). *Degree requirements:* For master's, thesis or alternative.

University of Mary, Program in Education, Bismarck, ND 58504-9652. Offers college teaching (MS Ed); curriculum and instruction (MS Ed); early childhood education (MS Ed); early childhood special education (MS Ed); elementary education administration (MS Ed); reading (MS Ed); secondary education administration (MS Ed); special education (MS Ed). Part-time programs available. *Faculty:* 8 full-time (4 women), 12 part-time/adjunct (7 women). *Students:* 2 full-time (1 woman), 34 part-time (25 women), 2 international. Average age 35. In 2006, 17 degrees awarded. *Degree requirements:* For master's, portfolio or thesis. *Entrance requirements:* For master's, interview, letters of reference. *Application deadline:* Applications are processed on a rolling basis. Application fee: $40. *Financial support:* In 2006–07, 1 teaching assistantship with full tuition reimbursement was awarded; career-related internships or fieldwork also available. Support available to part-time students. Financial award application deadline: 8/1; financial award applicants required to submit FAFSA. *Faculty research:* Innovative pedagogy in higher education, technology in education, content standards, children of poverty, children with diverse learning needs. *Unit head:* Dr. Rebecca Yunker Salveson, Director, 701-355-8186, E-mail: rysalves@umary.edu. *Application contact:* Leona Friedig, Administrative Secretary, 701-355-8058, E-mail: lfriedig@umary.edu.

University of Mary Hardin-Baylor, College of Education, Belton, TX 76513. Offers educational administration (M Ed, Ed D); educational psychology (M Ed); exercise and sport science (M Ed); general studies (M Ed); reading education (M Ed). Part-time and evening/weekend programs available. *Faculty:* 10 full-time (5 women), 1 part-time/adjunct (0 women). *Students:* 8 full-time (3 women), 36 part-time (26 women); includes 8 minority (3 African Americans, 5 Hispanic Americans). Average age 24. In 2006, 18 degrees awarded. *Degree requirements:* For master's, comprehensive exam, registration. *Entrance requirements:* For master's, GRE General Test, minimum GPA of 2.75, Texas teaching certificate. *Application deadline:* For fall admission, 6/1 priority date for domestic students; for spring admission, 11/1 for domestic students. Applications are processed on a rolling basis. Application fee: $35 ($135 for international students). Electronic applications accepted. *Expenses:* Tuition: Full-time $8,910; part-time $495 per hour. Required fees: $906; $47 per hour. $30 per term. Tuition and fees vary according to course load. *Financial support:* Federal Work-Study, scholarships/grants, and scholarships (for some active duty military personnel only) available. Support available to part-time students. Financial award application deadline: 6/1; financial award applicants required to submit FAFSA. *Unit head:* Dr. Marlene Zipperlen, Dean, 254-295-4572, Fax: 254-295-4480, E-mail: mzipperlen@umhb.edu. *Application contact:* Dr. Shirley Dahl, Director, Graduate Programs in Education, 254-295-4185, Fax: 254-295-4480, E-mail: sdahl@umhb.edu.

University of Maryland, College Park, Graduate Studies, College of Education, Department of Counseling and Personnel Services, College Park, MD 20742. Offers college student personnel (M Ed, MA); college student personnel administration (PhD); community counseling (CAGS); community/career counseling (M Ed, MA); counseling and personnel services (M Ed, MA, PhD); counseling psychology (PhD); counselor education (PhD); rehabilitation counseling (M Ed, MA); school counseling (M Ed, MA); school psychology (M Ed, MA, PhD). *Accreditation:* ACA (one or more programs are accredited); APA (one or more programs are accredited); CORE (one or more programs are accredited); NCATE. Part-time and evening/weekend programs available. Postbaccalaureate distance learning degree programs offered (no on-campus study). *Faculty:* 41 full-time (26 women), 6 part-time/adjunct (5 women). *Students:* 169 full-time (124 women), 21 part-time (15 women); includes 76 minority (42 African Americans, 1 American Indian/Alaska Native, 14 Asian Americans or Pacific Islanders, 19 Hispanic Americans), 11 international. 382 applicants, 15% accepted, 31 enrolled. In 2006, 57 master's, 13 doctorates, 10 other advanced degrees awarded. *Degree requirements:* For master's, thesis (for some programs); for doctorate, thesis/dissertation. *Entrance requirements:* For master's, GRE General Test or MAT, minimum GPA of 3.0, 3 letters of recommendation; for doctorate, GRE General Test or MAT, minimum GPA of 3.5, 3 letters of recommendation. Additional exam requirements/recommendations for international students: Required—TOEFL. *Application deadline:* For fall admission, 3/1 for domestic students, 2/1 for international students; for spring admission, 9/1 for domestic students, 6/1 for international students. Applications are processed on a rolling basis. Application fee: $60. Electronic applications accepted. *Financial support:* In 2006–07, 11 fellowships with full tuition reimbursements (averaging $8,799 per year), 14 research assistantships (averaging $12,849 per year), 100 teaching assistantships with tuition reimbursements (averaging $14,265 per year) were awarded; career-related internships or fieldwork, Federal Work-Study, and scholarships/grants also available. Support available to part-time students. Financial award applicants required to submit FAFSA. *Faculty research:* Educational psychology, counseling, health. Total annual research expenditures: $2.1 million. *Unit head:* Dr. Ruth Fassingel, Dean, 301-405-2860, Fax: 301-405-9995, E-mail: rfassing@umd.edu. *Application contact:* Dean of Graduate School, 301-405-0358, Fax: 301-314-9305.

University of Maryland, College Park, Graduate Studies, College of Education, Department of Education Policy and Leadership, College Park, MD 20742. Offers curriculum and educational communications (M Ed, MA, Ed D, PhD); social foundations of education (M Ed, MA, Ed D, PhD, CAGS). *Accreditation:* NCATE. Part-time and evening/weekend programs available. Postbaccalaureate distance learning degree programs offered (minimal on-campus study). *Faculty:* 17 full-time (11 women), 6 part-time/adjunct (4 women). *Students:* 180 full-time (127 women), 145 part-time (105 women); includes 107 minority (69 African Americans, 1 American Indian/Alaska Native, 20 Asian Americans or Pacific Islanders, 17 Hispanic Americans), 23 international. 167 applicants, 40% accepted, 25 enrolled. In 2006, 37 master's, 15 doctorates, 1 other advanced degree awarded. *Degree requirements:* For master's, thesis or alternative, internship and/or field experience; for doctorate, thesis/dissertation, practicum or internship, comprehensive exam. *Entrance requirements:* For master's, GRE General Test or MAT, minimum GPA of 3.0, scholarly writing sample, 3 letters of recommendation; for doctorate, GRE General Test or MAT, scholarly writing sample, minimum undergraduate GPA of 3.0, minimum graduate GPA of 3.5. *Application deadline:* For fall admission, 2/1 for domestic and international students; for spring admission, 9/1 for domestic students, 6/1 for international students. Applications are processed on a rolling basis. Application fee: $60. Electronic applications accepted. *Financial support:* In 2006–07, 6 fellowships with full tuition reimbursements (averaging $13,118 per year), 2 research assistantships with tuition reimbursements (averaging $15,252 per year), 47 teaching assistantships with tuition reimbursements (averaging $14,510 per year) were awarded; career-related internships or fieldwork, Federal Work-Study, and scholarships/grants also available. Support available to part-time students. Financial award applicants required to submit FAFSA. *Faculty research:* Educational technology, adult and higher education. Total annual research expenditures: $314,050. *Unit head:* Dr. Thomas Weible, Acting Chair, 301-405-3589, Fax: 301-405-3573, E-mail: tweible@umd.edu. *Application contact:* Dean of Graduate School, 301-405-4190, Fax: 301-314-9305.

University of Maryland Eastern Shore, Graduate Programs, Department of Education, Program in Education Leadership, Princess Anne, MD 21853-1299. Offers Ed D. Evening/weekend programs available. *Faculty:* 8 part-time/adjunct (1 woman). *Students:* 9 full-time (5 women), 20 part-time (15 women); includes 10 minority (all African Americans) Average age 43. In 2006, 1 degree awarded. *Degree requirements:* For doctorate, thesis/dissertation, internship, comprehensive exam. *Entrance requirements:* For doctorate, interview, writing sample, state certification in a standard area, 3 years recent teaching or successful professional experience in a k-12 school setting. Additional exam requirements/recommendations for international students: Required—TOEFL (minimum score 213 computer-based; 79 iBT). *Application deadline:* For fall admission, 4/1 for domestic and international students. Applications are processed on a rolling basis. Application fee: $30. Electronic applications accepted. *Financial support:* Application deadline: 3/1. *Unit head:* Dr. Harry Hoffer, Director, 410-651-8361, Fax: 410-651-8414, E-mail: hehoffer@umes.edu.

University of Massachusetts Amherst, Graduate School, School of Education, Program in Education, Amherst, MA 01003. Offers cultural diversity and curriculum reform (M Ed, Ed D, CAGS); early childhood education and development (M Ed, Ed D, CAGS); educational administration (M Ed, Ed D, CAGS); elementary teacher education (M Ed, Ed D, CAGS); higher education (M Ed, Ed D, CAGS); international education (M Ed, Ed D, CAGS); mathematics, science, and instructional technology (M Ed, Ed D, CAGS); physical education teacher education (M Ed, Ed D, CAGS); reading and writing (M Ed, Ed D, CAGS); research and evaluation methods (M Ed, Ed D, CAGS); school psychology and school counseling (M Ed, Ed D, CAGS); secondary teacher education (M Ed, Ed D, CAGS); social justice education (M Ed, Ed D, CAGS); special education (M Ed, Ed D, CAGS). *Accreditation:* NCATE. *Students:* 418 full-time (286 women), 447 part-time (319 women); includes 147 minority (70 African Americans, 4 American Indian/Alaska Native, 28 Asian Americans or Pacific Islanders, 45 Hispanic Americans), 81 international. Average age 36. In 2006, 260 master's, 30 doctorates awarded. *Degree requirements:* For doctorate, thesis/dissertation. *Entrance requirements:* For master's and doctorate, GRE General Test. Additional exam requirements/recommendations for international students: Required—TOEFL (minimum score 530 paper-based; 197 computer-based). *Application deadline:* For fall admission, 1/15 for domestic and international students; for spring admission, 10/1 for domestic and international students. Applications are processed on a rolling basis. Application fee: $40 ($65 for international students). Electronic applications accepted. *Expenses:* Tuition, state resident: full-time $2,640; part-time $110 per credit. Tuition, nonresident: full-time $9,936; part-time $414 per credit. Required fees: $8,969; $3,129 per term. One-time fee: $257 full-time. Tuition and fees vary according to class time, course load, campus/location and reciprocity agreements. *Financial support:* Fellowships with full tuition reimbursements, research assistantships with full tuition reimbursements, teaching assistantships with full tuition reimbursements, career-related internships or fieldwork, Federal Work-Study, scholarships/grants, traineeships, and unspecified assistantships available. Support available to part-time students. Financial award application deadline: 1/15. *Unit head:* Linda L. Griffin, Professor, 413-545-6984.

University of Massachusetts Boston, Office of Graduate Studies, Graduate College of Education, School Organization, Curriculum and Instruction Department, Program in Educational Administration, Boston, MA 02125-3393. Offers M Ed, CAGS. Part-time and evening/weekend programs available. *Students:* Average age 34. 31 applicants, 68% accepted, 19 enrolled. In 2006, 9 master's, 6 other advanced degrees awarded. *Median time to degree:* Master's–3 years full-time. *Degree requirements:* For master's, practicum. *Entrance requirements:* For master's, GRE General Test or MAT, 2 years of teaching experience, minimum GPA of 2.75; for CAGS, minimum GPA of 2.75. *Application deadline:* For fall admission, 3/1 priority date for domestic students; for spring admission, 11/1 for domestic students. Application fee: $25 ($40 for international students). *Expenses:* Tuition, state resident: full-time $2,590; part-time $301 per credit. Tuition, nonresident: full-time $9,758; part-time $427 per credit. One-time fee: $495 full-time. *Financial support:* In 2006–07, 1 research assistantship with full tuition reimbursement (averaging $13,000 per year) was awarded; teaching assistantships with full tuition reimbursements, career-related internships or fieldwork, Federal Work-Study, and unspecified assistantships also available. Support available to part-time students. Financial award application deadline: 3/1; financial award applicants required to submit FAFSA. *Faculty research:* Power in the classroom, teacher leadership, professional development schools. *Unit head:* Dr. Joseph Check, Director, 617-287-7655, E-mail: joseph.check@umb.edu. *Application contact:* Peggy Roldan, Graduate Admissions Coordinator, 617-287-6400, Fax: 617-287-6236, E-mail: bos.gadm@dpc.umassp.edu.

University of Massachusetts Boston, Office of Graduate Studies, Graduate College of Education, School Organization, Curriculum and Instruction Department, Program in Education, Track in Higher Education Administration, Boston, MA 02125-3393. Offers Ed D. *Accreditation:* NCATE. Part-time and evening/weekend programs available. *Students:* 2 full-time (both women), 107 part-time (77 women); includes 29 minority (15 African Americans, 4 Asian Americans or Pacific Islanders, 10 Hispanic Americans), 1 international. Average age 48. 26 applicants, 42% accepted, 9 enrolled. In 2006, 2 degrees awarded. *Median time to degree:* Doctorate–12 years full-time. *Degree requirements:* For doctorate, thesis/dissertation, comprehensive exam. *Entrance requirements:* For doctorate, GRE General Test or MAT, minimum GPA of 2.75. *Application deadline:* For fall admission, 3/1 for domestic students. Application fee: $25 ($40 for international students). *Expenses:* Tuition, state resident: full-time $2,590; part-time $301 per credit. Tuition, nonresident: full-time $9,758; part-time $427 per credit. One-time fee: $495 full-time. *Financial support:* In 2006–07, research assistantships with full tuition reimbursements (averaging $13,000 per year); teaching assistantships, career-related internships or fieldwork, Federal Work-Study, and unspecified assistantships also available. Support available to part-time students. Financial award application deadline: 3/1; financial award applicants required to submit FAFSA. *Faculty research:* Women, higher education and professionalization, school reform, urban classroom, higher education policy. *Unit head:* Dr. Dwight Giles, Coordinator, 617-287-7621, E-mail: dwight.giles@umb.edu. *Application contact:* Peggy Roldan, Graduate Admissions Coordinator, 617-287-6400, Fax: 617-287-6236, E-mail: bos.gadm@dpc.umassp.edu.

University of Massachusetts Boston, Office of Graduate Studies, Graduate College of Education, School Organization, Curriculum and Instruction Department, Program in Education, Track in Urban School Leadership, Boston, MA 02125-3393. Offers Ed D. *Accreditation:* NCATE. Part-time and evening/weekend programs available. *Students:* 2 full-time (both women),

Educational Administration

University of Massachusetts Boston (continued)
46 part-time (32 women); includes 22 minority (12 African Americans, 1 American Indian/Alaska Native, 3 Asian Americans or Pacific Islanders, 6 Hispanic Americans), 1 international. Average age 41. 26 applicants, 46% accepted, 8 enrolled. In 2006, 5 degrees awarded. *Median time to degree:* Doctorate–8 years full-time. *Degree requirements:* For doctorate, thesis/dissertation, comprehensive exam. *Entrance requirements:* For doctorate, GRE General Test or MAT, minimum GPA of 2.75. *Application deadline:* For fall admission, 3/1 for domestic students. Application fee: $25 ($40 for international students). *Expenses:* Tuition, state resident: full-time $2,590; part-time $301 per credit. Tuition, nonresident: full-time $9,758; part-time $427 per credit. One-time fee: $495 full-time. *Financial support:* In 2006–07, 4 research assistantships with full tuition reimbursements (averaging $13,000 per year) were awarded; teaching assistantships with full tuition reimbursements, career-related internships or fieldwork, Federal Work-Study, and unspecified assistantships also available. Support available to part-time students. Financial award application deadline: 3/1; financial award applicants required to submit FAFSA. *Faculty research:* School reform, race and culture in schools, race and higher education, language, literacy and writing. *Unit head:* Dr. Joseph Check, Director, 617-287-7655, E-mail: joseph.check@umb.edu. *Application contact:* Peggy Roldan, Graduate Admissions Coordinator, 617-287-6400, Fax: 617-287-6236, E-mail: bos.gadm@dpc.umassp.edu.

University of Massachusetts Lowell, Graduate School, Graduate School of Education, Lowell, MA 01854-2881. Offers administration, planning, and policy (CAGS); curriculum and instruction (M Ed, CAGS); educational administration (M Ed); language arts and literacy (Ed D); leadership in schooling (Ed D); math and science education (Ed D); reading and language (M Ed, CAGS). *Accreditation:* NCATE. Part-time and evening/weekend programs available. Postbaccalaureate distance learning degree programs offered (no on-campus study). Terminal master's awarded for partial completion of doctoral program. *Degree requirements:* For doctorate, thesis/dissertation. *Entrance requirements:* For master's and doctorate, GRE General Test. Additional exam requirements/recommendations for international students: Required—TOEFL. Electronic applications accepted.

University of Memphis, Graduate School, College of Education, Department of Counseling, Educational Psychology and Research, Memphis, TN 38152. Offers counseling and personnel services (MS, Ed D), including community agency counseling (MS), rehabilitation counseling (MS), school counseling (MS), student personnel services (MS); counseling psychology (PhD); educational psychology and research (MS, Ed D, PhD), including educational psychology (MS, Ed D), educational research (MS, Ed D). *Accreditation:* ACA (one or more programs are accredited); APA (one or more programs are accredited); CORE (one or more programs are accredited); NCATE. *Degree requirements:* For master's, thesis or alternative, comprehensive exam; for doctorate, thesis/dissertation, comprehensive exam. *Entrance requirements:* For master's, GRE General Test or MAT, minimum GPA of 2.5; for doctorate, GRE General Test. *Faculty research:* Anger management, aging and disability, supervision, multicultural counseling.

University of Memphis, Graduate School, College of Education, Department of Leadership, Memphis, TN 38152. Offers adult education (Ed D); community education (Ed D); education (Ed S); educational leadership (Ed D); higher education (Ed D); leadership (MS); policy studies (Ed D); school administration and supervision (MS). *Accreditation:* NCATE. *Degree requirements:* For master's, thesis optional; for doctorate, thesis/dissertation, comprehensive exam; for Ed S, thesis or alternative, comprehensive exam. *Entrance requirements:* For master's, GRE General Test or MAT; for doctorate, GRE General Test, GRE Subject Test, 3 years of teaching experience; for Ed S, GRE General Test. *Faculty research:* Organizational learning, gender issues, leadership, technology and learning, principal preparation.

University of Miami, Graduate School, School of Education, Department of Educational and Psychological Studies, Program in Higher Education Administration, Coral Gables, FL 33124. Offers higher education administration (MS Ed), including enrollment management, student life and development; higher education administration/enrollment management (Certificate). *Accreditation:* NCATE. *Students:* 5 full-time (4 women), 11 part-time (10 women); includes 9 minority (4 African Americans, 1 Asian American or Pacific Islander, 4 Hispanic Americans). Average age 33. 8 applicants, 100% accepted, 5 enrolled. In 2006, 2 degrees awarded. *Entrance requirements:* For master's, GRE General Test. Additional exam requirements/recommendations for international students: Required—TOEFL (minimum score 550 paper-based; 212 computer-based). *Application deadline:* Applications are processed on a rolling basis. Application fee: $50. Electronic applications accepted. *Financial support:* In 2006–07, 16 students received support; fellowships with partial tuition reimbursements available, research assistantships with partial tuition reimbursements available, career-related internships or fieldwork, Federal Work-Study, institutionally sponsored loans, scholarships/grants, and unspecified assistantships available. Financial award application deadline: 3/1; financial award applicants required to submit FAFSA. *Unit head:* Dr. Carol Anne Phekoo, Coordinator, 305-284-5013, Fax: 305-284-3003, E-mail: cphekoo@miami.edu. *Application contact:* Shelley Lue Foung, Senior Administrative Assistant, 305-284-3001, Fax: 305-284-3003, E-mail: sluefoung@miami.edu.

University of Michigan, Horace H. Rackham School of Graduate Studies, School of Education, Center for the Study of Higher and Postsecondary Education, Ann Arbor, MI 48109. Offers academic affairs and student development (PhD); education (AM); higher education (AM); individually designed concentration (PhD); organizational behavior and management (PhD); public policy (PhD); research, evaluation, and assessment (PhD); MBA/MA; MPP/MA. *Students:* 674 applicants, 41% accepted, 175 enrolled. In 2006, 134 master's, 43 doctorates awarded. Terminal master's awarded for partial completion of doctoral program. *Median time to degree:* Of those who began their doctoral program in fall 1998, 58% received their degree in 8 years or less. *Degree requirements:* For master's, thesis optional; for doctorate, thesis/dissertation, comprehensive exam. *Entrance requirements:* For master's and doctorate, GRE General Test. Additional exam requirements/recommendations for international students: Required—TOEFL (minimum score 600 paper-based; 250 computer-based). *Application deadline:* For fall admission, 12/1 priority date for domestic students, 12/1 for international students. Application fee: $60 ($75 for international students). Electronic applications accepted. *Financial support:* In 2006–07, 215 fellowships (averaging $5,852 per year), 109 research assistantships with full tuition reimbursements (averaging $14,695 per year), 32 teaching assistantships with full tuition reimbursements (averaging $14,756 per year) were awarded; career-related internships or fieldwork, Federal Work-Study, health care benefits, and tuition waivers also available. Support available to part-time students. Financial award applicants required to submit FAFSA. *Unit head:* Dr. Deborah Carter, Chairperson, 734-647-1981, Fax: 734-764-2510, E-mail: dfcarter@umich.edu. *Application contact:* Roberta Perry, Office of Student Services, 734-764-7563, Fax: 734-763-1495, E-mail: ed.grad.admit@umich.edu.

University of Michigan, Horace H. Rackham School of Graduate Studies, School of Education, Programs in Educational Studies, Ann Arbor, MI 48109. Offers curriculum development (MA); early childhood education (MA, PhD); educational administration and policy (MA, PhD); educational foundation, administration, policy, and research methods (MA); educational foundations and policy (MA, PhD); elementary education (MA-Certification); English education (MA); English language learning in school settings (MA); learning technologies (MA, PhD); literacy, language, and culture (MA, PhD); mathematics education (MA, PhD); research methods (MA); science education (MA, PhD); secondary education (MA-Certification); social studies education (MA); special education (PhD); teaching and teacher education (PhD); MA-Certification; MBA/MA; PhD/MA. Terminal master's awarded for partial completion of doctoral program. *Degree requirements:* For master's, thesis (for some programs); for doctorate, thesis/dissertation, comprehensive exam. *Entrance requirements:* For master's and doctorate, GRE General Test. Additional exam requirements/recommendations for international students: Required—TOEFL (minimum score 600 paper-based; 250 computer-based). *Application deadline:* For fall admission, 12/1 priority date for domestic students, 12/1 for international students. Application fee: $60 ($75 for international students). Electronic applications accepted. *Financial support:* Applicants required to submit FAFSA. *Unit head:* Dr. Addison Stone, Chairperson, 734-763-7500, Fax: 734-615-1290, E-mail: addison@umich.edu. *Application contact:* Roberta Perry, Office of Student Services, 734-764-7563, Fax: 734-763-1495, E-mail: ed.grad.admit@umich.edu.

University of Michigan–Dearborn, School of Education, Division of Public Administration, Dearborn, MI 48128-1491. Offers educational administration (Certificate), including assistant principalship, central office administration, principalship; nonprofit leadership (Certificate); public administration (MPA). Part-time and evening/weekend programs available. *Entrance requirements:* For master's, GRE or minimum undergraduate GPA of 3.0. Additional exam requirements/recommendations for international students: Required—TOEFL, TWE. Electronic applications accepted. *Faculty research:* Federal, state, and local agency management; independent sector management; educational administration.

University of Minnesota, Twin Cities Campus, Graduate School, College of Education and Human Development, Department of Educational Policy and Administration, Program in Educational Administration, Minneapolis, MN 55455-0213. Offers MA, Ed D, PhD. *Students:* 55 full-time (33 women), 187 part-time (110 women); includes 28 minority (9 African Americans, 10 American Indian/Alaska Native, 5 Asian Americans or Pacific Islanders, 4 Hispanic Americans), 7 international. Average age 42. 56 applicants, 73% accepted, 31 enrolled. In 2006, 12 master's, 29 doctorates awarded. *Expenses:* Tuition, state resident: full-time $9,302; part-time $775 per credit. Tuition, nonresident: full-time $16,400; part-time $1,367 per credit. Full-time tuition and fees vary according to class time, course load, program, reciprocity agreements and student level. *Application contact:* Dr. Mary Bents, Associate Dean, 612-625-6501, Fax: 612-626-1580, E-mail: mbents@tc.umn.edu.

University of Minnesota, Twin Cities Campus, Graduate School, College of Education and Human Development, Department of Work and Human Resource Education, Minneapolis, MN 55455-0213. Offers adult education (M Ed, MA, Ed D, PhD, Certificate); agricultural, food and environmental education (M Ed, MA, Ed D, PhD); business and industry education (M Ed, MA, Ed D, PhD); business education (M Ed); human resource development (M Ed, MA, Ed D, PhD, Certificate); marketing education (M Ed); postsecondary administration (Ed D); school-to-work (Certificate); technical education (Certificate); technology education (M Ed, MA); work and human resource education (M Ed, MA, Ed D, PhD); youth development leadership (M Ed). *Faculty:* 10 full-time (3 women). *Students:* 160 full-time (98 women), 215 part-time (143 women); includes 42 minority (24 African Americans, 2 American Indian/Alaska Native, 10 Asian Americans or Pacific Islanders, 6 Hispanic Americans), 56 international. Average age 38. 168 applicants, 80% accepted, 104 enrolled. In 2006, 79 master's, 23 doctorates, 50 other advanced degrees awarded. *Expenses:* Tuition, state resident: full-time $9,302; part-time $775 per credit. Tuition, nonresident: full-time $16,400; part-time $1,367 per credit. Full-time tuition and fees vary according to class time, course load, program, reciprocity agreements and student level. *Financial support:* In 2006–07, 9 research assistantships with full tuition reimbursements (averaging $24,775 per year), 16 teaching assistantships with full tuition reimbursements (averaging $24,775 per year) were awarded; fellowships also available. *Faculty research:* Assessment of career and technical education; adult education literacy; international human resource development; technology education; education and leadership related to agriculture, food, and the environment. Total annual research expenditures: $2.1 million. *Unit head:* Ken Bartlett, Chair, 612-624-4935, Fax: 612-624-2231. *Application contact:* Dr. Mary Bents, Associate Dean, 612-625-6501, Fax: 612-626-1580, E-mail: mbents@tc.umn.edu.

University of Mississippi, Graduate School, School of Education, Department of Educational Leadership and Counselor Education, Oxford, University, MS 38677. Offers counselor education (M Ed, PhD, Specialist); educational leadership (PhD); educational leadership and counselor education (M Ed, MA, Ed D, Ed S); higher education/student personnel (MA). *Accreditation:* ACA; NCATE. *Faculty:* 14 full-time (9 women), 4 part-time/adjunct (2 women). *Students:* 171 full-time (113 women), 158 part-time (110 women); includes 93 minority (88 African Americans, 2 Asian Americans or Pacific Islanders, 3 Hispanic Americans), 11 international. In 2006, 76 master's, 9 doctorates, 22 other advanced degrees awarded. *Degree requirements:* For doctorate, thesis/dissertation. *Entrance requirements:* For master's, GRE General Test, minimum GPA of 3.0; for doctorate, GRE General Test. Additional exam requirements/recommendations for international students: Required—TOEFL. *Application deadline:* For fall admission, 4/1 for domestic students; for spring admission, 10/1 for domestic students. Applications are processed on a rolling basis. Application fee: $25. Electronic applications accepted. *Expenses:* Tuition, state resident: full-time $4,602; part-time $256 per credit hour. Tuition, nonresident: full-time $10,566; part-time $587 per credit hour. *Financial support:* Scholarships/grants available. Financial award application deadline: 3/1; financial award applicants required to submit FAFSA. *Unit head:* Dr. Timothy Letzring, Acting Chair, 662-915-7069, E-mail: fdl@olemiss.edu.

University of Missouri–Columbia, Graduate School, College of Education, Department of Educational Leadership and Policy Analysis, Columbia, MO 65211. Offers education administration (M Ed, MA, Ed D, PhD, Ed S); higher and adult education (M Ed, MA, Ed D, PhD, Ed S). Part-time programs available. *Faculty:* 17 full-time (11 women). *Students:* 224 full-time (136 women), 133 part-time (86 women); includes 41 minority (25 African Americans, 5 American Indian/Alaska Native, 3 Asian Americans or Pacific Islanders, 8 Hispanic Americans), 16 international. In 2006, 27 master's, 31 doctorates, 9 other advanced degrees awarded. *Degree requirements:* For doctorate, variable foreign language requirement, thesis/dissertation. *Entrance requirements:* For master's, GRE General Test, minimum GPA of 3.0; for doctorate, GRE General Test, GRE Subject Test, minimum GPA of 3.5; for Ed S, GRE General Test, GRE Subject Test, minimum GPA of 3.25. *Application deadline:* For fall admission, 12/15 priority date for domestic students. Applications are processed on a rolling basis. Application fee: $45 ($60 for international students). *Financial support:* Fellowships, research assistantships, teaching assistantships, institutionally sponsored loans and scholarships/grants available. *Faculty research:* Administrative communication and behavior, middle schools leadership, administration of special education. *Unit head:* Dr. Margaret M. Grogan, Director of Graduate Studies, 573-882-8221, E-mail: groganm@missouri.edu.

University of Missouri–Kansas City, School of Education, Kansas City, MO 64110-2499. Offers administration (Ed D); counseling and guidance (MA, Ed S); counseling psychology (PhD); curriculum and instruction (MA, Ed S); education (PhD); educational administration (Ed S); reading education (MA, Ed S); special education (MA). *Accreditation:* NCATE. Part-time and evening/weekend programs available. *Faculty:* 59 full-time (46 women), 39 part-time/adjunct (29 women). *Students:* 182 full-time (151 women), 470 part-time (344 women); includes 148 minority (117 African Americans, 5 American Indian/Alaska Native, 8 Asian Americans or Pacific Islanders, 18 Hispanic Americans), 9 international. Average age 34. 560 applicants, 79% accepted, 253 enrolled. In 2006, 196 master's, 4 doctorates, 41 other advanced degrees awarded. *Degree requirements:* For doctorate, thesis/dissertation, internship, practicum. *Entrance requirements:* For master's, GRE, minimum GPA of 2.75, 2 letters of references, a written statement of purpose; for doctorate, GRE, minimum GPA of 3.0; for Ed S, minimum GPA of 3.0. Additional exam requirements/recommendations for international students: Required—TOEFL (minimum score 550 paper-based; 213 computer-based). *Application deadline:* For fall admission, 4/1 priority date for domestic students, 4/1 for international students; for winter admission, 10/1 priority date for domestic students, 10/1 for international students; for spring admission, 10/1 priority date for domestic students, 10/1 for international students. Applications are processed on a rolling basis. Application fee: $35 ($50 for international students). *Expenses:* Tuition, state resident: full-time $4,975; part-time $276 per credit. Tuition, nonresident: full-time $12,847; part-time $713 per credit. Required fees: $595; $595 per year. *Financial support:* In 2006–07, 361 students received support, including 13 research assistantships with partial tuition reimbursements available (averaging $10,560 per year); fellowships with full tuition reimbursements available, teaching assistantships, career-related internships or fieldwork, Federal Work-Study, institutionally sponsored loans, and tuition waivers (full and partial) also available. Support available to part-time students. Financial award application deadline: 3/1. *Faculty research:* Urban education, inquiry-based field study, theories of counseling and psychotherapy, school literacy, educational technology. Total annual research expenditures: $94,515. *Unit head:* Dr. Linda Edwards, Dean, 816-235-2236, Fax: 816-235-5270, E-mail: edwardsli@umkc.edu. *Application contact:* Dr. Lori Reesor, Assistant Dean, 816-235-1473, Fax: 816-235-5270, E-mail: reesorl@umkc.edu.

University of Missouri–St. Louis, College of Education, Division of Educational Leadership and Policy Studies, St. Louis, MO 63121. Offers adult and higher education (M Ed, Ed D); educational administration (M Ed, Ed D, Ed S), including community education (M Ed), elementary education (M Ed), secondary education (M Ed); educational leadership and policy studies (PhD); institutional research (Certificate). *Accreditation:* NCATE. *Faculty:* 15 full-time (8 women), 2 part-time/adjunct (0 women). *Students:* 37 full-time (27 women), 325 part-time (214 women); includes 130 minority (118 African Americans, 1 American Indian/Alaska Native, 4 Asian Americans or Pacific Islanders, 7 Hispanic Americans), 4 international. Average age 39. In 2006, 64 master's, 12 doctorates, 32 other advanced degrees awarded. *Entrance requirements:* For doctorate, GRE, 3 letters of recommendation. Additional exam requirements/recommendations for international students: Required—TOEFL (minimum score 550 paper-based; 213 computer-based). *Application deadline:* Applications are processed on a rolling basis. Application fee: $35 ($40 for international students). Electronic applications accepted. *Expenses:* Tuition, state resident: part-time $332 per credit hour. Tuition, nonresident: part-time $770 per credit hour. *Financial support:* In 2006–07, 6 research assistantships (averaging $8,235 per year) were awarded. *Faculty research:* Educational policy research; philosophy of education; higher, adult, and vocational education; school initiatives, change, and reform. *Unit head:* Dr. E. Paulette Savage, Chair, 514-516-5944. *Application contact:* 314-516-5458, Fax: 314-516-6996, E-mail: gradadm@umsl.edu.

The University of Montana, Graduate School, School of Education, Department of Educational Leadership and Counseling, Program in Educational Leadership, Missoula, MT 59812-0002. Offers M Ed, Ed D, Ed S. *Degree requirements:* For doctorate and Ed S, thesis/dissertation. *Entrance requirements:* For master's and Ed S, GRE General Test. Additional exam requirements/recommendations for international students: Required—TOEFL.

University of Montevallo, College of Education, Program in Educational Administration, Montevallo, AL 35115. Offers M Ed, Ed S. *Accreditation:* NCATE. Part-time and evening/weekend programs available. *Degree requirements:* For master's and Ed S, comprehensive exam. *Entrance requirements:* For master's, GRE General Test, MAT, minimum undergraduate GPA of 2.75 in last 60 hours or 2.5 overall; for Ed S, minimum GPA of 3.0. Additional exam requirements/recommendations for international students: Required—TOEFL (minimum score 550 paper-based).

University of Montevallo, College of Education, Program in Teacher Leader, Montevallo, AL 35115. Offers Ed S. Part-time programs available. *Entrance requirements:* For degree, minimum graduate GPA of 3.0.

University of Nebraska at Kearney, College of Graduate Study, College of Education, Department of Educational Administration, Kearney, NE 68849-0001. Offers educational administration (MA Ed, Ed S); supervisor (MA Ed). *Accreditation:* NCATE. Part-time and evening/weekend programs available. *Faculty:* 3 full-time (2 women). *Students:* 3 full-time (2 women), 104 part-time (26 women); includes 3 minority (all Hispanic Americans), 1 international. 18 applicants, 83% accepted. In 2006, 29 master's, 11 other advanced degrees awarded. *Degree requirements:* For master's, thesis optional; for Ed S, thesis. *Entrance requirements:* For master's, letters of recommendation, departmental application. Additional exam requirements/recommendations for international students: Required—TOEFL (minimum score 550 paper-based; 213 computer-based). *Application deadline:* For fall admission, 5/1 priority date for domestic students, 5/1 for international students; for spring admission, 8/15 priority date for domestic students, 8/1 for international students. Applications are processed on a rolling basis. Application fee: $45. Electronic applications accepted. *Expenses:* Tuition, state resident: part-time $161 per hour. Tuition, nonresident: part-time $332 per hour. Required fees: $57 per hour. *Financial support:* In 2006–07, 3 research assistantships with full tuition reimbursements (averaging $8,200 per year) were awarded; career-related internships or fieldwork and scholarships/grants also available. Support available to part-time students. Financial award application deadline: 3/1; financial award applicants required to submit FAFSA. *Faculty research:* Leadership and organizational behavior. *Unit head:* Dr. Patricia Hoehner, Chair, 308-865-8512, E-mail: hoehnerp@unk.edu.

University of Nebraska at Omaha, Graduate Studies and Research, College of Education, Department of Counseling, Omaha, NE 68182. Offers community counseling (MA, MS); counseling gerontology (MA, MS); school counseling-elementary (MA, MS); school counseling-secondary (MA, MS); student affairs practice in higher education (MA, MS). *Accreditation:* ACA (one or more programs are accredited); NCATE. Part-time and evening/weekend programs available. *Faculty:* 6 full-time (2 women). *Students:* 42 full-time (30 women), 114 part-time (98 women); includes 9 minority (6 African Americans, 2 Asian Americans or Pacific Islanders, 1 Hispanic American), 1 international. Average age 33. 55 applicants, 64% accepted, 23 enrolled. In 2006, 55 degrees awarded. *Degree requirements:* For master's, thesis (for some programs), comprehensive exam. *Entrance requirements:* For master's, GRE General Test, MAT, department test, interview, minimum GPA of 3.0. Additional exam requirements/recommendations for international students: Required—TOEFL (minimum score 550 paper-based; 213 computer-based; 80 iBT). *Application deadline:* For fall admission, 3/1 for domestic students; for spring admission, 10/1 for domestic students. Applications are processed on a rolling basis. Application fee: $45. Electronic applications accepted. *Financial support:* In 2006–07, 89 students received support, including 2 research assistantships with tuition reimbursements available; fellowships, Federal Work-Study, institutionally sponsored loans, scholarships/grants, tuition waivers (partial), and unspecified assistantships also available. Support available to part-time students. Financial award application deadline: 3/1; financial award applicants required to submit FAFSA. *Unit head:* Dr. Jeanette Seaberry, Chairperson, 402-554-2727.

University of Nebraska at Omaha, Graduate Studies and Research, College of Education, Department of Educational Administration and Supervision, Omaha, NE 68182. Offers MS, Ed D, Ed S. *Accreditation:* NCATE. Part-time and evening/weekend programs available. *Faculty:* 5 full-time (2 women). *Students:* 4 full-time (3 women), 146 part-time (81 women); includes 18 minority (13 African Americans, 2 Asian Americans or Pacific Islanders, 3 Hispanic Americans). Average age 38. 48 applicants, 48% accepted, 16 enrolled. In 2006, 45 master's, 6 doctorates, 3 other advanced degrees awarded. *Degree requirements:* For master's, thesis (for some programs), comprehensive exam; for doctorate and Ed S, thesis/dissertation, comprehensive exam. *Entrance requirements:* For master's, minimum GPA of 3.0; for doctorate, GRE General Test, resumé, 3 samples of research/written work, letters of recommendation. Additional exam requirements/recommendations for international students: Required—TOEFL (minimum score 500 paper-based; 173 computer-based; 61 iBT). *Application deadline:* For fall admission, 2/1 priority date for domestic students; for spring admission, 10/15 priority date for domestic students. Applications are processed on a rolling basis. Application fee: $45. Electronic applications accepted. *Financial support:* In 2006–07, 40 students received support; research assistantships with tuition reimbursements available, Federal Work-Study, institutionally sponsored loans, scholarships/grants, tuition waivers (partial), and unspecified assistantships available. Support available to part-time students. Financial award application deadline: 3/1. *Unit head:* Dr. John Hill, Chairperson, 402-554-2721.

University of Nebraska–Lincoln, Graduate College, College of Education and Human Services, Department of Educational Administration, Lincoln, NE 68588. Offers M Ed, MA, Ed D, Certificate. *Accreditation:* NCATE. *Degree requirements:* For master's, thesis optional; for doctorate, thesis/dissertation, comprehensive exam. *Entrance requirements:* For master's, GRE or MAT; for doctorate, GRE General Test, administrative certification. Additional exam requirements/recommendations for international students: Required—TOEFL (minimum score 550 paper-based; 213 computer-based). Electronic applications accepted. *Faculty research:* Educational policy, school finance, school law, school restructuring, leadership behavior.

University of Nebraska–Lincoln, Graduate College, College of Education and Human Services, Interdepartmental Area of Administration, Curriculum and Instruction, Lincoln, NE 68588. Offers Ed D, PhD, JD/PhD. *Accreditation:* NCATE. Postbaccalaureate distance learning degree programs offered. *Degree requirements:* For doctorate, thesis/dissertation, comprehensive exam. *Entrance requirements:* For doctorate, GRE, writing samples, curriculum vitae. Additional exam requirements/recommendations for international students: Required—TOEFL (minimum score 550 paper-based; 213 computer-based). Electronic applications accepted.

University of Nevada, Las Vegas, Graduate College, College of Education, Department of Curriculum and Instruction, Las Vegas, NV 89154-9900. Offers curriculum and instruction (Ed D, PhD, Ed S); elementary education (M Ed, MS); English education (M Ed, MS); library science (M Ed, MS); literacy education (M Ed, MS); mathematics education (M Ed, MS); multicultural education (M Ed, MS); reading specialist (M Ed, MS); secondary education (M Ed, MS); teacher leadership (M Ed, MS); teaching English as a second language (M Ed, MS); technology integration and leadership (M Ed, MS). *Accreditation:* NCATE. Part-time and evening/weekend programs available. *Faculty:* 40 full-time (19 women), 21 part-time/adjunct (14 women). *Students:* 257 full-time (189 women), 387 part-time (296 women); includes 114 minority (28 African Americans, 5 American Indian/Alaska Native, 34 Asian Americans or Pacific Islanders, 47 Hispanic Americans), 7 international. 261 applicants, 70% accepted, 168 enrolled. In 2006, 231 master's, 5 doctorates awarded. *Degree requirements:* For master's, thesis (for some programs), comprehensive exam (for some programs); for doctorate, thesis/dissertation, oral exam. *Entrance requirements:* For master's, minimum GPA of 3.0; for doctorate, GRE General Test, minimum graduate GPA of 3.0. Additional exam requirements/recommendations for international students: Required—TOEFL (minimum score 550 paper-based; 213 computer-based; 80 iBT). *Application deadline:* For fall admission, 2/15 for domestic and international students; for spring admission, 9/30 for domestic and international students. Application fee: $60 ($75 for international students). Electronic applications accepted. *Financial support:* In 2006–07, 30 research assistantships with partial tuition reimbursements (averaging $10,000 per year), 7 teaching assistantships with partial tuition reimbursements (averaging $12,000 per year) were awarded; career-related internships or fieldwork, Federal Work-Study, institutionally sponsored loans, scholarships/grants, health care benefits, and unspecified assistantships also available. Support available to part-time students. Financial award application deadline: 3/1. *Unit head:* Dr. Greg Levitt, Chair, 702-895-3241. *Application contact:* Graduate College Admissions Evaluator, 702-895-3320, E-mail: gradcollege@unlv.edu.

University of Nevada, Las Vegas, Graduate College, College of Education, Department of Educational Leadership, Las Vegas, NV 89154-9900. Offers educational administration (M Ed, Ed D, PhD, Ed S); educational leadership (M Ed, MS). *Accreditation:* NCATE. Part-time and evening/weekend programs available. *Faculty:* 16 full-time (6 women), 16 part-time/adjunct (6 women). *Students:* 48 full-time (31 women), 261 part-time (169 women); includes 71 minority (30 African Americans, 3 American Indian/Alaska Native, 19 Asian Americans or Pacific Islanders, 19 Hispanic Americans), 5 international. 193 applicants, 67% accepted, 104 enrolled. In 2006, 106 master's, 11 doctorates awarded. *Degree requirements:* For master's, thesis (for some programs), comprehensive exam (for some programs); for doctorate, thesis/dissertation, oral exam. *Entrance requirements:* For master's, MAT or GRE General Test, minimum GPA of 3.0 during previous 2 years, 2.75 overall; for doctorate, GRE General Test, minimum graduate GPA of 3.0; for Ed S, M Ed or equivalent. Additional exam requirements/recommendations for international students: Required—TOEFL (minimum score 550 paper-based; 213 computer-based; 80 iBT). *Application deadline:* For fall admission, 3/15 for domestic students, 3/1 for international students; for spring admission, 11/15 for domestic students, 10/1 for international students. Application fee: $60 ($75 for international students). Electronic applications accepted. *Financial support:* In 2006–07, 13 research assistantships with partial tuition reimbursements (averaging $11,000 per year) were awarded; teaching assistantships, career-related internships or fieldwork, Federal Work-Study, institutionally sponsored loans, scholarships/grants, health care benefits, and unspecified assistantships also available. Support available to part-time students. Financial award application deadline: 3/1. *Unit head:* Dr. Sterling Saddler, Chair, 702-895-3491. *Application contact:* Graduate College Admissions Evaluator, 702-895-3320, Fax: 702-895-4180, E-mail: gradcollege@unlv.edu.

University of Nevada, Reno, Graduate School, College of Education, Department of Educational Leadership, Reno, NV 89557. Offers M Ed, MA, MS, Ed D, PhD, Ed S. *Accreditation:* NCATE. *Faculty:* 8. *Students:* 38 full-time (23 women), 85 part-time (48 women); includes 8 minority (2 African Americans, 2 Asian Americans or Pacific Islanders, 4 Hispanic Americans). Average age 40. 54 applicants, 81% accepted, 32 enrolled. In 2006, 21 master's, 2 doctorates, 1 other advanced degree awarded. Terminal master's awarded for partial completion of doctoral program. *Degree requirements:* For master's, thesis optional; for doctorate, thesis/dissertation, comprehensive exam. *Entrance requirements:* For master's, GRE General Test, minimum GPA of 2.75; for doctorate, GRE General Test, minimum GPA of 3.0. Additional exam requirements/recommendations for international students: Required—TOEFL. *Application deadline:* For fall admission, 3/1 priority date for domestic students. Applications are processed on a rolling basis. Application fee: $60 ($95 for international students). *Financial support:* In 2006–07, 6 research assistantships were awarded; teaching assistantships, Federal Work-Study and institutionally sponsored loans also available. Financial award application deadline: 3/1. *Faculty research:* Law, finance, supervision, organizational theory, principalship. *Unit head:* Dr. William Wallace, Graduate Program Director, 775-784-6828.

University of New England, College of Arts and Sciences, Program in Educational Leadership, Biddeford, ME 04005-9526. Offers CAGS. Part-time programs available. Postbaccalaureate distance learning degree programs offered (minimal on-campus study). *Faculty:* 3 full-time (2 women), 6 part-time/adjunct (3 women). *Students:* Average age 41. 13 applicants, 100% accepted, 8 enrolled. In 2006, 11 degrees awarded. *Degree requirements:* For degree, registration. *Entrance requirements:* For degree, 3 years of teaching experience in an accredited school, master's degree. *Application deadline:* For fall admission, 8/15 priority date for domestic students; for winter admission, 11/15 priority date for domestic students; for spring admission, 4/15 priority date for domestic students. Applications are processed on a rolling basis. Application fee: $40. Electronic applications accepted. *Expenses: Contact institution. Financial support:* Application deadline: 5/1; *Unit head:* Dr. Susan Hillman, Chair of Education Department, 207-283-0171 Ext. 2888, E-mail: shillman@une.edu. *Application contact:* Lucille Smith, Program Assistant, 207-283-0171 Ext. 2692, Fax: 207-602-5998, E-mail: lsmith@une.edu.

University of New Hampshire, Graduate School, College of Liberal Arts, Department of Education, Program in Educational Administration, Durham, NH 03824. Offers M Ed, CAGS. Part-time programs available. *Faculty:* 32 full-time. *Students:* 1 (woman) full-time, 41 part-time (20 women); includes 3 minority (1 American Indian/Alaska Native, 1 Asian American or Pacific Islander, 1 Hispanic American). Average age 40. 7 applicants, 86% accepted, 4 enrolled. In 2006, 7 master's, 4 other advanced degrees awarded. *Degree requirements:* For master's, thesis or alternative. *Entrance requirements:* For master's and CAGS, GRE General Test. Additional exam requirements/recommendations for international students: Required—TOEFL (minimum score 550 paper-based; 213 computer-based). *Application deadline:* For fall admission, 4/1 priority date for domestic students, 4/1 for international students; for winter admission, 12/1 for domestic students. Applications are processed on a rolling basis. Application fee: $60. *Expenses:* Tuition, state resident: full-time $8,540; part-time $474 per credit hour. Tuition, nonresident: full-time $20,990; part-time $862 per credit hour. Required fees: $1,343; $356 per term. Tuition and fees vary according to course load, program and reciprocity agreements. *Financial support:* In 2006–07, 6 fellowships were awarded; research assistantships, teaching assistantships, career-related internships or fieldwork, Federal Work-Study, scholarships/grants, and tuition waivers (full and partial) also available. Support available to part-time students. Financial award application deadline: 2/15. *Faculty research:* School principalship, supervision, superintendency. *Unit head:* Dr. Virginia Garland, Coordinator, 603-862-1731, E-mail: education.department@unh.edu.

University of New Hampshire, Graduate School, College of Liberal Arts, Department of Education, Program in Teacher Leadership, Durham, NH 03824. Offers M Ed. Part-time

Educational Administration

University of New Hampshire (continued)

programs available. *Faculty:* 32 full-time. *Students:* 1 (woman) full-time, 17 part-time (10 women); includes 1 minority (Hispanic American) 6 applicants, 100% accepted, 5 enrolled. In 2006, 5 degrees awarded. *Degree requirements:* For master's, oral exam or thesis. *Entrance requirements:* For master's, GRE. Additional exam requirements/recommendations for international students: Required—TOEFL (minimum score 550 paper-based; 213 computer-based). *Application deadline:* For fall admission, 3/1 for domestic and international students; for winter admission, 11/15 for domestic students; for spring admission, 4/1 for domestic students. Applications are processed on a rolling basis. Application fee: $60. Electronic applications accepted. *Expenses:* Tuition, state resident: full-time $8,540; part-time $474 per credit hour. Tuition, nonresident: full-time $20,990; part-time $862 per credit hour. Required fees: $1,343; $356 per term. Tuition and fees vary according to course load, program and reciprocity agreements. *Financial support:* In 2006–07, 1 fellowship was awarded; research assistantships, teaching assistantships, Federal Work-Study and scholarships/grants also available. Support available to part-time students. Financial award application deadline: 2/15. *Unit head:* Dr. Michael D. Andrew, Coordinator, 603-862-2371, E-mail: education.department@unh.edu.

University of New Hampshire at Manchester, Center for Graduate and Professional Studies, Manchester, NH 03101-1113. Offers business administration (MBA); counseling (M Ed); education (M Ed, MAT); educational administration and supervision (M Ed, CAGS); industrial statistics (Certificate); public administration (MPA); public health (MPH, Certificate); social work (MSW).

University of New Mexico, Graduate School, College of Education, Department of Educational Leadership and Organizational Learning, Program in Educational Leadership, Albuquerque, NM 87131-2039. Offers MA, Ed D, EDSPC. *Accreditation:* NCATE. Part-time and evening/weekend programs available. *Students:* 9 full-time (8 women), 78 part-time (46 women); includes 34 minority (1 African American, 7 American Indian/Alaska Native, 26 Hispanic Americans). Average age 44. 41 applicants, 41% accepted, 15 enrolled. In 2006, 18 master's, 1 doctorate, 15 other advanced degrees awarded. *Degree requirements:* For master's, comprehensive exam; for doctorate, thesis/dissertation, comprehensive exam. *Entrance requirements:* For master's, bachelor's degree; for doctorate, GRE, master's degree. *Application deadline:* For fall admission, 6/1 for domestic students; for spring admission, 10/1 for domestic students. Applications are processed on a rolling basis. Application fee: $50. Electronic applications accepted. *Financial support:* In 2006–07, 28 students received support, including 16 fellowships (averaging $24,356 per year), 7 teaching assistantships with tuition reimbursements available (averaging $7,371 per year). Financial award application deadline: 3/1; financial award applicants required to submit FAFSA. *Faculty research:* K-20 educational and organizational leadership, individual and organizational learning, policy, legal and political contexts. *Unit head:* Steve Preskill, Head, 505-277-7784, E-mail: preskill@unm.edu. *Application contact:* Linda Wood, Information Contact, 505-277-0441, Fax: 505-277-5553, E-mail: woodl@unm.edu.

University of New Orleans, Graduate School, College of Education and Human Development, Department of Educational Leadership, Counseling, and Foundations, Program in Educational Leadership, New Orleans, LA 70148. Offers M Ed, PhD, GCE. *Accreditation:* NCATE. Evening/weekend programs available. *Students:* 120 (89 women). Average age 40. In 2006, 33 master's, 3 doctorates awarded. Terminal master's awarded for partial completion of doctoral program. *Degree requirements:* For doctorate, variable foreign language requirement, thesis/dissertation. *Entrance requirements:* For master's and doctorate, GRE General Test. Additional exam requirements/recommendations for international students: Required—TOEFL (minimum score 550 paper-based; 213 computer-based). *Application deadline:* For fall admission, 7/1 priority date for domestic students, 6/1 for international students; for spring admission, 11/15 priority date for domestic students, 10/1 for international students. Applications are processed on a rolling basis. Application fee: $40. Electronic applications accepted. *Expenses:* Tuition, state resident: full-time $3,292. Tuition, nonresident: full-time $10,336. Required fees: $158. *Financial support:* Fellowships, research assistantships, teaching assistantships, career-related internships or fieldwork and tuition waivers (partial) available. Financial award application deadline: 3/15; financial award applicants required to submit FAFSA. *Unit head:* Dr. Juanita Haydel, Graduate Coordinator, 504-280-6450, E-mail: jbhaydel@uno.edu.

University of North Alabama, College of Education, Department of Secondary Education, Program in Education Leadership, Florence, AL 35632-0001. Offers Ed S. *Accreditation:* NCATE. Part-time and evening/weekend programs available. *Faculty:* 2 part-time/adjunct (1 woman). *Students:* 2 full-time (0 women), 24 part-time (12 women); includes 8 minority (7 African Americans, 1 Hispanic American). Average age 39. In 2006, 7 degrees awarded. *Application deadline:* For fall admission, 7/1 priority date for domestic students; for spring admission, 12/1 for domestic students. Applications are processed on a rolling basis. Application fee: $25. Electronic applications accepted. *Expenses:* Tuition, state resident: full-time $4,080. Tuition, nonresident: full-time $8,160. Required fees: $764. *Financial support:* Application deadline: 4/1. *Application contact:* Dr. Sue Wilson, Dean of Enrollment Management, 256-765-4316, Fax: 256-765-4349, E-mail: sjwilson@una.edu.

University of North Alabama, College of Education, Department of Secondary Education, Programs in Principalship, Superintendency, and Supervision of Instruction, Florence, AL 35632-0001. Offers principalship (MA Ed); superintendency (MA Ed); supervision of instruction (MA Ed). *Accreditation:* NCATE. Part-time and evening/weekend programs available. *Faculty:* 2 part-time/adjunct (1 woman). *Students:* 4 full-time (1 woman), 18 part-time (8 women); includes 3 African Americans. Average age 37. In 2006, 27 degrees awarded. *Degree requirements:* For master's, comprehensive exam. *Entrance requirements:* For master's, GRE, MAT, or NTE, minimum GPA of 2.5, Alabama Class B Certificate or equivalent, teaching experience. *Application deadline:* For fall admission, 7/1 priority date for domestic students; for spring admission, 12/1 for domestic students. Applications are processed on a rolling basis. Application fee: $25. Electronic applications accepted. *Expenses:* Tuition, state resident: full-time $4,080. Tuition, nonresident: full-time $8,160. Required fees: $764. *Financial support:* Federal Work-Study available. Support available to part-time students. Financial award application deadline: 4/1. *Application contact:* Dr. Sue Wilson, Dean of Enrollment Management, 256-765-4316, Fax: 256-765-4349, E-mail: sjwilson@una.edu.

The University of North Carolina at Chapel Hill, Graduate School, School of Education, Programs in Educational Leadership and School Administration, Chapel Hill, NC 27599. Offers educational leadership (Ed D); school administration (MSA). *Accreditation:* NCATE. Part-time programs available. *Degree requirements:* For master's, comprehensive exam; for doctorate, thesis/dissertation, comprehensive exam. *Entrance requirements:* For master's, GRE General Test or MAT, minimum GPA of 3.2 during last 2 years of undergraduate course work, 3 years of school-based professional experience; for doctorate, GRE General Test, minimum GPA of 3.2 during last 2 years of undergraduate course work, 3 years of school-based professional experience. Additional exam requirements/recommendations for international students: Required—TOEFL (minimum score 550 paper-based; 213 computer-based). *Application deadline:* For fall admission, 1/1 priority date for domestic and international students. Applications are processed on a rolling basis. Application fee: $60. *Financial support:* Application deadline: 3/1; *Faculty research:* Gender, race, and class issues; school leadership; school finance and reform. *Unit head:* Dr. Kathleen Brown, Chair, 919-966-1354, Fax: 919-962-1533. *Application contact:* Janet Carroll, Registrar, 919-962-8690, Fax: 919-962-1533, E-mail: jscarrol@email.unc.edu.

The University of North Carolina at Charlotte, Graduate School, College of Education, Department of Educational Leadership, Charlotte, NC 28223-0001. Offers curriculum and supervision (M Ed); educational administration (CAS); educational leadership (Ed D); instructional systems technology (M Ed); school administration (MSA). Part-time and evening/weekend programs available. *Faculty:* 17 full-time (4 women), 10 part-time/adjunct (5 women). *Students:* 67 full-time (55 women), 158 part-time (112 women); includes 68 minority (63 African Americans, 1 American Indian/Alaska Native, 1 Asian American or Pacific Islander, 3 Hispanic Americans), 1 international. Average age 38. 149 applicants, 71% accepted, 90 enrolled. In 2006, 61 degrees awarded. *Entrance requirements:* For master's and doctorate, GRE or MAT. Additional exam requirements/recommendations for international students: Required—TOEFL (minimum score 550 paper-based; 220 computer-based). *Application deadline:* For fall admission, 7/1 for domestic students, 5/1 for international students; for spring admission, 11/1 for domestic students, 10/1 for international students. Applications are processed on a rolling basis. Application fee: $55. Electronic applications accepted. *Expenses:* Tuition, state resident: full-time $2,719; part-time $170 per credit. Tuition, nonresident: full-time $12,926; part-time $808 per credit. Required fees: $1,555. *Financial support:* In 2006–07, 3 teaching assistantships (averaging $8,027 per year) were awarded; fellowships, research assistantships, career-related internships or fieldwork, Federal Work-Study, institutionally sponsored loans, scholarships/grants, and unspecified assistantships also available. Support available to part-time students. Financial award application deadline: 4/1; financial award applicants required to submit FAFSA. *Faculty research:* Educational leadership theory and practice, instructional systems technology, educational research methodology, curriculum and supervision in the schools, school law and finance. Total annual research expenditures: $800,000. *Unit head:* Dr. Dawson R. Hancock, Interim Chair, 704-687-8730, Fax: 704-687-3493. *Application contact:* Kathy B. Giddings, Director of Graduate Admissions, 704-687-3366, Fax: 704-687-3279, E-mail: gradadm@email.uncc.edu.

The University of North Carolina at Greensboro, Graduate School, School of Education, Department of Curriculum and Instruction, Greensboro, NC 27412-5001. Offers college teaching and adult learning (Certificate); curriculum and instruction (M Ed), including chemistry education, elementary education, English as a second language, French education, instructional technology, mathematics education, middle grades education, reading education, science education, social studies education, Spanish education; curriculum and teaching (PhD), including higher education, teacher education and development; English as a second language (Certificate); higher education (M Ed); supervision (M Ed). *Accreditation:* NCATE. Part-time programs available. *Faculty:* 27 full-time (18 women), 8 part-time/adjunct (3 women). *Students:* 137 full-time (114 women), 231 part-time (195 women); includes 63 minority (52 African Americans, 2 American Indian/Alaska Native, 5 Asian Americans or Pacific Islanders, 4 Hispanic Americans). 146 applicants, 32% accepted. *Degree requirements:* For doctorate, thesis/dissertation. *Entrance requirements:* For master's and doctorate, GRE General Test. Additional exam requirements/recommendations for international students: Required—TOEFL. Application fee: $45. Electronic applications accepted. *Expenses:* Tuition, state resident: full-time $2,692. Tuition, nonresident: full-time $13,742. *Financial support:* Fellowships, research assistantships with full tuition reimbursements, teaching assistantships with full tuition reimbursements, career-related internships or fieldwork, Federal Work-Study, scholarships/grants, traineeships, and unspecified assistantships available. Support available to part-time students. *Faculty research:* Community college literacy program, middle school mathematics/computer mathematics. *Unit head:* Dr. Sam Miller, Chair, 336-334-3445, Fax: 336-334-4120, E-mail: sdmille2@uncg.edu. *Application contact:* Michelle Harkleroad, Director of Graduate Admissions, 336-334-4884, Fax: 336-334-4424, E-mail: mbharkle@uncg.edu.

The University of North Carolina at Greensboro, Graduate School, School of Education, Department of Educational Leadership and Cultural Foundations, Greensboro, NC 27412-5001. Offers curriculum and teaching (PhD), including cultural studies; educational leadership (Ed D, Ed S); school administration (MSA). *Accreditation:* NCATE. *Faculty:* 12 full-time (7 women), 1 part-time/adjunct (0 women). *Students:* 100 full-time (71 women), 113 part-time (79 women); includes 74 minority (70 African Americans, 1 American Indian/Alaska Native, 1 Asian American or Pacific Islander, 2 Hispanic Americans). 124 applicants, 35% accepted. *Degree requirements:* For doctorate, thesis/dissertation. *Entrance requirements:* For master's, doctorate, and Ed S, GRE General Test. Additional exam requirements/recommendations for international students: Required—TOEFL. *Application deadline:* For fall admission, 1/1 priority date for domestic students; for spring admission, 11/1 for domestic students. Applications are processed on a rolling basis. Application fee: $45. Electronic applications accepted. *Expenses:* Tuition, state resident: full-time $2,692. Tuition, nonresident: full-time $13,742. *Financial support:* Fellowships with full tuition reimbursements, research assistantships with full tuition reimbursements, teaching assistantships with full tuition reimbursements, career-related internships or fieldwork, Federal Work-Study, scholarships/grants, and traineeships available. Support available to part-time students. *Unit head:* Dr. Ulrich Reitzug, Chair, 336-334-3490, Fax: 336-334-4120, E-mail: ucreitzu@uncg.edu. *Application contact:* Michelle Harkleroad, Director of Graduate Admissions, 336-334-4884, Fax: 336-334-4424, E-mail: mbharkle@uncg.edu.

The University of North Carolina at Pembroke, Graduate Studies, School of Education, Program in School Administration, Pembroke, NC 28372-1510. Offers MSA. Part-time and evening/weekend programs available. *Faculty:* 4 full-time (1 woman). *Students:* Average age 34. 83 applicants, 100% accepted, 83 enrolled. In 2006, 55 degrees awarded. *Degree requirements:* For master's, internship. *Entrance requirements:* For master's, GRE General Test or MAT, minimum GPA of 3.0 in major, 2.5 overall; 3 years teaching experience. Additional exam requirements/recommendations for international students: Required—TOEFL. *Application deadline:* For fall admission, 7/15 priority date for domestic and international students; for spring admission, 12/1 priority date for domestic students, 12/15 priority date for international students. Applications are processed on a rolling basis. Application fee: $40. *Expenses:* Tuition, state resident: full-time $3,516; part-time $1,091 per semester. Tuition, nonresident: full-time $12,924; part-time $4,619 per semester. Tuition and fees vary according to class time, course load, degree level and campus/location. *Financial support:* In 2006–07, research assistantships with full tuition reimbursements (averaging $6,000 per year); unspecified assistantships also available. Support available to part-time students. Financial award application deadline: 4/15; financial award applicants required to submit FAFSA. *Unit head:* Dr. Carol L. Higy, Director, 910-521-6449, Fax: 910-521-6165, E-mail: carol.higy@uncp.edu. *Application contact:* Dr. Kathleen C. Hilton, Dean of Graduate Studies, 910-521-6271, Fax: 910-521-6751, E-mail: grad@uncp.edu.

The University of North Carolina Wilmington, School of Education, Department of Educational Leadership, Program in Educational Leadership, Wilmington, NC 28403-3297. Offers MSA. *Students:* 26 full-time (19 women), 18 part-time (12 women); includes 10 minority (6 African Americans, 2 American Indian/Alaska Native, 2 Hispanic Americans). 19 applicants, 74% accepted, 12 enrolled. In 2006, 23 degrees awarded. *Degree requirements:* For master's, comprehensive exam. *Application deadline:* For fall admission, 6/1 for domestic students. Applications are processed on a rolling basis. Application fee: $45. *Financial support:* Application deadline: 3/15. *Unit head:* Dr. Marc Sosne, Director, 910-962-7995. *Application contact:* Dr. Robert D. Roer, Dean, Graduate School, 910-962-4117, Fax: 910-962-3787, E-mail: roer@uncw.edu.

University of North Dakota, Graduate School, College of Education and Human Development, Program in Educational Leadership, Grand Forks, ND 58202. Offers M Ed, MS, Ed D, PhD, Specialist. *Accreditation:* NCATE. Part-time and evening/weekend programs available. Postbaccalaureate distance learning degree programs offered (minimal on-campus study). *Faculty:* 8 full-time (3 women). *Students:* 47 applicants, 62% accepted, 28 enrolled. In 2006, 18 master's, 14 doctorates, 2 other advanced degrees awarded. *Degree requirements:* For master's and Specialist, thesis or alternative, comprehensive exam; for doctorate, thesis/dissertation, final exam, comprehensive exam. *Entrance requirements:* For master's, minimum GPA of 3.0; for doctorate, minimum GPA of 3.5. Additional exam requirements/recommendations for international students: Required—TOEFL (minimum score 550 paper-based; 213 computer-based). *Application deadline:* For fall admission, 2/15 priority date for domestic and international students; for spring admission, 10/15 priority date for domestic and international students. Application fee: $35. Electronic applications accepted. *Expenses:* Tuition, state resident: full-time $5,650; part-time $214 per credit. Tuition, nonresident: full-time $14,248; part-time $572 per credit. Required fees: $1,008; $42 per credit. Tuition and fees vary according to reciprocity agreements. *Financial support:* In 2006–07, 9 students received support, including 2 research assistantships (averaging $9,111 per year), 3 teaching assistantships with full tuition reimbursements available (averaging $10,413 per year); fellowships, career-related internships or fieldwork, Federal Work-Study, institutionally sponsored loans, scholarships/grants, tuition waivers (full and partial), and unspecified assistantships also available. Support available to part-time students. Financial award application deadline: 3/15; financial award applicants required to submit FAFSA. *Unit head:* Dr. Margaret Healy, Chairperson, 701-777-3577, Fax: 701-777-4365, E-mail: margaret.healy@und.nodak.edu. *Application contact:* Linda M. Baeza, Admissions Officer, 701-777-2945, Fax: 701-777-3619, E-mail: gradschool@mail.und.nodak.edu.

University of Northern Colorado, Graduate School, College of Education and Behavioral Sciences, School of Educational Research, Leadership and Technology, Educational Leadership and Policy Studies, Greeley, CO 80639. Offers educational leadership (MA, Ed D, Ed S). *Accreditation:* NCATE. Part-time and evening/weekend programs available. Postbaccalaureate distance learning degree programs offered. *Faculty:* 5 full-time (4 women). *Students:* 38 full-time (22 women), 50 part-time (32 women); includes 13 minority (4 African Americans, 1 American Indian/Alaska Native, 1 Asian American or Pacific Islander, 7 Hispanic Americans), 2 international. Average age 37. 19 applicants, 84% accepted, 11 enrolled. In 2006, 13 master's, 3 doctorates, 8 other advanced degrees awarded. *Degree requirements:* For master's, thesis or alternative, comprehensive exam; for doctorate and Ed S, thesis/dissertation, comprehensive exam. *Entrance requirements:* For master's, resumé, interview; for doctorate, GRE General Test, resumé, interview; for Ed S, resumé. *Application deadline:* For fall admission, 5/1 for domestic and international students. Applications are processed on a rolling basis. Application fee: $50 ($60 for international students). Electronic applications accepted. *Expenses:* Tuition, state resident: full-time $5,118; part-time $213 per credit hour. Tuition, nonresident: full-time $14,832; part-time $618 per credit hour. Required fees: $674; $34 per credit hour. *Financial support:* In 2006–07, 38 students received support, including 5 fellowships (averaging $2,440 per year), 17 research assistantships (averaging $16,165 per year); teaching assistantships, unspecified assistantships also available. Financial award application deadline: 3/1; financial award applicants required to submit FAFSA. *Unit head:* Dr. Rachard King, Program Coordinator, 970-351-2861, E-mail: elps@unco.edu.

University of Northern Iowa, Graduate College, College of Education, Department of Educational Leadership, Counseling, and Postsecondary Education, Program in Educational Leadership, Cedar Falls, IA 50614. Offers educational administration (Ed D); elementary principal (MAE); secondary principal (MAE). Part-time and evening/weekend programs available. *Students:* 3 full-time (2 women), 110 part-time (46 women); includes 6 minority (5 African Americans, 1 Asian American or Pacific Islander), 2 international. 52 applicants, 75% accepted, 37 enrolled. In 2006, 26 master's, 9 doctorates awarded. *Degree requirements:* For master's, thesis or alternative, comprehensive exam; for doctorate, thesis/dissertation. *Entrance requirements:* For master's, 3 years of educational experience, minimum GPA of 3.5; for doctorate, GRE, 3 years of educational experience, master's degree, minimum GPA of 3.2. Additional exam requirements/recommendations for international students: Required—TOEFL (minimum score 500 paper-based; 180 computer-based; 61 iBT). *Application deadline:* For fall admission, 8/1 priority date for domestic students. Applications are processed on a rolling basis. Application fee: $30 ($50 for international students). Electronic applications accepted. *Expenses:* Tuition, state resident: full-time $5,936. Tuition, nonresident: full-time $14,074. *Financial support:* Career-related internships or fieldwork, Federal Work-Study, and tuition waivers (full and partial) available. Support available to part-time students. Financial award application deadline: 2/1. *Unit head:* Dr. David Else, Coordinator, 319-273-3358, E-mail: david.else@uni.edu.

University of Northern Virginia, Graduate Programs, Manassas, VA 20109. Offers accountancy (MS); accounting (MBA); business administration (DBA); computer science (MS); counseling education (M Ed); early childhood education (M Ed); educational communication and instructional technology (M Ed); educational leadership (M Ed); finance (MBA); information systems technology (MS); management (MBA); marketing (MBA); project management (MBA); public administration (MPA); teaching English to speakers of other languages (M Ed). Part-time and evening/weekend programs available. Postbaccalaureate distance learning degree programs offered (no on-campus study). *Degree requirements:* For doctorate, thesis/dissertation, comprehensive exam, registration. *Entrance requirements:* Additional exam requirements/recommendations for international students: Required—TOEFL (minimum score 550 paper-based; 230 computer-based), IELTS (minimum score 6). Electronic applications accepted.

University of North Florida, College of Education and Human Services, Department of Counseling and Educational Leadership, Program in Educational Leadership, Jacksonville, FL 32224-2645. Offers educational leadership (M Ed, Ed D); instructional leadership (M Ed). *Accreditation:* NCATE. Part-time and evening/weekend programs available. *Faculty:* 15 full-time (9 women). *Students:* 25 full-time (17 women), 221 part-time (146 women); includes 64 minority (51 African Americans, 1 American Indian/Alaska Native, 3 Asian Americans or Pacific Islanders, 9 Hispanic Americans), 2 international. Average age 39. 71 applicants, 49% accepted, 33 enrolled. In 2006, 73 master's, 13 doctorates awarded. *Degree requirements:* For doctorate, thesis/dissertation. *Entrance requirements:* For master's, GRE General Test, minimum GPA of 3.0 in last 60 hours, interview, 3 letters of recommendation; for doctorate, GRE General Test, master's degree, interview, 3 letters of recommendation, writing sample. Additional exam requirements/recommendations for international students: Required—TOEFL (minimum score 500 paper-based; 173 computer-based). *Application deadline:* For fall admission, 7/1 priority date for domestic students, 5/1 for international students; for spring admission, 11/1 priority date for domestic students, 10/1 for international students. Applications are processed on a rolling basis. Application fee: $30. Electronic applications accepted. *Expenses:* Tuition, state resident: full-time $4,948; part-time $206 per semester hour. Tuition, nonresident: full-time $19,140; part-time $408 per semester hour. *Financial support:* In 2006–07, 69 students received support; teaching assistantships, career-related internships or fieldwork, Federal Work-Study, and tuition waivers (partial) available. Support available to part-time students. Financial award application deadline: 4/1; financial award applicants required to submit FAFSA. *Faculty research:* Site-based management, supervision, assessment, policy, finance. *Application contact:* Dr. Russell Mays, Graduate Coordinator for M Ed Program, 904-620-1819, E-mail: rmays@unf.edu.

University of North Texas, Robert B. Toulouse School of Graduate Studies, College of Education, Department of Teacher Education and Administration, Program in Educational Administration, Denton, TX 76203. Offers M Ed, Ed D, PhD. *Accreditation:* NCATE. *Students:* 35 full-time (25 women), 303 part-time (192 women); includes 100 minority (55 African Americans, 2 American Indian/Alaska Native, 3 Asian Americans or Pacific Islanders, 40 Hispanic Americans), 1 international. Average age 36. 87 applicants, 55% accepted, 42 enrolled. In 2006, 97 master's, 7 doctorates awarded. *Degree requirements:* For doctorate, thesis/dissertation. *Entrance requirements:* For master's and doctorate, GRE General Test. Additional exam requirements/recommendations for international students: Recommended—TOEFL (minimum score 550 paper-based; 213 computer-based). *Application deadline:* For fall admission, 7/15 for domestic students. Application fee: $50 ($75 for international students). *Expenses:* Tuition, state resident: full-time $3,573; part-time $198 per credit. Tuition, nonresident: full-time $8,577; part-time $476 per credit. Required fees: $1,258; $126 per credit. One-time fee: $150 full-time. Tuition and fees vary according to course load. *Financial support:* Fellowships, research assistantships, teaching assistantships, career-related internships or fieldwork, Federal Work-Study, and institutionally sponsored loans available. Financial award application deadline: 4/1. *Application contact:* Robert Trevino, Graduate Advisor, 940-565-2940, Fax: 940-565-4952, E-mail: rtrevino@coe.unt.edu.

University of Oklahoma, Graduate College, College of Education, Department of Educational Leadership and Policy Studies, Program in Educational Administration, Curriculum and Supervision, Norman, OK 73019-0390. Offers M Ed, Ed D, PhD. *Accreditation:* NCATE. Part-time and evening/weekend programs available. *Students:* 32 full-time (22 women), 80 part-time (53 women); includes 37 minority (15 African Americans, 18 American Indian/Alaska Native, 1 Asian American or Pacific Islander, 3 Hispanic Americans). 15 applicants, 73% accepted, 9 enrolled. In 2006, 38 master's, 5 doctorates awarded. *Degree requirements:* For master's, thesis optional; for doctorate, variable foreign language requirement, thesis/dissertation, general exam. *Entrance requirements:* For master's, 12 hours of course work in education; for doctorate, GRE General Test, master's degree, 3 letters of reference, writing sample. Additional exam requirements/recommendations for international students: Required—TOEFL (minimum score 550 paper-based; 213 computer-based). *Application deadline:* For fall admission, 6/1 priority date for domestic students, 4/1 for international students; for spring admission, 10/1 for domestic students, 9/1 for international students. Application fee: $40 ($90 for international students). *Expenses:* Tuition, state resident: full-time $3,180; part-time $133 per credit hour. Tuition, nonresident: full-time $11,347; part-time $473 per credit hour. Required fees: $1,729; $62 per credit hour. $117 per semester. Tuition and fees vary according to course load and program. *Financial support:* Research assistantships with partial tuition reimbursements, teaching assistantships with partial tuition reimbursements, unspecified assistantships available. Financial award applicants required to submit FAFSA. *Faculty research:* Law of education, ethics, technology in K-12 curriculum, instruction, supervision in K-12. *Application contact:* Geri Evans, Programs Officer, 405-325-5978, Fax: 405-325-2403, E-mail: gevans@ou.edu.

University of Pennsylvania, Graduate School of Education, Division of Foundations and Practices in Education, Program in Educational Policy and Leadership, Philadelphia, PA 19104. Offers MS Ed, Ed D, PhD. Part-time programs available. *Degree requirements:* For master's, thesis, comprehensive exam; for doctorate, thesis/dissertation, oral exams, comprehensive exam. *Entrance requirements:* For master's, GRE or MAT; for doctorate, GRE. Electronic applications accepted. Expenses: Contact institution. *Faculty research:* Public policy, curriculum and instruction, organization theory/leadership, school reform.

University of Pennsylvania, Graduate School of Education, Division of Policy, Management and Evaluation, Philadelphia, PA 19104. Offers MS Ed, Ed D, PhD. Part-time programs available. Terminal master's awarded for partial completion of doctoral program. *Degree requirements:* For master's, comprehensive exam; for doctorate, thesis/dissertation, comprehensive exam. *Entrance requirements:* For master's and doctorate, GRE. Electronic applications accepted. Expenses: Contact institution. *Faculty research:* Institutional research, strategic planning, governance and administration, public policy, budgeting and finance.

University of Phoenix–Central Florida Campus, The Artemis School, College of Education, Maitland, FL 32751-7057. Offers administration and supervision (MA Ed); curriculum and instruction (MA Ed); elementary teacher education (MA Ed); secondary teacher education (MA Ed). Evening/weekend programs available. *Faculty:* 10 full-time (9 women), 16 part-time/adjunct (6 women). *Students:* 20 full-time (18 women); includes 5 minority (3 African Americans, 2 Hispanic Americans), 1 international. Average age 38. In 2006, 7 degrees awarded. *Degree requirements:* For master's, thesis (for some programs), registration. *Entrance requirements:* For master's, 3 years of work experience, minimum undergraduate GPA of 2.5. Additional exam requirements/recommendations for international students: Required—TOEFL (minimum score 550 paper-based; 213 computer-based; 79 iBT). *Application deadline:* Applications are processed on a rolling basis. Application fee: $45. Electronic applications accepted. *Expenses:* Tuition: Full-time $9,450. Required fees: $760. *Financial support:* Institutionally sponsored loans and scholarships/grants available. Financial award applicants required to submit FAFSA. *Unit head:* Dr. Marla LaRue, Dean/Executive Director, 480-557-1218. *Application contact:* Chair, 407-667-0555, Fax: 407-667-0560.

University of Phoenix–Denver Campus, The Artemis School, College of Education, Lone Tree, CO 80124-5453. Offers administration and supervision (MAEd); curriculum instruction (MAEd); elementary teacher education (MAEd); school counseling (MSC); secondary teacher education (MAEd). Evening/weekend programs available. *Faculty:* 19 full-time (14 women), 141 part-time/adjunct (84 women). *Students:* 738 full-time (513 women); includes 72 minority (27 African Americans, 4 American Indian/Alaska Native, 9 Asian Americans or Pacific Islanders, 32 Hispanic Americans), 66 international. Average age 37. In 2006, 435 master's awarded. *Degree requirements:* For master's, thesis (for some programs), registration. *Entrance requirements:* For master's, minimum undergraduate GPA of 2.5, 3 years work experience. Additional exam requirements/recommendations for international students: Required—TOEFL (minimum score 550 paper-based; 213 computer-based; 79 iBT). *Application deadline:* Applications are processed on a rolling basis. Application fee: $45. Electronic applications accepted. *Expenses:* Tuition: Full-time $10,032. Required fees: $760. *Financial support:* Institutionally sponsored loans and scholarships/grants available. Financial award applicants required to submit FAFSA. *Unit head:* Dr. Marla LaRue, Dean/Executive Director, 480-557-1218, E-mail: marla.larue@phoenix.edu. *Application contact:* Chair, 303-694-9093, Fax: 303-662-0911.

University of Phoenix–Fort Lauderdale Campus, The Artemis School, College of Education, Fort Lauderdale, FL 33309. Offers administration and supervision (MA Ed); computer education (MA Ed); curriculum and instruction (MA Ed); elementary teacher education (MA Ed); secondary teacher education (MA Ed). Evening/weekend programs available. *Faculty:* 10 full-time (5 women), 17 part-time/adjunct (7 women). *Students:* 132 full-time (114 women); includes 60 minority (52 African Americans, 1 Asian American or Pacific Islander, 7 Hispanic Americans), 5 international. Average age 39. In 2006, 25 degrees awarded. *Degree requirements:* For master's, thesis (for some programs), registration. *Entrance requirements:* For master's, 3 years of work experience, minimum undergraduate GPA of 2.5. Additional exam requirements/recommendations for international students: Required—TOEFL (minimum score 550 paper-based; 213 computer-based; 79 iBT). *Application deadline:* Applications are processed on a rolling basis. Application fee: $45. Electronic applications accepted. *Expenses:* Tuition: Full-time $9,450. Required fees: $760. *Financial support:* Institutionally sponsored loans and scholarships/grants available. Financial award applicants required to submit FAFSA. *Unit head:* Dr. Marla LaRue, Dean/Executive Director, 480-557-1218. *Application contact:* Chair, 954-382-5303, Fax: 954-382-5304.

University of Phoenix–Hawaii Campus, The Artemis School, College of Education, Honolulu, HI 96813-4317. Offers administration and supervision (MA Ed); curriculum and instruction (MA Ed); elementary education (MA Ed); secondary education (MA Ed); teacher education for elementary licensure (MA Ed). Evening/weekend programs available. *Faculty:* 10 full-time (7 women), 58 part-time/adjunct (34 women). *Students:* 261 full-time (176 women); includes 61 minority (1 African American, 1 American Indian/Alaska Native, 53 Asian Americans or Pacific Islanders, 6 Hispanic Americans), 106 international. Average age 36. In 2006, 151 degrees awarded. *Degree requirements:* For master's, thesis (for some programs), registration. *Entrance requirements:* For master's, minimum undergraduate GPA of 2.5, 3 years of work experience. Additional exam requirements/recommendations for international students: Required—TOEFL (minimum score 550 paper-based; 213 computer-based; 79 iBT). *Application deadline:* Applications are processed on a rolling basis. Application fee: $45. Electronic applications accepted. *Expenses:* Tuition: Full-time $11,520. Required fees: $760. *Financial support:* Institutionally sponsored loans and scholarships/grants available. Financial award applicants required to submit FAFSA. *Unit head:* Dr. Marla LaRue, Dean/Executive Director, 480-557-1309, E-mail: marla.larue@phoenix.edu. *Application contact:* Chair, 580-536-2686, Fax: 808-536-3848.

University of Phoenix–Las Vegas Campus, The Artemis School, College of Education, Las Vegas, NV 89128. Offers administration and supervision (MA Ed); curriculum and instruction (MA Ed); school counseling (MSC); teacher education-elementary licensure (MA Ed). Evening/weekend programs available. *Faculty:* 9 full-time (8 women), 45 part-time/adjunct (27 women). *Students:* 494 full-time (388 women); includes 105 minority (51 African Americans, 2 American Indian/Alaska Native, 18 Asian Americans or Pacific Islanders, 34 Hispanic Americans), 9 international. Average age 35. In 2006, 227 degrees awarded. *Degree requirements:* For master's, thesis (for some programs), registration. *Entrance requirements:* For master's, minimum undergraduate GPA of 2.5, 3 years of work experience. Additional exam requirements/recommendations for international students: Required—TOEFL (minimum score 550 paper-based; 213 computer-based; 79 iBT). *Application deadline:* Applications are processed on a rolling basis. Application fee: $45. Electronic applications accepted. *Expenses:* Tuition: Full-

Educational Administration

University of Phoenix–Las Vegas Campus (continued)
time $9,576. Required fees: $760. *Financial support:* Institutionally sponsored loans and scholarships/grants available. Financial award applicants required to submit FAFSA. *Unit head:* Dr. Marla LaRue, Dean/Executive Director, 480-557-1218, E-mail: marla.larue@phoenix. edu. *Application contact:* Chair, 702-638-7249, Fax: 702-638-8085.

University of Phoenix–Metro Detroit Campus, The Artemis School, College of Education, Troy, MI 48098-2623. Offers administration and supervision (MA Ed); adult education and distance learning (MA Ed); curriculum and development (MA Ed); special education (MA Ed); teacher education elementary (MA Ed). Evening/weekend programs available. *Faculty:* 8 full-time (3 women), 27 part-time/adjunct (21 women). *Students:* 102 full-time (75 women); includes 59 minority (57 African Americans, 1 American Indian/Alaska Native, 1 Asian American or Pacific Islander), 1 international. Average age 40. In 2006, 30 master's awarded. *Degree requirements:* For master's, thesis (for some programs), registration. *Entrance requirements:* For master's, 3 years of work experience, minimum undergraduate GPA of 2.5. Additional exam requirements/recommendations for international students: Required—TOEFL (minimum score 550 paper-based; 213 computer-based; 79 iBT). *Application deadline:* Applications are processed on a rolling basis. Application fee: $45. Electronic applications accepted. *Expenses:* Tuition: Full-time $12,168. Required fees: $760. *Financial support:* Institutionally sponsored loans and scholarships/grants available. Financial award applicants required to submit FAFSA. *Unit head:* Dr. Marla LaRue, Dean/Executive Director, 480-557-1218. *Application contact:* Chair, 800-834-2438, Fax: 248-267-0147.

University of Phoenix–Nashville Campus, The Artemis School, College of Education, Nashville, TN 37214-5048. Offers administration and supervision (MA Ed); curriculum and instruction (MA Ed); elementary teacher education (MA Ed); secondary teacher education (MA Ed). Evening/weekend programs available. *Degree requirements:* For master's, thesis (for some programs), registration. *Entrance requirements:* For master's, minimum undergraduate GPA of 2.5, 3 years work experience. Additional exam requirements/recommendations for international students: Required—TOEFL (minimum score 500 paper-based; 213 computer-based; 79 iBT). *Application deadline:* Applications are processed on a rolling basis. Application fee: $45. Electronic applications accepted. *Expenses:* Tuition: Full-time $10,104. Required fees: $760. *Financial support:* Institutionally sponsored loans and scholarships/grants available. Financial award applicants required to submit FAFSA. *Unit head:* Dr. Marla LaRue, Dean/Executive Director, 480-557-1218, E-mail: marla.larue@phoenix. edu. *Application contact:* Chair, 615-872-0188.

University of Phoenix–New Mexico Campus, The Artemis School, College of Education, Albuquerque, NM 87109-4645. Offers administration (MAEd); curriculum and instruction (MAEd); teacher education (MAEd), including elementary, secondary. Evening/weekend programs available. *Faculty:* 9 full-time (5 women), 62 part-time/adjunct (40 women). *Students:* 234 full-time (181 women); includes 116 minority (5 African Americans, 1 Asian American or Pacific Islander, 110 Hispanic Americans), 10 international. Average age 39. In 2006, 131 degrees awarded. *Degree requirements:* For master's, thesis (for some programs), registration. *Entrance requirements:* For master's, minimum undergraduate GPA of 2.5, 3 years of work experience. Additional exam requirements/recommendations for international students: Required—TOEFL (minimum score 550 paper-based; 213 computer-based; 79 iBT). *Application deadline:* Applications are processed on a rolling basis. Application fee: $45. Electronic applications accepted. *Expenses:* Tuition: Full-time $9,005. Required fees: $760. *Financial support:* Institutionally sponsored loans and scholarships/grants available. Financial award applicants required to submit FAFSA. *Unit head:* Dr. Marla LaRue, Dean/Executive Director, 480-557-1218, E-mail: marla.larue@phoenix.edu. *Application contact:* Chair, 505-821-4800, Fax: 505-821-5551.

University of Phoenix—Northern Nevada Campus, College of Education, Reno, NV 89511. Offers administration and supervision (MA Ed); elementary teacher educatino (MA Ed).

University of Phoenix–Northern Virginia Campus, College of Education, Reston, VA 20190. Offers administration and supervision (MA Ed).

University of Phoenix–North Florida Campus, The Artemis School, College of Education, Jacksonville, FL 32216-0959. Offers administration (MA Ed); curriculum and instruction (MA Ed); curriculum and instruction—computer education (MA Ed); elementary teacher education (MA Ed); secondary teacher education (MA Ed). Evening/weekend programs available. *Faculty:* 9 full-time (5 women), 10 part-time/adjunct (4 women). *Students:* 98 full-time (78 women); includes 41 minority (37 African Americans, 4 Hispanic Americans), 1 international. Average age 37. In 2006, 22 master's awarded. *Degree requirements:* For master's, thesis (for some programs), registration. *Entrance requirements:* For master's, 3 years of work experience, minimum undergraduate GPA of 2.5. Additional exam requirements/recommendations for international students: Required—TOEFL (minimum score 550 paper-based; 213 computer-based; 49 iBT). *Application deadline:* Applications are processed on a rolling basis. Application fee: $45. Electronic applications accepted. *Financial support:* Institutionally sponsored loans and scholarships/grants available. Financial award applicants required to submit FAFSA. *Unit head:* Dr. Marla LaRue, Dean, 480-557-1218, E-mail: marla.larue@phoenix.edu. *Application contact:* Chair, 904-636-6645, Fax: 904-636-0998.

University of Phoenix–Omaha Campus, College of Education, Omaha, NE 68154-5240. Offers administration and supervision (MA Ed); curriculum and instruction (MA Ed); curriculum and instruction—English and language arts education (MA Ed); curriculum and instruction—adult education (MA Ed); curriculum and instruction—computer education (MA Ed); curriculum and instruction—English as a second language (MA Ed); curriculum and instruction—mathematics education (MA Ed); elementary teacher education (MA Ed); secondary teacher education (MA Ed); special education (MA Ed).

University of Phoenix Online Campus, The Artemis School, College of Education, Phoenix, AZ 85034-7209. Offers administration and supervision (MAEd); adult education and training (MAEd); curriculum and instruction-adult education (MAEd); curriculum and instruction-English and language arts education (MAEd); curriculum and instruction-mathematics education (MAEd); curriculum education (MAEd); curriculum instruction (MAEd); early childhood (MAEd); English as a second language (MAEd); teacher education elementary (MAEd); teacher education secondary (MAEd). Evening/weekend programs available. Postbaccalaureate distance learning degree programs offered (no on-campus study). *Faculty:* 12 full-time (5 women), 8,196 part-time/adjunct (6,937 women). *Students:* 11,937 full-time (9,375 women); includes 2,972 minority (2,210 African Americans, 74 American Indian/Alaska Native, 205 Asian Americans or Pacific Islanders, 483 Hispanic Americans), 906 international. Average age 36. *Degree requirements:* For master's, thesis (for some programs), registration. *Entrance requirements:* For master's, 3 years of work experience, minimum GPA of 2.5. Additional exam requirements/recommendations for international students: Required—TOEFL (minimum score 550 paper-based; 213 computer-based; 79 iBT). *Application deadline:* Applications are processed on a rolling basis. Application fee: $45. Electronic applications accepted. *Expenses:* Tuition: Full-time $12,664. Required fees: $760. *Financial support:* Institutionally sponsored loans and scholarships/grants available. Financial award applicants required to submit FAFSA. *Unit head:* Dr. Marla LaRue, Dean/Executive Director, 480-557-1218, E-mail: marla.larue@phoenix. edu. *Application contact:* Dr. Marla LaRue, Dean/Executive Director, 480-557-1218, E-mail: marla.larue@phoenix.edu.

University of Phoenix–Phoenix Campus, The Artemis School, College of Education, Phoenix, AZ 85040-1958. Offers administration and supervision (MA Ed); curriculum and instruction (MA Ed); elementary licensure (MA Ed); secondary licensure (MA Ed). Evening/weekend programs available. *Faculty:* 39 full-time (23 women), 422 part-time/adjunct (255 women). *Students:* 850 full-time (614 women); includes 135 minority (45 African Americans, 7 American Indian/Alaska Native, 20 Asian Americans or Pacific Islanders, 63 Hispanic Americans), 15 international. Average age 35. In 2006, 500 degrees awarded. *Degree requirements:* For master's, thesis (for some programs), registration. *Entrance requirements:* For master's, 3

years of work experience, minimum undergraduate GPA of 2.5. Additional exam requirements/recommendations for international students: Required—TOEFL (minimum score 550 paper-based; 213 computer-based; 79 iBT). *Application deadline:* Applications are processed on a rolling basis. Application fee: $45. Electronic applications accepted. *Financial support:* Institutionally sponsored loans and scholarships/grants available. Financial award applicants required to submit FAFSA. *Unit head:* Dr. Marla LaRue, Dean/Executive Director, 480-557-1218, E-mail: marla.larue@phoenix.edu. *Application contact:* College Chair, 480-804-7400, Fax: 480-557-2320.

University of Phoenix–Puerto Rico Campus, The Artemis School, College of Education, Guaynabo, PR 00968. Offers administration and supervision (MA Ed); early childhood education (MA Ed); school counselor (MSC). Evening/weekend programs available. *Faculty:* 8 full-time (all women), 28 part-time/adjunct (21 women). *Students:* 186 full-time (156 women); includes 91 minority (1 African American, 1 American Indian/Alaska Native, 89 Hispanic Americans), 4 international. Average age 37. In 2006, 39 degrees awarded. *Degree requirements:* For master's, thesis (for some programs), registration. *Entrance requirements:* For master's, minimum undergraduate GPA of 2.5, 3 years work experience. Additional exam requirements/recommendations for international students: Required—TOEFL (minimum score 550 paper-based; 213 computer-based; 79 iBT). *Application deadline:* Applications are processed on a rolling basis. Application fee: $45. Electronic applications accepted. *Expenses:* Tuition: Full-time $5,816. Required fees: $760. *Financial support:* Institutionally sponsored loans and scholarships/grants available. Financial award applicants required to submit FAFSA. *Unit head:* Dr. Marla LaRue, Dean/Executive Director, 480-557-1218, E-mail: marla.larue@phoenix. edu. *Application contact:* Chair, 787-731-5400, Fax: 787-731-1510.

University of Phoenix–Southern Colorado Campus, The Artemis School, College of Education, Colorado Springs, CO 80919-2335. Offers administration and supervision (MA Ed); curriculum and instruction (MA Ed); elementary licensure (MA Ed); principal licensure certification (Certificate); school counseling (MSC); secondary licensure (MA Ed). Evening/weekend programs available. *Faculty:* 7 full-time (3 women), 90 part-time/adjunct (53 women). *Students:* 220 full-time (162 women); includes 22 minority (7 African Americans, 1 American Indian/ Alaska Native, 4 Asian Americans or Pacific Islanders, 10 Hispanic Americans), 15 international. Average age 37. In 2006, 122 degrees awarded. *Degree requirements:* For master's, thesis (for some programs), registration. *Entrance requirements:* For master's, minimum undergraduate GPA of 2.5, 3 years of work experience. Additional exam requirements/recommendations for international students: Required—TOEFL (minimum score 550 paper-based; 213 computer-based; 79 iBT). *Application deadline:* Applications are processed on a rolling basis. Application fee: $45. Electronic applications accepted. *Expenses:* Tuition: Full-time $10,291. Required fees: $760. *Financial support:* Institutionally sponsored loans and scholarships/grants available. Financial award applicants required to submit FAFSA. *Unit head:* Dr. Marla LaRue, Dean/Executive Director, 480-557-1218, E-mail: marla.larue@phoenix.edu. *Application contact:* Chair, 719-599-5282, Fax: 719-599-7973.

University of Phoenix–Springfield Campus, College of Education, Springfield, MO 65804-7211. Offers administration and supervision (MA Ed); curriculum and instruction (MA Ed); curriculum and instruction/adult education (MA Ed); curriculum and instruction/computer education (MA Ed); curriculum and instruction/English as a second language (MA Ed); English and language arts education (MA Ed); mathematics education (MA Ed).

University of Phoenix–Utah Campus, The Artemis School, College of Education, Salt Lake City, UT 84123-4617. Offers administration and supervision (MA Ed); curriculum and instruction (MA Ed); elementary education (MA Ed); school counseling (MSC); secondary education (MA Ed). Evening/weekend programs available. *Faculty:* 14 full-time (8 women), 78 part-time/adjunct (39 women). *Students:* 395 full-time (246 women); includes 20 minority (2 African Americans, 1 American Indian/Alaska Native, 8 Asian Americans or Pacific Islanders, 9 Hispanic Americans), 4 international. Average age 37. In 2006, 233 degrees awarded. *Degree requirements:* For master's, thesis (for some programs), registration. *Entrance requirements:* For master's, minimum undergraduate GPA of 2.5, 3 years work experience. Additional exam requirements/recommendations for international students: Required—TOEFL (minimum score 550 paper-based; 213 computer-based; 79 iBT). *Application deadline:* Applications are processed on a rolling basis. Application fee: $45. Electronic applications accepted. *Expenses:* Tuition: Full-time $9,104. Required fees: $760. *Financial support:* Institutionally sponsored loans and scholarships/grants available. Financial award applicants required to submit FAFSA. *Unit head:* Dr. Marla LaRue, Dean/Executive Director, 480-557-1218, E-mail: marla.larue@phoenix. edu. *Application contact:* Chair, 801-263-1444, Fax: 801-269-9766.

University of Phoenix–Vancouver Campus, The Artemis School, College of Education, Burnaby, BC V5C 6G9, Canada. Offers administration and supervision (MA Ed); curriculum and instruction (MA Ed). Evening/weekend programs available. *Faculty:* 25. *Students:* 131 full-time (79 women); includes 6 minority (all Asian Americans or Pacific Islanders) Average age 40. In 2006, 49 degrees awarded. *Degree requirements:* For master's, thesis (for some programs), registration. *Entrance requirements:* For master's, minimum undergraduate GPA of 2.5, 3 years work experience. Additional exam requirements/recommendations for international students: Required—TOEFL (minimum score 550 paper-based; 213 computer-based; 79 iBT). *Application deadline:* Applications are processed on a rolling basis. Application fee: $45. Electronic applications accepted. *Expenses:* Tuition: Full-time $12,840. Required fees: $760. *Financial support:* Institutionally sponsored loans and scholarships/ grants available. *Unit head:* Dr. Marla LaRue, Dean/Executive Director, 480-557-1218, E-mail: marla.larue@phoenix.edu. *Application contact:* Chair, 404-205-6999.

University of Phoenix–West Florida Campus, The Artemis School, College of Education, Temple Terrace, FL 33637. Offers administration and supervision (MA Ed); curriculum and instruction (MA Ed); curriculum and technology (MA Ed); elementary teacher education (MA Ed); secondary teacher education (MA Ed). Evening/weekend programs available. *Faculty:* 10 full-time (8 women), 15 part-time/adjunct (7 women). *Students:* 67 full-time (61 women); includes 24 minority (20 African Americans, 1 American Indian/Alaska Native, 3 Hispanic Americans), 3 international. Average age 40. In 2006, 8 degrees awarded. *Degree requirements:* For master's, thesis (for some programs), registration. *Entrance requirements:* For master's, 3 years of work experience, minimum undergraduate GPA of 2.5. Additional exam requirements/ recommendations for international students: Required—TOEFL (minimum score 550 paper-based; 213 computer-based; 79 iBT). Application fee: $45. *Expenses:* Tuition: Full-time $9,450. Required fees: $760. *Financial support:* Institutionally sponsored loans and scholarships/ grants available. Financial award applicants required to submit FAFSA. *Unit head:* Dr. Marla LaRue, Dean, 480-557-1218, E-mail: marla.larue@phoenix.edu. *Application contact:* Chair, 813-626-7911, Fax: 813-977-1449.

University of Phoenix–West Michigan Campus, The Artemis School, College of Education, Walker, MI 49544. Offers administration and supervision (MA Ed); curriculum and instruction (MA Ed). Evening/weekend programs available. *Faculty:* 5 full-time (1 woman), 15 part-time/adjunct (9 women). In 2006, 5 master's awarded. *Degree requirements:* For master's, thesis (for some programs), registration. *Entrance requirements:* For master's, 3 years of work experience, minimum undergraduate GPA of 2.5. Additional exam requirements/ recommendations for international students: Required—TOEFL (minimum score 550 paper-based; 213 computer-based; 79 iBT). *Application deadline:* Applications are processed on a rolling basis. Application fee: $45. Electronic applications accepted. *Expenses:* Tuition: Full-time $12,043. Required fees: $760. *Financial support:* Institutionally sponsored loans and scholarships/grants available. Financial award applicants required to submit FAFSA. *Unit head:* Dr. Marla LaRue, Dean/Executive Director, 480-557-1218, E-mail: marla.larue@phoenix.edu. *Application contact:* Chair, 888-345-9699, Fax: 616-784-5300.

University of Pittsburgh, School of Education, Department of Administrative and Policy Studies, Program in School Leadership, Pittsburgh, PA 15260. Offers M Ed, Ed D. Part-time and evening/weekend programs available. *Students:* 17 full-time (10 women), 169 part-time (99 women); includes 14 minority (13 African Americans, 1 Hispanic American), 1 international.

80 applicants, 85% accepted, 61 enrolled. In 2006, 17 master's, 15 doctorates awarded. *Degree requirements:* For master's and doctorate, thesis/dissertation. *Entrance requirements:* For doctorate, GRE General Test. Additional exam requirements/recommendations for international students: Required—TOEFL. *Application deadline:* For fall admission, 2/1 priority date for domestic students; for spring admission, 11/1 priority date for domestic students. Applications are processed on a rolling basis. Application fee: $50. Electronic applications accepted. *Financial support:* Fellowships, Federal Work-Study and tuition waivers (partial) available. Support available to part-time students. Financial award application deadline: 3/15; financial award applicants required to submit FAFSA. *Application contact:* Joan M. Cutone, Director, School of Education Student Service Center, 412-648-2230, Fax: 412-648-1899, E-mail: soeinfo@pitt.edu.

University of Prince Edward Island, Faculty of Education, Charlottetown, PE C1A 4P3, Canada. Offers leadership and learning (M Ed). Part-time programs available. *Students:* 9 full-time (8 women), 110 part-time (85 women). 106 applicants, 55% accepted, 56 enrolled. In 2006, 72 degrees awarded. *Degree requirements:* For master's, thesis. *Entrance requirements:* For master's, 2 years of professional experience, bachelor of education, professional certificate. Additional exam requirements/recommendations for international students: Required—TOEFL (minimum score 550 paper-based; 213 computer-based; 80 iBT), Canadian Academic English Language Assessment, Michigan English Language Assessment Battery, Canadian Test of English for Scholars and Trainees. *Application deadline:* For fall admission, 1/15 for domestic and international students. Application fee: $75 ($100 for international students). *Faculty research:* Distance learning, aboriginal communities and education leadership development, international development, immersion language learning. *Unit head:* Dr. Graham Pike, Dean, 902-566-0731, Fax: 902-566-0416. *Application contact:* Dr. Gerald Hopkirk, Graduate Studies Coordinator, 902-566-0622, Fax: 902-566-0416, E-mail: ghopkirk@upei.ca.

University of Puerto Rico, Río Piedras, College of Education, Program in School Administration and Supervision, San Juan, PR 00931-3300. Offers M Ed, Ed D. Part-time programs available. *Students:* 46 full-time (38 women), 42 part-time (26 women); all minorities (all Hispanic Americans) In 2006, 7 master's, 3 doctorates awarded. *Degree requirements:* For master's, thesis; for doctorate, thesis/dissertation, internship. *Entrance requirements:* For master's, PAEG or GRE, minimum GPA of 3.0, letter of recommendation; for doctorate, GRE or PAEG, interview, master's degree, minimum GPA of 3.0, letter of recommendation. *Application deadline:* For fall admission, 2/1 for domestic and international students. Application fee: $17. *Expenses:* Tuition, state resident: part-time $100 per credit. Tuition, nonresident: part-time $291 per credit. Required fees: $72 per semester. *Financial support:* Fellowships, research assistantships, teaching assistantships, career-related internships or fieldwork, Federal Work-Study, institutionally sponsored loans, and tuition waivers (partial) available. Financial award application deadline: 5/31. *Faculty research:* Secondary education and administration. *Unit head:* Dr. Loyda Martinez, Coordinator, 787-764-0000 Ext. 4361, Fax: 787-763-4130.

University of Regina, Faculty of Graduate Studies and Research, Faculty of Education, Department of Educational Administration, Regina, SK S4S 0A2, Canada. Offers M Ed. *Faculty:* 3 full-time (1 woman), 1 (woman) part-time/adjunct. *Students:* 6 full-time (3 women), 61 part-time (21 women). 25 applicants, 92% accepted. In 2006, 23 degrees awarded. *Degree requirements:* For master's, practicum, project, or thesis. *Entrance requirements:* For master's, bachelor's degree in education, 2 years of teaching experience. Additional exam requirements/recommendations for international students: Required—TOEFL (minimum score 580 paper-based; 237 computer-based; 88 iBT). *Application deadline:* For fall admission, 2/15 for domestic students; for winter admission, 2/15 for domestic students; for spring admission, 2/15 for domestic students. Application fee: $60 ($100 for international students). *Financial support:* Fellowships, research assistantships, teaching assistantships available. Financial award application deadline: 6/15. *Faculty research:* Administration, policy. *Application contact:* Vicki Minhinnick, Graduate Program Coordinator, 306-585-4506, Fax: 306-585-5387, E-mail: edgrad@uregina.ca.

University of St. Francis, College of Education, Joliet, IL 60435-6169. Offers curriculum and instruction (MS); educational leadership (MS), including reading, special education; elementary education certification (M Ed); secondary education certification (M Ed), including English education, math education, science education, social studies education; special education (M Ed); teaching and learning (MS). Part-time and evening/weekend programs available. *Faculty:* 11 full-time (10 women), 25 part-time/adjunct (12 women). *Students:* 52 full-time (38 women), 381 part-time (293 women); includes 38 minority (21 African Americans, 1 American Indian/Alaska Native, 4 Asian Americans or Pacific Islanders, 12 Hispanic Americans). Average age 33. 194 applicants, 80% accepted, 117 enrolled. In 2006, 165 degrees awarded. *Degree requirements:* For master's, comprehensive exam (for some programs), registration. *Entrance requirements:* For master's, minimum undergraduate GPA of 2.75, 2 letters of recommendation, computer competency. Additional exam requirements/recommendations for international students: Required—TOEFL (minimum score 550 paper-based; 213 computer-based). *Application deadline:* Applications are processed on a rolling basis. Application fee: $30. Electronic applications accepted. *Expenses:* Contact institution. Part-time tuition and fees vary according to campus/location and program. *Financial support:* In 2006–07, 272 students received support. Scholarships/grants, tuition waivers (partial), and unspecified assistantships available. Support available to part-time students. Financial award applicants required to submit FAFSA. *Unit head:* Dr. John Gambro, Dean, 815-740-3456, Fax: 815-740-2264, E-mail: jgambro@stfrancis.edu. *Application contact:* Sandra Sloka, Director of Admissions for Graduate and Degree Completion Programs, 800-735-7500, Fax: 815-740-5032, E-mail: ssloka@stfrancis.edu.

University of St. Thomas, Graduate Studies, School of Education, Department of Leadership, Policy and Administration, St. Paul, MN 55105-1096. Offers athletics and activities administration (MA); community education administration (MA); educational leadership (Ed S); educational leadership and administration (MA); leadership (Ed D); leadership in student affairs (MA, Certificate); police leadership (MA); public policy and leadership (MA, Certificate). Part-time and evening/weekend programs available. *Faculty:* 6 full-time (3 women), 24 part-time/adjunct (9 women). *Students:* 22 full-time (19 women), 327 part-time (156 women); includes 32 minority (17 African Americans, 3 American Indian/Alaska Native, 8 Asian Americans or Pacific Islanders, 4 Hispanic Americans), 3 international. Average age 38. 140 applicants, 93% accepted, 123 enrolled. In 2006, 14 master's, 8 doctorates, 2 other advanced degrees awarded. Terminal master's awarded for partial completion of doctoral program. *Degree requirements:* For master's, thesis (for some programs), registration; for doctorate, thesis/dissertation, registration; for other advanced degree, thesis or alternative, registration. *Entrance requirements:* For master's, minimum GPA of 2.75 or MAT; for doctorate, MAT, minimum graduate GPA of 3.5; for other advanced degree, MAT, minimum graduate GPA of 3.25. Additional exam requirements/recommendations for international students: Required—TOEFL (minimum score 550 paper-based; 213 computer-based). *Application deadline:* For fall admission, 6/1 priority date for domestic students; for spring admission, 11/1 priority date for domestic students. Applications are processed on a rolling basis. Application fee: $50. *Expenses:* Contact institution. *Financial support:* In 2006–07, 124 students received support; fellowships, research assistantships, institutionally sponsored loans and scholarships/grants available. Support available to part-time students. Financial award applicants required to submit FAFSA. *Unit head:* Dr. Donald R. LaMagdeleine, Chair, 651-962-4893, Fax: 651-962-4169, E-mail: drlamagdelei@stthomas.edu. *Application contact:* Jackie Grossklaus, Department Assistant, 651-962-4885, Fax: 651-962-4169, E-mail: jmgrossklaus@stthomas.edu.

University of San Diego, School of Leadership and Education Sciences, Program in Leadership Studies, San Diego, CA 92110-2492. Offers educational leadership (M Ed); leadership studies (MA, PhD); nonprofit leadership and management (Certificate). Part-time programs available. *Faculty:* 6 full-time (4 women), 13 part-time/adjunct (8 women). *Students:* 16 full-time (10 women), 136 part-time (91 women); includes 39 minority (10 African Americans, 7 Asian Americans or Pacific Islanders, 22 Hispanic Americans), 7 international. Average age 38. 115 applicants, 64% accepted, 53 enrolled. In 2006, 38 master's, 8 doctorates awarded. *Degree requirements:* For master's, thesis (for some programs), portfolio; for doctorate, thesis/dissertation, comprehensive exam. *Entrance requirements:* For master's, minimum GPA of 3.0, interview; for doctorate, master's degree, minimum GPA of 3.5 (recommended), master's course work, interview, writing sample, resumé. Additional exam requirements/recommendations for international students: Required—TOEFL (minimum score 580 paper-based; 237 computer-based), TWE. *Application deadline:* For fall admission, 7/1 priority date for domestic students; for spring admission, 11/15 priority date for domestic students. Application fee: $45. Electronic applications accepted. *Financial support:* Career-related internships or fieldwork, Federal Work-Study, institutionally sponsored loans, tuition waivers (partial), unspecified assistantships, and stipends available. Support available to part-time students. Financial award application deadline: 5/1; financial award applicants required to submit FAFSA. *Unit head:* Dr. Edward DeRoche, Graduate Program Director, 619-260-2250, Fax: 619-260-6835, E-mail: deroche@sandiego.edu. *Application contact:* Stephen Pultz, Director of Admissions, 619-260-4524, Fax: 619-260-4158, E-mail: grads@sandiego.edu.

University of San Francisco, School of Education, Department of Catholic Educational Leadership, San Francisco, CA 94117-1080. Offers Catholic school leadership (MA, Ed D); Catholic school teaching (MA); private school administration (Ed D). *Faculty:* 1 (woman) full-time, 3 part-time/adjunct (2 women). *Students:* 9 full-time (5 women), 32 part-time (18 women); includes 10 minority (6 Asian Americans or Pacific Islanders, 4 Hispanic Americans), 3 international. Average age 37. 33 applicants, 97% accepted, 13 enrolled. In 2006, 4 master's, 6 doctorates awarded. *Degree requirements:* For doctorate, thesis/dissertation. Application fee: $55 ($65 for international students). *Expenses:* Tuition: Full-time $17,370; part-time $965 per unit. Tuition and fees vary according to degree level, campus/location and program. *Financial support:* In 2006–07, 14 students received support; fellowships, research assistantships, teaching assistantships available. Financial award application deadline: 3/2; financial award applicants required to submit FAFSA. *Unit head:* Br. Ray Vercruysse, Chair, 415-422-6226.

University of San Francisco, School of Education, Department of Organization and Leadership, San Francisco, CA 94117-1080. Offers digital media and learning (MA); organization and leadership (MA, Ed D). *Faculty:* 5 full-time (4 women), 9 part-time/adjunct (5 women). *Students:* 167 full-time (116 women), 120 part-time (78 women); includes 105 minority (32 African Americans, 1 American Indian/Alaska Native, 37 Asian Americans or Pacific Islanders, 35 Hispanic Americans), 5 international. Average age 35. 188 applicants, 87% accepted, 84 enrolled. In 2006, 91 master's, 19 doctorates awarded. *Degree requirements:* For doctorate, thesis/dissertation. Application fee: $55 ($65 for international students). *Expenses:* Tuition: Full-time $17,370; part-time $965 per unit. Tuition and fees vary according to degree level, campus/location and program. *Financial support:* In 2006–07, 178 students received support; fellowships, research assistantships, teaching assistantships available. Financial award application deadline: 3/2; financial award applicants required to submit FAFSA. *Unit head:* Br. Ray Vercruysse, Chair, 415-422-6551.

University of Saskatchewan, College of Graduate Studies and Research, College of Education, Department of Educational Administration, Saskatoon, SK S7N 5A2, Canada. Offers M Ed, PhD, Diploma. Part-time programs available. *Degree requirements:* For master's, thesis (for some programs), registration; for doctorate, thesis/dissertation, registration. *Entrance requirements:* Additional exam requirements/recommendations for international students: Required—TOEFL.

The University of Scranton, Graduate School, Department of Education, Program in Educational Administration, Scranton, PA 18510. Offers MS. *Accreditation:* NCATE. Part-time and evening/weekend programs available. Postbaccalaureate distance learning degree programs offered (no on-campus study). *Students:* 2 full-time (0 women), 333 part-time (197 women); includes 45 minority (33 African Americans, 1 Asian American or Pacific Islander, 11 Hispanic Americans), 2 international. Average age 35. 127 applicants, 97% accepted. In 2006, 4 degrees awarded. *Degree requirements:* For master's, capstone experience. *Entrance requirements:* For master's, minimum GPA of 2.75. Additional exam requirements/recommendations for international students: Required—TOEFL (minimum score 500 paper-based; 173 computer-based), IELTS (minimum score 6). *Application deadline:* Applications are processed on a rolling basis. Application fee: $50. *Expenses:* Tuition: Part-time $684 per credit. Required fees: $25 per term. *Financial support:* Teaching assistantships, career-related internships or fieldwork, Federal Work-Study, and unspecified assistantships available. Support available to part-time students. Financial award application deadline: 3/1. *Unit head:* Dr. Derry Stufft, Director, 570-941-7421, Fax: 570-941-7401, E-mail: stufftda@scranton.edu.

University of Sioux Falls, Program in Education, Sioux Falls, SD 57105-1699. Offers leadership (M Ed); reading (M Ed); superintendent (Ed S); teaching (M Ed); technology (M Ed). Summer admission only. *Accreditation:* NCATE. Part-time and evening/weekend programs available. Postbaccalaureate distance learning degree programs offered (minimal on-campus study). *Faculty:* 12 full-time (8 women), 13 part-time/adjunct (7 women). *Students:* 9 applicants, 100% accepted, 7 enrolled. In 2006, 46 master's, 26 other advanced degrees awarded. *Median time to degree:* Master's–2.5 years part-time; Ed S–2 years part-time. *Degree requirements:* For master's, research application project; for Ed S, portfolio. *Entrance requirements:* For master's, minimum GPA of 3.0, 1 year of teaching experience; for Ed S, administrative exam, minimum 3 years of teaching experience, minimum cumulative GPA of 3.5. Additional exam requirements/recommendations for international students: Required—TOEFL. *Application deadline:* Applications are processed on a rolling basis. Application fee: $25. *Expenses:* Tuition: Part-time $300 per semester hour. Required fees: $15 per term. Part-time tuition and fees vary according to program. *Financial support:* In 2006–07, 58 students received support. Scholarships/grants available. Support available to part-time students. *Unit head:* Dawn Olson, Director of Graduate Education, 605-575-2063, Fax: 605-575-2079, E-mail: dawn.olson@usiouxfalls.edu.

University of South Alabama, Graduate School, College of Education, Department of Leadership and Teacher Education, Mobile, AL 36688-0002. Offers early childhood education (M Ed); educational administration (Ed S); educational leadership (M Ed); elementary education (M Ed); reading education (M Ed); science education (M Ed); secondary education (M Ed); special education (M Ed, Ed S). *Accreditation:* NCATE. Part-time programs available. *Faculty:* 22 full-time (13 women). *Students:* 287 full-time (251 women), 229 part-time (194 women); includes 137 minority (125 African Americans, 8 American Indian/Alaska Native, 3 Asian Americans or Pacific Islanders, 1 Hispanic American), 4 international. 43 applicants, 84% accepted, 20 enrolled. In 2006, 169 master's, 12 other advanced degrees awarded. *Degree requirements:* For master's, comprehensive exam. *Entrance requirements:* For master's, GRE General Test or MAT, minimum GPA of 3.0. *Application deadline:* For fall admission, 9/1 priority date for domestic students. Applications are processed on a rolling basis. Application fee: $25. *Financial support:* In 2006–07, 6 research assistantships were awarded; career-related internships or fieldwork also available. Support available to part-time students. Financial award application deadline: 4/1. *Unit head:* Dr. David L. Gray, Chair, 251-380-2894.

University of South Carolina, The Graduate School, College of Education, Department of Educational Leadership and Policies, Program in Educational Administration, Columbia, SC 29208. Offers M Ed, MA, PhD, Ed S. *Accreditation:* NCATE. Part-time and evening/weekend programs available. *Degree requirements:* For master's, thesis (for some programs), foreign language (MA), comprehensive exam; for doctorate, thesis/dissertation, comprehensive exam. *Entrance requirements:* For master's and Ed S, GRE General Test or MAT; for doctorate, GRE General Test or MAT, interview. Electronic applications accepted.

The University of South Dakota, Graduate School, School of Education, Division of Educational Administration, Vermillion, SD 57069-2390. Offers MA, Ed D, Ed S. *Accreditation:* NCATE. Part-time and evening/weekend programs available. Postbaccalaureate distance learning degree programs offered (no on-campus study). *Faculty:* 8 full-time (4 women), 2 part-time/adjunct (0 women). *Students:* 244 (131 women). In 2006, 21 master's, 32 doctorates, 15 other advanced degrees awarded. *Degree requirements:* For master's and Ed S, thesis or alternative, comprehensive exam; for doctorate, thesis/dissertation, comprehensive exam. *Entrance*

Educational Administration

The University of South Dakota *(continued)*
requirements: For master's and doctorate, GRE General Test, MAT, minimum GPA of 2.7. Additional exam requirements/recommendations for international students: Required—TOEFL (minimum score 550 paper-based; 213 computer-based; 79 iBT). *Application deadline:* Applications are processed on a rolling basis. Application fee: $35. Electronic applications accepted. *Expenses:* Tuition, state resident: part-time $120 per credit hour. Tuition, nonresident: part-time $355 per credit hour. Required fees: $90 per credit hour. *Financial support:* In 2006–07, research assistantships with partial tuition reimbursements (averaging $4,626 per year), teaching assistantships with partial tuition reimbursements (averaging $4,626 per year) were awarded; Federal Work-Study, traineeships, and unspecified assistantships also available. Financial award applicants required to submit FAFSA. *Unit head:* Dr. Mark Baron, Chair and Graduate Director, 605-677-5260, Fax: 605-677-5438, E-mail: mbaron@usd.edu.

University of Southern Maine, College of Education and Human Development, Educational Leadership Program, Portland, ME 04104-9300. Offers assistant principal (Certificate); athletic administration (Certificate); educational leadership (MS Ed, CAS); middle-level education (Certificate). *Accreditation:* NCATE. Part-time and evening/weekend programs available. Postbaccalaureate distance learning degree programs offered (minimal on-campus study). *Faculty:* 7 full-time (1 woman), 5 part-time/adjunct (2 women). *Students:* 4 full-time (3 women), 111 part-time (63 women), 1 international. 20 applicants, 65% accepted, 8 enrolled. In 2006, 36 master's, 23 CASs awarded. *Degree requirements:* For master's, thesis or alternative, practicum; for other advanced degree, thesis or alternative. *Entrance requirements:* For master's, GRE General Test or MAT; for other advanced degree, master's degree. Additional exam requirements/recommendations for international students: Required—TOEFL. *Application deadline:* For fall admission, 2/1 for domestic students; for spring admission, 9/15 for domestic students. Application fee: $50. Electronic applications accepted. *Expenses:* Tuition, state resident: full-time $4,860; part-time $270 per credit hour. Tuition, nonresident: full-time $13,572; part-time $754 per credit hour. Required fees: $222 per semester. Tuition and fees vary according to course load. *Financial support:* In 2006–07, 3 students received support, including 2 research assistantships with tuition reimbursements available (averaging $4,500 per year); career-related internships or fieldwork, Federal Work-Study, institutionally sponsored loans, scholarships/grants, and unspecified assistantships also available. Financial award application deadline: 3/1; financial award applicants required to submit FAFSA. *Unit head:* Dr. James Curry, Chair, Professional Education Department, 270-780-5400, Fax: 270-780-5674, E-mail: jcurry@usm.maine.edu. *Application contact:* Robin Audesse, Associate Director of Graduate Admissions, 207-780-5306, Fax: 207-780-5193, E-mail: raudesse@usm.maine.edu.

University of Southern Mississippi, Graduate School, College of Education and Psychology, Department of Educational Leadership and Research, Hattiesburg, MS 39406-0001. Offers adult education (M Ed, Ed D, PhD, Ed S); educational administration (M Ed, Ed D, PhD, Ed S); higher education (PhD). *Faculty:* 19 full-time (7 women). *Students:* 86 full-time (66 women), 250 part-time (173 women); includes 102 minority (97 African Americans, 1 American Indian/Alaska Native, 2 Asian Americans or Pacific Islanders, 2 Hispanic Americans), 4 international. Average age 38. 123 applicants, 62% accepted, 72 enrolled. In 2006, 56 master's, 25 doctorates, 41 other advanced degrees awarded. *Degree requirements:* For master's, thesis (for some programs), internship, comprehensive exam, registration; for doctorate, thesis/dissertation, comprehensive exam, registration; for Ed S, thesis (for some programs), comprehensive exam, registration. *Entrance requirements:* For master's, GRE General Test, minimum GPA of 2.75; for doctorate, GRE General Test, minimum GPA of 3.5; for Ed S, GRE General Test, minimum GPA of 3.25. Additional exam requirements/recommendations for international students: Required—TOEFL. *Application deadline:* For fall admission, 3/1 priority date for domestic students, 3/1 for international students. Applications are processed on a rolling basis. Application fee: $25 ($30 for international students). *Financial support:* In 2006–07, 12 research assistantships with full tuition reimbursements (averaging $5,571 per year), 1 teaching assistantship (averaging $5,571 per year) were awarded; career-related internships or fieldwork, Federal Work-Study, and institutionally sponsored loans also available. Financial award application deadline: 3/15. *Faculty research:* Supervision, learning styles, education finance, higher education organization. Total annual research expenditures: $88,500. *Unit head:* Dr. Gaylynn Parker, Interim Chair, 601-266-4589, Fax: 601-266-5141.

University of South Florida, Graduate School, College of Education, Department of Educational Leadership and Policy Studies, Tampa, FL 33620-9951. Offers educational leadership (M Ed, Ed D, Ed S). Part-time and evening/weekend programs available. *Faculty:* 11 full-time (6 women), 18 part-time/adjunct (8 women). *Students:* 133 full-time (95 women), 313 part-time (217 women); includes 101 minority (46 African Americans, 4 Asian Americans or Pacific Islanders, 51 Hispanic Americans), 1 international. 251 applicants, 77% accepted, 150 enrolled. In 2006, 139 master's, 3 doctorates awarded. *Degree requirements:* For doctorate, thesis/dissertation, 2 tools of research in foreign language, statistics, and/or computers. *Entrance requirements:* For master's, GRE General Test, minimum GPA of 3.0 in last 60 hours. *Application deadline:* For fall admission, 12/1 for domestic students. Application fee: $30. Electronic applications accepted. *Financial support:* Unspecified assistantships available. Financial award application deadline: 3/22. Total annual research expenditures: $1,891. *Unit head:* Judith Ponticell, Chairperson, 813-974-4078, Fax: 813-974-5423, E-mail: bojap@tempest.coedu.usf.edu.

The University of Tennessee, Graduate School, College of Education, Health and Human Sciences, Program in Education, Knoxville, TN 37996. Offers art education (MS); counseling education (PhD); cultural studies in education (PhD); curriculum (MS, Ed S); curriculum, educational research and evaluation (Ed D, PhD); early childhood education (PhD); early childhood special education (MS); education of deaf and hard of hearing (MS); educational administration and policy studies (Ed D, PhD); educational administration and supervision (Ed S); educational psychology (Ed D, PhD); elementary education (MS, Ed S); elementary teaching (MS); English education (MS, Ed S); exercise science (PhD); foreign language/ESL education (MS, Ed S); instructional technology (MS, Ed D, PhD, Ed S); literacy, language and ESL education (PhD); literacy, language education, and ESL education (Ed D); mathematics education (MS, Ed S); modified and comprehensive special education (MS); reading education (MS, Ed S); school counseling (Ed S); school psychology (PhD, Ed S); science education (MS, Ed S); secondary teaching (MS); social foundations (MS); social science education (MS, Ed S); socio-cultural foundations of sports and education (PhD); special education (Ed S); teacher education (Ed D, PhD). *Accreditation:* NCATE. Part-time and evening/weekend programs available. *Students:* 529 (401 women); includes 39 minority (23 African Americans, 2 American Indian/Alaska Native, 9 Asian Americans or Pacific Islanders, 5 Hispanic Americans) 34 international. 420 applicants, 50% accepted. In 2006, 258 master's, 28 doctorates awarded. *Degree requirements:* For master's and Ed S, thesis optional; for doctorate, variable foreign language requirement, thesis/dissertation. *Entrance requirements:* For master's, minimum GPA of 2.7; for doctorate and Ed S, GRE General Test, minimum GPA of 2.7. Additional exam requirements/recommendations for international students: Required—TOEFL. *Application deadline:* For fall admission, 2/1 priority date for domestic students. Applications are processed on a rolling basis. Application fee: $35. Electronic applications accepted. *Expenses:* Tuition, state resident: full-time $5,574. Tuition, nonresident: full-time $16,840. Required fees: $792. *Financial support:* In 2006–07, 4 fellowships, 9 teaching assistantships were awarded; career-related internships or fieldwork, Federal Work-Study, institutionally sponsored loans, and unspecified assistantships also available. Financial award application deadline: 2/1; financial award applicants required to submit FAFSA. *Unit head:* Dr. Lester Knight, Head, 865-974-0907, Fax: 865-974-8718, E-mail: lknight@utk.edu.

The University of Tennessee, Graduate School, College of Education, Health and Human Sciences, Program in Educational Administration and Policy Studies, Knoxville, TN 37996. Offers educational administration and policy studies (Ed D); educational administration and supervision (MS). *Accreditation:* NCATE. Part-time and evening/weekend programs available. Postbaccalaureate distance learning degree programs offered (no on-campus study). *Students:* 21 (14 women); includes 1 African American. In 2006, 5 master's, 10 doctorates awarded.

Degree requirements: For master's, thesis optional. *Entrance requirements:* For master's, minimum GPA of 2.7. Additional exam requirements/recommendations for international students: Required—TOEFL. *Application deadline:* For fall admission, 2/1 priority date for domestic students. Applications are processed on a rolling basis. Application fee: $35. Electronic applications accepted. *Expenses:* Tuition, state resident: full-time $5,574. Tuition, nonresident: full-time $16,840. Required fees: $792. *Financial support:* In 2006–07, 2 teaching assistantships were awarded. Financial award application deadline: 2/1; financial award applicants required to submit FAFSA. *Unit head:* Dr. Joy Desensi, Head, 865-974-2216, Fax: 865-974-6146, E-mail: desensi@utk.edu.

The University of Tennessee at Chattanooga, Graduate School, College of Health, Education and Professional Studies, Graduate Studies Division of Education, Chattanooga, TN 37403-2598. Offers counseling (M Ed); educational leadership (Ed D); educational specialist (Ed S), including educational technology, school psychology; elementary education (M Ed); school leadership (M Ed); secondary education (M Ed); special education (M Ed). *Accreditation:* ACA; NCATE. Part-time and evening/weekend programs available. *Faculty:* 28 full-time (18 women), 7 part-time/adjunct (3 women). *Students:* 166 full-time (123 women), 309 part-time (238 women); includes 57 minority (46 African Americans, 2 American Indian/Alaska Native, 7 Asian Americans or Pacific Islanders, 2 Hispanic Americans). Average age 33. 138 applicants, 95% accepted, 66 enrolled. In 2006, 133 master's, 25 other advanced degrees awarded. *Degree requirements:* For master's, thesis optional; for doctorate, thesis/dissertation, comprehensive exam. *Entrance requirements:* For master's, GRE General Test or MAT, teaching certificate. *Application deadline:* For fall admission, 8/1 for domestic students; for spring admission, 12/1 for domestic students. Applications are processed on a rolling basis. Application fee: $30. *Expenses:* Tuition, state resident: full-time $5,434; part-time $339 per hour. Tuition, nonresident: full-time $14,830; part-time $861 per hour. Required fees: $940; $178 per hour. *Financial support:* Fellowships, research assistantships, Federal Work-Study and institutionally sponsored loans available. Support available to part-time students. Financial award application deadline: 4/1; financial award applicants required to submit FAFSA. *Faculty research:* School counseling, community counseling, elementary and secondary education, school leadership and administration. Total annual research expenditures: $258,901. *Unit head:* Dr. Anthony Lease, Head, 423-425-4211, Fax: 423-425-5380, E-mail: tony-lease@utc.edu. *Application contact:* Dr. Deborah E. Arfken, Dean of Graduate Studies, 423-425-4666, Fax: 423-425-5223, E-mail: deborah-arfken@utc.edu.

The University of Tennessee at Martin, Graduate Programs, College of Education and Behavioral Sciences, Program in Educational Administration and Supervision, Martin, TN 38238-1000. Offers MS Ed. Part-time programs available. Postbaccalaureate distance learning degree programs offered. *Students:* 106 (81 women); includes 13 African Americans. 22 applicants, 45% accepted, 4 enrolled. In 2006, 36 degrees awarded. *Degree requirements:* For master's, comprehensive exam. *Entrance requirements:* For master's, GRE General Test, minimum GPA of 2.5, letters of reference, teaching license, resumé. Additional exam requirements/recommendations for international students: Required—TOEFL (minimum score 525 paper-based; 197 computer-based). *Application deadline:* For fall admission, 8/1 priority date for domestic students, 8/1 for international students; for spring admission, 1/1 priority date for domestic students, 1/1 for international students. Applications are processed on a rolling basis. Application fee: $30 ($50 for international students). Electronic applications accepted. *Expenses:* Tuition, state resident: part-time $303 per credit hour. Tuition, nonresident: part-time $829 per credit hour. *Financial support:* Research assistantships with full tuition reimbursements, teaching assistantships with full tuition reimbursements, career-related internships or fieldwork, scholarships/grants, and unspecified assistantships available. *Unit head:* Dr. Suzanne Maniss, Coordinator, 731-881-7163, Fax: 731-881-7975, E-mail: smaniss@utm.edu.

The University of Texas at Arlington, Graduate School, College of Education, Arlington, TX 76019. Offers curriculum and instruction (M Ed); educational leadership and policy studies (M Ed); physiology of exercise (MS); teaching (M Ed T). *Accreditation:* NCATE. Part-time and evening/weekend programs available. Postbaccalaureate distance learning degree programs offered (minimal on-campus study). *Faculty:* 19 full-time (11 women), 3 part-time/adjunct (2 women). *Students:* 171 full-time (107 women), 579 part-time (474 women); includes 278 minority (130 African Americans, 6 American Indian/Alaska Native, 20 Asian Americans or Pacific Islanders, 122 Hispanic Americans), 40 international. Average age 36. 579 applicants, 88% accepted, 368 enrolled. In 2006, 101 degrees awarded. *Degree requirements:* For master's, thesis (for some programs), comprehensive activity, research project, comprehensive exam (for some programs), registration. *Entrance requirements:* For master's, GRE General Test, minimum undergraduate GPA of 3.0 in last 60 hours of course work, writing sample, 3 letters of recommendation. Additional exam requirements/recommendations for international students: Required—TOEFL (minimum score 550 paper-based; 213 computer-based). *Application deadline:* For fall admission, 6/16 priority date for domestic students, 4/9 priority date for international students; for winter admission, 10/22 priority date for domestic students, 9/10 priority date for international students; for spring admission, 3/25 priority date for domestic and international students. Applications are processed on a rolling basis. Application fee: $35 ($50 for international students). Electronic applications accepted. *Expenses:* Tuition, state resident: full-time $5,528. Tuition, nonresident: full-time $10,478. International tuition: $10,608 full-time. *Financial support:* In 2006–07, 11 fellowships (averaging $1,000 per year), teaching assistantships with tuition reimbursements (averaging $9,000 per year) were awarded; career-related internships or fieldwork, Federal Work-Study, scholarships/grants, and unspecified assistantships also available. Financial award application deadline: 6/1; financial award applicants required to submit FAFSA. *Unit head:* Dr. Jeanne M. Gerlach, Dean, 817-272-2591, Fax: 817-272-2530, E-mail: soeadvising@uta.edu. *Application contact:* Brendan Hardy, Graduate Advisor, 817-272-2956, Fax: 817-272-7624, E-mail: coedadvising@uta.edu.

The University of Texas at Austin, Graduate School, College of Education, Department of Educational Administration, Austin, TX 78712-1111. Offers M Ed, Ed D, PhD. *Degree requirements:* For doctorate, thesis/dissertation. *Entrance requirements:* For master's and doctorate, GRE General Test. Electronic applications accepted.

The University of Texas at Brownsville, Graduate Studies, School of Education, Brownsville, TX 78520-4991. Offers bilingual education (M Ed); counseling and guidance (M Ed); curriculum and instruction (M Ed); early childhood education (M Ed); educational administration (M Ed); educational technology (M Ed); English as a second language (M Ed); reading specialist (M Ed); special education/educational diagnostician (M Ed). Part-time and evening/weekend programs available. Postbaccalaureate distance learning degree programs offered (minimal on-campus study). *Degree requirements:* For master's, thesis optional. *Entrance requirements:* For master's, GRE General Test. Additional exam requirements/recommendations for international students: Required—TOEFL.

The University of Texas at El Paso, Graduate School, College of Education, Department of Educational Administration, El Paso, TX 79968-0001. Offers M Ed, MA, Ed D. Part-time and evening/weekend programs available. *Degree requirements:* For master's, thesis optional; for doctorate, thesis/dissertation. *Entrance requirements:* For doctorate, GRE General Test, minimum graduate GPA of 3.0. Additional exam requirements/recommendations for international students: Required—TOEFL. Electronic applications accepted.

The University of Texas at San Antonio, College of Education and Human Development, Department of Educational Leadership and Policy Studies, San Antonio, TX 78249-0617. Offers educational leadership (Ed D); educational leadership and policy studies (MA). Part-time and evening/weekend programs available. *Faculty:* 10 full-time (4 women), 16 part-time/adjunct (6 women). *Students:* 25 full-time (15 women), 330 part-time (237 women); includes 189 minority (19 African Americans, 1 American Indian/Alaska Native, 5 Asian Americans or Pacific Islanders, 164 Hispanic Americans). Average age 36. 96 applicants, 95% accepted, 91 enrolled. In 2006, 91 master's, 8 doctorates awarded. *Degree requirements:* For master's, thesis optional; for doctorate, thesis/dissertation, comprehensive exam, registration. *Entrance requirements:* For master's and doctorate, GRE General Test. Additional exam requirements/

recommendations for international students: Required—TOEFL (minimum score 500 paper-based; 173 computer-based). *Application deadline:* For fall admission, 7/1 for domestic students, 4/1 for international students; for spring admission, 11/1 for domestic students, 9/1 for international students. Applications are processed on a rolling basis. Application fee: $45 ($80 for international students). Electronic applications accepted. *Expenses:* Tuition, state resident: full-time $1,730; part-time $192 per credit hour. Tuition, nonresident: full-time $6,680; part-time $742 per credit hour. Required fees: $733; $308,359 per credit hour. *Financial support:* Career-related internships or fieldwork, Federal Work-Study, scholarships/grants, and unspecified assistantships available. *Unit head:* Dr. David P. Thompson, Chair, 210-458-5436, Fax: 210-458-5848, E-mail: david.thompson@utsa.edu.

The University of Texas at Tyler, College of Education and Psychology, Department of Educational Leadership, Tyler, TX 75799-0001. Offers M Ed. Part-time and evening/weekend programs available. *Faculty:* 5 full-time (2 women). *Students:* 2 full-time (1 woman), 76 part-time (50 women); includes 17 minority (13 African Americans, 4 Hispanic Americans). Average age 36. 3 applicants, 2 enrolled. In 2006, 43 degrees awarded. *Degree requirements:* For master's, 2 years of teaching experience. *Entrance requirements:* For master's, GRE General Test. *Application deadline:* Applications are processed on a rolling basis. Application fee: $0 ($50 for international students). *Expenses:* Tuition, state resident: part-time $50 per credit hour. Tuition, nonresident: part-time $328 per credit hour. Required fees: $107 per credit hour. $426 per term. *Financial support:* Fellowships, research assistantships, teaching assistantships, scholarships/grants available. Financial award application deadline: 7/1. *Faculty research:* Effective schools, restructuring of schools, leadership. Total annual research expenditures: $516,000. *Unit head:* Dr. Ross Sherman, Chair, 903-566-7218, Fax: 903-566-5527, E-mail: rsherman@mail.uttyl.edu. *Application contact:* Bonnie Purser, Office of Graduate Studies, 903-566-7142, Fax: 903-566-7068, E-mail: bpurser@uttyler.edu.

The University of Texas of the Permian Basin, Office of Graduate Studies, School of Education, Program in Educational Leadership, Odessa, TX 79762-0001. Offers MA. *Degree requirements:* For master's, thesis (for some programs), comprehensive exam (for some programs), registration. *Entrance requirements:* For master's, GRE General Test. Additional exam requirements/recommendations for international students: Required—TOEFL (minimum score 550 paper-based; 213 computer-based).

The University of Texas–Pan American, College of Education, Department of Educational Leadership, Edinburg, TX 78541-2999. Offers M Ed, Ed D. Part-time and evening/weekend programs available. *Degree requirements:* For master's, thesis optional; for doctorate, thesis/dissertation, comprehensive exam. *Entrance requirements:* For master's, GRE; for doctorate, master's degree. Additional exam requirements/recommendations for international students: Required—TOEFL. Electronic applications accepted. *Expenses:* Tuition, state resident: full-time $2,577; part-time $143 per credit hour. Tuition, nonresident: full-time $7,527; part-time $418 per credit hour. Required fees: $561. *Faculty research:* Community perceptions of education, leadership and gender studies, continuous improvement processes, leadership.

University of the Cumberlands, Graduate Programs in Education, Program in Elementary/Secondary Principalship, Williamsburg, KY 40769-1372. Offers MA Ed, Certificate. *Entrance requirements:* For degree, 3 years of teaching experience, master's degree.

University of the Pacific, School of Education, Department of Educational Administration and Leadership, Stockton, CA 95211-0197. Offers educational administration (MA, Ed D). *Accreditation:* NCATE. *Faculty:* 6 full-time (3 women). *Students:* 32 full-time (18 women), 69 part-time (40 women); includes 33 minority (8 African Americans, 1 American Indian/Alaska Native, 11 Asian Americans or Pacific Islanders, 13 Hispanic Americans), 3 international. Average age 38. 47 applicants, 70% accepted, 21 enrolled. In 2006, 19 master's, 5 doctorates awarded. *Degree requirements:* For master's, thesis (for some programs); for doctorate, thesis/dissertation. *Entrance requirements:* For master's and doctorate, GRE General Test, GRE Subject Test. Additional exam requirements/recommendations for international students: Required—TOEFL (minimum score 475 paper-based; 150 computer-based). *Application deadline:* For fall admission, 3/1 priority date for domestic students; for spring admission, 10/1 priority date for domestic students. Applications are processed on a rolling basis. Application fee: $75. *Expenses:* Tuition: Full-time $26,920. Required fees: $430. Tuition and fees vary according to course load. *Financial support:* Application deadline: 3/1; *Unit head:* Dr. Dennis Brennan, Chairperson, 209-946-2580, E-mail: dbrennan@pacific.edu.

The University of Toledo, College of Graduate Studies, College of Education, Department of Educational Leadership, Program in Educational Administration and Supervision, Toledo, OH 43606-3390. Offers ME, DE, Ed S. *Accreditation:* NCATE. Evening/weekend programs available. *Students:* 9 full-time (5 women), 85 part-time (46 women); includes 15 minority (12 African Americans, 3 Hispanic Americans). Average age 37. 23 applicants, 87% accepted, 16 enrolled. In 2006, 12 degrees awarded. *Degree requirements:* For master's, thesis or alternative, comprehensive exam; for doctorate, thesis/dissertation, comprehensive exams; for Ed S, thesis optional. *Entrance requirements:* For master's, minimum GPA of 2.7; for doctorate, GRE General Test, interview; minimum GPA of 2.7 (undergraduate), 3.0 (graduate); for Ed S, minimum GPA of 2.7 (undergraduate), 3.0 (graduate). *Application deadline:* For fall admission, 8/15 priority date for domestic students. Applications are processed on a rolling basis. Electronic applications accepted. *Financial support:* Career-related internships or fieldwork, Federal Work-Study, and institutionally sponsored loans available. Support available to part-time students. Financial award application deadline: 4/1; financial award applicants required to submit FAFSA. *Faculty research:* School learning organizations, equity, access and equality in schools. *Application contact:* Doctoral Program Director, 419-530-2461, Fax: 419-530-4912, E-mail: edleadr@utnet.utoledo.edu.

University of Utah, The Graduate School, College of Education, Department of Educational Leadership and Policy, Salt Lake City, UT 84112-1107. Offers M Ed, M Phil, Ed D, PhD, MPA/Ed D, MPA/PhD. Part-time programs available. *Faculty:* 12 full-time (7 women), 5 part-time/adjunct (2 women). *Students:* 44 full-time (27 women), 73 part-time (41 women); includes 11 minority (1 African American, 3 Asian Americans or Pacific Islanders, 7 Hispanic Americans), 5 international. Average age 39. 64 applicants, 66% accepted, 40 enrolled. In 2006, 31 master's, 9 doctorates awarded. *Median time to degree:* Of those who began their doctoral program in fall 1998, 30% received their degree in 8 years or less. *Degree requirements:* For master's, internship; for doctorate, thesis/dissertation, qualifying exam. *Entrance requirements:* For master's, GRE General Test, minimum undergraduate GPA of 3.0, 2 years teaching experience, valid teaching certificate; for doctorate, GRE General Test, minimum undergraduate GPA of 3.0. Additional exam requirements/recommendations for international students: Required—TOEFL (minimum score 500 paper-based; 173 computer-based). *Application deadline:* For fall admission, 2/1 for domestic and international students. Application fee: $45 ($65 for international students). Electronic applications accepted. *Expenses:* Tuition, state resident: full-time $3,208. Tuition, nonresident: full-time $11,326. Required fees: $608. Tuition and fees vary according to class time and program. *Financial support:* In 2006–07, 4 fellowships (averaging $3,500 per year), 4 teaching assistantships with full tuition reimbursements (averaging $10,000 per year) were awarded; career-related internships or fieldwork, scholarships/grants, and unspecified assistantships also available. Financial award application deadline: 4/12; financial award applicants required to submit FAFSA. *Faculty research:* Education accountability, college student diversity, social principalship, middle school teaming, comparative higher education. Total annual research expenditures: $50,000. *Unit head:* Dr. Diana Pounder, Chair, 801-581-5714, Fax: 801-585-6756, E-mail: diana.pounder@ed.utah.edu. *Application contact:* Amber D. Locher, Academic Program Specialist, 801-581-6714, Fax: 801-585-6756, E-mail: amber.locher@ed.utah.edu.

University of Vermont, Graduate College, College of Education and Social Services, Department of Educational Leadership and Policy Studies, Burlington, VT 05405. Offers Ed D. *Accreditation:* NCATE. *Students:* 74 (52 women); includes 3 minority (all African Americans) 1 international. 48 applicants, 44% accepted, 16 enrolled. In 2006, 12 degrees awarded. *Degree requirements:* For doctorate, thesis/dissertation. *Entrance requirements:* Additional exam

requirements/recommendations for international students: Required—TOEFL (minimum score 550 paper-based; 213 computer-based). *Application deadline:* For fall admission, 2/1 priority date for domestic students. Application fee: $40. Electronic applications accepted. *Expenses:* Tuition, state resident: part-time $434 per credit. Tuition, nonresident: part-time $1,096 per credit. *Financial support:* Research assistantships, teaching assistantships available. *Unit head:* Dr. Susan Hasazi, Chairperson, 802-656-1442.

University of Vermont, Graduate College, College of Education and Social Services, Department of Education, Program in Educational Leadership, Burlington, VT 05405. Offers M Ed. *Accreditation:* NCATE. *Students:* 28 (19 women); includes 2 minority (1 African American, 1 Hispanic American). 20 applicants, 75% accepted, 11 enrolled. In 2006, 14 degrees awarded. *Degree requirements:* For master's, thesis or alternative. *Entrance requirements:* Additional exam requirements/recommendations for international students: Required—TOEFL (minimum score 550 paper-based; 213 computer-based). *Application deadline:* For fall admission, 4/1 priority date for domestic students; for spring admission, 11/1 priority date for domestic students. Application fee: $40. *Expenses:* Tuition, state resident: part-time $434 per credit. Tuition, nonresident: part-time $1,096 per credit. *Financial support:* Research assistantships, teaching assistantships, career-related internships or fieldwork available. Financial award application deadline: 3/1. *Unit head:* Dr. Susan Hasazi, Coordinator, 802-656-2936.

University of Vermont, Graduate College, College of Education and Social Services, Department of Integrated Professional Studies, Program in Higher Education and Student Affairs Administration, Burlington, VT 05405. Offers M Ed. *Accreditation:* NCATE. *Students:* 36 (20 women); includes 12 minority (2 African Americans, 2 American Indian/Alaska Native, 6 Asian Americans or Pacific Islanders, 2 Hispanic Americans) 2 international. 105 applicants, 31% accepted, 16 enrolled. In 2006, 16 degrees awarded. *Degree requirements:* For master's, thesis or alternative. *Entrance requirements:* For master's, GRE General Test. Additional exam requirements/recommendations for international students: Required—TOEFL (minimum score 550 paper-based; 213 computer-based). *Application deadline:* For fall admission, 1/1 priority date for domestic students. Applications are processed on a rolling basis. Application fee: $40. Electronic applications accepted. *Expenses:* Tuition, state resident: part-time $434 per credit. Tuition, nonresident: part-time $1,096 per credit. *Financial support:* Application deadline: 1/1. *Unit head:* Dr. D. Hunter, Coordinator, 802-656-2030.

University of Victoria, Faculty of Graduate Studies, Faculty of Education, Department of Educational Psychology and Leadership Studies, Victoria, BC V8W 2Y2, Canada. Offers counseling (M Ed, MA); educational psychology (M Ed, MA, PhD), including counseling psychology (M Ed, MA), learning and development (PhD), learning development (MA), measurement and evaluation (PhD), measurement evaluation (M Ed, MA), special education (M Ed, MA); leadership studies (M Ed, MA). Part-time programs available. *Degree requirements:* For master's, thesis (for some programs), comprehensive exam (M Ed); for doctorate, thesis/dissertation, candidacy exam, comprehensive exam, registration. *Entrance requirements:* For master's, 2 years of work experience in a relevant field, minimum B average; for doctorate, GRE, 2 years of work experience in a relevant field, minimum B average. Additional exam requirements/recommendations for international students: Required—TOEFL (minimum score 575 paper-based; 233 computer-based), IELTS (minimum score 7). *Faculty research:* Learning and development (child, adolescent and adult), special education and exceptional children, evaluation and measurement.

University of Virginia, Curry School of Education, Department of Leadership, Foundations and Policy, Program in Administration and Supervision, Charlottesville, VA 22903. Offers M Ed, Ed D, Ed S. *Students:* 26 full-time (14 women), 34 part-time (16 women); includes 2 minority (1 African American, 1 Asian American or Pacific Islander). Average age 39. 21 applicants, 76% accepted, 8 enrolled. In 2006, 54 master's, 16 doctorates, 26 other advanced degrees awarded. *Degree requirements:* For master's, thesis (for some programs), comprehensive exam (for some programs); for doctorate, thesis/dissertation, comprehensive exam (for some programs). *Entrance requirements:* For master's, doctorate, and Ed S, GRE General Test. *Application deadline:* Applications are processed on a rolling basis. Application fee: $60. Electronic applications accepted. *Financial support:* Fellowships, research assistantships, teaching assistantships available. Financial award applicants required to submit FAFSA. *Unit head:* Cheryl Henig, Professor and Program Coordinator, 434-924-3160. *Application contact:* Student Enrollment Coordinator, 434-924-3160, E-mail: dwf9w@virginia.edu.

University of Washington, Graduate School, College of Education, Seattle, WA 98195. Offers curriculum and instruction (M Ed, Ed D, PhD), including educational technology, general curriculum (Ed D, PhD), language, literacy, and culture, mathematics education, multicultural education, reading and language arts education (Ed D), science education, social studies education, teaching and curriculum (M Ed); educational leadership and policy studies (M Ed, Ed D, PhD), including administration, educational organization and policy, higher education, school district leadership (Ed D), social/cultural foundations; educational psychology (M Ed, PhD), including human development and cognition, measurement and research, school counseling (M Ed), school psychology; special education (M Ed, Ed D, PhD), including early childhood education, elementary special education, emotional and behavioral disabilities (M Ed), general special education, severe disabilities; teacher education (MIT). *Accreditation:* APA. Part-time and evening/weekend programs available. *Degree requirements:* For master's, thesis optional; for doctorate, thesis/dissertation. *Entrance requirements:* For master's and doctorate, GRE General Test, minimum GPA of 3.0. Additional exam requirements/recommendations for international students: Required—TOEFL. Electronic applications accepted. *Faculty research:* School restructuring/effective schools, special education interventions, literacy and writing, technology, school partnerships, teacher preparation.

University of Washington, Graduate School, Education Programs, Tacoma Campus, Seattle, WA 98195. Offers education (M Ed, Professional Certificate); K-8 education (Certificate); principalship (Certificate); school administration (Certificate). Part-time and evening/weekend programs available. *Degree requirements:* For master's, final project. *Entrance requirements:* For master's, GRE General Test; for other advanced degree, Washington Educator Skills Test - Basic. Electronic applications accepted. *Faculty research:* Special education, technology, literacy, children's literature, science.

The University of West Alabama, School of Graduate Studies, College of Education, Department of Teacher Education, Program in School Administration, Livingston, AL 35470. Offers M Ed. *Accreditation:* NCATE. Part-time programs available. *Faculty:* 2 full-time (1 woman). *Students:* 10 full-time (5 women), 33 part-time (21 women); includes 27 minority (all African Americans) In 2006, 15 degrees awarded. *Entrance requirements:* For master's, GRE General Test, MAT, minimum GPA of 2.75. *Application deadline:* For fall admission, 9/10 priority date for domestic students; for spring admission, 3/24 for domestic students. Applications are processed on a rolling basis. Application fee: $20 ($50 for international students). *Financial support:* Career-related internships or fieldwork, Federal Work-Study, scholarships/grants, and unspecified assistantships available. Support available to part-time students. *Unit head:* Dr. Alvin Marson, Coordinator, 205-652-3445.

University of West Florida, College of Professional Studies, Division of Graduate Education, Program in Educational Leadership, Pensacola, FL 32514-5750. Offers M Ed, Ed S. *Accreditation:* NCATE. Part-time and evening/weekend programs available. *Students:* 23 full-time (13 women), 66 part-time (45 women); includes 17 minority (13 African Americans, 1 American Indian/Alaska Native, 3 Asian Americans or Pacific Islanders), 1 international. Average age 38. 59 applicants, 54% accepted, 24 enrolled. In 2006, 43 master's, 10 other advanced degrees awarded. *Degree requirements:* For master's, thesis optional. *Entrance requirements:* For master's, GRE General Test or minimum GPA of 3.0. Additional exam requirements/recommendations for international students: Required—TOEFL (minimum score 550 paper-based; 213 computer-based). *Application deadline:* For fall admission, 6/1 for domestic students, 5/15 for international students; for spring admission, 11/1 for domestic students, 10/1 for international students. Applications are processed on a rolling basis. Application fee: $30. *Expenses:* Tuition, state resident: full-time $5,871; part-time $245 per credit hour.

Educational Administration

University of West Florida (continued)

Tuition, nonresident: full-time $21,241; part-time $885 per credit hour. *Financial support:* Fellowships, career-related internships or fieldwork, scholarships/grants, and unspecified assistantships available. Support available to part-time students. Financial award application deadline: 4/15; financial award applicants required to submit FAFSA. *Unit head:* Dr. Thomas J. Kramer, Chairperson, Division of Graduate Education, 850-474-2768.

University of West Georgia, Graduate School, College of Education, Department of Educational Leadership and Professional Studies, Carrollton, GA 30118. Offers administration and supervision (M Ed, Ed S). *Accreditation:* NCATE. Part-time and evening/weekend programs available. Postbaccalaureate distance learning degree programs offered (minimal on-campus study). *Faculty:* 16 full-time (5 women), 2 part-time/adjunct (1 woman). *Students:* 13 full-time (8 women), 176 part-time (141 women); includes 82 minority (80 African Americans, 2 Hispanic Americans). Average age 33. In 2006, 43 master's, 36 other advanced degrees awarded. *Degree requirements:* For master's, internship; for Ed S, research project. *Entrance requirements:* For master's, GRE General Test, minimum GPA of 2.7 in field, 3.0 overall; 3 letters of reference; for Ed S, GRE General Test, master's degree, minimum graduate GPA of 3.0, letters of recommendation. *Application deadline:* For fall admission, 8/1 priority date for domestic students; for spring admission, 12/18 for domestic students. Application fee: $20. Electronic applications accepted. *Expenses:* Tuition, state resident: full-time $2,286; part-time $127 per credit. Tuition, nonresident: full-time $9,144; part-time $508 per credit. Required fees: $494; $27 per credit. $121 per semester. *Financial support:* In 2006–07, 4 research assistantships with full tuition reimbursements (averaging $12,000 per year) were awarded; career-related internships or fieldwork, scholarships/grants, and unspecified assistantships also available. Support available to part-time students. Financial award applicants required to submit FAFSA. *Faculty research:* Legal issues in schooling, school violence, transforming leadership, action research in professional practice. *Unit head:* Dr. Roy D. Nichols, Chair (Interim), 678-839-6557, Fax: 678-839-6097, E-mail: rnichols@westga.edu. *Application contact:* Dr. Charles W. Clark, Chair, 678-839-6508, E-mail: cclark@westga.edu.

University of Wisconsin–Madison, Graduate School, School of Education, Department of Educational Leadership and Policy Analysis, Madison, WI 53706-1380. Offers administration (Certificate); educational policy (MS, PhD). *Degree requirements:* For doctorate, thesis/dissertation. *Entrance requirements:* For master's and doctorate, GRE General Test. *Application deadline:* For fall admission, 1/15 for domestic and international students. Application fee: $45. Electronic applications accepted. *Financial support:* Fellowships with full tuition reimbursements, research assistantships with full tuition reimbursements, teaching assistantships with full tuition reimbursements, project assistantships available. *Unit head:* Dr. Carolyn Kelley, Chair, 608-262-3106.

University of Wisconsin–Milwaukee, Graduate School, School of Education, Department of Administrative Leadership, Milwaukee, WI 53201-0413. Offers administrative leadership (Certificate); administrative leadership and supervision in education (MS). Part-time programs available. *Faculty:* 9 full-time (6 women). *Students:* 12 full-time (8 women), 85 part-time (49 women); includes 30 minority (21 African Americans, 4 American Indian/Alaska Native, 2 Asian Americans or Pacific Islanders, 3 Hispanic Americans). 59 applicants, 49% accepted, 26 enrolled. In 2006, 30 degrees awarded. *Degree requirements:* For master's, thesis or alternative. *Application deadline:* For fall admission, 1/1 priority date for domestic students; for spring admission, 9/1 for domestic students. Applications are processed on a rolling basis. Application fee: $45 ($75 for international students). *Expenses:* Tuition, state resident: part-time $510 per credit. Tuition, nonresident: part-time $1,408 per credit. Tuition and fees vary according to program. *Financial support:* Fellowships, research assistantships, teaching assistantships, career-related internships or fieldwork and unspecified assistantships available. Support available to part-time students. Financial award application deadline: 4/15. *Unit head:* Barbara J. Daley, Chair, 414-229-4740, Fax: 414-229-5300.

University of Wisconsin–Oshkosh, The School of Graduate Studies, College of Education and Human Services, Department of Professional Leadership and Human Services, Oshkosh, WI 54901. Offers educational leadership (MS). Part-time and evening/weekend programs available. *Degree requirements:* For master's, thesis optional. *Entrance requirements:* For master's, bachelor's degree in education or related field. Additional exam requirements/recommendations for international students: Required—TOEFL (minimum score 550 paper-based; 213 computer-based). Electronic applications accepted. *Faculty research:* Supervision models, learning styles, total quality management, cooperative learning, school choice.

University of Wisconsin–Stevens Point, College of Professional Studies, School of Education, Program in Educational Administration, Stevens Point, WI 54481-3897. Offers MSE. *Degree requirements:* For master's, thesis or alternative, comprehensive exam. *Application deadline:* For fall admission, 5/1 priority date for domestic students. Applications are processed on a rolling basis. Application fee: $45. *Expenses:* Tuition, state resident: full-time $5,910; part-time $328 per credit. Tuition, nonresident: full-time $16,520; part-time $918 per credit. Required fees: $756; $73 per credit. *Financial support:* Application deadline: 5/1. *Application contact:* Dr. Patricia Caro, Director, 715-346-4403, Fax: 715-346-4846, E-mail: pcaro@uwsp.edu.

University of Wisconsin–Superior, Graduate Division, Department of Educational Administration, Superior, WI 54880-4500. Offers MSE, Ed S. Part-time and evening/weekend programs available. Postbaccalaureate distance learning degree programs offered (minimal on-campus study). *Degree requirements:* For master's, thesis or alternative, research project or position paper, written exam; for Ed S, thesis, internship, oral and written exams. *Entrance requirements:* For master's, GRE General Test or MAT, minimum GPA of 2.75, teaching license, 3 years teaching experience; for Ed S, MAT, GRE, master's degree, 3 years of teaching experience, teaching license. *Faculty research:* Postsecondary disabilities, educational partnerships, K-12.

University of Wisconsin–Whitewater, School of Graduate Studies, College of Business and Economics, Program in School Business Management, Whitewater, WI 53190-1790. Offers MS Ed. Part-time and evening/weekend programs available. Postbaccalaureate distance learning degree programs offered (no on-campus study). *Students:* 4 full-time (1 woman), 54 part-time (29 women); includes 6 minority (1 African American, 4 Asian Americans or Pacific Islanders, 1 Hispanic American). Average age 33. 25 applicants, 92% accepted, 18 enrolled. In 2006, 12 degrees awarded. *Degree requirements:* For master's, thesis or alternative. *Entrance requirements:* For master's, minimum GPA of 2.75 or MAT. Additional exam requirements/recommendations for international students: Required—TOEFL (minimum score 550 paper-based; 213 computer-based). *Application deadline:* For fall admission, 7/15 priority date for domestic students; for spring admission, 12/1 priority date for domestic students. Applications are processed on a rolling basis. Application fee: $45. Electronic applications accepted. *Expenses:* Tuition, state resident: full-time $3,311. Tuition, nonresident: full-time $8,616. Required fees: $368 per credit. *Financial support:* Research assistantships, Federal Work-Study, unspecified assistantships, and out-of-state fee waivers available. Support available to part-time students. Financial award application deadline: 3/15; financial award applicants required to submit FAFSA. *Unit head:* Dr. Bambi Statz, Coordinator, 262-472-1350, E-mail: statzb@uww.edu. *Application contact:* Sally A. Lange, School of Graduate Studies, 262-472-1006, Fax: 262-472-5027, E-mail: gradschl@uww.edu.

University of Wyoming, Graduate School, College of Education, Department of Educational Leadership, Laramie, WY 82070. Offers MA, Ed D, PhD, Ed S. Part-time programs available. Postbaccalaureate distance learning degree programs offered (minimal on-campus study). *Faculty:* 6 full-time (3 women). *Students:* 1 (woman) full-time, 99 part-time (39 women); includes 4 minority (3 American Indian/Alaska Native, 1 Asian American or Pacific Islander). Average age 45. In 2006, 8 master's, 1 doctorate awarded. *Median time to degree:* Of those who began their doctoral program in fall 1998, 95% received their degree in 8 years or less. *Degree requirements:* For master's, thesis, portfolio; for doctorate, thesis/dissertation, paper. *Entrance requirements:* For master's, GRE; for doctorate, MA. Additional exam requirements/recommendations for international students: Required—TOEFL (minimum score 520 paper-based). Application fee: $50. *Faculty research:* School leadership, leadership preparation, leadership skills. *Unit head:* Dr. William G. Berube, Professor and Head, 307-766-6825, Fax: 307-766-5638, E-mail: berube@uwyo.edu.

Ursuline College, School of Graduate Studies, Program in Educational Administration, Pepper Pike, OH 44124-4398. Offers MA. Part-time programs available. *Faculty:* 2 full-time (1 woman), 8 part-time/adjunct (3 women). *Students:* 6 full-time (all women), 63 part-time (38 women); includes 8 minority (all African Americans) Average age 36. 8 applicants, 100% accepted, 8 enrolled. In 2006, 18 degrees awarded. *Degree requirements:* For master's, thesis or alternative. *Entrance requirements:* For master's, minimum undergraduate GPA of 3.0, teaching certificate, professional experience. Additional exam requirements/recommendations for international students: Required—TOEFL (minimum score 500 paper-based; 173 computer-based). *Application deadline:* For fall admission, 8/1 priority date for domestic students. Applications are processed on a rolling basis. Application fee: $25. *Expenses: Contact institution. Financial support:* In 2006–07, 39 students received support. Federal Work-Study available. Financial award application deadline: 3/1; financial award applicants required to submit FAFSA. *Unit head:* Martin Kane, Director, 440-646-8148, Fax: 440-646-8328, E-mail: mkane@ursuline.edu. *Application contact:* Jo Mann, Secretary, 440-646-8119, Fax: 440-684-6088, E-mail: gradsch@ursuline.edu.

Valdosta State University, Graduate School, College of Education, Department of Educational Leadership, Valdosta, GA 31698. Offers M Ed, Ed D, Ed S. *Accreditation:* NCATE. *Degree requirements:* For master's, thesis (for some programs), comprehensive written and/or oral exams; for doctorate and Ed S, thesis/dissertation, comprehensive written and/or oral exams; for Ed S, thesis. *Entrance requirements:* For master's and Ed S, GRE General Test or MAT; for doctorate, GRE General Test, minimum GPA of 3.5, 3 years experience. Additional exam requirements/recommendations for international students: Required—TOEFL (minimum score 523 paper-based; 193 computer-based). Electronic applications accepted. *Faculty research:* Student transition, mentoring in higher education, contemporary issues in higher education.

Vanderbilt University, Graduate School, Program in Leadership and Policy Studies, Nashville, TN 37240-1001. Offers PhD. Part-time programs available. *Faculty:* 18 full-time (5 women). *Students:* 41 full-time (22 women); includes 7 minority (5 African Americans, 1 Asian American or Pacific Islander, 1 Hispanic American), 6 international. 53 applicants, 23% accepted, 8 enrolled. In 2006, 13 degrees awarded. *Application deadline:* For fall admission, 1/15 for domestic and international students. Application fee: $0. Electronic applications accepted. *Expenses:* Tuition: Full-time $24,462. Required fees: $2,515. One-time fee: $30 full-time. Full-time tuition and fees vary according to course load, degree level and program. *Financial support:* Fellowships with tuition reimbursements, research assistantships with full tuition reimbursements, teaching assistantships with full tuition reimbursements, Federal Work-Study, institutionally sponsored loans, and traineeships available. Financial award application deadline: 1/15. *Unit head:* James W. Guthrie, Chair, 615-322-8000, Fax: 615-343-7094, E-mail: james.w.guthrie@vanderbilt.edu. *Application contact:* Dr. Robert L. Crowson, Director of Graduate Studies, 615-322-8000, Fax: 615-343-7094, E-mail: robert.l.crowson@vanderbilt.edu.

Vanderbilt University, Peabody College, Department of Leadership and Organizations, Nashville, TN 37240-1001. Offers education policy (MPP); educational leadership and policy (Ed D); higher education (M Ed); higher education, leadership and policy (Ed D); human resource development (M Ed); international education policy and management (M Ed); organizational leadership (M Ed); school administration (M Ed). Part-time and evening/weekend programs available. *Faculty:* 21 full-time (6 women), 9 part-time/adjunct (3 women). *Students:* 131 full-time (88 women), 85 part-time (39 women); includes 35 minority (30 African Americans, 4 Asian Americans or Pacific Islanders, 1 Hispanic American), 11 international. Average age 31. 214 applicants, 63% accepted, 64 enrolled. In 2006, 43 master's, 12 doctorates awarded. *Median time to degree:* Of those who began their doctoral program in fall 1998, 62% received their degree in 8 years or less. *Degree requirements:* For master's, thesis optional; for doctorate, thesis/dissertation, qualifying exams, residency. *Entrance requirements:* For master's and doctorate, GRE General Test. Additional exam requirements/recommendations for international students: Required—TOEFL (minimum score 550 paper-based; 213 computer-based). *Application deadline:* For fall admission, 12/31 priority date for domestic and international students; for spring admission, 11/1 priority date for domestic and international students. Applications are processed on a rolling basis. Application fee: $0. Electronic applications accepted. *Expenses:* Tuition: Full-time $24,462. Required fees: $2,515. One-time fee: $30 full-time. Full-time tuition and fees vary according to course load, degree level and program. *Financial support:* In 2006–07, 90 students received support, including 50 fellowships with full and partial tuition reimbursements available, 38 research assistantships with full and partial tuition reimbursements available, 2 teaching assistantships with full and partial tuition reimbursements available; Federal Work-Study, institutionally sponsored loans, scholarships/grants, tuition waivers (partial), and unspecified assistantships also available. Support available to part-time students. Financial award application deadline: 2/1; financial award applicants required to submit FAFSA. *Faculty research:* Education policy, education finances, economics of education, education leadership and management, higher education leadership and policy; educator pay for performance. *Unit head:* James W. Guthrie, Chair, 615-322-8000, Fax: 615-343-7094, E-mail: james.w.guthrie@vanderbilt.edu. *Application contact:* Rosie Moody, Educational Coordinator, 615-322-8019, Fax: 615-343-7094, E-mail: rosie.moody@vanderbilt.edu.

Vanderbilt University, Peabody College, Department of Teaching and Learning, Nashville, TN 37240-1001. Offers curriculum and instructional leadership (M Ed); early childhood education (M Ed); early childhood leadership (Ed D); elementary education (M Ed); English education (M Ed); English language learners (M Ed); mathematics education (M Ed); reading education (M Ed); science education (M Ed); secondary education (M Ed). *Accreditation:* NCATE. *Faculty:* 23 full-time (13 women), 28 part-time/adjunct (19 women). *Students:* 71 full-time (62 women), 21 part-time (15 women); includes 9 minority (8 African Americans, 1 Hispanic American), 2 international. Average age 27. 102 applicants, 60% accepted, 27 enrolled. In 2006, 53 master's, 3 doctorates awarded. *Degree requirements:* For master's, thesis optional. *Entrance requirements:* For master's, GRE General Test, MAT. Additional exam requirements/recommendations for international students: Required—TOEFL (minimum score 550 paper-based; 213 computer-based). *Application deadline:* For fall admission, 12/31 priority date for domestic and international students; for spring admission, 11/1 priority date for domestic and international students. Applications are processed on a rolling basis. Application fee: $0. Electronic applications accepted. *Expenses:* Tuition: Full-time $24,462. Required fees: $2,515. One-time fee: $30 full-time. Full-time tuition and fees vary according to course load, degree level and program. *Financial support:* In 2006–07, 62 students received support, including 36 fellowships with full and partial tuition reimbursements available, 13 research assistantships with full and partial tuition reimbursements available, 13 teaching assistantships with full and partial tuition reimbursements available; Federal Work-Study, institutionally sponsored loans, scholarships/grants, tuition waivers (partial), and unspecified assistantships also available. Support available to part-time students. Financial award application deadline: 2/1; financial award applicants required to submit FAFSA. *Faculty research:* Teaching and learning; development of subject matter knowledge; learning and policy; development students' mathematical and scientific knowledge, development of literacy. *Unit head:* Leona Schauble, Chair, 615-322-8100, Fax: 615-322-8999, E-mail: leona.schauble@vanderbilt.edu. *Application contact:* Angela Saylor, Educational Coordinator, 615-322-8092, Fax: 615-322-8999.

Villanova University, Graduate School of Liberal Arts and Sciences, Department of Education and Human Services, Program in Educational Leadership, Villanova, PA 19085-1699. Offers MA. Part-time and evening/weekend programs available. *Students:* 2 full-time (both women), 24 part-time (9 women); includes 2 minority (1 African American, 1 American Indian/Alaska Native), 1 international. Average age 31. In 2006, 8 degrees awarded. *Degree requirements:* For master's, comprehensive exam. *Entrance requirements:* For master's, GRE or MAT, minimum GPA of 3.0. Additional exam requirements/recommendations for international students: Required—TOEFL. *Application deadline:* For fall admission, 8/1 priority date for domestic students; for spring admission, 12/1 for domestic students. Applications are processed on a rolling basis. Application fee: $50. Electronic applications accepted. *Expenses:* Tuition: Part-time $565 per credit. *Financial support:* Career-related internships or fieldwork and Federal Work-Study available. Financial award applicants required to submit FAFSA. *Unit head:* Dr. Connie Titone, Chairperson, 610-519-4620.

Virginia Commonwealth University, Graduate School, School of Education, Doctoral Program in Education, Richmond, VA 23284-9005. Offers educational leadership (PhD); instructional leadership (PhD); research and evaluation (PhD); urban services leadership (PhD). *Accreditation:* NCATE. Part-time programs available. *Students:* 53 full-time (44 women), 112 part-time (77 women); includes 38 minority (35 African Americans, 1 American Indian/Alaska Native, 2 Hispanic Americans), 5 international. 39 applicants, 67% accepted, 22 enrolled. In 2006, 13 degrees awarded. *Degree requirements:* For doctorate, thesis/dissertation. *Entrance requirements:* For doctorate, GRE, interview, master's degree, writing sample. *Application deadline:* For fall admission, 3/15 for domestic students. Application fee: $50. *Financial support:* Fellowships, research assistantships, career-related internships or fieldwork, Federal Work-Study, and institutionally sponsored loans available. Financial award application deadline: 3/1. *Unit head:* Dr. Henry Clark, Director, Graduate Studies, 804-828-3382. *Application contact:* Patricia Willard, Administrative Assistant, 804-828-6530, E-mail: pawillar@vcu.edu.

See Close-Up on page 1135.

Virginia Polytechnic Institute and State University, Graduate School, College of Liberal Arts and Human Sciences, School of Education, Department of Educational Leadership and Policy Studies, Program in Administration and Supervision of Special Education, Blacksburg, VA 24061. Offers Ed D, PhD, Ed S. *Accreditation:* NCATE. Postbaccalaureate distance learning degree programs offered (minimal on-campus study). *Degree requirements:* For doctorate, thesis/dissertation, internship. *Entrance requirements:* For doctorate and Ed S, GRE General Test, teaching experience. Additional exam requirements/recommendations for international students: Required—TOEFL. *Application deadline:* Applications are processed on a rolling basis. Application fee: $45. Electronic applications accepted. *Expenses:* Tuition, state resident: full-time $7,017; part-time $390 per credit hour. Tuition, nonresident: full-time $12,414; part-time $690 per credit hour. International tuition: $11,296 full-time. Required fees: $1,523; $256 per term. *Financial support:* In 2006–07, research assistantships with full tuition reimbursements (averaging $11,250 per year); career-related internships or fieldwork and unspecified assistantships also available. Financial award application deadline: 4/1. *Unit head:* Jean B. Crockett, Program Area Leader and Associate Professor, 540-231-4546, Fax: 540-231-7845, E-mail: crocketj@vt.edu.

Virginia State University, School of Graduate Studies, Research, and Outreach, School of Liberal Arts and Education, Department of Educational Leadership and Administrative Systems Management, Program in Educational Administration and Supervision, Petersburg, VA 23806-0001. Offers M Ed, MS. *Accreditation:* NCATE. *Degree requirements:* For master's, thesis optional.

Wagner College, Division of Graduate Studies, Department of Education, Program in Educational Leadership, Staten Island, NY 10301-4495. Offers school building leader (Certificate); school district leader (Certificate). *Expenses:* Tuition: Full-time $15,120; part-time $840 per credit. *Application contact:* Susan Rosenberg, Office of Graduate Studies, 718-390-3106, Fax: 718-390-3456, E-mail: graduate@wagner.edu.

Walla Walla College, Graduate School, School of Education and Psychology, Specialization in Educational Leadership, College Place, WA 99324-1198. Offers M Ed, MA, MAT. Part-time programs available. *Faculty:* 8 full-time (3 women), 3 part-time/adjunct (1 woman). *Degree requirements:* For master's, thesis (for some programs). *Entrance requirements:* For master's, GRE General Test, minimum GPA of 2.75; undergraduate major in psychology, sociology, or equivalent. *Application deadline:* For fall admission, 4/1 priority date for domestic students. Applications are processed on a rolling basis. Application fee: $50. Electronic applications accepted. *Expenses:* Tuition: Full-time $20,124; part-time $516 per quarter hour. *Financial support:* Teaching assistantships with partial tuition reimbursements available. Financial award application deadline: 4/1; financial award applicants required to submit FAFSA. *Faculty research:* Instructional psychology. *Application contact:* Dr. Joe G. Galusha, Dean of Graduate Studies, 509-527-2421, Fax: 509-527-2237, E-mail: galujo@wwc.edu.

Washburn University, College of Arts and Sciences, Department of Education, Program in Educational Leadership, Topeka, KS 66621. Offers M Ed. *Accreditation:* NCATE. *Degree requirements:* For master's, portfolio. *Expenses:* Tuition, state resident: full-time $4,338; part-time $241 per credit hour. Tuition, nonresident: full-time $8,820; part-time $490 per credit hour. Required fees: $62; $31 per semester. *Application contact:* Tara Porter, Licensure Officer, 785-670-1434, Fax: 785-670-1046, E-mail: tara.porter@washburn.edu.

Washington State University, Graduate School, College of Education, Department of Educational Leadership and Counseling Psychology, Program in Educational Leadership, Pullman, WA 99164. Offers M Ed, MA, Ed D, PhD. *Accreditation:* NCATE. *Faculty:* 15. *Students:* 53 full-time (26 women), 37 part-time (21 women); includes 17 minority (7 African Americans, 4 Asian Americans or Pacific Islanders, 6 Hispanic Americans), 5 international. 263 applicants, 27% accepted, 30 enrolled. In 2006, 37 master's, 9 doctorates awarded. *Degree requirements:* For master's, thesis (for some programs), oral or written exam, comprehensive exam (for some programs); for doctorate, thesis/dissertation, oral exam, written exam, comprehensive exam. *Entrance requirements:* For master's, minimum GPA of 3.0, 3 letters of recommendation; for doctorate, GRE General Test, minimum GPA of 3.0, 3 letters of recommendation. Additional exam requirements/recommendations for international students: Recommended—TOEFL (minimum score 550 paper-based; 213 computer-based). *Application deadline:* For fall admission, 3/15 for domestic students, 3/1 for international students; for spring admission, 10/1 for domestic students, 7/1 for international students. Application fee: $50. Electronic applications accepted. *Expenses:* Tuition, state resident: full-time $7,066. Tuition, nonresident: full-time $17,204. *Financial support:* In 2006–07, research assistantships with partial tuition reimbursements (averaging $13,917 per year), teaching assistantships with partial tuition reimbursements (averaging $13,056 per year) were awarded; career-related internships or fieldwork, Federal Work-Study, institutionally sponsored loans, scholarships/grants, and unspecified assistantships also available. Financial award application deadline:4/1. *Faculty research:* Cross cultural personality study, language, learning school as community. *Unit head:* Dr. Gail Furman, Area Coordinator, 509-335-8412. *Application contact:* Graduate School Admissions, 800-GRADWSU, Fax: 509-335-1949, E-mail: gradsch@wsu.edu.

Washington State University Spokane, Graduate Programs, Program in Education, Spokane, WA 99210-1495. Offers educational leadership (Ed M, MA); principal (Certificate); professional certification for teachers (Certificate); program administrator (Certificate); school psychologist (Certificate); superintendent (Certificate); teaching (MIT). *Faculty:* 9. *Students:* 24 full-time (15 women), 50 part-time (25 women); includes 8 minority (3 African Americans, 2 Asian Americans or Pacific Islanders, 3 Hispanic Americans). 22 applicants, 73% accepted, 8 enrolled. *Degree requirements:* For master's, thesis (for some programs), comprehensive exam (for some programs). *Entrance requirements:* For master's, GRE or GMAT, minimum GPA of 3.0, 3 letters of recommendation, resumé. Additional exam requirements/recommendations for international students: Required—TOEFL (minimum score 550 paper-based; 213 computer-based). *Application deadline:* For fall admission, 3/1 for international students; for spring admission, 10/1 for domestic students, 7/1 for international students. Application fee: $50. *Expenses:* Tuition, state resident: full-time $7,066. Tuition, nonresident: full-time $17,204. Tuition and fees vary according to program. *Financial support:* In 2006–07, 33 students received support, including 1 fellowship (averaging $4,296 per year), 1 teaching assistantship (averaging $13,056 per year). Total annual research expenditures: $16,557. *Unit head:* Dr. Joan Kingrey, Director, 509-358-7939, Fax: 509-358-7900, E-mail: kingrey@wsu.edu. *Application contact:* Graduate School Admissions, 800-GRADWSU, Fax: 509-335-1949, E-mail: gradsch@wsu.edu.

Washington State University Tri-Cities, Graduate Programs, Program in Education, Richland, WA 99352-1671. Offers counseling (Ed M); educational leadership (Ed M, Ed D); literacy (Ed M); secondary certification (Ed M); teaching (MIT). Part-time programs available. *Faculty:* 23. *Students:* 27 full-time (20 women), 82 part-time (68 women); includes 11 minority (all Hispanic Americans) Average age 36. 77 applicants, 71% accepted, 34 enrolled. *Degree requirements:* For master's, thesis or alternative, comprehensive exam, registration; for doctorate, thesis/dissertation, comprehensive exam. *Entrance requirements:* For master's, GRE, minimum GPA of 3.0, Working with Youth form, Character and Fitness form, 3 letters of recommendation. Additional exam requirements/recommendations for international students: Required—TOEFL. *Application deadline:* For fall admission, 2/1 priority date for domestic students, 3/1 for international students; for spring admission, 9/1 priority date for domestic students, 7/1 for international students. Applications are processed on a rolling basis. Application fee: $50. Electronic applications accepted. *Expenses:* Tuition, state resident: full-time $7,066. Tuition, nonresident: full-time $17,204. *Financial support:* In 2006–07, 59 students received support, including 1 fellowship (averaging $7,950 per year), teaching assistantships (averaging $13,056 per year); Federal Work-Study, scholarships/grants, and unspecified assistantships also available. *Faculty research:* Multicultural counseling, socio-cultural influences in schools, diverse learners, teacher education, K-12 educational leadership. *Unit head:* Dr. Nancy Kyle, Director, 509-372-7396.

Wayne State College, School of Education and Counseling, Department of Educational Foundations and Leadership, Program in Educational Administration, Wayne, NE 68787. Offers educational administration (Ed S); elementary administration (MSE); elementary and secondary administration (MSE); secondary administration (MSE). *Accreditation:* NCATE. Part-time and evening/weekend programs available. *Faculty:* 3 part-time/adjunct (1 woman). *Students:* 2 full-time (0 women), 63 part-time (18 women); includes 4 minority (3 African Americans, 1 American Indian/Alaska Native), 1 international. Average age 38. In 2006, 8 master's, 8 other advanced degrees awarded. *Degree requirements:* For master's, research paper, thesis optional. *Entrance requirements:* For master's, GRE General Test, minimum GPA of 2.5; for Ed S, GRE General Test, minimum GPA of 3.2. Additional exam requirements/recommendations for international students: Required—TOEFL (minimum score 550 paper-based; 213 computer-based). *Application deadline:* Applications are processed on a rolling basis. Application fee: $30. Electronic applications accepted. *Expenses:* Tuition, state resident: full-time $3,114; part-time $130 per credit hour. Tuition, nonresident: full-time $6,228; part-time $260 per credit hour. Required fees: $894; $37 per credit hour. Tuition and fees vary according to course load. *Financial support:* Teaching assistantships available. Financial award applicants required to submit FAFSA.

Wayne State University, College of Education, Division of Administrative and Organizational Studies, Detroit, MI 48202. Offers administration and supervision-secondary (Ed S); college and university teaching (Certificate); curriculum and instruction (PhD); educational leadership (M Ed, Ed S); educational leadership and policy studies (Ed D, PhD); elementary education curriculum and instruction (MA, Ed S); general administration and supervision (Ed D, PhD, Ed S); higher education (Ed D, PhD); instructional technology (M Ed, Ed D, PhD, Ed S); secondary curriculum and instruction (M Ed, Ed S). *Faculty:* 24 full-time (13 women), 1 (woman) part-time/adjunct. *Students:* 153 full-time (103 women), 389 part-time (266 women); includes 252 minority (223 African Americans, 6 American Indian/Alaska Native, 8 Asian Americans or Pacific Islanders, 15 Hispanic Americans), 19 international. Average age 38. 138 applicants, 79% accepted, 74 enrolled. In 2006, 116 master's, 30 doctorates, 64 other advanced degrees awarded. *Degree requirements:* For doctorate, thesis/dissertation. *Entrance requirements:* For doctorate, interview, minimum GPA of 3.0. Additional exam requirements/recommendations for international students: Required—TOEFL (minimum score 550 paper-based; 213 computer-based), TWE (minimum score 6). *Application deadline:* For fall admission, 7/1 for domestic students, 6/1 for international students; for winter admission, 10/1 for international students; for spring admission, 2/1 for international students. Application fee: $30 ($50 for international students). Electronic applications accepted. *Financial support:* In 2006–07, 4 research assistantships (averaging $12,797 per year) were awarded; career-related internships or fieldwork, Federal Work-Study, and institutionally sponsored loans also available. Support available to part-time students. *Faculty research:* Total quality management, participatory management, administering educational technology, school improvement, principalship. Total annual research expenditures: $344,504. *Unit head:* Dr. JoAnne Holbert, Assistant Dean, 313-577-1721, E-mail: jholbert@wayne.edu.

Webster University, School of Education, Department of Multidisciplinary Studies, St. Louis, MO 63119-3194. Offers administrative leadership (Ed S); education leadership (Ed S); educational technology (MAT); mathematics (MAT); multidisciplinary studies (MAT); school systems, superintendency and leadership (Ed S); social science (MAT); special education (MAT). Part-time programs available. *Students:* 97 full-time (83 women), 687 part-time (573 women); includes 173 minority (142 African Americans, 2 American Indian/Alaska Native, 13 Asian Americans or Pacific Islanders, 16 Hispanic Americans), 6 international. Average age 34. In 2006, 14 degrees awarded. *Entrance requirements:* For master's, minimum GPA of 2.5. *Application deadline:* Applications are processed on a rolling basis. Application fee: $25 ($50 for international students). *Expenses:* Tuition: Full-time $8,820; part-time $490 per credit. Tuition and fees vary according to degree level, campus/location and program. *Financial support:* Federal Work-Study available. Support available to part-time students. Financial award application deadline: 4/1; financial award applicants required to submit FAFSA. *Unit head:* Dr. Donna Campbell, Chair, 314-961-2660 Ext. 7042, Fax: 314-968-7118. *Application contact:* Director of Graduate and Evening Student Admissions, Fax: 314-968-7116, E-mail: gadmit@webster.edu.

Western Carolina University, Graduate School, College of Education and Allied Professions, Department of Educational Leadership and Foundations, Program in Educational Leadership, Cullowhee, NC 28723. Offers Ed D, Ed S. *Accreditation:* NCATE. Part-time and evening/weekend programs available. *Degree requirements:* For doctorate, thesis/dissertation, comprehensive exam. *Entrance requirements:* For doctorate and Ed S, GRE General Test, minimum graduate GPA of 3.5. Additional exam requirements/recommendations for international students: Required—TOEFL (minimum score 550 paper-based; 213 computer-based).

Western Carolina University, Graduate School, College of Education and Allied Professions, Department of Educational Leadership and Foundations, Program in Educational Supervision, Cullowhee, NC 28723. Offers MA Ed. *Accreditation:* NCATE. Part-time and evening/weekend programs available. *Degree requirements:* For master's, comprehensive exam. *Entrance requirements:* For master's, GRE General Test or MAT. Additional exam requirements/recommendations for international students: Required—TOEFL (minimum score 550 paper-based; 213 computer-based).

Western Carolina University, Graduate School, College of Education and Allied Professions, Department of Educational Leadership and Foundations, Program in School Administration, Cullowhee, NC 28723. Offers MSA. *Accreditation:* NCATE. Part-time and evening/weekend programs available. *Degree requirements:* For master's, comprehensive exam. *Entrance requirements:* For master's, GRE General Test. Additional exam requirements/recommendations for international students: Required—TOEFL (minimum score 550 paper-based; 213 computer-based).

Western Connecticut State University, Division of Graduate Studies, School of Professional Studies, Program in Instructional Leadership, Danbury, CT 06810-6885. Offers Ed D. *Students:* Average age 44.*Unit head:* Dr. Marcia A. Delcourt, Coordinator, 203-837-9121.

Western Governors University, Teachers College, Salt Lake City, UT 84107. Offers English language learning (K-12) (MA); learning and technology (M Ed, MA); management and evaluation (M Ed); management and innovation (M Ed); mathematics education (5-12) (MA); mathematics education (5-9) (MA); mathematics education (K-6) (MA); science (5-12) (MA), including biology, geology; science education (509) (MA); technology (M Ed); technology for

Educational Administration

Western Governors University (continued)
principals (Post-Graduate Certificate). *Accreditation:* NCATE. Part-time and evening/weekend programs available. Postbaccalaureate distance learning degree programs offered (no on-campus study). *Degree requirements:* For master's, comprehensive exam, registration. *Entrance requirements:* Additional exam requirements/recommendations for international students: Required—TOEFL (minimum score 450 paper-based). Electronic applications accepted. Expenses: Contact institution.

Western Illinois University, School of Graduate Studies, College of Education and Human Services, Department of Educational Leadership, Macomb, IL 61455-1390. Offers MS Ed, Ed D, Ed S. *Accreditation:* NCATE. Part-time and evening/weekend programs available. *Students:* 16 full-time (9 women), 243 part-time (112 women); includes 11 minority (7 African Americans, 4 Hispanic Americans), 1 international. Average age 38. 47 applicants, 68% accepted. In 2006, 45 master's, 7 other advanced degrees awarded. *Degree requirements:* For master's, thesis or alternative; for doctorate, thesis/dissertation, electronic portfolio, comprehensive exam. *Entrance requirements:* For master's and Ed S, interview; for doctorate, GRE General Test. Additional exam requirements/recommendations for international students: Required—TOEFL (minimum score 575 paper-based; 233 computer-based; 89 iBT). *Application deadline:* Applications are processed on a rolling basis. Application fee: $30. Electronic applications accepted. *Expenses:* Tuition, state resident: part-time $200 per credit hour. Tuition, nonresident: part-time $400 per credit hour. *Financial support:* In 2006–07, research assistantships (averaging $6,568 per year). Financial award applicants required to submit FAFSA. *Unit head:* Dr. Robert Hall, Chairperson, 309-298-1070. *Application contact:* Dr. Barbara Baily, Director of Graduate Studies/Associate Provost, 309-298-1806, Fax: 309-298-2345, E-mail: grad-office@wiu.edu.

Western Kentucky University, Graduate Studies, College of Education and Behavioral Sciences, Department of Educational Administration Leadership and Research, Bowling Green, KY 42101. Offers educational administration (MAE); school administration (Ed S). *Accreditation:* NCATE. Part-time and evening/weekend programs available. *Faculty:* 10 full-time (4 women), 3 part-time/adjunct (1 woman). *Students:* 13 full-time (6 women), 110 part-time (52 women); includes 11 minority (9 African Americans, 1 American Indian/Alaska Native, 1 Asian American or Pacific Islander). Average age 34. 10 applicants, 70% accepted, 7 enrolled. In 2006, 30 degrees awarded. *Degree requirements:* For master's, thesis or applied project and oral defense, thesis optional; for Ed S, thesis. *Entrance requirements:* For master's, GRE General Test, minimum GPA of 2.75. Additional exam requirements/recommendations for international students: Required—TOEFL (minimum score 555 paper-based; 213 computer-based; 79 iBT). *Application deadline:* For fall admission, 7/1 priority date for domestic students, 4/1 for international students; for spring admission, 11/1 for domestic students, 9/1 for international students. Applications are processed on a rolling basis. Application fee: $35. *Expenses:* Tuition, state resident: full-time $6,520; part-time $226 per hour. Tuition, nonresident: full-time $7,140; part-time $357 per hour. International tuition: $15,820 full-time. *Financial support:* Research assistantships with partial tuition reimbursements, teaching assistantships, Federal Work-Study, institutionally sponsored loans, and service awards available. Support available to part-time students. Financial award application deadline: 4/1; financial award applicants required to submit FAFSA. *Faculty research:* Principal internship, superintendent assessment, administrative leadership, group training for residential workers. Total annual research expenditures: $3,946. *Unit head:* Dr. Jeanne R Fiene, Head, 270-745-4997, Fax: 270-745-5445, E-mail: jeanne.fiene@wku.edu.

Western Michigan University, Graduate College, College of Education, Department of Teaching, Learning, and Leadership, Kalamazoo, MI 49008-5202. Offers early childhood education (MA); education and professional development (MA); educational leadership (MA, Ed D, PhD, Ed S); educational technology (MA); elementary education (MA); human resources development (MA); middle school education (MA); reading (MA); socio-cultural foundations and educational thought (MA). *Degree requirements:* For doctorate and Ed S, thesis/dissertation, oral exams. *Entrance requirements:* For doctorate and Ed S, GRE General Test.

Western New Mexico University, Graduate Division, School of Education, Silver City, NM 88062-0680. Offers counselor education (MA); elementary education (MAT); reading education (MAT); school administration (MA); secondary education (MAT); special education (MAT). *Accreditation:* NCATE. *Degree requirements:* For master's, comprehensive exam. *Entrance requirements:* For master's, GRE General Test, GRE Subject Test, minimum GPA of 3.2 in last 64 hours of undergraduate study. Additional exam requirements/recommendations for international students: Required—TOEFL (minimum score 550 paper-based; 213 computer-based). Electronic applications accepted. *Expenses:* Tuition, state resident: full-time $1,329. Tuition, nonresident: full-time $4,779.

Western Washington University, Graduate School, Woodring College of Education, Department of Educational Leadership, Educational Administration Program, Bellingham, WA 98225-5996. Offers M Ed. *Accreditation:* NCATE. Part-time programs available. *Faculty:* 9. *Students:* 17 full-time (12 women), 20 part-time (8 women); includes 4 minority (1 American Indian/Alaska Native, 3 Asian Americans or Pacific Islanders), 1 international. 45 applicants, 98% accepted. In 2006, 36 degrees awarded. *Degree requirements:* For master's, thesis optional. *Entrance requirements:* For master's, GRE General Test or MAT, minimum GPA of 3.0 in last 60 semester hours or last 90 quarter hours, certification. Additional exam requirements/recommendations for international students: Required—TOEFL (minimum score 567 paper-based; 227 computer-based). *Application deadline:* For fall admission, 6/1 for domestic students; for winter admission, 10/1 for domestic students; for spring admission, 2/1 for domestic students. Applications are processed on a rolling basis. Application fee: $50. *Expenses:* Tuition, state resident: full-time $6,609; part-time $199 per credit. Tuition, nonresident: full-time $16,845; part-time $540 per credit. *Financial support:* In 2006–07, 2 teaching assistantships with partial tuition reimbursements (averaging $9,339 per year) were awarded; career-related internships or fieldwork, Federal Work-Study, institutionally sponsored loans, scholarships/grants, tuition waivers (partial), and unspecified assistantships also available. Support available to part-time students. Financial award application deadline: 2/15; financial award applicants required to submit FAFSA. *Unit head:* Dr. Kristine McDuffy, Director, 360-650-2546, E-mail: kristine.mcduffy@wwu.edu. *Application contact:* Judy Gramm, Program Manager, 360-650-3708.

Western Washington University, Graduate School, Woodring College of Education, Department of Educational Leadership, Program in Student Affairs Administration, Bellingham, WA 98225-5996. Offers M Ed. *Accreditation:* NCATE. Part-time programs available. *Faculty:* 1. *Students:* 11 full-time (9 women), 3 part-time (2 women), 1 international. In 2006, 15 degrees awarded. *Degree requirements:* For master's, research project, thesis optional. *Entrance requirements:* For master's, GRE General Test or MAT, minimum GPA of 3.0 in last 60 semester hours or last 90 quarter hours. Additional exam requirements/recommendations for international students: Required—TOEFL (minimum score 567 paper-based; 227 computer-based). *Application deadline:* For fall admission, 3/1 priority date for domestic students. Application fee: $50. *Expenses:* Tuition, state resident: full-time $6,609; part-time $199 per credit. Tuition, nonresident: full-time $16,845; part-time $540 per credit. *Financial support:* In 2006–07, 1 teaching assistantship with partial tuition reimbursement (averaging $9,339 per year) was awarded; career-related internships or fieldwork, Federal Work-Study, institutionally sponsored loans, scholarships/grants, tuition waivers (partial), and unspecified assistantships also available. Support available to part-time students. Financial award application deadline: 2/15; financial award applicants required to submit FAFSA. *Application contact:* Sherry Haskins, Graduate Coordinator, 360-650-3190.

Westfield State College, Division of Graduate and Continuing Education, Department of Education, Program in School Administration, Westfield, MA 01086. Offers M Ed, CAGS. Part-time and evening/weekend programs available. *Degree requirements:* For master's, practicum; for CAGS, research-based field internship. *Entrance requirements:* For master's, GRE General Test or MAT, minimum undergraduate GPA of 2.7; for CAGS, master's degree. *Faculty research:* Collaborative teacher education, developmental early childhood education.

Westminster College, Programs in Education, Program in Administration, New Wilmington, PA 16172-0001. Offers M Ed, Certificate. Part-time and evening/weekend programs available. *Degree requirements:* For master's, comprehensive exam. *Entrance requirements:* For master's, GRE or MAT, minimum GPA of 3.0.

West Texas A&M University, College of Education and Social Sciences, Division of Education, Program in Administration, Canyon, TX 79016-0001. Offers M Ed. Part-time and evening/weekend programs available. Postbaccalaureate distance learning degree programs offered (minimal on-campus study). *Degree requirements:* For master's, thesis optional. *Entrance requirements:* For master's, GRE General Test. Additional exam requirements/recommendations for international students: Required—TOEFL (minimum score 550 paper-based). Electronic applications accepted. *Faculty research:* Teacher quality, leadership, recruitment, retention.

West Virginia University, College of Human Resources and Education, Department of Educational Leadership Studies, Morgantown, WV 26506. Offers educational leadership (Ed D); higher education administration (MA); public school administration (MA). *Accreditation:* NCATE. Part-time programs available. *Faculty:* 6 full-time (2 women). *Students:* 78 full-time (38 women), 129 part-time (84 women); includes 20 minority (15 African Americans, 1 American Indian/Alaska Native, 1 Asian American or Pacific Islander, 3 Hispanic Americans), 5 international. Average age 38. 91 applicants, 79% accepted, 43 enrolled. In 2006, 10 master's, 2 doctorates awarded. *Degree requirements:* For master's, content exams; for doctorate, thesis/dissertation, comprehensive exam. *Entrance requirements:* For master's, minimum GPA of 2.75 or MA Degree or MAT of 4107; for doctorate, GRE General Test or MAT, minimum GPA of 3.25. Additional exam requirements/recommendations for international students: Required—TOEFL. *Application deadline:* Applications are processed on a rolling basis. Application fee: $50. *Expenses:* Tuition, state resident: full-time $4,926; part-time $276 per credit hour. Tuition, nonresident: full-time $14,278; part-time $796 per credit hour. Tuition and fees vary according to program. *Financial support:* In 2006–07, 131 students received support, including 1 research assistantship (averaging $8,730 per year), 4 teaching assistantships with full tuition reimbursements available (averaging $8,264 per year); career-related internships or fieldwork, Federal Work-Study, institutionally sponsored loans, and tuition waivers (partial) also available. Financial award application deadline: 2/1; financial award applicants required to submit FAFSA. *Faculty research:* Evaluation, collective bargaining, educational law, international higher education, superintendency. *Unit head:* Dr. Richard Hartnett, Chairperson, 304-293-3708, Fax: 304-293-2279, E-mail: richard.hartnett@mail.wvu.edu.

Wheelock College, Graduate Programs, Division of Education, Boston, MA 02215-4176. Offers early childhood education (MS); education leadership (MS); elementary education (MS); language, literacy, and reading (MS); teaching students with moderate disabilities (MS). *Accreditation:* NCATE. Postbaccalaureate distance learning degree programs offered (minimal on-campus study). *Degree requirements:* For master's, comprehensive exam. *Entrance requirements:* Additional exam requirements/recommendations for international students: Required—TOEFL. Electronic applications accepted. *Faculty research:* Symbolic learning, emergent literacy, diversity inclusion, beginning reading language and culture, math education.

Whittier College, Graduate Programs, Department of Education and Child Development, Program in Educational Administration, Whittier, CA 90608-0634. Offers MA Ed. Part-time and evening/weekend programs available. *Degree requirements:* For master's, thesis, registration. *Entrance requirements:* For master's, GRE General Test, MAT. *Faculty research:* Candidate leadership development.

Whitworth University, School of Education, Graduate Studies in Education, Program in Administration, Spokane, WA 99251-0001. Offers M Ed. *Accreditation:* NCATE. Part-time and evening/weekend programs available. *Students:* 35. *Degree requirements:* For master's, internship, practicum, research project, or thesis. *Entrance requirements:* For master's, GRE General Test, MAT. *Application deadline:* For fall admission, 9/1 priority date for domestic students; for spring admission, 2/1 for domestic students. Applications are processed on a rolling basis. Application fee: $35. *Financial support:* Career-related internships or fieldwork available. Financial award application deadline: 2/1. *Faculty research:* Rural staff development. *Application contact:* Pat Bailey, Program Assistant, 509-777-3228, Fax: 509-777-4753, E-mail: gse@whitworth.edu.

Wichita State University, Graduate School, College of Education, Department of Administration, Counseling, Educational and School Psychology, Wichita, KS 67260. Offers counseling (M Ed); education administration (M Ed, Ed D); educational psychology (M Ed); school psychology (Ed S). *Accreditation:* NCATE. Part-time and evening/weekend programs available. *Degree requirements:* For master's, thesis optional; for doctorate, one foreign language, thesis/dissertation; for Ed S, internship, practicum. *Entrance requirements:* For master's, minimum GPA of 2.75; for doctorate, GRE General Test. Additional exam requirements/recommendations for international students: Required—TOEFL. Electronic applications accepted.

Widener University, School of Human Service Professions, Center for Education, Chester, PA 19013-5792. Offers adult education (M Ed); counseling in higher education (M Ed); counselor education (M Ed); early childhood education (M Ed); educational foundations (M Ed); educational leadership (M Ed); educational psychology (M Ed); elementary education (M Ed); English and language arts (M Ed); health education (M Ed); higher education leadership (Ed D); home and school visitor (M Ed); human sexuality (M Ed); mathematics education (M Ed); middle school education (M Ed); principalship (M Ed); reading and language arts (Ed D); reading education (M Ed); school administration (Ed D); science education (M Ed); social studies education (M Ed); special education (M Ed); technology education (M Ed). Part-time and evening/weekend programs available. Terminal master's awarded for partial completion of doctoral program. *Degree requirements:* For doctorate, thesis/dissertation. *Entrance requirements:* For master's, minimum GPA of 2.5; for doctorate, GRE or MAT, minimum GPA of 2.0 (undergraduate), 3.5 (graduate). Electronic applications accepted. Expenses: Contact institution. *Faculty research:* Reading and cognition, adult education, technology education, educational leadership, special education.

Wilkes University, Graduate Studies and Continued Learning, College of Arts, Humanities and Social Sciences, Program in Teacher Education, Wilkes-Barre, PA 18766-0002. Offers classroom technology (MS Ed); educational computing (MS Ed); educational development and strategies (MS Ed); educational leadership (MS Ed); elementary education (MS Ed); instructional technology (MS Ed); school business leadership (MS Ed); secondary education (MS Ed), including biology, chemistry, English, history; special education (MS Ed). Part-time and evening/weekend programs available. Postbaccalaureate distance learning degree programs offered (minimal on-campus study). *Students:* 32 full-time (21 women), 1,588 part-time (1,106 women); includes 29 minority (6 African Americans, 2 American Indian/Alaska Native, 4 Asian Americans or Pacific Islanders, 17 Hispanic Americans). Average age 33. In 2006, 754 degrees awarded. *Entrance requirements:* Additional exam requirements/recommendations for international students: Required—TOEFL (minimum score 500 paper-based; 173 computer-based). *Application deadline:* Applications are processed on a rolling basis. Application fee: $40. *Expenses: Contact institution. Financial support:* Federal Work-Study and unspecified assistantships available. Financial award application deadline: 3/1; financial award applicants required to submit FAFSA. *Unit head:* Dr. Michael Speziale, Interim Dean, 570-408-4679, Fax: 570-408-4905, E-mail: michael.speziale@wilkes.edu. *Application contact:* Kathleen Houlihan, Director of Graduate Studies, 570-408-3235, Fax: 570-408-7846, E-mail: kathleen.houlihan@wilkes.edu.

William Paterson University of New Jersey, College of Education, Program in Educational Leadership, Wayne, NJ 07470-8420. Offers M Ed. *Students:* 13 full-time (9 women), 22 part-time (14 women); includes 5 African Americans, 5 Hispanic Americans. Application fee: $50. *Unit head:* Dr. Michael Chirichello, Program Director, 973-720-2130. *Application contact:* Danielle Liautaud, Director, 973-720-3579, Fax: 973-720-2035, E-mail: liautaudd@wpunj.edu.

William Woods University, Graduate and Adult Studies, Fulton, MO 65251-1098. Offers administration (M Ed, Ed S); agribusiness (MBA); curriculum/instruction (M Ed); health management (MBA); human services (MBA); instructional leadership (Ed S). Evening/weekend programs available. *Faculty:* 38 full-time (14 women), 174 part-time/adjunct (50 women). *Students:* 1,944 full-time (1,230 women); includes 71 minority (43 African Americans, 16 American Indian/Alaska Native, 7 Asian Americans or Pacific Islanders, 5 Hispanic Americans), 41 international. 824 applicants, 86% accepted, 631 enrolled. In 2006, 919 master's, 112 other advanced degrees awarded. *Median time to degree:* Master's–1.5 years full-time; Ed S–1.5 years full-time. *Degree requirements:* For master's, capstone course (MBA), action research (M Ed); for Ed S, field experience. *Entrance requirements:* For master's, 2 recommendations, resumé, BA/BS; teaching certification (M Ed); course work in economics and accounting (MBA); for Ed S, M Ed, 2 letters of recommendation, resumé, teaching certification. Additional exam requirements/recommendations for international students: Required—TOEFL (minimum score 550 paper-based). *Application deadline:* Applications are processed on a rolling basis. Application fee: $25. Electronic applications accepted. *Expenses:* Tuition: Part-time $255 per credit hour. Tuition and fees vary according to program. *Financial support:* Institutionally sponsored loans available. Financial award applicants required to submit FAFSA. *Unit head:* Sean Siebert, Dean of Graduate and Adult Studies Enrollment Services, 573-592-4383, Fax: 573-592-1164. *Application contact:* Linda Rembish, Administrative Assistant, 800-995-3199, Fax: 573-592-1164, E-mail: cgas@williamwoods.edu.

Wilmington College, Division of Education, New Castle, DE 19720-6491. Offers applied education technology (M Ed); career and technical education (M Ed); elementary and secondary school counseling (M Ed); elementary special education (M Ed); elementary studies (M Ed); instruction: gifted and talented (M Ed); instruction: teaching and learning (M Ed); literacy (M Ed); reading (M Ed); school leadership (M Ed); secondary teaching (MAT). Part-time and evening/weekend programs available. *Faculty:* 7 full-time (4 women). *Students:* 609 full-time (447 women), 1,350 part-time (1,013 women); includes 144 minority (131 African Americans, 3 American Indian/Alaska Native, 1 Asian American or Pacific Islander, 9 Hispanic Americans). Average age 34. 818 applicants, 100% accepted, 599 enrolled. In 2006, 737 degrees awarded. *Entrance requirements:* For master's, 2 letters of recommendation, interview. Additional exam requirements/recommendations for international students: Required—TOEFL (minimum score 500 paper-based; 173 computer-based). *Application deadline:* For fall admission, 4/30 for domestic students. Applications are processed on a rolling basis. Application fee: $25. *Financial support:* Applicants required to submit FAFSA. *Unit head:* Dr. Richard Gochnauer, Chair, 302-328-6795 Ext. 163, Fax: 302-328-7081. *Application contact:* Chris Ferguson, Director of Admissions and Financial Aid, 302-328-9407 Ext. 256, Fax: 302-328-5164, E-mail: inquire@wilmcoll.edu.

Wilmington College, Division of Nursing, New Castle, DE 19720-6491. Offers adult nurse practitioner (MSN); family nurse practitioner (MSN); gerontology (MSN); leadership (MSN); nursing (MSN); women's nurse practitioner (MSN). *Accreditation:* AACN; NLN. Part-time programs available. *Students:* 30 full-time (28 women), 195 part-time (176 women); includes 24 minority (19 African Americans, 3 Asian Americans or Pacific Islanders, 2 Hispanic Americans). Average age 39. 54 applicants, 100% accepted, 48 enrolled. In 2006, 58 degrees awarded. *Degree requirements:* For master's, thesis. *Entrance requirements:* For master's, BSN, RN license, interview, 3 letters of recommendation. Additional exam requirements/recommendations for international students: Required—TOEFL (minimum score 500 paper-based; 173 computer-based). *Application deadline:* For fall admission, 3/31 priority date for domestic students. Applications are processed on a rolling basis. Application fee: $25. *Financial support:* In 2006–07, 28 fellowships with tuition reimbursements (averaging $2,200 per year) were awarded; traineeships also available. Financial award applicants required to submit FAFSA. *Faculty research:* Outcomes assessment, student writing ability. *Unit head:* Dr. Mary Letitia Gallagher, Chair, 302-328-9401 Ext. 161, Fax: 302-328-7081, E-mail: tgall@wilmcoll.edu. *Application contact:* Chris Ferguson, Director of Admissions and Financial Aid, 302-328-9407 Ext. 256, Fax: 302-328-5164, E-mail: inquire@wilmcoll.edu.

Wilmington College, Program in Innovation and Leadership, New Castle, DE 19720-6491. Offers education innovation (Ed D); organizational leadership (Ed D). Part-time programs available. *Students:* 263 full-time (159 women); includes 60 minority (52 African Americans, 2 Asian Americans or Pacific Islanders, 6 Hispanic Americans). Average age 41. 141 applicants, 101 enrolled. In 2006, 45 degrees awarded. *Degree requirements:* For doctorate, thesis/dissertation. *Entrance requirements:* For doctorate, 3 letters of recommendation. Additional exam requirements/recommendations for international students: Required—TOEFL (minimum score 500 paper-based; 173 computer-based). Application fee: $25. *Unit head:* Dr. Joe Deardorff, Head, 302-328-9401 Ext. 351. *Application contact:* 302-328-9407.

Wingate University, Program in Education, Wingate, NC 28174-0159. Offers educational leadership (MA Ed); elementary education (MA Ed, MAT); physical education (MA Ed); sport administration (MA Ed). *Accreditation:* NCATE. Part-time and evening/weekend programs available. *Faculty:* 4 full-time (3 women), 4 part-time/adjunct (1 woman). *Students:* 1 (woman) full-time, 127 part-time (96 women); includes 2 minority (both African Americans) Average age 35. 19 applicants, 58% accepted, 11 enrolled. In 2006, 12 degrees awarded. *Degree requirements:* For master's, portfolio. *Entrance requirements:* For master's, GRE General Test or MAT, teaching certificate (MA Ed). *Application deadline:* For fall admission, 8/15 priority date for domestic students; for spring admission, 12/15 for domestic students. Applications are processed on a rolling basis. Application fee: $0. *Expenses:* Tuition: Full-time $3,330; part-time $185 per credit hour. *Financial support:* In 2006–07, 20 students received support. Scholarships/grants available. Support available to part-time students. Financial award applicants required to submit FAFSA. *Faculty research:* Teaching/learning styles, principles of teaching, homework, stress management, student's rights. *Unit head:* Dr. Robert Shaw, Dean, Thayer School of Education, 704-233-8128, Fax: 704-233-8273, E-mail: rshaw@wingate.edu. *Application contact:* Marsha Luke, Secretary, Thayer School of Education, 704-233-8127, Fax: 704-233-8273, E-mail: mluke@wingate.edu.

Winona State University, Graduate Studies, College of Education, Department of Educational Leadership, Winona, MN 55987-5838. Offers educational leadership (Ed S); general school leadership (MS); K-12 principalship (MS); teacher leadership (MS). *Accreditation:* NCATE. Part-time and evening/weekend programs available. *Faculty:* 3 full-time (1 woman). *Students:* 1 (woman) full-time, 61 part-time (27 women). 23 applicants, 91% accepted, 18 enrolled. In 2006, 20 master's, 5 other advanced degrees awarded. *Degree requirements:* For master's, thesis or alternative. *Application deadline:* For fall admission, 8/8 priority date for domestic students; for spring admission, 2/17 for domestic students. Applications are processed on a rolling basis. Application fee: $20. *Financial support:* Federal Work-Study available. Support available to part-time students. Financial award applicants required to submit FAFSA. *Unit head:* Dr. Lee Gray, Director of Graduate Studies, 507-457-5346, E-mail: lgray@winona.edu.

Winthrop University, College of Education, Program in Educational Leadership, Rock Hill, SC 29733. Offers M Ed. *Students:* 13 full-time (5 women), 66 part-time (50 women); includes 35 minority (34 African Americans, 1 Hispanic American). Average age 34. In 2006, 30 degrees awarded. *Entrance requirements:* For master's, GRE General Test or MAT, 3 years of experience, South Carolina Class III Teaching Certificate. *Application deadline:* For fall admission, 7/15 priority date for domestic students; for spring admission, 12/1 for domestic students. Applications are processed on a rolling basis. Application fee: $35. Electronic applications accepted. *Expenses:* Tuition, state resident: full-time $9,148; part-time $383 per hour. Tuition, nonresident: full-time $16,864; part-time $704 per hour. *Financial support:* Application deadline: 2/1; *Unit head:* Dr. Mary Martin, Acting Chair, 803-323-4725. *Application contact:* 800-411-7041, Fax: 803-323-2204, E-mail: graduatestu@winthrop.edu.

Worcester State College, Graduate Studies, Department of Education, Concentration in Leadership and Administration, Worcester, MA 01602-2597. Offers M Ed. Part-time programs available. *Students:* Average age 43. 23 applicants, 83% accepted, 9 enrolled. In 2006, 17 degrees awarded. *Degree requirements:* For master's, thesis optional. *Entrance requirements:* For master's, GRE General Test or MAT, teaching certificate. Additional exam requirements/recommendations for international students: Required—TOEFL (minimum score 550 paper-based; 213 computer-based). *Application deadline:* Applications are processed on a rolling basis. Application fee: $30. *Expenses:* Tuition, state resident: full-time $4,518; part-time $251 per credit hour. Tuition, nonresident: full-time $4,518; part-time $251 per credit hour. *Financial support:* Career-related internships or fieldwork, Federal Work-Study, scholarships/grants, and unspecified assistantships available. Support available to part-time students. Financial award application deadline: 3/1; financial award applicants required to submit FAFSA. *Unit head:* Dr. Audrey Wright, Coordinator, 508-929-8594, Fax: 508-929-8164, E-mail: awright1@worcester.edu. *Application contact:* Nicole Brown, Assistant Dean of Graduate and Continuing Education, 508-929-8787, Fax: 508-929-8100, E-mail: nbrown@worcester.edu.

Wright State University, School of Graduate Studies, College of Education and Human Services, Department of Educational Leadership, Program in Advanced Educational Leadership, Dayton, OH 45435. Offers advanced curriculum and instruction (Ed S); higher education-adult education (Ed S); superintendent (Ed S). *Accreditation:* NCATE. *Students:* 6 full-time (4 women), 10 part-time (6 women); includes 3 minority (all African Americans) Average age 35. 3 applicants, 100% accepted. In 2006, 1 degree awarded. *Degree requirements:* For Ed S, thesis. *Entrance requirements:* For degree, GRE General Test, MAT. Additional exam requirements/recommendations for international students: Required—TOEFL. Application fee: $25. *Financial support:* Available to part-time students. Applicants required to submit FAFSA. *Unit head:* Dr. Thomas Diamantes, Director, 937-775-3008, Fax: 937-775-2405, E-mail: thomas.diamantes@wright.edu. *Application contact:* John Kimble, Associate Director of Graduate Admissions and Records, 937-775-2957, Fax: 937-775-2453, E-mail: john.kimble@wright.edu.

Wright State University, School of Graduate Studies, College of Education and Human Services, Department of Educational Leadership, Programs in Educational Leadership, Dayton, OH 45435. Offers curriculum and instruction: teacher leader (MA); educational administrative specialist: teacher leader (M Ed); educational administrative specialist: vocational education administration (M Ed, MA); student affairs in higher education-administration (M Ed, MA). *Accreditation:* NCATE. *Students:* 26 full-time (22 women), 430 part-time (344 women); includes 10 minority (8 African Americans, 1 American Indian/Alaska Native, 1 Hispanic American), 1 international. Average age 33. 179 applicants, 97% accepted. In 2006, 211 degrees awarded. *Degree requirements:* For master's, thesis (for some programs). *Entrance requirements:* For master's, GRE General Test, MAT. Additional exam requirements/recommendations for international students: Required—TOEFL. Application fee: $25. *Financial support:* Available to part-time students. Applicants required to submit FAFSA. *Unit head:* Dr. Charles W. Ryan, Director and Director of Graduate Programs in Education, 937-775-3286, Fax: 937-775-2405, E-mail: charles.ryan@wright.edu. *Application contact:* John Kimble, Associate Director of Graduate Admissions and Records, 937-775-2957, Fax: 937-775-2453, E-mail: john.kimble@wright.edu.

Xavier University, College of Social Sciences, Health and Education, School of Education, Program in Educational Administration, Cincinnati, OH 45207. Offers M Ed. Part-time and evening/weekend programs available. *Faculty:* 2 full-time (0 women), 8 part-time/adjunct (1 woman). *Students:* 4 full-time (2 women), 118 part-time (77 women); includes 11 minority (all African Americans), 1 international. Average age 33. 52 applicants, 60% accepted, 26 enrolled. In 2006, 84 degrees awarded. *Degree requirements:* For master's, thesis, research project, comprehensive exam, registration. *Entrance requirements:* For master's, MAT or GRE, minimum GPA of 2.8. Additional exam requirements/recommendations for international students: Required—TOEFL (minimum score 550 paper-based; 213 computer-based). *Application deadline:* For fall admission, 8/15 priority date for domestic students. Applications are processed on a rolling basis. Application fee: $35. Electronic applications accepted. *Expenses:* Tuition: Part-time $462 per credit hour. Part-time tuition and fees vary according to degree level, campus/location and program. *Financial support:* Scholarships/grants and unspecified assistantships available. Support available to part-time students. Financial award applicants required to submit FAFSA. *Faculty research:* Total quality management for school, ethics in administration, fiscal-social equity in schools, hidden curriculum, curriculum leadership theory/research, school law. *Unit head:* Dr. Leo Bradley, Director, 513-745-2982, Fax: 513-745-1052, E-mail: bradley@xavier.edu. *Application contact:* Roger Bosse, Interim Director of Graduate Studies, 513-745-3357, Fax: 513-745-1048, E-mail: bosse@xavier.edu.

Xavier University of Louisiana, Graduate School, Programs in Education, New Orleans, LA 70125-1098. Offers curriculum and instruction (MA); education administration and supervision (MA); guidance and counseling (MA). *Accreditation:* NCATE. Part-time and evening/weekend programs available. *Degree requirements:* For master's, thesis or alternative, comprehensive exam. *Entrance requirements:* For master's, GRE General Test, MAT, minimum GPA of 2.5. Additional exam requirements/recommendations for international students: Required—TOEFL.

Yeshiva University, Azrieli Graduate School of Jewish Education and Administration, New York, NY 10033-4391. Offers MS, Ed D, Specialist. Part-time and evening/weekend programs available. Terminal master's awarded for partial completion of doctoral program. *Degree requirements:* For master's, one foreign language; for doctorate, one foreign language, thesis/dissertation, certifying exams, internship, comprehensive exam; for Specialist, one foreign language, comprehensive exam, certifying exams, internship. *Entrance requirements:* For master's, GRE General Test, BA in Jewish studies or equivalent; for doctorate and Specialist, GRE General Test, master's degree in Jewish education, 2 years of teaching experience. Expenses: Contact institution. *Faculty research:* Social patterns of American and Israeli Jewish population, special education, adult education, technology in education, return to religious values.

Youngstown State University, Graduate School, College of Education, Department of Educational Administration, Research, and Foundations, Youngstown, OH 44555-0001. Offers educational administration (MS Ed); educational leadership (Ed D). *Accreditation:* NCATE. Part-time and evening/weekend programs available. *Degree requirements:* For master's, comprehensive exam; for doctorate, thesis/dissertation, comprehensive exam. *Entrance requirements:* For master's, GRE, MAT, or teaching certificate; minimum GPA of 2.7; for doctorate, GRE General Test, GRE Subject Test, interview, minimum GPA of 3.5. Additional exam requirements/recommendations for international students: Required—TOEFL. *Faculty research:* Administrative theory, computer applications, education law, school and community relations, finance principalship.

Educational Measurement and Evaluation

Abilene Christian University, Graduate School, College of Education and Human Services, Graduate Studies in Education, Educational Diagnostician Program, Abilene, TX 79699-9100. Offers M Ed. Part-time programs available. *Faculty:* 9 part-time/adjunct (6 women). *Students:* 1 applicant, 100% accepted, 1 enrolled. In 2006, 1 degree awarded. *Degree requirements:* For master's, comprehensive exam. *Entrance requirements:* For master's, GRE General Test or MAT. *Application deadline:* For fall admission, 4/1 priority date for domestic students; for spring admission, 11/1 for domestic students. Applications are processed on a rolling basis. Application fee: $40 ($45 for international students). Electronic applications accepted. *Expenses:* Tuition: Full-time $12,504; part-time $521 per hour. Required fees: $700; $34 per hour. *Financial support:* Federal Work-Study available. Support available to part-time students. Financial award application deadline: 4/1. *Application contact:* William Horn, Graduate Admissions Counselor, 325-674-2656, Fax: 325-674-6717, E-mail: gradinfo@acu.edu.

American InterContinental University Online, Program in Education, Hoffman Estates, IL 60192. Offers curriculum and instruction (M Ed); educational assessment and evaluation (M Ed); instructional technology (M Ed); leadership of educational organizations (M Ed). Evening/weekend programs available. Postbaccalaureate distance learning degree programs offered (no on-campus study). *Entrance requirements:* Additional exam requirements/recommendations for international students: Required—TOEFL (minimum score 550 paper-based; 213 computer-based). *Application deadline:* Applications are processed on a rolling basis. Application fee: $50. Electronic applications accepted. *Financial support:* Institutionally sponsored loans and scholarships/grants available. Financial award applicants required to submit FAFSA. *Unit head:* Kerri J Holloway, Vice President of Academic Affairs, 847-851-5000 Ext. 15399, Fax: 847-586-6309, E-mail: kholloway@aivonline.edu. *Application contact:* 877-701-3800, E-mail: info@aiuonline.edu.

Angelo State University, College of Graduate Studies, College of Education, Department of Teacher Education, Program in Educational Diagnostics, San Angelo, TX 76909. Offers M Ed. Part-time and evening/weekend programs available. *Faculty:* 17 full-time (12 women). *Students:* Average age 39. 7 applicants, 71% accepted, 3 enrolled. In 2006, 9 degrees awarded. *Degree requirements:* For master's, comprehensive exam. *Entrance requirements:* For master's, GRE General Test. Additional exam requirements/recommendations for international students: Required—TOEFL or IELTS. *Application deadline:* For fall admission, 7/15 priority date for domestic students, 6/15 for international students; for spring admission, 12/8 for domestic students, 11/1 for international students. Applications are processed on a rolling basis. Application fee: $40 ($50 for international students). Electronic applications accepted. *Expenses:* Tuition, state resident: full-time $2,340; part-time $130 per hour. Tuition, nonresident: full-time $7,290; part-time $405 per hour. Required fees: $906; $56 per hour. *Financial support:* In 2006–07, 3 students received support. Career-related internships or fieldwork, Federal Work-Study, scholarships/grants, and unspecified assistantships available. Support available to part-time students. Financial award application deadline: 3/1; financial award applicants required to submit FAFSA. *Application contact:* Dr. Mary E. Sanders, Graduate Advisor, 325-942-2052 Ext. 265, E-mail: mary.sanders@angelo.edu.

Arkansas State University, Graduate School, College of Education, Department of Psychology and Counseling, Jonesboro, State University, AR 72467. Offers college student personnel services (MS); counselor education (Ed S), including college student personnel services, psychoeducational diagnosis, school counseling; rehabilitation counseling (MRC); school counseling (MSE); student affairs (Certificate). *Accreditation:* ACA (one or more programs are accredited); CORE (one or more programs are accredited); NCATE. Part-time programs available. *Faculty:* 13 full-time (6 women), 3 part-time/adjunct (1 woman). *Students:* 61 full-time (41 women), 56 part-time (43 women); includes 25 minority (22 African Americans, 3 Hispanic Americans). Average age 30. 74 applicants, 69% accepted, 40 enrolled. In 2006, 26 master's, 11 other advanced degrees awarded. *Degree requirements:* For master's and other advanced degree, thesis or alternative, comprehensive exam. *Entrance requirements:* For master's, GRE General Test or MAT (MSE), appropriate bachelor's degree, interview, letters of reference, official transcript; for other advanced degree, GRE General Test, interview, master's degree, letters of reference, official transcript. Additional exam requirements/recommendations for international students: Required—TOEFL (minimum score 213 computer-based). *Application deadline:* Applications are processed on a rolling basis. Application fee: $30 ($40 for international students). Electronic applications accepted. *Expenses:* Tuition, state resident: full-time $3,393; part-time $189 per hour. Tuition, nonresident: full-time $8,577; part-time $477 per hour. Required fees: $752; $39 per hour. $25 per semester. *Financial support:* Teaching assistantships, career-related internships or fieldwork, scholarships/grants, and unspecified assistantships available. Financial award application deadline: 7/1; financial award applicants required to submit FAFSA. *Unit head:* Dr. Loretta McGregor, Chair, 870-972-3064, Fax: 870-972-3962, E-mail: lmcgregor@astate.edu.

Boston College, Lynch Graduate School of Education, Department of Educational Research, Measurement, and Evaluation, Chestnut Hill, MA 02467-3800. Offers M Ed, PhD. *Students:* 34 full-time (24 women), 9 part-time (7 women); includes 8 minority (2 African Americans, 3 Asian Americans or Pacific Islanders, 3 Hispanic Americans), 13 international. 51 applicants, 53% accepted, 12 enrolled. In 2006, 5 master's, 1 doctorate awarded. Terminal master's awarded for partial completion of doctoral program. *Degree requirements:* For master's, comprehensive exam; for doctorate, thesis/dissertation, comprehensive exam. *Entrance requirements:* For master's, GRE General Test or MAT; for doctorate, GRE General Test. Additional exam requirements/recommendations for international students: Required—TOEFL. Application fee: $60. *Financial support:* Fellowships with full and partial tuition reimbursements, research assistantships with full and partial tuition reimbursements, teaching assistantships with full and partial tuition reimbursements, career-related internships or fieldwork, Federal Work-Study, institutionally sponsored loans, scholarships/grants, traineeships, tuition waivers (full and partial), and unspecified assistantships available. Support available to part-time students. Financial award applicants required to submit FAFSA. *Faculty research:* Classroom assessment, effects and uses of tests in public policy, history of testing, national and international assessment and surveys, high stakes testing. *Unit head:* Dr. Larry Ludlow, Chairperson, 617-552-4214, Fax: 617-552-0812. *Application contact:* Timothy P. Blackman, Director, Graduate Admission and Financial Aid, 617-552-4214, Fax: 617-552-0398, E-mail: timothy.blackman.1@bc.edu.

Bucknell University, Graduate Studies, College of Arts and Sciences, Department of Education, Specialization in Educational Research, Lewisburg, PA 17837. Offers MS Ed. *Degree requirements:* For master's, thesis or alternative. *Entrance requirements:* For master's, GRE General Test, minimum GPA of 2.8. Additional exam requirements/recommendations for international students: Required—TOEFL.

Claremont Graduate University, Graduate Programs, School of Educational Studies, Claremont, CA 91711-6160. Offers Africana education (Certificate); education policy issues (MA, PhD); higher education (PhD); higher education administration (MA); human development (MA, PhD); public school administration (MA, PhD); teacher education (MA, PhD); teaching and learning (MA, PhD); urban education administration (MA, PhD); MBA/PhD. Part-time programs available. *Faculty:* 15 full-time (9 women), 11 part-time/adjunct (9 women). *Students:* 236 full-time (155 women), 168 part-time (117 women); includes 177 minority (34 African Americans, 2 American Indian/Alaska Native, 43 Asian Americans or Pacific Islanders, 98 Hispanic Americans), 7 international. Average age 38. In 2006, 90 master's, 20 doctorates awarded. Terminal master's awarded for partial completion of doctoral program. *Degree requirements:* For master's, thesis or alternative, comprehensive exam (for some programs); for doctorate, thesis/dissertation, comprehensive exam. *Entrance requirements:* For master's and doctorate, GRE General Test. *Application deadline:* For fall admission, 2/15 priority date for domestic students. Applications are processed on a rolling basis. Electronic applications accepted. *Financial support:* Fellowships, research assistantships, Federal Work-Study and institutionally sponsored loans available. Support available to part-time students. Financial award application deadline: 2/15; financial award applicants required to submit FAFSA. *Faculty research:* Education administration, K–12 and higher education, multicultural education, education policy, diversity in higher education, faculty issues. *Unit head:* Philip H. Dreyer, Dean, 909-621-8075, Fax: 909-621-8734, E-mail: philip.dreyer@cgu.edu. *Application contact:* Cece Gaddy, Administrative Director, 909-621-8317, Fax: 909-621-8734, E-mail: cece.gaddy@cgu.edu.

College of the Southwest, School of Education, Hobbs, NM 88240-9129. Offers curriculum and instruction (MS); educational administration (MS); educational counseling (MS); educational diagnostician (MS). Part-time and evening/weekend programs available. Postbaccalaureate distance learning degree programs offered. *Faculty:* 2 full-time (both women), 6 part-time/adjunct (1 woman). *Students:* 41 full-time (28 women), 43 part-time (35 women); includes 24 minority (1 African American, 1 American Indian/Alaska Native, 1 Asian American or Pacific Islander, 21 Hispanic Americans), 1 international. Average age 38. 119 applicants, 29% accepted, 34 enrolled. In 2006, 26 degrees awarded. *Degree requirements:* For master's, comprehensive exam. *Entrance requirements:* For master's, GRE General Test. Additional exam requirements/recommendations for international students: Recommended—TOEFL (minimum score 550 paper-based; 213 computer-based). *Application deadline:* For fall admission, 3/1 priority date for domestic students; for spring admission, 10/1 for domestic students. Applications are processed on a rolling basis. Application fee: $50. *Expenses:* Tuition: Part-time $375 per credit hour. *Financial support:* In 2006–07, 58 students received support, including 1 research assistantship; Federal Work-Study, scholarships/grants, and tuition waivers (partial) also available. Support available to part-time students. Financial award application deadline: 4/1; financial award applicants required to submit FAFSA. *Unit head:* Dr. Dennis Atherton, Dean, 505-392-6561 Ext. 1069, Fax: 505-392-6006, E-mail: datherton@csw.edu. *Application contact:* Kerrie Mitchell, Coordinator of Financial Aid and Admissions Operations, 505-392-6563 Ext. 1048, Fax: 505-392-6006, E-mail: kmitchell@csw.edu.

Florida State University, Graduate Studies, College of Education, Department of Educational Leadership and Policy Studies, Program in Program Evaluation, Tallahassee, FL 32306. Offers MS, PhD. *Faculty:* 1 (woman) full-time. *Students:* 1 (woman) full-time, 7 part-time (6 women); includes 5 minority (4 African Americans, 1 Hispanic American). 2 applicants, 0% accepted. In 2006, 1 degree awarded. *Application deadline:* For fall admission, 7/1 for domestic students; for spring admission, 11/1 for domestic students. Application fee: $30. *Expenses:* Tuition, state resident: full-time $5,822; part-time $243 per credit hour. Tuition, nonresident: full-time $20,976; part-time $874 per credit hour. Tuition and fees vary according to program. *Financial support:* Fellowships with partial tuition reimbursements, research assistantships with partial tuition reimbursements, teaching assistantships with partial tuition reimbursements, career-related internships or fieldwork, scholarships/grants, and unspecified assistantships available. *Unit head:* Dr. Linda Schrader, Head, 850-644-6777, Fax: 850-644-1258, E-mail: lschrade@coe.fsu.edu. *Application contact:* Jimmy Pastrano, Program Assistant, 850-644-6777, Fax: 850-644-1258, E-mail: pastrano@coe.fsu.edu.

Florida State University, Graduate Studies, College of Education, Department of Educational Psychology and Learning Systems, Program in Measurement and Statistics, Tallahassee, FL 32306. Offers MS, PhD. *Faculty:* 3 full-time (1 woman), 2 part-time/adjunct (0 women). *Students:* 17 full-time (9 women), 7 part-time (4 women); includes 13 minority (4 African Americans, 8 Asian Americans or Pacific Islanders, 1 Hispanic American). Average age 20. 10 applicants, 60% accepted, 3 enrolled. In 2006, 5 master's, 2 doctorates awarded. *Application deadline:* For fall admission, 7/1 for domestic students; for spring admission, 11/1 for domestic students. Application fee: $30. *Expenses:* Tuition, state resident: full-time $5,822; part-time $243 per credit hour. Tuition, nonresident: full-time $20,976; part-time $874 per credit hour. Tuition and fees vary according to program. *Financial support:* In 2006–07, fellowships with partial tuition reimbursements (averaging $5,000 per year), research assistantships with partial tuition reimbursements (averaging $18,000 per year), teaching assistantships with partial tuition reimbursements (averaging $18,000 per year) were awarded. *Unit head:* Dr. Betsy Becker, Program Leader, 850-645-2371, Fax: 850-644-8776, E-mail: bjbecker@coe.fsu.edu. *Application contact:* Sally Gadson, Program Assistant, 850-644-8046, Fax: 850-644-5067, E-mail: gadson@coe.fsu.edu.

Gallaudet University, The Graduate School, School of Education and Human Services, Department of Educational Foundations and Research, Washington, DC 20002-3625. Offers integrating technology in the classroom (Certificate). *Accreditation:* NCATE. *Degree requirements:* For Certificate, thesis optional. *Entrance requirements:* For degree, GRE General Test or MAT.

George Mason University, Graduate School of Education, Initiatives in Educational Transformation Program, Fairfax, VA 22030. Offers MA. *Faculty:* 7 full-time (4 women), 3 part-time/adjunct (all women). *Students:* 4 full-time (all women), 250 part-time (216 women); includes 32 minority (18 African Americans, 7 Asian Americans or Pacific Islanders, 7 Hispanic Americans), 1 international. Average age 36. 156 applicants, 89% accepted, 119 enrolled. In 2006, 127 degrees awarded. *Entrance requirements:* For master's, minimum GPA of 3.0 in last 60 hours. Application fee: $60 ($75 for international students). *Expenses:* Tuition, state resident: full-time $5,724; part-time $238 per credit. Tuition, nonresident: full-time $16,896; part-time $704 per credit. Required fees: $1,656; $69 per credit. *Financial support:* Application deadline: 3/1; *Unit head:* Betsy De Mulder, Director, 703-993-8323, Fax: 703-993-8321, E-mail: iet@gmu.edu.

Georgia State University, College of Education, Department of Educational Policy Studies, Program in Educational Research, Atlanta, GA 30303-3083. Offers educational research (MS); research, measurements and statistics (PhD). *Accreditation:* NCATE. *Students:* 11 full-time (9 women), 13 part-time (10 women); includes 10 minority (9 African Americans, 1 Hispanic American), 5 international. Average age 35. 7 applicants, 100% accepted. In 2006, 3 master's, 4 doctorates awarded. *Degree requirements:* For master's, thesis or project; for doctorate, thesis/dissertation, comprehensive exam. *Entrance requirements:* For master's, GRE General Test, minimum GPA of 2.5; for doctorate, GRE General Test or MAT, minimum GPA of 3.3. Application fee: $25. *Financial support:* Research assistantships available. *Faculty research:* Educational statistics, item response theory, instructional computing, measurement. *Unit head:* Dr. Asa G. Hilliard, Chair, Department of Educational Policy Studies, 404-651-1269, Fax: 404-651-1009, E-mail: ahilliard@gsu.edu.

Harvard University, Graduate School of Education, Doctoral Program in Education, Cambridge, MA 02138. Offers culture, communities and education (Ed D); education policy (Ed D); education policy, leadership and instructional practice (Ed D); higher education (Ed D); human development and education (Ed D); quantitative policy analysis in education (Ed D); urban superintendency (Ed D). Part-time programs available. *Faculty:* 58 full-time (25 women), 40 part-time/adjunct (22 women). *Students:* 306 full-time (216 women), 35 part-time (26 women); includes 95 minority (38 African Americans, 4 American Indian/Alaska Native, 35 Asian Americans or Pacific Islanders, 18 Hispanic Americans), 46 international. Average age 35. 494 applicants, 12% accepted, 48 enrolled. In 2006, 70 degrees awarded. Terminal master's awarded for partial completion of doctoral program. *Degree requirements:* For doctorate, thesis/dissertation. *Entrance requirements:* For doctorate, GRE General Test, 3 letters of recommendation, official transcripts, statement of purpose. Additional exam requirements/recommendations for international students: Required—TOEFL (minimum score 600 paper-based; 250 computer-based; 100 iBT), TWE (minimum score 5). *Application deadline:* For fall admission, 12/14 for domestic and international students. Application fee: $85. Electronic applications accepted. *Expenses:* Contact institution. *Financial support:* In 2006–07, 171 fellowships with full and partial tuition reimbursements (averaging $11,489 per year), 47 research assistantships (averaging $9,340 per year), 153 teaching assistantships (averaging $7,710 per year) were awarded; career-related internships or fieldwork, Federal Work-Study, institutionally sponsored loans, scholarships/grants, health care benefits, tuition waivers (full and partial), and unspecified assistantships also available. Support available to part-time students. Financial award application deadline: 2/2; financial award applicants required to submit FAFSA. *Faculty research:* Learning and development; educational leadership and organizations; education policy analysis. Total annual research expenditures: $4.8 million. *Unit head:* Dr. James Stiles, Associate Dean for Degree Programs. *Application contact:* Information Contact, 617-495-3414, Fax: 617-496-3577, E-mail: gseadmissions@harvard.edu.

Hofstra University, School of Education and Allied Human Services, Department of Counseling, Research, Special Education and Rehabilitation, Program in Program Evaluation, Hempstead, NY 11549. Offers MS Ed. Part-time and evening/weekend programs available. *Degree requirements:* For master's, thesis, registration. *Entrance requirements:* For master's, GRE, 2 letters of recommendation, interview, essay. Additional exam requirements/recommendations for international students: Required—TOEFL (minimum score 550 paper-based; 213 computer-based). *Application deadline:* Applications are processed on a rolling basis. Application fee: $60. Electronic applications accepted. *Expenses:* Tuition: Full-time $13,320; part-time $740 per credit. Required fees: $930; $155 per term. *Financial support:* Fellowships with tuition reimbursements, research assistantships with full and partial tuition reimbursements, career-related internships or fieldwork, scholarships/grants, tuition waivers (full and partial), and unspecified assistantships available. Support available to part-time students. Financial award applicants required to submit FAFSA. *Faculty research:* Faculty evaluation, faculty collective bargaining. *Unit head:* Dr. Estelle Gellman, Program Director, 516-463-5753, Fax: 516-463-6415, E-mail: cpresg@hofstra.edu. *Application contact:* Carol Drummer, Dean of Graduate Admissions, 516-463-4876, Fax: 516-463-4664, E-mail: gradstudent@hofstra.edu.

Houston Baptist University, College of Education and Behavioral Sciences, Programs in Education, Houston, TX 77074-3298. Offers bilingual education (M Ed); counselor education (M Ed); curriculum and instruction (M Ed); educational administration (M Ed); educational diagnostician (M Ed); reading education (M Ed). Part-time programs available. *Degree requirements:* For master's, registration. *Entrance requirements:* For master's, GRE General Test or MAT. Additional exam requirements/recommendations for international students: Required—TOEFL (minimum score 550 paper-based; 213 computer-based).

Iowa State University of Science and Technology, Graduate College, College of Human Sciences, Department of Educational Leadership and Policy Studies, Ames, IA 50011. Offers counselor education (M Ed, MS); educational administration (M Ed, MS); educational leadership (PhD); higher education (M Ed, MS); organizational learning and human resource development (M Ed, MS); research and evaluation (MS). *Faculty:* 19 full-time, 9 part-time/adjunct. *Students:* 82 full-time (53 women), 191 part-time (109 women); includes 40 minority (23 African Americans, 4 American Indian/Alaska Native, 5 Asian Americans or Pacific Islanders, 8 Hispanic Americans), 5 international. 156 applicants, 70% accepted, 76 enrolled. In 2006, 95 master's, 13 doctorates awarded. *Degree requirements:* For master's, thesis or alternative; for doctorate, thesis/dissertation. *Entrance requirements:* For doctorate, GRE General Test. Additional exam requirements/recommendations for international students: Required—TOEFL (paper-based 560; computer-based 220; iBT 79) or IELTS (6.0). *Application deadline:* For fall admission, 1/1 priority date for domestic and international students. Applications are processed on a rolling basis. Application fee: $30 ($70 for international students). Electronic applications accepted. *Expenses:* Tuition, state resident: full-time $5,936; part-time $330 per credit. Tuition, nonresident: full-time $16,350; part-time $330 per credit. *Financial support:* In 2006–07, 17 research assistantships with full and partial tuition reimbursements (averaging $16,419 per year) were awarded; fellowships, teaching assistantships with full and partial tuition reimbursements, scholarships/grants, health care benefits, and unspecified assistantships also available. *Unit head:* Dr. Laura Rendon, Chair, 515-294-7093, E-mail: lrendon@iastate.edu. *Application contact:* Dr. Daniel Robinson, Information Contact, 515-294-1241, E-mail: eldrshp@iastate.edu.

Kent State University, Graduate School of Education, Health, and Human Services, Department of Educational Foundations and Special Services, Program in Evaluation and Measurement, Kent, OH 44242-0001. Offers M Ed, MA, PhD. *Faculty:* 4 full-time (2 women), 4 part-time/adjunct (3 women). *Students:* 11 full-time (5 women), 35 part-time (27 women); includes 3 minority (2 African Americans, 1 Asian American or Pacific Islander), 5 international. 22 applicants, 100% accepted. In 2006, 3 degrees awarded. *Entrance requirements:* For doctorate, GRE. Application fee: $30. *Financial support:* In 2006–07, fellowships (averaging $8,497 per year); research assistantships, teaching assistantships, career-related internships or fieldwork, Federal Work-Study, institutionally sponsored loans, scholarships/grants, health care benefits, and unspecified assistantships also available. Support available to part-time students. *Unit head:* Dr. Shawn Fitzgerald, Coordinator, 330-672-2294, E-mail: smfitzge@kent.edu. *Application contact:* Nancy Miller, Academic Program Coordinator, Office of Graduate Student Services, 330-672-2576, Fax: 330-672-9162, E-mail: ogs@kent.edu.

Louisiana State University and Agricultural and Mechanical College, Graduate School, College of Education, Department of Educational Theory, Policy and Practice, Baton Rouge, LA 70803. Offers counseling (M Ed, MA, Ed S); educational administration (M Ed, MA, PhD, Ed S); educational technology (MA); elementary education (M Ed); higher education (PhD); research methodology (PhD); secondary education (M Ed). *Accreditation:* ACA (one or more programs are accredited); NCATE. Part-time and evening/weekend programs available. *Faculty:* 39 full-time (24 women). *Students:* 147 full-time (115 women), 183 part-time (143 women); includes 63 minority (51 African Americans, 3 American Indian/Alaska Native, 3 Asian Americans or Pacific Islanders, 6 Hispanic Americans), 14 international. Average age 35. 110 applicants, 58% accepted, 15 enrolled. In 2006, 93 master's, 24 doctorates awarded. Terminal master's awarded for partial completion of doctoral program. *Degree requirements:* For doctorate, thesis/dissertation; for Ed S, thesis optional. *Entrance requirements:* For master's and doctorate, GRE General Test, minimum GPA of 3.0. Additional exam requirements/recommendations for international students: Required—TOEFL (minimum score 550 paper-based; 213 computer-based; 79 iBT). *Application deadline:* For fall admission, 1/25 priority date for domestic students, 5/15 for international students; for spring admission, 10/15 for international students. Applications are processed on a rolling basis. Application fee: $25. Electronic applications accepted. *Financial support:* In 2006–07, 82 students received support, including 6 fellowships with full tuition reimbursements available (averaging $26,273 per year), 24 research assistantships with full and partial tuition reimbursements available (averaging $9,812 per year), teaching assistantships with full and partial tuition reimbursements available (averaging $11,693 per year); career-related internships or fieldwork, Federal Work-Study, institutionally sponsored loans, and unspecified assistantships also available. Support available to part-time students. Financial award applicants required to submit FAFSA. *Faculty research:* Literary, curriculum studies, science education, K-12 leadership, higher education. Total annual research expenditures: $335,618. *Unit head:* Dr. Earl Cheek, Chair, 225-578-6897, Fax: 225-578-1045, E-mail: echeek@lsu.edu.

Loyola University Chicago, School of Education, Program in Research Methods, Chicago, IL 60611-2196. Offers M Ed, MA, PhD. MA and PhD offered through the Graduate School. Part-time and evening/weekend programs available. *Faculty:* 2 full-time (both women), 2 part-time/adjunct (both women). *Students:* 17. Average age 25. 8 applicants, 50% accepted, 2 enrolled. In 2006, 1 master's, 2 doctorates awarded. *Degree requirements:* For master's, comprehensive exam (M Ed), thesis (MA); for doctorate, thesis/dissertation, comprehensive exam. *Entrance requirements:* For master's, GRE General Test, letters of recommendation, resumé, minimum GPA of 3.0; for doctorate, GRE General Test, interview. Additional exam requirements/recommendations for international students: Required—TOEFL (minimum score 550 paper-based; 213 computer-based; 79 iBT). *Application deadline:* For fall admission, 2/15 for domestic and international students. Applications are processed on a rolling basis. Application fee: $50. Electronic applications accepted. *Financial support:* In 2006–07, 1 research assistantship with full tuition reimbursement (averaging $11,000 per year) was awarded. Financial award application deadline: 2/15; financial award applicants required to submit FAFSA. *Faculty research:* Circular statistics, program evaluation, psychological measurement, infant attachment, adolescent development. *Unit head:* Dr. Pamela Fenning, Director, 312-915-6803, E-mail: pfennin@luc.edu. *Application contact:* Marie Rosin-Dittmar, Information Contact, 312-915-6800, E-mail: schleduc@luc.edu.

Michigan State University, The Graduate School, College of Education, Department of Counseling, Educational Psychology and Special Education, East Lansing, MI 48824. Offers counseling (MA); educational psychology and educational technology (PhD); educational technology (MA); measurement and quantitative methods (PhD); rehabilitation counseling (MA); rehabilitation counselor education (PhD); school psychology (MA, PhD, Ed S); special education (MA, PhD). *Accreditation:* APA (one or more programs are accredited); CORE (one or more programs are accredited). Part-time programs available. *Faculty:* 36 full-time (13 women). *Students:* 218 full-time (149 women), 75 part-time (60 women); includes 38 minority (31 African Americans, 4 Asian Americans or Pacific Islanders, 3 Hispanic Americans), 63 international. Average age 31. 243 applicants, 44% accepted. In 2006, 136 master's, 34 doctorates awarded. *Entrance requirements:* Additional exam requirements/recommendations for international students: Required—TOEFL. Electronic applications accepted. *Expenses:* Tuition, state resident: part-time $346 per credit hour. Tuition, nonresident: part-time $730 per credit hour. Tuition and fees vary according to program. *Financial support:* In 2006–07, 125 fellowships with tuition reimbursements, 87 research assistantships with tuition reimbursements (averaging $13,854 per year), 67 teaching assistantships with tuition reimbursements (averaging $13,722 per year) were awarded. Total annual research expenditures: $3.4 million. *Unit head:* Dr. Richard S. Prawat, Chairperson, 517-353-6417, E-mail: rsprawat@msu.edu. *Application contact:* Kathy Dimoff, Admissions Coordinator, 517-355-6683, E-mail: dimoff@msu.edu.

New York University, Steinhardt School of Culture, Education and Human Development, Department of Applied Psychology, Program in Educational and Developmental Psychology, New York, NY 10012-1019. Offers educational psychology (MA), including general educational psychology, psychological measurement and evaluation, psychology of parenthood; psychological development (PhD); school psychology (PhD). *Accreditation:* APA (one or more programs are accredited). Part-time and evening/weekend programs available. *Faculty:* 23 full-time (15 women). *Students:* 58 full-time (54 women), 74 part-time (72 women); includes 37 minority (14 African Americans, 8 Asian Americans or Pacific Islanders, 15 Hispanic Americans), 18 international. 238 applicants, 47% accepted, 46 enrolled. In 2006, 22 master's, 13 doctorates awarded. Terminal master's awarded for partial completion of doctoral program. *Degree requirements:* For master's, thesis (for some programs); for doctorate, thesis/dissertation. *Entrance requirements:* For doctorate, GRE General Test, interview. Additional exam requirements/recommendations for international students: Required—TOEFL. *Application deadline:* For fall admission, 12/15 priority date for domestic and international students; for spring admission, 11/1 for domestic and international students. Applications are processed on a rolling basis. Application fee: $50. *Expenses:* Tuition: Part-time $1,080 per unit. Required fees: $56 per unit. $329 per term. Tuition and fees vary according to program. *Financial support:* Teaching assistantships with partial tuition reimbursements, career-related internships or fieldwork, Federal Work-Study, institutionally sponsored loans, and tuition waivers (partial) available. Support available to part-time students. Financial award application deadline: 2/1; financial award applicants required to submit FAFSA. *Faculty research:* High risk children and youth; child and adolescent developments; families and schooling; infant cognition; exploration, language, and symbolic play in toddlerhood. *Unit head:* Dr. Barbara Hummel-Rossi, Director, 212-998-5360, Fax: 212-995-4358. *Application contact:* 212-998-5030, Fax: 212-995-4328, E-mail: steinhardt.gradadmissions@nyu.edu.

North Carolina State University, Graduate School, College of Education, Department of Educational Research, Leadership and Counselor Education, Program in Educational Research and Policy Analysis, Raleigh, NC 27695. Offers PhD. *Degree requirements:* For doctorate, thesis/dissertation. *Entrance requirements:* For doctorate, GRE General Test, minimum GPA of 3.0, interview, sample of work. Electronic applications accepted.

Ohio University, Graduate Studies, College of Education, Department of Educational Studies, Athens, OH 45701-2979. Offers computer education and technology (M Ed); educational administration (M Ed, Ed D); educational research and evaluation (M Ed, PhD); instructional technology (PhD). Part-time and evening/weekend programs available. Postbaccalaureate distance learning degree programs offered (minimal on-campus study). *Faculty:* 13 full-time (7 women), 1 (woman) part-time/adjunct. *Students:* 77 full-time (41 women), 120 part-time (55 women); includes 5 minority (3 African Americans, 1 Asian American or Pacific Islander, 1 Hispanic American), 79 international. 121 applicants, 69% accepted, 49 enrolled. In 2006, 12 master's, 14 doctorates awarded. *Median time to degree:* Of those who began their doctoral program in fall 1998, 92% received their degree in 8 years or less. *Degree requirements:* For master's, thesis or alternative, registration; for doctorate, thesis/dissertation, comprehensive exam, registration. *Entrance requirements:* For master's, GRE General Test if GPA is less than 2.8; for doctorate, GRE General Test, minimum GPA of 3.4, work experience, 3 letters of reference, autobiography. Additional exam requirements/recommendations for international students: Required—TOEFL (minimum score 550 paper-based; 213 computer-based). *Application deadline:* For fall admission, 4/1 priority date for domestic and international students. Applications are processed on a rolling basis. Application fee: $45. Electronic applications accepted. *Financial support:* In 2006–07, 26 research assistantships with full tuition reimbursements (averaging $6,500 per year), 2 teaching assistantships with full tuition reimbursements (averaging $7,200 per year) were awarded; Federal Work-Study, institutionally sponsored loans, tuition waivers (full), and unspecified assistantships also available. Financial award application deadline: 3/15. *Faculty research:* Race, class and gender; computer programs; development and organization theory; evaluation/development of instruments, leadership. Total annual research expenditures: $158,037. *Unit head:* Dr. Catherine H. Glascock, Chair, 740-593-4464, Fax: 740-593-0477, E-mail: glascock@ohio.edu. *Application contact:* Floyd J. Doney, Director of Student Affairs, 740-593-4400, Fax: 740-593-9310, E-mail: doney@ohio.edu.

Rutgers, The State University of New Jersey, New Brunswick, Graduate School of Education, Department of Educational Psychology, Program in Educational Statistics, Measurement and Evaluation, New Brunswick, NJ 08901-1281. Offers Ed M. Part-time and evening/weekend programs available. *Faculty:* 4 full-time (0 women). *Students:* 3 full-time (2 women), 10 part-time (5 women). 12 applicants, 58% accepted, 4 enrolled. In 2006, 2 degrees awarded. *Entrance requirements:* For master's, GRE General Test, 3 letters of recommendation. Additional exam requirements/recommendations for international students: Required—TOEFL (minimum score 550 paper-based; 233 computer-based; 83 iBT). *Application deadline:* For fall admission, 2/1 for domestic and international students; for spring admission, 11/1 for domestic and international students. Application fee: $60. Electronic applications accepted. *Financial support:* Application deadline: 3/15; *Faculty research:* Program evaluation of student assessment, Type I error and power comparisons, test performance factors, theory building in participatory program evaluation, test validity in higher education admissions. *Unit head:* Dr. Douglas A. Penfield, Coordinator, 732-932-7496 Ext. 8324, Fax: 732-932-6829, E-mail: dougpen@rci.rutgers.edu.

Southern Connecticut State University, School of Graduate Studies, School of Education, Program in Research, Measurement and Quantitative Analysis, New Haven, CT 06515-1355. Offers MS. *Faculty:* 2 full-time (0 women). *Students:* 4 full-time (2 women), 18 part-time (16 women); includes 4 minority (2 African Americans, 2 Asian Americans or Pacific Islanders). 6 applicants, 83% accepted, 5 enrolled. In 2006, 12 degrees awarded. *Degree requirements:* For master's, thesis. *Entrance requirements:* For master's, interview. *Application deadline:* For fall admission, 7/15 priority date for domestic students. Applications are processed on a rolling basis. Application fee: $50. Electronic applications accepted. *Financial support:* Application deadline: 4/15; *Unit head:* Dr. Brian Perkins, Chairperson, 203-392-5345, E-mail: perkinsb1@southernct.edu. *Application contact:* Dr. William Diffley, Coordinator, 203-392-5911, E-mail: diffleyw1@southernct.edu.

Educational Measurement and Evaluation

Southern Illinois University Carbondale, Graduate School, College of Education, Department of Educational Psychology and Special Education, Program in Educational Psychology, Carbondale, IL 62901-4701. Offers counselor education (MS Ed, PhD); educational psychology (PhD); human learning and development (MS Ed); measurement and statistics (PhD). *Accreditation:* NCATE. *Faculty:* 19 full-time (9 women), 7 part-time/adjunct (2 women). *Students:* 42 full-time (32 women), 61 part-time (46 women); includes 10 minority (7 African Americans, 1 Asian American or Pacific Islander, 2 Hispanic Americans), 12 international. Average age 36. 54 applicants, 56% accepted, 3 enrolled. In 2006, 20 master's, 5 doctorates awarded. *Degree requirements:* For master's and doctorate, thesis/dissertation. *Entrance requirements:* For master's, GRE General Test, minimum GPA of 2.7; for doctorate, minimum GPA of 3.25. Additional exam requirements/recommendations for international students: Required—TOEFL. *Application deadline:* For fall admission, 6/15 priority date for domestic students. Applications are processed on a rolling basis. Application fee: $20. *Financial support:* In 2006–07, 36 students received support, including 2 fellowships with full tuition reimbursements available, 4 research assistantships with full tuition reimbursements available, teaching assistantships with full tuition reimbursements available, career-related internships or fieldwork, Federal Work-Study, institutionally sponsored loans, and tuition waivers (full) also available. Support available to part-time students. Financial award application deadline: 5/1. *Faculty research:* Career development, problem solving, learning and instruction, cognitive development, family assessment. Total annual research expenditures: $10,000. *Application contact:* Cathy Earnhart, Administrative Clerk, 618-453-6932, E-mail: pern@siu.edu.

See Close-Up on page 1125.

Southwestern Oklahoma State University, College of Professional and Graduate Studies, School of Behavioral Sciences and Education, Specialization in School Psychometry, Weatherford, OK 73096-3098. Offers M Ed. M Ed distance learning degree program offered to Oklahoma residents only. *Accreditation:* NCATE. Part-time and evening/weekend programs available. *Degree requirements:* For master's, exam. *Entrance requirements:* For master's, GRE General Test or minimum undergraduate GPA of 3.0, portfolio. Additional exam requirements/recommendations for international students: Required—TOEFL.

Stanford University, School of Education, Program in Social Sciences, Policy, and Educational Practice, Stanford, CA 94305-9991. Offers administration and policy analysis (Ed D, PhD); anthropology of education (PhD); economics of education (PhD); educational linguistics (PhD); evaluation (MA), including interdisciplinary studies; higher education (PhD); history of education (PhD); interdisciplinary studies (PhD); international comparative education (MA, PhD); international education administration and policy analysis (MA); philosophy of education (PhD); policy analysis (MA); prospective principal's program (MA); sociology of education (PhD). *Degree requirements:* For master's, thesis (for some programs); for doctorate, thesis/dissertation. *Entrance requirements:* For master's and doctorate, GRE General Test. Electronic applications accepted.

Sul Ross State University, Rio Grande College of Sul Ross State University, Alpine, TX 79832. Offers business administration (MBA); teacher education (M Ed), including bilingual education, counseling, educational diagnostics, elementary education, general education, reading, school administration, secondary education. Part-time and evening/weekend programs available. *Degree requirements:* For master's, thesis optional. *Entrance requirements:* For master's, GMAT or GRE General Test, minimum GPA of 2.5 in last 60 hours of undergraduate work. *Faculty research:* Drug and substance abuse counseling, U.S.-Mexico border economic development.

Sul Ross State University, School of Professional Studies, Department of Teacher Education, Program in Educational Diagnostics, Alpine, TX 79832. Offers M Ed. Part-time and evening/weekend programs available. *Degree requirements:* For master's, thesis optional. *Entrance requirements:* For master's, GMAT or GRE General Test, minimum GPA of 2.5 in last 60 hours of undergraduate work.

Syracuse University, Graduate School, School of Education, Instructional Design, Development, and Evaluation Program, Syracuse, NY 13244. Offers MS, PhD, CAS. Part-time programs available. *Students:* 44 full-time (21 women), 36 part-time (23 women); includes 8 minority (4 African Americans, 1 American Indian/Alaska Native, 2 Asian Americans or Pacific Islanders, 1 Hispanic American), 20 international. 35 applicants, 57% accepted, 11 enrolled. *Degree requirements:* For master's, thesis or alternative; for doctorate, thesis/dissertation. *Entrance requirements:* For master's, GRE; for doctorate and CAS, GRE, interview. *Application deadline:* For fall admission, 2/1 for domestic students. Applications are processed on a rolling basis. Application fee: $65. Electronic applications accepted. *Expenses:* Tuition: Full-time $16,920; part-time $940 per credit hour. Required fees: $930; $930 per year. *Financial support:* Fellowships with full tuition reimbursements, research assistantships with full and partial tuition reimbursements, teaching assistantships with full tuition reimbursements available. *Faculty research:* Cultural pluralism and instructional design, corrections training, aging and learning, the University and social change, investigative evaluation. *Unit head:* Dr. Gerald Mager, Chair, 315-443-2685, E-mail: gmmager@syr.edu. *Application contact:* Liza Rochelson, Graduate Admission Recruiter, 315-443-2505, Fax: 315-443-2258, E-mail: gradcrt@gwmail.syr.edu.

Teachers College Columbia University, Graduate Faculty of Education, Department of Human Development, Program in Measurement, Evaluation, and Statistics, New York, NY 10027-6696. Offers MA, MS, Ed D, PhD. *Faculty:* 4 full-time (2 women), 4 part-time/adjunct. *Students:* 9 full-time (8 women), 20 part-time (19 women); includes 12 minority (11 Asian Americans or Pacific Islanders, 1 Hispanic American), 8 international. Average age 32. 19 applicants, 84% accepted, 5 enrolled. In 2006, 6 master's, 1 doctorate awarded. *Entrance requirements:* For master's and doctorate, GRE. *Application deadline:* For fall admission, 5/15 for domestic students; for spring admission, 12/1 for domestic students. Application fee: $65. *Expenses:* Tuition: Full-time $23,400; part-time $975 per credit. Required fees: $320 per term. *Financial support:* Career-related internships or fieldwork, Federal Work-Study, institutionally sponsored loans, and tuition waivers (full and partial) available. Support available to part-time students. Financial award application deadline: 2/1. *Faculty research:* Probability and inference, potentially biased test items, research design, clustering and scaling methods for multivariate data. *Application contact:* Melba Remice, Assistant Director of Admission, 212-678-4035, Fax: 212-678-4171, E-mail: ms2545@columbia.edu.

Texas A&M University, College of Education and Human Development, Department of Educational Psychology, College Station, TX 77843. Offers counseling psychology (PhD); educational psychology (PhD); educational technology (M Ed); gifted and talented education (M Ed, MS); Hispanic bilingual education (M Ed, PhD); human learning and development (MS); intelligence, creativity, and giftedness (PhD); learning, development, and instruction (PhD); research, measurement and statistics (MS); research, measurement, and statistics (PhD); school counseling (M Ed); school psychology (PhD); special education (M Ed, PhD). *Accreditation:* APA (one or more programs are accredited); NCATE. Part-time and evening/weekend programs available. Postbaccalaureate distance learning degree programs offered (no on-campus study). *Faculty:* 25 full-time (11 women), 5 part-time/adjunct (2 women). *Students:* 156 full-time (123 women), 109 part-time (89 women); includes 66 minority (20 African Americans, 1 American Indian/Alaska Native, 7 Asian Americans or Pacific Islanders, 38 Hispanic Americans), 36 international. 159 applicants, 52% accepted, 51 enrolled. In 2006, 59 master's, 21 doctorates awarded. *Median time to degree:* Of those who began their doctoral program in fall 1998, 89% received their degree in 8 years or less. *Degree requirements:* For master's, thesis optional; for doctorate, thesis/dissertation. *Entrance requirements:* For master's and doctorate, GRE General Test. Additional exam requirements/recommendations for international students: Required—TOEFL. Application fee: $50 ($75 for international students). Electronic applications accepted. *Expenses:* Tuition, state resident: full-time $4,697. Tuition, nonresident: full-time $11,297. Required fees: $2,272. *Financial support:* In 2006–07, fellowships (averaging $12,000 per year), research assistantships (averaging $9,000 per year), teaching assistantships (averaging $9,000 per year) were awarded; career-related internships

or fieldwork, institutionally sponsored loans, scholarships/grants, and unspecified assistantships also available. Financial award applicants required to submit FAFSA. *Unit head:* Dr. Michael R. Benz, Head, 979-845-1394, Fax: 979-862-1256, E-mail: mbanz@tamu.edu. *Application contact:* Carol A. Wagner, Director of Advising, 979-845-1833, Fax: 979-862-1256, E-mail: c-wagner@tamu.edu.

Texas Christian University, School of Education, Program in Educational Foundations, Fort Worth, TX 76129-0002. Offers M Ed. Part-time and evening/weekend programs available. *Entrance requirements:* For master's, interview. Additional exam requirements/recommendations for international students: Required—TOEFL. *Application deadline:* For fall admission, 3/1 for domestic students; for spring admission, 12/1 for domestic students. Applications are processed on a rolling basis. Application fee: $0. *Expenses:* Tuition: Part-time $800 per credit hour. *Financial support:* Unspecified assistantships available. Financial award application deadline: 3/1. *Application contact:* Director of Graduate Studies, 817-257-7664.

Texas Southern University, Graduate School, College of Education, Department of Educational Administration and Foundation, Houston, TX 77004-4584. Offers educational administration (M Ed, Ed D); higher education administration (Ed D); mid-management superintending (Ed D); research education and certification (Ed D); research education and education (Ed D). Part-time and evening/weekend programs available. *Faculty:* 7 full-time (3 women), 5 part-time/adjunct (1 woman). *Students:* 40 full-time (29 women), 72 part-time (53 women); includes 109 minority (105 African Americans, 1 Asian American or Pacific Islander, 3 Hispanic Americans). Average age 37. 45 applicants, 80% accepted, 30 enrolled. In 2006, 32 degrees awarded. *Degree requirements:* For master's, comprehensive exam; for doctorate, thesis/dissertation, comprehensive exam. *Entrance requirements:* For master's, GRE General Test, minimum GPA of 2.5; for doctorate, GRE General Test or MAT, master's degree, minimum B+ average. Additional exam requirements/recommendations for international students: Required—TOEFL. *Application deadline:* For fall admission, 7/15 priority date for domestic students. Applications are processed on a rolling basis. Application fee: $50 ($75 for international students). *Financial support:* In 2006–07, 2 fellowships (averaging $1,750 per year) were awarded; Federal Work-Study and institutionally sponsored loans also available. Financial award application deadline: 5/1. *Unit head:* Dr. Emmanuel Nwagwu, Chairperson, 713-313-1055, E-mail: nwagwu_ec@tsu.edu.

Université Laval, Faculty of Education, Department of Foundations and Interventions in Education, Québec, QC G1K 7P4, Canada. Offers educational administration and evaluation (MA, PhD); educational practice (Diploma), including educational pedagogy, pedagogy management and development, school adaptation; orientation sciences (MA, PhD). *Degree requirements:* For doctorate, thesis/dissertation, comprehensive exam. Electronic applications accepted.

University at Albany, State University of New York, School of Education, Department of Educational and Counseling Psychology, Albany, NY 12222-0001. Offers counseling psychology (MS, PhD, CAS); educational psychology (Ed D); educational psychology and statistics (MS); measurements and evaluation (Ed D); rehabilitation counseling (MS), including counseling psychology; school counselor (CAS); school psychology (Psy D, CAS); special education (MS); statistics and research design (Ed D). *Accreditation:* APA (one or more programs are accredited). Evening/weekend programs available. *Students:* 75 full-time (59 women), 25 part-time (21 women). Average age 28. In 2006, 33 master's, 8 doctorates, 12 other advanced degrees awarded. *Degree requirements:* For doctorate, thesis/dissertation. *Entrance requirements:* For doctorate, GRE General Test. Additional exam requirements/recommendations for international students: Required—TOEFL (minimum score 550 paper-based; 213 computer-based). Application fee: $75. Electronic applications accepted. *Expenses:* Tuition, state resident: full-time $6,900; part-time $288 per credit. Tuition, nonresident: full-time $10,920; part-time $455 per credit. Required fees: $1,139. *Financial support:* Fellowships, career-related internships or fieldwork available. *Unit head:* Deborah May, Chair, 518-442-5050.

The University of British Columbia, Faculty of Graduate Studies, Faculty of Education, Department of Educational and Counseling Psychology, and Special Education, Vancouver, BC V6T 1Z1, Canada. Offers counseling psychology (M Ed, MA, PhD); development, learning and culture (MA, PhD); guidance studies (Diploma); measurement and evaluation and research methodology (M Ed); measurement, evaluation and research methodology (MA); measurement, evaluation, and research methodology (PhD); school psychology (M Ed, MA, PhD); special education (M Ed, MA, PhD, Diploma). Part-time programs available. *Faculty:* 39 full-time (26 women). *Students:* 304 full-time (247 women), 82 part-time (77 women). 266 applicants, 39% accepted. In 2006, 100 master's, 10 doctorates awarded. *Median time to degree:* Of those who began their doctoral program in fall 1998, 95% received their degree in 8 years or less. *Degree requirements:* For master's, thesis (for some programs); registration; for doctorate, thesis/dissertation, comprehensive exam, registration. *Entrance requirements:* For master's, GRE General Test (counseling psychology MA); for doctorate, GRE General Test. Additional exam requirements/recommendations for international students: Required—TOEFL. *Application deadline:* For fall admission, 12/1 for domestic and international students. Application fee: $90 Canadian dollars ($150 Canadian dollars for international students). Electronic applications accepted. *Financial support:* In 2006–07, 20 fellowships (averaging $19,000 per year), 50 research assistantships (averaging $12,000 per year), 30 teaching assistantships (averaging $5,000 per year) were awarded; career-related internships or fieldwork, Federal Work-Study, institutionally sponsored loans, scholarships/grants, health care benefits, tuition waivers (full and partial), and unspecified assistantships also available. *Faculty research:* Women, family, social problems, career transition, stress and coping problems. *Unit head:* Dr. Sandra Mathison, Head, 604-822-6352, Fax: 604-822-3302, E-mail: sandra.mathison@ubc.ca. *Application contact:* Lynda McDicken, Graduate Admissions, 604-822-5351, Fax: 604-822-3302, E-mail: lynda.mcdicken@ubc.ca.

University of Calgary, Faculty of Graduate Studies, Faculty of Education, Graduate Division of Educational Research, Calgary, AB T2N 1N4, Canada. Offers community rehabilitation and disability studies (M Ed, M Sc, Ed D, PhD, Graduate Certificate, Graduate Diploma); curriculum, teaching and learning (M Ed, M Sc, MA, Ed D, PhD, Graduate Certificate, Graduate Diploma); educational contexts (M Ed, MA, Ed D, PhD, Graduate Certificate, Graduate Diploma); educational leadership (M Ed, MA, Ed D, PhD, Graduate Certificate, Graduate Diploma); educational technology (M Ed, M Sc, MA, Ed D, PhD, Graduate Certificate, Graduate Diploma); gifted education (M Sc, MA, Ed D, PhD, Graduate Certificate, Graduate Diploma); higher education administration (Ed D); interpretive studies in education (M Ed, M Sc, MA, Ed D, PhD, Graduate Certificate, Graduate Diploma); second language teaching (M Ed, Ed D, PhD, Graduate Certificate, Graduate Diploma); teaching English as a second language (M Ed, M Sc, MA, Ed D, PhD, Graduate Certificate, Graduate Diploma); workplace and adult learning (M Ed, MA, Ed D, PhD, Graduate Certificate, Graduate Diploma). Ed D in both higher education administration and educational leadership offered via distance delivery. Part-time and evening/weekend programs available. Postbaccalaureate distance learning degree programs offered (minimal on-campus study). *Faculty:* 44 full-time, 52 part-time/adjunct. *Students:* 488 full-time, 550 part-time. 400 applicants, 50% accepted. In 2006, 102 master's, 18 doctorates awarded. *Degree requirements:* For master's, thesis (for some programs); for doctorate, thesis/dissertation, candidacy exam. *Entrance requirements:* For master's, minimum GPA of 3.0, 3 letters of reference; for doctorate, minimum GPA of 3.5, 3 letters of reference; for other advanced degree, minimum GPA of 3.0. Additional exam requirements/recommendations for international students: Required—TOEFL, IELTS. *Application deadline:* For fall admission, 2/15 for domestic students, 2/5 for international students; for winter admission, 6/15 for domestic and international students. Application fee: $100. Electronic applications accepted. *Financial support:* In 2006–07, research assistantships (averaging $3,920 per year); teaching assistantships, career-related internships or fieldwork, scholarships/grants, and unspecified assistantships also available. Financial award application deadline: 2/1. *Faculty research:* Curriculum, leadership, technology, contexts, gifted, second language teaching, work place and adult learning. *Unit head:* Dr. Charles F. Webber, Associate Dean, 403-220-5675, Fax: 403-282-3005, E-mail: cwebber@ucalgary.ca. *Application contact:* Patricia A. Brown, Program

Officer, Graduate Division of Educational Research, 403-220-3178, Fax: 403-282-3005, E-mail: brownp@ucalgary.ca.

University of California, Berkeley, Graduate Division, School of Education, Division of Policy, Organization, Measurement and Evaluation, Berkeley, CA 94720-1500. Offers educational leadership (Ed D); policy and organizational research (MA, PhD); principal leadership (MA); program evaluation and assessment (Ed D); quantitative methods and evaluation (MA, PhD); PhD/MA. Terminal master's awarded for partial completion of doctoral program. *Degree requirements:* For master's, exam or thesis; for doctorate, thesis/dissertation, oral qualifying exam (PhD). *Entrance requirements:* For master's and doctorate, GRE General Test, minimum undergraduate GPA of 3.0 during last 2 years. *Application deadline:* For fall admission, 12/15 for domestic and international students. Application fee: $60 ($80 for international students). Electronic applications accepted. *Financial support:* Fellowships, research assistantships, teaching assistantships, unspecified assistantships available. *Application contact:* Admissions Office, 510-642-0841, Fax: 510-642-4808, E-mail: gse_info@uclink.berkeley.edu.

University of California, Santa Barbara, Graduate Division, Gevirtz Graduate School of Education, Santa Barbara, CA 93106. Offers counseling, clinical and school psychology (PhD), including clinical psychology, counseling psychology; education (M Ed, MA, PhD), including child and adolescent development (MA, PhD), cultural perspectives and comparative education (MA, PhD), educational leadership and organizations (MA, PhD), research methodology (MA, PhD), special education disabilities and risk studies (MA), special education, disabilities and risk studies (PhD), teaching and learning (MA, PhD); educational leadership (Ed D). *Accreditation:* APA (one or more programs are accredited). Postbaccalaureate distance learning degree programs offered (minimal on-campus study). *Faculty:* 39 full-time (18 women). *Students:* 375 full-time (285 women); includes 111 minority (13 African Americans, 2 American Indian/Alaska Native, 33 Asian Americans or Pacific Islanders, 63 Hispanic Americans), 14 international. Average age 29. 777 applicants, 36% accepted, 154 enrolled. In 2006, 151 master's, 31 doctorates awarded. Terminal master's awarded for partial completion of doctoral program. *Median time to degree:* Master's–1.5 years full-time; doctorate–5.5 years full-time. *Degree requirements:* For master's, thesis optional; for doctorate, thesis/dissertation, qualifying exam, comprehensive exam (for some programs), registration; for degree. *Entrance requirements:* For master's, GRE, MAT (M Ed); for doctorate, GRE. Additional exam requirements/recommendations for international students: Required—TOEFL (minimum score 550 paper-based; 213 computer-based; 80 iBT). *Application deadline:* For fall admission, 12/15 for domestic and international students. Application fee: $60. Electronic applications accepted. *Financial support:* In 2006–07, 181 fellowships with full and partial tuition reimbursements (averaging $4,200 per year), 64 research assistantships with full and partial tuition reimbursements (averaging $6,200 per year), 75 teaching assistantships with partial tuition reimbursements (averaging $7,500 per year) were awarded; career-related internships or fieldwork, Federal Work-Study, institutionally sponsored loans, scholarships/grants, traineeships, health care benefits, and unspecified assistantships also available. Support available to part-time students. Financial award application deadline: 12/15; financial award applicants required to submit FAFSA. Total annual research expenditures: $4 million. *Unit head:* Dr. Jane Conoley, Chair, 805-893-3917, E-mail: jane_conoley@education.ucsb.edu. *Application contact:* Student Affairs Office, 805-893-2137, E-mail: sao@education.ucsb.edu.

University of Colorado at Boulder, Graduate School, School of Education, Division of Research and Evaluation Methodology, Boulder, CO 80309. Offers PhD. *Accreditation:* NCATE. *Students:* 9 full-time (6 women), 3 part-time (2 women); includes 2 minority (1 Asian American or Pacific Islander, 1 Hispanic American). Average age 34. 6 applicants, 67% accepted. *Degree requirements:* For doctorate, one foreign language, thesis/dissertation, comprehensive exam. *Entrance requirements:* For doctorate, GRE General Test, minimum undergraduate GPA of 2.75. *Application deadline:* For fall admission, 2/1 priority date for domestic students, 12/1 for international students; for spring admission, 9/1 for domestic students, 12/1 for international students. Application fee: $40 ($60 for international students). *Financial support:* In 2006–07, 2 fellowships (averaging $21,656 per year), 6 research assistantships (averaging $7,989 per year), 2 teaching assistantships (averaging $11,730 per year) were awarded; career-related internships or fieldwork, Federal Work-Study, and scholarships/grants also available. Financial award application deadline: 2/1. *Application contact:* 303-492-6555, Fax: 303-492-5839, E-mail: edadvise@colorado.edu.

University of Connecticut, Graduate School, Neag School of Education, Department of Educational Psychology, Storrs, CT 06269. Offers educational psychology (MA, PhD), including cognition and instruction, counseling psychology, gifted and talented education, learning technology, measurement, evaluation, and assessment, school psychology, special education. *Faculty:* 34 full-time (16 women). *Students:* 154 full-time (127 women), 147 part-time (114 women); includes 35 minority (15 African Americans, 2 American Indian/Alaska Native, 7 Asian Americans or Pacific Islanders, 11 Hispanic Americans), 20 international. Average age 34. 331 applicants, 48% accepted, 139 enrolled. In 2006, 115 master's, 20 doctorates awarded. *Degree requirements:* For master's, comprehensive exam; for doctorate, thesis/dissertation. *Entrance requirements:* For doctorate, GRE General Test. Additional exam requirements/recommendations for international students: Required—TOEFL (minimum score 550 paper-based; 213 computer-based). *Application deadline:* For fall admission, 2/1 priority date for domestic and international students; for spring admission, 11/1 for domestic students, 10/1 for international students. Applications are processed on a rolling basis. Application fee: $55. Electronic applications accepted. *Financial support:* In 2006–07, 87 research assistantships with full tuition reimbursements, 1 teaching assistantship with full tuition reimbursement were awarded; fellowships, Federal Work-Study, scholarships/grants, health care benefits, and unspecified assistantships also available. Financial award application deadline: 2/1; financial award applicants required to submit FAFSA. *Unit head:* Sally Reis, Head, 860-486-4031, Fax: 860-486-0210. *Application contact:* Lisa Rasicot, Graduate Coordinator, 860-486-3065, Fax: 860-486-0210, E-mail: soeadm02@uconnvm.uconn.edu.

University of Connecticut, Graduate School, Neag School of Education, Department of Educational Psychology, Field of Educational Psychology, Program in Measurement, Evaluation, and Assessment, Storrs, CT 06269. Offers MA, PhD. *Faculty:* 8 full-time (2 women). *Students:* 7 full-time (5 women), 4 international. Average age 33. 15 applicants, 27% accepted, 4 enrolled. In 2006, 1 degree awarded. Terminal master's awarded for partial completion of doctoral program. *Degree requirements:* For master's, thesis or alternative, comprehensive exam; for doctorate, thesis/dissertation. *Entrance requirements:* For doctorate, GRE General Test. Additional exam requirements/recommendations for international students: Required—TOEFL (minimum score 550 paper-based; 213 computer-based). *Application deadline:* For fall admission, 2/1 priority date for domestic and international students; for spring admission, 11/1 for domestic students, 10/1 for international students. Applications are processed on a rolling basis. Application fee: $55. Electronic applications accepted. *Financial support:* In 2006–07, 5 research assistantships with full tuition reimbursements were awarded; fellowships, teaching assistantships with full tuition reimbursements, Federal Work-Study, scholarships/grants, health care benefits, and unspecified assistantships also available. Financial award application deadline: 2/1; financial award applicants required to submit FAFSA. *Application contact:* Lisa Rasicot, Graduate Coordinator, 860-486-3065, Fax: 860-486-0210, E-mail: soeadm02@uconnvm.uconn.edu.

University of Denver, College of Education, Denver, CO 80208. Offers counseling psychology (MA, PhD); curriculum and instruction (MA, PhD, Certificate), including curriculum leadership (MA, PhD); educational administration and policy studies (Certificate); educational psychology (MA, PhD, Ed S), including child and family studies (MA, PhD), quantitative research methods (MA, PhD), school psychology (PhD, Ed S); higher education and adult studies (MA, PhD); library and information science (MLIS); library and information sciences (Certificate); school administration (PhD). *Accreditation:* ALA; APA (one or more programs are accredited). Part-time and evening/weekend programs available. Postbaccalaureate distance learning degree programs offered (no on-campus study). *Faculty:* 28 full-time (18 women). *Students:* 293 full-time (240 women), 439 part-time (357 women); includes 102 minority (28 African Americans, 7 American Indian/Alaska Native, 14 Asian Americans or Pacific Islanders, 53 Hispanic Americans), 11 international. Average age 34. 574 applicants, 72% accepted. In 2006, 168 master's, 28 doctorates, 67 other advanced degrees awarded. Terminal master's awarded for partial completion of doctoral program. *Degree requirements:* For master's, comprehensive exam; for doctorate, 2 foreign languages, thesis/dissertation, comprehensive exam. *Entrance requirements:* For master's, GRE General Test or MAT (for most programs); for doctorate, GRE General Test or MAT. *Application deadline:* Applications are processed on a rolling basis. Application fee: $50. Electronic applications accepted. *Expenses:* Tuition: Full-time $29,628; part-time $823 per credit. *Financial support:* In 2006–07, 51 teaching assistantships with full and partial tuition reimbursements (averaging $6,700 per year) were awarded; career-related internships or fieldwork, Federal Work-Study, institutionally sponsored loans, and scholarships/grants also available. Support available to part-time students. Financial award application deadline: 3/1; financial award applicants required to submit FAFSA. *Faculty research:* Parkinson's disease, personnel training, development and assessments, gifted education, service learning, transportation, public schools. Total annual research expenditures: $172,000. *Unit head:* Dr. Virginia Maloney, Dean, 303-871-2509. *Application contact:* Linda McCarthy, Contact, 303-871-2509, E-mail: edinfo@du.edu.

University of Florida, Graduate School, College of Education, Department of Educational Psychology, Gainesville, FL 32611. Offers educational psychology (M Ed, MAE, Ed D, PhD, Ed S); research and evaluation methodology (M Ed, MAE, Ed D, PhD, Ed S); school psychology (M Ed, MAE, Ed D, PhD, Ed S). *Accreditation:* NCATE. *Faculty:* 15 full-time (6 women). *Students:* 95 (77 women); includes 27 minority (7 African Americans, 1 American Indian/Alaska Native, 4 Asian Americans or Pacific Islanders, 15 Hispanic Americans) 11 international. In 2006, 17 master's, 5 doctorates awarded. Terminal master's awarded for partial completion of doctoral program. *Degree requirements:* For master's, thesis (MAE); for doctorate, variable foreign language requirement, thesis/dissertation. *Entrance requirements:* For master's and doctorate, GRE General Test, minimum GPA of 3.0; for Ed S, GRE General Test. Additional exam requirements/recommendations for international students: Required—TOEFL (minimum score 550 paper-based; 213 computer-based). *Application deadline:* For fall admission, 6/1 priority date for domestic students. Applications are processed on a rolling basis. Application fee: $30. Electronic applications accepted. *Expenses:* Tuition, state resident: full-time $6,827. Tuition, nonresident: full-time $21,951. Required fees: $999. *Financial support:* In 2006–07, 12 teaching assistantships (averaging $8,768 per year) were awarded; fellowships, research assistantships, career-related internships or fieldwork and unspecified assistantships also available. Financial award application deadline: 4/30. *Faculty research:* School improvement, teaching and learning, item response theory. *Unit head:* Tina Smith-Bonahue, Interim Chair, 352-392-0725 Ext. 224. *Application contact:* Dr. Bridget Franks, Coordinator, 352-395-0723 Ext. 234, Fax: 352-392-5929, E-mail: bfranks@coe.ufl.edu.

The University of Iowa, Graduate College, College of Education, Department of Psychological and Quantitative Foundations, Iowa City, IA 52242-1316. Offers counseling psychology (PhD); educational measurement and statistics (MA, PhD); educational psychology (MA, PhD); school psychology (PhD, Ed S); JD/PhD. *Accreditation:* APA. *Faculty:* 21 full-time, 8 part-time/adjunct. *Students:* 97 full-time (71 women), 65 part-time (50 women); includes 30 minority (9 African Americans, 1 American Indian/Alaska Native, 8 Asian Americans or Pacific Islanders, 12 Hispanic Americans), 39 international. 119 applicants, 36% accepted, 23 enrolled. In 2006, 8 master's, 15 doctorates, 3 other advanced degrees awarded. *Degree requirements:* For master's, exam, thesis optional; for doctorate, thesis/dissertation, comprehensive exam, registration; for Ed S, exam. *Entrance requirements:* For master's, doctorate, and Ed S, GRE General Test, minimum GPA of 3.0. Additional exam requirements/recommendations for international students: Required—TOEFL (minimum score 550 paper-based; 213 computer-based; 81 iBT). Application fee: $60 ($85 for international students). Electronic applications accepted. *Financial support:* In 2006–07, 7 fellowships, 89 research assistantships with partial tuition reimbursements, 21 teaching assistantships with partial tuition reimbursements were awarded. Financial award applicants required to submit FAFSA. *Unit head:* Timothy Ansley, Chair, 319-335-5411, Fax: 319-335-6145.

University of Kansas, Graduate Studies, School of Education, Department of Psychology and Research in Education, Program in Educational Psychology and Research, Lawrence, KS 66045. Offers MS Ed, PhD. *Faculty:* 6 full-time (1 woman), 2 part-time/adjunct (1 woman). *Students:* 9 full-time (7 women), 10 part-time (7 women); includes 2 minority (1 African American, 1 Asian American or Pacific Islander), 6 international. Average age 33. 13 applicants, 54% accepted. In 2006, 2 master's, 6 doctorates awarded. *Degree requirements:* For master's, thesis/dissertation; for doctorate, thesis/dissertation, comprehensive exam. *Entrance requirements:* For master's, GRE General Test, minimum GPA of 3.0; for doctorate, GRE General Test. Additional exam requirements/recommendations for international students: Required—TOEFL. *Application deadline:* For fall admission, 4/1 for domestic students; for spring admission, 11/1 for domestic students. Application fee: $55 ($60 for international students). Electronic applications accepted. *Expenses:* Tuition, area resident: Part-time $227 per credit. Tuition, state resident: part-time $543 per credit. Tuition and fees vary according to course load, campus/location, program and reciprocity agreements. *Financial support:* Fellowships, research assistantships with full and partial tuition reimbursements, teaching assistantships with full and partial tuition reimbursements, career-related internships or fieldwork, institutionally sponsored loans, scholarships/grants, traineeships, health care benefits, tuition waivers (full and partial), and unspecified assistantships available. Support available to part-time students. Financial award application deadline: 2/1. *Faculty research:* Educational measurement, applied statistics, research design, program evaluation, learning and development. *Unit head:* Bruce Frey, Faculty Coordinator, 785-864-3931, E-mail: bfrey@ku.edu. *Application contact:* Admissions Coordinator, 785-864-3931, Fax: 785-864-3820, E-mail: preadmit@ku.edu.

University of Kentucky, Graduate School, College of Education, Program in Educational Policy Studies and Evaluation, Lexington, KY 40506-0032. Offers educational policy studies and evaluation (Ed D); higher education (MS Ed, PhD). *Accreditation:* NCATE. *Students:* 50 full-time (37 women), 30 part-time (19 women); includes 7 minority (all African Americans), 2 international. Average age 38. In 2006, 9 master's, 3 doctorates awarded. Terminal master's awarded for partial completion of doctoral program. *Median time to degree:* Of those who began their doctoral program in fall 1998, 46% received their degree in 8 years or less. *Degree requirements:* For master's, thesis optional; for doctorate, thesis/dissertation, comprehensive exam. *Entrance requirements:* For master's, GRE General Test, minimum undergraduate GPA of 2.75; for doctorate, GRE General Test, minimum graduate GPA of 3.0. Additional exam requirements/recommendations for international students: Required—TOEFL (minimum score 550 paper-based; 213 computer-based). *Application deadline:* For fall admission, 7/17 priority date for domestic students, 2/1 priority date for international students; for spring admission, 12/13 priority date for domestic students, 6/15 priority date for international students. Application fee: $40 ($55 for international students). Electronic applications accepted. *Expenses:* Tuition, state resident: full-time $7,670; part-time $401 per credit hour. Tuition, nonresident: full-time $16,158; part-time $873 per credit hour. *Financial support:* In 2006–07, 9 students received support, including 1 fellowship with full tuition reimbursement available (averaging $4,500 per year), 2 research assistantships with full tuition reimbursements available (averaging $16,748 per year), 6 teaching assistantships with full tuition reimbursements available (averaging $950 per year); career-related internships or fieldwork, Federal Work-Study, institutionally sponsored loans, scholarships/grants, traineeships, health care benefits, tuition waivers (partial), and unspecified assistantships also available. Support available to part-time students. Financial award application deadline: 3/15. *Faculty research:* Studies in higher education; comparative and international education; evaluation of educational programs, policies, and reform; student, teacher, and faculty cultures; gender and education. *Unit head:* Richard Angelo, Director of Graduate Studies, 859-257-3993, Fax: 859-257-4243, E-mail: angelo@pop.uky.edu. *Application contact:* Dr. Brian Jackson, Senior Associate Dean, 859-257-4667, Fax: 859-257-4676, E-mail: brian.jackson@uky.edu.

University of Maryland, College Park, Graduate Studies, College of Education, Department of Measurement, Statistics, and Evaluation, College Park, MD 20742. Offers measurement

Educational Measurement and Evaluation

University of Maryland, College Park (continued)
(MA, PhD); program evaluation (MA, PhD); statistics (MA, PhD). *Accreditation:* NCATE. Part-time and evening/weekend programs available. Postbaccalaureate distance learning degree programs offered (minimal on-campus study). *Faculty:* 7 full-time (0 women), 2 part-time/adjunct (both women). *Students:* 45 full-time (33 women), 8 part-time (4 women); includes 4 minority (2 African Americans, 1 American Indian/Alaska Native, 1 Asian American or Pacific Islander), 32 international. In 2006, 8 master's, 2 doctorates awarded. *Median time to degree:* Of those who began their doctoral program in fall 1998, 67% received their degree in 8 years or less. *Degree requirements:* For master's, thesis optional; for doctorate, thesis/dissertation, preliminary and comprehensive written exams. *Entrance requirements:* For master's and doctorate, GRE General Test or MAT, minimum GPA of 3.0, 3 letters of recommendation. Additional exam requirements/recommendations for international students: Required—TOEFL. *Application deadline:* For fall admission, 1/15 for domestic and international students; for spring admission, 10/31 for domestic students, 6/1 for international students. Applications are processed on a rolling basis. Application fee: $60. Electronic applications accepted. *Financial support:* In 2006–07, 1 fellowship with tuition reimbursement (averaging $13,000 per year), 2 research assistantships with tuition reimbursements (averaging $13,768 per year), 25 teaching assistantships with tuition reimbursements (averaging $14,636 per year) were awarded; Federal Work-Study and scholarships/grants also available. Support available to part-time students. Financial award applicants required to submit FAFSA. Total annual research expenditures: $731,408. *Unit head:* Dr. C. Mitchell Dayton, Chair, 301-405-3624, Fax: 301-314-9245, E-mail: cdayton@umd.edu. *Application contact:* Dean of Graduate School, 301-405-0358, Fax: 301-314-9305.

University of Massachusetts Amherst, Graduate School, School of Education, Program in Education, Amherst, MA 01003. Offers cultural diversity and curriculum reform (M Ed, Ed D, CAGS); early childhood education and development (M Ed, Ed D, CAGS); educational administration (M Ed, Ed D, CAGS); elementary teacher education (M Ed, Ed D, CAGS); higher education (M Ed, Ed D, CAGS); international education (M Ed, Ed D, CAGS); mathematics, science, and instructional technology (M Ed, Ed D, CAGS); physical education teacher education (M Ed, Ed D, CAGS); reading and writing (M Ed, Ed D, CAGS); research and evaluation methods (M Ed, Ed D, CAGS); school psychology and school counseling (M Ed, Ed D, CAGS); secondary teacher education (M Ed, Ed D, CAGS); social justice education (M Ed, Ed D, CAGS); special education (M Ed, Ed D, CAGS). *Accreditation:* NCATE. *Students:* 418 full-time (286 women), 447 part-time (319 women); includes 147 minority (70 African Americans, 4 American Indian/Alaska Native, 28 Asian Americans or Pacific Islanders, 45 Hispanic Americans), 81 international. Average age 36. In 2006, 260 master's, 30 doctorates awarded. *Degree requirements:* For doctorate, thesis/dissertation. *Entrance requirements:* For master's and doctorate, GRE General Test. Additional exam requirements/recommendations for international students: Required—TOEFL (minimum score 530 paper-based; 197 computer-based). *Application deadline:* For fall admission, 1/15 for domestic and international students; for spring admission, 10/1 for domestic and international students. Applications are processed on a rolling basis. Application fee: $40 ($65 for international students). Electronic applications accepted. *Expenses:* Tuition, state resident: full-time $2,640; part-time $110 per credit. Tuition, nonresident: full-time $9,936; part-time $414 per credit. Required fees: $8,969; $3,129 per term. One-time fee: $257 full-time. Tuition and fees vary according to class time, course load, campus/location and reciprocity agreements. *Financial support:* Fellowships with full tuition reimbursements, research assistantships with full tuition reimbursements, teaching assistantships with full tuition reimbursements, career-related internships or fieldwork, Federal Work-Study, scholarships/grants, traineeships, and unspecified assistantships available. Support available to part-time students. Financial award application deadline: 1/15. *Unit head:* Linda L. Griffin, Professor, 413-545-6984.

University of Memphis, Graduate School, College of Education, Department of Counseling, Educational Psychology and Research, Memphis, TN 38152. Offers counseling and personnel services (MS, Ed D), including community agency counseling (MS), rehabilitation counseling (MS), school counseling (MS), student personnel services (MS); counseling psychology (PhD); educational psychology and research (MS, Ed D, PhD), including educational psychology (MS, Ed D), educational research (MS, Ed D). *Accreditation:* ACA (one or more programs are accredited); APA (one or more programs are accredited); CORE (one or more programs are accredited); NCATE. *Degree requirements:* For master's, thesis or alternative, comprehensive exam; for doctorate, thesis/dissertation, comprehensive exam. *Entrance requirements:* For master's, GRE General Test or MAT, minimum GPA of 2.5; for doctorate, GRE General Test. *Faculty research:* Anger management, aging and disability, supervision, multicultural counseling.

University of Miami, Graduate School, School of Education, Department of Educational and Psychological Studies, Program in Research, Measurement, and Evaluation, Coral Gables, FL 33124. Offers MS Ed, PhD. *Accreditation:* NCATE. Part-time and evening/weekend programs available. *Faculty:* 3 full-time (1 woman). *Students:* 1 (woman) full-time, 4 part-time (3 women); includes 1 minority (Hispanic American) Average age 28. 6 applicants, 67% accepted, 2 enrolled. In 2006, 1 degree awarded. *Degree requirements:* For master's, 36 credits of required courses, thesis optional; for doctorate, thesis/dissertation, 63 credits of graduate courses, comprehensive exam. *Entrance requirements:* For master's and doctorate, GRE General Test. Additional exam requirements/recommendations for international students: Required—TOEFL. *Application deadline:* Applications are processed on a rolling basis. Application fee: $50. Electronic applications accepted. *Financial support:* In 2006–07, 3 students received support; fellowships with partial tuition reimbursements available, research assistantships with partial tuition reimbursements available, teaching assistantships with partial tuition reimbursements available, career-related internships or fieldwork, Federal Work-Study, institutionally sponsored loans, and unspecified assistantships available. Support available to part-time students. Financial award application deadline: 3/1; financial award applicants required to submit FAFSA. *Faculty research:* Psychometric theory, computer-based testing, quantitative research methods. *Unit head:* Dr. Randall D. Penfield, Coordinator, 305-284-8340, Fax: 305-284-3003, E-mail: penfield@miami.edu. *Application contact:* Shelley Lue Foung, Senior Administrative Assistant, 305-284-3001, Fax: 305-284-3003, E-mail: sluefoung@miami.edu.

University of Michigan, Horace H. Rackham School of Graduate Studies, School of Education, Center for the Study of Higher and Postsecondary Education, Ann Arbor, MI 48109. Offers academic affairs and student development (PhD); education (AM); higher education (AM); individually designed concentration (PhD); organizational behavior and management (PhD); public policy (PhD); research, evaluation, and assessment (PhD); MBA/MA; MPP/MA. *Students:* 674 applicants, 41% accepted, 175 enrolled. In 2006, 134 master's, 43 doctorates awarded. Terminal master's awarded for partial completion of doctoral program. *Median time to degree:* Of those who began their doctoral program in fall 1998, 51% received their degree in 8 years or less. *Degree requirements:* For master's, thesis optional; for doctorate, thesis/dissertation, comprehensive exam. *Entrance requirements:* For master's and doctorate, GRE General Test. Additional exam requirements/recommendations for international students: Required—TOEFL (minimum score 600 paper-based; 250 computer-based). *Application deadline:* For fall admission, 12/1 priority date for domestic students, 12/1 for international students. Application fee: $60 ($75 for international students). Electronic applications accepted. *Financial support:* In 2006–07, 215 fellowships (averaging $5,852 per year), 109 research assistantships with full tuition reimbursements (averaging $14,695 per year), 32 teaching assistantships with full tuition reimbursements (averaging $14,756 per year) were awarded; career-related internships or fieldwork, Federal Work-Study, health care benefits, and tuition waivers also available. Support available to part-time students. Financial award applicants required to submit FAFSA. *Unit head:* Dr. Deborah Carter, Chairperson, 734-647-1981, Fax: 734-764-2510, E-mail: dfcarter@umich.edu. *Application contact:* Roberta Perry, Office of Student Services, 734-764-7563, Fax: 734-763-1495, E-mail: ed.grad.admit@umich.edu.

University of Minnesota, Twin Cities Campus, Graduate School, College of Education and Human Development, Department of Educational Policy and Administration, Program in Evaluation Studies, Minneapolis, MN 55455-0213. Offers MA, PhD. *Students:* 22 full-time (18 women), 18 part-time (17 women); includes 5 minority (1 African American, 3 American Indian/Alaska Native, 1 Asian American or Pacific Islander), 3 international. Average age 37. 6 applicants, 83% accepted, 3 enrolled. In 2006, 4 master's, 3 doctorates awarded. *Expenses:* Tuition, state resident: full-time $9,302; part-time $775 per credit. Tuition, nonresident: full-time $16,400; part-time $1,367 per credit. Full-time tuition and fees vary according to class time, course load, program, reciprocity agreements and student level. *Application contact:* Dr. Mary Bents, Associate Dean, 612-625-6501, Fax: 612-626-1580, E-mail: mbents@tc.umn.edu.

University of Missouri–St. Louis, College of Education, Division of Educational Leadership and Policy Studies, St. Louis, MO 63121. Offers adult and higher education (M Ed, Ed D); educational administration (M Ed, Ed D, Ed S), including community education (M Ed), elementary education (M Ed), secondary education (M Ed); educational leadership and policy studies (PhD); institutional research (Certificate). *Accreditation:* NCATE. *Faculty:* 15 full-time (8 women), 2 part-time/adjunct (0 women). *Students:* 37 full-time (27 women), 325 part-time (214 women); includes 130 minority (118 African Americans, 1 American Indian/Alaska Native, 4 Asian Americans or Pacific Islanders, 7 Hispanic Americans), 4 international. Average age 39. In 2006, 64 master's, 12 doctorates, 32 other advanced degrees awarded. *Entrance requirements:* For doctorate, GRE, 3 letters of recommendation. Additional exam requirements/recommendations for international students: Required—TOEFL (minimum score 550 paper-based; 213 computer-based). *Application deadline:* Applications are processed on a rolling basis. Application fee: $35 ($40 for international students). Electronic applications accepted. *Expenses:* Tuition, state resident: part-time $332 per credit hour. Tuition, nonresident: part-time $770 per credit hour. *Financial support:* In 2006–07, 6 research assistantships (averaging $8,235 per year) were awarded. *Faculty research:* Educational policy research; philosophy of education; higher, adult, and vocational education; school initiatives, change, and reform. *Unit head:* Dr. E. Paulette Savage, Chair, 514-516-5944. *Application contact:* 314-516-5458, Fax: 314-516-6996, E-mail: gradadm@umsl.edu.

University of New England, College of Arts and Sciences, Program in Education, Biddeford, ME 04005-9526. Offers general studies (MS Ed); literacy (MS Ed); teaching methodologies (MS Ed). Part-time programs available. Postbaccalaureate distance learning degree programs offered (minimal on-campus study). *Faculty:* 4 full-time (2 women), 22 part-time/adjunct (13 women). *Students:* 12 full-time (9 women), 435 part-time (322 women); includes 11 minority (3 African Americans, 1 American Indian/Alaska Native, 3 Asian Americans or Pacific Islanders, 4 Hispanic Americans), 1 international. Average age 36. 148 applicants, 100% accepted, 116 enrolled. In 2006, 241 degrees awarded. *Degree requirements:* For master's, collaborative action research project, integrative seminar portfolio. *Entrance requirements:* For master's, teaching certificate, 2 years of teaching experience. Additional exam requirements/recommendations for international students: Required—TOEFL. *Application deadline:* For fall admission, 9/15 for domestic students; for spring admission, 1/15 for domestic students. Applications are processed on a rolling basis. Application fee: $40. Electronic applications accepted. *Expenses: Contact institution. Financial support:* Application deadline: 5/1; *Faculty research:* Distance learning, effective teaching, transition planning, adult learning. *Unit head:* Dr. Susan Hillman, Chair of Education Department, 207-283-0171 Ext. 2888, E-mail: shillman@une.edu. *Application contact:* Robert Pecchia, Associate Dean of Admissions, 207-283-0171 Ext. 2297, Fax: 207-602-5900, E-mail: admissions@une.edu.

The University of North Carolina at Chapel Hill, Graduate School, School of Education, Program in Education, Chapel Hill, NC 27599. Offers culture, curriculum and change (PhD); culture, curriculum, and change (MA); early childhood, families, and literacy studies (MA, PhD); educational psychology measurements, and evaluation (PhD); educational psychology, measurement, and evaluation (MA). *Accreditation:* NCATE. In 2006, 11 master's, 10 doctorates awarded. *Degree requirements:* For master's, thesis/dissertation; for doctorate, thesis/dissertation, comprehensive exam, registration. *Entrance requirements:* For master's, GRE General Test, minimum GPA of 3.0 during last 2 years of undergraduates course work; for doctorate, GRE General Test, minimum GPA of 3.0 during last 2 years of undergraduate course work. Additional exam requirements/recommendations for international students: Required—TOEFL (minimum score 550 paper-based; 213 computer-based). *Application deadline:* For fall admission, 1/1 priority date for domestic and international students. Applications are processed on a rolling basis. Application fee: $60. Electronic applications accepted. *Financial support:* Federal Work-Study available. Support available to part-time students. Financial award application deadline: 3/1; financial award applicants required to submit FAFSA. *Application contact:* Janet Carroll, Registrar, 919-962-8690, Fax: 919-962-1533, E-mail: jscarrol@email.unc.edu.

The University of North Carolina at Greensboro, Graduate School, School of Education, Department of Educational Research Methodology, Greensboro, NC 27412-5001. Offers educational research, measurement and evaluation (PhD); MS/PhD. *Accreditation:* NCATE. *Faculty:* 6 full-time (1 woman), 6 part-time/adjunct (4 women). *Students:* 22 full-time (11 women), 5 part-time (all women); includes 6 minority (2 African Americans, 4 Asian Americans or Pacific Islanders). 24 applicants, 29% accepted. *Degree requirements:* For doctorate, thesis/dissertation. *Entrance requirements:* For doctorate, GRE General Test. Additional exam requirements/recommendations for international students: Required—TOEFL. *Application deadline:* For fall admission, 7/1 priority date for domestic students; for spring admission, 11/1 for domestic students. Applications are processed on a rolling basis. Application fee: $45. Electronic applications accepted. *Expenses:* Tuition, state resident: full-time $2,692. Tuition, nonresident: full-time $13,742. *Financial support:* Fellowships with full tuition reimbursements, research assistantships with full tuition reimbursements, teaching assistantships with full tuition reimbursements, career-related internships or fieldwork, Federal Work-Study, scholarships/grants, and traineeships available. Support available to part-time students. *Unit head:* Dr. Terry Ackerman, Chair, 336-334-3471, Fax: 336-334-4120, E-mail: taackerm@uncg.edu. *Application contact:* Michelle Harkleroad, Director of Graduate Admissions, 336-334-4884, Fax: 336-334-4424, E-mail: mbharkle@uncg.edu.

University of North Dakota, Graduate School, College of Education and Human Development, Teaching and Learning Program, Grand Forks, ND 58202. Offers elementary education (Ed D, PhD); measurement and statistics (Ed D, PhD); secondary education (Ed D, PhD); special education (Ed D, PhD). *Accreditation:* NCATE. *Faculty:* 19 full-time (16 women), 2 part-time/adjunct (1 woman). *Students:* 9 applicants, 0% accepted. In 2006, 18 degrees awarded. *Degree requirements:* For doctorate, thesis/dissertation, final exam, comprehensive exam. *Entrance requirements:* For doctorate, minimum GPA of 3.5. Additional exam requirements/recommendations for international students: Required—TOEFL (minimum score 550 paper-based; 213 computer-based; 79 iBT), IELTS (minimum score 6). *Application deadline:* For fall admission, 2/15 priority date for domestic and international students; for spring admission, 10/15 priority date for domestic and international students. Application fee: $35. Electronic applications accepted. *Expenses:* Tuition, state resident: full-time $5,650; part-time $214 per credit. Tuition, nonresident: full-time $14,248; part-time $572 per credit. Required fees: $1,008; $42 per credit. Tuition and fees vary according to reciprocity agreements. *Financial support:* In 2006–07, 17 students received support, including 1 research assistantship with full tuition reimbursement available (averaging $4,877 per year), 4 teaching assistantships with full tuition reimbursements available (averaging $7,609 per year); fellowships, career-related internships or fieldwork, Federal Work-Study, institutionally sponsored loans, scholarships/grants, tuition waivers (full and partial), and unspecified assistantships also available. Support available to part-time students. Financial award application deadline: 3/15; financial award applicants required to submit FAFSA. *Application contact:* Linda M. Baeza, Admissions Officer, 701-777-2945, Fax: 701-777-3619, E-mail: gradschool@mail.und.nodak.edu.

University of Northern Colorado, Graduate School, College of Education and Behavioral Sciences, School of Educational Research, Leadership and Technology, Program in Applied Statistics and Research Methods, Greeley, CO 80639. Offers MS, PhD. *Faculty:* 6 full-time (2 women). *Students:* 26 full-time (10 women), 13 part-time (7 women); includes 6 minority (2 African Americans, 1 American Indian/Alaska Native, 2 Asian Americans or Pacific Islanders, 1

Hispanic American), 1 international. Average age 37. 17 applicants, 88% accepted, 4 enrolled. In 2006, 8 master's, 2 doctorates awarded. *Degree requirements:* For master's, comprehensive exam; for doctorate, thesis/dissertation, comprehensive exam. *Entrance requirements:* For master's, 3 letters of reference; for doctorate, GRE General Test, 3 letters of reference. *Application deadline:* Applications are processed on a rolling basis. Application fee: $50 ($60 for international students). Electronic applications accepted. *Expenses:* Tuition, state resident: full-time $5,118; part-time $213 per credit hour. Tuition, nonresident: full-time $14,832; part-time $618 per credit hour. Required fees: $674; $34 per credit hour. *Financial support:* In 2006–07, 29 students received support, including 4 fellowships (averaging $1,525 per year), 11 research assistantships (averaging $9,303 per year), 12 teaching assistantships (averaging $13,918 per year). Financial award application deadline: 3/1. *Unit head:* Dr. Susan Hutchinson, Program Coordinator, 970-351-2807, Fax: 970-351-1669.

University of North Texas, Robert B. Toulouse School of Graduate Studies, College of Education, Department of Technology and Cognition, Program in Educational Research, Denton, TX 76203. Offers PhD. *Accreditation:* NCATE. *Students:* 2 full-time (both women), 11 part-time (10 women); includes 3 minority (1 Asian American or Pacific Islander, 2 Hispanic Americans), 1 international. Average age 37. 2 applicants, 0% accepted. In 2006, 1 degree awarded. *Degree requirements:* For doctorate, one foreign language, thesis/dissertation, internship. *Entrance requirements:* For doctorate, GRE General Test, admissions exam. Additional exam requirements/recommendations for international students: Recommended—TOEFL (minimum score 550 paper-based; 213 computer-based). *Application deadline:* For fall admission, 7/17 for domestic students. Application fee: $50 ($75 for international students). *Expenses:* Tuition, state resident: full-time $3,573; part-time $198 per credit. Tuition, nonresident: full-time $8,577; part-time $476 per credit. Required fees: $1,258; $126 per credit. One-time fee: $150 full-time. Tuition and fees vary according to course load. *Financial support:* Fellowships, research assistantships, teaching assistantships, career-related internships or fieldwork, Federal Work-Study, and institutionally sponsored loans available. Financial award application deadline: 4/1. *Unit head:* Coordinator, 940-369-8385, Fax: 940-565-2185. *Application contact:* Dr. Kyle Roberts, Graduate Adviser, 940-369-7168, E-mail: kroberts@tac.coe.unt.edu.

University of Pennsylvania, Graduate School of Education, Division of Policy, Management and Evaluation, Philadelphia, PA 19104. Offers MS Ed, Ed D, PhD. Part-time programs available. Terminal master's awarded for partial completion of doctoral program. *Degree requirements:* For master's, comprehensive exam; for doctorate, thesis/dissertation, comprehensive exam. *Entrance requirements:* For master's and doctorate, GRE. Electronic applications accepted. Expenses: Contact institution. *Faculty research:* Institutional research, strategic planning, governance and administration, public policy, budgeting and finance.

University of Pittsburgh, School of Education, Department of Psychology in Education, Program in Research Methodology, Pittsburgh, PA 15260. Offers M Ed, MA, PhD. Part-time and evening/weekend programs available. *Students:* 23 full-time (18 women), 12 part-time (10 women), 16 international. 28 applicants, 89% accepted, 15 enrolled. In 2006, 7 degrees awarded. Terminal master's awarded for partial completion of doctoral program. *Degree requirements:* For master's and doctorate, thesis/dissertation. *Entrance requirements:* For doctorate, GRE General Test. Additional exam requirements/recommendations for international students: Required—TOEFL. *Application deadline:* For fall admission, 2/1 for domestic students. Application fee: $50. Electronic applications accepted. *Financial support:* In 2006–07, fellowships (averaging $2,500 per year), research assistantships with partial tuition reimbursements (averaging $8,000 per year) were awarded; Federal Work-Study, tuition waivers (partial), and unspecified assistantships also available. Support available to part-time students. Financial award application deadline: 3/15; financial award applicants required to submit FAFSA. *Application contact:* Joan M. Cutone, Director, School of Education Student Service Center, 412-648-2230, Fax: 412-648-1899, E-mail: soeinfo@pitt.edu.

University of Puerto Rico, Río Piedras, College of Education, Program in Educational Research and Evaluation, San Juan, PR 00931-3300. Offers M Ed. Part-time programs available. *Students:* 10 full-time (9 women), 10 part-time (6 women); all minorities (all Hispanic Americans) *Degree requirements:* For master's, thesis. *Entrance requirements:* For master's, PAEG or GRE, interview, minimum GPA of 3.0, letter of recommendation. *Application deadline:* For fall admission, 2/1 for domestic and international students. Application fee: $17. *Expenses:* Tuition, state resident: part-time $100 per credit. Tuition, nonresident: part-time $291 per credit. Required fees: $72 per semester. *Financial support:* Fellowships, research assistantships, teaching assistantships, career-related internships or fieldwork, Federal Work-Study, institutionally sponsored loans, and tuition waivers (partial) available. Financial award application deadline: 5/31. *Faculty research:* Adolescent sexuality. *Unit head:* Dr. Loyda Martinez, Coordinator, 787-764-0000 Ext. 4361, Fax: 787-763-4130. *Application contact:* Information Contact, 787-764-0000 Ext. 4368, Fax: 787-763-4130.

University of South Carolina, The Graduate School, College of Education, Department of Educational Studies, Program in Educational Psychology, Research, Columbia, SC 29208. Offers M Ed, PhD. *Accreditation:* NCATE. *Degree requirements:* For master's, thesis (for some programs), comprehensive exam; for doctorate, thesis/dissertation, comprehensive exam. *Entrance requirements:* For master's, GRE General Test; for doctorate, GRE General Test, interview. Electronic applications accepted. *Faculty research:* Problem solving, higher order thinking skills, psychometric research, methodology.

University of South Florida, Graduate School, College of Education, Department of Educational Measurement and Research, Tampa, FL 33620-9951. Offers M Ed, PhD, Ed S. *Accreditation:* NCATE. *Faculty:* 11 full-time (3 women), 2 part-time/adjunct (both women). *Students:* 15 full-time (9 women), 22 part-time (12 women); includes 2 minority (1 African American, 1 Hispanic American), 4 international. 11 applicants, 91% accepted, 7 enrolled. In 2006, 1 master's, 2 doctorates awarded. *Degree requirements:* For doctorate, thesis/dissertation. *Entrance requirements:* For master's, GRE General Test, minimum GPA of 3.0 in last 60 hours; for doctorate, GRE General Test, minimum undergraduate GPA of 3.5. *Application deadline:* For fall admission, 5/1 for domestic and international students; for spring admission, 9/1 for domestic and international students. Application fee: $30. Electronic applications accepted. *Financial support:* Career-related internships or fieldwork, scholarships/grants, and unspecified assistantships available. Financial award application deadline: 6/1; financial award applicants required to submit FAFSA. Total annual research expenditures: $35,966. *Unit head:* Dr. Jeffrey D. Kromrey, Chairperson, 813-974-5739, Fax: 813-974-4495, E-mail: kromrey@tempest.usf.edu. *Application contact:* Lou Carey, Application Contact, 813-974-5247, Fax: 813-974-4495, E-mail: carey@tempest.cordu.usf.edu.

The University of Tennessee, Graduate School, College of Education, Health and Human Sciences, Program in Education, Knoxville, TN 37996. Offers art education (MS); counseling education (PhD); cultural studies in education (PhD); curriculum (MS, Ed S); curriculum, educational research and evaluation (Ed D, PhD); early childhood education (PhD); early childhood special education (MS); education of deaf and hard of hearing (MS); educational administration and policy studies (Ed D, PhD); educational administration and supervision (Ed S); educational psychology (Ed D, PhD); elementary education (MS, Ed S); elementary teaching (MS); English education (MS, Ed S); exercise science (PhD); foreign language/ESL education (MS, Ed S); instructional technology (MS, Ed D, PhD, Ed S); literacy, language and ESL education (PhD); literacy, language education, and ESL education (Ed D); mathematics education (MS, Ed S); modified and comprehensive special education (MS); reading education (MS, Ed S); school counseling (Ed S); school psychology (PhD, Ed S); science education (MS, Ed S); secondary teaching (MS); social foundations (MS); social science education (MS, Ed S); socio-cultural foundations of sports and education (PhD); special education (Ed S); teacher education (Ed D, PhD). *Accreditation:* NCATE. Part-time and evening/weekend programs available. *Students:* 529 (401 women); includes 39 minority (23 African Americans, 2 American Indian/Alaska Native, 9 Asian Americans or Pacific Islanders, 5 Hispanic Americans) 34 international. 420 applicants, 50% accepted. In 2006, 258 master's, 28 doctorates awarded. *Degree requirements:* For master's and Ed S, thesis optional; for doctorate, variable foreign language requirement, thesis/dissertation. *Entrance requirements:* For master's, minimum GPA of 2.7; for doctorate and Ed S, GRE General Test, minimum GPA of 2.7. Additional exam requirements/recommendations for international students: Required—TOEFL. *Application deadline:* For fall admission, 2/1 priority date for domestic students. Applications are processed on a rolling basis. Application fee: $35. Electronic applications accepted. *Expenses:* Tuition, state resident: full-time $5,574. Tuition, nonresident: full-time $16,840. Required fees: $792. *Financial support:* In 2006–07, 4 fellowships, 9 teaching assistantships were awarded; career-related internships or fieldwork, Federal Work-Study, institutionally sponsored loans, and unspecified assistantships also available. Financial award application deadline: 2/1; financial award applicants required to submit FAFSA. *Unit head:* Dr. Lester Knight, Head, 865-974-0907, Fax: 865-974-8718, E-mail: lknight@utk.edu.

The University of Texas–Pan American, College of Education, Department of Educational Psychology, Edinburg, TX 78541-2999. Offers counseling (M Ed); educational diagnostician (M Ed); gifted education (M Ed); school psychology (MA); special education (M Ed). Part-time and evening/weekend programs available. *Degree requirements:* For master's, thesis (for some programs), comprehensive exam (for some programs). *Entrance requirements:* For master's, GRE General Test, interview. *Expenses:* Tuition, state resident: full-time $2,577; part-time $143 per credit hour. Tuition, nonresident: full-time $7,527; part-time $418 per credit hour. Required fees: $561. *Faculty research:* Reading instruction, assessment practice, behavior interventions consultation, mental retardation.

The University of Toledo, College of Graduate Studies, College of Education, Department of Foundations of Education, Program in Educational Research and Measurement, Toledo, OH 43606-3390. Offers ME, PhD. *Students:* 4 full-time (all women), 3 international. Average age 39. 5 applicants, 40% accepted, 2 enrolled. *Financial support:* Research assistantships, teaching assistantships available. *Unit head:* Dr. Dale Snauwaert, Chair, Department of Foundations of Education, 419-530-2478, Fax: 419-530-8337.

University of Virginia, Curry School of Education, Department of Leadership, Foundations and Policy, Program in Educational Policy and Evaluation, Charlottesville, VA 22903. Offers M Ed, Ed D. *Students:* 1 full-time (0 women), 1 part-time. Average age 42. In 2006, 1 degree awarded. *Degree requirements:* For master's, thesis (for some programs), comprehensive exam (for some programs); for doctorate, thesis/dissertation, comprehensive exam (for some programs). *Entrance requirements:* For master's and doctorate, GRE General Test. Additional exam requirements/recommendations for international students: Required—TOEFL (minimum score 600 paper-based; 250 computer-based). *Application deadline:* Applications are processed on a rolling basis. Application fee: $60. Electronic applications accepted. *Financial support:* Fellowships, research assistantships, teaching assistantships available. Financial award applicants required to submit FAFSA.

University of Washington, Graduate School, College of Education, Program in Educational Psychology, Seattle, WA 98195. Offers human development and cognition (M Ed, PhD); measurement and research (M Ed, PhD); school counseling (M Ed, PhD); school psychology (M Ed, PhD). *Accreditation:* APA. *Degree requirements:* For master's, thesis optional; for doctorate, thesis/dissertation. *Entrance requirements:* For master's and doctorate, GRE General Test, minimum GPA of 3.0. Additional exam requirements/recommendations for international students: Required—TOEFL.

University of West Georgia, Graduate School, College of Education, Program in School Improvement, Carrollton, GA 30118. Offers Ed D. Part-time and evening/weekend programs available. *Students:* Average age 37. 68 applicants, 26% accepted, 18 enrolled. In 2006, 8 degrees awarded. *Degree requirements:* For doctorate, thesis/dissertation, research project, professional portfolio. *Entrance requirements:* For doctorate, GRE, curriculum vitae, minimum GPA of 3.0 in graduate education, interview, references, 2 writing samples. *Application deadline:* For spring admission, 2/28 for domestic students. Application fee: $20. Electronic applications accepted. *Expenses:* Tuition, state resident: full-time $2,286; part-time $127 per credit. Tuition, nonresident: full-time $9,144; part-time $508 per credit. Required fees: $494; $27 per credit. $121 per semester. *Financial support:* In 2006–07, 1 student received support, including 1 research assistantship with full tuition reimbursement available (averaging $6,000 per year). Financial award application deadline: 4/30; financial award applicants required to submit FAFSA. *Faculty research:* School-based partnerships, school change, action research, teacher leadership, teacher certification. *Unit head:* Dr. Cher Hendricks, Director, 678-839-6134, Fax: 678-839-6063, E-mail: cher@westga.edu. *Application contact:* Dr. Charles W. Clark, Chair, 678-839-6508, E-mail: cclark@westga.edu.

Utah State University, School of Graduate Studies, College of Education and Human Services, Department of Psychology, Logan, UT 84322. Offers clinical/counseling/school psychology (PhD); research and evaluation methodology (PhD); school counseling (MS); school psychology (MS). *Accreditation:* APA (one or more programs are accredited). Part-time and evening/weekend programs available. Postbaccalaureate distance learning degree programs offered (no on-campus study). *Faculty:* 21 full-time (10 women), 35 part-time/adjunct (13 women). *Students:* 145 full-time (89 women), 24 part-time (16 women); includes 14 minority (3 African Americans, 3 American Indian/Alaska Native, 3 Asian Americans or Pacific Islanders, 5 Hispanic Americans), 14 international. Average age 34. 290 applicants, 66% accepted, 169 enrolled. In 2006, 44 master's, 5 doctorates awarded. Terminal master's awarded for partial completion of doctoral program. *Degree requirements:* For master's, thesis (for some programs); for doctorate, thesis/dissertation. *Entrance requirements:* For master's, GRE General Test (school psychology), MAT (school counseling), minimum GPA of 3.5; for doctorate, GRE General Test, minimum GPA of 3.5. Additional exam requirements/recommendations for international students: Required—TOEFL. *Application deadline:* For fall admission, 1/15 for domestic and international students; for spring admission, 10/15 for domestic and international students. Applications are processed on a rolling basis. Application fee: $50 ($60 for international students). *Financial support:* In 2006–07, 5 fellowships with full and partial tuition reimbursements (averaging $12,600 per year), 24 research assistantships with full and partial tuition reimbursements (averaging $11,500 per year), 12 teaching assistantships with full and partial tuition reimbursements (averaging $7,000 per year) were awarded; career-related internships or fieldwork, Federal Work-Study, institutionally sponsored loans, scholarships/grants, tuition waivers (partial), and unspecified assistantships also available. Financial award application deadline: 2/1. *Faculty research:* Hearing loss detection in infancy, ADHD, eating disorders, domestic violence, neuropsychology, bilingual/Spanish speaking students/parents. *Unit head:* David M. Stein, Head, 435-797-1460, Fax: 435-797-1448, E-mail: davids@coe.usu.edu. *Application contact:* Sheila Jessie, Staff Assistant IV, 435-797-1449, Fax: 435-797-1448, E-mail: sheilaj@coe.usu.edu.

Utah State University, School of Graduate Studies, College of Education and Human Services, Doctoral Program in Education, Logan, UT 84322. Offers business information systems (Ed D, PhD); curriculum and instruction (Ed D, PhD); research and evaluation (PhD). *Accreditation:* NCATE. *Faculty:* 61 full-time (19 women). *Students:* 107 full-time (75 women), 100 part-time (60 women); includes 6 minority (3 African Americans, 3 Hispanic Americans), 18 international. Average age 36. 43 applicants, 49% accepted, 12 enrolled. In 2006, 14 degrees awarded. *Degree requirements:* For doctorate, thesis/dissertation, comprehensive exam, registration. *Entrance requirements:* For doctorate, GRE General Test, minimum GPA of 3.0, master's degree. Additional exam requirements/recommendations for international students: Required—TOEFL. *Application deadline:* For fall admission, 6/15 priority date for domestic and international students; for spring admission, 10/15 priority date for domestic and international students. Applications are processed on a rolling basis. Application fee: $50 ($60 for international students). Electronic applications accepted. *Financial support:* In 2006–07, 7 fellowships were awarded; research assistantships with partial tuition reimbursements, teaching assistantships with partial tuition reimbursements, career-related internships or fieldwork, Federal Work-Study, and institutionally sponsored loans also available. Financial award application deadline: 2/1. *Faculty research:* Language and literacy development, math and science education, instructional technology, hearing problems/deafness, domestic violence and

Educational Measurement and Evaluation

Utah State University (continued)
animal abuse. Total annual research expenditures: $30.6 million. *Application contact:* Shannon Johnson, Staff Assistant, 435-797-1470, Fax: 435-797-3939, E-mail: shannon.johnson@usu.edu.

Vanderbilt University, Graduate School, Department of Physics and Astronomy, Nashville, TN 37240-1001. Offers astronomy (MS); physics (MA, MAT, MS, PhD). *Faculty:* 65 full-time (3 women). *Students:* 74 full-time (18 women); includes 4 minority (3 African Americans, 1 Hispanic American), 36 international. 180 applicants, 13% accepted, 13 enrolled. In 2006, 8 master's, 5 doctorates awarded. *Degree requirements:* For master's, thesis; for doctorate, thesis/dissertation, final and qualifying exams. *Entrance requirements:* For master's, GRE General Test; for doctorate, GRE General Test, GRE Subject Test. *Application deadline:* For fall admission, 1/15 for domestic and international students. Application fee: $0. Electronic applications accepted. *Expenses:* Tuition: Full-time $24,462. Required fees: $2,515. One-time fee: $30 full-time. Full-time tuition and fees vary according to course load, degree level and program. *Financial support:* Fellowships with full and partial tuition reimbursements, research assistantships with full tuition reimbursements, teaching assistantships with full tuition reimbursements, career-related internships or fieldwork, Federal Work-Study, and institutionally sponsored loans available. Financial award application deadline: 1/15. *Faculty research:* Experimental and theoretical physics, free electron laser, living-state physics, heavy-ion physics, nuclear structure. *Unit head:* Robert J. Scherrer, Chair, 615-322-2828, Fax: 615-343-7263. *Application contact:* Vicky Greene, Director of Graduate Studies, 615-322-2828, Fax: 615-343-7263, E-mail: senta.greene@vanderbilt.edu.

Virginia Commonwealth University, Graduate School, School of Education, Doctoral Program in Education, Richmond, VA 23284-9005. Offers educational leadership (PhD); instructional leadership (PhD); research and evaluation (PhD); urban services leadership (PhD). *Accreditation:* NCATE. Part-time programs available. *Students:* 53 full-time (44 women), 112 part-time (77 women); includes 38 minority (35 African Americans, 1 American Indian/Alaska Native, 2 Hispanic Americans), 5 international. 39 applicants, 67% accepted, 22 enrolled. In 2006, 13 degrees awarded. *Degree requirements:* For doctorate, thesis/dissertation. *Entrance requirements:* For doctorate, GRE, interview, master's degree, writing sample. *Application deadline:* For fall admission, 3/15 for domestic students. Application fee: $50. *Financial support:* Fellowships, research assistantships, career-related internships or fieldwork, Federal Work-Study, and institutionally sponsored loans available. Financial award application deadline: 3/1. *Unit head:* Dr. Henry Clark, Director, Graduate Studies, 804-828-3382. *Application contact:* Patricia Willard, Administrative Assistant, 804-828-6530, E-mail: pawillar@vcu.edu.

See Close-Up on page 1135.

Virginia Polytechnic Institute and State University, Graduate School, College of Liberal Arts and Human Sciences, School of Education, Department of Educational Leadership and Policy Studies, Program in Educational Research and Evaluation, Blacksburg, VA 24061. Offers PhD. *Accreditation:* NCATE. *Degree requirements:* For doctorate, thesis/dissertation. *Entrance requirements:* Additional exam requirements/recommendations for international students: Required—TOEFL. *Application deadline:* Applications are processed on a rolling basis. Application fee: $45. Electronic applications accepted. *Expenses:* Tuition, state resident: full-time $7,017; part-time $390 per credit hour. Tuition, nonresident: full-time $12,414; part-time $690 per credit hour. International tuition: $11,296 full-time. Required fees: $1,523; $256 per term. *Financial support:* In 2006–07, research assistantships with full tuition reimbursements (averaging $10,370 per year). Financial award application deadline: 4/1. *Unit head:* Kusum Singh, Program Area Leader and Professor, 540-231-9729, Fax: 540-231-7845, E-mail: ksingh@vt.edu.

Washington University in St. Louis, Graduate School of Arts and Sciences, Department of Education, Program in Educational Research, St. Louis, MO 63130-4899. Offers PhD. *Entrance requirements:* For doctorate, GRE General Test. Electronic applications accepted.

Wayne State University, College of Education, Division of Theoretical and Behavioral Foundations, Detroit, MI 48202. Offers counseling (M Ed, MA, Ed D, PhD, Ed S); education evaluation and research (M Ed, Ed D, PhD); educational psychology (M Ed, Ed D, PhD, Ed S); educational sociology (M Ed, Ed D, PhD, Ed S); history and philosophy of education (M Ed, Ed D, PhD); rehabilitation counseling and community inclusion (MA, Ed S); school and community psychology (MA, Ed S); school clinical psychology (Ed S). *Accreditation:* ACA (one or more programs are accredited); CORE (one or more programs are accredited). Evening/weekend programs available. *Faculty:* 51 full-time (18 women), 11 part-time/adjunct (7 women). *Students:* 156 full-time (125 women), 232 part-time (191 women); includes 146 minority (140 African Americans, 1 American Indian/Alaska Native, 5 Hispanic Americans), 14 international. Average age 35. 146 applicants, 38% accepted, 39 enrolled. In 2006, 84 master's, 8 doctorates awarded. *Degree requirements:* For doctorate, thesis/dissertation. *Entrance requirements:* For master's, GRE (school and community psychology); for doctorate, GRE (educational psychology), interview, minimum GPA of 3.0. Additional exam requirements/recommendations for international students: Required—TOEFL (minimum score 550 paper-based; 213 computer-based), TWE (minimum score 6). *Application deadline:* For fall admission, 7/1 for domestic students, 6/1 for international students; for winter admission, 10/1 for international students; for spring admission, 2/1 for international students. Application fee: $20 ($30 for international students). Electronic applications accepted. *Financial support:* In 2006–07, 2 research assistantships (averaging $12,797 per year) were awarded; fellowships, career-related internships or fieldwork, Federal Work-Study, and institutionally sponsored loans also available. *Faculty research:* Adolescents at risk, supervision of counseling. *Unit head:* Dr. JoAnne Holbert, Assistant Dean, 313-577-1721, E-mail: jholbert@wayne.edu.

West Chester University of Pennsylvania, Graduate Studies, School of Education, Department of Professional and Secondary Education, West Chester, PA 19383. Offers educational research (MS); secondary education (M Ed). Part-time and evening/weekend programs available. *Students:* 23 full-time (17 women), 50 part-time (30 women); includes 2 Asian Americans or Pacific Islanders. Average age 31. 55 applicants, 93% accepted, 28 enrolled. In 2006, 14 degrees awarded. *Degree requirements:* For master's, thesis (for some programs), comprehensive exam. *Entrance requirements:* For master's, GRE or MAT, teaching certificate. *Application deadline:* For fall admission, 4/15 priority date for domestic students; for spring admission, 10/15 priority date for domestic students. Applications are processed on a rolling basis. Application fee: $35. *Financial support:* In 2006–07, 1 research assistantship with full tuition reimbursement (averaging $5,000 per year) was awarded; unspecified assistantships also available. Support available to part-time students. Financial award application deadline: 2/15; financial award applicants required to submit FAFSA. *Faculty research:* Technology integration: preparing our teachers for the 21st century. *Unit head:* Dr. Lesley Welsh, Chair, 610-436-2958, E-mail: lwelsh@wcupa.edu. *Application contact:* Dr. Cynthia Haggard, Graduate Coordinator, 610-436-6934, E-mail: chaggard@wcupa.edu.

Western Governors University, Teachers College, Salt Lake City, UT 84107. Offers English language learning (K-12) (MA); learning and technology (M Ed, MA); management and evaluation (M Ed); management and innovation (M Ed); mathematics education (5-12) (MA); mathematics education (5-9) (MA); mathematics education (K-6) (MA); science (5-12) (MA), including biology, geology; science education (509) (MA); technology (M Ed); technology for principals (Post-Graduate Certificate). *Accreditation:* NCATE. Part-time and evening/weekend programs available. Postbaccalaureate distance learning degree programs offered (no on-campus study). *Degree requirements:* For master's, comprehensive exam, registration. *Entrance requirements:* Additional exam requirements/recommendations for international students: Required—TOEFL (minimum score 450 paper-based). Electronic applications accepted. Expenses: Contact institution.

Western Michigan University, Graduate College, College of Education, Department of Educational Studies, Kalamazoo, MI 49008-5202. Offers educational studies (MA, Ed D); evaluation, measurement, and research (MA, PhD). *Accreditation:* NCATE. *Degree requirements:* For master's, written exams; for doctorate, thesis/dissertation, internships. *Entrance requirements:* For doctorate, GRE General Test.

West Texas A&M University, College of Education and Social Sciences, Division of Education, Program in Educational Diagnostician, Canyon, TX 79016-0001. Offers M Ed. Part-time programs available. Postbaccalaureate distance learning degree programs offered (minimal on-campus study). *Degree requirements:* For master's, thesis optional. *Entrance requirements:* For master's, GRE General Test, 3 years teaching experience, competency in diagnosis and prescription. Additional exam requirements/recommendations for international students: Required—TOEFL (minimum score 550 paper-based). Electronic applications accepted. *Faculty research:* Teacher preparation through web-based instruction, developmental disabilities.

Wilkes University, Graduate Studies and Continued Learning, College of Arts, Humanities and Social Sciences, Program in Teacher Education, Wilkes-Barre, PA 18766-0002. Offers classroom technology (MS Ed); educational computing (MS Ed); educational development and strategies (MS Ed); educational leadership (MS Ed); elementary education (MS Ed); instructional technology (MS Ed); school business leadership (MS Ed); secondary education (MS Ed), including biology, chemistry, English, history; special education (MS Ed). Part-time and evening/weekend programs available. Postbaccalaureate distance learning degree programs offered (minimal on-campus study). *Students:* 32 full-time (21 women), 1,588 part-time (1,106 women); includes 29 minority (6 African Americans, 2 American Indian/Alaska Native, 4 Asian Americans or Pacific Islanders, 17 Hispanic Americans). Average age 33. In 2006, 754 degrees awarded. *Entrance requirements:* Additional exam requirements/recommendations for international students: Required—TOEFL (minimum score 500 paper-based; 173 computer-based). *Application deadline:* Applications are processed on a rolling basis. Application fee: $40. *Expenses:* Contact institution. *Financial support:* Federal Work-Study and unspecified assistantships available. Financial award application deadline: 3/1; financial award applicants required to submit FAFSA. *Unit head:* Dr. Michael Speziale, Interim Dean, 570-408-4679, Fax: 570-408-4905, E-mail: michael.speziale@wilkes.edu. *Application contact:* Kathleen Houlihan, Director of Graduate Studies, 570-408-3235, Fax: 570-408-7846, E-mail: kathleen.houlihan@wilkes.edu.

Educational Media/Instructional Technology

Acadia University, Faculty of Professional Studies, School of Education, Program in Curriculum Studies, Wolfville, NS B4P 2R6, Canada. Offers cultural and media studies (M Ed); inclusive education (M Ed); learning and technology (M Ed); science, math and technology (M Ed). Evening/weekend programs available. *Faculty:* 12 full-time (5 women). *Students:* 2 full-time (both women), 27 part-time (19 women). In 2006, 25 degrees awarded. *Degree requirements:* For master's, thesis optional. *Entrance requirements:* For master's, B Ed or the equivalent, minimum B average in undergraduate course work, 2 years of teaching experience. Additional exam requirements/recommendations for international students: Required—TOEFL (minimum score 580 paper-based; 237 computer-based). *Application deadline:* For fall admission, 3/15 priority date for domestic and international students. Application fee: $50. Electronic applications accepted. *Financial support:* Teaching assistantships available. Financial award application deadline: 2/1. *Faculty research:* Literacy development, postmodern philosophy and curriculum theory, historiography, philosophy of education, learning and technology. *Application contact:* Sheila Langille, Secretary, 902-585-1229, Fax: 902-585-1071, E-mail: sheila.langille@acadiau.ca.

Adelphi University, School of Education, Program in Educational Leadership and Technology, Garden City, NY 11530-0701. Offers MA, Certificate. *Students:* 7 full-time (6 women), 50 part-time (40 women); includes 25 minority (16 African Americans, 3 Asian Americans or Pacific Islanders, 6 Hispanic Americans). Average age 40. In 2006, 25 master's, 2 other advanced degrees awarded. *Entrance requirements:* For master's, 2 letters of recommendation, resumé, letter attesting to teaching experience (3 years full-time K-12). Additional exam requirements/recommendations for international students: Required—TOEFL (minimum score 550 paper-based; 213 computer-based). *Application deadline:* For fall admission, 8/15 priority date for domestic students; for spring admission, 1/15 priority date for domestic students. Applications are processed on a rolling basis. Application fee: $50. Electronic applications accepted. *Financial support:* Research assistantships with partial tuition reimbursements, institutionally sponsored loans available. Financial award application deadline: 2/15; financial award applicants required to submit FAFSA. *Faculty research:* Technology methodology focusing on in-service and pre-service curriculum. *Unit head:* Dr. Devin Thornburg, Director, 516-877-4026, E-mail: thornburg@adelphi.edu. *Application contact:* Christine Murphy, Director of Admissions, 516-877-3050, Fax: 516-877-3039, E-mail: graduateadmissions@adelphi.edu.

Alabama State University, School of Graduate Studies, College of Education, Department of Instructional Support, Library Education Media Program, Montgomery, AL 36101-0271. Offers M Ed, Ed S. Part-time programs available. *Students:* 19 full-time (18 women), 50 part-time (all women); includes 26 minority (all African Americans) In 2006, 17 master's, 1 other advanced degree awarded. *Degree requirements:* For master's, comprehensive exam; for Ed S, thesis, comprehensive exam. *Entrance requirements:* For master's, GRE General Test or MAT, graduate writing competency test, 2 letters of recommendation; for Ed S, graduate writing competency test, GRE or MAT, 2 letters of recommendation. Additional exam requirements/recommendations for international students: Required—TOEFL (minimum score 500 paper-based; 173 computer-based). *Application deadline:* For fall admission, 7/15 for domestic students; for spring admission, 12/15 for domestic students. Applications are processed on a rolling basis. Application fee: $10. *Expenses:* Tuition, state resident: full-time $1,728; part-time $192 per hour. Tuition, nonresident: full-time $3,456; part-time $334 per hour. *Financial support:* In 2006–07, research assistantships (averaging $9,450 per year). *Faculty research:* Developing research capabilities through media, computer and media usage for teaching young children, use of media for in-service. *Unit head:* Dr. Agnes Helen Bellel, Coordinator, 334-229-8801, E-mail: abellel@alasu.edu.

Alliant International University–Irvine, Graduate School of Education, Teacher Education Programs, Irvine, CA 92612. Offers auditory oral education (Certificate); CLAD (Certificate); preliminary multiple subject (Credential); preliminary multiple subject with BCLAD (Credential); preliminary single subject (Credential); professional clear multiple subject (Credential); professional clear single subject (Credential); teaching (MA, Credential); technology and learning (MA). Part-time and evening/weekend programs available. *Students:* 4. In 2006, 6 degrees awarded. *Entrance requirements:* For degree, California Basic Educational Skills Test, minimum GPA of 2.5. Additional exam requirements/recommendations for international students: Required—TOEFL (minimum score 550 paper-based; 213 computer-based), TWE.

Application deadline: For fall admission, 7/1 priority date for domestic and international students; for spring admission, 12/1 priority date for domestic and international students. Applications are processed on a rolling basis. Application fee: $55. Electronic applications accepted. *Financial support:* Career-related internships or fieldwork, Federal Work-Study, institutionally sponsored loans, and scholarships/grants available. Financial award applicants required to submit FAFSA. *Unit head:* Dr. Trudy Day, Assistant Dean, 866-825-5426, Fax: 949-833-3507, E-mail: admissions@alliant.edu. *Application contact:* Alliant International University Central Contact Center, 866-U-ALLIANT, Fax: 858-635-4555, E-mail: admissions@alliant.edu.

Alverno College, School of Education, Milwaukee, WI 53234-3922. Offers adaptive education (MA); administrative leadership (MA); adult education and organizational development (MA); adult educational and instructional design (MA); adult educational and instructional technology (MA); instructional leadership (MA); instructional technology for K-12 settings (MA); professional development (MA); reading education (MA); reading education with adaptive education (MA); science education (MA); teaching in alternative schools (MA). *Accreditation:* NCATE. Part-time and evening/weekend programs available. *Faculty:* 12 full-time (11 women), 12 part-time/adjunct (10 women). *Students:* 83 full-time (68 women), 74 part-time (60 women); includes 37 minority (32 African Americans, 2 American Indian/Alaska Native, 3 Hispanic Americans). Average age 35. 61 applicants, 82% accepted, 41 enrolled. In 2006, 46 degrees awarded. *Degree requirements:* For master's, presentation/defense of proposal, conference presentation of inquiry projects. *Entrance requirements:* For master's, bachelor's degree in related field, communication samples from work setting, 3 letters of recommendation. Additional exam requirements/recommendations for international students: Required—TOEFL. *Application deadline:* For fall admission, 8/1 priority date for domestic and international students; for spring admission, 12/15 priority date for domestic and international students. Applications are processed on a rolling basis. Application fee: $20. Electronic applications accepted. *Expenses:* Tuition: Full-time $9,288; part-time $516 per credit. Required fees: $250; $125 per semester. Tuition and fees vary according to program. *Financial support:* In 2006–07, 92 students received support. Federal Work-Study available. Support available to part-time students. Financial award application deadline: 4/15; financial award applicants required to submit FAFSA. *Faculty research:* Student self-assessment, self-reflection, integration of curriculum, identifying needs of students in strategic situations and designing appropriate classroom strategies, implementing guided. *Unit head:* Dr. Mary Diez, Graduate Dean, 414-382-6214, Fax: 414-382-6332, E-mail: mary.diez@alverno.edu. *Application contact:* Sarajane Kennedy, Associate Director, Admissions Graduate Programs, 414-382-6104, Fax: 414-382-6332, E-mail: sarajane.kennedy@alverno.edu.

American InterContinental University, Program in Education, Los Angeles, CA 90066. Offers instructional technology (M Ed). Part-time and evening/weekend programs available. *Faculty:* 2 full-time (1 woman). *Students:* 4 full-time (3 women); includes 1 minority (African American) Average age 33. In 2006, 4 degrees awarded. *Entrance requirements:* For master's, interview, proof of Baccalaureate. Additional exam requirements/recommendations for international students: Required—TOEFL (minimum score 550 paper-based; 79 iBT), IELTS (minimum score 7). *Application deadline:* Applications are processed on a rolling basis. Application fee: $50. Electronic applications accepted. *Expenses:* Tuition: Full-time $26,400. *Financial support:* Institutionally sponsored loans, scholarships/grants, and health care benefits available. Support available to part-time students. Financial award applicants required to submit FAFSA. *Faculty research:* Curriculum and instructional technology, educational psychology, computer and information technology. *Unit head:* Dr. Eleanore Miller, Associate Dean of Education, 310-302-2634, E-mail: emiller@la.aiuniv.edu. *Application contact:* Admissions Advisor, Fax: 310-302-2001.

American InterContinental University, Program in Instructional Technology, Weston, FL 33326. Offers M Ed. Part-time and evening/weekend programs available. *Faculty:* 3 full-time (1 woman), 1 part-time/adjunct (0 women). *Students:* 11 full-time; includes 7 minority (3 African Americans, 1 Asian American or Pacific Islander, 3 Hispanic Americans). In 2006, 12 degrees awarded. *Entrance requirements:* Additional exam requirements/recommendations for international students: Required—TOEFL (minimum score 670 paper-based). *Application deadline:* Applications are processed on a rolling basis. Application fee: $50. Electronic applications accepted. *Financial support:* Federal Work-Study and scholarships/grants available. Financial award application deadline: 1/15; financial award applicants required to submit FAFSA. *Unit head:* Dr. Fabian Cone, Director of Institutional Effectiveness, 954-446-6118, Fax: 954-446-6392, E-mail: fcone@aiufl.edu.

American InterContinental University Online, Program in Education, Hoffman Estates, IL 60192. Offers curriculum and instruction (M Ed); educational assessment and evaluation (M Ed); instructional technology (M Ed); leadership of educational organizations (M Ed). Evening/weekend programs available. Postbaccalaureate distance learning degree programs offered (no on-campus study). *Entrance requirements:* Additional exam requirements/recommendations for international students: Required—TOEFL (minimum score 550 paper-based; 213 computer-based). *Application deadline:* Applications are processed on a rolling basis. Application fee: $50. Electronic applications accepted. *Financial support:* Institutionally sponsored loans and scholarships/grants available. Financial award applicants required to submit FAFSA. *Unit head:* Kerri J Holloway, Vice President of Academic Affairs, 847-851-5000 Ext. 15399, Fax: 847-586-6309, E-mail: kholloway@aivonline.edu. *Application contact:* 877-701-3800, E-mail: info@aiuonline.edu.

American University, College of Arts and Sciences, School of Education, Teaching, and Health, Program in Education, Washington, DC 20016-8001. Offers education (PhD); educational leadership (MA); educational technology (MA). Part-time and evening/weekend programs available. In 2006, 6 degrees awarded. *Entrance requirements:* For doctorate, GRE General Test or MAT, minimum GPA of 3.0. *Application deadline:* For fall admission, 2/1 priority date for domestic students; for spring admission, 10/1 priority date for domestic students. Applications are processed on a rolling basis. Application fee: $50. *Expenses:* Tuition: Full-time $18,864; part-time $1,048 per credit. Required fees: $380. Tuition and fees vary according to program. *Financial support:* Fellowships with full tuition reimbursements, research assistantships with partial tuition reimbursements, teaching assistantships, career-related internships or fieldwork, Federal Work-Study, and institutionally sponsored loans available. Support available to part-time students. Financial award application deadline: 2/1; financial award applicants required to submit FAFSA.

Appalachian State University, Cratis D. Williams Graduate School, College of Education, Department of Curriculum and Instruction, Boone, NC 28608. Offers curriculum specialist (MA); educational media (MA); elementary education (MA); secondary education (MA). *Accreditation:* NCATE. Part-time and evening/weekend programs available. Postbaccalaureate distance learning degree programs offered (minimal on-campus study). *Faculty:* 32 full-time (21 women). *Students:* 7 full-time (5 women), 206 part-time (172 women); includes 2 minority (both African Americans), 2 international. 100 applicants, 97% accepted, 95 enrolled. In 2006, 96 degrees awarded. *Degree requirements:* For master's, thesis or alternative, comprehensive exam, registration. *Entrance requirements:* For master's, GRE General Test or MAT. Additional exam requirements/recommendations for international students: Required—TOEFL (minimum score 570 paper-based; 230 computer-based). *Application deadline:* For fall admission, 7/1 priority date for domestic students, 1/1 for international students; for spring admission, 11/1 for domestic students, 6/1 for international students. Application fee: $50. *Expenses:* Tuition, state resident: full-time $2,600; part-time $127 per hour. Tuition, nonresident: full-time $13,200; part-time $597 per hour. Required fees: $2,000; $546 per term. *Financial support:* In 2006–07, 6 teaching assistantships (averaging $7,000 per year) were awarded; fellowships, research assistantships, career-related internships or fieldwork, Federal Work-Study, scholarships/grants, and unspecified assistantships also available. Support available to part-time students. Financial award application deadline: 7/1; financial award applicants required to submit FAFSA. Total annual research expenditures: $366,043. *Unit head:* Dr. Michael Jacobson, Chairperson, 828-262-2224.

Appalachian State University, Cratis D. Williams Graduate School, College of Education, Department of Leadership and Educational Studies, Program in Educational Media, Boone, NC 28608. Offers MA. Part-time and evening/weekend programs available. Postbaccalaureate distance learning degree programs offered (minimal on-campus study). *Students:* 2 full-time (1 woman), 126 part-time (94 women); includes 4 minority (2 African Americans, 2 Hispanic Americans), 3 international. 27 applicants, 100% accepted, 26 enrolled. In 2006, 86 degrees awarded. *Degree requirements:* For master's, comprehensive exam. *Entrance requirements:* For master's, GRE, MAT. *Application deadline:* For fall admission, 7/1 for domestic students; for winter admission, 11/1 for domestic students. Applications are processed on a rolling basis. Application fee: $50. *Expenses:* Tuition, state resident: full-time $2,600; part-time $127 per hour. Tuition, nonresident: full-time $13,200; part-time $597 per hour. Required fees: $2,000; $546 per term. *Financial support:* Research assistantships, career-related internships or fieldwork, Federal Work-Study, scholarships/grants, and unspecified assistantships available. Financial award application deadline: 7/1. *Faculty research:* Mixed media, web-based case analysis. *Unit head:* Dr. Richard Riedl, Director, 828-262-3112, E-mail: reidlr@appstate.edu.

Arcadia University, Graduate Studies, Department of Education, Glenside, PA 19038-3295. Offers art education (M Ed, MA Ed); biology education (MA Ed); chemistry education (MA Ed); child development (CAS); computer education (M Ed, CAS); computer education 7–12 (MA Ed); early childhood education (M Ed, CAS), including individualized (M Ed), master teacher (M Ed), research in child development (M Ed); educational leadership (M Ed, CAS); educational psychology (CAS); elementary education (M Ed, CAS); English education (MA Ed); environmental education (MA Ed, CAS); history education (MA Ed); language arts (M Ed, CAS); mathematics education (M Ed, MA Ed, CAS); music education (MA Ed); psychology (MA Ed); pupil personnel services (CAS); reading (M Ed, CAS); school library science (M Ed); science education (M Ed, CAS); secondary education (M Ed, CAS); special education (M Ed, Ed D, CAS); theater arts (MA Ed); written communication (MA Ed). *Accreditation:* NASAD. Part-time and evening/weekend programs available. Postbaccalaureate distance learning degree programs offered (minimal on-campus study). *Faculty:* 12 full-time (8 women), 38 part-time/adjunct (26 women). *Students:* 60 full-time (56 women), 419 part-time (324 women); includes 70 minority (57 African Americans, 1 American Indian/Alaska Native, 6 Asian Americans or Pacific Islanders, 6 Hispanic Americans), 1 international. In 2006, 257 master's, 4 doctorates awarded. *Application deadline:* Applications are processed on a rolling basis. Application fee: $35. Electronic applications accepted. *Financial support:* Career-related internships or fieldwork, tuition waivers (partial), and unspecified assistantships available. *Unit head:* Dr. Steven P. Gulkus, Chair, 215-572-2120. *Application contact:* 215-572-2925, Fax: 215-572-2126, E-mail: grad@arcadia.edu.

Argosy University, Denver Campus, College of Education, Denver, CO 80203. Offers educational leadership (MA Ed, Ed D), including higher education adminstration (Ed D), K-12 education (Ed D); instructional leadership (MA Ed, Ed D), including higher education (Ed D), K-12 education (Ed D).

See Close-Up on page 829.

Argosy University, Nashville Campus, College of Education, Program in Instructional Leadership, Franklin, TN 37067-7226. Offers higher education administration (Ed D); instructional leadership (MA Ed); K-12 education (Ed D).

Argosy University, Orange County Campus, College of Education, Santa Ana, CA 92704. Offers community college executive leadership (Ed D); educational leadership (MA Ed, Ed D), including higher education administration (Ed D), K-12 education (Ed D); instructional leadership (MA Ed, Ed D), including educational technology (Ed D), higher education (Ed D), K-12 education (Ed D), multiple subject teacher credential preparation (MA Ed), multiple subject teacher credential preparation with BCLAD (MA Ed), single subject teacher credential preparation (MA Ed), single subject teacher credential preparation with BCLAD (MA Ed). Part-time and evening/weekend programs available. *Faculty:* 3 full-time (2 women), 33 part-time/adjunct (15 women). *Students:* 185 full-time (112 women), 49 part-time (28 women). Average age 37. 91 applicants, 76 enrolled. In 2006, 58 master's, 17 doctorates awarded. Terminal master's awarded for partial completion of doctoral program. *Degree requirements:* For master's, comprehensive exam; for doctorate, thesis/dissertation, preliminary and final dissertation defense, comprehensive exam. *Entrance requirements:* For master's, minimum GPA of 3.0 in final 2 years of course work, 3 letters of recommendation, resumé; for doctorate, minimum GPA of 3.0 in graduate study, 3 letters of recommendation, resumé. Additional exam requirements/recommendations for international students: Required—TOEFL. *Application deadline:* Applications are processed on a rolling basis. Application fee: $50. Electronic applications accepted. *Financial support:* Federal Work-Study and scholarships/grants available. Support available to part-time students. Financial award applicants required to submit FAFSA. *Faculty research:* Educational leadership, higher education, qualitative research, K-12 education, multicultural education. *Unit head:* Dr. Christine Zeppos, Dean, 800-7196-9598, Fax: 714-437-1287, E-mail: czeppos@argosy.edu. *Application contact:* Mark Betz, Director of Admissions, 800-716-9598, Fax: 714-437-1697, E-mail: mbetz@argosy.edu.

See Close-Up on page 833.

Argosy University, Sarasota Campus, College of Education, Sarasota, FL 34235-8246. Offers community college educational leadership (Ed D); educational leadership (MA Ed, Ed D, Ed S), including higher education administration (Ed D), K-12 education (Ed D); instructional leadership (MA Ed, Ed D, Ed S), including education technology (Ed D), higher education (Ed D), K-12 education (Ed D). Part-time and evening/weekend programs available. Postbaccalaureate distance learning degree programs offered (minimal on-campus study). *Faculty:* 15 full-time (8 women), 49 part-time/adjunct (21 women). *Students:* 149 applicants, 96% accepted, 121 enrolled. In 2006, 9 master's, 141 doctorates awarded. *Degree requirements:* For doctorate, thesis/dissertation, comprehensive exam. *Entrance requirements:* For doctorate, minimum undergraduate GPA of 3.0. Additional exam requirements/recommendations for international students: Required—TOEFL. *Application deadline:* Applications are processed on a rolling basis. Application fee: $50. Electronic applications accepted. *Expenses:* Contact institution. *Financial support:* Federal Work-Study available. Support available to part-time students. Financial award application deadline: 4/1; financial award applicants required to submit FAFSA. *Unit head:* Dr. Chuck Mlynarczyk, Dean, 800-331-5995, Fax: 941-371-9464, E-mail: cmlynarczyk@argosy.edu. *Application contact:* Admissions Representative, 800-331-5995 Ext. 221, Fax: 941-371-8910.

See Close-Up on page 843.

Argosy University, Seattle Campus, College of Education, Seattle, WA 98121. Offers community college executive leadership (Ed D); education (MA Ed); educational leadership (MA Ed, Ed D), including higher education administration (Ed D), K-12 education (Ed D); instructional leadership (MA Ed, Ed D), including education technology (Ed D), higher education (Ed D), K-12 education (Ed D). Part-time and evening/weekend programs available. *Students:* 29 full-time, 15 part-time. *Degree requirements:* For master's, thesis or alternative, capstone project; for doctorate, thesis/dissertation, comprehensive exam, registration. *Entrance requirements:* For master's, minimum GPA of 3.0 in last 60 hours of course work or minimum cumulative GPA of 2.7; for doctorate, minimum GPA of 3.0. Additional exam requirements/recommendations for international students: Required—TOEFL (minimum score 550 paper-based; 213 computer-based). *Application deadline:* For fall admission, 4/15 priority date for domestic students, 4/15 for international students. Application fee: $50. *Expenses:* Contact institution. *Financial support:* Teaching assistantships with partial tuition reimbursements, Federal Work-Study, scholarships/grants, and unspecified assistantships available. Support available to part-time students. Financial award application deadline: 4/19; financial award applicants required to submit FAFSA. *Unit head:* Dr. Leslie Aune Oja, Chair of Education, 206-393-3570, Fax: 206-283-5777, E-mail: ioja@argosy.edu. *Application contact:* Josh Pond, Director of Admissions, 206-283-4500, Fax: 206-283-5777, E-mail: jpond@argosyu.edu.

See Close-Up on page 847.

Educational Media/Instructional Technology

Argosy University, Twin Cities Campus, College of Education, Eagan, MN 55121. Offers educational leadership (MA Ed, Ed D, Ed S), including higher education administration (Ed D), K-12 education (Ed D); instructional leadership (MA Ed, Ed D, Ed S), including education technology (Ed D), higher education (Ed D), K-12 education (Ed D). Part-time and evening/weekend programs available. *Faculty:* 1 full-time (0 women), 10 part-time/adjunct (4 women). *Students:* 30 full-time (22 women), 12 part-time (9 women); includes 3 minority (1 African American, 1 American Indian/Alaska Native, 1 Asian American or Pacific Islander). Average age 45. 35 applicants, 86% accepted, 12 enrolled. In 2006, 1 master's, 6 doctorates awarded. *Degree requirements:* For doctorate, thesis/dissertation, comprehensive exam. *Entrance requirements:* For master's, 3 letters of recommendation, minimum undergraduate GPA of 3.0, resumé; for doctorate, 3 letters of recommendation, master's degree, minimum GPA of 3.0, resumé. Additional exam requirements/recommendations for international students: Required—TOEFL (minimum score 550 paper-based; 213 computer-based). *Application deadline:* For fall admission, 5/15 priority date for domestic students, 5/15 for international students; for spring admission, 10/15 priority date for domestic students, 10/15 for international students. Applications are processed on a rolling basis. Application fee: $50. Electronic applications accepted. *Financial support:* In 2006–07, 12 fellowships with partial tuition reimbursements, 3 teaching assistantships with partial tuition reimbursements were awarded; Federal Work-Study and scholarships/grants also available. Financial award applicants required to submit FAFSA. *Unit head:* Dr. David Lange, Program Chair, 888-844-2004. *Application contact:* Jennifer Radke, 2nd Director of Graduate Admissions, 651-846-3300, Fax: 651-994-7954, E-mail: tcadmissions@argosy.edu.

See Close-Up on page 851.

Arizona State University, Division of Graduate Studies, College of Education, Division of Psychology in Education, Academic Program of Learning and Instructional Technology, Tempe, AZ 85287. Offers M Ed, MA, PhD. *Degree requirements:* For master's, thesis or alternative; for doctorate, thesis/dissertation. *Entrance requirements:* For master's and doctorate, GRE General Test or MAT.

Ashland University, College of Education, Graduate Studies in Education, Department of Curriculum and Instruction, Ashland, OH 44805-3702. Offers educational technology (M Ed); intervention specialist-mild/moderate (M Ed); intervention specialist-moderate/intensive (M Ed); middle school education (M Ed); talent development (M Ed). *Accreditation:* NCATE. Part-time and evening/weekend programs available. *Faculty:* 11 full-time (7 women), 93 part-time/adjunct (54 women). *Students:* 188 full-time (161 women), 354 part-time (314 women); includes 25 minority (19 African Americans, 3 Asian Americans or Pacific Islanders, 3 Hispanic Americans), 1 international. Average age 32. In 2006, 220 degrees awarded. *Degree requirements:* For master's, thesis or alternative, internship, practicum, seminar. *Entrance requirements:* For master's, GRE General Test or MAT, teaching certificate, minimum GPA of 2.75 (or 2.5 with 2.75 in education or major subject field). Additional exam requirements/recommendations for international students: Required—TOEFL. *Application deadline:* For fall admission, 8/27 for domestic students; for spring admission, 1/14 for domestic students. Applications are processed on a rolling basis. Application fee: $30. *Expenses:* Tuition: Part-time $403 per credit. Tuition and fees vary according to degree level and program. *Financial support:* In 2006–07, 189 students received support. Institutionally sponsored loans and scholarships/grants available. Financial award application deadline: 4/15. *Faculty research:* Gender equity, postmodern children's and young adult literature, outdoor/experimental education, re-examining literature study in middle grades, morality and giftedness. *Unit head:* Dr. James P. Van Keuren, Chair, 419-289-5377, Fax: 419-207-4949, E-mail: jvankeu1@ashland.edu.

Auburn University, Graduate School, College of Education, Department of Educational Foundations, Leadership, and Technology, Auburn University, AL 36849. Offers adult education (M Ed, MS, Ed D); curriculum and instruction (M Ed, MS, Ed D, Ed S); curriculum supervision (M Ed, MS, Ed D, Ed S); educational psychology (PhD); higher education administration (M Ed, MS, Ed D, Ed S); media instructional design (MS); media specialist (M Ed); school administration (M Ed, MS, Ed D, Ed S). *Accreditation:* NCATE. Part-time programs available. *Faculty:* 23 full-time (11 women). *Students:* 40 full-time (26 women), 148 part-time (93 women); includes 64 minority (60 African Americans, 3 American Indian/Alaska Native, 1 Asian American or Pacific Islander), 6 international. Average age 38. 99 applicants, 57% accepted, 37 enrolled. In 2006, 32 master's, 10 doctorates, 7 other advanced degrees awarded. *Degree requirements:* For master's, thesis (for some programs); for doctorate, thesis/dissertation; for Ed S, field project. *Entrance requirements:* For master's, doctorate, and Ed S, GRE General Test. *Application deadline:* For fall admission, 7/7 for domestic students; for spring admission, 11/24 for domestic students. Applications are processed on a rolling basis. Application fee: $25 ($50 for international students). Electronic applications accepted. *Expenses:* Tuition, state resident: full-time $5,000. Tuition, nonresident: full-time $15,000. Required fees: $416. Tuition and fees vary according to program. *Financial support:* Teaching assistantships, Federal Work-Study available. Support available to part-time students. Financial award application deadline: 3/15. *Unit head:* Dr. William A. Spencer, Head, 334-844-4460. *Application contact:* Dr. Joe Pittman, Interim Dean of the Graduate School, 334-844-4700.

Azusa Pacific University, School of Education, Department of Advanced Studies, Program in Educational Technology, Azusa, CA 91702-7000. Offers M Ed. Part-time and evening/weekend programs available. In 2006, 48 degrees awarded. *Degree requirements:* For master's, core exam, oral presentation. *Entrance requirements:* For master's, 12 units of course work in education, minimum GPA of 3.0. Application fee: $45 ($65 for international students). *Expenses:* Tuition: Part-time $475 per credit. *Unit head:* Joanne Gilbreath, Director, 626-815-5059, E-mail: jgilbreath@apu.edu.

Baldwin-Wallace College, Graduate Programs, Division of Education, Specialization in Educational Technology, Berea, OH 44017-2088. Offers MA Ed. *Students:* 15 full-time (9 women), 54 part-time (39 women); includes 8 minority (3 African Americans, 4 Asian Americans or Pacific Islanders, 1 Hispanic American). Average age 32. 54 applicants, 83% accepted, 31 enrolled. In 2006, 29 degrees awarded. *Degree requirements:* For master's, comprehensive exam. *Entrance requirements:* For master's, bachelor's degree in field, MAT or minimum GPA of 2.75. *Application deadline:* For fall admission, 8/15 priority date for domestic students; for spring admission, 12/15 priority date for domestic students. Applications are processed on a rolling basis. Application fee: $25. Electronic applications accepted. *Expenses:* Tuition: Part-time $760 per credit hour. Tuition and fees vary according to program. *Application contact:* Winifred W. Gerhardt, Director of Admission for the Evening and Weekend College, 440-826-2222, Fax: 440-826-3830, E-mail: admission@bw.edu.

Barry University, School of Education, Graduate Certificate Programs, Miami Shores, FL 33161-6695. Offers advanced teaching and learning with technology (Certificate); distance education (Certificate); higher education technology integration (Certificate); human resources: not for profit and religious organizations (Certificate); K-12 technology integration (Certificate). *Application contact:* Dave Fletcher, Director of Graduate Admissions, 305-899-3113, Fax: 305-899-2971, E-mail: dfletcher@mail.barry.edu.

Barry University, School of Education, Program in Educational Technology Applications, Miami Shores, FL 33161-6695. Offers educational computing and technology (MS, Ed S). Part-time and evening/weekend programs available. Postbaccalaureate distance learning degree programs offered (minimal on-campus study). *Students:* 1 (woman) full-time, 30 part-time (20 women); includes 20 minority (6 African Americans, 14 Hispanic Americans). 35 applicants, 66% accepted, 10 enrolled. In 2006, 15 master's, 2 other advanced degrees awarded. *Degree requirements:* For master's and Ed S, comprehensive exam. *Entrance requirements:* For master's, GRE General Test or MAT, minimum GPA of 3.0; for Ed S, GRE General Test, minimum GPA of 3.0. *Application deadline:* For fall admission, 5/1 for domestic students. Applications are processed on a rolling basis. Application fee: $30. *Unit head:* Dr. Joel Levine, Director, 305-899-3608, Fax: 305-899-4708, E-mail: jlevine@mail.barry.edu. *Application contact:* Dave Fletcher, Director of Graduate Admissions, 305-899-3113, Fax: 305-899-2971, E-mail: dfletcher@mail.barry.edu.

Barry University, School of Education, Program in Leadership and Education, Miami Shores, FL 33161-6695. Offers educational technology (PhD); exceptional student education (PhD); higher education administration (PhD); human resource development (PhD); leadership (PhD). Part-time and evening/weekend programs available. *Students:* 15 full-time (7 women), 233 part-time (147 women); includes 97 minority (52 African Americans, 45 Hispanic Americans), 7 international. 58 applicants, 34% accepted, 18 enrolled. In 2006, 23 degrees awarded. *Degree requirements:* For doctorate, thesis/dissertation. *Entrance requirements:* For doctorate, GRE General Test, minimum GPA of 3.25. *Application deadline:* For fall admission, 5/1 priority date for domestic students. Applications are processed on a rolling basis. Application fee: $30. Electronic applications accepted. *Unit head:* Dr. Carmen McCrink, Director, 305-899-3702, Fax: 305-899-4708, E-mail: cmccrink@mail.barry.edu. *Application contact:* Dave Fletcher, Director of Graduate Admissions, 305-899-3113, Fax: 305-899-2971, E-mail: dfletcher@mail.barry.edu.

Barry University, School of Education, Program in Technology and TESOL, Miami Shores, FL 33161-6695. Offers MS, Ed S. *Unit head:* Dr. Rita Oates, Director, 305-899-3740, Fax: 305-899-4708, E-mail: roates@mail.barry.edu. *Application contact:* Dave Fletcher, Director of Graduate Admissions, 305-899-3113, Fax: 305-899-2971, E-mail: dfletcher@mail.barry.edu.

Belmont University, College of Arts and Sciences, School of Education, Nashville, TN 37212-3757. Offers education (MAT); elementary education (M Ed), including early childhood education, elementary education, gifted education, language arts education; English (M Ed); history (M Ed); mathematics (M Ed); middle grade education (M Ed); science (M Ed); secondary education (M Ed), including gifted education; sports administration (MSA); technology (M Ed). *Accreditation:* NCATE. Part-time and evening/weekend programs available. *Faculty:* 9 full-time (7 women), 20 part-time/adjunct (15 women). *Students:* 50 full-time (36 women), 116 part-time (76 women); includes 23 minority (20 African Americans, 1 Asian American or Pacific Islander, 2 Hispanic Americans), 1 international. Average age 30. 55 applicants, 60% accepted, 30 enrolled. In 2006, 82 degrees awarded. *Degree requirements:* For master's, thesis, comprehensive exam. *Entrance requirements:* For master's, MAT or GRE, minimum GPA of 2.75. Additional exam requirements/recommendations for international students: Required—TOEFL. *Application deadline:* For fall admission, 8/1 priority date for domestic students, 5/1 for international students; for spring admission, 12/1 priority date for domestic students, 9/1 for international students. Applications are processed on a rolling basis. Application fee: $50. *Expenses: Contact institution. Financial support:* In 2006–07, 25 students received support; fellowships with partial tuition reimbursements available, institutionally sponsored loans and tuition waivers (partial) available. Financial award application deadline: 4/15; financial award applicants required to submit FAFSA. *Faculty research:* Technology grant, professional development schools. Total annual research expenditures: $6,500. *Unit head:* Dr. Trevor F. Hutchins, Associate Dean, 615-460-6232, Fax: 615-460-6414, E-mail: hutchinst@mail.belmont.edu. *Application contact:* Julie Hullett, Admission/Licensure Officer, 615-460-6879, Fax: 615-460-5556, E-mail: hullettj@email.belmont.edu.

Bloomsburg University of Pennsylvania, School of Graduate Studies, College of Science and Technology, Department of Instructional Technology, Bloomsburg, PA 17815-1301. Offers instructional technology (MS), including corporate track, education track, eLearning certificate. Postbaccalaureate distance learning degree programs offered (no on-campus study). *Faculty:* 4 full-time (1 woman). *Students:* 39 full-time (17 women), 73 part-time (45 women); includes 9 minority (6 African Americans, 1 Asian American or Pacific Islander, 2 Hispanic Americans), 11 international. Average age 31. 53 applicants, 100% accepted, 43 enrolled. In 2006, 53 degrees awarded. *Degree requirements:* For master's, thesis or alternative. *Entrance requirements:* For master's, minimum QPA of 3.0, 3 letters of recommendation. Additional exam requirements/recommendations for international students: Required—TOEFL (minimum score 550 paper-based; 213 computer-based; 79 iBT). *Application deadline:* Applications are processed on a rolling basis. Application fee: $30. Electronic applications accepted. *Expenses:* Tuition, state resident: full-time $6,048; part-time $336 per credit. Tuition, nonresident: full-time $9,678; part-time $538 per credit. Required fees: $1,415. *Financial support:* Career-related internships or fieldwork and unspecified assistantships available. *Faculty research:* Instructional design and computing, interactive graphics, authoring tools. *Unit head:* Dr. Timothy Phillips, Coordinator, 570-389-4506, Fax: 570-389-4943, E-mail: tphillip@bloomu.edu.

Boise State University, Graduate College, College of Education, Programs in Teacher Education, Department of Educational Technology, Boise, ID 83725-0399. Offers MET, MS, MS Ed. *Accreditation:* NCATE. Part-time programs available. Postbaccalaureate distance learning degree programs offered (no on-campus study). *Faculty:* 3 full-time (2 women), 5 part-time/adjunct (3 women). *Students:* 2 full-time (both women), 129 part-time (70 women); includes 5 minority (1 African American, 2 Asian Americans or Pacific Islanders, 2 Hispanic Americans). Average age 37. 25 applicants, 96% accepted, 10 enrolled. In 2006, 32 degrees awarded. *Degree requirements:* For master's, thesis optional. *Entrance requirements:* For master's, minimum GPA of 3.0. *Application deadline:* For fall admission, 7/1 priority date for domestic students; for spring admission, 11/15 priority date for domestic students. Applications are processed on a rolling basis. Application fee: $0. Electronic applications accepted. *Financial support:* Career-related internships or fieldwork, Federal Work-Study, institutionally sponsored loans, and unspecified assistantships available. Support available to part-time students. Financial award application deadline: 3/1. *Unit head:* Dr. Lisa Dawley, Chair, 208-426-5430, E-mail: lisadawley@boisestate.edu.

Boise State University, Graduate College, College of Engineering, Department of Instructional and Performance Technology, Boise, ID 83725-0399. Offers MS. Part-time programs available. Postbaccalaureate distance learning degree programs offered (no on-campus study). *Faculty:* 5 full-time (1 woman), 23 part-time/adjunct (12 women). *Students:* 14 full-time (9 women), 181 part-time (103 women); includes 18 minority (10 African Americans, 1 American Indian/Alaska Native, 5 Asian Americans or Pacific Islanders, 2 Hispanic Americans), 7 international. Average age 40. 52 applicants, 98% accepted, 34 enrolled. In 2006, 55 degrees awarded. *Degree requirements:* For master's, thesis optional. *Entrance requirements:* For master's, minimum GPA of 3.0. *Application deadline:* For fall admission, 3/1 priority date for domestic students; for spring admission, 10/1 priority date for domestic students. Applications are processed on a rolling basis. Application fee: $0. Electronic applications accepted. *Financial support:* In 2006–07, 5 students received support, including 4 research assistantships with full tuition reimbursements available (averaging $8,633 per year); career-related internships or fieldwork, Federal Work-Study, institutionally sponsored loans, tuition waivers (full), and unspecified assistantships also available. Support available to part-time students. Financial award application deadline: 3/1. *Unit head:* Donald Stepich, Chair, 208-426-3840, Fax: 208-426-1970.

Boston University, School of Education, Department of Curriculum and Teaching, Program in Educational Media and Technology, Boston, MA 02215. Offers Ed M, Ed D, CAGS. *Students:* 6 full-time (5 women), 16 part-time (12 women); includes 2 minority (1 Asian American or Pacific Islander, 1 Hispanic American), 5 international. Average age 31. 47 applicants, 87% accepted. In 2006, 18 master's, 1 other advanced degree awarded. *Degree requirements:* For master's, thesis optional; for doctorate, thesis/dissertation, comprehensive exam. *Entrance requirements:* For master's, doctorate, and CAGS, GRE General Test or MAT. Additional exam requirements/recommendations for international students: Required—TOEFL. *Application deadline:* For fall admission, 2/15 priority date for domestic students; for winter admission, 11/1 priority date for domestic students. Applications are processed on a rolling basis. Application fee: $70. Electronic applications accepted. *Expenses:* Tuition: Full-time $33,330; part-time $1,042 per credit. Required fees: $462; $40. *Financial support:* Application deadline: 2/15. *Faculty research:* Facilities design, program evaluation, human factors, computer-based technologies. *Unit head:* Dr. David Whittier, Coordinator, 617-353-3181, E-mail: whittier@bu.edu. *Application contact:* 617-353-4237, Fax: 617-353-8937, E-mail: sedgrad@bu.edu.

Bowling Green State University, Graduate College, College of Education and Human Development, School of Education and Intervention Services, Intervention Services Division, Program in Special Education, Bowling Green, OH 43403. Offers assistive technology (M Ed); early childhood intervention (M Ed); gifted education (M Ed); hearing impaired intervention (M Ed); mild/moderate intervention (M Ed); moderate/intensive intervention (M Ed). *Accreditation:* NCATE. Part-time programs available. *Students:* 26 full-time (21 women), 84 part-time (78 women); includes 4 minority (all African Americans) Average age 35. 39 applicants, 87% accepted, 12 enrolled. In 2006, 47 degrees awarded. *Degree requirements:* For master's, thesis or alternative. *Entrance requirements:* For master's, GRE General Test. Additional exam requirements/recommendations for international students: Required—TOEFL. *Application deadline:* For fall admission, 3/1 priority date for domestic students. Applications are processed on a rolling basis. Application fee: $30. Electronic applications accepted. *Expenses:* Tuition, state resident: part-time $535 per hour. Tuition, nonresident: part-time $884 per hour. *Financial support:* In 2006–07, 16 research assistantships with full tuition reimbursements (averaging $5,202 per year) were awarded; teaching assistantships with full tuition reimbursements, Federal Work-Study and unspecified assistantships also available. Financial award applicants required to submit FAFSA. *Faculty research:* Reading and special populations, deafness, early childhood, gifted and talented, behavior disorders. *Application contact:* Dr. Lessie Cochran, Graduate Coordinator, 419-372-7298.

Bowling Green State University, Graduate College, College of Education and Human Development, School of Education and Intervention Services, Teacher and Learning Division, Program in Classroom Technology, Bowling Green, OH 43403. Offers M Ed. *Accreditation:* NCATE. Part-time and evening/weekend programs available. *Students:* Average age 34. 11 applicants, 100% accepted, 7 enrolled. In 2006, 27 degrees awarded. *Degree requirements:* For master's, thesis or alternative. *Entrance requirements:* For master's, GRE General Test. Additional exam requirements/recommendations for international students: Required—TOEFL. *Application deadline:* Applications are processed on a rolling basis. Application fee: $30. Electronic applications accepted. *Expenses:* Tuition, state resident: part-time $535 per hour. Tuition, nonresident: part-time $884 per hour. *Financial support:* Research assistantships with full tuition reimbursements, teaching assistantships with full tuition reimbursements, career-related internships or fieldwork, Federal Work-Study, and institutionally sponsored loans available. Financial award applicants required to submit FAFSA. *Unit head:* Dr. Gregg Brownell, Graduate Coordinator, 419-372-9546.

Bridgewater State College, School of Graduate Studies, School of Education and Allied Science, Department of Secondary Education and Professional Programs, Program in Instructional Technology, Bridgewater, MA 02325-0001. Offers M Ed. Part-time and evening/weekend programs available. *Entrance requirements:* For master's, GRE General Test or Massachusetts Test for Educator Licensure. *Application deadline:* For fall admission, 3/1 priority date for domestic students; for spring admission, 10/1 priority date for domestic students. Application fee: $50. *Financial support:* Career-related internships or fieldwork, health care benefits, and unspecified assistantships available. Support available to part-time students. *Application contact:* Dr. Raymond Charles Guillette, Assistant Dean School of Graduate Studies, 508-531-2919, Fax: 508-531-6162, E-mail: rguillette@bridgew.edu.

Brigham Young University, Graduate Studies, David O. McKay School of Education, Department of Instructional Psychology and Technology, Provo, UT 84602-1001. Offers MS, PhD. *Faculty:* 9 full-time (0 women), 10 part-time/adjunct (2 women). *Students:* 48 full-time (24 women), 24 part-time (10 women); includes 1 minority (Asian American or Pacific Islander), 13 international. Average age 36. 43 applicants, 42% accepted, 14 enrolled. In 2006, 5 master's, 6 doctorates awarded. *Median time to degree:* Of those who began their doctoral program in fall 1998, 50% received their degree in 8 years or less. *Degree requirements:* For master's, thesis/dissertation; for doctorate, thesis/dissertation, comprehensive exam. *Entrance requirements:* For master's and doctorate, GRE General Test. Additional exam requirements/recommendations for international students: Required—TOEFL. *Application deadline:* For fall and winter admission, 2/1 for domestic and international students. Application fee: $50. Electronic applications accepted. *Financial support:* In 2006–07, 23 students received support, including 6 research assistantships with full and partial tuition reimbursements available (averaging $10,000 per year), 14 teaching assistantships with full and partial tuition reimbursements available (averaging $6,000 per year); career-related internships or fieldwork, tuition waivers (full and partial), and unspecified assistantships also available. Support available to part-time students. *Faculty research:* Interactive learning, learning theory, instructional designed development, research and evaluation, measurement. Total annual research expenditures: $2,520. *Unit head:* Dr. Andrew S. Gibbons, Chair, 801-422-5097, Fax: 801-422-0314, E-mail: andy_gibbons@byu.edu. *Application contact:* Michele Bray, Department Secretary, 801-422-2746, Fax: 801-422-0314, E-mail: michele_bray@byu.edu.

Brigham Young University, Graduate Studies, Ira A. Fulton College of Engineering and Technology, School of Technology, Provo, UT 84602-1001. Offers construction management (MS); information technology (MS); manufacturing systems (MS); technology teacher education (MS). *Faculty:* 25 full-time (0 women). *Students:* 30 full-time (1 woman), 15 part-time (1 woman); includes 3 minority (1 American Indian/Alaska Native, 1 Asian American or Pacific Islander, 1 Hispanic American). Average age 25. 14 applicants, 71% accepted, 8 enrolled. In 2006, 19 degrees awarded. *Degree requirements:* For master's, thesis. *Entrance requirements:* For master's, GRE General Test, GMAT (construction management), minimum GPA of 3.0 in last 60 hours of course work. Additional exam requirements/recommendations for international students: Required—TOEFL (minimum score 580 paper-based; 237 computer-based; 85 iBT). *Application deadline:* For fall admission, 2/15 for domestic and international students; for winter admission, 9/15 for domestic and international students. Application fee: $50. Electronic applications accepted. *Financial support:* In 2006–07, 35 students received support, including 5 research assistantships (averaging $2,530 per year), 9 teaching assistantships (averaging $3,600 per year); fellowships, career-related internships or fieldwork also available. Financial award application deadline: 3/15. *Faculty research:* Real time process control in IT, electronic physical design, processing and non-linear systems, networking, computerized systems in CM. Total annual research expenditures: $52,110. *Unit head:* Val D. Hawks, Director, 801-422-6300, Fax: 801-422-0490, E-mail: hawksv@byu.edu. *Application contact:* Barry M. Lunt, Graduate Coordinator, 801-422-2264, Fax: 801-422-0490, E-mail: ralowe@byu.edu.

Buffalo State College, State University of New York, Graduate Studies and Research, Faculty of Applied Science and Education, Department of Computer Information Systems, Program in Educational Computing, Buffalo, NY 14222-1095. Offers MS Ed. *Accreditation:* NCATE. Part-time and evening/weekend programs available. *Degree requirements:* For master's, thesis, project. *Entrance requirements:* Additional exam requirements/recommendations for international students: Required—TOEFL (minimum score 550 paper-based; 213 computer-based).

Cabrini College, Graduate and Professional Studies, Radnor, PA 19087-3698. Offers biotechnology (Certificate); education (M Ed); educational leadership (Certificate); instructional systems technology (MS); organization leadership (MS); project management (Certificate). Part-time and evening/weekend programs available. *Faculty:* 11 full-time (7 women), 25 part-time/adjunct (11 women). *Students:* 91 full-time (63 women), 484 part-time (364 women); includes 43 minority (28 African Americans, 6 Asian Americans or Pacific Islanders, 9 Hispanic Americans), 6 international. Average age 32. In 2006, 143 degrees awarded. *Degree requirements:* For master's, thesis optional. *Entrance requirements:* For master's, GRE and/or MAT (in some cases), letter of recommendation, minimum GPA of 2.5. *Application deadline:* For fall admission, 7/29 priority date for domestic students; for spring admission, 12/9 for domestic students. Applications are processed on a rolling basis. Application fee: $50. Electronic applications accepted. *Expenses:* Tuition: Part-time $310 per credit. Required fees: $45 per term. Tuition and fees vary according to course load. *Financial support:* Career-related internships or fieldwork and unspecified assistantships available. Support available to part-time students. Financial award applicants required to submit FAFSA. *Faculty research:* Qualitative research in reading, ethnographic studies. *Unit head:* Dr. Michael W. Markowitz, Dean for Graduate and Professional Studies, 610-902-8501, Fax: 610-902-8522, E-mail: michael.w.markowitz@cabrini.edu. *Application contact:* Bruce D. Bryde, Director of Enrollment and Recruiting, 610-902-8291, Fax: 610-902-8522, E-mail: bruce.d.bryde@cabrini.edu.

California Baptist University, Program in Education, Riverside, CA 92504-3206. Offers cross-cultural language and academic development (MA Ed); educational leadership (MS Ed); educational technology (MS Ed); instructional computer applications (MS Ed); reading (MS Ed); special education (MS Ed); teaching (MS Ed). Part-time programs available. *Faculty:* 16 full-time (10 women), 16 part-time/adjunct (13 women). *Students:* 77 full-time (64 women), 408 part-time (342 women); includes 157 minority (41 African Americans, 12 American Indian/Alaska Native, 18 Asian Americans or Pacific Islanders, 86 Hispanic Americans), 2 international. 282 applicants, 70% accepted, 171 enrolled. In 2006, 63 degrees awarded. *Degree requirements:* For master's, thesis optional. *Entrance requirements:* For master's, minimum undergraduate GPA of 2.75, 12 semester hours of course work in education. Additional exam requirements/recommendations for international students: Required—TOEFL (minimum score 575 paper-based; 230 computer-based), IELTS (minimum score 7). *Application deadline:* For fall admission, 9/1 for domestic students, 7/15 priority date for international students; for spring admission, 1/3 for domestic students, 11/1 priority date for international students. Applications are processed on a rolling basis. Application fee: $45. Electronic applications accepted. *Expenses:* Tuition: Full-time $7,812; part-time $434 per unit. Required fees: $120 per semester. Tuition and fees vary according to program. *Financial support:* In 2006–07, 19 students received support. Career-related internships or fieldwork, Federal Work-Study, and scholarships/grants available. Support available to part-time students. Financial award applicants required to submit FAFSA. *Unit head:* Dr. Mary Crist, Dean, School of Education, 951-343-4313, Fax: 951-343-4516, E-mail: mcrist@calbaptist.edu. *Application contact:* Gail Ronveaux, Dean of Graduate Enrollment, 951-343-5045, Fax: 951-343-5095, E-mail: graduateadmissions@calbaptist.edu.

California State University, Chico, Graduate School, College of Communication and Education, Department of Communication Design, Chico, CA 95929-0504. Offers instructional technology (MS). *Students:* 5 full-time (1 woman), 4 part-time (2 women); includes 1 minority (Asian American or Pacific Islander) Average age 38. 1 applicant, 0% accepted. In 2006, 32 degrees awarded. *Degree requirements:* For master's, thesis or alternative, oral exam. *Entrance requirements:* For master's, GRE General Test or MAT, portfolio or sample of written or media work, 3 letters of recommendation. Additional exam requirements/recommendations for international students: Required—TOEFL (minimum score 550 paper-based; 213 computer-based). *Application deadline:* For fall admission, 3/1 for domestic and international students; for spring admission, 9/15 for domestic and international students. Applications are processed on a rolling basis. Application fee: $55. Electronic applications accepted. *Financial support:* Career-related internships or fieldwork available. *Unit head:* Dr. John Long, Chair, 530-898-4048. *Application contact:* Tom Welsh, Graduate Coordinator, 530-898-6048.

California State University, East Bay, Academic Programs and Graduate Studies, College of Education and Allied Studies, Department of Teacher Education, Hayward, CA 94542-3000. Offers education (MS), including curriculum, educational technology leadership, reading. *Faculty:* 8 full-time, 9 part-time/adjunct. *Students:* 58 full-time (41 women), 153 part-time (115 women); includes 67 minority (18 African Americans, 3 American Indian/Alaska Native, 21 Asian Americans or Pacific Islanders, 25 Hispanic Americans), 3 international. Average age 37. 98 applicants, 74% accepted, 54 enrolled. In 2006, 65 degrees awarded. *Degree requirements:* For master's, project or thesis. *Entrance requirements:* For master's, minimum GPA of 3.0 in field, 2.5 overall; teaching experience. Additional exam requirements/recommendations for international students: Required—TOEFL (minimum score 550 paper-based; 213 computer-based). *Application deadline:* For fall admission, 5/31 for domestic students, 4/30 for international students; for winter admission, 9/30 for domestic and international students; for spring admission, 12/31 for domestic students, 11/30 for international students. Application fee: $55. Electronic applications accepted. *Financial support:* Career-related internships or fieldwork, Federal Work-Study, and institutionally sponsored loans available. Support available to part-time students. Financial award application deadline: 3/2. *Unit head:* Dr. James Zarillo, Chair, 510-885-7439, E-mail: james.zarillo@csueastbay.edu. *Application contact:* My Huynh, Graduate Prospect Specialist, 510-885-2989, Fax: 510-885-4059, E-mail: my.huynh@csueastbay.edu.

California State University, Fullerton, Graduate Studies, College of Education, Program of Instructional Design and Technology, Fullerton, CA 92834-9480. Offers MS. *Students:* 1 (woman) full-time, 43 part-time (21 women); includes 10 minority (1 African American, 5 Asian Americans or Pacific Islanders, 4 Hispanic Americans). Average age 39. 42 applicants, 62% accepted, 25 enrolled. In 2006, 17 degrees awarded. Application fee: $55. *Expenses:* Tuition, nonresident: part-time $339 per unit. Required fees: $1,155 per semester. *Unit head:* Dr. Jo Ann Carter-Wells, Chair.

California State University, Los Angeles, Graduate Studies, Charter College of Education, Division of Applied and Advanced Studies in Education, Major in Instructional Technology, Los Angeles, CA 90032-8530. Offers MA. *Students:* 2 full-time (1 woman), 11 part-time (6 women); includes 6 minority (1 Asian American or Pacific Islander, 5 Hispanic Americans), 3 international. In 2006, 14 degrees awarded. *Entrance requirements:* For master's, minimum GPA of 2.75 in last 90 units of course work, teaching certificate. Additional exam requirements/recommendations for international students: Required—TOEFL. *Application deadline:* For fall admission, 6/30 for domestic students; for spring admission, 2/1 for domestic students. Applications are processed on a rolling basis. Application fee: $55. *Expenses:* Tuition, nonresident: part-time $226 per unit. *Financial support:* Application deadline: 3/1. *Unit head:* Dr. Chogollah Maroufi, Chair, Division of Applied and Advanced Studies in Education, 323-343-4330, Fax: 323-343-5336.

California State University, San Bernardino, Graduate Studies, College of Education, Program in Instructional Technology, San Bernardino, CA 92407-2397. Offers MA. *Students:* 23 full-time (14 women), 28 part-time (11 women); includes 21 minority (4 African Americans, 1 American Indian/Alaska Native, 6 Asian Americans or Pacific Islanders, 10 Hispanic Americans). Average age 32. 19 applicants, 58% accepted, 5 enrolled. In 2006, 17 degrees awarded. *Application deadline:* For fall admission, 8/31 priority date for domestic students. Application fee: $55. *Unit head:* Dr. Herbert Brunkhorst, Chair, 909-537-5290, Fax: 909-537-7522, E-mail: hkbrunkh@csusb.edu.

Cape Breton University, School of Education, Health, and Wellness, Sydney, NS B1P 6L2, Canada. Offers educational counseling (Diploma); educational studies-arts education (Certificate); educational technology (Diploma). Part-time and evening/weekend programs available. Postbaccalaureate distance learning degree programs offered (no on-campus study). Electronic applications accepted.

Capella University, School of Education, Minneapolis, MN 55402. Offers college teaching (Certificate); curriculum and instruction (MS, PhD); education (MS); enrollment management (MS); instructional design for online learning (MS, PhD); k-12 studies in education (MS, PhD); leadership for higher education (MS, PhD); leadership in education administration (Certificate); leadership in educational administration (MS, PhD); postsecondary and adult education (MS, PhD); professional studies in education (MS, PhD); reading and literacy (MS); training and performance improvement (MS, PhD). Part-time and evening/weekend programs available. Postbaccalaureate distance learning degree programs offered (minimal on-campus study). Terminal master's awarded for partial completion of doctoral program. *Degree requirements:* For master's, integrative project, thesis optional; for doctorate, thesis/dissertation, comprehensive exam, registration. *Entrance requirements:* Additional exam requirements/recommendations for international students: Required—TOEFL (minimum score 550 paper-based; 213 computer-based), TWE (minimum score 4). Electronic applications accepted. *Faculty research:* Higher education administration, distance learning, adult education, training and curriculum design.

Carlow University, School of Education, Program in Education, Pittsburgh, PA 15213-3165. Offers elementary education (M Ed); instructional technology specialist (M Ed); secondary education (M Ed); special education (M Ed). Part-time and evening/weekend programs available. *Entrance requirements:* For master's, resumé, 3 letters of recommendation, minimum GPA of 3.0, interview. Electronic applications accepted.

Central Connecticut State University, School of Graduate Studies, School of Education and Professional Studies, Department of Educational Leadership, Program in Educational Technol-

Educational Media/Instructional Technology

Central Connecticut State University (continued)

ogy and Media, New Britain, CT 06050-4010. Offers MS. Part-time and evening/weekend programs available. *Students:* 18 applicants, 89% accepted, 12 enrolled. In 2006, 19 degrees awarded. *Degree requirements:* For master's, thesis or alternative, comprehensive exam or special project. *Entrance requirements:* For master's, minimum GPA of 2.7. Additional exam requirements/recommendations for international students: Required—TOEFL. *Application deadline:* For fall admission, 7/1 for domestic students; for spring admission, 12/1 for domestic students. Applications are processed on a rolling basis. Application fee: $50. Electronic applications accepted. *Expenses:* Tuition, area resident: Full-time $3,970; part-time $380 per credit. Tuition, state resident: full-time $5,955; part-time $380 per credit. Tuition, nonresident: full-time $11,061; part-time $380 per credit. Required fees: $3,189. One-time fee: $62 part-time. Tuition and fees vary according to degree level and program. *Faculty research:* Design and development of multimedia packages, semiotics, perceptual theories, integrated media presentations, distance teaching.

Central Michigan University, Central Michigan University Off-Campus Programs, Program in Education, Mount Pleasant, MI 48859. Offers education (MA); educational technology (MA); reading and literacy (MA). Part-time and evening/weekend programs available. *Entrance requirements:* For master's, minimum GPA of 2.7 in major. Additional exam requirements/recommendations for international students: Required—TOEFL. *Application deadline:* Applications are processed on a rolling basis. Application fee: $50. Electronic applications accepted. *Financial support:* Scholarships/grants available. Support available to part-time students. *Unit head:* Jennifer Cochran, Director, 989-774-2584, E-mail: jennifer.cochran@cmich.edu. *Application contact:* 877-268-4636, E-mail: cmuoffcampus@cmich.edu.

Central Michigan University, College of Graduate Studies, College of Education and Human Services, Department of Teacher Education and Professional Development, Mount Pleasant, MI 48859. Offers educational technology (MA); elementary education (MA), including classroom teaching, early childhood education, reading in the elementary school; library, media, and technology (MA), including library media, media and technology; middle level education (MA); reading improvement (MA); secondary education (MA); teaching senior high (MA). *Accreditation:* NCATE. *Degree requirements:* For master's, thesis or alternative, registration. *Faculty research:* Reading instruction and reading disabilities, teaching and learning styles, school and business partnerships, school restructuring and improvement, mathematics learning and instruction.

Central State University, Program in Education, Wilberforce, OH 45384. Offers educational technology (M Ed); leadership (M Ed); literacy (M Ed). Part-time and evening/weekend programs available. *Degree requirements:* For master's, thesis or alternative. *Entrance requirements:* For master's, GRE.

Chestnut Hill College, School of Graduate Studies, Department of Computer Science and Information Technology, Philadelphia, PA 19118-2693. Offers e-communication (CAS); education and technology (CAS); instructional design (CAS); instructional technology specialist (CAS); instructional technology/instruction design (MS); instructional technology/leadership and technology (MS); instructional technology/technology and education (MS); leadership and technology (CAS); multimedia design (CAS); online learning (CAS); restructured environments (CAS); video (CAS). Part-time and evening/weekend programs available. Postbaccalaureate distance learning degree programs offered (minimal on-campus study). *Faculty:* 1 full-time (0 women), 5 part-time/adjunct (3 women). *Students:* 1 full-time (0 women), 16 part-time (12 women); includes 2 minority (1 African American, 1 Asian American or Pacific Islander). Average age 36. In 2006, 5 degrees awarded. *Degree requirements:* For master's, thesis optional. *Entrance requirements:* For master's, GRE General Test or MAT, writing sample. Additional exam requirements/recommendations for international students: Required—TOEFL (minimum score 500 paper-based). *Application deadline:* For fall admission, 7/17 priority date for domestic students, 7/17 for international students; for spring admission, 12/15 priority date for domestic students, 12/15 for international students. Applications are processed on a rolling basis. Application fee: $50. *Expenses:* Tuition: Part-time $470 per credit hour. Required fees: $30 per semester. Tuition and fees vary according to degree level. *Financial support:* Institutionally sponsored loans available. Financial award application deadline: 7/15; financial award applicants required to submit FAFSA. *Faculty research:* E-learning/e-training, motivation: A technology perspective, technology and restructured environments, restructured environments and learning: K-12 perspective. *Unit head:* Dr. Ralph Swan, Chair, 215-248-7008, Fax: 215-248-7155. *Application contact:* Jayne Mashett, Director of Graduate Admissions, 215-248-7020, Fax: 215-248-7161, E-mail: mashehj@chc.edu.

Chicago State University, School of Graduate and Professional Studies, College of Education, Department of Reading, Elementary Education, Library Information and Media Studies, Program in Library Information and Media Studies, Chicago, IL 60628. Offers MS Ed. *Entrance requirements:* For master's, minimum GPA of 2.75.

Chicago State University, School of Graduate and Professional Studies, College of Education, Department of Technology and Education, Chicago, IL 60628. Offers secondary education (MAT); technology and education (MS Ed). Postbaccalaureate distance learning degree programs offered. *Degree requirements:* For master's, thesis optional. *Entrance requirements:* For master's, minimum GPA of 2.75.

City University, Graduate Division, Gordon Albright School of Education, Bellevue, WA 98005. Offers curriculum and instruction (M Ed); educational leadership (M Ed); educational leadership: principal certification (M Ed, Certificate); educational leadership: principal/program administrator certification (Certificate); educational leadership: program administrator certification (M Ed, Certificate); guidance and counseling (M Ed, Certificate); integrated arts and performance learning (M Ed); professional certification-teachers (Certificate); reading (Certificate); reading and literacy (M Ed); reading. literacy, and ESL/ELL (M Ed); teacher certification (MIT); technology, curriculum and instruction (M Ed). Part-time and evening/weekend programs available. Postbaccalaureate distance learning degree programs offered (no on-campus study). *Entrance requirements:* Additional exam requirements/recommendations for international students: Required—TOEFL (minimum score 540 paper-based; 207 computer-based); Recommended—IELTS. Electronic applications accepted.

Clarke College, Program in Education, Dubuque, IA 52001-3198. Offers early childhood/special education (MA); educational administration: elementary and secondary (MA); educational media: elementary and secondary (MA); multi-categorical resource K–12 (MA); multidisciplinary studies (MA); reading: elementary (MA); technology in education (MA). Part-time and evening/weekend programs available. Postbaccalaureate distance learning degree programs offered (minimal on-campus study). *Degree requirements:* For master's, thesis optional. *Entrance requirements:* For master's, GRE General Test or MAT, minimum GPA of 2.75. Electronic applications accepted.

College of Mount Saint Vincent, School of Professional and Continuing Studies, Department of Teacher Education, Riverdale, NY 10471-1093. Offers instructional technology and global perspectives (Certificate); middle level education (Certificate); multicultural studies (Certificate); urban and multicultural education (MS Ed). *Accreditation:* Teacher Education Accreditation Council. Part-time programs available. *Faculty:* 1 full-time (0 women), 18 part-time/adjunct (12 women). *Students:* 20 full-time (13 women), 239 part-time (172 women); includes 101 minority (50 African Americans, 11 Asian Americans or Pacific Islanders, 40 Hispanic Americans). Average age 38. 35 applicants, 57% accepted. In 2006, 124 degrees awarded. *Degree requirements:* For master's, comprehensive exam, registration. *Entrance requirements:* For master's, interview, New York teaching certificate. Additional exam requirements/recommendations for international students: Required—TOEFL. *Application deadline:* For fall admission, 9/1 priority date for domestic students, 7/1 priority date for international students; for winter admission, 11/1 priority date for domestic students, 10/1 priority date for international students; for spring admission, 12/1 priority date for domestic students, 11/1 priority date for international students. Applications are processed on a rolling basis. Application fee: $50. *Financial support:* Career-related internships or fieldwork available. Financial award applicants required to submit FAFSA. *Unit head:* Mary Ellen Sullivan, Chair, 718-405-3281, Fax: 718-601-6392. *Application contact:* Beigica Collado, Executive Assistant, 718-405-3322, Fax: 718-405-3764, E-mail: beigica.collado@mountsaintvincent.edu.

The College of New Jersey, Graduate Division, School of Education, Department of Special Education, Language and Literacy, Program in Educational Technology, Ewing, NJ 08628. Offers MS. Part-time and evening/weekend programs available. *Students:* 1 (woman) full-time, 27 part-time (19 women); includes 3 minority (2 Asian Americans or Pacific Islanders, 1 Hispanic American). 11 applicants, 91% accepted. In 2006, 17 degrees awarded. *Entrance requirements:* For master's, GRE, minimum GPA of 3.0 in field or 2.75 overall. Additional exam requirements/recommendations for international students: Required—TOEFL. *Application deadline:* For fall admission, 4/15 for domestic students; for spring admission, 10/15 for domestic students. Application fee: $60. Electronic applications accepted. *Financial support:* Unspecified assistantships available. Financial award application deadline: 5/1; financial award applicants required to submit FAFSA. *Unit head:* Dr. Amy Dell, Coordinator, 609-771-2308. *Application contact:* Susan L. Hydro, Office of Graduate Studies, Assistant Dean, 609-771-2300, Fax: 609-637-5105, E-mail: graduate@tcnj.edu.

College of Saint Elizabeth, Department of Education, Morristown, NJ 07960-6989. Offers accelerated certification for teachers (Certificate); assistive technology (Certificate); education: human services leadership (MA); educational technology (MA). Part-time and evening/weekend programs available. *Faculty:* 8 full-time (3 women), 14 part-time/adjunct (8 women). *Students:* 69 full-time (58 women), 354 part-time (303 women); includes 21 minority (10 African Americans, 4 Asian Americans or Pacific Islanders, 7 Hispanic Americans). Average age 36. In 2006, 82 master's, 31 other advanced degrees awarded. *Degree requirements:* For master's, thesis or alternative, portfolio. *Entrance requirements:* For master's, interview, minimum undergraduate GPA of 3.0. *Application deadline:* For fall admission, 6/30 priority date for domestic students; for spring admission, 11/30 for domestic students. Applications are processed on a rolling basis. Application fee: $35. Electronic applications accepted. *Financial support:* Career-related internships or fieldwork, Federal Work-Study, tuition waivers (partial), and unspecified assistantships available. Support available to part-time students. Financial award application deadline: 3/15; financial award applicants required to submit FAFSA. *Faculty research:* Developmental stages for teaching and human services professionals, effectiveness of humanities core curriculum. *Unit head:* Dr. Alan H. Markowitz, Director of Graduate Education Programs, 973-290-4374, Fax: 973-290-4389, E-mail: amarkowitz@cse.edu. *Application contact:* Michael Szarek, Director of Enrollment Management, 973-290-4112, Fax: 973-290-4167, E-mail: mszarek@cse.edu.

The College of Saint Rose, Graduate Studies, School of Education, Educational and School Psychology Department, Albany, NY 12203-1419. Offers applied technology education (MS Ed); educational psychology (MS Ed); school psychology (MS, Adv C). Part-time and evening/weekend programs available. *Entrance requirements:* For master's, minimum undergraduate GPA of 3.0. Additional exam requirements/recommendations for international students: Required—TOEFL (minimum score 550 paper-based; 213 computer-based). Electronic applications accepted.

The College of St. Scholastica, Graduate Studies, Program in Educational Media and Technology, Duluth, MN 55811-4199. Offers M Ed. Part-time and evening/weekend programs available. Postbaccalaureate distance learning degree programs offered (no on-campus study). *Faculty:* 2 full-time (both women). *Students:* 8 full-time (7 women), 6 part-time (all women); includes 1 minority (African American) Average age 42. 5 applicants, 80% accepted, 4 enrolled. In 2006, 3 degrees awarded. *Degree requirements:* For master's, thesis. *Entrance requirements:* For master's, interview, minimum GPA of 2.7. Additional exam requirements/recommendations for international students: Required—TOEFL (minimum score 550 paper-based; 213 computer-based; 79 iBT). *Application deadline:* For fall admission, 8/1 priority date for domestic students, 8/1 for international students; for spring admission, 11/1 priority date for domestic students, 11/1 for international students. Applications are processed on a rolling basis. Application fee: $50. Electronic applications accepted. *Expenses:* Contact institution. *Financial support:* In 2006–07, 9 students received support. Scholarships/grants available. Support available to part-time students. Financial award applicants required to submit FAFSA. *Faculty research:* The current standards environment. *Unit head:* Dr. Marie Kelsey, Director, 218-723-6155, E-mail: mkelsey@css.edu. *Application contact:* Tonya J. Roth, Graduate Recruitment Counselor, 218-723-6285, Fax: 218-733-2275, E-mail: gradstudies@css.edu.

The College of William and Mary, School of Education, Program in Education Policy, Planning, and Leadership, Williamsburg, VA 23187-8795. Offers curriculum and educational technology (Ed D, PhD); curriculum leadership (Ed D, PhD); educational leadership (M Ed), including higher education administration (M Ed, Ed D, PhD), K-12 administration and supervision; educational policy, planning, and leadership (Ed D, PhD), including general education administration, gifted education administration, higher education administration (M Ed, Ed D, PhD), special education administration; gifted education administration (M Ed). *Accreditation:* NCATE. Part-time and evening/weekend programs available. *Faculty:* 10 full-time (5 women), 4 part-time/adjunct (2 women). *Students:* 51 full-time (44 women), 101 part-time (64 women); includes 28 minority (27 African Americans, 1 Hispanic American), 7 international. Average age 28. 114 applicants, 55% accepted, 42 enrolled. In 2006, 38 master's, 12 doctorates awarded. *Degree requirements:* For doctorate, thesis/dissertation, comprehensive exam. *Entrance requirements:* For master's, GRE or MAT, minimum GPA of 2.5; for doctorate, GRE or MAT, minimum GPA of 3.0. Additional exam requirements/recommendations for international students: Required—TOEFL. *Application deadline:* For fall admission, 2/1 for domestic and international students; for spring admission, 10/1 for domestic and international students. Application fee: $30. *Expenses:* Tuition, state resident: full-time $6,100; part-time $260 per credit. Tuition, nonresident: full-time $18,790; part-time $725 per credit. Required fees: $3,314. Tuition and fees vary according to program. *Financial support:* In 2006–07, 41 research assistantships with full and partial tuition reimbursements (averaging $13,300 per year) were awarded; career-related internships or fieldwork, Federal Work-Study, institutionally sponsored loans, scholarships/grants, and unspecified assistantships also available. Support available to part-time students. Financial award application deadline: 2/1; financial award applicants required to submit FAFSA. *Faculty research:* Higher education policy, faculty incentives, history of adversity, resilience, leadership. *Unit head:* Dr. Megan Tschannen-Moran, Area Coordinator, 757-221-2187, E-mail: mxtsch@wm.edu. *Application contact:* Patricia Burleson, Director of Admissions, 757-221-2317, E-mail: paburl@wm.edu.

Columbia International University, Columbia Graduate School, Columbia, SC 29230-3122. Offers Bible teaching (MABT); Christian higher education leadership (Ed D); Christian school educational leadership (Ed D); counseling (MACN); curriculum and instruction (M Ed), including Christian school guidance, English as a second language, learning disabilities, school technology; early childhood and elementary education (MAT); educational administration (M Ed); teaching English as a foreign language (Certificate); teaching English as a foreign language and intercultural studies (MATF). Part-time and evening/weekend programs available. *Faculty:* 11 full-time (4 women), 7 part-time/adjunct (5 women). *Students:* 52 full-time (44 women), 93 part-time (59 women); includes 17 minority (11 African Americans, 2 Asian Americans or Pacific Islanders, 4 Hispanic Americans), 10 international. Average age 35. 107 applicants, 56% accepted, 41 enrolled. In 2006, 62 degrees awarded. *Degree requirements:* For master's, internships, professional project. *Entrance requirements:* For master's, Minnesota Multiphasic Personality Inventory, MAT, minimum GPA of 2.7. Additional exam requirements/recommendations for international students: Required—TOEFL. *Application deadline:* For fall admission, 8/1 priority date for domestic and international students; for winter admission, 12/15 priority date for domestic and international students; for spring admission, 1/15 priority date for domestic and international students. Applications are processed on a rolling basis. Application fee: $45. Electronic applications accepted. *Expenses:* Tuition: Part-time $400 per semester hour. Tuition and fees vary according to course load and program. *Financial support:*

In 2006–07, 35 students received support. Career-related internships or fieldwork, Federal Work-Study, institutionally sponsored loans, and scholarships/grants available. Financial award application deadline: 3/17; financial award applicants required to submit FAFSA. *Unit head:* Dr. Milton Uecker, Dean, 803-807-5319, Fax: 803-786-4209, E-mail: muecker@ciu.edu. *Application contact:* Michelle MacGregor, Director of Admissions, 800-777-2227 Ext. 5335, Fax: 803-786-4209, E-mail: yescbs@ciu.edu.

Concordia University, School of Graduate Studies, Faculty of Arts and Science, Department of Education, Program in Educational Technology, Montréal, QC H3G 1M8, Canada. Offers MA, PhD. *Students:* 69 full-time (41 women), 49 part-time (31 women). 60 applicants, 47% accepted, 14 enrolled. In 2006, 28 master's, 4 doctorates awarded. *Degree requirements:* For master's, one foreign language, internship, thesis optional; for doctorate, thesis/dissertation, comprehensive exam. *Entrance requirements:* For doctorate, MA in educational technology or equivalent. *Application deadline:* For fall admission, 3/31 priority date for domestic students; for winter admission, 9/30 for domestic students; for spring admission, 3/31 for domestic students. Application fee: $50. *Financial support:* Career-related internships or fieldwork available. *Faculty research:* Instructional design and tele-education, educational cybernetics and systems analysis, media research and theory development, distance education. *Unit head:* Dr. Dennis Dicks, Director, 514-848-2424 Ext. 2030, Fax: 514-848-4250.

Concordia University, School of Graduate Studies, Faculty of Arts and Science, Department of Education, Program in Instructional Technology, Montréal, QC H3G 1M8, Canada. Offers Diploma. *Students:* 8 full-time (7 women), 12 part-time (5 women). 19 applicants, 79% accepted, 9 enrolled. In 2006, 6 degrees awarded. *Entrance requirements:* For degree, BA in related field. *Application deadline:* For fall admission, 3/31 priority date for domestic students; for winter admission, 9/30 for domestic students; for spring admission, 3/31 for domestic students. Application fee: $50. *Unit head:* Dr. Dennis Dicks, Director, 514-848-2424 Ext. 2030, Fax: 514-848-4250.

Dakota State University, College of Education, Madison, SD 57042-1799. Offers instructional technology (MSET). *Accreditation:* NCATE. Part-time programs available. Postbaccalaureate distance learning degree programs offered (minimal on-campus study). *Faculty:* 6 full-time (1 woman), 3 part-time/adjunct (1 woman). *Students:* Average age 36. 40 applicants, 95% accepted, 34 enrolled. In 2006, 9 degrees awarded. *Degree requirements:* For master's, thesis, electronic portfolio. *Entrance requirements:* For master's, GRE General Test, demonstration of technology skills, minimum GPA of 2.7. Additional exam requirements/recommendations for international students: Required—TOEFL. *Application deadline:* For fall admission, 8/1 for domestic students, 6/1 for international students. Applications are processed on a rolling basis. Application fee: $35 ($85 for international students). Electronic applications accepted. *Expenses:* Tuition, state resident: part-time $120 per credit hour. Tuition, nonresident: part-time $355 per credit hour. Required fees: $89 per credit hour. Tuition and fees vary according to course load, campus/location, program and reciprocity agreements. *Financial support:* In 2006–07, 17 students received support, including 1 research assistantship (averaging $4,812 per year); teaching assistantships, Federal Work-Study, scholarships/grants, tuition waivers (partial), unspecified assistantships, and administrative assistantships also available. Support available to part-time students. Financial award applicants required to submit FAFSA. *Faculty research:* Educational technology evaluation, computer supported collaborative learning, cognitive theory and visual representation of the effects of ambiquitous wireless computing on student learning and productivity. *Unit head:* Dr. Judy Dittman, Dean (Interim), 605-256-5177, Fax: 605-256-7300, E-mail: judy.dittman@dsu.edu. *Application contact:* Jennifer Maher, Program Assistant II, Office of Studies and Research, 605-256-5799, Fax: 605-256-5093, E-mail: jennifer.maher@dsu.edu.

DeSales University, Graduate Division, Program in Education, Center Valley, PA 18034-9568. Offers academic standards and information (Certificate); bilingual/ESL studies (Certificate); biology (M Ed); chemistry (M Ed); computers in education (K-12) (M Ed); computers in education (K-8) (M Ed); English (M Ed); instructional technology specialist (Certificate); mathematics (M Ed); special education (M Ed, Certificate); TESOL (M Ed). Part-time and evening/weekend programs available. Postbaccalaureate distance learning degree programs offered (minimal on-campus study). *Students:* 34 full-time, 190 part-time. In 2006, 30 degrees awarded. *Degree requirements:* For master's, thesis project. *Entrance requirements:* For master's, teaching certificate. *Application deadline:* Applications are processed on a rolling basis. Application fee: $35. Electronic applications accepted. *Expenses: Contact institution. Financial support:* Unspecified assistantships available. Support available to part-time students. Financial award application deadline: 5/1. *Faculty research:* Effective teaching, computer interfacing in chemistry labs, computer applications to teaching, history of philosophy, aesthetics multidrug-resistant cancer. *Unit head:* Dr. Lujean Baab, Director of M.Ed. Program, 610-282-1100 Ext. 1739, Fax: 610-282-3734, E-mail: lujean.baab@desales.edu. *Application contact:* Donna L. Cressman, Program Secretary, 610-282-1100 Ext. 1461, Fax: 610-282-3734, E-mail: med@desales.edu.

Dowling College, Graduate Programs in Education, Oakdale, NY 11769-1999. Offers educational administration (Ed D, PD), including computers in education (PD), educational administration (Ed D), school administration and supervision (PD), school district administration (PD); human development and learning (MS Ed); literacy (MS Ed); literacy/special education (MS Ed); secondary education (MS Ed); special education (MS Ed). *Accreditation:* NCATE. Part-time and evening/weekend programs available. Postbaccalaureate distance learning degree programs offered. *Faculty:* 29 full-time (13 women), 91 part-time/adjunct (60 women). *Students:* 496 full-time (364 women), 1,083 part-time (827 women); includes 119 minority (37 African Americans, 20 Asian Americans or Pacific Islanders, 62 Hispanic Americans), 2 international. Average age 38. 618 applicants, 86% accepted, 300 enrolled. In 2006, 641 master's, 25 doctorates awarded. *Degree requirements:* For master's and PD, comprehensive exam; for doctorate, thesis/dissertation. *Entrance requirements:* For master's, minimum GPA of 3.0; for doctorate, GRE, master's degree; for PD, teaching certificate. Additional exam requirements/recommendations for international students: Required—TOEFL (minimum score 550 paper-based). *Application deadline:* For fall admission, 9/1 priority date for domestic students; for winter admission, 1/1 priority date for domestic students; for spring admission, 2/1 priority date for domestic students. Applications are processed on a rolling basis. Application fee: $25. Electronic applications accepted. *Expenses:* Tuition: Full-time $16,008; part-time $667 per credit. Tuition and fees vary according to course load. *Financial support:* In 2006–07, 358 students received support, including 20 research assistantships with tuition reimbursements available (averaging $3,150 per year); career-related internships or fieldwork, Federal Work-Study, scholarships/grants, tuition waivers (partial), and unspecified assistantships also available. Support available to part-time students. Financial award application deadline: 6/30; financial award applicants required to submit FAFSA. *Faculty research:* Natural readers, Korean styles and learning strategies, mothers of children with disabilities, computers in instruction, cultural background and organizational roadblocks to problem solving. *Unit head:* Dr. Clyde Payne, Associate Provost, 631-244-3404, Fax: 631-589-6644, E-mail: paynec@dowling.edu. *Application contact:* Franks S. Pizzardi, Director of Admissions Operations, 631-244-3227, Fax: 631-244-1059, E-mail: pizzardf@dowling.edu.

Drexel University, School of Education, Program in Educational Leadership and Learning Technology, Philadelphia, PA 19104-2875. Offers PhD. *Degree requirements:* For doctorate, thesis/dissertation. Electronic applications accepted.

Duquesne University, School of Education, Department of Instruction and Leadership, Program in Instructional Technology, Pittsburgh, PA 15282-0001. Offers MS Ed, Ed D. Part-time programs available. Postbaccalaureate distance learning degree programs offered (minimal on-campus study). *Faculty:* 3 full-time (1 woman), 4 part-time/adjunct (2 women). *Students:* 78. 19 applicants, 95% accepted, 15 enrolled. In 2006, 17 master's, 3 doctorates awarded. *Entrance requirements:* For master's, MAT, minimum GPA of 3.0; for doctorate, GRE. Additional exam requirements/recommendations for international students: Required—TOEFL. *Application deadline:* For fall admission, 8/1 priority date for domestic students; for spring admission, 12/1 priority date for domestic students. Applications are processed on a rolling basis. Application fee: $50. *Expenses:* Tuition: Part-time $723 per credit. Required fees: $71 per credit. Tuition and fees vary according to degree level and program. *Financial support:* Available to part-time students. *Unit head:* Dr. David Carbonara, Coordinator, 412-396-4039, Fax: 412-396-5388, E-mail: carbonara@duq.edu.

East Carolina University, Graduate School, College of Education, Department of Library Science and Instructional Technology, Greenville, NC 27858-4353. Offers instruction technology specialist (MA Ed); library science (MLS, CAS). *Accreditation:* NCATE. Part-time and evening/weekend programs available. Postbaccalaureate distance learning degree programs offered (no on-campus study). *Students:* 26 full-time (21 women), 314 part-time (284 women); includes 33 minority (24 African Americans, 1 American Indian/Alaska Native, 5 Asian Americans or Pacific Islanders, 3 Hispanic Americans), 1 international. Average age 37. 56 applicants, 20% accepted, 10 enrolled. In 2006, 104 master's, 2 other advanced degrees awarded. *Degree requirements:* For master's, thesis optional. *Entrance requirements:* For master's, GRE General Test or MAT, interview, minimum GPA of 2.5, bachelor's degree in related field, teaching license (MA Ed). Additional exam requirements/recommendations for international students: Required—TOEFL. *Application deadline:* For fall admission, 6/1 priority date for domestic students. Applications are processed on a rolling basis. Application fee: $50. *Financial support:* Research assistantships, teaching assistantships, Federal Work-Study available. Support available to part-time students. Financial award application deadline: 6/1. *Unit head:* Dr. William Suger, Interim Chair, 252-328-4373, Fax: 252-328-4368, E-mail: sugerw@ecu.edu. *Application contact:* Dean of Graduate School, 252-328-6012, Fax: 252-328-6071, E-mail: gradschool@ecu.edu.

Eastern Connecticut State University, School of Education and Professional Studies/ Graduate Division, Program in Educational Technology, Willimantic, CT 06226-2295. Offers MS. Part-time and evening/weekend programs available. *Faculty:* 2 full-time (1 woman). *Students:* 1 full-time (0 women), 31 part-time (22 women); includes 1 minority (Hispanic American) Average age 40. 4 applicants, 100% accepted, 3 enrolled. In 2006, 13 degrees awarded. *Degree requirements:* For master's, comprehensive exam or thesis. *Entrance requirements:* For master's, minimum GPA of 2.7. Additional exam requirements/recommendations for international students: Required—TOEFL (minimum score 550 paper-based; 213 computer-based). *Application deadline:* For fall admission, 7/6 priority date for domestic and international students; for spring admission, 11/3 priority date for domestic and international students. Applications are processed on a rolling basis. Application fee: $50. Electronic applications accepted. *Expenses:* Tuition, state resident: full-time $3,970. Tuition, nonresident: full-time $11,061; part-time $336 per credit. Required fees: $35 per credit. *Financial support:* Career-related internships or fieldwork, scholarships/grants, and unspecified assistantships available. Support available to part-time students. Financial award application deadline: 3/15. *Unit head:* Dr. Catherine Tannahill, Advisor, 860-465-5098, Fax: 860-465-5099, E-mail: tannahillc@easternct.edu. *Application contact:* Dr. Tuesday L. Cooper, Associate Dean, 860-465-4543, Fax: 860-465-4538, E-mail: coopert@easternct.edu.

Eastern Michigan University, Graduate School, College of Education, Department of Teacher Education, Program in Educational Media and Technology, Ypsilanti, MI 48197. Offers MA. Part-time and evening/weekend programs available. Postbaccalaureate distance learning degree programs offered (minimal on-campus study). *Students:* 1 (woman) full-time, 65 part-time (41 women); includes 10 minority (6 African Americans, 4 Hispanic Americans), 2 international. Average age 35. In 2006, 10 degrees awarded. *Entrance requirements:* Additional exam requirements/recommendations for international students: Required—TOEFL. *Application deadline:* For fall admission, 5/15 priority date for domestic students, 5/1 priority date for international students; for winter admission, 10/15 priority date for domestic students, 10/1 priority date for international students; for spring admission, 3/15 priority date for domestic students, 3/1 priority date for international students. Applications are processed on a rolling basis. Application fee: $35. *Expenses:* Tuition, state resident: part-time $341 per credit hour. Tuition, nonresident: full-time $16,104; part-time $671 per credit hour. Required fees: $816; $34 per credit hour. $40 per term. One-time fee: $82 full-time. Tuition and fees vary according to course level, course load, degree level and reciprocity agreements. *Financial support:* Fellowships, research assistantships with full tuition reimbursements, teaching assistantships with full tuition reimbursements, career-related internships or fieldwork, Federal Work-Study, institutionally sponsored loans, scholarships/grants, tuition waivers (partial), and unspecified assistantships available. Support available to part-time students. Financial award applicants required to submit FAFSA.

Eastern Washington University, Graduate Studies, College of Education and Human Development, Department of Education, Program in Instructional Media and Technology, Cheney, WA 99004-2431. Offers M Ed.

East Stroudsburg University of Pennsylvania, Graduate School, School of Professional Studies, Department of Media Communications and Technology, East Stroudsburg, PA 18301-2999. Offers instructional technology (M Ed). Part-time and evening/weekend programs available. *Faculty:* 3 full-time (2 women), 1 part-time/adjunct (0 women). *Students:* 2 full-time (1 woman), 11 part-time (4 women); includes 1 minority (Hispanic American), 1 international. Average age 34. In 2006, 6 degrees awarded. *Degree requirements:* For master's, comprehensive exam. *Entrance requirements:* For master's, letter of recommendation, portfolio, Pennsylvania Department of Education certification requirements. Additional exam requirements/ recommendations for international students: Required—TOEFL (minimum score 560 paper-based; 220 computer-based; 83 iBT). *Application deadline:* For fall admission, 7/31 priority date for domestic students, 5/1 priority date for international students; for spring admission, 11/30 for domestic students, 10/1 for international students. Application fee: $50. *Expenses:* Tuition, state resident: full-time $6,048; part-time $336 per credit. Tuition, nonresident: full-time $9,678; part-time $538 per credit. Required fees: $1,353; $67 per credit. One-time fee: $37 part-time. *Financial support:* In 2006–07, 2 research assistantships with full and partial tuition reimbursements were awarded; career-related internships or fieldwork, Federal Work-Study, and institutionally sponsored loans also available. Financial award application deadline: 3/1; financial award applicants required to submit FAFSA. *Unit head:* Dr. Elzar Camper, Graduate Coordinator, 570-423-3646, Fax: 570-422-3506, E-mail: ecamper@po-box.esu.edu.

East Tennessee State University, School of Graduate Studies, College of Education, Department of Curriculum and Instruction, Johnson City, TN 37614. Offers 7-12 (MAT); classroom technology (M Ed); educational communication (M Ed); educational media/educational technology (M Ed); elementary education (M Ed, MAT); K-12 (MAT); reading and storytelling (M Ed, MA); reading education (M Ed, MA); school library media (M Ed); secondary education (M Ed, MAT). *Accreditation:* NCATE. Part-time and evening/weekend programs available. *Degree requirements:* For master's, thesis (for some programs). *Entrance requirements:* For master's, GRE, minimum GPA of 3.0. Additional exam requirements/recommendations for international students: Required—TOEFL (minimum score 550 paper-based; 213 computer-based). *Faculty research:* Critical thinking, curriculum development, cultural diversity, cognitive processes, effective teaching strategies.

Emporia State University, School of Graduate Studies, The Teachers College, Department of Instructional Design and Technology, Emporia, KS 66801-5087. Offers MS. *Accreditation:* NCATE. Part-time programs available. Postbaccalaureate distance learning degree programs offered (minimal on-campus study). *Faculty:* 6 full-time (2 women). *Students:* 12 full-time (3 women), 103 part-time (76 women); includes 6 minority (3 African Americans, 1 Asian American or Pacific Islander, 2 Hispanic Americans), 1 international. In 2006, 36 degrees awarded. *Degree requirements:* For master's, thesis (for some programs), project, comprehensive exam (for some programs). *Entrance requirements:* For master's, appropriate bachelor's degree, letters of recommendation. Additional exam requirements/recommendations for international students: Required—TOEFL. *Application deadline:* For fall admission, 8/15 priority date for domestic students. Applications are processed on a rolling basis. Application fee: $30 ($75 for international students). Electronic applications accepted. *Expenses:* Tuition, state resident:

Educational Media/Instructional Technology

Emporia State University (continued)
full-time $3,438; part-time $143 per credit hour. Tuition, nonresident: full-time $10,398; part-time $433 per credit hour. Required fees: $724; $44 per credit hour. *Financial support:* In 2006–07, research assistantships with full tuition reimbursements (averaging $6,752 per year), 6 teaching assistantships with full tuition reimbursements (averaging $6,752 per year) were awarded; Federal Work-Study, institutionally sponsored loans, health care benefits, and unspecified assistantships also available. Financial award application deadline: 3/15; financial award applicants required to submit FAFSA. *Unit head:* Dr. Marcus Childress, Chair, 620-341-5627, E-mail: mchildre@emporia.edu.

Fairfield University, Graduate School of Education and Allied Professions, Department of Media/Educational Technology, Fairfield, CT 06824-5195. Offers computers in education (MA, CAS); educational media (MA, CAS); school media specialist (MA, CAS). Part-time and evening/weekend programs available. Postbaccalaureate distance learning degree programs offered. *Faculty:* 1 (woman) full-time, 4 part-time/adjunct (1 woman). *Students:* 4 full-time (all women), 36 part-time (24 women). Average age 32. 13 applicants, 77% accepted, 9 enrolled. In 2006, 25 master's, 1 other advanced degree awarded. *Degree requirements:* For master's, comprehensive exam. *Entrance requirements:* For master's, PRAXIS I (PPST), minimum QPA of 2.67, 2 recommendations, resumè. Additional exam requirements/recommendations for international students: Required—TOEFL (minimum score 550 paper-based; 213 computer-based; 79 iBT). *Application deadline:* Applications are processed on a rolling basis. Application fee: $55. Electronic applications accepted. *Financial support:* Tuition waivers (partial) and unspecified assistantships available. Financial award applicants required to submit FAFSA. *Faculty research:* Television, advertising, children in television, multimedia applications. *Application contact:* Marianne Gumpper, Director of Graduate and Continuing Studies Admissions, 203-254-4184, Fax: 203-254-4073, E-mail: gradadmis@mail.fairfield.edu.

Fairleigh Dickinson University, College at Florham, University College: Arts, Sciences, and Professional Studies, Peter Sammartino School of Education, Madison, NJ 07940-1099. Offers education for certified teachers (MA, Certificate); educational leadership (MA); instructional technology (Certificate); literacy/reading (Certificate); teaching (MAT). *Students:* 62 full-time (52 women), 58 part-time (41 women). Average age 29. 77 applicants, 83% accepted, 58 enrolled. In 2006, 86 degrees awarded. *Application deadline:* Applications are processed on a rolling basis. Application fee: $40.

Fairleigh Dickinson University, Metropolitan Campus, University College: Arts, Sciences, and Professional Studies, Peter Sammartino School of Education, Teaneck, NJ 07666-1914. Offers dyslexia specialist (Certificate); education for certified teachers (MA); educational leadership (MA); instructional technology (Certificate); learning disabilities (MA); literacy/reading (Certificate); multilingual education (MA); teacher of the handicapped (Certificate); teaching (MAT). Part-time programs available. *Students:* 70 full-time (54 women), 515 part-time (424 women), 14 international. Average age 36. 290 applicants, 92% accepted, 130 enrolled. In 2006, 106 degrees awarded. *Degree requirements:* For master's, research project (MAT). *Application deadline:* Applications are processed on a rolling basis. Application fee: $40. *Unit head:* Dr. Vicki Cohen, Director, 201-692-2525, Fax: 201-692-2603, E-mail: vicki_cohen@fdu.edu.

See Close-Up on page 877.

Ferris State University, College of Education and Human Services, School of Education, Big Rapids, MI 49307. Offers administration (MSCTE); curriculum and instruction (M Ed), including administration, elementary education, philanthropic education, reading, secondary education, special education, subject matter option; education technology (MSCTE); instructor (MSCTE); post-secondary administration (MSCTE); training and development (MSCTE). Part-time and evening/weekend programs available. Postbaccalaureate distance learning degree programs offered (no on-campus study). *Faculty:* 13 full-time (9 women), 26 part-time/adjunct (19 women). *Students:* 38 full-time (27 women), 254 part-time (164 women); includes 30 minority (22 African Americans, 1 American Indian/Alaska Native, 2 Asian Americans or Pacific Islanders, 5 Hispanic Americans), 1 international. Average age 37. 171 applicants, 99% accepted. In 2006, 92 degrees awarded. *Degree requirements:* For master's, thesis, research paper. *Entrance requirements:* For master's, 2 years of work experience, minimum GPA of 3.0. *Application deadline:* For fall admission, 6/1 priority date for domestic students; for winter admission, 12/10 priority date for domestic students. Applications are processed on a rolling basis. Application fee: $30. *Expenses:* Tuition, state resident: part-time $355 per credit hour. Tuition, nonresident: part-time $687 per credit hour. *Financial support:* Career-related internships or fieldwork and tuition waivers (full and partial) available. Support available to part-time students. Financial award applicants required to submit FAFSA. *Faculty research:* Suicide prevention, reading, women in education, special needs, administration. *Unit head:* Interim Director, 231-591-5362, Fax: 231-591-2041. *Application contact:* Sigrid Robertson, Secretary, 231-591-3511, Fax: 231-591-2041, E-mail: robertss@ferris.edu.

Fitchburg State College, Division of Graduate and Continuing Education, Program in Applied Communications, Fitchburg, MA 01420-2697. Offers applied communications (MS, Certificate); library media (MS); media technology (MS); technical and professional writing (MS). Part-time and evening/weekend programs available. *Students:* 7 full-time (6 women), 21 part-time (11 women); includes 5 minority (2 African Americans, 1 Asian American or Pacific Islander, 2 Hispanic Americans), 2 international. Average age 35. 15 applicants, 100% accepted, 9 enrolled. In 2006, 7 degrees awarded. *Entrance requirements:* For master's, GRE General Test or MAT, minimum 2 years of related experience, letters of recommendation, resumé. Additional exam requirements/recommendations for international students: Required—TOEFL (minimum score 550 paper-based; 213 computer-based; 79 iBT). *Application deadline:* Applications are processed on a rolling basis. Application fee: $25 ($50 for international students). *Expenses:* Tuition, state resident: part-time $150 per credit. Tuition, nonresident: part-time $150 per credit. Required fees: $90 per credit. *Financial support:* In 2006–07, research assistantships with partial tuition reimbursements (averaging $5,500 per year); Federal Work-Study, scholarships/grants, and unspecified assistantships also available. Support available to part-time students. Financial award application deadline: 3/1; financial award applicants required to submit FAFSA. *Unit head:* Dr. John Chetro-Szivos, Chair, 978-665-3257, Fax: 978-665-3658, E-mail: gce@fsc.edu. *Application contact:* Director of Admissions, 978-665-3144, Fax: 978-665-4540, E-mail: admissions@fsc.edu.

Florida Atlantic University, College of Education, Department of Instructional Technology and Research, Boca Raton, FL 33431-0991. Offers educational research (MSF); educational technology (MSF); foundations-educational research (M Ed); foundations-educational technology (M Ed). *Accreditation:* NCATE. Part-time programs available. *Faculty:* 12 full-time (3 women), 2 part-time/adjunct (1 woman). *Students:* 17 full-time (12 women), 40 part-time (30 women); includes 17 minority (7 African Americans, 10 Hispanic Americans), 3 international. Average age 33. 25 applicants, 56% accepted, 12 enrolled. In 2006, 21 degrees awarded. *Degree requirements:* For master's, registration. *Entrance requirements:* For master's, GRE General Test, minimum GPA of 3.0 in last 60 hours of course work. *Application deadline:* Applications are processed on a rolling basis. Application fee: $30. *Expenses:* Tuition, area resident: Full-time $4,394. Tuition, nonresident: full-time $16,441. *Financial support:* In 2006–07, 3 research assistantships with tuition reimbursements (averaging $11,250 per year) were awarded; fellowships, career-related internships or fieldwork also available. *Faculty research:* Cognition, statistics, research design. *Unit head:* Dr. Don Torok, Chair, 561-297-3602, Fax: 561-297-2309.

Florida Gulf Coast University, College of Education, Program in Curriculum and Instruction, Fort Myers, FL 33965-6565. Offers educational technology (M Ed, MA). Part-time and evening/weekend programs available. Postbaccalaureate distance learning degree programs offered (minimal on-campus study). *Faculty:* 31 full-time (21 women), 30 part-time/adjunct (24 women). *Students:* 41 full-time (23 women), 7 part-time (3 women); includes 7 minority (2 African Americans, 5 Hispanic Americans). Average age 39. 16 applicants, 81% accepted, 8 enrolled. In 2006, 11 degrees awarded. *Degree requirements:* For master's, final project or portfolio. *Entrance requirements:* For master's, GRE General Test, MAT, minimum undergraduate GPA of 3.0 in last 2 years. Additional exam requirements/recommendations for international students: Required—TOEFL (minimum score 550 paper-based; 213 computer-based). *Application deadline:* For fall admission, 7/1 priority date for domestic students; for spring admission, 10/15 for domestic students. Applications are processed on a rolling basis. Application fee: $30. Electronic applications accepted. *Expenses:* Tuition, state resident: full-time $4,326. Tuition, nonresident: full-time $18,523. Required fees: $1,211. One-time fee: $5 full-time. *Faculty research:* Internet in schools, technology in pre-service and in-service teacher training. *Unit head:* Dr. Pat Wachholz, Associate Dean, 239-590-7808, Fax: 239-590-7801, E-mail: wachhol@fgcu.edu.

Florida International University, College of Education, Department of Curriculum and Instruction, Miami, FL 33199. Offers art education (MAT, MS, Ed D); curriculum and instruction (Ed S); curriculum development (MS); curriculum studies (PhD); early childhood education (MS, Ed D); elementary education (MS, Ed D); English education (MAT, MS, Ed D); foreign language education—teaching English to speakers of other languages (TESOL) (Certificate), including foreign language education; foreign language education- teaching English to speakers of other languages (TESOL) (MS), including teaching English; French education—initial teacher preparation (MAT); international and intercultural development education (Ed D); international and intercultural developmental education (MS); language, literacy and culture (PhD); learning technologies (MS, Ed D, PhD); mathematics education (MAT, MS, Ed D, PhD); modern language education/bilingual education (MS, Ed D); physical education (MS); reading education (MS, Ed D); science education (MAT, MS, Ed D, PhD); social studies education (MAT, MS, Ed D); Spanish education—initial teacher preparation (MAT); special education (MS). Part-time and evening/weekend programs available. *Faculty:* 19 full-time (11 women). *Students:* 89 full-time (66 women), 258 part-time (221 women); includes 99 minority (72 African Americans, 10 Asian Americans or Pacific Islanders, 17 Hispanic Americans). Average age 35. 167 applicants, 50% accepted, 81 enrolled. In 2006, 141 master's, 8 doctorates, 1 other advanced degree awarded. *Degree requirements:* For doctorate, thesis/dissertation, comprehensive exam, registration. *Entrance requirements:* For master's, GRE General Test, Florida General Knowledge Test or Florida College Level Academic Skills Test; for doctorate and other advanced degree, GRE General Test. Additional exam requirements/recommendations for international students: Required—TOEFL (minimum score 550 paper-based; 213 computer-based; 80 iBT), IELTS (minimum score 6). *Application deadline:* For fall admission, 6/1 priority date for domestic students, 4/1 for international students; for winter admission, 10/1 priority date for domestic students, 9/1 for international students; for spring admission, 3/1 priority date for domestic students, 2/1 for international students. Applications are processed on a rolling basis. Application fee: $30. Electronic applications accepted. *Expenses:* Tuition, state resident: part-time $249 per credit hour. Tuition, nonresident: part-time $753 per credit hour. Tuition and fees vary according to program. *Financial support:* Research assistantships with full and partial tuition reimbursements, teaching assistantships with full and partial tuition reimbursements available. *Unit head:* Dr. Lisbeth Dixon-Krauss, Interim Chairperson, 305-348-3609, Fax: 305-348-2086, E-mail: kraussl@fiu.edu. *Application contact:* Marisa Salazar, Student Recruiter, 305-348-3002, Fax: 305-348-3227, E-mail: marisa.salazar@fiu.edu.

Florida State University, Graduate Studies, College of Education, Department of Educational Psychology and Learning Systems, Program in Instructional Systems, Tallahassee, FL 32306. Offers instructional systems (MS, PhD, Ed S); open and distance learning (MS). *Faculty:* 6 full-time (2 women), 4 part-time/adjunct (1 woman). *Students:* 51 full-time (30 women), 78 part-time (46 women); includes 41 minority (10 African Americans, 22 Asian Americans or Pacific Islanders, 9 Hispanic Americans). Average age 20. 106 applicants, 41% accepted, 41 enrolled. In 2006, 35 master's, 6 doctorates awarded. *Degree requirements:* For master's and Ed S, thesis optional; for doctorate, thesis/dissertation, comprehensive exam. *Entrance requirements:* For master's, doctorate, and Ed S, GRE General Test, minimum GPA of 3.0. *Application deadline:* For fall admission, 7/1 priority date for domestic students; for spring admission, 11/1 for domestic students. Applications are processed on a rolling basis. Application fee: $30. *Expenses:* Tuition, state resident: full-time $5,822; part-time $243 per credit hour. Tuition, nonresident: full-time $20,976; part-time $874 per credit hour. Tuition and fees vary according to program. *Financial support:* In 2006–07, fellowships with partial tuition reimbursements (averaging $5,000 per year), research assistantships with partial tuition reimbursements (averaging $18,000 per year), teaching assistantships with partial tuition reimbursements (averaging $18,000 per year) were awarded; career-related internships or fieldwork also available. Financial award applicants required to submit FAFSA. *Unit head:* Dr. Robert Reiser, Program Leader, 850-644-4592, Fax: 850-644-8776, E-mail: rreiser@mailer.fsu.edu. *Application contact:* Mary Kate McKee, Program Coordinator, 850-644-8792, Fax: 850-644-8776, E-mail: mmckee@oddl.fsu.edu.

Fort Hays State University, Graduate School, College of Education and Technology, Department of Technology Studies, Hays, KS 67601-4099. Offers instructional technology (MS). *Faculty:* 3 full-time (1 woman). *Students:* 3 full-time (1 woman), 19 part-time (6 women); includes 3 minority (1 African American, 1 American Indian/Alaska Native, 1 Asian American or Pacific Islander). 5 applicants, 100% accepted. In 2006, 10 degrees awarded. *Degree requirements:* For master's, thesis or alternative, comprehensive exam. *Entrance requirements:* Additional exam requirements/recommendations for international students: Required—TOEFL (minimum score 550 paper-based; 213 computer-based). *Application deadline:* For fall admission, 7/1 priority date for domestic students. Applications are processed on a rolling basis. Application fee: $35. Electronic applications accepted. *Unit head:* Dr. Fred Ruda, Chair, 785-628-4315, Fax: 785-628-4267, E-mail: fruda@fhsu.edu.

Framingham State College, Division of Graduate and Continuing Education, Program in Curriculum and Instructional Technology, Framingham, MA 01701-9101. Offers M Ed. *Students:* 60. In 2006, 30 degrees awarded. *Unit head:* Dr. Claire Graham, Coordinator, 508-224-1550, Fax: 508-626-4030, E-mail: czgraham@hotmail.com. *Application contact:* 508-626-4550, Fax: 508-626-4030, E-mail: dgce@frc.mass.edu.

Fresno Pacific University, Graduate Programs, Programs in Education, Fresno, CA 93702-4709. Offers administration (MA Ed), including administrative services; foundations, curriculum and teaching (MA Ed), including curriculum and teaching, school library and information technology; language, literacy, and culture (MA Ed), including bilingual/cross-cultural education, language development, multilingual contexts, reading; mathematics/science/computer education (MA Ed), including educational technology, integrated mathematics/science education, mathematics education; pupil personnel services (MA Ed), including school counseling, school psychology; special education (MA Ed), including mild/moderate, moderate/severe, physical and health impairments. Part-time and evening/weekend programs available. *Faculty:* 12 full-time (5 women), 19 part-time/adjunct (9 women). *Students:* 73 full-time (59 women), 399 part-time (295 women); includes 136 minority (9 African Americans, 5 American Indian/Alaska Native, 12 Asian Americans or Pacific Islanders, 110 Hispanic Americans), 2 international. Average age 39. 124 applicants, 73% accepted, 10 enrolled. In 2006, 128 degrees awarded. *Degree requirements:* For master's, thesis (for some programs), registration. *Entrance requirements:* For master's, interview; GMAT, GRE, MAT, or 6 units of course work with a faculty recommendation. Additional exam requirements/recommendations for international students: Required—TOEFL (minimum score 550 paper-based; 213 computer-based). *Application deadline:* For fall admission, 7/15 for domestic and international students; for spring admission, 11/15 for domestic and international students. Applications are processed on a rolling basis. Application fee: $90. Electronic applications accepted. *Expenses:* Tuition: Full-time $7,470; part-time $415 per credit. *Financial support:* In 2006–07, 260 students received support. Career-related internships or fieldwork, scholarships/grants, and tuition waivers (full and partial) available. Support available to part-time students. Financial award applicants required to submit FAFSA.

Fresno Pacific University, Graduate Programs, Programs in Education, Division of Foundations, Curriculum and Teaching, Program in School Library and Information Technology, Fresno,

CA 93702-4709. Offers MA Ed. Part-time and evening/weekend programs available. *Students:* Average age 43. 10 applicants, 60% accepted, 0 enrolled. In 2006, 3 degrees awarded. *Degree requirements:* For master's, thesis or alternative, registration. *Entrance requirements:* Additional exam requirements/recommendations for international students: Required—TOEFL (minimum score 550 paper-based; 213 computer-based). *Application deadline:* For fall admission, 7/15 for domestic and international students; for spring admission, 11/15 for domestic and international students. Applications are processed on a rolling basis. Application fee: $90. Electronic applications accepted. *Expenses:* Tuition: Full-time $7,470; part-time $415 per credit. *Financial support:* In 2006–07, 2 students received support. Scholarships/grants and tuition waivers (full and partial) available. Support available to part-time students. Financial award applicants required to submit FAFSA.

Fresno Pacific University, Graduate Programs, Programs in Education, Division of Mathematics/Science/Computer Education, Program in Educational Technology, Fresno, CA 93702-4709. Offers MA Ed. Part-time and evening/weekend programs available. *Students:* 1 (woman) full-time, 29 part-time (14 women); includes 4 minority (1 Asian American or Pacific Islander, 3 Hispanic Americans). Average age 42. 2 applicants, 100% accepted, 0 enrolled. In 2006, 23 degrees awarded. *Degree requirements:* For master's, thesis or alternative, registration. *Entrance requirements:* Additional exam requirements/recommendations for international students: Required—TOEFL (minimum score 550 paper-based; 213 computer-based). *Application deadline:* For fall admission, 7/15 for domestic and international students; for spring admission, 11/15 for domestic and international students. Applications are processed on a rolling basis. Application fee: $90. *Expenses:* Tuition: Full-time $7,470; part-time $415 per credit. *Financial support:* In 2006–07, 22 students received support. Scholarships/grants and tuition waivers (full and partial) available. Support available to part-time students. Financial award applicants required to submit FAFSA. *Unit head:* Terry Bese, Acting Director, 559-453-3687, Fax: 559-453-2001, E-mail: tlbese@fresno.edu.

Frostburg State University, Graduate School, College of Education, Department of Educational Professions, Program in Curriculum and Instruction, Frostburg, MD 21532-1099. Offers educational technology (M Ed); elementary education (M Ed); secondary education (M Ed). Part-time and evening/weekend programs available. *Degree requirements:* For master's, thesis or alternative. *Entrance requirements:* For master's, teaching certificate. Electronic applications accepted.

Gallaudet University, The Graduate School, School of Education and Human Services, Department of Educational Foundations and Research, Washington, DC 20002-3625. Offers integrating technology in the classroom (Certificate). *Accreditation:* NCATE. *Degree requirements:* For Certificate, thesis optional. *Entrance requirements:* For degree, GRE General Test or MAT.

Gannon University, School of Graduate Studies, College of Humanities, Business, and Education, School of Education, Program in Educational Computing Technology, Erie, PA 16541-0001. Offers M Ed. Part-time and evening/weekend programs available. *Students:* Average age 37. In 2006, 3 degrees awarded. *Degree requirements:* For master's, thesis, comprehensive exam. *Entrance requirements:* For master's, GRE or MAT, interview, teaching certificate. Additional exam requirements/recommendations for international students: Required—TOEFL (minimum score 500 paper-based; 173 computer-based). *Application deadline:* Applications are processed on a rolling basis. Application fee: $25. *Expenses:* Tuition: Full-time $12,240; part-time $680 per credit. Required fees: $496; $16 per credit. Tuition and fees vary according to course load, degree level, campus/location and program. *Financial support:* Available to part-time students. Application deadline: 7/1; *Application contact:* Debra Meszaros, Director of Graduate Recruitment, 814-871-5819, Fax: 814-871-5827, E-mail: cfal@gannon.edu.

Gannon University, School of Graduate Studies, College of Humanities, Business, and Education, School of Education, Program in Instructional Technology Specialist, Erie, PA 16541-0001. Offers Certificate. Part-time and evening/weekend programs available. In 2006, 1 degree awarded. *Entrance requirements:* Additional exam requirements/recommendations for international students: Required—TOEFL (minimum score 500 paper-based; 173 computer-based). *Application deadline:* Applications are processed on a rolling basis. Application fee: $25. *Expenses:* Tuition: Full-time $12,240; part-time $680 per credit. Required fees: $496; $16 per credit. Tuition and fees vary according to course load, degree level, campus/location and program. *Financial support:* Application deadline: 7/1; *Application contact:* Debra Meszaros, Director of Graduate Recruitment, 814-871-5819, Fax: 814-871-5827, E-mail: cfal@gannon.edu.

George Mason University, Graduate School of Education, Programs in Curriculum and Instruction, Fairfax, VA 22030. Offers bilingual/multicultural/English as a second language education (M Ed); early childhood education (M Ed); instructional technology (M Ed); middle education (M Ed); reading (M Ed); secondary education (M Ed); special education (M Ed). Part-time and evening/weekend programs available. *Faculty:* 108 full-time (70 women), 193 part-time/adjunct (140 women). *Students:* 185 full-time (144 women), 816 part-time (683 women); includes 148 minority (46 African Americans, 2 American Indian/Alaska Native, 44 Asian Americans or Pacific Islanders, 56 Hispanic Americans), 28 international. Average age 34. 822 applicants, 72% accepted, 473 enrolled. In 2006, 606 master's awarded. *Entrance requirements:* For master's, minimum GPA of 3.0 in last 60 hours. *Application deadline:* For fall admission, 5/1 for domestic students; for spring admission, 11/1 for domestic students. Application fee: $60 ($75 for international students). Electronic applications accepted. *Expenses:* Tuition, state resident: full-time $5,724; part-time $238 per credit. Tuition, nonresident: full-time $16,896; part-time $704 per credit. Required fees: $1,656; $69 per credit. *Financial support:* Career-related internships or fieldwork available. Support available to part-time students. Financial award application deadline: 3/1; financial award applicants required to submit FAFSA. *Unit head:* Martin E. Ford, Senior Associate Dean, 703-993-2008.

The George Washington University, Graduate School of Education and Human Development, Department of Educational Leadership, Program in Educational Technology Leadership, Washington, DC 20052. Offers MA Ed. *Accreditation:* NCATE. Part-time and evening/weekend programs available. *Degree requirements:* For master's, thesis or alternative, comprehensive exam. *Entrance requirements:* For master's, GRE General Test or MAT, minimum GPA of 2.75. Expenses: Contact institution. *Faculty research:* Interactive multimedia, distance education, federal technology policy.

Georgia College & State University, Graduate School, School of Education, Department of Foundations and Secondary Education, Milledgeville, GA 31061. Offers English education (M Ed); instructional technology (M Ed); mathematics education (M Ed); natural science education (M Ed, Ed S); secondary education (MAT); social science education (M Ed, Ed S). *Accreditation:* NCATE. *Students:* 49 full-time (33 women), 66 part-time (47 women); includes 13 minority (11 African Americans, 2 Hispanic Americans), 2 international. Average age 32. 75 applicants, 27% accepted, 9 enrolled. In 2006, 83 master's awarded. *Degree requirements:* For master's and Ed S, comprehensive exam. *Entrance requirements:* For master's, GRE General Test or MAT, 2 letters of recommendation; for Ed S, GRE General Test or MAT, master's degree, 2 letters of recommendation, 2 years teaching experience. Additional exam requirements/recommendations for international students: Required—TOEFL. *Application deadline:* For fall admission, 7/1 priority date for domestic students. Applications are processed on a rolling basis. Application fee: $25. Electronic applications accepted. *Expenses:* Tuition, state resident: full-time $3,222; part-time $179 per credit hour. Tuition, nonresident: full-time $12,870; part-time $715 per credit hour. Required fees: $391 per semester. Tuition and fees vary according to course load. *Financial support:* In 2006–07, 10 research assistantships (averaging $3,800 per year) were awarded; career-related internships or fieldwork and Federal Work-Study also available. Support available to part-time students. Financial award application deadline: 3/15. *Unit head:* Dr. Cynthia Alby, Chair/MAT Cohort Leader, 478-445-2513, Fax: 478-445-7362, E-mail: cynthia.alby@gcsu.edu.

Georgian Court University, School of Education, Lakewood, NJ 08701-2697. Offers administration, supervision, and curriculum planning (MA); early intervention studies (Certificate); education (MA); instructional technology (MA, Certificate); special education (MA); substance awareness coordinator (Certificate). Part-time and evening/weekend programs available. *Faculty:* 25 full-time (14 women), 41 part-time/adjunct (23 women). *Students:* 128 full-time (110 women), 594 part-time (495 women); includes 56 minority (17 African Americans, 8 Asian Americans or Pacific Islanders, 31 Hispanic Americans), 1 international. Average age 34. 676 applicants, 80% accepted, 312 enrolled. In 2006, 130 master's, 4 other advanced degrees awarded. *Degree requirements:* For master's, thesis (for some programs), comprehensive exam (for some programs). *Entrance requirements:* For master's, GRE, MAT or NTE/PRAXIS, 3 letters of recommendation. Additional exam requirements/recommendations for international students: Required—TOEFL (minimum score 550 paper-based; 213 computer-based). *Application deadline:* For fall admission, 8/1 priority date for domestic students, 4/1 for international students; for spring admission, 1/1 priority date for domestic students, 7/1 for international students. Applications are processed on a rolling basis. Application fee: $40. Electronic applications accepted. *Financial support:* In 2006–07, 183 students received support. Scholarships/grants, health care benefits, and unspecified assistantships available. Financial award application deadline: 4/15; financial award applicants required to submit FAFSA. *Unit head:* Sr. Mary Gurley, OSF, Dean, 732-987-2525, E-mail: garleym@gergian.edu. *Application contact:* Eugene Soltys, Director of Graduate Admissions, 732-987-2760 Ext. 2760, Fax: 732-987-2000, E-mail: admissions@georgian.edu.

Georgia Southern University, Jack N. Averitt College of Graduate Studies, College of Education, Department of Leadership, Technology, and Human Development, Program in Instructional Technology, Statesboro, GA 30460. Offers M Ed. Part-time and evening/weekend programs available. *Students:* 7 full-time (6 women), 64 part-time (55 women); includes 4 minority (all African Americans) Average age 33. 21 applicants, 90% accepted, 15 enrolled. In 2006, 9 degrees awarded. *Degree requirements:* For master's, portfolio. *Entrance requirements:* For master's, GRE General Test or MAT, minimum GPA of 2.5. Additional exam requirements/recommendations for international students: Required—TOEFL (minimum score 550 paper-based; 213 computer-based; 80 iBT). *Application deadline:* For fall admission, 3/1 priority date for domestic students, 3/1 for international students; for spring admission, 10/1 priority date for domestic students, 10/1 for international students. Applications are processed on a rolling basis. Application fee: $50. Electronic applications accepted. *Financial support:* In 2006–07, 25 students received support, including research assistantships with partial tuition reimbursements available (averaging $5,500 per year), teaching assistantships with partial tuition reimbursements available (averaging $5,500 per year); career-related internships or fieldwork, Federal Work-Study, scholarships/grants, tuition waivers (partial), and unspecified assistantships also available. Support available to part-time students. Financial award application deadline: 4/15; financial award applicants required to submit FAFSA. *Unit head:* Dr. Elizabeth Downs, Coordinator, 912-681-5634, Fax: 912-486-7194, E-mail: edowns@georgiasouthern.edu. *Application contact:* 912-681-5384, Fax: 912-681-0740, E-mail: gradadmissions@georgiasouthern.edu.

Georgia State University, College of Education, Department of Middle-Secondary Education and Instructional Technology, Library Science/Media Unit, Atlanta, GA 30303-3083. Offers instructional technology (MS, PhD, Ed S); library media technology (MLM, PhD, Ed S). Part-time and evening/weekend programs available. *Students:* 30 full-time (24 women), 104 part-time (81 women); includes 31 minority (24 African Americans, 3 Asian Americans or Pacific Islanders, 4 Hispanic Americans), 2 international. Average age 37. 52 applicants, 87% accepted. In 2006, 27 master's, 5 doctorates, 12 other advanced degrees awarded. *Degree requirements:* For master's, comprehensive exam; for doctorate, thesis/dissertation, comprehensive exam; for Ed S, project/exam. *Entrance requirements:* For master's, GRE General Test, minimum GPA of 2.5; for doctorate, GRE General Test or MAT, minimum GPA of 3.3; for Ed S, GRE General Test or MAT, minimum graduate GPA of 3.25. Application fee: $25. *Financial support:* Federal Work-Study and institutionally sponsored loans available. *Faculty research:* Automation, children's literature, cataloging, electronic resources.

Governors State University, College of Arts and Sciences, Program in Communication and Training, University Park, IL 60466-0975. Offers communication studies (MA); instructional and training technology (MA); media communication (MA). Part-time and evening/weekend programs available. *Students:* 30 full-time, 78 part-time. Average age 35. *Degree requirements:* For master's, thesis or alternative. *Application deadline:* For fall admission, 7/15 priority date for domestic students; for spring admission, 11/10 for domestic students. Applications are processed on a rolling basis. Application fee: $25. *Expenses:* Tuition, state resident: full-time $4,104; part-time $171 per hour. Tuition, nonresident: part-time $513 per hour. *Financial support:* Research assistantships, Federal Work-Study, institutionally sponsored loans, and scholarships/grants available. Support available to part-time students. Financial award application deadline: 5/1. *Unit head:* Dr. Eric V. Martin, Interim Dean, College of Arts and Sciences, 708-534-4101.

Grand Valley State University, College of Education, Programs in General Education, Allendale, MI 49401-9403. Offers adult and higher education (M Ed); early childhood education (M Ed); education of the gifted and talented (M Ed); educational leadership (M Ed); educational technology (M Ed); elementary education (M Ed); middle and high school education (M Ed); teaching English to speakers of other languages (M Ed). Part-time and evening/weekend programs available. Postbaccalaureate distance learning degree programs offered (minimal on-campus study). *Faculty:* 82 full-time (42 women), 43 part-time/adjunct (25 women). *Students:* 136 full-time (97 women), 828 part-time (565 women); includes 55 minority (26 African Americans, 7 American Indian/Alaska Native, 5 Asian Americans or Pacific Islanders, 17 Hispanic Americans). Average age 33. 280 applicants, 94% accepted, 188 enrolled. In 2006, 322 degrees awarded. *Degree requirements:* For master's, thesis. *Entrance requirements:* For master's, GRE General Test or minimum GPA of 3.0. Additional exam requirements/recommendations for international students: Required—TOEFL. *Application deadline:* Applications are processed on a rolling basis. Application fee: $30. Electronic applications accepted. *Expenses:* Tuition, state resident: full-time $5,850; part-time $325 per credit. Tuition, nonresident: full-time $10,800; part-time $600 per credit. Tuition and fees vary according to course load. *Financial support:* In 2006–07, 2 research assistantships with full and partial tuition reimbursements (averaging $8,000 per year) were awarded; career-related internships or fieldwork, Federal Work-Study, scholarships/grants, and unspecified assistantships also available. *Faculty research:* Effectiveness of technology in education, parental involvement, effective teaching, effective schools research. *Unit head:* Dr. Linda McCrea, Director, 616-331-2080, E-mail: mccreal@gvsu.edu. *Application contact:* Dr. Douglas Busman, Director, Student Information and Services, 616-331-6831, Fax: 616-331-6217, E-mail: busmando@gvsu.edu.

Harvard University, Extension School, Cambridge, MA 02138-3722. Offers applied sciences (CAS); biotechnology (ALM); educational technologies (ALM); educational technology (CET); English for graduate and professional studies (DGP); environmental management (ALM, CEM); information technology (ALM); journalism (ALM); liberal arts (ALM); management (ALM, CM); mathematics for teaching (ALM); museum studies (ALM); premedical studies (Diploma); publication and communication (CPC). Part-time and evening/weekend programs available. *Faculty:* 236 part-time/adjunct. *Students:* 101 full-time (56 women), 564 part-time (278 women); includes 167 minority (35 African Americans, 1 American Indian/Alaska Native, 84 Asian Americans or Pacific Islanders, 47 Hispanic Americans). Average age 36. In 2006, 112 master's, 184 Diplomas awarded. *Degree requirements:* For master's, thesis. *Entrance requirements:* For master's, 3 completed graduate courses with grade of B or higher. Additional exam requirements/recommendations for international students: Required—TOEFL (minimum score 600 paper-based; 250 computer-based), TWE (minimum score 5). *Application deadline:* Applications are processed on a rolling basis. Application fee: $75. *Expenses: Contact institution.* Full-time tuition and fees vary according to program and student level. *Financial support:* In 2006–07, 268 students received support. Scholarships/grants available. Support available to part-time students. Financial award application deadline: 8/6; financial award applicants required

Educational Media/Instructional Technology

Harvard University *(continued)*

to submit FAFSA. *Unit head:* Michael Shinagel, Dean. *Application contact:* Program Director, 617-495-4024, Fax: 617-495-9176.

Harvard University, Graduate School of Education, Master's Programs in Education, Cambridge, MA 02138. Offers arts in education (Ed M); education policy and management (Ed M); higher education (Ed M); human development and psychology (Ed M); international education policy (Ed M); language and literacy (Ed M); learning and teaching (Ed M); mid-career mathematics and science (teaching certificate) (Ed M); mind brain and education (Ed M); risk and prevention (Ed M); school leadership (Ed M); special studies (Ed M); teaching and curriculum (teaching certificate) (Ed M); technology innovation and education (Ed M). Part-time programs available. *Faculty:* 58 full-time (25 women), 40 part-time/adjunct (22 women). *Students:* 540 full-time (412 women), 90 part-time (70 women); includes 137 minority (49 African Americans, 2 American Indian/Alaska Native, 61 Asian Americans or Pacific Islanders, 25 Hispanic Americans), 70 international. Average age 29. 1,211 applicants, 61% accepted, 585 enrolled. In 2006, 591 degrees awarded. *Entrance requirements:* For master's, GRE General Test, 3 letters of recommendation, official transcripts, statement of purpose. Additional exam requirements/recommendations for international students: Required—TOEFL (minimum score 600 paper-based; 250 computer-based; 100 iBT), TWE (minimum score 5). *Application deadline:* For fall admission, 1/2 for domestic and international students. Application fee: $85. Electronic applications accepted. *Expenses: Contact institution. Financial support:* In 2006–07, 392 students received support, including 23 fellowships (averaging $15,870 per year); career-related internships or fieldwork, Federal Work-Study, institutionally sponsored loans, scholarships/grants, health care benefits, tuition waivers (full and partial), and unspecified assistantships also available. Support available to part-time students. Financial award application deadline: 2/2; financial award applicants required to submit FAFSA. *Faculty research:* Learning and development; educational leadership and organizations; educational policy analysis. Total annual research expenditures: $14.8 million. *Unit head:* Dr. James Stiles, Associate Dean for Degree Programs. *Application contact:* Information Contact, 617-495-3414, Fax: 617-496-3577, E-mail: gseadmissions@harvard.edu.

Hofstra University, School of Education and Allied Human Services, Department of Curriculum and Teaching, Program in Elementary Education-Math/Science/Technology, Hempstead, NY 11549. Offers MA. *Accreditation:* NCATE. Part-time and evening/weekend programs available. *Students:* 8 full-time (7 women), 30 part-time (27 women); includes 5 minority (2 African Americans, 3 Hispanic Americans). Average age 25. 8 applicants, 88% accepted, 4 enrolled. In 2006, 26 degrees awarded. *Degree requirements:* For master's, thesis, BA or BS in elementary education. *Entrance requirements:* For master's, 2 letters of recommendation, interview, teaching certificate (MA), essay. Additional exam requirements/recommendations for international students: Required—TOEFL (minimum score 550 paper-based; 213 computer-based). *Application deadline:* Applications are processed on a rolling basis. Application fee: $60. Electronic applications accepted. *Expenses:* Tuition: Full-time $13,320; part-time $740 per credit. Required fees: $930; $155 per term. *Financial support:* In 2006–07, 5 students received support, including 4 fellowships with tuition reimbursements available (averaging $300 per year); research assistantships with tuition reimbursements available, scholarships/grants, tuition waivers (full and partial), and unspecified assistantships also available. Support available to part-time students. Financial award applicants required to submit FAFSA. *Faculty research:* Constructivism, mathematical reasoning, concept formation, science of learning, interdisciplinary curriculum. *Unit head:* Dr. Jacqueline Grennon Brooks, Program Director, 516-463-5371, Fax: 516-463-6196, E-mail: catjzk@hofstra.edu. *Application contact:* Carol Drummer, Dean of Graduate Admissions, 516-463-4876, Fax: 516-463-4664, E-mail: gradstudent@hofstra.edu.

Idaho State University, Office of Graduate Studies, College of Education, Department of Educational Leadership, Pocatello, ID 83209. Offers educational administration (6th Year Certificate, Ed S); educational leadership (Ed D), including education training and development, educational administration, educational technology, higher education administration. Part-time and evening/weekend programs available. Postbaccalaureate distance learning degree programs offered (no on-campus study). *Faculty:* 5 full-time (2 women). *Students:* 12 full-time (5 women), 93 part-time (39 women); includes 8 minority (2 African Americans, 3 American Indian/Alaska Native, 1 Asian American or Pacific Islander, 2 Hispanic Americans), 13 international. Average age 44. In 2006, 17 doctorates, 1 other advanced degree awarded. *Degree requirements:* For doctorate, thesis/dissertation, written exam, comprehensive exam, registration; for other advanced degree, thesis (for some programs), written and oral exam, comprehensive exam, registration (for some programs). *Entrance requirements:* For doctorate, GRE General Test or MAT, minimum GPA of 3.0 (undergraduate), 3.5 (graduate), departmental interview; for other advanced degree, GRE General Test, minimum GPA of 3.0, master's degree. Additional exam requirements/recommendations for international students: Required—TOEFL (minimum score 550 paper-based; 213 computer-based; 80 iBT). *Application deadline:* For fall admission, 7/1 for domestic students, 6/1 for international students; for spring admission, 12/1 for domestic students, 11/1 for international students. Applications are processed on a rolling basis. Application fee: $55. *Expenses:* Tuition, state resident: part-time $251 per credit. Tuition, nonresident: part-time $366 per credit. Tuition and fees vary according to degree level, program and reciprocity agreements. *Financial support:* In 2006–07, teaching assistantships with full and partial tuition reimbursements (averaging $8,694 per year); career-related internships or fieldwork, Federal Work-Study, institutionally sponsored loans, scholarships/grants, tuition waivers, and unspecified assistantships also available. Support available to part-time students. Financial award application deadline: 1/1. *Faculty research:* Educational leadership, gender issues in education and sport, staff development. *Unit head:* Dr. E.E. 'Gene" Davis, Chair, 208-282-3202, Fax: 208-282-4697.

Idaho State University, Office of Graduate Studies, College of Education, Department of Instructional Methods and Technology, Pocatello, ID 83209. Offers instructional design (PhD); instructional technology (M Ed). Part-time programs available. *Faculty:* 4 full-time (2 women). *Students:* 4 full-time (3 women), 14 part-time (10 women). Average age 49. In 2006, 3 degrees awarded. *Degree requirements:* For master's, minimum 36 credits, thesis optional; for doctorate, thesis/dissertation (for some programs), minimum 3.0 GPA, comprehensive exam, registration. *Entrance requirements:* For master's, GRE or MAT, bachelor's degree; for doctorate, GRE or MAT, Master's degree. Additional exam requirements/recommendations for international students: Required—TOEFL (minimum score 550 paper-based; 213 computer-based; 80 iBT). *Application deadline:* For fall admission, 7/1 for domestic students, 6/1 for international students; for spring admission, 12/1 for domestic students, 11/1 for international students. Applications are processed on a rolling basis. Application fee: $55. *Expenses:* Tuition, state resident: part-time $251 per credit. Tuition, nonresident: part-time $366 per credit. Tuition and fees vary according to degree level, program and reciprocity agreements. *Unit head:* Dr. Dotty Sammons-Lohse, Chairman, 208-282-2569, Fax: 208-282-4697, E-mail: sammdott@isu.edu. *Application contact:* Dr. Peter Denner, Assistant Dean, 208-282-3807, Fax: 208-282-4697, E-mail: dennpete@isu.edu.

Indiana State University, School of Graduate Studies, College of Education, Department of Curriculum and Instruction and Media Technology, Terre Haute, IN 47809-1401. Offers curriculum and instruction (M Ed, PhD); educational technology (MS). *Accreditation:* NCATE. *Faculty:* 7 full-time (3 women). *Students:* 45 full-time (22 women), 131 part-time (96 women); includes 13 minority (7 African Americans, 3 Asian Americans or Pacific Islanders, 3 Hispanic Americans), 37 international. Average age 37. 54 applicants, 96% accepted, 17 enrolled. In 2006, 25 master's, 11 doctorates awarded. *Degree requirements:* For doctorate, thesis/dissertation. *Entrance requirements:* For doctorate, GRE General Test. *Application deadline:* For fall admission, 7/1 priority date for domestic students; for spring admission, 11/1 priority date for domestic students. Applications are processed on a rolling basis. Application fee: $20. Electronic applications accepted. *Expenses:* Tuition, state resident: part-time $278 per credit. Tuition, nonresident: part-time $552 per credit. *Financial support:* In 2006–07, 7 research assistantships with partial tuition reimbursements (averaging $7,000 per year) were awarded; fellowships with partial tuition reimbursements, teaching assistantships with partial tuition

reimbursements, tuition waivers (partial) also available. Financial award application deadline: 3/1; financial award applicants required to submit FAFSA. *Faculty research:* Discipline FERPA reading, teacher strengths and needs. *Unit head:* Dr. Susan Kiger, Interim Chairperson, 812-237-2960.

Indiana University Bloomington, School of Education, Department of Instructional Systems Technology, Bloomington, IN 47405-7000. Offers MS, PhD, Ed S. PhD offered through the University Graduate School. *Students:* 37 full-time (19 women), 103 part-time (54 women); includes 16 minority (6 African Americans, 4 Asian Americans or Pacific Islanders, 6 Hispanic Americans), 50 international. Average age 36. In 2006, 18 master's, 2 doctorates awarded. *Degree requirements:* For master's, portfolio; for doctorate, thesis/dissertation, portfolio. *Entrance requirements:* For master's and doctorate, GRE General Test, minimum GPA of 2.75. Additional exam requirements/recommendations for international students: Required—TOEFL. *Application deadline:* For fall admission, 6/1 for domestic students, 3/1 for international students; for winter admission, 11/1 for domestic students; for spring admission, 9/1 for international students. Application fee: $50 ($60 for international students). *Expenses:* Tuition, state resident: full-time $5,791; part-time $241 per credit hour. Tuition, nonresident: full-time $16,866; part-time $703 per credit hour. *Financial support:* Fellowships with partial tuition reimbursements, research assistantships, teaching assistantships with full tuition reimbursements, career-related internships or fieldwork, Federal Work-Study, institutionally sponsored loans, and unspecified assistantships available. Financial award application deadline: 2/15. *Faculty research:* Instructional design and development, high technology applications, computer-assisted instruction. *Unit head:* Dr. Elizabeth Boling, Chairperson, 812-856-8450. *Application contact:* Ruth Teh, Office Manager, 812-856-8455.

Indiana University of Pennsylvania, School of Graduate Studies and Research, College of Education and Educational Technology, Department of Adult and Community Education, Program in Adult Education and Communication Technology, Indiana, PA 15705-1087. Offers communications technology (MA). Part-time and evening/weekend programs available. *Faculty:* 7 full-time (0 women). *Students:* 30 full-time (13 women), 45 part-time (36 women); includes 4 minority (3 African Americans, 1 Asian American or Pacific Islander), 6 international. Average age 34. 45 applicants, 64% accepted. In 2006, 35 degrees awarded. *Degree requirements:* For master's, thesis optional. *Entrance requirements:* For master's, letters of recommendation (2), writing sample. Additional exam requirements/recommendations for international students: Required—TOEFL. *Application deadline:* For fall admission, 7/1 priority date for domestic students; for spring admission, 11/1 for domestic students. Applications are processed on a rolling basis. Application fee: $30. *Expenses:* Tuition, state resident: full-time $6,048; part-time $336 per credit. Tuition, nonresident: full-time $9,678; part-time $538 per credit. Required fees: $1,069; $148 per year. *Financial support:* In 2006–07, 11 research assistantships with full and partial tuition reimbursements (averaging $2,495 per year) were awarded; career-related internships or fieldwork and Federal Work-Study also available. Support available to part-time students. Financial award application deadline: 3/15; financial award applicants required to submit FAFSA.

Instituto Tecnológico y de Estudios Superiores de Monterrey, Campus Central de Veracruz, Graduate Programs, Córdoba, Mexico. Offers administration (MA); administration of information technologies (MTI); computer sciences (MCC); education (MEE); educational institution administration (MAD); educational technology (MTE); electronic commerce (MCE); finance (MAF); humanistic studies (MEH); international business for Latin America (MNL); marketing (MMT); science (MCP); technology management (MTT). Part-time and evening/weekend programs available. Postbaccalaureate distance learning degree programs offered (minimal on-campus study). *Degree requirements:* For master's, thesis (for some programs). *Entrance requirements:* For master's, PAEP College Board. Electronic applications accepted.

Instituto Tecnológico y de Estudios Superiores de Monterrey, Campus Ciudad de México, Virtual University Division, Ciudad de Mexico, Mexico. Offers administration of information technologies (MA); computer sciences (MA); education (MA, PhD); educational technology (MA); environmental engineering (MA); environmental systems (MA); humanistic studies (MA); industrial engineering (MA); international business for Latin America (MA); quality systems (MA); quality systems and productivity (MA). Part-time and evening/weekend programs available. Postbaccalaureate distance learning degree programs offered (minimal on-campus study). *Entrance requirements:* For master's and doctorate, Instituto entrance exam. Additional exam requirements/recommendations for international students: Required—TOEFL.

Instituto Tecnológico y de Estudios Superiores de Monterrey, Campus Estado de México, Professional and Graduate Division, Estado de Mexico, Mexico. Offers administration of information technologies (MITA); architecture (M Arch); business administration (GMBA, MBA); computer sciences (MCS, PhD); education (M Ed); educational institution administration (MAD); educational technology and innovation (PhD); electronic commerce (MEC); environmental systems (MS); finance (MAF); humanistic studies (MHS); information sciences and knowledge management (MISKM); information systems (MS); manufacturing systems (MS); marketing (MEM); quality systems and productivity (MS); science and materials engineering (PhD); telecommunications management (MTM). Part-time programs available. Postbaccalaureate distance learning degree programs offered (minimal on-campus study). *Degree requirements:* For master's, one foreign language, thesis (for some programs), registration; for doctorate, one foreign language, thesis/dissertation, registration (for some programs). *Entrance requirements:* For master's, E-PAEP 500, interview; for doctorate, E-PAEP 500, research proposal. Additional exam requirements/recommendations for international students: Required—TOEFL (minimum score 550 paper-based). *Faculty research:* Surface treatments by plasmas, mechanical properties, robotics, graphical computing, mechatronics security protocols.

Instituto Tecnológico y de Estudios Superiores de Monterrey, Campus Irapuato, Graduate Programs, Irapuato, Mexico. Offers administration (MBA); administration of information technology (MAIT); administration of telecommunications (MAT); architecture (M Arch); computer science (MCS); education (M Ed); educational administration (MEA); educational innovation and technology (DEIT); educational technology (MET); electronic commerce (MBA); environmental administration and planning (MEAP); environmental systems (MES); finances (MBA); humanistic studies (MHS); international management for Latin American executives (MIMLAE); library and information science (MLIS); manufacturing quality management (MMQM); marketing research (MBA).

Inter American University of Puerto Rico, Metropolitan Campus, Faculty of Science and Technology, Program in Educational Computing, San Juan, PR 00919-1293. Offers MA. *Degree requirements:* For master's, portfolio. *Entrance requirements:* For master's, GRE or EXADEP, minimum GPA of 2.5. Electronic applications accepted. *Faculty research:* Effectiveness of multimedia, World Wide Web for distance learning.

Iona College, School of Arts and Science, Program in Educational Technology, New Rochelle, NY 10801-1890. Offers MS, Certificate. Part-time and evening/weekend programs available. *Faculty:* 11 full-time (4 women), 7 part-time/adjunct (2 women). *Students:* Average age 29. 6 applicants, 67% accepted, 2 enrolled. In 2006, 15 degrees awarded. *Degree requirements:* For master's, thesis or alternative. *Entrance requirements:* For master's, minimum GPA of 3.0. Additional exam requirements/recommendations for international students: Required—TOEFL (minimum score 550 paper-based; 213 computer-based). *Application deadline:* Applications are processed on a rolling basis. Application fee: $50. Electronic applications accepted. *Expenses:* Tuition: Part-time $665 per credit. Required fees: $150 per term. *Financial support:* Tuition waivers (partial) and unspecified assistantships available. Support available to part-time students. *Faculty research:* Human factors in computing, use of advanced workstations in education, use of authoring languages for educational software, multimedia, educational computing. *Unit head:* Dr. Lubomir Ivanov, Chair, 914-633-2342, E-mail: livanov@iona.edu. *Application contact:* Veronica Jarek-Prinz, Graduate Admissions, 914-633-2289, Fax: 914-633-2012, E-mail: vjarekprinz@iona.edu.

Iowa State University of Science and Technology, Graduate College, College of Human Sciences, Department of Curriculum and Instruction, Ames, IA 50011. Offers curriculum and instructional technology (M Ed, MS, PhD); elementary education (M Ed, MS); historical, philosophical, and comparative studies in education (M Ed, MS); special education (M Ed, MS). *Faculty:* 28 full-time, 3 part-time/adjunct. *Students:* 54 full-time (40 women), 78 part-time (54 women); includes 11 minority (3 African Americans, 4 Asian Americans or Pacific Islanders, 4 Hispanic Americans), 26 international. 64 applicants, 69% accepted, 32 enrolled. In 2006, 31 master's, 10 doctorates awarded. *Degree requirements:* For master's, thesis or alternative; for doctorate, thesis/dissertation. *Entrance requirements:* For doctorate, GRE General Test. Additional exam requirements/recommendations for international students: Required—TOEFL (paper-based 560; computer-based 220; iBT 83) or IELTS (6.5). *Application deadline:* For fall admission, 1/1 priority date for domestic and international students; for spring admission, 9/1 for domestic and international students. Application fee: $30 ($70 for international students). Electronic applications accepted. *Expenses:* Tuition, state resident: full-time $5,936; part-time $330 per credit. Tuition, nonresident: full-time $16,350; part-time $330 per credit. *Financial support:* In 2006–07, 22 research assistantships with full and partial tuition reimbursements (averaging $17,457 per year), 17 teaching assistantships with full and partial tuition reimbursements (averaging $17,788 per year) were awarded; fellowships, scholarships/grants, health care benefits, and unspecified assistantships also available. *Unit head:* Dr. Carl Smith, Chair, 515-294-7021, E-mail: cigrad@iastate.edu. *Application contact:* Dr. Patricia Leigh, Director of Graduate Education, 515-294-7021, E-mail: cigrad@iastate.edu.

Jackson State University, Graduate School, School of Education, Department of Educational Foundations and Leadership, Jackson, MS 39217. Offers education administration (Ed S); educational administration (MS Ed, PhD); secondary education (MS Ed, Ed S), including educational technology (MS Ed). *Accreditation:* NCATE. Part-time and evening/weekend programs available. *Faculty:* 21 full-time (10 women), 5 part-time/adjunct (1 woman). *Students:* 43 full-time (24 women), 58 part-time (34 women); includes 82 minority (all African Americans), 2 international. In 2006, 38 master's, 5 doctorates, 5 other advanced degrees awarded. *Degree requirements:* For master's, thesis or alternative, comprehensive exam; for doctorate and Ed S, thesis/dissertation, comprehensive exam. *Entrance requirements:* For master's, GRE General Test; for doctorate, MAT, GRE, teaching experience. Additional exam requirements/recommendations for international students: Required—TOEFL. *Application deadline:* For fall admission, 3/1 priority date for domestic students; for spring admission, 10/1 for domestic students. Applications are processed on a rolling basis. Application fee: $20. *Financial support:* In 2006–07, 33 students received support. Career-related internships or fieldwork, Federal Work-Study, scholarships/grants, and unspecified assistantships available. Support available to part-time students. Financial award application deadline: 3/1; financial award applicants required to submit FAFSA. *Unit head:* Dr. Carrine Bishop, Interim Chair, 601-968-2351, Fax: 601-968-2213, E-mail: carrine.h.bishop@jsums.edu. *Application contact:* Curtis Gore, Director of Graduate Admissions, 601-979-2455, Fax: 601-974-4325, E-mail: cgore@ccaix.jsums.edu.

Jacksonville State University, College of Graduate Studies and Continuing Education, College of Education and Professional Studies, Program in Instructional Media, Jacksonville, AL 36265-1602. Offers MS Ed. Part-time and evening/weekend programs available. *Faculty:* 3 full-time (2 women), 1 part-time/adjunct (0 women). *Students:* 6 full-time (5 women), 24 part-time (22 women); includes 3 minority (1 African American, 2 Hispanic Americans). In 2006, 23 degrees awarded. *Entrance requirements:* For master's, GRE General Test or MAT. *Application deadline:* Applications are processed on a rolling basis. Application fee: $20. *Expenses:* Tuition, state resident: full-time $5,400; part-time $225 per credit hour. Tuition, nonresident: full-time $10,800; part-time $450 per credit hour. One-time fee: $20 full-time. *Financial support:* In 2006–07, 1 research assistantship was awarded. Support available to part-time students. Financial award application deadline: 4/1. *Unit head:* Dr. Martha Merrill, Head, 256-782-5011. *Application contact:* 256-782-5329.

Jacksonville University, College of Arts and Sciences, School of Education, Program in Integrated Learning with Educational Technology, Jacksonville, FL 32211-3394. Offers MAT. *Degree requirements:* For master's, comprehensive exam. *Entrance requirements:* For master's, GRE General Test, minimum GPA of 3.0. Additional exam requirements/recommendations for international students: Required—TOEFL.

The Johns Hopkins University, School of Professional Studies in Business and Education, School of Education, Department of Teacher Development and Leadership, Baltimore, MD 21218-2699. Offers adult learning (Certificate); business leadership for independent schools (Certificate); earth/space science (Certificate); educational leadership for independent schools (Certificate); educational studies (MS); effective teaching of reading (Certificate); ESL instruction (Certificate); gifted education (Certificate); leadership for school, family and community collaboration (Certificate); reading (MS); school administration and supervision (MS, Certificate); teacher development and leadership (Ed D); teacher leadership (Certificate); technology for educators (MS); urban education (Certificate). Part-time and evening/weekend programs available. Postbaccalaureate distance learning degree programs offered (minimal on-campus study). *Students:* 19 full-time (18 women), 535 part-time (413 women); includes 98 minority (76 African Americans, 1 American Indian/Alaska Native, 18 Asian Americans or Pacific Islanders, 3 Hispanic Americans), 2 international. Average age 31. 544 applicants, 79% accepted, 374 enrolled. In 2006, 151 master's, 180 other advanced degrees awarded. *Degree requirements:* For master's and Certificate, portfolio; for doctorate, thesis/dissertation, comprehensive exam, registration. *Entrance requirements:* For master's and Certificate, minimum GPA of 3.0; for doctorate, GRE, interview, master's degree, minimum GPA of 3.0, resumé, letters of recommendation. Additional exam requirements/recommendations for international students: Required—TOEFL (minimum score 600 paper-based; 250 computer-based; 100 iBT). *Application deadline:* For fall admission, 5/1 for international students; for spring admission, 10/15 for international students. Applications are processed on a rolling basis. Application fee: $60. *Expenses:* Tuition: Full-time $32,976. Tuition and fees vary according to degree level and program. *Financial support:* Scholarships/grants available. Support available to part-time students. Financial award application deadline: 6/1; financial award applicants required to submit FAFSA. *Unit head:* Dr. Edward Pajak, Chair, 410-309-1265, Fax: 410-290-0467. *Application contact:* Carol Herrman, Admissions Coordinator, 410-872-1234, Fax: 410-872-1251, E-mail: onestop.admissions@jhu.edu.

Johnson Bible College, Teacher Education Program, Knoxville, TN 37998-1001. Offers Bible and educational technology (MA); holistic education (MA). Part-time programs available. *Faculty:* 1 (woman) full-time, 7 part-time/adjunct (3 women). *Students:* 12 full-time (all women), 13 part-time (10 women), 1 international. Average age 30. 18 applicants, 100% accepted, 18 enrolled. In 2006, 18 degrees awarded. *Degree requirements:* For master's, multimedia action research presentation. *Entrance requirements:* For master's, interview, minimum GPA of 3.0, portfolio, teaching license. Additional exam requirements/recommendations for international students: Required—TOEFL. *Application deadline:* For fall admission, 7/1 priority date for domestic and international students; for spring admission, 12/1 priority date for domestic and international students. Applications are processed on a rolling basis. Application fee: $50. *Expenses:* Tuition: Full-time $6,100. Required fees: $730. *Financial support:* Career-related internships or fieldwork available. Support available to part-time students. Financial award application deadline: 5/1; financial award applicants required to submit FAFSA. *Faculty research:* Instructional technology. *Unit head:* Dr. Chris Templar, Graduate Program Coordinator, 865-251-2348, Fax: 865-251-3438, E-mail: ctemplar@jbc.edu.

Jones International University, Graduate School of Education, Centennial, CO 80112. Offers adult education (M Ed); corporate training and knowledge management (M Ed); curriculum and instruction (M Ed), including elementary teacher licensure, secondary teacher licensure; e-learning technology and design (M Ed); educational leadership and administration (M Ed); educational leadership and administration: principal and administrator licensure (M Ed); elementary curriculum instruction and assessment (M Ed); higher education leadership and administration (M Ed); K-12 instructional technology (M Ed); K-12 instructional technology: teacher licensure (M Ed); secondary curriculum instruction and assessment (M Ed); technology and design (M Ed). Part-time and evening/weekend programs available. Postbaccalaureate distance learning degree programs offered (no on-campus study). *Entrance requirements:* For master's, minimum cumulative GPA of 2.5. Additional exam requirements/recommendations for international students: Recommended—TOEFL (minimum score 550 paper-based; 213 computer-based). Electronic applications accepted.

Kean University, College of Education, Program in Classroom Instruction and Curriculum, Union, NJ 07083. Offers bilingual/bicultural education (MA); classroom instruction (MA); earth science (MA); educational technology (MA); elementary education (MA); mathematics/science/computer education (MA); teaching (MA); teaching English as a second language (MA). *Accreditation:* NCATE. Part-time and evening/weekend programs available. *Faculty:* 19 full-time (10 women). *Students:* 34 full-time (29 women), 174 part-time (139 women); includes 73 minority (9 African Americans, 7 Asian Americans or Pacific Islanders, 57 Hispanic Americans), 4 international. Average age 34. 103 applicants, 93% accepted, 67 enrolled. In 2006, 82 degrees awarded. *Degree requirements:* For master's, 2 foreign languages, thesis, comprehensive exam. *Entrance requirements:* For master's, GRE General Test or MAT, PRAXIS, minimum GPA of 2.75, 2 letters of recommendation, interview. *Application deadline:* For fall admission, 5/1 for domestic students; for spring admission, 11/1 for domestic students. Application fee: $60 ($150 for international students). Electronic applications accepted. *Expenses:* Tuition, state resident: full-time $8,856; part-time $369 per credit. Tuition, nonresident: full-time $11,256; part-time $469 per credit. *Financial support:* In 2006–07, 2 research assistantships with full tuition reimbursements (averaging $3,217 per year) were awarded; unspecified assistantships also available. *Unit head:* Dr. Frank H. Osborn, Program Coordinator, 908-737-4289, E-mail: fosborne@kean.edu. *Application contact:* Joanne Morris, Director of Graduate Admissions, 908-737-3355, Fax: 908-737-3354, E-mail: grad-adm@kean.edu.

Kean University, College of Education, Program in Educational Media Specialist, Union, NJ 07083. Offers MA. Part-time and evening/weekend programs available. *Faculty:* 10 full-time (8 women). *Students:* 3 full-time (2 women), 37 part-time (34 women); includes 12 minority (11 African Americans, 1 Asian American or Pacific Islander). Average age 42. 10 applicants, 80% accepted, 8 enrolled. In 2006, 10 degrees awarded. *Degree requirements:* For master's, thesis, research. *Entrance requirements:* For master's, GRE General Test or MAT, interview, 2 letters of reference, minimum GPA of 2.75. *Application deadline:* For fall admission, 5/1 for domestic students; for spring admission, 11/1 for domestic students. Application fee: $60 ($150 for international students). Electronic applications accepted. *Expenses:* Tuition, state resident: full-time $8,856; part-time $369 per credit. Tuition, nonresident: full-time $11,256; part-time $469 per credit. *Financial support:* In 2006–07, 1 research assistantship with full tuition reimbursement (averaging $3,217 per year) was awarded; career-related internships or fieldwork and unspecified assistantships also available. *Unit head:* Dr. Joan M. Kastner, Program Coordinator, 908-737-3942, E-mail: jkastner@kean.edu. *Application contact:* Joanne Morris, Director of Graduate Admissions, 908-737-3355, Fax: 908-737-3354, E-mail: grad-adm@kean.edu.

Kent State University, Graduate School of Education, Health, and Human Services, Department of Educational Foundations and Special Services, Program in Instructional Technology, Kent, OH 44242-0001. Offers computer technology (M Ed, MA); instructional technology general (M Ed, MA); library media (M Ed, MA). *Accreditation:* NCATE. *Faculty:* 9 full-time (5 women), 1 (woman) part-time/adjunct. *Students:* 8 full-time (7 women), 45 part-time (26 women); includes 3 minority (2 African Americans, 1 American Indian/Alaska Native), 1 international. 12 applicants, 58% accepted. In 2006, 18 degrees awarded. *Degree requirements:* For master's, thesis (for some programs), registration. *Entrance requirements:* For master's, GRE General Test. Additional exam requirements/recommendations for international students: Required—TOEFL. *Application deadline:* Applications are processed on a rolling basis. Application fee: $30. *Financial support:* In 2006–07, fellowships with full tuition reimbursements (averaging $7,210 per year); research assistantships with full tuition reimbursements, teaching assistantships with full tuition reimbursements, career-related internships or fieldwork, Federal Work-Study, institutionally sponsored loans, scholarships/grants, health care benefits, and unspecified assistantships also available. Support available to part-time students. Financial award application deadline: 4/1; financial award applicants required to submit FAFSA. *Faculty research:* Cooperative learning, aesthetics, computers in schools. *Unit head:* Dr. Albert Ingram, Coordinator, 330-672-2294, E-mail: aingram@kent.edu. *Application contact:* Nancy Miller, Academic Program Coordinator, Office of Graduate Student Services, 330-672-2576, Fax: 330-672-9162, E-mail: ogs@kent.edu.

Kutztown University of Pennsylvania, College of Graduate Studies and Extended Learning, College of Education, Program in Instructional Technology, Kutztown, PA 19530-0730. Offers M Ed, Certificate. Part-time and evening/weekend programs available. *Faculty:* 3 full-time (1 woman). *Students:* 2 full-time (0 women), 30 part-time (16 women); includes 1 minority (African American) Average age 33. 31 applicants, 84% accepted, 12 enrolled. In 2006, 3 degrees awarded. *Degree requirements:* For master's, comprehensive exam. *Entrance requirements:* Additional exam requirements/recommendations for international students: Required—TOEFL. *Application deadline:* Applications are processed on a rolling basis. Application fee: $35. Electronic applications accepted. *Expenses:* Tuition, state resident: full-time $6,048; part-time $336 per credit. Tuition, nonresident: full-time $9,678; part-time $538 per credit. *Financial support:* Career-related internships or fieldwork, Federal Work-Study, and unspecified assistantships available. Financial award application deadline: 3/15; financial award applicants required to submit FAFSA. *Unit head:* Dr. Lynn Milet, Graduate Coordinator, 610-683-1598, E-mail: milet@kutztown.edu.

Lamar University, College of Graduate Studies, College of Education and Human Development, Department of Educational Leadership, Beaumont, TX 77710. Offers counseling and development (M Ed, Certificate); education administration (M Ed); educational leadership (DE); principal (Certificate); school superintendent (Certificate); supervision (M Ed); technology application (Certificate). Part-time and evening/weekend programs available. *Faculty:* 11 full-time (5 women), 4 part-time/adjunct (1 woman). *Students:* 44 full-time (34 women), 113 part-time (86 women); includes 34 minority (27 African Americans, 2 Asian Americans or Pacific Islanders, 5 Hispanic Americans), 2 international. Average age 35. 301 applicants, 33% accepted, 32 enrolled. In 2006, 68 degrees awarded. Terminal master's awarded for partial completion of doctoral program. *Degree requirements:* For master's, thesis optional; for doctorate, thesis/dissertation, registration. *Entrance requirements:* For master's, GRE General Test, minimum GPA of 2.5; for doctorate, GRE. Additional exam requirements/recommendations for international students: Required—TOEFL. *Application deadline:* For fall admission, 8/1 priority date for domestic students; for spring admission, 12/1 priority date for domestic students. Applications are processed on a rolling basis. Application fee: $25 ($50 for international students). *Expenses:* Tuition, nonresident: part-time $33 per hour. Required fees: $43 per hour. $110 per semester. *Financial support:* In 2006–07, 3 fellowships (averaging $20,000 per year), 1 research assistantship with tuition reimbursement (averaging $6,500 per year) were awarded; teaching assistantships with tuition reimbursements, career-related internships or fieldwork and scholarships/grants also available. Support available to part-time students. Financial award application deadline: 4/1. *Faculty research:* School dropouts, suicide prevention in public school students, school climate and gifted performance, teacher evaluation. *Unit head:* Dr. Carolyn Crawford, Chair, 409-880-8689, Fax: 409-880-8685.

Lawrence Technological University, College of Arts and Sciences, Southfield, MI 48075-1058. Offers computer science (MS); educational technology (MET); science education (MSE); technical communication (MS). Part-time and evening/weekend programs available. *Faculty:* 9 full-time (3 women), 8 part-time/adjunct (0 women). *Students:* 5 full-time (0 women), 100 part-time (59 women); includes 21 minority (8 African Americans, 13 Asian Americans or Pacific Islanders), 2 international. Average age 33. 87 applicants, 87% accepted, 39 enrolled. In 2006, 42 degrees awarded. *Entrance requirements:* For master's, GRE. Additional exam requirements/recommendations for international students: Required—TOEFL (minimum score 550 paper-based; 213 computer-based). *Application deadline:* For fall admission, 8/1 priority date for domestic students; for winter admission, 12/1 priority date for domestic students; for

Educational Media/Instructional Technology

Lawrence Technological University (continued)

spring admission, 5/1 for domestic students. Applications are processed on a rolling basis. Application fee: $50. Electronic applications accepted. *Financial support:* Application deadline: 3/1; *Unit head:* Dr. Hsiao-Ping Moore, Interim Dean, 248-204-3500, Fax: 248-204-3518, E-mail: scidean@ltu.edu. *Application contact:* Jane Rohrback, Director of Admissions, 248-204-3160, Fax: 248-204-3188, E-mail: admissions@ltu.edu.

Lehigh University, College of Education, Department of Education and Human Services, Program in Educational Technology, Bethlehem, PA 18015-3094. Offers educational technology (Ed D, PhD); instructional technology (MS); learning sciences and technology (PhD); project management (Certificate); technology use in schools (Certificate). Part-time and evening/weekend programs available. *Faculty:* 29 full-time (16 women), 17 part-time/adjunct (9 women). *Students:* 12 full-time (8 women), 32 part-time (18 women); includes 4 minority (2 African Americans, 1 Asian American or Pacific Islander, 1 Hispanic American), 10 international. 24 applicants, 58% accepted, 11 enrolled. In 2006, 9 degrees awarded. Terminal master's awarded for partial completion of doctoral program. *Degree requirements:* For doctorate, thesis/dissertation. *Entrance requirements:* For master's, minimum GPA of 3.0; for doctorate, GRE General Test or MAT, minimum graduate GPA of 3.0. Additional exam requirements/recommendations for international students: Required—TOEFL (minimum score 600 paper-based; 250 computer-based). *Application deadline:* Applications are processed on a rolling basis. Application fee: $60. Electronic applications accepted. *Financial support:* Career-related internships or fieldwork, Federal Work-Study, institutionally sponsored loans, scholarships/grants, and tuition waivers (full and partial) available. Financial award application deadline: 1/31. *Unit head:* Dr. H. Lynn Columba, Head, 610-758-3230, Fax: 610-758-3243, E-mail: hlc0@lehigh.edu.

Lehigh University, College of Education, Department of Education and Human Services, Program in Technology–Based Teacher Education, Bethlehem, PA 18015-3094. Offers elementary education (M Ed); learning sciences and technology (PhD); secondary education (M Ed, MA). Part-time and evening/weekend programs available. *Faculty:* 29 full-time (16 women), 17 part-time/adjunct (9 women). *Students:* 36 full-time (30 women), 34 part-time (22 women); includes 2 minority (both Asian Americans or Pacific Islanders), 2 international. 27 applicants, 85% accepted, 10 enrolled. In 2006, 53 master's, 1 doctorate awarded. *Entrance requirements:* For master's, minimum GPA of 3.0; for doctorate, GRE General Test, minimum GPA of 3.0. Additional exam requirements/recommendations for international students: Required—TOEFL (minimum score 600 paper-based; 250 computer-based). *Application deadline:* Applications are processed on a rolling basis. Application fee: $60. Electronic applications accepted. *Financial support:* Career-related internships or fieldwork, Federal Work-Study, institutionally sponsored loans, scholarships/grants, and tuition waivers (full and partial) available. Financial award application deadline: 1/31. *Unit head:* Dr. H. Lynn Columba, Head, 610-758-3230, Fax: 610-758-3243, E-mail: hlc0@lehigh.edu.

Lindenwood University, Graduate Programs, Division of Education, St. Charles, MO 63301-1695. Offers education (MA); educational administration (MA, Ed D, Ed S); instructional leadership (Ed D, Ed S); library media (MA); professional and school counseling (MA); professional counseling (MA); school counseling (MA); teaching (MA). Part-time and evening/weekend programs available. *Faculty:* 15 full-time (6 women), 16 part-time/adjunct (11 women). *Students:* 569 full-time (446 women), 1,869 part-time (1,433 women); includes 526 minority (494 African Americans, 8 American Indian/Alaska Native, 9 Asian Americans or Pacific Islanders, 15 Hispanic Americans), 8 international. Average age 35. In 2006, 747 master's, 19 other advanced degrees awarded. *Degree requirements:* For master's, thesis (for some programs); for doctorate, thesis/dissertation; for Ed S, specialist project. *Entrance requirements:* For master's, interview, minimum GPA of 3.0, writing sample; for Ed S, master's degree in education, relevant work experience. Additional exam requirements/recommendations for international students: Required—TOEFL (minimum score 550 paper-based; 213 computer-based). *Application deadline:* For fall admission, 8/30 priority date for domestic and international students; for spring admission, 12/30 priority date for domestic and international students. Applications are processed on a rolling basis. Application fee: $30 ($100 for international students). Electronic applications accepted. *Expenses:* Tuition: Part-time $340 per credit hour. Tuition and fees vary according to course level, course load, degree level and program. *Financial support:* Career-related internships or fieldwork, institutionally sponsored loans, and tuition waivers (partial) available. Financial award application deadline: 6/30; financial award applicants required to submit FAFSA. *Unit head:* Dr. John Dougherty, Dean of Education, 636-949-4937, E-mail: jdougherty@lindenwood.edu. *Application contact:* Brett Barger, Dean, Adult, Corporate and Graduate Admissions, 636-949-4934, Fax: 636-949-4109, E-mail: adultadmissions@lindenwood.edu.

Long Island University, Brooklyn Campus, School of Education, Department of Teaching and Learning, Program in Computers in Education, Brooklyn, NY 11201-8423. Offers MS. *Degree requirements:* For master's, thesis optional. *Entrance requirements:* For master's, 2 letters of recommendation. Additional exam requirements/recommendations for international students: Required—TOEFL (minimum score 500 paper-based; 173 computer-based).

Long Island University, C.W. Post Campus, School of Education, Department of Educational Technology, Brookville, NY 11548-1300. Offers computers in education (MS). Part-time and evening/weekend programs available. *Degree requirements:* For master's, research project. *Entrance requirements:* For master's, interview; minimum GPA of 2.75 in major, 2.5 overall. Electronic applications accepted. *Faculty research:* Desktop publishing, higher-order thinking skills, interactive learning environments.

Longwood University, Office of Graduate Studies, College of Education and Human Services, Farmville, VA 23909. Offers communication sciences and disorders (MS); community and college counseling (MS); curriculum and instruction specialist-elementary (MS), including mild disabilities, modern languages; curriculum and instruction specialist-secondary (MS), including English, mild disabilities, modern languages; educational leadership (MS); guidance and counseling (MS); literacy and culture (MS); school library media (MS). *Accreditation:* NCATE. Part-time and evening/weekend programs available. *Degree requirements:* For master's, thesis optional. *Entrance requirements:* For master's, GRE (communication sciences and disorders), minimum GPA of 2.75. Additional exam requirements/recommendations for international students: Required—TOEFL (minimum score 550 paper-based; 213 computer-based).

Louisiana State University and Agricultural and Mechanical College, Graduate School, College of Education, Department of Educational Theory, Policy and Practice, Baton Rouge, LA 70803. Offers counseling (M Ed, MA, Ed S); educational administration (M Ed, MA, PhD, Ed S); educational technology (MA); elementary education (M Ed); higher education (PhD); research methodology (PhD); secondary education (M Ed). *Accreditation:* ACA (one or more programs are accredited); NCATE. Part-time and evening/weekend programs available. *Faculty:* 39 full-time (24 women). *Students:* 147 full-time (115 women), 183 part-time (143 women); includes 63 minority (51 African Americans, 3 American Indian/Alaska Native, 3 Asian Americans or Pacific Islanders, 6 Hispanic Americans), 14 international. Average age 35. 110 applicants, 58% accepted, 15 enrolled. In 2006, 93 master's, 24 doctorates awarded. Terminal master's awarded for partial completion of doctoral program. *Degree requirements:* For doctorate, thesis/dissertation; for Ed S, thesis optional. *Entrance requirements:* For master's and doctorate, GRE General Test, minimum GPA of 3.0. Additional exam requirements/recommendations for international students: Required—TOEFL (minimum score 550 paper-based; 213 computer-based; 79 iBT). *Application deadline:* For fall admission, 1/25 priority date for domestic students, 5/15 for international students; for spring admission, 10/15 for international students. Applications are processed on a rolling basis. Application fee: $25. Electronic applications accepted. *Financial support:* In 2006–07, 82 students received support, including 6 fellowships with full tuition reimbursements available (averaging $26,273 per year), 24 research assistantships with full and partial tuition reimbursements available (averaging $9,812 per year), teaching assistantships with full and partial tuition reimbursements available (averaging

$11,693 per year); career-related internships or fieldwork, Federal Work-Study, institutionally sponsored loans, and unspecified assistantships also available. Support available to part-time students. Financial award applicants required to submit FAFSA. *Faculty research:* Literary, curriculum studies, science education, K-12 leadership, higher education. Total annual research expenditures: $335,618. *Unit head:* Dr. Earl Cheek, Chair, 225-578-6897, Fax: 225-578-1045, E-mail: echeek@lsu.edu.

Lourdes College, School of Graduate and Professional Studies, Program in Education, Sylvania, OH 43560-2898. Offers endorsement in computer technology (M Ed). Evening/weekend programs available. *Entrance requirements:* Additional exam requirements/recommendations for international students: Required—TOEFL.

Loyola College in Maryland, Graduate Programs, College of Arts and Sciences, Department of Education, Program in Educational Technology, Baltimore, MD 21210-2699. Offers M Ed. *Students:* 3 full-time (2 women), 31 part-time (24 women); includes 4 minority (2 African Americans, 1 Asian American or Pacific Islander, 1 Hispanic American). Average age 29. In 2006, 10 degrees awarded. *Entrance requirements:* For master's, GRE General Test, GRE Subject Test (recommended). Additional exam requirements/recommendations for international students: Required—TOEFL (minimum score 550 paper-based; 213 computer-based). *Application deadline:* For fall admission, 7/1 for domestic students. Applications are processed on a rolling basis. Application fee: $50. *Financial support:* Applicants required to submit FAFSA. *Unit head:* Dr. David Marcovitz, Director, 410-617-2250, E-mail: marco@loyola.edu.

Loyola University Chicago, School of Education, Program in Initial Teacher Preparation, Chicago, IL 60611-2196. Offers elementary education (M Ed); reading specialist (M Ed); school technology (M Ed); science education (M Ed); secondary education (M Ed); special education (M Ed). *Accreditation:* NCATE. *Faculty:* 11 full-time (9 women), 6 part-time/adjunct (4 women). *Students:* 138. Average age 28. 95 applicants, 65% accepted, 39 enrolled. In 2006, 84 degrees awarded. *Degree requirements:* For master's, comprehensive exam. *Entrance requirements:* For master's, Illinois Basic Skills Test, 3 letters of recommendation, minimum GPA of 3.0, resumé. Additional exam requirements/recommendations for international students: Required—TOEFL (minimum score 550 paper-based; 213 computer-based; 79 iBT). *Application deadline:* For fall admission, 7/1 priority date for domestic and international students; for spring admission, 11/1 priority date for domestic and international students. Applications are processed on a rolling basis. Application fee: $50. Electronic applications accepted. *Financial support:* In 2006–07, 2 research assistantships with full tuition reimbursements (averaging $8,500 per year), 1 teaching assistantship were awarded. Financial award application deadline: 2/15. *Faculty research:* Positive behavior support, school reform, school improvement. *Unit head:* Dr. Dorothy Giroux, Director, 312-915-7027, E-mail: dgiroux@luc.edu. *Application contact:* Marie Rosin-Dittmar, Information Contact, 312-915-6800, E-mail: schleduc@luc.edu.

Malone College, School of Education, Graduate Program in Education, Canton, OH 44709-3897. Offers curriculum and instruction (MA); curriculum, instruction, and professional development (MA); instructional technology (MA); intervention specialist (MA); reading (MA). Part-time and evening/weekend programs available. *Faculty:* 11 full-time (4 women), 12 part-time/adjunct (9 women). *Students:* 4 full-time (2 women), 96 part-time (78 women); includes 5 minority (1 African American, 2 Asian Americans or Pacific Islanders, 2 Hispanic Americans). Average age 33. In 2006, 26 degrees awarded. *Degree requirements:* For master's, research project. *Entrance requirements:* For master's, minimum GPA of 3.0, teaching license. *Application deadline:* Applications are processed on a rolling basis. Application fee: $25. *Expenses:* Tuition: Part-time $399 per credit hour. *Financial support:* Tuition waivers (partial) available. Support available to part-time students. Financial award application deadline: 6/30. *Faculty research:* The Bible as children's literature, special needs students and literacy development, middle level education, school/university partnerships and professional development, child/adolescent literature and popular culture. *Unit head:* Dr. Donald Williams, Director, 330-471-8509, Fax: 330-471-8563, E-mail: dwilliams@malone.edu. *Application contact:* Dr. David Kleffman, Recruiter, 330-471-8447, Fax: 330-471-8343, E-mail: dkleffman@malone.edu.

McDaniel College, Graduate and Professional Studies, Program in Media/Library Science, Westminster, MD 21157-4390. Offers MS. Part-time and evening/weekend programs available. *Degree requirements:* For master's, thesis optional. *Entrance requirements:* For master's, GRE General Test, MAT, or NTE/PRAXIS I, letters of reference (3). Additional exam requirements/recommendations for international students: Required—TOEFL (minimum score 213 computer-based).

McNeese State University, Graduate School, College of Education, Department of Educational Leadership and Instructional Technology, Program in Educational Technology Leadership, Lake Charles, LA 70609. Offers M Ed. Evening/weekend programs available. *Faculty:* 4 full-time (3 women), 1 (woman) part-time/adjunct. *Students:* 10 full-time (7 women), 29 part-time (26 women); includes 10 minority (all African Americans), 1 international. In 2006, 22 degrees awarded. *Entrance requirements:* For master's, GRE, teaching certificate. *Application deadline:* For fall admission, 5/15 priority date for domestic students. Applications are processed on a rolling basis. Application fee: $20 ($30 for international students). *Expenses:* Tuition, area resident: Full-time $2,226; part-time $193 per hour. Required fees: $919; $106 per hour. *Financial support:* Fellowships available. Financial award application deadline: 5/1. *Unit head:* Dr. Sharon Van Metre, Head, Department of Educational Leadership and Instructional Technology, 337-475-5423, Fax: 337-475-5402, E-mail: svanmetr@mcneese.edu.

McNeese State University, Graduate School, College of Education, Program in Instructional Technology, Lake Charles, LA 70609. Offers MS. Evening/weekend programs available. *Faculty:* 4 full-time (3 women), 1 (woman) part-time/adjunct. *Students:* 7 full-time (4 women), 13 part-time (10 women); includes 4 African Americans, 1 Hispanic American, 4 international. In 2006, 4 degrees awarded. *Entrance requirements:* For master's, GRE, Teaching Certificate. *Application deadline:* For fall admission, 5/15 for domestic students. Applications are processed on a rolling basis. Application fee: $20 ($30 for international students). *Expenses:* Tuition, area resident: Full-time $2,226; part-time $193 per hour. Required fees: $919; $106 per hour. *Financial support:* Application deadline: 5/1. *Unit head:* Dr. Wayne R Fetter, Dean, College of Education, 337-475-5432, Fax: 337-475-5467, E-mail: wfetter@mcneese.edu.

Memorial University of Newfoundland, School of Graduate Studies, Faculty of Education, St. John's, NL A1C 5S7, Canada. Offers counseling psychology (M Ed); curriculum, teaching, and learning studies (M Ed); education (PhD); educational leadership studies (M Ed); information technology (M Ed); post-secondary studies (M Ed, Diploma), including health professional education (Diploma). Part-time programs available. *Degree requirements:* For master's, internship, paper folio, project, thesis optional; for doctorate, thesis/dissertation, thesis seminar, oral defense of thesis, comprehensive exam. *Entrance requirements:* For master's, undergraduate degree with at least 2nd class standing, 1-2 years work experience; for doctorate, minimum A average in graduate course work, MA in education, 2 years professional experience; for Diploma, 2nd class degree, 2 years of work experience with adult learners, appropriate academic qualifications and work experience in a health-related field. Electronic applications accepted. *Faculty research:* Critical thinking, literacy, cognitive studies and counseling, educational change, technology in instruction.

Mercy College, Division of Education, Dobbs Ferry, NY 10522-1189. Offers adolescence education: grades 7-12 (MS); applied behavior analysis (MS); bilingual education (MS); childhood education: grades 1-6 (MS); early childhood education: birth—grade 2 (MS); education (MS); elementary education (MS); learning technology (MS); middle childhood education: grades 5-9 (MS); reading (MS); school administration and supervision (MS); school building leadership (MS); school business administration (MS); secondary education (MS); special education (MS); students with disabilities: grades 5-9 (MS); students with disabilities: grades 7-12 (MS); teaching English to speakers of other languages (MS); teaching literacy: birth—grade 6 (MS); teaching literacy: grades 5-12 (MS); urban education (MS). *Students:* 572

full-time (467 women), 1,719 part-time (1,287 women); includes 943 minority (470 African Americans, 7 American Indian/Alaska Native, 48 Asian Americans or Pacific Islanders, 418 Hispanic Americans), 6 international. Average age 33. In 2006, 1090 degrees awarded. *Entrance requirements:* For master's, teaching certificate. *Application deadline:* For fall admission, 2/1 for domestic students. Applications are processed on a rolling basis. Application fee: $37. *Expenses: Contact institution.* Tuition and fees vary according to program. *Financial support:* Institutionally sponsored loans, scholarships/grants, and unspecified assistantships available. Support available to part-time students. *Faculty research:* Distance learning, literacy, assessment, community schools, impact of staff development. *Unit head:* Dr. William Prattella, Chairperson, 914-674-7555, Fax: 914-674-7352, E-mail: wprattella@mercy.edu. *Application contact:* Kathleen Jackson, Director of Admissions, 800-Mercy-NY, Fax: 914-674-7382, E-mail: admissions@mercy.edu.

Michigan State University, The Graduate School, College of Education, Department of Counseling, Educational Psychology and Special Education, East Lansing, MI 48824. Offers counseling (MA); educational psychology and educational technology (PhD); educational technology (MA); measurement and quantitative methods (PhD); rehabilitation counseling (MA); rehabilitation counselor education (PhD); school psychology (MA, PhD, Ed S); special education (MA, PhD). *Accreditation:* APA (one or more programs are accredited); CORE (one or more programs are accredited). Part-time programs available. *Faculty:* 36 full-time (13 women). *Students:* 218 full-time (149 women), 75 part-time (60 women); includes 38 minority (31 African Americans, 4 Asian Americans or Pacific Islanders, 3 Hispanic Americans), 63 international. Average age 31. 243 applicants, 44% accepted. In 2006, 136 master's, 34 doctorates awarded. *Entrance requirements:* Additional exam requirements/recommendations for international students: Required—TOEFL. Electronic applications accepted. *Expenses:* Tuition, state resident: part-time $346 per credit hour. Tuition, nonresident: part-time $730 per credit hour. Tuition and fees vary according to program. *Financial support:* In 2006–07, 125 fellowships with tuition reimbursements, 87 research assistantships with tuition reimbursements (averaging $13,854 per year), 67 teaching assistantships with tuition reimbursements (averaging $13,722 per year) were awarded. Total annual research expenditures: $3.4 million. *Unit head:* Dr. Richard S. Prawat, Chairperson, 517-353-6417, E-mail: rsprawat@msu.edu. *Application contact:* Kathy Dimoff, Admissions Coordinator, 517-355-6683, E-mail: dimoff@msu.edu.

MidAmerica Nazarene University, Graduate Studies in Education, Olathe, KS 66062-1899. Offers curriculum and instruction (M Ed); educational technology (MET); special education (MA). *Accreditation:* NCATE. Evening/weekend programs available. *Degree requirements:* For master's, thesis or alternative, creative project, technology leadership practicum. *Entrance requirements:* For master's, minimum undergraduate GPA of 2.8, 2 years of teaching experience. Expenses: Contact institution.

Midwestern State University, Graduate Studies, College of Education, Program in Educational Leadership and Technology, Wichita Falls, TX 76308. Offers ME. Part-time and evening/weekend programs available. *Faculty:* 11 full-time (7 women), 3 part-time/adjunct (2 women). *Students:* 1 full-time (0 women), 28 part-time (15 women); includes 3 minority (1 African American, 2 Hispanic Americans). Average age 38. 5 applicants, 80% accepted, 1 enrolled. In 2006, 23 degrees awarded. *Degree requirements:* For master's, comprehensive exam. *Entrance requirements:* For master's, GRE General Test or MAT. Additional exam requirements/recommendations for international students: Required—TOEFL (minimum score 550 paper-based; 213 computer-based). *Application deadline:* For fall admission, 7/1 for domestic students, 4/1 for international students; for spring admission, 11/1 for domestic students, 8/1 for international students. Applications are processed on a rolling basis. Application fee: $35 ($50 for international students). Electronic applications accepted. *Financial support:* In 2006–07, 17 students received support. Career-related internships or fieldwork, Federal Work-Study, institutionally sponsored loans, scholarships/grants, tuition waivers (partial), and unspecified assistantships available. Support available to part-time students. Financial award application deadline: 5/1; financial award applicants required to submit FAFSA. *Unit head:* Dr. Michael Land, Chair, 940-397-4139, Fax: 940-397-4694, E-mail: michael.land@mwsu.edu. *Application contact:* Dr. Martha Burger, Admissions Office, 940-397-6220, Fax: 940-397-4694, E-mail: martha.burger@mwsu.edu.

Minnesota State University Mankato, College of Graduate Studies, College of Education, Educational Studies: K–12 and Secondary Programs, Program in Library Media Education, Mankato, MN 56001. Offers MS, Certificate, SP. *Accreditation:* NCATE. Part-time programs available. *Students:* 3 full-time (all women), 31 part-time (27 women). Average age 40. In 2006, 12 degrees awarded. *Degree requirements:* For master's, thesis or alternative, comprehensive exam; for other advanced degree, thesis, comprehensive exam. *Entrance requirements:* For master's, GRE General Test (if GPA is below 3.0), minimum GPA of 3.0 during previous 2 years; for other advanced degree, minimum GPA of 3.0. Additional exam requirements/recommendations for international students: Required—TOEFL. *Application deadline:* For fall admission, 7/1 priority date for domestic students; for spring admission, 11/1 for domestic students. Applications are processed on a rolling basis. Application fee: $40. Electronic applications accepted. *Financial support:* Research assistantships with full tuition reimbursements, teaching assistantships with full tuition reimbursements, career-related internships or fieldwork, Federal Work-Study, and institutionally sponsored loans available. Support available to part-time students. Financial award application deadline: 3/15; financial award applicants required to submit FAFSA. *Unit head:* Dr. Linda Underwood, Graduate Coordinator, 507-389-5650. *Application contact:* 507-389-2321, E-mail: grad@mnsu.edu.

Mississippi State University, College of Education, Department of Instructional Systems, Leadership, and Workforce Development, Mississippi State, MS 39762. Offers instructional technology (MSIT); technology (MS, Ed D, PhD, Ed S); workforce education leadership (MS). *Faculty:* 20 full-time (7 women), 1 (woman) part-time/adjunct. *Students:* 48 full-time (30 women), 62 part-time (48 women); includes 54 minority (53 African Americans, 1 Hispanic American). Average age 34. 28 applicants, 75% accepted, 17 enrolled. In 2006, 65 master's, 8 doctorates awarded. *Degree requirements:* For master's, comprehensive oral or written exam, thesis optional; for doctorate, thesis/dissertation, comprehensive oral and written exam. *Entrance requirements:* For master's, GRE, minimum GPA of 2.75 in junior and senior courses; for doctorate, GRE. Additional exam requirements/recommendations for international students: Required—TOEFL. *Application deadline:* For fall admission, 7/1 for domestic students; for spring admission, 11/1 for domestic students. Applications are processed on a rolling basis. Application fee: $30. *Expenses:* Tuition, state resident: full-time $4,550; part-time $253 per hour. Tuition, nonresident: full-time $10,552; part-time $584 per hour. International tuition: $10,882 full-time. Tuition and fees vary according to course load. *Financial support:* In 2006–07, 6 teaching assistantships with full tuition reimbursements (averaging $8,923 per year) were awarded; Federal Work-Study, institutionally sponsored loans, and unspecified assistantships also available. Financial award applicants required to submit FAFSA. *Faculty research:* Computer technology, nontraditional students, interactive video, instructional technology, educational leadership. *Unit head:* Dr. Linda Cornelius, Interim Head, 662-325-2281, Fax: 662-325-7599, E-mail: lcornelius@colled.msstate.edu. *Application contact:* Dr. Phil Bonfanti, Director of Admissions, 662-325-4104, Fax: 662-325-8872, E-mail: admit@msstate.edu.

Mississippi University for Women, Graduate School, Division of Education and Human Sciences, Columbus, MS 39701-9998. Offers gifted studies (M Ed); instructional management (M Ed); speech/language pathology (MS). *Accreditation:* ASHA; NCATE. Part-time programs available. *Degree requirements:* For master's, thesis optional. *Entrance requirements:* For master's, GRE General Test or NTE (M Ed in gifted education or MS in speech/language pathology), MAT (M Ed in instructional management), minimum QPA of 3.0.

Missouri State University, Graduate College, College of Education, School of Teacher Education, Program in Instructional Media Technology, Springfield, MO 65804-0094. Offers MS Ed. *Students:* Average age 35. 3 applicants, 100% accepted, 3 enrolled. In 2006, 7 degrees awarded. *Degree requirements:* For master's, thesis or alternative, comprehensive exam. *Entrance requirements:* Additional exam requirements/recommendations for international students: Required—TOEFL (minimum score 550 paper-based; 213 computer-based; 79 iBT). *Application deadline:* For fall admission, 7/20 for domestic students; for spring admission, 12/20 for domestic students. Application fee: $35. *Expenses:* Tuition, state resident: full-time $3,582; part-time $199 per credit hour. Tuition, nonresident: full-time $6,984; part-time $199 per credit hour. Required fees: $548. Full-time tuition and fees vary according to course level, course load, program and reciprocity agreements. *Financial support:* Teaching assistantships with full tuition reimbursements, Federal Work-Study available. Financial award application deadline: 3/31; financial award applicants required to submit FAFSA.

Montana State University–Billings, College of Education and Human Services, Department of Educational Theory and Practice, Option in Educational Technology, Billings, MT 59101-0298. Offers M Ed. *Accreditation:* NCATE. Part-time programs available. *Students:* 1. In 2006, 1 degree awarded. *Degree requirements:* For master's, professional paper or thesis, thesis optional. *Entrance requirements:* For master's, GRE General Test or MAT, minimum GPA of 3.0 (undergraduate), 3.25 (graduate). *Application deadline:* Applications are processed on a rolling basis. Application fee: $40. *Expenses:* Tuition, state resident: full-time $4,599. Tuition, nonresident: full-time $10,786. *Financial support:* Teaching assistantships, career-related internships or fieldwork, Federal Work-Study, institutionally sponsored loans, scholarships/grants, tuition waivers (partial), and unspecified assistantships available. Support available to part-time students. Financial award application deadline: 5/1; financial award applicants required to submit FAFSA. *Application contact:* David M. Sullivan, Graduate Studies Counselor, 406-657-2053, Fax: 406-657-2299, E-mail: dsullivan@msubillings.edu.

Montclair State University, The Graduate School, College of Education and Human Services, Department of Curriculum and Teaching, Montclair, NJ 07043-1624. Offers education (M Ed); educational technology (M Ed); school library media specialist (Certificate); teaching (MAT, Certificate), including art (MAT), biological science (MAT), early childhood education (P-3) (MAT), earth science (MAT), elementary education (K-8) (MAT), English (MAT), French (MAT), health and physical education (MAT), health education (MAT), home economics (MAT), mathematics (MAT), music (MAT), physical education (MAT), physical science (MAT), social studies (MAT), Spanish (MAT), teacher of ESL (MAT), teacher of students with disabilities (MAT). Part-time and evening/weekend programs available. *Faculty:* 16 full-time (12 women), 13 part-time/adjunct (8 women). *Students:* 147 full-time (113 women), 230 part-time (188 women); includes 58 minority (33 African Americans, 1 American Indian/Alaska Native, 12 Asian Americans or Pacific Islanders, 12 Hispanic Americans), 4 international. Average age 33. 118 applicants, 38% accepted, 37 enrolled. In 2006, 166 master's, 11 other advanced degrees awarded. *Degree requirements:* For master's, field experience. *Entrance requirements:* For master's, PRAXIS II, minimum GPA of 2.67, 2 letters of recommendation. Additional exam requirements/recommendations for international students: Required—TOEFL (minimum score 83 computer-based). *Application deadline:* For fall admission, 2/15 for domestic and international students; for spring admission, 9/15 for domestic and international students. Applications are processed on a rolling basis. Application fee: $60. Electronic applications accepted. *Expenses:* Tuition, state resident: part-time $450 per credit. Tuition, nonresident: part-time $682 per credit. Tuition and fees vary according to degree level and program. *Financial support:* In 2006–07, 7 research assistantships with full tuition reimbursements (averaging $7,000 per year) were awarded; Federal Work-Study, scholarships/grants, and unspecified assistantships also available. Support available to part-time students. Financial award application deadline: 3/1; financial award applicants required to submit FAFSA. *Unit head:* Dr. Deborah Eldridge, Chairperson, 973-655-5187.

National-Louis University, National College of Education, Program in Technology in Education, Chicago, IL 60603. Offers M Ed, MS Ed, CAS. Part-time and evening/weekend programs available. *Students:* Average age 39. 24 applicants, 100% accepted. In 2006, 46 master's, 8 other advanced degrees awarded. *Degree requirements:* For master's, thesis (for some programs). *Entrance requirements:* For master's, GRE or MAT, minimum GPA of 3.0, teaching certificate; for CAS, master's degree, teaching certificate. *Application deadline:* Applications are processed on a rolling basis. Application fee: $25. *Expenses:* Tuition: Full-time $17,685. One-time fee: $40 full-time. *Financial support:* Fellowships, career-related internships or fieldwork, Federal Work-Study, institutionally sponsored loans, and scholarships/grants available. Support available to part-time students. Financial award applicants required to submit FAFSA. *Unit head:* Dr. Marianne Handler, Coordinator, 847-475-1100 Ext. 5155. *Application contact:* David McCulloch, Vice President for University Services, 800-443-5522 Ext. 5127, Fax: 847-465-0593, E-mail: dmcc@wheeling1.nl.edu.

National University, Academic Affairs, School of Education, Department of Special Education and Technology, La Jolla, CA 92037-1011. Offers deaf and hard of hearing education (MS); educational technology (MS); exceptional student education (MS); special education (MS). Part-time and evening/weekend programs available. Postbaccalaureate distance learning degree programs offered (no on-campus study). *Faculty:* 15 full-time (12 women), 389 part-time/adjunct (232 women). *Students:* 1,039 full-time (706 women), 2,426 part-time (1,549 women); includes 997 minority (337 African Americans, 27 American Indian/Alaska Native, 179 Asian Americans or Pacific Islanders, 454 Hispanic Americans), 19 international. Average age 38. 1,579 applicants, 1481 enrolled. In 2006, 215 degrees awarded. *Degree requirements:* For master's, thesis (for some programs). *Entrance requirements:* For master's, interview, minimum GPA of 2.5. Additional exam requirements/recommendations for international students: Required—TOEFL (minimum score 550 paper-based; 213 computer-based; 80 iBT), IELTS (minimum score 6). *Application deadline:* Applications are processed on a rolling basis. Application fee: $60 ($65 for international students). Electronic applications accepted. *Expenses:* Tuition: Full-time $7,722; part-time $286 per unit. One-time fee: $60. *Financial support:* Career-related internships or fieldwork, institutionally sponsored loans, scholarships/grants, and tuition waivers (partial) available. Support available to part-time students. Financial award application deadline: 6/30; financial award applicants required to submit FAFSA. *Unit head:* Dr. Jane Duckett, Chair, 858-642-8346, Fax: 858-642-8724, E-mail: jduckett@nu.edu. *Application contact:* Dominick Giovanniello, Associate Regional Dean—San Diego, 800-NAT-UNIV, Fax: 858-642-8709, E-mail: dgiovann@nu.edu.

National University, Academic Affairs, School of Media and Communication, Department of Media, La Jolla, CA 92037-1011. Offers digital cinema (MFA); educational and instructional technology (MS); video game production and design (MFA). Part-time and evening/weekend programs available. Postbaccalaureate distance learning degree programs offered (no on-campus study). *Faculty:* 11 full-time (5 women), 23 part-time/adjunct (8 women). *Students:* 71 full-time (31 women), 138 part-time (66 women); includes 54 minority (22 African Americans, 1 American Indian/Alaska Native, 13 Asian Americans or Pacific Islanders, 18 Hispanic Americans). Average age 39. 179 applicants, 167 enrolled. In 2006, 29 degrees awarded. *Degree requirements:* For master's, thesis. *Entrance requirements:* For master's, interview, minimum GPA of 2.5. Additional exam requirements/recommendations for international students: Required—TOEFL (minimum score 550 paper-based; 213 computer-based; 80 iBT), IELTS (minimum score 6). *Application deadline:* Applications are processed on a rolling basis. Application fee: $60 ($65 for international students). Electronic applications accepted. *Expenses:* Tuition: Full-time $7,722; part-time $286 per unit. One-time fee: $60. *Financial support:* Career-related internships or fieldwork, institutionally sponsored loans, scholarships/grants, and tuition waivers (partial) available. Support available to part-time students. Financial award application deadline: 6/30; financial award applicants required to submit FAFSA. *Unit head:* Dr. Timothy Langdell, Department Chair, 858-642-8466, Fax: 858-642-8743, E-mail: tlangdell@nu.edu. *Application contact:* Dominick Giovanniello, Associate Regional Dean—San Diego, 800-NAT-UNIV, Fax: 858-642-8709, E-mail: dgiovann@nu.edu.

Nazareth College of Rochester, Graduate Studies, Department of Education, Program in Educational Technology/Computer Education, Rochester, NY 14618-3790. Offers MS Ed. Part-time and evening/weekend programs available. *Faculty:* 2 full-time (1 woman), 4 part-time/adjunct (all women). *Students:* Average age 33. 6 applicants, 100% accepted, 4 enrolled. In 2006, 16 degrees awarded. *Entrance requirements:* For master's, minimum GPA of 3.0.

Educational Media/Instructional Technology

Nazareth College of Rochester (continued)
Application deadline: For fall admission, 4/1 for domestic students; for spring admission, 10/1 for domestic students. Application fee: $40. *Financial support:* Research assistantships with partial tuition reimbursements available. Financial award application deadline: 3/1; financial award applicants required to submit FAFSA. *Unit head:* Dr. James Fenwick, Director, 585-389-2815, Fax: 585-389-2817, E-mail: jfenwic3@naz.edu. *Application contact:* Judith G. Baker, Director, Graduate Admissions, 585-389-2050, Fax: 585-389-2817, E-mail: gradstudies@naz.edu.

New Jersey City University, Graduate and Continuing Education, College of Education, Concentration in Educational Technology, Jersey City, NJ 07305-1597. Offers MA. *Accreditation:* NCATE. Part-time and evening/weekend programs available. Postbaccalaureate distance learning degree programs offered (minimal on-campus study). *Faculty:* 10. *Students:* Average age 38. In 2006, 24 degrees awarded. *Degree requirements:* For master's, internship. *Entrance requirements:* For master's, GRE General Test or MAT. Additional exam requirements/recommendations for international students: Required—TOEFL. *Application deadline:* For fall admission, 8/1 priority date for domestic students; for spring admission, 12/1 for domestic students. Applications are processed on a rolling basis. Application fee: $0. *Expenses:* Tuition, state resident: full-time $7,038; part-time $391 per credit. Tuition, nonresident: full-time $12,510; part-time $695 per credit. Required fees: $65 per credit. *Financial support:* Unspecified assistantships available. *Unit head:* Dr. Cordelia Twomey, Chairperson, 201-200-3421, E-mail: ctwomey@njcu.edu.

New York Institute of Technology, Graduate Division, School of Education and Professional Services, Program in Instructional Technology, Old Westbury, NY 11568-8000. Offers distance learning (Advanced Certificate); instructional technology (MS); multimedia (Advanced Certificate). Part-time and evening/weekend programs available. Postbaccalaureate distance learning degree programs offered. *Students:* 13 full-time (8 women), 240 part-time (132 women); includes 33 minority (17 African Americans, 1 American Indian/Alaska Native, 2 Asian Americans or Pacific Islanders, 13 Hispanic Americans), 5 international. Average age 33. 79 applicants, 73% accepted, 47 enrolled. In 2006, 98 degrees awarded. *Degree requirements:* For master's, thesis. *Entrance requirements:* For master's, minimum QPA of 3.0; for Advanced Certificate, master's degree, minimum GPA of 3.0, 3 years of teaching experience, New York teaching certificate, 2 letters of recommendation. Additional exam requirements/recommendations for international students: Required—TOEFL. *Application deadline:* For fall admission, 7/1 priority date for domestic students; for spring admission, 12/1 priority date for domestic students. Applications are processed on a rolling basis. Application fee: $50. Electronic applications accepted. *Expenses:* Tuition: Full-time $16,800; part-time $700 per credit. *Financial support:* Research assistantships with partial tuition reimbursements, career-related internships or fieldwork, institutionally sponsored loans, and tuition waivers (full and partial) available. Support available to part-time students. Financial award applicants required to submit FAFSA. *Faculty research:* Distance learning, teacher training resources and strategies. *Unit head:* Dr. Joanne Clemente, Coordinator, 516-686-7494, Fax: 516-686-7655, E-mail: jclement@nyit.edu. *Application contact:* Jacquelyn Nealon, Dean of Admissions and Financial Aid, 516-686-7925, Fax: 516-686-7613, E-mail: jnealon@nyit.edu.

New York Institute of Technology, Graduate Division, School of Education and Professional Services, Program in Leadership and Technology, Old Westbury, NY 11568-8000. Offers district leadership and technology (Professional Diploma); school leadership and technology (Professional Diploma). Part-time and evening/weekend programs available. *Students:* 2 applicants, 50% accepted, 0 enrolled. In 2006, 2 degrees awarded. *Degree requirements:* For Professional Diploma, internship. *Entrance requirements:* For degree, must be full-time teacher with 3 years experience, permanent teacher certification in New York state. *Application deadline:* For fall admission, 7/1 for domestic students; for spring admission, 12/1 for domestic students. Application fee: $50. *Expenses:* Tuition: Full-time $16,800; part-time $700 per credit. *Financial support:* Career-related internships or fieldwork available. Financial award applicants required to submit FAFSA. *Application contact:* Jacquelyn Nealon, Dean of Admissions and Financial Aid, 516-686-7925, Fax: 516-686-7613, E-mail: jnealon@nyit.edu.

New York University, Steinhardt School of Culture, Education and Human Development, Department of Administration, Leadership, and Technology, Program in Educational Communication and Technology, New York, NY 10012-1019. Offers MA, PhD, Advanced Certificate. Part-time and evening/weekend programs available. *Faculty:* 4 full-time (2 women). *Students:* 21 full-time (12 women), 38 part-time (23 women); includes 15 minority (7 African Americans, 2 Asian Americans or Pacific Islanders, 6 Hispanic Americans), 17 international. 56 applicants, 52% accepted, 17 enrolled. In 2006, 15 master's, 2 doctorates, 1 other advanced degree awarded. Terminal master's awarded for partial completion of doctoral program. *Degree requirements:* For master's, thesis (for some programs); for doctorate, thesis/dissertation. *Entrance requirements:* For doctorate, GRE General Test, interview; for Advanced Certificate, master's degree. Additional exam requirements/recommendations for international students: Required—TOEFL. *Application deadline:* For fall admission, 12/15 priority date for domestic and international students; for spring admission, 11/1 for domestic and international students. Applications are processed on a rolling basis. Application fee: $50. *Expenses:* Tuition: Part-time $1,080 per unit. Required fees: $56 per unit. $329 per term. Tuition and fees vary according to program. *Financial support:* Fellowships with full and partial tuition reimbursements, research assistantships with full and partial tuition reimbursements, teaching assistantships with partial tuition reimbursements, career-related internships or fieldwork, Federal Work-Study, institutionally sponsored loans, scholarships/grants, tuition waivers (partial), and unspecified assistantships available. Support available to part-time students. Financial award application deadline: 2/1; financial award applicants required to submit FAFSA. *Faculty research:* Instructional design for video and interactive video programs, critical evaluation of instructional materials, multimedia, cognitive science, individual differences in multimedia learning. *Unit head:* Dr. Michael Reed, Director, 212-998-5520, Fax: 212-995-4047, E-mail: w.michael.reed@nyu.edu. *Application contact:* 212-998-5030, Fax: 212-995-4328, E-mail: steinhardt.gradadmissions@nyu.edu.

North Carolina Agricultural and Technical State University, Graduate School, School of Education, Department of Curriculum and Instruction, Greensboro, NC 27411. Offers early childhood education (MS); educational media (MS); elementary education (MS); intermediate education (MS), including biology education, chemistry education, English education, history education, social science education; reading (MS). *Accreditation:* NCATE. Part-time and evening/weekend programs available. *Degree requirements:* For master's, qualifying exam. *Entrance requirements:* For master's, GRE General Test, minimum GPA of 3.0.

North Carolina Central University, Division of Academic Affairs, School of Education, Program in Educational Technology, Durham, NC 27707-3129. Offers instructional media (MA). *Accreditation:* NCATE. Part-time and evening/weekend programs available. *Degree requirements:* For master's, thesis or alternative, comprehensive exam. *Entrance requirements:* For master's, GRE, minimum GPA of 3.0 in major, 2.5 overall. Additional exam requirements/recommendations for international students: Required—TOEFL. *Faculty research:* Role of media in school libraries, media and implications for educational gerontology.

North Carolina State University, Graduate School, College of Education, Department of Mathematics, Science, and Technology Education, Program in Technology Education, Raleigh, NC 27695. Offers M Ed, MS, Ed D. *Degree requirements:* For master's, thesis (for some programs); for doctorate, thesis/dissertation. *Entrance requirements:* For master's, GRE or MAT; for doctorate, GRE General Test or MAT, minimum GPA of 3.0, interview. Electronic applications accepted.

Northeastern State University, Graduate College, College of Education, Program in Library Media and Information Technology, Tahlequah, OK 74464-2399. Offers MS Ed. *Students:* 8 full-time (7 women), 45 part-time (all women); includes 12 minority (9 American Indian/Alaska Native, 3 Hispanic Americans), 1 international. In 2006, 10 degrees awarded. *Entrance requirements:* Additional exam requirements/recommendations for international students: Required—TOEFL (minimum score 213 computer-based). *Application deadline:* For fall admission, 6/1 for domestic students. Application fee: $0 ($25 for international students). *Unit head:* Dr. Barbara Ray, Head, 918-449-6000 Ext. 6451.

Northern Arizona University, Graduate College, College of Education, Program in Career and Technical Education, Flagstaff, AZ 86011. Offers administration (M Ed); educational technology (M Ed); teaching (M Ed). *Degree requirements:* For master's, final oral exam, project, thesis optional.

Northern Arizona University, Graduate College, College of Education, Program in Educational Technology, Flagstaff, AZ 86011. Offers M Ed, Certificate. Part-time and evening/weekend programs available.

Northern Illinois University, Graduate School, College of Education, Department of Educational Technology, Research and Assessment, De Kalb, IL 60115-2854. Offers educational research and evaluation (MS); instructional technology (MS Ed, Ed D). Part-time and evening/weekend programs available. *Faculty:* 13 full-time (7 women). *Students:* 32 full-time (21 women), 134 part-time (87 women); includes 41 minority (21 African Americans, 11 Asian Americans or Pacific Islanders, 9 Hispanic Americans), 11 international. Average age 41. 58 applicants, 64% accepted, 26 enrolled. In 2006, 37 master's, 9 doctorates awarded. Terminal master's awarded for partial completion of doctoral program. *Degree requirements:* For master's, thesis optional; for doctorate, thesis/dissertation, candidacy exam, dissertation defense. *Entrance requirements:* For master's, GRE General Test or MAT, minimum GPA of 2.75; for doctorate, GRE General Test or MAT, minimum undergraduate GPA of 2.75, 3.2 graduate. Additional exam requirements/recommendations for international students: Required—TOEFL (minimum score 550 paper-based; 213 computer-based). *Application deadline:* For fall admission, 6/1 for domestic students, 5/1 for international students; for spring admission, 11/1 for domestic students, 10/1 for international students. Applications are processed on a rolling basis. Application fee: $30. Electronic applications accepted. *Financial support:* In 2006–07, 3 research assistantships with full tuition reimbursements, 2 teaching assistantships with full tuition reimbursements were awarded; fellowships with full tuition reimbursements, career-related internships or fieldwork, Federal Work-Study, scholarships/grants, tuition waivers (full), and unspecified assistantships also available. Support available to part-time students. Financial award applicants required to submit FAFSA. *Faculty research:* Distance education, web based training, copyright assessment during student teaching, instructional software. *Unit head:* Dr. Jeffrey Hecht, Chair, 815-753-9939, E-mail: jbhecht@niu.edu.

Northern State University, Division of Graduate Studies in Education, Center for Statewide E-Learning, Aberdeen, SD 57401-7198. Offers e-learning design and instruction (MS Ed); e-learning technology and administration (MS). Part-time and evening/weekend programs available. *Faculty:* 2 full-time (1 woman), 1 part-time/adjunct (0 women). *Students:* 1 (woman) full-time, 5 part-time (2 women); includes 1 minority (Hispanic American) Average age 32. In 2006, 3 degrees awarded. *Degree requirements:* For master's, thesis optional. *Entrance requirements:* For master's, minimum GPA of 2.75. Additional exam requirements/recommendations for international students: Required—TOEFL (minimum score 550 paper-based; 213 computer-based). *Application deadline:* For fall admission, 8/15 priority date for domestic students; for spring admission, 12/15 for domestic students. Applications are processed on a rolling basis. Application fee: $35. Electronic applications accepted. *Expenses:* Tuition, state resident: full-time $3,373; part-time $120 per credit. Tuition, nonresident: full-time $9,943; part-time $355 per credit. International tuition: $13,000 full-time. Required fees: $86 per credit. One-time fee: $35 full-time. Tuition and fees vary according to course load, degree level and reciprocity agreements. *Financial support:* In 2006–07, 5 teaching assistantships with partial tuition reimbursements (averaging $4,812 per year) were awarded; career-related internships or fieldwork, Federal Work-Study, institutionally sponsored loans, scholarships/grants, and unspecified assistantships also available. Support available to part-time students. Financial award application deadline: 3/1; financial award applicants required to submit FAFSA. *Application contact:* Tammy K. Griffith, Senior Secretary, 605-626-2558, Fax: 605-626-2542, E-mail: griffith@northern.edu.

Northwestern State University of Louisiana, Graduate Studies and Research, College of Education, Program in Educational Technology Leadership, Natchitoches, LA 71497. Offers M Ed. *Students:* 3 full-time (all women), 10 part-time (8 women); includes 3 minority (all African Americans) Average age 35.*Application contact:* Dr. Steven G. Horton, Associate Provost/Dean, Graduate Studies, Research, and Information Systems, 318-357-5851, Fax: 318-357-5019, E-mail: grad_school@nsula.edu.

Northwestern State University of Louisiana, Graduate Studies and Research, College of Education, Programs in Education, Natchitoches, LA 71497. Offers business and distributive education (M Ed); counseling (M Ed); early childhood education (M Ed); education (M Ed); education leadership (M Ed); educational technology (M Ed); elementary teaching (M Ed); English education (M Ed); home economics education (M Ed); mathematics education (M Ed); reading (M Ed); science education (M Ed); secondary teaching (M Ed); social sciences education (M Ed). *Students:* 49 full-time (41 women), 245 part-time (206 women); includes 78 minority (70 African Americans, 5 American Indian/Alaska Native, 2 Asian Americans or Pacific Islanders, 1 Hispanic American). Average age 35. In 2006, 158 degrees awarded. *Degree requirements:* For master's, thesis or alternative, comprehensive exam, registration. *Entrance requirements:* For master's, GRE General Test, minimum undergraduate GPA of 2.5. *Application contact:* Dr. Steven G. Horton, Associate Provost/Dean, Graduate Studies, Research, and Information Systems, 318-357-5851, Fax: 318-357-5019, E-mail: grad_school@nsula.edu.

Northwestern State University of Louisiana, Graduate Studies and Research, College of Education, Programs in Educational Leadership and Instruction, Natchitoches, LA 71497. Offers counseling (Ed S); educational leadership (Ed S); educational technology (Ed S); elementary teaching (Ed S); reading (Ed S); secondary teaching (Ed S); special education (Ed S). *Students:* 17 full-time (15 women), 114 part-time (87 women); includes 55 minority (51 African Americans, 1 Asian American or Pacific Islander, 3 Hispanic Americans). Average age 39. In 2006, 11 degrees awarded. *Entrance requirements:* For degree, GRE General Test. *Application contact:* Dr. Steven G. Horton, Associate Provost/Dean, Graduate Studies, Research, and Information Systems, 318-357-5851, Fax: 318-357-5019, E-mail: grad_school@nsula.edu.

Northwestern University, The Graduate School, School of Education and Social Policy, Program in Learning Sciences, Evanston, IL 60208. Offers MA, PhD. Admissions and degrees offered through The Graduate School. *Faculty:* 18 full-time (4 women), 13 part-time/adjunct (7 women). *Students:* 40 full-time (23 women); includes 7 minority (4 African Americans, 2 Asian Americans or Pacific Islanders, 1 Hispanic American), 8 international. Average age 32. 88 applicants, 35% accepted, 9 enrolled. In 2006, 6 master's, 7 doctorates awarded. Terminal master's awarded for partial completion of doctoral program. *Degree requirements:* For master's, thesis or alternative, portfolio; for doctorate, thesis/dissertation, qualifying exam. *Entrance requirements:* For master's, GRE General Test (recommended); for doctorate, GRE General Test. Additional exam requirements/recommendations for international students: Required—TOEFL (minimum score 600 paper-based; 250 computer-based; 100 iBT). *Application deadline:* For winter admission, 12/31 for domestic and international students. Application fee: $75. Electronic applications accepted. *Financial support:* In 2006–07, 40 students received support, including 11 fellowships, 20 research assistantships; teaching assistantships with full tuition reimbursements available, institutionally sponsored loans, scholarships/grants, and unspecified assistantships also available. Financial award application deadline: 12/31; financial award applicants required to submit FAFSA. *Faculty research:* Technologically supported learning environments; inquiry based learning in mathematics, science, and literacy; learning social contexts; cognitive models of learning and problem solving; changing roles for teachers involved in innovative design and practice. *Unit head:* Louis Gomez, Coordinator of Doctoral

Program, 847-491-7494, Fax: 847-491-8999. *Application contact:* Dapne Nwankpa, Department Assistant, 847-491-7494, Fax: 847-491-8999, E-mail: lsprograms@mail.sesp.northwestern.edu.

See Close-Up on page 901.

Northwest Missouri State University, Graduate School, Melvin and Valorie Booth College of Business and Professional Studies, Department of Computer Science and Information Systems, Program in Teaching Instructional Technology, Maryville, MO 64468-6001. Offers MS Ed. Part-time programs available. *Faculty:* 8 full-time (3 women). *Students:* 1 full-time (0 women), 16 part-time (12 women). 11 applicants, 100% accepted, 2 enrolled. In 2006, 10 degrees awarded. *Degree requirements:* For master's, comprehensive exam. *Entrance requirements:* For master's, GRE General Test, GRE Subject Test, minimum GPA of 2.5, teaching certificate, writing sample. Additional exam requirements/recommendations for international students: Required—TOEFL (minimum score 550 paper-based; 213 computer-based). *Application deadline:* For fall admission, 7/1 for domestic and international students; for spring admission, 12/1 for domestic students, 11/15 for international students. Applications are processed on a rolling basis. Application fee: $0 ($50 for international students). *Financial support:* Application deadline: 3/1; *Unit head:* Dr. Cheryl Malm, Director, 660-562-1206. *Application contact:* Dr. Frances Shipley, Dean of Graduate School, 660-562-1145, Fax: 660-562-1096, E-mail: gradsch@nwmissouri.edu.

Notre Dame de Namur University, Division of Academic Affairs, School of Education and Leadership, Program in Education in Technology Leadership, Belmont, CA 94002-1908. Offers MA, Certificate. *Degree requirements:* For master's, thesis. *Application deadline:* For fall admission, 8/1 priority date for domestic students; for spring admission, 12/1 priority date for domestic students. Applications are processed on a rolling basis. Application fee: $50. Electronic applications accepted. *Expenses:* Tuition: Part-time $655 per credit. *Financial support:* Applicants required to submit FAFSA. *Unit head:* Dr. Diane Guay, Director, 650-508-3702. *Application contact:* Helen Valine, Director of Graduate Admissions, 650-508-3534, Fax: 650-508-3426, E-mail: grad.admit@ndnu.edu.

Nova Southeastern University, Fischler School of Education and Human Services, Graduate Teacher Education Program, Fort Lauderdale, FL 33314-7796. Offers athletic administration (MS); cognitive and behavioral disabilities (MS); computer science education (Ed S); computer science education (K-12) (MS); curriculum and teaching (Ed S); curriculum, instruction and technology (MS); curriculum, instruction, management and administration (Ed S); early childhood special education (MS); early literacy and reading (Ed S); early literacy education (MS); education technology (MS); educational leadership (administration K–12) (MS, Ed S); educational media (Ed S); educational media (K-12) (MS); elementary education (MS, Ed S), including ESOL endorsement (MS); English (MS, Ed S); exceptional student education (MS), including ESOL endorsement; gifted education (MS, Ed S); interdisciplinary arts education (MS); management and administration of educational programs (MS); mathematics (MS, Ed S); multicultural early intervention (MS); pre-kindergarten/primary (MS); preschool education (MS); reading (MS, Ed S); science (MS, Ed S); secondary education (MS); social studies (MS, Ed S); Spanish language (MS); teaching and learning (MA, MS), including curriculum and instruction (MA), elementary mathematics (MA), elementary reading (MA), K-12 technology integration (MA); teaching English to speakers of other languages (MS, Ed S); technology management and administration (Ed S); urban studies education (MS); varying exceptionalities (Ed S). Part-time and evening/weekend programs available. Postbaccalaureate distance learning degree programs offered. *Faculty:* 131 full-time (78 women), 548 part-time/adjunct (342 women). *Students:* 1,418 full-time (1,139 women), 3,464 part-time (2,877 women); includes 2,462 minority (1,732 African Americans, 13 American Indian/Alaska Native, 44 Asian Americans or Pacific Islanders, 673 Hispanic Americans), 77 international. Average age 38. 1,771 applicants, 80% accepted, 1419 enrolled. In 2006, 2,078 master's, 425 other advanced degrees awarded. *Degree requirements:* For master's and Ed S, thesis, practicum, internship. *Entrance requirements:* For master's, MAT, GRE, CLAST, CBEST, PRAXIS I, GKT, minimum GPA of 2.5; for Ed S, MAT or GRE, master's degree, teaching certificate, minimum GPA of 3.0. Additional exam requirements/recommendations for international students: Recommended—TOEFL (minimum score 550 paper-based; 213 computer-based), IELTS (minimum score 6). *Application deadline:* For fall admission, 8/11 priority date for domestic and international students; for winter admission, 12/28 priority date for domestic and international students; for spring admission, 4/22 priority date for domestic and international students. Applications are processed on a rolling basis. Application fee: $50. Electronic applications accepted. *Financial support:* Federal Work-Study available. Support available to part-time students. Financial award application deadline: 1/7. *Faculty research:* School effectiveness, critical thinking, leadership skills acquisition, child education, multicultural education. *Unit head:* Dr. Meline Kevorkian, Associate Dean of Master's and Educational Programs, 954-262-8500, Fax: 954-262-3606, E-mail: melinek@nova.edu. *Application contact:* Jennifer Quiñones Nottingham, Dean of Student Affairs, 800-986-3223 Ext. 8624, Fax: 954-262-3911, E-mail: jlquinon@nova.edu.

Nova Southeastern University, Fischler School of Education and Human Services, Program in Education, Fort Lauderdale, FL 33314-7796. Offers educational leadership (Ed D); health care education (Ed D); higher education (Ed D); human serviced administration (Ed D); instructional leadership (Ed D); instructional technology distance education (Ed D); organizational leadership (Ed D); special education (Ed D); speech language pathology (Ed D). *Students:* 619 full-time (452 women), 615 part-time (473 women); includes 737 minority (616 African Americans, 2 American Indian/Alaska Native, 14 Asian Americans or Pacific Islanders, 105 Hispanic Americans), 8 international. Average age 38. 480 applicants, 83% accepted, 398 enrolled. *Degree requirements:* For doctorate, thesis/dissertation. *Entrance requirements:* For doctorate, MAT or GRE, master's degree, 2 letters of recommendation, work experience. Additional exam requirements/recommendations for international students: Required—TSE (recommended) with a minimum score of 50; Recommended—TOEFL (minimum score 550 paper-based; 213 computer-based), IELTS (minimum score 6). *Application deadline:* For fall admission, 8/11 priority date for domestic and international students; for winter admission, 12/28 priority date for domestic and international students; for spring admission, 4/22 priority date for domestic and international students. Applications are processed on a rolling basis. Application fee: $50. Electronic applications accepted. *Financial support:* In 2006–07, 2 fellowships (averaging $9,375 per year) were awarded; scholarships/grants and tuition waivers (full) also available. Support available to part-time students. Financial award application deadline: 1/7; financial award applicants required to submit FAFSA. *Unit head:* Dr. Karen D. Bowser, Associate Dean of Doctoral Programs, 954-262-8500, Fax: 954-262-3912, E-mail: bowserk@nova.edu. *Application contact:* Jennifer Quiñones Nottingham, Dean of Student Affairs, 800-986-3223 Ext. 8624, Fax: 954-262-3911, E-mail: jlquinon@nova.edu.

Nova Southeastern University, Fischler School of Education and Human Services, Programs in Instructional Technology and Distance Education, Fort Lauderdale, FL 33314-7796. Offers MS, Ed D. Part-time and evening/weekend programs available. Postbaccalaureate distance learning degree programs offered. *Faculty:* 6 full-time (2 women), 22 part-time/adjunct (14 women). *Students:* 6 full-time (5 women), 234 part-time (150 women); includes 87 minority (17 African Americans, 1 American Indian/Alaska Native, 2 Asian Americans or Pacific Islanders, 67 Hispanic Americans), 68 international. In 2006, 4 master's, 21 doctorates awarded. *Degree requirements:* For master's, practicum; for doctorate, thesis/dissertation, practicum. *Entrance requirements:* For master's, interview, current employment in a position using technology; for doctorate, MAT, minimum GPA of 3.0, interview, current employment in a position using technology. *Application deadline:* Applications are processed on a rolling basis. Application fee: $50. *Financial support:* Fellowships available. *Unit head:* Dr. Maryellen Maher, Executive Dean, 954-262-8554, Fax: 954-262-3905, E-mail: maherm@nova.edu. *Application contact:* Dr. Marsha Burmeister, Head, 800-986-3223 Ext. 8572, Fax: 954-262-3905, E-mail: burmeist@nova.edu.

Nova Southeastern University, Graduate School of Computer and Information Sciences, Program in Computing Technology in Education, Fort Lauderdale, FL 33314-7796. Offers MS, PhD. Part-time and evening/weekend programs available. Postbaccalaureate distance learning degree programs offered (no on-campus study). *Students:* 44 full-time (23 women), 104 part-time (70 women); includes 37 minority (22 African Americans, 1 Asian American or Pacific Islander, 14 Hispanic Americans), 2 international. In 2006, 20 master's, 22 doctorates awarded. *Degree requirements:* For master's, thesis optional; for doctorate, thesis/dissertation. *Application deadline:* Applications are processed on a rolling basis. *Financial support:* Application deadline: 5/1; *Application contact:* 954-262-2000, Fax: 954-262-3915, E-mail: scisinfo@nova.edu.

Oakland University, Graduate Study and Lifelong Learning, School of Education and Human Services, Program in Microcomputer Applications in Education, Rochester, MI 48309-4401. Offers advanced microcomputer applications (Certificate); microcomputer applications (Certificate). In 2006, 1 degree awarded. *Entrance requirements:* Additional exam requirements/recommendations for international students: Required—TOEFL (minimum score 550 paper-based; 213 computer-based). *Application deadline:* For fall admission, 8/1 priority date for domestic students, 5/1 priority date for international students; for winter admission, 12/1 priority date for domestic students, 9/1 priority date for international students; for spring admission, 4/1 priority date for domestic students. Application fee: $35. Electronic applications accepted. *Expenses:* Tuition, state resident: full-time $9,936; part-time $414 per credit. Tuition, nonresident: full-time $17,202; part-time $716 per credit. *Financial support:* Federal Work-Study, institutionally sponsored loans, and tuition waivers (full) available. Financial award application deadline: 3/1; financial award applicants required to submit FAFSA. *Unit head:* Dr. Anne E. Porter, Coordinator, 248-370-3074, Fax: 248-370-4367, E-mail: porter@oakland.edu.

Ohio University, Graduate Studies, College of Education, Department of Educational Studies, Athens, OH 45701-2979. Offers computer education and technology (M Ed); educational administration (M Ed, Ed D); educational research and evaluation (M Ed, PhD); instructional technology (PhD). Part-time and evening/weekend programs available. Postbaccalaureate distance learning degree programs offered (minimal on-campus study). *Faculty:* 13 full-time (7 women), 1 (woman) part-time/adjunct. *Students:* 77 full-time (41 women), 120 part-time (55 women); includes 5 minority (3 African Americans, 1 Asian American or Pacific Islander, 1 Hispanic American), 79 international. 121 applicants, 69% accepted, 49 enrolled. In 2006, 12 master's, 14 doctorates awarded. *Median time to degree:* Of those who began their doctoral program in fall 1998, 92% received their degree in 8 years or less. *Degree requirements:* For master's, thesis or alternative, registration; for doctorate, thesis/dissertation, comprehensive exam, registration. *Entrance requirements:* For master's, GRE General Test if GPA is less than 2.8; for doctorate, GRE General Test, minimum GPA of 3.4, work experience, 3 letters of reference, autobiography. Additional exam requirements/recommendations for international students: Required—TOEFL (minimum score 550 paper-based; 213 computer-based). *Application deadline:* For fall admission, 4/1 priority date for domestic and international students. Applications are processed on a rolling basis. Application fee: $45. Electronic applications accepted. *Financial support:* In 2006–07, 26 research assistantships with full tuition reimbursements (averaging $6,500 per year), 2 teaching assistantships with full tuition reimbursements (averaging $7,200 per year) were awarded; Federal Work-Study, institutionally sponsored loans, tuition waivers (full), and unspecified assistantships also available. Financial award application deadline: 3/15. *Faculty research:* Race, class and gender; computer programs; development and organization theory; evaluation/development of instruments, leadership. Total annual research expenditures: $158,037. *Unit head:* Dr. Catherine H. Glascock, Chair, 740-593-4464, Fax: 740-593-0477, E-mail: glascock@ohio.edu. *Application contact:* Floyd J. Doney, Director of Student Affairs, 740-593-4400, Fax: 740-593-9310, E-mail: doney@ohio.edu.

Old Dominion University, Darden College of Education, Program in Elementary/Middle Education, Norfolk, VA 23529. Offers educational media (MS Ed); elementary education (MS Ed); instructional technology (MS Ed); library science (MS Ed); middle school education (MS Ed). *Accreditation:* NCATE. Part-time and evening/weekend programs available. Postbaccalaureate distance learning degree programs offered (no on-campus study). *Faculty:* 20 full-time (9 women). *Students:* 116 full-time (103 women), 217 part-time (178 women); includes 32 minority (22 African Americans, 2 American Indian/Alaska Native, 3 Asian Americans or Pacific Islanders, 5 Hispanic Americans). Average age 35. 127 applicants, 56% accepted, 61 enrolled. In 2006, 167 degrees awarded. *Degree requirements:* For master's, comprehensive exam. *Entrance requirements:* For master's, GRE General Test or MAT and PRAXIS I or SAT or ACT, minimum GPA of 2.8. *Application deadline:* For fall admission, 6/1 priority date for domestic students; for winter admission, 11/1 priority date for domestic students; for spring admission, 3/1 priority date for domestic students. Applications are processed on a rolling basis. Application fee: $40. Electronic applications accepted. *Expenses:* Tuition, area resident: Part-time $285 per credit hour. Tuition, nonresident: part-time $715 per credit hour. Required fees: $94 per semester. *Financial support:* In 2006–07, 180 students received support, including 4 research assistantships with tuition reimbursements available (averaging $9,000 per year), teaching assistantships (averaging $8,000 per year); fellowships, career-related internships or fieldwork, Federal Work-Study, institutionally sponsored loans, scholarships/grants, and tuition waivers (partial) also available. Support available to part-time students. Financial award application deadline: 2/15; financial award applicants required to submit FAFSA. *Faculty research:* Education pre-K to 6, school librarianship. *Unit head:* Dr. Gail S. Taylor, Graduate Program Director, 757-683-4180, E-mail: eciegpd@odu.edu.

Old Dominion University, Darden College of Education, Program in Instructional Design and Technology, Norfolk, VA 23529. Offers PhD. Part-time and evening/weekend programs available. Postbaccalaureate distance learning degree programs offered (no on-campus study). *Faculty:* 3 full-time (1 woman). *Students:* 7 full-time (5 women), 6 part-time (2 women); includes 3 minority (all African Americans) Average age 43. 8 applicants, 75% accepted, 6 enrolled. *Degree requirements:* For doctorate, thesis/dissertation, comprehensive exam, registration. *Entrance requirements:* For doctorate, GRE, references, interview. Additional exam requirements/recommendations for international students: Required—TOEFL (minimum score 550 paper-based; 213 computer-based). *Application deadline:* For fall admission, 6/1 priority date for domestic and international students; for winter admission, 11/1 priority date for domestic and international students. Applications are processed on a rolling basis. Application fee: $40. Electronic applications accepted. *Expenses:* Tuition, area resident: Part-time $285 per credit hour. Tuition, nonresident: part-time $715 per credit hour. Required fees: $94 per semester. *Financial support:* In 2006–07, 4 students received support, including 3 research assistantships with full tuition reimbursements available (averaging $12,500 per year); career-related internships or fieldwork and unspecified assistantships also available. Financial award application deadline: 2/15; financial award applicants required to submit FAFSA. *Faculty research:* Instructional design, cognitive load, distance education, pedagogical agents, human performance technology. Total annual research expenditures: $2 million. *Unit head:* Dr. Gary R. Morrison, Graduate Program Director, 757-683-3284, Fax: 757-683-5862, E-mail: gmorriso@odu.edu.

Old Dominion University, Darden College of Education, Programs in Secondary Education, Norfolk, VA 23529. Offers biology (MS Ed); chemistry (MS Ed); English (MS Ed); instructional technology (MS Ed); library science (MS Ed); secondary education (MS Ed). *Accreditation:* NCATE. Part-time and evening/weekend programs available. Postbaccalaureate distance learning degree programs offered (minimal on-campus study). *Faculty:* 28 full-time (11 women). *Students:* 61 full-time (45 women), 119 part-time (72 women); includes 21 minority (13 African Americans, 4 Asian Americans or Pacific Islanders, 4 Hispanic Americans), 1 international. Average age 35. 47 applicants, 87% accepted. In 2006, 119 degrees awarded. *Degree requirements:* For master's, thesis optional. *Entrance requirements:* For master's, GRE General Test, or MAT, PRAXIS I for master's with licensure, minimum GPA of 2.8, teaching certificate. Additional exam requirements/recommendations for international students: Required—TOEFL. *Application deadline:* Applications are processed on a rolling basis. Application fee: $40. Electronic applications accepted. *Expenses:* Tuition, area resident: Part-time $285 per credit hour. Tuition, nonresident: part-time $715 per credit hour. Required fees: $94 per semester. *Financial support:* In 2006–07, 58 students received support, including 2 research assistantships with tuition reimbursements available (averaging $6,777 per year), 3 teaching assistantships with

Educational Media/Instructional Technology

Old Dominion University (continued)

tuition reimbursements available (averaging $5,333 per year); fellowships, career-related internships or fieldwork, Federal Work-Study, institutionally sponsored loans, scholarships/grants, and tuition waivers (partial) also available. Support available to part-time students. Financial award application deadline: 2/15; financial award applicants required to submit FAFSA. *Faculty research:* Mathematics retraining, writing project for teachers, geography teaching, reading. *Unit head:* Dr. Robert Lucking, Graduate Program Director, 757-683-5545, Fax: 757-683-5862, E-mail: rlucking@odu.edu.

Ottawa University, Graduate Studies-Arizona, Program in Education, Ottawa, KS 66067-3399. Offers community college counseling (MA); curriculum and instruction (MA); early childhood (MA); education intervention (MA); education leadership (MA); education technology (MA); Montessori early childhood education (MA); Montessori elementary education (MA); professional development (MA); school guidance counseling (MA); special education—cross categorical (MA). Programs offered in Mesa, Phoenix, Tempe and West Valley, AZ. *Accreditation:* NCATE. Part-time programs available. *Faculty:* 7 full-time (3 women), 24 part-time/adjunct (11 women). *Students:* 14 full-time (9 women), 162 part-time (128 women); includes 31 minority (13 African Americans, 2 American Indian/Alaska Native, 1 Asian American or Pacific Islander, 15 Hispanic Americans), 1 international. Average age 38. In 2006, 56 degrees awarded. *Degree requirements:* For master's, thesis or alternative, registration. *Entrance requirements:* For master's, minimum undergraduate GPA of 3.0, copy of current state certification or teaching license. Additional exam requirements/recommendations for international students: Required—TOEFL (minimum score 550 paper-based; 213 computer-based). *Application deadline:* For fall admission, 7/1 priority date for domestic students; for winter admission, 11/1 priority date for domestic students; for spring admission, 2/1 priority date for domestic students. Applications are processed on a rolling basis. Application fee: $50. Electronic applications accepted. *Expenses:* Contact institution. *Application contact:* Bunny Simpson, Secretary, 602-371-1188, Fax: 602-371-0035, E-mail: bunny.simpson@ottawa.edu.

Our Lady of the Lake University of San Antonio, School of Education and Clinical Studies, Program in Learning Resources, San Antonio, TX 78207-4689. Offers M Ed. Part-time and evening/weekend programs available. *Degree requirements:* For master's, comprehensive exam. *Entrance requirements:* For master's, GRE General Test or MAT. Additional exam requirements/recommendations for international students: Required—TOEFL. Electronic applications accepted. *Faculty research:* Automation and libraries, electronic books.

Penn State Great Valley, Graduate Studies, Education Division, Malvern, PA 19355-1488. Offers curriculum and instruction (M Ed); instructional systems (M Ed, MS); special education (M Ed, MS). *Unit head:* Dr. Arlene Mitchell, Academic Division Head, 610-648-3355, E-mail: ahm13@psu.edu. *Application contact:* Dr. Arlene Mitchell, Academic Division Head, 610-648-3355, E-mail: ahm13@psu.edu.

Penn State University Park, Graduate School, College of Education, Department of Curriculum and Instruction, State College, University Park, PA 16802-1503. Offers bilingual education (M Ed, MS, PhD); early childhood education (M Ed, MS, PhD); elementary education (M Ed, MS, PhD); instructional systems (M Ed, MS, PhD); language arts and reading (M Ed, MS, PhD); science education (M Ed, MS, PhD); social studies education (MS, PhD); supervisor and curriculum development (M Ed, MS, PhD). *Accreditation:* NCATE. *Unit head:* Dr. Murry R. Nelson, Head, 814-865-6321, Fax: 814-863-7602, E-mail: mrn2@psu.edu. *Application contact:* Judy Nastase, Graduate Staff Assistant, 814-865-2168, E-mail: jcn3@psu.edu.

Penn State University Park, Graduate School, College of Education, Department of Learning and Performance Systems, State College, University Park, PA 16802-1503. Offers adult education (M Ed, D Ed, PhD); instructional systems (M Ed, MS, D Ed, PhD); workforce education and development (M Ed, MS, D Ed, PhD). *Unit head:* Dr. Edgar I. Farmer, Head, 814-863-3858, Fax: 814-865-2632, E-mail: eif1@psu.edu.

Pepperdine University, Graduate School of Education and Psychology, Division of Education, Program in Educational Technology, Los Angeles, CA 90045. Offers Ed D. Part-time and evening/weekend programs available. Postbaccalaureate distance learning degree programs offered (minimal on-campus study). *Students:* 21 full-time (15 women), 93 part-time (47 women); includes 20 minority (6 African Americans, 6 Asian Americans or Pacific Islanders, 8 Hispanic Americans), 1 international. 9 applicants, 0% accepted. In 2006, 8 degrees awarded. *Degree requirements:* For doctorate, thesis/dissertation. *Entrance requirements:* For doctorate, GMAT, GRE General Test, MAT. Additional exam requirements/recommendations for international students: Required—TOEFL. *Application deadline:* For fall admission, 5/1 priority date for domestic students. Applications are processed on a rolling basis. Application fee: $50. *Expenses:* Contact institution. *Financial support:* Research assistantships, teaching assistantships, institutionally sponsored loans and scholarships/grants available. Support available to part-time students. Financial award application deadline: 7/1; financial award applicants required to submit FAFSA. *Unit head:* Dr. Linda Polin, Director, 310-568-5641, E-mail: linda.polin@pepperdine.edu. *Application contact:* Alexis Burdick, Program Administrator, 310-568-2849, E-mail: aburdick@pepperdine.edu.

Philadelphia University, School of Design and Media, Program in Instructional Design and Technology, Philadelphia, PA 19144-5497. Offers MS, MBA/MS. Part-time and evening/weekend programs available. *Faculty:* 3 full-time (0 women), 12 part-time/adjunct (3 women). *Students:* 36 applicants, 78% accepted, 24 enrolled. In 2006, 22 degrees awarded. *Entrance requirements:* For master's, GRE or MAT. Additional exam requirements/recommendations for international students: Required—TOEFL (minimum score 550 paper-based; 213 computer-based; 79 iBT). *Application deadline:* Applications are processed on a rolling basis. Application fee: $35. Electronic applications accepted. *Expenses:* Contact institution. *Financial support:* In 2006–07, research assistantships with full tuition reimbursements (averaging $2,500 per year); career-related internships or fieldwork, Federal Work-Study, and unspecified assistantships also available. Support available to part-time students. Financial award applicants required to submit FAFSA. *Unit head:* Dr. Timothy McGee, Director, 215-951-2872, Fax: 215-951-2615, E-mail: mcgeet@philau.edu. *Application contact:* Jack A. Klett, Director of Graduate Admissions, 215-951-2943, Fax: 215-951-2907, E-mail: gradadm@philau.edu.

See Close-Up on page 1119.

Pittsburg State University, Graduate School, College of Education, Department of Special Services and Leadership Studies, Program in Educational Leadership, Pittsburg, KS 66762. Offers educational technology (MS). *Accreditation:* NCATE. *Students:* 109. *Degree requirements:* For master's, thesis or alternative. *Entrance requirements:* For master's, GRE General Test or MAT. Application fee: $35 ($60 for international students). *Expenses:* Tuition, state resident: full-time $2,144; part-time $181 per credit hour. Tuition, nonresident: full-time $5,273; part-time $442 per credit hour. Tuition and fees vary according to course load and campus/location. *Financial support:* In 2006–07, teaching assistantships (averaging $5,000 per year); career-related internships or fieldwork, Federal Work-Study, and unspecified assistantships also available. *Application contact:* Marvene Darraugh, Administrative Officer, 620-235-4220, Fax: 620-235-4219, E-mail: mdarraug@pittstate.edu.

Pontifical Catholic University of Puerto Rico, College of Education, Ponce, PR 00717-0777. Offers commercial education (MRE); curriculum instruction (M Ed); education (PhD); education-general (MRE); English as a second language (MRE); religious education (MA Ed); scholar psychology (MRE). Part-time and evening/weekend programs available. *Degree requirements:* For master's, thesis (for some programs), comprehensive exam. *Entrance requirements:* For master's, GRE, 2 letters of recommendation, interview, minimum GPA of 2.75; for doctorate, EXADEP, GRE or MAT, 3 letters of recommendation. *Faculty research:* Teaching English as a second language, learning styles, leadership styles.

Portland State University, Graduate Studies, School of Education, Department of Curriculum and Instruction, Portland, OR 97207-0751. Offers early childhood education (MA, MS); education (M Ed, MA, MS); educational leadership: curriculum and instruction (Ed D); educational media/school librarianship (MA, MS); elementary education (M Ed, MAT, MST); reading (MA, MS); secondary education (M Ed, MAT, MST). *Accreditation:* NCATE. Part-time programs available. *Faculty:* 20 full-time (14 women), 18 part-time/adjunct (9 women). *Students:* 185 full-time (135 women), 209 part-time (160 women); includes 53 minority (7 African Americans, 4 American Indian/Alaska Native, 13 Asian Americans or Pacific Islanders, 29 Hispanic Americans), 13 international. Average age 32. 372 applicants, 87% accepted, 171 enrolled. In 2006, 352 master's, 4 doctorates awarded. *Degree requirements:* For master's, special project or thesis, written exam; for doctorate, thesis/dissertation. *Entrance requirements:* For master's, California Basic Educational Skills Test, minimum GPA of 3.0 in upper-division course work or 2.75 overall. Additional exam requirements/recommendations for international students: Required—TOEFL (minimum score 550 paper-based; 213 computer-based). *Application deadline:* For fall admission, 4/1 for domestic and international students; for winter admission, 9/1 for domestic and international students; for spring admission, 11/1 for domestic and international students. Applications are processed on a rolling basis. Application fee: $50. *Expenses:* Tuition, state resident: full-time $6,426; part-time $238 per credit. Tuition, nonresident: full-time $11,016; part-time $408 per credit. Tuition and fees vary according to course load. *Financial support:* In 2006–07, 5 research assistantships with full tuition reimbursements (averaging $5,508 per year) were awarded; teaching assistantships with full tuition reimbursements, career-related internships or fieldwork, Federal Work-Study, and institutionally sponsored loans also available. Support available to part-time students. Financial award application deadline: 3/1; financial award applicants required to submit FAFSA. *Faculty research:* Early literacy, characteristics of successful teachers of at-risk students, participation of women/minorities in technology courses, selection of cooperating teachers. Total annual research expenditures: $308,420. *Unit head:* Steven Lee, Head, 503-725-4689, Fax: 503-725-8475. *Application contact:* Majken Elek, Department Secretary, 503-725-4756, Fax: 503-725-8475, E-mail: majkene@pdx.edu.

Purdue University, Graduate School, School of Education, Department of Curriculum and Instruction, West Lafayette, IN 47907. Offers agricultural and extension education (PhD, Ed S); agriculture and extension education (MS, MS Ed); art education (PhD); consumer and family sciences and extension education (MS Ed, PhD, Ed S); curriculum studies (MS Ed, PhD, Ed S); educational technology (MS Ed, PhD, Ed S); elementary education (MS Ed); foreign language education (MS Ed, PhD, Ed S); industrial technology (PhD, Ed S); language arts (MS Ed, PhD, Ed S); literacy (MS Ed, PhD, Ed S); mathematics/science education (MS, MS Ed, PhD, Ed S); social studies (MS Ed, PhD); social studies education (Ed S); vocational/industrial education (MS Ed, PhD, Ed S); vocational/technical education (MS Ed, PhD, Ed S). *Accreditation:* NCATE. Part-time and evening/weekend programs available. *Faculty:* 26 full-time (13 women), 3 part-time/adjunct (all women). *Students:* 59 full-time (37 women), 112 part-time (70 women); includes 24 minority (13 African Americans, 3 American Indian/Alaska Native, 4 Asian Americans or Pacific Islanders, 4 Hispanic Americans), 38 international. Average age 35. 92 applicants, 68% accepted, 38 enrolled. In 2006, 52 master's, 23 doctorates awarded. *Degree requirements:* For master's, thesis optional; for doctorate, thesis/dissertation, oral and written exams; for Ed S, oral presentation, project. *Entrance requirements:* For master's, GRE General Test, minimum B average; for doctorate, GRE General Test; for Ed S, GRE, minimum B average. Additional exam requirements/recommendations for international students: Required—TOEFL. *Application deadline:* For fall admission, 1/15 priority date for domestic students, 1/15 for international students; for spring admission, 9/15 for domestic and international students. Applications are processed on a rolling basis. Application fee: $55. Electronic applications accepted. *Financial support:* In 2006–07, 3 fellowships with full tuition reimbursements (averaging $10,500 per year), 11 research assistantships with full tuition reimbursements (averaging $11,500 per year), 43 teaching assistantships with full tuition reimbursements (averaging $10,800 per year) were awarded; career-related internships or fieldwork and tuition waivers (full) also available. Support available to part-time students. Financial award application deadline: 3/1; financial award applicants required to submit FAFSA. *Faculty research:* Literacy acquisition and development, teacher beliefs and knowledge, recruitment and retention of underrepresented students, economic education, literacy discourse. *Unit head:* Dr. James D Lehman, Head, 765-494-7935, Fax: 765-496-1622. *Application contact:* Patricia Mason, Coordinator of Graduate Studies, 765-494-2345, Fax: 765-494-5832, E-mail: gradoffice@soe.purdue.edu.

Purdue University Calumet, Graduate School, School of Education, Program in Media Sciences, Hammond, IN 46323-2094. Offers MS Ed. *Entrance requirements:* Additional exam requirements/recommendations for international students: Required—TOEFL.

Regis University, School for Professional Studies, Program in Teacher Education, Denver, CO 80221-1099. Offers adult learning, training, and development (M Ed); curriculum, instruction, and assessment (M Ed); early childhood (M Ed); educational technology (Certificate); elementary (M Ed); ESL (M Ed); fine arts (M Ed), including arts, music; instructional technology (M Ed); professional leadership (M Ed); reading (M Ed); secondary (M Ed); self-designed (M Ed); space studies (M Ed); special education (M Ed); teacher licensure (M Ed). Program also offered in Henderson and Las Vegas (Summerlin), NV. Postbaccalaureate distance learning degree programs offered. *Unit head:* Dr. Suzie Perry, Dean, 303-458-4302. *Application contact:* Partick Lowenthal, Assistant Director, 303-458-4300 Ext. 4314, E-mail: masters@regis.edu.

The Richard Stockton College of New Jersey, Graduate Programs, Program in Instructional Technology, Pomona, NJ 08240-0195. Offers MA. Part-time programs available. *Faculty:* 3 full-time (2 women), 5 part-time/adjunct (3 women). *Students:* 1 full-time (0 women), 78 part-time (45 women); includes 11 minority (5 African Americans, 3 Asian Americans or Pacific Islanders, 3 Hispanic Americans). Average age 42. In 2006, 31 degrees awarded. *Degree requirements:* For master's, final project. *Entrance requirements:* For master's, GRE, minimum GPA of 3.0. Additional exam requirements/recommendations for international students: Required—TOEFL. *Application deadline:* For fall admission, 5/1 priority date for domestic students. Applications are processed on a rolling basis. Application fee: $50. Electronic applications accepted. *Expenses:* Tuition, state resident: full-time $9,746. Tuition, nonresident: full-time $14,462. Required fees: $2,340. *Financial support:* Career-related internships or fieldwork, Federal Work-Study, and scholarships/grants available. Support available to part-time students. Financial award application deadline: 3/1; financial award applicants required to submit FAFSA. *Faculty research:* Ethics, digital imaging, virtual reality in the classroom, 3-D art in multimedia, technology projects for job-skills training, community computing networks. *Unit head:* Dr. Douglas Harvey, Head, 609-652-4949, E-mail: mait@stockton.edu. *Application contact:* Alison Henry, Associate Director of Admissions, 609-652-4261, Fax: 609-626-5541, E-mail: admissions@stockton.edu.

Rochester Institute of Technology, Graduate Enrollment Services, Golisano College of Computing and Information Sciences, Department of Information Technology, Program in Learning and Knowledge Management Systems, Rochester, NY 14623-5603. Offers MS. *Students:* 1 (woman) full-time, 7 part-time (6 women); includes 1 African American. 6 applicants, 67% accepted, 4 enrolled. *Entrance requirements:* For master's, GRE, 3.0 GPA. *Expenses:* Tuition: Full-time $28,491; part-time $800 per credit. Required fees: $201. *Application contact:* Diane Bills, Graduate Coordinator, 585-475-6791, E-mail: dpb@it.rit.edu.

Rosemont College, Graduate School, Program in Technology and Education, Rosemont, PA 19010-1699. Offers technology in education (M Ed). Part-time and evening/weekend programs available. *Degree requirements:* For master's, thesis or alternative. *Entrance requirements:* Additional exam requirements/recommendations for international students: Required—TOEFL. Electronic applications accepted. Expenses: Contact institution.

Rowan University, Graduate School, College of Education, Department of Foundations of Education, Glassboro, NJ 08028-1701. Offers school and public librarianship (MA); teaching-secondary (MST). *Accreditation:* NCATE. Part-time and evening/weekend programs available. *Students:* 11 full-time (8 women), 39 part-time (36 women); includes 5 minority (4 African Americans, 1 Hispanic American). Average age 36. 10 applicants, 60% accepted, 5 enrolled.

In 2006, 20 degrees awarded. *Degree requirements:* For master's, thesis, comprehensive exam. *Entrance requirements:* For master's, GRE General Test, minimum GPA of 2.8. Additional exam requirements/recommendations for international students: Required—TOEFL. *Application deadline:* Applications are processed on a rolling basis. Application fee: $50. Electronic applications accepted. *Expenses:* Tuition, state resident: full-time $9,882; part-time $549 per credit. Tuition, nonresident: full-time $9,882; part-time $549 per credit. Tuition and fees vary according to degree level. *Financial support:* Career-related internships or fieldwork, Federal Work-Study, and unspecified assistantships available. Support available to part-time students. *Unit head:* Dr. Frank Orlando, 856-256-4728.

Royal Roads University, Graduate Studies, Organizational Leadership and Training Program, Victoria, BC V9B 5Y2, Canada. Offers distributed learning (MA); leadership and training (MA). Postbaccalaureate distance learning degree programs offered (minimal on-campus study). *Degree requirements:* For master's, thesis. *Entrance requirements:* For master's, 5-7 years of related work experience. Additional exam requirements/recommendations for international students: Required—TOEFL (paper-based 570; computer-based 233) or IELTS (paper-based 7) (recommended). Electronic applications accepted. Expenses: Contact institution. *Faculty research:* Approaches to leadership development, professional learning, problem-based learning, effective leadership styles, use of self-knowledge instruments in leadership development.

Sacred Heart University, Graduate Studies, College of Education and Health Professions, Department of Education, Fairfield, CT 06825-1000. Offers administration (CAS); educational technology (MAT); elementary education (MAT); reading (CAS); secondary education (MAT); teaching (CAS). Part-time and evening/weekend programs available. Postbaccalaureate distance learning degree programs offered (minimal on-campus study). *Faculty:* 23 full-time (10 women). *Students:* 360 full-time (285 women), 710 part-time (520 women); includes 39 minority (15 African Americans, 4 American Indian/Alaska Native, 5 Asian Americans or Pacific Islanders, 15 Hispanic Americans), 4 international. Average age 34. 335 applicants, 87% accepted, 270 enrolled. In 2006, 312 master's, 59 other advanced degrees awarded. *Degree requirements:* For master's, thesis or alternative. *Entrance requirements:* For master's, PRAXIS (teacher certification/MAT); for CAS, PRAXIS I. Additional exam requirements/recommendations for international students: Required—TOEFL (minimum score 550 paper-based; 213 computer-based). *Application deadline:* Applications are processed on a rolling basis. Application fee: $50 ($100 for international students). Electronic applications accepted. *Expenses: Contact institution.* Full-time tuition and fees vary according to degree level and program. *Financial support:* Teaching assistantships with partial tuition reimbursements, career-related internships or fieldwork, institutionally sponsored loans, traineeships, tuition waivers (partial), and unspecified assistantships available. Support available to part-time students. Financial award applicants required to submit FAFSA. *Faculty research:* Reading education, learning theory, teacher preparation, education of underachievers. *Unit head:* Dr. Edward Malin, Director, 203-371-7800, Fax: 203-365-7513. *Application contact:* Alexis Haakonsen, Dean of Graduate Admissions, 203-365-7619, Fax: 203-365-4732, E-mail: haakonsena@sacredheart.edu.

Saginaw Valley State University, College of Education, Program in Instructional Technology, University Center, MI 48710. Offers MAT. Part-time and evening/weekend programs available. *Students:* 1 full-time (0 women), 24 part-time (15 women); includes 1 minority (Asian American or Pacific Islander) Average age 32. 10 applicants, 100% accepted, 8 enrolled. In 2006, 8 degrees awarded. Application fee: $25. *Expenses:* Tuition, state resident: full-time $7,225; part-time $301 per credit hour. Tuition, nonresident: full-time $13,888; part-time $579 per credit hour. Required fees: $330; $14 per credit hour. Tuition and fees vary according to course load. *Financial support:* Applicants required to submit FAFSA. *Application contact:* Jeanne Chipman, Certification Officer, 989-964-4083, Fax: 989-964-4385, E-mail: jdc@svsu.edu.

St. Cloud State University, School of Graduate Studies, College of Education, Center for Information Media, St. Cloud, MN 56301-4498. Offers MS. *Faculty:* 11 full-time (5 women), 6 part-time/adjunct (3 women). *Students:* 6 full-time (4 women), 30 part-time (22 women); includes 2 minority (1 African American, 1 American Indian/Alaska Native), 1 international. 6 applicants, 100% accepted. In 2006, 13 degrees awarded. *Degree requirements:* For master's, thesis or alternative, comprehensive exam. *Entrance requirements:* For master's, GRE General Test, minimum GPA of 2.75. Additional exam requirements/recommendations for international students: Required—MELAB; Recommended—TOEFL (minimum score 550 paper-based; 213 computer-based), IELTS (minimum score 7). *Application deadline:* For fall admission, 6/1 priority date for domestic students, 4/1 for international students; for spring admission, 10/1 priority date for domestic students, 8/1 for international students. Applications are processed on a rolling basis. Application fee: $35. Electronic applications accepted. *Financial support:* Federal Work-Study, scholarships/grants, and unspecified assistantships available. Financial award application deadline: 3/1. *Unit head:* Dr. Kristi Tornquist, Dean, 320-308-2022, E-mail: kmtornquist@stcloudstate.edu. *Application contact:* Linda Lou Krueger, School of Graduate Studies, 320-308-2113, Fax: 320-308-5371, E-mail: lekrueger@stcloudstate.edu.

Saint Joseph's University, College of Arts and Sciences, Department of Education, Philadelphia, PA 19131-1395. Offers educational leadership (Ed D); elementary education (MS); instructional technology (MS); professional education (MS); reading (MS); secondary education (MS); special education (MS); training and organizational development (MS, Certificate). Part-time and evening/weekend programs available. *Faculty:* 18 full-time (9 women), 67 part-time/adjunct (34 women). *Students:* 77 full-time (63 women), 551 part-time (417 women); includes 115 minority (94 African Americans, 2 American Indian/Alaska Native, 8 Asian Americans or Pacific Islanders, 11 Hispanic Americans), 12 international. In 2006, 286 master's, 5 doctorates awarded. *Entrance requirements:* For master's, 2 letters of recommendation, minimum GPA of 3.0; for doctorate, GRE/MAT, 2 letters of recommendation, resumé. Additional exam requirements/recommendations for international students: Required—TOEFL. *Application deadline:* For fall admission, 7/15 for domestic students. Application fee: $35. *Expenses: Contact institution. Financial support:* Fellowships, research assistantships, career-related internships or fieldwork and Federal Work-Study available. Support available to part-time students. *Unit head:* Dr. Encarnacion Rodriguez, Director of Graduate Education, 610-660-3348.

Saint Michael's College, Graduate Programs, Program in Education, Colchester, VT 05439. Offers administration (M Ed, CAGS); arts in education (CAGS); curriculum and instruction (M Ed, CAGS); information technology (CAGS); reading (M Ed); special education (M Ed, CAGS); technology (M Ed). Part-time and evening/weekend programs available. *Faculty:* 5 full-time (3 women), 35 part-time/adjunct (29 women). *Students:* 26 full-time (18 women), 114 part-time (86 women), 2 international. Average age 34. 48 applicants, 81% accepted, 36 enrolled. In 2006, 46 degrees awarded. *Degree requirements:* For master's, thesis. *Entrance requirements:* For master's, minimum GPA of 3.0. *Application deadline:* Applications are processed on a rolling basis. Application fee: $35. Electronic applications accepted. *Financial support:* Fellowships, scholarships/grants available. Support available to part-time students. Financial award applicants required to submit FAFSA. *Faculty research:* Integrative curriculum, moral and spiritual dimensions of education, learning styles, multiple intelligences, integrating technology into the curriculum. *Unit head:* Dr. Anne P. Judson, Director, 802-654-2649, Fax: 802-654-2664, E-mail: ajudson@smcvt.edu.

Saint Vincent College, Program in Education, Latrobe, PA 15650-2690. Offers curriculum and instruction (MS); environmental education (MS); library media management (MS); school administration (MS); special education (MS). Part-time and evening/weekend programs available. *Degree requirements:* For master's, comprehensive exam. *Entrance requirements:* For master's, GRE (if undergraduate GPA is below 3.0). Additional exam requirements/recommendations for international students: Required—TOEFL (minimum score 550 paper-based; 213 computer-based). *Faculty research:* Assessment and instructional technology.

Salem International University, School of Education, Salem, WV 26426-0500. Offers curriculum and instruction (M Ed), including curriculum and instruction, educational technology leadership, physical education/health, teaching English as a second language; educational administration (M Ed). Part-time and evening/weekend programs available. Postbaccalaureate distance learning degree programs offered. *Faculty:* 5 full-time (4 women), 17 part-time/adjunct (8 women). *Students:* 74 full-time (45 women), 154 part-time (75 women); includes 7 minority (2 African Americans, 5 Asian Americans or Pacific Islanders), 28 international. Average age 41. 200 applicants, 75% accepted, 130 enrolled. In 2006, 18 degrees awarded. *Degree requirements:* For master's, thesis (for some programs), comprehensive exam (for some programs), registration. *Entrance requirements:* For master's, GRE, MAT, NTE, 3 letters of recommendation. Additional exam requirements/recommendations for international students: Required—TOEFL (minimum score 550 paper-based; 213 computer-based). *Application deadline:* Applications are processed on a rolling basis. Application fee: $25. Electronic applications accepted. *Expenses: Contact institution.* One-time fee: $25 part-time. Tuition and fees vary according to program. *Financial support:* Application deadline: 4/15; *Faculty research:* Improved classroom effectiveness. *Unit head:* Dean, School of Education, 304-326-1253, Fax: 304-326-1246. *Application contact:* Thomas White, Director of Admissions, 304-326-1549, Fax: 304-326-1246, E-mail: admission@salemiu.edu.

Salem State College, Graduate School, Program in Library Media Studies, Salem, MA 01970-5353. Offers M Ed. *Accreditation:* NCATE. Part-time and evening/weekend programs available. *Faculty:* 3 part-time/adjunct (2 women). *Students:* 1 full-time (0 women), 16 part-time (15 women). Average age 42. In 2006, 5 degrees awarded. *Entrance requirements:* For master's, GRE General Test, MAT. *Application deadline:* Applications are processed on a rolling basis. Application fee: $35. *Unit head:* Elizabeth Dole, Coordinator, 978-542-6477, Fax: 978-744-6596, E-mail: edole@salemstate.edu.

Salem State College, Graduate School, Program in Technology in Education, Salem, MA 01970-5353. Offers M Ed. Part-time and evening/weekend programs available. *Students:* 1 (woman) full-time, 10 part-time (6 women), 1 international. Average age 45. In 2006, 9 degrees awarded. *Entrance requirements:* For master's, GRE General Test, MAT. *Application deadline:* Applications are processed on a rolling basis. Application fee: $35. *Unit head:* Sneila Smith-McAdams, Professor, 978-542 Ext. 6322, E-mail: ssmithmcadams@salemsatate.edu.

Salisbury University, Graduate Division, Department of Education, Salisbury, MD 21801-6837. Offers art (MAT); biology (MAT); business education (MAT); chemistry (MAT); early childhood education (M Ed); educational administration (M Ed); elementary education (M Ed); English (M Ed, MAT); French (MAT); geography (MAT); history (MAT); mathematics (MAT); media and technology (MAT); music (MAT); psychology (MAT); reading education (MAT); science (MAT); secondary education (MAT); social studies (MAT); Spanish (MAT). *Accreditation:* NCATE. Part-time and evening/weekend programs available. *Faculty:* 12 full-time (6 women), 10 part-time/adjunct (8 women). *Students:* 17 full-time (9 women), 84 part-time (72 women); includes 6 minority (5 African Americans, 1 Hispanic American). Average age 30. 15 applicants, 73% accepted, 11 enrolled. In 2006, 63 degrees awarded. *Degree requirements:* For master's, comprehensive exam (for some programs). *Entrance requirements:* For master's, PRAXIS, minimum GPA of 2.75. Additional exam requirements/recommendations for international students: Required—TOEFL (minimum score 550 paper-based; 213 computer-based). *Application deadline:* For fall admission, 8/1 priority date for domestic students; for spring admission, 1/1 for domestic students. Applications are processed on a rolling basis. Application fee: $45. *Expenses:* Tuition, state resident: part-time $260 per credit hour. Tuition, nonresident: part-time $546 per credit hour. Required fees: $52 per credit hour. *Financial support:* In 2006–07, 3 teaching assistantships with full tuition reimbursements were awarded; career-related internships or fieldwork and scholarships/grants also available. Support available to part-time students. Financial award applicants required to submit FAFSA. *Faculty research:* Middle-level education, student outcomes. *Unit head:* Dr. Edward C. Robeck, Program Coordinator, 410-543-6292, Fax: 410-548-2593, E-mail: ecrobeck@salisbury.edu. *Application contact:* Debra J. Clark, Administrative Assistant I, 410-543-6281, Fax: 410-548-2593, E-mail: djclark@salisbury.edu.

San Diego State University, Graduate and Research Affairs, College of Education, Department of Educational Technology, San Diego, CA 92182. Offers educational technology (MA); educational technology and teaching and learning (Ed D). *Accreditation:* NCATE. Evening/weekend programs available. *Students:* 19 full-time (14 women), 43 part-time (31 women); includes 9 minority (2 African Americans, 1 Asian American or Pacific Islander, 6 Hispanic Americans), 7 international. 48 applicants, 69% accepted, 5 enrolled. In 2006, 38 master's, 1 doctorate awarded. *Entrance requirements:* For master's, GRE General Test, letters of reference. Additional exam requirements/recommendations for international students: Required—TOEFL. *Application deadline:* For fall admission, 5/1 for domestic and international students; for spring admission, 11/1 for domestic students, 10/1 for international students. Applications are processed on a rolling basis. Application fee: $55. Electronic applications accepted. *Financial support:* In 2006–07, 11 teaching assistantships were awarded. Financial award applicants required to submit FAFSA. Total annual research expenditures: $535,067. *Unit head:* Marcie Bober, Chair, 619-594-6718, Fax: 619-594-6376.

San Francisco State University, Division of Graduate Studies, College of Education, Department of Instructional Technologies, San Francisco, CA 94132-1722. Offers educational technology (MA); training systems development (AC). Part-time programs available. *Students:* 128 (79 women). *Entrance requirements:* For master's, minimum GPA of 2.5 in last 60 units. *Application deadline:* For fall admission, 11/30 priority date for domestic students. Applications are processed on a rolling basis. Application fee: $55. *Financial support:* Career-related internships or fieldwork available. Financial award application deadline: 3/1. *Unit head:* Dr. Gene Michaels, Chair, 415-338-6384.

San Jose State University, Graduate Studies and Research, College of Education, Department of Instructional Technology, San Jose, CA 95192-0001. Offers MA, Certificate. *Accreditation:* NCATE. Evening/weekend programs available. *Students:* 12 full-time (7 women), 96 part-time (62 women); includes 23 minority (3 African Americans, 17 Asian Americans or Pacific Islanders, 3 Hispanic Americans), 8 international. Average age 37. 58 applicants, 84% accepted, 36 enrolled. In 2006, 60 degrees awarded. *Application deadline:* For fall admission, 6/29 for domestic students; for spring admission, 11/30 for domestic students. Applications are processed on a rolling basis. Application fee: $59. Electronic applications accepted. *Financial support:* Career-related internships or fieldwork available. Financial award applicants required to submit FAFSA. *Unit head:* Roberta Barba, Chair, 408-924-3613, Fax: 408-924-3713.

Seton Hall University, College of Education and Human Services, Department of Educational Studies, Program in Instructional Design, South Orange, NJ 07079-2697. Offers MA. Part-time and evening/weekend programs available. *Faculty:* 10 full-time (7 women). *Students:* 3 full-time (2 women), 6 part-time (5 women); includes 2 minority (1 African American, 1 Hispanic American), 1 international. Average age 38. 3 applicants, 100% accepted, 2 enrolled. In 2006, 2 master's awarded. *Degree requirements:* For master's, comprehensive exam. *Entrance requirements:* For master's, GRE General Test or MAT, minimum GPA of 2.75. *Application deadline:* For fall admission, 5/1 for domestic students; for spring admission, 10/1 for domestic students. Applications are processed on a rolling basis. Application fee: $50. *Financial support:* Application deadline: 2/1. *Unit head:* Dr. Rosemary Skeele, Head, 973-761-9393, E-mail: skeelero@shu.edu. *Application contact:* 973-761-9393.

Seton Hill University, Program in Instructional Design, Greensburg, PA 15601. Offers M Ed. Part-time and evening/weekend programs available. *Faculty:* 3 full-time (2 women), 3 part-time/adjunct (2 women). *Students:* 6 full-time (3 women), 7 part-time (all women); includes 2 minority (1 African American, 1 Hispanic American). Average age 36. 12 applicants, 75% accepted, 7 enrolled. In 2006, 3 degrees awarded. *Degree requirements:* For master's, thesis optional. *Entrance requirements:* For master's, minimum GPA of 3.0. Additional exam requirements/recommendations for international students: Required—TOEFL. *Application deadline:* For fall admission, 8/15 priority date for domestic students; for spring admission, 12/15 for domestic students. Applications are processed on a rolling basis. Application fee: $35. Electronic applications accepted. *Expenses:* Tuition: Part-time $620 per credit. Required fees: $100 per semester. *Financial support:* In 2006–07, 7 students received support.

Educational Media/Instructional Technology

Seton Hill University (continued)
Scholarships/grants, tuition waivers (partial), and unspecified assistantships available. Support available to part-time students. Financial award application deadline: 8/15; financial award applicants required to submit FAFSA. *Faculty research:* Use of technology for teaching and learning, problem-based theories in education and instruction. *Unit head:* Dr. Shirley Campbell, Director, 724-830-1007, Fax: 724-830-1294. *Application contact:* Dane Zimmer, Advisor, 724-838-4209, Fax: 724-830-1891, E-mail: zimmer@setonhill.edu.

Simmons College, Graduate School, College of Arts and Sciences Graduate Studies, Department of Education, Program in Special Education, Boston, MA 02115. Offers applied behavior analysis (PhD); assistive technology (MS Ed, Ed S); behavioral education (MS Ed, Ed S); health professions education (PhD); language and literacy (MS Ed, Ed S); moderate disabilities (Ed S); moderate special needs (MS Ed); severe disabilities (Ed S); severe special needs (MS Ed); special education administration (MS Ed, PhD, Ed S). Part-time and evening/weekend programs available. *Faculty:* 9 full-time (7 women), 34 part-time/adjunct (23 women). *Students:* 51 full-time (46 women), 405 part-time (339 women); includes 31 minority (13 African Americans, 2 American Indian/Alaska Native, 7 Asian Americans or Pacific Islanders, 9 Hispanic Americans), 2 international. Average age 28. 155 applicants, 91% accepted, 121 enrolled. In 2006, 122 master's, 27 other advanced degrees awarded. *Degree requirements:* For master's, practicum; for doctorate, thesis/dissertation. *Entrance requirements:* For doctorate, GRE, research proposal interview. Additional exam requirements/recommendations for international students: Required—TOEFL (minimum score 600 paper-based; 250 computer-based; 100 iBT). *Application deadline:* For fall admission, 8/1 priority date for domestic students; for spring admission, 12/1 priority date for domestic students. Applications are processed on a rolling basis. Application fee: $35. Electronic applications accepted. *Expenses: Contact institution. Financial support:* Career-related internships or fieldwork, Federal Work-Study, institutionally sponsored loans, scholarships/grants, and tuition waivers (partial) available. Support available to part-time students. Financial award application deadline: 3/1; financial award applicants required to submit FAFSA. *Faculty research:* Classroom-based research, inclusion strategies, beginning teacher development. *Unit head:* Dr. Cathryn Mercier, Associate Dean, 617-521-2091. *Application contact:* Kristen Haack, Director, Graduate Studies Admission, 617-521-2915, Fax: 617-521-3058, E-mail: gsa@simmons.edu.

Simmons College, Graduate School of Library and Information Science, Program in School Library Teacher, Boston, MA 02115. Offers MS, Certificate. *Faculty:* 3 full-time (2 women), 4 part-time/adjunct (3 women). *Students:* 2 full-time (both women), 39 part-time (37 women); includes 2 minority (1 African American, 1 Hispanic American). 28 applicants, 75% accepted, 14 enrolled. *Degree requirements:* For master's, two practica: (elementary; secondary and technology competencies). *Entrance requirements:* For degree, GRE General Test or minimum GPA of 3.0, interview. Additional exam requirements/recommendations for international students: Required—TOEFL (minimum score 550 paper-based; 213 computer-based; 79 iBT). *Application deadline:* For fall admission, 3/1 priority date for domestic students; for spring admission, 7/1 priority date for domestic students. Applications are processed on a rolling basis. Application fee: $35. Electronic applications accepted. *Expenses: Contact institution. Faculty research:* Student achievement, curriculum studies. *Unit head:* James C. Baughman, Director, 617-521-2791, Fax: 617-521-3192, E-mail: baughman@simmons.edu. *Application contact:* Denise Davis, Assistant Dean for Admission and Recruitment, 617-521-2801, Fax: 617-521-3192, E-mail: denise.davis@simmons.edu.

Southeastern Oklahoma State University, Graduate School, School of Education, Durant, OK 74701-0609. Offers educational administration (M Ed); educational instruction and leadership (M Ed); educational technology (M Ed); elementary education (M Ed); school counseling (M Ed); secondary education (M Ed). *Accreditation:* NCATE. Part-time and evening/weekend programs available. *Degree requirements:* For master's, portfolio (M Ed), thesis optional. *Entrance requirements:* For master's, GRE General Test (MBS), minimum GPA of 3.0 in last 60 hours or 2.75 overall. Additional exam requirements/recommendations for international students: Required—TOEFL (minimum score 550 paper-based; 213 computer-based). Electronic applications accepted.

Southern Connecticut State University, School of Graduate Studies, School of Communication, Information and Library Science, Department of Library Science and Instructional Technology, New Haven, CT 06515-1355. Offers instructional technology (MS); library science (MLS); library/information studies (Diploma); JD/MLS; MLS/MA; MLS/MS. Part-time and evening/weekend programs available. Postbaccalaureate distance learning degree programs offered (no on-campus study). *Faculty:* 12 full-time, 5 part-time/adjunct. *Students:* 50 full-time (38 women), 255 part-time (223 women); includes 18 minority (5 African Americans, 10 Asian Americans or Pacific Islanders, 3 Hispanic Americans). 139 applicants, 86% accepted, 104 enrolled. In 2006, 127 master's, 12 other advanced degrees awarded. *Degree requirements:* For master's and Diploma, thesis or alternative. *Entrance requirements:* For master's, GRE General Test, interview, minimum QPA of 2.7, introductory computer science course; for Diploma, master's degree in library science or information science. *Application deadline:* For fall admission, 7/15 priority date for domestic students. Applications are processed on a rolling basis. Application fee: $50. Electronic applications accepted. *Financial support:* Research assistantships available. Financial award application deadline: 4/15; financial award applicants required to submit FAFSA. *Unit head:* Dr. Josephine Sche, Chairperson, 203-392-5710, Fax: 203-392-5780, E-mail: schej1@southernct.edu.

Southern Illinois University Edwardsville, Graduate Studies and Research, School of Education, Department of Educational Leadership, Program in Instructional Design and Learning Technologies, Edwardsville, IL 62026-0001. Offers MS Ed. *Accreditation:* NCATE. Part-time and evening/weekend programs available. *Students:* 1 (woman) full-time, 23 part-time (14 women). Average age 33. 5 applicants, 40% accepted. In 2006, 33 degrees awarded. *Degree requirements:* For master's, thesis or alternative, portfolio. *Entrance requirements:* For master's, MAT. Additional exam requirements/recommendations for international students: Required—TOEFL. *Application deadline:* For fall admission, 7/23 for domestic students, 6/15 for international students; for spring admission, 12/10 for domestic students, 10/1 for international students. Application fee: $30. *Financial support:* Fellowships, research assistantships, teaching assistantships, Federal Work-Study, institutionally sponsored loans, and unspecified assistantships available. Support available to part-time students. Financial award application deadline: 3/1; financial award applicants required to submit FAFSA. *Unit head:* Dr. Yuliang Liu, Program Director, 618-650-3293, E-mail: ylu@siue.edu.

Southern University and Agricultural and Mechanical College, Graduate School, College of Education, Department of Curriculum and Instruction, Baton Rouge, LA 70813. Offers elementary education (M Ed); media (M Ed); secondary education (M Ed). *Degree requirements:* For master's, thesis optional. *Entrance requirements:* For master's, GMAT or GRE General Test. Additional exam requirements/recommendations for international students: Required—TOEFL (minimum score 525 paper-based; 193 computer-based).

State University of New York College at Potsdam, School of Education, Program in Educational Technology, Potsdam, NY 13676. Offers MS Ed. Part-time and evening/weekend programs available. Postbaccalaureate distance learning degree programs offered. *Faculty:* 4 full-time (1 woman), 3 part-time/adjunct (1 woman). *Students:* 39 full-time (19 women), 14 part-time (7 women), 22 international. In 2006, 40 degrees awarded. *Degree requirements:* For master's, culminating experience, thesis optional. *Entrance requirements:* For master's, minimum GPA of 2.75 in last 60 hours of course work. Additional exam requirements/recommendations for international students: Required—TOEFL (minimum score 550 paper-based; 213 computer-based). *Application deadline:* Applications are processed on a rolling basis. Application fee: $50. *Financial support:* Fellowships, teaching assistantships, career-related internships or fieldwork, Federal Work-Study, and scholarships/grants available. Support available to part-time students. Financial award application deadline: 3/1. *Unit head:* Dr. Tony Betrus, Chairperson, Information and Communication Technology Department, 315-267-2535, Fax: 315-267-4802, E-mail: betrusak@potsdam.edu. *Application contact:* Peter Cutler, Graduate Admissions Counselor, 315-267-3154, Fax: 315-267-4802, E-mail: cutlerpj@potsdam.edu.

Stony Brook University, State University of New York, Graduate School, College of Engineering and Applied Sciences, Department of Technology and Society, Program in Educational Technology, Stony Brook, NY 11794. Offers MS. *Accreditation:* NCATE. *Application deadline:* For fall admission, 6/1 for domestic students; for spring admission, 12/1 for domestic students. *Expenses:* Tuition, state resident: full-time $6,900; part-time $288 per credit. Tuition, nonresident: full-time $10,920; part-time $455 per credit. *Financial support:* Research assistantships, teaching assistantships available.

See Close-Up on page 1613.

Stony Brook University, State University of New York, School of Professional Development, Stony Brook, NY 11794. Offers adolescence education: mathematics (Certificate); biology 7-12 (MAT); chemistry-grade 7-12 (MAT); coaching (Certificate); computer integrated engineering (Certificate); cultural studies (Certificate); earth science-grade 7-12 (MAT); educational computing (Advanced Certificate, Certificate); English-grade 7-12 (MAT); environmental and waste management (MS, Advanced Certificate); environmental systems management (Certificate); environmental/occupational health and safety (Certificate); French-grade 7-12 (MAT); German-grade 7-12 (MAT); human resource management (Certificate); industrial management (Certificate); information systems management (Certificate); Italian-grade 7-12 (MAT); liberal studies (MA); liberal studies online (MA); Long Island regional studies (Certificate); operation research (Certificate); physics-grade 7-12 (MAT); Russian-grade 7-12 (MAT); school administration and supervision (Certificate); school district administration (Certificate); social science and the professions (MPS), including human resources management, labor management, public affairs, waste management; social studies 7-12 (MAT); waste management (Certificate); women's studies (Certificate). Part-time and evening/weekend programs available. Postbaccalaureate distance learning degree programs offered. *Faculty:* 1 full-time (0 women), 118 part-time/adjunct (45 women). *Students:* 322 full-time (202 women), 1,188 part-time (728 women); includes 164 minority (69 African Americans, 2 American Indian/Alaska Native, 29 Asian Americans or Pacific Islanders, 64 Hispanic Americans), 11 international. Average age 28. In 2006, 738 master's, 405 other advanced degrees awarded. *Degree requirements:* For master's, one foreign language, thesis or alternative. *Application deadline:* Applications are processed on a rolling basis. Application fee: $62. *Expenses:* Tuition, state resident: full-time $6,900; part-time $288 per credit. Tuition, nonresident: full-time $10,920; part-time $455 per credit. *Financial support:* In 2006–07, 5 teaching assistantships were awarded; fellowships, research assistantships, career-related internships or fieldwork also available. Support available to part-time students. *Unit head:* Dr. Paul J. Edelson, Dean, 631-632-7052, Fax: 631-632-9046, E-mail: paul.edelson@sunysb.edu. *Application contact:* Sandra Romansky, Director of Admissions and Advisement, 631-632-7050, Fax: 631-632-9046, E-mail: sandra.romansky@sunysb.edu.

Syracuse University, Graduate School, School of Information Studies, Library and Information Science Program, Syracuse, NY 13244. Offers library and information science (MS); school media (MS). *Accreditation:* ALA. Part-time and evening/weekend programs available. Postbaccalaureate distance learning degree programs offered (minimal on-campus study). *Students:* 64 full-time (49 women), 232 part-time (204 women); includes 24 African Americans, 5 Asian Americans or Pacific Islanders, 10 Hispanic Americans, 10 international. 112 applicants, 85% accepted, 33 enrolled. *Degree requirements:* For master's, fieldwork or research paper. *Entrance requirements:* For master's, GRE General Test. Additional exam requirements/recommendations for international students: Required—TOEFL. *Application deadline:* For fall admission, 2/14 priority date for domestic students; for spring admission, 11/1 priority date for domestic students. Application fee: $65. Electronic applications accepted. *Expenses:* Tuition: Full-time $16,920; part-time $940 per credit hour. Required fees: $930; $930 per year. *Unit head:* Dr. Gisela von Dran, Head, 315-443-2086, Fax: 315-443-6886, E-mail: gmvondra@syr.edu. *Application contact:* Susan Corieri, Director of Enrollment Management, 315-443-6885, E-mail: ist@syr.edu.

See Close-Up on page 2135.

Syracuse University, Graduate School, School of Information Studies, Program in School Library Media, Syracuse, NY 13244. Offers CAS. Part-time and evening/weekend programs available. Postbaccalaureate distance learning degree programs offered. *Students:* 4 applicants, 75% accepted, 3 enrolled. *Entrance requirements:* Additional exam requirements/recommendations for international students: Required—TOEFL. *Application deadline:* For fall admission, 2/14 for domestic students. Application fee: $65. Electronic applications accepted. *Expenses:* Tuition: Full-time $16,920; part-time $940 per credit hour. Required fees: $930; $930 per year. *Unit head:* Ruth Small, Head, 315-443-4511. *Application contact:* Susan Corieri, Director of Enrollment Management, 315-443-6885, E-mail: ist@syr.edu.

Teachers College Columbia University, Graduate Faculty of Education, Department of Math, Science and Technology, Program in Educational Media/Instructional Technology, New York, NY 10027-6696. Offers Ed M, MA, Ed D. *Faculty:* 4 full-time (2 women), 4 part-time/adjunct. *Students:* 44 full-time (28 women), 105 part-time (69 women); includes 46 minority (13 African Americans, 28 Asian Americans or Pacific Islanders, 5 Hispanic Americans), 39 international. Average age 34. 70 applicants, 93% accepted, 30 enrolled. In 2006, 28 master's, 6 doctorates awarded. *Degree requirements:* For doctorate, thesis/dissertation. *Entrance requirements:* For doctorate, GRE General Test or MAT. *Application deadline:* For fall admission, 5/15 for domestic students; for spring admission, 12/1 for domestic students. Application fee: $65. *Expenses:* Tuition: Full-time $23,400; part-time $975 per credit. Required fees: $320 per term. *Financial support:* Career-related internships or fieldwork, Federal Work-Study, institutionally sponsored loans, and tuition waivers (full and partial) available. Support available to part-time students. Financial award application deadline: 2/1. *Faculty research:* Video and interactive learning. *Application contact:* Deanna Ghozati, Assistant Director of Admission, 212-678-4018, Fax: 212-678-4171, E-mail: ghozati@tc.edu.

See Close-Up on page 1615.

Texas A&M University, College of Education and Human Development, Department of Educational Psychology, College Station, TX 77843. Offers counseling psychology (PhD); educational psychology (PhD); educational technology (M Ed); gifted and talented education (M Ed, MS); Hispanic bilingual education (M Ed, PhD); human learning and development (MS); intelligence, creativity, and giftedness (PhD); learning, development, and instruction (PhD); research, measurement and statistics (MS); research, measurement, and statistics (PhD); school counseling (M Ed); school psychology (PhD); special education (M Ed, PhD). *Accreditation:* APA (one or more programs are accredited); NCATE. Part-time and evening/weekend programs available. Postbaccalaureate distance learning degree programs offered (no on-campus study). *Faculty:* 25 full-time (11 women), 5 part-time/adjunct (2 women). *Students:* 156 full-time (123 women), 109 part-time (89 women); includes 66 minority (20 African Americans, 1 American Indian/Alaska Native, 7 Asian Americans or Pacific Islanders, 38 Hispanic Americans), 36 international. 159 applicants, 52% accepted, 51 enrolled. In 2006, 59 master's, 21 doctorates awarded. *Median time to degree:* Of those who began their doctoral program in fall 1998, 89% received their degree in 8 years or less. *Degree requirements:* For master's, thesis optional; for doctorate, thesis/dissertation. *Entrance requirements:* For master's and doctorate, GRE General Test. Additional exam requirements/recommendations for international students: Required—TOEFL. Application fee: $50 ($75 for international students). Electronic applications accepted. *Expenses:* Tuition, state resident: full-time $4,697. Tuition, nonresident: full-time $11,297. Required fees: $2,272. *Financial support:* In 2006–07, fellowships (averaging $12,000 per year), research assistantships (averaging $9,000 per year), teaching assistantships (averaging $9,000 per year) were awarded; career-related internships or fieldwork, institutionally sponsored loans, scholarships/grants, and unspecified assistantships also available. Financial award applicants required to submit FAFSA. *Unit head:* Dr.

Michael R. Benz, Head, 979-845-1394, Fax: 979-862-1256, E-mail: mbanz@tamu.edu. *Application contact:* Carol A. Wagner, Director of Advising, 979-845-1833, Fax: 979-862-1256, E-mail: c-wagner@tamu.edu.

Texas A&M University–Commerce, Graduate School, College of Education and Human Services, Department of Secondary and Higher Education, Commerce, TX 75429-3011. Offers higher education (MS), including administration, teaching; learning technology and information systems (M Ed, MS), including educational computing, library and information science, media and technology; secondary education (M Ed, MS); supervision, curriculum, and instruction (Ed D); training and development (MS). Part-time programs available. Terminal master's awarded for partial completion of doctoral program. *Degree requirements:* For master's, thesis (for some programs), comprehensive exam; for doctorate, thesis/dissertation, departmental qualifying exam. *Entrance requirements:* For master's and doctorate, GRE General Test. Electronic applications accepted. *Faculty research:* Deviance, migration.

Texas A&M University–Corpus Christi, Graduate Studies and Research, College of Education, Corpus Christi, TX 78412-5503. Offers counseling (MS, PhD), including counseling (MS), counselor education (PhD); curriculum and instruction (MS, Ed D); early childhood education (MS); educational administration (MS); educational leadership (Ed D); educational technology (MS); elementary education (MS); kinesiology (MS); occupational training and development (MS); reading (MS); secondary education (MS); special education (MS). Part-time and evening/weekend programs available. *Degree requirements:* For master's, thesis (for some programs), comprehensive exam, registration; for doctorate, thesis/dissertation, comprehensive exam, registration. *Entrance requirements:* For master's, GRE General Test. Additional exam requirements/recommendations for international students: Required—TOEFL. Electronic applications accepted.

Texas A&M University–Texarkana, Graduate Studies and Research, College of Arts and Sciences and Education, Texarkana, TX 75505-5518. Offers adult education (MS); curriculum and instruction (MS); education (MS); educational administration (M Ed); English (MA); history (MS); instructional technology (MS); interdisciplinary studies (MA, MS); special education (M Ed, MS). Part-time and evening/weekend programs available. *Students:* 285. Average age 32. 41 applicants, 76% accepted. In 2006, 51 degrees awarded. *Degree requirements:* For master's, thesis optional. *Entrance requirements:* For master's, minimum GPA of 2.5 on last 60 hours of bachelor's degree. Additional exam requirements/recommendations for international students: Required—TOEFL. *Application deadline:* For fall admission, 7/15 priority date for domestic students; for spring admission, 12/1 priority date for domestic students. Applications are processed on a rolling basis. Application fee: $0 ($25 for international students). Electronic applications accepted. *Expenses:* Tuition, state resident: part-time $112 per credit hour. Tuition, nonresident: part-time $387 per credit hour. Required fees: $8 per credit hour. $8 per term. *Financial support:* Career-related internships or fieldwork and scholarships/grants available. Financial award applicants required to submit FAFSA. *Unit head:* Dr. Rosannce Stripling, Dean, 903-223-3073, E-mail: rosanne.stripling@tamut.edu. *Application contact:* Patricia E. Black, Director of Admissions and Registrar, 903-223-3068, Fax: 903-223-3140, E-mail: pat.black@tamut.edu.

Texas Tech University, Graduate School, College of Education, Department of Educational Psychology and Leadership, Lubbock, TX 79409. Offers counselor (Certificate); counselor education (M Ed, PhD); education diagnostician (Certificate); educational leadership (M Ed, Ed D); educational psychology (M Ed, PhD); gifted and talented (Certificate); higher education (M Ed, Ed D, PhD); information processing technologist (Certificate); instructional technology (M Ed, Ed D); principal (Certificate); special education (M Ed, Ed D); special education counselor (Certificate); superintendent (Certificate); visually handicapped (Certificate). *Accreditation:* ACA; NCATE. Part-time programs available. *Students:* 128 full-time (88 women), 321 part-time (233 women); includes 67 minority (23 African Americans, 1 American Indian/Alaska Native, 5 Asian Americans or Pacific Islanders, 38 Hispanic Americans), 22 international. Average age 38. 347 applicants, 49% accepted, 61 enrolled. In 2006, 110 master's, 16 doctorates awarded. *Degree requirements:* For master's, thesis optional; for doctorate, thesis/dissertation. *Entrance requirements:* For master's and doctorate, GRE General Test. Additional exam requirements/recommendations for international students: Required—TOEFL (minimum score 550 paper-based; 213 computer-based). *Application deadline:* For fall admission, 3/1 priority date for international students; for spring admission, 11/1 priority date for international students. Applications are processed on a rolling basis. Application fee: $50 ($60 for international students). Electronic applications accepted. *Expenses:* Tuition, state resident: full-time $4,440. Tuition, nonresident: full-time $11,040. Required fees: $2,136. *Financial support:* In 2006–07, 242 students received support; research assistantships with partial tuition reimbursements available, teaching assistantships with partial tuition reimbursements available, career-related internships or fieldwork, Federal Work-Study, and institutionally sponsored loans available. Support available to part-time students. Financial award application deadline: 4/15; financial award applicants required to submit FAFSA. *Faculty research:* Psychological processes of teaching and learning, teaching populations with special needs, instructional technology, educational administration in education, theories and practice in counseling and counselor education K-12 and higher. *Unit head:* Dr. Fred Hartmeister, Chair, 806-742-1998 Ext. 436, Fax: 806-742-2179, E-mail: fred.hartmeister@ttu.edu. *Application contact:* Graduate Adviser, 806-742-1998, Fax: 806-742-2179.

Thomas Edison State College, Heavin School of Arts and Sciences, Program in Liberal Studies, Trenton, NJ 08608-1176. Offers human resource management (MALS); online learning and teaching (MALS); organizational leadership (MALS). Part-time programs available. Postbaccalaureate distance learning degree programs offered (no on-campus study). *Students:* Average age 45. 34 applicants, 25 enrolled. In 2006, 12 degrees awarded. *Degree requirements:* For master's, capstone project. *Entrance requirements:* Additional exam requirements/recommendations for international students: Required—TOEFL (minimum score 550 paper-based; 213 computer-based). *Application deadline:* For fall admission, 8/15 priority date for domestic and international students; for winter admission, 11/15 priority date for domestic and international students; for spring admission, 2/15 priority date for domestic and international students. Applications are processed on a rolling basis. Application fee: $75. Electronic applications accepted. *Expenses:* Tuition, nonresident: part-time $422 per credit. Part-time tuition and fees vary according to program. *Financial support:* Applicants required to submit FAFSA. *Unit head:* Dr. Esther Taitsman, Director of Graduate School, 609-984-1168, Fax: 609-633-8593, E-mail: graduateschool@tesc.edu. *Application contact:* Renee San Giacomo, Director of Admissions, 888-442-8372, Fax: 609-984-8447, E-mail: admissions@tesc.edu.

Thomas Edison State College, School of Business and Management, Program in Management, Trenton, NJ 08608-1176. Offers human resource management (MSM); online learning and teaching (MSM); organizational leadership (MSM); public sector auditing (MSM); public service leadership (MSM). Part-time programs available. Postbaccalaureate distance learning degree programs offered (minimal on-campus study). *Students:* Average age 42. 77 applicants, 60 enrolled. In 2006, 55 degrees awarded. *Degree requirements:* For master's, capstone/thesis, applied project. *Entrance requirements:* For master's, 3-5 years of work experience. Additional exam requirements/recommendations for international students: Required—TOEFL (minimum score 550 paper-based; 213 computer-based). *Application deadline:* For fall admission, 8/15 priority date for domestic and international students; for winter admission, 11/15 priority date for domestic and international students; for spring admission, 2/15 priority date for domestic and international students. Applications are processed on a rolling basis. Application fee: $75. Electronic applications accepted. *Expenses:* Tuition, nonresident: part-time $422 per credit. Part-time tuition and fees vary according to program. *Financial support:* Applicants required to submit FAFSA. *Application contact:* Renee San Giacomo, Director of Admissions, 888-442-8372, Fax: 609-984-8447, E-mail: admissions@tesc.edu.

Touro University International, College of Education, Program in Educational Leadership, Cypress, CA 90630. Offers e-learning leadership (MA Ed, PhD); educational leadership (MA Ed); higher education leadership (PhD); K-12 leadership (PhD). Part-time and evening/weekend programs available. Postbaccalaureate distance learning degree programs offered (no on-campus study). In 2006, 13 degrees awarded. *Degree requirements:* For doctorate, thesis/dissertation, defense of dissertation, comprehensive exam. *Entrance requirements:* For doctorate, minimum GPA of 3.4, course work in research methods or statistics. Additional exam requirements/recommendations for international students: Required—TOEFL (minimum score 550 paper-based). Application fee: $75. *Expenses:* Tuition: Part-time $300 per credit hour. Tuition and fees vary according to course level and program. *Unit head:* Dr. Edith Neumann, Vice President for Academic Affairs, College of Education, 714-816-0366 Ext. 2030, Fax: 714-226-9844, E-mail: eneumann@tourou.edu.

Towson University, Graduate School, Program in Instructional Technology, Towson, MD 21252-0001. Offers educational technology (MS); instructional design and training (MS); instructional technology (Ed D); school library media (MS). Part-time and evening/weekend programs available. *Faculty:* 7 full-time (3 women), 3 part-time/adjunct (1 woman). *Students:* 19 full-time (16 women), 176 part-time (147 women); includes 22 minority (15 African Americans, 3 Asian Americans or Pacific Islanders, 4 Hispanic Americans), 5 international. 59 applicants, 76% accepted, 23 enrolled. In 2006, 69 master's, 1 doctorate awarded. *Degree requirements:* For master's, thesis optional; for doctorate, thesis/dissertation, comprehensive exam. *Entrance requirements:* For master's, minimum GPA of 3.0, technological literacy; for doctorate, GRE, writing sample, letters of recommendation. Additional exam requirements/recommendations for international students: Required—TOEFL (minimum score 600 paper-based). *Application deadline:* For fall admission, 8/1 priority date for domestic students, 7/15 priority date for international students. Applications are processed on a rolling basis. Application fee: $50. Electronic applications accepted. *Expenses:* Tuition, state resident: part-time $275 per unit. Tuition, nonresident: part-time $577 per unit. Required fees: $72 per unit. *Financial support:* In 2006–07, 1 fellowship with tuition reimbursement, 3 research assistantships with tuition reimbursements (averaging $4,000 per year) were awarded; career-related internships or fieldwork, Federal Work-Study, and unspecified assistantships also available. Financial award application deadline: 4/1; financial award applicants required to submit FAFSA. *Faculty research:* Training and commercial vehicle inspections. Total annual research expenditures: $840,000. *Unit head:* Jeff Kenton, Graduate Program Director, 410-704-4226. *Application contact:* 410-704-2501, Fax: 410-704-4675, E-mail: grads@towson.edu.

Université Laval, Faculty of Education, Department of Teaching and Learning Studies, Programs in Teaching Technology, Québec, QC G1K 7P4, Canada. Offers MA, PhD. Terminal master's awarded for partial completion of doctoral program. *Degree requirements:* For master's, thesis (for some programs); for doctorate, thesis/dissertation, comprehensive exam. *Entrance requirements:* For master's and doctorate, English exam (comprehension of written English), knowledge of French. Electronic applications accepted.

University at Albany, State University of New York, School of Education, Department of Educational Theory and Practice, Albany, NY 12222-0001. Offers curriculum and instruction (MS, Ed D, CAS); curriculum planning and development (MA); educational communications (MS, CAS). Evening/weekend programs available. *Students:* 169 full-time (114 women), 213 part-time (147 women). Average age 33. 144 applicants, 53% accepted, 41 enrolled. In 2006, 151 master's, 8 doctorates awarded. *Degree requirements:* For doctorate, one foreign language, thesis/dissertation. *Entrance requirements:* For doctorate, GRE General Test. Additional exam requirements/recommendations for international students: Required—TOEFL (minimum score 550 paper-based; 213 computer-based). *Application deadline:* For fall admission, 2/1 for domestic students, 1/31 for international students. Application fee: $75. Electronic applications accepted. *Expenses:* Tuition, state resident: full-time $6,900; part-time $288 per credit. Tuition, nonresident: full-time $10,920; part-time $455 per credit. Required fees: $1,139. *Financial support:* Fellowships available. *Unit head:* Arthur Appleby, Chair, 518-442-5020.

The University of Akron, Graduate School, College of Education, Department of Educational Foundations and Leadership, Program in Technical Education, Akron, OH 44325. Offers technical education guidance (MS); technical education instructional technology (MS); technical education teaching (MS); technical education training (MS). *Accreditation:* NCATE. *Students:* 3 full-time (2 women), 15 part-time (13 women); includes 4 minority (all African Americans), 1 international. Average age 40. 4 applicants, 100% accepted, 3 enrolled. In 2006, 7 degrees awarded. *Degree requirements:* For master's, cumulative portfolio. *Entrance requirements:* For master's, minimum GPA of 2.75. Additional exam requirements/recommendations for international students: Required—TOEFL (minimum score 550 paper-based; 213 computer-based; 79 iBT). *Application deadline:* For fall admission, 8/15 for domestic students. Applications are processed on a rolling basis. Application fee: $30 ($40 for international students). Electronic applications accepted. *Expenses:* Tuition, state resident: full-time $6,164; part-time $342 per credit. Tuition, nonresident: full-time $10,575; part-time $588 per credit. Required fees: $806; $43 per credit. $12 per term. Tuition and fees vary according to course load, degree level and program. *Financial support:* Fellowships with full tuition reimbursements, research assistantships with full tuition reimbursements, teaching assistantships with full tuition reimbursements, Federal Work-Study and unspecified assistantships available. *Unit head:* Dr. Qetler Jensrud, Head, 330-972-6403.

University of Alaska Southeast, Graduate Programs, Program in Education, Juneau, AK 99801. Offers early childhood education (M Ed, MAT); educational technology (M Ed); elementary education (MAT); reading (M Ed); secondary education (MAT). *Accreditation:* NCATE. Part-time and evening/weekend programs available. Postbaccalaureate distance learning degree programs offered (minimal on-campus study). *Faculty:* 12 full-time (7 women), 6 part-time/adjunct (5 women). *Students:* 81 full-time (49 women), 109 part-time (88 women); includes 24 minority (3 African Americans, 11 American Indian/Alaska Native, 5 Asian Americans or Pacific Islanders, 5 Hispanic Americans), 6 international. Average age 34. In 2006, 84 degrees awarded. *Degree requirements:* For master's, comprehensive exam or project, portfolio. *Entrance requirements:* For master's, PRAXIS, minimum GPA of 3.0, writing sample, letters of recommendation. *Application deadline:* For fall admission, 3/8 for domestic students. Applications are processed on a rolling basis. Application fee: $50. Electronic applications accepted. *Financial support:* Federal Work-Study, scholarships/grants, and tuition waivers (full and partial) available. Support available to part-time students. Financial award applicants required to submit FAFSA. *Faculty research:* Applied classroom research, culturally responsive practices, action research, teaching effectiveness. *Unit head:* Dr. Larry Harris, Dean, 907-796-6551, Fax: 907-796-6550, E-mail: larry.harris@uas.alaska.edu. *Application contact:* Susan A. Stuck, Administrative Assistant, 866-465-6424, Fax: 866-465-5159, E-mail: jnsas@uas.alaska.edu.

University of Alberta, Faculty of Graduate Studies and Research, Department of Educational Psychology, Edmonton, AB T6G 2E1, Canada. Offers counseling psychology (M Ed, PhD); educational psychology (M Ed, PhD); instructional technology (M Ed); school counseling (M Ed); school psychology (M Ed, PhD); special education (M Ed, PhD); special education-deafness studies (M Ed); teaching English as a second language (M Ed). Part-time programs available. *Faculty:* 34 full-time (14 women), 12 part-time/adjunct (6 women). *Students:* 117 full-time (93 women), 173 part-time (121 women), 15 international. Average age 36. 252 applicants, 34% accepted. In 2006, 30 master's, 10 doctorates awarded. *Degree requirements:* For master's, thesis optional; for doctorate, thesis/dissertation, comprehensive exam. *Entrance requirements:* For master's and doctorate, minimum GPA of 3.0. Additional exam requirements/recommendations for international students: Required—TOEFL. *Application deadline:* For fall admission, 2/1 priority date for domestic and international students. Applications are processed on a rolling basis. *Financial support:* In 2006–07, 10 fellowships with full tuition reimbursements (averaging $16,120 per year), 36 research assistantships with full tuition reimbursements (averaging $12,614 per year), 46 teaching assistantships with full tuition reimbursements (averaging $5,462 per year) were awarded; career-related internships or fieldwork and scholarships/grants also available. *Faculty research:* Human learning, development and assessment. *Unit head:* Dr. Linda M. McDonald, Chair, 780-492-1149, Fax: 780-492-1318, E-mail: linda.mcdonald@ualberta.ca. *Application contact:* Judy Maynes, Information Contact, 780-492-1149, Fax: 780-492-1318, E-mail: edpygrad@ualberta.ca.

Educational Media/Instructional Technology

University of Arkansas, Graduate School, College of Education and Health Professions, Department of Educational Leadership, Counseling and Foundations, Program in Educational Technology, Fayetteville, AR 72701-1201. Offers M Ed. *Accreditation:* NCATE. Part-time and evening/weekend programs available. *Students:* 3 full-time (0 women), 7 part-time (4 women), 1 international. 10 applicants, 50% accepted. In 2006, 9 degrees awarded. *Entrance requirements:* For master's, GRE General Test, MAT or minimum GPA of 3.0. Application fee: $40 ($50 for international students). *Financial support:* In 2006–07, 2 teaching assistantships were awarded; fellowships with tuition reimbursements, research assistantships, career-related internships or fieldwork and Federal Work-Study also available. Support available to part-time students. Financial award application deadline: 4/1; financial award applicants required to submit FAFSA. *Application contact:* Dr. Carl Holt, Graduate Coordinator, 479-575-2207, E-mail: cholt@uark.edu.

University of Arkansas at Little Rock, Graduate School, College of Education, Department of Educational Leadership, Program in Learning Systems Technology, Little Rock, AR 72204-1099. Offers M Ed. *Degree requirements:* For master's, comprehensive exam or defense of portfolio. *Entrance requirements:* For master's, GRE General Test, interview, minimum GPA of 2.75. *Faculty research:* Instructional program development, educational technology product development, educational technology management.

University of Calgary, Faculty of Graduate Studies, Faculty of Education, Graduate Division of Educational Research, Calgary, AB T2N 1N4, Canada. Offers community rehabilitation and disability studies (M Ed, M Sc, Ed D, PhD, Graduate Certificate, Graduate Diploma); curriculum, teaching and learning (M Ed, M Sc, MA, Ed D, PhD, Graduate Certificate, Graduate Diploma); educational contexts (M Ed, MA, Ed D, PhD, Graduate Certificate, Graduate Diploma); educational leadership (M Ed, MA, Ed D, PhD, Graduate Certificate, Graduate Diploma); educational technology (M Ed, M Sc, MA, Ed D, PhD, Graduate Certificate, Graduate Diploma); gifted education (M Sc, MA, Ed D, PhD, Graduate Certificate, Graduate Diploma); higher education administration (Ed D); interpretive studies in education (M Ed, M Sc, MA, Ed D, PhD, Graduate Certificate, Graduate Diploma); second language teaching (M Ed, Ed D, PhD, Graduate Certificate, Graduate Diploma); teaching English as a second language (M Ed, M Sc, MA, Ed D, PhD, Graduate Certificate, Graduate Diploma); workplace and adult learning (M Ed, MA, Ed D, PhD, Graduate Certificate, Graduate Diploma). Ed D in both higher education administration and educational leadership offered via distance delivery. Part-time and evening/weekend programs available. Postbaccalaureate distance learning degree programs offered (minimal on-campus study). *Faculty:* 44 full-time, 52 part-time/adjunct. *Students:* 488 full-time, 550 part-time. 400 applicants, 50% accepted. In 2006, 102 master's, 18 doctorates awarded. *Degree requirements:* For master's, thesis (for some programs); for doctorate, thesis/dissertation, candidacy exam. *Entrance requirements:* For master's, minimum GPA of 3.0, 3 letters of reference; for doctorate, minimum GPA of 3.5, 3 letters of reference; for other advanced degree, minimum GPA of 3.0. Additional exam requirements/recommendations for international students: Required—TOEFL, IELTS. *Application deadline:* For fall admission, 2/15 for domestic students, 2/5 for international students; for winter admission, 6/15 for domestic and international students. Application fee: $100. Electronic applications accepted. *Financial support:* In 2006–07, research assistantships (averaging $3,920 per year); teaching assistantships, career-related internships or fieldwork, scholarships/grants, and unspecified assistantships also available. Financial award application deadline: 2/1. *Faculty research:* Curriculum, leadership, technology, contexts, gifted, second language teaching, work place and adult learning. *Unit head:* Dr. Charles F. Webber, Associate Dean, 403-220-5675, Fax: 403-282-3005, E-mail: cwebber@ucalgary.ca. *Application contact:* Patricia A. Brown, Program Officer, Graduate Division of Educational Research, 403-220-3178, Fax: 403-282-3005, E-mail: brownp@ucalgary.ca.

University of Central Arkansas, Graduate School, College of Education, Department of Middle/Secondary Education and Instructional Technologies, Program in Education Media and Library Science, Conway, AR 72035-0001. Offers MS. Part-time programs available. *Students:* 9 full-time (all women), 96 part-time (93 women); includes 15 minority (6 African Americans, 9 Asian Americans or Pacific Islanders). In 2006, 22 degrees awarded. *Degree requirements:* For master's, comprehensive exam. *Entrance requirements:* For master's, GRE General Test, minimum GPA of 2.7. Additional exam requirements/recommendations for international students: Required—TOEFL (minimum score 550 paper-based; 213 computer-based). *Application deadline:* For fall admission, 3/1 priority date for domestic and international students; for spring admission, 10/1 priority date for domestic and international students. Applications are processed on a rolling basis. Application fee: $25 ($40 for international students). *Expenses:* Tuition, state resident: full-time $4,194; part-time $233 per semester. Tuition, nonresident: full-time $5,963; part-time $429 per semester. International tuition: $6,162 full-time. Required fees: $65; $23 per semester. One-time fee: $65 part-time. *Financial support:* Federal Work-Study, scholarships/grants, and tuition waivers (partial) available. Financial award application deadline: 2/15; financial award applicants required to submit FAFSA. *Unit head:* Stephanie Huffman, Head, 501-450-5430, Fax: 501-450-5680, E-mail: stephanieh@uca.edu. *Application contact:* Brenda Herring, Admissions Assistant, 501-450-5065, Fax: 501-450-5678, E-mail: bherring@uca.edu.

University of Central Arkansas, Graduate School, College of Education, Department of Middle/Secondary Education and Instructional Technologies, Program in Training Systems, Conway, AR 72035-0001. Offers MSE. Part-time programs available. *Students:* 14 full-time (8 women), 14 part-time (12 women); includes 5 minority (4 African Americans, 1 Asian American or Pacific Islander), 1 international. In 2006, 5 degrees awarded. *Degree requirements:* For master's, thesis optional. *Entrance requirements:* For master's, GRE General Test, minimum GPA of 2.7. Additional exam requirements/recommendations for international students: Required—TOEFL (minimum score 550 paper-based; 213 computer-based). *Application deadline:* For fall admission, 3/1 priority date for domestic and international students; for spring admission, 10/1 priority date for domestic and international students. Applications are processed on a rolling basis. Application fee: $25 ($40 for international students). *Expenses:* Tuition, state resident: full-time $4,194; part-time $233 per semester. Tuition, nonresident: full-time $5,963; part-time $429 per semester. International tuition: $6,162 full-time. Required fees: $65; $23 per semester. One-time fee: $65 part-time. *Financial support:* Federal Work-Study, scholarships/grants, tuition waivers (partial), and unspecified assistantships available. Support available to part-time students. Financial award application deadline: 2/15; financial award applicants required to submit FAFSA. *Unit head:* Cheryl Wiedmaier, Assistant Professor, 501-852-5151, Fax: 501-450-5680, E-mail: cherylw@uca.edu. *Application contact:* Brenda Herring, Admissions Assistant, 501-450-5065, Fax: 501-450-5678, E-mail: bherring@uca.edu.

University of Central Florida, College of Education, Department of Educational Research, Technology and Leadership, Program in Educational Technology, Orlando, FL 32816. Offers MA. *Students:* 3 full-time (2 women), 19 part-time (14 women); includes 4 minority (1 African American, 1 American Indian/Alaska Native, 2 Hispanic Americans). 11 applicants, 91% accepted, 7 enrolled. In 2006, 10 master's awarded. *Degree requirements:* For master's, thesis or alternative. *Application deadline:* For fall admission, 7/15 for domestic students; for spring admission, 12/1 for domestic students. Application fee: $30. Electronic applications accepted. *Expenses:* Tuition, state resident: full-time $6,167; part-time $257 per credit hour. Tuition, nonresident: full-time $22,790; part-time $950 per credit hour. *Financial support:* In 2006–07, 1 research assistantship with partial tuition reimbursement (averaging $7,500 per year) was awarded; fellowships with partial tuition reimbursements, career-related internships or fieldwork, Federal Work-Study, institutionally sponsored loans, tuition waivers (partial), and unspecified assistantships also available. *Unit head:* Dr. Glenda Gunter, Coordinator, 407-823-3502, E-mail: ggunter@pegasus.cc.ucf.edu.

University of Central Florida, College of Education, Department of Educational Research, Technology and Leadership, Program in e-Learning, Orlando, FL 32816. Offers e-learning professional development (Certificate); instructional technology/media and e-learning (MA). *Students:* 3 full-time (0 women), 6 part-time (3 women); includes 3 minority (1 American Indian/Alaska Native, 2 Hispanic Americans), 1 international. *Expenses:* Tuition, state resident: full-time $6,167; part-time $257 per credit hour. Tuition, nonresident: full-time $22,790; part-time $950 per credit hour. *Financial support:* In 2006–07, 1 research assistantship (averaging $6,200 per year) was awarded.

University of Central Florida, College of Education, Department of Educational Research, Technology and Leadership, Program in Instructional Systems, Orlando, FL 32816. Offers MA. *Students:* 5 full-time (3 women), 20 part-time (14 women); includes 3 minority (all Hispanic Americans), 1 international. Average age 34. In 2006, 7 master's awarded. Application fee: $30. Electronic applications accepted. *Expenses:* Tuition, state resident: full-time $6,167; part-time $257 per credit hour. Tuition, nonresident: full-time $22,790; part-time $950 per credit hour. *Financial support:* In 2006–07, 2 research assistantships with partial tuition reimbursements (averaging $7,200 per year) were awarded; fellowships with partial tuition reimbursements, teaching assistantships with partial tuition reimbursements also available. *Unit head:* Dr. Atusi Hirumi, Coordinator, 407-823-1760, E-mail: hirumi@mail.ucf.edu.

University of Central Florida, College of Education, Department of Teaching and Learning Principles, Program in Educational Media, Orlando, FL 32816. Offers M Ed. *Students:* 1 (woman) full-time, 30 part-time (28 women); includes 2 minority (both Hispanic Americans), 2 international. Average age 38. In 2006, 7 degrees awarded. Application fee: $30. Electronic applications accepted. *Expenses:* Tuition, state resident: full-time $6,167; part-time $257 per credit hour. Tuition, nonresident: full-time $22,790; part-time $950 per credit hour. *Financial support:* Fellowships, research assistantships available. *Unit head:* Dr. Judy R. Lee, Coordinator, 407-823-6139, E-mail: jlee@mail.ucf.edu.

University of Central Florida, College of Education, Doctoral Program in Education, Orlando, FL 32816. Offers communication sciences and disorders (PhD); counselor education (PhD); curriculum and instruction (PhD); elementary education (PhD); exceptional education (PhD); hospitality education (PhD); instructional technology (PhD); mathematics education (PhD). *Students:* 86 full-time (63 women), 9 part-time (4 women); includes 21 minority (15 African Americans, 2 Asian Americans or Pacific Islanders, 4 Hispanic Americans), 19 international. Average age 39. In 2006, 16 degrees awarded. Application fee: $30. Electronic applications accepted. *Expenses:* Tuition, state resident: full-time $6,167; part-time $257 per credit hour. Tuition, nonresident: full-time $22,790; part-time $950 per credit hour. *Financial support:* In 2006–07, 44 fellowships with partial tuition reimbursements (averaging $3,700 per year), 54 research assistantships with partial tuition reimbursements (averaging $7,000 per year), 9 teaching assistantships with partial tuition reimbursements (averaging $7,000 per year) were awarded.

University of Central Missouri, The Graduate School, College of Education, Department of Educational Leadership and Human Development, Program in Educational Technology, Warrensburg, MO 64093. Offers MSE. Part-time programs available. *Students:* 3 full-time (all women), 18 part-time (14 women); includes 1 minority (African American), 2 international. Average age 32. 5 applicants. In 2006, 13 degrees awarded. *Degree requirements:* For master's, portfolio, research project. *Entrance requirements:* For master's, interview, minimum GPA of 2.75. Additional exam requirements/recommendations for international students: Required—TOEFL (minimum score 500 paper-based; 173 computer-based). *Application deadline:* For fall admission, 6/1 priority date for domestic students, 5/1 priority date for international students; for spring admission, 10/1 priority date for domestic students, 10/1 for international students. Applications are processed on a rolling basis. Application fee: $30 ($50 for international students). *Expenses:* Tuition, state resident: full-time $5,448; part-time $227 per credit hour. Tuition, nonresident: full-time $10,896; part-time $454 per credit hour. Required fees: $336; $14 per credit hour. *Financial support:* Career-related internships or fieldwork, Federal Work-Study, scholarships/grants, unspecified assistantships, and administrative and laboratory assistantships available. Support available to part-time students. Financial award application deadline: 3/1; financial award applicants required to submit FAFSA.

University of Central Oklahoma, College of Graduate Studies and Research, College of Education, Department of Curriculum and Instruction, Program in Instructional Media, Edmond, OK 73034-5209. Offers M Ed. *Accreditation:* NCATE. Part-time programs available. *Entrance requirements:* For master's, GRE General Test. Additional exam requirements/recommendations for international students: Required—TOEFL (minimum score 550 paper-based; 213 computer-based). Electronic applications accepted.

University of Colorado at Denver and Health Sciences Center, School of Education and Human Development, Program in Professional Learning and Advancement Networks (PLAN), Denver, CO 80217-3364. Offers MA. *Students:* 8 full-time (6 women), 108 part-time (76 women); includes 17 minority (1 African American, 7 Asian Americans or Pacific Islanders, 9 Hispanic Americans). Average age 38. 27 applicants, 89% accepted, 16 enrolled. In 2006, 72 degrees awarded. *Degree requirements:* For master's, thesis or alternative. *Entrance requirements:* For master's, GRE, MAT, minimum GPA of 2.75. Additional exam requirements/recommendations for international students: Required—TOEFL (minimum score 525 paper-based; 197 computer-based). *Application deadline:* For fall admission, 4/15 for domestic students; for spring admission, 9/15 for domestic students. Applications are processed on a rolling basis. Application fee: $50 ($75 for international students). Electronic applications accepted. *Financial support:* Research assistantships, teaching assistantships, Federal Work-Study available. Financial award application deadline: 4/1; financial award applicants required to submit FAFSA. *Unit head:* Nancy Shanklin, Program Coordinator, 303-556-8446, Fax: 303-556-4479, E-mail: nancy.shanklin@cudenver.edu. *Application contact:* 303-556-2717, Fax: 303-556-4479, E-mail: education@cudenver.edu.

University of Connecticut, Graduate School, Neag School of Education, Department of Educational Psychology, Storrs, CT 06269. Offers educational psychology (MA, PhD), including cognition and instruction, counseling psychology, gifted and talented education, learning technology, measurement, evaluation, and assessment, school psychology, special education. *Faculty:* 34 full-time (16 women). *Students:* 154 full-time (127 women), 147 part-time (114 women); includes 35 minority (15 African Americans, 2 American Indian/Alaska Native, 7 Asian Americans or Pacific Islanders, 11 Hispanic Americans), 20 international. Average age 34. 331 applicants, 48% accepted, 139 enrolled. In 2006, 115 master's, 20 doctorates awarded. *Degree requirements:* For master's, comprehensive exam; for doctorate, thesis/dissertation. *Entrance requirements:* For doctorate, GRE General Test. Additional exam requirements/recommendations for international students: Required—TOEFL (minimum score 550 paper-based; 213 computer-based). *Application deadline:* For fall admission, 2/1 priority date for domestic and international students; for spring admission, 11/1 for domestic students, 10/1 for international students. Applications are processed on a rolling basis. Application fee: $55. Electronic applications accepted. *Financial support:* In 2006–07, 87 research assistantships with full tuition reimbursements, 1 teaching assistantship with full tuition reimbursement were awarded; fellowships, Federal Work-Study, scholarships/grants, health care benefits, and unspecified assistantships also available. Financial award application deadline: 2/1; financial award applicants required to submit FAFSA. *Unit head:* Sally Reis, Head, 860-486-4031, Fax: 860-486-0210. *Application contact:* Lisa Rasicot, Graduate Coordinator, 860-486-3065, Fax: 860-486-0210, E-mail: soeadm02@uconnvm.uconn.edu.

University of Connecticut, Graduate School, Neag School of Education, Department of Educational Psychology, Field of Educational Psychology, Program in Learning Technology, Storrs, CT 06269. Offers MA, PhD. *Accreditation:* NCATE. *Faculty:* 7 full-time (1 woman). *Students:* 14 full-time (12 women), 11 part-time (2 women); includes 3 minority (all Asian Americans or Pacific Islanders), 4 international. Average age 34. 29 applicants, 55% accepted, 11 enrolled. In 2006, 2 degrees awarded. Terminal master's awarded for partial completion of doctoral program. *Degree requirements:* For master's, thesis or alternative, comprehensive exam; for doctorate, thesis/dissertation. *Entrance requirements:* For master's and doctorate, GRE General Test. Additional exam requirements/recommendations for international students: Required—TOEFL (minimum score 550 paper-based; 213 computer-based). *Application deadline:* For fall admission, 2/1 priority date for domestic and international students; for spring admission, 11/1 for domestic students, 10/1 for international students. Applications are processed on a rolling basis. Application fee: $55. Electronic applications accepted. *Financial support:*

Fellowships, research assistantships with full tuition reimbursements, teaching assistantships with full tuition reimbursements, Federal Work-Study, scholarships/grants, health care benefits, and unspecified assistantships available. Financial award application deadline: 2/1; financial award applicants required to submit FAFSA. *Application contact:* Lisa Rasicot, Graduate Coordinator, 860-486-3065, Fax: 860-486-0210, E-mail: soeadm02@uconnvm.uconn.edu.

University of Dayton, Graduate School, School of Education and Allied Professions, Department of Teacher Education, Dayton, OH 45469-1300. Offers adolescent/young adult (MS Ed); art education (MS Ed); early childhood education (MS Ed); inclusive early childhood (MS Ed); interdisciplinary education (MS Ed); intervention specialist education, mild/moderate (MS Ed); literacy (MS Ed); middle childhood (MS Ed); multi-age education (MS Ed); music education (MS Ed); teacher as leader (MS Ed); technology in education (MS Ed). Part-time and evening/weekend programs available. *Faculty:* 13 full-time (9 women), 33 part-time/adjunct (25 women). *Students:* 149 full-time (120 women), 284 part-time (241 women); includes 37 minority (31 African Americans, 3 Asian Americans or Pacific Islanders, 3 Hispanic Americans), 3 international. Average age 33. 201 applicants, 58% accepted, 31 enrolled. In 2006, 150 degrees awarded. *Degree requirements:* For master's, thesis, capstone research project. *Entrance requirements:* For master's, GRE General Test, minimum GPA of 2.75. Additional exam requirements/recommendations for international students: Required—TOEFL (minimum score 550 paper-based; 213 computer-based). *Application deadline:* For fall admission, 3/15 priority date for domestic students, 3/1 priority date for international students. Applications are processed on a rolling basis. Application fee: $0. Electronic applications accepted. *Expenses: Contact institution.* *Financial support:* In 2006–07, 8 teaching assistantships with partial tuition reimbursements (averaging $7,600 per year) were awarded; career-related internships or fieldwork, institutionally sponsored loans, health care benefits, and unspecified assistantships also available. Financial award applicants required to submit FAFSA. *Faculty research:* Diversity, literacy, art representation by young children, preservice teacher preparation. Total annual research expenditures: $330,000. *Unit head:* Dr. Katie A. Kinnucan-Welsch, Chair, 937-229-3346. *Application contact:* Erika Eavers, Graduate Admission Processor, 937-229-3065, Fax: 937-229-4729, E-mail: erika.eavers@notes.udayton.edu.

The University of Findlay, Graduate and Professional Studies, College of Education, Findlay, OH 45840-3653. Offers administration (MA Ed); early childhood (MA Ed); elementary education (MA Ed); human resource development (MA Ed); leadership (MA Ed); special education (MA Ed); technology (MA Ed); web instruction (MA Ed). *Accreditation:* NCATE. Part-time and evening/weekend programs available. *Faculty:* 12 full-time, 6 part-time/adjunct. *Students:* 84 full-time (65 women), 223 part-time (169 women); includes 11 minority (3 African Americans, 2 American Indian/Alaska Native, 1 Asian American or Pacific Islander, 5 Hispanic Americans), 13 international. Average age 35. 91 applicants, 97% accepted, 76 enrolled. In 2006, 146 degrees awarded. *Degree requirements:* For master's, thesis, cumulative project. *Entrance requirements:* For master's, minimum undergraduate GPA of 3.0 in last 60 hours of course work. Additional exam requirements/recommendations for international students: Required—TOEFL. *Application deadline:* Applications are processed on a rolling basis. Application fee: $25. Electronic applications accepted. *Expenses: Contact institution.* *Financial support:* In 2006–07, 6 students received support, including 6 teaching assistantships with full tuition reimbursements available (averaging $6,000 per year); unspecified assistantships also available. Financial award application deadline: 4/1; financial award applicants required to submit FAFSA. *Faculty research:* Children's literature, books and artwork, educational technology, professional development. *Unit head:* Dr. Melissa A. Cain, Dean, 419-434-4840, Fax: 419-434-4822. *Application contact:* Heather Riffle, Director, Graduate and Special Programs, 419-434-4642, Fax: 419-434-5517, E-mail: riffle@findlay.edu.

University of Georgia, Graduate School, College of Education, Department of Educational Psychology and Instructional Technology, Athens, GA 30602. Offers M Ed, MA, Ed D, PhD, Ed S. *Accreditation:* NCATE. *Faculty:* 25 full-time (13 women). *Students:* 123 full-time (85 women), 142 part-time (111 women); includes 21 minority (15 African Americans, 1 American Indian/Alaska Native, 4 Asian Americans or Pacific Islanders, 1 Hispanic American), 49 international. 278 applicants, 45% accepted, 60 enrolled. In 2006, 43 master's, 23 doctorates, 26 other advanced degrees awarded. *Entrance requirements:* For master's and Ed S, GRE General Test or MAT; for doctorate, GRE General Test. *Application deadline:* For fall admission, 7/1 priority date for domestic students; for spring admission, 11/15 for domestic students. Application fee: $50. Electronic applications accepted. *Financial support:* Fellowships, research assistantships, teaching assistantships, unspecified assistantships available. *Unit head:* Dr. Randy W. Kamphaus, Head, 706-542-4253, Fax: 706-542-4240.

University of Hartford, College of Education, Nursing, and Health Professions, Program in Educational Technology, West Hartford, CT 06117-1599. Offers M Ed. *Accreditation:* NCATE. Part-time and evening/weekend programs available. *Faculty:* 5 full-time (1 woman), 2 part-time/adjunct (both women). *Students:* 1 (woman) full-time, 22 part-time (15 women); includes 4 minority (all African Americans) Average age 35. 16 applicants, 94% accepted, 11 enrolled. In 2006, 7 degrees awarded. *Degree requirements:* For master's, comprehensive exam. *Entrance requirements:* For master's, interview, 2 letters of recommendation. Additional exam requirements/recommendations for international students: Required—TOEFL (minimum score 550 paper-based; 213 computer-based). *Application deadline:* For fall admission, 8/15 for domestic students; for winter admission, 12/1 for domestic students; for spring admission, 12/1 for domestic students. Applications are processed on a rolling basis. Application fee: $40 ($55 for international students). Electronic applications accepted. *Expenses:* Tuition: Part-time $515 per credit. Required fees: $200 per term. *Financial support:* Teaching assistantships, institutionally sponsored loans and unspecified assistantships available. Financial award application deadline: 6/1; financial award applicants required to submit FAFSA. *Unit head:* Dr. Frederick King, Director, 860-768-5190, Fax: 860-768-5043, E-mail: rking@hartford.edu. *Application contact:* Susan Brown, Assistant Dean of Academic Services, 860-768-4692, Fax: 860-768-5043, E-mail: brown@hartford.edu.

University of Hawaii at Manoa, Graduate Division, College of Education, Department of Educational Technology, Honolulu, HI 96822. Offers M Ed. Part-time programs available. *Faculty:* 10 full-time (4 women). *Students:* 30 full-time (18 women), 26 part-time (14 women); includes 17 minority (15 Asian Americans or Pacific Islanders, 2 Hispanic Americans), 3 international. Average age 36. 58 applicants, 72% accepted, 36 enrolled. In 2006, 14 degrees awarded. *Degree requirements:* For master's, thesis optional. *Entrance requirements:* Additional exam requirements/recommendations for international students: Required—TOEFL (minimum score 650 paper-based; 280 computer-based; 114 iBT). *Application deadline:* For fall admission, 3/1 for domestic and international students. Application fee: $50. *Financial support:* In 2006–07, 4 research assistantships (averaging $16,998 per year) were awarded; tuition waivers (full and partial) also available. *Faculty research:* Distance education-interaction via electronic means. Total annual research expenditures: $24,720. *Application contact:* Catherine Fulford, Information Contact, 808-956-7671, Fax: 808-956-3905.

University of Houston–Clear Lake, School of Education, Program in Curriculum and Instruction, Houston, TX 77058-1098. Offers curriculum and instruction (MS); early childhood education (MS); reading (MS); school library and information science (MS). Part-time and evening/weekend programs available. *Faculty:* 17 full-time (15 women), 9 part-time/adjunct (7 women). *Students:* 40 full-time (39 women), 185 part-time (176 women); includes 66 minority (32 African Americans, 7 Asian Americans or Pacific Islanders, 27 Hispanic Americans), 6 international. Average age 34. In 2006, 80 degrees awarded. *Degree requirements:* For master's, thesis (for some programs). *Entrance requirements:* For master's, GRE or minimum GPA of 3.0 in last 60 hours. Additional exam requirements/recommendations for international students: Required—TOEFL (minimum score 550 paper-based; 213 computer-based). *Application deadline:* For fall admission, 7/1 for domestic students, 6/1 for international students; for spring admission, 10/1 for domestic and international students. Applications are processed on a rolling basis. Application fee: $35 ($75 for international students). Electronic applications accepted. *Financial support:* Career-related internships or fieldwork, Federal Work-Study, institutionally sponsored loans, and scholarships/grants available. Support available to part-time students. Financial award application deadline: 5/1; financial award applicants required to submit FAFSA. *Unit head:* Dr. Suzanne Brown, Chair, 281-283-3540, E-mail: brownsue@uhcl.edu. *Application contact:* Janis S. Bigelow, Assistant Director of Admissions, Recruitment and Communications, 281-283-2540, Fax: 281-283-2530, E-mail: bigelow@uhcl.edu.

University of Houston–Clear Lake, School of Education, Program in Foundations and Professional Studies, Houston, TX 77058-1098. Offers counseling (MS); instructional technology (MS); multicultural studies (MS). Part-time and evening/weekend programs available. *Faculty:* 15 full-time (11 women), 11 part-time/adjunct (6 women). *Students:* 35 full-time (29 women), 283 part-time (239 women); includes 111 minority (58 African Americans, 1 American Indian/Alaska Native, 10 Asian Americans or Pacific Islanders, 42 Hispanic Americans), 10 international. Average age 35. In 2006, 86 degrees awarded. *Degree requirements:* For master's, thesis optional. *Entrance requirements:* For master's, GRE or minimum GPA of 3.0 in last 60 hours. Additional exam requirements/recommendations for international students: Required—TOEFL (minimum score 550 paper-based; 213 computer-based). *Application deadline:* For fall admission, 7/1 for domestic students, 6/1 for international students; for spring admission, 10/1 for domestic and international students. Applications are processed on a rolling basis. Application fee: $35 ($75 for international students). Electronic applications accepted. *Financial support:* Career-related internships or fieldwork, Federal Work-Study, institutionally sponsored loans, and scholarships/grants available. Support available to part-time students. Financial award application deadline: 5/1; financial award applicants required to submit FAFSA. *Unit head:* Dr. Judy Marquez, Chair, 281-283-3580, E-mail: marquez@uhcl.edu. *Application contact:* Janis S. Bigelow, Assistant Director of Admissions, Recruitment and Communications, 281-283-2540, Fax: 281-283-2530, E-mail: bigelow@uhcl.edu.

University of Kentucky, Graduate School, College of Education, Program in Curriculum and Instruction, Lexington, KY 40506-0032. Offers curriculum and instruction (MA Ed, Ed D); instruction and administration (Ed D); instruction system design (MS Ed); middle school education (MS Ed). *Accreditation:* NCATE. *Faculty:* 22 full-time (13 women), 2 part-time/adjunct (both women). *Students:* 116 full-time (85 women), 84 part-time (70 women); includes 26 minority (19 African Americans, 6 Asian Americans or Pacific Islanders, 1 Hispanic American), 6 international. Average age 34. 179 applicants, 51% accepted, 36 enrolled. In 2006, 72 master's, 4 doctorates awarded. *Degree requirements:* For master's, thesis optional; for doctorate, thesis/dissertation, comprehensive exam. *Entrance requirements:* For master's, GRE General Test, minimum undergraduate GPA of 2.75; for doctorate, GRE General Test, minimum graduate GPA of 3.0. Additional exam requirements/recommendations for international students: Required—TOEFL (minimum score 550 paper-based; 213 computer-based). *Application deadline:* For fall admission, 7/18 for domestic students, 2/1 priority date for international students; for spring admission, 12/15 for domestic students, 6/16 priority date for international students. Application fee: $35 ($45 for international students). Electronic applications accepted. *Expenses:* Tuition, state resident: full-time $7,670; part-time $401 per credit hour. Tuition, nonresident: full-time $16,158; part-time $873 per credit hour. *Financial support:* In 2006–07, 4 fellowships (averaging $8,018 per year), 13 research assistantships (averaging $15,000 per year), 11 teaching assistantships (averaging $9,384 per year) were awarded; career-related internships or fieldwork, Federal Work-Study, and institutionally sponsored loans also available. Support available to part-time students. *Faculty research:* Educational reform, multicultural education, classroom instructional practices, performance based assessment, primary school programs. *Unit head:* Dr. Mary Shake, Director of Graduate Studies, 859-257-5676, Fax: 859-257-1602. *Application contact:* Dr. Brian Jackson, Senior Associate Dean, 859-257-4667, Fax: 859-257-4676, E-mail: brian.jackson@uky.edu.

University of Louisville, Graduate School, College of Education and Human Development, Department of Teaching and Learning, Program in Instructional Technology, Louisville, KY 40292-0001. Offers M Ed. *Students:* 2 full-time (both women), 36 part-time (20 women); includes 1 minority (Hispanic American), 4 international. Average age 41. In 2006, 16 degrees awarded. Application fee: $50. *Unit head:* Dr. Sara Kajder, Director, 502-852-0586, Fax: 502-852-1497, E-mail: sara.kajder@louisville.edu.

University of Maine, Graduate School, College of Education and Human Development, Program in Instructional Technology, Orono, ME 04469. Offers M Ed. Part-time and evening/weekend programs available. *Students:* 7 full-time (4 women), 9 part-time (5 women); includes 1 minority (Asian American or Pacific Islander), 2 international. Average age 42. 4 applicants, 75% accepted, 3 enrolled. In 2006, 4 degrees awarded. *Degree requirements:* For master's, thesis or alternative. *Entrance requirements:* For master's, MAT. Additional exam requirements/recommendations for international students: Required—TOEFL. *Application deadline:* Applications are processed on a rolling basis. Application fee: $50. Electronic applications accepted. *Financial support:* In 2006–07, teaching assistantships (averaging $9,010 per year). Financial award application deadline: 3/1. *Unit head:* Dr. Dorothy Breen, Coordinator, 207-581-2444, Fax: 207-581-2423. *Application contact:* Scott G. Delcourt, Associate Dean of the Graduate School, 207-581-3219, Fax: 207-581-3232, E-mail: graduate@maine.edu.

University of Maryland, Baltimore County, Graduate School, College of Arts, Humanities and Social Sciences, Department of Education, Program in Instructional Systems Development, Baltimore, MD 21250. Offers ESOL/bilingual education (Postbaccalaureate Certificate); ESOL/bilingual training systems (MA). Part-time and evening/weekend programs available. *Faculty:* 3 full-time (2 women), 3 part-time/adjunct (all women). *Students:* 39 full-time (34 women), 149 part-time (119 women); includes 39 minority (25 African Americans, 10 Asian Americans or Pacific Islanders, 4 Hispanic Americans), 12 international. Average age 37. *Degree requirements:* For master's, thesis (for some programs), comprehensive exam, registration. *Entrance requirements:* Additional exam requirements/recommendations for international students: Required—TOEFL. *Application deadline:* Applications are processed on a rolling basis. Application fee: $50. Electronic applications accepted. *Expenses:* Tuition, state resident: part-time $412 per credit hour. Tuition, nonresident: part-time $681 per credit hour. Required fees: $91 per credit hour. One-time fee: $75 part-time. *Financial support:* Research assistantships, career-related internships or fieldwork, Federal Work-Study, scholarships/grants, tuition waivers, and unspecified assistantships available. Financial award application deadline: 3/1. *Faculty research:* Cross-cultural communication, culturally sensitive pedagogy. *Unit head:* Dr. John Nelson, Coordinator, 410-455-3056.

University of Maryland, College Park, Graduate Studies, College of Education, Department of Education Policy and Leadership, College Park, MD 20742. Offers curriculum and educational communications (M Ed, MA, Ed D, PhD); social foundations of education (M Ed, MA, Ed D, PhD, CAGS). *Accreditation:* NCATE. Part-time and evening/weekend programs available. Postbaccalaureate distance learning degree programs offered (minimal on-campus study). *Faculty:* 17 full-time (11 women), 6 part-time/adjunct (4 women). *Students:* 180 full-time (127 women), 145 part-time (105 women); includes 107 minority (69 African Americans, 1 American Indian/Alaska Native, 20 Asian Americans or Pacific Islanders, 17 Hispanic Americans), 23 international. 167 applicants, 40% accepted, 25 enrolled. In 2006, 37 master's, 15 doctorates, 1 other advanced degree awarded. *Degree requirements:* For master's, thesis or alternative, internship and/or field experience; for doctorate, thesis/dissertation, practicum or internship, comprehensive exam. *Entrance requirements:* For master's, GRE General Test or MAT, minimum GPA of 3.0, scholarly writing sample, 3 letters of recommendation; for doctorate, GRE General Test or MAT, scholarly writing sample, minimum undergraduate GPA of 3.0, minimum graduate GPA of 3.5. *Application deadline:* For fall admission, 2/1 for domestic and international students; for spring admission, 9/1 for domestic students, 6/1 for international students. Applications are processed on a rolling basis. Application fee: $60. Electronic applications accepted. *Financial support:* In 2006–07, 6 fellowships with full tuition reimbursements (averaging $13,118 per year), 2 research assistantships with tuition reimbursements (averaging $15,252 per year), 47 teaching assistantships with tuition reimbursements (averaging $14,510 per year) were awarded; career-related internships or fieldwork, Federal Work-Study, and scholarships/grants also available. Support available to part-time students. Financial award applicants required to submit FAFSA. *Faculty research:* Educational technology, adult and higher education. Total annual research expenditures: $314,050. *Unit head:* Dr. Thomas Weible, Acting Chair, 301-

Educational Media/Instructional Technology

University of Maryland, College Park (continued)
405-3589, Fax: 301-405-3573, E-mail: tweible@umd.edu. *Application contact:* Dean of Graduate School, 301-405-4190, Fax: 301-314-9305.

University of Massachusetts Amherst, Graduate School, School of Education, Program in Education, Amherst, MA 01003. Offers cultural diversity and curriculum reform (M Ed, Ed D, CAGS); early childhood education and development (M Ed, Ed D, CAGS); educational administration (M Ed, Ed D, CAGS); elementary teacher education (M Ed, Ed D, CAGS); higher education (M Ed, Ed D, CAGS); international education (M Ed, Ed D, CAGS); mathematics, science, and instructional technology (M Ed, Ed D, CAGS); physical education teacher education (M Ed, Ed D, CAGS); reading and writing (M Ed, Ed D, CAGS); research and evaluation methods (M Ed, Ed D, CAGS); school psychology and school counseling (M Ed, Ed D, CAGS); secondary teacher education (M Ed, Ed D, CAGS); social justice education (M Ed, Ed D, CAGS); special education (M Ed, Ed D, CAGS). *Accreditation:* NCATE. *Students:* 418 full-time (286 women), 447 part-time (319 women); includes 147 minority (70 African Americans, 4 American Indian/Alaska Native, 28 Asian Americans or Pacific Islanders, 45 Hispanic Americans), 81 international. Average age 36. In 2006, 260 master's, 30 doctorates awarded. *Degree requirements:* For doctorate, thesis/dissertation. *Entrance requirements:* For master's and doctorate, GRE General Test. Additional exam requirements/recommendations for international students: Required—TOEFL (minimum score 530 paper-based; 197 computer-based). *Application deadline:* For fall admission, 1/15 for domestic and international students; for spring admission, 10/1 for domestic and international students. Applications are processed on a rolling basis. Application fee: $40 ($65 for international students). Electronic applications accepted. *Expenses:* Tuition, state resident: full-time $2,640; part-time $110 per credit. Tuition, nonresident: full-time $9,936; part-time $414 per credit. Required fees: $8,969; $3,129 per term. One-time fee: $257 full-time. Tuition and fees vary according to class time, course load, campus/location and reciprocity agreements. *Financial support:* Fellowships with full tuition reimbursements, research assistantships with full tuition reimbursements, teaching assistantships with full tuition reimbursements, career-related internships or fieldwork, Federal Work-Study, scholarships/grants, traineeships, and unspecified assistantships available. Support available to part-time students. Financial award application deadline: 1/15. *Unit head:* Linda L. Griffin, Professor, 413-545-6984.

University of Memphis, Graduate School, College of Education, Department of Instruction and Curriculum Leadership, Memphis, TN 38152. Offers early childhood education (MAT, MS, Ed D); elementary education (MAT); instruction and curriculum (MS, Ed D); instruction design and technology (MS, Ed D); reading (MS, Ed D); secondary education (MAT); special education (MAT, MS, Ed D). *Accreditation:* NCATE (one or more programs are accredited). Part-time programs available. Terminal master's awarded for partial completion of doctoral program. *Degree requirements:* For master's, thesis or alternative, comprehensive exam; for doctorate, thesis/dissertation, comprehensive exam. *Entrance requirements:* For master's, GRE General Test, minimum GPA of 2.5; for doctorate, GRE General Test, GRE Subject Test, 2 years of teaching experience. Electronic applications accepted. *Faculty research:* Effective urban teachers, preparation and retention of urban teachers, technology utilization in schools, field-based preparation teacher preparation programs, effective use of online instruction.

University of Michigan, Horace H. Rackham School of Graduate Studies, School of Education, Programs in Educational Studies, Ann Arbor, MI 48109. Offers curriculum development (MA); early childhood education (MA, PhD); educational administration and policy (MA, PhD); educational foundation, administration, policy, and research methods (MA); educational foundations and policy (MA, PhD); elementary education (MA-Certification); English education (MA); English language learning in school settings (MA); learning technologies (MA, PhD); literacy, language, and culture (MA, PhD); mathematics education (MA, PhD); research methods (MA); science education (MA, PhD); secondary education (MA-Certification); social studies education (MA); special education (PhD); teaching and teacher education (PhD); MA-Certification; MBA/MA; PhD/MA. Terminal master's awarded for partial completion of doctoral program. *Degree requirements:* For master's, thesis (for some programs); for doctorate, thesis/dissertation, comprehensive exam. *Entrance requirements:* For master's and doctorate, GRE General Test. Additional exam requirements/recommendations for international students: Required—TOEFL (minimum score 600 paper-based; 250 computer-based). *Application deadline:* For fall admission, 12/1 priority date for domestic students, 12/1 for international students. Application fee: $60 ($75 for international students). Electronic applications accepted. *Financial support:* Applicants required to submit FAFSA. *Unit head:* Dr. Addison Stone, Chairperson, 734-763-7500, Fax: 734-615-1290, E-mail: addison@umich.edu. *Application contact:* Roberta Perry, Office of Student Services, 734-764-7563, Fax: 734-763-1495, E-mail: ed.grad.admit@umich.edu.

University of Michigan–Flint, School of Education and Human Services, Program in Technology in Education, Flint, MI 48502-1950. Offers MA. Part-time programs available. *Students:* 22 full-time (18 women), 7 part-time (6 women); includes 5 minority (4 African Americans, 1 American Indian/Alaska Native). Average age 35. *Entrance requirements:* Additional exam requirements/recommendations for international students: Required—TOEFL (minimum score 550 paper-based; 220 computer-based), IELTS (minimum score 7). *Application deadline:* For fall admission, 8/1 priority date for domestic students, 3/1 priority date for international students; for winter admission, 11/15 priority date for domestic students, 7/15 priority date for international students; for spring admission, 3/15 priority date for domestic students, 11/15 priority date for international students. Applications are processed on a rolling basis. Application fee: $55. Electronic applications accepted. *Expenses:* Contact institution. *Unit head:* Dr. Beverly Schumer, Director, 810-424-5215, E-mail: bschumer@umflint.edu. *Application contact:* Beulah Alexander, Executive Secretary, 810-766-6879, Fax: 810-766-6891, E-mail: beulaha@umflint.edu.

See Close-Up on page 1133.

University of Minnesota, Twin Cities Campus, Graduate School, College of Education and Human Development, Department of Curriculum and Instruction, Minneapolis, MN 55455-0213. Offers art education (M Ed, MA, PhD); children's literature (M Ed, MA, PhD); curriculum and instruction (MA, PhD); early childhood education (M Ed, PhD); elementary education (M Ed, MA, PhD); English education (MA, PhD); environmental education (M Ed); family education (M Ed, MA, Ed D, PhD); instructional systems and technology (M Ed, MA, PhD); language arts (MA, PhD); language immersion education (Certificate); literacy education (MA); mathematics education (MA, PhD); reading education (MA, PhD); science education (MA, PhD); second languages and cultures education (MA, PhD); social studies education (MA, PhD); teaching (M Ed), including Chinese, earth science, elementary special education, English, English as a second language, French, German, Hebrew, Japanese, life sciences, mathematics, middle school science, science, second languages and cultures, social studies, Spanish; technology enhanced learning (Certificate); writing education (M Ed, MA, PhD). *Faculty:* 30 full-time (18 women). *Students:* 496 full-time (363 women), 338 part-time (235 women); includes 89 minority (26 African Americans, 4 American Indian/Alaska Native, 42 Asian Americans or Pacific Islanders, 17 Hispanic Americans), 33 international. Average age 29. 734 applicants, 66% accepted, 425 enrolled. In 2006, 644 master's, 18 doctorates, 11 other advanced degrees awarded. *Expenses:* Tuition, state resident: full-time $9,302; part-time $775 per credit. Tuition, nonresident: full-time $16,400; part-time $1,367 per credit. Full-time tuition and fees vary according to class time, course load, program, reciprocity agreements and student level. *Financial support:* In 2006–07, 7 fellowships (averaging $24,775 per year), 22 research assistantships with full tuition reimbursements (averaging $24,775 per year), 52 teaching assistantships with full tuition reimbursements (averaging $24,775 per year) were awarded. *Faculty research:* Educational practice for a democratic and just society; curriculum history and development/assessment; teacher preparation/induction/mentoring/development; cultural, linguistic, social, political, technological, and economic factors that influence teaching and learning. Total annual research expenditures: $1.2 million. *Unit head:* Dr. Ruth Thomas, Chair, 612-624-4772, Fax: 612-624-8277, E-mail: thoma006@umn.edu. *Application contact:* Dr. Mary Bents, Associate Dean, 612-625-6501, Fax: 612-626-1580, E-mail: mbents@tc.umn.edu.

University of Missouri–Columbia, Graduate School, College of Education, School of Information Science and Learning Technologies, Columbia, MO 65211. Offers educational technology (M Ed, Ed S); information science and learning technology (PhD); library science (MA). *Accreditation:* ALA (one or more programs are accredited). Part-time and evening/weekend programs available. *Faculty:* 15 full-time (7 women). *Students:* 140 full-time (105 women), 260 part-time (200 women); includes 15 minority (5 African Americans, 4 American Indian/Alaska Native, 3 Asian Americans or Pacific Islanders, 3 Hispanic Americans), 37 international. In 2006, 175 master's, 7 doctorates, 3 other advanced degrees awarded. *Entrance requirements:* For master's, GRE General Test or MAT, minimum GPA of 3.0. *Application deadline:* For fall admission, 3/1 priority date for domestic students; for winter admission, 10/1 priority date for domestic students; for spring admission, 3/1 priority date for domestic students. Applications are processed on a rolling basis. Application fee: $45 ($60 for international students). *Financial support:* Fellowships, teaching assistantships available. *Unit head:* Dr. John Wedman, Director of Graduate Studies, 573-882-9424, E-mail: wedmanj@missouri.edu.

University of Nebraska at Kearney, College of Graduate Study, College of Education, Department of Teacher Education, Kearney, NE 68849-0001. Offers curriculum and instruction (MS Ed); instructional technology (MS Ed); reading education (MA Ed); special education (MA Ed). Part-time and evening/weekend programs available. *Faculty:* 9 full-time (5 women). *Students:* 15 full-time (10 women), 226 part-time (173 women); includes 5 minority (1 African American, 1 Asian American or Pacific Islander, 3 Hispanic Americans), 4 international. 46 applicants, 78% accepted. In 2006, 66 degrees awarded. *Degree requirements:* For master's, thesis optional. *Entrance requirements:* For master's, portfolio or GRE. Additional exam requirements/recommendations for international students: Required—TOEFL (minimum score 550 paper-based; 213 computer-based). *Application deadline:* For fall admission, 5/1 for domestic and international students; for spring admission, 8/15 for domestic students, 8/1 for international students. Applications are processed on a rolling basis. Application fee: $45. Electronic applications accepted. *Expenses:* Tuition, state resident: part-time $161 per hour. Tuition, nonresident: part-time $332 per hour. Required fees: $57 per hour. *Financial support:* In 2006–07, 8 research assistantships with full tuition reimbursements (averaging $8,200 per year) were awarded; career-related internships or fieldwork, scholarships/grants, and unspecified assistantships also available. Support available to part-time students. *Unit head:* Dr. Dennis Pottnoff, Chair, 308-865-8513, E-mail: pottnoffd@unk.edu.

University of Nebraska at Omaha, Graduate Studies and Research, College of Education, Department of Teacher Education, Omaha, NE 68182. Offers elementary education (MA, MS); instruction in urban schools (Certificate); instructional technology (Certificate); reading education (MS); secondary education (MA, MS). Part-time and evening/weekend programs available. *Faculty:* 24 full-time (15 women). *Students:* 33 full-time (28 women), 277 part-time (236 women); includes 18 minority (11 African Americans, 2 Asian Americans or Pacific Islanders, 5 Hispanic Americans), 1 international. Average age 32. 85 applicants, 84% accepted, 46 enrolled. In 2006, 101 master's, 5 other advanced degrees awarded. *Degree requirements:* For master's, thesis (for some programs), comprehensive exam. *Entrance requirements:* For master's, minimum GPA of 3.0. Additional exam requirements/recommendations for international students: Required—TOEFL (minimum score 550 paper-based; 213 computer-based; 80 iBT). *Application deadline:* For fall admission, 7/1 priority date for domestic students; for spring admission, 12/1 priority date for domestic students. Applications are processed on a rolling basis. Application fee: $45. Electronic applications accepted. *Financial support:* In 2006–07, 116 students received support; fellowships, teaching assistantships with tuition reimbursements available, Federal Work-Study, institutionally sponsored loans, scholarships/grants, tuition waivers (partial), and unspecified assistantships available. Support available to part-time students. Financial award application deadline: 3/1; financial award applicants required to submit FAFSA. *Unit head:* Dr. Lana Danielson, Advisor, 402-554-2212. *Application contact:* Dr. Wilma Kuhlman, Student Contact, 402-554-2212.

University of Nevada, Las Vegas, Graduate College, College of Education, Department of Curriculum and Instruction, Las Vegas, NV 89154-9900. Offers curriculum and instruction (Ed D, PhD, Ed S); elementary education (M Ed, MS); English education (M Ed, MS); library science (M Ed, MS); literacy education (M Ed, MS); mathematics education (M Ed, MS); multicultural education (M Ed, MS); reading specialist (M Ed, MS); secondary education (M Ed, MS); teacher leadership (M Ed, MS); teaching English as a second language (M Ed, MS); technology integration and leadership (M Ed, MS). *Accreditation:* NCATE. Part-time and evening/weekend programs available. *Faculty:* 40 full-time (19 women), 21 part-time/adjunct (14 women). *Students:* 257 full-time (189 women), 387 part-time (296 women); includes 114 minority (28 African Americans, 5 American Indian/Alaska Native, 34 Asian Americans or Pacific Islanders, 47 Hispanic Americans), 7 international. 261 applicants, 70% accepted, 168 enrolled. In 2006, 231 master's, 5 doctorates awarded. *Degree requirements:* For master's, thesis (for some programs), comprehensive exam (for some programs); for doctorate, thesis/dissertation, oral exam. *Entrance requirements:* For master's, minimum GPA of 3.0; for doctorate, GRE General Test, minimum graduate GPA of 3.0. Additional exam requirements/recommendations for international students: Required—TOEFL (minimum score 550 paper-based; 213 computer-based; 80 iBT). *Application deadline:* For fall admission, 2/15 for domestic and international students; for spring admission, 9/30 for domestic and international students. Application fee: $60 ($75 for international students). Electronic applications accepted. *Financial support:* In 2006–07, 30 research assistantships with partial tuition reimbursements (averaging $10,000 per year), 7 teaching assistantships with partial tuition reimbursements (averaging $12,000 per year) were awarded; career-related internships or fieldwork, Federal Work-Study, institutionally sponsored loans, scholarships/grants, health care benefits, and unspecified assistantships also available. Support available to part-time students. Financial award application deadline: 3/1. *Unit head:* Dr. Greg Levitt, Chair, 702-895-3241. *Application contact:* Graduate College Admissions Evaluator, 702-895-3320, E-mail: gradcollege@unlv.edu.

University of Nevada, Las Vegas, Graduate College, College of Education, Department of Educational Psychology, Las Vegas, NV 89154-9900. Offers education psychology (MS); educational psychology (PhD); learning and technology (PhD); school counseling (M Ed); school counselor education (PhD); school psychology (PhD, Ed S). *Accreditation:* ACA (one or more programs are accredited); NCATE. Part-time and evening/weekend programs available. *Faculty:* 21 full-time (10 women), 1 (woman) part-time/adjunct. *Students:* 70 full-time (55 women), 95 part-time (68 women); includes 36 minority (18 African Americans, 12 Asian Americans or Pacific Islanders, 6 Hispanic Americans), 7 international. 104 applicants, 53% accepted, 47 enrolled. In 2006, 23 master's, 3 doctorates, 17 other advanced degrees awarded. *Degree requirements:* For master's, thesis (for some programs), comprehensive exam (for some programs); for doctorate, thesis/dissertation, oral exam, comprehensive exam. *Entrance requirements:* For master's, GRE General Test, minimum GPA of 3.0 during previous 2 years, 2.75 overall; for doctorate, GRE General Test, minimum GPA of 3.0. Additional exam requirements/recommendations for international students: Required—TOEFL (minimum score 550 paper-based; 213 computer-based; 80 iBT). *Application deadline:* For fall admission, 2/1 for domestic and international students. Application fee: $60 ($75 for international students). Electronic applications accepted. *Financial support:* In 2006–07, 17 research assistantships with partial tuition reimbursements (averaging $11,000 per year), 10 teaching assistantships with partial tuition reimbursements (averaging $12,000 per year) were awarded; career-related internships or fieldwork, Federal Work-Study, institutionally sponsored loans, scholarships/grants, health care benefits, and unspecified assistantships also available. Support available to part-time students. Financial award application deadline: 3/1. *Unit head:* Dr. Ralph E. Reynolds, Chair, 702-895-3787, E-mail: ralph.reynolds@unlv.edu. *Application contact:* Graduate College Admissions Evaluator, 702-895-3320, Fax: 702-895-4180, E-mail: gradcollege@unlv.edu.

University of Nevada, Las Vegas, Graduate College, College of Education, Department of Special Education, Las Vegas, NV 89154-9900. Offers assistive technology (Ed S); emotional disturbance (Ed D); general special education (Ed D); gifted and talented education (Ed D); learning disabilities (Ed D); mental retardation (Ed D); special education (M Ed, MS, PhD, Ed S). *Accreditation:* NCATE. Part-time and evening/weekend programs available. *Faculty:* 21

full-time (15 women), 23 part-time/adjunct (20 women). *Students:* 161 full-time (119 women), 119 part-time (105 women); includes 44 minority (18 African Americans, 2 American Indian/Alaska Native, 11 Asian Americans or Pacific Islanders, 13 Hispanic Americans), 4 international. 187 applicants, 70% accepted, 117 enrolled. In 2006, 129 master's, 9 doctorates awarded. *Degree requirements:* For master's, thesis (for some programs), oral exam, comprehensive exam (for some programs); for doctorate, thesis/dissertation, oral exam, comprehensive exam. *Entrance requirements:* For master's, minimum GPA of 3.0; for doctorate, GRE General Test, minimum graduate GPA of 3.0; for Ed S, GRE General Test or MAT, minimum graduate GPA of 3.0. Additional exam requirements/recommendations for international students: Required—TOEFL (minimum score 550 paper-based; 213 computer-based; 80 iBT). *Application deadline:* For fall admission, 2/12 for domestic and international students; for spring admission, 11/15 for domestic students, 10/1 for international students. Application fee: $60 ($75 for international students). Electronic applications accepted. *Financial support:* In 2006–07, 14 research assistantships with partial tuition reimbursements (averaging $10,000 per year), 3 teaching assistantships with partial tuition reimbursements (averaging $12,000 per year) were awarded; career-related internships or fieldwork, Federal Work-Study, institutionally sponsored loans, scholarships/grants, health care benefits, and unspecified assistantships also available. Support available to part-time students. Financial award application deadline: 3/1. *Unit head:* Dr. Tom Pierce, Chair, 702-895-3205. *Application contact:* Graduate College Admissions Evaluator, 702-895-3320, Fax: 702-895-4180, E-mail: gradcollege@unlv.edu.

University of New Mexico, Graduate School, College of Education, Department of Educational Leadership and Organizational Learning, Program in Organizational Learning and Instructional Technologies, Albuquerque, NM 87131-2039. Offers MA, PhD, EDSPC. *Accreditation:* NCATE. Part-time programs available. *Students:* 20 full-time (11 women), 67 part-time (44 women); includes 20 minority (4 African Americans, 1 American Indian/Alaska Native, 15 Hispanic Americans), 1 international. Average age 44. 24 applicants, 67% accepted, 15 enrolled. In 2006, 10 master's, 5 doctorates awarded. *Degree requirements:* For master's, thesis; for doctorate, variable foreign language requirement, thesis/dissertation optional. *Entrance requirements:* For master's, GRE General Test, MAT, minimum GPA of 3.0 in last 60 hours of course work, bachelor's degree; for doctorate, GRE General Test, MAT, master's degree, minimum GPA of 3.5. Additional exam requirements/recommendations for international students: Required—TOEFL. *Application deadline:* For fall admission, 6/15 for domestic students; for spring admission, 10/15 for domestic students. Application fee: $40. Electronic applications accepted. *Financial support:* In 2006–07, 16 fellowships (averaging $24,356 per year), 7 teaching assistantships with tuition reimbursements (averaging $7,371 per year) were awarded. Financial award application deadline: 3/1; financial award applicants required to submit FAFSA. *Faculty research:* Workplace and learning environment factors that enhance learning and productivity, program and organization evaluation and reform, effects of technology on learning and problem solving. *Unit head:* Steve Preskill, Head, 505-277-7784, E-mail: preskill@unm.edu. *Application contact:* Loretta Brown, Administrative Assistant, 505-277-4131, Fax: 505-277-5553, E-mail: loribrwn@unm.edu.

The University of North Carolina at Charlotte, Graduate School, College of Education, Department of Educational Leadership, Charlotte, NC 28223-0001. Offers curriculum and supervision (M Ed); educational administration (CAS); educational leadership (Ed D); instructional systems technology (M Ed); school administration (MSA). Part-time and evening/weekend programs available. *Faculty:* 17 full-time (4 women), 10 part-time/adjunct (5 women). *Students:* 67 full-time (55 women), 158 part-time (112 women); includes 68 minority (63 African Americans, 1 American Indian/Alaska Native, 1 Asian American or Pacific Islander, 3 Hispanic Americans), 1 international. Average age 38. 149 applicants, 71% accepted, 90 enrolled. In 2006, 61 degrees awarded. *Entrance requirements:* For master's and doctorate, GRE or MAT. Additional exam requirements/recommendations for international students: Required—TOEFL (minimum score 550 paper-based; 220 computer-based). *Application deadline:* For fall admission, 7/1 for domestic students, 5/1 for international students; for spring admission, 11/1 for domestic students, 10/1 for international students. Applications are processed on a rolling basis. Application fee: $55. Electronic applications accepted. *Expenses:* Tuition, state resident: full-time $2,719; part-time $170 per credit. Tuition, nonresident: full-time $12,926; part-time $808 per credit. Required fees: $1,555. *Financial support:* In 2006–07, 3 teaching assistantships (averaging $8,027 per year) were awarded; fellowships, research assistantships, career-related internships or fieldwork, Federal Work-Study, institutionally sponsored loans, scholarships/grants, and unspecified assistantships also available. Support available to part-time students. Financial award application deadline: 4/1; financial award applicants required to submit FAFSA. *Faculty research:* Educational leadership theory and practice, instructional systems technology, educational research methodology, curriculum and supervision in the schools, school law and finance. Total annual research expenditures: $800,000. *Unit head:* Dr. Dawson R. Hancock, Interim Chair, 704-687-8730, Fax: 704-687-3493. *Application contact:* Kathy B. Giddings, Director of Graduate Admissions, 704-687-3366, Fax: 704-687-3279, E-mail: gradadm@email.uncc.edu.

The University of North Carolina at Greensboro, Graduate School, School of Education, Department of Curriculum and Instruction, Greensboro, NC 27412-5001. Offers college teaching and adult learning (Certificate); curriculum and instruction (M Ed), including chemistry education, elementary education, English as a second language, French education, instructional technology, mathematics education, middle grades education, reading education, science education, social studies education, Spanish education; curriculum and teaching (PhD), including higher education, teacher education and development; English as a second language (Certificate); higher education (M Ed); supervision (M Ed). *Accreditation:* NCATE. Part-time programs available. *Faculty:* 27 full-time (18 women), 8 part-time/adjunct (3 women). *Students:* 137 full-time (114 women), 231 part-time (195 women); includes 63 minority (52 African Americans, 2 American Indian/Alaska Native, 5 Asian Americans or Pacific Islanders, 4 Hispanic Americans). 146 applicants, 32% accepted. *Degree requirements:* For doctorate, thesis/dissertation. *Entrance requirements:* For master's and doctorate, GRE General Test. Additional exam requirements/recommendations for international students: Required—TOEFL. Application fee: $45. Electronic applications accepted. *Expenses:* Tuition, state resident: full-time $2,692. Tuition, nonresident: full-time $13,742. *Financial support:* Fellowships, research assistantships with full tuition reimbursements, teaching assistantships with full tuition reimbursements, career-related internships or fieldwork, Federal Work-Study, scholarships/grants, traineeships, and unspecified assistantships available. Support available to part-time students. *Faculty research:* Community college literacy program, middle school mathematics/computer mathematics. *Unit head:* Dr. Sam Miller, Chair, 336-334-3445, Fax: 336-334-4120, E-mail: sdmille2@uncg.edu. *Application contact:* Michelle Harkleroad, Director of Graduate Admissions, 336-334-4884, Fax: 336-334-4424, E-mail: mbharkle@uncg.edu.

The University of North Carolina Wilmington, School of Education, Department of Instructional Technology, Foundations and Secondary Education, Program in Instructional Technology, Wilmington, NC 28403-3297. Offers MS. *Students:* 4 full-time (2 women), 17 part-time (13 women); includes 1 minority (African American), 1 international. 8 applicants, 100% accepted, 5 enrolled. In 2006, 6 degrees awarded. *Degree requirements:* For master's, comprehensive exam. *Application deadline:* For fall admission, 6/1 for domestic students. Applications are processed on a rolling basis. Application fee: $45. *Unit head:* Dr. Mahnaz Moaller, Coordinator, 910-962-4183. *Application contact:* Dr. Robert D. Roer, Dean, Graduate School, 910-962-4117, Fax: 910-962-3787, E-mail: roer@uncw.edu.

University of North Dakota, Graduate School, College of Business and Public Administration, Department of Technology Education, Grand Forks, ND 58202. Offers MS. *Faculty:* 5 full-time (1 woman). *Students:* 1 (woman) full-time. *Degree requirements:* For master's, thesis or alternative, final exam, comprehensive exam. *Entrance requirements:* For master's, minimum GPA of 3.0. Additional exam requirements/recommendations for international students: Required—TOEFL (minimum score 550 paper-based; 213 computer-based; 79 iBT), IELTS (minimum score 6). *Application deadline:* For fall admission, 2/15 priority date for domestic and international students; for spring admission, 10/15 priority date for domestic and international students. Application fee: $35. Electronic applications accepted. *Expenses:* Tuition, state resident: full-time $5,650; part-time $214 per credit. Tuition, nonresident: full-time $14,248; part-time $572 per credit. Required fees: $1,008; $42 per credit. Tuition and fees vary according to reciprocity agreements. *Financial support:* In 2006–07, 1 student received support; fellowships, research assistantships, teaching assistantships with full tuition reimbursements available, Federal Work-Study, scholarships/grants, tuition waivers (full and partial), and unspecified assistantships available. Support available to part-time students. Financial award application deadline: 3/15; financial award applicants required to submit FAFSA. *Faculty research:* Graphic communications, photography, design, drafting, computers. *Unit head:* Dr. Ronald Holten, Graduate Director, 701-777-2249, Fax: 701-777-4320, E-mail: ronald_holten@nodak.edu. *Application contact:* Linda M. Baeza, Admissions Officer, 701-777-2945, Fax: 701-777-3619, E-mail: gradschool@mail.und.nodak.edu.

University of North Dakota, Graduate School, College of Education and Human Development, Department of Instructional Design and Technology, Grand Forks, ND 58202. Offers M Ed, MS. *Faculty:* 1 full-time (0 women). *Students:* 7 applicants, 71% accepted, 5 enrolled. In 2006, 2 degrees awarded. *Degree requirements:* For master's, thesis or alternative, comprehensive exam. *Entrance requirements:* For master's, minimum GPA of 3.0. Additional exam requirements/recommendations for international students: Required—TOEFL (minimum score 550 paper-based; 213 computer-based; 79 iBT), IELTS (minimum score 6). *Application deadline:* For fall admission, 2/15 priority date for domestic and international students; for spring admission, 10/15 priority date for domestic and international students. Applications are processed on a rolling basis. Application fee: $35. Electronic applications accepted. *Expenses:* Tuition, state resident: full-time $5,650; part-time $214 per credit. Tuition, nonresident: full-time $14,248; part-time $572 per credit. Required fees: $1,008; $42 per credit. Tuition and fees vary according to reciprocity agreements. *Financial support:* In 2006–07, 1 teaching assistantship with full tuition reimbursement (averaging $2,603 per year) was awarded; fellowships, research assistantships, Federal Work-Study, institutionally sponsored loans, scholarships/grants, and unspecified assistantships also available. Support available to part-time students. Financial award application deadline: 3/15; financial award applicants required to submit FAFSA. *Unit head:* Dr. Richard Van Eck, Graduate Director, 701-777-3239, Fax: 701-777-4365, E-mail: richard.vaneck@und.edu. *Application contact:* Linda M. Baeza, Admissions Officer, 701-777-2945, Fax: 701-777-3619, E-mail: gradschool@mail.und.nodak.edu.

University of Northern Colorado, Graduate School, College of Education and Behavioral Sciences, School of Educational Research, Leadership and Technology, Program in Educational Technology, Greeley, CO 80639. Offers educational media (MA); educational technology (MA, PhD). *Accreditation:* NCATE. Part-time programs available. Postbaccalaureate distance learning degree programs offered (minimal on-campus study). *Faculty:* 5 full-time (2 women). *Students:* 54 full-time (37 women), 22 part-time (11 women); includes 6 minority (1 African American, 4 Asian Americans or Pacific Islanders, 1 Hispanic American), 12 international. Average age 36. 22 applicants, 100% accepted, 16 enrolled. In 2006, 12 master's, 4 doctorates awarded. *Degree requirements:* For master's, thesis or alternative, comprehensive exam; for doctorate, thesis/dissertation, comprehensive exam. *Entrance requirements:* For master's and doctorate, GRE General Test, 3 letters of reference. *Application deadline:* For fall admission, 2/10 for domestic and international students; for spring admission, 10/10 for domestic and international students. Applications are processed on a rolling basis. Application fee: $50 ($60 for international students). Electronic applications accepted. *Expenses:* Tuition, state resident: full-time $5,118; part-time $213 per credit hour. Tuition, nonresident: full-time $14,832; part-time $618 per credit hour. Required fees: $674; $34 per credit hour. *Financial support:* In 2006–07, 45 students received support, including 4 fellowships (averaging $2,300 per year), 7 research assistantships (averaging $9,950 per year), 4 teaching assistantships (averaging $9,086 per year); unspecified assistantships also available. Financial award application deadline: 3/1; financial award applicants required to submit FAFSA. *Unit head:* Dr. Heng-Yu Ku, Program Coordinator, 970-351-2816.

University of Northern Iowa, Graduate College, College of Education, Department of Curriculum and Instruction, Program in Educational Technology, Cedar Falls, IA 50614. Offers communication and training technology (MA); educational media (MA). *Students:* 10 full-time (4 women), 15 part-time (7 women); includes 5 minority (all African Americans) 11 applicants, 82% accepted, 6 enrolled. In 2006, 4 degrees awarded. *Degree requirements:* For master's, thesis or alternative, comprehensive exam. *Entrance requirements:* For master's, 3 years of educational experience, minimum GPA of 3.5. Additional exam requirements/recommendations for international students: Required—TOEFL (minimum score 500 paper-based; 180 computer-based; 61 iBT). *Application deadline:* For fall admission, 8/1 priority date for domestic students. Applications are processed on a rolling basis. Application fee: $30 ($50 for international students). Electronic applications accepted. *Expenses:* Tuition, state resident: full-time $5,936. Tuition, nonresident: full-time $14,074. *Financial support:* Application deadline: 2/1. *Unit head:* Dr. Mary Herring, Coordinator, 319-273-3250, Fax: 319-273-5886, E-mail: mary.herring@uni.edu.

University of Northern Iowa, Graduate College, College of Education, Department of Curriculum and Instruction, Program in School Library Media Studies, Cedar Falls, IA 50614. Offers MA. Part-time and evening/weekend programs available. *Students:* 5 full-time (all women), 24 part-time (22 women). 7 applicants, 86% accepted, 3 enrolled. In 2006, 9 degrees awarded. *Degree requirements:* For master's, thesis or alternative. *Entrance requirements:* For master's, minimum GPA of 3.5, 3 years of educational experience. Additional exam requirements/recommendations for international students: Required—TOEFL (minimum score 500 paper-based; 180 computer-based; 61 iBT). *Application deadline:* For fall admission, 8/1 priority date for domestic students. Applications are processed on a rolling basis. Application fee: $30 ($50 for international students). Electronic applications accepted. *Expenses:* Tuition, state resident: full-time $5,936. Tuition, nonresident: full-time $14,074. *Financial support:* Career-related internships or fieldwork, Federal Work-Study, scholarships/grants, and tuition waivers (full and partial) available. Support available to part-time students. Financial award application deadline: 2/1. *Unit head:* Dr. Barbara R. Safford, Coordinator, 319-273-2551, Fax: 319-273-2913, E-mail: barbara.safford@uni.edu.

University of Northern Virginia, Graduate Programs, Manassas, VA 20109. Offers accountancy (MS); accounting (MBA); business administration (DBA); computer science (MS); counseling education (M Ed); early childhood education (M Ed); educational communication and instructional technology (M Ed); educational leadership (M Ed); finance (MBA); information systems technology (MS); management (MBA); marketing (MBA); project management (MBA); public administration (MPA); teaching English to speakers of other languages (M Ed). Part-time and evening/weekend programs available. Postbaccalaureate distance learning degree programs offered (no on-campus study). *Degree requirements:* For doctorate, thesis/dissertation, comprehensive exam, registration. *Entrance requirements:* Additional exam requirements/recommendations for international students: Required—TOEFL (minimum score 550 paper-based; 230 computer-based), IELTS (minimum score 6). Electronic applications accepted.

University of Phoenix Online Campus, The Artemis School, College of Education, Phoenix, AZ 85034-7209. Offers administration and supervision (MAEd); adult education and training (MAEd); curriculum and instruction-adult education (MAEd); curriculum and instruction-English and language arts education (MAEd); curriculum and instruction-mathematics education (MAEd); curriculum education (MAEd); curriculum instruction (MAEd); early childhood (MAEd); English as a second language (MAEd); teacher education elementary (MAEd); teacher education secondary (MAEd). Evening/weekend programs available. Postbaccalaureate distance learning degree programs offered (no on-campus study). *Faculty:* 12 full-time (5 women), 8,196 part-time/adjunct (6,937 women). *Students:* 11,937 full-time (9,375 women); includes 2,972 minority (2,210 African Americans, 74 American Indian/Alaska Native, 205 Asian Americans or Pacific Islanders, 483 Hispanic Americans), 906 international. Average age 36. *Degree requirements:* For master's, thesis (for some programs), registration. *Entrance requirements:* For master's, 3 years of work experience, minimum GPA of 2.5. Additional exam requirements/recommendations for international students: Required—TOEFL (minimum score 550 paper-based; 213 computer-based; 79 iBT). *Application deadline:* Applications are processed on a rolling basis. Application fee: $45. Electronic applications accepted. *Expenses:* Tuition: Full-

Educational Media/Instructional Technology

University of Phoenix Online Campus (continued)
time $12,664. Required fees: $760. *Financial support:* Institutionally sponsored loans and scholarships/grants available. Financial award applicants required to submit FAFSA. *Unit head:* Dr. Marla LaRue, Dean/Executive Director, 480-557-1218, E-mail: marla.larue@phoenix.edu. *Application contact:* Dr. Marla LaRue, Dean/Executive Director, 480-557-1218, E-mail: marla.larue@phoenix.edu.

University of Phoenix–West Florida Campus, The Artemis School, College of Education, Temple Terrace, FL 33637. Offers administration and supervision (MA Ed); curriculum and instruction (MA Ed); curriculum and technology (MA Ed); elementary teacher education (MA Ed); secondary teacher education (MA Ed). Evening/weekend programs available. *Faculty:* 10 full-time (8 women), 15 part-time/adjunct (7 women). *Students:* 67 full-time (61 women); includes 24 minority (20 African Americans, 1 American Indian/Alaska Native, 3 Hispanic Americans), 3 international. Average age 40. In 2006, 8 degrees awarded. *Degree requirements:* For master's, thesis (for some programs), registration. *Entrance requirements:* For master's, 3 years of work experience, minimum undergraduate GPA of 2.5. Additional exam requirements/recommendations for international students: Required—TOEFL (minimum score 550 paper-based; 213 computer-based; 79 iBT). Application fee: $45. *Expenses:* Tuition: Full-time $9,450. Required fees: $760. *Financial support:* Institutionally sponsored loans and scholarships/grants available. Financial award applicants required to submit FAFSA. *Unit head:* Dr. Marla LaRue, Dean, 480-557-1218, E-mail: marla.larue@phoenix.edu. *Application contact:* Chair, 813-626-7911, Fax: 813-977-1449.

University of St. Thomas, Graduate Studies, School of Education, Department of Curriculum and Instruction, St. Paul, MN 55105-1096. Offers critical pedagogy (Ed D); curriculum and instruction (MA, Ed S), including elementary (MA), K-12 (MA), secondary (MA); gifted, creative, and talented education (MA, Certificate); learning technology (MA, Certificate); reading (MA). Part-time and evening/weekend programs available. Postbaccalaureate distance learning degree programs offered (minimal on-campus study). *Students:* 5 full-time (all women), 109 part-time (91 women); includes 12 minority (7 African Americans, 1 American Indian/Alaska Native, 2 Asian Americans or Pacific Islanders, 2 Hispanic Americans), 2 international. Average age 35. 103 applicants, 91% accepted, 89 enrolled. In 2006, 13 master's, 7 doctorates, 11 other advanced degrees awarded. *Degree requirements:* For master's, thesis (for some programs), registration; for doctorate and other advanced degree, thesis/dissertation, registration. *Entrance requirements:* For master's, minimum GPA of 2.75 or MAT; for doctorate, minimum 3 years of experience as an educator; master's degree; minimum graduate GPA of 2.75, interview, writing sample; for other advanced degree, MAT, minimum graduate GPA of 2.75. Additional exam requirements/recommendations for international students: Required—TOEFL (minimum score 550 paper-based; 213 computer-based). *Application deadline:* For fall admission, 6/1 priority date for domestic students; for spring admission, 11/1 priority date for domestic students. Applications are processed on a rolling basis. Application fee: $50. *Financial support:* In 2006–07, 59 students received support; fellowships, research assistantships, institutionally sponsored loans and scholarships/grants available. Support available to part-time students. *Faculty research:* Multicultural education for gifted children, education plans for gifted children, globalization and adult learning, best gifted practices in Minnesota, exploring cultural tools. *Unit head:* Dr. Karen L. Westberg, Department Chair, 651-962-4985, Fax: 651-962-4169, E-mail: klwestberg@stthomas.edu. *Application contact:* Daniel Vevang, Department Assistant, 651-962-4460, Fax: 651-962-4169, E-mail: dvevang@stthomas.edu.

University of San Francisco, School of Education, Department of Organization and Leadership, San Francisco, CA 94117-1080. Offers digital media and learning (MA); organization and leadership (MA, Ed D). *Faculty:* 5 full-time (4 women), 9 part-time/adjunct (5 women). *Students:* 167 full-time (116 women), 120 part-time (78 women); includes 105 minority (32 African Americans, 1 American Indian/Alaska Native, 37 Asian Americans or Pacific Islanders, 35 Hispanic Americans), 5 international. Average age 35. 188 applicants, 87% accepted, 84 enrolled. In 2006, 91 master's, 19 doctorates awarded. *Degree requirements:* For doctorate, thesis/dissertation. Application fee: $55 ($65 for international students). *Expenses:* Tuition: Full-time $17,370; part-time $965 per unit. Tuition and fees vary according to degree level, campus/location and program. *Financial support:* In 2006–07, 178 students received support; fellowships, research assistantships, teaching assistantships available. Financial award application deadline: 3/2; financial award applicants required to submit FAFSA. *Unit head:* Br. Ray Vercruysse, Chair, 415-422-6551.

University of Sioux Falls, Program in Education, Sioux Falls, SD 57105-1699. Offers leadership (M Ed); reading (M Ed); superintendent (Ed S); teaching (M Ed); technology (M Ed). Summer admission only. *Accreditation:* NCATE. Part-time and evening/weekend programs available. Postbaccalaureate distance learning degree programs offered (minimal on-campus study). *Faculty:* 12 full-time (8 women), 13 part-time/adjunct (7 women). *Students:* 9 applicants, 100% accepted, 7 enrolled. In 2006, 46 master's, 26 other advanced degrees awarded. *Median time to degree:* Master's–2.5 years part-time; Ed S–2 years part-time. *Degree requirements:* For master's, research application project; for Ed S, portfolio. *Entrance requirements:* For master's, minimum GPA of 3.0, 1 year of teaching experience; for Ed S, administrative exam, minimum 3 years of teaching experience, minimum cumulative GPA of 3.5. Additional exam requirements/recommendations for international students: Required—TOEFL. *Application deadline:* Applications are processed on a rolling basis. Application fee: $25. *Expenses:* Tuition: Part-time $300 per semester hour. Required fees: $15 per term. Part-time tuition and fees vary according to program. *Financial support:* In 2006–07, 58 students received support. Scholarships/grants available. Support available to part-time students. *Unit head:* Dawn Olson, Director of Graduate Education, 605-575-2063, Fax: 605-575-2079, E-mail: dawn.olson@usiouxfalls.edu.

University of South Alabama, Graduate School, College of Education, Department of Professional Studies, Mobile, AL 36688-0002. Offers community counseling (MS); educational media (M Ed, MS); instructional design and development (MS, PhD); rehabilitation counseling (MS); school counseling (M Ed); school psychometry (M Ed). *Accreditation:* NCATE. Part-time programs available. *Faculty:* 19 full-time (7 women). *Students:* 131 full-time (106 women), 192 part-time (155 women); includes 83 minority (74 African Americans, 5 American Indian/Alaska Native, 3 Asian Americans or Pacific Islanders, 1 Hispanic American), 10 international. 98 applicants, 69% accepted, 38 enrolled. In 2006, 59 master's, 2 doctorates awarded. *Degree requirements:* For master's, comprehensive exam. *Entrance requirements:* For master's, GRE General Test or MAT, minimum GPA of 3.0. *Application deadline:* For fall admission, 9/1 priority date for domestic students. Applications are processed on a rolling basis. Application fee: $25. *Financial support:* In 2006–07, 5 research assistantships were awarded; career-related internships or fieldwork also available. Support available to part-time students. Financial award application deadline: 4/1. *Faculty research:* Agency counseling, rehabilitation counseling, school psychometry. *Unit head:* Dr. Charles Guest, Chair, 251-380-2861.

University of South Carolina, The Graduate School, College of Education, Department of Educational Studies, Program in Educational Technology, Columbia, SC 29208. Offers M Ed. *Accreditation:* NCATE. *Degree requirements:* For master's, comprehensive exam. *Entrance requirements:* For master's, GRE or MAT, interview.

University of South Carolina Aiken, School of Education, Program in Educational Technology, Aiken, SC 29801-6309. Offers M Ed. Part-time and evening/weekend programs available. *Faculty:* 3 full-time (1 woman), 1 part-time/adjunct (0 women). *Students:* 1 (woman) full-time, 21 part-time (15 women); includes 2 minority (1 African American, 1 Asian American or Pacific Islander). In 2006, 8 degrees awarded. *Entrance requirements:* For master's, GRE or MAT. *Application deadline:* Applications are processed on a rolling basis. Application fee: $40. Electronic applications accepted. *Expenses:* Tuition, state resident: full-time $8,288; part-time $411 per hour. Tuition, nonresident: full-time $17,916; part-time $874 per hour. Required fees: $230; $8 per hour. $15 per hour. *Financial support:* Federal Work-Study available. Support available to part-time students. Financial award application deadline: 3/15; financial award applicants required to submit FAFSA. *Unit head:* Dr. Tom Smyth, Unit Head, 803-641-3527. *Application contact:* Karen Morris, Graduate Studies Coordinator, 803-641-3489, E-mail: karenm@usca.edu.

The University of South Dakota, Graduate School, School of Education, Division of Technology for Education and Training, Vermillion, SD 57069-2390. Offers MS, Ed S. Part-time and evening/weekend programs available. Postbaccalaureate distance learning degree programs offered (no on-campus study). *Faculty:* 8 full-time (4 women), 1 part-time/adjunct (0 women). *Students:* 57 (42 women). In 2006, 12 master's, 2 other advanced degrees awarded. *Degree requirements:* For master's and Ed S, thesis or alternative, comprehensive exam. *Entrance requirements:* For master's and Ed S, GRE, minimum GPA of 2.7. Additional exam requirements/recommendations for international students: Required—TOEFL (minimum score 550 paper-based; 213 computer-based; 79 iBT). *Application deadline:* Applications are processed on a rolling basis. Application fee: $35. Electronic applications accepted. *Expenses:* Tuition, state resident: part-time $120 per credit hour. Tuition, nonresident: part-time $355 per credit hour. Required fees: $90 per credit hour. *Financial support:* In 2006–07, research assistantships with partial tuition reimbursements (averaging $4,626 per year), teaching assistantships with partial tuition reimbursements (averaging $4,626 per year) were awarded; career-related internships or fieldwork, Federal Work-Study, and unspecified assistantships also available. Financial award applicants required to submit FAFSA. *Unit head:* Dr. Leslie I. Moller, Division Chair/Graduate Director, 605-677-5448, Fax: 605-677-5438, E-mail: cfjohnson@usd.edu.

University of South Florida, Graduate School, College of Education, Department of Secondary Education, Tampa, FL 33620-9951. Offers English education (M Ed, MA, PhD); foreign language education (M Ed, MA); instructional technology (M Ed); mathematics education (M Ed, MA, PhD, Ed S); middle school education (M Ed); science education (M Ed, MA, MAT, PhD); second language acquisition/instructional technology (PhD); secondary education (PhD); social science education (M Ed, MA). *Accreditation:* NCATE. Part-time and evening/weekend programs available. *Faculty:* 29 full-time (16 women), 15 part-time/adjunct (8 women). *Students:* 136 full-time (95 women), 279 part-time (188 women); includes 85 minority (35 African Americans, 1 American Indian/Alaska Native, 13 Asian Americans or Pacific Islanders, 36 Hispanic Americans), 19 international. 212 applicants, 71% accepted, 96 enrolled. In 2006, 87 master's, 12 doctorates awarded. *Entrance requirements:* For master's and doctorate, GRE General Test, minimum GPA of 3.5; for Ed S, GRE General Test. *Application deadline:* For fall admission, 6/1 for domestic students; for spring admission, 10/15 for domestic students. Application fee: $30. Electronic applications accepted. *Financial support:* Scholarships/grants and unspecified assistantships available. Total annual research expenditures: $477,202. *Unit head:* Dr. Jane H. Applegate, Interim Chairperson, 813-974-3533, Fax: 813-974-3837, E-mail: applegat@tempest.coedu.usf.edu.

The University of Tennessee, Graduate School, College of Education, Health and Human Sciences, Program in Education, Knoxville, TN 37996. Offers art education (MS); counseling education (PhD); cultural studies in education (PhD); curriculum (MS, Ed S); curriculum, educational research and evaluation (Ed D, PhD); early childhood education (PhD); early childhood special education (MS); education of deaf and hard of hearing (MS); educational administration and policy studies (Ed D, PhD); educational administration and supervision (Ed S); educational psychology (Ed D, PhD); elementary education (MS, Ed S); elementary teaching (MS); English education (MS, Ed S); exercise science (PhD); foreign language/ESL education (MS, Ed S); instructional technology (MS, Ed D, PhD, Ed S); literacy, language and ESL education (PhD); literacy, language education, and ESL education (Ed D); mathematics education (MS, Ed S); modified and comprehensive special education (MS); reading education (MS, Ed S); school counseling (Ed S); school psychology (PhD, Ed S); science education (MS, Ed S); secondary teaching (MS); social foundations (MS); social science education (MS, Ed S); socio-cultural foundations of sports and education (PhD); special education (Ed S); teacher education (Ed D, PhD). *Accreditation:* NCATE. Part-time and evening/weekend programs available. *Students:* 529 (401 women); includes 39 minority (23 African Americans, 2 American Indian/Alaska Native, 9 Asian Americans or Pacific Islanders, 5 Hispanic Americans) 34 international. 420 applicants, 50% accepted. In 2006, 258 master's, 28 doctorates awarded. *Degree requirements:* For master's and Ed S, thesis optional; for doctorate, variable foreign language requirement, thesis/dissertation. *Entrance requirements:* For master's, minimum GPA of 2.7; for doctorate and Ed S, GRE General Test, minimum GPA of 2.7. Additional exam requirements/recommendations for international students: Required—TOEFL. *Application deadline:* For fall admission, 2/1 priority date for domestic students. Applications are processed on a rolling basis. Application fee: $35. Electronic applications accepted. *Expenses:* Tuition, state resident: full-time $5,574. Tuition, nonresident: full-time $16,840. Required fees: $792. *Financial support:* In 2006–07, 4 fellowships, 9 teaching assistantships were awarded; career-related internships or fieldwork, Federal Work-Study, institutionally sponsored loans, and unspecified assistantships also available. Financial award application deadline: 2/1; financial award applicants required to submit FAFSA. *Unit head:* Dr. Lester Knight, Head, 865-974-0907, Fax: 865-974-8718, E-mail: lknight@utk.edu.

The University of Tennessee at Chattanooga, Graduate School, College of Health, Education and Professional Studies, Graduate Studies Division of Education, Program for Educational Specialist, Chattanooga, TN 37403-2598. Offers educational technology (Ed S); school psychology (Ed S). *Faculty:* 6 full-time (3 women), 1 part-time/adjunct (0 women). *Students:* 18 full-time (15 women), 20 part-time (16 women). Average age 34. 15 applicants, 100% accepted, 4 enrolled. In 2006, 23 degrees awarded. *Application deadline:* For fall admission, 8/1 priority date for domestic students; for spring admission, 12/1 priority date for domestic students. Application fee: $30. *Expenses:* Tuition, state resident: full-time $5,434; part-time $339 per hour. Tuition, nonresident: full-time $14,830; part-time $861 per hour. Required fees: $940; $178 per hour. *Financial support:* Applicants required to submit FAFSA. *Faculty research:* Educational technology; using technology in the classroom; interactive media; distance learning; instructional design technological implementation. *Unit head:* Dr. Lloyd D. Davis, Coordinator, 423-425-4161, Fax: 423-425-5380, E-mail: lloyd-davis@utc.edu. *Application contact:* Dr. Deborah E. Arfken, Dean of Graduate Studies, 423-425-4666, Fax: 423-425-5223, E-mail: deborah-arfken@utc.edu.

The University of Texas at Brownsville, Graduate Studies, School of Education, Brownsville, TX 78520-4991. Offers bilingual education (M Ed); counseling and guidance (M Ed); curriculum and instruction (M Ed); early childhood education (M Ed); educational administration (M Ed); educational technology (M Ed); English as a second language (M Ed); reading specialist (M Ed); special education/educational diagnostician (M Ed). Part-time and evening/weekend programs available. Postbaccalaureate distance learning degree programs offered (minimal on-campus study). *Degree requirements:* For master's, thesis optional. *Entrance requirements:* For master's, GRE General Test. Additional exam requirements/recommendations for international students: Required—TOEFL.

The University of Texas at San Antonio, College of Education and Human Development, Department of Interdisciplinary Learning and Teaching, San Antonio, TX 78249-0617. Offers curriculum and instruction (MA); early childhood and elementary education (MA); educational psychology/special education (MA); instructional technology (MA); reading and literacy (MA). Part-time and evening/weekend programs available. *Faculty:* 26 full-time (all women), 1 part-time/adjunct (0 women). *Students:* 40 full-time (32 women), 240 part-time (207 women); includes 155 minority (20 African Americans, 1 American Indian/Alaska Native, 6 Asian Americans or Pacific Islanders, 128 Hispanic Americans), 3 international. Average age 35. 94 applicants, 100% accepted, 94 enrolled. In 2006, 61 degrees awarded. *Degree requirements:* For master's, thesis optional. *Entrance requirements:* For master's, GRE General Test. Additional exam requirements/recommendations for international students: Required—TOEFL (minimum score 500 paper-based; 173 computer-based). *Application deadline:* For fall admission, 7/1 for domestic students, 4/1 for international students; for spring admission, 11/1 for domestic students, 9/1 for international students. Applications are processed on a rolling basis. Application fee: $45 ($80 for international students). Electronic applications accepted. *Expenses:* Tuition, state resident: full-time $1,730; part-time $192 per credit hour. Tuition, nonresident: full-time $6,680; part-time $742 per credit hour. Required fees: $733; $308,359 per credit hour.

Financial support: In 2006–07, 3 research assistantships (averaging $28,891 per year) were awarded; career-related internships or fieldwork, Federal Work-Study, scholarships/grants, and unspecified assistantships also available. *Faculty research:* Early childhood, reading, special education, foundations, curriculum and instruction. Total annual research expenditures: $570,791. *Unit head:* Dr. Belinda B. Flores, Chair, 210-458-5969, Fax: 210-458-7281, E-mail: belinda.flores@utsa.edu.

University of the Incarnate Word, School of Graduate Studies and Research, Dreeben School of Education, Programs in Education, San Antonio, TX 78209-6397. Offers adult education (M Ed, MA); diversity education (M Ed, MA); early childhood education (M Ed, MA); instructional technology (M Ed, MA); international education and entrepreneurship (PhD); kinesiology (M Ed, MA); mathematics education (PhD); organizational leadership (PhD); organizational learning (M Ed, MA); reading (M Ed, MA); special education (M Ed, MA). *Students:* 15 full-time (8 women), 179 part-time (117 women); includes 70 minority (20 African Americans, 1 American Indian/Alaska Native, 1 Asian American or Pacific Islander, 48 Hispanic Americans), 54 international. Average age 39. In 2006, 15 degrees awarded. Application fee: $20. *Expenses:* Tuition: Part-time $570 per credit hour. Required fees: $54 per credit hour. One-time fee: $195 part-time. Tuition and fees vary according to degree level. *Financial support:* Federal Work-Study and scholarships/grants available. *Unit head:* Dr. Richard Gray, Director, 210-829-3138, Fax: 210-829-3134, E-mail: gray@uiwtx.edu. *Application contact:* Andrea Cyterski-Acosta, Dean of Enrollment, 210-829-6005, Fax: 210-829-3921, E-mail: cyterski@uiwtx.edu.

University of the Incarnate Word, School of Graduate Studies and Research, H-E-B School of Business and Administration, Programs in Administration, San Antonio, TX 78209-6397. Offers adult education (MAA); applied administration (MAA); communication arts (MAA); English (MAA); instructional technology (MAA); international business (Certificate); multidisciplinary sciences (MAA); nutrition (MAA); organizational development (MAA, Certificate); project management (Certificate); sports management (MAA); urban administration (MAA). *Students:* 1 (woman) full-time, 161 part-time (102 women); includes 17 African Americans, 1 American Indian/Alaska Native, 82 Hispanic Americans, 18 international. Average age 34. In 2006, 78 degrees awarded. *Entrance requirements:* For master's, GMAT, GRE, MAT. Additional exam requirements/recommendations for international students: Required—TOEFL. *Application deadline:* For fall admission, 8/15 priority date for domestic students; for spring admission, 12/31 for domestic students. Applications are processed on a rolling basis. Application fee: $20. *Expenses:* Tuition: Part-time $570 per credit hour. Required fees: $54 per credit hour. One-time fee: $195 part-time. Tuition and fees vary according to degree level. *Financial support:* Federal Work-Study and scholarships/grants available. *Unit head:* Dr. Dan Dominguez, MAA Director, 210-829-3180, Fax: 210-805-3564, E-mail: domingue@uiwtx.edu. *Application contact:* Andrea Cyterski-Acosta, Dean of Enrollment, 210-829-6005, Fax: 210-829-3921, E-mail: cyterski@uiwtx.edu.

University of the Sacred Heart, Graduate Programs, Department of Education, Program in Instruction Systems and Education Technology, San Juan, PR 00914-0383. Offers M Ed. Part-time and evening/weekend programs available. *Degree requirements:* For master's, thesis. *Entrance requirements:* For master's, EXADEP, interview, minimum undergraduate GPA of 2.75.

The University of Toledo, College of Graduate Studies, College of Education, Department of Curriculum and Instruction, Program in Educational Media, Toledo, OH 43606-3390. Offers DE, PhD, Ed S. *Students:* 5 full-time (1 woman), 5 part-time (1 woman), 3 international. Average age 44. 2 applicants, 50% accepted, 1 enrolled. In 2006, 1 degree awarded.

The University of Toledo, College of Graduate Studies, College of Education, Department of Curriculum and Instruction, Program in Educational Technology, Toledo, OH 43606-3390. Offers ME. *Students:* 2 full-time (1 woman), 17 part-time (9 women); includes 3 minority (1 African American, 1 Asian American or Pacific Islander, 1 Hispanic American). Average age 33. 8 applicants, 100% accepted, 7 enrolled. In 2006, 12 degrees awarded.

University of Washington, Graduate School, College of Education, Seattle, WA 98195. Offers curriculum and instruction (M Ed, Ed D, PhD), including educational technology, general curriculum (Ed D, PhD), language, literacy, and culture, mathematics education, multicultural education, reading and language arts education (Ed D), science education, social studies education, teaching and curriculum (M Ed); educational leadership and policy studies (M Ed, Ed D, PhD), including administration, educational organization and policy, higher education, school district leadership (Ed D), social/cultural foundations; educational psychology (M Ed, PhD), including human development and cognition, measurement and research, school counseling (M Ed), school psychology; special education (M Ed, Ed D, PhD), including early childhood education, elementary special education, emotional and behavioral disabilities (M Ed), general special education, severe disabilities; teacher education (MIT). *Accreditation:* APA. Part-time and evening/weekend programs available. *Degree requirements:* For master's, thesis optional; for doctorate, thesis/dissertation. *Entrance requirements:* For master's and doctorate, GRE General Test, minimum GPA of 3.0. Additional exam requirements/recommendations for international students: Required—TOEFL. Electronic applications accepted. *Faculty research:* School restructuring/effective schools, special education interventions, literacy and writing, technology, school partnerships, teacher preparation.

The University of West Alabama, School of Graduate Studies, College of Education, Department of Teacher Education, Program in Library Media, Livingston, AL 35470. Offers M Ed. Part-time programs available. *Faculty:* 1 full-time (0 women), 4 part-time/adjunct (3 women). *Students:* 59 full-time (55 women), 99 part-time (97 women); includes 35 minority (31 African Americans, 1 American Indian/Alaska Native, 1 Asian American or Pacific Islander, 2 Hispanic Americans), 1 international. In 2006, 10 degrees awarded. *Entrance requirements:* For master's, GRE General Test, MAT, minimum GPA of 2.75. *Application deadline:* For fall admission, 9/10 priority date for domestic students; for spring admission, 3/24 for domestic students. Applications are processed on a rolling basis. Application fee: $20 ($50 for international students). *Financial support:* Career-related internships or fieldwork, Federal Work-Study, scholarships/grants, and unspecified assistantships available. Support available to part-time students. *Unit head:* Dr. Neil Snider, Director, 205-652-3614.

University of West Florida, College of Professional Studies, Division of Graduate Education, Program in Instructional Technology, Pensacola, FL 32514-5750. Offers M Ed. *Students:* 8 full-time (4 women), 24 part-time (16 women); includes 6 minority (3 African Americans, 1 American Indian/Alaska Native, 2 Asian Americans or Pacific Islanders). Average age 37. 11 applicants, 91% accepted, 10 enrolled. In 2006, 5 degrees awarded. *Entrance requirements:* Additional exam requirements/recommendations for international students: Required—TOEFL (minimum score 550 paper-based; 213 computer-based). *Application deadline:* For fall admission, 6/1 for domestic students, 5/15 for international students; for spring admission, 11/1 for domestic students, 10/1 for international students. Application fee: $30. *Expenses:* Tuition, state resident: full-time $5,871; part-time $245 per credit hour. Tuition, nonresident: full-time $21,241; part-time $885 per credit hour. *Financial support:* Application deadline: 4/15; *Unit head:* Dr. Thomas J. Kramer, Chairperson, Division of Graduate Education, 850-474-2768.

University of West Georgia, Graduate School, College of Education, Department of Media and Instructional Technology, Carrollton, GA 30118. Offers media (M Ed, Ed S). Part-time programs available. Postbaccalaureate distance learning degree programs offered. *Faculty:* 8 full-time (all women), 3 part-time/adjunct (2 women). *Students:* 18 full-time (16 women), 218 part-time (197 women); includes 40 minority (39 African Americans, 1 Hispanic American). Average age 31. 77 applicants, 97% accepted, 75 enrolled. In 2006, 48 master's, 35 other advanced degrees awarded. *Degree requirements:* For master's, comprehensive exam, registration; for Ed S, research project. *Entrance requirements:* For master's, GRE General Test, minimum GPA of 2.7, teaching certificate; for Ed S, GRE General Test, master's degree, minimum graduate GPA of 3.0. *Application deadline:* For fall admission, 8/2 priority date for domestic and international students; for spring admission, 12/17 priority date for domestic and international students. Application fee: $20. Electronic applications accepted. *Expenses:* Tuition, state resident: full-time $2,286; part-time $127 per credit. Tuition, nonresident: full-time $9,144; part-time $508 per credit. Required fees: $494; $27 per credit. $121 per semester. *Financial support:* In 2006–07, 2 students received support, including 2 research assistantships with full tuition reimbursements available (averaging $6,000 per year); career-related internships or fieldwork, scholarships/grants, and unspecified assistantships also available. Support available to part-time students. Financial award applicants required to submit FAFSA. *Faculty research:* Distance education, technology integration, collaboration, e-books for children, instructional design. Total annual research expenditures: $180,455. *Unit head:* Dr. Barbara K. McKenzie, Chair, 678-839-6558, Fax: 678-839-6153, E-mail: bmckenzi@westga.edu. *Application contact:* Dr. Charles W. Clark, Chair, 678-839-6508, E-mail: cclark@westga.edu.

University of Wyoming, Graduate School, College of Education, Department of Adult Learning and Technology, Laramie, WY 82070. Offers adult and post secondary education (Ed S); adult and postsecondary education (MA, Ed D, PhD); distance education (Ed D, PhD); instructional technology (MS, Ed D, PhD). Part-time programs available. Postbaccalaureate distance learning degree programs offered (no on-campus study). *Faculty:* 6 full-time (3 women), 11 part-time/adjunct (5 women). *Students:* 14 full-time (10 women), 91 part-time (52 women); includes 10 minority (2 African Americans, 1 American Indian/Alaska Native, 2 Asian Americans or Pacific Islanders, 5 Hispanic Americans), 4 international. Average age 44. 26 applicants, 85% accepted, 20 enrolled. In 2006, 24 master's, 5 doctorates awarded. *Degree requirements:* For master's, thesis or alternative; for doctorate, thesis/dissertation, comprehensive exam. *Entrance requirements:* For master's, GRE, minimum GPA of 3.0; for doctorate, MS or MA, minimum GPA of 3.0. Additional exam requirements/recommendations for international students: Required—TOEFL. *Application deadline:* For fall admission, 2/1 for domestic and international students; for spring admission, 10/1 for domestic and international students. Application fee: $50. Electronic applications accepted. *Financial support:* In 2006–07, 1 student received support, including 1 teaching assistantship with tuition reimbursement available (averaging $14,400 per year); scholarships/grants also available. Financial award application deadline: 2/1. *Faculty research:* Web based instruction, instructional decision, adult education history, literacy in adults, international distance education. *Unit head:* Dr. John J. Cochenour, Head, 307-766-3608, Fax: 307-766-3237, E-mail: johncoc@uwyo.edu. *Application contact:* Jeannete A. Skinner, Office Associate, 307-766-3247, Fax: 307-766-3237, E-mail: ask-alt@uwyo.edu.

Utah State University, School of Graduate Studies, College of Education and Human Services, Department of Instructional Technology, Logan, UT 84322. Offers M Ed, MS, PhD, Ed S. *Accreditation:* NCATE. Part-time and evening/weekend programs available. Postbaccalaureate distance learning degree programs offered (minimal on-campus study). *Faculty:* 9 full-time (4 women). *Students:* 133 full-time (51 women), 27 part-time (12 women); includes 1 minority (Hispanic American), 21 international. Average age 28. 145 applicants, 64% accepted, 64 enrolled. In 2006, 56 master's, 4 doctorates awarded. Terminal master's awarded for partial completion of doctoral program. *Median time to degree:* Of those who began their doctoral program in fall 1998, 100% received their degree in 8 years or less. *Degree requirements:* For master's, thesis (for some programs), registration; for doctorate, thesis/dissertation, comprehensive exam, registration. *Entrance requirements:* For master's, GRE General Test or MAT, minimum GPA of 3.0, 3 recommendation letters, transcripts; for doctorate, GRE General Test, minimum GPA of 3.0, 3 recommendation letters, transcripts, letter of intent; for Ed S, GRE General Test, GRE Subject Test, minimum GPA of 3.0. Additional exam requirements/recommendations for international students: Required—TOEFL (minimum score 550 paper-based; 213 computer-based). *Application deadline:* For spring admission, 1/31 for domestic and international students. Application fee: $50 ($60 for international students). Electronic applications accepted. *Financial support:* In 2006–07, 2 fellowships with partial tuition reimbursements (averaging $12,000 per year), 10 research assistantships with partial tuition reimbursements (averaging $10,320 per year), 9 teaching assistantships with partial tuition reimbursements (averaging $10,320 per year) were awarded; career-related internships or fieldwork, Federal Work-Study, and institutionally sponsored loans also available. Financial award application deadline: 7/1. *Faculty research:* Interactive learning environments, computer-assisted instruction, learning, distance education, corporate training. Total annual research expenditures: $800,000. *Unit head:* Mike Freeman, Interim Head, 435-797-1474, Fax: 435-797-2693, E-mail: michael.freeman@usu.edu. *Application contact:* Katie McKay, Staff Assistant, 435-797-2694, Fax: 435-797-2693, E-mail: katie.mckay@usu.edu.

Valdosta State University, Graduate School, College of Education, Department of Curriculum and Instructional Technology, Valdosta, GA 31698. Offers curriculum and instruction (Ed D); instructional technology (M Ed, Ed S), including library/media technology (M Ed), technology application (M Ed).

Virginia Polytechnic Institute and State University, Graduate School, College of Liberal Arts and Human Sciences, School of Education, Department of Teaching and Learning, Instructional Technology Program Area, Blacksburg, VA 24061. Offers ITMA. Postbaccalaureate distance learning degree programs offered (no on-campus study). *Entrance requirements:* For master's, professional experience, 3 letters of recommendation. Additional exam requirements/recommendations for international students: Required—TOEFL (minimum score 550 paper-based). *Expenses:* Tuition, state resident: full-time $7,017; part-time $390 per credit hour. Tuition, nonresident: full-time $12,414; part-time $690 per credit hour. International tuition: $11,296 full-time. Required fees: $1,523; $256 per term.

Wayne State University, College of Education, Division of Administrative and Organizational Studies, Detroit, MI 48202. Offers administration and supervision-secondary (Ed S); college and university teaching (Certificate); curriculum and instruction (PhD); educational leadership (M Ed, Ed S); educational leadership and policy studies (Ed D, PhD); elementary education curriculum and instruction (MA, Ed S); general administration and supervision (Ed D, PhD, Ed S); higher education (Ed D, PhD); instructional technology (M Ed, Ed D, PhD, Ed S); secondary curriculum and instruction (M Ed, Ed S). *Faculty:* 24 full-time (13 women), 1 (woman) part-time/adjunct. *Students:* 153 full-time (103 women), 389 part-time (266 women); includes 252 minority (223 African Americans, 6 American Indian/Alaska Native, 8 Asian Americans or Pacific Islanders, 15 Hispanic Americans), 19 international. Average age 38. 138 applicants, 79% accepted, 74 enrolled. In 2006, 116 master's, 30 doctorates, 64 other advanced degrees awarded. *Degree requirements:* For doctorate, thesis/dissertation. *Entrance requirements:* For doctorate, interview, minimum GPA of 3.0. Additional exam requirements/recommendations for international students: Required—TOEFL (minimum score 550 paper-based; 213 computer-based), TWE (minimum score 6). *Application deadline:* For fall admission, 7/1 for domestic students, 6/1 for international students; for winter admission, 10/1 for international students; for spring admission, 2/1 for international students. Application fee: $30 ($50 for international students). Electronic applications accepted. *Financial support:* In 2006–07, 4 research assistantships (averaging $12,797 per year) were awarded; career-related internships or fieldwork, Federal Work-Study, and institutionally sponsored loans also available. Support available to part-time students. *Faculty research:* Total quality management, participatory management, administering educational technology, school improvement, principalship. Total annual research expenditures: $344,504. *Unit head:* Dr. JoAnne Holbert, Assistant Dean, 313-577-1721, E-mail: jholbert@wayne.edu.

Wayne State University, College of Education, Division of Teacher Education, Detroit, MI 48202. Offers adult and continuing education (M Ed); art education (M Ed); bilingual/bicultural education (M Ed, MAT); business education (M Ed, MAT); career and technical education (M Ed, Ed D, PhD, Ed S); curriculum and instruction (Ed D, PhD, Ed S); distributive education (M Ed, MAT); early childhood education (M Ed); elementary education (M Ed, MAT, Ed D, PhD, Ed S); elementary education curriculum and instruction (M Ed); English education (M Ed); English education-secondary (M Ed, Ed S); foreign language education (M Ed); general education (Ed D, Ed S); health occupations education (M Ed); industrial education (M Ed); mathematics education (M Ed, Ed S); pre-school and parent education (M Ed); reading (M Ed, Ed D, Ed S); reading, languages and literature (Ed D); school music-vocal (M Ed); science education (M Ed, MAT, Ed S); secondary education (MAT); secondary school reading (M Ed);

Educational Media/Instructional Technology

Wayne State University (continued)
social studies education (M Ed, Ed S), including education-secondary (M Ed); special education (M Ed, Ed D, PhD, Ed S); teacher education (MAT, Ed D, PhD). *Faculty:* 41 full-time (22 women), 2 part-time/adjunct (both women). *Students:* 401 full-time (295 women), 1,021 part-time (784 women); includes 527 minority (452 African Americans, 6 American Indian/Alaska Native, 32 Asian Americans or Pacific Islanders, 37 Hispanic Americans), 18 international. Average age 36. 296 applicants, 81% accepted, 132 enrolled. In 2006, 386 master's, 1 doctorate awarded. *Degree requirements:* For doctorate, thesis/dissertation. *Entrance requirements:* For master's, minimum GPA of 2.6; for doctorate, minimum undergraduate GPA of 3.0, graduate 3.5; interview. Additional exam requirements/recommendations for international students: Required—TOEFL (minimum score 550 paper-based; 213 computer-based), TWE (minimum score 6). *Application deadline:* For fall admission, 7/1 for domestic students, 6/1 for international students; for winter admission, 10/1 for international students; for spring admission, 2/1 for international students. Application fee: $30 ($50 for international students). Electronic applications accepted. *Financial support:* In 2006–07, 1 fellowship (averaging $34,919 per year) was awarded; research assistantships. *Faculty research:* Reading and writing literacy and literature. Total annual research expenditures: $209,400. *Unit head:* Dr. Joann Snyder, Academic Director, 313-577-1644, E-mail: joanne.snyder@wayne.edu. *Application contact:* Sharon Elliott, Assistant Dean, 313-577-0902, E-mail: sharon.elliott@wayne.edu.

Webster University, School of Education, Department of Multidisciplinary Studies, St. Louis, MO 63119-3194. Offers administrative leadership (Ed S); education leadership (Ed S); educational technology (MAT); mathematics (MAT); multidisciplinary studies (MAT); school systems, superintendency and leadership (Ed S); social science (MAT); special education (MAT). Part-time programs available. *Students:* 97 full-time (83 women), 687 part-time (573 women); includes 173 minority (142 African Americans, 2 American Indian/Alaska Native, 13 Asian Americans or Pacific Islanders, 16 Hispanic Americans), 6 international. Average age 34. In 2006, 14 degrees awarded. *Entrance requirements:* For master's, minimum GPA of 2.5. *Application deadline:* Applications are processed on a rolling basis. Application fee: $25 ($50 for international students). *Expenses:* Tuition: Full-time $8,820; part-time $490 per credit. Tuition and fees vary according to degree level, campus/location and program. *Financial support:* Federal Work-Study available. Support available to part-time students. Financial award application deadline: 4/1; financial award applicants required to submit FAFSA. *Unit head:* Dr. Donna Campbell, Chair, 314-961-2660 Ext. 7042, Fax: 314-968-7118. *Application contact:* Director of Graduate and Evening Student Admissions, Fax: 314-968-7116, E-mail: gadmit@webster.edu.

West Chester University of Pennsylvania, Graduate Studies, School of Education, West Chester, PA 19383. Offers counseling and educational psychology (M Ed, MS), including elementary school counseling (M Ed), higher education counseling (MS), secondary school counseling (M Ed); early childhood and special education (M Ed), including special education; elementary education (M Ed); literacy (M Ed), including reading; professional and secondary education (M Ed, MS), including educational research (MS), secondary education (M Ed); teaching and learning with technology (Certificate). *Accreditation:* NCATE. Part-time and evening/weekend programs available. *Students:* 189 full-time (159 women), 536 part-time (460 women); includes 31 African Americans, 3 Asian Americans or Pacific Islanders, 7 Hispanic Americans, 2 international. Average age 29. 309 applicants, 94% accepted, 157 enrolled. In 2006, 173 degrees awarded. *Degree requirements:* For master's, thesis (for some programs), comprehensive exam. *Entrance requirements:* For master's, MAT. *Application deadline:* For fall admission, 4/15 priority date for domestic students; for spring admission, 10/15 for domestic students. Applications are processed on a rolling basis. Application fee: $35. *Financial support:* In 2006–07, 25 research assistantships with full tuition reimbursements (averaging $5,000 per year) were awarded; unspecified assistantships also available. Support available to part-time students. Financial award application deadline: 2/15; financial award applicants required to submit FAFSA. *Unit head:* Dr. Joseph Malak, Dean, 610-436-2428, E-mail: jmalak@wcupa.edu.

Western Connecticut State University, Division of Graduate Studies, School of Professional Studies, Department of Education and Educational Psychology, Instructional Technology Option, Danbury, CT 06810-6885. Offers MS. Part-time and evening/weekend programs available. *Students:* 2 full-time (1 woman), 34 part-time (14 women); includes 2 minority (both Hispanic Americans), 1 international. Average age 32. In 2006, 22 degrees awarded. *Degree requirements:* For master's, thesis or research project. *Entrance requirements:* For master's, minimum GPA of 2.8, teaching certificate. *Application deadline:* For fall admission, 8/1 priority date for domestic students. Applications are processed on a rolling basis. Application fee: $40. *Financial support:* Fellowships, career-related internships or fieldwork available. Support available to part-time students. Financial award application deadline: 5/1; financial award applicants required to submit FAFSA. *Application contact:* Chris Shankle, Associate Director of Graduate Admissions, 203-837-8244, Fax: 203-837-8338, E-mail: shanklec@wcsu.edu.

Western Governors University, Teachers College, Salt Lake City, UT 84107. Offers English language learning (K-12) (MA); learning and technology (M Ed, MA); management and evaluation (M Ed); management and innovation (M Ed); mathematics education (5-12) (MA); mathematics education (5-9) (MA); mathematics education (K-6) (MA); science (5-12) (MA), including biology, geology; science education (509) (MA); technology (M Ed); technology for principals (Post-Graduate Certificate). *Accreditation:* NCATE. Part-time and evening/weekend programs available. Postbaccalaureate distance learning degree programs offered (no on-campus study). *Degree requirements:* For master's, comprehensive exam, registration. *Entrance requirements:* Additional exam requirements/recommendations for international students: Required—TOEFL (minimum score 450 paper-based). Electronic applications accepted. Expenses: Contact institution.

Western Illinois University, School of Graduate Studies, College of Education and Human Services, Department of Instructional Design and Technology, Macomb, IL 61455-1390. Offers distance learning (Certificate); graphic applications (Certificate); instructional technology and telecommunications (MS); multimedia (Certificate); technology integration in education (Certificate); training development (Certificate). Part-time programs available. Postbaccalaureate distance learning degree programs offered (no on-campus study). *Students:* 17 full-time (7 women), 68 part-time (42 women); includes 8 minority (4 African Americans, 4 Asian Americans or Pacific Islanders), 6 international. Average age 36. 18 applicants, 61% accepted. In 2006, 17 master's, 1 other advanced degree awarded. *Degree requirements:* For master's, thesis or alternative. *Entrance requirements:* For master's, minimum GPA of 2.75. Additional exam requirements/recommendations for international students: Required—TOEFL (minimum score 550 paper-based; 213 computer-based; 80 iBT). *Application deadline:* Applications are processed on a rolling basis. Application fee: $30. Electronic applications accepted. *Expenses:* Tuition, state resident: part-time $200 per credit hour. Tuition, nonresident: part-time $400 per credit hour. *Financial support:* In 2006–07, 13 students received support, including 11 research assistantships with full tuition reimbursements available (averaging $6,568 per year), 2 teaching assistantships with full tuition reimbursements available (averaging $7,576 per year). Financial award applicants required to submit FAFSA. *Unit head:* Dr. Hoyet Hemphill, Chairperson, 309-298-1952. *Application contact:* Dr. Barbara Baily, Director of Graduate Studies/Associate Provost, 309-298-1806, Fax: 309-298-2345, E-mail: grad-office@wiu.edu.

Western Kentucky University, Graduate Studies, College of Education and Behavioral Sciences, Department of Special Instructional Programs, Bowling Green, KY 42101. Offers exceptional child education (MAE); interdisciplinary early child education (MAE); library media education (MS); literacy (MAE). Part-time and evening/weekend programs available. Postbaccalaureate distance learning degree programs offered (minimal on-campus study). *Faculty:* 15 full-time (12 women), 1 (woman) part-time/adjunct. *Students:* 38 full-time (35 women), 347 part-time (296 women); includes 18 minority (8 African Americans, 2 American Indian/Alaska Native, 1 Asian American or Pacific Islander, 7 Hispanic Americans), 2 international. Average age 33. 131 applicants, 66% accepted, 57 enrolled. In 2006, 146 degrees awarded. *Degree requirements:* For master's, comprehensive exam. *Entrance requirements:* For master's, GRE General Test. Additional exam requirements/recommendations for international students: Required—TOEFL (minimum score 555 paper-based; 213 computer-based; 79 iBT). *Application deadline:* For fall admission, 7/1 for domestic students, 4/1 for international students; for spring admission, 11/1 for domestic students, 9/1 for international students. Application fee: $35. *Expenses:* Tuition, state resident: full-time $6,520; part-time $226 per hour. Tuition, nonresident: full-time $7,140; part-time $357 per hour. International tuition: $15,820 full-time. *Financial support:* In 2006–07, 2 research assistantships with partial tuition reimbursements (averaging $8,000 per year) were awarded; tuition waivers (partial) and unspecified assistantships also available. *Faculty research:* Teacher preparation in moderate/severe disabilities. Total annual research expenditures: $125,538. *Unit head:* Dr. Sherry Powers, Department Head, 270-745-4607, Fax: 270-745-3441, E-mail: sherry.powers@wku.edu.

Western Oregon University, Graduate Programs, College of Education, Division of Teacher Education, Program in Information Technology, Monmouth, OR 97361-1394. Offers MS Ed. *Accreditation:* NCATE. Part-time and evening/weekend programs available. Postbaccalaureate distance learning degree programs offered (minimal on-campus study). *Faculty:* 13 part-time/adjunct (9 women). *Students:* 4 full-time (3 women), 57 part-time (39 women). Average age 40. In 2006, 48 degrees awarded. *Degree requirements:* For master's, written exams. *Entrance requirements:* For master's, interview, minimum GPA of 3.0, teaching license. *Application deadline:* Applications are processed on a rolling basis. Application fee: $50. *Expenses:* Tuition, state resident: full-time $8,250; part-time $250 per credit. Tuition, nonresident: full-time $14,025; part-time $250 per credit. Required fees: $1,173. *Financial support:* Research assistantships with full tuition reimbursements, teaching assistantships with full tuition reimbursements, career-related internships or fieldwork, Federal Work-Study, and tuition waivers (full and partial) available. Support available to part-time students. Financial award application deadline: 3/1; financial award applicants required to submit FAFSA. *Faculty research:* Impact of technology on teaching and learning. *Unit head:* Dr. Mary Bucy, Unit Head, 503-838-8794, Fax: 503-838-8228. *Application contact:* Dr. David McDonald, Dean of Admissions, Retention and Enrollment Management, 503-838-8919, Fax: 503-838-8067, E-mail: mcdonald@wou.edu.

Westfield State College, Division of Graduate and Continuing Education, Department of Education, Program in Technology for Educators, Westfield, MA 01086. Offers M Ed. Part-time and evening/weekend programs available. *Degree requirements:* For master's, comprehensive exam or project. *Entrance requirements:* For master's, GRE General Test or MAT, minimum undergraduate GPA of 2.7.

West Texas A&M University, College of Education and Social Sciences, Division of Education, Program in Educational Technology, Canyon, TX 79016-0001. Offers M Ed. Part-time and evening/weekend programs available. Postbaccalaureate distance learning degree programs offered (minimal on-campus study). *Degree requirements:* For master's, thesis optional. *Entrance requirements:* For master's, GRE General Test, approval from the instructional technology admissions committee. Additional exam requirements/recommendations for international students: Required—TOEFL (minimum score 550 paper-based). Electronic applications accepted. *Faculty research:* Mathematics and science instruction, technology, developing online courses for freshmen, integrity of online courses.

Widener University, School of Human Service Professions, Center for Education, Chester, PA 19013-5792. Offers adult education (M Ed); counseling in higher education (M Ed); counselor education (M Ed); early childhood education (M Ed); educational foundations (M Ed); educational leadership (M Ed); educational psychology (M Ed); elementary education (M Ed); English and language arts (M Ed); health education (M Ed); higher education leadership (Ed D); home and school visitor (M Ed); human sexuality (M Ed); mathematics education (M Ed); middle school education (M Ed); principalship (M Ed); reading and language arts (Ed D); reading education (M Ed); school administration (Ed D); science education (M Ed); social studies education (M Ed); special education (M Ed); technology education (M Ed). Part-time and evening/weekend programs available. Terminal master's awarded for partial completion of doctoral program. *Degree requirements:* For doctorate, thesis/dissertation. *Entrance requirements:* For master's, minimum GPA of 2.5; for doctorate, GRE or MAT, minimum GPA of 2.0 (undergraduate), 3.5 (graduate). Electronic applications accepted. Expenses: Contact institution. *Faculty research:* Reading and cognition, adult education, technology education, educational leadership, special education.

Wilkes University, Graduate Studies and Continued Learning, College of Arts, Humanities and Social Sciences, Program in Teacher Education, Wilkes-Barre, PA 18766-0002. Offers classroom technology (MS Ed); educational computing (MS Ed); educational development and strategies (MS Ed); educational leadership (MS Ed); elementary education (MS Ed); instructional technology (MS Ed); school business leadership (MS Ed); secondary education (MS Ed), including biology, chemistry, English, history; special education (MS Ed). Part-time and evening/weekend programs available. Postbaccalaureate distance learning degree programs offered (minimal on-campus study). *Students:* 32 full-time (21 women), 1,588 part-time (1,106 women); includes 29 minority (6 African Americans, 2 American Indian/Alaska Native, 4 Asian Americans or Pacific Islanders, 17 Hispanic Americans). Average age 33. In 2006, 754 degrees awarded. *Entrance requirements:* Additional exam requirements/recommendations for international students: Required—TOEFL (minimum score 500 paper-based; 173 computer-based). *Application deadline:* Applications are processed on a rolling basis. Application fee: $40. *Expenses:* Contact institution. *Financial support:* Federal Work-Study and unspecified assistantships available. Financial award application deadline: 3/1; financial award applicants required to submit FAFSA. *Unit head:* Dr. Michael Speziale, Interim Dean, 570-408-4679, Fax: 570-408-4905, E-mail: michael.speziale@wilkes.edu. *Application contact:* Kathleen Houlihan, Director of Graduate Studies, 570-408-3235, Fax: 570-408-7846, E-mail: kathleen.houlihan@wilkes.edu.

Wilmington College, Division of Education, New Castle, DE 19720-6491. Offers applied education technology (M Ed); career and technical education (M Ed); elementary and secondary school counseling (M Ed); elementary special education (M Ed); elementary studies (M Ed); instruction: gifted and talented (M Ed); instruction: teaching and learning (M Ed); literacy (M Ed); reading (M Ed); school leadership (M Ed); secondary teaching (MAT). Part-time and evening/weekend programs available. *Faculty:* 7 full-time (4 women). *Students:* 609 full-time (447 women), 1,350 part-time (1,013 women); includes 144 minority (131 African Americans, 3 American Indian/Alaska Native, 1 Asian American or Pacific Islander, 9 Hispanic Americans). Average age 34. 818 applicants, 100% accepted, 599 enrolled. In 2006, 737 degrees awarded. *Entrance requirements:* For master's, 2 letters of recommendation, interview. Additional exam requirements/recommendations for international students: Required—TOEFL (minimum score 500 paper-based; 173 computer-based). *Application deadline:* For fall admission, 4/30 for domestic students. Applications are processed on a rolling basis. Application fee: $25. *Financial support:* Applicants required to submit FAFSA. *Unit head:* Dr. Richard Gochnauer, Chair, 302-328-6795 Ext. 163, Fax: 302-328-7081. *Application contact:* Chris Ferguson, Director of Admissions and Financial Aid, 302-328-9407 Ext. 256, Fax: 302-328-5164, E-mail: inquire@wilmcoll.edu.

Educational Policy

Alabama State University, School of Graduate Studies, College of Education, Department of Instructional Support, Program in Educational Administration, Montgomery, AL 36101-0271. Offers educational administration (M Ed, Ed S); educational leadership, policy and law (Ed D). Part-time programs available. *Students:* 16 full-time (11 women), 128 part-time (84 women); includes 108 minority (all African Americans) Average age 45. In 2006, 31 master's, 4 other advanced degrees awarded. *Degree requirements:* For master's, thesis optional; for Ed S, thesis. *Entrance requirements:* For master's, GRE General Test, MAT, graduate writing competency test; for Ed S, graduate writing competency test, GRE, MAT. Additional exam requirements/recommendations for international students: Required—TOEFL (minimum score 500 paper-based; 173 computer-based). *Application deadline:* For fall admission, 7/15 for domestic students; for spring admission, 12/15 for domestic students. Applications are processed on a rolling basis. Application fee: $10. *Expenses:* Tuition, state resident: full-time $1,728; part-time $192 per hour. Tuition, nonresident: full-time $3,456; part-time $334 per hour. *Financial support:* In 2006–07, research assistantships (averaging $9,450 per year). *Faculty research:* Nontraditional roles, computer applications for principals, women in educational administration. *Unit head:* Dr. Hyacinth Findlay, Coordinator, 334-229-4417, E-mail: hfindlay@alasu.edu.

The College of William and Mary, School of Education, Program in Education Policy, Planning, and Leadership, Williamsburg, VA 23187-8795. Offers curriculum and educational technology (Ed D, PhD); curriculum leadership (Ed D, PhD); educational leadership (M Ed), including higher education administration (M Ed, Ed D, PhD), K-12 administration and supervision; educational policy, planning, and leadership (Ed D, PhD), including general education administration, gifted education administration, higher education administration (M Ed, Ed D, PhD), special education administration; gifted education administration (M Ed). *Accreditation:* NCATE. Part-time and evening/weekend programs available. *Faculty:* 10 full-time (5 women), 4 part-time/adjunct (2 women). *Students:* 51 full-time (44 women), 101 part-time (64 women); includes 28 minority (27 African Americans, 1 Hispanic American), 7 international. Average age 28. 114 applicants, 55% accepted, 42 enrolled. In 2006, 38 master's, 12 doctorates awarded. *Degree requirements:* For doctorate, thesis/dissertation, comprehensive exam. *Entrance requirements:* For master's, GRE or MAT, minimum GPA of 2.5; for doctorate, GRE or MAT, minimum GPA of 3.0. Additional exam requirements/recommendations for international students: Required—TOEFL. *Application deadline:* For fall admission, 2/1 for domestic and international students; for spring admission, 10/1 for domestic and international students. Application fee: $30. *Expenses:* Tuition, state resident: full-time $6,100; part-time $260 per credit. Tuition, nonresident: full-time $18,790; part-time $725 per credit. Required fees: $3,314. Tuition and fees vary according to program. *Financial support:* In 2006–07, 41 research assistantships with full and partial tuition reimbursements (averaging $13,300 per year) were awarded; career-related internships or fieldwork, Federal Work-Study, institutionally sponsored loans, scholarships/grants, and unspecified assistantships also available. Support available to part-time students. Financial award application deadline: 2/1; financial award applicants required to submit FAFSA. *Faculty research:* Higher education policy, faculty incentives, history of adversity, resilience, leadership. *Unit head:* Dr. Megan Tschannen-Moran, Area Coordinator, 757-221-2187, E-mail: mxtsch@wm.edu. *Application contact:* Patricia Burleson, Director of Admissions, 757-221-2317, E-mail: paburl@wm.edu.

DeSales University, Graduate Division, Program in Education, Center Valley, PA 18034-9568. Offers academic standards and information (Certificate); bilingual/ESL studies (Certificate); biology (M Ed); chemistry (M Ed); computers in education (K-12) (M Ed); computers in education (K-8) (M Ed); English (M Ed); instructional technology specialist (Certificate); mathematics (M Ed); special education (M Ed, Certificate); TESOL (M Ed). Part-time and evening/weekend programs available. Postbaccalaureate distance learning degree programs offered (minimal on-campus study). *Students:* 34 full-time, 190 part-time. In 2006, 30 degrees awarded. *Degree requirements:* For master's, thesis project. *Entrance requirements:* For master's, teaching certificate. *Application deadline:* Applications are processed on a rolling basis. Application fee: $35. Electronic applications accepted. *Expenses: Contact institution. Financial support:* Unspecified assistantships available. Support available to part-time students. Financial award application deadline: 5/1. *Faculty research:* Effective teaching, computer interfacing in chemistry labs, computer applications to teaching, history of philosophy, aesthetics multidrug-resistant cancer. *Unit head:* Dr. Lujean Baab, Director of M.Ed. Program, 610-282-1100 Ext. 1739, Fax: 610-282-3734, E-mail: lujean.baab@desales.edu. *Application contact:* Donna L. Cressman, Program Secretary, 610-282-1100 Ext. 1461, Fax: 610-282-3734, E-mail: med@desales.edu.

The George Washington University, Graduate School of Education and Human Development, Department of Educational Leadership, Program in Educational Administration and Policy Studies, Washington, DC 20052. Offers Ed D. *Accreditation:* NCATE. *Degree requirements:* For doctorate, thesis/dissertation, comprehensive exam. *Entrance requirements:* For doctorate, GRE General Test or MAT, interview, minimum GPA of 3.3.

The George Washington University, Graduate School of Education and Human Development, Department of Educational Leadership, Program in Education Policy Studies, Washington, DC 20052. Offers MA Ed. *Accreditation:* NCATE. *Degree requirements:* For master's, comprehensive exam. *Entrance requirements:* For master's, GRE General Test or MAT, interview, minimum GPA of 2.75.

Georgia State University, College of Education, Department of Educational Policy Studies, Atlanta, GA 30303-3083. Offers educational leadership (M Ed, PhD, Ed S); educational research (MS, PhD), including educational research (MS), research, measurements and statistics (PhD); social foundations of education (MS, PhD). Part-time and evening/weekend programs available. *Faculty:* 22 full-time (10 women), 4 part-time/adjunct (1 woman). *Students:* 69 full-time (51 women), 122 part-time (84 women); includes 66 minority (58 African Americans, 2 American Indian/Alaska Native, 3 Asian Americans or Pacific Islanders, 3 Hispanic Americans), 10 international. Average age 37. 66 applicants, 70% accepted. In 2006, 39 master's, 14 doctorates, 13 other advanced degrees awarded. *Entrance requirements:* For master's, GRE General Test, minimum GPA of 2.5; for doctorate, GRE General Test or MAT, minimum GPA of 3.3; for Ed S, GRE General Test or MAT, minimum GPA of 3.25. Application fee: $25. *Financial support:* In 2006–07, 22 research assistantships, 5 teaching assistantships were awarded; career-related internships or fieldwork, Federal Work-Study, institutionally sponsored loans, and tuition waivers (partial) also available. Support available to part-time students. *Faculty research:* Policy studies, organizational studies, education and culture. Total annual research expenditures: $7,500. *Unit head:* Dr. Asa G. Hilliard, Chair, 404-651-1269, Fax: 404-651-1009, E-mail: ahilliard@gsu.edu.

Harvard University, Graduate School of Education, Doctoral Program in Education, Cambridge, MA 02138. Offers culture, communities and education (Ed D); education policy (Ed D); education policy, leadership and instructional practice (Ed D); higher education (Ed D); human development and education (Ed D); quantitative policy analysis in education (Ed D); urban superintendency (Ed D). Part-time programs available. *Faculty:* 58 full-time (25 women), 40 part-time/adjunct (22 women). *Students:* 306 full-time (216 women), 35 part-time (26 women); includes 95 minority (38 African Americans, 4 American Indian/Alaska Native, 35 Asian Americans or Pacific Islanders, 18 Hispanic Americans), 46 international. Average age 35. 494 applicants, 12% accepted, 48 enrolled. In 2006, 70 degrees awarded. Terminal master's awarded for partial completion of doctoral program. *Degree requirements:* For doctorate, thesis/dissertation. *Entrance requirements:* For doctorate, GRE General Test, 3 letters of recommendation, official transcripts, statement of purpose. Additional exam requirements/recommendations for international students: Required—TOEFL (minimum score 600 paper-based; 250 computer-based; 100 iBT), TWE (minimum score 5). *Application deadline:* For fall admission, 12/14 for domestic and international students. Application fee: $85. Electronic applications accepted. *Expenses: Contact institution. Financial support:* In 2006–07, 171 fellowships with full and partial tuition reimbursements (averaging $11,489 per year), 47 research assistantships (averaging $9,340 per year), 153 teaching assistantships (averaging $7,710 per year) were awarded; career-related internships or fieldwork, Federal Work-Study, institutionally sponsored loans, scholarships/grants, health care benefits, tuition waivers (full and partial), and unspecified assistantships also available. Support available to part-time students. Financial award application deadline: 2/2; financial award applicants required to submit FAFSA. *Faculty research:* Learning and development; educational leadership and organizations; education policy analysis. Total annual research expenditures: $4.8 million. *Unit head:* Dr. James Stiles, Associate Dean for Degree Programs. *Application contact:* Information Contact, 617-495-3414, Fax: 617-496-3577, E-mail: gseadmissions@harvard.edu.

Harvard University, Graduate School of Education, Master's Programs in Education, Cambridge, MA 02138. Offers arts in education (Ed M); education policy and management (Ed M); higher education (Ed M); human development and psychology (Ed M); international education policy (Ed M); language and literacy (Ed M); learning and teaching (Ed M); mid-career mathematics and science (teaching certificate) (Ed M); mind brain and education (Ed M); risk and prevention (Ed M); school leadership (Ed M); special studies (Ed M); teaching and curriculum (teaching certificate) (Ed M); technology innovation and education (Ed M). Part-time programs available. *Faculty:* 58 full-time (25 women), 40 part-time/adjunct (22 women). *Students:* 540 full-time (412 women), 90 part-time (70 women); includes 137 minority (49 African Americans, 2 American Indian/Alaska Native, 61 Asian Americans or Pacific Islanders, 25 Hispanic Americans), 70 international. Average age 29. 1,211 applicants, 61% accepted, 585 enrolled. In 2006, 591 degrees awarded. *Entrance requirements:* For master's, GRE General Test, 3 letters of recommendation, official transcripts, statement of purpose. Additional exam requirements/recommendations for international students: Required—TOEFL (minimum score 600 paper-based; 250 computer-based; 100 iBT), TWE (minimum score 5). *Application deadline:* For fall admission, 1/2 for domestic and international students. Application fee: $85. Electronic applications accepted. *Expenses: Contact institution. Financial support:* In 2006–07, 392 students received support, including 23 fellowships (averaging $15,870 per year); career-related internships or fieldwork, Federal Work-Study, institutionally sponsored loans, scholarships/grants, health care benefits, tuition waivers (full and partial), and unspecified assistantships also available. Support available to part-time students. Financial award application deadline: 2/2; financial award applicants required to submit FAFSA. *Faculty research:* Learning and development; educational leadership and organizations; educational policy analysis. Total annual research expenditures: $14.8 million. *Unit head:* Dr. James Stiles, Associate Dean for Degree Programs. *Application contact:* Information Contact, 617-495-3414, Fax: 617-496-3577, E-mail: gseadmissions@harvard.edu.

Illinois State University, Graduate School, College of Education, Department of Curriculum and Instruction, Normal, IL 61790-2200. Offers curriculum and instruction (MS, MS Ed, Ed D); educational policies (Ed D); postsecondary education (Ed D); reading (MS Ed); supervision (Ed D). *Accreditation:* NCATE. *Faculty:* 28 full-time (13 women). *Students:* 21 full-time (16 women), 157 part-time (123 women); includes 20 minority (11 African Americans, 5 Asian Americans or Pacific Islanders, 4 Hispanic Americans), 11 international. 26 applicants, 73% accepted. In 2006, 60 master's, 14 doctorates awarded. *Degree requirements:* For master's, variable foreign language requirement, thesis or alternative; for doctorate, variable foreign language requirement, thesis/dissertation, 2 terms of residency, internship. *Entrance requirements:* For master's, GRE General Test, minimum GPA of 3.0 in last 60 hours of course work; for doctorate, GRE General Test. *Application deadline:* Applications are processed on a rolling basis. Application fee: $40. *Expenses:* Tuition, state resident: full-time $3,330; part-time $185 per credit hour. Tuition, nonresident: full-time $6,948; part-time $438 per credit hour. Required fees: $1,259; $52 per credit hour. *Financial support:* In 2006–07, 15 research assistantships (averaging $7,056 per year), 5 teaching assistantships (averaging $9,675 per year) were awarded; tuition waivers (full) and unspecified assistantships also available. Financial award application deadline: 4/1. *Faculty research:* In-service and pre-service teacher education for teachers of English language learners; teachers for all children: developing a model for alternative, bilingual elementary certification for paraprofessionals in Illinois; Illinois Geographic Alliance. Total annual research expenditures: $1 million. *Unit head:* Dr. Barbara Nourie, Acting Chairperson, 309-438-5425.

Indiana University Bloomington, School of Education, Department of Educational Leadership and Policy Studies, Bloomington, IN 47405-7000. Offers education policy studies (PhD); educational leadership (MS, Ed D, PhD, Ed S); higher education (MS, Ed D, PhD); history and philosophy of education (MS); history of education (PhD); international and comparative education (MS, PhD); philosophy of education (PhD); student affairs administration (MS). PhD offered through the University Graduate School. *Accreditation:* NCATE. Part-time and evening/weekend programs available. *Students:* 12 full-time (5 women), 28 part-time (14 women). Average age 35. In 2006, 32 master's, 4 doctorates awarded. *Degree requirements:* For master's, thesis optional; for doctorate, thesis/dissertation; for Ed S, comprehensive exam or project. *Entrance requirements:* For master's, doctorate, and Ed S, GRE General Test. *Application deadline:* For fall admission, 6/1 for domestic students, 3/1 for international students; for spring admission, 9/1 for international students. Application fee: $45 ($55 for international students). *Expenses:* Tuition, state resident: full-time $5,791; part-time $241 per credit hour. Tuition, nonresident: full-time $16,866; part-time $703 per credit hour. *Financial support:* Fellowships, research assistantships, teaching assistantships, career-related internships or fieldwork, Federal Work-Study, institutionally sponsored loans, and tuition waivers (full and partial) available. Support available to part-time students. *Unit head:* Martha McCarthy, Chair, 812-856-8377. *Application contact:* Sandy Strain, Department Secretary, 812-856-8360, Fax: 812-856-8394, E-mail: strain@indiana.edu.

Loyola University Chicago, School of Education, Program in Cultural and Educational Policy Studies, Chicago, IL 60611-2196. Offers M Ed, MA, Ed D, PhD. Part-time programs available. *Faculty:* 3 full-time (0 women), 4 part-time/adjunct (3 women). *Students:* 89. Average age 30. 28 applicants, 82% accepted, 13 enrolled. In 2006, 2 master's, 16 doctorates awarded. *Degree requirements:* For master's, comprehensive exam (M Ed), thesis (MA); for doctorate, thesis/dissertation, oral candidacy exam, comprehensive exam. *Entrance requirements:* For master's, letters of recommendation, minimum GPA of 3.0; for doctorate, GRE General Test or MAT, interview, letter of recommendation, resumé, minimum GPA of 3.0. Additional exam requirements/recommendations for international students: Required—TOEFL (minimum score 550 paper-based; 218 computer-based; 79 iBT). *Application deadline:* For fall admission, 7/1 for domestic and international students; for winter admission, 3/1 for domestic and international students; for spring admission, 11/1 for domestic and international students. Applications are processed on a rolling basis. Application fee: $50. *Financial support:* In 2006–07, 2 students received support, including 2 research assistantships with full tuition reimbursements available (averaging $11,000 per year); career-related internships or fieldwork, Federal Work-Study, institutionally sponsored loans, and tuition waivers (partial) also available. Support available to part-time students. Financial award application deadline: 2/1; financial award applicants required to submit FAFSA. *Faculty research:* Politics of education, cultural foundations, policy studies, qualitative research methods, multicultural diversity. *Unit head:* Dr. Robert Roemer, Director, 312-915-6883. *Application contact:* Marie Rosin-Dittmar, Information Contact, 312-915-6800, E-mail: schleduc@luc.edu.

Michigan State University, The Graduate School, College of Education, Program in Educational Policy, East Lansing, MI 48824. Offers PhD. *Students:* 24 full-time (13 women), 1 (woman) part-time; includes 5 minority (4 African Americans, 1 Hispanic American), 8 international. Average age 32. 27 applicants, 37% accepted. In 2006, 2 degrees awarded. *Entrance requirements:* Additional exam requirements/recommendations for international students: Required—TOEFL. Electronic applications accepted. *Expenses:* Tuition, state resident: part-time $346 per credit hour. Tuition, nonresident: part-time $730 per credit hour. Tuition and fees vary according to program. *Financial support:* In 2006–07, 21 fellowships with tuition reimbursements, 19 research assistantships with tuition reimbursements (averaging $13,644 per year),

Educational Policy

Michigan State University (continued)

2 teaching assistantships with tuition reimbursements (averaging $13,158 per year) were awarded. *Unit head:* Dr. Michael Sedlak, Associate Dean, 517-432-1260, Fax: 517-353-6393, E-mail: msedlak@msu.edu. *Application contact:* Program Information, 517-432-1260, E-mail: edacadaf@msu.edu.

New York University, Steinhardt School of Culture, Education and Human Development, Department of Humanities and Social Sciences in the Professions, Program in Sociology of Education, New York, NY 10012-1019. Offers education policy (MA); social and cultural studies of education (MA); sociology of education (PhD). Part-time and evening/weekend programs available. *Faculty:* 5 full-time (2 women). *Students:* 21 full-time (19 women), 9 part-time (6 women); includes 11 minority (2 African Americans, 2 Asian Americans or Pacific Islanders, 7 Hispanic Americans), 1 international. 65 applicants, 71% accepted, 15 enrolled. In 2006, 6 master's, 2 doctorates awarded. Terminal master's awarded for partial completion of doctoral program. *Degree requirements:* For master's, thesis (for some programs); for doctorate, thesis/dissertation. *Entrance requirements:* For master's, letters of recommendation; for doctorate, GRE General Test, interview. Additional exam requirements/recommendations for international students: Required—TOEFL. *Application deadline:* For fall admission, 12/15 priority date for domestic and international students; for spring admission, 11/1 for domestic and international students. Applications are processed on a rolling basis. Application fee: $50. *Expenses:* Tuition: Part-time $1,080 per unit. Required fees: $56 per unit. $329 per term. Tuition and fees vary according to program. *Financial support:* Fellowships with full and partial tuition reimbursements, Federal Work-Study, institutionally sponsored loans, scholarships/grants, and tuition waivers (partial) available. Support available to part-time students. Financial award application deadline: 2/1; financial award applicants required to submit FAFSA. *Faculty research:* Legal and institutional environments of schools; social inequality; high school reform and achievement; education's link with occupations, professions and inequality. *Unit head:* Dr. Floyd M. Hammack, Program Director, 212-992-9475, Fax: 212-995-4832, E-mail: fmhl@nyu.edu. *Application contact:* 212-998-5030, Fax: 212-995-4328, E-mail: steinhardt.gradadmissions@nyu.edu.

The Ohio State University, Graduate School, College of Education and Human Ecology, School of Educational Policy and Leadership, Columbus, OH 43210. Offers M Ed, MA, PhD. *Accreditation:* NCATE. *Faculty:* 41. *Students:* 137 full-time (98 women), 206 part-time (133 women); includes 70 minority (58 African Americans, 1 American Indian/Alaska Native, 8 Asian Americans or Pacific Islanders, 3 Hispanic Americans), 30 international. Average age 33. 401 applicants, 51% accepted, 77 enrolled. In 2006, 76 master's, 19 doctorates awarded. *Degree requirements:* For master's, thesis optional; for doctorate, thesis/dissertation. *Entrance requirements:* For master's, GRE (for some MA applicants); for doctorate, GRE General Test. Additional exam requirements/recommendations for international students: Required—TOEFL (minimum score 600 paper-based; 250 computer-based). *Application deadline:* For fall admission, 8/15 priority date for domestic students, 7/1 priority date for international students; for winter admission, 12/1 priority date for domestic students, 11/1 priority date for international students; for spring admission, 3/1 priority date for domestic students, 2/1 priority date for international students. Applications are processed on a rolling basis. Application fee: $40 ($50 for international students). Electronic applications accepted. *Expenses:* Tuition, state resident: full-time $9,438. Tuition, nonresident: full-time $22,791. Tuition and fees vary according to course load, campus/location and program. *Financial support:* Fellowships, research assistantships, teaching assistantships, Federal Work-Study, institutionally sponsored loans, and unspecified assistantships available. Support available to part-time students. *Unit head:* Philip L. Smith, Graduate Studies Committee Chair, 614-688-4791, Fax: 614-292-2581, E-mail: smith.133@osu.edu. *Application contact:* 614-292-9444, Fax: 614-292-3895, E-mail: domestic.grad@osu.edu.

Portland State University, Graduate Studies, School of Education, Department of Educational Policy, Foundations, and Administrative Studies, Portland, OR 97207-0751. Offers educational leadership (MA, MS, Ed D); postsecondary, adult and continuing education (Ed D). *Accreditation:* NCATE. Part-time and evening/weekend programs available. *Faculty:* 11 full-time (5 women), 10 part-time/adjunct (4 women). *Students:* 62 full-time (51 women), 227 part-time (149 women); includes 41 minority (7 African Americans, 10 American Indian/Alaska Native, 8 Asian Americans or Pacific Islanders, 16 Hispanic Americans), 10 international. Average age 40. 234 applicants, 91% accepted, 67 enrolled. In 2006, 69 master's, 4 doctorates awarded. *Degree requirements:* For master's, thesis or alternative, written exam; for doctorate, thesis/dissertation, comprehensive exam. *Entrance requirements:* For master's, California Basic Educational Skills Test, minimum GPA of 3.0 in upper-division course work or 2.75 overall; for doctorate, GRE General Test or MAT. Additional exam requirements/recommendations for international students: Required—TOEFL (minimum score 550 paper-based; 213 computer-based). *Application deadline:* For fall admission, 4/1 for domestic and international students; for winter admission, 9/1 for domestic and international students; for spring admission, 11/1 for domestic and international students. Applications are processed on a rolling basis. Application fee: $50. *Expenses:* Tuition, state resident: full-time $6,426; part-time $238 per credit. Tuition, nonresident: full-time $11,016; part-time $408 per credit. Tuition and fees vary according to course load. *Financial support:* In 2006–07, 10 research assistantships with full tuition reimbursements (averaging $5,453 per year) were awarded; teaching assistantships with full tuition reimbursements, career-related internships or fieldwork, Federal Work-Study, and institutionally sponsored loans also available. Support available to part-time students. Financial award application deadline: 3/1; financial award applicants required to submit FAFSA. *Faculty research:* Leadership development and research, principals and urban schools, accelerated schools, cooperative learning, family involvement in schools. Total annual research expenditures: $322,962. *Unit head:* Dilafroz Williams, Head, 503-725-4676, Fax: 503-725-8475. *Application contact:* Kellie Walker, Admission Secretary, 503-725-4716, Fax: 503-725-8475.

Rutgers, The State University of New Jersey, Camden, Graduate School of Arts and Sciences, Department of Public Policy and Administration, Camden, NJ 08102-1401. Offers education policy and leadeship (MPA); international public service and development (MPA); public management (MPA); JD/MPA. *Accreditation:* NASPAA. Part-time and evening/weekend programs available. *Faculty:* 14 full-time (6 women). *Students:* 50 full-time (33 women), 32 part-time (26 women); includes 30 minority (19 African Americans, 1 Asian American or Pacific Islander, 10 Hispanic Americans), 2 international. Average age 27. 79 applicants, 70% accepted, 31 enrolled. In 2006, 39 degrees awarded. *Degree requirements:* For master's, directed study, research workshop. *Entrance requirements:* For master's, GRE General Test, GMAT or LSAT. Additional exam requirements/recommendations for international students: Required—TOEFL (minimum score 550 paper-based; 213 computer-based). *Application deadline:* For fall admission, 5/1 priority date for domestic students; for spring admission, 12/1 priority date for domestic students. Applications are processed on a rolling basis. Application fee: $50. Electronic applications accepted. *Financial support:* In 2006–07, 14 students received support, including 5 fellowships (averaging $1,000 per year), 2 research assistantships with full tuition reimbursements available (averaging $6,000 per year), 1 teaching assistantship with full tuition reimbursement available (averaging $12,186 per year); career-related internships or fieldwork, Federal Work-Study, and scholarships/grants also available. Financial award application deadline: 3/15; financial award applicants required to submit FAFSA. *Faculty research:* Nonprofit management, county and municipal administration, health and human services, government communication, administrative law, educational finance. *Unit head:* Dr. Richard Harris, Chair, 856-225-6339, Fax: 856-225-6559, E-mail: raharris@camden.rutgers.edu. *Application contact:* Sandra J. Cheesman, Department Administrator, 856-225-6860, Fax: 856-225-6559, E-mail: scheesma@camden.rutgers.edu.

Rutgers, The State University of New Jersey, New Brunswick, Graduate School of Education, Doctoral Program in Education, New Brunswick, NJ 08901-1281. Offers educational policy (PhD); educational psychology (PhD); literacy education (PhD); mathematics education (PhD). Part-time programs available. *Faculty:* 63 full-time (30 women). *Students:* 29 full-time (21 women), 45 part-time (34 women); includes 7 minority (4 African Americans, 3 Asian Americans or Pacific Islanders), 15 international. 85 applicants, 33% accepted, 13 enrolled. In 2006, 8 degrees awarded. *Degree requirements:* For doctorate, thesis/dissertation, qualifying exam. *Entrance requirements:* For doctorate, GRE General Test, GRE Subject Test (for mathematics education). Additional exam requirements/recommendations for international students: Required—TOEFL (minimum score 575 paper-based; 233 computer-based). *Application deadline:* For fall admission, 2/1 for domestic and international students. Application fee: $60. Electronic applications accepted. *Financial support:* In 2006–07, research assistantships with full tuition reimbursements (averaging $15,730 per year). Financial award application deadline: 3/15. *Faculty research:* Literacy education, math education, educational psychology, educational policy. *Unit head:* Prof. Clark Chinn, Director, 732-932-7496 Ext. 8319, Fax: 732-932-6829, E-mail: cchinn@rci.rutgers.edu. *Application contact:* Kristine Spaventa, Administrative Assistant, 732-932-7496 Ext. 8104, Fax: 732-932-8206, E-mail: sparenta@rci.rutgers.edu.

University of Alberta, Faculty of Graduate Studies and Research, Department of Educational Policy Studies, Edmonton, AB T6G 2E1, Canada. Offers adult education (M Ed, Ed D, PhD); educational administration and leadership (M Ed, Ed D, PhD, Postgraduate Diploma); First Nations education (M Ed, Ed D, PhD); theoretical, cultural and international studies in education (M Ed, Ed D, PhD). *Faculty:* 19 full-time (10 women), 5 part-time/adjunct (1 woman). *Students:* 73 full-time (47 women), 144 part-time (86 women). 141 applicants, 44% accepted. In 2006, 52 master's, 20 doctorates awarded. *Degree requirements:* For master's, thesis (for some programs); for doctorate, thesis/dissertation. *Entrance requirements:* For master's, minimum GPA of 6.5 on a 9.0 scale; for doctorate, minimum GPA of 7.5 on a 9.0 scale. Additional exam requirements/recommendations for international students: Required—TOEFL (minimum score 580 paper-based; 237 computer-based). *Application deadline:* For spring admission, 2/1 for domestic and international students. Electronic applications accepted. *Financial support:* In 2006–07, 7 fellowships with partial tuition reimbursements, 10 research assistantships with partial tuition reimbursements (averaging $6,936 per year), 30 teaching assistantships with partial tuition reimbursements (averaging $11,130 per year) were awarded; scholarships/grants and unspecified assistantships also available. *Unit head:* Dr. Frank Peters, Graduate Coordinator, 780-492-3679, Fax: 780-492-2024, E-mail: epscoord@ualberta.ca. *Application contact:* Joan A. White, Secretary, 780-492-3679, Fax: 780-492-2024, E-mail: joan.white@ualberta.ca.

The University of British Columbia, Faculty of Graduate Studies, Faculty of Education, Department of Educational Studies, Vancouver, BC V6T 1Z1, Canada. Offers adult education (M Ed, MA); adult learning and global change (M Ed); educational administration (M Ed, MA); educational leadership and policy (Ed D); educational studies (M Ed, PhD), including history of education (M Ed), philosophy of education (M Ed), sociology of education (M Ed); higher education (M Ed, MA); society, culture and politics in education (M Ed, MA). Part-time and evening/weekend programs available. *Faculty:* 30 full-time (15 women), 9 part-time/adjunct (6 women). *Students:* 308 full-time (217 women), 45 part-time (31 women). Average age 35. 211 applicants, 60% accepted. In 2006, 128 master's, 15 doctorates awarded. Terminal master's awarded for partial completion of doctoral program. *Degree requirements:* For master's, thesis (MA); for doctorate, thesis/dissertation. *Entrance requirements:* Additional exam requirements/recommendations for international students: Required—TOEFL, TOEFL or IELTS. Electronic applications accepted. *Financial support:* Fellowships, research assistantships, teaching assistantships available. *Faculty research:* Educational leadership educational administration adult education politics in education, global change and adult learning. Total annual research expenditures: $547,440. *Unit head:* Dr. Tara Fenwick, Head, 604-822-5359, Fax: 604-82-4244. *Application contact:* Christine Adams, Graduate Secretary, 604-822-6647, Fax: 604-822-4244, E-mail: grad.edst@ubc.ca.

University of Georgia, Graduate School, College of Education, Department of Lifelong Education, Administration and Policy, Athens, GA 30602. Offers M Ed, MA, Ed D, PhD, Ed S. *Accreditation:* NCATE. *Faculty:* 21 full-time (13 women). *Students:* 68 full-time (45 women), 248 part-time (159 women); includes 62 minority (54 African Americans, 1 American Indian/Alaska Native, 5 Asian Americans or Pacific Islanders, 2 Hispanic Americans), 21 international. 205 applicants, 63% accepted, 97 enrolled. In 2006, 61 master's, 12 doctorates, 15 other advanced degrees awarded. *Entrance requirements:* For master's and Ed S, GRE General Test or MAT; for doctorate, GRE General Test. *Application deadline:* For fall admission, 7/1 priority date for domestic students; for spring admission, 11/15 for domestic students. Application fee: $50. Electronic applications accepted. *Unit head:* Dr. Ronald M. Cervero, Head, 706-542-2221, Fax: 706-542-4024, E-mail: rcervero@coe.uga.edu.

University of Hawaii at Manoa, Graduate Division, College of Education, Education Program, Honolulu, HI 96822. Offers curriculum and instruction (PhD); educational administration (PhD); educational foundations (PhD); educational policy studies (PhD); exceptionalities (PhD). Evening/weekend programs available. *Faculty:* 78 full-time (44 women), 1 part-time/adjunct (0 women). *Students:* 54 full-time (37 women), 97 part-time (66 women); includes 28 minority (6 African Americans, 1 American Indian/Alaska Native, 19 Asian Americans or Pacific Islanders, 2 Hispanic Americans), 3 international. Average age 45. 63 applicants, 52% accepted, 24 enrolled. In 2006, 17 degrees awarded. *Median time to degree:* Of those who began their doctoral program in fall 1998, 35% received their degree in 8 years or less. *Degree requirements:* For doctorate, thesis/dissertation. *Entrance requirements:* For doctorate, GRE General Test, sample of written work. Additional exam requirements/recommendations for international students: Required—TOEFL (minimum score 600 paper-based; 250 computer-based; 100 iBT). *Application deadline:* For fall admission, 2/1 for domestic students, 1/15 for international students. Application fee: $50. *Financial support:* In 2006–07, 12 research assistantships (averaging $16,565 per year), 5 teaching assistantships (averaging $13,964 per year) were awarded; career-related internships or fieldwork, Federal Work-Study, and tuition waivers (full and partial) also available. *Application contact:* Dr. Helen Slaughter, Chairperson, 808-956-7913, Fax: 808-956-9100, E-mail: slaughte@hawaii.edu.

University of Illinois at Chicago, Graduate College, College of Education, Department of Curriculum and Instruction, Chicago, IL 60607-7128. Offers curriculum and instruction (PhD); educational psychology (PhD); instructional leadership (M Ed), including elementary education, reading, secondary education; leadership and administration (M Ed); policy and administration (PhD); policy studies in urban education (PhD). Part-time and evening/weekend programs available. *Degree requirements:* For doctorate, thesis/dissertation. *Entrance requirements:* For master's, minimum GPA of 2.75; for doctorate, GRE General Test, minimum GPA of 2.75. Additional exam requirements/recommendations for international students: Required—TOEFL. Electronic applications accepted. *Faculty research:* Curriculum theory, curriculum development, research on teaching, curriculum and context, reading/literacy.

University of Illinois at Urbana–Champaign, Graduate College, College of Education, Department of Educational Policy Studies, Champaign, IL 61820. Offers Ed M, MA, Ed D, PhD. Part-time programs available. *Faculty:* 15 full-time (5 women). *Students:* 89 full-time (62 women), 64 part-time (39 women); includes 69 minority (36 African Americans, 6 American Indian/Alaska Native, 9 Asian Americans or Pacific Islanders, 18 Hispanic Americans), 20 international. 85 applicants, 40% accepted, 17 enrolled. In 2006, 9 master's, 16 doctorates awarded. *Degree requirements:* For doctorate, thesis/dissertation. *Application deadline:* For fall admission, 4/1 for domestic students; for spring admission, 4/1 for domestic students. Applications are processed on a rolling basis. Application fee: $50 ($60 for international students). Electronic applications accepted. *Financial support:* In 2006–07, 29 fellowships, 44 research assistantships, 41 teaching assistantships were awarded; tuition waivers (full and partial) also available. Financial award application deadline: 2/15. *Unit head:* James D. Anderson, Head, 217-333-7404, Fax: 217-244-7064, E-mail: janders@uiuc.edu. *Application contact:* Arnita Althaus, Secretary, 217-244-3370, Fax: 217-244-7064, E-mail: althaus@uiuc.edu.

The University of Iowa, Graduate College, College of Education, Department of Educational Policy and Leadership Studies, Iowa City, IA 52242-1316. Offers educational administration (MA, PhD, Ed S); higher education (MA, PhD, Ed S); social foundations (MA, PhD); JD/PhD.

Faculty: 15 full-time, 2 part-time/adjunct. *Students:* 39 full-time (22 women), 87 part-time (47 women); includes 11 minority (6 African Americans, 1 American Indian/Alaska Native, 1 Asian American or Pacific Islander, 3 Hispanic Americans), 20 international. 59 applicants, 68% accepted, 22 enrolled. In 2006, 12 master's, 2 doctorates, 2 other advanced degrees awarded. *Degree requirements:* For master's and Ed S, exam; for doctorate, thesis/dissertation, comprehensive exam, registration. *Entrance requirements:* For master's, doctorate, and Ed S, GRE General Test, minimum GPA of 3.0. Additional exam requirements/recommendations for international students: Required—TOEFL (minimum score 550 paper-based; 213 computer-based; 81 iBT). Application fee: $60 ($85 for international students). Electronic applications accepted. *Financial support:* In 2006–07, 3 fellowships, 19 research assistantships with partial tuition reimbursements, 15 teaching assistantships with partial tuition reimbursements were awarded; career-related internships or fieldwork also available. Financial award applicants required to submit FAFSA. *Unit head:* Dr. Larry Bartlett, Chair, 319-335-5302, Fax: 319-384-0587.

University of Kansas, Graduate Studies, School of Education, Department of Educational Leadership and Policy Studies, Program in Policy Studies, Lawrence, KS 66045. Offers foundations (Ed D, PhD); higher education (Ed D, PhD); school administration (Ed D, PhD). Part-time and evening/weekend programs available. *Faculty:* 19. *Students:* 18 full-time (10 women), 133 part-time (69 women); includes 17 minority (7 African Americans, 4 American Indian/Alaska Native, 2 Asian Americans or Pacific Islanders, 4 Hispanic Americans), 5 international. Average age 40. 17 applicants, 59% accepted. In 2006, 21 degrees awarded. *Degree requirements:* For doctorate, thesis/dissertation, comprehensive exam. *Entrance requirements:* For doctorate, GRE General Test, minimum graduate GPA of 3.5. Additional exam requirements/recommendations for international students: Required—TOEFL. *Application deadline:* For fall admission, 7/1 priority date for domestic and international students; for spring admission, 11/1 priority date for domestic and international students. Applications are processed on a rolling basis. Application fee: $55 ($60 for international students). Electronic applications accepted. *Expenses:* Tuition, area resident: Part-time $227 per credit. Tuition, state resident: part-time $543 per credit. Tuition and fees vary according to course load, campus/location, program and reciprocity agreements. *Financial support:* Fellowships, research assistantships with full and partial tuition reimbursements, teaching assistantships with full and partial tuition reimbursements available. Financial award application deadline: 3/15. *Faculty research:* Policy studies in higher education, policy studies in foundations, policy studies in educational leaderships. *Application contact:* Denise Brubaker, Admissions Coordinator, 785-864-4458, Fax: 785-864-4697, E-mail: elps@ku.edu.

University of Kentucky, Graduate School, College of Education, Program in Educational Policy Studies and Evaluation, Lexington, KY 40506-0032. Offers educational policy studies and evaluation (Ed D); higher education (MS Ed, PhD). *Accreditation:* NCATE. *Students:* 50 full-time (37 women), 30 part-time (19 women); includes 7 minority (all African Americans), 2 international. Average age 38. In 2006, 9 master's, 3 doctorates awarded. Terminal master's awarded for partial completion of doctoral program. *Median time to degree:* Of those who began their doctoral program in fall 1998, 46% received their degree in 8 years or less. *Degree requirements:* For master's, thesis optional; for doctorate, thesis/dissertation, comprehensive exam. *Entrance requirements:* For master's, GRE General Test, minimum undergraduate GPA of 2.75; for doctorate, GRE General Test, minimum graduate GPA of 3.0. Additional exam requirements/recommendations for international students: Required—TOEFL (minimum score 550 paper-based; 213 computer-based). *Application deadline:* For fall admission, 7/17 priority date for domestic students, 2/1 priority date for international students; for spring admission, 12/13 priority date for domestic students, 6/15 priority date for international students. Application fee: $40 ($55 for international students). Electronic applications accepted. *Expenses:* Tuition, state resident: full-time $7,670; part-time $401 per credit hour. Tuition, nonresident: full-time $16,158; part-time $873 per credit hour. *Financial support:* In 2006–07, 9 students received support, including 1 fellowship with full tuition reimbursement available (averaging $4,500 per year), 2 research assistantships with full tuition reimbursements available (averaging $16,748 per year), 6 teaching assistantships with full tuition reimbursements available (averaging $950 per year); career-related internships or fieldwork, Federal Work-Study, institutionally sponsored loans, scholarships/grants, traineeships, health care benefits, tuition waivers (partial), and unspecified assistantships also available. Support available to part-time students. Financial award application deadline: 3/15. *Faculty research:* Studies in higher education; comparative and international education; evaluation of educational programs, policies, and reform; student, teacher, and faculty cultures; gender and education. *Unit head:* Richard Angelo, Director of Graduate Studies, 859-257-3993, Fax: 859-257-4243, E-mail: angelo@pop.uky.edu. *Application contact:* Dr. Brian Jackson, Senior Associate Dean, 859-257-4667, Fax: 859-257-4676, E-mail: brian.jackson@uky.edu.

University of Minnesota, Twin Cities Campus, Graduate School, College of Education and Human Development, Department of Educational Policy and Administration, Minneapolis, MN 55455-0213. Offers comparative and international development education (MA, PhD); disability policy and services (Certificate); educational administration (MA, Ed D, PhD); evaluation studies (MA, PhD); higher education (MA, PhD); postsecondary administration (Ed D); program evaluation (Certificate); staff development (Certificate); teacher leadership (M Ed); youth development leadership (M Ed). *Faculty:* 16 full-time (6 women). *Students:* 211 full-time (140 women), 326 part-time (203 women); includes 58 minority (25 African Americans, 16 American Indian/Alaska Native, 8 Asian Americans or Pacific Islanders, 9 Hispanic Americans), 63 international. Average age 38. 179 applicants, 69% accepted, 84 enrolled. In 2006, 46 master's, 45 doctorates, 20 other advanced degrees awarded. *Expenses:* Tuition, state resident: full-time $9,302; part-time $775 per credit. Tuition, nonresident: full-time $16,400; part-time $1,367 per credit. Full-time tuition and fees vary according to class time, course load, program, reciprocity agreements and student level. *Financial support:* In 2006–07, fellowships (averaging $24,775 per year), 32 research assistantships with full tuition reimbursements (averaging $24,775 per year), 10 teaching assistantships with full tuition reimbursements (averaging $24,775 per year) were awarded. *Faculty research:* Organizational effects of schools and postsecondary institutions on the effects of leadership in school-based settings; program evaluation in shaping education reform; effects of institutional initiatives on the development of intercultural sensitivity and global awareness; the development of theory, technology, and pedagogy of a knowledge producing paradigm suitable for pre-k through graduate school. Total annual research expenditures: $560,163. *Unit head:* Dr. R. Michael Paige, Chair, 612-626-7456, Fax: 612-624-3377, E-mail: r-paig@umn.edu. *Application contact:* Dr. Mary Bents, Associate Dean, 612-625-6501, Fax: 612-626-1580, E-mail: mbents@tc.umn.edu.

University of Pennsylvania, Graduate School of Education, Division of Foundations and Practices in Education, Program in Educational Policy and Leadership, Philadelphia, PA 19104. Offers MS Ed, Ed D, PhD. Part-time programs available. *Degree requirements:* For master's, thesis, comprehensive exam; for doctorate, thesis/dissertation, oral exams, comprehensive exam. *Entrance requirements:* For master's, GRE or MAT; for doctorate, GRE. Electronic applications accepted. Expenses: Contact institution. *Faculty research:* Public policy, curriculum and instruction, organization theory/leadership, school reform.

University of St. Thomas, Graduate Studies, School of Education, Department of Leadership, Policy and Administration, St. Paul, MN 55105-1096. Offers athletics and activities administration (MA); community education administration (MA); educational leadership (Ed S); educational leadership and administration (MA); leadership (Ed D); leadership in student affairs (MA, Certificate); police leadership (MA); public policy and leadership (MA, Certificate). Part-time and evening/weekend programs available. *Faculty:* 6 full-time (3 women), 24 part-time/adjunct (9 women). *Students:* 22 full-time (19 women), 327 part-time (156 women); includes 32 minority (17 African Americans, 3 American Indian/Alaska Native, 8 Asian Americans or Pacific Islanders, 4 Hispanic Americans), 3 international. Average age 38. 140 applicants, 93% accepted, 123 enrolled. In 2006, 14 master's, 8 doctorates, 2 other advanced degrees awarded. Terminal master's awarded for partial completion of doctoral program. *Degree requirements:* For master's, thesis (for some programs), registration; for doctorate, thesis/dissertation, registration; for other advanced degree, thesis or alternative, registration. *Entrance requirements:* For master's, minimum GPA of 2.75 or MAT; for doctorate, MAT, minimum graduate GPA of 3.5; for other advanced degree, MAT, minimum graduate GPA of 3.25. Additional exam requirements/recommendations for international students: Required—TOEFL (minimum score 550 paper-based; 213 computer-based). *Application deadline:* For fall admission, 6/1 priority date for domestic students; for spring admission, 11/1 priority date for domestic students. Applications are processed on a rolling basis. Application fee: $50. *Expenses:* Contact institution. *Financial support:* In 2006–07, 124 students received support; fellowships, research assistantships, institutionally sponsored loans and scholarships/grants available. Support available to part-time students. Financial award applicants required to submit FAFSA. *Unit head:* Dr. Donald R. LaMagdeleine, Chair, 651-962-4893, Fax: 651-962-4169, E-mail: drlamagdelei@stthomas.edu. *Application contact:* Jackie Grossklaus, Department Assistant, 651-962-4885, Fax: 651-962-4169, E-mail: jmgrossklaus@stthomas.edu.

University of Virginia, Curry School of Education, Department of Leadership, Foundations and Policy, Program in Educational Policy and Evaluation, Charlottesville, VA 22903. Offers M Ed, Ed D. *Students:* 1 full-time (0 women), 1 part-time. Average age 42. In 2006, 1 degree awarded. *Degree requirements:* For master's, thesis (for some programs), comprehensive exam (for some programs); for doctorate, thesis/dissertation, comprehensive exam (for some programs). *Entrance requirements:* For master's and doctorate, GRE General Test. Additional exam requirements/recommendations for international students: Required—TOEFL (minimum score 600 paper-based; 250 computer-based). *Application deadline:* Applications are processed on a rolling basis. Application fee: $60. Electronic applications accepted. *Financial support:* Fellowships, research assistantships, teaching assistantships available. Financial award applicants required to submit FAFSA.

University of Washington, Graduate School, College of Education, Seattle, WA 98195. Offers curriculum and instruction (M Ed, Ed D, PhD), including educational technology, general curriculum (Ed D, PhD), language, literacy, and culture, mathematics education, multicultural education, reading and language arts education (Ed D), science education, social studies education, teaching and curriculum (M Ed); educational leadership and policy studies (M Ed, Ed D, PhD), including administration, educational organization and policy, higher education, school district leadership (Ed D), social/cultural foundations; educational psychology (M Ed, PhD), including human development and cognition, measurement and research, school counseling (M Ed), school psychology; special education (M Ed, Ed D, PhD), including early childhood education, elementary special education, emotional and behavioral disabilities (M Ed), general special education, severe disabilities; teacher education (MIT). *Accreditation:* APA. Part-time and evening/weekend programs available. *Degree requirements:* For master's, thesis optional; for doctorate, thesis/dissertation. *Entrance requirements:* For master's and doctorate, GRE General Test, minimum GPA of 3.0. Additional exam requirements/recommendations for international students: Required—TOEFL. Electronic applications accepted. *Faculty research:* School restructuring/effective schools, special education interventions, literacy and writing, technology, school partnerships, teacher preparation.

The University of Western Ontario, Faculty of Graduate Studies, Social Sciences Division, Faculty of Education, Program in Educational Studies, London, ON N6A 5B8, Canada. Offers curriculum studies (M Ed); educational policy studies (M Ed); educational psychology/special education (M Ed). Part-time programs available. *Application deadline:* For fall admission, 2/1 for domestic students. Application fee: $50. *Financial support:* Research assistantships, teaching assistantships available. Financial award application deadline: 4/1. *Faculty research:* Reflective practice, gender and schooling, feminist pedagogy, narrative inquiry, second language, multiculturalism in Canada, education and law. *Unit head:* Allan Pitman, Graduate Chair, 519-661-2111 Ext. 88870, Fax: 519-661-3833, E-mail: pitman@uwo.ca. *Application contact:* L. Kulak, Graduate Supervisor, 519-661-2099, Fax: 519-661-3833, E-mail: kulak@edu.uwo.ca.

University of Wisconsin–Madison, Graduate School, School of Education, Department of Educational Leadership and Policy Analysis, Madison, WI 53706-1380. Offers administration (Certificate); educational policy (MS, PhD). *Degree requirements:* For doctorate, thesis/dissertation. *Entrance requirements:* For master's and doctorate, GRE General Test. *Application deadline:* For fall admission, 1/15 for domestic and international students. Application fee: $45. Electronic applications accepted. *Financial support:* Fellowships with full tuition reimbursements, research assistantships with full tuition reimbursements, teaching assistantships with full tuition reimbursements, project assistantships available. *Unit head:* Dr. Carolyn Kelley, Chair, 608-262-3106.

University of Wisconsin–Madison, Graduate School, School of Education, Department of Educational Policy Studies, Madison, WI 53706-1380. Offers MA, PhD. *Degree requirements:* For doctorate, thesis/dissertation. *Entrance requirements:* For master's and doctorate, GRE General Test. *Application deadline:* For fall admission, 1/1 for domestic and international students; for spring admission, 10/15 for domestic and international students. Application fee: $38. Electronic applications accepted. *Financial support:* Project assistantships available. *Unit head:* Dr. Michael Fultz, Chair, 608-262-1760.

University of Wisconsin–Milwaukee, Graduate School, School of Education, Department of Educational Policy and Community Studies, Milwaukee, WI 53201-0413. Offers cultural foundations of education (MS). Part-time programs available. *Faculty:* 9 full-time (3 women). *Students:* 5 full-time (3 women), 21 part-time (18 women); includes 12 minority (9 African Americans, 1 American Indian/Alaska Native, 2 Asian Americans or Pacific Islanders). 13 applicants, 62% accepted, 5 enrolled. In 2006, 7 degrees awarded. *Degree requirements:* For master's, thesis or alternative. *Application deadline:* For fall admission, 1/1 priority date for domestic students; for spring admission, 9/1 for domestic students. Applications are processed on a rolling basis. Application fee: $45 ($75 for international students). *Expenses:* Tuition, state resident: part-time $510 per credit. Tuition, nonresident: part-time $1,408 per credit. Tuition and fees vary according to program. *Financial support:* Fellowships, research assistantships, teaching assistantships, career-related internships or fieldwork available. Support available to part-time students. Financial award application deadline: 4/15. *Faculty research:* Human relations in education, international and multicultural education. *Unit head:* Michael Bonds, Representative, 414-229-2256, Fax: 414-229-3700.

Vanderbilt University, Peabody College, Department of Leadership and Organizations, Nashville, TN 37240-1001. Offers education policy (MPP); educational leadership and policy (Ed D); higher education (M Ed); higher education, leadership and policy (Ed D); human resource development (M Ed); international education policy and management (M Ed); organizational leadership (M Ed); school administration (M Ed). Part-time and evening/weekend programs available. *Faculty:* 21 full-time (6 women), 9 part-time/adjunct (3 women). *Students:* 131 full-time (88 women), 85 part-time (39 women); includes 35 minority (30 African Americans, 4 Asian Americans or Pacific Islanders, 1 Hispanic American), 11 international. Average age 31. 214 applicants, 63% accepted, 64 enrolled. In 2006, 43 master's, 12 doctorates awarded. *Median time to degree:* Of those who began their doctoral program in fall 1998, 62% received their degree in 8 years or less. *Degree requirements:* For master's, thesis optional; for doctorate, thesis/dissertation, qualifying exams, residency. *Entrance requirements:* For master's and doctorate, GRE General Test. Additional exam requirements/recommendations for international students: Required—TOEFL (minimum score 550 paper-based; 213 computer-based). *Application deadline:* For fall admission, 12/31 priority date for domestic and international students; for spring admission, 11/1 priority date for domestic and international students. Applications are processed on a rolling basis. Application fee: $0. Electronic applications accepted. *Expenses:* Tuition: Full-time $24,462. Required fees: $2,515. One-time fee: $30 full-time. Full-time tuition and fees vary according to course load, degree level and program. *Financial support:* In 2006–07, 90 students received support, including 50 fellowships with full and partial tuition reimbursements available, 38 research assistantships with full and partial tuition reimbursements available, 2 teaching assistantships with full and partial tuition reimbursements available; Federal Work-Study, institutionally sponsored loans, scholarships/grants, tuition waivers (partial), and unspecified assistantships also available. Support available to part-time students. Financial award application deadline: 2/1; financial award applicants required

Educational Policy

Vanderbilt University (continued)
to submit FAFSA. *Faculty research:* Education policy, education finances, economics of education, education leadership and management, higher education leadership and policy; educator pay for performance. *Unit head:* James W. Guthrie, Chair, 615-322-8000, Fax: 615-343-7094, E-mail: james.w.guthrie@vanderbilt.edu. *Application contact:* Rosie Moody, Educational Coordinator, 615-322-8019, Fax: 615-343-7094, E-mail: rosie.moody@vanderbilt.edu.

Wayne State University, College of Education, Division of Administrative and Organizational Studies, Detroit, MI 48202. Offers administration and supervision-secondary (Ed S); college and university teaching (Certificate); curriculum and instruction (PhD); educational leadership (M Ed, Ed S); educational leadership and policy studies (Ed D, PhD); elementary education curriculum and instruction (MA, Ed S); general administration and supervision (Ed D, PhD, Ed S); higher education (Ed D, PhD); instructional technology (M Ed, Ed D, PhD, Ed S); secondary curriculum and instruction (M Ed, Ed S). *Faculty:* 24 full-time (13 women), 1 (woman) part-time/adjunct. *Students:* 153 full-time (103 women), 389 part-time (266 women); includes 252 minority (223 African Americans, 6 American Indian/Alaska Native, 8 Asian Americans or Pacific Islanders, 15 Hispanic Americans), 19 international. Average age 38. 138 applicants, 79% accepted, 74 enrolled. In 2006, 116 master's, 30 doctorates, 64 other advanced degrees awarded. *Degree requirements:* For doctorate, thesis/dissertation. *Entrance requirements:* For doctorate, interview, minimum GPA of 3.0. Additional exam requirements/recommendations for international students: Required—TOEFL (minimum score 550 paper-based; 213 computer-based), TWE (minimum score 6). *Application deadline:* For fall admission, 7/1 for domestic students, 6/1 for international students; for winter admission, 10/1 for international students; for spring admission, 2/1 for international students. Application fee: $30 ($50 for international students). Electronic applications accepted. *Financial support:* In 2006–07, 4 research assistantships (averaging $12,797 per year) were awarded; career-related internships or fieldwork, Federal Work-Study, and institutionally sponsored loans also available. Support available to part-time students. *Faculty research:* Total quality management, participatory management, administering educational technology, school improvement, principalship. Total annual research expenditures: $344,504. *Unit head:* Dr. JoAnne Holbert, Assistant Dean, 313-577-1721, E-mail: jholbert@wayne.edu.

Educational Psychology

Alliant International University–Irvine, Graduate School of Education, Educational Psychology Programs, Irvine, CA 92612. Offers educational psychology (Psy D); pupil personnel services (Credential); school psychology (MA). Part-time programs available. *Students:* 27 full-time (24 women), 29 part-time (26 women); includes 18 minority (3 African Americans, 5 Asian Americans or Pacific Islanders, 10 Hispanic Americans). Average age 31. 39 applicants, 59% accepted, 22 enrolled. In 2006, 11 master's, 1 doctorate awarded. *Degree requirements:* For doctorate, thesis/dissertation. *Entrance requirements:* For master's, minimum GPA of 3.0, letters of recommendation; for doctorate, interview, minimum GPA of 3.0, letters of recommendation. Additional exam requirements/recommendations for international students: Required—TOEFL (minimum score 550 paper-based; 213 computer-based), TWE (minimum score 5). *Application deadline:* For fall admission, 7/1 priority date for domestic and international students; for spring admission, 12/1 priority date for domestic and international students. Application fee: $55. *Financial support:* Career-related internships or fieldwork, Federal Work-Study, institutionally sponsored loans, and scholarships/grants available. Financial award application deadline: 2/15; financial award applicants required to submit FAFSA. *Faculty research:* School based mental health. *Unit head:* Dr. Don Wofford, Systemwide Program Director, Fax: 949-833-3507, E-mail: admissions@alliant.edu. *Application contact:* Alliant International University Central Contact Center, 866-U-ALLIANT, Fax: 858-635-4555, E-mail: admissions@alliant.edu.

See Close-Up on page 1099.

Alliant International University–Los Angeles, Graduate School of Education, Educational Psychology Programs, Alhambra, CA 91803-1360. Offers educational psychology (Psy D); pupil personnel services (Credential); school psychology (MA). Part-time programs available. *Students:* 26 full-time (16 women), 23 part-time (15 women); includes 10 African Americans, 5 Asian Americans or Pacific Islanders, 18 Hispanic Americans, 1 international. Average age 43. 21 applicants, 67% accepted, 9 enrolled. In 2006, 3 doctorates awarded. *Degree requirements:* For doctorate, thesis/dissertation. *Entrance requirements:* For master's, minimum GPA of 3.0, letters of recommendation; for doctorate, interview, minimum GPA of 3.0, letters of recommendation. Additional exam requirements/recommendations for international students: Required—TOEFL (minimum score 550 paper-based; 213 computer-based), TWE (minimum score 5). *Application deadline:* For fall admission, 7/1 priority date for domestic and international students; for spring admission, 12/1 priority date for domestic and international students. Applications are processed on a rolling basis. Application fee: $55. Electronic applications accepted. *Financial support:* Career-related internships or fieldwork, Federal Work-Study, institutionally sponsored loans, and scholarships/grants available. Financial award application deadline: 2/15; financial award applicants required to submit FAFSA. *Faculty research:* Early identification and intervention with high-risk preschoolers, pediatric neuropsychology, interpersonal violence, ADHD, learning theories. *Unit head:* Dr. Carlton Parks, Program Director, 866-825-5426, Fax: 626-284-0550, E-mail: admissions@alliant.edu. *Application contact:* Alliant International University Central Contact Center, 866-U-ALLIANT, Fax: 858-635-4555, E-mail: admissions@alliant.edu.

See Close-Up on page 1099.

Alliant International University–San Diego, Graduate School of Education, Educational Psychology Programs, San Diego, CA 92131-1799. Offers educational psychology (Psy D); pupil personnel services (Credential); school psychology (MA); student personnel services (Certificate). Part-time programs available. *Students:* 30 full-time (25 women), 16 part-time (12 women); includes 11 minority (1 African American, 1 American Indian/Alaska Native, 2 Asian Americans or Pacific Islanders, 7 Hispanic Americans), 2 international. Average age 31. 38 applicants, 61% accepted, 18 enrolled. In 2006, 13 master's, 1 doctorate awarded. *Degree requirements:* For doctorate, thesis/dissertation. *Entrance requirements:* For master's, minimum GPA of 3.0, letters of recommendation; for doctorate, interview, letters of recommendation. Additional exam requirements/recommendations for international students: Required—TOEFL (minimum score 550 paper-based; 213 computer-based), TWE (minimum score 5). *Application deadline:* For fall admission, 7/1 priority date for domestic and international students; for spring admission, 12/1 priority date for domestic and international students. Applications are processed on a rolling basis. Application fee: $55. Electronic applications accepted. *Expenses:* Tuition: Part-time $825 per unit. Tuition and fees vary according to course load, degree level and program. *Financial support:* In 2006–07, 42 students received support. Career-related internships or fieldwork, Federal Work-Study, institutionally sponsored loans, and scholarships/grants available. Financial award application deadline: 2/15; financial award applicants required to submit FAFSA. *Unit head:* Dr. Don Wofford, Systemwide Program Director, 866-825-5426, Fax: 858-635-4739, E-mail: admissions@alliant.edu. *Application contact:* Alliant International University Central Contact Center, 866-U-ALLIANT, Fax: 858-635-4555, E-mail: admissions@alliant.edu.

See Close-Up on page 1099.

Alliant International University–San Francisco, Graduate School of Education, Educational Psychology Programs, San Francisco, CA 94133-1221. Offers educational psychology (Psy D); pupil personnel services (Credential); school psychology (MA). Part-time programs available. *Faculty:* 6. *Students:* 12 full-time (11 women), 6 part-time (5 women); includes 5 minority (4 African Americans, 1 Asian American or Pacific Islander). Average age 39. 21 applicants, 33% accepted, 6 enrolled. In 2006, 8 degrees awarded. *Degree requirements:* For doctorate, thesis/dissertation. *Entrance requirements:* For master's, minimum GPA of 3.0, letters of recommendation; for doctorate, interview, minimum GPA of 3.0, letters of recommendation. Additional exam requirements/recommendations for international students: Required—TOEFL (minimum score 550 paper-based; 213 computer-based), TWE (minimum score 5). *Application deadline:* For fall admission, 7/1 priority date for domestic and international students; for spring admission, 12/1 priority date for domestic and international students. Applications are processed on a rolling basis. Application fee: $55. Electronic applications accepted. *Expenses:* Tuition: Part-time $825 per unit. Tuition and fees vary according to course load, degree level and program. *Financial support:* Career-related internships or fieldwork, Federal Work-Study, institutionally sponsored loans, and scholarships/grants available. Financial award application deadline: 2/15; financial award applicants required to submit FAFSA. *Faculty research:* Social skills, ADHD, effects of sightedness on areas of knowledge. *Unit head:* Dr. James Hiromto, Systemwide Program Director, 866-825-5426, Fax: 415-955-2179, E-mail: admissions@alliant.edu. *Application contact:* Alliant International University Central Contact Center, 866-U-ALLIANT, Fax: 858-635-4555, E-mail: admissions@alliant.edu.

See Close-Up on page 1099.

American International College, School of Psychology and Education, Department of Education, Springfield, MA 01109-3189. Offers administration (M Ed, CAGS); child development (MA, Ed D), including educational psychology; elementary education (M Ed, CAGS); reading (M Ed, CAGS); secondary education (M Ed, CAGS); special education (M Ed, CAGS); teaching (MAT). Part-time and evening/weekend programs available. *Faculty:* 5 full-time (3 women), 15 part-time/adjunct (9 women). *Students:* 31 full-time (27 women), 268 part-time (217 women); includes 25 minority (13 African Americans, 4 Asian Americans or Pacific Islanders, 8 Hispanic Americans), 2 international. Average age 39. In 2006, 38 master's, 2 doctorates, 5 other advanced degrees awarded. Terminal master's awarded for partial completion of doctoral program. *Degree requirements:* For master's, thesis (for some programs), practicum, comprehensive exam (for some programs), registration; for doctorate, thesis/dissertation, comprehensive exam (for some programs), registration; for CAGS, practicum. *Entrance requirements:* For master's, minimum B- average in undergraduate course work; for doctorate, GRE General Test, interview. Additional exam requirements/recommendations for international students: Required—TOEFL. *Application deadline:* For fall admission, 7/1 priority date for domestic and international students; for spring admission, 12/1 priority date for domestic and international students. Applications are processed on a rolling basis. Application fee: $50. *Expenses:* Tuition: Part-time $585 per semester hour. Required fees: $100 per year. Full-time tuition and fees vary according to program. *Financial support:* Career-related internships or fieldwork and institutionally sponsored loans available. Financial award applicants required to submit FAFSA. *Unit head:* Dr. Barbara Dautrich, Chair, 413-205-3407, Fax: 413-205-3943, E-mail: barbara.dautrich@aic.edu. *Application contact:* Keshawn Dodds, Associate Director of Graduate Admissions, 413-205-3549, Fax: 413-205-3911, E-mail: keshawn.dodds@aic.edu.

American International College, School of Psychology and Education, Department of Psychology, Springfield, MA 01109-3189. Offers child development (MA, Ed D), including educational psychology; clinical psychology (MA); forensic psychology (MS). Part-time and evening/weekend programs available. *Faculty:* 8 full-time (3 women), 12 part-time/adjunct (5 women). *Students:* 50 full-time (43 women), 57 part-time (51 women); includes 22 minority (12 African Americans, 4 Asian Americans or Pacific Islanders, 6 Hispanic Americans), 2 international. Average age 35. In 2006, 33 master's, 2 doctorates awarded. *Degree requirements:* For master's, thesis (for some programs), practicum, comprehensive exam (for some programs), registration. *Entrance requirements:* For master's, minimum GPA of 3.0; for doctorate, GRE General Test, interview. Additional exam requirements/recommendations for international students: Required—TOEFL. *Application deadline:* For fall admission, 4/1 for domestic students, 4/15 for international students. Applications are processed on a rolling basis. Application fee: $50. Electronic applications accepted. *Expenses:* Tuition: Part-time $585 per semester hour. Required fees: $100 per year. Full-time tuition and fees vary according to program. *Financial support:* In 2006–07, 6 fellowships were awarded; career-related internships or fieldwork and institutionally sponsored loans also available. Financial award applicants required to submit FAFSA. *Unit head:* Dr. Richard Sprinthall, Chair, 413-205-3315, Fax: 413-205-3943, E-mail: richard.sprinthall@aic.edu. *Application contact:* Keshawn Dodds, Associate Director of Graduate Admissions, 413-205-3549, Fax: 413-205-3911, E-mail: keshawn.dodds@aic.edu.

Andrews University, School of Graduate Studies, School of Education, Department of Educational and Counseling Psychology, Program in Educational and Developmental Psychology, Berrien Springs, MI 49104. Offers educational and developmental psychology (MA); educational psychology (Ed D, PhD). *Degree requirements:* For master's, thesis optional.

Arcadia University, Graduate Studies, Department of Education, Glenside, PA 19038-3295. Offers art education (M Ed, MA Ed); biology education (MA Ed); chemistry education (MA Ed); child development (CAS); computer education (M Ed, CAS); computer education 7–12 (MA Ed); early childhood education (M Ed, CAS), including individualized (M Ed), master teacher (M Ed), research in child development (M Ed); educational leadership (M Ed, CAS); educational psychology (CAS); elementary education (M Ed, CAS); English education (MA Ed); environmental education (MA Ed, CAS); history education (MA Ed); language arts (M Ed, CAS); mathematics education (M Ed, MA Ed, CAS); music education (MA Ed); psychology (MA Ed); pupil personnel services (CAS); reading (M Ed, CAS); school library science (M Ed); science education (M Ed, CAS); secondary education (M Ed, CAS); special education (M Ed, Ed D, CAS); theater arts (MA Ed); written communication (MA Ed). *Accreditation:* NASAD. Part-time and evening/weekend programs available. Postbaccalaureate distance learning degree programs offered (minimal on-campus study). *Faculty:* 12 full-time (8 women), 38 part-time/adjunct (26 women). *Students:* 60 full-time (56 women), 419 part-time (324 women); includes 70 minority (57 African Americans, 1 American Indian/Alaska Native, 6 Asian Americans or Pacific Islanders, 6 Hispanic Americans), 1 international. In 2006, 257 master's, 4 doctorates awarded. *Application deadline:* Applications are processed on a rolling basis. Application fee: $35. Electronic applications accepted. *Financial support:* Career-related internships or fieldwork, tuition waivers (partial), and unspecified assistantships available. *Unit head:* Dr. Steven P. Gulkus, Chair, 215-572-2120. *Application contact:* 215-572-2925, Fax: 215-572-2126, E-mail: grad@arcadia.edu.

Arizona State University, Division of Graduate Studies, College of Education, Division of Psychology in Education, Academic Program in Educational Psychology, Tempe, AZ 85287. Offers M Ed, MA, PhD. *Accreditation:* APA. *Degree requirements:* For master's and doctorate, thesis/dissertation. *Entrance requirements:* For master's and doctorate, GRE General Test or MAT.

Educational Psychology

Auburn University, Graduate School, College of Education, Department of Educational Foundations, Leadership, and Technology, Auburn University, AL 36849. Offers adult education (M Ed, MS, Ed D); curriculum and instruction (M Ed, MS, Ed D, Ed S); curriculum supervision (M Ed, MS, Ed D, Ed S); educational psychology (PhD); higher education administration (M Ed, MS, Ed D, Ed S); media instructional design (MS); media specialist (M Ed); school administration (M Ed, MS, Ed D, Ed S). *Accreditation:* NCATE. Part-time programs available. *Faculty:* 23 full-time (11 women). *Students:* 40 full-time (26 women), 148 part-time (93 women); includes 64 minority (60 African Americans, 3 American Indian/Alaska Native, 1 Asian American or Pacific Islander), 6 international. Average age 38. 99 applicants, 57% accepted, 37 enrolled. In 2006, 32 master's, 10 doctorates, 7 other advanced degrees awarded. *Degree requirements:* For master's, thesis (for some programs); for doctorate, thesis/dissertation; for Ed S, field project. *Entrance requirements:* For master's, doctorate, and Ed S, GRE General Test. *Application deadline:* For fall admission, 7/7 for domestic students; for spring admission, 11/24 for domestic students. Applications are processed on a rolling basis. Application fee: $25 ($50 for international students). Electronic applications accepted. *Expenses:* Tuition, state resident: full-time $5,000. Tuition, nonresident: full-time $15,000. Required fees: $416. Tuition and fees vary according to program. *Financial support:* Teaching assistantships, Federal Work-Study available. Support available to part-time students. Financial award application deadline: 3/15. *Unit head:* Dr. William A. Spencer, Head, 334-844-4460. *Application contact:* Dr. Joe Pittman, Interim Dean of the Graduate School, 334-844-4700.

Ball State University, Graduate School, Teachers College, Department of Educational Psychology, Program in Educational Psychology, Muncie, IN 47306-1099. Offers MA, PhD, Ed S. *Accreditation:* NCATE. *Students:* 5 full-time (3 women), 14 part-time (13 women); includes 1 minority (African American), 1 international. Average age 27. 25 applicants, 36% accepted, 6 enrolled. In 2006, 4 degrees awarded. *Degree requirements:* For doctorate and Ed S, thesis/dissertation. *Entrance requirements:* For master's and Ed S, GRE General Test; for doctorate, GRE General Test, minimum graduate GPA of 3.2. Application fee: $25 ($35 for international students). *Financial support:* Application deadline: 3/1. *Unit head:* Dr. Felicia Dixon, Head, 785-285-8500, Fax: 785-285-3653.

Baylor University, Graduate School, School of Education, Department of Educational Psychology, Waco, TX 76798. Offers MA, MS Ed, PhD, Ed S. *Accreditation:* NCATE. Part-time programs available. *Faculty:* 6 full-time (3 women), 2 part-time/adjunct (1 woman). *Students:* 26 full-time (23 women), 22 part-time (18 women); includes 8 minority (7 African Americans, 1 Asian American or Pacific Islander), 3 international. In 2006, 12 master's, 1 doctorate, 1 other advanced degree awarded. *Degree requirements:* For doctorate, thesis/dissertation. *Entrance requirements:* For master's, GRE General Test; for doctorate, GRE General Test, master's degree. *Application deadline:* For fall admission, 8/1 for domestic students. Applications are processed on a rolling basis. Application fee: $25. *Financial support:* Federal Work-Study and institutionally sponsored loans available. *Faculty research:* Medical education, cross-cultural learning disabilities, characteristics of an ideal special education teacher, verbal following behavior in adult counseling groups. *Unit head:* Dr. Terrill Saxon, Chair, 254-710-3112, Fax: 254-710-3987, E-mail: terrill_saxon@baylor.edu. *Application contact:* Suzanne Keener, Administrative Assistant, 254-710-3588, Fax: 254-710-3870.

Boston College, Lynch Graduate School of Education, Department of Counseling Psychology, Developmental, and Educational Psychology, Program in Developmental and Educational Psychology, Chestnut Hill, MA 02467-3800. Offers MA, PhD. *Students:* 31 full-time (28 women), 6 part-time (5 women); includes 3 minority (1 African American, 1 Asian American or Pacific Islander, 1 Hispanic American), 7 international. 102 applicants, 34% accepted, 16 enrolled. In 2006, 21 master's, 3 doctorates awarded. Terminal master's awarded for partial completion of doctoral program. *Degree requirements:* For master's, comprehensive exam; for doctorate, thesis/dissertation, comprehensive exam. *Entrance requirements:* For master's, GRE General Test or MAT; for doctorate, GRE General Test. Additional exam requirements/recommendations for international students: Required—TOEFL. Application fee: $60. *Financial support:* Fellowships with full and partial tuition reimbursements, research assistantships with full and partial tuition reimbursements, teaching assistantships with full and partial tuition reimbursements, career-related internships or fieldwork, Federal Work-Study, scholarships/grants, traineeships, tuition waivers (full and partial), and unspecified assistantships available. Support available to part-time students. Financial award applicants required to submit FAFSA. *Faculty research:* Cognitive learning and culture, effects of social policy reform on children and families, youth empowerment, impact of poverty and violence on families and communities, psychosocial trauma, human rights and international justice. *Application contact:* Timothy P. Blackman, Director, Graduate Admission and Financial Aid, 617-552-4214, Fax: 617-552-0398, E-mail: timothy.blackman.1@bc.edu.

Brigham Young University, Graduate Studies, David O. McKay School of Education, Department of Instructional Psychology and Technology, Provo, UT 84602-1001. Offers MS, PhD. *Faculty:* 9 full-time (0 women), 10 part-time/adjunct (2 women). *Students:* 48 full-time (24 women), 24 part-time (10 women); includes 1 minority (Asian American or Pacific Islander), 13 international. Average age 36. 43 applicants, 42% accepted, 14 enrolled. In 2006, 5 master's, 6 doctorates awarded. *Median time to degree:* Of those who began their doctoral program in fall 1998, 50% received their degree in 8 years or less. *Degree requirements:* For master's, thesis/dissertation; for doctorate, thesis/dissertation, comprehensive exam. *Entrance requirements:* For master's and doctorate, GRE General Test. Additional exam requirements/recommendations for international students: Required—TOEFL. *Application deadline:* For fall and winter admission, 2/1 for domestic and international students. Application fee: $50. Electronic applications accepted. *Financial support:* In 2006–07, 23 students received support, including 6 research assistantships with full and partial tuition reimbursements available (averaging $10,000 per year), 14 teaching assistantships with full and partial tuition reimbursements available (averaging $6,000 per year); career-related internships or fieldwork, tuition waivers (full and partial), and unspecified assistantships also available. Support available to part-time students. *Faculty research:* Interactive learning, learning theory, instructional designed development, research and evaluation, measurement. Total annual research expenditures: $2,520. *Unit head:* Dr. Andrew S. Gibbons, Chair, 801-422-5097, Fax: 801-422-0314, E-mail: andy_gibbons@byu.edu. *Application contact:* Michele Bray, Department Secretary, 801-422-2746, Fax: 801-422-0314, E-mail: michele_bray@byu.edu.

California State University, Northridge, Graduate Studies, College of Education, Department of Educational Psychology and Counseling, Northridge, CA 91330. Offers counseling (MS), including career counseling, college counseling and student services, marriage and family therapy, school counseling, school psychology; educational psychology (MA Ed), including development, learning, and instruction, early childhood education; genetic counseling (MS). *Accreditation:* ACA (one or more programs are accredited); NCATE. Part-time and evening/weekend programs available. *Faculty:* 19 full-time (11 women), 57 part-time/adjunct (39 women). *Students:* 344 full-time (50 women), 135 part-time (19 women); includes 210 minority (26 African Americans, 3 American Indian/Alaska Native, 40 Asian Americans or Pacific Islanders, 141 Hispanic Americans), 11 international. Average age 32. 244 applicants, 62% accepted, 116 enrolled. In 2006, 176 degrees awarded. *Entrance requirements:* For master's, GRE General Test, MAT, or minimum GPA of 3.0. Additional exam requirements/recommendations for international students: Required—TOEFL. *Application deadline:* For fall admission, 11/30 for domestic students. Application fee: $55. *Expenses:* Tuition, nonresident: full-time $8,136; part-time $4,068 per year. Required fees: $3,624; $1,161 per term. *Financial support:* Scholarships/grants available. Support available to part-time students. Financial award application deadline: 3/1. *Unit head:* Dr. Beverly Cabello, Chair, 818-677-2599. *Application contact:* Todd Wolfe, Graduate Advisor, 818-677-5719.

California State University, San Bernardino, Graduate Studies, College of Education, San Bernardino, CA 92407-2397. Offers bilingual/cross-cultural education (MA); curriculum and instruction (MA); educational administration (MA); educational psychology and counseling (MA, MS), including counseling and guidance (MS), rehabilitation counseling (MA); elementary education (MA); English as a second language (MA); environmental education (MA); history and English for secondary teachers (MA); instructional technology (MA); reading (MA); secondary education (MA); special education and rehabilitation counseling (MA), including rehabilitation counseling, special education; teaching of science (MA); vocational and career education (MA). *Accreditation:* NCATE. Part-time and evening/weekend programs available. *Faculty:* 69 full-time, 145 part-time/adjunct. *Students:* 692 full-time (515 women), 345 part-time (245 women); includes 479 minority (145 African Americans, 12 American Indian/Alaska Native, 45 Asian Americans or Pacific Islanders, 277 Hispanic Americans), 17 international. Average age 33. 450 applicants, 82% accepted, 147 enrolled. In 2006, 349 degrees awarded. *Entrance requirements:* For master's, minimum GPA of 3.0 in education. *Application deadline:* For fall admission, 8/31 priority date for domestic students. Application fee: $55. *Financial support:* Career-related internships or fieldwork and Federal Work-Study available. Support available to part-time students. *Faculty research:* Multicultural education, brain-based learning, science education, social studies/global education. *Unit head:* Dr. Patricia Arlin, Dean, 909-537-5600, Fax: 909-537-7011, E-mail: parlin@csusb.edu.

Capella University, Harold Abel School of Psychology, Minneapolis, MN 55402. Offers clinical psychology (MS); counseling psychology (MS); educational psychology (MS, PhD); general psychology (MS, PhD); industrial/organizational psychology (MS, PhD); school psychology (MS, Certificate); sport psychology (MS). Part-time and evening/weekend programs available. Postbaccalaureate distance learning degree programs offered (minimal on-campus study). Terminal master's awarded for partial completion of doctoral program. *Degree requirements:* For master's, project, thesis optional; for doctorate, thesis/dissertation. *Entrance requirements:* For degree, master's degree in school psychology. Additional exam requirements/recommendations for international students: Required—TOEFL (minimum score 550 paper-based; 213 computer-based), TWE (minimum score 4). Electronic applications accepted. *Faculty research:* Correctional mental health delivery, community mental health, attachment and caregiving in adult and family relationships, influence of encouragement on motivation, and moral dilemmas in business.

The Catholic University of America, School of Arts and Sciences, Department of Education, Washington, DC 20064. Offers administration, curriculum, and policy studies (MA); Catholic school leadership (MA); counselor education (MA); educational administration (PhD); educational psychology (PhD); English as a second language (MA); learning and instruction (MA); policy studies (PhD); teacher education (MA). *Accreditation:* NCATE. Part-time programs available. *Faculty:* 11 full-time (8 women), 3 part-time/adjunct (2 women). *Students:* 11 full-time (8 women), 52 part-time (34 women); includes 13 minority (9 African Americans, 1 Asian American or Pacific Islander, 3 Hispanic Americans), 2 international. Average age 35. 67 applicants, 55% accepted, 13 enrolled. In 2006, 19 master's, 2 doctorates awarded. *Degree requirements:* For master's, thesis or alternative, comprehensive exam; for doctorate, thesis/dissertation, comprehensive exam. *Entrance requirements:* For master's and doctorate, GRE General Test or MAT, 3 letters of recommendation. Additional exam requirements/recommendations for international students: Required—TOEFL (minimum score 580 paper-based; 237 computer-based). *Application deadline:* For fall admission, 2/1 priority date for domestic students; for spring admission, 11/15 priority date for domestic students. Applications are processed on a rolling basis. Application fee: $55. Electronic applications accepted. *Expenses:* Tuition: Full-time $27,700; part-time $1,045 per credit hour. Required fees: $1,290. Part-time tuition and fees vary according to campus/location and program. *Financial support:* Research assistantships, teaching assistantships, career-related internships or fieldwork, Federal Work-Study, scholarships/grants, tuition waivers (full and partial), and unspecified assistantships available. Support available to part-time students. Financial award application deadline: 2/1; financial award applicants required to submit FAFSA. *Faculty research:* Catholic school issues, reflective teaching, cognitive psychology, urban education. *Unit head:* Dr. Merylann Schuttloffel, Chair, 202-319-5805, Fax: 202-319-5815, E-mail: schuttloffel@cua.edu.

Chapman University, Graduate Studies, School of Education, Program in Educational Psychology, Orange, CA 92866. Offers educational psychology (MA); school psychology (Ed S). Part-time and evening/weekend programs available. *Faculty:* 16 full-time (11 women), 25 part-time/adjunct (14 women). *Students:* 45 full-time (35 women), 11 part-time (6 women); includes 2 African Americans, 4 Asian Americans or Pacific Islanders. Average age 27. 60 applicants, 25% accepted, 8 enrolled. In 2006, 43 degrees awarded. *Degree requirements:* For master's, comprehensive exam, registration. *Entrance requirements:* For master's, GRE General Test, MAT, or California Subject Examinations for Teachers, minimum undergraduate GPA of 2.75. Additional exam requirements/recommendations for international students: Required—TOEFL (minimum score 550 paper-based). *Application deadline:* Applications are processed on a rolling basis. Application fee: $55. Electronic applications accepted. *Expenses:* Contact institution. *Financial support:* In 2006–07, 52 students received support, including 18 fellowships (averaging $2,000 per year); Federal Work-Study also available. Financial award application deadline: 6/30; financial award applicants required to submit FAFSA. *Unit head:* Dr. Michael Hass, Coordinator, 714-997-6781, E-mail: hass@chapman.edu. *Application contact:* Rika Judd, Information Contact, 714-997-6786, Fax: 714-997-6713, E-mail: rjudd@chapman.edu.

Clark Atlanta University, School of Education, Department of Counseling and Psychological Services, Atlanta, GA 30314. Offers counseling (MA, PhD); education psychology (MA). *Degree requirements:* For master's, one foreign language, thesis; for doctorate, 2 foreign languages, thesis/dissertation. *Entrance requirements:* For master's, GRE General Test, minimum undergraduate GPA of 2.5; for doctorate, GRE General Test, minimum graduate GPA of 3.0.

The College of Saint Rose, Graduate Studies, School of Education, Educational and School Psychology Department, Albany, NY 12203-1419. Offers applied technology education (MS Ed); educational psychology (MS Ed); school psychology (MS, Adv C). Part-time and evening/weekend programs available. *Entrance requirements:* For master's, minimum undergraduate GPA of 3.0. Additional exam requirements/recommendations for international students: Required—TOEFL (minimum score 550 paper-based; 213 computer-based). Electronic applications accepted.

Eastern Michigan University, Graduate School, College of Education, Department of Teacher Education, Programs in Educational Psychology, Ypsilanti, MI 48197. Offers MA. *Accreditation:* NCATE. Part-time and evening/weekend programs available. Postbaccalaureate distance learning degree programs offered (minimal on-campus study). *Students:* Average age 34. In 2006, 5 degrees awarded. *Degree requirements:* For master's, thesis or alternative. *Entrance requirements:* For master's, GRE. Additional exam requirements/recommendations for international students: Required—TOEFL. *Application deadline:* For fall admission, 5/15 priority date for domestic students, 5/1 priority date for international students; for winter admission, 10/15 priority date for domestic students, 10/1 priority date for international students; for spring admission, 3/15 priority date for domestic students, 3/1 priority date for international students. Applications are processed on a rolling basis. Application fee: $35. *Expenses:* Tuition, state resident: part-time $341 per credit hour. Tuition, nonresident: full-time $16,104; part-time $671 per credit hour. Required fees: $816; $34 per credit hour. $40 per term. One-time fee: $82 full-time. Tuition and fees vary according to course level, course load, degree level and reciprocity agreements. *Financial support:* Fellowships, research assistantships with full tuition reimbursements, teaching assistantships with full tuition reimbursements, career-related internships or fieldwork, Federal Work-Study, institutionally sponsored loans, scholarships/grants, tuition waivers (partial), and unspecified assistantships available. Support available to part-time students. Financial award applicants required to submit FAFSA.

Eastern University, Programs in Counseling, Program in Educational Counseling, St. Davids, PA 19087-3696. Offers school counseling (MA); school psychology (MS). *Degree requirements:* For master's, internship. *Entrance requirements:* For master's, minimum GPA of 2.5. Additional exam requirements/recommendations for international students: Required—TOEFL.

Edinboro University of Pennsylvania, Graduate Studies and Research, School of Education, Department of Special Education and School Psychology, Program in Educational Psychology, Edinboro, PA 16444. Offers M Ed. Part-time and evening/weekend programs available.

Educational Psychology

Edinboro University of Pennsylvania (continued)

Students: 18 full-time (16 women), 5 part-time (all women). Average age 29. In 2006, 19 degrees awarded. *Degree requirements:* For master's, thesis or alternative, competency exam. *Entrance requirements:* For master's, GRE or MAT, minimum QPA of 2.5. *Application deadline:* Applications are processed on a rolling basis. Application fee: $30. *Expenses:* Tuition, state resident: full-time $6,048; part-time $336 per credit. Tuition, nonresident: full-time $9,678; part-time $538 per credit. Required fees: $1,849; $42 per credit. *Financial support:* In 2006–07, 8 research assistantships with full and partial tuition reimbursements (averaging $3,850 per year) were awarded; career-related internships or fieldwork, Federal Work-Study, scholarships/grants, and unspecified assistantships also available. Support available to part-time students. Financial award application deadline: 2/15; financial award applicants required to submit FAFSA. *Unit head:* Dr. Edward Snyder, Coordinator, 814-732-1099, Fax: 814-732-2268, E-mail: esnyder@edinboro.edu. *Application contact:* Dr. R. Scott Baldwin, Dean, 814-732-2752, Fax: 814-732-2268, E-mail: sbaldwin@edinboro.edu.

Florida Atlantic University, College of Education, Department of Teacher Education, Boca Raton, FL 33431-0991. Offers art teacher education (M Ed); curriculum and instruction (M Ed, Ed D, Ed S); educational psychology (MSF); elementary education (M Ed); foundations of education (M Ed); multicultural education (MSF); reading teacher education (M Ed). *Accreditation:* NCATE. Part-time and evening/weekend programs available. *Faculty:* 29 full-time (23 women), 75 part-time/adjunct (50 women). *Students:* 78 full-time (65 women), 176 part-time (159 women); includes 50 minority (20 African Americans, 1 American Indian/Alaska Native, 6 Asian Americans or Pacific Islanders, 23 Hispanic Americans), 1 international. Average age 35. 132 applicants, 64% accepted, 62 enrolled. In 2006, 95 master's, 2 doctorates awarded. *Degree requirements:* For master's, registration; for doctorate, thesis/dissertation, departmental qualifying exam, comprehensive exam, registration; for Ed S, departmental qualifying exam. *Entrance requirements:* For master's, GRE General Test, minimum GPA of 3.0 in last 2 years of undergraduate course work; for doctorate, GRE General Test, GRE Subject Test, minimum graduate GPA of 3.2, 3.0 in last 2 years of undergraduate course work; for Ed S, GRE General Test. Additional exam requirements/recommendations for international students: Required—TOEFL. *Application deadline:* Applications are processed on a rolling basis. Application fee: $30. *Expenses:* Tuition, area resident: Full-time $4,394. Tuition, nonresident: full-time $16,441. *Financial support:* In 2006–07, 4 research assistantships with partial tuition reimbursements (averaging $8,000 per year), 3 teaching assistantships with partial tuition reimbursements (averaging $8,000 per year) were awarded; fellowships with partial tuition reimbursements, career-related internships or fieldwork, scholarships/grants, and unspecified assistantships also available. *Faculty research:* Technology, teaching English to speakers of other languages, math teaching, electronic portfolio assessment, global perspectives through social studies. *Unit head:* Dr. Penelope Fritzer, Chairperson, 561-297-3584.

Florida State University, Graduate Studies, College of Education, Department of Educational Psychology and Learning Systems, Program in Educational Psychology, Tallahassee, FL 32306. Offers learning and cognition (MS, PhD); sports psychology (MS, PhD). *Faculty:* 6 full-time (3 women), 4 part-time/adjunct (2 women). *Students:* 33 full-time (20 women), 25 part-time (14 women); includes 13 minority (5 African Americans, 4 Asian Americans or Pacific Islanders, 4 Hispanic Americans). Average age 20. 82 applicants, 43% accepted, 16 enrolled. In 2006, 2 master's, 2 doctorates awarded. *Degree requirements:* For master's, thesis optional; for doctorate, thesis/dissertation, comprehensive exam. *Entrance requirements:* For master's and doctorate, GRE General Test, minimum GPA of 3.0. *Application deadline:* For fall admission, 7/1 priority date for domestic students; for spring admission, 11/1 for domestic students. Applications are processed on a rolling basis. Application fee: $30. *Expenses:* Tuition, state resident: full-time $5,822; part-time $243 per credit hour. Tuition, nonresident: full-time $20,976; part-time $874 per credit hour. Tuition and fees vary according to program. *Financial support:* In 2006–07, fellowships with partial tuition reimbursements (averaging $5,000 per year), research assistantships with partial tuition reimbursements (averaging $18,000 per year), teaching assistantships with partial tuition reimbursements (averaging $18,000 per year) were awarded; career-related internships or fieldwork also available. Financial award applicants required to submit FAFSA. *Unit head:* Dr. Susan Losh, Program Leader, 850-644-8776, Fax: 850-644-8776, E-mail: slosh@coe.fsu.edu. *Application contact:* Sally Gadson, Program Assistant, 850-644-8046, Fax: 850-644-5067, E-mail: gadson@coe.fsu.edu.

Fordham University, Graduate School of Education, Division of Psychological and Educational Services, New York, NY 10023. Offers counseling and personnel services (MSE, Adv C); counseling psychology (PhD); educational psychology (MSE, PhD); school psychology (PhD); urban and urban bilingual school psychology (Adv C). *Accreditation:* APA (one or more programs are accredited); NCATE. *Faculty:* 18 full-time (11 women), 23 part-time/adjunct (14 women). *Students:* 118 full-time (90 women), 272 part-time (206 women); includes 106 minority (39 African Americans, 20 Asian Americans or Pacific Islanders, 47 Hispanic Americans), 1 international. Average age 30. 503 applicants, 58% accepted, 102 enrolled. In 2006, 117 master's, 18 doctorates, 6 other advanced degrees awarded. *Degree requirements:* For doctorate, thesis/dissertation. *Entrance requirements:* For doctorate, GRE General Test. Application fee: $65. *Financial support:* Applicants required to submit FAFSA. *Unit head:* Dr. Mitch Rabinowitz, Chairman, 212-636-6461.

Georgian Court University, School of Sciences and Mathematics, Lakewood, NJ 08701-2697. Offers biology (MS); counseling psychology (MA); holistic health (Certificate); holistic health studies (MA); mathematics (MA); professional counselor (Certificate); school psychology (Certificate). Part-time and evening/weekend programs available. *Faculty:* 17 full-time (10 women), 6 part-time/adjunct (3 women). *Students:* 35 full-time (31 women), 109 part-time (94 women); includes 13 minority (7 African Americans, 1 American Indian/Alaska Native, 3 Asian Americans or Pacific Islanders, 2 Hispanic Americans), 1 international. Average age 36. 80 applicants, 71% accepted, 44 enrolled. In 2006, 33 master's, 11 other advanced degrees awarded. *Degree requirements:* For master's, thesis (for some programs), comprehensive exam (for some programs). *Entrance requirements:* For master's, GRE General Test, GRE Subject Test in biology (MS), 3 letters of recommendation. Additional exam requirements/recommendations for international students: Required—TOEFL (minimum score 550 paper-based; 213 computer-based). *Application deadline:* For fall admission, 8/1 priority date for domestic students, 4/1 for international students; for spring admission, 1/1 priority date for domestic students, 7/1 for international students. Applications are processed on a rolling basis. Application fee: $40. Electronic applications accepted. *Financial support:* Scholarships/grants, health care benefits, and unspecified assistantships available. Financial award application deadline: 4/15; financial award applicants required to submit FAFSA. *Unit head:* Dr. Linda James, Dean, 732-987-2617. *Application contact:* Eugene Soltys, Director of Graduate Admissions, 732-987-2760 Ext. 2760, Fax: 732-987-2000, E-mail: admissions@georgian.edu.

Georgia State University, College of Education, Department of Educational Psychology and Special Education, Program in Educational Psychology, Atlanta, GA 30303-3083. Offers MS, PhD. *Accreditation:* NCATE. Part-time and evening/weekend programs available. *Students:* 20 full-time (16 women), 22 part-time (17 women); includes 12 minority (10 African Americans, 2 Asian Americans or Pacific Islanders). Average age 36. 17 applicants, 65% accepted. In 2006, 2 master's, 2 doctorates awarded. *Degree requirements:* For master's, thesis or project; for doctorate, thesis/dissertation, comprehensive exam. *Entrance requirements:* For master's, GRE General Test, minimum GPA of 2.5; for doctorate, GRE General Test, minimum GPA of 3.3. Application fee: $25. *Financial support:* Research assistantships, teaching assistantships available. *Faculty research:* Cognitive and language development, language development of deaf children, reading in adult populations. *Unit head:* Dr. Ron P. Colarusso, Dean, College of Education, 404-651-2310.

Graduate School and University Center of the City University of New York, Graduate Studies, Program in Educational Psychology, New York, NY 10016-4039. Offers PhD. *Accreditation:* APA. *Faculty:* 19 full-time (9 women). *Students:* 106 full-time (82 women), 22 part-time (18 women); includes 13 minority (5 African Americans, 5 Asian Americans or Pacific Islanders, 3 Hispanic Americans), 12 international. Average age 35. 75 applicants, 36% accepted, 18 enrolled. In 2006, 3 degrees awarded. *Degree requirements:* For doctorate, 2 foreign languages, thesis/dissertation. *Entrance requirements:* For doctorate, GRE General Test, interview, minimum GPA of 3.0. Additional exam requirements/recommendations for international students: Required—TOEFL. *Application deadline:* For fall admission, 4/15 for domestic students. Application fee: $125. Electronic applications accepted. *Financial support:* In 2006–07, 45 students received support, including 36 fellowships, 4 research assistantships, 2 teaching assistantships; career-related internships or fieldwork, Federal Work-Study, institutionally sponsored loans, and tuition waivers (full and partial) also available. Financial award application deadline: 2/1; financial award applicants required to submit FAFSA. *Unit head:* Dr. Alan Gross, Executive Officer, 212-817-8286, Fax: 212-817-1516.

Harvard University, Graduate School of Education, Master's Programs in Education, Cambridge, MA 02138. Offers arts in education (Ed M); education policy and management (Ed M); higher education (Ed M); human development and psychology (Ed M); international education policy (Ed M); language and literacy (Ed M); learning and teaching (Ed M); mid-career mathematics and science (teaching certificate) (Ed M); mind brain and education (Ed M); risk and prevention (Ed M); school leadership (Ed M); special studies (Ed M); teaching and curriculum (teaching certificate) (Ed M); technology innovation and education (Ed M). Part-time programs available. *Faculty:* 58 full-time (25 women), 40 part-time/adjunct (22 women). *Students:* 540 full-time (412 women), 90 part-time (70 women); includes 137 minority (49 African Americans, 2 American Indian/Alaska Native, 61 Asian Americans or Pacific Islanders, 25 Hispanic Americans), 70 international. Average age 29. 1,211 applicants, 61% accepted, 585 enrolled. In 2006, 591 degrees awarded. *Entrance requirements:* For master's, GRE General Test, 3 letters of recommendation, official transcripts, statement of purpose. Additional exam requirements/recommendations for international students: Required—TOEFL (minimum score 600 paper-based; 250 computer-based; 100 iBT), TWE (minimum score 5). *Application deadline:* For fall admission, 1/2 for domestic and international students. Application fee: $85. Electronic applications accepted. *Expenses:* Contact institution. *Financial support:* In 2006–07, 392 students received support, including 23 fellowships (averaging $15,870 per year); career-related internships or fieldwork, Federal Work-Study, institutionally sponsored loans, scholarships/grants, health care benefits, tuition waivers (full and partial), and unspecified assistantships also available. Support available to part-time students. Financial award application deadline: 2/2; financial award applicants required to submit FAFSA. *Faculty research:* Learning and development; educational leadership and organizations; educational policy analysis. Total annual research expenditures: $14.8 million. *Unit head:* Dr. James Stiles, Associate Dean for Degree Programs. *Application contact:* Information Contact, 617-495-3414, Fax: 617-496-3577, E-mail: gseadmissions@harvard.edu.

Holy Names University, Graduate Division, Department of Education, Oakland, CA 94619-1699. Offers advanced curriculum studies (M Ed); educational therapy (M Ed); mild/moderate disabilities (Ed S); multiple subject credential (M Ed); single subject credential (M Ed); special education (M Ed); teaching English as a second language (M Ed, Certificate); urban education (M Ed). Part-time programs available. *Faculty:* 6 full-time (all women), 9 part-time/adjunct (all women). *Students:* 17 full-time (14 women), 131 part-time (90 women); includes 58 minority (36 African Americans, 1 American Indian/Alaska Native, 11 Asian Americans or Pacific Islanders, 10 Hispanic Americans). Average age 40. 75 applicants, 80% accepted, 49 enrolled. In 2006, 11 master's, 29 Certificates awarded. *Degree requirements:* For master's, research paper, thesis or project. *Entrance requirements:* For master's, minimum undergraduate GPA of 2.6 overall, 3.0 in major. Additional exam requirements/recommendations for international students: Required—TOEFL. *Application deadline:* For fall admission, 8/1 priority date for domestic students; for spring admission, 12/1 priority date for domestic students. Applications are processed on a rolling basis. Application fee: $50. *Expenses:* Tuition: Full-time $10,800; part-time $600 per unit. Required fees: $240; $120 per term. *Financial support:* In 2006–07, 67 students received support. Scholarships/grants available. Support available to part-time students. Financial award application deadline: 3/2; financial award applicants required to submit FAFSA. *Faculty research:* Cognitive development, language development, learning handicaps. *Unit head:* Dr. Zaida McCall-Perez, Chairperson, 510-436-1288, E-mail: mccall-perez@hnu.edu. *Application contact:* 800-430-1351, Fax: 510-436-1325, E-mail: admissions@hnu.edu.

Howard University, School of Education, Department of Human Development and Psychoeducational Studies, Program in Educational Psychology, Washington, DC 20059-0002. Offers M Ed, MA, Ed D, PhD, CAGS. MA and PhD offered through the Graduate School of Arts and Sciences. Part-time programs available. *Faculty:* 4 full-time (2 women). *Students:* 11 full-time (8 women), 15 part-time (12 women); includes 22 minority (all African Americans), 1 international. Average age 31. 20 applicants, 55% accepted, 3 enrolled. In 2006, 1 master's, 3 doctorates awarded. Terminal master's awarded for partial completion of doctoral program. *Degree requirements:* For master's, thesis (for some programs), expository writing exam, comprehensive exam; for doctorate, one foreign language, thesis/dissertation, expository writing exam, internship, comprehensive exam. *Entrance requirements:* For master's, GRE General Test, minimum GPA of 2.7; for doctorate, GRE General Test, minimum GPA of 3.4; for CAGS, GRE General Test, minimum graduate GPA of 3.0. *Application deadline:* For fall admission, 4/1 priority date for domestic students; for spring admission, 11/1 for domestic students. Applications are processed on a rolling basis. Application fee: $45. *Financial support:* In 2006–07, 8 students received support; fellowships, research assistantships, teaching assistantships, career-related internships or fieldwork, Federal Work-Study, institutionally sponsored loans, and scholarships/grants available. Financial award application deadline: 4/1. *Unit head:* Dr. Kimberly E. Freeman, Assistant Professor/Coordinator, 202-865-0612, Fax: 202-806-5205, E-mail: kefreeman@howard.edu.

Illinois State University, Graduate School, College of Arts and Sciences, Department of Psychology, Normal, IL 61790-2200. Offers psychology (MA, MS), including clinical psychology, counseling psychology, developmental psychology, educational psychology, experimental psychology, measurement-evaluation, organizational-industrial psychology; school psychology (PhD, SSP). *Accreditation:* APA. *Faculty:* 38 full-time (15 women). *Students:* 53 full-time (34 women), 20 part-time (12 women); includes 3 minority (1 African American, 1 Asian American or Pacific Islander, 1 Hispanic American), 8 international. 148 applicants, 30% accepted. In 2006, 16 degrees awarded. *Degree requirements:* For master's, thesis or alternative; for doctorate, variable foreign language requirement, thesis/dissertation, 2 terms of residency, internship, practicum. *Entrance requirements:* For master's, GRE General Test, GRE Subject Test, minimum GPA of 3.0 in last 60 hours of course work; for doctorate, GRE General Test. *Application deadline:* Applications are processed on a rolling basis. Application fee: $40. *Expenses:* Tuition, state resident: full-time $3,330; part-time $185 per credit hour. Tuition, nonresident: full-time $6,948; part-time $438 per credit hour. Required fees: $1,259; $52 per credit hour. *Financial support:* In 2006–07, 7 research assistantships (averaging $5,406 per year), 25 teaching assistantships (averaging $4,230 per year) were awarded; tuition waivers (full) and unspecified assistantships also available. Financial award application deadline: 4/1. *Faculty research:* The autism project Jumpstart: providing low-income preschool children with early literary experiences, internship in clinical counseling psychology. Total annual research expenditures: $292,085. *Unit head:* Dr. David Barone, Chairperson, 309-438-8651.

Indiana State University, School of Graduate Studies, College of Education, Department of Educational and School Psychology, Terre Haute, IN 47809-1401. Offers school psychology (M Ed, PhD, Ed S). *Accreditation:* APA (one or more programs are accredited); NCATE. *Faculty:* 5 full-time (2 women), 7 part-time/adjunct (4 women). *Students:* 24 full-time (20 women), 22 part-time (21 women); includes 5 minority (2 African Americans, 1 Asian American or Pacific Islander, 2 Hispanic Americans), 1 international. Average age 29. 38 applicants, 50% accepted, 7 enrolled. In 2006, 14 master's, 2 doctorates, 6 other advanced degrees awarded. *Degree requirements:* For doctorate, thesis/dissertation, comprehensive exam, registration; for Ed S, research project. *Entrance requirements:* For master's, GRE General Test, minimum undergraduate GPA of 2.5; for doctorate, GRE General Test, minimum graduate GPA of 3.5;

for Ed S, GRE General Test, minimum graduate GPA of 3.25. *Application deadline:* For fall admission, 7/1 priority date for domestic students; for spring admission, 11/1 priority date for domestic students. Applications are processed on a rolling basis. Application fee: $35. Electronic applications accepted. *Expenses:* Tuition, state resident: part-time $278 per credit. Tuition, nonresident: part-time $552 per credit. *Financial support:* In 2006–07, 18 research assistantships with partial tuition reimbursements (averaging $5,340 per year) were awarded; fellowships with partial tuition reimbursements, teaching assistantships with partial tuition reimbursements, career-related internships or fieldwork, Federal Work-Study, institutionally sponsored loans, and unspecified assistantships also available. Financial award application deadline: 3/1; financial award applicants required to submit FAFSA. *Faculty research:* Cognitive behavior modification, moral development, emotional handicaps, personality assessments, human development. *Unit head:* Dr. Eric Hampton, Interim Chairperson, 812-237-2884.

Indiana University Bloomington, School of Education, Department of Counseling and Educational Psychology, Bloomington, IN 47405-7000. Offers counseling (MS, PhD, Ed S); counseling psychology (PhD); counselor education (MS, Ed S); educational psychology (MS, PhD); learning and developmental sciences (MS, PhD); school psychology (PhD, Ed S). PhD offered through the University Graduate School. *Accreditation:* ACA (one or more programs are accredited); APA (one or more programs are accredited); NCATE. *Students:* 96 full-time (72 women), 79 part-time (56 women); includes 16 minority (10 African Americans, 4 Asian Americans or Pacific Islanders, 2 Hispanic Americans), 38 international. Average age 29. In 2006, 50 degrees awarded. Terminal master's awarded for partial completion of doctoral program. *Degree requirements:* For master's, thesis optional; for doctorate, thesis/dissertation; for Ed S, comprehensive exam or project. *Entrance requirements:* For master's, doctorate, and Ed S, GRE General Test. *Application deadline:* For fall admission, 6/1 for domestic students, 3/1 for international students; for winter admission, 11/1 for domestic students; for spring admission, 9/1 for international students. Applications are processed on a rolling basis. Application fee: $50 ($60 for international students). Electronic applications accepted. *Expenses:* Tuition, state resident: full-time $5,791; part-time $241 per credit hour. Tuition, nonresident: full-time $16,866; part-time $703 per credit hour. *Financial support:* Fellowships with partial tuition reimbursements, research assistantships with partial tuition reimbursements, teaching assistantships with partial tuition reimbursements, career-related internships or fieldwork, Federal Work-Study, institutionally sponsored loans, tuition waivers (full and partial), and unspecified assistantships available. Support available to part-time students. *Faculty research:* Affective and maturational factors in learning complex cognitive tasks, children's strategies for representing depth, prime time evaluation, rural school psychology. *Unit head:* Dr. Joyce Alexander, Chairperson, 812-856-8300.

Indiana University of Pennsylvania, School of Graduate Studies and Research, College of Education and Educational Technology, Department of Educational and School Psychology, Program in Educational Psychology, Indiana, PA 15705-1087. Offers M Ed, Certificate. *Accreditation:* NCATE. Part-time and evening/weekend programs available. *Faculty:* 5 full-time (2 women). *Students:* 15 full-time (12 women), 6 part-time (5 women); includes 1 minority (African American), 1 international. Average age 24. 50 applicants, 42% accepted. In 2006, 12 degrees awarded. *Degree requirements:* For master's, thesis optional. *Entrance requirements:* For master's, GRE General Test, GRE Subject Test, 2 letters of recommendation. Additional exam requirements/recommendations for international students: Required—TOEFL. *Application deadline:* For fall admission, 7/1 priority date for domestic students; for spring admission, 11/1 for domestic students. Applications are processed on a rolling basis. Application fee: $30. *Expenses:* Tuition, state resident: full-time $6,048; part-time $336 per credit. Tuition, nonresident: full-time $9,678; part-time $538 per credit. Required fees: $1,069; $148 per year. *Financial support:* In 2006–07, 2 fellowships (averaging $500 per year), 12 research assistantships with full and partial tuition reimbursements (averaging $4,990 per year) were awarded; career-related internships or fieldwork and Federal Work-Study also available. Support available to part-time students. Financial award application deadline: 3/15; financial award applicants required to submit FAFSA. *Unit head:* Dr. Victoria Damiani, Graduate Coordinator, 724-357-3783, E-mail: vdamiani@iup.edu.

John Carroll University, Graduate School, Department of Education and Allied Studies, Program in Educational and School Psychology, University Heights, OH 44118-4581. Offers M Ed, MA. *Accreditation:* NCATE. Part-time and evening/weekend programs available. *Faculty:* 2 full-time (1 woman). *Students:* 19 full-time (18 women), 10 part-time (9 women); includes 1 minority (African American) Average age 31. 7 applicants, 43% accepted, 2 enrolled. In 2006, 7 degrees awarded. *Degree requirements:* For master's, research essay or thesis (MA only). *Entrance requirements:* For master's, GRE General Test or MAT, minimum GPA of 2.75. *Application deadline:* For fall admission, 8/15 priority date for domestic students; for spring admission, 1/3 for domestic students. Applications are processed on a rolling basis. Application fee: $25 ($35 for international students). *Expenses:* Tuition: Full-time $9,675; part-time $645 per credit hour. Tuition and fees vary according to program. *Financial support:* Teaching assistantships available. Financial award application deadline: 3/1; financial award applicants required to submit FAFSA. *Unit head:* Dr. Jeanne E. Jenkins, Coordinator, 216-397-4656, Fax: 216-397-3045, E-mail: jjenkins@jcu.edu.

Johnson State College, Graduate Program in Education, Program in Applied Behavior Analysis, Johnson, VT 05656-9405. Offers children's mental health (MA Ed); developmental disabilities (MA Ed). *Faculty:* 6 part-time/adjunct (3 women). *Students:* 3 full-time (all women), 9 part-time (6 women). *Entrance requirements:* Additional exam requirements/recommendations for international students: Required—TOEFL. *Application deadline:* For fall admission, 7/1 priority date for domestic students, 4/15 priority date for international students; for winter admission, 11/1 priority date for domestic students; for spring admission, 4/1 priority date for domestic students, 8/15 priority date for international students. Applications are processed on a rolling basis. Application fee: $35. *Application contact:* Catherine H. Higley, Administrative Assistant for Graduate Programs, 800-635-2356 Ext. 1244, Fax: 802-635-1248, E-mail: higleyc@jsc.vsc.edu.

Kansas State University, Graduate School, College of Education, Department of Counseling and Educational Psychology, Manhattan, KS 66506. Offers counseling and student development-college student personnel work (MS); counseling and student development-school counseling (MS); counselor education and supervisors (PhD); school counseling (Ed D); student affairs in higher education (PhD). *Accreditation:* ACA; NCATE. *Faculty:* 12 full-time (6 women). *Students:* 104 full-time (63 women), 30 part-time (16 women); includes 14 minority (10 African Americans, 1 American Indian/Alaska Native, 2 Asian Americans or Pacific Islanders, 1 Hispanic American), 1 international. 45 applicants, 67% accepted, 25 enrolled. In 2006, 37 master's, 3 doctorates awarded. *Degree requirements:* For master's, thesis or alternative, final written exam; for doctorate, thesis/dissertation, comprehensive exam. *Entrance requirements:* For master's, GRE General Test, MAT; for doctorate, GRE General Test. *Application deadline:* For fall admission, 3/1 priority date for domestic students, 2/1 priority date for international students; for spring admission, 10/1 priority date for domestic students, 8/1 priority date for international students. Applications are processed on a rolling basis. Application fee: $30 ($55 for international students). Electronic applications accepted. *Expenses:* Tuition, state resident: full-time $6,352; part-time $240 per credit hour. Tuition, nonresident: full-time $14,296; part-time $571 per credit hour. Required fees: $585. *Financial support:* In 2006–07, 1 research assistantship (averaging $10,868 per year), 3 teaching assistantships with full tuition reimbursements (averaging $11,568 per year) were awarded; career-related internships or fieldwork, institutionally sponsored loans, and scholarships/grants also available. Support available to part-time students. Financial award application deadline: 3/1; financial award applicants required to submit FAFSA. *Faculty research:* College student mental health, college student development, school counselor education, role of religion in student life, multicultural counseling. *Unit head:* Stephen Benton, Head, 785-532-5784, Fax: 785-532-7304, E-mail: leroy@ksu.edu. *Application contact:* Linda Thurston, Director, 785-532-5595, Fax: 785-532-7304, E-mail: coegrads@ksu.edu.

Kean University, College of Humanities and Social Sciences, Program in Educational Psychology, Union, NJ 07083. Offers MA. Part-time and evening/weekend programs available. *Faculty:* 18 full-time (10 women). *Students:* 2 full-time (both women), 8 part-time (all women); includes 1 minority (Hispanic American) Average age 28. 10 applicants, 60% accepted, 3 enrolled. In 2006, 23 degrees awarded. *Degree requirements:* For master's, thesis, research, comprehensive exam. *Entrance requirements:* For master's, GRE General Test, interview, 3 letters of recommendation, prerequisites in psychology. *Application deadline:* For fall admission, 3/15 for domestic students. Applications are processed on a rolling basis. Application fee: $60 ($150 for international students). Electronic applications accepted. *Expenses:* Tuition, state resident: full-time $8,856; part-time $369 per credit. Tuition, nonresident: full-time $11,256; part-time $469 per credit. *Financial support:* In 2006–07, 1 research assistantship with full tuition reimbursement (averaging $3,217 per year) was awarded. *Unit head:* Dr. Dennis Finger, Program Coordinator, 908-737-4024, E-mail: dfinger@kean.edu. *Application contact:* Joanne Morris, Director of Graduate Admissions, 908-737-3355, Fax: 908-737-3354, E-mail: gradadm@kean.edu.

Kent State University, Graduate School of Education, Health, and Human Services, Department of Educational Foundations and Special Services, Program in Educational Psychology, Kent, OH 44242-0001. Offers M Ed, MA, PhD. *Faculty:* 3 full-time (2 women). *Students:* 18 full-time (11 women), 11 part-time (5 women); includes 1 minority (American Indian/Alaska Native), 6 international. 12 applicants, 42% accepted. In 2006, 1 degree awarded. *Entrance requirements:* For doctorate, GRE. *Application deadline:* Applications are processed on a rolling basis. Application fee: $30. Electronic applications accepted. *Financial support:* In 2006–07, fellowships (averaging $8,497 per year); career-related internships or fieldwork, Federal Work-Study, institutionally sponsored loans, scholarships/grants, health care benefits, and unspecified assistantships also available. Support available to part-time students. *Unit head:* Dr. Albert Ingram, Coordinator, 330-672-2294, E-mail: aingram@kent.edu. *Application contact:* Nancy Miller, Academic Program Coordinator, Office of Graduate Student Services, 330-672-2576, Fax: 330-672-9162, E-mail: ogs@kent.edu.

La Sierra University, School of Education, Department of Educational Psychology and Counseling, Riverside, CA 92515. Offers counseling (MA); educational psychology (Ed S); school psychology (Ed S). Part-time and evening/weekend programs available. *Degree requirements:* For master's, thesis optional; for Ed S, practicum (educational psychology). *Entrance requirements:* For master's, California Basic Educational Skills Test, NTE, minimum GPA of 3.0; for Ed S, minimum GPA of 3.3. *Faculty research:* Equivalent score scales, self perception.

Long Island University, Westchester Graduate Campus, Program in Education-School Counselor and School Psychology, Purchase, NY 10577. Offers school counselor (MS Ed); school psychologist (MS Ed). Part-time and evening/weekend programs available. *Faculty:* 2 full-time (both women), 12 part-time/adjunct (8 women). *Students:* 84 (72 women). 40 applicants, 73% accepted, 21 enrolled. In 2006, 21 degrees awarded. *Application deadline:* Applications are processed on a rolling basis. Application fee: $30. *Expenses:* Tuition: Part-time $790 per credit. *Financial support:* In 2006–07, 22 students received support. Scholarships/grants, tuition waivers (partial), and unspecified assistantships available. *Unit head:* Prof. Beth Weiner, Director, 914-831-2717, Fax: 914-251-5959, E-mail: beth.weiner@liu.edu. *Application contact:* Ellen Brief, Coordinator of Admissions, Marketing, Student Services and Public Relations, 914-831-2701, Fax: 914-251-5959, E-mail: westchester@liu.edu.

Loyola Marymount University, Graduate Division, School of Education, Program in Educational Psychology, Los Angeles, CA 90045-2659. Offers school psychology (MA). Part-time and evening/weekend programs available. *Students:* 39 full-time (37 women); includes 24 minority (3 African Americans, 5 Asian Americans or Pacific Islanders, 16 Hispanic Americans). Average age 26. In 2006, 17 degrees awarded. *Degree requirements:* For master's, comprehensive exam. *Entrance requirements:* For master's, GRE General Test, interview. Additional exam requirements/recommendations for international students: Required—TOEFL (minimum score 600 paper-based; 250 computer-based). *Application deadline:* For fall admission, 7/15 for domestic students; for spring admission, 11/15 for domestic students. Application fee: $50. Electronic applications accepted. *Financial support:* In 2006–07, 37 students received support. Scholarships/grants available. Support available to part-time students. Financial award application deadline: 6/1; financial award applicants required to submit FAFSA. *Unit head:* Dr. Brian Leung, Coordinator, 310-338-1707, E-mail: bleung@lmu.edu.

Loyola University Chicago, School of Education, Program in Educational Psychology, Chicago, IL 60611-2196. Offers M Ed. Part-time and evening/weekend programs available. *Faculty:* 5 full-time (3 women), 4 part-time/adjunct (3 women). *Students:* 35. Average age 28. 22 applicants, 64% accepted, 8 enrolled. In 2006, 25 master's awarded. Terminal master's awarded for partial completion of doctoral program. *Degree requirements:* For master's, thesis (for some programs), comprehensive exam. *Entrance requirements:* For master's, GRE General Test, letters of recommendation, minimum GPA of 3.0. Additional exam requirements/recommendations for international students: Required—TOEFL (minimum score 550 paper-based; 213 computer-based; 79 iBT). *Application deadline:* For fall admission, 12/15 for domestic and international students. Application fee: $50. Electronic applications accepted. *Financial support:* In 2006–07, 7 students received support. Institutionally sponsored loans, scholarships/grants, and tuition waivers (full and partial) available. Financial award application deadline: 2/15. *Faculty research:* Research methodology; learning theory and teaching; cognitive, social, and cultural constructivism; school reform; workplace training and adult education. *Unit head:* Dr. Pamela Fenning, Director, 312-915-6803, E-mail: pfennin@luc.edu. *Application contact:* Marie Rosin-Dittmar, Information Contact, 312-915-6800, E-mail: schleduc@luc.edu.

Marist College, Graduate Programs, School of Social and Behavioral Sciences, Poughkeepsie, NY 12601-1387. Offers counseling psychology (MA); education (M Ed); education psychology (MA); school psychology (MA, Adv C). Part-time and evening/weekend programs available. *Faculty:* 21 full-time (9 women), 25 part-time/adjunct (14 women). *Students:* 98 full-time (81 women), 120 part-time (98 women); includes 21 minority (9 African Americans, 2 Asian Americans or Pacific Islanders, 10 Hispanic Americans), 4 international. Average age 30. 105 applicants, 72% accepted, 52 enrolled. In 2006, 105 master's, 4 other advanced degrees awarded. *Degree requirements:* For master's, thesis optional. *Entrance requirements:* For master's, GRE General Test, letters of recommendation, minimum undergraduate GPA of 3.0, interview, essay, official transcript. Additional exam requirements/recommendations for international students: Required—TOEFL (minimum score 550 paper-based; 213 computer-based; 80 iBT); Recommended—IELTS (minimum score 6). *Application deadline:* For fall admission, 8/1 for domestic students, 6/1 for international students; for spring admission, 12/1 for domestic students, 10/15 for international students. Applications are processed on a rolling basis. Application fee: $50. Electronic applications accepted. *Expenses:* Tuition: Full-time $11,340; part-time $630 per credit. Required fees: $60; $30 per semester. *Financial support:* In 2006–07, 146 students received support. Career-related internships or fieldwork, scholarships/grants, and unspecified assistantships available. Support available to part-time students. Financial award application deadline: 8/15; financial award applicants required to submit FAFSA. *Faculty research:* AIDS prevention, educational intervention, humanistic counseling research, aging and development, neuroimaging. *Unit head:* Margaret Calista, Dean, 845-575-3000 Ext. 2960, E-mail: margaret.calista@marist.edu. *Application contact:* Anu R. Ailawadhi, Director of Graduate Admissions, 845-575-3800, Fax: 845-575-3166, E-mail: graduate@marist.edu.

McGill University, Faculty of Graduate and Postdoctoral Studies, Faculty of Education, Department of Educational and Counseling Psychology, Program in Educational Psychology, Montréal, QC H3A 2T5, Canada. Offers M Ed, MA, PhD. Part-time and evening/weekend programs available. *Degree requirements:* For master's, thesis (for some programs), registration; for doctorate, thesis/dissertation, comprehensive exam, registration. *Entrance requirements:* For master's, minimum GPA of 3.0. Additional exam requirements/recommendations for international students: Required—TOEFL (minimum score 550 paper-based; 213 computer-based), IELTS (minimum score 7). *Faculty research:* Cognitive, instructional design, special education, computers in education.

Memorial University of Newfoundland, School of Graduate Studies, Faculty of Education, St. John's, NL A1C 5S7, Canada. Offers counseling psychology (M Ed); curriculum, teaching,

Educational Psychology

Memorial University of Newfoundland (continued)

and learning studies (M Ed); education (PhD); educational leadership studies (M Ed); information technology (M Ed); post-secondary studies (M Ed, Diploma), including health professional education (Diploma). Part-time programs available. *Degree requirements:* For master's, internship, paper folio, project, thesis optional; for doctorate, thesis/dissertation, thesis seminar, oral defense of thesis, comprehensive exam. *Entrance requirements:* For master's, undergraduate degree with at least 2nd class standing, 1-2 years work experience; for doctorate, minimum A average in graduate course work, MA in education, 2 years professional experience; for Diploma, 2nd class degree, 2 years of work experience with adult learners, appropriate academic qualifications and work experience in a health-related field. Electronic applications accepted. *Faculty research:* Critical thinking, literacy, cognitive studies and counseling, educational change, technology in instruction.

Miami University, Graduate School, School of Education and Allied Professions, Department of Educational Psychology, Oxford, OH 45056. Offers educational psychology (M Ed); school psychology (MS, Ed S); special education (M Ed). *Accreditation:* NCATE. *Degree requirements:* For master's, oral or written exam, thesis optional; for Ed S, oral or written exam. *Entrance requirements:* For master's, GRE General Test or MAT, minimum undergraduate GPA of 3.0 during previous 2 years or 2.75 overall; for Ed S, GRE General Test or MAT. Additional exam requirements/recommendations for international students: Required—TOEFL (minimum score 550 paper-based; 213 computer-based), TWE (minimum score 4).

Michigan School of Professional Psychology, Programs in Humanistic and Clinical Psychology, Farmington Hills, MI 48334. Offers humanistic and clinical psychology (MA, Psy D). *Faculty:* 4 full-time (2 women), 13 part-time/adjunct (6 women). *Students:* 125 full-time; includes 18 minority (13 African Americans, 5 Asian Americans or Pacific Islanders). Average age 38. 200 applicants, 40% accepted. In 2006, 30 master's, 16 doctorates awarded. *Median time to degree:* Master's–1 year full-time; doctorate–4 years full-time. Of those who began their doctoral program in fall 1998, 100% received their degree in 8 years or less. *Degree requirements:* For master's, thesis, practicum; for doctorate, thesis/dissertation, internship, practicum. *Entrance requirements:* For master's, 1 year of work experience, interview, minimum GPA of 3.0, curriculum vitae, personal essay; for doctorate, 3 years of work experience, 2 interviews, minimum graduate GPA of 3.0, scholarly writing sample, curriculum vitae, personal essay. Additional exam requirements/recommendations for international students: Required—TOEFL. *Application deadline:* For fall admission, 1/15 priority date for domestic students. Applications are processed on a rolling basis. Application fee: $75. Electronic applications accepted. *Expenses:* Tuition: Full-time $21,255. Required fees: $1,500. Full-time tuition and fees vary according to class time, course level, course load, degree level, program and student level. *Financial support:* In 2006–07, 39 students received support. Application deadline: 6/30; *Faculty research:* Qualitative research, existential-phenomenological psychology, applications to clinical practice. *Unit head:* Dr. Kerry Moustakas, President, 248-476-1122, Fax: 248-476-1125, E-mail: kmoustakas@mispp.edu. *Application contact:* Linda Potter-Gallant, Admissions Advisor, 248-476-1122, Fax: 248-476-1125, E-mail: lpgallant@mispp.edu.

Michigan State University, The Graduate School, College of Education, Department of Counseling, Educational Psychology and Special Education, East Lansing, MI 48824. Offers counseling (MA); educational psychology and educational technology (PhD); educational technology (MA); measurement and quantitative methods (PhD); rehabilitation counseling (MA); rehabilitation counselor education (PhD); school psychology (MA, PhD, Ed S); special education (MA, PhD). *Accreditation:* APA (one or more programs are accredited); CORE (one or more programs are accredited). Part-time programs available. *Faculty:* 36 full-time (13 women). *Students:* 218 full-time (149 women), 75 part-time (60 women); includes 38 minority (31 African Americans, 4 Asian Americans or Pacific Islanders, 3 Hispanic Americans), 63 international. Average age 31. 243 applicants, 44% accepted. In 2006, 136 master's, 34 doctorates awarded. *Entrance requirements:* Additional exam requirements/recommendations for international students: Required—TOEFL. Electronic applications accepted. *Expenses:* Tuition, state resident: part-time $346 per credit hour. Tuition, nonresident: part-time $730 per credit hour. Tuition and fees vary according to program. *Financial support:* In 2006–07, 125 fellowships with tuition reimbursements, 87 research assistantships with tuition reimbursements (averaging $13,854 per year), 67 teaching assistantships with tuition reimbursements (averaging $13,722 per year) were awarded. Total annual research expenditures: $3.4 million. *Unit head:* Dr. Richard S. Prawat, Chairperson, 517-353-6417, E-mail: rsprawat@msu.edu. *Application contact:* Kathy Dimoff, Admissions Coordinator, 517-355-6683, E-mail: dimoff@msu.edu.

Mississippi State University, College of Education, Department of Counseling, Educational Psychology, and Special Education, Mississippi State, MS 39762. Offers counselor education (MS, PhD, Ed S); educational psychology (MS, PhD, Ed S); special education (MS, Ed S). *Accreditation:* ACA (one or more programs are accredited); APA; CORE (one or more programs are accredited); NCATE. Part-time programs available. Postbaccalaureate distance learning degree programs offered (minimal on-campus study). *Faculty:* 24 full-time (13 women), 10 part-time/adjunct (8 women). *Students:* 120 full-time (94 women), 72 part-time (62 women); includes 68 minority (66 African Americans, 2 Asian Americans or Pacific Islanders), 4 international. Average age 29. 61 applicants, 72% accepted, 32 enrolled. In 2006, 73 master's, 2 doctorates awarded. Terminal master's awarded for partial completion of doctoral program. *Degree requirements:* For master's, thesis optional; for doctorate, thesis/dissertation, comprehensive oral and written exam. *Entrance requirements:* For master's, GRE, minimum QPA of 3.0; for doctorate, GRE, interview, minimum GPA of 3.4. Additional exam requirements/recommendations for international students: Required—TOEFL. *Application deadline:* For fall admission, 3/15 for domestic students. Application fee: $30. *Expenses:* Tuition, state resident: full-time $4,550; part-time $253 per hour. Tuition, nonresident: full-time $10,552; part-time $584 per hour. International tuition: $10,882 full-time. Tuition and fees vary according to course load. *Financial support:* In 2006–07, 30 students received support, including 6 teaching assistantships with full tuition reimbursements available (averaging $7,554 per year); research assistantships with full tuition reimbursements available, career-related internships or fieldwork, Federal Work-Study, institutionally sponsored loans, and unspecified assistantships also available. Financial award application deadline: 2/1; financial award applicants required to submit FAFSA. *Faculty research:* HIV-AIDS in college population, substance abuse in youth and college students, ADHD and conduct disorders in youth, assessment and identification of early childhood disabilities, assessment and vocational transition of the disabled. *Unit head:* Dr. Thomas W. Hosie, Head, 662-325-3426, Fax: 662-325-3263, E-mail: hosie@colled.msstate.edu. *Application contact:* Dr. Phil Bonfanti, Director of Admissions, 662-325-4104, Fax: 662-325-8872, E-mail: admit@msstate.edu.

Montclair State University, The Graduate School, College of Humanities and Social Sciences, Department of Psychology, Montclair, NJ 07043-1624. Offers educational psychology (MA), including child/adolescent clinical psychology, clinical psychology for Spanish/English bilinguals; psychology (MA), including industrial and organizational psychology; school psychologist (Certificate). Part-time and evening/weekend programs available. *Faculty:* 27 full-time (11 women), 27 part-time/adjunct (20 women). *Students:* 29 full-time (23 women), 63 part-time (57 women); includes 26 minority (7 African Americans, 4 Asian Americans or Pacific Islanders, 15 Hispanic Americans), 3 international. 87 applicants, 26% accepted, 14 enrolled. In 2006, 29 master's, 10 other advanced degrees awarded. *Degree requirements:* For master's, thesis or alternative, comprehensive exam. *Entrance requirements:* For master's, GRE General Test, GRE Subject Test, previous course work in psychology, interview, 2 letters of recommendation. Additional exam requirements/recommendations for international students: Required—TOEFL (minimum score 83 computer-based). *Application deadline:* For fall admission, 2/1 for domestic and international students; for spring admission, 10/1 for domestic and international students. Applications are processed on a rolling basis. Application fee: $60. Electronic applications accepted. *Expenses:* Tuition, state resident: part-time $450 per credit. Tuition, nonresident: part-time $682 per credit. Tuition and fees vary according to degree level and program. *Financial support:* In 2006–07, 10 research assistantships with full tuition reimbursements (averaging $7,000 per year) were awarded; Federal Work-Study, scholarships/grants, and unspecified assistantships also available. Support available to part-time students. Financial award application deadline: 3/1; financial award applicants required to submit FAFSA. *Faculty research:* Engaged learning, academic and civic development. Total annual research expenditures: $10,000. *Unit head:* Dr. Saundra Collins, Chairperson, 973-655-5201. *Application contact:* Dr. Paul Locher, Adviser, 973-655-7381, E-mail: locherp@mail.montclair.edu.

Mount Saint Vincent University, Graduate Programs, Faculty of Education, Program in Educational Psychology, Halifax, NS B3M 2J6, Canada. Offers education of the blind or visually impaired (M Ed, MA Ed); education of the deaf or hard of hearing (M Ed, MA Ed); educational psychology (MA-R); human relations (M Ed, MA Ed). Part-time and evening/weekend programs available. Postbaccalaureate distance learning degree programs offered (minimal on-campus study). *Degree requirements:* For master's, thesis (for some programs). *Entrance requirements:* For master's, bachelor's degree in related field, 1 year of teaching experience. Electronic applications accepted. *Faculty research:* Personality measurement, values reasoning, aggression and sexuality, power and control, quantitative and qualitative research methodologies.

National-Louis University, National College of Education, Doctoral Programs in Education, Program in Educational Psychology/School Psychology, Chicago, IL 60603. Offers Ed D. Part-time and evening/weekend programs available. *Students:* 6 full-time (all women), 10 part-time (all women); includes 3 minority (1 African American, 2 Hispanic Americans). Average age 37. 3 applicants, 100% accepted. *Degree requirements:* For doctorate, thesis/dissertation, internship, comprehensive exam. *Entrance requirements:* For doctorate, GRE General Test, minimum GPA of 3.25, interview, resumé, writing sample. *Application deadline:* For fall admission, 5/1 for domestic students; for spring admission, 1/15 for domestic students. Application fee: $25. *Expenses:* Tuition: Full-time $17,685. One-time fee: $40 full-time. *Financial support:* Fellowships, research assistantships, teaching assistantships, career-related internships or fieldwork, Federal Work-Study, institutionally sponsored loans, and scholarships/grants available. Support available to part-time students. Financial award application deadline: 4/15; financial award applicants required to submit FAFSA. *Application contact:* David McCulloch, Vice President for University Services, 800-443-5522 Ext. 5127, Fax: 847-465-0593, E-mail: dmcc@wheeling1.nl.edu.

National-Louis University, National College of Education, Program in Educational Psychology/Human Learning and Development, Chicago, IL 60603. Offers educational psychology (CAS, Ed S); educational psychology/human learning and development (M Ed, MS Ed). Part-time and evening/weekend programs available. *Students:* 36 full-time (34 women), 44 part-time (40 women); includes 9 minority (2 African Americans, 7 Hispanic Americans). Average age 33. 17 applicants, 94% accepted. In 2006, 10 master's, 1 other advanced degree awarded. *Degree requirements:* For master's, thesis (for some programs). *Entrance requirements:* For master's, MAT or GRE, minimum GPA of 3.0, teaching certificate; for other advanced degree, master's degree, teaching certificate. *Application deadline:* Applications are processed on a rolling basis. Application fee: $25. Electronic applications accepted. *Expenses:* Tuition: Full-time $17,685. One-time fee: $40 full-time. *Financial support:* Fellowships, career-related internships or fieldwork, Federal Work-Study, institutionally sponsored loans, and scholarships/grants available. Support available to part-time students. Financial award applicants required to submit FAFSA. *Unit head:* Dr. Philip Garber, Coordinator, 847-475-1100 Ext. 2553. *Application contact:* David McCulloch, Vice President for University Services, 800-443-5522 Ext. 5127, Fax: 847-465-0593, E-mail: dmcc@wheeling1.nl.edu.

National-Louis University, National College of Education, Programs in School Psychology, Chicago, IL 60603. Offers M Ed, Ed S. *Students:* 18 full-time (17 women), 34 part-time (31 women); includes 6 minority (1 African American, 5 Hispanic Americans). Average age 32. 5 applicants, 100% accepted. In 2006, 20 degrees awarded. *Degree requirements:* For master's and Ed S, internship. *Entrance requirements:* For master's, MAT or GRE, minimum GPA of 3.0; for Ed S, GRE, interview, master's degree, writing sample. *Application deadline:* Applications are processed on a rolling basis. *Expenses:* Tuition: Full-time $17,685. One-time fee: $40 full-time. *Financial support:* Fellowships, career-related internships or fieldwork, Federal Work-Study, scholarships/grants, and tuition waivers available. Support available to part-time students. *Unit head:* Dr. Diane Salmon, Coordinator, 847-475-1100 Ext. 2726. *Application contact:* David McCulloch, Vice President for University Services, 800-443-5522 Ext. 5127, Fax: 847-465-0593, E-mail: dmcc@wheeling1.nl.edu.

New Jersey City University, Graduate and Continuing Education, College of Arts and Sciences, Department of Psychology, Program in Educational Psychology, Jersey City, NJ 07305-1597. Offers educational psychology (MA); school psychology (PD). *Faculty:* 12. *Students:* 11 full-time (8 women), 33 part-time (30 women); includes 10 minority (3 African Americans, 1 Asian American or Pacific Islander, 6 Hispanic Americans), 1 international. Average age 30. In 2006, 15 master's, 5 other advanced degrees awarded. *Degree requirements:* For PD, summer internship or externship. *Entrance requirements:* For master's, GRE General Test or MAT; for PD, GRE General Test. Additional exam requirements/recommendations for international students: Required—TOEFL. *Application deadline:* For fall admission, 8/1 priority date for domestic students; for spring admission, 12/1 for domestic students. Applications are processed on a rolling basis. Application fee: $0. *Expenses:* Tuition, state resident: full-time $7,038; part-time $391 per credit. Tuition, nonresident: full-time $12,510; part-time $695 per credit. Required fees: $65 per credit. *Financial support:* Unspecified assistantships available. *Unit head:* Dr. James Lennon, Director, 201-200-3309, E-mail: jlennon@njcu.edu.

New York University, Steinhardt School of Culture, Education and Human Development, Department of Applied Psychology, Program in Educational and Developmental Psychology, New York, NY 10012-1019. Offers educational psychology (MA), including general educational psychology, psychological measurement and evaluation, psychology of parenthood; psychological development (PhD); school psychology (PhD). *Accreditation:* APA (one or more programs are accredited). Part-time and evening/weekend programs available. *Faculty:* 23 full-time (15 women). *Students:* 58 full-time (54 women), 74 part-time (72 women); includes 37 minority (14 African Americans, 8 Asian Americans or Pacific Islanders, 15 Hispanic Americans), 18 international. 238 applicants, 47% accepted, 46 enrolled. In 2006, 22 master's, 13 doctorates awarded. Terminal master's awarded for partial completion of doctoral program. *Degree requirements:* For master's, thesis (for some programs); for doctorate, thesis/dissertation. *Entrance requirements:* For doctorate, GRE General Test, interview. Additional exam requirements/recommendations for international students: Required—TOEFL. *Application deadline:* For fall admission, 12/15 priority date for domestic and international students; for spring admission, 11/1 for domestic and international students. Applications are processed on a rolling basis. Application fee: $50. *Expenses:* Tuition: Part-time $1,080 per unit. Required fees: $56 per unit. $329 per term. Tuition and fees vary according to program. *Financial support:* Teaching assistantships with partial tuition reimbursements, career-related internships or fieldwork, Federal Work-Study, institutionally sponsored loans, and tuition waivers (partial) available. Support available to part-time students. Financial award application deadline: 2/1; financial award applicants required to submit FAFSA. *Faculty research:* High risk children and youth; child and adolescent developments; families and schooling; infant cognition; exploration, language, and symbolic play in toddlerhood. *Unit head:* Dr. Barbara Hummel-Rossi, Director, 212-998-5360, Fax: 212-995-4358. *Application contact:* 212-998-5030, Fax: 212-995-4328, E-mail: steinhardt.gradadmissions@nyu.edu.

Northeastern University, Bouvé College of Health Sciences Graduate School, Department of Counseling and Applied Educational Psychology, Program in Applied Educational Psychology, Boston, MA 02115-5096. Offers school counseling (MS); school psychology (MS). Part-time programs available. *Faculty:* 5 full-time (3 women), 4 part-time/adjunct (2 women). *Students:* 53 full-time (48 women), 4 part-time (all women). Average age 26. 146 applicants, 71% accepted. In 2006, 39 degrees awarded. *Entrance requirements:* For master's, GRE General Test or MAT. Additional exam requirements/recommendations for international students: Required—TOEFL. *Application deadline:* Applications are processed on a rolling basis. Application fee: $50. *Financial support:* Career-related internships or fieldwork, Federal Work-Study, tuition waivers (partial), and unspecified assistantships available. Support available to part-time students. Financial award application deadline: 3/1; financial award applicants required to submit FAFSA. *Faculty research:* Multicultural issues, assessment, early intervention, bilingual education. *Application contact:* Margaret Schnabel, Director of Graduate Admissions, 617-373-2708, Fax: 617-373-4704, E-mail: bouvegrad@neu.edu.

Northern Arizona University, Graduate College, College of Education, Program in Educational Psychology, Flagstaff, AZ 86011. Offers counseling psychology (Ed D); learning and instruction (Ed D); school psychology (Ed D). *Degree requirements:* For doctorate, thesis/dissertation, internship, comprehensive exam. *Entrance requirements:* For doctorate, GRE General Test.

Northern Illinois University, Graduate School, College of Education, Department of Leadership, Educational Psychology and Foundations, De Kalb, IL 60115-2854. Offers educational administration (MS Ed, Ed D, Ed S); educational psychology (MS Ed, Ed D); foundations of education (MS Ed); school business management (MS Ed). Part-time and evening/weekend programs available. Postbaccalaureate distance learning degree programs offered (minimal on-campus study). *Faculty:* 23 full-time (12 women). *Students:* 15 full-time (7 women), 499 part-time (289 women); includes 75 minority (53 African Americans, 2 American Indian/Alaska Native, 6 Asian Americans or Pacific Islanders, 14 Hispanic Americans), 2 international. Average age 37. 186 applicants, 62% accepted, 92 enrolled. In 2006, 171 master's, 10 doctorates, 50 other advanced degrees awarded. *Degree requirements:* For master's, thesis optional; for doctorate, thesis/dissertation, candidacy exam, dissertation defense. *Entrance requirements:* For master's, minimum undergraduate GPA of 2.75; for doctorate, GRE General Test, minimum undergraduate GPA of 2.75, 3.2 graduate; for Ed S, GRE General Test, minimum GPA of 2.75 (undergraduate), 3.2 (graduate). Additional exam requirements/recommendations for international students: Required—TOEFL (minimum score 550 paper-based; 213 computer-based). *Application deadline:* For fall admission, 6/1 for domestic students, 5/1 for international students; for spring admission, 11/1 for domestic students, 10/1 for international students. Applications are processed on a rolling basis. Application fee: $30. Electronic applications accepted. *Financial support:* In 2006–07, 3 research assistantships with full tuition reimbursements, 8 teaching assistantships with full tuition reimbursements were awarded; fellowships with full tuition reimbursements, career-related internships or fieldwork, Federal Work-Study, scholarships/grants, tuition waivers (full), and unspecified assistantships also available. Support available to part-time students. Financial award applicants required to submit FAFSA. *Faculty research:* Interpersonal forgiveness, learner-centered education, psychedelic studies, senior theory, professional growth. *Unit head:* Dr. Wilma Miranda, Chair, 815-753-1562, E-mail: wmiranda@niu.edu.

Oklahoma City University, Petree College of Arts and Sciences, Division of Education and Kinesiology Exercise Studies, Programs in Education, Oklahoma City, OK 73106-1402. Offers applied behavioral studies (M Ed); early childhood education (M Ed); elementary education (M Ed). Part-time and evening/weekend programs available. *Faculty:* 4 full-time (3 women), 13 part-time/adjunct (8 women). *Students:* 15 full-time (14 women), 14 part-time (11 women); includes 7 minority (4 African Americans, 2 Asian Americans or Pacific Islanders, 1 Hispanic American). Average age 33. 25 applicants, 76% accepted. In 2006, 23 degrees awarded. *Degree requirements:* For master's, thesis optional. *Entrance requirements:* For master's, minimum GPA of 3.0. *Application deadline:* For fall admission, 8/22 for domestic students; for spring admission, 1/15 for domestic students. Applications are processed on a rolling basis. Application fee: $30 ($70 for international students). *Expenses:* Tuition: Full-time $12,780; part-time $710 per hour. Required fees: $89 per hour. *Financial support:* Fellowships with partial tuition reimbursements, career-related internships or fieldwork, Federal Work-Study, institutionally sponsored loans, and tuition waivers (partial) available. Support available to part-time students. Financial award application deadline: 8/1; financial award applicants required to submit FAFSA. *Faculty research:* Adult literacy, cognition, reading strategies. *Application contact:* Leslie McKenzie, Director, Graduate Admissions, 800-633-7242, Fax: 405-208-5356, E-mail: gadmissions@okcu.edu.

Oklahoma State University, College of Education, School of Applied Health and Educational Psychology, Stillwater, OK 74078. Offers applied behavioral studies (MS, Ed D, PhD); counseling and student personnel (MS, PhD); educational psychology (PhD); health (MS, Ed D); leisure sciences (MS, Ed D); physical education (MS, Ed D); physical education and leisure sciences (Ed D); school psychology (Ed S). *Accreditation:* APA (one or more programs are accredited). Part-time programs available. *Faculty:* 37 full-time (17 women), 12 part-time/adjunct (8 women). *Students:* 189 full-time (137 women), 180 part-time (113 women); includes 75 minority (25 African Americans, 34 American Indian/Alaska Native, 5 Asian Americans or Pacific Islanders, 11 Hispanic Americans), 27 international. Average age 33. 275 applicants, 28% accepted, 64 enrolled. In 2006, 45 master's, 21 doctorates awarded. *Degree requirements:* For master's, thesis or alternative; for doctorate, thesis/dissertation. *Entrance requirements:* For master's, GRE or MAT; for doctorate, GRE (PhD). Additional exam requirements/recommendations for international students: Required—TOEFL. *Application deadline:* For fall admission, 7/1 priority date for domestic students, 3/1 priority date for international students; for spring admission, 8/1 priority date for international students. Applications are processed on a rolling basis. Application fee: $40 ($75 for international students). Electronic applications accepted. *Expenses:* Tuition, state resident: part-time $146 per credit hour. Tuition, nonresident: part-time $516 per credit hour. Required fees: $44 per credit hour. Tuition and fees vary according to program. *Financial support:* In 2006–07, 29 research assistantships (averaging $6,452 per year), 64 teaching assistantships (averaging $8,263 per year) were awarded; career-related internships or fieldwork, Federal Work-Study, scholarships/grants, health care benefits, tuition waivers (partial), and unspecified assistantships also available. Support available to part-time students. Financial award application deadline: 3/1. *Unit head:* Dr. John Romans, Head, 405-744-6040.

Penn State University Park, Graduate School, College of Education, Department of Educational and School Psychology and Special Education, State College, University Park, PA 16802-1503. Offers educational psychology (MS, PhD); school psychology (M Ed, MS, PhD); special education (M Ed, MS, PhD). *Unit head:* Dr. Kathy L. Ruhl, Head, 814-865-6072, Fax: 814-865-7066, E-mail: klr3@psu.edu. *Application contact:* Bobbi Jo Robison, Department Head Secretary, 814-863-4450, E-mail: bjb9@psu.edu.

Purdue University, Graduate School, School of Education, Department of Educational Studies, West Lafayette, IN 47907. Offers administration (MS Ed, PhD, Ed S); counseling and development (MS Ed, PhD); education of the gifted (MS Ed); educational psychology (MS Ed, PhD); foundations of education (MS Ed, PhD); higher education administration (MS Ed, PhD); special education (MS Ed, PhD). *Accreditation:* ACA (one or more programs are accredited); NCATE (one or more programs are accredited). Part-time and evening/weekend programs available. *Faculty:* 28 full-time (18 women). *Students:* 100 full-time (71 women), 126 part-time (77 women); includes 32 minority (19 African Americans, 2 American Indian/Alaska Native, 6 Asian Americans or Pacific Islanders, 5 Hispanic Americans), 33 international. Average age 36. 152 applicants, 62% accepted, 56 enrolled. In 2006, 51 master's, 17 doctorates awarded. *Degree requirements:* For master's, thesis optional; for doctorate, thesis/dissertation, oral and written exams; for Ed S, oral presentation, project. *Entrance requirements:* For master's, GRE General Test, minimum undergraduate GPA of 3.0; for doctorate, GRE General Test; for Ed S, GRE, minimum B average. Additional exam requirements/recommendations for international students: Required—TOEFL. *Application deadline:* For fall admission, 1/15 for domestic students; for spring admission, 9/15 for domestic students. Applications are processed on a rolling basis. Application fee: $55. Electronic applications accepted. *Financial support:* In 2006–07, 6 fellowships with full tuition reimbursements (averaging $13,300 per year), 23 research assistantships with full tuition reimbursements (averaging $11,500 per year), 33 teaching assistantships with full tuition reimbursements (averaging $10,800 per year) were awarded; career-related internships or fieldwork and tuition waivers (full) also available. Support available to part-time students. Financial award application deadline: 3/1; financial award applicants required to submit FAFSA. *Faculty research:* Motivation, learning disabilities, school learning, group processes, cognitive development. *Unit head:* Dr. Kevin R Kelly, Head, 765-494-9170, Fax: 765-496-1228. *Application contact:* Patricia Mason, Coordinator of Graduate Studies, 765-494-2346, Fax: 765-494-5832, E-mail: gradoffice@soe.purdue.edu.

Rutgers, The State University of New Jersey, New Brunswick, Graduate School of Education, Department of Educational Psychology, Program in Learning, Cognition and Development, New Brunswick, NJ 08901-1281. Offers Ed M. Part-time and evening/weekend programs available. *Faculty:* 7 full-time (5 women). *Students:* 3 full-time (all women), 14 part-time (12 women). 13 applicants, 69% accepted, 8 enrolled. In 2006, 4 master's awarded. *Entrance requirements:* For master's, GRE General Test, 3 letters of recommendation. Additional exam requirements/recommendations for international students: Required—TOEFL (minimum score 550 paper-based; 233 computer-based; 83 iBT). *Application deadline:* For fall admission, 2/1 for domestic and international students; for spring admission, 11/1 for domestic and international students. Application fee: $60. Electronic applications accepted. *Financial support:* Application deadline: 3/15; *Faculty research:* Cognitive development, gender roles, cognition and instruction, peer learning, infancy and early childhood. *Unit head:* Dr. Susan Golbeck, Coordinator, 732-932-7496 Ext. 8323, Fax: 732-932-6829, E-mail: golbeck@rutgers.edu.

Rutgers, The State University of New Jersey, New Brunswick, Graduate School of Education, Doctoral Program in Education, New Brunswick, NJ 08901-1281. Offers educational policy (PhD); educational psychology (PhD); literacy education (PhD); mathematics education (PhD). Part-time programs available. *Faculty:* 63 full-time (30 women). *Students:* 29 full-time (21 women), 45 part-time (34 women); includes 7 minority (4 African Americans, 3 Asian Americans or Pacific Islanders), 15 international. 85 applicants, 33% accepted, 13 enrolled. In 2006, 8 degrees awarded. *Degree requirements:* For doctorate, thesis/dissertation, qualifying exam. *Entrance requirements:* For doctorate, GRE General Test, GRE Subject Test (for mathematics education). Additional exam requirements/recommendations for international students: Required—TOEFL (minimum score 575 paper-based; 233 computer-based). *Application deadline:* For fall admission, 2/1 for domestic and international students. Application fee: $60. Electronic applications accepted. *Financial support:* In 2006–07, research assistantships with full tuition reimbursements (averaging $15,730 per year). Financial award application deadline: 3/15. *Faculty research:* Literacy education, math education, educational psychology, educational policy. *Unit head:* Prof. Clark Chinn, Director, 732-932-7496 Ext. 8319, Fax: 732-932-6829, E-mail: cchinn@rci.rutgers.edu. *Application contact:* Kristine Spaventa, Administrative Assistant, 732-932-7496 Ext. 8104, Fax: 732-932-8206, E-mail: sparenta@rci.rutgers.edu.

Simon Fraser University, Graduate Studies, Faculty of Education, Program in Educational Psychology, Burnaby, BC V5A 1S6, Canada. Offers M Ed, MA, PhD. *Degree requirements:* For master's, project or thesis; for doctorate, thesis/dissertation. *Entrance requirements:* For master's, minimum GPA of 3.0; for doctorate, GRE, master's degree or exceptional record in a bachelor's degree, minimum GPA of 3.5. Additional exam requirements/recommendations for international students: Required—TOEFL or IELTS.

Southern Illinois University Carbondale, Graduate School, College of Education, Department of Educational Psychology and Special Education, Program in Educational Psychology, Carbondale, IL 62901-4701. Offers counselor education (MS Ed, PhD); educational psychology (PhD); human learning and development (MS Ed); measurement and statistics (PhD). *Accreditation:* NCATE. *Faculty:* 19 full-time (9 women), 7 part-time/adjunct (2 women). *Students:* 42 full-time (32 women), 61 part-time (46 women); includes 10 minority (7 African Americans, 1 Asian American or Pacific Islander, 2 Hispanic Americans), 12 international. Average age 36. 54 applicants, 56% accepted, 3 enrolled. In 2006, 20 master's, 5 doctorates awarded. *Degree requirements:* For master's and doctorate, thesis/dissertation. *Entrance requirements:* For master's, GRE General Test, minimum GPA of 2.7; for doctorate, minimum GPA of 3.25. Additional exam requirements/recommendations for international students: Required—TOEFL. *Application deadline:* For fall admission, 6/15 priority date for domestic students. Applications are processed on a rolling basis. Application fee: $20. *Financial support:* In 2006–07, 36 students received support, including 2 fellowships with full tuition reimbursements available, 4 research assistantships with full tuition reimbursements available; teaching assistantships with full tuition reimbursements available, career-related internships or fieldwork, Federal Work-Study, institutionally sponsored loans, and tuition waivers (full) also available. Support available to part-time students. Financial award application deadline: 5/1. *Faculty research:* Career development, problem solving, learning and instruction, cognitive development, family assessment. Total annual research expenditures: $10,000. *Application contact:* Cathy Earnhart, Administrative Clerk, 618-453-6932, E-mail: pern@siu.edu.

Announcement: The MS Ed and PhD programs offer specialties in counselor education and human learning and development. The PhD is also offered in special education and statistics and measurement. Graduates have taken a variety of positions in universities, state educational agencies, industrial organizations, private and public research centers, and public school systems as well as industrial, military, or rehabilitation settings. Teaching, instructional design, and instructional evaluation are also career options.

See Close-Up on page 1125.

Stanford University, School of Education, Program in Psychological Studies in Education, Stanford, CA 94305-9991. Offers child and adolescent development (PhD); counseling psychology (PhD); educational psychology (PhD). *Degree requirements:* For doctorate, thesis/dissertation. *Entrance requirements:* For doctorate, GRE General Test. Electronic applications accepted.

State University of New York College at Oneonta, Graduate Studies, Division of Education, Department of Educational Psychology and Counseling, Oneonta, NY 13820-4015. Offers school counselor K-12 (MS Ed, CAS). *Accreditation:* NCATE. Part-time and evening/weekend programs available. *Degree requirements:* For master's, comprehensive exam. *Entrance requirements:* For master's, GRE General Test.

Teachers College Columbia University, Graduate Faculty of Education, Department of Health and Behavioral Studies, Program in Applied Educational Psychology – School Psychology, New York, NY 10027-6696. Offers Ed M, MA, Ed D, PhD. *Accreditation:* APA (one or more programs are accredited). *Faculty:* 2 full-time (1 woman), 3 part-time/adjunct. *Students:* 49 full-time (44 women), 50 part-time (44 women); includes 20 minority (6 African Americans, 11 Asian Americans or Pacific Islanders, 3 Hispanic Americans). Average age 31. 219 applicants, 22% accepted, 23 enrolled. In 2006, 24 master's, 5 doctorates awarded. *Degree requirements:* For master's, integrative paper; for doctorate, thesis/dissertation, integrative project. *Entrance requirements:* For doctorate, GRE General Test. *Application deadline:* For fall admission, 5/15 for domestic students. Application fee: $65. *Expenses:* Tuition: Full-time $23,400; part-time $975 per credit. Required fees: $320 per term. *Financial support:* Fellowships, research assistantships, career-related internships or fieldwork, Federal Work-Study, institutionally sponsored loans, and tuition waivers (full and partial) available. Support available to part-time students. Financial award application deadline: 2/1. *Faculty research:* Psychoeducational assessment, observation and concept acquisition in young children, reading, mathematical thinking, memory. *Application contact:* Peter Shon, Assistant Director of Admission, 212-678-3305, Fax: 212-678-4171, E-mail: shon@exchange.tc.columbia.edu.

See Close-Up on page 1129.

Teachers College Columbia University, Graduate Faculty of Education, Department of Human Development, Program in Educational Psychology-Human Cognition and Learning, New York, NY 10027-6696. Offers Ed M, MA, Ed D, PhD. *Accreditation:* APA (one or more programs are accredited). Part-time programs available. *Faculty:* 4 full-time (2 women). *Students:* 16 full-time (12 women), 68 part-time (50 women); includes 24 minority (3 African Americans, 17 Asian Americans or Pacific Islanders, 4 Hispanic Americans), 13 international. Average age 34. 44 applicants, 68% accepted, 15 enrolled. In 2006, 12 master's, 4 doctorates awarded. Terminal master's awarded for partial completion of doctoral program. *Degree requirements:*

Educational Psychology

Teachers College Columbia University (continued)

For master's, integrative paper; for doctorate, thesis/dissertation, integrative project. *Entrance requirements:* For doctorate, GRE General Test. *Application deadline:* For fall admission, 5/15 for domestic students; for spring admission, 12/1 for domestic students. Application fee: $65. *Expenses:* Tuition: Full-time $23,400; part-time $975 per credit. Required fees: $320 per term. *Financial support:* Fellowships, research assistantships, career-related internships or fieldwork, Federal Work-Study, institutionally sponsored loans, and tuition waivers (full and partial) available. Support available to part-time students. Financial award application deadline: 2/1. *Faculty research:* Early reading, text comprehension, learning disabilities, mathematical thinking, reasoning. *Application contact:* Melba Remice, Assistant Director of Admission, 212-678-4035, Fax: 212-678-4171, E-mail: ms2545@columbia.edu.

Temple University, Graduate School, College of Education, Department of Psychological Studies in Education, Program in Educational Psychology, Philadelphia, PA 19122-6096. Offers Ed M, PhD. *Accreditation:* NCATE. Part-time and evening/weekend programs available. *Faculty:* 9 full-time (2 women). *Students:* 20 full-time (17 women), 89 part-time (59 women). 14 applicants, 36% accepted. In 2006, 20 master's, 10 doctorates awarded. Terminal master's awarded for partial completion of doctoral program. *Degree requirements:* For master's, thesis or alternative; for doctorate, thesis/dissertation. *Entrance requirements:* For master's and doctorate, GRE General Test or MAT, minimum GPA of 3.0. Additional exam requirements/recommendations for international students: Required—TOEFL (minimum score 550 paper-based; 213 computer-based; 79 iBT). *Application deadline:* For fall admission, 5/1 for domestic students, 12/15 for international students; for spring admission, 11/1 for domestic students, 8/1 for international students. Applications are processed on a rolling basis. Application fee: $50. Electronic applications accepted. *Expenses:* Tuition, state resident: full-time $12,264; part-time $511 per credit. Tuition, nonresident: full-time $17,904; part-time $746 per credit. Required fees: $84 per course. Tuition and fees vary according to program. *Financial support:* Fellowships, research assistantships with full tuition reimbursements, teaching assistantships with full tuition reimbursements available. Financial award application deadline: 1/15; financial award applicants required to submit FAFSA. *Faculty research:* Computers in education, student motivation, school improvement in city schools, individual differences in learning, teaching strategies. *Unit head:* Dr. William Fullard, Head, 215-204-6022, E-mail: william.fullard@temple.edu.

Tennessee Technological University, Graduate School, College of Education, Department of Counseling and Psychology, Cookeville, TN 38505. Offers educational psychology (MA, Ed S); educational psychology and student personnel (MA, Ed S). *Accreditation:* NCATE (one or more programs are accredited). Part-time and evening/weekend programs available. *Faculty:* 24 full-time (6 women). *Students:* 43 full-time (34 women), 35 part-time (27 women); includes 7 minority (6 African Americans, 1 Asian American or Pacific Islander). Average age 27. 44 applicants, 82% accepted, 27 enrolled. In 2006, 23 master's, 19 other advanced degrees awarded. *Degree requirements:* For Ed S, thesis or alternative. *Entrance requirements:* For master's, MAT; for Ed S, MAT, NTE. Additional exam requirements/recommendations for international students: Required—TOEFL. *Application deadline:* For fall admission, 3/1 priority date for domestic students; for spring admission, 8/1 for domestic students. Application fee: $25 ($30 for international students). Electronic applications accepted. *Expenses:* Tuition, state resident: full-time $8,748; part-time $319 per hour. Tuition, nonresident: full-time $23,524; part-time $740 per hour. *Financial support:* In 2006–07, 1 fellowship (averaging $8,000 per year), 8 research assistantships (averaging $4,000 per year), 3 teaching assistantships (averaging $4,000 per year) were awarded; career-related internships or fieldwork also available. Financial award application deadline: 4/1. *Unit head:* Dr. Michael Rohr, Chairperson, 931-372-3457, Fax: 931-372-6319. *Application contact:* Dr. Francis O. Otuonye, Associate Vice President for Research and Graduate Studies, 931-372-3233, Fax: 931-372-3497, E-mail: fotuonye@tntech.edu.

Texas A&M University, College of Education and Human Development, Department of Educational Psychology, College Station, TX 77843. Offers counseling psychology (PhD); educational psychology (PhD); educational technology (M Ed); gifted and talented education (M Ed, MS); Hispanic bilingual education (M Ed, PhD); human learning and development (MS); intelligence, creativity, and giftedness (PhD); learning, development, and instruction (PhD); research, measurement and statistics (MS); research, measurement, and statistics (PhD); school counseling (M Ed); school psychology (PhD); special education (M Ed, PhD). *Accreditation:* APA (one or more programs are accredited); NCATE. Part-time and evening/weekend programs available. Postbaccalaureate distance learning degree programs offered (no on-campus study). *Faculty:* 25 full-time (11 women), 5 part-time/adjunct (2 women). *Students:* 156 full-time (123 women), 109 part-time (89 women); includes 66 minority (20 African Americans, 1 American Indian/Alaska Native, 7 Asian Americans or Pacific Islanders, 38 Hispanic Americans), 36 international. 159 applicants, 52% accepted, 51 enrolled. In 2006, 59 master's, 21 doctorates awarded. *Median time to degree:* Of those who began their doctoral program in fall 1998, 89% received their degree in 8 years or less. *Degree requirements:* For master's, thesis optional; for doctorate, thesis/dissertation. *Entrance requirements:* For master's and doctorate, GRE General Test. Additional exam requirements/recommendations for international students: Required—TOEFL. Application fee: $50 ($75 for international students). Electronic applications accepted. *Expenses:* Tuition, state resident: full-time $4,697. Tuition, nonresident: full-time $11,297. Required fees: $2,272. *Financial support:* In 2006–07, fellowships (averaging $12,000 per year), research assistantships (averaging $9,000 per year), teaching assistantships (averaging $9,000 per year) were awarded; career-related internships or fieldwork, institutionally sponsored loans, scholarships/grants, and unspecified assistantships also available. Financial award applicants required to submit FAFSA. *Unit head:* Dr. Michael R. Benz, Head, 979-845-1394, Fax: 979-862-1256, E-mail: mbanz@tamu.edu. *Application contact:* Carol A. Wagner, Director of Advising, 979-845-1833, Fax: 979-862-1256, E-mail: c-wagner@tamu.edu.

Texas A&M University–Commerce, Graduate School, College of Education and Human Services, Department of Psychology and Special Education, Commerce, TX 75429-3011. Offers educational psychology (PhD); psychology (MA, MS); special education (M Ed, MA, MS). Part-time programs available. Terminal master's awarded for partial completion of doctoral program. *Degree requirements:* For master's, thesis (for some programs), comprehensive exam; for doctorate, thesis/dissertation, departmental qualifying exam. *Entrance requirements:* For master's, GRE General Test; for doctorate, GRE General Test, 3 letters of recommendation. Electronic applications accepted. *Faculty research:* Human learning, study skills, multicultural bilingual, diversity and special education, educationally handicapped.

Texas Christian University, School of Education, Program in Counseling, Fort Worth, TX 76129-0002. Offers counseling (M Ed); school counseling (Certificate). Part-time and evening/weekend programs available. *Application deadline:* For fall admission, 3/1 for domestic students; for spring admission, 12/1 for domestic students. Applications are processed on a rolling basis. Application fee: $0. *Expenses:* Tuition: Part-time $800 per credit hour. *Financial support:* Application deadline: 3/1. *Application contact:* Director of Graduate Studies, 817-257-7664.

Texas Tech University, Graduate School, College of Education, Department of Educational Psychology and Leadership, Lubbock, TX 79409. Offers counselor (Certificate); counselor education (M Ed, PhD); education diagnostician (Certificate); educational leadership (M Ed, Ed D); educational psychology (M Ed, PhD); gifted and talented (Certificate); higher education (M Ed, Ed D, PhD); information processing technologist (Certificate); instructional technology (M Ed, Ed D); principal (Certificate); special education (M Ed, Ed D); special education counselor (Certificate); superintendent (Certificate); visually handicapped (Certificate). *Accreditation:* ACA; NCATE. Part-time programs available. *Students:* 128 full-time (88 women), 321 part-time (233 women); includes 67 minority (23 African Americans, 1 American Indian/Alaska Native, 5 Asian Americans or Pacific Islanders, 38 Hispanic Americans), 22 international. Average age 38. 347 applicants, 49% accepted, 61 enrolled. In 2006, 110 master's, 16 doctorates awarded. *Degree requirements:* For master's, thesis optional; for doctorate, thesis/dissertation. *Entrance requirements:* For master's and doctorate, GRE General Test. Additional exam requirements/recommendations for international students: Required—TOEFL (minimum score 550 paper-based; 213 computer-based). *Application deadline:* For fall admission, 3/1 priority date for international students; for spring admission, 11/1 priority date for international students. Applications are processed on a rolling basis. Application fee: $50 ($60 for international students). Electronic applications accepted. *Expenses:* Tuition, state resident: full-time $4,440. Tuition, nonresident: full-time $11,040. Required fees: $2,136. *Financial support:* In 2006–07, 242 students received support; research assistantships with partial tuition reimbursements available, teaching assistantships with partial tuition reimbursements available, career-related internships or fieldwork, Federal Work-Study, and institutionally sponsored loans available. Support available to part-time students. Financial award application deadline: 4/15; financial award applicants required to submit FAFSA. *Faculty research:* Psychological processes of teaching and learning, teaching populations with special needs, instructional technology, educational administration in education, theories and practice in counseling and counselor education K-12 and higher. *Unit head:* Dr. Fred Hartmeister, Chair, 806-742-1998 Ext. 436, Fax: 806-742-2179, E-mail: fred.hartmeister@ttu.edu. *Application contact:* Graduate Adviser, 806-742-1998, Fax: 806-742-2179.

Universidad de Iberoamerica, Graduate School, San Jose, Costa Rica. Offers clinical psychology (M Psych); educational psychology (M Psych); hospital and health services management (MHA); intensive care nursing (MN); medicine (MD). *Entrance requirements:* For master's, 2 letters of recommendation, interview.

Université de Moncton, Faculty of Education, Graduate Studies in Education, Moncton, NB E1A 3E9, Canada. Offers educational psychology (M Ed, MA Ed); guidance (M Ed, MA Ed); school administration (M Ed, MA Ed); teaching (M Ed, MA Ed). Part-time programs available. *Degree requirements:* For master's, proficiency in English and French. *Entrance requirements:* For master's, minimum GPA of 3.0. *Faculty research:* Guidance, ethnolinguistic vitality, children's rights, ecological education, entrepreneurship.

Université de Montréal, Faculty of Graduate Studies, Faculty of Education, Department of Psychopedagogy and Andragogy, Montréal, QC H3C 3J7, Canada. Offers M Ed, MA, PhD, DESS. Part-time and evening/weekend programs available. *Faculty:* 27 full-time (19 women), 9 part-time/adjunct (6 women). *Students:* 101 full-time (62 women), 57 part-time (48 women). 55 applicants, 25% accepted, 14 enrolled. In 2006, 6 master's, 6 doctorates, 3 other advanced degrees awarded. Terminal master's awarded for partial completion of doctoral program. *Degree requirements:* For master's, thesis (for some programs); for doctorate, thesis/dissertation, general exam. *Entrance requirements:* For doctorate, MA or M Ed. *Application deadline:* For fall admission, 2/1 priority date for domestic students; for winter admission, 11/1 priority date for domestic students; for spring admission, 2/1 priority date for domestic students. Application fee: $30. Electronic applications accepted. *Financial support:* Teaching assistantships available. *Unit head:* Manon Théręt, Director, 514-343-7035, Fax: 514-343-7660. *Application contact:* Jacques Viens, Information Contact, 514-343-7266, Fax: 514-343-7660.

Université du Québec à Trois-Rivières, Graduate Programs, Program in Psychoeducation, Trois-Rivières, QC G9A 5H7, Canada. Offers M Ed. *Entrance requirements:* For master's, appropriate bachelor's degree, proficiency in French. *Faculty research:* Troubled youth intervention.

Université du Québec en Outaouais, Graduate Programs, Program in Psychoéducation, Gatineau, QC J8X 3X7, Canada. Offers M Ed, MA. Part-time programs available. *Students:* 33 full-time, 15 part-time. *Entrance requirements:* For master's, appropriate bachelor's degree, proficiency in French. *Application deadline:* For fall admission, 6/1 priority date for domestic students, 3/1 for international students; for winter admission, 11/1 priority date for domestic students, 10/1 for international students. Application fee: $30 Canadian dollars. *Financial support:* Fellowships, research assistantships, teaching assistantships available. *Unit head:* Sylvain Coutu, Director, 819-595-3900 Ext. 2289, Fax: 819-595-2250, E-mail: sylvain.coutu@ugo.ca. *Application contact:* Registrar's Office, 819-773-1850, Fax: 819-773-1835, E-mail: registraire@ugo.ca.

Université Laval, Faculty of Education, Department of Teaching and Learning Studies, Programs in Educational Psychology, Québec, QC G1K 7P4, Canada. Offers MA, PhD. Terminal master's awarded for partial completion of doctoral program. *Degree requirements:* For master's, thesis (for some programs); for doctorate, thesis/dissertation, comprehensive exam. *Entrance requirements:* For master's and doctorate, English exam (comprehension of written English), knowledge of French. Electronic applications accepted. *Faculty research:* Emotional, social, and cognitive development; learning and motivation in school; language development; reading acquisition; computer and learning strategies.

University at Albany, State University of New York, School of Education, Department of Educational and Counseling Psychology, Albany, NY 12222-0001. Offers counseling psychology (MS, PhD, CAS); educational psychology (Ed D); educational psychology and statistics (MS); measurements and evaluation (Ed D); rehabilitation counseling (MS), including counseling psychology; school counselor (CAS); school psychology (Psy D, CAS); special education (MS); statistics and research design (Ed D). *Accreditation:* APA (one or more programs are accredited). Evening/weekend programs available. *Students:* 75 full-time (59 women), 25 part-time (21 women). Average age 28. In 2006, 33 master's, 8 doctorates, 12 other advanced degrees awarded. *Degree requirements:* For doctorate, thesis/dissertation. *Entrance requirements:* For doctorate, GRE General Test. Additional exam requirements/recommendations for international students: Required—TOEFL (minimum score 550 paper-based; 213 computer-based). Application fee: $75. Electronic applications accepted. *Expenses:* Tuition, state resident: full-time $6,900; part-time $288 per credit. Tuition, nonresident: full-time $10,920; part-time $455 per credit. Required fees: $1,139. *Financial support:* Fellowships, career-related internships or fieldwork available. *Unit head:* Deborah May, Chair, 518-442-5050.

University at Buffalo, the State University of New York, Graduate School, Graduate School of Education, Department of Counseling, School, and Educational Psychology, Buffalo, NY 14260. Offers counseling/school psychology (PhD); counselor education (PhD); educational psychology (MA, PhD); mental health counseling (MS); rehabilitation counseling (MS); school counseling (Ed M, Certificate); school psychology (MA). *Accreditation:* CORE (one or more programs are accredited). *Faculty:* 19 full-time (9 women), 11 part-time/adjunct (8 women). *Students:* 183 full-time (145 women), 63 part-time (46 women); includes 26 minority (15 African Americans, 1 American Indian/Alaska Native, 6 Asian Americans or Pacific Islanders, 4 Hispanic Americans), 20 international. Average age 25. 398 applicants, 36% accepted, 123 enrolled. In 2006, 57 master's, 20 doctorates, 12 other advanced degrees awarded. *Degree requirements:* For master's, thesis (for some programs), comprehensive exam (for some programs), registration; for doctorate, thesis/dissertation, comprehensive exam, registration. *Entrance requirements:* For master's and doctorate, GRE General Test, interview, letters of reference. Additional exam requirements/recommendations for international students: Required—TOEFL. *Application deadline:* For fall admission, 2/1 priority date for domestic students. Application fee: $50. Electronic applications accepted. *Financial support:* In 2006–07, 40 students received support, including 5 fellowships with full tuition reimbursements available (averaging $10,000 per year), 16 research assistantships with full tuition reimbursements available (averaging $9,000 per year), teaching assistantships with tuition reimbursements available (averaging $9,000 per year); career-related internships or fieldwork, Federal Work-Study, institutionally sponsored loans, and unspecified assistantships also available. Financial award application deadline: 2/1; financial award applicants required to submit FAFSA. *Faculty research:* Multicultural counseling, class size effects, quality of life, eating disorders, outcome assessment. Total annual research expenditures: $1.5 million. *Unit head:* Dr. Scott T. Meier, Chair, 716-645-2484 Ext. 1066, Fax: 716-645-6616, E-mail: stmeier@buffalo.edu. *Application contact:* Rochelle Cohen, Admissions Assistant, 716-645-2110 Ext. 1256, Fax: 716-645-7937, E-mail: recohen@buffalo.edu.

University of Alberta, Faculty of Graduate Studies and Research, Department of Educational Psychology, Edmonton, AB T6G 2E1, Canada. Offers counseling psychology (M Ed, PhD); educational psychology (M Ed, PhD); instructional technology (M Ed); school counseling (M Ed); school psychology (M Ed, PhD); special education (M Ed, PhD); special education-deafness studies (M Ed); teaching English as a second language (M Ed). Part-time programs available. *Faculty:* 34 full-time (14 women), 12 part-time/adjunct (6 women). *Students:* 117 full-time (93 women), 173 part-time (121 women), 15 international. Average age 36. 252 applicants, 34% accepted. In 2006, 30 master's, 10 doctorates awarded. *Degree requirements:* For master's, thesis optional; for doctorate, thesis/dissertation, comprehensive exam. *Entrance requirements:* For master's and doctorate, minimum GPA of 3.0. Additional exam requirements/recommendations for international students: Required—TOEFL. *Application deadline:* For fall admission, 2/1 priority date for domestic and international students. Applications are processed on a rolling basis. *Financial support:* In 2006–07, 10 fellowships with full tuition reimbursements (averaging $16,120 per year), 36 research assistantships with full tuition reimbursements (averaging $12,614 per year), 46 teaching assistantships with full tuition reimbursements (averaging $5,462 per year) were awarded; career-related internships or fieldwork and scholarships/grants also available. *Faculty research:* Human learning, development and assessment. *Unit head:* Dr. Linda M. McDonald, Chair, 780-492-1149, Fax: 780-492-1318, E-mail: linda.mcdonald@ualberta.ca. *Application contact:* Judy Maynes, Information Contact, 780-492-1149, Fax: 780-492-1318, E-mail: edpygrad@ualberta.ca.

The University of Arizona, Graduate College, College of Education, Department of Educational Psychology, Tucson, AZ 85721. Offers educational psychology (MA, PhD); school counseling and guidance (M Ed). *Accreditation:* APA (one or more programs are accredited). Part-time programs available. *Faculty:* 10 full-time (4 women), 2 part-time/adjunct (1 woman). *Students:* 39 full-time (34 women), 34 part-time (26 women); includes 18 minority (5 African Americans, 2 American Indian/Alaska Native, 2 Asian Americans or Pacific Islanders, 9 Hispanic Americans), 6 international. Average age 35. 28 applicants, 57% accepted, 11 enrolled. In 2006, 13 master's, 3 doctorates awarded. Terminal master's awarded for partial completion of doctoral program. *Degree requirements:* For master's, thesis optional; for doctorate, thesis/dissertation, comprehensive exam, registration. *Entrance requirements:* For doctorate, GRE General Test. Additional exam requirements/recommendations for international students: Required—TOEFL (minimum score 600 paper-based; 250 computer-based). *Application deadline:* For fall admission, 2/1 priority date for domestic students, 12/1 for international students; for spring admission, 10/1 priority date for domestic students, 6/1 for international students. Applications are processed on a rolling basis. Application fee: $50. *Financial support:* In 2006–07, 7 fellowships with partial tuition reimbursements (averaging $2,500 per year), 1 research assistantship with partial tuition reimbursement (averaging $5,811 per year), 6 teaching assistantships with partial tuition reimbursements (averaging $5,811 per year) were awarded; career-related internships or fieldwork, scholarships/grants, tuition waivers (partial), and unspecified assistantships also available. *Faculty research:* School reform, motivational learning in classroom settings, measurement and evaluation of learning outcomes, student resilience, preadolesent and adolescent development. *Unit head:* Dr. Thomas Good, Head, 520-621-7828, Fax: 520-621-2909, E-mail: goodt@u.arizona.edu. *Application contact:* Toni Sollars, Administrative Associate, 520-621-7828, Fax: 520-621-2909, E-mail: tsollars@u.arizona.edu.

University of Calgary, Faculty of Graduate Studies, Faculty of Education, Division of Applied Psychology, Calgary, AB T2N 1N4, Canada. Offers counseling psychology (M Ed, M Sc, PhD); human development and learning (M Ed, M Sc, PhD); school psychology (M Ed, M Sc, PhD); special education (M Ed, M Sc, PhD). Part-time programs available. *Faculty:* 16 full-time, 25 part-time/adjunct. *Students:* 130 full-time, 29 part-time. Average age 36. 117 applicants, 19% accepted. In 2006, 35 master's, 13 doctorates awarded. *Degree requirements:* For master's, thesis (for some programs), final oral exam; for doctorate, thesis/dissertation, candidacy exam, final oral exam. *Entrance requirements:* For master's, minimum GPA of 3.0, 3 letters of reference; for doctorate, minimum GPA of 3.5, 3 letters of reference. *Application deadline:* For winter admission, 2/1 for domestic students. Application fee: $60. *Financial support:* In 2006–07, research assistantships (averaging $3,920 per year), teaching assistantships (averaging $5,651 per year) were awarded; fellowships, scholarships/grants also available. Financial award application deadline: 2/1. *Faculty research:* Counselor education, family life studies, learning and cognition. *Unit head:* Dr. Vicki Schean, Associate Dean, 403-220-5651. *Application contact:* Dr. John Mueller, Graduate Coordinator, 403-220-5664, Fax: 403-282-9244, E-mail: mueller@ucalgary.ca.

University of California, Davis, Graduate Studies, Graduate Group in Education, Davis, CA 95616. Offers education (MA, Ed D); instructional studies (PhD); psychological studies (PhD); sociocultural studies (PhD). Terminal master's awarded for partial completion of doctoral program. *Degree requirements:* For master's, thesis (for some programs), comprehensive exam (for some programs); for doctorate, thesis/dissertation. *Entrance requirements:* For master's and doctorate, GRE. Additional exam requirements/recommendations for international students: Required—TOEFL (minimum score 550 paper-based; 213 computer-based). Electronic applications accepted. *Faculty research:* Language and literacy, mathematics education, science education, teacher development, school psychology.

University of Colorado at Boulder, Graduate School, School of Education, Division of Educational and Psychological Studies, Boulder, CO 80309. Offers MA, PhD. *Accreditation:* NCATE. Part-time programs available. *Students:* 10 full-time (8 women), 7 part-time (6 women); includes 1 minority (Hispanic American) Average age 35. In 2006, 1 degree awarded. *Degree requirements:* For master's, thesis or alternative, comprehensive exam; for doctorate, one foreign language, thesis/dissertation, comprehensive exam. *Entrance requirements:* For master's, GRE General Test or MAT, minimum undergraduate GPA of 2.75; for doctorate, GRE General Test. *Application deadline:* For fall admission, 2/1 priority date for domestic students, 12/1 for international students; for spring admission, 9/1 for domestic students, 12/1 for international students. Application fee: $50 ($60 for international students). *Financial support:* In 2006–07, 2 fellowships (averaging $8,360 per year), 4 research assistantships (averaging $13,593 per year), 3 teaching assistantships (averaging $8,294 per year) were awarded. Financial award application deadline: 2/1. *Unit head:* Jennifer Whitcomb, Assistant Dean, 303-735-3029, Fax: 303-492-7090, E-mail: jennie.whitcomb@colorado.edu. *Application contact:* 303-492-6555, Fax: 303-492-5839, E-mail: edadvise@colorado.edu.

University of Colorado at Denver and Health Sciences Center, School of Education and Human Development, Programs in Educational Psychology and Early Childhood Education, Denver, CO 80217-3364. Offers early childhood education (MA); educational psychology (MA). *Accreditation:* NCATE. Part-time and evening/weekend programs available. *Faculty:* 7 full-time (3 women). *Students:* 17 full-time (15 women), 52 part-time (44 women); includes 5 minority (1 African American, 1 American Indian/Alaska Native, 1 Asian American or Pacific Islander, 2 Hispanic Americans), 2 international. Average age 32. 37 applicants, 84% accepted, 13 enrolled. In 2006, 127 degrees awarded. *Degree requirements:* For master's, thesis optional. *Entrance requirements:* For master's, GRE, minimum GPA of 2.75 or MAT. Additional exam requirements/recommendations for international students: Required—TOEFL (minimum score 525 paper-based; 197 computer-based). *Application deadline:* For fall admission, 4/15 for domestic students; for spring admission, 9/15 for domestic students. Applications are processed on a rolling basis. Application fee: $50 ($75 for international students). Electronic applications accepted. *Financial support:* Research assistantships, teaching assistantships, Federal Work-Study available. Financial award application deadline: 4/1; financial award applicants required to submit FAFSA. *Faculty research:* Early childhood growth and development, faculty development, adult learning, gender and equity issues, research methodology. *Unit head:* William Goodwin, Area Coordinator, 303-556-3355, Fax: 303-556-4479, E-mail: william_goodwin@ceo.cudenver.edu. *Application contact:* Meredith Lopez, Application Contact, 303-556-2717, Fax: 303-556-4479.

University of Connecticut, Graduate School, Neag School of Education, Department of Educational Psychology, Field of Educational Psychology, Storrs, CT 06269. Offers cognition and instruction (MA, PhD); counseling psychology (MA, PhD), including counseling psychology (PhD), school counseling (MA); gifted and talented education (MA, PhD); learning technology (MA, PhD); measurement, evaluation, and assessment (MA, PhD); school psychology (MA, PhD); special education (MA, PhD). *Accreditation:* NCATE. *Faculty:* 22 full-time (11 women). *Students:* 154 full-time (127 women), 147 part-time (114 women); includes 35 minority (15 African Americans, 2 American Indian/Alaska Native, 7 Asian Americans or Pacific Islanders, 11 Hispanic Americans), 20 international. Average age 34. 331 applicants, 48% accepted, 139 enrolled. In 2006, 115 master's, 20 doctorates awarded. Terminal master's awarded for partial completion of doctoral program. *Degree requirements:* For master's, thesis or alternative, comprehensive exam; for doctorate, thesis/dissertation. *Entrance requirements:* For master's and doctorate, GRE General Test. Additional exam requirements/recommendations for international students: Required—TOEFL (minimum score 550 paper-based; 213 computer-based). *Application deadline:* For fall admission, 2/1 priority date for domestic and international students; for spring admission, 11/1 for domestic students, 10/1 for international students. Applications are processed on a rolling basis. Application fee: $55. Electronic applications accepted. *Financial support:* In 2006–07, 87 research assistantships with full tuition reimbursements, 1 teaching assistantship with full tuition reimbursement were awarded; fellowships, Federal Work-Study, scholarships/grants, health care benefits, and unspecified assistantships also available. Financial award application deadline: 2/1; financial award applicants required to submit FAFSA. *Application contact:* Lisa Rasicot, Graduate Coordinator, 860-486-3065, Fax: 860-486-0210, E-mail: soeadm02@uconnvm.uconn.edu.

University of Denver, College of Education, Denver, CO 80208. Offers counseling psychology (MA, PhD); curriculum and instruction (MA, PhD, Certificate), including curriculum leadership (MA, PhD); educational administration and policy studies (Certificate); educational psychology (MA, PhD, Ed S), including child and family studies (MA, PhD), quantitative research methods (MA, PhD), school psychology (PhD, Ed S); higher education and adult studies (MA, PhD); library and information science (MLIS); library and information sciences (Certificate); school administration (PhD). *Accreditation:* ALA; APA (one or more programs are accredited). Part-time and evening/weekend programs available. Postbaccalaureate distance learning degree programs offered (no on-campus study). *Faculty:* 28 full-time (18 women). *Students:* 293 full-time (240 women), 439 part-time (357 women); includes 102 minority (28 African Americans, 7 American Indian/Alaska Native, 14 Asian Americans or Pacific Islanders, 53 Hispanic Americans), 11 international. Average age 34. 574 applicants, 72% accepted. In 2006, 168 master's, 28 doctorates, 67 other advanced degrees awarded. Terminal master's awarded for partial completion of doctoral program. *Degree requirements:* For master's, comprehensive exam; for doctorate, 2 foreign languages, thesis/dissertation, comprehensive exam. *Entrance requirements:* For master's, GRE General Test or MAT (for most programs); for doctorate, GRE General Test or MAT. *Application deadline:* Applications are processed on a rolling basis. Application fee: $50. Electronic applications accepted. *Expenses:* Tuition: Full-time $29,628; part-time $823 per credit. *Financial support:* In 2006–07, 51 teaching assistantships with full and partial tuition reimbursements (averaging $6,700 per year) were awarded; career-related internships or fieldwork, Federal Work-Study, institutionally sponsored loans, and scholarships/grants also available. Support available to part-time students. Financial award application deadline: 3/1; financial award applicants required to submit FAFSA. *Faculty research:* Parkinson's disease, personnel training, development and assessments, gifted education, service learning, transportation, public schools. Total annual research expenditures: $172,000. *Unit head:* Dr. Virginia Maloney, Dean, 303-871-2509. *Application contact:* Linda McCarthy, Contact, 303-871-2509, E-mail: edinfo@du.edu.

University of Florida, Graduate School, College of Education, Department of Educational Psychology, Gainesville, FL 32611. Offers educational psychology (M Ed, MAE, Ed D, PhD, Ed S); research and evaluation methodology (M Ed, MAE, Ed D, PhD, Ed S); school psychology (M Ed, MAE, Ed D, PhD, Ed S). *Accreditation:* NCATE. *Faculty:* 15 full-time (6 women). *Students:* 95 (77 women); includes 27 minority (7 African Americans, 1 American Indian/Alaska Native, 4 Asian Americans or Pacific Islanders, 15 Hispanic Americans) 11 international. In 2006, 17 master's, 5 doctorates awarded. Terminal master's awarded for partial completion of doctoral program. *Degree requirements:* For master's, thesis (MAE); for doctorate, variable foreign language requirement, thesis/dissertation. *Entrance requirements:* For master's and doctorate, GRE General Test, minimum GPA of 3.0; for Ed S, GRE General Test. Additional exam requirements/recommendations for international students: Required—TOEFL (minimum score 550 paper-based; 213 computer-based). *Application deadline:* For fall admission, 6/1 priority date for domestic students. Applications are processed on a rolling basis. Application fee: $30. Electronic applications accepted. *Expenses:* Tuition, state resident: full-time $6,827. Tuition, nonresident: full-time $21,951. Required fees: $999. *Financial support:* In 2006–07, 12 teaching assistantships (averaging $8,768 per year) were awarded; fellowships, research assistantships, career-related internships or fieldwork and unspecified assistantships also available. Financial award application deadline: 4/30. *Faculty research:* School improvement, teaching and learning, item response theory. *Unit head:* Tina Smith-Bonahue, Interim Chair, 352-392-0725 Ext. 224. *Application contact:* Dr. Bridget Franks, Coordinator, 352-395-0723 Ext. 234, Fax: 352-392-5929, E-mail: bfranks@coe.ufl.edu.

University of Georgia, Graduate School, College of Education, Department of Educational Psychology and Instructional Technology, Athens, GA 30602. Offers M Ed, MA, Ed D, PhD, Ed S. *Accreditation:* NCATE. *Faculty:* 25 full-time (13 women). *Students:* 123 full-time (85 women), 142 part-time (111 women); includes 21 minority (15 African Americans, 1 American Indian/Alaska Native, 4 Asian Americans or Pacific Islanders, 1 Hispanic American), 49 international. 278 applicants, 45% accepted, 60 enrolled. In 2006, 43 master's, 23 doctorates, 26 other advanced degrees awarded. *Entrance requirements:* For master's and Ed S, GRE General Test or MAT; for doctorate, GRE General Test. *Application deadline:* For fall admission, 7/1 priority date for domestic students; for spring admission, 11/15 for domestic students. Application fee: $50. Electronic applications accepted. *Financial support:* Fellowships, research assistantships, teaching assistantships, unspecified assistantships available. *Unit head:* Dr. Randy W. Kamphaus, Head, 706-542-4253, Fax: 706-542-4240.

University of Hawaii at Manoa, Graduate Division, College of Education, Department of Educational Psychology, Honolulu, HI 96822. Offers M Ed, PhD. *Faculty:* 11 full-time (7 women), 3 part-time/adjunct (1 woman). *Students:* 18 full-time (11 women), 35 part-time (27 women); includes 5 minority (1 African American, 3 Asian Americans or Pacific Islanders, 1 Hispanic American), 6 international. Average age 36. 37 applicants, 54% accepted, 12 enrolled. In 2006, 8 master's, 2 doctorates awarded. *Median time to degree:* Of those who began their doctoral program in fall 1998, 50% received their degree in 8 years or less. *Degree requirements:* For master's, thesis optional; for doctorate, thesis/dissertation, comprehensive exam. *Entrance requirements:* Additional exam requirements/recommendations for international students: Required—TOEFL (minimum score 600 paper-based; 250 computer-based; 100 iBT). *Application deadline:* For fall admission, 2/1 for domestic students, 1/15 for international students. Application fee: $50. *Financial support:* In 2006–07, 11 students received support, including 3 research assistantships (averaging $17,290 per year), 1 teaching assistantship (averaging $14,382 per year); career-related internships or fieldwork, institutionally sponsored loans, and tuition waivers (full) also available. Financial award application deadline: 3/1; financial award applicants required to submit FAFSA. *Faculty research:* Human learning and development, measurement, research methods, statistics. *Application contact:* Marie Iding, Information, 808-956-7775, Fax: 808-956-6615.

University of Houston, College of Education, Department of Educational Psychology, Houston, TX 77204. Offers counseling psychology (M Ed, PhD); educational psychology (M Ed); educational psychology and individual differences (PhD); special education (M Ed, Ed D). *Accreditation:* NCATE. Part-time and evening/weekend programs available. *Faculty:* 17 full-time (9 women), 9 part-time/adjunct (6 women). *Students:* 104 full-time (95 women), 119 part-time (107 women); includes 66 minority (24 African Americans, 1 American Indian/Alaska Native, 15 Asian Americans or Pacific Islanders, 26 Hispanic Americans), 4 international. Average age 33. 107 applicants, 39% accepted, 27 enrolled. In 2006, 47 master's, 11 doctorates awarded. *Degree requirements:* For master's, comprehensive exam or thesis; for doctorate, thesis/dissertation, comprehensive exam. *Entrance requirements:* For master's, GRE

Educational Psychology

University of Houston (continued)

General Test or MAT, interview (counseling psychology); for doctorate, GRE General Test, interview. *Application deadline:* For fall admission, 2/1 for domestic students. Application fee: $35 ($75 for international students). *Expenses:* Tuition, state resident: full-time $5,429; part-time $226 per credit. Tuition, nonresident: full-time $12,029; part-time $501 per credit. Required fees: $2,454. *Financial support:* In 2006–07, 1 fellowship with full tuition reimbursement (averaging $9,500 per year), 3 research assistantships with full tuition reimbursements (averaging $10,225 per year), 35 teaching assistantships with full tuition reimbursements (averaging $10,225 per year) were awarded; career-related internships or fieldwork, Federal Work-Study, institutionally sponsored loans, scholarships/grants, health care benefits, and unspecified assistantships also available. Support available to part-time students. Financial award application deadline: 3/10. *Faculty research:* Cross-cultural assessment and counseling, cognitive and psychosocial development, learning and emotional disturbances. *Unit head:* Dr. Jacqueline Hawkins, Chairperson, 713-743-9827, Fax: 713-743-4996, E-mail: jhawkins@uh.edu. *Application contact:* Graduate Adviser, 713-743-5019, Fax: 713-743-4996, E-mail: epsy@uh.edu.

University of Illinois at Chicago, Graduate College, College of Education, Department of Curriculum and Instruction, Chicago, IL 60607-7128. Offers curriculum and instruction (PhD); educational psychology (PhD); instructional leadership (M Ed), including elementary education, reading, secondary education; leadership and administration (M Ed); policy and administration (PhD); policy studies in urban education (PhD). Part-time and evening/weekend programs available. *Degree requirements:* For doctorate, thesis/dissertation. *Entrance requirements:* For master's, minimum GPA of 2.75; for doctorate, GRE General Test, minimum GPA of 2.75. Additional exam requirements/recommendations for international students: Required—TOEFL. Electronic applications accepted. *Faculty research:* Curriculum theory, curriculum development, research on teaching, curriculum and context, reading/literacy.

University of Illinois at Urbana–Champaign, Graduate College, College of Education, Department of Educational Psychology, Champaign, IL 61820. Offers Ed M, MA, MS, PhD, CAS. *Accreditation:* APA (one or more programs are accredited). Part-time programs available. *Faculty:* 24 full-time (16 women), 1 (woman) part-time/adjunct. *Students:* 92 full-time (66 women), 70 part-time (44 women); includes 25 minority (12 African Americans, 8 Asian Americans or Pacific Islanders, 5 Hispanic Americans), 53 international. 154 applicants, 32% accepted, 21 enrolled. In 2006, 30 master's, 12 doctorates awarded. *Degree requirements:* For doctorate, thesis/dissertation. *Entrance requirements:* For master's and doctorate, GRE General Test, minimum GPA of 3.5. *Application deadline:* Applications are processed on a rolling basis. Application fee: $50 ($60 for international students). Electronic applications accepted. *Financial support:* In 2006–07, 17 fellowships, 52 research assistantships, 51 teaching assistantships were awarded; tuition waivers (full and partial) also available. Financial award application deadline: 1/15. *Unit head:* Michelle Perry, Chair, 217-244-7766, Fax: 217-244-7620, E-mail: mperry@uiuc.edu. *Application contact:* Helen Katz, Secretary, 217-333-5242, Fax: 217-244-7620, E-mail: hnkatz@uiuc.edu.

The University of Iowa, Graduate College, College of Education, Department of Psychological and Quantitative Foundations, Iowa City, IA 52242-1316. Offers counseling psychology (PhD); educational measurement and statistics (MA, PhD); educational psychology (MA, PhD); school psychology (PhD, Ed S); JD/PhD. *Accreditation:* APA. *Faculty:* 21 full-time, 8 part-time/adjunct. *Students:* 97 full-time (71 women), 65 part-time (50 women); includes 30 minority (9 African Americans, 1 American Indian/Alaska Native, 8 Asian Americans or Pacific Islanders, 12 Hispanic Americans), 39 international. 119 applicants, 36% accepted, 23 enrolled. In 2006, 8 master's, 15 doctorates, 3 other advanced degrees awarded. *Degree requirements:* For master's, exam, thesis optional; for doctorate, thesis/dissertation, comprehensive exam, registration; for Ed S, exam. *Entrance requirements:* For master's, doctorate, and Ed S, GRE General Test, minimum GPA of 3.0. Additional exam requirements/recommendations for international students: Required—TOEFL (minimum score 550 paper-based; 213 computer-based; 81 iBT). Application fee: $60 ($85 for international students). Electronic applications accepted. *Financial support:* In 2006–07, 7 fellowships, 89 research assistantships with partial tuition reimbursements, 21 teaching assistantships with partial tuition reimbursements were awarded. Financial award applicants required to submit FAFSA. *Unit head:* Timothy Ansley, Chair, 319-335-5411, Fax: 319-335-6145.

University of Kansas, Graduate Studies, School of Education, Department of Psychology and Research in Education, Program in Educational Psychology and Research, Lawrence, KS 66045. Offers MS Ed, PhD. *Faculty:* 6 full-time (1 woman), 2 part-time/adjunct (1 woman). *Students:* 9 full-time (7 women), 10 part-time (7 women); includes 2 minority (1 African American, 1 Asian American or Pacific Islander), 6 international. Average age 33. 13 applicants, 54% accepted. In 2006, 2 master's, 6 doctorates awarded. *Degree requirements:* For master's, thesis/dissertation; for doctorate, thesis/dissertation, comprehensive exam. *Entrance requirements:* For master's, GRE General Test, minimum GPA of 3.0; for doctorate, GRE General Test. Additional exam requirements/recommendations for international students: Required—TOEFL. *Application deadline:* For fall admission, 4/1 for domestic students; for spring admission, 11/1 for domestic students. Application fee: $55 ($60 for international students). Electronic applications accepted. *Expenses:* Tuition, area resident: Part-time $227 per credit. Tuition, state resident: part-time $543 per credit. Tuition and fees vary according to course load, campus/location, program and reciprocity agreements. *Financial support:* Fellowships, research assistantships with full and partial tuition reimbursements, teaching assistantships with full and partial tuition reimbursements, career-related internships or fieldwork, institutionally sponsored loans, scholarships/grants, traineeships, health care benefits, tuition waivers (full and partial), and unspecified assistantships available. Support available to part-time students. Financial award application deadline: 2/1. *Faculty research:* Educational measurement, applied statistics, research design, program evaluation, learning and development. *Unit head:* Bruce Frey, Faculty Coordinator, 785-864-3931, E-mail: bfrey@ku.edu. *Application contact:* Admissions Coordinator, 785-864-3931, Fax: 785-864-3820, E-mail: preadmit@ku.edu.

University of Kentucky, Graduate School, College of Education, Program in Educational and Counseling Psychology, Lexington, KY 40506-0032. Offers counseling psychology (MS Ed, PhD, Ed S); educational and counseling psychology (MS Ed); educational psychology (Ed D, PhD, Ed S); school psychometrist and school psychology (MA Ed). *Accreditation:* APA (one or more programs are accredited); NCATE. *Students:* 111 full-time (89 women), 22 part-time (15 women); includes 18 minority (16 African Americans, 1 Asian American or Pacific Islander, 1 Hispanic American), 7 international. Average age 33. 204 applicants, 30% accepted, 33 enrolled. In 2006, 24 master's, 15 doctorates, 37 other advanced degrees awarded. *Degree requirements:* For master's, thesis optional; for doctorate, thesis/dissertation, comprehensive exam. *Entrance requirements:* For master's, GRE General Test, minimum undergraduate GPA of 2.75; for doctorate, GRE General Test, minimum graduate GPA of 3.0; for Ed S, GRE General Test. Additional exam requirements/recommendations for international students: Required—TOEFL (minimum score 550 paper-based; 213 computer-based). *Application deadline:* For fall admission, 7/17 priority date for domestic students, 2/1 priority date for international students; for spring admission, 12/13 priority date for domestic students, 6/15 priority date for international students. Application fee: $40 ($55 for international students). Electronic applications accepted. *Expenses:* Tuition, state resident: full-time $7,670; part-time $401 per credit hour. Tuition, nonresident: full-time $16,158; part-time $873 per credit hour. *Financial support:* In 2006–07, 58 students received support, including 9 fellowships with full tuition reimbursements available (averaging $4,821 per year), 22 research assistantships with full tuition reimbursements available (averaging $13,906 per year), 27 teaching assistantships with full tuition reimbursements available (averaging $9,500 per year); career-related internships or fieldwork, Federal Work-Study, institutionally sponsored loans, scholarships/grants, traineeships, health care benefits, tuition waivers (partial), and unspecified assistantships also available. Support available to part-time students. Financial award application deadline: 3/15. *Unit head:* Dr. Lynley Anderman, Director of Graduate Studies, 859-257-8647, Fax: 859-257-5662, E-mail: lynley.anderman@uky.edu. *Application contact:* Dr. Brian Jackson, Senior Associate Dean, 859-257-4667, Fax: 859-257-4676, E-mail: brian.jackson@uky.edu.

University of Louisville, Graduate School, College of Education and Human Development, Department of Educational and Counseling Psychology, Louisville, KY 40292-0001. Offers college student personnel services (M Ed); counseling and personnel services (M Ed, PhD), including school counseling and guidance; counseling psychology (M Ed, PhD); expressive therapies (M Ed); mental health counseling (PhD). *Accreditation:* APA; NCATE. *Students:* 122 full-time (90 women), 125 part-time (100 women); includes 54 minority (48 African Americans, 1 American Indian/Alaska Native, 5 Asian Americans or Pacific Islanders), 6 international. Average age 35. In 2006, 78 master's, 9 doctorates awarded. *Degree requirements:* For doctorate, thesis/dissertation. *Entrance requirements:* For master's and doctorate, GRE General Test. *Application deadline:* Applications are processed on a rolling basis. Application fee: $50. Electronic applications accepted. *Financial support:* Fellowships, research assistantships, teaching assistantships, Federal Work-Study and scholarships/grants available. *Unit head:* Dr. Samuel C Stringfield, Acting Chair, 502-852-6884, Fax: 502-852-0629, E-mail: sam.stringfield@louisville.edu.

University of Manitoba, Faculty of Graduate Studies, Faculty of Education, Department of Educational Administration, Foundations and Psychology, Winnipeg, MB R3T 2N2, Canada. Offers adult education (M Ed); educational administration (M Ed); guidance and counseling (M Ed); inclusive special education (M Ed); special foundations education (M Ed). *Degree requirements:* For master's, thesis or alternative.

University of Mary Hardin-Baylor, College of Education, Belton, TX 76513. Offers educational administration (M Ed, Ed D); educational psychology (M Ed); exercise and sport science (M Ed); general studies (M Ed); reading education (M Ed). Part-time and evening/weekend programs available. *Faculty:* 10 full-time (5 women), 1 part-time/adjunct (0 women). *Students:* 8 full-time (3 women), 36 part-time (26 women); includes 8 minority (3 African Americans, 5 Hispanic Americans). Average age 24. In 2006, 18 degrees awarded. *Degree requirements:* For master's, comprehensive exam, registration. *Entrance requirements:* For master's, GRE General Test, minimum GPA of 2.75, Texas teaching certificate. *Application deadline:* For fall admission, 6/1 priority date for domestic students; for spring admission, 11/1 for domestic students. Applications are processed on a rolling basis. Application fee: $35 ($135 for international students). Electronic applications accepted. *Expenses:* Tuition: Full-time $8,910; part-time $495 per hour. Required fees: $906; $47 per hour. $30 per term. Tuition and fees vary according to course load. *Financial support:* Federal Work-Study, scholarships/grants, and scholarships (for some active duty military personnel only) available. Support available to part-time students. Financial award application deadline: 6/1; financial award applicants required to submit FAFSA. *Unit head:* Dr. Marlene Zipperlen, Dean, 254-295-4572, Fax: 254-295-4480, E-mail: mzipperlen@umhb.edu. *Application contact:* Dr. Shirley Dahl, Director, Graduate Programs in Education, 254-295-4185, Fax: 254-295-4480, E-mail: sdahl@umhb.edu.

University of Maryland, College Park, Graduate Studies, College of Education, Department of Human Development, College Park, MD 20742. Offers early childhood/elementary education (M Ed, MA, Ed D, PhD); human development (M Ed, MA, Ed D, PhD). *Accreditation:* NCATE. Part-time and evening/weekend programs available. Postbaccalaureate distance learning degree programs offered. *Faculty:* 43 full-time (37 women), 16 part-time/adjunct (12 women). *Students:* 61 full-time (54 women), 39 part-time (32 women); includes 19 minority (11 African Americans, 5 Asian Americans or Pacific Islanders, 3 Hispanic Americans), 7 international. 97 applicants, 51% accepted, 29 enrolled. In 2006, 16 master's, 9 doctorates awarded. *Median time to degree:* Of those who began their doctoral program in fall 1998, 57% received their degree in 8 years or less. *Degree requirements:* For master's, thesis optional; for doctorate, thesis/dissertation, essay, exam, research paper, comprehensive exam. *Entrance requirements:* For master's, GRE General Test, minimum GPA of 3.0, 3 letters of recommendation; for doctorate, GRE General Test or MAT, minimum undergraduate GPA of 3.0, graduate 3.5; 3 letters of recommendation. Additional exam requirements/recommendations for international students: Required—TOEFL. *Application deadline:* For fall admission, 5/1 for domestic students, 11/15 for international students; for spring admission, 10/1 for domestic and international students. Applications are processed on a rolling basis. Application fee: $60. Electronic applications accepted. *Financial support:* In 2006–07, 18 fellowships with full tuition reimbursements (averaging $13,943 per year), 2 research assistantships with tuition reimbursements (averaging $15,766 per year), 35 teaching assistantships with tuition reimbursements (averaging $15,881 per year) were awarded; Federal Work-Study and scholarships/grants also available. Support available to part-time students. Financial award applicants required to submit FAFSA. *Faculty research:* Developmental science, educational psychology, cognitive development, language development. Total annual research expenditures: $3.2 million. *Unit head:* Dr. Alan L. Wigfield, Chair, 301-405-1659, Fax: 301-405-2891, E-mail: awigfield@umd.edu. *Application contact:* Dean of Graduate School, 301-405-0358, Fax: 301-314-9305.

University of Memphis, Graduate School, College of Education, Department of Counseling, Educational Psychology and Research, Memphis, TN 38152. Offers counseling and personnel services (MS, Ed D), including community agency counseling (MS), rehabilitation counseling (MS), school counseling (MS), student personnel services (MS); counseling psychology (PhD); educational psychology and research (MS, Ed D, PhD), including educational psychology (MS, Ed D), educational research (MS, Ed D). *Accreditation:* ACA (one or more programs are accredited); APA (one or more programs are accredited); CORE (one or more programs are accredited); NCATE. *Degree requirements:* For master's, thesis or alternative, comprehensive exam; for doctorate, thesis/dissertation, comprehensive exam. *Entrance requirements:* For master's, GRE General Test or MAT, minimum GPA of 2.5; for doctorate, GRE General Test. *Faculty research:* Anger management, aging and disability, supervision, multicultural counseling.

University of Minnesota, Twin Cities Campus, Graduate School, College of Education and Human Development, Department of Educational Psychology, Minneapolis, MN 55455-0213. Offers counseling and student personnel psychology (MA, PhD, Ed S); early childhood education (M Ed, MA, PhD); educational psychology (PhD); psychological foundations of education (MA, PhD, Ed S); school psychology (MA, PhD, Ed S); special education (M Ed, MA, PhD, Ed S); talent development and gifted education (Certificate). *Accreditation:* APA (one or more programs are accredited). *Faculty:* 33 full-time (11 women). *Students:* 323 full-time (260 women), 118 part-time (95 women); includes 39 minority (15 African Americans, 4 American Indian/Alaska Native, 14 Asian Americans or Pacific Islanders, 6 Hispanic Americans), 56 international. Average age 32. 334 applicants, 53% accepted, 122 enrolled. In 2006, 112 master's, 20 doctorates, 10 other advanced degrees awarded. *Expenses:* Tuition, state resident: full-time $9,302; part-time $775 per credit. Tuition, nonresident: full-time $16,400; part-time $1,367 per credit. Full-time tuition and fees vary according to class time, course load, program, reciprocity agreements and student level. *Financial support:* In 2006–07, 8 fellowships (averaging $24,775 per year), 72 research assistantships (averaging $24,775 per year), 40 teaching assistantships (averaging $24,775 per year) were awarded. *Faculty research:* Social psychology and development in education, multicultural education and counseling, international psychology, learning and readiness processes, measurement and statistical processes. Total annual research expenditures: $2.5 million. *Unit head:* Dr. John Romano, Chair, 612-624-1099, Fax: 612-624-8241, E-mail: roman001@umn.edu. *Application contact:* Dr. Mary Bents, Associate Dean, 612-625-6501, Fax: 612-626-1580, E-mail: mbents@tc.umn.edu.

University of Missouri–Columbia, Graduate School, College of Education, Department of Educational, School, and Counseling Psychology, Columbia, MO 65211. Offers counseling psychology (M Ed, MA, PhD, Ed S); educational psychology (M Ed, MA, PhD, Ed S); learning and instruction (M Ed); school psychology (M Ed, MA, PhD, Ed S). *Accreditation:* APA (one or more programs are accredited); CORE. Part-time programs available. *Faculty:* 31 full-time (10 women), 1 (woman) part-time/adjunct. *Students:* 134 full-time (99 women), 59 part-time (45 women); includes 33 minority (20 African Americans, 2 American Indian/Alaska Native, 6 Asian Americans or Pacific Islanders, 5 Hispanic Americans), 23 international. In 2006, 56 master's,

13 doctorates, 13 other advanced degrees awarded. *Degree requirements:* For doctorate, thesis/dissertation. *Entrance requirements:* For master's, doctorate, and Ed S, GRE General Test, minimum GPA of 3.0. *Application deadline:* For fall admission, 1/8 priority date for domestic students. Applications are processed on a rolling basis. Application fee: $45 ($60 for international students). *Financial support:* Fellowships, research assistantships, teaching assistantships, institutionally sponsored loans available. *Unit head:* Dr. David Bergin, Director of Graduate Studies, 573-882-1303, E-mail: bergind@missouri.edu.

University of Missouri–St. Louis, College of Education, Division of Educational Psychology, Research, and Evaluation, St. Louis, MO 63121. Offers education (Ed D); educational psychology (PhD); school psychology (Certificate, Ed S). *Faculty:* 10 full-time (2 women), 2 part-time/adjunct (1 woman). *Students:* 15 full-time (13 women), 21 part-time (18 women); includes 1 minority (African American), 2 international. Average age 33. In 2006, 5 degrees awarded. *Degree requirements:* For doctorate, thesis/dissertation. *Entrance requirements:* For doctorate, GRE General Test, 3 letters of recommendation. Additional exam requirements/recommendations for international students: Required—TOEFL (minimum score 550 paper-based; 213 computer-based). *Application deadline:* For fall admission, 2/15 for domestic students; for spring admission, 9/15 for domestic students. Application fee: $35 ($40 for international students). Electronic applications accepted. *Expenses:* Tuition, state resident: part-time $332 per credit hour. Tuition, nonresident: part-time $770 per credit hour. *Financial support:* In 2006–07, 1 research assistantship (averaging $25,500 per year) was awarded; teaching assistantships. *Faculty research:* Child/adolescent psychology, quantitative and qualitative methodology, evaluation processes, measurement and assessment. *Unit head:* Dr. Matthew Keefer, Chairperson, 314-516-5783, Fax: 314-516-5784, E-mail: keefer@umsl.edu. *Application contact:* 314-516-5458, Fax: 314-516-6996, E-mail: gradadm@umsl.edu.

University of Nebraska at Omaha, Graduate Studies and Research, College of Arts and Sciences, Department of Psychology, Omaha, NE 68182. Offers developmental psychology (PhD); industrial/organizational psychology (MS, PhD); psychobiology (PhD); psychology (MA); school psychology (MS, Ed S). Part-time programs available. *Faculty:* 19 full-time (9 women). *Students:* 40 full-time (30 women), 25 part-time (19 women); includes 4 minority (2 African Americans, 1 Asian American or Pacific Islander, 1 Hispanic American), 3 international. Average age 29. 93 applicants, 44% accepted, 27 enrolled. In 2006, 11 master's, 2 other advanced degrees awarded. *Degree requirements:* For master's, thesis (for some programs), comprehensive exam. *Entrance requirements:* For master's, GRE General Test, GRE Subject Test, previous course work in psychology, including statistics and a laboratory course; minimum GPA of 3.0, 3 letters of recommendation; for doctorate, GRE General Test. Additional exam requirements/recommendations for international students: Required—TOEFL (minimum score 500 paper-based; 173 computer-based; 61 iBT). *Application deadline:* For fall admission, 1/5 for domestic students. Application fee: $45. Electronic applications accepted. *Financial support:* In 2006–07, 56 students received support; fellowships, research assistantships with tuition reimbursements available, teaching assistantships with tuition reimbursements available, career-related internships or fieldwork, Federal Work-Study, institutionally sponsored loans, scholarships/grants, tuition waivers (partial), and unspecified assistantships available. Support available to part-time students. Financial award application deadline: 3/1; financial award applicants required to submit FAFSA. *Unit head:* Dr. Kenneth Deffenbacher, Chairperson, 402-554-2592. *Application contact:* Dr. Joseph Brown, Student Contact, 402-554-2592.

University of Nebraska–Lincoln, Graduate College, College of Education and Human Services, Department of Educational Psychology, Lincoln, NE 68588. Offers MA, Ed S. *Accreditation:* APA (one or more programs are accredited); NCATE. *Degree requirements:* For master's, thesis optional. *Entrance requirements:* For master's, GRE General Test. Additional exam requirements/recommendations for international students: Required—TOEFL (minimum score 500 paper-based; 173 computer-based). Electronic applications accepted. *Faculty research:* Measurement and assessment, metacognition, academic skills, child development, multicultural education and counseling.

University of Nevada, Las Vegas, Graduate College, College of Education, Department of Educational Psychology, Las Vegas, NV 89154-9900. Offers education psychology (MS); educational psychology (PhD); learning and technology (PhD); school counseling (M Ed); school counselor education (PhD); school psychology (PhD, Ed S). *Accreditation:* ACA (one or more programs are accredited); NCATE. Part-time and evening/weekend programs available. *Faculty:* 21 full-time (10 women), 1 (woman) part-time/adjunct. *Students:* 70 full-time (55 women), 95 part-time (68 women); includes 36 minority (18 African Americans, 12 Asian Americans or Pacific Islanders, 6 Hispanic Americans), 7 international. 104 applicants, 53% accepted, 47 enrolled. In 2006, 23 master's, 3 doctorates, 17 other advanced degrees awarded. *Degree requirements:* For master's, thesis (for some programs), comprehensive exam (for some programs); for doctorate, thesis/dissertation, oral exam, comprehensive exam. *Entrance requirements:* For master's, GRE General Test, minimum GPA of 3.0 during previous 2 years, 2.75 overall; for doctorate, GRE General Test, minimum GPA of 3.0. Additional exam requirements/recommendations for international students: Required—TOEFL (minimum score 550 paper-based; 213 computer-based; 80 iBT). *Application deadline:* For fall admission, 2/1 for domestic and international students. Application fee: $60 ($75 for international students). Electronic applications accepted. *Financial support:* In 2006–07, 17 research assistantships with partial tuition reimbursements (averaging $11,000 per year), 10 teaching assistantships with partial tuition reimbursements (averaging $12,000 per year) were awarded; career-related internships or fieldwork, Federal Work-Study, institutionally sponsored loans, scholarships/grants, health care benefits, and unspecified assistantships also available. Support available to part-time students. Financial award application deadline: 3/1. *Unit head:* Dr. Ralph E. Reynolds, Chair, 702-895-3787, E-mail: ralph.reynolds@unlv.edu. *Application contact:* Graduate College Admissions Evaluator, 702-895-3320, Fax: 702-895-4180, E-mail: gradcollege@unlv.edu.

University of Nevada, Reno, Graduate School, College of Education, Department of Counseling and Educational Psychology, Reno, NV 89557. Offers M Ed, MA, MS, Ed D, PhD, Ed S. *Accreditation:* ACA (one or more programs are accredited); NCATE. *Faculty:* 17. *Students:* 71 full-time (50 women), 64 part-time (52 women); includes 20 minority (4 African Americans, 5 American Indian/Alaska Native, 2 Asian Americans or Pacific Islanders, 9 Hispanic Americans), 5 international. Average age 36. 53 applicants, 85% accepted, 32 enrolled. In 2006, 24 master's, 10 doctorates, 4 other advanced degrees awarded. Terminal master's awarded for partial completion of doctoral program. *Degree requirements:* For master's, thesis optional; for doctorate, thesis/dissertation, qualifying exam, comprehensive exam. *Entrance requirements:* For master's, GRE, minimum GPA of 2.75; for doctorate, GRE, minimum GPA of 3.0. Additional exam requirements/recommendations for international students: Required—TOEFL. *Application deadline:* For fall admission, 2/15 priority date for domestic students; for spring admission, 9/15 for domestic students. Application fee: $60 ($95 for international students). *Financial support:* In 2006–07, 2 research assistantships with tuition reimbursements, 9 teaching assistantships with tuition reimbursements were awarded; Federal Work-Study, institutionally sponsored loans, and scholarships/grants also available. Financial award application deadline: 3/1. *Faculty research:* Marriage and family counseling, substance abuse attitudes of teachers, current supply of counseling educators, HIV-positive services for patients, family counseling for youth at risk. *Unit head:* Dr. Thomas Harrison, Chair, 775-784-6637.

University of New Mexico, Graduate School, College of Education, Department of Individual, Family and Community Education, Program in Educational Psychology, Albuquerque, NM 87131-2039. Offers MA, PhD. *Accreditation:* NCATE. Part-time and evening/weekend programs available. *Students:* 11 full-time (9 women), 23 part-time (16 women); includes 13 minority (2 African Americans, 3 American Indian/Alaska Native, 8 Hispanic Americans). Average age 43. 11 applicants, 36% accepted, 4 enrolled. In 2006, 6 degrees awarded. *Degree requirements:* For master's, thesis (for some programs), comprehensive exam (for some programs), registration; for doctorate, thesis/dissertation, comprehensive exam, registration. *Entrance requirements:* For master's, GRE General Test or MAT, minimum GPA of 3.0 in last 2 years of undergraduate study, 3 letters of reference, interview with 3 faculty; for doctorate, GRE General Test or MAT, minimum GPA of 3.0 in last 2 years of undergraduate study, 3 letters of reference. *Application deadline:* For fall admission, 3/15 priority date for domestic students; for spring admission, 10/15 priority date for domestic students. Applications are processed on a rolling basis. Application fee: $50. Electronic applications accepted. *Financial support:* In 2006–07, 6 research assistantships (averaging $6,057 per year), 12 teaching assistantships with full and partial tuition reimbursements (averaging $12,804 per year) were awarded. Financial award application deadline: 3/1; financial award applicants required to submit FAFSA. *Faculty research:* Measurement and assessment, cognitive strategies, accountability, motivation, instructional technology. *Unit head:* Dr. Deborah Rifenbary, Program Coordinator, 505-277-4535, Fax: 505-277-8361, E-mail: edpsy@unm.edu. *Application contact:* Cynthia Salas, Information Contact, 505-277-4535, Fax: 505-277-8361, E-mail: casalas@unm.edu.

The University of North Carolina at Chapel Hill, Graduate School, School of Education, Program in Education, Chapel Hill, NC 27599. Offers culture, curriculum and change (PhD); culture, curriculum, and change (MA); early childhood, families, and literacy studies (MA, PhD); educational psychology measurements, and evaluation (PhD); educational psychology, measurement, and evaluation (MA). *Accreditation:* NCATE. In 2006, 11 master's, 10 doctorates awarded. *Degree requirements:* For master's, thesis/dissertation; for doctorate, thesis/dissertation, comprehensive exam, registration. *Entrance requirements:* For master's, GRE General Test, minimum GPA of 3.0 during last 2 years of undergraduates course work; for doctorate, GRE General Test, minimum GPA of 3.0 during last 2 years of undergraduate course work. Additional exam requirements/recommendations for international students: Required—TOEFL (minimum score 550 paper-based; 213 computer-based). *Application deadline:* For fall admission, 1/1 priority date for domestic and international students. Applications are processed on a rolling basis. Application fee: $60. Electronic applications accepted. *Financial support:* Federal Work-Study available. Support available to part-time students. Financial award application deadline: 3/1; financial award applicants required to submit FAFSA. *Application contact:* Janet Carroll, Registrar, 919-962-8690, Fax: 919-962-1533, E-mail: jscarrol@email.unc.edu.

University of Northern Colorado, Graduate School, College of Education and Behavioral Sciences, School of Psychological Sciences, Program in Educational Psychology, Greeley, CO 80639. Offers early childhood education (MA); educational psychology (MA, PhD). *Accreditation:* NCATE. Part-time programs available. *Faculty:* 13 full-time (6 women). *Students:* 22 full-time (19 women), 5 part-time (2 women); includes 2 minority (both Hispanic Americans), 2 international. Average age 37. 16 applicants, 94% accepted, 6 enrolled. In 2006, 3 master's, 3 doctorates awarded. *Degree requirements:* For master's, thesis or alternative, comprehensive exam; for doctorate, thesis/dissertation, comprehensive exam. *Entrance requirements:* For master's, GRE General Test, letters of recommendation; for doctorate, GRE General Test, letters of recommendation, resumé. *Application deadline:* Applications are processed on a rolling basis. Application fee: $50 ($60 for international students). Electronic applications accepted. *Expenses:* Tuition, state resident: full-time $5,118; part-time $213 per credit hour. Tuition, nonresident: full-time $14,832; part-time $618 per credit hour. Required fees: $674; $34 per credit hour. *Financial support:* In 2006–07, 26 students received support, including 8 fellowships (averaging $2,327 per year), 2 research assistantships (averaging $14,477 per year), 11 teaching assistantships (averaging $7,813 per year); unspecified assistantships also available. Financial award application deadline: 3/1; financial award applicants required to submit FAFSA.

University of Northern Iowa, Graduate College, College of Education, Department of Educational Psychology and Foundations, Cedar Falls, IA 50614. Offers educational psychology (MAE), including professional development for teachers; school psychology (Ed S). Part-time and evening/weekend programs available. *Faculty:* 22 full-time (9 women). *Students:* 15 full-time (11 women), 20 part-time (18 women); includes 1 minority (African American), 2 international. 35 applicants, 71% accepted, 15 enrolled. In 2006, 16 degrees awarded. *Degree requirements:* For master's and Ed S, thesis or alternative. *Entrance requirements:* For master's, GRE General Test, 3 years of educational experience, minimum GPA of 3.5; for Ed S, GRE General Test. Additional exam requirements/recommendations for international students: Required—TOEFL (minimum score 500 paper-based; 180 computer-based; 61 iBT). *Application deadline:* For fall admission, 8/1 priority date for domestic students. Applications are processed on a rolling basis. Application fee: $30 ($50 for international students). Electronic applications accepted. *Expenses:* Tuition, state resident: full-time $5,936. Tuition, nonresident: full-time $14,074. *Financial support:* Career-related internships or fieldwork, Federal Work-Study, scholarships/grants, and tuition waivers (full and partial) available. Support available to part-time students. Financial award application deadline: 2/1. *Unit head:* Dr. Michael D. Waggoner, Coordinator, 319-273-2605, Fax: 319-273-5175, E-mail: mike.waggoner@uni.edu.

University of Oklahoma, Graduate College, College of Education, Department of Educational Psychology, Program in Instructional Psychology, Norman, OK 73019-0390. Offers M Ed, PhD. Part-time programs available. *Students:* 21 full-time (15 women), 30 part-time (21 women); includes 7 minority (5 African Americans, 2 American Indian/Alaska Native), 6 international. 11 applicants, 82% accepted, 5 enrolled. In 2006, 7 master's, 3 doctorates awarded. *Degree requirements:* For master's, thesis optional; for doctorate, thesis/dissertation, general exam. *Entrance requirements:* For master's, minimum GPA of 3.0; for doctorate, GRE General Test, master's degree, minimum graduate GPA of 3.25. Additional exam requirements/recommendations for international students: Required—TOEFL (minimum score 550 paper-based; 213 computer-based). *Application deadline:* For fall admission, 2/1 for domestic and international students; for spring admission, 10/15 for domestic and international students. Applications are processed on a rolling basis. Application fee: $40 ($90 for international students). *Expenses:* Tuition, state resident: full-time $3,180; part-time $133 per credit hour. Tuition, nonresident: full-time $11,347; part-time $473 per credit hour. Required fees: $1,729; $62 per credit hour. $117 per semester. Tuition and fees vary according to course load and program. *Financial support:* In 2006–07, 18 students received support; fellowships with tuition reimbursements available, research assistantships with partial tuition reimbursements available, teaching assistantships with partial tuition reimbursements available, institutionally sponsored loans, scholarships/grants, health care benefits, and unspecified assistantships available. Financial award applicants required to submit FAFSA. *Faculty research:* Student motivation and engagement in learning, measurement of motivation, visual literacy, scaffolding problem solving with technology. *Unit head:* Dr. Ray Miller, Program Coordinator, 405-325-5974, Fax: 405-325-6655, E-mail: rmiller@ou.edu. *Application contact:* Applications Officer, 405-325-4525, Fax: 405-325-6655, E-mail: gpoedpsych@ou.edu.

University of Pennsylvania, Graduate School of Education, Division of Applied Psychology and Human Development, Philadelphia, PA 19104. Offers MS Ed, Ed D, PhD. Part-time programs available. Terminal master's awarded for partial completion of doctoral program. *Degree requirements:* For master's, exam; for doctorate, thesis/dissertation, exam. *Entrance requirements:* For master's, GRE General Test; for doctorate, GRE General Test, GRE Subject Test. Electronic applications accepted. Expenses: Contact institution. *Faculty research:* Multivariate analysis, therapeutic intervention at a preschool level, actuarial systems for assessment of children.

University of Phoenix–Southern Arizona Campus, The Artemis School, College of Education, Tucson, AZ 85712-2732. Offers curriculum instruction (MA Ed); educational counseling (MA Ed); elementary licensure (MA Ed); school counseling (MSC); secondary licensure (MA Ed); special education (Certificate). Evening/weekend programs available. *Faculty:* 101. *Students:* 75 full-time (55 women); includes 16 minority (2 African Americans, 1 American Indian/Alaska Native, 1 Asian American or Pacific Islander, 12 Hispanic Americans), 2 international. Average age 38. In 2006, 113 degrees awarded. *Degree requirements:* For master's, thesis (for some programs), registration. *Entrance requirements:* For master's, minimum undergraduate GPA of 2.5, 3 years of work experience. Additional exam requirements/recommendations for international students: Required—TOEFL (minimum score 550 paper-based; 213 computer-based; 79 iBT). *Application deadline:* Applications are processed on a rolling basis. Application fee: $45. Electronic applications accepted. *Expenses:* Tuition: Full-time $8,669.

Educational Psychology

University of Phoenix–Southern Arizona Campus (continued)

Required fees: $760. *Financial support:* Institutionally sponsored loans and scholarships/grants available. Financial award applicants required to submit FAFSA. *Unit head:* Dr. Marla LaRue, Dean/Executive Director, 480-557-1218, E-mail: marla.larue@phoenix.edu. *Application contact:* Campus College Chair, 520-881-6512, Fax: 520-795-6177.

University of Regina, Faculty of Graduate Studies and Research, Faculty of Education, Department of Educational Psychology, Regina, SK S4S 0A2, Canada. Offers M Ed. Part-time programs available. *Faculty:* 5 full-time (3 women), 1 part-time/adjunct (0 women). *Students:* 10 full-time (6 women), 45 part-time (42 women). 37 applicants, 68% accepted. In 2006, 15 degrees awarded. *Degree requirements:* For master's, practicum, project, or thesis. *Entrance requirements:* For master's, bachelor's degree in education. Additional exam requirements/recommendations for international students: Required—TOEFL (minimum score 580 paper-based; 237 computer-based; 88 iBT). *Application deadline:* For fall admission, 2/15 for domestic students; for winter admission, 2/15 for domestic students; for spring admission, 2/15 for domestic students. Application fee: $60 ($100 for international students). *Financial support:* Fellowships, research assistantships, teaching assistantships, career-related internships or fieldwork available. Financial award application deadline: 6/15. *Application contact:* Vicki Minhinnick, Graduate Program Coordinator, 306-585-4506, Fax: 306-585-5387, E-mail: edgrad@uregina.ca.

University of Saskatchewan, College of Graduate Studies and Research, College of Education, Department of Educational Psychology and Special Education, Saskatoon, SK S7N 5A2, Canada. Offers M Ed, PhD, Diploma. *Degree requirements:* For master's, thesis (for some programs), registration; for doctorate, thesis/dissertation, registration. *Entrance requirements:* Additional exam requirements/recommendations for international students: Required—TOEFL.

University of South Carolina, The Graduate School, College of Education, Department of Educational Studies, Program in Educational Psychology, Research, Columbia, SC 29208. Offers M Ed, PhD. *Accreditation:* NCATE. *Degree requirements:* For master's, thesis (for some programs), comprehensive exam; for doctorate, thesis/dissertation, comprehensive exam. *Entrance requirements:* For master's, GRE General Test; for doctorate, GRE General Test, interview. Electronic applications accepted. *Faculty research:* Problem solving, higher order thinking skills, psychometric research, methodology.

The University of South Dakota, Graduate School, School of Education, Division of Counseling and Psychology in Education, Vermillion, SD 57069-2390. Offers MA, PhD, Ed S. *Accreditation:* ACA (one or more programs are accredited); NCATE. Part-time programs available. *Faculty:* 14 full-time (7 women), 2 part-time/adjunct (1 woman). *Students:* 135 (102 women). In 2006, 20 master's, 3 doctorates, 7 other advanced degrees awarded. *Degree requirements:* For master's and Ed S, thesis or alternative, comprehensive exam; for doctorate, thesis/dissertation, comprehensive exam. *Entrance requirements:* For master's and doctorate, GRE General Test, minimum GPA of 3.0. Additional exam requirements/recommendations for international students: Required—TOEFL (minimum score 550 paper-based; 213 computer-based; 79 iBT). *Application deadline:* Applications are processed on a rolling basis. Application fee: $35. Electronic applications accepted. *Expenses:* Tuition, state resident: part-time $120 per credit hour. Tuition, nonresident: part-time $355 per credit hour. Required fees: $90 per credit hour. *Financial support:* In 2006–07, research assistantships with partial tuition reimbursements (averaging $4,626 per year), teaching assistantships with partial tuition reimbursements (averaging $4,626 per year) were awarded; career-related internships or fieldwork, Federal Work-Study, and unspecified assistantships also available. Financial award applicants required to submit FAFSA. *Unit head:* Dr. Frank Main, Chair, 605-677-5250, Fax: 605-677-5438, E-mail: fmain@usd.edu.

The University of Tennessee, Graduate School, College of Education, Health and Human Sciences, Department of Educational Psychology and Counseling, Knoxville, TN 37996. Offers adult education (MS); applied educational psychology (MS); collaborative learning (Ed D); college student personnel (MS); mental health counseling (MS); rehabilitation counseling (MS); school counseling (MS). *Accreditation:* ACA (one or more programs are accredited); CORE (one or more programs are accredited); NCATE. Part-time and evening/weekend programs available. *Students:* 27 (20 women); includes 2 African Americans, 1 American Indian/Alaska Native 1 international. 69 applicants, 33% accepted. In 2006, 36 degrees awarded. *Degree requirements:* For master's, thesis optional. *Entrance requirements:* For master's, GRE General Test, minimum GPA of 2.7. Additional exam requirements/recommendations for international students: Required—TOEFL. *Application deadline:* For fall admission, 2/1 priority date for domestic students. Applications are processed on a rolling basis. Application fee: $35. Electronic applications accepted. *Expenses:* Tuition, state resident: full-time $5,574. Tuition, nonresident: full-time $16,840. Required fees: $792. *Financial support:* In 2006–07, 1 research assistantship, 2 teaching assistantships were awarded. Financial award application deadline: 2/1; financial award applicants required to submit FAFSA. *Unit head:* Dr. Olga Welch, Head, 865-974-5131, Fax: 865-974-8674, E-mail: owelch@utk.edu.

The University of Tennessee, Graduate School, College of Education, Health and Human Sciences, Program in Education, Knoxville, TN 37996. Offers art education (MS); counseling education (PhD); cultural studies in education (PhD); curriculum (MS, Ed S); curriculum, educational research and evaluation (Ed D, PhD); early childhood education (PhD); early childhood special education (MS); education of deaf and hard of hearing (MS); educational administration and policy studies (Ed D, PhD); educational administration and supervision (Ed S); educational psychology (Ed D, PhD); elementary education (MS, Ed S); elementary teaching (MS); English education (MS, Ed S); exercise science (PhD); foreign language/ESL education (MS, Ed S); instructional technology (MS, Ed D, PhD, Ed S); literacy, language and ESL education (PhD); literacy, language education, and ESL education (Ed D); mathematics education (MS, Ed S); modified and comprehensive special education (MS); reading education (MS, Ed S); school counseling (Ed S); school psychology (PhD, Ed S); science education (MS, Ed S); secondary teaching (MS); social foundations (MS); social science education (MS, Ed S); socio-cultural foundations of sports and education (PhD); special education (Ed S); teacher education (Ed D, PhD). *Accreditation:* NCATE. Part-time and evening/weekend programs available. *Students:* 529 (401 women); includes 39 minority (23 African Americans, 2 American Indian/Alaska Native, 9 Asian Americans or Pacific Islanders, 5 Hispanic Americans) 34 international. 420 applicants, 50% accepted. In 2006, 258 master's, 28 doctorates awarded. *Degree requirements:* For master's and Ed S, thesis optional; for doctorate, variable foreign language requirement, thesis/dissertation. *Entrance requirements:* For master's, minimum GPA of 2.7; for doctorate and Ed S, GRE General Test, minimum GPA of 2.7. Additional exam requirements/recommendations for international students: Required—TOEFL. *Application deadline:* For fall admission, 2/1 priority date for domestic students. Applications are processed on a rolling basis. Application fee: $35. Electronic applications accepted. *Expenses:* Tuition, state resident: full-time $5,574. Tuition, nonresident: full-time $16,840. Required fees: $792. *Financial support:* In 2006–07, 4 fellowships, 9 teaching assistantships were awarded; career-related internships or fieldwork, Federal Work-Study, institutionally sponsored loans, and unspecified assistantships also available. Financial award application deadline: 2/1; financial award applicants required to submit FAFSA. *Unit head:* Dr. Lester Knight, Head, 865-974-0907, Fax: 865-974-8718, E-mail: lknight@utk.edu.

The University of Texas at Austin, Graduate School, College of Education, Department of Educational Psychology, Austin, TX 78712-1111. Offers academic educational psychology (M Ed, MA); counseling education (M Ed); counseling psychology (PhD); human development and education (PhD); learning cognition and instruction (PhD); quantitative methods (PhD); school psychology (PhD). *Accreditation:* APA (one or more programs are accredited). *Degree requirements:* For master's, thesis optional; for doctorate, thesis/dissertation. *Entrance requirements:* For master's and doctorate, GRE General Test, 3 letters of recommendation. Additional exam requirements/recommendations for international students: Required—TOEFL.

The University of Texas at San Antonio, College of Education and Human Development, Department of Interdisciplinary Learning and Teaching, San Antonio, TX 78249-0617. Offers curriculum and instruction (MA); early childhood and elementary education (MA); educational psychology/special education (MA); instructional technology (MA); reading and literacy (MA). Part-time and evening/weekend programs available. *Faculty:* 26 full-time (all women), 1 part-time/adjunct (0 women). *Students:* 40 full-time (32 women), 240 part-time (207 women); includes 155 minority (20 African Americans, 1 American Indian/Alaska Native, 6 Asian Americans or Pacific Islanders, 128 Hispanic Americans), 3 international. Average age 35. 94 applicants, 100% accepted, 94 enrolled. In 2006, 61 degrees awarded. *Degree requirements:* For master's, thesis optional. *Entrance requirements:* For master's, GRE General Test. Additional exam requirements/recommendations for international students: Required—TOEFL (minimum score 500 paper-based; 173 computer-based). *Application deadline:* For fall admission, 7/1 for domestic students, 4/1 for international students; for spring admission, 11/1 for domestic students, 9/1 for international students. Applications are processed on a rolling basis. Application fee: $45 ($80 for international students). Electronic applications accepted. *Expenses:* Tuition, state resident: full-time $1,730; part-time $192 per credit hour. Tuition, nonresident: full-time $6,680; part-time $742 per credit hour. Required fees: $733; $308,359 per credit hour. *Financial support:* In 2006–07, 3 research assistantships (averaging $28,891 per year) were awarded; career-related internships or fieldwork, Federal Work-Study, scholarships/grants, and unspecified assistantships also available. *Faculty research:* Early childhood, reading, special education, foundations, curriculum and instruction. Total annual research expenditures: $570,791. *Unit head:* Dr. Belinda B. Flores, Chair, 210-458-5969, Fax: 210-458-7281, E-mail: belinda.flores@utsa.edu.

The University of Texas–Pan American, College of Education, Department of Educational Psychology, Edinburg, TX 78541-2999. Offers counseling (M Ed); educational diagnostician (M Ed); gifted education (M Ed); school psychology (MA); special education (M Ed). Part-time and evening/weekend programs available. *Degree requirements:* For master's, thesis (for some programs), comprehensive exam (for some programs). *Entrance requirements:* For master's, GRE General Test, interview. *Expenses:* Tuition, state resident: full-time $2,577; part-time $143 per credit hour. Tuition, nonresident: full-time $7,527; part-time $418 per credit hour. Required fees: $561. *Faculty research:* Reading instruction, assessment practice, behavior interventions consultation, mental retardation.

University of the Pacific, School of Education, Department of Educational and School Psychology, Stockton, CA 95211-0197. Offers educational psychology (MA, Ed D); school psychology (Ed S). *Accreditation:* NCATE. *Faculty:* 3 full-time (2 women), 4 part-time/adjunct (2 women). *Students:* 15 full-time (13 women), 15 part-time (10 women); includes 10 minority (1 African American, 4 Asian Americans or Pacific Islanders, 5 Hispanic Americans), 1 international. Average age 30. 27 applicants, 37% accepted, 6 enrolled. In 2006, 4 degrees awarded. *Degree requirements:* For master's, thesis (for some programs); for doctorate, thesis/dissertation. *Entrance requirements:* For master's and doctorate, GRE General Test, GRE Subject Test. Additional exam requirements/recommendations for international students: Required—TOEFL (minimum score 475 paper-based; 150 computer-based). *Application deadline:* For fall admission, 3/1 priority date for domestic students; for spring admission, 10/1 priority date for domestic students. Applications are processed on a rolling basis. Application fee: $75. *Expenses:* Tuition: Full-time $26,920. Required fees: $430. Tuition and fees vary according to course load. *Financial support:* In 2006–07, 6 teaching assistantships were awarded. Financial award application deadline: 3/1; financial award applicants required to submit FAFSA. *Unit head:* Dr. Linda Webster, Chairperson, 209-946-2559, E-mail: lwebster@pacific.edu.

The University of Toledo, College of Graduate Studies, College of Education, Department of Foundations of Education, Program in Educational Psychology, Toledo, OH 43606-3390. Offers ME, DE, PhD. *Students:* 2 full-time (both women), 3 part-time (all women). Average age 43. 2 applicants, 0% accepted. In 2006, 2 degrees awarded. *Unit head:* Dr. Dale Snauwaert, Chair, Department of Foundations of Education, 419-530-2478, Fax: 419-530-8337.

University of Utah, The Graduate School, College of Education, Department of Educational Psychology, Salt Lake City, UT 84112-1107. Offers counseling psychology (PhD); educational psychology (MA); professional counseling (MS); professional psychology (M Ed); school counseling (M Ed, MS); statistics (M Stat). *Accreditation:* APA (one or more programs are accredited). Evening/weekend programs available. *Faculty:* 16 full-time (7 women), 9 part-time/adjunct (3 women). *Students:* 83 full-time (55 women), 90 part-time (59 women); includes 24 minority (3 African Americans, 6 American Indian/Alaska Native, 3 Asian Americans or Pacific Islanders, 12 Hispanic Americans), 4 international. Average age 32. 166 applicants, 45% accepted, 32 enrolled. In 2006, 44 master's, 14 doctorates awarded. *Degree requirements:* For master's, variable foreign language requirement, thesis (for some programs), comprehensive exam; for doctorate, variable foreign language requirement, thesis/dissertation, oral exam. *Entrance requirements:* For master's and doctorate, GRE General Test, minimum GPA of 3.0. Additional exam requirements/recommendations for international students: Required—TOEFL (minimum score 500 paper-based; 173 computer-based). *Application deadline:* For fall admission, 4/1 for domestic and international students; for spring admission, 11/1 for domestic and international students. Applications are processed on a rolling basis. Application fee: $45 ($65 for international students). Electronic applications accepted. *Expenses:* Tuition, state resident: full-time $3,208. Tuition, nonresident: full-time $11,326. Required fees: $608. Tuition and fees vary according to class time and program. *Financial support:* Fellowships with full tuition reimbursements, research assistantships with full tuition reimbursements, teaching assistantships with partial tuition reimbursements, career-related internships or fieldwork, Federal Work-Study, institutionally sponsored loans, scholarships/grants, and unspecified assistantships available. Financial award application deadline: 2/1; financial award applicants required to submit FAFSA. *Faculty research:* Autism, computer technology and instruction, cognitive behavior, aging, group counseling. Total annual research expenditures: $37,452. *Unit head:* Dr. Robert D. Hill, Chair, 801-581-7148, Fax: 801-581-5566, E-mail: bob.hill@ed.utah.edu. *Application contact:* Sherrill Christensen, Academic Program Specialist, 801-581-7148, Fax: 801-581-5566, E-mail: sherrill.christensen@ed.utah.edu.

University of Victoria, Faculty of Graduate Studies, Faculty of Education, Department of Educational Psychology and Leadership Studies, Victoria, BC V8W 2Y2, Canada. Offers counseling (M Ed, MA); educational psychology (M Ed, MA, PhD), including counseling psychology (M Ed, MA), learning and development (PhD), learning development (MA), measurement and evaluation (PhD), measurement evaluation (M Ed, MA), special education (M Ed, MA); leadership studies (M Ed, MA). Part-time programs available. *Degree requirements:* For master's, thesis (for some programs), comprehensive exam (M Ed); for doctorate, thesis/dissertation, candidacy exam, comprehensive exam, registration. *Entrance requirements:* For master's, 2 years of work experience in a relevant field, minimum B average; for doctorate, GRE, 2 years of work experience in a relevant field, minimum B average. Additional exam requirements/recommendations for international students: Required—TOEFL (minimum score 575 paper-based; 233 computer-based), IELTS (minimum score 7). *Faculty research:* Learning and development (child, adolescent and adult), special education and exceptional children, evaluation and measurement.

University of Virginia, Curry School of Education, Department of Leadership, Foundations and Policy, Program in Educational Psychology, Charlottesville, VA 22903. Offers M Ed, Ed D, Ed S. *Students:* 43 full-time (34 women), 8 part-time (4 women); includes 6 minority (4 African Americans, 1 Asian American or Pacific Islander, 1 Hispanic American), 7 international. Average age 30. 214 applicants, 23% accepted, 26 enrolled. In 2006, 55 degrees awarded. *Degree requirements:* For master's, thesis (for some programs), comprehensive exam (for some programs); for doctorate, thesis/dissertation, comprehensive exam (for some programs). *Entrance requirements:* For master's and doctorate, GRE General Test. Additional exam requirements/recommendations for international students: Required—TOEFL (minimum score 600 paper-based; 250 computer-based). *Application deadline:* Applications are processed on a rolling basis. Application fee: $60. Electronic applications accepted. *Financial support:*

Fellowships, research assistantships, teaching assistantships available. Financial award applicants required to submit FAFSA.

University of Washington, Graduate School, College of Education, Program in Educational Psychology, Seattle, WA 98195. Offers human development and cognition (M Ed, PhD); measurement and research (M Ed, PhD); school counseling (M Ed, PhD); school psychology (M Ed, PhD). *Accreditation:* APA. *Degree requirements:* For master's, thesis optional; for doctorate, thesis/dissertation. *Entrance requirements:* For master's and doctorate, GRE General Test, minimum GPA of 3.0. Additional exam requirements/recommendations for international students: Required—TOEFL.

The University of Western Ontario, Faculty of Graduate Studies, Social Sciences Division, Faculty of Education, Program in Educational Studies, London, ON N6A 5B8, Canada. Offers curriculum studies (M Ed); educational policy studies (M Ed); educational psychology/special education (M Ed). Part-time programs available. *Application deadline:* For fall admission, 2/1 for domestic students. Application fee: $50. *Financial support:* Research assistantships, teaching assistantships available. Financial award application deadline: 4/1. *Faculty research:* Reflective practice, gender and schooling, feminist pedagogy, narrative inquiry, second language, multiculturalism in Canada, education and law. *Unit head:* Allan Pitman, Graduate Chair, 519-661-2111 Ext. 88870, Fax: 519-661-3833, E-mail: pitman@uwo.ca. *Application contact:* L. Kulak, Graduate Supervisor, 519-661-2099, Fax: 519-661-3833, E-mail: kulak@edu.uwo.ca.

University of Wisconsin–Madison, Graduate School, School of Education, Department of Educational Psychology, Madison, WI 53706-1380. Offers MS, PhD. *Accreditation:* APA (one or more programs are accredited). *Degree requirements:* For doctorate, thesis/dissertation. *Entrance requirements:* For master's and doctorate, GRE General Test. *Application deadline:* For fall admission, 12/1 for domestic and international students; for spring admission, 10/1 for domestic and international students. Application fee: $45. Electronic applications accepted. *Financial support:* Fellowships with full tuition reimbursements, research assistantships with full tuition reimbursements, teaching assistantships with full tuition reimbursements, project assistantships available. *Unit head:* Dr. Ronald Serlin, Chair, 608-262-9920.

University of Wisconsin–Milwaukee, Graduate School, School of Education, Department of Educational Psychology, Milwaukee, WI 53201-0413. Offers MS, Ed S. *Accreditation:* APA. Part-time programs available. *Faculty:* 22 full-time (12 women). *Students:* 115 full-time (97 women), 72 part-time (60 women); includes 26 minority (13 African Americans, 1 American Indian/Alaska Native, 3 Asian Americans or Pacific Islanders, 9 Hispanic Americans). 228 applicants, 43% accepted, 52 enrolled. In 2006, 57 degrees awarded. *Entrance requirements:* For master's, minimum GPA of 3.0. *Application deadline:* For fall admission, 1/1 priority date for domestic students; for spring admission, 9/1 for domestic students. Applications are processed on a rolling basis. Application fee: $45 ($75 for international students). *Expenses:* Tuition, state resident: part-time $510 per credit. Tuition, nonresident: part-time $1,408 per credit. Tuition and fees vary according to program. *Financial support:* In 2006–07, 6 teaching assistantships were awarded; fellowships, research assistantships, career-related internships or fieldwork and unspecified assistantships also available. Support available to part-time students. Financial award application deadline: 4/15. *Unit head:* Anthony Hains, Chair, 414-229-4590, Fax: 414-229-4939.

Washington State University, Graduate School, College of Education, Department of Educational Leadership and Counseling Psychology, Pullman, WA 99164. Offers counseling psychology (Ed M, MA, PhD); educational leadership (M Ed, MA, Ed D, PhD); educational psychology (Ed M, MA, PhD); higher education (Ed M, MA, Ed D, PhD), including higher education administration (PhD), sport management (PhD), student affairs (PhD); higher education with sport management (Ed M). *Accreditation:* NCATE. *Faculty:* 25. *Students:* 109 full-time (63 women), 54 part-time (34 women); includes 42 minority (11 African Americans, 2 American Indian/Alaska Native, 12 Asian Americans or Pacific Islanders, 17 Hispanic Americans). Average age 34. 107 applicants, 67% accepted, 30 enrolled. In 2006, 33 master's, 20 doctorates awarded. Terminal master's awarded for partial completion of doctoral program. *Degree requirements:* For master's, thesis (for some programs), oral exam or written exam, comprehensive exam (for some programs); for doctorate, thesis/dissertation, oral and written exams, comprehensive exam. *Entrance requirements:* For master's and doctorate, GRE General Test, minimum GPA of 3.0, 3 letters of recommendation. Additional exam requirements/recommendations for international students: Required—TOEFL (minimum score 550 paper-based; 213 computer-based). *Application deadline:* For fall admission, 3/1 for domestic and international students; for spring admission, 10/1 for domestic students, 7/1 for international students. Application fee: $50. *Expenses:* Tuition, state resident: full-time $7,066. Tuition, nonresident: full-time $17,204. *Financial support:* In 2006–07, research assistantships (averaging $13,917 per year), teaching assistantships (averaging $13,056 per year) were awarded; career-related internships or fieldwork, Federal Work-Study, institutionally sponsored loans, scholarships/grants, tuition waivers (partial), and unspecified assistantships also available. Financial award application deadline: 4/1; financial award applicants required to submit FAFSA. *Faculty research:* Attentional processes, cross cultural psychology, faculty development in higher education. Total annual research expenditures: $854,827. *Unit head:* Dr. Phyllis Erdman, Chair, 509-335-9117. *Application contact:* Graduate School Admissions, 800-GRADWSU, Fax: 509-335-1949, E-mail: gradsch@wsu.edu.

Wayne State University, College of Education, Division of Theoretical and Behavioral Foundations, Detroit, MI 48202. Offers counseling (M Ed, MA, Ed D, PhD, Ed S); education evaluation and research (M Ed, Ed D, PhD); educational psychology (M Ed, Ed D, PhD, Ed S); educational sociology (M Ed, Ed D, PhD, Ed S); history and philosophy of education (M Ed, Ed D, PhD); rehabilitation counseling and community inclusion (MA, Ed S); school and community psychology (MA, Ed S); school clinical psychology (Ed S). *Accreditation:* ACA (one or more programs are accredited); CORE (one or more programs are accredited). Evening/weekend programs available. *Faculty:* 51 full-time (18 women), 11 part-time/adjunct (7 women). *Students:* 156 full-time (125 women), 232 part-time (191 women); includes 146 minority (140 African Americans, 1 American Indian/Alaska Native, 5 Hispanic Americans), 14 international. Average age 35. 146 applicants, 38% accepted, 39 enrolled. In 2006, 84 master's, 8 doctorates awarded. *Degree requirements:* For doctorate, thesis/dissertation. *Entrance requirements:* For master's, GRE (school and community psychology); for doctorate, GRE (educational psychology), interview, minimum GPA of 3.0. Additional exam requirements/recommendations for international students: Required—TOEFL (minimum score 550 paper-based; 213 computer-based), TWE (minimum score 6). *Application deadline:* For fall admission, 7/1 for domestic students, 6/1 for international students; for winter admission, 10/1 for international students; for spring admission, 2/1 for international students. Application fee: $20 ($30 for international students). Electronic applications accepted. *Financial support:* In 2006–07, 2 research assistantships (averaging $12,797 per year) were awarded; fellowships, career-related internships or fieldwork, Federal Work-Study, and institutionally sponsored loans also available. *Faculty research:* Adolescents at risk, supervision of counseling. *Unit head:* Dr. JoAnne Holbert, Assistant Dean, 313-577-1721, E-mail: jholbert@wayne.edu.

Western Kentucky University, Graduate Studies, College of Education and Behavioral Sciences, Department of Counseling and Student Affairs, Bowling Green, KY 42101. Offers business and marketing education (MA Ed); counseling (MA Ed); counselor education (Ed S); education and behavioral science (MA Ed); elementary education (MA Ed, Ed S); middle years education (MA Ed); secondary education (MA Ed, Ed S); student affairs (MA Ed). *Accreditation:* ACA; NCATE. Part-time and evening/weekend programs available. *Faculty:* 11 full-time (5 women), 9 part-time/adjunct (3 women). *Students:* 59 full-time (47 women), 157 part-time (126 women); includes 18 minority (13 African Americans, 1 American Indian/Alaska Native, 2 Asian Americans or Pacific Islanders, 2 Hispanic Americans), 1 international. Average age 31. 49 applicants, 67% accepted, 27 enrolled. In 2006, 89 master's, 4 other advanced degrees awarded. *Degree requirements:* For master's, thesis optional. *Entrance requirements:* For master's, GRE General Test. Additional exam requirements/recommendations for international students: Required—TOEFL (minimum score 555 paper-based; 213 computer-based; 79 iBT). *Application deadline:* For fall admission, 8/1 priority date for domestic students, 4/1 for international students; for spring admission, 12/1 for domestic students, 9/1 for international students. Applications are processed on a rolling basis. Application fee: $35. *Expenses:* Tuition, state resident: full-time $6,520; part-time $226 per hour. Tuition, nonresident: full-time $7,140; part-time $357 per hour. International tuition: $15,820 full-time. *Financial support:* In 2006–07, 1 research assistantship with partial tuition reimbursement (averaging $8,000 per year) was awarded; Federal Work-Study, institutionally sponsored loans, and service awards also available. Financial award application deadline: 4/1; financial award applicants required to submit FAFSA. *Faculty research:* Counselor education, research for residential workers. *Unit head:* Dr. Aaron W Hughey, Department Head, 270-745-4953, E-mail: aaron.hughey@wku.edu.

West Virginia University, College of Human Resources and Education, Department of Technology, Learning and Culture, Program in Educational Psychology, Morgantown, WV 26506. Offers MA. *Accreditation:* NCATE. Evening/weekend programs available. *Students:* 14 full-time (8 women), 9 part-time (7 women); includes 3 minority (1 African American, 1 American Indian/Alaska Native, 1 Hispanic American), 4 international. Average age 37. 10 applicants, 30% accepted, 3 enrolled. *Degree requirements:* For master's, thesis, content exams. *Entrance requirements:* For master's, GRE General Test, minimum GPA of 3.0, interview. Additional exam requirements/recommendations for international students: Required—TOEFL. *Application deadline:* Applications are processed on a rolling basis. Application fee: $50. *Expenses:* Tuition, state resident: full-time $4,926; part-time $276 per credit hour. Tuition, nonresident: full-time $14,278; part-time $796 per credit hour. Tuition and fees vary according to program. *Financial support:* In 2006–07, 17 students received support, including 1 research assistantship with full tuition reimbursement available (averaging $12,000 per year), 7 teaching assistantships with full tuition reimbursements available (averaging $8,264 per year); fellowships, career-related internships or fieldwork, Federal Work-Study, institutionally sponsored loans, and tuition waivers (full and partial) also available. Financial award application deadline: 2/1; financial award applicants required to submit FAFSA. *Faculty research:* Learning, development, instructional design, stimulus control, rehabilitation.

Wichita State University, Graduate School, College of Education, Department of Administration, Counseling, Educational and School Psychology, Wichita, KS 67260. Offers counseling (M Ed); education administration (M Ed, Ed D); educational psychology (M Ed); school psychology (Ed S). *Accreditation:* NCATE. Part-time and evening/weekend programs available. *Degree requirements:* For master's, thesis optional; for doctorate, one foreign language, thesis/dissertation; for Ed S, internship, practicum. *Entrance requirements:* For master's, minimum GPA of 2.75; for doctorate, GRE General Test. Additional exam requirements/recommendations for international students: Required—TOEFL. Electronic applications accepted.

Widener University, School of Human Service Professions, Center for Education, Chester, PA 19013-5792. Offers adult education (M Ed); counseling in higher education (M Ed); counselor education (M Ed); early childhood education (M Ed); educational foundations (M Ed); educational leadership (M Ed); educational psychology (M Ed); elementary education (M Ed); English and language arts (M Ed); health education (M Ed); higher education leadership (Ed D); home and school visitor (M Ed); human sexuality (M Ed); mathematics education (M Ed); middle school education (M Ed); principalship (M Ed); reading and language arts (Ed D); reading education (M Ed); school administration (Ed D); science education (M Ed); social studies education (M Ed); special education (M Ed); technology education (M Ed). Part-time and evening/weekend programs available. Terminal master's awarded for partial completion of doctoral program. *Degree requirements:* For doctorate, thesis/dissertation. *Entrance requirements:* For master's, minimum GPA of 2.5; for doctorate, GRE or MAT, minimum GPA of 2.0 (undergraduate), 3.5 (graduate). Electronic applications accepted. Expenses: Contact institution. *Faculty research:* Reading and cognition, adult education, technology education, educational leadership, special education.

Foundations and Philosophy of Education

Antioch University New England, Graduate School, Department of Education, Experienced Educators Program, Keene, NH 03431-3552. Offers M Ed. *Faculty:* 10 full-time (5 women), 11 part-time/adjunct (7 women). *Students:* 25 full-time (23 women), 21 part-time (19 women), 1 international. Average age 39. 28 applicants, 100% accepted, 26 enrolled. In 2006, 36 degrees awarded. *Degree requirements:* For master's, thesis, practicum. *Entrance requirements:* For master's, previous course work and work experience in education. Additional exam requirements/recommendations for international students: Required—TOEFL (minimum score 600 paper-based; 250 computer-based). *Application deadline:* For fall admission, 8/1 for domestic and international students; for spring admission, 12/1 for domestic and international students. Applications are processed on a rolling basis. Application fee: $50. Electronic applications accepted. *Expenses: Contact institution.* Tuition and fees vary according to program and student level. *Financial support:* In 2006–07, 39 students received support, including 1 fellowship (averaging $900 per year); Federal Work-Study also available. Financial award applicants required to submit FAFSA. *Faculty research:* Classroom action research, school restructuring, problem-based learning, brain-based learning. *Unit head:* Dr. Tom Julius, Director, 603-283-2309, Fax: 603-357-0718, E-mail: tjulius@antiochne.edu. *Application contact:* Leatrice A. Oram, Co-Director of Admissions, 800-490-3310, Fax: 603-357-0718, E-mail: admissions@antiochne.edu.

Arizona State University, Division of Graduate Studies, College of Education, Division of Educational Leadership and Policy Studies, Academic Program in Social and Philosophical Foundations of Education, Tempe, AZ 85287. Offers MA. *Degree requirements:* For master's, thesis or alternative. *Entrance requirements:* For master's, GRE General Test or MAT.

Arkansas State University, Graduate School, College of Education, Department of Educational Leadership, Curriculum, and Special Education, Jonesboro, State University, AR 72467. Offers community college administration education (SCCT); education theory and practice (MSE); educational leadership (MSE, Ed D, Ed S), including curriculum and instruction (Ed S), elementary curriculum and instruction (MSE), elementary principalship (Ed S), secondary principalship (Ed S), superintendency (Ed S); special education (MSE), including emotionally disturbed, gifted, talented and creative, instructional specialist 4-12, instructional specialist P-4; special education program administration (Ed S). *Accreditation:* NCATE. Part-time programs available. *Faculty:* 14 full-time (7 women), 5 part-time/adjunct (2 women). *Students:* 28 full-time (21 women), 328 part-time (233 women); includes 63 minority (58 African Americans, 3 American Indian/Alaska Native, 1 Asian American or Pacific Islander, 1 Hispanic American), 2 international. Average age 36. 181 applicants, 78% accepted, 70 enrolled. In 2006, 70 master's, 13 doctorates, 14 other advanced degrees awarded. *Degree requirements:* For master's, thesis or alternative, comprehensive exam; for doctorate, thesis/dissertation,

Foundations and Philosophy of Education

Arkansas State University (continued)
comprehensive exam. *Entrance requirements:* For master's, GRE General Test or MAT, appropriate bachelor's degree, letters of reference, interview, official transcript; for doctorate and other advanced degree, GRE General Test or MAT, interview, master's degree, letters of reference, official transcript. Additional exam requirements/recommendations for international students: Required—TOEFL (minimum score 213 computer-based). *Application deadline:* Applications are processed on a rolling basis. Application fee: $30 ($40 for international students). Electronic applications accepted. *Expenses:* Tuition, state resident: full-time $3,393; part-time $189 per hour. Tuition, nonresident: full-time $8,577; part-time $477 per hour. Required fees: $752; $39 per hour. $25 per semester. *Financial support:* Teaching assistantships, career-related internships or fieldwork, scholarships/grants, and unspecified assistantships available. Financial award application deadline: 7/1; financial award applicants required to submit FAFSA. *Unit head:* Dr. Mitchell Holifield, Chair, 870-972-3062, Fax: 870-680-8130, E-mail: hfield@astate.edu.

Ashland University, College of Education, Graduate Studies in Education, Department of Educational Foundations, Ashland, OH 44805-3702. Offers classroom instruction (M Ed). Part-time and evening/weekend programs available. *Faculty:* 15 full-time (9 women), 67 part-time/adjunct (36 women). *Students:* 88 full-time (72 women), 216 part-time (171 women); includes 18 minority (13 African Americans, 1 American Indian/Alaska Native, 2 Asian Americans or Pacific Islanders, 2 Hispanic Americans), 8 international. Average age 34. In 2006, 217 degrees awarded. *Degree requirements:* For master's, thesis or alternative. *Entrance requirements:* For master's, GRE General Test or MAT, teaching certificate, minimum GPA of 2.75. Additional exam requirements/recommendations for international students: Required—TOEFL. Application fee: $30. *Expenses:* Tuition: Part-time $403 per credit. Tuition and fees vary according to degree level and program. *Financial support:* In 2006–07, 103 students received support. Application deadline: 4/15. *Faculty research:* Character education, teacher reflection, religion and education, professional education, environmental education. *Unit head:* Dr. Kathleen Flanagan Hudson, Chair, 419-289-5356, E-mail: kflanag@ashland.edu.

Ball State University, Graduate School, Teachers College, Department of Educational Studies, Program in Educational Studies, Muncie, IN 47306-1099. Offers PhD. *Students:* 1 full-time (0 women), 8 part-time (5 women); includes 2 minority (1 American Indian/Alaska Native, 1 Asian American or Pacific Islander), 2 international. 10 applicants, 30% accepted, 2 enrolled. *Unit head:* Dr. Theresa Richardson, Chairman, Department of Educational Studies, 765-285-5400, Fax: 765-285-5489.

Bank Street College of Education, Graduate School, Studies in Education, New York, NY 10025. Offers Ed M, MS Ed. *Students:* 4 full-time (all women), 6 part-time (all women); includes 1 minority (African American), 2 international. Average age 29. 10 applicants, 80% accepted, 6 enrolled. In 2006, 13 degrees awarded. *Degree requirements:* For master's, thesis, registration. *Entrance requirements:* For master's, interview. Additional exam requirements/recommendations for international students: Required—TOEFL (minimum score 600 paper-based; 250 computer-based). *Application deadline:* For fall admission, 3/1 priority date for domestic students; for spring admission, 11/1 priority date for domestic students. Applications are processed on a rolling basis. Application fee: $50. *Expenses:* Tuition: Part-time $940 per credit. Required fees: $100 per term. *Financial support:* Career-related internships or fieldwork, Federal Work-Study, scholarships/grants, and unspecified assistantships available. Support available to part-time students. Financial award application deadline: 4/15; financial award applicants required to submit FAFSA. *Unit head:* Lia Gelb, Head, 212-875-4489, Fax: 212-875-4753, E-mail: liag@bankstreet.edu. *Application contact:* Ann Morgan, Director of Graduate Admissions, 212-875-4403, Fax: 212-875-4678, E-mail: amorgan@bankstreet.edu.

Brigham Young University, Graduate Studies, David O. McKay School of Education, Department of Educational Leadership and Foundations, Provo, UT 84602-1001. Offers M Ed, PhD. *Accreditation:* NCATE. Part-time and evening/weekend programs available. *Faculty:* 12 full-time (4 women), 3 part-time/adjunct (1 woman). *Students:* 37 full-time (18 women), 56 part-time (28 women); includes 15 minority (1 African American, 12 Asian Americans or Pacific Islanders, 2 Hispanic Americans), 8 international. Average age 38. 73 applicants, 81% accepted, 44 enrolled. In 2006, 28 master's, 6 doctorates awarded. *Median time to degree:* Of those who began their doctoral program in fall 1998, 50% received their degree in 8 years or less. *Degree requirements:* For master's, thesis or alternative, comprehensive exam, registration; for doctorate, thesis/dissertation, comprehensive exam, registration. *Entrance requirements:* For master's and doctorate, GRE. Additional exam requirements/recommendations for international students: Required—TOEFL (minimum score 580 paper-based; 237 computer-based). *Application deadline:* For fall admission, 2/15 for domestic and international students; for spring admission, 2/1 for domestic and international students. Application fee: $50. Electronic applications accepted. *Financial support:* In 2006–07, 11 students received support, including 9 research assistantships (averaging $5,000 per year), 2 teaching assistantships (averaging $2,500 per year); career-related internships or fieldwork, scholarships/grants, and unspecified assistantships also available. *Faculty research:* Mentoring, pre-service training of administrators, policy development, cross cultural studies of educational leadership. *Unit head:* Dr. A. LeGrand Richards, Chair, 801-422-5073, Fax: 801-422-0196, E-mail: buddy_richards@byu.edu. *Application contact:* Bonnie Bennett, Department Secretary, 801-422-4291, Fax: 801-422-0196, E-mail: bonnie_bennett@byu.edu.

California State University, Los Angeles, Graduate Studies, Charter College of Education, Division of Applied and Advanced Studies in Education, Major in Educational Foundations, Los Angeles, CA 90032-8530. Offers psychological foundations (MA); social foundations (MA). *Accreditation:* NCATE. Part-time and evening/weekend programs available. *Students:* 7 full-time (6 women), 28 part-time (17 women); includes 25 minority (5 African Americans, 1 American Indian/Alaska Native, 2 Asian Americans or Pacific Islanders, 17 Hispanic Americans), 3 international. *Degree requirements:* For master's, project or thesis. *Entrance requirements:* For master's, minimum GPA of 2.75 in last 90 units of course work, teaching certificate. Additional exam requirements/recommendations for international students: Required—TOEFL. *Application deadline:* For fall admission, 6/30 for domestic students; for spring admission, 2/1 for domestic students. Applications are processed on a rolling basis. Application fee: $55. *Expenses:* Tuition, nonresident: part-time $226 per unit. *Financial support:* Career-related internships or fieldwork and Federal Work-Study available. Support available to part-time students. Financial award application deadline: 3/1. *Unit head:* Dr. Chogollah Maroufi, Chair, Division of Applied and Advanced Studies in Education, 323-343-4330, Fax: 323-343-5336.

Central Connecticut State University, School of Graduate Studies, School of Education and Professional Studies, Department of Teacher Education, Program in Educational Foundations Policy/Secondary Education, New Britain, CT 06050-4010. Offers MS. Part-time and evening/weekend programs available. *Students:* 2 full-time (both women), 22 part-time (15 women); includes 2 minority (1 African American, 1 Hispanic American). 13 applicants, 54% accepted, 5 enrolled. In 2006, 12 degrees awarded. *Degree requirements:* For master's, thesis or alternative, comprehensive exam. *Entrance requirements:* For master's, minimum GPA of 2.7. Additional exam requirements/recommendations for international students: Required—TOEFL. *Application deadline:* For fall admission, 7/1 for domestic students; for spring admission, 12/1 for domestic students. Applications are processed on a rolling basis. Application fee: $50. Electronic applications accepted. *Expenses:* Tuition, area resident: Full-time $3,970; part-time $380 per credit. Tuition, state resident: full-time $5,955; part-time $380 per credit. Tuition, nonresident: full-time $11,061; part-time $380 per credit. Required fees: $3,189. One-time fee: $62 part-time. Tuition and fees vary according to degree level and program.

Chicago State University, School of Graduate and Professional Studies, College of Education, Department of Educational Leadership, Curriculum and Foundations, Program in Curriculum and Instruction, Chicago, IL 60628. Offers instructional foundations (MS Ed). *Degree requirements:* For master's, thesis optional. *Entrance requirements:* For master's, minimum GPA of 2.75.

Curry College, Division of Continuing Education and Graduate Studies, Program in Education, Milton, MA 02186-9984. Offers adult education (Certificate); educational administration (M Ed); educational therapy (Certificate); elementary education (M Ed); foundations (non-license) (M Ed); learning disabilities across the lifespan (Certificate); reading (M Ed, Certificate); special education (M Ed). Part-time and evening/weekend programs available. *Faculty:* 6 full-time (4 women), 11 part-time/adjunct (7 women). *Degree requirements:* For master's, research project. *Entrance requirements:* For master's, MAT, interview, recommendations, resumé. Additional exam requirements/recommendations for international students: Required—TOEFL (minimum score 550 paper-based). *Application deadline:* For fall admission, 8/1 priority date for domestic students; for spring admission, 1/1 for domestic students. Applications are processed on a rolling basis. Application fee: $50. *Expenses:* *Contact institution.* *Financial support:* Career-related internships or fieldwork and tuition waivers (partial) available. *Faculty research:* Classroom trauma, therapeutic writing, inclusionary practices. *Unit head:* Dr. Donald Gratz, Director and Associate Professor, 617-333-2243, E-mail: dgratz0703@curry.edu. *Application contact:* John Bresnahan, Director of Graduate Enrollment and Student Services, 617-333-2243, Fax: 617-333-2045, E-mail: jbresnah0104@curry.edu.

Duquesne University, School of Education, Department of Foundations and Leadership, Program in Educational Studies, Pittsburgh, PA 15282-0001. Offers MS Ed. Part-time and evening/weekend programs available. Postbaccalaureate distance learning degree programs offered (minimal on-campus study). *Faculty:* 9 full-time (4 women), 6 part-time/adjunct (3 women). *Students:* 13. 6 applicants, 50% accepted, 2 enrolled. In 2006, 9 degrees awarded. *Degree requirements:* For master's, thesis optional. *Entrance requirements:* For master's, MAT, minimum GPA of 3.0. *Application deadline:* For fall admission, 8/1 for domestic students; for spring admission, 12/1 for domestic students. Applications are processed on a rolling basis. Application fee: $50. *Expenses:* Tuition: Part-time $723 per credit. Required fees: $71 per credit. Tuition and fees vary according to degree level and program. *Financial support:* In 2006–07, 1 research assistantship with full and partial tuition reimbursement (averaging $5,200 per year) was awarded. Support available to part-time students. *Unit head:* Dr. Connie Marie Moss, Coordinator, 412-396-4778, Fax: 412-396-5585.

Eastern Michigan University, Graduate School, College of Education, Department of Teacher Education, Program in Social Foundations, Ypsilanti, MI 48197. Offers MA. *Accreditation:* NCATE. Part-time and evening/weekend programs available. Postbaccalaureate distance learning degree programs offered (minimal on-campus study). *Students:* Average age 35. *Entrance requirements:* For master's, GRE. Additional exam requirements/recommendations for international students: Required—TOEFL. *Application deadline:* For fall admission, 5/15 priority date for domestic students, 5/1 priority date for international students; for winter admission, 10/15 priority date for domestic students, 10/1 priority date for international students; for spring admission, 3/15 priority date for domestic students, 3/1 priority date for international students. Applications are processed on a rolling basis. Application fee: $35. *Expenses:* Tuition, state resident: part-time $341 per credit hour. Tuition, nonresident: full-time $16,104; part-time $671 per credit hour. Required fees: $816; $34 per credit hour. $40 per term. One-time fee: $82 full-time. Tuition and fees vary according to course level, course load, degree level and reciprocity agreements. *Financial support:* Fellowships, research assistantships with full tuition reimbursements, teaching assistantships with full tuition reimbursements, career-related internships or fieldwork, Federal Work-Study, institutionally sponsored loans, scholarships/grants, tuition waivers (partial), and unspecified assistantships available. Support available to part-time students. Financial award applicants required to submit FAFSA.

Eastern Washington University, Graduate Studies, College of Education and Human Development, Department of Education, Program in Foundations of Education, Cheney, WA 99004-2431. Offers M Ed. *Accreditation:* NCATE. *Degree requirements:* For master's, comprehensive exam. *Entrance requirements:* For master's, minimum GPA of 3.0.

Fairfield University, Graduate School of Education and Allied Professions, Department of Curriculum and Instruction, Fairfield, CT 06824-5195. Offers elementary education (MA); secondary education (MA); teaching and foundations (MA, CAS). Part-time and evening/weekend programs available. *Faculty:* 5 full-time (4 women), 5 part-time/adjunct (3 women). *Students:* 58 full-time (43 women), 98 part-time (81 women). Average age 28. 49 applicants, 55% accepted, 20 enrolled. In 2006, 45 master's, 1 other advanced degree awarded. *Degree requirements:* For master's, thesis or alternative, educational technology course, comprehensive exam. *Entrance requirements:* For master's, PRAXIS I (PPST), minimum QPA of 2.67, 2 recommendations, resumé. Additional exam requirements/recommendations for international students: Required—TOEFL (minimum score 550 paper-based; 213 computer-based). *Application deadline:* For fall admission, 3/1 for domestic students; for spring admission, 10/15 for domestic students. Applications are processed on a rolling basis. Application fee: $55. Electronic applications accepted. *Financial support:* Tuition waivers (partial) and unspecified assistantships available. Support available to part-time students. Financial award applicants required to submit FAFSA. *Faculty research:* Participatory action research, adolescent homosexuality, assessment of student teachers, supervision and staff development, writing process, Piaget. *Unit head:* Dr. Wendy R. Kohli, Chair, 203-254-4000 Ext. 2286, Fax: 203-254-4047, E-mail: wkohli@mail.fairfield.edu. *Application contact:* Marianne Gumpper, Director of Graduate and Continuing Studies Admissions, 203-254-4184, Fax: 203-254-4073, E-mail: gradadmis@mail.fairfield.edu.

Fairleigh Dickinson University, Metropolitan Campus, University College: Arts, Sciences, and Professional Studies, School of Computer Sciences and Engineering, Program in Mathematical Foundation, Teaneck, NJ 07666-1914. Offers MS. *Students:* Average age 38. 2 applicants, 100% accepted, 2 enrolled. *Application deadline:* Applications are processed on a rolling basis. Application fee: $40. *Unit head:* Dr. Alfredo Tan, Director, School of Computer Sciences and Engineering, 201-692-2000.

Florida Atlantic University, College of Education, Department of Teacher Education, Boca Raton, FL 33431-0991. Offers art teacher education (M Ed); curriculum and instruction (M Ed, Ed D, Ed S); educational psychology (MSF); elementary education (M Ed); foundations of education (M Ed); multicultural education (MSF); reading teacher education (M Ed). *Accreditation:* NCATE. Part-time and evening/weekend programs available. *Faculty:* 29 full-time (23 women), 75 part-time/adjunct (50 women). *Students:* 78 full-time (65 women), 176 part-time (159 women); includes 50 minority (20 African Americans, 1 American Indian/Alaska Native, 6 Asian Americans or Pacific Islanders, 23 Hispanic Americans), 1 international. Average age 35. 132 applicants, 64% accepted, 62 enrolled. In 2006, 95 master's, 2 doctorates awarded. *Degree requirements:* For master's, registration; for doctorate, thesis/dissertation, departmental qualifying exam, comprehensive exam, registration; for Ed S, departmental qualifying exam. *Entrance requirements:* For master's, GRE General Test, minimum GPA of 3.0 in last 2 years of undergraduate course work; for doctorate, GRE General Test, GRE Subject Test, minimum graduate GPA of 3.2, 3.0 in last 2 years of undergraduate course work; for Ed S, GRE General Test. Additional exam requirements/recommendations for international students: Required—TOEFL. *Application deadline:* Applications are processed on a rolling basis. Application fee: $30. *Expenses:* Tuition, area resident: Full-time $4,394. Tuition, nonresident: full-time $16,441. *Financial support:* In 2006–07, 4 research assistantships with partial tuition reimbursements (averaging $8,000 per year), 3 teaching assistantships with partial tuition reimbursements (averaging $8,000 per year) were awarded; fellowships with partial tuition reimbursements, career-related internships or fieldwork, scholarships/grants, and unspecified assistantships also available. *Faculty research:* Technology, teaching English to speakers of other languages, math teaching, electronic portfolio assessment, global perspectives through social studies. *Unit head:* Dr. Penelope Fritzer, Chairperson, 561-297-3584.

Florida State University, Graduate Studies, College of Education, Department of Educational Leadership and Policy Studies, Program in Social, History and Philosophy of Education, Tallahassee, FL 32306. Offers history and philosophy of education (MS, PhD, Ed S); international and intercultural education (MS, PhD, Ed S). *Faculty:* 4 full-time (0 women), 2 part-time/adjunct (1 woman). *Students:* 11 full-time (6 women), 17 part-time (8 women);

includes 7 minority (1 African American, 6 Asian Americans or Pacific Islanders). 16 applicants, 69% accepted, 4 enrolled. In 2006, 1 master's, 1 doctorate awarded. *Degree requirements:* For master's and Ed S, thesis optional; for doctorate, thesis/dissertation, comprehensive exam. *Entrance requirements:* For master's, doctorate, and Ed S, GRE General Test, minimum GPA of 3.0. *Application deadline:* For fall admission, 7/1 priority date for domestic students; for spring admission, 11/1 for domestic students. Applications are processed on a rolling basis. Application fee: $20. *Expenses:* Tuition, state resident: full-time $5,822; part-time $243 per credit hour. Tuition, nonresident: full-time $20,976; part-time $874 per credit hour. Tuition and fees vary according to program. *Financial support:* Fellowships with partial tuition reimbursements, research assistantships with partial tuition reimbursements, teaching assistantships with partial tuition reimbursements, career-related internships or fieldwork, scholarships/grants, and unspecified assistantships available. Financial award applicants required to submit FAFSA. *Unit head:* Dr. Jeffrey Milligan, Assistant Professor and Program Coordinator, 850-644-8171, Fax: 850-644-1258, E-mail: milligan@coe.fsu.edu. *Application contact:* Jimmy Pastrano, Program Assistant, 850-644-6777, Fax: 850-644-1258, E-mail: pastrano@coe.fsu.edu.

George Fox University, School of Education, Newberg, OR 97132-2697. Offers counseling (MA, MS, Certificate), including counseling (MA), marriage and family therapy (MA, Certificate), school counseling (MA), school psychology (MS, Certificate), trauma (Certificate); educational foundations and leadership (M Ed, Ed D); teaching (MAT). Evening/weekend programs available. Postbaccalaureate distance learning degree programs offered (minimal on-campus study). *Faculty:* 34 full-time (18 women), 27 part-time/adjunct (19 women). *Students:* 157 full-time (125 women), 312 part-time (225 women); includes 15 minority (2 African Americans, 3 American Indian/Alaska Native, 3 Asian Americans or Pacific Islanders, 7 Hispanic Americans), 3 international. Average age 36. 165 applicants, 76% accepted, 106 enrolled. In 2006, 208 master's, 11 doctorates, 1 other advanced degree awarded. *Degree requirements:* For master's, thesis (for some programs). *Entrance requirements:* For master's, California Basic Educational Skills Test, PRAXIS II, minimum undergraduate GPA of 3.0 during previous 2 years. *Application deadline:* For fall admission, 2/1 for domestic students. Applications are processed on a rolling basis. Application fee: $40. Electronic applications accepted. *Expenses:* Contact institution. *Financial support:* Career-related internships or fieldwork available. Financial award applicants required to submit FAFSA. *Unit head:* Dr. James Worthington, Dean, 503-554-2871, E-mail: jworthington@georgefox.edu. *Application contact:* Beth Molzahn, Admissions Counselor, 800-631-0921, Fax: 503-554-3856, E-mail: bmolzahn@georgefox.edu.

Georgia State University, College of Education, Department of Educational Policy Studies, Program in Social Foundations of Education, Atlanta, GA 30303-3083. Offers MS, PhD. *Accreditation:* NCATE. Part-time and evening/weekend programs available. *Students:* 7 full-time (3 women), 19 part-time (14 women); includes 6 minority (5 African Americans, 1 Asian American or Pacific Islander), 2 international. Average age 37. 7 applicants, 57% accepted. In 2006, 2 master's, 3 doctorates awarded. *Degree requirements:* For master's, thesis or project; for doctorate, thesis/dissertation, comprehensive exam. *Entrance requirements:* For master's, GRE General Test, minimum GPA of 2.5; for doctorate, GRE General Test or MAT, minimum GPA of 3.3. Application fee: $25. *Financial support:* Teaching assistantships, career-related internships or fieldwork available. *Faculty research:* Teacher unionism, African and African-American history and culture, multicultural and workplace education, teacher autonomy and epistemology. *Unit head:* Dr. Asa G. Hilliard, Chair, Department of Educational Policy Studies, 404-651-1269, Fax: 404-651-1009, E-mail: ahilliard@gsu.edu.

Harvard University, Extension School, Cambridge, MA 02138-3722. Offers applied sciences (CAS); biotechnology (ALM); educational technologies (ALM); educational technology (CET); English for graduate and professional studies (DGP); environmental management (ALM, CEM); information technology (ALM); journalism (ALM); liberal arts (ALM); management (ALM, CM); mathematics for teaching (ALM); museum studies (ALM); premedical studies (Diploma); publication and communication (CPC). Part-time and evening/weekend programs available. *Faculty:* 236 part-time/adjunct. *Students:* 101 full-time (56 women), 564 part-time (278 women); includes 167 minority (35 African Americans, 1 American Indian/Alaska Native, 84 Asian Americans or Pacific Islanders, 47 Hispanic Americans). Average age 36. In 2006, 112 master's, 184 Diplomas awarded. *Degree requirements:* For master's, thesis. *Entrance requirements:* For master's, 3 completed graduate courses with grade of B or higher. Additional exam requirements/recommendations for international students: Required—TOEFL (minimum score 600 paper-based; 250 computer-based), TWE (minimum score 5). *Application deadline:* Applications are processed on a rolling basis. Application fee: $75. *Expenses:* Contact institution. Full-time tuition and fees vary according to program and student level. *Financial support:* In 2006–07, 268 students received support. Scholarships/grants available. Support available to part-time students. Financial award application deadline: 8/6; financial award applicants required to submit FAFSA. *Unit head:* Michael Shinagel, Dean. *Application contact:* Program Director, 617-495-4024, Fax: 617-495-9176.

Hofstra University, School of Education and Allied Human Services, Department of Foundations, Leadership, and Policy Studies, Program in Foundations of Education, Hempstead, NY 11549. Offers MA, CAS. *Accreditation:* NCATE. Part-time and evening/weekend programs available. *Students:* 2 full-time (1 woman), 6 part-time (5 women); includes 1 minority (Hispanic American) Average age 27. 5 applicants, 100% accepted, 2 enrolled. In 2006, 9 degrees awarded. *Degree requirements:* For master's, thesis or alternative, comprehensive exam, registration. *Entrance requirements:* For master's and CAS, interview, writing sample, essay. Additional exam requirements/recommendations for international students: Required—TOEFL (minimum score 550 paper-based; 213 computer-based). *Application deadline:* Applications are processed on a rolling basis. Application fee: $60. Electronic applications accepted. *Expenses:* Tuition: Full-time $13,320; part-time $740 per credit. Required fees: $930; $155 per term. *Financial support:* In 2006–07, 3 students received support; fellowships with tuition reimbursements available, research assistantships with full and partial tuition reimbursements available, scholarships/grants and tuition waivers (full and partial) available. Financial award applicants required to submit FAFSA. *Faculty research:* Philosophy of education, race and class and gender, museum education and aesthetics, aesthetics in cross cultural perspectives, children and games: historical and cross-cultural. *Unit head:* Dr. Donna R. Barnes, Director, 516-463-5781, Fax: 516-463-5949, E-mail: edadrb@hofstra.edu. *Application contact:* Carol Drummer, Dean of Graduate Admissions, 516-463-4876, Fax: 516-463-4664, E-mail: gradstudent@hofstra.edu.

Indiana University Bloomington, School of Education, Department of Educational Leadership and Policy Studies, Bloomington, IN 47405-7000. Offers education policy studies (PhD); educational leadership (MS, Ed D, PhD, Ed S); higher education (MS, Ed D, PhD); history and philosophy of education (MS); history of education (PhD); international and comparative education (MS, PhD); philosophy of education (PhD); student affairs administration (MS). PhD offered through the University Graduate School. *Accreditation:* NCATE. Part-time and evening/weekend programs available. *Students:* 12 full-time (5 women), 28 part-time (14 women). Average age 35. In 2006, 32 master's, 4 doctorates awarded. *Degree requirements:* For master's, thesis optional; for doctorate, thesis/dissertation; for Ed S, comprehensive exam or project. *Entrance requirements:* For master's, doctorate, and Ed S, GRE General Test. *Application deadline:* For fall admission, 6/1 for domestic students, 3/1 for international students; for spring admission, 9/1 for international students. Application fee: $45 ($55 for international students). *Expenses:* Tuition, state resident: full-time $5,791; part-time $241 per credit hour. Tuition, nonresident: full-time $16,866; part-time $703 per credit hour. *Financial support:* Fellowships, research assistantships, teaching assistantships, career-related internships or fieldwork, Federal Work-Study, institutionally sponsored loans, and tuition waivers (full and partial) available. Support available to part-time students. *Unit head:* Martha McCarthy, Chair, 812-856-8377. *Application contact:* Sandy Strain, Department Secretary, 812-856-8360, Fax: 812-856-8394, E-mail: strain@indiana.edu.

Iowa State University of Science and Technology, Graduate College, College of Human Sciences, Department of Curriculum and Instruction, Ames, IA 50011. Offers curriculum and instructional technology (M Ed, MS, PhD); elementary education (M Ed, MS); historical, philosophical, and comparative studies in education (M Ed, MS); special education (M Ed, MS). *Faculty:* 28 full-time, 3 part-time/adjunct. *Students:* 54 full-time (40 women), 78 part-time (54 women); includes 11 minority (3 African Americans, 4 Asian Americans or Pacific Islanders, 4 Hispanic Americans), 26 international. 64 applicants, 69% accepted, 32 enrolled. In 2006, 31 master's, 10 doctorates awarded. *Degree requirements:* For master's, thesis or alternative; for doctorate, thesis/dissertation. *Entrance requirements:* For doctorate, GRE General Test. Additional exam requirements/recommendations for international students: Required—TOEFL (paper-based 560; computer-based 220; iBT 83) or IELTS (6.5). *Application deadline:* For fall admission, 1/1 priority date for domestic and international students; for spring admission, 9/1 for domestic and international students. Application fee: $30 ($70 for international students). Electronic applications accepted. *Expenses:* Tuition, state resident: full-time $5,936; part-time $330 per credit. Tuition, nonresident: full-time $16,350; part-time $330 per credit. *Financial support:* In 2006–07, 22 research assistantships with full and partial tuition reimbursements (averaging $17,457 per year), 17 teaching assistantships with full and partial tuition reimbursements (averaging $17,788 per year) were awarded; fellowships, scholarships/grants, health care benefits, and unspecified assistantships also available. *Unit head:* Dr. Carl Smith, Chair, 515-294-7021, E-mail: cigrad@iastate.edu. *Application contact:* Dr. Patricia Leigh, Director of Graduate Education, 515-294-7021, E-mail: cigrad@iastate.edu.

Kent State University, Graduate School of Education, Health, and Human Services, Department of Educational Foundations and Special Services, Program in Cultural Foundations, Kent, OH 44242-0001. Offers M Ed, MA, PhD. *Accreditation:* NCATE. *Faculty:* 8 full-time (4 women). *Students:* 21 full-time (18 women), 26 part-time (24 women); includes 8 minority (3 African Americans, 5 Hispanic Americans), 1 international. 13 applicants, 100% accepted. In 2006, 3 master's, 2 doctorates awarded. *Degree requirements:* For master's, thesis (for some programs), registration; for doctorate, thesis/dissertation, comprehensive exam, registration. *Entrance requirements:* For master's and doctorate, GRE General Test. Additional exam requirements/recommendations for international students: Required—TOEFL. *Application deadline:* Applications are processed on a rolling basis. Application fee: $30. Electronic applications accepted. *Financial support:* In 2006–07, fellowships with full tuition reimbursements (averaging $8,497 per year); research assistantships with full tuition reimbursements, teaching assistantships with full tuition reimbursements, career-related internships or fieldwork, Federal Work-Study, institutionally sponsored loans, scholarships/grants, health care benefits, and unspecified assistantships also available. Support available to part-time students. Financial award application deadline: 4/1; financial award applicants required to submit FAFSA. *Faculty research:* Public politics, intercultural communication and training, research paradigms, comparative and international education. *Unit head:* Dr. Averil McClelland, Coordinator, 330-672-2294, E-mail: amcclell@kent.edu. *Application contact:* Nancy Miller, Academic Program Coordinator, Office of Graduate Student Services, 330-672-2576, Fax: 330-672-9162, E-mail: ogs@kent.edu.

McGill University, Faculty of Graduate and Postdoctoral Studies, Faculty of Education, Department of Integrated Studies in Education, Montréal, QC H3A 2T5, Canada. Offers culture and values in education (MA, PhD); curriculum (MA); educational leadership (Certificate, Diploma); educational studies (PhD); integrated studies in education (M Ed); leadership (MA); second language education (MA, PhD). *Degree requirements:* For master's, thesis (for some programs), registration; for doctorate, thesis/dissertation, comprehensive exam, registration. *Entrance requirements:* For master's, 2 years of relevant experience, minimum GPA of 3.0; for doctorate, minimum GPA of 3.0, acquisition of prospective supervisor; for other advanced degree, minimum GPA of 3.0. Additional exam requirements/recommendations for international students: Required—TOEFL (minimum score 580 paper-based; 237 computer-based).

Millersville University of Pennsylvania, Graduate School, School of Education, Department of Educational Foundations, Millersville, PA 17551-0302. Offers leadership for teaching and learning (M Ed). Part-time and evening/weekend programs available. *Faculty:* 13 full-time (10 women), 11 part-time/adjunct (3 women). *Students:* Average age 32. 7 applicants, 100% accepted, 5 enrolled. In 2006, 14 degrees awarded. *Degree requirements:* For master's, qualifying exam. *Entrance requirements:* For master's, GRE or MAT, 5 years of experience, Pennsylvania teacher's certification, interview, letters of recommendation. *Application deadline:* For fall admission, 3/1 priority date for domestic students; for winter admission, 10/1 priority date for domestic students; for spring admission, 10/1 priority date for domestic students. Applications are processed on a rolling basis. Application fee: $35. *Expenses:* Tuition, state resident: full-time $6,048; part-time $336 per credit. Tuition, nonresident: full-time $9,678; part-time $538 per credit. Required fees: $1,244. Tuition and fees vary according to course load. *Financial support:* Research assistantships with full tuition reimbursements, career-related internships or fieldwork, Federal Work-Study, institutionally sponsored loans, and unspecified assistantships available. Support available to part-time students. Financial award application deadline: 3/15; financial award applicants required to submit FAFSA. *Faculty research:* Teacher reflection, administrator development, motivation, multicultural education, first year students. *Unit head:* Dr. John K. Ward, Chair, 717-871-3835, Fax: 717-872-3856, E-mail: john.ward@millersville.edu. *Application contact:* Dr. Victor S. DeSantis, Dean of Graduate Studies, 717-872-3099, Fax: 717-871-2022, E-mail: victor.desantis@millersville.edu.

Montclair State University, The Graduate School, College of Education and Human Services, Department of Educational Foundations, Montclair, NJ 07043-1624. Offers critical thinking (M Ed); mathematics education (Ed D); philosophy for children (M Ed, Ed D, Certificate). Part-time and evening/weekend programs available. *Faculty:* 9 full-time (3 women), 7 part-time/adjunct (3 women). *Students:* 12 full-time (6 women), 42 part-time (29 women); includes 10 minority (7 African Americans, 1 Asian American or Pacific Islander, 2 Hispanic Americans), 8 international. Average age 33. 11 applicants, 27% accepted, 2 enrolled. In 2006, 18 master's, 4 doctorates, 1 other advanced degree awarded. *Degree requirements:* For master's, field experience; for doctorate, thesis/dissertation, comprehensive exam. *Entrance requirements:* For master's, GRE or MAT, minimum GPA of 2.67, 2 letters of recommendation, teaching certificate; for doctorate, GRE General Test, 3 years of classroom teaching experience, interview, writing sample. Additional exam requirements/recommendations for international students: Required—TOEFL (minimum score 117 computer-based). *Application deadline:* For fall admission, 2/1 for domestic students, 2/15 for international students; for spring admission, 10/15 for domestic and international students. Applications are processed on a rolling basis. Application fee: $60. Electronic applications accepted. *Expenses:* Tuition, state resident: part-time $450 per credit. Tuition, nonresident: part-time $682 per credit. Tuition and fees vary according to degree level and program. *Financial support:* In 2006–07, 1 research assistantship with full tuition reimbursement (averaging $7,000 per year) was awarded; Federal Work-Study and scholarships/grants also available. Support available to part-time students. Financial award application deadline: 3/1; financial award applicants required to submit FAFSA. *Unit head:* Dr. Mark Weinstein, Chairperson, 973-655-5170.

Mount Saint Vincent University, Graduate Programs, Faculty of Education, Program in Educational Foundations, Halifax, NS B3M 2J6, Canada. Offers M Ed, MA Ed, MA-R. Part-time and evening/weekend programs available. *Degree requirements:* For master's, thesis (for some programs). *Entrance requirements:* For master's, bachelor's degree in related field, minimum B average. Electronic applications accepted. *Faculty research:* Research paradigms, moral aspects of education and teaching, private/independent schools, theory of critical thinking, teachers as workers and as agents of social change.

New York University, Steinhardt School of Culture, Education and Human Development, Department of Humanities and Social Sciences in the Professions, Program in History of Education, New York, NY 10012-1019. Offers MA, PhD. Part-time and evening/weekend programs available. *Faculty:* 3 full-time (1 woman). *Students:* 4 full-time (2 women), 3 part-time (2 women); includes 2 minority (both African Americans) 10 applicants, 60% accepted, 3 enrolled. In 2006, 2 degrees awarded. Terminal master's awarded for partial completion of doctoral program. *Degree requirements:* For master's, thesis (for some programs); for doctor-

Foundations and Philosophy of Education

New York University (continued)

ate, thesis/dissertation. *Entrance requirements:* For doctorate, GRE General Test, interview. Additional exam requirements/recommendations for international students: Required—TOEFL. *Application deadline:* For fall admission, 12/15 priority date for domestic and international students; for spring admission, 11/1 for domestic and international students. Applications are processed on a rolling basis. Application fee: $50. *Expenses:* Tuition: Part-time $1,080 per unit. Required fees: $56 per unit. $329 per term. Tuition and fees vary according to program. *Financial support:* Fellowships with full and partial tuition reimbursements, Federal Work-Study, institutionally sponsored loans, scholarships/grants, and tuition waivers (partial) available. Support available to part-time students. Financial award application deadline: 2/1; financial award applicants required to submit FAFSA. *Faculty research:* American educational thought, democratic community and education, twentieth century history of education. *Unit head:* Dr. Jonathan Zimmerman, Director, 212-992-9475, Fax: 212-995-4832, E-mail: jlzimm@aol.com. *Application contact:* 212-998-5030, Fax: 212-995-4328, E-mail: steinhardt.gradadmissions@nyu.edu.

New York University, Steinhardt School of Culture, Education and Human Development, Department of Humanities and Social Sciences in the Professions, Program in Philosophy of Education, New York, NY 10012-1019. Offers MA, PhD. *Faculty:* 2 full-time (0 women). *Students:* 1 full-time (0 women). 2 applicants, 0% accepted. In 2006, 1 degree awarded. *Degree requirements:* For master's, thesis (for some programs); for doctorate, thesis/dissertation. *Entrance requirements:* For doctorate, GRE General Test, interview. Additional exam requirements/recommendations for international students: Required—TOEFL. *Application deadline:* For fall admission, 12/15 priority date for domestic and international students; for spring admission, 11/1 for domestic and international students. Applications are processed on a rolling basis. Application fee: $50. *Expenses:* Tuition: Part-time $1,080 per unit. Required fees: $56 per unit. $329 per term. Tuition and fees vary according to program. *Financial support:* Fellowships with full and partial tuition reimbursements, Federal Work-Study, institutionally sponsored loans, scholarships/grants, and tuition waivers (partial) available. Support available to part-time students. Financial award application deadline: 2/1; financial award applicants required to submit FAFSA. *Faculty research:* Foundations in education, liberal learning, modernism, ethics. *Unit head:* Gabriel Moran, Director, 212-998-5652, E-mail: gm3@nyu.edu. *Application contact:* 212-998-5030, Fax: 212-995-4328, E-mail: steinhardt.gradadmissions@nyu.edu.

Niagara University, Graduate Division of Education, Concentration in Foundations of Teaching, Niagara Falls, Niagara University, NY 14109. Offers MA, MS Ed. *Accreditation:* NCATE. Part-time and evening/weekend programs available. *Faculty:* 1 full-time (0 women), 7 part-time/adjunct (4 women). *Students:* 5 full-time (4 women), 9 part-time (7 women), 1 international. In 2006, 18 degrees awarded. *Degree requirements:* For master's, thesis. *Entrance requirements:* For master's, GRE General Test or MAT. *Application deadline:* For fall admission, 8/1 for domestic students. Applications are processed on a rolling basis. Application fee: $30. *Expenses:* Contact institution. *Financial support:* Application deadline: 3/15. *Unit head:* Dr. Chandra Foote, Chair, 716-286-8549. *Application contact:* Dr. Debra A. Colley, Dean of Education, 716-286-8560, Fax: 716-286-8560, E-mail: dcolley@niagara.edu.

Northeastern State University, Graduate College, College of Education, Department of Educational Foundation and Leadership, Tahlequah, OK 74464-2399. Offers collegiate scholarship and services (MS); school administration (M Ed); teaching (M Ed). Part-time and evening/weekend programs available. *Students:* 32 full-time (26 women), 200 part-time (126 women); includes 68 minority (12 African Americans, 48 American Indian/Alaska Native, 8 Asian Americans or Pacific Islanders). In 2006, 89 degrees awarded. *Degree requirements:* For master's, thesis. *Entrance requirements:* For master's, MAT or GRE. Additional exam requirements/recommendations for international students: Required—TOEFL (minimum score 213 computer-based). *Application deadline:* For fall admission, 6/1 priority date for domestic students. Applications are processed on a rolling basis. Application fee: $0 ($25 for international students). Electronic applications accepted. *Financial support:* Teaching assistantships, Federal Work-Study available. Financial award application deadline: 3/1. *Unit head:* Dr. Marion Morgan, Head, 918-449-6000 Ext. 6589.

Northern Illinois University, Graduate School, College of Education, Department of Leadership, Educational Psychology and Foundations, De Kalb, IL 60115-2854. Offers educational administration (MS Ed, Ed D, Ed S); educational psychology (MS Ed, Ed D); foundations of education (MS Ed); school business management (MS Ed). Part-time and evening/weekend programs available. Postbaccalaureate distance learning degree programs offered (minimal on-campus study). *Faculty:* 23 full-time (12 women). *Students:* 15 full-time (7 women), 499 part-time (289 women); includes 75 minority (53 African Americans, 2 American Indian/Alaska Native, 6 Asian Americans or Pacific Islanders, 14 Hispanic Americans), 2 international. Average age 37. 186 applicants, 62% accepted, 92 enrolled. In 2006, 171 master's, 10 doctorates, 50 other advanced degrees awarded. *Degree requirements:* For master's, thesis optional; for doctorate, thesis/dissertation, candidacy exam, dissertation defense. *Entrance requirements:* For master's, minimum undergraduate GPA of 2.75; for doctorate, GRE General Test, minimum undergraduate GPA of 2.75, 3.2 graduate; for Ed S, GRE General Test, minimum GPA of 2.75 (undergraduate), 3.2 (graduate). Additional exam requirements/recommendations for international students: Required—TOEFL (minimum score 550 paper-based; 213 computer-based). *Application deadline:* For fall admission, 6/1 for domestic students, 5/1 for international students; for spring admission, 11/1 for domestic students, 10/1 for international students. Applications are processed on a rolling basis. Application fee: $30. Electronic applications accepted. *Financial support:* In 2006–07, 3 research assistantships with full tuition reimbursements, 8 teaching assistantships with full tuition reimbursements were awarded; fellowships with full tuition reimbursements, career-related internships or fieldwork, Federal Work-Study, scholarships/grants, tuition waivers (full), and unspecified assistantships also available. Support available to part-time students. Financial award applicants required to submit FAFSA. *Faculty research:* Interpersonal forgiveness, learner-centered education, psychedelic studies, senior theory, professional growth. *Unit head:* Dr. Wilma Miranda, Chair, 815-753-1562, E-mail: wmiranda@niu.edu.

Oakland University, Graduate Study and Lifelong Learning, School of Education and Human Services, Department of Teacher Development and Educational Studies, Rochester, MI 48309-4401. Offers education studies (M Ed); secondary education (MAT). *Accreditation:* NCATE. *Faculty:* 6 full-time (5 women), 2 part-time/adjunct (both women). *Students:* 190 full-time (158 women), 170 part-time (130 women); includes 24 minority (13 African Americans, 1 American Indian/Alaska Native, 8 Asian Americans or Pacific Islanders, 2 Hispanic Americans). Average age 32. 146 applicants, 97% accepted, 125 enrolled. In 2006, 57 degrees awarded. *Entrance requirements:* For master's, minimum GPA of 3.0 for unconditional admission. *Application deadline:* For fall admission, 3/1 for domestic students. Application fee: $35. Electronic applications accepted. *Expenses:* Tuition, state resident: full-time $9,936; part-time $414 per credit. Tuition, nonresident: full-time $17,202; part-time $716 per credit. *Financial support:* Federal Work-Study, institutionally sponsored loans, and tuition waivers (full) available. Financial award application deadline: 3/1; financial award applicants required to submit FAFSA. *Faculty research:* Earth science for middle and high school teachers through real world connections, learning communities, content enrichment. *Unit head:* Dr. Dyanne M Tracy, Chair, 248-370-3064, Fax: 248-370-4605, E-mail: dtracy@oakland.edu.

Penn State University Park, Graduate School, College of Education, Department of Education Policy Studies, State College, University Park, PA 16802-1503. Offers college student affairs (M Ed); educational leadership (M Ed, MS, D Ed, PhD); educational theory and policy (MA, PhD); higher education (M Ed, D Ed, PhD). *Accreditation:* NCATE. *Unit head:* Dr. Jacqueline A. Stefkovich, Head, 814-863-0619, E-mail: jas71@psu.edu.

Purdue University, Graduate School, School of Education, Department of Educational Studies, West Lafayette, IN 47907. Offers administration (MS Ed, PhD, Ed S); counseling and development (MS Ed, PhD); education of the gifted (MS Ed); educational psychology (MS Ed, PhD); foundations of education (MS Ed, PhD); higher education administration (MS Ed, PhD); special education (MS Ed, PhD). *Accreditation:* ACA (one or more programs are accredited); NCATE (one or more programs are accredited). Part-time and evening/weekend programs available. *Faculty:* 28 full-time (18 women). *Students:* 100 full-time (71 women), 126 part-time (77 women); includes 32 minority (19 African Americans, 2 American Indian/Alaska Native, 6 Asian Americans or Pacific Islanders, 5 Hispanic Americans), 33 international. Average age 36. 152 applicants, 62% accepted, 56 enrolled. In 2006, 51 master's, 17 doctorates awarded. *Degree requirements:* For master's, thesis optional; for doctorate, thesis/dissertation, oral and written exams; for Ed S, oral presentation, project. *Entrance requirements:* For master's, GRE General Test, minimum undergraduate GPA of 3.0; for doctorate, GRE General Test; for Ed S, GRE, minimum B average. Additional exam requirements/recommendations for international students: Required—TOEFL. *Application deadline:* For fall admission, 1/15 for domestic students; for spring admission, 9/15 for domestic students. Applications are processed on a rolling basis. Application fee: $55. Electronic applications accepted. *Financial support:* In 2006–07, 6 fellowships with full tuition reimbursements (averaging $13,300 per year), 23 research assistantships with full tuition reimbursements (averaging $11,500 per year), 33 teaching assistantships with full tuition reimbursements (averaging $10,800 per year) were awarded; career-related internships or fieldwork and tuition waivers (full) also available. Support available to part-time students. Financial award application deadline: 3/1; financial award applicants required to submit FAFSA. *Faculty research:* Motivation, learning disabilities, school learning, group processes, cognitive development. *Unit head:* Dr. Kevin R Kelly, Head, 765-494-9170, Fax: 765-496-1228. *Application contact:* Patricia Mason, Coordinator of Graduate Studies, 765-494-2346, Fax: 765-494-5832, E-mail: gradoffice@soe.purdue.edu.

Regis University, School for Professional Studies, Program in Teacher Education, Denver, CO 80221-1099. Offers adult learning, training, and development (M Ed); curriculum, instruction, and assessment (M Ed); early childhood (M Ed); educational technology (Certificate); elementary (M Ed); ESL (M Ed); fine arts (M Ed), including arts, music; instructional technology (M Ed); professional leadership (M Ed); reading (M Ed); secondary (M Ed); self-designed (M Ed); space studies (M Ed); special education (M Ed); teacher licensure (M Ed). Program also offered in Henderson and Las Vegas (Summerlin), NV. Postbaccalaureate distance learning degree programs offered. *Unit head:* Dr. Suzie Perry, Dean, 303-458-4302. *Application contact:* Partick Lowenthal, Assistant Director, 303-458-4300 Ext. 4314, E-mail: masters@regis.edu.

Rutgers, The State University of New Jersey, New Brunswick, Graduate School of Education, Department of Educational Theory, Policy and Administration, Program in Social and Philosophical Foundations of Education, New Brunswick, NJ 08901-1281. Offers Ed M, Ed D. Part-time and evening/weekend programs available. *Faculty:* 5 full-time (1 woman). *Students:* 11 full-time (6 women), 48 part-time (38 women). Average age 33. 33 applicants, 24% accepted, 5 enrolled. In 2006, 3 master's, 3 doctorates awarded. *Degree requirements:* For doctorate, thesis/dissertation, qualifying exam. *Entrance requirements:* For master's, GRE General Test; for doctorate, GRE General Test, writing sample. Additional exam requirements/recommendations for international students: Required—TOEFL. *Application deadline:* For fall admission, 2/1 for domestic and international students; for spring admission, 11/1 for domestic and international students. Application fee: $60. Electronic applications accepted. *Financial support:* Fellowships, research assistantships, teaching assistantships available. Financial award application deadline: 3/15; financial award applicants required to submit FAFSA. *Unit head:* Dr. James M. Giarelli, Coordinator, 732-932-7496 Ext. 8239, Fax: 732-932-6803, E-mail: giarelli@rci.rutgers.edu. *Application contact:* Sandy Chubrick, Administrative Assistant, 732-932-7496 Ext. 8239, Fax: 732-932-6803, E-mail: chubrick@rci.rutgers.edu.

Saint Louis University, Graduate School, College of Public Service and Graduate School, Department of Educational Studies, St. Louis, MO 63103-2097. Offers curriculum and instruction (MA, Ed D, PhD); educational foundations (MA, Ed D, PhD); special education (MA); teaching (MAT). *Accreditation:* NCATE. Part-time programs available. *Faculty:* 12 full-time (8 women), 18 part-time/adjunct (12 women). *Students:* 15 full-time (10 women), 53 part-time (42 women); includes 3 minority (1 African American, 2 Asian Americans or Pacific Islanders), 4 international. Average age 36. 25 applicants, 80% accepted, 14 enrolled. In 2006, 2 master's, 5 doctorates awarded. *Degree requirements:* For master's, comprehensive exam, registration; for doctorate, thesis/dissertation, preliminary oral and written exams, comprehensive exam, registration. *Entrance requirements:* For master's, GRE General Test or MAT, letters of recommendation, resumé; for doctorate, GRE General Test, letters of recommendation, resumé. Additional exam requirements/recommendations for international students: Required—TOEFL (minimum score 525 paper-based; 194 computer-based). *Application deadline:* For fall admission, 7/1 for domestic and international students; for spring admission, 11/1 for domestic and international students. Applications are processed on a rolling basis. Application fee: $40. *Expenses:* Tuition: Part-time $800 per credit hour. Required fees: $105 per semester. *Financial support:* In 2006–07, 24 students received support, including 4 teaching assistantships with full tuition reimbursements available (averaging $11,000 per year); Federal Work-Study, scholarships/grants, traineeships, health care benefits, and unspecified assistantships also available. Support available to part-time students. Financial award application deadline: 6/1; financial award applicants required to submit FAFSA. *Faculty research:* Teacher preparation, multicultural issues, children with special needs, qualitative research in education, inclusion. *Unit head:* Dr. Mary Chittooran, Interim Chairperson, 314-977-4062, Fax: 314-977-3214, E-mail: chittomm@slu.edu. *Application contact:* Gary Behrman, Associate Dean of the Graduate School, 314-977-3827, E-mail: behrmang@slu.edu.

Southeast Missouri State University, School of Graduate Studies, Department of Middle and Secondary Education, Cape Girardeau, MO 63701-4799. Offers educational studies (MA); middle level education (MA). *Accreditation:* NCATE. Part-time and evening/weekend programs available. *Faculty:* 3 full-time (all women). *Students:* Average age 35. 16 applicants, 88% accepted. In 2006, 6 degrees awarded. *Degree requirements:* For master's, thesis or alternative. *Entrance requirements:* For master's, GRE General Test, MAT, PRAXIS II, minimum GPA of 2.75. Additional exam requirements/recommendations for international students: Required—TOEFL (minimum score 550 paper-based; 213 computer-based). *Application deadline:* For fall admission, 8/1 for domestic students, 4/1 for international students; for spring admission, 11/21 for domestic students, 10/1 for international students. Applications are processed on a rolling basis. Application fee: $20 ($100 for international students). Electronic applications accepted. *Financial support:* In 2006–07, 6 students received support. Applicants required to submit FAFSA. *Unit head:* Dr. Simin Cwick, Interim Chair, 573-651-2008, Fax: 573-651-6141, E-mail: scwick@semo.edu. *Application contact:* Marsha L. Arant, Senior Administrative Assistant, Office of Graduate Studies, 573-651-2192, Fax: 573-651-2001, E-mail: marant@semo.edu.

Southern Connecticut State University, School of Graduate Studies, School of Education, Department of Educational Foundations, New Haven, CT 06515-1355. Offers foundational studies (Diploma). Part-time and evening/weekend programs available. *Faculty:* 2 full-time, 2 part-time/adjunct. *Students:* 4 full-time (1 woman), 26 part-time (17 women); includes 3 minority (all African Americans) 19 applicants, 32% accepted, 4 enrolled. In 2006, 20 degrees awarded. *Entrance requirements:* For degree, master's degree. *Application deadline:* For fall admission, 7/15 priority date for domestic students. Applications are processed on a rolling basis. Application fee: $50. Electronic applications accepted. *Financial support:* Teaching assistantships available. Financial award application deadline: 4/15; financial award applicants required to submit FAFSA. *Unit head:* Dr. Bernard Hayford, Coordinator, 203-392-6443, Fax: 203-392-6473, E-mail: hayfordb1@southernct.edu.

Southern Illinois University Edwardsville, Graduate Studies and Research, School of Education, Department of Educational Leadership, Program in Learning, Culture, and Society, Edwardsville, IL 62026-0001. Offers MS Ed. *Students:* 1 (woman) full-time, 1 (woman) part-time. 2 applicants, 100% accepted. *Degree requirements:* For master's, thesis or alternative, project oral defense. *Entrance requirements:* Additional exam requirements/recommendations for international students: Required—TOEFL. *Application deadline:* For fall admission, 7/20 for domestic students, 6/1 for international students; for spring admission, 12/14 for domestic students, 10/1 for international students. Applications are processed on a rolling basis. Application fee: $30. Electronic applications accepted. *Unit head:* Dr. Laurel Puchner, Director, 618-650-3286.

Stanford University, School of Education, Program in Social Sciences, Policy, and Educational Practice, Stanford, CA 94305-9991. Offers administration and policy analysis (Ed D, PhD); anthropology of education (PhD); economics of education (PhD); educational linguistics (PhD); evaluation (MA), including interdisciplinary studies; higher education (PhD); history of education (PhD); interdisciplinary studies (PhD); international comparative education (MA, PhD); international education administration and policy analysis (MA); philosophy of education (PhD); policy analysis (MA); prospective principal's program (MA); sociology of education (PhD). *Degree requirements:* For master's, thesis (for some programs); for doctorate, thesis/dissertation. *Entrance requirements:* For master's and doctorate, GRE General Test. Electronic applications accepted.

State University of New York at Binghamton, Graduate School, School of Education, Program in Educational Theory and Practice, Binghamton, NY 13902-6000. Offers Ed D. *Students:* 11 full-time (9 women), 33 part-time (24 women); includes 4 minority (1 African American, 1 American Indian/Alaska Native, 1 Asian American or Pacific Islander, 1 Hispanic American), 4 international. Average age 43. 13 applicants, 46% accepted. In 2006, 5 degrees awarded. *Degree requirements:* For doctorate, thesis/dissertation. *Entrance requirements:* For doctorate, GRE General Test, writing sample. Additional exam requirements/recommendations for international students: Required—TOEFL. *Application deadline:* For fall admission, 4/15 priority date for domestic students, 1/15 priority date for international students; for spring admission, 11/1 for domestic students, 10/1 for international students. Applications are processed on a rolling basis. Application fee: $60. Electronic applications accepted. *Financial support:* In 2006–07, 14 students received support, including 6 fellowships (averaging $8,837 per year), 8 teaching assistantships with full tuition reimbursements available (averaging $8,300 per year); research assistantships, career-related internships or fieldwork, Federal Work-Study, institutionally sponsored loans, and unspecified assistantships also available. Support available to part-time students. Financial award application deadline: 2/15. *Unit head:* Dr. James Carpenter, Coordinator, 607-777-4678, E-mail: jcarpent@binghamton.edu.

Suffolk University, College of Arts and Sciences, Department of Education and Human Services, Program in Foundations of Education, Boston, MA 02108-2770. Offers administration of higher education (M Ed); foundations of education (M Ed), including administration of higher education; leadership (CAGS). Part-time and evening/weekend programs available. *Entrance requirements:* For master's, GRE General Test or MAT. *Application deadline:* For fall admission, 6/15 priority date for domestic students, 6/15 for international students; for spring admission, 11/15 priority date for domestic students, 11/15 for international students. Applications are processed on a rolling basis. Application fee: $35. *Financial support:* Fellowships, career-related internships or fieldwork, Federal Work-Study, and institutionally sponsored loans available. Support available to part-time students. Financial award application deadline: 4/1; financial award applicants required to submit FAFSA. *Faculty research:* History of medieval education, history of universities, philosophy of education. *Unit head:* Dr. Sarah M. Carroll, Program Director, 617-573-8262, Fax: 617-722-9440, E-mail: scaroll@suffolk.edu. *Application contact:* Judith Reynolds, Director of Graduate Admissions, 617-573-8302, Fax: 617-523-0116, E-mail: grad.admission@suffolk.edu.

Syracuse University, Graduate School, School of Education, Program in Cultural Foundations of Education, Syracuse, NY 13244. Offers cultural foundations of education (MS, PhD). Part-time and evening/weekend programs available. *Faculty:* 7 full-time (3 women), 1 part-time/adjunct (0 women). *Students:* 43 full-time (32 women), 30 part-time (20 women); includes 19 minority (10 African Americans, 3 American Indian/Alaska Native, 1 Asian American or Pacific Islander, 5 Hispanic Americans), 15 international. 42 applicants, 79% accepted, 18 enrolled. *Degree requirements:* For master's, thesis or alternative; for doctorate, thesis/dissertation. *Entrance requirements:* For doctorate, GRE. Additional exam requirements/recommendations for international students: Required—TOEFL. *Application deadline:* For fall admission, 2/1 for domestic students. Applications are processed on a rolling basis. Application fee: $65. Electronic applications accepted. *Expenses:* Tuition: Full-time $16,920; part-time $940 per credit hour. Required fees: $930; $930 per year. *Financial support:* Fellowships with full tuition reimbursements, research assistantships with full tuition reimbursements, teaching assistantships with full and partial tuition reimbursements available. *Faculty research:* Gender and education, history of women's education, the role of science in liberal education, student attrition. *Unit head:* Dr. Sari Knopp Biklen, Chair, 315-443-9075. *Application contact:* Liza Rochelson, Graduate Admission Recruiter, 315-443-2505, Fax: 315-443-2258, E-mail: gradcrt@gwmail.syr.edu.

Teachers College Columbia University, Graduate Faculty of Education, Department of Arts and Humanities, Program in Philosophy and Education, New York, NY 10027-6696. Offers Ed M, MA, Ed D, PhD. *Faculty:* 2 full-time (1 woman). *Students:* 12 full-time (9 women), 33 part-time (17 women); includes 8 minority (3 African Americans, 3 Asian Americans or Pacific Islanders, 2 Hispanic Americans), 5 international. Average age 35. 28 applicants, 54% accepted, 8 enrolled. In 2006, 9 master's, 3 doctorates awarded. *Degree requirements:* For doctorate, thesis/dissertation. *Entrance requirements:* For master's, previous course work in philosophy; for doctorate, previous course work in philosophy (Ed D), undergraduate degree in philosophy (PhD). *Application deadline:* For fall admission, 5/15 for domestic students; for spring admission, 12/1 for domestic students. Application fee: $65. *Expenses:* Tuition: Full-time $23,400; part-time $975 per credit. Required fees: $320 per term. *Financial support:* Career-related internships or fieldwork, Federal Work-Study, institutionally sponsored loans, and tuition waivers (full and partial) available. Support available to part-time students. Financial award application deadline: 2/1. *Faculty research:* Philosophy and its relationship to educational thought, ethics and education, social theory and ideology. *Application contact:* Mark E. Stearns, Associate Director of Admission, 212-678-3710, Fax: 212-678-4171.

Texas A&M University, College of Education and Human Development, Department of Teaching, Learning, and Culture, College Station, TX 77843. Offers curriculum and instruction (M Ed, MS, PhD); mathematics education (M Ed, MS, PhD); multicultural/urban/ESL/international education (M Ed, MS, PhD); reading/language arts (M Ed, MS, PhD); science education (M Ed, MS, PhD); social studies education (M Ed, MS, PhD). *Accreditation:* NCATE. Part-time programs available. *Faculty:* 25 full-time (9 women), 2 part-time/adjunct (both women). *Students:* 156 full-time (115 women), 226 part-time (191 women); includes 95 minority (43 African Americans, 1 American Indian/Alaska Native, 9 Asian Americans or Pacific Islanders, 42 Hispanic Americans), 36 international. Average age 36. 137 applicants, 83% accepted, 80 enrolled. In 2006, 69 master's, 15 doctorates awarded. *Median time to degree:* Of those who began their doctoral program in fall 1998, 77% received their degree in 8 years or less. *Degree requirements:* For master's, thesis (for some programs), comprehensive exam; for doctorate, thesis/dissertation, comprehensive exam. *Entrance requirements:* For master's, GRE General Test, minimum GPA of 3.0; for doctorate, GRE General Test, 3 years of teaching experience. Additional exam requirements/recommendations for international students: Required—TOEFL (minimum score 550 paper-based; 213 computer-based). *Application deadline:* For fall admission, 1/15 priority date for domestic and international students; for spring admission, 9/15 priority date for domestic and international students. Applications are processed on a rolling basis. Application fee: $50 ($75 for international students). Electronic applications accepted. *Expenses:* Tuition, state resident: full-time $4,697. Tuition, nonresident: full-time $11,297. Required fees: $2,272. *Financial support:* In 2006–07, fellowships with partial tuition reimbursements (averaging $3,000 per year), teaching assistantships with partial tuition reimbursements (averaging $7,200 per year) were awarded; research assistantships with partial tuition reimbursements, career-related internships or fieldwork, Federal Work-Study, institutionally sponsored loans, scholarships/grants, tuition waivers (partial), and unspecified assistantships also available. Support available to part-time students. Financial award application deadline: 4/1; financial award applicants required to submit FAFSA. *Unit head:* Dr. Dennie Smith, Head, 979-845-8384, Fax: 979-845-9663. *Application contact:* Graduate Admissions Supervisor, 979-845-8382, Fax: 979-845-9663.

University of Arkansas, Graduate School, College of Education and Health Professions, Department of Educational Leadership, Counseling and Foundations, Program in Educational Foundations, Fayetteville, AR 72701-1201. Offers MS, PhD. *Students:* 3 full-time (2 women), 3 part-time (all women). 1 applicant, 0% accepted.Application fee: $40 ($50 for international students). *Financial support:* In 2006–07, 1 fellowship was awarded; research assistantships, teaching assistantships. *Application contact:* Dr. Carl Holt, Graduate Coordinator, 479-575-2207, E-mail: cholt@uark.edu.

The University of British Columbia, Faculty of Graduate Studies, Faculty of Education, Department of Educational Studies, Vancouver, BC V6T 1Z1, Canada. Offers adult education (M Ed, MA); adult learning and global change (M Ed); educational administration (M Ed, MA); educational leadership and policy (Ed D); educational studies (M Ed, PhD), including history of education (M Ed), philosophy of education (M Ed), sociology of education (M Ed); higher education (M Ed, MA); society, culture and politics in education (M Ed, MA). Part-time and evening/weekend programs available. *Faculty:* 30 full-time (15 women), 9 part-time/adjunct (6 women). *Students:* 308 full-time (217 women), 45 part-time (31 women). Average age 35. 211 applicants, 60% accepted. In 2006, 128 master's, 15 doctorates awarded. Terminal master's awarded for partial completion of doctoral program. *Degree requirements:* For master's, thesis (MA); for doctorate, thesis/dissertation. *Entrance requirements:* Additional exam requirements/recommendations for international students: Required—TOEFL, TOEFL or IELTS. Electronic applications accepted. *Financial support:* Fellowships, research assistantships, teaching assistantships available. *Faculty research:* Educational leadership educational administration adult education politics in education, global change and adult learning. Total annual research expenditures: $547,440. *Unit head:* Dr. Tara Fenwick, Head, 604-822-5359, Fax: 604-82-4244. *Application contact:* Christine Adams, Graduate Secretary, 604-822-6647, Fax: 604-822-4244, E-mail: grad.edst@ubc.ca.

University of Calgary, Faculty of Graduate Studies, Faculty of Education, Graduate Division of Educational Research, Calgary, AB T2N 1N4, Canada. Offers community rehabilitation and disability studies (M Ed, M Sc, Ed D, PhD, Graduate Certificate, Graduate Diploma); curriculum, teaching and learning (M Ed, M Sc, MA, Ed D, PhD, Graduate Certificate, Graduate Diploma); educational contexts (M Ed, MA, Ed D, PhD, Graduate Certificate, Graduate Diploma); educational leadership (M Ed, MA, Ed D, PhD, Graduate Certificate, Graduate Diploma); educational technology (M Ed, M Sc, MA, Ed D, PhD, Graduate Certificate, Graduate Diploma); gifted education (M Sc, MA, Ed D, PhD, Graduate Certificate, Graduate Diploma); higher education administration (Ed D); interpretive studies in education (M Ed, M Sc, MA, Ed D, PhD, Graduate Certificate, Graduate Diploma); second language teaching (M Ed, Ed D, PhD, Graduate Certificate, Graduate Diploma); teaching English as a second language (M Ed, M Sc, MA, Ed D, PhD, Graduate Certificate, Graduate Diploma); workplace and adult learning (M Ed, MA, Ed D, PhD, Graduate Certificate, Graduate Diploma). Ed D in both higher education administration and educational leadership offered via distance delivery. Part-time and evening/weekend programs available. Postbaccalaureate distance learning degree programs offered (minimal on-campus study). *Faculty:* 44 full-time, 52 part-time/adjunct. *Students:* 488 full-time, 550 part-time. 400 applicants, 50% accepted. In 2006, 102 master's, 18 doctorates awarded. *Degree requirements:* For master's, thesis (for some programs); for doctorate, thesis/dissertation, candidacy exam. *Entrance requirements:* For master's, minimum GPA of 3.0, 3 letters of reference; for doctorate, minimum GPA of 3.5, 3 letters of reference; for other advanced degree, minimum GPA of 3.0. Additional exam requirements/recommendations for international students: Required—TOEFL, IELTS. *Application deadline:* For fall admission, 2/15 for domestic students, 2/5 for international students; for winter admission, 6/15 for domestic and international students. Application fee: $100. Electronic applications accepted. *Financial support:* In 2006–07, research assistantships (averaging $3,920 per year); teaching assistantships, career-related internships or fieldwork, scholarships/grants, and unspecified assistantships also available. Financial award application deadline: 2/1. *Faculty research:* Curriculum, leadership, technology, contexts, gifted, second language teaching, work place and adult learning. *Unit head:* Dr. Charles F. Webber, Associate Dean, 403-220-5675, Fax: 403-282-3005, E-mail: cwebber@ucalgary.ca. *Application contact:* Patricia A. Brown, Program Officer, Graduate Division of Educational Research, 403-220-3178, Fax: 403-282-3005, E-mail: brownp@ucalgary.ca.

University of California, Berkeley, Graduate Division, School of Education, Division of Language and Literacy, Society and Culture, Program in Social and Cultural Studies in Education, Berkeley, CA 94720-1500. Offers MA, PhD. *Degree requirements:* For master's, exam or thesis; for doctorate, thesis/dissertation, oral qualifying exam. *Entrance requirements:* For master's and doctorate, GRE General Test, minimum GPA of 3.0 during last 2 years of undergraduate course work. *Application deadline:* For fall admission, 12/1 for domestic students. Application fee: $60 ($80 for international students). Electronic applications accepted. *Financial support:* Unspecified assistantships available. *Unit head:* Dr. Harley Shaiken, Professor, 510-643-5363. *Application contact:* Admissions Office, 510-642-0841, Fax: 510-642-4808, E-mail: gse_info@uclink.berkeley.edu.

University of Cincinnati, Division of Research and Advanced Studies, College of Education, Criminal Justice, and Human Services, Division of Educational Studies, Program in Educational Studies, Cincinnati, OH 45221. Offers M Ed, PhD. *Accreditation:* NCATE. Part-time programs available. *Students:* 47. *Degree requirements:* For master's, thesis optional; for doctorate, thesis/dissertation, comprehensive exam. *Entrance requirements:* For master's, GRE General Test; for doctorate, GRE General Test, GRE Subject Test. Additional exam requirements/recommendations for international students: Required—TOEFL (minimum score 520 paper-based; 190 computer-based), OEPT 3. *Application deadline:* For fall admission, 2/15 for domestic students. Application fee: $40. Electronic applications accepted. *Financial support:* Teaching assistantships with full tuition reimbursements, tuition waivers (full) and unspecified assistantships available. *Unit head:* Wei Pan, Head, 513-556-2610, Fax: 513-556-3535, E-mail: wei.pan@uc.edu.

University of Colorado at Boulder, Graduate School, School of Education, Division of Educational Foundations, Policy, and Practice, Boulder, CO 80309. Offers MA, PhD. *Application contact:* Graduate Program Assistant, 303-492-6555, Fax: 303-492-5839, E-mail: edadvise@colorado.edu.

University of Connecticut, Graduate School, Neag School of Education, Department of Educational Leadership, Center for Education Policy Analysis, Storrs, CT 06269. Offers PhD. *Accreditation:* NCATE. *Faculty:* 8 full-time (4 women). *Degree requirements:* For doctorate, thesis/dissertation. *Entrance requirements:* For doctorate, GRE General Test. Additional exam requirements/recommendations for international students: Required—TOEFL (minimum score 550 paper-based; 213 computer-based). *Application deadline:* For fall admission, 2/1 priority date for domestic and international students; for spring admission, 11/1 for domestic students, 10/1 for international students. Applications are processed on a rolling basis. Application fee: $55. Electronic applications accepted. *Financial support:* In 2006–07, 1 research assistantship with full tuition reimbursement, 1 teaching assistantship with full tuition reimbursement were awarded; fellowships, Federal Work-Study, scholarships/grants, health care benefits, and unspecified assistantships also available. Financial award application deadline: 2/1; financial award applicants required to submit FAFSA. *Application contact:* Lisa Rasicot, Graduate Coordinator, 860-486-3065, Fax: 860-486-0210, E-mail: soeadm02@uconnvm.uconn.edu.

University of Florida, Graduate School, College of Education, School of Teaching and Learning, Gainesville, FL 32611. Offers bilingual/ESOL education (M Ed, MAE, Ed D, PhD, Ed S); curriculum and instruction (M Ed, MAE, Ed D, PhD, Ed S); early childhood education (Ed D, PhD, Ed S); elementary education (M Ed, MAE); English education (M Ed, MAE); mathematics education (M Ed, MAE); reading education (M Ed, MAE); science education (M Ed, MAE); social foundations (M Ed, MAE, Ed D, PhD); social studies education (M Ed, MAE). *Accreditation:* NCATE. *Faculty:* 29 full-time (20 women). *Students:* 506 (406 women); includes

Foundations and Philosophy of Education

University of Florida (continued)
87 minority (20 African Americans, 3 American Indian/Alaska Native, 13 Asian Americans or Pacific Islanders, 51 Hispanic Americans) 34 international. In 2006, 278 master's, 8 doctorates awarded. *Degree requirements:* For master's, thesis optional; for doctorate, variable foreign language requirement, thesis/dissertation. *Entrance requirements:* For master's and doctorate, GRE General Test, minimum GPA of 3.0; for Ed S, GRE General Test. Additional exam requirements/recommendations for international students: Required—TOEFL (minimum score 550 paper-based; 213 computer-based). *Application deadline:* For fall admission, 6/1 for domestic students. Applications are processed on a rolling basis. Application fee: $30. Electronic applications accepted. *Expenses:* Tuition, state resident: full-time $6,827. Tuition, nonresident: full-time $21,951. Required fees: $999. *Financial support:* In 2006–07, 5 research assistantships (averaging $11,947 per year), 22 teaching assistantships (averaging $9,709 per year) were awarded; fellowships, career-related internships or fieldwork and unspecified assistantships also available. *Faculty research:* Teacher education, inclusive education, classroom processes, curriculum and technology. *Unit head:* Dr. Tom Dana, Director, 352-392-9191 Ext. 200, Fax: 352-392-9193, E-mail: tdana@coe.ufl.edu. *Application contact:* Dr. Linda C. Jones, Coordinator, 352-392-0761 Ext. 267, Fax: 352-392-9193, E-mail: lcjones@coe.ufl.edu.

University of Georgia, Graduate School, College of Education, Department of Elementary and Social Studies Education, Athens, GA 30602. Offers early childhood education (M Ed, PhD, Ed S); elementary and middle school education (M Ed, PhD, Ed S), including elementary education (PhD), middle school education; social foundations of education (PhD). *Faculty:* 15 full-time (8 women). *Students:* 113 full-time (88 women), 122 part-time (95 women); includes 25 minority (19 African Americans, 4 Asian Americans or Pacific Islanders, 2 Hispanic Americans), 14 international. 170 applicants, 69% accepted, 88 enrolled. In 2006, 77 master's, 6 doctorates, 6 other advanced degrees awarded. *Entrance requirements:* For master's and Ed S, GRE General Test or MAT; for doctorate, GRE General Test. *Application deadline:* For fall admission, 7/1 priority date for domestic students; for spring admission, 11/15 for domestic students. Application fee: $50. Electronic applications accepted. *Financial support:* Fellowships, research assistantships, teaching assistantships, unspecified assistantships available. *Unit head:* Dr. Ronald J. Vansickle, Head, 706-542-7265, Fax: 706-542-6506, E-mail: rvansick@uga.edu. *Application contact:* Dr. John D. Hoge, Graduate Coordinator, 706-542-4416, Fax: 706-542-4277, E-mail: jdhoge@uga.edu.

University of Georgia, Graduate School, College of Education, Department of Workforce Education, Leadership and Social Foundations, Athens, GA 30602. Offers M Ed, MA, MAT, Ed D, PhD, Ed S. *Accreditation:* NCATE. *Faculty:* 19 full-time (10 women). *Students:* 45 full-time (27 women), 181 part-time (109 women); includes 37 minority (34 African Americans, 1 American Indian/Alaska Native, 1 Asian American or Pacific Islander, 1 Hispanic American), 5 international. 139 applicants, 72% accepted, 62 enrolled. In 2006, 52 master's, 18 doctorates, 7 other advanced degrees awarded. *Entrance requirements:* For master's, GRE General Test, MAT; for doctorate, GRE General Test; for Ed S, GRE General Test or MAT. *Application deadline:* For fall admission, 7/1 priority date for domestic students; for spring admission, 11/15 for domestic students. Application fee: $50. Electronic applications accepted. *Financial support:* Fellowships, research assistantships, teaching assistantships, unspecified assistantships available. *Unit head:* Dr. Roger B. Hill, Head, 706-542-4100, Fax: 706-542-4054, E-mail: rbhill@uga.edu. *Application contact:* Dr. Mura N. Womble, Graduate Coordinator, 706-542-4503, Fax: 706-542-4054, E-mail: mwomble@uga.edu.

University of Hawaii at Manoa, Graduate Division, College of Education, Department of Educational Foundations, Honolulu, HI 96822. Offers M Ed. Evening/weekend programs available. *Faculty:* 9 full-time (5 women), 5 part-time/adjunct (2 women). *Students:* 15 full-time (10 women), 54 part-time (38 women); includes 15 minority (13 Asian Americans or Pacific Islanders, 2 Hispanic Americans), 2 international. Average age 39. 27 applicants, 63% accepted, 10 enrolled. In 2006, 27 degrees awarded. *Degree requirements:* For master's, thesis optional. *Entrance requirements:* Additional exam requirements/recommendations for international students: Required—TOEFL (minimum score 580 paper-based; 237 computer-based; 92 iBT). *Application deadline:* For fall admission, 3/1 for domestic students, 1/15 for international students; for spring admission, 9/1 for domestic students, 8/1 for international students. Applications are processed on a rolling basis. Application fee: $50. *Financial support:* In 2006–07, 5 research assistantships (averaging $16,306 per year) were awarded; teaching assistantships, institutionally sponsored loans and tuition waivers (full and partial) also available. Support available to part-time students. Financial award application deadline: 9/26. *Faculty research:* Multicultural-ethnic education, comparative education, educational policy, interdisciplinary inquiry, moral/political education. *Application contact:* Eileen Tamura, Information Contact, 808-956-7817, Fax: 808-956-9100.

University of Hawaii at Manoa, Graduate Division, College of Education, Education Program, Honolulu, HI 96822. Offers curriculum and instruction (PhD); educational administration (PhD); educational foundations (PhD); educational policy studies (PhD); exceptionalities (PhD). Evening/weekend programs available. *Faculty:* 78 full-time (44 women), 1 part-time/adjunct (0 women). *Students:* 54 full-time (37 women), 97 part-time (66 women); includes 28 minority (6 African Americans, 1 American Indian/Alaska Native, 19 Asian Americans or Pacific Islanders, 2 Hispanic Americans), 3 international. Average age 45. 63 applicants, 52% accepted, 24 enrolled. In 2006, 17 degrees awarded. *Median time to degree:* Of those who began their doctoral program in fall 1998, 35% received their degree in 8 years or less. *Degree requirements:* For doctorate, thesis/dissertation. *Entrance requirements:* For doctorate, GRE General Test, sample of written work. Additional exam requirements/recommendations for international students: Required—TOEFL (minimum score 600 paper-based; 250 computer-based; 100 iBT). *Application deadline:* For fall admission, 2/1 for domestic students, 1/15 for international students. Application fee: $50. *Financial support:* In 2006–07, 12 research assistantships (averaging $16,565 per year), 5 teaching assistantships (averaging $13,964 per year) were awarded; career-related internships or fieldwork, Federal Work-Study, and tuition waivers (full and partial) also available. *Application contact:* Dr. Helen Slaughter, Chairperson, 808-956-7913, Fax: 808-956-9100, E-mail: slaughte@hawaii.edu.

University of Houston, College of Education, Department of Educational Leadership and Cultural Studies, Houston, TX 77204. Offers educational administration (M Ed, Ed D); higher education (M Ed); historical, social, and cultural foundations of education (M Ed, Ed D). *Accreditation:* NCATE. Part-time and evening/weekend programs available. *Faculty:* 8 full-time (6 women), 8 part-time/adjunct (3 women). *Students:* 19 full-time (12 women), 169 part-time (110 women); includes 72 minority (39 African Americans, 10 Asian Americans or Pacific Islanders, 23 Hispanic Americans), 3 international. Average age 36. 89 applicants, 60% accepted, 43 enrolled. In 2006, 31 master's, 5 doctorates awarded. *Degree requirements:* For master's, comprehensive exam or thesis; for doctorate, thesis/dissertation, comprehensive exam. *Entrance requirements:* For master's, GRE General Test or MAT, minimum GPA of 3.0 in last 60 hours of course work; for doctorate, GRE General Test, interview, minimum GPA of 3.0 in last 60 hours. *Application deadline:* For fall admission, 7/18 priority date for domestic students; for spring admission, 12/18 for domestic students. Applications are processed on a rolling basis. Application fee: $35 ($75 for international students). *Expenses:* Tuition, state resident: full-time $5,429; part-time $226 per credit. Tuition, nonresident: full-time $12,029; part-time $501 per credit. Required fees: $2,454. *Financial support:* In 2006–07, 1 fellowship with full tuition reimbursement (averaging $9,500 per year), 1 research assistantship with full tuition reimbursement (averaging $9,500 per year), 1 teaching assistantship with full tuition reimbursement (averaging $9,500 per year) were awarded; career-related internships or fieldwork, Federal Work-Study, institutionally sponsored loans, scholarships/grants, health care benefits, and unspecified assistantships also available. Support available to part-time students. Financial award application deadline: 3/10; financial award applicants required to submit FAFSA. *Faculty research:* Change, supervision, multiculturalism, evaluation, policy. *Unit head:* Robert McPherson, Interim Dean, 713-743-5003, Fax: 713-743-8650, E-mail: bmcph@uh.edu. *Application contact:* Rose L. Hernandez, Office Assistant, 713-743-5044, Fax: 713-743-4979.

University of Houston–Clear Lake, School of Education, Program in Foundations and Professional Studies, Houston, TX 77058-1098. Offers counseling (MS); instructional technology (MS); multicultural studies (MS). Part-time and evening/weekend programs available. *Faculty:* 15 full-time (11 women), 11 part-time/adjunct (6 women). *Students:* 35 full-time (29 women), 283 part-time (239 women); includes 111 minority (58 African Americans, 1 American Indian/Alaska Native, 10 Asian Americans or Pacific Islanders, 42 Hispanic Americans), 10 international. Average age 35. In 2006, 86 degrees awarded. *Degree requirements:* For master's, thesis optional. *Entrance requirements:* For master's, GRE or minimum GPA of 3.0 in last 60 hours. Additional exam requirements/recommendations for international students: Required—TOEFL (minimum score 550 paper-based; 213 computer-based). *Application deadline:* For fall admission, 7/1 for domestic students, 6/1 for international students; for spring admission, 10/1 for domestic and international students. Applications are processed on a rolling basis. Application fee: $35 ($75 for international students). Electronic applications accepted. *Financial support:* Career-related internships or fieldwork, Federal Work-Study, institutionally sponsored loans, and scholarships/grants. Support available to part-time students. Financial award application deadline: 5/1; financial award applicants required to submit FAFSA. *Unit head:* Dr. Judy Marquez, Chair, 281-283-3580, E-mail: marquez@uhcl.edu. *Application contact:* Janis S. Bigelow, Assistant Director of Admissions, Recruitment and Communications, 281-283-2540, Fax: 281-283-2530, E-mail: bigelow@uhcl.edu.

The University of Iowa, Graduate College, College of Education, Department of Educational Policy and Leadership Studies, Program in Social Foundations, Iowa City, IA 52242-1316. Offers MA, PhD. *Faculty:* 5 full-time. *Students:* 15 full-time (10 women), 29 part-time (21 women); includes 6 minority (3 African Americans, 1 American Indian/Alaska Native, 2 Hispanic Americans), 9 international. 20 applicants, 75% accepted, 6 enrolled. In 2006, 3 degrees awarded. *Degree requirements:* For master's, exam, thesis optional; for doctorate, thesis/dissertation, comprehensive exam, registration. *Entrance requirements:* For master's and doctorate, GRE General Test, minimum GPA of 3.0. Additional exam requirements/recommendations for international students: Required—TOEFL (minimum score 550 paper-based; 213 computer-based; 81 iBT). *Application deadline:* For fall admission, 4/15 priority date for domestic students. Applications are processed on a rolling basis. Application fee: $60 ($85 for international students). Electronic applications accepted. *Financial support:* In 2006–07, 1 fellowship, 9 research assistantships with partial tuition reimbursements, 8 teaching assistantships with partial tuition reimbursements were awarded. Financial award applicants required to submit FAFSA. *Unit head:* Dr. Scott McNabb, Coordinator, 319-335-5372, Fax: 319-384-0587.

The University of Iowa, Graduate College, College of Education, Department of Psychological and Quantitative Foundations, Iowa City, IA 52242-1316. Offers counseling psychology (PhD); educational measurement and statistics (MA, PhD); educational psychology (MA, PhD); school psychology (PhD, Ed S); JD/PhD. *Accreditation:* APA. *Faculty:* 21 full-time, 8 part-time/adjunct. *Students:* 97 full-time (71 women), 65 part-time (50 women); includes 30 minority (9 African Americans, 1 American Indian/Alaska Native, 8 Asian Americans or Pacific Islanders, 12 Hispanic Americans), 39 international. 119 applicants, 36% accepted, 23 enrolled. In 2006, 8 master's, 15 doctorates, 3 other advanced degrees awarded. *Degree requirements:* For master's, exam, thesis optional; for doctorate, thesis/dissertation, comprehensive exam, registration; for Ed S, exam. *Entrance requirements:* For master's, doctorate, and Ed S, GRE General Test, minimum GPA of 3.0. Additional exam requirements/recommendations for international students: Required—TOEFL (minimum score 550 paper-based; 213 computer-based; 81 iBT). Application fee: $60 ($85 for international students). Electronic applications accepted. *Financial support:* In 2006–07, 7 fellowships, 89 research assistantships with partial tuition reimbursements, 21 teaching assistantships with partial tuition reimbursements were awarded. Financial award applicants required to submit FAFSA. *Unit head:* Timothy Ansley, Chair, 319-335-5411, Fax: 319-335-6145.

University of Kansas, Graduate Studies, School of Education, Department of Educational Leadership and Policy Studies, Program in Policy Studies, Lawrence, KS 66045. Offers foundations (Ed D, PhD); higher education (Ed D, PhD); school administration (Ed D, PhD). Part-time and evening/weekend programs available. *Faculty:* 19. *Students:* 18 full-time (10 women), 133 part-time (69 women); includes 17 minority (7 African Americans, 4 American Indian/Alaska Native, 2 Asian Americans or Pacific Islanders, 4 Hispanic Americans), 5 international. Average age 40. 17 applicants, 59% accepted. In 2006, 21 degrees awarded. *Degree requirements:* For doctorate, thesis/dissertation, comprehensive exam. *Entrance requirements:* For doctorate, GRE General Test, minimum graduate GPA of 3.5. Additional exam requirements/recommendations for international students: Required—TOEFL. *Application deadline:* For fall admission, 7/1 priority date for domestic and international students; for spring admission, 11/1 priority date for domestic and international students. Applications are processed on a rolling basis. Application fee: $55 ($60 for international students). Electronic applications accepted. *Expenses:* Tuition, area resident: Part-time $227 per credit. Tuition, state resident: part-time $543 per credit. Tuition and fees vary according to course load, campus/location, program and reciprocity agreements. *Financial support:* Fellowships, research assistantships with full and partial tuition reimbursements, teaching assistantships with full and partial tuition reimbursements available. Financial award application deadline: 3/15. *Faculty research:* Policy studies in higher education, policy studies in foundations, policy studies in educational leaderships. *Application contact:* Denise Brubaker, Admissions Coordinator, 785-864-4458, Fax: 785-864-4697, E-mail: elps@ku.edu.

University of Manitoba, Faculty of Graduate Studies, Faculty of Education, Department of Educational Administration, Foundations and Psychology, Winnipeg, MB R3T 2N2, Canada. Offers adult education (M Ed); educational administration (M Ed); guidance and counseling (M Ed); inclusive special education (M Ed); special foundations education (M Ed). *Degree requirements:* For master's, thesis or alternative.

University of Maryland, College Park, Graduate Studies, College of Education, Department of Education Policy and Leadership, College Park, MD 20742. Offers curriculum and educational communications (M Ed, MA, Ed D, PhD); social foundations of education (M Ed, MA, Ed D, PhD, CAGS). *Accreditation:* NCATE. Part-time and evening/weekend programs available. Postbaccalaureate distance learning degree programs offered (minimal on-campus study). *Faculty:* 17 full-time (11 women), 6 part-time/adjunct (4 women). *Students:* 180 full-time (127 women), 145 part-time (105 women); includes 107 minority (69 African Americans, 1 American Indian/Alaska Native, 20 Asian Americans or Pacific Islanders, 17 Hispanic Americans), 23 international. 167 applicants, 40% accepted, 25 enrolled. In 2006, 37 master's, 15 doctorates, 1 other advanced degree awarded. *Degree requirements:* For master's, thesis or alternative, internship and/or field experience; for doctorate, thesis/dissertation, practicum or internship, comprehensive exam. *Entrance requirements:* For master's, GRE General Test or MAT, minimum GPA of 3.0, scholarly writing sample, 3 letters of recommendation; for doctorate, GRE General Test or MAT, scholarly writing sample, minimum undergraduate GPA of 3.0, minimum graduate GPA of 3.5. *Application deadline:* For fall admission, 2/1 for domestic and international students; for spring admission, 9/1 for domestic students, 6/1 for international students. Applications are processed on a rolling basis. Application fee: $60. Electronic applications accepted. *Financial support:* In 2006–07, 6 fellowships with full tuition reimbursements (averaging $13,118 per year), 2 research assistantships with tuition reimbursements (averaging $15,252 per year), 47 teaching assistantships with tuition reimbursements (averaging $14,510 per year) were awarded; career-related internships or fieldwork, Federal Work-Study, and scholarships/grants also available. Support available to part-time students. Financial award applicants required to submit FAFSA. *Faculty research:* Educational technology, adult and higher education. Total annual research expenditures: $314,050. *Unit head:* Dr. Thomas Weible, Acting Chair, 301-405-3589, Fax: 301-405-3573, E-mail: tweible@umd.edu. *Application contact:* Dean of Graduate School, 301-405-4190, Fax: 301-314-9305.

University of Michigan, Horace H. Rackham School of Graduate Studies, School of Education, Programs in Educational Studies, Ann Arbor, MI 48109. Offers curriculum development (MA); early childhood education (MA, PhD); educational administration and policy (MA, PhD); educational foundation, administration, policy, and research methods (MA); educational foundations and policy (MA, PhD); elementary education (MA-Certification); English education (MA); English language learning in school settings (MA); learning technologies (MA, PhD); literacy, language, and culture (MA, PhD); mathematics education (MA, PhD); research methods (MA); science education (MA, PhD); secondary education (MA-Certification); social studies education (MA); special education (PhD); teaching and teacher education (PhD); MA-Certification; MBA/MA; PhD/MA. Terminal master's awarded for partial completion of doctoral program. *Degree requirements:* For master's, thesis (for some programs); for doctorate, thesis/dissertation, comprehensive exam. *Entrance requirements:* For master's and doctorate, GRE General Test. Additional exam requirements/recommendations for international students: Required—TOEFL (minimum score 600 paper-based; 250 computer-based). *Application deadline:* For fall admission, 12/1 priority date for domestic students, 12/1 for international students. Application fee: $60 ($75 for international students). Electronic applications accepted. *Financial support:* Applicants required to submit FAFSA. *Unit head:* Dr. Addison Stone, Chairperson, 734-763-7500, Fax: 734-615-1290, E-mail: addison@umich.edu. *Application contact:* Roberta Perry, Office of Student Services, 734-764-7563, Fax: 734-763-1495, E-mail: ed.grad.admit@umich.edu.

University of Minnesota, Twin Cities Campus, Graduate School, College of Education and Human Development, Department of Educational Psychology, Program in Psychological Foundations of Education, Minneapolis, MN 55455-0213. Offers MA, PhD, Ed S. *Students:* 53 full-time (35 women), 32 part-time (24 women); includes 7 minority (3 African Americans, 3 Asian Americans or Pacific Islanders, 1 Hispanic American), 21 international. Average age 37. 47 applicants, 57% accepted, 13 enrolled. In 2006, 10 master's, 9 doctorates awarded. *Expenses:* Tuition, state resident: full-time $9,302; part-time $775 per credit. Tuition, nonresident: full-time $16,400; part-time $1,367 per credit. Full-time tuition and fees vary according to class time, course load, program, reciprocity agreements and student level. *Application contact:* Dr. Mary Bents, Associate Dean, 612-625-6501, Fax: 612-626-1580, E-mail: mbents@tc.umn.edu.

University of New Mexico, Graduate School, College of Education, Department of Language, Literacy and Sociocultural Studies, Program in Language, Literacy and Sociocultural Studies, Albuquerque, NM 87131-2039. Offers MA, Ed D, PhD. Part-time programs available. *Students:* 44 full-time (33 women), 145 part-time (118 women); includes 76 minority (4 African Americans, 19 American Indian/Alaska Native, 7 Asian Americans or Pacific Islanders, 46 Hispanic Americans), 19 international. Average age 40. 63 applicants, 73% accepted, 33 enrolled. In 2006, 34 master's, 12 doctorates awarded. *Degree requirements:* For master's, thesis optional; for doctorate, thesis/dissertation, research skills, comprehensive exam. *Entrance requirements:* For master's, letter of intent, 3 letters of recommendation, resumé; for doctorate, writing sample, letter of intent, 3 letters of recommendation, resumé. Additional exam requirements/recommendations for international students: Required—TOEFL. *Application deadline:* For fall admission, 12/1 for domestic students; for spring admission, 9/15 priority date for domestic students. Application fee: $50. Electronic applications accepted. *Financial support:* In 2006–07, 137 students received support, including 35 fellowships (averaging $16,435 per year), 3 research assistantships (averaging $10,862 per year), 17 teaching assistantships with tuition reimbursements available (averaging $4,562 per year); career-related internships or fieldwork, institutionally sponsored loans, scholarships/grants, and unspecified assistantships also available. Support available to part-time students. Financial award application deadline: 3/1; financial award applicants required to submit FAFSA. *Faculty research:* School reform, professional development, history of education, Native American education, politics of education, feminism and issues of sexual identity, critical race theory, language maintenance, bilingualism, literacy reading, adolescent literature, second language acquisition, critical theory and schooling. *Application contact:* Debra Schaffer, Administrative Assistant, 505-277-0437, Fax: 505-277-8362, E-mail: schaffer@unm.edu.

University of New Orleans, Graduate School, College of Education and Human Development, Department of Educational Leadership, Counseling, and Foundations, New Orleans, LA 70148. Offers counselor education (M Ed, PhD, GCE); educational leadership (M Ed, PhD, GCE). *Accreditation:* ACA (one or more programs are accredited); NCATE. Evening/weekend programs available. *Students:* 211 (160 women). Average age 37. In 2006, 70 master's, 10 doctorates awarded. Terminal master's awarded for partial completion of doctoral program. *Degree requirements:* For doctorate, thesis/dissertation. *Entrance requirements:* For master's and doctorate, GRE General Test. Additional exam requirements/recommendations for international students: Required—TOEFL (minimum score 550 paper-based; 213 computer-based). *Application deadline:* For fall admission, 7/1 priority date for domestic students, 6/1 for international students; for spring admission, 11/15 priority date for domestic students, 10/1 for international students. Applications are processed on a rolling basis. Application fee: $40. Electronic applications accepted. *Expenses:* Tuition, state resident: full-time $3,292. Tuition, nonresident: full-time $10,336. Required fees: $158. *Financial support:* Fellowships, research assistantships, teaching assistantships, career-related internships or fieldwork and tuition waivers (partial) available. Financial award application deadline: 3/15; financial award applicants required to submit FAFSA. *Unit head:* Dr. Lorelei Cropley, Chairperson, 504-280-6661, Fax: 504-280-6453, E-mail: lcropley@uno.edu. *Application contact:* Dr. Lorelei Cropley, Chairperson, 504-280-6661, Fax: 504-280-6453, E-mail: lcropley@uno.edu.

University of Oklahoma, Graduate College, College of Education, Department of Educational Leadership and Policy Studies, Norman, OK 73019-0390. Offers adult and higher education (M Ed, PhD); educational administration, curriculum and supervision (M Ed, Ed D, PhD); educational studies (M Ed, PhD); historical, philosophical, and social foundations of education (M Ed, PhD). *Accreditation:* NCATE. Part-time programs available. *Faculty:* 41 full-time (21 women), 29 part-time/adjunct (14 women). *Students:* 101 full-time (67 women), 208 part-time (133 women); includes 87 minority (44 African Americans, 31 American Indian/Alaska Native, 2 Asian Americans or Pacific Islanders, 10 Hispanic Americans), 4 international. 62 applicants, 89% accepted, 36 enrolled. In 2006, 84 master's, 16 doctorates awarded. Terminal master's awarded for partial completion of doctoral program. *Degree requirements:* For master's, comprehensive exam; for doctorate, thesis/dissertation, general exam. *Entrance requirements:* For master's, 12 hours of course work in education; for doctorate, GRE General Test, master's degree, minimum graduate GPA of 3.25. Additional exam requirements/recommendations for international students: Required—TOEFL (minimum score 550 paper-based; 213 computer-based). *Application deadline:* For fall admission, 6/1 for domestic students, 4/1 for international students; for spring admission, 10/1 for domestic students, 9/1 for international students. Application fee: $40 ($90 for international students). *Expenses:* Tuition, state resident: full-time $3,180; part-time $133 per credit hour. Tuition, nonresident: full-time $11,347; part-time $473 per credit hour. Required fees: $1,729; $62 per credit hour. $117 per semester. Tuition and fees vary according to course load and program. *Financial support:* In 2006–07, 150 students received support, including 31 research assistantships with partial tuition reimbursements available (averaging $9,581 per year), 1 teaching assistantship with partial tuition reimbursement available (averaging $9,900 per year); Federal Work-Study, institutionally sponsored loans, and tuition waivers (full) also available. Financial award applicants required to submit FAFSA. Total annual research expenditures: $869,594. *Unit head:* Dr. Grayson B. Noley, Chair, 405-325-4202, Fax: 405-325-2403, E-mail: gnoley@ou.edu. *Application contact:* Geri Evans, Programs Officer, 405-325-5978, Fax: 405-325-2403, E-mail: gevans@ou.edu.

University of Pittsburgh, School of Education, Department of Administrative and Policy Studies, Program in Social and Comparative Analysis in Education, Pittsburgh, PA 15260. Offers international development education (MA, PhD); international developmental education (M Ed); social, philosophical, and historical foundations of education (M Ed, MA, PhD). Evening/weekend programs available. *Students:* 45 full-time (27 women), 36 part-time (31 women); includes 12 minority (8 African Americans, 3 Asian Americans or Pacific Islanders, 1 Hispanic American), 21 international. 70 applicants, 86% accepted, 30 enrolled. In 2006, 5 master's, 9 doctorates awarded. *Degree requirements:* For master's and doctorate, thesis/dissertation. *Entrance requirements:* For doctorate, GRE General Test. Additional exam requirements/recommendations for international students: Required—TOEFL. *Application deadline:* For fall admission, 2/1 priority date for domestic students; for spring admission, 11/15 priority date for domestic students. Applications are processed on a rolling basis. Application fee: $50. Electronic applications accepted. *Financial support:* Research assistantships, teaching assistantships, Federal Work-Study, institutionally sponsored loans, and tuition waivers (partial) available. Support available to part-time students. Financial award application deadline: 3/15; financial award applicants required to submit FAFSA. *Application contact:* Joan M. Cutone, Director, School of Education Student Service Center, 412-648-2230, Fax: 412-648-1899, E-mail: soeinfo@pitt.edu.

University of Saskatchewan, College of Graduate Studies and Research, College of Education, Department of Educational Foundations, Saskatoon, SK S7N 5A2, Canada. Offers M Ed, MC Ed, PhD, Diploma. Part-time programs available. *Degree requirements:* For master's, thesis (for some programs), registration; for doctorate, thesis/dissertation, registration. *Entrance requirements:* Additional exam requirements/recommendations for international students: Required—TOEFL. *Faculty research:* Indian and northern education, adult and continuing education, international education.

University of South Carolina, The Graduate School, College of Education, Department of Educational Studies, Program in Foundations in Education, Columbia, SC 29208. Offers PhD. *Accreditation:* NCATE. *Degree requirements:* For doctorate, thesis/dissertation, comprehensive exam. *Entrance requirements:* For doctorate, GRE General Test or MAT, interview. Electronic applications accepted. *Faculty research:* Oral history, educational biography, home schooling, international education.

The University of Tennessee, Graduate School, College of Education, Health and Human Sciences, Program in Education, Knoxville, TN 37996. Offers art education (MS); counseling education (PhD); cultural studies in education (PhD); curriculum (MS, Ed S); curriculum, educational research and evaluation (Ed D, PhD); early childhood education (PhD); early childhood special education (MS); education of deaf and hard of hearing (MS); educational administration and policy studies (Ed D, PhD); educational administration and supervision (Ed S); educational psychology (Ed D, PhD); elementary education (MS, Ed S); elementary teaching (MS); English education (MS, Ed S); exercise science (PhD); foreign language/ESL education (MS, Ed S); instructional technology (MS, Ed D, PhD, Ed S); literacy, language and ESL education (PhD); literacy, language education, and ESL education (Ed D); mathematics education (MS, Ed S); modified and comprehensive special education (MS); reading education (MS, Ed S); school counseling (Ed S); school psychology (PhD, Ed S); science education (MS, Ed S); secondary teaching (MS); social foundations (MS); social science education (MS, Ed S); socio-cultural foundations of sports and education (PhD); special education (Ed S); teacher education (Ed D, PhD). *Accreditation:* NCATE. Part-time and evening/weekend programs available. *Students:* 529 (401 women); includes 39 minority (23 African Americans, 2 American Indian/Alaska Native, 9 Asian Americans or Pacific Islanders, 5 Hispanic Americans) 34 international. 420 applicants, 50% accepted. In 2006, 258 master's, 28 doctorates awarded. *Degree requirements:* For master's and Ed S, thesis optional; for doctorate, variable foreign language requirement, thesis/dissertation. *Entrance requirements:* For master's, minimum GPA of 2.7; for doctorate and Ed S, GRE General Test, minimum GPA of 2.7. Additional exam requirements/recommendations for international students: Required—TOEFL. *Application deadline:* For fall admission, 2/1 priority date for domestic students. Applications are processed on a rolling basis. Application fee: $35. Electronic applications accepted. *Expenses:* Tuition, state resident: full-time $5,574. Tuition, nonresident: full-time $16,840. Required fees: $792. *Financial support:* In 2006–07, 4 fellowships, 9 teaching assistantships were awarded; career-related internships or fieldwork, Federal Work-Study, institutionally sponsored loans, and unspecified assistantships also available. Financial award application deadline: 2/1; financial award applicants required to submit FAFSA. *Unit head:* Dr. Lester Knight, Head, 865-974-0907, Fax: 865-974-8718, E-mail: lknight@utk.edu.

The University of Texas of the Permian Basin, Office of Graduate Studies, School of Education, Program in Professional Education, Odessa, TX 79762-0001. Offers MA. *Degree requirements:* For master's, thesis (for some programs), comprehensive exam (for some programs), registration. *Entrance requirements:* For master's, GRE General Test. Additional exam requirements/recommendations for international students: Required—TOEFL (minimum score 550 paper-based; 213 computer-based).

The University of Toledo, College of Graduate Studies, College of Education, Department of Foundations of Education, Program in Educational Sociology, Toledo, OH 43606-3390. Offers DE, PhD. *Students:* 3 full-time (all women), 3 part-time (2 women); includes 1 minority (African American), 2 international. Average age 35. 11 applicants, 9% accepted, 1 enrolled. In 2006, 1 degree awarded. *Unit head:* Dr. Dale Snauwaert, Chair, Department of Foundations of Education, 419-530-2478, Fax: 419-530-8337.

The University of Toledo, College of Graduate Studies, College of Education, Department of Foundations of Education, Program in Educational Theory and Social Foundations, Toledo, OH 43606-3390. Offers ME. *Students:* 1 full-time (0 women), 5 part-time (all women); includes 3 minority (2 African Americans, 1 Hispanic American). Average age 31. In 2006, 2 degrees awarded. *Unit head:* Dr. Dale Snauwaert, Chair, Department of Foundations of Education, 419-530-2478, Fax: 419-530-8337.

The University of Toledo, College of Graduate Studies, College of Education, Department of Foundations of Education, Program in Foundations of Education, Toledo, OH 43606-3390. Offers DE, PhD. *Students:* 4 full-time (1 woman), 3 part-time (1 woman); includes 2 minority (1 African American, 1 Hispanic American), 2 international. Average age 36. 2 applicants, 50% accepted, 0 enrolled. In 2006, 1 degree awarded. *Financial support:* In 2006–07, 6 research assistantships (averaging $8,000 per year), 5 teaching assistantships (averaging $9,600 per year) were awarded. *Unit head:* Dr. Dale Snauwaert, Chair, Department of Foundations of Education, 419-530-2478, Fax: 419-530-8337.

The University of Toledo, College of Graduate Studies, College of Education, Department of Foundations of Education, Program in History of Education, Toledo, OH 43606-3390. Offers DE, PhD. *Unit head:* Dr. Dale Snauwaert, Chair, Department of Foundations of Education, 419-530-2478, Fax: 419-530-8337.

The University of Toledo, College of Graduate Studies, College of Education, Department of Foundations of Education, Program in Philosophy of Education, Toledo, OH 43606-3390. Offers DE, PhD. *Students:* 2 full-time (0 women); includes 1 minority (African American), 1 international. Average age 29. 3 applicants, 33% accepted, 1 enrolled. *Financial support:* Fellowships, teaching assistantships available. *Unit head:* Dr. Dale Snauwaert, Chair, Department of Foundations of Education, 419-530-2478, Fax: 419-530-8337.

University of Utah, The Graduate School, College of Education, Department of Education, Culture, and Society, Salt Lake City, UT 84112-1107. Offers M Ed, MA, MS, PhD. Evening/weekend programs available. *Faculty:* 12 full-time (6 women). *Students:* 36 full-time (21 women), 39 part-time (31 women); includes 28 minority (8 African Americans, 6 American Indian/Alaska Native, 3 Asian Americans or Pacific Islanders, 11 Hispanic Americans), 1 international. Average age 37. 26 applicants, 92% accepted, 16 enrolled. In 2006, 8 master's, 5 doctorates awarded. *Degree requirements:* For master's, professional experience; for doctorate, thesis/dissertation. *Entrance requirements:* For master's and doctorate, minimum GPA of 3.0. Additional exam requirements/recommendations for international students: Required—TOEFL (minimum score 650 paper-based; 278 computer-based). *Application deadline:* For fall admission, 2/15 priority date for domestic and international students; for spring admission, 9/15 priority date for domestic students, 10/15 priority date for international students. Applications are processed on a rolling basis. Application fee: $45 ($65 for international students). *Expenses:* Tuition, state resident: full-time $3,208. Tuition, nonresident: full-time $11,326. Required fees: $608. Tuition and fees vary according to class time and program. *Financial support:* In 2006–07, 4 teaching assistantships with full tuition reimbursements (averaging $11,500 per year) were awarded; career-related internships or fieldwork and tuition waivers (full) also available. Financial award application deadline: 2/1; financial award applicants required to submit FAFSA. *Faculty research:* History, philosophy and sociology of education,

Foundations and Philosophy of Education

University of Utah (continued)
language, culture and curriculum. Total annual research expenditures: $16,458. *Unit head:* Dr. Harvey Kantor, Chair, 801-581-7805, Fax: 801-587-7801, E-mail: kantor@ed.utah.edu. *Application contact:* Dr. Audrey Thompson, Advisor, 801-581-7803, Fax: 801-587-7801, E-mail: thompson@ed.utah.edu.

University of Victoria, Faculty of Graduate Studies, Faculty of Education, Department of Curriculum and Instruction, Victoria, BC V8W 2Y2, Canada. Offers art (M Ed, MA, PhD); curriculum studies (M Ed, MA, PhD); early childhood (M Ed, MA, PhD); language and literacy (M Ed, MA, PhD); mathematics (M Ed, MA, PhD); music (M Ed, MA); music education (PhD); science (M Ed, MA, PhD); social studies (M Ed, MA); social, cultural and foundational studies (PhD); technology and environmental education (PhD). Part-time programs available. *Degree requirements:* For master's, thesis, project (M Ed); for doctorate, thesis/dissertation, comprehensive exam, registration. *Entrance requirements:* For master's, minimum B average. Additional exam requirements/recommendations for international students: Required—TOEFL (minimum score 575 paper-based; 233 computer-based), IELTS (minimum score 7). Electronic applications accepted. *Faculty research:* Elementary and secondary English, language arts, curriculum theory and practice, educational media and technology, educational administration and leadership, history and philosophy of education.

University of Washington, Graduate School, College of Education, Seattle, WA 98195. Offers curriculum and instruction (M Ed, Ed D, PhD), including educational technology, general curriculum (Ed D, PhD), language, literacy, and culture, mathematics education, multicultural education, reading and language arts education (Ed D), science education, social studies education, teaching and curriculum (M Ed); educational leadership and policy studies (M Ed, Ed D, PhD), including administration, educational organization and policy, higher education, school district leadership (Ed D), social/cultural foundations; educational psychology (M Ed, PhD), including human development and cognition, measurement and research, school counseling (M Ed), school psychology; special education (M Ed, Ed D, PhD), including early childhood education, elementary special education, emotional and behavioral disabilities (M Ed), general special education, severe disabilities; teacher education (MIT). *Accreditation:* APA. Part-time and evening/weekend programs available. *Degree requirements:* For master's, thesis optional; for doctorate, thesis/dissertation. *Entrance requirements:* For master's and doctorate, GRE General Test, minimum GPA of 3.0. Additional exam requirements/recommendations for international students: Required—TOEFL. Electronic applications accepted. *Faculty research:* School restructuring/effective schools, special education interventions, literacy and writing, technology, school partnerships, teacher preparation.

The University of West Alabama, School of Graduate Studies, College of Education, Department of Teacher Education, Livingston, AL 35470. Offers continuing education (MSCE); early childhood education (M Ed); elementary education (M Ed); guidance and counseling (M Ed, MSCE), including continuing education (MSCE), guidance and counseling (M Ed); library media (M Ed); school administration (M Ed); secondary education (MAT); special education (M Ed). *Accreditation:* NCATE. Part-time programs available. *Students:* 137. *Degree requirements:* For master's, comprehensive exam. *Entrance requirements:* For master's, GRE General Test, MAT, minimum GPA of 2.75. *Application deadline:* For fall admission, 9/10 priority date for domestic students; for spring admission, 3/24 for domestic students. Applications are processed on a rolling basis. Application fee: $20 ($50 for international students). *Financial support:* Career-related internships or fieldwork, Federal Work-Study, scholarships/grants, and unspecified assistantships available. Support available to part-time students. *Unit head:* Dr. Louis R. Smith, Associate Dean, 205-652-3439, Fax: 205-652-3706, E-mail: lsmith@uwa.edu.

University of Wisconsin–Milwaukee, Graduate School, School of Education, Department of Educational Policy and Community Studies, Milwaukee, WI 53201-0413. Offers cultural foundations of education (MS). Part-time programs available. *Faculty:* 9 full-time (3 women). *Students:* 5 full-time (3 women), 21 part-time (18 women); includes 12 minority (9 African Americans, 1 American Indian/Alaska Native, 2 Asian Americans or Pacific Islanders). 13 applicants, 62% accepted, 5 enrolled. In 2006, 7 degrees awarded. *Degree requirements:* For master's, thesis or alternative. *Application deadline:* For fall admission, 1/1 priority date for domestic students; for spring admission, 9/1 for domestic students. Applications are processed on a rolling basis. Application fee: $45 ($75 for international students). *Expenses:* Tuition, state resident: part-time $510 per credit. Tuition, nonresident: part-time $1,408 per credit. Tuition and fees vary according to program. *Financial support:* Fellowships, research assistantships, teaching assistantships, career-related internships or fieldwork available. Support available to part-time students. Financial award application deadline: 4/15. *Faculty research:* Human relations in education, international and multicultural education. *Unit head:* Michael Bonds, Representative, 414-229-2256, Fax: 414-229-3700.

Wayne State University, College of Education, Division of Theoretical and Behavioral Foundations, Detroit, MI 48202. Offers counseling (M Ed, MA, Ed D, PhD, Ed S); education evaluation and research (M Ed, Ed D, PhD); educational psychology (M Ed, Ed D, PhD, Ed S); educational sociology (M Ed, Ed D, PhD, Ed S); history and philosophy of education (M Ed, Ed D, PhD); rehabilitation counseling and community inclusion (MA, Ed S); school and community psychology (MA, Ed S); school clinical psychology (Ed S). *Accreditation:* ACA (one or more programs are accredited); CORE (one or more programs are accredited). Evening/weekend programs available. *Faculty:* 51 full-time (18 women), 11 part-time/adjunct (7 women). *Students:* 156 full-time (125 women), 232 part-time (191 women); includes 146 minority (140 African Americans, 1 American Indian/Alaska Native, 5 Hispanic Americans), 14 international. Average age 35. 146 applicants, 38% accepted, 39 enrolled. In 2006, 84 master's, 8 doctorates awarded. *Degree requirements:* For doctorate, thesis/dissertation. *Entrance requirements:* For master's, GRE (school and community psychology); for doctorate, GRE (educational psychology), interview, minimum GPA of 3.0. Additional exam requirements/recommendations for international students: Required—TOEFL (minimum score 550 paper-based; 213 computer-based), TWE (minimum score 6). *Application deadline:* For fall admission, 7/1 for domestic students, 6/1 for international students; for winter admission, 10/1 for international students; for spring admission, 2/1 for international students. Application fee: $20 ($30 for international students). Electronic applications accepted. *Financial support:* In 2006–07, 2 research assistantships (averaging $12,797 per year) were awarded; fellowships, career-related internships or fieldwork, Federal Work-Study, and institutionally sponsored loans also available. *Faculty research:* Adolescents at risk, supervision of counseling. *Unit head:* Dr. JoAnne Holbert, Assistant Dean, 313-577-1721, E-mail: jholbert@wayne.edu.

Western Illinois University, School of Graduate Studies, College of Education and Human Services, Department of Educational and Interdisciplinary Studies, Program in Educational and Interdisciplinary Studies, Macomb, IL 61455-1390. Offers MS Ed. *Accreditation:* NCATE. Part-time programs available. *Students:* 15 full-time (11 women), 36 part-time (25 women); includes 5 minority (2 African Americans, 3 Hispanic Americans), 1 international. Average age 34. 12 applicants, 75% accepted. In 2006, 28 degrees awarded. *Degree requirements:* For master's, thesis or alternative. *Entrance requirements:* For master's, minimum GPA of 2.75, interview. Additional exam requirements/recommendations for international students: Required—TOEFL (minimum score 550 paper-based; 213 computer-based; 80 iBT). *Application deadline:* Applications are processed on a rolling basis. Application fee: $30. Electronic applications accepted. *Expenses:* Tuition, state resident: part-time $200 per credit hour. Tuition, nonresident: part-time $400 per credit hour. *Financial support:* In 2006–07, 8 students received support, including 8 research assistantships with full tuition reimbursements available (averaging $6,568 per year). Financial award applicants required to submit FAFSA. *Unit head:* Dr. Tom Cody, Graduate Committee Chairperson, 309-298-1183. *Application contact:* Dr. Barbara Baily, Director of Graduate Studies/Associate Provost, 309-298-1806, Fax: 309-298-2345, E-mail: grad-office@wiu.edu.

Widener University, School of Human Service Professions, Center for Education, Chester, PA 19013-5792. Offers adult education (M Ed); counseling in higher education (M Ed); counselor education (M Ed); early childhood education (M Ed); educational foundations (M Ed); educational leadership (M Ed); educational psychology (M Ed); elementary education (M Ed); English and language arts (M Ed); health education (M Ed); higher education leadership (Ed D); home and school visitor (M Ed); human sexuality (M Ed); mathematics education (M Ed); middle school education (M Ed); principalship (M Ed); reading and language arts (Ed D); reading education (M Ed); school administration (Ed D); science education (M Ed); social studies education (M Ed); special education (M Ed); technology education (M Ed). Part-time and evening/weekend programs available. Terminal master's awarded for partial completion of doctoral program. *Degree requirements:* For doctorate, thesis/dissertation. *Entrance requirements:* For master's, minimum GPA of 2.5; for doctorate, GRE or MAT, minimum GPA of 2.0 (undergraduate), 3.5 (graduate). Electronic applications accepted. Expenses: Contact institution. *Faculty research:* Reading and cognition, adult education, technology education, educational leadership, special education.

Wilfrid Laurier University, Faculty of Graduate Studies, Faculty of Arts, Cultural Analysis and Social Theory Program, Waterloo, ON N2L 3C5, Canada. Offers MA. *Faculty:* 13 full-time. *Entrance requirements:* For master's, honours BA in humanities, social science or interdisciplinary program with social theory, minimum B+ in final year of full-time study. Additional exam requirements/recommendations for international students: Required—TOEFL (minimum score 230 computer-based; 89 iBT). *Application deadline:* For fall admission, 2/1 priority date for domestic students. Application fee: $75. Electronic applications accepted. *Financial support:* Fellowships, research assistantships, teaching assistantships available. *Faculty research:* Globalization, identify and social movements, body politics: gender, sexuality and embodiment, cultural representation and social theory. *Unit head:* Dr. Andrew Lyons, Head, 519-884-1970 Ext. 3660, E-mail: alyons@uiu.ca. *Application contact:* Dianne Duffy, Student Contact, 519-884-0710 Ext. 3127, Fax: 519-884-1020, E-mail: gradstudies@wlu.ca.

Youngstown State University, Graduate School, College of Education, Department of Educational Administration, Research, and Foundations, Youngstown, OH 44555-0001. Offers educational administration (MS Ed); educational leadership (Ed D). *Accreditation:* NCATE. Part-time and evening/weekend programs available. *Degree requirements:* For master's, comprehensive exam; for doctorate, thesis/dissertation, comprehensive exam. *Entrance requirements:* For master's, GRE, MAT, or teaching certificate; minimum GPA of 2.7; for doctorate, GRE General Test, GRE Subject Test, interview, minimum GPA of 3.5. Additional exam requirements/recommendations for international students: Required—TOEFL. *Faculty research:* Administrative theory, computer applications, education law, school and community relations, finance principalship.

International and Comparative Education

American University, College of Arts and Sciences, School of Education, Teaching, and Health, Program in International Education, Washington, DC 20016-8001. Offers MA. *Students:* 15 full-time (12 women), 21 part-time (18 women); includes 6 minority (2 African Americans, 1 Asian American or Pacific Islander, 3 Hispanic Americans), 2 international. Average age 28. In 2006, 21 degrees awarded. *Degree requirements:* For master's, one foreign language, comprehensive exam. *Entrance requirements:* For master's, GRE General Test or MAT, minimum GPA of 3.0. *Application deadline:* For fall admission, 2/1 priority date for domestic students; for spring admission, 10/1 priority date for domestic students. Applications are processed on a rolling basis. Application fee: $50. *Expenses:* Tuition: Full-time $18,864; part-time $1,048 per credit. Required fees: $380. Tuition and fees vary according to program. *Financial support:* Application deadline: 2/1.

Boston University, School of Education, Department of Administration, Training, and Policy Studies, International Educational Development Program, Boston, MA 02215. Offers Ed M. Part-time programs available. *Students:* 13 full-time (12 women), 7 part-time (5 women); includes 1 minority (African American), 13 international. Average age 30. 27 applicants, 63% accepted, 12 enrolled. In 2006, 6 degrees awarded. *Degree requirements:* For master's, thesis. *Entrance requirements:* For master's, GRE General Test or MAT. Additional exam requirements/recommendations for international students: Required—TOEFL. *Application deadline:* For fall admission, 2/15 priority date for domestic students; for winter admission, 10/1 for domestic students. Applications are processed on a rolling basis. Application fee: $70. Electronic applications accepted. *Expenses:* Tuition: Full-time $33,330; part-time $1,042 per credit. Required fees: $462; $40. *Financial support:* Application deadline: 2/15; *Faculty research:* Formal and nonformal education for social and economic development, industrialized and agrarian societies. *Unit head:* Karen Boatman, Coordinator, 617-353-3187, E-mail: kboats@bu.edu. *Application contact:* 617-353-4237, Fax: 617-353-8937, E-mail: sedgrad@bu.edu.

California State University, Dominguez Hills, College of Extended and International Education, Carson, CA 90747-0001. Offers MA, MS. Part-time and evening/weekend programs available. Postbaccalaureate distance learning degree programs offered. *Faculty:* 8 full-time (4 women), 52 part-time/adjunct (17 women). *Students:* 12 full-time (3 women), 793 part-time (363 women); includes 139 minority (47 African Americans, 6 American Indian/Alaska Native, 42 Asian Americans or Pacific Islanders, 44 Hispanic Americans), 39 international. Average age 41. 158 applicants, 88% accepted, 106 enrolled. In 2006, 74 degrees awarded. *Degree requirements:* For master's, thesis, registration. *Entrance requirements:* Additional exam requirements/recommendations for international students: Required—TOEFL. Application fee: $55. Electronic applications accepted. *Expenses:* Contact institution. *Unit head:* Dr. Margaret Gordon, Dean, 310-243-3737, Fax: 310-516-4423, E-mail: mgordon@csudh.edu.

The College of New Jersey, Graduate Division, Office of Global Programs, Program in Overseas Education, Ewing, NJ 08628. Offers M Ed, Certificate. *Students:* 38 applicants, 100% accepted. In 2006, 54 degrees awarded. *Entrance requirements:* For master's, GRE, minimum GPA of 3.0 in field or 2.75 overall. Additional exam requirements/recommendations for international students: Required—TOEFL. *Application deadline:* For fall admission, 4/15 for domestic students; for spring admission, 10/15 for domestic students. Application fee: $60. Electronic applications accepted. *Unit head:* Dr. Stuart Carroll, Coordinator, 609-771-2221. *Application contact:* Susan L. Hydro, Office of Graduate Studies, Assistant Dean, 609-771-2300, Fax: 609-637-5105, E-mail: graduate@tcnj.edu.

Drexel University, School of Education, Program in Global and International Education, Philadelphia, PA 19104-2875. Offers MS.

Endicott College, Van Loan School of Graduate and Professional Studies, Program in International Education, Beverly, MA 01915-2096. Offers international education (M Ed); organizational management (M Ed). Part-time and evening/weekend programs available. Postbaccalaureate distance learning degree programs offered. *Faculty:* 2 part-time/adjunct (1 woman). *Students:* Average age 35. 23 applicants, 100% accepted, 23 enrolled. In 2006, 9 degrees awarded. *Degree requirements:* For master's, thesis, practicum. *Entrance requirements:* For master's, MAT or GRE, 2 letters of recommendation. *Application deadline:* For fall admission, 7/15 priority date for domestic students; for winter admission, 12/15 priority date for domestic students. Applications are processed on a rolling basis. Application fee: $50. *Expenses:* Tuition: Part-time $279 per credit. Tuition and fees vary according to program. *Financial support:* In 2006–07, 10 students received support. Career-related internships or fieldwork and scholarships/grants available. Financial award application deadline: 12/15. *Unit head:* Dr. April Burriss, Dean of School of International Studies, 978-232-2272, E-mail: aburriss@endicott.edu.

Florida International University, College of Education, Department of Curriculum and Instruction, Program in International and Intercultural Development Education, Miami, FL 33199. Offers MS, Ed D. *Accreditation:* NCATE. Part-time and evening/weekend programs available. *Students:* 8 applicants. *Entrance requirements:* Additional exam requirements/recommendations for international students: Required—TOEFL. *Application deadline:* Applications are processed on a rolling basis. Application fee: $25. *Expenses:* Tuition, state resident: part-time $249 per credit hour. Tuition, nonresident: part-time $753 per credit hour. Tuition and fees vary according to program. *Unit head:* Dr. Hilary Landorf, Assistant Professor, 305-348-2410, E-mail: landorf@fiu.edu.

Florida State University, Graduate Studies, College of Education, Department of Educational Leadership and Policy Studies, Program in Social, History and Philosophy of Education, Tallahassee, FL 32306. Offers history and philosophy of education (MS, PhD, Ed S); international and intercultural education (MS, PhD, Ed S). *Faculty:* 4 full-time (0 women), 2 part-time/adjunct (1 woman). *Students:* 11 full-time (6 women), 17 part-time (8 women); includes 7 minority (1 African American, 6 Asian Americans or Pacific Islanders). 16 applicants, 69% accepted, 4 enrolled. In 2006, 1 master's, 1 doctorate awarded. *Degree requirements:* For master's and Ed S, thesis optional; for doctorate, thesis/dissertation, comprehensive exam. *Entrance requirements:* For master's, doctorate, and Ed S, GRE General Test, minimum GPA of 3.0. *Application deadline:* For fall admission, 7/1 priority date for domestic students; for spring admission, 11/1 for domestic students. Applications are processed on a rolling basis. Application fee: $20. *Expenses:* Tuition, state resident: full-time $5,822; part-time $243 per credit hour. Tuition, nonresident: full-time $20,976; part-time $874 per credit hour. Tuition and fees vary according to program. *Financial support:* Fellowships with partial tuition reimbursements, research assistantships with partial tuition reimbursements, teaching assistantships with partial tuition reimbursements, career-related internships or fieldwork, scholarships/grants, and unspecified assistantships available. Financial award applicants required to submit FAFSA. *Unit head:* Dr. Jeffrey Milligan, Assistant Professor and Program Coordinator, 850-644-8171, Fax: 850-644-1258, E-mail: milligan@coe.fsu.edu. *Application contact:* Jimmy Pastrano, Program Assistant, 850-644-6777, Fax: 850-644-1258, E-mail: pastrano@coe.fsu.edu.

The George Washington University, Graduate School of Education and Human Development, Department of Educational Leadership, Program in International Education, Washington, DC 20052. Offers MA Ed. *Accreditation:* NCATE. *Degree requirements:* For master's, comprehensive exam. *Entrance requirements:* For master's, GRE General Test or MAT, minimum GPA of 2.75. *Faculty research:* Education and development.

Harvard University, Graduate School of Education, Master's Programs in Education, Cambridge, MA 02138. Offers arts in education (Ed M); education policy and management (Ed M); higher education (Ed M); human development and psychology (Ed M); international education policy (Ed M); language and literacy (Ed M); learning and teaching (Ed M); mid-career mathematics and science (teaching certificate) (Ed M); mind brain and education (Ed M); risk and prevention (Ed M); school leadership (Ed M); special studies (Ed M); teaching and curriculum (teaching certificate) (Ed M); technology innovation and education (Ed M). Part-time programs available. *Faculty:* 58 full-time (25 women), 40 part-time/adjunct (22 women). *Students:* 540 full-time (412 women), 90 part-time (70 women); includes 137 minority (49 African Americans, 2 American Indian/Alaska Native, 61 Asian Americans or Pacific Islanders, 25 Hispanic Americans), 70 international. Average age 29. 1,211 applicants, 61% accepted, 585 enrolled. In 2006, 591 degrees awarded. *Entrance requirements:* For master's, GRE General Test, 3 letters of recommendation, official transcripts, statement of purpose. Additional exam requirements/recommendations for international students: Required—TOEFL (minimum score 600 paper-based; 250 computer-based; 100 iBT), TWE (minimum score 5). *Application deadline:* For fall admission, 1/2 for domestic and international students. Application fee: $85. Electronic applications accepted. *Expenses:* Contact institution. *Financial support:* In 2006–07, 392 students received support, including 23 fellowships (averaging $15,870 per year); career-related internships or fieldwork, Federal Work-Study, institutionally sponsored loans, scholarships/grants, health care benefits, tuition waivers (full and partial), and unspecified assistantships also available. Support available to part-time students. Financial award application deadline: 2/2; financial award applicants required to submit FAFSA. *Faculty research:* Learning and development; educational leadership and organizations; educational policy analysis. Total annual research expenditures: $14.8 million. *Unit head:* Dr. James Stiles, Associate Dean for Degree Programs. *Application contact:* Information Contact, 617-495-3414, Fax: 617-496-3577, E-mail: gseadmissions@harvard.edu.

Indiana University Bloomington, School of Education, Department of Educational Leadership and Policy Studies, Bloomington, IN 47405-7000. Offers education policy studies (PhD); educational leadership (MS, Ed D, PhD, Ed S); higher education (MS, Ed D, PhD); history and philosophy of education (MS); history of education (PhD); international and comparative education (MS, PhD); philosophy of education (PhD); student affairs administration (MS). PhD offered through the University Graduate School. *Accreditation:* NCATE. Part-time and evening/weekend programs available. *Students:* 12 full-time (5 women), 28 part-time (14 women). Average age 35. In 2006, 32 master's, 4 doctorates awarded. *Degree requirements:* For master's, thesis optional; for doctorate, thesis/dissertation; for Ed S, comprehensive exam or project. *Entrance requirements:* For master's, doctorate, and Ed S, GRE General Test. *Application deadline:* For fall admission, 6/1 for domestic students, 3/1 for international students; for spring admission, 9/1 for international students. Application fee: $45 ($55 for international students). *Expenses:* Tuition, state resident: full-time $5,791; part-time $241 per credit hour. Tuition, nonresident: full-time $16,866; part-time $703 per credit hour. *Financial support:* Fellowships, research assistantships, teaching assistantships, career-related internships or fieldwork, Federal Work-Study, institutionally sponsored loans, and tuition waivers (full and partial) available. Support available to part-time students. *Unit head:* Martha McCarthy, Chair, 812-856-8377. *Application contact:* Sandy Strain, Department Secretary, 812-856-8360, Fax: 812-856-8394, E-mail: strain@indiana.edu.

Louisiana State University and Agricultural and Mechanical College, Graduate School, College of Agriculture, School of Human Resource Education and Workforce Development, Baton Rouge, LA 70803. Offers comprehensive vocational education (MS, PhD); extension and international education (MS, PhD); industrial education (MS); vocational agriculture education (MS, PhD); vocational business education (MS); vocational home economics education (MS). *Accreditation:* NCATE. Part-time programs available. *Faculty:* 13 full-time (6 women). *Students:* 39 full-time (24 women), 68 part-time (42 women); includes 12 African Americans, 3 Hispanic Americans, 9 international. Average age 38. 20 applicants, 60% accepted, 3 enrolled. In 2006, 18 master's, 33 doctorates awarded. Terminal master's awarded for partial completion of doctoral program. *Degree requirements:* For master's, thesis (for some programs); for doctorate, thesis/dissertation. *Entrance requirements:* For master's and doctorate, GRE General Test, minimum GPA of 3.0. Additional exam requirements/recommendations for international students: Required—TOEFL (minimum score 550 paper-based; 213 computer-based; 79 iBT). *Application deadline:* For fall admission, 1/25 priority date for domestic students, 5/15 for international students; for spring admission, 10/15 for international students. Applications are processed on a rolling basis. Application fee: $25. Electronic applications accepted. *Financial support:* In 2006–07, 23 students received support, including 1 fellowship with full and partial tuition reimbursement available (averaging $23,678 per year), 10 research assistantships with full and partial tuition reimbursements available (averaging $11,750 per year), 5 teaching assistantships with partial tuition reimbursements available (averaging $10,210 per year); career-related internships or fieldwork, institutionally sponsored loans, tuition waivers (full and partial), and unspecified assistantships also available. Financial award application deadline: 3/1; financial award applicants required to submit FAFSA. *Faculty research:* Adult education, history and philosophy of vocational education, curriculum and instruction, career decision making. *Unit head:* Dr. Michael F. Burnett, Director, 225-578-5748, Fax: 225-578-2526, E-mail: vocbur@lsu.edu.

Lynn University, College of Business and Management, Boca Raton, FL 33431-5598. Offers aviation management (MBA); financial valuation and investment management (MBA); global leadership (PhD); hospitality management (MBA); international business (MBA); marketing (MBA); mass communication and media management (MBA); sports and athletics administration (MBA). Part-time and evening/weekend programs available. Postbaccalaureate distance learning degree programs offered. *Faculty:* 13 full-time (5 women), 7 part-time/adjunct (3 women). *Students:* 71 full-time (37 women), 113 part-time (47 women); includes 35 minority (13 African Americans, 6 Asian Americans or Pacific Islanders, 16 Hispanic Americans), 55 international. Average age 32. 114 applicants, 88% accepted, 71 enrolled. In 2006, 83 master's, 9 doctorates awarded. *Degree requirements:* For master's, project; for doctorate, thesis/dissertation, qualifying paper. *Entrance requirements:* For master's, GMAT or GRE, minimum undergraduate GPA of 3.0, resumé, 2 letters of recommendation; for doctorate, GRE or GMAT, minimum graduate GPA of 3.25, resumé, 2 letters of recommendation. Additional exam requirements/recommendations for international students: Required—TOEFL (minimum score 550 paper-based; 213 computer-based). *Application deadline:* Applications are processed on a rolling basis. Application fee: $50. Electronic applications accepted. *Expenses:* Tuition: Full-time $26,200. Required fees: $1,500. Tuition and fees vary according to class time, course load and degree level. *Financial support:* In 2006–07, 160 students received support. Career-related internships or fieldwork, Federal Work-Study, institutionally sponsored loans, scholarships/grants, tuition waivers (full and partial), and unspecified assistantships available. Support available to part-time students. Financial award application deadline: 8/1; financial award applicants required to submit FAFSA. *Faculty research:* Labor relations, dynamic balance in leisure-time skills, ethics in athletics, hotel development. *Unit head:* Dr. Russell Boisjoly, Dean, 561-237-7458, Fax: 561-237-7014, E-mail: rboisjoly@lynn.edu. *Application contact:* Dr. Larissa Baia, Assistant Director of Graduate Admissions, 561-237-7916, Fax: 561-237-7100, E-mail: admissionpm@lynn.edu.

Lynn University, Donald and Helen Ross College of Education, Boca Raton, FL 33431-5598. Offers exceptional student education (M Ed); global leadership (PhD). Part-time and evening/weekend programs available. *Faculty:* 5 full-time (3 women), 8 part-time/adjunct (4 women). *Students:* 29 full-time (22 women), 88 part-time (61 women); includes 30 minority (18 African Americans, 1 Asian American or Pacific Islander, 11 Hispanic Americans), 10 international. Average age 36. 48 applicants, 79% accepted, 33 enrolled. In 2006, 69 master's, 6 doctorates awarded. *Degree requirements:* For master's, thesis (for some programs); for doctorate, thesis/dissertation, qualifying paper. *Entrance requirements:* For master's, GRE, minimum undergraduate GPA of 3.0, resumé, 2 letters of recommendation; for doctorate, GRE or GMAT, minimum GPA of 3.25, resumé, 2 letters of recommendation. Additional exam requirements/recommendations for international students: Required—TOEFL (minimum score 550 paper-based; 213 computer-based). *Application deadline:* Applications are processed on a rolling basis. Application fee: $50. Electronic applications accepted. *Expenses:* Tuition: Full-time $26,200. Required fees: $1,500. Tuition and fees vary according to class time, course load and degree level. *Financial support:* Career-related internships or fieldwork, Federal Work-Study, institutionally sponsored loans, scholarships/grants, tuition waivers (partial), and unspecified assistantships available. Support available to part-time students. Financial award application deadline: 8/1; financial award applicants required to submit FAFSA. *Faculty research:* Non-traditional education, innovative curricula, multicultural education, simulation games. *Unit head:* Dr. Patrick Hartwick, Dean, 561-237-7441, Fax: 561-237-7792, E-mail: phartwick@lynn.edu. *Application contact:* Dr. Larissa Baia, Assistant Director of Graduate Admissions, 561-237-7916, Fax: 561-237-7100, E-mail: lbaia@lynn.edu.

Morehead State University, Graduate Programs, College of Education, Department of Curriculum and Instruction, Program in Elementary Education, Morehead, KY 40351. Offers elementary education (MA Ed); international education (MA Ed); middle school education (MA Ed, MAT); reading (MA Ed). *Accreditation:* NCATE. Part-time and evening/weekend programs available. *Students:* 2 full-time (both women), 84 part-time (80 women); includes 1 minority (American Indian/Alaska Native). Average age 32. In 2006, 52 degrees awarded. *Degree requirements:* For master's, thesis optional. *Entrance requirements:* For master's, GRE General Test, minimum GPA of 2.75, teaching certificate. Additional exam requirements/recommendations for international students: Required—TOEFL (minimum score 500 paper-based; 173 computer-based). *Application deadline:* For fall admission, 8/1 priority date for domestic and international students; for spring admission, 12/1 priority date for domestic and international students. Applications are processed on a rolling basis. Application fee: $0 ($55 for international students). Electronic applications accepted. *Financial support:* In 2006–07, teaching assistantships (averaging $6,000 per year); career-related internships or fieldwork, Federal Work-Study, and unspecified assistantships also available. Financial award application deadline: 4/1; financial award applicants required to submit FAFSA. *Faculty research:* Teaching through journal writing, gifted children, reading instruction in elementary schools, teaching social studies in elementary schools, ungraded elementary schools. *Application contact:* Michelle Barber, Graduate Admissions Counselor, 606-783-2039, Fax: 606-783-5061, E-mail: m.barber@moreheadstate.edu.

New York University, Steinhardt School of Culture, Education and Human Development, Department of Humanities and Social Sciences in the Professions, Program in International Education, New York, NY 10012-1019. Offers MA, PhD, Advanced Certificate. Part-time and evening/weekend programs available. *Faculty:* 4 full-time (2 women). *Students:* 37 full-time (31 women), 46 part-time (41 women); includes 19 minority (5 African Americans, 9 Asian Americans or Pacific Islanders, 5 Hispanic Americans), 8 international. 116 applicants, 78% accepted, 32 enrolled. In 2006, 28 master's, 4 doctorates awarded. *Degree requirements:* For master's, thesis (for some programs); for doctorate, thesis/dissertation. *Entrance requirements:* For doctorate, GRE General Test, interview; for Advanced Certificate, master's degree. Additional exam requirements/recommendations for international students: Required—TOEFL. *Application deadline:* For fall admission, 12/15 priority date for domestic and international students; for spring admission, 11/1 for domestic and international students. Application fee: $50. *Expenses:* Tuition: Part-time $1,080 per unit. Required fees: $56 per unit. $329 per term. Tuition and fees vary according to program. *Financial support:* Fellowships with full and partial tuition reimbursements, career-related internships or fieldwork, Federal Work-Study, institutionally sponsored loans, and scholarships/grants available. Support available to part-time students. Financial award application deadline: 2/1; financial award applicants required to submit FAFSA. *Faculty research:* Civic education, ethnic identity among students and teachers, comparative education. *Unit head:* Dr. Philip Hosay, Director, 212-992-9475, Fax: 212-995-4832, E-mail: pmh2@nyu.edu. *Application contact:* 212-998-5030, Fax: 212-995-4328, E-mail: steinhardt.gradadmissions@nyu.edu.

School for International Training, Graduate Programs, Master's Programs in Intercultural Service, Leadership, and Management, Brattleboro, VT 05302-0676. Offers conflict transformation (MA); intercultural service, leadership, and management (MA); international education (MA); management (MS); social justice in intercultural relations (MA); sustainable development (MA). Postbaccalaureate distance learning degree programs offered (minimal on-campus study). *Students:* 182 full-time (116 women), 298 part-time (215 women); includes 60 minority (27 African Americans, 1 American Indian/Alaska Native, 14 Asian Americans or Pacific Islanders, 18 Hispanic Americans), 96 international. Average age 30. 634 applicants,

International and Comparative Education

School for International Training (continued)
73% accepted, 157 enrolled. In 2006, 84 master's awarded. *Degree requirements:* For master's, one foreign language, thesis. *Entrance requirements:* For master's, 3 letters of reference. Additional exam requirements/recommendations for international students: Required—TOEFL. *Application deadline:* Applications are processed on a rolling basis. Application fee: $50. *Expenses:* Tuition: Full-time $27,355; part-time $638 per credit hour. Required fees: $1,092. *Financial support:* Career-related internships or fieldwork, Federal Work-Study, institutionally sponsored loans, and scholarships/grants available. Financial award application deadline: 3/1; financial award applicants required to submit FAFSA. *Faculty research:* Intercultural communication, conflict resolution, advising and training, world issues, international business. *Unit head:* Marla Solomon, Graduate Dean, 802-258-3325, Fax: 802-258-3241, E-mail: marla. solomon@sit.edu. *Application contact:* Information Contact, 800-336-1616, Fax: 802-258-3500, E-mail: admissions@sit.edu.

Stanford University, School of Education, Program in Social Sciences, Policy, and Educational Practice, Stanford, CA 94305-9991. Offers administration and policy analysis (Ed D, PhD); anthropology of education (PhD); economics of education (PhD); educational linguistics (PhD); evaluation (MA), including interdisciplinary studies; higher education (PhD); history of education (PhD); interdisciplinary studies (PhD); international comparative education (MA, PhD); international education administration and policy analysis (MA); philosophy of education (PhD); policy analysis (MA); prospective principal's program (MA); sociology of education (PhD). *Degree requirements:* For master's, thesis (for some programs); for doctorate, thesis/dissertation. *Entrance requirements:* For master's and doctorate, GRE General Test. Electronic applications accepted.

Teachers College Columbia University, Graduate Faculty of Education, Department of International and Transcultural Studies, Program in Comparative and International Education, New York, NY 10027-6696. Offers Ed M, MA, Ed D, PhD. *Faculty:* 1 (woman) full-time, 1 part-time/adjunct. *Students:* 15 full-time (10 women), 42 part-time (30 women); includes 20 minority (5 African Americans, 9 Asian Americans or Pacific Islanders, 6 Hispanic Americans), 10 international. Average age 33. 61 applicants, 41% accepted, 12 enrolled. In 2006, 15 master's, 3 doctorates awarded. *Degree requirements:* For doctorate, thesis/dissertation. *Application deadline:* For fall admission, 5/15 for domestic students; for spring admission, 12/1 for domestic students. Application fee: $65. *Expenses:* Tuition: Full-time $23,400; part-time $975 per credit. Required fees: $320 per term. *Financial support:* Career-related internships or fieldwork, Federal Work-Study, institutionally sponsored loans, and tuition waivers (full and partial) available. Support available to part-time students. Financial award application deadline: 2/1. *Faculty research:* Comparative analysis of national educational systems, identity and community in local and transcultural settings. *Application contact:* Deanna Ghozati, Assistant Director of Admission, 212-678-4018, Fax: 212-678-4171, E-mail: ghozati@tc.edu.

Teachers College Columbia University, Graduate Faculty of Education, Department of International and Transcultural Studies, Program in International Educational Development, New York, NY 10027-6696. Offers Ed M, MA, Ed D, PhD. *Faculty:* 5 full-time (4 women), 2 part-time/adjunct. *Students:* 70 full-time (58 women), 156 part-time (123 women); includes 65 minority (16 African Americans, 1 American Indian/Alaska Native, 33 Asian Americans or Pacific Islanders, 15 Hispanic Americans), 61 international. Average age 34. 245 applicants, 63% accepted, 64 enrolled. In 2006, 76 master's, 11 doctorates awarded. *Degree requirements:* For doctorate, thesis/dissertation. *Application deadline:* For fall admission, 5/15 for domestic students; for spring admission, 12/1 for domestic students. Application fee: $65. *Expenses:* Tuition: Full-time $23,400; part-time $975 per credit. Required fees: $320 per term. *Financial support:* Career-related internships or fieldwork, Federal Work-Study, institutionally sponsored loans, and tuition waivers (full and partial) available. Support available to part-time students. Financial award application deadline: 2/1. *Faculty research:* Application of formal and nonformal education to programs of social and economic development in Third World countries. *Application contact:* Deanna Ghozati, Assistant Director of Admission, 212-678-4018, Fax: 212-678-4171, E-mail: ghozati@tc.edu.

Tufts University, Fletcher School of Law and Diplomacy, Medford, MA 02155. Offers MA, MAHA, MALD, PhD, DVM/MA, JD/MALD, MALD/MA, MALD/MBA, MALD/MS, MD/MA. Postbaccalaureate distance learning degree programs offered (minimal on-campus study). *Faculty:* 34 full-time (7 women), 31 part-time/adjunct (8 women). *Students:* 527 full-time (268 women), 9 part-time (4 women); includes 61 minority (12 African Americans, 1 American Indian/Alaska Native, 32 Asian Americans or Pacific Islanders, 16 Hispanic Americans), 212 international. Average age 31. 1,605 applicants, 40% accepted, 234 enrolled. In 2006, 203 master's, 10 doctorates awarded. *Median time to degree:* Of those who began their doctoral program in fall 1998, 75% received their degree in 8 years or less. *Degree requirements:* For master's, one foreign language, thesis, registration; for doctorate, one foreign language, thesis/dissertation, dissertation defense, comprehensive exam, registration. *Entrance requirements:* For master's and doctorate, GMAT or GRE General Test. Additional exam requirements/recommendations for international students: Required—TOEFL (minimum score 600 paper-based; 250 computer-based; 100 iBT), IELTS (minimum score 7). *Application deadline:* For fall admission, 1/15 for domestic and international students; for spring admission, 10/15 for domestic and international students. Application fee: $65. Electronic applications accepted. *Expenses:* Contact institution. Tuition and fees vary according to degree level and program. *Financial support:* Federal Work-Study, institutionally sponsored loans, scholarships/grants, and tuition waivers (partial) available. Financial award application deadline: 1/15; financial award applicants required to submit FAFSA. *Faculty research:* Negotiation and conflict resolution, international organizations, international business and economic law, security studies, development economics. *Unit head:* Stephen W. Bosworth, Dean, 617-627-3050, Fax: 617-627-3712. *Application contact:* Laurie A. Hurley, Director of Admissions and Financial Aid, 617-627-2410, Fax: 617-627-3712, E-mail: fletcheradmissions@tufts.edu.

University of Bridgeport, School of Education and Human Resources, Division of Education, Program in Secondary Education, Bridgeport, CT 06604. Offers computer specialist (Diploma); international education (Diploma); reading specialist (MS, Diploma); secondary education (MS, Diploma). Part-time and evening/weekend programs available. *Faculty:* 12 full-time (5 women), 72 part-time/adjunct (44 women). *Students:* 1 full-time (0 women), 5 part-time (all women). Average age 37. 8 applicants, 63% accepted, 1 enrolled. In 2006, 4 degrees awarded. *Degree requirements:* For master's, final exam, final project, or thesis; for Diploma, thesis or alternative, final project. *Entrance requirements:* For master's, GRE General Test, MAT, minimum undergraduate QPA of 2.5; for Diploma, GRE General Test or MAT, minimum graduate QPA of 3.0. *Application deadline:* For fall admission, 8/1 priority date for domestic students; for spring admission, 12/1 priority date for domestic students. Applications are processed on a rolling basis. Application fee: $25 ($35 for international students). Electronic applications accepted. *Financial support:* Career-related internships or fieldwork, Federal Work-Study, and institutionally sponsored loans available. Support available to part-time students. Financial award application deadline: 6/1; financial award applicants required to submit FAFSA. *Faculty research:* Self-concept, internship assessment, stress and situational development, follow-up of graduation, trend analysis. *Unit head:* Dr. Allen P. Cook, Associate Dean, Division of Education, 203-576-4206, Fax: 203-576-4200, E-mail: acook@bridgeport.edu.

University of California, Santa Barbara, Graduate Division, Gevirtz Graduate School of Education, Santa Barbara, CA 93106. Offers counseling, clinical and school psychology (PhD), including clinical psychology, counseling psychology; education (M Ed, MA, PhD), including child and adolescent development (MA, PhD), cultural perspectives and comparative education (MA, PhD), educational leadership and organizations (MA, PhD), research methodology (MA, PhD), special education disabilities and risk studies (MA), special education, disabilities and risk studies (PhD), teaching and learning (MA, PhD); educational leadership (Ed D). *Accreditation:* APA (one or more programs are accredited). Postbaccalaureate distance learning degree programs offered (minimal on-campus study). *Faculty:* 39 full-time (18 women). *Students:* 375 full-time (285 women); includes 111 minority (13 African Americans, 2 American Indian/Alaska Native, 33 Asian Americans or Pacific Islanders, 63 Hispanic Americans), 14 international. Average age 29. 777 applicants, 36% accepted, 154 enrolled. In 2006, 151 master's, 31 doctorates awarded. Terminal master's awarded for partial completion of doctoral program. *Median time to degree:* Master's–1.5 years full-time; doctorate–5.5 years full-time. *Degree requirements:* For master's, thesis optional; for doctorate, thesis/dissertation, qualifying exam, comprehensive exam (for some programs), registration; for degree. *Entrance requirements:* For master's, GRE, MAT (M Ed); for doctorate, GRE. Additional exam requirements/recommendations for international students: Required—TOEFL (minimum score 550 paper-based; 213 computer-based; 80 iBT). *Application deadline:* For fall admission, 12/15 for domestic and international students. Application fee: $60. Electronic applications accepted. *Financial support:* In 2006–07, 181 fellowships with full and partial tuition reimbursements (averaging $4,200 per year), 64 research assistantships with full and partial tuition reimbursements (averaging $6,200 per year), 75 teaching assistantships with partial tuition reimbursements (averaging $7,500 per year) were awarded; career-related internships or fieldwork, Federal Work-Study, institutionally sponsored loans, scholarships/grants, traineeships, health care benefits, and unspecified assistantships also available. Support available to part-time students. Financial award application deadline: 12/15; financial award applicants required to submit FAFSA. Total annual research expenditures: $4 million. *Unit head:* Dr. Jane Conoley, Chair, 805-893-3917, E-mail: jane_conoley@education.ucsb.edu. *Application contact:* Student Affairs Office, 805-893-2137, E-mail: sao@education.ucsb.edu.

University of Massachusetts Amherst, Graduate School, School of Education, Program in Education, Amherst, MA 01003. Offers cultural diversity and curriculum reform (M Ed, Ed D, CAGS); early childhood education and development (M Ed, Ed D, CAGS); educational administration (M Ed, Ed D, CAGS); elementary teacher education (M Ed, Ed D, CAGS); higher education (M Ed, Ed D, CAGS); international education (M Ed, Ed D, CAGS); mathematics, science, and instructional technology (M Ed, Ed D, CAGS); physical education teacher education (M Ed, Ed D, CAGS); reading and writing (M Ed, Ed D, CAGS); research and evaluation methods (M Ed, Ed D, CAGS); school psychology and school counseling (M Ed, Ed D, CAGS); secondary teacher education (M Ed, Ed D, CAGS); social justice education (M Ed, Ed D, CAGS); special education (M Ed, Ed D, CAGS). *Accreditation:* NCATE. *Students:* 418 full-time (286 women), 447 part-time (319 women); includes 147 minority (70 African Americans, 4 American Indian/Alaska Native, 28 Asian Americans or Pacific Islanders, 45 Hispanic Americans), 81 international. Average age 36. In 2006, 260 master's, 30 doctorates awarded. *Degree requirements:* For doctorate, thesis/dissertation. *Entrance requirements:* For master's and doctorate, GRE General Test. Additional exam requirements/recommendations for international students: Required—TOEFL (minimum score 530 paper-based; 197 computer-based). *Application deadline:* For fall admission, 1/15 for domestic and international students; for spring admission, 10/1 for domestic and international students. Applications are processed on a rolling basis. Application fee: $40 ($65 for international students). Electronic applications accepted. *Expenses:* Tuition, state resident: full-time $2,640; part-time $110 per credit. Tuition, nonresident: full-time $9,936; part-time $414 per credit. Required fees: $8,969; $3,129 per term. One-time fee: $257 full-time. Tuition and fees vary according to class time, course load, campus/location and reciprocity agreements. *Financial support:* Fellowships with full tuition reimbursements, research assistantships with full tuition reimbursements, teaching assistantships with full tuition reimbursements, career-related internships or fieldwork, Federal Work-Study, scholarships/grants, traineeships, and unspecified assistantships available. Support available to part-time students. Financial award application deadline: 1/15. *Unit head:* Linda L. Griffin, Professor, 413-545-6984.

University of Minnesota, Twin Cities Campus, Graduate School, College of Education and Human Development, Department of Educational Policy and Administration, Program in Comparative and International Development Education, Minneapolis, MN 55455-0213. Offers MA, PhD. *Students:* 67 full-time (46 women), 39 part-time (29 women); includes 8 minority (5 African Americans, 1 American Indian/Alaska Native, 1 Asian American or Pacific Islander, 1 Hispanic American), 31 international. Average age 33. 57 applicants, 58% accepted, 16 enrolled. In 2006, 18 master's, 8 doctorates awarded. *Expenses:* Tuition, state resident: full-time $9,302; part-time $775 per credit. Tuition, nonresident: full-time $16,400; part-time $1,367 per credit. Full-time tuition and fees vary according to class time, course load, program, reciprocity agreements and student level. *Application contact:* Dr. Mary Bents, Associate Dean, 612-625-6501, Fax: 612-626-1580, E-mail: mbents@tc.umn.edu.

University of Pennsylvania, Graduate School of Education, Division of Foundations and Practices in Education, Programs in Education, Culture and Society, Philadelphia, PA 19104. Offers MS Ed, PhD.

University of Pittsburgh, School of Education, Department of Administrative and Policy Studies, Program in Social and Comparative Analysis in Education, Pittsburgh, PA 15260. Offers international development education (MA, PhD); international developmental education (M Ed); social, philosophical, and historical foundations of education (M Ed, MA, PhD). Evening/weekend programs available. *Students:* 45 full-time (27 women), 36 part-time (31 women); includes 12 minority (8 African Americans, 3 Asian Americans or Pacific Islanders, 1 Hispanic American), 21 international. 70 applicants, 86% accepted, 30 enrolled. In 2006, 5 master's, 9 doctorates awarded. *Degree requirements:* For master's and doctorate, thesis/dissertation. *Entrance requirements:* For doctorate, GRE General Test. Additional exam requirements/recommendations for international students: Required—TOEFL. *Application deadline:* For fall admission, 2/1 priority date for domestic students; for spring admission, 11/15 priority date for domestic students. Applications are processed on a rolling basis. Application fee: $50. Electronic applications accepted. *Financial support:* Research assistantships, teaching assistantships, Federal Work-Study, institutionally sponsored loans, and tuition waivers (partial) available. Support available to part-time students. Financial award application deadline: 3/15; financial award applicants required to submit FAFSA. *Application contact:* Joan M. Cutone, Director, School of Education Student Service Center, 412-648-2230, Fax: 412-648-1899, E-mail: soeinfo@pitt.edu.

University of San Francisco, School of Education, Department of International and Multicultural Education, San Francisco, CA 94117-1080. Offers international and multicultural education (MA, Ed D); multicultural literature for children and young adults (MA); teaching English as a second language (MA). *Faculty:* 6 full-time (4 women), 8 part-time/adjunct (6 women). *Students:* 102 full-time (80 women), 71 part-time (64 women); includes 74 minority (16 African Americans, 24 Asian Americans or Pacific Islanders, 34 Hispanic Americans), 37 international. Average age 34. 163 applicants, 88% accepted, 50 enrolled. In 2006, 37 master's, 11 doctorates awarded. *Degree requirements:* For doctorate, thesis/dissertation. Application fee: $55 ($65 for international students). *Expenses:* Tuition: Full-time $17,370; part-time $965 per unit. Tuition and fees vary according to degree level, campus/location and program. *Financial support:* In 2006–07, 93 students received support; fellowships, research assistantships, teaching assistantships available. Financial award application deadline: 3/2; financial award applicants required to submit FAFSA. *Unit head:* Dr. Rosita Galang, Chair, 415-422-6878.

Vanderbilt University, Peabody College, Department of Leadership and Organizations, Nashville, TN 37240-1001. Offers education policy (MPP); educational leadership and policy (Ed D); higher education (M Ed); higher education, leadership and policy (Ed D); human resource development (M Ed); international education policy and management (M Ed); organizational leadership (M Ed); school administration (M Ed). Part-time and evening/weekend programs available. *Faculty:* 21 full-time (6 women), 9 part-time/adjunct (3 women). *Students:* 131 full-time (88 women), 85 part-time (39 women); includes 35 minority (30 African Americans, 4 Asian Americans or Pacific Islanders, 1 Hispanic American), 11 international. Average age 31. 214 applicants, 63% accepted, 64 enrolled. In 2006, 43 master's, 12 doctorates awarded. *Median time to degree:* Of those who began their doctoral program in fall 1998, 62% received their degree in 8 years or less. *Degree requirements:* For master's, thesis optional; for doctorate, thesis/dissertation, qualifying exams, residency. *Entrance requirements:* For master's and doctorate, GRE General Test. Additional exam requirements/recommendations for international students: Required—TOEFL (minimum score 550 paper-based; 213 computer-based). *Application deadline:* For fall admission, 12/31 priority date for domestic and international students; for spring admission, 11/1 priority date for domestic and international students. Applications are processed on a rolling basis. Application fee: $0. Electronic applications accepted. *Expenses:* Tuition: Full-time $24,462. Required fees: $2,515. One-time fee: $30 full-time. Full-time tuition and fees vary according to course load, degree level and program. *Financial support:* In 2006–07, 90 students received support, including 50 fellowships with full and partial tuition reimbursements available, 38 research assistantships with full and partial tuition reimbursements available, 2 teaching assistantships with full and partial tuition reimbursements available; Federal Work-Study, institutionally sponsored loans, scholarships/grants, tuition waivers (partial), and unspecified assistantships also available. Support available to part-time students. Financial award application deadline: 2/1; financial award applicants required to submit FAFSA. *Faculty research:* Education policy, education finances, economics of education, education leadership and management, higher education leadership and policy; educator pay for performance. *Unit head:* James W. Guthrie, Chair, 615-322-8000, Fax: 615-343-7094, E-mail: james.w.guthrie@vanderbilt.edu. *Application contact:* Rosie Moody, Educational Coordinator, 615-322-8019, Fax: 615-343-7094, E-mail: rosie.moody@vanderbilt.edu.

Wright State University, School of Graduate Studies, College of Liberal Arts, Program in Applied Behavioral Science, Dayton, OH 45435. Offers criminal justice and social problems (MA); international and comparative politics (MA). *Students:* 18 full-time (12 women), 14 part-time (11 women); includes 6 minority (5 African Americans, 1 Hispanic American). Average age 32. 20 applicants, 95% accepted. In 2006, 17 degrees awarded. *Degree requirements:* For master's, thesis optional. *Entrance requirements:* Additional exam requirements/recommendations for international students: Required—TOEFL. Application fee: $25. *Financial support:* Fellowships, research assistantships, unspecified assistantships available. Support available to part-time students. Financial award applicants required to submit FAFSA. *Faculty research:* Training and development, criminal justice and social problems, community systems, human factors, industrial/organizational psychology. *Unit head:* Dr. David M. Orenstein, Director, 937-775-2667, Fax: 937-775-4228, E-mail: david.orenstein@wright.edu.

Student Affairs

Alliant International University–Los Angeles, Graduate School of Education, Educational Psychology Programs, Alhambra, CA 91803-1360. Offers educational psychology (Psy D); pupil personnel services (Credential); school psychology (MA). Part-time programs available. *Students:* 26 full-time (16 women), 23 part-time (15 women); includes 10 African Americans, 5 Asian Americans or Pacific Islanders, 18 Hispanic Americans, 1 international. Average age 43. 21 applicants, 67% accepted, 9 enrolled. In 2006, 3 doctorates awarded. *Degree requirements:* For doctorate, thesis/dissertation. *Entrance requirements:* For master's, minimum GPA of 3.0, letters of recommendation; for doctorate, interview, minimum GPA of 3.0, letters of recommendation. Additional exam requirements/recommendations for international students: Required—TOEFL (minimum score 550 paper-based; 213 computer-based), TWE (minimum score 5). *Application deadline:* For fall admission, 7/1 priority date for domestic and international students; for spring admission, 12/1 priority date for domestic and international students. Applications are processed on a rolling basis. Application fee: $55. Electronic applications accepted. *Financial support:* Career-related internships or fieldwork, Federal Work-Study, institutionally sponsored loans, and scholarships/grants available. Financial award application deadline: 2/15; financial award applicants required to submit FAFSA. *Faculty research:* Early identification and intervention with high-risk preschoolers, pediatric neuropsychology, interpersonal violence, ADHD, learning theories. *Unit head:* Dr. Carlton Parks, Program Director, 866-825-5426, Fax: 626-284-0550, E-mail: admissions@alliant.edu. *Application contact:* Alliant International University Central Contact Center, 866-U-ALLIANT, Fax: 858-635-4555, E-mail: admissions@alliant.edu.

See Close-Up on page 1099.

Alliant International University–San Diego, Graduate School of Education, Educational Psychology Programs, San Diego, CA 92131-1799. Offers educational psychology (Psy D); pupil personnel services (Credential); school psychology (MA); student personnel services (Certificate). Part-time programs available. *Students:* 30 full-time (25 women), 16 part-time (12 women); includes 11 minority (1 African American, 1 American Indian/Alaska Native, 2 Asian Americans or Pacific Islanders, 7 Hispanic Americans), 2 international. Average age 31. 38 applicants, 61% accepted, 18 enrolled. In 2006, 13 master's, 1 doctorate awarded. *Degree requirements:* For doctorate, thesis/dissertation. *Entrance requirements:* For master's, minimum GPA of 3.0, letters of recommendation; for doctorate, interview, letters of recommendation. Additional exam requirements/recommendations for international students: Required—TOEFL (minimum score 550 paper-based; 213 computer-based), TWE (minimum score 5). *Application deadline:* For fall admission, 7/1 priority date for domestic and international students; for spring admission, 12/1 priority date for domestic and international students. Applications are processed on a rolling basis. Application fee: $55. Electronic applications accepted. *Expenses:* Tuition: Part-time $825 per unit. Tuition and fees vary according to course load, degree level and program. *Financial support:* In 2006–07, 42 students received support. Career-related internships or fieldwork, Federal Work-Study, institutionally sponsored loans, and scholarships/grants available. Financial award application deadline: 2/15; financial award applicants required to submit FAFSA. *Unit head:* Dr. Don Wofford, Systemwide Program Director, 866-825-5426, Fax: 858-635-4739, E-mail: admissions@alliant.edu. *Application contact:* Alliant International University Central Contact Center, 866-U-ALLIANT, Fax: 858-635-4555, E-mail: admissions@alliant.edu.

See Close-Up on page 1099.

Arkansas State University, Graduate School, College of Education, Department of Psychology and Counseling, Jonesboro, State University, AR 72467. Offers college student personnel services (MS); counselor education (Ed S), including college student personnel services, psychoeducational diagnosis, school counseling; rehabilitation counseling (MRC); school counseling (MSE); student affairs (Certificate). *Accreditation:* ACA (one or more programs are accredited); CORE (one or more programs are accredited); NCATE. Part-time programs available. *Faculty:* 13 full-time (6 women), 3 part-time/adjunct (1 woman). *Students:* 61 full-time (41 women), 56 part-time (43 women); includes 25 minority (22 African Americans, 3 Hispanic Americans). Average age 30. 74 applicants, 69% accepted, 40 enrolled. In 2006, 26 master's, 11 other advanced degrees awarded. *Degree requirements:* For master's and other advanced degree, thesis or alternative, comprehensive exam. *Entrance requirements:* For master's, GRE General Test or MAT (MSE), appropriate bachelor's degree, interview, letters of reference, official transcript; for other advanced degree, GRE General Test, interview, master's degree, letters of reference, official transcript. Additional exam requirements/recommendations for international students: Required—TOEFL (minimum score 213 computer-based). *Application deadline:* Applications are processed on a rolling basis. Application fee: $30 ($40 for international students). Electronic applications accepted. *Expenses:* Tuition, state resident: full-time $3,393; part-time $189 per hour. Tuition, nonresident: full-time $8,577; part-time $477 per hour. Required fees: $752; $39 per hour. $25 per semester. *Financial support:* Teaching assistantships, career-related internships or fieldwork, scholarships/grants, and unspecified assistantships available. Financial award application deadline: 7/1; financial award applicants required to submit FAFSA. *Unit head:* Dr. Loretta McGregor, Chair, 870-972-3064, Fax: 870-972-3962, E-mail: lmcgregor@astate.edu.

Arkansas Tech University, Graduate School, School of Education, Russellville, AR 72801. Offers college student personnel (MSE); educational leadership (M Ed, Ed S); English education (M Ed); gifted education (MSE); instructional improvement (M Ed); secondary education (M Ed); teaching, learning and leadership (M Ed). *Accreditation:* NCATE. Part-time programs available. *Students:* 44 full-time (33 women), 244 part-time (181 women); includes 20 minority (14 African Americans, 1 American Indian/Alaska Native, 3 Asian Americans or Pacific Islanders, 2 Hispanic Americans), 18 international. Average age 34. In 2006, 72 master's, 4 other advanced degrees awarded. *Degree requirements:* For master's, action research project, thesis optional. *Entrance requirements:* For master's, GRE General Test or MAT. Additional exam requirements/recommendations for international students: Required—TOEFL (minimum score 500 paper-based; 173 computer-based). *Application deadline:* For fall admission, 3/1 priority date for domestic students, 5/1 priority date for international students; for winter admission, 10/1 priority date for international students; for spring admission, 10/1 priority date for domestic and international students. Applications are processed on a rolling basis. Application fee: $0 ($30 for international students). Electronic applications accepted. *Expenses:* Tuition, state resident: full-time $3,060; part-time $170 per hour. Tuition, nonresident: full-time $6,120; part-time $340 per hour. Required fees: $312; $4 per hour. $84 per term. Part-time tuition and fees vary according to course load. *Financial support:* In 2006–07, teaching assistantships with full tuition reimbursements (averaging $4,000 per year); career-related internships or fieldwork, Federal Work-Study, scholarships/grants, health care benefits, and unspecified assistantships also available. Support available to part-time students. Financial award application deadline: 4/15; financial award applicants required to submit FAFSA. *Unit head:* Dr. C. Glenn Sheets, Dean, 479-968-0350, Fax: 479-968-0350, E-mail: glenn.sheets@atu.edu. *Application contact:* Dr. Eldon G. Clary, Dean of Graduate School, 479-968-0398, Fax: 479-964-0542, E-mail: graduate.school@atu.edu.

Ashland University, College of Education, Graduate Studies in Education, Program in Educational Administration, Ashland, OH 44805-3702. Offers administration (M Ed); business manager (M Ed); curriculum specialist (M Ed); principalship (M Ed); pupil services (M Ed); school treasurer (M Ed); superintendency (M Ed). Part-time programs available. *Faculty:* 10 full-time (3 women), 23 part-time/adjunct (6 women). *Students:* 134 full-time (76 women), 220 part-time (121 women); includes 27 minority (23 African Americans, 1 Asian American or Pacific Islander, 3 Hispanic Americans), 2 international. Average age 33. 68 applicants, 100% accepted, 68 enrolled. In 2006, 144 degrees awarded. *Degree requirements:* For master's, thesis or alternative, internship. *Entrance requirements:* For master's, teaching certificate, minimum GPA of 2.75. Additional exam requirements/recommendations for international students: Required—TOEFL. *Application deadline:* Applications are processed on a rolling basis. Application fee: $30. *Expenses:* Tuition: Part-time $403 per credit. Tuition and fees vary according to degree level and program. *Financial support:* In 2006–07, 116 students received support. Institutionally sponsored loans and scholarships/grants available. Financial award application deadline: 4/15. *Faculty research:* Gender and religious considerations in employment, ISLLC standards, adjunct faculty training, politics of school finance, ethnicity and employment. *Unit head:* Dr. John Bailey, Chair, 419-289-5396, Fax: 419-207-6702, E-mail: jbailey@ashland.edu. *Application contact:* Fred Slater, Director, Graduate Education, 419-289-5367, Fax: 419-207-4942, E-mail: fslater@ashland.edu.

Azusa Pacific University, School of Behavioral and Applied Sciences, Department of Higher Education and Organizational Leadership, Program in College Student Affairs, Azusa, CA 91702-7000. Offers M Ed. Part-time and evening/weekend programs available. *Students:* 1 (woman) full-time, 62 part-time (43 women); includes 12 minority (4 African Americans, 1 Asian American or Pacific Islander, 7 Hispanic Americans), 1 international. In 2006, 14 degrees awarded. *Degree requirements:* For master's, exam. *Entrance requirements:* For master's, 12 units of course work in social science, minimum GPA of 3.0. Application fee: $45 ($65 for international students). *Expenses:* Tuition: Part-time $475 per credit. *Application contact:* Grace Barnes, Coordinator, 626-815-3848, Fax: 626-815-3868.

Azusa Pacific University, School of Education, Department of Education, Program in Pupil Personnel Services, Azusa, CA 91702-7000. Offers MA. Part-time and evening/weekend programs available. *Students:* 1 (woman) full-time, 2 part-time (1 woman); includes 2 minority (both Hispanic Americans) In 2006, 2 degrees awarded. *Degree requirements:* For master's, core exams, oral presentation. *Entrance requirements:* For master's, 12 units of course work in education, minimum GPA of 3.0. Application fee: $45 ($65 for international students). *Expenses:* Tuition: Part-time $475 per credit. *Unit head:* Dr. Barbara W. Sorenson, Director, 626-815-5362.

Bloomsburg University of Pennsylvania, School of Graduate Studies, College of Professional Studies, School of Education, Department of Educational Studies and Secondary Education, Program in Guidance Counseling and Student Affairs, Bloomsburg, PA 17815-1301. Offers M Ed. *Faculty:* 8 full-time (3 women). *Entrance requirements:* For master's, GRE, 3 letters of recommendation, resumé. *Expenses:* Tuition, state resident: full-time $6,048; part-time $336 per credit. Tuition, nonresident: full-time $9,678; part-time $538 per credit. Required fees: $1,415. *Unit head:* Dr. Robert Gates, Coordinator, Department of Educational Studies and Secondary Education, 570-389-4961, Fax: 570-389-3894, E-mail: rgates@bloomu.edu.

Bob Jones University, Graduate Programs, Greenville, SC 29614. Offers accountancy (MS); Bible (MA); Bible translation (MA); Biblical studies (Certificate); broadcast management (MS); business administration (MBA); church history (MA, PhD); church ministries (MA); church music (MM); cinema and video production (MA); counseling (MS); curriculum and instruction (Ed D); divinity (M Div); dramatic production (MA); educational leadership (MS, Ed D, Ed S); elementary education (M Ed, MAT); English (M Ed, MA, MAT); fine arts (MA); graphic design (MA); history (M Ed, MA); illustration (MA); interpretative speech (MA); mathematics (M Ed, MAT); medical missions (Certificate); ministry (MM, D Min); multi-categorical special education (M Ed, MAT); music (M Ed); New Testament interpretation (PhD); Old Testament interpretation (PhD); orchestral instrument performance (MM); organ performance (MM); pastoral studies (MA); personnel services (MS, Ed S); piano pedagogy (MM); piano performance (MM); platform arts (MA); radio and television broadcasting (MS); rhetoric and public address (MA); secondary education (M Ed); studio art (MA); teaching Bible (MA); theology (MA, PhD); voice performance (MM); youth ministries (MA); M Div/MM.

Bowling Green State University, Graduate College, College of Education and Human Development, School of Leadership and Policy Studies, Program in College Student Personnel, Bowling Green, OH 43403. Offers MA. Part-time programs available. *Students:* 80 full-time (57 women), 2 part-time (both women); includes 10 minority (6 African Americans, 2 Asian Americans or Pacific Islanders, 2 Hispanic Americans), 1 international. Average age 25. 141 applicants, 16% accepted, 22 enrolled. In 2006, 39 degrees awarded. *Degree requirements:* For master's, thesis or alternative. *Entrance requirements:* For master's, GRE General Test, interview. Additional exam requirements/recommendations for international students: Required—TOEFL. *Application deadline:* For fall admission, 1/1 for domestic students. Application fee: $30. Electronic applications accepted. *Expenses:* Tuition, state resident: part-time $535 per hour. Tuition, nonresident: part-time $884 per hour. *Financial support:* In 2006–07, 34 research

Student Affairs

Bowling Green State University (continued)
assistantships with full tuition reimbursements (averaging $8,120 per year), 2 teaching assistantships with full tuition reimbursements (averaging $8,120 per year) were awarded; career-related internships or fieldwork, institutionally sponsored loans, and unspecified assistantships also available. Financial award applicants required to submit FAFSA. *Faculty research:* Adult learning, legal issues, moral and ethical development. *Application contact:* Dr. Michael Coomes, Graduate Coordinator, 419-372-7157.

Buffalo State College, State University of New York, Graduate Studies and Research, Faculty of Applied Science and Education, Department of Educational Foundations, Program in Student Personnel Administration, Buffalo, NY 14222-1095. Offers MS. *Degree requirements:* For master's, comprehensive exam. *Entrance requirements:* For master's, minimum GPA of 2.75 in last 60 hours of undergraduate course work. Additional exam requirements/recommendations for international students: Required—TOEFL (minimum score 550 paper-based; 213 computer-based).

Canisius College, Graduate Division, School of Education and Human Services, Department of Graduate Education, Buffalo, NY 14208-1098. Offers business education (MS); childhood education (MS); college student personnel (MS); differentiated instruction (MS Ed); early childhood education (MS); education administration (MS); education of the deaf and hard of hearing (MS); general education (MS Ed); literacy education (MS Ed); reading education (MS Ed); secondary education (MS); special education (MS). *Accreditation:* NCATE. Part-time and evening/weekend programs available. *Faculty:* 13 full-time (12 women), 74 part-time/adjunct (44 women). *Students:* 377 full-time (267 women), 303 part-time (219 women); includes 43 minority (27 African Americans, 2 American Indian/Alaska Native, 6 Asian Americans or Pacific Islanders, 8 Hispanic Americans), 187 international. Average age 30. In 2006, 296 degrees awarded. Application fee: $25. *Expenses:* Tuition: Part-time $645 per credit hour. Required fees: $19 per credit hour. Tuition and fees vary according to program. *Financial support:* Research assistantships with full tuition reimbursements, career-related internships or fieldwork, institutionally sponsored loans, scholarships/grants, health care benefits, tuition waivers (full and partial), and unspecified assistantships available. *Faculty research:* Autism, Asperger's disease, private higher education, reading strategies. *Unit head:* Rev. Paul Nochelski, Chair of Graduate Education and Leadership, 716-888-3297, Fax: 716-888-3299. *Application contact:* James D. Bagwell, Director of Graduate Recruitment and Admissions, 716-888-2544, Fax: 716-888-3290, E-mail: bagwellj@canisius.edu.

Cleveland State University, College of Graduate Studies, College of Education and Human Services, Department of Counseling, Administration, Supervision and Adult Learning, Cleveland, OH 44115. Offers adult learning and development (M Ed); community agency counseling (M Ed); counseling and pupil personnel administration (Ed S); educational administration (Ed S); educational administration and supervision (M Ed); school counseling (M Ed). *Accreditation:* ACA (one or more programs are accredited). Part-time programs available. *Faculty:* 15 full-time (9 women), 8 part-time/adjunct (5 women). *Students:* 43 full-time (33 women), 304 part-time (236 women); includes 91 minority (78 African Americans, 2 Asian Americans or Pacific Islanders, 11 Hispanic Americans). Average age 35. 205 applicants, 36% accepted, 54 enrolled. In 2006, 136 master's, 6 other advanced degrees awarded. *Degree requirements:* For master's, thesis optional; for Ed S, internship, thesis optional. *Entrance requirements:* For master's, GRE General Test or MAT, letter of recommendation, minimum GPA of 2.75. Additional exam requirements/recommendations for international students: Required—TOEFL (minimum score 525 paper-based; 197 computer-based), IELTS (minimum score 6). *Application deadline:* For fall admission, 6/21 for domestic students; for spring admission, 8/31 for domestic students. Application fee: $30. *Financial support:* In 2006–07, 8 students received support, including research assistantships with full and partial tuition reimbursements available (averaging $3,287 per year), teaching assistantships with full and partial tuition reimbursements available (averaging $3,480 per year); career-related internships or fieldwork, scholarships/grants, tuition waivers (full), and unspecified assistantships also available. Support available to part-time students. *Faculty research:* Education law, career development, women in school administration, psychopharmacology, counseling and spirituality. Total annual research expenditures: $478,265. *Unit head:* Dr. Rollin D. Nordgren, Interim Chairperson, 216-523-7499, Fax: 216-687-5378, E-mail: r.nordgren@csuohio.edu.

College of Saint Elizabeth, Department of Psychology, Morristown, NJ 07960-6989. Offers counseling psychology (MA); student affairs in higher education (Certificate). Part-time and evening/weekend programs available. *Faculty:* 5 full-time (2 women), 8 part-time/adjunct (5 women). *Students:* 5 full-time (all women), 46 part-time (43 women); includes 12 minority (6 African Americans, 1 Asian American or Pacific Islander, 5 Hispanic Americans), 2 international. Average age 35. In 2006, 2 degrees awarded. *Degree requirements:* For master's, thesis or alternative, portfolio. *Entrance requirements:* For master's, minimum GPA of 3.0, BA in psychology (preferred), 12 credits of course work in psychology. *Application deadline:* For fall admission, 4/14 priority date for domestic students; for spring admission, 11/15 for domestic students. Applications are processed on a rolling basis. Application fee: $35. Electronic applications accepted. *Financial support:* Career-related internships or fieldwork, tuition waivers (partial), and unspecified assistantships available. Support available to part-time students. Financial award application deadline: 3/15; financial award applicants required to submit FAFSA. *Faculty research:* Family systems, dissociative identity disorder, multicultural counseling, outcomes assessment. *Unit head:* Dr. Valerie Scott, Director of the Graduate Program in Counseling Psychology, 973-290-4102, Fax: 973-290-4676, E-mail: vscott@cse.edu. *Application contact:* Michael Szarek, Director of Enrollment Management, 973-290-4112, Fax: 973-290-4167, E-mail: mszarek@cse.edu.

The College of Saint Rose, Graduate Studies, School of Education, Department of Counseling and Educational Administration, Program in Counseling, Albany, NY 12203-1419. Offers college student personnel (MS Ed); community counseling (MS Ed); school counseling (MS Ed). *Accreditation:* NCATE. Part-time and evening/weekend programs available. *Degree requirements:* For master's, comprehensive exam or thesis. *Entrance requirements:* For master's, interview, minimum undergraduate GPA of 3.0, 9 hours of psychology coursework. Additional exam requirements/recommendations for international students: Required—TOEFL (minimum score 550 paper-based; 213 computer-based). Electronic applications accepted.

The College of Saint Rose, Graduate Studies, School of Education, Department of Counseling and Educational Administration, Program in Educational Administration and Supervision, Albany, NY 12203-1419. Offers college student services administration (MS Ed); educational administration and supervision (MS Ed, Certificate); school administrator and supervisor (Certificate). Part-time and evening/weekend programs available. *Degree requirements:* For master's, comprehensive exam or thesis. *Entrance requirements:* For master's, minimum undergraduate GPA of 3.0, timed writing sample, interview, permanent certification or 3 years teaching experience. Additional exam requirements/recommendations for international students: Required—TOEFL (minimum score 550 paper-based; 213 computer-based). Electronic applications accepted.

Colorado State University, Graduate School, College of Applied Human Sciences, School of Education, Fort Collins, CO 80523-0015. Offers education and human resource studies (M Ed, PhD); student affairs in higher education (MS). PhD is offered in conjunction with the Department of Occupational Therapy. *Accreditation:* ACA; NCATE. Part-time programs available. Postbaccalaureate distance learning degree programs offered. *Faculty:* 19 full-time (8 women). *Students:* 137 full-time (96 women), 487 part-time (301 women); includes 91 minority (28 African Americans, 7 American Indian/Alaska Native, 15 Asian Americans or Pacific Islanders, 41 Hispanic Americans), 16 international. Average age 38. 349 applicants, 53% accepted, 143 enrolled. In 2006, 134 master's, 38 doctorates awarded. *Degree requirements:* For master's, thesis optional; for doctorate, thesis/dissertation, comprehensive exam, registration. *Entrance requirements:* For master's, GRE, minimum undergraduate GPA of 3.0, 3 letters of recommendation, curriculum vitae/resumé, additional School of Education application; for doctorate, minimum GPA of 3.0, 3 letters of recommendation, curriculum vitae. Additional exam requirements/recommendations for international students: Required—TOEFL (minimum score 550 paper-based; 213 computer-based). *Application deadline:* For fall admission, 3/15 for domestic and international students. Applications are processed on a rolling basis. Application fee: $50. Electronic applications accepted. *Expenses:* Tuition, state resident: full-time $4,248; part-time $236 per credit. Tuition, nonresident: full-time $15,642; part-time $869 per credit. Required fees: $66 per credit. Tuition and fees vary according to program. *Financial support:* In 2006–07, 6 fellowships (averaging $3,833 per year), 4 research assistantships with full tuition reimbursements (averaging $10,225 per year), 13 teaching assistantships with full tuition reimbursements (averaging $9,000 per year) were awarded; career-related internships or fieldwork, Federal Work-Study, institutionally sponsored loans, and traineeships also available. *Faculty research:* Innovative instruction, diverse learners, transition, scientifically-based evaluation methods, leadership and organizational development. Total annual research expenditures: $926,884. *Unit head:* Dr. Jean P. Lehmann, Interim Director, 970-491-6317, Fax: 970-491-1317, E-mail: jean.lehmann@colostate.edu. *Application contact:* Randi Fuller, Administrative Assistant, 970-491-0545, Fax: 970-491-1317, E-mail: fuller@cahs.colostate.edu.

Concordia University Wisconsin, Graduate Programs, School of Business and Legal Studies, Program in Student Personnel Administration, Mequon, WI 53097-2402. Offers MSSPA. *Students:* 41 (25 women). In 2006, 4 degrees awarded. *Degree requirements:* For master's, thesis or alternative, comprehensive exam. *Entrance requirements:* Additional exam requirements/recommendations for international students: Required—TOEFL. Application fee: $35 ($125 for international students). *Financial support:* Application deadline: 8/1. *Unit head:* Dr. Andrew Luptak, Director, 262-243-4331, E-mail: andy.luptak@cuw.edu.

Eastern Illinois University, Graduate School, College of Education and Professional Studies, Department of Counseling and Student Development, Charleston, IL 61920-3099. Offers college student affairs (MS); community counseling (MS); school counseling (MS). *Accreditation:* ACA; NCATE. Part-time and evening/weekend programs available. *Faculty:* 8 full-time (2 women). In 2006, 61 degrees awarded. *Degree requirements:* For master's, comprehensive exam. *Entrance requirements:* For master's, GRE General Test or MAT. *Application deadline:* For fall admission, 7/31 priority date for domestic students. Applications are processed on a rolling basis. Application fee: $30. *Expenses:* Tuition, state resident: part-time $169 per semester hour. Tuition, nonresident: part-time $508 per semester hour. Required fees: $60 per semester hour. *Financial support:* In 2006–07, research assistantships with tuition reimbursements (averaging $7,200 per year), 4 teaching assistantships with tuition reimbursements (averaging $7,200 per year) were awarded. *Unit head:* Dr. Rick Roberts, Chairperson, 217-581-2400, Fax: 217-581-7417, E-mail: rlroberts@eiu.edu.

Fresno Pacific University, Graduate Programs, Programs in Education, Division of Pupil Personnel Services, Fresno, CA 93702-4709. Offers school counseling (MA Ed); school psychology (MA Ed). *Faculty:* 1 (woman) full-time, 7 part-time/adjunct (3 women). *Students:* 55 full-time (44 women), 37 part-time (27 women); includes 39 minority (5 African Americans, 3 Asian Americans or Pacific Islanders, 31 Hispanic Americans). Average age 35. 10 applicants, 50% accepted, 1 enrolled. In 2006, 24 degrees awarded. *Degree requirements:* For master's, thesis or alternative, registration. *Entrance requirements:* Additional exam requirements/recommendations for international students: Required—TOEFL (minimum score 550 paper-based; 213 computer-based). *Application deadline:* For fall admission, 7/15 for domestic and international students; for spring admission, 11/15 for domestic and international students. Applications are processed on a rolling basis. Application fee: $90. *Expenses:* Tuition: Full-time $7,470; part-time $415 per credit. *Financial support:* In 2006–07, 65 students received support. Applicants required to submit FAFSA. *Unit head:* Dr. Diane Talbot, Head, 559-453-7166, Fax: 559-453-2001, E-mail: dtalbot@fresno.edu.

Hampton University, Graduate College, Department of Education, Program in Counseling, Hampton, VA 23668. Offers college student development (MA); community agency counseling (MA). *Accreditation:* NCATE. Part-time and evening/weekend programs available. *Entrance requirements:* For master's, GRE General Test.

Kansas State University, Graduate School, College of Education, Department of Counseling and Educational Psychology, Manhattan, KS 66506. Offers counseling and student development-college student personnel work (MS); counseling and student development-school counseling (MS); counselor education and supervisors (PhD); school counseling (Ed D); student affairs in higher education (PhD). *Accreditation:* ACA; NCATE. *Faculty:* 12 full-time (6 women). *Students:* 104 full-time (63 women), 30 part-time (16 women); includes 14 minority (10 African Americans, 1 American Indian/Alaska Native, 2 Asian Americans or Pacific Islanders, 1 Hispanic American), 1 international. 45 applicants, 67% accepted, 25 enrolled. In 2006, 37 master's, 3 doctorates awarded. *Degree requirements:* For master's, thesis or alternative, final written exam; for doctorate, thesis/dissertation, comprehensive exam. *Entrance requirements:* For master's, GRE General Test, MAT; for doctorate, GRE General Test. *Application deadline:* For fall admission, 3/1 priority date for domestic students, 2/1 priority date for international students; for spring admission, 10/1 priority date for domestic students, 8/1 priority date for international students. Applications are processed on a rolling basis. Application fee: $30 ($55 for international students). Electronic applications accepted. *Expenses:* Tuition, state resident: full-time $6,352; part-time $240 per credit hour. Tuition, nonresident: full-time $14,296; part-time $571 per credit hour. Required fees: $585. *Financial support:* In 2006–07, 1 research assistantship (averaging $10,868 per year), 3 teaching assistantships with full tuition reimbursements (averaging $11,568 per year) were awarded; career-related internships or fieldwork, institutionally sponsored loans, and scholarships/grants also available. Support available to part-time students. Financial award application deadline: 3/1; financial award applicants required to submit FAFSA. *Faculty research:* College student mental health, college student development, school counselor education, role of religion in student life, multicultural counseling. *Unit head:* Stephen Benton, Head, 785-532-5784, Fax: 785-532-7304, E-mail: leroy@ksu.edu. *Application contact:* Linda Thurston, Director, 785-532-5595, Fax: 785-532-7304, E-mail: coegrads@ksu.edu.

Kent State University, Graduate School of Education, Health, and Human Services, Department of Teaching, Leadership, and Curriculum Studies, Program in Higher Education Administration and Student Personnel, Kent, OH 44242-0001. Offers M Ed, MA. *Accreditation:* NCATE. *Faculty:* 6 full-time (2 women), 2 part-time/adjunct (both women). *Students:* 52 full-time (41 women), 30 part-time (21 women); includes 8 minority (7 African Americans, 1 Asian American or Pacific Islander), 1 international. 65 applicants, 55% accepted. In 2006, 31 degrees awarded. *Degree requirements:* For master's, thesis (for some programs), registration. *Entrance requirements:* Additional exam requirements/recommendations for international students: Required—TOEFL. *Application deadline:* Applications are processed on a rolling basis. Application fee: $30. Electronic applications accepted. *Financial support:* In 2006–07, fellowships with full tuition reimbursements (averaging $7,210 per year); research assistantships with full tuition reimbursements, teaching assistantships with full tuition reimbursements, career-related internships or fieldwork, Federal Work-Study, institutionally sponsored loans, scholarships/grants, health care benefits, and unspecified assistantships also available. Support available to part-time students. Financial award application deadline: 4/1; financial award applicants required to submit FAFSA. *Faculty research:* History/sociology of higher education, organization and administration in higher education. *Unit head:* Dr. Mark Kretovics, Coordinator, 330-672-2477, E-mail: mkretov1@kent.edu. *Application contact:* Nancy Miller, Academic Program Coordinator, Office of Graduate Student Services, 330-672-2576, Fax: 330-672-9162, E-mail: ogs@kent.edu.

Lewis University, College of Arts and Sciences, Program in Organizational Leadership, Romeoville, IL 60446. Offers higher education/student services (MA); organizational management (MA); public administration (MA); training and development (MA). Part-time and evening/weekend programs available. *Entrance requirements:* For master's, bachelor's degree, at least 25 years of age, minimum of 3 years of work experience, minimum GPA of 3.0 (provisional admission possible), letter of recommendation, interview. Additional exam requirements/

recommendations for international students: Required—TOEFL (minimum score 550 paper-based; 213 computer-based). Electronic applications accepted.

Miami University, Graduate School, School of Education and Allied Professions, Department of Educational Leadership, Program in College Student Personnel Services, Oxford, OH 45056. Offers MS. *Accreditation:* NCATE. *Degree requirements:* For master's, thesis or alternative, oral or written exam. *Entrance requirements:* For master's, MAT, minimum undergraduate GPA of 3.0 during previous 2 years or 2.75 overall. Additional exam requirements/recommendations for international students: Required—TOEFL (minimum score 550 paper-based; 213 computer-based), TWE (minimum score 4).

Minnesota State University Mankato, College of Graduate Studies, College of Education, Department of Counseling and Student Personnel, Mankato, MN 56001. Offers college student affairs (MS); marriage and family (Certificate); professional community counseling (MS); professional school counseling (MS). *Accreditation:* ACA (one or more programs are accredited); NCATE. *Students:* 70 full-time (59 women), 39 part-time (34 women). Average age 30. In 2006, 49 degrees awarded. *Degree requirements:* For master's, thesis or alternative, comprehensive exam. *Entrance requirements:* For master's, GRE General Test or MAT (if GPA is below 3.0 for last 2 years), minimum GPA of 3.0 during previous 2 years, 3 letters of reference. Additional exam requirements/recommendations for international students: Required—TOEFL. *Application deadline:* For fall admission, 3/15 priority date for domestic students; for spring admission, 11/20 for domestic students. Applications are processed on a rolling basis. Application fee: $40. Electronic applications accepted. *Financial support:* Research assistantships with full tuition reimbursements, teaching assistantships with full tuition reimbursements, career-related internships or fieldwork, Federal Work-Study, institutionally sponsored loans, and unspecified assistantships available. Support available to part-time students. Financial award application deadline: 3/15; financial award applicants required to submit FAFSA. *Unit head:* Dr. Richard Auger, Chairperson, 507-389-5658. *Application contact:* 507-389-2321, E-mail: grad@mnsu.edu.

New York University, Steinhardt School of Culture, Education and Human Development, Department of Administration, Leadership, and Technology, Program in Higher Education, New York, NY 10012-1019. Offers higher education administration (PhD); student personnel administration higher education (MA). *Accreditation:* Teacher Education Accreditation Council. Part-time and evening/weekend programs available. *Faculty:* 7 full-time (3 women). *Students:* 42 full-time (31 women), 67 part-time (49 women); includes 32 minority (14 African Americans, 9 Asian Americans or Pacific Islanders, 9 Hispanic Americans), 3 international. 148 applicants, 25% accepted, 31 enrolled. In 2006, 27 master's, 7 doctorates awarded. Terminal master's awarded for partial completion of doctoral program. *Degree requirements:* For master's, thesis (for some programs); for doctorate, thesis/dissertation. *Entrance requirements:* For master's, interview, 2 letters of recommendation; for doctorate, GRE General Test, interview. Additional exam requirements/recommendations for international students: Required—TOEFL. *Application deadline:* For fall admission, 12/15 priority date for domestic and international students; for spring admission, 11/1 for domestic and international students. Applications are processed on a rolling basis. Application fee: $50. *Expenses:* Tuition: Part-time $1,080 per unit. Required fees: $56 per unit. $329 per term. Tuition and fees vary according to program. *Financial support:* Fellowships with full and partial tuition reimbursements, career-related internships or fieldwork, Federal Work-Study, institutionally sponsored loans, scholarships/grants, tuition waivers (partial), and unspecified assistantships available. Support available to part-time students. Financial award application deadline: 2/1; financial award applicants required to submit FAFSA. *Faculty research:* Organizational theory and culture, systemic change, leadership development, access, equity and diversity. *Unit head:* Dr. Ann Marcus, Head, 212-998-4041, Fax: 212-995-4041. *Application contact:* 212-998-5030, Fax: 212-995-4328, E-mail: steinhardt.gradadmissions@nyu.edu.

Northeastern University, Bouvé College of Health Sciences Graduate School, Department of Counseling and Applied Educational Psychology, Program in College Student Development and Counseling, Boston, MA 02115-5096. Offers MS. Part-time and evening/weekend programs available. *Faculty:* 1 (woman) full-time, 4 part-time/adjunct (all women). *Students:* 41 full-time (32 women), 18 part-time (15 women). Average age 27. 34 applicants, 76% accepted. In 2006, 18 degrees awarded. *Entrance requirements:* For master's, GRE General Test or MAT. Additional exam requirements/recommendations for international students: Required—TOEFL. Application fee: $50. *Financial support:* Career-related internships or fieldwork, Federal Work-Study, tuition waivers (partial), and unspecified assistantships available. Support available to part-time students. Financial award application deadline: 3/1; financial award applicants required to submit FAFSA. *Unit head:* Dr. Vanessa Johnson, Director, 617-373-5937, E-mail: v.johnson@neu.edu. *Application contact:* Margaret Schnabel, Director of Graduate Admissions, 617-373-2708, Fax: 617-373-4704, E-mail: bouvegrad@neu.edu.

Northwestern State University of Louisiana, Graduate Studies and Research, College of Education, Program in Student Personnel Services, Natchitoches, LA 71497. Offers counseling and guidance (M Ed, Ed S); special education (M Ed, Ed S); student personnel services (MA). *Accreditation:* NCATE (one or more programs are accredited). *Faculty:* 3 full-time (2 women), 2 part-time/adjunct (1 woman). *Students:* 39 full-time (31 women), 12 part-time (all women); includes 29 minority (27 African Americans, 2 American Indian/Alaska Native). Average age 29. In 2006, 13 degrees awarded. *Degree requirements:* For master's, thesis or alternative, comprehensive exam, registration. *Entrance requirements:* For master's, GRE General Test, GRE Subject Test, minimum undergraduate GPA of 2.5. *Application deadline:* For fall admission, 8/1 priority date for domestic students; for spring admission, 1/10 for domestic students. Applications are processed on a rolling basis. Application fee: $20 ($30 for international students). *Financial support:* Application deadline: 7/15. *Application contact:* Dr. Steven G. Horton, Associate Provost/Dean, Graduate Studies, Research, and Information Systems, 318-357-5851, Fax: 318-357-5019, E-mail: grad_school@nsula.edu.

Nova Southeastern University, Graduate School of Humanities and Social Sciences, Department of Conflict Analysis and Resolution, Master's Program in Conflict Analysis and Resolution, Fort Lauderdale, FL 33314-7796. Offers college student affairs (MS); community solutions and partnership (MS); conflict analysis and resolution (MS); JD/MS. *Faculty:* 9 full-time (5 women), 10 part-time/adjunct (4 women). *Students:* 40 full-time (32 women), 64 part-time (53 women); includes 48 minority (32 African Americans, 1 American Indian/Alaska Native, 3 Asian Americans or Pacific Islanders, 12 Hispanic Americans), 9 international. 67 applicants, 63% accepted, 40 enrolled. In 2006, 19 degrees awarded. *Median time to degree:* Master's–2 years full-time, 3 years part-time. *Degree requirements:* For master's, thesis optional. *Entrance requirements:* For master's, interview, minimum GPA of 3.0, writing sample. Application fee: $50. *Faculty research:* International conflict, violence prevention, communication and conflict facilitation, mediation. *Application contact:* Marcia Arango, Student Recruitment Coordinator, 954-262-3006, Fax: 954-262-3968, E-mail: marango@nsu.nova.edu.

Nova Southeastern University, Graduate School of Humanities and Social Sciences, Program in Cross-Disciplinary Studies, Fort Lauderdale, FL 33314-7796. Offers MA. Part-time programs available. Postbaccalaureate distance learning degree programs offered (no on-campus study). *Faculty:* 1 part-time/adjunct (0 women). *Students:* 2 full-time (both women), 28 part-time (26 women); includes 18 minority (12 African Americans, 6 Hispanic Americans), 2 international. 10 applicants, 70% accepted, 7 enrolled. In 2006, 1 degree awarded. *Median time to degree:* Master's–2 years full-time, 3 years part-time. *Degree requirements:* For master's, thesis optional. *Entrance requirements:* For master's, interview, minimum GPA of 3.0. Additional exam requirements/recommendations for international students: Required—TOEFL. *Application deadline:* For fall admission, 7/1 priority date for domestic and international students; for winter admission, 11/1 priority date for domestic and international students; for spring admission, 3/1 priority date for domestic and international students. Applications are processed on a rolling basis. Electronic applications accepted. *Financial support:* Career-related internships or fieldwork, Federal Work-Study, institutionally sponsored loans, and scholarships/grants available. Financial award applicants required to submit CSS PROFILE. *Unit head:* Dr. Suzanne Marshall, Senior Associate Dean, 954-262-3014, Fax: 954-262-3893, E-mail: msuzanne@nsu.nova.edu. *Application contact:* Marcia Arango, Student Recruitment Coordinator, 954-262-3006, Fax: 954-262-3968, E-mail: marango@nsu.nova.edu.

The Ohio State University, Graduate School, College of Education and Human Ecology, Program in Education, Columbus, OH 43210. Offers higher education and student affairs (MA). *Students:* Average age 47. *Application deadline:* Applications are processed on a rolling basis. Application fee: $40 ($50 for international students). Electronic applications accepted. *Expenses:* Tuition, state resident: full-time $9,438. Tuition, nonresident: full-time $22,791. Tuition and fees vary according to course load, campus/location and program. *Unit head:* Sonora Stroot, Graduate Studies Committee Chair, 614-292-8368, Fax: 614-292-2581, E-mail: stroot.1@osu.edu. *Application contact:* Graduate Admissions, 614-292-9444, Fax: 614-292-3985, E-mail: domestic.grad@osu.edu.

Ohio University, Graduate Studies, College of Education, Department of Counseling and Higher Education, Athens, OH 45701-2979. Offers college student personnel (M Ed); community/agency counseling (M Ed); counselor education (PhD); higher education (M Ed, PhD); rehabilitation counseling (M Ed); school counseling (M Ed). *Accreditation:* ACA; CORE. Part-time and evening/weekend programs available. *Faculty:* 12 full-time (5 women), 6 part-time/adjunct (0 women). *Students:* 123 full-time (89 women), 111 part-time (73 women); includes 20 minority (18 African Americans, 2 Hispanic Americans), 42 international. 209 applicants, 62% accepted, 106 enrolled. In 2006, 40 master's, 7 doctorates awarded. *Median time to degree:* Of those who began their doctoral program in fall 1998, 92% received their degree in 8 years or less. *Degree requirements:* For master's, thesis or alternative, registration; for doctorate, thesis/dissertation, comprehensive exam, registration. *Entrance requirements:* For master's, GRE General Test or MAT (if GPA below 2.9), 3 letters of reference, 5-page biography, statement of purpose; for doctorate, GRE General Test, work experience, minimum GPA of 3.4. Additional exam requirements/recommendations for international students: Required—TOEFL (minimum score 550 paper-based; 213 computer-based). *Application deadline:* For fall admission, 3/1 for domestic and international students. Applications are processed on a rolling basis. Application fee: $45. Electronic applications accepted. *Financial support:* In 2006–07, 66 students received support, including 35 research assistantships with full tuition reimbursements available (averaging $6,500 per year), 6 teaching assistantships with full tuition reimbursements available (averaging $7,200 per year); Federal Work-Study, institutionally sponsored loans, and unspecified assistantships also available. Financial award application deadline: 3/15. *Faculty research:* Youth violence, gender studies, student affairs, chemical dependency, disabilities issues. Total annual research expenditures: $527,983. *Unit head:* Dr. Jerry Olsheski, Chair, 740-593-0032, Fax: 740-593-0477, E-mail: olsheski@ohio.edu. *Application contact:* Floyd J. Doney, Director of Student Affairs, 740-593-4400, Fax: 740-593-9310, E-mail: doney@ohio.edu.

Oklahoma State University, College of Education, School of Applied Health and Educational Psychology, Stillwater, OK 74078. Offers applied behavioral studies (MS, Ed D, PhD); counseling and student personnel (MS, PhD); educational psychology (PhD); health (MS, Ed D); leisure sciences (MS, Ed D); physical education (MS, Ed D); physical education and leisure sciences (Ed D); school psychology (Ed S). *Accreditation:* APA (one or more programs are accredited). Part-time programs available. *Faculty:* 37 full-time (17 women), 12 part-time/adjunct (8 women). *Students:* 189 full-time (137 women), 180 part-time (113 women); includes 75 minority (25 African Americans, 34 American Indian/Alaska Native, 5 Asian Americans or Pacific Islanders, 11 Hispanic Americans), 27 international. Average age 33. 275 applicants, 28% accepted, 64 enrolled. In 2006, 45 master's, 21 doctorates awarded. *Degree requirements:* For master's, thesis or alternative; for doctorate, thesis/dissertation. *Entrance requirements:* For master's, GRE or MAT; for doctorate, GRE (PhD). Additional exam requirements/recommendations for international students: Required—TOEFL. *Application deadline:* For fall admission, 7/1 priority date for domestic students, 3/1 priority date for international students; for spring admission, 8/1 priority date for international students. Applications are processed on a rolling basis. Application fee: $40 ($75 for international students). Electronic applications accepted. *Expenses:* Tuition, state resident: part-time $146 per credit hour. Tuition, nonresident: part-time $516 per credit hour. Required fees: $44 per credit hour. Tuition and fees vary according to program. *Financial support:* In 2006–07, 29 research assistantships (averaging $6,452 per year), 64 teaching assistantships (averaging $8,263 per year) were awarded; career-related internships or fieldwork, Federal Work-Study, scholarships/grants, health care benefits, tuition waivers (partial), and unspecified assistantships also available. Support available to part-time students. Financial award application deadline: 3/1. *Unit head:* Dr. John Romans, Head, 405-744-6040.

Oregon State University, Graduate School, College of Education, Program in College Student Service Administration, Corvallis, OR 97331. Offers Ed M, MS. *Students:* 33 full-time (27 women), 9 part-time (6 women); includes 10 minority (3 African Americans, 1 American Indian/Alaska Native, 4 Asian Americans or Pacific Islanders, 2 Hispanic Americans), 1 international. Average age 28. In 2006, 23 degrees awarded. *Degree requirements:* For master's, thesis or alternative. *Entrance requirements:* For master's, minimum GPA of 3.0 in last 90 hours of course work. Additional exam requirements/recommendations for international students: Required—TOEFL. *Application deadline:* For fall admission, 3/1 for domestic students. Applications are processed on a rolling basis. Application fee: $50. *Financial support:* Teaching assistantships, career-related internships or fieldwork, Federal Work-Study, and institutionally sponsored loans available. Support available to part-time students. Financial award application deadline: 2/1. *Faculty research:* Improvement of student activities, administering recreational sports programs. *Unit head:* Dr. Richard Shintaku, Head, 541-737-9324. *Application contact:* Lloye A. Liedtke, Program Associate, Fax: 541-737-8725, E-mail: lloye.liedtke@orst.edu.

Penn State University Park, Graduate School, College of Education, Department of Education Policy Studies, State College, University Park, PA 16802-1503. Offers college student affairs (M Ed); educational leadership (M Ed, MS, D Ed, PhD); educational theory and policy (MA, PhD); higher education (M Ed, D Ed, PhD). *Accreditation:* NCATE. *Unit head:* Dr. Jacqueline A. Stefkovich, Head, 814-863-0619, E-mail: jas71@psu.edu.

Providence College and Theological Seminary, Theological Seminary, Otterburne, MB R0A 1G0, Canada. Offers children's ministry (Certificate); Christian studies (MA, Certificate); counseling (MA); cross-cultural discipleship (Certificate); divinity (M Div); educational studies (MA), including counseling psychology, educational ministries, student development, teaching English to speakers of other languages, training teachers of English to speakers of other languages; global studies (MA); lay counseling (Diploma); ministry (D Min); teaching English to speakers of other languages (Certificate); theological studies (MA); training teacher of English to speakers of other languages (Certificate); youth ministry (Certificate). *Accreditation:* ATS. Part-time programs available. *Degree requirements:* For M Div, 2 foreign languages, thesis (for some programs), comprehensive exam; for master's, variable foreign language requirement, thesis (for some programs); for doctorate, thesis/dissertation. *Entrance requirements:* Additional exam requirements/recommendations for international students: Recommended—TOEFL (minimum score 550 paper-based; 213 computer-based). *Faculty research:* Studies in Isaiah, theology of sin.

St. Cloud State University, School of Graduate Studies, College of Education, Department of Counselor Education and Educational Psychology, Program in College Counseling and Student Development, St. Cloud, MN 56301-4498. Offers MS. *Faculty:* 12 full-time (5 women). *Students:* 11 full-time (8 women), 4 part-time (all women); includes 1 minority (Asian American or Pacific Islander) 21 applicants, 81% accepted. In 2006, 11 degrees awarded. *Degree requirements:* For master's, thesis or alternative, comprehensive exam. *Entrance requirements:* For master's, GRE General Test, minimum GPA of 2.75. Additional exam requirements/recommendations for international students: Required—MELAB; Recommended—TOEFL (minimum score 550 paper-based; 213 computer-based), IELTS (minimum score 7). *Application deadline:* For fall admission, 3/1 for domestic and international students. Application fee: $35. Electronic applications accepted. *Financial support:* Federal Work-Study, scholarships/grants, and unspecified

Student Affairs

St. Cloud State University (continued)

assistantships available. Financial award application deadline: 3/1. *Unit head:* Dr. Dan Macari, Coordinator, 320-308-1044, E-mail: dpmacari@stcloudstate.edu. *Application contact:* Linda Lou Krueger, School of Graduate Studies, 320-308-2113, Fax: 320-308-5371, E-mail: lekrueger@stcloudstate.edu.

Saint Louis University, Graduate School, College of Public Service and Graduate School, Department of Educational Leadership and Higher Education, St. Louis, MO 63103-2097. Offers Catholic school leadership (MA); educational administration (MA, Ed D, PhD, Ed S); higher education (MA, Ed D, PhD); student personnel administration (MA). *Accreditation:* NCATE. *Faculty:* 11 full-time (4 women), 13 part-time/adjunct (4 women). *Students:* 43 full-time (26 women), 280 part-time (148 women); includes 38 minority (33 African Americans, 1 American Indian/Alaska Native, 3 Asian Americans or Pacific Islanders, 1 Hispanic American). Average age 38. 157 applicants, 79% accepted, 88 enrolled. In 2006, 18 master's, 55 doctorates, 16 other advanced degrees awarded. *Degree requirements:* For master's, comprehensive written and oral exam; for doctorate, thesis/dissertation, preliminary oral and written exams, comprehensive exam, registration. *Entrance requirements:* For master's, GRE General Test, MAT, LSAT, GMAT, MCAT, letters of recommendation, resumé; for doctorate and Ed S, GRE General Test, LSAT, GMAT, MCAT, letters of recommendation, resumé. Additional exam requirements/recommendations for international students: Required—TOEFL (minimum score 525 paper-based; 194 computer-based). *Application deadline:* For fall admission, 7/1 for domestic and international students; for spring admission, 11/1 for domestic and international students. Applications are processed on a rolling basis. Application fee: $40. *Expenses:* Tuition: Part-time $800 per credit hour. Required fees: $105 per semester. *Financial support:* In 2006–07, 84 students received support, including 6 teaching assistantships with full tuition reimbursements available (averaging $11,000 per year); Federal Work-Study, scholarships/grants, traineeships, health care benefits, tuition waivers (partial), and unspecified assistantships also available. Support available to part-time students. Financial award application deadline: 6/1; financial award applicants required to submit FAFSA. *Faculty research:* Superintendent of schools, school finance, school facilities, student personal administration, building leadership. Total annual research expenditures: $100,000. *Unit head:* Dr. William T. Rebore, Chairperson, 314-977-2508, E-mail: reborewt@slu.edu. *Application contact:* Gary Behrman, Associate Dean of the Graduate School, 314-977-3827, E-mail: behrmang@slu.edu.

San Jose State University, Graduate Studies and Research, College of Education, Department of Counselor Education, San Jose, CA 95192-0001. Offers education (counseling and student personnel) (MA). *Accreditation:* NCATE. Evening/weekend programs available. *Students:* 134 full-time (107 women), 64 part-time (52 women); includes 117 minority (22 African Americans, 2 American Indian/Alaska Native, 23 Asian Americans or Pacific Islanders, 70 Hispanic Americans), 2 international. Average age 31. 128 applicants, 78% accepted, 75 enrolled. In 2006, 62 degrees awarded. *Degree requirements:* For master's, thesis or alternative. *Application deadline:* For fall admission, 6/29 for domestic students; for spring admission, 11/30 for domestic students. Applications are processed on a rolling basis. Application fee: $59. Electronic applications accepted. *Financial support:* Career-related internships or fieldwork available. Financial award applicants required to submit FAFSA. *Unit head:* Dr. Xialou Hu, Chair, 408-924-3636, Fax: 408-924-3713.

Seton Hall University, College of Education and Human Services, Department of Education Leadership, Management and Policy, Program in College Student Personnel Administration, South Orange, NJ 07079-2697. Offers MA. Part-time and evening/weekend programs available. *Faculty:* 12 full-time (4 women), 1 part-time/adjunct (0 women). *Students:* 44 full-time (24 women), 158 part-time (65 women); includes 13 minority (9 African Americans, 1 Asian American or Pacific Islander, 3 Hispanic Americans). Average age 33. 63 applicants, 100% accepted, 39 enrolled. In 2006, 164 degrees awarded. *Degree requirements:* For master's, registration. *Entrance requirements:* For master's, GRE or MAT (within past 5 years), minimum GPA of 3.0. *Application deadline:* Applications are processed on a rolling basis. Application fee: $50. *Unit head:* Dr. Charles Mitchell, Chair, 973-275-2446, E-mail: mitchca@shu.edu. *Application contact:* Information Contact, 973-761-9668.

Slippery Rock University of Pennsylvania, Graduate Studies (Recruitment), College of Education, Department of Counseling and Development, Slippery Rock, PA 16057-1383. Offers community counseling (MA), including addiction, adult, child and adolescent; elementary guidance and counseling (M Ed); secondary guidance and counseling (M Ed); student personnel (MA). *Accreditation:* ACA (one or more programs are accredited); NCATE. Part-time and evening/weekend programs available. *Degree requirements:* For master's, thesis (for some programs), oral comprehensive exam. *Entrance requirements:* For master's, GRE General Test, MAT, minimum GPA of 2.75. Additional exam requirements/recommendations for international students: Required—TOEFL (minimum score 550 paper-based; 213 computer-based). *Application deadline:* For fall admission, 7/1 priority date for domestic and international students; for spring admission, 11/1 priority date for domestic and international students. Applications are processed on a rolling basis. Application fee: $25. Electronic applications accepted. *Expenses:* Tuition, state resident: part-time $336 per credit. Tuition, nonresident: part-time $538 per credit. Required fees: $84 per credit. $37 per semester. *Financial support:* Career-related internships or fieldwork, Federal Work-Study, scholarships/grants, and unspecified assistantships available. Support available to part-time students. Financial award application deadline: 5/1; financial award applicants required to submit FAFSA. *Unit head:* Dr. Donald Strano, Graduate Coordinator, 724-738-2035, Fax: 724-738-2880, E-mail: donald.strano@sru.edu. *Application contact:* April Longwell, Interim Director of Graduate Studies, 724-738-2051 Ext. 2116, Fax: 724-738-2146, E-mail: graduate.studies@sru.edu.

Springfield College, Graduate Programs, Programs in Psychology and Counseling, Springfield, MA 01109-3797. Offers athletic counseling (M Ed, MS, CAS); general counseling (M Ed); industrial/organizational psychology (MS, CAS); marriage and family therapy (M Ed, MS, CAS); mental health counseling (M Ed, MS, CAS); school guidance and counseling (M Ed, MS, CAS); student personnel in higher education (M Ed, MS, CAS). Part-time and evening/weekend programs available. *Faculty:* 14 full-time (8 women), 17 part-time/adjunct (7 women). *Students:* 213. Average age 28. 161 applicants, 84% accepted, 77 enrolled. In 2006, 93 master's, 1 other advanced degree awarded. *Degree requirements:* For master's, thesis (for some programs), research project, internship, comprehensive exam. *Entrance requirements:* For master's and CAS, interview. Additional exam requirements/recommendations for international students: Required—TOEFL (minimum score 550 paper-based; 213 computer-based). *Application deadline:* For fall admission, 1/15 priority date for domestic students; for winter admission, 11/1 for domestic students; for spring admission, 12/1 for domestic students. Applications are processed on a rolling basis. Application fee: $50. Electronic applications accepted. *Expenses:* Tuition: Full-time $12,222; part-time $679 per credit. Required fees: $25; $25 per year. One-time fee: $25 full-time. *Financial support:* In 2006–07, 8 fellowships with partial tuition reimbursements (averaging $2,000 per year), 2 research assistantships (averaging $4,000 per year), 7 teaching assistantships (averaging $1,800 per year) were awarded; career-related internships or fieldwork, Federal Work-Study, institutionally sponsored loans, scholarships/grants, and tuition waivers (full and partial) also available. Financial award application deadline: 3/1. *Faculty research:* Sport psychology, leadership and emotional intelligence, violence and terrorism, performance enhancement, cognitive function. Total annual research expenditures: $715,109. *Unit head:* Dr. Anna L. Moriarty, Director, 413-748-3322, Fax: 413-748-3854, E-mail: anna_l_moriarty@spfldcol.edu. *Application contact:* Donald James Shaw, Director of Graduate Admissions, 413-748-3060, Fax: 413-748-3069, E-mail: donald_shaw_jr@spfldcol.edu.

Teachers College Columbia University, Graduate Faculty of Education, Department of Organization and Leadership, New York, NY 10027-6696. Offers adult education (MA, Ed D); education leadership (Ed M, MA, Ed D, PhD), including education leadership (PhD), education leadership studies (Ed M, MA, Ed D), leadership, policy and politics, private school leadership (Ed M, MA, Ed D), public school and school district leadership (Ed M, MA, Ed D); educational administration (Ed M, MA, Ed D, PhD); higher education (Ed M, MA, Ed D, PhD); inquiry in education leadership (Ed D); nurse executive (Ed M, MA, Ed D); politics and education (Ed M, MA, Ed D, PhD); social and organizational psychology (MA, Ed D, PhD), including organizational psychology, social psychology (Ed D, PhD); student personnel administration (Ed M, MA, Ed D); MBA/Ed D. Part-time and evening/weekend programs available. *Faculty:* 23 full-time (12 women). *Students:* 349 full-time (203 women), 503 part-time (265 women); includes 249 minority (109 African Americans, 2 American Indian/Alaska Native, 83 Asian Americans or Pacific Islanders, 55 Hispanic Americans), 53 international. Average age 35. 839 applicants, 61% accepted, 261 enrolled. In 2006, 210 master's, 97 doctorates awarded. *Degree requirements:* For doctorate, thesis/dissertation. *Application deadline:* For fall admission, 5/15 for domestic students. Application fee: $65. *Expenses:* Tuition: Full-time $23,400; part-time $975 per credit. Required fees: $320 per term. *Financial support:* Fellowships, research assistantships, career-related internships or fieldwork, Federal Work-Study, institutionally sponsored loans, and tuition waivers (full and partial) available. Support available to part-time students. Financial award application deadline: 2/1. *Unit head:* Warner Burke, Chair, 212-678-3258. *Application contact:* Debbie Lesperance, Assistant Director of Admission, 212-678-3710, Fax: 212-678-4171.

See Close-Up on page 1131.

Tennessee Technological University, Graduate School, College of Education, Department of Counseling and Psychology, Cookeville, TN 38505. Offers educational psychology (MA, Ed S); educational psychology and student personnel (MA, Ed S). *Accreditation:* NCATE (one or more programs are accredited). Part-time and evening/weekend programs available. *Faculty:* 24 full-time (6 women). *Students:* 43 full-time (34 women), 35 part-time (27 women); includes 7 minority (6 African Americans, 1 Asian American or Pacific Islander). Average age 27. 44 applicants, 82% accepted, 27 enrolled. In 2006, 23 master's, 19 other advanced degrees awarded. *Degree requirements:* For Ed S, thesis or alternative. *Entrance requirements:* For master's, MAT; for Ed S, MAT, NTE. Additional exam requirements/recommendations for international students: Required—TOEFL. *Application deadline:* For fall admission, 3/1 priority date for domestic students; for spring admission, 8/1 for domestic students. Application fee: $25 ($30 for international students). Electronic applications accepted. *Expenses:* Tuition, state resident: full-time $8,748; part-time $319 per hour. Tuition, nonresident: full-time $23,524; part-time $740 per hour. *Financial support:* In 2006–07, 1 fellowship (averaging $8,000 per year), 8 research assistantships (averaging $4,000 per year), 3 teaching assistantships (averaging $4,000 per year) were awarded; career-related internships or fieldwork also available. Financial award application deadline: 4/1. *Unit head:* Dr. Michael Rohr, Chairperson, 931-372-3457, Fax: 931-372-6319. *Application contact:* Dr. Francis O. Otuonye, Associate Vice President for Research and Graduate Studies, 931-372-3233, Fax: 931-372-3497, E-mail: fotuonye@tntech.edu.

University of Bridgeport, School of Education and Human Resources, Division of Human Resources, Bridgeport, CT 06604. Offers college student personnel (MS); community counseling (MS); human resource development (MS). Part-time and evening/weekend programs available. *Faculty:* 6 full-time (3 women), 14 part-time/adjunct (9 women). *Students:* 27 full-time (21 women), 76 part-time (59 women); includes 42 minority (30 African Americans, 1 American Indian/Alaska Native, 1 Asian American or Pacific Islander, 10 Hispanic Americans), 23 international. Average age 34. 84 applicants, 70% accepted, 37 enrolled. In 2006, 25 degrees awarded. *Degree requirements:* For master's, thesis optional. *Application deadline:* For fall admission, 8/1 priority date for domestic students; for spring admission, 12/1 priority date for domestic students. Applications are processed on a rolling basis. Application fee: $25 ($35 for international students). Electronic applications accepted. *Financial support:* In 2006–07, 27 students received support; fellowships, research assistantships, teaching assistantships, career-related internships or fieldwork, Federal Work-Study, and institutionally sponsored loans available. Support available to part-time students. Financial award application deadline: 6/1; financial award applicants required to submit FAFSA. *Faculty research:* Corporate elder care programs. *Unit head:* Dr. Joseph T. Cullen, Head, 203-576-4175.

University of Central Arkansas, Graduate School, Graduate School of Management, Leadership, and Administration, Program in College Student Personnel, Conway, AR 72035-0001. Offers MS. *Students:* 37 full-time (23 women), 14 part-time (10 women); includes 15 minority (12 African Americans, 1 American Indian/Alaska Native, 1 Asian American or Pacific Islander, 1 Hispanic American), 3 international. 26 applicants, 100% accepted, 26 enrolled. In 2006, 13 degrees awarded. *Degree requirements:* For master's, thesis, comprehensive exam. *Entrance requirements:* For master's, GRE General Test, minimum GPA of 2.7. Additional exam requirements/recommendations for international students: Required—TOEFL (minimum score 550 paper-based; 213 computer-based). *Application deadline:* For fall admission, 3/1 priority date for domestic students; for spring admission, 10/1 priority date for domestic students. Applications are processed on a rolling basis. Application fee: $25 ($40 for international students). *Expenses:* *Contact institution.* One-time fee: $65 part-time. *Financial support:* Applicants required to submit FAFSA. *Unit head:* Dr. John Smith, Coordinator, 501-450-5303, Fax: 501-450-5469, E-mail: johns@uca.edu. *Application contact:* Nanette Fitzhugh, Administrative Assistant, 501-450-5063, Fax: 501-450-5678, E-mail: fitzhugh@uca.edu.

University of Central Missouri, The Graduate School, College of Education, Department of Educational Leadership and Human Development, Program in College Student Personnel Administration, Warrensburg, MO 64093. Offers MS. *Accreditation:* NCATE. Part-time programs available. *Students:* 39 full-time (29 women), 153 part-time (95 women); includes 17 minority (12 African Americans, 1 American Indian/Alaska Native, 1 Asian American or Pacific Islander, 3 Hispanic Americans), 1 international. Average age 34. 41 applicants, 68% accepted, 25 enrolled. In 2006, 39 degrees awarded. *Degree requirements:* For master's, thesis, internship. *Entrance requirements:* For master's, minimum GPA of 2.75, teaching certificate. Additional exam requirements/recommendations for international students: Required—TOEFL (minimum score 500 paper-based; 173 computer-based). *Application deadline:* For fall admission, 6/1 priority date for domestic students, 5/1 priority date for international students; for spring admission, 10/1 priority date for domestic students, 10/1 for international students. Applications are processed on a rolling basis. Application fee: $30 ($50 for international students). *Expenses:* Tuition, state resident: full-time $5,448; part-time $227 per credit hour. Tuition, nonresident: full-time $10,896; part-time $454 per credit hour. Required fees: $336; $14 per credit hour. *Financial support:* Teaching assistantships with full tuition reimbursements, career-related internships or fieldwork, Federal Work-Study, and scholarships/grants available. Support available to part-time students. Financial award application deadline: 3/1; financial award applicants required to submit FAFSA. *Faculty research:* Theories of college student development, higher education administration, counseling skills, university residence hall administration, higher education law. *Unit head:* Dr. Doug Thomas, Chair, 660-543-8834, Fax: 660-543-4164, E-mail: thomas@ucmo.edu.

University of Dayton, Graduate School, School of Education and Allied Professions, Department of Counselor Education and Human Services, Dayton, OH 45469-1300. Offers college student personnel (MS Ed); community counseling (MS Ed); higher education administration (MS Ed); human development services (MS Ed); school counseling (MS Ed); school psychology (MS Ed, Ed S); teacher as child/youth development specialist (MS Ed). *Accreditation:* NCATE. Part-time and evening/weekend programs available. *Faculty:* 11 full-time (7 women), 32 part-time/adjunct (17 women). *Students:* 271 full-time (234 women), 316 part-time (263 women); includes 85 minority (69 African Americans, 3 American Indian/Alaska Native, 13 Hispanic Americans), 1 international. Average age 32. 363 applicants, 47% accepted, 121 enrolled. In 2006, 267 degrees awarded. *Degree requirements:* For master's, exit exam, thesis optional. *Entrance requirements:* For master's, MAT or GRE (if GPA is below 2.75), interview. Additional exam requirements/recommendations for international students: Required—TOEFL (minimum score 550 paper-based; 213 computer-based). *Application deadline:* For fall admission, 2/15 priority date for domestic students, 4/10 priority date for international students; for winter admission, 9/10 priority date for international students; for spring admission, 1/10 priority date for international students. Applications are processed on a rolling basis. Application fee: $0. Electronic applications accepted. *Expenses:* Tuition: Part-time $601 per semester hour. Tuition and fees vary according to degree level and program. *Financial support:* In 2006–07, 1 research assistantship with partial tuition reimbursement (averaging $7,400 per year), 4 teaching assistantships with partial tuition reimbursements (averaging $7,600 per year) were awarded; career-related internships or fieldwork, institutionally sponsored loans, health care benefits, and unspecified assistantships also available. Financial award applicants required to submit FAFSA. *Faculty research:* Anger as part of the grief process, inclusion of children with severe disabilities, comparisons of school counselors in Bosnia and the U. S., graduate and professional student socialization, use of cohort groups in doctoral programs. *Unit head:* Dr. Thomas W. Rueth, Chairperson, 937-229-3644, Fax: 937-229-1055, E-mail: thomas.rueth@notes.udayton.edu. *Application contact:* Erika Eavers, Graduate Admission Processor, 937-229-3065, Fax: 937-229-4729, E-mail: erika.eavers@notes.udayton.edu.

University of Florida, Graduate School, College of Education, Department of Educational Administration and Policy, Gainesville, FL 32611. Offers curriculum and instruction (Ed D, PhD); educational leadership (M Ed, MAE, Ed D, PhD, Ed S); higher education administration (Ed D, PhD, Ed S); student personnel in higher education (M Ed, MAE); PhD/JD. *Accreditation:* NCATE. *Faculty:* 10 full-time (3 women). *Degree requirements:* For master's, thesis optional; for doctorate, variable foreign language requirement, thesis/dissertation. *Entrance requirements:* For master's, GRE General Test, minimum GPA of 3.0, teaching experience; for doctorate and Ed S, GRE General Test, minimum GPA of 3.0. Additional exam requirements/recommendations for international students: Required—TOEFL (minimum score 550 paper-based; 213 computer-based). *Application deadline:* For fall admission, 6/1 priority date for domestic students. Applications are processed on a rolling basis. Application fee: $30. Electronic applications accepted. *Expenses:* Tuition, state resident: full-time $6,827. Tuition, nonresident: full-time $21,951. Required fees: $999. *Financial support:* In 2006–07, 2 research assistantships (averaging $9,424 per year) were awarded; fellowships, teaching assistantships, career-related internships or fieldwork and unspecified assistantships also available. *Faculty research:* Educational finance, community education, middle school curriculum, community college administration. *Unit head:* Linda Hagedorn, Chair, 352-392-2391 Ext. 275. *Application contact:* Dr. Katherine Gratto, Coordinator, 352-392-2391 Ext. 274, Fax: 352-392-0038, E-mail: kgratto@coe.ufl.edu.

The University of Iowa, Graduate College, College of Education, Department of Counseling, Rehabilitation, and Student Development, Iowa City, IA 52242-1316. Offers administration and research (PhD); counselor education and supervision (PhD); rehabilitation counseling (MA); rehabilitation counselor education (PhD); school counseling (MA); student development (MA, PhD). *Accreditation:* ACA (one or more programs are accredited); CORE (one or more programs are accredited). *Faculty:* 14 full-time, 3 part-time/adjunct. *Students:* 86 full-time (67 women), 31 part-time (21 women); includes 20 minority (15 African Americans, 2 Asian Americans or Pacific Islanders, 3 Hispanic Americans), 7 international. 63 applicants, 60% accepted, 25 enrolled. In 2006, 34 master's, 4 doctorates awarded. *Degree requirements:* For master's, exam, thesis optional; for doctorate, thesis/dissertation, comprehensive exam, registration. *Entrance requirements:* For master's and doctorate, GRE General Test, minimum GPA of 3.0. Additional exam requirements/recommendations for international students: Required—TOEFL (minimum score 550 paper-based; 213 computer-based; 81 iBT). Application fee: $60 ($85 for international students). Electronic applications accepted. *Financial support:* In 2006–07, 1 fellowship, 21 research assistantships with partial tuition reimbursements, 37 teaching assistantships with partial tuition reimbursements were awarded. Financial award applicants required to submit FAFSA. *Unit head:* Dr. Dennis R. Maki, Chair, 319-335-5275, Fax: 319-335-5291.

University of Louisville, Graduate School, College of Education and Human Development, Department of Educational and Counseling Psychology, Louisville, KY 40292-0001. Offers college student personnel services (M Ed); counseling and personnel services (M Ed, PhD), including school counseling and guidance; counseling psychology (M Ed, PhD); expressive therapies (M Ed); mental health counseling (PhD). *Accreditation:* APA; NCATE. *Students:* 122 full-time (90 women), 125 part-time (100 women); includes 54 minority (48 African Americans, 1 American Indian/Alaska Native, 5 Asian Americans or Pacific Islanders), 6 international. Average age 35. In 2006, 78 master's, 9 doctorates awarded. *Degree requirements:* For doctorate, thesis/dissertation. *Entrance requirements:* For master's and doctorate, GRE General Test. *Application deadline:* Applications are processed on a rolling basis. Application fee: $50. Electronic applications accepted. *Financial support:* Fellowships, research assistantships, teaching assistantships, Federal Work-Study and scholarships/grants available. *Unit head:* Dr. Samuel C Stringfield, Acting Chair, 502-852-6884, Fax: 502-852-0629, E-mail: sam.stringfield@louisville.edu.

University of Maryland, College Park, Graduate Studies, College of Education, Department of Counseling and Personnel Services, College Park, MD 20742. Offers college student personnel (M Ed, MA); college student personnel administration (PhD); community counseling (CAGS); community/career counseling (M Ed, MA); counseling and personnel services (M Ed, MA, PhD); counseling psychology (PhD); counselor education (PhD); rehabilitation counseling (M Ed, MA); school counseling (M Ed, MA); school psychology (M Ed, MA, PhD). *Accreditation:* ACA (one or more programs are accredited); APA (one or more programs are accredited); CORE (one or more programs are accredited); NCATE. Part-time and evening/weekend programs available. Postbaccalaureate distance learning degree programs offered (no on-campus study). *Faculty:* 41 full-time (26 women), 6 part-time/adjunct (5 women). *Students:* 169 full-time (124 women), 21 part-time (15 women); includes 76 minority (42 African Americans, 1 American Indian/Alaska Native, 14 Asian Americans or Pacific Islanders, 19 Hispanic Americans), 11 international. 382 applicants, 15% accepted, 31 enrolled. In 2006, 57 master's, 13 doctorates, 10 other advanced degrees awarded. *Degree requirements:* For master's, thesis (for some programs); for doctorate, thesis/dissertation. *Entrance requirements:* For master's, GRE General Test or MAT, minimum GPA of 3.0, 3 letters of recommendation; for doctorate, GRE General Test or MAT, minimum GPA of 3.5, 3 letters of recommendation. Additional exam requirements/recommendations for international students: Required—TOEFL. *Application deadline:* For fall admission, 3/1 for domestic students, 2/1 for international students; for spring admission, 9/1 for domestic students, 6/1 for international students. Applications are processed on a rolling basis. Application fee: $60. Electronic applications accepted. *Financial support:* In 2006–07, 11 fellowships with full tuition reimbursements (averaging $8,799 per year), 14 research assistantships (averaging $12,849 per year), 100 teaching assistantships with tuition reimbursements (averaging $14,265 per year) were awarded; career-related internships or fieldwork, Federal Work-Study, and scholarships/grants also available. Support available to part-time students. Financial award applicants required to submit FAFSA. *Faculty research:* Educational psychology, counseling, health. Total annual research expenditures: $2.1 million. *Unit head:* Dr. Ruth Fassingel, Dean, 301-405-2860, Fax: 301-405-9995, E-mail: rfassing@umd.edu. *Application contact:* Dean of Graduate School, 301-405-0358, Fax: 301-314-9305.

University of Miami, Graduate School, School of Education, Department of Educational and Psychological Studies, Program in Higher Education Administration, Coral Gables, FL 33124. Offers higher education administration (MS Ed), including enrollment management, student life and development; higher education administration/enrollment management (Certificate). *Accreditation:* NCATE. *Students:* 5 full-time (4 women), 11 part-time (10 women); includes 9 minority (4 African Americans, 1 Asian American or Pacific Islander, 4 Hispanic Americans). Average age 33. 8 applicants, 100% accepted, 5 enrolled. In 2006, 2 degrees awarded. *Entrance requirements:* For master's, GRE General Test. Additional exam requirements/recommendations for international students: Required—TOEFL (minimum score 550 paper-based; 212 computer-based). *Application deadline:* Applications are processed on a rolling basis. Application fee: $50. Electronic applications accepted. *Financial support:* In 2006–07, 16 students received support; fellowships with partial tuition reimbursements available, research assistantships with partial tuition reimbursements available, career-related internships or fieldwork, Federal Work-Study, institutionally sponsored loans, scholarships/grants, and unspecified assistantships available. Financial award application deadline: 3/1; financial award applicants required to submit FAFSA. *Unit head:* Dr. Carol Anne Phekoo, Coordinator, 305-284-5013, Fax: 305-284-3003, E-mail: cphekoo@miami.edu. *Application contact:* Shelley Lue Foung, Senior Administrative Assistant, 305-284-3001, Fax: 305-284-3003, E-mail: sluefoung@miami.edu.

University of Minnesota, Twin Cities Campus, Graduate School, College of Education and Human Development, Department of Educational Psychology, Program in Counseling and Student Personnel Psychology, Minneapolis, MN 55455-0213. Offers MA, PhD, Ed S. *Students:* 109 full-time (88 women), 11 part-time (7 women); includes 16 minority (5 African Americans, 2 American Indian/Alaska Native, 7 Asian Americans or Pacific Islanders, 2 Hispanic Americans), 16 international. Average age 30. 127 applicants, 48% accepted, 39 enrolled. In 2006, 33 master's, 4 doctorates awarded. *Expenses:* Tuition, state resident: full-time $9,302; part-time $775 per credit. Tuition, nonresident: full-time $16,400; part-time $1,367 per credit. Full-time tuition and fees vary according to class time, course load, program, reciprocity agreements and student level. *Application contact:* Dr. Mary Bents, Associate Dean, 612-625-6501, Fax: 612-626-1580, E-mail: mbents@tc.umn.edu.

University of Mississippi, Graduate School, School of Education, Department of Educational Leadership and Counselor Education, Oxford, University, MS 38677. Offers counselor education (M Ed, PhD, Specialist); educational leadership (PhD); educational leadership and counselor education (M Ed, MA, Ed D, Ed S); higher education/student personnel (MA). *Accreditation:* ACA; NCATE. *Faculty:* 14 full-time (9 women), 4 part-time/adjunct (2 women). *Students:* 171 full-time (113 women), 158 part-time (110 women); includes 93 minority (88 African Americans, 2 Asian Americans or Pacific Islanders, 3 Hispanic Americans), 11 international. In 2006, 76 master's, 9 doctorates, 22 other advanced degrees awarded. *Degree requirements:* For doctorate, thesis/dissertation. *Entrance requirements:* For master's, GRE General Test, minimum GPA of 3.0; for doctorate, GRE General Test. Additional exam requirements/recommendations for international students: Required—TOEFL. *Application deadline:* For fall admission, 4/1 for domestic students; for spring admission, 10/1 for domestic students. Applications are processed on a rolling basis. Application fee: $25. Electronic applications accepted. *Expenses:* Tuition, state resident: full-time $4,602; part-time $256 per credit hour. Tuition, nonresident: full-time $10,566; part-time $587 per credit hour. *Financial support:* Scholarships/grants available. Financial award application deadline: 3/1; financial award applicants required to submit FAFSA. *Unit head:* Dr. Timothy Letzring, Acting Chair, 662-915-7069, E-mail: fdl@olemiss.edu.

University of Northern Iowa, Graduate College, College of Education, Department of Educational Leadership, Counseling, and Postsecondary Education, Program in Postsecondary Education, Cedar Falls, IA 50614. Offers student affairs (MAE). *Students:* 19 full-time (13 women), 10 part-time (6 women); includes 7 minority (5 African Americans, 1 American Indian/Alaska Native, 1 Asian American or Pacific Islander). 32 applicants, 66% accepted, 11 enrolled. In 2006, 19 degrees awarded. *Degree requirements:* For master's, research paper. *Entrance requirements:* For master's, 3 years of educational experience, minimum GPA of 3.5. Additional exam requirements/recommendations for international students: Required—TOEFL (minimum score 500 paper-based; 180 computer-based; 61 iBT). *Application deadline:* For fall admission, 8/1 priority date for domestic students. Applications are processed on a rolling basis. Application fee: $30 ($50 for international students). Electronic applications accepted. *Expenses:* Tuition, state resident: full-time $5,936. Tuition, nonresident: full-time $14,074. *Financial support:* Career-related internships or fieldwork, Federal Work-Study, scholarships/grants, and tuition waivers (full) available. Financial award application deadline: 2/1.

University of Rhode Island, Graduate School, College of Human Science and Services, Department of Human Development and Family Studies, Kingston, RI 02881. Offers college student personnel (MS); human development and family studies (MS); marriage and family therapy (MS). *Accreditation:* AAMFT/COAMFTE. Evening/weekend programs available. *Entrance requirements:* For master's, GRE or MAT. *Application deadline:* For fall admission, 4/15 priority date for domestic students; for spring admission, 11/15 for domestic students. Applications are processed on a rolling basis. Application fee: $35. *Expenses:* Tuition, state resident: full-time $6,032; part-time $335 per credit. Tuition, nonresident: full-time $17,288; part-time $960 per credit. Required fees: $65 per credit. $30 per semester. One-time fee: $80 part-time. *Financial support:* Career-related internships or fieldwork available. *Unit head:* Dr. Jerome Adams, Chair, 401-874-5962.

University of St. Thomas, Graduate Studies, School of Education, Department of Leadership, Policy and Administration, St. Paul, MN 55105-1096. Offers athletics and activities administration (MA); community education administration (MA); educational leadership (Ed S); educational leadership and administration (MA); leadership (Ed D); leadership in student affairs (MA, Certificate); police leadership (MA); public policy and leadership (MA, Certificate). Part-time and evening/weekend programs available. *Faculty:* 6 full-time (3 women), 24 part-time/adjunct (9 women). *Students:* 22 full-time (19 women), 327 part-time (156 women); includes 32 minority (17 African Americans, 3 American Indian/Alaska Native, 8 Asian Americans or Pacific Islanders, 4 Hispanic Americans), 3 international. Average age 38. 140 applicants, 93% accepted, 123 enrolled. In 2006, 14 master's, 8 doctorates, 2 other advanced degrees awarded. Terminal master's awarded for partial completion of doctoral program. *Degree requirements:* For master's, thesis (for some programs), registration; for doctorate, thesis/dissertation, registration; for other advanced degree, thesis or alternative, registration. *Entrance requirements:* For master's, minimum GPA of 2.75 or MAT; for doctorate, MAT, minimum graduate GPA of 3.5; for other advanced degree, MAT, minimum graduate GPA of 3.25. Additional exam requirements/recommendations for international students: Required—TOEFL (minimum score 550 paper-based; 213 computer-based). *Application deadline:* For fall admission, 6/1 priority date for domestic students; for spring admission, 11/1 priority date for domestic students. Applications are processed on a rolling basis. Application fee: $50. *Expenses:* Contact institution. *Financial support:* In 2006–07, 124 students received support; fellowships, research assistantships, institutionally sponsored loans and scholarships/grants available. Support available to part-time students. Financial award applicants required to submit FAFSA. *Unit head:* Dr. Donald R. LaMagdeleine, Chair, 651-962-4893, Fax: 651-962-4169, E-mail: drlamagdelei@stthomas.edu. *Application contact:* Jackie Grossklaus, Department Assistant, 651-962-4885, Fax: 651-962-4169, E-mail: jmgrossklaus@stthomas.edu.

University of South Carolina, The Graduate School, College of Education, Department of Educational Leadership and Policies, Program in Higher Education and Student Affairs, Columbia, SC 29208. Offers M Ed. *Accreditation:* NCATE. Part-time and evening/weekend programs available. *Degree requirements:* For master's, thesis (for some programs), comprehensive exam. *Entrance requirements:* For master's, GRE General Test or MAT. Electronic applications accepted. *Faculty research:* Minorities in higher education, community college transfer problem, federal role in educational research.

University of South Florida, Graduate School, College of Education, Department of Psychological and Social Foundations of Education, Tampa, FL 33620-9951. Offers college student affairs (M Ed); counselor education (MA, PhD); interdisciplinary education (PhD, Ed S); school psychology (PhD, Ed S). Part-time and evening/weekend programs available. *Faculty:* 28 full-time (15 women), 8 part-time/adjunct (4 women). *Students:* 151 full-time (118 women), 113 part-time (95 women); includes 75 minority (37 African Americans, 2 American Indian/Alaska Native, 7 Asian Americans or Pacific Islanders, 29 Hispanic Americans), 6 international. 253 applicants, 45% accepted, 91 enrolled. In 2006, 70 master's, 18 doctorates awarded. *Degree requirements:* For doctorate, thesis/dissertation. *Entrance requirements:* For master's, GRE General Test, minimum GPA of 3.5 in last 60 hours; for doctorate, GRE General Test, minimum GPA of 3.5 in last 60 hours of coursework; for Ed S, GRE General Test. *Application deadline:* For fall admission, 1/15 for domestic and international students. Application fee: $30. Electronic applications accepted. *Financial support:* Career-related internships or fieldwork, scholarships/grants, and unspecified assistantships available. Financial award applicants required to submit CSS PROFILE. Total annual research expenditures: $2.2 million. *Unit head:* Dr. Harold R.

Student Affairs

University of South Florida (continued)
Keller, Chairperson, 813-974-6709, Fax: 813-974-5814, E-mail: hkeller@tempest.coedu.usf. edu. *Application contact:* Dr. Kathy Bradley, Faculty Program Coordinator, 813-974-9486, Fax: 813-974-5814, E-mail: kbradley@tempest.coedu.usf.edu.

The University of Tennessee, Graduate School, College of Education, Health and Human Sciences, Department of Educational Psychology and Counseling, Program in College Student Personnel, Knoxville, TN 37996. Offers MS. *Accreditation:* NCATE. Part-time programs available. *Students:* 36 (20 women); includes 3 African Americans. 26 applicants, 69% accepted. In 2006, 13 degrees awarded. *Degree requirements:* For master's, thesis optional. *Entrance requirements:* For master's, GRE General Test, minimum GPA of 2.7. Additional exam requirements/recommendations for international students: Required—TOEFL. *Application deadline:* For fall admission, 2/1 priority date for domestic students. Applications are processed on a rolling basis. Application fee: $35. Electronic applications accepted. *Expenses:* Tuition, state resident: full-time $5,574. Tuition, nonresident: full-time $16,840. Required fees: $792. *Financial support:* Application deadline: 2/1; *Unit head:* Dr. Joy Desensi, Head, 865-974-2216, Fax: 865-974-6146, E-mail: desensi@utk.edu.

University of Wisconsin–La Crosse, Office of University Graduate Studies, College of Liberal Studies, Department of Educational Studies, La Crosse, WI 54601-3742. Offers college student development and administration (MS Ed); professional development (MEPD), including elementary education, K–12, professional development, secondary education; reading (MS Ed); special education (MS Ed), including emotional disturbance, learning disabilities. Part-time programs available. *Faculty:* 18 full-time (6 women), 49 part-time/adjunct (35 women). *Students:* 34 full-time (24 women), 712 part-time (516 women); includes 20 minority (5 African Americans, 1 American Indian/Alaska Native, 10 Asian Americans or Pacific Islanders, 4 Hispanic Americans). Average age 35. 234 applicants, 91% accepted, 198 enrolled. In 2006, 236 degrees awarded. *Degree requirements:* For master's, thesis optional. *Entrance requirements:* For master's, minimum GPA of 2.85. Additional exam requirements/recommendations for international students: Required—TOEFL (minimum score 550 paper-based; 213 computer-based). *Application deadline:* Applications are processed on a rolling basis. Application fee: $45. Electronic applications accepted. *Financial support:* In 2006–07, 60 students received support; research assistantships, career-related internships or fieldwork, Federal Work-Study, institutionally sponsored loans, health care benefits, unspecified assistantships, and grant-funded positions available. Support available to part-time students. Financial award application deadline: 3/15; financial award applicants required to submit FAFSA. *Faculty research:* Reading techniques, diversity and social justice, special education services. Total annual research expenditures: $200,000. *Unit head:* Dr. Jon Davies, Chair, 608-785-5411, Fax: 608-785-8128, E-mail: davies.jon@uwlax.edu. *Application contact:* Kathryn Kiefer, Associate Director of Admissions, 608-785-8939, E-mail: admissions@uwlax.edu.

University of Wisconsin–La Crosse, Office of University Graduate Studies, College of Liberal Studies, Department of Psychology, Program in College Student Development and Administration, La Crosse, WI 54601-3742. Offers MS Ed. Part-time programs available. *Faculty:* 9 part-time/adjunct (5 women). *Students:* 25 full-time (20 women), 9 part-time (5 women); includes 5 minority (1 African American, 3 Asian Americans or Pacific Islanders, 1 Hispanic American), 1 international. Average age 26. 39 applicants, 51% accepted, 14 enrolled. In 2006, 20 degrees awarded. *Degree requirements:* For master's, thesis optional. *Entrance requirements:* For master's, interview, writing sample, references, experience in the field. Additional exam requirements/recommendations for international students: Required—TOEFL (minimum score 550 paper-based; 213 computer-based). *Application deadline:* For fall admission, 3/1 priority date for domestic students. Applications are processed on a rolling basis. Application fee: $45. Electronic applications accepted. *Financial support:* In 2006–07, 27 research assistantships with tuition reimbursements (averaging $7,748 per year) were awarded; career-related internships or fieldwork, Federal Work-Study, health care benefits, and unspecified assistantships also available. Support available to part-time students. Financial award application deadline: 3/15; financial award applicants required to submit FAFSA. *Faculty research:* College student personnel standards, campus ecology, standard testing and admissions, student development theory, diversity/inclusion practices. *Unit head:* Dr. Christine S. Bakkum, Director, 608-785-8953, Fax: 608-785-6575, E-mail: bakkum.chri@uwlax.edu. *Application contact:* Kathryn Kiefer, Associate Director of Admissions, 608-785-8939, E-mail: admissions@uwlax.edu.

Washington State University, Graduate School, College of Education, Department of Educational Leadership and Counseling Psychology, Pullman, WA 99164. Offers counseling psychology (Ed M, MA, PhD); educational leadership (M Ed, MA, Ed D, PhD); educational psychology (Ed M, MA, PhD); higher education (Ed M, MA, Ed D, PhD), including higher education administration (PhD), sport management (PhD), student affairs (PhD); higher education with sport management (Ed M). *Accreditation:* NCATE. *Faculty:* 25. *Students:* 109 full-time (63 women), 54 part-time (34 women); includes 42 minority (11 African Americans, 2 American Indian/Alaska Native, 12 Asian Americans or Pacific Islanders, 17 Hispanic Americans). Average age 34. 107 applicants, 67% accepted, 30 enrolled. In 2006, 33 master's, 20 doctorates awarded. Terminal master's awarded for partial completion of doctoral program. *Degree requirements:* For master's, thesis (for some programs), oral exam or written exam, comprehensive exam (for some programs); for doctorate, thesis/dissertation, oral and written exams, comprehensive exam. *Entrance requirements:* For master's and doctorate, GRE General Test, minimum GPA of 3.0, 3 letters of recommendation. Additional exam requirements/recommendations for international students: Required—TOEFL (minimum score 550 paper-based; 213 computer-based). *Application deadline:* For fall admission, 3/1 for domestic and international students; for spring admission, 10/1 for domestic students, 7/1 for international students. Application fee: $50. *Expenses:* Tuition, state resident: full-time $7,066. Tuition, nonresident: full-time $17,204. *Financial support:* In 2006–07, research assistantships (averaging $13,917 per year), teaching assistantships (averaging $13,056 per year) were awarded; career-related internships or fieldwork, Federal Work-Study, institutionally sponsored loans, scholarships/grants, tuition waivers (partial), and unspecified assistantships also available. Financial award application deadline: 4/1; financial award applicants required to submit FAFSA. *Faculty research:* Attentional processes, cross cultural psychology, faculty development in higher education. Total annual research expenditures: $854,827. *Unit head:* Dr. Phyllis Erdman, Chair, 509-335-9117. *Application contact:* Graduate School Admissions, 800-GRADWSU, Fax: 509-335-1949, E-mail: gradsch@wsu.edu.

Western Illinois University, School of Graduate Studies, College of Education and Human Services, Department of Educational and Interdisciplinary Studies, Program in College Student Personnel, Macomb, IL 61455-1390. Offers MS. *Accreditation:* NCATE. Part-time programs available. *Students:* 39 full-time (28 women), 1 part-time; includes 5 minority (3 African Americans, 2 Hispanic Americans), 6 international. Average age 24. 53 applicants, 38% accepted. In 2006, 18 degrees awarded. *Degree requirements:* For master's, thesis or alternative. *Entrance requirements:* For master's, interview. Additional exam requirements/recommendations for international students: Required—TOEFL (minimum score 550 paper-based; 213 computer-based; 80 iBT). *Application deadline:* Applications are processed on a rolling basis. Application fee: $30. Electronic applications accepted. *Expenses:* Tuition, state resident: part-time $200 per credit hour. Tuition, nonresident: part-time $400 per credit hour. *Financial support:* In 2006–07, 39 students received support, including 39 research assistantships with full tuition reimbursements available (averaging $6,568 per year). Financial award applicants required to submit FAFSA. *Unit head:* Dr. Tracy Davis, Coordinator, 309-298-1183. *Application contact:* Dr. Barbara Baily, Director of Graduate Studies/Associate Provost, 309-298-1806, Fax: 309-298-2345, E-mail: grad-office@wiu.edu.

Western Kentucky University, Graduate Studies, College of Education and Behavioral Sciences, Department of Counseling and Student Affairs, Bowling Green, KY 42101. Offers business and marketing education (MA Ed); counseling (MA Ed); counselor education (Ed S); education and behavioral science (MA Ed); elementary education (MA Ed, Ed S); middle years education (MA Ed); secondary education (MA Ed, Ed S); student affairs (MA Ed). *Accreditation:* ACA; NCATE. Part-time and evening/weekend programs available. *Faculty:* 11 full-time (5 women), 9 part-time/adjunct (3 women). *Students:* 59 full-time (47 women), 157 part-time (126 women); includes 18 minority (13 African Americans, 1 American Indian/Alaska Native, 2 Asian Americans or Pacific Islanders, 2 Hispanic Americans), 1 international. Average age 31. 49 applicants, 67% accepted, 27 enrolled. In 2006, 89 master's, 4 other advanced degrees awarded. *Degree requirements:* For master's, thesis optional. *Entrance requirements:* For master's, GRE General Test. Additional exam requirements/recommendations for international students: Required—TOEFL (minimum score 555 paper-based; 213 computer-based; 79 iBT). *Application deadline:* For fall admission, 8/1 priority date for domestic students, 4/1 for international students; for spring admission, 12/1 for domestic students, 9/1 for international students. Applications are processed on a rolling basis. Application fee: $35. *Expenses:* Tuition, state resident: full-time $6,520; part-time $226 per hour. Tuition, nonresident: full-time $7,140; part-time $357 per hour. International tuition: $15,820 full-time. *Financial support:* In 2006–07, 1 research assistantship with partial tuition reimbursement (averaging $8,000 per year) was awarded; Federal Work-Study, institutionally sponsored loans, and service awards also available. Financial award application deadline: 4/1; financial award applicants required to submit FAFSA. *Faculty research:* Counselor education, research for residential workers. *Unit head:* Dr. Aaron W Hughey, Department Head, 270-745-4953, E-mail: aaron.hughey@wku.edu.

ALLIANT INTERNATIONAL UNIVERSITY

Graduate School of Education
Educational Leadership and Management Program

Program of Study	The Graduate School of Education (GSOE) at Alliant International University offers the M.A.E. in educational administration with the Preliminary Administrative Services (PAS) Credential at the Irvine, Los Angeles, Sacramento, San Diego, and San Francisco campuses. This degree and credential will meet all California requirements for K–12 administration, and the degree will qualify graduates to teach or administrate at the community college level. The Ed.D. is offered at the Fresno, Irvine, Los Angeles, Sacramento, San Diego, and San Francisco campuses. This executive management program prepares the doctoral candidate for executive leadership and administration in the community college or university setting. It is particularly attuned to settings that are characterized by diverse student body populations. Candidates who complete the program are well versed in multicultural and global educational trends and practice, curriculum theory and ethical issues, organizational and governance practices, higher education finance, business and human resources, mergers and acquisitions, student and personnel services, applied technology, and research practices and methods. Two Ed.D. degrees are available: a doctorate in educational leadership and management, K–12, and a doctorate in educational leadership and management, higher education. Students take four thematically linked courses (12 units) in an emphasis area such as cross-cultural studies or technology and learning; students can also design their own emphasis area under the guidance of a faculty member. All course work, with the exception of dissertation classes, must be completed before a student writes the comprehensive examination paper. The exam may be taken concurrently with the last semester of course work. All Ed.D. candidates must successfully complete the comprehensive exam prior to enrolling in the dissertation sequence. The exam or any section may be taken a maximum of two times.
Research Facilities	Alliant International offers excellent research facilities throughout the system. The Alliant libraries maintain a diverse available collection of more than 160,000 books, 1,150 current print journal subscriptions, 12 electronic database subscriptions, approximately 995 psychological test titles, 1,700 audiotapes, and more than 1,200 videotapes. Each campus library is a resource for a variety of research topics and works in cooperation with several other four-year institutions in the immediate area. Each academic school or college has research clusters, labs, and/or other resources to support original scholarly and applied research. The Computer Lab and Learning Center has a number of computers available for student use. The computers are loaded with current versions of word processing, statistical, and other software programs and are connected to laser printers. Further, Alliant maintains partnerships with area university libraries that allow students to access material.
Financial Aid	Most students interested in school-based financial aid pursue college work-study. Students work as teaching or research assistants to core faculty members. In addition, students can work on campus in a number of departments, including admissions and field placement. Stipends generally average about $1000 per assistantship per semester. For complete information, students should contact the Financial Aid Office.
Cost of Study	Master's programs are $500 per semester unit; doctoral programs cost $900 per semester unit. Fees are additional.
Living and Housing Costs	On-campus housing is not available on the Fresno, Irvine, Los Angeles, and San Francisco campuses. Most Alliant students live in communities adjacent to the campuses. The estimated cost of living for a graduate student (including housing and food, transportation, and personal expenses) for the nine-month academic year is $17,262. Room and board on the San Diego campus cost $9820 for the academic year for a private room and $7430 for double occupancy. Students can expect to pay between $700 and $1000 per month plus utilities (gas and electricity) for an off-campus unfurnished, one-bedroom apartment. The estimated cost for books and supplies is $1500 per year.
Student Group	Alliant ranked first in international students in *U.S. News & World Report*'s 2007 nationwide survey. *Diverse* magazine ranked Alliant sixth for awarding doctorates to minority women and fourteenth for doctorates to minorities (all disciplines combined). Alliant International University has students from almost every state plus 407 international students from sixty-nine countries, including Botswana, Cameroon, Greece, Iceland, Portugal, and Turkey.
Location	The Los Angeles-area campus is in Alhambra, conveniently located 6 miles east of downtown Los Angeles and Hollywood and easily accessible from the San Bernardino and Long Beach freeways. The Alhambra complex features 24-hour gated security and plenty of parking spaces for students and faculty and staff members. Famous Venice Beach, Malibu, and Santa Monica are 20 minutes away. The Irvine campus is a friendly, conveniently-located center that caters to the needs of working adults, with evening classes and free on-site parking. Small class sizes offer personalized learning, and quiet classrooms, computer labs, and a comfortable student lounge provide a conductive learning environment. An hour south of Los Angeles and conveniently accessible to two major freeways and the John Wayne Airport, Irvine is within easy driving distance of beautiful Corona Del Mar and the sun drenched sand of Laguna Beach and Newport Beach. Even closer at hand is an extensive system nature preserves, wilderness parks and trails that offers get-aways to hikers, bicyclists, equestrians, and photographers. The ambience on the Fresno campus is friendly and warm, a reflection of its Central Valley location. Blessed with abundant sunshine and mild temperatures, the region brims with orchards and blossoms. Conveniently located adjacent to Fresno's Yosemite International Airport, Alliant's Fresno campus serves one of the fastest growing cities in California. The San Diego campus is located in what is often called "America's Finest City." San Diego is a dynamic, multicultural location in which to study. A vibrant, metropolitan city with a laid-back, small-town feel, the area is filled with an incredible selection of activities and attractions. There are many cultural and historic attractions, shopping centers, fine dining establishments, and places to relax and reenergize. From the beautiful beaches to the inland mountains, the views are spectacular, and San Diego has a climate unmatched for mildness nationwide. Alliant's San Francisco's campus is located on the waterfront, with the restaurants and amusements of Pier 39 just across the street. The music, food, art, and politics of this city provide a dynamic backdrop to graduate studies.
The University and The School	Alliant International University focuses on preparing students for professional careers. Alliant International University was officially formed in 2001 by the combination of the California School of Professional Psychology (CSPP), founded in 1969, and United States International University (USIU), founded in 1967. But their history goes back more than the forty plus years since USIU's founding. USIU was the successor to two other institutions: California Western University, founded in 1952, and Balboa College, founded in 1924. The Graduate School of Education trains professionals who make a difference in the lives of others through teaching, counseling, leadership, advocacy, administration, management, and community work. GSOE infuses its curricula with multicultural content and emphasizes student achievement, instructional technology, assessment, neuropsychology, mentoring of diverse populations, and comprehensive community service. At the core of its professional practitioner model is the cohort structure, which supports learning while students are enrolled in advanced studies and provides a professional support system of colleagues throughout their career.
Applying	Applicants must have a master's degree, with a minimum GPA of 2.5. In general, applicants should submit the completed application, the $70 application fee, all official transcripts, a personal essay, a resume, and three letters of recommendation. MAT or GRE scores are optional. International students must also submit TOEFL scores.
Correspondence and Information	Alliant Admissions Alliant International University 10455 Pomerado Road San Diego, California 92131 Phone: 866-U-ALLIANT (toll-free) E-mail: admissions@alliant.edu Web site: http://alliant.edu/gsoe

Alliant International University

THE FACULTY AND THEIR RESEARCH

Core and Noncore Faculty

Joseph Adwere-Boamah, Assistant Professor and Program Coordinator, Educational Leadership (San Diego); Ph.D., Berkeley, 1970.

Hassana Alidou, Professor and Program Coordinator, TESOL (San Diego and Irvine); Ph.D., Illinois at Urbana–Champaign, 1997. Sociolinguistics, teacher training in TESOL.

Frederick Ansoff, Assistant Professor, Educational Leadership and Management (San Diego); Ph.D., Georgetown, 1998. Statistical analyses.

Shirley Baker, Instructor, TESOL (Fresno) and Director, International Language and Cultural Center; M.A., Kentucky, 1987; M.A., US International, 1999. TESOL program description, TESOL teacher preparation.

Suzanne Borman, Professor (San Diego); Ed.D., Columbia Teachers College, 1983. Curriculum and instructional planning.

Mary Ellen Butler-Pascoe, Professor and Systemwide Program Director, TESOL (San Diego); Ph.D., US International, 1990. ESL/EFL teacher training, integration of technology and second-language instruction, program and curriculum design.

Ana Guisela Chupina, Assistant Professor, Teacher Education, Higher Education (San Francisco); Ph.D., Iowa State, 2004. Immigrant women as adult learners, first-generation and culturally diverse students in higher education, methodological issues in cross-cultural research.

Geoffrey M. Cox, Professor of Higher Education (San Francisco) and President, Alliant International University; Ph.D., Chicago, 1987. Social and political philosophy, leadership in higher education.

Trudy Day, Assistant Professor, Teacher Education, Higher Education (San Francisco); Systemwide Assistant Dean, Graduate School of Education; and Systemwide Director, TeachersCHOICE; Ed.D., Louisville, 1996. Leadership and crisis, first-year teachers, shared governance, instructional strategies for the university professor.

Steven Fisher, Assistant Professor and Program Director, School and Educational Psychology (San Diego); Ph.D., US International, 1998. Clinical psychology.

Xuanning Fu, Assistant Professor and Program Coordinator, Educational Leadership and Management (Fresno); Ph.D., Brigham Young, 1993. Program analysis and evaluation.

James F. Hiramoto, Principal Lecturer and Program Coordinator, School and Educational Psychology (San Francisco); Ph.D., Berkeley, 2004. Effects of sightedness on areas of knowledge, social skills, and perceptions of self; ADHD.

Kenneth Kelch, Assistant Professor of TESOL and Director, International Languages and Cultural Center (San Diego); Ed.D., Alliant International, 2005. TESOL pedagogy.

Jerry Kill, Assistant Professor and Coordinator, Educational Leadership and Management (Irvine); Ed.D., California Coast, 2005. Educational leadership, school administration.

Yury Kostin, Assistant Professor (Fresno); Ed.D., California State, Fresno, 2003. Technological applications.

Robert D. Kreger, Associate Professor (San Francisco); Ph.D., Michigan, 1980. Teacher preparation, child development and disorder issues in education, special education.

Irving Leung, Assistant Professor and Field Services Coordinator, Teacher Education–Early Completion Option (San Francisco); Ed.D., San Francisco, 1998. Bilingual education, special education.

Estela C. Matriano, Professor and Secretary, World Council for Curriculum and Instruction (San Diego); Ed.D., Indiana, 1968. Global education.

Jerold D. Miller, Professor; Program Director, Teacher Education; and Director, Partners for Success Tech and Media Center (San Diego); Ed.D., US International, 1985. Technology planning and curriculum development.

Beverly J. Palley, Field Services Coordinator, Teacher Education; Ed.D., Fielding Graduate University, 2003. Teacher-training programs, improving alternative certification approaches in teacher internship programs.

Carlton Parks, Professor and Campus Program Director, Educational Psychology (Los Angeles); Ph.D., Minnesota, 1986. Interpersonal relations, interpersonal violence, sexual and ethnic minorities, psychosocial aspects of HIV infection/AIDS, feminist studies, spirituality and mental health.

Connell Persico, University Professor and Systemwide Program Director, Educational Leadership, Educational Administration; Ph.D., Stanford, 1974. Education leadership, higher education organization, politics of education.

Debra Reeves-Gutierrez, Assistant Professor, Teacher Education–Early Completion Option (San Francisco); Ed.D., University of the Pacific, 2005. Pedagogy.

Robert Reyes, Assistant Professor and Program Coordinator, Educational Leadership and Management (Los Angeles); Ph.D., Berne, 2001. English language development, educational leadership, global education.

Karen Schuster Webb, Professor of Higher Education and TESOL and Systemwide Dean, Graduate School of Education (San Francisco); Ph.D., Indiana–Bloomington, 1980. Language and cognition, discourse pragmatics, inclusive pedagogy.

Ed Shenk, Associate Professor and Program Director, Educational Leadership and Management, Higher Education (San Francisco); Ed.D., Oregon, 1981. Student services, student discipline, leadership, organizational structures.

George Stamos, Associate Professor; Ed.D., Northern Arizona, 1996. Teacher education reform.

Barbara Stein-Stover, Assistant Professor and Program Director, Teacher Education–Early Completion Option (Los Angeles and San Diego); Ed.D., Alliant International, 2006. Adolescent mental health issues, pedagogy.

Holly Wilson, Associate Professor (San Diego); Ph.D., New Mexico, 1999. Second-language-learner errors, grammar instruction, proposed use of covert grammar.

Donald Wofford, Assistant Professor and Interim Systemwide Director, Educational and School Psychology (Irvine); Psy.D., California School of Professional Psychology, 2002. School-based mental health.

Adjunct Faculty

Christine Alexander (San Diego); Ed.D., US International, 2001.

Remijio Alvarez, Lecturer (Irvine); M.A., Pepperdine, 1976.

Robert Appenzeller (San Diego); M.A., US International, 1987.

Theresa M. Ashby (Los Angeles); Ph.D., Alliant International, 2002.

Tomiko Lynn Bobo (Los Angeles), PPS Credential in School Counseling, National.

Celeste Cusumano, Senior Lecturer (Fresno); Ed.D., University of the Pacific, 1984.

Diane DeBoer (Los Angeles); Ph.D., US International, 1997.

Greg Dhuyvettor, Lecturer (Irvine); M.A., US International, 2002.

Diane di Bari (San Francisco); M.S., California State, Fresno, 1976.

Richard G. Duke (Fresno); Ed.D., Brigham Young, 1981.

Krystel Edmonds-Biglow (Los Angeles); Psy.D., Alliant International, 2001.

Joe Fox (Irvine); M.A., Northern Colorado, 1966.

La Faune Yvette Gordon (Los Angeles); Ph.D., California School of Professional Psychology, 1993.

Michelyn Gould (Los Angeles); Psy.D., California School of Professional Psychology, 1999.

Mary Lou Hamaker, Lecturer (Irvine), Ph.D., USC, 1986.

Leanne Harmon-Doyle (Los Angeles); Psy.D., Alliant International, 2003.

Christine A. Hoffman (Irvine); Ed.D., Northern Arizona, 1997.

Erica L. Holmes (Los Angeles); Psy.D., US International, 2001.

Elena M. Ingrao (San Diego); M.S., National, 1993.

Adi´na Janzen (Fresno); J.D., San Joaquin College of Law, 1985.

Vallarie Johnson (Los Angeles); Psy.D., Alliant International, 2004.

Dan Kettlehake (San Diego); Ph.D., Bowling Green State, 1997.

Lori Lambertson, Lecturer (San Francisco); M.A., San Francisco State, 1993.

Susan Lees (Los Angeles); Psy.D., Alliant International, 2003.

Bill Madigan (San Diego); M.A., San Diego State, 1990.

Sally Madruga (San Diego); M.A., San Diego State, 1981.

N. Bert McIntosh Jr. (San Diego); M.A., San Diego State, 1969.

Erv Metzgar (San Diego); M.A., San Diego State.

Susan Moore (San Diego); Ed.D., Alliant International, 2005.

Emil Nolte, Lecturer (Irvine).

Romelia Orozco (San Diego); Ed.D., Alliant International, 2002.

Cyndi Paik, Lecturer (Irvine); M.A., US International, 2002.

Walter T. Parry (San Diego); M.A., Stanford, 1964.

Ernest Proud (Los Angeles); Ph.D., California School of Professional Psychology.

Thomas Ryerson (Los Angeles); Psy.D., Alliant International, 2004.

Jerry Salazar, Lecturer (Irvine); M.A., California State, Long Beach, 1972.

Marilyn Shepherd (Fresno); Ed.D., California, Davis, 1996.

Erlinda Teisinger (Fresno); Ed.D., USC, 2000.

Marvin Warner (San Diego); M.A., Azusa Pacific, 1978.

Gary E. Warren (Los Angeles); Ed.D., US International, 1987.

Lori Williams (Los Angeles); Psy.D., Alliant International, 2004.

ALLIANT INTERNATIONAL UNIVERSITY

Graduate School of Education
Educational Psychology Programs

Programs of Study

The Graduate School of Education (GSOE) at Alliant International University offers master's and doctoral degrees at the Irvine, Los Angeles, San Diego, and San Francisco campuses. The Master of Arts in Education (M.A.E.) in school psychology with a Pupil Personnel Services (PPS) Credential program gives students the education, skills, and qualifications required by the State of California to be practicing school psychologists. This program is for recent college graduates with bachelor's degrees, current teachers, school personnel, and professionals in other related fields. Typically, students complete course work in the first two years and the PPS internship in the third year. Upon completion of 43 semester units (including 450 practicum hours), candidates qualify for the degree. Most students seeking the PPS credential in school psychology complete and additional 17 units (7 units of course work and practicum, plus 10 units of a 1,200-hour internship). Paid internships depend on the budgets and policies of individual school district.

The 61-credit Advanced Standing Doctor of Psychology (Psy.D.) program is designed for those who already possess an M.A.E. in school psychology and a PPS credential. This program is for practicing school psychologists who are interested in conducting groundbreaking research, becoming faculty members, or being experts in the field. Graduates are prepared for leadership in a variety of institutions, including K–12 public schools as well as other private and public organizations. Classes meet in the evenings and on weekends to accommodate working professionals. Students must complete course work, a Psy.D. project, and additional research/applied work to qualify for the degree. In addition, during each semester, students take a course in a special-interest area, such as adolescent stress, coping, and resilience; multicultural counseling; pediatric psychology; infant and preschool mental health, including assessment and intervention; child neuropsychology; and provision of services for children and adolescents in alternative placements. Most students finish the advanced standing doctoral program in three years while working full-time.

Research Facilities

Alliant International offers excellent research facilities throughout the system. The Alliant libraries maintain a diverse available collection of more than 160,000 books, 1,150 current print journal subscriptions, 12 electronic database subscriptions, approximately 995 psychological test titles, 1,700 audiotapes, and more than 1,200 videotapes. Each campus library is a resource for a variety of research topics and works in cooperation with several other four-year institutions in the immediate area. Each academic school or college has research clusters, labs, and/or other resources to support original scholarly and applied research. The Computer Lab and Learning Center has a number of computers available for student use. The computers are loaded with current versions of word processing, statistical, and other software programs and are connected to laser printers. Further, Alliant maintains partnerships with area university libraries that allow students to access material.

Financial Aid

Most students interested in school-based financial aid pursue college work-study. Students work as teaching or research assistants to core faculty members. In addition, students can work on campus in a number of departments, including admissions and field placement. Stipends generally average about $1000 per assistantship per semester. For complete information, students should contact the Financial Aid Office.

Cost of Study

Master's programs are $500 per semester unit; doctoral programs cost $900 per semester unit. Fees are additional.

Living and Housing Costs

On-campus housing is not available on the Irvine, Los Angeles, and San Francisco campuses. Most Alliant students live in communities adjacent to the campuses. The estimated cost of living for a graduate student (including housing and food, transportation, and personal expenses) for the nine-month academic year is $17,262. Room and board on the San Diego campus cost $9820 for the academic year for a private room and $7430 for double occupancy. Students can expect to pay between $700 and $1000 per month plus utilities (gas and electricity) for an off-campus unfurnished, one-bedroom apartment. The estimated cost for books and supplies is $1500 per year.

Student Group

Alliant ranked first in international students in *U.S. News & World Report*'s 2007 nationwide survey. *Diverse* magazine ranked Alliant sixth for awarding doctorates to minority women and fourteenth for doctorates to minorities (all disciplines combined). Alliant International University has students from almost every state plus 407 international students from sixty-nine countries, including Botswana, Cameroon, Greece, Iceland, Portugal, and Turkey.

Location

The Los Angeles–area campus is in Alhambra, conveniently located 6 miles east of downtown Los Angeles and Hollywood and easily accessible from the San Bernardino and Long Beach freeways. The Alhambra complex features 24-hour gated security and plenty of parking spaces for students and faculty and staff members. Famous Venice Beach, Malibu, and Santa Monica are 20 minutes away. The Irvine campus is a friendly, conveniently-located center that caters to the needs of working adults, with evening classes and free on-site parking. Small class sizes offer personalized learning, and quiet classrooms, computer labs, and a comfortable student lounge provide a conductive learning environment. An hour south of Los Angeles and conveniently accessible to two major freeways and the John Wayne Airport, Irvine is within easy driving distance of beautiful Corona Del Mar and the sun drenched sand of Laguna Beach and Newport Beach. Even closer at hand is an extensive system nature preserves, wilderness parks and trails that offers get-aways to hikers, bicyclists, equestrians, and photographers. The San Diego campus is located in what is often called "America's Finest City." San Diego is a dynamic, multicultural location in which to study. A vibrant, metropolitan city with a laid-back, small-town feel, the area is filled with an incredible selection of activities and attractions. There are many cultural and historic attractions, shopping centers, fine dining establishments, and places to relax and reenergize. From the beautiful beaches to the inland mountains, the views are spectacular, and San Diego has a climate unmatched for mildness nationwide. Alliant's San Francisco's campus is located on the waterfront, with the restaurants and amusements of Pier 39 just across the street. The music, food, art, and politics of this city provide a dynamic backdrop to graduate studies.

The University and The School

Alliant International University focuses on preparing students for professional careers. Alliant International University was officially formed in 2001 by the combination of the California School of Professional Psychology (CSPP), founded in 1969 and United States International University (USIU), founded in 1967. But their history goes back more than the forty plus years since USIU's founding. USIU was the successor to two other institutions: California Western University, founded in 1952, and Balboa College, founded in 1924.

The Graduate School of Education trains professionals who make a difference in the lives of others through teaching, counseling, leadership, advocacy, administration, management, and community work. GSOE infuses its curricula with multicultural content and emphasizes student achievement, instructional technology, assessment, neuropsychology, mentoring of diverse populations, and comprehensive community service. At the core of its professional practitioner model is the cohort structure, which supports learning while students are enrolled in advanced studies and provides a professional support system of colleagues throughout their career.

Applying

Applicants must possess a bachelor's degree or a master's degree for the master's and doctoral programs, respectively, and have a minimum GPA of 3.0. In general, applicants should submit the completed application, the application fee ($55 for master's programs, $70 for doctoral programs), all official transcripts, a personal essay, and letters of recommendation (two for master's students, three for doctoral). For doctoral students, a resume is required, but MAT or GRE scores are optional. Candidates for the Advanced Standing Psy.D. in educational psychology must be practicing, credentialed school psychologists. International students must also submit TOEFL scores.

Correspondence and Information

Admissions Office
Alliant International University
10455 Pomerado Road
San Diego, California 92131

Phone: 866-U-ALLIANT (toll-free)
E-mail: admissions@alliant.edu
Web site: http://www.alliant.edu/gsoe

Alliant International University

THE FACULTY

Core and Noncore Faculty

Joseph Adwere-Boamah, Assistant Professor and Program Coordinator, Educational Leadership (San Diego); Ph.D., Berkeley, 1970.

Hassana Alidou, Professor and Program Coordinator, TESOL (San Diego and Irvine); Ph.D., Illinois at Urbana–Champaign, 1997. Sociolinguistics, teacher training in TESOL.

Frederick Ansoff, Assistant Professor, Educational Leadership and Management (San Diego); Ph.D., Georgetown, 1998. Statistical analyses.

Shirley Baker, Instructor, TESOL (Fresno) and Director, International Language and Cultural Center; M.A., Kentucky, 1987; M.A., US International, 1999. TESOL program description, TESOL teacher preparation.

Suzanne Borman, Professor (San Diego); Ed.D., Columbia Teachers College, 1983. Curriculum and instructional planning.

Mary Ellen Butler-Pascoe, Professor and Systemwide Program Director, TESOL (San Diego); Ph.D., US International, 1990. ESL/EFL teacher training, integration of technology and second-language instruction, program and curriculum design.

Ana Guisela Chupina, Assistant Professor, Teacher Education, Higher Education (San Francisco); Ph.D., Iowa State, 2004. Immigrant women as adult learners, first-generation and culturally diverse students in higher education, methodological issues in cross-cultural research.

Geoffrey M. Cox, Professor of Higher Education (San Francisco) and President, Alliant International University; Ph.D., Chicago, 1987. Social and political philosophy, leadership in higher education.

Trudy Day, Assistant Professor, Teacher Education, Higher Education (San Francisco); Systemwide Assistant Dean, Graduate School of Education; and Systemwide Director, TeachersCHOICE; Ed.D., Louisville, 1996. Leadership and crisis, first-year teachers, shared governance, instructional strategies for the university professor.

Steven Fisher, Assistant Professor and Program Director, School and Educational Psychology (San Diego); Ph.D., US International, 1998. Clinical psychology.

Xuanning Fu, Assistant Professor and Program Coordinator, Educational Leadership and Management (Fresno); Ph.D., Brigham Young, 1993. Program analysis and evaluation.

James F. Hiramoto, Principal Lecturer and Program Coordinator, School and Educational Psychology (San Francisco); Ph.D., Berkeley, 2004. Effects of sightedness on areas of knowledge, social skills, and perceptions of self; ADHD.

Kenneth Kelch, Assistant Professor of TESOL and Director, International Languages and Cultural Center (San Diego); Ed.D., Alliant International, 2005. TESOL pedagogy.

Jerry Kill, Assistant Professor and Coordinator, Educational Leadership and Management (Irvine); Ed.D., California Coast, 2005. Educational leadership, school administration.

Yury Kostin, Assistant Professor (Fresno); Ed.D., California State, Fresno, 2003. Technological applications.

Robert D. Kreger, Associate Professor (San Francisco); Ph.D., Michigan, 1980. Teacher preparation, child development and disorder issues in education, special education.

Irving Leung, Assistant Professor and Field Services Coordinator, Teacher Education–Early Completion Option (San Francisco); Ed.D., San Francisco, 1998. Bilingual education, special education.

Estela C. Matriano, Professor and Secretary, World Council for Curriculum and Instruction (San Diego); Ed.D., Indiana, 1968. Global education.

Jerold D. Miller, Professor; Program Director, Teacher Education; and Director, Partners for Success Tech and Media Center (San Diego); Ed.D., US International, 1985. Technology planning and curriculum development.

Beverly J. Palley, Field Services Coordinator, Teacher Education; Ed.D., Fielding Graduate University, 2003. Teacher-training programs, improving alternative certification approaches in teacher internship programs.

Carlton Parks, Professor and Campus Program Director, Educational Psychology (Los Angeles); Ph.D., Minnesota, 1986. Interpersonal relations, interpersonal violence, sexual and ethnic minorities, psychosocial aspects of HIV infection/AIDS, feminist studies, spirituality and mental health.

Connell Persico, University Professor and Systemwide Program Director, Educational Leadership, Educational Administration; Ph.D., Stanford, 1974. Education leadership, higher education organization, politics of education.

Debra Reeves-Gutierrez, Assistant Professor, Teacher Education–Early Completion Option (San Francisco); Ed.D., University of the Pacific, 2005. Pedagogy.

Robert Reyes, Assistant Professor and Program Coordinator, Educational Leadership and Management (Los Angeles); Ph.D., Berne, 2001. English language development, educational leadership, global education.

Karen Schuster Webb, Professor of Higher Education and TESOL and Systemwide Dean, Graduate School of Education (San Francisco); Ph.D., Indiana–Bloomington, 1980. Language and cognition, discourse pragmatics, inclusive pedagogy.

Ed Shenk, Associate Professor and Program Director, Educational Leadership and Management, Higher Education (San Francisco); Ed.D., Oregon, 1981. Student services, student discipline, leadership, organizational structures.

George Stamos, Associate Professor; Ed.D., Northern Arizona, 1996. Teacher education reform.

Barbara Stein-Stover, Assistant Professor and Program Director, Teacher Education–Early Completion Option (Los Angeles and San Diego); Ed.D., Alliant International, 2006. Adolescent mental health issues, pedagogy.

Holly Wilson, Associate Professor (San Diego); Ph.D., New Mexico, 1999. Second-language-learner errors, grammar instruction, proposed use of covert grammar.

Donald Wofford, Assistant Professor and Interim Systemwide Director, Educational and School Psychology (Irvine); Psy.D., California School of Professional Psychology, 2002. School-based mental health.

Adjunct Faculty

Christine Alexander (San Diego); Ed.D., US International, 2001.

Remijio Alvarez, Lecturer (Irvine); M.A., Pepperdine, 1976.

Robert Appenzeller (San Diego); M.A., US International, 1987.

Theresa M. Ashby (Los Angeles); Ph.D., Alliant International, 2002.

Tomiko Lynn Bobo (Los Angeles), PPS Credential in School Counseling, National.

Celeste Cusumano, Senior Lecturer (Fresno); Ed.D., University of the Pacific, 1984.

Diane DeBoer (Los Angeles); Ph.D., US International, 1997.

Greg Dhuyvettor, Lecturer (Irvine); M.A., US International, 2002.

Diane di Bari (San Francisco); M.S., California State, Fresno, 1976.

Richard G. Duke (Fresno); Ed.D., Brigham Young, 1981.

Krystel Edmonds-Biglow (Los Angeles); Psy.D., Alliant International, 2001.

Joe Fox (Irvine); M.A., Northern Colorado, 1966.

La Faune Yvette Gordon (Los Angeles); Ph.D., California School of Professional Psychology, 1993.

Michelyn Gould (Los Angeles); Psy.D., California School of Professional Psychology, 1999.

Mary Lou Hamaker, Lecturer (Irvine), Ph.D., USC, 1986.

Leanne Harmon-Doyle (Los Angeles); Psy.D., Alliant International, 2003.

Christine A. Hoffman (Irvine); Ed.D., Northern Arizona, 1997.

Erica L. Holmes (Los Angeles); Psy.D., US International, 2001.

Elena M. Ingrao (San Diego); M.S., National, 1993.

Adi´na Janzen (Fresno); J.D., San Joaquin College of Law, 1985.

Vallarie Johnson (Los Angeles); Psy.D., Alliant International, 2004.

Dan Kettlehake (San Diego); Ph.D., Bowling Green State, 1997.

Lori Lambertson, Lecturer (San Francisco); M.A., San Francisco State, 1993.

Susan Lees (Los Angeles); Psy.D., Alliant International, 2003.

Bill Madigan (San Diego); M.A., San Diego State, 1990.

Sally Madruga (San Diego); M.A., San Diego State, 1981.

N. Bert McIntosh Jr. (San Diego); M.A., San Diego State, 1969.

Erv Metzgar (San Diego); M.A., San Diego State.

Susan Moore (San Diego); Ed.D., Alliant International, 2005.

Emil Nolte, Lecturer (Irvine).

Romelia Orozco (San Diego); Ed.D., Alliant International, 2002.

Cyndi Paik, Lecturer (Irvine); M.A., US International, 2002.

Walter T. Parry (San Diego); M.A., Stanford, 1964.

Ernest Proud (Los Angeles); Ph.D., California School of Professional Psychology.

Thomas Ryerson (Los Angeles); Psy.D., Alliant International, 2004.

Jerry Salazar, Lecturer (Irvine); M.A., California State, Long Beach, 1972.

Marilyn Shepherd (Fresno); Ed.D., California, Davis, 1996.

Erlinda Teisinger (Fresno); Ed.D., USC, 2000.

Marvin Warner (San Diego); M.A., Azusa Pacific, 1978.

Gary E. Warren (Los Angeles); Ed.D., US International, 1987.

Lori Williams (Los Angeles); Psy.D., Alliant International, 2004.

ARGOSY UNIVERSITY, ATLANTA CAMPUS

ARGOSY UNIVERSITY

College of Education

Programs of Study
Argosy University, Atlanta Campus, offers the Master of Arts in Education (M.A.Ed.), the Education Specialist (Ed.S.), and the Doctor of Education (Ed.D.) degrees in educational leadership or instructional leadership.

The M.A.Ed. in Educational Leadership program is designed to instill key philosophies, theories, and values that impact education. It prepares students to improve policies and practices within organizations through the motivation and supervision of others. Students develop skills needed to design, implement, and evaluate educational programs and curricula. Courses include educational law, educational finance, organizational communication, human resource management, instruction supervision, and organizational management.

The M.A.Ed. in Instructional Leadership program examines the challenges and problems encountered in today's educational environment. Course work encompasses the historical, philosophical, psychological, social, technical, and theoretical aspects of education. Students develop skills in analysis, oral and written communication, problem solving, critical thinking, team building, and computer technology. The program is designed for those who wish to develop or enhance classroom skills, become curriculum supervisors, or become educational leaders with a focus on instruction.

The Ed.S. in Educational Leadership program concentrates on applied organizational theory within the context of educational organizations. This specialized program develops the competencies required to secure educational administrator positions at the elementary or secondary school level.

The Ed.S. in Instructional Leadership program enables experienced teachers to become more effective practitioners and educational leaders with a focus on instruction. Course work is designed to satisfy the requirements of students seeking career advancement and those who are working toward a doctoral degree.

The Ed.D. in Educational Leadership program is designed to enhance educational leadership strengths. Students learn innovative and collaborative techniques used to manage and govern educational institutions. The program prepares students for leadership positions at the district, regional, state, or national level. Students must choose a concentration in higher education administration or K–12 education.

The Ed.D. in Instructional Leadership program draws upon educational theories and practices to help students discover new learning techniques for diverse audiences. Students enrolled in this program master teaching methodologies, hone classroom skills, and gain the knowledge required to become curriculum administrators or educational leaders with a focus on instruction. Students must choose a concentration in higher education or K–12 education.

Research Facilities
Argosy University libraries provide curriculum support and educational resources, including current text materials, diagnostic training documents, reference materials and databases, journals and dissertations, and major and current titles in program areas. They provide an online public-access catalog of library resources throughout the Argosy University system. Students enjoy full remote access to their campus library database, enabling them to study and conduct research at home. Academic databases offer dissertation abstracts, academic journals, and professional periodicals. All library computers are Internet accessible. Software applications include Word, Excel, PowerPoint, SPSS, and various test-scoring programs.

Financial Aid
A wide range of financial aid options is available to students who qualify. Argosy University's Atlanta Campus offers access to federal and state aid programs, merit-based awards, grants, loans, and a work-study program. As a first step, students should complete the Free Application for Federal Student Aid (FAFSA). Prospective students can apply electronically at http://www.fafsa.ed.gov or at the campus. To receive consideration for the maximum amount of aid and ensure timely receipt of funds, it is best to submit an application promptly.

Cost of Study
Tuition varies by program. Students should contact Argosy University's Atlanta Campus for tuition information.

Living and Housing Costs
Students typically live in apartments in the metropolitan Atlanta area. Living expenses vary according to each student's preferred standard of living, housing, and transportation. The University does not offer or operate student housing. Most of the students are full-time working professionals who live within driving distance of the campus. Several nearby hotels offer special rates for those who commute from long distances. The Admissions Department also maintains a list of housing options, including contact information for University students who wish to share housing. For more information, students should contact the Admissions Department.

Student Group
Admission to Argosy University's Atlanta Campus is selective to ensure a highly qualified student body. It encourages diversity in academic and employment backgrounds and promotes integration of the student body into professional life through established connections with local and national professional associations. Argosy University offers a professionally oriented education with rich opportunities to gain practical experience in class, field placements, and internships. Full-time students and working professionals gain the extensive knowledge and range of skills necessary for effective performance in their chosen fields.

Student Outcomes
Students can register with the University's online career-services system and use select services from a distance, such as degree-specific career e-mail lists, national job posts, and virtual job fairs. Students should contact the University for more information.

Location
The Argosy University, Atlanta Campus, is housed in a modern building in Sandy Springs, a northern suburb of Atlanta. The campus features a cafe and outdoor lakeside terrace. Beyond the University, students find a wide selection of affordable housing options. This major metropolitan area offers many social and recreational opportunities, from clubs and concerts to galleries and museums, from a growing restaurant scene to Braves baseball games and rollerblading in Piedmont Park.

Many educational institutions and agencies in the area provide excellent opportunities for student training. Atlanta's thriving business environment includes high-technology companies such as EarthLink and Macquarium, as well as corporate giants such as the Coca-Cola Company, CNN, Delta Air Lines, AT&T, and Georgia Pacific.

The University
Argosy University is a private institution with eighteen locations across the nation. Argosy University's Atlanta Campus provides students with a career resources office, an academic resources center, and extensive information access for research. It offers the resources of a large university, plus the friendliness and personal attention of a small campus. Argosy University's Atlanta Campus is closely associated with the Franklin, Tennessee, campus, an approved degree site near Nashville.

The innovative programs feature dynamic, relevant, and practical curricula delivered in flexible class formats. Students enjoy scheduling options that make it easier to fit school into their busy lives, choosing from day and evening courses, on campus or online. Many students find a combination of class formats to be an ideal way of continuing their education while meeting family and professional demands.

Argosy University is accredited by the Higher Learning Commission and is a member of the North Central Association (NCA, 30 North LaSalle Street, Suite 2400, Chicago, Illinois 60602; 800-621-7440 (toll-free); http://www.ncahlc.org).

Applying
Argosy University, Atlanta Campus, accepts students year-round on a rolling admissions basis, depending on availability of required courses. Applications for admission are available online or by contacting the campus.

Correspondence and Information
Argosy University, the Atlanta Campus
990 Hammond Drive, Suite 100
Atlanta, Georgia 30328
Phone: 770-671-1200
        888-671-4777 (toll-free)
Fax: 770-671-0476
E-mail: auadmissions@argosy.edu
Web site: http://www.argosy.edu/atlanta

Argosy University, Atlanta Campus

THE FACULTY

The Argosy University faculty comprises working professionals who are eager to help students succeed. Members bring real-world experience and the latest practice innovations to the academic setting. The diverse faculty members of the College of Education are widely recognized for contributions to the field. Many are published scholars, and most hold doctoral degrees. They provide a substantive education that combines comprehensive knowledge with critical skills and practical workplace relevance. Above all, faculty members are committed to their students' personal and professional development.

ARGOSY UNIVERSITY

ARGOSY UNIVERSITY, INLAND EMPIRE CAMPUS

College of Education

Programs of Study
Argosy University, Inland Empire Campus, offers the Master of Arts in Education (M.A.Ed.) degree in educational leadership and instructional leadership and the Doctor of Education (Ed.D.) degree in community college executive leadership, educational leadership, and instructional leadership.

The M.A.Ed. in Educational Leadership program is designed to instill key philosophies, theories, and values that impact education. It prepares students to improve policies and practices within organizations through the motivation and supervision of others. Students develop skills needed to design, implement, and evaluate educational programs and curricula. Courses include educational law, educational finance, organizational communication, human resource management, instruction supervision, and organizational management.

The M.A.Ed. in Instructional Leadership program examines the challenges and problems encountered in today's educational environment. Course work encompasses the historical, philosophical, psychological, social, technical, and theoretical aspects of education. Students develop skills in analysis, oral and written communication, problem solving, critical thinking, team building, and computer technology. The program is designed for those who wish to develop or enhance classroom skills, become curriculum supervisors, or become educational leaders with a focus on instruction. Students may choose one of four optional concentrations: single or multiple subject teacher credential preparation or single or multiple subject teacher credential preparation with bilingual cross-cultural language and academic development (BCLAD).

The Ed.D. in Community College Executive Leadership program offers an accelerated course of study intended to meet the needs of community college administrators who are looking to move into senior administrative positions (such as president, vice president, dean, and director) in community colleges.

The Ed.D. in Educational Leadership program is designed to enhance educational leadership strengths. Students learn innovative and collaborative techniques used to manage and govern educational institutions. The program prepares students for administrative leadership positions at the district, regional, state, or national level. Students must choose a concentration in higher education administration or K–12 education.

The Ed.D. in Instructional Leadership program draws upon educational theories and practices to help students discover new learning techniques for diverse audiences. Students enrolled in this program master teaching methodologies, hone classroom skills, and gain the knowledge required to become curriculum administrators or educational leaders with a focus on instruction. Students must choose a concentration in higher education or K–12 education.

Research Facilities
Argosy University libraries provide curriculum support and educational resources, including current text materials, diagnostic training documents, reference materials and databases, journals and dissertations, and major and current titles in program areas. They provide an online public-access catalog of library resources throughout the Argosy University system. Students enjoy full remote access to their campus library database, enabling them to study and conduct research at home. Academic databases offer dissertation abstracts, academic journals, and professional periodicals. All library computers are Internet accessible. Software applications include Word, Excel, PowerPoint, SPSS, and various test-scoring programs.

Financial Aid
A wide range of financial aid options is available to students who qualify. Argosy University's Inland Empire Campus offers access to federal and state aid programs, merit-based awards, grants, loans, and a work-study program. As a first step, students should complete the Free Application for Federal Student Aid (FAFSA). Prospective students can apply electronically at http://www.fafsa.ed.gov or at the campus. To receive consideration for the maximum amount of aid and ensure timely receipt of funds, it is best to submit an application promptly.

Cost of Study
Tuition varies by program. Students should contact Argosy University's Inland Empire Campus for tuition information.

Living and Housing Costs
Students typically live in apartments in the metropolitan area. Living expenses vary according to each student's preferred standard of living, housing, and transportation. The University does not offer or operate student housing. Most of the students are full-time working professionals who live within driving distance of the campus. Several nearby hotels offer special rates for those who commute from long distances. The Admissions Department also maintains a list of housing options, including contact information for University students who wish to share housing. For more information, students should contact the Admissions Department.

Student Group
Admission to Argosy University's Inland Empire Campus is selective to ensure a highly qualified student body. It encourages diversity in academic and employment backgrounds and promotes integration of the student body into professional life through established connections with local and national professional associations. Argosy University offers a professionally oriented education with rich opportunities to gain practical experience in class, field placements, and internships. Full-time students and working professionals gain the extensive knowledge and range of skills necessary for effective performance in their chosen fields.

Student Outcomes
Students can register with the University's online career-services system and use select services from a distance, such as degree-specific career e-mail lists, national job posts, and virtual job fairs. Students should contact the University for more information.

Location
Argosy University's Inland Empire Campus is located in the Hospitality Lane section of San Bernardino, California. The facility features classrooms, computer labs, a resource center with Internet access, a student lounge, staff and faculty offices, and proximity to the region's many cultural and recreational attractions. Argosy University provides a supportive educational environment with convenient class options that enable students to earn a degree while fulfilling other life responsibilities. All of the programs are thoroughly oriented to the real working world. The University focuses on developing technical proficiency in each student's field, as well as an overall professional career approach. Many educational institutions and agencies in the area provide excellent opportunities for student training.

The University
Argosy University is a private institution with eighteen locations across the nation. Argosy University's Inland Empire Campus provides students with a career resources office, an academic resources center, and extensive information access for research. It offers the resources of a large university, plus the friendliness and personal attention of a small campus.

The innovative programs feature dynamic, relevant, and practical curricula delivered in flexible class formats. Students enjoy scheduling options that make it easier to fit school into their busy lives, choosing from day and evening courses, on campus or online. Many students find a combination of class formats to be an ideal way of continuing their education while meeting family and professional demands.

Argosy University is accredited by the Higher Learning Commission and is a member of the North Central Association (NCA, 30 North LaSalle Street, Suite 2400, Chicago, Illinois 60602; 800-621-7440 (toll-free); http://www.ncahlc.org).

Applying
Argosy University, Inland Empire Campus, accepts students year-round on a rolling admissions basis, depending on availability of required courses. Applications for admission are available online or by contacting the campus.

Correspondence and Information
Argosy University, Inland Empire Campus
636 East Brier Drive, Suite 235
San Bernardino, California 92408
Phone: 909-915-3800
          866-217-9075 (toll-free)
Fax: 909-915-3810
E-mail: auadmissions@argosy.edu
Web site: http://www.argosy.edu/inlandempire

Argosy University, Inland Empire Campus

THE FACULTY

The Argosy University faculty comprises working professionals who are eager to help students succeed. Members bring real-world experience and the latest practice innovations to the academic setting. The diverse faculty members of the College of Education are widely recognized for contributions to the field. Most hold doctoral degrees. They provide a substantive education that combines comprehensive knowledge with critical skills and practical workplace relevance. Above all, faculty members are committed to their students' personal and professional development.

ARGOSY UNIVERSITY, NASHVILLE CAMPUS

College of Education

ARGOSY UNIVERSITY

Programs of Study   Argosy University, Nashville Campus, offers the Master of Arts in Education (M.A.Ed.), the Education Specialist (Ed.S.), and the Doctor of Education (Ed.D.) degrees in educational leadership and instructional leadership.

The M.A.Ed. in Educational Leadership program is designed to instill key philosophies, theories, and values that impact education. It prepares students to improve policies and practices within organizations through the motivation and supervision of others. Students develop skills needed to design, implement, and evaluate educational programs and curricula. Courses include educational law, educational finance, organizational communication, human resource management, instruction supervision, and organizational management.

The M.A.Ed. in Instructional Leadership program examines the challenges and problems encountered in today's educational environment. Course work encompasses the historical, philosophical, psychological, social, technical, and theoretical aspects of education. Students develop skills in analysis, oral and written communication, problem solving, critical thinking, team building, and computer technology. The program is designed for those who wish to develop or enhance classroom skills, become curriculum supervisors, or become educational leaders with a focus on instruction.

The Ed.S. in Educational Leadership program concentrates on applied organizational theory within the context of educational organizations. This specialized program develops the competencies required to secure educational administrator positions at the elementary or secondary school level.

The Ed.S. in Instructional Leadership program enables experienced teachers to become more effective practitioners and educational leaders with a focus on instruction. Course work is designed to satisfy the requirements of students seeking career advancement and those who are working toward a doctoral degree.

The Ed.D. in Educational Leadership program is designed to enhance educational leadership strengths. Students learn innovative and collaborative techniques used to manage and govern educational institutions. The program prepares students for administrative leadership positions at the district, regional, state, or national level. Students must choose a concentration in higher education administration or K–12 education.

The Ed.D. in Instructional Leadership program draws upon educational theories and practices to help students discover new learning techniques for diverse audiences. Students enrolled in this program master teaching methodologies, hone classroom skills, and gain the knowledge required to become curriculum administrators or educational leaders with a focus on instruction. Students must choose a concentration in higher education administration or K–12 education.

Research Facilities   Argosy University libraries provide curriculum support and educational resources, including current text materials, diagnostic training documents, reference materials and databases, journals and dissertations, and major and current titles in program areas. They provide an online public-access catalog of library resources throughout the Argosy University system. Students enjoy full remote access to their campus library database, enabling them to study and conduct research at home. Academic databases offer dissertation abstracts, academic journals, and professional periodicals. All library computers are Internet accessible. Software applications include Word, Excel, PowerPoint, SPSS, and various test-scoring programs.

Financial Aid   A wide range of financial aid options is available to students who qualify. Argosy University's Nashville Campus offers access to federal and state aid programs, merit-based awards, grants, loans, and a work-study program. As a first step, students should complete the Free Application for Federal Student Aid (FAFSA). Prospective students can apply electronically at http://www.fafsa.ed.gov or at the campus. To receive consideration for the maximum amount of aid and ensure timely receipt of funds, it is best to submit an application promptly.

Cost of Study   Tuition varies by program. Students should contact Argosy University's Nashville Campus for tuition information.

Living and Housing Costs   Students typically live in apartments in the metropolitan Nashville area. Living expenses vary according to each student's preferred standard of living, housing, and transportation. The University does not offer or operate student housing. Most of the students are full-time working professionals who live within driving distance of the campus. Several nearby hotels offer special rates for those who commute from long distances. The Admissions Department also maintains a list of housing options, including contact information, for University students who wish to share housing. For more information, students should contact the Admissions Department.

Student Group   Admission to Argosy University's Nashville Campus is selective to ensure a highly qualified student body. It encourages diversity in academic and employment backgrounds and promotes integration of the student body into professional life through established connections with local and national professional associations. Argosy University offers a professionally oriented education with rich opportunities to gain practical experience in class, field placements, and internships. Full-time students and working professionals gain the extensive knowledge and range of skills necessary for effective performance in their chosen fields.

Student Outcomes   Students can register with the University's online career-services system and use select services from a distance, such as degree-specific career e-mail lists, national job posts, and virtual job fairs. Students should contact the University for more information.

Location   Argosy University's Nashville Campus is located at 100 Centerview Drive in Nashville, Tennessee. This growing city offers a variety of recreational activities, including the ballet and symphony, the newly established Frist Museum of Art, and professional sports. Nashville is known as Music City, USA, and is home to the Country Music Hall of Fame. Many educational institutions and agencies in the area provide excellent opportunities for student training. The thriving business environment includes companies such as Moses Cone Health Systems, Inc., and Novant Health, Inc.

The University   Argosy University is a private institution with eighteen locations across the nation. Argosy University's Nashville Campus provides students with a career resources office, an academic resources center, and extensive information access for research. It offers the resources of a large university, plus the friendliness and personal attention of a small campus. The innovative programs feature dynamic, relevant, and practical curricula delivered in flexible class formats. Students enjoy scheduling options that make it easier to fit school into their busy lives, choosing from day and evening courses, on campus or online. Many students find a combination of class formats to be an ideal way of continuing their education while meeting family and professional demands.

Argosy University is accredited by the Higher Learning Commission and is a member of the North Central Association (NCA, 30 North LaSalle Street, Suite 2400, Chicago, Illinois 60602; 800-621-7440 (toll-free); http://www.ncahlc.org).

Applying   Argosy University, Nashville Campus, accepts students year-round on a rolling admissions basis, depending on availability of required courses. Applications for admission are available online or by contacting the campus.

Correspondence and Information
Argosy University, Nashville Campus
100 Centerview Drive, Suite 225
Nashville, Tennessee 37214
Phone: 615-525-2800
        866-833-6598 (toll-free)
Fax: 615-525-2900
E-mail: auadmissions@argosy.edu
Web site: http://www.argosy.edu/nashville

Argosy University, Nashville Campus

THE FACULTY

The Argosy University faculty comprises working professionals who are eager to help students succeed. Members bring real-world experience and the latest practice innovations to the academic setting. The diverse faculty members of the College of Education are widely recognized for contributions to the field. Most hold doctoral degrees. They provide a substantive education that combines comprehensive knowledge with critical skills and practical workplace relevance. Above all, faculty members are committed to their students' personal and professional development.

CLEMSON UNIVERSITY

Master's Program in Administration and Supervision

Program of Study

The Department of Leadership, Technology, and Counselor Education at Clemson University offers a program of graduate study leading to the Master of Education degree in educational administration and supervision. The program is accredited by the National Council for Accreditation of Teacher Education (NCATE), and it fulfills the requirements of the South Carolina State Department of Education for certification as a school principal and supervisor.

Classes are held at the University Center of Greenville in Greenville, South Carolina. The program requires 42 credit hours of study. Required classes include the following: EDL 700, Introduction to Educational Administration, 3 hours; EDL 710, Organization Theory for School Administrators, 3 hours; EDL 720, School Personnel Administration, 3 hours; EDL 730, Techniques of Supervision, 3 hours; EDL 735, Educational Evaluation, 3 hours; EDL 740, Curriculum Planning and Improvement, 3 hours; EDL 745, School Finance, 3 hours; EDL 725, Legal Phases of School Administration and Supervision, 3 hours; EDL 705, The Principalship, 3 hours; EDL 715, School and Community Relations, 3 hours; EDL 795, Leadership Information Systems, 3 hours; and EDL 750, Field Experience in Elementary Administration and Supervision, 6 hours, or EDL 755, Field Experience in Secondary Administration and Supervision, 6 hours (students should take 3 practicum hours at the beginning of the program and 3 at the end). In addition, there is a 3-hour Education Research requirement, in which courses must be taken in sequence within three levels: Level I consists of EDL 730, EDL 700, EDL 710, EDL 795, EDL 735, and EDL750/755. The practicum plus two of the four Level I courses must be completed before attempting Level II or Level III. Level II consists of EDL 705, EDL 720, EDL 725, and EDL 778. Two of the four Level II courses must be completed before attempting Level III. Level III consists of EDL 750/755, EDL 745, EDL 715, and EDL 740.

A comprehensive written examination is required for graduation, and students must complete the program within six years; however, most students earn their degrees much sooner.

Research Facilities

The program allows students to participate in internships and research projects via practicums and internships. Students also have full access to the University libraries and their hard copy and online holdings.

Financial Aid

Financial aid in the form of competitive University fellowships is available, as are student loans. For more information about financial aid, students should visit the financial aid office at http://virtual.clemson.edu/groups/finaid/.

Cost of Study

Tuition for 2007–08 is $3641 per semester for in-state students and $7285 per semester for nonresidents. Off-campus rates are $330 per hour for in-state students and $660 per hour for nonresidents. Graduate assistants pay a flat fee of $950 per semester and $315 per summer session. Graduate fellows pay South Carolina resident fees.

Living and Housing Costs

On-campus housing is available. For information, students should visit http://www.housing.clemson.edu. The cost of living in Clemson is quite low compared to the national average. Students who choose to live off the campus typically spend $300–$400 per month for rent, depending on location, amenities, roommates, and other factors.

Student Outcomes

Graduates are prepared to become principals and administrators in a variety of educational settings.

Location

Clemson is a small, beautiful college town near the Blue Ridge Mountains and Lake Hartwell in upstate South Carolina. The Upstate is one of the country's fastest-growing areas and is an important part of the I-85 corridor, a multi-state area along Interstate 85 that runs from metro Atlanta to Richmond, Virginia, and encompasses Charlotte, North Carolina, and North Carolina's Research Triangle. Atlanta and Charlotte are each a two-hour drive. Many financial institutions and other industries have a national headquarters or a major presence in the Upstate, including Wachovia, Bank of America, BMW, Bon Secours St. Francis Health System, Bosch North America, Bowater, Charter Communications, Ernst and Young, Fluor Corporation, IBM, Microsoft, Michelin of North America, and many others.

The University

Clemson is classified by the Carnegie Foundation as an RU/H: Research University (high research activity), a category comprising just 10 percent of all graduate degree-granting universities in America. The University's mission is to fulfill the covenant between its founder and the people of South Carolina to establish a "high seminary of learning" through its responsibilities of teaching, research, and extended public service. The University has identified eight areas of academic emphasis that create collaborations that, in turn, help fulfill the University's mission.

Applying

Applicants may apply on the Web at http://www.grad.clemson.edu/p_apply.html. Applications with a $50 nonrefundable fee should be received no later than five weeks prior to registration. Every required item in support of the application must be on file by that date. Students are advised to contact the department for the deadlines of the program of proposed study.

Correspondence and Information

David S. Fleming, Ph.D.
Graduate Coordinator
Eugene T. Moore School of Education
G-01 Tillman Hall
Clemson University
Clemson, South Carolina 29634
Phone: 864-656-1881
Fax: 864-656-0311
E-mail: dflemin@clemson.edu
Web site: http://www.hehd.clemson.edu/schoolofed/g-admin.htm

Clemson University

THE FACULTY AND THEIR RESEARCH

Jackson L. Flanigan, Professor; Ed.D., Virginia Tech. Education administration; school law, principals, and superintendents.

Edward A. Grandpre, Assistant Professor; Ph.D., Ohio State. Higher education student affairs; research and evaluation, higher education finance, higher education legal principles, legal and ethical issues in student affairs practice, counselor education.

Jane C. Lindle, Professor; Ph.D., Wisconsin–Madison. Educational administration; school and community relations, parent involvement, micropolitical aspects of schooling, research methodology, school policy and governance.

Russell A. Marion, Professor; Ph.D., North Carolina. Education administration; leadership, organizational theory, business management, facility planning, leadership information systems.

Patricia Diane Ricciardi, Assistant Professor; Ph.D., South Carolina. Educational leadership; public school administration, instructional leadership, school personnel management, curriculum organization.

Frankie Keels Williams, Assistant Professor; Ph.D., South Carolina. Education administration; women in educational leadership, diversity issues and experiences, community colleges, supervision techniques, history of higher education, research in higher education.

CLEMSON UNIVERSITY

Curriculum and Instruction

Program of Study

The Doctor of Philosophy (Ph.D.) degree in curriculum and instruction at Clemson University is a research degree program. The intent of the program is to prepare students to make significant contributions to knowledge in a specialized field related to education. Programs are available in the following areas: elementary education, English education, mathematics education, reading and literacy education, science education, social studies education, and special education. These areas provide a general structure of course work and research emphases. However, students are encouraged to work with faculty members to design programs that are uniquely suited to their areas of interest and to obtain guidance in developing research expertise.

The goals of the program are for students to critically analyze the social, historical, psychological, personal, and policy dimensions of curriculum and instruction, particularly in their chosen area of concentration; to acquire an understanding of the research processes appropriate to their field of study, including designing research studies, analyzing data, and reporting results in scholarly outlets; and to analyze and evaluate critically the literature of the field.

Doctoral students must satisfy requirements pertaining to course work and internships. They must pass a comprehensive exam, successfully defend a dissertation proposal, and complete a dissertation. The degree typically requires at least 70 credit hours beyond the master's degree. However, a student's program of study is designed with and approved by a dissertation committee made up of faculty members. A minimum of 3 semester hours of internship credit is required in the area of specialization, and a minimum of 6 semester hours must be completed in programs outside the School of Education.

Research Facilities

The teacher education department has two specialized computer labs for instruction and a curriculum lab with a host of curriculum materials. In addition, faculty members and students are supported by the South Carolina Center of Excellence for Instructional Technology Training that is housed in the teacher education department. There are also excellent collaborations for research and projects with schools and school districts across the state.

Financial Aid

There are typically a number of grant-funded assistantships, as well as several graduate teaching assistantships for students enrolled in Clemson's teacher education programs, available for approximately $14,000 per year or more.

Cost of Study

Tuition for 2007–08 is $3641 per semester for in-state students and $7285 per semester for nonresidents. Off-campus rates are $330 per hour for in-state students and $660 per hour for nonresidents. Graduate assistants pay a flat fee of $950 per semester. Graduate fellows pay South Carolina resident fees.

Living and Housing Costs

On-campus housing is available; for information, students should visit http://www.housing.clemson.edu. The cost of living in Clemson is quite low compared to the national average; students who choose to live off campus typically spend $300–$400 per month for rent, depending on location, amenities, roommates, and other factors.

Student Group

The program has approximately 30 students; 85 percent are women, 66 percent attend on a part-time basis, and 6 percent are international students.

Student Outcomes

Graduate students are prepared to continue teaching as master teachers, to function in school/district curriculum leadership positions, or to succeed as higher education faculty members in teacher education preparation programs, capable of handling any mixture of teaching, research, and service demands.

Location

Clemson is a small, beautiful college town near the Blue Ridge Mountains and Lake Hartwell in Upstate South Carolina. The Upstate is one of the country's fastest-growing areas and is an important part of the I-85 corridor, a multistate area along Interstate 85 that runs from metro Atlanta to Richmond, Virginia, and encompasses Charlotte, North Carolina, and North Carolina's Research Triangle. Atlanta and Charlotte are each a 2-hour drive away. Many financial institutions and other industries have national headquarters for a major presence in the Upstate, including Wachovia, Bank of America, BMW, Bon Secours St. Francis Health System, Bosch North America, Bowater, Charter Communications, Ernst & Young, Fluor Corporation, IBM, Microsoft, Michelin of North America, and many others.

The University

Clemson is classified by the Carnegie Foundation as an RU/H: Research University (high research activity), a category comprising just 10 percent of all graduate degree–granting universities in America. The University's mission is to fulfill the covenant between its founder and the people of South Carolina to establish a "high seminary of learning" through its responsibilities of teaching, research, and extended public service. The University has identified eight areas of academic emphasis that create collaborations that, in turn, help fulfill the University's mission.

Applying

Successful candidates typically have a master's degree, a minimum GPA of 3.5, acceptable GRE scores, relevant experiences, and a successful interview. Applicants may apply on the Web at http://www.grad.clemson.edu/p_apply.html. Applications with a $50 nonrefundable fee should be received no later than five weeks prior to registration. Every required item in support of the application must be on file by that date. Students are advised to contact the department for the deadlines of the program of proposed study.

Correspondence and Information

David S. Fleming, Ph.D.
Graduate Coordinator
Eugene T. Moore School of Education
G-01 Tillman Hall
Clemson University
Clemson, South Carolina 29634-0702
Phone: 864-656-1881
Fax: 864-656-0311
E-mail: dflemin@clemson.edu
Web site: http://www.hehd.clemson.edu/schoolofed/

Clemson University

THE FACULTY AND THEIR RESEARCH

Beatrice Naff Bailey, Professor; Ed.D., Virginia Tech. Curriculum and instruction.

David E. Barrett, Professor; Ph.D., USC. Education psychology.

Wanda Calvert, Clinical Faculty; Ph.D., South Carolina. Elementary education.

Megan Che, Assistant Professor; Ph.D., Oklahoma. Instructional leadership and academic curriculum.

Michelle Cook, Assistant Professor; Ph.D., North Carolina State. Science education.

Vivian Correa, Distinguished Professor; Ph.D., Vanderbilt. Special education.

Chrystal Dean, Assistant Professor; Ph.D., Vanderbilt. Teaching and learning, math education.

Gail C. Delicio, Associate Professor; Ph.D., Florida State. Education psychology.

Pamela J. Dunston, Associate Professor; Ph.D., Georgia. Reading education.

Angela Eckhoff, Assistant Professor; Ph.D., Colorado. Educational psychology and cognitive science.

Lienne C. Federico, Assistant Professor; Ph.D., East Carolina. Educational leadership/English education.

William R. Fisk, Professor and Department Chair; Ph.D., Florida State. School psychology.

David S. Fleming, Assistant Professor; Ph.D., USC. Physical education/pedagogy.

Susan King Fullerton, Associate Professor; Ph.D., Maryland. Curriculum and instruction, reading.

Linda Gambrell, Full Professor; Ph.D., Maryland. Curriculum and instruction, reading.

Robert P. Green Jr., Alumni Professor; Ed.D., Virginia. Curriculum and instruction.

Kathy Neal Headley, Professor; Ed.D., Auburn. Reading.

Martha J. Hodge, Associate Professor; Ph.D., Vanderbilt. Special education.

Robert M. Horton, Associate Professor; Ed.D., Cincinnati. Curriculum and instruction.

Larry Brent Igo, Assistant Professor; Ph.D., Nebraska–Lincoln. Educational psychology.

Rebecca Kaminski, Clinical Faculty; Ed.D., Pittsburgh. Instruction and learning.

Antonis Katsiyannis, Professor; Ed.D., William and Mary. Education administration, special education–behavior disorders.

Charles C. Linnell, Associate Professor; Ed.D., North Carolina State. Industrial arts education.

Agida Manizade, Assistant Professor; Ph.D., Virginia. Mathematics education.

Jeff Marshall, Assistant Professor; Ph.D., Indiana. Curriculum and instruction.

William Paige, Professor; Ph.D., Ohio State. Industrial technology education.

Kimberly McDuffie, Assistant Professor; Ph.D., George Mason. Special education.

Jonda Cecole McNair, Assistant Professor; Ph.D., Ohio State. Language, literacy, and culture.

Susan J. Pass, Assistant Professor; Ed.D., Houston. Social studies.

Chris L. Peters, Associate Professor; Ed.D., Georgia. Instructional technology.

Cheryl Poston, Associate Professor; Ed.D., Georgia. Vocational education.

David Paul Reinking, Named Professor; Ph.D., Minnesota, Twin Cities. Reading education.

Paul J. Riccomini, Assistant Professor; Ph.D., Penn State. Special education.

Victoria G. Ridgeway, Associate Professor; Ph.D., Georgia. Reading education.

Suzanne N. Rosenblith, Assistant Professor; Ph.D., Wisconsin–Madison. Educational policy studies.

Joseph Ryan, Assistant Professor; Ph.D., Nebraska–Lincoln. Special education.

Deborah A. Smith, Associate Professor; Ed.D., Tennessee. Physical education.

Mindy Spearman, Assistant Professor; Ph.D., Texas. Curriculum and instruction.

Pamela M. Stecker, Associate Professor; Ph.D., Vanderbilt. Education and human development.

Dolores A. Stegelin, Professor; Ph.D., Florida. Early childhood development and interdisciplinary research.

Deborah M. Switzer, Professor; Ph.D., Illinois. Educational psychology.

Rachelle Washington, Assistant Professor; Ph.D., Georgia. Language and literacy.

Carol G. Weatherford, Associate Professor; Ed.D., North Carolina State. Occupational education.

Elaine Mumbauer Wiegert, Assistant Professor; Ph.D., Clemson. Curriculum and instruction.

Seal Wilson, Clinical Faculty; Ph.D., Southern Mississippi. Special education.

CLEMSON UNIVERSITY

Ph.D. in Educational Leadership

Program of Study

The Ph.D. in educational leadership program is designed to provide students with a strong background in five domains: leadership, research, policy, ethics, and diversity. As the highest academic degree granted by Clemson University, the Ph.D. is designed to prepare students to become scholars who can discover, integrate, and apply knowledge as leaders in schools and postsecondary and community educational institutions and agencies. This is accomplished through close association with and apprenticeship to faculty members experienced in research, teaching, and a variety of leadership roles in the field of education.

Candidates must take a minimum of 58 graduate-level course credits beyond the master's degree and complete an 18-hour dissertation project. The program core consists of 15 hours, culminating in a preliminary exam and the confirmation of their doctoral advising committee members. Research and assessment methodology compose another 13 hours, while the specialty area comprises 18 hours. The field of specialization may be in either public school leadership or higher education. All students must complete an internship for 6 hours of credit. (Students focusing on public leadership may complete additional internships as required for state licensing.) Internships are supervised by a practicing educational leader and by a faculty member. The internship experience is designed to acquaint the student with the practical applications of education theory as well as develop a research agenda. Cognates are courses from another area of study, and each student must complete a minimum of 6 graduate semester hours in a supporting academic discipline beyond educational leadership. At the completion of this program of studies (research, specialization, internship, and cognate courses), students achieve candidacy toward completion of their dissertation by successfully completing a comprehensive examination. Candidates then proceed through three courses of proposal development and guided residency courses for completing the dissertation and a successful defense.

A student admitted to the educational leadership doctoral program must begin course work within one year from the semester of acceptance or reapply for admission. Students are discouraged from taking more than 6 hours of doctoral course work prior to being admitted to the program. This does not preclude the use of courses completed in the Ed.S. degree in educational administration.

Research Facilities

The Clemson University libraries have a collection of more than 7,000 serial titles and 1.5 million volumes that were developed to support the undergraduate and graduate curricula and research. Several commercial bibliographic databases and locally created full-text databases may be searched online from local and remote computers. The library is linked electronically through OCLC, Inc., to more than 11,000 other libraries worldwide for cataloging and interlibrary loan services.

The Houston Center for the Study of Black Experience Affecting Higher Education assists in developing programs to increase the number of African-American students and faculty members in education. Programs are developed in cooperation with public schools, community-based organizations, federal and state government, and private foundations. The center also participates in designing evaluation strategies for twenty-first-century after-school projects. The International Center for Service-Learning and Teacher Education integrates service learning and teacher education with an international perspective. The Eugene T. Moore School of Education embraces a commitment to service learning, civic engagement, and social responsibility. Center activities focus on four areas—professional development and technical assistance, collection and dissemination of information and resources, collaborations and partnerships, and research and evaluation.

Financial Aid

Graduate students may receive two types of appointments—a graduate assistantship requiring University employment or a fellowship requiring no service to the University. Fellowships and assistantships are administered by the respective colleges or departments, and applicants should contact their department for more details.

The Federal Stafford Loan is the only form of federal aid available to graduate students through the financial aid office. Students must be accepted into a degree-granting graduate program and be enrolled at least half-time.

Cost of Study

Tuition for 2007–08 is $3641 per semester for in-state students and $7285 per semester for nonresidents. Off-campus rates are $330 per hour for in-state students and $660 per hour for nonresidents. Graduate assistants pay a flat fee of $950 per semester. Graduate fellows pay South Carolina resident fees.

Living and Housing Costs

On-campus housing is available; for information, students should visit http://www.housing.clemson.edu. The cost of living in Clemson is quite low compared to the national average; students who choose to live off-campus typically spend $300–$400 per month for rent, depending on location, amenities, roommates, and other factors.

Student Group

There are 6 full-time (4 women) and 37 part-time (18 women) students. These figures include 3 African American students.

Location

Clemson is a small, beautiful college town near the Blue Ridge Mountains and Lake Hartwell in upstate South Carolina. The Upstate is one of the country's fastest-growing areas and is an important part of the I-85 corridor, a multistate area along Interstate 85 that runs from metro Atlanta to Richmond, Virginia, and encompasses Charlotte, North Carolina, and North Carolina's Research Triangle. Atlanta and Charlotte are each a two-hour's drive away. Many financial institutions and other industries have national headquarters for a major presence in the Upstate, including Wachovia, Bank of America, BMW, Bon Secours St. Francis Health System, Bosch North America, Bowater, Charter Communications, Ernst and Young, Fluor Corporation, IBM, Microsoft, Michelin of North America, and many others.

The University

Clemson is classified by the Carnegie Foundation as an RU/H: Research University (high research activity), a category comprising just 10 percent of all graduate degree-granting universities in America. The University's mission is to fulfill the covenant between its founder and the people of South Carolina to establish a "high seminary of learning" through its responsibilities of teaching, research, and extended public service. The University has identified eight areas of academic emphasis that create collaborations that, in turn, help fulfill the University's mission.

Applying

Applicants may apply on the Web at http://www.grad.clemson.edu/p_apply.html. Successful candidates have a master's degree in a related field as well as a minimum GRE composite score of 1450 (at least 500 on the verbal and quantitative sections). Applicants should complete the application form from the Graduate School and submit the $50 application fee, GRE scores, three letters of recommendation, and a two-page letter that discusses the reasons for pursuing the Ph.D. This letter may be used as a writing sample. Interviews are optional. The application deadline is June 1.

Correspondence and Information

David S. Fleming, Ph.D.
Graduate Coordinator
Eugene T. Moore School of Education
G-01 Tillman Hall
Clemson University
Clemson, South Carolina 29634-0702
Phone: 864-656-1881
Fax: 864-656-0311
E-mail: dflemin@clemson.edu
Web site: http://www.hehd.clemson.edu/schoolofed/

Clemson University

THE FACULTY AND THEIR RESEARCH

Faculty members of the Ph.D. in educational leadership program work to improve the quality of P–16 education by preparing leaders who develop and use research-based knowledge and practices about institutions, organizations, and instruction to create learning communities that improve the performance of all students.

Mike Campbell, Clinical Professor; Ph.D., Clemson. Superintendency.

Jackson L. Flanigan, Professor; Ed.D., Virginia Tech. Educational leadership, school law, finance.

Lamont Flowers, Distinguished Professor of Educational Leadership and Director of the Charles H. Houston Center; Ph.D., Iowa. Higher education administration, the professorate.

Jane C. Lindle, Eugene T. Moore Endowed Professor of Educational Leadership; Ph.D., Wisconsin–Madison. School and community relations, parent involvement, micropolitical aspects of schooling, research methodology, school policy, governance.

Russ Marion, Professor; Ph.D., North Carolina at Chapel Hill. Complexity leadership theory, leadership of learning organizations, leadership mechanisms, strategic leadership, modeling methodology.

Patricia Diane Ricciardi, Assistant Professor; Ph.D., South Carolina. Human resources, leadership development, mentoring, instructional leadership.

Frankie Keels Williams, Assistant Professor; Ph.D., South Carolina. Higher education administration, transitions and access to postsecondary education.

FIELDING GRADUATE UNIVERSITY

School of Educational Leadership & Change

Programs of Study

The School of Educational Leadership & Change offers a Doctor of Education (Ed.D.) program with optional concentrations in community college leadership and change, grounded theory and action, higher education systems, and media studies. A master's (M.A.) degree in collaborative educational leadership, with an optional concentration in charter school leadership, and a certificate in Teaching in the Virtual Classroom are also available.

The philosophy of the School is to enable teachers, community advocates, and educational administrators to work in their respective communities while simultaneously developing new competencies and leadership skills and acquiring a postgraduate education. Students strategically confront the complex realities and challenges facing schools and colleges today and in the future. These challenges are examined from a broad-based systems and equity perspective in a collaborative educational environment.

Doctoral students find a flexible, networked environment that enables them to pursue their course of study and develop competencies in required learning areas without relocating. Students begin the program by attending an orientation session; they then continue to work independently, with groups, and online. Regional student "cluster" groups meet on a regular basis, a national session takes place once a year, and regional research-intensive sessions occur three times a year. Cluster, national, and research sessions are not mandatory but are offered as opportunities for meaningful face-to-face interaction with faculty members and other students.

The master's program is a two-year, 36-credit course of study currently offered only in California, Georgia, Minnesota, and Wisconsin. Regional student groups gather five weekends per semester for four semesters without a summer school requirement. Students are in charge of their own professional development plan and immediately apply their study and research to their own classroom or work environments. They work with and learn from other professionals within their own geographic region and use Fielding's online tools to collaborate with those outside of their immediate area.

Research Facilities

Fielding's library services are designed to serve the complex needs of busy professionals by offering substantial research tools via the Web. The library collection and services include a database of Internet resources, a subsidized document delivery service, a catalog of available dissertations and electronic books, and access to numerous online library databases and journals.

Financial Aid

Fielding Graduate University participates in Veterans Assistance Programs and the Federal Stafford Student Loan program, which makes subsidized and unsubsidized loans available based on financial need. In 2006–07, Fielding Graduate University administered approximately $18 million in aid to about 75 percent of its graduate students.

Cost of Study

The 2007–08 tuition for the Ed.D. program is $17,640. Tuition for the master's program is $395 per credit, and tuition for the Teaching in the Virtual Classroom certificate program is $4000. Tuition and fee rates are subject to change each academic year. Current tuition information can be found at http://www.fielding.edu/tuition.

Living and Housing Costs

Because Fielding Graduate University students work independently and live in various parts of the United States and beyond, costs in addition to tuition vary. Considerations include computer equipment, books and materials, travel to orientation, and optional travel to national and research sessions and regional cluster meetings. There may be other costs related to a specific course of study.

Student Group

The Fielding Graduate University student community consists primarily of adult learners who have chosen a self-directed, independent learning program and are geographically dispersed, as are the members of the faculty. Fielding's total student population is more than 1,500. The 265 students in the School of Educational Leadership & Change are a diverse group of individuals who form a worldwide professional network. Fielding scholars are practitioners with varied work experience in areas such as higher education, nonprofit agencies, city and community schools, and colleges and agencies as well as business. The average student at Fielding Graduate University is 46 years old; the age range is from 22 to 74 years.

Location

Fielding's administrative offices are located in Santa Barbara, California. The students and faculty members create a global Fielding community representing the United States and thirty-one countries. Attendance at an orientation and planning session meets the doctoral program residency requirements. Optional national and regional sessions and student cluster meetings are offered throughout the year.

The University

Founded in 1974, Fielding Graduate University is a global leader in graduate-level networked education for professionals. Fielding is dedicated to providing high-quality accredited programs through a combination of face-to-face and online interactions between accomplished students and nationally recognized faculty members. The student-centered programs combine theory with practice and are designed to support flexible, independent learning and competency development. This flexibility allows students to apply their graduate studies to their professional work. The Fielding community is dedicated to lifelong learning, innovation, and change for individuals, communities, organizations, and social justice.

Applying

Applications for the Educational Leadership & Change doctoral programs are processed on a rolling basis. Students may enter the doctoral programs three times a year (spring, summer, or fall). Applications for the master's program are accepted continuously, and new cohorts begin as groups of 20 students and are formed in various geographic areas. All applicants must submit a $75 nonrefundable fee, an application form, and additional materials specific to their program of interest.

Correspondence and Information

Admission Office
Fielding Graduate University
2112 Santa Barbara Street
Santa Barbara, California 93105
Phone: 800-340-1099 (toll-free)
E-mail: admission@fielding.edu
Web site: http://www.fielding.edu

Fielding Graduate University

THE FACULTY

Ed.D. PROGRAM

Mentoring Faculty
Judy Witt, Ph.D., Dean.
Michael Suarez, Ph.D., Associate Dean.
Gloria Willingham, Ph.D., Associate Dean.

Rodney J. Beaulieu, Ph.D.
Malcolm Bonner, Ed.D.
Jenny Edwards, Ph.D.
Kitty Kelly Epstein, Ph.D.
Yolanda Gayol, Ed.D.
Sean Ginwright, Ph.D.
Sue Marquis Gordon, Ph.D.
Sheila T. Gregory, Ed.D.
Toni A. Gregory, Ed.D.
Lenneal Henderson Jr., Ph.D.
Anthony Holliday Jr., J.D., LL.M.
Szabi Ishtai-Zee, Ph.D.
Don Trent Jacobs, Ph.D., Ed.D.
Bernard Luskin, Ed.D.
Lee Mahon, Ed.D.
Barbara Mink, Ed.D.
Mark Scanlon-Greene, Ph.D.
Odis Simmons, Ph.D.
Nicola Smith, M.B.A., J.D.
Joyce Germaine Watts, Ed.D.

Adjunct Faculty
Burton A. Cohen, Ph.D.
Cynthia Heelan, Ph.D.
Nancy Holley, Ph.D.
Paul Jhin, Ed.D.
Irene McHenry, Ph.D.
Christopher Norris Oberg, Ph.D.
Gerald Patnode, Ed.D.
Geraldine Perri-Petruolo, Ph.D.
Keith Pratt, Ph.D.
Michael Raffanti, Ed.D.
Luis Reyes, Ph.D.
Harriet Robles, Ed.D.
Ting L. Sun, Ph.D.
Kathy Tiner, Ph.D.
Kara L. VanderLinden, Ed.D.
Yong-Kang Wei, Ph.D.

Program Consultants
Freda B. Garnanez, Ed.D.
Mary Maxwell, Ed.D.
Peter Park, Ph.D.

MASTER'S PROGRAM
Kathy Tiner, Ph.D., Program Director.

Consulting Faculty
Judy L. Jamieson, M.A.
Geraldine (Dene) Muller, M.E.P.D.
Ken Riley, M.E.

Faculty/Facilitators
James Adams, M.E.
JoAnna Birdsall, Ed.D.
Elisabeth Douglass, M.A.
Jackie Elliott, M.A.
Gary Garbe, M.E.
Martha Flores Gibson, Ed.D.
Gregory Kier, M.S.
Mary Maxwell, Ed.D.
Deborah Newbrand, Ed.D.
Gina Newton, M.A.
Joseph Peake, M.S.
Kaye Ragland, Ed.D.
Lois Rasberry, M.A.
Ref Rodriguez, M.A.
Bernard Slowey, M.S.
Bitsey Stark, Ed.D.
Gary Stebbins, Ed.D.
Monique Todd, M.A.
Gary Wilkins, Ed.D.
Roger Wistrcill, M.S.

MONTCLAIR STATE UNIVERSITY

Center of Pedagogy

Programs of Study

Montclair State University offers a doctoral (Ed.D.) program in pedagogy through the University's Center of Pedagogy. The Center is the first of its kind in the nation. The Center coordinates and oversees all aspects of teacher education. Its mission is to promote the continuous development of educators—new and experienced, field- and university-based—through the simultaneous renewal of schools and the education of educators. Policy making and governance in the Center rest on the collaboration of the tripartite: members of the faculty and administration from the schools, the College of Education and Human Services, and faculty members from the arts and sciences. The overarching goal is to support the abilities of current and new generations of teachers to engage actively and productively in a democratic community. Two areas of specialization are currently available: a specialization in mathematics education and a specialization in philosophy for children.

The Ed.D. at Montclair State University aims to mold and guide those who aspire to be models of teaching excellence, leaders among their colleagues, and spokespersons for education in the state. The Ed.D. is characterized by a strong theoretical base and a comprehensive perspective on the nature of schools and learning for social change. The Ed.D. provides the highest level of expertise in teaching, leadership, and education reform. The program also recognizes the indisputable role of teachers at all levels in renewing the education system and the critical importance of P–16 education. Four major themes give coherence to the program and represent the University's vision of teacher responsibility: to provide access to knowledge for all students, to create and sustain nurturing pedagogy, to enculturate students in multicultural political and social democracy, and to commit themselves to educational leadership based on the stewardship of best practice.

Although primarily designed for teachers who wish to remain in the classroom, the program can meet the needs of an educator with other career goals. The program is sensitive to the needs of classroom teachers and offers a part-time program that allows doctoral students to complete their course work at night and during the summer. Full-time students may be able to complete their course requirements in three years, while part-time students may be able to complete them in four. However, in addition to course work, students need to complete a qualifying assessment and a dissertation. The amount of time necessary to complete these depends on the student. Core courses for both the mathematics and philosophy for children disciplines are the same and cover democracy and education, pedagogy, access to knowledge and organizational change policy, and leadership. Elective core courses may cover teaching in multiple literacies, classroom community, or race and ethnicity issues.

Mathematics education is designed for those who already have a strong preparation in mathematics or mathematics education. The curriculum reflects both state and national recommendations. Doctoral candidates learn alternative approaches to the teaching of mathematics as well as methods of research in mathematics education. Specialization courses cover modeling for higher grades, mathematics educational leadership, specific subject teaching areas, critical thinking, and use of technology in the classroom teaching process. Other elective topics are available and are chosen depending on a student's interests and professional goals.

The philosophy for children program is designed for those who already have a strong preparation in philosophy. It builds on pedagogical knowledge and carries forward the major themes of the Ed.D. program. Students gain a thorough understanding of the role of philosophy in reasoning, critical-thinking skills, the use of philosophy-based children's literature, and research methods in philosophy for children. Specialization courses include philosophy for children and the educational experience, contemporary social and political philosophy, ethical inquiry through narrative, the role of logic in philosophy for children, and education for global citizenship. A complete list of required courses and electives can be found on the University's Web site.

Both the mathematics and the philosophy for children foci share a core of required courses. These include Advanced Pedagogical Studies; Democracy and Education; and Organizational Change, Policy, and Leadership. Both concentrations also require research method courses and a dissertation based on a chosen area of research.

Research Facilities

At the forefront of research and education at Montclair State University is the Center for Pedagogy, the first of its kind in the nation. The Center coordinates all aspects of teacher education, including the Ed.D. program in pedagogy, a network of twenty school district partnerships, and professional development for faculty members. Graduate students have the very latest techniques and theory to put into practice through academic partnerships.

Moreover, the ADP Center for Teacher Preparation and Learning Technologies functions as a hub of curriculum research, instructional planning, and educational technology within the Center of Pedagogy in the College of Education and Human Services at Montclair State University. The ADP mission is to improve the quality of education for teacher education students, practicing teachers, counselors, administrators, and others in professional careers in pre-K through secondary schools and in postsecondary education by providing access to the more than 30,000 curriculum and instructional technology resources as well as the requisite support in using them.

Doctoral students also make use of the Curriculum Resource Center (CRC), a central hub of curriculum research, instructional planning, and educational technology. More than 30,000 curriculum and instructional technology resources are available, including 10,000 guides, 25,000 books, 400 videos, sample tests, and more than 100 journals. Over 200 educational software titles and a range of state-of-the-art equipment are also part of the CRC. A videoconferencing center, the Classroom of the Future, enables students to join in multipoint distance learning programs as well as to experiment with current and emerging digital teaching tools.

Financial Aid

Student loans are the primary source of financial aid for graduate students. There are a limited number of doctoral assistantships available to defray the cost of tuition. A limited number of scholarships are available as well. Applications may be obtained through the Graduate School.

Cost of Study

Doctoral tuition and fees for in-state residents are $552.65 per credit. Out-of-state tuition is $745.75 per credit.

Living and Housing Costs

At Montclair State University, on-campus housing is available for a limited number of graduate students. Interested students should visit the Office of Residential Housing and Education Web site at http://www.montclair.edu/resed/residentialfacilities.html for up-to-date housing costs and information. Meal plans are also available in flexible package and court options, depending on individual needs.

Student Group

Montclair's doctoral candidates in education are educators who aspire to be leaders among their colleagues and spokespersons for education in their setting. They are teacher-leaders from local school districts, as well as from places as far away as Iceland, Brazil, Nigeria, and Indonesia.

Location

The University's easy access to New York City makes it a great place to study. The campus is near local bus and train service, major train transportation, and international airports. The availability of diverse cultural experiences, restaurants, shopping, recreation, and entertainment are limited only by a student's time and expense accounts. New Jersey is a microcosm of America, offering beautiful shoreline and beach areas, rural and park recreation, mountain skiing and hiking, and city culture and nightlife.

The University

Founded in 1908, Montclair State University was originally established for teacher training. In the 1930s, Montclair began offering master's degree programs and became accredited as a teachers' college—one of the first in the nation. The University now offers forty-four undergraduate majors, forty-two graduate majors, forty-six postbaccalaureate certificates and certifications, and five postmaster's certificates.

Applying

Candidates for the Ed.D. program should have completed a relevant master's degree. Teaching experience is preferred. Graduate students wishing to be considered as doctoral candidates must complete an application, which can be downloaded from the University's Web site at http://www.montclair.edu/graduate. Applicants must write a personal essay regarding the relevance of doctoral study to their personal and professional development, as well as an essay discussing an area of potential research interest. Official transcripts, writing samples, teacher reviews, GRE scores, Test of English as a Foreign Language (TOELF) scores if necessary, three letters of reference, and an application fee of $60 complete the process. Applicants to this program must complete a self-managed application, meaning the applicant gathers all required documentation and then submits it in one packet for University review. Admission also includes a personal interview.

Correspondence and Information

Montclair State University
One Normal Avenue
Montclair, New Jersey 07043
Phone: 973-655-4262
Fax: 973-655-7776
E-mail: sheehanbr@mail.montclair.edu
Web site: http://www.montclair.edu

Montclair State University

THE FACULTY AND THEIR RESEARCH

Ada Beth Cutler, Ed.D., Harvard. Teacher learning and professional development, education policy, school-university partnerships, school renewal.

Donna DeGennaro, Ph.D., Pennsylvania. Youth technology practices and interactions to inform innovative designs of learning environments.

Vanessa Domine, Ph.D., NYU. Educational technology, media literacy, uses of technology for educational renewal.

Deborah Eldridge, Ed.D., Boston University. Teacher preparation for literacy instruction, reading methods, primary and secondary discourse learning, home-school connections, integrating technology and aesthetics into teacher education.

Wandalyn Enix, Ed.D., Temple.

Juan-Miguel Fernandez-Balboa, Ed.D., Massachusetts Amherst. Qualitative research, educational reform, critical pedagogy.

Elaine Fine, Ed.D., Columbia. Assessment and methods on special education, learning strategies model, inclusion, postsecondary education for individuals with disabilities.

Jennifer L. Goeke, Ph.D., SUNY at Albany. Teacher education pedagogy, development of special educators, reasoning and instructional thought, conceptions of students with disabilities.

Rebecca A. Goldstein, Ph.D., Rochester. Urban education, school reform, teacher identity development in multicultural context and power in education.

David Lee Keiser, Ph.D., Berkeley. School/university partnerships, culturally responsive teaching, mindfulness.

Emily Klein, Ph.D., NYU. Professional development, school reform, professional communities of practice.

Cynthia Onore, Ph.D., NYU. Teacher education, urban education, multicultural education.

Jennifer Robinson, Ed.D., Columbia. Strategies for increasing the diversity of the teaching force, preservice teacher education, school/university partnerships.

Monica Taylor, Ph.D., Arizona.

Nancy R. Tumposky, Ed.D., SUNY at Albany. Second language learning and teaching, teaching for critical thinking.

Ana Maria Villegas, Ph.D., NYU. Culturally responsive teaching, preparing teachers for a diverse K–12 student population, increasing diversity and cultural knowledge/expertise of the teacher workforce.

Vincent J. Walencik, Ed.D., Rutgers. Distance learning, children engineering, critical thinking/problem solving, technology education, changing teacher/student behavior, preparing the workforce for the twenty-first century.

Richard Wolfson, Ph.D., Ohio State. Emerging trends in educational technology, university governance.

OAKLAND UNIVERSITY

Graduate Programs in Educational Leadership

Programs of Study

Oakland University offers three programs in educational leadership: a Master of Education (M.Ed.) degree in educational leadership, an Education Specialist in leadership, and a Doctor of Philosophy in education. Educational Leadership programs are designed to enrich the expertise and competence of teachers and other professional staff members in the research and theory of teaching, learning, and administration. The leadership program prepares educators for elementary and secondary principalships.

The Ph.D. program in education with a concentration in educational leadership is designed to develop individuals who can provide leadership to educational practice in the twenty-first century. Graduates are prepared to play roles in public and private schools, higher education administration, or research and teaching about educational policy and practice at the college or university level.

The Education Specialist program consists of a 36 semester hours of graduate-level courses that prepare students for the principalship and for central office administrative positions. The Interstate School Leaders Licensure Consortium (ISLLC) Standards for school leaders are endorsed throughout the students' course of study.

Research Facilities

The Office of Grants, Contracts, and Sponsored Research supports research and scholarship at Oakland University. In particular, the office acts as the coordinating office between Oakland University and the federal and state agencies, foundations, and public and private corporations that provide funds for research, education, training, and service programs.

Located in the center of campus, the Kresge Library houses collections of books, journals, reference works, government documents, musical scores, and recordings as well as a wireless network and computer workstations to access an array of digital resources. The Kresge Library's collections include over 727,000 books, approximately 1,400 print journal subscriptions and electronic access to more than 15,000 titles, over 240,000 federal and state documents, and more than 1.1 million microforms. The Library's homepage and online catalog serve as gateways to dozens of specialized and general research databases and hundreds of full-text electronic journals and e-books covering a wide range of disciplines and research areas.

Financial Aid

In order to assist eligible graduate students in financing their education, Oakland University participates in the Federal College Work-Study Program and the William Ford Federal Direct Loan Program.

The Department of Educational Leadership also awards the Jacqueline I. Lougheed Award.

Cost of Study

Graduate tuition in the 2007–08 academic year is $472.50 per credit hour for Michigan residents and $814.50 per credit hour for non-residents. For current tuition rates, interested students should visit http://www.oakland.edu/tuitionandfees.

Living and Housing Costs

The 2006–07 rate for room and board was $6385 for the academic year. Facilities with a limited number of single rooms are available to graduate students. For students with families, a limited number of two-bedroom town houses and two- to four-bedroom student apartments are available.

Student Group

Total enrollment at OU for fall 2006 was 17,737. Twenty-three percent of the total enrollment are graduate students. Within the graduate enrollment, 66 percent are women and 11.4 percent are members of ethnic minority groups. The diverse student body includes international students representing many different countries.

Location

Oakland University is located in Oakland County, the third-most-affluent county in the United States and the fastest growing county in Michigan. Rochester, Michigan, is OU's hometown. Rochester was named thirty-ninth in a list of top 100 cities in which to live, and the highest-ranking Michigan city in the survey, by *Money* magazine and *CNN Money* in 2005. Rochester and the surrounding area was ranked based on population, number of educational facilities, safety, environment, housing affordability, taxes, weather, commute times, and job market.

In addition, the area's rolling hills, wetlands, and woodlands provide beautiful neighborhoods and plenty of year-round recreation. The surrounding community also offers an abundance of entertainment, cultural, and social opportunities. Together, all this makes Oakland County and Rochester great places to live, work, and go to school.

The University

Oakland University, founded in 1957, is a comprehensive state-supported institution of higher education. The University is organized into the College of Arts and Sciences and the Schools of Business Administration, Education and Human Services, Engineering and Computer Science, Health Sciences, and Nursing.

Applying

Students applying to the educational leadership programs need to submit the Application for Admission to Graduate Study, the application processing fee, and supporting documents to Graduate Admissions. Both a paper and online application process are available. Information about application requirements and deadlines is available online at http://www.oakland.edu/grad/apply.

Correspondence and Information

Graduate Admissions
160 North Foundation Hall
Oakland University
Rochester, Michigan 48309
Phone: 248-370-3167
E-mail: gradmail@oakland.edu
Web site: http://www.oakland.edu/gograd

Oakland University

THE FACULTY

Brian Owen Clark, Ed.D., Wayne State (Michigan).
Shannon Flumerfelt, Ph.D., Oakland.
Eric Follo, Ed.D., Wayne State (Michigan).
Sarah Gibson, Ph.D., Wayne State (Michigan).
Ilene Ingram, Ed.D., Wayne State (Michigan).
Eileen Johnson, Ph.D., Houston.
William Keane, Ed.D., Columbia Teachers College.
Robert Maxfield, Ed.D., Wayne State (Michigan).
Sandra Packard, Ed.D., Indiana.
Julia Smith, Ed.D., Michigan.
Caryn Wells, Ph.D., Michigan State.

PHILADELPHIA UNIVERSITY

Master of Science in Instructional Design and Technology

Program of Study

Instructional technology is redefining the way in which people learn, teach, and communicate. The demand for professionals who understand the theory of instructional design and possess multimedia-development skills increases as information technologies proliferate in the workplace.

The Master of Science (M.S.) in Instructional Design and Technology Program (MSIDT) at Philadelphia University prepares professionals for careers in education, business, and industry by providing courses in learning theory, instructional design, change management, and multimedia development.

The MSIDT is a flexible and intensive program for individuals seeking professional development or a career change. While the curriculum offers a strong foundation in multimedia training and software analysis, the courses accommodate students with varied levels of computer experience. Features of the program include a unique blend of a theoretical classroom approach with real-world multimedia development, a hands-on approach to learning the fundamentals of technology and multimedia design, and meaningful real-life projects using the latest technologies.

The program offers three options: Instructional Design, Instructional Technology Specialist (ITS), and Systems Integration. The Instructional Design option provides students with an opportunity to design and develop multimedia educational tools for academic and corporate clients, culminating in a multimedia design exhibition held in May. The ITS option leads to Pennsylvania Department of Education certification for K–12 technology specialists, and the Systems Integration option provides students with both educational multimedia design expertise and the corresponding computer-programming skills.

Research Facilities

The Philadelphia University MSIDT program provides a hands-on approach to learning the fundamentals of technology and multimedia design in the state-of-the-art Instructional Technology Lab, a multimedia cross-platform lab, containing fifteen Macintosh computers and fifteen PCs. Students tackle meaningful, real-life projects using the latest professional multimedia development tools to produce interactive instructional content for CDs, DVDs, or the Internet.

Financial Aid

Eligible students who are enrolled on at least a half-time basis (4.5 credits per semester) may apply for Federal Stafford Student Loans and Unsubsidized Federal Stafford Loans. Philadelphia University requires that all students applying for financial aid file the Free Application for Federal Student Aid (FAFSA). A limited number of graduate assistantships are available to selected qualified incoming graduate students. Compensation is available to students enrolled on a full-time basis and includes tuition remission for 9 credits for each of the fall and spring semesters and a nine-month stipend of $2575.

Cost of Study

The estimated cost for full-time enrollment in 2006–07 was $6282 per semester ($698 per credit).

Location

The tree-lined, beautifully landscaped campus is located on the edge of Fairmount Park, about a 10-minute drive from Center City, Philadelphia.

The sixty-one buildings on the University's 100-acre campus range from historic Victorian mansions to contemporary facilities, including the Kanbar Student Center, the new 72,000-square-foot addition to the Philadelphia University campus where students come together for a bite to eat, to meet with fellow graduate students, or to connect with other students and faculty and staff members. In addition, the University features the Tuttleman Center, a high-technology academic building, and the Paul J. Gutman Library, a state-of-the-art, fully computerized resource center.

The University

Founded in 1884, Philadelphia University is an independent, career-oriented institution offering both graduate and undergraduate degree programs that blend academic theory with real-world experience.

Philadelphia University fosters close relationships between faculty members and its academically and culturally diverse students. Primarily a teaching institution, the University encourages research as a service to industry and as a vehicle for faculty and student development.

Applying

Anyone who holds, or is about to receive, a bachelor's degree from an accredited college or university is eligible to apply for admission.

Candidates who seek admission are reviewed based on the merit of their academic record, work experience, and the required scores on the Graduate Record Examinations (GRE) or Miller Analogies Test (MAT). Depending on the applicant's academic background, foundation courses may be required.

International students may begin in either the spring or fall semester. A minimum TOEFL score of 550 for the paper-based test, 213 for the computer-based test, or 79 for the Internet-based test is required for students for whom English is not their native language; international students must provide proof of adequate funds to cover the cost of tuition, room and board, and expenses.

Philadelphia University requires all international students to provide, as part of their application, an official transcript evaluation from World Education Services (WES). Students can learn more about WES at http://www.wes.org. The WES reports provide security for both the institution and the individual in that all transcripts are individually reviewed and verified for accuracy. This is particularly helpful in guaranteeing the applicant will receive full credit for all courses taken prior to their application to Philadelphia University. Another benefit to the applicant is that these reports are permanently on file with WES, and the applicant can have official evaluations sent anywhere at any time in the future. This is helpful not only for future academic endeavors but also for possible employment opportunities, as many employers require confirmation of academic degree completion.

Applications are accepted for fall, spring, and summer semesters and are reviewed on a rolling basis. International applicants to online programs may apply for the summer semester, but all other programs admit international students in the fall and spring terms only. International applicants should send completed applications by June 1 for the fall semester and October 1 for the spring semester.

Correspondence and Information

William H. Firman Jr.
Director, Graduate Admissions
Philadelphia University
School House Lane and Henry Avenue
Philadelphia, Pennsylvania 19144
Phone: 215-951-2943
Fax: 215-951-2907
E-mail: gradadm@philau.edu
Web site: http://www.philau.edu/graduate

Philadelphia University

THE FACULTY

Philadelphia University is a teaching institution where the primary focus is on the students. Classes are small—the average class size is 18 students—allowing for extensive faculty-student interaction. The MSIDT faculty combines both full-time professors and leading IT professionals from the Philadelphia area. This unique combination provides a mix of real-world experience and applied research in the classroom. Their academic credentials and business experience make them uniquely qualified to provide students with the knowledge to become successful professionals in their chosen fields.

Gail Austin, M.Ed., West Chester.
Hellene Bankowski, M.S., Temple.
Mary Beans, M.A., Gratz.
Dolly Bernard-Marks, M.S.I.T., Philadelphia University.
Rebecca Britt, M.S., Capella.
Jeanne Buckley, Ed.D., Columbia.
Jill Carney, M.S., Philadelphia University.
Jennifer Celano, M.S., Philadelphia University.
Phil Charron, M.S.I.T., Temple.
Paul Choitz, M.Ed., Penn State.
Thomas Craven, M.B.A., Phoenix.
David Dubble, M.S., Nova Southeastern.
Nicholas Florentino, M.S., Bloomsburg.
Karen Girton-Snyder, M.S., Bloomsburg.
George Heake, M.S., Wilmington (Delaware).
Michael Hermann, M.S., Philadelphia University.
John Kahler, B.S., Temple.
Kenneth Kay, M.S., Pennsylvania.
R. Thomas Knorr, M.S., Philadelphia University.
Larry Kuenning, Ph.D., Westminster Theological Seminary (Philadelphia).
Jia Li, M.S., Philadelphia University.
Ruth List, M.S., Lehigh.
Brian Lownsbery, M.S., Philadelphia University.
Mary Malinconico, M.S., Ohio State.
Kristin Martin, M.S., Bloomsburg.
Tim McGee, Director; Ph.D., Berkeley.
Michele Mislevy, M.S., Philadelphia University.
Russell Pritchard, Ed.D., Wilmington (Delaware).
Charles Reisinger, M.S., Philadelphia University.
Jonathan Rowe, LL.M., Temple.
Janet Scannell, M.S., Stanford.
Mark Scott, B.S., Duke.
Janet Smith, Ph.D., Pennsylvania.
David Solon, M.S., Philadelphia University.
Russell Starke, M.S., Bloomsburg.
Mark Stauffer, M.S., Philadelphia University.
Brian Sutcliffe, M.S., Bloomsburg.
Rebecca Tunnell, M.A., Gratz.
Timothy Wetzel, M.S., Philadelphia University.
Peter Wolff, Ph.D., Bryn Mawr.

SOUTHERN ILLINOIS UNIVERSITY CARBONDALE

College of Education and Human Services
Department of Curriculum and Instruction
Ph.D. in Education

Program of Study	The Doctor of Philosophy (Ph.D.) in education in curriculum and instruction (CI) prepares research-oriented professionals who are capable of extending the knowledge base and assisting others to develop a comprehensive understanding of the discipline. It is designed for teachers and other educators who seek to improve their performance in general and specialized areas in either public schools or the private sector. This program is designed for students who desire positions requiring advanced preparation with emphasis on theories of curriculum and instruction and in-depth preparation in research. Students may choose from among ten different specialization options: curriculum and instruction, early childhood, elementary education, instructional technology, mathematics education, reading and language studies (including TESOL), science and environmental education, secondary education, social sciences education, and teacher leadership. The program requires 8 hours of college seminars; 9 hours of CI core courses; at least 23 hours of course work in the specialty area; and 24 hours of dissertation research. Twelve hours of written preliminary examinations precede the dissertation. Research tools are chosen in consultation with the student's doctoral committee. The program is usually completed in five to seven years.
Research Facilities	In addition to the University's 2.1-million-volume Morris Library, CI oversees several laboratories that provide research and learning opportunities for students. The Child Development Laboratory (CDL) is an age 0–5, on-campus, day-care facility that provides the context for innovative undergraduate early childhood preparation. CDL offers graduate students the chance to observe, interact with, and instruct children in a supervised environment. Action research as well as applied research opportunities abound. The Mathematics Laboratory is a newly renovated facility adjacent to classrooms that provides access to manipulatives, technology, and other materials relevant to mathematics education. In addition to a wide variety of science kits and other science and environmental education materials, the Science Laboratory also provides computer stations for the integration of technology into instruction. There are research opportunities available to graduate students to work with faculty members on the cutting edge of issue investigation. The Media Laboratory is primarily designed to provide technological assistance and research support for graduate students pursuing specializations in instructional design or technology.
Financial Aid	In addition to University-wide academic, financial need, and minority fellowships, CI offers limited financial aid in the form of graduate assistantships and scholarships. Teaching/research assistantships that provide a stipend and cover the cost of tuition are available by application each academic year. Successful applicants must meet the criteria for each assistantship.
Cost of Study	In-state graduate tuition is $275 per credit hour for fall 2007. Out-of-state tuition is 2.5 times the in-state tuition rate ($687.50 per credit hour). Graduate students with a graduate assistant appointment of at least 25 percent receive a tuition waiver. Fees vary from $490.11 (1 credit hour in-state) to $990.45 (15 credits hours out-of-state). Students with graduate assistantships must carry at least 6 hours of graduate credit each semester they hold the assistantship.
Living and Housing Costs	For married couples, students with families, and single graduate students, the University has 589 efficiency and one-, two-, and three-bedroom apartments that rent for $493 to $532 per month in 2007–08. Residence halls for single graduate students are also available, as are accessible residence hall rooms and apartments for students with disabilities.
Student Group	Graduates of the program work in a wide range of educational, governmental, and corporate settings. Approximately 70 percent hold teaching positions, primarily in postsecondary educational settings; 16 percent hold administrative positions; and 12 percent work in various other settings, including business and industry. Most doctoral students are part-time and attend classes in the evening. About 13 percent are international students.
Location	SIUC is 350 miles south of Chicago and 100 miles southeast of St. Louis. Nestled in rolling hills bordered by the Ohio and Mississippi Rivers and enhanced by a mild climate, the area has state parks, national forests and wildlife refuges, and large lakes for outdoor recreation. Cultural offerings include theater, opera, concerts, art exhibits, and cinema. Educational facilities for the families of students are excellent.
The University	Southern Illinois University Carbondale is a comprehensive public university with a variety of general and professional education programs. The University offers bachelor's and associate degrees, master's and doctoral degrees, the J.D. degree, and the M.D. degree. The University is fully accredited by the North Central Association of Colleges and Schools. The Graduate School has an essential role in the development and coordination of graduate instruction and research programs. The Graduate Council has academic responsibility for determining graduate standards, recommending new graduate programs and research centers, and establishing policies to facilitate the research effort.
Applying	Applicants must complete the departmental application materials and request that official transcripts from all higher education institutions previously attended be sent directly to the Department. Selection and review committees screen applicants on the basis of prior graduate work, grade point average (at least a 3.25 on a 4.0 scale for graduate work is required), standardized test scores (GRE), research ability, work experience, and letters of recommendation. A minimum TOEFL score of 550 is required for international students.
Correspondence and Information	To request or submit applications or for further information, students may contact: Coordinator of Graduate Studies Department of Curriculum and Instruction Mailcode 4610 Southern Illinois University 625 Wham Drive Carbondale, Illinois 62901-4610 Phone: 618-536-2441 Fax: 618-453-4244 E-mail: currinst@siu.edu

Southern Illinois University Carbondale

THE FACULTY AND THEIR RESEARCH

The Department of Curriculum and Instruction has 20 full-time graduate faculty members with expertise in a wide range of specialty areas. Research and grant activity is an integral part of the programming in CI, and the Department consistently secures more than $1 million in research funds. Faculty members work with graduate students to guide their development as effective consumers and producers of educational research. Students interested in participating in research and grant activities should discuss possible projects with their advisers.

Jerry Becker, Professor; Ph.D., Stanford. Mathematics education.
James Campbell, Associate Professor; Ph.D., Ohio State. Early childhood.
William Coscarelli, Professor; Ph.D., Indiana. Instructional design/technology.
Peter Fadde, Assistant Professor; Ph.D., Purdue. Instructional technology.
Kelly Glassett, Assistant Professor; Ph.D., Utah. Reading.
Joyce Killian, Professor; Ph.D., Penn State. Teacher education.
Cheng-Yao Lin, Assistant Professor; Ph.D., Illinois at Urbana-Champaign. Mathematics education.
C. Sebastian Loh, Assistant Professor; Ph.D., Georgia. Instructional technology.
Marla Mallette, Associate Professor; Ph.D., Nevada. Reading and early childhood.
John McIntyre, Professor; Ed.D., Syracuse. Teacher education, gifted education.
Grant Miller, Assistant Professor; Ph.D., Boston College. Social science education.
Catherine Mogharreban, Associate Professor; Ph.D., Southern Illinois. Early childhood.
Frackson Mumba, Assistant Professor; Ph.D., Illinois State. Science education.
Susan Pearlman, Associate Professor; Ph.D., Missouri–Columbia. Early childhood.
Donna Post, Associate Professor; Ph.D., Penn State. Teacher education, secondary education.
Edward Pultorak, Associate Professor; Ph.D., Indiana. Teacher education.
Sharon Shrock, Professor; Ph.D., Indiana. Instructional design/technology.
Lynn Smith, Associate Professor; Ph.D., Georgia. Elementary education, reading.
Stacy Thompson, Assistant Professor; Ph.D., Iowa State. Early childhood.
Jan Waggoner, Associate Professor; Ed.D., Memphis State. Middle-level, social studies, science education.
Kevin Wise, Associate Professor; Ed.D., Georgia. Science education.

SOUTHERN ILLINOIS UNIVERSITY CARBONDALE

Department of Educational Administration and Higher Education
Ph.D. in Education

Program of Study

The Department of Educational Administration and Higher Education of Southern Illinois University Carbondale (SIUC) offers the Ph.D. in education, with a concentration in educational administration. The Ph.D. program is 64 credit hours.

Research Facilities

The extensive holdings and wide array of bibliographic and instructional support services offered by SIUC's Morris Library place it among the foremost research institutions. The library is an active participant in the world's largest bibliographic network, Online Computer Library Center (OCLC), and is a member of ILLINET Online (IO), the statewide automated catalog, circulation, and interlibrary loan system, with records of more than 600 libraries. The library's general collection numbers 2.2 million volumes, 3.2 million microforms, and more than 12,500 serial subscriptions. Library users have access to nearly 900 electronic data files and CD-ROM products via multiple workstations located throughout the building.

Financial Aid

The Department assists students in their efforts to find financial support. For those in the K–12 administration program, the Department offers three graduate assistantships, in which students are primarily responsible for undergraduate teaching or research assistance. In the higher education programs, graduate assistantships are available in various administrative offices and residence halls throughout the campus. A stipend and tuition waiver are included. The Financial Aid Office also provides information on fellowships, scholarships, and other assistantship possibilities.

Cost of Study

In-state graduate tuition is $275 per credit hour in 2007–08. Out-of-state tuition is 2.5 times the in-state tuition rate ($687.50 per credit hour). Graduate students with at least a 25 percent appointment as a graduate assistant receive a tuition waiver. Fees vary from $490.11 (1 credit hour) to $1272.45 (12 credit hours).

Living and Housing Costs

For married couples, students with families, and single graduate students, the University has 690 efficiency and one-, two-, three-, and four-bedroom apartments that rent for $439 to $651 per month in 2007–08. Residence halls for single graduate students are also available, as are accessible residence hall rooms and apartments for students with disabilities.

Student Group

The Department has approximately 325 students and 7 full-time faculty members.

Location

SIUC is 350 miles south of Chicago and 100 miles southeast of St. Louis. Nestled in rolling hills bordered by the Ohio and Mississippi Rivers and enhanced by a mild climate, the area has state parks, national forests and wildlife refuges, and large lakes for outdoor recreation. Cultural offerings include theater, opera, concerts, art exhibits, and cinema. Educational facilities for the families of students are excellent.

The University

Southern Illinois University Carbondale is a comprehensive public university with a variety of general and professional education programs. The University offers associate, bachelor's, master's, and doctoral degrees. The University is fully accredited by the North Central Association of Colleges and Schools. The Graduate School has an essential role in the development and coordination of graduate instruction and research programs. The Graduate Council has academic responsibility for determining graduate standards, recommending new graduate programs and research centers, and establishing policies to facilitate the research effort.

Applying

Applicants must submit the standard application materials to the Department of Educational Administration and Higher Education. In addition to the application, each applicant must have on file a standardized test score (GRE or MAT) as well as letters of recommendation. A nonrefundable application fee of $45 must be submitted with the application.

Correspondence and Information

Debra Mibb, Administrative Clerk
Department of Educational Administration
and Higher Education
Pulliam Hall, Room 131–Mail Code 4606
Southern Illinois University Carbondale
Carbondale, Illinois 62901
Phone: 618-536-4434
E-mail: dmibb@siu.edu
Web site: http://www.siu.edu/departments/coe/eahe

Southern Illinois University Carbondale

THE FACULTY AND THEIR AREAS OF SPECIALIZATION

Brad Colwell, Professor and Department Chair; Ph.D., J.D., Illinois at Urbana-Champaign. Educational finance, collective bargaining, educational law and policy.

Larry Dietz, Associate Professor and Vice Chancellor for Student Affairs and Enrollment Management; Ph.D., Iowa State. Student affairs and higher education administration.

Patrick W. Dilley, Associate Professor; Ph.D., USC. Qualitative methods, student affairs administration, higher education administration.

Saran Donahoo, Assistant Professor; Ph.D., Illinois at Urbana-Champaign. History of education, legal issues in education, higher education policy, diversity in education, systemic educational transitions.

Judith Green, Associate Professor; Ph.D., Purdue. School leadership.

Kathy Hytten, Associate Professor; Ph.D., North Carolina at Chapel Hill. Philosophy of education, social foundations, cultural studies.

Marybelle Keim, Professor; Ph.D., Michigan State. Community college administration, higher education curriculum, college teaching, research/evaluation.

Elizabeth Lewin, Clinical Assistant Professor; Ed.D., South Florida. School leadership, principalship, superintendent.

Affiliated Faculty

Dr. Frank Barbre, Lecturer.

Ms. Paulette Curkin, Coordinator for Student Development.

Dr. Mary Ellen Grimes, Lecturer.

Dr. Cheryl Presley, Director of Student Health Programs.

Dr. Jennifer Presley, Research Associate Professor and Director of the Illinois Education Research Council.

SOUTHERN ILLINOIS UNIVERSITY CARBONDALE

College of Education and Human Services
Department of Educational Psychology and Special Education
Educational Psychology Doctoral Program

Program of Study

The Department of Educational Psychology and Special Education offers a Ph.D. in education with a concentration in educational psychology. Specialties include counselor education, human learning and development, special education, and statistics and measurement. The counselor education doctoral program prepares counselor educators and supervisors and is accredited by the Council for Accreditation of Counseling and Related Educational Programs (CACREP). Students are expected to develop competencies for leadership and instructional roles in counselor education and supervision, advanced counseling practice, and research. The doctoral program in human learning and development has as its goal the development of specialists in the field of human learning, and graduates of this specialty take a variety of positions in universities, state educational agencies, industrial organizations, private and public research centers, and public school systems. The special education emphasis offers three areas of concentration: research, college teaching, and special education administration. The program is suited for individuals with experience in teaching students with disabilities in general or special education classrooms, administrators of general or special education programs or related services, or persons who have professional experiences in fields related to special education (e.g., rehabilitation, speech-language pathology, social work). The doctoral program in educational statistics and measurement develops specialists in the fields of statistics, measurement, and evaluation. Students are exposed to the underlying mathematical models that serve as the basis for research and evaluation in education and psychology. Students become proficient in the use of statistical computer programs that are widely used to analyze research data.

Research Facilities

The extensive holdings and wide array of bibliographic and instructional support services offered by SIUC's Morris Library place it among the foremost research institutions. The library is a longtime member of the Association of Research Libraries and also holds membership in the Center of Research Libraries in Chicago. It is an active participant in the world's largest bibliographic network, OCLC (Online Computer Library Center), and is a member of ILLINET Online (IO), the statewide automated catalog, circulation, and interlibrary loan system with records of more than 600 libraries. The library's general collection numbers 2.4 million volumes, 3.1 million microforms, and more than 12,200 current serial subscriptions. Library users have access to nearly 900 electronic data files and CD-ROM products through multiple workstations located throughout the building. Up-to-date information about library services is available through the LINKS (Library Information Networks) component of the campuswide computer network. The library's many noteworthy holdings include depository collections of federal, state, and United Nations documents as well as the Instructional Materials Center, which includes current and historical children's literature, textbooks, and audiovisual teaching aids. Also part of Library Affairs is the Ulysses S. Grant Association's editorial project, which aims to publish the complete correspondence of President Grant. Educational Psychology, as part of the College of Education and Human Services (COEHS), has extensive resources to serve its graduate students. The College operates two computer labs to support students' research and academic endeavors. The state-of-the-art labs provide students with a variety of word processing, statistics, graphics, and multimedia software packages. The Multimedia Center for Teaching and Learning has an extensive array of media equipment to support students' professional development activities. The Statistics Laboratory provides students with opportunities for consulting with researchers from education, the behavioral and social sciences, and the biological sciences.

Financial Aid

A number of graduate assistantships are available for which students may make application through the Special Education Program. Students are advised to apply before February 1 to be considered for graduate assistantships or fellowships for the next academic year. Students may request application materials for assistantships and fellowships from the Graduate Secretary in the Department of Educational Psychology and Special Education. The COEHS grants a number of dissertation research awards to fund up to a full academic year of dissertation work for students who have been admitted to candidacy. Students interested in these awards should contact their academic advisers for the deadline and to prepare their application materials. The Graduate School also has a number of graduate study awards for students at the doctoral level. Information on the deadlines and application requirements are available from the Graduate School.

Cost of Study

In-state graduate tuition is $275 per credit hour in 2007–08. Out-of-state tuition is 2.5 times the in-state tuition rate ($687.50 per credit hour). Graduate students with at least a 25 percent appointment as a graduate assistant receive a tuition waiver. Fees vary from $490.11 (1 credit hour) to $1272.45 (12 credit hours).

Living and Housing Costs

For married couples, students with families, and single graduate students, the University has 690 efficiency and one-, two-, three-, and four-bedroom apartments that rent for $439 to $651 per month in 2007–08 (projected rates). Residence halls for single graduate students are also available, as are accessible residence hall rooms and apartments for students with disabilities.

Student Group

Master's program students include full-time and part-time students from a variety of educational backgrounds. The student body is culturally and ethnically diverse and includes a number of international students.

Student Outcomes

Individuals completing the doctoral program have taken positions as university faculty members, school administrators, community college instructors, and administrators of public human service agencies throughout the U.S. Graduates of the educational statistics and measurement specialty have been employed by universities, state education agencies, corporations, private and public research centers, testing companies, the military, and public school systems.

Location

SIUC is 350 miles south of Chicago and 100 miles southeast of St. Louis. Nestled in rolling hills bordered by the Ohio and Mississippi Rivers and enhanced by a mild climate, the area has state parks, national forests and wildlife refuges, and large lakes for outdoor recreation. Cultural offerings include theater, opera, concerts, art exhibits, and cinema. Educational facilities for the families of students are excellent.

The University

Southern Illinois University Carbondale is a comprehensive public university with a variety of general and professional education programs. The University offers bachelor's and associate degrees, master's and doctoral degrees, the J.D. degree, and the M.D. degree. The University is fully accredited by the North Central Association of Colleges and Schools. The Graduate School has an essential role in the development and coordination of graduate instruction and research programs. The Graduate Council has academic responsibility for determining graduate standards, recommending new graduate programs and research centers, and establishing policies to facilitate the research effort.

Applying

Application materials may be requested from the Department and are also available online at http://www.siu.edu/departments/coe/epse/. Each application must include an Application for Admission to Graduate Study, five letters of recommendation, a sample of writing skills, a short autobiography, a resume or curriculum vitae, official Graduate Record Examinations (GRE) scores, official transcripts from all colleges and universities previously attended (which must be submitted directly to the Department of Educational Psychology and Special Education by the registrar of each previously attended school), and a $35 application fee. Applications are considered throughout the academic year for admission the next academic semester. International students should refer to the *Graduate Catalog* for application and admission procedures.

Correspondence and Information

Graduate Secretary
Department of Educational Psychology and Special Education
223 Wham Education Building
Southern Illinois University Carbondale
Carbondale, Illinois 62901-4618
Phone: 618-536-7763
Web site: http://www.siu.edu/departments/coe/epse/

Southern Illinois University Carbondale

THE FACULTY AND THEIR RESEARCH

Kimberly Asner-Self, Assistant Professor; Ed.D., George Washington, 1999. Developmental indices among people from different cultures; effect of exposure to human-perpetrated traumatic events such as war, sexual assault, and incest on life-span human development; application of group counseling techniques in developing multicultural awareness.

Paul Bates, Professor; Ph.D. (special education), Wisconsin–Madison, 1978. Vocational development programs, curriculum for independent living, instruction and curriculum strategies to enhance generalization, social-interpersonal skill development, simulated versus naturalistic instruction of community living skills.

Beverly M. Brown, Professor; Ph.D., Iowa, 1974. Theory and practice of small group process as applied to counseling, laboratory education, and work environments; instruction and supervision of group counselors; the development of assessment instruments on group leadership; adaption of group process for inclusion of persons with disabilities.

Deborah A. Bruns, Assistant Professor; Ph.D. (special education), Illinois at Urbana-Champaign, 2000. Early childhood special education assessment and curriculum practices, parent-professional partnerships, early childhood transition, parenting education for at-risk populations.

Jane A. Cox, Associate Professor; Ph.D., Kent State, 1997. Applying the ideas of social construction to counseling practice and to the training of counselors, narrative and solution-focused therapy with couples and families, collaborative methods for supervision of counselors-in-training, use of current technology in counselor education.

Ronna F. Dillon, Professor; Ph.D., California, Riverside, 1978. Life-span human development; human learning, especially memory processes and strategies; new ways of measuring intellectual skills and predicting school achievement, including neuropsychological assessment and measurement of practical intelligence.

David Duys, Assistant Professor; Ph.D., Western Michigan, 1998. Counselor development and supervision, progressive career counseling intervention models, constructive-developmental approaches to school counseling.

Patricia B. Elmore, Professor and Associate Dean of the College of Education and Human Resources; Ph.D., Southern Illinois at Carbondale, 1970. Statistical methods in education and psychology, psychometric theory, test interpretation and use, development of a theoretical model of statistics achievement.

Norma J. Ewing, Associate Professor and Associate Dean, College of Education and Human Services; Ph.D. (special education), Southern Illinois at Carbondale, 1974. Special education administration, mild mental disability, multicultural education, reform in teacher training programs, issues associated with cultural diversity in classrooms, social skills training/behavior management for multicultural classrooms.

Regina M. Foley, Professor and Special Education Coordinator; Ed.D. (special education), Northern Illinois, 1989. Secondary school students with behavior disorders, collaboration-based instructional systems, effective instructional strategies for students with disabilities in inclusive classrooms.

Todd C. Headrick, Assistant Professor; Ph.D., Wayne State, 1997. Statistical science, computer simulations, rank tests.

Dennis W. Leitner, Associate Professor; Ph.D., Maryland, College Park, 1975. Monte Carlo methods, meta-analysis and computer applications, nonparametric statistics.

Ernest L. Lewis, Professor; Ph.D., Southern Illinois at Carbondale, 1971. Educational statistics and measurement, educational evaluation, research design.

Nancy A. Mundschenk, Associate Professor; Ph.D. (special education), Iowa, 1992. Emotional and behavioral disorders, autism, legal issues in special education, functional analysis, collaboration, social skills instruction.

Karen K. Prichard, Associate Professor; Ph.D., Kent State, 1981. Individual supervision, dual relationships in supervision, legal and ethical issues affecting counselors, counseling persons with disabilities.

James B. Schreiber, Assistant Professor; Ph.D., Indiana, 2000. Advanced mathematics achievement, Piercean reasoning, problem solving, hierarchical linear models.

Lyle J. White, Professor; Ph.D., Iowa, 1988. Applying the philosophy of social constructivism and cognitive linguistics to counseling, supervision, and consultation theory and practice; generating innovative approaches toward the delivery of school and rural community mental health service; pedagogy in counselor education.

TEACHERS COLLEGE COLUMBIA UNIVERSITY

Department of Curriculum and Teaching

Program of Study

The Department of Curriculum and Teaching at Teachers College, established in 1938, was the first department in the U.S. devoted to scholarly study of curriculum and teaching across all subjects and all levels of schooling. Continuing in that tradition, the Department offers master's and doctoral degree programs in the areas of early childhood, elementary, secondary, gifted, inclusive, and literacy education. All programs prepare teachers, administrators, teacher educators, and educational researchers as educational leaders committed to social justice. Through course work and teaching/research practicums, students gain understandings of teaching, curriculum, diversities, and schooling and design learning environments that are challenging and equitable. Students may complete all Department programs on a full-time or part-time basis.

The Department offers two Department-wide programs for advanced study. The Ed.D. program is designed for experienced educators interested in theory and inquiry in the field of curriculum and teaching. Students become part of a community of inquiry and develop the theoretical and methodological knowledge needed to study significant problems of curriculum and teaching across educational domains. The M.Ed. program, a flexible program of study for students with at least two years of teaching, offers students the opportunity to develop specialized understandings and a capacity for leadership in curriculum and pedagogy. Leadership is interpreted broadly in this program to include developing curricula, studying teaching, designing professional development, and engaging in action research.

The Department offers several in-service programs for certified teachers wishing to enhance their knowledge of teaching and curriculum, gifted education, and literacy education. Students in the elementary and secondary M.A. programs have opportunities to become experts in areas such as curriculum development, school change and reform initiatives, action research, and other school-based inquiry strategies and gain perspectives on teaching as a complex intellectual activity. Students in the M.A. program in gifted education develop additional expertise in designing curriculum and teaching for children identified as gifted learners. The literacy specialist M.A. program immerses students in the study of literacy practice, theory, and research (birth through grade 6). Students enrolled in this program have opportunities to work with the Teachers College Reading and Writing Project, which is a think tank and professional development organization that works in field-based ways with schools throughout New York City and the nation.

The Department offers graduate preservice teacher education programs for applicants with little or no teaching experience or preparation who seek initial certification as teachers. The early childhood and early childhood special education M.A. program prepares graduate students to teach in diverse and inclusive environments, including homes, schools, and other community settings that serve children from birth to 8 years of age as well as their families. Child-centered and culturally sensitive practices are emphasized throughout the program, focusing on the need for multiple methods of instruction to accommodate a broad range of learners. The inclusive elementary education M.A. program prepares graduate students to teach at elementary level, grades 1–6. The program includes a professional student-teaching sequence in New York City classrooms from September through May and emphasizes learning to teach in diverse, urban, and inclusive settings.

Research Facilities

The Gottesman Libraries, with more than a million books and materials, is one of the nation's largest and most comprehensive research libraries in education, psychology, and health services. Students have access to the 5.5 million volumes in the Columbia University library system. Organized research and service activities at Teachers College, in addition to being carried out by individual professors, are conducted through special projects and major institutes. Many of these research centers are listed in this description.

Data, voice, and video outlets are found in every classroom, office, and residence on the main portion of the campus, and laptops and projectors may be borrowed from Media Services. The Microcomputer Center provides students with PCs and Macs, software, printers, and other peripherals. The center's software library includes PC and Mac programs for word processing, Web development, graphics, statistical analysis, and qualitative analysis and databases. The Instructional Media Lab (IML) is a facility in which students and faculty members create rich content for classes, online learning, student teaching, and research. Digital cameras and other equipment are loaned. Workstations allow computer-based, full-motion video from a camera, VCR, or videodisk to be edited and integrated with animation, digitized voice, and music and to be written to a CD, DVD, or tape. IML also provides satellite downlink. Computer classrooms for hands-on instruction include both a PC and a Macintosh room, and the Goodman Family Computer Classroom suite includes a classroom equipped with thirty-two notebook computers on tables that can be reconfigured to accommodate varying work-group sizes.

Financial Aid

Each year, Teachers College awards approximately $5 million of its own funds in scholarship and stipend aid and $2 million of endowed funds to new and continuing students. There are no separate scholarship applications. Faculty members nominate new students for these scholarships based upon their admission application. Financial assistance is also available through federal aid programs. All students are encouraged to file a Free Application for Federal Student Aid (FAFSA), regardless of eligibility for federal aid. Fifty-one percent of students receive financial aid.

Cost of Study

For the 2006–07 academic year, tuition was $975 per point, with 12 or more points considered full-time. Fees included the Teachers College fee, $320; Teachers College research, $320; health service, $356; continuous doctoral advisement registration, $2925; and Ph.D. oral defense, $4319. The tuition deposit was $300. Medical insurance ranged from about $553 to $1218.

Living and Housing Costs

Teachers College offers a variety of on-campus housing options that are unique to the area and convenient to the campus. Housing for a single student ranges from $3100 to $8000 per semester, depending upon the type of setting selected. Family housing ranges from $6875 to $8200 per semester. Teachers College has approximately 705 spaces available for single students and 150 apartments for students with families. The buildings are located in the vibrant and historic urban neighborhood of Morningside Heights. Current residence halls are historic buildings similar to other apartment-style buildings that were in New York City in the early 1900s. A new residence hall opened in the fall 2004 semester.

Student Group

There are approximately 5,000 students enrolled at Teachers College. Of those, 77 percent are women and 23 percent are men; 12 percent are African American, 11 percent Asian American, and 7 percent are Latinos. The student body comprises 13 percent international students from eighty other countries and 87 percent domestic students from fifty different states.

Location

The College is located in the Morningside Heights section of Manhattan's Upper West Side, which is home to such venerable New York landmarks as Lincoln Center, the Cathedral of St. John the Divine, Grant's Tomb, Morningside Park, and the Manhattan School of Music. The Upper West Side is bounded by Central Park on the east and the Hudson River on the west. Located in New York City, students have access to an outstanding array of learning organizations, including museums, libraries, galleries, corporate learning centers, and K–12 schools.

The College and The University

Teachers College was founded in 1887 to provide a new form of schooling for teachers of children from low-income families of New York, one that combined a humanitarian concern to help others with a scientific approach to human development. For more than 100 years, Teachers College has conducted research on the central issues facing education, prepared generations of education leaders, and shaped debate and public policy in education. The College provides programs of study in administration, counseling, curriculum development, and school health care and continues its efforts to strengthen teaching skills, prepare leaders to develop and administer psychological and health-care programs, and develop new teaching software. In 1898, the College became affiliated with Columbia.

Columbia University was founded in 1754 as King's College by royal charter of King George II of England. It is the oldest institution of higher learning in the state of New York and the fifth-oldest in the United States. From its beginnings in a schoolhouse in lower Manhattan, the University has grown to encompass two principal campuses: the historic, neoclassical campus in Morningside Heights and the modern Medical Center in Washington Heights. Today, Columbia is one of the top academic and research institutions in the world, conducting research in medicine, science, the arts, and the humanities. It includes three undergraduate schools, thirteen graduate and professional schools, and a school of continuing education. Sixty-four Nobel laureates have taught or studied at Columbia. Each year, the faculty of approximately 4,000 teaches more than 23,000 students from more than 150 countries.

Applying

Teachers College welcomes applicants who wish to pursue graduate study associated with the education, psychological, and health service professions. All applicants receive consideration for admission without regard to race, color, creed, religion, sex, national origin, age, or disability. In order to be considered for scholarships, students must meet the priority deadline. Admissions applications received after the priority deadlines may be considered on a space available basis. Certain programs have special application deadlines. The 2007–08 final and early deadline for Ph.D. and all psychology doctoral programs is December 15. The early deadline for Ed.D. programs is January 2, with a final deadline of April 1. The early deadline for master's programs is January 15, with a final deadline of April 15. For applicants wishing to start in the spring semester, the early deadline is November 1. Teachers College requests that applicants collect the required documents for the application process and submit the entire package to the Office of Admission at one time. Admission application deadlines always refer to the date by which the Teachers College Office of Admissions must have received the application components and any other supporting material required by the Department. For more information as well as an online application, prospective students should visit http://www.tc.columbia.edu/admissions.

Correspondence and Information

Teachers College Columbia University
525 West 120th Street, Box 302
New York, New York 10027
Phone: 212-678-3710
Web site: http://www.tc.columbia.edu/discover
http://www.tc.columbia.edu/c&t

Teachers College Columbia University

THE FACULTY AND THEIR RESEARCH

Lynne Bejoian, Assistant Professor; Ph.D., USC. Disability studies in education, students with disabilities, graduate students with disabilities, inclusion, women and disability.

James Borland, Professor of Education; Ph.D., Columbia Teachers College. Education of gifted students, economically disadvantaged gifted students, conceptions of giftedness.

Alicia Broderick, Assistant Professor; Ph.D., Syracuse. Disability studies in education, students with disabilities, graduate students with disabilities.

Lucy Calkins, Robinson Professor of English Education; Ph.D., NYU. Teaching of reading and writing, reforming schools.

Celia Genishi, Professor of Education; Ph.D., Berkeley. Early childhood education, language in the classroom, qualitative research, childhood bilingualism.

A. Lin Goodwin, Professor of Education and Associate Dean of Teacher Education; Ed.D., Columbia Teachers College. Teacher education for urban and multicultural contexts, teachers' identities and their development and learning, multicultural understandings and curriculum enactments, Asian American socialization and education.

Britt Hamre, Assistant Professor; Ed.D., Columbia Teachers College. Teacher education, inclusive education, disability studies, curriculum, social justice education, action teacher research, collaborative research.

Thomas Hatch, Associate Professor of Education and Co-Director of the National Center for Restructuring Education, Schools, and Teaching (NCREST); Ed.D., Harvard. School reform, teaching and learning, teacher research, human development.

Stephanie Jones, Assistant Professor; Ed.D., Cincinnati. Issues of social class, gender, and race in public elementary schools; identity construction across contexts; critical literacy; teachers as ethnographers and activists.

Sharon Lynn Kagan, Virginia and Leonard Marx Professor of Early Childhood and Family Policy; Ed.D., Columbia Teachers College. Application of child and parent development research to the formation and implementation of public policies, the impact of institutions (family, childcare) on the development of low-income children.

Bonnie Keilty, Assistant Professor; Ed.D., George Washington. Early childhood education, early childhood special education, early intervention and inclusion.

Michelle Knight, Associate Professor of Education; Ph.D., UCLA. Equity issues in urban education, teacher education, multicultural feminisms and feminist pedagogies, African-American teaching practices with diverse populations.

Nancy Lesko, Professor of Education; Ph.D., Wisconsin–Madison. Curriculum theory and history, conceptions of children and youth in theory and practice, gender issues in education, citizenship education in times of war.

Celia Oyler, Associate Professor of Education; Ph.D., Illinois at Chicago. Classroom-based collaborative research on issues of social justice, equity, and accessible pedagogy; inclusion of students with disabilities in general education classrooms.

Susan Recchia, Associate Professor of Education; Ph.D., UCLA. Social and emotional development of young children, adult-child relationships across contexts, infants and preschoolers with special needs, early childhood professional development.

D. Kim Reid, Professor of Education; Ph.D., Temple. Sociohistorical construction of disability, inclusive instruction, classroom discourse.

Frances Schoonmaker, Professor of Education; Ed.D., Columbia Teachers College. Curriculum, teaching, and supervision: history, theory, and practice; teacher preparation; caring and values education; religious education.

Sam Shreyar, Assistant Professor of Education; Ed.D., Columbia Teachers College. Early childhood education, inquiry, classroom discussions in the area of mathematics.

Marjorie Siegel, Associate Professor of Education and Chair of the Department of Curriculum and Teaching; Ed.D., Indiana. Cultural and critical perspectives on literacy education, content area literacies, literacy and the arts, literacy and technology.

Leslie Williams, Professor of Education; Ed.D., Columbia Teachers College. Early childhood education, multicultural education, curriculum/program development and implementation, history of early childhood education.

Karen Zumwalt, Evenden Professor of Education; Ph.D., Chicago. Curriculum, teaching, teacher education, alternative routes to certification.

TEACHERS COLLEGE COLUMBIA UNIVERSITY

Department of Health and Behavior Studies

Programs of Study

Programs in the Department of Health and Behavior Studies share the common goal of helping people to realize their full potential as learners, to make informed decisions, and to attain the best possible quality of life. The best possible learning cannot take place in an atmosphere filled with physical, psychological, and social health problems. The same is true about optimal health, which cannot be achieved without skill in learning and literacy. The Department of Health and Behavior Studies offers graduate degrees in applied educational psychology, health studies, special education, and the teaching of American Sign Language as a foreign language.

The fields of study included in the applied educational psychology program are reading specialist and school psychology. Such study prepares students to serve as educators, scientists, and service providers in a variety of settings, including universities, schools, psychoeducational clinics, hospital-based child study clinics, and community agencies.

The health studies program includes health education, nursing education, and nutrition. These programs prepare students to serve in leadership roles in community-based organizations, government agencies, corporations, health-care settings, and educational settings. Current knowledge in behavioral science and education is integrated with field-based applications for health promotion and disease prevention. Nutrition includes programs in applied physiology and nutrition, community nutrition education, dietetic internship program, nutrition and program health, and nutrition education.

Among the programs included in special education are administration and supervision of special education programs, applied behavioral analysis, behavioral analysis, behavioral disorders, blindness and visual impairment, cross-categorical studies, deaf and hard of hearing, guidance and rehabilitation, instructional practice, mental retardation/autism, physical disabilities, research, and supervision of special education programs. These programs prepare students to serve as leaders and scholar-practitioners skilled in the development, evaluation, and application of practices that improve the life prospects of people with disabilities.

Teaching American Sign Language (ASL) as a foreign language prepares students to serve as scholar-practitioners who are skilled, knowledgeable, and practiced in the development, evaluation, and implementation of pedagogy that instructs and educates individuals unfamiliar with ASL, the deaf community, and the culture of individuals who are deaf or hard of hearing.

Typically, the population that these scholar-practitioners eventually instruct and educate consists of individuals who have hearing, are in regular education programs, and possess a wide range of cognitive, social, and academic abilities and cultural backgrounds.

Research Facilities

The Gottesman Libraries, with more than a million books and materials, is one of the nation's largest and most comprehensive research libraries in education, psychology, and health services. Students also have access to the 5.5 million volumes in the Columbia University library system. Organized research and service activities at Teachers College, in addition to being carried out by individual professors, are conducted through special projects and major institutes. Many of these centers of research are listed later.

Data, voice, and video outlets are found in every classroom, office, and residence on the main portion of the campus, and laptops and projectors may be borrowed from Media Services. The Microcomputer Center provides students with PCs and Macs, software, printers, and other peripherals. The center's software library includes PC and Mac programs for word processing, Web development, graphics, statistical analysis, and qualitative analysis and databases. The Instructional Media Lab (IML) is a facility in which students and faculty members create rich content for classes, online learning, student teaching, and research. Digital cameras and other equipment are loaned. Workstations allow computer-based full-motion video from camera, VCR, or videodisk to be edited and integrated with animation, digitized voice, and music and to be written to CD, DVD, or tape. IML also provides satellite downlink. Computer classrooms for hands-on instruction include both a PC and a Macintosh room, and the Goodman Family Computer Classroom suite includes a classroom with thirty-two notebook computers on tables that can be reconfigured for varying work groups.

Financial Aid

Each year, Teachers College awards approximately $5 million of its own funds in scholarship and stipend aid and $2 million of endowed funds to new and continuing students. There are no separate scholarship applications; faculty members nominate new students based upon their admission application. Financial assistance is also available through federal aid programs. All students are encouraged to file the FAFSA regardless of eligibility for aid; 51 percent of students receive financial aid.

Cost of Study

For the 2006–07 academic year, tuition was $975 per point, with 12 or more points considered full-time. Fees included the Teachers College, $320; Teachers College research, $320; health service, $356; continuous doctoral advisement registration, $2925; and Ph.D. oral defense, $4319. The tuition deposit was $300. Medical insurance ranged from about $553 to $1218.

Living and Housing Costs

Teachers College offers a variety of on-campus housing options that are unique to the area and convenient to the campus. Housing for a single student ranges from $3100 to $8000 per semester, depending upon the type of setting selected. Family housing ranges from $6875 to $8200 per semester. Teachers College has approximately 705 spaces available for single students and 150 apartments for students with families. The buildings are located in the vibrant and historic urban neighborhood of Morningside Heights. Current residence halls are historic buildings similar to other apartment-style buildings that were in New York City in the early 1900s. A new residence hall opened in the fall 2004 semester.

Student Group

There are approximately 5,000 students enrolled at Teachers College. About 77 percent are women, 12 percent are African American, 11 percent are Asian American, and 7 percent are Latino/a. The student body is composed of 13 percent international students from eighty different countries and 87 percent domestic students from all fifty states.

Location

The College is located in the Morningside Heights section of Manhattan's Upper West Side. Home to such venerable New York landmarks as Lincoln Center, the Cathedral of St. John the Divine, Grant's Tomb, Morningside Park, and the Manhattan School of Music, the Upper West Side is bounded by Central Park on the east and the Hudson River on the west. Because the College is located in New York City, students have access to an outstanding array of learning organizations, including museums, libraries, galleries, corporate learning centers, and K–12 schools.

The College and The University

Teachers College was founded in 1887 to provide a new form of schooling for teachers of children from low-income families of New York, one that combined a humanitarian concern to help others with a scientific approach to human development. For more than 100 years, Teachers College has conducted research on the central issues facing education, prepared generations of education leaders, and shaped debate and public policy in education. The College provides programs of study in administration, counseling, curriculum development, and school health care and continues its efforts to strengthen teaching skills, prepare leaders to develop and administer psychological and health-care programs, and develop new teaching software. In 1898, the College became affiliated with Columbia.

Columbia University was founded in 1754 as King's College by royal charter of King George II of England. It is the oldest institution of higher learning in the state of New York and the fifth oldest in the United States. From its beginnings in a schoolhouse in lower Manhattan, the University has grown to encompass two principal campuses: the historic, neoclassical campus in Morningside Heights and the modern Medical Center in Washington Heights. Today, Columbia is one of the top academic and research institutions in the world, conducting research in medicine, science, the arts, and the humanities. It includes three undergraduate schools, thirteen graduate and professional schools, and a school of continuing education. Sixty-four Nobel laureates have taught or studied at Columbia. Each year, the faculty of approximately 4,000 teaches more than 23,000 students from more than 150 countries.

Applying

Teachers College welcomes applicants who wish to pursue graduate study associated with the education, psychological, and health service professions. All applicants receive consideration for admission without regard to race, color, creed, religion, sex, national origin, age, or disability. In order to be considered for scholarships, students must meet the priority deadline. Admissions applications received after the priority deadlines may be considered on a space-available basis. Certain programs have special application deadlines. The 2007–08 final and early deadline for Ph.D. and all psychology doctoral programs is December 15. The early deadline for Ed.D. programs is January 2, with a final deadline of April 1. The early deadline for master's programs is January 15, with a final deadline of April 15. The early deadline is November 1 for the spring semester. Teachers College requests that applicants collect the required documents for the application process and submit the entire package to the Office of Admission at one time. Admission application deadlines always refer to the date by which the Teachers College Office of Admissions must have received the application components and any other supporting material required by the department.

Correspondence and Information

Teachers College Columbia University
525 West 120th Street, Box 302
New York, New York 10027

Phone: 212-678-3710
Web site: http://www.tc.columbia.edu/discover
http://www.tc.columbia.edu/hbs

Teachers College Columbia University

THE FACULTY AND THEIR RESEARCH

John Allegrante, Professor of Health Education; Ph.D., Illinois. Health education in multiple settings, health policy, interdisciplinary behavioral research, public health education workforce.

Charles Basch, Richard March Hoe Professor of Health Education and Chair of the Department of Health and Behavior Studies; Ph.D., Southern Illinois. Behavioral epidemiology, health education program planning and evaluation, urban and minority populations.

Marla Brassard, Associate Professor of Psychology and Education; Ph.D., Columbia. Psychological maltreatment—its assessment, the emotional injuries and behavioral problems that result, and the contextual factors that moderate the effect of maltreatment, particularly the role of schools, teachers, and peer relationships.

Isobel Contento, Mary Swartz Rose Professor of Nutrition and Education; Ph.D., Berkeley. Behavioral aspects of nutrition, use of psychosocial theory to study factors influencing food choice and decision-making processes.

Peg Cummins, Assistant Professor of Education; Ph.D., Vanderbilt. Blindness and visual impairment, new instructional strategies for orientation and mobility, services to individuals with severe mental and visual handicapping conditions.

R. Douglas Greer, Professor of Education and Psychology; Ph.D., Michigan. Comprehensive application of behavior analysis to schooling (CABAS®), teaching operations for the acquisition of verbal behavior by students with language deficits.

Linda Hickson, Professor of Education; Ph.D., Vanderbilt (Peabody). Education of children and adults with mental retardation and autism; cognitive, motivational, and emotional aspects of decision making.

Robert Kretschmer, Associate Professor of Education and Psychology; Ph.D., Kansas. Teaching of the deaf and hard of hearing, linguistics of English and ASL, literacy development, text structure, school psychology, auditory streaming.

Susan Masullo, Assistant Professor of Practice in Education; Ph.D., Fordham. Reading assessment and intervention, adult literacy, vocational and workplace literacy, learning disabilities.

Dennis Mithaug, Professor of Education; Ph.D., Washington (Seattle). Equal opportunity; empirical, moral, and policy theories; self-determination; self-regulation; social policy; special education leadership.

Kathleen O'Connell, Isabel Maitland Stewart Chair of Nursing Education; Ph.D., Kansas. Behavior change, smoking cessation and relapse, reversal theory, theory of self-control strength.

Delores Perin, Associate Professor of Psychology and Education; Ph.D., Essex (England). Reading and writing disabilities in children and adults, academic preparedness and remediation in community colleges.

Stephen Peverly, Associate Professor of Psychology and Education; Ph.D., Penn State. Cognitive processes that underlie reading comprehension and studying, cross-cultural differences between U.S. and Chinese children in mathematical performance and the reasons for differences in performance.

Russell Rosen, Adjunct Assistant Professor of Education and Psychology; Ph.D. Columbia Teachers College. American sign language as a second language and disability studies.

Denise Ross, Associate Professor of Psychology and Education; Ph.D., Columbia Teachers College. Autism, verbal behavior/communication, reading disabilities.

Philip Saigh, Professor of Psychology and Education; Ph.D., Georgia. Etiology, epidemiology, assessment, and cognitive-behavioral treatment of child-adolescent posttraumatic stress disorder.

Barbara Wallace, Associate Professor of Health Education; Ph.D., CUNY. Diversity training for multicultural competence; invisible, covert, and visible overt violence; primary, secondary, and tertiary violence prevention in school- and community-based settings; domestic violence; addictions and dependencies, especially to crack and cocaine.

Ye Wang, Assistant Professor of Education; Ph.D., Ohio State. Literacy and language, research methodology, multicultural education, child development, educational technology.

Randi Wolf, Associate Professor of Human Nutrition on the Vahlteich Endowment; Ph.D., Pittsburgh. Factors influencing colorectal cancer screening behaviors, nutrition and osteoporosis.

TEACHERS COLLEGE COLUMBIA UNIVERSITY

Department of Organization and Leadership

Programs of Study

The mission of the Department of Organization and Leadership is to educate, train, and support current and future leaders who work in schools, universities, and other organizations around the world as administrators, policy makers, researchers, psychologists, and educators from around the world. Students are or aspire to be in the fields of public and private education, higher and postsecondary education, adult education, health administration, organizational behavior, and organizational development and change. To accomplish this mission, the Department offers graduate degree programs in adult learning and leadership, education leadership, higher and postsecondary education, nurse executive studies, politics and education, and social-organizational psychology.

The adult learning and leadership program appeals to professionals who design, develop, and evaluate programs that meet the learning needs of adults in both face-to-face and online formats. Graduates serve in leadership positions in corporations, not-for-profit organizations, and a wide range of institutional settings.

The education leadership program concentrations prepare students for careers as successful scholars and practitioners who are capable of leading and transforming a wide variety of education organizations. Graduates serve in leadership positions as school and school district administrators, policy analysts and advocates, policy makers, and scholars of education and education leadership.

The higher and postsecondary education program creates knowledgeable practitioners and practicing scholars concerned with student affairs, teaching, learning, and scholarly and professional development; organizational and institutional analysis; and social and comparative perspectives. Across these domains the program examines the social, cultural, economic, and historic contexts of knowledge production, policy making, and institutional development while developing abilities to probe and develop the policies, structures, processes, and technologies of individual colleges and universities as well as state and national systems of tertiary education.

The program for nurse executives prepares students for leading roles in health-care organizations, in both service and education. These roles advance and implement the practice of nursing and health care, operating primarily in one-to-one relationships with clients. Graduates of this program influence other interdisciplinary health-care providers.

The politics and education program serves students who wish to study the ways in which governance institutions, political ideologies, and competing interests (within and outside the education community) influence the content, form, and functioning of schooling. Students study in depth the ways in which power and politics affect and are affected by such issues as reform and innovation, centralization and decentralization within federal systems of governance, privatization and school choice, race and ethnicity, poverty and inequality, and testing and accountability.

The social-organizational psychology program is concerned with the various contexts (interpersonal, group, intergroup, and interorganizational) in which human behavior occurs, the ways in which groups of individuals interact and influence these contexts, and how these interactions can be understood, studied, and modified through theory, research, and various types of interventions.

Courses in these programs are supplemented by other programs at Teachers College and Columbia University. With their faculty adviser's help, students select courses in their area of specialization, with consideration given to their academic backgrounds, work experiences, and career objectives

Research Facilities

The Gottesman Libraries, with more than a million books and materials, is one of the nation's largest and most comprehensive research libraries in education, psychology, and health services. Students also have access to the 5.5 million volumes in the Columbia University library system. Organized research and service activities at Teachers College, in addition to being carried out by individual professors, are conducted through special projects and major institutes.

Data, voice, and video outlets are found in every classroom, office, and residence on the main portion of the campus, and laptops and projectors may be borrowed from Media Services. The Microcomputer Center provides students with PCs and Macs, software, printers, and other peripherals. The center's software library includes PC and Macintosh programs for word processing, Web development, graphics, statistical analysis, and qualitative analysis and databases. The Instructional Media Lab (IML) is a facility in which students and faculty members create rich content for classes, online learning, student teaching, and research. Digital cameras and other equipment are loaned. IML also provides satellite downlink. Computer classrooms for hands-on instruction include both a PC and a Macintosh room, and the Goodman Family Computer Classroom suite includes a classroom with thirty-two notebook computers.

Financial Aid

Each year, Teachers College awards approximately $7 million of its own funds in scholarship and stipend aid and $2 million of endowed funds to new and continuing students. There are no separate scholarship applications; faculty members nominate new students based upon their admission application. Financial assistance is also available through federal aid programs. All students are encouraged to file the FAFSA regardless of eligibility for aid; 51 percent of students receive financial aid.

Cost of Study

For the 2006–07 academic year, tuition was $975 per point, with 12 or more points considered full-time. Fees included the Teachers College, $320; Teachers College research, $320; health service, $356; continuous doctoral advisement registration, $2925; and Ph.D. oral defense, $4319. The tuition deposit was $300. Medical insurance ranged from about $553 to $1218.

Living and Housing Costs

Teachers College offers a variety of on-campus housing options that are unique to the area and convenient to the campus. Housing for a single student ranges from $3100 to $8000 per semester, depending upon the type of setting selected. Family housing ranges from $6875 to $8200 per semester. Teachers College has approximately 705 spaces available for single students and 150 apartments for students with families. The buildings are located in the vibrant and historic urban neighborhood of Morningside Heights. Current residence halls are historic buildings similar to other apartment-style buildings that were in New York City in the early 1900s.

Student Group

There are approximately 5,000 students enrolled at Teachers College. About 77 percent are women, 12 percent are African American, 11 percent are Asian American, and 7 percent are Latino/a. The student body is composed of 13 percent international students from eighty different countries and 87 percent domestic students from all fifty states.

Location

The College is located in the Morningside Heights section of Manhattan's Upper West Side. Home to such venerable New York landmarks as Lincoln Center, the Cathedral of St. John the Divine, Grant's Tomb, Morningside Park, and the Manhattan School of Music, the Upper West Side is bounded by Central Park on the east and the Hudson River on the west. Because the College is located in New York City, students have access to an outstanding array of learning organizations, including museums, libraries, galleries, corporate learning centers, and K–12 schools.

The College and The University

Teachers College was founded in 1887 to provide a new form of schooling for teachers of children from low-income families of New York, one that combined a humanitarian concern to help others with a scientific approach to human development. For more than 100 years, Teachers College has conducted research on the central issues facing education, prepared generations of education leaders, and shaped debate and public policy in education. The College provides programs of study in administration, counseling, curriculum development, and school health care and continues its efforts to strengthen teaching skills, prepare leaders to develop and administer psychological and health-care programs, and develop new teaching software. In 1898, the College became affiliated with Columbia.

Columbia University was founded in 1754 as King's College by royal charter of King George II of England. It is the oldest institution of higher learning in the state of New York and the fifth oldest in the United States. From its beginnings in a schoolhouse in lower Manhattan, the University has grown to encompass two principal campuses: the historic, neoclassical campus in Morningside Heights and the modern Medical Center in Washington Heights. Today, Columbia is one of the top academic and research institutions in the world, conducting research in medicine, science, the arts, and the humanities. It includes three undergraduate schools, thirteen graduate and professional schools, and a school of continuing education. Sixty-four Nobel laureates have taught or studied at Columbia. Each year, the faculty of approximately 4,000 teaches more than 23,000 students from more than 150 countries.

Applying

Teachers College welcomes applicants who wish to pursue graduate study associated with the education, psychological, and health service professions. All applicants receive consideration for admission without regard to race, color, creed, religion, sex, national origin, age, or disability. In order to be considered for scholarships, students must meet the priority deadline. Admission applications received after the priority deadlines may be considered on a space-available basis. Certain programs have special application deadlines. The 2007–08 final and early deadline for Ph.D. and all psychology doctoral programs is December 15. The early deadline for Ed.D. programs is January 2, with a final deadline of April 1. The Adult Education Intensive Guided Study (AEGIS) Program has its own deadlines, posted on the Web site. A new cohort is accepted every two years. The early deadline for master's programs is January 15, with a final deadline of April 15. The priority deadline is November 1 for the spring semester. Admission application deadlines always refer to the date by which the Teachers College Office of Admissions must have received the application components and any other supporting material required by the Department. Teachers College requests that applicants collect the required documents for the application process and submit the entire package to the Office of Admissions at one time.

Correspondence and Information

Teachers College Columbia University
525 West 120th Street, Box 302
New York, New York 10027

Phone: 212-678-3710
Web site: http://www.tc.columbia.edu/discover
http://www.tc.columbia.edu/o&l

Teachers College Columbia University

THE FACULTY AND THEIR RESEARCH

Arlene Ackerman, Christian A. Johnson Professor of Outstanding Educational Practice, Ed.D., Harvard. Inquiry Program Director for the College's largest doctoral program for public school leaders, Superintendents' Work Conference.

Gregory Anderson, Associate Professor of Education and Minority Postdoctoral Fellow, Columbia Teachers College; Ph.D., CUNY. Higher-education policy and reform; race, access, and equity; compensatory/remedial education; comparative international topics in higher education (emphases on South Africa and the United States). Currently on leave.

William Baldwin, Associate Professor of Higher Education; Ed.D., Columbia Teachers College. College and university administration, financing higher education, technology in higher education, institutional research and planning.

Jeanne Bitterman, Lecturer of Adult and Continuing Education; Ed.D., Columbia. Cultivation of learning communities, distance learning, commitment to social action, basic and critical literacy.

Caryn Block, Associate Professor of Psychology and Education; Ph.D., NYU. Gender and racial issues in the workplace, motivation and performance.

Sarah Brazaitis, Senior Lecturer of Psychology and Education; Ph.D., Columbia Teachers College. Group dynamics and group relations, impact of social identities in groups and systems, racial identity.

Gina Buontempo, Lecturer of Psychology and Education; Ph.D., Columbia Teachers College. Emotional intelligence, decision making, leadership, and gender issues in the workplace.

W. Warner Burke, Edward L. Thorndike Professor of Psychology and Education; Ph.D., Texas at Austin. Behavioral practices associated with superior leaders and managers and their performance, empowerment in the workplace, leading and managing organization change.

Peter Coleman, Associate Professor of Psychology and Education and Director, International Center for Cooperation and Conflict Resolution (ICCCR); Ph.D., Columbia Teachers College. Conditions required for fostering constructive change in situations of protracted and intractable conflict, psychological processes and social conditions that foster the use of constructive social power.

Kevin Dougherty, Associate Professor of Higher Education and Senior Research Associate, Community College Research Center; Ph.D., Harvard. Higher-education policy and reform, higher-education finance, the community college, college students.

Eleanor Drago-Severson, Associate Professor of Education; Ed.D., Harvard. Leadership for adult learning and development; supporting teachers, principals, and other educational leaders in their professional development and growth in K–12 schools and adult education settings (domestically and internationally); adult learning and literacy; enhancing doctoral research training; qualitative research methodology.

Beth Fisher-Yoshida, Senior Lecturer and Associate Director, International Center for Cooperation and Conflict Resolution (ICCCR); Ph.D., Fielding Graduate University. Working with client organizations in supporting their change efforts through conflict resolution, negotiation, and mediation; diversity; communication and intercultural communication; team building; performance management; and leadership development.

Susan Fuhrman, President of Teachers College. Standards-based reform, research and policy.

Martha Gephart, Research Associate Professor of Education and Co-director, J. M. Huber Institute for Learning in Organizations; Ph.D., Columbia. Learning and performance in organizations, organizational assessment of organizational learning and links to performance in diverse organizational and inter-organizational settings.

Jeffrey Henig, Professor of Political Science and Education; Ph.D., Northwestern. The boundary between private action and public action in addressing social problems; privatization, race, and urban politics; the politics of urban education reform; school choice.

Jay Heubert, Professor of Education and Law; J.D., Ed.D., Harvard. Legal issues in education, equal educational opportunity, high-stakes testing, law and school reform, interprofessional collaboration.

Luis Huerta, Assistant Professor of Education; Ph.D., Berkeley. School choice and school reform policy, school finance, organizational theory.

Pearl Kane, Professor of Education and Klingenstein Family Chair for the Advancement of Independent School Education; Ed.D., Columbia Teachers College. Independent schools, private school governance, school choice and privatization, professional development of teachers and administrators.

Lee Knefelkamp, Professor of Psychology and Education; Ph.D., Minnesota. Theories and concepts of intercultural communications, the multicultural self in organizations, teaching to cognitive and cultural complexities in social-organizational psychology.

Hank Levin, William Heard Kilpatrick Professor of Economics and Education and Director, National Center for the Study of Privatization in Education; Ph.D., Rutgers. Economics of education, cost-effectiveness analysis, school reform, educational vouchers.

Terrence Maltbia, Senior Lecturer of Adult and Continuing Education; Ed.D., Columbia Teachers College. Strategic learning, leadership and organizational development, executive coaching and diversity.

Victoria Marsick, Professor of Education and Co-director, J. M. Huber Institute for Learning in Organizations; Ph.D., Berkeley. Informal workplace learning, team learning, action learning, strategic organizational learning and knowledge management, learning organizations, international models of management.

Robert Monson Jr., Senior Lecturer of Education and Director, Educational Policy Fellowship Program; Ph.D., Saint Louis. Accountability systems, public engagement, secondary schools, standards-based curriculum reform, professional development for teachers and leaders.

Anna Neumann, Professor of Higher Education; Ph.D., Michigan. Scholarly learning in life-span perspective, professors and their intellectual careers, learning and teaching in higher education, women's scholarly development.

Debra Noumair, Associate Professor of Psychology and Education; Ed.D., Columbia Teachers College. Group and organizational dynamics and the application of systems thinking to individual, team, and organizational performance.

Elissa Perry, Associate Professor of Psychology and Education; Ph.D., Carnegie Mellon. The role of personal characteristics (e.g., age, gender, race, disability) in human resource judgments and organizational behavior.

Patricia Raskin, Associate Professor of Psychology and Education; Ph.D., NYU. Career development of adults (especially women), work/family issues, executive coaching.

Douglas Ready, Assistant Professor of Education, Ph.D., Michigan. Influence of educational policies and practices on educational equity and access.

Michael Rebell, Professor of Law and Education and Executive Director, Campaign for Educational Equity; LL.B. Yale.

Craig Richards, Professor of Education and Director, Summer Principals Academy; Ph.D., Stanford. School finance, institutional incentives, market approaches to education, performance accountability systems, strategic management and organizational learning concepts.

Carolyn Riehl, Associate Professor of Education Leadership and Coordinator of the Education Leadership Program; Ph.D., Columbia Teachers College. Studies of school organization, studies of the practice of school administration and leadership, and scholarship on research, with diversity and equity stretching across all three clusters of research.

Elaine La Monica Rigolosi, Professor of Education; Ed.D., Massachusetts; J.D., Yeshiva. Health-care administration, health-care law, nursing administration and education, consumer satisfaction with health care, humanistic applications in health-care delivery.

Loriann Roberson, Professor of Psychology and Education; Ph.D., Minnesota. Employee motivation and work attitudes, workforce diversity issues, including diversity training and effects of stigmatization on performance.

Janice Robinson, Esq., Assistant Professor of Higher Education and General Counsel to the President, Office of the President–Diversity and Community; J.D., St. John's (New York). Affirmative action in higher education and legal education; legal issues in education; access and diversity in higher education; university and professional school leadership.

Thomas Sobol, Christian A. Johnson Professor of Outstanding Educational Practice; Ed.D., Columbia Teachers College. Education policy, elementary and secondary education reform, public school governance and finance, development of reflective education practitioners.

James Westaby, Associate Professor of Psychology and Education; Ph.D., Illinois. Employee attitudes, safety, and health; use of motivational reason measures in applied behavioral research; human resource management and survey research.

Lyle Yorks, Associate Professor of Adult and Continuing Education; Ed.D., Columbia Teachers College. Action learning, collaborative inquiry, qualitative research methods, strategic approaches to human resource development.

UNIVERSITY OF MICHIGAN–FLINT

Technology in Education Program

Program of Study

The Master of Arts in Education (M.A.Ed.) program at the University of Michigan–Flint, which is offered through the School of Education and Human Services, provides students an awareness of the unique characteristics and needs of diverse student populations, an understanding of the principles of motivation and learning, and an opportunity to examine classroom environments and develop strategies that can improve instruction.

The Technology in Education Program is one of five specializations available to M.A.Ed. students. This specialization is designed for students who wish to enhance their knowledge and skills in the use of technology as it relates to education. It provides opportunities for students to create individualized educational technology projects and emphasizes building a long-term network of innovative educators. The program is offered in a mixed-mode format, which blends Internet-based course work with limited on-campus meetings.

Students also have the option of applying to the Global Program of the Technology in Education specialization, beginning May 2007. This condensed fifteen-month program features convenient online courses and two 3-week summer residencies in Geneva, Switzerland. The Global Program emphasizes the innovative use of technology in science, civics, and social studies education. Course work is designed to support four activities that are at the heart of the program: the design of innovative, technology-mediated educational programs that are content-rich, pedagogically sound, socially responsible, and engaging for learners; acquisition of technology and design skills that support the creation of such programs; implementation and piloting of the programs in real-world settings; and documentation and dissemination of the cohort's work in ways that have an impact on broader educational communities. Through the World Federation of United Nations Associations and the Federation of International Institutions in Geneva, Global Cohort participants will work with a partner from an NGO or other organization on a topic of mutual interest. Participants will meet with partners during each Geneva residency, and will keep in contact electronically as project designs develop.

The degree requires the completion of 6 credits in core education courses, including a research seminar; 18 credits in technology courses, including 12 required credits and 6 elective credits; and 6 credits in cognate courses in another subject area that is relevant to the student's main area of interest. Students must select either the 36-credit-hour nonthesis option or the 33-credit-hour thesis option. The nonthesis option requires 6 additional elective credits. Students selecting the thesis option develop a research project or thesis, which is tailored to the area of specialization that the student has chosen. A final grade point average of at least 5.0 (B) on a 9.0 scale is required for successful completion of the degree.

Research Facilities

The Frances Willson Thompson Library's collection includes approximately 217,000 books and 35,000 bound magazines and journals. The library also contains over a half-million microforms, ranging from the *Times* of London to documents on education. The library subscribes to some 1,100 hardcopy periodicals, and it provides electronic access to approximately 13,000 more. The media collection includes music CDs, audio tapes, and other media, including CD-ROMs, DVDs, and videotapes.

Students in the Technology in Education Program have access to the human and technical resources of the Interactive Communications and Simulations (ICS) Group at the University of Michigan, which has supported the development and enactment of networked educational projects for over twenty years. ICS supports a dynamic assortment of innovative, educational online and computer-based programs. ICS activities focus on using computers and the Internet as tools to accentuate and improve classroom learning, often in the form of games and simulation activities.

Financial Aid

The Ralph and Emmalyn E. Freeman Master of Arts in Education Scholarship is awarded to students with a minimum GPA of 7.0 on a 9.0 scale (A-). The Dean's Graduate Student Scholarship is awarded to entering students with a minimum 3.5 undergraduate GPA or current students with a minimum A- GPA. The Carl and Sarah Morgan Graduate Student Scholarship is awarded to entering students with a GPA of at least 3.3 or to current students with a minimum B+ grade point average. Graduate research assistantships provide stipends for students who work with faculty members on a research project. Students may borrow up to $8500 in subsidized loans or $18,500 in unsubsidized loans. For more information, students should visit the Financial Aid Office Web site at http://www.umflint.edu/resources/offices/financial_aid/.

Cost of Study

In 2006–07, graduate tuition is $377.25 per credit for Michigan residents and $566 per credit for nonresidents. Other fees include a $50 registration fee, a $20 student activity fee, a $21 recreation fee, and a $76 technology fee.

Living and Housing Costs

Although the University does not provide housing for graduate students, there are many off-campus housing opportunities in Flint and the surrounding area. Apartments close to campus range from $370 per month for a studio to $750 for a two- or three-bedroom apartment. Further from campus, apartments range between $300 and $650 per month, depending on the size and location.

Student Group

Teachers, instructional technologists, educational administrators, and others who seek relevant, practical grounding in tools and concepts related to the use of technology in educational settings are prime candidates for this program. The University currently enrolls 153 full-time and 598 part-time graduate students.

Location

Although best known as the birthplace of General Motors, Flint has become better known for other activities in recent years, including the Crim Festival of Races and the Buick Open. A large cultural center occupies 30 acres near downtown, and more than fifty parks and four golf courses are interspersed throughout the city. Flint is located approximately 60 miles from Detroit, Ann Arbor, and Lansing.

The University

The University of Michigan–Flint was founded in 1956, when a two-year senior college was formed through public and private donations. Today, this four-year university offers 100 undergraduate and twenty-seven graduate degrees to more than 6,000 students. The programs have been designed to provide professional training in relationship to traditional study in the liberal arts and sciences, so that students develop the knowledge, intellectual skills, values, and attitudes they need to help them make thoughtful and informed judgments about their experiences.

Applying

To be considered for admission, applicants must submit an application form, a transcript showing an undergraduate GPA of 3.0 or higher, three letters of recommendation, a statement of purpose describing the applicant's experience and goals for entering the program, and a $55 application fee. The deadline to apply is November 15 for winter admission, March 15 for spring admission, May 15 for summer admission, and August 1 for fall admission. The deadline to apply for the Global Program that begins in May 2007 is December 15.

Correspondence and Information

For program information:
Beverly Schumer, Ed.D.
Education Program Director
Department of Education
430 David M. French Hall
University of Michigan–Flint
Flint, Michigan 48502-1950
Phone: 810-424-5215
E-mail: bschumer@umflint.edu
Web site: http://www.graduateprograms.umflint.edu/education.htm

Send applications to:
Office of Graduate Programs
251 Thompson Library
University of Michigan–Flint
Flint, Michigan 48502-1950
Phone: 810-762-3171
E-mail: gp@umflint.edu

University of Michigan–Flint

THE FACULTY AND THEIR RESEARCH

Judith Ableser, Assistant Professor of Special Education; Ph.D., Wayne State.

Wei Cao, Assistant Professor of Social Foundations. Ed.D., Cincinnati.

Rose Casement, Associate Professor of Literacy and Children's Literature; Ed.D., Maine. Diversity in children's literature; high-stakes testing.

Aviva Dorfman, Assistant Professor of Early Childhood Education; Ph.D., Michigan.

Mary Jo Finney, Associate Professor of Education Literacy; Ph.D., Oakland.

Patricia Gallant, Assistant Professor of Education Literacy; Ed.D., Vermont.

Jeff Kupperman, Assistant Professor of Educational Technology; Ph.D., Michigan.

Michael Pardales, Assistant Professor of Social Studies, Foundations of Education, and Curriculum Theory; Ph.D., Michigan State.

Sungho Park, Assistant Professor of Special Education; Ph.D., California, Santa Barbara.

Linda Pickett, Assistant Professor of Early Childhood Education; Ph.D., Mexico.

Beverly Schumer, Assistant Professor of Early Childhood Education and Director of Graduate Programs; Ed.D., Michigan.

Sharman Siebenthal Adams, Assistant Professor of Educational Technology and Social Foundations; Ph.D., Michigan State.

Sapna Taggar, Assistant Professor of Psychological Foundations; Ph.D., Michigan State.

Traki L Taylor, Associate Professor of Social Historical Foundations and Multicultural Education; Ph.D., Illinois.

Sue Woestehoff, Professor of Children's Literature; Ph.D., Minnesota. Literature for children and young adults.

VIRGINIA COMMONWEALTH UNIVERSITY

Programs in Educational Leadership

Programs of Study

Virginia Commonwealth University (VCU), through the Department of Educational Leadership, prepares critically reflective practitioners who are instructional leaders. Through course work and other experiences, the program prepares leaders who are able to develop positive school cultures that enhance student learning. The Department of Educational Leadership offers programs leading to the M.Ed. and a post-master's certificate. Individuals may also pursue the Ph.D. in education, specializing in the educational leadership track. Individuals who complete one or more those programs may qualify for endorsement by the Virginia Department of Education as a K–12 principal/supervisor.

The M.Ed. in educational leadership offers two tracks. The 30-credit leadership studies track is for individuals who wish to study leadership in educational settings but do not wish to seek a position as a school administrator. The 33-credit administration and supervision track is designed for individuals who aspire to positions as instructional leaders in schools.

The post-master's certificate is a 21-hour program for individuals who hold a master's degree in education and who seek certification in educational leadership. Students must take seven of the nine courses required for the M.Ed. in educational leadership, administration and supervision track. In addition, students must meet technology standards approved by the Virginia Board of Education, and they must supply proof of child-abuse and neglect-recognition training. Individuals successfully completing the program are eligible for the endorsement as a principal/supervisor K–12.

The doctoral program is designed primarily for line administrative personnel in public school units. Emphasis is placed on providing leadership training for superintendents, building principals, and assistant principals. Students must take a minimum of 18 credits in the educational leadership concentration.

Research Facilities

VCU libraries provide a combined capacity of more than 1.7 million volumes and 10,200 periodical titles and an online bibliographic search service accessing hundreds of databases. In addition, the Virginia State and Richmond Public libraries are within walking distance of both VCU campuses. Academic Computing provides a variety of microcomputer, minicomputer, and mainframe computing services to support the research and instructional endeavors of its faculty and students, including consultation, instruction, and computer acquisition.

The School of Education sponsors a variety of centers and institutes that connect students and faculty to the field of practice, including the Center for School Community Collaboration, the Center for Teacher Leadership, the Child Development Center, the Commonwealth Educational Policy Institute (CEPI), the Metropolitan Educational Research Consortium (MERC), the Partnership for People with Disabilities, the Virginia Department of Education's (VDOE) Training & Technical Assistance Center (T/TAC), the Rehabilitation Research and Training Center, the Virginia Adult Learning Resource Center, the Virginia Center for Teaching International Studies, and the Metropolitan Educational Training Alliance (META).

Financial Aid

Students may apply for need-based assistance through the University's Financial Aid Office. Current information on financial aid programs, policies, and procedures is available at http://www.vcu.edu/enroll/finaid.

Cost of Study

For full-time study (9–15 credits) in 2007–08, Virginia residents pay tuition and fees of $4452 per semester; nonresidents, $8876 per semester. For part-time study, Virginia residents pay tuition and fees of $465 per hour; nonresidents, $954 per hour. Some programs require additional fees. On the Medical College of Virginia (MCV) campus, tuition, fees, and other expenses vary in the medicine, pharmacy, nurse anesthesia, dentistry, and School of Allied Health programs.

Living and Housing Costs

Graduate student housing is available on both the MCV campus and the academic campus of Virginia Commonwealth University. Many graduate students live in off-campus housing, which is reasonably priced and readily available in a variety of styles and settings in nearby residential areas or within easy commuting distance. On- and off-campus housing information is available on the Web at http://www.housing.vcu.edu/.

Student Group

VCU enrolls 30,452 students, 7,611 of whom are graduate students. More than 200 clubs and organizations reflect the diverse social, recreational, educational, political, and religious interests of the student body.

Location

Richmond is Virginia's capital and a major East Coast financial and manufacturing center that offers students a wide range of cultural, educational, and recreational activities. Richmond is located in central Virginia at the intersection of Interstates 95 and 64, 2 hours south of Washington, D.C., and nestled between the Blue Ridge Mountains and the Atlantic coast. The Richmond region is easily accessible by plane, car, and train. With nearly 1 million residents, the historic city of Richmond combines big-city offerings with small-town hospitality. Applicants are encouraged to explore http://www.visit.richmond.com/ for more information on the city.

The University

VCU is a state-supported coeducational university with a graduate school, a major teaching hospital, and twelve academic and professional units that offer fifty-two undergraduate, twenty-two postbaccalaureate certificate, sixty-five master's, six post-master's certificate, and twenty-nine Ph.D. programs. VCU also offers M.D., D.D.S., D.P.T., and Pharm.D. programs as well as cooperative degree programs with other major Virginia colleges and universities. VCU has one of the largest evening colleges in the United States. The academic campus is located in Richmond's historic Fan District. The health sciences campus and hospital are located 2 miles east in the downtown business district. A University bus service provides free intercampus transportation for faculty members and students.

With more than $211 million in annual research funding, Virginia Commonwealth University is classified as one of the nation's top research universities by the Carnegie Foundation for the Advancement of Teaching. More than 29,000 undergraduate, certificate, graduate, post-master's, professional, and doctoral students are enrolled in 162 academic programs, forty of which are unique in the commonwealth of Virginia. The faculty members represent the finest American and international graduate institutions and enhance the University's position among the important institutions of higher learning in the United States and the world via their work in the classroom, laboratory, studio, and clinic and in their scholarly publications.

Applying

Admission procedures and program requirements are detailed in the *Graduate Bulletin*. Application deadlines and materials, including the application and the *Graduate Bulletin*, are available online at the Graduate School Web site at http://www.graduate.vcu.edu. Virginia Commonwealth University is an equal opportunity/affirmative action institution providing access to education and employment without regard to age, race, color, national origin, gender, religion, sexual orientation, veteran's status, political affiliation, or disability.

Correspondence and Information

Department of Educational Leadership
School of Education
1015 West Main Street
Virginia Commonwealth University
Richmond, Virginia 23284-2020
Phone: 804-828-3290
Fax: 804-828-1323
E-mail: soessc @vcu.edu
Web site: http://www.soe.vcu.edu/

Virginia Commonwealth University

THE FACULTY AND THEIR RESEARCH

Jonathan Becker, Assistant Professor; J.D., Boston College, 1997; Ph.D., Columbia Teachers College, 2003. Digital equity in education, educational equity as a multilevel organizational phenomenon, and the use of technology in data-driven decision making.

William C. Bosher Jr., Distinguished Professor; Ed.D., Virginia, 1974. Federal, state, and local policy development; school finance; educational accountability and leadership for reform.

Cheryl Magill, Assistant Professor; Ph.D., Virginia, 1999. Development of federal and state education law and policy, particularly by the development and implementation of the accountability components of the No Child Left Behind Act of 2001.

John Marshak, Associate Professor; Ph.D., Michigan, 1985. School finance policy development, court-ordered state educational finance reform, best practices in school leadership.

Martin Reardon, Assistant Professor; Ph.D., William and Mary, 2000. Improving the quality of supervision of instruction and personnel development in schools and school districts.

Charol Shakeshaft, Professor and Chair; Ph.D., Texas A&M. Gender patterns in educational delivery and classroom interactions.

Whitney Sherman, Assistant Professor, Ph.D. Women in leadership, leadership preparation and mentoring, social justice and equity issues in leadership.

VIRGINIA COMMONWEALTH UNIVERSITY

Programs in Teaching

Programs of Study	Virginia Commonwealth University (VCU), through the Department of Teaching and Learning, offers comprehensive programs of study in adult learning, early childhood/elementary education (pre-kindergarten through grade 6), ESL, instructional technology, middle education (grades 6 through 8), reading, and secondary education (grades 6 through 12). Using as its foundation the concept of the teacher as a reflective practitioner, the Department of Teaching and Learning both imparts knowledge and skills and asks that students question and inquire regarding pedagogy; curriculum; assessment; child, adolescent, and adult learners; and the school in society. The Master of Teaching programs are designed to incorporate eligibility for initial teaching licensure in Virginia in early childhood/elementary, middle, or secondary education (biology, chemistry, English, French, German, history, history and social studies, mathematics, physics, science, Spanish), or special education.
	In addition, the Department of Teaching and Learning offers a postbaccalaureate certificate, a 30-credit program for those who wish to become teachers in secondary schools, at the end of which students receive a certificate of study and are eligible to apply for teacher certification from the Commonwealth of Virginia. Persons completing the program are expected, among other attributes, to have an understanding of human development and learning theory appropriate to the age group they will teach, to demonstrate knowledge of the subjects they will teach, to develop an understanding of purposes for education and a defensible philosophical approach toward teaching, to acquire awareness of the diversity of the school-age population in cultural background and styles of learning, to demonstrate an ability to plan and implement effective teaching, and to measure student learning in ways that lead to sustained development and learning.
Research Facilities	VCU libraries provide a combined capacity of more than 1.7 million volumes and 10,200 periodical titles and an online bibliographic search service accessing hundreds of databases. In addition, the Virginia State and Richmond Public libraries are within walking distance of both VCU campuses. Academic Computing provides a variety of microcomputer, minicomputer, and mainframe computing services to support the research and instructional endeavors of its faculty and students, including consultation, instruction, and computer acquisition.
	The School of Education sponsors a variety of centers and institutes that connect students and faculty to the field of practice, including the Center for School Community Collaboration, the Center for Teacher Leadership, the Child Development Center, the Commonwealth Educational Policy Institute (CEPI), the Metropolitan Educational Research Consortium (MERC), the Partnership for People with Disabilities, the Virginia Department of Education's (VDOE) Training & Technical Assistance Center (T/TAC), the Rehabilitation Research and Training Center, the Virginia Adult Learning Resource Center, the Virginia Center for Teaching International Studies, and the Metropolitan Educational Training Alliance (META).
Financial Aid	Students may apply for need-based assistance through the University's Financial Aid Office. Current information on financial aid programs, policies, and procedures is available at http://www.vcu.edu/enroll/finaid.
Cost of Study	For full-time study (9–15 credits) in 2007–08, Virginia residents pay tuition and fees of $4452 per semester; nonresidents, $8876 per semester. For part-time study, Virginia residents pay tuition and fees of $465 per hour; nonresidents, $954 per hour. Some programs require additional fees. On the Medical College of Virginia (MCV) campus, tuition, fees, and other expenses vary in the medicine, pharmacy, nurse anesthesia, dentistry, and School of Allied Health programs.
Living and Housing Costs	Graduate student housing is available on both the MCV campus and the academic campus of Virginia Commonwealth University. Many graduate students live in off-campus housing, which is reasonably priced and readily available in a variety of styles and settings in nearby residential areas or within easy commuting distance. On- and off-campus housing information is available on the Web at http://www.housing.vcu.edu/.
Student Group	VCU enrolls 30,452 students, 7,611 of whom are graduate students. More than 200 clubs and organizations reflect the diverse social, recreational, educational, political, and religious interests of the student body.
Location	Richmond is Virginia's capital and a major East Coast financial and manufacturing center that offers students a wide range of cultural, educational, and recreational activities. Richmond is located in central Virginia at the intersection of Interstates 95 and 64, 2 hours south of Washington, D.C., and nestled between the Blue Ridge Mountains and the Atlantic coast. The Richmond region is easily accessible by plane, car, and train. With nearly 1 million residents, the historic city of Richmond combines big-city offerings with small-town hospitality. Applicants are encouraged to explore http://www.visit.richmond.com/ for more information on the city.
The University	VCU is a state-supported coeducational university with a graduate school, a major teaching hospital, and twelve academic and professional units that offer fifty-two undergraduate, twenty-two postbaccalaureate certificate, sixty-five master's, six post-master's certificate, and twenty-nine Ph.D. programs. VCU also offers M.D., D.D.S., D.P.T., and Pharm.D. programs as well as cooperative degree programs with other major Virginia colleges and universities. VCU has one of the largest evening colleges in the United States. The academic campus is located in Richmond's historic Fan District. The health sciences campus and hospital are located 2 miles east in the downtown business district. A University bus service provides free intercampus transportation for faculty members and students.
	With more than $211 million in annual research funding, Virginia Commonwealth University is classified as one of the nation's top research universities by the Carnegie Foundation for the Advancement of Teaching. More than 29,000 undergraduate, certificate, graduate, post-master's, professional, and doctoral students are enrolled in 162 academic programs, forty of which are unique in the commonwealth of Virginia. The faculty members represent the finest American and international graduate institutions and enhance the University's position among the important institutions of higher learning in the United States and the world via their work in the classroom, laboratory, studio, and clinic and in their scholarly publications.
Applying	Admission procedures and program requirements are detailed in the *Graduate Bulletin*. Application deadlines and materials, including the application and the *Graduate Bulletin*, are available online at the Graduate School Web site at http://www.graduate.vcu.edu. Virginia Commonwealth University is an equal opportunity/affirmative action institution providing access to education and employment without regard to age, race, color, national origin, gender, religion, sexual orientation, veteran's status, political affiliation, or disability.
Correspondence and Information	Michael Davis, Chair Department of Teaching and Learning School of Education 1015 West Main Street Virginia Commonwealth University Richmond, Virginia 23284-2020 Phone: 804-828-1305 Fax: 804-828-1323 E-mail: mddavis@vcu.edu Web site: http://www.soe.vcu.edu/

Virginia Commonwealth University

THE FACULTY AND THEIR RESEARCH

Nora Alder, Associate Professor; Ed.D., Nevada, 1996. Caring student/teacher relationships and urban schooling and teacher education.

Terry Carter, Assistant Professor; Ph.D., George Washington, 2001. Transformative learning among professionals in the workplace, learning through developmental relationships, including mentoring.

Seonhee Cho, Assistant Professor; Ph.D., Tennessee, 2005. ESL/international students' academic socialization issues that include relationships with peers and teachers, group work, institutional support, and access to academic resources.

Leila Christenbury, Professor; Ed.D., Virginia Tech, 1980. Classroom interaction strategies, specifically questioning; all aspects of young adult literature; the teaching of writing to secondary school students; approaches to teaching and learning in the secondary English classroom.

Michael Davis, Professor and Chair; Ph.D., Illinois, 1975. School change and teacher preparation.

Terry Dozier, Associate Professor and Director of the Center for Teacher Leadership; Ed.D., South Carolina. Promoting and supporting teacher leadership that enhances the quality of teaching and the teaching profession.

Ena Gross, Associate Professor; Ph.D., Georgia State, 1980. Math education.

Jacqueline McDonnough, Assistant Professor; Ph.D., Virginia, 2002. Assessing how pre-service teachers K-12 science experiences interact with their self-efficacy as future teachers of science.

Tammy Milby, Instructor; M.Ed., Radford, 1995. Struggling readers and writers, teacher quality/professional development practices, low-performing schools.

William Muth, Assistant Professor; Ph.D., George Mason, 2004. Thirdspace and reading components theories, especially as these apply to prison-based family literacy programs and children of incarcerated parents.

Gabriel Reich, Assistant Professor, Ph.D. Social studies teaching and learning, assessment, curriculum.

Joan Rhodes, Assistant Professor; Ph.D., Virginia Commonwealth, 1998. Early literacy development, using hypertext for increasing comprehension, instant messaging and social networking, electronic study skills, emerging and new literacies, assessment and instructional strategies for remediating reading difficulties.

Valerie Robnolt, Assistant Professor; Ph.D., Virginia, 2004. Assessment and instruction of reading comprehension, vocabulary, and fluency; the most effective methods of providing professional development to elementary teachers.

Gary Sarkozi, Assistant Professor; Ph.D., Virginia Commonwealth, 2001. Collect, analyzing, and evaluating data on activities related to technological integration in the many facets of today's global environment.

Loraine Stewart, Associate Professor; Ed.D., North Carolina at Greensboro, 1991. Examining strategies used by classroom teachers to integrate African American children's literature into the elementary curriculum and the impact this literature has on student achievement.

Doris White, Associate Professor; Ed.D., Illinois, 1971. Multicultural education, urban education, testing and achievement outcomes.

Section 24
Instructional Levels

This section contains a directory of institutions offering graduate work in instructional levels, followed by in-depth entries submitted by institutions that chose to prepare detailed program descriptions. Additional information about programs listed in the directory but not augmented by an in-depth entry may be obtained by writing directly to the dean of a graduate school or chair of a department at the address given in the directory.

For programs offering related work, see also in this book Administration, Instruction, and Theory; Education; Health-Related Professions; Leisure Studies and Recreation; Physical Education and Kinesiology; Special Focus; and Subject Areas; and in Book 2, Psychology and Counseling (School Psychology).

CONTENTS

Adult Education

Alverno College, School of Education, Milwaukee, WI 53234-3922. Offers adaptive education (MA); administrative leadership (MA); adult education and organizational development (MA); adult educational and instructional design (MA); adult educational and instructional technology (MA); instructional leadership (MA); instructional technology for K-12 settings (MA); professional development (MA); reading education (MA); reading education with adaptive education (MA); science education (MA); teaching in alternative schools (MA). *Accreditation:* NCATE. Part-time and evening/weekend programs available. *Faculty:* 12 full-time (11 women), 12 part-time/adjunct (10 women). *Students:* 83 full-time (68 women), 74 part-time (60 women); includes 37 minority (32 African Americans, 2 American Indian/Alaska Native, 3 Hispanic Americans). Average age 35. 61 applicants, 82% accepted, 41 enrolled. In 2006, 46 degrees awarded. *Degree requirements:* For master's, presentation/defense of proposal, conference presentation of inquiry projects. *Entrance requirements:* For master's, bachelor's degree in related field, communication samples from work setting, 3 letters of recommendation. Additional exam requirements/recommendations for international students: Required—TOEFL. *Application deadline:* For fall admission, 8/1 priority date for domestic and international students; for spring admission, 12/15 priority date for domestic and international students. Applications are processed on a rolling basis. Application fee: $20. Electronic applications accepted. *Expenses:* Tuition: Full-time $9,288; part-time $516 per credit. Required fees: $250; $125 per semester. Tuition and fees vary according to program. *Financial support:* In 2006–07, 92 students received support. Federal Work-Study available. Support available to part-time students. Financial award application deadline: 4/15; financial award applicants required to submit FAFSA. *Faculty research:* Student self-assessment, self-reflection, integration of curriculum, identifying needs of students in strategic situations and designing appropriate classroom strategies, implementing guided. *Unit head:* Dr. Mary Diez, Graduate Dean, 414-382-6214, Fax: 414-382-6332, E-mail: mary.diez@alverno.edu. *Application contact:* Sarajane Kennedy, Associate Director, Admissions Graduate Programs, 414-382-6104, Fax: 414-382-6332, E-mail: sarajane.kennedy@alverno.edu.

Armstrong Atlantic State University, School of Graduate Studies, Program in Education, Savannah, GA 31419-1997. Offers adult education (M Ed); early childhood education (M Ed); education (M Ed); elementary education (M Ed); middle grades education (M Ed); secondary education (M Ed), including business education, English education, mathematics education, science education, social science education; special education (M Ed), including behavioral disorders, curriculum and instruction, learning disabilities, speech-language pathology. *Accreditation:* NCATE. Part-time and evening/weekend programs available. Postbaccalaureate distance learning degree programs offered (minimal on-campus study). *Faculty:* 11 full-time (9 women), 13 part-time/adjunct (10 women). *Students:* 50 full-time (42 women), 219 part-time (175 women); includes 71 minority (67 African Americans, 3 Asian Americans or Pacific Islanders, 1 Hispanic American), 6 international. Average age 35. In 2006, 151 degrees awarded. *Degree requirements:* For master's, portfolio. *Entrance requirements:* For master's, GRE General Test or MAT, minimum GPA of 2.5, letters of recommendation. Additional exam requirements/recommendations for international students: Required—TOEFL (minimum score 523 paper-based; 193 computer-based). *Application deadline:* For fall admission, 7/1 priority date for domestic and international students; for spring admission, 11/15 priority date for domestic and international students. Applications are processed on a rolling basis. Application fee: $25. Electronic applications accepted. *Expenses:* Tuition, state resident: full-time $2,286; part-time $127 per credit. Tuition, nonresident: full-time $9,144; part-time $508 per credit. One-time fee: $257. *Financial support:* In 2006–07, research assistantships with partial tuition reimbursements (averaging $2,500 per year); career-related internships or fieldwork, Federal Work-Study, scholarships/grants, and unspecified assistantships also available. Support available to part-time students. Financial award applicants required to submit FAFSA. *Unit head:* Dr. Jane McHaney, College of Education Dean, 912-927-5398, Fax: 912-921-7425, E-mail: mchaneia@mail.armstrong.edu.

Athabasca University, Centre for Integrated Studies, Athabasca, AB T9S 3A3, Canada. Offers adult education (MA); community studies (MA); cultural studies (MA); educational studies (MA); global change (MA); work, organization, and leadership (MA). Part-time and evening/weekend programs available. Postbaccalaureate distance learning degree programs offered (no on-campus study). *Faculty:* 4 full-time (0 women), 50 part-time/adjunct (27 women). *Students:* Average age 39. 150 applicants, 87% accepted, 112 enrolled. In 2006, 40 degrees awarded. *Degree requirements:* For master's, project. *Entrance requirements:* For master's, 3- or 4-year BA. Additional exam requirements/recommendations for international students: Required—TOEFL or ENG 255 class (75) or Michigan English Language Assessment Battery (85) or IELTS (6.5) or CAEL (65); Recommended—TOEFL (minimum score 560 paper-based; 220 computer-based). *Application deadline:* For fall admission, 3/1 for domestic and international students; for winter admission, 10/1 for domestic and international students. Application fee: $65. Electronic applications accepted. *Faculty research:* Women's history, literature and culture studies, sustainable development, labor and education. *Unit head:* Dr. Derek Briton, Program Director, 780-675-6218, Fax: 780-675-6921, E-mail: derekb@athabascau.ca. *Application contact:* Derek Stovin, Program Administrator, 780-675-6236, Fax: 780-675-6921, E-mail: mais@athabascau.ca.

Auburn University, Graduate School, College of Education, Department of Educational Foundations, Leadership, and Technology, Auburn University, AL 36849. Offers adult education (M Ed, MS, Ed D); curriculum and instruction (M Ed, MS, Ed D, Ed S); curriculum supervision (M Ed, MS, Ed D, Ed S); educational psychology (PhD); higher education administration (M Ed, MS, Ed D, Ed S); media instructional design (MS); media specialist (M Ed); school administration (M Ed, MS, Ed D, Ed S). *Accreditation:* NCATE. Part-time programs available. *Faculty:* 23 full-time (11 women). *Students:* 40 full-time (26 women), 148 part-time (93 women); includes 64 minority (60 African Americans, 3 American Indian/Alaska Native, 1 Asian American or Pacific Islander), 6 international. Average age 38. 99 applicants, 57% accepted, 37 enrolled. In 2006, 32 master's, 10 doctorates, 7 other advanced degrees awarded. *Degree requirements:* For master's, thesis (for some programs); for doctorate, thesis/dissertation; for Ed S, field project. *Entrance requirements:* For master's, doctorate, and Ed S, GRE General Test. *Application deadline:* For fall admission, 7/7 for domestic students; for spring admission, 11/24 for domestic students. Applications are processed on a rolling basis. Application fee: $25 ($50 for international students). Electronic applications accepted. *Expenses:* Tuition, state resident: full-time $5,000. Tuition, nonresident: full-time $15,000. Required fees: $416. Tuition and fees vary according to program. *Financial support:* Teaching assistantships, Federal Work-Study available. Support available to part-time students. Financial award application deadline: 3/15. *Unit head:* Dr. William A. Spencer, Head, 334-844-4460. *Application contact:* Dr. Joe Pittman, Interim Dean of the Graduate School, 334-844-4700.

Ball State University, Graduate School, Teachers College, Department of Educational Studies, Program in Adult Education, Muncie, IN 47306-1099. Offers adult and community education (MA); adult, community, and higher education (Ed D). *Accreditation:* NCATE. *Students:* 16 full-time (10 women), 99 part-time (58 women); includes 11 minority (6 African Americans, 4 American Indian/Alaska Native, 1 Asian American or Pacific Islander), 11 international. Average age 34. 29 applicants, 76% accepted, 15 enrolled. In 2006, 6 degrees awarded. *Degree requirements:* For doctorate, thesis/dissertation. *Entrance requirements:* For doctorate, GRE General Test, minimum graduate GPA of 3.2. Application fee: $25 ($35 for international students). *Financial support:* Research assistantships with full tuition reimbursements, teaching assistantships with full tuition reimbursements, career-related internships or fieldwork available. Financial award application deadline: 3/1. *Faculty research:* Community education, executive development for public services, applied gerontology. *Unit head:* Joseph Armstrong, Director of Doctoral Program, 765-285-5348, Fax: 765-285-5489.

Buffalo State College, State University of New York, Graduate Studies and Research, Faculty of Applied Science and Education, Department of Educational Foundations, Program in Adult Education, Buffalo, NY 14222-1095. Offers adult education (MS, Certificate); human resources development (Certificate). Part-time and evening/weekend programs available. Postbaccalaureate distance learning degree programs offered (no on-campus study). *Degree requirements:* For master's, comprehensive exam. *Entrance requirements:* Additional exam requirements/recommendations for international students: Required—TOEFL (minimum score 550 paper-based; 213 computer-based).

Capella University, School of Education, Minneapolis, MN 55402. Offers college teaching (Certificate); curriculum and instruction (MS, PhD); education (MS); enrollment management (MS); instructional design for online learning (MS, PhD); k-12 studies in education (MS, PhD); leadership for higher education (MS, PhD); leadership in education administration (Certificate); leadership in educational administration (MS, PhD); postsecondary and adult education (MS, PhD); professional studies in education (MS, PhD); reading and literacy (MS); training and performance improvement (MS, PhD). Part-time and evening/weekend programs available. Postbaccalaureate distance learning degree programs offered (minimal on-campus study). Terminal master's awarded for partial completion of doctoral program. *Degree requirements:* For master's, integrative project, thesis optional; for doctorate, thesis/dissertation, comprehensive exam, registration. *Entrance requirements:* Additional exam requirements/recommendations for international students: Required—TOEFL (minimum score 550 paper-based; 213 computer-based), TWE (minimum score 4). Electronic applications accepted. *Faculty research:* Higher education administration, distance learning, adult education, training and curriculum design.

Cheyney University of Pennsylvania, School of Education, Program in Adult and Continuing Education, Cheyney, PA 19319-0200. Offers MS. Part-time and evening/weekend programs available. *Degree requirements:* For master's, thesis or alternative. *Entrance requirements:* For master's, GRE General Test, MAT, minimum GPA of 2.75. Electronic applications accepted.

Cheyney University of Pennsylvania, School of Education, Program in Educational Administration of Adult and Continuing Education, Cheyney, PA 19319-0200. Offers M Ed, MS. Part-time and evening/weekend programs available. *Degree requirements:* For master's, thesis or alternative. Electronic applications accepted.

Cleveland State University, College of Graduate Studies, College of Education and Human Services, Department of Counseling, Administration, Supervision and Adult Learning, Cleveland, OH 44115. Offers adult learning and development (M Ed); community agency counseling (M Ed); counseling and pupil personnel administration (Ed S); educational administration (Ed S); educational administration and supervision (M Ed); school counseling (M Ed). *Accreditation:* ACA (one or more programs are accredited). Part-time programs available. *Faculty:* 15 full-time (9 women), 8 part-time/adjunct (5 women). *Students:* 43 full-time (33 women), 304 part-time (236 women); includes 91 minority (78 African Americans, 2 Asian Americans or Pacific Islanders, 11 Hispanic Americans). Average age 35. 205 applicants, 36% accepted, 54 enrolled. In 2006, 136 master's, 6 other advanced degrees awarded. *Degree requirements:* For master's, thesis optional; for Ed S, internship, thesis optional. *Entrance requirements:* For master's, GRE General Test or MAT, letter of recommendation, minimum GPA of 2.75. Additional exam requirements/recommendations for international students: Required—TOEFL (minimum score 525 paper-based; 197 computer-based), IELTS (minimum score 6). *Application deadline:* For fall admission, 6/21 for domestic students; for spring admission, 8/31 for domestic students. Application fee: $30. *Financial support:* In 2006–07, 8 students received support, including research assistantships with full and partial tuition reimbursements available (averaging $3,287 per year), teaching assistantships with full and partial tuition reimbursements available (averaging $3,480 per year); career-related internships or fieldwork, scholarships/grants, tuition waivers (full), and unspecified assistantships also available. Support available to part-time students. *Faculty research:* Education law, career development, women in school administration, psychopharmacology, counseling and spirituality. Total annual research expenditures: $478,265. *Unit head:* Dr. Rollin D. Nordgren, Interim Chairperson, 216-523-7499, Fax: 216-687-5378, E-mail: r.nordgren@csuohio.edu.

Concordia University, School of Graduate Studies, Faculty of Arts and Science, Department of Education, Program in Adult Education, Montréal, QC H3G 1M8, Canada. Offers Diploma. *Students:* 6 applicants, 50% accepted, 1 enrolled. In 2006, 7 degrees awarded. *Degree requirements:* For Diploma, internship. *Entrance requirements:* For degree, interview. *Application deadline:* For fall admission, 3/1 for domestic students; for winter admission, 11/1 for domestic students. Application fee: $50. *Faculty research:* Staff development, human relations training, adult learning, professional development, learning in the workplace. *Unit head:* Dr. William Knitter, Director, 514-848-2424 Ext. 2017.

Concordia University, School of Graduate Studies, Faculty of Arts and Science, Department of Education, Program in Educational Studies, Montréal, QC H3G 1M8, Canada. Offers MA. *Students:* 23 full-time (15 women), 39 part-time (32 women). 43 applicants, 67% accepted, 11 enrolled. In 2006, 14 degrees awarded. *Degree requirements:* For master's, one foreign language, thesis optional. *Application deadline:* For fall admission, 6/1 for domestic students; for winter admission, 10/1 for domestic students; for spring admission, 2/1 for domestic students. Application fee: $50. *Faculty research:* Social aspects of microtechnology, gender and education, minorities and immigrants in Canadian education, professional development, political education. *Unit head:* Dr. William Knitter, Director, 514-848-2424 Ext. 2017.

Coppin State University, Division of Graduate Studies, Division of Education, Department of Adult and General Education, Baltimore, MD 21216-3698. Offers MS. Part-time and evening/weekend programs available. *Faculty:* 5 full-time (4 women), 4 part-time/adjunct (1 woman). *Students:* 8 full-time (7 women), 30 part-time (16 women); includes 33 minority (all African Americans) Average age 38. 28 applicants, 79% accepted, 19 enrolled. In 2006, 8 degrees awarded. *Degree requirements:* For master's, research paper, internship, thesis optional. *Entrance requirements:* For master's, GRE or PRAXIS, minimum GPA of 2.5, interview, resumé, references. *Application deadline:* For fall admission, 8/15 priority date for domestic students; for spring admission, 12/15 priority date for domestic students. Applications are processed on a rolling basis. Application fee: $45. *Financial support:* Federal Work-Study, institutionally sponsored loans, and scholarships/grants available. Support available to part-time students. Financial award application deadline: 6/30; financial award applicants required to submit FAFSA. *Unit head:* Dr. Geraldine Waters, Chair, 410-951-3027, E-mail: gwaters@coppin.edu.

Cornell University, Graduate School, Graduate Fields of Agriculture and Life Sciences, Field of Education, Ithaca, NY 14853-0001. Offers agricultural education (MAT); biology (7-12) (MAT); chemistry (7-12) (MAT); curriculum and instruction (MPS, MS, PhD); earth science (7-12) (MAT); extension, and adult education (MPS, MS, PhD); mathematics (7-12) (MAT); physics (7-12) (MAT). *Faculty:* 26 full-time (9 women). *Students:* 56 full-time (33 women); includes 10 minority (1 African American, 5 Asian Americans or Pacific Islanders, 4 Hispanic Americans), 4 international. Average age 31. 96 applicants, 40% accepted, 18 enrolled. In 2006, 22 master's, 8 doctorates awarded. Terminal master's awarded for partial completion of doctoral program. *Degree requirements:* For master's, thesis (MS); for doctorate, thesis/dissertation, comprehensive exam. *Entrance requirements:* For master's and doctorate, GRE General Test, sample of written work (recommended), 2 letters of recommendation. Additional exam requirements/recommendations for international students: Required—TOEFL (minimum score 550 paper-based; 213 computer-based). *Application deadline:* For fall admission, 2/15 for domestic students. Application fee: $60. Electronic applications accepted. *Expenses:* Tuition: Full-time $32,800. Full-time tuition and fees vary according to program. *Financial support:* In 2006–07, 31 students received support, including 4 fellowships with full tuition reimbursements available, 7 research assistantships with full tuition reimbursements available, 20 teaching assistantships with full tuition reimbursements available; institutionally sponsored loans, scholarships/grants, health care benefits, tuition waivers (full and partial), and unspecified assistantships also available. Financial award applicants required to submit FAFSA. *Faculty research:* Moral development and professional ethics; public issues education and community development; socio/political issues in public education; teacher education and curriculum in agricultural science, and mathematics; extension research. *Unit head:* Director of Graduate Studies, 607-255-4278, Fax: 607-255-7905. *Application contact:* Graduate Field Assistant, 607-255-4278, Fax: 607-255-7905, E-mail: rh22@cornell.edu.

Curry College, Division of Continuing Education and Graduate Studies, Program in Education, Milton, MA 02186-9984. Offers adult education (Certificate); educational administration (M Ed); educational therapy (Certificate); elementary education (M Ed); foundations (nonlicense) (M Ed); learning disabilities across the lifespan (Certificate); reading (M Ed, Certificate); special education (M Ed). Part-time and evening/weekend programs available. *Faculty:* 6 full-time (4 women), 11 part-time/adjunct (7 women). *Degree requirements:* For master's, research project. *Entrance requirements:* For master's, MAT, interview, recommendations, resumé. Additional exam requirements/recommendations for international students: Required—TOEFL (minimum score 550 paper-based). *Application deadline:* For fall admission, 8/1 priority date for domestic students; for spring admission, 1/1 for domestic students. Applications are processed on a rolling basis. Application fee: $50. *Expenses:* Contact institution. *Financial support:* Career-related internships or fieldwork and tuition waivers (partial) available. *Faculty research:* Classroom trauma, therapeutic writing, inclusionary practices. *Unit head:* Dr. Donald Gratz, Director and Associate Professor, 617-333-2243, E-mail: dgratz0703@curry.edu. *Application contact:* John Bresnahan, Director of Graduate Enrollment and Student Services, 617-333-2243, Fax: 617-333-2045, E-mail: jbresnah0104@curry.edu.

DePaul University, School for New Learning, Chicago, IL 60604-2287. Offers applied technology (MS); educating adults (MA); integrated professional studies (MA). Part-time and evening/weekend programs available. *Faculty:* 8 full-time (2 women), 9 part-time/adjunct (5 women). *Students:* 16 full-time (9 women), 139 part-time (96 women); includes 75 minority (42 African Americans, 1 American Indian/Alaska Native, 25 Asian Americans or Pacific Islanders, 7 Hispanic Americans), 1 international. Average age 42. 30 applicants, 80% accepted. In 2006, 20 master's awarded. *Degree requirements:* For master's, thesis or alternative. *Entrance requirements:* For master's, 3 years of work experience, current related employment. *Application deadline:* For fall admission, 9/1 priority date for domestic students; for spring admission, 3/1 priority date for domestic students. Applications are processed on a rolling basis. Application fee: $25. Electronic applications accepted. *Financial support:* In 2006–07, 7 students received support. Scholarships/grants and tuition waivers (partial) available. Financial award applicants required to submit FAFSA. *Faculty research:* Interactive problem-based learning, liberal learning and professional competence, effective instructional practice. *Unit head:* Dr. Barbara Radner, Program Director, 312-362-5515, Fax: 312-362-8809, E-mail: bradner@depaul.edu. *Application contact:* Berni Thomas, Assistant Director, 312-362-5744, Fax: 312-362-8809, E-mail: bthoma10@depaul.edu.

Drake University, School of Education, Department of Leadership, Counseling and Adult Development, Program in Adult Development, Des Moines, IA 50311-4516. Offers adult learning and performance development (MS). Part-time and evening/weekend programs available. *Faculty:* 10 full-time (3 women), 28 part-time/adjunct (16 women). *Students:* 33 applicants, 73% accepted. In 2006, 37 master's awarded. *Degree requirements:* For master's, comprehensive exam. *Entrance requirements:* For master's, GRE General Test, MAT, or Drake Writing Assessment, resumé, 2 letters of recommendation. Additional exam requirements/recommendations for international students: Required—TOEFL (minimum score 550 paper-based; 213 computer-based). *Application deadline:* For fall admission, 7/1 priority date for domestic students, 6/1 priority date for international students; for spring admission, 11/1 priority date for domestic students, 10/1 priority date for international students. Applications are processed on a rolling basis. Application fee: $25. Electronic applications accepted. *Financial support:* Career-related internships or fieldwork and unspecified assistantships available. Support available to part-time students. *Faculty research:* Counseling and rehabilitation, behavioral supports, inquiry-based science methods, teacher quality enhancements. Total annual research expenditures: $1.5 million. *Unit head:* Dr. Thomas West-Brook, Advisor, 515-271-3078, E-mail: thomas.westbrook@drake.edu. *Application contact:* Ann J. Martin, Graduate Coordinator, 515-271-2034, Fax: 515-271-2831, E-mail: ann.martin@drake.edu.

East Carolina University, Graduate School, College of Education, Department of Counselor and Adult Education, Greenville, NC 27858-4353. Offers adult education (MA Ed); counselor education (MS, Ed S). *Accreditation:* NCATE. Part-time and evening/weekend programs available. *Students:* 38 full-time (35 women), 59 part-time (50 women); includes 27 minority (24 African Americans, 2 American Indian/Alaska Native, 1 Hispanic American). Average age 32. 7 applicants, 57% accepted, 4 enrolled. In 2006, 41 master's, 3 other advanced degrees awarded. *Degree requirements:* For master's, thesis optional. *Entrance requirements:* For master's, GRE General Test or MAT, interview, minimum GPA of 2.5, bachelor's degree in related field, teaching license (MA Ed). Additional exam requirements/recommendations for international students: Required—TOEFL. *Application deadline:* For fall admission, 5/15 priority date for domestic students. Applications are processed on a rolling basis. Application fee: $50. *Financial support:* Research assistantships with partial tuition reimbursements, teaching assistantships with partial tuition reimbursements, Federal Work-Study available. Support available to part-time students. Financial award application deadline: 6/1. *Unit head:* Dr. Vivian Mott, Chair, 252-328-6177, Fax: 252-328-4368, E-mail: mottv@ecu.edu. *Application contact:* Dean of Graduate School, 252-328-6012, Fax: 252-328-6071, E-mail: gradschool@ecu.edu.

Eastern Washington University, Graduate Studies, College of Education and Human Development, Department of Education, Program in Adult Education, Cheney, WA 99004-2431. Offers M Ed. *Accreditation:* NCATE. *Degree requirements:* For master's, thesis or alternative, comprehensive exam. *Entrance requirements:* For master's, minimum GPA of 3.0.

Florida Agricultural and Mechanical University, Division of Graduate Studies, Research, and Continuing Education, College of Education, Department of Educational Leadership and Human Services, Tallahassee, FL 32307-3200. Offers administration and supervision (M Ed, MS Ed, PhD); adult education (M Ed, MS Ed); educational leadership (PhD); guidance and counseling (M Ed, MS Ed). *Accreditation:* NCATE. *Degree requirements:* For master's, thesis (for some programs); for doctorate, thesis/dissertation. *Entrance requirements:* For master's, GRE General Test, minimum GPA of 3.0. Additional exam requirements/recommendations for international students: Required—TOEFL.

Florida Atlantic University, College of Education, Department of Educational Leadership, Boca Raton, FL 33431-0991. Offers adult/community education (M Ed, PhD, Ed S); educational leadership (M Ed, PhD, Ed S); higher education management (M Ed, PhD). *Accreditation:* NCATE. Part-time and evening/weekend programs available. Postbaccalaureate distance learning degree programs offered (minimal on-campus study). *Faculty:* 19 full-time (8 women), 18 part-time/adjunct (11 women). *Students:* 65 full-time (43 women), 187 part-time (119 women); includes 81 minority (52 African Americans, 1 American Indian/Alaska Native, 4 Asian Americans or Pacific Islanders, 24 Hispanic Americans), 3 international. Average age 37. 114 applicants, 51% accepted, 50 enrolled. In 2006, 63 master's, 19 doctorates, 13 other advanced degrees awarded. *Degree requirements:* For master's, registration; for doctorate, thesis/dissertation, departmental qualifying exam, comprehensive exam, registration; for Ed S, departmental qualifying exam. *Entrance requirements:* For master's, GRE General Test, minimum GPA of 3.0 during previous 2 years; for doctorate, GRE General Test, minimum GPA of 3.5; for Ed S, GRE General Test. *Application deadline:* Applications are processed on a rolling basis. Application fee: $30. Electronic applications accepted. *Expenses:* Tuition, area resident: Full-time $4,394. Tuition, nonresident: full-time $16,441. *Financial support:* In 2006–07, 6 students received support, including 1 fellowship, 2 research assistantships, 2 teaching assistantships; career-related internships or fieldwork and tuition waivers (partial) also available. *Faculty research:* Self-directed learning, school reform issues, legal issues, mentoring, school leadership. *Unit head:* Dr. Anthony C. Townsend, Chairperson, 561-297-3550, Fax: 561-297-3618, E-mail: townsend@fau.edu. *Application contact:* Catherine Politi, Senior Secretary, 561-297-3550, Fax: 561-297-3618, E-mail: cpoliti@fau.edu.

Florida International University, College of Education, Department of Educational Leadership and Policy Studies, Program in Adult Education, Miami, FL 33199. Offers MS. *Accreditation:* NCATE. Part-time and evening/weekend programs available. *Faculty:* 2 full-time (1 woman), 3 part-time/adjunct (2 women). *Students:* 4 full-time (all women), 6 part-time (5 women); includes 7 minority (4 African Americans, 3 Hispanic Americans). 6 applicants, 17% accepted, 1 enrolled. In 2006, 6 degrees awarded. *Entrance requirements:* Additional exam requirements/recommendations for international students: Required—TOEFL (minimum score 550 paper-based; 213 computer-based; 80 iBT), IELTS (minimum score 6). *Application deadline:* For fall admission, 6/1 priority date for domestic students, 4/1 for international students; for winter admission, 10/1 priority date for domestic students, 9/1 for international students; for spring admission, 3/1 priority date for domestic students, 2/1 for international students. Applications are processed on a rolling basis. Application fee: $30. *Expenses:* Tuition, state resident: part-time $249 per credit hour. Tuition, nonresident: part-time $753 per credit hour. Tuition and fees vary according to program. *Financial support:* Fellowships, research assistantships, teaching assistantships, Federal Work-Study and tuition waivers (full and partial) available. Support available to part-time students. *Faculty research:* Adult education, family literacy, learning technology. *Unit head:* Dr. Jonette Rocco, Assistant Professor, 305-348-6151, E-mail: rocco@fiu.edu. *Application contact:* Marisa Salazar, Student Recruiter, 305-348-3002, Fax: 305-348-3227, E-mail: marisa.salazar@fiu.edu.

Florida International University, College of Education, Department of Educational Leadership and Policy Studies, Program in Adult Education in Human Resource Development, Miami, FL 33199. Offers Ed D. Part-time and evening/weekend programs available. *Faculty:* 2 full-time (1 woman), 3 part-time/adjunct (2 women). *Students:* 7 full-time (6 women), 31 part-time (23 women); includes 27 minority (13 African Americans, 4 Asian Americans or Pacific Islanders, 10 Hispanic Americans). Average age 44. 10 applicants, 30% accepted, 3 enrolled. In 2006, 4 degrees awarded. *Degree requirements:* For doctorate, thesis/dissertation, registration. *Entrance requirements:* For doctorate, GRE General Test. Additional exam requirements/recommendations for international students: Required—TOEFL (minimum score 550 paper-based; 213 computer-based; 80 iBT), IELTS (minimum score 6). *Application deadline:* For fall admission, 6/1 priority date for domestic students, 4/1 for international students; for winter admission, 10/1 priority date for domestic students, 9/1 for international students; for spring admission, 3/1 priority date for domestic students, 2/1 for international students. Applications are processed on a rolling basis. Application fee: $30. Electronic applications accepted. *Expenses:* Tuition, state resident: part-time $249 per credit hour. Tuition, nonresident: part-time $753 per credit hour. Tuition and fees vary according to program. *Financial support:* Fellowships, research assistantships with full and partial tuition reimbursements, teaching assistantships with full and partial tuition reimbursements, Federal Work-Study and tuition waivers (full and partial) available. Support available to part-time students. *Faculty research:* Adult education, family literacy, learning technologies. *Unit head:* Dr. Jonette Rocco, Assistant Professor, 305-348-6151, E-mail: rocco@fiu.edu. *Application contact:* Marisa Salazar, Student Recruiter, 305-348-3002, Fax: 305-348-3227, E-mail: marisa.salazar@fiu.edu.

Florida State University, Graduate Studies, College of Education, Department of Educational Leadership and Policy Studies, Program in Adult Education and Human Resource Development, Tallahassee, FL 32306. Offers MS, Ed D, PhD, Ed S. *Faculty:* 2 full-time (0 women). *Students:* 1 (woman) full-time, 27 part-time (22 women); includes 8 minority (6 African Americans, 1 Asian American or Pacific Islander, 1 Hispanic American). 30 applicants, 47% accepted, 13 enrolled. In 2006, 10 degrees awarded. *Degree requirements:* For master's and Ed S, thesis optional; for doctorate, thesis/dissertation, comprehensive exam. *Entrance requirements:* For master's, GRE General Test, minimum GPA of 3.0; for doctorate and Ed S, GRE General Test, minimum graduate GPA of 3.0. *Application deadline:* For fall admission, 7/1 priority date for domestic students; for spring admission, 11/1 for domestic students. Applications are processed on a rolling basis. Application fee: $30. *Expenses:* Tuition, state resident: full-time $5,822; part-time $243 per credit hour. Tuition, nonresident: full-time $20,976; part-time $874 per credit hour. Tuition and fees vary according to program. *Financial support:* Fellowships, research assistantships, teaching assistantships, career-related internships or fieldwork available. Financial award applicants required to submit FAFSA. *Unit head:* Dr. John Sample, Coordinator, 850-644-8176, Fax: 850-644-6401. *Application contact:* Jimmy Pastrano, Program Assistant, 850-644-6777, Fax: 850-644-1258, E-mail: pastrano@coe.fsu.edu.

Fordham University, Graduate School of Education, Division of Curriculum and Teaching, New York, NY 10023. Offers adult education (MS, MSE); bilingual teacher education (MSE); curriculum and teaching (MSE); early childhood education (MSE); elementary education (MST); language, literacy, and learning (PhD); reading education (MSE, Adv C); secondary education (MAT, MSE); special education (MSE, Adv C); teaching English as a second language (MSE). *Accreditation:* NCATE. *Faculty:* 22 full-time (18 women), 38 part-time/adjunct (28 women). *Students:* 68 full-time (51 women), 663 part-time (612 women); includes 200 minority (74 African Americans, 1 American Indian/Alaska Native, 37 Asian Americans or Pacific Islanders, 88 Hispanic Americans), 3 international. Average age 32. 636 applicants, 86% accepted, 322 enrolled. In 2006, 351 master's, 8 doctorates awarded. *Degree requirements:* For doctorate and Adv C, thesis/dissertation. *Entrance requirements:* For doctorate, MAT, GRE General Test. Application fee: $65. *Financial support:* Applicants required to submit FAFSA. *Unit head:* Dr. Terry Osborn, Chairperson, 212-636-6450.

Grand Valley State University, College of Education, Programs in General Education, Allendale, MI 49401-9403. Offers adult and higher education (M Ed); early childhood education (M Ed); education of the gifted and talented (M Ed); educational leadership (M Ed); educational technology (M Ed); elementary education (M Ed); middle and high school education (M Ed); teaching English to speakers of other languages (M Ed). Part-time and evening/weekend programs available. Postbaccalaureate distance learning degree programs offered (minimal on-campus study). *Faculty:* 82 full-time (42 women), 43 part-time/adjunct (25 women). *Students:* 136 full-time (97 women), 828 part-time (565 women); includes 55 minority (26 African Americans, 7 American Indian/Alaska Native, 5 Asian Americans or Pacific Islanders, 17 Hispanic Americans). Average age 33. 280 applicants, 94% accepted, 188 enrolled. In 2006, 322 degrees awarded. *Degree requirements:* For master's, thesis. *Entrance requirements:* For master's, GRE General Test or minimum GPA of 3.0. Additional exam requirements/recommendations for international students: Required—TOEFL. *Application deadline:* Applications are processed on a rolling basis. Application fee: $30. Electronic applications accepted. *Expenses:* Tuition, state resident: full-time $5,850; part-time $325 per credit. Tuition, nonresident: full-time $10,800; part-time $600 per credit. Tuition and fees vary according to course load. *Financial support:* In 2006–07, 2 research assistantships with full and partial tuition reimbursements (averaging $8,000 per year) were awarded; career-related internships or fieldwork, Federal Work-Study, scholarships/grants, and unspecified assistantships also available. *Faculty research:* Effectiveness of technology in education, parental involvement, effective teaching, effective schools research. *Unit head:* Dr. Linda McCrea, Director, 616-331-2080, E-mail: mccreal@gvsu.edu. *Application contact:* Dr. Douglas Busman, Director, Student Information and Services, 616-331-6831, Fax: 616-331-6217, E-mail: busmando@gvsu.edu.

Indiana University of Pennsylvania, School of Graduate Studies and Research, College of Education and Educational Technology, Department of Adult and Community Education, Program in Adult Education and Communication Technology, Indiana, PA 15705-1087. Offers communications technology (MA). Part-time and evening/weekend programs available. *Faculty:* 7 full-time (0 women). *Students:* 30 full-time (13 women), 45 part-time (36 women); includes 4 minority (3 African Americans, 1 Asian American or Pacific Islander), 6 international. Average age 34. 45 applicants, 64% accepted. In 2006, 35 degrees awarded. *Degree requirements:* For master's, thesis optional. *Entrance requirements:* For master's, letters of recommendation (2), writing sample. Additional exam requirements/recommendations for international students: Required—TOEFL. *Application deadline:* For fall admission, 7/1 priority date for domestic students; for spring admission, 11/1 for domestic students. Applications are processed on a rolling basis. Application fee: $30. *Expenses:* Tuition, state resident: full-time $6,048; part-time $336 per credit. Tuition, nonresident: full-time $9,678; part-time $538 per credit. Required fees: $1,069; $148 per year. *Financial support:* In 2006–07, 11 research assistantships with full and

Adult Education

Indiana University of Pennsylvania (continued)
partial tuition reimbursements (averaging $2,495 per year) were awarded; career-related internships or fieldwork and Federal Work-Study also available. Support available to part-time students. Financial award application deadline: 3/15; financial award applicants required to submit FAFSA.

Jones International University, Graduate School of Education, Centennial, CO 80112. Offers adult education (M Ed); corporate training and knowledge management (M Ed); curriculum and instruction (M Ed), including elementary teacher licensure, secondary teacher licensure; e-learning technology and design (M Ed); educational leadership and administration (M Ed); educational leadership and administration: principal and administrator licensure (M Ed); elementary curriculum instruction and assessment (M Ed); higher education leadership and administration (M Ed); K-12 instructional technology (M Ed); K-12 instructional technology: teacher licensure (M Ed); secondary curriculum instruction and assessment (M Ed); technology and design (M Ed). Part-time and evening/weekend programs available. Postbaccalaureate distance learning degree programs offered (no on-campus study). *Entrance requirements:* For master's, minimum cumulative GPA of 2.5. Additional exam requirements/recommendations for international students: Recommended—TOEFL (minimum score 550 paper-based; 213 computer-based). Electronic applications accepted.

Kansas State University, Graduate School, College of Education, Department of Educational Administration and Leadership, Manhattan, KS 66506. Offers adult and continuing education (MS, Ed D); educational administration (MS, Ed D). *Accreditation:* NCATE. *Faculty:* 10 full-time (5 women), 3 part-time/adjunct (0 women). *Students:* 36 full-time (23 women), 35 part-time (17 women); includes 8 minority (1 African American, 2 American Indian/Alaska Native, 2 Asian Americans or Pacific Islanders, 3 Hispanic Americans), 1 international. Average age 32. 64 applicants, 58% accepted, 29 enrolled. In 2006, 15 master's, 10 doctorates awarded. *Degree requirements:* For master's, thesis or alternative, final written exam; for doctorate, thesis/dissertation, preliminary exam, residency, comprehensive exam. *Entrance requirements:* For master's, GRE General Test, MAT, minimum undergraduate GPA of 3.0; for doctorate, GRE General Test, MAT, minimum GPA of 3.0. Additional exam requirements/recommendations for international students: Required—TOEFL. *Application deadline:* For fall admission, 3/1 priority date for domestic students, 2/1 priority date for international students; for spring admission, 10/1 priority date for domestic students, 8/1 priority date for international students. Applications are processed on a rolling basis. Application fee: $30 ($55 for international students). Electronic applications accepted. *Expenses:* Tuition, state resident: full-time $6,352; part-time $240 per credit hour. Tuition, nonresident: full-time $14,296; part-time $571 per credit hour. Required fees: $585. *Financial support:* In 2006–07, 5 research assistantships (averaging $8,552 per year), 2 teaching assistantships with full tuition reimbursements (averaging $12,172 per year) were awarded; career-related internships or fieldwork, institutionally sponsored loans, and scholarships/grants also available. Support available to part-time students. Financial award application deadline: 3/1; financial award applicants required to submit FAFSA. *Faculty research:* Educational law, finance, technology ethics, application, and leadership in education; distance learning/education; program evaluation. Total annual research expenditures: $42,204. *Unit head:* Dr. David C. Thompson, Head, 785-532-5543, Fax: 785-532-7304, E-mail: thomsond@ksu.edu. *Application contact:* Linda Thurston, Director, 785-532-5595, Fax: 785-532-7304, E-mail: coegrads@ksu.edu.

Kean University, College of Education, Program in Reading Specialization, Union, NJ 07083. Offers adult literacy (MA); basic skills (MA); reading specialization (MA). *Faculty:* 10 full-time (8 women). *Students:* 3 full-time (all women), 90 part-time (89 women); includes 10 minority (7 African Americans, 1 Asian American or Pacific Islander, 2 Hispanic Americans). Average age 33. 33 applicants, 97% accepted, 20 enrolled. In 2006, 20 degrees awarded. *Degree requirements:* For master's, thesis, practicum, clinic, research seminar. *Entrance requirements:* For master's, GRE General Test or MAT, 2 letters of recommendation, interview, teaching certification, minimum GPA of 2.75. *Application deadline:* For fall admission, 5/1 for domestic students; for spring admission, 11/1 for domestic students. Application fee: $60 ($150 for international students). Electronic applications accepted. *Expenses:* Tuition, state resident: full-time $8,856; part-time $369 per credit. Tuition, nonresident: full-time $11,256; part-time $469 per credit. *Financial support:* In 2006–07, 1 research assistantship with full tuition reimbursement (averaging $3,217 per year) was awarded. *Unit head:* Dr. Joan M. Kastner, Program Coordinator, 908-737-3942, E-mail: jkastner@kean.edu. *Application contact:* Joanne Morris, Director of Graduate Admissions, 908-737-3355, Fax: 908-737-3354, E-mail: gradadm@kean.edu.

Marshall University, Academic Affairs Division, College of Education and Human Services, Division of Human Development and Allied Technology, Program in Adult and Technical Education, Huntington, WV 25755. Offers MS. *Accreditation:* NCATE. Evening/weekend programs available. *Faculty:* 2 full-time (both women). *Students:* 146 full-time (87 women), 104 part-time (68 women); includes 38 minority (34 African Americans, 2 Asian Americans or Pacific Islanders, 2 Hispanic Americans), 53 international. Average age 34. In 2006, 59 degrees awarded. *Degree requirements:* For master's, comprehensive assessment, thesis optional. Application fee: $40. *Application contact:* Information Contact, 304-746-1900, Fax: 304-746-1902, E-mail: services@marshall.edu.

Marygrove College, Graduate Division, Education Unit, Program in Adult Learning, Detroit, MI 48221-2599. Offers MA.

Memorial University of Newfoundland, School of Graduate Studies, Faculty of Education, St. John's, NL A1C 5S7, Canada. Offers counseling psychology (M Ed); curriculum, teaching, and learning studies (M Ed); education (PhD); educational leadership studies (M Ed); information technology (M Ed); post-secondary studies (M Ed, Diploma), including health professional education (Diploma). Part-time programs available. *Degree requirements:* For master's, internship, paper folio, project, thesis optional; for doctorate, thesis/dissertation, thesis seminar, oral defense of thesis, comprehensive exam. *Entrance requirements:* For master's, undergraduate degree with at least 2nd class standing, 1-2 years work experience; for doctorate, minimum A average in graduate course work, MA in education, 2 years professional experience; for Diploma, 2nd class degree, 2 years of work experience with adult learners, appropriate academic qualifications and work experience in a health-related field. Electronic applications accepted. *Faculty research:* Critical thinking, literacy, cognitive studies and counseling, educational change, technology in instruction.

Michigan State University, The Graduate School, College of Education, Department of Educational Administration, East Lansing, MI 48824. Offers higher, adult and lifelong education (MA, PhD); K–12 educational administration (MA, PhD, Ed S); student affairs administration (MA). Part-time programs available. *Faculty:* 20 full-time (9 women). *Students:* 158 full-time (103 women), 181 part-time (95 women); includes 70 minority (42 African Americans, 4 American Indian/Alaska Native, 10 Asian Americans or Pacific Islanders, 14 Hispanic Americans), 44 international. Average age 35. 190 applicants, 54% accepted. In 2006, 109 master's, 29 doctorates awarded. *Entrance requirements:* Additional exam requirements/recommendations for international students: Required—TOEFL. Electronic applications accepted. *Expenses:* Tuition, state resident: part-time $346 per credit hour. Tuition, nonresident: part-time $730 per credit hour. Tuition and fees vary according to program. *Financial support:* In 2006–07, 40 fellowships with tuition reimbursements, 50 research assistantships with tuition reimbursements (averaging $13,143 per year), 6 teaching assistantships with tuition reimbursements (averaging $13,228 per year) were awarded. Total annual research expenditures: $1.5 million. *Unit head:* Dr. Marilyn J. Amey, Chairperson, 517-355-4538, Fax: 517-353-6393, E-mail: amey@msu.edu. *Application contact:* Graduate Admissions Assistant, E-mail: haleadm@msu.edu.

Morehead State University, Graduate Programs, College of Education, Department of Professional Programs in Education, Program in Adult and Higher Education, Morehead, KY 40351. Offers MA, Ed S. *Accreditation:* NCATE. Part-time and evening/weekend programs available.

Students: 12 full-time (6 women), 69 part-time (51 women); includes 9 minority (6 African Americans, 1 American Indian/Alaska Native, 1 Asian American or Pacific Islander, 1 Hispanic American). Average age 32. In 2006, 12 master's, 1 Ed S awarded. *Degree requirements:* For master's, oral and/or written comprehensive exams, thesis optional; for Ed S, thesis, oral exam. *Entrance requirements:* For master's, GRE General Test, minimum GPA of 2.5, 2 years of work experience; for Ed S, GRE General Test, interview, master's degree, minimum GPA of 3.5, work experience. Additional exam requirements/recommendations for international students: Required—TOEFL (minimum score 525 paper-based; 197 computer-based). *Application deadline:* For fall admission, 8/1 priority date for domestic and international students; for spring admission, 12/1 priority date for domestic and international students. Applications are processed on a rolling basis. Application fee: $0 ($55 for international students). Electronic applications accepted. *Financial support:* In 2006–07, teaching assistantships (averaging $6,000 per year); career-related internships or fieldwork, Federal Work-Study, and unspecified assistantships also available. Financial award application deadline: 4/1; financial award applicants required to submit FAFSA. *Faculty research:* Self-directed learning projects for nontraditional students, evaluation of adult educational programs, adult literacy, evaluation of homeless. *Application contact:* Michelle Barber, Graduate Admissions Counselor, 606-783-2039, Fax: 606-783-5061, E-mail: m.barber@moreheadstate.edu.

Mount Saint Vincent University, Graduate Programs, Faculty of Education, Program in Adult Education, Halifax, NS B3M 2J6, Canada. Offers M Ed, MA Ed, MA-R. Part-time and evening/weekend programs available. Postbaccalaureate distance learning degree programs offered (minimal on-campus study). *Degree requirements:* For master's, thesis (for some programs), practicum. *Entrance requirements:* For master's, bachelor's degree in related field, minimum B average. Electronic applications accepted.

National-Louis University, College of Arts and Sciences, Division of Language and Academic Development, Program in Adult, Continuing, and Literacy Education, Chicago, IL 60603. Offers M Ed, Certificate. Part-time and evening/weekend programs available. Postbaccalaureate distance learning degree programs offered (minimal on-campus study). *Students:* 2 full-time (both women), 26 part-time (21 women); includes 10 minority (all African Americans) Average age 41. 19 applicants, 100% accepted. In 2006, 16 degrees awarded. *Degree requirements:* For master's, thesis or alternative. *Entrance requirements:* For master's, GRE General Test, MAT, or Watson-Glaser Critical Thinking Appraisal, interview, minimum GPA of 3.0; for Certificate, GRE, MAT, or Watson-Glaser Critical Thinking Appraisal, interview, minimum GPA of 3.0. *Application deadline:* Applications are processed on a rolling basis. Application fee: $25. *Expenses:* Tuition: Full-time $17,685. One-time fee: $40 full-time. *Financial support:* Fellowships, research assistantships, Federal Work-Study, institutionally sponsored loans, scholarships/grants, and tuition waivers available. Support available to part-time students. Financial award application deadline: 4/15; financial award applicants required to submit FAFSA. *Unit head:* Dr. Scopio Colin, Associate Professor, 312-261-3326, E-mail: scolin@nl.edu. *Application contact:* David McCulloch, Vice President for University Services, 800-443-5522 Ext. 5127, Fax: 847-465-0593, E-mail: dmcc@wheeling1.nl.edu.

National-Louis University, College of Arts and Sciences, Division of Language and Academic Development, Program in Adult Literacy and Developmental Studies, Chicago, IL 60603. Offers M Ed, Certificate. Part-time and evening/weekend programs available. *Students:* Average age 40. 4 applicants, 100% accepted. In 2006, 7 master's, 2 Certificates awarded. *Entrance requirements:* For master's, GRE General Test, MAT, or Watson-Glaser Critical Thinking Appraisal, interview, minimum GPA of 3.0; for Certificate, GRE, MAT, or Watson-Glaser Critical Thinking Appraisal, interview, minimum GPA of 3.0. *Application deadline:* Applications are processed on a rolling basis. Application fee: $25. *Expenses:* Tuition: Full-time $17,685. One-time fee: $40 full-time. *Financial support:* Fellowships, career-related internships or fieldwork, Federal Work-Study, institutionally sponsored loans, scholarships/grants, and tuition waivers available. Support available to part-time students. Financial award application deadline: 4/15; financial award applicants required to submit FAFSA. *Faculty research:* Adult learning and development, learner-centered development, political and social foundations, reading development, curricular processes. *Application contact:* David McCulloch, Vice President for University Services, 800-443-5522 Ext. 5127, Fax: 847-465-0593, E-mail: dmcc@wheeling1.nl.edu.

National-Louis University, National College of Education, Doctoral Programs in Education, Program in Adult Education, Chicago, IL 60603. Offers Ed D. Part-time and evening/weekend programs available. *Students:* 1 applicant, 100% accepted. *Degree requirements:* For doctorate, thesis/dissertation. *Entrance requirements:* For doctorate, GRE General Test, MAT, or Watson-Glaser Critical Thinking Appraisal, 3 years of experience in field, interview, master's degree, resumé, writing sample. *Application deadline:* For fall admission, 12/1 for domestic students. Application fee: $25. *Expenses:* Tuition: Full-time $17,685. One-time fee: $40 full-time. *Financial support:* Federal Work-Study, institutionally sponsored loans, scholarships/grants, and tuition waivers available. Support available to part-time students. Financial award application deadline: 4/15; financial award applicants required to submit FAFSA. *Unit head:* Dr. Thomas Heaney, Coordinator, 847-475-1100 Ext. 3274. *Application contact:* David McCulloch, Vice President for University Services, 800-443-5522 Ext. 5127, Fax: 847-465-0593, E-mail: dmcc@wheeling1.nl.edu.

North Carolina Agricultural and Technical State University, Graduate School, School of Education, Department of Educational Leadership and Policy, Program in Adult Education, Greensboro, NC 27411. Offers MS. *Accreditation:* NCATE. Part-time and evening/weekend programs available. *Degree requirements:* For master's, thesis or alternative, qualifying exam, comprehensive exam. *Entrance requirements:* For master's, GRE General Test, minimum GPA of 2.6.

North Carolina State University, Graduate School, College of Education, Department of Adult and Community College Education, Program in Adult and Community College Education, Raleigh, NC 27695. Offers M Ed, MS, Ed D. *Degree requirements:* For master's, thesis (for some programs); for doctorate, thesis/dissertation. *Entrance requirements:* For master's and doctorate, GRE or MAT. Electronic applications accepted.

Northern Illinois University, Graduate School, College of Education, Department of Counseling, Adult and Higher Education, De Kalb, IL 60115-2854. Offers adult and higher education (MS Ed, Ed D); counseling (MS Ed, Ed D). *Accreditation:* ACA. Part-time and evening/weekend programs available. *Faculty:* 19 full-time (11 women), 2 part-time/adjunct (1 woman). *Students:* 102 full-time (73 women), 302 part-time (207 women); includes 110 minority (82 African Americans, 2 American Indian/Alaska Native, 7 Asian Americans or Pacific Islanders, 19 Hispanic Americans), 12 international. Average age 40. 124 applicants, 51% accepted, 51 enrolled. In 2006, 74 master's, 23 doctorates awarded. Terminal master's awarded for partial completion of doctoral program. *Degree requirements:* For master's, thesis optional; for doctorate, thesis/dissertation, candidacy exam, dissertation defense. *Entrance requirements:* For master's, GRE General Test or MAT, minimum undergraduate GPA of 2.75, interview (counseling); for doctorate, GRE General Test, minimum undergraduate GPA of 2.75, 3.2 graduate, interview (counseling). Additional exam requirements/recommendations for international students: Required—TOEFL (minimum score 550 paper-based; 213 computer-based). *Application deadline:* For fall admission, 6/1 for domestic students, 5/1 for international students; for spring admission, 11/1 for domestic students, 10/1 for international students. Applications are processed on a rolling basis. Application fee: $30. Electronic applications accepted. *Financial support:* In 2006–07, 14 teaching assistantships with full tuition reimbursements were awarded; fellowships with full tuition reimbursements, research assistantships with full tuition reimbursements, career-related internships or fieldwork, Federal Work-Study, scholarships/grants, tuition waivers (full), and unspecified assistantships also available. Support available to part-time students. Financial award applicants required to submit FAFSA. *Unit head:* Dr. Francesca Giordano, Chair, 815-753-9373, E-mail: watson@niu.edu.

Northwestern Oklahoma State University, School of Professional Studies, Program in Adult Education Management and Administration, Alva, OK 73717-2799. Offers adult education management and administration (M Ed); education: non-certificate option (M Ed). Part-time programs available. *Faculty:* 5 full-time (2 women). In 2006, 8 degrees awarded. *Degree requirements:* For master's, portfolio, thesis optional. *Entrance requirements:* For master's, GRE or MAT, min GPA of 2.75. *Application deadline:* Applications are processed on a rolling basis. Application fee: $15. *Expenses:* Tuition, state resident: part-time $700 per year. Tuition, nonresident: part-time $1,715 per year. *Unit head:* Dr. Rodney C. Murrow, Associate Dean of Graduate Studies, 580-327-8589, E-mail: rcmurrow@nwosu.edu.

Northwestern State University of Louisiana, Graduate Studies and Research, College of Education, Program in Adult and Continuing Education, Natchitoches, LA 71497. Offers M Ed. *Students:* 17 full-time (16 women), 62 part-time (47 women); includes 33 minority (31 African Americans, 1 American Indian/Alaska Native, 1 Hispanic American). Average age 37. In 2006, 11 degrees awarded. *Degree requirements:* For master's, thesis or alternative, comprehensive exam, registration. *Entrance requirements:* For master's, GRE General Test, minimum undergraduate GPA of 2.5. *Application contact:* Dr. Steven G. Horton, Associate Provost/Dean, Graduate Studies, Research, and Information Systems, 318-357-5851, Fax: 318-357-5019, E-mail: grad_school@nsula.edu.

Nova Southeastern University, Fischler School of Education and Human Services, Programs for Higher Education, Fort Lauderdale, FL 33314-7796. Offers adult education (Ed D); computing and information technology (Ed D); health care education (Ed D); higher education (Ed D); vocational, occupational and technical education (Ed D). Part-time and evening/weekend programs available. *Students:* 35 full-time (22 women), 321 part-time (222 women); includes 134 minority (116 African Americans, 1 American Indian/Alaska Native, 17 Hispanic Americans), 1 international. 4 applicants, 75% accepted, 3 enrolled. In 2006, 40 degrees awarded. *Degree requirements:* For doctorate, thesis/dissertation, practicum. *Entrance requirements:* For doctorate, MAT or GRE, master's degree, work experience in field, minimum GPA of 3.0. Additional exam requirements/recommendations for international students: Recommended—TOEFL (minimum score 550 paper-based; 213 computer-based), IELTS (minimum score 6). *Application deadline:* For fall admission, 8/11 priority date for domestic and international students; for winter admission, 12/28 priority date for domestic and international students; for spring admission, 4/22 priority date for domestic and international students. Applications are processed on a rolling basis. Application fee: $50. Electronic applications accepted. *Expenses:* Contact institution. *Financial support:* In 2006–07, 2 fellowships were awarded; career-related internships or fieldwork and tuition waivers (full) also available. Financial award application deadline: 1/7. *Unit head:* Dr. Karen D. Bowser, Associate Dean of Doctoral Programs, 954-262-8500, Fax: 954-262-3912, E-mail: bowserk@nova.edu. *Application contact:* Jennifer Quiñones Nottingham, Dean of Student Affairs, 800-986-3223 Ext. 8624, Fax: 954-262-3911, E-mail: jlquinon@nova.edu.

Oregon State University, Graduate School, College of Education, Program in Adult Education and Higher Education Leadership, Corvallis, OR 97331. Offers Ed M, MAIS. *Accreditation:* NCATE. Part-time programs available. *Students:* 2 full-time (both women), 50 part-time (38 women); includes 4 minority (2 African Americans, 1 Asian American or Pacific Islander, 1 Hispanic American). Average age 45. In 2006, 19 degrees awarded. *Degree requirements:* For master's, thesis or alternative. *Entrance requirements:* For master's, minimum GPA of 3.0 in last 90 hours. Additional exam requirements/recommendations for international students: Required—TOEFL. *Application deadline:* For fall admission, 3/1 for domestic students. Applications are processed on a rolling basis. Application fee: $50. *Financial support:* Research assistantships, teaching assistantships, career-related internships or fieldwork, Federal Work-Study, and institutionally sponsored loans available. Support available to part-time students. Financial award application deadline: 2/1. *Faculty research:* Adult training and developmental psychology, cross-cultural communication, leadership development and human relations, adult literacy. *Unit head:* Dr. Richard Shintaku, Head, 541-737-9324.

Penn State Harrisburg, Graduate School, School of Behavioral Sciences and Education, Middletown, PA 17057-4898. Offers adult education (D Ed); applied behavior analysis (MA); applied clinical psychology (MA); applied psychological research (MA); community psychology and social change (MA); health education (M Ed); teaching and curriculum (M Ed); training and development (M Ed). Part-time and evening/weekend programs available. *Expenses:* Tuition, state resident: full-time $13,224; part-time $551 per credit. Tuition, nonresident: full-time $18,652; part-time $777 per credit. Required fees: $84 per semester. *Financial support:* Career-related internships or fieldwork available. *Unit head:* Dr. William D. Milheim, Director, 717-948-6205, Fax: 717-948-6209, E-mail: wdm2@psu.edu.

Penn State University Park, Graduate School, College of Education, Department of Learning and Performance Systems, State College, University Park, PA 16802-1503. Offers adult education (M Ed, D Ed, PhD); instructional systems (M Ed, MS, D Ed, PhD); workforce education and development (M Ed, MS, D Ed, PhD). *Unit head:* Dr. Edgar I. Farmer, Head, 814-863-3858, Fax: 814-865-2632, E-mail: eif1@psu.edu.

Portland State University, Graduate Studies, School of Education, Department of Educational Policy, Foundations, and Administrative Studies, Portland, OR 97207-0751. Offers educational leadership (MA, MS, Ed D); postsecondary, adult and continuing education (Ed D). *Accreditation:* NCATE. Part-time and evening/weekend programs available. *Faculty:* 11 full-time (5 women), 10 part-time/adjunct (4 women). *Students:* 62 full-time (51 women), 227 part-time (149 women); includes 41 minority (7 African Americans, 10 American Indian/Alaska Native, 8 Asian Americans or Pacific Islanders, 16 Hispanic Americans), 10 international. Average age 40. 234 applicants, 91% accepted, 67 enrolled. In 2006, 69 master's, 4 doctorates awarded. *Degree requirements:* For master's, thesis or alternative, written exam; for doctorate, thesis/dissertation, comprehensive exam. *Entrance requirements:* For master's, California Basic Educational Skills Test, minimum GPA of 3.0 in upper-division course work or 2.75 overall; for doctorate, GRE General Test or MAT. Additional exam requirements/recommendations for international students: Required—TOEFL (minimum score 550 paper-based; 213 computer-based). *Application deadline:* For fall admission, 4/1 for domestic and international students; for winter admission, 9/1 for domestic and international students; for spring admission, 11/1 for domestic and international students. Applications are processed on a rolling basis. Application fee: $50. *Expenses:* Tuition, state resident: full-time $6,426; part-time $238 per credit. Tuition, nonresident: full-time $11,016; part-time $408 per credit. Tuition and fees vary according to course load. *Financial support:* In 2006–07, 10 research assistantships with full tuition reimbursements (averaging $5,453 per year) were awarded; teaching assistantships with full tuition reimbursements, career-related internships or fieldwork, Federal Work-Study, and institutionally sponsored loans also available. Support available to part-time students. Financial award application deadline: 3/1; financial award applicants required to submit FAFSA. *Faculty research:* Leadership development and research, principals and urban schools, accelerated schools, cooperative learning, family involvement in schools. Total annual research expenditures: $322,962. *Unit head:* Dilafroz Williams, Head, 503-725-4676, Fax: 503-725-8475. *Application contact:* Kellie Walker, Admission Secretary, 503-725-4716, Fax: 503-725-8475.

Regis University, School for Professional Studies, Program in Teacher Education, Denver, CO 80221-1099. Offers adult learning, training, and development (M Ed); curriculum, instruction, and assessment (M Ed); early childhood (M Ed); educational technology (Certificate); elementary (M Ed); ESL (M Ed); fine arts (M Ed), including arts, music; instructional technology (M Ed); professional leadership (M Ed); reading (M Ed); secondary (M Ed); self-designed (M Ed); space studies (M Ed); special education (M Ed); teacher licensure (M Ed). Program also offered in Henderson and Las Vegas (Summerlin), NV. Postbaccalaureate distance learning degree programs offered. *Unit head:* Dr. Suzie Perry, Dean, 303-458-4302. *Application contact:* Partick Lowenthal, Assistant Director, 303-458-4300 Ext. 4314, E-mail: masters@regis.edu.

Robert Morris University, Graduate Studies, School of Adult and Continuing Education, Moon Township, PA 15108-1189. Offers MS. Part-time and evening/weekend programs available. *Faculty:* 3 full-time (1 woman), 1 part-time/adjunct (0 women). *Students:* Average age 31. 36 applicants, 67% accepted, 23 enrolled. In 2006, 29 degrees awarded. *Entrance requirements:* For master's, letters of recommendation. Additional exam requirements/recommendations for international students: Required—TOEFL (minimum score 550 paper-based; 213 computer-based). *Application deadline:* For fall admission, 7/1 priority date for domestic and international students; for spring admission, 11/1 priority date for domestic and international students. Applications are processed on a rolling basis. Application fee: $35. Electronic applications accepted. *Expenses:* Contact institution. *Financial support:* Federal Work-Study, institutionally sponsored loans, and unspecified assistantships available. Financial award application deadline: 5/1. *Unit head:* Dr. Kathleen V. Davis, Dean, 412-397-6808, Fax: 412-397-5539, E-mail: daviska@rmu.edu. *Application contact:* Kellie L. Laurenzi, Dean of Enrollment, 412-262-8235, Fax: 412-299-2425, E-mail: laurenzi@rmu.edu.

Rutgers, The State University of New Jersey, New Brunswick, Graduate School of Education, Department of Educational Theory, Policy and Administration, Program in Adult and Continuing Education, New Brunswick, NJ 08901-1281. Offers Ed M. Part-time and evening/weekend programs available. *Faculty:* 1 full-time (0 women). *Students:* 3 full-time (all women), 4 part-time (3 women). Average age 35. 9 applicants, 67% accepted, 4 enrolled. In 2006, 5 degrees awarded. *Degree requirements:* For master's, comprehensive exam. *Entrance requirements:* For master's, GRE General Test. Additional exam requirements/recommendations for international students: Required—TOEFL. Application fee: $60. Electronic applications accepted. *Financial support:* Application deadline: 3/15; *Faculty research:* Adult literacy, popular education, continuing higher education, training and development. *Application contact:* Sandy Chubrick, Administrative Assistant, 732-932-7496 Ext. 8239, Fax: 732-932-6803, E-mail: chubrick@rci.rutgers.edu.

St. Francis Xavier University, Graduate Studies, Department of Adult Education, Antigonish, NS B2G 2W5, Canada. Offers M Ad Ed. Part-time programs available. Postbaccalaureate distance learning degree programs offered (minimal on-campus study). *Faculty:* 5 full-time (3 women), 2 part-time/adjunct (both women). *Students:* Average age 40. 52 applicants, 79% accepted. In 2006, 17 degrees awarded. *Degree requirements:* For master's, thesis, registration. *Entrance requirements:* For master's, minimum undergraduate B average, 2 years of work experience in field. Additional exam requirements/recommendations for international students: Required—TOEFL (minimum score 580 paper-based; 236 computer-based). *Application deadline:* Applications are processed on a rolling basis. Application fee: $40. *Faculty research:* Adult learning and development, religious education, women's issues, literacy, action research. Total annual research expenditures: $114,253. *Unit head:* Dr. Jane Dawson, Chairperson, 902-867-2393, Fax: 902-867-3765, E-mail: jdawson@stfx.ca. *Application contact:* 902-867-2219, Fax: 902-867-2329, E-mail: admit@stfx.ca.

San Francisco State University, Division of Graduate Studies, College of Education, Department of Administration and Interdisciplinary Studies, Program in Adult Education, San Francisco, CA 94132-1722. Offers MA Ed, AC. *Accreditation:* NCATE. Part-time programs available. *Faculty:* 1 full-time (0 women), 4 part-time/adjunct (3 women). *Students:* 39 (31 women). *Entrance requirements:* For master's, minimum GPA of 2.5 in last 60 units. *Application deadline:* For fall admission, 11/30 priority date for domestic students. Applications are processed on a rolling basis. Application fee: $55. *Financial support:* Application deadline: 3/1. *Application contact:* Dr. Ming-Yeh Lee, Assistant Professor, 415-338-1081, E-mail: mylee@sfsu.edu.

Seattle University, College of Education, Program in Adult Education and Training, Seattle, WA 98122-1090. Offers M Ed, MA, Certificate. *Accreditation:* NCATE. Part-time and evening/weekend programs available. *Students:* 2 full-time (1 woman), 31 part-time (23 women); includes 4 minority (1 African American, 2 Asian Americans or Pacific Islanders, 1 Hispanic American). Average age 40. 12 applicants, 92% accepted, 6 enrolled. In 2006, 16 degrees awarded. *Degree requirements:* For master's, comprehensive exam. *Entrance requirements:* For master's, GRE, MAT, or minimum GPA of 3.0; 1 year of related experience. Additional exam requirements/recommendations for international students: Required—TOEFL. *Application deadline:* For fall admission, 8/20 priority date for domestic students; for winter admission, 11/20 for domestic students; for spring admission, 2/20 for domestic students. Applications are processed on a rolling basis. Application fee: $55. *Financial support:* Career-related internships or fieldwork and Federal Work-Study available. Support available to part-time students. Financial award applicants required to submit FAFSA. *Unit head:* Dr. Carol Weaver, Director, 206-296-5908, E-mail: cweaver@seattleu.edu. *Application contact:* Janet Shandley, Associate Dean of Graduate Admissions, 206-296-5900, Fax: 206-298-5656, E-mail: grad_admissions@seattleu.edu.

Suffolk University, College of Arts and Sciences, Department of Education and Human Services, Program in Adult and Organizational Learning, Boston, MA 02108-2770. Offers adult and organizational learning (MS); human resources (MS, CAGS); instructional design (CAGS); organizational development (CAGS); organizational learning (CAGS). Part-time and evening/weekend programs available. *Entrance requirements:* For master's, GRE General Test or MAT. *Application deadline:* For fall admission, 6/15 priority date for domestic students, 6/15 for international students; for spring admission, 11/15 priority date for domestic students, 11/15 for international students. Applications are processed on a rolling basis. Application fee: $35. *Financial support:* Fellowships available. Financial award application deadline: 4/1. *Faculty research:* Adult training methods, adult learning theory, instructional design, learning and teaching styles, systems thinking. *Unit head:* Dr. Christine M. Westphal, Graduate Program Director, 617-994-6455, Fax: 617-722-9440, E-mail: cwestphal@suffolk.edu. *Application contact:* Judith Reynolds, Director of Graduate Admissions, 617-573-8302, Fax: 617-523-0116, E-mail: grad.admission@suffolk.edu.

Teachers College Columbia University, Graduate Faculty of Education, Department of Organization and Leadership, Program in Adult Education, New York, NY 10027-6696. Offers MA, Ed D. *Accreditation:* NCATE. *Faculty:* 3 full-time (2 women), 3 part-time/adjunct. *Students:* 42 full-time (26 women), 90 part-time (64 women); includes 43 minority (27 African Americans, 7 Asian Americans or Pacific Islanders, 9 Hispanic Americans), 16 international. Average age 46. 26 applicants, 65% accepted, 8 enrolled. In 2006, 9 master's, 8 doctorates awarded. *Degree requirements:* For doctorate, variable foreign language requirement, thesis/dissertation. *Entrance requirements:* For doctorate, 3-5 years of professional experience, master's degree. *Application deadline:* For fall admission, 5/15 for domestic students. Application fee: $65. *Expenses:* Tuition: Full-time $23,400; part-time $975 per credit. Required fees: $320 per term. *Financial support:* Career-related internships or fieldwork, Federal Work-Study, institutionally sponsored loans, and tuition waivers (full and partial) available. Support available to part-time students. Financial award application deadline: 2/1. *Faculty research:* Adult learning, perspective transformation, training and evaluation, workplace learning, theory to practice. *Application contact:* Debbie Lesperance, Assistant Director of Admission, 212-678-3710, Fax: 212-678-4171.

See Close-Up on page 1131.

Texas A&M University–Kingsville, College of Graduate Studies, College of Education, Department of Education, Program in Adult Education, Kingsville, TX 78363. Offers M Ed. Part-time and evening/weekend programs available. *Degree requirements:* For master's, mini-thesis. *Entrance requirements:* For master's, GRE General Test, MAT, minimum GPA of 3.0. *Faculty research:* Continuing education efforts in south Texas, adult education methodologies.

Texas A&M University–Texarkana, Graduate Studies and Research, College of Arts and Sciences and Education, Texarkana, TX 75505-5518. Offers adult education (MS); curriculum and instruction (MS); education (MS); educational administration (M Ed); English (MA); history (MS); instructional technology (MS); interdisciplinary studies (MA, MS); special education (M Ed, MS). Part-time and evening/weekend programs available. *Students:* 285. Average age 32. 41 applicants, 76% accepted. In 2006, 51 degrees awarded. *Degree requirements:* For master's, thesis optional. *Entrance requirements:* For master's, minimum GPA of 2.5 on last 60 hours of bachelor's degree. Additional exam requirements/recommendations for international students: Required—TOEFL. *Application deadline:* For fall admission, 7/15 priority date for domestic students; for spring admission, 12/1 priority date for domestic students. Applications are processed on a rolling basis. Application fee: $0 ($25 for international students).

Adult Education

Texas A&M University–Texarkana (continued)
Electronic applications accepted. *Expenses:* Tuition, state resident: part-time $112 per credit hour. Tuition, nonresident: part-time $387 per credit hour. Required fees: $8 per credit hour. $8 per term. *Financial support:* Career-related internships or fieldwork and scholarships/grants available. Financial award applicants required to submit FAFSA. *Unit head:* Dr. Rosannce Stripling, Dean, 903-223-3073, E-mail: rosanne.stripling@tamut.edu. *Application contact:* Patricia E. Black, Director of Admissions and Registrar, 903-223-3068, Fax: 903-223-3140, E-mail: pat.black@tamut.edu.

Touro University International, College of Education, Program in Education, Cypress, CA 90630. Offers adult education (MA Ed); aviation education (MA Ed); children's literacy development (MA Ed); e-learning (MA Ed); early childhood education (MA Ed); enrollment management (MA Ed); higher education (MA Ed); teaching and instruction (MA Ed); training and development (MA Ed). Part-time and evening/weekend programs available. Postbaccalaureate distance learning degree programs offered (no on-campus study). In 2006, 193 degrees awarded. *Degree requirements:* For master's, capstone project with integrative paper. *Entrance requirements:* For master's, minimum GPA of 3.0. Additional exam requirements/recommendations for international students: Required—TOEFL (minimum score 550 paper-based). Application fee: $75. *Expenses:* Tuition: Part-time $300 per credit hour. Tuition and fees vary according to course level and program. *Unit head:* Dr. Edith Neumann, Vice President for Academic Affairs, College of Education, 714-816-0366 Ext. 2030, Fax: 714-226-9844, E-mail: eneumann@tourou.edu.

Troy University, Graduate School, College of Education, Program in Adult Education, Troy, AL 36082. Offers MS. Part-time and evening/weekend programs available. *Students:* 5 full-time (4 women), 24 part-time (10 women); includes 12 minority (all African Americans) Average age 41. In 2006, 3 degrees awarded. *Degree requirements:* For master's, thesis or alternative, comprehensive exam, registration. *Entrance requirements:* Additional exam requirements/recommendations for international students: Required—TOEFL (minimum score 523 paper-based; 200 computer-based). *Application deadline:* Applications are processed on a rolling basis. Application fee: $50. Electronic applications accepted. *Expenses:* Tuition, state resident: full-time $4,368; part-time $182 per hour. Tuition, nonresident: full-time $8,736; part-time $364 per hour. Required fees: $50 per term. *Unit head:* Dr. Joe H. Reynolds, Coordinator, 334-241-8577, Fax: 334-240-7320, E-mail: jreynolds45@troy.edu. *Application contact:* Elizabeth Richmond, Graduate Actions Coordinator, 334-241-9707, Fax: 334-241-9586, E-mail: lizrichmond@troy.edu.

Troy University, Graduate School, College of Education, Program in Postsecondary Education, Troy, AL 36082. Offers M Ed. Also offered through the University College. *Accreditation:* NCATE. Part-time and evening/weekend programs available. *Students:* 493 full-time (385 women), 599 part-time (437 women); includes 509 minority (486 African Americans, 3 American Indian/Alaska Native, 7 Asian Americans or Pacific Islanders, 13 Hispanic Americans). Average age 34. In 2006, 1,187 master's awarded. *Degree requirements:* For master's, thesis, comprehensive exam, registration. *Entrance requirements:* For master's, minimum GPA of 2.5. Additional exam requirements/recommendations for international students: Required—TOEFL (minimum score 523 paper-based; 200 computer-based). *Application deadline:* Applications are processed on a rolling basis. Application fee: $50. Electronic applications accepted. *Expenses:* Tuition, state resident: full-time $4,368; part-time $182 per hour. Tuition, nonresident: full-time $8,736; part-time $364 per hour. Required fees: $50 per term. *Financial support:* Available to part-time students. Applicants required to submit FAFSA. *Unit head:* Dr. Andrew Creamer, Chair, 334-670-3350, Fax: 334-670-32961, E-mail: drcreamer@troy.edu. *Application contact:* Brenda K. Campbell, Director of Graduate Admissions, 334-670-3178, Fax: 334-670-3733, E-mail: bcamp@troy.edu.

Tusculum College, Graduate School, Program in Education, Greeneville, TN 37743-9997. Offers adult education (MA Ed); K–12 (MA Ed). Evening/weekend programs available. *Degree requirements:* For master's, thesis or alternative. *Entrance requirements:* For master's, GRE or MAT, NTE, 3 years of work experience, minimum GPA of 2.75.

Université du Québec en Outaouais, Graduate Programs, Program in Adult Education, Gatineau, QC J8X 3X7, Canada. Offers andragogy (DESS). Part-time programs available. *Students:* 2 full-time, 31 part-time, 1 international. *Entrance requirements:* For degree, appropriate bachelor's degree, proficiency in French. *Application deadline:* For fall admission, 6/1 for domestic students, 3/1 for international students; for winter admission, 11/1 for domestic students, 10/1 for international students. Application fee: $30 Canadian dollars. *Financial support:* Fellowships, research assistantships, teaching assistantships available. *Unit head:* Decanat des etudes, 819-595-3900 Ext. 3985, Fax: 819-595-3984. *Application contact:* Registrar's Office, 819-773-1850, Fax: 819-773-1835, E-mail: registraire@ugo.ca.

University of Alaska Anchorage, College of Education, Program in Adult Education, Anchorage, AK 99508-8060. Offers M Ed. Part-time programs available. *Students:* 1 full-time (0 women), 20 part-time (15 women); includes 7 minority (1 African American, 2 American Indian/Alaska Native, 1 Asian American or Pacific Islander, 3 Hispanic Americans), 2 international. 12 applicants, 50% accepted. In 2006, 10 degrees awarded. *Degree requirements:* For master's, thesis or alternative, registration. *Entrance requirements:* For master's, interview, minimum GPA of 3.0, writing exercise. Additional exam requirements/recommendations for international students: Required—TOEFL (minimum score 550 paper-based; 213 computer-based). *Application deadline:* For fall admission, 5/1 for domestic students; for spring admission, 11/1 for domestic students. Application fee: $45. *Expenses:* Tuition, state resident: part-time $268 per credit. Tuition, nonresident: part-time $547 per credit. Required fees: $124 per semester. Tuition and fees vary according to reciprocity agreements and student level. *Financial support:* Career-related internships or fieldwork and Federal Work-Study available. Support available to part-time students. Financial award application deadline: 4/1; financial award applicants required to submit FAFSA. *Unit head:* Dr. Carolyn Coe, Chair, 907-786-1654, Fax: 907-786-4445, E-mail: afcmc@uaa.alaska.edu. *Application contact:* Jane Jordan, Graduate Programs Assistant, 907-786-4401, Fax: 907-786-4445, E-mail: anjmj@uaa.alaska.edu.

University of Alberta, Faculty of Graduate Studies and Research, Department of Educational Policy Studies, Edmonton, AB T6G 2E1, Canada. Offers adult education (M Ed, Ed D, PhD); educational administration and leadership (M Ed, Ed D, PhD, Postgraduate Diploma); First Nations education (M Ed, Ed D, PhD); theoretical, cultural and international studies in education (M Ed, Ed D, PhD). *Faculty:* 19 full-time (10 women), 5 part-time/adjunct (1 woman). *Students:* 73 full-time (47 women), 144 part-time (86 women). 141 applicants, 44% accepted. In 2006, 52 master's, 20 doctorates awarded. *Degree requirements:* For master's, thesis (for some programs); for doctorate, thesis/dissertation. *Entrance requirements:* For master's, minimum GPA of 6.5 on a 9.0 scale; for doctorate, minimum GPA of 7.5 on a 9.0 scale. Additional exam requirements/recommendations for international students: Required—TOEFL (minimum score 580 paper-based; 237 computer-based). *Application deadline:* For spring admission, 2/1 for domestic and international students. Electronic applications accepted. *Financial support:* In 2006–07, 7 fellowships with partial tuition reimbursements, 10 research assistantships with partial tuition reimbursements (averaging $6,936 per year), 30 teaching assistantships with partial tuition reimbursements (averaging $11,130 per year) were awarded; scholarships/grants and unspecified assistantships also available. *Unit head:* Dr. Frank Peters, Graduate Coordinator, 780-492-3679, Fax: 780-492-2024, E-mail: epscoord@ualberta.ca. *Application contact:* Joan A. White, Secretary, 780-492-3679, Fax: 780-492-2024, E-mail: joan.white@ualberta.ca.

University of Arkansas, Graduate School, College of Education and Health Professions, Department of Rehabilitation, Human Resources and Communication Disorders, Fayetteville, AR 72701-1201. Offers adult education (M Ed, Ed D, Ed S); communication disorders (MS); rehabilitation (MS, PhD); vocational education (M Ed, MAT, Ed D, Ed S); workforce development education (M Ed). Part-time programs available. *Students:* 86 full-time (64 women), 165 part-time (119 women); includes 49 minority (41 African Americans, 6 American Indian/Alaska Native, 2 Hispanic Americans), 6 international. 110 applicants, 53% accepted. In 2006, 69 master's, 9 doctorates awarded. *Degree requirements:* For doctorate, thesis/dissertation. Application fee: $40 ($50 for international students). *Financial support:* In 2006–07, 10 fellowships with tuition reimbursements were awarded; research assistantships, teaching assistantships, career-related internships or fieldwork and Federal Work-Study also available. Support available to part-time students. Financial award application deadline: 4/1; financial award applicants required to submit FAFSA. *Unit head:* Dr. Barbara Hinton, Departmental Chairperson, 479-575-4758, Fax: 479-575-3319, E-mail: bhinton@uark.edu. *Application contact:* Dr. Brent Williams, Program Coordinator, 479-575-8696, E-mail: btwilli@uark.edu.

University of Arkansas, Graduate School, College of Education and Health Professions, Department of Vocational and Adult Education, Program in Adult Education, Fayetteville, AR 72701-1201. Offers M Ed, Ed D, Ed S. *Accreditation:* NCATE. Part-time and evening/weekend programs available. Postbaccalaureate distance learning degree programs offered. *Students:* 6 full-time (3 women), 26 part-time (15 women); includes 10 minority (7 African Americans, 3 American Indian/Alaska Native), 3 international. 15 applicants, 13% accepted. In 2006, 2 master's, 9 doctorates awarded. *Degree requirements:* For doctorate, thesis/dissertation. *Entrance requirements:* For doctorate, GRE General Test. Application fee: $40 ($50 for international students). *Financial support:* Fellowships with tuition reimbursements, research assistantships, teaching assistantships, career-related internships or fieldwork and Federal Work-Study available. Financial award application deadline: 4/1. *Application contact:* Dr. Frederick Nafukho, Graduate Coordinator, 479-575-4899, E-mail: nafukho@uark.edu.

University of Arkansas at Little Rock, Graduate School, College of Education, Department of Counseling and Rehabilitation Education, Program in Adult Education, Little Rock, AR 72204-1099. Offers M Ed. *Accreditation:* NCATE. Part-time programs available. *Degree requirements:* For master's, comprehensive exam. *Entrance requirements:* For master's, interview, minimum GPA of 2.75, GRE General Test or teaching certificate. *Faculty research:* Adult literacy, volunteer training, in-services education.

The University of British Columbia, Faculty of Graduate Studies, Faculty of Education, Department of Educational Studies, Vancouver, BC V6T 1Z1, Canada. Offers adult education (M Ed, MA); adult learning and global change (M Ed); educational administration (M Ed, MA); educational leadership and policy (Ed D); educational studies (M Ed, PhD), including history of education (M Ed), philosophy of education (M Ed), sociology of education (M Ed); higher education (M Ed, MA); society, culture and politics in education (M Ed, MA). Part-time and evening/weekend programs available. *Faculty:* 30 full-time (15 women), 9 part-time/adjunct (6 women). *Students:* 308 full-time (217 women), 45 part-time (31 women). Average age 35. 211 applicants, 60% accepted. In 2006, 128 master's, 15 doctorates awarded. Terminal master's awarded for partial completion of doctoral program. *Degree requirements:* For master's, thesis (MA); for doctorate, thesis/dissertation. *Entrance requirements:* Additional exam requirements/recommendations for international students: Required—TOEFL, TOEFL or IELTS. Electronic applications accepted. *Financial support:* Fellowships, research assistantships, teaching assistantships available. *Faculty research:* Educational leadership educational administration adult education politics in education, global change and adult learning. Total annual research expenditures: $547,440. *Unit head:* Dr. Tara Fenwick, Head, 604-822-5359, Fax: 604-82-4244. *Application contact:* Christine Adams, Graduate Secretary, 604-822-6647, Fax: 604-822-4244, E-mail: grad.edst@ubc.ca.

University of Central Oklahoma, College of Graduate Studies and Research, College of Education, Department of Occupational and Technical Education, Program in Adult Education, Edmond, OK 73034-5209. Offers community services (M Ed); gerontology (M Ed). *Accreditation:* NCATE. Part-time programs available. *Entrance requirements:* For master's, GRE General Test. Additional exam requirements/recommendations for international students: Required—TOEFL (minimum score 550 paper-based; 213 computer-based). Electronic applications accepted.

University of Cincinnati, Division of Research and Advanced Studies, College of Education, Criminal Justice, and Human Services, Division of Teacher Education, Cincinnati, OH 45221. Offers curriculum and instruction (M Ed, Ed D); deaf studies (Certificate); early childhood education (M Ed); middle childhood education (M Ed); postsecondary literacy instruction (Certificate); reading/literacy (M Ed, Ed D); secondary education (M Ed); special education (M Ed, Ed D); teaching English as a second language (M Ed, Ed D, Certificate); teaching science (MS). Part-time programs available. *Degree requirements:* For doctorate, thesis/dissertation. *Entrance requirements:* For master's, GRE General Test. *Application deadline:* For fall admission, 2/1 for domestic students. Application fee: $30. Electronic applications accepted. *Financial support:* Fellowships, career-related internships or fieldwork, tuition waivers (partial), and unspecified assistantships available. *Unit head:* David Naylor, Student Contact, 513-556-3563, Fax: 513-556-2483, E-mail: david.naylor@uc.edu. *Application contact:* Dr. Richard Kretschmer, Graduate Program Director, 513-556-4547, Fax: 513-556-1001, E-mail: richard.kretschmer@uc.edu.

University of Connecticut, Graduate School, Neag School of Education, Department of Educational Leadership, Field of Adult Learning, Storrs, CT 06269. Offers MA, PhD. *Accreditation:* NCATE. *Faculty:* 8 full-time (4 women). *Students:* 2 full-time (1 woman), 19 part-time (15 women); includes 2 minority (1 African American, 1 Hispanic American), 1 international. Average age 41. 7 applicants, 57% accepted, 4 enrolled. In 2006, 2 master's, 1 doctorate awarded. Terminal master's awarded for partial completion of doctoral program. *Degree requirements:* For master's, thesis or alternative, comprehensive exam; for doctorate, thesis/dissertation. *Entrance requirements:* For master's and doctorate, GRE General Test. Additional exam requirements/recommendations for international students: Required—TOEFL (minimum score 550 paper-based; 213 computer-based). *Application deadline:* For fall admission, 2/1 priority date for domestic and international students; for spring admission, 11/1 for domestic students, 10/1 for international students. Applications are processed on a rolling basis. Application fee: $55. Electronic applications accepted. *Financial support:* In 2006–07, 2 research assistantships with full tuition reimbursements were awarded; fellowships, teaching assistantships with full tuition reimbursements, Federal Work-Study, scholarships/grants, health care benefits, and unspecified assistantships also available. Financial award application deadline: 2/1; financial award applicants required to submit FAFSA. *Application contact:* Lisa Rasicot, Graduate Coordinator, 860-486-3065, Fax: 860-486-0210, E-mail: soeadm02@uconnvm.uconn.edu.

University of Denver, College of Education, Denver, CO 80208. Offers counseling psychology (MA, PhD); curriculum and instruction (MA, PhD, Certificate), including curriculum leadership (MA, PhD); educational administration and policy studies (Certificate); educational psychology (MA, PhD, Ed S), including child and family studies (MA, PhD), quantitative research methods (MA, PhD), school psychology (PhD, Ed S); higher education and adult studies (MA, PhD); library and information science (MLIS); library and information sciences (Certificate); school administration (PhD). *Accreditation:* ALA; APA (one or more programs are accredited). Part-time and evening/weekend programs available. Postbaccalaureate distance learning degree programs offered (no on-campus study). *Faculty:* 28 full-time (18 women). *Students:* 293 full-time (240 women), 439 part-time (357 women); includes 102 minority (28 African Americans, 7 American Indian/Alaska Native, 14 Asian Americans or Pacific Islanders, 53 Hispanic Americans), 11 international. Average age 34. 574 applicants, 72% accepted. In 2006, 168 master's, 28 doctorates, 67 other advanced degrees awarded. Terminal master's awarded for partial completion of doctoral program. *Degree requirements:* For master's, comprehensive exam; for doctorate, 2 foreign languages, thesis/dissertation, comprehensive exam. *Entrance requirements:* For master's, GRE General Test or MAT (for most programs); for doctorate, GRE General Test or MAT. *Application deadline:* Applications are processed on a rolling basis. Application fee: $50. Electronic applications accepted. *Expenses:* Tuition: Full-time $29,628; part-time $823 per credit. *Financial support:* In 2006–07, 51 teaching assistantships with full and partial tuition reimbursements (averaging $6,700 per year) were awarded; career-related internships or fieldwork, Federal Work-Study, institutionally sponsored loans, and scholarships/grants also available. Support available to part-time students. Financial award application deadline: 3/1; financial award applicants required to submit FAFSA. *Faculty research:* Parkinson's disease, personnel training, development and assessments, gifted education, service learning, transportation, public schools. Total annual research expenditures: $172,000. *Unit head:* Dr. Virginia Maloney, Dean, 303-871-2509. *Application contact:* Linda McCarthy, Contact, 303-871-2509, E-mail: edinfo@du.edu.

University of Georgia, Graduate School, College of Education, Department of Lifelong Education, Administration and Policy, Athens, GA 30602. Offers M Ed, MA, Ed D, PhD, Ed S. *Accreditation:* NCATE. *Faculty:* 21 full-time (13 women). *Students:* 68 full-time (45 women), 248 part-time (159 women); includes 62 minority (54 African Americans, 1 American Indian/Alaska Native, 5 Asian Americans or Pacific Islanders, 2 Hispanic Americans), 21 international. 205 applicants, 63% accepted, 97 enrolled. In 2006, 61 master's, 12 doctorates, 15 other advanced degrees awarded. *Entrance requirements:* For master's and Ed S, GRE General Test or MAT; for doctorate, GRE General Test. *Application deadline:* For fall admission, 7/1 priority date for domestic students; for spring admission, 11/15 for domestic students. Application fee: $50. Electronic applications accepted. *Unit head:* Dr. Ronald M. Cervero, Head, 706-542-2221, Fax: 706-542-4024, E-mail: rcervero@coe.uga.edu.

University of Idaho, College of Graduate Studies, College of Education, Department of Adult, Career, and Technology Education, Program in Adult and Organizational Learning, Moscow, ID 83844-2282. Offers MS, Ed S. *Accreditation:* NCATE. *Students:* 31 (22 women). Average age 42. In 2006, 24 master's, 5 other advanced degrees awarded. *Entrance requirements:* For master's, minimum GPA of 2.8. *Application deadline:* For fall admission, 8/1 for domestic students; for spring admission, 12/15 for domestic students. Application fee: $55 ($60 for international students). *Expenses:* Tuition, nonresident: full-time $9,600; part-time $140 per credit. Required fees: $4,740; $227 per credit. *Financial support:* Application deadline: 2/15. *Unit head:* Dr. James A. Gregson, Head, Department of Adult, Career, and Technology Education, 208-885-2768.

University of Idaho, College of Graduate Studies, College of Education, Doctoral Programs in Education, Moscow, ID 83844-2282. Offers adult and organizational learning (Ed D, PhD); counseliing and human services (PhD); counseling and human services (Ed D); curriculm and intstruction (Ed D); curriculum and instruction (PhD); educational leadership (Ed D, PhD); physical education (PhD); professional-technical and technology education (PhD); professional-technical and tecnology education (Ed D). *Students:* 208 (118 women). In 2006, 50 degrees awarded. *Expenses:* Tuition, nonresident: full-time $9,600; part-time $140 per credit. Required fees: $4,740; $227 per credit. *Application contact:* Shirley Green, Information Contact, 208-885-6773.

University of Manitoba, Faculty of Graduate Studies, Faculty of Education, Department of Curriculum, Teaching and Learning, Winnipeg, MB R3T 2N2, Canada. Offers general curriculum (M Ed); language and literacy (M Ed); post-secondary studies (M Ed); teaching English as a second language (M Ed). *Degree requirements:* For master's, thesis or alternative.

University of Manitoba, Faculty of Graduate Studies, Faculty of Education, Department of Educational Administration, Foundations and Psychology, Winnipeg, MB R3T 2N2, Canada. Offers adult education (M Ed); educational administration (M Ed); guidance and counseling (M Ed); inclusive special education (M Ed); special foundations education (M Ed). *Degree requirements:* For master's, thesis or alternative.

University of Memphis, Graduate School, College of Education, Department of Leadership, Memphis, TN 38152. Offers adult education (Ed D); community education (Ed D); education (Ed S); educational leadership (Ed D); higher education (Ed D); leadership (MS); policy studies (Ed D); school administration and supervision (MS). *Accreditation:* NCATE. *Degree requirements:* For master's, thesis optional; for doctorate, thesis/dissertation, comprehensive exam; for Ed S, thesis or alternative, comprehensive exam. *Entrance requirements:* For master's, GRE General Test or MAT; for doctorate, GRE General Test, GRE Subject Test, 3 years of teaching experience; for Ed S, GRE General Test. *Faculty research:* Organizational learning, gender issues, leadership, technology and learning, principal preparation.

University of Minnesota, Twin Cities Campus, Graduate School, College of Education and Human Development, Department of Work and Human Resource Education, Program in Adult Education, Minneapolis, MN 55455-0213. Offers M Ed, MA, Ed D, PhD, Certificate. *Students:* 20 full-time (18 women), 19 part-time (17 women); includes 4 minority (2 African Americans, 1 Asian American or Pacific Islander, 1 Hispanic American), 1 international. Average age 42. 33 applicants, 91% accepted, 26 enrolled. In 2006, 10 master's, 14 other advanced degrees awarded. *Expenses:* Tuition, state resident: full-time $9,302; part-time $775 per credit. Tuition, nonresident: full-time $16,400; part-time $1,367 per credit. Full-time tuition and fees vary according to class time, course load, program, reciprocity agreements and student level. *Application contact:* Dr. Mary Bents, Associate Dean, 612-625-6501, Fax: 612-626-1580, E-mail: mbents@tc.umn.edu.

University of Missouri–Columbia, Graduate School, College of Education, Department of Educational Leadership and Policy Analysis, Columbia, MO 65211. Offers education administration (M Ed, MA, Ed D, PhD, Ed S); higher and adult education (M Ed, MA, Ed D, PhD, Ed S). Part-time programs available. *Faculty:* 17 full-time (11 women). *Students:* 224 full-time (136 women), 133 part-time (86 women); includes 41 minority (25 African Americans, 5 American Indian/Alaska Native, 3 Asian Americans or Pacific Islanders, 8 Hispanic Americans), 16 international. In 2006, 27 master's, 31 doctorates, 9 other advanced degrees awarded. *Degree requirements:* For doctorate, variable foreign language requirement, thesis/dissertation. *Entrance requirements:* For master's, GRE General Test, minimum GPA of 3.0; for doctorate, GRE General Test, GRE Subject Test, minimum GPA of 3.5; for Ed S, GRE General Test, GRE Subject Test, minimum GPA of 3.25. *Application deadline:* For fall admission, 12/15 priority date for domestic students. Applications are processed on a rolling basis. Application fee: $45 ($60 for international students). *Financial support:* Fellowships, research assistantships, teaching assistantships, institutionally sponsored loans and scholarships/grants available. *Faculty research:* Administrative communication and behavior, middle schools leadership, administration of special education. *Unit head:* Dr. Margaret M. Grogan, Director of Graduate Studies, 573-882-8221, E-mail: groganm@missouri.edu.

University of Missouri–St. Louis, College of Education, Division of Educational Leadership and Policy Studies, St. Louis, MO 63121. Offers adult and higher education (M Ed, Ed D); educational administration (M Ed, Ed D, Ed S), including community education (M Ed), elementary education (M Ed), secondary education (M Ed); educational leadership and policy studies (PhD); institutional research (Certificate). *Accreditation:* NCATE. *Faculty:* 15 full-time (8 women), 2 part-time/adjunct (0 women). *Students:* 37 full-time (27 women), 325 part-time (214 women); includes 130 minority (118 African Americans, 1 American Indian/Alaska Native, 4 Asian Americans or Pacific Islanders, 7 Hispanic Americans), 4 international. Average age 39. In 2006, 64 master's, 12 doctorates, 32 other advanced degrees awarded. *Entrance requirements:* For doctorate, GRE, 3 letters of recommendation. Additional exam requirements/recommendations for international students: Required—TOEFL (minimum score 550 paper-based; 213 computer-based). *Application deadline:* Applications are processed on a rolling basis. Application fee: $35 ($40 for international students). Electronic applications accepted. *Expenses:* Tuition, state resident: part-time $332 per credit hour. Tuition, nonresident: part-time $770 per credit hour. *Financial support:* In 2006–07, 6 research assistantships (averaging $8,235 per year) were awarded. *Faculty research:* Educational policy research; philosophy of education; higher, adult, and vocational education; school initiatives, change, and reform. *Unit head:* Dr. E. Paulette Savage, Chair, 514-516-5944. *Application contact:* 314-516-5458, Fax: 314-516-6996, E-mail: gradadm@umsl.edu.

The University of North Carolina at Greensboro, Graduate School, School of Education, Department of Curriculum and Instruction, Greensboro, NC 27412-5001. Offers college teaching and adult learning (Certificate); curriculum and instruction (M Ed), including chemistry education, elementary education, English as a second language, French education, instructional technology, mathematics education, middle grades education, reading education, science education, social studies education, Spanish education; curriculum and teaching (PhD), including higher education, teacher education and development; English as a second language (Certificate); higher education (M Ed); supervision (M Ed). *Accreditation:* NCATE. Part-time programs available. *Faculty:* 27 full-time (18 women), 8 part-time/adjunct (3 women). *Students:* 137 full-time (114 women), 231 part-time (195 women); includes 63 minority (52 African Americans, 2 American Indian/Alaska Native, 5 Asian Americans or Pacific Islanders, 4 Hispanic Americans). 146 applicants, 32% accepted. *Degree requirements:* For doctorate, thesis/dissertation. *Entrance requirements:* For master's and doctorate, GRE General Test. Additional exam requirements/recommendations for international students: Required—TOEFL. Application fee: $45. Electronic applications accepted. *Expenses:* Tuition, state resident: full-time $2,692. Tuition, nonresident: full-time $13,742. *Financial support:* Fellowships, research assistantships with full tuition reimbursements, teaching assistantships with full tuition reimbursements, career-related internships or fieldwork, Federal Work-Study, scholarships/grants, traineeships, and unspecified assistantships available. Support available to part-time students. *Faculty research:* Community college literacy program, middle school mathematics/computer mathematics. *Unit head:* Dr. Sam Miller, Chair, 336-334-3445, Fax: 336-334-4120, E-mail: sdmille2@uncg.edu. *Application contact:* Michelle Harkleroad, Director of Graduate Admissions, 336-334-4884, Fax: 336-334-4424, E-mail: mbharkle@uncg.edu.

University of Oklahoma, Graduate College, College of Education, Department of Educational Leadership and Policy Studies, Program in Adult and Higher Education, Norman, OK 73019-0390. Offers M Ed, PhD. *Accreditation:* NCATE. Part-time and evening/weekend programs available. *Students:* 60 full-time (41 women), 103 part-time (62 women); includes 47 minority (27 African Americans, 12 American Indian/Alaska Native, 1 Asian American or Pacific Islander, 7 Hispanic Americans), 4 international. 46 applicants, 93% accepted, 26 enrolled. In 2006, 45 master's, 7 doctorates awarded. *Degree requirements:* For master's, comprehensive exam; for doctorate, variable foreign language requirement, thesis/dissertation, general exam. *Entrance requirements:* For master's, minimum GPA of 3.0 in last 60 hours of undergraduate course work; for doctorate, GRE General Test, resumé, 3 letters of reference, scholarly writing sample. Additional exam requirements/recommendations for international students: Required—TOEFL (minimum score 550 paper-based; 213 computer-based). *Application deadline:* For fall admission, 6/1 for domestic students, 4/1 for international students; for spring admission, 10/1 for domestic students, 9/1 for international students. Application fee: $40 ($90 for international students). *Expenses:* Tuition, state resident: full-time $3,180; part-time $133 per credit hour. Tuition, nonresident: full-time $11,347; part-time $473 per credit hour. Required fees: $1,729; $62 per credit hour. $117 per semester. Tuition and fees vary according to course load and program. *Financial support:* Research assistantships with partial tuition reimbursements, teaching assistantships with partial tuition reimbursements, career-related internships or fieldwork, scholarships/grants, health care benefits, tuition waivers (full), and unspecified assistantships available. Support available to part-time students. Financial award applicants required to submit FAFSA. *Faculty research:* Institutional research, student personnel administration, community college, distance education, instructional strategies. *Application contact:* Geri Evans, Programs Officer, 405-325-5978, Fax: 405-325-2403, E-mail: gevans@ou.edu.

University of Phoenix–Bay Area Campus, The Artemis School, College of Education, Pleasanton, CA 94588-3677. Offers curriculum instruction (MA Ed); curriculum instruction—adult education (MA Ed). Evening/weekend programs available. *Faculty:* 11 full-time (3 women), 100 part-time/adjunct (52 women). *Students:* 227 full-time (156 women); includes 50 minority (15 African Americans, 2 American Indian/Alaska Native, 19 Asian Americans or Pacific Islanders, 14 Hispanic Americans), 22 international. Average age 36. In 2006, 115 degrees awarded. *Degree requirements:* For master's, thesis (for some programs), registration. *Entrance requirements:* For master's, minimum undergraduate GPA of 2.5, 3 years of work experience. Additional exam requirements/recommendations for international students: Required—TOEFL (minimum score 550 paper-based; 213 computer-based; 79 iBT). *Application deadline:* Applications are processed on a rolling basis. Application fee: $45. Electronic applications accepted. *Expenses:* Tuition: Full-time $12,648. Required fees: $760. *Financial support:* Institutionally sponsored loans and scholarships/grants available. Financial award applicants required to submit FAFSA. *Unit head:* Dr. Marla LaRue, Dean/Executive Director, 480-557-1218, E-mail: marla.larue@phoenix.edu. *Application contact:* Chair, 408-435-8500, Fax: 408-435-8250.

University of Phoenix–Metro Detroit Campus, The Artemis School, College of Education, Troy, MI 48098-2623. Offers administration and supervision (MA Ed); adult education and distance learning (MA Ed); curriculum and development (MA Ed); special education (MA Ed); teacher education elementary (MA Ed). Evening/weekend programs available. *Faculty:* 8 full-time (3 women), 27 part-time/adjunct (21 women). *Students:* 102 full-time (75 women); includes 59 minority (57 African Americans, 1 American Indian/Alaska Native, 1 Asian American or Pacific Islander), 1 international. Average age 40. In 2006, 30 master's awarded. *Degree requirements:* For master's, thesis (for some programs), registration. *Entrance requirements:* For master's, 3 years of work experience, minimum undergraduate GPA of 2.5. Additional exam requirements/recommendations for international students: Required—TOEFL (minimum score 550 paper-based; 213 computer-based; 79 iBT). *Application deadline:* Applications are processed on a rolling basis. Application fee: $45. Electronic applications accepted. *Expenses:* Tuition: Full-time $12,168. Required fees: $760. *Financial support:* Institutionally sponsored loans and scholarships/grants available. Financial award applicants required to submit FAFSA. *Unit head:* Dr. Marla LaRue, Dean/Executive Director, 480-557-1218. *Application contact:* Chair, 800-834-2438, Fax: 248-267-0147.

University of Phoenix–Omaha Campus, College of Education, Omaha, NE 68154-5240. Offers administration and supervision (MA Ed); curriculum and instruction (MA Ed); curriculum and instruction—English and language arts education (MA Ed); curriculum and instruction—adult education (MA Ed); curriculum and instruction—computer education (MA Ed); curriculum and instruction—English as a second language (MA Ed); curriculum and instruction—mathematics education (MA Ed); elementary teacher education (MA Ed); secondary teacher education (MA Ed); special education (MA Ed).

University of Phoenix Online Campus, The Artemis School, College of Education, Phoenix, AZ 85034-7209. Offers administration and supervision (MAEd); adult education and training (MAEd); curriculum and instruction-adult education (MAEd); curriculum and instruction-English and language arts education (MAEd); curriculum and instruction-mathematics education (MAEd); curriculum education (MAEd); curriculum instruction (MAEd); early childhood (MAEd); English as a second language (MAEd); teacher education elementary (MAEd); teacher education secondary (MAEd). Evening/weekend programs available. Postbaccalaureate distance learning degree programs offered (no on-campus study). *Faculty:* 12 full-time (5 women), 8,196 part-time/adjunct (6,937 women). *Students:* 11,937 full-time (9,375 women); includes 2,972 minority (2,210 African Americans, 74 American Indian/Alaska Native, 205 Asian Americans or Pacific Islanders, 483 Hispanic Americans), 906 international. Average age 36. *Degree requirements:* For master's, thesis (for some programs), registration. *Entrance requirements:* For master's, 3 years of work experience, minimum GPA of 2.5. Additional exam requirements/recommendations for international students: Required—TOEFL (minimum score 550 paper-based; 213 computer-based; 79 iBT). *Application deadline:* Applications are processed on a rolling basis. Application fee: $45. Electronic applications accepted. *Expenses:* Tuition: Full-time $12,664. Required fees: $760. *Financial support:* Institutionally sponsored loans and scholarships/grants available. Financial award applicants required to submit FAFSA. *Unit head:* Dr. Marla LaRue, Dean/Executive Director, 480-557-1218, E-mail: marla.larue@phoenix.edu. *Application contact:* Dr. Marla LaRue, Dean/Executive Director, 480-557-1218, E-mail: marla.larue@phoenix.edu.

University of Phoenix–Sacramento Valley Campus, The Artemis School, College of Education, Sacramento, CA 95833-3632. Offers adult education (MA Ed); curriculum instruction

Adult Education

University of Phoenix–Sacramento Valley Campus (continued) (MA Ed); elementary education (MA Ed); secondary education (MA Ed); teacher education (Certificate). Evening/weekend programs available. *Faculty:* 9 full-time (5 women), 95 part-time/adjunct (41 women). *Students:* 234 full-time (161 women); includes 51 minority (20 African Americans, 2 American Indian/Alaska Native, 9 Asian Americans or Pacific Islanders, 20 Hispanic Americans), 15 international. Average age 36. In 2006, 80 degrees awarded. *Degree requirements:* For master's, thesis (for some programs), registration. *Entrance requirements:* For master's, 3 years of work experience, minimum undergraduate GPA of 2.5. Additional exam requirements/recommendations for international students: Required—TOEFL (minimum score 550 paper-based; 213 computer-based; 79 iBT). *Application deadline:* Applications are processed on a rolling basis. Application fee: $45. Electronic applications accepted. *Expenses:* Tuition: Full-time $12,024. Required fees: $760. *Financial support:* Institutionally sponsored loans and scholarships/grants available. Financial award applicants required to submit FAFSA. *Unit head:* Dr. Marla LaRue, Dean, 480-557-1218, E-mail: marla.larue@phoenix.edu. *Application contact:* Campus College Chair, 916-923-2107, Fax: 916-923-3914.

University of Phoenix–Springfield Campus, College of Education, Springfield, MO 65804-7211. Offers administration and supervision (MA Ed); curriculum and instruction (MA Ed); curriculum and instruction/adult education (MA Ed); curriculum and instruction/computer education (MA Ed); curriculum and instruction/English as a second language (MA Ed); English and language arts education (MA Ed); mathematics education (MA Ed).

University of Regina, Faculty of Graduate Studies and Research, Faculty of Education, Department of Adult Education, Regina, SK S4S 0A2, Canada. Offers M Ad Ed. Part-time programs available. *Faculty:* 2 full-time (1 woman). *Students:* 3 full-time (all women), 26 part-time (19 women). 10 applicants, 80% accepted. In 2006, 5 degrees awarded. *Degree requirements:* For master's, practicum, project, or thesis. *Entrance requirements:* For master's, bachelor's degree in education, 2 years of teaching experience. Additional exam requirements/recommendations for international students: Required—TOEFL (minimum score 580 paper-based; 237 computer-based; 88 iBT). *Application deadline:* For fall admission, 2/15 for domestic students; for winter admission, 2/15 for domestic students; for spring admission, 2/15 for domestic students. Application fee: $60 ($100 for international students). *Financial support:* Fellowships, research assistantships, teaching assistantships available. Financial award application deadline: 6/15. *Faculty research:* Program and instruction. *Application contact:* Vicki Minhinnick, Graduate Program Coordinator, 306-585-4506, Fax: 306-585-8387, E-mail: edgrad@uregina.ca.

University of Rhode Island, Graduate School, College of Human Science and Services, School of Education, Program in Adult Education, Kingston, RI 02881. Offers MA. *Accreditation:* NCATE. Evening/weekend programs available. In 2006, 1 degree awarded. *Entrance requirements:* For master's, GRE or MAT. Additional exam requirements/recommendations for international students: Required—TOEFL. *Application deadline:* For fall admission, 4/15 priority date for domestic students; for spring admission, 11/15 for domestic students. Applications are processed on a rolling basis. Application fee: $35. *Expenses:* Tuition, state resident: full-time $6,032; part-time $335 per credit. Tuition, nonresident: full-time $17,288; part-time $960 per credit. Required fees: $65 per credit. $30 per semester. One-time fee: $80 part-time. *Financial support:* Career-related internships or fieldwork available. *Unit head:* Dr. John Boulmetis, Coordinator, 401-874-4159.

University of St. Francis, College of Professional Studies, Joliet, IL 60435-6169. Offers health services administration (MS); training and development (MS). Part-time and evening/weekend programs available. Postbaccalaureate distance learning degree programs offered (no on-campus study). *Faculty:* 4 full-time (1 woman), 36 part-time/adjunct (19 women). *Students:* 95 full-time (78 women), 623 part-time (545 women); includes 98 minority (67 African Americans, 2 American Indian/Alaska Native, 13 Asian Americans or Pacific Islanders, 16 Hispanic Americans), 1 international. Average age 44. 215 applicants, 83% accepted, 136 enrolled. In 2006, 272 degrees awarded. *Degree requirements:* For master's, thesis (for some programs), comprehensive exam (for some programs), registration. *Entrance requirements:* For master's, minimum GPA of 2.75, 2 letters of recommendation, computer competency, 2 years of work experience. Additional exam requirements/recommendations for international students: Required—TOEFL (minimum score 550 paper-based; 213 computer-based). *Application deadline:* Applications are processed on a rolling basis. Application fee: $30. Electronic applications accepted. *Expenses: Contact institution.* Part-time tuition and fees vary according to campus/location and program. *Financial support:* In 2006–07, 163 students received support. Tuition waivers (partial) available. Support available to part-time students. Financial award applicants required to submit FAFSA. *Unit head:* Dr. Michael LaRocco, Dean, 815-740-3452, Fax: 815-774-2920, E-mail: mlarocco@stfrancis.edu. *Application contact:* Sandra Sloka, Director of Admissions for Graduate and Degree Completion Programs, 800-735-7500, Fax: 815-740-5032, E-mail: ssloka@stfrancis.edu.

University of Southern Maine, College of Education and Human Development, Program in Adult Education, Portland, ME 04104-9300. Offers adult education (MS); adult learning (CAS). *Accreditation:* NCATE. Part-time and evening/weekend programs available. Postbaccalaureate distance learning degree programs offered (minimal on-campus study). *Faculty:* 3 full-time (1 woman). *Students:* 14 applicants, 93% accepted, 9 enrolled. In 2006, 9 master's, 1 other advanced degree awarded. *Degree requirements:* For master's and CAS, thesis or alternative. *Entrance requirements:* For master's, GRE or MAT, interview; for CAS, master's degree. *Application deadline:* For fall admission, 2/1 for domestic students; for spring admission, 9/15 for domestic students. Application fee: $50. Electronic applications accepted. *Expenses:* Tuition, state resident: full-time $4,860; part-time $270 per credit hour. Tuition, nonresident: full-time $13,572; part-time $754 per credit hour. Required fees: $222 per semester. Tuition and fees vary according to course load. *Financial support:* In 2006–07, 5 students received support, including 3 research assistantships with tuition reimbursements available (averaging $4,500 per year); career-related internships or fieldwork, Federal Work-Study, institutionally sponsored loans, scholarships/grants, and unspecified assistantships also available. Support available to part-time students. Financial award application deadline: 3/1; financial award applicants required to submit FAFSA. *Faculty research:* Workplace education. *Unit head:* Dr. E. Michael Brady, Chair, Human Resource Development Department, 207-780-5316, Fax: 207-780-5043, E-mail: mbrady@usm.maine.edu. *Application contact:* Robin Audesse, Associate Director of Graduate Admissions, 207-780-5306, Fax: 207-780-5193, E-mail: raudesse@usm.maine.edu.

University of Southern Mississippi, Graduate School, College of Education and Psychology, Department of Educational Leadership and Research, Hattiesburg, MS 39406-0001. Offers adult education (M Ed, Ed D, PhD, Ed S); educational administration (M Ed, Ed D, PhD, Ed S); higher education (PhD). *Faculty:* 19 full-time (7 women). *Students:* 86 full-time (66 women), 250 part-time (173 women); includes 102 minority (97 African Americans, 1 American Indian/Alaska Native, 2 Asian Americans or Pacific Islanders, 2 Hispanic Americans), 4 international. Average age 38. 123 applicants, 62% accepted, 72 enrolled. In 2006, 56 master's, 25 doctorates, 41 other advanced degrees awarded. *Degree requirements:* For master's, thesis (for some programs), internship, comprehensive exam, registration; for doctorate, thesis/dissertation, comprehensive exam, registration; for Ed S, thesis (for some programs), comprehensive exam, registration. *Entrance requirements:* For master's, GRE General Test, minimum GPA of 2.75; for doctorate, GRE General Test, minimum GPA of 3.5; for Ed S, GRE General Test, minimum GPA of 3.25. Additional exam requirements/recommendations for international students: Required—TOEFL. *Application deadline:* For fall admission, 3/1 priority date for domestic students, 3/1 for international students. Applications are processed on a rolling basis. Application fee: $25 ($30 for international students). *Financial support:* In 2006–07, 12 research assistantships with full tuition reimbursements (averaging $5,571 per year), 1 teaching assistantship (averaging $5,571 per year) were awarded; career-related internships or fieldwork, Federal Work-Study, and institutionally sponsored loans also available. Financial award application deadline: 3/15. *Faculty research:* Supervision, learning styles, education finance, higher educa-

tion organization. Total annual research expenditures: $88,500. *Unit head:* Dr. Gaylynn Parker, Interim Chair, 601-266-4589, Fax: 601-266-5141.

University of South Florida, Graduate School, College of Education, Department of Adult, Career and Higher Education, Tampa, FL 33620-9951. Offers adult education (MA, Ed D, PhD, Ed S); career and technical education (MA); higher education/community college teaching (MA, PhD, Ed S); industrial-technical education (MA); vocational education (Ed D, PhD, Ed S). *Faculty:* 11 full-time (5 women), 2 part-time/adjunct (0 women). *Students:* 30 full-time (23 women), 176 part-time (121 women); includes 52 minority (32 African Americans, 1 American Indian/Alaska Native, 1 Asian American or Pacific Islander, 18 Hispanic Americans), 4 international. 104 applicants, 71% accepted, 55 enrolled. In 2006, 56 master's, 5 doctorates awarded. *Entrance requirements:* For master's, GRE General Test, minimum GPA of 3.0 in last 60 hours. *Application deadline:* For fall admission, 6/1 for domestic students; for spring admission, 10/15 for domestic students. Application fee: $30. *Financial support:* Career-related internships or fieldwork, scholarships/grants, and unspecified assistantships available. Total annual research expenditures: $191,880. *Unit head:* Robert Sullins, Interim Dean, E-mail: rsullins@ugs.usf.edu.

The University of Tennessee, Graduate School, College of Education, Health and Human Sciences, Department of Educational Psychology and Counseling, Knoxville, TN 37996. Offers adult education (MS); applied educational psychology (MS); collaborative learning (Ed D); college student personnel (MS); mental health counseling (MS); rehabilitation counseling (MS); school counseling (MS). *Accreditation:* ACA (one or more programs are accredited); CORE (one or more programs are accredited); NCATE. Part-time and evening/weekend programs available. *Students:* 27 (20 women); includes 2 African Americans, 1 American Indian/Alaska Native 1 international. 69 applicants, 33% accepted. In 2006, 36 degrees awarded. *Degree requirements:* For master's, thesis optional. *Entrance requirements:* For master's, GRE General Test, minimum GPA of 2.7. Additional exam requirements/recommendations for international students: Required—TOEFL. *Application deadline:* For fall admission, 2/1 priority date for domestic students. Applications are processed on a rolling basis. Application fee: $35. Electronic applications accepted. *Expenses:* Tuition, state resident: full-time $5,574. Tuition, nonresident: full-time $16,840. Required fees: $792. *Financial support:* In 2006–07, 1 research assistantship, 2 teaching assistantships were awarded. Financial award application deadline: 2/1; financial award applicants required to submit FAFSA. *Unit head:* Dr. Olga Welch, Head, 865-974-5131, Fax: 865-974-8674, E-mail: owelch@utk.edu.

The University of Texas at San Antonio, College of Education and Human Development, Department of Counseling, Educational Psychology, and Adult and Higher Education, San Antonio, TX 78249-0617. Offers counseling (MA); counselor education (PhD); education-adult and higher education (MA). Part-time programs available. *Faculty:* 17 full-time (9 women), 16 part-time/adjunct (4 women). *Students:* 154 full-time (125 women), 403 part-time (354 women); includes 299 minority (42 African Americans, 2 American Indian/Alaska Native, 7 Asian Americans or Pacific Islanders, 248 Hispanic Americans), 4 international. Average age 33. 210 applicants, 85% accepted, 172 enrolled. In 2006, 140 degrees awarded. *Degree requirements:* For master's, thesis optional. *Entrance requirements:* For master's, GRE General Test. Additional exam requirements/recommendations for international students: Required—TOEFL (minimum score 500 paper-based; 173 computer-based). *Application deadline:* For fall admission, 7/1 for domestic students, 4/1 for international students; for spring admission, 11/1 for domestic students, 9/1 for international students. Applications are processed on a rolling basis. Application fee: $45 ($80 for international students). Electronic applications accepted. *Expenses:* Tuition, state resident: full-time $1,730; part-time $192 per credit hour. Tuition, nonresident: full-time $6,680; part-time $742 per credit hour. Required fees: $733; $308,359 per credit hour. *Financial support:* In 2006–07, 1 research assistantship (averaging $18,720 per year) was awarded; career-related internships or fieldwork, Federal Work-Study, scholarships/grants, and unspecified assistantships also available. *Faculty research:* Early childhood, reading, special education, foundations, curriculum and instruction. *Unit head:* Dr. Marcheta P. Evans, Chair, 210-458-2600, Fax: 210-458-2605, E-mail: mevans@utsa.edu.

University of the Incarnate Word, School of Graduate Studies and Research, Dreeben School of Education, Programs in Education, San Antonio, TX 78209-6397. Offers adult education (M Ed, MA); diversity education (M Ed, MA); early childhood education (M Ed, MA); instructional technology (M Ed, MA); international education and entrepreneurship (PhD); kinesiology (M Ed, MA); mathematics education (PhD); organizational leadership (PhD); organizational learning (M Ed, MA); reading (M Ed, MA); special education (M Ed, MA). *Students:* 15 full-time (8 women), 179 part-time (117 women); includes 70 minority (20 African Americans, 1 American Indian/Alaska Native, 1 Asian American or Pacific Islander, 48 Hispanic Americans), 54 international. Average age 39. In 2006, 15 degrees awarded. Application fee: $20. *Expenses:* Tuition: Part-time $570 per credit hour. Required fees: $54 per credit hour. One-time fee: $195 part-time. Tuition and fees vary according to degree level. *Financial support:* Federal Work-Study and scholarships/grants available. *Unit head:* Dr. Richard Gray, Director, 210-829-3138, Fax: 210-829-3134, E-mail: gray@uiwtx.edu. *Application contact:* Andrea Cyterski-Acosta, Dean of Enrollment, 210-829-6005, Fax: 210-829-3921, E-mail: cyterski@uiwtx.edu.

University of the Incarnate Word, School of Graduate Studies and Research, H-E-B School of Business and Administration, Programs in Administration, San Antonio, TX 78209-6397. Offers adult education (MAA); applied administration (MAA); communication arts (MAA); English (MAA); instructional technology (MAA); international business (Certificate); multidisciplinary sciences (MAA); nutrition (MAA); organizational development (MAA, Certificate); project management (Certificate); sports management (MAA); urban administration (MAA). *Students:* 1 (woman) full-time, 161 part-time (102 women); includes 17 African Americans, 1 American Indian/Alaska Native, 82 Hispanic Americans, 18 international. Average age 34. In 2006, 78 degrees awarded. *Entrance requirements:* For master's, GMAT, GRE, MAT. Additional exam requirements/recommendations for international students: Required—TOEFL. *Application deadline:* For fall admission, 8/15 priority date for domestic students; for spring admission, 12/31 for domestic students. Applications are processed on a rolling basis. Application fee: $20. *Expenses:* Tuition: Part-time $570 per credit hour. Required fees: $54 per credit hour. One-time fee: $195 part-time. Tuition and fees vary according to degree level. *Financial support:* Federal Work-Study and scholarships/grants available. *Unit head:* Dr. Dan Dominguez, MAA Director, 210-829-3180, Fax: 210-805-3564, E-mail: domingue@uiwtx.edu. *Application contact:* Andrea Cyterski-Acosta, Dean of Enrollment, 210-829-6005, Fax: 210-829-3921, E-mail: cyterski@uiwtx.edu.

The University of West Alabama, School of Graduate Studies, College of Education, Department of Teacher Education, Program in Continuing Education, Livingston, AL 35470. Offers MSCE. *Accreditation:* NCATE. Part-time programs available. *Faculty:* 3 full-time (1 woman), 1 (woman) part-time/adjunct. *Students:* 1 (woman) full-time, 1 (woman) part-time; both minorities (both African Americans) 5 applicants, 100% accepted. In 2006, 96 degrees awarded. *Degree requirements:* For master's, comprehensive exam. *Entrance requirements:* For master's, GRE General Test, MAT, minimum GPA of 2.75. *Application deadline:* For fall admission, 9/10 priority date for domestic students; for spring admission, 3/24 for domestic students. Applications are processed on a rolling basis. Application fee: $20 ($50 for international students). *Financial support:* Career-related internships or fieldwork, Federal Work-Study, scholarships/grants, and unspecified assistantships available. Support available to part-time students. *Unit head:* Dr. Louis R. Smith, Coordinator, 205-652-3439, Fax: 205-652-3707, E-mail: livlrs@uwamail.westal.edu.

The University of West Alabama, School of Graduate Studies, College of Education, Department of Teacher Education, Program in Guidance and Counseling, Livingston, AL 35470. Offers continuing education (MSCE); guidance and counseling (M Ed). *Accreditation:* NCATE. Part-time and evening/weekend programs available. *Faculty:* 3 full-time, 16 part-time/adjunct. *Students:* 477 full-time (411 women), 529 part-time (459 women); includes 460 minority (436 African Americans, 5 American Indian/Alaska Native, 10 Asian Americans or Pacific Islanders, 9 Hispanic Americans), 1 international. Average age 25. 10 applicants, 100% accepted. In

2006, 116 degrees awarded. *Entrance requirements:* For master's, GRE General Test, MAT, minimum GPA of 2.75. *Application deadline:* For fall admission, 9/10 priority date for domestic students; for spring admission, 3/21 for domestic students. Applications are processed on a rolling basis. Application fee: $20 ($50 for international students). *Financial support:* Career-related internships or fieldwork, Federal Work-Study, scholarships/grants, and unspecified assistantships available. Support available to part-time students.

University of Wisconsin–Platteville, School of Graduate Studies, College of Liberal Arts and Education, School of Education, Platteville, WI 53818-3099. Offers adult education (MSE); elementary education (MSE); middle school education (MSE); secondary education (MSE); vocational and technical education (MSE). *Accreditation:* NCATE. Part-time programs available. *Faculty:* 8 part-time/adjunct (3 women). *Students:* 48 full-time (37 women), 103 part-time (72 women); includes 33 minority (27 African Americans, 1 Asian American or Pacific Islander, 5 Hispanic Americans), 39 international. 39 applicants, 72% accepted. In 2006, 55 degrees awarded. *Degree requirements:* For master's, thesis or alternative, comprehensive exam, registration. *Entrance requirements:* Additional exam requirements/recommendations for international students: Required—TOEFL (minimum score 500 paper-based; 173 computer-based). *Application deadline:* For fall admission, 7/1 priority date for domestic students; for spring admission, 11/1 for domestic students. Applications are processed on a rolling basis. Application fee: $45. Electronic applications accepted. *Expenses:* Tuition, state resident: part-time $365 per credit. Tuition, nonresident: part-time $955 per credit. *Financial support:* Research assistantships with partial tuition reimbursements, career-related internships or fieldwork, Federal Work-Study, institutionally sponsored loans, scholarships/grants, and unspecified assistantships available. Support available to part-time students. *Unit head:* Dr. Michael Anderson, Director, 608-342-1131, Fax: 608-342-1133, E-mail: andersonmi@uwplatt.edu. *Application contact:* Kristal Prohaska, Admissions and Enrollment Management, 608-342-1125, Fax: 608-342-1122, E-mail: admit@uwplatt.edu.

University of Wyoming, Graduate School, College of Education, Department of Adult Learning and Technology, Laramie, WY 82070. Offers adult and post secondary education (Ed S); adult and postsecondary education (MA, Ed D, PhD); distance education (Ed D, PhD); instructional technology (MS, Ed D, PhD). Part-time programs available. Postbaccalaureate distance learning degree programs offered (no on-campus study). *Faculty:* 6 full-time (3 women), 11 part-time/adjunct (5 women). *Students:* 14 full-time (10 women), 91 part-time (52 women); includes 10 minority (2 African Americans, 1 American Indian/Alaska Native, 2 Asian Americans or Pacific Islanders, 5 Hispanic Americans), 4 international. Average age 44. 26 applicants, 85% accepted, 20 enrolled. In 2006, 24 master's, 5 doctorates awarded. *Degree requirements:* For master's, thesis or alternative; for doctorate, thesis/dissertation, comprehensive exam. *Entrance requirements:* For master's, GRE, minimum GPA of 3.0; for doctorate, MS or MA, minimum GPA of 3.0. Additional exam requirements/recommendations for international students: Required—TOEFL. *Application deadline:* For fall admission, 2/1 for domestic and international students; for spring admission, 10/1 for domestic and international students. Application fee: $50. Electronic applications accepted. *Financial support:* In 2006–07, 1 student received support, including 1 teaching assistantship with tuition reimbursement available (averaging $14,400 per year); scholarships/grants also available. Financial award application deadline: 2/1. *Faculty research:* Web based instruction, instructional decision, adult education history, literacy in adults, international distance education. *Unit head:* Dr. John J. Cochenour, Head, 307-766-3608, Fax: 307-766-3237, E-mail: johncoc@uwyo.edu. *Application contact:* Jeannete A. Skinner, Office Associate, 307-766-3247, Fax: 307-766-3237, E-mail: ask-alt@uwyo.edu.

Valdosta State University, Graduate School, College of Education, Department of Adult and Career Education, Valdosta, GA 31698. Offers adult and career education (M Ed, Ed D); business education (M Ed). *Accreditation:* NCATE. Evening/weekend programs available. *Degree requirements:* For master's, portfolio; for doctorate, thesis/dissertation, comprehensive written and/or oral exams. *Entrance requirements:* For master's, GRE General Test or MAT, minimum GPA of 2.5; for doctorate, GRE General Test, minimum GPA of 3.5, 3 years of experience. Additional exam requirements/recommendations for international students: Required—TOEFL (minimum score 523 paper-based; 193 computer-based). Electronic applications accepted.

Virginia Commonwealth University, Graduate School, School of Education, Program in Adult and Organizational Learning, Richmond, VA 23284-9005. Offers adult literacy (M Ed); adults with disabilities (M Ed); human resource development (M Ed). *Accreditation:* NCATE. Part-time programs available. *Students:* 1 applicant, 0% accepted. In 2006, 14 degrees awarded. *Entrance requirements:* For master's, GRE General Test or MAT. *Application deadline:* For fall admission, 5/15 for domestic students; for spring admission, 11/15 for domestic students. Applications are processed on a rolling basis. Application fee: $50. *Financial support:* Career-related internships or fieldwork and Federal Work-Study available. Financial award application deadline: 3/1. *Faculty research:* Adult development and learning, program planning and evaluation. *Unit head:* James McMillan, Division Head, 804-828-1305. *Application contact:* Dr. Michael D. Davis, Director, Graduate Studies, 804-828-6530, Fax: 804-827-0676, E-mail: mddavis@vcu.edu.

See Close-Up on page 1279.

Virginia Polytechnic Institute and State University, Graduate School, College of Liberal Arts and Human Sciences, Department of Human Development, Blacksburg, VA 24061. Offers adult development and aging (MS, PhD); adult learning and human resource development (MS, PhD); child development (MS, PhD); family studies (MS, PhD); marriage and family therapy (MS, PhD). *Accreditation:* AAMFT/COAMFTE (one or more programs are accredited). *Faculty:* 23 full-time (17 women). *Students:* 54 full-time (43 women), 88 part-time (66 women); includes 27 minority (19 African Americans, 7 Asian Americans or Pacific Islanders, 1 Hispanic American), 9 international. Average age 37. 85 applicants, 45% accepted, 32 enrolled. In 2006, 27 master's, 17 doctorates awarded. *Entrance requirements:* For master's and doctorate, GRE General Test. Additional exam requirements/recommendations for international students: Required—TOEFL (minimum score 600 paper-based; 250 computer-based). *Application deadline:* For fall admission, 5/15 for international students; for spring admission, 10/15 for international students. Applications are processed on a rolling basis. Application fee: $45. Electronic applications accepted. *Expenses:* Tuition, state resident: full-time $7,017; part-time $390 per credit hour. Tuition, nonresident: full-time $12,414; part-time $690 per credit hour. International tuition: $11,296 full-time. Required fees: $1,523; $256 per term. *Financial support:* In 2006–07, 1 research assistantship with full tuition reimbursement, 16 teaching assistantships with full tuition reimbursements (averaging $9,911 per year) were awarded; career-related internships or fieldwork, Federal Work-Study, scholarships/grants, and unspecified assistantships also available. Financial award application deadline: 4/1. *Faculty research:* Stress management, children's play, dual-career families, social cognition, relationships of elderly. *Unit head:* Dr. Fred P. Piercy, Head, 540-231-4794, Fax: 540-231-7012, E-mail: piercy@vt.edu. *Application contact:* Kathy Surface, Information Contact, 540-231-6149, Fax: 540-231-7012, E-mail: ksurface@vt.edu.

Virginia Polytechnic Institute and State University, Graduate School, College of Liberal Arts and Human Sciences, School of Education, Department of Educational Leadership and Policy Studies, Blacksburg, VA 24061. Offers administration and supervision of special education (Ed D, PhD, Ed S); adult and continuing education (MA Ed, Ed D, PhD); educational counseling (MA Ed, Ed D, PhD, Ed S); educational leadership (MA Ed, Ed D, PhD); educational research and evaluation (PhD). *Accreditation:* ACA; NCATE. *Students:* 139 full-time (107 women), 301 part-time (200 women); includes 119 minority (101 African Americans, 2 American Indian/Alaska Native, 4 Asian Americans or Pacific Islanders, 12 Hispanic Americans), 10 international. Average age 40. 175 applicants, 48% accepted, 82 enrolled. In 2006, 72 master's, 35 doctorates, 28 other advanced degrees awarded. *Degree requirements:* For doctorate, thesis/dissertation, comprehensive exam. *Entrance requirements:* Additional exam requirements/recommendations for international students: Required—TOEFL (minimum score 550 paper-based; 213 computer-based). *Application deadline:* For fall admission, 5/15 for international students; for spring admission, 10/15 for international students. Applications are processed on a rolling basis. Application fee: $45. Electronic applications accepted. *Expenses:* Tuition, state resident: full-time $7,017; part-time $390 per credit hour. Tuition, nonresident: full-time $12,414; part-time $690 per credit hour. International tuition: $11,296 full-time. Required fees: $1,523; $256 per term. *Financial support:* Career-related internships or fieldwork, Federal Work-Study, scholarships/grants, and unspecified assistantships available. Financial award application deadline: 4/1. *Unit head:* Dr. M. David Alexander, Head, 540-231-5642, Fax: 540-231-7845, E-mail: mdavid@vt.edu. *Application contact:* Kathy Tickle, Information Contact, 540-231-9721, Fax: 540-231-7845, E-mail: ktickle@vt.edu.

Wayne State University, College of Education, Division of Teacher Education, Detroit, MI 48202. Offers adult and continuing education (M Ed); art education (M Ed); bilingual/bicultural education (M Ed, MAT); business education (M Ed, MAT); career and technical education (M Ed, Ed D, PhD, Ed S); curriculum and instruction (Ed D, PhD, Ed S); distributive education (M Ed, MAT); early childhood education (M Ed); elementary education (M Ed, MAT, Ed D, PhD, Ed S); elementary education curriculum and instruction (M Ed); English education (M Ed); English education-secondary (M Ed, Ed S); foreign language education (M Ed); general education (Ed D, Ed S); health occupations education (M Ed); industrial education (M Ed); mathematics education (M Ed, Ed S); pre-school and parent education (M Ed); reading (M Ed, Ed D, Ed S); reading, languages and literature (Ed D); school music-vocal (M Ed); science education (M Ed, MAT, Ed S); secondary education (MAT); secondary school reading (M Ed); social studies education (M Ed, Ed S), including education-secondary (M Ed); special education (M Ed, Ed D, PhD, Ed S); teacher education (MAT, Ed D, PhD). *Faculty:* 41 full-time (22 women), 2 part-time/adjunct (both women). *Students:* 401 full-time (295 women), 1,021 part-time (784 women); includes 527 minority (452 African Americans, 6 American Indian/Alaska Native, 32 Asian Americans or Pacific Islanders, 37 Hispanic Americans), 18 international. Average age 36. 296 applicants, 81% accepted, 132 enrolled. In 2006, 386 master's, 1 doctorate awarded. *Degree requirements:* For doctorate, thesis/dissertation. *Entrance requirements:* For master's, minimum GPA of 2.6; for doctorate, minimum undergraduate GPA of 3.0, graduate 3.5; interview. Additional exam requirements/recommendations for international students: Required—TOEFL (minimum score 550 paper-based; 213 computer-based), TWE (minimum score 6). *Application deadline:* For fall admission, 7/1 for domestic students, 6/1 for international students; for winter admission, 10/1 for international students; for spring admission, 2/1 for international students. Application fee: $30 ($50 for international students). Electronic applications accepted. *Financial support:* In 2006–07, 1 fellowship (averaging $34,919 per year) was awarded; research assistantships. *Faculty research:* Reading and writing literacy and literature. Total annual research expenditures: $209,400. *Unit head:* Dr. Joann Snyder, Academic Director, 313-577-1644, E-mail: joanne.snyder@wayne.edu. *Application contact:* Sharon Elliott, Assistant Dean, 313-577-0902, E-mail: sharon.elliott@wayne.edu.

Western Washington University, Graduate School, Woodring College of Education, Department of Educational Leadership, Program in Continuing and College Education, Bellingham, WA 98225-5996. Offers M Ed. Part-time and evening/weekend programs available. Postbaccalaureate distance learning degree programs offered (minimal on-campus study). *Faculty:* 4. *Students:* 11 full-time (8 women), 37 part-time (27 women). 17 applicants, 82% accepted, 4 enrolled. In 2006, 25 degrees awarded. *Degree requirements:* For master's, thesis optional. *Entrance requirements:* For master's, GRE General Test or MAT, minimum GPA of 3.0 in last 60 semester hours or last 90 quarter hours. Additional exam requirements/recommendations for international students: Required—TOEFL (minimum score 567 paper-based; 227 computer-based). *Application deadline:* For fall admission, 6/1 for domestic students; for winter admission, 10/1 for domestic students; for spring admission, 2/1 for domestic students. Applications are processed on a rolling basis. Application fee: $50. *Expenses:* Tuition, state resident: full-time $6,609; part-time $199 per credit. Tuition, nonresident: full-time $16,845; part-time $540 per credit. *Financial support:* In 2006–07, 1 teaching assistantship with partial tuition reimbursement (averaging $9,339 per year) was awarded; career-related internships or fieldwork, Federal Work-Study, institutionally sponsored loans, scholarships/grants, tuition waivers (partial), and unspecified assistantships also available. Support available to part-time students. Financial award application deadline: 2/15; financial award applicants required to submit FAFSA. *Faculty research:* Transfer of learning as a result of continuing professional education programs, postsecondary faculty development, action research as professional development, literacy education in community colleges. *Unit head:* Dr. Sandra Daffron, Program Director, 360-650-2977, E-mail: sandra.daffron@wwu.edu. *Application contact:* Sherry Haskins, Graduate Coordinator, 360-650-3190.

Widener University, School of Human Service Professions, Center for Education, Chester, PA 19013-5792. Offers adult education (M Ed); counseling in higher education (M Ed); counselor education (M Ed); early childhood education (M Ed); educational foundations (M Ed); educational leadership (M Ed); educational psychology (M Ed); elementary education (M Ed); English and language arts (M Ed); health education (M Ed); higher education leadership (Ed D); home and school visitor (M Ed); human sexuality (M Ed); mathematics education (M Ed); middle school education (M Ed); principalship (M Ed); reading and language arts (Ed D); reading education (M Ed); school administration (Ed D); science education (M Ed); social studies education (M Ed); special education (M Ed); technology education (M Ed). Part-time and evening/weekend programs available. Terminal master's awarded for partial completion of doctoral program. *Degree requirements:* For doctorate, thesis/dissertation. *Entrance requirements:* For master's, minimum GPA of 2.5; for doctorate, GRE or MAT, minimum GPA of 2.0 (undergraduate), 3.5 (graduate). Electronic applications accepted. Expenses: Contact institution. *Faculty research:* Reading and cognition, adult education, technology education, educational leadership, special education.

Wright State University, School of Graduate Studies, College of Education and Human Services, Department of Educational Leadership, Program in Advanced Educational Leadership, Dayton, OH 45435. Offers advanced curriculum and instruction (Ed S); higher education-adult education (Ed S); superintendent (Ed S). *Accreditation:* NCATE. *Students:* 6 full-time (4 women), 10 part-time (6 women); includes 3 minority (all African Americans) Average age 35. 3 applicants, 100% accepted. In 2006, 1 degree awarded. *Degree requirements:* For Ed S, thesis. *Entrance requirements:* For degree, GRE General Test, MAT. Additional exam requirements/recommendations for international students: Required—TOEFL. Application fee: $25. *Financial support:* Available to part-time students. Applicants required to submit FAFSA. *Unit head:* Dr. Thomas Diamantes, Director, 937-775-3008, Fax: 937-775-2405, E-mail: thomas.diamantes@wright.edu. *Application contact:* John Kimble, Associate Director of Graduate Admissions and Records, 937-775-2957, Fax: 937-775-2453, E-mail: john.kimble@wright.edu.

Community College Education

Argosy University, Chicago Campus, College of Education, Chicago, IL 60603. Offers community college executive leadership (Ed D); educational leadership (MA Ed, Ed D, Ed S), including administrative certification (MA Ed), district leadership (Ed D), higher education administration (Ed D), K-12 education (Ed D), principal/general (MA Ed), superintendent certification (Ed S); instructional leadership (MA Ed, Ed D, Ed S), including higher education (Ed D), K-12 education (Ed D). Part-time and evening/weekend programs available. *Faculty:* 3 full-time (1 woman), 7 part-time/adjunct (0 women). *Students:* 116 full-time (96 women), 42 part-time (32 women); includes 112 minority (108 African Americans, 1 Asian American or Pacific Islander, 3 Hispanic Americans). Average age 45. 56 applicants, 84% accepted, 45 enrolled. In 2006, 4 master's, 10 doctorates awarded. *Entrance requirements:* For master's and doctorate, minimum GPA of 3.0. Additional exam requirements/recommendations for international students: Required—TOEFL (minimum score 550 paper-based; 213 computer-based). *Application deadline:* For fall admission, 2/28 for domestic and international students; for spring admission, 10/30 for domestic and international students. Applications are processed on a rolling basis. Application fee: $50. Electronic applications accepted. *Financial support:* In 2006–07, 35 students received support. Scholarships/grants available. Financial award application deadline: 4/1. *Unit head:* Dr. Paul Busceni, Head, 800-626-4123, Fax: 312-777-7750, E-mail: pbusceni@argosy.edu. *Application contact:* Ashley Delaney, Director of Admissions, 800-626-4123, Fax: 312-777-7750, E-mail: argosyadmissions@argosy.edu.

See Close-Up on page 825.

Argosy University, Inland Empire Campus, College of Education, San Bernardino, CA 92408. Offers community college executive leadership (Ed D); educational leadership (MA Ed, Ed D), including higher education administration (Ed D), K-12 education (Ed D); instructional leadership (MA Ed, Ed D), including higher education (Ed D), K-12 education (Ed D), multiple subject teacher credential preparation (MA Ed), multiple subject teacher credntial preparation with BCLAD (MA Ed), single subject teacher credential preparation (MA Ed), single subject teacher credential preparation with BCLAD (MA Ed).

See Close-Up on page 1103.

Argosy University, Nashville Campus, College of Education, Franklin, TN 37067-7226. Offers community college executive leadership (Ed D); educational leadership (MA Ed, Ed D), including educational leadership (MA Ed), higher education administration (Ed D), K-12 education (Ed D); instructional leadership (MA Ed, Ed D), including higher education administration (Ed D), instructional leadership (MA Ed), K-12 education (Ed D).

Argosy University, Orange County Campus, College of Education, Santa Ana, CA 92704. Offers community college executive leadership (Ed D); educational leadership (MA Ed, Ed D), including higher education administration (Ed D), K-12 education (Ed D); instructional leadership (MA Ed, Ed D), including educational technology (Ed D), higher education (Ed D), K-12 education (Ed D), multiple subject teacher credential preparation (MA Ed), multiple subject teacher credential preparation with BCLAD (MA Ed), single subject teacher credential preparation (MA Ed), single subject teacher credential preparation with BCLAD (MA Ed). Part-time and evening/weekend programs available. *Faculty:* 3 full-time (2 women), 33 part-time/adjunct (15 women). *Students:* 185 full-time (112 women), 49 part-time (28 women). Average age 37. 91 applicants, 76 enrolled. In 2006, 58 master's, 17 doctorates awarded. Terminal master's awarded for partial completion of doctoral program. *Degree requirements:* For master's, comprehensive exam; for doctorate, thesis/dissertation, preliminary and final dissertation defense, comprehensive exam. *Entrance requirements:* For master's, minimum GPA of 3.0 in final 2 years of course work, 3 letters of recommendation, resumé; for doctorate, minimum GPA of 3.0 in graduate study, 3 letters of recommendation, resumé. Additional exam requirements/recommendations for international students: Required—TOEFL. *Application deadline:* Applications are processed on a rolling basis. Application fee: $50. Electronic applications accepted. *Financial support:* Federal Work-Study and scholarships/grants available. Support available to part-time students. Financial award applicants required to submit FAFSA. *Faculty research:* Educational leadership, higher education, qualitative research, K-12 education, multicultural education. *Unit head:* Dr. Christine Zeppos, Dean, 800-7196-9598, Fax: 714-437-1287, E-mail: czeppos@argosy.edu. *Application contact:* Mark Betz, Director of Admissions, 800-716-9598, Fax: 714-437-1697, E-mail: mbetz@argosy.edu.

See Close-Up on page 833.

Argosy University, Phoenix Campus, College of Education, Phoenix, AZ 85021. Offers community college executive leadership (Ed D); educational leadership (MA Ed, Ed D, Ed S), including higher education administration (Ed D), K-12 education (Ed D); instructional leadership (MA Ed, Ed D, Ed S), including higher education (Ed D), K-12 education (Ed D). Part-time and evening/weekend programs available. *Faculty:* 13 part-time/adjunct (4 women). *Students:* 26 full-time (17 women), 2 part-time (1 woman); includes 3 minority (2 African Americans, 1 Hispanic American). Average age 44. 10 applicants, 100% accepted, 9 enrolled. *Entrance requirements:* For doctorate, minimum GPA of 3.0, master's degree. Additional exam requirements/recommendations for international students: Required—TOEFL (minimum score 550 paper-based; 213 computer-based). *Application deadline:* Applications are processed on a rolling basis. Application fee: $50. Electronic applications accepted. *Financial support:* Federal Work-Study available. Financial award applicants required to submit FAFSA. *Unit head:* Dr. Gayle Schou, Director, 866-216-2777, E-mail: argosyadmissions@argosy.edu. *Application contact:* Andy Hughes, Director of Admissions, 866-216-2777, Fax: 602-216-2601, E-mail: ahughes@argosy.edu.

See Close-Up on page 835.

Argosy University, San Diego Campus, College of Education, San Diego, CA 92108. Offers community college executive leadership (Ed D); educational leadership (MA Ed, Ed D), including higher education administration (Ed D), K-12 education (Ed D); instructional leadership (MA Ed, Ed D), including higher education (Ed D), K-12 education (Ed D), multiple subject teacher credential preparation (MA Ed), multiple subject teacher credential preparation with BCLAD (MA Ed), single subject teacher credential preparation (MA Ed), single subject teacher credential preparation with BCLAD (MA Ed).

See Close-Up on page 837.

Argosy University, San Francisco Bay Area Campus, College of Education, Point Richmond, CA 94804-3547. Offers community college executive leadership (Ed D); educational leadership (MA Ed, Ed D), including higher education administration (Ed D), K–12 education (Ed D); instructional leadership (MA Ed, Ed D), including higher education (Ed D), K–12 education (Ed D), multiple subject teacher credential preparation (MA Ed), multiple subject teacher credential preparation with BCLAD (MA Ed), single subject teacher credential preparation (MA Ed), single subject teacher credential preparation with BCLAD (MA Ed). Part-time and evening/weekend programs available. Postbaccalaureate distance learning degree programs offered (minimal on-campus study). *Faculty:* 1 (woman) full-time, 14 part-time/adjunct. *Students:* 59 full-time (41 women), 30 part-time (14 women); includes 26 minority (11 African Americans, 11 Asian Americans or Pacific Islanders, 4 Hispanic Americans), 1 international. 34 applicants, 82% accepted, 20 enrolled. In 2006, 7 degrees awarded. *Degree requirements:* For master's, capstone project; for doctorate, thesis/dissertation, comprehensive exam, registration. *Entrance requirements:* For master's and doctorate, minimum GPA of 3.0. Additional exam requirements/recommendations for international students: Required—TOEFL (minimum score 550 paper-based; 213 computer-based). *Application deadline:* For fall admission, 7/1 priority date for domestic students, 7/1 for international students; for winter admission, 11/1 priority date for domestic and international students; for spring admission, 4/1 priority date for domestic and international students. Applications are processed on a rolling basis. Application fee: $50. Electronic applications accepted. *Financial support:* Career-related internships or fieldwork, Federal Work-Study, and scholarships/grants available. Support available to part-time students. Financial award application deadline: 4/20; financial award applicants required to submit FAFSA. *Unit head:* Dr. Keyes Kelly, 510-837-3740, E-mail: kkelly@argosy.edu. *Application contact:* John Vincent Stofan, Director, Admissions, 510-215-0277, Fax: 510-215-0299, E-mail: jstofan@argosy.edu.

See Close-Up on page 839.

Argosy University, Santa Monica Campus, College of Education, Santa Monica, CA 90405. Offers community college executive leadership (Ed D); educational leadership (MA Ed, Ed D), including higher education administration (Ed D), K-12 education (Ed D); instructional leadership (MA Ed, Ed D), including higher education (Ed D), K-12 education (Ed D), multiple subject teacher credential preparation (MA Ed), multiple subject teacher credential preparation with BCLAD (MA Ed), single subject teacher credential preparation (MA Ed), single subject teacher credential preparation with BCLAD (MA Ed).

See Close-Up on page 841.

Argosy University, Schaumburg Campus, College of Education, Schaumburg, IL 60173-5403. Offers community college executive leadership (Ed D); educational leadership (MA Ed, Ed D, Ed S), including administrative certification (MA Ed), higher education administration (Ed D), K-12 education (Ed D), principal/general (MA Ed), superintendent certification (Ed S); instructional leadership (MA Ed, Ed D, Ed S), including higher education (Ed D), K-12 education (Ed D). Part-time and evening/weekend programs available. *Faculty:* 1 (woman) full-time, 7 part-time/adjunct (3 women). *Students:* 19 full-time, 19 part-time. 15 applicants, 80% accepted, 10 enrolled. In 2006, 1 master's, 3 doctorates, 2 other advanced degrees awarded. *Degree requirements:* For doctorate, thesis/dissertation, comprehensive exam. *Entrance requirements:* For master's and doctorate, minimum GPA of 3.0. Additional exam requirements/recommendations for international students: Required—TOEFL. *Application deadline:* For fall admission, 3/15 priority date for domestic and international students; for spring admission, 10/15 priority date for domestic and international students. Applications are processed on a rolling basis. Application fee: $50. Electronic applications accepted. *Expenses:* Contact institution. *Financial support:* Federal Work-Study and scholarships/grants available. *Unit head:* Dr. Narjis Hyder, Program Chair, 866-290-7400, Fax: 847-598-6158, E-mail: nhyder@argosy.edu. *Application contact:* Jamal Scott, Application Contact, 866-290-7400, Fax: 630-598-6191, E-mail: jscott@argosy.edu.

See Close-Up on page 845.

Argosy University, Seattle Campus, College of Education, Seattle, WA 98121. Offers community college executive leadership (Ed D); education (MA Ed); educational leadership (MA Ed, Ed D), including higher education administration (Ed D), K-12 education (Ed D); instructional leadership (MA Ed, Ed D), including education technology (Ed D), higher education (Ed D), K-12 education (Ed D). Part-time and evening/weekend programs available. *Students:* 29 full-time, 15 part-time. *Degree requirements:* For master's, thesis or alternative, capstone project; for doctorate, thesis/dissertation, comprehensive exam, registration. *Entrance requirements:* For master's, minimum GPA of 3.0 in last 60 hours of course work or minimum cumulative GPA of 2.7; for doctorate, minimum GPA of 3.0. Additional exam requirements/recommendations for international students: Required—TOEFL (minimum score 550 paper-based; 213 computer-based). *Application deadline:* For fall admission, 4/15 priority date for domestic students, 4/15 for international students. Application fee: $50. *Expenses:* Contact institution. *Financial support:* Teaching assistantships with partial tuition reimbursements, Federal Work-Study, scholarships/grants, and unspecified assistantships available. Support available to part-time students. Financial award application deadline: 4/19; financial award applicants required to submit FAFSA. *Unit head:* Dr. Leslie Aune Oja, Chair of Education, 206-393-3570, Fax: 206-283-5777, E-mail: ioja@argosy.edu. *Application contact:* Josh Pond, Director of Admissions, 206-283-4500, Fax: 206-283-5777, E-mail: jpond@argosyu.edu.

See Close-Up on page 847.

Argosy University, Tampa Campus, College of Education, Tampa, FL 33614. Offers community college executive leadership (Ed D); educational leadership (MA Ed, Ed D, Ed S), including higher education administration (Ed D), K-12 education (Ed D); instructional leadership (MA Ed, Ed D, Ed S), including higher education (Ed D), K-12 education (Ed D). *Faculty:* 1 (woman) full-time, 8 part-time/adjunct (3 women). *Degree requirements:* For master's, capstone project; for doctorate, thesis/dissertation. *Entrance requirements:* For master's, minimum GPA of 3.0 in last 2 years of undergraduate course work, resumé, 3 letters of recommendation; for doctorate, minimum GPA of 3.0, 3 letters of recommendation, resumé. Additional exam requirements/recommendations for international students: Required—TOEFL (minimum score 550 paper-based; 213 computer-based). *Application deadline:* Applications are processed on a rolling basis. Application fee: $50. Electronic applications accepted. *Faculty research:* Reading methods, elementary education, educational leadership, instructional design and instructional technology. *Unit head:* Dr. Patty O'Grady, Head, 813-246-4419, Fax: 813-246-4045, E-mail: pogrady@argosy.edu.

See Close-Up on page 849.

Arkansas State University, Graduate School, College of Education, Department of Educational Leadership, Curriculum, and Special Education, Jonesboro, State University, AR 72467. Offers community college administration education (SCCT); education theory and practice (MSE); educational leadership (MSE, Ed D, Ed S), including curriculum and instruction (Ed S), elementary curriculum and instruction (MSE), elementary principalship (Ed S), secondary principalship (Ed S), superintendency (Ed S); special education (MSE), including emotionally disturbed, gifted, talented and creative, instructional specialist 4-12, instructional specialist P-4; special education program administration (Ed S). *Accreditation:* NCATE. Part-time programs available. *Faculty:* 14 full-time (7 women), 5 part-time/adjunct (2 women). *Students:* 28 full-time (21 women), 328 part-time (233 women); includes 63 minority (58 African Americans, 3 American Indian/Alaska Native, 1 Asian American or Pacific Islander, 1 Hispanic American), 2 international. Average age 36. 181 applicants, 78% accepted, 70 enrolled. In 2006, 70 master's, 13 doctorates, 14 other advanced degrees awarded. *Degree requirements:* For master's, thesis or alternative, comprehensive exam; for doctorate, thesis/dissertation, comprehensive exam. *Entrance requirements:* For master's, GRE General Test or MAT, appropriate bachelor's degree, letters of reference, interview, official transcript; for doctorate and other advanced degree, GRE General Test or MAT, interview, master's degree, letters of reference, official transcript. Additional exam requirements/recommendations for international students: Required—TOEFL (minimum score 213 computer-based). *Application deadline:* Applications are processed on a rolling basis. Application fee: $30 ($40 for international students). Electronic applications accepted. *Expenses:* Tuition, state resident: full-time $3,393; part-time $189 per hour. Tuition, nonresident: full-time $8,577; part-time $477 per hour. Required fees: $752; $39 per hour. $25 per semester. *Financial support:* Teaching assistantships, career-related internships or fieldwork, scholarships/grants, and unspecified assistantships available. Financial award application deadline: 7/1; financial award applicants required to submit FAFSA. *Unit head:* Dr. Mitchell Holifield, Chair, 870-972-3062, Fax: 870-680-8130, E-mail: hfield@astate.edu.

Eastern Washington University, Graduate Studies, College of Education and Human Development, Department of Education, Program in College Instruction, Cheney, WA 99004-2431. Offers MA, MS. *Accreditation:* NCATE. *Degree requirements:* For master's, internship. *Entrance requirements:* For master's, minimum GPA of 3.0.

George Mason University, College of Humanities and Social Sciences, The National Center for Community College Education, Fairfax, VA 22030. Offers DA Ed, Certificate. *Faculty:* 3 part-time/adjunct (2 women). *Students:* 4 full-time (3 women), 73 part-time (44 women);

includes 22 minority (14 African Americans, 5 Asian Americans or Pacific Islanders, 3 Hispanic Americans). Average age 48. 18 applicants, 67% accepted, 6 enrolled. In 2006, 8 doctorates, 3 other advanced degrees awarded. *Degree requirements:* For doctorate, thesis/dissertation, final project, internship, comprehensive exam. *Entrance requirements:* For doctorate, GRE or MAT, appropriate master's degree, interview. *Application deadline:* For fall admission, 5/1 for domestic students; for spring admission, 11/1 for domestic students. Application fee: $60 ($75 for international students). Electronic applications accepted. *Expenses:* Tuition, state resident: full-time $5,724; part-time $238 per credit. Tuition, nonresident: full-time $16,896; part-time $704 per credit. Required fees: $1,656; $69 per credit. *Financial support:* Fellowships available. Support available to part-time students. Financial award application deadline: 3/1; financial award applicants required to submit FAFSA. *Unit head:* Nance Lucas, Interim Director, 703-993-2310, Fax: 703-993-2307.

Morgan State University, School of Graduate Studies, School of Education and Urban Studies, Program in Higher Education-Community College Leadership, Baltimore, MD 21251. Offers Ed D. *Accreditation:* NCATE. Part-time and evening/weekend programs available. *Faculty:* 5 full-time (1 woman), 4 part-time/adjunct (1 woman). *Students:* 45. Average age 40. 29 applicants, 28% accepted. In 2006, 6 degrees awarded. *Degree requirements:* For doctorate, thesis/dissertation, comprehensive exam. *Entrance requirements:* For doctorate, GRE General Test or MAT. Additional exam requirements/recommendations for international students: Required—TOEFL (minimum score 550 paper-based; 213 computer-based). *Application deadline:* For fall admission, 2/1 priority date for domestic students; for spring admission, 10/1 priority date for domestic students. Applications are processed on a rolling basis. Application fee: $0. *Expenses:* Tuition, state resident: part-time $272 per credit. Tuition, nonresident: part-time $478 per credit. Required fees: $38 per credit. *Financial support:* Fellowships, research assistantships, teaching assistantships, career-related internships or fieldwork, Federal Work-Study, institutionally sponsored loans, scholarships/grants, health care benefits, and unspecified assistantships available. Support available to part-time students. Financial award application deadline: 2/1. *Faculty research:* Multicultural education, cooperative learning, psychology of cognition. *Unit head:* Dr. Christine Johnson McPhail, Coordinator, 443-885-1983. *Application contact:* Dr. Maurice C. Taylor, Dean, 443-885-3185, Fax: 443-885-8226, E-mail: mctaylor@moac.morgan.edu.

North Carolina State University, Graduate School, College of Education, Department of Adult and Community College Education, Program in Adult and Community College Education, Raleigh, NC 27695. Offers M Ed, MS, Ed D. *Degree requirements:* For master's, thesis (for some programs); for doctorate, thesis/dissertation. *Entrance requirements:* For master's and doctorate, GRE or MAT. Electronic applications accepted.

Northern Arizona University, Graduate College, College of Education, Program in Educational Leadership, Flagstaff, AZ 86011. Offers community college (M Ed); educational leadership (Ed D); school leadership (M Ed). Part-time programs available. *Degree requirements:* For master's, thesis optional; for doctorate, thesis/dissertation, comprehensive exam. *Faculty research:* Change processes, African education, law and education, program evaluation.

Old Dominion University, Darden College of Education, Program in Community College Leadership, Norfolk, VA 23529. Offers PhD. Part-time programs available. Postbaccalaureate distance learning degree programs offered (minimal on-campus study). *Faculty:* 3 full-time (2 women), 11 part-time/adjunct (2 women). *Students:* 4 full-time (3 women), 40 part-time (27 women); includes 3 minority (2 African Americans, 1 Hispanic American). Average age 46. 30 applicants, 60% accepted, 15 enrolled. *Median time to degree:* Doctorate–4 years part-time. *Degree requirements:* For doctorate, thesis/dissertation, internship, comprehensive exam, registration. *Entrance requirements:* For doctorate, GRE, master's degree, minimum GPA of 3.5, 3 letters of reference. Additional exam requirements/recommendations for international students: Required—TOEFL (minimum score 600 paper-based). *Application deadline:* For spring admission, 2/1 for domestic students, 2/1 priority date for international students. Application fee: $40. Electronic applications accepted. *Expenses:* Tuition, area resident: Part-time $285 per credit hour. Tuition, nonresident: part-time $715 per credit hour. Required fees: $94 per semester. *Financial support:* In 2006–07, 12 fellowships with full tuition reimbursements (averaging $2,500 per year), 1 research assistantship with full tuition reimbursement (averaging $18,000 per year) were awarded; career-related internships or fieldwork and unspecified assistantships also available. Financial award application deadline: 4/15. *Faculty research:* Legal issues, leadership, distance education. *Unit head:* Dr. Ted Raspiller, Graduate Program Director, 757-683-4344, Fax: 757-683-5756, E-mail: ccl@odu.edu.

Old Dominion University, Darden College of Education, Programs in Occupational and Technical Studies, Norfolk, VA 23529. Offers business and industry training (MS); career and technical education (PhD); community college teaching (MS); human resources training (PhD); middle and secondary teaching (MS); technology education (PhD). *Accreditation:* NCATE (one or more programs are accredited). Part-time and evening/weekend programs available. Postbaccalaureate distance learning degree programs offered (minimal on-campus study). *Faculty:* 7 full-time (1 woman), 5 part-time/adjunct (2 women). *Students:* 15 full-time (11 women), 68 part-time (39 women); includes 13 minority (9 African Americans, 2 American Indian/Alaska Native, 2 Asian Americans or Pacific Islanders), 1 international. Average age 39. 44 applicants, 95% accepted, 37 enrolled. In 2006, 29 degrees awarded. *Degree requirements:* For master's, writing exam, candidacy exam, thesis optional; for doctorate, thesis/dissertation, writing exam, candidacy exam, comprehensive exam, registration. *Entrance requirements:* For master's, GRE General Test or MAT, minimum GPA of 2.8; for doctorate, GRE, minimum GPA of 3.0, 3 letters of reference. Additional exam requirements/recommendations for international students: Required—TOEFL. *Application deadline:* For fall admission, 6/1 priority date for domestic students, 6/1 for international students; for winter admission, 11/1 priority date for domestic students, 11/1 for international students; for spring admission, 3/1 priority date for domestic students, 3/1 for international students. Applications are processed on a rolling basis. Application fee: $40. Electronic applications accepted. *Expenses:* Tuition, area resident: Part-time $285 per credit hour. Tuition, nonresident: part-time $715 per credit hour. Required fees: $94 per semester. *Financial support:* In 2006–07, 19 students received support, including 1 fellowship with full tuition reimbursement available (averaging $15,000 per year), 2 research assistantships with partial tuition reimbursements available (averaging $9,000 per year), 5 teaching assistantships with partial tuition reimbursements available (averaging $12,600 per year); career-related internships or fieldwork, scholarships/grants, tuition waivers (partial), and unspecified assistantships also available. Support available to part-time students. Financial award application deadline: 2/15; financial award applicants required to submit FAFSA. *Faculty research:* Training and development, marketing, technology, special populations, support of academic subjects. Total annual research expenditures: $799,773. *Unit head:* Dr. John M. Ritz, Graduate Program Director, 757-683-4305, Fax: 757-683-5227, E-mail: otsgpd@odu.edu.

Pittsburg State University, Graduate School, College of Education, Department of Special Services and Leadership Studies, Program in Community College and Higher Education, Pittsburg, KS 66762. Offers Ed S. *Accreditation:* NCATE. *Students:* 4. Application fee: $35 ($60 for international students). *Expenses:* Tuition, state resident: full-time $2,144; part-time $181 per credit hour. Tuition, nonresident: full-time $5,273; part-time $442 per credit hour. Tuition and fees vary according to course load and campus/location. *Financial support:* Teaching assistantships, career-related internships or fieldwork and Federal Work-Study available. *Application contact:* Jamie Vanderbeck, Assistant Director, 620-235-4223, Fax: 620-235-4219, E-mail: jvanderb@pittstate.edu.

Princeton University, Graduate School, Department of History, Princeton, NJ 08544-1019. Offers community college history teaching (PhD); history (PhD); history of science (PhD). *Degree requirements:* For doctorate, variable foreign language requirement, thesis/dissertation, comprehensive exam. *Entrance requirements:* For doctorate, GRE General Test, sample of written work. Additional exam requirements/recommendations for international students: Required—TOEFL (minimum score 600 paper-based; 250 computer-based). Electronic applications accepted. *Faculty research:* World comparative, Europe-early modern, modern, late antique, medieval.

University of Central Florida, College of Education, Department of Educational Studies, Orlando, FL 32816. Offers community college education (Certificate); educational studies (M Ed, MA, Ed D, Ed S). *Accreditation:* NCATE. Part-time and evening/weekend programs available. *Faculty:* 23 full-time (14 women), 11 part-time/adjunct (8 women). *Students:* 57 full-time (44 women), 155 part-time (121 women); includes 46 minority (22 African Americans, 1 American Indian/Alaska Native, 3 Asian Americans or Pacific Islanders, 20 Hispanic Americans), 6 international. 43 applicants, 91% accepted, 21 enrolled. In 2006, 7 master's, 18 doctorates, 39 Ed Ss awarded. *Degree requirements:* For other advanced degree, thesis or alternative, final exam. *Entrance requirements:* For degree, GRE General Test, minimum GPA of 3.0, resumé. Additional exam requirements/recommendations for international students: Required—TOEFL. *Application deadline:* For fall admission, 2/20 for domestic students; for spring admission, 9/20 for domestic students. Application fee: $30. Electronic applications accepted. *Expenses:* Tuition, state resident: full-time $6,167; part-time $257 per credit hour. Tuition, nonresident: full-time $22,790; part-time $950 per credit hour. *Financial support:* In 2006–07, 2 fellowships with partial tuition reimbursements (averaging $3,800 per year), 5 research assistantships with partial tuition reimbursements (averaging $7,600 per year), 1 teaching assistantship with partial tuition reimbursement (averaging $8,000 per year) were awarded; career-related internships or fieldwork, Federal Work-Study, institutionally sponsored loans, and unspecified assistantships also available. Financial award application deadline: 3/1; financial award applicants required to submit FAFSA. *Unit head:* Dr. Karen Biraimah, Chair, 407-823-2428, E-mail: biraimah@mail.ucf.edu.

University of South Florida, Graduate School, College of Education, Department of Adult, Career and Higher Education, Tampa, FL 33620-9951. Offers adult education (MA, Ed D, PhD, Ed S); career and technical education (MA); higher education/community college teaching (MA, PhD, Ed S); industrial-technical education (MA); vocational education (Ed D, PhD, Ed S). *Faculty:* 11 full-time (5 women), 2 part-time/adjunct (0 women). *Students:* 30 full-time (23 women), 176 part-time (121 women); includes 52 minority (32 African Americans, 1 American Indian/Alaska Native, 1 Asian American or Pacific Islander, 18 Hispanic Americans), 4 international. 104 applicants, 71% accepted, 55 enrolled. In 2006, 56 master's, 5 doctorates awarded. *Entrance requirements:* For master's, GRE General Test, minimum GPA of 3.0 in last 60 hours. *Application deadline:* For fall admission, 6/1 for domestic students; for spring admission, 10/15 for domestic students. Application fee: $30. *Financial support:* Career-related internships or fieldwork, scholarships/grants, and unspecified assistantships available. Total annual research expenditures: $191,880. *Unit head:* Robert Sullins, Interim Dean, E-mail: rsullins@ugs.usf.edu.

Western Carolina University, Graduate School, College of Education and Allied Professions, Department of Educational Leadership and Foundations, Program in Community College Education, Cullowhee, NC 28723. Offers MA Ed. *Accreditation:* NCATE. Part-time and evening/weekend programs available. *Degree requirements:* For master's, comprehensive exam. *Entrance requirements:* For master's, GRE General Test. Additional exam requirements/recommendations for international students: Required—TOEFL (minimum score 550 paper-based; 213 computer-based).

Early Childhood Education

Adelphi University, School of Education, Program in Early Childhood Education, Garden City, NY 11530-0701. Offers early childhood education (Certificate); in-service (MA); pre-certification (MA). *Students:* 1 (woman) full-time, 47 part-time (46 women); includes 5 minority (all African Americans) Average age 33. In 2006, 9 master's, 1 other advanced degree awarded. *Entrance requirements:* For master's, 2 letters of recommendation, resumé; for Certificate, 2 letters of recommendation, resumé, 6 credits in literacy. Additional exam requirements/recommendations for international students: Required—TOEFL (minimum score 550 paper-based; 213 computer-based). *Application deadline:* For fall admission, 4/1 for domestic students; for spring admission, 11/1 for domestic students. Application fee: $50. Electronic applications accepted. *Faculty research:* Gifted education; impact of family, culture and school in child development; teacher training; assessment of young children; classrooms as respectful communities. *Unit head:* Dr. Esther Kogan, Director, 516-877-4474, E-mail: kogan@adelphi.edu. *Application contact:* Christine Murphy, Director of Admissions, 516-877-3050, Fax: 516-877-3039, E-mail: graduateadmissions@adelphi.edu.

Adelphi University, School of Education, Program in Early Childhood Special Education, Garden City, NY 11530-0701. Offers birth through grade 2 (Certificate); in-service (MS); preservice (MS). *Students:* 12 full-time (all women), 45 part-time (44 women); includes 4 minority (1 African American, 3 Hispanic Americans). Average age 31. In 2006, 4 degrees awarded. *Entrance requirements:* For master's, 2 letters of recommendation, resumé, detailing paid/volunteer experience and organizational membership. Additional exam requirements/recommendations for international students: Required—TOEFL (minimum score 550 paper-based; 213 computer-based). *Application deadline:* For fall admission, 4/1 for domestic students; for spring admission, 11/1 for domestic students. Application fee: $50. *Faculty research:* Personnel preparation for: early intervention, early childhood special education teachers preparing to be interventionists for infants and young children with disabilities. *Unit head:* Dr. Crystal Kaiser, Director, 516-877-4064, E-mail: kaiser@adelphi.edu. *Application contact:* Christine Murphy, Director of Admissions, 516-877-3050, Fax: 516-877-3039, E-mail: graduateadmissions@adelphi.edu.

Alabama Agricultural and Mechanical University, School of Graduate Studies, School of Education, Department of Curriculum and Instruction, Area in Elementary and Early Childhood Education, Huntsville, AL 35811. Offers early childhood education (MS Ed, Ed S); elementary education (MS Ed, Ed S). *Accreditation:* NCATE. Evening/weekend programs available. *Faculty:* 3 full-time (all women), 3 part-time/adjunct (all women). *Students:* 4 full-time (all women), 18 part-time (all women); includes 12 minority (all African Americans) In 2006, 35 degrees awarded. *Degree requirements:* For master's, comprehensive exam; for Ed S, thesis. *Entrance requirements:* For master's, GRE General Test. *Application deadline:* For fall admission, 5/1 for domestic students. Applications are processed on a rolling basis. Application fee: $25. Electronic applications accepted. *Financial support:* In 2006–07, 2 research assistantships with tuition reimbursements (averaging $5,300 per year) were awarded; career-related internships or fieldwork also available. Financial award application deadline: 4/1. *Faculty research:* Multicultural education, learning styles, diagnostic-prescriptive instruction. *Unit head:* Dr. June Young, Head, 256-372-7272.

Alabama State University, School of Graduate Studies, College of Education, Department of Curriculum and Instruction, Program in Early Childhood Education, Montgomery, AL 36101-

Early Childhood Education

Alabama State University (continued)

0271. Offers M Ed, Ed S. Part-time programs available. *Faculty:* 3 full-time (2 women). *Students:* 9 full-time (all women), 80 part-time (77 women); includes 51 minority (all African Americans), 1 international. In 2006, 15 master's, 1 other advanced degree awarded. *Degree requirements:* For master's, comprehensive exam; for Ed S, thesis, comprehensive exam. *Entrance requirements:* For master's, GRE General Test, MAT or NTE, graduate writing competency test; for Ed S, graduate writing competency test, GRE, MAT. Additional exam requirements/recommendations for international students: Required—TOEFL (minimum score 500 paper-based; 173 computer-based). *Application deadline:* For fall admission, 7/15 for domestic students; for spring admission, 12/15 for domestic students. Applications are processed on a rolling basis. Application fee: $10. *Expenses:* Tuition, state resident: full-time $1,728; part-time $192 per hour. Tuition, nonresident: full-time $3,456; part-time $334 per hour. *Unit head:* Dr. Kathleen Tyler, Coordinator, 334-229-4268.

Albany State University, College of Education, Program in Early Childhood Education, Albany, GA 31705-2717. Offers M Ed. *Accreditation:* NCATE. Part-time programs available. *Degree requirements:* For master's, comprehensive exam. *Entrance requirements:* For master's, GRE General Test, MAT or NTE. Electronic applications accepted.

Albright College, Department of Education—Graduate Division, Reading, PA 19612-5234. Offers early childhood education (MS); elementary education (MS); English as a second language (MA); general education (MA); special education (MS). Part-time and evening/weekend programs available. *Degree requirements:* For master's, thesis. *Entrance requirements:* For master's, GRE General Test or MAT, minimum undergraduate GPA of 3.0, 2 letters of recommendation, interview. Additional exam requirements/recommendations for international students: Recommended—TOEFL (minimum score 525 paper-based; 197 computer-based). Electronic applications accepted.

Anna Maria College, Graduate Division, Program in Education, Paxton, MA 01612. Offers early childhood development (M Ed); education (CAGS); elementary education (M Ed); reading (M Ed). Part-time and evening/weekend programs available. *Faculty:* 6 full-time (5 women), 16 part-time/adjunct (15 women). *Students:* 13 full-time (all women), 84 part-time (82 women); includes 1 minority (Hispanic American) Average age 34. In 2006, 30 master's, 2 other advanced degrees awarded. *Degree requirements:* For master's, action research project. *Entrance requirements:* For master's, bachelor's degree in liberal arts or sciences, minimum GPA of 3.0. *Application deadline:* For fall admission, 3/1 priority date for domestic and international students; for spring admission, 11/1 priority date for domestic and international students. Applications are processed on a rolling basis. Application fee: $40. Electronic applications accepted. *Financial support:* Applicants required to submit FAFSA. *Unit head:* Christine Holmes, Director, 508-849-3418, Fax: 508-849-3343, E-mail: cholmes@annamaria.edu. *Application contact:* Janet LaPointe, Admissions Coordinator, Graduate and Continuing Education, 508-849-3234, Fax: 508-819-3362, E-mail: jlapointe@annamaria.edu.

Arcadia University, Graduate Studies, Department of Education, Glenside, PA 19038-3295. Offers art education (M Ed, MA Ed); biology education (MA Ed); chemistry education (MA Ed); child development (CAS); computer education (M Ed, CAS); computer education 7–12 (MA Ed); early childhood education (M Ed, CAS), including individualized (M Ed), master teacher (M Ed), research in child development (M Ed); educational leadership (M Ed, CAS); educational psychology (CAS); elementary education (M Ed, CAS); English education (MA Ed); environmental education (MA Ed, CAS); history education (MA Ed); language arts (M Ed, CAS); mathematics education (M Ed, MA Ed, CAS); music education (MA Ed); psychology (MA Ed); pupil personnel services (CAS); reading (M Ed, CAS); school library science (M Ed); science education (M Ed, CAS); secondary education (M Ed, CAS); special education (M Ed, Ed D, CAS); theater arts (MA Ed); written communication (MA Ed). *Accreditation:* NASAD. Part-time and evening/weekend programs available. Postbaccalaureate distance learning degree programs offered (minimal on-campus study). *Faculty:* 12 full-time (8 women), 38 part-time/adjunct (26 women). *Students:* 60 full-time (56 women), 419 part-time (324 women); includes 70 minority (57 African Americans, 1 American Indian/Alaska Native, 6 Asian Americans or Pacific Islanders, 6 Hispanic Americans), 1 international. In 2006, 257 master's, 4 doctorates awarded. *Application deadline:* Applications are processed on a rolling basis. Application fee: $35. Electronic applications accepted. *Financial support:* Career-related internships or fieldwork, tuition waivers (partial), and unspecified assistantships available. *Unit head:* Dr. Steven P. Gulkus, Chair, 215-572-2120. *Application contact:* 215-572-2925, Fax: 215-572-2126, E-mail: grad@arcadia.edu.

Arkansas State University, Graduate School, College of Education, Department of Teacher Education, Jonesboro, State University, AR 72467. Offers early childhood education (MSE); early childhood services (MS); elementary education (MSE); reading (MSE, SCCT). *Accreditation:* NCATE. Part-time programs available. *Faculty:* 6 full-time (3 women). *Students:* 2 full-time (both women), 30 part-time (29 women); includes 3 minority (2 African Americans, 1 Asian American or Pacific Islander). Average age 32. 22 applicants, 82% accepted, 12 enrolled. In 2006, 35 degrees awarded. *Degree requirements:* For master's, thesis or alternative, comprehensive exam. *Entrance requirements:* For master's, GRE General Test or MAT, appropriate bachelor's degree, official transcript; for SCCT, GRE General Test or MAT, interview, master's degree, official transcript. Additional exam requirements/recommendations for international students: Required—TOEFL (minimum score 213 computer-based). *Application deadline:* Applications are processed on a rolling basis. Application fee: $30 ($40 for international students). Electronic applications accepted. *Expenses:* Tuition, state resident: full-time $3,393; part-time $189 per hour. Tuition, nonresident: full-time $8,577; part-time $477 per hour. Required fees: $752; $39 per hour. $25 per semester. *Financial support:* Teaching assistantships, career-related internships or fieldwork, scholarships/grants, and unspecified assistantships available. Financial award application deadline: 7/1; financial award applicants required to submit FAFSA. *Unit head:* Dr. Dianne Lawler-Prince, Interim Chair, 870-972-3059, Fax: 870-972-3344, E-mail: dprince@astate.edu.

Armstrong Atlantic State University, School of Graduate Studies, Program in Education, Savannah, GA 31419-1997. Offers adult education (M Ed); early childhood education (M Ed); education (M Ed); elementary education (M Ed); middle grades education (M Ed); secondary education (M Ed), including business education, English education, mathematics education, science education, social science education; special education (M Ed), including behavioral disorders, curriculum and instruction, learning disabilities, speech-language pathology. *Accreditation:* NCATE. Part-time and evening/weekend programs available. Postbaccalaureate distance learning degree programs offered (minimal on-campus study). *Faculty:* 11 full-time (9 women), 13 part-time/adjunct (10 women). *Students:* 50 full-time (42 women), 219 part-time (175 women); includes 71 minority (67 African Americans, 3 Asian Americans or Pacific Islanders, 1 Hispanic American), 6 international. Average age 35. In 2006, 151 degrees awarded. *Degree requirements:* For master's, portfolio. *Entrance requirements:* For master's, GRE General Test or MAT, minimum GPA of 2.5, letters of recommendation. Additional exam requirements/recommendations for international students: Required—TOEFL (minimum score 523 paper-based; 193 computer-based). *Application deadline:* For fall admission, 7/1 priority date for domestic and international students; for spring admission, 11/15 priority date for domestic and international students. Applications are processed on a rolling basis. Application fee: $25. Electronic applications accepted. *Expenses:* Tuition, state resident: full-time $2,286; part-time $127 per credit. Tuition, nonresident: full-time $9,144; part-time $508 per credit. One-time fee: $257. *Financial support:* In 2006–07, research assistantships with partial tuition reimbursements (averaging $2,500 per year); career-related internships or fieldwork, Federal Work-Study, scholarships/grants, and unspecified assistantships also available. Support available to part-time students. Financial award applicants required to submit FAFSA. *Unit head:* Dr. Jane McHaney, College of Education Dean, 912-927-5398, Fax: 912-921-7425, E-mail: mchaneia@mail.armstrong.edu.

Ashland University, College of Education, Graduate Studies in Education, Program in Early Childhood Education, Ashland, OH 44805-3702. Offers early childhood education (M Ed); early childhood intervention (M Ed). Part-time and evening/weekend programs available. *Faculty:* 4 full-time (3 women), 52 part-time/adjunct (45 women). *Students:* 6 full-time (all women), 17 part-time (all women). Average age 30. In 2006, 9 degrees awarded. *Degree requirements:* For master's, thesis or alternative. *Entrance requirements:* For master's, GRE General Test or MAT, teaching certificate, minimum GPA of 2.75. Additional exam requirements/recommendations for international students: Required—TOEFL. Application fee: $30. *Expenses:* Tuition: Part-time $403 per credit. Tuition and fees vary according to degree level and program. *Financial support:* In 2006–07, 11 students received support. Application deadline: 4/15. *Faculty research:* Child behavior, literary technology, teacher licensure exams. *Unit head:* Dr. Linda Billman, Chair, 419-289-5369, Fax: 419-207-6702, E-mail: lbillman@ashland.edu.

Auburn University, Graduate School, College of Education, Department of Curriculum and Teaching, Auburn University, AL 36849. Offers business education (M Ed, MS, PhD); early childhood education (M Ed, MS, PhD, Ed S); elementary education (M Ed, MS, PhD, Ed S); foreign languages (M Ed, MS); music education (M Ed, MS, PhD, Ed S); postsecondary education (PhD); reading education (PhD, Ed S); secondary education (M Ed, MS, PhD, Ed S), including English language arts, mathematics, science, social studies. *Accreditation:* NASM (one or more programs are accredited); NCATE. Part-time programs available. *Faculty:* 26 full-time (19 women). *Students:* 51 full-time (36 women), 116 part-time (86 women); includes 24 minority (23 African Americans, 1 Asian American or Pacific Islander). Average age 33. 181 applicants, 56% accepted, 68 enrolled. In 2006, 63 master's, 12 doctorates, 14 other advanced degrees awarded. *Degree requirements:* For master's, thesis (for some programs); for doctorate, thesis/dissertation; for Ed S, field project. *Entrance requirements:* For master's, doctorate, and Ed S, GRE General Test. *Application deadline:* For fall admission, 7/7 for domestic students; for spring admission, 11/24 for domestic students. Applications are processed on a rolling basis. Application fee: $25 ($50 for international students). Electronic applications accepted. *Expenses:* Tuition, state resident: full-time $5,000. Tuition, nonresident: full-time $15,000. Required fees: $416. Tuition and fees vary according to program. *Financial support:* Fellowships, teaching assistantships, career-related internships or fieldwork and Federal Work-Study available. Support available to part-time students. Financial award application deadline: 3/15. *Faculty research:* Emerging literacy, reading attitudes, music for at-risk youth, portfolio assessment. *Unit head:* Dr. Andrew M. Weaver, Head, 334-844-4434, E-mail: weaveam@mail.auburn.edu. *Application contact:* Dr. Joe Pittman, Interim Dean of the Graduate School, 334-844-4700.

Auburn University, Graduate School, College of Education, Department of Rehabilitation and Special Education, Auburn University, AL 36849. Offers collaborative teacher special education (M Ed, MS); early childhood special education (M Ed, MS); rehabilitation counseling (M Ed, MS, PhD). *Accreditation:* CORE; NCATE. Part-time programs available. *Faculty:* 12 full-time (6 women). *Students:* 85 full-time (68 women), 45 part-time (36 women); includes 30 minority (24 African Americans, 3 American Indian/Alaska Native, 2 Asian Americans or Pacific Islanders, 1 Hispanic American). Average age 32. 69 applicants, 77% accepted, 41 enrolled. In 2006, 64 master's, 1 doctorate awarded. *Degree requirements:* For master's, thesis (for some programs); for doctorate, thesis/dissertation. *Entrance requirements:* For master's, GRE General Test; for doctorate, GRE General Test, interview. *Application deadline:* For fall admission, 7/17 for domestic students; for spring admission, 11/24 for domestic students. Applications are processed on a rolling basis. Application fee: $25 ($50 for international students). Electronic applications accepted. *Expenses:* Tuition, state resident: full-time $5,000. Tuition, nonresident: full-time $15,000. Required fees: $416. Tuition and fees vary according to program. *Financial support:* Research assistantships, teaching assistantships, Federal Work-Study available. Support available to part-time students. Financial award application deadline: 3/15. *Faculty research:* Emotional conflict/behavior disorders, gifted and talented, learning disabilities, mental retardation, multi-handicapped. *Unit head:* Dr. Philip L. Browning, Head, 334-844-5943. *Application contact:* Dr. Joe Pittman, Interim Dean of the Graduate School, 334-844-4700.

Auburn University Montgomery, School of Education, Department of Early Childhood, Elementary, and Reading Education, Montgomery, AL 36124-4023. Offers early childhood education (M Ed, Ed S); elementary education (M Ed, Ed S); reading education (M Ed, Ed S). *Accreditation:* NCATE. Part-time and evening/weekend programs available. *Faculty:* 6 full-time (all women). *Students:* 38 full-time (32 women), 88 part-time (83 women); includes 47 minority (43 African Americans, 1 American Indian/Alaska Native, 2 Asian Americans or Pacific Islanders, 1 Hispanic American), 1 international. Average age 32. In 2006, 33 master's, 5 other advanced degrees awarded. *Degree requirements:* For master's and Ed S, comprehensive exam. *Entrance requirements:* For master's, GRE General Test or MAT, certification, BS in teaching; for Ed S, GRE General Test or MAT, certification. *Application deadline:* Applications are processed on a rolling basis. Application fee: $25. Electronic applications accepted. *Financial support:* In 2006–07, 1 teaching assistantship was awarded; career-related internships or fieldwork and scholarships/grants also available. Support available to part-time students. Financial award application deadline: 3/1; financial award applicants required to submit FAFSA. *Unit head:* Dr. Lynne Mills, Head, 334-244-3283, Fax: 334-244-3835, E-mail: lmills@mail.aum.edu.

Bank Street College of Education, Graduate School, Department of Curriculum and Instruction, Program in Bilingual Education, New York, NY 10025. Offers bilingual childhood special education (Ed M, MS Ed); bilingual early childhood education (MS Ed); bilingual early childhood special and general education (MS Ed); bilingual early childhood special education (Ed M, MS Ed); bilingual elementary/childhood general education (MS Ed); bilingual elementary/childhood special and general education (MS Ed); bilingual middle school general education (MS Ed); bilingual middle school special and general education (Ed M, MS Ed); bilingual middle school special education (MS Ed). *Accreditation:* NCATE. *Faculty:* 2 full-time (both women), 5 part-time/adjunct (all women). *Students:* 8 full-time (7 women), 22 part-time (19 women); includes 21 minority (2 African Americans, 2 Asian Americans or Pacific Islanders, 17 Hispanic Americans). Average age 27. 19 applicants, 68% accepted, 10 enrolled. In 2006, 8 degrees awarded. *Degree requirements:* For master's, thesis, registration. *Entrance requirements:* For master's, interview. Additional exam requirements/recommendations for international students: Required—TOEFL (minimum score 600 paper-based; 250 computer-based). *Application deadline:* For fall admission, 3/1 priority date for domestic students; for spring admission, 11/1 priority date for domestic students. Applications are processed on a rolling basis. Application fee: $50. *Expenses:* Tuition: Part-time $940 per credit. Required fees: $100 per term. *Financial support:* Career-related internships or fieldwork, Federal Work-Study, scholarships/grants, and unspecified assistantships available. Support available to part-time students. Financial award application deadline: 4/15; financial award applicants required to submit FAFSA. *Faculty research:* Dual language education, language immersion, bilingual education in the urban classroom, community and school partnerships. Total annual research expenditures: $58,717. *Unit head:* Dr. Olga Romero, Director, 212-875-4468, Fax: 212-875-4753, E-mail: olgar@bankstreet.edu. *Application contact:* Ann Morgan, Director of Graduate Admissions, 212-875-4403, Fax: 212-875-4678, E-mail: amorgan@bankstreet.edu.

Bank Street College of Education, Graduate School, Department of Curriculum and Instruction, Program in Early Childhood Education, New York, NY 10025. Offers MS Ed. *Accreditation:* NCATE. *Students:* 25 full-time (23 women), 59 part-time (57 women); includes 16 minority (9 African Americans, 4 Asian Americans or Pacific Islanders, 3 Hispanic Americans). Average age 31. 49 applicants, 86% accepted, 38 enrolled. In 2006, 32 degrees awarded. *Degree requirements:* For master's, thesis, registration. *Entrance requirements:* For master's, interview. Additional exam requirements/recommendations for international students: Required—TOEFL (minimum score 600 paper-based; 250 computer-based). *Application deadline:* For fall admission, 3/1 priority date for domestic students; for spring admission, 11/1 priority date for domestic students. Applications are processed on a rolling basis. Application fee: $50. *Expenses:* Tuition: Part-time $940 per credit. Required fees: $100 per term. *Financial support:* Career-related internships or fieldwork, Federal Work-Study, scholarships/grants, and unspecified assistantships available. Support available to part-time students. Financial award application deadline: 4/15; financial award applicants required to submit FAFSA. *Faculty research:* Play in early childhood settings, early childhood learning environments, family-teacher interaction, child-centered education. *Unit head:* Adrianne Kamsler, Chairperson, 212-875-4571, Fax: 212-875-4753, E-mail: akamsler@bankstreet.edu. *Application contact:* Ann Morgan, Director of Graduate Admissions, 212-875-4403, Fax: 212-875-4678, E-mail: amorgan@bankstreet.edu.

Bank Street College of Education, Graduate School, Department of Curriculum and Instruction, Program in Elementary/Childhood Education, New York, NY 10025. Offers early childhood and elementary/childhood education (MS Ed); elementary/childhood education (MS Ed). *Accreditation:* NCATE. *Students:* 49 full-time (42 women), 82 part-time (73 women); includes 19 minority (8 African Americans, 7 Asian Americans or Pacific Islanders, 4 Hispanic Americans). Average age 27. 102 applicants, 67% accepted, 60 enrolled. In 2006, 73 degrees awarded. *Degree requirements:* For master's, thesis. *Entrance requirements:* For master's, interview. Additional exam requirements/recommendations for international students: Required—TOEFL (minimum score 600 paper-based; 250 computer-based). *Application deadline:* For fall admission, 3/1 priority date for domestic students; for spring admission, 11/1 priority date for domestic students. Applications are processed on a rolling basis. Application fee: $50. *Expenses:* Tuition: Part-time $940 per credit. Required fees: $100 per term. *Financial support:* Career-related internships or fieldwork, Federal Work-Study, scholarships/grants, and unspecified assistantships available. Support available to part-time students. Financial award application deadline: 4/15; financial award applicants required to submit FAFSA. *Faculty research:* Social studies in the elementary grades, urban education, experiential learning, child centered classrooms. *Unit head:* Adrianne Kamsler, Chairperson, 212-875-4571, Fax: 212-875-4753, E-mail: akamsler@bankstreet.edu. *Application contact:* Ann Morgan, Director of Graduate Admissions, 212-875-4403, Fax: 212-875-4678, E-mail: amorgan@bankstreet.edu.

See Close-Up on page 857.

Bank Street College of Education, Graduate School, Department of Curriculum and Instruction, Program in Infant and Parent Development and Early Intervention, New York, NY 10025. Offers infant and parent development and early intervention (MS Ed); infant and parent development and early intervention/early childhood special and general education (MS Ed); infant and parent development and early intervention/early childhood special education (Ed M). *Accreditation:* NCATE. *Students:* 14 full-time (all women), 29 part-time (27 women); includes 10 minority (3 African Americans, 7 Hispanic Americans). Average age 31. 27 applicants, 63% accepted, 12 enrolled. In 2006, 7 degrees awarded. *Degree requirements:* For master's, thesis, registration. *Entrance requirements:* For master's, interview. Additional exam requirements/recommendations for international students: Required—TOEFL (minimum score 600 paper-based; 250 computer-based). *Application deadline:* For fall admission, 3/1 priority date for domestic students; for spring admission, 11/1 priority date for domestic students. Applications are processed on a rolling basis. Application fee: $50. *Expenses:* Tuition: Part-time $940 per credit. Required fees: $100 per term. *Financial support:* Career-related internships or fieldwork, Federal Work-Study, scholarships/grants, and unspecified assistantships available. Support available to part-time students. Financial award application deadline: 4/15; financial award applicants required to submit FAFSA. *Faculty research:* Early intervention, early attachment practice in infant and toddler childcare, parenting skills in adolescents. *Unit head:* Carla Poole, Director, 212-875-4523, Fax: 212-875-4753, E-mail: @bankstreet.edu. *Application contact:* Ann Morgan, Director of Graduate Admissions, 212-875-4403, Fax: 212-875-4678, E-mail: amorgan@bankstreet.edu.

Bank Street College of Education, Graduate School, Department of Curriculum and Instruction, Program in Special Education, New York, NY 10025. Offers early childhood special and general education (MS Ed); early childhood special education (Ed M, MS Ed); elementary/childhood special and general education (MS Ed); elementary/childhood special education (MS Ed); elementary/childhood special education certification (Ed M); middle school special and general education (MS Ed); middle school special education (Ed M). *Students:* 98 full-time (86 women), 167 part-time (162 women); includes 57 minority (17 African Americans, 10 Asian Americans or Pacific Islanders, 30 Hispanic Americans), 1 international. Average age 31. 147 applicants, 78% accepted, 80 enrolled. In 2006, 68 degrees awarded. *Degree requirements:* For master's, thesis, registration. *Entrance requirements:* For master's, interview. Additional exam requirements/recommendations for international students: Required—TOEFL (minimum score 600 paper-based; 250 computer-based). *Application deadline:* For fall admission, 3/1 priority date for domestic students; for spring admission, 11/1 priority date for domestic students. Applications are processed on a rolling basis. Application fee: $50. *Expenses:* Tuition: Part-time $940 per credit. Required fees: $100 per term. *Financial support:* Career-related internships or fieldwork available. Financial award application deadline: 3/1; financial award applicants required to submit FAFSA. *Faculty research:* Inclusion, observation and assessment, early intervention, neurodevelopmental assessment. *Unit head:* Dr. Andrea (Penny) Spencer, Chairperson, 212-875-4602, Fax: 212-875-4753, E-mail: aspencer@bankstreet.edu. *Application contact:* Ann Morgan, Director of Graduate Admissions, 212-875-4403, Fax: 212-875-4678, E-mail: amorgan@bankstreet.edu.

See Close-Up on page 857.

Bank Street College of Education, Graduate School, Department of Educational Leadership, New York, NY 10025. Offers early childhood leadership (MS Ed); educational leadership (MS Ed); leadership for educational change (Ed M, MS Ed); leadership in mathematics education (MS Ed); leadership in museum education (MS Ed); leadership in the arts (MS Ed). *Students:* 59 full-time (35 women), 137 part-time (100 women); includes 75 minority (31 African Americans, 1 American Indian/Alaska Native, 10 Asian Americans or Pacific Islanders, 33 Hispanic Americans), 5 international. Average age 36. 107 applicants, 89% accepted, 89 enrolled. In 2006, 88 degrees awarded. *Degree requirements:* For master's, thesis, registration. *Entrance requirements:* For master's, interview, minimum of 2 years experience in the classroom. Additional exam requirements/recommendations for international students: Required—TOEFL (minimum score 600 paper-based; 250 computer-based). *Application deadline:* For fall admission, 3/1 priority date for domestic students; for spring admission, 11/1 priority date for domestic students. Applications are processed on a rolling basis. Application fee: $50. *Expenses:* Tuition: Part-time $940 per credit. Required fees: $100 per term. *Financial support:* Career-related internships or fieldwork, Federal Work-Study, scholarships/grants, and unspecified assistantships available. Support available to part-time students. Financial award application deadline: 4/15; financial award applicants required to submit FAFSA. *Faculty research:* Leadership in small schools, mathematics education in elementary schools, professional development in early childhood, leadership in arts education, leadership in special education. *Unit head:* Dr. Rima Shore, Chairperson, 212-875-4478, Fax: 212-875-8753, E-mail: rshore@bankstreet.edu. *Application contact:* Ann Morgan, Director of Graduate Admissions, 212-875-4403, Fax: 212-875-4678, E-mail: amorgan@bankstreet.edu.

Barry University, School of Education, Program in Curriculum and Instruction, Miami Shores, FL 33161-6695. Offers accomplished teacher (Ed S); culture, language and literacy (TESOL) (PhD); curriculum evaluation and research (PhD); early childhood (Ed S); early childhood education (PhD); elementary (Ed S); elementary education (PhD); ESOL (Ed S); gifted (Ed S); Montessori (Ed S); PKP/elementary (Ed S); reading (Ed S); reading, language and cognition (PhD). *Students:* 2 full-time (both women), 36 part-time (27 women); includes 21 minority (12 African Americans, 9 Hispanic Americans), 6 international. 45 applicants, 33% accepted, 4 enrolled. In 2006, 4 degrees awarded. *Entrance requirements:* For doctorate, GRE, minimum GPA of 3.25. Application fee: $30. *Unit head:* Dr. Jill Farrell, Director, 305-899-3198, Fax: 305-899-4708, E-mail: jfarrell@mail.barry.edu. *Application contact:* Dave Fletcher, Director of Graduate Admissions, 305-899-3113, Fax: 305-899-2971, E-mail: dfletcher@mail.barry.edu.

Barry University, School of Education, Program in Pre-Kindergarten and Primary Education, Miami Shores, FL 33161-6695. Offers pre-k/primary (MS); pre-k/primary/ESOL (MS). Part-time and evening/weekend programs available. *Students:* 4 full-time (all women), 12 part-time (all women); includes 9 minority (3 African Americans, 6 Hispanic Americans), 1 international. 7 applicants, 86% accepted, 5 enrolled. In 2006, 14 degrees awarded. *Degree requirements:* For master's, practicum. *Entrance requirements:* For master's, GRE General Test or MAT, minimum GPA of 3.0. *Application deadline:* For fall admission, 5/1 priority date for domestic students. Applications are processed on a rolling basis. Application fee: $30. Electronic applications accepted. *Unit head:* Dr. Lilia DiBello, Director, 305-899-4827, Fax: 305-899-4708, E-mail: ldibello@mail.barry.edu. *Application contact:* Dave Fletcher, Director of Graduate Admissions, 305-899-3113, Fax: 305-899-2971, E-mail: dfletcher@mail.barry.edu.

Bayamón Central University, Graduate Programs, Program in Education, Bayamón, PR 00960-1725. Offers administration and supervision (MA Ed); commercial education (MA Ed); education of the autistic (MA Ed); elementary education (K–3) (MA Ed); elementary education (K–6) (MA Ed); elementary physical education (MA Ed); guidance and counseling (MA Ed); pre-elementary teacher (MA Ed); special education (MA Ed), including attention deficit disorder, learning disabilities. Part-time and evening/weekend programs available. *Degree requirements:* For master's, comprehensive exam. *Entrance requirements:* For master's, EXADEP, bachelor's degree in education or related field.

Bellarmine University, Annsley Frazier Thornton School of Education, Louisville, KY 40205-0671. Offers early elementary education (MA, MAT); instructional leadership and school administration/school principal (MA); learning and behavior disorders (MA); middle school education (MA, MAT); reading and writing endorsement (MA); secondary school education (MAT); Waldorf inspired curriculum (MA);). *Accreditation:* NCATE. Part-time and evening/weekend programs available. *Faculty:* 10 full-time (8 women), 5 part-time/adjunct (all women). *Students:* 92 full-time (68 women), 140 part-time (104 women); includes 16 minority (11 African Americans, 1 Asian American or Pacific Islander, 4 Hispanic Americans). Average age 32. In 2006, 98 degrees awarded. *Degree requirements:* For master's, thesis (for some programs), comprehensive exam. *Entrance requirements:* For master's, minimum overall GPA of 2.75, 3.0 in major; letters of recommendation; valid Kentucky provisional or professional certificate. Additional exam requirements/recommendations for international students: Required—TOEFL (minimum score 550 paper-based; 213 computer-based; 80 iBT), GRE. *Application deadline:* Applications are processed on a rolling basis. Application fee: $25. Electronic applications accepted. *Expenses:* Contact institution. Tuition and fees vary according to program. *Faculty research:* Social justice, service learning dispositions, educational technology, special education. *Unit head:* Dr. Milton Brown, Dean (Interim), 502-452-8486, Fax: 502-452-8189, E-mail: mbrown@bellarmine.edu. *Application contact:* Theresa Klapheke, Director of Graduate Programs, 502-452-8033, Fax: 502-452-8189, E-mail: tklapheke@bellarmine.edu.

Belmont University, College of Arts and Sciences, School of Education, Nashville, TN 37212-3757. Offers education (MAT); elementary education (M Ed), including early childhood education, elementary education, gifted education, language arts education; English (M Ed); history (M Ed); mathematics (M Ed); middle grade education (M Ed); science (M Ed); secondary education (M Ed), including gifted education; sports administration (MSA); technology (M Ed). *Accreditation:* NCATE. Part-time and evening/weekend programs available. *Faculty:* 9 full-time (7 women), 20 part-time/adjunct (15 women). *Students:* 50 full-time (36 women), 116 part-time (76 women); includes 23 minority (20 African Americans, 1 Asian American or Pacific Islander, 2 Hispanic Americans), 1 international. Average age 30. 55 applicants, 60% accepted, 30 enrolled. In 2006, 82 degrees awarded. *Degree requirements:* For master's, thesis, comprehensive exam. *Entrance requirements:* For master's, MAT or GRE, minimum GPA of 2.75. Additional exam requirements/recommendations for international students: Required—TOEFL. *Application deadline:* For fall admission, 8/1 priority date for domestic students, 5/1 for international students; for spring admission, 12/1 priority date for domestic students, 9/1 for international students. Applications are processed on a rolling basis. Application fee: $50. *Expenses:* Contact institution. *Financial support:* In 2006–07, 25 students received support; fellowships with partial tuition reimbursements available, institutionally sponsored loans and tuition waivers (partial) available. Financial award application deadline: 4/15; financial award applicants required to submit FAFSA. *Faculty research:* Technology grant, professional development schools. Total annual research expenditures: $6,500. *Unit head:* Dr. Trevor F. Hutchins, Associate Dean, 615-460-6232, Fax: 615-460-6414, E-mail: hutchinst@mail.belmont.edu. *Application contact:* Julie Hullett, Admission/Licensure Officer, 615-460-6879, Fax: 615-460-5556, E-mail: hullettj@email.belmont.edu.

Bennington College, Graduate Programs, Program in Teaching, Bennington, VT 05201. Offers art education (MAT); early childhood (MAT); elementary education (MAT); English education (MAT); foreign language education (MAT); mathematics education (MAT); music education (MAT); science education (MAT); secondary education (MAT); social science education (MAT). *Faculty:* 4 part-time/adjunct (3 women). *Students:* 11 full-time (7 women), 1 (woman) part-time; includes 2 minority (both Hispanic Americans) Average age 31. 12 applicants, 75% accepted, 3 enrolled. In 2006, 13 degrees awarded. *Degree requirements:* For master's, 1 year teaching practicum, professional portfolio. *Entrance requirements:* For master's, interview. *Application deadline:* For fall admission, 3/1 for domestic students. Application fee: $60. *Expenses:* Contact institution. One-time fee: $75 full-time. Tuition and fees vary according to program. *Financial support:* In 2006–07, 10 students received support, including 4 fellowships (averaging $6,875 per year); scholarships/grants and unspecified assistantships also available. Financial award application deadline: 4/1; financial award applicants required to submit FAFSA. *Unit head:* George Kamberelis, Director of Center for Creative Teaching, 802-440-4863, E-mail: gkamberelis@bennington.edu. *Application contact:* Ken Himmelman, Dean of Admissions, 802-440-4312, Fax: 802-440-4320, E-mail: admissions@bennington.edu.

See Close-Up on page 861.

Berry College, Graduate Programs, Graduate Programs in Education, Program in Early Childhood Education, Mount Berry, GA 30149-0159. Offers M Ed. *Accreditation:* NCATE. Part-time programs available. *Faculty:* 10 part-time/adjunct (5 women). *Students:* 3 full-time (all women), 24 part-time (22 women); includes 1 minority (Hispanic American) Average age 33. In 2006, 16 degrees awarded. *Degree requirements:* For master's, oral exams, thesis optional. *Entrance requirements:* For master's, GRE General Test, MAT, or NTE, minimum GPA of 2.5. Additional exam requirements/recommendations for international students: Required—TOEFL (minimum score 550 paper-based; 213 computer-based). *Application deadline:* For fall admission, 5/1 for domestic students; for spring admission, 10/1 for domestic students. Applications are processed on a rolling basis. Application fee: $25 ($30 for international students). *Expenses:* Tuition: Full-time $6,174; part-time $343 per credit hour. *Financial support:* In 2006–07, 15 students received support; research assistantships with full tuition reimbursements available, unspecified assistantships available. Support available to part-time students. Financial award application deadline: 4/1; financial award applicants required to submit FAFSA. *Faculty research:* Curriculum development, teacher training, pedagogy. *Application contact:* Richard D. Paul, Dean of Admissions and Financial Aid, 706-236-2215, Fax: 706-290-2178, E-mail: dpaul@berry.edu.

Bloomsburg University of Pennsylvania, School of Graduate Studies, College of Professional Studies, School of Education, Department of Elementary and Early Childhood Education, Program in Early Childhood Education, Bloomsburg, PA 17815-1301. Offers MS. *Accreditation:* NCATE. *Faculty:* 10 full-time (5 women). *Students:* 2 full-time (both women). Average age 24. 3 applicants, 100% accepted, 1 enrolled. In 2006, 7 degrees awarded. *Degree requirements:* For master's, thesis optional. *Entrance requirements:* For master's, MAT, minimum QPA of 3.0. Additional exam requirements/recommendations for international students: Required—TOEFL. *Application deadline:* Applications are processed on a rolling basis. Application fee: $30. Electronic applications accepted. *Expenses:* Tuition, state resident: full-time $6,048; part-time $336 per credit. Tuition, nonresident: full-time $9,678; part-time $538 per credit. Required fees: $1,415. *Financial support:* Unspecified assistantships available. *Faculty research:* Child development, children's literature, theory, administration. *Unit head:* Dr. Michael Patte, Coordinator, 570-389-4026.

Boise State University, Graduate College, College of Education, Programs in Teacher Education, Program in Early Childhood Education, Boise, ID 83725-0399. Offers M Ed, MA. *Accreditation:* NCATE. Part-time programs available. *Faculty:* 3 full-time (all women), 2 part-

Early Childhood Education

Boise State University (continued)
time/adjunct (both women). *Students:* 3 full-time (all women), 10 part-time (all women); includes 1 minority (Hispanic American) Average age 38. 4 applicants, 100% accepted, 1 enrolled. In 2006, 5 degrees awarded. *Degree requirements:* For master's, thesis optional. *Entrance requirements:* For master's, minimum GPA of 3.0. *Application deadline:* For fall admission, 7/1 priority date for domestic students; for spring admission, 11/15 priority date for domestic students. Applications are processed on a rolling basis. Application fee: $0. Electronic applications accepted. *Financial support:* Career-related internships or fieldwork, Federal Work-Study, institutionally sponsored loans, and unspecified assistantships available. Support available to part-time students. Financial award application deadline: 3/1.

Boston College, Lynch Graduate School of Education, Department of Counseling Psychology, Developmental, and Educational Psychology, Program in Early Childhood/Specialist Option, Chestnut Hill, MA 02467-3800. Offers MA. Part-time programs available. *Students:* 1 (woman) full-time, 1 (woman) part-time. 14 applicants, 21% accepted, 1 enrolled. In 2006, 2 degrees awarded. *Degree requirements:* For master's, comprehensive exam. *Entrance requirements:* For master's, GRE General Test or MAT. Additional exam requirements/recommendations for international students: Required—TOEFL. *Application deadline:* For fall admission, 1/1 priority date for domestic students. Application fee: $60. *Financial support:* Fellowships with full and partial tuition reimbursements, research assistantships with full and partial tuition reimbursements, teaching assistantships with full and partial tuition reimbursements, career-related internships or fieldwork, Federal Work-Study, scholarships/grants, traineeships, tuition waivers (full and partial), and unspecified assistantships available. Support available to part-time students. Financial award applicants required to submit FAFSA. *Faculty research:* School preparedness, educational leadership in early childhood, dual language literacy in young children. *Application contact:* Timothy P. Blackman, Director, Graduate Admission and Financial Aid, 617-552-4214, Fax: 617-552-0398, E-mail: timothy.blackman.1@bc.edu.

Boston College, Lynch Graduate School of Education, Department of Teacher Education/Special Education and Curriculum and Instruction, Early Childhood Education/Teacher Option Program, Chestnut Hill, MA 02467-3800. Offers M Ed. *Students:* 8 full-time (all women); includes 2 minority (both African Americans) 25 applicants, 72% accepted, 4 enrolled. In 2006, 10 degrees awarded. *Degree requirements:* For master's, comprehensive exam. *Entrance requirements:* For master's, GRE General Test or MAT. Additional exam requirements/recommendations for international students: Required—TOEFL. *Application deadline:* For fall admission, 1/1 priority date for domestic students. Application fee: $60. *Financial support:* Fellowships with full and partial tuition reimbursements, research assistantships with full and partial tuition reimbursements, teaching assistantships with full and partial tuition reimbursements, career-related internships or fieldwork, Federal Work-Study, scholarships/grants, traineeships, tuition waivers (full and partial), and unspecified assistantships available. Support available to part-time students. Financial award applicants required to submit FAFSA. *Faculty research:* Early childhood testing and assessment, selective attention abilities in children, play therapy, problem-solving, dual language learning and literacy. *Application contact:* Timothy P. Blackman, Director, Graduate Admission and Financial Aid, 617-552-4214, Fax: 617-552-0398, E-mail: timothy.blackman.1@bc.edu.

Boston University, School of Education, Department of Curriculum and Teaching, Program in Early Childhood Education, Boston, MA 02215. Offers Ed M, Ed D, CAGS. *Students:* 5 full-time (all women), 4 part-time (all women), 1 international. Average age 28. 36 applicants, 50% accepted. *Degree requirements:* For master's, thesis optional; for doctorate, thesis/dissertation, comprehensive exam. *Entrance requirements:* For master's, doctorate, and CAGS, GRE General Test or MAT. Additional exam requirements/recommendations for international students: Required—TOEFL. *Application deadline:* For fall admission, 2/15 priority date for domestic students; for winter admission, 10/1 priority date for domestic students. Applications are processed on a rolling basis. Application fee: $70. Electronic applications accepted. *Expenses:* Tuition: Full-time $33,330; part-time $1,042 per credit. Required fees: $462; $40. *Financial support:* Application deadline: 2/15. *Faculty research:* Language acquisition, child development, needs of handicapped children. *Unit head:* Dr. Jane Lannak, Coordinator, 617-353-7258, E-mail: jlannak@bu.edu. *Application contact:* 617-353-4237, Fax: 617-353-8937, E-mail: sedgrad@bu.edu.

Bowling Green State University, Graduate College, College of Education and Human Development, School of Education and Intervention Services, Intervention Services Division, Program in Special Education, Bowling Green, OH 43403. Offers assistive technology (M Ed); early childhood intervention (M Ed); gifted education (M Ed); hearing impaired intervention (M Ed); mild/moderate intervention (M Ed); moderate/intensive intervention (M Ed). *Accreditation:* NCATE. Part-time programs available. *Students:* 26 full-time (21 women), 84 part-time (78 women); includes 4 minority (all African Americans) Average age 35. 39 applicants, 87% accepted, 12 enrolled. In 2006, 47 degrees awarded. *Degree requirements:* For master's, thesis or alternative. *Entrance requirements:* For master's, GRE General Test. Additional exam requirements/recommendations for international students: Required—TOEFL. *Application deadline:* For fall admission, 3/1 priority date for domestic students. Applications are processed on a rolling basis. Application fee: $30. Electronic applications accepted. *Expenses:* Tuition, state resident: part-time $535 per hour. Tuition, nonresident: part-time $884 per hour. *Financial support:* In 2006–07, 16 research assistantships with full tuition reimbursements (averaging $5,202 per year) were awarded; teaching assistantships with full tuition reimbursements, Federal Work-Study and unspecified assistantships also available. Financial award applicants required to submit FAFSA. *Faculty research:* Reading and special populations, deafness, early childhood, gifted and talented, behavior disorders. *Application contact:* Dr. Lessie Cochran, Graduate Coordinator, 419-372-7298.

Brenau University, Graduate Programs, School of Education, Gainesville, GA 30501. Offers early childhood education (M Ed, Ed S), including behavior disorders (M Ed); learning disabilities (M Ed), including special education; middle grades education (M Ed, Ed S). *Accreditation:* NCATE. Part-time and evening/weekend programs available. *Faculty:* 12 full-time (9 women), 17 part-time/adjunct (9 women). *Students:* 104 full-time (89 women), 160 part-time (140 women); includes 34 minority (28 African Americans, 3 Asian Americans or Pacific Islanders, 3 Hispanic Americans), 2 international. Average age 37. 187 applicants. In 2006, 92 master's, 24 other advanced degrees awarded. *Degree requirements:* For master's, comprehensive exam or applied research project, effective portfolio, thesis optional; for Ed S, applied research project. *Entrance requirements:* For master's, GRE, MAT, interview, minimum GPA of 3.0, teaching certificate, 3 references, writing samples; for Ed S, GRE, MAT, master's degree, minimum GPA of 3.0, writing sample, letters of reference. Additional exam requirements/recommendations for international students: Required—TOEFL (minimum score 550 paper-based). *Application deadline:* Applications are processed on a rolling basis. Application fee: $30. *Expenses:* Contact institution. *Financial support:* Career-related internships or fieldwork available. Financial award application deadline: 7/15; financial award applicants required to submit FAFSA. *Faculty research:* Environmental science literacy and awareness, curriculum integration for improved student success, teaching dispositions, impact of parent involvement on student success, grade inflation in higher education. *Unit head:* Dr. William B. Ware, Dean, 770-534-6220, Fax: 770-534-6221, E-mail: bware@brenau.edu. *Application contact:* Nathan Goss, Admissions Coordinator, 770-534-6162, Fax: 770-538-4701, E-mail: ngoss@brenau.edu.

Bridgewater State College, School of Graduate Studies, School of Education and Allied Science, Department of Elementary and Early Childhood Education, Program in Early Childhood Education, Bridgewater, MA 02325-0001. Offers M Ed. *Accreditation:* NCATE. Part-time and evening/weekend programs available. *Entrance requirements:* For master's, GRE General Test or Massachusetts Test for Educator Licensure. *Application deadline:* For fall admission, 3/1 priority date for domestic students; for spring admission, 10/1 priority date for domestic students. Application fee: $50. *Financial support:* Career-related internships or fieldwork, health care benefits, and unspecified assistantships available. Support available to part-time students.

Brooklyn College of the City University of New York, Division of Graduate Studies, School of Education, Program in Early Childhood Education, Brooklyn, NY 11210-2889. Offers birth-grade 2 (MS Ed). Part-time and evening/weekend programs available. *Students:* 7 full-time (6 women), 107 part-time (102 women); includes 68 minority (40 African Americans, 3 Asian Americans or Pacific Islanders, 25 Hispanic Americans), 4 international. 88 applicants, 72% accepted, 22 enrolled. In 2006, 50 degrees awarded. *Entrance requirements:* For master's, LAST, bachelor's degree in early childhood education, resumé, 2 letters of recommendation, essay. Additional exam requirements/recommendations for international students: Required—TOEFL. *Application deadline:* For fall admission, 3/1 priority date for domestic students, 2/1 priority date for international students; for spring admission, 11/1 priority date for domestic students, 10/1 priority date for international students. Applications are processed on a rolling basis. Application fee: $125. Electronic applications accepted. *Expenses:* Tuition, state resident: full-time $6,400; part-time $270 per credit. Tuition, nonresident: full-time $12,000; part-time $500 per credit. Required fees: $118 per semester. *Financial support:* Career-related internships or fieldwork, Federal Work-Study, institutionally sponsored loans, and scholarships/grants available. Support available to part-time students. Financial award application deadline: 5/1; financial award applicants required to submit FAFSA. *Faculty research:* Children's narrations, language acquisition, culture and education. *Unit head:* Dr. Mary DeBey, Program Head, 718-951-5214, Fax: 718-951-4816, E-mail: mdebey@brooklyn.cuny.edu. *Application contact:* Karen Alleyne-Pierre, Director of Admissions Services and Enrollment Communications, 718-951-5902, Fax: 718-951-4506, E-mail: grads@brooklyn.cuny.edu.

Buffalo State College, State University of New York, Graduate Studies and Research, Faculty of Applied Science and Education, Department of Elementary Education and Reading, Program in Elementary Education, Buffalo, NY 14222-1095. Offers childhood education (grades 1-6) (MS Ed); early childhood and childhood curriculum and instruction (MS Ed); early childhood education (birth-grade 2) (MS Ed). *Accreditation:* NCATE. Part-time programs available. *Degree requirements:* For master's, thesis or project. *Entrance requirements:* For master's, minimum GPA of 2.5 in last 60 hours, New York teaching certificate. Additional exam requirements/recommendations for international students: Required—TOEFL (minimum score 550 paper-based; 213 computer-based).

California State University, Fresno, Division of Graduate Studies, School of Education and Human Development, Department of Literacy and Early Education, Fresno, CA 93740-8027. Offers education (MA), including early childhood education, reading/language arts. *Accreditation:* NCATE. Part-time and evening/weekend programs available. *Degree requirements:* For master's, thesis or alternative. *Entrance requirements:* For master's, GRE General Test, MAT, minimum GPA of 2.75. Additional exam requirements/recommendations for international students: Required—TOEFL. Electronic applications accepted. *Faculty research:* Reading recovery, monitoring/tutoring programs, character and academics, professional ethics, low-performing partnership schools.

California State University, Northridge, Graduate Studies, College of Education, Department of Educational Psychology and Counseling, Northridge, CA 91330. Offers counseling (MS), including career counseling, college counseling and student services, marriage and family therapy, school counseling, school psychology; educational psychology (MA Ed), including development, learning, and instruction, early childhood education; genetic counseling (MS). *Accreditation:* ACA (one or more programs are accredited); NCATE. Part-time and evening/weekend programs available. *Faculty:* 19 full-time (11 women), 57 part-time/adjunct (39 women). *Students:* 344 full-time (50 women), 135 part-time (19 women); includes 210 minority (26 African Americans, 3 American Indian/Alaska Native, 40 Asian Americans or Pacific Islanders, 141 Hispanic Americans), 11 international. Average age 32. 244 applicants, 62% accepted, 116 enrolled. In 2006, 176 degrees awarded. *Entrance requirements:* For master's, GRE General Test, MAT, or minimum GPA of 3.0. Additional exam requirements/recommendations for international students: Required—TOEFL. *Application deadline:* For fall admission, 11/30 for domestic students. Application fee: $55. *Expenses:* Tuition, nonresident: full-time $8,136; part-time $4,068 per year. Required fees: $3,624; $1,161 per term. *Financial support:* Scholarships/grants available. Support available to part-time students. Financial award application deadline: 3/1. *Unit head:* Dr. Beverly Cabello, Chair, 818-677-2599. *Application contact:* Todd Wolfe, Graduate Advisor, 818-677-5719.

California State University, Sacramento, Graduate Studies, College of Education, Department of Teacher Education, Program in Early Childhood Education, Sacramento, CA 95819-6048. Offers MA. Part-time programs available. *Degree requirements:* For master's, thesis or alternative, writing proficiency exam. *Entrance requirements:* For master's, minimum GPA of 2.75, experience working with children. Additional exam requirements/recommendations for international students: Required—TOEFL. *Application deadline:* Applications are processed on a rolling basis. Application fee: $55. Electronic applications accepted. *Financial support:* Career-related internships or fieldwork and Federal Work-Study available. Support available to part-time students. Financial award application deadline: 3/1.

Canisius College, Graduate Division, School of Education and Human Services, Department of Graduate Education, Buffalo, NY 14208-1098. Offers business education (MS); childhood education (MS); college student personnel (MS); differentiated instruction (MS Ed); early childhood education (MS); education administration (MS); education of the deaf and hard of hearing (MS); general education (MS Ed); literacy education (MS Ed); reading education (MS Ed); secondary education (MS); special education (MS). *Accreditation:* NCATE. Part-time and evening/weekend programs available. *Faculty:* 13 full-time (12 women), 74 part-time/adjunct (44 women). *Students:* 377 full-time (267 women), 303 part-time (219 women); includes 43 minority (27 African Americans, 2 American Indian/Alaska Native, 6 Asian Americans or Pacific Islanders, 8 Hispanic Americans), 187 international. Average age 30. In 2006, 296 degrees awarded. Application fee: $25. *Expenses:* Tuition: Part-time $645 per credit hour. Required fees: $19 per credit hour. Tuition and fees vary according to program. *Financial support:* Research assistantships with full tuition reimbursements, career-related internships or fieldwork, institutionally sponsored loans, scholarships/grants, health care benefits, tuition waivers (full and partial), and unspecified assistantships available. *Faculty research:* Autism, Asperger's disease, private higher education, reading strategies. *Unit head:* Rev. Paul Nochelski, Chair of Graduate Education and Leadership, 716-888-3297, Fax: 716-888-3299. *Application contact:* James D. Bagwell, Director of Graduate Recruitment and Admissions, 716-888-2544, Fax: 716-888-3290, E-mail: bagwellj@canisius.edu.

Carlow University, School of Education, Program in Early Childhood Education, Pittsburgh, PA 15213-3165. Offers M Ed. Part-time and evening/weekend programs available. *Degree requirements:* For master's, thesis or alternative. *Entrance requirements:* For master's, interview, minimum GPA of 3.0, resumé, 1 year professional experience, 3 letters of recommendation. Additional exam requirements/recommendations for international students: Required—TOEFL. Electronic applications accepted. *Faculty research:* Understanding children's play, infant and toddler development, effects of violence on children, supervision and staff development.

Carlow University, School of Education, Program in Early Childhood Supervision, Pittsburgh, PA 15213-3165. Offers M Ed. Part-time and evening/weekend programs available. *Degree requirements:* For master's, thesis or alternative. *Entrance requirements:* For master's, interview, minimum GPA of 3.0, resumé, 1 year professional experience, current state certification as early childhood supervisor or teacher, 5 years of professional service in early childhood education prior to certification, 3 letters of recommendation. Additional exam requirements/recommendations for international students: Required—TOEFL. Electronic applications accepted. *Faculty research:* Leadership styles, learning styles, feminist pedagogy.

Central Connecticut State University, School of Graduate Studies, School of Education and Professional Studies, Department of Teacher Education, Program in Early Childhood Education, New Britain, CT 06050-4010. Offers MS. Part-time and evening/weekend programs available. *Students:* 1 (woman) full-time, 14 part-time (all women); includes 2 minority (1 African American, 1 Hispanic American), 1 international. 16 applicants, 69% accepted, 7 enrolled. In 2006, 13 degrees awarded. *Degree requirements:* For master's, thesis or alternative, comprehensive exam or special project. *Entrance requirements:* For master's, minimum GPA of 2.7. Additional exam requirements/recommendations for international students: Required—TOEFL. *Application deadline:* For fall admission, 7/1 for domestic students; for spring admission, 12/1 for domestic students. Applications are processed on a rolling basis. Application fee: $50. Electronic applications accepted. *Expenses:* Tuition, area resident: Full-time $3,970; part-time $380 per credit. Tuition, state resident: full-time $5,955; part-time $380 per credit. Tuition, nonresident: full-time $11,061; part-time $380 per credit. Required fees: $3,189. One-time fee: $62 part-time. Tuition and fees vary according to degree level and program. *Faculty research:* Pre-kindergarten and early learning research, early learning environments. *Unit head:* Dr. Susan Seider, Chair, Department of Teacher Education, 860-832-2415.

Central Michigan University, College of Graduate Studies, College of Education and Human Services, Department of Teacher Education and Professional Development, Mount Pleasant, MI 48859. Offers educational technology (MA); elementary education (MA), including classroom teaching, early childhood education, reading in the elementary school; library, media, and technology (MA), including library media, media and technology; middle level education (MA); reading improvement (MA); secondary education (MA); teaching senior high (MA). *Accreditation:* NCATE. *Degree requirements:* For master's, thesis or alternative, registration. *Faculty research:* Reading instruction and reading disabilities, teaching and learning styles, school and business partnerships, school restructuring and improvement, mathematics learning and instruction.

Chatham University, Program in Education, Pittsburgh, PA 15232-2826. Offers early childhood education (MAT); elementary education (MAT); English—secondary (MAT); environmental education (K-12) (MAT); secondary art (MAT); secondary biology education (MAT); secondary chemistry education (MAT); secondary English education (MAT); secondary math education (MAT); secondary physics education (MAT); secondary social studies education (MAT); special education (MAT). *Students:* 60 full-time (43 women), 23 part-time (22 women). Average age 29. 48 applicants, 77% accepted, 32 enrolled. In 2006, 59 degrees awarded. *Degree requirements:* For master's, thesis, teaching experience. *Entrance requirements:* For master's, PRAXIS I, minimum GPA of 3.0, sample of written work, recommendation letters. Additional exam requirements/recommendations for international students: Required—TOEFL (minimum score 600 paper-based; 250 computer-based; 100 iBT); Recommended—IELTS (minimum score 7), TWE (minimum score 5). *Application deadline:* For fall admission, 5/1 priority date for domestic and international students; for winter admission, 10/1 priority date for domestic and international students. Applications are processed on a rolling basis. Application fee: $45. Electronic applications accepted. *Financial support:* Career-related internships or fieldwork available. Financial award applicants required to submit FAFSA. *Faculty research:* Gifted education, environmental education, technology in education, writing as learning, class size and achievement. *Unit head:* Dr. Wendy Weiner, Director, 412-365-1146, Fax: 412-365-1505, E-mail: wweiner@chatham.edu. *Application contact:* 412-365-1825, Fax: 412-365-1609, E-mail: admissions@chatham.edu.

Chestnut Hill College, School of Graduate Studies, Department of Education, Program in Early Childhood Education, Philadelphia, PA 19118-2693. Offers M Ed. Part-time and evening/weekend programs available. *Faculty:* 33 part-time/adjunct (24 women). *Students:* 1 (woman) full-time, 11 part-time (all women); includes 1 minority (African American) Average age 34. In 2006, 1 degree awarded. *Degree requirements:* For master's, thesis optional. *Entrance requirements:* For master's, Pre-Professional Skills Test, writing sample. Additional exam requirements/recommendations for international students: Required—TOEFL (minimum score 500 paper-based). *Application deadline:* For fall admission, 7/15 priority date for domestic students, 7/15 for international students; for spring admission, 12/15 priority date for domestic students, 12/15 for international students. Applications are processed on a rolling basis. Application fee: $50. *Expenses:* Tuition: Part-time $470 per credit hour. Required fees: $30 per semester. Tuition and fees vary according to degree level. *Financial support:* Institutionally sponsored loans available. Financial award application deadline: 7/15; financial award applicants required to submit FAFSA. *Faculty research:* Emerging literacy practices, teacher preparation. *Application contact:* Jayne Mashett, Director of Graduate Admissions, 215-248-7020, Fax: 215-248-7161, E-mail: mashettj@chc.edu.

Cheyney University of Pennsylvania, School of Education, Program in Early Childhood Education, Cheyney, PA 19319-0200. Offers Certificate. Part-time and evening/weekend programs available. *Degree requirements:* For Certificate, thesis or alternative. *Entrance requirements:* For degree, GRE General Test, MAT, minimum GPA of 2.75. Electronic applications accepted.

Chicago State University, School of Graduate and Professional Studies, College of Education, Department of Special Education, Early Childhood Education and Bilingual Education, Program in Early Childhood Education, Chicago, IL 60628. Offers MAT, MS Ed. *Accreditation:* NCATE. *Degree requirements:* For master's, thesis optional. *Entrance requirements:* For master's, minimum GPA of 2.75.

City College of the City University of New York, Graduate School, School of Education, Department of Childhood Education, New York, NY 10031-9198. Offers MS. *Accreditation:* NCATE. *Students:* 29. 32 applicants, 91% accepted, 17 enrolled. In 2006, 117 degrees awarded. *Degree requirements:* For master's, thesis. *Entrance requirements:* For master's, Liberal Arts and Sciences Test (LAST), Content Specialty Test (CST). Additional exam requirements/recommendations for international students: Required—TOEFL. *Application deadline:* For fall admission, 3/15 for domestic students; for spring admission, 10/15 for domestic students. Application fee: $125. *Financial support:* Career-related internships or fieldwork available. *Unit head:* James Neujahr, Director, 212-650-6269, Fax: 212-650-7530, E-mail: jneujahr@ccny.cuny.edu. *Application contact:* Stacia Pusey, Graduate Admissions Adviser-Education, 212-650-5345, E-mail: spusey@ccny.cuny.edu.

Clarion University of Pennsylvania, Office of Research and Graduate Studies, College of Education and Human Services, Department of Education, Program in Education, Clarion, PA 16214. Offers curriculum and instruction (M Ed); early childhood (M Ed); English (M Ed); history (M Ed); literacy (M Ed); science (M Ed); technology (M Ed). *Accreditation:* NCATE. Part-time programs available. *Faculty:* 18 full-time (13 women). *Students:* 11 full-time (4 women), 54 part-time (37 women); includes 4 minority (3 African Americans, 1 Asian American or Pacific Islander). 50 applicants, 90% accepted. In 2006, 7 degrees awarded. *Degree requirements:* For master's, thesis or alternative, comprehensive exam. *Entrance requirements:* For master's, minimum QPA of 3.0, teacher certification. Additional exam requirements/recommendations for international students: Required—TOEFL (minimum score 550 paper-based; 213 computer-based; 80 iBT). *Application deadline:* For fall admission, 8/1 priority date for domestic students, 4/15 priority date for international students; for spring admission, 12/1 priority date for domestic students, 9/15 priority date for international students. Applications are processed on a rolling basis. Application fee: $30. Electronic applications accepted. *Expenses:* Tuition, state resident: part-time $336 per credit. Tuition, nonresident: part-time $538 per credit. *Financial support:* In 2006–07, 2 research assistantships with full tuition reimbursements (averaging $4,002 per year) were awarded. Support available to part-time students. Financial award application deadline: 3/1. *Application contact:* Dr. Brian Maguire, Coordinator, 814-393-2058, Fax: 814-393-2558, E-mail: bmaguire@clarion.edu.

Clarke College, Program in Education, Dubuque, IA 52001-3198. Offers early childhood/special education (MA); educational administration: elementary and secondary (MA); educational media: elementary and secondary (MA); multi-categorical resource K–12 (MA); multidisciplinary studies (MA); reading: elementary (MA); technology in education (MA). Part-time and evening/weekend programs available. Postbaccalaureate distance learning degree programs offered (minimal on-campus study). *Degree requirements:* For master's, thesis optional. *Entrance requirements:* For master's, GRE General Test or MAT, minimum GPA of 2.75. Electronic applications accepted.

Cleveland State University, College of Graduate Studies, College of Education and Human Services, Department of Teacher Education, Cleveland, OH 44115. Offers art education (M Ed); early childhood education (M Ed); foreign language education (M Ed); mathematics and science education (M Ed); middle childhood education (M Ed); special education (M Ed), including mild/moderate disabilities, moderate/intensive disabilities; teaching English to speakers of other languages (M Ed). Part-time and evening/weekend programs available. *Faculty:* 14 full-time (8 women), 5 part-time/adjunct (4 women). *Students:* 120 full-time (96 women), 592 part-time (485 women); includes 145 minority (123 African Americans, 7 Asian Americans or Pacific Islanders, 15 Hispanic Americans), 7 international. Average age 34. 526 applicants, 41% accepted, 144 enrolled. In 2006, 324 degrees awarded. *Degree requirements:* For master's, thesis or alternative, comprehensive exam (for some programs). *Entrance requirements:* For master's, GRE General Test or MAT, minimum GPA of 2.75. Additional exam requirements/recommendations for international students: Required—TOEFL (minimum score 525 paper-based; 197 computer-based), IELTS (minimum score 6). *Application deadline:* For fall admission, 7/15 priority date for domestic students. Applications are processed on a rolling basis. Application fee: $30. *Financial support:* In 2006–07, 12 research assistantships with full tuition reimbursements (averaging $3,480 per year) were awarded; tuition waivers (partial) and unspecified assistantships also available. *Faculty research:* Early literacy, professional development in reading, reading recovery, dual language, induction programs. Total annual research expenditures: $6.2 million. *Unit head:* Dr. Clifford T. Bennett, Chairperson, 216-523-7105, Fax: 216-687-5379, E-mail: c.t.bennett@csuohio.edu.

Coastal Carolina University, College of Education, Conway, SC 29528-6054. Offers early childhood education (M Ed); education (MAT); elementary education (M Ed); secondary education (M Ed). *Accreditation:* NCATE. Part-time and evening/weekend programs available. *Faculty:* 8 full-time (4 women), 16 part-time/adjunct (10 women). *Students:* 48 full-time (31 women), 45 part-time (33 women); includes 8 minority (6 African Americans, 2 Asian Americans or Pacific Islanders). Average age 30. In 2006, 70 degrees awarded. *Degree requirements:* For master's, comprehensive exam. *Entrance requirements:* For master's, GRE General Test, MAT, 2 letters of recommendation, copy of teaching credential. Additional exam requirements/recommendations for international students: Required—TOEFL. *Application deadline:* For fall admission, 8/15 priority date for domestic students. Applications are processed on a rolling basis. Application fee: $45. Electronic applications accepted. *Expenses:* Tuition, state resident: full-time $7,920; part-time $330 per credit hour. Tuition, nonresident: full-time $9,600; part-time $400 per credit hour. Required fees: $80; $40 per term. *Financial support:* Fellowships, research assistantships, unspecified assistantships available. Support available to part-time students. Financial award application deadline: 4/1; financial award applicants required to submit FAFSA. *Unit head:* Dr. Gilbert H. Hunt, Dean, 843-349-2607, Fax: 843-349-2332, E-mail: hunt@coastal.edu. *Application contact:* Dr. Judy W. Vogt, Vice President, Enrollment Services, 843-349-2037, Fax: 843-349-2127, E-mail: jvogt@coastal.edu.

College of Charleston, Graduate School, School of Education, Department of Elementary and Early Childhood Education, Program in Early Childhood Education, Charleston, SC 29424-0001. Offers M Ed, MAT. *Accreditation:* NCATE. Part-time and evening/weekend programs available. *Degree requirements:* For master's, thesis or alternative, written qualifying exam, student teaching experience (MAT). *Entrance requirements:* For master's, GRE, MAT, or NTE; South Carolina Education Entrance Exam (MAT), teaching certificate (M Ed). Additional exam requirements/recommendations for international students: Required—TOEFL. *Faculty research:* Teacher education and creative arts, integrated curriculum, multicultural awareness, teaching models, cooperative learning.

College of Mount St. Joseph, Graduate Education Program, Cincinnati, OH 45233-1670. Offers adolescent young adult education (MA); art (MA); inclusive early childhood education (MA); instructional leadership (MA); middle childhood education (MA); multicultural special education (MA); music (MA); reading (MA). *Accreditation:* Teacher Education Accreditation Council. Part-time and evening/weekend programs available. Postbaccalaureate distance learning degree programs offered (minimal on-campus study). *Faculty:* 22 full-time (14 women), 11 part-time/adjunct (6 women). *Students:* 68 full-time (54 women), 115 part-time (96 women); includes 21 minority (16 African Americans, 2 American Indian/Alaska Native, 1 Asian American or Pacific Islander, 2 Hispanic Americans). Average age 34. 91 applicants, 98% accepted, 62 enrolled. In 2006, 61 degrees awarded. *Degree requirements:* For master's, research project. *Entrance requirements:* For master's, GRE, PRAXIS II in teaching content area (math or science), 2 letters of recommendation, interview, resumé, prerequisite courses in communications, behavioral sciences and mathematics. Additional exam requirements/recommendations for international students: Required—TOEFL (minimum score 560 paper-based; 220 computer-based). *Application deadline:* Applications are processed on a rolling basis. Application fee: $50. Electronic applications accepted. *Expenses:* Contact institution. *Financial support:* In 2006–07, 3 students received support. Career-related internships or fieldwork and scholarships/grants available. Support available to part-time students. Financial award application deadline: 6/1; financial award applicants required to submit FAFSA. *Faculty research:* Foreign and second language learning problems/reading disabilities/hyperlexia, multicultural/bilingual special education, alternative educator licensure, science education, pedagogical content knowledge. *Unit head:* Dr. Mifrando Obach, Chair, 513-244-3263, Fax: 513-244-4867, E-mail: mifrando_obach@mail.msj.edu. *Application contact:* Marilyn Hoskins, Assistant Director of Admissions for Graduate Recruitment, 513-244-4723, Fax: 513-244-4629, E-mail: marilyn_hoskins@mail.msg.edu.

The College of New Jersey, Graduate Division, School of Education, Department of Elementary and Early Childhood Education, Program in School Personnel Licensure: Preschool-Grade 3, Ewing, NJ 08628. Offers M Ed, MAT. *Students:* 4 full-time (all women), 28 part-time (26 women); includes 10 minority (5 African Americans, 1 American Indian/Alaska Native, 4 Asian Americans or Pacific Islanders). 26 applicants, 81% accepted. In 2006, 22 degrees awarded. *Entrance requirements:* For master's, GRE, minimum GPA of 3.0 in field or 2.75 overall. Additional exam requirements/recommendations for international students: Required—TOEFL. *Application deadline:* For fall admission, 4/15 for domestic students; for spring admission, 10/15 for domestic students. Application fee: $60. Electronic applications accepted. *Unit head:* Dr. Arti Joshi, Coordinator, 609-771-2251. *Application contact:* Susan L. Hydro, Office of Graduate Studies, Assistant Dean, 609-771-2300, Fax: 609-637-5105, E-mail: graduate@tcnj.edu.

The College of New Rochelle, Graduate School, Division of Education, Program in Elementary Education/Early Childhood Education, New Rochelle, NY 10805-2308. Offers MS Ed. Part-time programs available. *Faculty:* 3 full-time (all women), 5 part-time/adjunct (3 women). *Students:* 13 full-time (12 women), 54 part-time (52 women); includes 19 minority (15 African Americans, 1 American Indian/Alaska Native, 3 Hispanic Americans). Average age 32. In 2006, 10 degrees awarded. *Degree requirements:* For master's, thesis (for some programs), practicum, comprehensive exam (for some programs), registration. *Entrance requirements:* For master's, interview, minimum GPA of 3.0 in field, 2.7 overall. *Application deadline:* For fall admission, 8/1 priority date for domestic students; for spring admission, 4/6 for domestic students. Applications are processed on a rolling basis. Application fee: $35. *Expenses:* Tuition: Part-time $575 per credit. Required fees: $90 per term. *Financial support:* Career-related internships or fieldwork, scholarships/grants, and unspecified assistantships available. *Unit head:* Dr. Marie Ribarich, Acting Division Head, Division of Education, 914-654-5333, Fax: 914-654-5593, E-mail: mribarich@cnr.edu.

The College of Saint Rose, Graduate Studies, School of Education, Teacher Education Department, Albany, NY 12203-1419. Offers business and marketing (MS Ed); childhood education (MS Ed); early childhood education (MS Ed); elementary education (K-6) (MS Ed); secondary education (MS Ed, Certificate); teacher education (MS Ed, Certificate), including bilingual pupil personnel services (Certificate). Part-time and evening/weekend programs available. *Entrance requirements:* For master's, minimum undergraduate GPA of 3.0. Additional exam requirements/recommendations for international students: Required—TOEFL (minimum score 550 paper-based; 213 computer-based). Electronic applications accepted.

Early Childhood Education

Columbia International University, Columbia Graduate School, Columbia, SC 29230-3122. Offers Bible teaching (MABT); Christian higher education leadership (Ed D); Christian school educational leadership (Ed D); counseling (MACN); curriculum and instruction (M Ed), including Christian school guidance, English as a second language, learning disabilities, school technology; early childhood and elementary education (MAT); educational administration (M Ed); teaching English as a foreign language (Certificate); teaching English as a foreign language and intercultural studies (MATF). Part-time and evening/weekend programs available. *Faculty:* 11 full-time (4 women), 7 part-time/adjunct (5 women). *Students:* 52 full-time (44 women), 93 part-time (59 women); includes 17 minority (11 African Americans, 2 Asian Americans or Pacific Islanders, 4 Hispanic Americans), 10 international. Average age 35. 107 applicants, 56% accepted, 41 enrolled. In 2006, 62 degrees awarded. *Degree requirements:* For master's, internships, professional project. *Entrance requirements:* For master's, Minnesota Multiphasic Personality Inventory, MAT, minimum GPA of 2.7. Additional exam requirements/recommendations for international students: Required—TOEFL. *Application deadline:* For fall admission, 8/1 priority date for domestic and international students; for winter admission, 12/15 priority date for domestic and international students; for spring admission, 1/15 priority date for domestic and international students. Applications are processed on a rolling basis. Application fee: $45. Electronic applications accepted. *Expenses:* Tuition: Part-time $400 per semester hour. Tuition and fees vary according to course load and program. *Financial support:* In 2006–07, 35 students received support. Career-related internships or fieldwork, Federal Work-Study, institutionally sponsored loans, and scholarships/grants available. Financial award application deadline: 3/17; financial award applicants required to submit FAFSA. *Unit head:* Dr. Milton Uecker, Dean, 803-807-5319, Fax: 803-786-4209, E-mail: muecker@ciu.edu. *Application contact:* Michelle MacGregor, Director of Admissions, 800-777-2227 Ext. 5335, Fax: 803-786-4209, E-mail: yescbs@ciu.edu.

Columbus State University, Graduate Studies, College of Education, Department of Teacher Education, Columbus, GA 31907-5645. Offers early childhood education (M Ed, Ed S); instructional technology (MS); middle grades education (M Ed, Ed S); physical education (M Ed); secondary education (M Ed, Ed S), including English/language arts, general science (M Ed), mathematics, science (Ed S), social science; special education (Ed S), including behavior disorders, learning disabilities, mental retardation. *Accreditation:* NCATE. Part-time and evening/weekend programs available. Postbaccalaureate distance learning degree programs offered (minimal on-campus study). *Faculty:* 16 full-time (8 women), 2 part-time/adjunct (1 woman). *Students:* 61 full-time (45 women), 128 part-time (89 women); includes 44 minority (36 African Americans, 3 Asian Americans or Pacific Islanders, 5 Hispanic Americans), 1 international. Average age 36. 77 applicants, 49% accepted, 26 enrolled. In 2006, 66 master's, 13 other advanced degrees awarded. *Degree requirements:* For master's, thesis, exit exam; for Ed S, thesis or alternative. *Entrance requirements:* For master's, GRE General Test, minimum GPA of 2.75; for Ed S, GRE General Test. Additional exam requirements/recommendations for international students: Required—TOEFL (minimum score 550 paper-based; 213 computer-based). *Application deadline:* For fall admission, 5/1 priority date for domestic students, 5/1 for international students; for spring admission, 11/1 for domestic and international students. Applications are processed on a rolling basis. Application fee: $25. Electronic applications accepted. *Expenses:* Tuition, state resident: part-time $127 per semester hour. Tuition, nonresident: part-time $508 per semester hour. Required fees: $264 per semester. Tuition and fees vary according to course load. *Financial support:* In 2006–07, 118 students received support, including 21 research assistantships with partial tuition reimbursements available (averaging $3,000 per year); career-related internships or fieldwork, Federal Work-Study, institutionally sponsored loans, scholarships/grants, tuition waivers (partial), and unspecified assistantships also available. Support available to part-time students. Financial award application deadline: 5/1; financial award applicants required to submit FAFSA. *Unit head:* Dr. Deborah Gober, Acting Chair, 706-568-2255, Fax: 706-568-3134, E-mail: gober_deborah@colstate.edu. *Application contact:* Katie Thornton, Graduate Admissions Specialist, 706-568-2035, Fax: 706-568-2462, E-mail: thornton_katie@colstate.edu.

Concordia University, College of Education, Program in Early Childhood Education, River Forest, IL 60305-1499. Offers MA, Ed D. Part-time and evening/weekend programs available. *Degree requirements:* For master's, thesis, comprehensive exam. *Entrance requirements:* For master's, minimum GPA of 2.9; for doctorate, MAT or GRE, minimum graduate GPA of 3.5. Additional exam requirements/recommendations for international students: Required—TOEFL (minimum score 550 paper-based; 195 computer-based). Electronic applications accepted. *Faculty research:* Child care training project, 'Children in Worship" project, ethical development of children.

Concordia University, Graduate Programs in Education, Program in Early Childhood Education, Seward, NE 68434-1599. Offers M Ed. *Accreditation:* NCATE. Part-time programs available. *Degree requirements:* For master's, thesis or alternative, comprehensive exam. *Entrance requirements:* For master's, GRE, MAT, or NTE, minimum GPA of 3.0, BS in education or equivalent. Additional exam requirements/recommendations for international students: Required—TOEFL.

Concordia University, St. Paul, College of Education, St. Paul, MN 55104-5494. Offers differentiated instruction (MA Ed); early childhood (MA Ed); family life education (MAHS); special education (Certificate). *Accreditation:* NCATE. Evening/weekend programs available. Postbaccalaureate distance learning degree programs offered (minimal on-campus study). *Faculty:* 8 full-time (7 women), 12 part-time/adjunct (7 women). *Students:* 101 full-time (95 women), 10 part-time (9 women); includes 29 minority (21 African Americans, 1 American Indian/Alaska Native, 6 Asian Americans or Pacific Islanders, 1 Hispanic American). Average age 34. In 2006, 59 master's, 8 other advanced degrees awarded. *Entrance requirements:* Additional exam requirements/recommendations for international students: Required—TOEFL. *Application deadline:* Applications are processed on a rolling basis. Application fee: $50. Electronic applications accepted. *Unit head:* Prof. Lonn Maly, Dean, 651-641-8278, Fax: 651-641-8807, E-mail: maly@csp.edu. *Application contact:* Kimberly Craig, Director of Graduate and Cohort Admission, 651-603-6223, Fax: 651-603-6320, E-mail: craig@csp.edu.

Concordia University Wisconsin, Graduate Programs, Department of Education, Program in Early Childhood, Mequon, WI 53097-2402. Offers MS Ed. *Students:* 26 (24 women). In 2006, 2 degrees awarded. *Degree requirements:* For master's, thesis or alternative, comprehensive exam. *Entrance requirements:* For master's, minimum GPA of 3.0, teaching license. Additional exam requirements/recommendations for international students: Required—TOEFL. Application fee: $35. *Financial support:* Application deadline: 8/1. *Unit head:* Dr. Candyce Seider, Head, 262-243-4221, E-mail: candyce.seider@cuw.edu. *Application contact:* Graduate Admissions, 262-243-4248, Fax: 262-243-4428, E-mail: candyce.seider@cuw.edu.

Converse College, School of Education and Graduate Studies, Spartanburg, SC 29302-0006. Offers art education (M Ed); early childhood education (MAT); education (Ed S), including administration and supervision, curriculum and instruction, marriage and family therapy; elementary education (M Ed, MAT); gifted education (M Ed); leadership (M Ed); liberal arts (MLA), including English (M Ed, MAT, MLA), history, political science; secondary education (M Ed, MAT), including biology (MAT), chemistry (MAT), English (M Ed, MAT, MLA), mathematics, natural sciences (M Ed), social sciences; special education (M Ed, MAT), including learning disabilities (MAT), mental disabilities (MAT), special education (M Ed). Part-time and evening/weekend programs available. *Faculty:* 13 full-time (8 women), 23 part-time/adjunct (16 women). *Students:* 156 full-time (136 women), 1,069 part-time (847 women). Average age 35. 115 applicants, 88% accepted. In 2006, 186 master's, 26 other advanced degrees awarded. *Entrance requirements:* For master's, PRAXIS II (M Ed), minimum GPA of 2.75; for Ed S, GRE or MAT, minimum GPA of 3.0. *Application deadline:* For fall admission, 8/1 for domestic and international students; for winter admission, 11/15 for domestic and international students; for spring admission, 1/15 for domestic and international students. Applications are processed on a rolling basis. Application fee: $40. Electronic applications accepted. *Expenses:* Tuition: Part-time $305 per credit hour. Required fees: $20 per term. *Financial support:* In 2006–07, 500 students received support; research assistantships, career-related internships or fieldwork

and scholarships/grants available. Support available to part-time students. Financial award applicants required to submit FAFSA. *Faculty research:* Motivation, classroom management, predictors of success in classroom teaching, sex equity in public education, gifted research. Total annual research expenditures: $50,000. *Unit head:* Thomas M. Faulkenberry, Dean of the School of Education and Graduate Studies, 864-596-9082, Fax: 864-596-9221, E-mail: tom.faulkenberry@converse.edu.

Daemen College, Education Department, Amherst, NY 14226-3592. Offers adolescence education (MS); childhood education (MS); childhood special education (MS). Part-time programs available. *Faculty:* 5 full-time (4 women), 53 part-time/adjunct (45 women). *Students:* 283 full-time (224 women), 238 part-time (202 women); includes 1 minority (African American), 192 international. Average age 33. 314 applicants, 71% accepted, 184 enrolled. In 2006, 284 degrees awarded. *Degree requirements:* For master's, thesis, registration. *Entrance requirements:* For master's, GRE, minimum GPA of 3.0, 3 letters of recommendation, proof of initial certification for licensure. Additional exam requirements/recommendations for international students: Required—TOEFL (minimum score 500 paper-based; 173 computer-based). *Application deadline:* For fall admission, 3/1 priority date for domestic and international students; for spring admission, 10/1 priority date for domestic and international students. Applications are processed on a rolling basis. Application fee: $25. Electronic applications accepted. *Expenses:* Tuition: Full-time $11,700; part-time $650 per credit hour. Required fees: $15 per credit hour. Tuition and fees vary according to course load. *Financial support:* In 2006–07, 48 students received support. Federal Work-Study, institutionally sponsored loans, traineeships, and tuition waivers (partial) available. Support available to part-time students. Financial award application deadline: 2/15; financial award applicants required to submit FAFSA. *Faculty research:* Transition for students with disabilities, early childhood special education, traumatic brain injury (TBI), reading assessment. *Unit head:* Dr. Mary H. Fox, Chair, 716-839-8530, Fax: 716-839-8516, E-mail: mfox@daemen.edu. *Application contact:* Karl Shallowhorn, Associate Director of Graduate Admissions, 716-839-8225, Fax: 716-839-8229, E-mail: kshallow@daemen.edu.

Dallas Baptist University, Dorothy M. Bush College of Education, Education Program, Dallas, TX 75211-9299. Offers early childhood education (M Ed); educational leadership (M Ed); elementary reading education (M Ed); general elementary education (M Ed); reading specialist (M Ed). Part-time and evening/weekend programs available. *Faculty:* 49 full-time (21 women), 112 part-time/adjunct (46 women). *Students:* 47 full-time, 149 part-time. 65 applicants, 58% accepted, 36 enrolled. In 2006, 67 degrees awarded. *Entrance requirements:* For master's, GRE General Test, minimum GPA of 3.0. Additional exam requirements/recommendations for international students: Required—TOEFL. *Application deadline:* Applications are processed on a rolling basis. Application fee: $25. Electronic applications accepted. *Expenses:* Tuition: Full-time $8,370; part-time $465 per credit hour. Required fees: $465 per credit hour. *Financial support:* Federal Work-Study, institutionally sponsored loans, scholarships/grants, and tuition waivers (full and partial) available. Support available to part-time students. *Faculty research:* Emerging literacy, self-directed schools. *Unit head:* Dr. Elaine Wilmore, Interim Director, 214-333-5413, Fax: 214-333-5551, E-mail: graduate@dbu.edu. *Application contact:* Kit P. Montgomery, Director of Graduate Programs, 214-333-5242, Fax: 214-333-5579, E-mail: graduate@dbu.edu.

Dominican University, School of Education, River Forest, IL 60305-1099. Offers curriculum and instruction (MA Ed); early childhood education (MS); education (MAT); educational administration (MA); literacy (MS); special education (MS). Part-time and evening/weekend programs available. *Faculty:* 17 full-time (14 women), 37 part-time/adjunct (24 women). *Students:* 65 full-time (46 women), 514 part-time (425 women); includes 78 minority (23 African Americans, 16 Asian Americans or Pacific Islanders, 39 Hispanic Americans), 2 international. Average age 34. 130 applicants, 89% accepted, 100 enrolled. In 2006, 203 degrees awarded. *Entrance requirements:* For master's, Illinois certification test of basic skills. Additional exam requirements/recommendations for international students: Required—TOEFL (minimum score 550 paper-based; 213 computer-based). *Application deadline:* Applications are processed on a rolling basis. Application fee: $25. *Expenses:* Contact institution. Tuition and fees vary according to campus/location and program. *Financial support:* In 2006–07, 63 students received support. Career-related internships or fieldwork, scholarships/grants, and tuition waivers (partial) available. Support available to part-time students. Financial award application deadline: 8/15; financial award applicants required to submit FAFSA. *Faculty research:* Governance of private education institutions, reading and language arts, inclusion, organizational planning, leadership and vision. *Unit head:* Sr. Colleen McNicholas, Dean, 708-524-6830, Fax: 708-524-6665, E-mail: educate@dom.edu. *Application contact:* Keven Hansen, Coordinator of Admissions and Recruitment, 708-524-6921, Fax: 708-524-6665, E-mail: educate@dom.edu.

Duquesne University, School of Education, Department of Instruction and Leadership, Program in Early Childhood Education, Pittsburgh, PA 15282-0001. Offers MS Ed. Part-time and evening/weekend programs available. *Faculty:* 1 (woman) full-time, 3 part-time/adjunct (all women). *Students:* 6. 3 applicants, 100% accepted, 3 enrolled. In 2006, 3 degrees awarded. *Degree requirements:* For master's, thesis optional. *Entrance requirements:* For master's, MAT, minimum GPA of 3.0. Additional exam requirements/recommendations for international students: Required—TOEFL. *Application deadline:* For fall admission, 8/1 priority date for domestic students; for spring admission, 12/1 priority date for domestic students. Applications are processed on a rolling basis. Application fee: $50. *Expenses:* Tuition: Part-time $723 per credit. Required fees: $71 per credit. Tuition and fees vary according to degree level and program. *Financial support:* Available to part-time students. *Unit head:* Julia Williams, Coordinator, 412-396-6098, Fax: 412-396-5388, E-mail: williamsj@duq.edu.

Eastern Connecticut State University, School of Education and Professional Studies/Graduate Division, Program in Early Childhood Education, Willimantic, CT 06226-2295. Offers MS. *Accreditation:* NCATE. Part-time and evening/weekend programs available. *Faculty:* 3 full-time (2 women), 4 part-time/adjunct (all women). *Students:* 12 full-time (all women), 22 part-time (21 women); includes 1 minority (Hispanic American). Average age 31. 12 applicants, 67% accepted, 6 enrolled. In 2006, 15 degrees awarded. *Degree requirements:* For master's, comprehensive exam or thesis. *Entrance requirements:* For master's, PRAXIS I, minimum GPA of 2.7. Additional exam requirements/recommendations for international students: Required—TOEFL (minimum score 550 paper-based; 213 computer-based). *Application deadline:* For fall admission, 7/6 priority date for domestic and international students; for spring admission, 11/3 priority date for domestic and international students. Applications are processed on a rolling basis. Application fee: $50. *Expenses:* Tuition, state resident: full-time $3,970. Tuition, nonresident: full-time $11,061; part-time $336 per credit. Required fees: $35 per credit. *Financial support:* In 2006–07, 1 student received support; teaching assistantships, career-related internships or fieldwork, scholarships/grants, and unspecified assistantships available. Support available to part-time students. Financial award application deadline: 3/15. *Unit head:* Dr. Theresa Bouley, Advisor, 860-465-4535, Fax: 860-465-5099. *Application contact:* Dr. Tuesday L. Cooper, Associate Dean, 860-465-4543, Fax: 860-465-4538, E-mail: coopert@easternct.edu.

Eastern Illinois University, Graduate School, College of Education and Professional Studies, Department of Early Childhood, Elementary and Middle Level Education, Charleston, IL 61920-3099. Offers elementary education (MS Ed). *Accreditation:* NCATE. Part-time programs available. *Faculty:* 14 full-time (6 women). In 2006, 55 degrees awarded. *Degree requirements:* For master's, comprehensive exam. *Application deadline:* For fall admission, 7/31 priority date for domestic students. Applications are processed on a rolling basis. Application fee: $30. *Expenses:* Tuition, state resident: part-time $169 per semester hour. Tuition, nonresident: part-time $508 per semester hour. Required fees: $60 per semester hour. *Financial support:* In 2006–07, research assistantships with tuition reimbursements (averaging $7,200 per year), 5 teaching assistantships with tuition reimbursements (averaging $7,200 per year) were awarded. *Unit head:* Dr. Joy Russell, Chairperson, 217-581-5728, E-mail: jlrussell@eiu.edu.

Eastern Michigan University, Graduate School, College of Education, Department of Teacher Education, Program in Early Childhood Education, Ypsilanti, MI 48197. Offers MA. *Accreditation:*

NCATE. Evening/weekend programs available. In 2006, 23 degrees awarded. *Degree requirements:* For master's, thesis optional. *Entrance requirements:* For master's, GRE. Additional exam requirements/recommendations for international students: Required—TOEFL. *Application deadline:* For fall admission, 5/15 priority date for domestic students, 5/1 priority date for international students; for winter admission, 10/15 priority date for domestic students, 10/1 priority date for international students; for spring admission, 3/15 priority date for domestic students, 3/1 priority date for international students. Applications are processed on a rolling basis. Application fee: $35. *Expenses:* Tuition, state resident: part-time $341 per credit hour. Tuition, nonresident: full-time $16,104; part-time $671 per credit hour. Required fees: $816; $34 per credit hour. $40 per term. One-time fee: $82 full-time. Tuition and fees vary according to course level, course load, degree level and reciprocity agreements. *Financial support:* Fellowships, teaching assistantships available. Support available to part-time students. Financial award applicants required to submit FAFSA. *Unit head:* Dr. Margo Dichfelmiller, Coordinator, 734-487-3260.

Eastern Nazarene College, Adult and Graduate Studies, Division of Education, Quincy, MA 02170-2999. Offers early childhood education (M Ed, Certificate); elementary education (M Ed, Certificate); English as a second language (M Ed, Certificate); instructional enrichment and development (M Ed, Certificate); middle school education (M Ed, Certificate); moderate special needs education (M Ed, Certificate); principal (Certificate); program development and supervision (M Ed, Certificate); secondary education (M Ed, Certificate); special education administrator (Certificate); supervisor (Certificate); teacher of reading (M Ed, Certificate). M Ed and Certificate also available through weekend program for administration, special needs, and reading only. Part-time and evening/weekend programs available. *Faculty:* 9 full-time (5 women), 11 part-time/adjunct (5 women). *Students:* 135. Average age 35. 20 applicants, 100% accepted. In 2006, 2 degrees awarded. *Entrance requirements:* Additional exam requirements/recommendations for international students: Required—TOEFL (minimum score 550 paper-based). *Application deadline:* Applications are processed on a rolling basis. Application fee: $35. *Financial support:* Career-related internships or fieldwork available. Support available to part-time students. Financial award applicants required to submit FAFSA. *Unit head:* Dr. Lorne Ranstrom, Chair, 617-745-3528, E-mail: randstrol@enc.edu. *Application contact:* Christine Galbraith, Graduate Studies Recruiter, 617-774-6703, Fax: 617-984-4901, E-mail: christine.galbraith@enc.edu.

Eastern Washington University, Graduate Studies, College of Education and Human Development, Department of Education, Cheney, WA 99004-2431. Offers adult education (M Ed); college instruction (MA, MS); curriculum and instruction (M Ed); early childhood education (M Ed); educational leadership (M Ed); elementary teaching (M Ed); foundations of education (M Ed); instructional media and technology (M Ed); literacy specialist (M Ed); school library media administration (M Ed); science education (M Ed); social science education (M Ed); supervising (clinic) teaching (M Ed). *Accreditation:* NCATE. Part-time programs available. *Degree requirements:* For master's, comprehensive exam. *Entrance requirements:* For master's, minimum GPA of 3.0.

East Tennessee State University, School of Graduate Studies, College of Education, Department of Human Development and Learning, Johnson City, TN 37614. Offers advanced practitioner (M Ed); community agency counseling (M Ed, MA); comprehensive concentration (M Ed); counseling (M Ed, MA); early childhood education (M Ed, MA); early childhood general (M Ed); early childhood special education (M Ed); early childhood teaching (M Ed); elementary and secondary (school counseling) (M Ed, MA); marriage and family therapy (M Ed, MA); modified concentration (M Ed). *Accreditation:* ACA; NCATE. Part-time programs available. *Degree requirements:* For master's, thesis (for some programs), comprehensive exam. *Entrance requirements:* For master's, GRE General Test, minimum GPA of 3.0. Additional exam requirements/recommendations for international students: Required—TOEFL (minimum score 550 paper-based; 213 computer-based). *Faculty research:* Drug and alcohol abuse, marriage and family counseling, severe mental retardation, parenting of children with disabilities.

Edinboro University of Pennsylvania, Graduate Studies and Research, School of Education, Department of Elementary Education, Program in Elementary Education, Edinboro, PA 16444. Offers character education (M Ed); early childhood education (M Ed); elementary education (M Ed), including language arts, mathematics, science, thesis focus. Part-time and evening/weekend programs available. *Students:* 31 full-time (26 women), 46 part-time (38 women). Average age 30. In 2006, 14 degrees awarded. *Degree requirements:* For master's, thesis or alternative, project, comprehensive exam. *Entrance requirements:* For master's, GRE or MAT, minimum QPA of 2.5, valid teaching certificate or current study to obtain certification. *Application deadline:* Applications are processed on a rolling basis. Application fee: $30. Electronic applications accepted. *Expenses:* Tuition, state resident: full-time $6,048; part-time $336 per credit. Tuition, nonresident: full-time $9,678; part-time $538 per credit. Required fees: $1,849; $42 per credit. *Financial support:* In 2006–07, 7 research assistantships with full and partial tuition reimbursements (averaging $3,850 per year) were awarded; career-related internships or fieldwork, Federal Work-Study, scholarships/grants, and unspecified assistantships also available. Support available to part-time students. Financial award application deadline: 2/15; financial award applicants required to submit FAFSA. *Unit head:* Dr. Kathleen Dailey, Coordinator, 814-732-2714, E-mail: dailey@edinboro.edu. *Application contact:* Dr. R. Scott Baldwin, Dean, 814-732-2752, Fax: 814-732-2268, E-mail: sbaldwin@edinboro.edu.

Elms College, Division of Education, Chicopee, MA 01013-2839. Offers early childhood education (MAT); education (M Ed, CAGS); elementary education (MAT); English as a second language (MAT); reading (MAT); secondary education (MAT), including biology education, English education, Spanish education; special education (MAT). Part-time and evening/weekend programs available. *Faculty:* 9 full-time (6 women), 4 part-time/adjunct (2 women). *Students:* 8 full-time (6 women), 97 part-time (89 women); includes 4 minority (2 Asian Americans or Pacific Islanders, 2 Hispanic Americans). Average age 36. 48 applicants, 90% accepted, 40 enrolled. In 2006, 37 master's, 8 other advanced degrees awarded. *Degree requirements:* For master's, thesis (for some programs). *Entrance requirements:* For master's, Massachusetts Educators Certification Test, minimum GPA of 3.0; for CAGS, master's degree in education. Additional exam requirements/recommendations for international students: Required—TOEFL. *Application deadline:* For fall admission, 7/1 priority date for domestic students; for spring admission, 11/1 priority date for domestic students. Applications are processed on a rolling basis. Application fee: $30. *Expenses:* Tuition: Full-time $9,180; part-time $510 per credit. Tuition and fees vary according to course load. *Financial support:* In 2006–07, 3 teaching assistantships with partial tuition reimbursements were awarded; tuition waivers (partial) also available. Support available to part-time students. Financial award application deadline: 4/15; financial award applicants required to submit FAFSA. *Unit head:* Dr. Mary Janeczek, Director, 413-594-2761, Fax: 413-592-4871, E-mail: janeczeke@elms.edu.

Emporia State University, School of Graduate Studies, The Teachers College, Department of Early Childhood/Elementary Teacher Education, Program in Early Childhood Education, Emporia, KS 66801-5087. Offers early childhood education (MS), including early childhood curriculum, early childhood special education. *Accreditation:* NCATE. *Students:* 5 full-time (all women), 42 part-time (41 women); includes 3 minority (2 African Americans, 1 Hispanic American), 2 international. 8 applicants, 75% accepted, 4 enrolled. In 2006, 9 degrees awarded. *Degree requirements:* For master's, comprehensive exam or thesis, practicum. *Entrance requirements:* For master's, GRE General Test or MAT, graduate essay exam, appropriate bachelor's degree, letters of recommendation. Additional exam requirements/recommendations for international students: Required—TOEFL. *Application deadline:* For fall admission, 8/15 priority date for domestic students. Applications are processed on a rolling basis. Application fee: $30 ($75 for international students). Electronic applications accepted. *Expenses:* Tuition, state resident: full-time $3,438; part-time $143 per credit hour. Tuition, nonresident: full-time $10,398; part-time $433 per credit hour. Required fees: $724; $44 per credit hour. *Financial support:* Federal Work-Study, institutionally sponsored loans, health care benefits, and unspecified assistantships available. Financial award application deadline: 3/15; financial award applicants required to submit FAFSA. *Unit head:* Dr. Jean Morrow, Chair, Department of Early Childhood/Elementary Teacher Education, 620-341-5766, E-mail: jmorrow@emporia.edu.

Erikson Institute, Erikson Institute, Chicago, IL 60611-5627. Offers child development (MS); early childhood education (M Ed, MS, PhD). PhD offered through the Graduate School. *Accreditation:* NCA. *Degree requirements:* For master's, internship; for doctorate, one foreign language, thesis/dissertation, comprehensive exam. *Entrance requirements:* For master's, experience working with young children, interview; for doctorate, GRE General Test, interview. *Faculty research:* Early childhood development, cognitive development, sociocultural contexts, early childhood education, family and culture, early literacy.

Erikson Institute, Academic Programs, Program in Early Childhood Education, Chicago, IL 60611-5627. Offers MS. *Degree requirements:* For master's, comprehensive exam. *Entrance requirements:* For master's, 3 letters of recommendation, minimum GPA of 2.75. Additional exam requirements/recommendations for international students: Required—TOEFL.

See Close-Up on page 1275.

Fitchburg State College, Division of Graduate and Continuing Education, Program in Early Childhood Education, Fitchburg, MA 01420-2697. Offers M Ed. *Accreditation:* NCATE. Part-time and evening/weekend programs available. *Students:* 2 full-time (both women), 26 part-time (25 women). Average age 33. 15 applicants, 93% accepted, 8 enrolled. In 2006, 6 degrees awarded. *Entrance requirements:* For master's, GRE General Test or MAT, teaching certificate, letters of recommendation, resumé. Additional exam requirements/recommendations for international students: Recommended—TOEFL (minimum score 550 paper-based; 213 computer-based; 79 iBT). *Application deadline:* Applications are processed on a rolling basis. Application fee: $25 ($50 for international students). *Expenses:* Tuition, state resident: part-time $150 per credit. Tuition, nonresident: part-time $150 per credit. Required fees: $90 per credit. *Financial support:* In 2006–07, research assistantships with partial tuition reimbursements (averaging $5,500 per year); Federal Work-Study, scholarships/grants, and unspecified assistantships also available. Support available to part-time students. Financial award application deadline: 3/1; financial award applicants required to submit FAFSA. *Unit head:* Dr. Ian Bothwell, Chair, 978-665-4657, Fax: 978-665-3658, E-mail: gce@fsc.edu. *Application contact:* Director of Admissions, 978-665-3144, Fax: 978-665-4540, E-mail: admissions@fsc.edu.

Five Towns College, Program in Childhood Education, Dix Hills, NY 11746-6055. Offers MS Ed. *Accreditation:* NCATE. Part-time and evening/weekend programs available. *Faculty:* 2 full-time (both women), 5 part-time/adjunct (4 women). *Students:* 2 full-time (both women), 5 part-time (4 women); includes 1 minority (African American) Average age 38. 34 applicants, 82% accepted. In 2006, 4 degrees awarded. Application fee: $50. *Unit head:* Patricia Schmidt, Director of Childhood Education, 631-424-7020, Fax: 631-656-2172.

Florida Agricultural and Mechanical University, Division of Graduate Studies, Research, and Continuing Education, College of Education, Department of Elementary Education, Tallahassee, FL 32307-3200. Offers early childhood and elementary education (M Ed, MS Ed). *Accreditation:* NCATE. *Degree requirements:* For master's, thesis (for some programs). *Entrance requirements:* For master's, GRE General Test, minimum GPA of 3.0. Additional exam requirements/recommendations for international students: Required—TOEFL.

Florida International University, College of Education, Department of Curriculum and Instruction, Program in Early Childhood Education, Miami, FL 33199. Offers MS, Ed D. *Accreditation:* NCATE. Part-time and evening/weekend programs available. *Faculty:* 3 full-time (2 women). *Students:* 3 full-time (2 women), 17 part-time (all women); includes 16 minority (1 African American, 15 Hispanic Americans), 2 international. Average age 31. 10 applicants, 50% accepted, 5 enrolled. In 2006, 5 degrees awarded. *Entrance requirements:* For master's, GRE General Test or minimum GPA of 3.0, teaching certificate. Additional exam requirements/recommendations for international students: Required—TOEFL (minimum score 550 paper-based; 213 computer-based; 80 iBT), IELTS (minimum score 6). *Application deadline:* For fall admission, 6/1 priority date for domestic students, 4/1 for international students; for winter admission, 10/1 priority date for domestic students, 9/1 for international students; for spring admission, 3/1 priority date for domestic students, 2/1 for international students. Applications are processed on a rolling basis. Application fee: $30. Electronic applications accepted. *Expenses:* Tuition, state resident: part-time $249 per credit hour. Tuition, nonresident: part-time $753 per credit hour. Tuition and fees vary according to program. *Faculty research:* Children's literature, parental involvement. *Unit head:* Dr. Charles Bleiker, Program Director, 305-348-0462, E-mail: bleikerc@fiu.edu. *Application contact:* Marisa Salazar, Student Recruiter, 305-348-3002, Fax: 305-348-3227, E-mail: marisa.salazar@fiu.edu.

Florida State University, Graduate Studies, College of Education, Department of Childhood Education, Reading, and Disability Services, Tallahassee, FL 32306. Offers early childhood education (MS, Ed D, PhD, Ed S); elementary education (MS, Ed D, PhD, Ed S); reading education/language arts (MS, Ed D, PhD, Ed S); special education (MS, PhD, Ed S), including emotional disturbance/learning disabilities (MS), mental retardation (MS), rehabilitation counseling, special education (PhD, Ed S), visual disabilities (MS). Part-time programs available. *Faculty:* 24 full-time (19 women), 3 part-time/adjunct (all women). *Students:* 85 full-time (73 women), 205 part-time (189 women); includes 60 minority (36 African Americans, 2 American Indian/Alaska Native, 13 Asian Americans or Pacific Islanders, 9 Hispanic Americans). 189 applicants, 61% accepted, 71 enrolled. In 2006, 76 master's, 7 doctorates, 5 other advanced degrees awarded. *Degree requirements:* For master's and Ed S, thesis optional; for doctorate, thesis/dissertation, comprehensive exam. *Entrance requirements:* For master's, doctorate, and Ed S, GRE General Test, minimum GPA of 3.0. *Application deadline:* For fall admission, 7/1 priority date for domestic students; for spring admission, 11/1 for domestic students. Applications are processed on a rolling basis. Application fee: $30. *Expenses:* Tuition, state resident: full-time $5,822; part-time $243 per credit hour. Tuition, nonresident: full-time $20,976; part-time $874 per credit hour. Tuition and fees vary according to program. *Financial support:* In 2006–07, 2 fellowships, 4 research assistantships, 12 teaching assistantships were awarded; career-related internships or fieldwork also available. Financial award applicants required to submit FAFSA. *Unit head:* Dr. Mary Frances Hanline, Chair, 850-644-5458, Fax: 850-644-7736, E-mail: mhanline@coe.fsu.edu. *Application contact:* Timolin Lynette Bodison-Baker, Program Assistant, 850-644-5458, Fax: 850-644-7736, E-mail: bodison@coe.fsu.edu.

Fordham University, Graduate School of Education, Division of Curriculum and Teaching, New York, NY 10023. Offers adult education (MS, MSE); bilingual teacher education (MSE); curriculum and teaching (MSE); early childhood education (MSE); elementary education (MST); language, literacy, and learning (PhD); reading education (MSE, Adv C); secondary education (MAT, MSE); special education (MSE, Adv C); teaching English as a second language (MSE). *Accreditation:* NCATE. *Faculty:* 22 full-time (18 women), 38 part-time/adjunct (28 women). *Students:* 68 full-time (51 women), 663 part-time (612 women); includes 200 minority (74 African Americans, 1 American Indian/Alaska Native, 37 Asian Americans or Pacific Islanders, 88 Hispanic Americans), 3 international. Average age 32. 636 applicants, 86% accepted, 322 enrolled. In 2006, 351 master's, 8 doctorates awarded. *Degree requirements:* For doctorate and Adv C, thesis/dissertation. *Entrance requirements:* For doctorate, MAT, GRE General Test. Application fee: $65. *Financial support:* Applicants required to submit FAFSA. *Unit head:* Dr. Terry Osborn, Chairperson, 212-636-6450.

Fort Valley State University, College of Graduate Studies and Extended Education, Department of Curriculum and Instruction, Program in Early Childhood Education, Fort Valley, GA 31030-4313. Offers MS. Part-time programs available. *Degree requirements:* For master's, thesis optional. *Entrance requirements:* For master's, GRE General Test or MAT.

Framingham State College, Division of Graduate and Continuing Education, Program in Early Childhood Education, Framingham, MA 01701-9101. Offers M Ed. *Students:* 20. In 2006, 4 degrees awarded. *Unit head:* Dr. Katherine Hibbard, Coordinator, 508-626-4830, Fax: 508-626-4030, E-mail: khibbard@frc.mass.edu. *Application contact:* Graduate Office, 508-626-4550, Fax: 508-626-4030, E-mail: dgce@frc.mass.edu.

Early Childhood Education

Francis Marion University, Graduate Programs, School of Education, Florence, SC 29501-0547. Offers early childhood education (M Ed); elementary education (M Ed); learning disabilities (M Ed, MAT); remedial education (M Ed); secondary education (M Ed). *Accreditation:* NCATE. Part-time programs available. *Faculty:* 19 full-time (11 women), 1 part-time/adjunct (0 women). *Students:* 11 full-time (8 women), 158 part-time (141 women); includes 54 minority (all African Americans), 1 international. Average age 34. 248 applicants, 100% accepted. In 2006, 91 degrees awarded. *Degree requirements:* For master's, comprehensive exam. *Entrance requirements:* For master's, GRE General Test, MAT, NTE, or PRAXIS II. *Application deadline:* For fall admission, 4/15 priority date for domestic students; for spring admission, 10/15 priority date for domestic students. Applications are processed on a rolling basis. Application fee: $30. *Expenses:* Tuition, state resident: full-time $6,527; part-time $326 per credit hour. Tuition, nonresident: full-time $13,054; part-time $653 per credit hour. Required fees: $185; $5 per credit hour. $45 per term. *Financial support:* In 2006–07, 3 research assistantships (averaging $6,000 per year) were awarded; unspecified assistantships also available. Support available to part-time students. Financial award application deadline: 3/1; financial award applicants required to submit FAFSA. *Faculty research:* Identification and alternate assessment of at-risk students. *Unit head:* Dr. James R. Faulkenberry, Dean, 843-661-1460, Fax: 843-661-4647.

Furman University, Graduate Division, Department of Education, Greenville, SC 29613. Offers early childhood education (MA); elementary education (MA); English as a second language (MA); middle school education (MA); reading (MA); school administration (MA); special education (MA). *Accreditation:* NCATE. Part-time and evening/weekend programs available. *Faculty:* 17 full-time (12 women), 19 part-time/adjunct (15 women). *Students:* 114 full-time (89 women), 72 part-time (59 women); includes 27 minority (23 African Americans, 4 Hispanic Americans). Average age 32. 36 applicants, 100% accepted, 36 enrolled. In 2006, 111 degrees awarded. *Degree requirements:* For master's, thesis (for some programs), comprehensive exam. *Entrance requirements:* For master's, GRE General Test or PRAXIS. *Application deadline:* For fall admission, 8/1 priority date for domestic and international students; for winter admission, 12/1 priority date for domestic and international students; for spring admission, 2/1 priority date for domestic and international students. Applications are processed on a rolling basis. Application fee: $50. *Expenses:* Tuition: Part-time $347 per credit. *Financial support:* In 2006–07, 97 students received support; fellowships, scholarships/grants and unspecified assistantships available. Financial award application deadline: 1/15; financial award applicants required to submit FAFSA. *Unit head:* Dr. Nelly Hecker, Head, 864-294-3385.

Gallaudet University, The Graduate School, School of Education and Human Services, Department of Education, Washington, DC 20002-3625. Offers early childhood education (MA, Ed S); education of deaf and hard of hearing students and multihandicapped deaf and hard of hearing students (MA, Ed S); elementary education (MA, Ed S); individualized program of study (PhD); parent/infant specialty (MA, Ed S); secondary education (MA, Ed S). *Accreditation:* NCATE. *Degree requirements:* For master's, thesis optional; for doctorate, thesis/dissertation. *Entrance requirements:* For master's, GRE General Test or MAT; for doctorate, GRE General Test or MAT, interview.

Gannon University, School of Graduate Studies, College of Humanities, Business, and Education, School of Education, Program in Early Intervention, Erie, PA 16541-0001. Offers MS, Certificate. Part-time and evening/weekend programs available. *Students:* Average age 34. In 2006, 3 degrees awarded. *Degree requirements:* For master's, research project. *Entrance requirements:* For master's, interview, teaching certificate. Additional exam requirements/recommendations for international students: Required—TOEFL (minimum score 500 paper-based; 173 computer-based). *Application deadline:* Applications are processed on a rolling basis. Application fee: $25. *Expenses:* Tuition: Full-time $12,240; part-time $680 per credit. Required fees: $496; $16 per credit. Tuition and fees vary according to course load, degree level, campus/location and program. *Financial support:* Career-related internships or fieldwork available. Support available to part-time students. Financial award application deadline: 7/1; financial award applicants required to submit FAFSA. *Application contact:* Debra Meszaros, Director of Graduate Recruitment, 814-871-5819, Fax: 814-871-5827, E-mail: cfal@gannon.edu.

George Mason University, Graduate School of Education, Programs in Curriculum and Instruction, Fairfax, VA 22030. Offers bilingual/multicultural/English as a second language education (M Ed); early childhood education (M Ed); instructional technology (M Ed); middle education (M Ed); reading (M Ed); secondary education (M Ed); special education (M Ed). Part-time and evening/weekend programs available. *Faculty:* 108 full-time (70 women), 193 part-time/adjunct (140 women). *Students:* 185 full-time (144 women), 816 part-time (683 women); includes 148 minority (46 African Americans, 2 American Indian/Alaska Native, 44 Asian Americans or Pacific Islanders, 56 Hispanic Americans), 28 international. Average age 34. 822 applicants, 72% accepted, 473 enrolled. In 2006, 606 master's awarded. *Entrance requirements:* For master's, minimum GPA of 3.0 in last 60 hours. *Application deadline:* For fall admission, 5/1 for domestic students; for spring admission, 11/1 for domestic students. Application fee: $60 ($75 for international students). Electronic applications accepted. *Expenses:* Tuition, state resident: full-time $5,724; part-time $238 per credit. Tuition, nonresident: full-time $16,896; part-time $704 per credit. Required fees: $1,656; $69 per credit. *Financial support:* Career-related internships or fieldwork available. Support available to part-time students. Financial award application deadline: 3/1; financial award applicants required to submit FAFSA. *Unit head:* Martin E. Ford, Senior Associate Dean, 703-993-2008.

The George Washington University, Graduate School of Education and Human Development, Department of Teacher Preparation and Special Education, Program in Early Childhood Special Education, Washington, DC 20052. Offers MA Ed. *Accreditation:* NCATE. *Degree requirements:* For master's, comprehensive exam. *Entrance requirements:* For master's, GRE General Test or MAT, minimum GPA of 2.75. *Faculty research:* Computer-assisted instruction and learning, disabled learner assessment of preschool, handicapped children.

The George Washington University, Graduate School of Education and Human Development, Department of Teacher Preparation and Special Education, Program in Infant Special Education, Washington, DC 20052. Offers MA Ed. *Accreditation:* NCATE. *Degree requirements:* For master's, comprehensive exam. *Entrance requirements:* For master's, GRE General Test or MAT, minimum GPA of 2.75. *Faculty research:* Assessment, early intervention.

Georgia College & State University, Graduate School, School of Education, Department of Early Childhood and Middle Grades Education, Milledgeville, GA 31061. Offers early childhood education (M Ed, Ed S); middle grades education (M Ed, Ed S). *Accreditation:* NCATE. *Students:* 5 full-time (4 women), 57 part-time (51 women); includes 12 minority (11 African Americans, 1 Hispanic American), 1 international. Average age 36. 67 applicants, 51% accepted, 9 enrolled. In 2006, 21 master's, 24 other advanced degrees awarded. *Degree requirements:* For master's, comprehensive exam; for Ed S, residency. *Entrance requirements:* For master's, GRE General Test or MAT, 2 professional recommendations; for Ed S, GRE General Test or MAT, master's degree, 2 years teaching experience, 2 professional recommendations. Additional exam requirements/recommendations for international students: Required—TOEFL. *Application deadline:* For fall admission, 7/1 priority date for domestic students. Applications are processed on a rolling basis. Application fee: $25. Electronic applications accepted. *Expenses:* Tuition, state resident: full-time $3,222; part-time $179 per credit hour. Tuition, nonresident: full-time $12,870; part-time $715 per credit hour. Required fees: $391 per semester. Tuition and fees vary according to course load. *Financial support:* Career-related internships or fieldwork, Federal Work-Study, and unspecified assistantships available. Support available to part-time students. Financial award application deadline: 3/1; financial award applicants required to submit FAFSA. *Unit head:* Dr. Charles Martin, Chair, 478-445-5479, E-mail: charles.martin@gcsu.edu.

Georgia Southern University, Jack N. Averitt College of Graduate Studies, College of Education, Department of Teaching and Learning, Program in Early Childhood Education, Statesboro, GA 30460. Offers M Ed. *Accreditation:* NCATE. Part-time and evening/weekend programs available. *Students:* 2 full-time (both women), 20 part-time (all women); includes 7 minority (4 African Americans, 1 American Indian/Alaska Native, 1 Asian American or Pacific Islander, 1 Hispanic American). Average age 27. 9 applicants, 78% accepted, 5 enrolled. In 2006, 2 degrees awarded. *Degree requirements:* For master's, exit assessment. *Entrance requirements:* For master's, GRE General Test or MAT, minimum GPA of 2.5. Additional exam requirements/recommendations for international students: Required—TOEFL (minimum score 550 paper-based; 213 computer-based; 80 iBT). *Application deadline:* For fall admission, 3/1 priority date for domestic students, 3/1 for international students; for spring admission, 10/1 priority date for domestic students, 10/1 for international students. Applications are processed on a rolling basis. Application fee: $50. Electronic applications accepted. *Financial support:* In 2006–07, 7 students received support, including research assistantships with partial tuition reimbursements available (averaging $5,500 per year), teaching assistantships with partial tuition reimbursements available (averaging $5,500 per year); career-related internships or fieldwork, Federal Work-Study, scholarships/grants, tuition waivers (partial), and unspecified assistantships also available. Support available to part-time students. Financial award application deadline: 4/15; financial award applicants required to submit FAFSA. *Faculty research:* Technology, effective instructional strategies, multiculturalism, children's literature, school violence. *Unit head:* Dr. Scott Beck, Coordinator, 912-681-0073, Fax: 912-681-0026. *Application contact:* 912-681-5384, Fax: 912-681-0740, E-mail: gradadmissions@georgiasouthern.edu.

Georgia Southwestern State University, Graduate Studies, School of Education, Americus, GA 31709-4693. Offers early childhood education (M Ed, Ed S); health and physical education (M Ed); middle grades education (M Ed, Ed S); reading (M Ed); secondary education (M Ed); special education (M Ed). *Accreditation:* NCATE. *Degree requirements:* For master's, comprehensive exam. *Entrance requirements:* For master's, GRE General Test or MAT, minimum GPA of 2.5; for Ed S, GRE General Test or MAT, minimum graduate GPA of 3.25, M Ed from accredited college or university, 3 years teaching experience. Electronic applications accepted.

Georgia State University, College of Education, Department of Early Childhood Education, Atlanta, GA 30303-3083. Offers M Ed, PhD, Ed S. *Accreditation:* NCATE. Evening/weekend programs available. *Faculty:* 19 full-time (17 women), 27 part-time/adjunct (26 women). *Students:* 73 full-time (70 women), 8 part-time (7 women); includes 7 minority (6 African Americans, 1 American Indian/Alaska Native). Average age 35. In 2006, 45 master's, 13 other advanced degrees awarded. *Degree requirements:* For master's, comprehensive exam; for doctorate, thesis/dissertation, comprehensive exam; for Ed S, project. *Entrance requirements:* For master's, GRE General Test, minimum GPA of 2.5; for doctorate, GRE General Test, minimum GPA of 3.3; for Ed S, GRE General Test or MAT, minimum graduate GPA of 3.25. Application fee: $25. *Financial support:* In 2006–07, 15 research assistantships were awarded; teaching assistantships, career-related internships or fieldwork and tuition waivers (partial) also available. *Faculty research:* Teacher training program evaluation, pre-kindergarten program evaluation, literacy development, children's literature, alternative assessment strategies, children in poverty. Total annual research expenditures: $2.2 million. *Unit head:* Dr. Barbara Meyers, Chair, 404-651-2584, E-mail: barbara@gsu.edu.

Golden Gate Baptist Theological Seminary, Graduate and Professional Programs, Mill Valley, CA 94941-3197. Offers divinity (M Div); early childhood education (Certificate); education leadership (MAEL, Diploma); ministry (D Min); theological studies (MTS); theology (Th M); youth ministry (Certificate). *Accreditation:* ACIPE; ATS (one or more programs are accredited). Part-time and evening/weekend programs available. *Degree requirements:* For M Div, 2 foreign languages; for master's, thesis (for some programs); for doctorate, 2 foreign languages, thesis/dissertation. *Entrance requirements:* For doctorate, MAT. Additional exam requirements/recommendations for international students: Required—TOEFL (minimum score 550 paper-based; 213 computer-based). Electronic applications accepted.

Governors State University, College of Education, Program in Early Childhood Education, University Park, IL 60466-0975. Offers MA. *Accreditation:* NCATE. *Students:* 6 full-time (all women), 20 part-time (all women). Average age 37. *Degree requirements:* For master's, practicum. *Entrance requirements:* For master's, minimum GPA of 2.75 in last 60 hours of undergraduate course work, minimum graduate GPA of 3.0. *Application deadline:* For fall admission, 7/15 priority date for domestic students; for spring admission, 11/10 for domestic students. Applications are processed on a rolling basis. Application fee: $25. *Expenses:* Tuition, state resident: full-time $4,104; part-time $171 per hour. Tuition, nonresident: part-time $513 per hour. *Financial support:* Application deadline: 5/1. *Application contact:* John Powers, Adviser, 708-534-6363.

Grambling State University, School of Graduate Studies and Research, College of Education, Department of Teacher Education, Grambling, LA 71245. Offers elementary/early childhood education (MS). *Accreditation:* NCATE. Part-time and evening/weekend programs available. Postbaccalaureate distance learning degree programs offered. *Faculty:* 9 full-time (7 women). *Students:* 4 full-time (3 women), 3 part-time (all women); all minorities (all African Americans) Average age 37. In 2006, 7 degrees awarded. *Degree requirements:* For master's, comprehensive exam. *Entrance requirements:* For master's, GRE. Additional exam requirements/recommendations for international students: Required—TOEFL. *Application deadline:* For fall admission, 7/1 for domestic students; for spring admission, 12/1 for domestic students. Application fee: $20 ($30 for international students). *Expenses:* Tuition, state resident: full-time $2,232; part-time $124 per credit hour. Tuition, nonresident: full-time $7,582; part-time $124 per credit hour. Required fees: $1,127. *Financial support:* In 2006–07, 6 students received support. Institutionally sponsored loans and unspecified assistantships available. Financial award application deadline: 5/31; financial award applicants required to submit FAFSA. *Unit head:* Dr. Doris Williams-Smith, Director, 318-394, Fax: 318-274-2799, E-mail: smithdo@gram.edu. *Application contact:* Melanie Monroe, Secretary II, 318-274-2238, Fax: 318-274-2799, E-mail: monroem@alpha0.gram.edu.

Grand Valley State University, College of Education, Program in Special Education, Allendale, MI 49401-9403. Offers early childhood developmental delay (M Ed); emotional impairment (M Ed); learning disabilities (M Ed); special education endorsements (M Ed). *Accreditation:* NCATE. Part-time and evening/weekend programs available. *Faculty:* 10 full-time (6 women), 6 part-time/adjunct (3 women). *Students:* 37 full-time (33 women), 289 part-time (252 women); includes 14 minority (8 African Americans, 3 American Indian/Alaska Native, 3 Hispanic Americans). Average age 36. 46 applicants, 93% accepted, 31 enrolled. In 2006, 77 degrees awarded. *Degree requirements:* For master's, thesis. *Entrance requirements:* For master's, GRE General Test or minimum GPA of 3.0. Additional exam requirements/recommendations for international students: Required—TOEFL. *Application deadline:* Applications are processed on a rolling basis. Application fee: $30. Electronic applications accepted. *Expenses:* Tuition, state resident: full-time $5,850; part-time $325 per credit. Tuition, nonresident: full-time $10,800; part-time $600 per credit. Tuition and fees vary according to course load. *Financial support:* In 2006–07, research assistantships with full and partial tuition reimbursements (averaging $8,000 per year); career-related internships or fieldwork, Federal Work-Study, scholarships/grants, and unspecified assistantships also available. *Faculty research:* Evaluation of special education program effects, adaptive behavior assessment, language development, writing disorders, comparative effects of presentation methods. *Unit head:* Dr. Sandy Miller, Director, 616-3344. *Application contact:* Dr. Douglas Busman, Director, Student Information and Services, 616-331-6831, Fax: 616-331-6217, E-mail: busmando@gvsu.edu.

Grand Valley State University, College of Education, Programs in General Education, Allendale, MI 49401-9403. Offers adult and higher education (M Ed); early childhood education (M Ed); education of the gifted and talented (M Ed); educational leadership (M Ed); educational technology (M Ed); elementary education (M Ed); middle and high school education (M Ed); teaching English to speakers of other languages (M Ed). Part-time and evening/weekend programs available. Postbaccalaureate distance learning degree programs offered (minimal on-campus study). *Faculty:* 82 full-time (42 women), 43 part-time/adjunct (25 women). *Students:* 136 full-time (97 women), 828 part-time (565 women); includes 55 minority (26 African Americans, 7 American Indian/Alaska Native, 5 Asian Americans or Pacific Islanders, 17 Hispanic Americans). Average age 33. 280 applicants, 94% accepted, 188 enrolled. In 2006, 322 degrees awarded.

Degree requirements: For master's, thesis. *Entrance requirements:* For master's, GRE General Test or minimum GPA of 3.0. Additional exam requirements/recommendations for international students: Required—TOEFL. *Application deadline:* Applications are processed on a rolling basis. Application fee: $30. Electronic applications accepted. *Expenses:* Tuition, state resident: full-time $5,850; part-time $325 per credit. Tuition, nonresident: full-time $10,800; part-time $600 per credit. Tuition and fees vary according to course load. *Financial support:* In 2006–07, 2 research assistantships with full and partial tuition reimbursements (averaging $8,000 per year) were awarded; career-related internships or fieldwork, Federal Work-Study, scholarships/grants, and unspecified assistantships also available. *Faculty research:* Effectiveness of technology in education, parental involvement, effective teaching, effective schools research. *Unit head:* Dr. Linda McCrea, Director, 616-331-2080, E-mail: mccreal@gvsu.edu. *Application contact:* Dr. Douglas Busman, Director, Student Information and Services, 616-331-6831, Fax: 616-331-6217, E-mail: busmando@gvsu.edu.

Harding University, College of Education, Searcy, AR 72149-0001. Offers advanced studies in teaching and learning (M Ed); art (MSE); behavioral science (MSE); Bible and religion (MSE); counseling (MS, Ed S); early childhood education (M Ed); early childhood special education (M Ed, MSE); education (MSE); educational leadership (M Ed, Ed S); elementary education (M Ed); English (MSE); family and consumer science (MSE); French (MSE); history/social science (MSE); kinesiology (MSE); math (MSE); physical science (MSE); reading (M Ed); secondary education (M Ed); Spanish (MSE); special education licensure (M Ed); teaching (MAT). *Accreditation:* NCATE. Part-time programs available. *Faculty:* 8 full-time (2 women), 45 part-time/adjunct (30 women). *Students:* 153 full-time (123 women), 469 part-time (341 women); includes 72 minority (63 African Americans, 4 American Indian/Alaska Native, 1 Asian American or Pacific Islander, 4 Hispanic Americans), 9 international. Average age 35. 175 applicants, 90% accepted, 147 enrolled. In 2006, 241 degrees awarded. *Degree requirements:* For master's, portfolio(s), thesis optional; for Ed S, portfolio, specialist project. *Entrance requirements:* For master's, GRE, MAT, PRAXIS; for Ed S, MAT or GRE. Additional exam requirements/recommendations for international students: Required—TOEFL (minimum score 550 paper-based). *Application deadline:* For fall admission, 8/1 for domestic and international students; for spring admission, 1/1 for domestic and international students. Applications are processed on a rolling basis. Application fee: $35. *Expenses:* Tuition: Part-time $455 per semester hour. Required fees: $20 per semester hour. Tuition and fees vary according to course load. *Financial support:* Scholarships/grants and unspecified assistantships available. Support available to part-time students. *Faculty research:* Reading, comprehension, school violence, educational technology, behavior, college choice, differentiated instruction, brain based teaching. *Unit head:* Pat Bashaw, Chair, 501-279-4183, Fax: 501-279-4051, E-mail: pbashaw@harding.edu.

Hebrew College, Shoolman Graduate School of Education, Newton Centre, MA 02459. Offers early childhood Jewish education (Certificate); Jewish day school education (Certificate); Jewish education (MJ Ed); Jewish family education (Certificate); Jewish special education (Certificate); Jewish youth education, informal education and camping (Certificate). Part-time and evening/weekend programs available. Postbaccalaureate distance learning degree programs offered. *Faculty:* 6 full-time (1 woman), 19 part-time/adjunct (7 women). *Students:* 51 (42 women). Average age 37. 33 applicants, 79% accepted, 19 enrolled. In 2006, 5 degrees awarded. *Degree requirements:* For master's, one foreign language. *Entrance requirements:* For master's, GRE, interview. Additional exam requirements/recommendations for international students: Required—TOEFL. *Application deadline:* For fall admission, 12/15 priority date for domestic and international students; for winter admission, 2/15 priority date for domestic and international students; for spring admission, 5/30 priority date for domestic and international students. Application fee: $50. *Financial support:* Fellowships, career-related internships or fieldwork and tuition waivers (partial) available. Support available to part-time students. Financial award application deadline: 4/15; financial award applicants required to submit FAFSA. *Unit head:* Dr. Barry Mesch, Provost, 617-559-8600, Fax: 617-559-8601, E-mail: bmesch@hebrewcollege.edu. *Application contact:* Kate Nachman, Director of Admissions, 617-559-8610, Fax: 617-559-8601, E-mail: admissions@hebrewcollege.edu.

Henderson State University, Graduate Studies, School of Education, Department of Curriculum, Instruction and Leadership, Arkadelphia, AR 71999-0001. Offers early childhood (P-4) (MSE); English (MSE); English as a second language (MSE, CP); math (MSE); middle school (MSE); reading (MSE); social science (MSE). *Accreditation:* NCATE. Part-time programs available. *Faculty:* 19 full-time (6 women), 4 part-time/adjunct (2 women). *Students:* 38 full-time (36 women), 49 part-time (47 women); includes 6 minority (5 African Americans, 1 Hispanic American), 16 international. Average age 37. In 2006, 31 degrees awarded. *Entrance requirements:* For master's, GRE General Test or MAT, minimum GPA of 2.7, teacher certification. *Application deadline:* For fall admission, 5/1 priority date for domestic students, 5/1 for international students; for winter admission, 10/1 for international students; for spring admission, 12/1 priority date for domestic students, 4/1 for international students. Applications are processed on a rolling basis. Application fee: $0 ($30 for international students). *Expenses:* Tuition, state resident: full-time $3,294; part-time $183 per credit hour. Tuition, nonresident: full-time $6,588; part-time $366 per credit hour. Required fees: $176 per term. *Financial support:* In 2006–07, 1 teaching assistantship with full tuition reimbursement (averaging $4,000 per year) was awarded; research assistantships, Federal Work-Study and institutionally sponsored loans also available. Support available to part-time students. Financial award application deadline: 7/31. *Unit head:* Dr. Kenneth Harris, Chairperson, 870-230-5203, Fax: 870-230-5455, E-mail: harris@hsu.edu. *Application contact:* Dr. Marck L. Beggs, Graduate Dean, 870-230-5126, Fax: 870-230-5479, E-mail: beggsm@hsu.edu.

Henderson State University, Graduate Studies, School of Education, Department of Educational Leadership and Special Education, Arkadelphia, AR 71999-0001. Offers early childhood special education (MSE); education (MAT); educational leadership (Ed S); instructional specialist (MSE); school administration (MSE). *Faculty:* 7 full-time (4 women), 3 part-time/adjunct (2 women). *Students:* 6 full-time (3 women), 144 part-time (113 women); includes 14 minority (all African Americans) Average age 35. In 2006, 18 degrees awarded. *Expenses:* Tuition, state resident: full-time $3,294; part-time $183 per credit hour. Tuition, nonresident: full-time $6,588; part-time $366 per credit hour. Required fees: $176 per term. *Unit head:* Dr. Bruce Smith, Chairperson, 870-230-5282. *Application contact:* Dr. Marck L. Beggs, Graduate Dean, 870-230-5126, Fax: 870-230-5479, E-mail: beggsm@hsu.edu.

Hofstra University, School of Education and Allied Human Services, Department of Counseling, Research, Special Education and Rehabilitation, Program in Special Education, Hempstead, NY 11549. Offers early childhood special education (MS Ed, Advanced Certificate); gifted education (Advanced Certificate); inclusive early childhood special education (MS Ed); inclusive elementary special education (MS Ed); inclusive secondary special education (MS Ed); literacy studies and special education (MS Ed); special education (MA, MS Ed, PD); special education assessment and diagnosis (Advanced Certificate); teaching students with severe/multiple disabilities (Advanced Certificate). *Accreditation:* NCATE. Part-time and evening/weekend programs available. Postbaccalaureate distance learning degree programs offered. *Students:* 87 full-time (82 women), 116 part-time (110 women); includes 21 minority (8 African Americans, 4 Asian Americans or Pacific Islanders, 9 Hispanic Americans). Average age 28. 110 applicants, 79% accepted, 61 enrolled. In 2006, 74 master's, 7 other advanced degrees awarded. *Degree requirements:* For master's, thesis (for some programs), seminars, student teaching, comprehensive exam (for some programs), registration; for other advanced degree, fieldwork. *Entrance requirements:* For master's, interview, 3 letters of reference, resumé, minimum GPA of 3.0; for other advanced degree, interview, 3 letters of recommendation, resumé. Additional exam requirements/recommendations for international students: Required—TOEFL (minimum score 550 paper-based; 213 computer-based). *Application deadline:* Applications are processed on a rolling basis. Application fee: $60. Electronic applications accepted. *Expenses:* Tuition: Full-time $13,320; part-time $740 per credit. Required fees: $930; $155 per term. *Financial support:* In 2006–07, 64 students received support, including 6 fellowships with tuition reimbursements available (averaging $2,552 per year), 4 research assistantships with full and partial tuition reimbursements available (averaging $4,378 per year); Federal Work-Study, scholarships/grants, tuition waivers (full and partial), and unspecified assistantships also available. Support available to part-time students. Financial award applicants required to submit FAFSA. *Faculty research:* Inclusive schooling, autism spectrum disorders related services, parent participation in the special education process, co-teaching student teaching. *Unit head:* Dr. George Guiliani, Director, 516-463-5778, Fax: 516-463-6184, E-mail: cprdcs@hofstra.edu. *Application contact:* Carol Drummer, Dean of Graduate Admissions, 516-463-4876, Fax: 516-463-4664, E-mail: gradstudent@hofstra.edu.

Hofstra University, School of Education and Allied Human Services, Department of Curriculum and Teaching, Program in Early Childhood Education, Hempstead, NY 11549. Offers early childhood and childhood education (MS Ed); early childhood education (MA, MS Ed). Part-time and evening/weekend programs available. *Students:* 30 full-time (28 women), 25 part-time (all women); includes 7 minority (1 African American, 6 Hispanic Americans). Average age 28. 40 applicants, 83% accepted, 20 enrolled. In 2006, 20 degrees awarded. *Degree requirements:* For master's, 35 semester hours; for degree. *Entrance requirements:* For master's, 2 letters of recommendation, teacher certification (MA), interview, essay. Additional exam requirements/recommendations for international students: Required—TOEFL (minimum score 550 paper-based; 213 computer-based). *Application deadline:* Applications are processed on a rolling basis. Application fee: $60. Electronic applications accepted. *Expenses:* Tuition: Full-time $13,320; part-time $740 per credit. Required fees: $930; $155 per term. *Financial support:* In 2006–07, 14 students received support, including 1 fellowship with tuition reimbursement available (averaging $3,000 per year), 2 research assistantships with full and partial tuition reimbursements available (averaging $4,300 per year); career-related internships or fieldwork, Federal Work-Study, scholarships/grants, health care benefits, tuition waivers (full and partial), and unspecified assistantships also available. Support available to part-time students. Financial award applicants required to submit FAFSA. *Faculty research:* Sociodramatic play; curriculum development, integrated curriculum. *Unit head:* Dr. Doris P. Fromberg, Program Director, 516-463-5768, Fax: 516-463-6196, E-mail: catdpf@hofstra.edu. *Application contact:* Carol Drummer, Dean of Graduate Admissions, 516-463-4876, Fax: 516-463-4664, E-mail: gradstudent@hofstra.edu.

Hood College, Graduate School, Department of Education, Frederick, MD 21701-8575. Offers curriculum and instruction (MS), including early childhood education, elementary education, elementary school science and mathematics, secondary education, special education; educational leadership (MS); reading specialization (MS); teaching the struggling reader (Certificate). Part-time and evening/weekend programs available. *Faculty:* 4 full-time (3 women), 32 part-time/adjunct (16 women). *Students:* 5 full-time (3 women), 371 part-time (313 women); includes 30 minority (23 African Americans, 4 Asian Americans or Pacific Islanders, 3 Hispanic Americans). Average age 32. 71 applicants, 99% accepted, 59 enrolled. In 2006, 67 degrees awarded. *Degree requirements:* For master's, action research project, portfolio (reading). *Entrance requirements:* For master's, minimum GPA of 2.5, teaching certification. *Application deadline:* Applications are processed on a rolling basis. Application fee: $35. *Expenses:* Tuition: Part-time $350 per credit. Required fees: $20 per semester. *Financial support:* Applicants required to submit FAFSA. *Faculty research:* Leadership, action research, brain research, learning styles. *Unit head:* Dr. John George, Chairperson, 301-696-3471, Fax: 301-696-3597, E-mail: george@hood.edu. *Application contact:* Dr. Kathleen C. Bands, Associate Dean of Graduate School, 301-696-3811, Fax: 301-696-3597, E-mail: gofurther@hood.edu.

Howard University, School of Education, Department of Curriculum and Instruction, Program in Early Childhood Education, Washington, DC 20059-0002. Offers M Ed, MA, MAT, CAGS. MA offered through the Graduate School of Arts and Sciences. *Accreditation:* NCATE. Part-time programs available. *Faculty:* 2 full-time (both women). *Students:* 1 (woman) full-time, 2 part-time (both women); all minorities (all African Americans) Average age 26. 13 applicants, 46% accepted, 2 enrolled. In 2006, 4 degrees awarded. *Degree requirements:* For master's, thesis (for some programs), expository writing exam, internships, practicum, comprehensive exam; for CAGS, thesis optional. *Entrance requirements:* For master's, GRE General Test (MA), minimum GPA of 2.7. *Application deadline:* For fall admission, 4/1 priority date for domestic students; for spring admission, 11/1 for domestic students. Applications are processed on a rolling basis. Application fee: $45. *Financial support:* In 2006–07, research assistantships (averaging $10,000 per year); fellowships, teaching assistantships, career-related internships or fieldwork, Federal Work-Study, institutionally sponsored loans, scholarships/grants, tuition waivers (full and partial), and unspecified assistantships also available. Financial award application deadline: 4/1. *Faculty research:* Parental factors on child development, early attachment, cross-culture. *Unit head:* Dr. Fang Wu, Assistant Professor/Coordinator, 202-806-4948, Fax: 202-806-5297, E-mail: f_wu@howard.edu.

Hunter College of the City University of New York, Graduate School, School of Education, Department of Curriculum and Teaching, New York, NY 10021-5085. Offers bilingual education (MS); corrective reading (K–12) (MS Ed); early childhood education (MS); educational supervision and administration (AC); elementary education (MS); literacy education (MS); teaching English as a second language (MA). *Faculty:* 84 full-time (68 women), 112 part-time/adjunct (79 women). *Students:* 272 full-time (238 women), 1,353 part-time (1,237 women); includes 393 minority (127 African Americans, 103 Asian Americans or Pacific Islanders, 163 Hispanic Americans). Average age 36. 778 applicants, 48% accepted, 256 enrolled. In 2006, 291 degrees awarded. *Degree requirements:* For master's, thesis; for AC, portfolio review. *Entrance requirements:* For degree, minimum B average in graduate course work, teaching certificate, minimum 3 years of full-time teaching experience, interview, 2 letters of support. Additional exam requirements/recommendations for international students: Required—TOEFL, TWE. *Application deadline:* For fall admission, 4/1 for domestic students; for spring admission, 11/1 for domestic students. Applications are processed on a rolling basis. Application fee: $125. *Expenses:* Tuition, state resident: part-time $270 per credit. Tuition, nonresident: part-time $500 per credit. Required fees: $45 per semester. *Financial support:* Federal Work-Study, scholarships/grants, and tuition waivers (partial) available. Support available to part-time students. *Faculty research:* Teacher opportunity corps-mentor program for first-year teachers, adult literacy, student literacy corporation. *Unit head:* Dr. Anne M. Ediger, Head, 212-777-4763, E-mail: anne.ediger@hunter.cuny.edu. *Application contact:* William Zlata, Director for Graduate Admissions, 212-772-4482, Fax: 212-650-3336, E-mail: admissions@hunter.cuny.edu.

Indiana State University, School of Graduate Studies, College of Education, Department of Elementary and Special Education, Terre Haute, IN 47809-1401. Offers early childhood education (M Ed); elementary education (M Ed); literacy (M Ed). *Accreditation:* NCATE. *Faculty:* 9 full-time (7 women), 5 part-time/adjunct (4 women). *Students:* 6 full-time (all women), 46 part-time (43 women); includes 3 minority (2 African Americans, 1 Asian American or Pacific Islander), 2 international. Average age 35. 26 applicants, 96% accepted, 12 enrolled. In 2006, 26 degrees awarded. *Application deadline:* For fall admission, 7/1 priority date for domestic students; for spring admission, 11/1 priority date for domestic students. Applications are processed on a rolling basis. Application fee: $35. Electronic applications accepted. *Expenses:* Tuition, state resident: part-time $278 per credit. Tuition, nonresident: part-time $552 per credit. *Financial support:* In 2006–07, research assistantships with partial tuition reimbursements (averaging $6,500 per year); teaching assistantships with partial tuition reimbursements, tuition waivers (partial) also available. Financial award application deadline: 3/1; financial award applicants required to submit FAFSA. *Unit head:* Dr. Diana Quatroche, Interim Chairperson, 812-237-2852.

Indiana University of Pennsylvania, School of Graduate Studies and Research, College of Education and Educational Technology, Department of Professional Studies in Education, Program in Early Childhood Education, Indiana, PA 15705-1087. Offers M Ed. *Accreditation:* NCATE. Part-time programs available. *Students:* 21 full-time (17 women), 13 part-time (10 women); includes 1 minority (African American) Average age 30. 59 applicants, 44% accepted. *Degree requirements:* For master's, thesis optional. *Entrance requirements:* For master's, 2 letters of recommendation. Additional exam requirements/recommendations for international students: Required—TOEFL. *Application deadline:* For fall admission, 7/1 priority date for

Early Childhood Education

Indiana University of Pennsylvania (continued)
domestic students; for spring admission, 11/1 for domestic students. Applications are processed on a rolling basis. Application fee: $30. *Expenses:* Tuition, state resident: full-time $6,048; part-time $336 per credit. Tuition, nonresident: full-time $9,678; part-time $538 per credit. Required fees: $1,069; $148 per year. *Financial support:* In 2006–07, research assistantships (averaging $6,000 per year); career-related internships or fieldwork and Federal Work-Study also available. Financial award application deadline: 3/15; financial award applicants required to submit FAFSA. *Unit head:* Dr. Mary R. Jalongo, Graduate Coordinator, 724-357-2417, E-mail: mjalongo@iup.edu.

Inter American University of Puerto Rico, Guayama Campus, Department of Education and Social Sciences, Guayama, PR 00785. Offers early childhood education (MA). *Entrance requirements:* For master's, GRE, MAT, EXADEP, letters of recommendation, minimum GPA of 2.5.

Jackson State University, Graduate School, School of Education, Department of Curriculum and Instruction, Jackson, MS 39217. Offers early childhood education (MS Ed, Ed D); elementary education (MS Ed, Ed S). *Accreditation:* NCATE. Evening/weekend programs available. *Faculty:* 10 full-time (7 women), 1 (woman) part-time/adjunct. *Students:* 12 full-time (9 women), 52 part-time (43 women); includes 59 minority (all African Americans) In 2006, 20 master's, 1 other advanced degree awarded. Terminal master's awarded for partial completion of doctoral program. *Degree requirements:* For master's, thesis or alternative, comprehensive exam; for doctorate, thesis/dissertation, comprehensive exam. *Entrance requirements:* For master's, GRE General Test; for doctorate, MAT, teaching experience. Additional exam requirements/recommendations for international students: Required—TOEFL. *Application deadline:* For fall admission, 3/1 priority date for domestic students; for spring admission, 10/1 for domestic students. Applications are processed on a rolling basis. Application fee: $20. *Financial support:* In 2006–07, 30 students received support. Career-related internships or fieldwork, Federal Work-Study, scholarships/grants, and unspecified assistantships available. Support available to part-time students. Financial award application deadline: 3/1; financial award applicants required to submit FAFSA. *Unit head:* Dr. Rodney Washington, Chair, 601-979-2336, Fax: 601-979-2178, E-mail: rodney.washington@jsums.edu. *Application contact:* Curtis Gore, Director of Graduate Admissions, 601-979-2455, Fax: 601-974-4325, E-mail: cgore@ccaix.jsums.edu.

Jacksonville State University, College of Graduate Studies and Continuing Education, College of Education and Professional Studies, Program in Early Childhood Education, Jacksonville, AL 36265-1602. Offers MS Ed. *Accreditation:* NCATE. *Faculty:* 2 full-time (both women). *Students:* 5 full-time (all women), 17 part-time (all women); includes 5 minority (4 African Americans, 1 American Indian/Alaska Native). In 2006, 9 degrees awarded. *Entrance requirements:* For master's, GRE General Test or MAT. *Application deadline:* Applications are processed on a rolling basis. Application fee: $20. *Expenses:* Tuition, state resident: full-time $5,400; part-time $225 per credit hour. Tuition, nonresident: full-time $10,800; part-time $450 per credit hour. One-time fee: $20 full-time. *Financial support:* In 2006–07, 1 research assistantship was awarded. Support available to part-time students. Financial award application deadline: 4/1. *Unit head:* Dr. Elizabeth Engley, Head, 256-782-5844. *Application contact:* 256-782-5329, Fax: 256-782-5321.

Jacksonville University, College of Arts and Sciences, School of Education, Jacksonville, FL 32211-3394. Offers computer sciences (MAT); early childhood education (Certificate); elementary education (MAT); integrated learning with educational technology (MAT); mathematics education (MAT); music education (MAT); reading education (MAT); second careers as a teacher (Certificate). Part-time and evening/weekend programs available. *Degree requirements:* For master's, comprehensive exam. *Entrance requirements:* For master's, GRE General Test, minimum GPA of 3.0. Additional exam requirements/recommendations for international students: Required—TOEFL (minimum score 550 paper-based), TWE. Expenses: Contact institution.

James Madison University, College of Graduate and Outreach Programs, College of Education, Early, Elementary, and Reading Education Department, Program in Early Childhood Education, Harrisonburg, VA 22807. Offers MAT. *Accreditation:* NCATE. Part-time programs available. *Students:* Average age 27. *Entrance requirements:* For master's, GRE General Test. Additional exam requirements/recommendations for international students: Required—TOEFL. *Application deadline:* For fall admission, 5/1 priority date for domestic students; for spring admission, 9/1 priority date for domestic students. Applications are processed on a rolling basis. Application fee: $55. Electronic applications accepted. *Expenses:* Tuition, state resident: full-time $6,336; part-time $264 per credit hour. Tuition, nonresident: full-time $17,832; part-time $743 per credit hour. *Financial support:* Career-related internships or fieldwork and unspecified assistantships available. Financial award application deadline: 3/1; financial award applicants required to submit FAFSA. *Unit head:* Dr. Martha Ross, Academic Unit Head, 540-568-6255.

John Carroll University, Graduate School, Department of Education and Allied Studies, Program in School Based Early Childhood Education, University Heights, OH 44118-4581. Offers M Ed. *Accreditation:* NCATE. *Faculty:* 1 (woman) full-time, 3 part-time/adjunct (all women). *Students:* 23 full-time (22 women); includes 2 minority (1 African American, 1 Asian American or Pacific Islander). Average age 29. 51 applicants, 45% accepted, 23 enrolled. In 2006, 23 degrees awarded. *Degree requirements:* For master's, comprehensive exam. *Entrance requirements:* For master's, GRE General Test or MAT, minimum GPA of 2.75. *Application deadline:* For spring admission, 5/15 for domestic students. Applications are processed on a rolling basis. Application fee: $25 ($35 for international students). *Expenses:* Tuition: Full-time $9,675; part-time $645 per credit hour. Tuition and fees vary according to program. *Financial support:* Application deadline: 3/1; *Unit head:* Dr. Barbara Garson, Coordinator, Teacher Education, 216-397-4689, Fax: 216-397-3045, E-mail: bgarson@jcu.edu.

Kean University, College of Education, Program in Early Childhood Education, Union, NJ 07083. Offers administration in early childhood and family studies (MA); advanced curriculum and teaching (MA); classroom instruction (MA, including preschool-third grade; early childhood education (MA); education for family living (MA). *Accreditation:* NCATE. Part-time and evening/weekend programs available. *Faculty:* 11 full-time (10 women). *Students:* 12 full-time (11 women), 90 part-time (88 women); includes 22 minority (11 African Americans, 1 Asian American or Pacific Islander, 10 Hispanic Americans), 2 international. Average age 31. 51 applicants, 82% accepted, 28 enrolled. In 2006, 27 degrees awarded. *Degree requirements:* For master's, thesis, portfolio, comprehensive exam. *Entrance requirements:* For master's, GRE General Test, 2 letters of recommendation, interview, writing sample, minimum GPA of 2.5. *Application deadline:* For fall admission, 5/1 for domestic students; for spring admission, 11/1 for domestic students. Application fee: $60 ($150 for international students). Electronic applications accepted. *Expenses:* Tuition, state resident: full-time $8,856; part-time $369 per credit. Tuition, nonresident: full-time $11,256; part-time $469 per credit. *Financial support:* Research assistantships with full tuition reimbursements, unspecified assistantships available. *Unit head:* Dr. Marjorie Kelly, Program Coordinator, 908-737-3789, E-mail: mkelly@kean.edu. *Application contact:* Joanne Morris, Director of Graduate Admissions, 908-737-3355, Fax: 908-737-3354, E-mail: grad-adm@kean.edu.

Kennesaw State University, Leland and Clarice C. Bagwell College of Education, Program in Graduate Education, Kennesaw, GA 30144-5591. Offers adolescent education (M Ed); early childhood education (M Ed); educational leadership (M Ed); special education (M Ed). *Accreditation:* NCATE. Part-time programs available. *Faculty:* 60 full-time (38 women), 12 part-time/adjunct (4 women). *Students:* 150 full-time (143 women), 489 part-time (371 women); includes 95 minority (85 African Americans, 1 American Indian/Alaska Native, 1 Asian American or Pacific Islander, 8 Hispanic Americans), 21 international. Average age 35. 165 applicants, 97% accepted, 142 enrolled. In 2006, 283 degrees awarded. *Degree requirements:* For master's, thesis or alternative. *Entrance requirements:* For master's, GRE General Test, T-4 state certification, minimum GPA of 2.75. Additional exam requirements/recommendations for

international students: Required—TOEFL (minimum score 550 paper-based; 213 computer-based; 80 iBT), IELTS (minimum score 6). *Application deadline:* For fall admission, 7/15 priority date for domestic students; for spring admission, 10/15 priority date for domestic students. Application fee: $50. Electronic applications accepted. *Expenses:* Tuition, state resident: full-time $3,044; part-time $127 per semester hour. Tuition, nonresident: full-time $12,172; part-time $508 per semester hour. Required fees: $353 per semester. Full-time tuition and fees vary according to campus/location and program. *Financial support:* Federal Work-Study and unspecified assistantships available. Support available to part-time students. Financial award application deadline: 6/15; financial award applicants required to submit FAFSA. *Application contact:* Alisha O'Brien, Administrative Coordinator, 770-423-6043, Fax: 770-420-4435, E-mail: aobrien@kennesaw.edu.

Kent State University, Graduate School of Education, Health, and Human Services, Department of Educational Foundations and Special Services, Program in Intervention Specialist, Kent, OH 44242-0001. Offers deaf education (M Ed, MA); early childhood education (M Ed, MA); educational interpreter (M Ed, MA); general special education (M Ed, MA); gifted (M Ed, MA); mild/moderate (M Ed, MA); moderate/intensive (M Ed, MA); transition to work (M Ed, MA). *Faculty:* 13 full-time (9 women), 15 part-time/adjunct (13 women). *Students:* 41 full-time (37 women), 103 part-time (91 women); includes 2 minority (1 African American, 1 American Indian/Alaska Native), 1 international. 30 applicants, 80% accepted. In 2006, 53 degrees awarded. *Entrance requirements:* For master's, GRE. Application fee: $30. *Financial support:* In 2006–07, fellowships with tuition reimbursements (averaging $7,210 per year); research assistantships with tuition reimbursements, teaching assistantships with tuition reimbursements, career-related internships or fieldwork, Federal Work-Study, institutionally sponsored loans, scholarships/grants, health care benefits, and unspecified assistantships also available. Support available to part-time students. *Unit head:* Dr. Penny Griffith, Coordinator, 330-672-2477, E-mail: pgriffith@kent.edu. *Application contact:* Nancy Miller, Academic Program Coordinator, Office of Graduate Student Services, 330-672-2576, Fax: 330-672-9162, E-mail: ogs@kent.edu.

Kent State University, Graduate School of Education, Health, and Human Services, Department of Teaching, Leadership, and Curriculum Studies, Program in Early Childhood Education, Kent, OH 44242-0001. Offers M Ed, MA, MAT. *Accreditation:* NCATE. *Faculty:* 20 full-time (17 women), 8 part-time/adjunct (7 women). *Students:* 16 full-time (15 women), 13 part-time (12 women); includes 3 minority (all African Americans) 21 applicants, 90% accepted. In 2006, 16 degrees awarded. *Degree requirements:* For master's, thesis (for some programs), registration. *Entrance requirements:* For master's, GRE General Test. Additional exam requirements/recommendations for international students: Required—TOEFL. *Application deadline:* For spring admission, 3/1 for domestic students. Application fee: $30. Electronic applications accepted. *Financial support:* In 2006–07, fellowships with full tuition reimbursements (averaging $7,210 per year); research assistantships with full tuition reimbursements, teaching assistantships with full tuition reimbursements, career-related internships or fieldwork, Federal Work-Study, institutionally sponsored loans, scholarships/grants, health care benefits, and unspecified assistantships also available. Support available to part-time students. Financial award application deadline: 4/1; financial award applicants required to submit FAFSA. *Faculty research:* Parent-child relationships, professional preparation, curriculum and assessment. *Unit head:* Carol Bersani, Coordinator, 330-672-2559, E-mail: cbersani@kent.edu. *Application contact:* Nancy Miller, Academic Program Coordinator, Office of Graduate Student Services, 330-672-2576, Fax: 330-672-9162, E-mail: ogs@kent.edu.

Keuka College, Program in Childhood Education, Keuka Park, NY 14478-0098. Offers MS. Part-time and evening/weekend programs available. *Faculty:* 4 part-time/adjunct (3 women). *Students:* 36 applicants, 100% accepted. In 2006, 49 degrees awarded. *Degree requirements:* For master's, thesis, research project, portfolio. *Entrance requirements:* For master's, minimum undergraduate GPA of 3.0, 2 letters of recommendation, provisional New York state certification. Additional exam requirements/recommendations for international students: Required—TOEFL (minimum score 550 paper-based; 213 computer-based). *Application deadline:* For fall admission, 8/15 priority date for domestic students; for winter admission, 12/15 priority date for domestic students; for spring admission, 4/15 priority date for domestic students. Applications are processed on a rolling basis. Application fee: $30. *Expenses:* Contact institution. *Faculty research:* Reading and writing across the curriculum, science education, elementary mathematics education; special education, critical thinking. *Unit head:* Dr. Diane Burke, Director of Graduate Program in Education, 315-279-5688.

Kutztown University of Pennsylvania, College of Graduate Studies and Extended Learning, College of Education, Program in Elementary Education, Kutztown, PA 19530-0730. Offers early childhood education (Certificate); elementary education (M Ed, Certificate); special education (Certificate). *Accreditation:* NCATE. Part-time and evening/weekend programs available. *Faculty:* 8 full-time (6 women), 1 (woman) part-time/adjunct. *Students:* 38 full-time (27 women), 64 part-time (54 women); includes 2 minority (both Hispanic Americans) Average age 29. 66 applicants, 85% accepted, 42 enrolled. In 2006, 15 degrees awarded. *Degree requirements:* For master's, comprehensive project, thesis optional. *Entrance requirements:* For master's, GRE General Test. Additional exam requirements/recommendations for international students: Required—TOEFL. *Application deadline:* Applications are processed on a rolling basis. Application fee: $35. Electronic applications accepted. *Expenses:* Tuition, state resident: full-time $6,048; part-time $336 per credit. Tuition, nonresident: full-time $9,678; part-time $538 per credit. *Financial support:* In 2006–07, research assistantships with full tuition reimbursements (averaging $5,000 per year); career-related internships or fieldwork, Federal Work-Study, and unspecified assistantships also available. Financial award application deadline: 3/15; financial award applicants required to submit FAFSA. *Faculty research:* Whole language, middle schools, cooperative learning discussion techniques, oral reading techniques, hemisphericity. *Unit head:* Dr. Elsa Geskus, Chairperson, 610-683-4262, Fax: 610-683-1327, E-mail: geskus@kutztown.edu.

Lehman College of the City University of New York, Division of Education, Department of Early Childhood and Elementary Education, Program in Early Childhood Education, Bronx, NY 10468-1589. Offers MS Ed. *Accreditation:* NCATE. Part-time and evening/weekend programs available. *Entrance requirements:* For master's, minimum GPA of 2.7. *Faculty research:* TV programming, literacy, children's trauma conceptualization.

Lenoir-Rhyne College, Graduate Programs, School of Education, Program in Birth through Kindergarten Education, Hickory, NC 28603. Offers MA. Part-time and evening/weekend programs available. *Degree requirements:* For master's, thesis optional. *Entrance requirements:* For master's, GRE General Test or MAT, minimum undergraduate GPA of 2.7, graduate 3.0. Additional exam requirements/recommendations for international students: Required—TOEFL (minimum score 600 paper-based). Electronic applications accepted.

Lesley University, School of Education, Cambridge, MA 02138-2790. Offers curriculum and instruction (M Ed, CAGS); early childhood education (M Ed); educational studies (PhD); elementary education (M Ed); individually designed (M Ed); middle school education (M Ed); moderate special needs (M Ed); reading (M Ed, CAGS); science in education (M Ed); severe special needs (M Ed); special needs (CAGS); technology in education (M Ed, CAGS). Part-time and evening/weekend programs available. Postbaccalaureate distance learning degree programs offered (no on-campus study). *Faculty:* 47 full-time (39 women), 208 part-time/adjunct (135 women). *Students:* 242 full-time (222 women), 2,903 part-time (2,495 women); includes 279 minority (179 African Americans, 7 American Indian/Alaska Native, 25 Asian Americans or Pacific Islanders, 68 Hispanic Americans), 10 international. Average age 36. 1,186 applicants, 96% accepted, 792 enrolled. In 2006, 1,724 master's, 6 doctorates, 17 other advanced degrees awarded. *Degree requirements:* For master's, practicum; for doctorate, thesis/dissertation. *Entrance requirements:* For doctorate, GRE General Test or MAT, interview, master's degree, resumé; for CAGS, interview, master's degree. Additional exam requirements/recommendations for international students: Required—TOEFL (minimum score 550 paper-based; 213 computer-based; 80 iBT). *Application deadline:* Applications are processed on a rolling basis. Application fee: $50. Electronic applications accepted. *Financial support:* In

2006–07, 26 students received support, including research assistantships (averaging $3,400 per year), teaching assistantships (averaging $3,400 per year); career-related internships or fieldwork, Federal Work-Study, scholarships/grants, and unspecified assistantships also available. Support available to part-time students. Financial award application deadline: 4/15; financial award applicants required to submit FAFSA. *Faculty research:* Assessment in literacy, mathematics and science; autism spectrum disorders; instructional technology and online learning; multicultural education and ELL. *Unit head:* Dr. Mario Borunda, Dean, 617-349-8375, Fax: 617-349-8607, E-mail: mborunda@lesley.edu. *Application contact:* Kristen Card, Associate Director of On-Campus Admissions, 617-349-8734, Fax: 617-349-8313, E-mail: kmcard@lesley.edu.

See Close-Up on page 893.

Liberty University, School of Education, Lynchburg, VA 24502. Offers administration and supervision (M Ed); curriculum and instruction (M Ed); early childhood education (M Ed); education specialist (Ed S); educational leadership (Ed D); elementary education (M Ed); gifted education (M Ed); reading specialist (M Ed); school counseling (M Ed); secondary education (M Ed); special education (M Ed). *Accreditation:* NCATE. Part-time programs available. Postbaccalaureate distance learning degree programs offered (minimal on-campus study). *Faculty:* 8 full-time (3 women), 7 part-time/adjunct (3 women). *Students:* 33 full-time (22 women), 308 part-time (180 women); includes 22 minority (12 African Americans, 2 American Indian/Alaska Native, 2 Asian Americans or Pacific Islanders, 6 Hispanic Americans), 5 international. Average age 39. 434 applicants, 77% accepted, 111 enrolled. In 2006, 39 master's, 12 doctorates, 16 other advanced degrees awarded. *Degree requirements:* For doctorate, thesis/dissertation, comprehensive exam. *Entrance requirements:* For master's, GRE General Test or MAT (if taken on or before 1999), 2 letters of recommendation, minimum undergraduate GPA of 3.0, curriculum vitae, graduate status record; for doctorate, GRE General Test or MAT (if taken before 1999), minimum master's GPA of 3.0, 3 years of teacher experience; for Ed S, GRE General Test or MAT (if taken before 1999), minimum master's GPA of 3.0, 3 years of teaching experience. Additional exam requirements/recommendations for international students: Required—TOEFL (minimum score 600 paper-based; 250 computer-based). *Application deadline:* For fall admission, 6/1 priority date for domestic students; for spring admission, 11/1 for domestic students. Applications are processed on a rolling basis. Application fee: $35. Electronic applications accepted. *Expenses:* Contact institution. *Financial support:* In 2006–07, 226 students received support. Federal Work-Study and tuition waivers (partial) available. *Faculty research:* Self-determination, character education, bibliotherapy, learning styles, distance education. *Unit head:* Dr. Karen L. Parker, Dean, 434-582-2195, Fax: 434-582-2468, E-mail: kparker@liberty.edu. *Application contact:* Kyle A Falce, Director of Graduate Admissions, 800-424-9596, Fax: 800-628-7977, E-mail: gradadmissions@liberty.edu.

Long Island University, C.W. Post Campus, School of Education, Department of Curriculum and Instruction, Brookville, NY 11548-1300. Offers adolescence education (MS); adolescence education: biology (MS); adolescence education: earth science (MS); adolescence education: English (MS); adolescence education: mathematics (MS); adolescence education: social studies (MS); adolescence education: Spanish (MS); art education (MS); bilingual education (MS); childhood education (MS); early childhood education (MS); middle childhood education (MS); music education (MS); teaching English to speakers of other languages (MS). Part-time and evening/weekend programs available. *Degree requirements:* For master's, comprehensive exam or thesis, student teaching. *Entrance requirements:* For master's, minimum GPA of 2.75 in major, 2.5 overall. Electronic applications accepted. *Faculty research:* Ethics and education, teaching strategies.

Long Island University, Southampton Graduate Campus, Education Division, Program in Childhood Education, Southampton, NY 11968-4198. Offers childhood education (MS Ed); elementary education (MS Ed). *Faculty:* 4 full-time, 6 part-time/adjunct. *Students:* 9 full-time (6 women), 35 part-time (29 women). Average age 31. 45 applicants, 100% accepted, 44 enrolled. In 2006, 10 degrees awarded. *Degree requirements:* For master's, thesis. *Entrance requirements:* For master's, minimum undergraduate GPA of 2.75, on-campus writing sample. Additional exam requirements/recommendations for international students: Required—TOEFL (minimum score 550 paper-based; 250 computer-based). *Application deadline:* For fall admission, 4/15 priority date for domestic and international students; for spring admission, 11/15 priority date for domestic and international students. Applications are processed on a rolling basis. Application fee: $30. Electronic applications accepted. *Expenses:* Tuition: Part-time $790 per credit. Required fees: $220 per semester. *Financial support:* In 2006–07, 1 research assistantship with full tuition reimbursement was awarded; scholarships/grants and unspecified assistantships also available. Support available to part-time students. Financial award applicants required to submit FAFSA. *Application contact:* Joyce Tuttle, Director of Graduate Admissions and Program Administration, 631-287-8010, Fax: 631-287-8253, E-mail: joyce.tuttle@liu.edu.

Long Island University, Westchester Graduate Campus, Programs in Education-Teaching, Program in Early Childhood Education, Purchase, NY 10577. Offers MS Ed. *Faculty:* 1 (woman) full-time, 3 part-time/adjunct (2 women). *Students:* 9 applicants, 100% accepted, 6 enrolled. In 2006, 2 degrees awarded. *Application deadline:* Applications are processed on a rolling basis. *Expenses:* Tuition: Part-time $790 per credit. *Financial support:* In 2006–07, 1 student received support. Scholarships/grants, tuition waivers (partial), and unspecified assistantships available. *Unit head:* Dr. Iris Goldberg, Director, 914-831-2710, Fax: 914-251-5959, E-mail: iris.goldberg@liu.edu. *Application contact:* Ellen Brief, Coordinator of Admissions, Marketing, Student Services and Public Relations, 914-831-2701, Fax: 914-251-5959, E-mail: ellen.brief@liu.edu.

Loyola College in Maryland, Graduate Programs, College of Arts and Sciences, Department of Education, Program in Montessori Education, Baltimore, MD 21210-2699. Offers M Ed, CAS. *Accreditation:* NCATE. Part-time and evening/weekend programs available. *Students:* 42 full-time (all women); includes 7 minority (5 African Americans, 1 Asian American or Pacific Islander, 1 Hispanic American), 6 international. Average age 31. In 2006, 115 degrees awarded. *Entrance requirements:* For master's and CAS, GRE General Test, GRE Subject Test (recommended). Additional exam requirements/recommendations for international students: Required—TOEFL (minimum score 550 paper-based; 213 computer-based). *Application deadline:* For fall admission, 5/1 priority date for domestic students; for spring admission, 10/1 priority date for domestic students. Applications are processed on a rolling basis. Application fee: $50. *Financial support:* Applicants required to submit FAFSA. *Unit head:* Dr. Sharon Dubble, Director, 410-617-2000 Ext. 1514, E-mail: sdubble@loyola.edu.

Manhattan College, Graduate Division, School of Education, Program in Special Education, Riverdale, NY 10471. Offers 5 year dual childhood/special education (MS Ed); dual childhood/special education (MS Ed); special education (MS Ed). Part-time and evening/weekend programs available. *Faculty:* 6 full-time (4 women), 9 part-time/adjunct (7 women). *Students:* 17 full-time (all women), 57 part-time (53 women). Average age 25. 39 applicants, 92% accepted, 35 enrolled. In 2006, 24 degrees awarded. *Degree requirements:* For master's, thesis, internship. *Entrance requirements:* For master's, minimum GPA of 3.0, NYSTE Last Test. Additional exam requirements/recommendations for international students: Required—TOEFL (minimum score 550 paper-based). *Application deadline:* For fall admission, 8/10 priority date for domestic students; for spring admission, 1/7 priority date for domestic students. Applications are processed on a rolling basis. Application fee: $50. *Expenses:* Contact institution. *Financial support:* Federal Work-Study, scholarships/grants, unspecified assistantships, and TOC/TLQP Grants—partial tuition available. Financial award application deadline: 2/1. *Faculty research:* Adapted physical education. *Unit head:* Dr. Elizabeth Mary Kosky, Director of Graduate Special Education Programs, 718-862-7969, Fax: 718-862-7816, E-mail: elizabeth.kosky@manhattan.edu. *Application contact:* Weldon Jackson.

Manhattanville College, Graduate Programs, School of Education, Program in Childhood Education, Purchase, NY 10577-2132. Offers childhood and special education (MPS); childhood education (MAT); special education childhood (MPS). Part-time and evening/weekend programs available. *Students:* 67 full-time (62 women), 150 part-time (120 women); includes 6 African Americans, 3 Asian Americans or Pacific Islanders, 10 Hispanic Americans, 2 international. In 2006, 65 degrees awarded. *Degree requirements:* For master's, comprehensive exam or research project, field experience. *Entrance requirements:* For master's, minimum undergraduate GPA of 3.0, 2 letters of recommendation. *Application deadline:* Applications are processed on a rolling basis. Application fee: $55. *Financial support:* Career-related internships or fieldwork and institutionally sponsored loans available. Support available to part-time students. *Application contact:* Alyce Ware Poli, Director of Admissions, 914-323-5142, Fax: 914-694-1732, E-mail: edschool@mville.edu.

Manhattanville College, Graduate Programs, School of Education, Program in Early Childhood Education, Purchase, NY 10577-2132. Offers childhood and early childhood education (MAT); early childhood education (birth-grade 2) (MAT); literacy (birth-grade 6) (MPS), including reading, writing; literacy (birth-grade 6) and special education (grades 1-6) (MPS); special education (birth-grade 2) (MPS); special education (birth-grade 6) (MPS). Part-time and evening/weekend programs available. *Students:* 43 full-time (42 women), 62 part-time (59 women); includes 1 African American, 1 Asian American or Pacific Islander, 7 Hispanic Americans. In 2006, 5 degrees awarded. *Degree requirements:* For master's, comprehensive exam or research project, field experience. *Entrance requirements:* For master's, minimum undergraduate GPA of 3.0, 2 letters of recommendation. *Application deadline:* Applications are processed on a rolling basis. Application fee: $55. *Financial support:* Career-related internships or fieldwork and institutionally sponsored loans available. Support available to part-time students. *Application contact:* Alyce Ware Poli, Director of Admissions, 914-323-5142, Fax: 914-694-1732, E-mail: edschool@mville.edu.

Marshall University, Academic Affairs Division, College of Education and Human Services, Graduate School of Education and Professional Development, Program in Early Childhood Education, Huntington, WV 25755. Offers MA. *Accreditation:* NCATE. Evening/weekend programs available. *Faculty:* 8 full-time (5 women). *Students:* 3 full-time (all women), 13 part-time (all women), 1 international. Average age 33. In 2006, 8 degrees awarded. *Degree requirements:* For master's, comprehensive or oral assessment, thesis optional. *Entrance requirements:* For master's, GRE General Test or MAT. Application fee: $40. *Unit head:* Dr. Calvin Meyer, Director, 304-746-1936, E-mail: meyer@marshall.edu. *Application contact:* Information Contact, 304-746-1900, Fax: 304-746-1902, E-mail: services@marshall.edu.

Maryville University of Saint Louis, School of Education, St. Louis, MO 63141-7299. Offers art education (MA Ed); early childhood education (MA Ed); education (Ed D); elementary education (MA Ed); elementary education/English (MA Ed); environmental education (MA Ed); gifted education (MA Ed); middle grades education (MA Ed); reading specialist (MA Ed); secondary education (MA Ed), including educational leadership, secondary teaching and inquiry. *Accreditation:* NASAD; NCATE. Part-time and evening/weekend programs available. *Students:* 17 full-time (14 women), 168 part-time (129 women); includes 20 African Americans, 2 Asian Americans or Pacific Islanders, 1 Hispanic American, 2 international. Average age 37. 39 applicants, 95% accepted, 24 enrolled. In 2006, 37 degrees awarded. *Degree requirements:* For master's, thesis, project. *Entrance requirements:* For master's and doctorate, minimum GPA of 3.0, 3 professional recommendations. Additional exam requirements/recommendations for international students: Required—TOEFL (minimum score 550 paper-based). *Application deadline:* Applications are processed on a rolling basis. Application fee: $35 ($50 for international students). Electronic applications accepted. *Expenses:* Tuition: Full-time $17,800; part-time $555 per credit. Required fees: $55 per semester. Tuition and fees vary according to degree level and program. *Financial support:* Career-related internships or fieldwork, Federal Work-Study, tuition waivers (partial), and professional educator discounts available. Financial award application deadline: 7/31; financial award applicants required to submit FAFSA. *Faculty research:* Collaboration with public schools, preservice program development, mathematics, diversity, literacy. *Unit head:* Dr. Sam Hausfather, Dean, 314-529-9466, Fax: 314-529-9921, E-mail: shausfather@maryville.edu. *Application contact:* Dr. Lillian Curtis, Graduate Admissions Coordinator, 314-529-9542, Fax: 314-529-9921, E-mail: teachered@maryville.edu.

Marywood University, Academic Affairs, College of Education and Human Development, Department of Education, Program in Early Childhood Intervention, Scranton, PA 18509-1598. Offers MS. *Accreditation:* NCATE. Part-time and evening/weekend programs available. *Students:* 1 (woman) full-time, 4 part-time (all women). Average age 38. 1 applicant, 0% accepted. *Degree requirements:* For master's, thesis or alternative, comprehensive exam. *Entrance requirements:* For master's, GRE or MAT. Additional exam requirements/recommendations for international students: Required—TOEFL (minimum score 550 paper-based; 213 computer-based). *Application deadline:* For fall admission, 4/15 priority date for domestic and international students; for spring admission, 11/15 priority date for domestic and international students. Applications are processed on a rolling basis. Application fee: $30. Electronic applications accepted. *Expenses:* Tuition: Part-time $672 per credit. Tuition and fees vary according to degree level, campus/location and program. *Financial support:* Research assistantships with tuition reimbursements, career-related internships or fieldwork, scholarships/grants, tuition waivers (partial), and unspecified assistantships available. Support available to part-time students. Financial award application deadline: 2/15; financial award applicants required to submit FAFSA. *Faculty research:* Montessori education, developmentally appropriate practice, child care environment. *Application contact:* Dr. Deborah M. Flynn, Coordinator of Graduate Advising (Enrollment Management), 570-348-6211, E-mail: flynn@ac.marywood.edu.

McNeese State University, Graduate School, College of Education, Department of Teacher Education, Program in Curriculum and Instruction, Lake Charles, LA 70609. Offers early childhood education (M Ed); elementary education (M Ed); secondary education (M Ed). Evening/weekend programs available. *Faculty:* 12 full-time (8 women), 2 part-time/adjunct (1 woman). *Students:* 7 full-time (6 women), 40 part-time (37 women); includes 20 minority (19 African Americans, 1 American Indian/Alaska Native). In 2006, 22 degrees awarded. *Entrance requirements:* For master's, GRE, teaching certificate. *Application deadline:* For fall admission, 5/15 priority date for domestic students. Applications are processed on a rolling basis. Application fee: $20 ($30 for international students). *Expenses:* Tuition, area resident: Full-time $2,226; part-time $193 per hour. Required fees: $919; $106 per hour. *Financial support:* Application deadline: 5/1. *Unit head:* Dr. Wayne R Fetter, Dean, College of Education, 337-475-5432, Fax: 337-475-5467, E-mail: wfetter@mcneese.edu.

Mercer University, Graduate Studies, Cecil B. Day Campus, Tift College of Education, Macon, GA 31207-0003. Offers early childhood education (M Ed, MAT); educational leadership (M Ed, PhD); middle grades education (M Ed, MAT); reading education (M Ed); secondary education (M Ed, MAT); teacher leadership (Ed S). Part-time and evening/weekend programs available. *Faculty:* 13 full-time (6 women), 7 part-time/adjunct (3 women). *Students:* 31 full-time (23 women), 211 part-time (174 women); includes 111 minority (101 African Americans, 2 American Indian/Alaska Native, 6 Asian Americans or Pacific Islanders, 2 Hispanic Americans), 2 international. Average age 33. In 2006, 57 master's, 4 other advanced degrees awarded. *Degree requirements:* For master's and Ed S, research project; for doctorate, thesis/dissertation. *Entrance requirements:* For master's, GRE or MAT, minimum undergraduate GPA of 2.75; for doctorate, GRE; for Ed S, GRE or MAT, minimum GPA of 3.25, 3 years of teaching experience. *Application deadline:* For fall admission, 8/1 for domestic and international students; for spring admission, 12/1 for domestic and international students. Applications are processed on a rolling basis. Application fee: $25. *Expenses:* Contact institution. *Financial support:* Federal Work-Study available. Support available to part-time students. Financial award application deadline: 5/1. *Faculty research:* Educational computing, content area reading, concept learning, importance of play for young children, multicultural literature. *Unit head:* Dr. Carl R. Martray, Dean, 478-301-5397, Fax: 478-301-2280, E-mail: martray_cr@mercer.edu. *Application contact:* Dr. Allison Gilmore, Associate Dean for Graduate Teacher Education, 678-547-6330, Fax: 678-547-6055, E-mail: gilmore_a@mercer.edu.

Mercy College, Division of Education, Dobbs Ferry, NY 10522-1189. Offers adolescence education: grades 7-12 (MS); applied behavior analysis (MS); bilingual education (MS); child-

Early Childhood Education

Mercy College (continued)

hood education: grades 1-6 (MS); early childhood education: birth—grade 2 (MS); education (MS); elementary education (MS); learning technology (MS); middle childhood education: grades 5-9 (MS); reading (MS); school administration and supervision (MS); school building leadership (MS); school business administration (MS); secondary education (MS); special education (MS); students with disabilities: grades 5-9 (MS); students with disabilities: grades 7-12 (MS); teaching English to speakers of other languages (MS); teaching literacy: birth—grade 6 (MS); teaching literacy: grades 5-12 (MS); urban education (MS). *Students:* 572 full-time (467 women), 1,719 part-time (1,287 women); includes 943 minority (470 African Americans, 7 American Indian/Alaska Native, 48 Asian Americans or Pacific Islanders, 418 Hispanic Americans), 6 international. Average age 33. In 2006, 1090 degrees awarded. *Entrance requirements:* For master's, teaching certificate. *Application deadline:* For fall admission, 2/1 for domestic students. Applications are processed on a rolling basis. Application fee: $37. *Expenses:* Contact institution. Tuition and fees vary according to program. *Financial support:* Institutionally sponsored loans, scholarships/grants, and unspecified assistantships available. Support available to part-time students. *Faculty research:* Distance learning, literacy, assessment, community schools, impact of staff development. *Unit head:* Dr. William Prattella, Chairperson, 914-674-7555, Fax: 914-674-7352, E-mail: wprattella@mercy.edu. *Application contact:* Kathleen Jackson, Director of Admissions, 800-Mercy-NY, Fax: 914-674-7382, E-mail: admissions@mercy.edu.

Miami University, Graduate School, School of Education and Allied Professions, Department of Teacher Education, Program in Secondary Education, Oxford, OH 45056. Offers adolescent education (MAT), including integrated English, integrated mathematics, integrated social studies, language arts; elementary mathematics education (M Ed); secondary education (M Ed, MAT). *Accreditation:* NCATE. Part-time programs available. *Degree requirements:* For master's, thesis (for some programs), final exam. *Entrance requirements:* For master's, MAT, minimum undergraduate GPA of 3.0 during previous 2 years or 2.75 overall. *Faculty research:* Teacher effectiveness, collaboration models.

Middle Tennessee State University, College of Graduate Studies, College of Education and Behavioral Science, Department of Elementary and Special Education, Major in Curriculum and Instruction, Murfreesboro, TN 37132. Offers early childhood education (M Ed); elementary education (M Ed, Ed S); middle school education (M Ed). *Accreditation:* NCATE. Part-time and evening/weekend programs available. Postbaccalaureate distance learning degree programs offered. *Students:* 13 full-time (12 women), 79 part-time (73 women); includes 7 minority (5 African Americans, 2 Asian Americans or Pacific Islanders). In 2006, 59 degrees awarded. *Degree requirements:* For master's, comprehensive exam; for Ed S, thesis. *Entrance requirements:* Additional exam requirements/recommendations for international students: Required—TOEFL (minimum score 525 paper-based; 195 computer-based). *Application deadline:* For fall admission, 8/1 priority date for domestic students. Applications are processed on a rolling basis. Application fee: $25. Electronic applications accepted. *Financial support:* Application deadline: 5/1. *Unit head:* Dr. Connie Jones, Chair, Department of Elementary and Special Education, 615-898-2680, Fax: 615-898-5309, E-mail: cojones@mtsu.edu.

Millersville University of Pennsylvania, Graduate School, School of Education, Department of Elementary and Early Childhood Education, Program in Early Childhood Education, Millersville, PA 17551-0302. Offers M Ed. Part-time and evening/weekend programs available. *Faculty:* 20 full-time (15 women), 11 part-time/adjunct (8 women). *Students:* Average age 31. 1 applicant, 100% accepted, 1 enrolled. In 2006, 10 degrees awarded. *Degree requirements:* For master's, exit test, thesis optional. *Entrance requirements:* For master's, MAT or GRE, minimum undergraduate GPA of 2.75, instructional certificate. *Application deadline:* For fall admission, 3/1 priority date for domestic students; for spring admission, 10/1 priority date for domestic students. Applications are processed on a rolling basis. Application fee: $35. *Expenses:* Tuition, state resident: full-time $6,048; part-time $336 per credit. Tuition, nonresident: full-time $9,678; part-time $538 per credit. Required fees: $1,244. Tuition and fees vary according to course load. *Financial support:* In 2006–07, 2 students received support, including 2 research assistantships (averaging $4,250 per year); career-related internships or fieldwork, Federal Work-Study, institutionally sponsored loans, and unspecified assistantships also available. Support available to part-time students. Financial award application deadline: 3/15; financial award applicants required to submit FAFSA. *Faculty research:* Alternative forms of early childhood education, parent education, Playland children's learning. *Unit head:* Dr. Alice Meckley, Coordinator, 717-872-3680, Fax: 717-871-5462, E-mail: alice.meckle@millersville.edu. *Application contact:* Dr. Victor S. DeSantis, Dean of Graduate Studies, 717-872-3099, Fax: 717-871-2022, E-mail: victor.desantis@millersville.edu.

Mills College, Graduate Studies, Education Department, Oakland, CA 94613-1000. Offers administration (Ed D); child life in health care settings (MA); early childhood education (MA); education (MA), including curriculum and instruction, elementary education, English education, mathematics education, science education, secondary education, social sciences education, teaching. Part-time and evening/weekend programs available. *Faculty:* 10 full-time (7 women), 15 part-time/adjunct (12 women). *Students:* 192 full-time (153 women), 41 part-time (36 women); includes 62 minority (28 African Americans, 13 Asian Americans or Pacific Islanders, 21 Hispanic Americans), 2 international. Average age 34. 160 applicants, 74% accepted, 73 enrolled. In 2006, 52 master's, 1 doctorate awarded. Terminal master's awarded for partial completion of doctoral program. *Degree requirements:* For master's, comprehensive exam. *Entrance requirements:* For doctorate, GRE General Test. Additional exam requirements/recommendations for international students: Required—TOEFL. *Application deadline:* For fall admission, 2/1 for domestic and international students; for spring admission, 11/1 for domestic and international students. Applications are processed on a rolling basis. Application fee: $50. Electronic applications accepted. *Financial support:* In 2006–07, 56 fellowships with tuition reimbursements (averaging $2,700 per year), 15 teaching assistantships (averaging $6,350 per year) were awarded; career-related internships or fieldwork, institutionally sponsored loans, scholarships/grants, and residence awards also available. Support available to part-time students. Financial award application deadline: 2/1; financial award applicants required to submit CSS PROFILE or FAFSA. *Faculty research:* Child development, gender and education, public policy, cross-cultural development, development of literacy. *Unit head:* Joseph Kahne, Chairperson, 510-430-3190, Fax: 510-430-3314, E-mail: grad-studies@mills.edu. *Application contact:* Randy McGlauthing, Director of Graduate Admissions, 510-430-2355, Fax: 510-430-2159, E-mail: rmglaut@mills.edu.

Minnesota State University Mankato, College of Graduate Studies, College of Education, Department of Educational Studies: Elementary and Early Childhood, Mankato, MN 56001. Offers MS. *Accreditation:* NCATE. Part-time programs available. *Students:* 3 full-time (2 women), 29 part-time (26 women). In 2006, 2 degrees awarded. *Degree requirements:* For master's, thesis or alternative, comprehensive exam. *Entrance requirements:* For master's, GRE General Test or MAT, minimum GPA of 3.0 during previous 2 years. Additional exam requirements/recommendations for international students: Required—TOEFL. *Application deadline:* For fall admission, 7/1 priority date for domestic students; for spring admission, 11/1 for domestic students. Applications are processed on a rolling basis. Application fee: $40. Electronic applications accepted. *Financial support:* Application deadline: 3/15; *Unit head:* Dr. Peg Ballard, Chairperson, 507-389-2431. *Application contact:* 507-389-2321, E-mail: grad@mnsu.edu.

Minot State University, Graduate School, Program in Special Education, Minot, ND 58707-0002. Offers education of the deaf (MS); learning disabilities (MS); special education strategist (MS), including early childhood special education, severe multiple handicaps. *Accreditation:* NCATE. *Faculty:* 11 full-time (7 women). *Students:* 68. In 2006, 15 degrees awarded. *Degree requirements:* For master's, thesis (for some programs), comprehensive exam (for some programs). *Entrance requirements:* For master's, GRE General Test or minimum GPA of 3.0. Application fee: $35. *Financial support:* Research assistantships with partial tuition reimbursements, teaching assistantships with partial tuition reimbursements, career-related internships or fieldwork, institutionally sponsored loans, scholarships/grants, traineeships, tuition waivers

(partial), and unspecified assistantships available. Support available to part-time students. Financial award application deadline: 4/1. *Faculty research:* Special education team diagnostic unit; individual diagnostic assessments of mentally retarded, learning-disabled, hearing-impaired, and speech-impaired youth; educational programming for the hearing impaired. *Unit head:* Dr. Lori Garnes, Chairperson, 701-858-3139. *Application contact:* Brenda Anderson, Administrative Assistant, 701-858-3250, Fax: 701-858-4286, E-mail: brenda.anderson@minotstateu.edu.

Missouri State University, Graduate College, College of Education, Department of Early Childhood and Family Development, Springfield, MO 65804-0094. Offers MS. *Faculty:* 3 full-time (all women), 1 (woman) part-time/adjunct. *Students:* Average age 29. 3 applicants, 100% accepted, 3 enrolled. *Degree requirements:* For master's, comprehensive exam. *Entrance requirements:* For master's, GRE, minimum GPA of 3.0. Additional exam requirements/recommendations for international students: Required—TOEFL (minimum score 550 paper-based; 213 computer-based; 79 iBT). *Application deadline:* For fall admission, 7/20 priority date for domestic students; for spring admission, 12/20 priority date for domestic students. Application fee: $35. *Expenses:* Tuition, state resident: full-time $3,582; part-time $199 per credit hour. Tuition, nonresident: full-time $6,984; part-time $199 per credit hour. Required fees: $548. Full-time tuition and fees vary according to course level, course load, program and reciprocity agreements. *Financial support:* Federal Work-Study, scholarships/grants, and unspecified assistantships available. Financial award applicants required to submit FAFSA. *Unit head:* Dr. Sue George, Head, 417-836-5984, Fax: 417-836-3263, E-mail: suegeorge@missouristate.edu.

Montana State University–Billings, College of Education and Human Services, Department of Special Education, Counseling, Reading and Early Childhood, Option in Early Childhood Education, Billings, MT 59101-0298. Offers M Ed. *Accreditation:* NCATE. Part-time programs available. *Students:* 3. Average age 42. In 2006, 1 degree awarded. *Degree requirements:* For master's, thesis or professional paper and/or field experience, thesis optional. *Entrance requirements:* For master's, GRE General Test or MAT, minimum GPA of 3.0 (undergraduate), 3.25 (graduate). *Application deadline:* Applications are processed on a rolling basis. Application fee: $40. *Expenses:* Tuition, state resident: full-time $4,599. Tuition, nonresident: full-time $10,786. *Financial support:* Teaching assistantships, career-related internships or fieldwork, Federal Work-Study, institutionally sponsored loans, scholarships/grants, tuition waivers (partial), and unspecified assistantships available. Support available to part-time students. Financial award application deadline: 5/1; financial award applicants required to submit FAFSA. *Faculty research:* Bilingual education. *Application contact:* David M. Sullivan, Graduate Studies Counselor, 406-657-2053, Fax: 406-657-2299, E-mail: dsullivan@msubillings.edu.

Montclair State University, The Graduate School, College of Education and Human Services, Department of Curriculum and Teaching, Montclair, NJ 07043-1624. Offers education (M Ed); educational technology (M Ed); school library media specialist (Certificate); teaching (MAT, Certificate), including art (MAT), biological science (MAT), early childhood education (P-3) (MAT), earth science (MAT), elementary education (K-8) (MAT), English (MAT), French (MAT), health and physical education (MAT), health education (MAT), home economics (MAT), mathematics (MAT), music (MAT), physical education (MAT), physical science (MAT), social studies (MAT), Spanish (MAT), teacher of ESL (MAT), teacher of students with disabilities (MAT). Part-time and evening/weekend programs available. *Faculty:* 16 full-time (12 women), 13 part-time/adjunct (8 women). *Students:* 147 full-time (113 women), 230 part-time (188 women); includes 58 minority (33 African Americans, 1 American Indian/Alaska Native, 12 Asian Americans or Pacific Islanders, 12 Hispanic Americans), 4 international. Average age 33. 118 applicants, 38% accepted, 37 enrolled. In 2006, 166 master's, 11 other advanced degrees awarded. *Degree requirements:* For master's, field experience. *Entrance requirements:* For master's, PRAXIS II, minimum GPA of 2.67, 2 letters of recommendation. Additional exam requirements/recommendations for international students: Required—TOEFL (minimum score 83 computer-based). *Application deadline:* For fall admission, 2/15 for domestic and international students; for spring admission, 9/15 for domestic and international students. Applications are processed on a rolling basis. Application fee: $60. Electronic applications accepted. *Expenses:* Tuition, state resident: part-time $450 per credit. Tuition, nonresident: part-time $682 per credit. Tuition and fees vary according to degree level and program. *Financial support:* In 2006–07, 7 research assistantships with full tuition reimbursements (averaging $7,000 per year) were awarded; Federal Work-Study, scholarships/grants, and unspecified assistantships also available. Support available to part-time students. Financial award application deadline: 3/1; financial award applicants required to submit FAFSA. *Unit head:* Dr. Deborah Eldridge, Chairperson, 973-655-5187.

Montclair State University, The Graduate School, College of Education and Human Services, Department of Early Childhood, Elementary and Literacy Education, Montclair, NJ 07043-1624. Offers early childhood /elementary education (M Ed); early childhood education and teaching students in disabilities (MAT); early childhood special education (M Ed, Certificate); elementary education with disabilities (MAT); elementary school teacher (Certificate); learning disabilities (Certificate); reading (MA, Certificate); reading specialist (Certificate). Part-time and evening/weekend programs available. *Faculty:* 15 full-time (13 women), 65 part-time/adjunct (52 women). *Students:* 27 full-time (24 women), 189 part-time (179 women); includes 24 minority (12 African Americans, 3 Asian Americans or Pacific Islanders, 9 Hispanic Americans), 1 international. 116 applicants, 47% accepted, 35 enrolled. In 2006, 40 master's, 53 other advanced degrees awarded. *Degree requirements:* For master's, clinical experience, portfolio. *Entrance requirements:* For master's, GRE, PRAXIS II, 2 letters of recommendation. Additional exam requirements/recommendations for international students: Required—TOEFL (minimum score 83 computer-based). *Application deadline:* For fall admission, 6/1 for international students; for spring admission, 10/1 for international students. Applications are processed on a rolling basis. Application fee: $60. Electronic applications accepted. *Expenses:* Tuition, state resident: part-time $450 per credit. Tuition, nonresident: part-time $682 per credit. Tuition and fees vary according to degree level and program. *Financial support:* In 2006–07, 15 research assistantships with full tuition reimbursements (averaging $7,000 per year) were awarded; Federal Work-Study, scholarships/grants, and unspecified assistantships also available. Support available to part-time students. Financial award application deadline: 3/1; financial award applicants required to submit FAFSA. *Unit head:* Dr. Nancy Lauter, Chairperson, 973-655-5407, E-mail: lautern@mail.montclair.edu. *Application contact:* Dr. Linda Luise, Adviser, 973-655-4247, E-mail: wisel@mail.montclair.edu.

Mount Saint Mary College, Division of Education, Newburgh, NY 12550-3494. Offers adolescence and special education (MS Ed); adolescence education (MS Ed); childhood and special education (MS Ed); childhood education (MS Ed); literacy and special education (MS Ed); literacy/childhood (MS Ed); middle school (5-6) (MS Ed); middle school (7-9) (MS Ed); special education (1-6) (MS Ed); special education (7-12) (MS Ed). *Accreditation:* NCATE.Part-time and evening/weekend programs available. *Faculty:* 11 full-time (8 women), 21 part-time/adjunct (18 women). *Students:* 87 full-time (74 women), 368 part-time (303 women); includes 38 minority (12 African Americans, 2 American Indian/Alaska Native, 5 Asian Americans or Pacific Islanders, 19 Hispanic Americans). Average age 31. 164 applicants, 45% accepted, 58 enrolled. In 2006, 131 degrees awarded. *Application deadline:* Applications are processed on a rolling basis. Application fee: $35. *Expenses:* Tuition: Full-time $11,880; part-time $660 per credit. *Financial support:* In 2006–07, 30 students received support. Unspecified assistantships available. Financial award application deadline: 3/15. *Faculty research:* Learning and teaching styles, computers in special education, language development. *Unit head:* Theresa Lewis, Coordinator, 845-569-3149, Fax: 845-569-3535, E-mail: tlewis@msmc.edu.

Murray State University, College of Education, Department of Early Childhood and Elementary Education, Program in Interdisciplinary Early Childhood Education, Murray, KY 42071. Offers MA Ed. Part-time programs available. *Faculty:* 2 part-time/adjunct (both women). *Students:* 43. 13 applicants, 100% accepted. In 2006, 17 master's awarded. *Median time to degree:* Of those who began their doctoral program in fall 1998, 100% received their degree in 8 years or less. *Degree requirements:* For master's, portfolio. *Entrance requirements:* For master's, minimum GPA of 2.5 for conditional admittance, 3.0 for unconditional. Application fee: $25. *Financial support:* Research assistantships, teaching assistantships, Federal Work-Study available.

National-Louis University, National College of Education, Program in Early Childhood Administration, Chicago, IL 60603. Offers M Ed, CAS. *Students:* Average age 40. 4 applicants, 100% accepted. In 2006, 10 degrees awarded. *Entrance requirements:* For master's, GRE or MAT, minimum GPA of 3.0, teaching certificate; for CAS, master's degree, teaching certificate. *Application deadline:* Applications are processed on a rolling basis. Application fee: $25. *Expenses:* Tuition: Full-time $17,685. One-time fee: $40 full-time. *Financial support:* Fellowships, career-related internships or fieldwork, Federal Work-Study, institutionally sponsored loans, and scholarships/grants available. Support available to part-time students. *Unit head:* Dr. Paula Jorde-Bloom, Coordinator, 847-475-1100 Ext. 5551. *Application contact:* David McCulloch, Vice President for University Services, 800-443-5522 Ext. 5127, Fax: 847-465-0593, E-mail: dmcc@wheeling1.nl.edu.

National-Louis University, National College of Education, Program in Early Childhood Education, Chicago, IL 60603. Offers early childhood curriculum and instruction specialist (M Ed, MS Ed, CAS); early childhood education (M Ed, MAT, CAS). Part-time and evening/weekend programs available. *Students:* 7 full-time (6 women), 75 part-time (73 women); includes 28 minority (21 African Americans, 1 Asian American or Pacific Islander, 6 Hispanic Americans). Average age 34. 14 applicants, 93% accepted. In 2006, 33 master's, 1 other advanced degree awarded. *Degree requirements:* For master's, thesis (for some programs), student teaching experience (MAT). *Entrance requirements:* For master's, GRE or MAT, minimum GPA of 3.0, teaching certificate (M Ed, MS Ed); for CAS, GRE or MAT, master's degree, teaching certificate. *Application deadline:* Applications are processed on a rolling basis. Application fee: $25. *Expenses:* Tuition: Full-time $17,685. One-time fee: $40 full-time. *Financial support:* Fellowships, career-related internships or fieldwork, Federal Work-Study, institutionally sponsored loans, and scholarships/grants available. Support available to part-time students. Financial award applicants required to submit FAFSA. *Faculty research:* Head Start training. Total annual research expenditures: $719,067. *Unit head:* Dr. Betty Hutchinson, Coordinator, 847-475-1100 Ext. 2227. *Application contact:* David McCulloch, Vice President for University Services, 800-443-5522 Ext. 5127, Fax: 847-465-0593, E-mail: dmcc@wheeling1.nl.edu.

Nazareth College of Rochester, Graduate Studies, Department of Education, Program in Inclusive Education-Early Childhood Level, Rochester, NY 14618-3790. Offers MS Ed. *Accreditation:* Teacher Education Accreditation Council. Part-time and evening/weekend programs available. *Students:* 29 full-time (28 women), 41 part-time (all women); includes 5 minority (2 African Americans, 2 American Indian/Alaska Native, 1 Hispanic American). Average age 33. 24 applicants, 100% accepted, 21 enrolled. In 2006, 17 degrees awarded. *Entrance requirements:* For master's, minimum GPA of 3.0. *Application deadline:* For fall admission, 4/1 for domestic students; for spring admission, 10/1 for domestic students. Application fee: $40. *Financial support:* Research assistantships with partial tuition reimbursements available. Financial award application deadline: 3/1; financial award applicants required to submit FAFSA. *Unit head:* Kathleen Russell, Director, 585-389-2595, Fax: 585-389-2452, E-mail: krussel6@naz.edu. *Application contact:* Judith G. Baker, Director, Graduate Admissions, 585-389-2050, Fax: 585-389-2817, E-mail: gradstudies@naz.edu.

New Jersey City University, Graduate and Continuing Education, College of Education, Department of Early Childhood Education, Jersey City, NJ 07305-1597. Offers MA. Evening/weekend programs available. *Faculty:* 13. *Students:* 7 full-time (6 women), 56 part-time (50 women); includes 29 minority (13 African Americans, 4 Asian Americans or Pacific Islanders, 12 Hispanic Americans), 1 international. Average age 34. In 2006, 58 degrees awarded. *Entrance requirements:* For master's, GRE General Test or MAT. Additional exam requirements/recommendations for international students: Required—TOEFL. *Application deadline:* For fall admission, 8/1 priority date for domestic students; for spring admission, 12/1 for domestic students. Applications are processed on a rolling basis. Application fee: $0. *Expenses:* Tuition, state resident: full-time $7,038; part-time $391 per credit. Tuition, nonresident: full-time $12,510; part-time $695 per credit. Required fees: $65 per credit. *Financial support:* Career-related internships or fieldwork and unspecified assistantships available. *Unit head:* Dr. Jo Anne Juncker, Coordinator, 201-200-3321, E-mail: jjuncker@njcu.edu.

New York University, Steinhardt School of Culture, Education and Human Development, Department of Teaching and Learning, Program in Early Childhood and Childhood Education, New York, NY 10012-1019. Offers childhood education (MA, PhD, Advanced Certificate); early childhood education (MA, PhD, Advanced Certificate). *Accreditation:* Teacher Education Accreditation Council. Part-time and evening/weekend programs available. *Faculty:* 12 full-time (10 women). *Students:* 120 full-time (113 women), 31 part-time (25 women); includes 39 minority (13 African Americans, 14 Asian Americans or Pacific Islanders, 12 Hispanic Americans), 5 international. 117 applicants, 79% accepted, 41 enrolled. In 2006, 78 master's, 1 doctorate awarded. Terminal master's awarded for partial completion of doctoral program. *Degree requirements:* For master's, thesis (for some programs); for doctorate, thesis/dissertation. *Entrance requirements:* For doctorate, GRE General Test, interview; for Advanced Certificate, master's degree. Additional exam requirements/recommendations for international students: Required—TOEFL. *Application deadline:* For fall admission, 12/15 priority date for domestic and international students; for spring admission, 11/1 for domestic and international students. Applications are processed on a rolling basis. Application fee: $50. *Expenses:* Tuition: Part-time $1,080 per unit. Required fees: $56 per unit. $329 per term. Tuition and fees vary according to program. *Financial support:* Fellowships with full and partial tuition reimbursements, career-related internships or fieldwork, Federal Work-Study, institutionally sponsored loans, scholarships/grants, tuition waivers (partial), and unspecified assistantships available. Support available to part-time students. Financial award application deadline: 2/1; financial award applicants required to submit FAFSA. *Faculty research:* Teacher evaluation and beliefs about teaching, early literacy development, language arts, child development and education, cultural differences. *Unit head:* Dr. Stephen Weiss, Co-Director, 212-998-5460, Fax: 212-995-4049. *Application contact:* 212-998-5030, Fax: 212-995-4328, E-mail: steinhardt.gradadmissions@nyu.edu.

Norfolk State University, School of Graduate Studies, School of Education, Department of Early Childhood and Elementary Education, Norfolk, VA 23504. Offers early childhood education (MAT); pre-elementary education (MA). *Accreditation:* NCATE. Part-time programs available. *Degree requirements:* For master's, thesis or alternative, comprehensive exam. *Entrance requirements:* For master's, PRAXIS I and II, minimum GPA of 2.5, letters of recommendation, interview. *Faculty research:* Parent involvement in education.

North Carolina Agricultural and Technical State University, Graduate School, School of Education, Department of Curriculum and Instruction, Greensboro, NC 27411. Offers early childhood education (MS); educational media (MS); elementary education (MS); intermediate education (MS), including biology education, chemistry education, English education, history education, social science education; reading (MS). *Accreditation:* NCATE. Part-time and evening/weekend programs available. *Degree requirements:* For master's, qualifying exam. *Entrance requirements:* For master's, GRE General Test, minimum GPA of 3.0.

Northeastern State University, Graduate College, College of Education, Department of Curriculum and Instruction, Program in Early Childhood Education, Tahlequah, OK 74464-2399. Offers M Ed. Part-time and evening/weekend programs available. *Students:* 5 full-time (all women), 20 part-time (18 women); includes 5 minority (2 African Americans, 3 American Indian/Alaska Native). In 2006, 7 degrees awarded. *Degree requirements:* For master's, thesis. *Entrance requirements:* For master's, GRE or MAT, minimum GPA of 2.5. Additional exam requirements/recommendations for international students: Required—TOEFL (minimum score 213 computer-based). *Application deadline:* For fall admission, 6/1 priority date for domestic students. Applications are processed on a rolling basis. Application fee: $0 ($25 for international students). Electronic applications accepted. *Financial support:* Teaching assistantships, Federal Work-Study available. Financial award application deadline: 3/1.

Northern Arizona University, Graduate College, College of Education, Program in Early Childhood Education, Flagstaff, AZ 86011. Offers M Ed. Part-time programs available. *Faculty research:* Multi-age education, early literacy, mathematical concepts development, integration of the arts, developmentally appropriate practices.

Northern Illinois University, Graduate School, College of Education, Department of Teaching and Learning, De Kalb, IL 60115-2854. Offers curriculum and instruction (MS Ed, Ed D), including curriculum leadership (Ed D), elementary education (Ed D), secondary education (Ed D); early childhood education (MS Ed); elementary education (MS Ed); special education (MS Ed). Part-time and evening/weekend programs available. *Faculty:* 22 full-time (14 women), 2 part-time/adjunct (both women). *Students:* 81 full-time (64 women), 534 part-time (417 women); includes 122 minority (21 African Americans, 12 Asian Americans or Pacific Islanders, 89 Hispanic Americans), 11 international. Average age 36. 92 applicants, 57% accepted, 43 enrolled. In 2006, 256 master's, 12 doctorates awarded. *Degree requirements:* For master's, thesis optional; for doctorate, thesis/dissertation, candidacy exam, dissertation defense. *Entrance requirements:* For master's, GRE General Test or MAT, minimum undergraduate GPA of 2.75; for doctorate, GRE General Test or MAT, minimum undergraduate GPA of 2.75, graduate 3.2. Additional exam requirements/recommendations for international students: Required—TOEFL (minimum score 550 paper-based; 213 computer-based). *Application deadline:* For fall admission, 6/1 for domestic students, 5/1 for international students; for spring admission, 11/1 for domestic students, 10/1 for international students. Applications are processed on a rolling basis. Application fee: $30. Electronic applications accepted. *Financial support:* In 2006–07, 27 research assistantships with full tuition reimbursements, 1 teaching assistantship with full tuition reimbursement were awarded; fellowships with full tuition reimbursements, career-related internships or fieldwork, Federal Work-Study, scholarships/grants, tuition waivers (full), and unspecified assistantships also available. Support available to part-time students. Financial award applicants required to submit FAFSA. *Faculty research:* Teacher certification, stress reduction during student teaching, teaching history, portfolios in student teaching. *Unit head:* Dr. Pamela Jackson, Acting Chair, 815-753-8452, E-mail: p30ngd1@wpo.cso.niu.edu.

North Georgia College & State University, Graduate Studies, Program in Teacher Education, Dahlonega, GA 30597. Offers early childhood education (M Ed); educational leadership (Ed S); middle grades education (M Ed); secondary education (M Ed), including art education, biology education, chemistry education, English education, history education, mathematics education, physical education, science education; special education (M Ed), including interrelated special education, learning disabilities. *Accreditation:* NCATE. Part-time and evening/weekend programs available. Postbaccalaureate distance learning degree programs offered (minimal on-campus study). *Faculty:* 35 full-time (18 women), 9 part-time/adjunct (6 women). *Students:* 260. Average age 32. 120 applicants, 63% accepted. In 2006, 134 degrees awarded. *Degree requirements:* For master's, thesis optional. *Entrance requirements:* For master's, GRE General Test or MAT, minimum GPA of 2.75; for Ed S, GRE General Test or MAT, 3 years of teaching experience, master's degree, minimum graduate GPA of 3.25. *Application deadline:* For fall admission, 7/1 priority date for domestic students; for spring admission, 12/10 priority date for domestic students. Applications are processed on a rolling basis. Application fee: $25. Electronic applications accepted. *Expenses:* Tuition, state resident: full-time $3,044; part-time $127 per credit hour. Tuition, nonresident: full-time $12,172; part-time $508 per credit hour. Required fees: $892; $458 per semester. *Financial support:* Teaching assistantships, career-related internships or fieldwork and scholarships/grants available. Support available to part-time students. Financial award application deadline: 5/1. *Faculty research:* Computers and teachers' attitudes, rural versus urban teacher attitudes, teacher leadership roles, minority recruitment in teaching force. *Unit head:* Dr. Bob Michael, Dean, School of Education, 706-864-1998, Fax: 706-867-2850, E-mail: bmichael@ngcsu.edu. *Application contact:* Dr. Donna A. Gessell, Director of Graduate Studies and External Programs, 706-864-1528, Fax: 706-867-2795, E-mail: dgessell@ngcsu.edu.

Northwestern State University of Louisiana, Graduate Studies and Research, College of Education, Program in Early Childhood Education, Natchitoches, LA 71497. Offers early childhood education and teaching (M Ed); teacher education and professional development, specific levels and methods (M Ed). *Students:* 1 (woman) full-time, 5 part-time (all women). *Application contact:* Dr. Steven G. Horton, Associate Provost/Dean, Graduate Studies, Research, and Information Systems, 318-357-5851, Fax: 318-357-5019, E-mail: grad_school@nsula.edu.

Northwestern State University of Louisiana, Graduate Studies and Research, College of Education, Programs in Education, Natchitoches, LA 71497. Offers business and distributive education (M Ed); counseling (M Ed); early childhood education (M Ed); education (M Ed); education leadership (M Ed); educational technology (M Ed); elementary teaching (M Ed); English education (M Ed); home economics education (M Ed); mathematics education (M Ed); reading (M Ed); science education (M Ed); secondary teaching (M Ed); social sciences education (M Ed). *Students:* 49 full-time (41 women), 245 part-time (206 women); includes 78 minority (70 African Americans, 5 American Indian/Alaska Native, 2 Asian Americans or Pacific Islanders, 1 Hispanic American). Average age 35. In 2006, 158 degrees awarded. *Degree requirements:* For master's, thesis or alternative, comprehensive exam, registration. *Entrance requirements:* For master's, GRE General Test, minimum undergraduate GPA of 2.5. *Application contact:* Dr. Steven G. Horton, Associate Provost/Dean, Graduate Studies, Research, and Information Systems, 318-357-5851, Fax: 318-357-5019, E-mail: grad_school@nsula.edu.

Northwest Missouri State University, Graduate School, College of Education and Human Services, Department of Curriculum and Instruction, Program in Teaching: Early Childhood, Maryville, MO 64468-6001. Offers MS Ed. *Accreditation:* NCATE. Part-time programs available. *Faculty:* 10 full-time (all women). *Students:* 7 applicants, 86% accepted, 1 enrolled. *Degree requirements:* For master's, comprehensive exam. *Entrance requirements:* For master's, GRE General Test, teaching certificate, minimum undergraduate GPA of 2.75, writing sample. Additional exam requirements/recommendations for international students: Required—TOEFL (minimum score 550 paper-based; 213 computer-based). *Application deadline:* For fall admission, 7/1 for domestic and international students; for spring admission, 11/15 for domestic and international students. Applications are processed on a rolling basis. Application fee: $0 ($50 for international students). *Financial support:* Teaching assistantships available. Financial award application deadline: 3/1; financial award applicants required to submit FAFSA. *Unit head:* Dr. Carolyn McCall, Director, 660-562-1236. *Application contact:* Dr. Frances Shipley, Dean of Graduate School, 660-562-1145, Fax: 660-562-1096, E-mail: gradsch@nwmissouri.edu.

Nova Southeastern University, Fischler School of Education and Human Services, Graduate Teacher Education Program, Fort Lauderdale, FL 33314-7796. Offers athletic administration (MS); cognitive and behavioral disabilities (MS); computer science education (Ed S); computer science education (K-12) (MS); curriculum and teaching (Ed S); curriculum, instruction and technology (MS); curriculum, instruction, management and administration (Ed S); early childhood special education (MS); early literacy and reading (Ed S); early literacy education (MS); education technology (MS); educational leadership (administration K–12) (MS, Ed S); educational media (Ed S); educational media (K-12) (MS); elementary education (MS, Ed S), including ESOL endorsement (MS); English (MS, Ed S); exceptional student education (MS), including ESOL endorsement; gifted education (MS, Ed S); interdisciplinary arts education (MS); management and administration of educational programs (MS); mathematics (MS, Ed S); multicultural early intervention (MS); pre-kindergarten/primary (MS); preschool education (MS); reading (MS, Ed S); science (MS, Ed S); secondary education (MS); social studies (MS, Ed S); Spanish language (MS); teaching and learning (MA, MS), including curriculum and instruction (MA), elementary mathematics (MA), elementary reading (MA), K-12 technology integration (MA); teaching English to speakers of other languages (MS, Ed S); technology management and administration (Ed S); urban studies education (MS); varying exceptionalities (Ed S). Part-time and evening/weekend programs available. Postbaccalaureate distance learning degree programs offered. *Faculty:* 131 full-time (78 women), 548 part-time/adjunct (342 women).

Early Childhood Education

Nova Southeastern University (continued)

Students: 1,418 full-time (1,139 women), 3,464 part-time (2,877 women); includes 2,462 minority (1,732 African Americans, 13 American Indian/Alaska Native, 44 Asian Americans or Pacific Islanders, 673 Hispanic Americans), 77 international. Average age 38. 1,771 applicants, 80% accepted, 1419 enrolled. In 2006, 2,078 master's, 425 other advanced degrees awarded. *Degree requirements:* For master's and Ed S, thesis, practicum, internship. *Entrance requirements:* For master's, MAT, GRE, CLAST, CBEST, PRAXIS I, GKT, minimum GPA of 2.5; for Ed S, MAT or GRE, master's degree, teaching certificate, minimum GPA of 3.0. Additional exam requirements/recommendations for international students: Recommended—TOEFL (minimum score 550 paper-based; 213 computer-based), IELTS (minimum score 6). *Application deadline:* For fall admission, 8/11 priority date for domestic and international students; for winter admission, 12/28 priority date for domestic and international students; for spring admission, 4/22 priority date for domestic and international students. Applications are processed on a rolling basis. Application fee: $50. Electronic applications accepted. *Financial support:* Federal Work-Study available. Support available to part-time students. Financial award application deadline: 1/7. *Faculty research:* School effectiveness, critical thinking, leadership skills acquisition, child education, multicultural education. *Unit head:* Dr. Meline Kevorkian, Associate Dean of Master's and Educational Programs, 954-262-8500, Fax: 954-262-3606, E-mail: melinek@nova.edu. *Application contact:* Jennifer Quiñones Nottingham, Dean of Student Affairs, 800-986-3223 Ext. 8624, Fax: 954-262-3911, E-mail: jlquinon@nova.edu.

Nova Southeastern University, Fischler School of Education and Human Services, Programs in Child, Youth and Family Studies, Fort Lauderdale, FL 33314-7796. Offers child and youth care administration (MS); child and youth studies (Ed D); early childhood education administration (MS); family support studies (MS); substance abuse counseling and education (MS). Part-time and evening/weekend programs available. *Students:* 50 full-time (42 women), 251 part-time (219 women); includes 166 minority (135 African Americans, 3 Asian Americans or Pacific Islanders, 28 Hispanic Americans), 5 international. Average age 38. 26 applicants, 77% accepted, 20 enrolled. In 2006, 14 master's, 49 doctorates awarded. *Degree requirements:* For master's and doctorate, thesis/dissertation, practicum. *Entrance requirements:* For master's, GRE or MAT, work experience in field, minimum GPA of 2.5; for doctorate, GRE or MAT, master's degree, minimum GPA of 3.0, work experience. Additional exam requirements/recommendations for international students: Recommended—TOEFL (minimum score 550 paper-based; 213 computer-based), IELTS (minimum score 6). *Application deadline:* For fall admission, 8/11 priority date for domestic and international students; for winter admission, 12/28 priority date for domestic and international students; for spring admission, 4/22 priority date for domestic and international students. Applications are processed on a rolling basis. Application fee: $50. Electronic applications accepted. *Expenses: Contact institution. Financial support:* Career-related internships or fieldwork and Federal Work-Study available. Support available to part-time students. Financial award application deadline: 1/7. *Unit head:* Dr. Michael Gaffley, Director, 954-262-8629, Fax: 954-262-3911, E-mail: gaffleym@nova.edu. *Application contact:* Jennifer Quiñones Nottingham, Dean of Student Affairs, 800-986-3223 Ext. 8624, Fax: 954-262-3911, E-mail: jlquinon@nova.edu.

Oakland University, Graduate Study and Lifelong Learning, School of Education and Human Services, Department of Human Development and Child Studies, Program in Early Childhood Education, Rochester, MI 48309-4401. Offers early childhood education (M Ed, PhD, Certificate); early mathematics education (Certificate). *Students:* 25 full-time (23 women), 149 part-time (142 women); includes 27 minority (23 African Americans, 1 American Indian/Alaska Native, 1 Asian American or Pacific Islander, 2 Hispanic Americans), 1 international. Average age 36. 43 applicants, 93% accepted, 28 enrolled. In 2006, 45 master's, 2 doctorates awarded. *Degree requirements:* For doctorate, thesis/dissertation. *Entrance requirements:* For master's, minimum GPA of 3.0 for unconditional admission; for doctorate, GRE General Test, minimum GPA of 3.0 for unconditional admission. Additional exam requirements/recommendations for international students: Required—TOEFL (minimum score 550 paper-based; 213 computer-based). *Application deadline:* For fall admission, 5/1 for domestic students, 5/1 priority date for international students; for winter admission, 2/1 for domestic students, 9/1 priority date for international students. Application fee: $35. *Expenses:* Tuition, state resident: full-time $9,936; part-time $414 per credit. Tuition, nonresident: full-time $17,202; part-time $716 per credit. *Financial support:* Career-related internships or fieldwork, Federal Work-Study, institutionally sponsored loans, and tuition waivers (full) available. Financial award application deadline: 3/1; financial award applicants required to submit FAFSA. *Unit head:* Dr. Sherri Oden, Coordinator, 248-370-3027, E-mail: oden@oakland.edu.

Oglethorpe University, Division of Education, Atlanta, GA 30319-2797. Offers early childhood education (MAT). Part-time programs available. *Degree requirements:* For master's, comprehensive exam. *Entrance requirements:* For master's, GRE General Test, PRAXIS, minimum GPA of 2.5.

The Ohio State University at Lima, Graduate Programs, Lima, OH 45804. Offers early childhood education (M Ed); education (MA); middle childhood education (M Ed); social work (MSW). *Students:* 46 full-time (37 women), 32 part-time (27 women), 1 international. Average age 30. *Degree requirements:* For master's, thesis (for some programs), comprehensive exam (for some programs). *Entrance requirements:* For master's, GRE, minimum GPA of 3.0. Additional exam requirements/recommendations for international students: Required—TOEFL, IELTS or Michigan English Language Assessment Battery. *Application deadline:* For fall admission, 8/15 priority date for domestic students, 7/1 priority date for international students; for winter admission, 12/1 priority date for domestic students, 11/1 priority date for international students; for spring admission, 3/1 priority date for domestic students, 2/1 priority date for international students. Applications are processed on a rolling basis. Application fee: $40 ($50 for international students). Electronic applications accepted. *Expenses:* Tuition, state resident: full-time $8,919. Tuition, nonresident: full-time $22,272. Tuition and fees vary according to course load, campus/location and program. *Unit head:* Dr. John Snyder, Dean/Director, 419-995-8481, E-mail: snyder.4@osu.edu. *Application contact:* Graduate Admissions, 614-292-9444, Fax: 614-292-3895, E-mail: domestic.grad@osu.edu.

The Ohio State University at Marion, Graduate Programs, Marion, OH 43302-5695. Offers early childhood education (pre-K to grade 3) (M Ed); integrated teaching and learning (MA); middle childhood education (grades 4-9) (M Ed); nursing (MS, PhD); social work (MSW); MS/PhD. *Students:* 63 full-time (56 women), 43 part-time (41 women); includes 2 minority (both African Americans), 1 international. Average age 32. *Degree requirements:* For master's, thesis (for some programs), comprehensive exam (for some programs). *Entrance requirements:* For master's and doctorate, GRE, minimum undergraduate GPA of 3.0. Additional exam requirements/recommendations for international students: Required—TOEFL, IELTS or Michigan English Language Assessment Battery. *Application deadline:* For fall admission, 8/15 priority date for domestic students, 7/1 priority date for international students; for winter admission, 12/1 priority date for domestic students, 11/1 priority date for international students; for spring admission, 3/1 priority date for domestic students, 2/1 priority date for international students. Applications are processed on a rolling basis. Application fee: $40 ($50 for international students). Electronic applications accepted. *Expenses:* Tuition, state resident: full-time $8,919. Tuition, nonresident: full-time $22,272. Tuition and fees vary according to course load, campus/location and program. *Unit head:* Gregory S. Rose, Dean/Director, 740-389-6786 Ext. 6218, E-mail: rose.9@osu.edu. *Application contact:* Graduate Admissions, 614-292-9444, Fax: 614-292-3895, E-mail: domestic.grad@osu.edu.

The Ohio State University–Mansfield Campus, Graduate Programs, Mansfield, OH 44906-1599. Offers early and middle childhood education (MA); early childhood education (M Ed); middle childhood education (M Ed); social work (MSW). *Faculty:* 8 full-time (4 women). *Students:* 35 full-time (32 women), 46 part-time (42 women); includes 4 minority (all African Americans), 1 international. Average age 32. *Degree requirements:* For master's, thesis (for some programs), comprehensive exam (for some programs). *Entrance requirements:* For master's, GRE, minimum GPA of 3.0. Additional exam requirements/recommendations for international students: Required—TOEFL (minimum score 550 paper-based; 213 computer-based). *Application deadline:* For fall admission, 8/15 priority date for domestic students, 7/1 priority date for international students; for winter admission, 12/1 priority date for domestic students, 11/1 priority date for international students; for spring admission, 3/1 priority date for domestic students, 2/1 priority date for international students. Applications are processed on a rolling basis. Application fee: $40 ($50 for international students). Electronic applications accepted. *Expenses:* Tuition, state resident: full-time $8,919. Tuition, nonresident: full-time $22,272. Tuition and fees vary according to course load, campus/location and program. *Financial support:* In 2006–07, 14 students received support, including 3 teaching assistantships with full tuition reimbursements available (averaging $9,000 per year); Federal Work-Study and scholarships/grants also available. Support available to part-time students. Financial award application deadline: 7/1. *Application contact:* Graduate Admissions, 614-292-9444, Fax: 614-292-3895, E-mail: domestic.grad@osu.edu.

The Ohio State University–Newark Campus, Graduate Programs, Newark, OH 43055-1797. Offers early/middle childhood education (M Ed); integrated teaching and learning (MA); social work (MSW). *Students:* 31 full-time (25 women), 39 part-time (34 women); includes 3 minority (1 African American, 1 Asian American or Pacific Islander, 1 Hispanic American), 1 international. Average age 33. *Degree requirements:* For master's, thesis (for some programs), comprehensive exam (for some programs). *Entrance requirements:* For master's, GRE, minimum GPA of 3.0. Additional exam requirements/recommendations for international students: Required—TOEFL, IELTS or Michigan English Language Assessment Battery. *Application deadline:* For fall admission, 8/15 priority date for domestic students, 7/1 priority date for international students; for winter admission, 12/1 priority date for domestic students, 11/1 priority date for international students; for spring admission, 3/1 priority date for domestic students, 2/1 priority date for international students. Applications are processed on a rolling basis. Application fee: $40 ($50 for international students). Electronic applications accepted. *Expenses:* Tuition, state resident: full-time $8,919. Tuition, nonresident: full-time $22,272. Tuition and fees vary according to course level, campus/location and program. *Unit head:* Dr. William L. MacDonald, Dean/Director, 740-366-9333 Ext. 330, E-mail: macdonald.24@osu.edu. *Application contact:* Graduate Admissions, 614-292-9444, Fax: 614-292-3985, E-mail: domestic.grad@osu.edu.

Ohio University, Graduate Studies, College of Health and Human Services, School of Human and Consumer Sciences, Athens, OH 45701-2979. Offers child development and family life (MSHCS); early childhood education (MSHCS); family studies (MSHCS); food and nutrition (MSHCS). Part-time programs available. *Faculty:* 13 full-time (9 women), 5 part-time/adjunct (all women). *Students:* 11 full-time (9 women), 5 part-time (4 women); includes 5 minority (2 African Americans, 3 Asian Americans or Pacific Islanders). Average age 26. 16 applicants, 69% accepted, 9 enrolled. In 2006, 8 degrees awarded. *Degree requirements:* For master's, thesis. *Entrance requirements:* For master's, GRE. Additional exam requirements/recommendations for international students: Required—TOEFL. *Application deadline:* For fall admission, 3/1 priority date for domestic students. Applications are processed on a rolling basis. Application fee: $45. Electronic applications accepted. *Financial support:* In 2006–07, 6 teaching assistantships (averaging $9,815 per year) were awarded; career-related internships or fieldwork, Federal Work-Study, institutionally sponsored loans, and unspecified assistantships also available. Financial award application deadline: 3/15. *Faculty research:* Diversity, developmentally appropriate activities, death and dying, gerontology, sexuality education. *Unit head:* Dr. V. Ann Paulins, Director, 740-593-2880, Fax: 740-593-0289, E-mail: paulins@ohio.edu.

Oklahoma City University, Petree College of Arts and Sciences, Division of Education and Kinesiology Exercise Studies, Programs in Education, Oklahoma City, OK 73106-1402. Offers applied behavioral studies (M Ed); early childhood education (M Ed); elementary education (M Ed). Part-time and evening/weekend programs available. *Faculty:* 4 full-time (3 women), 13 part-time/adjunct (8 women). *Students:* 15 full-time (14 women), 14 part-time (11 women); includes 7 minority (4 African Americans, 2 Asian Americans or Pacific Islanders, 1 Hispanic American). Average age 33. 25 applicants, 76% accepted. In 2006, 23 degrees awarded. *Degree requirements:* For master's, thesis optional. *Entrance requirements:* For master's, minimum GPA of 3.0. *Application deadline:* For fall admission, 8/22 for domestic students; for spring admission, 1/15 for domestic students. Applications are processed on a rolling basis. Application fee: $30 ($70 for international students). *Expenses:* Tuition: Full-time $12,780; part-time $710 per hour. Required fees: $89 per hour. *Financial support:* Fellowships with partial tuition reimbursements, career-related internships or fieldwork, Federal Work-Study, institutionally sponsored loans, and tuition waivers (partial) available. Support available to part-time students. Financial award application deadline: 8/1; financial award applicants required to submit FAFSA. *Faculty research:* Adult literacy, cognition, reading strategies. *Application contact:* Leslie McKenzie, Director, Graduate Admissions, 800-633-7242, Fax: 405-208-5356, E-mail: gadmissions@okcu.edu.

Old Dominion University, Darden College of Education, Program in Early Childhood Education, Norfolk, VA 23529. Offers MS Ed, PhD. *Accreditation:* NCATE. Part-time and evening/weekend programs available. *Faculty:* 4 full-time (3 women), 6 part-time/adjunct (5 women). *Students:* 29 full-time (28 women), 23 part-time (22 women); includes 1 minority (Asian American or Pacific Islander), 2 international. Average age 29. 35 applicants, 91% accepted. In 2006, 30 degrees awarded. *Degree requirements:* For master's, thesis or alternative, written exams, comprehensive exam. *Entrance requirements:* For master's, GRE General Test, PRAXIS I, minimum undergraduate GPA of 2.5; for doctorate, GRE General Test. Additional exam requirements/recommendations for international students: Required—TOEFL. *Application deadline:* For fall admission, 7/1 for domestic students; for winter admission, 7/1 for domestic students; for spring admission, 11/1 for domestic students. Applications are processed on a rolling basis. Application fee: $40. *Expenses:* Tuition, area resident: Part-time $285 per credit hour. Tuition, nonresident: part-time $715 per credit hour. Required fees: $94 per semester. *Financial support:* In 2006–07, 40 students received support, including 4 fellowships with full tuition reimbursements available (averaging $15,000 per year), 2 research assistantships with tuition reimbursements available (averaging $9,000 per year), 3 teaching assistantships with tuition reimbursements available (averaging $9,000 per year); career-related internships or fieldwork, scholarships/grants, and tuition waivers (partial) also available. Support available to part-time students. Financial award application deadline: 2/15; financial award applicants required to submit FAFSA. *Faculty research:* Child abuse, day care, parenting, discipline (positive), bullying. *Unit head:* Dr. Katharine Kersey, Graduate Program Director, 757-683-4121, Fax: 757-683-5593, E-mail: kkersey@odu.edu.

Ottawa University, Graduate Studies-Arizona, Program in Education, Ottawa, KS 66067-3399. Offers community college counseling (MA); curriculum and instruction (MA); early childhood (MA); education intervention (MA); education leadership (MA); education technology (MA); Montessori early childhood education (MA); Montessori elementary education (MA); professional development (MA); school guidance counseling (MA); special education—cross categorical (MA). Programs offered in Mesa, Phoenix, Tempe and West Valley, AZ. *Accreditation:* NCATE. Part-time programs available. *Faculty:* 7 full-time (3 women), 24 part-time/adjunct (11 women). *Students:* 14 full-time (9 women), 162 part-time (128 women); includes 31 minority (13 African Americans, 2 American Indian/Alaska Native, 1 Asian American or Pacific Islander, 15 Hispanic Americans), 1 international. Average age 38. In 2006, 56 degrees awarded. *Degree requirements:* For master's, thesis or alternative, registration. *Entrance requirements:* For master's, minimum undergraduate GPA of 3.0, copy of current state certification or teaching license. Additional exam requirements/recommendations for international students: Required—TOEFL (minimum score 550 paper-based; 213 computer-based). *Application deadline:* For fall admission, 7/1 priority date for domestic students; for winter admission, 11/1 priority date for domestic students; for spring admission, 2/1 priority date for domestic students. Applications are processed on a rolling basis. Application fee: $50. Electronic applications accepted. *Expenses: Contact institution. Application contact:* Bunny Simpson, Secretary, 602-371-1188, Fax: 602-371-0035, E-mail: bunny.simpson@ottawa.edu.

Pacific University, College of Education, Forest Grove, OR 97116-1797. Offers early childhood education (MAT); education (MAE); elementary education (MAT); high school education (MAT); middle school education (MAT); special education (MAT); visual function in learning (M Ed). Part-time and evening/weekend programs available. *Faculty:* 20 full-time (12 women), 40 part-time/adjunct (21 women). *Students:* 222 full-time (151 women), 115 part-time (90 women); includes 30 minority (3 African Americans, 5 American Indian/Alaska Native, 12 Asian Americans or Pacific Islanders, 10 Hispanic Americans). Average age 32. 92 applicants, 83% accepted, 69 enrolled. In 2006, 257 degrees awarded. *Degree requirements:* For master's, research project. *Entrance requirements:* For master's, California Basic Educational Skills Test, Praxis I, minimum undergraduate GPA of 2.75, 3.0 graduate. Additional exam requirements/recommendations for international students: Required—TOEFL. *Application deadline:* For fall admission, 6/15 priority date for domestic students; for spring admission, 10/15 for domestic students. Applications are processed on a rolling basis. Application fee: $35. Electronic applications accepted. *Expenses: Contact institution. Financial support:* In 2006–07, 287 students received support; fellowships, research assistantships, teaching assistantships, career-related internships or fieldwork, institutionally sponsored loans, and scholarships/grants available. Support available to part-time students. Financial award application deadline: 5/1; financial award applicants required to submit FAFSA. *Faculty research:* Defining a culturally competent classroom, technology in the k-12 classroom, Socratic seminars, social studies education. *Unit head:* Dr. Mark Ankeny, Acting Dean, 503-352-2102, E-mail: mankeny@pacificu.edu. *Application contact:* Diana Watkins, Assistant Director Graduate and Professional Admissions, 503-352-2958, Fax: 503-352-2907, E-mail: teach@pacificu.edu.

Penn State University Park, Graduate School, College of Education, Department of Curriculum and Instruction, State College, University Park, PA 16802-1503. Offers bilingual education (M Ed, MS, PhD); early childhood education (M Ed, MS, PhD); elementary education (M Ed, MS, PhD); instructional systems (M Ed, MS, PhD); language arts and reading (M Ed, MS, PhD); science education (M Ed, MS, PhD); social studies education (MS, PhD); supervisor and curriculum development (M Ed, MS, PhD). *Accreditation:* NCATE. *Unit head:* Dr. Murry R. Nelson, Head, 814-865-6321, Fax: 814-863-7602, E-mail: mrn2@psu.edu. *Application contact:* Judy Nastase, Graduate Staff Assistant, 814-865-2168, E-mail: jcn3@psu.edu.

Piedmont College, School of Education, Demorest, GA 30535-0010. Offers early childhood education (MA, MAT); instruction (Ed S); secondary education (MA, MAT). Part-time and evening/weekend programs available. *Faculty:* 20 full-time (17 women), 22 part-time/adjunct (5 women). *Students:* 210 full-time (158 women), 846 part-time (734 women); includes 95 minority (72 African Americans, 2 American Indian/Alaska Native, 10 Asian Americans or Pacific Islanders, 11 Hispanic Americans), 7 international. 327 applicants, 92% accepted, 235 enrolled. In 2006, 422 master's, 203 other advanced degrees awarded. *Degree requirements:* For master's, thesis, field experience in the teaching classroom. *Entrance requirements:* For master's, GRE General Test, MAT, minimum undergraduate GPA of 2.5; for Ed S, minimum graduate GPA of 3.5, valid teaching certificate. Additional exam requirements/recommendations for international students: Required—TOEFL (minimum score 550 paper-based; 213 computer-based). *Application deadline:* For fall admission, 7/15 for domestic students; for spring admission, 12/1 for domestic students. Application fee: $30. *Expenses:* Tuition: Part-time $310 per credit hour. *Financial support:* Career-related internships or fieldwork, Federal Work-Study, institutionally sponsored loans, and unspecified assistantships available. Support available to part-time students. Financial award applicants required to submit FAFSA. *Unit head:* Dr. Jane McFerrin, Dean, 706-778-3000 Ext. 1201, Fax: 706-776-9608, E-mail: jmcferrin@piedmont.edu. *Application contact:* Carol E. Kokesh, Director of Graduate Studies, 706-778-8500 Ext. 1181, Fax: 706-776-6635, E-mail: ckokesh@piedmont.edu.

Pittsburg State University, Graduate School, College of Education, Department of Curriculum and Instruction, Pittsburg, KS 66762. Offers classroom reading teacher (MS); early childhood education (MS); elementary education (MS); reading (MS); reading specialist (MS); secondary education (MS); teaching (MAT). *Accreditation:* NCATE. *Students:* 141. *Degree requirements:* For master's, thesis or alternative. *Entrance requirements:* For master's, GRE or MAT. Application fee: $35 ($60 for international students). *Expenses:* Tuition, state resident: full-time $2,144; part-time $181 per credit hour. Tuition, nonresident: full-time $5,273; part-time $442 per credit hour. Tuition and fees vary according to course load and campus/location. *Financial support:* In 2006–07, teaching assistantships (averaging $5,000 per year); career-related internships or fieldwork, Federal Work-Study, and unspecified assistantships also available. *Unit head:* Dr. V. June Taylor, Chairperson, 620-235-4508. *Application contact:* Jamie Vanderbeck, Assistant Director, 620-235-4223, Fax: 620-235-4219, E-mail: jvanderb@pittstate.edu.

Portland State University, Graduate Studies, School of Education, Department of Curriculum and Instruction, Portland, OR 97207-0751. Offers early childhood education (MA, MS); education (M Ed, MA, MS); educational leadership: curriculum and instruction (Ed D); educational media/school librarianship (MA, MS); elementary education (M Ed, MAT, MST); reading (MA, MS); secondary education (M Ed, MAT, MST). *Accreditation:* NCATE. Part-time programs available. *Faculty:* 20 full-time (14 women), 18 part-time/adjunct (9 women). *Students:* 185 full-time (135 women), 209 part-time (160 women); includes 53 minority (7 African Americans, 4 American Indian/Alaska Native, 13 Asian Americans or Pacific Islanders, 29 Hispanic Americans), 13 international. Average age 32. 372 applicants, 87% accepted, 171 enrolled. In 2006, 352 master's, 4 doctorates awarded. *Degree requirements:* For master's, special project or thesis, written exam; for doctorate, thesis/dissertation. *Entrance requirements:* For master's, California Basic Educational Skills Test, minimum GPA of 3.0 in upper-division course work or 2.75 overall. Additional exam requirements/recommendations for international students: Required—TOEFL (minimum score 550 paper-based; 213 computer-based). *Application deadline:* For fall admission, 4/1 for domestic and international students; for winter admission, 9/1 for domestic and international students; for spring admission, 11/1 for domestic and international students. Applications are processed on a rolling basis. Application fee: $50. *Expenses:* Tuition, state resident: full-time $6,426; part-time $238 per credit. Tuition, nonresident: full-time $11,016; part-time $408 per credit. Tuition and fees vary according to course load. *Financial support:* In 2006–07, 5 research assistantships with full tuition reimbursements (averaging $5,508 per year) were awarded; teaching assistantships with full tuition reimbursements, career-related internships or fieldwork, Federal Work-Study, and institutionally sponsored loans also available. Support available to part-time students. Financial award application deadline: 3/1; financial award applicants required to submit FAFSA. *Faculty research:* Early literacy, characteristics of successful teachers of at-risk students, participation of women/minorities in technology courses, selection of cooperating teachers. Total annual research expenditures: $308,420. *Unit head:* Steven Lee, Head, 503-725-4689, Fax: 503-725-8475. *Application contact:* Majken Elek, Department Secretary, 503-725-4756, Fax: 503-725-8475, E-mail: majkene@pdx.edu.

Queens College of the City University of New York, Division of Graduate Studies, Division of Education, Department of Elementary and Early Childhood Education, Flushing, NY 11367-1597. Offers bilingual education (MS Ed); childhood education (MA); early childhood education (MA); elementary education (MS Ed, AC); literacy (MS Ed). Part-time and evening/weekend programs available. *Faculty:* 31 full-time (25 women). *Students:* 87 full-time (80 women), 505 part-time (454 women). In 2006, 338 degrees awarded. *Degree requirements:* For master's, research project; for AC, thesis optional. *Entrance requirements:* For master's, minimum GPA of 3.0. Additional exam requirements/recommendations for international students: Required—TOEFL. *Application deadline:* For fall admission, 4/1 for domestic students; for spring admission, 11/1 for domestic students. Applications are processed on a rolling basis. Application fee: $125. *Financial support:* Career-related internships or fieldwork, Federal Work-Study, institutionally sponsored loans, and tuition waivers (partial) available. Support available to part-time students. Financial award application deadline: 4/1; financial award applicants required to submit FAFSA. *Unit head:* Dr. Myra Zarnowski, Chairperson, 718-997-5328.

Regis University, School for Professional Studies, Program in Teacher Education, Denver, CO 80221-1099. Offers adult learning, training, and development (M Ed); curriculum, instruction, and assessment (M Ed); early childhood (M Ed); educational technology (Certificate); elementary (M Ed); ESL (M Ed); fine arts (M Ed), including arts, music; instructional technology (M Ed); professional leadership (M Ed); reading (M Ed); secondary (M Ed); self-designed (M Ed); space studies (M Ed); special education (M Ed); teacher licensure (M Ed). Program also offered in Henderson and Las Vegas (Summerlin), NV. Postbaccalaureate distance learning degree programs offered. *Unit head:* Dr. Suzie Perry, Dean, 303-458-4302. *Application contact:* Partick Lowenthal, Assistant Director, 303-458-4300 Ext. 4314, E-mail: masters@regis.edu.

Rhode Island College, School of Graduate Studies, Feinstein School of Education and Human Development, Department of Elementary Education, Providence, RI 02908-1991. Offers early childhood education (M Ed); elementary education (M Ed, MAT); reading (M Ed). *Accreditation:* NCATE. Part-time and evening/weekend programs available. *Faculty:* 17 full-time (10 women), 5 part-time/adjunct (all women). *Students:* 33 full-time (28 women), 75 part-time (69 women); includes 4 minority (all Hispanic Americans) Average age 33. In 2006, 56 degrees awarded. *Entrance requirements:* For master's, GRE General Test or MAT, Praxis II (elementary content knowledge), 3 letters of recommendation, interview. *Application deadline:* For fall admission, 3/15 for domestic students; for spring admission, 11/1 for domestic students. Applications are processed on a rolling basis. Application fee: $50. *Expenses:* Tuition, state resident: part-time $244 per credit. Tuition, nonresident: part-time $512 per credit. Required fees: $12 per credit. $66 per term. Tuition and fees vary according to degree level, program and reciprocity agreements. *Financial support:* Teaching assistantships with full tuition reimbursements, Federal Work-Study, scholarships/grants, and health care benefits available. Support available to part-time students. Financial award application deadline: 5/15; financial award applicants required to submit FAFSA. *Unit head:* Dr. Lisa Owen, Chair, 401-456-8016, E-mail: lowen@ric.edu.

Rivier College, School of Graduate Studies, Department of Education, Nashua, NH 03060-5086. Offers curriculum and instruction (M Ed); early childhood education (M Ed); educational administration (M Ed); educational studies (M Ed); elementary education (M Ed); elementary education and general special education (M Ed); emotional and behavioral disorders (M Ed); general social education (M Ed); leadership and learning (CAGS); learning disabilities (M Ed); learning disabilities and reading (M Ed); mental health counseling (MA); reading (M Ed); school counseling (M Ed). Part-time and evening/weekend programs available. *Faculty:* 11 full-time (7 women), 40 part-time/adjunct (29 women). *Students:* 41 full-time (33 women), 221 part-time (192 women); includes 4 minority (2 African Americans, 2 Hispanic Americans). Average age 37. In 2006, 134 degrees awarded. *Degree requirements:* For master's, internships. *Entrance requirements:* For master's, GRE General Test or MAT. *Application deadline:* Applications are processed on a rolling basis. Application fee: $25. *Financial support:* Available to part-time students. Application deadline: 2/1; *Unit head:* Dr. Charles L. Mitsakos, Chairman, 603-888-1311 Ext. 8582. *Application contact:* Diane Monahan, Director of Graduate Admissions, 603-897-8129, Fax: 603-897-8810, E-mail: gradadm@rivier.edu.

Roberts Wesleyan College, Division of Teacher Education, Rochester, NY 14624-1997. Offers adolescence education (M Ed); childhood and special education (M Ed); literacy education (M Ed); urban education (M Ed). Part-time and evening/weekend programs available. *Faculty:* 17 part-time/adjunct (7 women). *Students:* 1 (woman) full-time, 66 part-time (47 women). Average age 33. 52 applicants, 63% accepted. In 2006, 20 degrees awarded. *Degree requirements:* For master's, thesis. *Application deadline:* For fall admission, 8/1 priority date for domestic students; for spring admission, 12/1 for domestic students. Applications are processed on a rolling basis. Application fee: $35. *Financial support:* In 2006–07, 7 students received support. Career-related internships or fieldwork available. Financial award application deadline: 9/1; financial award applicants required to submit FAFSA. *Unit head:* Dr. Richard Mace, Chair, 585-594-6934. *Application contact:* Paula Finch, Graduate Admissions Coordinator, 585-594-6683, E-mail: finch_paula@roberts.edu.

Roosevelt University, Graduate Division, College of Education, Program in Early Childhood Education/Early Childhood Professions, Chicago, IL 60605-1394. Offers MA. *Students:* 29 full-time (26 women), 40 part-time (39 women); includes 39 minority (30 African Americans, 3 Asian Americans or Pacific Islanders, 6 Hispanic Americans). Average age 33. 73 applicants, 59% accepted, 43 enrolled. In 2006, 19 degrees awarded. *Unit head:* Dr. Sharon Grant, Chair, 847-619-8831. *Application contact:* Joanne Canyon-Heller, Coordinator of Graduate Admission, 877-APPLY RU, Fax: 312-281-3356, E-mail: applyru@roosevelt.edu.

Rutgers, The State University of New Jersey, New Brunswick, Graduate School of Education, Department of Learning and Teaching, Program in Early Childhood/Elementary Education, New Brunswick, NJ 08901-1281. Offers Ed M, Ed D. Part-time programs available. *Faculty:* 4 full-time (all women). *Students:* 71 full-time (64 women), 26 part-time (24 women). 185 applicants, 45% accepted, 62 enrolled. In 2006, 71 master's, 1 doctorate awarded. Terminal master's awarded for partial completion of doctoral program. *Degree requirements:* For master's, comprehensive exam (for some programs); for doctorate, thesis/dissertation, qualifying exam. *Entrance requirements:* For master's, GRE General Test, minimum GPA of 3.0; for doctorate, GRE General Test, minimum GPA of 3.5. Additional exam requirements/recommendations for international students: Required—TOEFL. *Application deadline:* For fall admission, 2/1 for domestic and international students. Application fee: $60. Electronic applications accepted. *Financial support:* Application deadline: 3/15; *Unit head:* Dr. Sharon Ryan, Coordinator, 732-932-7496 Ext. 8114, E-mail: sr247@rci.rutgers.edu.

Saginaw Valley State University, College of Education, Program in Early Childhood Education, University Center, MI 48710. Offers MAT. *Accreditation:* NCATE. Part-time and evening/weekend programs available. *Students:* 2 full-time (both women), 131 part-time (129 women); includes 4 minority (1 African American, 2 Asian Americans or Pacific Islanders, 1 Hispanic American). Average age 33. 26 applicants, 100% accepted, 20 enrolled. In 2006, 46 degrees awarded. *Degree requirements:* For master's, practicum. *Entrance requirements:* For master's, minimum GPA of 3.0, teaching certificate. *Application deadline:* Applications are processed on a rolling basis. Application fee: $25. Electronic applications accepted. *Expenses:* Tuition, state resident: full-time $7,225; part-time $301 per credit hour. Tuition, nonresident: full-time $13,888; part-time $579 per credit hour. Required fees: $330; $14 per credit hour. Tuition and fees vary according to course load. *Financial support:* Applicants required to submit FAFSA. *Application contact:* Jeanne Chipman, Certification Officer, 989-964-4083, Fax: 989-964-4385, E-mail: jdc@svsu.edu.

St. John's University, The School of Education, Division of Early Childhood, Childhood and Adolescent Education, Program in Early Childhood Education, Queens, NY 11439. Offers MS Ed. *Students:* 10 full-time (all women), 142 part-time (138 women); includes 36 minority (11 African Americans, 10 Asian Americans or Pacific Islanders, 15 Hispanic Americans), 1 international. Average age 28. 83 applicants, 88% accepted, 47 enrolled. In 2006, 70 degrees awarded. *Entrance requirements:* Additional exam requirements/recommendations for international students: Required—TOEFL (minimum score 500 paper-based; 173 computer-based). *Application deadline:* For fall admission, 4/15 for domestic students, 5/1 priority date for international students; for spring admission, 11/1 priority date for international students. Applications are processed on a rolling basis. Application fee: $40. Electronic applications accepted. *Expenses:* Tuition: Full-time $18,480; part-time $770 per credit. Required fees: $125 per semester. Tuition and fees vary according to program. *Financial support:* Research assistantships available. *Application contact:* Kelly Ronayne, Assistant Dean, 718-990-2303, Fax: 718-990-6069, E-mail: graded@stjohns.edu.

Saint Joseph College, Graduate Division, Department of Education, West Hartford, CT 06117-2700. Offers early childhood education (MA); education (MA), including self-designed specializations; special education (MA). Part-time and evening/weekend programs available. *Degree requirements:* For master's, thesis or alternative, comprehensive exam. *Entrance requirements:* For master's, 2 letters of recommendation. Electronic applications accepted.

St. Joseph's College, New York, Graduate Programs, Program in Education, Field of Infant/Toddler Early Childhood Special Education, Brooklyn, NY 11205-3688. Offers MA.

See Close-Up on page 915.

Early Childhood Education

St. Joseph's College, Suffolk Campus, Program in Infant/Toddler Early Childhood Special Education, Patchogue, NY 11772-2399. Offers MA. Part-time and evening/weekend programs available. *Degree requirements:* For master's, thesis, full-time practicum experience. *Entrance requirements:* For master's, 1 course in child development, 2 courses in special education, minimum undergraduate GPA of 3.0, New York state teaching certificate, writing sample, interview. Additional exam requirements/recommendations for international students: Required—TOEFL (minimum score 550 paper-based; 213 computer-based).

Saint Mary's College of California, School of Education, Program in Early Childhood Education and Montessori Teacher Training, Moraga, CA 94575. Offers M Ed, MA. Part-time and evening/weekend programs available. *Faculty:* 2 full-time (both women), 2 part-time/adjunct (both women). *Students:* 19 full-time (all women), 42 part-time (all women); includes 10 minority (1 American Indian/Alaska Native, 5 Asian Americans or Pacific Islanders, 4 Hispanic Americans), 6 international. Average age 25. 28 applicants, 27 enrolled. In 2006, 4 degrees awarded. *Median time to degree:* Master's–2.5 years full-time. *Degree requirements:* For master's, thesis or alternative. *Entrance requirements:* For master's, interview, minimum GPA of 3.0. *Application deadline:* Applications are processed on a rolling basis. Application fee: $50. *Financial support:* Career-related internships or fieldwork available. Support available to part-time students. Financial award application deadline: 2/15. *Unit head:* Patricia Chambers, Coordinator, 925-631-4036, Fax: 925-376-8379, E-mail: pchambers@stmarys-ca.edu.

Saint Xavier University, Graduate Studies, School of Education, Chicago, IL 60655-3105. Offers counseling (MA); counselor education (MA); curriculum and instruction (MA); early childhood education (MA); education (CAS); educational administration (MA); elementary education (MA); field-based education (MA); general educational studies (MA); individualized program (MA); learning disabilities (MA); reading (MA); secondary education (MA). *Accreditation:* NCATE. Part-time and evening/weekend programs available. *Faculty:* 92. *Students:* 45 full-time (35 women), 1,529 part-time (1,309 women). In 2006, 474 degrees awarded. *Degree requirements:* For master's, thesis or project. *Entrance requirements:* For master's, minimum GPA of 3.0. *Application deadline:* For fall admission, 8/15 priority date for domestic students. Applications are processed on a rolling basis. Application fee: $35. *Expenses: Contact institution. Financial support:* Career-related internships or fieldwork available. Support available to part-time students. Financial award applicants required to submit FAFSA. *Unit head:* Dr. Beverly Gulley, Dean, 773-298-3221, Fax: 773-779-9061, E-mail: gulley@sxu.edu. *Application contact:* Beth Gierach, Managing Director of Admission, 773-298-3053, Fax: 773-298-3076, E-mail: gierach@sxu.edu.

Salem College, Department of Education, Winston-Salem, NC 27108-0548. Offers early education and leadership (MAT); elementary education (MAT); English as a second language (MAT); language and literacy (M Ed); middle school education (MAT); secondary education (MAT); special education (MAT). *Accreditation:* NCATE. Part-time and evening/weekend programs available. *Faculty:* 8 full-time (6 women), 5 part-time/adjunct (all women). *Students:* 8 full-time (all women), 250 part-time (238 women); includes 19 minority (16 African Americans, 1 Asian American or Pacific Islander, 2 Hispanic Americans). Average age 33. 110 applicants, 65% accepted, 68 enrolled. In 2006, 34 degrees awarded. *Degree requirements:* For master's, practicum (MAT), project (M Ed), oral and written comprehensive exams. *Entrance requirements:* For master's, GRE, minimum GPA of 2.5. *Application deadline:* Applications are processed on a rolling basis. Application fee: $30. *Financial support:* In 2006–07, 152 students received support. Federal Work-Study and scholarships/grants available. Support available to part-time students. Financial award applicants required to submit FAFSA. *Faculty research:* Content area reading strategies, literacy development, brain compatible instruction. *Unit head:* Dr. Paula Grubbs, Director of Teacher Education, 336-721-2610, Fax: 336-721-2683, E-mail: grubbs@salem.edu.

Salem State College, Graduate School, Program in Early Childhood Education, Salem, MA 01970-5353. Offers M Ed. *Accreditation:* NCATE. Part-time and evening/weekend programs available. *Faculty:* 3 part-time/adjunct (all women). *Students:* 3 full-time (all women), 25 part-time (24 women); includes 1 minority (Hispanic American) Average age 34. In 2006, 16 degrees awarded. *Entrance requirements:* For master's, GRE General Test or MAT. *Application deadline:* Applications are processed on a rolling basis. Application fee: $35. *Unit head:* Dr. Clarke Fowler, Coordinator, 978-542-7041, Fax: 978-542-7215, E-mail: rfowler@salemstate.edu.

Salisbury University, Graduate Division, Department of Education, Salisbury, MD 21801-6837. Offers art (MAT); biology (MAT); business education (MAT); chemistry (MAT); early childhood education (M Ed); educational administration (M Ed); elementary education (M Ed); English (M Ed, MAT); French (MAT); geography (MAT); history (MAT); mathematics (MAT); media and technology (MAT); music (MAT); psychology (MAT); reading education (MAT); science (MAT); secondary education (MAT); social studies (MAT); Spanish (MAT). *Accreditation:* NCATE. Part-time and evening/weekend programs available. *Faculty:* 12 full-time (6 women), 10 part-time/adjunct (8 women). *Students:* 17 full-time (9 women), 84 part-time (72 women); includes 6 minority (5 African Americans, 1 Hispanic American). Average age 30. 15 applicants, 73% accepted, 11 enrolled. In 2006, 63 degrees awarded. *Degree requirements:* For master's, comprehensive exam (for some programs). *Entrance requirements:* For master's, PRAXIS, minimum GPA of 2.75. Additional exam requirements/recommendations for international students: Required—TOEFL (minimum score 550 paper-based; 213 computer-based). *Application deadline:* For fall admission, 8/1 priority date for domestic students; for spring admission, 1/1 for domestic students. Applications are processed on a rolling basis. Application fee: $45. *Expenses:* Tuition, state resident: part-time $260 per credit hour. Tuition, nonresident: part-time $546 per credit hour. Required fees: $52 per credit hour. *Financial support:* In 2006–07, 3 teaching assistantships with full tuition reimbursements were awarded; career-related internships or fieldwork and scholarships/grants also available. Support available to part-time students. Financial award applicants required to submit FAFSA. *Faculty research:* Middle-level education, student outcomes. *Unit head:* Dr. Edward C. Robeck, Program Coordinator, 410-543-6292, Fax: 410-548-2593, E-mail: ecrobeck@salisbury.edu. *Application contact:* Debra J. Clark, Administrative Assistant I, 410-543-6281, Fax: 410-548-2593, E-mail: djclark@salisbury.edu.

Samford University, School of Education, Birmingham, AL 35229-0002. Offers early childhood education (Ed S); early childhood/elementary education (MS Ed); educational administration (Ed S); educational leadership (Ed D); elementary education (Ed S); gifted education (MS Ed); M Div/MS Ed. *Accreditation:* NCATE. Part-time programs available. *Faculty:* 12 full-time (7 women), 8 part-time/adjunct (4 women). *Students:* 16 full-time (14 women), 160 part-time (124 women); includes 25 minority (all African Americans) Average age 38. 45 applicants, 100% accepted, 17 enrolled. In 2006, 15 master's, 20 doctorates, 20 other advanced degrees awarded. *Entrance requirements:* For master's, GRE or MAT, minimum GPA of 3.0; for doctorate, minimum GPA of 3.7; for Ed S, GRE, master's degree, teaching certificate, minimum GPA of 3.25. Additional exam requirements/recommendations for international students: Required—TOEFL (minimum score 550 paper-based; 213 computer-based). *Application deadline:* Applications are processed on a rolling basis. Application fee: $25. *Expenses:* Tuition: Part-time $500 per credit. One-time fee: $25 part-time. Full-time tuition and fees vary according to program and student level. *Financial support:* In 2006–07, 54 students received support; research assistantships, career-related internships or fieldwork, Federal Work-Study, scholarships/grants, and tuition waivers (partial) available. Support available to part-time students. Financial award applicants required to submit FAFSA. *Faculty research:* School law, the characteristics of beginning teachers, the nature of school reform, school culture, quality improvement in education, K-12 student achievement. *Unit head:* Dr. Jean Ann Box, Dean, 205-726-2559, E-mail: jabox@samford.edu. *Application contact:* Dr. Maurice Persall, Director, Graduate Office, 205-726-2019, E-mail: jmpersal@samford.edu.

Sam Houston State University, College of Education and Applied Science, Department of Language, Literacy, and Special Populations, Huntsville, TX 77341. Offers early childhood education (M Ed); reading (M Ed, MA); special education (M Ed, MA). Part-time and evening/weekend programs available. *Faculty:* 6 full-time (4 women). *Students:* 2 full-time (both women), 104 part-time (100 women); includes 18 minority (6 African Americans, 1 American Indian/Alaska Native, 11 Hispanic Americans), 2 international. Average age 37. In 2006, 26 degrees awarded. *Entrance requirements:* For master's, GRE General Test, minimum GPA of 2.5. *Application deadline:* For fall admission, 8/1 for domestic students; for spring admission, 12/1 for domestic students. Application fee: $20. *Expenses:* Tuition, state resident: full-time $5,904; part-time $164 per semester hour. Tuition, nonresident: full-time $15,804; part-time $439 per semester hour. Required fees: $1,374; $462 per semester. *Financial support:* Teaching assistantships available. Financial award application deadline: 5/31; financial award applicants required to submit FAFSA. *Unit head:* Dr. Mary Robbins, Chair, 936-294-3890, Fax: 936-294-1131, E-mail: edu_mer@shsu.edu. *Application contact:* Molly Doughtie, Advisor, 936-294-1105, E-mail: edu_mxd@shsu.edu.

San Francisco State University, Division of Graduate Studies, College of Education, Department of Elementary Education, Program in Early Childhood Education, San Francisco, CA 94132-1722. Offers MA. *Accreditation:* NCATE. Part-time programs available. *Faculty:* 4 full-time (3 women), 2 part-time/adjunct (both women). *Students:* 35 (34 women). *Degree requirements:* For master's, thesis or alternative. *Entrance requirements:* For master's, minimum GPA of 2.5 in last 60 units. *Application deadline:* For fall admission, 11/30 priority date for domestic students. Applications are processed on a rolling basis. Application fee: $55. *Financial support:* Application deadline: 3/1. *Faculty research:* Play, social development, language and culture. *Application contact:* Barbara Henderson, Graduate Coordinator, 415-338-1319, E-mail: barbara@bungdabba.com.

Siena Heights University, Graduate College, Program in Teacher Education, Concentration in Early Childhood Education, Adrian, MI 49221-1796. Offers Montessori education (MA). Part-time programs available. *Degree requirements:* For master's, thesis, presentation. *Entrance requirements:* For master's, interview, minimum GPA of 3.0.

Slippery Rock University of Pennsylvania, Graduate Studies (Recruitment), College of Education, Department of Elementary Education and Early Childhood, Slippery Rock, PA 16057-1383. Offers early childhood education (M Ed); math/science (M Ed); reading (M Ed). *Accreditation:* NCATE. Part-time and evening/weekend programs available. *Degree requirements:* For master's, thesis (for some programs), reflective presentation, comprehensive exam (for some programs). *Entrance requirements:* For master's, GRE General Test, MAT, minimum GPA of 2.75 (minimum GPA of 3.0 for initial certification programs). Additional exam requirements/recommendations for international students: Required—TOEFL (minimum score 550 paper-based; 213 computer-based). *Application deadline:* For fall admission, 7/1 priority date for domestic and international students; for spring admission, 11/1 priority date for domestic and international students. Applications are processed on a rolling basis. Application fee: $25. Electronic applications accepted. *Expenses:* Tuition, state resident: part-time $336 per credit. Tuition, nonresident: part-time $538 per credit. Required fees: $84 per credit. $37 per semester. *Financial support:* Career-related internships or fieldwork, Federal Work-Study, scholarships/grants, and unspecified assistantships available. Support available to part-time students. Financial award application deadline: 5/1; financial award applicants required to submit FAFSA. *Unit head:* Dr. Suzanne Rose, Graduate Coordinator, 724-738-2863, Fax: 724-738-2880, E-mail: suzanne.rose@sn.edu. *Application contact:* April Longwell, Interim Director of Graduate Studies, 724-738-2051 Ext. 2116, Fax: 724-738-2146, E-mail: graduate.studies@sru.edu.

South Carolina State University, School of Graduate Studies, Department of Education, Orangeburg, SC 29117-0001. Offers early childhood and special education (M Ed); early childhood education (MAT); elementary education (M Ed, MAT); engineering (MAT); general science (MAT); mathematics (MAT); secondary education (M Ed), including biology education, business education, counselor education, English education, home economics education, industrial education, mathematics education, science education, social studies education; special education (M Ed), including emotionally handicapped, learning disabilities, mentally handicapped. *Accreditation:* NCATE. Part-time and evening/weekend programs available. *Faculty:* 21 full-time (10 women), 4 part-time/adjunct (0 women). *Students:* 34 full-time (28 women), 33 part-time (25 women); includes 63 minority (61 African Americans, 1 American Indian/Alaska Native, 1 Asian American or Pacific Islander). Average age 35. 46 applicants, 67% accepted, 19 enrolled. In 2006, 28 degrees awarded. *Degree requirements:* For master's, departmental qualifying exam, thesis optional. *Entrance requirements:* For master's, GRE General Test, NTE, interview, teaching certificate. *Application deadline:* For fall admission, 6/15 priority date for domestic students, 6/15 for international students; for spring admission, 11/1 for domestic and international students. Applications are processed on a rolling basis. Application fee: $25. Electronic applications accepted. *Expenses:* Tuition, state resident: full-time $7,278. Tuition, nonresident: full-time $14,322. *Financial support:* Fellowships, research assistantships, career-related internships or fieldwork, Federal Work-Study, and institutionally sponsored loans available. Financial award application deadline: 6/1. *Faculty research:* Critical thinking, child abuse, stress, test-taking skills, conflict resolution, mainstreaming. *Unit head:* Dr. Gail Joyner-Fleming, Interim Chair, 803-533-3769, Fax: 803-536-8492, E-mail: zf-gfleming@scsu.edu. *Application contact:* Annette Hazzard-Jones, Program Coordinator II, 803-536-8809, Fax: 803-536-8812, E-mail: zs_ahazzard@scsu.edu.

Southern Oregon University, Graduate Studies, School of Social Sciences, Department of Education, Ashland, OR 97520. Offers elementary education (MA Ed, MS Ed), including classroom teacher, early childhood, handicapped learner, reading, supervision; secondary education (MA Ed, MS Ed), including classroom teacher, handicapped learner, reading, supervision; teaching (MAT). *Degree requirements:* For master's, thesis optional. *Entrance requirements:* For master's, GRE General Test, minimum GPA of 3.0. Electronic applications accepted.

Southwestern Oklahoma State University, College of Professional and Graduate Studies, School of Behavioral Sciences and Education, Specialization in Early Childhood Education, Weatherford, OK 73096-3098. Offers M Ed. M Ed distance learning degree program offered to Oklahoma residents only. *Accreditation:* NCATE. Part-time and evening/weekend programs available. *Degree requirements:* For master's, exam. *Entrance requirements:* For master's, GRE General Test or minimum undergraduate GPA of 3.0. Additional exam requirements/recommendations for international students: Required—TOEFL.

Spring Hill College, Graduate Programs, Program in Education, Mobile, AL 36608-1791. Offers early childhood education (MAT, MS Ed); elementary education (MAT, MS Ed); secondary education (MAT, MS Ed). Part-time and evening/weekend programs available. *Faculty:* 2 full-time (both women), 7 part-time/adjunct (5 women). *Students:* 11 full-time (10 women), 44 part-time (34 women); includes 19 minority (all African Americans) Average age 33. In 2006, 21 degrees awarded. *Degree requirements:* For master's, comprehensive exam. *Entrance requirements:* For master's, GRE, MAT, NTE, or PRAXIS, minimum undergraduate GPA of 3.0. Additional exam requirements/recommendations for international students: Required—TOEFL (minimum score 550 paper-based; 213 computer-based). *Application deadline:* For fall admission, 8/1 priority date for domestic students, 6/1 priority date for international students; for spring admission, 12/1 priority date for domestic students, 11/1 priority date for international students. Applications are processed on a rolling basis. Application fee: $25 ($35 for international students). Electronic applications accepted. *Expenses: Contact institution. Financial support:* In 2006–07, 49 students received support. Career-related internships or fieldwork and scholarships/grants available. Support available to part-time students. Financial award applicants required to submit FAFSA. *Unit head:* Dr. Ann A. Adams, Chair of Teacher Education, 251-380-3479, Fax: 251-460-2184, E-mail: aadams@shc.edu. *Application contact:* Joyce Genz, Dean of Life Long Learning and Director of Graduate Programs, 251-380-3094, Fax: 251-460-2190, E-mail: grad@shc.edu.

State University of New York at Binghamton, Graduate School, School of Education, Program in Early Childhood and Elementary Education, Binghamton, NY 13902-6000. Offers MS Ed. *Accreditation:* Teacher Education Accreditation Council. Part-time and evening/weekend programs available. *Students:* 11 full-time (9 women), 11 part-time (9 women);

includes 1 minority (Hispanic American) Average age 29. 1 applicant, 0% accepted. In 2006, 8 degrees awarded. *Entrance requirements:* For master's, GRE General Test. Additional exam requirements/recommendations for international students: Required—TOEFL. *Application deadline:* For fall admission, 4/15 priority date for domestic students, 1/15 priority date for international students; for spring admission, 11/1 for domestic students, 10/1 priority date for international students. Applications are processed on a rolling basis. Application fee: $60. Electronic applications accepted. *Financial support:* In 2006–07, 10 students received support, including 10 teaching assistantships with full tuition reimbursements available (averaging $5,507 per year); fellowships, research assistantships with full tuition reimbursements available, career-related internships or fieldwork, Federal Work-Study, institutionally sponsored loans, and unspecified assistantships also available. Support available to part-time students. Financial award application deadline: 2/15. *Unit head:* Dr. Nicholas Paley, Coordinator, 607-777-2301, E-mail: npaley@binghamton.edu.

State University of New York at New Paltz, Graduate School, Faculty of Education, Department of Elementary Education, New Paltz, NY 12561. Offers childhood education (MS Ed); childhood education (1-6) (MST); early childhood education (B-2) (MST); literacy education (5-12) (MS Ed); literacy education (B-6) (MS Ed). *Accreditation:* NCATE. Part-time and evening/weekend programs available. *Faculty:* 10 full-time (6 women), 42 part-time/adjunct (33 women). *Students:* 53 full-time (47 women), 135 part-time (124 women); includes 11 minority (4 African Americans, 1 Asian American or Pacific Islander, 6 Hispanic Americans). Average age 30. 142 applicants. In 2006, 91 degrees awarded. *Degree requirements:* For master's, portfolio. *Entrance requirements:* For master's, GRE/MAT (MST), minimum GPA of 3.0, teaching certificate (MS Ed). Additional exam requirements/recommendations for international students: Required—TOEFL (minimum score 550 paper-based; 213 computer-based; 80 iBT). *Application deadline:* For fall admission, 4/1 for domestic and international students; for spring admission, 11/1 for domestic and international students. Application fee: $50. Electronic applications accepted. *Expenses:* Tuition, state resident: full-time $6,900; part-time $288 per credit hour. Tuition, nonresident: full-time $10,920; part-time $455 per credit hour. *Financial support:* Federal Work-Study and institutionally sponsored loans available. *Unit head:* Dr. Winifred Montgomery, Chair, 845-257-2860, E-mail: montgomw@newpaltz.edu.

State University of New York at New Paltz, Graduate School, Faculty of Education, Department of Special Education, New Paltz, NY 12561. Offers adolescence (7-12) (MS Ed); childhood (1-6) (MS Ed). *Accreditation:* NCATE. Part-time and evening/weekend programs available. *Faculty:* 11 full-time (9 women), 21 part-time/adjunct (15 women). *Students:* 40 full-time (38 women), 59 part-time (49 women); includes 5 minority (1 African American, 2 Asian Americans or Pacific Islanders, 2 Hispanic Americans), 1 international. Average age 29. 63 applicants. In 2006, 56 degrees awarded. *Degree requirements:* For master's, portfolio. *Entrance requirements:* For master's, minimum GPA of 3.0, teaching certificate. Additional exam requirements/recommendations for international students: Required—TOEFL (minimum score 550 paper-based; 213 computer-based; 80 iBT). *Application deadline:* For fall admission, 5/1 priority date for domestic students, 5/1 for international students; for spring admission, 11/15 for domestic and international students. Application fee: $50. Electronic applications accepted. *Expenses:* Tuition, state resident: full-time $6,900; part-time $288 per credit hour. Tuition, nonresident: full-time $10,920; part-time $455 per credit hour. *Financial support:* Career-related internships or fieldwork, Federal Work-Study, and institutionally sponsored loans available. *Unit head:* Dr. Spencer Salend, Coordinator, 845-257-2846, E-mail: salends@newpaltz.edu.

State University of New York College at Cortland, Graduate Studies, School of Education, Program in Childhood/Early Child Education, Cortland, NY 13045. Offers MS Ed, MST. *Accreditation:* NCATE.

State University of New York College at Geneseo, Graduate Studies, School of Education, Program in Early Childhood Education, Geneseo, NY 14454-1401. Offers MS Ed. *Faculty:* 6 full-time (4 women). *Students:* 1 (woman) full-time, 4 part-time (all women). Average age 24. 2 applicants, 100% accepted, 1 enrolled. *Entrance requirements:* For master's, GRE General Test. *Application deadline:* For fall admission, 6/1 priority date for domestic students; for spring admission, 10/1 for domestic students. Application fee: $50. *Financial support:* Fellowships, teaching assistantships available. Financial award application deadline: 4/1. *Unit head:* Dr. Osman Alawiye, Chairperson, School of Education, 585-245-5560, Fax: 585-245-5220.

Stephen F. Austin State University, Graduate School, College of Education, Department of Elementary Education, Program in Early Childhood Education, Nacogdoches, TX 75962. Offers M Ed. *Accreditation:* NCATE. *Degree requirements:* For master's, comprehensive exam. *Entrance requirements:* For master's, GRE General Test. Additional exam requirements/recommendations for international students: Required—TOEFL (minimum score 550 paper-based; 213 computer-based).

Sunbridge College, Programs in Education, Spring Valley, NY 10977. Offers Waldorf early childhood education (MS Ed); Waldorf elementary school education (MS Ed). Part-time programs available. *Entrance requirements:* For master's, interview.

Syracuse University, Graduate School, School of Education, Department of Teaching and Leadership, Program in Childhood Education: (1-6) Preparation, Syracuse, NY 13244. Offers MS. *Students:* 4 full-time (all women), 1 (woman) part-time; includes 1 minority (African American) *Entrance requirements:* Additional exam requirements/recommendations for international students: Required—TOEFL. *Application deadline:* For fall admission, 2/1 for domestic students. Application fee: $65. *Expenses:* Tuition: Full-time $16,920; part-time $940 per credit hour. Required fees: $930; $930 per year. *Unit head:* Dr. Patricia Tinto, Program Director, 315-443-2684, E-mail: pptinto@syr.edu. *Application contact:* Liza Rochelson, Graduate Admission Recruiter, 315-443-2505, Fax: 315-443-2258, E-mail: gradcrt@gwmail.syr.edu.

Syracuse University, Graduate School, School of Education, Department of Teaching and Leadership, Program in Early Childhood Special Education, Syracuse, NY 13244. Offers MS. *Students:* 13 full-time (11 women), 20 part-time (19 women); includes 2 African Americans, 1 Asian American or Pacific Islander, 1 international. *Entrance requirements:* For master's, interview. *Application deadline:* For fall admission, 2/1 for domestic students. *Expenses:* Tuition: Full-time $16,920; part-time $940 per credit hour. Required fees: $930; $930 per year. *Unit head:* Dr. Gail Ensher, Progarm Director, 315-443-9650. *Application contact:* Liza Rochelson, Graduate Admission Recruiter, 315-443-2505, Fax: 315-443-2258, E-mail: gradcrt@gwmail.syr.edu.

Teachers College Columbia University, Graduate Faculty of Education, Department of Curriculum and Teaching, Program in Early Childhood Education, New York, NY 10027-6696. Offers Ed M, MA, Ed D. *Accreditation:* NCATE. *Faculty:* 3 full-time (all women), 4 part-time/adjunct. *Students:* 14 full-time (12 women), 44 part-time (43 women); includes 25 minority (6 African Americans, 9 Asian Americans or Pacific Islanders, 10 Hispanic Americans), 4 international. Average age 31. 78 applicants, 47% accepted, 14 enrolled. In 2006, 5 master's, 1 doctorate awarded. *Degree requirements:* For doctorate, variable foreign language requirement, thesis/dissertation. *Entrance requirements:* For doctorate, GRE General Test or MAT. *Application deadline:* For fall admission, 5/15 for domestic students; for spring admission, 12/1 for domestic students. Application fee: $65. *Expenses:* Tuition: Full-time $23,400; part-time $975 per credit. Required fees: $320 per term. *Financial support:* Career-related internships or fieldwork, Federal Work-Study, institutionally sponsored loans, and tuition waivers (full and partial) available. Support available to part-time students. Financial award application deadline: 2/1. *Faculty research:* Infancy, child development, children and family, policy and program, childhood bilingualism. *Application contact:* Peter Shon, Assistant Director of Admission, 212-678-3305, Fax: 212-678-4171, E-mail: shon@exchange.tc.columbia.edu.

See Close-Up on page 1127.

Teachers College Columbia University, Graduate Faculty of Education, Department of Curriculum and Teaching, Program in Early Childhood Special Education, New York, NY 10027-6696. Offers Ed M, MA. *Accreditation:* NCATE. Evening/weekend programs available. *Faculty:* 1 (woman) full-time, 1 part-time/adjunct. *Students:* 13 full-time (all women), 35 part-time (all women); includes 18 minority (13 Asian Americans or Pacific Islanders, 5 Hispanic Americans), 6 international. Average age 30. 53 applicants, 53% accepted, 14 enrolled. In 2006, 23 degrees awarded. *Application deadline:* For fall admission, 5/15 for domestic students; for spring admission, 12/1 for domestic students. Application fee: $65. *Expenses:* Tuition: Full-time $23,400; part-time $975 per credit. Required fees: $320 per term. *Financial support:* Research assistantships, teaching assistantships, career-related internships or fieldwork, Federal Work-Study, institutionally sponsored loans, and tuition waivers (full and partial) available. Support available to part-time students. Financial award application deadline: 2/1. *Faculty research:* Curriculum development, infants, urban education, visually impaired infants. *Application contact:* Peter Shon, Assistant Director of Admission, 212-678-3305, Fax: 212-678-4171, E-mail: shon@exchange.tc.columbia.edu.

See Close-Up on page 1127.

Teachers College Columbia University, Graduate Faculty of Education, Department of Curriculum and Teaching, Program in Elementary/Childhood Education, Preservice, New York, NY 10027-6696. Offers MA. *Accreditation:* NCATE. *Faculty:* 3 full-time (all women), 9 part-time/adjunct. *Students:* 27 full-time (23 women), 51 part-time (48 women); includes 36 minority (9 African Americans, 24 Asian Americans or Pacific Islanders, 3 Hispanic Americans), 3 international. Average age 31. 170 applicants, 51% accepted, 44 enrolled. In 2006, 53 degrees awarded. *Application deadline:* For fall admission, 5/15 for domestic students; for spring admission, 12/1 for domestic students. Application fee: $65. *Expenses:* Tuition: Full-time $23,400; part-time $975 per credit. Required fees: $320 per term. *Financial support:* Career-related internships or fieldwork, Federal Work-Study, and tuition waivers (full and partial) available. Financial award application deadline: 2/1. *Faculty research:* Teaching of reading and writing, reforming schools, urban education, curriculum development. *Application contact:* Peter Shon, Assistant Director of Admission, 212-678-3305, Fax: 212-678-4171, E-mail: shon@exchange.tc.columbia.edu.

See Close-Up on page 1127.

Temple University, Graduate School, College of Education, Department of Curriculum, Instruction, and Technology in Education, Philadelphia, PA 19122-6096. Offers applied behavioral analysis (MS Ed); career and technical education (MS Ed); early childhood education and elementary education (MS Ed); English education (MS Ed); language arts education (Ed D); math/science education (Ed D); mathematics education (MS Ed); science education (MS Ed); second and foreign language education (MS Ed); special education (MS Ed); teaching English as a second language (MS Ed). Part-time and evening/weekend programs available. *Faculty:* 31 full-time (14 women). *Students:* 96 full-time (71 women), 482 part-time (336 women); includes 109 minority (67 African Americans, 3 American Indian/Alaska Native, 23 Asian Americans or Pacific Islanders, 16 Hispanic Americans), 28 international. 308 applicants, 64% accepted, 116 enrolled. In 2006, 225 master's, 21 doctorates awarded. Terminal master's awarded for partial completion of doctoral program. *Degree requirements:* For master's, thesis or alternative; for doctorate, thesis/dissertation. *Entrance requirements:* For master's and doctorate, GRE General Test or MAT, minimum GPA of 3.0. Additional exam requirements/recommendations for international students: Required—TOEFL (minimum score 550 paper-based; 213 computer-based; 79 iBT). *Application deadline:* For fall admission, 4/1 for domestic students, 12/15 for international students; for spring admission, 10/1 for domestic students, 8/1 for international students. Application fee: $50. Electronic applications accepted. *Expenses:* Tuition, state resident: full-time $12,264; part-time $511 per credit. Tuition, nonresident: full-time $17,904; part-time $746 per credit. Required fees: $84 per course. Tuition and fees vary according to program. *Financial support:* Fellowships, research assistantships with full tuition reimbursements, teaching assistantships with full tuition reimbursements available. Financial award application deadline: 1/15; financial award applicants required to submit FAFSA. *Faculty research:* School improvement, problem solving, literacy, language development. *Unit head:* Dr. Thomas Walker, Chair, 215-204-2117, Fax: 215-204-1414, E-mail: tjwalker@temple.edu.

Tennessee Technological University, Graduate School, College of Education, Department of Curriculum and Instruction, Program in Early Childhood Education, Cookeville, TN 38505. Offers MA, Ed S. *Accreditation:* NCATE. Part-time and evening/weekend programs available. *Faculty:* 2 full-time (both women). *Students:* 6 full-time (all women), 7 part-time (all women). Average age 27. 10 applicants, 80% accepted, 5 enrolled. In 2006, 2 degrees awarded. *Degree requirements:* For Ed S, thesis or alternative. *Entrance requirements:* For master's, MAT; for Ed S, MAT, NTE. Additional exam requirements/recommendations for international students: Required—TOEFL. *Application deadline:* For fall admission, 3/1 for domestic students; for spring admission, 8/1 for domestic students. Application fee: $25 ($30 for international students). *Expenses:* Tuition, state resident: full-time $8,748; part-time $319 per hour. Tuition, nonresident: full-time $23,524; part-time $740 per hour. *Financial support:* In 2006–07, research assistantships (averaging $4,000 per year), teaching assistantships (averaging $4,000 per year) were awarded; fellowships, career-related internships or fieldwork also available. Financial award application deadline: 4/1. *Application contact:* Dr. Francis O. Otuonye, Associate Vice President for Research and Graduate Studies, 931-372-3233, Fax: 931-372-3497, E-mail: fotuonye@tntech.edu.

Texas A&M International University, Office of Graduate Studies and Research, College of Education, Department of Curriculum and Instruction, Laredo, TX 78041-1900. Offers bilingual education (PhD); curriculum and instruction (MS, PhD); early childhood education (PhD); reading (MS). *Expenses:* Tuition, state resident: full-time $1,580. Tuition, nonresident: full-time $5,432. Required fees: $3,808. *Unit head:* Dr. Barbara Greybeck, Interim Chair, 956-326-2678, E-mail: bgreybeck@tamiu.edu. *Application contact:* Rosie Dickinson, Director of Admissions, 956-326-2200.

Texas A&M University–Commerce, Graduate School, College of Education and Human Services, Department of Elementary Education, Commerce, TX 75429-3011. Offers early childhood education (M Ed, MA, MS); elementary education (M Ed, MS); reading (M Ed, MA, MS); supervision of curriculum and instruction: elementary education (Ed D). Part-time programs available. Terminal master's awarded for partial completion of doctoral program. *Degree requirements:* For master's, thesis (for some programs), comprehensive exam; for doctorate, 2 foreign languages, thesis/dissertation, departmental qualifying exam. *Entrance requirements:* For master's and doctorate, GRE General Test. Electronic applications accepted. *Faculty research:* Literacy and learning, early childhood, preservice teacher education, technology.

Texas A&M University–Corpus Christi, Graduate Studies and Research, College of Education, Corpus Christi, TX 78412-5503. Offers counseling (MS, PhD), including counseling (MS), counselor education (PhD); curriculum and instruction (MS, Ed D); early childhood education (MS); educational administration (MS); educational leadership (Ed D); educational technology (MS); elementary education (MS); kinesiology (MS); occupational training and development (MS); reading (MS); secondary education (MS); special education (MS). Part-time and evening/weekend programs available. *Degree requirements:* For master's, thesis (for some programs), comprehensive exam, registration; for doctorate, thesis/dissertation, comprehensive exam, registration. *Entrance requirements:* For master's, GRE General Test. Additional exam requirements/recommendations for international students: Required—TOEFL. Electronic applications accepted.

Texas A&M University–Kingsville, College of Graduate Studies, College of Education, Department of Education, Program in Early Childhood Education, Kingsville, TX 78363. Offers M Ed. Part-time and evening/weekend programs available. *Degree requirements:* For master's, mini-thesis. *Entrance requirements:* For master's, GRE General Test, MAT, minimum GPA of 3.0.

Texas Southern University, Graduate School, College of Education, Area of Curriculum and Instruction, Houston, TX 77004-4584. Offers bilingual education (M Ed); curriculum, instruction, and urban education (Ed D); early childhood education (M Ed); elementary education (M Ed); reading education (M Ed); secondary education (M Ed); special education (M Ed). Part-time and evening/weekend programs available. *Faculty:* 8 full-time (6 women), 1 part-

Early Childhood Education

Texas Southern University (continued)
time/adjunct (0 women). *Students:* 41 full-time (36 women), 43 part-time (38 women); includes 82 minority (77 African Americans, 2 Asian Americans or Pacific Islanders, 3 Hispanic Americans). Average age 36. 34 applicants, 82% accepted, 24 enrolled. In 2006, 6 master's, 13 doctorates awarded. *Degree requirements:* For master's, comprehensive exam; for doctorate, thesis/dissertation, comprehensive exam. *Entrance requirements:* For master's, GRE General Test, minimum GPA of 2.5; for doctorate, GRE General Test or MAT, master's degree, minimum B+ average. Additional exam requirements/recommendations for international students: Required—TOEFL. *Application deadline:* For fall admission, 7/15 priority date for domestic students. Applications are processed on a rolling basis. Application fee: $50 ($75 for international students). *Financial support:* Federal Work-Study and institutionally sponsored loans available. Financial award application deadline: 5/1. *Unit head:* Dr. Cherry Gooden, Chair, 713-313-7496, Fax: 713-313-7496, E-mail: gooden_cr@tsu.edu.

Texas State University-San Marcos, Graduate School, College of Education, Department of Curriculum and Instruction, Program in Early Childhood Education, San Marcos, TX 78666. Offers M Ed, MA. *Faculty:* 2 part-time/adjunct (both women). *Students:* 10 full-time (8 women), 22 part-time (all women); includes 9 minority (5 African Americans, 4 Hispanic Americans). Average age 30. 1 applicant, 100% accepted, 1 enrolled. In 2006, 2 degrees awarded. *Degree requirements:* For master's, thesis optional. *Entrance requirements:* For master's, GRE General Test, minimum GPA of 2.75 in undergraduate work. Additional exam requirements/recommendations for international students: Required—TOEFL. *Application deadline:* For fall admission, 6/15 priority date for domestic students; for spring admission, 10/15 priority date for domestic students. Applications are processed on a rolling basis. Application fee: $40 ($90 for international students). *Financial support:* In 2006–07, 20 students received support. *Unit head:* Carolyn McCall, Graduate Advisor, 512-245-2041, Fax: 512-245-7911, E-mail: cm06@txstate.edu. *Application contact:* Dr. J. Michael Willoughby, Dean of Graduate School, 512-245-2581, Fax: 512-245-8365, E-mail: gradcollege@txstate.edu.

Texas Woman's University, Graduate School, College of Professional Education, Department of Family Sciences, Denton, TX 76201. Offers child development (MS, PhD); counseling and development (MS); early childhood education (M Ed, MA, MS, Ed D); family studies (MS, PhD); family therapy (MS, PhD). *Accreditation:* ACA (one or more programs are accredited). Part-time and evening/weekend programs available. *Students:* 102 full-time (96 women), 382 part-time (344 women); includes 157 minority (109 African Americans, 5 American Indian/Alaska Native, 11 Asian Americans or Pacific Islanders, 32 Hispanic Americans), 18 international. Average age 37. In 2006, 93 master's, 17 doctorates awarded. *Degree requirements:* For doctorate, thesis/dissertation, comprehensive exam. *Entrance requirements:* For master's, interview, writing sample, minimum GPA of 3.25 may be required; for doctorate, interview, writing sample may be required, GPA 3.25 last 60 hours of course work. Additional exam requirements/recommendations for international students: Required—TOEFL (minimum score 550 paper-based; 213 computer-based; 79 iBT). *Application deadline:* For fall admission, 4/1 for international students; for spring admission, 8/1 for international students. Applications are processed on a rolling basis. Application fee: $30 ($50 for international students). Electronic applications accepted. *Expenses:* Tuition, area resident: Part-time $168 per unit. Tuition, state resident: full-time $4,369. Tuition, nonresident: full-time $9,373; part-time $443 per unit. Required fees: $20 per unit. $177 per term. *Financial support:* In 2006–07, 11 research assistantships (averaging $10,494 per year), 12 teaching assistantships (averaging $10,494 per year) were awarded; career-related internships or fieldwork, Federal Work-Study, institutionally sponsored loans, scholarships/grants, traineeships, health care benefits, and unspecified assistantships also available. Support available to part-time students. Financial award application deadline: 3/1; financial award applicants required to submit FAFSA. *Faculty research:* Parenting/parent education, distance education, body image, family sexuality, diversity. *Unit head:* Dr. Larry LeFlore, Chair, 940-898-2685, Fax: 940-898-2676, E-mail: lleflore@twu.edu. *Application contact:* Samuel Wheeler, Coordinator of Graduate Admissions, 940-898-3188, Fax: 940-898-3081, E-mail: wheelersr@twu.edu.

Touro University International, College of Education, Program in Education, Cypress, CA 90630. Offers adult education (MA Ed); aviation education (MA Ed); children's literacy development (MA Ed); e-learning (MA Ed); early childhood education (MA Ed); enrollment management (MA Ed); higher education (MA Ed); teaching and instruction (MA Ed); training and development (MA Ed). Part-time and evening/weekend programs available. Postbaccalaureate distance learning degree programs offered (no on-campus study). In 2006, 193 degrees awarded. *Degree requirements:* For master's, capstone project with integrative paper. *Entrance requirements:* For master's, minimum GPA of 3.0. Additional exam requirements/recommendations for international students: Required—TOEFL (minimum score 550 paper-based). Application fee: $75. *Expenses:* Tuition: Part-time $300 per credit hour. Tuition and fees vary according to course level and program. *Unit head:* Dr. Edith Neumann, Vice President for Academic Affairs, College of Education, 714-816-0366 Ext. 2030, Fax: 714-226-9844, E-mail: eneumann@tourou.edu.

Towson University, Graduate School, Program in Early Childhood Education, Towson, MD 21252-0001. Offers M Ed, CAS. *Accreditation:* NCATE. Part-time and evening/weekend programs available. *Faculty:* 4 full-time (3 women), 1 (woman) part-time/adjunct. *Students:* 12 full-time (11 women), 120 part-time (115 women); includes 20 minority (all African Americans), 1 international. 41 applicants, 71% accepted, 20 enrolled. In 2006, 47 degrees awarded. *Degree requirements:* For master's, thesis optional. *Entrance requirements:* For master's, minimum GPA of 3.0, teacher certification, work experience or course work in early childhood education. *Application deadline:* Applications are processed on a rolling basis. Application fee: $50. Electronic applications accepted. *Expenses:* Tuition, state resident: part-time $275 per unit. Tuition, nonresident: part-time $577 per unit. Required fees: $72 per unit. *Financial support:* Federal Work-Study and unspecified assistantships available. Financial award application deadline: 4/1; financial award applicants required to submit FAFSA. *Faculty research:* Developmental programs, training caregivers for HIV/AIDS children. *Unit head:* Dr. Edyth Wheeler, Graduate Program Director, 410-704-2460, Fax: 410-704-2733, E-mail: ejwheeler@towson.edu. *Application contact:* 410-704-2501, Fax: 410-704-4675, E-mail: grads@towson.edu.

Trinity (Washington) University, School of Education, Washington, DC 20017-1094. Offers democracy, diversity, and social justice (M Ed); early childhood (MAT); educational administration (MSA); elementary education (MAT); English as a second language (M Ed, MAT); literacy and reading education (M Ed); school counseling (MA); secondary education (MAT), including English, math, science, social studies; special education (MAT). *Accreditation:* NCATE. Part-time and evening/weekend programs available. *Degree requirements:* For master's, thesis (for some programs), capstone project(s). *Entrance requirements:* For master's, PRAXIS I, minimum GPA of 2.8. Additional exam requirements/recommendations for international students: Required—TOEFL (minimum score 550 paper-based; 213 computer-based). *Faculty research:* Technology, literacy, special education, organizations, inclusion models.

Troy University, Graduate School, College of Education, Program in Early Childhood Education, Troy, AL 36082. Offers MS, MSE, Ed S. *Students:* 1 (woman) full-time, 4 part-time (all women); includes 1 minority (African American) Average age 39. In 2006, 13 master's, 1 other advanced degree awarded. *Degree requirements:* For master's, registration. *Entrance requirements:* For master's, GRE, MAT, or GMAT. Additional exam requirements/recommendations for international students: Required—TOEFL (minimum score 523 paper-based; 200 computer-based). Application fee: $50. *Expenses:* Tuition, state resident: full-time $4,368; part-time $182 per hour. Tuition, nonresident: full-time $8,736; part-time $364 per hour. Required fees: $50 per term. *Unit head:* Dr. Darrell Pearson, Interim Chair, 334-670-3444, Fax: 334-670-3474, E-mail: dpearson@troy.edu. *Application contact:* Brenda K. Campbell, Director of Graduate Admissions, 334-670-3178, Fax: 334-670-3733, E-mail: bcamp@troy.edu.

Tufts University, Graduate School of Arts and Sciences, Department of Child Development, Medford, MA 02155. Offers applied developmental psychology (PhD); child development (MA, CAGS); early childhood education (MAT). Part-time programs available. *Faculty:* 15 full-time, 8 part-time/adjunct. *Students:* 117 (107 women); includes 16 minority (7 African Americans, 3 Asian Americans or Pacific Islanders, 6 Hispanic Americans) 15 international. 152 applicants, 63% accepted, 49 enrolled. In 2006, 37 master's, 9 doctorates, 2 other advanced degrees awarded. *Degree requirements:* For master's, thesis (for some programs); for doctorate, thesis/dissertation. *Entrance requirements:* For master's and doctorate, GRE General Test. Additional exam requirements/recommendations for international students: Required—TOEFL (minimum score 550 paper-based; 213 computer-based; 80 iBT). *Application deadline:* For fall admission, 1/15 for domestic and international students. Applications are processed on a rolling basis. Application fee: $70. Electronic applications accepted. *Expenses:* Tuition: Full-time $33,672. Tuition and fees vary according to degree level and program. *Financial support:* Fellowships, research assistantships with full and partial tuition reimbursements, teaching assistantships with full and partial tuition reimbursements, career-related internships or fieldwork, Federal Work-Study, scholarships/grants, and tuition waivers (partial) available. Support available to part-time students. Financial award application deadline: 1/15; financial award applicants required to submit FAFSA. *Unit head:* Ellen Pinderhughes, Chair, 617-628-5000. *Application contact:* Janie Orthey Rockett, Information Contact, E-mail: janie.orthey@tufts.edu.

Universidad Metropolitana, Graduate Programs in Education, Program in Pre-School Education, San Juan, PR 00928-1150. Offers MA. *Degree requirements:* For master's, thesis or alternative. *Entrance requirements:* For master's, EXADEP, interview.

University at Buffalo, the State University of New York, Graduate School, Graduate School of Education, Department of Learning and Instruction, Buffalo, NY 14260. Offers adolescence education (Certificate); biology (Ed M); chemistry (Ed M); childhood education (Ed M); early childhood and childhood education with bilingual extension (Ed M); early childhood education (Ed M); earth science (Ed M); elementary education (Ed D, PhD); English (Ed M); English education (PhD); English for speakers of other languages (Ed M); foreign and second language education (PhD); French (Ed M); general education (Ed M); German (Ed M); Italian (Ed M); Japanese (Ed M); Latin (Ed M); literary specialist (Ed M); mathematics (Ed M); mathematics education (PhD); mentoring teachers (Certificate); music education (Ed M, Certificate); physics (Ed M); reading education (PhD); Russian (Ed M); school administrator and supervisor (Certificate); science education (PhD); social studies (Ed M); Spanish (Ed M); special education (PhD); teaching and leading for diversity (Certificate); teaching English to speakers of other languages (Ed M). Part-time and evening/weekend programs available. Postbaccalaureate distance learning degree programs offered (no on-campus study). *Faculty:* 30 full-time (20 women), 53 part-time/adjunct (38 women). *Students:* 368 full-time (269 women), 297 part-time (226 women); includes 50 minority (15 African Americans, 2 American Indian/Alaska Native, 14 Asian Americans or Pacific Islanders, 19 Hispanic Americans), 66 international. Average age 31. 638 applicants, 75% accepted, 298 enrolled. In 2006, 248 master's, 18 doctorates, 48 other advanced degrees awarded. Terminal master's awarded for partial completion of doctoral program. *Degree requirements:* For master's, comprehensive exam, registration; for doctorate, thesis/dissertation, research analysis exam, research experience component. *Entrance requirements:* For doctorate, GRE General Test or MAT, interview, writing sample, letters of recommendation. Additional exam requirements/recommendations for international students: Required—TOEFL (minimum score 600 paper-based; 250 computer-based). *Application deadline:* For fall admission, 2/1 priority date for domestic and international students; for spring admission, 11/15 priority date for domestic students, 10/1 for international students. Applications are processed on a rolling basis. Application fee: $50. Electronic applications accepted. *Financial support:* In 2006–07, 70 students received support, including 6 fellowships with full tuition reimbursements available (averaging $10,000 per year), 16 research assistantships with full tuition reimbursements available (averaging $9,000 per year), teaching assistantships with full tuition reimbursements available (averaging $9,000 per year); career-related internships or fieldwork, Federal Work-Study, institutionally sponsored loans, scholarships/grants, tuition waivers (partial), and unspecified assistantships also available. Financial award application deadline: 2/28; financial award applicants required to submit FAFSA. *Faculty research:* Science assessment, state-level testing, early learning, literacy, second language acquisition. Total annual research expenditures: $432,366. *Unit head:* Dr. Maria E. Runfola, Chair, 716-645-2455, Fax: 716-645-3161. *Application contact:* Barbara Belz, Admissions Secretary, 716-645-2110 Ext. 1159, Fax: 716-645-3161, E-mail: belz@buffalo.edu.

The University of Alabama at Birmingham, School of Education, Department of Curriculum and Instruction, Program in Early Childhood Education, Birmingham, AL 35294. Offers MA Ed, PhD. *Accreditation:* NCATE. *Students:* 27 full-time (25 women), 49 part-time (48 women); includes 20 minority (all African Americans), 9 international. 15 applicants, 93% accepted. In 2006, 57 master's, 2 doctorates awarded. *Degree requirements:* For master's, thesis optional; for doctorate, thesis/dissertation. *Entrance requirements:* For master's, GRE General Test, MAT, or NTE, minimum GPA of 3.0; for doctorate, GRE General Test, MAT, minimum GPA of 3.25. *Application deadline:* Applications are processed on a rolling basis. Application fee: $35 ($60 for international students). Electronic applications accepted. *Expenses:* Tuition, state resident: part-time $170 per credit hour. Tuition, nonresident: part-time $425 per credit hour. Required fees: $15 per credit hour. $122 per term. Tuition and fees vary according to program. *Unit head:* Dr. Charles Calhoun, Chair, Department of Curriculum and Instruction, 205-934-5371, Fax: 205-934-4792.

University of Alaska Anchorage, College of Education, Program in Special Education, Anchorage, AK 99508-8060. Offers early childhood special education (M Ed); special education (M Ed, Certificate). Part-time programs available. *Students:* 6 full-time (5 women), 26 part-time (24 women); includes 4 minority (2 American Indian/Alaska Native, 2 Asian Americans or Pacific Islanders), 1 international. 9 applicants, 56% accepted. In 2006, 16 degrees awarded. *Degree requirements:* For master's, thesis or alternative, comprehensive exam (for some programs), registration. *Entrance requirements:* For master's, GRE or MAT, interview, minimum GPA of 2.75. Additional exam requirements/recommendations for international students: Required—TOEFL (minimum score 550 paper-based; 213 computer-based). *Application deadline:* For fall admission, 3/15 for domestic students; for spring admission, 10/15 for domestic students. Application fee: $45. *Expenses:* Tuition, state resident: part-time $268 per credit. Tuition, nonresident: part-time $547 per credit. Required fees: $124 per semester. Tuition and fees vary according to reciprocity agreements and student level. *Financial support:* Career-related internships or fieldwork and Federal Work-Study available. Support available to part-time students. Financial award application deadline: 4/1; financial award applicants required to submit FAFSA. *Faculty research:* Mild disabilities, substance abuse issues for educators, partnerships to improve at-risk youth, analysis of planning models for teachers in special education. *Unit head:* Dr. Dean Konopasek, Chair, 907-786-4439, Fax: 907-786-4445, E-mail: dkonopasek@uaa.alaska.edu. *Application contact:* Jane Jordan, Graduate Programs Assistant, 907-786-4401, Fax: 907-786-4445, E-mail: anjmj@uaa.alaska.edu.

University of Alaska Southeast, Graduate Programs, Program in Education, Juneau, AK 99801. Offers early childhood education (M Ed, MAT); educational technology (M Ed); elementary education (MAT); reading (M Ed); secondary education (MAT). *Accreditation:* NCATE. Part-time and evening/weekend programs available. Postbaccalaureate distance learning degree programs offered (minimal on-campus study). *Faculty:* 12 full-time (7 women), 6 part-time/adjunct (5 women). *Students:* 81 full-time (49 women), 109 part-time (88 women); includes 24 minority (3 African Americans, 11 American Indian/Alaska Native, 5 Asian Americans or Pacific Islanders, 5 Hispanic Americans), 6 international. Average age 34. In 2006, 84 degrees awarded. *Degree requirements:* For master's, comprehensive exam or project, portfolio. *Entrance requirements:* For master's, PRAXIS, minimum GPA of 3.0, writing sample, letters of recommendation. *Application deadline:* For fall admission, 3/8 for domestic students. Applications are processed on a rolling basis. Application fee: $50. Electronic applications accepted. *Financial support:* Federal Work-Study, scholarships/grants, and tuition waivers (full and partial) available. Support available to part-time students. Financial award applicants required to submit FAFSA. *Faculty research:* Applied classroom research, culturally responsive practices, action research, teaching effectiveness. *Unit head:* Dr. Larry Harris, Dean, 907-796-6551, Fax: 907-796-6550, E-mail: larry.harris@uas.alaska.edu. *Application contact:* Susan A. Stuck, Administrative Assistant, 866-465-6424, Fax: 866-465-5159, E-mail: jnsas@uas.alaska.edu.

University of Arkansas, Graduate School, College of Education and Health Professions, Department of Curriculum and Instruction, Program in Childhood Education, Fayetteville, AR 72701-1201. Offers MAT. *Accreditation:* NCATE. *Students:* 49 full-time (45 women); includes 5 minority (4 African Americans, 1 Hispanic American). 4 applicants, 25% accepted. In 2006, 44 degrees awarded. Application fee: $40 ($50 for international students). *Financial support:* In 2006–07, 2 fellowships were awarded; research assistantships, teaching assistantships. *Unit head:* Unit Head, 479-575-4201.

University of Arkansas at Little Rock, Graduate School, College of Education, Department of Teacher Education, Program in Early Childhood Education, Little Rock, AR 72204-1099. Offers M Ed.

University of Bridgeport, School of Education and Human Resources, Division of Education, Program in Elementary Education, Bridgeport, CT 06604. Offers early childhood education (MS, Diploma); elementary education (MS, Diploma). Evening/weekend programs available. *Faculty:* 12 full-time (5 women), 72 part-time/adjunct (44 women). *Students:* 5 full-time (4 women), 21 part-time (all women); includes 2 minority (both African Americans), 1 international. Average age 36. 24 applicants, 63% accepted, 7 enrolled. In 2006, 10 degrees awarded. *Degree requirements:* For master's, final exam, final project, or thesis; for Diploma, thesis or alternative, final project. *Entrance requirements:* For master's, GRE General Test, MAT, minimum undergraduate QPA of 2.5; for Diploma, GRE General Test or MAT, minimum graduate QPA of 3.0. *Application deadline:* For fall admission, 8/1 priority date for domestic students; for spring admission, 12/1 priority date for domestic students. Applications are processed on a rolling basis. Application fee: $25 ($35 for international students). Electronic applications accepted. *Financial support:* Career-related internships or fieldwork, Federal Work-Study, and institutionally sponsored loans available. Support available to part-time students. Financial award application deadline: 6/1; financial award applicants required to submit FAFSA. *Faculty research:* Self-concept, internship assessment, stress and situational development, follow-up of graduation. *Unit head:* Dr. Allen P. Cook, Associate Dean, Division of Education, 203-576-4206, Fax: 203-576-4200, E-mail: acook@bridgeport.edu.

The University of British Columbia, Faculty of Graduate Studies, Faculty of Education, Centre for Cross-Faculty Inquiry in Education, Vancouver, BC V6T 1Z1, Canada. Offers curriculum and instruction (M Ed, MA, PhD); early childhood education (M Ed, MA). Part-time and evening/weekend programs available. *Faculty:* 50 full-time (22 women). *Students:* 88 full-time, 36 part-time. 41 applicants, 46% accepted, 18 enrolled. In 2006, 28 master's, 8 doctorates awarded. Terminal master's awarded for partial completion of doctoral program. *Degree requirements:* For master's, thesis (for some programs), thesis (MA); for doctorate, thesis/dissertation, registration. *Entrance requirements:* Additional exam requirements/recommendations for international students: Required—TOEFL (minimum score 567 paper-based; 227 computer-based). *Application deadline:* For fall admission, 1/1 for domestic and international students. Application fee: $90 Canadian dollars ($150 Canadian dollars for international students). Electronic applications accepted. *Financial support:* In 2006–07, 20 students received support; fellowships with tuition reimbursements available, research assistantships with tuition reimbursements available, teaching assistantships with tuition reimbursements available, institutionally sponsored loans, scholarships/grants, and tuition waivers (full and partial) available. *Unit head:* Dr. Graeme Chalmers, Director, 604-822-6502, Fax: 604-822-8234, E-mail: f.graeme.chalmers@ubc.ca. *Application contact:* Oliva dela-Cruz Cordero, Graduate Secretary, 604-822-6502, Fax: 604-822-8234, E-mail: oliva.dela.cruz-cordero@ubc.ca.

University of Central Arkansas, Graduate School, College of Education, Department of Early Childhood and Special Education, Program in Early Childhood Education, Conway, AR 72035-0001. Offers MSE. *Accreditation:* NCATE. Part-time programs available. *Students:* 3 full-time (all women), 60 part-time (53 women); includes 6 minority (all African Americans) 9 applicants, 100% accepted, 9 enrolled. In 2006, 9 degrees awarded. *Degree requirements:* For master's, thesis optional. *Entrance requirements:* For master's, GRE General Test, minimum GPA of 2.7. Additional exam requirements/recommendations for international students: Required—TOEFL (minimum score 550 paper-based; 213 computer-based). *Application deadline:* For fall admission, 3/1 priority date for domestic and international students; for spring admission, 10/1 priority date for domestic and international students. Applications are processed on a rolling basis. Application fee: $25 ($40 for international students). *Expenses:* Tuition, state resident: full-time $4,194; part-time $233 per semester. Tuition, nonresident: full-time $5,963; part-time $429 per semester. International tuition: $6,162 full-time. Required fees: $65; $23 per semester. One-time fee: $65 part-time. *Financial support:* Federal Work-Study, scholarships/grants, tuition waivers (partial), and unspecified assistantships available. Financial award application deadline: 2/15. *Unit head:* Dr. David Naylor, Coordinator, 501-450-3171, Fax: 501-450-5457, E-mail: davidn@uca.edu. *Application contact:* Brenda Herring, Admissions Assistant, 501-450-5065, Fax: 501-450-5678, E-mail: bherring@uca.edu.

University of Central Florida, College of Education, Department of Child, Family and Community Sciences, Program in Early Childhood Education, Orlando, FL 32816. Offers M Ed, MA. *Accreditation:* NCATE. *Students:* 10 full-time (all women), 37 part-time (all women); includes 7 minority (1 African American, 2 Asian Americans or Pacific Islanders, 4 Hispanic Americans). In 2006, 21 degrees awarded. Application fee: $30. Electronic applications accepted. *Expenses:* Tuition, state resident: full-time $6,167; part-time $257 per credit hour. Tuition, nonresident: full-time $22,790; part-time $950 per credit hour. *Financial support:* In 2006–07, 1 research assistantship (averaging $2,000 per year) was awarded; fellowships also available. *Unit head:* Dr. Roanne Brice, Coordinator, 407-823-0664, E-mail: robrice@mail.ucf.edu.

University of Central Oklahoma, College of Graduate Studies and Research, College of Education, Department of Curriculum and Instruction, Program in Early Childhood Education, Edmond, OK 73034-5209. Offers M Ed. *Accreditation:* NCATE. Part-time programs available. *Entrance requirements:* For master's, GRE General Test. Additional exam requirements/recommendations for international students: Required—TOEFL (minimum score 550 paper-based; 213 computer-based). Electronic applications accepted.

University of Cincinnati, Division of Research and Advanced Studies, College of Education, Criminal Justice, and Human Services, Division of Teacher Education, Program in Early Childhood Education, Cincinnati, OH 45221. Offers M Ed. *Accreditation:* NCATE. Part-time programs available. *Students:* 44. *Degree requirements:* For master's, thesis or alternative. *Entrance requirements:* For master's, GRE General Test. Additional exam requirements/recommendations for international students: Required—TOEFL (minimum score 610 paper-based), TWE (minimum score 5), OEPT. *Application deadline:* For fall admission, 2/1 for domestic students. Application fee: $40. Electronic applications accepted. *Financial support:* Fellowships, tuition waivers (partial) and unspecified assistantships available. *Application contact:* Linda Plevyak, Chair, 513-556-5106, Fax: 513-556-3764, E-mail: linda.plevyak@uc.edu.

University of Colorado at Denver and Health Sciences Center, School of Education and Human Development, Program in Initial Professional Teacher Education, Denver, CO 80217-3364. Offers special education (MA). *Accreditation:* NCATE. Part-time and evening/weekend programs available. *Faculty:* 26 full-time (20 women). *Students:* 177 full-time (142 women), 389 part-time (345 women); includes 58 minority (10 African Americans, 3 American Indian/Alaska Native, 14 Asian Americans or Pacific Islanders, 31 Hispanic Americans), 3 international. Average age 32. 170 applicants, 86% accepted, 91 enrolled. In 2006, 270 degrees awarded. *Degree requirements:* For master's, thesis or alternative. *Entrance requirements:* For master's, GRE, MAT, minimum GPA of 2.75, 3 letters of recommendation. Additional exam requirements/recommendations for international students: Required—TOEFL (minimum score 525 paper-based; 197 computer-based). *Application deadline:* For fall admission, 3/1 for domestic students; for spring admission, 9/15 for domestic students. Applications are processed on a rolling basis. Application fee: $50 ($75 for international students). Electronic applications accepted. *Financial support:* Research assistantships, teaching assistantships, Federal Work-Study available. Financial award application deadline: 4/1; financial award applicants required to submit FAFSA. *Unit head:* Carole Basile, Coordinator, 303-556-3336, Fax: 303-556-4479, E-mail: carole.basile@cudenver.edu. *Application contact:* Orlando Green, Academic Advisor, 303-556-5274, Fax: 303-556-4479, E-mail: orlando.green@cudenver.edu.

University of Colorado at Denver and Health Sciences Center, School of Education and Human Development, Programs in Educational Psychology and Early Childhood Education, Denver, CO 80217-3364. Offers early childhood education (MA); educational psychology (MA). *Accreditation:* NCATE. Part-time and evening/weekend programs available. *Faculty:* 7 full-time (3 women). *Students:* 17 full-time (15 women), 52 part-time (44 women); includes 5 minority (1 African American, 1 American Indian/Alaska Native, 1 Asian American or Pacific Islander, 2 Hispanic Americans), 2 international. Average age 32. 37 applicants, 84% accepted, 13 enrolled. In 2006, 127 degrees awarded. *Degree requirements:* For master's, thesis optional. *Entrance requirements:* For master's, GRE, minimum GPA of 2.75 or MAT. Additional exam requirements/recommendations for international students: Required—TOEFL (minimum score 525 paper-based; 197 computer-based). *Application deadline:* For fall admission, 4/15 for domestic students; for spring admission, 9/15 for domestic students. Applications are processed on a rolling basis. Application fee: $50 ($75 for international students). Electronic applications accepted. *Financial support:* Research assistantships, teaching assistantships, Federal Work-Study available. Financial award application deadline: 4/1; financial award applicants required to submit FAFSA. *Faculty research:* Early childhood growth and development, faculty development, adult learning, gender and equity issues, research methodology. *Unit head:* William Goodwin, Area Coordinator, 303-556-3355, Fax: 303-556-4479, E-mail: william_goodwin@ceo.cudenver.edu. *Application contact:* Meredith Lopez, Application Contact, 303-556-2717, Fax: 303-556-4479.

University of Dayton, Graduate School, School of Education and Allied Professions, Department of Teacher Education, Dayton, OH 45469-1300. Offers adolescent/young adult (MS Ed); art education (MS Ed); early childhood education (MS Ed); inclusive early childhood (MS Ed); interdisciplinary education (MS Ed); intervention specialist education, mild/moderate (MS Ed); literacy (MS Ed); middle childhood (MS Ed); multi-age education (MS Ed); music education (MS Ed); teacher as leader (MS Ed); technology in education (MS Ed). Part-time and evening/weekend programs available. *Faculty:* 13 full-time (9 women), 33 part-time/adjunct (25 women). *Students:* 149 full-time (120 women), 284 part-time (241 women); includes 37 minority (31 African Americans, 3 Asian Americans or Pacific Islanders, 3 Hispanic Americans), 3 international. Average age 33. 201 applicants, 58% accepted, 31 enrolled. In 2006, 150 degrees awarded. *Degree requirements:* For master's, thesis, capstone research project. *Entrance requirements:* For master's, GRE General Test, minimum GPA of 2.75. Additional exam requirements/recommendations for international students: Required—TOEFL (minimum score 550 paper-based; 213 computer-based). *Application deadline:* For fall admission, 3/15 priority date for domestic students, 3/1 priority date for international students. Applications are processed on a rolling basis. Application fee: $0. Electronic applications accepted. *Expenses: Contact institution. Financial support:* In 2006–07, 8 teaching assistantships with partial tuition reimbursements (averaging $7,600 per year) were awarded; career-related internships or fieldwork, institutionally sponsored loans, health care benefits, and unspecified assistantships also available. Financial award applicants required to submit FAFSA. *Faculty research:* Diversity, literacy, art representation by young children, preservice teacher preparation. Total annual research expenditures: $330,000. *Unit head:* Dr. Katie A. Kinnucan-Welsch, Chair, 937-229-3346. *Application contact:* Erika Eavers, Graduate Admission Processor, 937-229-3065, Fax: 937-229-4729, E-mail: erika.eavers@notes.udayton.edu.

University of Detroit Mercy, College of Liberal Arts and Education, Department of Education, Program in Early Childhood Education, Detroit, MI 48221. Offers MA. *Degree requirements:* For master's, thesis or alternative. *Entrance requirements:* For master's, minimum GPA of 2.75. *Expenses:* Tuition: Full-time $15,750; part-time $875 per credit hour. Required fees: $570.

The University of Findlay, Graduate and Professional Studies, College of Education, Findlay, OH 45840-3653. Offers administration (MA Ed); early childhood (MA Ed); elementary education (MA Ed); human resource development (MA Ed); leadership (MA Ed); special education (MA Ed); technology (MA Ed); web instruction (MA Ed). *Accreditation:* NCATE. Part-time and evening/weekend programs available. *Faculty:* 12 full-time, 6 part-time/adjunct. *Students:* 84 full-time (65 women), 223 part-time (169 women); includes 11 minority (3 African Americans, 2 American Indian/Alaska Native, 1 Asian American or Pacific Islander, 5 Hispanic Americans), 13 international. Average age 35. 91 applicants, 97% accepted, 76 enrolled. In 2006, 146 degrees awarded. *Degree requirements:* For master's, thesis, cumulative project. *Entrance requirements:* For master's, minimum undergraduate GPA of 3.0 in last 60 hours of course work. Additional exam requirements/recommendations for international students: Required—TOEFL. *Application deadline:* Applications are processed on a rolling basis. Application fee: $25. Electronic applications accepted. *Expenses: Contact institution. Financial support:* In 2006–07, 6 students received support, including 6 teaching assistantships with full tuition reimbursements available (averaging $6,000 per year); unspecified assistantships also available. Financial award application deadline: 4/1; financial award applicants required to submit FAFSA. *Faculty research:* Children's literature, books and artwork, educational technology, professional development. *Unit head:* Dr. Melissa A. Cain, Dean, 419-434-4840, Fax: 419-434-4822. *Application contact:* Heather Riffle, Director, Graduate and Special Programs, 419-434-4642, Fax: 419-434-5517, E-mail: riffle@findlay.edu.

University of Florida, Graduate School, College of Education, School of Teaching and Learning, Gainesville, FL 32611. Offers bilingual/ESOL education (M Ed, MAE, Ed D, PhD, Ed S); curriculum and instruction (M Ed, MAE, Ed D, PhD, Ed S); early childhood education (Ed D, PhD, Ed S); elementary education (M Ed, MAE); English education (M Ed, MAE); mathematics education (M Ed, MAE); reading education (M Ed, MAE); science education (M Ed, MAE); social foundations (M Ed, MAE, Ed D, PhD); social studies education (M Ed, MAE). *Accreditation:* NCATE. *Faculty:* 29 full-time (20 women). *Students:* 506 (406 women); includes 87 minority (20 African Americans, 3 American Indian/Alaska Native, 13 Asian Americans or Pacific Islanders, 51 Hispanic Americans) 34 international. In 2006, 278 master's, 8 doctorates awarded. *Degree requirements:* For master's, thesis optional; for doctorate, variable foreign language requirement, thesis/dissertation. *Entrance requirements:* For master's and doctorate, GRE General Test, minimum GPA of 3.0; for Ed S, GRE General Test. Additional exam requirements/recommendations for international students: Required—TOEFL (minimum score 550 paper-based; 213 computer-based). *Application deadline:* For fall admission, 6/1 for domestic students. Applications are processed on a rolling basis. Application fee: $30. Electronic applications accepted. *Expenses:* Tuition, state resident: full-time $6,827. Tuition, nonresident: full-time $21,951. Required fees: $999. *Financial support:* In 2006–07, 5 research assistantships (averaging $11,947 per year), 22 teaching assistantships (averaging $9,709 per year) were awarded; fellowships, career-related internships or fieldwork and unspecified assistantships also available. *Faculty research:* Teacher education, inclusive education, classroom processes, curriculum and technology. *Unit head:* Dr. Tom Dana, Director, 352-392-9191 Ext. 200, Fax: 352-392-9193, E-mail: tdana@coe.ufl.edu. *Application contact:* Dr. Linda C. Jones, Coordinator, 352-392-0761 Ext. 267, Fax: 352-392-9193, E-mail: lcjones@coe.ufl.edu.

University of Georgia, Graduate School, College of Education, Department of Elementary and Social Studies Education, Athens, GA 30602. Offers early childhood education (M Ed, PhD, Ed S); elementary and middle school education (M Ed, PhD, Ed S), including elementary education (PhD), middle school education; social foundations of education (PhD). *Faculty:* 15 full-time (8 women). *Students:* 113 full-time (88 women), 122 part-time (95 women); includes 25 minority (19 African Americans, 4 Asian Americans or Pacific Islanders, 2 Hispanic Americans), 14 international. 170 applicants, 69% accepted, 88 enrolled. In 2006, 77 master's, 6 doctorates, 6 other advanced degrees awarded. *Entrance requirements:* For master's and Ed S,

Early Childhood Education

University of Georgia (continued)

GRE General Test or MAT; for doctorate, GRE General Test. *Application deadline:* For fall admission, 7/1 priority date for domestic students; for spring admission, 11/15 for domestic students. Application fee: $50. Electronic applications accepted. *Financial support:* Fellowships, research assistantships, teaching assistantships, unspecified assistantships available. *Unit head:* Dr. Ronald J. Vansickle, Head, 706-542-7265, Fax: 706-542-6506, E-mail: rvansick@uga.edu. *Application contact:* Dr. John D. Hoge, Graduate Coordinator, 706-542-4416, Fax: 706-542-4277, E-mail: jdhoge@uga.edu.

University of Hartford, College of Education, Nursing, and Health Professions, Program in Early Childhood Education, West Hartford, CT 06117-1599. Offers M Ed. *Accreditation:* NCATE. Part-time and evening/weekend programs available. *Faculty:* 1 (woman) full-time, 1 (woman) part-time/adjunct. *Students:* 5 full-time (all women), 29 part-time (28 women); includes 5 minority (1 African American, 1 Asian American or Pacific Islander, 3 Hispanic Americans). Average age 32. 15 applicants, 93% accepted, 12 enrolled. In 2006, 6 degrees awarded. *Degree requirements:* For master's, comprehensive exam. *Entrance requirements:* For master's, PRAXIS I or waiver, interview, 2 letters of recommendation. Additional exam requirements/recommendations for international students: Required—TOEFL (minimum score 550 paper-based; 213 computer-based). *Application deadline:* For fall admission, 8/15 priority date for domestic students; for winter admission, 12/1 priority date for domestic students; for spring admission, 12/1 for domestic students. Applications are processed on a rolling basis. Application fee: $40 ($55 for international students). Electronic applications accepted. *Expenses:* Tuition: Part-time $515 per credit. Required fees: $200 per term. *Financial support:* In 2006–07, 1 teaching assistantship (averaging $2,000 per year) was awarded; institutionally sponsored loans and unspecified assistantships also available. Financial award application deadline: 6/1; financial award applicants required to submit FAFSA. *Unit head:* Dr. Regina Miller, Director, 860-768-4553, Fax: 860-768-5043, E-mail: remiller@hartford.edu. *Application contact:* Susan Brown, Assistant Dean of Academic Services, 860-768-4692, Fax: 860-768-5043, E-mail: brown@hartford.edu.

University of Hawaii at Manoa, Graduate Division, College of Education, Department of Curriculum Studies, Program in Early Childhood Education, Honolulu, HI 96822. Offers M Ed. *Accreditation:* NCATE. *Students:* 2 full-time (both women), 6 part-time (5 women); includes 5 minority (4 Asian Americans or Pacific Islanders, 1 Hispanic American), 1 international. In 2006, 1 degree awarded. *Degree requirements:* For master's, thesis optional. *Entrance requirements:* Additional exam requirements/recommendations for international students: Required—TOEFL (minimum score 580 paper-based; 237 computer-based; 92 iBT). *Application deadline:* For fall admission, 3/1 for domestic and international students. Application fee: $50. *Financial support:* In 2006–07, 1 research assistantship (averaging $16,176 per year) was awarded. *Application contact:* Neil Pateman, Graduate Chairperson, 808-956-4401, Fax: 808-956-9905.

University of Houston, College of Education, Department of Curriculum and Instruction, Houston, TX 77204. Offers art education (M Ed); bilingual education (M Ed); curriculum and instruction (Ed D); early childhood education (M Ed); education of the gifted (M Ed); elementary education (M Ed); mathematics education (M Ed); reading and language arts education (M Ed); science education (M Ed); second language education (M Ed); secondary education (M Ed); social studies education (M Ed); teaching (M Ed). *Accreditation:* NCATE. Part-time and evening/weekend programs available. *Faculty:* 24 full-time (11 women), 16 part-time/adjunct (14 women). *Students:* 134 full-time (102 women), 327 part-time (256 women); includes 142 minority (49 African Americans, 1 American Indian/Alaska Native, 29 Asian Americans or Pacific Islanders, 63 Hispanic Americans), 19 international. Average age 37. 113 applicants, 72% accepted, 61 enrolled. In 2006, 106 master's, 32 doctorates awarded. *Degree requirements:* For master's, comprehensive exam or thesis; for doctorate, thesis/dissertation, comprehensive exam. *Entrance requirements:* For master's, GRE General Test or MAT; for doctorate, GRE General Test, interview. *Application deadline:* For fall admission, 7/3 priority date for domestic students. Applications are processed on a rolling basis. Application fee: $35 ($75 for international students). *Expenses:* Tuition, state resident: full-time $5,429; part-time $226 per credit. Tuition, nonresident: full-time $12,029; part-time $501 per credit. Required fees: $2,454. *Financial support:* In 2006–07, 2 fellowships with full tuition reimbursements (averaging $9,500 per year), 6 research assistantships with full tuition reimbursements (averaging $8,800 per year), 25 teaching assistantships with full tuition reimbursements (averaging $8,800 per year) were awarded; career-related internships or fieldwork, Federal Work-Study, institutionally sponsored loans, scholarships/grants, health care benefits, and unspecified assistantships also available. Support available to part-time students. Financial award application deadline: 3/10. *Faculty research:* Teaching-learning process, instructional technology in schools, teacher education, classroom management, at-risk students. *Unit head:* Dr. Juanita Copley, Chairperson, 713-743-4950, Fax: 713-743-4990, E-mail: ncopley@aol.com.

University of Houston–Clear Lake, School of Education, Program in Curriculum and Instruction, Houston, TX 77058-1098. Offers curriculum and instruction (MS); early childhood education (MS); reading (MS); school library and information science (MS). Part-time and evening/weekend programs available. *Faculty:* 17 full-time (15 women), 9 part-time/adjunct (7 women). *Students:* 40 full-time (39 women), 185 part-time (176 women); includes 66 minority (32 African Americans, 7 Asian Americans or Pacific Islanders, 27 Hispanic Americans), 6 international. Average age 34. In 2006, 80 degrees awarded. *Degree requirements:* For master's, thesis (for some programs). *Entrance requirements:* For master's, GRE or minimum GPA of 3.0 in last 60 hours. Additional exam requirements/recommendations for international students: Required—TOEFL (minimum score 550 paper-based; 213 computer-based). *Application deadline:* For fall admission, 7/1 for domestic students, 6/1 for international students; for spring admission, 10/1 for domestic and international students. Applications are processed on a rolling basis. Application fee: $35 ($75 for international students). Electronic applications accepted. *Financial support:* Career-related internships or fieldwork, Federal Work-Study, institutionally sponsored loans, and scholarships/grants available. Support available to part-time students. Financial award application deadline: 5/1; financial award applicants required to submit FAFSA. *Unit head:* Dr. Suzanne Brown, Chair, 281-283-3540, E-mail: brownsue@uhcl.edu. *Application contact:* Janis S. Bigelow, Assistant Director of Admissions, Recruitment and Communications, 281-283-2540, Fax: 281-283-2530, E-mail: bigelow@uhcl.edu.

The University of Iowa, Graduate College, College of Education, Department of Teaching and Learning, Program in Early Childhood and Elementary Education, Iowa City, IA 52242-1316. Offers curriculum and supervision (MA, PhD); developmental reading (MA); early childhood education and care (MA); elementary education (MA, PhD); language, literature and culture (PhD). *Faculty:* 7 full-time, 4 part-time/adjunct. *Students:* 8 full-time (7 women), 23 part-time (all women); includes 2 minority (both African Americans), 5 international. 6 applicants, 67% accepted, 4 enrolled. In 2006, 11 master's, 1 doctorate awarded. *Degree requirements:* For master's, exam, thesis optional; for doctorate, thesis/dissertation, comprehensive exam, registration. *Entrance requirements:* For master's and doctorate, GRE General Test, minimum GPA of 3.0. Additional exam requirements/recommendations for international students: Required—TOEFL (minimum score 550 paper-based; 213 computer-based; 81 iBT). Application fee: $60 ($85 for international students). Electronic applications accepted. *Financial support:* In 2006–07, 1 fellowship, 2 research assistantships with partial tuition reimbursements, 8 teaching assistantships with partial tuition reimbursements were awarded. Financial award applicants required to submit FAFSA. *Unit head:* Gary Sasso, Chair, 319-335-5324, Fax: 319-335-5608.

University of Kentucky, Graduate School, College of Education, Program in Special Education, Lexington, KY 40506-0032. Offers early childhood special education (MS Ed); rehabilitation counseling (MRC); special education (MS Ed); special education leadership personnel preparation (Ed D). *Accreditation:* CORE; NCATE. *Faculty:* 38 full-time (24 women), 5 part-time/adjunct (4 women). *Students:* 108 full-time (76 women), 74 part-time (70 women); includes 28 minority (23 African Americans, 1 American Indian/Alaska Native, 3 Asian Americans or Pacific Islanders, 1 Hispanic American). Average age 37. 57 applicants, 65% accepted, 32 enrolled. In 2006, 48 master's, 2 doctorates awarded. Terminal master's awarded for partial completion of doctoral program. *Median time to degree:* Of those who began their doctoral program in fall 1998, 90% received their degree in 8 years or less. *Degree requirements:* For master's, thesis optional; for doctorate, thesis/dissertation, comprehensive exam. *Entrance requirements:* For master's, GRE General Test, minimum undergraduate GPA of 2.75; for doctorate, GRE General Test, minimum graduate GPA of 3.0. Additional exam requirements/recommendations for international students: Required—TOEFL (minimum score 550 paper-based; 213 computer-based). *Application deadline:* For fall admission, 7/17 priority date for domestic students, 2/1 priority date for international students; for spring admission, 12/13 priority date for domestic students, 6/15 priority date for international students. Application fee: $40 ($55 for international students). Electronic applications accepted. *Expenses:* Tuition, state resident: full-time $7,670; part-time $401 per credit hour. Tuition, nonresident: full-time $16,158; part-time $873 per credit hour. *Financial support:* In 2006–07, 10 fellowships with full tuition reimbursements (averaging $2,600 per year), 2 research assistantships with full tuition reimbursements (averaging $8,400 per year), 1 teaching assistantship with full tuition reimbursement (averaging $10,500 per year) were awarded; career-related internships or fieldwork, Federal Work-Study, institutionally sponsored loans, scholarships/grants, traineeships, health care benefits, tuition waivers (partial), and unspecified assistantships also available. Support available to part-time students. Financial award application deadline: 3/15. *Faculty research:* Applied behavior analysis applications in special education, single subject research design in classroom settings, transition research across life span, rural special education personnel. Total annual research expenditures: $1.6 million. *Unit head:* Dr. John Schuster, Director of Graduate Studies, 859-257-8594, Fax: 859-257-1325. *Application contact:* Dr. Brian Jackson, Senior Associate Dean, 859-257-4667, Fax: 859-257-4676, E-mail: brian.jackson@uky.edu.

University of Louisville, Graduate School, College of Education and Human Development, Department of Teaching and Learning, Program in Interdisciplinary Early Childhood Education, Louisville, KY 40292-0001. Offers M Ed. *Students:* 1 (woman) full-time, 19 part-time (all women); includes 1 minority (Asian American or Pacific Islander) Average age 35. In 2006, 9 degrees awarded. *Entrance requirements:* For master's, GRE General Test. *Application deadline:* Applications are processed on a rolling basis. Application fee: $50. *Financial support:* Fellowships, research assistantships, teaching assistantships, Federal Work-Study and scholarships/grants available. *Unit head:* Dr. Lora Bailey, Program Head, 502-852-2629, Fax: 502-852-1497, E-mail: l.bailey@louisville.edu.

University of Mary, Program in Education, Bismarck, ND 58504-9652. Offers college teaching (MS Ed); curriculum and instruction (MS Ed); early childhood education (MS Ed); early childhood special education (MS Ed); elementary education administration (MS Ed); reading (MS Ed); secondary education administration (MS Ed); special education (MS Ed). Part-time programs available. *Faculty:* 8 full-time (4 women), 12 part-time/adjunct (7 women). *Students:* 2 full-time (1 woman), 34 part-time (25 women), 2 international. Average age 35. In 2006, 17 degrees awarded. *Degree requirements:* For master's, portfolio or thesis. *Entrance requirements:* For master's, interview, letters of reference. *Application deadline:* Applications are processed on a rolling basis. Application fee: $40. *Financial support:* In 2006–07, 1 teaching assistantship with full tuition reimbursement was awarded; career-related internships or fieldwork also available. Support available to part-time students. Financial award application deadline: 8/1; financial award applicants required to submit FAFSA. *Faculty research:* Innovative pedagogy in higher education, technology in education, content standards, children of poverty, children with diverse learning needs. *Unit head:* Dr. Rebecca Yunker Salveson, Director, 701-355-8186, E-mail: rysalves@umary.edu. *Application contact:* Leona Friedig, Administrative Secretary, 701-355-8058, E-mail: lfriedig@umary.edu.

University of Maryland, Baltimore County, Graduate School, College of Arts, Humanities and Social Sciences, Department of Education, Program in Education, Baltimore, MD 21250. Offers early childhood education (MAT); elementary education (MAT); secondary education (MAT). Part-time and evening/weekend programs available. *Faculty:* 17 full-time (15 women), 3 part-time/adjunct (all women). *Students:* 49 full-time (43 women), 89 part-time (69 women); includes 11 minority (8 African Americans, 2 Asian Americans or Pacific Islanders, 1 Hispanic American). Average age 30. In 2006, 21 master's awarded. *Median time to degree:* Of those who began their doctoral program in fall 1998, 95% received their degree in 8 years or less. *Degree requirements:* For master's, thesis (for some programs), comprehensive exam, registration. *Entrance requirements:* For master's, PRAXIS I and II, minimum GPA of 3.0. *Application deadline:* Applications are processed on a rolling basis. Application fee: $50. Electronic applications accepted. *Expenses:* Tuition, state resident: part-time $412 per credit hour. Tuition, nonresident: part-time $681 per credit hour. Required fees: $91 per credit hour. One-time fee: $75 part-time. *Financial support:* In 2006–07, 6 students received support, including research assistantships with full tuition reimbursements available (averaging $12,000 per year); career-related internships or fieldwork, Federal Work-Study, scholarships/grants, tuition waivers, and unspecified assistantships also available. Financial award application deadline: 3/1. *Faculty research:* STEM teacher education, culturally sensitive pedagogy. Total annual research expenditures: $1.3 million. *Unit head:* Dr. Susan M. Blunck, Director, 410-455-2869, Fax: 410-455-3986, E-mail: blunck@umbc.edu. *Application contact:* Dr. Susan M. Blunck, Director, 410-455-2869, Fax: 410-455-3986, E-mail: blunck@umbc.edu.

University of Maryland, College Park, Graduate Studies, College of Education, Department of Human Development, College Park, MD 20742. Offers early childhood/elementary education (M Ed, MA, Ed D, PhD); human development (M Ed, MA, Ed D, PhD). *Accreditation:* NCATE. Part-time and evening/weekend programs available. Postbaccalaureate distance learning degree programs offered. *Faculty:* 43 full-time (37 women), 16 part-time/adjunct (12 women). *Students:* 61 full-time (54 women), 39 part-time (32 women); includes 19 minority (11 African Americans, 5 Asian Americans or Pacific Islanders, 3 Hispanic Americans), 7 international. 97 applicants, 51% accepted, 29 enrolled. In 2006, 16 master's, 9 doctorates awarded. *Median time to degree:* Of those who began their doctoral program in fall 1998, 57% received their degree in 8 years or less. *Degree requirements:* For master's, thesis optional; for doctorate, thesis/dissertation, essay, exam, research paper, comprehensive exam. *Entrance requirements:* For master's, GRE General Test, minimum GPA of 3.0, 3 letters of recommendation; for doctorate, GRE General Test or MAT, minimum undergraduate GPA of 3.0, graduate 3.5; 3 letters of recommendation. Additional exam requirements/recommendations for international students: Required—TOEFL. *Application deadline:* For fall admission, 5/1 for domestic students, 11/15 for international students; for spring admission, 10/1 for domestic and international students. Applications are processed on a rolling basis. Application fee: $60. Electronic applications accepted. *Financial support:* In 2006–07, 18 fellowships with full tuition reimbursements (averaging $13,943 per year), 2 research assistantships with tuition reimbursements (averaging $15,766 per year), 35 teaching assistantships with tuition reimbursements (averaging $15,881 per year) were awarded; Federal Work-Study and scholarships/grants also available. Support available to part-time students. Financial award applicants required to submit FAFSA. *Faculty research:* Developmental science, educational psychology, cognitive development, language development. Total annual research expenditures: $3.2 million. *Unit head:* Dr. Alan L. Wigfield, Chair, 301-405-1659, Fax: 301-405-2891, E-mail: awigfield@umd.edu. *Application contact:* Dean of Graduate School, 301-405-0358, Fax: 301-314-9305.

University of Massachusetts Amherst, Graduate School, School of Education, Program in Education, Amherst, MA 01003. Offers cultural diversity and curriculum reform (M Ed, Ed D, CAGS); early childhood education and development (M Ed, Ed D, CAGS); educational administration (M Ed, Ed D, CAGS); elementary teacher education (M Ed, Ed D, CAGS); higher education (M Ed, Ed D, CAGS); international education (M Ed, Ed D, CAGS); mathematics, science, and instructional technology (M Ed, Ed D, CAGS); physical education teacher education (M Ed, Ed D, CAGS); reading and writing (M Ed, Ed D, CAGS); research and evaluation methods (M Ed, Ed D, CAGS); school psychology and school counseling (M Ed, Ed D, CAGS); secondary teacher education (M Ed, Ed D, CAGS); social justice education (M Ed, Ed D, CAGS); special education (M Ed, Ed D, CAGS). *Accreditation:* NCATE. *Students:* 418 full-time (286 women), 447 part-time (319 women); includes 147 minority (70

African Americans, 4 American Indian/Alaska Native, 28 Asian Americans or Pacific Islanders, 45 Hispanic Americans), 81 international. Average age 36. In 2006, 260 master's, 30 doctorates awarded. *Degree requirements:* For doctorate, thesis/dissertation. *Entrance requirements:* For master's and doctorate, GRE General Test. Additional exam requirements/recommendations for international students: Required—TOEFL (minimum score 530 paper-based; 197 computer-based). *Application deadline:* For fall admission, 1/15 for domestic and international students; for spring admission, 10/1 for domestic and international students. Applications are processed on a rolling basis. Application fee: $40 ($65 for international students). Electronic applications accepted. *Expenses:* Tuition, state resident: full-time $2,640; part-time $110 per credit. Tuition, nonresident: full-time $9,936; part-time $414 per credit. Required fees: $8,969; $3,129 per term. One-time fee: $257 full-time. Tuition and fees vary according to class time, course load, campus/location and reciprocity agreements. *Financial support:* Fellowships with full tuition reimbursements, research assistantships with full tuition reimbursements, teaching assistantships with full tuition reimbursements, career-related internships or fieldwork, Federal Work-Study, scholarships/grants, traineeships, and unspecified assistantships available. Support available to part-time students. Financial award application deadline: 1/15. *Unit head:* Linda L. Griffin, Professor, 413-545-6984.

University of Memphis, Graduate School, College of Education, Department of Instruction and Curriculum Leadership, Memphis, TN 38152. Offers early childhood education (MAT, MS, Ed D); elementary education (MAT); instruction and curriculum (MS, Ed D); instruction design and technology (MS, Ed D); reading (MS, Ed D); secondary education (MAT); special education (MAT, MS, Ed D). *Accreditation:* NCATE (one or more programs are accredited). Part-time programs available. Terminal master's awarded for partial completion of doctoral program. *Degree requirements:* For master's, thesis or alternative, comprehensive exam; for doctorate, thesis/dissertation, comprehensive exam. *Entrance requirements:* For master's, GRE General Test, minimum GPA of 2.5; for doctorate, GRE General Test, GRE Subject Test, 2 years of teaching experience. Electronic applications accepted. *Faculty research:* Effective urban teachers, preparation and retention of urban teachers, technology utilization in schools, field-based preparation teacher preparation programs, effective use of online instruction.

University of Miami, Graduate School, School of Education, Department of Teaching and Learning, Program in Exceptional Student Education, Pre-K Disabilities and ESOL, Coral Gables, FL 33124. Offers MS Ed, Ed S. *Accreditation:* NCATE. Part-time and evening/weekend programs available. *Students:* 9 full-time (all women), 17 part-time (16 women); includes 9 minority (4 African Americans, 5 Hispanic Americans). 15 applicants, 67% accepted, 6 enrolled. In 2006, 9 degrees awarded. *Degree requirements:* For master's, electronic portfolio review; for Ed S, thesis optional. *Entrance requirements:* For master's and Ed S, GRE General Test. Additional exam requirements/recommendations for international students: Required—TOEFL (minimum score 550 paper-based; 212 computer-based). *Application deadline:* Applications are processed on a rolling basis. Application fee: $50. Electronic applications accepted. *Financial support:* In 2006–07, 25 students received support; teaching assistantships with tuition reimbursements available, Federal Work-Study available. Financial award application deadline: 3/1; financial award applicants required to submit FAFSA. *Faculty research:* Technology, social skills, inclusion, plan, evaluation. *Unit head:* Dr. Batya Elbaum, Advisor, 305-284-4218, Fax: 305-284-4439, E-mail: elbaum@miami.edu.

University of Michigan, Horace H. Rackham School of Graduate Studies, School of Education, Programs in Educational Studies, Ann Arbor, MI 48109. Offers curriculum development (MA); early childhood education (MA, PhD); educational administration and policy (MA, PhD); educational foundation, administration, policy, and research methods (MA); educational foundations and policy (MA, PhD); elementary education (MA-Certification); English education (MA); English language learning in school settings (MA); learning technologies (MA, PhD); literacy, language, and culture (MA, PhD); mathematics education (MA, PhD); research methods (MA); science education (MA, PhD); secondary education (MA-Certification); social studies education (MA); special education (PhD); teaching and teacher education (PhD); MA-Certification; MBA/MA; PhD/MA. Terminal master's awarded for partial completion of doctoral program. *Degree requirements:* For master's, thesis (for some programs); for doctorate, thesis/dissertation, comprehensive exam. *Entrance requirements:* For master's and doctorate, GRE General Test. Additional exam requirements/recommendations for international students: Required—TOEFL (minimum score 600 paper-based; 250 computer-based). *Application deadline:* For fall admission, 12/1 priority date for domestic students, 12/1 for international students. Application fee: $60 ($75 for international students). Electronic applications accepted. *Financial support:* Applicants required to submit FAFSA. *Unit head:* Dr. Addison Stone, Chairperson, 734-763-7500, Fax: 734-615-1290, E-mail: addison@umich.edu. *Application contact:* Roberta Perry, Office of Student Services, 734-764-7563, Fax: 734-763-1495, E-mail: ed.grad.admit@umich.edu.

University of Michigan–Flint, School of Education and Human Services, Department of Education, Flint, MI 48502-1950. Offers early childhood education (MA Ed); education (MA Ed); elementary education with teaching certificate (MA Ed); literacy (K-12) (MA Ed); special education (MA Ed); urban and multicultural education (MA Ed). Part-time programs available. *Faculty:* 19 full-time (15 women), 9 part-time/adjunct (6 women). *Students:* 20 full-time (18 women), 193 part-time (167 women); includes 15 minority (12 African Americans, 1 American Indian/Alaska Native, 2 Hispanic Americans), 2 international. 109 applicants, 80% accepted, 65 enrolled. In 2006, 54 degrees awarded. *Entrance requirements:* Additional exam requirements/recommendations for international students: Required—TOEFL (minimum score 550 paper-based; 220 computer-based), IELTS (minimum score 7). *Application deadline:* For fall admission, 8/1 priority date for domestic students, 3/1 priority date for international students; for winter admission, 11/15 priority date for domestic students, 7/15 priority date for international students; for spring admission, 3/15 priority date for domestic students, 11/15 priority date for international students. Application fee: $55. *Expenses:* Contact institution. *Unit head:* Dr. Beverly Schumer, Director, 810-424-5215, E-mail: bschumer@umflint.edu. *Application contact:* Beulah Alexander, Executive Secretary, 810-766-6879, Fax: 810-766-6891, E-mail: beulaha@umflint.edu.

University of Minnesota, Twin Cities Campus, Graduate School, College of Education and Human Development, Department of Curriculum and Instruction, Minneapolis, MN 55455-0213. Offers art education (M Ed, MA, PhD); children's literature (M Ed, MA, PhD); curriculum and instruction (MA, PhD); early childhood education (M Ed, PhD); elementary education (M Ed, MA, PhD); English education (MA, PhD); environmental education (M Ed); family education (M Ed, MA, Ed D, PhD); instructional systems and technology (M Ed, MA, PhD); language arts (MA, PhD); language immersion education (Certificate); literacy education (MA); mathematics education (MA, PhD); reading education (MA, PhD); science education (MA, PhD); second languages and cultures education (MA, PhD); social studies education (MA, PhD); teaching (M Ed), including Chinese, earth science, elementary special education, English, English as a second language, French, German, Hebrew, Japanese, life sciences, mathematics, middle school science, science, second languages and cultures, social studies, Spanish; technology enhanced learning (Certificate); writing education (M Ed, MA, PhD). *Faculty:* 30 full-time (18 women). *Students:* 496 full-time (363 women), 338 part-time (235 women); includes 89 minority (26 African Americans, 4 American Indian/Alaska Native, 42 Asian Americans or Pacific Islanders, 17 Hispanic Americans), 33 international. Average age 29. 734 applicants, 66% accepted, 425 enrolled. In 2006, 644 master's, 18 doctorates, 11 other advanced degrees awarded. *Expenses:* Tuition, state resident: full-time $9,302; part-time $775 per credit. Tuition, nonresident: full-time $16,400; part-time $1,367 per credit. Full-time tuition and fees vary according to class time, course load, program, reciprocity agreements and student level. *Financial support:* In 2006–07, 7 fellowships (averaging $24,775 per year), 22 research assistantships with full tuition reimbursements (averaging $24,775 per year), 52 teaching assistantships with full tuition reimbursements (averaging $24,775 per year) were awarded. *Faculty research:* Educational practice for a democratic and just society; curriculum history and development/assessment; teacher preparation/induction/mentoring/development; cultural, linguistic, social, political, technological, and economic factors that influence teaching and learning. Total annual research expenditures: $1.2 million. *Unit head:* Dr. Ruth Thomas, Chair, 612-624-4772, Fax: 612-624-8277, E-mail: thoma006@umn.edu. *Application contact:* Dr. Mary Bents, Associate Dean, 612-625-6501, Fax: 612-626-1580, E-mail: mbents@tc.umn.edu.

University of Minnesota, Twin Cities Campus, Graduate School, College of Education and Human Development, Department of Educational Psychology, Minneapolis, MN 55455-0213. Offers counseling and student personnel psychology (MA, PhD, Ed S); early childhood education (M Ed, MA, PhD); educational psychology (PhD); psychological foundations of education (MA, PhD, Ed S); school psychology (MA, PhD, Ed S); special education (M Ed, MA, PhD, Ed S); talent development and gifted education (Certificate). *Accreditation:* APA (one or more programs are accredited). *Faculty:* 33 full-time (11 women). *Students:* 323 full-time (260 women), 118 part-time (95 women); includes 39 minority (15 African Americans, 4 American Indian/Alaska Native, 14 Asian Americans or Pacific Islanders, 6 Hispanic Americans), 56 international. Average age 32. 334 applicants, 53% accepted, 122 enrolled. In 2006, 112 master's, 20 doctorates, 10 other advanced degrees awarded. *Expenses:* Tuition, state resident: full-time $9,302; part-time $775 per credit. Tuition, nonresident: full-time $16,400; part-time $1,367 per credit. Full-time tuition and fees vary according to class time, course load, program, reciprocity agreements and student level. *Financial support:* In 2006–07, 8 fellowships (averaging $24,775 per year), 72 research assistantships (averaging $24,775 per year), 40 teaching assistantships (averaging $24,775 per year) were awarded. *Faculty research:* Social psychology and development in education, multicultural education and counseling, international psychology, learning and readiness processes, measurement and statistical processes. Total annual research expenditures: $2.5 million. *Unit head:* Dr. John Romano, Chair, 612-624-1099, Fax: 612-624-8241, E-mail: roman001@umn.edu. *Application contact:* Dr. Mary Bents, Associate Dean, 612-625-6501, Fax: 612-626-1580, E-mail: mbents@tc.umn.edu.

University of Minnesota, Twin Cities Campus, Graduate School, College of Education and Human Development, Institute of Child Development, Minneapolis, MN 55455-0213. Offers child psychology (MA, PhD); early childhood education (M Ed, MA, PhD); school psychology (MA, PhD). *Faculty:* 17 full-time (6 women). *Students:* 100 full-time (92 women), 27 part-time (25 women); includes 12 minority (2 African Americans, 1 American Indian/Alaska Native, 5 Asian Americans or Pacific Islanders, 4 Hispanic Americans), 7 international. Average age 25. 131 applicants, 38% accepted, 38 enrolled. In 2006, 38 master's, 10 doctorates awarded. *Expenses:* Tuition, state resident: full-time $9,302; part-time $775 per credit. Tuition, nonresident: full-time $16,400; part-time $1,367 per credit. Full-time tuition and fees vary according to class time, course load, program, reciprocity agreements and student level. *Financial support:* In 2006–07, 24 fellowships (averaging $24,775 per year), 22 research assistantships with full tuition reimbursements (averaging $24,775 per year), 30 teaching assistantships with full tuition reimbursements (averaging $24,775 per year) were awarded. *Faculty research:* Developmental affective and cognitive neuroscience; developmental psychopathology; intervention and prevention science; social and emotional development; cognitive, language, and perceptual development. Total annual research expenditures: $3.7 million. *Unit head:* Dr. Nicki Crick, Director, 612-625-8879, Fax: 612-624-6373, E-mail: crick001@umn.edu. *Application contact:* Claudia Johnston, Information Contact, 612-624-2576, Fax: 612-624-6373, E-mail: johnstc@staff.tc.umn.edu.

University of Missouri–Columbia, Graduate School, College of Education, Department of Curriculum and Instruction, Columbia, MO 65211. Offers agricultural education (M Ed, PhD, Ed S); art education (M Ed, PhD, Ed S); business and office education (M Ed, PhD, Ed S); early childhood education (M Ed, PhD, Ed S); elementary education (M Ed, PhD, Ed S); English education (M Ed, PhD, Ed S); foreign language education (M Ed, PhD, Ed S); health education and promotion (M Ed, PhD); learning and instruction (M Ed); marketing education (M Ed, PhD, Ed S); mathematics education (M Ed, PhD, Ed S); music education (M Ed, PhD, Ed S); reading education (M Ed, PhD, Ed S); science education (M Ed, PhD, Ed S); social studies education (M Ed, PhD, Ed S); vocational education (M Ed, PhD, Ed S). Part-time programs available. *Faculty:* 24 full-time (12 women). *Students:* 195 full-time (148 women), 260 part-time (214 women); includes 27 minority (8 African Americans, 1 American Indian/Alaska Native, 10 Asian Americans or Pacific Islanders, 8 Hispanic Americans), 19 international. In 2006, 186 master's, 12 doctorates awarded. Terminal master's awarded for partial completion of doctoral program. *Degree requirements:* For doctorate, thesis/dissertation. *Entrance requirements:* For master's and Ed S, GRE General Test or MAT, minimum GPA of 3.0; for doctorate, GRE General Test, minimum GPA of 3.0. *Application deadline:* Applications are processed on a rolling basis. Application fee: $45 ($60 for international students). *Financial support:* Fellowships, research assistantships, teaching assistantships, institutionally sponsored loans available. *Unit head:* Dr. Lloyd H. Barrow, Director of Graduate Studies, 573-882-8247, E-mail: robinsonr@missouri.edu.

University of Montevallo, College of Education, Program in Early Childhood Education, Montevallo, AL 35115. Offers M Ed. *Accreditation:* NCATE. Part-time programs available. *Degree requirements:* For master's, comprehensive exam. *Entrance requirements:* For master's, GRE General Test, MAT, minimum undergraduate GPA of 2.5. Additional exam requirements/recommendations for international students: Required—TOEFL (minimum score 550 paper-based).

University of New Hampshire, Graduate School, College of Liberal Arts, Department of Education, Program in Early Childhood Education, Durham, NH 03824. Offers early childhood education (M Ed); special needs (M Ed). Part-time programs available. *Faculty:* 32 full-time. *Students:* 3 full-time (all women), 13 part-time (11 women); includes 1 minority (African American) Average age 31. 6 applicants, 100% accepted, 6 enrolled. In 2006, 10 degrees awarded. *Degree requirements:* For master's, thesis or alternative. *Entrance requirements:* For master's, GRE General Test. Additional exam requirements/recommendations for international students: Required—TOEFL (minimum score 550 paper-based; 213 computer-based). *Application deadline:* For fall admission, 4/1 priority date for domestic students, 4/1 for international students; for winter admission, 12/1 for domestic students. Applications are processed on a rolling basis. Application fee: $60. Electronic applications accepted. *Expenses:* Tuition, state resident: full-time $8,540; part-time $474 per credit hour. Tuition, nonresident: full-time $20,990; part-time $862 per credit hour. Required fees: $1,343; $356 per term. Tuition and fees vary according to course load, program and reciprocity agreements. *Financial support:* In 2006–07, 1 fellowship, 1 teaching assistantship were awarded; research assistantships, career-related internships or fieldwork, Federal Work-Study, scholarships/grants, and tuition waivers (full and partial) also available. Support available to part-time students. Financial award application deadline: 2/15. *Faculty research:* Young children with special needs. *Unit head:* Dr. John Hornstein, Coordinator, 603-862-2310, E-mail: education.department@unh.edu.

The University of North Carolina at Chapel Hill, Graduate School, School of Education, Program in Education, Chapel Hill, NC 27599. Offers culture, curriculum and change (PhD); culture, curriculum, and change (MA); early childhood, families, and literacy studies (MA, PhD); educational psychology measurements, and evaluation (PhD); educational psychology, measurement, and evaluation (MA). *Accreditation:* NCATE. In 2006, 11 master's, 10 doctorates awarded. *Degree requirements:* For master's, thesis/dissertation; for doctorate, thesis/dissertation, comprehensive exam, registration. *Entrance requirements:* For master's, GRE General Test, minimum GPA of 3.0 during last 2 years of undergraduates course work; for doctorate, GRE General Test, minimum GPA of 3.0 during last 2 years of undergraduate course work. Additional exam requirements/recommendations for international students: Required—TOEFL (minimum score 550 paper-based; 213 computer-based). *Application deadline:* For fall admission, 1/1 priority date for domestic and international students. Applications are processed on a rolling basis. Application fee: $60. Electronic applications accepted. *Financial support:* Federal Work-Study available. Support available to part-time students. Financial award application deadline: 3/1; financial award applicants required to submit FAFSA. *Application contact:* Janet Carroll, Registrar, 919-962-8690, Fax: 919-962-1533, E-mail: jscarrol@email.unc.edu.

Early Childhood Education

The University of North Carolina at Chapel Hill, Graduate School, School of Education, Program in Education for Experienced Teachers, Early Childhood Intervention and Family Studies (Birth-K), Chapel Hill, NC 27599. Offers M Ed. *Accreditation:* NCATE. *Degree requirements:* For master's, comprehensive exam. *Entrance requirements:* For master's, GRE General Test, minimum GPA of 3.0 during last 2 years of undergraduate course work. *Application deadline:* For fall admission, 1/1 for domestic students. Applications are processed on a rolling basis. Application fee: $55. *Financial support:* Application deadline: 1/1. *Faculty research:* Families of young children, ethics and early intervention, exceptional child development, assessment and evaluation. *Unit head:* Dr. Harriet Boone, Coordinator, 919-962-9371. *Application contact:* Janet Carroll, Registrar, 919-962-8690, Fax: 919-962-1533, E-mail: jscarrol@email.unc.edu.

The University of North Carolina at Greensboro, Graduate School, School of Education, Department of Specialized Education Services, Greensboro, NC 27412-5001. Offers cross-categorical special education (M Ed); interdisciplinary studies in special education (M Ed); leadership early care and education (Certificate); special education (M Ed, PhD). *Faculty:* 10 full-time (7 women), 1 (woman) part-time/adjunct. *Students:* 41 full-time (36 women), 36 part-time (33 women); includes 21 minority (18 African Americans, 3 Asian Americans or Pacific Islanders). 29 applicants, 45% accepted. *Degree requirements:* For master's, thesis or alternative. *Entrance requirements:* For master's, GRE General Test. Additional exam requirements/recommendations for international students: Required—TOEFL. Application fee: $45. Electronic applications accepted. *Expenses:* Tuition, state resident: full-time $2,692. Tuition, nonresident: full-time $13,742. *Financial support:* Fellowships, research assistantships with full tuition reimbursements, career-related internships or fieldwork, Federal Work-Study, scholarships/grants, and traineeships available. Support available to part-time students. *Unit head:* Dr. Marilyn Friend, Chair, 336-256-0153, E-mail: m_friend@uncg.edu. *Application contact:* Michelle Harkleroad, Director of Graduate Admissions, 336-334-4884, Fax: 336-334-4424, E-mail: mbharkle@uncg.edu.

University of North Dakota, Graduate School, College of Education and Human Development, Program in Early Childhood Education, Grand Forks, ND 58202. Offers MS. *Accreditation:* NCATE. Part-time programs available. *Faculty:* 6 full-time (3 women), 1 part-time/adjunct (0 women). *Students:* 2 applicants, 50% accepted, 1 enrolled. In 2006, 21 degrees awarded. *Degree requirements:* For master's, thesis or alternative, comprehensive exam. *Entrance requirements:* For master's, minimum GPA of 3.0. Additional exam requirements/recommendations for international students: Required—TOEFL (minimum score 550 paper-based; 213 computer-based; 79 iBT), IELTS (minimum score 6). *Application deadline:* For fall admission, 2/15 priority date for domestic and international students; for spring admission, 10/15 priority date for domestic and international students. Applications are processed on a rolling basis. Application fee: $35. Electronic applications accepted. *Expenses:* Tuition, state resident: full-time $5,650; part-time $214 per credit. Tuition, nonresident: full-time $14,248; part-time $572 per credit. Required fees: $1,008; $42 per credit. Tuition and fees vary according to reciprocity agreements. *Financial support:* In 2006–07, 1 student received support; fellowships, research assistantships, teaching assistantships, Federal Work-Study, institutionally sponsored loans, scholarships/grants, tuition waivers (full and partial), and unspecified assistantships available. Support available to part-time students. Financial award application deadline: 3/15; financial award applicants required to submit FAFSA. *Unit head:* Dr. Glenn W. Olsen, Director, 701-777-3145, Fax: 701-777-4393, E-mail: glenn.olsen@mail.und.nodak.edu. *Application contact:* Linda M. Baeza, Admissions Officer, 701-777-2945, Fax: 701-777-3619, E-mail: gradschool@mail.und.nodak.edu.

University of Northern Colorado, Graduate School, College of Education and Behavioral Sciences, School of Psychological Sciences, Program in Educational Psychology, Greeley, CO 80639. Offers early childhood education (MA); educational psychology (MA, PhD). *Accreditation:* NCATE. Part-time programs available. *Faculty:* 13 full-time (6 women). *Students:* 22 full-time (19 women), 5 part-time (2 women); includes 2 minority (both Hispanic Americans), 2 international. Average age 37. 16 applicants, 94% accepted, 6 enrolled. In 2006, 3 master's, 3 doctorates awarded. *Degree requirements:* For master's, thesis or alternative, comprehensive exam; for doctorate, thesis/dissertation, comprehensive exam. *Entrance requirements:* For master's, GRE General Test, letters of recommendation; for doctorate, GRE General Test, letters of recommendation, resumé. *Application deadline:* Applications are processed on a rolling basis. Application fee: $50 ($60 for international students). Electronic applications accepted. *Expenses:* Tuition, state resident: full-time $5,118; part-time $213 per credit hour. Tuition, nonresident: full-time $14,832; part-time $618 per credit hour. Required fees: $674; $34 per credit hour. *Financial support:* In 2006–07, 26 students received support, including 8 fellowships (averaging $2,327 per year), 2 research assistantships (averaging $14,477 per year), 11 teaching assistantships (averaging $7,813 per year); unspecified assistantships also available. Financial award application deadline: 3/1; financial award applicants required to submit FAFSA.

University of Northern Colorado, Graduate School, College of Education and Behavioral Sciences, School of Teacher Education, Program in Elementary Education and Early Childhood, Greeley, CO 80639. Offers educational studies (Ed D); elementary education (MAT). *Accreditation:* NCATE. Part-time and evening/weekend programs available. *Faculty:* 9 full-time (6 women). *Students:* 29 full-time (25 women), 29 part-time (27 women); includes 4 minority (1 African American, 1 American Indian/Alaska Native, 1 Asian American or Pacific Islander, 1 Hispanic American), 1 international. Average age 34. 7 applicants, 100% accepted, 4 enrolled. In 2006, 47 master's, 2 doctorates awarded. *Degree requirements:* For master's, thesis or alternative, comprehensive exam; for doctorate, thesis/dissertation, comprehensive exam. *Entrance requirements:* For master's, GRE General Test; for doctorate, GRE General Test, 3 letters of recommendation. *Application deadline:* Applications are processed on a rolling basis. Application fee: $50 ($60 for international students). Electronic applications accepted. *Expenses:* Tuition, state resident: full-time $5,118; part-time $213 per credit hour. Tuition, nonresident: full-time $14,832; part-time $618 per credit hour. Required fees: $674; $34 per credit hour. *Financial support:* In 2006–07, 36 students received support, including 1 teaching assistantship (averaging $5,424 per year); fellowships, research assistantships, unspecified assistantships also available. Financial award application deadline: 3/1; financial award applicants required to submit FAFSA. *Unit head:* Dr. Gary Fertig, Program Coordinator, 970-351-2908.

University of Northern Iowa, Graduate College, College of Education, Department of Curriculum and Instruction, Program in Early Childhood Education, Cedar Falls, IA 50614. Offers MAE. *Students:* 1 (woman) full-time, 7 part-time (all women), 1 international. 7 applicants, 100% accepted, 5 enrolled. In 2006, 1 degree awarded. *Degree requirements:* For master's, thesis or alternative, comprehensive exam. *Entrance requirements:* For master's, minimum GPA of 3.5, 3 years of educational experience. Additional exam requirements/recommendations for international students: Required—TOEFL (minimum score 500 paper-based; 180 computer-based; 61 iBT). *Application deadline:* For fall admission, 8/1 priority date for domestic students. Applications are processed on a rolling basis. Application fee: $30 ($50 for international students). Electronic applications accepted. *Expenses:* Tuition, state resident: full-time $5,936. Tuition, nonresident: full-time $14,074. *Financial support:* Application deadline: 2/1. *Unit head:* Dr. Charles R. May, Coordinator, 319-273-2795, Fax: 319-273-5886, E-mail: charles.may@uni.edu.

University of Northern Virginia, Graduate Programs, Manassas, VA 20109. Offers accountancy (MS); accounting (MBA); business administration (DBA); computer science (MS); counseling education (M Ed); early childhood education (M Ed); educational communication and instructional technology (M Ed); educational leadership (M Ed); finance (MBA); information systems technology (MS); management (MBA); marketing (MBA); project management (MBA); public administration (MPA); teaching English to speakers of other languages (M Ed). Part-time and evening/weekend programs available. Postbaccalaureate distance learning degree programs offered (no on-campus study). *Degree requirements:* For doctorate, thesis/dissertation, comprehensive exam, registration. *Entrance requirements:* Additional exam requirements/recommendations for international students: Required—TOEFL (minimum score 550 paper-based; 230 computer-based), IELTS (minimum score 6). Electronic applications accepted.

University of North Texas, Robert B. Toulouse School of Graduate Studies, College of Education, Department of Counseling, Development and Higher Education, Program in Development, Family Studies, and Early Childhood Education, Denton, TX 76203. Offers development and family studies (MS); early childhood education (MS, Ed D). Evening/weekend programs available. *Students:* 31 full-time (30 women), 49 part-time (45 women); includes 16 minority (7 African Americans, 1 American Indian/Alaska Native, 5 Asian Americans or Pacific Islanders, 3 Hispanic Americans), 14 international. Average age 33. 8 applicants, 50% accepted, 3 enrolled. In 2006, 19 master's, 3 doctorates awarded. *Degree requirements:* For master's, thesis optional. *Entrance requirements:* For master's and doctorate, GRE General Test. *Application deadline:* For fall admission, 7/15 for domestic students. Application fee: $50 ($75 for international students). *Expenses:* Tuition, state resident: full-time $3,573; part-time $198 per credit. Tuition, nonresident: full-time $8,577; part-time $476 per credit. Required fees: $1,258; $126 per credit. One-time fee: $150 full-time. Tuition and fees vary according to course load. *Financial support:* Teaching assistantships, career-related internships or fieldwork, Federal Work-Study, and institutionally sponsored loans available. Financial award application deadline: 4/1. *Application contact:* Dr. Linda Schertz, Graduate Adviser, 940-565-4646, E-mail: schertz@coe.unt.edu.

University of Oklahoma, Graduate College, College of Education, Department of Instructional Leadership and Academic Curriculum, Norman, OK 73019-0390. Offers education (Certificate); instructional leadership and academic curriculum (M Ed, PhD), including bilingual education, early childhood education, elementary education, English education, math education, reading education, science education, secondary education, social studies education. *Accreditation:* NCATE. Part-time and evening/weekend programs available. *Faculty:* 20 full-time (11 women), 6 part-time/adjunct (all women). *Students:* 76 full-time (63 women), 115 part-time (89 women); includes 25 minority (8 African Americans, 12 American Indian/Alaska Native, 4 Asian Americans or Pacific Islanders, 1 Hispanic American), 12 international. 72 applicants, 96% accepted, 56 enrolled. In 2006, 11 master's, 10 doctorates awarded. *Degree requirements:* For doctorate, thesis/dissertation. *Entrance requirements:* For master's, 12 hours of course work in education; for doctorate, GRE General Test, master's degree, minimum graduate GPA of 3.0. Additional exam requirements/recommendations for international students: Required—TOEFL (minimum score 550 paper-based; 213 computer-based). *Application deadline:* For fall admission, 6/1 priority date for domestic students, 4/1 for international students; for spring admission, 11/1 for domestic students, 9/1 for international students. Applications are processed on a rolling basis. Application fee: $40 ($90 for international students). *Expenses:* Tuition, state resident: full-time $3,180; part-time $133 per credit hour. Tuition, nonresident: full-time $11,347; part-time $473 per credit hour. Required fees: $1,729; $62 per credit hour. $117 per semester. Tuition and fees vary according to course load and program. *Financial support:* In 2006–07, 76 students received support, including 5 research assistantships with partial tuition reimbursements available (averaging $9,773 per year), 7 teaching assistantships with partial tuition reimbursements available (averaging $10,403 per year); scholarships/grants and unspecified assistantships also available. Financial award applicants required to submit FAFSA. *Faculty research:* Early literacy, learning cycle, social justice, teacher education. Total annual research expenditures: $119,917. *Unit head:* Dr. Priscilla Griffith, Chair and Graduate Liaison, 405-325-1498, Fax: 405-325-4061, E-mail: pgriffith@ou.edu.

University of Pennsylvania, Graduate School of Education, Division of Foundations and Practices in Education, Program in Early Childhood Education, Philadelphia, PA 19104. Offers MS Ed. Part-time programs available. *Degree requirements:* For master's, thesis/project. *Entrance requirements:* For master's, GRE General Test or MAT. Electronic applications accepted. Expenses: Contact institution. *Faculty research:* Early intervention, classification, and assessment on behalf of developmentally disabled children.

University of Phoenix–Louisiana Campus, The Artemis School, College of Education, Metairie, LA 70001-2082. Offers early childhood education (MA Ed). *Degree requirements:* For master's, thesis, registration (for some programs). *Entrance requirements:* For master's, minimum undergraduate GPA of 2.5, 3 years work experience. Additional exam requirements/recommendations for international students: Required—TOEFL (minimum score 550 paper-based; 213 computer-based; 79 iBT). Application fee: $45. *Expenses:* Tuition: Full-time $11,832. Required fees: $760. *Financial support:* Institutionally sponsored loans and scholarships/grants available. *Unit head:* Dr. Marla LaRue, Dean/Executive Director, 480-557-1218, E-mail: marla.larue@phoenix.edu. *Application contact:* Chair, 504-461-8852, Fax: 504-464-6373.

University of Phoenix Online Campus, The Artemis School, College of Education, Phoenix, AZ 85034-7209. Offers administration and supervision (MAEd); adult education and training (MAEd); curriculum and instruction-adult education (MAEd); curriculum and instruction-English and language arts education (MAEd); curriculum and instruction-mathematics education (MAEd); curriculum education (MAEd); curriculum instruction (MAEd); early childhood (MAEd); English as a second language (MAEd); teacher education elementary (MAEd); teacher education secondary (MAEd). Evening/weekend programs available. Postbaccalaureate distance learning degree programs offered (no on-campus study). *Faculty:* 12 full-time (5 women), 8,196 part-time/adjunct (6,937 women). *Students:* 11,937 full-time (9,375 women); includes 2,972 minority (2,210 African Americans, 74 American Indian/Alaska Native, 205 Asian Americans or Pacific Islanders, 483 Hispanic Americans), 906 international. Average age 36. *Degree requirements:* For master's, thesis (for some programs), registration. *Entrance requirements:* For master's, 3 years of work experience, minimum GPA of 2.5. Additional exam requirements/recommendations for international students: Required—TOEFL (minimum score 550 paper-based; 213 computer-based; 79 iBT). *Application deadline:* Applications are processed on a rolling basis. Application fee: $45. Electronic applications accepted. *Expenses:* Tuition: Full-time $12,664. Required fees: $760. *Financial support:* Institutionally sponsored loans and scholarships/grants available. Financial award applicants required to submit FAFSA. *Unit head:* Dr. Marla LaRue, Dean/Executive Director, 480-557-1218, E-mail: marla.larue@phoenix.edu. *Application contact:* Dr. Marla LaRue, Dean/Executive Director, 480-557-1218, E-mail: marla.larue@phoenix.edu.

University of Phoenix–Oregon Campus, The Artemis School, College of Education, Tigard, OR 97223. Offers early childhood and elementary education (MA Ed); secondary education (MA Ed). Evening/weekend programs available. *Faculty:* 3 full-time (2 women), 33 part-time/adjunct (14 women). *Students:* 90 full-time (59 women); includes 7 minority (4 African Americans, 1 American Indian/Alaska Native, 2 Hispanic Americans), 14 international. Average age 36. In 2006, 12 degrees awarded. *Degree requirements:* For master's, thesis (for some programs), registration. *Entrance requirements:* For master's, minimum undergraduate GPA of 2.5, 3 years work experience. Additional exam requirements/recommendations for international students: Required—TOEFL (minimum score 550 paper-based; 213 computer-based; 79 iBT). *Application deadline:* Applications are processed on a rolling basis. Application fee: $45. Electronic applications accepted. *Expenses:* Tuition: Full-time $10,200. Required fees: $760. *Financial support:* Institutionally sponsored loans and scholarships/grants available. Financial award applicants required to submit FAFSA. *Unit head:* Dr. Marla LaRue, Dean/Executive Director, 480-557-1218, E-mail: marla.larue@phoenix.edu. *Application contact:* Chair, 503-403-2500, Fax: 503-670-0614.

University of Phoenix–Puerto Rico Campus, The Artemis School, College of Education, Guaynabo, PR 00968. Offers administration and supervision (MA Ed); early childhood education (MA Ed); school counselor (MSC). Evening/weekend programs available. *Faculty:* 8 full-time (all women), 28 part-time/adjunct (21 women). *Students:* 186 full-time (156 women); includes 91 minority (1 African American, 1 American Indian/Alaska Native, 89 Hispanic Americans), 4 international. Average age 37. In 2006, 39 degrees awarded. *Degree requirements:* For master's, thesis (for some programs), registration. *Entrance requirements:* For master's, minimum undergraduate GPA of 2.5, 3 years work experience. Additional exam requirements/recommendations for international students: Required—TOEFL (minimum score

550 paper-based; 213 computer-based; 79 iBT). *Application deadline:* Applications are processed on a rolling basis. Application fee: $45. Electronic applications accepted. *Expenses:* Tuition: Full-time $5,816. Required fees: $760. *Financial support:* Institutionally sponsored loans and scholarships/grants available. Financial award applicants required to submit FAFSA. *Unit head:* Dr. Marla LaRue, Dean/Executive Director, 480-557-1218, E-mail: marla.larue@phoenix.edu. *Application contact:* Chair, 787-731-5400, Fax: 787-731-1510.

University of Pittsburgh, School of Education, Department of Instruction and Learning, Program in Early Childhood Education, Pittsburgh, PA 15260. Offers M Ed. Part-time and evening/weekend programs available. *Students:* 5 full-time (all women), 6 part-time (4 women); includes 1 minority (African American), 1 international. 11 applicants, 91% accepted, 9 enrolled. In 2006, 1 degree awarded. *Degree requirements:* For master's, thesis. *Entrance requirements:* For master's, PRAXIS I. Additional exam requirements/recommendations for international students: Required—TOEFL. *Application deadline:* For fall admission, 2/1 for domestic students. Application fee: $50. Electronic applications accepted. *Financial support:* Career-related internships or fieldwork, Federal Work-Study, institutionally sponsored loans, and tuition waivers (partial) available. Support available to part-time students. Financial award application deadline: 3/15; financial award applicants required to submit FAFSA. *Application contact:* Joan M. Cutone, Director, School of Education Student Service Center, 412-648-2230, Fax: 412-648-1899, E-mail: soeinfo@pitt.edu.

University of Portland, Graduate School, School of Education, Program in Elementary Education, Portland, OR 97203-5798. Offers early childhood education (M Ed, MA, MAT). *Degree requirements:* For master's, thesis optional. *Entrance requirements:* For master's, GRE General Test (MA); California Basic Educational Skills Test, PRAXIS (MAT); Oregon Educator Licensure Assessment; GRE General Test or MAT (M Ed), minimum GPA of 3.0, teaching certificate, resumé, letters of recommendation. Additional exam requirements/recommendations for international students: Required—TOEFL (minimum score 550 paper-based; 80 iBT). *Application deadline:* For fall admission, 8/1 priority date for domestic students; for spring admission, 12/1 for domestic students. Applications are processed on a rolling basis. Application fee: $50. *Expenses:* Tuition: Part-time $728 per semester hour. Required fees: $5 per semester hour. Tuition and fees vary according to program. *Financial support:* Federal Work-Study and scholarships/grants available. Financial award application deadline: 3/1; financial award applicants required to submit FAFSA. *Application contact:* Dr. Thomas G. Greene, Associate Dean, 503-943-7135, Fax: 503-943-7315, E-mail: greene@up.edu.

University of Puerto Rico, Río Piedras, College of Education, Program in Child Education, San Juan, PR 00931-3300. Offers M Ed. Part-time programs available. *Students:* 20 full-time (all women), 21 part-time (20 women); all minorities (all Hispanic Americans) In 2006, 10 degrees awarded. *Degree requirements:* For master's, thesis. *Entrance requirements:* For master's, EXADEP, GRE or PAEG, interview, minimum GPA of 3.0, letter of recommendation. *Application deadline:* For fall admission, 2/1 for domestic and international students. Application fee: $17. *Expenses:* Tuition: state resident: part-time $100 per credit. Tuition, nonresident: part-time $291 per credit. Required fees: $72 per semester. *Financial support:* Application deadline: 5/31. *Faculty research:* Children's literature in the classroom. *Unit head:* Dr. Loyda Martinez, Coordinator, 787-764-0000 Ext. 4361, Fax: 787-763-4130. *Application contact:* Information Contact, Fax: 787-763-4130.

The University of Scranton, Graduate School, Department of Education, Program in Early Childhood Education, Scranton, PA 18510. Offers MA, MS. Part-time and evening/weekend programs available. *Students:* 3 full-time (all women), 2 part-time (both women); all minorities (all Hispanic Americans) Average age 23. 1 applicant, 100% accepted. In 2006, 1 degree awarded. *Degree requirements:* For master's, thesis (for some programs), capstone experience, comprehensive exam, registration. *Entrance requirements:* For master's, minimum GPA of 2.75. Additional exam requirements/recommendations for international students: Required—TOEFL (minimum score 500 paper-based; 173 computer-based), IELTS (minimum score 6). *Application deadline:* Applications are processed on a rolling basis. Application fee: $50. *Expenses:* Tuition: Part-time $684 per credit. Required fees: $25 per term. *Financial support:* Unspecified assistantships available. Financial award application deadline: 3/1. *Unit head:* Dr. Derry Stufft, Director, 570-941-7421, Fax: 570-941-7401, E-mail: stufftda@scranton.edu.

University of South Alabama, Graduate School, College of Education, Department of Leadership and Teacher Education, Mobile, AL 36688-0002. Offers early childhood education (M Ed); educational administration (Ed S); educational leadership (M Ed); elementary education (M Ed); reading education (M Ed); science education (M Ed); secondary education (M Ed); special education (M Ed, Ed S). *Accreditation:* NCATE. Part-time programs available. *Faculty:* 22 full-time (13 women). *Students:* 287 full-time (251 women), 229 part-time (194 women); includes 137 minority (125 African Americans, 8 American Indian/Alaska Native, 3 Asian Americans or Pacific Islanders, 1 Hispanic American), 4 international. 43 applicants, 84% accepted, 20 enrolled. In 2006, 169 master's, 12 other advanced degrees awarded. *Degree requirements:* For master's, comprehensive exam. *Entrance requirements:* For master's, GRE General Test or MAT, minimum GPA of 3.0. *Application deadline:* For fall admission, 9/1 priority date for domestic students. Applications are processed on a rolling basis. Application fee: $25. *Financial support:* In 2006–07, 6 research assistantships were awarded; career-related internships or fieldwork also available. Support available to part-time students. Financial award application deadline: 4/1. *Unit head:* Dr. David L. Gray, Chair, 251-380-2894.

University of South Carolina, The Graduate School, College of Education, Department of Instruction and Teacher Education, Program in Early Childhood Education, Columbia, SC 29208. Offers M Ed, MAT, PhD. *Accreditation:* NCATE. *Degree requirements:* For master's, comprehensive exam; for doctorate, one foreign language, thesis/dissertation, comprehensive exam. *Entrance requirements:* For master's, GRE General Test, MAT, interview; for doctorate, GRE General Test, MAT, interview, teaching experience. *Faculty research:* Parent involvement, play, multicultural education, global education.

University of South Carolina Upstate, Graduate Programs, Spartanburg, SC 29303-4999. Offers early childhood education (M Ed); elementary education (M Ed); special education: visual impairment (M Ed). *Accreditation:* NCATE. Part-time and evening/weekend programs available. *Faculty:* 9 full-time (7 women). *Students:* 5 full-time (4 women), 29 part-time (26 women); includes 3 minority (all African Americans) Average age 34. 15 applicants, 100% accepted, 9 enrolled. In 2006, 9 degrees awarded. *Degree requirements:* For master's, graduate professional portfolio. *Entrance requirements:* For master's, GRE General Test, MAT, interview, minimum GPA of 2.5, teaching certificate. *Application deadline:* Applications are processed on a rolling basis. Application fee: $40. *Expenses:* Tuition, state resident: full-time $6,890; part-time $342 per semester hour. Tuition, nonresident: full-time $14,920; part-time $727 per semester hour. *Financial support:* Institutionally sponsored loans and institutional work-study available. Financial award application deadline: 7/15; financial award applicants required to submit FAFSA. *Faculty research:* Rough and tumble play, social justice education, American Indian literatures and cultures, diversity and multicultural education, science teaching strategy. *Unit head:* Dr. Rebecca L. Stevens, Director, 864-503-5521, Fax: 864-503-5574, E-mail: ystevens@uscupstate.edu. *Application contact:* Donette Stewart, Associate Vice Chancellor for Enrollment Services, 864-503-5280, E-mail: dstewart@uscupstate.edu.

University of Southern Mississippi, Graduate School, College of Education and Psychology, Department of Curriculum, Instruction, and Special Education, Hattiesburg, MS 39406-0001. Offers alternative secondary teacher education (MAT); early childhood education (M Ed, Ed S); education of the gifted (M Ed, Ed D, PhD, Ed S); elementary education (M Ed, Ed D, PhD, Ed S); reading (M Ed, MS, Ed S); secondary education (M Ed, MS, Ed D, PhD, Ed S); special education (M Ed, Ed D, PhD, Ed S). *Faculty:* 16 full-time (11 women). *Students:* 31 full-time (28 women), 54 part-time (51 women); includes 5 minority (4 African Americans, 1 Hispanic American), 1 international. Average age 35. 59 applicants, 27% accepted, 11 enrolled. In 2006, 43 master's, 3 doctorates, 4 other advanced degrees awarded. *Degree requirements:* For master's, thesis (for some programs), comprehensive exam, registration; for doctorate and Ed S, thesis/dissertation, comprehensive exam, registration. *Entrance requirements:* For

master's, GRE General Test, MAT, minimum GPA of 3.0; for doctorate, GRE General Test, minimum GPA of 3.5; for Ed S, GRE General Test, MAT, minimum GPA of 3.25. Additional exam requirements/recommendations for international students: Required—TOEFL. *Application deadline:* For fall admission, 3/1 priority date for domestic students, 3/1 for international students. Applications are processed on a rolling basis. Application fee: $25 ($30 for international students). *Financial support:* In 2006–07, 10 research assistantships with tuition reimbursements (averaging $22,333 per year), 2 teaching assistantships with full tuition reimbursements (averaging $22,333 per year) were awarded; Federal Work-Study, institutionally sponsored loans, and tuition waivers (partial) also available. Financial award application deadline: 3/15. *Faculty research:* Mathematical problem solving, integrative curriculum, writing process, teacher education models. Total annual research expenditures: $100,000. *Unit head:* Dr. Dana Thames, Chair, 601-266-4547, Fax: 601-266-4175. *Application contact:* B.J. Davis, Administrative Assistant, 601-266-6987, Fax: 601-266-4548.

University of South Florida, Graduate School, College of Education, Department of Childhood Education, Tampa, FL 33620-9951. Offers early childhood education (M Ed, MAT, PhD); elementary education (MA, Ed D, PhD, Ed S); reading education (M Ed, MA, PhD, Ed S). *Accreditation:* NCATE. Part-time and evening/weekend programs available. *Faculty:* 25 full-time (19 women), 8 part-time/adjunct (7 women). *Students:* 99 full-time (86 women), 328 part-time (310 women); includes 62 minority (21 African Americans, 2 American Indian/Alaska Native, 6 Asian Americans or Pacific Islanders, 33 Hispanic Americans), 25 international. 213 applicants, 77% accepted, 106 enrolled. In 2006, 136 master's, 8 doctorates awarded. *Degree requirements:* For doctorate, thesis/dissertation, 2 tools of research in foreign language, statistics, and/or computers. *Entrance requirements:* For master's, GRE General Test, minimum GPA of 3.5 in last 60 hours; for doctorate, GRE General Test, minimum GPA of 3.0 (undergraduate) or 3.5 (graduate); for Ed S, GRE General Test, interview. Additional exam requirements/recommendations for international students: Required—TOEFL (minimum score 550 paper-based; 213 computer-based). *Application deadline:* For fall admission, 6/1 for domestic students, 6/2 for international students; for spring admission, 10/15 for domestic students, 7/1 for international students. Application fee: $30. Electronic applications accepted. *Financial support:* Institutionally sponsored loans, scholarships/grants, and unspecified assistantships available. Financial award applicants required to submit FAFSA. Total annual research expenditures: $26,510. *Unit head:* Dr. Marcia Mann, Chairperson, 813-974-3460, Fax: 813-974-0938, E-mail: mmann@tempest.coedu.usf.edu. *Application contact:* Christine Miranda, Admissions/Registrar's Officer, 813-974-3463, Fax: 813-974-0936, E-mail: miranda@tempest.coedu.usf.edu.

The University of Tennessee, Graduate School, College of Education, Health and Human Sciences, Department of Child and Family Studies, Knoxville, TN 37996. Offers child and family studies (MS); early childhood education (MS). Part-time programs available. *Faculty:* 13 full-time (11 women). *Students:* 44 (39 women); includes 6 African Americans 3 international. In 2006, 31 degrees awarded. *Degree requirements:* For master's, thesis or alternative. *Entrance requirements:* For master's, GRE General Test, minimum GPA of 2.7. Additional exam requirements/recommendations for international students: Required—TOEFL. *Application deadline:* For fall admission, 2/1 priority date for domestic students. Applications are processed on a rolling basis. Application fee: $35. Electronic applications accepted. *Expenses:* Tuition, state resident: full-time $5,574. Tuition, nonresident: full-time $16,840. Required fees: $792. *Financial support:* In 2006–07, 1 fellowship, 23 teaching assistantships were awarded; research assistantships, Federal Work-Study, institutionally sponsored loans, and unspecified assistantships also available. Financial award application deadline: 2/1; financial award applicants required to submit FAFSA. *Unit head:* Dr. Gary Peterson, Head, 865-974-0748, Fax: 865-974-2617.

The University of Tennessee, Graduate School, College of Education, Health and Human Sciences, Program in Education, Knoxville, TN 37996. Offers art education (MS); counseling education (PhD); cultural studies in education (PhD); curriculum (MS, Ed S); curriculum, educational research and evaluation (Ed D, PhD); early childhood education (PhD); early childhood special education (MS); education of deaf and hard of hearing (MS); educational administration and policy studies (Ed D, PhD); educational administration and supervision (Ed S); educational psychology (Ed D, PhD); elementary education (MS, Ed S); elementary teaching (MS); English education (MS, Ed S); exercise science (PhD); foreign language/ESL education (MS, Ed S); instructional technology (MS, Ed D, PhD, Ed S); literacy, language and ESL education (PhD); literacy, language education, and ESL education (Ed D); mathematics education (MS, Ed S); modified and comprehensive special education (MS); reading education (MS, Ed S); school counseling (Ed S); school psychology (PhD, Ed S); science education (MS, Ed S); secondary teaching (MS); social foundations (MS); social science education (MS, Ed S); socio-cultural foundations of sports and education (PhD); special education (Ed S); teacher education (Ed D, PhD). *Accreditation:* NCATE. Part-time and evening/weekend programs available. *Students:* 529 (401 women); includes 39 minority (23 African Americans, 2 American Indian/Alaska Native, 9 Asian Americans or Pacific Islanders, 5 Hispanic Americans) 34 international. 420 applicants, 50% accepted. In 2006, 258 master's, 28 doctorates awarded. *Degree requirements:* For master's and Ed S, thesis optional; for doctorate, variable foreign language requirement, thesis/dissertation. *Entrance requirements:* For master's, minimum GPA of 2.7; for doctorate and Ed S GRE General Test, minimum GPA of 2.7. Additional exam requirements/recommendations for international students: Required—TOEFL. *Application deadline:* For fall admission, 2/1 priority date for domestic students. Applications are processed on a rolling basis. Application fee: $35. Electronic applications accepted. *Expenses:* Tuition, state resident: full-time $5,574. Tuition, nonresident: full-time $16,840. Required fees: $792. *Financial support:* In 2006–07, 4 fellowships, 9 teaching assistantships were awarded; career-related internships or fieldwork, Federal Work-Study, institutionally sponsored loans, and unspecified assistantships also available. Financial award application deadline: 2/1; financial award applicants required to submit FAFSA. *Unit head:* Dr. Lester Knight, Head, 865-974-0907, Fax: 865-974-8718, E-mail: lknight@utk.edu.

The University of Texas at Brownsville, Graduate Studies, School of Education, Brownsville, TX 78520-4991. Offers bilingual education (M Ed); counseling and guidance (M Ed); curriculum and instruction (M Ed); early childhood education (M Ed); educational administration (M Ed); educational technology (M Ed); English as a second language (M Ed); reading specialist (M Ed); special education/educational diagnostician (M Ed). Part-time and evening/weekend programs available. Postbaccalaureate distance learning degree programs offered (minimal on-campus study). *Degree requirements:* For master's, thesis optional. *Entrance requirements:* For master's, GRE General Test. Additional exam requirements/recommendations for international students: Required—TOEFL.

The University of Texas at San Antonio, College of Education and Human Development, Department of Interdisciplinary Learning and Teaching, San Antonio, TX 78249-0617. Offers curriculum and instruction (MA); early childhood and elementary education (MA); educational psychology/special education (MA); instructional technology (MA); reading and literacy (MA). Part-time and evening/weekend programs available. *Faculty:* 26 full-time (all women), 1 part-time/adjunct (0 women). *Students:* 40 full-time (32 women), 240 part-time (207 women); includes 155 minority (20 African Americans, 1 American Indian/Alaska Native, 6 Asian Americans or Pacific Islanders, 128 Hispanic Americans), 3 international. Average age 35. 94 applicants, 100% accepted, 94 enrolled. In 2006, 61 degrees awarded. *Degree requirements:* For master's, thesis optional. *Entrance requirements:* For master's, GRE General Test. Additional exam requirements/recommendations for international students: Required—TOEFL (minimum score 500 paper-based; 173 computer-based). *Application deadline:* For fall admission, 7/1 for domestic students, 4/1 for international students; for spring admission, 11/1 for domestic students, 9/1 for international students. Applications are processed on a rolling basis. Application fee: $45 ($80 for international students). Electronic applications accepted. *Expenses:* Tuition, state resident: full-time $1,730; part-time $192 per credit hour. Tuition, nonresident: full-time $6,680; part-time $742 per credit hour. Required fees: $733; $308,359 per credit hour. *Financial support:* In 2006–07, 3 research assistantships (averaging $28,891 per year) were awarded; career-related internships or fieldwork, Federal Work-Study, scholarships/grants, and unspecified assistantships also available. *Faculty research:* Early childhood, reading,

Early Childhood Education

The University of Texas at San Antonio (continued)
special education, foundations, curriculum and instruction. Total annual research expenditures: $570,791. *Unit head:* Dr. Belinda B. Flores, Chair, 210-458-5969, Fax: 210-458-7281, E-mail: belinda.flores@utsa.edu.

The University of Texas at Tyler, College of Education and Psychology, Department of Early Childhood Education, Reading and Special Education, Tyler, TX 75799-0001. Offers early childhood education (M Ed, MA); reading (M Ed, MA); special education (M Ed, MA). Part-time and evening/weekend programs available. *Faculty:* 13 full-time (11 women), 3 part-time/adjunct (2 women). *Students:* 9 full-time (8 women), 46 part-time (42 women); includes 8 minority (6 African Americans, 2 Hispanic Americans), 2 international. Average age 36. 5 applicants, 4 enrolled. In 2006, 16 degrees awarded. *Degree requirements:* For master's, thesis (for some programs), research project, comprehensive exam. *Entrance requirements:* For master's, GRE General Test. *Application deadline:* For fall admission, 11/1 for domestic students. Applications are processed on a rolling basis. Application fee: $0 ($50 for international students). Electronic applications accepted. *Expenses:* Tuition, state resident: part-time $50 per credit hour. Tuition, nonresident: part-time $328 per credit hour. Required fees: $107 per credit hour. $426 per term. *Financial support:* In 2006–07, 2 research assistantships (averaging $12,000 per year) were awarded; scholarships/grants also available. Financial award application deadline: 7/1. *Faculty research:* Improving quality in childcare settings, play and creativity, teacher interactions, effects of modeling on early childhood teachers, biofeedback, literacy instruction. *Unit head:* Dr. Brenda Gilliam, Head, 903-566-7087, Fax: 903-565-5527, E-mail: bgilliam@mail.uttyl.edu. *Application contact:* Bonnie Purser, Office of Graduate Studies, 903-566-7142, Fax: 903-566-7068, E-mail: bpurser@uttyler.edu.

The University of Texas of the Permian Basin, Office of Graduate Studies, School of Education, Program in Early Childhood Education, Odessa, TX 79762-0001. Offers MA. *Degree requirements:* For master's, thesis (for some programs), comprehensive exam (for some programs), registration. *Entrance requirements:* For master's, GRE General Test. Additional exam requirements/recommendations for international students: Required—TOEFL (minimum score 550 paper-based; 213 computer-based).

The University of Texas–Pan American, College of Education, Department of Curriculum and Instruction: Elementary and Secondary, Edinburg, TX 78541-2999. Offers bilingual education (M Ed); early childhood education (M Ed); elementary education (M Ed); reading (M Ed); secondary education (M Ed). Part-time programs available. *Degree requirements:* For master's, thesis optional. *Entrance requirements:* For master's, GRE. Additional exam requirements/recommendations for international students: Required—TOEFL, IELTS. *Expenses:* Tuition, state resident: full-time $2,577; part-time $143 per credit hour. Tuition, nonresident: full-time $7,527; part-time $418 per credit hour. Required fees: $561. *Faculty research:* Dual language instruction, literacy and technology, teacher education in diverse populations, mathematics and science education.

University of the Cumberlands, Graduate Programs in Education, Program in Early Childhood Education, Williamsburg, KY 40769-1372. Offers MA Ed. Part-time and evening/weekend programs available. *Degree requirements:* For master's, comprehensive exam. *Entrance requirements:* For master's, GRE or NTE, Kentucky teaching certificate.

University of the District of Columbia, College of Arts and Sciences, Department of Education, Program in Early Childhood Education, Washington, DC 20008-1175. Offers MA. *Accreditation:* NCATE. Part-time programs available. *Students:* Average age 35. 16 applicants, 94% accepted, 4 enrolled. In 2006, 4 degrees awarded. *Degree requirements:* For master's, research paper. *Entrance requirements:* For master's, GRE General Test, writing proficiency exam, minimum GPA of 3.0. *Application deadline:* For fall admission, 6/15 priority date for domestic students; for spring admission, 11/1 for domestic students. Applications are processed on a rolling basis. Application fee: $20. *Financial support:* Fellowships, research assistantships available. *Application contact:* LaVerne Hill Flannigan, Director of Admission, 202-274-6069.

University of the Incarnate Word, School of Graduate Studies and Research, Dreeben School of Education, Programs in Education, San Antonio, TX 78209-6397. Offers adult education (M Ed, MA); diversity education (M Ed, MA); early childhood education (M Ed, MA); instructional technology (M Ed, MA); international education and entrepreneurship (PhD); kinesiology (M Ed, MA); mathematics education (PhD); organizational leadership (PhD); organizational learning (M Ed, MA); reading (M Ed, MA); special education (M Ed, MA). *Students:* 15 full-time (8 women), 179 part-time (117 women); includes 70 minority (20 African Americans, 1 American Indian/Alaska Native, 1 Asian American or Pacific Islander, 48 Hispanic Americans), 54 international. Average age 39. In 2006, 15 degrees awarded. Application fee: $20. *Expenses:* Tuition: Part-time $570 per credit hour. Required fees: $54 per credit hour. One-time fee: $195 part-time. Tuition and fees vary according to degree level. *Financial support:* Federal Work-Study and scholarships/grants available. *Unit head:* Dr. Richard Gray, Director, 210-829-3138, Fax: 210-829-3134, E-mail: gray@uiwtx.edu. *Application contact:* Andrea Cyterski-Acosta, Dean of Enrollment, 210-829-6005, Fax: 210-829-3921, E-mail: cyterski@uiwtx.edu.

University of the Sacred Heart, Graduate Programs, Department of Education, San Juan, PR 00914-0383. Offers early childhood education (M Ed); instruction systems and education technology (M Ed). Part-time and evening/weekend programs available. *Degree requirements:* For master's, thesis. *Entrance requirements:* For master's, EXADEP, minimum undergraduate GPA of 2.75, interview.

The University of Toledo, College of Graduate Studies, College of Education, Department of Curriculum and Instruction, Program in Early Childhood Education, Toledo, OH 43606-3390. Offers ME. *Students:* 8 full-time (all women), 15 part-time (all women); includes 2 minority (both African Americans) Average age 29. 6 applicants, 100% accepted, 5 enrolled. In 2006, 7 degrees awarded.

The University of Toledo, College of Graduate Studies, College of Education, Department of Early Childhood, Physical and Special Education, Program in Early Childhood Education, Toledo, OH 43606-3390. Offers ME, Ed S. *Students:* Average age 30. 2 applicants, 100% accepted, 1 enrolled. *Unit head:* Dr. Laurie Dinnebeil, Chair, Department of Early Childhood, Physical and Special Education, 419-530-4330.

University of Victoria, Faculty of Graduate Studies, Faculty of Education, Department of Curriculum and Instruction, Victoria, BC V8W 2Y2, Canada. Offers art (M Ed, MA, PhD); curriculum studies (M Ed, MA, PhD); early childhood (M Ed, MA, PhD); language and literacy (M Ed, MA, PhD); mathematics (M Ed, MA, PhD); music (M Ed, MA); music education (PhD); science (M Ed, MA, PhD); social studies (M Ed, MA); social, cultural and foundational studies (PhD); technology and environmental education (PhD). Part-time programs available. *Degree requirements:* For master's, thesis, project (M Ed); for doctorate, thesis/dissertation, comprehensive exam, registration. *Entrance requirements:* For master's, minimum B average. Additional exam requirements/recommendations for international students: Required—TOEFL (minimum score 575 paper-based; 233 computer-based), IELTS (minimum score 7). Electronic applications accepted. *Faculty research:* Elementary and secondary English, language arts, curriculum theory and practice, educational media and technology, educational administration and leadership, history and philosophy of education.

The University of West Alabama, School of Graduate Studies, College of Education, Department of Teacher Education, Program in Early Childhood Education, Livingston, AL 35470. Offers M Ed. *Accreditation:* NCATE. Part-time programs available. *Faculty:* 1 (woman) full-time, 1 (woman) part-time/adjunct. *Students:* 17 full-time (16 women), 38 part-time (37 women); includes 29 minority (28 African Americans, 1 American Indian/Alaska Native). In 2006, 5 degrees awarded. *Entrance requirements:* For master's, GRE General Test, MAT, minimum GPA of 2.75. *Application deadline:* For fall admission, 9/10 priority date for domestic students; for spring admission, 3/24 for domestic students. Applications are processed on a rolling basis. Application fee: $20 ($50 for international students). *Financial support:* Career-related internships or fieldwork, Federal Work-Study, scholarships/grants, and unspecified assistantships available. Support available to part-time students. *Unit head:* Dr. Louis R. Smith, Associate Dean, Department of Teacher Education, 205-652-3439, Fax: 205-652-3706, E-mail: lsmith@uwa.edu.

University of West Florida, College of Professional Studies, Division of Teacher Education, Master's Program in Curriculum and Instruction, Specialization in Primary Education, Pensacola, FL 32514-5750. Offers M Ed. *Accreditation:* NCATE. Part-time and evening/weekend programs available. *Students:* Average age 41. 2 applicants, 100% accepted, 2 enrolled. *Degree requirements:* For master's, thesis or alternative. *Entrance requirements:* For master's, GRE General Test or minimum GPA of 3.0. Additional exam requirements/recommendations for international students: Required—TOEFL (minimum score 550 paper-based; 213 computer-based). *Application deadline:* For fall admission, 6/1 for domestic students, 5/15 for international students; for spring admission, 11/1 for domestic students, 10/1 for international students. Applications are processed on a rolling basis. Application fee: $30. *Expenses:* Tuition, state resident: full-time $5,871; part-time $245 per credit hour. Tuition, nonresident: full-time $21,241; part-time $885 per credit hour. *Financial support:* Fellowships, career-related internships or fieldwork, Federal Work-Study, scholarships/grants, and unspecified assistantships available. *Faculty research:* Diagnostic/prescriptive teaching, in-service teacher education, curriculum design and teaching methodology.

University of West Georgia, Graduate School, College of Education, Department of Curriculum and Instruction, Program in Early Childhood Education, Carrollton, GA 30118. Offers M Ed, Ed S. *Accreditation:* NCATE. Part-time and evening/weekend programs available. *Students:* 16 full-time (all women), 83 part-time (77 women); includes 6 minority (all African Americans) Average age 24. In 2006, 41 master's, 6 other advanced degrees awarded. *Degree requirements:* For master's, comprehensive exam; for Ed S, research project. *Entrance requirements:* For master's, GRE General Test or MAT, minimum GPA of 2.7; for Ed S, GRE General Test or MAT, master's degree, minimum graduate GPA of 3.0. *Application deadline:* For fall admission, 8/1 for domestic students. Applications are processed on a rolling basis. Application fee: $20. *Expenses:* Tuition, state resident: full-time $2,286; part-time $127 per credit. Tuition, nonresident: full-time $9,144; part-time $508 per credit. Required fees: $494; $27 per credit. $121 per semester. *Financial support:* In 2006–07, research assistantships with full tuition reimbursements (averaging $3,000 per year); career-related internships or fieldwork and unspecified assistantships also available. Support available to part-time students. Financial award applicants required to submit FAFSA. *Faculty research:* Critical thinking, cultural diversity, curriculum and instruction, character education. *Application contact:* Dr. Charles W. Clark, Chair, 678-839-6508, E-mail: cclark@westga.edu.

University of Wisconsin–Milwaukee, Graduate School, School of Education, Department of Curriculum and Instruction, Milwaukee, WI 53201-0413. Offers curriculum planning and instruction improvement (MS); early childhood education (MS); elementary education (MS); junior high/middle school education (MS); reading education (MS); secondary education (MS); teaching in an urban setting (MS). Part-time programs available. *Faculty:* 27 full-time (17 women). *Students:* 21 full-time (17 women), 67 part-time (54 women); includes 15 minority (8 African Americans, 3 Asian Americans or Pacific Islanders, 4 Hispanic Americans), 3 international. 44 applicants, 43% accepted, 19 enrolled. In 2006, 38 degrees awarded. *Degree requirements:* For master's, thesis or alternative. *Application deadline:* For fall admission, 1/1 priority date for domestic students; for spring admission, 9/1 for domestic students. Applications are processed on a rolling basis. Application fee: $45 ($75 for international students). *Expenses:* Tuition, state resident: part-time $510 per credit. Tuition, nonresident: part-time $1,408 per credit. Tuition and fees vary according to program. *Financial support:* Fellowships, research assistantships, teaching assistantships, career-related internships or fieldwork and unspecified assistantships available. Support available to part-time students. Financial award application deadline: 4/15. *Unit head:* Linda Post, Chair, 414-229-4884, Fax: 414-229-5571, E-mail: lpost@uwm.edu.

University of Wisconsin–Oshkosh, The School of Graduate Studies, College of Education and Human Services, Department of Special Education, Oshkosh, WI 54901. Offers cross-categorical (MSE); early childhood: exceptional education needs (MSE); non-licensure (MSE). *Accreditation:* NCATE. Part-time and evening/weekend programs available. *Degree requirements:* For master's, thesis or alternative, field report, comprehensive exam (for some programs), registration. *Entrance requirements:* For master's, interview, minimum GPA of 3.0, teaching license, letters of recommendation. Additional exam requirements/recommendations for international students: Required—TOEFL (minimum score 550 paper-based; 213 computer-based). Electronic applications accepted. *Faculty research:* Private agency contributions to the disabled, graduation requirements for exceptional education needs students, direct instruction in spelling for learning disabled, effects of behavioral parent training, secondary education programming issues.

Valdosta State University, Graduate School, College of Education, Department of Early Childhood and Reading Education, Valdosta, GA 31698. Offers early childhood education (M Ed, Ed S); reading education (M Ed). *Accreditation:* NCATE. Part-time and evening/weekend programs available. *Degree requirements:* For master's, comprehensive written and/or oral exams; for Ed S, thesis. *Entrance requirements:* For master's and Ed S, GRE General Test or MAT. Additional exam requirements/recommendations for international students: Required—TOEFL (minimum score 523 paper-based; 193 computer-based). Electronic applications accepted.

Vanderbilt University, Peabody College, Department of Teaching and Learning, Nashville, TN 37240-1001. Offers curriculum and instructional leadership (M Ed); early childhood education (M Ed); early childhood leadership (Ed D); elementary education (M Ed); English education (M Ed); English language learners (M Ed); mathematics education (M Ed); reading education (M Ed); science education (M Ed); secondary education (M Ed). *Accreditation:* NCATE. *Faculty:* 23 full-time (13 women), 28 part-time/adjunct (19 women). *Students:* 71 full-time (62 women), 21 part-time (15 women); includes 9 minority (8 African Americans, 1 Hispanic American), 2 international. Average age 27. 102 applicants, 60% accepted, 27 enrolled. In 2006, 53 master's, 3 doctorates awarded. *Degree requirements:* For master's, thesis optional. *Entrance requirements:* For master's, GRE General Test, MAT. Additional exam requirements/recommendations for international students: Required—TOEFL (minimum score 550 paper-based; 213 computer-based). *Application deadline:* For fall admission, 12/31 priority date for domestic and international students; for spring admission, 11/1 priority date for domestic and international students. Applications are processed on a rolling basis. Application fee: $0. Electronic applications accepted. *Expenses:* Tuition: Full-time $24,462. Required fees: $2,515. One-time fee: $30 full-time. Full-time tuition and fees vary according to course load, degree level and program. *Financial support:* In 2006–07, 62 students received support, including 36 fellowships with full and partial tuition reimbursements available, 13 research assistantships with full and partial tuition reimbursements available, 13 teaching assistantships with full and partial tuition reimbursements available; Federal Work-Study, institutionally sponsored loans, scholarships/grants, tuition waivers (partial), and unspecified assistantships also available. Support available to part-time students. Financial award application deadline: 2/1; financial award applicants required to submit FAFSA. *Faculty research:* Teaching and learning; development of subject matter knowledge; learning and policy; development students' mathematical and scientific knowledge, development of literacy. *Unit head:* Leona Schauble, Chair, 615-322-8100, Fax: 615-322-8999, E-mail: leona.schauble@vanderbilt.edu. *Application contact:* Angela Saylor, Educational Coordinator, 615-322-8092, Fax: 615-322-8999.

Virginia Commonwealth University, Graduate School, School of Education, Program in Special Education, Richmond, VA 23284-9005. Offers early childhood (M Ed); emotionally disturbed (M Ed, MT); learning disabilities (M Ed); mentally retarded (M Ed, MT); severely/profoundly handicapped (M Ed). *Accreditation:* NCATE. *Faculty:* 7 full-time (3 women). *Students:* 14 full-time (10 women), 78 part-time (71 women); includes 21 minority (19 African Americans, 2 American Indian/Alaska Native), 1 international. 21 applicants, 100% accepted.

In 2006, 29 degrees awarded. *Degree requirements:* For master's, comprehensive exam. *Entrance requirements:* For master's, GRE General Test or MAT. *Application deadline:* For fall admission, 5/15 for domestic students; for spring admission, 11/15 for domestic students. Applications are processed on a rolling basis. Application fee: $50. *Financial support:* Tuition waivers (partial) available. Financial award application deadline: 3/1. *Unit head:* Dr. John Kregel, Division Head, 804-828-1305. *Application contact:* Dr. Michael D. Davis, Director, Graduate Studies, 804-828-6530, Fax: 804-827-0676, E-mail: mddavis@vcu.edu.

See Close-Up on page 1371.

Virginia Commonwealth University, Graduate School, School of Education, Program in Teaching and Learning, Richmond, VA 23284-9005. Offers early education (MT); middle education (MT); secondary education (MT, Certificate); special education (MT). *Accreditation:* NCATE. Part-time programs available. *Faculty:* 22 full-time (12 women). *Students:* 152 full-time (130 women), 126 part-time (111 women); includes 42 minority (35 African Americans, 2 American Indian/Alaska Native, 4 Asian Americans or Pacific Islanders, 1 Hispanic American), 4 international. 551 applicants, 74% accepted. In 2006, 77 degrees awarded. *Entrance requirements:* For master's, GRE General Test or MAT. *Application deadline:* For fall admission, 5/15 for domestic students; for spring admission, 11/15 for domestic students. Applications are processed on a rolling basis. Application fee: $50. *Financial support:* Application deadline: 3/1. *Unit head:* Dr. Michael D. Davis, Director, Graduate Studies, 804-828-6530, Fax: 804-827-0676, E-mail: mddavis@vcu.edu. *Application contact:* Dr. Michael D. Davis, Director, Graduate Studies, 804-828-6530, Fax: 804-827-0676, E-mail: mddavis@vcu.edu.

See Close-Up on page 1137.

Wagner College, Division of Graduate Studies, Department of Education, Program in Early Childhood Education (Birth-Grade 2), Staten Island, NY 10301-4495. Offers MS Ed. Part-time and evening/weekend programs available. *Students:* 11 full-time (all women), 2 part-time (1 woman); includes 1 minority (Hispanic American) 9 applicants, 100% accepted, 9 enrolled. In 2006, 6 degrees awarded. *Degree requirements:* For master's, thesis. *Entrance requirements:* For master's, minimum GPA of 2.75. Additional exam requirements/recommendations for international students: Required—TOEFL (minimum score 550 paper-based; 217 computer-based). *Application deadline:* For fall admission, 8/1 priority date for domestic students, 10/30 priority date for international students; for spring admission, 12/10 for domestic students, 11/15 for international students. Applications are processed on a rolling basis. Application fee: $50 ($85 for international students). *Expenses:* Tuition: Full-time $15,120; part-time $840 per credit. *Financial support:* Fellowships, tuition waivers (partial) and unspecified assistantships available. Financial award applicants required to submit FAFSA. *Application contact:* Susan Rosenberg, Office of Graduate Studies, 718-390-3106, Fax: 718-390-3456, E-mail: graduate@wagner.edu.

Wayne State College, School of Education and Counseling, Department of Educational Foundations and Leadership, Program in Curriculum and Instruction, Wayne, NE 68787. Offers alternative education (MSE); business education (MSE); communication arts education (MSE); curriculum and instruction (MSE); early childhood education (MSE); elementary education (MSE); English as a second language (MSE); English education (MSE); family consumer science of education (MSE); industrial technology education (MSE); learning communities (MSE); mathematics education (MSE); music education (MSE); science education (MSE); social science education (MSE). *Accreditation:* NCATE. Part-time and evening/weekend programs available. *Faculty:* 17 part-time/adjunct (11 women). *Students:* 17 full-time (10 women), 307 part-time (248 women); includes 6 minority (2 African Americans, 1 American Indian/Alaska Native, 2 Asian Americans or Pacific Islanders, 1 Hispanic American), 1 international. Average age 35. In 2006, 167 degrees awarded. *Degree requirements:* For master's, thesis optional. *Entrance requirements:* For master's, GRE General Test. Additional exam requirements/recommendations for international students: Required—TOEFL (minimum score 550 paper-based; 213 computer-based). *Application deadline:* Applications are processed on a rolling basis. Application fee: $30. *Expenses:* Tuition, state resident: full-time $3,114; part-time $130 per credit hour. Tuition, nonresident: full-time $6,228; part-time $260 per credit hour. Required fees: $894; $37 per credit hour. Tuition and fees vary according to course load. *Financial support:* Applicants required to submit FAFSA.

Wayne State University, College of Education, Division of Teacher Education, Detroit, MI 48202. Offers adult and continuing education (M Ed); art education (M Ed); bilingual/bicultural education (M Ed, MAT); business education (M Ed, MAT); career and technical education (M Ed, Ed D, PhD, Ed S); curriculum and instruction (Ed D, PhD, Ed S); distributive education (M Ed, MAT); early childhood education (M Ed); elementary education (M Ed, MAT, Ed D, PhD, Ed S); elementary education curriculum and instruction (M Ed); English education (M Ed); English education-secondary (M Ed, Ed S); foreign language education (M Ed); general education (Ed D, Ed S); health occupations education (M Ed); industrial education (M Ed); mathematics education (M Ed, Ed S); pre-school and parent education (M Ed); reading (M Ed, Ed D, Ed S); reading, languages and literature (Ed D); school music-vocal (M Ed); science education (M Ed, MAT, Ed S); secondary education (MAT); secondary school reading (M Ed); social studies education (M Ed, Ed S), including education-secondary (M Ed); special education (M Ed, Ed D, PhD, Ed S); teacher education (MAT, Ed D, PhD). *Faculty:* 41 full-time (22 women), 2 part-time/adjunct (both women). *Students:* 401 full-time (295 women), 1,021 part-time (784 women); includes 527 minority (452 African Americans, 6 American Indian/Alaska Native, 32 Asian Americans or Pacific Islanders, 37 Hispanic Americans), 18 international. Average age 36. 296 applicants, 81% accepted, 132 enrolled. In 2006, 386 master's, 1 doctorate awarded. *Degree requirements:* For doctorate, thesis/dissertation. *Entrance requirements:* For master's, minimum GPA of 2.6; for doctorate, minimum undergraduate GPA of 3.0, graduate 3.5; interview. Additional exam requirements/recommendations for international students: Required—TOEFL (minimum score 550 paper-based; 213 computer-based), TWE (minimum score 6). *Application deadline:* For fall admission, 7/1 for domestic students, 6/1 for international students; for winter admission, 10/1 for international students; for spring admission, 2/1 for international students. Application fee: $30 ($50 for international students). Electronic applications accepted. *Financial support:* In 2006–07, 1 fellowship (averaging $34,919 per year) was awarded; research assistantships. *Faculty research:* Reading and writing literacy and literature. Total annual research expenditures: $209,400. *Unit head:* Dr. Joann Snyder, Academic Director, 313-577-1644, E-mail: joanne.snyder@wayne.edu. *Application contact:* Sharon Elliott, Assistant Dean, 313-577-0902, E-mail: sharon.elliott@wayne.edu.

Webster University, School of Education, Department of Communication Arts, Reading and Early Childhood, St. Louis, MO 63119-3194. Offers communications (MAT); early childhood education (MAT). *Students:* 47 full-time (44 women), 166 part-time (154 women); includes 35 minority (30 African Americans, 1 American Indian/Alaska Native, 3 Asian Americans or Pacific Islanders, 1 Hispanic American), 5 international. Average age 33. *Entrance requirements:* For master's, minimum GPA of 2.5. *Application deadline:* Applications are processed on a rolling basis. Application fee: $25 ($50 for international students). *Expenses:* Tuition: Full-time $8,820; part-time $490 per credit. Tuition and fees vary according to degree level, campus/location and program. *Financial support:* Federal Work-Study available. Support available to part-time students. Financial award application deadline: 4/1; financial award applicants required to submit FAFSA. *Unit head:* Phyllis Wilkinson, Chair, 314-968-7096, Fax: 314-968-7118. *Application contact:* Director of Graduate and Evening Student Admissions, Fax: 314-968-7116, E-mail: gadmit@webster.edu.

Wesleyan College, Department of Education, Program in Early Childhood Education, Macon, GA 31210-4462. Offers MA. Part-time programs available. *Faculty:* 4 full-time (3 women), 2 part-time/adjunct (both women). *Students:* 9 full-time (all women), 28 part-time (27 women); includes 13 minority (12 African Americans, 1 Asian American or Pacific Islander), 1 international. Average age 36. 5 applicants, 60% accepted, 3 enrolled. In 2006, 3 degrees awarded. *Degree requirements:* For master's, thesis or alternative, practicum, professional portfolio. *Entrance requirements:* For master's, GRE or MAT, interview, teaching certificate, 3 letters of recommendation. Additional exam requirements/recommendations for international students: Required—TOEFL. *Application deadline:* For fall admission, 7/1 priority date for domestic students; for spring admission, 12/1 priority date for domestic students. Applications are processed on a rolling basis. Application fee: $25. *Expenses:* Tuition: Full-time $14,500. Tuition and fees vary according to program. *Financial support:* Application deadline: 4/1;

Western Kentucky University, Graduate Studies, College of Education and Behavioral Sciences, Department of Special Instructional Programs, Bowling Green, KY 42101. Offers exceptional child education (MAE); interdisciplinary early child education (MAE); library media education (MS); literacy (MAE). Part-time and evening/weekend programs available. Postbaccalaureate distance learning degree programs offered (minimal on-campus study). *Faculty:* 15 full-time (12 women), 1 (woman) part-time/adjunct. *Students:* 38 full-time (35 women), 347 part-time (296 women); includes 18 minority (8 African Americans, 2 American Indian/Alaska Native, 1 Asian American or Pacific Islander, 7 Hispanic Americans), 2 international. Average age 33. 131 applicants, 66% accepted, 57 enrolled. In 2006, 146 degrees awarded. *Degree requirements:* For master's, comprehensive exam. *Entrance requirements:* For master's, GRE General Test. Additional exam requirements/recommendations for international students: Required—TOEFL (minimum score 555 paper-based; 213 computer-based; 79 iBT). *Application deadline:* For fall admission, 7/1 for domestic students, 4/1 for international students; for spring admission, 11/1 for domestic students, 9/1 for international students. Application fee: $35. *Expenses:* Tuition, state resident: full-time $6,520; part-time $226 per hour. Tuition, nonresident: full-time $7,140; part-time $357 per hour. International tuition: $15,820 full-time. *Financial support:* In 2006–07, 2 research assistantships with partial tuition reimbursements (averaging $8,000 per year) were awarded; tuition waivers (partial) and unspecified assistantships also available. *Faculty research:* Teacher preparation in moderate/severe disabilities. Total annual research expenditures: $125,538. *Unit head:* Dr. Sherry Powers, Department Head, 270-745-4607, Fax: 270-745-3441, E-mail: sherry.powers@wku.edu.

Western Michigan University, Graduate College, College of Education, Department of Teaching, Learning, and Leadership, Program in Early Childhood Education, Kalamazoo, MI 49008-5202. Offers MA. *Accreditation:* NCATE.

Western Oregon University, Graduate Programs, College of Education, Division of Teacher Education, Program in Early Childhood Education, Monmouth, OR 97361-1394. Offers MS Ed. *Accreditation:* NCATE. Part-time and evening/weekend programs available. *Faculty:* 1 full-time (0 women), 1 (woman) part-time/adjunct. *Students:* 1 (woman) full-time, 4 part-time (all women). Average age 34. In 2006, 2 degrees awarded. *Degree requirements:* For master's, written exam, thesis optional. *Entrance requirements:* For master's, minimum GPA of 3.0, teaching license. *Application deadline:* Applications are processed on a rolling basis. Application fee: $50. *Expenses:* Tuition, state resident: full-time $8,250; part-time $250 per credit. Tuition, nonresident: full-time $14,025; part-time $250 per credit. Required fees: $1,173. *Financial support:* Research assistantships with full tuition reimbursements, teaching assistantships with full tuition reimbursements, career-related internships or fieldwork, Federal Work-Study, and tuition waivers (full and partial) available. Support available to part-time students. Financial award application deadline: 3/1; financial award applicants required to submit FAFSA. *Faculty research:* High school through university articulation, career development for early childhood educators professional collaboration/cooperation. *Unit head:* Dr. Michelle Pardew, Coordinator, 503-838-8765, Fax: 503-838-8228. *Application contact:* Dr. David McDonald, Dean of Admissions, Retention and Enrollment Management, 503-838-8919, Fax: 503-838-8067, E-mail: mcdonald@wou.edu.

Westfield State College, Division of Graduate and Continuing Education, Department of Education, Program in Early Childhood Education, Westfield, MA 01086. Offers M Ed. *Accreditation:* NCATE. Part-time and evening/weekend programs available. *Degree requirements:* For master's, practicum. *Entrance requirements:* For master's, GRE General Test or MAT, minimum undergraduate GPA of 2.7.

West Virginia University, College of Human Resources and Education, Department of Special Education, Morgantown, WV 26506. Offers autism spectrum disorder (5-adult) (Ed D); autism spectrum disorder (K-6) (Ed D); early intervention (preschool) (MA); early intervention/early childhood special education (MA); gifted education (1-12) (MA); multicategorical special education (5-adult) (Ed D); multicategorical special education (K-6) (Ed D); severe/multiple disabilities (K-adult) (MA); special education (Ed D); vision impairments (PreK-adult) (Ed D). *Accreditation:* NCATE. Part-time and evening/weekend programs available. Postbaccalaureate distance learning degree programs offered (no on-campus study). *Faculty:* 5 full-time (4 women), 2 part-time/adjunct (both women). *Students:* 57 full-time (43 women), 193 part-time (159 women); includes 14 minority (8 African Americans, 1 American Indian/Alaska Native, 1 Asian American or Pacific Islander, 4 Hispanic Americans), 1 international. Average age 36. 119 applicants, 68% accepted, 44 enrolled. In 2006, 100 master's, 2 doctorates awarded. *Degree requirements:* For master's, thesis optional; for doctorate, thesis/dissertation, comprehensive exam, registration. *Entrance requirements:* For master's, minimum GPA of 2.75; for doctorate, GRE General Test or MAT. Additional exam requirements/recommendations for international students: Required—TOEFL. *Application deadline:* Applications are processed on a rolling basis. Application fee: $50. *Expenses:* Tuition, state resident: full-time $4,926; part-time $276 per credit hour. Tuition, nonresident: full-time $14,278; part-time $796 per credit hour. Tuition and fees vary according to program. *Financial support:* In 2006–07, 91 students received support, including 1 research assistantship with full tuition reimbursement available; teaching assistantships, career-related internships or fieldwork, Federal Work-Study, institutionally sponsored loans, tuition waivers (partial), and graduate resident hall assistantships also available. Financial award application deadline: 2/1; financial award applicants required to submit FAFSA. *Unit head:* Dr. Barbara Ludlow, Professor, 304-293-3450 Ext. 1127, Fax: 304-293-6834, E-mail: barbara.ludlow@mail.wvu.edu. *Application contact:* Sherilyn A. Bunner, Program Coordinator, 304-293-7143, Fax: 304-293-6834, E-mail: sherry.bunner@mail.wvu.edu.

Wheelock College, Graduate Programs, Division of Education, Boston, MA 02215-4176. Offers early childhood education (MS); education leadership (MS); elementary education (MS); language, literacy, and reading (MS); teaching students with moderate disabilities (MS). *Accreditation:* NCATE. Postbaccalaureate distance learning degree programs offered (minimal on-campus study). *Degree requirements:* For master's, comprehensive exam. *Entrance requirements:* Additional exam requirements/recommendations for international students: Required—TOEFL. Electronic applications accepted. *Faculty research:* Symbolic learning, emergent literacy, diversity inclusion, beginning reading language and culture, math education.

Widener University, School of Human Service Professions, Center for Education, Chester, PA 19013-5792. Offers adult education (M Ed); counseling in higher education (M Ed); counselor education (M Ed); early childhood education (M Ed); educational foundations (M Ed); educational leadership (M Ed); educational psychology (M Ed); elementary education (M Ed); English and language arts (M Ed); health education (M Ed); higher education leadership (Ed D); home and school visitor (M Ed); human sexuality (M Ed); mathematics education (M Ed); middle school education (M Ed); principalship (M Ed); reading and language arts (Ed D); reading education (M Ed); school administration (Ed D); science education (M Ed); social studies education (M Ed); special education (M Ed); technology education (M Ed). Part-time and evening/weekend programs available. Terminal master's awarded for partial completion of doctoral program. *Degree requirements:* For doctorate, thesis/dissertation. *Entrance requirements:* For master's, minimum GPA of 2.5; for doctorate, GRE or MAT, minimum GPA of 2.0 (undergraduate), 3.5 (graduate). Electronic applications accepted. Expenses: Contact institution. *Faculty research:* Reading and cognition, adult education, technology education, educational leadership, special education.

Worcester State College, Graduate Studies, Department of Education, Concentration in Early Childhood Education, Worcester, MA 01602-2597. Offers M Ed. *Students:* Average age 37. 6 applicants, 33% accepted, 1 enrolled. In 2006, 10 degrees awarded. *Degree requirements:* For master's, thesis optional. *Entrance requirements:* For master's, GRE General Test or MAT,

Early Childhood Education

Worcester State College (continued)
teaching certificate. Additional exam requirements/recommendations for international students: Required—TOEFL (minimum score 550 paper-based; 213 computer-based). *Application deadline:* For fall admission, 3/1 for domestic and international students. Application fee: $30. *Expenses:* Tuition, state resident: full-time $4,518; part-time $251 per credit hour. Tuition, nonresident: full-time $4,518; part-time $251 per credit hour. *Financial support:* Career-related internships or fieldwork, Federal Work-Study, institutionally sponsored loans, scholarships/grants, and unspecified assistantships available. Support available to part-time students. Financial award application deadline: 3/1; financial award applicants required to submit FAFSA. *Unit head:* Dr. Carol Donnelly, Coordinator, 508-929-8667, Fax: 508-929-8164, E-mail: cdonnelly@worcester.edu. *Application contact:* Nicole Brown, Assistant Dean of Graduate and Continuing Education, 508-929-8787, Fax: 508-929-8100, E-mail: nbrown@worcester.edu.

Wright State University, School of Graduate Studies, College of Education and Human Services, Department of Teacher Education, Program in Early Childhood Education, Dayton, OH 45435. Offers M Ed, MA. *Accreditation:* NCATE. *Students:* Average age 37. 8 applicants, 100% accepted. In 2006, 14 degrees awarded. *Degree requirements:* For master's, thesis (for some programs). *Entrance requirements:* For master's, GRE General Test, MAT. Additional exam requirements/recommendations for international students: Required—TOEFL. Application fee: $25. *Financial support:* Available to part-time students. Applicants required to submit FAFSA. *Unit head:* Dr. Deborah Hess, Program Advisor, 937-775-2024, Fax: 937-775-3308, E-mail: deborah.hess@wright.edu. *Application contact:* John Kimble, Associate Director of Graduate Admissions and Records, 937-775-2957, Fax: 937-775-2453, E-mail: john.kimble@wright.edu.

Xavier University, College of Social Sciences, Health and Education, School of Education, Montessori Program, Cincinnati, OH 45207. Offers M Ed. Part-time and evening/weekend programs available. *Faculty:* 3 full-time (all women), 20 part-time/adjunct (18 women). *Students:* 33 full-time (31 women), 38 part-time (37 women); includes 14 minority (11 African Americans, 2 Asian Americans or Pacific Islanders, 1 Hispanic American), 2 international. Average age 35. 24 applicants, 79% accepted, 17 enrolled. In 2006, 20 degrees awarded. *Degree requirements:* For master's, research project. *Entrance requirements:* For master's, MAT or GRE, minimum GPA of 2.7. Additional exam requirements/recommendations for international students: Required—TOEFL (minimum score 550 paper-based; 213 computer-based). *Application deadline:* For fall admission, 8/15 priority date for domestic students. Applications are processed on a rolling basis. Application fee: $35. Electronic applications accepted. *Expenses:* Tuition: Part-time $462 per credit hour. Part-time tuition and fees vary according to degree level, campus/location and program. *Financial support:* Career-related internships or fieldwork, scholarships/grants, and unspecified assistantships available. Support available to part-time students. Financial award applicants required to submit FAFSA. *Faculty research:* Montessori in junior high and high school, peace education, public school/standards versus Montessori curriculum, parent education, multiple age groupings. *Unit head:* Elizabeth Bronsil, Director, 513-745-3424, Fax: 513-745-4378, E-mail: bronsile@xavier.edu. *Application contact:* Roger Bosse, Interim Director of Graduate Studies, 513-745-3357, Fax: 513-745-1048, E-mail: bosse@xavier.edu.

Youngstown State University, Graduate School, College of Education, Department of Teacher Education, Program in Early and Middle Childhood Education, Youngstown, OH 44555-0001. Offers teaching—elementary education (MS Ed); teaching—secondary reading (MS Ed). *Accreditation:* NCATE. Part-time and evening/weekend programs available. *Degree requirements:* For master's, comprehensive exam. *Entrance requirements:* For master's, GRE, MAT, or teaching certificate; minimum GPA of 2.7. Additional exam requirements/recommendations for international students: Required—TOEFL.

Elementary Education

Adelphi University, School of Education, Program in Childhood Education, Garden City, NY 11530-0701. Offers elementary teachers pre K-6 (MA); grades 1-6 (MA). Part-time and evening/weekend programs available. *Students:* 92 full-time (87 women), 99 part-time (87 women); includes 26 minority (9 African Americans, 5 Asian Americans or Pacific Islanders, 12 Hispanic Americans). Average age 29. In 2006, 143 degrees awarded. *Entrance requirements:* For master's, 2 letters of recommendation, resumé. Additional exam requirements/recommendations for international students: Required—TOEFL (minimum score 550 paper-based; 213 computer-based). *Application deadline:* For fall admission, 4/1 priority date for domestic students; for spring admission, 11/1 priority date for domestic students. Application fee: $50. Electronic applications accepted. *Financial support:* Fellowships, research assistantships with partial tuition reimbursements, teaching assistantships, career-related internships or fieldwork, Federal Work-Study, institutionally sponsored loans, and tuition waivers (full) available. Support available to part-time students. Financial award application deadline: 2/15; financial award applicants required to submit FAFSA. *Faculty research:* Diversity; parental involvement; teacher education; psychoanalytic understanding of racial formation; relationships between ideology, language, culture and individual subject formation. *Unit head:* Dr. Renee White-Clark, Director, 516-877-4397, E-mail: whiteclark@adelphi.edu. *Application contact:* Christine Murphy, Director of Admissions, 516-877-3050, Fax: 516-877-3039, E-mail: graduateadmissions@adelphi.edu.

Alabama Agricultural and Mechanical University, School of Graduate Studies, School of Education, Department of Curriculum and Instruction, Area in Elementary and Early Childhood Education, Huntsville, AL 35811. Offers early childhood education (MS Ed, Ed S); elementary education (MS Ed, Ed S). *Accreditation:* NCATE. Evening/weekend programs available. *Faculty:* 3 full-time (all women), 3 part-time/adjunct (all women). *Students:* 4 full-time (all women), 18 part-time (all women); includes 12 minority (all African Americans) In 2006, 35 degrees awarded. *Degree requirements:* For master's, comprehensive exam; for Ed S, thesis. *Entrance requirements:* For master's, GRE General Test. *Application deadline:* For fall admission, 5/1 for domestic students. Applications are processed on a rolling basis. Application fee: $25. Electronic applications accepted. *Financial support:* In 2006–07, 2 research assistantships with tuition reimbursements (averaging $5,300 per year) were awarded; career-related internships or fieldwork also available. Financial award application deadline: 4/1. *Faculty research:* Multicultural education, learning styles, diagnostic-prescriptive instruction. *Unit head:* Dr. June Young, Head, 256-372-7272.

Alabama State University, School of Graduate Studies, College of Education, Department of Curriculum and Instruction, Program in Elementary Education, Montgomery, AL 36101-0271. Offers M Ed, Ed S. Part-time programs available. *Students:* 22 full-time (18 women), 149 part-time (131 women); includes 117 minority (116 African Americans, 1 Hispanic American), 1 international. In 2006, 21 degrees awarded. *Degree requirements:* For master's, thesis optional; for Ed S, thesis, comprehensive exam. *Entrance requirements:* For master's, GRE General Test, MAT, graduate writing competency test; for Ed S, graduate writing competency test, GRE, MAT. Additional exam requirements/recommendations for international students: Required—TOEFL (minimum score 500 paper-based; 173 computer-based). *Application deadline:* For fall admission, 7/15 for domestic students; for spring admission, 12/15 for domestic students. Applications are processed on a rolling basis. Application fee: $10. *Expenses:* Tuition, state resident: full-time $1,728; part-time $192 per hour. Tuition, nonresident: full-time $3,456; part-time $334 per hour. *Unit head:* Dr. Daniel Lucas, Coordinator, 334-229-4167, Fax: 334-229-4904, E-mail: dlucas@alasu.edu. *Application contact:* Dr. Allen Stewart, Chair, 334-229-6882, Fax: 334-229-6904, E-mail: astewart@alasu.edu.

Alaska Pacific University, Graduate Programs, Education Department, Program in Teaching, Anchorage, AK 99508-4672. Offers teaching (K-8) (MAT). *Faculty:* 3 full-time (2 women). *Students:* 10 full-time (8 women), 1 (woman) part-time. Average age 34. In 2006, 7 degrees awarded. *Degree requirements:* For master's, research project. *Entrance requirements:* For master's, GRE or MAT, PRAXIS, minimum GPA of 3.0. *Application deadline:* For fall admission, 4/15 for domestic students; for spring admission, 12/15 for domestic students. Applications are processed on a rolling basis. Application fee: $25. *Expenses:* Tuition: Part-time $550 per credit hour. Required fees: $100 per semester. Tuition and fees vary according to program. *Financial support:* Research assistantships, teaching assistantships, career-related internships or fieldwork and Federal Work-Study available. Support available to part-time students. Financial award application deadline: 4/15; financial award applicants required to submit FAFSA. *Unit head:* Dr. Theodore Munsch, Director, 907-564-8258, Fax: 907-564-8317, E-mail: edted@alaskapacific.edu. *Application contact:* Michael Warner, Director of Admissions, 907-564-8248, Fax: 907-564-8317, E-mail: mikew@alaskapacific.edu.

Albright College, Department of Education—Graduate Division, Reading, PA 19612-5234. Offers early childhood education (MS); elementary education (MS); English as a second language (MA); general education (MA); special education (MS). Part-time and evening/weekend programs available. *Degree requirements:* For master's, thesis. *Entrance requirements:* For master's, GRE General Test or MAT, minimum undergraduate GPA of 3.0, 2 letters of recommendation, interview. Additional exam requirements/recommendations for international students: Recommended—TOEFL (minimum score 525 paper-based; 197 computer-based). Electronic applications accepted.

Alcorn State University, School of Graduate Studies, School of Psychology and Education, Alcorn State, MS 39096-7500. Offers agricultural education (MS Ed); elementary education (MS Ed, Ed S); guidance and counseling (MS Ed); industrial education (MS Ed); secondary education (MS Ed), including health and physical education; special education (MS Ed). *Accreditation:* NCATE. *Faculty:* 14 full-time (9 women), 21 part-time/adjunct (13 women). *Students:* 76 full-time (44 women), 271 part-time (226 women); includes 333 minority (all African Americans) In 2006, 119 degrees awarded. *Degree requirements:* For master's, thesis optional. *Application deadline:* For fall admission, 7/15 priority date for domestic students; for spring admission, 11/25 for domestic students. Applications are processed on a rolling basis. Application fee: $0 ($10 for international students). *Financial support:* Career-related internships or fieldwork available. Support available to part-time students. *Unit head:* Dr. Josephine M. Posey, Dean, 601-877-6141, Fax: 601-877-3867.

American International College, School of Psychology and Education, Department of Education, Springfield, MA 01109-3189. Offers administration (M Ed, CAGS); child development (MA, Ed D), including educational psychology; elementary education (M Ed, CAGS); reading (M Ed, CAGS); secondary education (M Ed, CAGS); special education (M Ed, CAGS); teaching (MAT). Part-time and evening/weekend programs available. *Faculty:* 5 full-time (3 women), 15 part-time/adjunct (9 women). *Students:* 31 full-time (27 women), 268 part-time (217 women); includes 25 minority (13 African Americans, 4 Asian Americans or Pacific Islanders, 8 Hispanic Americans), 2 international. Average age 39. In 2006, 38 master's, 2 doctorates, 5 other advanced degrees awarded. Terminal master's awarded for partial completion of doctoral program. *Degree requirements:* For master's, thesis (for some programs), practicum, comprehensive exam (for some programs), registration; for doctorate, thesis/dissertation, comprehensive exam (for some programs), registration; for CAGS, practicum. *Entrance requirements:* For master's, minimum B- average in undergraduate course work; for doctorate, GRE General Test, interview. Additional exam requirements/recommendations for international students: Required—TOEFL. *Application deadline:* For fall admission, 7/1 priority date for domestic and international students; for spring admission, 12/1 priority date for domestic and international students. Applications are processed on a rolling basis. Application fee: $50. *Expenses:* Tuition: Part-time $585 per semester hour. Required fees: $100 per year. Full-time tuition and fees vary according to program. *Financial support:* Career-related internships or fieldwork and institutionally sponsored loans available. Financial award applicants required to submit FAFSA. *Unit head:* Dr. Barbara Dautrich, Chair, 413-205-3407, Fax: 413-205-3943, E-mail: barbara.dautrich@aic.edu. *Application contact:* Keshawn Dodds, Associate Director of Graduate Admissions, 413-205-3549, Fax: 413-205-3911, E-mail: keshawn.dodds@aic.edu.

American University, College of Arts and Sciences, School of Education, Teaching, and Health, Program in Elementary Education, Washington, DC 20016-8001. Offers MAT, Certificate. *Students:* 12 full-time (all women), 122 part-time (101 women); includes 38 minority (31 African Americans, 1 Asian American or Pacific Islander, 6 Hispanic Americans). Average age 28. In 2006, 73 master's, 3 other advanced degrees awarded. *Degree requirements:* For master's, PRAXIS II. *Entrance requirements:* For master's, GRE General Test or MAT, minimum GPA of 3.0. *Application deadline:* For fall admission, 2/1 priority date for domestic students; for spring admission, 10/1 priority date for domestic students. Applications are processed on a rolling basis. Application fee: $50. *Expenses:* Tuition: Full-time $18,864; part-time $1,048 per credit. Required fees: $380. Tuition and fees vary according to program. *Financial support:* Research assistantships with partial tuition reimbursements available. Financial award application deadline: 2/1.

American University of Puerto Rico, Program in Education, Bayamón, PR 00960-2037. Offers art history (M Ed); elementary education (4-6) (M Ed); elementary education (k-3) (M Ed); general science education (M Ed); physical education (k-12) (M Ed); special education at secondary level (transition) (M Ed). *Entrance requirements:* For master's, EXADEP or GRE or MAT, 2 letters of recommendation, minimum GPA of 2.5.

Andrews University, School of Graduate Studies, School of Education, Department of Teaching, Learning, and Curriculum, Berrien Springs, MI 49104. Offers curriculum and instruction (MA, Ed D, PhD, Ed S); elementary education (MAT); reading (MA); secondary education (MAT), including biology, education, English, English as a second language, French, history, physics; special education/learning disabilities (MS); teacher education (MAT). *Entrance requirements:* For master's, GRE Subject Test.

Anna Maria College, Graduate Division, Program in Education, Paxton, MA 01612. Offers early childhood development (M Ed); education (CAGS); elementary education (M Ed); reading (M Ed). Part-time and evening/weekend programs available. *Faculty:* 6 full-time (5 women), 16 part-time/adjunct (15 women). *Students:* 13 full-time (all women), 84 part-time (82 women); includes 1 minority (Hispanic American) Average age 34. In 2006, 30 master's, 2 other advanced degrees awarded. *Degree requirements:* For master's, action research project. *Entrance requirements:* For master's, bachelor's degree in liberal arts or sciences, minimum GPA of 3.0. *Application deadline:* For fall admission, 3/1 priority date for domestic and international students; for spring admission, 11/1 priority date for domestic and international students. Applications are processed on a rolling basis. Application fee: $40. Electronic applications accepted. *Financial support:* Applicants required to submit FAFSA. *Unit head:* Christine

Holmes, Director, 508-849-3418, Fax: 508-849-3343, E-mail: cholmes@annamaria.edu. *Application contact:* Janet LaPointe, Admissions Coordinator, Graduate and Continuing Education, 508-849-3234, Fax: 508-819-3362, E-mail: jlapointe@annamaria.edu.

Appalachian State University, Cratis D. Williams Graduate School, College of Education, Department of Curriculum and Instruction, Boone, NC 28608. Offers curriculum specialist (MA); educational media (MA); elementary education (MA); secondary education (MA). *Accreditation:* NCATE. Part-time and evening/weekend programs available. Postbaccalaureate distance learning degree programs offered (minimal on-campus study). *Faculty:* 32 full-time (21 women). *Students:* 7 full-time (5 women), 206 part-time (172 women); includes 2 minority (both African Americans), 2 international. 100 applicants, 97% accepted, 95 enrolled. In 2006, 96 degrees awarded. *Degree requirements:* For master's, thesis or alternative, comprehensive exam, registration. *Entrance requirements:* For master's, GRE General Test or MAT. Additional exam requirements/recommendations for international students: Required—TOEFL (minimum score 570 paper-based; 230 computer-based). *Application deadline:* For fall admission, 7/1 priority date for domestic students, 1/1 for international students; for spring admission, 11/1 for domestic students, 6/1 for international students. Application fee: $50. *Expenses:* Tuition, state resident: full-time $2,600; part-time $127 per hour. Tuition, nonresident: full-time $13,200; part-time $597 per hour. Required fees: $2,000; $546 per term. *Financial support:* In 2006–07, 6 teaching assistantships (averaging $7,000 per year) were awarded; fellowships, research assistantships, career-related internships or fieldwork, Federal Work-Study, scholarships/grants, and unspecified assistantships also available. Support available to part-time students. Financial award application deadline: 7/1; financial award applicants required to submit FAFSA. Total annual research expenditures: $366,043. *Unit head:* Dr. Michael Jacobson, Chairperson, 828-262-2224.

Arcadia University, Graduate Studies, Department of Education, Glenside, PA 19038-3295. Offers art education (M Ed, MA Ed); biology education (MA Ed); chemistry education (MA Ed); child development (CAS); computer education (M Ed, CAS); computer education 7–12 (MA Ed); early childhood education (M Ed, CAS), including individualized (M Ed), master teacher (M Ed), research in child development (M Ed); educational leadership (M Ed, CAS); educational psychology (CAS); elementary education (M Ed, CAS); English education (MA Ed); environmental education (MA Ed, CAS); history education (MA Ed); language arts (M Ed, CAS); mathematics education (M Ed, MA Ed, CAS); music education (MA Ed); psychology (MA Ed); pupil personnel services (CAS); reading (M Ed, CAS); school library science (M Ed); science education (M Ed, CAS); secondary education (M Ed, CAS); special education (M Ed, Ed D, CAS); theater arts (MA Ed); written communication (MA Ed). *Accreditation:* NASAD. Part-time and evening/weekend programs available. Postbaccalaureate distance learning degree programs offered (minimal on-campus study). *Faculty:* 12 full-time (8 women), 38 part-time/adjunct (26 women). *Students:* 60 full-time (56 women), 419 part-time (324 women); includes 70 minority (57 African Americans, 1 American Indian/Alaska Native, 6 Asian Americans or Pacific Islanders, 6 Hispanic Americans), 1 international. In 2006, 257 master's, 4 doctorates awarded. *Application deadline:* Applications are processed on a rolling basis. Application fee: $35. Electronic applications accepted. *Financial support:* Career-related internships or fieldwork, tuition waivers (partial), and unspecified assistantships available. *Unit head:* Dr. Steven P. Gulkus, Chair, 215-572-2120. *Application contact:* 215-572-2925, Fax: 215-572-2126, E-mail: grad@arcadia.edu.

Argosy University, Atlanta Campus, College of Education, Atlanta, GA 30328. Offers educational leadership (MAEd, Ed D, Ed S), including higher education administration (Ed D), k-12 administration (Ed D); instructional leadership (MAEd, Ed D, Ed S), including higher education (Ed D), K-12 education (Ed D). Evening/weekend programs available. *Students:* 459 full-time (377 women), 324 part-time (255 women); includes 388 minority (335 African Americans, 10 American Indian/Alaska Native, 14 Asian Americans or Pacific Islanders, 29 Hispanic Americans). *Entrance requirements:* For master's and doctorate, 3 letters of recommendation, minimum GPA of 3.0, resumé. Additional exam requirements/recommendations for international students: Required—TOEFL (minimum score 550 paper-based; 213 computer-based). *Application deadline:* For fall admission, 8/1 for domestic students; for spring admission, 10/1 for domestic students. Application fee: $50. *Financial support:* Teaching assistantships, Federal Work-Study available. *Unit head:* Jacqueline Jenkins, Department Chair, 770-407-1067, Fax: 770-671-0476, E-mail: jbeard@argosy.edu. *Application contact:* Christa Holton, Director of Admissions, 770-671-1200, Fax: 770-671-9050, E-mail: inquiry@argosy.edu.

See Close-Up on page 1101.

Argosy University, Chicago Campus, College of Education, Chicago, IL 60603. Offers community college executive leadership (Ed D); educational leadership (MA Ed, Ed D, Ed S), including administrative certification (MA Ed), district leadership (Ed D), higher education administration (Ed D), K-12 education (Ed D), principal/general (MA Ed), superintendent certification (Ed S); instructional leadership (MA Ed, Ed D, Ed S), including higher education (Ed D), K-12 education (Ed D). Part-time and evening/weekend programs available. *Faculty:* 3 full-time (1 woman), 7 part-time/adjunct (0 women). *Students:* 116 full-time (96 women), 42 part-time (32 women); includes 112 minority (108 African Americans, 1 Asian American or Pacific Islander, 3 Hispanic Americans). Average age 45. 56 applicants, 84% accepted, 45 enrolled. In 2006, 4 master's, 10 doctorates awarded. *Entrance requirements:* For master's and doctorate, minimum GPA of 3.0. Additional exam requirements/recommendations for international students: Required—TOEFL (minimum score 550 paper-based; 213 computer-based). *Application deadline:* For fall admission, 2/28 for domestic and international students; for spring admission, 10/30 for domestic and international students. Applications are processed on a rolling basis. Application fee: $50. Electronic applications accepted. *Financial support:* In 2006–07, 35 students received support. Scholarships/grants available. Financial award application deadline: 4/1. *Unit head:* Dr. Paul Busceni, Head, 800-626-4123, Fax: 312-777-7750, E-mail: pbusceni@argosy.edu. *Application contact:* Ashley Delaney, Director of Admissions, 800-626-4123, Fax: 312-777-7750, E-mail: argosyadmissions@argosy.edu.

See Close-Up on page 825.

Argosy University, Denver Campus, College of Education, Denver, CO 80203. Offers educational leadership (MA Ed, Ed D), including higher education adminstration (Ed D), K-12 education (Ed D); instructional leadership (MA Ed, Ed D), including higher education (Ed D), K-12 education (Ed D).

See Close-Up on page 829.

Argosy University, Hawai'i Campus, College of Education, Honolulu, HI 96813. Offers educational leadership (MAEd, Ed D), including higher education administration (Ed D), K-12 education (Ed D); instructional leadership (MAEd, Ed D), including higher education (Ed D), K-12 education (Ed D). *Faculty:* 9 part-time/adjunct (4 women). *Students:* 26 full-time (18 women), 4 part-time (all women); includes 16 minority (13 Asian Americans or Pacific Islanders, 3 Hispanic Americans). 17 applicants, 94% accepted, 14 enrolled. *Degree requirements:* For doctorate, thesis/dissertation. *Entrance requirements:* Additional exam requirements/recommendations for international students: Required—TOEFL (minimum score 550 paper-based; 214 computer-based). *Application deadline:* For fall admission, 1/15 priority date for domestic students; for spring admission, 10/15 for domestic students. Applications are processed on a rolling basis. Application fee: $50. Electronic applications accepted. *Unit head:* Dr. Kristine Lesperance, Chair, 888-323-2777, Fax: 808-536-5505, E-mail: klesperance@argosy.edu. *Application contact:* Cherie Andrade, Director of Admissions, 888-323-2777, Fax: 808-536-5505, E-mail: candrade@argosy.edu.

See Close-Up on page 831.

Argosy University, Inland Empire Campus, College of Education, San Bernardino, CA 92408. Offers community college executive leadership (Ed D); educational leadership (MA Ed, Ed D), including higher education administration (Ed D), K-12 education (Ed D); instructional leadership (MA Ed, Ed D), including higher education (Ed D), K-12 education (Ed D), multiple subject teacher credential preparation (MA Ed), multiple subject teacher credntial preparation with BCLAD (MA Ed), single subject teacher credential preparation (MA Ed), single subject teacher credential preparation with BCLAD (MA Ed).

See Close-Up on page 1103.

Argosy University, Nashville Campus, College of Education, Program in Educational Leadership, Franklin, TN 37067-7226. Offers educational leadership (MA Ed); higher education administration (Ed D); K-12 education (Ed D).

See Close-Up on page 1105.

Argosy University, Nashville Campus, College of Education, Program in Instructional Leadership, Franklin, TN 37067-7226. Offers higher education administration (Ed D); instructional leadership (MA Ed); K-12 education (Ed D).

Argosy University, Orange County Campus, College of Education, Santa Ana, CA 92704. Offers community college executive leadership (Ed D); educational leadership (MA Ed, Ed D), including higher education administration (Ed D), K-12 education (Ed D); instructional leadership (MA Ed, Ed D), including educational technology (Ed D), higher education (Ed D), K-12 education (Ed D), multiple subject teacher credential preparation (MA Ed), multiple subject teacher credential preparation with BCLAD (MA Ed), single subject teacher credential preparation (MA Ed), single subject teacher credential preparation with BCLAD (MA Ed). Part-time and evening/weekend programs available. *Faculty:* 3 full-time (2 women), 33 part-time/adjunct (15 women). *Students:* 185 full-time (112 women), 49 part-time (28 women). Average age 37. 91 applicants, 76 enrolled. In 2006, 58 master's, 17 doctorates awarded. Terminal master's awarded for partial completion of doctoral program. *Degree requirements:* For master's, comprehensive exam; for doctorate, thesis/dissertation, preliminary and final dissertation defense, comprehensive exam. *Entrance requirements:* For master's, minimum GPA of 3.0 in final 2 years of course work, 3 letters of recommendation, resumé; for doctorate, minimum GPA of 3.0 in graduate study, 3 letters of recommendation, resumé. Additional exam requirements/recommendations for international students: Required—TOEFL. *Application deadline:* Applications are processed on a rolling basis. Application fee: $50. Electronic applications accepted. *Financial support:* Federal Work-Study and scholarships/grants available. Support available to part-time students. Financial award applicants required to submit FAFSA. *Faculty research:* Educational leadership, higher education, qualitative research, K-12 education, multicultural education. *Unit head:* Dr. Christine Zeppos, Dean, 800-7196-9598, Fax: 714-437-1287, E-mail: czeppos@argosy.edu. *Application contact:* Mark Betz, Director of Admissions, 800-716-9598, Fax: 714-437-1697, E-mail: mbetz@argosy.edu.

See Close-Up on page 833.

Argosy University, Phoenix Campus, College of Education, Phoenix, AZ 85021. Offers community college executive leadership (Ed D); educational leadership (MA Ed, Ed D, Ed S), including higher education administration (Ed D), K-12 education (Ed D); instructional leadership (MA Ed, Ed D, Ed S), including higher education (Ed D), K-12 education (Ed D). Part-time and evening/weekend programs available. *Faculty:* 13 part-time/adjunct (4 women). *Students:* 26 full-time (17 women), 2 part-time (1 woman); includes 3 minority (2 African Americans, 1 Hispanic American). Average age 44. 10 applicants, 100% accepted, 9 enrolled. *Entrance requirements:* For doctorate, minimum GPA of 3.0, master's degree. Additional exam requirements/recommendations for international students: Required—TOEFL (minimum score 550 paper-based; 213 computer-based). *Application deadline:* Applications are processed on a rolling basis. Application fee: $50. Electronic applications accepted. *Financial support:* Federal Work-Study available. Financial award applicants required to submit FAFSA. *Unit head:* Dr. Gayle Schou, Director, 866-216-2777, E-mail: argosyadmissions@argosy.edu. *Application contact:* Andy Hughes, Director of Admissions, 866-216-2777, Fax: 602-216-2601, E-mail: ahughes@argosy.edu.

See Close-Up on page 835.

Argosy University, San Diego Campus, College of Education, San Diego, CA 92108. Offers community college executive leadership (Ed D); educational leadership (MA Ed, Ed D), including higher education administration (Ed D), K-12 education (Ed D); instructional leadership (MA Ed, Ed D), including higher education (Ed D), K-12 education (Ed D), multiple subject teacher credential preparation (MA Ed), multiple subject teacher credential preparation with BCLAD (MA Ed), single subject teacher credential preparation (MA Ed), single subject teacher credential preparation with BCLAD (MA Ed).

See Close-Up on page 837.

Argosy University, San Francisco Bay Area Campus, College of Education, Point Richmond, CA 94804-3547. Offers community college executive leadership (Ed D); educational leadership (MA Ed, Ed D), including higher education administration (Ed D), K–12 education (Ed D); instructional leadership (MA Ed, Ed D), including higher education (Ed D), K–12 education (Ed D), multiple subject teacher credential preparation (MA Ed), multiple subject teacher credential preparation with BCLAD (MA Ed), single subject teacher credential preparation (MA Ed), single subject teacher credential preparation with BCLAD (MA Ed). Part-time and evening/weekend programs available. Postbaccalaureate distance learning degree programs offered (minimal on-campus study). *Faculty:* 1 (woman) full-time, 14 part-time/adjunct. *Students:* 59 full-time (41 women), 30 part-time (14 women); includes 26 minority (11 African Americans, 11 Asian Americans or Pacific Islanders, 4 Hispanic Americans), 1 international. 34 applicants, 82% accepted, 20 enrolled. In 2006, 7 degrees awarded. *Degree requirements:* For master's, capstone project; for doctorate, thesis/dissertation, comprehensive exam, registration. *Entrance requirements:* For master's and doctorate, minimum GPA of 3.0. Additional exam requirements/recommendations for international students: Required—TOEFL (minimum score 550 paper-based; 213 computer-based). *Application deadline:* For fall admission, 7/1 priority date for domestic students, 7/1 for international students; for winter admission, 11/1 priority date for domestic and international students; for spring admission, 4/1 priority date for domestic and international students. Applications are processed on a rolling basis. Application fee: $50. Electronic applications accepted. *Financial support:* Career-related internships or fieldwork, Federal Work-Study, and scholarships/grants available. Support available to part-time students. Financial award application deadline: 4/20; financial award applicants required to submit FAFSA. *Unit head:* Dr. Keyes Kelly, 510-837-3740, E-mail: kkelly@argosy.edu. *Application contact:* John Vincent Stofan, Director, Admissions, 510-215-0277, Fax: 510-215-0299, E-mail: jstofan@argosy.edu.

See Close-Up on page 839.

Argosy University, Santa Monica Campus, College of Education, Santa Monica, CA 90405. Offers community college executive leadership (Ed D); educational leadership (MA Ed, Ed D), including higher education administration (Ed D), K-12 education (Ed D); instructional leadership (MA Ed, Ed D), including higher education (Ed D), K-12 education (Ed D), multiple subject teacher credential preparation (MA Ed), multiple subject teacher credential preparation with BCLAD (MA Ed), single subject teacher credential preparation (MA Ed), single subject teacher credential preparation with BCLAD (MA Ed).

See Close-Up on page 841.

Argosy University, Sarasota Campus, College of Education, Sarasota, FL 34235-8246. Offers community college educational leadership (Ed D); educational leadership (MA Ed, Ed D, Ed S), including higher education administration (Ed D), K-12 education (Ed D); instructional leadership (MA Ed, Ed D, Ed S), including education technology (Ed D), higher education (Ed D), K-12 education (Ed D). Part-time and evening/weekend programs available. Postbaccalaureate distance learning degree programs offered (minimal on-campus study). *Faculty:* 15 full-time (8 women), 49 part-time/adjunct (21 women). *Students:* 149 applicants, 96% accepted, 121 enrolled. In 2006, 9 master's, 141 doctorates awarded. *Degree requirements:* For doctorate, thesis/dissertation, comprehensive exam. *Entrance requirements:* For doctor-

Elementary Education

Argosy University, Sarasota Campus (continued)

ate, minimum undergraduate GPA of 3.0. Additional exam requirements/recommendations for international students: Required—TOEFL. *Application deadline:* Applications are processed on a rolling basis. Application fee: $50. Electronic applications accepted. *Expenses: Contact institution. Financial support:* Federal Work-Study available. Support available to part-time students. Financial award application deadline: 4/1; financial award applicants required to submit FAFSA. *Unit head:* Dr. Chuck Mlynarczyk, Dean, 800-331-5995, Fax: 941-371-9464, E-mail: cmlynarczyk@argosy.edu. *Application contact:* Admissions Representative, 800-331-5995 Ext. 221, Fax: 941-371-8910.

See Close-Up on page 843.

Argosy University, Schaumburg Campus, College of Education, Schaumburg, IL 60173-5403. Offers community college executive leadership (Ed D); educational leadership (MA Ed, Ed D, Ed S), including administrative certification (MA Ed), higher education administration (Ed D), K-12 education (Ed D), principal/general (MA Ed), superintendent certification (Ed S); instructional leadership (MA Ed, Ed D, Ed S), including higher education (Ed D), K-12 education (Ed D). Part-time and evening/weekend programs available. *Faculty:* 1 (woman) full-time, 7 part-time/adjunct (3 women). *Students:* 19 full-time, 19 part-time. 15 applicants, 80% accepted, 10 enrolled. In 2006, 1 master's, 3 doctorates, 2 other advanced degrees awarded. *Degree requirements:* For doctorate, thesis/dissertation, comprehensive exam. *Entrance requirements:* For master's and doctorate, minimum GPA of 3.0. Additional exam requirements/recommendations for international students: Required—TOEFL. *Application deadline:* For fall admission, 3/15 priority date for domestic and international students; for spring admission, 10/15 priority date for domestic and international students. Applications are processed on a rolling basis. Application fee: $50. Electronic applications accepted. *Expenses: Contact institution. Financial support:* Federal Work-Study and scholarships/grants available. *Unit head:* Dr. Narjis Hyder, Program Chair, 866-290-7400, Fax: 847-598-6158, E-mail: nhyder@argosy.edu. *Application contact:* Jamal Scott, Application Contact, 866-290-7400, Fax: 630-598-6191, E-mail: jscott@argosy.edu.

See Close-Up on page 845.

Argosy University, Seattle Campus, College of Education, Seattle, WA 98121. Offers community college executive leadership (Ed D); education (MA Ed); educational leadership (MA Ed, Ed D), including higher education administration (Ed D), K-12 education (Ed D); instructional leadership (MA Ed, Ed D), including education technology (Ed D), higher education (Ed D), K-12 education (Ed D). Part-time and evening/weekend programs available. *Students:* 29 full-time, 15 part-time. *Degree requirements:* For master's, thesis or alternative, capstone project; for doctorate, thesis/dissertation, comprehensive exam, registration. *Entrance requirements:* For master's, minimum GPA of 3.0 in last 60 hours of course work or minimum cumulative GPA of 2.7; for doctorate, minimum GPA of 3.0. Additional exam requirements/recommendations for international students: Required—TOEFL (minimum score 550 paper-based; 213 computer-based). *Application deadline:* For fall admission, 4/15 priority date for domestic students, 4/15 for international students. Application fee: $50. *Expenses: Contact institution. Financial support:* Teaching assistantships with partial tuition reimbursements, Federal Work-Study, scholarships/grants, and unspecified assistantships available. Support available to part-time students. Financial award application deadline: 4/19; financial award applicants required to submit FAFSA. *Unit head:* Dr. Leslie Aune Oja, Chair of Education, 206-393-3570, Fax: 206-283-5777, E-mail: ioja@argosy.edu. *Application contact:* Josh Pond, Director of Admissions, 206-283-4500, Fax: 206-283-5777, E-mail: jpond@argosyu.edu.

See Close-Up on page 847.

Argosy University, Tampa Campus, College of Education, Tampa, FL 33614. Offers community college executive leadership (Ed D); educational leadership (MA Ed, Ed D, Ed S), including higher education administration (Ed D), K-12 education (Ed D); instructional leadership (MA Ed, Ed D, Ed S), including higher education (Ed D), K-12 education (Ed D). *Faculty:* 1 (woman) full-time, 8 part-time/adjunct (3 women). *Degree requirements:* For master's, capstone project; for doctorate, thesis/dissertation. *Entrance requirements:* For master's, minimum GPA of 3.0 in last 2 years of undergraduate course work, resumé, 3 letters of recommendation; for doctorate, minimum GPA of 3.0, 3 letters of recommendation, resumé. Additional exam requirements/recommendations for international students: Required—TOEFL (minimum score 550 paper-based; 213 computer-based). *Application deadline:* Applications are processed on a rolling basis. Application fee: $50. Electronic applications accepted. *Faculty research:* Reading methods, elementary education, educational leadership, instructional design and instructional technology. *Unit head:* Dr. Patty O'Grady, Head, 813-246-4419, Fax: 813-246-4045, E-mail: pogrady@argosy.edu.

See Close-Up on page 849.

Argosy University, Twin Cities Campus, College of Education, Eagan, MN 55121. Offers educational leadership (MA Ed, Ed D, Ed S), including higher education administration (Ed D), K-12 education (Ed D); instructional leadership (MA Ed, Ed D, Ed S), including education technology (Ed D), higher education (Ed D), K-12 education (Ed D). Part-time and evening/weekend programs available. *Faculty:* 1 full-time (0 women), 10 part-time/adjunct (4 women). *Students:* 30 full-time (22 women), 12 part-time (9 women); includes 3 minority (1 African American, 1 American Indian/Alaska Native, 1 Asian American or Pacific Islander). Average age 45. 35 applicants, 86% accepted, 12 enrolled. In 2006, 1 master's, 6 doctorates awarded. *Degree requirements:* For doctorate, thesis/dissertation, comprehensive exam. *Entrance requirements:* For master's, 3 letters of recommendation, minimum undergraduate GPA of 3.0, resumé; for doctorate, 3 letters of recommendation, master's degree, minimum GPA of 3.0, resumé. Additional exam requirements/recommendations for international students: Required—TOEFL (minimum score 550 paper-based; 213 computer-based). *Application deadline:* For fall admission, 5/15 priority date for domestic students, 5/15 for international students; for spring admission, 10/15 priority date for domestic students, 10/15 for international students. Applications are processed on a rolling basis. Application fee: $50. Electronic applications accepted. *Financial support:* In 2006–07, 12 fellowships with partial tuition reimbursements, 3 teaching assistantships with partial tuition reimbursements were awarded; Federal Work-Study and scholarships/grants also available. Financial award applicants required to submit FAFSA. *Unit head:* Dr. David Lange, Program Chair, 888-844-2004. *Application contact:* Jennifer Radke, 2nd Director of Graduate Admissions, 651-846-3300, Fax: 651-994-7954, E-mail: tcadmissions@argosy.edu.

See Close-Up on page 851.

Argosy University, Washington DC Campus, College of Education, Arlington, VA 22209. Offers educational leadership (MA Ed, Ed D, Ed S), including higher education administration (Ed D), K-12 education (Ed D); instructional leadership (MA Ed, Ed D, Ed S), including higher education (Ed D), K-12 education (Ed D). Part-time and evening/weekend programs available. *Faculty:* 2 full-time (1 woman), 2 part-time/adjunct (0 women). *Students:* 22 full-time (16 women), 11 part-time (6 women); includes 24 minority (all African Americans) Average age 45. 16 applicants, 69% accepted, 9 enrolled. In 2006, 1 degree awarded. *Degree requirements:* For master's, thesis (for some programs), comprehensive exam (for some programs); for doctorate, thesis/dissertation, comprehensive exam. *Entrance requirements:* For master's and doctorate, minimum GPA of 3.0. Additional exam requirements/recommendations for international students: Required—TOEFL (minimum score 550 paper-based; 213 computer-based). *Application deadline:* For fall admission, 6/15 priority date for domestic and international students; for spring admission, 10/15 priority date for domestic and international students. Applications are processed on a rolling basis. Application fee: $50. Electronic applications accepted. *Financial support:* Federal Work-Study and scholarships/grants available. Financial award applicants required to submit FAFSA. *Unit head:* Dr. Colleen Logan, Academic Affairs Officer, 866-703-2777, Fax: 703-521-5850, E-mail: dcadmissions@argosy.edu. *Application contact:* Emily Peck, Director of Admissions, 866-703-2777 Ext. 5851, Fax: 703-526-5850, E-mail: dcadmissions@argosy.edu.

See Close-Up on page 853.

Arizona State University at the West campus, College of Teacher Education and Leadership, Phoenix, AZ 85069-7100. Offers educational administration and supervision (M Ed); elementary education (M Ed, Certificate); leadership/innovation (administration) (Ed D); leadership/innovation (teaching) (Ed D); secondary education (M Ed, Certificate); special education (M Ed). Part-time and evening/weekend programs available. *Faculty:* 25 full-time (18 women), 27 part-time/adjunct (21 women). *Students:* 169 full-time (133 women), 245 part-time (200 women); includes 76 minority (16 African Americans, 8 American Indian/Alaska Native, 7 Asian Americans or Pacific Islanders, 45 Hispanic Americans), 3 international. Average age 35. 308 applicants, 63% accepted, 171 enrolled. In 2006, 84 degrees awarded. *Degree requirements:* For master's, applied project or comprehensive exams; for doctorate, thesis/dissertation, comprehensive exam. *Entrance requirements:* For master's, 3 letters of recommendation; for doctorate, master's degree in education or related field, 3 professional references, resumé. Additional exam requirements/recommendations for international students: Required—TOEFL (minimum score 550 paper-based; 213 computer-based; 83 iBT), IELTS (minimum score 7). *Application deadline:* Applications are processed on a rolling basis. Application fee: $50. Electronic applications accepted. *Expenses:* Tuition, state resident: full-time $5,930. Tuition, nonresident: full-time $16,516. Tuition and fees vary according to course load. *Financial support:* In 2006–07, 2 research assistantships with partial tuition reimbursements (averaging $16,413 per year) were awarded; fellowships with tuition reimbursements, career-related internships or fieldwork, institutionally sponsored loans, scholarships/grants, tuition waivers (full and partial), and unspecified assistantships also available. Support available to part-time students. Financial award application deadline: 4/1; financial award applicants required to submit FAFSA. *Faculty research:* Self-regulated learning in students, collaboration and consultation skills for educators, school reform and restructuring, hands-on science and mathematics programs, educational technology. *Unit head:* Dr. Mari Koerner, Dean, 602-543-6352, Fax: 602-543-6350, E-mail: mari.koerner@asu.edu. *Application contact:* Marie Wright, Administrative Assistant, 602-543-3634, Fax: 602-543-6350, E-mail: marie.wright@asu.edu or ctelgrad@asu.edu.

Arkansas State University, Graduate School, College of Education, Department of Teacher Education, Jonesboro, State University, AR 72467. Offers early childhood education (MSE); early childhood services (MS); elementary education (MSE); reading (MSE, SCCT). *Accreditation:* NCATE. Part-time programs available. *Faculty:* 6 full-time (3 women). *Students:* 2 full-time (both women), 30 part-time (29 women); includes 3 minority (2 African Americans, 1 Asian American or Pacific Islander). Average age 32. 22 applicants, 82% accepted, 12 enrolled. In 2006, 35 degrees awarded. *Degree requirements:* For master's, thesis or alternative, comprehensive exam. *Entrance requirements:* For master's, GRE General Test or MAT, appropriate bachelor's degree, official transcript; for SCCT, GRE General Test or MAT, interview, master's degree, official transcript. Additional exam requirements/recommendations for international students: Required—TOEFL (minimum score 213 computer-based). *Application deadline:* Applications are processed on a rolling basis. Application fee: $30 ($40 for international students). Electronic applications accepted. *Expenses:* Tuition, state resident: full-time $3,393; part-time $189 per hour. Tuition, nonresident: full-time $8,577; part-time $477 per hour. Required fees: $752; $39 per hour. $25 per semester. *Financial support:* Teaching assistantships, career-related internships or fieldwork, scholarships/grants, and unspecified assistantships available. Financial award application deadline: 7/1; financial award applicants required to submit FAFSA. *Unit head:* Dr. Dianne Lawler-Prince, Interim Chair, 870-972-3059, Fax: 870-972-3344, E-mail: dprince@astate.edu.

Armstrong Atlantic State University, School of Graduate Studies, Program in Education, Savannah, GA 31419-1997. Offers adult education (M Ed); early childhood education (M Ed); education (M Ed); elementary education (M Ed); middle grades education (M Ed); secondary education (M Ed), including business education, English education, mathematics education, science education, social science education; special education (M Ed), including behavioral disorders, curriculum and instruction, learning disabilities, speech-language pathology. *Accreditation:* NCATE. Part-time and evening/weekend programs available. Postbaccalaureate distance learning degree programs offered (minimal on-campus study). *Faculty:* 11 full-time (9 women), 13 part-time/adjunct (10 women). *Students:* 50 full-time (42 women), 219 part-time (175 women); includes 71 minority (67 African Americans, 3 Asian Americans or Pacific Islanders, 1 Hispanic American), 6 international. Average age 35. In 2006, 151 degrees awarded. *Degree requirements:* For master's, portfolio. *Entrance requirements:* For master's, GRE General Test or MAT, minimum GPA of 2.5, letters of recommendation. Additional exam requirements/recommendations for international students: Required—TOEFL (minimum score 523 paper-based; 193 computer-based). *Application deadline:* For fall admission, 7/1 priority date for domestic and international students; for spring admission, 11/15 priority date for domestic and international students. Applications are processed on a rolling basis. Application fee: $25. Electronic applications accepted. *Expenses:* Tuition, state resident: full-time $2,286; part-time $127 per credit. Tuition, nonresident: full-time $9,144; part-time $508 per credit. One-time fee: $257. *Financial support:* In 2006–07, research assistantships with partial tuition reimbursements (averaging $2,500 per year); career-related internships or fieldwork, Federal Work-Study, scholarships/grants, and unspecified assistantships also available. Support available to part-time students. Financial award applicants required to submit FAFSA. *Unit head:* Dr. Jane McHaney, College of Education Dean, 912-927-5398, Fax: 912-921-7425, E-mail: mchaneia@mail.armstrong.edu.

Auburn University, Graduate School, College of Education, Department of Curriculum and Teaching, Auburn University, AL 36849. Offers business education (M Ed, MS, PhD); early childhood education (M Ed, MS, PhD, Ed S); elementary education (M Ed, MS, PhD, Ed S); foreign languages (M Ed, MS); music education (M Ed, MS, PhD, Ed S); postsecondary education (PhD); reading education (PhD, Ed S); secondary education (M Ed, MS, PhD, Ed S), including English language arts, mathematics, science, social studies. *Accreditation:* NASM (one or more programs are accredited); NCATE. Part-time programs available. *Faculty:* 26 full-time (19 women). *Students:* 51 full-time (36 women), 116 part-time (86 women); includes 24 minority (23 African Americans, 1 Asian American or Pacific Islander). Average age 33. 181 applicants, 56% accepted, 68 enrolled. In 2006, 63 master's, 12 doctorates, 14 other advanced degrees awarded. *Degree requirements:* For master's, thesis (for some programs); for doctorate, thesis/dissertation; for Ed S, field project. *Entrance requirements:* For master's, doctorate, and Ed S, GRE General Test. *Application deadline:* For fall admission, 7/7 for domestic students; for spring admission, 11/24 for domestic students. Applications are processed on a rolling basis. Application fee: $25 ($50 for international students). Electronic applications accepted. *Expenses:* Tuition, state resident: full-time $5,000. Tuition, nonresident: full-time $15,000. Required fees: $416. Tuition and fees vary according to program. *Financial support:* Fellowships, teaching assistantships, career-related internships or fieldwork and Federal Work-Study available. Support available to part-time students. Financial award application deadline: 3/15. *Faculty research:* Emerging literacy, reading attitudes, music for at-risk youth, portfolio assessment. *Unit head:* Dr. Andrew M. Weaver, Head, 334-844-4434, E-mail: weaveam@mail.auburn.edu. *Application contact:* Dr. Joe Pittman, Interim Dean of the Graduate School, 334-844-4700.

Auburn University Montgomery, School of Education, Department of Early Childhood, Elementary, and Reading Education, Montgomery, AL 36124-4023. Offers early childhood education (M Ed, Ed S); elementary education (M Ed, Ed S); reading education (M Ed, Ed S). *Accreditation:* NCATE. Part-time and evening/weekend programs available. *Faculty:* 6 full-time (all women). *Students:* 38 full-time (32 women), 88 part-time (83 women); includes 47 minority (43 African Americans, 1 American Indian/Alaska Native, 2 Asian Americans or Pacific Islanders, 1 Hispanic American), 1 international. Average age 32. In 2006, 33 master's, 5 other advanced degrees awarded. *Degree requirements:* For master's and Ed S, comprehensive exam. *Entrance requirements:* For master's, GRE General Test or MAT, certification, BS in teaching; for Ed S, GRE General Test or MAT, certification. *Application deadline:* Applications are processed on a rolling basis. Application fee: $25. Electronic applications accepted. *Financial support:* In 2006–07, 1 teaching assistantship was awarded; career-related internships or fieldwork and scholarships/grants also available. Support available to part-time students.

Financial award application deadline: 3/1; financial award applicants required to submit FAFSA. *Unit head:* Dr. Lynne Mills, Head, 334-244-3283, Fax: 334-244-3835, E-mail: lmills@mail.aum.edu.

Augustana College, Department of Education, Program in Education, Sioux Falls, SD 57197. Offers elementary (MA); secondary (MA). *Accreditation:* NCATE. Part-time programs available. *Degree requirements:* For master's, oral exam, paper, synthesis portfolio. *Entrance requirements:* For master's, appropriate bachelor's degree, minimum GPA of 3.0, teaching certificate. Additional exam requirements/recommendations for international students: Required—TOEFL.

Augusta State University, Graduate Studies, College of Education, Program in Elementary Education, Augusta, GA 30904-2200. Offers M Ed, Ed S. *Accreditation:* NCATE. Part-time and evening/weekend programs available. *Faculty:* 2 full-time (1 woman), 2 part-time/adjunct (both women). *Students:* 13 full-time (all women), 60 part-time (58 women); includes 9 minority (8 African Americans, 1 Asian American or Pacific Islander). Average age 37. 12 applicants, 100% accepted, 7 enrolled. In 2006, 7 degrees awarded. *Degree requirements:* For Ed S, thesis. *Entrance requirements:* For master's, GRE, MAT, minimum GPA of 2.5; for Ed S, GRE, MAT. *Application deadline:* For fall admission, 8/1 priority date for domestic students. Applications are processed on a rolling basis. Application fee: $20. *Expenses:* Tuition, state resident: full-time $3,044; part-time $127 per credit hour. Tuition, nonresident: full-time $12,172; part-time $508 per credit hour. *Financial support:* Career-related internships or fieldwork, Federal Work-Study, institutionally sponsored loans, and unspecified assistantships available. Support available to part-time students. Financial award application deadline: 4/15; financial award applicants required to submit FAFSA. *Faculty research:* Whole language, computers in teaching. *Unit head:* Dr. J. Gordon Eisenman, Chair, 706-737-1496, Fax: 706-667-4706, E-mail: geisenman@aug.edu. *Application contact:* Andrea M. Scott, Secretary to the Dean, 706-737-1499, Fax: 706-667-4706, E-mail: ascott1@aug.edu.

Austin College, Program in Education, Sherman, TX 75090-4400. Offers art education (MA); elementary education (MA); middle school education (MA); music education (MA); physical education and coaching (MA); secondary education (MA). Applicants must meet Austin College's undergraduate curriculum requirements. Part-time programs available. *Faculty:* 5 full-time (3 women), 1 (woman) part-time/adjunct. *Students:* 33 full-time (26 women); includes 3 minority (2 Asian Americans or Pacific Islanders, 1 Hispanic American). Average age 25. In 2006, 24 degrees awarded. *Degree requirements:* For master's, one foreign language, thesis or alternative. *Entrance requirements:* For master's, Texas Academic Skills Program Test. *Application deadline:* For fall admission, 5/1 priority date for domestic students; for spring admission, 1/15 priority date for domestic students. Applications are processed on a rolling basis. Application fee: $35. Electronic applications accepted. *Expenses:* Tuition: Full-time $27,385. Required fees: $160. *Financial support:* In 2006–07, 27 students received support. Career-related internships or fieldwork, Federal Work-Study, scholarships/grants, and unspecified assistantships available. Support available to part-time students. Financial award application deadline: 4/1; financial award applicants required to submit FAFSA. *Unit head:* Dr. Barbara Sylvester, Director of Teaching Program, 903-813-2498, Fax: 903-813-2326, E-mail: bsylvester@austincollege.edu.

Averett University, Graduate Studies in Education, Danville, VA 24541-3692. Offers art education (M Ed); biology (M Ed); chemistry (M Ed); curriculum and instruction (M Ed); elementary education (M Ed); English (M Ed); health and physical education (M Ed); history and social studies (M Ed); mathematics education (M Ed); physical science (M Ed); reading (M Ed); special education (learning disabilities specialization PK-12) (M Ed). Part-time and evening/weekend programs available. *Faculty:* 10 full-time (4 women), 7 part-time/adjunct (6 women). *Students:* 14 full-time (10 women), 85 part-time (67 women); includes 20 minority (18 African Americans, 2 Asian Americans or Pacific Islanders). Average age 33. 52 applicants, 100% accepted, 40 enrolled. In 2006, 48 degrees awarded. *Degree requirements:* For master's, thesis optional. *Entrance requirements:* For master's, PRAXIS, GRE General Test, MAT or NTE, writing proficiency exam, 3 letters of recommendation, current teacher's licensure or eligibility for licensure, minimum undergraduate GPA of 3.0 in previous 2 years. Additional exam requirements/recommendations for international students: Required—TOEFL (minimum score 600 paper-based; 200 computer-based). *Application deadline:* Applications are processed on a rolling basis. Application fee: $20. *Expenses:* Contact institution. *Financial support:* In 2006–07, 23 students received support. Federal Work-Study and scholarships/grants available. Financial award application deadline: 4/1; financial award applicants required to submit FAFSA. *Faculty research:* Literary assessment-PreK-6, handwriting instruction and assessment-PreK-6, written language instruction and assessment-PreK-6 and special needs students learning styles, curriculum and instruction processes. *Unit head:* Dr. Lynn H. Wolf, Chair, 434-793-3995, Fax: 434-791-4392, E-mail: lynn.wolf@averett.edu.

Ball State University, Graduate School, Teachers College, Department of Elementary Education, Muncie, IN 47306-1099. Offers MAE, Ed D, PhD. *Accreditation:* NCATE. *Faculty:* 21. *Students:* 11 full-time (10 women), 144 part-time (132 women); includes 6 minority (4 African Americans, 2 Hispanic Americans), 4 international. Average age 25. 68 applicants, 84% accepted, 42 enrolled. In 2006, 41 master's, 2 doctorates awarded. *Degree requirements:* For doctorate, thesis/dissertation. *Entrance requirements:* For doctorate, GRE General Test, interview, minimum graduate GPA of 3.2. Application fee: $25. *Financial support:* In 2006–07, 10 teaching assistantships (averaging $9,374 per year) were awarded; research assistantships with full tuition reimbursements. Financial award application deadline: 3/1. *Unit head:* Dr. Jill Miels, Chairperson, 765-285-8560, Fax: 765-285-8793.

Bank Street College of Education, Graduate School, Department of Curriculum and Instruction, Program in Bilingual Education, New York, NY 10025. Offers bilingual childhood special education (Ed M, MS Ed); bilingual early childhood education (MS Ed); bilingual early childhood special and general education (MS Ed); bilingual early childhood special education (Ed M, MS Ed); bilingual elementary/childhood general education (MS Ed); bilingual elementary/childhood special and general education (MS Ed); bilingual middle school general education (MS Ed); bilingual middle school special and general education (Ed M, MS Ed); bilingual middle school special education (MS Ed). *Accreditation:* NCATE. *Faculty:* 2 full-time (both women), 5 part-time/adjunct (all women). *Students:* 8 full-time (7 women), 22 part-time (19 women); includes 21 minority (2 African Americans, 2 Asian Americans or Pacific Islanders, 17 Hispanic Americans). Average age 27. 19 applicants, 68% accepted, 10 enrolled. In 2006, 8 degrees awarded. *Degree requirements:* For master's, thesis, registration. *Entrance requirements:* For master's, interview. Additional exam requirements/recommendations for international students: Required—TOEFL (minimum score 600 paper-based; 250 computer-based). *Application deadline:* For fall admission, 3/1 priority date for domestic students; for spring admission, 11/1 priority date for domestic students. Applications are processed on a rolling basis. Application fee: $50. *Expenses:* Tuition: Part-time $940 per credit. Required fees: $100 per term. *Financial support:* Career-related internships or fieldwork, Federal Work-Study, scholarships/grants, and unspecified assistantships available. Support available to part-time students. Financial award application deadline: 4/15; financial award applicants required to submit FAFSA. *Faculty research:* Dual language education, language immersion, bilingual education in the urban classroom, community and school partnerships. Total annual research expenditures: $58,717. *Unit head:* Dr. Olga Romero, Director, 212-875-4468, Fax: 212-875-4753, E-mail: olgar@bankstreet.edu. *Application contact:* Ann Morgan, Director of Graduate Admissions, 212-875-4403, Fax: 212-875-4678, E-mail: amorgan@bankstreet.edu.

Bank Street College of Education, Graduate School, Department of Curriculum and Instruction, Program in Elementary/Childhood Education, New York, NY 10025. Offers early childhood and elementary/childhood education (MS Ed); elementary/childhood education (MS Ed). *Accreditation:* NCATE. *Students:* 49 full-time (42 women), 82 part-time (73 women); includes 19 minority (8 African Americans, 7 Asian Americans or Pacific Islanders, 4 Hispanic Americans). Average age 27. 102 applicants, 67% accepted, 60 enrolled. In 2006, 73 degrees awarded. *Degree requirements:* For master's, thesis. *Entrance requirements:* For master's, interview. Additional exam requirements/recommendations for international students: Required—TOEFL (minimum score 600 paper-based; 250 computer-based). *Application deadline:* For fall admission, 3/1 priority date for domestic students; for spring admission, 11/1 priority date for domestic students. Applications are processed on a rolling basis. Application fee: $50. *Expenses:* Tuition: Part-time $940 per credit. Required fees: $100 per term. *Financial support:* Career-related internships or fieldwork, Federal Work-Study, scholarships/grants, and unspecified assistantships available. Support available to part-time students. Financial award application deadline: 4/15; financial award applicants required to submit FAFSA. *Faculty research:* Social studies in the elementary grades, urban education, experiential learning, child centered classrooms. *Unit head:* Adrianne Kamsler, Chairperson, 212-875-4571, Fax: 212-875-4753, E-mail: akamsler@bankstreet.edu. *Application contact:* Ann Morgan, Director of Graduate Admissions, 212-875-4403, Fax: 212-875-4678, E-mail: amorgan@bankstreet.edu.

See Close-Up on page 857.

Bank Street College of Education, Graduate School, Department of Curriculum and Instruction, Program in Museum Education, New York, NY 10025. Offers museum education (MS Ed); museum education: elementary education certification (MS Ed); museum education: middle school certification (MS Ed); museum studies (MS Ed). *Students:* 30 full-time (28 women), 27 part-time (all women); includes 8 minority (3 African Americans, 5 Asian Americans or Pacific Islanders). Average age 27. 37 applicants, 84% accepted, 23 enrolled. In 2006, 20 degrees awarded. *Degree requirements:* For master's, thesis, registration. *Entrance requirements:* For master's, interview. Additional exam requirements/recommendations for international students: Required—TOEFL (minimum score 600 paper-based; 250 computer-based). *Application deadline:* For fall admission, 3/1 priority date for domestic and international students; for spring admission, 11/1 priority date for domestic and international students. Applications are processed on a rolling basis. Application fee: $50. *Expenses:* Tuition: Part-time $940 per credit. Required fees: $100 per term. *Financial support:* Federal Work-Study and scholarships/grants available. Support available to part-time students. Financial award application deadline: 4/15; financial award applicants required to submit FAFSA. *Faculty research:* Equitable access and openness to diversity in museum settings, exhibition display and development, museum/school partnerships. *Unit head:* Nina Jensen, Director, 212-875-4491, Fax: 212-875-4753, E-mail: ninajensen@bankstreet.edu. *Application contact:* Ann Morgan, Director of Graduate Admissions, 212-875-4403, Fax: 212-875-4678, E-mail: amorgan@bankstreet.edu.

Bank Street College of Education, Graduate School, Department of Curriculum and Instruction, Program in Reading and Literacy, New York, NY 10025. Offers advanced literacy specialization (Ed M); reading and literacy (MS Ed); teaching literacy (MS Ed); teaching literacy and elementary education (MS Ed). *Accreditation:* NCATE. *Students:* 35 full-time (33 women), 71 part-time (70 women); includes 25 minority (9 African Americans, 6 Asian Americans or Pacific Islanders, 10 Hispanic Americans). Average age 30. 71 applicants, 75% accepted, 40 enrolled. In 2006, 30 degrees awarded. *Degree requirements:* For master's, thesis, registration. *Entrance requirements:* For master's, interview. Additional exam requirements/recommendations for international students: Required—TOEFL (minimum score 600 paper-based; 250 computer-based). *Application deadline:* For fall admission, 3/1 priority date for domestic students; for spring admission, 11/1 priority date for domestic students. Applications are processed on a rolling basis. Application fee: $50. *Expenses:* Tuition: Part-time $940 per credit. Required fees: $100 per term. *Financial support:* Career-related internships or fieldwork, Federal Work-Study, scholarships/grants, and unspecified assistantships available. Support available to part-time students. Financial award application deadline: 4/15; financial award applicants required to submit FAFSA. *Faculty research:* Language development, reading and the writing process, reading difficulties in multi-cultural classrooms. *Unit head:* Dr. Margaret McNamara, Director, 212-875-4586, Fax: 212-875-4753, E-mail: mam@bankstreet.edu. *Application contact:* Ann Morgan, Director of Graduate Admissions, 212-875-4403, Fax: 212-875-4678, E-mail: amorgan@bankstreet.edu.

Bank Street College of Education, Graduate School, Department of Curriculum and Instruction, Program in Special Education, New York, NY 10025. Offers early childhood special and general education (MS Ed); early childhood special education (Ed M, MS Ed); elementary/childhood special and general education (MS Ed); elementary/childhood special education (MS Ed); elementary/childhood special education certification (Ed M); middle school special and general education (MS Ed); middle school special education (Ed M). *Students:* 98 full-time (86 women), 167 part-time (162 women); includes 57 minority (17 African Americans, 10 Asian Americans or Pacific Islanders, 30 Hispanic Americans), 1 international. Average age 31. 147 applicants, 78% accepted, 80 enrolled. In 2006, 68 degrees awarded. *Degree requirements:* For master's, thesis, registration. *Entrance requirements:* For master's, interview. Additional exam requirements/recommendations for international students: Required—TOEFL (minimum score 600 paper-based; 250 computer-based). *Application deadline:* For fall admission, 3/1 priority date for domestic students; for spring admission, 11/1 priority date for domestic students. Applications are processed on a rolling basis. Application fee: $50. *Expenses:* Tuition: Part-time $940 per credit. Required fees: $100 per term. *Financial support:* Career-related internships or fieldwork available. Financial award application deadline: 3/1; financial award applicants required to submit FAFSA. *Faculty research:* Inclusion, observation and assessment, early intervention, neurodevelopmental assessment. *Unit head:* Dr. Andrea (Penny) Spencer, Chairperson, 212-875-4602, Fax: 212-875-4753, E-mail: aspencer@bankstreet.edu. *Application contact:* Ann Morgan, Director of Graduate Admissions, 212-875-4403, Fax: 212-875-4678, E-mail: amorgan@bankstreet.edu.

See Close-Up on page 857.

Barry University, School of Education, Program in Curriculum and Instruction, Miami Shores, FL 33161-6695. Offers accomplished teacher (Ed S); culture, language and literacy (TESOL) (PhD); curriculum evaluation and research (PhD); early childhood (Ed S); early childhood education (PhD); elementary (Ed S); elementary education (PhD); ESOL (Ed S); gifted (Ed S); Montessori (Ed S); PKP/elementary (Ed S); reading (Ed S); reading, language and cognition (PhD). *Students:* 2 full-time (both women), 36 part-time (27 women); includes 21 minority (12 African Americans, 9 Hispanic Americans), 6 international. 45 applicants, 33% accepted, 4 enrolled. In 2006, 4 degrees awarded. *Entrance requirements:* For doctorate, GRE, minimum GPA of 3.25. Application fee: $30. *Unit head:* Dr. Jill Farrell, Director, 305-899-3198, Fax: 305-899-4708, E-mail: jfarrell@mail.barry.edu. *Application contact:* Dave Fletcher, Director of Graduate Admissions, 305-899-3113, Fax: 305-899-2971, E-mail: dfletcher@mail.barry.edu.

Barry University, School of Education, Program in Elementary Education, Miami Shores, FL 33161-6695. Offers elementary education (MS); elementary education/ESOL (MS). Part-time and evening/weekend programs available. *Students:* 11 full-time (10 women), 11 part-time (8 women); includes 9 minority (2 African Americans, 1 Asian American or Pacific Islander, 6 Hispanic Americans), 2 international. 18 applicants, 67% accepted, 9 enrolled. In 2006, 3 degrees awarded. *Degree requirements:* For master's, practicum. *Entrance requirements:* For master's, GRE General Test or MAT, minimum GPA of 3.0. *Application deadline:* For fall admission, 5/1 priority date for domestic students. Applications are processed on a rolling basis. Application fee: $30. Electronic applications accepted. *Unit head:* Dr. Victoria Giordano, Director, 305-899-3613, Fax: 305-899-4708, E-mail: vgiordano@mail.barry.edu. *Application contact:* Dave Fletcher, Director of Graduate Admissions, 305-899-3113, Fax: 305-899-2971, E-mail: dfletcher@mail.barry.edu.

Bayamón Central University, Graduate Programs, Program in Education, Bayamón, PR 00960-1725. Offers administration and supervision (MA Ed); commercial education (MA Ed); education of the autistic (MA Ed); elementary education (K–3) (MA Ed); elementary education (K–6) (MA Ed); elementary physical education (MA Ed); guidance and counseling (MA Ed); pre-elementary teacher (MA Ed); special education (MA Ed), including attention deficit disorder, learning disabilities. Part-time and evening/weekend programs available. *Degree requirements:* For master's, comprehensive exam. *Entrance requirements:* For master's, EXADEP, bachelor's degree in education or related field.

Elementary Education

Belhaven College, School of Education, Jackson, MS 39202-1789. Offers elementary education (M Ed, MAT); secondary education (M Ed, MAT). *Degree requirements:* For master's, portfolio. *Entrance requirements:* For master's, PRAXIS I, PRAXIS II, minimum GPA of 2.8.

Belmont University, College of Arts and Sciences, School of Education, Nashville, TN 37212-3757. Offers education (MAT); elementary education (M Ed), including early childhood education, elementary education, gifted education, language arts education; English (M Ed); history (M Ed); mathematics (M Ed); middle grade education (M Ed); science (M Ed); secondary education (M Ed), including gifted education; sports administration (MSA); technology (M Ed). *Accreditation:* NCATE. Part-time and evening/weekend programs available. *Faculty:* 9 full-time (7 women), 20 part-time/adjunct (15 women). *Students:* 50 full-time (36 women), 116 part-time (76 women); includes 23 minority (20 African Americans, 1 Asian American or Pacific Islander, 2 Hispanic Americans), 1 international. Average age 30. 55 applicants, 60% accepted, 30 enrolled. In 2006, 82 degrees awarded. *Degree requirements:* For master's, thesis, comprehensive exam. *Entrance requirements:* For master's, MAT or GRE, minimum GPA of 2.75. Additional exam requirements/recommendations for international students: Required—TOEFL. *Application deadline:* For fall admission, 8/1 priority date for domestic students, 5/1 for international students; for spring admission, 12/1 priority date for domestic students, 9/1 for international students. Applications are processed on a rolling basis. Application fee: $50. *Expenses: Contact institution. Financial support:* In 2006–07, 25 students received support; fellowships with partial tuition reimbursements available, institutionally sponsored loans and tuition waivers (partial) available. Financial award application deadline: 4/15; financial award applicants required to submit FAFSA. *Faculty research:* Technology grant, professional development schools. Total annual research expenditures: $6,500. *Unit head:* Dr. Trevor F. Hutchins, Associate Dean, 615-460-6232, Fax: 615-460-6414, E-mail: hutchinst@mail.belmont.edu. *Application contact:* Julie Hullett, Admission/Licensure Officer, 615-460-6879, Fax: 615-460-5556, E-mail: hullettj@email.belmont.edu.

Benedictine University, Graduate Programs, Program in Education, Lisle, IL 60532-0900. Offers curriculum and instruction and collaborative teaching (M Ed); elementary education (MA Ed); leadership and administration (M Ed); reading and literacy (M Ed); secondary education (MA Ed); special education (MA Ed). Part-time and evening/weekend programs available. *Faculty:* 4 full-time (2 women), 52 part-time/adjunct (30 women). *Students:* 257 (196 women); includes 22 minority (4 African Americans, 1 American Indian/Alaska Native, 3 Asian Americans or Pacific Islanders, 14 Hispanic Americans) 2 international. Average age 33. 130 applicants, 93% accepted, 13 enrolled. In 2006, 181 degrees awarded. *Degree requirements:* For master's, thesis (for some programs), comprehensive exam. *Entrance requirements:* For master's, GRE or MAT. Additional exam requirements/recommendations for international students: Required—TOEFL (minimum score 550 paper-based; 213 computer-based). *Application deadline:* For fall admission, 9/1 for domestic students; for winter admission, 12/1 for domestic students; for spring admission, 2/15 for domestic students. Applications are processed on a rolling basis. Application fee: $40. Electronic applications accepted. *Expenses: Contact institution. Financial support:* Career-related internships or fieldwork and health care benefits available. Support available to part-time students. *Unit head:* Dr. Richard Campbell, Director, 630-829-6242, Fax: 630-960-1126, E-mail: rcampbell@ben.edu. *Application contact:* Kari Gibbons, Director, Admissions, 630-829-6200, Fax: 630-829-6584, E-mail: kgibbons@ben.edu.

Bennington College, Graduate Programs, Program in Teaching, Bennington, VT 05201. Offers art education (MAT); early childhood (MAT); elementary education (MAT); English education (MAT); foreign language education (MAT); mathematics education (MAT); music education (MAT); science education (MAT); secondary education (MAT); social science education (MAT). *Faculty:* 4 part-time/adjunct (3 women). *Students:* 11 full-time (7 women), 1 (woman) part-time; includes 2 minority (both Hispanic Americans) Average age 31. 12 applicants, 75% accepted, 3 enrolled. In 2006, 13 degrees awarded. *Degree requirements:* For master's, 1 year teaching practicum, professional portfolio. *Entrance requirements:* For master's, interview. *Application deadline:* For fall admission, 3/1 for domestic students. Application fee: $60. *Expenses: Contact institution.* One-time fee: $75 full-time. Tuition and fees vary according to program. *Financial support:* In 2006–07, 10 students received support, including 4 fellowships (averaging $6,875 per year); scholarships/grants and unspecified assistantships also available. Financial award application deadline: 4/1; financial award applicants required to submit FAFSA. *Unit head:* George Kamberelis, Director of Center for Creative Teaching, 802-440-4863, E-mail: gkamberelis@bennington.edu. *Application contact:* Ken Himmelman, Dean of Admissions, 802-440-4312, Fax: 802-440-4320, E-mail: admissions@bennington.edu.

See Close-Up on page 861.

Bethel College, Program in Education, McKenzie, TN 38201. Offers administration and supervision (MA Ed); biology education K8-12 (MAT); elementary education (MAT); English education K8-12 (MAT); history education K8-12 (MAT); physical education K8-12 (MAT); special education K8-12 (MAT). Part-time and evening/weekend programs available. *Degree requirements:* For master's, thesis (for some programs). *Entrance requirements:* For master's, GRE General Test or MAT, minimum undergraduate GPA of 2.5.

Bloomsburg University of Pennsylvania, School of Graduate Studies, College of Professional Studies, School of Education, Department of Elementary and Early Childhood Education, Program in Elementary Education, Bloomsburg, PA 17815-1301. Offers M Ed. *Accreditation:* NCATE. *Faculty:* 10 full-time (5 women). *Students:* 26 full-time (18 women), 26 part-time (23 women), 1 international. Average age 29. 14 applicants, 100% accepted, 8 enrolled. In 2006, 33 degrees awarded. *Degree requirements:* For master's, thesis or alternative. *Entrance requirements:* For master's, MAT or PRAXIS, minimum QPA of 3.0, teaching certificate. Additional exam requirements/recommendations for international students: Required—TOEFL (minimum score 550 paper-based; 213 computer-based; 79 iBT). *Application deadline:* Applications are processed on a rolling basis. Application fee: $30. Electronic applications accepted. *Expenses:* Tuition, state resident: full-time $6,048; part-time $336 per credit. Tuition, nonresident: full-time $9,678; part-time $538 per credit. Required fees: $1,415. *Financial support:* Unspecified assistantships available. *Faculty research:* Supervision, computing, measurement, mathematics, school law.

Bob Jones University, Graduate Programs, Greenville, SC 29614. Offers accountancy (MS); Bible (MA); Bible translation (MA); Biblical studies (Certificate); broadcast management (MS); business administration (MBA); church history (MA, PhD); church ministries (MA); church music (MM); cinema and video production (MA); counseling (MS); curriculum and instruction (Ed D); divinity (M Div); dramatic production (MA); educational leadership (MS, Ed D, Ed S); elementary education (M Ed, MAT); English (M Ed, MA, MAT); fine arts (MA); graphic design (MA); history (M Ed, MA); illustration (MA); interpretative speech (MA); mathematics (M Ed, MAT); medical missions (Certificate); ministry (MM, D Min); multi-categorical special education (M Ed, MAT); music (M Ed); New Testament interpretation (PhD); Old Testament interpretation (PhD); orchestral instrument performance (MM); organ performance (MM); pastoral studies (MA); personnel services (MS, Ed S); piano pedagogy (MM); piano performance (MM); platform arts (MA); radio and television broadcasting (MS); rhetoric and public address (MA); secondary education (M Ed); studio art (MA); teaching Bible (MA); theology (MA, PhD); voice performance (MM); youth ministries (MA); M Div/MM.

Boston College, Lynch Graduate School of Education, Department of Teacher Education/Special Education and Curriculum and Instruction, Program in Elementary Education, Chestnut Hill, MA 02467-3800. Offers M Ed. *Students:* 40 full-time (36 women), 28 part-time (26 women); includes 12 minority (6 African Americans, 6 Asian Americans or Pacific Islanders), 4 international. 102 applicants, 75% accepted, 31 enrolled. In 2006, 43 degrees awarded. *Degree requirements:* For master's, comprehensive exam. *Entrance requirements:* For master's, GRE General Test or MAT. Additional exam requirements/recommendations for international students: Required—TOEFL. *Application deadline:* For fall admission, 1/1 priority date for domestic students. Application fee: $60. *Financial support:* Fellowships with full and partial tuition reimbursements, research assistantships with full and partial tuition reimbursements, teaching assistantships with full and partial tuition reimbursements, career-related internships or fieldwork, Federal Work-Study, scholarships/grants, traineeships, tuition waivers (full and partial), and unspecified assistantships available. Support available to part-time students. Financial award applicants required to submit FAFSA. *Faculty research:* Cross-cultural studies in teaching, learning or supervision, curriculum design, teacher research. *Application contact:* Timothy P. Blackman, Director, Graduate Admission and Financial Aid, 617-552-4214, Fax: 617-552-0398, E-mail: timothy.blackman.1@bc.edu.

Boston University, School of Education, Department of Curriculum and Teaching, Program in Elementary Education, Boston, MA 02215. Offers Ed M. *Students:* 12 full-time (10 women), 2 part-time (both women). Average age 29. 85 applicants, 61% accepted. *Entrance requirements:* For master's, GRE General Test or MAT. Additional exam requirements/recommendations for international students: Required—TOEFL. *Application deadline:* For fall admission, 2/15 priority date for domestic students. Applications are processed on a rolling basis. Application fee: $70. Electronic applications accepted. *Expenses:* Tuition: Full-time $33,330; part-time $1,042 per credit. Required fees: $462; $40. *Financial support:* Application deadline: 2/15. *Faculty research:* Learning theory, program evaluation, preservice field experiences. *Unit head:* Dr. Carol Jenkins, Coordinator, 617-353-7103, E-mail: elemed@bu.edu. *Application contact:* 617-353-4237, Fax: 617-353-8937, E-mail: sedgrad@bu.edu.

Bowie State University, Graduate Programs, Program in Elementary Education, Bowie, MD 20715-9465. Offers M Ed. *Accreditation:* NCATE. Part-time and evening/weekend programs available. *Faculty:* 1 (woman) full-time. *Students:* Average age 33. 3 applicants, 100% accepted, 3 enrolled. In 2006, 6 degrees awarded. *Degree requirements:* For master's, research paper, thesis optional. *Entrance requirements:* For master's, minimum GPA of 2.5, teaching certificate, teaching experience. *Application deadline:* For fall admission, 4/1 priority date for domestic and international students; for spring admission, 11/1 priority date for domestic and international students. Applications are processed on a rolling basis. Application fee: $40. Electronic applications accepted. *Expenses:* Tuition, state resident: full-time $7,344; part-time $306 per credit. Tuition, nonresident: full-time $14,304; part-time $396 per credit. Required fees: $1,078; $77 per credit. $539 per term. One-time fee: $40. *Financial support:* Application deadline: 4/1. *Unit head:* Dr. Marion Amory, Coordinator, 301-860-3139, E-mail: mamory@bowiestate.edu. *Application contact:* Angela Issac, Information Contact.

Brandeis University, Graduate School of Arts and Sciences, Program in Elementary Education, Waltham, MA 02454-9110. Offers Jewish day school (MAT); public education elementary (MAT); secondary education (English, history, biology, Bible) (MAT). *Faculty:* 6 full-time (2 women), 9 part-time/adjunct (all women). *Students:* 7 full-time (5 women); includes 1 African American. Average age 27. In 2006, 9 degrees awarded. *Degree requirements:* For master's, research program MTEL. *Application deadline:* For fall admission, 1/15 priority date for domestic students, 1/15 for international students. Applications are processed on a rolling basis. Application fee: $55. Electronic applications accepted. *Financial support:* In 2006–07, 7 students received support, including 7 fellowships with tuition reimbursements available; scholarships/grants also available. Financial award applicants required to submit CSS PROFILE. *Faculty research:* Teacher education, induction, philosophy, education, democracy education. *Unit head:* Dr. Dirck Roosevelt, Director, MAT Program, 781-736-2020, Fax: 781-736-5020, E-mail: drooseve@brandeis.edu. *Application contact:* Marlene Mihalsky, Department Coordinator, 781-736-2022, Fax: 781-736-5020.

Bridgewater State College, School of Graduate Studies, School of Education and Allied Science, Department of Elementary and Early Childhood Education, Program in Elementary Education, Bridgewater, MA 02325-0001. Offers M Ed. *Accreditation:* NCATE. Part-time and evening/weekend programs available. *Entrance requirements:* For master's, GRE General Test or Massachusetts Test for Educator Licensure. *Application deadline:* For fall admission, 3/1 priority date for domestic students; for spring admission, 10/1 priority date for domestic students. Application fee: $50. *Financial support:* Career-related internships or fieldwork, health care benefits, and unspecified assistantships available. Support available to part-time students.

Brooklyn College of the City University of New York, Division of Graduate Studies, School of Education, Program in Childhood Education, Brooklyn, NY 11210-2889. Offers bilingual education (MS Ed); liberal arts (MS Ed); mathematics (MS Ed); science/environmental education (MS Ed). Part-time and evening/weekend programs available. *Students:* 10 full-time (9 women), 275 part-time (233 women); includes 130 minority (84 African Americans, 12 Asian Americans or Pacific Islanders, 34 Hispanic Americans), 11 international. 154 applicants, 81% accepted, 80 enrolled. In 2006, 214 degrees awarded. *Entrance requirements:* For master's, LAST, interview, previous course work in education, writing sample, resumé, 2 letters of recommendation. Additional exam requirements/recommendations for international students: Required—TOEFL. *Application deadline:* For fall admission, 3/1 priority date for domestic students, 2/1 priority date for international students; for spring admission, 11/1 priority date for domestic students, 10/1 priority date for international students. Applications are processed on a rolling basis. Application fee: $125. Electronic applications accepted. *Expenses:* Tuition, state resident: full-time $6,400; part-time $270 per credit. Tuition, nonresident: full-time $12,000; part-time $500 per credit. Required fees: $118 per semester. *Financial support:* Career-related internships or fieldwork, Federal Work-Study, institutionally sponsored loans, and scholarships/grants available. Support available to part-time students. Financial award application deadline: 5/1; financial award applicants required to submit FAFSA. *Faculty research:* Emotional intelligence, multiculturalism, arts immersion, the Holocaust. *Unit head:* Dr. Sharon O'Connor-Petruso, Program Head, 718-951-5214. *Application contact:* Karen Alleyne-Pierre, Director of Admissions Services and Enrollment Communications, 718-951-5902, Fax: 718-951-4506, E-mail: grads@brooklyn.cuny.edu.

Brown University, Graduate School, Department of Education, Providence, RI 02912. Offers elementary education 1-6 (MAT); secondary biology (MAT); secondary English (MAT); secondary social studies/history (MAT). *Faculty:* 4 full-time (2 women), 7 part-time/adjunct (all women). *Students:* 28 full-time (23 women); includes 5 minority (2 African Americans, 1 Asian American or Pacific Islander, 2 Hispanic Americans). Average age 25. 89 applicants, 61% accepted, 28 enrolled. In 2006, 35 degrees awarded. *Degree requirements:* For master's, student teaching, portfolio. *Entrance requirements:* For master's, GRE General Test (secondary only), PRAXIS II (elementary), letters of recommendation, interview. *Application deadline:* For winter admission, 1/3 for domestic students. Application fee: $70. Electronic applications accepted. *Financial support:* In 2006–07, 23 students received support, including 2 fellowships (averaging $7,000 per year); Federal Work-Study, institutionally sponsored loans, scholarships/grants, tuition waivers (partial), and proctorships also available. Financial award application deadline: 2/1; financial award applicants required to submit FAFSA. *Faculty research:* Literacy, performance-based assessment, teaching English as a foreign language. *Unit head:* Lawrence Wakeford, Chairman, 401-863-3428, Fax: 401-863-1276, E-mail: lawrence_wakeford@brown.edu. *Application contact:* Carin Algava, Assistant Director, 401-863-3364, Fax: 401-863-1276, E-mail: carin_algava@brown.edu.

Buffalo State College, State University of New York, Graduate Studies and Research, Faculty of Applied Science and Education, Department of Elementary Education and Reading, Program in Elementary Education, Buffalo, NY 14222-1095. Offers childhood education (grades 1-6) (MS Ed); early childhood and childhood curriculum and instruction (MS Ed); early childhood education (birth-grade 2) (MS Ed). *Accreditation:* NCATE. Part-time programs available. *Degree requirements:* For master's, thesis or project. *Entrance requirements:* For master's, minimum GPA of 2.5 in last 60 hours, New York teaching certificate. Additional exam requirements/recommendations for international students: Required—TOEFL (minimum score 550 paper-based; 213 computer-based).

Butler University, College of Education, Indianapolis, IN 46208-3485. Offers administration (MS); elementary education (MS); reading (MS); school counseling (MS); secondary education (MS); special education (MS). *Accreditation:* ACA; NCATE. Part-time and evening/weekend programs available. *Faculty:* 12 full-time (6 women), 11 part-time/adjunct (8 women). *Students:* 18 full-time (10 women), 156 part-time (125 women); includes 21 minority (16 African Americans,

2 Asian Americans or Pacific Islanders, 3 Hispanic Americans), 7 international. Average age 31. 56 applicants, 57% accepted, 29 enrolled. In 2006, 72 degrees awarded. *Entrance requirements:* For master's, GRE General Test, MAT, interview. *Application deadline:* For fall admission, 8/15 priority date for domestic students. Applications are processed on a rolling basis. Application fee: $35. Electronic applications accepted. *Expenses:* Tuition: Full-time $6,030; part-time $335 per credit. Tuition and fees vary according to program. *Financial support:* Institutionally sponsored loans available. Support available to part-time students. Financial award application deadline: 7/15; financial award applicants required to submit FAFSA. *Faculty research:* Ethics in cybercounseling, history of sports for disabled effect of fetal alcohol syndrome on perceptual learning, Reading Recovery's theoretical framework in teacher education. *Unit head:* Dr. Ena Shelley, Dean, 317-940-9752, Fax: 317-940-6481. *Application contact:* Karen Farrell, Department Secretary, 317-940-9220, E-mail: kfarrell@butler.edu.

California State University, Fullerton, Graduate Studies, College of Education, Department of Elementary and Bilingual Education, Fullerton, CA 92834-9480. Offers bilingual/bicultural education (MS); elementary curriculum and instruction (MS). *Accreditation:* NCATE. Part-time programs available. *Students:* 17 full-time (all women), 214 part-time (198 women); includes 95 minority (1 African American, 25 Asian Americans or Pacific Islanders, 69 Hispanic Americans), 2 international. Average age 31. 178 applicants, 90% accepted, 100 enrolled. In 2006, 70 degrees awarded. *Degree requirements:* For master's, project or thesis. *Entrance requirements:* For master's, minimum GPA of 2.5, teaching certificate. Application fee: $55. *Expenses:* Tuition, nonresident: part-time $339 per unit. Required fees: $1,155 per semester. *Financial support:* Teaching assistantships, career-related internships or fieldwork, Federal Work-Study, institutionally sponsored loans, and scholarships/grants available. Support available to part-time students. Financial award application deadline: 3/1. *Faculty research:* Teacher training and tracking, model for improvement of teaching. *Unit head:* Dr. Karen Ivers, Chair, 714-278-2470. *Application contact:* Dr. Ruth Yopp-Edwards, Co-Chair, 714-278-3411.

California State University, Los Angeles, Graduate Studies, Charter College of Education, Division of Curriculum and Instruction, Los Angeles, CA 90032-8530. Offers elementary teaching (MA); reading (MA); secondary teaching (MA). Part-time and evening/weekend programs available. *Faculty:* 13 full-time (8 women), 8 part-time/adjunct (all women). *Students:* 269 full-time (184 women), 572 part-time (406 women); includes 528 minority (48 African Americans, 1 American Indian/Alaska Native, 142 Asian Americans or Pacific Islanders, 337 Hispanic Americans), 20 international. In 2006, 134 degrees awarded. *Entrance requirements:* For master's, minimum GPA of 2.75 in last 90 units of course work, teaching certificate. Additional exam requirements/recommendations for international students: Required—TOEFL. *Application deadline:* For fall admission, 6/30 for domestic students; for spring admission, 2/1 for domestic students. Applications are processed on a rolling basis. Application fee: $55. *Expenses:* Tuition, nonresident: part-time $226 per unit. *Financial support:* Federal Work-Study available. Support available to part-time students. Financial award application deadline: 3/1. *Faculty research:* Media, language arts, mathematics, computers, drug-free schools. *Unit head:* Dr. Andrea Maxie, Chair, 323-343-4350, Fax: 323-343-5458.

California State University, Northridge, Graduate Studies, College of Education, Department of Elementary Education, Northridge, CA 91330. Offers MA. *Accreditation:* NCATE. Part-time and evening/weekend programs available. *Faculty:* 24 full-time (17 women), 53 part-time/adjunct (42 women). *Students:* 17 full-time (1 woman), 81 part-time (5 women); includes 44 minority (4 African Americans, 9 Asian Americans or Pacific Islanders, 31 Hispanic Americans), 1 international. Average age 33. 24 applicants, 79% accepted, 12 enrolled. In 2006, 21 degrees awarded. *Degree requirements:* For master's, comprehensive exam. *Entrance requirements:* For master's, GRE General Test or minimum GPA of 3.0. Additional exam requirements/recommendations for international students: Required—TOEFL. *Application deadline:* For fall admission, 11/30 for domestic students. Application fee: $55. *Expenses:* Tuition, nonresident: full-time $8,136; part-time $4,068 per year. Required fees: $3,624; $1,161 per term. *Financial support:* Federal Work-Study available. Financial award application deadline: 3/1. *Unit head:* Dr. David Kretschmer, Chair, 818-677-2621. *Application contact:* Thomas Potter, Graduate Coordinator, 818-677-2621.

California State University, San Bernardino, Graduate Studies, College of Education, Program in Elementary Education, San Bernardino, CA 92407-2397. Offers MA. *Accreditation:* NCATE. *Students:* 2 full-time (both women), 1 (woman) part-time; includes 2 minority (both Hispanic Americans) Average age 50. 2 applicants, 50% accepted, 1 enrolled. In 2006, 22 degrees awarded. *Application deadline:* For fall admission, 8/31 priority date for domestic students. Application fee: $55. *Unit head:* Dr. Ruth Norton, Interim Chair, 909-537-5603, Fax: 909-537-7510, E-mail: rnorton@csusb.edu.

California State University, Stanislaus, Graduate School, College of Education, Department of Teacher Education, Turlock, CA 95382. Offers curriculum and instruction (MA Ed), including elementary education, multilingual education, reading education, secondary education. Part-time and evening/weekend programs available. *Degree requirements:* For master's, thesis. *Entrance requirements:* For master's, MAT or GRE, minimum GPA of 3.0. Additional exam requirements/recommendations for international students: Required—TOEFL (minimum score 550 paper-based; 213 computer-based).

California University of Pennsylvania, School of Graduate Studies and Research, School of Education, Department of Elementary Education, California, PA 15419-1394. Offers reading specialist (M Ed). *Accreditation:* NCATE. Part-time and evening/weekend programs available. *Faculty:* 6 full-time (3 women). *Students:* 60 full-time (53 women), 29 part-time (24 women); includes 2 minority (1 African American, 1 Asian American or Pacific Islander). Average age 28. 25 applicants, 88% accepted, 22 enrolled. In 2006, 23 degrees awarded. *Median time to degree:* Master's–1.5 years full-time, 3 years part-time. *Degree requirements:* For master's, thesis optional. *Entrance requirements:* For master's, MAT, PRAXIS, minimum GPA of 3.0, state police clearances. Additional exam requirements/recommendations for international students: Required—TOEFL (minimum score 550 paper-based; 213 computer-based; 80 iBT). *Application deadline:* For fall admission, 8/1 priority date for domestic and international students; for winter admission, 12/1 priority date for domestic and international students; for spring admission, 5/1 priority date for domestic and international students. Applications are processed on a rolling basis. Application fee: $25. Electronic applications accepted. *Expenses:* Tuition, state resident: full-time $6,048; part-time $336 per credit. Tuition, nonresident: full-time $9,678; part-time $538 per credit. Required fees: $1,854; $263 per credit. Full-time tuition and fees vary according to course load, campus/location and program. *Financial support:* Career-related internships or fieldwork, scholarships/grants, traineeships, and unspecified assistantships available. Financial award applicants required to submit FAFSA. *Faculty research:* English as a second language, adult literacy, emerging literacy, diagnosis and remediation, phonemic awareness. Total annual research expenditures: $10,000. *Unit head:* Prof. Jane Bonari, Chairperson, 724-938-4569, Fax: 724-938-5873, E-mail: bonari@cup.edu.

Campbell University, Graduate and Professional Programs, School of Education, Buies Creek, NC 27506. Offers administration (MSA); community counseling (MA); elementary education (M Ed); English education (M Ed); interdisciplinary studies (M Ed); mathematics education (M Ed); middle grades education (M Ed); physical education (M Ed); school counseling (M Ed); secondary education (M Ed); social science education (M Ed). *Accreditation:* NCATE. Part-time and evening/weekend programs available. *Faculty:* 14 full-time (9 women), 12 part-time/adjunct (7 women). *Students:* 27 full-time (25 women), 183 part-time (146 women); includes 30 minority (24 African Americans, 3 American Indian/Alaska Native, 3 Hispanic Americans), 1 international. Average age 31. 112 applicants, 74% accepted, 74 enrolled. In 2006, 65 degrees awarded. *Degree requirements:* For master's, comprehensive exam. *Entrance requirements:* For master's, GRE General Test, minimum GPA of 2.7. *Application deadline:* For fall admission, 8/1 priority date for domestic students; for spring admission, 1/2 priority date for domestic students. Applications are processed on a rolling basis. Application fee: $65. *Expenses:* Tuition: Part-time $380 per semester hour. *Financial support:* In 2006–07, 67 students received support. Career-related internships or fieldwork and Federal Work-Study available. Financial award application deadline: 4/15; financial award applicants required to submit FAFSA. *Faculty research:* Spiritual values and wellness issues in counseling, stress and professional burnout among counselors, thinking strategies, leadership, adaptive technology. *Unit head:* Dr. Karen P. Nery, Dean, 910-893-1630, Fax: 910-893-1999, E-mail: nery@campbell.edu. *Application contact:* James S. Farthing, Director of Graduate Admissions for Business and Education, 910-893-1200 Ext. 1318, Fax: 910-814-4718, E-mail: farthing@campbell.edu.

Capella University, School of Education, Minneapolis, MN 55402. Offers college teaching (Certificate); curriculum and instruction (MS, PhD); education (MS); enrollment management (MS); instructional design for online learning (MS, PhD); k-12 studies in education (MS, PhD); leadership for higher education (MS, PhD); leadership in education administration (Certificate); leadership in educational administration (MS, PhD); postsecondary and adult education (MS, PhD); professional studies in education (MS, PhD); reading and literacy (MS); training and performance improvement (MS, PhD). Part-time and evening/weekend programs available. Postbaccalaureate distance learning degree programs offered (minimal on-campus study). Terminal master's awarded for partial completion of doctoral program. *Degree requirements:* For master's, integrative project, thesis optional; for doctorate, thesis/dissertation, comprehensive exam, registration. *Entrance requirements:* Additional exam requirements/recommendations for international students: Required—TOEFL (minimum score 550 paper-based; 213 computer-based), TWE (minimum score 4). Electronic applications accepted. *Faculty research:* Higher education administration, distance learning, adult education, training and curriculum design.

Carlow University, School of Education, Program in Education, Pittsburgh, PA 15213-3165. Offers elementary education (M Ed); instructional technology specialist (M Ed); secondary education (M Ed); special education (M Ed). Part-time and evening/weekend programs available. *Entrance requirements:* For master's, resumé, 3 letters of recommendation, minimum GPA of 3.0, interview. Electronic applications accepted.

Carson-Newman College, Graduate Program in Education, Jefferson City, TN 37760. Offers curriculum and instruction (M Ed); elementary education (MAT); school counseling (M Ed); secondary education (MAT); teaching English as a second language (MATESL). *Accreditation:* NCATE. Part-time and evening/weekend programs available. *Faculty:* 5 full-time (2 women), 10 part-time/adjunct (3 women). *Students:* 77 full-time (60 women), 41 part-time (29 women); includes 2 minority (both African Americans), 27 international. Average age 32. 65 applicants, 97% accepted. In 2006, 64 degrees awarded. *Degree requirements:* For master's, thesis or alternative. *Entrance requirements:* For master's, NTE, minimum GPA of 3.0 in major, 2.5 overall. *Application deadline:* For fall admission, 7/15 priority date for domestic students. Applications are processed on a rolling basis. Application fee: $25 ($50 for international students). *Expenses:* Tuition: Part-time $270 per credit hour. *Financial support:* In 2006–07, 86 students received support. Federal Work-Study and unspecified assistantships available. Financial award application deadline: 4/1; financial award applicants required to submit FAFSA. *Unit head:* Dr. Jean Love, Chair, 865-471-3461. *Application contact:* Graduate Admissions and Services Adviser, 865-471-3460, Fax: 865-471-3875.

Catawba College, Program in Education, Salisbury, NC 28144-2488. Offers elementary education (M Ed). *Accreditation:* NCATE. Part-time and evening/weekend programs available. *Faculty:* 3 full-time (2 women), 2 part-time/adjunct (1 woman). In 2006, 3 degrees awarded. *Degree requirements:* For master's, project, practicum, and portfolio. *Entrance requirements:* For master's, NTE, PRAXIS, minimum undergraduate GPA of 3.0, valid teaching license. *Application deadline:* For fall admission, 8/1 priority date for domestic students; for winter admission, 12/1 priority date for domestic students; for spring admission, 5/1 priority date for domestic students. Applications are processed on a rolling basis. Application fee: $0. *Expenses:* Tuition: Part-time $130 per credit hour. *Financial support:* Scholarships/grants available. *Faculty research:* Integrated arts in elementary schools, professional development schools. *Unit head:* Dr. James K. Stringfield, Chair, Department of Teacher Education, 704-637-4461, Fax: 704-637-4732, E-mail: jstringf@catawba.edu. *Application contact:* Dr. Lou W. Kasias, Director, Graduate Program, 704-637-4462, Fax: 704-637-4732, E-mail: lakasias@catawba.edu.

Centenary College of Louisiana, Graduate Programs, Department of Education, Shreveport, LA 71104. Offers administration (M Ed); elementary education (MAT); secondary education (MAT); supervision of instruction (M Ed). Part-time and evening/weekend programs available. *Degree requirements:* For master's, comprehensive exam. *Entrance requirements:* For master's, GRE General Test (M Ed), PRAXIS I and PRAXIS II (MAT), teacher certification (M Ed), minimum GPA of 2.5. Expenses: Contact institution. *Faculty research:* Teachers as advocates for teachers, portfolio assessment, disabled readers.

Central Connecticut State University, School of Graduate Studies, School of Education and Professional Studies, Department of Teacher Education, Program in Elementary Education, New Britain, CT 06050-4010. Offers MS, Certificate. Part-time and evening/weekend programs available. *Students:* 58 full-time (48 women), 95 part-time (79 women); includes 5 minority (3 African Americans, 2 Hispanic Americans). 72 applicants, 67% accepted, 28 enrolled. In 2006, 38 master's, 10 other advanced degrees awarded. *Degree requirements:* For master's, thesis or alternative, comprehensive exam or special project. *Entrance requirements:* For master's, minimum GPA of 2.7. Additional exam requirements/recommendations for international students: Required—TOEFL. *Application deadline:* For fall admission, 7/1 for domestic students; for spring admission, 12/1 for domestic students. Applications are processed on a rolling basis. Application fee: $50. Electronic applications accepted. *Expenses:* Tuition, area resident: Full-time $3,970; part-time $380 per credit. Tuition, state resident: full-time $5,955; part-time $380 per credit. Tuition, nonresident: full-time $11,061; part-time $380 per credit. Required fees: $3,189. One-time fee: $62 part-time. Tuition and fees vary according to degree level and program. *Faculty research:* Elementary school curriculum, changing school populations, multicultural education, professional development.

Central Michigan University, College of Graduate Studies, College of Education and Human Services, Department of Teacher Education and Professional Development, Mount Pleasant, MI 48859. Offers educational technology (MA); elementary education (MA), including classroom teaching, early childhood education, reading in the elementary school; library, media, and technology (MA), including library media, media and technology; middle level education (MA); reading improvement (MA); secondary education (MA); teaching senior high (MA). *Accreditation:* NCATE. *Degree requirements:* For master's, thesis or alternative, registration. *Faculty research:* Reading instruction and reading disabilities, teaching and learning styles, school and business partnerships, school restructuring and improvement, mathematics learning and instruction.

Chadron State College, School of Professional and Graduate Studies, Department of Education, Chadron, NE 69337. Offers business (MA Ed); community counseling (MA Ed); educational administration (MS Ed, Sp Ed); elementary education (MS Ed); history (MA Ed); language and literature (MA Ed); secondary administration (MS Ed); secondary education (MS Ed). *Accreditation:* NCATE. Part-time and evening/weekend programs available. Postbaccalaureate distance learning degree programs offered. *Degree requirements:* For master's, thesis optional. *Entrance requirements:* For master's, GRE General Test, GRE Writing Test, minimum GPA of 2.75 or 12 graduate hours at CSC with minimum GPA of 3.25. Additional exam requirements/recommendations for international students: Required—TOEFL. Electronic applications accepted. *Faculty research:* Rural education, technology, mental health.

Chapman University, Graduate Studies, School of Education, Program in Teaching: Elementary Education, Orange, CA 92866. Offers MA. Part-time and evening/weekend programs available. *Faculty:* 16 full-time (11 women), 25 part-time/adjunct (14 women). *Students:* 48 full-time (44 women), 43 part-time (39 women); includes 27 minority (9 Asian Americans or Pacific Islanders, 18 Hispanic Americans), 2 international. Average age 28. 23 applicants, 78% accepted, 16 enrolled. In 2006, 20 degrees awarded. *Degree requirements:* For master's, thesis, registration. *Entrance requirements:* For master's, GRE General Test, MAT, or California Subject Examinations for Teachers, minimum GPA of 2.75. Additional exam requirements/recommendations for international students: Required—TOEFL (minimum score 550 paper-

Elementary Education

Chapman University (continued)

based). *Application deadline:* Applications are processed on a rolling basis. Application fee: $55. Electronic applications accepted. *Expenses: Contact institution. Financial support:* In 2006–07, 88 students received support, including 8 fellowships (averaging $1,750 per year); Federal Work-Study also available. Financial award application deadline: 6/30; financial award applicants required to submit FAFSA. *Unit head:* Dr. Anaida Colon-Muniz, Coordinator, 714-997-6781, E-mail: acolon@chapman.edu. *Application contact:* Rika Judd, Graduate Admission Counselor, 714-997-6786, Fax: 714-997-6713, E-mail: rjudd@chapman.edu.

Charleston Southern University, Programs in Education, Charleston, SC 29423-8087. Offers administration and supervision (M Ed), including elementary, secondary; elementary education (M Ed); English (MAT); science (MAT); secondary education (M Ed); social studies (MAT). *Accreditation:* NCATE. Part-time and evening/weekend programs available. *Degree requirements:* For master's, thesis optional. *Entrance requirements:* For master's, GRE or MAT. Expenses: Contact institution. *Faculty research:* Economic education, multicultural education, restructuring teacher education, participation in mathematics and science by minorities and women, at-risk children.

Chatham University, Program in Education, Pittsburgh, PA 15232-2826. Offers early childhood education (MAT); elementary education (MAT); English—secondary (MAT); environmental education (K-12) (MAT); secondary art (MAT); secondary biology education (MAT); secondary chemistry education (MAT); secondary English education (MAT); secondary math education (MAT); secondary physics education (MAT); secondary social studies education (MAT); special education (MAT). *Students:* 60 full-time (43 women), 23 part-time (22 women). Average age 29. 48 applicants, 77% accepted, 32 enrolled. In 2006, 59 degrees awarded. *Degree requirements:* For master's, thesis, teaching experience. *Entrance requirements:* For master's, PRAXIS I, minimum GPA of 3.0, sample of written work, recommendation letters. Additional exam requirements/recommendations for international students: Required—TOEFL (minimum score 600 paper-based; 250 computer-based; 100 iBT); Recommended—IELTS (minimum score 7), TWE (minimum score 5). *Application deadline:* For fall admission, 5/1 priority date for domestic and international students; for winter admission, 10/1 priority date for domestic and international students. Applications are processed on a rolling basis. Application fee: $45. Electronic applications accepted. *Financial support:* Career-related internships or fieldwork available. Financial award applicants required to submit FAFSA. *Faculty research:* Gifted education, environmental education, technology in education, writing as learning, class size and achievement. *Unit head:* Dr. Wendy Weiner, Director, 412-365-1146, Fax: 412-365-1505, E-mail: wweiner@chatham.edu. *Application contact:* 412-365-1825, Fax: 412-365-1609, E-mail: admissions@chatham.edu.

Chestnut Hill College, School of Graduate Studies, Department of Education, Program in Elementary Education, Philadelphia, PA 19118-2693. Offers M Ed. Part-time and evening/weekend programs available. *Faculty:* 33 part-time/adjunct (24 women). *Students:* 39 full-time (30 women), 139 part-time (119 women); includes 32 minority (20 African Americans, 9 Asian Americans or Pacific Islanders, 3 Hispanic Americans). Average age 29. In 2006, 46 degrees awarded. *Degree requirements:* For master's, thesis optional. *Entrance requirements:* For master's, Pre-Professional Skills Test, writing sample. Additional exam requirements/recommendations for international students: Required—TOEFL (minimum score 500 paper-based). *Application deadline:* For fall admission, 7/15 priority date for domestic students, 7/15 for international students; for spring admission, 12/15 priority date for domestic students, 12/15 for international students. Applications are processed on a rolling basis. Application fee: $50. *Expenses: Contact institution.* Tuition and fees vary according to degree level. *Financial support:* Institutionally sponsored loans available. Financial award application deadline: 7/15; financial award applicants required to submit FAFSA. *Faculty research:* Effects of media on learning, use of on-line tests and virtual classrooms, literacy acquisition strategies, connections of media to literacy, electronic texts in the classroom. *Application contact:* Jayne Mashett, Director of Graduate Admissions, 215-248-7020, Fax: 215-248-7161, E-mail: mashettj@chc.edu.

Cheyney University of Pennsylvania, School of Education, Program in Elementary Education, Cheyney, PA 19319-0200. Offers M Ed, MAT. *Accreditation:* NCATE. Part-time and evening/weekend programs available. *Degree requirements:* For master's, thesis or alternative. *Entrance requirements:* For master's, GRE General Test, MAT, minimum GPA of 2.75. Electronic applications accepted.

Chicago State University, School of Graduate and Professional Studies, College of Education, Department of Reading, Elementary Education, Library Information and Media Studies, Program in Elementary Education, Chicago, IL 60628. Offers MAT. *Accreditation:* NCATE. *Degree requirements:* For master's, thesis optional. *Entrance requirements:* For master's, minimum GPA of 3.0 in last 60 hours.

Christopher Newport University, Graduate Studies, Department of Teacher Preparation, Newport News, VA 23606-2998. Offers art (PK-12) (MAT); biology (6-12) (MAT); computer science (6-12) (MAT); elementary (PK-6) (MAT); English (6-12) (MAT); French (PK-12) (MAT); history (6-12) (MAT); history and social science (MAT); mathematics (6-12) (MAT); music (PK-12) (MAT), including choral, instrumental; physics (6-12) (MAT); Spanish (PK-12) (MAT); theater (PK-12) (MAT). Part-time and evening/weekend programs available. *Degree requirements:* For master's, thesis or alternative, comprehensive exam. *Entrance requirements:* For master's, PRAXIS I, minimum GPA of 3.0. Electronic applications accepted. *Faculty research:* Early literacy development, instructional innovations, professional teaching standards, multicultural issues, aesthetic education.

City College of the City University of New York, Graduate School, School of Education, Program in Elementary Education, New York, NY 10031-9198. Offers MS. *Accreditation:* NCATE. *Degree requirements:* For master's, thesis. *Entrance requirements:* For master's, Liberal Arts and Sciences Test (LAST), Content Specialty Test (CST). Additional exam requirements/recommendations for international students: Required—TOEFL.

Clarion University of Pennsylvania, Office of Research and Graduate Studies, College of Education and Human Services, Department of Education, Program in Education, Clarion, PA 16214. Offers curriculum and instruction (M Ed); early childhood (M Ed); English (M Ed); history (M Ed); literacy (M Ed); science (M Ed); technology (M Ed). *Accreditation:* NCATE. Part-time programs available. *Faculty:* 18 full-time (13 women). *Students:* 11 full-time (4 women), 54 part-time (37 women); includes 4 minority (3 African Americans, 1 Asian American or Pacific Islander). 50 applicants, 90% accepted. In 2006, 7 degrees awarded. *Degree requirements:* For master's, thesis or alternative, comprehensive exam. *Entrance requirements:* For master's, minimum QPA of 3.0, teacher certification. Additional exam requirements/recommendations for international students: Required—TOEFL (minimum score 550 paper-based; 213 computer-based; 80 iBT). *Application deadline:* For fall admission, 8/1 priority date for domestic students, 4/15 priority date for international students; for spring admission, 12/1 priority date for domestic students, 9/15 priority date for international students. Applications are processed on a rolling basis. Application fee: $30. Electronic applications accepted. *Expenses:* Tuition, state resident: part-time $336 per credit. Tuition, nonresident: part-time $538 per credit. *Financial support:* In 2006–07, 2 research assistantships with full tuition reimbursements (averaging $4,002 per year) were awarded. Support available to part-time students. Financial award application deadline: 3/1. *Application contact:* Dr. Brian Maguire, Coordinator, 814-393-2058, Fax: 814-393-2558, E-mail: bmaguire@clarion.edu.

Clemson University, Graduate School, College of Health, Education, and Human Development, School of Education, Program in Elementary Education, Clemson, SC 29634. Offers M Ed. *Accreditation:* NCATE. *Students:* 4 full-time (all women), 3 part-time (all women), 1 international. 4 applicants, 100% accepted, 3 enrolled. In 2006, 4 degrees awarded. *Degree requirements:* For master's, comprehensive exam. *Entrance requirements:* For master's, GRE General Test, teaching certificate. Additional exam requirements/recommendations for international students: Required—TOEFL. *Application deadline:* For fall admission, 6/1 for domestic students. Applications are processed on a rolling basis. Application fee: $50. Electronic applications accepted. *Expenses:* Tuition, state resident: full-time $8,812; part-time $450 per hour. Tuition, nonresident: full-time $18,036; part-time $760 per hour. Required fees: $474; $5 per term. *Financial support:* Teaching assistantships available. Financial award application deadline: 6/1; financial award applicants required to submit FAFSA. *Unit head:* Dr. Dee Stegelin, Graduate Coordinator, 864-656-5119.

See Close-Up on page 1269.

Coastal Carolina University, College of Education, Conway, SC 29528-6054. Offers early childhood education (M Ed); education (MAT); elementary education (M Ed); secondary education (M Ed). *Accreditation:* NCATE. Part-time and evening/weekend programs available. *Faculty:* 8 full-time (4 women), 16 part-time/adjunct (10 women). *Students:* 48 full-time (31 women), 45 part-time (33 women); includes 8 minority (6 African Americans, 2 Asian Americans or Pacific Islanders). Average age 30. In 2006, 70 degrees awarded. *Degree requirements:* For master's, comprehensive exam. *Entrance requirements:* For master's, GRE General Test, MAT, 2 letters of recommendation, copy of teaching credential. Additional exam requirements/recommendations for international students: Required—TOEFL. *Application deadline:* For fall admission, 8/15 priority date for domestic students. Applications are processed on a rolling basis. Application fee: $45. Electronic applications accepted. *Expenses:* Tuition, state resident: full-time $7,920; part-time $330 per credit hour. Tuition, nonresident: full-time $9,600; part-time $400 per credit hour. Required fees: $80; $40 per term. *Financial support:* Fellowships, research assistantships, unspecified assistantships available. Support available to part-time students. Financial award application deadline: 4/1; financial award applicants required to submit FAFSA. *Unit head:* Dr. Gilbert H. Hunt, Dean, 843-349-2607, Fax: 843-349-2332, E-mail: hunt@coastal.edu. *Application contact:* Dr. Judy W. Vogt, Vice President, Enrollment Services, 843-349-2037, Fax: 843-349-2127, E-mail: jvogt@coastal.edu.

College of Charleston, Graduate School, School of Education, Department of Elementary and Early Childhood Education, Program in Elementary Education, Charleston, SC 29424-0001. Offers M Ed, MAT. *Accreditation:* NCATE. Part-time and evening/weekend programs available. *Degree requirements:* For master's, thesis or alternative, written qualifying exam, student teaching experience (MAT). *Entrance requirements:* For master's, GRE, MAT, or NTE; South Carolina Education Entrance Exam (MAT), teaching certificate (M Ed). Additional exam requirements/recommendations for international students: Required—TOEFL.

The College of New Jersey, Graduate Division, School of Education, Department of Elementary and Early Childhood Education, Program in Elementary Education, Ewing, NJ 08628. Offers M Ed, MAT. *Accreditation:* NCATE. Part-time and evening/weekend programs available. *Students:* 14 full-time (13 women), 40 part-time (33 women); includes 6 minority (4 African Americans, 2 Asian Americans or Pacific Islanders). 39 applicants, 77% accepted. In 2006, 42 degrees awarded. *Degree requirements:* For master's, comprehensive exam. *Entrance requirements:* For master's, GRE General Test, minimum GPA of 3.0 in field or 2.75 overall. Additional exam requirements/recommendations for international students: Required—TOEFL. *Application deadline:* For fall admission, 4/15 for domestic students; for spring admission, 10/15 for domestic students. Application fee: $60. Electronic applications accepted. *Financial support:* Unspecified assistantships available. Financial award application deadline: 5/1; financial award applicants required to submit FAFSA. *Unit head:* Dr. Brenda Leake, Coordinator, 609-771-2219, Fax: 609-637-5197. *Application contact:* Susan L. Hydro, Office of Graduate Studies, Assistant Dean, 609-771-2300, Fax: 609-637-5105, E-mail: graduate@tcnj.edu.

The College of New Rochelle, Graduate School, Division of Education, Program in Elementary Education/Early Childhood Education, New Rochelle, NY 10805-2308. Offers MS Ed. Part-time programs available. *Faculty:* 3 full-time (all women), 5 part-time/adjunct (3 women). *Students:* 13 full-time (12 women), 54 part-time (52 women); includes 19 minority (15 African Americans, 1 American Indian/Alaska Native, 3 Hispanic Americans). Average age 32. In 2006, 10 degrees awarded. *Degree requirements:* For master's, thesis (for some programs), practicum, comprehensive exam (for some programs), registration. *Entrance requirements:* For master's, interview, minimum GPA of 3.0 in field, 2.7 overall. *Application deadline:* For fall admission, 8/1 priority date for domestic students; for spring admission, 4/6 for domestic students. Applications are processed on a rolling basis. Application fee: $35. *Expenses:* Tuition: Part-time $575 per credit. Required fees: $90 per term. *Financial support:* Career-related internships or fieldwork, scholarships/grants, and unspecified assistantships available. *Unit head:* Dr. Marie Ribarich, Acting Division Head, Division of Education, 914-654-5333, Fax: 914-654-5593, E-mail: mribarich@cnr.edu.

College of St. Joseph, Graduate Program, Division of Education, Program in Elementary Education, Rutland, VT 05701-3899. Offers M Ed. Part-time and evening/weekend programs available. *Faculty:* 3 full-time (2 women), 8 part-time/adjunct (5 women). *Students:* 21 full-time, 14 part-time. Average age 32. 15 applicants, 87% accepted, 13 enrolled. In 2006, 13 degrees awarded. *Degree requirements:* For master's, comprehensive exam, registration. *Entrance requirements:* For master's, PRAXIS I (for initial licensure), 2 letters of reference, minimum GPA of 3.0 (initial licensure) or minimum GPA of 2.7 (nonlicensure), interview. *Application deadline:* Applications are processed on a rolling basis. Application fee: $35. *Expenses:* Tuition: Full-time $10,990; part-time $300 per credit. Part-time tuition and fees vary according to program. *Financial support:* Career-related internships or fieldwork, Federal Work-Study, and unspecified assistantships available. Support available to part-time students. Financial award application deadline: 3/1. *Application contact:* Tracy Gallipo, Director of Admissions, 802-773-5900 Ext. 3262, Fax: 802-773-5900, E-mail: tracygallipo@csj.edu.

The College of Saint Rose, Graduate Studies, School of Education, Teacher Education Department, Albany, NY 12203-1419. Offers business and marketing (MS Ed); childhood education (MS Ed); early childhood education (MS Ed); elementary education (K-6) (MS Ed); secondary education (MS Ed, Certificate); teacher education (MS Ed, Certificate), including bilingual pupil personnel services (Certificate). Part-time and evening/weekend programs available. *Entrance requirements:* For master's, minimum undergraduate GPA of 3.0. Additional exam requirements/recommendations for international students: Required—TOEFL (minimum score 550 paper-based; 213 computer-based). Electronic applications accepted.

College of Staten Island of the City University of New York, Graduate Programs, Department of Education, Program in Childhood Education, Staten Island, NY 10314-6600. Offers MS Ed. Part-time and evening/weekend programs available. *Faculty:* 4 full-time (2 women), 5 part-time/adjunct (3 women). *Students:* 25 full-time (23 women), 296 part-time (276 women); includes 36 minority (7 African Americans, 1 American Indian/Alaska Native, 8 Asian Americans or Pacific Islanders, 20 Hispanic Americans), 2 international. Average age 30. 68 applicants, 85% accepted, 42 enrolled. In 2006, 121 degrees awarded. *Degree requirements:* For master's, research project. *Entrance requirements:* For master's, minimum GPA of 2.75, 2 letters of recommendation. Additional exam requirements/recommendations for international students: Required—TOEFL (minimum score 550 paper-based; 213 computer-based; 79 iBT). *Application deadline:* For fall admission, 4/28 priority date for domestic and international students; for spring admission, 11/19 priority date for domestic and international students. Applications are processed on a rolling basis. Application fee: $125. *Expenses:* Tuition, state resident: full-time $6,400; part-time $270 per credit. Tuition, nonresident: part-time $500 per credit. Required fees: $53 per semester. *Financial support:* Applicants required to submit FAFSA. *Unit head:* Dr. Igor Arievitch, Coordinator, 718-982-4006, Fax: 718-982-3743, E-mail: arievitch@mail.csi.cuny.edu. *Application contact:* Emmanuel Esperance, Deputy Director of Office of Recruitment and Admissions, 718-982-2190, Fax: 718-982-2500, E-mail: admissions@mail.csi.cuny.edu.

The College of William and Mary, School of Education, Program in Curriculum and Instruction, Williamsburg, VA 23187-8795. Offers elementary education (MA Ed); gifted education (MA Ed); reading education (MA Ed); secondary education (MA Ed), including English education, mathematics education, modern foreign languages education, science education, social studies education; special education (MA Ed), including emotionally disturbed, learning disabled, mental retardation, resource collaborating teaching. *Accreditation:* NCATE. Part-time programs available. *Faculty:* 15 full-time (6 women), 13 part-time/adjunct (10 women). *Students:* 51 full-time (39 women), 51 part-time (45 women); includes 6 minority (all African Americans) Average age 29. 161 applicants, 68% accepted, 61 enrolled. In 2006, 68 degrees awarded. *Degree requirements:* For master's, master's project. *Entrance requirements:* For master's, GRE or MAT, minimum GPA of 2.5. Additional exam requirements/recommendations for international students: Required—TOEFL. *Application deadline:* For fall admission, 2/1 for domestic and international students; for spring admission, 10/1 for domestic and international students. Application fee: $30. *Expenses:* Tuition, state resident: full-time $6,100; part-time $260 per credit. Tuition, nonresident: full-time $18,790; part-time $725 per credit. Required fees: $3,314. Tuition and fees vary according to program. *Financial support:* In 2006–07, 10 research assistantships with full and partial tuition reimbursements (averaging $5,000 per year) were awarded; career-related internships or fieldwork, Federal Work-Study, institutionally sponsored loans, scholarships/grants, and unspecified assistantships also available. Financial award application deadline: 2/1; financial award applicants required to submit FAFSA. *Faculty research:* National Council of Teachers of Mathematics Standards, counseling, self-concept and self-esteem, special education, curriculum development. *Unit head:* Dr. John Moore, Area Coordinator, 757-221-2333, E-mail: jnmoor@wm.edu. *Application contact:* Dorothy Osborne, Director of Admissions, 757-221-2317, E-mail: dsosbo@wm.edu.

The Colorado College, Department of Education, Program in Elementary Education, Colorado Springs, CO 80903-3294. Offers elementary school teaching (MAT). *Faculty:* 4 full-time (2 women), 6 part-time/adjunct (3 women). *Students:* 9 full-time (7 women); includes 1 minority (Hispanic American) Average age 26. 19 applicants, 63% accepted, 9 enrolled. In 2006, 20 degrees awarded. *Degree requirements:* For master's, thesis, internship. *Entrance requirements:* For master's, PRAXIS II or PLACE. *Application deadline:* For fall admission, 2/1 for domestic and international students. Application fee: $50. *Expenses:* Tuition: Full-time $23,567. One-time fee: $1,485 full-time. *Financial support:* In 2006–07, 9 students received support, including 9 teaching assistantships (averaging $16,000 per year); career-related internships or fieldwork, institutionally sponsored loans, health care benefits, and tuition waivers (partial) also available. Financial award application deadline: 2/15; financial award applicants required to submit FAFSA. *Application contact:* Marsha E. Unruh, Director of Education Career Services, 719-389-6472, Fax: 719-389-6473, E-mail: munruh@coloradocollege.edu.

The Colorado College, Programs for Experienced Teachers, Colorado Springs, CO 80903-3294. Offers American Southwest studies for all teachers (MAT); arts and humanities for secondary school teachers and administrators (MAT); integrated natural science for all teachers (MAT); liberal arts for elementary school teachers and administrators (MAT). Programs offered during summer only. Part-time programs available. *Faculty:* 18 part-time/adjunct (8 women). *Students:* 78; includes 2 minority (both Hispanic Americans) Average age 31. In 2006, 28 degrees awarded. *Degree requirements:* For master's, thesis, oral exam, 50 page paper. *Application deadline:* Applications are processed on a rolling basis. Application fee: $50. *Expenses: Contact institution.* One-time fee: $1,485 full-time. *Financial support:* Institutionally sponsored loans and half-tuition waivers to teachers with a contract available. *Unit head:* Dr. Libby Rittenberg, Dean of Summer Programs, 719-389-6657, Fax: 719-389-6955. *Application contact:* Ann H. Van Horn, Assistant Dean of Summer Session, 719-389-6656, Fax: 719-389-6955, E-mail: avanhorn@coloradocollege.edu.

Columbia College, Graduate Programs, Department of Education, Columbia, SC 29203-5998. Offers divergent learning (M Ed). *Accreditation:* NCATE. Part-time and evening/weekend programs available. Postbaccalaureate distance learning degree programs offered (minimal on-campus study). *Faculty:* 4 full-time (2 women), 25 part-time/adjunct (15 women). *Students:* 234 full-time (219 women), 2 part-time (1 woman); includes 66 minority (64 African Americans, 2 Hispanic Americans). Average age 32. 144 applicants, 97% accepted, 122 enrolled. In 2006, 252 degrees awarded. *Degree requirements:* For master's, thesis. *Entrance requirements:* For master's, GRE General Test, MAT, 2 recommendations, current South Carolina teaching certificate, minimum GPA of 3.2. Additional exam requirements/recommendations for international students: Required—TOEFL. *Application deadline:* For fall admission, 7/15 for domestic and international students. Applications are processed on a rolling basis. Application fee: $50. Electronic applications accepted. *Expenses: Contact institution. Financial support:* Available to part-time students. Application deadline: 7/1; *Unit head:* Dr. Mary Steppling, Chair, 803-786-3782, Fax: 803-786-3034, E-mail: msteppling@colacoll.edu. *Application contact:* Carolyn Emeneker, Director of Graduate School and Evening College Admissions, 803-786-3766, Fax: 803-786-3674, E-mail: emeneker@colacoll.edu.

Columbia College Chicago, Graduate School, Department of Educational Studies, Chicago, IL 60605-1996. Offers elementary (MAT); English (MAT); interdisciplinary arts (MAT); multicultural education (MA); urban teaching (MA). Part-time and evening/weekend programs available. *Degree requirements:* For master's, thesis, student teaching experience, 100 preclinical hours. *Entrance requirements:* For master's, NTE, minimum GPA of 3.0, portfolio. Additional exam requirements/recommendations for international students: Required—TOEFL (minimum score 550 paper-based; 213 computer-based). Electronic applications accepted.

Columbia International University, Columbia Graduate School, Columbia, SC 29230-3122. Offers Bible teaching (MABT); Christian higher education leadership (Ed D); Christian school educational leadership (Ed D); counseling (MACN); curriculum and instruction (M Ed), including Christian school guidance, English as a second language, learning disabilities, school technology; early childhood and elementary education (MAT); educational administration (M Ed); teaching English as a foreign language (Certificate); teaching English as a foreign language and intercultural studies (MATF). Part-time and evening/weekend programs available. *Faculty:* 11 full-time (4 women), 7 part-time/adjunct (5 women). *Students:* 52 full-time (44 women), 93 part-time (59 women); includes 17 minority (11 African Americans, 2 Asian Americans or Pacific Islanders, 4 Hispanic Americans), 10 international. Average age 35. 107 applicants, 56% accepted, 41 enrolled. In 2006, 62 degrees awarded. *Degree requirements:* For master's, internships, professional project. *Entrance requirements:* For master's, Minnesota Multiphasic Personality Inventory, MAT, minimum GPA of 2.7. Additional exam requirements/recommendations for international students: Required—TOEFL. *Application deadline:* For fall admission, 8/1 priority date for domestic and international students; for winter admission, 12/15 priority date for domestic and international students; for spring admission, 1/15 priority date for domestic and international students. Applications are processed on a rolling basis. Application fee: $45. Electronic applications accepted. *Expenses:* Tuition: Part-time $400 per semester hour. Tuition and fees vary according to course load and program. *Financial support:* In 2006–07, 35 students received support. Career-related internships or fieldwork, Federal Work-Study, institutionally sponsored loans, and scholarships/grants available. Financial award application deadline: 3/17; financial award applicants required to submit FAFSA. *Unit head:* Dr. Milton Uecker, Dean, 803-807-5319, Fax: 803-786-4209, E-mail: muecker@ciu.edu. *Application contact:* Michelle MacGregor, Director of Admissions, 800-777-2227 Ext. 5335, Fax: 803-786-4209, E-mail: yescbs@ciu.edu.

Concordia University, College of Education, Portland, OR 97211-6099. Offers curriculum and instruction (elementary) (M Ed); educational administration (M Ed); elementary education (MAT); secondary education (MAT). Part-time programs available. Postbaccalaureate distance learning degree programs offered (no on-campus study). *Degree requirements:* For master's, work samples/portfolio. *Entrance requirements:* For master's, California Basic Educational Skills Test or PRAXIS I, minimum undergraduate GPA of 2.8, graduate 3.0; 2 letters of recommendation. Additional exam requirements/recommendations for international students: Required—TOEFL (minimum score 525 paper-based; 195 computer-based). Electronic applications accepted. *Faculty research:* Learner centered classroom, brain-based learning future of on-line learning.

Connecticut College, Graduate School, Programs in Education, Program in Elementary Education, New London, CT 06320-4196. Offers MAT. Part-time programs available. *Entrance requirements:* For master's, MAT.

Converse College, School of Education and Graduate Studies, Program in Elementary Education, Spartanburg, SC 29302-0006. Offers M Ed, MAT. Part-time programs available. *Faculty:* 2 full-time, 4 part-time/adjunct. *Students:* Average age 35. In 2006, 75 degrees awarded. *Degree requirements:* For master's, capstone paper. *Entrance requirements:* For master's, NTE or PRAXIS II (M Ed), minimum GPA of 2.75, 2 recommendations. *Application deadline:* For fall admission, 8/1 for domestic and international students; for winter admission, 11/15 for domestic and international students; for spring admission, 1/15 for domestic and international students. Applications are processed on a rolling basis. Application fee: $40. Electronic applications accepted. *Expenses:* Tuition: Part-time $305 per credit hour. Required fees: $20 per term. *Financial support:* Available to part-time students. Applicants required to submit FAFSA. *Unit head:* Dr. Deborah Haydon, Director, 864-596-9017. *Application contact:* Thomas M. Faulkenberry, Dean of the School of Education and Graduate Studies, 864-596-9082, Fax: 864-596-9221, E-mail: tom.faulkenberry@converse.edu.

Curry College, Division of Continuing Education and Graduate Studies, Program in Education, Milton, MA 02186-9984. Offers adult education (Certificate); educational administration (M Ed); educational therapy (Certificate); elementary education (M Ed); foundations (non-license) (M Ed); learning disabilities across the lifespan (Certificate); reading (M Ed, Certificate); special education (M Ed). Part-time and evening/weekend programs available. *Faculty:* 6 full-time (4 women), 11 part-time/adjunct (7 women). *Degree requirements:* For master's, research project. *Entrance requirements:* For master's, MAT, interview, recommendations, resumé. Additional exam requirements/recommendations for international students: Required—TOEFL (minimum score 550 paper-based). *Application deadline:* For fall admission, 8/1 priority date for domestic students; for spring admission, 1/1 for domestic students. Applications are processed on a rolling basis. Application fee: $50. *Expenses: Contact institution. Financial support:* Career-related internships or fieldwork and tuition waivers (partial) available. *Faculty research:* Classroom trauma, therapeutic writing, inclusionary practices. *Unit head:* Dr. Donald Gratz, Director and Associate Professor, 617-333-2243, E-mail: dgratz0703@curry.edu. *Application contact:* John Bresnahan, Director of Graduate Enrollment and Student Services, 617-333-2243, Fax: 617-333-2045, E-mail: jbresnah0104@curry.edu.

Dallas Baptist University, Dorothy M. Bush College of Education, Education Program, Dallas, TX 75211-9299. Offers early childhood education (M Ed); educational leadership (M Ed); elementary reading education (M Ed); general elementary education (M Ed); reading specialist (M Ed). Part-time and evening/weekend programs available. *Faculty:* 49 full-time (21 women), 112 part-time/adjunct (46 women). *Students:* 47 full-time, 149 part-time. 65 applicants, 58% accepted, 36 enrolled. In 2006, 67 degrees awarded. *Entrance requirements:* For master's, GRE General Test, minimum GPA of 3.0. Additional exam requirements/recommendations for international students: Required—TOEFL. *Application deadline:* Applications are processed on a rolling basis. Application fee: $25. Electronic applications accepted. *Expenses:* Tuition: Full-time $8,370; part-time $465 per credit hour. Required fees: $465 per credit hour. *Financial support:* Federal Work-Study, institutionally sponsored loans, scholarships/grants, and tuition waivers (full and partial) available. Support available to part-time students. *Faculty research:* Emerging literacy, self-directed schools. *Unit head:* Dr. Elaine Wilmore, Interim Director, 214-333-5413, Fax: 214-333-5551, E-mail: graduate@dbu.edu. *Application contact:* Kit P. Montgomery, Director of Graduate Programs, 214-333-5242, Fax: 214-333-5579, E-mail: graduate@dbu.edu.

Delta State University, Graduate Programs, College of Education, Division of Teacher Education, Program in Elementary Education, Cleveland, MS 38733-0001. Offers M Ed, MAT, Ed S. *Accreditation:* NCATE. Part-time and evening/weekend programs available. *Degree requirements:* For master's, thesis optional. *Entrance requirements:* For master's, GRE General Test; for Ed S, master's degree, teaching certificate. *Application deadline:* For fall admission, 8/1 priority date for domestic students; for spring admission, 12/1 priority date for domestic students. Applications are processed on a rolling basis. Application fee: $0. *Financial support:* Research assistantships, career-related internships or fieldwork, Federal Work-Study, and institutionally sponsored loans available. Support available to part-time students. Financial award application deadline: 6/1.

Delta State University, Graduate Programs, College of Education, Thad Cochran Center for Rural School Leadership and Research, Program in Administration and Supervision, Cleveland, MS 38733-0001. Offers educational administration and supervision (Ed S); educational leadership (M Ed); elementary education (Ed S); secondary education (Ed S). *Accreditation:* NCATE. Part-time and evening/weekend programs available. *Degree requirements:* For master's, thesis optional. *Entrance requirements:* For master's, GRE General Test or MAT; for Ed S, master's degree, teaching certificate. *Application deadline:* For fall admission, 8/1 priority date for domestic students; for spring admission, 12/1 priority date for domestic students. Applications are processed on a rolling basis. Application fee: $0. *Financial support:* Research assistantships, career-related internships or fieldwork, Federal Work-Study, and institutionally sponsored loans available. Support available to part-time students. Financial award application deadline: 6/1.

DePaul University, School of Education, Chicago, IL 60604-2287. Offers bilingual and bicultural education (M Ed, MA); curriculum studies (M Ed, MA); education (Ed D), including curriculum studies, educational leadership; educational leadership (M Ed, MA), including administration and supervision, Catholic school leadership, physical education; human development and learning (MA); human services and counseling (M Ed, MA), including agencies, family concerns, and higher education, elementary schools, human services management, secondary schools; reading and learning disabilities (M Ed, MA); social culture studies in education and development (M Ed, MA), including curriculum studies/development; teaching and learning (early childhood, elementary and secondary) (M Ed), including elementary education (M Ed, MA), secondary education (M Ed, MA); teaching and learning (early childhood, elementary, and secondary) (MA), including elementary education (M Ed, MA), secondary education (M Ed, MA). *Accreditation:* NCATE. Part-time and evening/weekend programs available. *Faculty:* 61 full-time (40 women), 76 part-time/adjunct (46 women). *Students:* 1,371 full-time (1,103 women), 474 part-time (362 women); includes 435 minority (144 African Americans, 7 American Indian/Alaska Native, 89 Asian Americans or Pacific Islanders, 195 Hispanic Americans), 11 international. Average age 30. 993 applicants, 80% accepted, 617 enrolled. In 2006, 324 master's, 7 doctorates awarded. *Degree requirements:* For doctorate, thesis/dissertation. *Entrance requirements:* For master's, interview, minimum GPA of 2.75, 2 letters of recommendation; for doctorate, interview, master's degree, 2 years of work experience (recommended), writing sample, 3 letters of recommendation. Application fee: $25. Electronic applications accepted. *Financial support:* In 2006–07, 16 research assistantships with tuition reimbursements (averaging $4,370 per year), 1 teaching assistantship (averaging $6,000 per year) were awarded; career-related internships or fieldwork also available. *Faculty research:* Reflective teaching, children at risk, loss, ethnicity, urban education. Total annual research expenditures: $556,194. *Unit head:* Dr. Clara Jennings, Dean, 773-325-7581, Fax: 773-325-7728, E-mail: cjennings@depaul.edu. *Application contact:* Dr. John Bollwark, Data Project Manager, 773-325-7582, Fax: 773-325-7713, E-mail: jbollwar@depaul.edu.

Drake University, School of Education, Department of Leadership, Counseling and Adult Development, Program in Counseling, Des Moines, IA 50311-4516. Offers community agency counseling (MSE); guidance counseling (MSE), including elementary, secondary. *Accreditation:* CORE. Part-time and evening/weekend programs available. *Faculty:* 10 full-time (3 women), 28 part-time/adjunct (16 women). *Students:* 137 applicants, 61% accepted. In 2006, 41 degrees awarded. *Degree requirements:* For master's, comprehensive exam. *Entrance requirements:* For master's, GRE General Test, MAT, or Drake Writing Assessment, resumé, 2 letters of recommendation. Additional exam requirements/recommendations for international students: Required—TOEFL (minimum score 550 paper-based; 213 computer-based). *Application deadline:* For fall admission, 7/1 priority date for domestic students, 6/1 priority date for international students; for spring admission, 11/1 priority date for domestic students, 10/1 priority date for international students. Applications are processed on a rolling basis. Application fee: $25. Electronic applications accepted. *Financial support:* Career-related internships or

Elementary Education

Drake University (continued)

fieldwork and unspecified assistantships available. Support available to part-time students. *Faculty research:* Counseling and rehabilitation, behavioral supports, inquiry-based science methods, teacher quality enhancements. Total annual research expenditures: $1.5 million. *Unit head:* Dr. Matt Bruinekool, Director, 515-271-4507, E-mail: matt.bruinekool@drake.edu. *Application contact:* Ann J. Martin, Graduate Coordinator, 515-271-2034, Fax: 515-271-2831, E-mail: ann.martin@drake.edu.

Drake University, School of Education, Department of Teaching and Learning, Program in Elementary Education, Des Moines, IA 50311-4516. Offers MST. Part-time programs available. *Faculty:* 10 full-time (3 women), 28 part-time/adjunct (16 women). *Students:* 15 full-time (10 women), 10 part-time (all women); includes 1 minority (Hispanic American), 1 international. 20 applicants, 50% accepted. In 2006, 11 degrees awarded. *Degree requirements:* For master's, thesis (for some programs), internships (s), comprehensive exam, registration. *Entrance requirements:* For master's, GRE General Test, MAT, or Drake SOE writing assessment, resumé, 2 letters of recommendation. Additional exam requirements/recommendations for international students: Required—TOEFL (minimum score 550 paper-based; 213 computer-based). *Application deadline:* For fall admission, 7/1 priority date for domestic students, 6/1 priority date for international students; for spring admission, 11/1 priority date for domestic students, 10/1 priority date for international students. Applications are processed on a rolling basis. Application fee: $25. Electronic applications accepted. *Financial support:* Career-related internships or fieldwork and unspecified assistantships available. Support available to part-time students. *Faculty research:* Counseling and rehabilitation, behavioral supports, inquiry-based science methods, teacher quality enhancement. Total annual research expenditures: $1.5 million. *Unit head:* Dr. Linda Espey, Head, 515-271-1954, E-mail: linda.espey@drake.edu. *Application contact:* Ann J. Martin, Graduate Coordinator, 515-271-2034, Fax: 515-271-2831, E-mail: ann.martin@drake.edu.

Drury University, Graduate Programs in Education, Program in Elementary Education, Springfield, MO 65802. Offers M Ed. *Accreditation:* NCATE. Part-time and evening/weekend programs available. *Degree requirements:* For master's, thesis. *Entrance requirements:* For master's, GRE or MAT, minimum GPA of 2.75. *Faculty research:* School climate, parent involvement, college/public school partnerships, technology.

Duquesne University, School of Education, Department of Instruction and Leadership, Program in Elementary Education, Pittsburgh, PA 15282-0001. Offers MS Ed. Part-time and evening/weekend programs available. *Faculty:* 6 full-time (4 women), 4 part-time/adjunct (2 women). *Students:* 81. 40 applicants, 93% accepted, 28 enrolled. In 2006, 41 degrees awarded. *Degree requirements:* For master's, thesis optional. *Entrance requirements:* For master's, MAT, minimum GPA of 3.0. *Application deadline:* For fall admission, 8/1 for domestic students; for spring admission, 12/1 for domestic students. Applications are processed on a rolling basis. Application fee: $50. *Expenses:* Tuition: Part-time $723 per credit. Required fees: $71 per credit. Tuition and fees vary according to degree level and program. *Financial support:* In 2006–07, 1 research assistantship with full and partial tuition reimbursement (averaging $5,200 per year) was awarded; Federal Work-Study also available. Support available to part-time students. *Unit head:* Dr. Kimberly Hyatt, Coordinator, 412-396-4794, Fax: 412-396-5388, E-mail: hyatt@duq.edu.

D'Youville College, Department of Education, Buffalo, NY 14201-1084. Offers elementary education (MS Ed, Teaching Certificate); secondary education (MS Ed, Teaching Certificate); special education (MS Ed). Part-time and evening/weekend programs available. *Faculty:* 31 full-time (18 women), 38 part-time/adjunct (25 women). *Students:* 613 full-time (434 women), 303 part-time (223 women); includes 26 minority (14 African Americans, 1 American Indian/Alaska Native, 2 Asian Americans or Pacific Islanders, 9 Hispanic Americans), 727 international. Average age 28. 1,092 applicants. In 2006, 328 master's, 401 other advanced degrees awarded. *Degree requirements:* For master's, project or thesis. *Entrance requirements:* For master's, minimum GPA of 3.0. Additional exam requirements/recommendations for international students: Required—TOEFL (minimum score 500 paper-based; 173 computer-based). *Application deadline:* For fall admission, 5/1 priority date for international students; for spring admission, 9/1 priority date for international students. Applications are processed on a rolling basis. Application fee: $25. Electronic applications accepted. *Financial support:* In 2006–07, 1 research assistantship with partial tuition reimbursement (averaging $3,000 per year) was awarded; career-related internships or fieldwork and scholarships/grants also available. Support available to part-time students. Financial award application deadline: 3/1; financial award applicants required to submit FAFSA. *Faculty research:* Developmentally disabled, multiculturalism, early childhood education. *Unit head:* Dr. David Gorlewski, Chair, 716-829-8140, Fax: 716-829-7660. *Application contact:* Linda Fisher, Graduate Admissions Director, 716-829-8400, Fax: 716-829-7900, E-mail: graduateadmissions@dyc.edu.

East Carolina University, Graduate School, College of Education, Department of Curriculum and Instruction, Greenville, NC 27858-4353. Offers behavior/emotional disabilities (MA Ed); elementary education (MA Ed); English education (MA Ed); learning disabilities (MA Ed); low incidence disabilities (MA Ed); mental retardation (MA Ed); middle grade education (MA Ed); reading education (MA Ed); social studies education (MA Ed). Part-time programs available. Postbaccalaureate distance learning degree programs offered. *Students:* 92 full-time (85 women), 233 part-time (211 women); includes 42 minority (39 African Americans, 1 American Indian/Alaska Native, 1 Asian American or Pacific Islander, 1 Hispanic American). Average age 30. 25 applicants, 100% accepted, 25 enrolled. In 2006, 195 degrees awarded. *Degree requirements:* For master's, thesis optional. *Entrance requirements:* For master's, GRE General Test or MAT, interview, bachelor's degree in related field, minimum GPA of 2.5, teaching license. Additional exam requirements/recommendations for international students: Required—TOEFL. *Application deadline:* For fall admission, 6/1 priority date for domestic students. Applications are processed on a rolling basis. Application fee: $50. *Financial support:* Research assistantships, teaching assistantships, Federal Work-Study available. Support available to part-time students. Financial award application deadline: 6/1; financial award applicants required to submit FAFSA. *Unit head:* Dr. Sandra H. Warren, Interim Chair, 252-328-2699, E-mail: warrens@ecu.edu. *Application contact:* Dean of Graduate School, 252-328-6012, Fax: 252-328-6071, E-mail: gradschool@ecu.edu.

Eastern Connecticut State University, School of Education and Professional Studies/Graduate Division, Program in Elementary Education, Willimantic, CT 06226-2295. Offers MS. *Accreditation:* NCATE. Part-time and evening/weekend programs available. *Faculty:* 8 full-time (5 women), 8 part-time/adjunct (1 woman). *Students:* 37 full-time (28 women), 55 part-time (48 women); includes 4 minority (1 African American, 3 Hispanic Americans). Average age 33. 20 applicants, 50% accepted, 9 enrolled. In 2006, 26 degrees awarded. *Degree requirements:* For master's, comprehensive exam or thesis. *Entrance requirements:* For master's, PRAXIS I, minimum GPA of 2.7, teaching certificate. Additional exam requirements/recommendations for international students: Required—TOEFL (minimum score 550 paper-based; 213 computer-based). *Application deadline:* For fall admission, 7/6 priority date for domestic and international students; for spring admission, 11/3 priority date for domestic and international students. Applications are processed on a rolling basis. Application fee: $50. *Expenses:* Tuition, state resident: full-time $3,970. Tuition, nonresident: full-time $11,061; part-time $336 per credit. Required fees: $35 per credit. *Financial support:* Teaching assistantships, career-related internships or fieldwork, scholarships/grants, and unspecified assistantships available. Support available to part-time students. Financial award application deadline: 3/15. *Unit head:* Dr. Delar Singh, Advisor, 860-465-4555, Fax: 860-465-5099, E-mail: singhd@easternct.edu. *Application contact:* Dr. Tuesday L. Cooper, Associate Dean, 860-465-4543, Fax: 860-465-4538, E-mail: coopert@easternct.edu.

Eastern Illinois University, Graduate School, College of Education and Professional Studies, Department of Early Childhood, Elementary and Middle Level Education, Charleston, IL 61920-3099. Offers elementary education (MS Ed). *Accreditation:* NCATE. Part-time programs available. *Faculty:* 14 full-time (6 women). In 2006, 55 degrees awarded. *Degree requirements:* For master's, comprehensive exam. *Application deadline:* For fall admission, 7/31 priority date for domestic students. Applications are processed on a rolling basis. Application fee: $30. *Expenses:* Tuition, state resident: part-time $169 per semester hour. Tuition, nonresident: part-time $508 per semester hour. Required fees: $60 per semester hour. *Financial support:* In 2006–07, research assistantships with tuition reimbursements (averaging $7,200 per year), 5 teaching assistantships with tuition reimbursements (averaging $7,200 per year) were awarded. *Unit head:* Dr. Joy Russell, Chairperson, 217-581-5728, E-mail: jlrussell@eiu.edu.

Eastern Kentucky University, The Graduate School, College of Education, Department of Curriculum and Instruction, Richmond, KY 40475-3102. Offers elementary education general (MA Ed), including early elementary education, elementary education general, reading; music education (MA Ed); secondary and higher education (MA Ed), including agricultural education, allied health sciences education, art education, biological sciences education, business education, chemistry education, earth science education, English education, general science education, geography education, history education, home economics education, industrial education, mathematical sciences education, physical education, physics education, political science education, psychology education, reading, school health education, sociology education. *Accreditation:* NCATE. Part-time programs available. *Faculty:* 22 full-time (13 women), 18 part-time/adjunct (14 women). *Students:* 62 full-time (51 women), 300 part-time (257 women); includes 9 minority (5 African Americans, 2 American Indian/Alaska Native, 1 Asian American or Pacific Islander, 1 Hispanic American), 1 international. Average age 32. 437 applicants, 22% accepted. In 2006, 166 degrees awarded. *Entrance requirements:* For master's, GRE General Test, minimum GPA of 2.5. Application fee: $35. *Expenses:* Tuition, state resident: full-time $5,610. Tuition, nonresident: full-time $15,910. *Financial support:* In 2006–07, research assistantships (averaging $6,500 per year), teaching assistantships (averaging $6,500 per year) were awarded; career-related internships or fieldwork and Federal Work-Study also available. Support available to part-time students. *Faculty research:* Technology in education, reading instruction, e-portfolios, induction to teacher education, dispositions of teachers. *Unit head:* Dr. Michael Martin, Chair, 859-622-2154, Fax: 859-622-2004.

Eastern Michigan University, Graduate School, College of Education, Department of Teacher Education, Program in Elementary Education, Ypsilanti, MI 48197. Offers MA. *Accreditation:* NCATE. Part-time and evening/weekend programs available. Postbaccalaureate distance learning degree programs offered (minimal on-campus study). *Students:* 1 (woman) full-time, 29 part-time (25 women); includes 2 minority (1 African American, 1 American Indian/Alaska Native), 2 international. Average age 32. In 2006, 3 degrees awarded. *Entrance requirements:* For master's, GRE. Additional exam requirements/recommendations for international students: Required—TOEFL. *Application deadline:* For fall admission, 5/15 priority date for domestic students, 5/1 priority date for international students; for winter admission, 10/15 priority date for domestic students, 10/1 priority date for international students; for spring admission, 3/15 priority date for domestic students, 3/1 priority date for international students. Applications are processed on a rolling basis. Application fee: $35. *Expenses:* Tuition, state resident: part-time $341 per credit hour. Tuition, nonresident: full-time $16,104; part-time $671 per credit hour. Required fees: $816; $34 per credit hour. $40 per term. One-time fee: $82 full-time. Tuition and fees vary according to course level, course load, degree level and reciprocity agreements. *Financial support:* Fellowships, research assistantships with full tuition reimbursements, teaching assistantships with full tuition reimbursements, career-related internships or fieldwork, Federal Work-Study, institutionally sponsored loans, scholarships/grants, tuition waivers (partial), and unspecified assistantships available. Support available to part-time students. Financial award applicants required to submit FAFSA.

Eastern Nazarene College, Adult and Graduate Studies, Division of Education, Quincy, MA 02170-2999. Offers early childhood education (M Ed, Certificate); elementary education (M Ed, Certificate); English as a second language (M Ed, Certificate); instructional enrichment and development (M Ed, Certificate); middle school education (M Ed, Certificate); moderate special needs education (M Ed, Certificate); principal (Certificate); program development and supervision (M Ed, Certificate); secondary education (M Ed, Certificate); special education administrator (Certificate); supervisor (Certificate); teacher of reading (M Ed, Certificate). M Ed and Certificate also available through weekend program for administration, special needs, and reading only. Part-time and evening/weekend programs available. *Faculty:* 9 full-time (5 women), 11 part-time/adjunct (5 women). *Students:* 135. Average age 35. 20 applicants, 100% accepted. In 2006, 2 degrees awarded. *Entrance requirements:* Additional exam requirements/recommendations for international students: Required—TOEFL (minimum score 550 paper-based). *Application deadline:* Applications are processed on a rolling basis. Application fee: $35. *Financial support:* Career-related internships or fieldwork available. Support available to part-time students. Financial award applicants required to submit FAFSA. *Unit head:* Dr. Lorne Ranstrom, Chair, 617-745-3528, E-mail: randstrol@enc.edu. *Application contact:* Christine Galbraith, Graduate Studies Recruiter, 617-774-6703, Fax: 617-984-4901, E-mail: christine.galbraith@enc.edu.

Eastern Oregon University, School of Education and Business, Program in Elementary Education, La Grande, OR 97850-2899. Offers MTE. Part-time programs available. Postbaccalaureate distance learning degree programs offered (minimal on-campus study). *Degree requirements:* For master's, thesis. *Entrance requirements:* For master's, NTE.

Eastern Washington University, Graduate Studies, College of Education and Human Development, Department of Education, Program in Elementary Teaching, Cheney, WA 99004-2431. Offers M Ed. *Accreditation:* NCATE. *Degree requirements:* For master's, comprehensive exam. *Entrance requirements:* For master's, minimum GPA of 3.0.

East Stroudsburg University of Pennsylvania, Graduate School, School of Professional Studies, Program in Elementary Education, East Stroudsburg, PA 18301-2999. Offers M Ed. Part-time and evening/weekend programs available. *Faculty:* 4 full-time (2 women), 5 part-time/adjunct (2 women). *Students:* 17 full-time (15 women), 64 part-time (55 women); includes 2 minority (both Hispanic Americans) Average age 32. In 2006, 12 degrees awarded. *Degree requirements:* For master's, comprehensive exam. *Entrance requirements:* For master's, PRAXIS/teacher certification, letter of recommendation, Pennsylvania Department of Education requirements. Additional exam requirements/recommendations for international students: Required—TOEFL (minimum score 560 paper-based; 220 computer-based; 83 iBT). *Application deadline:* For fall admission, 7/31 priority date for domestic students, 5/1 priority date for international students; for spring admission, 11/30 for domestic students, 10/1 for international students. Applications are processed on a rolling basis. Application fee: $50. *Expenses:* Tuition, state resident: full-time $6,048; part-time $336 per credit. Tuition, nonresident: full-time $9,678; part-time $538 per credit. Required fees: $1,353; $67 per credit. One-time fee: $37 part-time. *Financial support:* In 2006–07, 10 research assistantships with full and partial tuition reimbursements (averaging $2,900 per year) were awarded; Federal Work-Study and institutionally sponsored loans also available. Financial award application deadline: 3/1; financial award applicants required to submit FAFSA. *Unit head:* Dr. Paula Kelberman, Graduate Coordinator, 570-422-3365, Fax: 570-422-3942, E-mail: pkelberman@po-box.esu.edu.

East Tennessee State University, School of Graduate Studies, College of Education, Department of Curriculum and Instruction, Johnson City, TN 37614. Offers 7-12 (MAT); classroom technology (M Ed); educational communication (M Ed); educational media/educational technology (M Ed); elementary education (M Ed, MAT); K-12 (MAT); reading and storytelling (M Ed, MA); reading education (M Ed, MA); school library media (M Ed); secondary education (M Ed, MAT). *Accreditation:* NCATE. Part-time and evening/weekend programs available. *Degree requirements:* For master's, thesis (for some programs). *Entrance requirements:* For master's, GRE, minimum GPA of 3.0. Additional exam requirements/recommendations for international students: Required—TOEFL (minimum score 550 paper-based; 213 computer-based). *Faculty research:* Critical thinking, curriculum development, cultural diversity, cognitive processes, effective teaching strategies.

Edinboro University of Pennsylvania, Graduate Studies and Research, School of Education, Department of Elementary Education, Program in Elementary Education, Edinboro, PA

16444. Offers character education (M Ed); early childhood education (M Ed); elementary education (M Ed), including language arts, mathematics, science, thesis focus. Part-time and evening/weekend programs available. *Students:* 31 full-time (26 women), 46 part-time (38 women). Average age 30. In 2006, 14 degrees awarded. *Degree requirements:* For master's, thesis or alternative, project, comprehensive exam. *Entrance requirements:* For master's, GRE or MAT, minimum QPA of 2.5, valid teaching certificate or current study to obtain certification. *Application deadline:* Applications are processed on a rolling basis. Application fee: $30. Electronic applications accepted. *Expenses:* Tuition, state resident: full-time $6,048; part-time $336 per credit. Tuition, nonresident: full-time $9,678; part-time $538 per credit. Required fees: $1,849; $42 per credit. *Financial support:* In 2006–07, 7 research assistantships with full and partial tuition reimbursements (averaging $3,850 per year) were awarded; career-related internships or fieldwork, Federal Work-Study, scholarships/grants, and unspecified assistantships also available. Support available to part-time students. Financial award application deadline: 2/15; financial award applicants required to submit FAFSA. *Unit head:* Dr. Kathleen Dailey, Coordinator, 814-732-2714, E-mail: dailey@edinboro.edu. *Application contact:* Dr. R. Scott Baldwin, Dean, 814-732-2752, Fax: 814-732-2268, E-mail: sbaldwin@edinboro.edu.

Elizabeth City State University, Program in Elementary Education, Elizabeth City, NC 27909-7806. Offers M Ed. *Accreditation:* NCATE.

Elms College, Division of Education, Chicopee, MA 01013-2839. Offers early childhood education (MAT); education (M Ed, CAGS); elementary education (MAT); English as a second language (MAT); reading (MAT); secondary education (MAT), including biology education, English education, Spanish education; special education (MAT). Part-time and evening/weekend programs available. *Faculty:* 9 full-time (6 women), 4 part-time/adjunct (2 women). *Students:* 8 full-time (6 women), 97 part-time (89 women); includes 4 minority (2 Asian Americans or Pacific Islanders, 2 Hispanic Americans). Average age 36. 48 applicants, 90% accepted, 40 enrolled. In 2006, 37 master's, 8 other advanced degrees awarded. *Degree requirements:* For master's, thesis (for some programs). *Entrance requirements:* For master's, Massachusetts Educators Certification Test, minimum GPA of 3.0; for CAGS, master's degree in education. Additional exam requirements/recommendations for international students: Required—TOEFL. *Application deadline:* For fall admission, 7/1 priority date for domestic students; for spring admission, 11/1 priority date for domestic students. Applications are processed on a rolling basis. Application fee: $30. *Expenses:* Tuition: Full-time $9,180; part-time $510 per credit. Tuition and fees vary according to course load. *Financial support:* In 2006–07, 3 teaching assistantships with partial tuition reimbursements were awarded; tuition waivers (partial) also available. Support available to part-time students. Financial award application deadline: 4/15; financial award applicants required to submit FAFSA. *Unit head:* Dr. Mary Janeczek, Director, 413-594-2761, Fax: 413-592-4871, E-mail: janeczeke@elms.edu.

Elon University, Program in Education, Elon, NC 27244-2010. Offers elementary education (M Ed); gifted education (M Ed); special education (M Ed). *Accreditation:* NCATE. Part-time programs available. *Faculty:* 11 full-time (8 women), 5 part-time/adjunct (all women). *Students:* Average age 31. 62 applicants, 69% accepted, 30 enrolled. In 2006, 30 degrees awarded. *Entrance requirements:* For master's, GRE, MAT. Additional exam requirements/recommendations for international students: Required—TOEFL (minimum score 550 paper-based; 213 computer-based; 79 iBT). *Application deadline:* For winter admission, 6/1 priority date for domestic students. Applications are processed on a rolling basis. Application fee: $50. Electronic applications accepted. *Expenses: Contact institution. Financial support:* In 2006–07, 2 students received support, including 2 fellowships (averaging $2,635 per year); Federal Work-Study and scholarships/grants also available. Support available to part-time students. Financial award application deadline: 6/1; financial award applicants required to submit FAFSA. *Faculty research:* Teaching reading to low-achieving second and third graders; pre-and post-student teaching attitudes toward teaching; children's writing; whole language methodology; critical creative thinking. *Unit head:* Dr. Judith B. Howard, Director, 336-278-5885, Fax: 336-278-5919, E-mail: howardj@elon.edu. *Application contact:* Art Fadde, Director of Graduate Admissions, 800-334-8448 Ext. 3, Fax: 336-278-7699, E-mail: afadde@elon.edu.

Emmanuel College, Graduate Programs, Programs in Education, Boston, MA 02115. Offers educational leadership (CAGS); elementary education (MAT); school administration (M Ed); secondary education (MAT). Part-time and evening/weekend programs available. *Faculty:* 4 full-time (all women), 8 part-time/adjunct (4 women). *Students:* 5 full-time (all women), 34 part-time (24 women); includes 6 minority (3 African Americans, 1 Asian American or Pacific Islander, 2 Hispanic Americans). Average age 29. 44 applicants, 23% accepted, 10 enrolled. In 2006, 21 master's, 3 other advanced degrees awarded. *Entrance requirements:* For master's, interview, resumé, 2 letters of recommendation; for CAGS, interview, leadership statement, resumé, 2 letters of recommendation. Additional exam requirements/recommendations for international students: Required—TOEFL (minimum score 600 paper-based; 250 computer-based). *Application deadline:* For fall admission, 8/15 priority date for domestic students; for spring admission, 12/8 priority date for domestic students. Applications are processed on a rolling basis. Application fee: $50. Electronic applications accepted. *Expenses:* Tuition: Full-time $5,256. *Faculty research:* Literature/reading, history of education, multicultural education, special education. *Unit head:* Brian Minchello, Associate Director, Graduate and Professional Programs, 617-735-9928, Fax: 617-735-9708, E-mail: gpp@emmanuel.edu. *Application contact:* Kristin Balutis, Enrollment Counselor, 617-735-9859, Fax: 617-735-9708, E-mail: balutkr@emmanuel.edu.

Emporia State University, School of Graduate Studies, The Teachers College, Department of Early Childhood/Elementary Teacher Education, Program in Master Teacher, Emporia, KS 66801-5087. Offers master teacher (MS), including elementary subject matter, English as a second language, reading, secondary subject matter. *Accreditation:* NCATE. Part-time programs available. *Students:* 1 (woman) full-time, 83 part-time (82 women); includes 2 minority (1 American Indian/Alaska Native, 1 Hispanic American). 14 applicants, 93% accepted, 13 enrolled. In 2006, 23 degrees awarded. *Degree requirements:* For master's, comprehensive exam or thesis, practicum. *Entrance requirements:* For master's, GRE General Test or MAT, graduate essay exam, appropriate bachelor's degree, letters of recommendation. Additional exam requirements/recommendations for international students: Required—TOEFL. *Application deadline:* For fall admission, 8/15 priority date for domestic students. Applications are processed on a rolling basis. Application fee: $30 ($75 for international students). Electronic applications accepted. *Expenses:* Tuition, state resident: full-time $3,438; part-time $143 per credit hour. Tuition, nonresident: full-time $10,398; part-time $433 per credit hour. Required fees: $724; $44 per credit hour. *Financial support:* Federal Work-Study, institutionally sponsored loans, health care benefits, and unspecified assistantships available. Financial award application deadline: 3/15; financial award applicants required to submit FAFSA. *Unit head:* Dr. Jean Morrow, Chair, Department of Early Childhood/Elementary Teacher Education, 620-341-5766, E-mail: jmorrow@emporia.edu.

Endicott College, Van Loan School of Graduate and Professional Studies, Program in Elementary Education, Beverly, MA 01915-2096. Offers initial and professional licensure (M Ed). Part-time and evening/weekend programs available. In 2006, 26 degrees awarded. *Degree requirements:* For master's, comprehensive exam, registration. *Entrance requirements:* For master's, MAT or GRE, Massachusetts teaching certificate, 2 professional letters of recommendation. *Application deadline:* Applications are processed on a rolling basis. Application fee: $50. *Expenses:* Tuition: Part-time $279 per credit. Tuition and fees vary according to program. *Financial support:* Career-related internships or fieldwork, Federal Work-Study, and institutionally sponsored loans available. *Unit head:* Dr. John D. MacLean, Director of Licensure Programs, 978-232-2408, E-mail: jmaclean@endicott.edu.

Fairfield University, Graduate School of Education and Allied Professions, Department of Curriculum and Instruction, Fairfield, CT 06824-5195. Offers elementary education (MA); secondary education (MA); teaching and foundations (MA, CAS). Part-time and evening/weekend programs available. *Faculty:* 5 full-time (4 women), 5 part-time/adjunct (3 women). *Students:* 58 full-time (43 women), 98 part-time (81 women). Average age 28. 49 applicants, 55% accepted, 20 enrolled. In 2006, 45 master's, 1 other advanced degree awarded. *Degree requirements:* For master's, thesis or alternative, educational technology course, comprehensive exam. *Entrance requirements:* For master's, PRAXIS I (PPST), minimum QPA of 2.67, 2 recommendations, resumè. Additional exam requirements/recommendations for international students: Required—TOEFL (minimum score 550 paper-based; 213 computer-based). *Application deadline:* For fall admission, 3/1 for domestic students; for spring admission, 10/15 for domestic students. Applications are processed on a rolling basis. Application fee: $55. Electronic applications accepted. *Financial support:* Tuition waivers (partial) and unspecified assistantships available. Support available to part-time students. Financial award applicants required to submit FAFSA. *Faculty research:* Participatory action research, adolescent homosexuality, assessment of student teachers, supervision and staff development, writing process, Piaget. *Unit head:* Dr. Wendy R. Kohli, Chair, 203-254-4000 Ext. 2286, Fax: 203-254-4047, E-mail: wkohli@mail.fairfield.edu. *Application contact:* Marianne Gumpper, Director of Graduate and Continuing Studies Admissions, 203-254-4184, Fax: 203-254-4073, E-mail: gradadmis@mail.fairfield.edu.

Fayetteville State University, Graduate School, Program in Elementary Education, Fayetteville, NC 28301-4298. Offers MA Ed. *Accreditation:* NCATE. Part-time and evening/weekend programs available. *Faculty:* 5 full-time (3 women). *Students:* 7 full-time (all women), 25 part-time (all women); includes 13 minority (12 African Americans, 1 Hispanic American). Average age 39. 4 applicants, 100% accepted, 4 enrolled. In 2006, 32 degrees awarded. *Degree requirements:* For master's, internships. *Entrance requirements:* For master's, GRE or MAT, minimum GPA of 2.5, professional certification or waiver permission. *Application deadline:* For fall admission, 7/1 for domestic students; for spring admission, 12/1 for domestic students. Applications are processed on a rolling basis. Application fee: $25. Electronic applications accepted. *Expenses:* Tuition, state resident: full-time $2,118. Tuition, nonresident: full-time $11,708. Required fees: $1,099. Tuition and fees vary according to course load. *Faculty research:* Enhancing outcome based education for P-12 students, increasing males in teacher education, working with at risk students, working with families, developing playground for infants and toddlers. Total annual research expenditures: $21,000. *Unit head:* Dr. Saundra Shorter, Chairperson, 910-672-1257, E-mail: sshorter@uncfsu.edu.

Felician College, Program in Education, Lodi, NJ 07644-2117. Offers elementary education (MA); supervisory (MA); teacher for students with disabilities (MA). Part-time and evening/weekend programs available. *Students:* 18 applicants, 50% accepted, 9 enrolled. *Degree requirements:* For master's, project. *Entrance requirements:* For master's, MAT, minimum GPA of 3.0, 3 letters of recommendation. Additional exam requirements/recommendations for international students: Recommended—TOEFL (minimum score 550 paper-based; 213 computer-based). *Application deadline:* Applications are processed on a rolling basis. Application fee: $40. *Expenses:* Tuition: Part-time $675 per credit. Tuition and fees vary according to program. *Financial support:* Federal Work-Study available. *Unit head:* Dr. Julie Goods, Associate Dean, 201-559-3529, E-mail: goodj@felician.edu. *Application contact:* Wendy Lin-Cook, Director of Adult and Graduate Admission, 201-559-6077, Fax: 201-559-6138, E-mail: adultandgraduate@felician.edu.

See Close-Up on page 879.

Ferris State University, College of Education and Human Services, School of Education, Big Rapids, MI 49307. Offers administration (MSCTE); curriculum and instruction (M Ed), including administration, elementary education, philanthropic education, reading, secondary education, special education, subject matter option; education technology (MSCTE); instructor (MSCTE); post-secondary administration (MSCTE); training and development (MSCTE). Part-time and evening/weekend programs available. Postbaccalaureate distance learning degree programs offered (no on-campus study). *Faculty:* 13 full-time (9 women), 26 part-time/adjunct (19 women). *Students:* 38 full-time (27 women), 254 part-time (164 women); includes 30 minority (22 African Americans, 1 American Indian/Alaska Native, 2 Asian Americans or Pacific Islanders, 5 Hispanic Americans), 1 international. Average age 37. 171 applicants, 99% accepted. In 2006, 92 degrees awarded. *Degree requirements:* For master's, thesis, research paper. *Entrance requirements:* For master's, 2 years of work experience, minimum GPA of 3.0. *Application deadline:* For fall admission, 6/1 priority date for domestic students; for winter admission, 12/10 priority date for domestic students. Applications are processed on a rolling basis. Application fee: $30. *Expenses:* Tuition, state resident: part-time $355 per credit hour. Tuition, nonresident: part-time $687 per credit hour. *Financial support:* Career-related internships or fieldwork and tuition waivers (full and partial) available. Support available to part-time students. Financial award applicants required to submit FAFSA. *Faculty research:* Suicide prevention, reading, women in education, special needs, administration. *Unit head:* Interim Director, 231-591-5362, Fax: 231-591-2041. *Application contact:* Sigrid Robertson, Secretary, 231-591-3511, Fax: 231-591-2041, E-mail: robertss@ferris.edu.

Fitchburg State College, Division of Graduate and Continuing Education, Program in Elementary Education, Fitchburg, MA 01420-2697. Offers M Ed. *Accreditation:* NCATE. Part-time and evening/weekend programs available. *Students:* 2 full-time (both women), 50 part-time (47 women). Average age 36. 25 applicants, 100% accepted, 14 enrolled. In 2006, 27 degrees awarded. *Entrance requirements:* For master's, GRE General Test or MAT, teaching certificate, letters of recommendation, resumé. Additional exam requirements/recommendations for international students: Required—TOEFL (minimum score 550 paper-based; 213 computer-based; 79 iBT). *Application deadline:* Applications are processed on a rolling basis. Application fee: $25 ($50 for international students). *Expenses:* Tuition, state resident: part-time $150 per credit. Tuition, nonresident: part-time $150 per credit. Required fees: $90 per credit. *Financial support:* In 2006–07, research assistantships with partial tuition reimbursements (averaging $5,500 per year); Federal Work-Study, scholarships/grants, and unspecified assistantships also available. Support available to part-time students. Financial award application deadline: 3/1; financial award applicants required to submit FAFSA. *Unit head:* Dr. Ian Bothwell, Chair, 978-665-4657, Fax: 978-665-3658, E-mail: gce@fsc.edu. *Application contact:* Director of Admissions, 978-665-3144, Fax: 978-665-4540, E-mail: admissions@fsc.edu.

Florida Agricultural and Mechanical University, Division of Graduate Studies, Research, and Continuing Education, College of Education, Department of Elementary Education, Tallahassee, FL 32307-3200. Offers early childhood and elementary education (M Ed, MS Ed). *Accreditation:* NCATE. *Degree requirements:* For master's, thesis (for some programs). *Entrance requirements:* For master's, GRE General Test, minimum GPA of 3.0. Additional exam requirements/recommendations for international students: Required—TOEFL.

Florida Atlantic University, College of Education, Department of Teacher Education, Boca Raton, FL 33431-0991. Offers art teacher education (M Ed); curriculum and instruction (M Ed, Ed D, Ed S); educational psychology (MSF); elementary education (M Ed); foundations of education (M Ed); multicultural education (MSF); reading teacher education (M Ed). *Accreditation:* NCATE. Part-time and evening/weekend programs available. *Faculty:* 29 full-time (23 women), 75 part-time/adjunct (50 women). *Students:* 78 full-time (65 women), 176 part-time (159 women); includes 50 minority (20 African Americans, 1 American Indian/Alaska Native, 6 Asian Americans or Pacific Islanders, 23 Hispanic Americans), 1 international. Average age 35. 132 applicants, 64% accepted, 62 enrolled. In 2006, 95 master's, 2 doctorates awarded. *Degree requirements:* For master's, registration; for doctorate, thesis/dissertation, departmental qualifying exam, comprehensive exam, registration; for Ed S, departmental qualifying exam. *Entrance requirements:* For master's, GRE General Test, minimum GPA of 3.0 in last 2 years of undergraduate course work; for doctorate, GRE General Test, GRE Subject Test, minimum graduate GPA of 3.2, 3.0 in last 2 years of undergraduate course work; for Ed S, GRE General Test. Additional exam requirements/recommendations for international students: Required—TOEFL. *Application deadline:* Applications are processed on a rolling basis. Application fee: $30. *Expenses:* Tuition, area resident: Full-time $4,394. Tuition, nonresident: full-time $16,441. *Financial support:* In 2006–07, 4 research assistantships with partial tuition reimbursements (averaging $8,000 per year), 3 teaching assistantships with partial tuition reimbursements (averaging $8,000 per year) were awarded; fellowships with partial tuition reimbursements,

Elementary Education

Florida Atlantic University *(continued)*
career-related internships or fieldwork, scholarships/grants, and unspecified assistantships also available. *Faculty research:* Technology, teaching English to speakers of other languages, math teaching, electronic portfolio assessment, global perspectives through social studies. *Unit head:* Dr. Penelope Fritzer, Chairperson, 561-297-3584.

Florida Gulf Coast University, College of Education, Program in Elementary Education, Fort Myers, FL 33965-6565. Offers M Ed, MA. Part-time and evening/weekend programs available. Postbaccalaureate distance learning degree programs offered (minimal on-campus study). *Faculty:* 31 full-time (21 women), 30 part-time/adjunct (24 women). *Students:* 29 full-time (25 women), 4 part-time (3 women); includes 2 minority (both Asian Americans or Pacific Islanders), 1 international. Average age 33. 16 applicants, 94% accepted, 10 enrolled. In 2006, 2 degrees awarded. *Degree requirements:* For master's, thesis or alternative, final project, comprehensive exam. *Entrance requirements:* For master's, GRE General Test, MAT, minimum GPA of 3.0. Additional exam requirements/recommendations for international students: Required—TOEFL (minimum score 550 paper-based; 213 computer-based). *Application deadline:* For fall admission, 7/1 priority date for domestic students; for spring admission, 10/15 for domestic students. Applications are processed on a rolling basis. Application fee: $30. Electronic applications accepted. *Expenses:* Tuition, state resident: full-time $4,326. Tuition, nonresident: full-time $18,523. Required fees: $1,211. One-time fee: $5 full-time. *Faculty research:* Language acquisition, impact of literature on reading, action research in the classroom. *Unit head:* Dr. Patricia Wachholz, Head, 239-590-7808, Fax: 239-590-7801, E-mail: pwachhol@fgcu.edu.

Florida Institute of Technology, Graduate Programs, College of Science, Department of Science and Mathematics Education, Melbourne, FL 32901-6975. Offers computer education (MS); elementary science education (M Ed); environmental education (MS); mathematics education (MS, Ed D, PhD, Ed S); science and mathematics education (MAT); science education (MS, Ed D, PhD, Ed S). Part-time and evening/weekend programs available. *Faculty:* 4 full-time (1 woman), 2 part-time/adjunct (1 woman). *Students:* 11 full-time (6 women), 21 part-time (14 women); includes 2 minority (1 African American, 1 American Indian/Alaska Native), 7 international. Average age 38. 40 applicants, 58% accepted, 5 enrolled. In 2006, 7 master's, 2 doctorates, 1 other advanced degree awarded. Terminal master's awarded for partial completion of doctoral program. *Degree requirements:* For master's, thesis (for some programs), comprehensive exam (for some programs), registration; for doctorate, thesis/dissertation, oral defense of dissertation, comprehensive exam, registration. *Entrance requirements:* For master's, minimum GPA of 3.0, resumé, 3 letters of recommendation (elementary science education); for doctorate, minimum GPA of 3.2, resumé, 3 letters of recommendation; for Ed S, minimum GPA of 3.0, resumé, 3 letters of recommendation. Additional exam requirements/recommendations for international students: Required—TOEFL (minimum score 550 paper-based; 213 computer-based). *Application deadline:* Applications are processed on a rolling basis. Application fee: $50. Electronic applications accepted. *Expenses:* Tuition: Part-time $900 per credit. *Financial support:* In 2006–07, 1 student received support, including 1 research assistantship with full and partial tuition reimbursement available (averaging $5,346 per year); career-related internships or fieldwork and tuition remissions also available. Support available to part-time students. Financial award application deadline: 3/1; financial award applicants required to submit FAFSA. *Faculty research:* Measurement and evaluation, computers in education, educational technology. Total annual research expenditures: $6,000. *Unit head:* Dr. David E. Cook, Department Head, 321-674-8126, Fax: 321-674-7598, E-mail: dcook@fit.edu. *Application contact:* Carolyn P. Farrior, Director of Graduate Admissions, 321-674-7118, Fax: 321-723-9468, E-mail: cfarrior@fit.edu.

Florida International University, College of Education, Department of Curriculum and Instruction, Program in Elementary Education, Miami, FL 33199. Offers MS, Ed D. *Accreditation:* NCATE. Part-time and evening/weekend programs available. *Students:* Average age 28. 11 applicants, 0% accepted. In 2006, 4 degrees awarded. *Entrance requirements:* For master's, GRE General Test or minimum GPA of 3.0. Additional exam requirements/recommendations for international students: Required—TOEFL. *Application deadline:* For fall admission, 4/1 priority date for domestic students; for spring admission, 10/1 for domestic students. Applications are processed on a rolling basis. Application fee: $25. *Expenses:* Tuition, state resident: part-time $249 per credit hour. Tuition, nonresident: part-time $753 per credit hour. Tuition and fees vary according to program. *Faculty research:* Social studies, aerospace education, teacher training. *Unit head:* Dr. Alicia Mendoza, Head, 305-348-3607.

Florida State University, Graduate Studies, College of Education, Department of Childhood Education, Reading, and Disability Services, Program in Elementary Education, Tallahassee, FL 32306. Offers MS, Ed D, PhD, Ed S. Part-time programs available. *Faculty:* 6 full-time (5 women), 1 (woman) part-time/adjunct. *Students:* 17 full-time (14 women), 33 part-time (27 women); includes 5 minority (1 African American, 1 Asian American or Pacific Islander, 3 Hispanic Americans). 34 applicants, 44% accepted, 10 enrolled. In 2006, 13 master's, 1 doctorate awarded. *Degree requirements:* For master's and Ed S, thesis optional; for doctorate, thesis/dissertation, comprehensive exam. *Entrance requirements:* For master's, doctorate, and Ed S, GRE General Test, minimum GPA of 3.0. *Application deadline:* For fall admission, 7/1 priority date for domestic students; for spring admission, 11/1 for domestic students. Applications are processed on a rolling basis. Application fee: $30. *Expenses:* Tuition, state resident: full-time $5,822; part-time $243 per credit hour. Tuition, nonresident: full-time $20,976; part-time $874 per credit hour. Tuition and fees vary according to program. *Financial support:* In 2006–07, 1 fellowship, 5 teaching assistantships were awarded; research assistantships, career-related internships or fieldwork also available. Financial award applicants required to submit FAFSA. *Unit head:* Dr. Janice Flake, Head, 850-644-8481, Fax: 850-644-8715, E-mail: jflake@garnet.acns.fsu.edu. *Application contact:* Timolin Lynette Bodison-Baker, Program Assistant, 850-644-5458, Fax: 850-644-7736, E-mail: bodison@coe.fsu.edu.

Fordham University, Graduate School of Education, Division of Curriculum and Teaching, New York, NY 10023. Offers adult education (MS, MSE); bilingual teacher education (MSE); curriculum and teaching (MSE); early childhood education (MSE); elementary education (MST); language, literacy, and learning (PhD); reading education (MSE, Adv C); secondary education (MAT, MSE); special education (MSE, Adv C); teaching English as a second language (MSE). *Accreditation:* NCATE. *Faculty:* 22 full-time (18 women), 38 part-time/adjunct (28 women). *Students:* 68 full-time (51 women), 663 part-time (612 women); includes 200 minority (74 African Americans, 1 American Indian/Alaska Native, 37 Asian Americans or Pacific Islanders, 88 Hispanic Americans), 3 international. Average age 32. 636 applicants, 86% accepted, 322 enrolled. In 2006, 351 master's, 8 doctorates awarded. *Degree requirements:* For doctorate and Adv C, thesis/dissertation. *Entrance requirements:* For doctorate, MAT, GRE General Test. Application fee: $65. *Financial support:* Applicants required to submit FAFSA. *Unit head:* Dr. Terry Osborn, Chairperson, 212-636-6450.

Fort Hays State University, Graduate School, College of Education and Technology, Department of Teacher Education, Program in Elementary Education, Hays, KS 67601-4099. Offers MS. *Accreditation:* NCATE. *Faculty:* 8 full-time (6 women). *Students:* Average age 37. In 2006, 11 degrees awarded. *Degree requirements:* For master's, comprehensive exam. *Entrance requirements:* Additional exam requirements/recommendations for international students: Required—TOEFL (minimum score 550 paper-based; 213 computer-based). *Application deadline:* For fall admission, 7/1 priority date for domestic students. Applications are processed on a rolling basis. Application fee: $35. Electronic applications accepted. *Financial support:* In 2006–07, 2 teaching assistantships (averaging $5,000 per year) were awarded; research assistantships. *Faculty research:* Metric measurement (elementary and middle school), rural special education strategies for arithmetic mastery, word reading efficiency, textbooks on Great Plains, exceptional children. *Unit head:* Dr. Germaine Taggart, Interim Dean, Department of Teacher Education, 785-628-4204, E-mail: gtaggart@fhsu.edu.

Framingham State College, Division of Graduate and Continuing Education, Program in Elementary Education, Framingham, MA 01701-9101. Offers M Ed. *Students:* 55. In 2006, 12

degrees awarded. *Unit head:* Dr. Claire Graham, Coordinator, 508-224-1550, Fax: 508-626-4030, E-mail: czgraham@hotmail.com. *Application contact:* Graduate Office, 508-626-4550, Fax: 508-626-4030, E-mail: dgce@frc.mass.edu.

Francis Marion University, Graduate Programs, School of Education, Florence, SC 29501-0547. Offers early childhood education (M Ed); elementary education (M Ed); learning disabilities (M Ed, MAT); remedial education (M Ed); secondary education (M Ed). *Accreditation:* NCATE. Part-time programs available. *Faculty:* 19 full-time (11 women), 1 part-time/adjunct (0 women). *Students:* 11 full-time (8 women), 158 part-time (141 women); includes 54 minority (all African Americans), 1 international. Average age 34. 248 applicants, 100% accepted. In 2006, 91 degrees awarded. *Degree requirements:* For master's, comprehensive exam. *Entrance requirements:* For master's, GRE General Test, MAT, NTE, or PRAXIS II. *Application deadline:* For fall admission, 4/15 priority date for domestic students; for spring admission, 10/15 priority date for domestic students. Applications are processed on a rolling basis. Application fee: $30. *Expenses:* Tuition, state resident: full-time $6,527; part-time $326 per credit hour. Tuition, nonresident: full-time $13,054; part-time $653 per credit hour. Required fees: $185; $5 per credit hour. $45 per term. *Financial support:* In 2006–07, 3 research assistantships (averaging $6,000 per year) were awarded; unspecified assistantships also available. Support available to part-time students. Financial award application deadline: 3/1; financial award applicants required to submit FAFSA. *Faculty research:* Identification and alternate assessment of at-risk students. *Unit head:* Dr. James R. Faulkenberry, Dean, 843-661-1460, Fax: 843-661-4647.

Friends University, Graduate School, Division of Science, Arts, and Education, Program in Teaching, Wichita, KS 67213. Offers elementary education (MAT); secondary education (MAT). *Accreditation:* NCATE. Evening/weekend programs available. Postbaccalaureate distance learning degree programs offered (minimal on-campus study). *Faculty:* 1 (woman) full-time, 5 part-time/adjunct (2 women). *Students:* 79 full-time. In 2006, 32 degrees awarded. *Entrance requirements:* Additional exam requirements/recommendations for international students: Required—TOEFL (minimum score 560 paper-based; 220 computer-based). *Application deadline:* For fall admission, 3/15 priority date for domestic and international students; for spring admission, 12/15 priority date for domestic and international students. Applications are processed on a rolling basis. Application fee: $45 ($65 for international students). Electronic applications accepted. *Unit head:* Dr. Dona Gibson, Director, 800-794-6945 Ext. 5826. *Application contact:* Craig Davis, Executive Director of Recruitment-Adult and Graduate Studies, 800-794-6945 Ext. 5573, Fax: 316-295-5050, E-mail: cdavis@friends.edu.

Frostburg State University, Graduate School, College of Education, Department of Educational Professions, Program in Curriculum and Instruction, Frostburg, MD 21532-1099. Offers educational technology (M Ed); elementary education (M Ed); secondary education (M Ed). Part-time and evening/weekend programs available. *Degree requirements:* For master's, thesis or alternative. *Entrance requirements:* For master's, teaching certificate. Electronic applications accepted.

Frostburg State University, Graduate School, College of Education, Department of Educational Professions, Program in Elementary Teaching, Frostburg, MD 21532-1099. Offers MAT. *Accreditation:* NCATE. *Degree requirements:* For master's, thesis or alternative, PRAXIS II. *Entrance requirements:* For master's, PRAXIS I, entry portfolio. Electronic applications accepted.

Furman University, Graduate Division, Department of Education, Greenville, SC 29613. Offers early childhood education (MA); elementary education (MA); English as a second language (MA); middle school education (MA); reading (MA); school administration (MA); special education (MA). *Accreditation:* NCATE. Part-time and evening/weekend programs available. *Faculty:* 17 full-time (12 women), 19 part-time/adjunct (15 women). *Students:* 114 full-time (89 women), 72 part-time (59 women); includes 27 minority (23 African Americans, 4 Hispanic Americans). Average age 32. 36 applicants, 100% accepted, 36 enrolled. In 2006, 111 degrees awarded. *Degree requirements:* For master's, thesis (for some programs), comprehensive exam. *Entrance requirements:* For master's, GRE General Test or PRAXIS. *Application deadline:* For fall admission, 8/1 priority date for domestic and international students; for winter admission, 12/1 priority date for domestic and international students; for spring admission, 2/1 priority date for domestic and international students. Applications are processed on a rolling basis. Application fee: $50. *Expenses:* Tuition: Part-time $347 per credit. *Financial support:* In 2006–07, 97 students received support; fellowships, scholarships/grants and unspecified assistantships available. Financial award application deadline: 1/15; financial award applicants required to submit FAFSA. *Unit head:* Dr. Nelly Hecker, Head, 864-294-3385.

Gallaudet University, The Graduate School, School of Education and Human Services, Department of Education, Washington, DC 20002-3625. Offers early childhood education (MA, Ed S); education of deaf and hard of hearing students and multihandicapped deaf and hard of hearing students (MA, Ed S); elementary education (MA, Ed S); individualized program of study (PhD); parent/infant specialty (MA, Ed S); secondary education (MA, Ed S). *Accreditation:* NCATE. *Degree requirements:* For master's, thesis optional; for doctorate, thesis/dissertation. *Entrance requirements:* For master's, GRE General Test or MAT; for doctorate, GRE General Test or MAT, interview.

Gardner-Webb University, Graduate School, Department of Education, Program in Elementary Education, Boiling Springs, NC 28017. Offers MA. *Accreditation:* NCATE. Part-time and evening/weekend programs available. *Faculty:* 7 full-time (3 women), 2 part-time/adjunct (both women). *Students:* 1 (woman) full-time, 44 part-time (41 women); includes 7 minority (6 African Americans, 1 American Indian/Alaska Native). Average age 29. 17 applicants, 100% accepted, 16 enrolled. In 2006, 23 degrees awarded. *Degree requirements:* For master's, comprehensive exam. *Entrance requirements:* For master's, GRE General Test or NTE, PRAXIS, minimum GPA of 2.5. *Application deadline:* For fall admission, 8/1 priority date for domestic students. Applications are processed on a rolling basis. Application fee: $25. Electronic applications accepted. *Expenses:* Tuition: Full-time $3,144; part-time $262 per hour. *Financial support:* Unspecified assistantships available. *Unit head:* Dr. Donna Simmons, Chair, Department of Education, 704-406-4406, Fax: 704-406-3921, E-mail: dsimmons@gardner-webb.edu.

The George Washington University, Graduate School of Education and Human Development, Department of Teacher Preparation and Special Education, Program in Elementary Education, Washington, DC 20052. Offers M Ed. *Accreditation:* NCATE. Part-time programs available. *Degree requirements:* For master's, comprehensive exam. *Entrance requirements:* For master's, GRE General Test or MAT, minimum GPA of 2.75. *Faculty research:* Issues in teacher training.

Grambling State University, School of Graduate Studies and Research, College of Education, Department of Teacher Education, Grambling, LA 71245. Offers elementary/early childhood education (MS). *Accreditation:* NCATE. Part-time and evening/weekend programs available. Postbaccalaureate distance learning degree programs offered. *Faculty:* 9 full-time (7 women). *Students:* 4 full-time (3 women), 3 part-time (all women); all minorities (all African Americans). Average age 37. In 2006, 7 degrees awarded. *Degree requirements:* For master's, comprehensive exam. *Entrance requirements:* For master's, GRE. Additional exam requirements/recommendations for international students: Required—TOEFL. *Application deadline:* For fall admission, 7/1 for domestic students; for spring admission, 12/1 for domestic students. Application fee: $20 ($30 for international students). *Expenses:* Tuition, state resident: full-time $2,232; part-time $124 per credit hour. Tuition, nonresident: full-time $7,582; part-time $124 per credit hour. Required fees: $1,127. *Financial support:* In 2006–07, 6 students received support. Institutionally sponsored loans and unspecified assistantships available. Financial award application deadline: 5/31; financial award applicants required to submit FAFSA. *Unit head:* Dr. Doris Williams-Smith, Director, 318-394, Fax: 318-274-2799, E-mail: smithdo@gram.edu. *Application contact:* Melanie Monroe, Secretary II, 318-274-2238, Fax: 318-274-2799, E-mail: monroem@alpha0.gram.edu.

Grand Canyon University, College of Education, Phoenix, AZ 85017-1097. Offers elementary education (M Ed, MA); reading education (MA); secondary education (M Ed); teaching (MAT);

teaching English as a second language (MA). Part-time and evening/weekend programs available. Postbaccalaureate distance learning degree programs offered (no on-campus study). *Degree requirements:* For master's, publishable research paper (M Ed). *Entrance requirements:* For master's, MAT, GRE or minimum GPA of 3.0.

See Close-Up on page 885.

Grand Valley State University, College of Education, Programs in General Education, Allendale, MI 49401-9403. Offers adult and higher education (M Ed); early childhood education (M Ed); education of the gifted and talented (M Ed); educational leadership (M Ed); educational technology (M Ed); elementary education (M Ed); middle and high school education (M Ed); teaching English to speakers of other languages (M Ed). Part-time and evening/weekend programs available. Postbaccalaureate distance learning degree programs offered (minimal on-campus study). *Faculty:* 82 full-time (42 women), 43 part-time/adjunct (25 women). *Students:* 136 full-time (97 women), 828 part-time (565 women); includes 55 minority (26 African Americans, 7 American Indian/Alaska Native, 5 Asian Americans or Pacific Islanders, 17 Hispanic Americans). Average age 33. 280 applicants, 94% accepted, 188 enrolled. In 2006, 322 degrees awarded. *Degree requirements:* For master's, thesis. *Entrance requirements:* For master's, GRE General Test or minimum GPA of 3.0. Additional exam requirements/recommendations for international students: Required—TOEFL. *Application deadline:* Applications are processed on a rolling basis. Application fee: $30. Electronic applications accepted. *Expenses:* Tuition, state resident: full-time $5,850; part-time $325 per credit. Tuition, nonresident: full-time $10,800; part-time $600 per credit. Tuition and fees vary according to course load. *Financial support:* In 2006–07, 2 research assistantships with full and partial tuition reimbursements (averaging $8,000 per year) were awarded; career-related internships or fieldwork, Federal Work-Study, scholarships/grants, and unspecified assistantships also available. *Faculty research:* Effectiveness of technology in education, parental involvement, effective teaching, effective schools research. *Unit head:* Dr. Linda McCrea, Director, 616-331-2080, E-mail: mccreal@gvsu.edu. *Application contact:* Dr. Douglas Busman, Director, Student Information and Services, 616-331-6831, Fax: 616-331-6217, E-mail: busmando@gvsu.edu.

Greensboro College, Program in Education, Greensboro, NC 27401-1875. Offers elementary education (M Ed); special education (M Ed). Part-time and evening/weekend programs available. *Faculty:* 4 full-time (3 women). *Students:* 2 full-time (both women), 16 part-time (all women); includes 2 minority (1 African American, 1 Hispanic American). 5 applicants, 40% accepted, 2 enrolled. In 2006, 12 degrees awarded. *Degree requirements:* For master's, thesis. *Entrance requirements:* For master's, GRE, teacher license, 2 years of teaching experience, 2 letters of recommendation. Additional exam requirements/recommendations for international students: Required—TOEFL (minimum score 550 paper-based; 213 computer-based). *Application deadline:* For fall admission, 3/15 for domestic students. Applications are processed on a rolling basis. Application fee: $35. Electronic applications accepted. *Expenses:* Tuition: Part-time $275 per credit hour. Required fees: $30 per semester. *Financial support:* In 2006–07, 12 students received support. Scholarships/grants available. Support available to part-time students. *Unit head:* Dr. Rebecca Blomgren, Dean of Graduate and Professional Studies, 336-272-7102, Fax: 336-271-6634, E-mail: blomgrenr@gborocollege.edu.

Greenville College, Program in Education, Greenville, IL 62246-0159. Offers education (MAT); elementary education (MAE); secondary education (MAE). *Degree requirements:* For master's, thesis (for some programs). *Entrance requirements:* For master's, GRE, Illinois Basic Skills Test, teacher certification. Electronic applications accepted.

Hampton University, Graduate College, Department of Education, Program in Elementary Education, Hampton, VA 23668. Offers MA. *Accreditation:* NCATE. Part-time and evening/weekend programs available. *Entrance requirements:* For master's, GRE General Test.

Harding University, College of Education, Searcy, AR 72149-0001. Offers advanced studies in teaching and learning (M Ed); art (MSE); behavioral science (MSE); Bible and religion (MSE); counseling (MS, Ed S); early childhood education (M Ed); early childhood special education (M Ed, MSE); education (MSE); educational leadership (M Ed, Ed S); elementary education (M Ed); English (MSE); family and consumer science (MSE); French (MSE); history/social science (MSE); kinesiology (MSE); math (MSE); physical science (MSE); reading (M Ed); secondary education (M Ed); Spanish (MSE); special education licensure (M Ed); teaching (MAT). *Accreditation:* NCATE. Part-time programs available. *Faculty:* 8 full-time (2 women), 45 part-time/adjunct (30 women). *Students:* 153 full-time (123 women), 469 part-time (341 women); includes 72 minority (63 African Americans, 4 American Indian/Alaska Native, 1 Asian American or Pacific Islander, 4 Hispanic Americans), 9 international. Average age 35. 175 applicants, 90% accepted, 147 enrolled. In 2006, 241 degrees awarded. *Degree requirements:* For master's, portfolio(s), thesis optional; for Ed S, portfolio, specialist project. *Entrance requirements:* For master's, GRE, MAT, PRAXIS; for Ed S, MAT or GRE. Additional exam requirements/recommendations for international students: Required—TOEFL (minimum score 550 paper-based). *Application deadline:* For fall admission, 8/1 for domestic and international students; for spring admission, 1/1 for domestic and international students. Applications are processed on a rolling basis. Application fee: $35. *Expenses:* Tuition: Part-time $455 per semester hour. Required fees: $20 per semester hour. Tuition and fees vary according to course load. *Financial support:* Scholarships/grants and unspecified assistantships available. Support available to part-time students. *Faculty research:* Reading, comprehension, school violence, educational technology, behavior, college choice, differentiated instruction, brain based teaching. *Unit head:* Pat Bashaw, Chair, 501-279-4183, Fax: 501-279-4051, E-mail: pbashaw@harding.edu.

High Point University, Norcross Graduate School, High Point, NC 27262-3598. Offers business administration (MBA); educational leadership (M Ed); elementary education (M Ed); history (MA); nonprofit organizations (MPA); special education (M Ed); sport studies (MS). *Accreditation:* ACBSP; NCATE. Part-time and evening/weekend programs available. *Faculty:* 31 full-time (11 women), 1 part-time/adjunct (0 women). *Students:* 49 full-time (29 women), 202 part-time (130 women); includes 72 minority (66 African Americans, 1 American Indian/Alaska Native, 2 Asian Americans or Pacific Islanders, 3 Hispanic Americans), 11 international. Average age 33. 171 applicants, 71% accepted, 94 enrolled. In 2006, 95 degrees awarded. *Degree requirements:* For master's, thesis (for some programs), comprehensive exam (for some programs), registration. *Entrance requirements:* For master's, GMAT (MBA), GRE, MAT, minimum GPA of 3.0. Additional exam requirements/recommendations for international students: Required—TOEFL (minimum score 550 paper-based). *Application deadline:* For fall admission, 4/15 priority date for domestic and international students; for spring admission, 10/15 priority date for domestic and international students. Applications are processed on a rolling basis. Application fee: $50. Electronic applications accepted. *Expenses:* Tuition: Full-time $9,270; part-time $1,545 per course. *Financial support:* In 2006–07, 190 students received support. Federal Work-Study, scholarships/grants, and unspecified assistantships available. Support available to part-time students. Financial award application deadline: 3/1; financial award applicants required to submit FAFSA. *Application contact:* Dr. Alberta Haynes Herron, Dean of Norcross Graduate School, 336-841-9198, Fax: 336-888-6378, E-mail: aherron@highpoint.edu.

Hofstra University, School of Education and Allied Human Services, Department of Counseling, Research, Special Education and Rehabilitation, Program in Special Education, Hempstead, NY 11549. Offers early childhood special education (MS Ed, Advanced Certificate); gifted education (Advanced Certificate); inclusive early childhood special education (MS Ed); inclusive elementary special education (MS Ed); inclusive secondary special education (MS Ed); literacy studies and special education (MS Ed); special education (MA, MS Ed, PD); special education assessment and diagnosis (Advanced Certificate); teaching students with severe/multiple disabilities (Advanced Certificate). *Accreditation:* NCATE. Part-time and evening/weekend programs available. Postbaccalaureate distance learning degree programs offered. *Students:* 87 full-time (82 women), 116 part-time (110 women); includes 21 minority (8 African Americans, 4 Asian Americans or Pacific Islanders, 9 Hispanic Americans). Average age 28. 110 applicants, 79% accepted, 61 enrolled. In 2006, 74 master's, 7 other advanced degrees awarded. *Degree requirements:* For master's, thesis (for some programs), seminars, student teaching, comprehensive exam (for some programs), registration; for other advanced degree, fieldwork. *Entrance requirements:* For master's, interview, 3 letters of reference, resumé, minimum GPA of 3.0; for other advanced degree, interview, 3 letters of recommendation, resumé. Additional exam requirements/recommendations for international students: Required—TOEFL (minimum score 550 paper-based; 213 computer-based). *Application deadline:* Applications are processed on a rolling basis. Application fee: $60. Electronic applications accepted. *Expenses:* Tuition: Full-time $13,320; part-time $740 per credit. Required fees: $930; $155 per term. *Financial support:* In 2006–07, 64 students received support, including 6 fellowships with tuition reimbursements available (averaging $2,552 per year), 4 research assistantships with full and partial tuition reimbursements available (averaging $4,378 per year); Federal Work-Study, scholarships/grants, tuition waivers (full and partial), and unspecified assistantships also available. Support available to part-time students. Financial award applicants required to submit FAFSA. *Faculty research:* Inclusive schooling, autism spectrum disorders related services, parent participation in the special education process, co-teaching student teaching. *Unit head:* Dr. George Guiliani, Director, 516-463-5778, Fax: 516-463-6184, E-mail: cprdcs@hofstra.edu. *Application contact:* Carol Drummer, Dean of Graduate Admissions, 516-463-4876, Fax: 516-463-4664, E-mail: gradstudent@hofstra.edu.

Hofstra University, School of Education and Allied Human Services, Department of Curriculum and Teaching, Program in Elementary Education, Hempstead, NY 11549. Offers MA, MS Ed. *Accreditation:* NCATE. Part-time and evening/weekend programs available. *Students:* 84 full-time (73 women), 49 part-time (42 women); includes 27 minority (15 African Americans, 6 Asian Americans or Pacific Islanders, 6 Hispanic Americans). Average age 29. 117 applicants, 85% accepted, 45 enrolled. In 2006, 72 degrees awarded. *Degree requirements:* For master's, 39 semester hours. *Entrance requirements:* For master's, 2 letters of recommendation, teacher certification (MA), essay, interview. Additional exam requirements/recommendations for international students: Required—TOEFL (minimum score 550 paper-based; 213 computer-based). *Application deadline:* Applications are processed on a rolling basis. Application fee: $60. Electronic applications accepted. *Expenses:* Tuition: Full-time $13,320; part-time $740 per credit. Required fees: $930; $155 per term. *Financial support:* In 2006–07, 29 students received support, including 11 fellowships with tuition reimbursements available (averaging $3,000 per year), 4 research assistantships with full and partial tuition reimbursements available (averaging $3,944 per year); career-related internships or fieldwork, Federal Work-Study, scholarships/grants, tuition waivers (full and partial), and unspecified assistantships also available. Financial award applicants required to submit FAFSA. *Faculty research:* Curriculum development, integration; differentiated instruction; conceptual development; thematic instruction; assessment. *Unit head:* Dr. Esther Fusco, Program Director, 516-463-6566, E-mail: catezf@hofstra.edu. *Application contact:* Carol Drummer, Dean of Graduate Admissions, 516-463-4876, Fax: 516-463-4664, E-mail: gradstudent@hofstra.edu.

Holy Family University, Graduate School, School of Education, Philadelphia, PA 19114-2094. Offers education (M Ed); elementary education (M Ed); reading specialist (M Ed); secondary education (M Ed). Part-time and evening/weekend programs available. *Degree requirements:* For master's, thesis optional. *Entrance requirements:* For master's, GRE or MAT, interview. *Faculty research:* Cognition, developmental issues, sociological issues in education.

Hood College, Graduate School, Department of Education, Frederick, MD 21701-8575. Offers curriculum and instruction (MS), including early childhood education, elementary education, elementary school science and mathematics, secondary education, special education; educational leadership (MS); reading specialization (MS); teaching the struggling reader (Certificate). Part-time and evening/weekend programs available. *Faculty:* 4 full-time (3 women), 32 part-time/adjunct (16 women). *Students:* 5 full-time (3 women), 371 part-time (313 women); includes 30 minority (23 African Americans, 4 Asian Americans or Pacific Islanders, 3 Hispanic Americans). Average age 32. 71 applicants, 99% accepted, 59 enrolled. In 2006, 67 degrees awarded. *Degree requirements:* For master's, action research project, portfolio (reading). *Entrance requirements:* For master's, minimum GPA of 2.5, teaching certification. *Application deadline:* Applications are processed on a rolling basis. Application fee: $35. *Expenses:* Tuition: Part-time $350 per credit. Required fees: $20 per semester. *Financial support:* Applicants required to submit FAFSA. *Faculty research:* Leadership, action research, brain research, learning styles. *Unit head:* Dr. John George, Chairperson, 301-696-3471, Fax: 301-696-3597, E-mail: george@hood.edu. *Application contact:* Dr. Kathleen C. Bands, Associate Dean of Graduate School, 301-696-3811, Fax: 301-696-3597, E-mail: gofurther@hood.edu.

Howard University, School of Education, Department of Curriculum and Instruction, Program in Elementary Education, Washington, DC 20059-0002. Offers M Ed. *Accreditation:* NCATE. *Faculty:* 2 full-time (both women). *Students:* 3 full-time (2 women), 34 part-time (24 women); includes 33 minority (32 African Americans, 1 Asian American or Pacific Islander). Average age 25. 55 applicants, 80% accepted, 32 enrolled. In 2006, 15 degrees awarded. *Degree requirements:* For master's, expository writing exam, internships, seminar paper. *Entrance requirements:* For master's, PRAXIS I, minimum GPA of 2.7. *Application deadline:* For fall admission, 4/1 priority date for domestic students; for spring admission, 11/1 for domestic students. Applications are processed on a rolling basis. Application fee: $45. *Financial support:* Fellowships, research assistantships, teaching assistantships, career-related internships or fieldwork, Federal Work-Study, scholarships/grants, and unspecified assistantships available. Financial award application deadline: 4/1. *Unit head:* Dr. Helen Bond, Assistant Professor/Coordinator, 202-806-5299, Fax: 202-806-5297, E-mail: hbond@howard.edu.

Hunter College of the City University of New York, Graduate School, School of Education, Department of Curriculum and Teaching and Department of Educational Foundations and Counseling Programs, Program in Elementary Education, New York, NY 10021-5085. Offers MS. *Accreditation:* NCATE. *Faculty:* 8 full-time (all women), 20 part-time/adjunct (19 women). *Students:* 76 full-time (69 women), 575 part-time (528 women); includes 158 minority (43 African Americans, 51 Asian Americans or Pacific Islanders, 64 Hispanic Americans). Average age 30. 408 applicants, 63% accepted, 170 enrolled. In 2006, 200 degrees awarded. *Degree requirements:* For master's, thesis, completion of Integrative Seminar, New York State Teacher Certification Exams, student teaching. *Entrance requirements:* For master's, minimum undergraduate GPA of 2.8, writing sample. Additional exam requirements/recommendations for international students: Required—TOEFL, TWE. *Application deadline:* For fall admission, 4/1 for domestic students, 2/1 for international students; for spring admission, 11/1 for domestic students, 9/1 for international students. Application fee: $125. *Expenses:* Tuition, state resident: part-time $270 per credit. Tuition, nonresident: part-time $500 per credit. Required fees: $45 per semester. *Financial support:* Federal Work-Study, scholarships/grants, and tuition waivers (partial) available. Support available to part-time students. *Faculty research:* Urban education, multicultural education, gifted education, educational technology, cultural cognition. *Unit head:* Dr. Nancy Dela Cruz-Arroyo, Coordinator, 212-772-4667. *Application contact:* William Zlata, Director for Graduate Admissions, 212-772-4482, Fax: 212-650-3336, E-mail: admissions@hunter.cuny.edu.

Idaho State University, Office of Graduate Studies, College of Education, Department of Educational Foundations, Pocatello, ID 83209. Offers child and family studies (M Ed); curriculum leadership (M Ed); education (M Ed); educational administration (M Ed); educational foundations (5th Year Certificate); elementary education (M Ed), including K-12 education, literacy, secondary education. Part-time and evening/weekend programs available. Postbaccalaureate distance learning degree programs offered (no on-campus study). *Faculty:* 12 full-time (8 women). *Students:* 16 full-time (11 women), 161 part-time (102 women); includes 2 minority (1 Asian American or Pacific Islander, 1 Hispanic American), 2 international. Average age 40. In 2006, 15 degrees awarded. *Degree requirements:* For master's, oral exam, written exam, thesis optional; for 5th Year Certificate, thesis (for some programs), oral exam, written exam, comprehensive exam, registration (for some programs). *Entrance requirements:* For master's, GRE General Test or MAT, minimum undergraduate GPA of 3.0; for 5th Year Certificate, GRE General Test, minimum undergraduate GPA of 3.0, master's degree. Additional

Elementary Education

Idaho State University (continued)

exam requirements/recommendations for international students: Required—TOEFL (minimum score 550 paper-based; 213 computer-based; 80 iBT). *Application deadline:* For fall admission, 7/1 for domestic students, 6/1 for international students; for spring admission, 12/1 for domestic students, 11/1 for international students. Applications are processed on a rolling basis. Application fee: $55. *Expenses:* Tuition, state resident: part-time $251 per credit. Tuition, nonresident: part-time $366 per credit. Tuition and fees vary according to degree level, program and reciprocity agreements. *Financial support:* Career-related internships or fieldwork, Federal Work-Study, institutionally sponsored loans, scholarships/grants, tuition waivers, and unspecified assistantships available. Support available to part-time students. Financial award application deadline: 1/1. *Faculty research:* Child and families studies; business education; special education; math, science, and technology education. *Unit head:* Dr. Jack Newsome, Chair, 208-282-4838, E-mail: newsjack@isu.edu. *Application contact:* Dr. Peter Denner, Assistant Dean, 208-282-3807, Fax: 208-282-4697, E-mail: dennpete@isu.edu.

Immaculata University, College of Graduate Studies, Program in Educational Leadership and Administration, Immaculata, PA 19345. Offers educational leadership and administration (MA, Ed D); elementary education (Certificate); intermediate unit director (Certificate); school principal (Certificate); school superintendent (Certificate); secondary education (Certificate); special education (Certificate). Part-time and evening/weekend programs available. *Students:* 27 full-time (15 women), 510 part-time (353 women). Average age 33. 86 applicants, 74% accepted, 53 enrolled. In 2006, 47 master's, 27 doctorates awarded. *Degree requirements:* For master's, thesis optional; for doctorate, thesis/dissertation, comprehensive exam. *Entrance requirements:* For master's, GRE or MAT, minimum GPA of 3.0; for doctorate, GRE General Test, minimum GPA of 3.5. Additional exam requirements/recommendations for international students: Required—TOEFL. Application fee: $35. *Financial support:* Application deadline:5/1. *Faculty research:* Cooperative learning, school-based management, whole language, performance assessment. *Unit head:* Sr. Carol Anne Couchara, Chair, 610-647-4400 Ext. 3280, E-mail: ccouchara@immaculata.edu. *Application contact:* 610-647-4400 Ext. 3211, Fax: 610-993-8550, E-mail: graduate@immaculata.edu.

Indiana State University, School of Graduate Studies, College of Education, Department of Elementary and Special Education, Terre Haute, IN 47809-1401. Offers early childhood education (M Ed); elementary education (M Ed); literacy (M Ed). *Accreditation:* NCATE. *Faculty:* 9 full-time (7 women), 5 part-time/adjunct (4 women). *Students:* 6 full-time (all women), 46 part-time (43 women); includes 3 minority (2 African Americans, 1 Asian American or Pacific Islander), 2 international. Average age 35. 26 applicants, 96% accepted, 12 enrolled. In 2006, 26 degrees awarded. *Application deadline:* For fall admission, 7/1 priority date for domestic students; for spring admission, 11/1 priority date for domestic students. Applications are processed on a rolling basis. Application fee: $35. Electronic applications accepted. *Expenses:* Tuition, state resident: part-time $278 per credit. Tuition, nonresident: part-time $552 per credit. *Financial support:* In 2006–07, research assistantships with partial tuition reimbursements (averaging $6,500 per year); teaching assistantships with partial tuition reimbursements, tuition waivers (partial) also available. Financial award application deadline: 3/1; financial award applicants required to submit FAFSA. *Unit head:* Dr. Diana Quatroche, Interim Chairperson, 812-237-2852.

Indiana University Bloomington, School of Education, Department of Curriculum and Instruction, Bloomington, IN 47405-7000. Offers art education (MS, Ed D, PhD); curriculum studies (Ed D, PhD); elementary education (MS, Ed D, PhD, Ed S); mathematics education (MS, Ed D, PhD); science education (MS, Ed D, PhD); secondary education (MS, Ed D, PhD); social studies education (MS, PhD); special education (MS, Ed D, PhD, Ed S). PhD offered through the University Graduate School. *Accreditation:* NCATE. Part-time and evening/weekend programs available. *Students:* 39 full-time (28 women), 82 part-time (54 women); includes 15 minority (5 African Americans, 1 American Indian/Alaska Native, 6 Asian Americans or Pacific Islanders, 3 Hispanic Americans), 33 international. Average age 37. In 2006, 1 degree awarded. Terminal master's awarded for partial completion of doctoral program. *Degree requirements:* For doctorate, thesis/dissertation; for Ed S, comprehensive exam or project. *Entrance requirements:* For master's, doctorate, and Ed S, GRE General Test. *Application deadline:* For fall admission, 6/1 priority date for domestic students, 3/1 for international students; for winter admission, 11/1 priority date for domestic students; for spring admission, 9/1 for international students. Applications are processed on a rolling basis. Application fee: $50 ($60 for international students). Electronic applications accepted. *Expenses:* Tuition, state resident: full-time $5,791; part-time $241 per credit hour. Tuition, nonresident: full-time $16,866; part-time $703 per credit hour. *Financial support:* Fellowships with full and partial tuition reimbursements, research assistantships with full and partial tuition reimbursements, teaching assistantships with full and partial tuition reimbursements, career-related internships or fieldwork, Federal Work-Study, institutionally sponsored loans, and tuition waivers (partial) available. Support available to part-time students. *Unit head:* Cary Buzzelli, Chairperson, 812-856-8100. *Application contact:* Bobbie Partenheimer, Admissions Services Coordinator, 812-856-8127, Fax: 812-856-8333, E-mail: partenhe@indiana.edu.

Indiana University Kokomo, Division of Education, Kokomo, IN 46904-9003. Offers elementary education (MS); secondary education (MS). *Accreditation:* NCATE. Part-time and evening/weekend programs available. *Faculty:* 1 full-time (0 women). *Students:* Average age 32. In 2006, 3 degrees awarded. *Degree requirements:* For master's, research project, thesis optional. *Entrance requirements:* For master's, GRE General Test, minimum GPA of 2.5. *Application deadline:* For fall admission, 8/1 for domestic students; for spring admission, 12/1 for domestic students. Applications are processed on a rolling basis. Application fee: $40 ($50 for international students). *Expenses:* Tuition, state resident: full-time $4,391; part-time $183 per hour. Tuition, nonresident: full-time $10,043; part-time $418 per hour. Tuition and fees vary according to course load, campus/location and program. *Financial support:* Minority teacher scholarships available. *Faculty research:* Reading, teaching effectiveness, portfolio, curriculum development. *Unit head:* D. Antonio Cantu, Dean, 765-455-9287, Fax: 765-455-9503. *Application contact:* Charlotte Miller, Coordinator Educational/Student Resources, 765-455-9367, Fax: 765-455-9503, E-mail: cmiller@iuk.edu.

Indiana University Northwest, School of Education, Gary, IN 46408-1197. Offers elementary education (MS Ed); secondary education (MS Ed). *Accreditation:* NCATE. Part-time and evening/weekend programs available. *Faculty:* 5 full-time (2 women). *Students:* 3 full-time (all women), 64 part-time (49 women); includes 26 minority (23 African Americans, 3 Hispanic Americans). Average age 40. In 2006, 36 degrees awarded. *Degree requirements:* For master's, registration. *Entrance requirements:* For master's, GRE General Test or MAT, minimum GPA of 3.0. *Application deadline:* For fall admission, 7/15 priority date for domestic students; for spring admission, 11/15 for domestic students. Application fee: $25. *Expenses:* Tuition, state resident: full-time $4,332; part-time $181 per credit hour. Tuition, nonresident: full-time $10,081; part-time $420 per credit hour. Tuition and fees vary according to course load, campus/location and program. *Unit head:* Dr. Stanley E. Wigle, Dean, 219-980-6510, Fax: 219-981-4208, E-mail: amsanche@iun.edu.

Indiana University–Purdue University Fort Wayne, School of Education, Department of Educational Studies, Fort Wayne, IN 46805-1499. Offers elementary education (MS Ed); secondary education (MS Ed). *Accreditation:* NCATE. Part-time programs available. *Faculty:* 14 full-time (10 women). *Students:* 5 full-time (4 women), 117 part-time (93 women); includes 8 minority (5 African Americans, 3 Hispanic Americans), 1 international. Average age 40. 66 applicants, 100% accepted, 59 enrolled. In 2006, 37 degrees awarded. *Entrance requirements:* For master's, minimum GPA of 2.5. Additional exam requirements/recommendations for international students: Required—TOEFL (minimum score 600 paper-based; 260 computer-based). *Application deadline:* For fall admission, 7/1 priority date for domestic students; for spring admission, 12/1 for domestic students. Applications are processed on a rolling basis. Application fee: $30. *Expenses:* Tuition, state resident: full-time $4,039; part-time $224 per credit. Tuition, nonresident: full-time $9,220; part-time $512 per credit. Required fees: $429; $24 per credit. Tuition and fees vary according to course load. *Financial support:* Teaching assistantships with partial tuition reimbursements, scholarships/grants available. Support available to part-time students. Financial award application deadline: 3/1; financial award applicants required to submit FAFSA. *Unit head:* Dr. Joe Nichols, Chair, 260-481-6445, E-mail: nicholsj@ipfw.edu. *Application contact:* Vicky L. Schmidt, Graduate Recorder, 260-481-6450, Fax: 260-481-5408, E-mail: schmidt@ipfw.edu.

Indiana University South Bend, School of Education, South Bend, IN 46634-7111. Offers counseling and human services (MS Ed); elementary education (MS Ed); secondary education (MS Ed); special education (MS Ed). *Accreditation:* NCATE. Part-time and evening/weekend programs available. *Faculty:* 21 full-time (11 women), 9 part-time/adjunct (3 women). *Students:* 58 full-time (38 women), 237 part-time (186 women); includes 33 minority (22 African Americans, 1 American Indian/Alaska Native, 6 Asian Americans or Pacific Islanders, 4 Hispanic Americans), 5 international. Average age 35. 127 applicants, 100% accepted, 61 enrolled. In 2006, 141 degrees awarded. *Degree requirements:* For master's, thesis or alternative, exit project. *Entrance requirements:* For master's, letters of recommendation, GRE or minimum GPA of 3.0. Additional exam requirements/recommendations for international students: Required—TOEFL. *Application deadline:* For fall admission, 7/1 for domestic students; for spring admission, 11/1 for domestic students. Applications are processed on a rolling basis. Application fee: $45. Electronic applications accepted. *Expenses:* Tuition, state resident: full-time $4,450; part-time $185 per credit hour. Tuition, nonresident: full-time $10,954; part-time $456 per credit hour. Tuition and fees vary according to course load, campus/location and program. *Financial support:* Career-related internships or fieldwork available. Support available to part-time students. Financial award application deadline: 3/1; financial award applicants required to submit FAFSA. *Faculty research:* Professional dispositions, early childhood literacy, online learning, program assessments, problem-based learning. *Unit head:* Dr. Michael Horvath, Professor and Dean, School of Education, 574-520-4339, Fax: 574-520-4550. *Application contact:* Gil L. Martin, Graduate Admissions and Recruitment Officer, 574-520-4585, Fax: 574-520-5549, E-mail: marting@iusb.edu.

Indiana University Southeast, School of Education, New Albany, IN 47150-6405. Offers counselor education (MS Ed); elementary education (MS Ed); secondary education (MS Ed). *Accreditation:* NCATE. Part-time and evening/weekend programs available. *Students:* 5 full-time (4 women), 339 part-time (275 women); includes 19 minority (17 African Americans, 1 Asian American or Pacific Islander, 1 Hispanic American). Average age 32. In 2006, 176 degrees awarded. *Degree requirements:* For master's, registration. *Entrance requirements:* For master's, minimum undergraduate GPA of 2.5, graduate 3.0. *Application deadline:* Applications are processed on a rolling basis. Application fee: $30. *Expenses:* Tuition, state resident: full-time $4,458; part-time $186 per credit hour. Tuition, nonresident: full-time $10,196; part-time $425 per credit hour. Tuition and fees vary according to course load, campus/location and program. *Financial support:* In 2006–07, 29 students received support. Career-related internships or fieldwork, Federal Work-Study, and institutionally sponsored loans available. Support available to part-time students. Financial award applicants required to submit FAFSA. *Faculty research:* Learning styles, technology, constructivism, group process, innovative math strategies. *Unit head:* Dr. Gloria Murray, Dean, 812-941-2385, Fax: 812-941-2667, E-mail: soeinfo@ius.edu.

Inter American University of Puerto Rico, Aguadilla Campus, Graduate School, Aguadilla, PR 00605. Offers administration and supervision (MA); criminal justice (MA); elementary education (MA). Part-time and evening/weekend programs available. *Degree requirements:* For master's, comprehensive exam. *Entrance requirements:* For master's, EXADEP, 2 letters of recommendation, minimum GPA of 2.5. Electronic applications accepted.

Inter American University of Puerto Rico, Barranquitas Campus, Program in Education, Barranquitas, PR 00794. Offers educational administration and supervision (MA); elementary education (MA). *Degree requirements:* For master's, thesis optional. *Entrance requirements:* For master's, EXADEP, letter of recommendation. Electronic applications accepted.

Inter American University of Puerto Rico, Metropolitan Campus, Faculty of Education, Program in Elementary Education, San Juan, PR 00919-1293. Offers MA. *Degree requirements:* For master's, comprehensive exam. *Entrance requirements:* For master's, GRE or EXADEP, interview. Electronic applications accepted.

Inter American University of Puerto Rico, Ponce Campus, Graduate School, Mercedita, PR 00715-1602. Offers accounting (MBA); biology (M Ed); chemistry (M Ed); criminal justice (MA); elementary education (M Ed); English as a Second Language (M Ed); finance (MBA); history (M Ed); human resources (MBA); mathematics (M Ed); Spanish (M Ed); trade (MBA). *Entrance requirements:* For master's, minimum GPA of 2.5.

Inter American University of Puerto Rico, San Germán Campus, Graduate Studies Center, Graduate Program in Elementary Education, San Germán, PR 00683-5008. Offers MA. Part-time and evening/weekend programs available. *Faculty:* 8 full-time, 11 part-time/adjunct. *Students:* 42. In 2006, 23 degrees awarded. *Degree requirements:* For master's, comprehensive exam. *Entrance requirements:* For master's, GRE General Test or EXADEP, minimum GPA of 3.0. Application fee: $31. *Expenses:* Tuition: Part-time $175 per credit. Required fees: $238 per semester. Tuition and fees vary according to degree level. *Financial support:* Teaching assistantships, Federal Work-Study and unspecified assistantships available. *Application contact:* Dr. Aurora Graniela, Graduate Coordinator, 787-264-1912 Ext. 7355, Fax: 787-892-7510, E-mail: aurora@sg.inter.edu.

Iona College, School of Arts and Science, Program in Teaching Education, New Rochelle, NY 10801-1890. Offers MST. *Accreditation:* NCATE. *Faculty:* 11 full-time (6 women), 21 part-time/adjunct (13 women). *Students:* 7 full-time (all women), 50 part-time (44 women); includes 5 minority (3 African Americans, 2 Hispanic Americans). Average age 30. 29 applicants, 55% accepted, 13 enrolled. In 2006, 32 degrees awarded. *Entrance requirements:* For master's, GRE or minimum GPA of 2.75. Additional exam requirements/recommendations for international students: Required—TOEFL (minimum score 550 paper-based; 213 computer-based). *Application deadline:* Applications are processed on a rolling basis. Application fee: $50. Electronic applications accepted. *Expenses:* Tuition: Part-time $665 per credit. Required fees: $150 per term. *Financial support:* Unspecified assistantships available. *Faculty research:* Reading/writing assessment, multicultural education, administration, technology and education, early literacy assessment. *Unit head:* Dr. Patricia Antonacci, Chair, 914-633-2080, Fax: 914-633-2608, E-mail: pantonacci@iona.edu. *Application contact:* Veronica Jarek-Prinz, Graduate Admissions, 914-633-2289, Fax: 914-633-2012, E-mail: vjarekprinz@iona.edu.

Iowa State University of Science and Technology, Graduate College, College of Human Sciences, Department of Curriculum and Instruction, Ames, IA 50011. Offers curriculum and instructional technology (M Ed, MS, PhD); elementary education (M Ed, MS); historical, philosophical, and comparative studies in education (M Ed, MS); special education (M Ed, MS). *Faculty:* 28 full-time, 3 part-time/adjunct. *Students:* 54 full-time (40 women), 78 part-time (54 women); includes 11 minority (3 African Americans, 4 Asian Americans or Pacific Islanders, 4 Hispanic Americans), 26 international. 64 applicants, 69% accepted, 32 enrolled. In 2006, 31 master's, 10 doctorates awarded. *Degree requirements:* For master's, thesis or alternative; for doctorate, thesis/dissertation. *Entrance requirements:* For doctorate, GRE General Test. Additional exam requirements/recommendations for international students: Required—TOEFL (paper-based 560; computer-based 220; iBT 83) or IELTS (6.5). *Application deadline:* For fall admission, 1/1 priority date for domestic and international students; for spring admission, 9/1 for domestic and international students. Application fee: $30 ($70 for international students). Electronic applications accepted. *Expenses:* Tuition, state resident: full-time $5,936; part-time $330 per credit. Tuition, nonresident: full-time $16,350; part-time $330 per credit. *Financial support:* In 2006–07, 22 research assistantships with full and partial tuition reimbursements (averaging $17,457 per year), 17 teaching assistantships with full and partial tuition reimbursements (averaging $17,788 per year) were awarded; fellowships, scholarships/grants, health care benefits, and unspecified assistantships also available. *Unit head:* Dr. Carl Smith, Chair,

515-294-7021, E-mail: cigrad@iastate.edu. *Application contact:* Dr. Patricia Leigh, Director of Graduate Education, 515-294-7021, E-mail: cigrad@iastate.edu.

Jackson State University, Graduate School, School of Education, Department of Curriculum and Instruction, Jackson, MS 39217. Offers early childhood education (MS Ed, Ed D); elementary education (MS Ed, Ed S). *Accreditation:* NCATE. Evening/weekend programs available. *Faculty:* 10 full-time (7 women), 1 (woman) part-time/adjunct. *Students:* 12 full-time (9 women), 52 part-time (43 women); includes 59 minority (all African Americans) In 2006, 20 master's, 1 other advanced degree awarded. Terminal master's awarded for partial completion of doctoral program. *Degree requirements:* For master's, thesis or alternative, comprehensive exam; for doctorate, thesis/dissertation, comprehensive exam. *Entrance requirements:* For master's, GRE General Test; for doctorate, MAT, teaching experience. Additional exam requirements/recommendations for international students: Required—TOEFL. *Application deadline:* For fall admission, 3/1 priority date for domestic students; for spring admission, 10/1 for domestic students. Applications are processed on a rolling basis. Application fee: $20. *Financial support:* In 2006–07, 30 students received support. Career-related internships or fieldwork, Federal Work-Study, scholarships/grants, and unspecified assistantships available. Support available to part-time students. Financial award application deadline: 3/1; financial award applicants required to submit FAFSA. *Unit head:* Dr. Rodney Washington, Chair, 601-979-2336, Fax: 601-979-2178, E-mail: rodney.washington@jsums.edu. *Application contact:* Curtis Gore, Director of Graduate Admissions, 601-979-2455, Fax: 601-974-4325, E-mail: cgore@ccaix.jsums.edu.

Jacksonville State University, College of Graduate Studies and Continuing Education, College of Education and Professional Studies, Program in Elementary Education, Jacksonville, AL 36265-1602. Offers MS Ed. *Accreditation:* NCATE. *Faculty:* 5 full-time (all women). *Students:* 30 full-time (28 women), 114 part-time (113 women); includes 13 minority (10 African Americans, 3 American Indian/Alaska Native). In 2006, 46 degrees awarded. *Entrance requirements:* For master's, GRE General Test or MAT. *Application deadline:* Applications are processed on a rolling basis. Application fee: $20. *Expenses:* Tuition, state resident: full-time $5,400; part-time $225 per credit hour. Tuition, nonresident: full-time $10,800; part-time $450 per credit hour. One-time fee: $20 full-time. *Financial support:* In 2006–07, 1 research assistantship was awarded. Support available to part-time students. Financial award application deadline: 4/1. *Unit head:* Dr. Rita Boydston, Head, 256-782-5351. *Application contact:* 256-782-5329.

Jacksonville University, College of Arts and Sciences, School of Education, Program in Elementary Education, Jacksonville, FL 32211-3394. Offers MAT. Part-time and evening/weekend programs available. *Degree requirements:* For master's, comprehensive exam. *Entrance requirements:* For master's, GRE General Test, minimum GPA of 3.0. Additional exam requirements/recommendations for international students: Required—TOEFL.

The Johns Hopkins University, School of Professional Studies in Business and Education, School of Education, Department of Teacher Preparation, Baltimore, MD 21218-2699. Offers elementary education (MAT); English for speakers of other languages (MAT); secondary education (MAT). Part-time and evening/weekend programs available. *Students:* 234 full-time (173 women), 240 part-time (172 women); includes 87 minority (61 African Americans, 19 Asian Americans or Pacific Islanders, 7 Hispanic Americans), 4 international. Average age 27. 360 applicants, 71% accepted, 243 enrolled. In 2006, 218 degrees awarded. *Degree requirements:* For master's, portfolio. *Entrance requirements:* For master's, PRAXIS I, minimum GPA of 3.0, interview, resumé, letter of recommendation. Additional exam requirements/recommendations for international students: Required—TOEFL (minimum score 600 paper-based; 250 computer-based; 100 iBT). *Application deadline:* For fall admission, 4/1 priority date for domestic students, 4/1 for international students; for winter admission, 10/1 priority date for domestic students; for spring admission, 10/1 priority date for domestic students, 10/1 for international students. Applications are processed on a rolling basis. Application fee: $60. *Expenses:* Tuition: Full-time $32,976. Tuition and fees vary according to degree level and program. *Financial support:* Scholarships/grants available. Support available to part-time students. Financial award application deadline: 6/1; financial award applicants required to submit FAFSA. *Faculty research:* Professional development schools, data-informed instruction, alternative certification, dispositions. *Unit head:* Dr. Elaine Stotko, Chair, 410-309-1289, Fax: 410-290-0467, E-mail: matjhu@jhu.edu. *Application contact:* Carol Herrman, Admissions Coordinator, 410-872-1234, Fax: 410-872-1251, E-mail: onestop.admissions@jhu.edu.

Jones International University, Graduate School of Education, Centennial, CO 80112. Offers adult education (M Ed); corporate training and knowledge management (M Ed); curriculum and instruction (M Ed), including elementary teacher licensure, secondary teacher licensure; e-learning technology and design (M Ed); educational leadership and administration (M Ed); educational leadership and administration: principal and administrator licensure (M Ed); elementary curriculum instruction and assessment (M Ed); higher education leadership and administration (M Ed); K-12 instructional technology (M Ed); K-12 instructional technology: teacher licensure (M Ed); secondary curriculum instruction and assessment (M Ed); technology and design (M Ed). Part-time and evening/weekend programs available. Postbaccalaureate distance learning degree programs offered (no on-campus study). *Entrance requirements:* For master's, minimum cumulative GPA of 2.5. Additional exam requirements/recommendations for international students: Recommended—TOEFL (minimum score 550 paper-based; 213 computer-based). Electronic applications accepted.

Kansas State University, Graduate School, College of Education, Department of Elementary Education, Manhattan, KS 66506. Offers curriculum and instruction (MS, Ed D, PhD). *Faculty:* 8 full-time (6 women). *Application deadline:* For fall admission, 3/1 priority date for domestic students, 2/1 priority date for international students; for spring admission, 10/1 priority date for domestic students, 8/1 priority date for international students. Application fee: $30 ($55 for international students). *Expenses:* Tuition, state resident: full-time $6,352; part-time $240 per credit hour. Tuition, nonresident: full-time $14,296; part-time $571 per credit hour. Required fees: $585. *Financial support:* In 2006–07, 2 research assistantships (averaging $12,095 per year), 2 teaching assistantships (averaging $15,745 per year) were awarded. Total annual research expenditures: $297,757. *Unit head:* Dr. Paul R. Burden, Head, 785-532-5595, Fax: 785-532-7304, E-mail: burden@ksu.edu. *Application contact:* Linda Thurston, Director, 785-532-5595, Fax: 785-532-7304, E-mail: coegrads@ksu.edu.

Kent State University, Graduate School of Education, Health, and Human Services, Department of Teaching, Leadership, and Curriculum Studies, Program in K-12 Leadership, Kent, OH 44242-0001. Offers M Ed, MA, PhD, Ed S. *Faculty:* 5 full-time (3 women). *Students:* 10 full-time (6 women), 62 part-time (32 women); includes 4 minority (all African Americans), 1 international. 21 applicants, 52% accepted. In 2006, 40 master's, 2 doctorates, 3 other advanced degrees awarded. *Entrance requirements:* For doctorate and Ed S, GRE. Additional exam requirements/recommendations for international students: Required—TOEFL. *Application deadline:* Applications are processed on a rolling basis. Application fee: $30. Electronic applications accepted. *Financial support:* In 2006–07, fellowships (averaging $8,497 per year); research assistantships, teaching assistantships, career-related internships or fieldwork, Federal Work-Study, institutionally sponsored loans, scholarships/grants, health care benefits, and unspecified assistantships also available. Support available to part-time students. *Unit head:* Dr. Autumn Tooms, Coordinator, 330-672-2580, E-mail: atooms@kent.edu. *Application contact:* Nancy Miller, Academic Program Coordinator, Office of Graduate Student Services, 330-672-2576, Fax: 330-672-9162, E-mail: ogs@kent.edu.

Kutztown University of Pennsylvania, College of Graduate Studies and Extended Learning, College of Education, Program in Elementary Education, Kutztown, PA 19530-0730. Offers early childhood education (Certificate); elementary education (M Ed, Certificate); special education (Certificate). *Accreditation:* NCATE. Part-time and evening/weekend programs available. *Faculty:* 8 full-time (6 women), 1 (woman) part-time/adjunct. *Students:* 38 full-time (27 women), 64 part-time (54 women); includes 2 minority (both Hispanic Americans) Average age 29. 66 applicants, 85% accepted, 42 enrolled. In 2006, 15 degrees awarded. *Degree requirements:* For master's, comprehensive project, thesis optional. *Entrance requirements:* For master's, GRE General Test. Additional exam requirements/recommendations for international students: Required—TOEFL. *Application deadline:* Applications are processed on a rolling basis. Application fee: $35. Electronic applications accepted. *Expenses:* Tuition, state resident: full-time $6,048; part-time $336 per credit. Tuition, nonresident: full-time $9,678; part-time $538 per credit. *Financial support:* In 2006–07, research assistantships with full tuition reimbursements (averaging $5,000 per year); career-related internships or fieldwork, Federal Work-Study, and unspecified assistantships also available. Financial award application deadline: 3/15; financial award applicants required to submit FAFSA. *Faculty research:* Whole language, middle schools, cooperative learning discussion techniques, oral reading techniques, hemisphericity. *Unit head:* Dr. Elsa Geskus, Chairperson, 610-683-4262, Fax: 610-683-1327, E-mail: geskus@kutztown.edu.

Lander University, School of Education, Greenwood, SC 29649-2099. Offers elementary education (M Ed); teaching (MAT). *Accreditation:* NCATE. Part-time programs available. *Faculty:* 6 full-time (3 women), 4 part-time/adjunct (all women). *Students:* 11 full-time (8 women), 29 part-time (25 women); includes 5 minority (all African Americans) Average age 34. In 2006, 41 degrees awarded. *Degree requirements:* For master's, thesis or alternative, comprehensive exam. *Entrance requirements:* For master's, GRE General Test. Additional exam requirements/recommendations for international students: Required—TOEFL (minimum score 550 paper-based; 213 computer-based). *Application deadline:* Applications are processed on a rolling basis. Application fee: $35. Electronic applications accepted. *Expenses:* Tuition, state resident: full-time $7,824; part-time $326 per credit hour. Tuition, nonresident: full-time $14,932; part-time $622 per credit hour. Required fees: $550. *Financial support:* Federal Work-Study available. Support available to part-time students. Financial award application deadline: 4/15; financial award applicants required to submit FAFSA. *Unit head:* Dr. Sandra Lemoine, Dean, 864-388-8225, Fax: 864-388-8890. *Application contact:* Dr. Linda Neely, Director of Graduate Studies, 864-388-8268, Fax: 864-388-8144, E-mail: lneely@lander.edu.

Langston University, School of Education and Behavioral Sciences, Langston, OK 73050-0907. Offers bilingual/multicultural (M Ed); elementary education (M Ed); English as a second language (M Ed); rehabilitation counseling (M Sc); urban education (M Ed). *Accreditation:* CORE; NCATE (one or more programs are accredited). Part-time programs available. *Degree requirements:* For master's, thesis optional. *Entrance requirements:* For master's, GRE, writing skills test, minimum GPA of 2.5, 3 letters of recommendation. Additional exam requirements/recommendations for international students: Required—TOEFL, TWE. *Faculty research:* Bilingual/multicultural education, financing post-secondary education.

Lee University, Program in Education, Cleveland, TN 37320-3450. Offers classroom teaching (M Ed); educational leadership (M Ed); elementary/secondary education (MAT); special education (elementary) (M Ed); special education (secondary) (M Ed, MAT); special education (severe disabilities) (M Ed). *Faculty:* 25 full-time (11 women). *Students:* 103 full-time (66 women), 22 part-time (15 women); includes 43 minority (5 African Americans, 36 American Indian/Alaska Native, 2 Hispanic Americans), 3 international. 49 applicants, 100% accepted, 28 enrolled. In 2006, 75 degrees awarded. *Degree requirements:* For master's, variable foreign language requirement, thesis, internship, comprehensive exam. *Entrance requirements:* For master's, MAT or GRE General Test, minimum GPA of 2.75, 3 letters of recommendation, interview, writing sample. Additional exam requirements/recommendations for international students: Required—TOEFL. *Application deadline:* For fall admission, 4/1 for domestic students; for spring admission, 10/1 for domestic students. Applications are processed on a rolling basis. Application fee: $25. *Expenses:* Tuition: Part-time $412 per credit. Required fees: $10 per semester. Tuition and fees vary according to course load. *Financial support:* Career-related internships or fieldwork, Federal Work-Study, and institutionally sponsored loans available. *Unit head:* Dr. Gary Riggins, Director, 423-614-8193. *Application contact:* Vicki Glasscock, Graduate Admissions Director, 423-614-8059, E-mail: vglasscock@leeuniversity.edu.

Lehigh University, College of Education, Department of Education and Human Services, Program in Technology-Based Teacher Education, Bethlehem, PA 18015-3094. Offers elementary education (M Ed); learning sciences and technology (PhD); secondary education (M Ed, MA). Part-time and evening/weekend programs available. *Faculty:* 29 full-time (16 women), 17 part-time/adjunct (9 women). *Students:* 36 full-time (30 women), 34 part-time (22 women); includes 2 minority (both Asian Americans or Pacific Islanders), 2 international. 27 applicants, 85% accepted, 10 enrolled. In 2006, 53 master's, 1 doctorate awarded. *Entrance requirements:* For master's, minimum GPA of 3.0; for doctorate, GRE General Test, minimum GPA of 3.0. Additional exam requirements/recommendations for international students: Required—TOEFL (minimum score 600 paper-based; 250 computer-based). *Application deadline:* Applications are processed on a rolling basis. Application fee: $60. Electronic applications accepted. *Financial support:* Career-related internships or fieldwork, Federal Work-Study, institutionally sponsored loans, scholarships/grants, and tuition waivers (full and partial) available. Financial award application deadline: 1/31. *Unit head:* Dr. H. Lynn Columba, Head, 610-758-3230, Fax: 610-758-3243, E-mail: hlc0@lehigh.edu.

Lehman College of the City University of New York, Division of Education, Department of Early Childhood and Elementary Education, Program in Elementary Education, Bronx, NY 10468-1589. Offers MS Ed. *Accreditation:* NCATE. Part-time and evening/weekend programs available. *Degree requirements:* For master's, thesis, registration. *Entrance requirements:* For master's, minimum GPA of 3.0. *Faculty research:* POS network, emotional and intellectual learning, realistic picture books.

Lesley University, School of Education, Cambridge, MA 02138-2790. Offers curriculum and instruction (M Ed, CAGS); early childhood education (M Ed); educational studies (PhD); elementary education (M Ed); individually designed (M Ed); middle school education (M Ed); moderate special needs (M Ed); reading (M Ed, CAGS); science in education (M Ed); severe special needs (M Ed); special needs (CAGS); technology in education (M Ed, CAGS). Part-time and evening/weekend programs available. Postbaccalaureate distance learning degree programs offered (no on-campus study). *Faculty:* 47 full-time (39 women), 208 part-time/adjunct (135 women). *Students:* 242 full-time (222 women), 2,903 part-time (2,495 women); includes 279 minority (179 African Americans, 7 American Indian/Alaska Native, 25 Asian Americans or Pacific Islanders, 68 Hispanic Americans), 10 international. Average age 36. 1,186 applicants, 96% accepted, 792 enrolled. In 2006, 1,724 master's, 6 doctorates, 17 other advanced degrees awarded. *Degree requirements:* For master's, practicum; for doctorate, thesis/dissertation. *Entrance requirements:* For doctorate, GRE General Test or MAT, interview, master's degree, resumé; for CAGS, interview, master's degree. Additional exam requirements/recommendations for international students: Required—TOEFL (minimum score 550 paper-based; 213 computer-based; 80 iBT). *Application deadline:* Applications are processed on a rolling basis. Application fee: $50. Electronic applications accepted. *Financial support:* In 2006–07, 26 students received support, including research assistantships (averaging $3,400 per year), teaching assistantships (averaging $3,400 per year); career-related internships or fieldwork, Federal Work-Study, scholarships/grants, and unspecified assistantships also available. Support available to part-time students. Financial award application deadline: 4/15; financial award applicants required to submit FAFSA. *Faculty research:* Assessment in literacy, mathematics and science; autism spectrum disorders; instructional technology and online learning; multicultural education and ELL. *Unit head:* Dr. Mario Borunda, Dean, 617-349-8375, Fax: 617-349-8607, E-mail: mborunda@lesley.edu. *Application contact:* Kristen Card, Associate Director of On-Campus Admissions, 617-349-8734, Fax: 617-349-8313, E-mail: kmcard@lesley.edu.

See Close-Up on page 893.

Lewis & Clark College, Graduate School of Education and Counseling, Department of Education, Program in Early Childhood/Elementary Education, Portland, OR 97219-7899. Offers MAT. *Accreditation:* NCATE. *Faculty:* 6 full-time (4 women), 5 part-time/adjunct (4 women). *Students:* 58 full-time (44 women), 3 part-time (2 women); includes 6 minority (2 Asian Americans or Pacific Islanders, 4 Hispanic Americans). Average age 29. 84 applicants, 89% accepted, 59 enrolled. In 2006, 55 degrees awarded. *Entrance requirements:* For master's,

Elementary Education

Lewis & Clark College (continued)

minimum GPA of 2.75. Additional exam requirements/recommendations for international students: Required—TOEFL (minimum score 575 paper-based; 233 computer-based). *Application deadline:* For fall admission, 1/2 priority date for domestic and international students. Application fee: $50. Electronic applications accepted. *Expenses:* Tuition: Part-time $610 per semester hour. *Financial support:* In 2006–07, 50 students received support. Career-related internships or fieldwork, Federal Work-Study, institutionally sponsored loans, scholarships/grants, and tuition waivers (partial) available. Support available to part-time students. Financial award applicants required to submit FAFSA. *Faculty research:* Classroom ethnography, assessing student learning, reading, moral development, language arts. *Unit head:* Melanie Quinn, Coordinator, 503-768-6112, Fax: 503-768-7715, E-mail: lcteach@lclark.edu. *Application contact:* Becky Haas, Director of Admissions, 503-768-6200, Fax: 503-768-6205, E-mail: gseadmit@lclark.edu.

Liberty University, School of Education, Lynchburg, VA 24502. Offers administration and supervision (M Ed); curriculum and instruction (M Ed); early childhood education (M Ed); education specialist (Ed S); educational leadership (Ed D); elementary education (M Ed); gifted education (M Ed); reading specialist (M Ed); school counseling (M Ed); secondary education (M Ed); special education (M Ed). *Accreditation:* NCATE. Part-time programs available. Postbaccalaureate distance learning degree programs offered (minimal on-campus study). *Faculty:* 8 full-time (3 women), 7 part-time/adjunct (3 women). *Students:* 33 full-time (22 women), 308 part-time (180 women); includes 22 minority (12 African Americans, 2 American Indian/Alaska Native, 2 Asian Americans or Pacific Islanders, 6 Hispanic Americans), 5 international. Average age 39. 434 applicants, 77% accepted, 111 enrolled. In 2006, 39 master's, 12 doctorates, 16 other advanced degrees awarded. *Degree requirements:* For doctorate, thesis/dissertation, comprehensive exam. *Entrance requirements:* For master's, GRE General Test or MAT (if taken on or before 1999), 2 letters of recommendation, minimum undergraduate GPA of 3.0, curriculum vitae, graduate status record; for doctorate, GRE General Test or MAT (if taken before 1999), minimum master's GPA of 3.0, 3 years of teacher experience; for Ed S, GRE General Test or MAT (if taken before 1999), minimum master's GPA of 3.0, 3 years of teaching experience. Additional exam requirements/recommendations for international students: Required—TOEFL (minimum score 600 paper-based; 250 computer-based). *Application deadline:* For fall admission, 6/1 priority date for domestic students; for spring admission, 11/1 for domestic students. Applications are processed on a rolling basis. Application fee: $35. Electronic applications accepted. *Expenses:* Contact institution. *Financial support:* In 2006–07, 226 students received support. Federal Work-Study and tuition waivers (partial) available. *Faculty research:* Self-determination, character education, bibliotherapy, learning styles, distance education. *Unit head:* Dr. Karen L. Parker, Dean, 434-582-2195, Fax: 434-582-2468, E-mail: kparker@liberty.edu. *Application contact:* Kyle A Falce, Director of Graduate Admissions, 800-424-9596, Fax: 800-628-7977, E-mail: gradadmissions@liberty.edu.

Lincoln University, School of Graduate Studies and Continuing Education, College of Liberal Arts, Education and Journalism, Department of Education, Jefferson City, MO 65102. Offers educational leadership (Ed S), including elementary leadership, secondary leadership, superintendency; guidance and counseling (M Ed), including community/agency counseling, elementary school, secondary school; school administration and supervision (M Ed), including elementary school administration, secondary school administration, special education administration; school teaching (M Ed), including elementary school teaching, secondary school teaching. *Accreditation:* NCATE. Part-time and evening/weekend programs available. *Faculty:* 1 (woman) full-time, 10 part-time/adjunct (5 women). *Students:* 24 full-time (21 women), 62 part-time (51 women); includes 10 minority (8 African Americans, 2 Asian Americans or Pacific Islanders), 4 international. Average age 35. 13 applicants, 100% accepted, 10 enrolled. In 2006, 25 master's, 3 other advanced degrees awarded. *Degree requirements:* For master's and Ed S, portfolio. *Entrance requirements:* For master's, GRE or MAT, teaching certificate (school administration and supervision); background check; interview (elementary and secondary school teaching); for Ed S, GRE or MAT, principal certificate. Additional exam requirements/recommendations for international students: Required—TOEFL (minimum score 500 paper-based; 173 computer-based; 61 iBT). *Application deadline:* For fall admission, 7/1 priority date for domestic and international students; for spring admission, 12/1 priority date for domestic and international students. Applications are processed on a rolling basis. Application fee: $17. *Expenses:* Tuition, state resident: part-time $189 per credit hour. Tuition, nonresident: part-time $351 per credit hour. Required fees: $15 per credit hour. $20 per semester. *Financial support:* Federal Work-Study and scholarships/grants available. Financial award application deadline: 4/1; financial award applicants required to submit FAFSA. *Unit head:* Dr. Cynthia Chapel, Department Head, 573-681-5250, Fax: 573-681-5257, E-mail: chapelc@lincolnu.edu.

Lock Haven University of Pennsylvania, Office of Graduate Studies, Department of Education, Lock Haven, PA 17745-2390. Offers alternative education (M Ed); teaching and learning (M Ed). *Accreditation:* NCATE. Part-time and evening/weekend programs available. Postbaccalaureate distance learning degree programs offered. *Degree requirements:* For master's, thesis. *Entrance requirements:* For master's, minimum undergraduate GPA of 3.0. Additional exam requirements/recommendations for international students: Required—TOEFL. Electronic applications accepted.

Long Island University, Brentwood Campus, School of Education, Brentwood, NY 11717. Offers elementary education (MS); reading (MS); school counseling (MS); school district administration and supervision (MS); special education (MS). Part-time and evening/weekend programs available.

Long Island University, Brooklyn Campus, School of Education, Department of Teaching and Learning, Program in Elementary Education, Brooklyn, NY 11201-8423. Offers MS Ed. Part-time and evening/weekend programs available. *Degree requirements:* For master's, thesis optional. *Entrance requirements:* For master's, 2 letters of recommendation. Additional exam requirements/recommendations for international students: Required—TOEFL (minimum score 500 paper-based; 173 computer-based). Electronic applications accepted.

Long Island University, C.W. Post Campus, School of Education, Department of Curriculum and Instruction, Brookville, NY 11548-1300. Offers adolescence education (MS); adolescence education: biology (MS); adolescence education: earth science (MS); adolescence education: English (MS); adolescence education: mathematics (MS); adolescence education: social studies (MS); adolescence education: Spanish (MS); art education (MS); bilingual education (MS); childhood education (MS); early childhood education (MS); middle childhood education (MS); music education (MS); teaching English to speakers of other languages (MS). Part-time and evening/weekend programs available. *Degree requirements:* For master's, comprehensive exam or thesis, student teaching. *Entrance requirements:* For master's, minimum GPA of 2.75 in major, 2.5 overall. Electronic applications accepted. *Faculty research:* Ethics and education, teaching strategies.

Long Island University, Rockland Graduate Campus, Graduate School, Program in Curriculum and Instruction, Orangeburg, NY 10962. Offers childhood education (MS). *Entrance requirements:* For master's, GRE General Test.

Long Island University, Southampton Graduate Campus, Education Division, Program in Childhood Education, Southampton, NY 11968-4198. Offers childhood education (MS Ed); elementary education (MS Ed). *Faculty:* 4 full-time, 6 part-time/adjunct. *Students:* 9 full-time (6 women), 35 part-time (29 women). Average age 31. 45 applicants, 100% accepted, 44 enrolled. In 2006, 10 degrees awarded. *Degree requirements:* For master's, thesis. *Entrance requirements:* For master's, minimum undergraduate GPA of 2.75, on-campus writing sample. Additional exam requirements/recommendations for international students: Required—TOEFL (minimum score 550 paper-based; 250 computer-based). *Application deadline:* For fall admission, 4/15 priority date for domestic and international students; for spring admission, 11/15 priority date for domestic and international students. Applications are processed on a rolling

basis. Application fee: $30. Electronic applications accepted. *Expenses:* Tuition: Part-time $790 per credit. Required fees: $220 per semester. *Financial support:* In 2006–07, 1 research assistantship with full tuition reimbursement was awarded; scholarships/grants and unspecified assistantships also available. Support available to part-time students. Financial award applicants required to submit FAFSA. *Application contact:* Joyce Tuttle, Director of Graduate Admissions and Program Administration, 631-287-8010, Fax: 631-287-8253, E-mail: joyce.tuttle@liu.edu.

Long Island University, Westchester Graduate Campus, Programs in Education-Teaching, Purchase, NY 10577. Offers early childhood education (MS Ed); elementary education (MS Ed); literacy education (MS Ed); second language, TESOL, bilingual education (MS Ed); special education and secondary education (MS Ed). Part-time and evening/weekend programs available. *Faculty:* 4 full-time, 32 part-time/adjunct. *Students:* 50 applicants, 92% accepted, 42 enrolled. In 2006, 72 degrees awarded. *Degree requirements:* For master's, comprehensive exam. *Application deadline:* Applications are processed on a rolling basis. Application fee: $30. *Expenses:* Tuition: Part-time $790 per credit. *Financial support:* In 2006–07, 38 students received support. Scholarships/grants, tuition waivers (partial), and unspecified assistantships available. *Unit head:* Dr. Sylvia Blake, Academic Dean, Associate Provost, 914-831-2704, Fax: 914-251-5959, E-mail: sylvia.blake@liu.edu. *Application contact:* Ellen Brief, Coordinator of Admissions, Marketing, Student Services and Public Relations, 914-831-2701, Fax: 914-251-5959, E-mail: ellen.brief@liu.edu.

Longwood University, Office of Graduate Studies, College of Education and Human Services, Farmville, VA 23909. Offers communication sciences and disorders (MS); community and college counseling (MS); curriculum and instruction specialist-elementary (MS), including mild disabilities, modern languages; curriculum and instruction specialist-secondary (MS), including English, mild disabilities, modern languages; educational leadership (MS); guidance and counseling (MS); literacy and culture (MS); school library media (MS). *Accreditation:* NCATE. Part-time and evening/weekend programs available. *Degree requirements:* For master's, thesis optional. *Entrance requirements:* For master's, GRE (communication sciences and disorders), minimum GPA of 2.75. Additional exam requirements/recommendations for international students: Required—TOEFL (minimum score 550 paper-based; 213 computer-based).

Louisiana State University and Agricultural and Mechanical College, Graduate School, College of Education, Department of Educational Theory, Policy and Practice, Baton Rouge, LA 70803. Offers counseling (M Ed, MA, Ed S); educational administration (M Ed, MA, PhD, Ed S); educational technology (MA); elementary education (M Ed); higher education (PhD); research methodology (PhD); secondary education (M Ed). *Accreditation:* ACA (one or more programs are accredited); NCATE. Part-time and evening/weekend programs available. *Faculty:* 39 full-time (24 women). *Students:* 147 full-time (115 women), 183 part-time (143 women); includes 63 minority (51 African Americans, 3 American Indian/Alaska Native, 3 Asian Americans or Pacific Islanders, 6 Hispanic Americans), 14 international. Average age 35. 110 applicants, 58% accepted, 15 enrolled. In 2006, 93 master's, 24 doctorates awarded. Terminal master's awarded for partial completion of doctoral program. *Degree requirements:* For doctorate, thesis/dissertation; for Ed S, thesis optional. *Entrance requirements:* For master's and doctorate, GRE General Test, minimum GPA of 3.0. Additional exam requirements/recommendations for international students: Required—TOEFL (minimum score 550 paper-based; 213 computer-based; 79 iBT). *Application deadline:* For fall admission, 1/25 priority date for domestic students, 5/15 for international students; for spring admission, 10/15 for international students. Applications are processed on a rolling basis. Application fee: $25. Electronic applications accepted. *Financial support:* In 2006–07, 82 students received support, including 6 fellowships with full tuition reimbursements available (averaging $26,273 per year), 24 research assistantships with full and partial tuition reimbursements available (averaging $9,812 per year), teaching assistantships with full and partial tuition reimbursements available (averaging $11,693 per year); career-related internships or fieldwork, Federal Work-Study, institutionally sponsored loans, and unspecified assistantships also available. Support available to part-time students. Financial award applicants required to submit FAFSA. *Faculty research:* Literary, curriculum studies, science education, K-12 leadership, higher education. Total annual research expenditures: $335,618. *Unit head:* Dr. Earl Cheek, Chair, 225-578-6897, Fax: 225-578-1045, E-mail: echeek@lsu.edu.

Loyola Marymount University, Graduate Division, School of Education, Program in Elementary Education, Los Angeles, CA 90045-2659. Offers MA. Part-time and evening/weekend programs available. *Students:* 243 full-time (201 women), 27 part-time (21 women); includes 148 minority (17 African Americans, 2 American Indian/Alaska Native, 35 Asian Americans or Pacific Islanders, 94 Hispanic Americans). Average age 27. In 2006, 92 degrees awarded. *Degree requirements:* For master's, comprehensive exam. *Entrance requirements:* For master's, GRE General Test, interview. Additional exam requirements/recommendations for international students: Required—TOEFL (minimum score 600 paper-based; 250 computer-based). *Application deadline:* For fall admission, 7/15 for domestic students; for spring admission, 11/15 for domestic students. Application fee: $50. Electronic applications accepted. *Financial support:* Federal Work-Study and scholarships/grants available. Support available to part-time students. Financial award application deadline: 6/1; financial award applicants required to submit FAFSA. *Unit head:* Dr. Irene Oliver, Coordinator, 310-338-7302, Fax: 310-338-7302, E-mail: ioliver@lmu.edu.

Loyola University Chicago, School of Education, Program in Initial Teacher Preparation, Chicago, IL 60611-2196. Offers elementary education (M Ed); reading specialist (M Ed); school technology (M Ed); science education (M Ed); secondary education (M Ed); special education (M Ed). *Accreditation:* NCATE. *Faculty:* 11 full-time (9 women), 6 part-time/adjunct (4 women). *Students:* 138. Average age 28. 95 applicants, 65% accepted, 39 enrolled. In 2006, 84 degrees awarded. *Degree requirements:* For master's, comprehensive exam. *Entrance requirements:* For master's, Illinois Basic Skills Test, 3 letters of recommendation, minimum GPA of 3.0, resumé. Additional exam requirements/recommendations for international students: Required—TOEFL (minimum score 550 paper-based; 213 computer-based; 79 iBT). *Application deadline:* For fall admission, 7/1 priority date for domestic and international students; for spring admission, 11/1 priority date for domestic and international students. Applications are processed on a rolling basis. Application fee: $50. Electronic applications accepted. *Financial support:* In 2006–07, 2 research assistantships with full tuition reimbursements (averaging $8,500 per year), 1 teaching assistantship were awarded. Financial award application deadline: 2/15. *Faculty research:* Positive behavior support, school reform, school improvement. *Unit head:* Dr. Dorothy Giroux, Director, 312-915-7027, E-mail: dgiroux@luc.edu. *Application contact:* Marie Rosin-Dittmar, Information Contact, 312-915-6800, E-mail: schleduc@luc.edu.

Loyola University New Orleans, College of Arts and Sciences, Department of Education and Counseling, Program in Elementary Education, New Orleans, LA 70118-6195. Offers MS. Part-time and evening/weekend programs available. *Degree requirements:* For master's, comprehensive exam. *Entrance requirements:* For master's, GRE or MAT (preferred), interview, letters of recommendation, writing sample. Additional exam requirements/recommendations for international students: Required—TOEFL (minimum score 550 paper-based; 213 computer-based). Electronic applications accepted. *Faculty research:* Mathematics, methodology.

Lynchburg College, Graduate Studies, School of Education and Human Development, Program in Teaching and Learning, Lynchburg, VA 24501-3199. Offers M Ed. *Faculty:* 1 (woman) full-time, 1 (woman) part-time/adjunct. *Students:* 4 full-time (all women), 5 part-time (all women); includes 1 minority (Hispanic American) In 2006, 2 degrees awarded. *Median time to degree:* Master's–3 years full-time, 4 years part-time. *Expenses:* Tuition: Full-time $6,300; part-time $350 per credit. Required fees: $100. *Unit head:* Dr. Roger Jones, Program Coordinator, 434-544-8444.

Maharishi University of Management, Graduate Studies, Department of Education, Fairfield, IA 52557. Offers teaching elementary education (MA); teaching secondary education (MA).

Degree requirements: For master's, thesis or alternative. *Entrance requirements:* For master's, GRE, minimum GPA of 3.0. Additional exam requirements/recommendations for international students: Required—TOEFL. *Faculty research:* Unified field-based approach to education, moral climate, scientific study of teaching.

Manhattanville College, Graduate Programs, School of Education, Program in Child and Early Childhood Education, Purchase, NY 10577-2132. Offers MAT. Part-time and evening/weekend programs available. *Students:* 22 full-time (all women), 24 part-time (all women), 1 international. In 2006, 17 degrees awarded. *Degree requirements:* For master's, comprehensive exam or research project, field experience. *Entrance requirements:* For master's, minimum undergraduate GPA of 3.0, 2 letters of recommendation. *Application deadline:* Applications are processed on a rolling basis. Application fee: $55. *Financial support:* Career-related internships or fieldwork and institutionally sponsored loans available. Support available to part-time students. *Application contact:* Alyce Ware Poli, Director of Admissions, 914-323-5142, Fax: 914-694-1732, E-mail: edschool@mville.edu.

Manhattanville College, Graduate Programs, School of Education, Program in Childhood Education, Purchase, NY 10577-2132. Offers childhood and special education (MPS); childhood education (MAT); special education childhood (MPS). Part-time and evening/weekend programs available. *Students:* 67 full-time (62 women), 150 part-time (120 women); includes 6 African Americans, 3 Asian Americans or Pacific Islanders, 10 Hispanic Americans, 2 international. In 2006, 65 degrees awarded. *Degree requirements:* For master's, comprehensive exam or research project, field experience. *Entrance requirements:* For master's, minimum undergraduate GPA of 3.0, 2 letters of recommendation. *Application deadline:* Applications are processed on a rolling basis. Application fee: $55. *Financial support:* Career-related internships or fieldwork and institutionally sponsored loans available. Support available to part-time students. *Application contact:* Alyce Ware Poli, Director of Admissions, 914-323-5142, Fax: 914-694-1732, E-mail: edschool@mville.edu.

Mansfield University of Pennsylvania, Graduate Studies, Department of Education and Special Education, Mansfield, PA 16933. Offers elementary education (M Ed); secondary education (MS). *Accreditation:* NCATE (one or more programs are accredited). Part-time and evening/weekend programs available. Postbaccalaureate distance learning degree programs offered (no on-campus study). *Faculty:* 13 full-time (9 women), 1 (woman) part-time/adjunct. *Students:* 50 full-time (44 women), 72 part-time (52 women); includes 8 minority (4 African Americans, 1 Asian American or Pacific Islander, 3 Hispanic Americans). Average age 31. 130 applicants, 80% accepted, 34 enrolled. In 2006, 47 degrees awarded. *Degree requirements:* For master's, thesis optional. *Entrance requirements:* For master's, minimum GPA of 3.0. Additional exam requirements/recommendations for international students: Required—TOEFL (minimum score 550 paper-based; 220 computer-based). *Application deadline:* For fall admission, 8/1 priority date for domestic students, 8/1 for international students; for spring admission, 11/1 priority date for domestic students, 9/1 for international students. Applications are processed on a rolling basis. Application fee: $25. Electronic applications accepted. *Expenses:* Tuition, state resident: part-time $336 per credit. Tuition, nonresident: part-time $538 per credit. Tuition and fees vary according to course load and reciprocity agreements. *Financial support:* Career-related internships or fieldwork and unspecified assistantships available. Support available to part-time students. Financial award application deadline: 5/1; financial award applicants required to submit FAFSA. *Unit head:* Dr. Celeste Burns, Chairperson, 570-662-4563, E-mail: cburns@mnsfld.edu. *Application contact:* Judi Brayer, Assistant Director of Enrollment Management/Graduate Admissions, 570-662-4818, Fax: 570-662-4121, E-mail: jbrayer@mansfield.edu.

Marshall University, Academic Affairs Division, College of Education and Human Services, Graduate School of Education and Professional Development, Program in Elementary Education, Huntington, WV 25755. Offers MA. *Accreditation:* NCATE. Part-time and evening/weekend programs available. *Faculty:* 24 full-time (13 women). *Students:* 20 full-time (18 women), 100 part-time (95 women); includes 2 minority (both African Americans) Average age 35. In 2006, 26 degrees awarded. *Degree requirements:* For master's, comprehensive or oral assessment, research project, thesis optional. *Entrance requirements:* For master's, GRE General Test or MAT. Application fee: $40. *Financial support:* Federal Work-Study, tuition waivers (full and partial), and unspecified assistantships available. Support available to part-time students. Financial award applicants required to submit FAFSA. *Unit head:* Dr. Calvin Meyer, Director, 304-746-1936, E-mail: meyer@marshall.edu. *Application contact:* Information Contact, 304-746-1900, Fax: 304-746-1902, E-mail: services@marshall.edu.

Mary Baldwin College, Graduate Studies, Program in Teaching, Staunton, VA 24401-3610. Offers elementary education (MAT); middle grades education (MAT). *Faculty:* 5 full-time (3 women), 38 part-time/adjunct (20 women). *Students:* 104 full-time (76 women), 101 part-time (85 women). *Application deadline:* For fall admission, 7/15 priority date for domestic students; for spring admission, 11/15 priority date for domestic students. Application fee: $35. *Unit head:* Dr. Carole Grove, Program Director, 540-887-7134. *Application contact:* Lori Johnson, Administrative Assistant, 540-887-7333, E-mail: ljohnson@mbc.edu.

Marygrove College, Graduate Division, Education Unit, Program in Sage, Detroit, MI 48221-2599. Offers M Ed. *Entrance requirements:* For master's, Michigan Teacher Test for Certification.

Marymount University, School of Education and Human Services, Program in Education, Arlington, VA 22207-4299. Offers alternative teacher licensure (Certificate); elementary education (M Ed); English as a second language (M Ed); learning disabilities (M Ed); professional studies (M Ed); secondary education (M Ed). *Accreditation:* NCATE. Part-time and evening/weekend programs available. Postbaccalaureate distance learning degree programs offered (minimal on-campus study). *Faculty:* 10 full-time (8 women), 5 part-time/adjunct (2 women). *Students:* 75 full-time (65 women), 95 part-time (82 women); includes 25 minority (13 African Americans, 2 American Indian/Alaska Native, 6 Asian Americans or Pacific Islanders, 4 Hispanic Americans), 6 international. Average age 32. 58 applicants, 100% accepted, 45 enrolled. In 2006, 113 degrees awarded. *Degree requirements:* For master's, thesis or alternative. *Entrance requirements:* For master's, GRE General Test or MAT, PRAXIS I or SAT/ACT, interview, 2 letters of recommendation. Additional exam requirements/recommendations for international students: Required—TOEFL (minimum score 600 paper-based; 250 computer-based). *Application deadline:* Applications are processed on a rolling basis. Application fee: $40. Electronic applications accepted. *Expenses:* Tuition: Full-time $11,160; part-time $620 per credit. Required fees: $113; $630 per credit. *Financial support:* Research assistantships with full tuition reimbursements, career-related internships or fieldwork, scholarships/grants, and unspecified assistantships available. Support available to part-time students. Financial award applicants required to submit FAFSA. *Unit head:* Dr. Shelly Haser, Chair, 703-284-6955, Fax: 703-284-1631, E-mail: shelly.haser@marymount.edu.

Maryville University of Saint Louis, School of Education, St. Louis, MO 63141-7299. Offers art education (MA Ed); early childhood education (MA Ed); education (Ed D); elementary education (MA Ed); elementary education/English (MA Ed); environmental education (MA Ed); gifted education (MA Ed); middle grades education (MA Ed); reading specialist (MA Ed); secondary education (MA Ed), including educational leadership, secondary teaching and inquiry. *Accreditation:* NASAD; NCATE. Part-time and evening/weekend programs available. *Students:* 17 full-time (14 women), 168 part-time (129 women); includes 20 African Americans, 2 Asian Americans or Pacific Islanders, 1 Hispanic American, 2 international. Average age 37. 39 applicants, 95% accepted, 24 enrolled. In 2006, 37 degrees awarded. *Degree requirements:* For master's, thesis, project. *Entrance requirements:* For master's and doctorate, minimum GPA of 3.0, 3 professional recommendations. Additional exam requirements/recommendations for international students: Required—TOEFL (minimum score 550 paper-based). *Application deadline:* Applications are processed on a rolling basis. Application fee: $35 ($50 for international students). Electronic applications accepted. *Expenses:* Tuition: Full-time $17,800; part-time $555 per credit. Required fees: $55 per semester. Tuition and fees vary according to degree level and program. *Financial support:* Career-related internships or fieldwork, Federal Work-Study, tuition waivers (partial), and professional educator discounts available. Financial award application deadline: 7/31; financial award applicants required to submit FAFSA. *Faculty research:* Collaboration with public schools, preservice program development, mathematics, diversity, literacy. *Unit head:* Dr. Sam Hausfather, Dean, 314-529-9466, Fax: 314-529-9921, E-mail: shausfather@maryville.edu. *Application contact:* Dr. Lillian Curtis, Graduate Admissions Coordinator, 314-529-9542, Fax: 314-529-9921, E-mail: teachered@maryville.edu.

Marywood University, Academic Affairs, College of Education and Human Development, Department of Education, Program in Elementary Education, Scranton, PA 18509-1598. Offers MAT. *Accreditation:* NCATE. Part-time and evening/weekend programs available. *Students:* 13 full-time (all women), 23 part-time (20 women). Average age 31. In 2006, 18 degrees awarded. *Degree requirements:* For master's, thesis or alternative, internship/practicum. *Entrance requirements:* For master's, GRE or MAT. Additional exam requirements/recommendations for international students: Required—TOEFL (minimum score 550 paper-based; 213 computer-based). *Application deadline:* For fall admission, 4/15 priority date for domestic and international students; for spring admission, 11/15 priority date for domestic and international students. Applications are processed on a rolling basis. Application fee: $30. Electronic applications accepted. *Expenses:* Tuition: Part-time $672 per credit. Tuition and fees vary according to degree level, campus/location and program. *Financial support:* Research assistantships, career-related internships or fieldwork, scholarships/grants, and tuition waivers (partial) available. Support available to part-time students. Financial award application deadline: 2/15; financial award applicants required to submit FAFSA. *Application contact:* Dr. Deborah M. Flynn, Coordinator of Graduate Advising (Enrollment Management), 570-348-6211, E-mail: flynn@ac.marywood.edu.

McDaniel College, Graduate and Professional Studies, Program in Elementary and Secondary Education, Westminster, MD 21157-4390. Offers elementary education (MS); secondary education (MS). *Accreditation:* NCATE. Part-time and evening/weekend programs available. *Degree requirements:* For master's, thesis optional. *Entrance requirements:* For master's, GRE General Test, MAT, or NTE/PRAXIS I, letters of reference (3). Additional exam requirements/recommendations for international students: Required—TOEFL (minimum score 213 computer-based).

McNeese State University, Graduate School, College of Education, Department of Teacher Education, Program in Curriculum and Instruction, Lake Charles, LA 70609. Offers early childhood education (M Ed); elementary education (M Ed); secondary education (M Ed). Evening/weekend programs available. *Faculty:* 12 full-time (8 women), 2 part-time/adjunct (1 woman). *Students:* 7 full-time (6 women), 40 part-time (37 women); includes 20 minority (19 African Americans, 1 American Indian/Alaska Native). In 2006, 22 degrees awarded. *Entrance requirements:* For master's, GRE, teaching certificate. *Application deadline:* For fall admission, 5/15 priority date for domestic students. Applications are processed on a rolling basis. Application fee: $20 ($30 for international students). *Expenses:* Tuition, area resident: Full-time $2,226; part-time $193 per hour. Required fees: $919; $106 per hour. *Financial support:* Application deadline: 5/1. *Unit head:* Dr. Wayne R Fetter, Dean, College of Education, 337-475-5432, Fax: 337-475-5467, E-mail: wfetter@mcneese.edu.

Medaille College, Program in Education, Buffalo, NY 14214-2695. Offers curriculum and instruction (MS Ed); education preparation (MS Ed); literacy (MS Ed); special education (MS). Part-time and evening/weekend programs available. *Faculty:* 30 full-time (20 women), 28 part-time/adjunct (18 women). *Students:* 516 full-time (417 women), 334 part-time (276 women); includes 16 minority (13 African Americans, 2 Asian Americans or Pacific Islanders, 1 Hispanic American), 654 international. Average age 27. 725 applicants, 97% accepted, 655 enrolled. In 2006, 229 degrees awarded. *Degree requirements:* For master's, thesis or alternative. *Entrance requirements:* For master's, minimum undergraduate GPA of 2.7. Additional exam requirements/recommendations for international students: Required—TOEFL (minimum score 550 paper-based; 213 computer-based). *Application deadline:* For fall admission, 8/15 priority date for domestic students; for spring admission, 1/15 priority date for domestic students. Applications are processed on a rolling basis. Application fee: $35. Electronic applications accepted. *Expenses:* Tuition: Part-time $580 per credit hour. Full-time tuition and fees vary according to program. *Financial support:* In 2006–07, 390 students received support. Federal Work-Study available. Financial award applicants required to submit FAFSA. *Faculty research:* Curriculum planning, truancy, tracking minority students, curriculum design, mentoring students. *Unit head:* Dr. Robert DiSibio, Director of Graduate Programs, 716-635-5033 Ext. 2017, Fax: 716-634-2232, E-mail: rdisibio@medaille.edu. *Application contact:* Susan Greenwald, Executive Director of Admissions, 716-635-5033 Ext. 2011, Fax: 716-631-1380, E-mail: sgreenwald@medaille.edu.

Mercy College, Division of Education, Dobbs Ferry, NY 10522-1189. Offers adolescence education: grades 7-12 (MS); applied behavior analysis (MS); bilingual education (MS); childhood education: grades 1-6 (MS); early childhood education: birth—grade 2 (MS); education (MS); elementary education (MS); learning technology (MS); middle childhood education: grades 5-9 (MS); reading (MS); school administration and supervision (MS); school building leadership (MS); school business administration (MS); secondary education (MS); special education (MS); students with disabilities: grades 5-9 (MS); students with disabilities: grades 7-12 (MS); teaching English to speakers of other languages (MS); teaching literacy: birth—grade 6 (MS); teaching literacy: grades 5-12 (MS); urban education (MS). *Students:* 572 full-time (467 women), 1,719 part-time (1,287 women); includes 943 minority (470 African Americans, 7 American Indian/Alaska Native, 48 Asian Americans or Pacific Islanders, 418 Hispanic Americans), 6 international. Average age 33. In 2006, 1090 degrees awarded. *Entrance requirements:* For master's, teaching certificate. *Application deadline:* For fall admission, 2/1 for domestic students. Applications are processed on a rolling basis. Application fee: $37. *Expenses: Contact institution.* Tuition and fees vary according to program. *Financial support:* Institutionally sponsored loans, scholarships/grants, and unspecified assistantships available. Support available to part-time students. *Faculty research:* Distance learning, literacy, assessment, community schools, impact of staff development. *Unit head:* Dr. William Prattella, Chairperson, 914-674-7555, Fax: 914-674-7352, E-mail: wprattella@mercy.edu. *Application contact:* Kathleen Jackson, Director of Admissions, 800-Mercy-NY, Fax: 914-674-7382, E-mail: admissions@mercy.edu.

Metropolitan College of New York, Program in Childhood Education, New York, NY 10013-1919. Offers MS. *Faculty:* 7 full-time (5 women), 9 part-time/adjunct (6 women). *Students:* 36 full-time (30 women); includes 23 minority (16 African Americans, 3 Asian Americans or Pacific Islanders, 4 Hispanic Americans), 1 international. Average age 34. 44 applicants, 73% accepted, 17 enrolled. In 2006, 24 degrees awarded. *Median time to degree:* Master's–1 year full-time. *Degree requirements:* For master's, one foreign language. *Entrance requirements:* For master's, Liberal Arts and Sciences Test (LAST) recommended, minimum GPA of 3.0, 2 letters of reference, writing sample, interview. Additional exam requirements/recommendations for international students: Required—TOEFL (minimum score 600 paper-based; 250 computer-based). *Application deadline:* For fall admission, 8/1 priority date for domestic students, 7/1 for international students; for winter admission, 11/15 priority date for domestic students, 11/15 for international students; for spring admission, 4/15 priority date for domestic students, 3/15 for international students. Application fee: $45. *Expenses: Contact institution. Financial support:* In 2006–07, 35 students received support. Career-related internships or fieldwork, Federal Work-Study, institutionally sponsored loans, and scholarships/grants available. Financial award application deadline: 8/15; financial award applicants required to submit FAFSA. *Faculty research:* Classroom management, learner autonomy, teacher research, math and gender, intelligence. *Unit head:* Dr. Patrick Ianniello, Director, 212-343-1234 Ext. 2424, E-mail: pianniello@metropolitan.edu. *Application contact:* Sylvia Cameron, Graduate Admissions Coordinator, 212-343-1234 Ext. 2704, Fax: 212-343-7900, E-mail: scameron@mcny.edu.

Miami University, Graduate School, School of Education and Allied Professions, Department of Teacher Education, Program in Elementary Education, Oxford, OH 45056. Offers M Ed, MAT. *Accreditation:* NCATE. Part-time programs available. *Degree requirements:* For

Elementary Education

Miami University (continued)
master's, final exam. *Entrance requirements:* For master's, MAT, minimum undergraduate GPA of 3.0 during previous 2 years or 2.75 overall.

Miami University, Graduate School, School of Education and Allied Professions, Department of Teacher Education, Program in Secondary Education, Oxford, OH 45056. Offers adolescent education (MAT), including integrated English, integrated mathematics, integrated social studies, language arts; elementary mathematics education (M Ed); secondary education (M Ed, MAT). *Accreditation:* NCATE. Part-time programs available. *Degree requirements:* For master's, thesis (for some programs), final exam. *Entrance requirements:* For master's, MAT, minimum undergraduate GPA of 3.0 during previous 2 years or 2.75 overall. *Faculty research:* Teacher effectiveness, collaboration models.

Middle Tennessee State University, College of Graduate Studies, College of Education and Behavioral Science, Department of Elementary and Special Education, Major in Curriculum and Instruction, Murfreesboro, TN 37132. Offers early childhood education (M Ed); elementary education (M Ed, Ed S); middle school education (M Ed). *Accreditation:* NCATE. Part-time and evening/weekend programs available. Postbaccalaureate distance learning degree programs offered. *Students:* 13 full-time (12 women), 79 part-time (73 women); includes 7 minority (5 African Americans, 2 Asian Americans or Pacific Islanders). In 2006, 59 degrees awarded. *Degree requirements:* For master's, comprehensive exam; for Ed S, thesis. *Entrance requirements:* Additional exam requirements/recommendations for international students: Required—TOEFL (minimum score 525 paper-based; 195 computer-based). *Application deadline:* For fall admission, 8/1 priority date for domestic students. Applications are processed on a rolling basis. Application fee: $25. Electronic applications accepted. *Financial support:* Application deadline: 5/1. *Unit head:* Dr. Connie Jones, Chair, Department of Elementary and Special Education, 615-898-2680, Fax: 615-898-5309, E-mail: cojones@mtsu.edu.

Millersville University of Pennsylvania, Graduate School, School of Education, Department of Elementary and Early Childhood Education, Program in Elementary Education, Millersville, PA 17551-0302. Offers M Ed. *Accreditation:* NCATE. Part-time and evening/weekend programs available. *Faculty:* 20 full-time (15 women), 11 part-time/adjunct (6 women). *Students:* 9 full-time (all women), 23 part-time (19 women); includes 3 minority (all Hispanic Americans) Average age 31. 7 applicants, 100% accepted, 5 enrolled. In 2006, 20 degrees awarded. *Degree requirements:* For master's, exit test, thesis optional. *Entrance requirements:* For master's, MAT or GRE, instructional certificate, minimum undergraduate GPA of 2.75. *Application deadline:* For fall admission, 3/1 priority date for domestic students; for spring admission, 10/1 priority date for domestic students. Applications are processed on a rolling basis. Application fee: $35. *Expenses:* Tuition, state resident: full-time $6,048; part-time $336 per credit. Tuition, nonresident: full-time $9,678; part-time $538 per credit. Required fees: $1,244. Tuition and fees vary according to course load. *Financial support:* In 2006–07, 2 students received support, including 2 research assistantships with full tuition reimbursements available (averaging $4,250 per year); career-related internships or fieldwork, Federal Work-Study, institutionally sponsored loans, and unspecified assistantships also available. Support available to part-time students. Financial award application deadline: 3/15; financial award applicants required to submit FAFSA. *Unit head:* Dr. Jane F. Rudden, Coordinator, 717-872-3394, Fax: 717-871-5462, E-mail: jane.rudden@millersville.edu. *Application contact:* Dr. Victor S. DeSantis, Dean of Graduate Studies, 717-872-3099, Fax: 717-871-2022, E-mail: victor.desantis@millersville.edu.

Mills College, Graduate Studies, Education Department, Oakland, CA 94613-1000. Offers administration (Ed D); child life in health care settings (MA); early childhood education (MA); education (MA), including curriculum and instruction, elementary education, English education, mathematics education, science education, secondary education, social sciences education, teaching. Part-time and evening/weekend programs available. *Faculty:* 10 full-time (7 women), 15 part-time/adjunct (12 women). *Students:* 192 full-time (153 women), 41 part-time (36 women); includes 62 minority (28 African Americans, 13 Asian Americans or Pacific Islanders, 21 Hispanic Americans), 2 international. Average age 34. 160 applicants, 74% accepted, 73 enrolled. In 2006, 52 master's, 1 doctorate awarded. Terminal master's awarded for partial completion of doctoral program. *Degree requirements:* For master's, comprehensive exam. *Entrance requirements:* For doctorate, GRE General Test. Additional exam requirements/recommendations for international students: Required—TOEFL. *Application deadline:* For fall admission, 2/1 for domestic and international students; for spring admission, 11/1 for domestic and international students. Applications are processed on a rolling basis. Application fee: $50. Electronic applications accepted. *Financial support:* In 2006–07, 56 fellowships with tuition reimbursements (averaging $2,700 per year), 15 teaching assistantships (averaging $6,350 per year) were awarded; career-related internships or fieldwork, institutionally sponsored loans, scholarships/grants, and residence awards also available. Support available to part-time students. Financial award application deadline: 2/1; financial award applicants required to submit CSS PROFILE or FAFSA. *Faculty research:* Child development, gender and education, public policy, cross-cultural development, development of literacy. *Unit head:* Joseph Kahne, Chairperson, 510-430-3190, Fax: 510-430-3314, E-mail: grad-studies@mills.edu. *Application contact:* Randy McGlauthing, Director of Graduate Admissions, 510-430-2355, Fax: 510-430-2159, E-mail: rmglaut@mills.edu.

Minnesota State University Mankato, College of Graduate Studies, College of Education, Department of Educational Studies: Elementary and Early Childhood, Mankato, MN 56001. Offers MS. *Accreditation:* NCATE. Part-time programs available. *Students:* 3 full-time (2 women), 29 part-time (26 women). In 2006, 2 degrees awarded. *Degree requirements:* For master's, thesis or alternative, comprehensive exam. *Entrance requirements:* For master's, GRE General Test or MAT, minimum GPA of 3.0 during previous 2 years. Additional exam requirements/recommendations for international students: Required—TOEFL. *Application deadline:* For fall admission, 7/1 priority date for domestic students; for spring admission, 11/1 for domestic students. Applications are processed on a rolling basis. Application fee: $40. Electronic applications accepted. *Financial support:* Application deadline: 3/15; *Unit head:* Dr. Peg Ballard, Chairperson, 507-389-2431. *Application contact:* 507-389-2321, E-mail: grad@mnsu.edu.

Minot State University, Graduate School, Program in Education, Minot, ND 58707-0002. Offers elementary education (M Ed). *Accreditation:* NCATE. *Faculty:* 12 full-time (9 women), 9 part-time/adjunct (3 women). *Students:* 49. In 2006, 5 degrees awarded. *Degree requirements:* For master's, thesis. *Entrance requirements:* For master's, 2 years of teaching experience, bachelor's degree in education, minimum GPA of 2.75. Additional exam requirements/recommendations for international students: Required—TOEFL. *Application deadline:* Applications are processed on a rolling basis. Application fee: $35. *Financial support:* In 2006–07, 2 students received support, including 1 research assistantship with partial tuition reimbursement available (averaging $500 per year), 1 teaching assistantship with partial tuition reimbursement available (averaging $500 per year); career-related internships or fieldwork, institutionally sponsored loans, scholarships/grants, traineeships, tuition waivers (partial), and unspecified assistantships also available. Support available to part-time students. *Faculty research:* Technology, pergonel-teaching efficacy, reflective teaching. *Unit head:* Dr. Debra Jensen, Chairperson, 701-858-3028. *Application contact:* Brenda Anderson, Administrative Assistant, 701-858-3250, Fax: 701-858-4286, E-mail: brenda.anderson@minotstateu.edu.

Mississippi College, Graduate School, School of Education, Department of Teacher Education and Leadership, Clinton, MS 39058. Offers art (M Ed); biological science (M Ed); business education (M Ed); computer science (M Ed); dyslexia therapy (M Ed); educational leadership (M Ed, Ed S); elementary education (M Ed, Ed S); English (M Ed); higher education administration (MS); mathematics (M Ed); secondary education (M Ed); social studies (history) (M Ed); teaching arts (M Ed). Part-time programs available. *Faculty:* 9 full-time (5 women), 14 part-time/adjunct (10 women). *Students:* 52 full-time (36 women), 286 part-time (247 women); includes 173 minority (171 African Americans, 1 American Indian/Alaska Native, 1 Hispanic American), 1 international. Average age 32. In 2006, 131 degrees awarded. *Degree requirements:* For master's, thesis optional. *Entrance requirements:* For master's, NTE. Additional exam requirements/recommendations for international students: Recommended—IELTS. *Application deadline:* Applications are processed on a rolling basis. Application fee: $25. Electronic applications accepted. *Expenses:* Tuition: Full-time $7,290; part-time $405 per hour. Required fees: $150 per term. Tuition and fees vary according to campus/location and program. *Financial support:* Teaching assistantships, career-related internships or fieldwork, Federal Work-Study, scholarships/grants, and unspecified assistantships available. Support available to part-time students. Financial award applicants required to submit FAFSA. *Unit head:* Dr. Tom Williams, Chair, 601-925-3844, E-mail: twilliams@mc.edu.

Mississippi State University, College of Education, Department of Curriculum and Instruction, Mississippi State, MS 39762. Offers curriculum and instruction (PhD); elementary education (MS, Ed D, PhD, Ed S); secondary education (MS, Ed D, PhD, Ed S). *Accreditation:* NCATE. Part-time and evening/weekend programs available. *Faculty:* 23 full-time (20 women), 13 part-time/adjunct (9 women). *Students:* 15 full-time (8 women), 85 part-time (67 women); includes 23 minority (22 African Americans, 1 American Indian/Alaska Native). Average age 31. 10 applicants, 60% accepted, 4 enrolled. In 2006, 48 master's, 14 doctorates awarded. *Degree requirements:* For master's, comprehensive exam; for doctorate, thesis/dissertation; for Ed S, thesis or alternative, comprehensive exam. *Entrance requirements:* For master's, GRE, minimum GPA of 2.75 in junior and senior year, eligibility for initial teacher certification; for doctorate, GRE, minimum graduate GPA of 3.4; for Ed S, GRE, minimum graduate GPA of 3.2. *Application deadline:* For fall admission, 3/1 priority date for domestic students; for spring admission, 9/1 priority date for domestic students. Applications are processed on a rolling basis. Application fee: $30. Electronic applications accepted. *Expenses:* Tuition, state resident: full-time $4,550; part-time $253 per hour. Tuition, nonresident: full-time $10,552; part-time $584 per hour. International tuition: $10,882 full-time. Tuition and fees vary according to course load. *Financial support:* In 2006–07, 30 students received support; research assistantships with tuition reimbursements available, teaching assistantships with tuition reimbursements available, Federal Work-Study, institutionally sponsored loans, scholarships/grants, unspecified assistantships, and work on faculty secured grants available. Financial award applicants required to submit FAFSA. *Faculty research:* Early childhood education, reading, rural schools, multicultural education, use of technology in instruction. *Unit head:* Dr. Unda T. Coats, Interim Head, 662-325-3747, Fax: 662-325-7857, E-mail: ltc1@ra.msstate.edu. *Application contact:* Dr. Phil Bonfanti, Director of Admissions, 662-325-4104, Fax: 662-325-8872, E-mail: admit@msstate.edu.

Mississippi Valley State University, Department of Education, Itta Bena, MS 38941-1400. Offers education (MAT); elementary education (MA). *Accreditation:* NCATE.

Missouri State University, Graduate College, College of Education, Department of Educational Administration, Springfield, MO 65804-0094. Offers director of special education (Ed S); educational administration (MS Ed, Ed S); elementary education (MS Ed); elementary principal (Ed S); secondary education (MS Ed); secondary principal (Ed S); special education (MS Ed); superintendent (Ed S). Part-time and evening/weekend programs available. *Faculty:* 6 full-time (1 woman), 3 part-time/adjunct (0 women). *Students:* 10 full-time (8 women), 143 part-time (94 women); includes 1 minority (African American), 1 international. Average age 37. 13 applicants, 92% accepted, 10 enrolled. In 2006, 33 master's, 17 other advanced degrees awarded. *Degree requirements:* For master's and Ed S, thesis or alternative, comprehensive exam. *Entrance requirements:* For master's, minimum GPA of 2.75; for Ed S, GRE General Test, MAT, minimum GPA of 2.75. Additional exam requirements/recommendations for international students: Required—TOEFL (minimum score 550 paper-based; 213 computer-based; 79 iBT). *Application deadline:* For fall admission, 7/20 priority date for domestic students; for spring admission, 12/20 priority date for domestic students. Applications are processed on a rolling basis. Application fee: $35. Electronic applications accepted. *Expenses:* Tuition, state resident: full-time $3,582; part-time $199 per credit hour. Tuition, nonresident: full-time $6,984; part-time $199 per credit hour. Required fees: $548. Full-time tuition and fees vary according to course level, course load, program and reciprocity agreements. *Financial support:* In 2006–07, 1 teaching assistantship with full tuition reimbursement (averaging $6,780 per year) was awarded; career-related internships or fieldwork, Federal Work-Study, scholarships/grants, and unspecified assistantships also available. Financial award application deadline: 3/31; financial award applicants required to submit FAFSA. *Unit head:* Dr. Charles Barke, Acting Head, 417-836-5392, Fax: 417-836-6905, E-mail: edadmin@missouristate.edu.

Missouri State University, Graduate College, College of Education, School of Teacher Education, Program in Elementary Education, Springfield, MO 65804-0094. Offers MS Ed. Part-time and evening/weekend programs available. Postbaccalaureate distance learning degree programs offered (minimal on-campus study). *Students:* 29 full-time (26 women), 68 part-time (62 women); includes 2 minority (1 African American, 1 American Indian/Alaska Native). Average age 33. 18 applicants, 94% accepted, 12 enrolled. In 2006, 28 degrees awarded. *Degree requirements:* For master's, thesis or alternative, comprehensive exam. *Entrance requirements:* For master's, minimum GPA of 2.75, teaching certificate. Additional exam requirements/recommendations for international students: Required—TOEFL (minimum score 550 paper-based; 213 computer-based; 79 iBT). *Application deadline:* For fall admission, 7/20 priority date for domestic students; for spring admission, 12/20 priority date for domestic students. Applications are processed on a rolling basis. Application fee: $35. Electronic applications accepted. *Expenses:* Tuition, state resident: full-time $3,582; part-time $199 per credit hour. Tuition, nonresident: full-time $6,984; part-time $199 per credit hour. Required fees: $548. Full-time tuition and fees vary according to course level, course load, program and reciprocity agreements. *Financial support:* Teaching assistantships with full tuition reimbursements, Federal Work-Study, institutionally sponsored loans, and scholarships/grants available. Financial award application deadline: 3/31; financial award applicants required to submit FAFSA. *Unit head:* Dr. Cynthia Wilson, Graduate Director, 417-836-6065, E-mail: cindywilson@missouristate.edu.

Monmouth University, Graduate School, School of Education, West Long Branch, NJ 07764-1898. Offers educational counseling (MS Ed); elementary education (MAT), including certified teachers, non-certified teachers; learning disabilities-teacher consultant (Certificate); principal studies (MS Ed); reading specialist (MS Ed, Certificate); special education (MS Ed); supervisor (Certificate); teacher of the handicapped (Certificate). Part-time and evening/weekend programs available. *Faculty:* 24 full-time (15 women), 25 part-time/adjunct (17 women). *Students:* 169 full-time (133 women), 426 part-time (374 women); includes 45 minority (21 African Americans, 2 American Indian/Alaska Native, 2 Asian Americans or Pacific Islanders, 20 Hispanic Americans). Average age 31. 355 applicants, 96% accepted, 138 enrolled. In 2006, 209 degrees awarded. *Entrance requirements:* For master's, minimum GPA of 3.0 in major, 2.75 overall. Additional exam requirements/recommendations for international students: Required—TOEFL (minimum score 550 paper-based; 213 computer-based; 79 iBT), IELTS (minimum score 5), MELAB 77, Cambridge A, B, C. *Application deadline:* For fall admission, 7/15 priority date for domestic students; for spring admission, 11/15 priority date for domestic students. Applications are processed on a rolling basis. Application fee: $50. Electronic applications accepted. *Expenses:* Tuition: Full-time $12,780; part-time $710 per credit. Required fees: $628; $314 per term. *Financial support:* In 2006–07, 221 fellowships (averaging $2,053 per year), 17 research assistantships (averaging $6,527 per year) were awarded; career-related internships or fieldwork, scholarships/grants, tuition waivers (partial), and unspecified assistantships also available. Support available to part-time students. Financial award application deadline: 3/1; financial award applicants required to submit FAFSA. *Faculty research:* Multicultural literacy, science and mathematics teaching strategies, teacher as reflective practitioner, children with disabilities, varied contexts of learning. *Unit head:* Dr. Lynn Romeo, Program Director, 732-571-4484, Fax: 732-263-5277, E-mail: lromeo@monmouth.edu. *Application contact:* Kevin Roane, Director, Office of Graduate Admission, 732-571-3452, Fax: 732-263-5123, E-mail: gradadm@monmouth.edu.

Montclair State University, The Graduate School, College of Education and Human Services, Department of Curriculum and Teaching, Montclair, NJ 07043-1624. Offers education (M Ed); educational technology (M Ed); school library media specialist (Certificate); teaching (MAT,

Certificate), including art (MAT), biological science (MAT), early childhood education (P-3) (MAT), earth science (MAT), elementary education (K-8) (MAT), English (MAT), French (MAT), health and physical education (MAT), health education (MAT), home economics (MAT), mathematics (MAT), music (MAT), physical education (MAT), physical science (MAT), social studies (MAT), Spanish (MAT), teacher of ESL (MAT), teacher of students with disabilities (MAT). Part-time and evening/weekend programs available. *Faculty:* 16 full-time (12 women), 13 part-time/adjunct (8 women). *Students:* 147 full-time (113 women), 230 part-time (188 women); includes 58 minority (33 African Americans, 1 American Indian/Alaska Native, 12 Asian Americans or Pacific Islanders, 12 Hispanic Americans), 4 international. Average age 33. 118 applicants, 38% accepted, 37 enrolled. In 2006, 166 master's, 11 other advanced degrees awarded. *Degree requirements:* For master's, field experience. *Entrance requirements:* For master's, PRAXIS II, minimum GPA of 2.67, 2 letters of recommendation. Additional exam requirements/recommendations for international students: Required—TOEFL (minimum score 83 computer-based). *Application deadline:* For fall admission, 2/15 for domestic and international students; for spring admission, 9/15 for domestic and international students. Applications are processed on a rolling basis. Application fee: $60. Electronic applications accepted. *Expenses:* Tuition, state resident: part-time $450 per credit. Tuition, nonresident: part-time $682 per credit. Tuition and fees vary according to degree level and program. *Financial support:* In 2006–07, 7 research assistantships with full tuition reimbursements (averaging $7,000 per year) were awarded; Federal Work-Study, scholarships/grants, and unspecified assistantships also available. Support available to part-time students. Financial award application deadline: 3/1; financial award applicants required to submit FAFSA. *Unit head:* Dr. Deborah Eldridge, Chairperson, 973-655-5187.

Montclair State University, The Graduate School, College of Education and Human Services, Department of Early Childhood, Elementary and Literacy Education, Montclair, NJ 07043-1624. Offers early childhood /elementary education (M Ed); early childhood education and teaching students in disabilities (MAT); early childhood special education (M Ed, Certificate); elementary education with disabilities (MAT); elementary school teacher (Certificate); learning disabilities (Certificate); reading (MA, Certificate); reading specialist (Certificate). Part-time and evening/weekend programs available. *Faculty:* 15 full-time (13 women), 65 part-time/adjunct (52 women). *Students:* 27 full-time (24 women), 189 part-time (179 women); includes 24 minority (12 African Americans, 3 Asian Americans or Pacific Islanders, 9 Hispanic Americans), 1 international. 116 applicants, 47% accepted, 35 enrolled. In 2006, 40 master's, 53 other advanced degrees awarded. *Degree requirements:* For master's, clinical experience, portfolio. *Entrance requirements:* For master's, GRE, PRAXIS II, 2 letters of recommendation. Additional exam requirements/recommendations for international students: Required—TOEFL (minimum score 83 computer-based). *Application deadline:* For fall admission, 6/1 for international students; for spring admission, 10/1 for international students. Applications are processed on a rolling basis. Application fee: $60. Electronic applications accepted. *Expenses:* Tuition, state resident: part-time $450 per credit. Tuition, nonresident: part-time $682 per credit. Tuition and fees vary according to degree level and program. *Financial support:* In 2006–07, 15 research assistantships with full tuition reimbursements (averaging $7,000 per year) were awarded; Federal Work-Study, scholarships/grants, and unspecified assistantships also available. Support available to part-time students. Financial award application deadline: 3/1; financial award applicants required to submit FAFSA. *Unit head:* Dr. Nancy Lauter, Chairperson, 973-655-5407, E-mail: lautern@mail.montclair.edu. *Application contact:* Dr. Linda Luise, Adviser, 973-655-4247, E-mail: wisel@mail.montclair.edu.

Montreat College, School of Professional and Adult Studies, Montreat, NC 28757-1267. Offers business administration (MBA); K-6 education (MA Ed). Evening/weekend programs available. Postbaccalaureate distance learning degree programs offered. *Entrance requirements:* Additional exam requirements/recommendations for international students: Required—TOEFL (minimum score 500 paper-based; 190 computer-based).

Morehead State University, Graduate Programs, College of Education, Department of Curriculum and Instruction, Program in Elementary Education, Morehead, KY 40351. Offers elementary education (MA Ed); international education (MA Ed); middle school education (MA Ed, MAT); reading (MA Ed). *Accreditation:* NCATE. Part-time and evening/weekend programs available. *Students:* 2 full-time (both women), 84 part-time (80 women); includes 1 minority (American Indian/Alaska Native). Average age 32. In 2006, 52 degrees awarded. *Degree requirements:* For master's, thesis optional. *Entrance requirements:* For master's, GRE General Test, minimum GPA of 2.75, teaching certificate. Additional exam requirements/recommendations for international students: Required—TOEFL (minimum score 500 paper-based; 173 computer-based). *Application deadline:* For fall admission, 8/1 priority date for domestic and international students; for spring admission, 12/1 priority date for domestic and international students. Applications are processed on a rolling basis. Application fee: $0 ($55 for international students). Electronic applications accepted. *Financial support:* In 2006–07, teaching assistantships (averaging $6,000 per year); career-related internships or fieldwork, Federal Work-Study, and unspecified assistantships also available. Financial award application deadline: 4/1; financial award applicants required to submit FAFSA. *Faculty research:* Teaching through journal writing, gifted children, reading instruction in elementary schools, teaching social studies in elementary schools, ungraded elementary schools. *Application contact:* Michelle Barber, Graduate Admissions Counselor, 606-783-2039, Fax: 606-783-5061, E-mail: m.barber@moreheadstate.edu.

Morgan State University, School of Graduate Studies, School of Education and Urban Studies, Department of Teacher Education and Administration, Program in Elementary and Middle School Education, Baltimore, MD 21251. Offers elementary education (MS). *Accreditation:* NCATE. Part-time and evening/weekend programs available. *Students:* Average age 30. *Degree requirements:* For master's, thesis optional. *Application deadline:* For fall admission, 2/1 for domestic students; for spring admission, 10/1 for domestic students. Applications are processed on a rolling basis. Application fee: $0. *Expenses:* Tuition, state resident: part-time $272 per credit. Tuition, nonresident: part-time $478 per credit. Required fees: $38 per credit. *Financial support:* Application deadline: 4/1. *Faculty research:* Multicultural education, cooperative learning, psychology of cognition. *Application contact:* Dr. Maurice C. Taylor, Dean, 443-885-3185, Fax: 443-885-8226, E-mail: mctaylor@moac.morgan.edu.

Morgan State University, School of Graduate Studies, School of Education and Urban Studies, MAT Program, Baltimore, MD 21251. Offers elementary education (MAT); high school education (MAT); middle school education (MAT). Part-time programs available. *Students:* 1. Average age 30. In 2006, 4 degrees awarded. *Degree requirements:* For master's, comprehensive exam. *Entrance requirements:* For master's, GRE General Test or MAT. *Application deadline:* For fall admission, 2/1 priority date for domestic students; for spring admission, 10/1 priority date for domestic students. Applications are processed on a rolling basis. Application fee: $0. *Expenses:* Tuition, state resident: part-time $272 per credit. Tuition, nonresident: part-time $478 per credit. Required fees: $38 per credit. *Financial support:* Fellowships available. Financial award application deadline: 4/1. *Faculty research:* Multicultural education, cooperative learning, psychology of cognition. *Unit head:* Dr. Marlene Greer-Chase, Graduate Coordinator, 443-885-1984, Fax: 443-885-8240. *Application contact:* Dr. Maurice C. Taylor, Dean, 443-885-3185, Fax: 443-885-8226, E-mail: mctaylor@moac.morgan.edu.

Morningside College, Graduate Division, Department of Education, Program in Elementary Education, Sioux City, IA 51106. Offers MAT. Part-time and evening/weekend programs available. *Entrance requirements:* For master's, MAT, writing sample.

Mount Saint Mary College, Division of Education, Newburgh, NY 12550-3494. Offers adolescence and special education (MS Ed); adolescence education (MS Ed); childhood and special education (MS Ed); childhood education (MS Ed); literacy and special education (MS Ed); literacy/childhood (MS Ed); middle school (5-6) (MS Ed); middle school (7-9) (MS Ed); special education (1-6) (MS Ed); special education (7-12) (MS Ed). *Accreditation:* NCATE. Part-time and evening/weekend programs available. *Faculty:* 11 full-time (8 women), 21 part-time/adjunct (18 women). *Students:* 87 full-time (74 women), 368 part-time (303 women); includes 38 minority (12 African Americans, 2 American Indian/Alaska Native, 5 Asian Americans or Pacific Islanders, 19 Hispanic Americans). Average age 31. 164 applicants, 45% accepted, 58 enrolled. In 2006, 131 degrees awarded. *Application deadline:* Applications are processed on a rolling basis. Application fee: $35. *Expenses:* Tuition: Full-time $11,880; part-time $660 per credit. *Financial support:* In 2006–07, 30 students received support. Unspecified assistantships available. Financial award application deadline: 3/15. *Faculty research:* Learning and teaching styles, computers in special education, language development. *Unit head:* Theresa Lewis, Coordinator, 845-569-3149, Fax: 845-569-3535, E-mail: tlewis@msmc.edu.

Mount St. Mary's College, Graduate Division, Department of Education, Specialization in Elementary Education, Los Angeles, CA 90049-1599. Offers MS. *Students:* 31 full-time (29 women), 21 part-time (20 women); includes 4 African Americans, 3 Asian Americans or Pacific Islanders, 15 Hispanic Americans. Average age 33. *Degree requirements:* For master's, thesis, research project. *Entrance requirements:* For master's, MAT, minimum GPA of 3.0. Application fee: $50 ($75 for international students). *Expenses:* Tuition: Part-time $630 per unit. *Financial support:* Application deadline: 3/15; *Unit head:* Dr. Julie Feldman-Abe, Director, 213-477-2625. *Application contact:* Tom Hoener, Director, Graduate Recruitment, 213-477-2800, Fax: 213-477-2519, E-mail: thoener@msmc.la.edu.

Mount Saint Vincent University, Graduate Programs, Faculty of Education, Program in Elementary Education, Halifax, NS B3M 2J6, Canada. Offers M Ed, MA Ed, MA-R. Part-time and evening/weekend programs available. Postbaccalaureate distance learning degree programs offered (minimal on-campus study). *Degree requirements:* For master's, thesis (for some programs). *Entrance requirements:* For master's, bachelor's degree in education, 1 year of teaching experience. Electronic applications accepted. *Faculty research:* Curriculum theory, mathematics education, philosophy in teacher education, science education, literacy education.

Murray State University, College of Education, Department of Early Childhood and Elementary Education, Program in Elementary Education and Reading and Writing, Murray, KY 42071. Offers MA Ed, Ed S. *Accreditation:* NCATE. Part-time programs available. *Faculty:* 6 part-time/adjunct (5 women). *Students:* 108; includes 4 minority (all African Americans), 2 international. 18 applicants, 100% accepted, 18 enrolled. In 2006, 34 master's awarded. *Median time to degree:* Of those who began their doctoral program in fall 1998, 100% received their degree in 8 years or less. *Degree requirements:* For master's, thesis optional. *Entrance requirements:* For master's, minimum GPA of 2.5 for conditional admittance, 3.0 for unconditional; for Ed S, GRE General Test or MAT. Additional exam requirements/recommendations for international students: Required—TOEFL. *Application deadline:* Applications are processed on a rolling basis. Application fee: $25. *Financial support:* Research assistantships, teaching assistantships, Federal Work-Study available. Financial award application deadline: 4/1.

National-Louis University, National College of Education, Program in Elementary Education, Chicago, IL 60603. Offers MAT. Part-time and evening/weekend programs available. *Students:* 252 full-time (196 women), 612 part-time (514 women); includes 157 minority (87 African Americans, 2 American Indian/Alaska Native, 15 Asian Americans or Pacific Islanders, 53 Hispanic Americans). Average age 34. 84 applicants, 100% accepted. In 2006, 221 degrees awarded. *Degree requirements:* For master's, student teaching experience. *Entrance requirements:* For master's, GRE, minimum GPA of 3.0. *Application deadline:* Applications are processed on a rolling basis. Application fee: $25. *Expenses:* Tuition: Full-time $17,685. One-time fee: $40 full-time. *Financial support:* Fellowships, career-related internships or fieldwork, Federal Work-Study, institutionally sponsored loans, and scholarships/grants available. Support available to part-time students. Financial award applicants required to submit FAFSA. *Unit head:* Dr. Pennie Olson, Coordinator, 847-475-1100 Ext. 3403. *Application contact:* David McCulloch, Vice President for University Services, 800-443-5522 Ext. 5127, Fax: 847-465-0593, E-mail: dmcc@wheeling1.nl.edu.

Nazareth College of Rochester, Graduate Studies, Department of Education, Program in Inclusive Education-Childhood Level, Rochester, NY 14618-3790. Offers MS Ed. *Accreditation:* Teacher Education Accreditation Council. *Students:* 98 full-time (87 women), 80 part-time (65 women); includes 16 minority (8 African Americans, 3 American Indian/Alaska Native, 5 Asian Americans or Pacific Islanders). Average age 30. 75 applicants, 99% accepted, 45 enrolled. In 2006, 88 degrees awarded. *Entrance requirements:* For master's, minimum GPA of 3.0. *Application deadline:* For fall admission, 9/1 for domestic students; for spring admission, 10/1 for domestic students. Application fee: $40. *Financial support:* Research assistantships with partial tuition reimbursements available. Financial award application deadline: 3/1; financial award applicants required to submit FAFSA. *Unit head:* Dr. Kathleen DaBoll–Lavoie, Director, 585-389-2618, Fax: 585-389-2452, E-mail: kmdaboll9@naz.edu. *Application contact:* Judith G. Baker, Director, Graduate Admissions, 585-389-2050, Fax: 585-389-2817, E-mail: gradstudies@naz.edu.

New Jersey City University, Graduate and Continuing Education, College of Education, Department of Elementary and Secondary Education, Jersey City, NJ 07305-1597. Offers elementary education (MAT); secondary education (MAT). Part-time and evening/weekend programs available. *Faculty:* 11. *Students:* 1 (woman) full-time, 81 part-time (57 women); includes 13 minority (2 African Americans, 4 Asian Americans or Pacific Islanders, 7 Hispanic Americans). Average age 34. In 2006, 19 degrees awarded. *Application deadline:* For fall admission, 8/1 priority date for domestic students; for spring admission, 12/1 for domestic students. Applications are processed on a rolling basis. Application fee: $0. *Expenses:* Tuition, state resident: full-time $7,038; part-time $391 per credit. Tuition, nonresident: full-time $12,510; part-time $695 per credit. Required fees: $65 per credit. *Financial support:* Teaching assistantships, career-related internships or fieldwork and unspecified assistantships available. *Unit head:* Dr. Althea Hall, Coordinator, 201-200-2101.

New York Institute of Technology, Graduate Division, School of Education and Professional Services, Program in Elementary Education, Old Westbury, NY 11568-8000. Offers distance learning (Advanced Certificate); elementary education (MS). Part-time and evening/weekend programs available. Postbaccalaureate distance learning degree programs offered. *Students:* 2 full-time (both women), 14 part-time (12 women); includes 1 minority (Hispanic American) Average age 38. 10 applicants, 10% accepted, 1 enrolled. In 2006, 1 master's, 1 other advanced degree awarded. *Degree requirements:* For master's, thesis. *Entrance requirements:* For master's, minimum QPA of 3.0. Additional exam requirements/recommendations for international students: Required—TOEFL. *Application deadline:* For fall admission, 7/1 priority date for domestic students; for spring admission, 12/1 priority date for domestic students. Applications are processed on a rolling basis. Application fee: $50. Electronic applications accepted. *Expenses:* Tuition: Full-time $16,800; part-time $700 per credit. *Financial support:* Research assistantships with partial tuition reimbursements available. Financial award applicants required to submit FAFSA. *Faculty research:* Course development. *Unit head:* Dr. David Arneson, Chair, 516-686-7852, Fax: 516-686-7655, E-mail: darneson@nyit.edu. *Application contact:* Jacquelyn Nealon, Dean of Admissions and Financial Aid, 516-686-7925, Fax: 516-686-7613, E-mail: jnealon@nyit.edu.

New York University, Steinhardt School of Culture, Education and Human Development, Department of Teaching and Learning, Program in Early Childhood and Childhood Education, New York, NY 10012-1019. Offers childhood education (MA, PhD, Advanced Certificate); early childhood education (MA, PhD, Advanced Certificate). *Accreditation:* Teacher Education Accreditation Council. Part-time and evening/weekend programs available. *Faculty:* 12 full-time (10 women). *Students:* 120 full-time (113 women), 31 part-time (25 women); includes 39 minority (13 African Americans, 14 Asian Americans or Pacific Islanders, 12 Hispanic Americans), 5 international. 117 applicants, 79% accepted, 41 enrolled. In 2006, 78 master's, 1 doctorate awarded. Terminal master's awarded for partial completion of doctoral program. *Degree requirements:* For master's, thesis (for some programs); for doctorate, thesis/dissertation. *Entrance requirements:* For doctorate, GRE General Test, interview; for Advanced Certificate, master's degree. Additional exam requirements/recommendations for international students: Required—TOEFL. *Application deadline:* For fall admission, 12/15 priority date for domestic and international students; for spring admission, 11/1 for domestic and international students.

Elementary Education

New York University (continued)
Applications are processed on a rolling basis. Application fee: $50. *Expenses:* Tuition: Part-time $1,080 per unit. Required fees: $56 per unit. $329 per term. Tuition and fees vary according to program. *Financial support:* Fellowships with full and partial tuition reimbursements, career-related internships or fieldwork, Federal Work-Study, institutionally sponsored loans, scholarships/grants, tuition waivers (partial), and unspecified assistantships available. Support available to part-time students. Financial award application deadline: 2/1; financial award applicants required to submit FAFSA. *Faculty research:* Teacher evaluation and beliefs about teaching, early literacy development, language arts, child development and education, cultural differences. *Unit head:* Dr. Stephen Weiss, Co-Director, 212-998-5460, Fax: 212-995-4049. *Application contact:* 212-998-5030, Fax: 212-995-4328, E-mail: steinhardt.gradadmissions@nyu.edu.

Niagara University, Graduate Division of Education, Concentration in Teacher Education, Niagara Falls, Niagara University, NY 14109. Offers elementary education (MS Ed); secondary education (MS Ed). *Accreditation:* NCATE. *Faculty:* 4 full-time (1 woman), 6 part-time/adjunct (4 women). *Students:* 344 full-time (234 women), 3 part-time (all women); includes 14 minority (10 African Americans, 3 American Indian/Alaska Native, 1 Hispanic American), 259 international. Average age 25. In 2006, 206 degrees awarded. *Entrance requirements:* For master's, GRE General Test or MAT. *Application deadline:* For fall admission, 8/1 for domestic students. Applications are processed on a rolling basis. Application fee: $30. *Expenses:* Contact institution. *Financial support:* Career-related internships or fieldwork, Federal Work-Study, and scholarships/grants available. Financial award application deadline: 3/15. *Unit head:* Dr. Chandra Foote, Chair, 716-286-8549. *Application contact:* Dr. Debra A. Colley, Dean of Education, 716-286-8560, Fax: 716-286-8561, E-mail: dcolley@niagara.edu.

North Carolina Agricultural and Technical State University, Graduate School, School of Education, Department of Curriculum and Instruction, Program in Elementary Education, Greensboro, NC 27411. Offers MS. *Accreditation:* NCATE. Part-time and evening/weekend programs available. *Degree requirements:* For master's, thesis or alternative, qualifying exam, comprehensive exam. *Entrance requirements:* For master's, GRE General Test, minimum GPA of 3.0.

North Carolina Central University, Division of Academic Affairs, School of Education, Program in Elementary Education, Durham, NC 27707-3129. Offers M Ed, MA. *Accreditation:* NCATE. Part-time and evening/weekend programs available. *Degree requirements:* For master's, thesis or alternative, comprehensive exam. *Entrance requirements:* For master's, GRE, minimum GPA of 3.0 in major, 2.5 overall. Additional exam requirements/recommendations for international students: Required—TOEFL. *Faculty research:* Building self-image through contest application in middle grades education.

Northern Arizona University, Graduate College, College of Education, Program in Elementary Education, Flagstaff, AZ 86011. Offers M Ed. Part-time and evening/weekend programs available. *Degree requirements:* For master's, thesis optional. *Entrance requirements:* For master's, GRE General Test or minimum GPA of 3.0. *Faculty research:* Science/environmental education, whole language/literacy issues, technology education, school/university partnerships, school/museum partnerships.

Northern Illinois University, Graduate School, College of Education, Department of Teaching and Learning, De Kalb, IL 60115-2854. Offers curriculum and instruction (MS Ed, Ed D), including curriculum leadership (Ed D), elementary education (Ed D), secondary education (Ed D); early childhood education (MS Ed); elementary education (MS Ed); special education (MS Ed). Part-time and evening/weekend programs available. *Faculty:* 22 full-time (14 women), 2 part-time/adjunct (both women). *Students:* 81 full-time (64 women), 534 part-time (417 women); includes 122 minority (21 African Americans, 12 Asian Americans or Pacific Islanders, 89 Hispanic Americans), 11 international. Average age 36. 92 applicants, 57% accepted, 43 enrolled. In 2006, 256 master's, 12 doctorates awarded. *Degree requirements:* For master's, thesis optional; for doctorate, thesis/dissertation, candidacy exam, dissertation defense. *Entrance requirements:* For master's, GRE General Test or MAT, minimum undergraduate GPA of 2.75; for doctorate, GRE General Test or MAT, minimum undergraduate GPA of 2.75, graduate 3.2. Additional exam requirements/recommendations for international students: Required—TOEFL (minimum score 550 paper-based; 213 computer-based). *Application deadline:* For fall admission, 6/1 for domestic students, 5/1 for international students; for spring admission, 11/1 for domestic students, 10/1 for international students. Applications are processed on a rolling basis. Application fee: $30. Electronic applications accepted. *Financial support:* In 2006–07, 27 research assistantships with full tuition reimbursements, 1 teaching assistantship with full tuition reimbursement were awarded; fellowships with full tuition reimbursements, career-related internships or fieldwork, Federal Work-Study, scholarships/grants, tuition waivers (full), and unspecified assistantships also available. Support available to part-time students. Financial award applicants required to submit FAFSA. *Faculty research:* Teacher certification, stress reduction during student teaching, teaching history, portfolios in student teaching. *Unit head:* Dr. Pamela Jackson, Acting Chair, 815-753-8452, E-mail: p30ngd1@wpo.cso.niu.edu.

Northern Michigan University, College of Graduate Studies, College of Professional Studies, School of Education, Program in Elementary Education, Marquette, MI 49855-5301. Offers MA Ed. *Accreditation:* NCATE. Part-time programs available. *Degree requirements:* For master's, thesis or alternative. *Entrance requirements:* For master's, minimum GPA of 3.0. *Faculty research:* Whole language research, literature-based reading, essential elements of instruction, supervision and improvement of instruction.

Northern State University, Division of Graduate Studies in Education, Program in Teaching and Learning, Aberdeen, SD 57401-7198. Offers educational studies (MS Ed); elementary classroom teaching (MS Ed); health, physical education, and coaching (MS Ed); language and literacy (MS Ed); secondary classroom teaching (MS Ed); special education (MS Ed). *Accreditation:* NCATE. Part-time and evening/weekend programs available. *Faculty:* 69 full-time (19 women). *Students:* 5 full-time (3 women), 70 part-time (51 women); includes 3 minority (1 African American, 1 American Indian/Alaska Native, 1 Asian American or Pacific Islander). Average age 32. In 2006, 23 degrees awarded. *Degree requirements:* For master's, thesis optional. *Entrance requirements:* For master's, minimum GPA of 2.75. Additional exam requirements/recommendations for international students: Required—TOEFL (minimum score 550 paper-based; 213 computer-based). *Application deadline:* For fall admission, 8/15 priority date for domestic students; for spring admission, 12/15 for domestic students. Applications are processed on a rolling basis. Application fee: $35. Electronic applications accepted. *Expenses:* Tuition, state resident: full-time $3,373; part-time $120 per credit. Tuition, nonresident: full-time $9,943; part-time $355 per credit. International tuition: $13,000 full-time. Required fees: $86 per credit. One-time fee: $35 full-time. Tuition and fees vary according to course load, degree level and reciprocity agreements. *Financial support:* In 2006–07, 17 teaching assistantships with partial tuition reimbursements (averaging $4,812 per year) were awarded; career-related internships or fieldwork, Federal Work-Study, institutionally sponsored loans, scholarships/grants, and unspecified assistantships also available. Support available to part-time students. Financial award application deadline: 3/1; financial award applicants required to submit FAFSA. *Application contact:* Tammy K. Griffith, Senior Secretary, 605-626-2558, Fax: 605-626-2542, E-mail: griffith@northern.edu.

Northwestern Oklahoma State University, School of Professional Studies, Program in Elementary Education, Alva, OK 73717-2799. Offers M Ed. *Accreditation:* NCATE. Part-time programs available. *Faculty:* 6 full-time (5 women). In 2006, 1 degree awarded. *Degree requirements:* For master's, portfolio, thesis optional. *Entrance requirements:* For master's, GRE General Test or MAT, minimum GPA of 2.75. *Application deadline:* Applications are processed on a rolling basis. Application fee: $15. *Expenses:* Tuition, state resident: part-time $700 per year. Tuition, nonresident: part-time $1,715 per year. *Financial support:* Federal Work-Study available. Support available to part-time students. Financial award application deadline: 5/1. *Unit head:* Dr. Greg Seay, Coordinator, 580-327-8452.

Northwestern State University of Louisiana, Graduate Studies and Research, College of Education, Program in Elementary Education, Natchitoches, LA 71497. Offers MAT. *Students:* 3 full-time (all women), 15 part-time (all women); includes 2 minority (both African Americans) Average age 32. *Degree requirements:* For master's, thesis or alternative, comprehensive exam, registration. *Entrance requirements:* For master's, GRE General Test, minimum undergraduate GPA of 2.5. *Application contact:* Dr. Steven G. Horton, Associate Provost/Dean, Graduate Studies, Research, and Information Systems, 318-357-5851, Fax: 318-357-5019, E-mail: grad_school@nsula.edu.

Northwestern State University of Louisiana, Graduate Studies and Research, College of Education, Programs in Education, Natchitoches, LA 71497. Offers business and distributive education (M Ed); counseling (M Ed); early childhood education (M Ed); education (M Ed); education leadership (M Ed); educational technology (M Ed); elementary teaching (M Ed); English education (M Ed); home economics education (M Ed); mathematics education (M Ed); reading (M Ed); science education (M Ed); secondary teaching (M Ed); social sciences education (M Ed). *Students:* 49 full-time (41 women), 245 part-time (206 women); includes 78 minority (70 African Americans, 5 American Indian/Alaska Native, 2 Asian Americans or Pacific Islanders, 1 Hispanic American). Average age 35. In 2006, 158 degrees awarded. *Degree requirements:* For master's, thesis or alternative, comprehensive exam, registration. *Entrance requirements:* For master's, GRE General Test, minimum undergraduate GPA of 2.5. *Application contact:* Dr. Steven G. Horton, Associate Provost/Dean, Graduate Studies, Research, and Information Systems, 318-357-5851, Fax: 318-357-5019, E-mail: grad_school@nsula.edu.

Northwestern State University of Louisiana, Graduate Studies and Research, College of Education, Programs in Educational Leadership and Instruction, Natchitoches, LA 71497. Offers counseling (Ed S); educational leadership (Ed S); educational technology (Ed S); elementary teaching (Ed S); reading (Ed S); secondary teaching (Ed S); special education (Ed S). *Students:* 17 full-time (15 women), 114 part-time (87 women); includes 55 minority (51 African Americans, 1 Asian American or Pacific Islander, 3 Hispanic Americans). Average age 39. In 2006, 11 degrees awarded. *Entrance requirements:* For degree, GRE General Test. *Application contact:* Dr. Steven G. Horton, Associate Provost/Dean, Graduate Studies, Research, and Information Systems, 318-357-5851, Fax: 318-357-5019, E-mail: grad_school@nsula.edu.

Northwestern University, The Graduate School, School of Education and Social Policy, Master of Science in Education Program, Evanston, IL 60208. Offers advanced teaching (MS); elementary education and policy (MS); higher education administration (MS); secondary teaching (MS). Part-time and evening/weekend programs available. *Faculty:* 4 full-time (2 women), 33 part-time/adjunct (17 women). *Students:* 64 full-time (40 women), 90 part-time (66 women); includes 21 minority (3 African Americans, 13 Asian Americans or Pacific Islanders, 5 Hispanic Americans), 1 international. Average age 25. 88 applicants, 65% accepted, 36 enrolled. In 2006, 82 degrees awarded. *Degree requirements:* For master's, project. *Entrance requirements:* For master's, GRE General Test, State of Illinois Basic Skills Exam (secondary and elementary). *Application deadline:* For fall admission, 7/1 priority date for domestic students; for winter admission, 11/5 priority date for domestic students; for spring admission, 1/21 priority date for domestic students. Applications are processed on a rolling basis. Application fee: $45. *Financial support:* In 2006–07, 6 students received support. Career-related internships or fieldwork, Federal Work-Study, institutionally sponsored loans, scholarships/grants, tuition waivers (partial), and unspecified assistantships available. Financial award application deadline: 1/7; financial award applicants required to submit FAFSA. *Faculty research:* Discussion/questioning. *Unit head:* Dr. Sophie Haroutunian-Gordon, Director, 847-467-1458, Fax: 847-467-2495, E-mail: shg@northwestern.edu. *Application contact:* Patricia Rodriguez, Assistant Director, 847-491-7526, Fax: 847-467-2495.

Northwest Missouri State University, Graduate School, College of Education and Human Services, Department of Curriculum and Instruction, Program in Teaching: Elementary Self Contained, Maryville, MO 64468-6001. Offers MS Ed. *Accreditation:* NCATE. Part-time programs available. *Faculty:* 10 full-time (all women). *Students:* 1 (woman) full-time, 7 part-time (6 women); includes 1 minority (Hispanic American) 5 applicants, 80% accepted, 2 enrolled. In 2006, 2 degrees awarded. *Degree requirements:* For master's, comprehensive exam. *Entrance requirements:* For master's, GRE General Test, minimum undergraduate GPA of 2.75, teaching certificate, writing sample. Additional exam requirements/recommendations for international students: Required—TOEFL (minimum score 550 paper-based; 213 computer-based). *Application deadline:* For fall admission, 7/1 for domestic and international students; for spring admission, 11/15 for domestic and international students. Applications are processed on a rolling basis. Application fee: $0 ($50 for international students). Electronic applications accepted. *Financial support:* Application deadline: 3/1; *Unit head:* Dr. Carolyn McCall, Director, 660-562-1236. *Application contact:* Dr. Frances Shipley, Dean of Graduate School, 660-562-1145, Fax: 660-562-1096, E-mail: gradsch@nwmissouri.edu.

Northwest Missouri State University, Graduate School, College of Education and Human Services, Department of Educational Leadership, Program in Educational Leadership, Maryville, MO 64468-6001. Offers educational leadership: elementary (MS Ed); educational leadership: secondary (MS Ed); elementary principalship (Ed S); secondary principalship (Ed S); superintendency (Ed S). *Accreditation:* NCATE. Part-time programs available. *Faculty:* 12 full-time (4 women). *Students:* 13 full-time (7 women), 87 part-time (56 women); includes 5 minority (4 African Americans, 1 Asian American or Pacific Islander). 29 applicants, 93% accepted, 20 enrolled. In 2006, 42 master's, 17 other advanced degrees awarded. *Degree requirements:* For master's, comprehensive exam; for Ed S, thesis, comprehensive exam. *Entrance requirements:* For master's, GRE General Test, minimum undergraduate GPA of 2.75, teaching certificate, writing sample; for Ed S, minimum graduate GPA of 3.25. Additional exam requirements/recommendations for international students: Required—TOEFL (minimum score 550 paper-based; 213 computer-based). *Application deadline:* For fall admission, 7/1 for domestic and international students; for spring admission, 11/15 for domestic and international students. Application fee: $0 ($50 for international students). *Financial support:* In 2006–07, 3 research assistantships with full tuition reimbursements (averaging $6,000 per year), 2 teaching assistantships with full tuition reimbursements (averaging $6,000 per year) were awarded; unspecified assistantships also available. Financial award application deadline: 3/1; financial award applicants required to submit FAFSA. *Application contact:* Dr. Frances Shipley, Dean of Graduate School, 660-562-1145, Fax: 660-562-1096, E-mail: gradsch@nwmissouri.edu.

Nova Southeastern University, Fischler School of Education and Human Services, Graduate Teacher Education Program, Fort Lauderdale, FL 33314-7796. Offers athletic administration (MS); cognitive and behavioral disabilities (MS); computer science education (Ed S); computer science education (K-12) (MS); curriculum and teaching (Ed S); curriculum, instruction and technology (MS); curriculum, instruction, management and administration (Ed S); early childhood special education (MS); early literacy and reading (Ed S); early literacy education (MS); education technology (MS); educational leadership (administration K–12) (MS, Ed S); educational media (Ed S); educational media (K-12) (MS); elementary education (MS, Ed S), including ESOL endorsement (MS); English (MS, Ed S); exceptional student education (MS), including ESOL endorsement; gifted education (MS, Ed S); interdisciplinary arts education (MS); management and administration of educational programs (MS); mathematics (MS, Ed S); multicultural early intervention (MS); pre-kindergarten/primary (MS); preschool education (MS); reading (MS, Ed S); science (MS, Ed S); secondary education (MS); social studies (MS, Ed S); Spanish language (MS); teaching and learning (MA, MS), including curriculum and instruction (MA), elementary mathematics (MA), elementary reading (MA), K-12 technology integration (MA); teaching English to speakers of other languages (MS, Ed S); technology management and administration (Ed S); urban studies education (MS); varying exceptionalities (Ed S). Part-time and evening/weekend programs available. Postbaccalaureate distance learning degree programs offered. *Faculty:* 131 full-time (78 women), 548 part-time/adjunct (342 women).

Students: 1,418 full-time (1,139 women), 3,464 part-time (2,877 women); includes 2,462 minority (1,732 African Americans, 13 American Indian/Alaska Native, 44 Asian Americans or Pacific Islanders, 673 Hispanic Americans), 77 international. Average age 38. 1,771 applicants, 80% accepted, 1419 enrolled. In 2006, 2,078 master's, 425 other advanced degrees awarded. *Degree requirements:* For master's and Ed S, thesis, practicum, internship. *Entrance requirements:* For master's, MAT, GRE, CLAST, CBEST, PRAXIS I, GKT, minimum GPA of 2.5; for Ed S, MAT or GRE, master's degree, teaching certificate, minimum GPA of 3.0. Additional exam requirements/recommendations for international students: Recommended—TOEFL (minimum score 550 paper-based; 213 computer-based), IELTS (minimum score 6). *Application deadline:* For fall admission, 8/11 priority date for domestic and international students; for winter admission, 12/28 priority date for domestic and international students; for spring admission, 4/22 priority date for domestic and international students. Applications are processed on a rolling basis. Application fee: $50. Electronic applications accepted. *Financial support:* Federal Work-Study available. Support available to part-time students. Financial award application deadline: 1/7. *Faculty research:* School effectiveness, critical thinking, leadership skills acquisition, child education, multicultural education. *Unit head:* Dr. Meline Kevorkian, Associate Dean of Master's and Educational Programs, 954-262-8500, Fax: 954-262-3606, E-mail: melinek@nova.edu. *Application contact:* Jennifer Quiñones Nottingham, Dean of Student Affairs, 800-986-3223 Ext. 8624, Fax: 954-262-3911, E-mail: jlquinon@nova.edu.

Occidental College, Graduate Studies, Department of Education, Program in Elementary Education, Los Angeles, CA 90041-3314. Offers liberal studies (MAT). Part-time programs available. *Faculty:* 3 full-time (2 women), 2 part-time/adjunct (both women). *Students:* 3 full-time (2 women), 2 part-time (both women); includes 2 minority (1 Asian American or Pacific Islander, 1 Hispanic American). Average age 25. 5 applicants, 100% accepted, 3 enrolled. In 2006, 5 degrees awarded. *Degree requirements:* For master's, final exam, graduate synthesis paper. *Entrance requirements:* For master's, GRE General Test, minimum GPA of 3.0. Additional exam requirements/recommendations for international students: Required—TOEFL (minimum score 625 paper-based; 263 computer-based). *Application deadline:* For fall admission, 3/1 for domestic and international students; for spring admission, 10/1 for domestic and international students. Applications are processed on a rolling basis. Application fee: $50. *Expenses:* Contact institution. *Financial support:* Fellowships, Federal Work-Study, institutionally sponsored loans, and scholarships/grants available. Support available to part-time students. Financial award application deadline: 3/1; financial award applicants required to submit FAFSA. *Unit head:* Chair, 323-259-2781, E-mail: edudept@oxy.edu. *Application contact:* Angela Allen, Credential Analyst/Department Services Coordinator, 323-259-2781, E-mail: edudept@oxy.edu.

Oklahoma City University, Petree College of Arts and Sciences, Division of Education and Kinesiology Exercise Studies, Programs in Education, Oklahoma City, OK 73106-1402. Offers applied behavioral studies (M Ed); early childhood education (M Ed); elementary education (M Ed). Part-time and evening/weekend programs available. *Faculty:* 4 full-time (3 women), 13 part-time/adjunct (8 women). *Students:* 15 full-time (14 women), 14 part-time (11 women); includes 7 minority (4 African Americans, 2 Asian Americans or Pacific Islanders, 1 Hispanic American). Average age 33. 25 applicants, 76% accepted. In 2006, 23 degrees awarded. *Degree requirements:* For master's, thesis optional. *Entrance requirements:* For master's, minimum GPA of 3.0. *Application deadline:* For fall admission, 8/22 for domestic students; for spring admission, 1/15 for domestic students. Applications are processed on a rolling basis. Application fee: $30 ($70 for international students). *Expenses:* Tuition: Full-time $12,780; part-time $710 per hour. Required fees: $89 per hour. *Financial support:* Fellowships with partial tuition reimbursements, career-related internships or fieldwork, Federal Work-Study, institutionally sponsored loans, and tuition waivers (partial) available. Support available to part-time students. Financial award application deadline: 8/1; financial award applicants required to submit FAFSA. *Faculty research:* Adult literacy, cognition, reading strategies. *Application contact:* Leslie McKenzie, Director, Graduate Admissions, 800-633-7242, Fax: 405-208-5356, E-mail: gadmissions@okcu.edu.

Old Dominion University, Darden College of Education, Program in Elementary/Middle Education, Norfolk, VA 23529. Offers educational media (MS Ed); elementary education (MS Ed); instructional technology (MS Ed); library science (MS Ed); middle school education (MS Ed). *Accreditation:* NCATE. Part-time and evening/weekend programs available. Postbaccalaureate distance learning degree programs offered (no on-campus study). *Faculty:* 20 full-time (9 women). *Students:* 116 full-time (103 women), 217 part-time (178 women); includes 32 minority (22 African Americans, 2 American Indian/Alaska Native, 3 Asian Americans or Pacific Islanders, 5 Hispanic Americans). Average age 35. 127 applicants, 56% accepted, 61 enrolled. In 2006, 167 degrees awarded. *Degree requirements:* For master's, comprehensive exam. *Entrance requirements:* For master's, GRE General Test or MAT and PRAXIS I or SAT or ACT, minimum GPA of 2.8. *Application deadline:* For fall admission, 6/1 priority date for domestic students; for winter admission, 11/1 priority date for domestic students; for spring admission, 3/1 priority date for domestic students. Applications are processed on a rolling basis. Application fee: $40. Electronic applications accepted. *Expenses:* Tuition, area resident: Part-time $285 per credit hour. Tuition, nonresident: part-time $715 per credit hour. Required fees: $94 per semester. *Financial support:* In 2006–07, 180 students received support, including 4 research assistantships with tuition reimbursements available (averaging $9,000 per year), teaching assistantships (averaging $8,000 per year); fellowships, career-related internships or fieldwork, Federal Work-Study, institutionally sponsored loans, scholarships/grants, and tuition waivers (partial) also available. Support available to part-time students. Financial award application deadline: 2/15; financial award applicants required to submit FAFSA. *Faculty research:* Education pre-K to 6, school librarianship. *Unit head:* Dr. Gail S. Taylor, Graduate Program Director, 757-683-4180, E-mail: eciegpd@odu.edu.

Olivet Nazarene University, Graduate School, Division of Education, Program in Elementary Education, Bourbonnais, IL 60914-2271. Offers MAT. *Accreditation:* NCATE. Evening/weekend programs available. *Degree requirements:* For master's, thesis or alternative.

Oregon State University, Graduate School, College of Education, Program in Elementary Education, Corvallis, OR 97331. Offers MAT. *Accreditation:* NCATE. In 2006, 30 degrees awarded. *Entrance requirements:* For master's, NTE, minimum GPA of 3.0 in last 90 hours of course work. Additional exam requirements/recommendations for international students: Required—TOEFL. *Application deadline:* For fall admission, 3/1 priority date for domestic students. Applications are processed on a rolling basis. Application fee: $50. *Financial support:* Fellowships, Federal Work-Study and institutionally sponsored loans available. Support available to part-time students. Financial award application deadline: 2/1. *Faculty research:* Kindergarten curriculum, the reading-writing connection, authentic assessment, classroom management. *Unit head:* Dr. Kenneth J. Winograd, Chair, 541-737-4661.

Ottawa University, Graduate Studies-Arizona, Program in Education, Ottawa, KS 66067-3399. Offers community college counseling (MA); curriculum and instruction (MA); early childhood (MA); education intervention (MA); education leadership (MA); education technology (MA); Montessori early childhood education (MA); Montessori elementary education (MA); professional development (MA); school guidance counseling (MA); special education—cross categorical (MA). Programs offered in Mesa, Phoenix, Tempe and West Valley, AZ. *Accreditation:* NCATE. Part-time programs available. *Faculty:* 7 full-time (3 women), 24 part-time/adjunct (11 women). *Students:* 14 full-time (9 women), 162 part-time (128 women); includes 31 minority (13 African Americans, 2 American Indian/Alaska Native, 1 Asian American or Pacific Islander, 15 Hispanic Americans), 1 international. Average age 38. In 2006, 56 degrees awarded. *Degree requirements:* For master's, thesis or alternative, registration. *Entrance requirements:* For master's, minimum undergraduate GPA of 3.0, copy of current state certification or teaching license. Additional exam requirements/recommendations for international students: Required—TOEFL (minimum score 550 paper-based; 213 computer-based). *Application deadline:* For fall admission, 7/1 priority date for domestic students; for winter admission, 11/1 priority date for domestic students; for spring admission, 2/1 priority date for domestic students. Applications are processed on a rolling basis. Application fee: $50. Electronic applications accepted. *Expenses:* Contact institution. *Application contact:* Bunny Simpson, Secretary, 602-371-1188, Fax: 602-371-0035, E-mail: bunny.simpson@ottawa.edu.

Pacific University, College of Education, Forest Grove, OR 97116-1797. Offers early childhood education (MAT); education (MAE); elementary education (MAT); high school education (MAT); middle school education (MAT); special education (MAT); visual function in learning (M Ed). Part-time and evening/weekend programs available. *Faculty:* 20 full-time (12 women), 40 part-time/adjunct (21 women). *Students:* 222 full-time (151 women), 115 part-time (90 women); includes 30 minority (3 African Americans, 5 American Indian/Alaska Native, 12 Asian Americans or Pacific Islanders, 10 Hispanic Americans). Average age 32. 92 applicants, 83% accepted, 69 enrolled. In 2006, 257 degrees awarded. *Degree requirements:* For master's, research project. *Entrance requirements:* For master's, California Basic Educational Skills Test, Praxis I, minimum undergraduate GPA of 2.75, 3.0 graduate. Additional exam requirements/recommendations for international students: Required—TOEFL. *Application deadline:* For fall admission, 6/15 priority date for domestic students; for spring admission, 10/15 for domestic students. Applications are processed on a rolling basis. Application fee: $35. Electronic applications accepted. *Expenses:* Contact institution. *Financial support:* In 2006–07, 287 students received support; fellowships, research assistantships, teaching assistantships, career-related internships or fieldwork, institutionally sponsored loans, and scholarships/grants available. Support available to part-time students. Financial award application deadline: 5/1; financial award applicants required to submit FAFSA. *Faculty research:* Defining a culturally competent classroom, technology in the k-12 classroom, Socratic seminars, social studies education. *Unit head:* Dr. Mark Ankeny, Acting Dean, 503-352-2102, E-mail: mankeny@pacificu.edu. *Application contact:* Diana Watkins, Assistant Director Graduate and Professional Admissions, 503-352-2958, Fax: 503-352-2907, E-mail: teach@pacificu.edu.

Palm Beach Atlantic University, School of Education and Behavioral Studies, West Palm Beach, FL 33416-4708. Offers counseling psychology (MSCP), including addictions/mental health, marriage and family therapy, mental health counseling, school guidance counseling; elementary education (M Ed). Part-time and evening/weekend programs available. *Faculty:* 13 full-time (3 women), 6 part-time/adjunct (5 women). *Students:* 211 full-time (169 women), 66 part-time (55 women); includes 103 minority (61 African Americans, 4 Asian Americans or Pacific Islanders, 38 Hispanic Americans), 7 international. Average age 36. 98 applicants, 71% accepted, 51 enrolled. In 2006, 49 degrees awarded. *Entrance requirements:* For master's, GRE General Test, minimum GPA of 3.0 in last 60 hours of course work. Additional exam requirements/recommendations for international students: Required—TOEFL (minimum score 550 paper-based; 213 computer-based). *Application deadline:* For fall admission, 7/15 priority date for domestic students; for spring admission, 11/15 priority date for domestic students. Applications are processed on a rolling basis. Application fee: $35. Electronic applications accepted. *Expenses:* Tuition: Full-time $10,665; part-time $395 per credit. Required fees: $90 per semester. *Financial support:* Unspecified assistantships available. Support available to part-time students. Financial award applicants required to submit FAFSA. *Unit head:* Dr. Melise Bunker, Dean, 561-803-2350, Fax: 561-803-2186, E-mail: melise_bunker@pba.edu. *Application contact:* Laura A. Leinweber, Director of Graduate and Evening Admissions, 888-468-6722, Fax: 561-803-2115, E-mail: grad@pba.edu.

Penn State University Park, Graduate School, College of Education, Department of Curriculum and Instruction, State College, University Park, PA 16802-1503. Offers bilingual education (M Ed, MS, PhD); early childhood education (M Ed, MS, PhD); elementary education (M Ed, MS, PhD); instructional systems (M Ed, MS, PhD); language arts and reading (M Ed, MS, PhD); science education (M Ed, MS, PhD); social studies education (MS, PhD); supervisor and curriculum development (M Ed, MS, PhD). *Accreditation:* NCATE. *Unit head:* Dr. Murry R. Nelson, Head, 814-865-6321, Fax: 814-863-7602, E-mail: mrn2@psu.edu. *Application contact:* Judy Nastase, Graduate Staff Assistant, 814-865-2168, E-mail: jcn3@psu.edu.

Pfeiffer University, School of Education, Misenheimer, NC 28109-0960. Offers elementary education (MS); teaching (MAT). *Accreditation:* NCATE. *Faculty:* 4 full-time (3 women), 2 part-time/adjunct (1 woman). *Students:* 5 full-time (all women), 60 part-time (52 women); includes 22 minority (21 African Americans, 1 Hispanic American), 1 international. Average age 39. In 2006, 29 degrees awarded. *Entrance requirements:* For master's, GRE, MAT, minimum GPA of 2.75. *Application deadline:* Applications are processed on a rolling basis. Application fee: $75. *Expenses:* Tuition: Part-time $380 per semester hour. Tuition and fees vary according to campus/location. *Financial support:* Unspecified assistantships available. Support available to part-time students. Financial award applicants required to submit FAFSA. *Unit head:* Dr. Sandra Loehr, Director of Teacher Education, 704-521-9116 Ext. 239.

Pittsburg State University, Graduate School, College of Education, Department of Curriculum and Instruction, Pittsburg, KS 66762. Offers classroom reading teacher (MS); early childhood education (MS); elementary education (MS); reading (MS); reading specialist (MS); secondary education (MS); teaching (MAT). *Accreditation:* NCATE. *Students:* 141. *Degree requirements:* For master's, thesis or alternative. *Entrance requirements:* For master's, GRE or MAT. Application fee: $35 ($60 for international students). *Expenses:* Tuition, state resident: full-time $2,144; part-time $181 per credit hour. Tuition, nonresident: full-time $5,273; part-time $442 per credit hour. Tuition and fees vary according to course load and campus/location. *Financial support:* In 2006–07, teaching assistantships (averaging $5,000 per year); career-related internships or fieldwork, Federal Work-Study, and unspecified assistantships also available. *Unit head:* Dr. V. June Taylor, Chairperson, 620-235-4508. *Application contact:* Jamie Vanderbeck, Assistant Director, 620-235-4223, Fax: 620-235-4219, E-mail: jvanderb@pittstate.edu.

Plymouth State University, College of Graduate Studies, Graduate Studies in Education, Program in Elementary Education, Plymouth, NH 03264-1595. Offers M Ed. *Accreditation:* NCATE. Part-time and evening/weekend programs available. *Students:* 2 full-time (both women), 137 part-time (122 women); includes 4 minority (1 African American, 2 Asian Americans or Pacific Islanders, 1 Hispanic American). Average age 37. 31 applicants, 100% accepted, 31 enrolled. In 2006, 42 degrees awarded. *Entrance requirements:* For master's, MAT, minimum GPA of 3.0. *Application deadline:* Applications are processed on a rolling basis. Application fee: $75. *Expenses:* Tuition, state resident: part-time $369 per credit. Tuition, nonresident: part-time $407 per credit. Tuition and fees vary according to course level. *Financial support:* Career-related internships or fieldwork, scholarships/grants, and unspecified assistantships available. Support available to part-time students. Financial award application deadline: 3/1; financial award applicants required to submit FAFSA. *Unit head:* Dr. Kathleen Norris, Director of Graduate Admissions, Programs and Certification, 603-535-3023, Fax: 603-535-2572, E-mail: knorris@plymouth.edu.

Plymouth State University, College of Graduate Studies, Graduate Studies in Education, Program in K-12 Education, Plymouth, NH 03264-1595. Offers M Ed. *Accreditation:* NCATE. Part-time and evening/weekend programs available. *Students:* 1 (woman) full-time, 222 part-time (168 women); includes 7 minority (2 African Americans, 3 Asian Americans or Pacific Islanders, 2 Hispanic Americans). Average age 39. 48 applicants, 100% accepted, 48 enrolled. In 2006, 59 degrees awarded. *Degree requirements:* For master's, PRAXIS. *Entrance requirements:* For master's, MAT, minimum GPA of 3.0. *Application deadline:* Applications are processed on a rolling basis. Application fee: $75. *Expenses:* Tuition, state resident: part-time $369 per credit. Tuition, nonresident: part-time $407 per credit. Tuition and fees vary according to course level. *Financial support:* Career-related internships or fieldwork, scholarships/grants, and unspecified assistantships available. Support available to part-time students. Financial award applicants required to submit FAFSA. *Unit head:* Dr. Kathleen Norris, Director of Graduate Admissions, Programs and Certification, 603-535-3023, Fax: 603-535-2572, E-mail: knorris@plymouth.edu.

Portland State University, Graduate Studies, School of Education, Department of Curriculum and Instruction, Portland, OR 97207-0751. Offers early childhood education (MA, MS); education (M Ed, MA, MS); educational leadership: curriculum and instruction (Ed D); educational media/school librarianship (MA, MS); elementary education (M Ed, MAT, MST); reading (MA,

Elementary Education

Portland State University (continued)
MS); secondary education (M Ed, MAT, MST). *Accreditation:* NCATE. Part-time programs available. *Faculty:* 20 full-time (14 women), 18 part-time/adjunct (9 women). *Students:* 185 full-time (135 women), 209 part-time (160 women); includes 53 minority (7 African Americans, 4 American Indian/Alaska Native, 13 Asian Americans or Pacific Islanders, 29 Hispanic Americans), 13 international. Average age 32. 372 applicants, 87% accepted, 171 enrolled. In 2006, 352 master's, 4 doctorates awarded. *Degree requirements:* For master's, special project or thesis, written exam; for doctorate, thesis/dissertation. *Entrance requirements:* For master's, California Basic Educational Skills Test, minimum GPA of 3.0 in upper-division course work or 2.75 overall. Additional exam requirements/recommendations for international students: Required—TOEFL (minimum score 550 paper-based; 213 computer-based). *Application deadline:* For fall admission, 4/1 for domestic and international students; for winter admission, 9/1 for domestic and international students; for spring admission, 11/1 for domestic and international students. Applications are processed on a rolling basis. Application fee: $50. *Expenses:* Tuition, state resident: full-time $6,426; part-time $238 per credit. Tuition, nonresident: full-time $11,016; part-time $408 per credit. Tuition and fees vary according to course load. *Financial support:* In 2006–07, 5 research assistantships with full tuition reimbursements (averaging $5,508 per year) were awarded; teaching assistantships with full tuition reimbursements, career-related internships or fieldwork, Federal Work-Study, and institutionally sponsored loans also available. Support available to part-time students. Financial award application deadline: 3/1; financial award applicants required to submit FAFSA. *Faculty research:* Early literacy, characteristics of successful teachers of at-risk students, participation of women/minorities in technology courses, selection of cooperating teachers. Total annual research expenditures: $308,420. *Unit head:* Steven Lee, Head, 503-725-4689, Fax: 503-725-8475. *Application contact:* Majken Elek, Department Secretary, 503-725-4756, Fax: 503-725-8475, E-mail: majkene@pdx.edu.

Purdue University, Graduate School, School of Education, Department of Curriculum and Instruction, West Lafayette, IN 47907. Offers agricultural and extension education (PhD, Ed S); agriculture and extension education (MS, MS Ed); art education (PhD); consumer and family sciences and extension education (MS Ed, PhD, Ed S); curriculum studies (MS Ed, PhD, Ed S); educational technology (MS Ed, PhD, Ed S); elementary education (MS Ed); foreign language education (MS Ed, PhD, Ed S); industrial technology (PhD, Ed S); language arts (MS Ed, PhD, Ed S); literacy (MS Ed, PhD, Ed S); mathematics/science education (MS, MS Ed, PhD, Ed S); social studies (MS Ed, PhD); social studies education (Ed S); vocational/industrial education (MS Ed, PhD, Ed S); vocational/technical education (MS Ed, PhD, Ed S). *Accreditation:* NCATE. Part-time and evening/weekend programs available. *Faculty:* 26 full-time (13 women), 3 part-time/adjunct (all women). *Students:* 59 full-time (37 women), 112 part-time (70 women); includes 24 minority (13 African Americans, 3 American Indian/Alaska Native, 4 Asian Americans or Pacific Islanders, 4 Hispanic Americans), 38 international. Average age 35. 92 applicants, 68% accepted, 38 enrolled. In 2006, 52 master's, 23 doctorates awarded. *Degree requirements:* For master's, thesis optional; for doctorate, thesis/dissertation, oral and written exams; for Ed S, oral presentation, project. *Entrance requirements:* For master's, GRE General Test, minimum B average; for doctorate, GRE General Test; for Ed S, GRE, minimum B average. Additional exam requirements/recommendations for international students: Required—TOEFL. *Application deadline:* For fall admission, 1/15 priority date for domestic students, 1/15 for international students; for spring admission, 9/15 for domestic and international students. Applications are processed on a rolling basis. Application fee: $55. Electronic applications accepted. *Financial support:* In 2006–07, 3 fellowships with full tuition reimbursements (averaging $10,500 per year), 11 research assistantships with full tuition reimbursements (averaging $11,500 per year), 43 teaching assistantships with full tuition reimbursements (averaging $10,800 per year) were awarded; career-related internships or fieldwork and tuition waivers (full) also available. Support available to part-time students. Financial award application deadline: 3/1; financial award applicants required to submit FAFSA. *Faculty research:* Literacy acquisition and development, teacher beliefs and knowledge, recruitment and retention of underrepresented students, economic education, literacy discourse. *Unit head:* Dr. James D Lehman, Head, 765-494-7935, Fax: 765-496-1622. *Application contact:* Patricia Mason, Coordinator of Graduate Studies, 765-494-2345, Fax: 765-494-5832, E-mail: gradoffice@soe.purdue.edu.

Purdue University Calumet, Graduate School, School of Education, Program in Elementary Education, Hammond, IN 46323-2094. Offers MS Ed. *Accreditation:* NCATE. *Entrance requirements:* Additional exam requirements/recommendations for international students: Required—TOEFL.

Purdue University North Central, Program in Education, Westville, IN 46391-9542. Offers elementary education (MS Ed). *Accreditation:* NCATE. Part-time and evening/weekend programs available. *Degree requirements:* For master's, one foreign language. *Entrance requirements:* For master's, GRE, minimum GPA of 3.0. *Faculty research:* Diversity, integration.

Queens College of the City University of New York, Division of Graduate Studies, Division of Education, Department of Elementary and Early Childhood Education, Flushing, NY 11367-1597. Offers bilingual education (MS Ed); childhood education (MA); early childhood education (MA); elementary education (MS Ed, AC); literacy (MS Ed). Part-time and evening/weekend programs available. *Faculty:* 31 full-time (25 women). *Students:* 87 full-time (80 women), 505 part-time (454 women). In 2006, 338 degrees awarded. *Degree requirements:* For master's, research project; for AC, thesis optional. *Entrance requirements:* For master's, minimum GPA of 3.0. Additional exam requirements/recommendations for international students: Required—TOEFL. *Application deadline:* For fall admission, 4/1 for domestic students; for spring admission, 11/1 for domestic students. Applications are processed on a rolling basis. Application fee: $125. *Financial support:* Career-related internships or fieldwork, Federal Work-Study, institutionally sponsored loans, and tuition waivers (partial) available. Support available to part-time students. Financial award application deadline: 4/1; financial award applicants required to submit FAFSA. *Unit head:* Dr. Myra Zarnowski, Chairperson, 718-997-5328.

Queens University of Charlotte, Hayworth College, Department of Education, Charlotte, NC 28274-0002. Offers elementary education (MAT). *Accreditation:* NCATE. Part-time and evening/weekend programs available. *Faculty:* 5 full-time (3 women). *Students:* 16 full-time (15 women), 74 part-time (69 women); includes 8 minority (4 African Americans, 1 American Indian/Alaska Native, 3 Hispanic Americans). Average age 27. 49 applicants, 80% accepted, 24 enrolled. In 2006, 42 degrees awarded. *Degree requirements:* For master's, comprehensive exam. *Entrance requirements:* For master's, GRE General Test. *Application deadline:* Applications are processed on a rolling basis. Application fee: $40. *Expenses:* Contact institution. *Financial support:* Institutionally sponsored loans available. *Unit head:* Dr. Patrice D. Petroff, Chair, 704-337-2575, Fax: 704-337-2477. *Application contact:* Lori Morrow, Director of Admissions, 704-337-2580, Fax: 704-337-2415.

Quinnipiac University, Division of Education, Program in Elementary Education, Hamden, CT 06518-1940. Offers MAT. *Faculty:* 7 full-time (5 women), 23 part-time/adjunct (14 women). *Students:* 83 full-time (75 women); includes 5 minority (1 African American, 4 Hispanic Americans), 1 international. Average age 25. 82 applicants, 94% accepted, 68 enrolled. In 2006, 64 degrees awarded. *Entrance requirements:* For master's, PRAXIS I, minimum GPA of 2.67, interview. Additional exam requirements/recommendations for international students: Required—TOEFL (minimum score 575 paper-based; 233 computer-based; 90 iBT), IELTS (minimum score 7). *Application deadline:* For fall admission, 3/15 priority date for domestic students, 1/15 for international students. Applications are processed on a rolling basis. Application fee: $45. Electronic applications accepted. *Expenses:* Tuition: Part-time $675 per credit. Required fees: $30 per credit. *Financial support:* Career-related internships or fieldwork and tuition waivers (partial) available. Financial award application deadline: 4/15; financial award applicants required to submit FAFSA. *Faculty research:* Multicultural and urban education, challenges of teaching diverse learners, soci-cultural nature of learning. *Unit head:* Dr. Bernadine Krawczyk, Assistant Dean, Division of Education, 203-582-3510, Fax: 203-582-3473, E-mail: bernadine.krawczyk@quinnipiac.edu. *Application contact:* Office of Graduate Admissions, 800-462-1944, Fax: 203-582-3443, E-mail: graduate@quinnipiac.edu.

See Close-Up on page 911.

Regent University, Graduate School, School of Education, Virginia Beach, VA 23464-9800. Offers Christian school program (M Ed); cross-categorical special education (M Ed); education (M Ed, Ed D); educational leadership (M Ed); elementary education (M Ed); individual degree plan (M Ed); master teacher (M Ed); special education leadership (Ed S); TESOL (M Ed). Part-time and evening/weekend programs available. Postbaccalaureate distance learning degree programs offered (minimal on-campus study). *Faculty:* 25 full-time (11 women), 132 part-time/adjunct (90 women). *Students:* 220 full-time (176 women), 501 part-time (374 women); includes 264 minority (229 African Americans, 9 Asian Americans or Pacific Islanders, 26 Hispanic Americans), 13 international. Average age 38. 472 applicants, 79% accepted, 256 enrolled. In 2006, 185 master's, 5 doctorates awarded. *Degree requirements:* For master's, thesis or alternative; for doctorate, thesis/dissertation, comprehensive exam. *Entrance requirements:* For master's, MAT, minimum undergraduate GPA of 2.75, writing sample, resumé; for doctorate, GRE, writing sample, 3 years of relevant professional experience, master's-level paper, copies of published work. Additional exam requirements/recommendations for international students: Required—TOEFL (minimum score 577 paper-based; 233 computer-based). *Application deadline:* For fall admission, 4/1 priority date for domestic students; for spring admission, 10/15 priority date for domestic students. Applications are processed on a rolling basis. Application fee: $50. Electronic applications accepted. *Expenses:* Contact institution. *Financial support:* In 2006–07, 721 students received support; fellowships, career-related internships or fieldwork, scholarships/grants, tuition waivers (full and partial), and unspecified assistantships available. Support available to part-time students. Financial award application deadline: 4/1; financial award applicants required to submit FAFSA. *Faculty research:* Character development and discipline for children, education leadership development, diversity in schools, classroom management, technology in education settings. *Unit head:* Dr. Alan A. Arroyo, Dean, 757-226-4261, Fax: 757-226-4318, E-mail: alanarr@regent.edu. *Application contact:* Althea Bishard, Registrar and Executive Director of Enrollment and Academic Services, 800-373-5504, Fax: 757-226-4381, E-mail: admissions@regent.edu.

Regis University, School for Professional Studies, Program in Teacher Education, Denver, CO 80221-1099. Offers adult learning, training, and development (M Ed); curriculum, instruction, and assessment (M Ed); early childhood (M Ed); educational technology (Certificate); elementary (M Ed); ESL (M Ed); fine arts (M Ed), including arts, music; instructional technology (M Ed); professional leadership (M Ed); reading (M Ed); secondary (M Ed); self-designed (M Ed); space studies (M Ed); special education (M Ed); teacher licensure (M Ed). Program also offered in Henderson and Las Vegas (Summerlin), NV. Postbaccalaureate distance learning degree programs offered. *Unit head:* Dr. Suzie Perry, Dean, 303-458-4302. *Application contact:* Partick Lowenthal, Assistant Director, 303-458-4300 Ext. 4314, E-mail: masters@regis.edu.

Rhode Island College, School of Graduate Studies, Feinstein School of Education and Human Development, Department of Elementary Education, Providence, RI 02908-1991. Offers early childhood education (M Ed); elementary education (M Ed, MAT); reading (M Ed). *Accreditation:* NCATE. Part-time and evening/weekend programs available. *Faculty:* 17 full-time (10 women), 5 part-time/adjunct (all women). *Students:* 33 full-time (28 women), 75 part-time (69 women); includes 4 minority (all Hispanic Americans) Average age 33. In 2006, 56 degrees awarded. *Entrance requirements:* For master's, GRE General Test or MAT, Praxis II (elementary content knowledge), 3 letters of recommendation, interview. *Application deadline:* For fall admission, 3/15 for domestic students; for spring admission, 11/1 for domestic students. Applications are processed on a rolling basis. Application fee: $50. *Expenses:* Tuition, state resident: part-time $244 per credit. Tuition, nonresident: part-time $512 per credit. Required fees: $12 per credit. $66 per term. Tuition and fees vary according to degree level, program and reciprocity agreements. *Financial support:* Teaching assistantships with full tuition reimbursements, Federal Work-Study, scholarships/grants, and health care benefits available. Support available to part-time students. Financial award application deadline: 5/15; financial award applicants required to submit FAFSA. *Unit head:* Dr. Lisa Owen, Chair, 401-456-8016, E-mail: lowen@ric.edu.

Rider University, Department of Graduate Education, Leadership and Counseling, Lawrenceville, NJ 08648-3001. Offers counseling services (MA, Ed S); curriculum, instruction and supervision (MA); director of school counseling services (Certificate); educational administration (MA); organizational leadership (MA); principal (Certificate); reading/language arts (MA, Certificate), including reading specialist (Certificate), reading/language arts (MA); school business administrator (Certificate); school counseling services (Certificate); school psychology (Ed S); special education (MA); supervisor (Certificate); teacher certification (Certificate), including business education, elementary education, English as a second language, English education, mathematics education, preschool to grade 3, science education, social studies education, world languages; teaching (MA). *Accreditation:* NCATE. Part-time and evening/weekend programs available. *Faculty:* 24 full-time (12 women), 30 part-time/adjunct (15 women). *Students:* 90 full-time (75 women), 457 part-time (369 women); includes 73 minority (50 African Americans, 2 American Indian/Alaska Native, 6 Asian Americans or Pacific Islanders, 15 Hispanic Americans), 1 international. Average age 32. 314 applicants, 61% accepted, 138 enrolled. In 2006, 116 master's, 19 other advanced degrees awarded. *Degree requirements:* For master's, thesis or alternative, internship, portfolios, comprehensive exam (for some programs); for other advanced degree, internship, professional portfolio. *Entrance requirements:* For master's, GRE (counseling, school psychology), MAT, interview, resumé, letters of recommendation; for other advanced degree, PRAXIS. Additional exam requirements/recommendations for international students: Required—TOEFL (minimum score 550 paper-based; 213 computer-based). *Application deadline:* For fall admission, 5/1 priority date for domestic students, 6/1 priority date for international students; for spring admission, 11/1 priority date for domestic and international students. Applications are processed on a rolling basis. Application fee: $50. Electronic applications accepted. *Expenses:* Tuition: Part-time $525 per credit. Required fees: $35 per course. $30 per semester. *Financial support:* In 2006–07, 271 students received support. Career-related internships or fieldwork, Federal Work-Study, institutionally sponsored loans, and unspecified assistantships available. Support available to part-time students. Financial award applicants required to submit FAFSA. *Faculty research:* Gifted students, self-esteem, hope and mental health, conflicts in group work, cultural diversity and counseling assessment of special needs in children. *Unit head:* Dr. Dennis C. Buss, Chair, 609-895-5353, Fax: 609-896-5362, E-mail: dbuss@rider.edu. *Application contact:* Jamie L Mitchell, Director of Graduate Admissions, 609-896-5036, Fax: 609-895-5680, E-mail: jmitchell@rider.edu.

See Close-Up on page 913.

Rivier College, School of Graduate Studies, Department of Education, Nashua, NH 03060-5086. Offers curriculum and instruction (M Ed); early childhood education (M Ed); educational administration (M Ed); educational studies (M Ed); elementary education (M Ed); elementary education and general special education (M Ed); emotional and behavioral disorders (M Ed); general social education (M Ed); leadership and learning (CAGS); learning disabilities (M Ed); learning disabilities and reading (M Ed); mental health counseling (MA); reading (M Ed); school counseling (M Ed). Part-time and evening/weekend programs available. *Faculty:* 11 full-time (7 women), 40 part-time/adjunct (29 women). *Students:* 41 full-time (33 women), 221 part-time (192 women); includes 4 minority (2 African Americans, 2 Hispanic Americans). Average age 37. In 2006, 134 degrees awarded. *Degree requirements:* For master's, internships. *Entrance requirements:* For master's, GRE General Test or MAT. *Application deadline:* Applications are processed on a rolling basis. Application fee: $25. *Financial support:* Available to part-time students. Application deadline: 2/1; *Unit head:* Dr. Charles L. Mitsakos, Chairman, 603-888-1311 Ext. 8582. *Application contact:* Diane Monahan, Director of Graduate Admissions, 603-897-8129, Fax: 603-897-8810, E-mail: gradadm@rivier.edu.

Rockford College, Graduate Studies, Department of Education, Program in Elementary Education, Rockford, IL 61108-2393. Offers MAT. Part-time and evening/weekend programs available. *Degree requirements:* For master's, thesis optional. *Entrance requirements:* For master's, GRE General Test.

Roger Williams University, School of Education, Program in Elementary Education, Bristol, RI 02809. Offers MAT. Part-time programs available. *Faculty:* 8 full-time (5 women), 2 part-time/adjunct (both women). *Students:* 18 full-time (15 women), 49 part-time (43 women); includes 2 minority (1 Asian American or Pacific Islander, 1 Hispanic American). Average age 34. 10 applicants, 80% accepted, 4 enrolled. In 2006, 37 degrees awarded. *Degree requirements:* For master's, state-mandated exams. *Entrance requirements:* For master's, GRE or MAT. *Application deadline:* Applications are processed on a rolling basis. Application fee: $50. Electronic applications accepted. *Expenses:* Tuition: Part-time $362 per credit. Tuition and fees vary according to program. *Financial support:* In 2006–07, 41 students received support. Career-related internships or fieldwork and health care benefits available. Financial award applicants required to submit FAFSA. *Faculty research:* Assistive technology; standards-based curricular development; professional development strategies, instruction, and assessment. *Application contact:* Suzanne Faubl, Director of Graduate Admissions, 401-254-3809, Fax: 401-254-3557, E-mail: sfaubl@rwu.edu.

Rollins College, Hamilton Holt School, Program in Education, Winter Park, FL 32789-4499. Offers elementary education (M Ed, MAT); secondary education (MAT), including English, mathematics, music. Part-time and evening/weekend programs available. *Students:* 14 full-time (12 women), 36 part-time (32 women); includes 5 minority (2 African Americans, 1 Asian American or Pacific Islander, 2 Hispanic Americans), 1 international. Average age 35. In 2006, 14 degrees awarded. *Degree requirements:* For master's, comprehensive exam. *Entrance requirements:* For master's, GRE or MAT, interview. Additional exam requirements/recommendations for international students: Required—TOEFL. *Application deadline:* For fall admission, 7/16 for domestic students; for winter admission, 12/3 for domestic students; for spring admission, 4/22 for domestic students. Applications are processed on a rolling basis. Application fee: $50. Electronic applications accepted. *Expenses:* Contact institution. *Financial support:* Teaching assistantships, scholarships/grants available. Support available to part-time students. *Unit head:* Dr. J. Scott Hewit, Director, 407-646-2300, E-mail: jhewit@rollins.edu. *Application contact:* Rebecca Cordray, Coordinator of Records and Registration, 407-646-1568, Fax: 407-975-6430, E-mail: rcordray@rollins.edu.

Roosevelt University, Graduate Division, College of Education, Program in Elementary Education, Chicago, IL 60605-1394. Offers MA. *Students:* 32 full-time (30 women), 132 part-time (113 women); includes 38 minority (25 African Americans, 4 Asian Americans or Pacific Islanders, 9 Hispanic Americans). Average age 33. 155 applicants, 66% accepted, 95 enrolled. In 2006, 60 degrees awarded. *Unit head:* Dr. Sharon Grant, Chair, 847-619-8831. *Application contact:* Joanne Canyon-Heller, Coordinator of Graduate Admission, 877-APPLY RU, Fax: 312-281-3356, E-mail: applyru@roosevelt.edu.

Rosemont College, Graduate School, Program in Curriculum and Instruction, Rosemont, PA 19010-1699. Offers elementary certification (MA). Part-time and evening/weekend programs available. *Entrance requirements:* Additional exam requirements/recommendations for international students: Required—TOEFL. Electronic applications accepted.

Rutgers, The State University of New Jersey, New Brunswick, Graduate School of Education, Department of Learning and Teaching, Program in Early Childhood/Elementary Education, New Brunswick, NJ 08901-1281. Offers Ed M, Ed D. Part-time programs available. *Faculty:* 4 full-time (all women). *Students:* 71 full-time (64 women), 26 part-time (24 women). 185 applicants, 45% accepted, 62 enrolled. In 2006, 71 master's, 1 doctorate awarded. Terminal master's awarded for partial completion of doctoral program. *Degree requirements:* For master's, comprehensive exam (for some programs); for doctorate, thesis/dissertation, qualifying exam. *Entrance requirements:* For master's, GRE General Test, minimum GPA of 3.0; for doctorate, GRE General Test, minimum GPA of 3.5. Additional exam requirements/recommendations for international students: Required—TOEFL. *Application deadline:* For fall admission, 2/1 for domestic and international students. Application fee: $60. Electronic applications accepted. *Financial support:* Application deadline: 3/15; *Unit head:* Dr. Sharon Ryan, Coordinator, 732-932-7496 Ext. 8114, E-mail: sr247@rci.rutgers.edu.

Sacred Heart University, Graduate Studies, College of Education and Health Professions, Department of Education, Fairfield, CT 06825-1000. Offers administration (CAS); educational technology (MAT); elementary education (MAT); reading (CAS); secondary education (MAT); teaching (CAS). Part-time and evening/weekend programs available. Postbaccalaureate distance learning degree programs offered (minimal on-campus study). *Faculty:* 23 full-time (10 women). *Students:* 360 full-time (285 women), 710 part-time (520 women); includes 39 minority (15 African Americans, 4 American Indian/Alaska Native, 5 Asian Americans or Pacific Islanders, 15 Hispanic Americans), 4 international. Average age 34. 335 applicants, 87% accepted, 270 enrolled. In 2006, 312 master's, 59 other advanced degrees awarded. *Degree requirements:* For master's, thesis or alternative. *Entrance requirements:* For master's, PRAXIS (teacher certification/MAT); for CAS, PRAXIS I. Additional exam requirements/recommendations for international students: Required—TOEFL (minimum score 550 paper-based; 213 computer-based). *Application deadline:* Applications are processed on a rolling basis. Application fee: $50 ($100 for international students). Electronic applications accepted. *Expenses:* Contact institution. Full-time tuition and fees vary according to degree level and program. *Financial support:* Teaching assistantships with partial tuition reimbursements, career-related internships or fieldwork, institutionally sponsored loans, traineeships, tuition waivers (partial), and unspecified assistantships available. Support available to part-time students. Financial award applicants required to submit FAFSA. *Faculty research:* Reading education, learning theory, teacher preparation, education of underachievers. *Unit head:* Dr. Edward Malin, Director, 203-371-7800, Fax: 203-365-7513. *Application contact:* Alexis Haakonsen, Dean of Graduate Admissions, 203-365-7619, Fax: 203-365-4732, E-mail: haakonsena@sacredheart.edu.

Sage Graduate School, Graduate School, Division of Education, Program in Childhood Education, Troy, NY 12180-4115. Offers MS Ed. *Accreditation:* NCATE. Part-time and evening/weekend programs available. *Faculty:* 11 full-time (8 women), 20 part-time/adjunct (15 women). *Students:* 26 full-time (21 women), 27 part-time (20 women); includes 5 minority (1 African American, 3 Asian Americans or Pacific Islanders, 1 Hispanic American). Average age 28. 30 applicants, 63% accepted, 12 enrolled. In 2006, 29 degrees awarded. *Degree requirements:* For master's, thesis. *Entrance requirements:* For master's, minimum GPA of 2.75. Additional exam requirements/recommendations for international students: Required—TOEFL (minimum score 550 paper-based; 213 computer-based). *Application deadline:* Applications are processed on a rolling basis. Application fee: $40. *Expenses:* Tuition: Full-time $9,270; part-time $515 per credit hour. *Financial support:* Career-related internships or fieldwork, scholarships/grants, and unspecified assistantships available. Support available to part-time students. Financial award application deadline: 3/1; financial award applicants required to submit FAFSA. *Faculty research:* The effects of teachers' personal characteristics on the instructional process. *Application contact:* Shannon K. Easton, Director of Graduate and Adult Admission, 518-244-2443, Fax: 518-244-6880, E-mail: sgsadm@sage.edu.

Sage Graduate School, Graduate School, Division of Education, Program in Childhood Education/Literacy, Troy, NY 12180-4115. Offers MS. Part-time and evening/weekend programs available. *Faculty:* 11 full-time (8 women), 20 part-time/adjunct (15 women). *Students:* 7 full-time (all women), 12 part-time (all women). Average age 27. 15 applicants, 73% accepted, 6 enrolled. In 2006, 3 degrees awarded. *Degree requirements:* For master's, thesis optional. *Entrance requirements:* Additional exam requirements/recommendations for international students: Required—TOEFL (minimum score 550 paper-based; 213 computer-based). *Application deadline:* Applications are processed on a rolling basis. Application fee: $40. *Expenses:* Tuition: Full-time $9,270; part-time $515 per credit hour. *Financial support:* Career-related internships or fieldwork, scholarships/grants, and unspecified assistantships available. Support available to part-time students. Financial award application deadline: 3/1. *Application contact:* Shannon K. Easton, Director of Graduate and Adult Admission, 518-244-2443, Fax: 518-244-6880, E-mail: sgsadm@sage.edu.

Sage Graduate School, Graduate School, Division of Education, Program in Childhood Special Education, Troy, NY 12180-4115. Offers MS Ed. *Accreditation:* NCATE. Part-time and evening/weekend programs available. *Faculty:* 11 full-time (8 women), 20 part-time/adjunct (15 women). *Students:* 7 full-time (all women), 31 part-time (all women); includes 2 minority (1 African American, 1 Asian American or Pacific Islander). Average age 29. 16 applicants, 69% accepted, 7 enrolled. In 2006, 17 degrees awarded. *Degree requirements:* For master's, thesis optional. *Entrance requirements:* For master's, minimum GPA of 2.75. Additional exam requirements/recommendations for international students: Required—TOEFL (minimum score 550 paper-based; 213 computer-based). *Application deadline:* Applications are processed on a rolling basis. Application fee: $40. *Expenses:* Tuition: Full-time $9,270; part-time $515 per credit hour. *Financial support:* Career-related internships or fieldwork, scholarships/grants, and unspecified assistantships available. Support available to part-time students. Financial award application deadline: 3/1; financial award applicants required to submit FAFSA. *Faculty research:* Effective behavioral strategies for classroom instruction. *Application contact:* Shannon K. Easton, Director of Graduate and Adult Admission, 518-244-2443, Fax: 518-244-6880, E-mail: sgsadm@sage.edu.

Saginaw Valley State University, College of Education, Program in Elementary Classroom Teaching, University Center, MI 48710. Offers MAT. *Accreditation:* NCATE. Part-time and evening/weekend programs available. *Students:* 2 full-time (both women), 121 part-time (107 women); includes 1 minority (Hispanic American) Average age 33. 26 applicants, 100% accepted, 21 enrolled. In 2006, 33 degrees awarded. *Degree requirements:* For master's, capstone course. *Entrance requirements:* For master's, minimum GPA of 3.0, teaching certificate. *Application deadline:* Applications are processed on a rolling basis. Application fee: $25. Electronic applications accepted. *Expenses:* Tuition, state resident: full-time $7,225; part-time $301 per credit hour. Tuition, nonresident: full-time $13,888; part-time $579 per credit hour. Required fees: $330; $14 per credit hour. Tuition and fees vary according to course load. *Financial support:* Applicants required to submit FAFSA. *Faculty research:* Reading, writing, and speaking about persistent civic issues. *Application contact:* Jeanne Chipman, Certification Officer, 989-964-4083, Fax: 989-964-4385, E-mail: jdc@svsu.edu.

Saginaw Valley State University, College of Education, Program in Natural Science Teaching, University Center, MI 48710. Offers elementary (MAT); middle school (MAT); secondary school (MAT). *Accreditation:* NCATE. Part-time and evening/weekend programs available. *Students:* 1 (woman) full-time, 22 part-time (16 women). Average age 36. 3 applicants, 100% accepted, 3 enrolled. In 2006, 15 degrees awarded. *Degree requirements:* For master's, capstone course. *Entrance requirements:* For master's, minimum GPA of 3.0, teaching certificate. *Application deadline:* Applications are processed on a rolling basis. Application fee: $25. Electronic applications accepted. *Expenses:* Tuition, state resident: full-time $7,225; part-time $301 per credit hour. Tuition, nonresident: full-time $13,888; part-time $579 per credit hour. Required fees: $330; $14 per credit hour. Tuition and fees vary according to course load. *Financial support:* Applicants required to submit FAFSA. *Application contact:* Jeanne Chipman, Certification Officer, 989-964-4083, Fax: 989-964-4385, E-mail: jdc@svsu.edu.

St. John Fisher College, Office of the Provost, Ralph C. Wilson Jr. School of Education, Childhood Education Program, Rochester, NY 14618-3597. Offers MS Ed. Part-time and evening/weekend programs available. *Faculty:* 10 full-time (6 women), 2 part-time/adjunct (1 woman). *Students:* 17 full-time (13 women), 27 part-time (25 women); includes 3 African Americans, 2 Asian Americans or Pacific Islanders, 1 Hispanic American. Average age 31. 37 applicants, 81% accepted, 18 enrolled. In 2006, 26 degrees awarded. *Degree requirements:* For master's, student teaching, field experience. *Entrance requirements:* For master's, GRE (if GPA is below 3.0), minimum GPA of 3.0, letters of reference, personal statement, 30 hours in content area. Additional exam requirements/recommendations for international students: Required—TOEFL (minimum score 575 paper-based; 233 computer-based; 80 iBT). *Application deadline:* For fall admission, 4/1 for domestic students; for spring admission, 10/30 for domestic students. Applications are processed on a rolling basis. Application fee: $30. *Expenses:* Tuition: Part-time $615 per credit. Tuition and fees vary according to program. *Financial support:* Federal Work-Study and scholarships/grants available. Financial award application deadline: 2/15; financial award applicants required to submit FAFSA. *Faculty research:* Professional development; science assessment; multi-cultural; educational technology. *Unit head:* Dr. Michelle Erklenz-Watts, Director, 585-385-8404, E-mail: merklenz-watts@sjfc.edu. *Application contact:* Shannon Cleverley, Director of Graduate Admissions, 585-385-8161, Fax: 585-385-8344, E-mail: scleverley@sjfc.edu.

St. John's University, The School of Education, Division of Early Childhood, Childhood and Adolescent Education, Program in Childhood Education, Queens, NY 11439. Offers MS Ed. *Students:* 30 full-time (27 women), 250 part-time (222 women); includes 50 minority (22 African Americans, 10 Asian Americans or Pacific Islanders, 18 Hispanic Americans), 7 international. Average age 29. 190 applicants, 75% accepted, 62 enrolled. In 2006, 66 degrees awarded. *Degree requirements:* For master's, comprehensive exam. *Entrance requirements:* Additional exam requirements/recommendations for international students: Required—TOEFL (minimum score 500 paper-based; 173 computer-based). *Application deadline:* For fall admission, 4/15 for domestic students, 5/1 priority date for international students; for spring admission, 11/1 priority date for international students. Applications are processed on a rolling basis. Application fee: $40. Electronic applications accepted. *Expenses:* Tuition: Full-time $18,480; part-time $770 per credit. Required fees: $125 per semester. Tuition and fees vary according to program. *Financial support:* Research assistantships available. *Faculty research:* Self determination in special education setting. *Application contact:* Kelly Ronayne, Assistant Dean, 718-990-2303, Fax: 718-990-6069, E-mail: graded@stjohns.edu.

Saint Joseph's University, College of Arts and Sciences, Department of Education, Philadelphia, PA 19131-1395. Offers educational leadership (Ed D); elementary education (MS); instructional technology (MS); professional education (MS); reading (MS); secondary education (MS); special education (MS); training and organizational development (MS, Certificate). Part-time and evening/weekend programs available. *Faculty:* 18 full-time (9 women), 67 part-time/adjunct (34 women). *Students:* 77 full-time (63 women), 551 part-time (417 women); includes 115 minority (94 African Americans, 2 American Indian/Alaska Native, 8 Asian Americans or Pacific Islanders, 11 Hispanic Americans), 12 international. In 2006, 286 master's, 5 doctorates awarded. *Entrance requirements:* For master's, 2 letters of recommendation, minimum GPA of 3.0; for doctorate, GRE/MAT, 2 letters of recommendation, resumé. Additional exam requirements/recommendations for international students: Required—TOEFL. *Application deadline:* For fall admission, 7/15 for domestic students. Application fee: $35. *Expenses:* Contact institution. *Financial support:* Fellowships, research assistantships, career-related internships or fieldwork and Federal Work-Study available. Support available to part-time students. *Unit head:* Dr. Encarnacion Rodriguez, Director of Graduate Education, 610-660-3348.

Saint Mary's University of Minnesota, School of Graduate and Professional Programs, Program in Instruction, Winona, MN 55987-1399. Offers MA, Certificate. *Unit head:* Rebecca Hopkins, Director, 507-457-6620, E-mail: rhopkins@smumn.edu.

Saint Peter's College, Graduate Programs in Education, Program in Teaching, Jersey City, NJ 07306-5997. Offers elementary teacher (Certificate); supervisor of instruction (Certificate); teaching (MA). Part-time and evening/weekend programs available. *Degree requirements:* For master's, departmental qualifying exam. *Entrance requirements:* For master's, GRE General Test or MAT.

St. Thomas Aquinas College, Division of Teacher Education, Sparkill, NY 10976. Offers adolescence education (MST); childhood and special education (MST); childhood education (MST); reading (MS Ed, PMC); special education (MS Ed, PMC); teaching (MS Ed), including elementary education, middle school education, secondary education. *Accreditation:* NCATE.

Elementary Education

St. Thomas Aquinas College (continued)
Part-time and evening/weekend programs available. *Degree requirements:* For master's, comprehensive professional portfolio; for PMC, action research project. *Entrance requirements:* For master's, New York State Qualifying Exam, GRE General Test or minimum GPA of 3.0, teaching certificate; for PMC, GRE General Test or minimum GPA of 3.0. Electronic applications accepted. *Faculty research:* Computer applications in education, adolescent special education students, literacy development, inclusive practices for special education students.

See Close-Up on page 917.

St. Thomas University, School of Graduate Studies, Department of Education, Miami Gardens, FL 33054-6459. Offers educational administration (MS, Certificate); educational leadership (Ed D); elementary education (MS); reading (MS); special education (MS). Part-time and evening/weekend programs available. *Degree requirements:* For master's, comprehensive exam; for doctorate, thesis/dissertation, comprehensive exam. *Entrance requirements:* For master's, interview, minimum GPA of 3.0 or GRE; for doctorate, GRE or MAT. Additional exam requirements/recommendations for international students: Required—TOEFL. Electronic applications accepted.

Saint Xavier University, Graduate Studies, School of Education, Chicago, IL 60655-3105. Offers counseling (MA); counselor education (MA); curriculum and instruction (MA); early childhood education (MA); education (CAS); educational administration (MA); elementary education (MA); field-based education (MA); general educational studies (MA); individualized program (MA); learning disabilities (MA); reading (MA); secondary education (MA). *Accreditation:* NCATE. Part-time and evening/weekend programs available. *Faculty:* 92. *Students:* 45 full-time (35 women), 1,529 part-time (1,309 women). In 2006, 474 degrees awarded. *Degree requirements:* For master's, thesis or project. *Entrance requirements:* For master's, minimum GPA of 3.0. *Application deadline:* For fall admission, 8/15 priority date for domestic students. Applications are processed on a rolling basis. Application fee: $35. *Expenses: Contact institution. Financial support:* Career-related internships or fieldwork available. Support available to part-time students. Financial award applicants required to submit FAFSA. *Unit head:* Dr. Beverly Gulley, Dean, 773-298-3221, Fax: 773-779-9061, E-mail: gulley@sxu.edu. *Application contact:* Beth Gierach, Managing Director of Admission, 773-298-3053, Fax: 773-298-3076, E-mail: gierach@sxu.edu.

Salem College, Department of Education, Winston-Salem, NC 27108-0548. Offers early education and leadership (MAT); elementary education (MAT); English as a second language (MAT); language and literacy (M Ed); middle school education (MAT); secondary education (MAT); special education (MAT). *Accreditation:* NCATE. Part-time and evening/weekend programs available. *Faculty:* 8 full-time (6 women), 5 part-time/adjunct (all women). *Students:* 8 full-time (all women), 250 part-time (238 women); includes 19 minority (16 African Americans, 1 Asian American or Pacific Islander, 2 Hispanic Americans). Average age 33. 110 applicants, 65% accepted, 68 enrolled. In 2006, 34 degrees awarded. *Degree requirements:* For master's, practicum (MAT), project (M Ed), oral and written comprehensive exams. *Entrance requirements:* For master's, GRE, minimum GPA of 2.5. *Application deadline:* Applications are processed on a rolling basis. Application fee: $30. *Financial support:* In 2006–07, 152 students received support. Federal Work-Study and scholarships/grants available. Support available to part-time students. Financial award applicants required to submit FAFSA. *Faculty research:* Content area reading strategies, literacy development, brain compatible instruction. *Unit head:* Dr. Paula Grubbs, Director of Teacher Education, 336-721-2610, Fax: 336-721-2683, E-mail: grubbs@salem.edu.

Salem State College, Graduate School, Professional Studies—Physical Education K-9, Salem, MA 01970-5353. Offers M Ed. Part-time and evening/weekend programs available. *Students:* Average age 32. In 2006, 2 degrees awarded. *Application deadline:* Applications are processed on a rolling basis. Application fee: $35. *Unit head:* MaryLou Breitborde, Associate Dean of Education, 978-542-6262, E-mail: mbreitborde@salemstate.edu.

Salem State College, Graduate School, Program in Elementary Education, Salem, MA 01970-5353. Offers M Ed. *Accreditation:* NCATE. *Faculty:* 2 part-time/adjunct (1 woman). *Students:* 21 full-time (18 women), 117 part-time (109 women); includes 2 minority (both Hispanic Americans) Average age 31. In 2006, 57 degrees awarded. *Entrance requirements:* For master's, GRE General Test, MAT. *Application deadline:* Applications are processed on a rolling basis. Application fee: $35. *Unit head:* Greg Carroll, Chairperson, 978-542-6075, Fax: 978-542-7215, E-mail: gcarroll@salemstate.edu.

Salem State College, Graduate School, Program in Spanish, Salem, MA 01970-5353. Offers MAT. Part-time and evening/weekend programs available. *Students:* Average age 33. In 2006, 1 degree awarded. Application fee: $35. *Unit head:* Dr. Nicole Sherf, Coordinator, 978-542-6468, E-mail: nsherf@salemstate.edu.

Salisbury University, Graduate Division, Department of Education, Salisbury, MD 21801-6837. Offers art (MAT); biology (MAT); business education (MAT); chemistry (MAT); early childhood education (M Ed); educational administration (M Ed); elementary education (M Ed); English (M Ed, MAT); French (MAT); geography (MAT); history (MAT); mathematics (MAT); media and technology (MAT); music (MAT); psychology (MAT); reading education (MAT); science (MAT); secondary education (MAT); social studies (MAT); Spanish (MAT). *Accreditation:* NCATE. Part-time and evening/weekend programs available. *Faculty:* 12 full-time (6 women), 10 part-time/adjunct (8 women). *Students:* 17 full-time (9 women), 84 part-time (72 women); includes 6 minority (5 African Americans, 1 Hispanic American). Average age 30. 15 applicants, 73% accepted, 11 enrolled. In 2006, 63 degrees awarded. *Degree requirements:* For master's, comprehensive exam (for some programs). *Entrance requirements:* For master's, PRAXIS, minimum GPA of 2.75. Additional exam requirements/recommendations for international students: Required—TOEFL (minimum score 550 paper-based; 213 computer-based). *Application deadline:* For fall admission, 8/1 priority date for domestic students; for spring admission, 1/1 for domestic students. Applications are processed on a rolling basis. Application fee: $45. *Expenses:* Tuition, state resident: part-time $260 per credit hour. Tuition, nonresident: part-time $546 per credit hour. Required fees: $52 per credit hour. *Financial support:* In 2006–07, 3 teaching assistantships with full tuition reimbursements were awarded; career-related internships or fieldwork and scholarships/grants also available. Support available to part-time students. Financial award applicants required to submit FAFSA. *Faculty research:* Middle-level education, student outcomes. *Unit head:* Dr. Edward C. Robeck, Program Coordinator, 410-543-6292, Fax: 410-548-2593, E-mail: ecrobeck@salisbury.edu. *Application contact:* Debra J. Clark, Administrative Assistant I, 410-543-6281, Fax: 410-548-2593, E-mail: djclark@salisbury.edu.

Samford University, School of Education, Birmingham, AL 35229-0002. Offers early childhood education (Ed S); early childhood/elementary education (MS Ed); educational administration (Ed S); educational leadership (Ed D); elementary education (Ed S); gifted education (MS Ed); M Div/MS Ed. *Accreditation:* NCATE. Part-time programs available. *Faculty:* 12 full-time (7 women), 8 part-time/adjunct (4 women). *Students:* 16 full-time (14 women), 160 part-time (124 women); includes 25 minority (all African Americans) Average age 38. 45 applicants, 100% accepted, 17 enrolled. In 2006, 15 master's, 20 doctorates, 20 other advanced degrees awarded. *Entrance requirements:* For master's, GRE or MAT, minimum GPA of 3.0; for doctorate, minimum GPA of 3.7; for Ed S, GRE, master's degree, teaching certificate, minimum GPA of 3.25. Additional exam requirements/recommendations for international students: Required—TOEFL (minimum score 550 paper-based; 213 computer-based). *Application deadline:* Applications are processed on a rolling basis. Application fee: $25. *Expenses:* Tuition: Part-time $500 per credit. One-time fee: $25 part-time. Full-time tuition and fees vary according to program and student level. *Financial support:* In 2006–07, 54 students received support; research assistantships, career-related internships or fieldwork, Federal Work-Study, scholarships/grants, and tuition waivers (partial) available. Support available to part-time students. Financial award applicants required to submit FAFSA. *Faculty research:* School law, the characteristics of beginning teachers, the nature of school reform, school culture, quality improvement in education, K-12 student achievement. *Unit head:* Dr. Jean Ann Box, Dean, 205-726-2559, E-mail: jabox@samford.edu. *Application contact:* Dr. Maurice Persall, Director, Graduate Office, 205-726-2019, E-mail: jmpersal@samford.edu.

Sam Houston State University, College of Education and Applied Science, Department of Curriculum and Instruction, Huntsville, TX 77341. Offers elementary education (M Ed, MA); secondary education (M Ed, MA). *Accreditation:* NCATE. Part-time and evening/weekend programs available. *Faculty:* 4 full-time (3 women). *Students:* 26 full-time (21 women), 86 part-time (61 women); includes 19 minority (11 African Americans, 1 American Indian/Alaska Native, 2 Asian Americans or Pacific Islanders, 5 Hispanic Americans), 3 international. Average age 32. In 2006, 35 degrees awarded. *Entrance requirements:* For master's, GRE General Test. *Application deadline:* For fall admission, 8/1 for domestic students; for spring admission, 12/1 for domestic students. Application fee: $20. *Expenses:* Tuition, state resident: full-time $5,904; part-time $164 per semester hour. Tuition, nonresident: full-time $15,804; part-time $439 per semester hour. Required fees: $1,374; $462 per semester. *Financial support:* Teaching assistantships, institutionally sponsored loans available. Financial award application deadline: 5/31; financial award applicants required to submit FAFSA. *Unit head:* Dr. Charlene Crocker, Chair, 936-294-1136, Fax: 936-294-1056, E-mail: csc001@shsu.edu. *Application contact:* Dr. Eren Johnson, Advisor, 936-294-1140, E-mail: edu_mej@shsu.edu.

San Diego State University, Graduate and Research Affairs, College of Education, School of Teacher Education, Program in Elementary Curriculum and Instruction, San Diego, CA 92182. Offers MA. *Accreditation:* NCATE. Evening/weekend programs available. *Students:* 16 full-time (12 women), 38 part-time (36 women); includes 14 minority (1 African American, 2 American Indian/Alaska Native, 6 Asian Americans or Pacific Islanders, 5 Hispanic Americans). Average age 29. 34 applicants, 71% accepted, 2 enrolled. In 2006, 68 degrees awarded. *Entrance requirements:* For master's, GRE General Test, letters of reference. Additional exam requirements/recommendations for international students: Required—TOEFL. *Application deadline:* For fall admission, 5/1 for domestic and international students; for spring admission, 11/1 for domestic students, 10/1 for international students. Applications are processed on a rolling basis. Application fee: $55. Electronic applications accepted. *Financial support:* Applicants required to submit FAFSA. *Unit head:* Dr. Valerie Pang, Graduate Advisor, 619-594-6286, Fax: 619-594-7828.

San Francisco State University, Division of Graduate Studies, College of Education, Department of Elementary Education, Program in Elementary Education, San Francisco, CA 94132-1722. Offers MA. *Accreditation:* NCATE. Part-time programs available. *Students:* 22 (19 women). *Degree requirements:* For master's, thesis or alternative. *Entrance requirements:* For master's, minimum GPA of 2.5 in last 60 units. *Application deadline:* For fall admission, 11/30 priority date for domestic students. Applications are processed on a rolling basis. Application fee: $55. *Financial support:* Application deadline: 3/1. *Application contact:* Dr. Jane Bernard-Powers, Professor, 415-338-2299, E-mail: jbp@sfsu.edu.

San Jose State University, Graduate Studies and Research, College of Education, Department of Elementary Education, San Jose, CA 95192-0001. Offers MA, Certificate. *Accreditation:* NCATE. *Students:* 380 full-time (311 women), 154 part-time (136 women); includes 170 minority (7 African Americans, 93 Asian Americans or Pacific Islanders, 70 Hispanic Americans), 5 international. Average age 31. 318 applicants, 94% accepted, 244 enrolled. In 2006, 55 degrees awarded. *Degree requirements:* For master's, thesis or alternative. *Application deadline:* For fall admission, 6/29 for domestic students; for spring admission, 11/30 for domestic students. Applications are processed on a rolling basis. Application fee: $59. Electronic applications accepted. *Financial support:* Career-related internships or fieldwork available. Financial award applicants required to submit FAFSA. *Unit head:* Dr. Carolyn Nelson, Chair, 408-924-3760, Fax: 408-924-3775.

Seton Hill University, Program in Elementary Education, Greensburg, PA 15601. Offers MA, Teaching Certificate. Part-time and evening/weekend programs available. *Faculty:* 7 full-time (5 women), 4 part-time/adjunct (2 women). *Students:* 15 full-time (13 women), 28 part-time (25 women); includes 1 minority (Asian American or Pacific Islander) Average age 31. 21 applicants, 90% accepted, 14 enrolled. In 2006, 12 master's awarded. *Degree requirements:* For master's, thesis optional. *Entrance requirements:* For master's, minimum GPA of 3.0. Additional exam requirements/recommendations for international students: Required—TOEFL (minimum score 600 paper-based; 250 computer-based). *Application deadline:* For fall admission, 8/15 priority date for domestic students; for spring admission, 12/15 for domestic students. Applications are processed on a rolling basis. Application fee: $35. Electronic applications accepted. *Expenses:* Tuition: Part-time $620 per credit. Required fees: $100 per semester. *Financial support:* In 2006–07, 36 students received support. Scholarships/grants, tuition waivers (partial), and unspecified assistantships available. Support available to part-time students. Financial award application deadline: 8/15; financial award applicants required to submit FAFSA. *Faculty research:* Second language acquisition, curriculum development, distance education, Holocaust studies. *Unit head:* Dr. Michele H. Conway, Director, 724-830-4732, Fax: 724-830-1294, E-mail: conway@setonhill.edu. *Application contact:* Dane Zimmer, Advisor, 724-838-4209, Fax: 724-830-1891, E-mail: zimmer@setonhill.edu.

Shenandoah University, College of Arts and Sciences, Winchester, VA 22601-5195. Offers administrative leadership (D Ed); advanced professional teaching English to speakers of other languages (Certificate); education (MSE); elementary education (Certificate); middle school education (Certificate); professional studies (Certificate); professional teaching English to speakers of other languages (Certificate); public management (Certificate); secondary education (Certificate); women's studies (Certificate). Part-time and evening/weekend programs available. Postbaccalaureate distance learning degree programs offered (minimal on-campus study). *Faculty:* 14 full-time (9 women), 7 part-time/adjunct (4 women). *Students:* 28 full-time (16 women), 283 part-time (208 women); includes 8 minority (3 African Americans, 1 American Indian/Alaska Native, 3 Asian Americans or Pacific Islanders, 1 Hispanic American), 26 international. Average age 40. 182 applicants, 68% accepted, 98 enrolled. In 2006, 96 master's, 6 doctorates, 22 other advanced degrees awarded. *Degree requirements:* For master's, thesis (for some programs), internship, comprehensive exam (for some programs); for doctorate, thesis/dissertation, comprehensive exam. *Entrance requirements:* For master's, minimum GPA of 3.0 or satisfactory GRE, 3 letters of recommendation, valid teaching license; for doctorate, minimum GPA of 3.5 in master's, 3 years of teaching experience, 3 letters of recommendation, writing samples. Additional exam requirements/recommendations for international students: Required—TOEFL (minimum score 527 paper-based; 197 computer-based; 71 iBT). *Application deadline:* For fall admission, 7/15 for domestic students; for spring admission, 10/15 for domestic students. Applications are processed on a rolling basis. Application fee: $30. Electronic applications accepted. *Expenses:* Tuition: Full-time $12,200; part-time $610 per credit. Required fees: $150. Full-time tuition and fees vary according to course load and program. *Financial support:* In 2006–07, fellowships with partial tuition reimbursements (averaging $2,581 per year); career-related internships or fieldwork, institutionally sponsored loans, and unspecified assistantships also available. Support available to part-time students. Financial award application deadline: 3/15; financial award applicants required to submit FAFSA. *Faculty research:* Nanotechnology, writing pedagogy and writing centers, violence in schools, Virginia/Shenandoah Valley history and culture, stress in children. *Unit head:* Dr. Calvin Allen, Dean, 540-665-4587, Fax: 540-665-4644, E-mail: callen@su.edu. *Application contact:* David Anthony, Dean of Admissions, 540-665-4581, Fax: 540-665-4627, E-mail: admit@su.edu.

See Close-Up on page 919.

Siena Heights University, Graduate College, Program in Teacher Education, Concentration in Elementary Education, Adrian, MI 49221-1796. Offers elementary education/reading (MA). Part-time programs available. *Degree requirements:* For master's, thesis, presentation. *Entrance requirements:* For master's, interview, minimum GPA of 3.0.

Sierra Nevada College, Teacher Education Program, Incline Village, NV 89451. Offers elementary education (MAT); secondary education (MAT). Part-time and evening/weekend programs available. *Faculty:* 2 full-time (both women), 26 part-time/adjunct (16 women). *Students:* 179 full-time (136 women), 85 part-time (58 women); includes 21 minority (6 African Americans, 1 American Indian/Alaska Native, 2 Asian Americans or Pacific Islanders, 12 Hispanic Americans). Average age 35. In 2006, 29 degrees awarded. *Median time to degree:* Master's–2.5 years full-time, 3.5 years part-time. *Degree requirements:* For master's, thesis, PRAXIS I and II, comprehensive exam, registration. *Entrance requirements:* For master's, 2 letters of recommendation, minimum GPA of 3.0. *Application deadline:* For fall admission, 8/16 priority date for domestic students; for winter admission, 1/10 priority date for domestic students; for spring admission, 5/25 priority date for domestic students. Applications are processed on a rolling basis. Application fee: $50. *Expenses:* Tuition: Full-time $3,590; part-time $350 per credit. *Financial support:* In 2006–07, 230 students received support. Federal Work-Study available. Support available to part-time students. Financial award application deadline: 8/16; financial award applicants required to submit FAFSA. *Unit head:* Dr. Francesca Bero, Statewide Director, 775-831-1314, Fax: 775-832-1686, E-mail: fbero@sierranevada.edu. *Application contact:* Katrina Midgley, Teacher Education Admissions Counselor, 775-831-1314 Ext. 7517, Fax: 775-832-1694, E-mail: kmidgley@sierranevada.edu.

Simmons College, Graduate School, College of Arts and Sciences Graduate Studies, Department of Education, Program in Teacher Preparation, Boston, MA 02115. Offers educational leadership (MS Ed, CAGS); elementary education (MAT, CAGS); general education (CAGS); general purposes (MS); middle school education (MAT, CAGS); professional license (CAGS); professional license: elementary (MS Ed); professional license: middle/high (MS Ed); secondary education (MAT, CAGS); urban education (MS Ed, CAGS). *Faculty:* 4 full-time (3 women), 22 part-time/adjunct (13 women). *Students:* 61 full-time (53 women), 141 part-time (128 women); includes 33 minority (13 African Americans, 10 Asian Americans or Pacific Islanders, 10 Hispanic Americans), 1 international. Average age 24. 86 applicants, 77% accepted, 39 enrolled. In 2006, 128 master's, 12 other advanced degrees awarded. *Degree requirements:* For master's, student teaching experience or internship. *Entrance requirements:* For master's, GRE General Test, MAT or Massachusetts Tests for Educator Licensure (MTEL). Additional exam requirements/recommendations for international students: Required—TOEFL (minimum score 600 paper-based; 250 computer-based; 100 iBT). *Application deadline:* For fall admission, 8/1 priority date for domestic and international students; for spring admission, 12/15 priority date for domestic and international students. Applications are processed on a rolling basis. Application fee: $35. Electronic applications accepted. *Expenses: Contact institution. Financial support:* Teaching assistantships, career-related internships or fieldwork, Federal Work-Study, institutionally sponsored loans, scholarships/grants, and tuition waivers (partial) available. Support available to part-time students. Financial award application deadline: 3/1; financial award applicants required to submit FAFSA. *Faculty research:* Putting standards/frameworks into practice, restructuring middle and high schools, interactive teaching and learning developing curriculum for Third World countries. Total annual research expenditures: $110,000. *Unit head:* Lynda Johnson, Assistant Dean, 617-521-2576, Fax: 617-521-3133, E-mail: gsa@simmons.edu. *Application contact:* Kristen Haack, Director, Graduate Studies Admission, 617-521-2915, Fax: 617-521-3058, E-mail: gsa@simmons.edu.

Sinte Gleska University, Graduate Education Program, Rosebud, SD 57555. Offers elementary education (M Ed). Part-time and evening/weekend programs available. *Degree requirements:* For master's, thesis. *Entrance requirements:* For master's, 2 years of experience in elementary education, minimum GPA of 2.5, South Dakota elementary education certification. *Faculty research:* American Indian graduate education, teaching of Native American students.

Slippery Rock University of Pennsylvania, Graduate Studies (Recruitment), College of Education, Department of Elementary Education and Early Childhood, Slippery Rock, PA 16057-1383. Offers early childhood education (M Ed); math/science (M Ed); reading (M Ed). *Accreditation:* NCATE. Part-time and evening/weekend programs available. *Degree requirements:* For master's, thesis (for some programs), reflective presentation, comprehensive exam (for some programs). *Entrance requirements:* For master's, GRE General Test, MAT, minimum GPA of 2.75 (minimum GPA of 3.0 for initial certification programs). Additional exam requirements/recommendations for international students: Required—TOEFL (minimum score 550 paper-based; 213 computer-based). *Application deadline:* For fall admission, 7/1 priority date for domestic and international students; for spring admission, 11/1 priority date for domestic and international students. Applications are processed on a rolling basis. Application fee: $25. Electronic applications accepted. *Expenses:* Tuition, state resident: part-time $336 per credit. Tuition, nonresident: part-time $538 per credit. Required fees: $84 per credit. $37 per semester. *Financial support:* Career-related internships or fieldwork, Federal Work-Study, scholarships/grants, and unspecified assistantships available. Support available to part-time students. Financial award application deadline: 5/1; financial award applicants required to submit FAFSA. *Unit head:* Dr. Suzanne Rose, Graduate Coordinator, 724-738-2863, Fax: 724-738-2880, E-mail: suzanne.rose@sn.edu. *Application contact:* April Longwell, Interim Director of Graduate Studies, 724-738-2051 Ext. 2116, Fax: 724-738-2146, E-mail: graduate.studies@sru.edu.

Smith College, Graduate Programs, Department of Education and Child Study, Program in Elementary Education, Northampton, MA 01063. Offers middle school education (Ed M). Part-time programs available. *Faculty:* 6 full-time (4 women), 3 part-time/adjunct (2 women). *Students:* 11 full-time (7 women), 3 part-time (all women), 1 international. Average age 28. 23 applicants, 78% accepted, 14 enrolled. In 2006, 9 degrees awarded. *Entrance requirements:* For master's, GRE General Test or MAT. *Application deadline:* For fall admission, 4/1 for domestic students, 1/15 for international students; for spring admission, 12/1 for domestic students. Application fee: $60. *Expenses:* Tuition: Full-time $32,320; part-time $1,010 per credit. Tuition and fees vary according to course load. *Financial support:* In 2006–07, 14 students received support, including 6 teaching assistantships with full tuition reimbursements available (averaging $11,150 per year); fellowships, research assistantships, career-related internships or fieldwork, institutionally sponsored loans, and scholarships/grants also available. Support available to part-time students. Financial award application deadline: 1/15. *Unit head:* Alan Rudnitsky, Graduate Student Adviser, 413-585-3261, E-mail: arudnits@smith.edu.

Sonoma State University, School of Education, Department of Literacy Studies and Elementary Education, Rohnert Park, CA 94928-3609. Offers MA. Part-time and evening/weekend programs available. *Faculty:* 5 full-time (3 women). *Degree requirements:* For master's, thesis or alternative. *Entrance requirements:* For master's, GRE General Test, minimum GPA of 2.5. Application fee: $55. *Expenses:* Tuition, nonresident: part-time $339 per unit. Required fees: $1,464 per term. *Financial support:* Application deadline: 3/2. *Unit head:* Dr. Charles Elster, Chair, 707-664-3115, E-mail: elster@sonoma.edu.

South Carolina State University, School of Graduate Studies, Department of Education, Orangeburg, SC 29117-0001. Offers early childhood and special education (M Ed); early childhood education (MAT); elementary education (M Ed, MAT); engineering (MAT); general science (MAT); mathematics (MAT); secondary education (M Ed), including biology education, business education, counselor education, English education, home economics education, industrial education, mathematics education, science education, social studies education; special education (M Ed), including emotionally handicapped, learning disabilities, mentally handicapped. *Accreditation:* NCATE. Part-time and evening/weekend programs available. *Faculty:* 21 full-time (10 women), 4 part-time/adjunct (0 women). *Students:* 34 full-time (28 women), 33 part-time (25 women); includes 63 minority (61 African Americans, 1 American Indian/Alaska Native, 1 Asian American or Pacific Islander). Average age 35. 46 applicants, 67% accepted, 19 enrolled. In 2006, 28 degrees awarded. *Degree requirements:* For master's, departmental qualifying exam, thesis optional. *Entrance requirements:* For master's, GRE General Test, NTE, interview, teaching certificate. *Application deadline:* For fall admission, 6/15 priority date for domestic students, 6/15 for international students; for spring admission, 11/1 for domestic and international students. Applications are processed on a rolling basis. Application fee: $25. Electronic applications accepted. *Expenses:* Tuition, state resident: full-time $7,278. Tuition, nonresident: full-time $14,322. *Financial support:* Fellowships, research assistantships, career-related internships or fieldwork, Federal Work-Study, and institutionally sponsored loans available. Financial award application deadline: 6/1. *Faculty research:* Critical thinking, child abuse, stress, test-taking skills, conflict resolution, mainstreaming. *Unit head:* Dr. Gail Joyner-Fleming, Interim Chair, 803-533-3769, Fax: 803-536-8492, E-mail: zf-gfleming@scsu.edu. *Application contact:* Annette Hazzard-Jones, Program Coordinator II, 803-536-8809, Fax: 803-536-8812, E-mail: zs_ahazzard@scsu.edu.

Southeastern Louisiana University, College of Education and Human Development, Department of Teaching and Learning, Hammond, LA 70402. Offers curriculum and instruction (M Ed); elementary education (MAT); secondary education (MAT); special education (M Ed, MAT). *Accreditation:* NCATE. Part-time programs available. *Faculty:* 23 full-time (18 women), 1 (woman) part-time/adjunct. *Students:* 31 full-time (27 women), 300 part-time (269 women); includes 50 minority (39 African Americans, 2 Asian Americans or Pacific Islanders, 9 Hispanic Americans), 3 international. Average age 33. 47 applicants, 100% accepted, 31 enrolled. In 2006, 101 degrees awarded. *Degree requirements:* For master's, comprehensive exam (for some programs). *Entrance requirements:* For master's, GRE, PRAXIS (MAT), minimum GPA of 2.5. Additional exam requirements/recommendations for international students: Required—TOEFL (minimum score 500 paper-based; 173 computer-based). *Application deadline:* For fall admission, 7/15 priority date for domestic students, 6/1 priority date for international students; for spring admission, 12/1 priority date for domestic students, 10/1 priority date for international students. Applications are processed on a rolling basis. Application fee: $20 ($30 for international students). Electronic applications accepted. *Expenses:* Tuition, state resident: full-time $2,216; part-time $123 per credit. Tuition, nonresident: full-time $6,212; part-time $345 per credit. Required fees: $986; $55 per credit. Part-time tuition and fees vary according to course load. *Financial support:* Federal Work-Study, institutionally sponsored loans, unspecified assistantships, and administrative assistantship available. Support available to part-time students. Financial award application deadline: 5/1; financial award applicants required to submit FAFSA. *Faculty research:* Reading, instructional methodology, science education, math education, early childhood. *Unit head:* Dr. Shirley Jacob, Department Head, 985-549-2221, Fax: 985-549-5009, E-mail: sjacob@selu.edu. *Application contact:* Sandra Meyers, Graduate Admissions Analyst, 985-549-2066, Fax: 985-549-5632, E-mail: admissions@selu.edu.

Southeastern Oklahoma State University, Graduate School, School of Education, Durant, OK 74701-0609. Offers educational administration (M Ed); educational instruction and leadership (M Ed); educational technology (M Ed); elementary education (M Ed); school counseling (M Ed); secondary education (M Ed). *Accreditation:* NCATE. Part-time and evening/weekend programs available. *Degree requirements:* For master's, portfolio (M Ed), thesis optional. *Entrance requirements:* For master's, GRE General Test (MBS), minimum GPA of 3.0 in last 60 hours or 2.75 overall. Additional exam requirements/recommendations for international students: Required—TOEFL (minimum score 550 paper-based; 213 computer-based). Electronic applications accepted.

Southeast Missouri State University, School of Graduate Studies, Department of Elementary and Special Education, Program in Elementary Education, Cape Girardeau, MO 63701-4799. Offers MA. *Accreditation:* NCATE. Part-time and evening/weekend programs available. *Faculty:* 9 full-time (7 women). *Students:* 3 full-time (all women), 68 part-time (67 women); includes 1 minority (African American) Average age 34. 36 applicants, 86% accepted. In 2006, 1 degree awarded. *Degree requirements:* For master's, thesis or alternative. *Entrance requirements:* For master's, GRE General Test, MAT, PRAXIS, minimum GPA of 2.75. Additional exam requirements/recommendations for international students: Required—TOEFL (minimum score 550 paper-based; 213 computer-based). *Application deadline:* For fall admission, 8/1 for domestic students, 4/1 for international students; for spring admission, 11/21 for domestic students, 10/1 for international students. Applications are processed on a rolling basis. Application fee: $20 ($100 for international students). Electronic applications accepted. *Financial support:* In 2006–07, 10 students received support. Career-related internships or fieldwork available. Financial award applicants required to submit FAFSA. *Application contact:* Marsha L. Arant, Senior Administrative Assistant Office of Graduate Studies, 573-651-2192, Fax: 573-651-2001, E-mail: marant@semo.edu.

Southern Arkansas University–Magnolia, Graduate Programs, Magnolia, AR 71753. Offers computer and information sciences (MS); counseling (MS); education (M Ed), including counseling and development, educational administration and supervision, elementary education, secondary education; kinesiology (MS); library media and information specialist (M Ed); school counseling (M Ed); teaching (MAT). *Accreditation:* NCATE. Part-time and evening/weekend programs available. *Degree requirements:* For master's, thesis optional. *Entrance requirements:* For master's, GRE or MAT, minimum GPA of 2.75. *Faculty research:* Alternative certification for teachers, supervision of instruction, instructional leadership, counseling.

Southern Connecticut State University, School of Graduate Studies, School of Education, Department of Education, New Haven, CT 06515-1355. Offers classroom teacher specialist (Diploma); elementary education (MS). *Accreditation:* NCATE. Part-time and evening/weekend programs available. *Faculty:* 14 full-time, 12 part-time/adjunct. *Students:* 123 full-time (108 women), 253 part-time (211 women); includes 22 minority (10 African Americans, 1 American Indian/Alaska Native, 3 Asian Americans or Pacific Islanders, 8 Hispanic Americans). 81 applicants, 74% accepted, 53 enrolled. In 2006, 109 degrees awarded. *Degree requirements:* For master's, thesis or alternative. *Entrance requirements:* For master's, interview, minimum QPA of 2.5; for Diploma, master's degree. *Application deadline:* For fall admission, 7/15 priority date for domestic students. Applications are processed on a rolling basis. Application fee: $50. Electronic applications accepted. *Financial support:* Application deadline: 4/15. *Unit head:* Dr. Maria Diamantis, Graduate Coordinator, 203-392-6143, Fax: 203-392-6473, E-mail: diamantism1@southernct.edu.

Southern Illinois University Edwardsville, Graduate Studies and Research, School of Education, Department of Curriculum and Instruction, Program in Elementary Education, Edwardsville, IL 62026-0001. Offers MS Ed. *Accreditation:* NCATE. Part-time and evening/weekend programs available. *Students:* 2 full-time (both women), 71 part-time (67 women); includes 2 minority (both African Americans) Average age 33. 33 applicants, 64% accepted. In 2006, 65 degrees awarded. *Degree requirements:* For master's, thesis or alternative, final exam. *Entrance requirements:* For master's, MAT, teaching certificate. Additional exam requirements/recommendations for international students: Required—TOEFL. *Application deadline:* For fall admission, 7/20 for domestic students, 6/1 for international students; for spring admission, 12/14 for domestic students, 10/1 for international students. Application fee: $30. Electronic applications accepted. *Financial support:* Fellowships, research assistantships, teaching assistantships, Federal Work-Study, institutionally sponsored loans, and unspecified assistantships available. Support available to part-time students. Financial award application deadline: 3/1; financial award applicants required to submit FAFSA. *Unit head:* Dr. Ann Taylor, Director, 618-650-3446, E-mail: ataylor@siue.edu.

Southern New Hampshire University, School of Education, Manchester, NH 03106-1045. Offers business education (MS); child development (M Ed); computer technology education (Certificate); curriculum and instruction (M Ed); education (M Ed, CAS); elementary education (M Ed); general special education (Certificate); school business administrator (Certificate); school counseling (M Ed); school psychology (M Ed); secondary education (M Ed); training and development (Certificate). Part-time and evening/weekend programs available. Post-baccalaureate distance learning degree programs offered. *Faculty:* 6 full-time (3 women), 9 part-time/adjunct (7 women). *Students:* Average age 35. In 2006, 52 degrees awarded. *Degree requirements:* For master's, thesis or alternative, comprehensive exam (for some programs). *Entrance requirements:* For master's, GRE General Test or MAT, minimum GPA of 3.0. Additional exam requirements/recommendations for international students: Required—TOEFL (minimum score 550 paper-based; 213 computer-based). *Application deadline:* Applications are processed on a rolling basis. Application fee: $25. Electronic applications accepted. *Expenses: Contact institution. Financial support:* Institutionally sponsored loans available. Financial award applicants required to submit FAFSA. *Unit head:* Dr. Patrick J. Hartwick, Dean, 603-668-2211 Ext. 4698, Fax: 603-629-4673, E-mail: p.hartwick@snhu.edu. *Application*

Elementary Education

Southern New Hampshire University (continued)

contact: Scott Durand, Director of Graduate Enrollment Services, 603-644-3102 Ext. 3338, Fax: 603-644-3144, E-mail: s.durand@snhu.edu.

Southern Oregon University, Graduate Studies, School of Social Sciences, Department of Education, Ashland, OR 97520. Offers elementary education (MA Ed, MS Ed), including classroom teacher, early childhood, handicapped learner, reading, supervision; secondary education (MA Ed, MS Ed), including classroom teacher, handicapped learner, reading, supervision; teaching (MAT). *Degree requirements:* For master's, thesis optional. *Entrance requirements:* For master's, GRE General Test, minimum GPA of 3.0. Electronic applications accepted.

Southern University and Agricultural and Mechanical College, Graduate School, College of Education, Department of Curriculum and Instruction, Baton Rouge, LA 70813. Offers elementary education (M Ed); media (M Ed); secondary education (M Ed). *Degree requirements:* For master's, thesis optional. *Entrance requirements:* For master's, GMAT or GRE General Test. Additional exam requirements/recommendations for international students: Required—TOEFL (minimum score 525 paper-based; 193 computer-based).

Southwestern Adventist University, Education Department, Graduate Program, Keene, TX 76059. Offers elementary education (M Ed). Part-time and evening/weekend programs available. *Degree requirements:* For master's, thesis or alternative, professional paper. *Entrance requirements:* For master's, GRE General Test.

Southwestern Oklahoma State University, College of Professional and Graduate Studies, School of Behavioral Sciences and Education, Specialization in Elementary Education, Weatherford, OK 73096-3098. Offers M Ed. M Ed distance learning degree program offered to Oklahoma residents only. *Accreditation:* NCATE. Part-time and evening/weekend programs available. *Degree requirements:* For master's, exam. *Entrance requirements:* For master's, GRE General Test or minimum undergraduate GPA of 3.0. Additional exam requirements/recommendations for international students: Required—TOEFL.

Spalding University, Graduate Studies, College of Education, Programs in Education, Louisville, KY 40203-2188. Offers elementary school education (MAT); general education (MA); high school education (MAT); middle school education (MAT); school administration (MA); special education (learning and behavioral disorders) (MAT). MAT degree programs offered for first teaching certificate/license students. *Accreditation:* NCATE. Part-time and evening/weekend programs available. *Degree requirements:* For master's, portfolio, final project, clinical experience. *Entrance requirements:* For master's, GRE General Test or MAT, interview, recommendations, resumé. Additional exam requirements/recommendations for international students: Required—TOEFL. Electronic applications accepted. *Faculty research:* Instructional technology, achievement gap, classroom management, assessment.

Spring Hill College, Graduate Programs, Program in Education, Mobile, AL 36608-1791. Offers early childhood education (MAT, MS Ed); elementary education (MAT, MS Ed); secondary education (MAT, MS Ed). Part-time and evening/weekend programs available. *Faculty:* 2 full-time (both women), 7 part-time/adjunct (5 women). *Students:* 11 full-time (10 women), 44 part-time (34 women); includes 19 minority (all African Americans) Average age 33. In 2006, 21 degrees awarded. *Degree requirements:* For master's, comprehensive exam. *Entrance requirements:* For master's, GRE, MAT, NTE, or PRAXIS, minimum undergraduate GPA of 3.0. Additional exam requirements/recommendations for international students: Required—TOEFL (minimum score 550 paper-based; 213 computer-based). *Application deadline:* For fall admission, 8/1 priority date for domestic students, 6/1 priority date for international students; for spring admission, 12/1 priority date for domestic students, 11/1 priority date for international students. Applications are processed on a rolling basis. Application fee: $25 ($35 for international students). Electronic applications accepted. *Expenses: Contact institution. Financial support:* In 2006–07, 49 students received support. Career-related internships or fieldwork and scholarships/grants available. Support available to part-time students. Financial award applicants required to submit FAFSA. *Unit head:* Dr. Ann A. Adams, Chair of Teacher Education, 251-380-3479, Fax: 251-460-2184, E-mail: aadams@shc.edu. *Application contact:* Joyce Genz, Dean of Life Long Learning and Director of Graduate Programs, 251-380-3094, Fax: 251-460-2190, E-mail: grad@shc.edu.

State University of New York at Binghamton, Graduate School, School of Education, Program in Early Childhood and Elementary Education, Binghamton, NY 13902-6000. Offers MS Ed. *Accreditation:* Teacher Education Accreditation Council. Part-time and evening/weekend programs available. *Students:* 11 full-time (9 women), 11 part-time (9 women); includes 1 minority (Hispanic American) Average age 29. 1 applicant, 0% accepted. In 2006, 8 degrees awarded. *Entrance requirements:* For master's, GRE General Test. Additional exam requirements/recommendations for international students: Required—TOEFL. *Application deadline:* For fall admission, 4/15 priority date for domestic students, 1/15 priority date for international students; for spring admission, 11/1 for domestic students, 10/1 priority date for international students. Applications are processed on a rolling basis. Application fee: $60. Electronic applications accepted. *Financial support:* In 2006–07, 10 students received support, including 10 teaching assistantships with full tuition reimbursements available (averaging $5,507 per year); fellowships, research assistantships with full tuition reimbursements available, career-related internships or fieldwork, Federal Work-Study, institutionally sponsored loans, and unspecified assistantships also available. Support available to part-time students. Financial award application deadline: 2/15. *Unit head:* Dr. Nicholas Paley, Coordinator, 607-777-2301, E-mail: npaley@binghamton.edu.

State University of New York at Fredonia, Graduate Studies, College of Education, Program in Elementary Education, Fredonia, NY 14063-1136. Offers MS Ed. *Accreditation:* NCATE. Part-time and evening/weekend programs available. *Faculty:* 7 full-time (4 women), 4 part-time/adjunct (0 women). *Students:* 21 full-time (18 women), 39 part-time (27 women). Average age 27. In 2006, 51 degrees awarded. *Degree requirements:* For master's, thesis optional. *Application deadline:* For fall admission, 8/5 for domestic students; for spring admission, 12/1 for domestic students. Application fee: $50. *Expenses:* Tuition, state resident: full-time $6,900; part-time $288 per credit hour. Tuition, nonresident: full-time $10,920; part-time $455 per credit hour. Required fees: $1,132; $47 per credit hour. *Financial support:* In 2006–07, 4 teaching assistantships (averaging $6,500 per year) were awarded; research assistantships, career-related internships or fieldwork and tuition waivers (full and partial) also available. Support available to part-time students. Financial award application deadline: 3/15. *Unit head:* Dr. Christine Givner, Dean, College of Education, 716-673-3311, E-mail: christine.givner@fredonia.edu.

State University of New York at New Paltz, Graduate School, Faculty of Education, Department of Elementary Education, New Paltz, NY 12561. Offers childhood education (MS Ed); childhood education (1-6) (MST); early childhood education (B-2) (MST); literacy education (5-12) (MS Ed); literacy education (B-6) (MS Ed). *Accreditation:* NCATE. Part-time and evening/weekend programs available. *Faculty:* 10 full-time (6 women), 42 part-time/adjunct (33 women). *Students:* 53 full-time (47 women), 135 part-time (124 women); includes 11 minority (4 African Americans, 1 Asian American or Pacific Islander, 6 Hispanic Americans). Average age 30. 142 applicants. In 2006, 91 degrees awarded. *Degree requirements:* For master's, portfolio. *Entrance requirements:* For master's, GRE/MAT (MST), minimum GPA of 3.0, teaching certificate (MS Ed). Additional exam requirements/recommendations for international students: Required—TOEFL (minimum score 550 paper-based; 213 computer-based; 80 iBT). *Application deadline:* For fall admission, 4/1 for domestic and international students; for spring admission, 11/1 for domestic and international students. Application fee: $50. Electronic applications accepted. *Expenses:* Tuition, state resident: full-time $6,900; part-time $288 per credit hour. Tuition, nonresident: full-time $10,920; part-time $455 per credit hour. *Financial support:* Federal Work-Study and institutionally sponsored loans available. *Unit head:* Dr. Winifred Montgomery, Chair, 845-257-2860, E-mail: montgomw@newpaltz.edu.

State University of New York at Oswego, Graduate Studies, School of Education, Department of Curriculum and Instruction, Oswego, NY 13126. Offers art education (MAT); elementary education (MS Ed); literacy education (MS Ed); secondary education (MS Ed); special education (MS Ed). Part-time and evening/weekend programs available. *Faculty:* 23 full-time, 45 part-time/adjunct. *Students:* 184 full-time (139 women), 220 part-time (185 women); includes 12 minority (5 African Americans, 1 American Indian/Alaska Native, 1 Asian American or Pacific Islander, 5 Hispanic Americans), 1 international. Average age 33. 266 applicants, 89% accepted. In 2006, 255 degrees awarded. *Degree requirements:* For master's, thesis optional. *Entrance requirements:* For master's, GRE General Test, minimum GPA of 2.7, provisional teaching certificate. Additional exam requirements/recommendations for international students: Required—TOEFL (minimum score 560 paper-based; 220 computer-based). *Application deadline:* For fall admission, 3/1 for domestic students; for spring admission, 10/1 for domestic students. Application fee: $50. *Expenses:* Tuition, state resident: part-time $288 per credit. Tuition, nonresident: part-time $455 per credit. Tuition and fees vary according to program. *Financial support:* In 2006–07, 9 students received support, including 3 fellowships, 6 teaching assistantships with full tuition reimbursements available; career-related internships or fieldwork, Federal Work-Study, institutionally sponsored loans, scholarships/grants, and unspecified assistantships also available. Support available to part-time students. Financial award application deadline: 4/1; financial award applicants required to submit FAFSA. *Faculty research:* Classroom applications for microcomputers; classroom questioning, wait-time, and achievement; values clarification and academic achievement. *Unit head:* Dr. Pamela Michel, Chair, 315-312-4052. *Application contact:* Dr. Joyce Smith, Coordinator, Graduate Education, 315-312-4052.

State University of New York at Plattsburgh, Division of Education, Health, and Human Services, Department of Adolescence Education/Health, Plattsburgh, NY 12901-2681. Offers adolescence education (MST); biology 7-12 (MST); chemistry 7-12 (MST); earth science 7-12 (MST); English 7-12 (MST); French 7-12 (MST); mathematics 7-12 (MST); physics 7-12 (MST); social studies 7-12 (MST); Spanish 7-12 (MST). *Faculty:* 4 full-time (3 women), 2 part-time/adjunct (0 women). *Students:* 58 full-time (38 women), 14 part-time (10 women); includes 5 minority (1 African American, 4 Hispanic Americans). Average age 30. 49 applicants, 78% accepted, 32 enrolled. In 2006, 30 degrees awarded. *Degree requirements:* For master's, comprehensive exam or research project. *Entrance requirements:* For master's, GRE General Test or MAT, minimum GPA of 2.5. *Application deadline:* For fall admission, 2/15 priority date for domestic students; for spring admission, 10/15 priority date for domestic students. Applications are processed on a rolling basis. Application fee: $50. *Expenses:* Tuition, state resident: full-time $6,900; part-time $288 per credit hour. Tuition, nonresident: full-time $10,920; part-time $455 per credit hour. *Financial support:* Application deadline: 4/15; *Unit head:* Dr. Lois Beach, Chair, 578-564-5750, E-mail: lois.beach@plattsburgh.edu. *Application contact:* Sharon Derr, Assistant Director, Graduate Admission, 518-564-4723, Fax: 518-564-4722, E-mail: derrsl@plattsburgh.edu.

State University of New York at Plattsburgh, Division of Education, Health, and Human Services, Department of Childhood Education, Plattsburgh, NY 12901-2681. Offers childhood education (grades 1-6) (MST). *Faculty:* 8 full-time (6 women), 6 part-time/adjunct (2 women). *Students:* 28 full-time (22 women), 3 part-time (2 women); includes 28 minority (1 American Indian/Alaska Native, 27 Hispanic Americans). Average age 30. 19 applicants, 95% accepted, 11 enrolled. In 2006, 19 degrees awarded. *Degree requirements:* For master's, comprehensive exam or research project, thesis optional. *Entrance requirements:* For master's, GRE General Test or MAT, minimum GPA of 2.5. *Application deadline:* For fall admission, 2/15 priority date for domestic students; for spring admission, 10/15 priority date for domestic students. Applications are processed on a rolling basis. Application fee: $50. *Expenses:* Tuition, state resident: full-time $6,900; part-time $288 per credit hour. Tuition, nonresident: full-time $10,920; part-time $455 per credit hour. *Financial support:* In 2006–07, 30 students received support. Federal Work-Study available. Support available to part-time students. Financial award application deadline: 4/15; financial award applicants required to submit FAFSA. *Unit head:* Dr. Michael Morgan, Interim Chair, 518-564-5748, Fax: 518-564-4069. *Application contact:* Sharon Derr, Assistant Director, Graduate Admission, 518-564-4723, Fax: 518-564-4722, E-mail: derrsl@plattsburgh.edu.

State University of New York College at Geneseo, Graduate Studies, School of Education, Program in Elementary Education, Geneseo, NY 14454-1401. Offers MS Ed. Part-time and evening/weekend programs available. *Faculty:* 3 full-time (2 women). *Students:* Average age 24. In 2006, 21 degrees awarded. *Degree requirements:* For master's, thesis optional. *Entrance requirements:* For master's, GRE General Test. *Application deadline:* For fall admission, 6/1 priority date for domestic students; for spring admission, 10/1 for domestic students. *Financial support:* Fellowships, teaching assistantships, career-related internships or fieldwork, Federal Work-Study, and institutionally sponsored loans available. Financial award application deadline: 4/1; financial award applicants required to submit FAFSA. *Unit head:* Dr. Osman Alawiye, Chairperson, School of Education, 585-245-5560, Fax: 585-245-5220.

State University of New York College at Oneonta, Graduate Studies, Division of Education, Department of Elementary and Reading Education, Oneonta, NY 13820-4015. Offers childhood education (MS Ed); literacy education (MS Ed). *Accreditation:* NCATE. Part-time and evening/weekend programs available. *Entrance requirements:* For master's, GRE General Test.

State University of New York College at Potsdam, School of Education, Program in Elementary Education, Potsdam, NY 13676. Offers MS Ed, MST. *Accreditation:* NCATE. Part-time and evening/weekend programs available. Postbaccalaureate distance learning degree programs offered. *Faculty:* 5 full-time (4 women), 5 part-time/adjunct (all women). *Students:* 251 full-time (196 women), 44 part-time (28 women), 235 international. In 2006, 200 degrees awarded. *Degree requirements:* For master's, variable foreign language requirement, culminating experience, thesis optional. *Entrance requirements:* For master's, minimum GPA of 2.75 in last 60 hours of course work. Additional exam requirements/recommendations for international students: Required—TOEFL (minimum score 550 paper-based; 213 computer-based). *Application deadline:* Applications are processed on a rolling basis. Application fee: $50. *Financial support:* Fellowships, teaching assistantships, career-related internships or fieldwork, Federal Work-Study, and scholarships/grants available. Support available to part-time students. Financial award application deadline: 3/1. *Unit head:* Dr. Sandra Chadwick, Chairperson, Early Childhood, Childhood and General Professional Education Department, 315-267-2502, Fax: 315-267-4802, E-mail: chadwisc@potsdam.edu. *Application contact:* Peter Cutler, Graduate Admissions Counselor, 315-267-3154, Fax: 315-267-4802, E-mail: cutlerpj@potsdam.edu.

Stephen F. Austin State University, Graduate School, College of Education, Department of Elementary Education, Program in Elementary Education, Nacogdoches, TX 75962. Offers M Ed. *Accreditation:* NCATE. *Degree requirements:* For master's, comprehensive exam. *Entrance requirements:* For master's, GRE General Test. Additional exam requirements/recommendations for international students: Required—TOEFL.

Sul Ross State University, Rio Grande College of Sul Ross State University, Alpine, TX 79832. Offers business administration (MBA); teacher education (M Ed), including bilingual education, counseling, educational diagnostics, elementary education, general education, reading, school administration, secondary education. Part-time and evening/weekend programs available. *Degree requirements:* For master's, thesis optional. *Entrance requirements:* For master's, GMAT or GRE General Test, minimum GPA of 2.5 in last 60 hours of undergraduate work. *Faculty research:* Drug and substance abuse counseling, U.S.-Mexico border economic development.

Sul Ross State University, School of Professional Studies, Department of Teacher Education, Program in Elementary Education, Alpine, TX 79832. Offers M Ed. Part-time and evening/weekend programs available. *Degree requirements:* For master's, thesis optional. *Entrance requirements:* For master's, GMAT or GRE General Test, minimum GPA of 2.5 in last 60 hours of undergraduate work.

Sunbridge College, Programs in Education, Spring Valley, NY 10977. Offers Waldorf early childhood education (MS Ed); Waldorf elementary school education (MS Ed). Part-time programs available. *Entrance requirements:* For master's, interview.

Teachers College Columbia University, Graduate Faculty of Education, Department of Curriculum and Teaching, Program in Elementary/Childhood Education, Preservice, New York, NY 10027-6696. Offers MA. *Accreditation:* NCATE. *Faculty:* 3 full-time (all women), 9 part-time/adjunct. *Students:* 27 full-time (23 women), 51 part-time (48 women); includes 36 minority (9 African Americans, 24 Asian Americans or Pacific Islanders, 3 Hispanic Americans), 3 international. Average age 31. 170 applicants, 51% accepted, 44 enrolled. In 2006, 53 degrees awarded. *Application deadline:* For fall admission, 5/15 for domestic students; for spring admission, 12/1 for domestic students. Application fee: $65. *Expenses:* Tuition: Full-time $23,400; part-time $975 per credit. Required fees: $320 per term. *Financial support:* Career-related internships or fieldwork, Federal Work-Study, and tuition waivers (full and partial) available. Financial award application deadline: 2/1. *Faculty research:* Teaching of reading and writing, reforming schools, urban education, curriculum development. *Application contact:* Peter Shon, Assistant Director of Admission, 212-678-3305, Fax: 212-678-4171, E-mail: shon@exchange.tc.columbia.edu.

See Close-Up on page 1127.

Temple University, Graduate School, College of Education, Department of Curriculum, Instruction, and Technology in Education, Philadelphia, PA 19122-6096. Offers applied behavioral analysis (MS Ed); career and technical education (MS Ed); early childhood education and elementary education (MS Ed); English education (MS Ed); language arts education (Ed D); math/science education (Ed D); mathematics education (MS Ed); science education (MS Ed); second and foreign language education (MS Ed); special education (MS Ed); teaching English as a second language (MS Ed). Part-time and evening/weekend programs available. *Faculty:* 31 full-time (14 women). *Students:* 96 full-time (71 women), 482 part-time (336 women); includes 109 minority (67 African Americans, 3 American Indian/Alaska Native, 23 Asian Americans or Pacific Islanders, 16 Hispanic Americans), 28 international. 308 applicants, 64% accepted, 116 enrolled. In 2006, 225 master's, 21 doctorates awarded. Terminal master's awarded for partial completion of doctoral program. *Degree requirements:* For master's, thesis or alternative; for doctorate, thesis/dissertation. *Entrance requirements:* For master's and doctorate, GRE General Test or MAT, minimum GPA of 3.0. Additional exam requirements/recommendations for international students: Required—TOEFL (minimum score 550 paper-based; 213 computer-based; 79 iBT). *Application deadline:* For fall admission, 4/1 for domestic students, 12/15 for international students; for spring admission, 10/1 for domestic students, 8/1 for international students. Application fee: $50. Electronic applications accepted. *Expenses:* Tuition, state resident: full-time $12,264; part-time $511 per credit. Tuition, nonresident: full-time $17,904; part-time $746 per credit. Required fees: $84 per course. Tuition and fees vary according to program. *Financial support:* Fellowships, research assistantships with full tuition reimbursements, teaching assistantships with full tuition reimbursements available. Financial award application deadline: 1/15; financial award applicants required to submit FAFSA. *Faculty research:* School improvement, problem solving, literacy, language development. *Unit head:* Dr. Thomas Walker, Chair, 215-204-2117, Fax: 215-204-1414, E-mail: tjwalker@temple.edu.

Tennessee State University, The School of Graduate Studies and Research, College of Education, Department of Teaching and Learning, Program in Elementary Education, Nashville, TN 37209-1561. Offers M Ed, MA Ed, Ed D. *Accreditation:* NCATE. *Degree requirements:* For master's, project; for doctorate, thesis/dissertation, comprehensive exam. *Entrance requirements:* For master's, GRE General Test, GRE Subject Test, or MAT, minimum GPA of 2.5; for doctorate, GRE General Test, GRE Subject Test, or MAT, master's degree, minimum GPA of 3.25, teaching certificate. *Application deadline:* Applications are processed on a rolling basis. *Financial support:* Application deadline: 5/1. *Faculty research:* Multicultural education, middle school education, curriculum development. *Application contact:* Dr. Helen Barrett, Dean, 615-963-5139, Fax: 615-963-5963, E-mail: hbarrett@tnstate.edu.

Tennessee Technological University, Graduate School, College of Education, Department of Curriculum and Instruction, Program in Elementary Education, Cookeville, TN 38505. Offers MA, Ed S. *Accreditation:* NCATE. Part-time and evening/weekend programs available. *Faculty:* 8 full-time (2 women). *Students:* 17 full-time (14 women), 18 part-time (14 women); includes 1 minority (African American) Average age 27. 15 applicants, 80% accepted, 6 enrolled. In 2006, 12 degrees awarded. *Degree requirements:* For Ed S, thesis or alternative. *Entrance requirements:* For master's, MAT; for Ed S, MAT, NTE. Additional exam requirements/recommendations for international students: Required—TOEFL. *Application deadline:* For fall admission, 3/1 priority date for domestic students; for spring admission, 8/1 for domestic students. Application fee: $25 ($30 for international students). *Expenses:* Tuition, state resident: full-time $8,748; part-time $319 per hour. Tuition, nonresident: full-time $23,524; part-time $740 per hour. *Financial support:* In 2006–07, 1 fellowship (averaging $8,000 per year), research assistantships (averaging $4,000 per year), 1 teaching assistantship (averaging $4,000 per year) were awarded; career-related internships or fieldwork also available. Financial award application deadline: 4/1. *Faculty research:* Educational television art program. *Application contact:* Dr. Francis O. Otuonye, Associate Vice President for Research and Graduate Studies, 931-372-3233, Fax: 931-372-3497, E-mail: fotuonye@tntech.edu.

Texas A&M University–Commerce, Graduate School, College of Education and Human Services, Department of Elementary Education, Commerce, TX 75429-3011. Offers early childhood education (M Ed, MA, MS); elementary education (M Ed, MS); reading (M Ed, MA, MS); supervision of curriculum and instruction: elementary education (Ed D). Part-time programs available. Terminal master's awarded for partial completion of doctoral program. *Degree requirements:* For master's, thesis (for some programs), comprehensive exam; for doctorate, 2 foreign languages, thesis/dissertation, departmental qualifying exam. *Entrance requirements:* For master's and doctorate, GRE General Test. Electronic applications accepted. *Faculty research:* Literacy and learning, early childhood, preservice teacher education, technology.

Texas A&M University–Corpus Christi, Graduate Studies and Research, College of Education, Program in Elementary Education, Corpus Christi, TX 78412-5503. Offers MS. Part-time and evening/weekend programs available. *Degree requirements:* For master's, thesis (for some programs), comprehensive exam, registration. *Entrance requirements:* For master's, GRE General Test. Additional exam requirements/recommendations for international students: Required—TOEFL. Electronic applications accepted.

Texas A&M University–Kingsville, College of Graduate Studies, College of Education, Department of Education, Program in Elementary Education, Kingsville, TX 78363. Offers MA, MS. Part-time and evening/weekend programs available. *Degree requirements:* For master's, thesis or alternative, comprehensive exam. *Entrance requirements:* For master's, GRE General Test, MAT, minimum GPA of 3.0. *Faculty research:* Strategies in elementary science, manipulatives in the classroom, latest developments.

Texas Christian University, School of Education, Program in Elementary Education, Fort Worth, TX 76129-0002. Offers M Ed, Certificate. Part-time and evening/weekend programs available. *Degree requirements:* For master's, thesis optional. *Entrance requirements:* Additional exam requirements/recommendations for international students: Required—TOEFL. *Application deadline:* For fall admission, 3/1 for domestic students; for spring admission, 12/1 for domestic students. Applications are processed on a rolling basis. Application fee: $0. *Expenses:* Tuition: Part-time $800 per credit hour. *Financial support:* Application deadline: 3/1. *Application contact:* Director of Graduate Studies, 817-257-7664.

Texas Southern University, Graduate School, College of Education, Area of Curriculum and Instruction, Houston, TX 77004-4584. Offers bilingual education (M Ed); curriculum, instruction, and urban education (Ed D); early childhood education (M Ed); elementary education (M Ed); reading education (M Ed); secondary education (M Ed); special education (M Ed). Part-time and evening/weekend programs available. *Faculty:* 8 full-time (6 women), 1 part-time/adjunct (0 women). *Students:* 41 full-time (36 women), 43 part-time (38 women); includes 82 minority (77 African Americans, 2 Asian Americans or Pacific Islanders, 3 Hispanic Americans). Average age 36. 34 applicants, 82% accepted, 24 enrolled. In 2006, 6 master's, 13 doctorates awarded. *Degree requirements:* For master's, comprehensive exam; for doctorate, thesis/dissertation, comprehensive exam. *Entrance requirements:* For master's, GRE General Test, minimum GPA of 2.5; for doctorate, GRE General Test or MAT, master's degree, minimum B+ average. Additional exam requirements/recommendations for international students: Required—TOEFL. *Application deadline:* For fall admission, 7/15 priority date for domestic students. Applications are processed on a rolling basis. Application fee: $50 ($75 for international students). *Financial support:* Federal Work-Study and institutionally sponsored loans available. Financial award application deadline: 5/1. *Unit head:* Dr. Cherry Gooden, Chair, 713-313-7496, Fax: 713-313-7496, E-mail: gooden_cr@tsu.edu.

Texas State University-San Marcos, Graduate School, College of Education, Department of Curriculum and Instruction, Program in Elementary Education, San Marcos, TX 78666. Offers M Ed, MA. Part-time and evening/weekend programs available. *Faculty:* 14 full-time (10 women), 4 part-time/adjunct (2 women). *Students:* 94 full-time (86 women), 161 part-time (144 women); includes 59 minority (8 African Americans, 1 American Indian/Alaska Native, 8 Asian Americans or Pacific Islanders, 42 Hispanic Americans), 6 international. Average age 31. In 2006, 115 degrees awarded. *Degree requirements:* For master's, thesis (for some programs), comprehensive exam. *Entrance requirements:* For master's, GRE General Test, minimum GPA of 2.75 in last 60 hours of course work, teaching experience. Additional exam requirements/recommendations for international students: Required—TOEFL. *Application deadline:* For fall admission, 6/15 priority date for domestic students; for spring admission, 10/15 priority date for domestic students. Applications are processed on a rolling basis. Application fee: $40 ($90 for international students). *Financial support:* In 2006–07, 142 students received support, including 11 research assistantships (averaging $6,750 per year), 2 teaching assistantships (averaging $2,697 per year); career-related internships or fieldwork, Federal Work-Study, and institutionally sponsored loans also available. Support available to part-time students. Financial award application deadline: 4/1; financial award applicants required to submit FAFSA. *Faculty research:* Bilingual, general elementary, and early childhood education; gifted and talented education. *Unit head:* Carolyn McCall, Graduate Advisor, 512-245-2041, Fax: 512-245-7911, E-mail: cm06@txstate.edu.

Texas State University-San Marcos, Graduate School, College of Education, Department of Curriculum and Instruction, Program in Elementary Education-Bilingual/Bicultural, San Marcos, TX 78666. Offers M Ed, MA. *Faculty:* 1 (woman) part-time/adjunct. *Students:* 2 full-time (1 woman), 5 part-time (all women); includes 5 minority (all Hispanic Americans), 1 international. Average age 33. 3 applicants, 100% accepted, 2 enrolled. In 2006, 10 degrees awarded. *Degree requirements:* For master's, comprehensive exam. *Entrance requirements:* For master's, GRE General Test, minimum GPA of 2.75 in last 60 hours of course work, teaching experience. Additional exam requirements/recommendations for international students: Required—TOEFL. *Application deadline:* For fall admission, 6/15 priority date for domestic students; for spring admission, 10/15 priority date for domestic students. Applications are processed on a rolling basis. Application fee: $40 ($90 for international students). *Financial support:* In 2006–07, 7 students received support. *Unit head:* Carolyn McCall, Graduate Advisor, 512-245-2041, Fax: 512-245-7911, E-mail: cm06@txstate.edu.

Texas State University-San Marcos, Graduate School, Interdisciplinary Studies Program in Elementary Mathematics, Science, and Technology, San Marcos, TX 78666. Offers MSIS. *Students:* 3 applicants, 0% accepted. In 2006, 2 degrees awarded. *Degree requirements:* For master's, comprehensive exam. *Application deadline:* For fall admission, 6/15 priority date for domestic students; for spring admission, 10/15 priority date for domestic students. Applications are processed on a rolling basis. Application fee: $40 ($90 for international students). *Financial support:* Application deadline: 4/1; *Unit head:* Dr. Sandra Mody, Acting Dean, 512-245-3381, Fax: 512-245-8095, E-mail: sw04@txstate.edu.

Texas Tech University, Graduate School, College of Education, Division of Curriculum and Instruction, Lubbock, TX 79409. Offers bilingual education (M Ed); curriculum and instruction (M Ed, PhD); elementary education (M Ed); language and literacy education (M Ed); secondary education (M Ed). *Accreditation:* NCATE. Part-time programs available. *Students:* 68 full-time (48 women), 99 part-time (82 women); includes 35 minority (6 African Americans, 1 Asian American or Pacific Islander, 28 Hispanic Americans), 10 international. Average age 34. 165 applicants, 59% accepted, 10 enrolled. In 2006, 61 master's, 7 doctorates awarded. *Degree requirements:* For master's, thesis optional; for doctorate, thesis/dissertation. *Entrance requirements:* For master's and doctorate, GRE General Test. Additional exam requirements/recommendations for international students: Required—TOEFL (minimum score 550 paper-based; 213 computer-based). *Application deadline:* For fall admission, 3/1 priority date for international students; for spring admission, 11/1 priority date for international students. Applications are processed on a rolling basis. Application fee: $50 ($60 for international students). Electronic applications accepted. *Expenses:* Tuition, state resident: full-time $4,440. Tuition, nonresident: full-time $11,040. Required fees: $2,136. *Financial support:* In 2006–07, 100 students received support; research assistantships with partial tuition reimbursements available, teaching assistantships with partial tuition reimbursements available, career-related internships or fieldwork, Federal Work-Study, and institutionally sponsored loans available. Support available to part-time students. Financial award application deadline: 4/15; financial award applicants required to submit FAFSA. *Faculty research:* Multicultural foundations of education, teacher education, instruction and pedagogy in subject areas, curriculum theory, language and literary. *Unit head:* Dr. Peggy Johnson, Associate Dean, 806-742-1988 Ext. 437, Fax: 806-742-2179, E-mail: peggy.johnson@ttu.edu.

Texas Woman's University, Graduate School, College of Professional Education, Department of Teacher Education, Denton, TX 76201. Offers education administration (M Ed, MA); elementary education (M Ed, MA); special education (M Ed, MA, PhD), including educational diagnostician (M Ed, MA), mental retardation (M Ed, MA), physically handicapped (M Ed, MA); teaching (MAT). Part-time programs available. *Students:* 45 full-time (30 women), 226 part-time (194 women); includes 95 minority (53 African Americans, 1 American Indian/Alaska Native, 5 Asian Americans or Pacific Islanders, 36 Hispanic Americans), 11 international. Average age 37. In 2006, 106 master's, 6 doctorates awarded. Terminal master's awarded for partial completion of doctoral program. *Degree requirements:* For master's, professional paper (M Ed); for doctorate, thesis/dissertation, comprehensive exam. *Entrance requirements:* For master's, 3 letters of reference, curriculum vitae, copy of certifications, Teacher Service Record; for doctorate, minimum graduate GPA of 3.5, 3 reference letters, resumé, copy of certifications, Teacher Service Record. Additional exam requirements/recommendations for international students: Required—TOEFL (minimum score 550 paper-based; 213 computer-based; 79 iBT). *Application deadline:* For fall admission, 4/1 for international students; for spring admission, 8/1 for international students. Applications are processed on a rolling basis. Application fee: $30 ($50 for international students). Electronic applications accepted. *Expenses:* Tuition, area resident: Part-time $168 per unit. Tuition, state resident: full-time $4,369. Tuition, nonresident: full-time $9,373; part-time $443 per unit. Required fees: $20 per unit. $177 per term. *Financial support:* In 2006–07, 3 research assistantships (averaging $10,206 per year), teaching assistantships (averaging $10,206 per year) were awarded; career-related internships or fieldwork, Federal Work-Study, institutionally sponsored loans, scholarships/grants, traineeships, health care benefits, tuition waivers (partial), and unspecified assistantships also available. Support available to part-time students. Financial award application deadline: 3/1; financial award applicants required to submit FAFSA. *Faculty research:* Classroom management, learning disabilities, staff and professional development, leadership assessment. *Application contact:* Samuel Wheeler, Coordinator of Graduate Admissions, 940-898-3188, Fax: 940-898-3081, E-mail: wheelersr@twu.edu.

Towson University, Graduate School, Program in Elementary Education, Towson, MD 21252-0001. Offers M Ed. *Accreditation:* NCATE. Part-time and evening/weekend programs avail-

Elementary Education

Towson University (continued)

able. *Faculty:* 4 full-time (2 women), 7 part-time/adjunct (4 women). *Students:* 2 full-time (both women), 89 part-time (78 women); includes 11 minority (7 African Americans, 2 Asian Americans or Pacific Islanders, 2 Hispanic Americans). 12 applicants, 83% accepted, 5 enrolled. In 2006, 24 degrees awarded. *Degree requirements:* For master's, capstone project or thesis. *Entrance requirements:* For master's, minimum GPA of 3.0, bachelor's degree in education, certified in teaching or eligibility for certification. Additional exam requirements/recommendations for international students: Required—TOEFL. *Application deadline:* Applications are processed on a rolling basis. Application fee: $50. Electronic applications accepted. *Expenses:* Tuition, state resident: part-time $275 per unit. Tuition, nonresident: part-time $577 per unit. Required fees: $72 per unit. *Financial support:* Federal Work-Study and unspecified assistantships available. Financial award application deadline: 4/1; financial award applicants required to submit FAFSA. *Faculty research:* Professional development schools, values education, teacher development, reading, academic underachievement. *Unit head:* Dr. Linda Emerick, Graduate Program Director, 410-704-4251, Fax: 410-704-2733, E-mail: lemerick@towson.edu. *Application contact:* 410-704-2501, Fax: 410-704-4675, E-mail: grads@towson.edu.

Trevecca Nazarene University, Graduate Division, School of Education, Major in Teaching, Nashville, TN 37210-2877. Offers teaching 7-12 (MAT); teaching K-6 (MAT). Part-time and evening/weekend programs available. *Students:* 185 full-time (153 women), 37 part-time (24 women); includes 64 minority (59 African Americans, 1 American Indian/Alaska Native, 2 Asian Americans or Pacific Islanders, 2 Hispanic Americans), 2 international. In 2006, 63 degrees awarded. *Degree requirements:* For master's, exit assessment, student teaching. *Entrance requirements:* For master's, GRE General Test, MAT, Praxis I: Pre-Professional Skills Test, minimum GPA of 2.7, 2 letters of reference. Additional exam requirements/recommendations for international students: Required—TOEFL (minimum score 500 paper-based; 173 computer-based). *Application deadline:* Applications are processed on a rolling basis. Application fee: $25. *Expenses: Contact institution.* Tuition and fees vary according to degree level and program. *Financial support:* Applicants required to submit FAFSA. *Application contact:* Admissions Office, 615-248-1201, Fax: 615-248-1597, E-mail: admissions_ged@trevecca.edu.

Trinity (Washington) University, School of Education, Washington, DC 20017-1094. Offers democracy, diversity, and social justice (M Ed); early childhood (MAT); educational administration (MSA); elementary education (MAT); English as a second language (M Ed, MAT); literacy and reading education (M Ed); school counseling (MA); secondary education (MAT), including English, math, science, social studies; special education (MAT). *Accreditation:* NCATE. Part-time and evening/weekend programs available. *Degree requirements:* For master's, thesis (for some programs), capstone project(s). *Entrance requirements:* For master's, PRAXIS I, minimum GPA of 2.8. Additional exam requirements/recommendations for international students: Required—TOEFL (minimum score 550 paper-based; 213 computer-based). *Faculty research:* Technology, literacy, special education, organizations, inclusion models.

Troy University, Graduate School, College of Education, Program in K–6 Elementary and Collaborative Education, Troy, AL 36082. Offers MS, MSE, Ed S. *Accreditation:* NCATE. Part-time and evening/weekend programs available. *Students:* 200 full-time (185 women), 211 part-time (203 women); includes 176 minority (169 African Americans, 2 American Indian/Alaska Native, 2 Asian Americans or Pacific Islanders, 3 Hispanic Americans). Average age 34. In 2006, 177 master's, 115 other advanced degrees awarded. *Degree requirements:* For master's, thesis, comprehensive exam, registration. *Entrance requirements:* For master's, minimum GPA of 2.5; for Ed S, GRE General Test or MAT, Alabama Class A certificate or equivalent, minimum graduate GPA of 3.0. Additional exam requirements/recommendations for international students: Required—TOEFL (minimum score 523 paper-based; 200 computer-based). *Application deadline:* Applications are processed on a rolling basis. Application fee: $50. Electronic applications accepted. *Expenses:* Tuition, state resident: full-time $4,368; part-time $182 per hour. Tuition, nonresident: full-time $8,736; part-time $364 per hour. Required fees: $50 per term. *Financial support:* Available to part-time students. Applicants required to submit FAFSA. *Unit head:* Dr. Darrell Pearson, Interim Chair, 334-670-3444, Fax: 334-670-3474, E-mail: dpearson@troy.edu. *Application contact:* Brenda K. Campbell, Director of Graduate Admissions, 334-670-3178, Fax: 334-670-3733, E-mail: bcamp@troy.edu.

Tufts University, Graduate School of Arts and Sciences, Department of Education, Program in Education, Medford, MA 02155. Offers education (MS, PhD); elementary education (MAT); middle and secondary education (MA, MAT); secondary education (MA). *Faculty:* 13 full-time, 9 part-time/adjunct. *Students:* 114 (77 women); includes 22 minority (9 African Americans, 4 Asian Americans or Pacific Islanders, 9 Hispanic Americans) 7 international. 199 applicants, 79% accepted, 75 enrolled. In 2006, 72 degrees awarded. *Degree requirements:* For master's, thesis optional; for doctorate, thesis/dissertation. *Entrance requirements:* For master's, GRE General Test. Additional exam requirements/recommendations for international students: Required—TOEFL (minimum score 550 paper-based; 213 computer-based; 80 iBT). *Application deadline:* For fall admission, 2/1 for domestic students, 12/30 for international students; for spring admission, 10/15 for domestic students, 9/15 for international students. Applications are processed on a rolling basis. Application fee: $70. Electronic applications accepted. *Expenses:* Tuition: Full-time $33,672. Tuition and fees vary according to degree level and program. *Financial support:* Teaching assistantships with full and partial tuition reimbursements, Federal Work-Study, scholarships/grants, and tuition waivers (full and partial) available. Financial award application deadline: 2/1. *Unit head:* Analucia Schliemann, Chair, Department of Education, 617-627-3244, Fax: 617-627-3901.

Union College, Graduate Programs, Department of Education, Program in Elementary Education, Barbourville, KY 40906-1499. Offers MA. *Degree requirements:* For master's, thesis optional. *Entrance requirements:* For master's, GRE General Test, NTE.

Universidad del Este, Graduate School, Carolina, PR 00983. Offers accounting (MBA); administration (M Ed); criminal justice and criminology (MA); education (M Ed); elementary education (M Ed); human resources (MBA); management (MBA); social work (MA); teaching English (M Ed); teaching Spanish (M Ed).

Université de Sherbrooke, Faculty of Education, Program in Elementary Education, Sherbrooke, QC J1K 2R1, Canada. Offers M Ed, Diploma. Part-time and evening/weekend programs available. *Degree requirements:* For master's, thesis.

University at Buffalo, the State University of New York, Graduate School, Graduate School of Education, Department of Learning and Instruction, Buffalo, NY 14260. Offers adolescence education (Certificate); biology (Ed M); chemistry (Ed M); childhood education (Ed M); early childhood and childhood education with bilingual extension (Ed M); early childhood education (Ed M); earth science (Ed M); elementary education (Ed D, PhD); English (Ed M); English education (PhD); English for speakers of other languages (Ed M); foreign and second language education (PhD); French (Ed M); general education (Ed M); German (Ed M); Italian (Ed M); Japanese (Ed M); Latin (Ed M); literary specialist (Ed M); mathematics (Ed M); mathematics education (PhD); mentoring teachers (Certificate); music education (Ed M, Certificate); physics (Ed M); reading education (PhD); Russian (Ed M); school administrator and supervisor (Certificate); science education (PhD); social studies (Ed M); Spanish (Ed M); special education (PhD); teaching and leading for diversity (Certificate); teaching English to speakers of other languages (Ed M). Part-time and evening/weekend programs available. Postbaccalaureate distance learning degree programs offered (no on-campus study). *Faculty:* 30 full-time (20 women), 53 part-time/adjunct (38 women). *Students:* 368 full-time (269 women), 297 part-time (226 women); includes 50 minority (15 African Americans, 2 American Indian/Alaska Native, 14 Asian Americans or Pacific Islanders, 19 Hispanic Americans), 66 international. Average age 31. 638 applicants, 75% accepted, 298 enrolled. In 2006, 248 master's, 18 doctorates, 48 other advanced degrees awarded. Terminal master's awarded for partial completion of doctoral program. *Degree requirements:* For master's, comprehensive exam, registration; for doctorate, thesis/dissertation, research analysis exam, research experience component. *Entrance requirements:* For doctorate, GRE General Test or MAT, interview, writing sample, letters of recommendation. Additional exam requirements/recommendations for international students: Required—TOEFL (minimum score 600 paper-based; 250 computer-based). *Application deadline:* For fall admission, 2/1 priority date for domestic and international students; for spring admission, 11/15 priority date for domestic students, 10/1 for international students. Applications are processed on a rolling basis. Application fee: $50. Electronic applications accepted. *Financial support:* In 2006–07, 70 students received support, including 6 fellowships with full tuition reimbursements available (averaging $10,000 per year), 16 research assistantships with full tuition reimbursements available (averaging $9,000 per year), teaching assistantships with full tuition reimbursements available (averaging $9,000 per year); career-related internships or fieldwork, Federal Work-Study, institutionally sponsored loans, scholarships/grants, tuition waivers (partial), and unspecified assistantships also available. Financial award application deadline: 2/28; financial award applicants required to submit FAFSA. *Faculty research:* Science assessment, state-level testing, early learning, literacy, second language acquisition. Total annual research expenditures: $432,366. *Unit head:* Dr. Maria E. Runfola, Chair, 716-645-2455, Fax: 716-645-3161. *Application contact:* Barbara Belz, Admissions Secretary, 716-645-2110 Ext. 1159, Fax: 716-645-3161, E-mail: belz@buffalo.edu.

The University of Akron, Graduate School, College of Education, Department of Curricular and Instructional Studies, Program in Elementary Education, Akron, OH 44325. Offers elementary education (PhD); elementary education—literacy (MA); elementary education with licensure (MS). *Accreditation:* NCATE. *Students:* 17 full-time (all women), 134 part-time (124 women); includes 12 minority (10 African Americans, 2 Asian Americans or Pacific Islanders), 2 international. Average age 37. 27 applicants, 74% accepted, 14 enrolled. In 2006, 24 master's, 4 doctorates awarded. *Degree requirements:* For master's, thesis optional; for doctorate, one foreign language, thesis/dissertation, written and oral exams, other language alternatives, comprehensive exam. *Entrance requirements:* For master's, minimum GPA of 2.75; for doctorate, MAT or GRE, interview, minimum GPA of 3.5, writing sample, letters of reference. Additional exam requirements/recommendations for international students: Required—TOEFL (minimum score 550 paper-based; 213 computer-based; 79 iBT). *Application deadline:* For fall admission, 3/1 for domestic students. Applications are processed on a rolling basis. Application fee: $30 ($40 for international students). Electronic applications accepted. *Expenses:* Tuition, state resident: full-time $6,164; part-time $342 per credit. Tuition, nonresident: full-time $10,575; part-time $588 per credit. Required fees: $806; $43 per credit. $12 per term. Tuition and fees vary according to course load, degree level and program.

The University of Alabama at Birmingham, School of Education, Department of Curriculum and Instruction, Program in Elementary Education, Birmingham, AL 35294. Offers MA Ed. *Accreditation:* NCATE. *Students:* 42 full-time (37 women), 64 part-time (62 women); includes 23 minority (22 African Americans, 1 Hispanic American), 1 international. 24 applicants, 100% accepted. In 2006, 97 degrees awarded. *Degree requirements:* For master's, thesis optional. *Entrance requirements:* For master's, GRE General Test, MAT, or NTE, minimum GPA of 3.0. *Application deadline:* Applications are processed on a rolling basis. Application fee: $35 ($60 for international students). Electronic applications accepted. *Expenses:* Tuition, state resident: part-time $170 per credit hour. Tuition, nonresident: part-time $425 per credit hour. Required fees: $15 per credit hour. $122 per term. Tuition and fees vary according to program. *Unit head:* Dr. Charles Calhoun, Chair, Department of Curriculum and Instruction, 205-934-5371, Fax: 205-934-4792.

University of Alaska Southeast, Graduate Programs, Program in Education, Juneau, AK 99801. Offers early childhood education (M Ed, MAT); educational technology (M Ed); elementary education (MAT); reading (M Ed); secondary education (MAT). *Accreditation:* NCATE. Part-time and evening/weekend programs available. Postbaccalaureate distance learning degree programs offered (minimal on-campus study). *Faculty:* 12 full-time (7 women), 6 part-time/adjunct (5 women). *Students:* 81 full-time (49 women), 109 part-time (88 women); includes 24 minority (3 African Americans, 11 American Indian/Alaska Native, 5 Asian Americans or Pacific Islanders, 5 Hispanic Americans), 6 international. Average age 34. In 2006, 84 degrees awarded. *Degree requirements:* For master's, comprehensive exam or project, portfolio. *Entrance requirements:* For master's, PRAXIS, minimum GPA of 3.0, writing sample, letters of recommendation. *Application deadline:* For fall admission, 3/8 for domestic students. Applications are processed on a rolling basis. Application fee: $50. Electronic applications accepted. *Financial support:* Federal Work-Study, scholarships/grants, and tuition waivers (full and partial) available. Support available to part-time students. Financial award applicants required to submit FAFSA. *Faculty research:* Applied classroom research, culturally responsive practices, action research, teaching effectiveness. *Unit head:* Dr. Larry Harris, Dean, 907-796-6551, Fax: 907-796-6550, E-mail: larry.harris@uas.alaska.edu. *Application contact:* Susan A. Stuck, Administrative Assistant, 866-465-6424, Fax: 866-465-5159, E-mail: jnsas@uas.alaska.edu.

University of Alberta, Faculty of Graduate Studies and Research, Department of Elementary Education, Edmonton, AB T6G 2E1, Canada. Offers M Ed, Ed D, PhD. Part-time and evening/weekend programs available. Postbaccalaureate distance learning degree programs offered (minimal on-campus study). *Faculty:* 26 full-time (18 women). *Students:* 32 full-time (26 women), 146 part-time (121 women), 7 international. Average age 38. 51 applicants, 80% accepted. In 2006, 28 master's, 11 doctorates awarded. *Degree requirements:* For master's, thesis (for some programs); for doctorate, thesis/dissertation. *Entrance requirements:* For master's and doctorate, 1 year of teaching experience, minimum GPA of 6.5 on a 9.0 scale. *Application deadline:* For fall admission, 4/1 for domestic students; for winter admission, 10/1 for domestic students; for spring admission, 4/1 for domestic students. Application fee: $0. *Financial support:* In 2006–07, 23 students received support, including 3 fellowships with full tuition reimbursements available, 9 research assistantships with partial tuition reimbursements available, 6 teaching assistantships with full tuition reimbursements available; career-related internships or fieldwork and scholarships/grants also available. Financial award application deadline: 6/1. *Faculty research:* Literacy education, early childhood education, teacher education, curriculum studies, instructional studies. Total annual research expenditures: $100,000. *Unit head:* Dr. Jill McClay, Graduate Coordinator, 780-492-2267, Fax: 780-492-7622. *Application contact:* Gwen Parker, 780-492-4273 Ext. 225, Fax: 780-492-7622, E-mail: educ.elem@ualberta.ca.

The University of Arizona, Graduate College, College of Education, Department of Teaching and Teacher Education, Concentration in Elementary Education, Tucson, AZ 85721. Offers M Ed, Ed D. *Degree requirements:* For master's, thesis optional; for doctorate, thesis/dissertation. *Entrance requirements:* For master's, minimum GPA of 3.0, 5 units of education course work; for doctorate, GRE General Test, 15 units of education course work, 2 years of teaching experience, minimum graduate GPA of 3.0. Additional exam requirements/recommendations for international students: Required—TOEFL. *Faculty research:* Mathematics diagnosis, middle schools, teacher effectiveness, curriculum design.

University of Arkansas, Graduate School, College of Education and Health Professions, Department of Curriculum and Instruction, Program in Elementary Education, Fayetteville, AR 72701-1201. Offers M Ed, Ed S. *Accreditation:* NCATE. *Students:* 4 full-time (3 women), 12 part-time (11 women); includes 2 minority (1 African American, 1 American Indian/Alaska Native), 4 international. 16 applicants, 44% accepted.Application fee: $40 ($50 for international students). *Financial support:* Fellowships, research assistantships, teaching assistantships, career-related internships or fieldwork and Federal Work-Study available. Support available to part-time students. Financial award application deadline: 4/1; financial award applicants required to submit FAFSA. *Unit head:* Unit Head, 479-575-4201.

University of Arkansas at Pine Bluff, Program in Education, Pine Bluff, AR 71601-2799. Offers elementary education (M Ed); secondary education (M Ed), including English, general science, mathematics, physical education, social studies. Part-time and evening/weekend programs available. *Degree requirements:* For master's, comprehensive exam. *Entrance requirements:* For master's, GRE, minimum GPA of 2.75, NTE or Standard Arkansas Teaching Certificate. *Faculty research:* Teacher certification, accreditation, assessment, standards, portfolio development, rehabilitation, technology.

University of Bridgeport, School of Education and Human Resources, Division of Education, Program in Elementary Education, Bridgeport, CT 06604. Offers early childhood education (MS, Diploma); elementary education (MS, Diploma). Evening/weekend programs available. *Faculty:* 12 full-time (5 women), 72 part-time/adjunct (44 women). *Students:* 5 full-time (4 women), 21 part-time (all women); includes 2 minority (both African Americans), 1 international. Average age 36. 24 applicants, 63% accepted, 7 enrolled. In 2006, 10 degrees awarded. *Degree requirements:* For master's, final exam, final project, or thesis; for Diploma, thesis or alternative, final project. *Entrance requirements:* For master's, GRE General Test, MAT, minimum undergraduate QPA of 2.5; for Diploma, GRE General Test or MAT, minimum graduate QPA of 3.0. *Application deadline:* For fall admission, 8/1 priority date for domestic students; for spring admission, 12/1 priority date for domestic students. Applications are processed on a rolling basis. Application fee: $25 ($35 for international students). Electronic applications accepted. *Financial support:* Career-related internships or fieldwork, Federal Work-Study, and institutionally sponsored loans available. Support available to part-time students. Financial award application deadline: 6/1; financial award applicants required to submit FAFSA. *Faculty research:* Self-concept, internship assessment, stress and situational development, follow-up of graduation. *Unit head:* Dr. Allen P. Cook, Associate Dean, Division of Education, 203-576-4206, Fax: 203-576-4200, E-mail: acook@bridgeport.edu.

University of California, Irvine, Office of Graduate Studies, Department of Education, Irvine, CA 92697. Offers educational administration (Ed D); educational administration and leadership (Ed D); elementary and secondary education (MAT). Part-time and evening/weekend programs available. *Students:* 138 full-time (95 women), 3 part-time (all women); includes 61 minority (14 African Americans, 1 American Indian/Alaska Native, 26 Asian Americans or Pacific Islanders, 20 Hispanic Americans). Average age 34. In 2006, 67 master's, 8 doctorates awarded. *Degree requirements:* For doctorate, thesis/dissertation. *Entrance requirements:* For master's, GRE, minimum GPA of 3.0; for doctorate, GRE General Test, minimum GPA of 3.0. Additional exam requirements/recommendations for international students: Required—TOEFL (minimum score 550 paper-based; 213 computer-based). *Application deadline:* For fall admission, 4/1 priority date for domestic students. Application fee: $60. Electronic applications accepted. *Financial support:* Fellowships, research assistantships with full tuition reimbursements, institutionally sponsored loans, traineeships, health care benefits, and unspecified assistantships available. Financial award application deadline: 3/1; financial award applicants required to submit FAFSA. *Faculty research:* Education technology, learning theory, social theory, cultural diversity, postmodernism. *Unit head:* David Brant, Interim Chair, 949-824-7840, E-mail: dbrant@uci.edu. *Application contact:* Sarah K. Singh, Student Affairs Officer, 949-824-7832, Fax: 949-824-2965, E-mail: sksingh@uci.edu.

University of Central Florida, College of Education, Department of Teaching and Learning Principles, Program in Elementary Education, Orlando, FL 32816. Offers M Ed, MA. *Accreditation:* NCATE. *Students:* 29 full-time (28 women), 62 part-time (59 women); includes 11 minority (5 African Americans, 4 Asian Americans or Pacific Islanders, 2 Hispanic Americans), 2 international. 24 applicants, 83% accepted, 13 enrolled. In 2006, 38 degrees awarded. *Degree requirements:* For master's, thesis or alternative. *Application deadline:* For fall admission, 7/15 for domestic students; for spring admission, 12/15 for domestic students. Application fee: $30. Electronic applications accepted. *Expenses:* Tuition, state resident: full-time $6,167; part-time $257 per credit hour. Tuition, nonresident: full-time $22,790; part-time $950 per credit hour. *Financial support:* In 2006–07, 1 fellowship with tuition reimbursement (averaging $5,000 per year), 2 research assistantships with tuition reimbursements (averaging $4,100 per year) were awarded; teaching assistantships, career-related internships or fieldwork, Federal Work-Study, institutionally sponsored loans, tuition waivers (partial), and unspecified assistantships also available. *Unit head:* Dr. Rosie Joels, Coordinator, 407-823-2008, E-mail: rjoels@mail.ucf.edu.

University of Central Florida, College of Education, Doctoral Program in Education, Orlando, FL 32816. Offers communication sciences and disorders (PhD); counselor education (PhD); curriculum and instruction (PhD); elementary education (PhD); exceptional education (PhD); hospitality education (PhD); instructional technology (PhD); mathematics education (PhD). *Students:* 86 full-time (63 women), 9 part-time (4 women); includes 21 minority (15 African Americans, 2 Asian Americans or Pacific Islanders, 4 Hispanic Americans), 19 international. Average age 39. In 2006, 16 degrees awarded. Application fee: $30. Electronic applications accepted. *Expenses:* Tuition, state resident: full-time $6,167; part-time $257 per credit hour. Tuition, nonresident: full-time $22,790; part-time $950 per credit hour. *Financial support:* In 2006–07, 44 fellowships with partial tuition reimbursements (averaging $3,700 per year), 54 research assistantships with partial tuition reimbursements (averaging $7,000 per year), 9 teaching assistantships with partial tuition reimbursements (averaging $7,000 per year) were awarded.

University of Central Missouri, The Graduate School, College of Education, Department of Curriculum and Instruction, Warrensburg, MO 64093. Offers curriculum and instruction (Ed S); elementary education (MSE); K–12 education (MSE); literacy education (MSE); secondary education (MSE). *Accreditation:* NCATE. Part-time programs available. *Faculty:* 22 full-time (14 women). *Students:* 43 full-time (33 women), 309 part-time (237 women); includes 27 minority (23 African Americans, 1 Asian American or Pacific Islander, 3 Hispanic Americans), 3 international. Average age 33. 81 applicants, 81% accepted, 65 enrolled. In 2006, 70 master's, 1 other advanced degree awarded. *Degree requirements:* For master's, comprehensive exam or thesis; for Ed S, thesis, comprehensive exam. *Entrance requirements:* For master's, GRE General Test, minimum GPA of 2.75, teaching certificate; for Ed S, GRE General Test, minimum GPA of 3.25, teaching certificate. Additional exam requirements/recommendations for international students: Required—TOEFL (minimum score 500 paper-based; 173 computer-based). *Application deadline:* For fall admission, 6/1 priority date for domestic students, 5/1 priority date for international students; for spring admission, 10/1 priority date for domestic students, 10/1 for international students. Applications are processed on a rolling basis. Application fee: $30 ($50 for international students). *Expenses:* Tuition, state resident: full-time $5,448; part-time $227 per credit hour. Tuition, nonresident: full-time $10,896; part-time $454 per credit hour. Required fees: $336; $14 per credit hour. *Financial support:* In 2006–07, 4 students received support. Federal Work-Study, scholarships/grants, unspecified assistantships, and administrative and laboratory assistantships available. Support available to part-time students. Financial award application deadline: 3/1; financial award applicants required to submit FAFSA. *Faculty research:* Reading maturity, student and faculty evaluation, online teaching and learning, video documentation, teacher candidates' assessment of student thinking and learning. *Unit head:* Dr. Sharon Lamson, Chair, 660-543-4235, Fax: 660-543-4167, E-mail: lamson@ucmo.edu.

University of Central Oklahoma, College of Graduate Studies and Research, College of Education, Department of Curriculum and Instruction, Program in Elementary Education, Edmond, OK 73034-5209. Offers M Ed. *Accreditation:* NCATE. Part-time programs available. *Entrance requirements:* For master's, GRE General Test. Additional exam requirements/recommendations for international students: Required—TOEFL (minimum score 550 paper-based; 213 computer-based). Electronic applications accepted. *Faculty research:* Science education.

University of Cincinnati, Division of Research and Advanced Studies, College of Education, Criminal Justice, and Human Services, Division of Teacher Education, Program in Middle Childhood Education, Cincinnati, OH 45221. Offers M Ed. *Accreditation:* NCATE. Part-time programs available. *Students:* 83. *Degree requirements:* For master's, thesis or alternative. *Entrance requirements:* For master's, GRE General Test. Additional exam requirements/recommendations for international students: Required—TOEFL (minimum score 550 paper-based; 213 computer-based), TWE (minimum score 4.5), OEPT. *Application deadline:* For fall admission, 2/1 for domestic students. Application fee: $40. Electronic applications accepted. *Financial support:* Fellowships, tuition waivers (partial) and unspecified assistantships available. *Application contact:* Haly Johnson, Chair, 513-556-3600, Fax: 513-556-1001, E-mail: holly.johnson@uc.edu.

University of Connecticut, Graduate School, Neag School of Education, Department of Curriculum and Instruction, Storrs, CT 06269. Offers curriculum and instruction (MA, PhD), including agriculture education, bilingual and bicultural education, elementary education, English education, history and social sciences education, mathematics education, reading education, science education, secondary education, world languages education. *Accreditation:* NCATE. *Faculty:* 28 full-time (12 women). *Students:* 158 full-time (120 women), 54 part-time (44 women); includes 24 minority (3 African Americans, 1 American Indian/Alaska Native, 3 Asian Americans or Pacific Islanders, 17 Hispanic Americans), 2 international. Average age 27. 268 applicants, 76% accepted, 203 enrolled. In 2006, 181 master's, 4 doctorates awarded. Terminal master's awarded for partial completion of doctoral program. *Degree requirements:* For master's, thesis or alternative, comprehensive exam; for doctorate, thesis/dissertation. *Entrance requirements:* For doctorate, GRE General Test. Additional exam requirements/recommendations for international students: Required—TOEFL (minimum score 550 paper-based; 213 computer-based). *Application deadline:* For fall admission, 2/1 priority date for domestic and international students; for spring admission, 11/1 for domestic students, 10/1 for international students. Applications are processed on a rolling basis. Application fee: $55. Electronic applications accepted. *Financial support:* In 2006–07, 14 research assistantships with full tuition reimbursements, 4 teaching assistantships with full tuition reimbursements were awarded; fellowships, Federal Work-Study, scholarships/grants, health care benefits, and unspecified assistantships also available. Financial award application deadline: 2/1; financial award applicants required to submit FAFSA. *Unit head:* Mary Anne Doyle, Head, 860-486-2433, Fax: 860-486-0280. *Application contact:* Lisa Rasicot, Graduate Coordinator, 860-486-3065, Fax: 860-486-0210, E-mail: soeadm02@uconnvm.uconn.edu.

University of Connecticut, Graduate School, Neag School of Education, Department of Curriculum and Instruction, Field of Curriculum and Instruction, Program in Elementary Education, Storrs, CT 06269. Offers MA, PhD. *Accreditation:* NCATE. *Faculty:* 16 full-time (9 women). *Students:* 14 full-time (all women), 4 part-time (3 women); includes 3 minority (1 African American, 1 Asian American or Pacific Islander, 1 Hispanic American). Average age 25. 19 applicants, 89% accepted, 17 enrolled. In 2006, 6 degrees awarded. Terminal master's awarded for partial completion of doctoral program. *Degree requirements:* For master's, thesis or alternative, comprehensive exam; for doctorate, thesis/dissertation. *Entrance requirements:* For doctorate, GRE General Test. Additional exam requirements/recommendations for international students: Required—TOEFL (minimum score 550 paper-based; 214 computer-based). *Application deadline:* For fall admission, 2/1 priority date for domestic and international students; for spring admission, 11/1 for domestic students, 10/1 for international students. Applications are processed on a rolling basis. Application fee: $55. Electronic applications accepted. *Financial support:* Fellowships, research assistantships with full tuition reimbursements, teaching assistantships with full tuition reimbursements, Federal Work-Study, scholarships/grants, health care benefits, and unspecified assistantships available. Financial award application deadline: 2/1; financial award applicants required to submit FAFSA. *Application contact:* Lisa Rasicot, Graduate Coordinator, 860-486-3065, Fax: 860-486-0210, E-mail: soeadm02@uconnvm.uconn.edu.

The University of Findlay, Graduate and Professional Studies, College of Education, Findlay, OH 45840-3653. Offers administration (MA Ed); early childhood (MA Ed); elementary education (MA Ed); human resource development (MA Ed); leadership (MA Ed); special education (MA Ed); technology (MA Ed); web instruction (MA Ed). *Accreditation:* NCATE. Part-time and evening/weekend programs available. *Faculty:* 12 full-time, 6 part-time/adjunct. *Students:* 84 full-time (65 women), 223 part-time (169 women); includes 11 minority (3 African Americans, 2 American Indian/Alaska Native, 1 Asian American or Pacific Islander, 5 Hispanic Americans), 13 international. Average age 35. 91 applicants, 97% accepted, 76 enrolled. In 2006, 146 degrees awarded. *Degree requirements:* For master's, thesis, cumulative project. *Entrance requirements:* For master's, minimum undergraduate GPA of 3.0 in last 60 hours of course work. Additional exam requirements/recommendations for international students: Required—TOEFL. *Application deadline:* Applications are processed on a rolling basis. Application fee: $25. Electronic applications accepted. *Expenses:* Contact institution. *Financial support:* In 2006–07, 6 students received support, including 6 teaching assistantships with full tuition reimbursements available (averaging $6,000 per year); unspecified assistantships also available. Financial award application deadline: 4/1; financial award applicants required to submit FAFSA. *Faculty research:* Children's literature, books and artwork, educational technology, professional development. *Unit head:* Dr. Melissa A. Cain, Dean, 419-434-4840, Fax: 419-434-4822. *Application contact:* Heather Riffle, Director, Graduate and Special Programs, 419-434-4642, Fax: 419-434-5517, E-mail: riffle@findlay.edu.

University of Florida, Graduate School, College of Education, School of Teaching and Learning, Gainesville, FL 32611. Offers bilingual/ESOL education (M Ed, MAE, Ed D, PhD, Ed S); curriculum and instruction (M Ed, MAE, Ed D, PhD, Ed S); early childhood education (Ed D, PhD, Ed S); elementary education (M Ed, MAE); English education (M Ed, MAE); mathematics education (M Ed, MAE); reading education (M Ed, MAE); science education (M Ed, MAE); social foundations (M Ed, MAE, Ed D, PhD); social studies education (M Ed, MAE). *Accreditation:* NCATE. *Faculty:* 29 full-time (20 women). *Students:* 506 (406 women); includes 87 minority (20 African Americans, 3 American Indian/Alaska Native, 13 Asian Americans or Pacific Islanders, 51 Hispanic Americans) 34 international. In 2006, 278 master's, 8 doctorates awarded. *Degree requirements:* For master's, thesis optional; for doctorate, variable foreign language requirement, thesis/dissertation. *Entrance requirements:* For master's and doctorate, GRE General Test, minimum GPA of 3.0; for Ed S, GRE General Test. Additional exam requirements/recommendations for international students: Required—TOEFL (minimum score 550 paper-based; 213 computer-based). *Application deadline:* For fall admission, 6/1 for domestic students. Applications are processed on a rolling basis. Application fee: $30. Electronic applications accepted. *Expenses:* Tuition, state resident: full-time $6,827. Tuition, nonresident: full-time $21,951. Required fees: $999. *Financial support:* In 2006–07, 5 research assistantships (averaging $11,947 per year), 22 teaching assistantships (averaging $9,709 per year) were awarded; fellowships, career-related internships or fieldwork and unspecified assistantships also available. *Faculty research:* Teacher education, inclusive education, classroom processes, curriculum and technology. *Unit head:* Dr. Tom Dana, Director, 352-392-9191 Ext. 200, Fax: 352-392-9193, E-mail: tdana@coe.ufl.edu. *Application contact:* Dr. Linda C. Jones, Coordinator, 352-392-0761 Ext. 267, Fax: 352-392-9193, E-mail: lcjones@coe.ufl.edu.

University of Georgia, Graduate School, College of Education, Department of Elementary and Social Studies Education, Athens, GA 30602. Offers early childhood education (M Ed, PhD, Ed S); elementary and middle school education (M Ed, PhD, Ed S), including elementary education (PhD), middle school education; social foundations of education (PhD). *Faculty:* 15 full-time (8 women). *Students:* 113 full-time (88 women), 122 part-time (95 women); includes 25 minority (19 African Americans, 4 Asian Americans or Pacific Islanders, 2 Hispanic Americans), 14 international. 170 applicants, 69% accepted, 88 enrolled. In 2006, 77 master's, 6 doctorates, 6 other advanced degrees awarded. *Entrance requirements:* For master's and Ed S, GRE General Test or MAT; for doctorate, GRE General Test. *Application deadline:* For fall admission, 7/1 priority date for domestic students; for spring admission, 11/15 for domestic students. Application fee: $50. Electronic applications accepted. *Financial support:* Fellowships, research assistantships, teaching assistantships, unspecified assistantships available. *Unit head:* Dr. Ronald J. Vansickle, Head, 706-542-7265, Fax: 706-542-6506, E-mail: rvansick@uga.edu. *Application contact:* Dr. John D. Hoge, Graduate Coordinator, 706-542-4416, Fax: 706-542-4277, E-mail: jdhoge@uga.edu.

University of Hartford, College of Education, Nursing, and Health Professions, Program in Elementary and Special Education, West Hartford, CT 06117-1599. Offers elementary education (M Ed). *Accreditation:* NCATE. Part-time and evening/weekend programs available. *Faculty:* 2 full-time (both women), 2 part-time/adjunct (both women). *Students:* 32 full-time (24 women), 29 part-time (23 women); includes 1 minority (African American) Average age 35. 17 applicants, 53% accepted, 9 enrolled. In 2006, 24 degrees awarded. *Degree requirements:* For master's, comprehensive exam. *Entrance requirements:* For master's, PRAXIS I or waiver, interview, 2 letters of recommendation. Additional exam requirements/recommendations for international

Elementary Education

University of Hartford (continued)
students: Required—TOEFL (minimum score 550 paper-based; 213 computer-based). *Application deadline:* For fall admission, 8/15 for domestic students; for winter admission, 12/1 for domestic students; for spring admission, 12/1 for domestic students. Applications are processed on a rolling basis. Application fee: $40 ($55 for international students). Electronic applications accepted. *Expenses:* Tuition: Part-time $515 per credit. Required fees: $200 per term. *Financial support:* In 2006–07, 1 teaching assistantship (averaging $2,000 per year) was awarded; institutionally sponsored loans and unspecified assistantships also available. Financial award application deadline: 6/1; financial award applicants required to submit FAFSA. *Unit head:* Dr. Janet P. Kremenitzer, Director, 860-768-4084, Fax: 860-768-5043, E-mail: kremenitzer@hartford.edu. *Application contact:* Susan Brown, Assistant Dean of Academic Services, 860-768-4692, Fax: 860-768-5043, E-mail: brown@hartford.edu.

University of Houston, College of Education, Department of Curriculum and Instruction, Houston, TX 77204. Offers art education (M Ed); bilingual education (M Ed); curriculum and instruction (Ed D); early childhood education (M Ed); education of the gifted (M Ed); elementary education (M Ed); mathematics education (M Ed); reading and language arts education (M Ed); science education (M Ed); second language education (M Ed); secondary education (M Ed); social studies education (M Ed); teaching (M Ed). *Accreditation:* NCATE. Part-time and evening/weekend programs available. *Faculty:* 24 full-time (11 women), 16 part-time/adjunct (14 women). *Students:* 134 full-time (102 women), 327 part-time (256 women); includes 142 minority (49 African Americans, 1 American Indian/Alaska Native, 29 Asian Americans or Pacific Islanders, 63 Hispanic Americans), 19 international. Average age 37. 113 applicants, 72% accepted, 61 enrolled. In 2006, 106 master's, 32 doctorates awarded. *Degree requirements:* For master's, comprehensive exam or thesis; for doctorate, thesis/dissertation, comprehensive exam. *Entrance requirements:* For master's, GRE General Test or MAT; for doctorate, GRE General Test, interview. *Application deadline:* For fall admission, 7/3 priority date for domestic students. Applications are processed on a rolling basis. Application fee: $35 ($75 for international students). *Expenses:* Tuition, state resident: full-time $5,429; part-time $226 per credit. Tuition, nonresident: full-time $12,029; part-time $501 per credit. Required fees: $2,454. *Financial support:* In 2006–07, 2 fellowships with full tuition reimbursements (averaging $9,500 per year), 6 research assistantships with full tuition reimbursements (averaging $8,800 per year), 25 teaching assistantships with full tuition reimbursements (averaging $8,800 per year) were awarded; career-related internships or fieldwork, Federal Work-Study, institutionally sponsored loans, scholarships/grants, health care benefits, and unspecified assistantships also available. Support available to part-time students. Financial award application deadline: 3/10. *Faculty research:* Teaching-learning process, instructional technology in schools, teacher education, classroom management, at-risk students. *Unit head:* Dr. Juanita Copley, Chairperson, 713-743-4950, Fax: 713-743-4990, E-mail: ncopley@aol.com.

University of Illinois at Chicago, Graduate College, College of Education, Department of Curriculum and Instruction, Chicago, IL 60607-7128. Offers curriculum and instruction (PhD); educational psychology (PhD); instructional leadership (M Ed), including elementary education, reading, secondary education; leadership and administration (M Ed); policy and administration (PhD); policy studies in urban education (PhD). Part-time and evening/weekend programs available. *Degree requirements:* For doctorate, thesis/dissertation. *Entrance requirements:* For master's, minimum GPA of 2.75; for doctorate, GRE General Test, minimum GPA of 2.75. Additional exam requirements/recommendations for international students: Required—TOEFL. Electronic applications accepted. *Faculty research:* Curriculum theory, curriculum development, research on teaching, curriculum and context, reading/literacy.

University of Indianapolis, Graduate Programs, School of Education, Indianapolis, IN 46227-3697. Offers art education (MAT); biology (MAT); chemistry (MAT); curriculum and instruction (MA); earth sciences (MAT); education (MA, MAT); educational leadership (MA); elementary education (MA); English (MAT); French (MAT); math (MAT); physical education (MAT); physics (MAT); secondary education (MA), including art education, education, English education, social studies education; social studies (MAT); Spanish (MAT). *Accreditation:* NCATE. Part-time and evening/weekend programs available. *Faculty:* 4 full-time (2 women), 6 part-time/adjunct (2 women). *Students:* 32 full-time (16 women), 70 part-time (42 women); includes 2 minority (1 African American, 1 Hispanic American). Average age 31. In 2006, 51 degrees awarded. *Entrance requirements:* For master's, GRE Subject Test, minimum GPA of 2.5, 3 letters of recommendation, interview, Praxis I, writing exercise, be within 9 hours of completing content requirements. Additional exam requirements/recommendations for international students: Required—TOEFL (minimum score 550 paper-based; 213 computer-based). *Application deadline:* Applications are processed on a rolling basis. Application fee: $50. *Financial support:* Federal Work-Study available. Financial award application deadline: 5/1; financial award applicants required to submit FAFSA. *Faculty research:* Assessment of teacher education, perceptions of prospective teachers by parents. *Unit head:* Dr. E. Lynne Weisenbach, Dean, 317-788-3446, Fax: 317-788-3300, E-mail: weisenbach@uindy.edu.

The University of Iowa, Graduate College, College of Education, Department of Teaching and Learning, Program in Early Childhood and Elementary Education, Iowa City, IA 52242-1316. Offers curriculum and supervision (MA, PhD); developmental reading (MA); early childhood education and care (MA); elementary education (MA, PhD); language, literature and culture (PhD). *Faculty:* 7 full-time, 4 part-time/adjunct. *Students:* 8 full-time (7 women), 23 part-time (all women); includes 2 minority (both African Americans), 5 international. 6 applicants, 67% accepted, 4 enrolled. In 2006, 11 master's, 1 doctorate awarded. *Degree requirements:* For master's, exam, thesis optional; for doctorate, thesis/dissertation, comprehensive exam, registration. *Entrance requirements:* For master's and doctorate, GRE General Test, minimum GPA of 3.0. Additional exam requirements/recommendations for international students: Required—TOEFL (minimum score 550 paper-based; 213 computer-based; 81 iBT). Application fee: $60 ($85 for international students). Electronic applications accepted. *Financial support:* In 2006–07, 1 fellowship, 2 research assistantships with partial tuition reimbursements, 8 teaching assistantships with partial tuition reimbursements were awarded. Financial award applicants required to submit FAFSA. *Unit head:* Gary Sasso, Chair, 319-335-5324, Fax: 319-335-5608.

University of Louisiana at Monroe, Graduate Studies and Research, College of Education and Human Development, Department of Curriculum and Instruction, Program in Elementary Education, Monroe, LA 71209-0001. Offers M Ed, MAT. *Accreditation:* NCATE. Part-time and evening/weekend programs available. *Students:* 15 full-time (13 women), 92 part-time (76 women); includes 35 minority (all African Americans) Average age 33. In 2006, 72 degrees awarded. *Degree requirements:* For master's, thesis optional. *Entrance requirements:* For master's, GRE General Test, minimum GPA of 2.5. *Application deadline:* For fall admission, 7/1 for domestic students; for spring admission, 11/1 for domestic students. Application fee: $20 ($30 for international students). *Expenses:* Tuition, state resident: part-time $124 per credit hour. Tuition, nonresident: part-time $124 per credit hour. *Financial support:* Research assistantships, teaching assistantships, career-related internships or fieldwork and unspecified assistantships available. Financial award application deadline: 7/1. *Faculty research:* Student attitudes. *Unit head:* Dr. Gary Stringer, Head, Department of Curriculum and Instruction, 318-342-1266, Fax: 318-342-1240, E-mail: stringer@ulm.edu.

University of Louisville, Graduate School, College of Education and Human Development, Department of Teaching and Learning, Program in Early Elementary Education, Louisville, KY 40292-0001. Offers M Ed, MAT. *Accreditation:* NCATE. *Students:* 70 full-time (67 women), 29 part-time (26 women); includes 16 minority (15 African Americans, 1 Asian American or Pacific Islander), 1 international. Average age 33. In 2006, 62 degrees awarded. *Entrance requirements:* For master's, GRE General Test. *Application deadline:* Applications are processed on a rolling basis. Application fee: $50. Electronic applications accepted. *Financial support:* Fellowships, research assistantships, teaching assistantships, Federal Work-Study and scholarships/grants available. *Unit head:* Dr. Chuck Thompson, Head, 502-852-0583, Fax: 502-852-1497, E-mail: chuck@louisville.edu.

University of Maine, Graduate School, College of Education and Human Development, Program in Elementary Education, Orono, ME 04469. Offers M Ed, MAT, MS, CAS. *Accreditation:* NCATE. Part-time and evening/weekend programs available. *Students:* 17 full-time (13 women), 3 part-time (all women); includes 2 minority (1 American Indian/Alaska Native, 1 Asian American or Pacific Islander). Average age 33. 1 applicant, 100% accepted, 1 enrolled. In 2006, 11 degrees awarded. *Degree requirements:* For master's, thesis or alternative. *Entrance requirements:* For master's, MAT; for CAS, MA, M Ed, or MS. Additional exam requirements/recommendations for international students: Required—TOEFL. *Application deadline:* For fall admission, 2/1 priority date for domestic students. Applications are processed on a rolling basis. Application fee: $50. Electronic applications accepted. *Financial support:* Research assistantships with tuition reimbursements, teaching assistantships with tuition reimbursements, career-related internships or fieldwork, Federal Work-Study, institutionally sponsored loans, tuition waivers (full and partial), and unspecified assistantships available. Financial award application deadline: 3/1. *Unit head:* Dr. Dorothy Breen, Coordinator, 207-581-2444, Fax: 207-581-2423. *Application contact:* Scott G. Delcourt, Associate Dean of the Graduate School, 207-581-3219, Fax: 207-581-3232, E-mail: graduate@maine.edu.

University of Maryland, Baltimore County, Graduate School, College of Arts, Humanities and Social Sciences, Department of Education, Program in Education, Baltimore, MD 21250. Offers early childhood education (MAT); elementary education (MAT); secondary education (MAT). Part-time and evening/weekend programs available. *Faculty:* 17 full-time (15 women), 3 part-time/adjunct (all women). *Students:* 49 full-time (43 women), 89 part-time (69 women); includes 11 minority (8 African Americans, 2 Asian Americans or Pacific Islanders, 1 Hispanic American). Average age 30. In 2006, 21 master's awarded. *Median time to degree:* Of those who began their doctoral program in fall 1998, 95% received their degree in 8 years or less. *Degree requirements:* For master's, thesis (for some programs), comprehensive exam, registration. *Entrance requirements:* For master's, PRAXIS I and II, minimum GPA of 3.0. *Application deadline:* Applications are processed on a rolling basis. Application fee: $50. Electronic applications accepted. *Expenses:* Tuition, state resident: part-time $412 per credit hour. Tuition, nonresident: part-time $681 per credit hour. Required fees: $91 per credit hour. One-time fee: $75 part-time. *Financial support:* In 2006–07, 6 students received support, including research assistantships with full tuition reimbursements available (averaging $12,000 per year); career-related internships or fieldwork, Federal Work-Study, scholarships/grants, tuition waivers, and unspecified assistantships also available. Financial award application deadline: 3/1. *Faculty research:* STEM teacher education, culturally sensitive pedagogy. Total annual research expenditures: $1.3 million. *Unit head:* Dr. Susan M. Blunck, Director, 410-455-2869, Fax: 410-455-3986, E-mail: blunck@umbc.edu. *Application contact:* Dr. Susan M. Blunck, Director, 410-455-2869, Fax: 410-455-3986, E-mail: blunck@umbc.edu.

University of Massachusetts Amherst, Graduate School, School of Education, Program in Education, Amherst, MA 01003. Offers cultural diversity and curriculum reform (M Ed, Ed D, CAGS); early childhood education and development (M Ed, Ed D, CAGS); educational administration (M Ed, Ed D, CAGS); elementary teacher education (M Ed, Ed D, CAGS); higher education (M Ed, Ed D, CAGS); international education (M Ed, Ed D, CAGS); mathematics, science, and instructional technology (M Ed, Ed D, CAGS); physical education teacher education (M Ed, Ed D, CAGS); reading and writing (M Ed, Ed D, CAGS); research and evaluation methods (M Ed, Ed D, CAGS); school psychology and school counseling (M Ed, Ed D, CAGS); secondary teacher education (M Ed, Ed D, CAGS); social justice education (M Ed, Ed D, CAGS); special education (M Ed, Ed D, CAGS). *Accreditation:* NCATE. *Students:* 418 full-time (286 women), 447 part-time (319 women); includes 147 minority (70 African Americans, 4 American Indian/Alaska Native, 28 Asian Americans or Pacific Islanders, 45 Hispanic Americans), 81 international. Average age 36. In 2006, 260 master's, 30 doctorates awarded. *Degree requirements:* For doctorate, thesis/dissertation. *Entrance requirements:* For master's and doctorate, GRE General Test. Additional exam requirements/recommendations for international students: Required—TOEFL (minimum score 530 paper-based; 197 computer-based). *Application deadline:* For fall admission, 1/15 for domestic and international students; for spring admission, 10/1 for domestic and international students. Applications are processed on a rolling basis. Application fee: $40 ($65 for international students). Electronic applications accepted. *Expenses:* Tuition, state resident: full-time $2,640; part-time $110 per credit. Tuition, nonresident: full-time $9,936; part-time $414 per credit. Required fees: $8,969; $3,129 per term. One-time fee: $257 full-time. Tuition and fees vary according to class time, course load, campus/location and reciprocity agreements. *Financial support:* Fellowships with full tuition reimbursements, research assistantships with full tuition reimbursements, teaching assistantships with full tuition reimbursements, career-related internships or fieldwork, Federal Work-Study, scholarships/grants, traineeships, and unspecified assistantships available. Support available to part-time students. Financial award application deadline: 1/15. *Unit head:* Linda L. Griffin, Professor, 413-545-6984.

University of Massachusetts Boston, Office of Graduate Studies, Graduate College of Education, School Organization, Curriculum and Instruction Department, Boston, MA 02125-3393. Offers education (M Ed, Ed D), including elementary and secondary education/certification (M Ed), higher education administration (Ed D), teacher certification (M Ed), urban school leadership (Ed D); educational administration (M Ed, CAGS); special education (M Ed). *Students:* 141 full-time (103 women), 403 part-time (291 women); includes 81 minority (44 African Americans, 1 American Indian/Alaska Native, 13 Asian Americans or Pacific Islanders, 23 Hispanic Americans), 7 international. Average age 37. 381 applicants, 72% accepted, 178 enrolled. In 2006, 117 master's, 18 doctorates, 10 other advanced degrees awarded. *Degree requirements:* For master's and CAGS, comprehensive exam; for doctorate, thesis/dissertation, comprehensive exam. *Entrance requirements:* For master's, GRE General Test or MAT; for doctorate, GRE General Test or MAT, minimum GPA of 2.75; for CAGS, minimum GPA of 2.75. *Application deadline:* For fall admission, 3/1 for domestic students. Application fee: $25 ($35 for international students). *Expenses:* Tuition, state resident: full-time $2,590; part-time $301 per credit. Tuition, nonresident: full-time $9,758; part-time $427 per credit. One-time fee: $495 full-time. *Financial support:* In 2006–07, 37 research assistantships with full tuition reimbursements (averaging $2,000 per year), teaching assistantships with full tuition reimbursements (averaging $2,000 per year) were awarded; unspecified assistantships also available. Financial award application deadline: 3/1; financial award applicants required to submit FAFSA. *Unit head:* Dr. Lisa Coonsalves, Director, 617-287-7642, E-mail: lisa.gonsalves@umb.edu. *Application contact:* Peggy Roldan, Graduate Admissions Coordinator, 617-287-6400, Fax: 617-287-6236, E-mail: bos.gadm@dpc.umassp.edu.

University of Massachusetts Boston, Office of Graduate Studies, Graduate College of Education, School Organization, Curriculum and Instruction Department, Program in Education, Track in Elementary and Secondary Education/Certification, Boston, MA 02125-3393. Offers M Ed. *Accreditation:* NCATE. Part-time and evening/weekend programs available. *Students:* 113 full-time (86 women), 241 part-time (182 women); includes 38 minority (21 African Americans, 7 Asian Americans or Pacific Islanders, 10 Hispanic Americans), 2 international. Average age 31. 259 applicants, 80% accepted, 124 enrolled. In 2006, 98 degrees awarded. *Degree requirements:* For master's, practicum, thesis optional. *Entrance requirements:* For master's, GRE General Test or MAT, minimum GPA of 3.0, 2 years of teaching experience. *Application deadline:* For fall admission, 3/1 priority date for domestic students; for spring admission, 11/1 for domestic students. Application fee: $25 ($40 for international students). *Expenses:* Tuition, state resident: full-time $2,590; part-time $301 per credit. Tuition, nonresident: full-time $9,758; part-time $427 per credit. One-time fee: $495 full-time. *Financial support:* In 2006–07, 30 research assistantships with full tuition reimbursements (averaging $4,000 per year), teaching assistantships with full tuition reimbursements (averaging $4,000 per year) were awarded; career-related internships or fieldwork, Federal Work-Study, and unspecified assistantships also available. Support available to part-time students. Financial award application deadline: 3/1; financial award applicants required to submit FAFSA. *Faculty research:* Anti-bias education, inclusionary curriculum and instruction, creativity and learning, science, technology and society, teaching of reading. *Unit head:* Dr. Joseph Check, Director, 617-287-7655, E-mail: joseph.check@umb.edu. *Application contact:*

Peggy Roldan, Graduate Admissions Coordinator, 617-287-6400, Fax: 617-287-6236, E-mail: bos.gadm@dpc.umassp.edu.

University of Memphis, Graduate School, College of Education, Department of Instruction and Curriculum Leadership, Memphis, TN 38152. Offers early childhood education (MAT, MS, Ed D); elementary education (MAT); instruction and curriculum (MS, Ed D); instruction design and technology (MS, Ed D); reading (MS, Ed D); secondary education (MAT); special education (MAT, MS, Ed D). *Accreditation:* NCATE (one or more programs are accredited). Part-time programs available. Terminal master's awarded for partial completion of doctoral program. *Degree requirements:* For master's, thesis or alternative, comprehensive exam; for doctorate, thesis/dissertation, comprehensive exam. *Entrance requirements:* For master's, GRE General Test, minimum GPA of 2.5; for doctorate, GRE General Test, GRE Subject Test, 2 years of teaching experience. Electronic applications accepted. *Faculty research:* Effective urban teachers, preparation and retention of urban teachers, technology utilization in schools, field-based preparation teacher preparation programs, effective use of online instruction.

University of Miami, Graduate School, School of Education, Department of Teaching and Learning, Program in Elementary Education/TESOL, Coral Gables, FL 33124. Offers MS Ed. *Accreditation:* NCATE. Part-time and evening/weekend programs available. *Students:* 10 full-time (9 women), 8 part-time (all women); includes 3 minority (all Hispanic Americans), 2 international. 9 applicants, 56% accepted, 4 enrolled. In 2006, 7 degrees awarded. *Degree requirements:* For master's, electronic portfolio review. *Entrance requirements:* For master's, GRE General Test. Additional exam requirements/recommendations for international students: Required—TOEFL (minimum score 550 paper-based; 212 computer-based). *Application deadline:* Applications are processed on a rolling basis. Application fee: $50. Electronic applications accepted. *Financial support:* In 2006–07, 12 students received support. Federal Work-Study and tuition waivers (partial) available. Financial award application deadline: 3/1; financial award applicants required to submit FAFSA. *Faculty research:* Mathematics, technology. *Unit head:* Dr. Cory Buxton, Advisor, 305-284-5946, Fax: 305-284-4439, E-mail: cbuxton@miami.edu.

University of Michigan, Horace H. Rackham School of Graduate Studies, School of Education, Programs in Educational Studies, Ann Arbor, MI 48109. Offers curriculum development (MA); early childhood education (MA, PhD); educational administration and policy (MA, PhD); educational foundation, administration, policy, and research methods (MA); educational foundations and policy (MA, PhD); elementary education (MA-Certification); English education (MA); English language learning in school settings (MA); learning technologies (MA, PhD); literacy, language, and culture (MA, PhD); mathematics education (MA, PhD); research methods (MA); science education (MA, PhD); secondary education (MA-Certification); social studies education (MA); special education (PhD); teaching and teacher education (PhD); MA-Certification; MBA/MA; PhD/MA. Terminal master's awarded for partial completion of doctoral program. *Degree requirements:* For master's, thesis (for some programs); for doctorate, thesis/dissertation, comprehensive exam. *Entrance requirements:* For master's and doctorate, GRE General Test. Additional exam requirements/recommendations for international students: Required—TOEFL (minimum score 600 paper-based; 250 computer-based). *Application deadline:* For fall admission, 12/1 priority date for domestic students, 12/1 for international students. Application fee: $60 ($75 for international students). Electronic applications accepted. *Financial support:* Applicants required to submit FAFSA. *Unit head:* Dr. Addison Stone, Chairperson, 734-763-7500, Fax: 734-615-1290, E-mail: addison@umich.edu. *Application contact:* Roberta Perry, Office of Student Services, 734-764-7563, Fax: 734-763-1495, E-mail: ed.grad.admit@umich.edu.

University of Michigan–Flint, School of Education and Human Services, Department of Education, Flint, MI 48502-1950. Offers early childhood education (MA Ed); education (MA Ed); elementary education with teaching certificate (MA Ed); literacy (K-12) (MA Ed); special education (MA Ed); urban and multicultural education (MA Ed). Part-time programs available. *Faculty:* 19 full-time (15 women), 9 part-time/adjunct (6 women). *Students:* 20 full-time (18 women), 193 part-time (167 women); includes 15 minority (12 African Americans, 1 American Indian/Alaska Native, 2 Hispanic Americans), 2 international. 109 applicants, 80% accepted, 65 enrolled. In 2006, 54 degrees awarded. *Entrance requirements:* Additional exam requirements/recommendations for international students: Required—TOEFL (minimum score 550 paper-based; 220 computer-based), IELTS (minimum score 7). *Application deadline:* For fall admission, 8/1 priority date for domestic students, 3/1 priority date for international students; for winter admission, 11/15 priority date for domestic students, 7/15 priority date for international students; for spring admission, 3/15 priority date for domestic students, 11/15 priority date for international students. Application fee: $55. *Expenses:* Contact institution. *Unit head:* Dr. Beverly Schumer, Director, 810-424-5215, E-mail: bschumer@umflint.edu. *Application contact:* Beulah Alexander, Executive Secretary, 810-766-6879, Fax: 810-766-6891, E-mail: beulaha@umflint.edu.

University of Minnesota, Twin Cities Campus, Graduate School, College of Education and Human Development, Department of Curriculum and Instruction, Minneapolis, MN 55455-0213. Offers art education (M Ed, MA, PhD); children's literature (M Ed, MA, PhD); curriculum and instruction (MA, PhD); early childhood education (M Ed, PhD); elementary education (M Ed, MA, PhD); English education (MA, PhD); environmental education (M Ed); family education (M Ed, MA, Ed D, PhD); instructional systems and technology (M Ed, MA, PhD); language arts (MA, PhD); language immersion education (Certificate); literacy education (MA); mathematics education (MA, PhD); reading education (MA, PhD); science education (MA, PhD); second languages and cultures education (MA, PhD); social studies education (MA, PhD); teaching (M Ed), including Chinese, earth science, elementary special education, English, English as a second language, French, German, Hebrew, Japanese, life sciences, mathematics, middle school science, science, second languages and cultures, social studies, Spanish; technology enhanced learning (Certificate); writing education (M Ed, MA, PhD). *Faculty:* 30 full-time (18 women). *Students:* 496 full-time (363 women), 338 part-time (235 women); includes 89 minority (26 African Americans, 4 American Indian/Alaska Native, 42 Asian Americans or Pacific Islanders, 17 Hispanic Americans), 33 international. Average age 29. 734 applicants, 66% accepted, 425 enrolled. In 2006, 644 master's, 18 doctorates, 11 other advanced degrees awarded. *Expenses:* Tuition, state resident: full-time $9,302; part-time $775 per credit. Tuition, nonresident: full-time $16,400; part-time $1,367 per credit. Full-time tuition and fees vary according to class time, course load, program, reciprocity agreements and student level. *Financial support:* In 2006–07, 7 fellowships (averaging $24,775 per year), 22 research assistantships with full tuition reimbursements (averaging $24,775 per year), 52 teaching assistantships with full tuition reimbursements (averaging $24,775 per year) were awarded. *Faculty research:* Educational practice for a democratic and just society; curriculum history and development/assessment; teacher preparation/induction/mentoring/development; cultural, linguistic, social, political, technological, and economic factors that influence teaching and learning. Total annual research expenditures: $1.2 million. *Unit head:* Dr. Ruth Thomas, Chair, 612-624-4772, Fax: 612-624-8277, E-mail: thoma006@umn.edu. *Application contact:* Dr. Mary Bents, Associate Dean, 612-625-6501, Fax: 612-626-1580, E-mail: mbents@tc.umn.edu.

University of Missouri–Columbia, Graduate School, College of Education, Department of Curriculum and Instruction, Columbia, MO 65211. Offers agricultural education (M Ed, PhD, Ed S); art education (M Ed, PhD, Ed S); business and office education (M Ed, PhD, Ed S); early childhood education (M Ed, PhD, Ed S); elementary education (M Ed, PhD, Ed S); English education (M Ed, PhD, Ed S); foreign language education (M Ed, PhD, Ed S); health education and promotion (M Ed, PhD); learning and instruction (M Ed); marketing education (M Ed, PhD, Ed S); mathematics education (M Ed, PhD, Ed S); music education (M Ed, PhD, Ed S); reading education (M Ed, PhD, Ed S); science education (M Ed, PhD, Ed S); social studies education (M Ed, PhD, Ed S); vocational education (M Ed, PhD, Ed S). Part-time programs available. *Faculty:* 24 full-time (12 women). *Students:* 195 full-time (148 women), 260 part-time (214 women); includes 27 minority (8 African Americans, 1 American Indian/Alaska Native, 10 Asian Americans or Pacific Islanders, 8 Hispanic Americans), 19 international. In 2006, 186 master's, 12 doctorates awarded. Terminal master's awarded for partial completion of doctoral program. *Degree requirements:* For doctorate, thesis/dissertation. *Entrance requirements:* For master's and Ed S, GRE General Test or MAT, minimum GPA of 3.0; for doctorate, GRE General Test, minimum GPA of 3.0. *Application deadline:* Applications are processed on a rolling basis. Application fee: $45 ($60 for international students). *Financial support:* Fellowships, research assistantships, teaching assistantships, institutionally sponsored loans available. *Unit head:* Dr. Lloyd H. Barrow, Director of Graduate Studies, 573-882-8247, E-mail: robinsonr@missouri.edu.

University of Missouri–St. Louis, College of Education, Division of Teaching and Learning, St. Louis, MO 63121. Offers elementary education (M Ed), including reading; secondary education (M Ed), including curriculum and instruction, middle school, reading; special education (M Ed), including behavioral disorders, early childhood special education, learning disabilities, mentally retardation; teaching-learning processes (Ed D, PhD). *Faculty:* 20 full-time (13 women), 5 part-time/adjunct (4 women). *Students:* 118 full-time (84 women), 353 part-time (311 women); includes 90 minority (75 African Americans, 1 American Indian/Alaska Native, 3 Asian Americans or Pacific Islanders, 11 Hispanic Americans), 4 international. Average age 36. In 2006, 136 master's, 3 doctorates awarded. *Entrance requirements:* For doctorate, GRE General Test, 3 letters of recommendation. *Application deadline:* For fall admission, 7/15 for domestic students; for spring admission, 12/15 for domestic students. *Expenses:* Tuition, state resident: part-time $332 per credit hour. Tuition, nonresident: part-time $770 per credit hour. *Financial support:* In 2006–07, 9 teaching assistantships (averaging $14,250 per year) were awarded; research assistantships. *Unit head:* Dr. Gayle Wilkinson, Chair, 314-516-5791. *Application contact:* 314-516-5458, Fax: 314-516-6996, E-mail: gadadm@umsl.edu.

University of Montevallo, College of Education, Program in Elementary Education, Montevallo, AL 35115. Offers M Ed. *Accreditation:* NCATE. Part-time programs available. *Degree requirements:* For master's, comprehensive exam. *Entrance requirements:* For master's, GRE General Test, MAT, minimum undergraduate GPA of 2.5. Additional exam requirements/recommendations for international students: Required—TOEFL (minimum score 550 paper-based).

University of Nebraska at Omaha, Graduate Studies and Research, College of Education, Department of Teacher Education, Program in Elementary Education, Omaha, NE 68182. Offers MA, MS. *Accreditation:* NCATE. Part-time and evening/weekend programs available. *Faculty:* 10 full-time (7 women). *Students:* 3 full-time (all women), 113 part-time (106 women); includes 7 minority (4 African Americans, 1 Asian American or Pacific Islander, 2 Hispanic Americans). Average age 31. 36 applicants, 81% accepted, 14 enrolled. In 2006, 48 degrees awarded. *Degree requirements:* For master's, thesis (for some programs), comprehensive exam. *Entrance requirements:* For master's, minimum GPA of 3.0. Additional exam requirements/recommendations for international students: Required—TOEFL (minimum score 550 paper-based; 213 computer-based; 80 iBT). *Application deadline:* For fall admission, 7/1 priority date for domestic students; for spring admission, 12/1 priority date for domestic students. Applications are processed on a rolling basis. Application fee: $45. Electronic applications accepted. *Financial support:* In 2006–07, 48 students received support; fellowships, teaching assistantships, Federal Work-Study, institutionally sponsored loans, scholarships/grants, tuition waivers (full), and unspecified assistantships available. Support available to part-time students. Financial award application deadline: 3/1.

University of Nevada, Las Vegas, Graduate College, College of Education, Department of Curriculum and Instruction, Las Vegas, NV 89154-9900. Offers curriculum and instruction (Ed D, PhD, Ed S); elementary education (M Ed, MS); English education (M Ed, MS); library science (M Ed, MS); literacy education (M Ed, MS); mathematics education (M Ed, MS); multicultural education (M Ed, MS); reading specialist (M Ed, MS); secondary education (M Ed, MS); teacher leadership (M Ed, MS); teaching English as a second language (M Ed, MS); technology integration and leadership (M Ed, MS). *Accreditation:* NCATE. Part-time and evening/weekend programs available. *Faculty:* 40 full-time (19 women), 21 part-time/adjunct (14 women). *Students:* 257 full-time (189 women), 387 part-time (296 women); includes 114 minority (28 African Americans, 5 American Indian/Alaska Native, 34 Asian Americans or Pacific Islanders, 47 Hispanic Americans), 7 international. 261 applicants, 70% accepted, 168 enrolled. In 2006, 231 master's, 5 doctorates awarded. *Degree requirements:* For master's, thesis (for some programs), comprehensive exam (for some programs); for doctorate, thesis/dissertation, oral exam. *Entrance requirements:* For master's, minimum GPA of 3.0; for doctorate, GRE General Test, minimum graduate GPA of 3.0. Additional exam requirements/recommendations for international students: Required—TOEFL (minimum score 550 paper-based; 213 computer-based; 80 iBT). *Application deadline:* For fall admission, 2/15 for domestic and international students; for spring admission, 9/30 for domestic and international students. Application fee: $60 ($75 for international students). Electronic applications accepted. *Financial support:* In 2006–07, 30 research assistantships with partial tuition reimbursements (averaging $10,000 per year), 7 teaching assistantships with partial tuition reimbursements (averaging $12,000 per year) were awarded; career-related internships or fieldwork, Federal Work-Study, institutionally sponsored loans, scholarships/grants, health care benefits, and unspecified assistantships also available. Support available to part-time students. Financial award application deadline: 3/1. *Unit head:* Dr. Greg Levitt, Chair, 702-895-3241. *Application contact:* Graduate College Admissions Evaluator, 702-895-3320, E-mail: gradcollege@unlv.edu.

University of Nevada, Reno, Graduate School, College of Education, Department of Curriculum, Teaching and Learning, Reno, NV 89557. Offers curriculum, teaching and learning (Ed D, PhD); elementary education (M Ed, MA, Ed S); secondary education (M Ed, MA, MS, Ed S); special education and disability studies (PhD). *Students:* 82 full-time (65 women), 74 part-time (58 women); includes 12 minority (1 African American, 3 American Indian/Alaska Native, 5 Asian Americans or Pacific Islanders, 3 Hispanic Americans), 2 international. Average age 35. 66 applicants, 85% accepted, 0 enrolled. In 2006, 51 degrees awarded. *Degree requirements:* For master's, thesis optional. *Entrance requirements:* For master's, GRE General Test, minimum GPA of 2.75. Additional exam requirements/recommendations for international students: Required—TOEFL (minimum score 500 paper-based; 173 computer-based). *Application deadline:* For fall admission, 3/1 priority date for domestic students; for spring admission, 10/1 for domestic students. Applications are processed on a rolling basis. Application fee: $60 ($95 for international students). Electronic applications accepted. *Unit head:* Dr. Margaret Ferrara, Program Director, 775-682-7530, E-mail: ferrara@unr.edu.

University of New Hampshire, Graduate School, College of Liberal Arts, Department of Education, Program in Elementary Education, Durham, NH 03824. Offers M Ed, MAT. Part-time programs available. *Faculty:* 32 full-time. *Students:* 48 full-time (44 women), 33 part-time (all women); includes 3 minority (1 African American, 1 Asian American or Pacific Islander, 1 Hispanic American). Average age 29. 30 applicants, 63% accepted, 18 enrolled. In 2006, 69 degrees awarded. *Degree requirements:* For master's, thesis or alternative. *Entrance requirements:* For master's, GRE General Test. Additional exam requirements/recommendations for international students: Required—TOEFL (minimum score 550 paper-based; 213 computer-based). *Application deadline:* For fall admission, 4/1 priority date for domestic students, 4/1 for international students; for winter admission, 12/1 for domestic students. Applications are processed on a rolling basis. Application fee: $60. *Expenses:* Tuition, state resident: full-time $8,540; part-time $474 per credit hour. Tuition, nonresident: full-time $20,990; part-time $862 per credit hour. Required fees: $1,343; $356 per term. Tuition and fees vary according to course load, program and reciprocity agreements. *Financial support:* In 2006–07, 1 fellowship, 1 teaching assistantship were awarded; research assistantships, career-related internships or fieldwork, Federal Work-Study, scholarships/grants, and tuition waivers (full and partial) also available. Support available to part-time students. Financial award application deadline: 2/15. *Faculty research:* Pre-service teacher education. *Unit head:* Dr. Michael D. Andrew, Coordinator, 603-862-2371, E-mail: education.department@unh.edu.

University of New Mexico, Graduate School, College of Education, Department of Teacher Education, Program in Elementary Education, Albuquerque, NM 87131-2039. Offers MA,

Elementary Education

University of New Mexico (continued)

EDSPC. Part-time and evening/weekend programs available. *Students:* 20 full-time (15 women), 129 part-time (105 women); includes 50 minority (2 African Americans, 22 American Indian/Alaska Native, 2 Asian Americans or Pacific Islanders, 24 Hispanic Americans). Average age 38. 42 applicants, 57% accepted, 22 enrolled. *Degree requirements:* For master's, thesis optional. *Entrance requirements:* For master's, overall GPA of 3.0, some experience working with students, 3 letters of reference, 1 letter of intent, International students: Above information plus I-20; for EDSPC, master's degree required, overall GPA of 3.0, experience working with students, 3 letters of reference, 1 letter of intent, International students: Above information plus I-20. Additional exam requirements/recommendations for international students: Required—TOEFL (minimum score 550 paper-based; 213 computer-based). *Application deadline:* For fall admission, 3/1 priority date for domestic students; for spring admission, 10/1 priority date for domestic students. Applications are processed on a rolling basis. Application fee: $50. Electronic applications accepted. *Financial support:* In 2006–07, 2 teaching assistantships with partial tuition reimbursements (averaging $11,641 per year) were awarded; career-related internships or fieldwork, scholarships/grants, and unspecified assistantships also available. Financial award applicants required to submit FAFSA. *Unit head:* Dr. Rosalita Mitchell, Chair, 505-277-9611, Fax: 505-277-0455, E-mail: rosalita@unm.edu. *Application contact:* Mary Francis, Administrative Assistant, 505-277-9439, Fax: 505-277-4532, E-mail: mfrancis@unm.edu.

University of North Alabama, College of Education, Department of Elementary Education, Program in Elementary Education, Florence, AL 35632-0001. Offers MA Ed, Ed S. *Accreditation:* NCATE. Part-time and evening/weekend programs available. *Faculty:* 3 part-time/adjunct (all women). *Students:* 8 full-time (all women), 61 part-time (57 women); includes 6 minority (3 African Americans, 2 American Indian/Alaska Native, 1 Hispanic American). Average age 33. In 2006, 35 degrees awarded. *Degree requirements:* For master's, comprehensive exam. *Entrance requirements:* For master's, GRE, MAT, or NTE, minimum GPA of 2.5, Alabama Class B Certificate or equivalent, teaching experience. *Application deadline:* For fall admission, 7/1 priority date for domestic students; for spring admission, 12/1 for domestic students. Applications are processed on a rolling basis. Application fee: $25. Electronic applications accepted. *Expenses:* Tuition, state resident: full-time $4,080. Tuition, nonresident: full-time $8,160. Required fees: $764. *Financial support:* Federal Work-Study available. Support available to part-time students. Financial award application deadline: 4/1. *Application contact:* Dr. Sue Wilson, Dean of Enrollment Management, 256-765-4316, Fax: 256-765-4349, E-mail: sjwilson@una.edu.

The University of North Carolina at Charlotte, Graduate School, College of Education, Department of Reading and Elementary Education, Charlotte, NC 28223-0001. Offers elementary education (M Ed); reading education (M Ed). Part-time and evening/weekend programs available. Postbaccalaureate distance learning degree programs offered (no on-campus study). *Faculty:* 17 full-time (8 women), 2 part-time/adjunct (0 women). *Students:* 4 full-time (all women), 80 part-time (78 women); includes 4 minority (3 African Americans, 1 American Indian/Alaska Native). Average age 30. 28 applicants, 89% accepted, 20 enrolled. In 2006, 28 degrees awarded. *Entrance requirements:* For master's, GRE or MAT. Additional exam requirements/recommendations for international students: Required—TOEFL (minimum score 557 paper-based; 220 computer-based). *Application deadline:* For fall admission, 7/1 for domestic students, 5/1 for international students; for spring admission, 11/1 for domestic students, 10/1 for international students. Applications are processed on a rolling basis. Application fee: $55. Electronic applications accepted. *Expenses:* Tuition, state resident: full-time $2,719; part-time $170 per credit. Tuition, nonresident: full-time $12,926; part-time $808 per credit. Required fees: $1,555. *Financial support:* In 2006–07, 4 teaching assistantships (averaging $8,500 per year) were awarded; fellowships, research assistantships, career-related internships or fieldwork, Federal Work-Study, institutionally sponsored loans, scholarships/grants, and unspecified assistantships also available. Support available to part-time students. Financial award application deadline: 4/1; financial award applicants required to submit FAFSA. *Unit head:* Dr. Robert J. Rickelman, Chair, 704-687-8889, Fax: 704-687-3749, E-mail: rjrickel@email.uncc.edu. *Application contact:* Kathy B. Giddings, Director of Graduate Admissions, 704-687-3366, Fax: 704-687-3279, E-mail: gradadm@email.uncc.edu.

The University of North Carolina at Charlotte, Graduate School, College of Education, Program in Teacher Education, Charlotte, NC 28223-0001. Offers art education (K-12) (MAT); dance education (K-12) (MAT); elementary education (K-6) (MAT); English as a second language (K-12) (MAT); foreign language education (K-12) (MAT); general teacher education (MAT); middle grades education (6-9) (MAT); music education (K-12) (MAT); secondary education (9-12) (MAT); special education (K-12) (MAT); theatre education (K-12) (MAT). *Students:* 16 full-time (12 women), 200 part-time (170 women); includes 30 minority (22 African Americans, 2 American Indian/Alaska Native, 2 Asian Americans or Pacific Islanders, 4 Hispanic Americans), 2 international. Average age 33. 74 applicants, 85% accepted, 49 enrolled. In 2006, 43 degrees awarded. *Entrance requirements:* For master's, GRE or MAT. Additional exam requirements/recommendations for international students: Required—TOEFL (minimum score 557 paper-based; 220 computer-based). *Application deadline:* For fall admission, 7/1 for domestic students, 5/1 for international students; for spring admission, 11/1 for domestic students, 10/1 for international students. Applications are processed on a rolling basis. Application fee: $55. Electronic applications accepted. *Expenses:* Tuition, state resident: full-time $2,719; part-time $170 per credit. Tuition, nonresident: full-time $12,926; part-time $808 per credit. Required fees: $1,555. *Financial support:* Fellowships, research assistantships, teaching assistantships, career-related internships or fieldwork, Federal Work-Study, institutionally sponsored loans, scholarships/grants, and unspecified assistantships available. Support available to part-time students. Financial award application deadline: 4/1; financial award applicants required to submit FAFSA. *Unit head:* Dr. Kimberly J. Hartman, Coordinator, 704-687-8883, Fax: 704-687-6430, E-mail: khartman@email.uncc.edu. *Application contact:* Kathy B. Giddings, Director of Graduate Admissions, 704-687-3366, Fax: 704-687-3279, E-mail: gradadm@email.uncc.edu.

The University of North Carolina at Greensboro, Graduate School, School of Education, Department of Curriculum and Instruction, Program in Curriculum and Teaching, Greensboro, NC 27412-5001. Offers higher education (PhD); teacher education and development (PhD). *Accreditation:* NCATE. *Students:* 50 full-time (39 women), 51 part-time (37 women); includes 24 minority (21 African Americans, 1 American Indian/Alaska Native, 2 Asian Americans or Pacific Islanders). *Degree requirements:* For doctorate, thesis/dissertation, comprehensive exam. *Entrance requirements:* For doctorate, GRE General Test. Additional exam requirements/recommendations for international students: Required—TOEFL. *Application deadline:* For fall admission, 3/1 for domestic students; for spring admission, 11/1 for domestic students. Applications are processed on a rolling basis. Application fee: $45. Electronic applications accepted. *Expenses:* Tuition, state resident: full-time $2,692. Tuition, nonresident: full-time $13,742. *Financial support:* In 2006–07, 16 students received support; fellowships, research assistantships, teaching assistantships available. *Unit head:* Dr. Barbara B Levin, Director of Graduate Studies, 336-334-3434, E-mail: bblevin@uncg.edu. *Application contact:* Michelle Harkleroad, Director of Graduate Admissions, 336-334-4884, Fax: 336-334-4424, E-mail: mbharkle@uncg.edu.

The University of North Carolina at Pembroke, Graduate Studies, School of Education, Program in Elementary Education, Pembroke, NC 28372-1510. Offers MA Ed. *Accreditation:* NCATE. Part-time and evening/weekend programs available. *Faculty:* 8 full-time (2 women), 1 part-time/adjunct (0 women). *Students:* Average age 34. 27 applicants, 100% accepted, 27 enrolled. In 2006, 12 degrees awarded. *Degree requirements:* For master's, thesis optional. *Entrance requirements:* For master's, GRE General Test or MAT, minimum GPA of 3.0 in major, 2.5 overall; teaching license. Additional exam requirements/recommendations for international students: Required—TOEFL. *Application deadline:* For fall admission, 7/15 priority date for domestic and international students; for spring admission, 12/1 priority date for domestic and international students. Applications are processed on a rolling basis. Application fee: $40. *Expenses:* Tuition, state resident: full-time $3,516; part-time $1,091 per semester. Tuition, nonresident: full-time $12,924; part-time $4,619 per semester. Tuition and fees vary according to class time, course load, degree level and campus/location. *Financial support:* In 2006–07, research assistantships with full tuition reimbursements (averaging $6,000 per year); unspecified assistantships also available. Support available to part-time students. Financial award application deadline: 4/15; financial award applicants required to submit FAFSA. *Unit head:* Dr. Sharon Sharp, Director, 910-521-6362, Fax: 910-521-6165, E-mail: sharon.sharp@uncp.edu. *Application contact:* Dr. Kathleen C. Hilton, Dean of Graduate Studies, 910-521-6271, Fax: 910-521-6751, E-mail: grad@uncp.edu.

The University of North Carolina Wilmington, School of Education, Department of Elementary, Middle Level and Literacy Education, Program in Elementary Education, Wilmington, NC 28403-3297. Offers M Ed. *Accreditation:* NCATE. Part-time and evening/weekend programs available. *Students:* 3 full-time (all women), 12 part-time (all women). Average age 28. 16 applicants, 63% accepted, 7 enrolled. In 2006, 8 degrees awarded. *Degree requirements:* For master's, comprehensive exam. *Entrance requirements:* For master's, GRE General Test, MAT, minimum B average in upper-division undergraduate course work, bachelor's degree in elementary education. *Application deadline:* For fall admission, 6/1 for domestic students. Applications are processed on a rolling basis. Application fee: $45. *Financial support:* Career-related internships or fieldwork, Federal Work-Study, and unspecified assistantships available. Support available to part-time students. Financial award application deadline: 3/15. *Unit head:* Dr. Tracy Hargrove, Coordinator, 910-962-7646. *Application contact:* Dr. Robert D. Roer, Dean, Graduate School, 910-962-4117, Fax: 910-962-3787, E-mail: roer@uncw.edu.

University of North Dakota, Graduate School, College of Education and Human Development, Program in Elementary Education, Grand Forks, ND 58202. Offers M Ed, MS. *Accreditation:* NCATE. Part-time programs available. *Faculty:* 4 full-time (3 women). *Students:* 5 applicants, 40% accepted, 2 enrolled. In 2006, 24 degrees awarded. *Degree requirements:* For master's, thesis or alternative, comprehensive exam. *Entrance requirements:* For master's, minimum GPA of 3.0. Additional exam requirements/recommendations for international students: Required—TOEFL (minimum score 550 paper-based; 213 computer-based; 79 iBT), IELTS (minimum score 6). *Application deadline:* For fall admission, 2/15 priority date for domestic and international students; for spring admission, 10/15 priority date for domestic and international students. Applications are processed on a rolling basis. Application fee: $35. Electronic applications accepted. *Expenses:* Tuition, state resident: full-time $5,650; part-time $214 per credit. Tuition, nonresident: full-time $14,248; part-time $572 per credit. Required fees: $1,008; $42 per credit. Tuition and fees vary according to reciprocity agreements. *Financial support:* In 2006–07, 13 teaching assistantships (averaging $10,553 per year) were awarded; fellowships, research assistantships with full tuition reimbursements, career-related internships or fieldwork, Federal Work-Study, institutionally sponsored loans, scholarships/grants, tuition waivers (full and partial), and unspecified assistantships also available. Support available to part-time students. Financial award application deadline: 3/15; financial award applicants required to submit FAFSA. *Faculty research:* Whole language, multicultural education, child-focused learning, experiential science, cooperative learning. *Unit head:* Dr. Bonni Gourneau, Graduate Director, 701-777-3239, Fax: 701-777-4393, E-mail: bonni.gourneau@nodak.edu. *Application contact:* Linda M. Baeza, Admissions Officer, 701-777-2945, Fax: 701-777-3619, E-mail: gradschool@mail.und.nodak.edu.

University of North Dakota, Graduate School, College of Education and Human Development, Teaching and Learning Program, Grand Forks, ND 58202. Offers elementary education (Ed D, PhD); measurement and statistics (Ed D, PhD); secondary education (Ed D, PhD); special education (Ed D, PhD). *Accreditation:* NCATE. *Faculty:* 19 full-time (16 women), 2 part-time/adjunct (1 woman). *Students:* 9 applicants, 0% accepted. In 2006, 18 degrees awarded. *Degree requirements:* For doctorate, thesis/dissertation, final exam, comprehensive exam. *Entrance requirements:* For doctorate, minimum GPA of 3.5. Additional exam requirements/recommendations for international students: Required—TOEFL (minimum score 550 paper-based; 213 computer-based; 79 iBT), IELTS (minimum score 6). *Application deadline:* For fall admission, 2/15 priority date for domestic and international students; for spring admission, 10/15 priority date for domestic and international students. Application fee: $35. Electronic applications accepted. *Expenses:* Tuition, state resident: full-time $5,650; part-time $214 per credit. Tuition, nonresident: full-time $14,248; part-time $572 per credit. Required fees: $1,008; $42 per credit. Tuition and fees vary according to reciprocity agreements. *Financial support:* In 2006–07, 17 students received support, including 1 research assistantship with full tuition reimbursement available (averaging $4,877 per year), 4 teaching assistantships with full tuition reimbursements available (averaging $7,609 per year); fellowships, career-related internships or fieldwork, Federal Work-Study, institutionally sponsored loans, scholarships/grants, tuition waivers (full and partial), and unspecified assistantships also available. Support available to part-time students. Financial award application deadline: 3/15; financial award applicants required to submit FAFSA. *Application contact:* Linda M. Baeza, Admissions Officer, 701-777-2945, Fax: 701-777-3619, E-mail: gradschool@mail.und.nodak.edu.

University of Northern Colorado, Graduate School, College of Education and Behavioral Sciences, School of Teacher Education, Program in Elementary Education and Early Childhood, Greeley, CO 80639. Offers educational studies (Ed D); elementary education (MAT). *Accreditation:* NCATE. Part-time and evening/weekend programs available. *Faculty:* 9 full-time (6 women). *Students:* 29 full-time (25 women), 29 part-time (27 women); includes 4 minority (1 African American, 1 American Indian/Alaska Native, 1 Asian American or Pacific Islander, 1 Hispanic American), 1 international. Average age 34. 7 applicants, 100% accepted, 4 enrolled. In 2006, 47 master's, 2 doctorates awarded. *Degree requirements:* For master's, thesis or alternative, comprehensive exam; for doctorate, thesis/dissertation, comprehensive exam. *Entrance requirements:* For master's, GRE General Test; for doctorate, GRE General Test, 3 letters of recommendation. *Application deadline:* Applications are processed on a rolling basis. Application fee: $50 ($60 for international students). Electronic applications accepted. *Expenses:* Tuition, state resident: full-time $5,118; part-time $213 per credit hour. Tuition, nonresident: full-time $14,832; part-time $618 per credit hour. Required fees: $674; $34 per credit hour. *Financial support:* In 2006–07, 36 students received support, including 1 teaching assistantship (averaging $5,424 per year); fellowships, research assistantships, unspecified assistantships also available. Financial award application deadline: 3/1; financial award applicants required to submit FAFSA. *Unit head:* Dr. Gary Fertig, Program Coordinator, 970-351-2908.

University of Northern Iowa, Graduate College, College of Education, Department of Curriculum and Instruction, Program in Elementary Education, Cedar Falls, IA 50614. Offers MAE. Part-time and evening/weekend programs available. *Students:* 2 full-time (both women), 13 part-time (12 women); includes 1 minority (Hispanic American), 1 international. 4 applicants, 75% accepted, 2 enrolled. In 2006, 8 degrees awarded. *Degree requirements:* For master's, thesis or alternative, comprehensive exam. *Entrance requirements:* For master's, minimum GPA of 3.5, 3 years of educational experience. Additional exam requirements/recommendations for international students: Required—TOEFL (minimum score 500 paper-based; 180 computer-based; 61 iBT). *Application deadline:* For fall admission, 8/1 priority date for domestic students. Applications are processed on a rolling basis. Application fee: $30 ($50 for international students). *Expenses:* Tuition, state resident: full-time $5,936. Tuition, nonresident: full-time $14,074. *Financial support:* Career-related internships or fieldwork, Federal Work-Study, and tuition waivers (full and partial) available. Support available to part-time students. Financial award application deadline: 2/1. *Unit head:* Lynn E. Nielsen, Coordinator, 319-273-7759, Fax: 319-273-5886, E-mail: lynn.nielsen@uni.edu.

University of North Florida, College of Education and Human Services, Division of Curriculum and Instruction, Program in Elementary Education, Jacksonville, FL 32224-2645. Offers M Ed. *Accreditation:* NCATE. Part-time and evening/weekend programs available. *Faculty:* 31 full-time (17 women). *Students:* 15 full-time (13 women), 52 part-time (51 women); includes 4 minority (2 African Americans, 1 American Indian/Alaska Native, 1 Hispanic American). Average age 33. 50 applicants, 60% accepted, 19 enrolled. In 2006, 27 degrees awarded. *Entrance requirements:* For master's, GRE General Test, minimum GPA of 3.0 in last 60 hours, 3 letters of recommendation, interview. Additional exam requirements/recommendations for international students: Required—TOEFL (minimum score 500 paper-based; 173 computer-based). *Application deadline:* For fall admission, 7/1 priority date for domestic students, 5/1 for international students; for spring admission, 11/1 priority date for domestic students, 10/1 for international students. Applications are processed on a rolling basis. Application fee: $30. Electronic applications accepted. *Expenses:* Tuition, state resident: full-time $4,948; part-time $206 per semester hour. Tuition, nonresident: full-time $19,140; part-time $408 per semester hour. *Financial support:* In 2006–07, 14 students received support. Federal Work-Study and tuition waivers (partial) available. Support available to part-time students. Financial award application deadline: 4/1; financial award applicants required to submit FAFSA. *Faculty research:* The social context of and processes in learning, inter-disciplinary instruction, cross-cultural conflict resolution, the Vygotskian perspective on literacy diagnosis and instruction, performance poetry and teaching the language arts through drama.

University of Oklahoma, Graduate College, College of Education, Department of Instructional Leadership and Academic Curriculum, Norman, OK 73019-0390. Offers education (Certificate); instructional leadership and academic curriculum (M Ed, PhD), including bilingual education, early childhood education, elementary education, English education, math education, reading education, science education, secondary education, social studies education. *Accreditation:* NCATE. Part-time and evening/weekend programs available. *Faculty:* 20 full-time (11 women), 6 part-time/adjunct (all women). *Students:* 76 full-time (63 women), 115 part-time (89 women); includes 25 minority (8 African Americans, 12 American Indian/Alaska Native, 4 Asian Americans or Pacific Islanders, 1 Hispanic American), 12 international. 72 applicants, 96% accepted, 56 enrolled. In 2006, 11 master's, 10 doctorates awarded. *Degree requirements:* For doctorate, thesis/dissertation. *Entrance requirements:* For master's, 12 hours of course work in education; for doctorate, GRE General Test, master's degree, minimum graduate GPA of 3.0. Additional exam requirements/recommendations for international students: Required—TOEFL (minimum score 550 paper-based; 213 computer-based). *Application deadline:* For fall admission, 6/1 priority date for domestic students, 4/1 for international students; for spring admission, 11/1 for domestic students, 9/1 for international students. Applications are processed on a rolling basis. Application fee: $40 ($90 for international students). *Expenses:* Tuition, state resident: full-time $3,180; part-time $133 per credit hour. Tuition, nonresident: full-time $11,347; part-time $473 per credit hour. Required fees: $1,729; $62 per credit hour. $117 per semester. Tuition and fees vary according to course load and program. *Financial support:* In 2006–07, 76 students received support, including 5 research assistantships with partial tuition reimbursements available (averaging $9,773 per year), 7 teaching assistantships with partial tuition reimbursements available (averaging $10,403 per year); scholarships/grants and unspecified assistantships also available. Financial award applicants required to submit FAFSA. *Faculty research:* Early literacy, learning cycle, social justice, teacher education. Total annual research expenditures: $119,917. *Unit head:* Dr. Priscilla Griffith, Chair and Graduate Liaison, 405-325-1498, Fax: 405-325-4061, E-mail: pgriffith@ou.edu.

University of Pennsylvania, Graduate School of Education, Division of Foundations and Practices in Education, Program in Elementary Education, Philadelphia, PA 19104. Offers MS Ed. *Degree requirements:* For master's, comprehensive exam or portfolio. *Entrance requirements:* For master's, GRE General Test, MAT. Electronic applications accepted. Expenses: Contact institution.

University of Phoenix–Central Florida Campus, The Artemis School, College of Education, Maitland, FL 32751-7057. Offers administration and supervision (MA Ed); curriculum and instruction (MA Ed); elementary teacher education (MA Ed); secondary teacher education (MA Ed). Evening/weekend programs available. *Faculty:* 10 full-time (9 women), 16 part-time/adjunct (6 women). *Students:* 20 full-time (18 women); includes 5 minority (3 African Americans, 2 Hispanic Americans), 1 international. Average age 38. In 2006, 7 degrees awarded. *Degree requirements:* For master's, thesis (for some programs), registration. *Entrance requirements:* For master's, 3 years of work experience, minimum undergraduate GPA of 2.5. Additional exam requirements/recommendations for international students: Required—TOEFL (minimum score 550 paper-based; 213 computer-based; 79 iBT). *Application deadline:* Applications are processed on a rolling basis. Application fee: $45. Electronic applications accepted. *Expenses:* Tuition: Full-time $9,450. Required fees: $760. *Financial support:* Institutionally sponsored loans and scholarships/grants available. Financial award applicants required to submit FAFSA. *Unit head:* Dr. Marla LaRue, Dean/Executive Director, 480-557-1218. *Application contact:* Chair, 407-667-0555, Fax: 407-667-0560.

University of Phoenix–Central Valley Campus, College of Education, Fresno, CA 93720. Offers curriculum and instruction (MA Ed); elementary teacher education (MA Ed); secondary teacher education (MA Ed).

University of Phoenix–Denver Campus, The Artemis School, College of Education, Lone Tree, CO 80124-5453. Offers administration and supervision (MAEd); curriculum instruction (MAEd); elementary teacher education (MAEd); school counseling (MSC); secondary teacher education (MAEd). Evening/weekend programs available. *Faculty:* 19 full-time (14 women), 141 part-time/adjunct (84 women). *Students:* 738 full-time (513 women); includes 72 minority (27 African Americans, 4 American Indian/Alaska Native, 9 Asian Americans or Pacific Islanders, 32 Hispanic Americans), 66 international. Average age 37. In 2006, 435 master's awarded. *Degree requirements:* For master's, thesis (for some programs), registration. *Entrance requirements:* For master's, minimum undergraduate GPA of 2.5, 3 years work experience. Additional exam requirements/recommendations for international students: Required—TOEFL (minimum score 550 paper-based; 213 computer-based; 79 iBT). *Application deadline:* Applications are processed on a rolling basis. Application fee: $45. Electronic applications accepted. *Expenses:* Tuition: Full-time $10,032. Required fees: $760. *Financial support:* Institutionally sponsored loans and scholarships/grants available. Financial award applicants required to submit FAFSA. *Unit head:* Dr. Marla LaRue, Dean/Executive Director, 480-557-1218, E-mail: marla.larue@phoenix.edu. *Application contact:* Chair, 303-694-9093, Fax: 303-662-0911.

University of Phoenix–Fort Lauderdale Campus, The Artemis School, College of Education, Fort Lauderdale, FL 33309. Offers administration and supervision (MA Ed); computer education (MA Ed); curriculum and instruction (MA Ed); elementary teacher education (MA Ed); secondary teacher education (MA Ed). Evening/weekend programs available. *Faculty:* 10 full-time (5 women), 17 part-time/adjunct (7 women). *Students:* 132 full-time (114 women); includes 60 minority (52 African Americans, 1 Asian American or Pacific Islander, 7 Hispanic Americans), 5 international. Average age 39. In 2006, 25 degrees awarded. *Degree requirements:* For master's, thesis (for some programs), registration. *Entrance requirements:* For master's, 3 years of work experience, minimum undergraduate GPA of 2.5. Additional exam requirements/recommendations for international students: Required—TOEFL (minimum score 550 paper-based; 213 computer-based; 79 iBT). *Application deadline:* Applications are processed on a rolling basis. Application fee: $45. Electronic applications accepted. *Expenses:* Tuition: Full-time $9,450. Required fees: $760. *Financial support:* Institutionally sponsored loans and scholarships/grants available. Financial award applicants required to submit FAFSA. *Unit head:* Dr. Marla LaRue, Dean/Executive Director, 480-557-1218. *Application contact:* Chair, 954-382-5303, Fax: 954-382-5304.

University of Phoenix–Hawaii Campus, The Artemis School, College of Education, Honolulu, HI 96813-4317. Offers administration and supervision (MA Ed); curriculum and instruction (MA Ed); elementary education (MA Ed); secondary education (MA Ed); teacher education for elementary licensure (MA Ed). Evening/weekend programs available. *Faculty:* 10 full-time (7 women), 58 part-time/adjunct (34 women). *Students:* 261 full-time (176 women); includes 61 minority (1 African American, 1 American Indian/Alaska Native, 53 Asian Americans or Pacific Islanders, 6 Hispanic Americans), 106 international. Average age 36. In 2006, 151 degrees awarded. *Degree requirements:* For master's, thesis (for some programs), registration. *Entrance requirements:* For master's, minimum undergraduate GPA of 2.5, 3 years of work experience. Additional exam requirements/recommendations for international students: Required—TOEFL (minimum score 550 paper-based; 213 computer-based; 79 iBT). *Application deadline:* Applications are processed on a rolling basis. Application fee: $45. Electronic applications accepted. *Expenses:* Tuition: Full-time $11,520. Required fees: $760. *Financial support:* Institutionally sponsored loans and scholarships/grants available. Financial award applicants required to submit FAFSA. *Unit head:* Dr. Marla LaRue, Dean/Executive Director, 480-557-1309, E-mail: marla.larue@phoenix.edu. *Application contact:* Chair, 580-536-2686, Fax: 808-536-3848.

University of Phoenix–Las Vegas Campus, The Artemis School, College of Education, Las Vegas, NV 89128. Offers administration and supervision (MA Ed); curriculum and instruction (MA Ed); school counseling (MSC); teacher education-elementary licensure (MA Ed). Evening/weekend programs available. *Faculty:* 9 full-time (8 women), 45 part-time/adjunct (27 women). *Students:* 494 full-time (388 women); includes 105 minority (51 African Americans, 2 American Indian/Alaska Native, 18 Asian Americans or Pacific Islanders, 34 Hispanic Americans), 9 international. Average age 35. In 2006, 227 degrees awarded. *Degree requirements:* For master's, thesis (for some programs), registration. *Entrance requirements:* For master's, minimum undergraduate GPA of 2.5, 3 years of work experience. Additional exam requirements/recommendations for international students: Required—TOEFL (minimum score 550 paper-based; 213 computer-based; 79 iBT). *Application deadline:* Applications are processed on a rolling basis. Application fee: $45. Electronic applications accepted. *Expenses:* Tuition: Full-time $9,576. Required fees: $760. *Financial support:* Institutionally sponsored loans and scholarships/grants available. Financial award applicants required to submit FAFSA. *Unit head:* Dr. Marla LaRue, Dean/Executive Director, 480-557-1218, E-mail: marla.larue@phoenix.edu. *Application contact:* Chair, 702-638-7249, Fax: 702-638-8085.

University of Phoenix–Metro Detroit Campus, The Artemis School, College of Education, Troy, MI 48098-2623. Offers administration and supervision (MA Ed); adult education and distance learning (MA Ed); curriculum and development (MA Ed); special education (MA Ed); teacher education elementary (MA Ed). Evening/weekend programs available. *Faculty:* 8 full-time (3 women), 27 part-time/adjunct (21 women). *Students:* 102 full-time (75 women); includes 59 minority (57 African Americans, 1 American Indian/Alaska Native, 1 Asian American or Pacific Islander), 1 international. Average age 40. In 2006, 30 master's awarded. *Degree requirements:* For master's, thesis (for some programs), registration. *Entrance requirements:* For master's, 3 years of work experience, minimum undergraduate GPA of 2.5. Additional exam requirements/recommendations for international students: Required—TOEFL (minimum score 550 paper-based; 213 computer-based; 79 iBT). *Application deadline:* Applications are processed on a rolling basis. Application fee: $45. Electronic applications accepted. *Expenses:* Tuition: Full-time $12,168. Required fees: $760. *Financial support:* Institutionally sponsored loans and scholarships/grants available. Financial award applicants required to submit FAFSA. *Unit head:* Dr. Marla LaRue, Dean/Executive Director, 480-557-1218. *Application contact:* Chair, 800-834-2438, Fax: 248-267-0147.

University of Phoenix–Nashville Campus, The Artemis School, College of Education, Nashville, TN 37214-5048. Offers administration and supervision (MA Ed); curriculum and instruction (MA Ed); elementary teacher education (MA Ed); secondary teacher education (MA Ed). Evening/weekend programs available. *Degree requirements:* For master's, thesis (for some programs), registration. *Entrance requirements:* For master's, minimum undergraduate GPA of 2.5, 3 years work experience. Additional exam requirements/recommendations for international students: Required—TOEFL (minimum score 500 paper-based; 213 computer-based; 79 iBT). *Application deadline:* Applications are processed on a rolling basis. Application fee: $45. Electronic applications accepted. *Expenses:* Tuition: Full-time $10,104. Required fees: $760. *Financial support:* Institutionally sponsored loans and scholarships/grants available. Financial award applicants required to submit FAFSA. *Unit head:* Dr. Marla LaRue, Dean/Executive Director, 480-557-1218, E-mail: marla.larue@phoenix.edu. *Application contact:* Chair, 615-872-0188.

University of Phoenix–New Mexico Campus, The Artemis School, College of Education, Albuquerque, NM 87109-4645. Offers administration (MAEd); curriculum and instruction (MAEd); teacher education (MAEd), including elementary, secondary. Evening/weekend programs available. *Faculty:* 9 full-time (5 women), 62 part-time/adjunct (40 women). *Students:* 234 full-time (181 women); includes 116 minority (5 African Americans, 1 Asian American or Pacific Islander, 110 Hispanic Americans), 10 international. Average age 39. In 2006, 131 degrees awarded. *Degree requirements:* For master's, thesis (for some programs), registration. *Entrance requirements:* For master's, minimum undergraduate GPA of 2.5, 3 years of work experience. Additional exam requirements/recommendations for international students: Required—TOEFL (minimum score 550 paper-based; 213 computer-based; 79 iBT). *Application deadline:* Applications are processed on a rolling basis. Application fee: $45. Electronic applications accepted. *Expenses:* Tuition: Full-time $9,005. Required fees: $760. *Financial support:* Institutionally sponsored loans and scholarships/grants available. Financial award applicants required to submit FAFSA. *Unit head:* Dr. Marla LaRue, Dean/Executive Director, 480-557-1218, E-mail: marla.larue@phoenix.edu. *Application contact:* Chair, 505-821-4800, Fax: 505-821-5551.

University of Phoenix—Northern Nevada Campus, College of Education, Reno, NV 89511. Offers administration and supervision (MA Ed); elementary teacher educatino (MA Ed).

University of Phoenix–North Florida Campus, The Artemis School, College of Education, Jacksonville, FL 32216-0959. Offers administration (MA Ed); curriculum and instruction (MA Ed); curriculum and instruction—computer education (MA Ed); elementary teacher education (MA Ed); secondary teacher education (MA Ed). Evening/weekend programs available. *Faculty:* 9 full-time (5 women), 10 part-time/adjunct (4 women). *Students:* 98 full-time (78 women); includes 41 minority (37 African Americans, 4 Hispanic Americans), 1 international. Average age 37. In 2006, 22 master's awarded. *Degree requirements:* For master's, thesis (for some programs), registration. *Entrance requirements:* For master's, 3 years of work experience, minimum undergraduate GPA of 2.5. Additional exam requirements/recommendations for international students: Required—TOEFL (minimum score 550 paper-based; 213 computer-based; 49 iBT). *Application deadline:* Applications are processed on a rolling basis. Application fee: $45. Electronic applications accepted. *Financial support:* Institutionally sponsored loans and scholarships/grants available. Financial award applicants required to submit FAFSA. *Unit head:* Dr. Marla LaRue, Dean, 480-557-1218, E-mail: marla.larue@phoenix.edu. *Application contact:* Chair, 904-636-6645, Fax: 904-636-0998.

University of Phoenix–Omaha Campus, College of Education, Omaha, NE 68154-5240. Offers administration and supervision (MA Ed); curriculum and instruction (MA Ed); curriculum and instruction—English and language arts education (MA Ed); curriculum and instruction—adult education (MA Ed); curriculum and instruction—computer education (MA Ed); curriculum and instruction—English as a second language (MA Ed); curriculum and instruction—mathematics education (MA Ed); elementary teacher education (MA Ed); secondary teacher education (MA Ed); special education (MA Ed).

University of Phoenix Online Campus, The Artemis School, College of Education, Phoenix, AZ 85034-7209. Offers administration and supervision (MAEd); adult education and training (MAEd); curriculum and instruction-adult education (MAEd); curriculum and instruction-English and language arts education (MAEd); curriculum and instruction-mathematics education (MAEd); curriculum education (MAEd); curriculum instruction (MAEd); early childhood (MAEd); English as a second language (MAEd); teacher education elementary (MAEd); teacher education secondary (MAEd). Evening/weekend programs available. Postbaccalaureate distance learning degree programs offered (no on-campus study). *Faculty:* 12 full-time (5 women), 8,196 part-time/adjunct (6,937 women). *Students:* 11,937 full-time (9,375 women); includes 2,972 minority (2,210 African Americans, 74 American Indian/Alaska Native, 205 Asian Americans or Pacific Islanders, 483 Hispanic Americans), 906 international. Average age 36. *Degree requirements:* For master's, thesis (for some programs), registration. *Entrance requirements:* For master's, 3 years of work experience, minimum GPA of 2.5. Additional exam requirements/recommendations for international students: Required—TOEFL (minimum score 550 paper-based; 213 computer-based; 79 iBT). *Application deadline:* Applications are processed on a rolling basis. Application fee: $45. Electronic applications accepted. *Expenses:* Tuition: Full-time $12,664. Required fees: $760. *Financial support:* Institutionally sponsored loans and

Elementary Education

University of Phoenix Online Campus (continued)
scholarships/grants available. Financial award applicants required to submit FAFSA. *Unit head:* Dr. Marla LaRue, Dean/Executive Director, 480-557-1218, E-mail: marla.larue@phoenix.edu. *Application contact:* Dr. Marla LaRue, Dean/Executive Director, 480-557-1218, E-mail: marla.larue@phoenix.edu.

University of Phoenix–Oregon Campus, The Artemis School, College of Education, Tigard, OR 97223. Offers early childhood and elementary education (MA Ed); secondary education (MA Ed). Evening/weekend programs available. *Faculty:* 3 full-time (2 women), 33 part-time/adjunct (14 women). *Students:* 90 full-time (59 women); includes 7 minority (4 African Americans, 1 American Indian/Alaska Native, 2 Hispanic Americans), 14 international. Average age 36. In 2006, 12 degrees awarded. *Degree requirements:* For master's, thesis (for some programs), registration. *Entrance requirements:* For master's, minimum undergraduate GPA of 2.5, 3 years work experience. Additional exam requirements/recommendations for international students: Required—TOEFL (minimum score 550 paper-based; 213 computer-based; 79 iBT). *Application deadline:* Applications are processed on a rolling basis. Application fee: $45. Electronic applications accepted. *Expenses:* Tuition: Full-time $10,200. Required fees: $760. *Financial support:* Institutionally sponsored loans and scholarships/grants available. Financial award applicants required to submit FAFSA. *Unit head:* Dr. Marla LaRue, Dean/Executive Director, 480-557-1218, E-mail: marla.larue@phoenix.edu. *Application contact:* Chair, 503-403-2500, Fax: 503-670-0614.

University of Phoenix–Phoenix Campus, The Artemis School, College of Education, Phoenix, AZ 85040-1958. Offers administration and supervision (MA Ed); curriculum and instruction (MA Ed); elementary licensure (MA Ed); secondary licensure (MA Ed). Evening/weekend programs available. *Faculty:* 39 full-time (23 women), 422 part-time/adjunct (255 women). *Students:* 850 full-time (614 women); includes 135 minority (45 African Americans, 7 American Indian/Alaska Native, 20 Asian Americans or Pacific Islanders, 63 Hispanic Americans), 15 international. Average age 35. In 2006, 500 degrees awarded. *Degree requirements:* For master's, thesis (for some programs), registration. *Entrance requirements:* For master's, 3 years of work experience, minimum undergraduate GPA of 2.5. Additional exam requirements/recommendations for international students: Required—TOEFL (minimum score 550 paper-based; 213 computer-based; 79 iBT). *Application deadline:* Applications are processed on a rolling basis. Application fee: $45. Electronic applications accepted. *Financial support:* Institutionally sponsored loans and scholarships/grants available. Financial award applicants required to submit FAFSA. *Unit head:* Dr. Marla LaRue, Dean/Executive Director, 480-557-1218, E-mail: marla.larue@phoenix.edu. *Application contact:* College Chair, 480-804-7400, Fax: 480-557-2320.

University of Phoenix–Sacramento Valley Campus, The Artemis School, College of Education, Sacramento, CA 95833-3632. Offers adult education (MA Ed); curriculum instruction (MA Ed); elementary education (MA Ed); secondary education (MA Ed); teacher education (Certificate). Evening/weekend programs available. *Faculty:* 9 full-time (5 women), 95 part-time/adjunct (41 women). *Students:* 234 full-time (161 women); includes 51 minority (20 African Americans, 2 American Indian/Alaska Native, 9 Asian Americans or Pacific Islanders, 20 Hispanic Americans), 15 international. Average age 36. In 2006, 80 degrees awarded. *Degree requirements:* For master's, thesis (for some programs), registration. *Entrance requirements:* For master's, 3 years of work experience, minimum undergraduate GPA of 2.5. Additional exam requirements/recommendations for international students: Required—TOEFL (minimum score 550 paper-based; 213 computer-based; 79 iBT). *Application deadline:* Applications are processed on a rolling basis. Application fee: $45. Electronic applications accepted. *Expenses:* Tuition: Full-time $12,024. Required fees: $760. *Financial support:* Institutionally sponsored loans and scholarships/grants available. Financial award applicants required to submit FAFSA. *Unit head:* Dr. Marla LaRue, Dean, 480-557-1218, E-mail: marla.larue@phoenix.edu. *Application contact:* Campus College Chair, 916-923-2107, Fax: 916-923-3914.

University of Phoenix–San Diego Campus, The Artemis School, College of Education, San Diego, CA 92123. Offers curriculum and instruction (MA Ed); elementary education (MA Ed); secondary education (MA Ed). Evening/weekend programs available. *Faculty:* 6 full-time (3 women), 69 part-time/adjunct (36 women). *Students:* 165 full-time (110 women); includes 42 minority (9 African Americans, 8 Asian Americans or Pacific Islanders, 25 Hispanic Americans), 12 international. Average age 34. In 2006, 81 degrees awarded. *Degree requirements:* For master's, thesis (for some programs), registration. *Entrance requirements:* For master's, 3 years of work experience, minimum undergraduate GPA of 3.0. Additional exam requirements/recommendations for international students: Required—TOEFL (minimum score 550 paper-based; 213 computer-based; 79 iBT). *Application deadline:* Applications are processed on a rolling basis. Application fee: $45. Electronic applications accepted. *Expenses:* Tuition: Full-time $11,419. Required fees: $760. *Financial support:* Institutionally sponsored loans and scholarships/grants available. Financial award applicants required to submit FAFSA. *Unit head:* Dr. Marla LaRue, Dean/Executive Director, 480-557-1218, E-mail: marla.larue@phoenix.edu. *Application contact:* Campus College Chair, 888-UOP-INFO, Fax: 858-509-4399.

University of Phoenix–Southern Arizona Campus, The Artemis School, College of Education, Tucson, AZ 85712-2732. Offers curriculum instruction (MA Ed); educational counseling (MA Ed); elementary licensure (MA Ed); school counseling (MSC); secondary licensure (MA Ed); special education (Certificate). Evening/weekend programs available. *Faculty:* 101. *Students:* 75 full-time (55 women); includes 16 minority (2 African Americans, 1 American Indian/Alaska Native, 1 Asian American or Pacific Islander, 12 Hispanic Americans), 2 international. Average age 38. In 2006, 113 degrees awarded. *Degree requirements:* For master's, thesis (for some programs), registration. *Entrance requirements:* For master's, minimum undergraduate GPA of 2.5, 3 years of work experience. Additional exam requirements/recommendations for international students: Required—TOEFL (minimum score 550 paper-based; 213 computer-based; 79 iBT). *Application deadline:* Applications are processed on a rolling basis. Application fee: $45. Electronic applications accepted. *Expenses:* Tuition: Full-time $8,669. Required fees: $760. *Financial support:* Institutionally sponsored loans and scholarships/grants available. Financial award applicants required to submit FAFSA. *Unit head:* Dr. Marla LaRue, Dean/Executive Director, 480-557-1218, E-mail: marla.larue@phoenix.edu. *Application contact:* Campus College Chair, 520-881-6512, Fax: 520-795-6177.

University of Phoenix–Southern California Campus, The Artemis School, College of Education, Costa Mesa, CA 92626. Offers curriculum and instruction (MA Ed); elementary education (MA Ed); secondary education (MA Ed). Evening/weekend programs available. *Faculty:* 22 full-time (9 women), 195 part-time/adjunct (108 women). *Students:* 1,152 full-time (858 women); includes 420 minority (135 African Americans, 7 American Indian/Alaska Native, 59 Asian Americans or Pacific Islanders, 219 Hispanic Americans), 78 international. Average age 34. In 2006, 359 degrees awarded. *Degree requirements:* For master's, thesis (for some programs), registration. *Entrance requirements:* For master's, minimum undergraduate GPA of 2.5, 3 years work experience. Additional exam requirements/recommendations for international students: Required—TOEFL (minimum score 550 paper-based; 213 computer-based; 79 iBT). *Application deadline:* Applications are processed on a rolling basis. Application fee: $45. Electronic applications accepted. *Expenses:* Tuition: Full-time $13,512. Required fees: $760. *Financial support:* Institutionally sponsored loans and scholarships/grants available. Financial award applicants required to submit FAFSA. *Unit head:* Dr. Marla LaRue, Dean/Executive Director, 480-557-1218, E-mail: marla.larue@phoenix.edu. *Application contact:* Campus College Chair, 714-378-1878, Fax: 714-378-5875.

University of Phoenix–Southern Colorado Campus, The Artemis School, College of Education, Colorado Springs, CO 80919-2335. Offers administration and supervision (MA Ed); curriculum and instruction (MA Ed); elementary licensure (MA Ed); principal licensure certification (Certificate); school counseling (MSC); secondary licensure (MA Ed). Evening/weekend programs available. *Faculty:* 7 full-time (3 women), 90 part-time/adjunct (53 women). *Students:* 220 full-time (162 women); includes 22 minority (7 African Americans, 1 American Indian/Alaska Native, 4 Asian Americans or Pacific Islanders, 10 Hispanic Americans), 15 international. Average age 37. In 2006, 122 degrees awarded. *Degree requirements:* For master's, thesis (for some programs), registration. *Entrance requirements:* For master's, minimum undergraduate GPA of 2.5, 3 years of work experience. Additional exam requirements/recommendations for international students: Required—TOEFL (minimum score 550 paper-based; 213 computer-based; 79 iBT). *Application deadline:* Applications are processed on a rolling basis. Application fee: $45. Electronic applications accepted. *Expenses:* Tuition: Full-time $10,291. Required fees: $760. *Financial support:* Institutionally sponsored loans and scholarships/grants available. Financial award applicants required to submit FAFSA. *Unit head:* Dr. Marla LaRue, Dean/Executive Director, 480-557-1218, E-mail: marla.larue@phoenix.edu. *Application contact:* Chair, 719-599-5282, Fax: 719-599-7973.

University of Phoenix–Utah Campus, The Artemis School, College of Education, Salt Lake City, UT 84123-4617. Offers administration and supervision (MA Ed); curriculum and instruction (MA Ed); elementary education (MA Ed); school counseling (MSC); secondary education (MA Ed). Evening/weekend programs available. *Faculty:* 14 full-time (8 women), 78 part-time/adjunct (39 women). *Students:* 395 full-time (246 women); includes 20 minority (2 African Americans, 1 American Indian/Alaska Native, 8 Asian Americans or Pacific Islanders, 9 Hispanic Americans), 4 international. Average age 37. In 2006, 233 degrees awarded. *Degree requirements:* For master's, thesis (for some programs), registration. *Entrance requirements:* For master's, minimum undergraduate GPA of 2.5, 3 years work experience. Additional exam requirements/recommendations for international students: Required—TOEFL (minimum score 550 paper-based; 213 computer-based; 79 iBT). *Application deadline:* Applications are processed on a rolling basis. Application fee: $45. Electronic applications accepted. *Expenses:* Tuition: Full-time $9,104. Required fees: $760. *Financial support:* Institutionally sponsored loans and scholarships/grants available. Financial award applicants required to submit FAFSA. *Unit head:* Dr. Marla LaRue, Dean/Executive Director, 480-557-1218, E-mail: marla.larue@phoenix.edu. *Application contact:* Chair, 801-263-1444, Fax: 801-269-9766.

University of Phoenix–West Florida Campus, The Artemis School, College of Education, Temple Terrace, FL 33637. Offers administration and supervision (MA Ed); curriculum and instruction (MA Ed); curriculum and technology (MA Ed); elementary teacher education (MA Ed); secondary teacher education (MA Ed). Evening/weekend programs available. *Faculty:* 10 full-time (8 women), 15 part-time/adjunct (7 women). *Students:* 67 full-time (61 women); includes 24 minority (20 African Americans, 1 American Indian/Alaska Native, 3 Hispanic Americans), 3 international. Average age 40. In 2006, 8 degrees awarded. *Degree requirements:* For master's, thesis (for some programs), registration. *Entrance requirements:* For master's, 3 years of work experience, minimum undergraduate GPA of 2.5. Additional exam requirements/recommendations for international students: Required—TOEFL (minimum score 550 paper-based; 213 computer-based; 79 iBT). Application fee: $45. *Expenses:* Tuition: Full-time $9,450. Required fees: $760. *Financial support:* Institutionally sponsored loans and scholarships/grants available. Financial award applicants required to submit FAFSA. *Unit head:* Dr. Marla LaRue, Dean, 480-557-1218, E-mail: marla.larue@phoenix.edu. *Application contact:* Chair, 813-626-7911, Fax: 813-977-1449.

University of Pittsburgh, School of Education, Department of Instruction and Learning, Program in Elementary Education, Pittsburgh, PA 15260. Offers M Ed, MAT. *Students:* 98 full-time (83 women), 25 part-time (22 women); includes 7 minority (6 African Americans, 1 Hispanic American). 70 applicants, 81% accepted, 50 enrolled. In 2006, 65 degrees awarded. *Degree requirements:* For master's, thesis. *Entrance requirements:* For master's, PRAXIS I. Additional exam requirements/recommendations for international students: Required—TOEFL. *Application deadline:* For fall admission, 2/1 for domestic students. Application fee: $50. Electronic applications accepted. *Financial support:* In 2006–07, fellowships (averaging $1,000 per year); career-related internships or fieldwork, Federal Work-Study, traineeships, and tuition waivers (partial) also available. Support available to part-time students. Financial award application deadline: 3/15; financial award applicants required to submit FAFSA. *Application contact:* Joan M. Cutone, Director, School of Education Student Service Center, 412-648-2230, Fax: 412-648-1899, E-mail: soeinfo@pitt.edu.

University of Puget Sound, Graduate Studies, School of Education, Program in Teaching, Tacoma, WA 98416. Offers elementary education (MAT); middle school education (MAT); secondary education (MAT). *Accreditation:* NASM; NCATE. *Faculty:* 10 full-time (6 women), 2 part-time/adjunct (both women). *Students:* 53 full-time (35 women), 1 (woman) part-time; includes 7 minority (2 African Americans, 2 American Indian/Alaska Native, 3 Asian Americans or Pacific Islanders), 1 international. Average age 26. 96 applicants, 88% accepted, 51 enrolled. In 2006, 41 degrees awarded. *Median time to degree:* Master's–1 year full-time. *Entrance requirements:* For master's, GRE General Test, West-B for WA residents, PRAXIS I, minimum GPA of 3.0. Additional exam requirements/recommendations for international students: Required—TOEFL (minimum score 550 paper-based; 213 computer-based; 80 iBT). *Application deadline:* For fall admission, 3/1 priority date for domestic and international students. Applications are processed on a rolling basis. Application fee: $65. Electronic applications accepted. *Expenses:* Tuition: Full-time $26,390. Tuition and fees vary according to course load. *Financial support:* In 2006–07, 24 students received support, including 16 fellowships (averaging $7,575 per year); career-related internships or fieldwork and scholarships/grants also available. Support available to part-time students. Financial award application deadline: 3/31; financial award applicants required to submit FAFSA. *Faculty research:* Economic support for schools, teacher thinking/student understanding, self-reflection in teacher education, civics and decision making. Total annual research expenditures: $11,005. *Application contact:* Dr. George H. Mills, Vice President for Enrollment, 253-879-3211, Fax: 253-879-3993, E-mail: admission@ups.edu.

University of Rhode Island, Graduate School, College of Human Science and Services, School of Education, Program in Elementary Education, Kingston, RI 02881. Offers MA. *Accreditation:* NCATE. *Entrance requirements:* For master's, GRE or MAT. Additional exam requirements/recommendations for international students: Required—TOEFL. *Application deadline:* For fall admission, 4/15 priority date for domestic students; for spring admission, 11/15 for domestic students. Applications are processed on a rolling basis. Application fee: $35. *Expenses:* Tuition, state resident: full-time $6,032; part-time $335 per credit. Tuition, nonresident: full-time $17,288; part-time $960 per credit. Required fees: $65 per credit. $30 per semester. One-time fee: $80 part-time. *Financial support:* Career-related internships or fieldwork available. *Unit head:* Dr. Peter Adamy, Team Leader, 401-874-7036.

University of St. Francis, College of Education, Joliet, IL 60435-6169. Offers curriculum and instruction (MS); educational leadership (MS), including reading, special education; elementary education certification (M Ed); secondary education certification (M Ed), including English education, math education, science education, social studies education; special education (M Ed); teaching and learning (MS). Part-time and evening/weekend programs available. *Faculty:* 11 full-time (10 women), 25 part-time/adjunct (12 women). *Students:* 52 full-time (38 women), 381 part-time (293 women); includes 38 minority (21 African Americans, 1 American Indian/Alaska Native, 4 Asian Americans or Pacific Islanders, 12 Hispanic Americans). Average age 33. 194 applicants, 80% accepted, 117 enrolled. In 2006, 165 degrees awarded. *Degree requirements:* For master's, comprehensive exam (for some programs), registration. *Entrance requirements:* For master's, minimum undergraduate GPA of 2.75, 2 letters of recommendation, computer competency. Additional exam requirements/recommendations for international students: Required—TOEFL (minimum score 550 paper-based; 213 computer-based). *Application deadline:* Applications are processed on a rolling basis. Application fee: $30. Electronic applications accepted. *Expenses:* *Contact institution.* Part-time tuition and fees vary according to campus/location and program. *Financial support:* In 2006–07, 272 students received support. Scholarships/grants, tuition waivers (partial), and unspecified assistantships available. Support available to part-time students. Financial award applicants required to submit FAFSA. *Unit head:* Dr. John Gambro, Dean, 815-740-3456, Fax: 815-740-2264, E-mail: jgambro@stfrancis.edu. *Application contact:* Sandra Sloka, Director of Admissions for Graduate and Degree Completion Programs, 800-735-7500, Fax: 815-740-5032, E-mail: ssloka@stfrancis.edu.

The University of Scranton, Graduate School, Department of Education, Program in Elementary Education, Scranton, PA 18510. Offers MS. *Accreditation:* NCATE. Part-time and evening/weekend programs available. *Students:* 6 full-time (all women), 14 part-time (12 women). Average age 32. 11 applicants, 91% accepted. In 2006, 8 degrees awarded. *Degree requirements:* For master's, capstone experience. *Entrance requirements:* For master's, minimum GPA of 2.75. Additional exam requirements/recommendations for international students: Required—TOEFL (minimum score 500 paper-based; 173 computer-based), IELTS (minimum score 6). *Application deadline:* Applications are processed on a rolling basis. Application fee: $50. *Expenses:* Tuition: Part-time $684 per credit. Required fees: $25 per term. *Financial support:* Fellowships, teaching assistantships, career-related internships or fieldwork, Federal Work-Study, and unspecified assistantships available. Support available to part-time students. Financial award application deadline: 3/1. *Unit head:* Dr. Derry Stufft, Director, 570-941-7421, Fax: 570-941-7401, E-mail: stufftda@scranton.edu.

University of South Alabama, Graduate School, College of Education, Department of Leadership and Teacher Education, Mobile, AL 36688-0002. Offers early childhood education (M Ed); educational administration (Ed S); educational leadership (M Ed); elementary education (M Ed); reading education (M Ed); science education (M Ed); secondary education (M Ed); special education (M Ed, Ed S). *Accreditation:* NCATE. Part-time programs available. *Faculty:* 22 full-time (13 women). *Students:* 287 full-time (251 women), 229 part-time (194 women); includes 137 minority (125 African Americans, 8 American Indian/Alaska Native, 3 Asian Americans or Pacific Islanders, 1 Hispanic American), 4 international. 43 applicants, 84% accepted, 20 enrolled. In 2006, 169 master's, 12 other advanced degrees awarded. *Degree requirements:* For master's, comprehensive exam. *Entrance requirements:* For master's, GRE General Test or MAT, minimum GPA of 3.0. *Application deadline:* For fall admission, 9/1 priority date for domestic students. Applications are processed on a rolling basis. Application fee: $25. *Financial support:* In 2006–07, 6 research assistantships were awarded; career-related internships or fieldwork also available. Support available to part-time students. Financial award application deadline: 4/1. *Unit head:* Dr. David L. Gray, Chair, 251-380-2894.

University of South Carolina, The Graduate School, College of Education, Department of Instruction and Teacher Education, Program in Elementary Education, Columbia, SC 29208. Offers M Ed, MAT, PhD. *Accreditation:* NCATE. *Degree requirements:* For master's, comprehensive exam; for doctorate, one foreign language, thesis/dissertation, comprehensive exam. *Entrance requirements:* For master's, GRE General Test, MAT, teaching certificate (M Ed), interview; for doctorate, GRE General Test, MAT, interview. *Faculty research:* Children's conception of science, whole language, middle school curriculum.

University of South Carolina Aiken, School of Education, Program in Elementary Education, Aiken, SC 29801-6309. Offers M Ed. *Accreditation:* NCATE. Part-time and evening/weekend programs available. *Faculty:* 3 full-time (2 women), 3 part-time/adjunct (2 women). In 2006, 2 degrees awarded. *Degree requirements:* For master's, comprehensive evaluation. *Entrance requirements:* For master's, GRE General Test or MAT. *Application deadline:* For fall admission, 8/1 priority date for domestic students. Applications are processed on a rolling basis. Application fee: $40. Electronic applications accepted. *Expenses:* Tuition, state resident: full-time $8,288; part-time $411 per hour. Tuition, nonresident: full-time $17,916; part-time $874 per hour. Required fees: $230; $8 per hour. $15 per hour. *Financial support:* Federal Work-Study available. Support available to part-time students. Financial award application deadline: 3/15; financial award applicants required to submit FAFSA. *Unit head:* Dr. Audrey Skrupskelis, Unit Head, 803-641-3240. *Application contact:* Karen Morris, Graduate Studies Coordinator, 803-641-3489, E-mail: karenm@usca.edu.

University of South Carolina Upstate, Graduate Programs, Spartanburg, SC 29303-4999. Offers early childhood education (M Ed); elementary education (M Ed); special education: visual impairment (M Ed). *Accreditation:* NCATE. Part-time and evening/weekend programs available. *Faculty:* 9 full-time (7 women). *Students:* 5 full-time (4 women), 29 part-time (26 women); includes 3 minority (all African Americans) Average age 34. 15 applicants, 100% accepted, 9 enrolled. In 2006, 9 degrees awarded. *Degree requirements:* For master's, graduate professional portfolio. *Entrance requirements:* For master's, GRE General Test, MAT, interview, minimum GPA of 2.5, teaching certificate. *Application deadline:* Applications are processed on a rolling basis. Application fee: $40. *Expenses:* Tuition, state resident: full-time $6,890; part-time $342 per semester hour. Tuition, nonresident: full-time $14,920; part-time $727 per semester hour. *Financial support:* Institutionally sponsored loans and institutional work-study available. Financial award application deadline: 7/15; financial award applicants required to submit FAFSA. *Faculty research:* Rough and tumble play, social justice education, American Indian literatures and cultures, diversity and multicultural education, science teaching strategy. *Unit head:* Dr. Rebecca L. Stevens, Director, 864-503-5521, Fax: 864-503-5574, E-mail: ystevens@uscupstate.edu. *Application contact:* Donette Stewart, Associate Vice Chancellor for Enrollment Services, 864-503-5280, E-mail: dstewart@uscupstate.edu.

The University of South Dakota, Graduate School, School of Education, Division of Curriculum and Instruction, Program in Elementary Education, Vermillion, SD 57069-2390. Offers MA. *Accreditation:* NCATE. Part-time programs available. Postbaccalaureate distance learning degree programs offered. *Students:* 19 (17 women). In 2006, 10 degrees awarded. *Degree requirements:* For master's, thesis or alternative, comprehensive exam. *Entrance requirements:* For master's, GRE General Test, MAT, minimum GPA of 2.7. Additional exam requirements/recommendations for international students: Required—TOEFL (minimum score 550 paper-based; 213 computer-based; 79 iBT). *Application deadline:* Applications are processed on a rolling basis. Application fee: $35. Electronic applications accepted. *Expenses:* Tuition, state resident: part-time $120 per credit hour. Tuition, nonresident: part-time $355 per credit hour. Required fees: $90 per credit hour. *Financial support:* In 2006–07, research assistantships with partial tuition reimbursements (averaging $4,626 per year), teaching assistantships with partial tuition reimbursements (averaging $4,626 per year) were awarded; career-related internships or fieldwork, Federal Work-Study, and unspecified assistantships also available. Financial award applicants required to submit FAFSA.

University of Southern Indiana, Graduate Studies, College of Education and Human Services, Department of Teacher Education, Program in Elementary Education, Evansville, IN 47712-3590. Offers MS. *Accreditation:* NCATE. Part-time and evening/weekend programs available. *Faculty:* 13 full-time (5 women), 4 part-time/adjunct (1 woman). *Students:* 1 (woman) full-time, 58 part-time (51 women); includes 1 minority (American Indian/Alaska Native). Average age 36. 34 applicants, 100% accepted, 17 enrolled. In 2006, 26 degrees awarded. *Entrance requirements:* For master's, GRE General Test, NTE or Praxis I, minimum GPA of 3.0, teaching license. Additional exam requirements/recommendations for international students: Required—TOEFL (minimum score 500 paper-based; 173 computer-based). *Application deadline:* For fall admission, 7/1 priority date for domestic students. Applications are processed on a rolling basis. Application fee: $25. *Expenses:* Tuition, state resident: full-time $3,888; part-time $216 per credit hour. Tuition, nonresident: full-time $7,688; part-time $426 per credit hour. Required fees: $220; $23 per term. Tuition and fees vary according to course load and reciprocity agreements. *Financial support:* In 2006–07, 14 students received support. Federal Work-Study, scholarships/grants, tuition waivers (full and partial), and unspecified assistantships available. Financial award application deadline: 3/1; financial award applicants required to submit FAFSA. *Unit head:* Dr. Michael L. Slavkin, Coordinator, 812-465-1858, E-mail: mslavkin@usi.edu.

University of Southern Mississippi, Graduate School, College of Education and Psychology, Department of Curriculum, Instruction, and Special Education, Hattiesburg, MS 39406-0001. Offers alternative secondary teacher education (MAT); early childhood education (M Ed, Ed S); education of the gifted (M Ed, Ed D, PhD, Ed S); elementary education (M Ed, Ed D, PhD, Ed S); reading (M Ed, MS, Ed S); secondary education (M Ed, MS, Ed D, PhD, Ed S); special education (M Ed, Ed D, PhD, Ed S). *Faculty:* 16 full-time (11 women). *Students:* 31 full-time (28 women), 54 part-time (51 women); includes 5 minority (4 African Americans, 1 Hispanic American), 1 international. Average age 35. 59 applicants, 27% accepted, 11 enrolled. In 2006, 43 master's, 3 doctorates, 4 other advanced degrees awarded. *Degree requirements:* For master's, thesis (for some programs), comprehensive exam, registration; for doctorate and Ed S, thesis/dissertation, comprehensive exam, registration. *Entrance requirements:* For master's, GRE General Test, MAT, minimum GPA of 3.0; for doctorate, GRE General Test, minimum GPA of 3.5; for Ed S, GRE General Test, MAT, minimum GPA of 3.25. Additional exam requirements/recommendations for international students: Required—TOEFL. *Application deadline:* For fall admission, 3/1 priority date for domestic students, 3/1 for international students. Applications are processed on a rolling basis. Application fee: $25 ($30 for international students). *Financial support:* In 2006–07, 10 research assistantships with tuition reimbursements (averaging $22,333 per year), 2 teaching assistantships with full tuition reimbursements (averaging $22,333 per year) were awarded; Federal Work-Study, institutionally sponsored loans, and tuition waivers (partial) also available. Financial award application deadline: 3/15. *Faculty research:* Mathematical problem solving, integrative curriculum, writing process, teacher education models. Total annual research expenditures: $100,000. *Unit head:* Dr. Dana Thames, Chair, 601-266-4547, Fax: 601-266-4175. *Application contact:* B.J. Davis, Administrative Assistant, 601-266-6987, Fax: 601-266-4548.

University of South Florida, Graduate School, College of Education, Department of Childhood Education, Tampa, FL 33620-9951. Offers early childhood education (M Ed, MAT, PhD); elementary education (MA, Ed D, PhD, Ed S); reading education (M Ed, MA, PhD, Ed S). *Accreditation:* NCATE. Part-time and evening/weekend programs available. *Faculty:* 25 full-time (19 women), 8 part-time/adjunct (7 women). *Students:* 99 full-time (86 women), 328 part-time (310 women); includes 62 minority (21 African Americans, 2 American Indian/Alaska Native, 6 Asian Americans or Pacific Islanders, 33 Hispanic Americans), 25 international. 213 applicants, 77% accepted, 106 enrolled. In 2006, 136 master's, 8 doctorates awarded. *Degree requirements:* For doctorate, thesis/dissertation, 2 tools of research in foreign language, statistics, and/or computers. *Entrance requirements:* For master's, GRE General Test, minimum GPA of 3.5 in last 60 hours; for doctorate, GRE General Test, minimum GPA of 3.0 (undergraduate) or 3.5 (graduate); for Ed S, GRE General Test, interview. Additional exam requirements/recommendations for international students: Required—TOEFL (minimum score 550 paper-based; 213 computer-based). *Application deadline:* For fall admission, 6/1 for domestic students, 6/2 for international students; for spring admission, 10/15 for domestic students, 7/1 for international students. Application fee: $30. Electronic applications accepted. *Financial support:* Institutionally sponsored loans, scholarships/grants, and unspecified assistantships available. Financial award applicants required to submit FAFSA. Total annual research expenditures: $26,510. *Unit head:* Dr. Marcia Mann, Chairperson, 813-974-3460, Fax: 813-974-0938, E-mail: mmann@tempest.coedu.usf.edu. *Application contact:* Christine Miranda, Admissions/Registrar's Officer, 813-974-3463, Fax: 813-974-0936, E-mail: miranda@tempest.coedu.usf.edu.

The University of Tennessee, Graduate School, College of Education, Health and Human Sciences, Program in Education, Knoxville, TN 37996. Offers art education (MS); counseling education (PhD); cultural studies in education (PhD); curriculum (MS, Ed S); curriculum, educational research and evaluation (Ed D, PhD); early childhood education (PhD); early childhood special education (MS); education of deaf and hard of hearing (MS); educational administration and policy studies (Ed D, PhD); educational administration and supervision (Ed S); educational psychology (Ed D, PhD); elementary education (MS, Ed S); elementary teaching (MS); English education (MS, Ed S); exercise science (PhD); foreign language/ESL education (MS, Ed S); instructional technology (MS, Ed D, PhD, Ed S); literacy, language and ESL education (PhD); literacy, language education, and ESL education (Ed D); mathematics education (MS, Ed S); modified and comprehensive special education (MS); reading education (MS, Ed S); school counseling (Ed S); school psychology (PhD, Ed S); science education (MS, Ed S); secondary teaching (MS); social foundations (MS); social science education (MS, Ed S); socio-cultural foundations of sports and education (PhD); special education (Ed S); teacher education (Ed D, PhD). *Accreditation:* NCATE. Part-time and evening/weekend programs available. *Students:* 529 (401 women); includes 39 minority (23 African Americans, 2 American Indian/Alaska Native, 9 Asian Americans or Pacific Islanders, 5 Hispanic Americans) 34 international. 420 applicants, 50% accepted. In 2006, 258 master's, 28 doctorates awarded. *Degree requirements:* For master's and Ed S, thesis optional; for doctorate, variable foreign language requirement, thesis/dissertation. *Entrance requirements:* For master's, minimum GPA of 2.7; for doctorate and Ed S, GRE General Test, minimum GPA of 2.7. Additional exam requirements/recommendations for international students: Required—TOEFL. *Application deadline:* For fall admission, 2/1 priority date for domestic students. Applications are processed on a rolling basis. Application fee: $35. Electronic applications accepted. *Expenses:* Tuition, state resident: full-time $5,574. Tuition, nonresident: full-time $16,840. Required fees: $792. *Financial support:* In 2006–07, 4 fellowships, 9 teaching assistantships were awarded; career-related internships or fieldwork, Federal Work-Study, institutionally sponsored loans, and unspecified assistantships also available. Financial award application deadline: 2/1; financial award applicants required to submit FAFSA. *Unit head:* Dr. Lester Knight, Head, 865-974-0907, Fax: 865-974-8718, E-mail: lknight@utk.edu.

The University of Tennessee at Chattanooga, Graduate School, College of Health, Education and Professional Studies, Graduate Studies Division of Education, Chattanooga, TN 37403-2598. Offers counseling (M Ed); educational leadership (Ed D); educational specialist (Ed S), including educational technology, school psychology; elementary education (M Ed); school leadership (M Ed); secondary education (M Ed); special education (M Ed). *Accreditation:* ACA; NCATE. Part-time and evening/weekend programs available. *Faculty:* 28 full-time (18 women), 7 part-time/adjunct (3 women). *Students:* 166 full-time (123 women), 309 part-time (238 women); includes 57 minority (46 African Americans, 2 American Indian/Alaska Native, 7 Asian Americans or Pacific Islanders, 2 Hispanic Americans). Average age 33. 138 applicants, 95% accepted, 66 enrolled. In 2006, 133 master's, 25 other advanced degrees awarded. *Degree requirements:* For master's, thesis optional; for doctorate, thesis/dissertation, comprehensive exam. *Entrance requirements:* For master's, GRE General Test or MAT, teaching certificate. *Application deadline:* For fall admission, 8/1 for domestic students; for spring admission, 12/1 for domestic students. Applications are processed on a rolling basis. Application fee: $30. *Expenses:* Tuition, state resident: full-time $5,434; part-time $339 per hour. Tuition, nonresident: full-time $14,830; part-time $861 per hour. Required fees: $940; $178 per hour. *Financial support:* Fellowships, research assistantships, Federal Work-Study and institutionally sponsored loans available. Support available to part-time students. Financial award application deadline: 4/1; financial award applicants required to submit FAFSA. *Faculty research:* School counseling, community counseling, elementary and secondary education, school leadership and administration. Total annual research expenditures: $258,901. *Unit head:* Dr. Anthony Lease, Head, 423-425-4211, Fax: 423-425-5380, E-mail: tony-lease@utc.edu. *Application contact:* Dr. Deborah E. Arfken, Dean of Graduate Studies, 423-425-4666, Fax: 423-425-5223, E-mail: deborah-arfken@utc.edu.

The University of Tennessee at Martin, Graduate Programs, College of Education and Behavioral Sciences, Program in Teaching, Martin, TN 38238-1000. Offers advanced elementary (MS Ed); advanced secondary (MS Ed); initial licensure comprehensive (MS Ed); initial licensure elementary (MS Ed); initial licensure secondary (MS Ed). Part-time programs available. *Students:* 176 (129 women); includes 28 African Americans. 69 applicants, 71% accepted, 34 enrolled. In 2006, 46 degrees awarded. *Degree requirements:* For master's, comprehensive exam. *Entrance requirements:* For master's, GRE General Test, minimum GPA of 2.5. Additional exam requirements/recommendations for international students: Required—TOEFL (minimum score 525 paper-based; 197 computer-based). *Application deadline:* For fall admission, 8/1 priority date for domestic students, 8/1 for international students; for spring admission, 1/1 priority date for domestic students, 1/1 for international students. Applications are processed on a rolling basis. Application fee: $30 ($50 for international students). Electronic applications accepted. *Expenses:* Tuition, state resident: part-time $303 per credit hour. Tuition, nonresident: part-time $829 per credit hour. *Financial support:* Research assistantships with full tuition reimbursements, teaching assistantships with full tuition reimbursements, career-related internships or fieldwork, scholarships/grants, tuition waivers (partial), and unspecified assistantships available. Financial award application deadline: 3/1. *Faculty research:* Special

Elementary Education

The University of Tennessee at Martin (continued)
education, science/math/technology, school reform, reading. *Unit head:* Dr. Suzanne Maniss, Coordinator, 731-881-7163, Fax: 731-881-7975, E-mail: smaniss@utm.edu.

The University of Texas at San Antonio, College of Education and Human Development, Department of Interdisciplinary Learning and Teaching, San Antonio, TX 78249-0617. Offers curriculum and instruction (MA); early childhood and elementary education (MA); educational psychology/special education (MA); instructional technology (MA); reading and literacy (MA). Part-time and evening/weekend programs available. *Faculty:* 26 full-time (all women), 1 part-time/adjunct (0 women). *Students:* 40 full-time (32 women), 240 part-time (207 women); includes 155 minority (20 African Americans, 1 American Indian/Alaska Native, 6 Asian Americans or Pacific Islanders, 128 Hispanic Americans), 3 international. Average age 35. 94 applicants, 100% accepted, 94 enrolled. In 2006, 61 degrees awarded. *Degree requirements:* For master's, thesis optional. *Entrance requirements:* For master's, GRE General Test. Additional exam requirements/recommendations for international students: Required—TOEFL (minimum score 500 paper-based; 173 computer-based). *Application deadline:* For fall admission, 7/1 for domestic students, 4/1 for international students; for spring admission, 11/1 for domestic students, 9/1 for international students. Applications are processed on a rolling basis. Application fee: $45 ($80 for international students). Electronic applications accepted. *Expenses:* Tuition, state resident: full-time $1,730; part-time $192 per credit hour. Tuition, nonresident: full-time $6,680; part-time $742 per credit hour. Required fees: $733; $308,359 per credit hour. *Financial support:* In 2006–07, 3 research assistantships (averaging $28,891 per year) were awarded; career-related internships or fieldwork, Federal Work-Study, scholarships/grants, and unspecified assistantships also available. *Faculty research:* Early childhood, reading, special education, foundations, curriculum and instruction. Total annual research expenditures: $570,791. *Unit head:* Dr. Belinda B. Flores, Chair, 210-458-5969, Fax: 210-458-7281, E-mail: belinda.flores@utsa.edu.

The University of Texas–Pan American, College of Education, Department of Curriculum and Instruction: Elementary and Secondary, Edinburg, TX 78541-2999. Offers bilingual education (M Ed); early childhood education (M Ed); elementary education (M Ed); reading (M Ed); secondary education (M Ed). Part-time programs available. *Degree requirements:* For master's, thesis optional. *Entrance requirements:* For master's, GRE. Additional exam requirements/recommendations for international students: Required—TOEFL, IELTS. *Expenses:* Tuition, state resident: full-time $2,577; part-time $143 per credit hour. Tuition, nonresident: full-time $7,527; part-time $418 per credit hour. Required fees: $561. *Faculty research:* Dual language instruction, literacy and technology, teacher education in diverse populations, mathematics and science education.

University of the Cumberlands, Graduate Programs in Education, Program in Elementary Education, Williamsburg, KY 40769-1372. Offers elementary (P-5) (MA Ed, MAT); middle school (5-9) (MA Ed, MAT). Part-time and evening/weekend programs available. *Degree requirements:* For master's, comprehensive exam. *Entrance requirements:* For master's, GRE or NTE, Kentucky teaching certificate.

University of the Cumberlands, Graduate Programs in Education, Program in Elementary/Secondary Teaching, Williamsburg, KY 40769-1372. Offers MA Ed, MAT, Certificate. *Entrance requirements:* For degree, master's degree, 3 years of teaching experience.

University of the Incarnate Word, School of Graduate Studies and Research, Dreeben School of Education, Program in Teaching, San Antonio, TX 78209-6397. Offers elementary teaching (MAT); secondary teaching (MAT). *Students:* 11 full-time (9 women), 90 part-time (64 women); includes 57 minority (8 African Americans, 2 Asian Americans or Pacific Islanders, 47 Hispanic Americans), 2 international. Average age 35. In 2006, 15 degrees awarded. Application fee: $20. *Expenses:* Tuition: Part-time $570 per credit hour. Required fees: $54 per credit hour. One-time fee: $195 part-time. Tuition and fees vary according to degree level. *Financial support:* Federal Work-Study and scholarships/grants available. *Unit head:* Dr. Elda Martinez, Director of Teacher Education, 210-832-3297, Fax: 210-829-3134, E-mail: eemartin@uiwtx.edu. *Application contact:* Andrea Cyterski-Acosta, Dean of Enrollment, 210-829-6005, Fax: 210-829-3921, E-mail: cyterski@uiwtx.edu.

The University of Toledo, College of Graduate Studies, College of Education, Department of Curriculum and Instruction, Program in Elementary, Toledo, OH 43606-3390. Offers PhD. *Students:* 5 full-time (all women). 1 applicant, 100% accepted, 1 enrolled. *Entrance requirements:* For doctorate, GRE, minimum undergraduate GPA of 2.7.

The University of Toledo, College of Graduate Studies, College of Education, Department of Early Childhood, Physical and Special Education, Program in Elementary, Toledo, OH 43606-3390. Offers Ed S. *Students:* 2 full-time (both women). Average age 38. 2 applicants, 100% accepted, 2 enrolled. *Unit head:* Dr. Laurie Dinnebeil, Chair, Department of Early Childhood, Physical and Special Education, 419-530-4330.

University of Utah, The Graduate School, College of Education, Department of Teaching and Learning, Salt Lake City, UT 84112-1107. Offers elementary education (MAT); secondary education (MAT); teaching and learning (M Ed, M Phil, MA, MS, PhD). Part-time and evening/weekend programs available. *Faculty:* 10 full-time (8 women). *Students:* 71 full-time (59 women), 109 part-time (88 women); includes 9 minority (1 American Indian/Alaska Native, 4 Asian Americans or Pacific Islanders, 4 Hispanic Americans), 1 international. Average age 35. 50 applicants, 62% accepted, 26 enrolled. In 2006, 100 master's, 3 doctorates awarded. *Degree requirements:* For master's, thesis optional; for doctorate, thesis/dissertation. *Entrance requirements:* For master's, GRE General Test or MAT, GRE Subject Test, minimum GPA of 3.0; for doctorate, GRE General Test, minimum graduate GPA of 3.5, minimum undergraduate GPA of 3.0. Additional exam requirements/recommendations for international students: Required—TOEFL (minimum score 500 paper-based; 173 computer-based). *Application deadline:* For fall admission, 3/1 for domestic students, 4/1 for international students; for spring admission, 10/15 for domestic students, 11/1 for international students. Applications are processed on a rolling basis. Application fee: $45 ($65 for international students). *Expenses:* Tuition, state resident: full-time $3,208. Tuition, nonresident: full-time $11,326. Required fees: $608. Tuition and fees vary according to class time and program. *Financial support:* Fellowships, research assistantships with full and partial tuition reimbursements, teaching assistantships with full and partial tuition reimbursements, career-related internships or fieldwork and tuition waivers (partial) available. Financial award application deadline: 2/1; financial award applicants required to submit FAFSA. *Faculty research:* Teacher development, teacher education, reading instruction, math instruction, technology. Total annual research expenditures: $1,111. *Unit head:* Lynne Schrum, Department Chair, 801-587-7800, Fax: 801-581-3609, E-mail: lynne.schrum@ed.utah.edu. *Application contact:* Becky Owen, Graduate Academic Program Specialist, 801-581-7158, Fax: 801-581-3609, E-mail: becky.owen@ed.utah.edu.

The University of West Alabama, School of Graduate Studies, College of Education, Department of Teacher Education, Program in Elementary Education, Livingston, AL 35470. Offers M Ed. *Accreditation:* NCATE. Part-time programs available. *Faculty:* 3 full-time (all women), 4 part-time/adjunct (all women). *Students:* 90 full-time (84 women), 109 part-time (103 women); includes 87 minority (84 African Americans, 3 Hispanic Americans). In 2006, 53 degrees awarded. *Entrance requirements:* For master's, GRE General Test, MAT, minimum GPA of 2.75. *Application deadline:* For fall admission, 9/10 priority date for domestic students; for spring admission, 3/24 for domestic students. Applications are processed on a rolling basis. Application fee: $20 ($50 for international students). *Financial support:* Career-related internships or fieldwork, Federal Work-Study, scholarships/grants, and unspecified assistantships available. Support available to part-time students. *Unit head:* Dr. Louis R. Smith, Associate Dean, Department of Teacher Education, 205-652-3439, Fax: 205-652-3706, E-mail: lsmith@uwa.edu.

University of West Florida, College of Professional Studies, Division of Teacher Education, Master's Program in Curriculum and Instruction, Specialization in Elementary Education, Pensacola, FL 32514-5750. Offers M Ed. *Accreditation:* NCATE. Part-time and evening/weekend programs available. *Students:* 14 full-time (all women), 19 part-time (all women); includes 7 minority (4 African Americans, 1 American Indian/Alaska Native, 1 Asian American or Pacific Islander, 1 Hispanic American). Average age 36. 8 applicants, 88% accepted, 7 enrolled. In 2006, 18 degrees awarded. *Degree requirements:* For master's, thesis or alternative. *Entrance requirements:* For master's, GRE General Test or minimum GPA of 3.0. Additional exam requirements/recommendations for international students: Required—TOEFL (minimum score 550 paper-based; 213 computer-based). *Application deadline:* For fall admission, 6/1 for domestic students, 5/15 for international students; for spring admission, 11/1 for domestic students, 10/1 for international students. Applications are processed on a rolling basis. Application fee: $30. *Expenses:* Tuition, state resident: full-time $5,871; part-time $245 per credit hour. Tuition, nonresident: full-time $21,241; part-time $885 per credit hour. *Financial support:* Fellowships, career-related internships or fieldwork, Federal Work-Study, scholarships/grants, and unspecified assistantships available. Financial award application deadline: 4/15; financial award applicants required to submit FAFSA. *Faculty research:* Curriculum development, in-service teacher education, teaching methodologies.

University of Wisconsin–Eau Claire, College of Education and Human Sciences, Program in Elementary Education, Eau Claire, WI 54702-4004. Offers MST. *Faculty:* 9 full-time (6 women). *Students:* Average age 45. 1 applicant, 0% accepted. *Degree requirements:* For master's, thesis optional. *Application deadline:* For fall admission, 7/1 for domestic students; for spring admission, 12/1 for domestic students. Applications are processed on a rolling basis. Application fee: $45. *Expenses:* Tuition, state resident: full-time $6,533; part-time $363 per credit. Tuition, nonresident: full-time $17,143; part-time $952 per credit. Tuition and fees vary according to program and reciprocity agreements. *Financial support:* Career-related internships or fieldwork and Federal Work-Study available. Financial award application deadline: 3/1; financial award applicants required to submit FAFSA. *Unit head:* Dr. Tamara Lindsey, Chair, 715-836-4737, Fax: 715-836-4868, E-mail: lindsetp@uwec.edu.

University of Wisconsin–La Crosse, Office of University Graduate Studies, College of Liberal Studies, Department of Educational Studies, Program in Professional Development, La Crosse, WI 54601-3742. Offers elementary education (MEPD), including grades 1 through 6, grades 1 through 9; K–12 (MEPD); professional development (MEPD); secondary education (MEPD), including grades 6 through 12. Part-time programs available. *Students:* 26 full-time (18 women), 691 part-time (498 women); includes 20 minority (5 African Americans, 1 American Indian/Alaska Native, 10 Asian Americans or Pacific Islanders, 4 Hispanic Americans). Average age 32. 219 applicants, 93% accepted, 189 enrolled. In 2006, 221 degrees awarded. *Degree requirements:* For master's, thesis optional. *Entrance requirements:* For master's, PPST, minimum GPA of 2.85; minimum cumulative GPA of 3.0 in subject area. Additional exam requirements/recommendations for international students: Required—TOEFL (minimum score 550 paper-based; 213 computer-based). *Application deadline:* Applications are processed on a rolling basis. Application fee: $45. Electronic applications accepted. *Financial support:* In 2006–07, 9 research assistantships with partial tuition reimbursements (averaging $8,109 per year) were awarded; career-related internships or fieldwork, Federal Work-Study, health care benefits, unspecified assistantships, and grant-funded positions also available. Support available to part-time students. Financial award application deadline: 3/15; financial award applicants required to submit FAFSA. *Faculty research:* Professional development, adult learning theory, transformative learning, learning in community, teacher leadership. *Unit head:* Dr. Teri Staloch, Director, 608-785-8146, Fax: 608-785-6560, E-mail: staloch.teri@uwlax.edu. *Application contact:* Kathryn Kiefer, Associate Director of Admissions, 608-785-8939, E-mail: admissions@uwlax.edu.

University of Wisconsin–Milwaukee, Graduate School, School of Education, Department of Curriculum and Instruction, Milwaukee, WI 53201-0413. Offers curriculum planning and instruction improvement (MS); early childhood education (MS); elementary education (MS); junior high/middle school education (MS); reading education (MS); secondary education (MS); teaching in an urban setting (MS). Part-time programs available. *Faculty:* 27 full-time (17 women). *Students:* 21 full-time (17 women), 67 part-time (54 women); includes 15 minority (8 African Americans, 3 Asian Americans or Pacific Islanders, 4 Hispanic Americans), 3 international. 44 applicants, 43% accepted, 19 enrolled. In 2006, 38 degrees awarded. *Degree requirements:* For master's, thesis or alternative. *Application deadline:* For fall admission, 1/1 priority date for domestic students; for spring admission, 9/1 for domestic students. Applications are processed on a rolling basis. Application fee: $45 ($75 for international students). *Expenses:* Tuition, state resident: part-time $510 per credit. Tuition, nonresident: part-time $1,408 per credit. Tuition and fees vary according to program. *Financial support:* Fellowships, research assistantships, teaching assistantships, career-related internships or fieldwork and unspecified assistantships available. Support available to part-time students. Financial award application deadline: 4/15. *Unit head:* Linda Post, Chair, 414-229-4884, Fax: 414-229-5571, E-mail: lpost@uwm.edu.

University of Wisconsin–Platteville, School of Graduate Studies, College of Liberal Arts and Education, School of Education, Platteville, WI 53818-3099. Offers adult education (MSE); elementary education (MSE); middle school education (MSE); secondary education (MSE); vocational and technical education (MSE). *Accreditation:* NCATE. Part-time programs available. *Faculty:* 8 part-time/adjunct (3 women). *Students:* 48 full-time (37 women), 103 part-time (72 women); includes 33 minority (27 African Americans, 1 Asian American or Pacific Islander, 5 Hispanic Americans), 39 international. 39 applicants, 72% accepted. In 2006, 55 degrees awarded. *Degree requirements:* For master's, thesis or alternative, comprehensive exam, registration. *Entrance requirements:* Additional exam requirements/recommendations for international students: Required—TOEFL (minimum score 500 paper-based; 173 computer-based). *Application deadline:* For fall admission, 7/1 priority date for domestic students; for spring admission, 11/1 for domestic students. Applications are processed on a rolling basis. Application fee: $45. Electronic applications accepted. *Expenses:* Tuition, state resident: part-time $365 per credit. Tuition, nonresident: part-time $955 per credit. *Financial support:* Research assistantships with partial tuition reimbursements, career-related internships or fieldwork, Federal Work-Study, institutionally sponsored loans, scholarships/grants, and unspecified assistantships available. Support available to part-time students. *Unit head:* Dr. Michael Anderson, Director, 608-342-1131, Fax: 608-342-1133, E-mail: andersonmi@uwplatt.edu. *Application contact:* Kristal Prohaska, Admissions and Enrollment Management, 608-342-1125, Fax: 608-342-1122, E-mail: admit@uwplatt.edu.

University of Wisconsin–River Falls, Outreach and Graduate Studies, College of Education and Professional Studies, Department of Teacher Education, River Falls, WI 54022-5001. Offers elementary education (MSE); reading (MSE). *Accreditation:* NCATE. Part-time programs available. *Degree requirements:* For master's, thesis or alternative, comprehensive exam, registration. *Entrance requirements:* For master's, minimum GPA of 2.75. Electronic applications accepted.

University of Wisconsin–Stevens Point, College of Professional Studies, School of Education, Program in Elementary Education, Stevens Point, WI 54481-3897. Offers MSE. Part-time programs available. *Faculty:* 13 full-time (11 women). *Students:* 1 (woman) full-time, 8 part-time (7 women). In 2006, 8 degrees awarded. *Degree requirements:* For master's, thesis or alternative, comprehensive exam. *Entrance requirements:* For master's, teacher certification, minimum undergraduate GPA of 3.0. Additional exam requirements/recommendations for international students: Required—TOEFL (minimum score 523 paper-based). *Application deadline:* For fall admission, 5/1 priority date for domestic students. Applications are processed on a rolling basis. Application fee: $45. *Expenses:* Tuition, state resident: full-time $5,910; part-time $328 per credit. Tuition, nonresident: full-time $16,520; part-time $918 per credit. Required fees: $756; $73 per credit. *Financial support:* In 2006–07, 4 research assistantships with partial tuition reimbursements (averaging $9,807 per year) were awarded; Federal Work-Study also available. Support available to part-time students. Financial award application deadline: 5/1. *Faculty research:* Gifted education, early childhood special education, curriculum and instruction, standards-based education. *Application contact:* Dr. Patricia Caro, Director, 715-346-4403, Fax: 715-346-4846, E-mail: pcaro@uwsp.edu.

Utah State University, School of Graduate Studies, College of Education and Human Services, Department of Elementary Education, Logan, UT 84322. Offers M Ed, MA, MS. *Accreditation:* NCATE. Part-time programs available. Postbaccalaureate distance learning degree programs offered (no on-campus study). *Faculty:* 16 full-time (7 women). *Students:* 24 full-time (21 women), 44 part-time (42 women); includes 1 minority (Hispanic American), 12 international. Average age 39. 91 applicants, 64% accepted, 55 enrolled. In 2006, 42 degrees awarded. *Degree requirements:* For master's, thesis (for some programs), comprehensive exam (for some programs), registration. *Entrance requirements:* For master's, GRE General Test or MAT, minimum GPA of 3.0, teaching certificate, 3 recommendations, 1 year teaching department record. Additional exam requirements/recommendations for international students: Required—TOEFL. *Application deadline:* For fall admission, 6/15 priority date for domestic students, 6/15 for international students; for spring admission, 10/15 for domestic and international students. Applications are processed on a rolling basis. Application fee: $50 ($60 for international students). *Financial support:* In 2006–07, 1 research assistantship with partial tuition reimbursement, 2 teaching assistantships with partial tuition reimbursements (averaging $6,400 per year) were awarded; fellowships, career-related internships or fieldwork, institutionally sponsored loans, and tuition waivers (partial) also available. *Faculty research:* Teacher education, supervision, gifted and talented education, language arts/writing, early childhood education. Total annual research expenditures: $126,000. *Unit head:* Dr. Jim Dorward, Interim Head, 435-797-0385, Fax: 435-797-0372, E-mail: jim.dorward@usu.edu. *Application contact:* Stephanie Lenard, Staff Assistant III, 435-797-0389, Fax: 435-797-0372, E-mail: stephanie.leonard@usu.edu.

Vanderbilt University, Peabody College, Department of Teaching and Learning, Nashville, TN 37240-1001. Offers curriculum and instructional leadership (M Ed); early childhood education (M Ed); early childhood leadership (Ed D); elementary education (M Ed); English education (M Ed); English language learners (M Ed); mathematics education (M Ed); reading education (M Ed); science education (M Ed); secondary education (M Ed). *Accreditation:* NCATE. *Faculty:* 23 full-time (13 women), 28 part-time/adjunct (19 women). *Students:* 71 full-time (62 women), 21 part-time (15 women); includes 9 minority (8 African Americans, 1 Hispanic American), 2 international. Average age 27. 102 applicants, 60% accepted, 27 enrolled. In 2006, 53 master's, 3 doctorates awarded. *Degree requirements:* For master's, thesis optional. *Entrance requirements:* For master's, GRE General Test, MAT. Additional exam requirements/recommendations for international students: Required—TOEFL (minimum score 550 paper-based; 213 computer-based). *Application deadline:* For fall admission, 12/31 priority date for domestic and international students; for spring admission, 11/1 priority date for domestic and international students. Applications are processed on a rolling basis. Application fee: $0. Electronic applications accepted. *Expenses:* Tuition: Full-time $24,462. Required fees: $2,515. One-time fee: $30 full-time. Full-time tuition and fees vary according to course load, degree level and program. *Financial support:* In 2006–07, 62 students received support, including 36 fellowships with full and partial tuition reimbursements available, 13 research assistantships with full and partial tuition reimbursements available, 13 teaching assistantships with full and partial tuition reimbursements available; Federal Work-Study, institutionally sponsored loans, scholarships/grants, tuition waivers (partial), and unspecified assistantships also available. Support available to part-time students. Financial award application deadline: 2/1; financial award applicants required to submit FAFSA. *Faculty research:* Teaching and learning; development of subject matter knowledge; learning and policy; development students' mathematical and scientific knowledge, development of literacy. *Unit head:* Leona Schauble, Chair, 615-322-8100, Fax: 615-322-8999, E-mail: leona.schauble@vanderbilt.edu. *Application contact:* Angela Saylor, Educational Coordinator, 615-322-8092, Fax: 615-322-8999.

Villanova University, Graduate School of Liberal Arts and Sciences, Department of Education and Human Services, Program in Elementary Teacher Education, Villanova, PA 19085-1699. Offers MA. Part-time and evening/weekend programs available. *Students:* 2 full-time (both women), 14 part-time (all women). Average age 28. In 2006, 5 degrees awarded. *Degree requirements:* For master's, comprehensive exam. *Entrance requirements:* For master's, GRE or MAT, minimum GPA of 3.0. *Application deadline:* For fall admission, 8/1 priority date for domestic students; for spring admission, 12/1 for domestic students. Applications are processed on a rolling basis. Application fee: $50. Electronic applications accepted. *Expenses:* Tuition: Part-time $565 per credit. *Financial support:* Career-related internships or fieldwork and Federal Work-Study available. Financial award applicants required to submit FAFSA. *Unit head:* Fr. Robert Murray, Coordinator, 610-519-4620.

Wagner College, Division of Graduate Studies, Department of Education, Program in Childhood Education, Staten Island, NY 10301-4495. Offers MS Ed. Part-time and evening/weekend programs available. *Students:* 30 full-time (24 women), 10 part-time (9 women); includes 13 minority (3 African Americans, 1 Asian American or Pacific Islander, 9 Hispanic Americans). Average age 23. 19 applicants, 84% accepted, 15 enrolled. In 2006, 11 degrees awarded. *Entrance requirements:* For master's, New York State Teacher Certification Examinations (NYSTCE), Liberal Arts and Sciences Test (LAST), minimum GPA of 2.75. Additional exam requirements/recommendations for international students: Required—TOEFL (minimum score 550 paper-based; 217 computer-based). *Application deadline:* For fall admission, 8/1 priority date for domestic students, 6/30 priority date for international students; for spring admission, 12/10 for domestic students, 11/15 for international students. Applications are processed on a rolling basis. Application fee: $50 ($80 for international students). *Expenses:* Tuition: Full-time $15,120; part-time $840 per credit. *Financial support:* Fellowships, tuition waivers (partial) and unspecified assistantships available. Financial award applicants required to submit FAFSA. *Application contact:* Susan Rosenberg, Office of Graduate Studies, 718-390-3106, Fax: 718-390-3456, E-mail: graduate@wagner.edu.

Washington State University, Graduate School, College of Education, Department of Teaching and Learning, Pullman, WA 99164. Offers curriculum and instruction (Ed D, PhD); diverse languages (M Ed, MA); elementary education (M Ed, MA, MIT); exercise science (MS); literacy education (M Ed, MA, PhD); math education (PhD); secondary education (M Ed, MA). *Accreditation:* NCATE. *Faculty:* 27. *Students:* 54 full-time (43 women), 20 part-time (14 women); includes 13 minority (4 African Americans, 2 American Indian/Alaska Native, 2 Asian Americans or Pacific Islanders, 5 Hispanic Americans), 5 international. Average age 34. 244 applicants, 16% accepted, 11 enrolled. In 2006, 20 master's, 3 doctorates awarded. *Degree requirements:* For master's, thesis (for some programs), oral or written exam, comprehensive exam (for some programs); for doctorate, thesis/dissertation, oral, written exam, comprehensive exam. *Entrance requirements:* For master's and doctorate, GRE General Test, minimum GPA of 3.0, 3 letters of recommendation. Additional exam requirements/recommendations for international students: Required—TOEFL. *Application deadline:* For fall admission, 2/1 for domestic students, 3/1 for international students; for spring admission, 9/1 for domestic students, 7/1 for international students. Applications are processed on a rolling basis. Application fee: $50. *Expenses:* Tuition, state resident: full-time $7,066. Tuition, nonresident: full-time $17,204. *Financial support:* In 2006–07, 13 research assistantships with partial tuition reimbursements (averaging $13,917 per year), 22 teaching assistantships with partial tuition reimbursements (averaging $13,056 per year) were awarded; career-related internships or fieldwork, Federal Work-Study, institutionally sponsored loans, tuition waivers (partial), unspecified assistantships, and staff assistantships, teaching associateships also available. Financial award application deadline: 4/1. *Faculty research:* Evolution of middle school education issues in special education, computer-assisted language learning. Total annual research expenditures: $1.1 million. *Unit head:* Dr. Corinne Mantle-Bromley, Chair, 509-335-5027. *Application contact:* Graduate School Admissions, 800-GRADWSU, Fax: 509-335-1949, E-mail: gradsch@wsu.edu.

Washington University in St. Louis, Graduate School of Arts and Sciences, Department of Education, Program in Elementary Education, St. Louis, MO 63130-4899. Offers MA Ed. *Degree requirements:* For master's, thesis or alternative. *Entrance requirements:* For master's, GRE General Test or MAT. Electronic applications accepted.

Wayne State College, School of Education and Counseling, Department of Educational Foundations and Leadership, Program in Curriculum and Instruction, Wayne, NE 68787. Offers alternative education (MSE); business education (MSE); communication arts education (MSE); curriculum and instruction (MSE); early childhood education (MSE); elementary education (MSE); English as a second language (MSE); English education (MSE); family consumer science of education (MSE); industrial technology education (MSE); learning communities (MSE); mathematics education (MSE); music education (MSE); science education (MSE); social science education (MSE). *Accreditation:* NCATE. Part-time and evening/weekend programs available. *Faculty:* 17 part-time/adjunct (11 women). *Students:* 17 full-time (10 women), 307 part-time (248 women); includes 6 minority (2 African Americans, 1 American Indian/Alaska Native, 2 Asian Americans or Pacific Islanders, 1 Hispanic American), 1 international. Average age 35. In 2006, 167 degrees awarded. *Degree requirements:* For master's, thesis optional. *Entrance requirements:* For master's, GRE General Test. Additional exam requirements/recommendations for international students: Required—TOEFL (minimum score 550 paper-based; 213 computer-based). *Application deadline:* Applications are processed on a rolling basis. Application fee: $30. *Expenses:* Tuition, state resident: full-time $3,114; part-time $130 per credit hour. Tuition, nonresident: full-time $6,228; part-time $260 per credit hour. Required fees: $894; $37 per credit hour. Tuition and fees vary according to course load. *Financial support:* Applicants required to submit FAFSA.

Wayne State University, College of Education, Division of Administrative and Organizational Studies, Detroit, MI 48202. Offers administration and supervision-secondary (Ed S); college and university teaching (Certificate); curriculum and instruction (PhD); educational leadership (M Ed, Ed S); educational leadership and policy studies (Ed D, PhD); elementary education curriculum and instruction (MA, Ed S); general administration and supervision (Ed D, PhD, Ed S); higher education (Ed D, PhD); instructional technology (M Ed, Ed D, PhD, Ed S); secondary curriculum and instruction (M Ed, Ed S). *Faculty:* 24 full-time (13 women), 1 (woman) part-time/adjunct. *Students:* 153 full-time (103 women), 389 part-time (266 women); includes 252 minority (223 African Americans, 6 American Indian/Alaska Native, 8 Asian Americans or Pacific Islanders, 15 Hispanic Americans), 19 international. Average age 38. 138 applicants, 79% accepted, 74 enrolled. In 2006, 116 master's, 30 doctorates, 64 other advanced degrees awarded. *Degree requirements:* For doctorate, thesis/dissertation. *Entrance requirements:* For doctorate, interview, minimum GPA of 3.0. Additional exam requirements/recommendations for international students: Required—TOEFL (minimum score 550 paper-based; 213 computer-based), TWE (minimum score 6). *Application deadline:* For fall admission, 7/1 for domestic students, 6/1 for international students; for winter admission, 10/1 for international students; for spring admission, 2/1 for international students. Application fee: $30 ($50 for international students). Electronic applications accepted. *Financial support:* In 2006–07, 4 research assistantships (averaging $12,797 per year) were awarded; career-related internships or fieldwork, Federal Work-Study, and institutionally sponsored loans also available. Support available to part-time students. *Faculty research:* Total quality management, participatory management, administering educational technology, school improvement, principalship. Total annual research expenditures: $344,504. *Unit head:* Dr. JoAnne Holbert, Assistant Dean, 313-577-1721, E-mail: jholbert@wayne.edu.

Wayne State University, College of Education, Division of Teacher Education, Detroit, MI 48202. Offers adult and continuing education (M Ed); art education (M Ed); bilingual/bicultural education (M Ed, MAT); business education (M Ed, MAT); career and technical education (M Ed, Ed D, PhD, Ed S); curriculum and instruction (Ed D, PhD, Ed S); distributive education (M Ed, MAT); early childhood education (M Ed); elementary education (M Ed, MAT, Ed D, PhD, Ed S); elementary education curriculum and instruction (M Ed); English education (M Ed); English education-secondary (M Ed, Ed S); foreign language education (M Ed); general education (Ed D, Ed S); health occupations education (M Ed); industrial education (M Ed); mathematics education (M Ed, Ed S); pre-school and parent education (M Ed); reading (M Ed, Ed D, Ed S); reading, languages and literature (Ed D); school music-vocal (M Ed); science education (M Ed, MAT, Ed S); secondary education (MAT); secondary school reading (M Ed); social studies education (M Ed, Ed S), including education-secondary (M Ed); special education (M Ed, Ed D, PhD, Ed S); teacher education (MAT, Ed D, PhD). *Faculty:* 41 full-time (22 women), 2 part-time/adjunct (both women). *Students:* 401 full-time (295 women), 1,021 part-time (784 women); includes 527 minority (452 African Americans, 6 American Indian/Alaska Native, 32 Asian Americans or Pacific Islanders, 37 Hispanic Americans), 18 international. Average age 36. 296 applicants, 81% accepted, 132 enrolled. In 2006, 386 master's, 1 doctorate awarded. *Degree requirements:* For doctorate, thesis/dissertation. *Entrance requirements:* For master's, minimum GPA of 2.6; for doctorate, minimum undergraduate GPA of 3.0, graduate 3.5; interview. Additional exam requirements/recommendations for international students: Required—TOEFL (minimum score 550 paper-based; 213 computer-based), TWE (minimum score 6). *Application deadline:* For fall admission, 7/1 for domestic students, 6/1 for international students; for winter admission, 10/1 for international students; for spring admission, 2/1 for international students. Application fee: $30 ($50 for international students). Electronic applications accepted. *Financial support:* In 2006–07, 1 fellowship (averaging $34,919 per year) was awarded; research assistantships. *Faculty research:* Reading and writing literacy and literature. Total annual research expenditures: $209,400. *Unit head:* Dr. Joann Snyder, Academic Director, 313-577-1644, E-mail: joanne.snyder@wayne.edu. *Application contact:* Sharon Elliott, Assistant Dean, 313-577-0902, E-mail: sharon.elliott@wayne.edu.

West Chester University of Pennsylvania, Graduate Studies, School of Education, Department of Elementary Education, West Chester, PA 19383. Offers M Ed. *Accreditation:* NCATE. Part-time and evening/weekend programs available. *Students:* 51 full-time (39 women), 156 part-time (131 women); includes 1 African American, 1 Asian American or Pacific Islander, 2 Hispanic Americans, 1 international. Average age 30. 61 applicants, 97% accepted, 38 enrolled. In 2006, 26 degrees awarded. *Degree requirements:* For master's, thesis optional. *Entrance requirements:* For master's, GRE or MAT, instructional certificate, interview. *Application deadline:* For fall admission, 4/15 priority date for domestic students; for spring admission, 10/15 for domestic students. Applications are processed on a rolling basis. Application fee: $35. *Financial support:* In 2006–07, 1 research assistantship with full tuition reimbursement (averaging $5,000 per year) was awarded; unspecified assistantships also available. Support available to part-time students. Financial award application deadline: 2/15; financial award applicants required to submit FAFSA. *Faculty research:* Cooperative learning, peer mediation in schools, creative thinking and questioning. *Unit head:* Dr. Martha Drobnak, Chair, 610-436-3319, E-mail: mdrobnak@wcupa.edu. *Application contact:* Dr. Connie DiLucchio, Graduate Coordinator, 610-436-2994, E-mail: cdilucchio@wcupa.edu.

Western Carolina University, Graduate School, College of Education and Allied Professions, Department of Birth-Kindergarten, Elementary and Middle Grades Education, Program in Elementary Education, Cullowhee, NC 28723. Offers comprehensive education-elementary education (MA Ed). *Accreditation:* NCATE. Part-time and evening/weekend programs available. *Degree requirements:* For master's, comprehensive exam. *Entrance requirements:* For master's, GRE General Test. Additional exam requirements/recommendations for international students: Required—TOEFL (minimum score 550 paper-based; 213 computer-based).

Western Illinois University, School of Graduate Studies, College of Education and Human Services, Department of Curriculum and Instruction, Program in Elementary Education, Macomb, IL 61455-1390. Offers MS Ed. *Accreditation:* NCATE. Part-time programs available. *Students:* 4 full-time (all women), 117 part-time (105 women); includes 3 minority (all Hispanic Americans) Average age 35. 25 applicants, 60% accepted. In 2006, 33 degrees awarded. *Degree requirements:* For master's, thesis or alternative. *Entrance requirements:* For master's, minimum GPA of 2.75. Additional exam requirements/recommendations for international students: Required—TOEFL (minimum score 550 paper-based; 213 computer-based; 80 iBT). *Application deadline:* Applications are processed on a rolling basis. Application fee: $30. Electronic applications accepted. *Expenses:* Tuition, state resident: part-time $200 per credit hour. Tuition, nonresident: part-time $400 per credit hour. *Financial support:* In 2006–07, 1 student received support, including 1 research assistantship with full tuition reimbursement available (averaging $6,568 per year). Financial award applicants required to submit FAFSA. *Unit head:* Dr. Angela Ferree, Graduate Committee Chairperson, 309-298-1961. *Application contact:* Dr. Barbara

Elementary Education

Western Illinois University *(continued)*
Baily, Director of Graduate Studies/Associate Provost, 309-298-1806, Fax: 309-298-2345, E-mail: grad-office@wiu.edu.

Western Kentucky University, Graduate Studies, College of Education and Behavioral Sciences, Department of Counseling and Student Affairs, Bowling Green, KY 42101. Offers business and marketing education (MA Ed); counseling (MA Ed); counselor education (Ed S); education and behavioral science (MA Ed); elementary education (MA Ed, Ed S); middle years education (MA Ed); secondary education (MA Ed, Ed S); student affairs (MA Ed). *Accreditation:* ACA; NCATE. Part-time and evening/weekend programs available. *Faculty:* 11 full-time (5 women), 9 part-time/adjunct (3 women). *Students:* 59 full-time (47 women), 157 part-time (126 women); includes 18 minority (13 African Americans, 1 American Indian/Alaska Native, 2 Asian Americans or Pacific Islanders, 2 Hispanic Americans), 1 international. Average age 31. 49 applicants, 67% accepted, 27 enrolled. In 2006, 89 master's, 4 other advanced degrees awarded. *Degree requirements:* For master's, thesis optional. *Entrance requirements:* For master's, GRE General Test. Additional exam requirements/recommendations for international students: Required—TOEFL (minimum score 555 paper-based; 213 computer-based; 79 iBT). *Application deadline:* For fall admission, 8/1 priority date for domestic students, 4/1 for international students; for spring admission, 12/1 for domestic students, 9/1 for international students. Applications are processed on a rolling basis. Application fee: $35. *Expenses:* Tuition, state resident: full-time $6,520; part-time $226 per hour. Tuition, nonresident: full-time $7,140; part-time $357 per hour. International tuition: $15,820 full-time. *Financial support:* In 2006–07, 1 research assistantship with partial tuition reimbursement (averaging $8,000 per year) was awarded; Federal Work-Study, institutionally sponsored loans, and service awards also available. Financial award application deadline: 4/1; financial award applicants required to submit FAFSA. *Faculty research:* Counselor education, research for residential workers. *Unit head:* Dr. Aaron W Hughey, Department Head, 270-745-4953, E-mail: aaron.hughey@wku.edu.

Western Kentucky University, Graduate Studies, College of Education and Behavioral Sciences, Department of Curriculum and Instruction, Bowling Green, KY 42101. Offers business and marketing education (MAE); elementary education (MAE, Ed S); middle grades education (MAE); secondary education (MAE, Ed S). *Faculty:* 10 full-time (7 women), 1 (woman) part-time/adjunct. *Students:* 7 full-time (3 women), 133 part-time (109 women); includes 2 minority (1 African American, 1 Hispanic American), 1 international. Average age 31. 30 applicants, 63% accepted, 14 enrolled. In 2006, 56 degrees awarded. *Degree requirements:* For master's, comprehensive exam; for Ed S, thesis. *Entrance requirements:* For master's, GRE. Additional exam requirements/recommendations for international students: Required—TOEFL (minimum score 555 paper-based; 213 computer-based; 79 iBT). *Application deadline:* For fall admission, 7/1 priority date for domestic students, 5/15 for international students; for spring admission, 11/1 for domestic students, 9/15 for international students. Applications are processed on a rolling basis. Application fee: $35. *Expenses:* Tuition, state resident: full-time $6,520; part-time $226 per hour. Tuition, nonresident: full-time $7,140; part-time $357 per hour. International tuition: $15,820 full-time. *Financial support:* In 2006–07, 1 research assistantship with partial tuition reimbursement (averaging $7,200 per year) was awarded. Total annual research expenditures: $17,998. *Unit head:* Dr. Tabitha Daniel, Head, 270-745-2157, E-mail: tabitha.daniel@wku.edu.

Western Michigan University, Graduate College, College of Education, Department of Teaching, Learning, and Leadership, Program in Elementary Education, Kalamazoo, MI 49008-5202. Offers MA. *Accreditation:* NCATE.

Western New England College, School of Arts and Sciences, Program in Elementary Education, Springfield, MA 01119. Offers M Ed. Part-time and evening/weekend programs available.

Western New Mexico University, Graduate Division, School of Education, Silver City, NM 88062-0680. Offers counselor education (MA); elementary education (MAT); reading education (MAT); school administration (MA); secondary education (MAT); special education (MAT). *Accreditation:* NCATE. *Degree requirements:* For master's, comprehensive exam. *Entrance requirements:* For master's, GRE General Test, GRE Subject Test, minimum GPA of 3.2 in last 64 hours of undergraduate study. Additional exam requirements/recommendations for international students: Required—TOEFL (minimum score 550 paper-based; 213 computer-based). Electronic applications accepted. *Expenses:* Tuition, state resident: full-time $1,329. Tuition, nonresident: full-time $4,779.

Western Washington University, Graduate School, Woodring College of Education, Department of Elementary Education, Bellingham, WA 98225-5996. Offers M Ed. *Accreditation:* NCATE. Part-time programs available. *Faculty:* 9. In 2006, 2 degrees awarded. *Degree requirements:* For master's, thesis optional. *Entrance requirements:* For master's, GRE General Test or MAT, minimum GPA of 3.0 in last 60 semester hours or last 90 quarter hours, elementary teaching certificate. Additional exam requirements/recommendations for international students: Required—TOEFL (minimum score 567 paper-based; 227 computer-based). *Application deadline:* For fall admission, 6/1 for domestic students; for winter admission, 10/1 for domestic students; for spring admission, 2/1 for domestic students. Applications are processed on a rolling basis. Application fee: $50. *Expenses:* Tuition, state resident: full-time $6,609; part-time $199 per credit. Tuition, nonresident: full-time $16,845; part-time $540 per credit. *Financial support:* In 2006–07, 2 teaching assistantships with partial tuition reimbursements (averaging $9,339 per year) were awarded; career-related internships or fieldwork, Federal Work-Study, institutionally sponsored loans, scholarships/grants, tuition waivers (partial), and unspecified assistantships also available. Support available to part-time students. Financial award application deadline: 2/15; financial award applicants required to submit FAFSA. *Faculty research:* Teacher learning through National Board certification. *Unit head:* Dr. Chris Ohana, Chair, 360-650-6533, E-mail: chris.ohana@wwu.edu. *Application contact:* Dr. Marsha Riddle Buly, Graduate Program Director, 360-650-7348.

Westfield State College, Division of Graduate and Continuing Education, Department of Education, Program in Elementary Education, Westfield, MA 01086. Offers M Ed. *Accreditation:* NCATE. Part-time and evening/weekend programs available. *Degree requirements:* For master's, practicum. *Entrance requirements:* For master's, GRE General Test or MAT, minimum undergraduate GPA of 2.7.

West Virginia University, College of Human Resources and Education, Department of Curriculum and Instruction-Literacy, Program in Elementary Education, Morgantown, WV 26506. Offers MA. Students enter program as undergraduates. *Accreditation:* NCATE. Part-time programs available. *Students:* 136 full-time (119 women), 40 part-time (39 women); includes 7 minority (4 African Americans, 1 American Indian/Alaska Native, 2 Hispanic Americans), 5 international. Average age 28. 81 applicants, 88% accepted, 44 enrolled. In 2006, 82 degrees awarded. *Degree requirements:* For master's, content exams, thesis optional. *Entrance requirements:* For master's, minimum GPA of 2.75. Additional exam requirements/recommendations for international students: Required—TOEFL. *Application deadline:* Applications are processed on a rolling basis. Application fee: $50. Electronic applications accepted. *Expenses:* Tuition, state resident: full-time $4,926; part-time $276 per credit hour. Tuition, nonresident: full-time $14,278; part-time $796 per credit hour. Tuition and fees vary according to program. *Financial support:* In 2006–07, 114 students received support, including 1 research assistantship with full tuition reimbursement available (averaging $8,264 per year), 2 teaching assistantships with full tuition reimbursements available (averaging $8,264 per year); career-related internships or fieldwork, Federal Work-Study, institutionally sponsored loans, and tuition waivers (full and partial) also available. Financial award application deadline: 2/1; financial award applicants required to submit FAFSA. *Faculty research:* Teacher education, school reform, teacher and student attitudes, curriculum development, education technology. *Application contact:* Dr. Elizabeth A. Dooley, Chair, 304-293-3441, Fax: 304-293-3802, E-mail: elizabeth.dooley@mail.wvu.edu.

Wheaton College, Graduate School, Department of Education, Wheaton, IL 60187-5593. Offers elementary level (MAT); secondary level (MAT). *Accreditation:* NCATE. *Students:* 9. 10 applicants, 80% accepted, 4 enrolled. *Degree requirements:* For master's, thesis or alternative. *Entrance requirements:* For master's, GRE General Test. *Application deadline:* For fall admission, 3/1 priority date for domestic students; for spring admission, 11/1 for domestic students. Applications are processed on a rolling basis. Application fee: $30. *Financial support:* Career-related internships or fieldwork and Federal Work-Study available. Financial award application deadline: 3/1; financial award applicants required to submit FAFSA. *Unit head:* Dr. Andrew Brulle, Chair, 630-752-5763, E-mail: andrew.brulle@wheaton.edu. *Application contact:* Julie A. Huebner, Director of Graduate Admissions, 630-752-5195, Fax: 630-752-5935, E-mail: gradadm@wheaton.edu.

Wheelock College, Graduate Programs, Division of Education, Boston, MA 02215-4176. Offers early childhood education (MS); education leadership (MS); elementary education (MS); language, literacy, and reading (MS); teaching students with moderate disabilities (MS). *Accreditation:* NCATE. Postbaccalaureate distance learning degree programs offered (minimal on-campus study). *Degree requirements:* For master's, comprehensive exam. *Entrance requirements:* Additional exam requirements/recommendations for international students: Required—TOEFL. Electronic applications accepted. *Faculty research:* Symbolic learning, emergent literacy, diversity inclusion, beginning reading language and culture, math education.

Whittier College, Graduate Programs, Department of Education and Child Development, Program in Elementary Education, Whittier, CA 90608-0634. Offers MA Ed. Part-time and evening/weekend programs available. *Degree requirements:* For master's, thesis, registration. *Entrance requirements:* For master's, GRE General Test, MAT.

Whitworth University, School of Education, Graduate Studies in Education, Spokane, WA 99251-0001. Offers administration (M Ed); counseling (M Ed), including school counselors, social agency/church setting; elementary education (M Ed); gifted and talented (MAT); secondary education (M Ed); special education (MAT); teaching (MIT). *Accreditation:* NCATE. Part-time and evening/weekend programs available. *Faculty:* 2 full-time (both women), 25 part-time/adjunct (15 women). *Degree requirements:* For master's, thesis (for some programs), comprehensive exam. *Entrance requirements:* For master's, GRE General Test, MAT. Additional exam requirements/recommendations for international students: Required—TOEFL. *Application deadline:* For fall admission, 9/1 priority date for domestic students; for spring admission, 2/1 priority date for domestic students. Applications are processed on a rolling basis. Application fee: $35. *Financial support:* Fellowships with partial tuition reimbursements, career-related internships or fieldwork, institutionally sponsored loans, and scholarships/grants available. Financial award application deadline: 2/1. *Faculty research:* Rural program development, mainstreaming, special needs learners. *Unit head:* Dr. Sharon Mowry, Director, 509-777-4393, Fax: 509-777-3785, E-mail: smowry@whitworth.edu. *Application contact:* Pat Bailey, Program Assistant, 509-777-3228, Fax: 509-777-4753, E-mail: gse@whitworth.edu.

Widener University, School of Human Service Professions, Center for Education, Chester, PA 19013-5792. Offers adult education (M Ed); counseling in higher education (M Ed); counselor education (M Ed); early childhood education (M Ed); educational foundations (M Ed); educational leadership (M Ed); educational psychology (M Ed); elementary education (M Ed); English and language arts (M Ed); health education (M Ed); higher education leadership (Ed D); home and school visitor (M Ed); human sexuality (M Ed); mathematics education (M Ed); middle school education (M Ed); principalship (M Ed); reading and language arts (Ed D); reading education (M Ed); school administration (Ed D); science education (M Ed); social studies education (M Ed); special education (M Ed); technology education (M Ed). Part-time and evening/weekend programs available. Terminal master's awarded for partial completion of doctoral program. *Degree requirements:* For doctorate, thesis/dissertation. *Entrance requirements:* For master's, minimum GPA of 2.5; for doctorate, GRE or MAT, minimum GPA of 2.0 (undergraduate), 3.5 (graduate). Electronic applications accepted. Expenses: Contact institution. *Faculty research:* Reading and cognition, adult education, technology education, educational leadership, special education.

Wilkes University, Graduate Studies and Continued Learning, College of Arts, Humanities and Social Sciences, Program in Teacher Education, Wilkes-Barre, PA 18766-0002. Offers classroom technology (MS Ed); educational computing (MS Ed); educational development and strategies (MS Ed); educational leadership (MS Ed); elementary education (MS Ed); instructional technology (MS Ed); school business leadership (MS Ed); secondary education (MS Ed), including biology, chemistry, English; history; special education (MS Ed). Part-time and evening/weekend programs available. Postbaccalaureate distance learning degree programs offered (minimal on-campus study). *Students:* 32 full-time (21 women), 1,588 part-time (1,106 women); includes 29 minority (6 African Americans, 2 American Indian/Alaska Native, 4 Asian Americans or Pacific Islanders, 17 Hispanic Americans). Average age 33. In 2006, 754 degrees awarded. *Entrance requirements:* Additional exam requirements/recommendations for international students: Required—TOEFL (minimum score 500 paper-based; 173 computer-based). *Application deadline:* Applications are processed on a rolling basis. Application fee: $40. *Expenses:* Contact institution. *Financial support:* Federal Work-Study and unspecified assistantships available. Financial award application deadline: 3/1; financial award applicants required to submit FAFSA. *Unit head:* Dr. Michael Speziale, Interim Dean, 570-408-4679, Fax: 570-408-4905, E-mail: michael.speziale@wilkes.edu. *Application contact:* Kathleen Houlihan, Director of Graduate Studies, 570-408-3235, Fax: 570-408-7846, E-mail: kathleen.houlihan@wilkes.edu.

William Carey University, Graduate Studies, School of Education, Hattiesburg, MS 39401-5499. Offers art education (M Ed); art of teaching (M Ed); elementary education (M Ed, Ed S); English education (M Ed); gifted education (M Ed); history and social science (M Ed); mild/moderate disabilities (M Ed); secondary education (M Ed). Part-time programs available. *Faculty:* 19 full-time (12 women), 25 part-time/adjunct (17 women). *Students:* 142 full-time (111 women), 412 part-time (343 women); includes 123 minority (121 African Americans, 1 Asian American or Pacific Islander, 1 Hispanic American). In 2006, 305 master's, 2 other advanced degrees awarded. *Degree requirements:* For master's, comprehensive exam. *Entrance requirements:* For master's, GRE, MAT, minimum GPA of 2.5, Class A teacher's license. Additional exam requirements/recommendations for international students: Required—TOEFL (minimum score 550 paper-based; 213 computer-based). *Application deadline:* For fall admission, 8/7 for domestic and international students; for winter admission, 10/30 for domestic and international students; for spring admission, 2/12 for domestic and international students. Application fee: $25. *Expenses:* Tuition: Full-time $5,040; part-time $240 per credit hour. Tuition and fees vary according to course load. *Financial support:* In 2006–07, 371 students received support. Federal Work-Study and scholarships/grants available. Support available to part-time students. *Unit head:* Dr. Patty Ward, Dean, 601-318-6139, Fax: 601-318-6185, E-mail: patty.ward@wmcarey.edu. *Application contact:* Jason Douglas, Clerical Assistant, Graduate Admissions, 601-318-6774, Fax: 601-318-6765, E-mail: jason.douglas@wmcarey.edu.

William Paterson University of New Jersey, College of Education, Program in Elementary Education, Wayne, NJ 07470-8420. Offers M Ed, MAT. *Accreditation:* NCATE. *Students:* 197; includes 20 minority (6 African Americans, 3 Asian Americans or Pacific Islanders, 11 Hispanic Americans). 145 applicants, 49% accepted, 58 enrolled. *Degree requirements:* For master's, research design. *Entrance requirements:* For master's, GRE General Test, MAT, minimum GPA of 2.75, teaching certificate. *Application deadline:* Applications are processed on a rolling basis. Application fee: $50. Electronic applications accepted. *Financial support:* Research assistantships with full tuition reimbursements, career-related internships or fieldwork and unspecified assistantships available. Support available to part-time students. Financial award application deadline: 4/1; financial award applicants required to submit FAFSA. *Unit head:* Dr. Rochelle Kaplan, Director, 973-720-2598. *Application contact:* Danielle Liautaud, Director, 973-720-3579, Fax: 973-720-2035, E-mail: liautaudd@wpunj.edu.

Wilmington College, Division of Education, New Castle, DE 19720-6491. Offers applied education technology (M Ed); career and technical education (M Ed); elementary and secondary school counseling (M Ed); elementary special education (M Ed); elementary studies (M Ed); instruction: gifted and talented (M Ed); instruction: teaching and learning (M Ed); literacy (M Ed); reading (M Ed); school leadership (M Ed); secondary teaching (MAT). Part-time and evening/weekend programs available. *Faculty:* 7 full-time (4 women). *Students:* 609 full-time (447 women), 1,350 part-time (1,013 women); includes 144 minority (131 African Americans, 3 American Indian/Alaska Native, 1 Asian American or Pacific Islander, 9 Hispanic Americans). Average age 34. 818 applicants, 100% accepted, 599 enrolled. In 2006, 737 degrees awarded. *Entrance requirements:* For master's, 2 letters of recommendation, interview. Additional exam requirements/recommendations for international students: Required—TOEFL (minimum score 500 paper-based; 173 computer-based). *Application deadline:* For fall admission, 4/30 for domestic students. Applications are processed on a rolling basis. Application fee: $25. *Financial support:* Applicants required to submit FAFSA. *Unit head:* Dr. Richard Gochnauer, Chair, 302-328-6795 Ext. 163, Fax: 302-328-7081. *Application contact:* Chris Ferguson, Director of Admissions and Financial Aid, 302-328-9407 Ext. 256, Fax: 302-328-5164, E-mail: inquire@wilmcoll.edu.

Wingate University, Program in Education, Wingate, NC 28174-0159. Offers educational leadership (MA Ed); elementary education (MA Ed, MAT); physical education (MA Ed); sport administration (MA Ed). *Accreditation:* NCATE. Part-time and evening/weekend programs available. *Faculty:* 4 full-time (3 women), 4 part-time/adjunct (1 woman). *Students:* 1 (woman) full-time, 127 part-time (96 women); includes 2 minority (both African Americans) Average age 35. 19 applicants, 58% accepted, 11 enrolled. In 2006, 12 degrees awarded. *Degree requirements:* For master's, portfolio. *Entrance requirements:* For master's, GRE General Test or MAT, teaching certificate (MA Ed). *Application deadline:* For fall admission, 8/15 priority date for domestic students; for spring admission, 12/15 for domestic students. Applications are processed on a rolling basis. Application fee: $0. *Expenses:* Tuition: Full-time $3,330; part-time $185 per credit hour. *Financial support:* In 2006–07, 20 students received support. Scholarships/grants available. Support available to part-time students. Financial award applicants required to submit FAFSA. *Faculty research:* Teaching/learning styles, principles of teaching, homework, stress management, student's rights. *Unit head:* Dr. Robert Shaw, Dean, Thayer School of Education, 704-233-8128, Fax: 704-233-8273, E-mail: rshaw@wingate.edu. *Application contact:* Marsha Luke, Secretary, Thayer School of Education, 704-233-8127, Fax: 704-233-8273, E-mail: mluke@wingate.edu.

Winston-Salem State University, Program in Elementary Education, Winston-Salem, NC 27110-0003. Offers M Ed. *Accreditation:* NCATE. Part-time and evening/weekend programs available. Postbaccalaureate distance learning degree programs offered (minimal on-campus study). *Faculty:* 4 full-time (1 woman). *Students:* 14 applicants, 71% accepted, 9 enrolled. In 2006, 9 degrees awarded. *Entrance requirements:* For master's, GRE, MAT, NC Teacher 'A" Licensure. *Application deadline:* For fall admission, 7/15 for domestic and international students. Applications are processed on a rolling basis. Application fee: $40. Electronic applications accepted. *Expenses:* Tuition, state resident: full-time $2,010. Tuition, nonresident: full-time $10,502. Tuition and fees vary according to course load. *Financial support:* Research assistantships, teaching assistantships, career-related internships or fieldwork and institutionally sponsored loans available. *Faculty research:* Action research on issues in elementary classroom. *Unit head:* Dr. Cathy Griffin-Famble, Chair, Education, 336-750-2550, Fax: 336-750-2335, E-mail: famblecg@wssu.edu. *Application contact:* Graduate Studies and Research, 336-750-2102, Fax: 336-750-3042, E-mail: graduate@wssu.edu.

Worcester State College, Graduate Studies, Department of Education, Concentration in Elementary Education, Worcester, MA 01602-2597. Offers M Ed. Part-time and evening/weekend programs available. *Students:* 1 (woman) full-time, 31 part-time (29 women). Average age 29. 25 applicants, 64% accepted, 6 enrolled. In 2006, 13 degrees awarded. *Degree requirements:* For master's, thesis optional. *Entrance requirements:* For master's, GRE General Test or MAT, elementary teaching certificate. Additional exam requirements/recommendations for international students: Required—TOEFL (minimum score 550 paper-based; 213 computer-based). *Application deadline:* Applications are processed on a rolling basis. Application fee: $30. *Expenses:* Tuition, state resident: full-time $4,518; part-time $251 per credit hour. Tuition, nonresident: full-time $4,518; part-time $251 per credit hour. *Financial support:* Career-related internships or fieldwork, Federal Work-Study, institutionally sponsored loans, scholarships/grants, and unspecified assistantships available. Support available to part-time students. Financial award application deadline: 3/1; financial award applicants required to submit FAFSA. *Faculty research:* Contemporary elementary education, social studies in the elementary school. *Unit head:* Dr. Elaine Tateronis, Coordinator, 508-929-8823. *Application contact:* Nicole Brown, Assistant Dean of Graduate and Continuing Education, 508-929-8787, Fax: 508-929-8100, E-mail: nbrown@worcester.edu.

Wright State University, School of Graduate Studies, College of Education and Human Services, Department of Teacher Education, Programs in Classroom Teacher Education, Dayton, OH 45435. Offers M Ed, MA. *Accreditation:* NCATE. *Students:* 51 full-time (36 women), 54 part-time (47 women); includes 8 minority (7 African Americans, 1 Hispanic American). Average age 34. 30 applicants, 97% accepted. In 2006, 59 degrees awarded. *Degree requirements:* For master's, thesis (for some programs). *Entrance requirements:* For master's, GRE General Test, MAT, PRAXIS II. Additional exam requirements/recommendations for international students: Required—TOEFL. Application fee: $25. *Financial support:* Available to part-time students. Applicants required to submit FAFSA. *Application contact:* John Kimble, Associate Director of Graduate Admissions and Records, 937-775-2957, Fax: 937-775-2453, E-mail: john.kimble@wright.edu.

Xavier University, College of Social Sciences, Health and Education, School of Education, Program in Elementary Education, Cincinnati, OH 45207. Offers M Ed. Part-time and evening/weekend programs available. *Faculty:* 5 full-time (3 women), 5 part-time/adjunct (3 women). *Students:* 48 full-time (40 women), 61 part-time (51 women); includes 8 minority (6 African Americans, 2 Hispanic Americans). Average age 31. 45 applicants, 67% accepted, 27 enrolled. In 2006, 41 degrees awarded. *Degree requirements:* For master's, research project. *Entrance requirements:* For master's, GRE or MAT, minimum GPA of 2.8. Additional exam requirements/recommendations for international students: Required—TOEFL (minimum score 550 paper-based; 213 computer-based). *Application deadline:* For fall admission, 8/15 priority date for domestic students. Applications are processed on a rolling basis. Application fee: $35. Electronic applications accepted. *Expenses:* Tuition: Part-time $462 per credit hour. Part-time tuition and fees vary according to degree level, campus/location and program. *Financial support:* Scholarships/grants available. Support available to part-time students. Financial award applicants required to submit FAFSA. *Faculty research:* Reading/language arts, multicultural elementary education, science teaching strategies' effectiveness, technology in the classroom, math anxiety. *Unit head:* Dr. Cynthia Geer, Chair, 513-745-3262, Fax: 513-745-1052. *Application contact:* Roger Bosse, Interim Director of Graduate Studies, 513-745-3357, Fax: 513-745-1048, E-mail: bosse@xavier.edu.

Youngstown State University, Graduate School, College of Education, Department of Teacher Education, Program in Early and Middle Childhood Education, Youngstown, OH 44555-0001. Offers teaching—elementary education (MS Ed); teaching—secondary reading (MS Ed). *Accreditation:* NCATE. Part-time and evening/weekend programs available. *Degree requirements:* For master's, comprehensive exam. *Entrance requirements:* For master's, GRE, MAT, or teaching certificate; minimum GPA of 2.7. Additional exam requirements/recommendations for international students: Required—TOEFL.

Higher Education

Abilene Christian University, Graduate School, College of Education and Human Services, Graduate Studies in Education, Program in Higher Education, Abilene, TX 79699-9100. Offers M Ed. *Faculty:* 6 part-time/adjunct (2 women). *Students:* 6 full-time (2 women), 2 part-time. 17 applicants, 59% accepted. *Expenses:* Tuition: Full-time $12,504; part-time $521 per hour. Required fees: $700; $34 per hour. *Financial support:* Application deadline: 4/1. *Unit head:* Dr. Jason Morris, Graduate Advisor, 325-674-2838, Fax: 325-674-3707, E-mail: morrisj@acu.edu.

Alliant International University–Irvine, Graduate School of Education, Educational Leadership Programs, Irvine, CA 92612. Offers educational administration (MA, Credential); educational leadership and management (K-12) (Ed D); higher education (Ed D); preliminary administrative services (Credential). Part-time programs available. *Students:* 11. In 2006, 8 master's, 4 doctorates awarded. *Entrance requirements:* For master's and doctorate, minimum GPA of 3.0, letters of recommendation. Additional exam requirements/recommendations for international students: Required—TOEFL (minimum score 550 paper-based; 213 computer-based), TWE (minimum score 5). *Application deadline:* For fall admission, 7/1 priority date for domestic and international students; for spring admission, 12/1 priority date for domestic and international students. Applications are processed on a rolling basis. Application fee: $55. Electronic applications accepted. *Financial support:* Federal Work-Study, institutionally sponsored loans, and scholarships/grants available. Financial award application deadline: 2/15. *Unit head:* Dr. Suzanne Power, Acting Director, 866-825-5426, Fax: 949-833-3507, E-mail: admissions@alliant.edu. *Application contact:* Alliant International University Central Contact Center, 866-U-ALLIANT, Fax: 858-635-4555, E-mail: admissions@alliant.edu.

See Close-Up on page 1097.

Alliant International University–Los Angeles, Graduate School of Education, Educational Leadership Programs, Alhambra, CA 91803-1360. Offers educational administration (MA); educational leadership and management (K-12) (Ed D); higher education (Ed D); preliminary administrative services (Credential). Part-time programs available. *Students:* 14 (9 women). In 2006, 13 degrees awarded. *Entrance requirements:* For master's and doctorate, minimum GPA of 3.0, letters of recommendation. Additional exam requirements/recommendations for international students: Required—TOEFL (minimum score 550 paper-based; 213 computer-based), TWE (minimum score 5). *Application deadline:* For fall admission, 7/1 priority date for domestic students, 7/1 for international students; for spring admission, 12/1 priority date for domestic students, 12/1 for international students. Application fee: $55. *Financial support:* Federal Work-Study, institutionally sponsored loans, and scholarships/grants available. Financial award application deadline: 2/15; financial award applicants required to submit FAFSA. *Unit head:* Dr. Suzanne Power, Acting Director, 866-825-5426, Fax: 620-284-0550, E-mail: admissions@alliant.edu. *Application contact:* Alliant International University Central Contact Center, 866-U-ALLIANT, Fax: 858-635-4555, E-mail: admissions@alliant.edu.

See Close-Up on page 1097.

Alliant International University–San Diego, Graduate School of Education, Educational Leadership Programs, San Diego, CA 92131-1799. Offers educational administration (MA); educational leadership and management (K-12) (Ed D); higher education (Ed D, Certificate); preliminary administrative services (Credential). Part-time programs available. *Faculty:* 2 full-time (0 women), 15 part-time/adjunct (6 women). *Students:* 39 full-time (30 women), 44 part-time (33 women); includes 28 minority (14 African Americans, 2 American Indian/Alaska Native, 4 Asian Americans or Pacific Islanders, 8 Hispanic Americans), 4 international. In 2006, 4 master's, 10 doctorates awarded. *Entrance requirements:* For master's and doctorate, minimum GPA of 3.0, letters of recommendation. Additional exam requirements/recommendations for international students: Required—TOEFL (minimum score 550 paper-based; 213 computer-based), TWE (minimum score 5). *Application deadline:* For fall admission, 7/1 priority date for domestic and international students; for spring admission, 12/1 priority date for domestic and international students. Applications are processed on a rolling basis. Application fee: $55. Electronic applications accepted. *Expenses:* Tuition: Part-time $825 per unit. Tuition and fees vary according to course load, degree level and program. *Financial support:* In 2006–07, 75 students received support. Federal Work-Study, institutionally sponsored loans, and scholarships/grants available. Financial award application deadline: 2/15; financial award applicants required to submit FAFSA. *Unit head:* Dr. Suzanne Borman, Acting Director, 866-825-5426, Fax: 858-635-4739, E-mail: admissions@alliant.edu. *Application contact:* Alliant International University Central Contact Center, 866-U-ALLIANT, Fax: 858-635-4555, E-mail: admissions@alliant.edu.

See Close-Up on page 1097.

Alliant International University–San Francisco, Graduate School of Education, Educational Leadership Programs, San Francisco, CA 94133-1221. Offers community college administration (Ed D); educational administration (MA); educational leadership and management (K-12) (Ed D); higher education (Ed D); preliminary administrative services (Credential); university administration (Ed D). Part-time programs available. *Faculty:* 2 full-time (0 women), 4 part-time/adjunct. *Students:* 1 (woman) full-time, 21 part-time (11 women); includes 9 minority (3 African Americans, 1 American Indian/Alaska Native, 1 Asian American or Pacific Islander, 4 Hispanic Americans), 2 international. Average age 45. 5 applicants, 60% accepted, 3 enrolled. In 2006, 2 degrees awarded. *Entrance requirements:* For master's and doctorate, minimum GPA of 3.0, letters of recommendation. Additional exam requirements/recommendations for international students: Required—TOEFL (minimum score 550 paper-based; 213 computer-based), TWE (minimum score 5). *Application deadline:* For fall admission, 7/1 priority date for domestic and international students; for spring admission, 12/1 priority date for domestic and international students. Applications are processed on a rolling basis. Application fee: $70. Electronic applications accepted. *Expenses:* Tuition: Part-time $825 per unit. Tuition and fees vary according to course load, degree level and program. *Financial support:* Federal Work-Study, institutionally sponsored loans, and scholarships/grants available. Financial award application deadline: 2/15; financial award applicants required to submit FAFSA. *Faculty research:* Leadership in higher education, community colleges. *Unit head:* Dr. Joseph Adwere-Boamah, Program Coordinator, 415-955-2103, Fax: 415-955-2179, E-mail: admissions@alliant.edu. *Application contact:* Jen Kulbeck, Alliant International University Central Contact Center, 866-U-ALLIANT, Fax: 858-635-4555, E-mail: admissions@alliant.edu.

See Close-Up on page 1097.

Angelo State University, College of Graduate Studies, College of Education, Department of Curriculum and Instruction, Program in Student Development and Leadership in Higher Education, San Angelo, TX 76909. Offers M Ed. Part-time and evening/weekend programs available. *Faculty:* 17 full-time (12 women). *Students:* 4 full-time (2 women), 7 part-time (5 women); includes 2 minority (1 Asian American or Pacific Islander, 1 Hispanic American). Average age 40. 5 applicants, 100% accepted, 5 enrolled. In 2006, 1 degree awarded. *Degree requirements:* For master's, comprehensive exam. *Entrance requirements:* For master's, GRE General Test.

Higher Education

Angelo State University (continued)

Additional exam requirements/recommendations for international students: Required—TOEFL or IELTS. *Application deadline:* For fall admission, 7/15 priority date for domestic students, 6/15 for international students; for spring admission, 12/1 priority date for domestic students, 11/1 for international students. Applications are processed on a rolling basis. Application fee: $40 ($50 for international students). Electronic applications accepted. *Expenses:* Tuition, state resident: full-time $2,340; part-time $130 per hour. Tuition, nonresident: full-time $7,290; part-time $405 per hour. Required fees: $906; $56 per hour. *Financial support:* In 2006–07, 7 students received support. Federal Work-Study, scholarships/grants, and unspecified assistantships available. Support available to part-time students. Financial award application deadline: 3/1; financial award applicants required to submit FAFSA. *Application contact:* Dr. David J. Tarver, Graduate Advisor, 325-942-2052 Ext. 262, E-mail: david.tarver@angelo.edu.

Appalachian State University, Cratis D. Williams Graduate School, College of Education, Department of Leadership and Educational Studies, Program in Higher Education, Boone, NC 28608. Offers MA, Ed S. *Accreditation:* NCATE. *Students:* 18 full-time (10 women), 97 part-time (64 women); includes 11 minority (all African Americans), 4 international. 55 applicants, 96% accepted, 50 enrolled. In 2006, 24 degrees awarded. *Degree requirements:* For master's, thesis or alternative, comprehensive exam; for Ed S, thesis optional. *Entrance requirements:* For master's and Ed S, GRE General Test. *Application deadline:* For fall admission, 7/1 for domestic students, 1/1 for international students; for spring admission, 11/1 for domestic students, 6/1 for international students. Application fee: $50. *Expenses:* Tuition, state resident: full-time $2,600; part-time $127 per hour. Tuition, nonresident: full-time $13,200; part-time $597 per hour. Required fees: $2,000; $546 per term. *Financial support:* Fellowships, research assistantships, teaching assistantships, Federal Work-Study, scholarships/grants, and unspecified assistantships available. Financial award application deadline: 7/1. *Faculty research:* Developmental education, college student personnel. *Unit head:* Dr. Barbara Bonham, Coordinator, E-mail: bonhambs@appstate.edu.

Argosy University, Atlanta Campus, College of Education, Atlanta, GA 30328. Offers educational leadership (MAEd, Ed D, Ed S), including higher education administration (Ed D), k-12 administration (Ed D); instructional leadership (MAEd, Ed D, Ed S), including higher education (Ed D), K-12 education (Ed D). Evening/weekend programs available. *Students:* 459 full-time (377 women), 324 part-time (255 women); includes 388 minority (335 African Americans, 10 American Indian/Alaska Native, 14 Asian Americans or Pacific Islanders, 29 Hispanic Americans). *Entrance requirements:* For master's and doctorate, 3 letters of recommendation, minimum GPA of 3.0, resumé. Additional exam requirements/recommendations for international students: Required—TOEFL (minimum score 550 paper-based; 213 computer-based). *Application deadline:* For fall admission, 8/1 for domestic students; for spring admission, 10/1 for domestic students. Application fee: $50. *Financial support:* Teaching assistantships, Federal Work-Study available. *Unit head:* Jacqueline Jenkins, Department Chair, 770-407-1067, Fax: 770-671-0476, E-mail: jbeard@argosy.edu. *Application contact:* Christa Holton, Director of Admissions, 770-671-1200, Fax: 770-671-9050, E-mail: inquiry@argosy.edu.

See Close-Up on page 1101.

Argosy University, Chicago Campus, College of Education, Chicago, IL 60603. Offers community college executive leadership (Ed D); educational leadership (MA Ed, Ed D, Ed S), including administrative certification (MA Ed), district leadership (Ed D), higher education administration (Ed D), K-12 education (Ed D), principal/general (MA Ed), superintendent certification (Ed S); instructional leadership (MA Ed, Ed D, Ed S), including higher education (Ed D), K-12 education (Ed D). Part-time and evening/weekend programs available. *Faculty:* 3 full-time (1 woman), 7 part-time/adjunct (0 women). *Students:* 116 full-time (96 women), 42 part-time (32 women); includes 112 minority (108 African Americans, 1 Asian American or Pacific Islander, 3 Hispanic Americans). Average age 45. 56 applicants, 84% accepted, 45 enrolled. In 2006, 4 master's, 10 doctorates awarded. *Entrance requirements:* For master's and doctorate, minimum GPA of 3.0. Additional exam requirements/recommendations for international students: Required—TOEFL (minimum score 550 paper-based; 213 computer-based). *Application deadline:* For fall admission, 2/28 for domestic and international students; for spring admission, 10/30 for domestic and international students. Applications are processed on a rolling basis. Application fee: $50. Electronic applications accepted. *Financial support:* In 2006–07, 35 students received support. Scholarships/grants available. Financial award application deadline: 4/1. *Unit head:* Dr. Paul Busceni, Head, 800-626-4123, Fax: 312-777-7750, E-mail: pbusceni@argosy.edu. *Application contact:* Ashley Delaney, Director of Admissions, 800-626-4123, Fax: 312-777-7750, E-mail: argosyadmissions@argosy.edu.

See Close-Up on page 825.

Argosy University, Denver Campus, College of Education, Denver, CO 80203. Offers educational leadership (MA Ed, Ed D), including higher education adminstration (Ed D), K-12 education (Ed D); instructional leadership (MA Ed, Ed D), including higher education (Ed D), K-12 education (Ed D).

See Close-Up on page 829.

Argosy University, Hawai'i Campus, College of Education, Honolulu, HI 96813. Offers educational leadership (MAEd, Ed D), including higher education administration (Ed D), K-12 education (Ed D); instructional leadership (MAEd, Ed D), including higher education (Ed D), K-12 education (Ed D). *Faculty:* 9 part-time/adjunct (4 women). *Students:* 26 full-time (18 women), 4 part-time (all women); includes 16 minority (13 Asian Americans or Pacific Islanders, 3 Hispanic Americans). 17 applicants, 94% accepted, 14 enrolled. *Degree requirements:* For doctorate, thesis/dissertation. *Entrance requirements:* Additional exam requirements/recommendations for international students: Required—TOEFL (minimum score 550 paper-based; 214 computer-based). *Application deadline:* For fall admission, 1/15 priority date for domestic students; for spring admission, 10/15 for domestic students. Applications are processed on a rolling basis. Application fee: $50. Electronic applications accepted. *Unit head:* Dr. Kristine Lesperance, Chair, 888-323-2777, Fax: 808-536-5505, E-mail: klesperance@argosy.edu. *Application contact:* Cherie Andrade, Director of Admissions, 888-323-2777, Fax: 808-536-5505, E-mail: candrade@argosy.edu.

See Close-Up on page 831.

Argosy University, Inland Empire Campus, College of Education, San Bernardino, CA 92408. Offers community college executive leadership (Ed D); educational leadership (MA Ed, Ed D), including higher education administration (Ed D), K-12 education (Ed D); instructional leadership (MA Ed, Ed D), including higher education (Ed D), K-12 education (Ed D), multiple subject teacher credential preparation (MA Ed), multiple subject teacher credntial preparation with BCLAD (MA Ed), single subject teacher credential preparation (MA Ed), single subject teacher credential preparation with BCLAD (MA Ed).

See Close-Up on page 1103.

Argosy University, Nashville Campus, College of Education, Program in Educational Leadership, Franklin, TN 37067-7226. Offers educational leadership (MA Ed); higher education administration (Ed D); K-12 education (Ed D).

See Close-Up on page 1105.

Argosy University, Nashville Campus, College of Education, Program in Instructional Leadership, Franklin, TN 37067-7226. Offers higher education administration (Ed D); instructional leadership (MA Ed); K-12 education (Ed D).

Argosy University, Orange County Campus, College of Education, Santa Ana, CA 92704. Offers community college executive leadership (Ed D); educational leadership (MA Ed, Ed D), including higher education administration (Ed D), K-12 education (Ed D); instructional leadership (MA Ed, Ed D), including educational technology (Ed D), higher education (Ed D), K-12 education (Ed D), multiple subject teacher credential preparation (MA Ed), multiple subject teacher credential preparation with BCLAD (MA Ed), single subject teacher credential preparation (MA Ed), single subject teacher credential preparation with BCLAD (MA Ed). Part-time and evening/weekend programs available. *Faculty:* 3 full-time (2 women), 33 part-time/adjunct (15 women). *Students:* 185 full-time (112 women), 49 part-time (28 women). Average age 37. 91 applicants, 76 enrolled. In 2006, 58 master's, 17 doctorates awarded. Terminal master's awarded for partial completion of doctoral program. *Degree requirements:* For master's, comprehensive exam; for doctorate, thesis/dissertation, preliminary and final dissertation defense, comprehensive exam. *Entrance requirements:* For master's, minimum GPA of 3.0 in final 2 years of course work, 3 letters of recommendation, resumé; for doctorate, minimum GPA of 3.0 in graduate study, 3 letters of recommendation, resumé. Additional exam requirements/recommendations for international students: Required—TOEFL. *Application deadline:* Applications are processed on a rolling basis. Application fee: $50. Electronic applications accepted. *Financial support:* Federal Work-Study and scholarships/grants available. Support available to part-time students. Financial award applicants required to submit FAFSA. *Faculty research:* Educational leadership, higher education, qualitative research, K-12 education, multicultural education. *Unit head:* Dr. Christine Zeppos, Dean, 800-7196-9598, Fax: 714-437-1287, E-mail: czeppos@argosy.edu. *Application contact:* Mark Betz, Director of Admissions, 800-716-9598, Fax: 714-437-1697, E-mail: mbetz@argosy.edu.

See Close-Up on page 833.

Argosy University, Phoenix Campus, College of Education, Phoenix, AZ 85021. Offers community college executive leadership (Ed D); educational leadership (MA Ed, Ed D, Ed S), including higher education administration (Ed D), K-12 education (Ed D); instructional leadership (MA Ed, Ed D, Ed S), including higher education (Ed D), K-12 education (Ed D). Part-time and evening/weekend programs available. *Faculty:* 13 part-time/adjunct (4 women). *Students:* 26 full-time (17 women), 2 part-time (1 woman); includes 3 minority (2 African Americans, 1 Hispanic American). Average age 44. 10 applicants, 100% accepted, 9 enrolled. *Entrance requirements:* For doctorate, minimum GPA of 3.0, master's degree. Additional exam requirements/recommendations for international students: Required—TOEFL (minimum score 550 paper-based; 213 computer-based). *Application deadline:* Applications are processed on a rolling basis. Application fee: $50. Electronic applications accepted. *Financial support:* Federal Work-Study available. Financial award applicants required to submit FAFSA. *Unit head:* Dr. Gayle Schou, Director, 866-216-2777, E-mail: argosyadmissions@argosy.edu. *Application contact:* Andy Hughes, Director of Admissions, 866-216-2777, Fax: 602-216-2601, E-mail: ahughes@argosy.edu.

See Close-Up on page 835.

Argosy University, San Diego Campus, College of Education, San Diego, CA 92108. Offers community college executive leadership (Ed D); educational leadership (MA Ed, Ed D), including higher education administration (Ed D), K-12 education (Ed D); instructional leadership (MA Ed, Ed D), including higher education (Ed D), K-12 education (Ed D), multiple subject teacher credential preparation (MA Ed), multiple subject teacher credential preparation with BCLAD (MA Ed), single subject teacher credential preparation (MA Ed), single subject teacher credential preparation with BCLAD (MA Ed).

See Close-Up on page 837.

Argosy University, San Francisco Bay Area Campus, College of Education, Point Richmond, CA 94804-3547. Offers community college executive leadership (Ed D); educational leadership (MA Ed, Ed D), including higher education administration (Ed D), K–12 education (Ed D); instructional leadership (MA Ed, Ed D), including higher education (Ed D), K–12 education (Ed D), multiple subject teacher credential preparation (MA Ed), multiple subject teacher credential preparation with BCLAD (MA Ed), single subject teacher credential preparation (MA Ed), single subject teacher credential preparation with BCLAD (MA Ed). Part-time and evening/weekend programs available. Postbaccalaureate distance learning degree programs offered (minimal on-campus study). *Faculty:* 1 (woman) full-time, 14 part-time/adjunct. *Students:* 59 full-time (41 women), 30 part-time (14 women); includes 26 minority (11 African Americans, 11 Asian Americans or Pacific Islanders, 4 Hispanic Americans), 1 international. 34 applicants, 82% accepted, 20 enrolled. In 2006, 7 degrees awarded. *Degree requirements:* For master's, capstone project; for doctorate, thesis/dissertation, comprehensive exam, registration. *Entrance requirements:* For master's and doctorate, minimum GPA of 3.0. Additional exam requirements/recommendations for international students: Required—TOEFL (minimum score 550 paper-based; 213 computer-based). *Application deadline:* For fall admission, 7/1 priority date for domestic students, 7/1 for international students; for winter admission, 11/1 priority date for domestic and international students; for spring admission, 4/1 priority date for domestic and international students. Applications are processed on a rolling basis. Application fee: $50. Electronic applications accepted. *Financial support:* Career-related internships or fieldwork, Federal Work-Study, and scholarships/grants available. Support available to part-time students. Financial award application deadline: 4/20; financial award applicants required to submit FAFSA. *Unit head:* Dr. Keyes Kelly, 510-837-3740, E-mail: kkelly@argosy.edu. *Application contact:* John Vincent Stofan, Director, Admissions, 510-215-0277, Fax: 510-215-0299, E-mail: jstofan@argosy.edu.

See Close-Up on page 839.

Argosy University, Santa Monica Campus, College of Education, Santa Monica, CA 90405. Offers community college executive leadership (Ed D); educational leadership (MA Ed, Ed D), including higher education administration (Ed D), K-12 education (Ed D); instructional leadership (MA Ed, Ed D), including higher education (Ed D), K-12 education (Ed D), multiple subject teacher credential preparation (MA Ed), multiple subject teacher credential preparation with BCLAD (MA Ed), single subject teacher credential preparation (MA Ed), single subject teacher credential preparation with BCLAD (MA Ed).

See Close-Up on page 841.

Argosy University, Sarasota Campus, College of Education, Sarasota, FL 34235-8246. Offers community college educational leadership (Ed D); educational leadership (MA Ed, Ed D, Ed S), including higher education administration (Ed D), K-12 education (Ed D); instructional leadership (MA Ed, Ed D, Ed S), including education technology (Ed D), higher education (Ed D), K-12 education (Ed D). Part-time and evening/weekend programs available. Postbaccalaureate distance learning degree programs offered (minimal on-campus study). *Faculty:* 15 full-time (8 women), 49 part-time/adjunct (21 women). *Students:* 149 applicants, 96% accepted, 121 enrolled. In 2006, 9 master's, 141 doctorates awarded. *Degree requirements:* For doctorate, thesis/dissertation, comprehensive exam. *Entrance requirements:* For doctorate, minimum undergraduate GPA of 3.0. Additional exam requirements/recommendations for international students: Required—TOEFL. *Application deadline:* Applications are processed on a rolling basis. Application fee: $50. Electronic applications accepted. *Expenses: Contact institution. Financial support:* Federal Work-Study available. Support available to part-time students. Financial award application deadline: 4/1; financial award applicants required to submit FAFSA. *Unit head:* Dr. Chuck Mlynarczyk, Dean, 800-331-5995, Fax: 941-371-9464, E-mail: cmlynarczyk@argosy.edu. *Application contact:* Admissions Representative, 800-331-5995 Ext. 221, Fax: 941-371-8910.

See Close-Up on page 843.

Argosy University, Schaumburg Campus, College of Education, Schaumburg, IL 60173-5403. Offers community college executive leadership (Ed D); educational leadership (MA Ed, Ed D, Ed S), including administrative certification (MA Ed), higher education administration (Ed D), K-12 education (Ed D), principal/general (MA Ed), superintendent certification (Ed S); instructional leadership (MA Ed, Ed D, Ed S), including higher education (Ed D), K-12 education (Ed D). Part-time and evening/weekend programs available. *Faculty:* 1 (woman) full-time, 7 part-time/adjunct (3 women). *Students:* 19 full-time, 19 part-time. 15 applicants, 80% accepted, 10 enrolled. In 2006, 1 master's, 3 doctorates, 2 other advanced degrees awarded. *Degree* *requirements:* For doctorate, thesis/dissertation, comprehensive exam. *Entrance requirements:* For master's and doctorate, minimum GPA of 3.0. Additional exam requirements/ recommendations for international students: Required—TOEFL. *Application deadline:* For fall admission, 3/15 priority date for domestic and international students; for spring admission, 10/15 priority date for domestic and international students. Applications are processed on a rolling basis. Application fee: $50. Electronic applications accepted. *Expenses: Contact institution. Financial support:* Federal Work-Study and scholarships/grants available. *Unit head:* Dr. Narjis Hyder, Program Chair, 866-290-7400, Fax: 847-598-6158, E-mail: nhyder@argosy.edu. *Application contact:* Jamal Scott, Application Contact, 866-290-7400, Fax: 630-598-6191, E-mail: jscott@argosy.edu.

See Close-Up on page 845.

Argosy University, Seattle Campus, College of Education, Seattle, WA 98121. Offers community college executive leadership (Ed D); education (MA Ed); educational leadership (MA Ed, Ed D), including higher education administration (Ed D), K-12 education (Ed D); instructional leadership (MA Ed, Ed D), including education technology (Ed D), higher education (Ed D), K-12 education (Ed D). Part-time and evening/weekend programs available. *Students:* 29 full-time, 15 part-time. *Degree requirements:* For master's, thesis or alternative, capstone project; for doctorate, thesis/dissertation, comprehensive exam, registration. *Entrance requirements:* For master's, minimum GPA of 3.0 in last 60 hours of course work or minimum cumulative GPA of 2.7; for doctorate, minimum GPA of 3.0. Additional exam requirements/ recommendations for international students: Required—TOEFL (minimum score 550 paper-based; 213 computer-based). *Application deadline:* For fall admission, 4/15 priority date for domestic students, 4/15 for international students. Application fee: $50. *Expenses: Contact institution. Financial support:* Teaching assistantships with partial tuition reimbursements, Federal Work-Study, scholarships/grants, and unspecified assistantships available. Support available to part-time students. Financial award application deadline: 4/19; financial award applicants required to submit FAFSA. *Unit head:* Dr. Leslie Aune Oja, Chair of Education, 206-393-3570, Fax: 206-283-5777, E-mail: ioja@argosy.edu. *Application contact:* Josh Pond, Director of Admissions, 206-283-4500, Fax: 206-283-5777, E-mail: jpond@argosyu.edu.

See Close-Up on page 847.

Argosy University, Tampa Campus, College of Education, Tampa, FL 33614. Offers community college executive leadership (Ed D); educational leadership (MA Ed, Ed D, Ed S), including higher education administration (Ed D), K-12 education (Ed D); instructional leadership (MA Ed, Ed D, Ed S), including higher education (Ed D), K-12 education (Ed D). *Faculty:* 1 (woman) full-time, 8 part-time/adjunct (3 women). *Degree requirements:* For master's, capstone project; for doctorate, thesis/dissertation. *Entrance requirements:* For master's, minimum GPA of 3.0 in last 2 years of undergraduate course work, resumé, 3 letters of recommendation; for doctorate, minimum GPA of 3.0, 3 letters of recommendation, resumé. Additional exam requirements/recommendations for international students: Required—TOEFL (minimum score 550 paper-based; 213 computer-based). *Application deadline:* Applications are processed on a rolling basis. Application fee: $50. Electronic applications accepted. *Faculty research:* Reading methods, elementary education, educational leadership, instructional design and instructional technology. *Unit head:* Dr. Patty O'Grady, Head, 813-246-4419, Fax: 813-246-4045, E-mail: pogrady@argosy.edu.

See Close-Up on page 849.

Argosy University, Twin Cities Campus, College of Education, Eagan, MN 55121. Offers educational leadership (MA Ed, Ed D, Ed S), including higher education administration (Ed D), K-12 education (Ed D); instructional leadership (MA Ed, Ed D, Ed S), including education technology (Ed D), higher education (Ed D), K-12 education (Ed D). Part-time and evening/ weekend programs available. *Faculty:* 1 full-time (0 women), 10 part-time/adjunct (4 women). *Students:* 30 full-time (22 women), 12 part-time (9 women); includes 3 minority (1 African American, 1 American Indian/Alaska Native, 1 Asian American or Pacific Islander). Average age 45. 35 applicants, 86% accepted, 12 enrolled. In 2006, 1 master's, 6 doctorates awarded. *Degree requirements:* For doctorate, thesis/dissertation, comprehensive exam. *Entrance requirements:* For master's, 3 letters of recommendation, minimum undergraduate GPA of 3.0, resumé; for doctorate, 3 letters of recommendation, master's degree, minimum GPA of 3.0, resumé. Additional exam requirements/recommendations for international students: Required—TOEFL (minimum score 550 paper-based; 213 computer-based). *Application deadline:* For fall admission, 5/15 priority date for domestic students, 5/15 for international students; for spring admission, 10/15 priority date for domestic students, 10/15 for international students. Applications are processed on a rolling basis. Application fee: $50. Electronic applications accepted. *Financial support:* In 2006–07, 12 fellowships with partial tuition reimbursements, 3 teaching assistantships with partial tuition reimbursements were awarded; Federal Work-Study and scholarships/grants also available. Financial award applicants required to submit FAFSA. *Unit head:* Dr. David Lange, Program Chair, 888-844-2004. *Application contact:* Jennifer Radke, 2nd Director of Graduate Admissions, 651-846-3300, Fax: 651-994-7954, E-mail: tcadmissions@argosy.edu.

See Close-Up on page 851.

Argosy University, Washington DC Campus, College of Education, Arlington, VA 22209. Offers educational leadership (MA Ed, Ed D, Ed S), including higher education administration (Ed D), K-12 education (Ed D); instructional leadership (MA Ed, Ed D, Ed S), including higher education (Ed D), K-12 education (Ed D). Part-time and evening/weekend programs available. *Faculty:* 2 full-time (1 woman), 2 part-time/adjunct (0 women). *Students:* 22 full-time (16 women), 11 part-time (6 women); includes 24 minority (all African Americans) Average age 45. 16 applicants, 69% accepted, 9 enrolled. In 2006, 1 degree awarded. *Degree requirements:* For master's, thesis (for some programs), comprehensive exam (for some programs); for doctorate, thesis/dissertation, comprehensive exam. *Entrance requirements:* For master's and doctorate, minimum GPA of 3.0. Additional exam requirements/recommendations for international students: Required—TOEFL (minimum score 550 paper-based; 213 computer-based). *Application deadline:* For fall admission, 6/15 priority date for domestic and international students; for spring admission, 10/15 priority date for domestic and international students. Applications are processed on a rolling basis. Application fee: $50. Electronic applications accepted. *Financial support:* Federal Work-Study and scholarships/grants available. Financial award applicants required to submit FAFSA. *Unit head:* Dr. Colleen Logan, Academic Affairs Officer, 866-703-2777, Fax: 703-521-5850, E-mail: dcadmissions@argosy.edu. *Application contact:* Emily Peck, Director of Admissions, 866-703-2777 Ext. 5851, Fax: 703-526-5850, E-mail: dcadmissions@argosy.edu.

See Close-Up on page 853.

Arizona State University, Division of Graduate Studies, College of Education, Division of Educational Leadership and Policy Studies, Academic Program of Higher and Post-Secondary Education, Tempe, AZ 85287. Offers M Ed, Ed D. *Degree requirements:* For doctorate, thesis/dissertation. *Entrance requirements:* For master's and doctorate, GRE General Test or MAT.

Auburn University, Graduate School, College of Education, Department of Curriculum and Teaching, Auburn University, AL 36849. Offers business education (M Ed, MS, PhD); early childhood education (M Ed, MS, PhD, Ed S); elementary education (M Ed, MS, PhD, Ed S); foreign languages (M Ed, MS); music education (M Ed, MS, PhD, Ed S); postsecondary education (PhD); reading education (PhD, Ed S); secondary education (M Ed, MS, PhD, Ed S), including English language arts, mathematics, science, social studies. *Accreditation:* NASM (one or more programs are accredited); NCATE. Part-time programs available. *Faculty:* 26 full-time (19 women). *Students:* 51 full-time (36 women), 116 part-time (86 women); includes 24 minority (23 African Americans, 1 Asian American or Pacific Islander). Average age 33. 181 applicants, 56% accepted, 68 enrolled. In 2006, 63 master's, 12 doctorates, 14 other advanced degrees awarded. *Degree requirements:* For master's, thesis (for some programs); for doctorate, thesis/dissertation; for Ed S, field project. *Entrance requirements:* For master's, doctorate, and Ed S, GRE General Test. *Application deadline:* For fall admission, 7/7 for domestic students; for spring admission, 11/24 for domestic students. Applications are processed on a rolling basis. Application fee: $25 ($50 for international students). Electronic applications accepted. *Expenses:* Tuition, state resident: full-time $5,000. Tuition, nonresident: full-time $15,000. Required fees: $416. Tuition and fees vary according to program. *Financial support:* Fellowships, teaching assistantships, career-related internships or fieldwork and Federal Work-Study available. Support available to part-time students. Financial award application deadline: 3/15. *Faculty research:* Emerging literacy, reading attitudes, music for at-risk youth, portfolio assessment. *Unit head:* Dr. Andrew M. Weaver, Head, 334-844-4434, E-mail: weaveam@mail.auburn.edu. *Application contact:* Dr. Joe Pittman, Interim Dean of the Graduate School, 334-844-4700.

Auburn University, Graduate School, College of Education, Department of Educational Foundations, Leadership, and Technology, Auburn University, AL 36849. Offers adult education (M Ed, MS, Ed D); curriculum and instruction (M Ed, MS, Ed D, Ed S); curriculum supervision (M Ed, MS, Ed D, Ed S); educational psychology (PhD); higher education administration (M Ed, MS, Ed D, Ed S); media instructional design (MS); media specialist (M Ed); school administration (M Ed, MS, Ed D, Ed S). *Accreditation:* NCATE. Part-time programs available. *Faculty:* 23 full-time (11 women). *Students:* 40 full-time (26 women), 148 part-time (93 women); includes 64 minority (60 African Americans, 3 American Indian/Alaska Native, 1 Asian American or Pacific Islander), 6 international. Average age 38. 99 applicants, 57% accepted, 37 enrolled. In 2006, 32 master's, 10 doctorates, 7 other advanced degrees awarded. *Degree requirements:* For master's, thesis (for some programs); for doctorate, thesis/dissertation; for Ed S, field project. *Entrance requirements:* For master's, doctorate, and Ed S, GRE General Test. *Application deadline:* For fall admission, 7/7 for domestic students; for spring admission, 11/24 for domestic students. Applications are processed on a rolling basis. Application fee: $25 ($50 for international students). Electronic applications accepted. *Expenses:* Tuition, state resident: full-time $5,000. Tuition, nonresident: full-time $15,000. Required fees: $416. Tuition and fees vary according to program. *Financial support:* Teaching assistantships, Federal Work-Study available. Support available to part-time students. Financial award application deadline: 3/15. *Unit head:* Dr. William A. Spencer, Head, 334-844-4460. *Application contact:* Dr. Joe Pittman, Interim Dean of the Graduate School, 334-844-4700.

Azusa Pacific University, School of Behavioral and Applied Sciences, Department of Higher Education and Organizational Leadership, Azusa, CA 91702-7000. Offers college student affairs (M Ed); higher education leadership (Ed D); leadership and organizational studies (MLOS); organizational leadership (MA). *Faculty:* 7 full-time (5 women). *Students:* 17 full-time (9 women), 271 part-time (137 women); includes 49 minority (16 African Americans, 10 Asian Americans or Pacific Islanders, 23 Hispanic Americans), 36 international. In 2006, 95 master's, 3 doctorates awarded. Application fee: $45 ($65 for international students). *Expenses:* Tuition: Part-time $475 per credit. *Unit head:* Dr. Dennis A. Sheridan, Director, 626-815-5485, Fax: 626-815-3868.

Ball State University, Graduate School, Teachers College, Department of Educational Studies, Program in Adult Education, Muncie, IN 47306-1099. Offers adult and community education (MA); adult, community, and higher education (Ed D). *Accreditation:* NCATE. *Students:* 16 full-time (10 women), 99 part-time (58 women); includes 11 minority (6 African Americans, 4 American Indian/Alaska Native, 1 Asian American or Pacific Islander), 11 international. Average age 34. 29 applicants, 76% accepted, 15 enrolled. In 2006, 6 degrees awarded. *Degree requirements:* For doctorate, thesis/dissertation. *Entrance requirements:* For doctorate, GRE General Test, minimum graduate GPA of 3.2. Application fee: $25 ($35 for international students). *Financial support:* Research assistantships with full tuition reimbursements, teaching assistantships with full tuition reimbursements, career-related internships or fieldwork available. Financial award application deadline: 3/1. *Faculty research:* Community education, executive development for public services, applied gerontology. *Unit head:* Joseph Armstrong, Director of Doctoral Program, 765-285-5348, Fax: 765-285-5489.

Ball State University, Graduate School, Teachers College, Department of Educational Studies, Program in Student Affairs Administration in Higher Education, Muncie, IN 47306-1099. Offers MA. *Accreditation:* NCATE. *Students:* 28 full-time (13 women), 7 part-time (all women); includes 6 minority (4 African Americans, 1 Asian American or Pacific Islander, 1 Hispanic American), 2 international. Average age 22. 105 applicants, 41% accepted, 25 enrolled. In 2006, 27 degrees awarded. *Entrance requirements:* For master's, GRE General Test, interview. Application fee: $25 ($35 for international students). *Financial support:* In 2006–07, 24 research assistantships with full tuition reimbursements (averaging $6,150 per year) were awarded. Financial award application deadline: 3/1. *Unit head:* Dr. Randy Hyman, Director, 765-285-5343, Fax: 765-285-2464.

Barry University, School of Education, Program in Higher Education Administration, Miami Shores, FL 33161-6695. Offers higher education administration (MS). Part-time and evening/ weekend programs available. *Students:* 4 full-time (3 women), 6 part-time (5 women); includes 4 minority (3 African Americans, 1 Hispanic American), 1 international. 7 applicants, 29% accepted, 1 enrolled. In 2006, 2 degrees awarded. *Degree requirements:* For master's, comprehensive exam. *Entrance requirements:* For master's, GRE General Test or MAT, minimum GPA of 3.0. *Application deadline:* For fall admission, 5/1 priority date for domestic students. Applications are processed on a rolling basis. Application fee: $30. Electronic applications accepted. *Unit head:* Dr. Carmen McCrink, Director, 305-899-3702, Fax: 305-899-4708, E-mail: cmccrink@mail.barry.edu. *Application contact:* Dave Fletcher, Director of Graduate Admissions, 305-899-3113, Fax: 305-899-2971, E-mail: dfletcher@mail.barry.edu.

Barry University, School of Education, Program in Leadership and Education, Miami Shores, FL 33161-6695. Offers educational technology (PhD); exceptional student education (PhD); higher education administration (PhD); human resource development (PhD); leadership (PhD). Part-time and evening/weekend programs available. *Students:* 15 full-time (7 women), 233 part-time (147 women); includes 97 minority (52 African Americans, 45 Hispanic Americans), 7 international. 58 applicants, 34% accepted, 18 enrolled. In 2006, 23 degrees awarded. *Degree requirements:* For doctorate, thesis/dissertation. *Entrance requirements:* For doctorate, GRE General Test, minimum GPA of 3.25. *Application deadline:* For fall admission, 5/1 priority date for domestic students. Applications are processed on a rolling basis. Application fee: $30. Electronic applications accepted. *Unit head:* Dr. Carmen McCrink, Director, 305-899-3702, Fax: 305-899-4708, E-mail: cmccrink@mail.barry.edu. *Application contact:* Dave Fletcher, Director of Graduate Admissions, 305-899-3113, Fax: 305-899-2971, E-mail: dfletcher@mail.barry.edu.

Benedictine University, Graduate Programs, Program in Higher Education and Organizational Change, Lisle, IL 60532-0900. Offers Ed D. *Expenses:* Tuition: Full-time $12,150; part-time $450 per credit hour. *Unit head:* Dr. Donald Fouts, Director, 630-829-6343.

Bernard M. Baruch College of the City University of New York, School of Public Affairs, Program in Higher Education Administration, New York, NY 10010-5585. Offers MS Ed. Part-time and evening/weekend programs available. *Students:* 3 full-time (2 women), 68 part-time (44 women); includes 38 minority (17 African Americans, 4 Asian Americans or Pacific Islanders, 17 Hispanic Americans). Average age 34. 51 applicants, 57% accepted, 22 enrolled. In 2006, 31 degrees awarded. *Degree requirements:* For master's, internship. *Entrance requirements:* For master's, GRE General Test, minimum GPA of 3.0. Additional exam requirements/recommendations for international students: Required—TOEFL (minimum score 650 paper-based; 257 computer-based). *Application deadline:* For fall admission, 4/1 priority date for domestic and international students; for spring admission, 11/1 priority date for domestic and international students. Applications are processed on a rolling basis. Application fee: $125. Electronic applications accepted. *Expenses: Contact institution. Financial support:* In 2006–07, 8 students received support, including 7 fellowships (averaging $3,000 per year), 1 research assistantship (averaging $9,800 per year); teaching assistantships, career-related internships or fieldwork, Federal Work-Study, scholarships/grants, tuition waivers (partial), and

Higher Education

Bernard M. Baruch College of the City University of New York (continued)
unspecified assistantships also available. Support available to part-time students. Financial award application deadline: 5/30; financial award applicants required to submit FAFSA. *Application contact:* Michael J. Lovaglio, Director of Graduate Admissions and Student Services, 646-660-6750, Fax: 646-660-6751, E-mail: michael_lovaglio@baruch.cuny.edu.

Bethel University, Graduate School, Department of Communication, St. Paul, MN 55112-6999. Offers communication (MA); postsecondary teaching (Certificate). Evening/weekend programs available. *Faculty:* 8 full-time (3 women), 4 part-time/adjunct (2 women). *Students:* 53 full-time (38 women), 6 part-time (5 women); includes 7 minority (3 African Americans, 1 American Indian/Alaska Native, 1 Asian American or Pacific Islander, 2 Hispanic Americans), 1 international. Average age 37. In 2006, 17 master's, 9 other advanced degrees awarded. *Degree requirements:* For master's, thesis, comprehensive exam. *Entrance requirements:* For master's, MAT, interview, minimum GPA of 3.0, course work in communication and statistics, references. Additional exam requirements/recommendations for international students: Required—TOEFL (minimum score 550 paper-based; 213 computer-based). *Application deadline:* For fall admission, 5/15 priority date for domestic students; for spring admission, 3/15 for domestic students. Applications are processed on a rolling basis. Application fee: $25. Electronic applications accepted. *Expenses:* Tuition: Part-time $395 per credit. Tuition and fees vary according to program. *Financial support:* Institutionally sponsored loans and scholarships/grants available. *Unit head:* Dr. Leta J. Frazier, Director, 651-638-6260, Fax: 651-635-8004, E-mail: leta-frazier@bethel.edu. *Application contact:* Michael Price, Director of Admissions, 651-635-8000 Ext. 8017, Fax: 651-635-8004, E-mail: m_price@bethel.edu.

Boston College, Lynch Graduate School of Education, Department of Educational Administration and Higher Education, Higher Education Specialization, Chestnut Hill, MA 02467-3800. Offers MA, PhD, JD/MA, MBA/MA. *Students:* 63 full-time (38 women), 43 part-time (30 women); includes 16 minority (6 African Americans, 7 Asian Americans or Pacific Islanders, 3 Hispanic Americans), 12 international. 198 applicants, 47% accepted, 33 enrolled. In 2006, 43 master's, 6 doctorates awarded. Terminal master's awarded for partial completion of doctoral program. *Degree requirements:* For master's, comprehensive exam; for doctorate, thesis/dissertation, comprehensive exam. *Entrance requirements:* For master's, GRE General Test or MAT; for doctorate, GRE General Test. Additional exam requirements/recommendations for international students: Required—TOEFL. Application fee: $60. *Financial support:* Fellowships with full and partial tuition reimbursements, research assistantships with full and partial tuition reimbursements, teaching assistantships with full and partial tuition reimbursements, career-related internships or fieldwork, Federal Work-Study, scholarships/grants, traineeships, tuition waivers (full and partial), and unspecified assistantships available. Support available to part-time students. Financial award applicants required to submit FAFSA. *Faculty research:* Administration and leadership theory, change process in policy making, organizational analysis, comparative education, higher education in developing countries. *Application contact:* Timothy P. Blackman, Director, Graduate Admission and Financial Aid, 617-552-4214, Fax: 617-552-0398, E-mail: timothy.blackman.1@bc.edu.

Bowling Green State University, Graduate College, College of Education and Human Development, School of Leadership and Policy Studies, Program in Higher Education Administration, Bowling Green, OH 43403. Offers PhD. *Accreditation:* NCATE. Part-time programs available. *Students:* 20 full-time (16 women), 19 part-time (17 women); includes 7 minority (4 African Americans, 2 Asian Americans or Pacific Islanders, 1 Hispanic American), 1 international. Average age 38. 17 applicants, 71% accepted, 8 enrolled. In 2006, 4 degrees awarded. *Degree requirements:* For doctorate, thesis/dissertation, comprehensive exam. *Entrance requirements:* For doctorate, GRE General Test. Additional exam requirements/recommendations for international students: Required—TOEFL. *Application deadline:* For fall admission, 1/15 for domestic students. Application fee: $30. Electronic applications accepted. *Expenses:* Tuition, state resident: part-time $535 per hour. Tuition, nonresident: part-time $884 per hour. *Financial support:* In 2006–07, 17 research assistantships with full tuition reimbursements (averaging $11,207 per year) were awarded; teaching assistantships, career-related internships or fieldwork, Federal Work-Study, institutionally sponsored loans, and unspecified assistantships also available. Support available to part-time students. Financial award applicants required to submit FAFSA. *Faculty research:* Adult learners, legal issues, intellectual development. *Application contact:* Dr. Michael Coomes, Graduate Coordinator, 419-372-7157.

Capella University, School of Education, Minneapolis, MN 55402. Offers college teaching (Certificate); curriculum and instruction (MS, PhD); education (MS); enrollment management (MS); instructional design for online learning (MS, PhD); k-12 studies in education (MS, PhD); leadership for higher education (MS, PhD); leadership in education administration (Certificate); leadership in educational administration (MS, PhD); postsecondary and adult education (MS, PhD); professional studies in education (MS, PhD); reading and literacy (MS); training and performance improvement (MS, PhD). Part-time and evening/weekend programs available. Postbaccalaureate distance learning degree programs offered (minimal on-campus study). Terminal master's awarded for partial completion of doctoral program. *Degree requirements:* For master's, integrative project, thesis optional; for doctorate, thesis/dissertation, comprehensive exam, registration. *Entrance requirements:* Additional exam requirements/recommendations for international students: Required—TOEFL (minimum score 550 paper-based; 213 computer-based), TWE (minimum score 4). Electronic applications accepted. *Faculty research:* Higher education administration, distance learning, adult education, training and curriculum design.

Chicago State University, School of Graduate and Professional Studies, College of Education, Department of Educational Leadership, Curriculum and Foundations, Program in Educational Leadership, Chicago, IL 60628. Offers educational leadership (Ed D); general administration (MA); higher education administration (MA). *Accreditation:* NCATE. *Degree requirements:* For master's, thesis optional. *Entrance requirements:* For master's, minimum GPA of 2.75.

Claremont Graduate University, Graduate Programs, School of Educational Studies, Claremont, CA 91711-6160. Offers Africana education (Certificate); education policy issues (MA, PhD); higher education (PhD); higher education administration (MA); human development (MA, PhD); public school administration (MA, PhD); teacher education (MA, PhD); teaching and learning (MA, PhD); urban education administration (MA, PhD); MBA/PhD. Part-time programs available. *Faculty:* 15 full-time (9 women), 11 part-time/adjunct (9 women). *Students:* 236 full-time (155 women), 168 part-time (117 women); includes 177 minority (34 African Americans, 2 American Indian/Alaska Native, 43 Asian Americans or Pacific Islanders, 98 Hispanic Americans), 7 international. Average age 38. In 2006, 90 master's, 20 doctorates awarded. Terminal master's awarded for partial completion of doctoral program. *Degree requirements:* For master's, thesis or alternative, comprehensive exam (for some programs); for doctorate, thesis/dissertation, comprehensive exam. *Entrance requirements:* For master's and doctorate, GRE General Test. *Application deadline:* For fall admission, 2/15 priority date for domestic students. Applications are processed on a rolling basis. Electronic applications accepted. *Financial support:* Fellowships, research assistantships, Federal Work-Study and institutionally sponsored loans available. Support available to part-time students. Financial award application deadline: 2/15; financial award applicants required to submit FAFSA. *Faculty research:* Education administration, K–12 and higher education, multicultural education, education policy, diversity in higher education, faculty issues. *Unit head:* Philip H. Dreyer, Dean, 909-621-8075, Fax: 909-621-8734, E-mail: philip.dreyer@cgu.edu. *Application contact:* Cece Gaddy, Administrative Director, 909-621-8317, Fax: 909-621-8734, E-mail: cece.gaddy@cgu.edu.

College of Saint Elizabeth, Department of Psychology, Morristown, NJ 07960-6989. Offers counseling psychology (MA); student affairs in higher education (Certificate). Part-time and evening/weekend programs available. *Faculty:* 5 full-time (2 women), 8 part-time/adjunct (5 women). *Students:* 5 full-time (all women), 46 part-time (43 women); includes 12 minority (6 African Americans, 1 Asian American or Pacific Islander, 5 Hispanic Americans), 2 international. Average age 35. In 2006, 2 degrees awarded. *Degree requirements:* For master's, thesis or alternative, portfolio. *Entrance requirements:* For master's, minimum GPA of 3.0, BA in psychology (preferred), 12 credits of course work in psychology. *Application deadline:* For fall admission, 4/14 priority date for domestic students; for spring admission, 11/15 for domestic students. Applications are processed on a rolling basis. Application fee: $35. Electronic applications accepted. *Financial support:* Career-related internships or fieldwork, tuition waivers (partial), and unspecified assistantships available. Support available to part-time students. Financial award application deadline: 3/15; financial award applicants required to submit FAFSA. *Faculty research:* Family systems, dissociative identity disorder, multicultural counseling, outcomes assessment. *Unit head:* Dr. Valerie Scott, Director of the Graduate Program in Counseling Psychology, 973-290-4102, Fax: 973-290-4676, E-mail: vscott@cse.edu. *Application contact:* Michael Szarek, Director of Enrollment Management, 973-290-4112, Fax: 973-290-4167, E-mail: mszarek@cse.edu.

Columbia International University, Columbia Graduate School, Columbia, SC 29230-3122. Offers Bible teaching (MABT); Christian higher education leadership (Ed D); Christian school educational leadership (Ed D); counseling (MACN); curriculum and instruction (M Ed), including Christian school guidance, English as a second language, learning disabilities, school technology; early childhood and elementary education (MAT); educational administration (M Ed); teaching English as a foreign language (Certificate); teaching English as a foreign language and intercultural studies (MATF). Part-time and evening/weekend programs available. *Faculty:* 11 full-time (4 women), 7 part-time/adjunct (5 women). *Students:* 52 full-time (44 women), 93 part-time (59 women); includes 17 minority (11 African Americans, 2 Asian Americans or Pacific Islanders, 4 Hispanic Americans), 10 international. Average age 35. 107 applicants, 56% accepted, 41 enrolled. In 2006, 62 degrees awarded. *Degree requirements:* For master's, internships, professional project. *Entrance requirements:* For master's, Minnesota Multiphasic Personality Inventory, MAT, minimum GPA of 2.7. Additional exam requirements/recommendations for international students: Required—TOEFL. *Application deadline:* For fall admission, 8/1 priority date for domestic and international students; for winter admission, 12/15 priority date for domestic and international students; for spring admission, 1/15 priority date for domestic and international students. Applications are processed on a rolling basis. Application fee: $45. Electronic applications accepted. *Expenses:* Tuition: Part-time $400 per semester hour. Tuition and fees vary according to course load and program. *Financial support:* In 2006–07, 35 students received support. Career-related internships or fieldwork, Federal Work-Study, institutionally sponsored loans, and scholarships/grants available. Financial award application deadline: 3/17; financial award applicants required to submit FAFSA. *Unit head:* Dr. Milton Uecker, Dean, 803-807-5319, Fax: 803-786-4209, E-mail: muecker@ciu.edu. *Application contact:* Michelle MacGregor, Director of Admissions, 800-777-2227 Ext. 5335, Fax: 803-786-4209, E-mail: yescbs@ciu.edu.

Dallas Baptist University, College of Adult Education, Professional Development Program, Dallas, TX 75211-9299. Offers accounting (MA); business (MA); church leadership (MA); corporate management (MA); counseling (MA); criminal justice (MA); English as a second language (MA); finance (MA); higher education (MA); leadership studies (MA); management (MA); management information systems (MA); marketing (MA); missions (MA). Part-time and evening/weekend programs available. *Faculty:* 49 full-time (21 women), 112 part-time/adjunct (46 women). *Students:* 31 full-time, 65 part-time. 51 applicants, 49% accepted, 15 enrolled. In 2006, 41 degrees awarded. Application fee: $25. *Expenses:* Tuition: Full-time $8,370; part-time $465 per credit hour. Required fees: $465 per credit hour. *Financial support:* Tuition waivers (full and partial) available. *Unit head:* Lynda Jackson, Director, 214-333-6830, Fax: 214-333-5558, E-mail: graduate@dbu.edu. *Application contact:* Kit P. Montgomery, Director of Graduate Programs, 214-333-5242, Fax: 214-333-5579, E-mail: graduate@dbu.edu.

Dallas Baptist University, School of Leadership and Christian Education, Higher Education Program, Dallas, TX 75211-9299. Offers M Ed. Part-time and evening/weekend programs available. *Faculty:* 49 full-time (21 women), 112 part-time/adjunct (46 women). *Students:* 10 full-time, 29 part-time. 29 applicants, 55% accepted, 14 enrolled. In 2006, 7 degrees awarded. *Entrance requirements:* For master's, GRE General Test, minimum GPA of 3.0. Additional exam requirements/recommendations for international students: Required—TOEFL. *Application deadline:* Applications are processed on a rolling basis. Application fee: $25. Electronic applications accepted. *Expenses:* Tuition: Full-time $8,370; part-time $465 per credit hour. Required fees: $465 per credit hour. *Financial support:* Federal Work-Study, institutionally sponsored loans, scholarships/grants, and tuition waivers (full and partial) available. Support available to part-time students. *Faculty research:* Enrollment management, portfolio assessment, servant leadership. *Unit head:* Dr. Jeremy B. Dutschke, Director, 214-333-6758, Fax: 214-333-5673, E-mail: graduate@dbu.edu. *Application contact:* Kit P. Montgomery, Director of Graduate Programs, 214-333-5242, Fax: 214-333-5579, E-mail: graduate@dbu.edu.

Drexel University, School of Education, Program in Higher Education, Philadelphia, PA 19104-2875. Offers MS. Postbaccalaureate distance learning degree programs offered (no on-campus study). *Degree requirements:* For master's, co-op experience. *Entrance requirements:* For master's, bachelor's degree from an accredited institution, minimum GPA of 3.0 or GRE. Additional exam requirements/recommendations for international students: Required—TOEFL (minimum score 550 paper-based). *Faculty research:* Governance and administration, financial management, enrollment management, institutional research, strategic planning, advancement, academic development, technology, and instruction.

Eastern Kentucky University, The Graduate School, College of Education, Department of Curriculum and Instruction, Program in Secondary and Higher Education, Richmond, KY 40475-3102. Offers agricultural education (MA Ed); allied health sciences education (MA Ed); art education (MA Ed); biological sciences education (MA Ed); business education (MA Ed); chemistry education (MA Ed); earth science education (MA Ed); English education (MA Ed); general science education (MA Ed); geography education (MA Ed); history education (MA Ed); home economics education (MA Ed); industrial education (MA Ed); mathematical sciences education (MA Ed); physical education (MA Ed); physics education (MA Ed); political science education (MA Ed); psychology education (MA Ed); reading (MA Ed); school health education (MA Ed); sociology education (MA Ed). *Accreditation:* NCATE. Part-time programs available. *Students:* 16 full-time (8 women), 63 part-time (43 women); includes 5 minority (2 African Americans, 2 American Indian/Alaska Native, 1 Asian American or Pacific Islander). Average age 32. *Entrance requirements:* For master's, GRE General Test, minimum GPA of 2.5. Application fee: $30. *Expenses:* Tuition, state resident: full-time $5,610. Tuition, nonresident: full-time $15,910. *Financial support:* Research assistantships, teaching assistantships, Federal Work-Study available. Support available to part-time students. *Unit head:* Dr. Michael Martin, Chair, Department of Curriculum and Instruction, 859-622-2154, Fax: 859-622-2004.

Eastern Washington University, Graduate Studies, College of Education and Human Development, Department of Education, Program in College Instruction, Cheney, WA 99004-2431. Offers MA, MS. *Accreditation:* NCATE. *Degree requirements:* For master's, internship. *Entrance requirements:* For master's, minimum GPA of 3.0.

Fitchburg State College, Division of Graduate and Continuing Education, Program in Educational Leadership and Management, Fitchburg, MA 01420-2697. Offers educational technology (Certificate); higher education administration (CAGS); non-licensure (M Ed, CAGS); professional mentoring for teachers (Certificate); school principal (M Ed, CAGS); supervisor director (M Ed, CAGS); technology leader (M Ed, CAGS). *Accreditation:* NCATE. Part-time and evening/weekend programs available. *Students:* 19 full-time (14 women), 44 part-time (30 women); includes 2 minority (both African Americans), 1 international. Average age 39. 33 applicants, 97% accepted, 15 enrolled. In 2006, 24 master's, 20 other advanced degrees awarded. *Degree requirements:* For master's, thesis or alternative, comprehensive exam. *Entrance requirements:* For master's, GRE General Test or MAT, 3 years of teaching experience, teaching certificate, letters of recommendation, resumé; for other advanced degree, master's degree, letters of recommendation, resumé. Additional exam requirements/recommendations for international students: Required—TOEFL (minimum score 550 paper-based; 213 computer-based; 79 iBT). *Application deadline:* Applications are processed on a rolling basis. Application fee: $25 ($50 for international students). *Expenses:* Tuition, state resident: part-time $150 per credit. Tuition, nonresident: part-time $150 per credit. Required fees: $90 per credit. *Financial support:* In 2006–07, research assistantships with partial tuition reimbursements (averaging $5,500 per year); Federal Work-Study, scholarships/grants, and unspecified assistantships also available. Support available to part-time students. Financial award application deadline: 3/1; financial award applicants required to submit FAFSA. *Unit head:* Dr. Randy Howe, Chair, 978-665-3544, Fax: 978-665-3658, E-mail: gce@fsc.edu. *Application contact:* Director of Admissions, 978-665-3144, Fax: 978-665-4540, E-mail: admissions@fsc.edu.

Florida Atlantic University, College of Education, Department of Educational Leadership, Boca Raton, FL 33431-0991. Offers adult/community education (M Ed, PhD, Ed S); educational leadership (M Ed, PhD, Ed S); higher education management (M Ed, PhD). *Accreditation:* NCATE. Part-time and evening/weekend programs available. Postbaccalaureate distance learning degree programs offered (minimal on-campus study). *Faculty:* 19 full-time (8 women), 18 part-time/adjunct (11 women). *Students:* 65 full-time (43 women), 187 part-time (119 women); includes 81 minority (52 African Americans, 1 American Indian/Alaska Native, 4 Asian Americans or Pacific Islanders, 24 Hispanic Americans), 3 international. Average age 37. 114 applicants, 51% accepted, 50 enrolled. In 2006, 63 master's, 19 doctorates, 13 other advanced degrees awarded. *Degree requirements:* For master's, registration; for doctorate, thesis/dissertation, departmental qualifying exam, comprehensive exam, registration; for Ed S, departmental qualifying exam. *Entrance requirements:* For master's, GRE General Test, minimum GPA of 3.0 during previous 2 years; for doctorate, GRE General Test, minimum GPA of 3.5; for Ed S, GRE General Test. *Application deadline:* Applications are processed on a rolling basis. Application fee: $30. Electronic applications accepted. *Expenses:* Tuition, area resident: Full-time $4,394. Tuition, nonresident: full-time $16,441. *Financial support:* In 2006–07, 6 students received support, including 1 fellowship, 2 research assistantships, 2 teaching assistantships; career-related internships or fieldwork and tuition waivers (partial) also available. *Faculty research:* Self-directed learning, school reform issues, legal issues, mentoring, school leadership. *Unit head:* Dr. Anthony C. Townsend, Chairperson, 561-297-3550, Fax: 561-297-3618, E-mail: townsend@fau.edu. *Application contact:* Catherine Politi, Senior Secretary, 561-297-3550, Fax: 561-297-3618, E-mail: cpoliti@fau.edu.

Florida International University, College of Education, Department of Educational Leadership and Policy Studies, Program in Higher Education, Miami, FL 33199. Offers Ed D. Part-time and evening/weekend programs available. *Faculty:* 4 full-time (2 women), 5 part-time/adjunct (3 women). *Students:* 32 full-time (5 women), 39 part-time (all women); includes 43 minority (16 African Americans, 2 Asian Americans or Pacific Islanders, 25 Hispanic Americans). 14 applicants, 43% accepted, 5 enrolled. In 2006, 2 degrees awarded. *Degree requirements:* For doctorate, thesis/dissertation, registration. *Entrance requirements:* For doctorate, GRE General Test. Additional exam requirements/recommendations for international students: Required—TOEFL (minimum score 550 paper-based; 213 computer-based; 80 iBT), IELTS (minimum score 6). *Application deadline:* For fall admission, 6/1 priority date for domestic students, 4/1 for international students; for winter admission, 10/1 priority date for domestic students, 9/1 for international students; for spring admission, 3/1 priority date for domestic students, 2/1 for international students. Applications are processed on a rolling basis. Application fee: $30. Electronic applications accepted. *Expenses:* Tuition, state resident: part-time $249 per credit hour. Tuition, nonresident: part-time $753 per credit hour. Tuition and fees vary according to program. *Financial support:* Fellowships, research assistantships with full and partial tuition reimbursements, teaching assistantships with full and partial tuition reimbursements, Federal Work-Study and tuition waivers (full and partial) available. Support available to part-time students. *Faculty research:* Access and equity in college admission, social justice, higher education law, faculty and tenure issues for individuals of color. *Unit head:* Dr. Benjamin Baez, Associate Professor, 305-348-5214, E-mail: baezb@fiu.edu. *Application contact:* Marisa Salazar, Student Recruiter, 305-348-3002, Fax: 305-348-3227, E-mail: marisa.salazar@fiu.edu.

Florida State University, Graduate Studies, College of Education, Department of Educational Leadership and Policy Studies, Program in Higher Education, Tallahassee, FL 32306. Offers higher education (MS, Ed D, PhD, Ed S); institutional research (MS, Ed D, PhD, Ed S). *Faculty:* 6 full-time (2 women), 3 part-time/adjunct (1 woman). *Students:* 46 full-time (35 women), 45 part-time (22 women); includes 31 minority (19 African Americans, 7 Asian Americans or Pacific Islanders, 5 Hispanic Americans). 93 applicants, 65% accepted, 22 enrolled. In 2006, 32 master's, 5 doctorates awarded. Terminal master's awarded for partial completion of doctoral program. *Degree requirements:* For master's and Ed S, thesis optional; for doctorate, thesis/dissertation, comprehensive exam. *Entrance requirements:* For master's, GRE General Test, minimum GPA of 3.0; for doctorate and Ed S, GRE General Test, minimum graduate GPA of 3.0. *Application deadline:* For fall admission, 7/1 priority date for domestic students; for spring admission, 11/1 for domestic students. Applications are processed on a rolling basis. Application fee: $30. *Expenses:* Tuition, state resident: full-time $5,822; part-time $243 per credit hour. Tuition, nonresident: full-time $20,976; part-time $874 per credit hour. Tuition and fees vary according to program. *Financial support:* Fellowships with partial tuition reimbursements, research assistantships with partial tuition reimbursements, teaching assistantships with partial tuition reimbursements, career-related internships or fieldwork, scholarships/grants, and unspecified assistantships available. Financial award applicants required to submit FAFSA. *Unit head:* Dr. Beverly Bower, Associate Professor and Program Coordinator, 850-644-6777, Fax: 850-644-1258, E-mail: bower@coe.fsu.edu. *Application contact:* Jimmy Pastrano, Program Assistant, 850-644-6777, Fax: 850-644-1258, E-mail: pastrano@coe.fsu.edu.

Geneva College, Program in Higher Education, Beaver Falls, PA 15010-3599. Offers campus ministry (MA); college teaching (MA); educational leadership (MA); student affairs administration (MA). Part-time and evening/weekend programs available. Postbaccalaureate distance learning degree programs offered (minimal on-campus study). *Degree requirements:* For master's, research seminar. *Entrance requirements:* For master's, minimum GPA of 2.8, writing sample, letters of recommendation (3). Additional exam requirements/recommendations for international students: Required—TOEFL. Electronic applications accepted. *Faculty research:* Student development, learning theories, church-related higher education, assessment, organizational culture.

The George Washington University, Graduate School of Education and Human Development, Department of Educational Leadership, Program in Higher Education Administration, Washington, DC 20052. Offers MA Ed, Ed D, Ed S. *Accreditation:* NCATE. *Degree requirements:* For master's and Ed S, comprehensive exam; for doctorate, thesis/dissertation, comprehensive exam. *Entrance requirements:* For master's, GRE General Test or MAT, minimum GPA of 2.75; for doctorate, GRE General Test or MAT, interview, minimum GPA of 3.3; for Ed S, GRE General Test or MAT, minimum GPA of 3.3. *Faculty research:* Technology in higher education administration.

Georgia Southern University, Jack N. Averitt College of Graduate Studies, College of Education, Department of Leadership, Technology, and Human Development, Program in Higher Education, Statesboro, GA 30460. Offers M Ed. *Accreditation:* NCATE. Part-time and evening/weekend programs available. *Students:* 12 full-time (6 women), 11 part-time (9 women); includes 8 minority (all African Americans), 1 international. Average age 30. 8 applicants, 100% accepted, 8 enrolled. In 2006, 7 degrees awarded. *Degree requirements:* For master's, portfolio. *Entrance requirements:* For master's, GRE General Test or MAT, minimum GPA of 2.5. Additional exam requirements/recommendations for international students: Required—TOEFL (minimum score 550 paper-based; 213 computer-based; 80 iBT). *Application deadline:* For fall admission, 3/1 priority date for domestic students, 3/1 for international students; for spring admission, 10/1 priority date for domestic students, 10/1 for international students. Applications are processed on a rolling basis. Application fee: $50. Electronic applications accepted. *Financial support:* In 2006–07, 16 students received support, including research assistantships with partial tuition reimbursements available (averaging $5,500 per year), teaching assistantships with partial tuition reimbursements available (averaging $5,500 per year); career-related internships or fieldwork, Federal Work-Study, scholarships/grants, tuition waivers (partial), and unspecified assistantships also available. Support available to part-time students. Financial award application deadline: 4/15; financial award applicants required to submit FAFSA. *Application contact:* 912-681-5384, Fax: 912-681-0740, E-mail: gradadmissions@georgiasouthern.edu.

Grand Valley State University, College of Education, Program in College Student Affairs Leadership, Allendale, MI 49401-9403. Offers M Ed. Part-time programs available. *Students:* 9 full-time (6 women), 13 part-time (10 women); includes 7 minority (all African Americans) Average age 31. In 2006, 15 degrees awarded. *Entrance requirements:* For master's, GRE General Test or minimum GPA of 3.0. *Expenses:* Tuition, state resident: full-time $5,850; part-time $325 per credit. Tuition, nonresident: full-time $10,800; part-time $600 per credit. Tuition and fees vary according to course load. *Financial support:* In 2006–07, research assistantships with full and partial tuition reimbursements (averaging $8,000 per year); unspecified assistantships also available. *Faculty research:* Adult learners, diversity and multiculturalism. *Unit head:* Dr. Lorraine Alston, Associate Professor of Education, 616-331-6591, E-mail: alstonl@gvsu.edu. *Application contact:* Ginger Randall, Associate Dean of Students, 616-331-3585, E-mail: randallg@gvsu.edu.

Grand Valley State University, College of Education, Programs in General Education, Allendale, MI 49401-9403. Offers adult and higher education (M Ed); early childhood education (M Ed); education of the gifted and talented (M Ed); educational leadership (M Ed); educational technology (M Ed); elementary education (M Ed); middle and high school education (M Ed); teaching English to speakers of other languages (M Ed). Part-time and evening/weekend programs available. Postbaccalaureate distance learning degree programs offered (minimal on-campus study). *Faculty:* 82 full-time (42 women), 43 part-time/adjunct (25 women). *Students:* 136 full-time (97 women), 828 part-time (565 women); includes 55 minority (26 African Americans, 7 American Indian/Alaska Native, 5 Asian Americans or Pacific Islanders, 17 Hispanic Americans). Average age 33. 280 applicants, 94% accepted, 188 enrolled. In 2006, 322 degrees awarded. *Degree requirements:* For master's, thesis. *Entrance requirements:* For master's, GRE General Test or minimum GPA of 3.0. Additional exam requirements/recommendations for international students: Required—TOEFL. *Application deadline:* Applications are processed on a rolling basis. Application fee: $30. Electronic applications accepted. *Expenses:* Tuition, state resident: full-time $5,850; part-time $325 per credit. Tuition, nonresident: full-time $10,800; part-time $600 per credit. Tuition and fees vary according to course load. *Financial support:* In 2006–07, 2 research assistantships with full and partial tuition reimbursements (averaging $8,000 per year) were awarded; career-related internships or fieldwork, Federal Work-Study, scholarships/grants, and unspecified assistantships also available. *Faculty research:* Effectiveness of technology in education, parental involvement, effective teaching, effective schools research. *Unit head:* Dr. Linda McCrea, Director, 616-331-2080, E-mail: mccreal@gvsu.edu. *Application contact:* Dr. Douglas Busman, Director, Student Information and Services, 616-331-6831, Fax: 616-331-6217, E-mail: busmando@gvsu.edu.

Harvard University, Graduate School of Education, Doctoral Program in Education, Cambridge, MA 02138. Offers culture, communities and education (Ed D); education policy (Ed D); education policy, leadership and instructional practice (Ed D); higher education (Ed D); human development and education (Ed D); quantitative policy analysis in education (Ed D); urban superintendency (Ed D). Part-time programs available. *Faculty:* 58 full-time (25 women), 40 part-time/adjunct (22 women). *Students:* 306 full-time (216 women), 35 part-time (26 women); includes 95 minority (38 African Americans, 4 American Indian/Alaska Native, 35 Asian Americans or Pacific Islanders, 18 Hispanic Americans), 46 international. Average age 35. 494 applicants, 12% accepted, 48 enrolled. In 2006, 70 degrees awarded. Terminal master's awarded for partial completion of doctoral program. *Degree requirements:* For doctorate, thesis/dissertation. *Entrance requirements:* For doctorate, GRE General Test, 3 letters of recommendation, official transcripts, statement of purpose. Additional exam requirements/recommendations for international students: Required—TOEFL (minimum score 600 paper-based; 250 computer-based; 100 iBT), TWE (minimum score 5). *Application deadline:* For fall admission, 12/14 for domestic and international students. Application fee: $85. Electronic applications accepted. *Expenses:* Contact institution. *Financial support:* In 2006–07, 171 fellowships with full and partial tuition reimbursements (averaging $11,489 per year), 47 research assistantships (averaging $9,340 per year), 153 teaching assistantships (averaging $7,710 per year) were awarded; career-related internships or fieldwork, Federal Work-Study, institutionally sponsored loans, scholarships/grants, health care benefits, tuition waivers (full and partial), and unspecified assistantships also available. Support available to part-time students. Financial award application deadline: 2/2; financial award applicants required to submit FAFSA. *Faculty research:* Learning and development; educational leadership and organizations; education policy analysis. Total annual research expenditures: $4.8 million. *Unit head:* Dr. James Stiles, Associate Dean for Degree Programs. *Application contact:* Information Contact, 617-495-3414, Fax: 617-496-3577, E-mail: gseadmissions@harvard.edu.

Illinois State University, Graduate School, College of Education, Department of Curriculum and Instruction, Normal, IL 61790-2200. Offers curriculum and instruction (MS, MS Ed, Ed D); educational policies (Ed D); postsecondary education (Ed D); reading (MS Ed); supervision (Ed D). *Accreditation:* NCATE. *Faculty:* 28 full-time (13 women). *Students:* 21 full-time (16 women), 157 part-time (123 women); includes 20 minority (11 African Americans, 5 Asian Americans or Pacific Islanders, 4 Hispanic Americans), 11 international. 26 applicants, 73% accepted. In 2006, 60 master's, 14 doctorates awarded. *Degree requirements:* For master's, variable foreign language requirement, thesis or alternative; for doctorate, variable foreign language requirement, thesis/dissertation, 2 terms of residency, internship. *Entrance requirements:* For master's, GRE General Test, minimum GPA of 3.0 in last 60 hours of course work; for doctorate, GRE General Test. *Application deadline:* Applications are processed on a rolling basis. Application fee: $40. *Expenses:* Tuition, state resident: full-time $3,330; part-time $185 per credit hour. Tuition, nonresident: full-time $6,948; part-time $438 per credit hour. Required fees: $1,259; $52 per credit hour. *Financial support:* In 2006–07, 15 research assistantships (averaging $7,056 per year), 5 teaching assistantships (averaging $9,675 per year) were awarded; tuition waivers (full) and unspecified assistantships also available. Financial award application deadline: 4/1. *Faculty research:* In-service and pre-service teacher education for teachers of English language learners; teachers for all children: developing a model for alternative, bilingual elementary certification for paraprofessionals in Illinois; Illinois Geographic Alliance. Total annual research expenditures: $1 million. *Unit head:* Dr. Barbara Nourie, Acting Chairperson, 309-438-5425.

Indiana University Bloomington, School of Education, Department of Educational Leadership and Policy Studies, Bloomington, IN 47405-7000. Offers education policy studies (PhD); educational leadership (MS, Ed D, PhD, Ed S); higher education (MS, Ed D, PhD); history and philosophy of education (MS); history of education (PhD); international and comparative education (MS, PhD); philosophy of education (PhD); student affairs administration (MS). PhD offered through the University Graduate School. *Accreditation:* NCATE. Part-time and evening/weekend programs available. *Students:* 12 full-time (5 women), 28 part-time (14 women). Average age 35. In 2006, 32 master's, 4 doctorates awarded. *Degree requirements:* For master's, thesis optional; for doctorate, thesis/dissertation; for Ed S, comprehensive exam or project. *Entrance requirements:* For master's, doctorate, and Ed S, GRE General Test. *Application deadline:* For fall admission, 6/1 for domestic students, 3/1 for international students; for spring admission, 9/1 for international students. Application fee: $45 ($55 for international students). *Expenses:* Tuition, state resident: full-time $5,791; part-time $241 per credit hour. Tuition, nonresident: full-time $16,866; part-time $703 per credit hour. *Financial support:* Fellowships, research assistantships, teaching assistantships, career-related internships or fieldwork, Federal Work-Study, institutionally sponsored loans, and tuition waivers (full and partial) available. Support available to part-time students. *Unit head:* Martha McCarthy, Chair, 812-856-8377. *Application contact:* Sandy Strain, Department Secretary, 812-856-8360, Fax: 812-856-8394, E-mail: strain@indiana.edu.

Indiana University of Pennsylvania, School of Graduate Studies and Research, College of Education and Educational Technology, Department of Student Affairs in Higher Education,

Higher Education

Indiana University of Pennsylvania (continued)
Indiana, PA 15705-1087. Offers MA. *Accreditation:* NCATE. Part-time programs available. *Faculty:* 4 full-time (2 women). *Students:* 55 full-time (33 women), 10 part-time (7 women); includes 6 minority (3 African Americans, 2 Asian Americans or Pacific Islanders, 1 Hispanic American), 1 international. Average age 24. 110 applicants, 38% accepted. In 2006, 34 degrees awarded. *Degree requirements:* For master's, thesis optional. *Entrance requirements:* For master's, resumé, interview, 2 letters of recommendation, writing sample. Additional exam requirements/recommendations for international students: Required—TOEFL. *Application deadline:* For fall admission, 7/1 priority date for domestic students; for spring admission, 11/1 for domestic students. Applications are processed on a rolling basis. Application fee: $30. *Expenses:* Tuition, state resident: full-time $6,048; part-time $336 per credit. Tuition, nonresident: full-time $9,678; part-time $538 per credit. Required fees: $1,069; $148 per year. *Financial support:* In 2006–07, 1 fellowship (averaging $500 per year), 21 research assistantships with full and partial tuition reimbursements (averaging $4,900 per year) were awarded; career-related internships or fieldwork and Federal Work-Study also available. Support available to part-time students. Financial award application deadline: 3/15; financial award applicants required to submit FAFSA. *Unit head:* Dr. Ronald W. Lunardini, Chairperson and Graduate Coordinator, 724-357-4535, E-mail: lunar@iup.edu.

Inter American University of Puerto Rico, Metropolitan Campus, Faculty of Education, Program in Higher Education, San Juan, PR 00919-1293. Offers MA Ed. *Degree requirements:* For master's, comprehensive exam. *Entrance requirements:* For master's, GRE or EXADEP, interview. Electronic applications accepted.

Iowa State University of Science and Technology, Graduate College, College of Human Sciences, Department of Educational Leadership and Policy Studies, Ames, IA 50011. Offers counselor education (M Ed, MS); educational administration (M Ed, MS); educational leadership (PhD); higher education (M Ed, MS); organizational learning and human resource development (M Ed, MS); research and evaluation (MS). *Faculty:* 19 full-time, 9 part-time/adjunct. *Students:* 82 full-time (53 women), 191 part-time (109 women); includes 40 minority (23 African Americans, 4 American Indian/Alaska Native, 5 Asian Americans or Pacific Islanders, 8 Hispanic Americans), 5 international. 156 applicants, 70% accepted, 76 enrolled. In 2006, 95 master's, 13 doctorates awarded. *Degree requirements:* For master's, thesis or alternative; for doctorate, thesis/dissertation. *Entrance requirements:* For doctorate, GRE General Test. Additional exam requirements/recommendations for international students: Required—TOEFL (paper-based 560; computer-based 220; iBT 79) or IELTS (6.0). *Application deadline:* For fall admission, 1/1 priority date for domestic and international students. Applications are processed on a rolling basis. Application fee: $30 ($70 for international students). Electronic applications accepted. *Expenses:* Tuition, state resident: full-time $5,936; part-time $330 per credit. Tuition, nonresident: full-time $16,350; part-time $330 per credit. *Financial support:* In 2006–07, 17 research assistantships with full and partial tuition reimbursements (averaging $16,419 per year) were awarded; fellowships, teaching assistantships with full and partial tuition reimbursements, scholarships/grants, health care benefits, and unspecified assistantships also available. *Unit head:* Dr. Laura Rendon, Chair, 515-294-7093, E-mail: lrendon@iastate.edu. *Application contact:* Dr. Daniel Robinson, Information Contact, 515-294-1241, E-mail: eldrshp@iastate.edu.

Jones International University, Graduate School of Education, Centennial, CO 80112. Offers adult education (M Ed); corporate training and knowledge management (M Ed); curriculum and instruction (M Ed), including elementary teacher licensure, secondary teacher licensure; e-learning technology and design (M Ed); educational leadership and administration (M Ed); educational leadership and administration: principal and administrator licensure (M Ed); elementary curriculum instruction and assessment (M Ed); higher education leadership and administration (M Ed); K-12 instructional technology (M Ed); K-12 instructional technology: teacher licensure (M Ed); secondary curriculum instruction and assessment (M Ed); technology and design (M Ed). Part-time and evening/weekend programs available. Postbaccalaureate distance learning degree programs offered (no on-campus study). *Entrance requirements:* For master's, minimum cumulative GPA of 2.5. Additional exam requirements/recommendations for international students: Recommended—TOEFL (minimum score 550 paper-based; 213 computer-based). Electronic applications accepted.

Kent State University, Graduate School of Education, Health, and Human Services, Department of Teaching, Leadership, and Curriculum Studies, Program in Higher Education Administration and Student Personnel, Kent, OH 44242-0001. Offers M Ed, MA. *Accreditation:* NCATE. *Faculty:* 6 full-time (2 women), 2 part-time/adjunct (both women). *Students:* 52 full-time (41 women), 30 part-time (21 women); includes 8 minority (7 African Americans, 1 Asian American or Pacific Islander), 1 international. 65 applicants, 55% accepted. In 2006, 31 degrees awarded. *Degree requirements:* For master's, thesis (for some programs), registration. *Entrance requirements:* Additional exam requirements/recommendations for international students: Required—TOEFL. *Application deadline:* Applications are processed on a rolling basis. Application fee: $30. Electronic applications accepted. *Financial support:* In 2006–07, fellowships with full tuition reimbursements (averaging $7,210 per year); research assistantships with full tuition reimbursements, teaching assistantships with full tuition reimbursements, career-related internships or fieldwork, Federal Work-Study, institutionally sponsored loans, scholarships/grants, health care benefits, and unspecified assistantships also available. Support available to part-time students. Financial award application deadline: 4/1; financial award applicants required to submit FAFSA. *Faculty research:* History/sociology of higher education, organization and administration in higher education. *Unit head:* Dr. Mark Kretovics, Coordinator, 330-672-2477, E-mail: mkretov1@kent.edu. *Application contact:* Nancy Miller, Academic Program Coordinator, Office of Graduate Student Services, 330-672-2576, Fax: 330-672-9162, E-mail: ogs@kent.edu.

Louisiana State University and Agricultural and Mechanical College, Graduate School, College of Education, Department of Educational Theory, Policy and Practice, Baton Rouge, LA 70803. Offers counseling (M Ed, MA, Ed S); educational administration (M Ed, MA, PhD, Ed S); educational technology (MA); elementary education (M Ed); higher education (PhD); research methodology (PhD); secondary education (M Ed). *Accreditation:* ACA (one or more programs are accredited); NCATE. Part-time and evening/weekend programs available. *Faculty:* 39 full-time (24 women). *Students:* 147 full-time (115 women), 183 part-time (143 women); includes 63 minority (51 African Americans, 3 American Indian/Alaska Native, 3 Asian Americans or Pacific Islanders, 6 Hispanic Americans), 14 international. Average age 35. 110 applicants, 58% accepted, 15 enrolled. In 2006, 93 master's, 24 doctorates awarded. Terminal master's awarded for partial completion of doctoral program. *Degree requirements:* For doctorate, thesis/dissertation; for Ed S, thesis optional. *Entrance requirements:* For master's and doctorate, GRE General Test, minimum GPA of 3.0. Additional exam requirements/recommendations for international students: Required—TOEFL (minimum score 550 paper-based; 213 computer-based; 79 iBT). *Application deadline:* For fall admission, 1/25 priority date for domestic students, 5/15 for international students; for spring admission, 10/15 for international students. Applications are processed on a rolling basis. Application fee: $25. Electronic applications accepted. *Financial support:* In 2006–07, 82 students received support, including 6 fellowships with full tuition reimbursements available (averaging $26,273 per year), 24 research assistantships with full and partial tuition reimbursements available (averaging $9,812 per year), teaching assistantships with full and partial tuition reimbursements available (averaging $11,693 per year); career-related internships or fieldwork, Federal Work-Study, institutionally sponsored loans, and unspecified assistantships also available. Support available to part-time students. Financial award applicants required to submit FAFSA. *Faculty research:* Literary, curriculum studies, science education, K-12 leadership, higher education. Total annual research expenditures: $335,618. *Unit head:* Dr. Earl Cheek, Chair, 225-578-6897, Fax: 225-578-1045, E-mail: echeek@lsu.edu.

Loyola University Chicago, School of Education, Program in Higher Education, Chicago, IL 60611-2196. Offers M Ed, PhD. PhD offered through the Graduate School. *Accreditation:* NCATE. Part-time programs available. *Faculty:* 3 full-time (2 women), 6 part-time/adjunct (4 women). *Students:* 114. Average age 38. 117 applicants, 74% accepted, 26 enrolled. In 2006, 32 master's, 6 doctorates awarded. *Degree requirements:* For doctorate, thesis/dissertation, dissertation defense, oral candidacy exam, comprehensive exam. *Entrance requirements:* For master's, letters of recommendation, minimum GPA of 3.0, resumé, transcripts; for doctorate, GMAT, GRE General Test, or MAT, 5 years of higher education work experience, interview. Additional exam requirements/recommendations for international students: Required—TOEFL (minimum score 550 paper-based; 213 computer-based; 79 iBT). *Application deadline:* For fall admission, 4/1 for domestic and international students; for winter admission, 2/1 for domestic and international students; for spring admission, 11/1 for domestic and international students. Applications are processed on a rolling basis. Application fee: $50. Electronic applications accepted. *Financial support:* In 2006–07, 6 students received support, including 2 research assistantships with full tuition reimbursements available (averaging $8,500 per year); career-related internships or fieldwork also available. Support available to part-time students. Financial award application deadline: 2/15; financial award applicants required to submit FAFSA. *Faculty research:* Church-affiliated higher education, enrollment management, academic programs, program evaluation/quality. *Unit head:* Dr. Terry E. Williams, Director, 312-915-7002, Fax: 312-915-6660, E-mail: twillia@luc.edu. *Application contact:* Marie Rosin-Dittmar, Information Contact, 312-915-6800, E-mail: schleduc@luc.edu.

Marywood University, Academic Affairs, College of Education and Human Development, Department of Education, Program in Higher Education Administration, Scranton, PA 18509-1598. Offers MS. Part-time and evening/weekend programs available. *Students:* 2 full-time (both women), 8 part-time (4 women). Average age 30. 6 applicants, 100% accepted. In 2006, 4 degrees awarded. *Degree requirements:* For master's, thesis or alternative, internship/practicum. *Entrance requirements:* For master's, GRE or MAT. Additional exam requirements/recommendations for international students: Required—TOEFL (minimum score 550 paper-based; 213 computer-based). *Application deadline:* For fall admission, 4/15 priority date for domestic and international students; for spring admission, 11/15 priority date for domestic and international students. Applications are processed on a rolling basis. Application fee: $30. Electronic applications accepted. *Expenses:* Tuition: Part-time $672 per credit. Tuition and fees vary according to degree level, campus/location and program. *Financial support:* Research assistantships with tuition reimbursements, career-related internships or fieldwork, scholarships/grants, tuition waivers (partial), and unspecified assistantships available. Support available to part-time students. Financial award application deadline: 2/15; financial award applicants required to submit FAFSA. *Faculty research:* Integrated thematic instruction. *Application contact:* Dr. Deborah M. Flynn, Coordinator of Graduate Advising (Enrollment Management), 570-348-6211, E-mail: flynn@ac.marywood.edu.

Marywood University, Academic Affairs, College of Education and Human Development, Department of Human Development, Emphasis in Higher Education Administration, Scranton, PA 18509-1598. Offers PhD. *Students:* 2 full-time (1 woman), 20 part-time (14 women); includes 1 minority (Hispanic American), 2 international. Average age 37. *Expenses:* Tuition: Part-time $672 per credit. Tuition and fees vary according to degree level, campus/location and program. *Unit head:* Dr. Marie Loftus, Director, Department of Human Development, 570-348-6292, E-mail: loftus@es.marywood.edu.

Michigan State University, The Graduate School, College of Education, Department of Educational Administration, East Lansing, MI 48824. Offers higher, adult and lifelong education (MA, PhD); K–12 educational administration (MA, PhD, Ed S); student affairs administration (MA). Part-time programs available. *Faculty:* 20 full-time (9 women). *Students:* 158 full-time (103 women), 181 part-time (95 women); includes 70 minority (42 African Americans, 4 American Indian/Alaska Native, 10 Asian Americans or Pacific Islanders, 14 Hispanic Americans), 44 international. Average age 35. 190 applicants, 54% accepted. In 2006, 109 master's, 29 doctorates awarded. *Entrance requirements:* Additional exam requirements/recommendations for international students: Required—TOEFL. Electronic applications accepted. *Expenses:* Tuition, state resident: part-time $346 per credit hour. Tuition, nonresident: part-time $730 per credit hour. Tuition and fees vary according to program. *Financial support:* In 2006–07, 40 fellowships with tuition reimbursements, 50 research assistantships with tuition reimbursements (averaging $13,143 per year), 6 teaching assistantships with tuition reimbursements (averaging $13,228 per year) were awarded. Total annual research expenditures: $1.5 million. *Unit head:* Dr. Marilyn J. Amey, Chairperson, 517-355-4538, Fax: 517-353-6393, E-mail: amey@msu.edu. *Application contact:* Graduate Admissions Assistant, E-mail: haleadm@msu.edu.

Minnesota State University Mankato, College of Graduate Studies, College of Education, Department of Educational Leadership, Mankato, MN 56001. Offers computer services administration (MS); educational administration (Certificate); educational leadership (MS); elementary school administration (MS, SP); experiential education (MS, Certificate, SP), including educational administration (Certificate), elementary school administration (SP), experiential education (MS), secondary administration (SP); general school administration (MS); higher education administration (MS); secondary administration (MS, SP); vocational-technical administration (MS). *Accreditation:* NCATE. Part-time and evening/weekend programs available. *Students:* 45 full-time (26 women), 102 part-time (53 women). Average age 38. In 2006, 29 master's, 44 other advanced degrees awarded. *Degree requirements:* For master's, thesis or alternative, comprehensive exam; for other advanced degree, thesis. *Entrance requirements:* For master's, minimum GPA of 3.0 during previous 2 years or GRE; for other advanced degree, minimum GPA of 3.0. Additional exam requirements/recommendations for international students: Required—TOEFL. *Application deadline:* For fall admission, 7/1 priority date for domestic students; for spring admission, 11/1 for domestic students. Applications are processed on a rolling basis. Application fee: $40. Electronic applications accepted. *Financial support:* Research assistantships with full tuition reimbursements, teaching assistantships with full tuition reimbursements, career-related internships or fieldwork, Federal Work-Study, and unspecified assistantships available. Support available to part-time students. Financial award application deadline: 3/15; financial award applicants required to submit FAFSA. *Unit head:* Dr. Jean Haar, Graduate Coordinator, 507-389-5434, Fax: 507-389-5863. *Application contact:* 507-389-2321, E-mail: grad@mnsu.edu.

Mississippi College, Graduate School, School of Education, Department of Teacher Education and Leadership, Clinton, MS 39058. Offers art (M Ed); biological science (M Ed); business education (M Ed); computer science (M Ed); dyslexia therapy (M Ed); educational leadership (M Ed, Ed S); elementary education (M Ed, Ed S); English (M Ed); higher education administration (MS); mathematics (M Ed); secondary education (M Ed); social studies (history) (M Ed); teaching arts (M Ed). Part-time programs available. *Faculty:* 9 full-time (5 women), 14 part-time/adjunct (10 women). *Students:* 52 full-time (36 women), 286 part-time (247 women); includes 173 minority (171 African Americans, 1 American Indian/Alaska Native, 1 Hispanic American), 1 international. Average age 32. In 2006, 131 degrees awarded. *Degree requirements:* For master's, thesis optional. *Entrance requirements:* For master's, NTE. Additional exam requirements/recommendations for international students: Recommended—IELTS. *Application deadline:* Applications are processed on a rolling basis. Application fee: $25. Electronic applications accepted. *Expenses:* Tuition: Full-time $7,290; part-time $405 per hour. Required fees: $150 per term. Tuition and fees vary according to campus/location and program. *Financial support:* Teaching assistantships, career-related internships or fieldwork, Federal Work-Study, scholarships/grants, and unspecified assistantships available. Support available to part-time students. Financial award applicants required to submit FAFSA. *Unit head:* Dr. Tom Williams, Chair, 601-925-3844, E-mail: twilliams@mc.edu.

Morehead State University, Graduate Programs, College of Education, Department of Professional Programs in Education, Program in Adult and Higher Education, Morehead, KY 40351. Offers MA, Ed S. *Accreditation:* NCATE. Part-time and evening/weekend programs available. *Students:* 12 full-time (6 women), 69 part-time (51 women); includes 9 minority (6 African Americans, 1 American Indian/Alaska Native, 1 Asian American or Pacific Islander, 1 Hispanic American). Average age 32. In 2006, 12 master's, 1 Ed S awarded. *Degree* *requirements:* For master's, oral and/or written comprehensive exams, thesis optional; for Ed S, thesis, oral exam. *Entrance requirements:* For master's, GRE General Test, minimum GPA of 2.5, 2 years of work experience; for Ed S, GRE General Test, interview, master's degree, minimum GPA of 3.5, work experience. Additional exam requirements/recommendations for international students: Required—TOEFL (minimum score 525 paper-based; 197 computer-based). *Application deadline:* For fall admission, 8/1 priority date for domestic and international students; for spring admission, 12/1 priority date for domestic and international students. Applications are processed on a rolling basis. Application fee: $0 ($55 for international students). Electronic applications accepted. *Financial support:* In 2006–07, teaching assistantships (averaging $6,000 per year); career-related internships or fieldwork, Federal Work-Study, and unspecified assistantships also available. Financial award application deadline: 4/1; financial award applicants required to submit FAFSA. *Faculty research:* Self-directed learning projects for nontraditional students, evaluation of adult educational programs, adult literacy, evaluation of homeless. *Application contact:* Michelle Barber, Graduate Admissions Counselor, 606-783-2039, Fax: 606-783-5061, E-mail: m.barber@moreheadstate.edu.

Morgan State University, School of Graduate Studies, School of Education and Urban Studies, Program in Higher Education Administration, Baltimore, MD 21251. Offers PhD. *Students:* 23. In 2006, 2 degrees awarded. *Degree requirements:* For doctorate, thesis/dissertation, comprehensive exam. *Entrance requirements:* For doctorate, GRE General Test or MAT, minimum GPA of 3.0. *Application deadline:* For fall admission, 2/1 priority date for domestic students; for spring admission, 10/1 priority date for domestic students. Applications are processed on a rolling basis. Application fee: $0. *Expenses:* Tuition, state resident: part-time $272 per credit. Tuition, nonresident: part-time $478 per credit. Required fees: $38 per credit. *Financial support:* Fellowships, research assistantships, teaching assistantships, career-related internships or fieldwork, Federal Work-Study, institutionally sponsored loans, scholarships/grants, health care benefits, tuition waivers (full and partial), and unspecified assistantships available. Support available to part-time students. Financial award application deadline: 2/1. *Unit head:* Dr. Howard Simmons, Chairperson, Advanced Studies Leadership and Policy, 443-885-1969, E-mail: hsimmons@moac.morgan.edu. *Application contact:* Dr. Maurice C. Taylor, Dean, 443-885-3185, Fax: 443-885-8226, E-mail: mctaylor@moac.morgan.edu.

Morgan State University, School of Graduate Studies, School of Education and Urban Studies, Program in Higher Education-Community College Leadership, Baltimore, MD 21251. Offers Ed D. *Accreditation:* NCATE. Part-time and evening/weekend programs available. *Faculty:* 5 full-time (1 woman), 4 part-time/adjunct (1 woman). *Students:* 45. Average age 40. 29 applicants, 28% accepted. In 2006, 6 degrees awarded. *Degree requirements:* For doctorate, thesis/dissertation, comprehensive exam. *Entrance requirements:* For doctorate, GRE General Test or MAT. Additional exam requirements/recommendations for international students: Required—TOEFL (minimum score 550 paper-based; 213 computer-based). *Application deadline:* For fall admission, 2/1 priority date for domestic students; for spring admission, 10/1 priority date for domestic students. Applications are processed on a rolling basis. Application fee: $0. *Expenses:* Tuition, state resident: part-time $272 per credit. Tuition, nonresident: part-time $478 per credit. Required fees: $38 per credit. *Financial support:* Fellowships, research assistantships, teaching assistantships, career-related internships or fieldwork, Federal Work-Study, institutionally sponsored loans, scholarships/grants, health care benefits, and unspecified assistantships available. Support available to part-time students. Financial award application deadline: 2/1. *Faculty research:* Multicultural education, cooperative learning, psychology of cognition. *Unit head:* Dr. Christine Johnson McPhail, Coordinator, 443-885-1983. *Application contact:* Dr. Maurice C. Taylor, Dean, 443-885-3185, Fax: 443-885-8226, E-mail: mctaylor@moac.morgan.edu.

New York University, Steinhardt School of Culture, Education and Human Development, Department of Administration, Leadership, and Technology, Program in Higher Education, New York, NY 10012-1019. Offers higher education administration (PhD); student personnel administration higher education (MA). *Accreditation:* Teacher Education Accreditation Council. Part-time and evening/weekend programs available. *Faculty:* 7 full-time (3 women). *Students:* 42 full-time (31 women), 67 part-time (49 women); includes 32 minority (14 African Americans, 9 Asian Americans or Pacific Islanders, 9 Hispanic Americans), 3 international. 148 applicants, 25% accepted, 31 enrolled. In 2006, 27 master's, 7 doctorates awarded. Terminal master's awarded for partial completion of doctoral program. *Degree requirements:* For master's, thesis (for some programs); for doctorate, thesis/dissertation. *Entrance requirements:* For master's, interview, 2 letters of recommendation; for doctorate, GRE General Test, interview. Additional exam requirements/recommendations for international students: Required—TOEFL. *Application deadline:* For fall admission, 12/15 priority date for domestic and international students; for spring admission, 11/1 for domestic and international students. Applications are processed on a rolling basis. Application fee: $50. *Expenses:* Tuition: Part-time $1,080 per unit. Required fees: $56 per unit. $329 per term. Tuition and fees vary according to program. *Financial support:* Fellowships with full and partial tuition reimbursements, career-related internships or fieldwork, Federal Work-Study, institutionally sponsored loans, scholarships/grants, tuition waivers (partial), and unspecified assistantships available. Support available to part-time students. Financial award application deadline: 2/1; financial award applicants required to submit FAFSA. *Faculty research:* Organizational theory and culture, systemic change, leadership development, access, equity and diversity. *Unit head:* Dr. Ann Marcus, Head, 212-998-4041, Fax: 212-995-4041. *Application contact:* 212-998-5030, Fax: 212-995-4328, E-mail: steinhardt.gradadmissions@nyu.edu.

North Carolina State University, Graduate School, College of Education, Department of Adult and Community College Education, Program in Higher Education Administration, Raleigh, NC 27695. Offers M Ed, MS, Ed D. *Degree requirements:* For master's, thesis (for some programs); for doctorate, thesis/dissertation. *Entrance requirements:* For master's and doctorate, GRE General Test or MAT, minimum GPA of 3.0 in major. Electronic applications accepted.

Northeastern State University, Graduate College, College of Education, Department of Educational Foundation and Leadership, Program in Collegiate Scholarship and Services, Tahlequah, OK 74464-2399. Offers MS. Part-time and evening/weekend programs available. *Students:* 9 full-time (7 women), 34 part-time (27 women); includes 14 minority (2 African Americans, 8 American Indian/Alaska Native, 4 Asian Americans or Pacific Islanders). In 2006, 12 degrees awarded. *Degree requirements:* For master's, thesis. *Entrance requirements:* For master's, MAT or GRE, minimum GPA of 3.0. Additional exam requirements/recommendations for international students: Required—TOEFL (minimum score 213 computer-based). *Application deadline:* For fall admission, 6/1 priority date for domestic students. Applications are processed on a rolling basis. Application fee: $0 ($25 for international students). Electronic applications accepted. *Financial support:* Federal Work-Study available. Financial award application deadline: 3/1. *Unit head:* Dr. Swen Digranes, Coordinator, 918-456-5511 Ext. 3719, E-mail: digranes@nsuok.edu.

Northern Illinois University, Graduate School, College of Education, Department of Counseling, Adult and Higher Education, De Kalb, IL 60115-2854. Offers adult and higher education (MS Ed, Ed D); counseling (MS Ed, Ed D). *Accreditation:* ACA. Part-time and evening/weekend programs available. *Faculty:* 19 full-time (11 women), 2 part-time/adjunct (1 woman). *Students:* 102 full-time (73 women), 302 part-time (207 women); includes 110 minority (82 African Americans, 2 American Indian/Alaska Native, 7 Asian Americans or Pacific Islanders, 19 Hispanic Americans), 12 international. Average age 40. 124 applicants, 51% accepted, 51 enrolled. In 2006, 74 master's, 23 doctorates awarded. Terminal master's awarded for partial completion of doctoral program. *Degree requirements:* For master's, thesis optional; for doctorate, thesis/dissertation, candidacy exam, dissertation defense. *Entrance requirements:* For master's, GRE General Test or MAT, minimum undergraduate GPA of 2.75, interview (counseling); for doctorate, GRE General Test, minimum undergraduate GPA of 2.75, 3.2 graduate, interview (counseling). Additional exam requirements/recommendations for international students: Required—TOEFL (minimum score 550 paper-based; 213 computer-based). *Application deadline:* For fall admission, 6/1 for domestic students, 5/1 for international students; for spring admission, 11/1 for domestic students, 10/1 for international students. Applications are processed on a rolling basis. Application fee: $30. Electronic applications accepted. *Financial support:* In 2006–07, 14 teaching assistantships with full tuition reimbursements were awarded; fellowships with full tuition reimbursements, research assistantships with full tuition reimbursements, career-related internships or fieldwork, Federal Work-Study, scholarships/grants, tuition waivers (full), and unspecified assistantships also available. Support available to part-time students. Financial award applicants required to submit FAFSA. *Unit head:* Dr. Francesca Giordano, Chair, 815-753-9373, E-mail: watson@niu.edu.

Northwestern University, The Graduate School, School of Education and Social Policy, Master of Science in Education Program, Evanston, IL 60208. Offers advanced teaching (MS); elementary education and policy (MS); higher education administration (MS); secondary teaching (MS). Part-time and evening/weekend programs available. *Faculty:* 4 full-time (2 women), 33 part-time/adjunct (17 women). *Students:* 64 full-time (40 women), 90 part-time (66 women); includes 21 minority (3 African Americans, 13 Asian Americans or Pacific Islanders, 5 Hispanic Americans), 1 international. Average age 25. 88 applicants, 65% accepted, 36 enrolled. In 2006, 82 degrees awarded. *Degree requirements:* For master's, project. *Entrance requirements:* For master's, GRE General Test, State of Illinois Basic Skills Exam (secondary and elementary). *Application deadline:* For fall admission, 7/1 priority date for domestic students; for winter admission, 11/5 priority date for domestic students; for spring admission, 1/21 priority date for domestic students. Applications are processed on a rolling basis. Application fee: $45. *Financial support:* In 2006–07, 6 students received support. Career-related internships or fieldwork, Federal Work-Study, institutionally sponsored loans, scholarships/grants, tuition waivers (partial), and unspecified assistantships available. Financial award application deadline: 1/7; financial award applicants required to submit FAFSA. *Faculty research:* Discussion/questioning. *Unit head:* Dr. Sophie Haroutunian-Gordon, Director, 847-467-1458, Fax: 847-467-2495, E-mail: shg@northwestern.edu. *Application contact:* Patricia Rodriguez, Assistant Director, 847-491-7526, Fax: 847-467-2495.

Nova Southeastern University, Fischler School of Education and Human Services, Program in Education, Fort Lauderdale, FL 33314-7796. Offers educational leadership (Ed D); health care education (Ed D); higher education (Ed D); human serviced administration (Ed D); instructional leadership (Ed D); instructional technology distance education (Ed D); organizational leadership (Ed D); special education (Ed D); speech language pathology (Ed D). *Students:* 619 full-time (452 women), 615 part-time (473 women); includes 737 minority (616 African Americans, 2 American Indian/Alaska Native, 14 Asian Americans or Pacific Islanders, 105 Hispanic Americans), 8 international. Average age 38. 480 applicants, 83% accepted, 398 enrolled. *Degree requirements:* For doctorate, thesis/dissertation. *Entrance requirements:* For doctorate, MAT or GRE, master's degree, 2 letters of recommendation, work experience. Additional exam requirements/recommendations for international students: Required—TSE (recommended) with a minimum score of 50; Recommended—TOEFL (minimum score 550 paper-based; 213 computer-based), IELTS (minimum score 6). *Application deadline:* For fall admission, 8/11 priority date for domestic and international students; for winter admission, 12/28 priority date for domestic and international students; for spring admission, 4/22 priority date for domestic and international students. Applications are processed on a rolling basis. Application fee: $50. Electronic applications accepted. *Financial support:* In 2006–07, 2 fellowships (averaging $9,375 per year) were awarded; scholarships/grants and tuition waivers (full) also available. Support available to part-time students. Financial award application deadline: 1/7; financial award applicants required to submit FAFSA. *Unit head:* Dr. Karen D. Bowser, Associate Dean of Doctoral Programs, 954-262-8500, Fax: 954-262-3912, E-mail: bowserk@nova.edu. *Application contact:* Jennifer Quiñones Nottingham, Dean of Student Affairs, 800-986-3223 Ext. 8624, Fax: 954-262-3911, E-mail: jlquinon@nova.edu.

Nova Southeastern University, Fischler School of Education and Human Services, Programs for Higher Education, Fort Lauderdale, FL 33314-7796. Offers adult education (Ed D); computing and information technology (Ed D); health care education (Ed D); higher education (Ed D); vocational, occupational and technical education (Ed D). Part-time and evening/weekend programs available. *Students:* 35 full-time (22 women), 321 part-time (222 women); includes 134 minority (116 African Americans, 1 American Indian/Alaska Native, 17 Hispanic Americans), 1 international. 4 applicants, 75% accepted, 3 enrolled. In 2006, 40 degrees awarded. *Degree requirements:* For doctorate, thesis/dissertation, practicum. *Entrance requirements:* For doctorate, MAT or GRE, master's degree, work experience in field, minimum GPA of 3.0. Additional exam requirements/recommendations for international students: Recommended—TOEFL (minimum score 550 paper-based; 213 computer-based), IELTS (minimum score 6). *Application deadline:* For fall admission, 8/11 priority date for domestic and international students; for winter admission, 12/28 priority date for domestic and international students; for spring admission, 4/22 priority date for domestic and international students. Applications are processed on a rolling basis. Application fee: $50. Electronic applications accepted. *Expenses:* Contact institution. *Financial support:* In 2006–07, 2 fellowships were awarded; career-related internships or fieldwork and tuition waivers (full) also available. Financial award application deadline: 1/7. *Unit head:* Dr. Karen D. Bowser, Associate Dean of Doctoral Programs, 954-262-8500, Fax: 954-262-3912, E-mail: bowserk@nova.edu. *Application contact:* Jennifer Quiñones Nottingham, Dean of Student Affairs, 800-986-3223 Ext. 8624, Fax: 954-262-3911, E-mail: jlquinon@nova.edu.

Oakland University, Graduate Study and Lifelong Learning, School of Education and Human Services, Department of Educational Leadership, Rochester, MI 48309-4401. Offers educational leadership (M Ed, PhD); higher education (Certificate); higher education administration (Certificate); school administration (Ed S). *Faculty:* 10 full-time (6 women), 2 part-time/adjunct (0 women). *Students:* 13 full-time (9 women), 287 part-time (200 women); includes 37 minority (31 African Americans, 1 American Indian/Alaska Native, 2 Asian Americans or Pacific Islanders, 3 Hispanic Americans), 2 international. Average age 38. 125 applicants, 89% accepted, 96 enrolled. In 2006, 29 master's, 6 doctorates, 139 Certificates awarded. *Entrance requirements:* Additional exam requirements/recommendations for international students: Required—TOEFL (minimum score 550 paper-based; 213 computer-based). *Application deadline:* For fall admission, 7/15 for domestic students, 5/1 priority date for international students; for winter admission, 9/1 priority date for international students. Application fee: $35. *Expenses:* Tuition, state resident: full-time $9,936; part-time $414 per credit. Tuition, nonresident: full-time $17,202; part-time $716 per credit. *Financial support:* Federal Work-Study, institutionally sponsored loans, and tuition waivers (full) available. Financial award application deadline: 3/1; financial award applicants required to submit FAFSA. *Unit head:* Dr. William G. Keane, Chair, 248-370-3070, Fax: 248-370-4605. *Application contact:* Information Contact, 248-370-3070.

See Close-Up on page 1117.

The Ohio State University, Graduate School, College of Education and Human Ecology, Program in Education, Columbus, OH 43210. Offers higher education and student affairs (MA). *Students:* Average age 47. *Application deadline:* Applications are processed on a rolling basis. Application fee: $40 ($50 for international students). Electronic applications accepted. *Expenses:* Tuition, state resident: full-time $9,438. Tuition, nonresident: full-time $22,791. Tuition and fees vary according to course load, campus/location and program. *Unit head:* Sonora Stroot, Graduate Studies Committee Chair, 614-292-8368, Fax: 614-292-2581, E-mail: stroot.1@osu.edu. *Application contact:* Graduate Admissions, 614-292-9444, Fax: 614-292-3985, E-mail: domestic.grad@osu.edu.

Ohio University, Graduate Studies, College of Education, Department of Counseling and Higher Education, Athens, OH 45701-2979. Offers college student personnel (M Ed); community/agency counseling (M Ed); counselor education (PhD); higher education (M Ed, PhD); rehabilitation counseling (M Ed); school counseling (M Ed). *Accreditation:* ACA; CORE. Part-time and evening/weekend programs available. *Faculty:* 12 full-time (5 women), 6 part-time/adjunct (0 women). *Students:* 123 full-time (89 women), 111 part-time (73 women); includes 20 minority

Higher Education

Ohio University (continued)

(18 African Americans, 2 Hispanic Americans), 42 international. 209 applicants, 62% accepted, 106 enrolled. In 2006, 40 master's, 7 doctorates awarded. *Median time to degree:* Of those who began their doctoral program in fall 1998, 92% received their degree in 8 years or less. *Degree requirements:* For master's, thesis or alternative, registration; for doctorate, thesis/dissertation, comprehensive exam, registration. *Entrance requirements:* For master's, GRE General Test or MAT (if GPA below 2.9), 3 letters of reference, 5-page biography, statement of purpose; for doctorate, GRE General Test, work experience, minimum GPA of 3.4. Additional exam requirements/recommendations for international students: Required—TOEFL (minimum score 550 paper-based; 213 computer-based). *Application deadline:* For fall admission, 3/1 for domestic and international students. Applications are processed on a rolling basis. Application fee: $45. Electronic applications accepted. *Financial support:* In 2006–07, 66 students received support, including 35 research assistantships with full tuition reimbursements available (averaging $6,500 per year), 6 teaching assistantships with full tuition reimbursements available (averaging $7,200 per year); Federal Work-Study, institutionally sponsored loans, and unspecified assistantships also available. Financial award application deadline: 3/15. *Faculty research:* Youth violence, gender studies, student affairs, chemical dependency, disabilities issues. Total annual research expenditures: $527,983. *Unit head:* Dr. Jerry Olsheski, Chair, 740-593-0032, Fax: 740-593-0477, E-mail: olsheski@ohio.edu. *Application contact:* Floyd J. Doney, Director of Student Affairs, 740-593-4400, Fax: 740-593-9310, E-mail: doney@ohio.edu.

Oklahoma State University, College of Education, School of Educational Studies, Stillwater, OK 74078. Offers educational administration (MS); higher education (MS, Ed D); technical education (MS, Ed D); trade and industrial education (MS, Ed D). *Faculty:* 28 full-time (10 women), 25 part-time/adjunct (6 women). *Students:* 40 full-time (28 women), 160 part-time (93 women); includes 34 minority (14 African Americans, 11 American Indian/Alaska Native, 5 Asian Americans or Pacific Islanders, 4 Hispanic Americans), 8 international. Average age 40. 124 applicants, 43% accepted, 37 enrolled. In 2006, 34 master's, 29 doctorates awarded. *Degree requirements:* For master's, thesis or alternative; for doctorate, thesis/dissertation. *Entrance requirements:* For master's and doctorate, GRE or MAT. Additional exam requirements/recommendations for international students: Required—TOEFL. *Application deadline:* For fall admission, 7/1 priority date for domestic students, 3/1 priority date for international students; for spring admission, 8/1 priority date for international students. Applications are processed on a rolling basis. Application fee: $40 ($75 for international students). Electronic applications accepted. *Expenses:* Tuition, state resident: part-time $146 per credit hour. Tuition, nonresident: part-time $516 per credit hour. Required fees: $44 per credit hour. Tuition and fees vary according to program. *Financial support:* In 2006–07, 13 research assistantships (averaging $8,838 per year), 7 teaching assistantships (averaging $7,586 per year) were awarded; career-related internships or fieldwork, Federal Work-Study, and tuition waivers (partial) also available. Support available to part-time students. Financial award application deadline: 3/1. *Unit head:* Dr. Bert Jacobson, Head, 405-744-6275.

Old Dominion University, Darden College of Education, Doctoral Programs in Higher Education, Norfolk, VA 23529. Offers PhD. Part-time programs available. Postbaccalaureate distance learning degree programs offered (minimal on-campus study). *Faculty:* 3 full-time (1 woman), 10 part-time/adjunct (5 women). *Students:* 4 full-time (all women), 8 part-time (7 women); includes 3 minority (1 African American, 1 American Indian/Alaska Native, 1 Hispanic American). Average age 40. *Degree requirements:* For doctorate, thesis/dissertation, comprehensive exam, registration. *Entrance requirements:* For doctorate, GRE, master's degree, minimum graduate GPA of 3.5. Additional exam requirements/recommendations for international students: Required—TOEFL. *Application deadline:* For spring admission, 2/1 for domestic and international students. Application fee: $40. Electronic applications accepted. *Expenses:* Tuition, area resident: Part-time $285 per credit hour. Tuition, nonresident: part-time $715 per credit hour. Required fees: $94 per semester. *Financial support:* In 2006–07, 3 fellowships with tuition reimbursements (averaging $15,000 per year), 2 research assistantships with full tuition reimbursements (averaging $15,000 per year), 2 teaching assistantships with full tuition reimbursements (averaging $15,000 per year) were awarded; career-related internships or fieldwork, tuition waivers (full), and unspecified assistantships also available. Financial award application deadline: 2/1. *Faculty research:* Law leadership, student development, research administration, international higher education administration. *Unit head:* Dr. Dennis Edward Gregory, Graduate Program Director, 757-683-3702, Fax: 757-683-5756, E-mail: dgregory@odu.edu.

Old Dominion University, Darden College of Education, Programs in Higher Education, Norfolk, VA 23529. Offers educational leadership (MS Ed, Ed S), including higher education. Part-time programs available. *Faculty:* 3 full-time (1 woman), 10 part-time/adjunct (5 women). *Students:* 37 full-time (22 women), 13 part-time (12 women); includes 10 minority (9 African Americans, 1 American Indian/Alaska Native), 1 international. Average age 25. 50 applicants, 70% accepted, 27 enrolled. In 2006, 10 degrees awarded. *Degree requirements:* For master's, comprehensive exam, registration. *Entrance requirements:* For master's, GRE or MAT, minimum undergraduate GPA of 2.8; for Ed S, GRE or MAT, 2 letters of reference, minimum GPA of 3.5, master's degree. Additional exam requirements/recommendations for international students: Required—TOEFL. *Application deadline:* For fall admission, 5/1 for domestic and international students; for winter admission, 10/1 for domestic and international students; for spring admission, 3/1 for domestic and international students. Applications are processed on a rolling basis. Application fee: $40. Electronic applications accepted. *Expenses:* Tuition, area resident: Part-time $285 per credit hour. Tuition, nonresident: part-time $715 per credit hour. Required fees: $94 per semester. *Financial support:* Research assistantships with partial tuition reimbursements, career-related internships or fieldwork, scholarships/grants, and unspecified assistantships available. *Faculty research:* Law leadership, student development, research administration, international higher education administration. *Unit head:* Dr. Dennis Edward Gregory, Graduate Program Director, 757-683-3702, Fax: 757-683-5756, E-mail: dgregory@odu.edu.

Oral Roberts University, School of Education, Tulsa, OK 74171-0001. Offers Christian school administration (MA Ed, Ed D); Christian school administration (K-12) (MA Ed, Ed D); Christian school curriculum development (MA Ed); college and higher education administration (MA Ed, Ed D); public school administration (K-12) (MA Ed, Ed D); public school teaching (MA Ed); teaching English as a second language (MA Ed). *Accreditation:* NCATE. Part-time programs available. Postbaccalaureate distance learning degree programs offered (minimal on-campus study). *Faculty:* 9 full-time (2 women), 9 part-time/adjunct (4 women). *Students:* 331 full-time (217 women); includes 118 minority (96 African Americans, 7 American Indian/Alaska Native, 10 Asian Americans or Pacific Islanders, 5 Hispanic Americans). 125 applicants, 96% accepted, 116 enrolled. In 2006, 25 master's, 10 doctorates awarded. *Degree requirements:* For master's, thesis (for some programs), comprehensive exam; for doctorate, thesis/dissertation, comprehensive exam. *Entrance requirements:* For master's, GRE General Test or MAT, minimum GPA of 3.0; for doctorate, minimum GPA of 3.0. Additional exam requirements/recommendations for international students: Required—TOEFL (minimum score 500 paper-based; 173 computer-based). *Application deadline:* For fall admission, 7/1 priority date for domestic students, 5/1 priority date for international students; for spring admission, 12/1 priority date for domestic students, 10/1 priority date for international students. Applications are processed on a rolling basis. Application fee: $35. *Expenses:* Contact institution. *Financial support:* In 2006–07, 4 research assistantships (averaging $5,000 per year) were awarded; scholarships/grants and unspecified assistantships also available. Financial award application deadline: 6/1; financial award applicants required to submit FAFSA. *Faculty research:* Teacher effectiveness, college success in high achieving, African-Americans, professional development practices. *Unit head:* Dr. David Hand, Dean, 918-495-7084, Fax: 918-495-6050, E-mail: dhand@oru.edu. *Application contact:* Kim Schmeisser, Graduate Admissions, 918-495-6058, Fax: 918-495-6222, E-mail: gradeducation@oru.edu.

Penn State University Park, Graduate School, College of Education, Department of Education Policy Studies, State College, University Park, PA 16802-1503. Offers college student

affairs (M Ed); educational leadership (M Ed, MS, D Ed, PhD); educational theory and policy (MA, PhD); higher education (M Ed, D Ed, PhD). *Accreditation:* NCATE. *Unit head:* Dr. Jacqueline A. Stefkovich, Head, 814-863-0619, E-mail: jas71@psu.edu.

Phillips Theological Seminary, Programs in Theology, Tulsa, OK 74116. Offers administration of church agencies (M Div); campus ministry (M Div); church-related social work (M Div); college and seminary teaching (M Div); global mission work (M Div); institutional chaplaincy (M Div); ministerial vocations in Christian education (M Div); ministry (D Min), including parish ministry, pastoral counseling, practices of ministry; ministry and culture (MAMC), including Christian education, congregational leadership, history and practice of Christian spirituality, theology, ethics, and culture; ministry of music (M Div); pastoral care and counseling (M Div); pastoral ministry (M Div); theological studies (MTS). *Accreditation:* ATS. Part-time programs available. Postbaccalaureate distance learning degree programs offered (minimal on-campus study). *Degree requirements:* For master's, thesis (for some programs); for doctorate, thesis/dissertation. *Entrance requirements:* For master's, minimum GPA of 2.5; for doctorate, M Div, minimum GPA of 3.0. *Faculty research:* Biblical studies, historical studies, theology and culture, practical theology, theology and film.

Pittsburg State University, Graduate School, College of Education, Department of Special Services and Leadership Studies, Pittsburg, KS 66762. Offers community college and higher education (Ed S); educational leadership (MS), including educational technology; special education teaching (MS), including behavioral disorders, learning disabilities, mentally retarded. *Students:* 274. *Degree requirements:* For master's, thesis or alternative. *Entrance requirements:* For master's, GRE General Test or MAT. Application fee: $35 ($60 for international students). *Expenses:* Tuition, state resident: full-time $2,144; part-time $181 per credit hour. Tuition, nonresident: full-time $5,273; part-time $442 per credit hour. Tuition and fees vary according to course load and campus/location. *Financial support:* In 2006–07, teaching assistantships (averaging $5,000 per year); career-related internships or fieldwork, Federal Work-Study, and unspecified assistantships also available. *Application contact:* Jamie Vanderbeck, Assistant Director, 620-235-4223, Fax: 620-235-4219, E-mail: jvanderb@pittstate.edu.

Portland State University, Graduate Studies, School of Education, Department of Educational Policy, Foundations, and Administrative Studies, Portland, OR 97207-0751. Offers educational leadership (MA, MS, Ed D); postsecondary, adult and continuing education (Ed D). *Accreditation:* NCATE. Part-time and evening/weekend programs available. *Faculty:* 11 full-time (5 women), 10 part-time/adjunct (4 women). *Students:* 62 full-time (51 women), 227 part-time (149 women); includes 41 minority (7 African Americans, 10 American Indian/Alaska Native, 8 Asian Americans or Pacific Islanders, 16 Hispanic Americans), 10 international. Average age 40. 234 applicants, 91% accepted, 67 enrolled. In 2006, 69 master's, 4 doctorates awarded. *Degree requirements:* For master's, thesis or alternative, written exam; for doctorate, thesis/dissertation, comprehensive exam. *Entrance requirements:* For master's, California Basic Educational Skills Test, minimum GPA of 3.0 in upper-division course work or 2.75 overall; for doctorate, GRE General Test or MAT. Additional exam requirements/recommendations for international students: Required—TOEFL (minimum score 550 paper-based; 213 computer-based). *Application deadline:* For fall admission, 4/1 for domestic and international students; for winter admission, 9/1 for domestic and international students; for spring admission, 11/1 for domestic and international students. Applications are processed on a rolling basis. Application fee: $50. *Expenses:* Tuition, state resident: full-time $6,426; part-time $238 per credit. Tuition, nonresident: full-time $11,016; part-time $408 per credit. Tuition and fees vary according to course load. *Financial support:* In 2006–07, 10 research assistantships with full tuition reimbursements (averaging $5,453 per year) were awarded; teaching assistantships with full tuition reimbursements, career-related internships or fieldwork, Federal Work-Study, and institutionally sponsored loans also available. Support available to part-time students. Financial award application deadline: 3/1; financial award applicants required to submit FAFSA. *Faculty research:* Leadership development and research, principals and urban schools, accelerated schools, cooperative learning, family involvement in schools. Total annual research expenditures: $322,962. *Unit head:* Dilafroz Williams, Head, 503-725-4676, Fax: 503-725-8475. *Application contact:* Kellie Walker, Admission Secretary, 503-725-4716, Fax: 503-725-8475.

Purdue University, Graduate School, School of Education, Department of Educational Studies, West Lafayette, IN 47907. Offers administration (MS Ed, PhD, Ed S); counseling and development (MS Ed, PhD); education of the gifted (MS Ed); educational psychology (MS Ed, PhD); foundations of education (MS Ed, PhD); higher education administration (MS Ed, PhD); special education (MS Ed, PhD). *Accreditation:* ACA (one or more programs are accredited); NCATE (one or more programs are accredited). Part-time and evening/weekend programs available. *Faculty:* 28 full-time (18 women). *Students:* 100 full-time (71 women), 126 part-time (77 women); includes 32 minority (19 African Americans, 2 American Indian/Alaska Native, 6 Asian Americans or Pacific Islanders, 5 Hispanic Americans), 33 international. Average age 36. 152 applicants, 62% accepted, 56 enrolled. In 2006, 51 master's, 17 doctorates awarded. *Degree requirements:* For master's, thesis optional; for doctorate, thesis/dissertation, oral and written exams; for Ed S, oral presentation, project. *Entrance requirements:* For master's, GRE General Test, minimum undergraduate GPA of 3.0; for doctorate, GRE General Test; for Ed S, GRE, minimum B average. Additional exam requirements/recommendations for international students: Required—TOEFL. *Application deadline:* For fall admission, 1/15 for domestic students; for spring admission, 9/15 for domestic students. Applications are processed on a rolling basis. Application fee: $55. Electronic applications accepted. *Financial support:* In 2006–07, 6 fellowships with full tuition reimbursements (averaging $13,300 per year), 23 research assistantships with full tuition reimbursements (averaging $11,500 per year), 33 teaching assistantships with full tuition reimbursements (averaging $10,800 per year) were awarded; career-related internships or fieldwork and tuition waivers (full) also available. Support available to part-time students. Financial award application deadline: 3/1; financial award applicants required to submit FAFSA. *Faculty research:* Motivation, learning disabilities, school learning, group processes, cognitive development. *Unit head:* Dr. Kevin R Kelly, Head, 765-494-9170, Fax: 765-496-1228. *Application contact:* Patricia Mason, Coordinator of Graduate Studies, 765-494-2346, Fax: 765-494-5832, E-mail: gradoffice@soe.purdue.edu.

Rowan University, Graduate School, College of Education, Department of Educational Leadership, Program in Higher Education Administration, Glassboro, NJ 08028-1701. Offers MA. *Accreditation:* NCATE. Part-time and evening/weekend programs available. *Students:* 12 full-time (7 women), 20 part-time (17 women); includes 28 minority (4 African Americans, 1 Asian American or Pacific Islander, 23 Hispanic Americans). Average age 31. 11 applicants, 45% accepted, 5 enrolled. In 2006, 15 degrees awarded. *Degree requirements:* For master's, thesis, comprehensive exam. *Entrance requirements:* For master's, GRE General Test, minimum GPA of 2.8, 2 years of teaching experience. Additional exam requirements/recommendations for international students: Required—TOEFL. *Application deadline:* Applications are processed on a rolling basis. Application fee: $50. Electronic applications accepted. *Expenses:* Tuition, state resident: full-time $9,882; part-time $549 per credit. Tuition, nonresident: full-time $9,882; part-time $549 per credit. Tuition and fees vary according to degree level. *Financial support:* Career-related internships or fieldwork and unspecified assistantships available. Support available to part-time students. *Unit head:* Dr. Burton Sisko, Advisor, 856-256-4500 Ext. 3717.

St. Cloud State University, School of Graduate Studies, College of Education, Department of Educational Leadership and Community Psychology, Program in Higher Education Administration, St. Cloud, MN 56301-4498. Offers MS. *Students:* 11 full-time (6 women), 4 part-time (all women), 1 international. In 2006, 6 degrees awarded. Application fee: $35. *Unit head:* Dr. Christine Imbra, Head, 320-308-4909, E-mail: cmimbra@stcloudstate.edu.

St. John's University, The School of Education, Division of Human Services and Counseling, Program in Student Development Practice in Higher Education, Queens, NY 11439. Offers PD. Part-time and evening/weekend programs available. *Students:* 1 (woman) full-time, 5 part-time (4 women); includes 2 minority (1 African American, 1 Hispanic American). Average age 29. In 2006, 1 PD awarded. *Entrance requirements:* For degree, minimum GPA of 3.0. Additional exam requirements/recommendations for international students: Required—TOEFL (minimum score 500 paper-based). *Application deadline:* For fall admission, 4/1 for domestic students, 5/1 priority date for international students; for spring admission, 11/1 for domestic students, 11/1 priority date for international students. Applications are processed on a rolling basis. Application fee: $40. Electronic applications accepted. *Expenses:* Tuition: Full-time $18,480; part-time $770 per credit. Required fees: $125 per semester. Tuition and fees vary according to program. *Financial support:* Research assistantships, career-related internships or fieldwork and scholarships/grants available. Support available to part-time students. Financial award application deadline: 3/1; financial award applicants required to submit FAFSA. *Faculty research:* Counseling techniques, communication skills, American college student, college retention. *Application contact:* Kelly Ronayne, Assistant Dean, 718-990-2303, Fax: 718-990-6069, E-mail: graded@stjohns.edu.

Saint Louis University, Graduate School, College of Public Service and Graduate School, Department of Educational Leadership and Higher Education, St. Louis, MO 63103-2097. Offers Catholic school leadership (MA); educational administration (MA, Ed D, PhD, Ed S); higher education (MA, Ed D, PhD); student personnel administration (MA). *Accreditation:* NCATE. *Faculty:* 11 full-time (4 women), 13 part-time/adjunct (4 women). *Students:* 43 full-time (26 women), 280 part-time (148 women); includes 38 minority (33 African Americans, 1 American Indian/Alaska Native, 3 Asian Americans or Pacific Islanders, 1 Hispanic American). Average age 38. 157 applicants, 79% accepted, 88 enrolled. In 2006, 18 master's, 55 doctorates, 16 other advanced degrees awarded. *Degree requirements:* For master's, comprehensive written and oral exam; for doctorate, thesis/dissertation, preliminary oral and written exams, comprehensive exam, registration. *Entrance requirements:* For master's, GRE General Test, MAT, LSAT, GMAT, MCAT, letters of recommendation, resumé; for doctorate and Ed S, GRE General Test, LSAT, GMAT, MCAT, letters of recommendation, resumé. Additional exam requirements/recommendations for international students: Required—TOEFL (minimum score 525 paper-based; 194 computer-based). *Application deadline:* For fall admission, 7/1 for domestic and international students; for spring admission, 11/1 for domestic and international students. Applications are processed on a rolling basis. Application fee: $40. *Expenses:* Tuition: Part-time $800 per credit hour. Required fees: $105 per semester. *Financial support:* In 2006–07, 84 students received support, including 6 teaching assistantships with full tuition reimbursements available (averaging $11,000 per year); Federal Work-Study, scholarships/grants, traineeships, health care benefits, tuition waivers (partial), and unspecified assistantships also available. Support available to part-time students. Financial award application deadline: 6/1; financial award applicants required to submit FAFSA. *Faculty research:* Superintendent of schools, school finance, school facilities, student personal administration, building leadership. Total annual research expenditures: $100,000. *Unit head:* Dr. William T. Rebore, Chairperson, 314-977-2508, E-mail: reborewt@slu.edu. *Application contact:* Gary Behrman, Associate Dean of the Graduate School, 314-977-3827, E-mail: behrmang@slu.edu.

Salem State College, Graduate School, Program in Higher Education in Student Affairs, Salem, MA 01970-5353. Offers M Ed. Part-time and evening/weekend programs available. *Students:* 7 full-time (6 women), 21 part-time (17 women); includes 1 African American, 1 Hispanic American, 1 international. Average age 32. In 2006, 15 degrees awarded. Application fee: $35. *Unit head:* Lee Brossoit, 978-542-6401, E-mail: lbrossoit@salemstate.edu.

San Diego State University, Graduate and Research Affairs, College of Education, Department of Administration, Rehabilitation and Post-Secondary Education, San Diego, CA 92182. Offers educational leadership in post-secondary education (MA); rehabilitation counseling (MS), including deafness. Evening/weekend programs available. Postbaccalaureate distance learning degree programs offered. *Students:* 56 full-time (41 women), 4 part-time (1 woman); includes 21 minority (7 African Americans, 1 American Indian/Alaska Native, 4 Asian Americans or Pacific Islanders, 9 Hispanic Americans), 1 international. 50 applicants, 72% accepted, 11 enrolled. In 2006, 41 degrees awarded. *Degree requirements:* For master's, thesis (for some programs), comprehensive exam (for some programs). *Entrance requirements:* For master's, GRE General Test, letters of reference. Additional exam requirements/recommendations for international students: Required—TOEFL. *Application deadline:* For fall admission, 5/1 for domestic and international students; for spring admission, 11/1 for domestic students, 10/1 for international students. Applications are processed on a rolling basis. Application fee: $55. Electronic applications accepted. *Financial support:* Career-related internships or fieldwork available. Financial award applicants required to submit FAFSA. *Faculty research:* Rehabilitation in cultural diversity, distance learning technology. Total annual research expenditures: $3.3 million. *Unit head:* Fred McFarlane, Chair, 619-594-6115, Fax: 619-594-4208, E-mail: fmcfarla@mail.sdsu.edu.

San Jose State University, Graduate Studies and Research, College of Education, Department of Educational Leadership, San Jose, CA 95192-0001. Offers educational administration (MA); higher education administration (MA); school business management (Certificate). *Accreditation:* NCATE. *Students:* 286 full-time (201 women), 69 part-time (54 women); includes 110 minority (9 African Americans, 25 Asian Americans or Pacific Islanders, 76 Hispanic Americans), 2 international. Average age 38. 330 applicants, 88% accepted, 169 enrolled. In 2006, 263 degrees awarded. *Degree requirements:* For master's, thesis or alternative. *Application deadline:* For fall admission, 6/29 for domestic students; for spring admission, 11/30 for domestic students. Applications are processed on a rolling basis. Application fee: $59. Electronic applications accepted. *Financial support:* Career-related internships or fieldwork available. Financial award applicants required to submit FAFSA. *Unit head:* Dr. Noni Reis, Chair, 408-924-3622, Fax: 408-924-3713.

Seton Hall University, College of Education and Human Services, Department of Education Leadership, Management and Policy, Program in Higher Education Administration, South Orange, NJ 07079-2697. Offers PhD. *Accreditation:* NCATE. Part-time and evening/weekend programs available. *Faculty:* 12 full-time (4 women), 1 part-time/adjunct (0 women). *Students:* 5 full-time (1 woman), 52 part-time (29 women); includes 7 minority (3 African Americans, 3 Asian Americans or Pacific Islanders, 1 Hispanic American), 1 international. Average age 41. 12 applicants, 50% accepted, 5 enrolled. In 2006, 4 degrees awarded. *Degree requirements:* For doctorate, thesis/dissertation, internship, comprehensive exam. *Entrance requirements:* For doctorate, GRE or MAT, interview, minimum GPA of 3.5. *Application deadline:* For fall admission, 2/1 priority date for domestic students; for spring admission, 10/1 for domestic students. Applications are processed on a rolling basis. Application fee: $50. *Financial support:* Application deadline: 2/1. *Unit head:* Charles Mitchell, Chair, 973-275-2056.

Southeast Missouri State University, School of Graduate Studies, Department of Educational Leadership and Counseling, Cape Girardeau, MO 63701-4799. Offers educational administration (MA, Ed S); guidance and counseling (MA, Ed S), including community counseling (MA), counseling education (Ed S), school counseling (MA); higher education (MA). *Accreditation:* NCATE. Part-time and evening/weekend programs available. *Faculty:* 13 full-time (7 women). *Students:* 53 full-time (39 women), 222 part-time (164 women); includes 8 minority (5 African Americans, 3 Asian Americans or Pacific Islanders), 1 international. Average age 35. 97 applicants, 89% accepted. In 2006, 51 master's, 16 other advanced degrees awarded. *Degree requirements:* For master's, thesis or alternative. *Entrance requirements:* For master's, GRE General Test, PRAXIS or MAT, minimum undergraduate GPA of 2.75; for Ed S, GRE General Test, PRAXIS or MAT, minimum graduate GPA of 3.5. Additional exam requirements/recommendations for international students: Required—TOEFL (minimum score 550 paper-based; 213 computer-based). *Application deadline:* For fall admission, 8/1 for domestic students, 4/1 for international students; for spring admission, 11/21 for domestic students, 10/1 for international students. Applications are processed on a rolling basis. Application fee: $20 ($100 for international students). Electronic applications accepted. *Financial support:* In 2006–07, 80 students received support, including 19 research assistantships with full tuition reimbursements available (averaging $7,100 per year); career-related internships or fieldwork and unspecified assistantships also available. Financial award applicants required to submit FAFSA. *Unit head:* Dr. Zaidy MohdZain, Chairperson, 573-651-2417, Fax: 573-986-6812, E-mail:

zmohdzain@semo.edu. *Application contact:* Marsha L. Arant, Senior Administrative Assistant Office of Graduate Studies, 573-651-2192, Fax: 573-651-2001, E-mail: marant@semo.edu.

Southern Illinois University Carbondale, Graduate School, College of Education, Department of Educational Administration and Higher Education, Program in Higher Education, Carbondale, IL 62901-4701. Offers MS Ed. *Accreditation:* NCATE. Part-time programs available. *Faculty:* 9 full-time (3 women). *Students:* 22 full-time (16 women), 14 part-time (9 women); includes 4 minority (3 African Americans, 1 Hispanic American), 8 international. Average age 26. 29 applicants, 76% accepted, 6 enrolled. In 2006, 12 degrees awarded. *Degree requirements:* For master's, thesis. *Entrance requirements:* For master's, GRE General Test or MAT, minimum GPA of 2.7. Additional exam requirements/recommendations for international students: Required—TOEFL. *Application deadline:* For fall admission, 5/15 for domestic students; for spring admission, 9/15 for domestic students. Applications are processed on a rolling basis. Application fee: $20. *Financial support:* In 2006–07, 15 students received support; fellowships with full tuition reimbursements available, research assistantships with full tuition reimbursements available, teaching assistantships with full tuition reimbursements available, Federal Work-Study, institutionally sponsored loans, tuition waivers (full), and unspecified assistantships available. Support available to part-time students. Financial award application deadline: 4/1. *Faculty research:* Student affairs administration, international education, community college teaching. *Application contact:* Debra Mibb, Admissions Secretary, 618-536-4434, Fax: 618-453-4338, E-mail: dmibb@siu.edu.

Stanford University, School of Education, Program in Social Sciences, Policy, and Educational Practice, Stanford, CA 94305-9991. Offers administration and policy analysis (Ed D, PhD); anthropology of education (PhD); economics of education (PhD); educational linguistics (PhD); evaluation (MA), including interdisciplinary studies; higher education (PhD); history of education (PhD); interdisciplinary studies (PhD); international comparative education (MA, PhD); international education administration and policy analysis (MA); philosophy of education (PhD); policy analysis (MA); prospective principal's program (MA); sociology of education (PhD). *Degree requirements:* For master's, thesis (for some programs); for doctorate, thesis/dissertation. *Entrance requirements:* For master's and doctorate, GRE General Test. Electronic applications accepted.

Syracuse University, Graduate School, College of Arts and Sciences, Program in College Science Teaching, Syracuse, NY 13244. Offers PhD. Part-time programs available. Postbaccalaureate distance learning degree programs offered. *Students:* 3 full-time (2 women), 6 part-time (4 women); includes 1 minority (Asian American or Pacific Islander) *Entrance requirements:* For doctorate, GRE General Test, GRE Subject Test. *Application deadline:* For fall admission, 1/10 priority date for domestic students. Applications are processed on a rolling basis. Application fee: $65. Electronic applications accepted. *Expenses:* Tuition: Full-time $16,920; part-time $940 per credit hour. Required fees: $930; $930 per year. *Financial support:* Fellowships with full tuition reimbursements, teaching assistantships with full and partial tuition reimbursements available. *Unit head:* Dr. Marvin Druger, Chair, 315-443-3820, Fax: 315-443-1140, E-mail: mdruger@syr.edu. *Application contact:* Cynthia Daley, 315-443-2586.

Syracuse University, Graduate School, School of Education, Higher Education Program, Syracuse, NY 13244. Offers MS, PhD. Part-time programs available. *Students:* 22 full-time (17 women), 39 part-time (25 women); includes 7 minority (5 African Americans, 2 Hispanic Americans), 2 international. 64 applicants, 78% accepted, 19 enrolled. *Degree requirements:* For master's, thesis or alternative; for doctorate, thesis/dissertation. *Entrance requirements:* For master's, resumé; for doctorate, GRE. Additional exam requirements/recommendations for international students: Required—TOEFL. *Application deadline:* For fall admission, 2/1 priority date for domestic students. Applications are processed on a rolling basis. Application fee: $65. Electronic applications accepted. *Expenses:* Tuition: Full-time $16,920; part-time $940 per credit hour. Required fees: $930; $930 per year. *Financial support:* Fellowships with full tuition reimbursements, research assistantships with full tuition reimbursements, teaching assistantships with full tuition reimbursements, career-related internships or fieldwork, Federal Work-Study, and unspecified assistantships available. Support available to part-time students. *Faculty research:* Faculty evaluation, teaching portfolios, student culture, college student personnel development, organizational culture. *Unit head:* Dr. Vince Tinto, Chair, 315-443-4763. *Application contact:* Liza Rochelson, Graduate Admission Recruiter, 315-443-2505, Fax: 315-443-2258, E-mail: gradcrt@gwmail.syr.edu.

Teachers College Columbia University, Graduate Faculty of Education, Department of Organization and Leadership, Program in Higher Education, New York, NY 10027-6696. Offers Ed M, MA, Ed D, PhD. *Accreditation:* NCATE. *Faculty:* 4 full-time (2 women), 6 part-time/adjunct. *Students:* 39 full-time (36 women), 80 part-time (59 women); includes 51 minority (14 African Americans, 19 Asian Americans or Pacific Islanders, 18 Hispanic Americans), 1 international. Average age 40. 164 applicants, 62% accepted, 41 enrolled. In 2006, 37 master's, 6 doctorates awarded. *Degree requirements:* For doctorate, variable foreign language requirement, thesis/dissertation. *Entrance requirements:* For doctorate, master's degree, 2 years of professional experience. *Application deadline:* For fall admission, 5/15 for domestic students. Application fee: $65. *Expenses:* Tuition: Full-time $23,400; part-time $975 per credit. Required fees: $320 per term. *Financial support:* Career-related internships or fieldwork, Federal Work-Study, institutionally sponsored loans, and tuition waivers (full and partial) available. Support available to part-time students. Financial award application deadline: 2/1. *Faculty research:* Educational leadership, general management issues, finance and planning, organizational analysis and development, higher education issues. *Application contact:* Debbie Lesperance, Assistant Director of Admission, 212-678-3710, Fax: 212-678-4171.

See Close-Up on page 1131.

Texas A&M University–Commerce, Graduate School, College of Education and Human Services, Department of Secondary and Higher Education, Commerce, TX 75429-3011. Offers higher education (MS), including administration, teaching; learning technology and information systems (M Ed, MS), including educational computing, library and information science, media and technology; secondary education (M Ed, MS); supervision, curriculum, and instruction (Ed D); training and development (MS). Part-time programs available. Terminal master's awarded for partial completion of doctoral program. *Degree requirements:* For master's, thesis (for some programs), comprehensive exam; for doctorate, thesis/dissertation, departmental qualifying exam. *Entrance requirements:* For master's and doctorate, GRE General Test. Electronic applications accepted. *Faculty research:* Deviance, migration.

Texas A&M University–Kingsville, College of Graduate Studies, College of Education, Department of Education, Program in Higher Education Administration Leadership, Kingsville, TX 78363. Offers PhD. *Degree requirements:* For doctorate, one foreign language, thesis/dissertation, comprehensive exam. *Entrance requirements:* For doctorate, GRE General Test, MAT, minimum GPA of 3.25.

Texas Southern University, Graduate School, College of Education, Department of Educational Administration and Foundation, Houston, TX 77004-4584. Offers educational administration (M Ed, Ed D); higher education administration (Ed D); mid-management superintending (Ed D); research education and certification (Ed D); research education and education (Ed D). Part-time and evening/weekend programs available. *Faculty:* 7 full-time (3 women), 5 part-time/adjunct (1 woman). *Students:* 40 full-time (29 women), 72 part-time (53 women); includes 109 minority (105 African Americans, 1 Asian American or Pacific Islander, 3 Hispanic Americans). Average age 37. 45 applicants, 80% accepted, 30 enrolled. In 2006, 32 degrees awarded. *Degree requirements:* For master's, comprehensive exam; for doctorate, thesis/dissertation, comprehensive exam. *Entrance requirements:* For master's, GRE General Test, minimum GPA of 2.5; for doctorate, GRE General Test or MAT, master's degree, minimum B+ average. Additional exam requirements/recommendations for international students: Required—TOEFL. *Application deadline:* For fall admission, 7/15 priority date for domestic students. Applications are processed on a rolling basis. Application fee: $50 ($75 for international students). *Financial*

Higher Education

Texas Southern University (continued)
support: In 2006–07, 2 fellowships (averaging $1,750 per year) were awarded; Federal Work-Study and institutionally sponsored loans also available. Financial award application deadline: 5/1. *Unit head:* Dr. Emmanuel Nwagwu, Chairperson, 713-313-1055, E-mail: nwagwu_ec@tsu.edu.

Texas Tech University, Graduate School, College of Education, Department of Educational Psychology and Leadership, Lubbock, TX 79409. Offers counselor (Certificate); counselor education (M Ed, PhD); education diagnostician (Certificate); educational leadership (M Ed, Ed D); educational psychology (M Ed, PhD); gifted and talented (Certificate); higher education (M Ed, Ed D, PhD); information processing technologist (Certificate); instructional technology (M Ed, Ed D); principal (Certificate); special education (M Ed, Ed D); special education counselor (Certificate); superintendent (Certificate); visually handicapped (Certificate). *Accreditation:* ACA; NCATE. Part-time programs available. *Students:* 128 full-time (88 women), 321 part-time (233 women); includes 67 minority (23 African Americans, 1 American Indian/Alaska Native, 5 Asian Americans or Pacific Islanders, 38 Hispanic Americans), 22 international. Average age 38. 347 applicants, 49% accepted, 61 enrolled. In 2006, 110 master's, 16 doctorates awarded. *Degree requirements:* For master's, thesis optional; for doctorate, thesis/dissertation. *Entrance requirements:* For master's and doctorate, GRE General Test. Additional exam requirements/recommendations for international students: Required—TOEFL (minimum score 550 paper-based; 213 computer-based). *Application deadline:* For fall admission, 3/1 priority date for international students; for spring admission, 11/1 priority date for international students. Applications are processed on a rolling basis. Application fee: $50 ($60 for international students). Electronic applications accepted. *Expenses:* Tuition, state resident: full-time $4,440. Tuition, nonresident: full-time $11,040. Required fees: $2,136. *Financial support:* In 2006–07, 242 students received support; research assistantships with partial tuition reimbursements available, teaching assistantships with partial tuition reimbursements available, career-related internships or fieldwork, Federal Work-Study, and institutionally sponsored loans available. Support available to part-time students. Financial award application deadline: 4/15; financial award applicants required to submit FAFSA. *Faculty research:* Psychological processes of teaching and learning, teaching populations with special needs, instructional technology, educational administration in education, theories and practice in counseling and counselor education K-12 and higher. *Unit head:* Dr. Fred Hartmeister, Chair, 806-742-1998 Ext. 436, Fax: 806-742-2179, E-mail: fred.hartmeister@ttu.edu. *Application contact:* Graduate Adviser, 806-742-1998, Fax: 806-742-2179.

Touro University International, College of Education, Program in Education, Cypress, CA 90630. Offers adult education (MA Ed); aviation education (MA Ed); children's literacy development (MA Ed); e-learning (MA Ed); early childhood education (MA Ed); enrollment management (MA Ed); higher education (MA Ed); teaching and instruction (MA Ed); training and development (MA Ed). Part-time and evening/weekend programs available. Postbaccalaureate distance learning degree programs offered (no on-campus study). In 2006, 193 degrees awarded. *Degree requirements:* For master's, capstone project with integrative paper. *Entrance requirements:* For master's, minimum GPA of 3.0. Additional exam requirements/recommendations for international students: Required—TOEFL (minimum score 550 paper-based). Application fee: $75. *Expenses:* Tuition: Part-time $300 per credit hour. Tuition and fees vary according to course level and program. *Unit head:* Dr. Edith Neumann, Vice President for Academic Affairs, College of Education, 714-816-0366 Ext. 2030, Fax: 714-226-9844, E-mail: eneumann@tourou.edu.

Touro University International, College of Education, Program in Educational Leadership, Cypress, CA 90630. Offers e-learning leadership (MA Ed, PhD); educational leadership (MA Ed); higher education leadership (PhD); K-12 leadership (PhD). Part-time and evening/weekend programs available. Postbaccalaureate distance learning degree programs offered (no on-campus study). In 2006, 13 degrees awarded. *Degree requirements:* For doctorate, thesis/dissertation, defense of dissertation, comprehensive exam. *Entrance requirements:* For doctorate, minimum GPA of 3.4, course work in research methods or statistics. Additional exam requirements/recommendations for international students: Required—TOEFL (minimum score 550 paper-based). Application fee: $75. *Expenses:* Tuition: Part-time $300 per credit hour. Tuition and fees vary according to course level and program. *Unit head:* Dr. Edith Neumann, Vice President for Academic Affairs, College of Education, 714-816-0366 Ext. 2030, Fax: 714-226-9844, E-mail: eneumann@tourou.edu.

Union University, School of Education, Jackson, TN 38305-3697. Offers education (M Ed, MA Ed); education administration generalist (Ed S); educational leadership (Ed D); educational supervision (Ed S); higher education (Ed D). M Ed also available at Germantown campus. *Accreditation:* NCATE. Part-time and evening/weekend programs available. *Faculty:* 19 full-time (11 women), 18 part-time/adjunct (12 women). *Students:* 254 full-time (207 women), 161 part-time (120 women); includes 197 minority (193 African Americans, 1 American Indian/Alaska Native, 1 Asian American or Pacific Islander, 2 Hispanic Americans). Average age 32. In 2006, 184 master's, 22 doctorates, 77 other advanced degrees awarded. *Degree requirements:* For master's, thesis (for some programs), capstone research course; for doctorate, thesis/dissertation, comprehensive exam; for Ed S, thesis or alternative. *Entrance requirements:* For master's, MAT, PRAXIS II or GRE, minimum GPA of 3.0, teaching license, writing sample; for doctorate, GRE, minimum graduate GPA of 3.2, writing sample; for Ed S, PRAXIS II, minimum graduate GPA of 3.2, writing sample. *Application deadline:* Applications are processed on a rolling basis. Application fee: $25 ($50 for international students). *Financial support:* In 2006–07, 117 students received support. Application deadline: 2/15; *Faculty research:* Mathematics education, direct instruction, language disorders and special education, brain compatible learning, empathy and school leadership. *Unit head:* Dr. Tom R. Rosebrough, Dean, 731-661-5523, Fax: 731-661-5468, E-mail: trosebro@uu.edu. *Application contact:* Helen F. Fowler, Assistant to the Dean, 731-661-5374, Fax: 731-661-5468, E-mail: hfowler@uu.edu.

Université de Sherbrooke, Faculty of Education, Program in Postsecondary Education Training, Sherbrooke, QC J1K 2R1, Canada. Offers M Ed, Diploma. *Degree requirements:* For master's, thesis.

University at Buffalo, the State University of New York, Graduate School, Graduate School of Education, Department of Educational Leadership and Policy, Buffalo, NY 14260. Offers educational administration (Ed M, Ed D, PhD); general education (Ed M); higher education (PhD); higher education administration (Ed M); school business and human resource administration (Certificate); social foundations (PhD); specialist in education administration (Certificate). Part-time and evening/weekend programs available. *Faculty:* 12 full-time (7 women), 6 part-time/adjunct (3 women). *Students:* 107 full-time (73 women), 141 part-time (89 women); includes 50 minority (35 African Americans, 1 American Indian/Alaska Native, 7 Asian Americans or Pacific Islanders, 7 Hispanic Americans), 25 international. Average age 37. 262 applicants, 36% accepted, 58 enrolled. In 2006, 28 master's, 17 doctorates, 12 other advanced degrees awarded. Terminal master's awarded for partial completion of doctoral program. *Median time to degree:* Master's–2 years full-time, 4 years part-time; doctorate–4 years full-time, 6 years part-time; Certificate–2 years part-time. *Degree requirements:* For master's, thesis optional; for doctorate, thesis/dissertation, comprehensive exam, registration. *Entrance requirements:* For doctorate, GRE General Test or MAT, writing sample. Additional exam requirements/recommendations for international students: Required—TOEFL (minimum score 550 paper-based; 213 computer-based). *Application deadline:* For fall admission, 3/1 priority date for domestic students, 3/1 for international students; for spring admission, 11/15 priority date for domestic students, 10/1 for international students. Applications are processed on a rolling basis. Application fee: $50. Electronic applications accepted. *Financial support:* In 2006–07, 50 students received support, including 1 fellowship with full tuition reimbursement available (averaging $10,000 per year), 10 research assistantships with full tuition reimbursements available (averaging $9,000 per year); career-related internships or fieldwork, Federal Work-Study, institutionally sponsored loans, health care benefits, tuition waivers (full and partial), and unspecified assistantships also available. Financial award application deadline: 3/15; financial award applicants required to submit FAFSA. *Faculty research:* Academic collective bargaining, faculty governance, educational technology, educational policy studies, multicultural issues. Total annual research expenditures: $326,191. *Unit head:* Dr. William C. Barba, Chairman, 716-645-2471 Ext. 1097, Fax: 716-645-2481, E-mail: barba@buffalo.edu. *Application contact:* Bonnie Fisher, Secretary, 716-645-2110 Ext. 1255, Fax: 716-645-2481, E-mail: brfisher@buffalo.edu.

The University of Akron, Graduate School, College of Education, Department of Educational Foundations and Leadership, Program in Higher Education Administration, Akron, OH 44325. Offers MA, MS. *Accreditation:* NCATE. *Students:* 42 full-time (28 women), 34 part-time (20 women); includes 20 minority (19 African Americans, 1 Hispanic American), 3 international. Average age 30. 47 applicants, 83% accepted, 26 enrolled. In 2006, 35 degrees awarded. *Degree requirements:* For master's, written comprehensive exam or portfolio assessment. *Entrance requirements:* For master's, minimum GPA of 2.75. Additional exam requirements/recommendations for international students: Required—TOEFL (minimum score 550 paper-based; 213 computer-based; 79 iBT). *Application deadline:* For fall admission, 8/15 for domestic students. Applications are processed on a rolling basis. Application fee: $30 ($40 for international students). Electronic applications accepted. *Expenses:* Tuition, state resident: full-time $6,164; part-time $342 per credit. Tuition, nonresident: full-time $10,575; part-time $588 per credit. Required fees: $806; $43 per credit. $12 per term. Tuition and fees vary according to course load, degree level and program. *Financial support:* Fellowships with full tuition reimbursements, research assistantships with full tuition reimbursements, teaching assistantships with full tuition reimbursements, career-related internships or fieldwork and unspecified assistantships available. *Unit head:* Dr. Sandra Coyner, Coordinator, 330-972-5822, E-mail: scoyner@uakron.edu.

The University of Alabama, Graduate School, College of Education, Department of Educational Leadership, Policy, and Technology Studies, Higher Education Administration Program, Tuscaloosa, AL 35487. Offers MA, Ed D, PhD. Evening/weekend programs available. *Students:* 4 full-time (3 women), 15 part-time (3 women); includes 4 minority (3 African Americans, 1 Hispanic American). Terminal master's awarded for partial completion of doctoral program. *Degree requirements:* For master's, comprehensive exam, registration; for doctorate, thesis/dissertation, comprehensive exam, registration. *Entrance requirements:* For master's, GRE, MAT or GMAT; for doctorate, GRE or MAT. Application fee: $25. Electronic applications accepted. *Financial support:* In 2006–07, 5 students received support. Career-related internships or fieldwork, scholarships/grants, and unspecified assistantships available. *Unit head:* Dr. Claire H. Major, Coordinator and Associate Professor, 205-348-6871, Fax: 205-348-2161, E-mail: bea@bamaed.ua.edu. *Application contact:* Donna Smith, Administration Assistant, 205-348-6871, Fax: 205-348-2161, E-mail: dbsmith@bamaed.ua.edu.

The University of Arizona, Graduate College, College of Education, Program in Higher Education, Tucson, AZ 85721. Offers MA, PhD. Terminal master's awarded for partial completion of doctoral program. *Degree requirements:* For master's, thesis (MA); for doctorate, thesis/dissertation, comprehensive exam. *Entrance requirements:* For master's and doctorate, GRE General Test. Additional exam requirements/recommendations for international students: Required—TOEFL. *Faculty research:* Technology transfer, higher education policy, finance, curricular change.

University of Arkansas, Graduate School, College of Education and Health Professions, Department of Educational Leadership, Counseling and Foundations, Program in Higher Education, Fayetteville, AR 72701-1201. Offers M Ed, Ed D, Ed S. *Accreditation:* NCATE. Part-time and evening/weekend programs available. *Students:* 27 full-time (16 women), 68 part-time (42 women); includes 21 minority (15 African Americans, 3 American Indian/Alaska Native, 3 Hispanic Americans), 2 international. 58 applicants, 38% accepted. In 2006, 24 master's, 10 doctorates awarded. *Degree requirements:* For master's, thesis optional; for doctorate, thesis/dissertation. *Entrance requirements:* For master's, GRE General Test, MAT or minimum GPA of 3.0; for doctorate, GRE General Test or MAT. Application fee: $40 ($50 for international students). *Financial support:* In 2006–07, 6 research assistantships, 4 teaching assistantships were awarded; fellowships with tuition reimbursements, career-related internships or fieldwork and Federal Work-Study also available. Support available to part-time students. Financial award application deadline: 4/1; financial award applicants required to submit FAFSA. *Application contact:* Dr. Carl Holt, Graduate Coordinator, 479-575-2207, E-mail: cholt@uark.edu.

University of Arkansas at Little Rock, Graduate School, College of Education, Department of Educational Leadership, Program in Higher Education Administration, Little Rock, AR 72204-1099. Offers Ed D. *Degree requirements:* For doctorate, oral defense of dissertation, residency. *Entrance requirements:* For doctorate, GRE General Test or MAT, interview, minimum graduate GPA of 3.0, teaching certificate, work experience.

The University of British Columbia, Faculty of Graduate Studies, Faculty of Education, Department of Educational Studies, Vancouver, BC V6T 1Z1, Canada. Offers adult education (M Ed, MA); adult learning and global change (M Ed); educational administration (M Ed, MA); educational leadership and policy (Ed D); educational studies (M Ed, PhD), including history of education (M Ed), philosophy of education (M Ed), sociology of education (M Ed); higher education (M Ed, MA); society, culture and politics in education (M Ed, MA). Part-time and evening/weekend programs available. *Faculty:* 30 full-time (15 women), 9 part-time/adjunct (6 women). *Students:* 308 full-time (217 women), 45 part-time (31 women). Average age 35. 211 applicants, 60% accepted. In 2006, 128 master's, 15 doctorates awarded. Terminal master's awarded for partial completion of doctoral program. *Degree requirements:* For master's, thesis (MA); for doctorate, thesis/dissertation. *Entrance requirements:* Additional exam requirements/recommendations for international students: Required—TOEFL, TOEFL or IELTS. Electronic applications accepted. *Financial support:* Fellowships, research assistantships, teaching assistantships available. *Faculty research:* Educational leadership educational administration adult education politics in education, global change and adult learning. Total annual research expenditures: $547,440. *Unit head:* Dr. Tara Fenwick, Head, 604-822-5359, Fax: 604-82-4244. *Application contact:* Christine Adams, Graduate Secretary, 604-822-6647, Fax: 604-822-4244, E-mail: grad.edst@ubc.ca.

University of Calgary, Faculty of Graduate Studies, Faculty of Education, Graduate Division of Educational Research, Calgary, AB T2N 1N4, Canada. Offers community rehabilitation and disability studies (M Ed, M Sc, Ed D, PhD, Graduate Certificate, Graduate Diploma); curriculum, teaching and learning (M Ed, M Sc, MA, Ed D, PhD, Graduate Certificate, Graduate Diploma); educational contexts (M Ed, MA, Ed D, PhD, Graduate Certificate, Graduate Diploma); educational leadership (M Ed, MA, Ed D, PhD, Graduate Certificate, Graduate Diploma); educational technology (M Ed, M Sc, MA, Ed D, PhD, Graduate Certificate, Graduate Diploma); gifted education (M Sc, MA, Ed D, PhD, Graduate Certificate, Graduate Diploma); higher education administration (Ed D); interpretive studies in education (M Ed, M Sc, MA, Ed D, PhD, Graduate Certificate, Graduate Diploma); second language teaching (M Ed, Ed D, PhD, Graduate Certificate, Graduate Diploma); teaching English as a second language (M Ed, M Sc, MA, Ed D, PhD, Graduate Certificate, Graduate Diploma); workplace and adult learning (M Ed, MA, Ed D, PhD, Graduate Certificate, Graduate Diploma). Ed D in both higher education administration and educational leadership offered via distance delivery. Part-time and evening/weekend programs available. Postbaccalaureate distance learning degree programs offered (minimal on-campus study). *Faculty:* 44 full-time, 52 part-time/adjunct. *Students:* 488 full-time, 550 part-time. 400 applicants, 50% accepted. In 2006, 102 master's, 18 doctorates awarded. *Degree requirements:* For master's, thesis (for some programs); for doctorate, thesis/dissertation, candidacy exam. *Entrance requirements:* For master's, minimum GPA of 3.0, 3 letters of reference; for doctorate, minimum GPA of 3.5, 3 letters of reference; for other advanced degree, minimum GPA of 3.0. Additional exam requirements/recommendations for international students: Required—TOEFL, IELTS. *Application deadline:* For fall admission, 2/15 for domestic students, 2/5 for international students; for winter admission, 6/15 for domestic and international students. Application fee: $100. Electronic applications accepted.

Financial support: In 2006–07, research assistantships (averaging $3,920 per year); teaching assistantships, career-related internships or fieldwork, scholarships/grants, and unspecified assistantships also available. Financial award application deadline: 2/1. *Faculty research:* Curriculum, leadership, technology, contexts, gifted, second language teaching, work place and adult learning. *Unit head:* Dr. Charles F. Webber, Associate Dean, 403-220-5675, Fax: 403-282-3005, E-mail: cwebber@ucalgary.ca. *Application contact:* Patricia A. Brown, Program Officer, Graduate Division of Educational Research, 403-220-3178, Fax: 403-282-3005, E-mail: brownp@ucalgary.ca.

University of Central Oklahoma, College of Graduate Studies and Research, College of Education, Department of Occupational and Technical Education, Program in General Education, Edmond, OK 73034-5209. Offers M Ed. *Accreditation:* NCATE. Part-time programs available. *Entrance requirements:* For master's, GRE General Test. Additional exam requirements/recommendations for international students: Required—TOEFL (minimum score 550 paper-based; 213 computer-based). Electronic applications accepted. *Faculty research:* Community college education.

University of Connecticut, Graduate School, Neag School of Education, Department of Educational Leadership, Field of Higher Education and Student Affairs, Storrs, CT 06269. Offers MA. *Accreditation:* NCATE. *Faculty:* 5 full-time (2 women). *Degree requirements:* For master's, thesis or alternative, comprehensive exam. *Entrance requirements:* Additional exam requirements/recommendations for international students: Required—TOEFL (minimum score 550 paper-based; 213 computer-based). *Application deadline:* For fall admission, 2/1 priority date for domestic and international students; for spring admission, 11/1 for domestic students, 10/1 for international students. Applications are processed on a rolling basis. Application fee: $55. Electronic applications accepted. *Financial support:* In 2006–07, 28 research assistantships with full tuition reimbursements, 3 teaching assistantships with full tuition reimbursements were awarded; fellowships, Federal Work-Study, scholarships/grants, health care benefits, and unspecified assistantships also available. Financial award application deadline: 2/1; financial award applicants required to submit FAFSA. *Application contact:* Lisa Rasicot, Graduate Coordinator, 860-486-3065, Fax: 860-486-0210, E-mail: soeadm02@uconnvm.uconn.edu.

University of Delaware, College of Human Services, Education and Public Policy and Department of Individual and Family Studies, Program in Counseling in Higher Education, Newark, DE 19716. Offers M Ed, MA. *Accreditation:* NCATE. *Degree requirements:* For master's, comprehensive exam. *Entrance requirements:* For master's, GRE (quantitative and verbal), on-campus interview, letters of recommendation. Additional exam requirements/recommendations for international students: Required—TOEFL (minimum score 600 paper-based). Electronic applications accepted. *Faculty research:* Counseling outcomes, student culture, group counseling.

University of Denver, College of Education, Denver, CO 80208. Offers counseling psychology (MA, PhD); curriculum and instruction (MA, PhD, Certificate), including curriculum leadership (MA, PhD); educational administration and policy studies (Certificate); educational psychology (MA, PhD, Ed S), including child and family studies (MA, PhD), quantitative research methods (MA, PhD); school psychology (PhD, Ed S); higher education and adult studies (MA, PhD); library and information science (MLIS); library and information sciences (Certificate); school administration (PhD). *Accreditation:* ALA; APA (one or more programs are accredited). Part-time and evening/weekend programs available. Postbaccalaureate distance learning degree programs offered (no on-campus study). *Faculty:* 28 full-time (18 women). *Students:* 293 full-time (240 women), 439 part-time (357 women); includes 102 minority (28 African Americans, 7 American Indian/Alaska Native, 14 Asian Americans or Pacific Islanders, 53 Hispanic Americans), 11 international. Average age 34. 574 applicants, 72% accepted. In 2006, 168 master's, 28 doctorates, 67 other advanced degrees awarded. Terminal master's awarded for partial completion of doctoral program. *Degree requirements:* For master's, comprehensive exam; for doctorate, 2 foreign languages, thesis/dissertation, comprehensive exam. *Entrance requirements:* For master's, GRE General Test or MAT (for most programs); for doctorate, GRE General Test or MAT. *Application deadline:* Applications are processed on a rolling basis. Application fee: $50. Electronic applications accepted. *Expenses:* Tuition: Full-time $29,628; part-time $823 per credit. *Financial support:* In 2006–07, 51 teaching assistantships with full and partial tuition reimbursements (averaging $6,700 per year) were awarded; career-related internships or fieldwork, Federal Work-Study, institutionally sponsored loans, and scholarships/grants also available. Support available to part-time students. Financial award application deadline: 3/1; financial award applicants required to submit FAFSA. *Faculty research:* Parkinson's disease, personnel training, development and assessments, gifted education, service learning, transportation, public schools. Total annual research expenditures: $172,000. *Unit head:* Dr. Virginia Maloney, Dean, 303-871-2509. *Application contact:* Linda McCarthy, Contact, 303-871-2509, E-mail: edinfo@du.edu.

University of Florida, Graduate School, College of Education, Department of Educational Administration and Policy, Gainesville, FL 32611. Offers curriculum and instruction (Ed D, PhD); educational leadership (M Ed, MAE, Ed D, PhD, Ed S); higher education administration (Ed D, PhD, Ed S); student personnel in higher education (M Ed, MAE); PhD/JD. *Accreditation:* NCATE. *Faculty:* 10 full-time (3 women). *Degree requirements:* For master's, thesis optional; for doctorate, variable foreign language requirement, thesis/dissertation. *Entrance requirements:* For master's, GRE General Test, minimum GPA of 3.0, teaching experience; for doctorate and Ed S, GRE General Test, minimum GPA of 3.0. Additional exam requirements/recommendations for international students: Required—TOEFL (minimum score 550 paper-based; 213 computer-based). *Application deadline:* For fall admission, 6/1 priority date for domestic students. Applications are processed on a rolling basis. Application fee: $30. Electronic applications accepted. *Expenses:* Tuition, state resident: full-time $6,827. Tuition, nonresident: full-time $21,951. Required fees: $999. *Financial support:* In 2006–07, 2 research assistantships (averaging $9,424 per year) were awarded; fellowships, teaching assistantships, career-related internships or fieldwork and unspecified assistantships also available. *Faculty research:* Educational finance, community education, middle school curriculum, community college administration. *Unit head:* Linda Hagedorn, Chair, 352-392-2391 Ext. 275. *Application contact:* Dr. Katherine Gratto, Coordinator, 352-392-2391 Ext. 274, Fax: 352-392-0038, E-mail: kgratto@coe.ufl.edu.

University of Georgia, Graduate School, College of Education, Program in Higher Education, Athens, GA 30602. Offers Ed D, PhD. *Accreditation:* NCATE. *Faculty:* 11 full-time (4 women). *Students:* 15 full-time (11 women), 33 part-time (17 women); includes 7 minority (6 African Americans, 1 Hispanic American), 2 international. 23 applicants, 43% accepted, 6 enrolled. *Degree requirements:* For doctorate, thesis/dissertation. *Entrance requirements:* For doctorate, GRE General Test. *Application deadline:* For fall admission, 7/1 priority date for domestic students; for spring admission, 11/15 for domestic students. Application fee: $50. Electronic applications accepted. *Financial support:* Fellowships, research assistantships, teaching assistantships, unspecified assistantships available. *Unit head:* Dr. Libby V. Morris, Director, 706-542-0580, Fax: 706-542-7588, E-mail: lvmorris@uga.edu. *Application contact:* Dr. Christopher Morphew, Graduate Coordinator, 706-542-573, Fax: 706-542-7588, E-mail: morphew@uga.edu.

University of Houston, College of Education, Department of Educational Leadership and Cultural Studies, Houston, TX 77204. Offers educational administration (M Ed, Ed D); higher education (M Ed); historical, social, and cultural foundations of education (M Ed, Ed D). *Accreditation:* NCATE. Part-time and evening/weekend programs available. *Faculty:* 8 full-time (6 women), 8 part-time/adjunct (3 women). *Students:* 19 full-time (12 women), 169 part-time (110 women); includes 72 minority (39 African Americans, 10 Asian Americans or Pacific Islanders, 23 Hispanic Americans), 3 international. Average age 36. 89 applicants, 60% accepted, 43 enrolled. In 2006, 31 master's, 5 doctorates awarded. *Degree requirements:* For master's, comprehensive exam or thesis; for doctorate, thesis/dissertation, comprehensive exam. *Entrance requirements:* For master's, GRE General Test or MAT, minimum GPA of 3.0 in last 60 hours of course work; for doctorate, GRE General Test, interview, minimum GPA of 3.0 in

last 60 hours. *Application deadline:* For fall admission, 7/18 priority date for domestic students; for spring admission, 12/18 for domestic students. Applications are processed on a rolling basis. Application fee: $35 ($75 for international students). *Expenses:* Tuition, state resident: full-time $5,429; part-time $226 per credit. Tuition, nonresident: full-time $12,029; part-time $501 per credit. Required fees: $2,454. *Financial support:* In 2006–07, 1 fellowship with full tuition reimbursement (averaging $9,500 per year), 1 research assistantship with full tuition reimbursement (averaging $9,500 per year), 1 teaching assistantship with full tuition reimbursement (averaging $9,500 per year) were awarded; career-related internships or fieldwork, Federal Work-Study, institutionally sponsored loans, scholarships/grants, health care benefits, and unspecified assistantships also available. Support available to part-time students. Financial award application deadline: 3/10; financial award applicants required to submit FAFSA. *Faculty research:* Change, supervision, multiculturalism, evaluation, policy. *Unit head:* Robert McPherson, Interim Dean, 713-743-5003, Fax: 713-743-8650, E-mail: bmcph@uh.edu. *Application contact:* Rose L. Hernandez, Office Assistant, 713-743-5044, Fax: 713-743-4979.

University of Illinois at Urbana–Champaign, Graduate College, College of Education, Department of Education, Organization and Leadership, Champaign, IL 61820. Offers Ed M, MA, MS, Ed D, PhD, CAS. Part-time programs available. *Faculty:* 8 full-time (2 women), 1 part-time/adjunct (0 women). *Students:* 32 full-time (17 women), 172 part-time (116 women); includes 29 minority (22 African Americans, 3 Asian Americans or Pacific Islanders, 4 Hispanic Americans), 1 international. 100 applicants, 68% accepted, 31 enrolled. In 2006, 18 master's, 15 doctorates, 4 other advanced degrees awarded. *Degree requirements:* For doctorate, thesis/dissertation. *Entrance requirements:* For master's, GRE or MAT, interview, minimum GPA of 3.0; for doctorate, GRE General Test or MAT, interview, minimum GPA of 3.0. *Application deadline:* For fall admission, 1/15 for domestic students; for spring admission, 4/15 for domestic students. Applications are processed on a rolling basis. Application fee: $50 ($60 for international students). Electronic applications accepted. *Financial support:* In 2006–07, 4 fellowships, 8 research assistantships, 2 teaching assistantships were awarded; tuition waivers (full and partial) also available. Financial award application deadline: 1/15. *Unit head:* Carolyn M. Shields, Head, 217-333-2155, Fax: 217-244-3378, E-mail: cshields@uiuc.edu. *Application contact:* Jean Bettridge, Assistant to the Head, 217-333-2155, Fax: 217-244-3378, E-mail: jeanb@uiuc.edu.

The University of Iowa, Graduate College, College of Education, Department of Educational Policy and Leadership Studies, Program in Higher Education, Iowa City, IA 52242-1316. Offers MA, PhD, Ed S, JD/PhD. *Faculty:* 6 full-time. *Students:* 16 full-time (8 women), 30 part-time (18 women); includes 2 minority (1 African American, 1 Asian American or Pacific Islander), 8 international. 22 applicants, 73% accepted, 10 enrolled. In 2006, 3 master's, 1 doctorate, 1 other advanced degree awarded. *Degree requirements:* For master's and Ed S, exam; for doctorate, thesis/dissertation, comprehensive exam, registration. *Entrance requirements:* For master's, doctorate, and Ed S, GRE General Test, minimum GPA of 3.0. Additional exam requirements/recommendations for international students: Required—TOEFL (minimum score 550 paper-based; 213 computer-based; 81 iBT). *Application deadline:* For fall admission, 4/15 for domestic students. Application fee: $60 ($85 for international students). Electronic applications accepted. *Financial support:* In 2006–07, 2 fellowships, 9 research assistantships with partial tuition reimbursements, 7 teaching assistantships with partial tuition reimbursements were awarded; career-related internships or fieldwork also available. Financial award applicants required to submit FAFSA. *Unit head:* Chris Ogren, Program Coordinator, 319-335-5202, Fax: 319-384-0587.

University of Kansas, Graduate Studies, School of Education, Department of Educational Leadership and Policy Studies, Program in Higher Education Administration, Lawrence, KS 66045. Offers MS Ed. Part-time and evening/weekend programs available. *Faculty:* 19. *Students:* 43 full-time (30 women), 16 part-time (13 women); includes 6 minority (4 African Americans, 2 Hispanic Americans), 3 international. Average age 28. 47 applicants, 66% accepted. In 2006, 19 degrees awarded. *Degree requirements:* For master's, comprehensive exam. *Entrance requirements:* For master's, minimum GPA of 3.0. Additional exam requirements/recommendations for international students: Required—TOEFL. *Application deadline:* For fall admission, 3/9 for domestic and international students; for winter admission, 7/1 for domestic and international students; for spring admission, 11/1 for domestic and international students. Application fee: $55 ($60 for international students). Electronic applications accepted. *Expenses:* Tuition, area resident: Part-time $227 per credit. Tuition, state resident: part-time $543 per credit. Tuition and fees vary according to course load, campus/location, program and reciprocity agreements. *Financial support:* Fellowships with full and partial tuition reimbursements, career-related internships or fieldwork available. Financial award application deadline: 3/15. *Faculty research:* Institutional drift, higher education policy, faculty issues, research on college students. *Application contact:* Denise Brubaker, Admissions Coordinator, 785-864-4458, Fax: 785-864-4697, E-mail: elps@ku.edu.

University of Kansas, Graduate Studies, School of Education, Department of Educational Leadership and Policy Studies, Program in Policy Studies, Lawrence, KS 66045. Offers foundations (Ed D, PhD); higher education (Ed D, PhD); school administration (Ed D, PhD). Part-time and evening/weekend programs available. *Faculty:* 19. *Students:* 18 full-time (10 women), 133 part-time (69 women); includes 17 minority (7 African Americans, 4 American Indian/Alaska Native, 2 Asian Americans or Pacific Islanders, 4 Hispanic Americans), 5 international. Average age 40. 17 applicants, 59% accepted. In 2006, 21 degrees awarded. *Degree requirements:* For doctorate, thesis/dissertation, comprehensive exam. *Entrance requirements:* For doctorate, GRE General Test, minimum graduate GPA of 3.5. Additional exam requirements/recommendations for international students: Required—TOEFL. *Application deadline:* For fall admission, 7/1 priority date for domestic and international students; for spring admission, 11/1 priority date for domestic and international students. Applications are processed on a rolling basis. Application fee: $55 ($60 for international students). Electronic applications accepted. *Expenses:* Tuition, area resident: Part-time $227 per credit. Tuition, state resident: part-time $543 per credit. Tuition and fees vary according to course load, campus/location, program and reciprocity agreements. *Financial support:* Fellowships, research assistantships with full and partial tuition reimbursements, teaching assistantships with full and partial tuition reimbursements available. Financial award application deadline: 3/15. *Faculty research:* Policy studies in higher education, policy studies in foundations, policy studies in educational leaderships. *Application contact:* Denise Brubaker, Admissions Coordinator, 785-864-4458, Fax: 785-864-4697, E-mail: elps@ku.edu.

University of Kentucky, Graduate School, College of Education, Program in Educational Policy Studies and Evaluation, Lexington, KY 40506-0032. Offers educational policy studies and evaluation (Ed D); higher education (MS Ed, PhD). *Accreditation:* NCATE. *Students:* 50 full-time (37 women), 30 part-time (19 women); includes 7 minority (all African Americans), 2 international. Average age 38. In 2006, 9 master's, 3 doctorates awarded. Terminal master's awarded for partial completion of doctoral program. *Median time to degree:* Of those who began their doctoral program in fall 1998, 46% received their degree in 8 years or less. *Degree requirements:* For master's, thesis optional; for doctorate, thesis/dissertation, comprehensive exam. *Entrance requirements:* For master's, GRE General Test, minimum undergraduate GPA of 2.75; for doctorate, GRE General Test, minimum graduate GPA of 3.0. Additional exam requirements/recommendations for international students: Required—TOEFL (minimum score 550 paper-based; 213 computer-based). *Application deadline:* For fall admission, 7/17 priority date for domestic students, 2/1 priority date for international students; for spring admission, 12/13 priority date for domestic students, 6/15 priority date for international students. Application fee: $40 ($55 for international students). Electronic applications accepted. *Expenses:* Tuition, state resident: full-time $7,670; part-time $401 per credit hour. Tuition, nonresident: full-time $16,158; part-time $873 per credit hour. *Financial support:* In 2006–07, 9 students received support, including 1 fellowship with full tuition reimbursement available (averaging $4,500 per year), 2 research assistantships with full tuition reimbursements available (averaging $16,748 per year), 6 teaching assistantships with full tuition reimbursements available (averaging $950 per year); career-related internships or fieldwork, Federal Work-Study, institutionally sponsored loans, scholarships/grants, traineeships, health care benefits, tuition waivers

Higher Education

University of Kentucky (continued)

(partial), and unspecified assistantships also available. Support available to part-time students. Financial award application deadline: 3/15. *Faculty research:* Studies in higher education; comparative and international education; evaluation of educational programs, policies, and reform; student, teacher, and faculty cultures; gender and education. *Unit head:* Richard Angelo, Director of Graduate Studies, 859-257-3993, Fax: 859-257-4243, E-mail: angelo@pop.uky.edu. *Application contact:* Dr. Brian Jackson, Senior Associate Dean, 859-257-4667, Fax: 859-257-4676, E-mail: brian.jackson@uky.edu.

University of Louisville, Graduate School, College of Education and Human Development, Department of Leadership, Foundations and Human Resource Education, Program in Higher Education, Louisville, KY 40292-0001. Offers MA, Ed S. *Accreditation:* NCATE. *Students:* 15 full-time (11 women), 50 part-time (29 women); includes 6 minority (all African Americans), 1 international. Average age 34. In 2006, 15 degrees awarded. *Entrance requirements:* For master's and Ed S, GRE General Test. *Application deadline:* Applications are processed on a rolling basis. Application fee: $50. Electronic applications accepted. *Financial support:* Fellowships, research assistantships, teaching assistantships, Federal Work-Study and scholarships/grants available. *Unit head:* Dr. John F. Welsh, Director, 502-852-0606, Fax: 502-852-4563, E-mail: john.welsh@louisville.edu.

University of Maine, Graduate School, College of Education and Human Development, Program in Higher Education, Orono, ME 04469. Offers M Ed, MA, MS, Ed D, CAS. *Accreditation:* NCATE. Part-time and evening/weekend programs available. *Students:* 27 full-time (19 women), 25 part-time (16 women); includes 1 minority (Hispanic American), 2 international. Average age 32. 28 applicants, 86% accepted, 15 enrolled. In 2006, 16 master's, 1 doctorate, 2 other advanced degrees awarded. *Degree requirements:* For master's, thesis or alternative. *Entrance requirements:* For master's, MAT; for doctorate, GRE General Test, MA, M Ed, or MS; for CAS, MA, M Ed, or MS. Additional exam requirements/recommendations for international students: Required—TOEFL. *Application deadline:* For fall admission, 2/1 priority date for domestic students. Applications are processed on a rolling basis. Application fee: $50. Electronic applications accepted. *Financial support:* Research assistantships with tuition reimbursements, teaching assistantships, Federal Work-Study, institutionally sponsored loans, tuition waivers (full and partial), and unspecified assistantships available. Financial award application deadline: 3/1. *Unit head:* Dr. Dorothy Breen, Coordinator, 207-581-2444, Fax: 207-581-2423. *Application contact:* Scott G. Delcourt, Associate Dean of the Graduate School, 207-581-3219, Fax: 207-581-3232, E-mail: graduate@maine.edu.

University of Mary, Program in Education, Bismarck, ND 58504-9652. Offers college teaching (MS Ed); curriculum and instruction (MS Ed); early childhood education (MS Ed); early childhood special education (MS Ed); elementary education administration (MS Ed); reading (MS Ed); secondary education administration (MS Ed); special education (MS Ed). Part-time programs available. *Faculty:* 8 full-time (4 women), 12 part-time/adjunct (7 women). *Students:* 2 full-time (1 woman), 34 part-time (25 women), 2 international. Average age 35. In 2006, 17 degrees awarded. *Degree requirements:* For master's, portfolio or thesis. *Entrance requirements:* For master's, interview, letters of reference. *Application deadline:* Applications are processed on a rolling basis. Application fee: $40. *Financial support:* In 2006–07, 1 teaching assistantship with full tuition reimbursement was awarded; career-related internships or fieldwork also available. Support available to part-time students. Financial award application deadline: 8/1; financial award applicants required to submit FAFSA. *Faculty research:* Innovative pedagogy in higher education, technology in education, content standards, children of poverty, children with diverse learning needs. *Unit head:* Dr. Rebecca Yunker Salveson, Director, 701-355-8186, E-mail: rysalves@umary.edu. *Application contact:* Leona Friedig, Administrative Secretary, 701-355-8058, E-mail: lfriedig@umary.edu.

University of Massachusetts Amherst, Graduate School, School of Education, Program in Education, Amherst, MA 01003. Offers cultural diversity and curriculum reform (M Ed, Ed D, CAGS); early childhood education and development (M Ed, Ed D, CAGS); educational administration (M Ed, Ed D, CAGS); elementary teacher education (M Ed, Ed D, CAGS); higher education (M Ed, Ed D, CAGS); international education (M Ed, Ed D, CAGS); mathematics, science, and instructional technology (M Ed, Ed D, CAGS); physical education teacher education (M Ed, Ed D, CAGS); reading and writing (M Ed, Ed D, CAGS); research and evaluation methods (M Ed, Ed D, CAGS); school psychology and school counseling (M Ed, Ed D, CAGS); secondary teacher education (M Ed, Ed D, CAGS); social justice education (M Ed, Ed D, CAGS); special education (M Ed, Ed D, CAGS). *Accreditation:* NCATE. *Students:* 418 full-time (286 women), 447 part-time (319 women); includes 147 minority (70 African Americans, 4 American Indian/Alaska Native, 28 Asian Americans or Pacific Islanders, 45 Hispanic Americans), 81 international. Average age 36. In 2006, 260 master's, 30 doctorates awarded. *Degree requirements:* For doctorate, thesis/dissertation. *Entrance requirements:* For master's and doctorate, GRE General Test. Additional exam requirements/recommendations for international students: Required—TOEFL (minimum score 530 paper-based; 197 computer-based). *Application deadline:* For fall admission, 1/15 for domestic and international students; for spring admission, 10/1 for domestic and international students. Applications are processed on a rolling basis. Application fee: $40 ($65 for international students). Electronic applications accepted. *Expenses:* Tuition, state resident: full-time $2,640; part-time $110 per credit. Tuition, nonresident: full-time $9,936; part-time $414 per credit. Required fees: $8,969; $3,129 per term. One-time fee: $257 full-time. Tuition and fees vary according to class time, course load, campus/location and reciprocity agreements. *Financial support:* Fellowships with full tuition reimbursements, research assistantships with full tuition reimbursements, teaching assistantships with full tuition reimbursements, career-related internships or fieldwork, Federal Work-Study, scholarships/grants, traineeships, and unspecified assistantships available. Support available to part-time students. Financial award application deadline: 1/15. *Unit head:* Linda L. Griffin, Professor, 413-545-6984.

University of Massachusetts Boston, Office of Graduate Studies, Graduate College of Education, School Organization, Curriculum and Instruction Department, Boston, MA 02125-3393. Offers education (M Ed, Ed D), including elementary and secondary education/certification (M Ed), higher education administration (Ed D), teacher certification (M Ed), urban school leadership (Ed D); educational administration (M Ed, CAGS); special education (M Ed). *Students:* 141 full-time (103 women), 403 part-time (291 women); includes 81 minority (44 African Americans, 1 American Indian/Alaska Native, 13 Asian Americans or Pacific Islanders, 23 Hispanic Americans), 7 international. Average age 37. 381 applicants, 72% accepted, 178 enrolled. In 2006, 117 master's, 18 doctorates, 10 other advanced degrees awarded. *Degree requirements:* For master's and CAGS, comprehensive exam; for doctorate, thesis/dissertation, comprehensive exam. *Entrance requirements:* For master's, GRE General Test or MAT; for doctorate, GRE General Test or MAT, minimum GPA of 2.75; for CAGS, minimum GPA of 2.75. *Application deadline:* For fall admission, 3/1 for domestic students. Application fee: $25 ($35 for international students). *Expenses:* Tuition, state resident: full-time $2,590; part-time $301 per credit. Tuition, nonresident: full-time $9,758; part-time $427 per credit. One-time fee: $495 full-time. *Financial support:* In 2006–07, 37 research assistantships with full tuition reimbursements (averaging $2,000 per year), teaching assistantships with full tuition reimbursements (averaging $2,000 per year) were awarded; unspecified assistantships also available. Financial award application deadline: 3/1; financial award applicants required to submit FAFSA. *Unit head:* Dr. Lisa Coonsalves, Director, 617-287-7642, E-mail: lisa.gonsalves@umb.edu. *Application contact:* Peggy Roldan, Graduate Admissions Coordinator, 617-287-6400, Fax: 617-287-6236, E-mail: bos.gadm@dpc.umassp.edu.

University of Massachusetts Boston, Office of Graduate Studies, Graduate College of Education, School Organization, Curriculum and Instruction Department, Program in Education, Track in Higher Education Administration, Boston, MA 02125-3393. Offers Ed D. *Accreditation:* NCATE. Part-time and evening/weekend programs available. *Students:* 2 full-time (both women), 107 part-time (77 women); includes 29 minority (15 African Americans, 4 Asian Americans or Pacific Islanders, 10 Hispanic Americans), 1 international. Average age

48. 26 applicants, 42% accepted, 9 enrolled. In 2006, 2 degrees awarded. *Median time to degree:* Doctorate–12 years full-time. *Degree requirements:* For doctorate, thesis/dissertation, comprehensive exam. *Entrance requirements:* For doctorate, GRE General Test or MAT, minimum GPA of 2.75. *Application deadline:* For fall admission, 3/1 for domestic students. Application fee: $25 ($40 for international students). *Expenses:* Tuition, state resident: full-time $2,590; part-time $301 per credit. Tuition, nonresident: full-time $9,758; part-time $427 per credit. One-time fee: $495 full-time. *Financial support:* In 2006–07, research assistantships with full tuition reimbursements (averaging $13,000 per year); teaching assistantships, career-related internships or fieldwork, Federal Work-Study, and unspecified assistantships also available. Support available to part-time students. Financial award application deadline: 3/1; financial award applicants required to submit FAFSA. *Faculty research:* Women, higher education and professionalization, school reform, urban classroom, higher education policy. *Unit head:* Dr. Dwight Giles, Coordinator, 617-287-7621, E-mail: dwight.giles@umb.edu. *Application contact:* Peggy Roldan, Graduate Admissions Coordinator, 617-287-6400, Fax: 617-287-6236, E-mail: bos.gadm@dpc.umassp.edu.

University of Memphis, Graduate School, College of Education, Department of Leadership, Memphis, TN 38152. Offers adult education (Ed D); community education (Ed D); education (Ed S); educational leadership (Ed D); higher education (Ed D); leadership (MS); policy studies (Ed D); school administration and supervision (MS). *Accreditation:* NCATE. *Degree requirements:* For master's, thesis optional; for doctorate, thesis/dissertation, comprehensive exam; for Ed S, thesis or alternative, comprehensive exam. *Entrance requirements:* For master's, GRE General Test or MAT; for doctorate, GRE General Test, GRE Subject Test, 3 years of teaching experience; for Ed S, GRE General Test. *Faculty research:* Organizational learning, gender issues, leadership, technology and learning, principal preparation.

University of Miami, Graduate School, School of Education, Department of Educational and Psychological Studies, Program in Higher Education Administration, Coral Gables, FL 33124. Offers higher education administration (MS Ed), including enrollment management, student life and development; higher education administration/enrollment management (Certificate). *Accreditation:* NCATE. *Students:* 5 full-time (4 women), 11 part-time (10 women); includes 9 minority (4 African Americans, 1 Asian American or Pacific Islander, 4 Hispanic Americans). Average age 33. 8 applicants, 100% accepted, 5 enrolled. In 2006, 2 degrees awarded. *Entrance requirements:* For master's, GRE General Test. Additional exam requirements/recommendations for international students: Required—TOEFL (minimum score 550 paper-based; 212 computer-based). *Application deadline:* Applications are processed on a rolling basis. Application fee: $50. Electronic applications accepted. *Financial support:* In 2006–07, 16 students received support; fellowships with partial tuition reimbursements available, research assistantships with partial tuition reimbursements available, career-related internships or fieldwork, Federal Work-Study, institutionally sponsored loans, scholarships/grants, and unspecified assistantships available. Financial award application deadline: 3/1; financial award applicants required to submit FAFSA. *Unit head:* Dr. Carol Anne Phekoo, Coordinator, 305-284-5013, Fax: 305-284-3003, E-mail: cphekoo@miami.edu. *Application contact:* Shelley Lue Foung, Senior Administrative Assistant, 305-284-3001, Fax: 305-284-3003, E-mail: sluefoung@miami.edu.

University of Michigan, Horace H. Rackham School of Graduate Studies, School of Education, Center for the Study of Higher and Postsecondary Education, Ann Arbor, MI 48109. Offers academic affairs and student development (PhD); education (AM); higher education (AM); individually designed concentration (PhD); organizational behavior and management (PhD); public policy (PhD); research, evaluation, and assessment (PhD); MBA/MA; MPP/MA. *Students:* 674 applicants, 41% accepted, 175 enrolled. In 2006, 134 master's, 43 doctorates awarded. Terminal master's awarded for partial completion of doctoral program. *Median time to degree:* Of those who began their doctoral program in fall 1998, 51% received their degree in 8 years or less. *Degree requirements:* For master's, thesis optional; for doctorate, thesis/dissertation, comprehensive exam. *Entrance requirements:* For master's and doctorate, GRE General Test. Additional exam requirements/recommendations for international students: Required—TOEFL (minimum score 600 paper-based; 250 computer-based). *Application deadline:* For fall admission, 12/1 priority date for domestic students, 12/1 for international students. Application fee: $60 ($75 for international students). Electronic applications accepted. *Financial support:* In 2006–07, 215 fellowships (averaging $5,852 per year), 109 research assistantships with full tuition reimbursements (averaging $14,695 per year), 32 teaching assistantships with full tuition reimbursements (averaging $14,756 per year) were awarded; career-related internships or fieldwork, Federal Work-Study, health care benefits, and tuition waivers also available. Support available to part-time students. Financial award applicants required to submit FAFSA. *Unit head:* Dr. Deborah Carter, Chairperson, 734-647-1981, Fax: 734-764-2510, E-mail: dfcarter@umich.edu. *Application contact:* Roberta Perry, Office of Student Services, 734-764-7563, Fax: 734-763-1495, E-mail: ed.grad.admit@umich.edu.

University of Minnesota, Twin Cities Campus, Graduate School, College of Education and Human Development, Department of Educational Policy and Administration, Program in Higher Education, Minneapolis, MN 55455-0213. Offers MA, PhD. *Students:* 67 full-time (43 women), 82 part-time (47 women); includes 17 minority (10 African Americans, 2 American Indian/Alaska Native, 1 Asian American or Pacific Islander, 4 Hispanic Americans), 22 international. Average age 38. 60 applicants, 73% accepted, 34 enrolled. In 2006, 12 master's, 5 doctorates awarded. *Expenses:* Tuition, state resident: full-time $9,302; part-time $775 per credit. Tuition, nonresident: full-time $16,400; part-time $1,367 per credit. Full-time tuition and fees vary according to class time, course load, program, reciprocity agreements and student level. *Application contact:* Dr. Mary Bents, Associate Dean, 612-625-6501, Fax: 612-626-1580, E-mail: mbents@tc.umn.edu.

University of Mississippi, Graduate School, School of Education, Department of Educational Leadership and Counselor Education, Oxford, University, MS 38677. Offers counselor education (M Ed, PhD, Specialist); educational leadership (PhD); educational leadership and counselor education (M Ed, MA, Ed D, Ed S); higher education/student personnel (MA). *Accreditation:* ACA; NCATE. *Faculty:* 14 full-time (9 women), 4 part-time/adjunct (2 women). *Students:* 171 full-time (113 women), 158 part-time (110 women); includes 93 minority (88 African Americans, 2 Asian Americans or Pacific Islanders, 3 Hispanic Americans), 11 international. In 2006, 76 master's, 9 doctorates, 22 other advanced degrees awarded. *Degree requirements:* For doctorate, thesis/dissertation. *Entrance requirements:* For master's, GRE General Test, minimum GPA of 3.0; for doctorate, GRE General Test. Additional exam requirements/recommendations for international students: Required—TOEFL. *Application deadline:* For fall admission, 4/1 for domestic students; for spring admission, 10/1 for domestic students. Applications are processed on a rolling basis. Application fee: $25. Electronic applications accepted. *Expenses:* Tuition, state resident: full-time $4,602; part-time $256 per credit hour. Tuition, nonresident: full-time $10,566; part-time $587 per credit hour. *Financial support:* Scholarships/grants available. Financial award application deadline: 3/1; financial award applicants required to submit FAFSA. *Unit head:* Dr. Timothy Letzring, Acting Chair, 662-915-7069, E-mail: fdl@olemiss.edu.

University of Missouri–Columbia, Graduate School, College of Education, Department of Educational Leadership and Policy Analysis, Columbia, MO 65211. Offers education administration (M Ed, MA, Ed D, PhD, Ed S); higher and adult education (M Ed, MA, Ed D, PhD, Ed S). Part-time programs available. *Faculty:* 17 full-time (11 women). *Students:* 224 full-time (136 women), 133 part-time (86 women); includes 41 minority (25 African Americans, 5 American Indian/Alaska Native, 3 Asian Americans or Pacific Islanders, 8 Hispanic Americans), 16 international. In 2006, 27 master's, 31 doctorates, 9 other advanced degrees awarded. *Degree requirements:* For doctorate, variable foreign language requirement, thesis/dissertation. *Entrance requirements:* For master's, GRE General Test, minimum GPA of 3.0; for doctorate, GRE General Test, GRE Subject Test, minimum GPA of 3.5; for Ed S, GRE General Test, GRE Subject Test, minimum GPA of 3.25. *Application deadline:* For fall admission, 12/15 priority date for domestic students. Applications are processed on a rolling basis. Application fee: $45 ($60 for international students). *Financial support:* Fellowships, research assistantships, teaching assistantships, institutionally sponsored loans and scholarships/grants available. *Faculty* *research:* Administrative communication and behavior, middle schools leadership, administration of special education. *Unit head:* Dr. Margaret M. Grogan, Director of Graduate Studies, 573-882-8221, E-mail: groganm@missouri.edu.

University of Missouri–St. Louis, College of Education, Division of Educational Leadership and Policy Studies, St. Louis, MO 63121. Offers adult and higher education (M Ed, Ed D); educational administration (M Ed, Ed D, Ed S), including community education (M Ed), elementary education (M Ed), secondary education (M Ed); educational leadership and policy studies (PhD); institutional research (Certificate). *Accreditation:* NCATE. *Faculty:* 15 full-time (8 women), 2 part-time/adjunct (0 women). *Students:* 37 full-time (27 women), 325 part-time (214 women); includes 130 minority (118 African Americans, 1 American Indian/Alaska Native, 4 Asian Americans or Pacific Islanders, 7 Hispanic Americans), 4 international. Average age 39. In 2006, 64 master's, 12 doctorates, 32 other advanced degrees awarded. *Entrance requirements:* For doctorate, GRE, 3 letters of recommendation. Additional exam requirements/recommendations for international students: Required—TOEFL (minimum score 550 paper-based; 213 computer-based). *Application deadline:* Applications are processed on a rolling basis. Application fee: $35 ($40 for international students). Electronic applications accepted. *Expenses:* Tuition, state resident: part-time $332 per credit hour. Tuition, nonresident: part-time $770 per credit hour. *Financial support:* In 2006–07, 6 research assistantships (averaging $8,235 per year) were awarded. *Faculty research:* Educational policy research; philosophy of education; higher, adult, and vocational education; school initiatives, change, and reform. *Unit head:* Dr. E. Paulette Savage, Chair, 514-516-5944. *Application contact:* 314-516-5458, Fax: 314-516-6996, E-mail: gradadm@umsl.edu.

University of New Hampshire, Graduate School, Interdisciplinary Programs, Program in College Teaching, Durham, NH 03824. Offers MST. Program offered in summer only. Part-time programs available. *Faculty:* 32 full-time. In 2006, 3 degrees awarded. *Entrance requirements:* Additional exam requirements/recommendations for international students: Required—TOEFL (minimum score 550 paper-based; 213 computer-based). *Application deadline:* For fall admission, 4/1 priority date for domestic students, 4/1 for international students; for winter admission, 12/1 priority date for domestic students. Applications are processed on a rolling basis. Application fee: $60. Electronic applications accepted. *Expenses:* Tuition, state resident: full-time $8,540; part-time $474 per credit hour. Tuition, nonresident: full-time $20,990; part-time $862 per credit hour. Required fees: $1,343; $356 per term. Tuition and fees vary according to course load, program and reciprocity agreements. *Financial support:* Fellowships, research assistantships, teaching assistantships available. Financial award application deadline: 2/15. *Unit head:* Dr. Harry J. Richards, Dean, 603-862-3005, Fax: 603-862-0275, E-mail: harry.richards@unh.edu. *Application contact:* Sharon Andrews, Senior Administrative Assistant, 603-862-3005, E-mail: college.teaching@unh.edu.

The University of North Carolina at Greensboro, Graduate School, School of Education, Department of Curriculum and Instruction, Program in Curriculum and Teaching, Greensboro, NC 27412-5001. Offers higher education (PhD); teacher education and development (PhD). *Accreditation:* NCATE. *Students:* 50 full-time (39 women), 51 part-time (37 women); includes 24 minority (21 African Americans, 1 American Indian/Alaska Native, 2 Asian Americans or Pacific Islanders). *Degree requirements:* For doctorate, thesis/dissertation, comprehensive exam. *Entrance requirements:* For doctorate, GRE General Test. Additional exam requirements/recommendations for international students: Required—TOEFL. *Application deadline:* For fall admission, 3/1 for domestic students; for spring admission, 11/1 for domestic students. Applications are processed on a rolling basis. Application fee: $45. Electronic applications accepted. *Expenses:* Tuition, state resident: full-time $2,692. Tuition, nonresident: full-time $13,742. *Financial support:* In 2006–07, 16 students received support; fellowships, research assistantships, teaching assistantships available. *Unit head:* Dr. Barbara B Levin, Director of Graduate Studies, 336-334-3434, E-mail: bblevin@uncg.edu. *Application contact:* Michelle Harkleroad, Director of Graduate Admissions, 336-334-4884, Fax: 336-334-4424, E-mail: mbharkle@uncg.edu.

University of Northern Iowa, Graduate College, College of Education, Department of Educational Leadership, Counseling, and Postsecondary Education, Program in Postsecondary Education, Cedar Falls, IA 50614. Offers student affairs (MAE). *Students:* 19 full-time (13 women), 10 part-time (6 women); includes 7 minority (5 African Americans, 1 American Indian/Alaska Native, 1 Asian American or Pacific Islander). 32 applicants, 66% accepted, 11 enrolled. In 2006, 19 degrees awarded. *Degree requirements:* For master's, research paper. *Entrance requirements:* For master's, 3 years of educational experience, minimum GPA of 3.5. Additional exam requirements/recommendations for international students: Required—TOEFL (minimum score 500 paper-based; 180 computer-based; 61 iBT). *Application deadline:* For fall admission, 8/1 priority date for domestic students. Applications are processed on a rolling basis. Application fee: $30 ($50 for international students). Electronic applications accepted. *Expenses:* Tuition, state resident: full-time $5,936. Tuition, nonresident: full-time $14,074. *Financial support:* Career-related internships or fieldwork, Federal Work-Study, scholarships/grants, and tuition waivers (full) available. Financial award application deadline: 2/1.

University of North Texas, Robert B. Toulouse School of Graduate Studies, College of Education, Department of Counseling, Development and Higher Education, Program in Higher Education, Denton, TX 76203. Offers M Ed, MS, Ed D, PhD. *Accreditation:* NCATE. Evening/weekend programs available. *Students:* 41 full-time (16 women), 87 part-time (56 women); includes 45 minority (28 African Americans, 5 American Indian/Alaska Native, 3 Asian Americans or Pacific Islanders, 9 Hispanic Americans), 8 international. Average age 35. 46 applicants, 35% accepted, 11 enrolled. In 2006, 10 master's, 12 doctorates awarded. *Degree requirements:* For doctorate, thesis/dissertation. *Entrance requirements:* For doctorate, GRE General Test, admissions exam. *Application deadline:* For fall admission, 7/15 for domestic students. Application fee: $50 ($75 for international students). *Expenses:* Tuition, state resident: full-time $3,573; part-time $198 per credit. Tuition, nonresident: full-time $8,577; part-time $476 per credit. Required fees: $1,258; $126 per credit. One-time fee: $150 full-time. Tuition and fees vary according to course load. *Financial support:* Teaching assistantships, career-related internships or fieldwork, Federal Work-Study, and institutionally sponsored loans available. Financial award application deadline: 4/1. *Application contact:* Dr. Barbara Bush, Graduate Adviser, 940-565-2045, E-mail: bbush@coe.unt.edu.

University of Oklahoma, Graduate College, College of Education, Department of Educational Leadership and Policy Studies, Program in Adult and Higher Education, Norman, OK 73019-0390. Offers M Ed, PhD. *Accreditation:* NCATE. Part-time and evening/weekend programs available. *Students:* 60 full-time (41 women), 103 part-time (62 women); includes 47 minority (27 African Americans, 12 American Indian/Alaska Native, 1 Asian American or Pacific Islander, 7 Hispanic Americans), 4 international. 46 applicants, 93% accepted, 26 enrolled. In 2006, 45 master's, 7 doctorates awarded. *Degree requirements:* For master's, comprehensive exam; for doctorate, variable foreign language requirement, thesis/dissertation, general exam. *Entrance requirements:* For master's, minimum GPA of 3.0 in last 60 hours of undergraduate course work; for doctorate, GRE General Test, resumé, 3 letters of reference, scholarly writing sample. Additional exam requirements/recommendations for international students: Required—TOEFL (minimum score 550 paper-based; 213 computer-based). *Application deadline:* For fall admission, 6/1 for domestic students, 4/1 for international students; for spring admission, 10/1 for domestic students, 9/1 for international students. Application fee: $40 ($90 for international students). *Expenses:* Tuition, state resident: full-time $3,180; part-time $133 per credit hour. Tuition, nonresident: full-time $11,347; part-time $473 per credit hour. Required fees: $1,729; $62 per credit hour. $117 per semester. Tuition and fees vary according to course load and program. *Financial support:* Research assistantships with partial tuition reimbursements, teaching assistantships with partial tuition reimbursements, career-related internships or fieldwork, scholarships/grants, health care benefits, tuition waivers (full), and unspecified assistantships available. Support available to part-time students. Financial award applicants required to submit FAFSA. *Faculty research:* Institutional research, student personnel administration, community college, distance education, instructional strategies. *Application contact:* Geri Evans, Programs Officer, 405-325-5978, Fax: 405-325-2403, E-mail: gevans@ou.edu.

University of Pittsburgh, School of Education, Department of Administrative and Policy Studies, Program in Higher Education Management, Pittsburgh, PA 15260. Offers higher education (M Ed, Ed D). Part-time and evening/weekend programs available. *Students:* 18 full-time (12 women), 66 part-time (40 women); includes 11 minority (all African Americans), 2 international. 40 applicants, 53% accepted, 14 enrolled. In 2006, 15 master's, 8 doctorates awarded. *Degree requirements:* For master's and doctorate, thesis/dissertation. *Entrance requirements:* For doctorate, GRE General Test. Additional exam requirements/recommendations for international students: Required—TOEFL. *Application deadline:* For fall admission, 2/1 priority date for domestic students; for spring admission, 11/1 priority date for domestic students. Applications are processed on a rolling basis. Application fee: $50. Electronic applications accepted. *Financial support:* Fellowships, Federal Work-Study and tuition waivers (partial) available. Support available to part-time students. Financial award application deadline: 3/15; financial award applicants required to submit FAFSA. *Application contact:* Joan M. Cutone, Director, School of Education Student Service Center, 412-648-2230, Fax: 412-648-1899, E-mail: soeinfo@pitt.edu.

University of South Carolina, The Graduate School, College of Education, Department of Educational Leadership and Policies, Program in Higher Education and Student Affairs, Columbia, SC 29208. Offers M Ed. *Accreditation:* NCATE. Part-time and evening/weekend programs available. *Degree requirements:* For master's, thesis (for some programs), comprehensive exam. *Entrance requirements:* For master's, GRE General Test or MAT. Electronic applications accepted. *Faculty research:* Minorities in higher education, community college transfer problem, federal role in educational research.

University of Southern Mississippi, Graduate School, College of Education and Psychology, Department of Educational Leadership and Research, Hattiesburg, MS 39406-0001. Offers adult education (M Ed, Ed D, PhD, Ed S); educational administration (M Ed, Ed D, PhD, Ed S); higher education (PhD). *Faculty:* 19 full-time (7 women). *Students:* 86 full-time (66 women), 250 part-time (173 women); includes 102 minority (97 African Americans, 1 American Indian/Alaska Native, 2 Asian Americans or Pacific Islanders, 2 Hispanic Americans), 4 international. Average age 38. 123 applicants, 62% accepted, 72 enrolled. In 2006, 56 master's, 25 doctorates, 41 other advanced degrees awarded. *Degree requirements:* For master's, thesis (for some programs), internship, comprehensive exam, registration; for doctorate, thesis/dissertation, comprehensive exam, registration; for Ed S, thesis (for some programs), comprehensive exam, registration. *Entrance requirements:* For master's, GRE General Test, minimum GPA of 2.75; for doctorate, GRE General Test, minimum GPA of 3.5; for Ed S, GRE General Test, minimum GPA of 3.25. Additional exam requirements/recommendations for international students: Required—TOEFL. *Application deadline:* For fall admission, 3/1 priority date for domestic students, 3/1 for international students. Applications are processed on a rolling basis. Application fee: $25 ($30 for international students). *Financial support:* In 2006–07, 12 research assistantships with full tuition reimbursements (averaging $5,571 per year), 1 teaching assistantship (averaging $5,571 per year) were awarded; career-related internships or fieldwork, Federal Work-Study, and institutionally sponsored loans also available. Financial award application deadline: 3/15. *Faculty research:* Supervision, learning styles, education finance, higher education organization. Total annual research expenditures: $88,500. *Unit head:* Dr. Gaylynn Parker, Interim Chair, 601-266-4589, Fax: 601-266-5141.

University of South Florida, Graduate School, College of Education, Department of Adult, Career and Higher Education, Tampa, FL 33620-9951. Offers adult education (MA, Ed D, PhD, Ed S); career and technical education (MA); higher education/community college teaching (MA, PhD, Ed S); industrial-technical education (MA); vocational education (Ed D, PhD, Ed S). *Faculty:* 11 full-time (5 women), 2 part-time/adjunct (0 women). *Students:* 30 full-time (23 women), 176 part-time (121 women); includes 52 minority (32 African Americans, 1 American Indian/Alaska Native, 1 Asian American or Pacific Islander, 18 Hispanic Americans), 4 international. 104 applicants, 71% accepted, 55 enrolled. In 2006, 56 master's, 5 doctorates awarded. *Entrance requirements:* For master's, GRE General Test, minimum GPA of 3.0 in last 60 hours. *Application deadline:* For fall admission, 6/1 for domestic students; for spring admission, 10/15 for domestic students. Application fee: $30. *Financial support:* Career-related internships or fieldwork, scholarships/grants, and unspecified assistantships available. Total annual research expenditures: $191,880. *Unit head:* Robert Sullins, Interim Dean, E-mail: rsullins@ugs.usf.edu.

The University of Texas at San Antonio, College of Education and Human Development, Department of Counseling, Educational Psychology, and Adult and Higher Education, San Antonio, TX 78249-0617. Offers counseling (MA); counselor education (PhD); education-adult and higher education (MA). Part-time programs available. *Faculty:* 17 full-time (9 women), 16 part-time/adjunct (4 women). *Students:* 154 full-time (125 women), 403 part-time (354 women); includes 299 minority (42 African Americans, 2 American Indian/Alaska Native, 7 Asian Americans or Pacific Islanders, 248 Hispanic Americans), 4 international. Average age 33. 210 applicants, 85% accepted, 172 enrolled. In 2006, 140 degrees awarded. *Degree requirements:* For master's, thesis optional. *Entrance requirements:* For master's, GRE General Test. Additional exam requirements/recommendations for international students: Required—TOEFL (minimum score 500 paper-based; 173 computer-based). *Application deadline:* For fall admission, 7/1 for domestic students, 4/1 for international students; for spring admission, 11/1 for domestic students, 9/1 for international students. Applications are processed on a rolling basis. Application fee: $45 ($80 for international students). Electronic applications accepted. *Expenses:* Tuition, state resident: full-time $1,730; part-time $192 per credit hour. Tuition, nonresident: full-time $6,680; part-time $742 per credit hour. Required fees: $733; $308,359 per credit hour. *Financial support:* In 2006–07, 1 research assistantship (averaging $18,720 per year) was awarded; career-related internships or fieldwork, Federal Work-Study, scholarships/grants, and unspecified assistantships also available. *Faculty research:* Early childhood, reading, special education, foundations, curriculum and instruction. *Unit head:* Dr. Marcheta P. Evans, Chair, 210-458-2600, Fax: 210-458-2605, E-mail: mevans@utsa.edu.

The University of Toledo, College of Graduate Studies, College of Education, Department of Educational Leadership, Program in Higher Education, Toledo, OH 43606-3390. Offers ME, PhD. *Accreditation:* NCATE. *Students:* 40 full-time (24 women), 70 part-time (47 women); includes 29 minority (25 African Americans, 4 Hispanic Americans), 1 international. Average age 37. 52 applicants, 87% accepted, 33 enrolled. In 2006, 5 master's, 7 doctorates awarded. *Degree requirements:* For master's, thesis or alternative, comprehensive exam; for doctorate, thesis/dissertation, comprehensive exams. *Entrance requirements:* For master's, minimum GPA of 2.7; for doctorate, GRE General Test, minimum GPA of 2.7 (undergraduate), 3.0 (graduate). *Application deadline:* For fall admission, 8/15 priority date for domestic students. Applications are processed on a rolling basis. *Financial support:* Career-related internships or fieldwork, Federal Work-Study, and institutionally sponsored loans available. Support available to part-time students. Financial award application deadline: 4/1; financial award applicants required to submit FAFSA. *Application contact:* Doctoral Program Director, 419-530-2461, Fax: 419-530-4912, E-mail: edleadr@utnet.utoledo.edu.

University of Virginia, Curry School of Education, Department of Leadership, Foundations and Policy, Program in Higher Education, Charlottesville, VA 22903. Offers Ed D, Ed S. *Students:* 3 full-time (0 women), 5 part-time (3 women). Average age 43. 3 applicants, 33% accepted, 1 enrolled. *Degree requirements:* For doctorate, thesis/dissertation, comprehensive exam (for some programs). *Entrance requirements:* For doctorate and Ed S, GRE General Test. Additional exam requirements/recommendations for international students: Required—TOEFL (minimum score 600 paper-based; 250 computer-based). *Application deadline:* Applications are processed on a rolling basis. Application fee: $60. Electronic applications accepted. *Financial support:* Fellowships, research assistantships, teaching assistantships available. Financial award applicants required to submit FAFSA. *Unit head:* Margaret A. Miller, Professor and Director, 434-924-7782, E-mail: highered@virginia.edu.

University of Washington, Graduate School, College of Education, Seattle, WA 98195. Offers curriculum and instruction (M Ed, Ed D, PhD), including educational technology, general

Higher Education

University of Washington (continued)

curriculum (Ed D, PhD), language, literacy, and culture, mathematics education, multicultural education, reading and language arts education (Ed D), science education, social studies education, teaching and curriculum (M Ed); educational leadership and policy studies (M Ed, Ed D, PhD), including administration, educational organization and policy, higher education, school district leadership (Ed D), social/cultural foundations; educational psychology (M Ed, PhD), including human development and cognition, measurement and research, school counseling (M Ed), school psychology; special education (M Ed, Ed D, PhD), including early childhood education, elementary special education, emotional and behavioral disabilities (M Ed), general special education, severe disabilities; teacher education (MIT). *Accreditation:* APA. Part-time and evening/weekend programs available. *Degree requirements:* For master's, thesis optional; for doctorate, thesis/dissertation. *Entrance requirements:* For master's and doctorate, GRE General Test, minimum GPA of 3.0. Additional exam requirements/recommendations for international students: Required—TOEFL. Electronic applications accepted. *Faculty research:* School restructuring/effective schools, special education interventions, literacy and writing, technology, school partnerships, teacher preparation.

University of Wisconsin–Whitewater, School of Graduate Studies, College of Business and Economics, Department of Business Education, Whitewater, WI 53190-1790. Offers general business education (MS); post-secondary business education (MS); secondary business education (MS). *Accreditation:* NCATE. Part-time and evening/weekend programs available. Post-baccalaureate distance learning degree programs offered (no on-campus study). *Students:* 5 full-time (1 woman), 14 part-time (10 women); includes 1 minority (African American) Average age 33. 8 applicants, 75% accepted, 4 enrolled. In 2006, 11 degrees awarded. *Degree requirements:* For master's, thesis or alternative. *Entrance requirements:* For master's, interview, teaching license. Additional exam requirements/recommendations for international students: Required—TOEFL (minimum score 550 paper-based; 213 computer-based). *Application deadline:* For fall admission, 7/15 priority date for domestic and international students; for spring admission, 12/1 priority date for domestic and international students. Applications are processed on a rolling basis. Application fee: $45. Electronic applications accepted. *Expenses:* Tuition, state resident: full-time $3,311. Tuition, nonresident: full-time $8,616. Required fees: $368 per credit. *Financial support:* In 2006–07, 2 research assistantships (averaging $7,385 per year) were awarded; Federal Work-Study, unspecified assistantships, and out of state fee waiver also available. Support available to part-time students. Financial award application deadline: 3/15; financial award applicants required to submit FAFSA. *Faculty research:* Active learning and performance strategies, technology-enhanced formative assessment, computer-supported cooperative work, privacy surveillance. *Unit head:* Dr. Lila Waldman, Coordinator, 262-472-5475. *Application contact:* Sally A. Lange, School of Graduate Studies, 262-472-1006, Fax: 262-472-5027, E-mail: gradschl@uww.edu.

University of Wisconsin–Whitewater, School of Graduate Studies, College of Education, Department of Counselor Education, Whitewater, WI 53190-1790. Offers community counseling (MS Ed); higher education (MS Ed); school counseling (MS Ed). *Accreditation:* ACA; NCATE. Part-time and evening/weekend programs available. *Students:* 36 full-time (31 women), 91 part-time (76 women); includes 8 minority (2 African Americans, 1 Asian American or Pacific Islander, 5 Hispanic Americans). Average age 25. 52 applicants, 31% accepted, 13 enrolled. In 2006, 40 degrees awarded. *Degree requirements:* For master's, thesis or alternative. *Entrance requirements:* For master's, resumé, 2 letters of reference. Additional exam requirements/recommendations for international students: Required—TOEFL (minimum score 550 paper-based; 213 computer-based). *Application deadline:* For fall admission, 2/1 for domestic and international students. Application fee: $45. Electronic applications accepted. *Expenses:* Tuition, state resident: full-time $3,311. Tuition, nonresident: full-time $8,616. Required fees: $368 per credit. *Financial support:* In 2006–07, 1 research assistantship (averaging $9,875 per year) was awarded; Federal Work-Study, unspecified assistantships, and out of state fee waiver also available. Support available to part-time students. Financial award application deadline: 3/15; financial award applicants required to submit FAFSA. *Faculty research:* Alcohol and other drugs, counseling effectiveness, teacher mentoring. *Unit head:* Dr. Brenda O'Beirne, Coordinator, 262-472-1452, Fax: 262-472-2841, E-mail: obeirneb@uww.edu. *Application contact:* Sally A. Lange, School of Graduate Studies, 262-472-1006, Fax: 262-472-5027, E-mail: gradschl@uww.edu.

Vanderbilt University, Peabody College, Department of Leadership and Organizations, Nashville, TN 37240-1001. Offers education policy (MPP); educational leadership and policy (Ed D); higher education (M Ed); higher education, leadership and policy (Ed D); human resource development (M Ed); international education policy and management (M Ed); organizational leadership (M Ed); school administration (M Ed). Part-time and evening/weekend programs available. *Faculty:* 21 full-time (6 women), 9 part-time/adjunct (3 women). *Students:* 131 full-time (88 women), 85 part-time (39 women); includes 35 minority (30 African Americans, 4 Asian Americans or Pacific Islanders, 1 Hispanic American), 11 international. Average age 31. 214 applicants, 63% accepted, 64 enrolled. In 2006, 43 master's, 12 doctorates awarded. *Median time to degree:* Of those who began their doctoral program in fall 1998, 62% received their degree in 8 years or less. *Degree requirements:* For master's, thesis optional; for doctorate, thesis/dissertation, qualifying exams, residency. *Entrance requirements:* For master's and doctorate, GRE General Test. Additional exam requirements/recommendations for international students: Required—TOEFL (minimum score 550 paper-based; 213 computer-based). *Application deadline:* For fall admission, 12/31 priority date for domestic and international students; for spring admission, 11/1 priority date for domestic and international students. Applications are processed on a rolling basis. Application fee: $0. Electronic applications accepted. *Expenses:* Tuition: Full-time $24,462. Required fees: $2,515. One-time fee: $30 full-time. Full-time tuition and fees vary according to course load, degree level and program. *Financial support:* In 2006–07, 90 students received support, including 50 fellowships with full and partial tuition reimbursements available, 38 research assistantships with full and partial tuition reimbursements available, 2 teaching assistantships with full and partial tuition reimbursements available; Federal Work-Study, institutionally sponsored loans, scholarships/grants, tuition waivers (partial), and unspecified assistantships also available. Support available to part-time students. Financial award application deadline: 2/1; financial award applicants required to submit FAFSA. *Faculty research:* Education policy, education finances, economics of education, education leadership and management, higher education leadership and policy; educator pay for performance. *Unit head:* James W. Guthrie, Chair, 615-322-8000, Fax: 615-343-7094, E-mail: james.w.guthrie@vanderbilt.edu. *Application contact:* Rosie Moody, Educational Coordinator, 615-322-8019, Fax: 615-343-7094, E-mail: rosie.moody@vanderbilt.edu.

Washington State University, Graduate School, College of Education, Department of Educational Leadership and Counseling Psychology, Pullman, WA 99164. Offers counseling psychology (Ed M, MA, PhD); educational leadership (M Ed, MA, Ed D, PhD); educational psychology (Ed M, MA, PhD); higher education (Ed M, MA, Ed D, PhD), including higher education administration (PhD), sport management (PhD), student affairs (PhD); higher education with sport management (Ed M). *Accreditation:* NCATE. *Faculty:* 25. *Students:* 109 full-time (63 women), 54 part-time (34 women); includes 42 minority (11 African Americans, 2 American Indian/Alaska Native, 12 Asian Americans or Pacific Islanders, 17 Hispanic Americans). Average age 34. 107 applicants, 67% accepted, 30 enrolled. In 2006, 33 master's, 20 doctorates awarded. Terminal master's awarded for partial completion of doctoral program. *Degree requirements:* For master's, thesis (for some programs), oral exam or written exam, comprehensive exam (for some programs); for doctorate, thesis/dissertation, oral and written exams, comprehensive exam. *Entrance requirements:* For master's and doctorate, GRE General Test, minimum GPA of 3.0, 3 letters of recommendation. Additional exam requirements/recommendations for international students: Required—TOEFL (minimum score 550 paper-based; 213 computer-based). *Application deadline:* For fall admission, 3/1 for domestic and international students; for spring admission, 10/1 for domestic students, 7/1 for international students. Application fee: $50. *Expenses:* Tuition, state resident: full-time $7,066. Tuition, nonresident: full-time $17,204. *Financial support:* In 2006–07, research assistantships (averaging $13,917 per year), teaching assistantships (averaging $13,056 per year) were awarded;

career-related internships or fieldwork, Federal Work-Study, institutionally sponsored loans, scholarships/grants, tuition waivers (partial), and unspecified assistantships also available. Financial award application deadline: 4/1; financial award applicants required to submit FAFSA. *Faculty research:* Attentional processes, cross cultural psychology, faculty development in higher education. Total annual research expenditures: $854,827. *Unit head:* Dr. Phyllis Erdman, Chair, 509-335-9117. *Application contact:* Graduate School Admissions, 800-GRADWSU, Fax: 509-335-1949, E-mail: gradsch@wsu.edu.

Wayne State University, College of Education, Division of Administrative and Organizational Studies, Detroit, MI 48202. Offers administration and supervision-secondary (Ed S); college and university teaching (Certificate); curriculum and instruction (PhD); educational leadership (M Ed, Ed S); educational leadership and policy studies (Ed D, PhD); elementary education curriculum and instruction (MA, Ed S); general administration and supervision (Ed D, PhD, Ed S); higher education (Ed D, PhD); instructional technology (M Ed, Ed D, PhD, Ed S); secondary curriculum and instruction (M Ed, Ed S). *Faculty:* 24 full-time (13 women), 1 (woman) part-time/adjunct. *Students:* 153 full-time (103 women), 389 part-time (266 women); includes 252 minority (223 African Americans, 6 American Indian/Alaska Native, 8 Asian Americans or Pacific Islanders, 15 Hispanic Americans), 19 international. Average age 38. 138 applicants, 79% accepted, 74 enrolled. In 2006, 116 master's, 30 doctorates, 64 other advanced degrees awarded. *Degree requirements:* For doctorate, thesis/dissertation. *Entrance requirements:* For doctorate, interview, minimum GPA of 3.0. Additional exam requirements/recommendations for international students: Required—TOEFL (minimum score 550 paper-based; 213 computer-based), TWE (minimum score 6). *Application deadline:* For fall admission, 7/1 for domestic students, 6/1 for international students; for winter admission, 10/1 for international students; for spring admission, 2/1 for international students. Application fee: $30 ($50 for international students). Electronic applications accepted. *Financial support:* In 2006–07, 4 research assistantships (averaging $12,797 per year) were awarded; career-related internships or fieldwork, Federal Work-Study, and institutionally sponsored loans also available. Support available to part-time students. *Faculty research:* Total quality management, participatory management, administering educational technology, school improvement, principalship. Total annual research expenditures: $344,504. *Unit head:* Dr. JoAnne Holbert, Assistant Dean, 313-577-1721, E-mail: jholbert@wayne.edu.

Western Governors University, Teachers College, Salt Lake City, UT 84107. Offers English language learning (K-12) (MA); learning and technology (M Ed, MA); management and evaluation (M Ed); management and innovation (M Ed); mathematics education (5-12) (MA); mathematics education (5-9) (MA); mathematics education (K-6) (MA); science (5-12) (MA), including biology, geology; science education (509) (MA); technology (M Ed); technology for principals (Post-Graduate Certificate). *Accreditation:* NCATE. Part-time and evening/weekend programs available. Postbaccalaureate distance learning degree programs offered (no on-campus study). *Degree requirements:* For master's, comprehensive exam, registration. *Entrance requirements:* Additional exam requirements/recommendations for international students: Required—TOEFL (minimum score 450 paper-based). Electronic applications accepted. Expenses: Contact institution.

Western Washington University, Graduate School, Woodring College of Education, Department of Educational Leadership, Program in Continuing and College Education, Bellingham, WA 98225-5996. Offers M Ed. Part-time and evening/weekend programs available. Postbaccalaureate distance learning degree programs offered (minimal on-campus study). *Faculty:* 4. *Students:* 11 full-time (8 women), 37 part-time (27 women). 17 applicants, 82% accepted, 4 enrolled. In 2006, 25 degrees awarded. *Degree requirements:* For master's, thesis optional. *Entrance requirements:* For master's, GRE General Test or MAT, minimum GPA of 3.0 in last 60 semester hours or last 90 quarter hours. Additional exam requirements/recommendations for international students: Required—TOEFL (minimum score 567 paper-based; 227 computer-based). *Application deadline:* For fall admission, 6/1 for domestic students; for winter admission, 10/1 for domestic students; for spring admission, 2/1 for domestic students. Applications are processed on a rolling basis. Application fee: $50. *Expenses:* Tuition, state resident: full-time $6,609; part-time $199 per credit. Tuition, nonresident: full-time $16,845; part-time $540 per credit. *Financial support:* In 2006–07, 1 teaching assistantship with partial tuition reimbursement (averaging $9,339 per year) was awarded; career-related internships or fieldwork, Federal Work-Study, institutionally sponsored loans, scholarships/grants, tuition waivers (partial), and unspecified assistantships also available. Support available to part-time students. Financial award application deadline: 2/15; financial award applicants required to submit FAFSA. *Faculty research:* Transfer of learning as a result of continuing professional education programs, postsecondary faculty development, action research as professional development, literacy education in community colleges. *Unit head:* Dr. Sandra Daffron, Program Director, 360-650-2977, E-mail: sandra.daffron@wwu.edu. *Application contact:* Sherry Haskins, Graduate Coordinator, 360-650-3190.

West Virginia University, College of Human Resources and Education, Department of Curriculum and Instruction-Literacy, Program in Secondary Education, Morgantown, WV 26506. Offers higher education curriculum and teaching (MA); secondary education (MA). Students enter program as undergraduates. *Accreditation:* NCATE. Part-time programs available. *Students:* 134 full-time (84 women), 28 part-time (19 women); includes 14 minority (6 African Americans, 2 Asian Americans or Pacific Islanders, 6 Hispanic Americans), 9 international. Average age 29. 88 applicants, 90% accepted, 50 enrolled. In 2006, 80 degrees awarded. *Degree requirements:* For master's, content exams, thesis optional. *Entrance requirements:* For master's, minimum GPA of 2.75. Additional exam requirements/recommendations for international students: Required—TOEFL. *Application deadline:* Applications are processed on a rolling basis. Application fee: $50. Electronic applications accepted. *Expenses:* Tuition, state resident: full-time $4,926; part-time $276 per credit hour. Tuition, nonresident: full-time $14,278; part-time $796 per credit hour. Tuition and fees vary according to program. *Financial support:* In 2006–07, 117 students received support, including 2 teaching assistantships with full tuition reimbursements available (averaging $8,264 per year); research assistantships, career-related internships or fieldwork, Federal Work-Study, institutionally sponsored loans, and tuition waivers (full and partial) also available. Financial award application deadline: 2/1; financial award applicants required to submit FAFSA. *Faculty research:* Teacher education, school reform, curriculum development, education technology. *Application contact:* Dr. Elizabeth A. Dooley, Chair, 304-293-3441, Fax: 304-293-3802, E-mail: elizabeth.dooley@mail.wvu.edu.

West Virginia University, College of Human Resources and Education, Department of Educational Leadership Studies, Morgantown, WV 26506. Offers educational leadership (Ed D); higher education administration (MA); public school administration (MA). *Accreditation:* NCATE. Part-time programs available. *Faculty:* 6 full-time (2 women). *Students:* 78 full-time (38 women), 129 part-time (84 women); includes 20 minority (15 African Americans, 1 American Indian/Alaska Native, 1 Asian American or Pacific Islander, 3 Hispanic Americans), 5 international. Average age 38. 91 applicants, 79% accepted, 43 enrolled. In 2006, 10 master's, 2 doctorates awarded. *Degree requirements:* For master's, content exams; for doctorate, thesis/dissertation, comprehensive exam. *Entrance requirements:* For master's, minimum GPA of 2.75 or MA Degree or MAT of 4107; for doctorate, GRE General Test or MAT, minimum GPA of 3.25. Additional exam requirements/recommendations for international students: Required—TOEFL. *Application deadline:* Applications are processed on a rolling basis. Application fee: $50. *Expenses:* Tuition, state resident: full-time $4,926; part-time $276 per credit hour. Tuition, nonresident: full-time $14,278; part-time $796 per credit hour. Tuition and fees vary according to program. *Financial support:* In 2006–07, 131 students received support, including 1 research assistantship (averaging $8,730 per year), 4 teaching assistantships with full tuition reimbursements available (averaging $8,264 per year); career-related internships or fieldwork, Federal Work-Study, institutionally sponsored loans, and tuition waivers (partial) also available. Financial award application deadline: 2/1; financial award applicants required to submit FAFSA. *Faculty research:* Evaluation, collective bargaining, educational law, international higher education, superintendency. *Unit head:* Dr. Richard Hartnett, Chairperson, 304-293-3708, Fax: 304-293-2279, E-mail: richard.hartnett@mail.wvu.edu.

Wright State University, School of Graduate Studies, College of Education and Human Services, Department of Educational Leadership, Program in Advanced Educational Leadership, Dayton, OH 45435. Offers advanced curriculum and instruction (Ed S); higher education-adult education (Ed S); superintendent (Ed S). *Accreditation:* NCATE. *Students:* 6 full-time (4 women), 10 part-time (6 women); includes 3 minority (all African Americans) Average age 35. 3 applicants, 100% accepted. In 2006, 1 degree awarded. *Degree requirements:* For Ed S, thesis. *Entrance requirements:* For degree, GRE General Test, MAT. Additional exam requirements/recommendations for international students: Required—TOEFL. Application fee: $25. *Financial support:* Available to part-time students. Applicants required to submit FAFSA. *Unit head:* Dr. Thomas Diamantes, Director, 937-775-3008, Fax: 937-775-2405, E-mail: thomas.diamantes@wright.edu. *Application contact:* John Kimble, Associate Director of Graduate Admissions and Records, 937-775-2957, Fax: 937-775-2453, E-mail: john.kimble@wright.edu.

Wright State University, School of Graduate Studies, College of Education and Human Services, Department of Educational Leadership, Programs in Educational Leadership, Dayton, OH 45435. Offers curriculum and instruction: teacher leader (MA); educational administrative specialist: teacher leader (M Ed); educational administrative specialist: vocational education administration (M Ed, MA); student affairs in higher education-administration (M Ed, MA). *Accreditation:* NCATE. *Students:* 26 full-time (22 women), 430 part-time (344 women); includes 10 minority (8 African Americans, 1 American Indian/Alaska Native, 1 Hispanic American), 1 international. Average age 33. 179 applicants, 97% accepted. In 2006, 211 degrees awarded. *Degree requirements:* For master's, thesis (for some programs). *Entrance requirements:* For master's, GRE General Test, MAT. Additional exam requirements/recommendations for international students: Required—TOEFL. Application fee: $25. *Financial support:* Available to part-time students. Applicants required to submit FAFSA. *Unit head:* Dr. Charles W. Ryan, Director and Director of Graduate Programs in Education, 937-775-3286, Fax: 937-775-2405, E-mail: charles.ryan@wright.edu. *Application contact:* John Kimble, Associate Director of Graduate Admissions and Records, 937-775-2957, Fax: 937-775-2453, E-mail: john.kimble@wright.edu.

Middle School Education

Alaska Pacific University, Graduate Programs, Education Department, Program in Teaching, Anchorage, AK 99508-4672. Offers teaching (K-8) (MAT). *Faculty:* 3 full-time (2 women). *Students:* 10 full-time (8 women), 1 (woman) part-time. Average age 34. In 2006, 7 degrees awarded. *Degree requirements:* For master's, research project. *Entrance requirements:* For master's, GRE or MAT, PRAXIS, minimum GPA of 3.0. *Application deadline:* For fall admission, 4/15 for domestic students; for spring admission, 12/15 for domestic students. Applications are processed on a rolling basis. Application fee: $25. *Expenses:* Tuition: Part-time $550 per credit hour. Required fees: $100 per semester. Tuition and fees vary according to program. *Financial support:* Research assistantships, teaching assistantships, career-related internships or fieldwork and Federal Work-Study available. Support available to part-time students. Financial award application deadline: 4/15; financial award applicants required to submit FAFSA. *Unit head:* Dr. Theodore Munsch, Director, 907-564-8258, Fax: 907-564-8317, E-mail: edted@alaskapacific.edu. *Application contact:* Michael Warner, Director of Admissions, 907-564-8248, Fax: 907-564-8317, E-mail: mikew@alaskapacific.edu.

Albany State University, College of Education, Program in Middle Grades Education, Albany, GA 31705-2717. Offers M Ed. *Accreditation:* NCATE. Part-time programs available. *Degree requirements:* For master's, comprehensive exam. *Entrance requirements:* For master's, GRE General Test, MAT or NTE. Electronic applications accepted.

Armstrong Atlantic State University, School of Graduate Studies, Program in Education, Savannah, GA 31419-1997. Offers adult education (M Ed); early childhood education (M Ed); education (M Ed); elementary education (M Ed); middle grades education (M Ed); secondary education (M Ed), including business education, English education, mathematics education, science education, social science education; special education (M Ed), including behavioral disorders, curriculum and instruction, learning disabilities, speech-language pathology. *Accreditation:* NCATE. Part-time and evening/weekend programs available. Postbaccalaureate distance learning degree programs offered (minimal on-campus study). *Faculty:* 11 full-time (9 women), 13 part-time/adjunct (10 women). *Students:* 50 full-time (42 women), 219 part-time (175 women); includes 71 minority (67 African Americans, 3 Asian Americans or Pacific Islanders, 1 Hispanic American), 6 international. Average age 35. In 2006, 151 degrees awarded. *Degree requirements:* For master's, portfolio. *Entrance requirements:* For master's, GRE General Test or MAT, minimum GPA of 2.5, letters of recommendation. Additional exam requirements/recommendations for international students: Required—TOEFL (minimum score 523 paper-based; 193 computer-based). *Application deadline:* For fall admission, 7/1 priority date for domestic and international students; for spring admission, 11/15 priority date for domestic and international students. Applications are processed on a rolling basis. Application fee: $25. Electronic applications accepted. *Expenses:* Tuition, state resident: full-time $2,286; part-time $127 per credit. Tuition, nonresident: full-time $9,144; part-time $508 per credit. One-time fee: $257. *Financial support:* In 2006–07, research assistantships with partial tuition reimbursements (averaging $2,500 per year); career-related internships or fieldwork, Federal Work-Study, scholarships/grants, and unspecified assistantships also available. Support available to part-time students. Financial award applicants required to submit FAFSA. *Unit head:* Dr. Jane McHaney, College of Education Dean, 912-927-5398, Fax: 912-921-7425, E-mail: mchaneia@mail.armstrong.edu.

Ashland University, College of Education, Graduate Studies in Education, Department of Curriculum and Instruction, Ashland, OH 44805-3702. Offers educational technology (M Ed); intervention specialist-mild/moderate (M Ed); intervention specialist-moderate/intensive (M Ed); middle school education (M Ed); talent development (M Ed). *Accreditation:* NCATE. Part-time and evening/weekend programs available. *Faculty:* 11 full-time (7 women), 93 part-time/adjunct (54 women). *Students:* 188 full-time (161 women), 354 part-time (314 women); includes 25 minority (19 African Americans, 3 Asian Americans or Pacific Islanders, 3 Hispanic Americans), 1 international. Average age 32. In 2006, 220 degrees awarded. *Degree requirements:* For master's, thesis or alternative, internship, practicum, seminar. *Entrance requirements:* For master's, GRE General Test or MAT, teaching certificate, minimum GPA of 2.75 (or 2.5 with 2.75 in education or major subject field). Additional exam requirements/recommendations for international students: Required—TOEFL. *Application deadline:* For fall admission, 8/27 for domestic students; for spring admission, 1/14 for domestic students. Applications are processed on a rolling basis. Application fee: $30. *Expenses:* Tuition: Part-time $403 per credit. Tuition and fees vary according to degree level and program. *Financial support:* In 2006–07, 189 students received support. Institutionally sponsored loans and scholarships/grants available. Financial award application deadline: 4/15. *Faculty research:* Gender equity, postmodern children's and young adult literature, outdoor/experimental education, re-examining literature study in middle grades, morality and giftedness. *Unit head:* Dr. James P. Van Keuren, Chair, 419-289-5377, Fax: 419-207-4949, E-mail: jvankeu1@ashland.edu.

Augusta State University, Graduate Studies, College of Education, Program in Middle Grades Education, Augusta, GA 30904-2200. Offers M Ed, Ed S. *Accreditation:* NCATE. Part-time and evening/weekend programs available. *Faculty:* 2 full-time (1 woman), 1 (woman) part-time/adjunct. *Students:* 2 full-time (1 woman), 34 part-time (30 women); includes 7 African Americans, 1 Hispanic American. Average age 35. 5 applicants, 100% accepted, 5 enrolled. In 2006, 3 master's, 6 other advanced degrees awarded. *Degree requirements:* For Ed S, thesis. *Entrance requirements:* For master's, GRE, MAT, minimum GPA of 2.5; for Ed S, GRE, MAT. *Application deadline:* For fall admission, 8/1 priority date for domestic students. Applications are processed on a rolling basis. Application fee: $20. *Expenses:* Tuition, state resident: full-time $3,044; part-time $127 per credit hour. Tuition, nonresident: full-time $12,172; part-time $508 per credit hour. *Financial support:* Career-related internships or fieldwork, Federal Work-Study, and institutionally sponsored loans available. Support available to part-time students. Financial award application deadline: 4/15; financial award applicants required to submit FAFSA. *Unit head:* Dr. J. Gordon Eisenman, Chair, 706-737-1496, Fax: 706-667-4706, E-mail: geisenman@aug.edu. *Application contact:* Andrea M. Scott, Secretary to the Dean, 706-737-1499, Fax: 706-667-4706, E-mail: ascott1@aug.edu.

Austin College, Program in Education, Sherman, TX 75090-4400. Offers art education (MA); elementary education (MA); middle school education (MA); music education (MA); physical education and coaching (MA); secondary education (MA). Applicants must meet Austin College's undergraduate curriculum requirements. Part-time programs available. *Faculty:* 5 full-time (3 women), 1 (woman) part-time/adjunct. *Students:* 33 full-time (26 women); includes 3 minority (2 Asian Americans or Pacific Islanders, 1 Hispanic American). Average age 25. In 2006, 24 degrees awarded. *Degree requirements:* For master's, one foreign language, thesis or alternative. *Entrance requirements:* For master's, Texas Academic Skills Program Test. *Application deadline:* For fall admission, 5/1 priority date for domestic students; for spring admission, 1/15 priority date for domestic students. Applications are processed on a rolling basis. Application fee: $35. Electronic applications accepted. *Expenses:* Tuition: Full-time $27,385. Required fees: $160. *Financial support:* In 2006–07, 27 students received support. Career-related internships or fieldwork, Federal Work-Study, scholarships/grants, and unspecified assistantships available. Support available to part-time students. Financial award application deadline: 4/1; financial award applicants required to submit FAFSA. *Unit head:* Dr. Barbara Sylvester, Director of Teaching Program, 903-813-2498, Fax: 903-813-2326, E-mail: bsylvester@austincollege.edu.

Bank Street College of Education, Graduate School, Department of Curriculum and Instruction, Program in Bilingual Education, New York, NY 10025. Offers bilingual childhood special education (Ed M, MS Ed); bilingual early childhood education (MS Ed); bilingual early childhood special and general education (MS Ed); bilingual early childhood special education (Ed M, MS Ed); bilingual elementary/childhood general education (MS Ed); bilingual elementary/childhood special and general education (MS Ed); bilingual middle school general education (MS Ed); bilingual middle school special and general education (Ed M, MS Ed); bilingual middle school special education (MS Ed). *Accreditation:* NCATE. *Faculty:* 2 full-time (both women), 5 part-time/adjunct (all women). *Students:* 8 full-time (7 women), 22 part-time (19 women); includes 21 minority (2 African Americans, 2 Asian Americans or Pacific Islanders, 17 Hispanic Americans). Average age 27. 19 applicants, 68% accepted, 10 enrolled. In 2006, 8 degrees awarded. *Degree requirements:* For master's, thesis, registration. *Entrance requirements:* For master's, interview. Additional exam requirements/recommendations for international students: Required—TOEFL (minimum score 600 paper-based; 250 computer-based). *Application deadline:* For fall admission, 3/1 priority date for domestic students; for spring admission, 11/1 priority date for domestic students. Applications are processed on a rolling basis. Application fee: $50. *Expenses:* Tuition: Part-time $940 per credit. Required fees: $100 per term. *Financial support:* Career-related internships or fieldwork, Federal Work-Study, scholarships/grants, and unspecified assistantships available. Support available to part-time students. Financial award application deadline: 4/15; financial award applicants required to submit FAFSA. *Faculty research:* Dual language education, language immersion, bilingual education in the urban classroom, community and school partnerships. Total annual research expenditures: $58,717. *Unit head:* Dr. Olga Romero, Director, 212-875-4468, Fax: 212-875-4753, E-mail: olgar@bankstreet.edu. *Application contact:* Ann Morgan, Director of Graduate Admissions, 212-875-4403, Fax: 212-875-4678, E-mail: amorgan@bankstreet.edu.

Bank Street College of Education, Graduate School, Department of Curriculum and Instruction, Program in Middle School Education, New York, NY 10025. Offers MS Ed. *Accreditation:* NCATE. *Students:* 16 full-time (13 women), 10 part-time (7 women); includes 4 minority (3 African Americans, 1 Hispanic American). Average age 28. 22 applicants, 86% accepted, 15 enrolled. In 2006, 12 degrees awarded. *Degree requirements:* For master's, thesis. *Entrance requirements:* For master's, academic background in middle school level subjects, interview. Additional exam requirements/recommendations for international students: Required—TOEFL (minimum score 600 paper-based; 250 computer-based). *Application deadline:* For fall admission, 3/1 priority date for domestic students; for spring admission, 11/1 priority date for domestic students. Applications are processed on a rolling basis. Application fee: $50. *Expenses:* Tuition: Part-time $940 per credit. Required fees: $100 per term. *Financial support:* Career-related internships or fieldwork, Federal Work-Study, scholarships/grants, and unspecified assistantships available. Support available to part-time students. Financial award application deadline: 4/15; financial award applicants required to submit FAFSA. *Faculty research:* Collaborative learning in middle school settings, the interdisciplinary middle school classroom, experiential learning in middle school, adolescent development. *Unit head:* Dr. Sue Ruskin-Mayher, Director, 212-875-4780, Fax: 212-875-4753, E-mail: sruskin-mayher@bankstreet.edu. *Application contact:* Ann Morgan, Director of Graduate Admissions, 212-875-4403, Fax: 212-875-4678, E-mail: amorgan@bankstreet.edu.

Bank Street College of Education, Graduate School, Department of Curriculum and Instruction, Program in Museum Education, New York, NY 10025. Offers museum education (MS Ed); museum education: elementary education certification (MS Ed); museum education: middle school certification (MS Ed); museum studies (MS Ed). *Students:* 30 full-time (28 women), 27 part-time (all women); includes 8 minority (3 African Americans, 5 Asian Americans or Pacific Islanders). Average age 27. 37 applicants, 84% accepted, 23 enrolled. In 2006, 20 degrees awarded. *Degree requirements:* For master's, thesis, registration. *Entrance requirements:* For master's, interview. Additional exam requirements/recommendations for international students: Required—TOEFL (minimum score 600 paper-based; 250 computer-based). *Application deadline:* For fall admission, 3/1 priority date for domestic and international students; for spring admission, 11/1 priority date for domestic and international students. Applications are processed on a rolling basis. Application fee: $50. *Expenses:* Tuition: Part-time $940 per credit. Required fees: $100 per term. *Financial support:* Federal Work-Study and scholarships/grants available. Support available to part-time students. Financial award application deadline: 4/15; financial award applicants required to submit FAFSA. *Faculty research:* Equitable access and openness to diversity in museum settings, exhibition display and development, museum/school partnerships. *Unit head:* Nina Jensen, Director, 212-875-4491, Fax: 212-875-4753, E-mail: ninajensen@bankstreet.edu. *Application contact:* Ann Morgan, Director of Graduate Admissions, 212-875-4403, Fax: 212-875-4678, E-mail: amorgan@bankstreet.edu.

Bank Street College of Education, Graduate School, Department of Curriculum and Instruction, Program in Special Education, New York, NY 10025. Offers early childhood special and general education (MS Ed); early childhood special education (Ed M, MS Ed); elementary/childhood special and general education (MS Ed); elementary/childhood special education (MS Ed); elementary/childhood special education certification (Ed M); middle school special and general education (MS Ed); middle school special education (Ed M). *Students:* 98 full-time

Middle School Education

Bank Street College of Education (continued)
(86 women), 167 part-time (162 women); includes 57 minority (17 African Americans, 10 Asian Americans or Pacific Islanders, 30 Hispanic Americans), 1 international. Average age 31. 147 applicants, 78% accepted, 80 enrolled. In 2006, 68 degrees awarded. *Degree requirements:* For master's, thesis, registration. *Entrance requirements:* For master's, interview. Additional exam requirements/recommendations for international students: Required—TOEFL (minimum score 600 paper-based; 250 computer-based). *Application deadline:* For fall admission, 3/1 priority date for domestic students; for spring admission, 11/1 priority date for domestic students. Applications are processed on a rolling basis. Application fee: $50. *Expenses:* Tuition: Part-time $940 per credit. Required fees: $100 per term. *Financial support:* Career-related internships or fieldwork available. Financial award application deadline: 3/1; financial award applicants required to submit FAFSA. *Faculty research:* Inclusion, observation and assessment, early intervention, neurodevelopmental assessment. *Unit head:* Dr. Andrea (Penny) Spencer, Chairperson, 212-875-4602, Fax: 212-875-4753, E-mail: aspencer@bankstreet.edu. *Application contact:* Ann Morgan, Director of Graduate Admissions, 212-875-4403, Fax: 212-875-4678, E-mail: amorgan@bankstreet.edu.

See Close-Up on page 857.

Bellarmine University, Annsley Frazier Thornton School of Education, Louisville, KY 40205-0671. Offers early elementary education (MA, MAT); instructional leadership and school administration/school principal (MA); learning and behavior disorders (MA); middle school education (MA, MAT); reading and writing endorsement (MA); secondary school education (MAT); Waldorf inspired curriculum (MA);). *Accreditation:* NCATE. Part-time and evening/weekend programs available. *Faculty:* 10 full-time (8 women), 5 part-time/adjunct (all women). *Students:* 92 full-time (68 women), 140 part-time (104 women); includes 16 minority (11 African Americans, 1 Asian American or Pacific Islander, 4 Hispanic Americans). Average age 32. In 2006, 98 degrees awarded. *Degree requirements:* For master's, thesis (for some programs), comprehensive exam. *Entrance requirements:* For master's, minimum overall GPA of 2.75, 3.0 in major; letters of recommendation; valid Kentucky provisional or professional certificate. Additional exam requirements/recommendations for international students: Required—TOEFL (minimum score 550 paper-based; 213 computer-based; 80 iBT), GRE. *Application deadline:* Applications are processed on a rolling basis. Application fee: $25. Electronic applications accepted. *Expenses: Contact institution.* Tuition and fees vary according to program. *Faculty research:* Social justice, service learning dispositions, educational technology, special education. *Unit head:* Dr. Milton Brown, Dean (Interim), 502-452-8486, Fax: 502-452-8189, E-mail: mbrown@bellarmine.edu. *Application contact:* Theresa Klapheke, Director of Graduate Programs, 502-452-8033, Fax: 502-452-8189, E-mail: tklapheke@bellarmine.edu.

Belmont University, College of Arts and Sciences, School of Education, Nashville, TN 37212-3757. Offers education (MAT); elementary education (M Ed), including early childhood education, elementary education, gifted education, language arts education; English (M Ed); history (M Ed); mathematics (M Ed); middle grade education (M Ed); science (M Ed); secondary education (M Ed), including gifted education; sports administration (MSA); technology (M Ed). *Accreditation:* NCATE. Part-time and evening/weekend programs available. *Faculty:* 9 full-time (7 women), 20 part-time/adjunct (15 women). *Students:* 50 full-time (36 women), 116 part-time (76 women); includes 23 minority (20 African Americans, 1 Asian American or Pacific Islander, 2 Hispanic Americans), 1 international. Average age 30. 55 applicants, 60% accepted, 30 enrolled. In 2006, 82 degrees awarded. *Degree requirements:* For master's, thesis, comprehensive exam. *Entrance requirements:* For master's, MAT or GRE, minimum GPA of 2.75. Additional exam requirements/recommendations for international students: Required—TOEFL. *Application deadline:* For fall admission, 8/1 priority date for domestic students, 5/1 for international students; for spring admission, 12/1 priority date for domestic students, 9/1 for international students. Applications are processed on a rolling basis. Application fee: $50. *Expenses: Contact institution. Financial support:* In 2006–07, 25 students received support; fellowships with partial tuition reimbursements available, institutionally sponsored loans and tuition waivers (partial) available. Financial award application deadline: 4/15; financial award applicants required to submit FAFSA. *Faculty research:* Technology grant, professional development schools. Total annual research expenditures: $6,500. *Unit head:* Dr. Trevor F. Hutchins, Associate Dean, 615-460-6232, Fax: 615-460-6414, E-mail: hutchinst@mail.belmont.edu. *Application contact:* Julie Hullett, Admission/Licensure Officer, 615-460-6879, Fax: 615-460-5556, E-mail: hullettj@email.belmont.edu.

Berry College, Graduate Programs, Graduate Programs in Education, Program in Middle-Grades Education and Reading, Mount Berry, GA 30149-0159. Offers M Ed. *Accreditation:* NCATE. Part-time programs available. *Faculty:* 9 part-time/adjunct (5 women). *Students:* 1 full-time (0 women), 30 part-time (23 women); includes 1 Hispanic American. Average age 34. In 2006, 11 degrees awarded. *Degree requirements:* For master's, oral exams, thesis optional. *Entrance requirements:* For master's, GRE General Test, MAT, or NTE, minimum GPA of 2.5. Additional exam requirements/recommendations for international students: Required—TOEFL (minimum score 550 paper-based; 213 computer-based). *Application deadline:* For fall admission, 5/1 for domestic students; for spring admission, 10/1 for domestic students. Applications are processed on a rolling basis. Application fee: $25 ($30 for international students). *Expenses: Contact institution. Financial support:* In 2006–07, 27 students received support, including 2 research assistantships with full tuition reimbursements available (averaging $3,500 per year); scholarships/grants, tuition waivers (partial), and unspecified assistantships also available. Support available to part-time students. Financial award application deadline: 4/1; financial award applicants required to submit FAFSA. *Faculty research:* Curriculum development, teacher training, pedagogy. *Application contact:* Richard D. Paul, Dean of Admissions and Financial Aid, 706-236-2215, Fax: 706-290-2178, E-mail: dpaul@berry.edu.

Brenau University, Graduate Programs, School of Education, Gainesville, GA 30501. Offers early childhood education (M Ed, Ed S), including behavior disorders (M Ed); learning disabilities (M Ed), including special education; middle grades education (M Ed, Ed S). *Accreditation:* NCATE. Part-time and evening/weekend programs available. *Faculty:* 12 full-time (9 women), 17 part-time/adjunct (9 women). *Students:* 104 full-time (89 women), 160 part-time (140 women); includes 34 minority (28 African Americans, 3 Asian Americans or Pacific Islanders, 3 Hispanic Americans), 2 international. Average age 37. 187 applicants. In 2006, 92 master's, 24 other advanced degrees awarded. *Degree requirements:* For master's, comprehensive exam or applied research project, effective portfolio, thesis optional; for Ed S, applied research project. *Entrance requirements:* For master's, GRE, MAT, interview, minimum GPA of 3.0, teaching certificate, 3 references, writing samples; for Ed S, GRE, MAT, master's degree, minimum GPA of 3.0, writing sample, letters of reference. Additional exam requirements/recommendations for international students: Required—TOEFL (minimum score 550 paper-based). *Application deadline:* Applications are processed on a rolling basis. Application fee: $30. *Expenses: Contact institution. Financial support:* Career-related internships or fieldwork available. Financial award application deadline: 7/15; financial award applicants required to submit FAFSA. *Faculty research:* Environmental science literacy and awareness, curriculum integration for improved student success, teaching dispositions, impact of parent involvement on student success, grade inflation in higher education. *Unit head:* Dr. William B. Ware, Dean, 770-534-6220, Fax: 770-534-6221, E-mail: bware@brenau.edu. *Application contact:* Nathan Goss, Admissions Coordinator, 770-534-6162, Fax: 770-538-4701, E-mail: ngoss@brenau.edu.

Brooklyn College of the City University of New York, Division of Graduate Studies, School of Education, Program in Middle Childhood Education (Math), Brooklyn, NY 11210-2889. Offers MS Ed. *Students:* 7 full-time (3 women), 194 part-time (102 women); includes 95 minority (60 African Americans, 25 Asian Americans or Pacific Islanders, 10 Hispanic Americans), 10 international. 84 applicants, 87% accepted, 59 enrolled. In 2006, 52 degrees awarded. *Entrance requirements:* For master's, LAST, 2 letters of recommendation, essay, resumé. Additional exam requirements/recommendations for international students: Required—TOEFL. *Application deadline:* For fall admission, 3/1 priority date for domestic students, 2/1 priority date for international students; for spring admission, 11/1 priority date for domestic students, 10/1 priority date for international students. Applications are processed on a rolling basis. Electronic applications accepted. *Expenses:* Tuition, state resident: full-time $6,400; part-time $270 per credit. Tuition, nonresident: full-time $12,000; part-time $500 per credit. Required fees: $118 per semester. *Financial support:* Federal Work-Study, institutionally sponsored loans, and scholarships/grants available. Support available to part-time students. Financial award application deadline: 5/1; financial award applicants required to submit FAFSA. *Unit head:* Prof. Mary Chiusano, Program Head, 718-951-5214, E-mail: mchiusano@brooklyn.cuny.edu. *Application contact:* Karen Alleyne-Pierre, Director of Admissions Services and Enrollment Communications, 718-951-5902, Fax: 718-951-4506, E-mail: grads@brooklyn.cuny.edu.

Brooklyn College of the City University of New York, Division of Graduate Studies, School of Education, Program in Middle Childhood Education (Science), Brooklyn, NY 11210-2889. Offers MS Ed. Part-time and evening/weekend programs available. *Students:* 19 applicants, 100% accepted, 11 enrolled. In 2006, 10 degrees awarded. *Entrance requirements:* For master's, LAST, interview, previous course work in education and mathematics, resumé, 2 letters of recommendation, essay. Additional exam requirements/recommendations for international students: Required—TOEFL. *Application deadline:* For fall admission, 3/1 priority date for domestic students, 2/1 priority date for international students; for spring admission, 11/1 priority date for domestic students, 10/1 priority date for international students. Applications are processed on a rolling basis. Application fee: $125. Electronic applications accepted. *Expenses:* Tuition, state resident: full-time $6,400; part-time $270 per credit. Tuition, nonresident: full-time $12,000; part-time $500 per credit. Required fees: $118 per semester. *Financial support:* Federal Work-Study, institutionally sponsored loans, and scholarships/grants available. Support available to part-time students. Financial award application deadline: 5/1; financial award applicants required to submit FAFSA. *Faculty research:* Geometric thinking, mastery of basic facts, problem-solving strategies, history of mathematics. *Unit head:* Dr. Eleanor Miele, Program Head, 718-951-5214, E-mail: emiele@brooklyn.cuny.edu. *Application contact:* Karen Alleyne-Pierre, Director of Admissions Services and Enrollment Communications, 718-951-5902, Fax: 718-951-4506, E-mail: grads@brooklyn.cuny.edu.

California State University, Fullerton, Graduate Studies, College of Education, Department of Secondary Education, Fullerton, CA 92834-9480. Offers middle school mathematics (MS); secondary education (MS); teacher induction (MS). *Students:* 2 full-time (both women), 30 part-time (20 women); includes 12 minority (7 Asian Americans or Pacific Islanders, 5 Hispanic Americans). Average age 31. 43 applicants, 70% accepted, 25 enrolled. In 2006, 28 degrees awarded. *Expenses:* Tuition, nonresident: part-time $339 per unit. Required fees: $1,155 per semester. *Unit head:* Dr. Victoria Costa, Head, 714-278-7037.

Campbell University, Graduate and Professional Programs, School of Education, Buies Creek, NC 27506. Offers administration (MSA); community counseling (MA); elementary education (M Ed); English education (M Ed); interdisciplinary studies (M Ed); mathematics education (M Ed); middle grades education (M Ed); physical education (M Ed); school counseling (M Ed); secondary education (M Ed); social science education (M Ed). *Accreditation:* NCATE. Part-time and evening/weekend programs available. *Faculty:* 14 full-time (9 women), 12 part-time/adjunct (7 women). *Students:* 27 full-time (25 women), 183 part-time (146 women); includes 30 minority (24 African Americans, 3 American Indian/Alaska Native, 3 Hispanic Americans), 1 international. Average age 31. 112 applicants, 74% accepted, 74 enrolled. In 2006, 65 degrees awarded. *Degree requirements:* For master's, comprehensive exam. *Entrance requirements:* For master's, GRE General Test, minimum GPA of 2.7. *Application deadline:* For fall admission, 8/1 priority date for domestic students; for spring admission, 1/2 priority date for domestic students. Applications are processed on a rolling basis. Application fee: $65. *Expenses:* Tuition: Part-time $380 per semester hour. *Financial support:* In 2006–07, 67 students received support. Career-related internships or fieldwork and Federal Work-Study available. Financial award application deadline: 4/15; financial award applicants required to submit FAFSA. *Faculty research:* Spiritual values and wellness issues in counseling, stress and professional burnout among counselors, thinking strategies, leadership, adaptive technology. *Unit head:* Dr. Karen P. Nery, Dean, 910-893-1630, Fax: 910-893-1999, E-mail: nery@campbell.edu. *Application contact:* James S. Farthing, Director of Graduate Admissions for Business and Education, 910-893-1200 Ext. 1318, Fax: 910-814-4718, E-mail: farthing@campbell.edu.

Capella University, School of Education, Minneapolis, MN 55402. Offers college teaching (Certificate); curriculum and instruction (MS, PhD); education (MS); enrollment management (MS); instructional design for online learning (MS, PhD); k-12 studies in education (MS, PhD); leadership for higher education (MS, PhD); leadership in education administration (Certificate); leadership in educational administration (MS, PhD); postsecondary and adult education (MS, PhD); professional studies in education (MS, PhD); reading and literacy (MS); training and performance improvement (MS, PhD). Part-time and evening/weekend programs available. Postbaccalaureate distance learning degree programs offered (minimal on-campus study). Terminal master's awarded for partial completion of doctoral program. *Degree requirements:* For master's, integrative project, thesis optional; for doctorate, thesis/dissertation, comprehensive exam, registration. *Entrance requirements:* Additional exam requirements/recommendations for international students: Required—TOEFL (minimum score 550 paper-based; 213 computer-based), TWE (minimum score 4). Electronic applications accepted. *Faculty research:* Higher education administration, distance learning, adult education, training and curriculum design.

Central Michigan University, College of Graduate Studies, College of Education and Human Services, Department of Teacher Education and Professional Development, Program in Middle Level Education, Mount Pleasant, MI 48859. Offers MA. *Accreditation:* NCATE. *Degree requirements:* For master's, thesis or alternative, registration. *Entrance requirements:* For master's, minimum GPA of 2.7, Michigan teaching certificate.

Chicago State University, School of Graduate and Professional Studies, College of Education, Department of Reading, Elementary Education, Library Information and Media Studies, Program in Middle School Education, Chicago, IL 60628. Offers MAT.

City College of the City University of New York, Graduate School, School of Education, Department of Secondary Education, New York, NY 10031-9198. Offers adolescent mathematics education (MA, AC); English education (MA); middle school mathematics education (MS); science education (MA); social studies education (AC). *Accreditation:* NCATE. *Students:* 286 applicants, 94% accepted, 219 enrolled. *Entrance requirements:* For master's, Liberal Arts and Sciences Test (LAST), Content Specialty Test (CST). Additional exam requirements/recommendations for international students: Required—TOEFL. *Application deadline:* For fall admission, 3/15 for domestic students; for spring admission, 10/15 for domestic students. Application fee: $125. *Unit head:* Susan Semel, Chair, 212-650-7262, E-mail: ssemel@ccny.cuny.edu. *Application contact:* Stacia Pusey, Graduate Admissions Adviser-Education, 212-650-5345, E-mail: spusey@ccny.cuny.edu.

Clemson University, Graduate School, College of Health, Education, and Human Development, School of Education, Program in Middle Grades Education, Clemson, SC 29634. Offers MAT. *Students:* 37 full-time (27 women), 11 part-time (7 women); includes 11 minority (9 African Americans, 2 Hispanic Americans), 1 international. 11 applicants, 91% accepted, 8 enrolled. In 2006, 36 degrees awarded. *Entrance requirements:* For master's, GRE, PRAXIS II. *Expenses:* Tuition, state resident: full-time $8,812; part-time $450 per hour. Tuition, nonresident: full-time $18,036; part-time $760 per hour. Required fees: $474; $5 per term. *Unit head:* Dr. Lienne Medford, Coordinator, 864-250-8891, E-mail: lienne@clemson.edu.

See Close-Up on page 1271.

Cleveland State University, College of Graduate Studies, College of Education and Human Services, Department of Teacher Education, Cleveland, OH 44115. Offers art education (M Ed); early childhood education (M Ed); foreign language education (M Ed); mathematics and science education (M Ed); middle childhood education (M Ed); special education (M Ed), including mild/moderate disabilities, moderate/intensive disabilities; teaching English to speakers of other languages (M Ed). Part-time and evening/weekend programs available. *Faculty:* 14 full-time (8 women), 5 part-time/adjunct (4 women). *Students:* 120 full-time (96 women),

592 part-time (485 women); includes 145 minority (123 African Americans, 7 Asian Americans or Pacific Islanders, 15 Hispanic Americans), 7 international. Average age 34. 526 applicants, 41% accepted, 144 enrolled. In 2006, 324 degrees awarded. *Degree requirements:* For master's, thesis or alternative, comprehensive exam (for some programs). *Entrance requirements:* For master's, GRE General Test or MAT, minimum GPA of 2.75. Additional exam requirements/recommendations for international students: Required—TOEFL (minimum score 525 paper-based; 197 computer-based), IELTS (minimum score 6). *Application deadline:* For fall admission, 7/15 priority date for domestic students. Applications are processed on a rolling basis. Application fee: $30. *Financial support:* In 2006–07, 12 research assistantships with full tuition reimbursements (averaging $3,480 per year) were awarded; tuition waivers (partial) and unspecified assistantships also available. *Faculty research:* Early literacy, professional development in reading, reading recovery, dual language, induction programs. Total annual research expenditures: $6.2 million. *Unit head:* Dr. Clifford T. Bennett, Chairperson, 216-523-7105, Fax: 216-687-5379, E-mail: c.t.bennett@csuohio.edu.

College of Mount St. Joseph, Graduate Education Program, Cincinnati, OH 45233-1670. Offers adolescent young adult education (MA); art (MA); inclusive early childhood education (MA); instructional leadership (MA); middle childhood education (MA); multicultural special education (MA); music (MA); reading (MA). *Accreditation:* Teacher Education Accreditation Council. Part-time and evening/weekend programs available. Postbaccalaureate distance learning degree programs offered (minimal on-campus study). *Faculty:* 22 full-time (14 women), 11 part-time/adjunct (6 women). *Students:* 68 full-time (54 women), 115 part-time (96 women); includes 21 minority (16 African Americans, 2 American Indian/Alaska Native, 1 Asian American or Pacific Islander, 2 Hispanic Americans). Average age 34. 91 applicants, 98% accepted, 62 enrolled. In 2006, 61 degrees awarded. *Degree requirements:* For master's, research project. *Entrance requirements:* For master's, GRE, PRAXIS II in teaching content area (math or science), 2 letters of recommendation, interview, resumé, prerequisite courses in communications, behavioral sciences and mathematics. Additional exam requirements/recommendations for international students: Required—TOEFL (minimum score 560 paper-based; 220 computer-based). *Application deadline:* Applications are processed on a rolling basis. Application fee: $50. Electronic applications accepted. *Expenses:* Contact institution. *Financial support:* In 2006–07, 3 students received support. Career-related internships or fieldwork and scholarships/grants available. Support available to part-time students. Financial award application deadline: 6/1; financial award applicants required to submit FAFSA. *Faculty research:* Foreign and second language learning problems/reading disabilities/hyperlexia, multicultural/bilingual special education, alternative educator licensure, science education, pedagogical content knowledge. *Unit head:* Dr. Mifrando Obach, Chair, 513-244-3263, Fax: 513-244-4867, E-mail: mifrando_obach@mail.msj.edu. *Application contact:* Marilyn Hoskins, Assistant Director of Admissions for Graduate Recruitment, 513-244-4723, Fax: 513-244-4629, E-mail: marilyn_hoskins@mail.msg.edu.

College of Mount Saint Vincent, School of Professional and Continuing Studies, Department of Teacher Education, Riverdale, NY 10471-1093. Offers instructional technology and global perspectives (Certificate); middle level education (Certificate); multicultural studies (Certificate); urban and multicultural education (MS Ed). *Accreditation:* Teacher Education Accreditation Council. Part-time programs available. *Faculty:* 1 full-time (0 women), 18 part-time/adjunct (12 women). *Students:* 20 full-time (13 women), 239 part-time (172 women); includes 101 minority (50 African Americans, 11 Asian Americans or Pacific Islanders, 40 Hispanic Americans). Average age 38. 35 applicants, 57% accepted. In 2006, 124 degrees awarded. *Degree requirements:* For master's, comprehensive exam, registration. *Entrance requirements:* For master's, interview, New York teaching certificate. Additional exam requirements/recommendations for international students: Required—TOEFL. *Application deadline:* For fall admission, 9/1 priority date for domestic students, 7/1 priority date for international students; for winter admission, 11/1 priority date for domestic students, 10/1 priority date for international students; for spring admission, 12/1 priority date for domestic students, 11/1 priority date for international students. Applications are processed on a rolling basis. Application fee: $50. *Financial support:* Career-related internships or fieldwork available. Financial award applicants required to submit FAFSA. *Unit head:* Mary Ellen Sullivan, Chair, 718-405-3281, Fax: 718-601-6392. *Application contact:* Beigica Collado, Executive Assistant, 718-405-3322, Fax: 718-405-3764, E-mail: beigica.collado@mountsaintvincent.edu.

Columbus State University, Graduate Studies, College of Education, Department of Teacher Education, Columbus, GA 31907-5645. Offers early childhood education (M Ed, Ed S); instructional technology (MS); middle grades education (M Ed, Ed S); physical education (M Ed); secondary education (M Ed, Ed S), including English/language arts, general science (M Ed), mathematics, science (Ed S), social science; special education (Ed S), including behavior disorders, learning disabilities, mental retardation. *Accreditation:* NCATE. Part-time and evening/weekend programs available. Postbaccalaureate distance learning degree programs offered (minimal on-campus study). *Faculty:* 16 full-time (8 women), 2 part-time/adjunct (1 woman). *Students:* 61 full-time (45 women), 128 part-time (89 women); includes 44 minority (36 African Americans, 3 Asian Americans or Pacific Islanders, 5 Hispanic Americans), 1 international. Average age 36. 77 applicants, 49% accepted, 26 enrolled. In 2006, 66 master's, 13 other advanced degrees awarded. *Degree requirements:* For master's, thesis, exit exam; for Ed S, thesis or alternative. *Entrance requirements:* For master's, GRE General Test, minimum GPA of 2.75; for Ed S, GRE General Test. Additional exam requirements/recommendations for international students: Required—TOEFL (minimum score 550 paper-based; 213 computer-based). *Application deadline:* For fall admission, 5/1 priority date for domestic students, 5/1 for international students; for spring admission, 11/1 for domestic and international students. Applications are processed on a rolling basis. Application fee: $25. Electronic applications accepted. *Expenses:* Tuition, state resident: part-time $127 per semester hour. Tuition, nonresident: part-time $508 per semester hour. Required fees: $264 per semester. Tuition and fees vary according to course load. *Financial support:* In 2006–07, 118 students received support, including 21 research assistantships with partial tuition reimbursements available (averaging $3,000 per year); career-related internships or fieldwork, Federal Work-Study, institutionally sponsored loans, scholarships/grants, tuition waivers (partial), and unspecified assistantships also available. Support available to part-time students. Financial award application deadline: 5/1; financial award applicants required to submit FAFSA. *Unit head:* Dr. Deborah Gober, Acting Chair, 706-568-2255, Fax: 706-568-3134, E-mail: gober_deborah@colstate.edu. *Application contact:* Katie Thornton, Graduate Admissions Specialist, 706-568-2035, Fax: 706-568-2462, E-mail: thornton_katie@colstate.edu.

Daemen College, Education Department, Amherst, NY 14226-3592. Offers adolescence education (MS); childhood education (MS); childhood special education (MS). Part-time programs available. *Faculty:* 5 full-time (4 women), 53 part-time/adjunct (45 women). *Students:* 283 full-time (224 women), 238 part-time (202 women); includes 1 minority (African American), 192 international. Average age 33. 314 applicants, 71% accepted, 184 enrolled. In 2006, 284 degrees awarded. *Degree requirements:* For master's, thesis, registration. *Entrance requirements:* For master's, GRE, minimum GPA of 3.0, 3 letters of recommendation, proof of initial certification for licensure. Additional exam requirements/recommendations for international students: Required—TOEFL (minimum score 500 paper-based; 173 computer-based). *Application deadline:* For fall admission, 3/1 priority date for domestic and international students; for spring admission, 10/1 priority date for domestic and international students. Applications are processed on a rolling basis. Application fee: $25. Electronic applications accepted. *Expenses:* Tuition: Full-time $11,700; part-time $650 per credit hour. Required fees: $15 per credit hour. Tuition and fees vary according to course load. *Financial support:* In 2006–07, 48 students received support. Federal Work-Study, institutionally sponsored loans, traineeships, and tuition waivers (partial) available. Support available to part-time students. Financial award application deadline: 2/15; financial award applicants required to submit FAFSA. *Faculty research:* Transition for students with disabilities, early childhood special education, traumatic brain injury (TBI), reading assessment. *Unit head:* Dr. Mary H. Fox, Chair, 716-839-8530, Fax: 716-839-8516, E-mail: mfox@daemen.edu. *Application contact:* Karl Shallowhorn, Associate Director of Graduate Admissions, 716-839-8225, Fax: 716-839-8229, E-mail: kshallow@daemen.edu.

Drury University, Graduate Programs in Education, Program in Middle School Teaching, Springfield, MO 65802. Offers M Ed. *Accreditation:* NCATE. Part-time and evening/weekend programs available. *Degree requirements:* For master's, thesis. *Entrance requirements:* For master's, GRE or MAT, minimum GPA of 2.75. *Faculty research:* Public school higher education partnerships, reading.

East Carolina University, Graduate School, College of Education, Department of Curriculum and Instruction, Greenville, NC 27858-4353. Offers behavior/emotional disabilities (MA Ed); elementary education (MA Ed); English education (MA Ed); learning disabilities (MA Ed); low incidence disabilities (MA Ed); mental retardation (MA Ed); middle grade education (MA Ed); reading education (MA Ed); social studies education (MA Ed). Part-time programs available. Postbaccalaureate distance learning degree programs offered. *Students:* 92 full-time (85 women), 233 part-time (211 women); includes 42 minority (39 African Americans, 1 American Indian/Alaska Native, 1 Asian American or Pacific Islander, 1 Hispanic American). Average age 30. 25 applicants, 100% accepted, 25 enrolled. In 2006, 195 degrees awarded. *Degree requirements:* For master's, thesis optional. *Entrance requirements:* For master's, GRE General Test or MAT, interview, bachelor's degree in related field, minimum GPA of 2.5, teaching license. Additional exam requirements/recommendations for international students: Required—TOEFL. *Application deadline:* For fall admission, 6/1 priority date for domestic students. Applications are processed on a rolling basis. Application fee: $50. *Financial support:* Research assistantships, teaching assistantships, Federal Work-Study available. Support available to part-time students. Financial award application deadline: 6/1; financial award applicants required to submit FAFSA. *Unit head:* Dr. Sandra H. Warren, Interim Chair, 252-328-2699, E-mail: warrens@ecu.edu. *Application contact:* Dean of Graduate School, 252-328-6012, Fax: 252-328-6071, E-mail: gradschool@ecu.edu.

Eastern Illinois University, Graduate School, College of Education and Professional Studies, Department of Early Childhood, Elementary and Middle Level Education, Charleston, IL 61920-3099. Offers elementary education (MS Ed). *Accreditation:* NCATE. Part-time programs available. *Faculty:* 14 full-time (6 women). In 2006, 55 degrees awarded. *Degree requirements:* For master's, comprehensive exam. *Application deadline:* For fall admission, 7/31 priority date for domestic students. Applications are processed on a rolling basis. Application fee: $30. *Expenses:* Tuition, state resident: part-time $169 per semester hour. Tuition, nonresident: part-time $508 per semester hour. Required fees: $60 per semester hour. *Financial support:* In 2006–07, research assistantships with tuition reimbursements (averaging $7,200 per year), 5 teaching assistantships with tuition reimbursements (averaging $7,200 per year) were awarded. *Unit head:* Dr. Joy Russell, Chairperson, 217-581-5728, E-mail: jlrussell@eiu.edu.

Eastern Michigan University, Graduate School, College of Education, Department of Teacher Education, Program in Middle School Education, Ypsilanti, MI 48197. Offers MA. *Accreditation:* NCATE. Part-time and evening/weekend programs available. Postbaccalaureate distance learning degree programs offered (minimal on-campus study). *Students:* Average age 30. In 2006, 9 degrees awarded. *Entrance requirements:* For master's, GRE. Additional exam requirements/recommendations for international students: Required—TOEFL. *Application deadline:* For fall admission, 5/15 priority date for domestic students, 5/1 priority date for international students; for winter admission, 10/15 priority date for domestic students, 10/1 priority date for international students; for spring admission, 3/15 priority date for domestic students, 3/1 priority date for international students. Applications are processed on a rolling basis. Application fee: $35. *Expenses:* Tuition, state resident: part-time $341 per credit hour. Tuition, nonresident: full-time $16,104; part-time $671 per credit hour. Required fees: $816; $34 per credit hour. $40 per term. One-time fee: $82 full-time. Tuition and fees vary according to course level, course load, degree level and reciprocity agreements. *Financial support:* Fellowships, research assistantships with full tuition reimbursements, teaching assistantships with full tuition reimbursements, career-related internships or fieldwork, Federal Work-Study, institutionally sponsored loans, scholarships/grants, tuition waivers (partial), and unspecified assistantships available. Support available to part-time students. Financial award applicants required to submit FAFSA.

Eastern Nazarene College, Adult and Graduate Studies, Division of Education, Quincy, MA 02170-2999. Offers early childhood education (M Ed, Certificate); elementary education (M Ed, Certificate); English as a second language (M Ed, Certificate); instructional enrichment and development (M Ed, Certificate); middle school education (M Ed, Certificate); moderate special needs education (M Ed, Certificate); principal (Certificate); program development and supervision (M Ed, Certificate); secondary education (M Ed, Certificate); special education administrator (Certificate); supervisor (Certificate); teacher of reading (M Ed, Certificate). M Ed and Certificate also available through weekend program for administration, special needs, and reading only. Part-time and evening/weekend programs available. *Faculty:* 9 full-time (5 women), 11 part-time/adjunct (5 women). *Students:* 135. Average age 35. 20 applicants, 100% accepted. In 2006, 2 degrees awarded. *Entrance requirements:* Additional exam requirements/recommendations for international students: Required—TOEFL (minimum score 550 paper-based). *Application deadline:* Applications are processed on a rolling basis. Application fee: $35. *Financial support:* Career-related internships or fieldwork available. Support available to part-time students. Financial award applicants required to submit FAFSA. *Unit head:* Dr. Lorne Ranstrom, Chair, 617-745-3528, E-mail: randstrol@enc.edu. *Application contact:* Christine Galbraith, Graduate Studies Recruiter, 617-774-6703, Fax: 617-984-4901, E-mail: christine.galbraith@enc.edu.

Emory University, Graduate School of Arts and Sciences, Division of Educational Studies, Atlanta, GA 30322-1100. Offers educational studies (MA, PhD, DAST); middle grades teaching (M Ed, MAT); secondary teaching (M Ed, MAT). *Accreditation:* NCATE. Terminal master's awarded for partial completion of doctoral program. *Degree requirements:* For master's, thesis/dissertation, registration; for doctorate, thesis/dissertation, comprehensive exam, registration. *Entrance requirements:* For master's and doctorate, GRE General Test, minimum GPA of 3.0. Additional exam requirements/recommendations for international students: Required—TOEFL. Electronic applications accepted. *Expenses:* Tuition: Full-time $30,246. *Faculty research:* Educational policy, educational measurement, urban and multicultural education, mathematics and science education, comparative education.

Fayetteville State University, Graduate School, Program in Middle Grades, Secondary and Special Education, Fayetteville, NC 28301-4298. Offers biology (MA Ed); history (MA Ed); mathematics (MA Ed); middle grades (MA Ed); political science (MA Ed); reading (MA Ed); sociology (MA Ed); special education (MA Ed), including behavioral-emotional handicaps, mentally handicapped, specific training disability. *Accreditation:* NCATE. Part-time and evening/weekend programs available. *Faculty:* 19 full-time (12 women), 3 part-time/adjunct (2 women). *Students:* 14 full-time (10 women), 48 part-time (40 women); includes 44 minority (40 African Americans, 2 American Indian/Alaska Native, 1 Asian American or Pacific Islander, 1 Hispanic American). Average age 39. 16 applicants, 100% accepted, 16 enrolled. In 2006, 33 degrees awarded. *Degree requirements:* For master's, internship. *Application deadline:* For fall admission, 7/1 for domestic students; for spring admission, 12/1 for domestic students. Applications are processed on a rolling basis. Application fee: $25. Electronic applications accepted. *Expenses:* Tuition, state resident: full-time $2,118. Tuition, nonresident: full-time $11,708. Required fees: $1,099. Tuition and fees vary according to course load. *Unit head:* Dr. Charletta Barringer-Brown, Interim Chair, 910-672-1182, E-mail: cbarringerbrown@uncfsu.edu.

Fitchburg State College, Division of Graduate and Continuing Education, Program in Middle School Education, Fitchburg, MA 01420-2697. Offers M Ed. *Accreditation:* NCATE. Part-time and evening/weekend programs available. *Students:* 2 full-time (0 women), 28 part-time (18 women). Average age 35. 11 applicants, 100% accepted, 9 enrolled. In 2006, 15 degrees awarded. *Entrance requirements:* For master's, GRE General Test or MAT, teaching certificate. Additional exam requirements/recommendations for international students: Required—TOEFL (minimum score 550 paper-based; 213 computer-based; 79 iBT). *Application deadline:* Applications are processed on a rolling basis. Application fee: $25 ($50 for international students). *Expenses:* Tuition, state resident: part-time $150 per credit. Tuition, nonresident: part-time $150 per credit. Required fees: $90 per credit. *Financial support:* In 2006–07, research assistantships with partial tuition reimbursements (averaging $5,500 per year); Federal Work-Study,

Middle School Education

Fitchburg State College (continued)
scholarships/grants, and unspecified assistantships also available. Support available to part-time students. Financial award application deadline: 3/1; financial award applicants required to submit FAFSA. *Unit head:* Dr. Ian Bothwell, Chair, 978-665-4657, Fax: 978-665-3658, E-mail: gce@fsc.edu. *Application contact:* Director of Admissions, 978-665-3144, Fax: 978-665-4540, E-mail: admissions@fsc.edu.

Fort Valley State University, College of Graduate Studies and Extended Education, Department of Curriculum and Instruction, Program in Middle Grades Education, Fort Valley, GA 31030-4313. Offers MS. Part-time programs available. *Degree requirements:* For master's, thesis optional. *Entrance requirements:* For master's, GRE General Test or MAT.

Furman University, Graduate Division, Department of Education, Greenville, SC 29613. Offers early childhood education (MA); elementary education (MA); English as a second language (MA); middle school education (MA); reading (MA); school administration (MA); special education (MA). *Accreditation:* NCATE. Part-time and evening/weekend programs available. *Faculty:* 17 full-time (12 women), 19 part-time/adjunct (15 women). *Students:* 114 full-time (89 women), 72 part-time (59 women); includes 27 minority (23 African Americans, 4 Hispanic Americans). Average age 32. 36 applicants, 100% accepted, 36 enrolled. In 2006, 111 degrees awarded. *Degree requirements:* For master's, thesis (for some programs), comprehensive exam. *Entrance requirements:* For master's, GRE General Test or PRAXIS. *Application deadline:* For fall admission, 8/1 priority date for domestic and international students; for winter admission, 12/1 priority date for domestic and international students; for spring admission, 2/1 priority date for domestic and international students. Applications are processed on a rolling basis. Application fee: $50. *Expenses:* Tuition: Part-time $347 per credit. *Financial support:* In 2006–07, 97 students received support; fellowships, scholarships/grants and unspecified assistantships available. Financial award application deadline: 1/15; financial award applicants required to submit FAFSA. *Unit head:* Dr. Nelly Hecker, Head, 864-294-3385.

Gardner-Webb University, Graduate School, Department of Education, Program in Middle Grades Education, Boiling Springs, NC 28017. Offers MA. *Accreditation:* NCATE. Part-time and evening/weekend programs available. *Faculty:* 7 full-time (3 women), 2 part-time/adjunct (both women). *Students:* Average age 29. 6 applicants, 100% accepted, 6 enrolled. In 2006, 4 degrees awarded. *Degree requirements:* For master's, comprehensive exam. *Entrance requirements:* For master's, GRE General Test or NTE, PRAXIS, minimum GPA of 2.5. *Application deadline:* For fall admission, 8/1 priority date for domestic students. Applications are processed on a rolling basis. Application fee: $25. Electronic applications accepted. *Expenses:* Tuition: Full-time $3,144; part-time $262 per hour. *Financial support:* Unspecified assistantships available. *Unit head:* Dr. Donna Simmons, Chair, Department of Education, 704-406-4406, Fax: 704-406-3921, E-mail: dsimmons@gardner-webb.edu.

George Mason University, Graduate School of Education, Programs in Curriculum and Instruction, Fairfax, VA 22030. Offers bilingual/multicultural/English as a second language education (M Ed); early childhood education (M Ed); instructional technology (M Ed); middle education (M Ed); reading (M Ed); secondary education (M Ed); special education (M Ed). Part-time and evening/weekend programs available. *Faculty:* 108 full-time (70 women), 193 part-time/adjunct (140 women). *Students:* 185 full-time (144 women), 816 part-time (683 women); includes 148 minority (46 African Americans, 2 American Indian/Alaska Native, 44 Asian Americans or Pacific Islanders, 56 Hispanic Americans), 28 international. Average age 34. 822 applicants, 72% accepted, 473 enrolled. In 2006, 606 master's awarded. *Entrance requirements:* For master's, minimum GPA of 3.0 in last 60 hours. *Application deadline:* For fall admission, 5/1 for domestic students; for spring admission, 11/1 for domestic students. Application fee: $60 ($75 for international students). Electronic applications accepted. *Expenses:* Tuition, state resident: full-time $5,724; part-time $238 per credit. Tuition, nonresident: full-time $16,896; part-time $704 per credit. Required fees: $1,656; $69 per credit. *Financial support:* Career-related internships or fieldwork available. Support available to part-time students. Financial award application deadline: 3/1; financial award applicants required to submit FAFSA. *Unit head:* Martin E. Ford, Senior Associate Dean, 703-993-2008.

Georgia College & State University, Graduate School, School of Education, Department of Early Childhood and Middle Grades Education, Milledgeville, GA 31061. Offers early childhood education (M Ed, Ed S); middle grades education (M Ed, Ed S). *Accreditation:* NCATE. *Students:* 5 full-time (4 women), 57 part-time (51 women); includes 12 minority (11 African Americans, 1 Hispanic American), 1 international. Average age 36. 67 applicants, 51% accepted, 9 enrolled. In 2006, 21 master's, 24 other advanced degrees awarded. *Degree requirements:* For master's, comprehensive exam; for Ed S, residency. *Entrance requirements:* For master's, GRE General Test or MAT, 2 professional recommendations; for Ed S, GRE General Test or MAT, master's degree, 2 years teaching experience, 2 professional recommendations. Additional exam requirements/recommendations for international students: Required—TOEFL. *Application deadline:* For fall admission, 7/1 priority date for domestic students. Applications are processed on a rolling basis. Application fee: $25. Electronic applications accepted. *Expenses:* Tuition, state resident: full-time $3,222; part-time $179 per credit hour. Tuition, nonresident: full-time $12,870; part-time $715 per credit hour. Required fees: $391 per semester. Tuition and fees vary according to course load. *Financial support:* Career-related internships or fieldwork, Federal Work-Study, and unspecified assistantships available. Support available to part-time students. Financial award application deadline: 3/1; financial award applicants required to submit FAFSA. *Unit head:* Dr. Charles Martin, Chair, 478-445-5479, E-mail: charles.martin@gcsu.edu.

Georgia Southern University, Jack N. Averitt College of Graduate Studies, College of Education, Department of Teaching and Learning, Program in Middle Grades Education, Statesboro, GA 30460. Offers M Ed, MAT. *Accreditation:* NCATE. Part-time and evening/weekend programs available. *Students:* 4 full-time (3 women), 25 part-time (22 women); includes 4 minority (all African Americans) Average age 30. 11 applicants, 82% accepted, 4 enrolled. In 2006, 14 degrees awarded. *Degree requirements:* For master's, exit assessment. *Entrance requirements:* For master's, GRE General Test or MAT, minimum GPA of 2.5. Additional exam requirements/recommendations for international students: Required—TOEFL (minimum score 550 paper-based; 213 computer-based; 80 iBT). *Application deadline:* For fall admission, 3/1 priority date for domestic students, 3/1 for international students; for spring admission, 10/1 priority date for domestic students, 10/1 for international students. Applications are processed on a rolling basis. Application fee: $50. Electronic applications accepted. *Financial support:* In 2006–07, 19 students received support, including research assistantships with partial tuition reimbursements available (averaging $5,500 per year), teaching assistantships with partial tuition reimbursements available (averaging $5,500 per year); career-related internships or fieldwork, Federal Work-Study, and tuition waivers (partial) also available. Support available to part-time students. Financial award application deadline: 4/15; financial award applicants required to submit FAFSA. *Faculty research:* Teacher teams, gender, technology applications. *Unit head:* Dr. Deborah Thomas, Associate Professor, 912-486-7691, Fax: 912-681-0026, E-mail: debthom@georgiasouthern.edu. *Application contact:* 912-681-5384, Fax: 912-681-0740, E-mail: gradadmissions@georgiasouthern.edu.

Georgia Southwestern State University, Graduate Studies, School of Education, Americus, GA 31709-4693. Offers early childhood education (M Ed, Ed S); health and physical education (M Ed); middle grades education (M Ed, Ed S); reading (M Ed); secondary education (M Ed); special education (M Ed). *Accreditation:* NCATE. *Degree requirements:* For master's, comprehensive exam. *Entrance requirements:* For master's, GRE General Test or MAT, minimum GPA of 2.5; for Ed S, GRE General Test or MAT, minimum graduate GPA of 3.25, M Ed from accredited college or university, 3 years teaching experience. Electronic applications accepted.

Georgia State University, College of Education, Department of Middle-Secondary Education and Instructional Technology, Program in Middle Childhood Education, Atlanta, GA 30303-3083. Offers M Ed, Ed S. *Accreditation:* NCATE. Part-time and evening/weekend programs available. *Students:* 3 full-time (all women), 23 part-time (17 women); includes 6 minority (all African Americans), 1 international. Average age 35. 7 applicants, 86% accepted. In 2006, 11 master's, 3 other advanced degrees awarded. *Degree requirements:* For master's, comprehensive exam; for Ed S, project/exam. *Entrance requirements:* For master's, GRE General Test, minimum GPA of 2.5; for Ed S, GRE General Test or MAT, minimum graduate GPA of 3.25. *Application deadline:* For fall admission, 7/15 for domestic students; for spring admission, 1/15 for domestic students. Application fee: $25. *Financial support:* Federal Work-Study and institutionally sponsored loans available. *Unit head:* Dr. Ruth Hough, Acting Chair, Department of Middle-Secondary Education and Instructional Technology, 404-651-2510.

Grand Valley State University, College of Education, Programs in General Education, Allendale, MI 49401-9403. Offers adult and higher education (M Ed); early childhood education (M Ed); education of the gifted and talented (M Ed); educational leadership (M Ed); educational technology (M Ed); elementary education (M Ed); middle and high school education (M Ed); teaching English to speakers of other languages (M Ed). Part-time and evening/weekend programs available. Postbaccalaureate distance learning degree programs offered (minimal on-campus study). *Faculty:* 82 full-time (42 women), 43 part-time/adjunct (25 women). *Students:* 136 full-time (97 women), 828 part-time (565 women); includes 55 minority (26 African Americans, 7 American Indian/Alaska Native, 5 Asian Americans or Pacific Islanders, 17 Hispanic Americans). Average age 33. 280 applicants, 94% accepted, 188 enrolled. In 2006, 322 degrees awarded. *Degree requirements:* For master's, thesis. *Entrance requirements:* For master's, GRE General Test or minimum GPA of 3.0. Additional exam requirements/recommendations for international students: Required—TOEFL. *Application deadline:* Applications are processed on a rolling basis. Application fee: $30. Electronic applications accepted. *Expenses:* Tuition, state resident: full-time $5,850; part-time $325 per credit. Tuition, nonresident: full-time $10,800; part-time $600 per credit. Tuition and fees vary according to course load. *Financial support:* In 2006–07, 2 research assistantships with full and partial tuition reimbursements (averaging $8,000 per year) were awarded; career-related internships or fieldwork, Federal Work-Study, scholarships/grants, and unspecified assistantships also available. *Faculty research:* Effectiveness of technology in education, parental involvement, effective teaching, effective schools research. *Unit head:* Dr. Linda McCrea, Director, 616-331-2080, E-mail: mccreal@gvsu.edu. *Application contact:* Dr. Douglas Busman, Director, Student Information and Services, 616-331-6831, Fax: 616-331-6217, E-mail: busmando@gvsu.edu.

Hebrew College, Shoolman Graduate School of Education, Newton Centre, MA 02459. Offers early childhood Jewish education (Certificate); Jewish day school education (Certificate); Jewish education (MJ Ed); Jewish family education (Certificate); Jewish special education (Certificate); Jewish youth education, informal education and camping (Certificate). Part-time and evening/weekend programs available. Postbaccalaureate distance learning degree programs offered. *Faculty:* 6 full-time (1 woman), 19 part-time/adjunct (7 women). *Students:* 51 (42 women). Average age 37. 33 applicants, 79% accepted, 19 enrolled. In 2006, 5 degrees awarded. *Degree requirements:* For master's, one foreign language. *Entrance requirements:* For master's, GRE, interview. Additional exam requirements/recommendations for international students: Required—TOEFL. *Application deadline:* For fall admission, 12/15 priority date for domestic and international students; for winter admission, 2/15 priority date for domestic and international students; for spring admission, 5/30 priority date for domestic and international students. Application fee: $50. *Financial support:* Fellowships, career-related internships or fieldwork and tuition waivers (partial) available. Support available to part-time students. Financial award application deadline: 4/15; financial award applicants required to submit FAFSA. *Unit head:* Dr. Barry Mesch, Provost, 617-559-8600, Fax: 617-559-8601, E-mail: bmesch@hebrewcollege.edu. *Application contact:* Kate Nachman, Director of Admissions, 617-559-8610, Fax: 617-559-8601, E-mail: admissions@hebrewcollege.edu.

Henderson State University, Graduate Studies, School of Education, Department of Curriculum, Instruction and Leadership, Arkadelphia, AR 71999-0001. Offers early childhood (P-4) (MSE); English (MSE); English as a second language (MSE, CP); math (MSE); middle school (MSE); reading (MSE); social science (MSE). *Accreditation:* NCATE. Part-time programs available. *Faculty:* 19 full-time (6 women), 4 part-time/adjunct (2 women). *Students:* 38 full-time (36 women), 49 part-time (47 women); includes 6 minority (5 African Americans, 1 Hispanic American), 16 international. Average age 37. In 2006, 31 degrees awarded. *Entrance requirements:* For master's, GRE General Test or MAT, minimum GPA of 2.7, teacher certification. *Application deadline:* For fall admission, 5/1 priority date for domestic students, 5/1 for international students; for winter admission, 10/1 for international students; for spring admission, 12/1 priority date for domestic students, 4/1 for international students. Applications are processed on a rolling basis. Application fee: $0 ($30 for international students). *Expenses:* Tuition, state resident: full-time $3,294; part-time $183 per credit hour. Tuition, nonresident: full-time $6,588; part-time $366 per credit hour. Required fees: $176 per term. *Financial support:* In 2006–07, 1 teaching assistantship with full tuition reimbursement (averaging $4,000 per year) was awarded; research assistantships, Federal Work-Study and institutionally sponsored loans also available. Support available to part-time students. Financial award application deadline: 7/31. *Unit head:* Dr. Kenneth Harris, Chairperson, 870-230-5203, Fax: 870-230-5455, E-mail: harris@hsu.edu. *Application contact:* Dr. Marck L. Beggs, Graduate Dean, 870-230-5126, Fax: 870-230-5479, E-mail: beggsm@hsu.edu.

Hofstra University, School of Education and Allied Human Services, Department of Curriculum and Teaching, Program in Middle Level Education, Hempstead, NY 11549. Offers middle school extension (grades 5-6) (CAS); middle school extension (grades 7-9) (CAS). Part-time and evening/weekend programs available. *Students:* 1 (woman) full-time. Average age 43. 11 applicants, 91% accepted, 1 enrolled. In 2006, 12 degrees awarded. *Degree requirements:* For degree, registration. *Entrance requirements:* For degree, interview, teacher certificate. Additional exam requirements/recommendations for international students: Required—TOEFL (minimum score 550 paper-based; 213 computer-based). *Application deadline:* Applications are processed on a rolling basis. Application fee: $60. Electronic applications accepted. *Expenses:* Tuition: Full-time $13,320; part-time $740 per credit. Required fees: $930; $155 per term. *Financial support:* Fellowships with tuition reimbursements, research assistantships with full and partial tuition reimbursements, tuition waivers (full and partial) available. Financial award applicants required to submit FAFSA. *Faculty research:* Teaming, gender issues, after school programs, advisories, authentic assessment. *Unit head:* Dr. Sandra L. Stacki, Director, 516-463-5783, Fax: 516-463-6196, E-mail: catsls@hofstra.edu. *Application contact:* Carol Drummer, Dean of Graduate Admissions, 516-463-4876, Fax: 516-463-4664, E-mail: gradstudent@hofstra.edu.

James Madison University, College of Graduate and Outreach Programs, College of Education, Middle, Secondary, and Mathematics Education Department, Program in Middle Education, Harrisonburg, VA 22807. Offers MAT. *Accreditation:* NCATE. Part-time and evening/weekend programs available. *Students:* Average age 27. *Entrance requirements:* For master's, GRE General Test. Additional exam requirements/recommendations for international students: Required—TOEFL. *Application deadline:* For fall admission, 5/1 priority date for domestic students; for spring admission, 9/1 priority date for domestic students. Applications are processed on a rolling basis. Application fee: $55. Electronic applications accepted. *Expenses:* Tuition, state resident: full-time $6,336; part-time $264 per credit hour. Tuition, nonresident: full-time $17,832; part-time $743 per credit hour. *Financial support:* Federal Work-Study and unspecified assistantships available. Financial award application deadline: 3/1; financial award applicants required to submit FAFSA. *Unit head:* Dr. Lou Ann Lovin, Academic Unit Head, 540-568-6701.

John Carroll University, Graduate School, Department of Education and Allied Studies, Program in School Based Middle Childhood Education, University Heights, OH 44118-4581. Offers M Ed. *Accreditation:* NCATE. *Faculty:* 1 (woman) full-time, 4 part-time/adjunct (3 women). *Students:* 6 full-time (3 women). Average age 29. 15 applicants, 40% accepted, 6 enrolled. In 2006, 5 degrees awarded. *Degree requirements:* For master's, research essay or thesis. *Entrance requirements:* For master's, GRE General Test or MAT, minimum GPA of 2.75. *Application deadline:* For spring admission, 5/15 for domestic students. Applications are processed on a rolling basis. Application fee: $25 ($35 for international students). *Expenses:* Tuition: Full-time $9,675; part-time $645 per credit hour. Tuition and fees vary according to program. *Financial support:* Application deadline: 3/1; *Unit head:* Dr. Barbara Garson, Coordinator, Teacher Education, 216-397-4689, Fax: 216-397-3045, E-mail: bgarson@jcu.edu.

John Carroll University, Graduate School, Program in Integrated Science, University Heights, OH 44118-4581. Offers MA. Part-time programs available. *Students:* 18 applicants, 94% accepted, 16 enrolled. In 2006, 15 degrees awarded. *Median time to degree:* Master's–2 years part-time. *Degree requirements:* For master's, thesis optional. *Entrance requirements:* For master's, minimum GPA of 2.5. Application fee: $25 ($35 for international students). *Expenses:* Tuition: Full-time $9,675; part-time $645 per credit hour. Tuition and fees vary according to program. *Financial support:* Tuition waivers (partial) available. Support available to part-time students. *Unit head:* Michael Kimmel, Director, Integrated Science Program, 216-397-1507, Fax: 216-397-1835, E-mail: mkimmel@jcu.edu.

Kennesaw State University, Leland and Clarice C. Bagwell College of Education, Program in Graduate Education, Kennesaw, GA 30144-5591. Offers adolescent education (M Ed); early childhood education (M Ed); educational leadership (M Ed); special education (M Ed). *Accreditation:* NCATE. Part-time programs available. *Faculty:* 60 full-time (38 women), 12 part-time/adjunct (4 women). *Students:* 150 full-time (143 women), 489 part-time (371 women); includes 95 minority (85 African Americans, 1 American Indian/Alaska Native, 1 Asian American or Pacific Islander, 8 Hispanic Americans), 21 international. Average age 35. 165 applicants, 97% accepted, 142 enrolled. In 2006, 283 degrees awarded. *Degree requirements:* For master's, thesis or alternative. *Entrance requirements:* For master's, GRE General Test, T-4 state certification, minimum GPA of 2.75. Additional exam requirements/recommendations for international students: Required—TOEFL (minimum score 550 paper-based; 213 computer-based; 80 iBT), IELTS (minimum score 6). *Application deadline:* For fall admission, 7/15 priority date for domestic students; for spring admission, 10/15 priority date for domestic students. Application fee: $50. Electronic applications accepted. *Expenses:* Tuition, state resident: full-time $3,044; part-time $127 per semester hour. Tuition, nonresident: full-time $12,172; part-time $508 per semester hour. Required fees: $353 per semester. Full-time tuition and fees vary according to campus/location and program. *Financial support:* Federal Work-Study and unspecified assistantships available. Support available to part-time students. Financial award application deadline: 6/15; financial award applicants required to submit FAFSA. *Application contact:* Alisha O'Brien, Administrative Coordinator, 770-423-6043, Fax: 770-420-4435, E-mail: aobrien@kennesaw.edu.

Kent State University, Graduate School of Education, Health, and Human Services, Department of Teaching, Leadership, and Curriculum Studies, Program in Junior High/Middle School, Kent, OH 44242-0001. Offers M Ed, MA. Part-time programs available. *Faculty:* 14 full-time (10 women). *Students:* 7 full-time (3 women), 7 part-time (6 women); includes 2 minority (both African Americans) In 2006, 6 degrees awarded. *Degree requirements:* For master's, registration. *Entrance requirements:* For master's, GRE. Additional exam requirements/recommendations for international students: Required—TOEFL. Electronic applications accepted. *Financial support:* In 2006–07, fellowships with full tuition reimbursements (averaging $7,210 per year); research assistantships with full tuition reimbursements, teaching assistantships with full tuition reimbursements, career-related internships or fieldwork, Federal Work-Study, institutionally sponsored loans, scholarships/grants, health care benefits, and unspecified assistantships also available. Support available to part-time students. Financial award applicants required to submit FAFSA. *Faculty research:* Middle school reform, teacher action research. *Unit head:* Dr. Alexa Sandmann, Coordinator, 330-672-2580, E-mail: asandman@kent.edu. *Application contact:* Nancy Miller, Academic Program Coordinator, Office of Graduate Student Services, 330-672-2576, Fax: 330-672-9162, E-mail: ogs@kent.edu.

Lesley University, School of Education, Cambridge, MA 02138-2790. Offers curriculum and instruction (M Ed, CAGS); early childhood education (M Ed); educational studies (PhD); elementary education (M Ed); individually designed (M Ed); middle school education (M Ed); moderate special needs (M Ed); reading (M Ed, CAGS); science in education (M Ed); severe special needs (M Ed); special needs (CAGS); technology in education (M Ed, CAGS). Part-time and evening/weekend programs available. Postbaccalaureate distance learning degree programs offered (no on-campus study). *Faculty:* 47 full-time (39 women), 208 part-time/adjunct (135 women). *Students:* 242 full-time (222 women), 2,903 part-time (2,495 women); includes 279 minority (179 African Americans, 7 American Indian/Alaska Native, 25 Asian Americans or Pacific Islanders, 68 Hispanic Americans), 10 international. Average age 36. 1,186 applicants, 96% accepted, 792 enrolled. In 2006, 1,724 master's, 6 doctorates, 17 other advanced degrees awarded. *Degree requirements:* For master's, practicum; for doctorate, thesis/dissertation. *Entrance requirements:* For doctorate, GRE General Test or MAT, interview, master's degree, resumé; for CAGS, interview, master's degree. Additional exam requirements/recommendations for international students: Required—TOEFL (minimum score 550 paper-based; 213 computer-based; 80 iBT). *Application deadline:* Applications are processed on a rolling basis. Application fee: $50. Electronic applications accepted. *Financial support:* In 2006–07, 26 students received support, including research assistantships (averaging $3,400 per year), teaching assistantships (averaging $3,400 per year); career-related internships or fieldwork, Federal Work-Study, scholarships/grants, and unspecified assistantships also available. Support available to part-time students. Financial award application deadline: 4/15; financial award applicants required to submit FAFSA. *Faculty research:* Assessment in literacy, mathematics and science; autism spectrum disorders; instructional technology and online learning; multicultural education and ELL. *Unit head:* Dr. Mario Borunda, Dean, 617-349-8375, Fax: 617-349-8607, E-mail: mborunda@lesley.edu. *Application contact:* Kristen Card, Associate Director of On-Campus Admissions, 617-349-8734, Fax: 617-349-8313, E-mail: kmcard@lesley.edu.

See Close-Up on page 893.

Long Island University, C.W. Post Campus, School of Education, Department of Curriculum and Instruction, Brookville, NY 11548-1300. Offers adolescence education (MS); adolescence education: biology (MS); adolescence education: earth science (MS); adolescence education: English (MS); adolescence education: mathematics (MS); adolescence education: social studies (MS); adolescence education: Spanish (MS); art education (MS); bilingual education (MS); childhood education (MS); early childhood education (MS); middle childhood education (MS); music education (MS); teaching English to speakers of other languages (MS). Part-time and evening/weekend programs available. *Degree requirements:* For master's, comprehensive exam or thesis, student teaching. *Entrance requirements:* For master's, minimum GPA of 2.75 in major, 2.5 overall. Electronic applications accepted. *Faculty research:* Ethics and education, teaching strategies.

Manhattanville College, Graduate Programs, School of Education, Program in Middle Childhood/Adolescence Education (Grades 5-12), Purchase, NY 10577-2132. Offers biology (MAT); biology and special education (MPS); chemistry (MAT); chemistry and special education (MPS); English (MAT); English and special education (MPS); literacy (MPS), including reading and writing, writing; literacy and special education (MPS); math (MAT); math and special education (MPS); second language (MAT), including French, Italian, Latin, Spanish; social studies (MAT); social studies and special education (MPS); special education (MPS). Part-time and evening/weekend programs available. *Students:* 76 full-time (53 women), 109 part-time (68 women); includes 8 African Americans, 1 Asian American or Pacific Islander, 10 Hispanic Americans, 1 international. In 2006, 165 degrees awarded. *Degree requirements:* For master's, comprehensive exam or research project, field experience. *Entrance requirements:* For master's, minimum undergraduate GPA of 3.0, 2 letters of recommendation. *Application deadline:* Applications are processed on a rolling basis. Application fee: $55. *Financial support:* Career-related internships or fieldwork and institutionally sponsored loans available. Support available to part-time students. *Application contact:* Alyce Ware Poli, Director of Admissions, 914-323-5142, Fax: 914-694-1732, E-mail: edschool@mville.edu.

Mary Baldwin College, Graduate Studies, Program in Teaching, Staunton, VA 24401-3610. Offers elementary education (MAT); middle grades education (MAT). *Faculty:* 5 full-time (3 women), 38 part-time/adjunct (20 women). *Students:* 104 full-time (76 women), 101 part-time (85 women). *Application deadline:* For fall admission, 7/15 priority date for domestic students; for spring admission, 11/15 priority date for domestic students. Application fee: $35. *Unit head:* Dr. Carole Grove, Program Director, 540-887-7134. *Application contact:* Lori Johnson, Administrative Assistant, 540-887-7333, E-mail: ljohnson@mbc.edu.

Maryville University of Saint Louis, School of Education, St. Louis, MO 63141-7299. Offers art education (MA Ed); early childhood education (MA Ed); education (Ed D); elementary education (MA Ed); elementary education/English (MA Ed); environmental education (MA Ed); gifted education (MA Ed); middle grades education (MA Ed); reading specialist (MA Ed); secondary education (MA Ed), including educational leadership, secondary teaching and inquiry. *Accreditation:* NASAD; NCATE. Part-time and evening/weekend programs available. *Students:* 17 full-time (14 women), 168 part-time (129 women); includes 20 African Americans, 2 Asian Americans or Pacific Islanders, 1 Hispanic American, 2 international. Average age 37. 39 applicants, 95% accepted, 24 enrolled. In 2006, 37 degrees awarded. *Degree requirements:* For master's, thesis, project. *Entrance requirements:* For master's and doctorate, minimum GPA of 3.0, 3 professional recommendations. Additional exam requirements/recommendations for international students: Required—TOEFL (minimum score 550 paper-based). *Application deadline:* Applications are processed on a rolling basis. Application fee: $35 ($50 for international students). Electronic applications accepted. *Expenses:* Tuition: Full-time $17,800; part-time $555 per credit. Required fees: $55 per semester. Tuition and fees vary according to degree level and program. *Financial support:* Career-related internships or fieldwork, Federal Work-Study, tuition waivers (partial), and professional educator discounts available. Financial award application deadline: 7/31; financial award applicants required to submit FAFSA. *Faculty research:* Collaboration with public schools, preservice program development, mathematics, diversity, literacy. *Unit head:* Dr. Sam Hausfather, Dean, 314-529-9466, Fax: 314-529-9921, E-mail: shausfather@maryville.edu. *Application contact:* Dr. Lillian Curtis, Graduate Admissions Coordinator, 314-529-9542, Fax: 314-529-9921, E-mail: teachered@maryville.edu.

Mercer University, Graduate Studies, Cecil B. Day Campus, Tift College of Education, Macon, GA 31207-0003. Offers early childhood education (M Ed, MAT); educational leadership (M Ed, PhD); middle grades education (M Ed, MAT); reading education (M Ed); secondary education (M Ed, MAT); teacher leadership (Ed S). Part-time and evening/weekend programs available. *Faculty:* 13 full-time (6 women), 7 part-time/adjunct (3 women). *Students:* 31 full-time (23 women), 211 part-time (174 women); includes 111 minority (101 African Americans, 2 American Indian/Alaska Native, 6 Asian Americans or Pacific Islanders, 2 Hispanic Americans), 2 international. Average age 33. In 2006, 57 master's, 4 other advanced degrees awarded. *Degree requirements:* For master's and Ed S, research project; for doctorate, thesis/dissertation. *Entrance requirements:* For master's, GRE or MAT, minimum undergraduate GPA of 2.75; for doctorate, GRE; for Ed S, GRE or MAT, minimum GPA of 3.25, 3 years of teaching experience. *Application deadline:* For fall admission, 8/1 for domestic and international students; for spring admission, 12/1 for domestic and international students. Applications are processed on a rolling basis. Application fee: $25. *Expenses: Contact institution. Financial support:* Federal Work-Study available. Support available to part-time students. Financial award application deadline: 5/1. *Faculty research:* Educational computing, content area reading, concept learning, importance of play for young children, multicultural literature. *Unit head:* Dr. Carl R. Martray, Dean, 478-301-5397, Fax: 478-301-2280, E-mail: martray_cr@mercer.edu. *Application contact:* Dr. Allison Gilmore, Associate Dean for Graduate Teacher Education, 678-547-6330, Fax: 678-547-6055, E-mail: gilmore_a@mercer.edu.

Mercy College, Division of Education, Dobbs Ferry, NY 10522-1189. Offers adolescence education: grades 7-12 (MS); applied behavior analysis (MS); bilingual education (MS); childhood education: grades 1-6 (MS); early childhood education: birth—grade 2 (MS); education (MS); elementary education (MS); learning technology (MS); middle childhood education: grades 5-9 (MS); reading (MS); school administration and supervision (MS); school building leadership (MS); school business administration (MS); secondary education (MS); special education (MS); students with disabilities: grades 5-9 (MS); students with disabilities: grades 7-12 (MS); teaching English to speakers of other languages (MS); teaching literacy: birth—grade 6 (MS); teaching literacy: grades 5-12 (MS); urban education (MS). *Students:* 572 full-time (467 women), 1,719 part-time (1,287 women); includes 943 minority (470 African Americans, 7 American Indian/Alaska Native, 48 Asian Americans or Pacific Islanders, 418 Hispanic Americans), 6 international. Average age 33. In 2006, 1090 degrees awarded. *Entrance requirements:* For master's, teaching certificate. *Application deadline:* For fall admission, 2/1 for domestic students. Applications are processed on a rolling basis. Application fee: $37. *Expenses: Contact institution.* Tuition and fees vary according to program. *Financial support:* Institutionally sponsored loans, scholarships/grants, and unspecified assistantships available. Support available to part-time students. *Faculty research:* Distance learning, literacy, assessment, community schools, impact of staff development. *Unit head:* Dr. William Prattella, Chairperson, 914-674-7555, Fax: 914-674-7352, E-mail: wprattella@mercy.edu. *Application contact:* Kathleen Jackson, Director of Admissions, 800-Mercy-NY, Fax: 914-674-7382, E-mail: admissions@mercy.edu.

Middle Tennessee State University, College of Graduate Studies, College of Education and Behavioral Science, Department of Elementary and Special Education, Major in Curriculum and Instruction, Murfreesboro, TN 37132. Offers early childhood education (M Ed); elementary education (M Ed, Ed S); middle school education (M Ed). *Accreditation:* NCATE. Part-time and evening/weekend programs available. Postbaccalaureate distance learning degree programs offered. *Students:* 13 full-time (12 women), 79 part-time (73 women); includes 7 minority (5 African Americans, 2 Asian Americans or Pacific Islanders). In 2006, 59 degrees awarded. *Degree requirements:* For master's, comprehensive exam; for Ed S, thesis. *Entrance requirements:* Additional exam requirements/recommendations for international students: Required—TOEFL (minimum score 525 paper-based; 195 computer-based). *Application deadline:* For fall admission, 8/1 priority date for domestic students. Applications are processed on a rolling basis. Application fee: $25. Electronic applications accepted. *Financial support:* Application deadline: 5/1. *Unit head:* Dr. Connie Jones, Chair, Department of Elementary and Special Education, 615-898-2680, Fax: 615-898-5309, E-mail: cojones@mtsu.edu.

Montclair State University, The Graduate School, College of Science and Mathematics, Department of Mathematics, Montclair, NJ 07043-1624. Offers mathematics (MS), including mathematics education, pure and applied mathematics, statistics; teaching middle grades math (Certificate). Part-time and evening/weekend programs available. *Faculty:* 29 full-time (10 women), 26 part-time/adjunct (11 women). *Students:* 20 full-time (15 women), 146 part-time (104 women); includes 26 minority (11 African Americans, 9 Asian Americans or Pacific Islanders, 6 Hispanic Americans), 6 international. 60 applicants, 55% accepted, 24 enrolled. In 2006, 21 master's, 15 other advanced degrees awarded. *Degree requirements:* For master's, comprehensive exam. *Entrance requirements:* For master's, GRE General Test, minimum GPA of 2.67, 2 letters of recommendation. Additional exam requirements/recommendations for international students: Required—TOEFL (minimum score 83 computer-based). *Application deadline:* For fall admission, 6/1 for international students; for spring admission, 10/1 for international students. Applications are processed on a rolling basis. Application fee: $60. *Expenses:* Tuition, state resident: part-time $450 per credit. Tuition, nonresident: part-time $682 per credit. Tuition and fees vary according to degree level and program. *Financial support:* In 2006–07, 8 research assistantships with full tuition reimbursements (averaging $7,000 per year) were awarded; Federal Work-Study, scholarships/grants, and unspecified assistantships also available. Support available to part-time students. Financial award application deadline: 3/1; financial award applicants required to submit FAFSA. *Faculty research:* Infectious disease. Total annual research expenditures: $130,000. *Unit head:* Dr. Helen Roberts, Chairperson, 973-655-5132. *Application contact:* Dr. Ted Williamson, Advisor, 973-655-5146, E-mail: williamsont@mail.montclair.edu.

Morehead State University, Graduate Programs, College of Education, Department of Curriculum and Instruction, Program in Elementary Education, Morehead, KY 40351. Offers elementary education (MA Ed); international education (MA Ed); middle school education (MA Ed, MAT); reading (MA Ed). *Accreditation:* NCATE. Part-time and evening/weekend

Middle School Education

Morehead State University *(continued)*
programs available. *Students:* 2 full-time (both women), 84 part-time (80 women); includes 1 minority (American Indian/Alaska Native). Average age 32. In 2006, 52 degrees awarded. *Degree requirements:* For master's, thesis optional. *Entrance requirements:* For master's, GRE General Test, minimum GPA of 2.75, teaching certificate. Additional exam requirements/recommendations for international students: Required—TOEFL (minimum score 500 paper-based; 173 computer-based). *Application deadline:* For fall admission, 8/1 priority date for domestic and international students; for spring admission, 12/1 priority date for domestic and international students. Applications are processed on a rolling basis. Application fee: $0 ($55 for international students). Electronic applications accepted. *Financial support:* In 2006–07, teaching assistantships (averaging $6,000 per year); career-related internships or fieldwork, Federal Work-Study, and unspecified assistantships also available. Financial award application deadline: 4/1; financial award applicants required to submit FAFSA. *Faculty research:* Teaching through journal writing, gifted children, reading instruction in elementary schools, teaching social studies in elementary schools, ungraded elementary schools. *Application contact:* Michelle Barber, Graduate Admissions Counselor, 606-783-2039, Fax: 606-783-5061, E-mail: m.barber@moreheadstate.edu.

Morgan State University, School of Graduate Studies, School of Education and Urban Studies, Department of Teacher Education and Administration, Baltimore, MD 21251. Offers educational administration and supervision (MS); elementary and middle school education (MS), including elementary education. *Accreditation:* NCATE. Part-time and evening/weekend programs available. *Degree requirements:* For master's, thesis optional. *Entrance requirements:* For master's, GRE General Test or MAT. Additional exam requirements/recommendations for international students: Required—TOEFL. *Application deadline:* For fall admission, 2/1 priority date for domestic students; for spring admission, 10/1 priority date for domestic students. Applications are processed on a rolling basis. Application fee: $0. *Expenses:* Tuition, state resident: part-time $272 per credit. Tuition, nonresident: part-time $478 per credit. Required fees: $38 per credit. *Financial support:* Fellowships, research assistantships available. Financial award application deadline: 2/1. *Faculty research:* Multicultural education, cooperative learning, psychology of cognition. *Unit head:* Dr. Iola Ragins Smith, Chairperson, 443-885-3292, Fax: 443-319-3871. *Application contact:* Dr. Maurice C. Taylor, Dean, 443-885-3185, Fax: 443-885-8226, E-mail: mctaylor@moac.morgan.edu.

Morgan State University, School of Graduate Studies, School of Education and Urban Studies, MAT Program, Baltimore, MD 21251. Offers elementary education (MAT); high school education (MAT); middle school education (MAT). Part-time programs available. *Students:* 1. Average age 30. In 2006, 4 degrees awarded. *Degree requirements:* For master's, comprehensive exam. *Entrance requirements:* For master's, GRE General Test or MAT. *Application deadline:* For fall admission, 2/1 priority date for domestic students; for spring admission, 10/1 priority date for domestic students. Applications are processed on a rolling basis. Application fee: $0. *Expenses:* Tuition, state resident: part-time $272 per credit. Tuition, nonresident: part-time $478 per credit. Required fees: $38 per credit. *Financial support:* Fellowships available. Financial award application deadline: 4/1. *Faculty research:* Multicultural education, cooperative learning, psychology of cognition. *Unit head:* Dr. Marlene Greer-Chase, Graduate Coordinator, 443-885-1984, Fax: 443-885-8240. *Application contact:* Dr. Maurice C. Taylor, Dean, 443-885-3185, Fax: 443-885-8226, E-mail: mctaylor@moac.morgan.edu.

Mount Saint Mary College, Division of Education, Newburgh, NY 12550-3494. Offers adolescence and special education (MS Ed); adolescence education (MS Ed); childhood and special education (MS Ed); childhood education (MS Ed); literacy and special education (MS Ed); literacy/childhood (MS Ed); middle school (5-6) (MS Ed); middle school (7-9) (MS Ed); special education (1-6) (MS Ed); special education (7-12) (MS Ed). *Accreditation:* NCATE.Part-time and evening/weekend programs available. *Faculty:* 11 full-time (8 women), 21 part-time/adjunct (18 women). *Students:* 87 full-time (74 women), 368 part-time (303 women); includes 38 minority (12 African Americans, 2 American Indian/Alaska Native, 5 Asian Americans or Pacific Islanders, 19 Hispanic Americans). Average age 31. 164 applicants, 45% accepted, 58 enrolled. In 2006, 131 degrees awarded. *Application deadline:* Applications are processed on a rolling basis. Application fee: $35. *Expenses:* Tuition: Full-time $11,880; part-time $660 per credit. *Financial support:* In 2006–07, 30 students received support. Unspecified assistantships available. Financial award application deadline: 3/15. *Faculty research:* Learning and teaching styles, computers in special education, language development. *Unit head:* Theresa Lewis, Coordinator, 845-569-3149, Fax: 845-569-3535, E-mail: tlewis@msmc.edu.

Mount Saint Vincent University, Graduate Programs, Faculty of Education, Program in Curriculum Studies, Halifax, NS B3M 2J6, Canada. Offers education of young adolescents (M Ed, MA Ed, MA-R); general studies (M Ed, MA Ed, MA-R); teaching English as a second language (M Ed, MA Ed, MA-R). Part-time and evening/weekend programs available. Postbaccalaureate distance learning degree programs offered (minimal on-campus study). *Degree requirements:* For master's, thesis (for some programs). *Entrance requirements:* For master's, bachelor's degree in related field, minimum B average, 1 year of teaching experience. Electronic applications accepted. *Faculty research:* Science education, cultural studies, international education, curriculum development.

Murray State University, College of Education, Department of Adolescent, Career and Special Education, Program in Middle School Education, Murray, KY 42071. Offers MA Ed, Ed S. *Accreditation:* NCATE. *Students:* 23. 3 applicants, 100% accepted. *Degree requirements:* For master's, thesis optional. *Entrance requirements:* Additional exam requirements/recommendations for international students: Required—TOEFL. *Application deadline:* Applications are processed on a rolling basis. Application fee: $25. *Financial support:* Research assistantships, teaching assistantships, Federal Work-Study available. Financial award application deadline: 4/1. *Unit head:* Dr. Bill Koenecke, Graduate Coordinator, 270-809-4669, Fax: 270-809-2540.

Nazareth College of Rochester, Graduate Studies, Department of Education, Program in Inclusive Education-Adolescence Level, Rochester, NY 14618-3790. Offers MS Ed. *Accreditation:* Teacher Education Accreditation Council. *Students:* 52 full-time (34 women), 29 part-time (18 women); includes 5 minority (2 African Americans, 2 Asian Americans or Pacific Islanders, 1 Hispanic American). Average age 30. 64 applicants, 97% accepted. In 2006, 35 degrees awarded. *Entrance requirements:* For master's, minimum GPA of 3.0. *Application deadline:* For fall admission, 4/1 for domestic students; for spring admission, 10/1 for domestic students. Application fee: $35. *Financial support:* Research assistantships with partial tuition reimbursements available. Financial award application deadline: 3/1; financial award applicants required to submit FAFSA. *Unit head:* Dr. James W. Black, Director, 585-389-2619, Fax: 585-389-2452, E-mail: jblack8@naz.edu. *Application contact:* Judith G. Baker, Director, Graduate Admissions, 585-389-2050, Fax: 585-389-2817, E-mail: gradstudies@naz.edu.

North Carolina Agricultural and Technical State University, Graduate School, School of Education, Department of Curriculum and Instruction, Program in Intermediate Education, Greensboro, NC 27411. Offers biology education (MS); chemistry education (MS); English education (MS); history education (MS); social science education (MS). *Accreditation:* NCATE. Part-time and evening/weekend programs available. *Degree requirements:* For master's, thesis (for some programs), qualifying exam, comprehensive exam. *Entrance requirements:* For master's, GRE General Test, minimum GPA of 3.0.

North Carolina State University, Graduate School, College of Education, Department of Curriculum and Instruction, Program in Middle Grades Education, Raleigh, NC 27695. Offers M Ed, MS. *Accreditation:* NCATE. *Degree requirements:* For master's, thesis optional. *Entrance requirements:* For master's, GRE General Test or MAT, minimum GPA of 3.0 in major.

North Georgia College & State University, Graduate Studies, Program in Teacher Education, Dahlonega, GA 30597. Offers early childhood education (M Ed); educational leadership (Ed S); middle grades education (M Ed); secondary education (M Ed), including art education, biology education, chemistry education, English education, history education, mathematics education, physical education, science education; special education (M Ed), including inter-related special education, learning disabilities. *Accreditation:* NCATE. Part-time and evening/weekend programs available. Postbaccalaureate distance learning degree programs offered (minimal on-campus study). *Faculty:* 35 full-time (18 women), 9 part-time/adjunct (6 women). *Students:* 260. Average age 32. 120 applicants, 63% accepted. In 2006, 134 degrees awarded. *Degree requirements:* For master's, thesis optional. *Entrance requirements:* For master's, GRE General Test or MAT, minimum GPA of 2.75; for Ed S, GRE General Test or MAT, 3 years of teaching experience, master's degree, minimum graduate GPA of 3.25. *Application deadline:* For fall admission, 7/1 priority date for domestic students; for spring admission, 12/10 priority date for domestic students. Applications are processed on a rolling basis. Application fee: $25. Electronic applications accepted. *Expenses:* Tuition, state resident: full-time $3,044; part-time $127 per credit hour. Tuition, nonresident: full-time $12,172; part-time $508 per credit hour. Required fees: $892; $458 per semester. *Financial support:* Teaching assistantships, career-related internships or fieldwork and scholarships/grants available. Support available to part-time students. Financial award application deadline: 5/1. *Faculty research:* Computers and teachers' attitudes, rural versus urban teacher attitudes, teacher leadership roles, minority recruitment in teaching force. *Unit head:* Dr. Bob Michael, Dean, School of Education, 706-864-1998, Fax: 706-867-2850, E-mail: bmichael@ngcsu.edu. *Application contact:* Dr. Donna A. Gessell, Director of Graduate Studies and External Programs, 706-864-1528, Fax: 706-867-2795, E-mail: dgessell@ngcsu.edu.

Northwestern State University of Louisiana, Graduate Studies and Research, College of Education, Program in Middle School Education, Natchitoches, LA 71497. Offers MAT. *Students:* 1 (woman) full-time, 11 part-time (9 women). Average age 29. In 2006, 1 degree awarded. *Degree requirements:* For master's, thesis or alternative, comprehensive exam, registration. *Entrance requirements:* For master's, GRE General Test, minimum undergraduate GPA of 2.5. *Application contact:* Dr. Steven G. Horton, Associate Provost/Dean, Graduate Studies, Research, and Information Systems, 318-357-5851, Fax: 318-357-5019, E-mail: grad_school@nsula.edu.

Northwest Missouri State University, Graduate School, College of Education and Human Services, Department of Curriculum and Instruction, Program in Teaching: Middle School, Maryville, MO 64468-6001. Offers MS Ed. *Accreditation:* NCATE. *Faculty:* 10 full-time (all women). *Students:* 1 applicant, 100% accepted, 1 enrolled. In 2006, 1 degree awarded. *Degree requirements:* For master's, comprehensive exam. *Entrance requirements:* For master's, GRE General Test, minimum undergraduate GPA of 2.75, teaching certificate, writing sample. Additional exam requirements/recommendations for international students: Required—TOEFL. *Application deadline:* For fall admission, 7/1 for domestic and international students; for spring admission, 11/15 for domestic and international students. Applications are processed on a rolling basis. Application fee: $0 ($50 for international students). *Financial support:* Application deadline: 3/1; *Unit head:* Pat Thompson, Director, 660-562-1775. *Application contact:* Dr. Frances Shipley, Dean of Graduate School, 660-562-1145, Fax: 660-562-1096, E-mail: gradsch@nwmissouri.edu.

The Ohio State University at Lima, Graduate Programs, Lima, OH 45804. Offers early childhood education (M Ed); education (MA); middle childhood education (M Ed); social work (MSW). *Students:* 46 full-time (37 women), 32 part-time (27 women), 1 international. Average age 30. *Degree requirements:* For master's, thesis (for some programs), comprehensive exam (for some programs). *Entrance requirements:* For master's, GRE, minimum GPA of 3.0. Additional exam requirements/recommendations for international students: Required—TOEFL, IELTS or Michigan English Language Assessment Battery. *Application deadline:* For fall admission, 8/15 priority date for domestic students, 7/1 priority date for international students; for winter admission, 12/1 priority date for domestic students, 11/1 priority date for international students; for spring admission, 3/1 priority date for domestic students, 2/1 priority date for international students. Applications are processed on a rolling basis. Application fee: $40 ($50 for international students). Electronic applications accepted. *Expenses:* Tuition, state resident: full-time $8,919. Tuition, nonresident: full-time $22,272. Tuition and fees vary according to course load, campus/location and program. *Unit head:* Dr. John Snyder, Dean/Director, 419-995-8481, E-mail: snyder.4@osu.edu. *Application contact:* Graduate Admissions, 614-292-9444, Fax: 614-292-3895, E-mail: domestic.grad@osu.edu.

The Ohio State University at Marion, Graduate Programs, Marion, OH 43302-5695. Offers early childhood education (pre-K to grade 3) (M Ed); integrated teaching and learning (MA); middle childhood education (grades 4-9) (M Ed); nursing (MS, PhD); social work (MSW); MS/PhD. *Students:* 63 full-time (56 women), 43 part-time (41 women); includes 2 minority (both African Americans), 1 international. Average age 32. *Degree requirements:* For master's, thesis (for some programs), comprehensive exam (for some programs). *Entrance requirements:* For master's and doctorate, GRE, minimum undergraduate GPA of 3.0. Additional exam requirements/recommendations for international students: Required—TOEFL, IELTS or Michigan English Language Assessment Battery. *Application deadline:* For fall admission, 8/15 priority date for domestic students, 7/1 priority date for international students; for winter admission, 12/1 priority date for domestic students, 11/1 priority date for international students; for spring admission, 3/1 priority date for domestic students, 2/1 priority date for international students. Applications are processed on a rolling basis. Application fee: $40 ($50 for international students). Electronic applications accepted. *Expenses:* Tuition, state resident: full-time $8,919. Tuition, nonresident: full-time $22,272. Tuition and fees vary according to course load, campus/location and program. *Unit head:* Gregory S. Rose, Dean/Director, 740-389-6786 Ext. 6218, E-mail: rose.9@osu.edu. *Application contact:* Graduate Admissions, 614-292-9444, Fax: 614-292-3895, E-mail: domestic.grad@osu.edu.

The Ohio State University–Mansfield Campus, Graduate Programs, Mansfield, OH 44906-1599. Offers early and middle childhood education (MA); early childhood education (M Ed); middle childhood education (M Ed); social work (MSW). *Faculty:* 8 full-time (4 women). *Students:* 35 full-time (32 women), 46 part-time (42 women); includes 4 minority (all African Americans), 1 international. Average age 32. *Degree requirements:* For master's, thesis (for some programs), comprehensive exam (for some programs). *Entrance requirements:* For master's, GRE, minimum GPA of 3.0. Additional exam requirements/recommendations for international students: Required—TOEFL (minimum score 550 paper-based; 213 computer-based). *Application deadline:* For fall admission, 8/15 priority date for domestic students, 7/1 priority date for international students; for winter admission, 12/1 priority date for domestic students, 11/1 priority date for international students; for spring admission, 3/1 priority date for domestic students, 2/1 priority date for international students. Applications are processed on a rolling basis. Application fee: $40 ($50 for international students). Electronic applications accepted. *Expenses:* Tuition, state resident: full-time $8,919. Tuition, nonresident: full-time $22,272. Tuition and fees vary according to course load, campus/location and program. *Financial support:* In 2006–07, 14 students received support, including 3 teaching assistantships with full tuition reimbursements available (averaging $9,000 per year); Federal Work-Study and scholarships/grants also available. Support available to part-time students. Financial award application deadline: 7/1. *Application contact:* Graduate Admissions, 614-292-9444, Fax: 614-292-3895, E-mail: domestic.grad@osu.edu.

The Ohio State University–Newark Campus, Graduate Programs, Newark, OH 43055-1797. Offers early/middle childhood education (M Ed); integrated teaching and learning (MA); social work (MSW). *Students:* 31 full-time (25 women), 39 part-time (34 women); includes 3 minority (1 African American, 1 Asian American or Pacific Islander, 1 Hispanic American), 1 international. Average age 33. *Degree requirements:* For master's, thesis (for some programs), comprehensive exam (for some programs). *Entrance requirements:* For master's, GRE, minimum GPA of 3.0. Additional exam requirements/recommendations for international students: Required—TOEFL, IELTS or Michigan English Language Assessment Battery. *Application deadline:* For fall admission, 8/15 priority date for domestic students, 7/1 priority date for international students; for winter admission, 12/1 priority date for domestic students, 11/1 priority date for international students; for spring admission, 3/1 priority date for domestic students, 2/1 priority date for international students. Applications are processed on a rolling basis. Application fee: $40 ($50 for international students). Electronic applications accepted. *Expenses:* Tuition, state resident: full-time $8,919. Tuition, nonresident: full-time $22,272. Tuition and fees vary according to course level, campus/location and program. *Unit head:* Dr. William L. MacDonald, Dean/Director, 740-366-9333 Ext. 330, E-mail: macdonald.24@osu.edu. *Application contact:* Graduate Admissions, 614-292-9444, Fax: 614-292-3985, E-mail: domestic.grad@osu.edu.

Ohio University, Graduate Studies, College of Education, Department of Teacher Education, Athens, OH 45701-2979. Offers adolescent to young adult education (M Ed); curriculum and instruction (M Ed, PhD); mathematics education (PhD); middle child education (M Ed); reading and language arts (PhD); reading education (M Ed); social studies education (PhD); special education (M Ed, PhD). Part-time and evening/weekend programs available. *Faculty:* 21 full-time (13 women), 7 part-time/adjunct (all women). *Students:* 57 full-time (44 women), 61 part-time (46 women); includes 4 minority (2 African Americans, 1 Asian American or Pacific Islander, 1 Hispanic American), 36 international. 93 applicants, 61% accepted, 37 enrolled. *Median time to degree:* Of those who began their doctoral program in fall 1998, 92% received their degree in 8 years or less. *Degree requirements:* For master's, thesis or alternative, registration; for doctorate, thesis/dissertation, comprehensive exam, registration. *Entrance requirements:* For master's, GRE General Test or MAT if GPA is less than 2.9; for doctorate, GRE General Test, minimum GPA of 3.4, work experience. Additional exam requirements/recommendations for international students: Required—TOEFL (minimum score 550 paper-based; 213 computer-based). *Application deadline:* For fall admission, 4/1 priority date for domestic and international students. Applications are processed on a rolling basis. Application fee: $45. Electronic applications accepted. *Financial support:* In 2006–07, 52 students received support, including 31 research assistantships with full tuition reimbursements available (averaging $6,500 per year), teaching assistantships with full tuition reimbursements available (averaging $7,200 per year); Federal Work-Study, institutionally sponsored loans, tuition waivers (full), and unspecified assistantships also available. Financial award application deadline: 3/15. *Faculty research:* Cognition literacy, character education, teacher's education reform, disabilities. Total annual research expenditures: $605,070. *Unit head:* Dr. William Earl Smith, Chair, 740-593-4483, Fax: 740-593-0477, E-mail: smithw@ohio.edu. *Application contact:* Floyd J. Doney, Director of Student Affairs, 740-593-4400, Fax: 740-593-9310, E-mail: doney@ohio.edu.

Old Dominion University, Darden College of Education, Program in Elementary/Middle Education, Norfolk, VA 23529. Offers educational media (MS Ed); elementary education (MS Ed); instructional technology (MS Ed); library science (MS Ed); middle school education (MS Ed). *Accreditation:* NCATE. Part-time and evening/weekend programs available. Postbaccalaureate distance learning degree programs offered (no on-campus study). *Faculty:* 20 full-time (9 women). *Students:* 116 full-time (103 women), 217 part-time (178 women); includes 32 minority (22 African Americans, 2 American Indian/Alaska Native, 3 Asian Americans or Pacific Islanders, 5 Hispanic Americans). Average age 35. 127 applicants, 56% accepted, 61 enrolled. In 2006, 167 degrees awarded. *Degree requirements:* For master's, comprehensive exam. *Entrance requirements:* For master's, GRE General Test or MAT and PRAXIS I or SAT or ACT, minimum GPA of 2.8. *Application deadline:* For fall admission, 6/1 priority date for domestic students; for winter admission, 11/1 priority date for domestic students; for spring admission, 3/1 priority date for domestic students. Applications are processed on a rolling basis. Application fee: $40. Electronic applications accepted. *Expenses:* Tuition, area resident: Part-time $285 per credit hour. Tuition, nonresident: part-time $715 per credit hour. Required fees: $94 per semester. *Financial support:* In 2006–07, 180 students received support, including 4 research assistantships with tuition reimbursements available (averaging $9,000 per year), teaching assistantships (averaging $8,000 per year); fellowships, career-related internships or fieldwork, Federal Work-Study, institutionally sponsored loans, scholarships/grants, and tuition waivers (partial) also available. Support available to part-time students. Financial award application deadline: 2/15; financial award applicants required to submit FAFSA. *Faculty research:* Education pre-K to 6, school librarianship. *Unit head:* Dr. Gail S. Taylor, Graduate Program Director, 757-683-4180, E-mail: eciegpd@odu.edu.

Old Dominion University, Darden College of Education, Programs in Occupational and Technical Studies, Norfolk, VA 23529. Offers business and industry training (MS); career and technical education (PhD); community college teaching (MS); human resources training (PhD); middle and secondary teaching (MS); technology education (PhD). *Accreditation:* NCATE (one or more programs are accredited). Part-time and evening/weekend programs available. Postbaccalaureate distance learning degree programs offered (minimal on-campus study). *Faculty:* 7 full-time (1 woman), 5 part-time/adjunct (2 women). *Students:* 15 full-time (11 women), 68 part-time (39 women); includes 13 minority (9 African Americans, 2 American Indian/Alaska Native, 2 Asian Americans or Pacific Islanders), 1 international. Average age 39. 44 applicants, 95% accepted, 37 enrolled. In 2006, 29 degrees awarded. *Degree requirements:* For master's, writing exam, candidacy exam, thesis optional; for doctorate, thesis/dissertation, writing exam, candidacy exam, comprehensive exam, registration. *Entrance requirements:* For master's, GRE General Test or MAT, minimum GPA of 2.8; for doctorate, GRE, minimum GPA of 3.0, 3 letters of reference. Additional exam requirements/recommendations for international students: Required—TOEFL. *Application deadline:* For fall admission, 6/1 priority date for domestic students, 6/1 for international students; for winter admission, 11/1 priority date for domestic students, 11/1 for international students; for spring admission, 3/1 priority date for domestic students, 3/1 for international students. Applications are processed on a rolling basis. Application fee: $40. Electronic applications accepted. *Expenses:* Tuition, area resident: Part-time $285 per credit hour. Tuition, nonresident: part-time $715 per credit hour. Required fees: $94 per semester. *Financial support:* In 2006–07, 19 students received support, including 1 fellowship with full tuition reimbursement available (averaging $15,000 per year), 2 research assistantships with partial tuition reimbursements available (averaging $9,000 per year), 5 teaching assistantships with partial tuition reimbursements available (averaging $12,600 per year); career-related internships or fieldwork, scholarships/grants, tuition waivers (partial), and unspecified assistantships also available. Support available to part-time students. Financial award application deadline: 2/15; financial award applicants required to submit FAFSA. *Faculty research:* Training and development, marketing, technology, special populations, support of academic subjects. Total annual research expenditures: $799,773. *Unit head:* Dr. John M. Ritz, Graduate Program Director, 757-683-4305, Fax: 757-683-5227, E-mail: otsgpd@odu.edu.

Pacific University, College of Education, Forest Grove, OR 97116-1797. Offers early childhood education (MAT); education (MAE); elementary education (MAT); high school education (MAT); middle school education (MAT); special education (MAT); visual function in learning (M Ed). Part-time and evening/weekend programs available. *Faculty:* 20 full-time (12 women), 40 part-time/adjunct (21 women). *Students:* 222 full-time (151 women), 115 part-time (90 women); includes 30 minority (3 African Americans, 5 American Indian/Alaska Native, 12 Asian Americans or Pacific Islanders, 10 Hispanic Americans). Average age 32. 92 applicants, 83% accepted, 69 enrolled. In 2006, 257 degrees awarded. *Degree requirements:* For master's, research project. *Entrance requirements:* For master's, California Basic Educational Skills Test, Praxis I, minimum undergraduate GPA of 2.75, 3.0 graduate. Additional exam requirements/recommendations for international students: Required—TOEFL. *Application deadline:* For fall admission, 6/15 priority date for domestic students; for spring admission, 10/15 for domestic students. Applications are processed on a rolling basis. Application fee: $35. Electronic applications accepted. *Expenses:* Contact institution. *Financial support:* In 2006–07, 287 students received support; fellowships, research assistantships, teaching assistantships, career-related internships or fieldwork, institutionally sponsored loans, and scholarships/grants available. Support available to part-time students. Financial award application deadline: 5/1; financial award applicants required to submit FAFSA. *Faculty research:* Defining a culturally competent classroom, technology in the k-12 classroom, Socratic seminars, social studies education. *Unit head:* Dr. Mark Ankeny, Acting Dean, 503-352-2102, E-mail: mankeny@pacificu.edu. *Application contact:* Diana Watkins, Assistant Director Graduate and Professional Admissions, 503-352-2958, Fax: 503-352-2907, E-mail: teach@pacificu.edu.

Park University, College of Graduate and Professional Studies, Kansas City, MO 54105. Offers adult education (M Ed); at-risk students (M Ed); disaster and emergency management (MPA); educational administration (M Ed); entrepreneurship (MBA); general business (MBA); general education (M Ed); government/business relations (MPA); healthcare/services management (MBA, MPA); international business (MBA); K-12 certification (MAT); management information systems (MBA); management of information systems (MPA); middle school certification (MAT); multi-cultural education (M Ed); nonprofit management (MPA); public management (MPA); school law (M Ed); secondary school certification (MAT); special education (M Ed). Part-time and evening/weekend programs available. Postbaccalaureate distance learning degree programs offered (no on-campus study). *Degree requirements:* For master's, thesis (for some programs), comprehensive exam, registration. *Entrance requirements:* For master's, GRE, GMAT, teacher certification (M Ed). Additional exam requirements/recommendations for international students: Required—TOEFL (minimum score 550 paper-based). Electronic applications accepted. *Faculty research:* Literacy, leadership, brain based research, multicultural education, diversity.

Plymouth State University, College of Graduate Studies, Graduate Studies in Education, Program in K-12 Education, Plymouth, NH 03264-1595. Offers M Ed. *Accreditation:* NCATE. Part-time and evening/weekend programs available. *Students:* 1 (woman) full-time, 222 part-time (168 women); includes 7 minority (2 African Americans, 3 Asian Americans or Pacific Islanders, 2 Hispanic Americans). Average age 39. 48 applicants, 100% accepted, 48 enrolled. In 2006, 59 degrees awarded. *Degree requirements:* For master's, PRAXIS. *Entrance requirements:* For master's, MAT, minimum GPA of 3.0. *Application deadline:* Applications are processed on a rolling basis. Application fee: $75. *Expenses:* Tuition, state resident: part-time $369 per credit. Tuition, nonresident: part-time $407 per credit. Tuition and fees vary according to course level. *Financial support:* Career-related internships or fieldwork, scholarships/grants, and unspecified assistantships available. Support available to part-time students. Financial award applicants required to submit FAFSA. *Unit head:* Dr. Kathleen Norris, Director of Graduate Admissions, Programs and Certification, 603-535-3023, Fax: 603-535-2572, E-mail: knorris@plymouth.edu.

Quinnipiac University, Division of Education, Program in Secondary Education, Hamden, CT 06518-1940. Offers biology (MAT); chemistry (MAT); English (MAT); French (MAT); history/social studies (MAT); mathematics (MAT); physics (MAT); Spanish (MAT). *Faculty:* 7 full-time (5 women), 23 part-time/adjunct (14 women). *Students:* 64 full-time (41 women); includes 5 minority (1 African American, 4 Hispanic Americans). Average age 26. 63 applicants, 87% accepted, 42 enrolled. In 2006, 37 degrees awarded. *Entrance requirements:* For master's, PRAXIS I, minimum GPA of 2.67, interview. Additional exam requirements/recommendations for international students: Required—TOEFL (minimum score 575 paper-based; 233 computer-based; 90 iBT), IELTS (minimum score 7). *Application deadline:* For fall admission, 3/15 priority date for domestic students. Applications are processed on a rolling basis. Application fee: $45. Electronic applications accepted. *Expenses:* Tuition: Part-time $675 per credit. Required fees: $30 per credit. *Financial support:* Career-related internships or fieldwork and tuition waivers (partial) available. Financial award application deadline: 4/15; financial award applicants required to submit FAFSA. *Faculty research:* Multicultural and urban education, role of technology in education, challenges of teaching divers learners, socio-cultural nature of learning. *Unit head:* Dr. Bernadine Krawczyk, Assistant Dean, Division of Education, 203-582-3510, Fax: 203-582-3473, E-mail: bernadine.krawczyk@quinnipiac.edu. *Application contact:* 800-462-1944, Fax: 203-582-3443, E-mail: graduate@quinnipiac.edu.

See Close-Up on page 911.

Roberts Wesleyan College, Division of Teacher Education, Rochester, NY 14624-1997. Offers adolescence education (M Ed); childhood and special education (M Ed); literacy education (M Ed); urban education (M Ed). Part-time and evening/weekend programs available. *Faculty:* 17 part-time/adjunct (7 women). *Students:* 1 (woman) full-time, 66 part-time (47 women). Average age 33. 52 applicants, 63% accepted. In 2006, 20 degrees awarded. *Degree requirements:* For master's, thesis. *Application deadline:* For fall admission, 8/1 priority date for domestic students; for spring admission, 12/1 for domestic students. Applications are processed on a rolling basis. Application fee: $35. *Financial support:* In 2006–07, 7 students received support. Career-related internships or fieldwork available. Financial award application deadline: 9/1; financial award applicants required to submit FAFSA. *Unit head:* Dr. Richard Mace, Chair, 585-594-6934. *Application contact:* Paula Finch, Graduate Admissions Coordinator, 585-594-6683, E-mail: finch_paula@roberts.edu.

Rosemont College, Graduate School, Program in Middle Level Education, Rosemont, PA 19010-1699. Offers M Ed. *Degree requirements:* For master's, thesis or alternative. *Entrance requirements:* Additional exam requirements/recommendations for international students: Required—TOEFL. Electronic applications accepted.

Saginaw Valley State University, College of Education, Program in Middle School Classroom Teaching, University Center, MI 48710. Offers MAT. *Accreditation:* NCATE. Part-time and evening/weekend programs available. *Students:* 1 (woman) full-time, 31 part-time (20 women); includes 1 minority (Asian American or Pacific Islander) Average age 32. 5 applicants, 100% accepted, 3 enrolled. In 2006, 11 degrees awarded. *Degree requirements:* For master's, capstone course. *Entrance requirements:* For master's, minimum GPA of 3.0, teaching certificate. *Application deadline:* Applications are processed on a rolling basis. Application fee: $25. Electronic applications accepted. *Expenses:* Tuition, state resident: full-time $7,225; part-time $301 per credit hour. Tuition, nonresident: full-time $13,888; part-time $579 per credit hour. Required fees: $330; $14 per credit hour. Tuition and fees vary according to course load. *Financial support:* Applicants required to submit FAFSA. *Faculty research:* Pre-service, middle school, secondary teacher, literacy education. *Application contact:* Jeanne Chipman, Certification Officer, 989-964-4083, Fax: 989-964-4385, E-mail: jdc@svsu.edu.

Saginaw Valley State University, College of Education, Program in Natural Science Teaching, University Center, MI 48710. Offers elementary (MAT); middle school (MAT); secondary school (MAT). *Accreditation:* NCATE. Part-time and evening/weekend programs available. *Students:* 1 (woman) full-time, 22 part-time (16 women). Average age 36. 3 applicants, 100% accepted, 3 enrolled. In 2006, 15 degrees awarded. *Degree requirements:* For master's, capstone course. *Entrance requirements:* For master's, minimum GPA of 3.0, teaching certificate. *Application deadline:* Applications are processed on a rolling basis. Application fee: $25. Electronic applications accepted. *Expenses:* Tuition, state resident: full-time $7,225; part-time $301 per credit hour. Tuition, nonresident: full-time $13,888; part-time $579 per credit hour. Required fees: $330; $14 per credit hour. Tuition and fees vary according to course load. *Financial support:* Applicants required to submit FAFSA. *Application contact:* Jeanne Chipman, Certification Officer, 989-964-4083, Fax: 989-964-4385, E-mail: jdc@svsu.edu.

St. John Fisher College, Office of the Provost, Ralph C. Wilson Jr. School of Education, Adolescence Education Program, Rochester, NY 14618-3597. Offers adolescence English (MS Ed); adolescence French (MS Ed); adolescence social studies (MS Ed); adolescence Spanish (MS Ed). Part-time and evening/weekend programs available. *Faculty:* 4 full-time (2 women), 2 part-time/adjunct (1 woman). *Students:* Average age 31. 35 applicants, 91% accepted, 25 enrolled. In 2006, 13 degrees awarded. *Degree requirements:* For master's, student teaching, capstone project, field experiences; for degree. *Entrance requirements:* For master's, GRE (if GPA is below 3.0), minimum GPA of 3.0, 30 hours in certification area, 2 letters of reference, personal statement. Additional exam requirements/recommendations for international students: Required—TOEFL (minimum score 575 paper-based; 233 computer-based; 80 iBT). *Application deadline:* For fall admission, 4/1 for domestic students; for spring admission, 10/30 for domestic students. Applications are processed on a rolling basis. Application fee: $30. *Expenses:* Tuition: Part-time $615 per credit. Tuition and fees vary according to program. *Financial support:* In 2006–07, 1 student received support. Federal Work-Study and scholarships/grants available. Financial award application deadline: 2/15; financial award applicants required to submit FAFSA. *Faculty research:* Arts and humanities, urban schools, constructivist learning, at risk students, mentoring. *Unit head:* Dr. Russell Coward, Director,

Middle School Education

St. John Fisher College (continued)
585-385-8114, E-mail: rcoward@sjfc.edu. *Application contact:* Shannon Cleverley, Director of Graduate Admissions, 585-385-8161, Fax: 585-385-8344, E-mail: scleverley@sjfc.edu.

St. Thomas Aquinas College, Division of Teacher Education, Sparkill, NY 10976. Offers adolescence education (MST); childhood and special education (MST); childhood education (MST); reading (MS Ed, PMC); special education (MS Ed, PMC); teaching (MS Ed), including elementary education, middle school education, secondary education. *Accreditation:* NCATE. Part-time and evening/weekend programs available. *Degree requirements:* For master's, comprehensive professional portfolio; for PMC, action research project. *Entrance requirements:* For master's, New York State Qualifying Exam, GRE General Test or minimum GPA of 3.0, teaching certificate; for PMC, GRE General Test or minimum GPA of 3.0. Electronic applications accepted. *Faculty research:* Computer applications in education, adolescent special education students, literacy development, inclusive practices for special education students.

See Close-Up on page 917.

Salem College, Department of Education, Winston-Salem, NC 27108-0548. Offers early education and leadership (MAT); elementary education (MAT); English as a second language (MAT); language and literacy (M Ed); middle school education (MAT); secondary education (MAT); special education (MAT). *Accreditation:* NCATE. Part-time and evening/weekend programs available. *Faculty:* 8 full-time (6 women), 5 part-time/adjunct (all women). *Students:* 8 full-time (all women), 250 part-time (238 women); includes 19 minority (16 African Americans, 1 Asian American or Pacific Islander, 2 Hispanic Americans). Average age 33. 110 applicants, 65% accepted, 68 enrolled. In 2006, 34 degrees awarded. *Degree requirements:* For master's, practicum (MAT), project (M Ed), oral and written comprehensive exams. *Entrance requirements:* For master's, GRE, minimum GPA of 2.5. *Application deadline:* Applications are processed on a rolling basis. Application fee: $30. *Financial support:* In 2006–07, 152 students received support. Federal Work-Study and scholarships/grants available. Support available to part-time students. Financial award applicants required to submit FAFSA. *Faculty research:* Content area reading strategies, literacy development, brain compatible instruction. *Unit head:* Dr. Paula Grubbs, Director of Teacher Education, 336-721-2610, Fax: 336-721-2683, E-mail: grubbs@salem.edu.

Salem State College, Graduate School, Program in Middle School Education, Salem, MA 01970-5353. Offers M Ed, MAT. Part-time and evening/weekend programs available. *Students:* 3 full-time (2 women), 27 part-time (15 women); includes 1 minority (African American) Average age 37. In 2006, 16 degrees awarded. *Entrance requirements:* For master's, GRE General Test, MAT. *Application deadline:* Applications are processed on a rolling basis. Application fee: $35. *Unit head:* Steve Prodanas, Coordinator, 978-542-7079, Fax: 978-542-7215, E-mail: spondanas@salemstate.edu.

Shenandoah University, College of Arts and Sciences, Winchester, VA 22601-5195. Offers administrative leadership (D Ed); advanced professional teaching English to speakers of other languages (Certificate); education (MSE); elementary education (Certificate); middle school education (Certificate); professional studies (Certificate); professional teaching English to speakers of other languages (Certificate); public management (Certificate); secondary education (Certificate); women's studies (Certificate). Part-time and evening/weekend programs available. Postbaccalaureate distance learning degree programs offered (minimal on-campus study). *Faculty:* 14 full-time (9 women), 7 part-time/adjunct (4 women). *Students:* 28 full-time (16 women), 283 part-time (208 women); includes 8 minority (3 African Americans, 1 American Indian/Alaska Native, 3 Asian Americans or Pacific Islanders, 1 Hispanic American), 26 international. Average age 40. 182 applicants, 68% accepted, 98 enrolled. In 2006, 96 master's, 6 doctorates, 22 other advanced degrees awarded. *Degree requirements:* For master's, thesis (for some programs), internship, comprehensive exam (for some programs); for doctorate, thesis/dissertation, comprehensive exam. *Entrance requirements:* For master's, minimum GPA of 3.0 or satisfactory GRE, 3 letters of recommendation, valid teaching license; for doctorate, minimum GPA of 3.5 in master's, 3 years of teaching experience, 3 letters of recommendation, writing samples. Additional exam requirements/recommendations for international students: Required—TOEFL (minimum score 527 paper-based; 197 computer-based; 71 iBT). *Application deadline:* For fall admission, 7/15 for domestic students; for spring admission, 10/15 for domestic students. Applications are processed on a rolling basis. Application fee: $30. Electronic applications accepted. *Expenses:* Tuition: Full-time $12,200; part-time $610 per credit. Required fees: $150. Full-time tuition and fees vary according to course load and program. *Financial support:* In 2006–07, fellowships with partial tuition reimbursements (averaging $2,581 per year); career-related internships or fieldwork, institutionally sponsored loans, and unspecified assistantships also available. Support available to part-time students. Financial award application deadline: 3/15; financial award applicants required to submit FAFSA. *Faculty research:* Nanotechnology, writing pedagogy and writing centers, violence in schools, Virginia/Shenandoah Valley history and culture, stress in children. *Unit head:* Dr. Calvin Allen, Dean, 540-665-4587, Fax: 540-665-4644, E-mail: callen@su.edu. *Application contact:* David Anthony, Dean of Admissions, 540-665-4581, Fax: 540-665-4627, E-mail: admit@su.edu.

See Close-Up on page 919.

Siena Heights University, Graduate College, Program in Teacher Education, Concentration in Middle School Education, Adrian, MI 49221-1796. Offers MA. Part-time programs available. *Degree requirements:* For master's, thesis, presentation. *Entrance requirements:* For master's, minimum GPA of 3.0, interview.

Simmons College, Graduate School, College of Arts and Sciences Graduate Studies, Department of Education, Program in Teacher Preparation, Boston, MA 02115. Offers educational leadership (MS Ed, CAGS); elementary education (MAT, CAGS); general education (CAGS); general purposes (MS); middle school education (MAT, CAGS); professional license (CAGS); professional license: elementary (MS Ed); professional license: middle/high (MS Ed); secondary education (MAT, CAGS); urban education (MS Ed, CAGS). *Faculty:* 4 full-time (3 women), 22 part-time/adjunct (13 women). *Students:* 61 full-time (53 women), 141 part-time (128 women); includes 33 minority (13 African Americans, 10 Asian Americans or Pacific Islanders, 10 Hispanic Americans), 1 international. Average age 24. 86 applicants, 77% accepted, 39 enrolled. In 2006, 128 master's, 12 other advanced degrees awarded. *Degree requirements:* For master's, student teaching experience or internship. *Entrance requirements:* For master's, GRE General Test, MAT or Massachusetts Tests for Educator Licensure (MTEL). Additional exam requirements/recommendations for international students: Required—TOEFL (minimum score 600 paper-based; 250 computer-based; 100 iBT). *Application deadline:* For fall admission, 8/1 priority date for domestic and international students; for spring admission, 12/15 priority date for domestic and international students. Applications are processed on a rolling basis. Application fee: $35. Electronic applications accepted. *Expenses:* Contact institution. *Financial support:* Teaching assistantships, career-related internships or fieldwork, Federal Work-Study, institutionally sponsored loans, scholarships/grants, and tuition waivers (partial) available. Support available to part-time students. Financial award application deadline: 3/1; financial award applicants required to submit FAFSA. *Faculty research:* Putting standards/frameworks into practice, restructuring middle and high schools, interactive teaching and learning developing curriculum for Third World countries. Total annual research expenditures: $110,000. *Unit head:* Lynda Johnson, Assistant Dean, 617-521-2576, Fax: 617-521-3133, E-mail: gsa@simmons.edu. *Application contact:* Kristen Haack, Director, Graduate Studies Admission, 617-521-2915, Fax: 617-521-3058, E-mail: gsa@simmons.edu.

Smith College, Graduate Programs, Department of Education and Child Study, Program in Elementary Education, Northampton, MA 01063. Offers middle school education (Ed M). Part-time programs available. *Faculty:* 6 full-time (4 women), 3 part-time/adjunct (2 women). *Students:* 11 full-time (7 women), 3 part-time (all women), 1 international. Average age 28. 23 applicants, 78% accepted, 14 enrolled. In 2006, 9 degrees awarded. *Entrance requirements:* For master's, GRE General Test or MAT. *Application deadline:* For fall admission, 4/1 for domestic students, 1/15 for international students; for spring admission, 12/1 for domestic

students. Application fee: $60. *Expenses:* Tuition: Full-time $32,320; part-time $1,010 per credit. Tuition and fees vary according to course load. *Financial support:* In 2006–07, 14 students received support, including 6 teaching assistantships with full tuition reimbursements available (averaging $11,150 per year); fellowships, research assistantships, career-related internships or fieldwork, institutionally sponsored loans, and scholarships/grants also available. Support available to part-time students. Financial award application deadline: 1/15. *Unit head:* Alan Rudnitsky, Graduate Student Adviser, 413-585-3261, E-mail: arudnits@smith.edu.

Southeast Missouri State University, School of Graduate Studies, Department of Middle and Secondary Education, Cape Girardeau, MO 63701-4799. Offers educational studies (MA); middle level education (MA). *Accreditation:* NCATE. Part-time and evening/weekend programs available. *Faculty:* 3 full-time (all women). *Students:* Average age 35. 16 applicants, 88% accepted. In 2006, 6 degrees awarded. *Degree requirements:* For master's, thesis or alternative. *Entrance requirements:* For master's, GRE General Test, MAT, PRAXIS II, minimum GPA of 2.75. Additional exam requirements/recommendations for international students: Required—TOEFL (minimum score 550 paper-based; 213 computer-based). *Application deadline:* For fall admission, 8/1 for domestic students, 4/1 for international students; for spring admission, 11/21 for domestic students, 10/1 for international students. Applications are processed on a rolling basis. Application fee: $20 ($100 for international students). Electronic applications accepted. *Financial support:* In 2006–07, 6 students received support. Applicants required to submit FAFSA. *Unit head:* Dr. Simin Cwick, Interim Chair, 573-651-2008, Fax: 573-651-6141, E-mail: scwick@semo.edu. *Application contact:* Marsha L. Arant, Senior Administrative Assistant, Office of Graduate Studies, 573-651-2192, Fax: 573-651-2001, E-mail: marant@semo.edu.

Spalding University, Graduate Studies, College of Education, Programs in Education, Louisville, KY 40203-2188. Offers elementary school education (MAT); general education (MA); high school education (MAT); middle school education (MAT); school administration (MA); special education (learning and behavioral disorders) (MAT). MAT degree programs offered for first teaching certificate/license students. *Accreditation:* NCATE. Part-time and evening/weekend programs available. *Degree requirements:* For master's, portfolio, final project, clinical experience. *Entrance requirements:* For master's, GRE General Test or MAT, interview, recommendations, resumé. Additional exam requirements/recommendations for international students: Required—TOEFL. Electronic applications accepted. *Faculty research:* Instructional technology, achievement gap, classroom management, assessment.

State University of New York College at Brockport, School of Professions, Department of Education and Human Development, Program in Adolescence Education, Brockport, NY 14420-2997. Offers biology education (MS Ed); chemistry education (MS Ed); earth science education (MS Ed); English education (MS Ed); mathematics education (MS Ed); physics education (MS Ed); social studies education (MS Ed). *Accreditation:* NCATE. Part-time programs available. *Students:* 39 full-time (21 women), 117 part-time (66 women); includes 6 minority (3 African Americans, 1 Asian American or Pacific Islander, 2 Hispanic Americans). 57 applicants, 61% accepted, 32 enrolled. In 2006, 91 degrees awarded. *Degree requirements:* For master's, thesis or alternative. *Entrance requirements:* For master's, minimum GPA of 3.0, letters of recommendation. Additional exam requirements/recommendations for international students: Required—TOEFL (minimum score 550 paper-based; 213 computer-based; 80 iBT). *Application deadline:* For fall admission, 2/15 for domestic and international students; for spring admission, 9/15 for domestic and international students. Application fee: $50. *Expenses:* Tuition, state resident: full-time $6,900; part-time $288 per credit. Tuition, nonresident: full-time $10,920; part-time $455 per credit. *Financial support:* Career-related internships or fieldwork, Federal Work-Study, scholarships/grants, and unspecified assistantships available. Support available to part-time students. Financial award application deadline: 3/15; financial award applicants required to submit FAFSA. *Application contact:* Coordinator of Certification and Graduate Advisement, 585-395-2344.

State University of New York College at Oneonta, Graduate Studies, Division of Education, Department of Adolescence Education, Oneonta, NY 13820-4015. Offers adolescence education (MS Ed); family and consumer science education (MS Ed). *Accreditation:* NCATE. Part-time and evening/weekend programs available. *Entrance requirements:* For master's, GRE General Test.

Tufts University, Graduate School of Arts and Sciences, Department of Education, Program in Education, Medford, MA 02155. Offers education (MS, PhD); elementary education (MAT); middle and secondary education (MA, MAT); secondary education (MA). *Faculty:* 13 full-time, 9 part-time/adjunct. *Students:* 114 (77 women); includes 22 minority (9 African Americans, 4 Asian Americans or Pacific Islanders, 9 Hispanic Americans) 7 international. 199 applicants, 79% accepted, 75 enrolled. In 2006, 72 degrees awarded. *Degree requirements:* For master's, thesis optional; for doctorate, thesis/dissertation. *Entrance requirements:* For master's, GRE General Test. Additional exam requirements/recommendations for international students: Required—TOEFL (minimum score 550 paper-based; 213 computer-based; 80 iBT). *Application deadline:* For fall admission, 2/1 for domestic students, 12/30 for international students; for spring admission, 10/15 for domestic students, 9/15 for international students. Applications are processed on a rolling basis. Application fee: $70. Electronic applications accepted. *Expenses:* Tuition: Full-time $33,672. Tuition and fees vary according to degree level and program. *Financial support:* Teaching assistantships with full and partial tuition reimbursements, Federal Work-Study, scholarships/grants, and tuition waivers (full and partial) available. Financial award application deadline: 2/1. *Unit head:* Analucia Schliemann, Chair, Department of Education, 617-627-3244, Fax: 617-627-3901.

Union College, Graduate Programs, Department of Education, Program in Middle Grades, Barbourville, KY 40906-1499. Offers MA. *Degree requirements:* For master's, thesis optional. *Entrance requirements:* For master's, GRE General Test, NTE.

University at Buffalo, the State University of New York, Graduate School, Graduate School of Education, Department of Learning and Instruction, Buffalo, NY 14260. Offers adolescence education (Certificate); biology (Ed M); chemistry (Ed M); childhood education (Ed M); early childhood and childhood education with bilingual extension (Ed M); early childhood education (Ed M); earth science (Ed M); elementary education (Ed D, PhD); English (Ed M); English education (PhD); English for speakers of other languages (Ed M); foreign and second language education (PhD); French (Ed M); general education (Ed M); German (Ed M); Italian (Ed M); Japanese (Ed M); Latin (Ed M); literary specialist (Ed M); mathematics (Ed M); mathematics education (PhD); mentoring teachers (Certificate); music education (Ed M, Certificate); physics (Ed M); reading education (PhD); Russian (Ed M); school administrator and supervisor (Certificate); science education (PhD); social studies (Ed M); Spanish (Ed M); special education (PhD); teaching and leading for diversity (Certificate); teaching English to speakers of other languages (Ed M). Part-time and evening/weekend programs available. Postbaccalaureate distance learning degree programs offered (no on-campus study). *Faculty:* 30 full-time (20 women), 53 part-time/adjunct (38 women). *Students:* 368 full-time (269 women), 297 part-time (226 women); includes 50 minority (15 African Americans, 2 American Indian/Alaska Native, 14 Asian Americans or Pacific Islanders, 19 Hispanic Americans), 66 international. Average age 31. 638 applicants, 75% accepted, 298 enrolled. In 2006, 248 master's, 18 doctorates, 48 other advanced degrees awarded. Terminal master's awarded for partial completion of doctoral program. *Degree requirements:* For master's, comprehensive exam, registration; for doctorate, thesis/dissertation, research analysis exam, research experience component. *Entrance requirements:* For doctorate, GRE General Test or MAT, interview, writing sample, letters of recommendation. Additional exam requirements/recommendations for international students: Required—TOEFL (minimum score 600 paper-based; 250 computer-based). *Application deadline:* For fall admission, 2/1 priority date for domestic and international students; for spring admission, 11/15 priority date for domestic students, 10/1 for international students. Applications are processed on a rolling basis. Application fee: $50. Electronic applications accepted. *Financial support:* In 2006–07, 70 students received support, including 6 fellowships with full tuition reimbursements available (averaging $10,000 per year), 16 research assistantships with full tuition reimbursements available (averaging $9,000 per year), teaching assistantships with full tuition reimbursements available (averaging $9,000 per year); career-related internships or fieldwork, Federal Work-Study, institutionally sponsored loans, scholarships/grants, tuition waivers (partial), and unspecified assistantships also available. Financial award application deadline: 2/28; financial award applicants required to submit FAFSA. *Faculty research:* Science assessment, state-level testing, early learning, literacy, second language acquisition. Total annual research expenditures: $432,366. *Unit head:* Dr. Maria E. Runfola, Chair, 716-645-2455, Fax: 716-645-3161. *Application contact:* Barbara Belz, Admissions Secretary, 716-645-2110 Ext. 1159, Fax: 716-645-3161, E-mail: belz@buffalo.edu.

University of Arkansas, Graduate School, College of Education and Health Professions, Department of Curriculum and Instruction, Fayetteville, AR 72701-1201. Offers childhood education (MAT); curriculum and instruction (PhD); elementary education (M Ed, Ed S); middle-level education (MAT); secondary education (M Ed, MAT, Ed S); special education (M Ed, MAT). *Accreditation:* NCATE. *Students:* 140 full-time (103 women), 85 part-time (77 women); includes 24 minority (19 African Americans, 1 American Indian/Alaska Native, 1 Asian American or Pacific Islander, 3 Hispanic Americans), 20 international. 94 applicants, 46% accepted. In 2006, 112 master's, 2 doctorates awarded. *Degree requirements:* For doctorate, thesis/dissertation. *Entrance requirements:* For doctorate, GRE General Test or MAT. *Application deadline:* Applications are processed on a rolling basis. Application fee: $40 ($50 for international students). *Financial support:* In 2006–07, 7 fellowships with tuition reimbursements, 1 research assistantship, 11 teaching assistantships were awarded; career-related internships or fieldwork and Federal Work-Study also available. Support available to part-time students. Financial award application deadline: 4/1; financial award applicants required to submit FAFSA. *Unit head:* Thomas E Smith, Departmental Chairperson, 479-575-4209, Fax: 479-575-6676, E-mail: tecsmith@uark.edu.

University of Arkansas at Little Rock, Graduate School, College of Education, Department of Teacher Education, Program in Middle Childhood Education, Little Rock, AR 72204-1099. Offers middle childhood education (M Ed); reading (M Ed).

University of Dayton, Graduate School, School of Education and Allied Professions, Department of Teacher Education, Dayton, OH 45469-1300. Offers adolescent/young adult (MS Ed); art education (MS Ed); early childhood (MS Ed); inclusive early childhood (MS Ed); interdisciplinary education (MS Ed); intervention specialist education, mild/moderate (MS Ed); literacy (MS Ed); middle childhood (MS Ed); multi-age education (MS Ed); music education (MS Ed); teacher as leader (MS Ed); technology in education (MS Ed). Part-time and evening/weekend programs available. *Faculty:* 13 full-time (9 women), 33 part-time/adjunct (25 women). *Students:* 149 full-time (120 women), 284 part-time (241 women); includes 37 minority (31 African Americans, 3 Asian Americans or Pacific Islanders, 3 Hispanic Americans), 3 international. Average age 33. 201 applicants, 58% accepted, 31 enrolled. In 2006, 150 degrees awarded. *Degree requirements:* For master's, thesis, capstone research project. *Entrance requirements:* For master's, GRE General Test, minimum GPA of 2.75. Additional exam requirements/recommendations for international students: Required—TOEFL (minimum score 550 paper-based; 213 computer-based). *Application deadline:* For fall admission, 3/15 priority date for domestic students, 3/1 priority date for international students. Applications are processed on a rolling basis. Application fee: $0. Electronic applications accepted. *Expenses: Contact institution. Financial support:* In 2006–07, 8 teaching assistantships with partial tuition reimbursements (averaging $7,600 per year) were awarded; career-related internships or fieldwork, institutionally sponsored loans, health care benefits, and unspecified assistantships also available. Financial award applicants required to submit FAFSA. *Faculty research:* Diversity, literacy, art representation by young children, preservice teacher preparation. Total annual research expenditures: $330,000. *Unit head:* Dr. Katie A. Kinnucan-Welsch, Chair, 937-229-3346. *Application contact:* Erika Eavers, Graduate Admission Processor, 937-229-3065, Fax: 937-229-4729, E-mail: erika.eavers@notes.udayton.edu.

University of Georgia, Graduate School, College of Education, Department of Elementary and Social Studies Education, Athens, GA 30602. Offers early childhood education (M Ed, PhD, Ed S); elementary and middle school education (M Ed, PhD, Ed S), including elementary education (PhD), middle school education; social foundations of education (PhD). *Faculty:* 15 full-time (8 women). *Students:* 113 full-time (88 women), 122 part-time (95 women); includes 25 minority (19 African Americans, 4 Asian Americans or Pacific Islanders, 2 Hispanic Americans), 14 international. 170 applicants, 69% accepted, 88 enrolled. In 2006, 77 master's, 6 doctorates, 6 other advanced degrees awarded. *Entrance requirements:* For master's and Ed S, GRE General Test or MAT; for doctorate, GRE General Test. *Application deadline:* For fall admission, 7/1 priority date for domestic students; for spring admission, 11/15 for domestic students. Application fee: $50. Electronic applications accepted. *Financial support:* Fellowships, research assistantships, teaching assistantships, unspecified assistantships available. *Unit head:* Dr. Ronald J. Vansickle, Head, 706-542-7265, Fax: 706-542-6506, E-mail: rvansick@uga.edu. *Application contact:* Dr. John D. Hoge, Graduate Coordinator, 706-542-4416, Fax: 706-542-4277, E-mail: jdhoge@uga.edu.

University of Kentucky, Graduate School, College of Education, Program in Curriculum and Instruction, Lexington, KY 40506-0032. Offers curriculum and instruction (MA Ed, Ed D); instruction and administration (Ed D); instruction system design (MS Ed); middle school education (MS Ed). *Accreditation:* NCATE. *Faculty:* 22 full-time (13 women), 2 part-time/adjunct (both women). *Students:* 116 full-time (85 women), 84 part-time (70 women); includes 26 minority (19 African Americans, 6 Asian Americans or Pacific Islanders, 1 Hispanic American), 6 international. Average age 34. 179 applicants, 51% accepted, 36 enrolled. In 2006, 72 master's, 4 doctorates awarded. *Degree requirements:* For master's, thesis optional; for doctorate, thesis/dissertation, comprehensive exam. *Entrance requirements:* For master's, GRE General Test, minimum undergraduate GPA of 2.75; for doctorate, GRE General Test, minimum graduate GPA of 3.0. Additional exam requirements/recommendations for international students: Required—TOEFL (minimum score 550 paper-based; 213 computer-based). *Application deadline:* For fall admission, 7/18 for domestic students, 2/1 priority date for international students; for spring admission, 12/15 for domestic students, 6/16 priority date for international students. Application fee: $35 ($45 for international students). Electronic applications accepted. *Expenses:* Tuition, state resident: full-time $7,670; part-time $401 per credit hour. Tuition, nonresident: full-time $16,158; part-time $873 per credit hour. *Financial support:* In 2006–07, 4 fellowships (averaging $8,018 per year), 13 research assistantships (averaging $15,000 per year), 11 teaching assistantships (averaging $9,384 per year) were awarded; career-related internships or fieldwork, Federal Work-Study, and institutionally sponsored loans also available. Support available to part-time students. *Faculty research:* Educational reform, multicultural education, classroom instructional practices, performance based assessment, primary school programs. *Unit head:* Dr. Mary Shake, Director of Graduate Studies, 859-257-5676, Fax: 859-257-1602. *Application contact:* Dr. Brian Jackson, Senior Associate Dean, 859-257-4667, Fax: 859-257-4676, E-mail: brian.jackson@uky.edu.

University of Louisville, Graduate School, College of Education and Human Development, Department of Teaching and Learning, Program in Middle School Education, Louisville, KY 40292-0001. Offers M Ed, MAT. *Accreditation:* NCATE. *Students:* 14 full-time (11 women), 66 part-time (48 women); includes 10 minority (8 African Americans, 2 Asian Americans or Pacific Islanders), 2 international. Average age 34. In 2006, 57 degrees awarded. *Entrance requirements:* For master's, GRE General Test. *Application deadline:* Applications are processed on a rolling basis. Application fee: $50. *Financial support:* Fellowships, research assistantships, teaching assistantships available. *Unit head:* Dr. Randall L. Wells, Head, 502-852-0598, Fax: 502-852-1497, E-mail: randy.wells@louisville.edu.

University of Missouri–St. Louis, College of Education, Division of Teaching and Learning, St. Louis, MO 63121. Offers elementary education (M Ed), including reading; secondary education (M Ed), including curriculum and instruction, middle school, reading; special education (M Ed), including behavioral disorders, early childhood special education, learning disabilities, mentally retardation; teaching-learning processes (Ed D, PhD). *Faculty:* 20 full-time (13 women), 5 part-time/adjunct (4 women). *Students:* 118 full-time (84 women), 353 part-time (311 women); includes 90 minority (75 African Americans, 1 American Indian/Alaska Native, 3 Asian Americans or Pacific Islanders, 11 Hispanic Americans), 4 international. Average age 36. In 2006, 136 master's, 3 doctorates awarded. *Entrance requirements:* For doctorate, GRE General Test, 3 letters of recommendation. *Application deadline:* For fall admission, 7/15 for domestic students; for spring admission, 12/15 for domestic students. *Expenses:* Tuition, state resident: part-time $332 per credit hour. Tuition, nonresident: part-time $770 per credit hour. *Financial support:* In 2006–07, 9 teaching assistantships (averaging $14,250 per year) were awarded; research assistantships. *Unit head:* Dr. Gayle Wilkinson, Chair, 314-516-5791. *Application contact:* 314-516-5458, Fax: 314-516-6996, E-mail: gadadm@umsl.edu.

The University of North Carolina at Charlotte, Graduate School, College of Education, Department of Middle, Secondary and K-12 Education, Charlotte, NC 28223-0001. Offers middle grades and secondary education (M Ed); teaching English as a second language (M Ed). *Faculty:* 16 full-time (10 women), 6 part-time/adjunct (all women). *Students:* 7 full-time (all women), 79 part-time (67 women); includes 12 minority (6 African Americans, 2 Asian Americans or Pacific Islanders, 4 Hispanic Americans), 3 international. Average age 32. 19 applicants, 89% accepted, 16 enrolled. In 2006, 16 degrees awarded. *Entrance requirements:* For master's, GRE or MAT. Additional exam requirements/recommendations for international students: Required—TOEFL (minimum score 557 paper-based; 220 computer-based). *Application deadline:* For fall admission, 7/1 for domestic students, 5/1 for international students; for spring admission, 11/1 for domestic students, 10/1 for international students. Applications are processed on a rolling basis. Application fee: $55. Electronic applications accepted. *Expenses:* Tuition, state resident: full-time $2,719; part-time $170 per credit. Tuition, nonresident: full-time $12,926; part-time $808 per credit. Required fees: $1,555. *Financial support:* In 2006–07, 7 teaching assistantships (averaging $8,475 per year) were awarded; fellowships, research assistantships, career-related internships or fieldwork, Federal Work-Study, institutionally sponsored loans, scholarships/grants, and unspecified assistantships also available. Support available to part-time students. Financial award application deadline: 4/1; financial award applicants required to submit FAFSA. *Unit head:* Melba Spooner, Chair, 704-687-8704, Fax: 704-687-6430. *Application contact:* Kathy B. Giddings, Director of Graduate Admissions, 704-687-3366, Fax: 704-687-3279, E-mail: gradadm@email.uncc.edu.

The University of North Carolina at Charlotte, Graduate School, College of Education, Program in Teacher Education, Charlotte, NC 28223-0001. Offers art education (K-12) (MAT); dance education (K-12) (MAT); elementary education (K-6) (MAT); English as a second language (K-12) (MAT); foreign language education (K-12) (MAT); general teacher education (MAT); middle grades education (6-9) (MAT); music education (K-12) (MAT); secondary education (9-12) (MAT); special education (K-12) (MAT); theatre education (K-12) (MAT). *Students:* 16 full-time (12 women), 200 part-time (170 women); includes 30 minority (22 African Americans, 2 American Indian/Alaska Native, 2 Asian Americans or Pacific Islanders, 4 Hispanic Americans), 2 international. Average age 33. 74 applicants, 85% accepted, 49 enrolled. In 2006, 43 degrees awarded. *Entrance requirements:* For master's, GRE or MAT. Additional exam requirements/recommendations for international students: Required—TOEFL (minimum score 557 paper-based; 220 computer-based). *Application deadline:* For fall admission, 7/1 for domestic students, 5/1 for international students; for spring admission, 11/1 for domestic students, 10/1 for international students. Applications are processed on a rolling basis. Application fee: $55. Electronic applications accepted. *Expenses:* Tuition, state resident: full-time $2,719; part-time $170 per credit. Tuition, nonresident: full-time $12,926; part-time $808 per credit. Required fees: $1,555. *Financial support:* Fellowships, research assistantships, teaching assistantships, career-related internships or fieldwork, Federal Work-Study, institutionally sponsored loans, scholarships/grants, and unspecified assistantships available. Support available to part-time students. Financial award application deadline: 4/1; financial award applicants required to submit FAFSA. *Unit head:* Dr. Kimberly J. Hartman, Coordinator, 704-687-8883, Fax: 704-687-6430, E-mail: khartman@email.uncc.edu. *Application contact:* Kathy B. Giddings, Director of Graduate Admissions, 704-687-3366, Fax: 704-687-3279, E-mail: gradadm@email.uncc.edu.

The University of North Carolina at Greensboro, Graduate School, School of Education, Department of Curriculum and Instruction, Greensboro, NC 27412-5001. Offers college teaching and adult learning (Certificate); curriculum and instruction (M Ed), including chemistry education, elementary education, English as a second language, French education, instructional technology, mathematics education, middle grades education, reading education, science education, social studies education, Spanish education; curriculum and teaching (PhD), including higher education, teacher education and development; English as a second language (Certificate); higher education (M Ed); supervision (M Ed). *Accreditation:* NCATE. Part-time programs available. *Faculty:* 27 full-time (18 women), 8 part-time/adjunct (3 women). *Students:* 137 full-time (114 women), 231 part-time (195 women); includes 63 minority (52 African Americans, 2 American Indian/Alaska Native, 5 Asian Americans or Pacific Islanders, 4 Hispanic Americans). 146 applicants, 32% accepted. *Degree requirements:* For doctorate, thesis/dissertation. *Entrance requirements:* For master's and doctorate, GRE General Test. Additional exam requirements/recommendations for international students: Required—TOEFL. Application fee: $45. Electronic applications accepted. *Expenses:* Tuition, state resident: full-time $2,692. Tuition, nonresident: full-time $13,742. *Financial support:* Fellowships, research assistantships with full tuition reimbursements, teaching assistantships with full tuition reimbursements, career-related internships or fieldwork, Federal Work-Study, scholarships/grants, traineeships, and unspecified assistantships available. Support available to part-time students. *Faculty research:* Community college literacy program, middle school mathematics/computer mathematics. *Unit head:* Dr. Sam Miller, Chair, 336-334-3445, Fax: 336-334-4120, E-mail: sdmille2@uncg.edu. *Application contact:* Michelle Harkleroad, Director of Graduate Admissions, 336-334-4884, Fax: 336-334-4424, E-mail: mbharkle@uncg.edu.

The University of North Carolina at Pembroke, Graduate Studies, School of Education, Program in Middle Grades Education, Pembroke, NC 28372-1510. Offers MA Ed, MAT. *Accreditation:* NCATE. Part-time and evening/weekend programs available. *Faculty:* 3 full-time (1 woman). *Students:* Average age 34. 10 applicants, 100% accepted, 10 enrolled. In 2006, 2 degrees awarded. *Degree requirements:* For master's, thesis optional. *Entrance requirements:* For master's, GRE General Test or MAT, minimum GPA of 3.0 in major, 2.5 overall. Additional exam requirements/recommendations for international students: Required—TOEFL. *Application deadline:* For fall admission, 7/15 priority date for domestic and international students; for spring admission, 12/1 priority date for domestic and international students. Applications are processed on a rolling basis. Application fee: $40. *Expenses:* Tuition, state resident: full-time $3,516; part-time $1,091 per semester. Tuition, nonresident: full-time $12,924; part-time $4,619 per semester. Tuition and fees vary according to class time, course load, degree level and campus/location. *Financial support:* In 2006–07, research assistantships with full tuition reimbursements (averaging $6,000 per year); unspecified assistantships also available. Support available to part-time students. Financial award application deadline: 4/15; financial award applicants required to submit FAFSA. *Unit head:* Dr. Olivia Oxendine, Director, 910-521-6894, Fax: 910-521-6165, E-mail: Olivia.oxendine@unip.edu. *Application contact:* Dr. Kathleen C. Hilton, Dean of Graduate Studies, 910-521-6271, Fax: 910-521-6751, E-mail: grad@uncp.edu.

The University of North Carolina Wilmington, School of Education, Department of Elementary, Middle Level and Literacy Education, Program in Middle Grades Education, Wilmington, NC 28403-3297. Offers M Ed. *Students:* 1 (woman) full-time, 5 part-time (all women). 5 applicants, 80% accepted, 3 enrolled. In 2006, 1 degree awarded. *Degree requirements:* For master's, comprehensive exam. *Application deadline:* For fall admission, 6/1 for domestic students. Applications are processed on a rolling basis. Application fee: $45. *Financial support:* Application deadline: 3/15. *Unit head:* Dr. Kathren Roney, Coordinator, 910-962-7195. *Application contact:* Dr. Robert D. Roer, Dean, Graduate School, 910-962-4117, Fax: 910-962-3787, E-mail: roer@uncw.edu.

University of Northern Iowa, Graduate College, College of Education, Department of Curriculum and Instruction, Program in Middle School/Junior High Education, Cedar Falls, IA

Middle School Education

University of Northern Iowa (continued)

50614. Offers MAE. *Students:* 1 (woman) full-time, 5 part-time (all women); includes 1 minority (African American), 1 international. 2 applicants, 100% accepted, 1 enrolled. In 2006, 2 degrees awarded. *Degree requirements:* For master's, thesis or alternative. *Entrance requirements:* For master's, minimum GPA of 3.5, 3 years of educational experience. Additional exam requirements/recommendations for international students: Required—TOEFL (minimum score 500 paper-based; 180 computer-based; 61 iBT). *Application deadline:* For fall admission, 8/1 priority date for domestic students. Applications are processed on a rolling basis. Application fee: $30 ($50 for international students). Electronic applications accepted. *Expenses:* Tuition, state resident: full-time $5,936. Tuition, nonresident: full-time $14,074. *Financial support:* Application deadline: 2/1. *Unit head:* Dr. Donna H. Schumacher-Douglas, Coordinator, 319-273-5880, Fax: 319-273-5886, E-mail: donna.schumacher@uni.edu.

University of Puget Sound, Graduate Studies, School of Education, Program in Teaching, Tacoma, WA 98416. Offers elementary education (MAT); middle school education (MAT); secondary education (MAT). *Accreditation:* NASM; NCATE. *Faculty:* 10 full-time (6 women), 2 part-time/adjunct (both women). *Students:* 53 full-time (35 women), 1 (woman) part-time; includes 7 minority (2 African Americans, 2 American Indian/Alaska Native, 3 Asian Americans or Pacific Islanders), 1 international. Average age 26. 96 applicants, 88% accepted, 51 enrolled. In 2006, 41 degrees awarded. *Median time to degree:* Master's–1 year full-time. *Entrance requirements:* For master's, GRE General Test, West-B for WA residents, PRAXIS I, minimum GPA of 3.0. Additional exam requirements/recommendations for international students: Required—TOEFL (minimum score 550 paper-based; 213 computer-based; 80 iBT). *Application deadline:* For fall admission, 3/1 priority date for domestic and international students. Applications are processed on a rolling basis. Application fee: $65. Electronic applications accepted. *Expenses:* Tuition: Full-time $26,390. Tuition and fees vary according to course load. *Financial support:* In 2006–07, 24 students received support, including 16 fellowships (averaging $7,575 per year); career-related internships or fieldwork and scholarships/grants also available. Support available to part-time students. Financial award application deadline: 3/31; financial award applicants required to submit FAFSA. *Faculty research:* Economic support for schools, teacher thinking/student understanding, self-reflection in teacher education, civics and decision making. Total annual research expenditures: $11,005. *Application contact:* Dr. George H. Mills, Vice President for Enrollment, 253-879-3211, Fax: 253-879-3993, E-mail: admission@ups.edu.

University of Southern Maine, College of Education and Human Development, Educational Leadership Program, Portland, ME 04104-9300. Offers assistant principal (Certificate); athletic administration (Certificate); educational leadership (MS Ed, CAS); middle-level education (Certificate). *Accreditation:* NCATE. Part-time and evening/weekend programs available. Postbaccalaureate distance learning degree programs offered (minimal on-campus study). *Faculty:* 7 full-time (1 woman), 5 part-time/adjunct (2 women). *Students:* 4 full-time (3 women), 111 part-time (63 women), 1 international. 20 applicants, 65% accepted, 8 enrolled. In 2006, 36 master's, 23 CASs awarded. *Degree requirements:* For master's, thesis or alternative, practicum; for other advanced degree, thesis or alternative. *Entrance requirements:* For master's, GRE General Test or MAT; for other advanced degree, master's degree. Additional exam requirements/recommendations for international students: Required—TOEFL. *Application deadline:* For fall admission, 2/1 for domestic students; for spring admission, 9/15 for domestic students. Application fee: $50. Electronic applications accepted. *Expenses:* Tuition, state resident: full-time $4,860; part-time $270 per credit hour. Tuition, nonresident: full-time $13,572; part-time $754 per credit hour. Required fees: $222 per semester. Tuition and fees vary according to course load. *Financial support:* In 2006–07, 3 students received support, including 2 research assistantships with tuition reimbursements available (averaging $4,500 per year); career-related internships or fieldwork, Federal Work-Study, institutionally sponsored loans, scholarships/grants, and unspecified assistantships also available. Financial award application deadline: 3/1; financial award applicants required to submit FAFSA. *Unit head:* Dr. James Curry, Chair, Professional Education Department, 270-780-5400, Fax: 270-780-5674, E-mail: jcurry@usm.maine.edu. *Application contact:* Robin Audesse, Associate Director of Graduate Admissions, 207-780-5306, Fax: 207-780-5193, E-mail: raudesse@usm.maine.edu.

University of South Florida, Graduate School, College of Education, Department of Secondary Education, Tampa, FL 33620-9951. Offers English education (M Ed, MA, PhD); foreign language education (M Ed, MA); instructional technology (M Ed); mathematics education (M Ed, MA, PhD, Ed S); middle school education (M Ed); science education (M Ed, MA, MAT, PhD); second language acquisition/instructional technology (PhD); secondary education (PhD); social science education (M Ed, MA). *Accreditation:* NCATE. Part-time and evening/weekend programs available. *Faculty:* 29 full-time (16 women), 15 part-time/adjunct (8 women). *Students:* 136 full-time (95 women), 279 part-time (188 women); includes 85 minority (35 African Americans, 1 American Indian/Alaska Native, 13 Asian Americans or Pacific Islanders, 36 Hispanic Americans), 19 international. 212 applicants, 71% accepted, 96 enrolled. In 2006, 87 master's, 12 doctorates awarded. *Entrance requirements:* For master's and doctorate, GRE General Test, minimum GPA of 3.5; for Ed S, GRE General Test. *Application deadline:* For fall admission, 6/1 for domestic students; for spring admission, 10/15 for domestic students. Application fee: $30. Electronic applications accepted. *Financial support:* Scholarships/grants and unspecified assistantships available. Total annual research expenditures: $477,202. *Unit head:* Dr. Jane H. Applegate, Interim Chairperson, 813-974-3533, Fax: 813-974-3837, E-mail: applegat@tempest.coedu.usf.edu.

University of the Cumberlands, Graduate Programs in Education, Program in Elementary Education, Williamsburg, KY 40769-1372. Offers elementary (P-5) (MA Ed, MAT); middle school (5-9) (MA Ed, MAT). Part-time and evening/weekend programs available. *Degree requirements:* For master's, comprehensive exam. *Entrance requirements:* For master's, GRE or NTE, Kentucky teaching certificate.

University of the Cumberlands, Graduate Programs in Education, Program in Middle School Education, Williamsburg, KY 40769-1372. Offers MA Ed, MAT. *Degree requirements:* For master's, comprehensive exam. *Entrance requirements:* For master's, GRE or NTE, Kentucky teaching certificate.

The University of Toledo, College of Graduate Studies, College of Education, Department of Curriculum and Instruction, Program in Middle Childhood Education, Toledo, OH 43606-3390. Offers ME. *Students:* 5 full-time (all women), 2 part-time (both women). Average age 26. 1 applicant, 0% accepted. In 2006, 7 degrees awarded.

University of West Florida, College of Professional Studies, Division of Teacher Education, Master's Program in Curriculum and Instruction, Specialization in Middle and Secondary Level Education, Pensacola, FL 32514-5750. Offers M Ed. *Accreditation:* NCATE. Part-time and evening/weekend programs available. *Students:* 39 full-time (29 women), 35 part-time (25 women); includes 29 minority (12 African Americans, 4 Asian Americans or Pacific Islanders, 13 Hispanic Americans). Average age 38. 27 applicants, 100% accepted, 27 enrolled. In 2006, 39 degrees awarded. *Degree requirements:* For master's, thesis or alternative. *Entrance requirements:* For master's, GRE General Test or minimum GPA of 3.0. Additional exam requirements/recommendations for international students: Required—TOEFL (minimum score 550 paper-based; 213 computer-based). *Application deadline:* For fall admission, 6/1 for domestic students, 5/15 for international students; for spring admission, 11/1 for domestic students, 10/1 for international students. Applications are processed on a rolling basis. Application fee: $30. *Expenses:* Tuition, state resident: full-time $5,871; part-time $245 per credit hour. Tuition, nonresident: full-time $21,241; part-time $885 per credit hour. *Financial support:* Fellowships, Federal Work-Study, scholarships/grants, and unspecified assistantships available.

University of West Georgia, Graduate School, College of Education, Department of Curriculum and Instruction, Program in Middle Grades Education, Carrollton, GA 30118. Offers M Ed, Ed S. *Accreditation:* NCATE. Part-time and evening/weekend programs available. *Students:* 4 full-time (all women), 46 part-time (42 women); includes 9 minority (8 African Americans, 1 Hispanic American). Average age 30. In 2006, 22 master's, 7 other advanced degrees awarded. *Degree requirements:* For master's, comprehensive exam; for Ed S, research project. *Entrance requirements:* For master's, GRE General Test or MAT, minimum GPA of 2.7; for Ed S, GRE General Test or MAT, master's degree, minimum graduate GPA of 3.0. *Application deadline:* For fall admission, 8/1 for domestic students. Applications are processed on a rolling basis. Application fee: $20. *Expenses:* Tuition, state resident: full-time $2,286; part-time $127 per credit. Tuition, nonresident: full-time $9,144; part-time $508 per credit. Required fees: $494; $27 per credit. $121 per semester. *Financial support:* In 2006–07, research assistantships with full tuition reimbursements (averaging $3,000 per year); career-related internships or fieldwork and unspecified assistantships also available. Support available to part-time students. Financial award applicants required to submit FAFSA. *Application contact:* Dr. Charles W. Clark, Chair, 678-839-6508, E-mail: cclark@westga.edu.

University of Wisconsin–Milwaukee, Graduate School, School of Education, Department of Curriculum and Instruction, Milwaukee, WI 53201-0413. Offers curriculum planning and instruction improvement (MS); early childhood education (MS); elementary education (MS); junior high/middle school education (MS); reading education (MS); secondary education (MS); teaching in an urban setting (MS). Part-time programs available. *Faculty:* 27 full-time (17 women). *Students:* 21 full-time (17 women), 67 part-time (54 women); includes 15 minority (8 African Americans, 3 Asian Americans or Pacific Islanders, 4 Hispanic Americans), 3 international. 44 applicants, 43% accepted, 19 enrolled. In 2006, 38 degrees awarded. *Degree requirements:* For master's, thesis or alternative. *Application deadline:* For fall admission, 1/1 priority date for domestic students; for spring admission, 9/1 for domestic students. Applications are processed on a rolling basis. Application fee: $45 ($75 for international students). *Expenses:* Tuition, state resident: part-time $510 per credit. Tuition, nonresident: part-time $1,408 per credit. Tuition and fees vary according to program. *Financial support:* Fellowships, research assistantships, teaching assistantships, career-related internships or fieldwork and unspecified assistantships available. Support available to part-time students. Financial award application deadline: 4/15. *Unit head:* Linda Post, Chair, 414-229-4884, Fax: 414-229-5571, E-mail: lpost@uwm.edu.

University of Wisconsin–Platteville, School of Graduate Studies, College of Liberal Arts and Education, School of Education, Platteville, WI 53818-3099. Offers adult education (MSE); elementary education (MSE); middle school education (MSE); secondary education (MSE); vocational and technical education (MSE). *Accreditation:* NCATE. Part-time programs available. *Faculty:* 8 part-time/adjunct (3 women). *Students:* 48 full-time (37 women), 103 part-time (72 women); includes 33 minority (27 African Americans, 1 Asian American or Pacific Islander, 5 Hispanic Americans), 39 international. 39 applicants, 72% accepted. In 2006, 55 degrees awarded. *Degree requirements:* For master's, thesis or alternative, comprehensive exam, registration. *Entrance requirements:* Additional exam requirements/recommendations for international students: Required—TOEFL (minimum score 500 paper-based; 173 computer-based). *Application deadline:* For fall admission, 7/1 priority date for domestic students; for spring admission, 11/1 for domestic students. Applications are processed on a rolling basis. Application fee: $45. Electronic applications accepted. *Expenses:* Tuition, state resident: part-time $365 per credit. Tuition, nonresident: part-time $955 per credit. *Financial support:* Research assistantships with partial tuition reimbursements, career-related internships or fieldwork, Federal Work-Study, institutionally sponsored loans, scholarships/grants, and unspecified assistantships available. Support available to part-time students. *Unit head:* Dr. Michael Anderson, Director, 608-342-1131, Fax: 608-342-1133, E-mail: andersonmi@uwplatt.edu. *Application contact:* Kristal Prohaska, Admissions and Enrollment Management, 608-342-1125, Fax: 608-342-1122, E-mail: admit@uwplatt.edu.

Valdosta State University, Graduate School, College of Education, Department of Middle Grades and Secondary Education, Valdosta, GA 31698. Offers middle grades education (M Ed, Ed S); secondary education (M Ed, Ed S). *Accreditation:* NCATE. Part-time and evening/weekend programs available. *Degree requirements:* For master's, thesis (for some programs), comprehensive written and/or oral exams; for Ed S, thesis. *Entrance requirements:* For master's, GRE General Test or MAT, minimum GPA of 2.5; for Ed S, GRE General Test or MAT, minimum GPA of 3.0. Additional exam requirements/recommendations for international students: Required—TOEFL (minimum score 523 paper-based; 193 computer-based). Electronic applications accepted. *Faculty research:* Distance education, learning styles, alternative assessment methods, interactive teaching strategies, learning styles of pre-service teachers.

Virginia Commonwealth University, Graduate School, School of Education, Program in Teaching and Learning, Richmond, VA 23284-9005. Offers early education (MT); middle education (MT); secondary education (MT, Certificate); special education (MT). *Accreditation:* NCATE. Part-time programs available. *Faculty:* 22 full-time (12 women). *Students:* 152 full-time (130 women), 126 part-time (111 women); includes 42 minority (35 African Americans, 2 American Indian/Alaska Native, 4 Asian Americans or Pacific Islanders, 1 Hispanic American), 4 international. 551 applicants, 74% accepted. In 2006, 77 degrees awarded. *Entrance requirements:* For master's, GRE General Test or MAT. *Application deadline:* For fall admission, 5/15 for domestic students; for spring admission, 11/15 for domestic students. Applications are processed on a rolling basis. Application fee: $50. *Financial support:* Application deadline: 3/1. *Unit head:* Dr. Michael D. Davis, Director, Graduate Studies, 804-828-6530, Fax: 804-827-0676, E-mail: mddavis@vcu.edu. *Application contact:* Dr. Michael D. Davis, Director, Graduate Studies, 804-828-6530, Fax: 804-827-0676, E-mail: mddavis@vcu.edu.

See Close-Up on page 1137.

Wagner College, Division of Graduate Studies, Department of Education, Program in Adolescent Education, Staten Island, NY 10301-4495. Offers MS Ed. Part-time and evening/weekend programs available. *Students:* 17 full-time (3 women), 4 part-time (2 women); includes 1 Asian American or Pacific Islander. 11 applicants, 100% accepted, 9 enrolled. In 2006, 11 degrees awarded. *Entrance requirements:* For master's, Liberal Arts and Sciences Test (LAST), New York State Teacher Certification Examinations (NYSTCE), minimum GPA of 2.75. Additional exam requirements/recommendations for international students: Required—TOEFL (minimum score 550 paper-based; 217 computer-based). *Application deadline:* For fall admission, 8/1 priority date for domestic students, 6/30 priority date for international students; for spring admission, 12/10 for domestic students, 11/15 for international students. Applications are processed on a rolling basis. Application fee: $50 ($85 for international students). *Expenses:* Tuition: Full-time $15,120; part-time $840 per credit. *Financial support:* Fellowships, tuition waivers (partial) and unspecified assistantships available. *Application contact:* Susan Rosenberg, Office of Graduate Studies, 718-390-3106, Fax: 718-390-3456, E-mail: graduate@wagner.edu.

Wagner College, Division of Graduate Studies, Department of Education, Program in Middle Level Education (5-9), Staten Island, NY 10301-4495. Offers MS Ed. *Students:* 2 full-time (1 woman), 1 (woman) part-time. 2 applicants, 100% accepted, 2 enrolled. In 2006, 4 degrees awarded. *Degree requirements:* For master's, thesis. *Entrance requirements:* For master's, minimum GPA of 2.75. Additional exam requirements/recommendations for international students: Required—TOEFL (minimum score 550 paper-based; 217 computer-based). *Application deadline:* For fall admission, 8/1 priority date for domestic students, 6/30 priority date for international students; for spring admission, 12/10 for domestic students, 11/15 for international students. Applications are processed on a rolling basis. Application fee: $50 ($85 for international students). *Expenses:* Tuition: Full-time $15,120; part-time $840 per credit. *Financial support:* Fellowships, unspecified assistantships available. Financial award applicants required to submit FAFSA. *Application contact:* Susan Rosenberg, Office of Graduate Studies, 718-390-3106, Fax: 718-390-3456, E-mail: graduate@wagner.edu.

Wesleyan College, Department of Education, Program in Middle-Level Mathematics and Middle-Level Science Education, Macon, GA 31210-4462. Offers MA. Offered during summer only. Part-time programs available. *Faculty:* 4 full-time (3 women), 2 part-time/adjunct (both women). *Students:* 4 full-time (3 women), 8 part-time (all women); includes 6 minority (all African Americans) Average age 32. 6 applicants, 67% accepted, 4 enrolled. In 2006, 2 degrees awarded. *Degree requirements:* For master's, thesis or alternative, practicum, professional portfolio. *Entrance requirements:* For master's, GRE or MAT. Additional exam requirements/recommendations for international students: Required—TOEFL. *Application deadline:* For fall admission, 7/1 priority date for domestic students; for spring admission, 12/1 priority date for domestic students. Applications are processed on a rolling basis. Application fee: $25. *Expenses:* Tuition: Full-time $14,500. Tuition and fees vary according to program. *Financial support:* Federal Work-Study available. Financial award application deadline: 4/1; financial award applicants required to submit FAFSA. *Faculty research:* Instructional technology, cognitive development, verbal classroom interactions.

Western Carolina University, Graduate School, College of Education and Allied Professions, Department of Birth-Kindergarten, Elementary and Middle Grades Education, Program in Middle Grades Education, Cullowhee, NC 28723. Offers MA Ed, MAT. *Accreditation:* NCATE. Part-time and evening/weekend programs available. *Degree requirements:* For master's, comprehensive exam. *Entrance requirements:* For master's, GRE General Test. Additional exam requirements/recommendations for international students: Required—TOEFL (minimum score 550 paper-based; 213 computer-based).

Western Kentucky University, Graduate Studies, College of Education and Behavioral Sciences, Department of Counseling and Student Affairs, Bowling Green, KY 42101. Offers business and marketing education (MA Ed); counseling (MA Ed); counselor education (Ed S); education and behavioral science (MA Ed); elementary education (MA Ed, Ed S); middle years education (MA Ed); secondary education (MA Ed, Ed S); student affairs (MA Ed). *Accreditation:* ACA; NCATE. Part-time and evening/weekend programs available. *Faculty:* 11 full-time (5 women), 9 part-time/adjunct (3 women). *Students:* 59 full-time (47 women), 157 part-time (126 women); includes 18 minority (13 African Americans, 1 American Indian/Alaska Native, 2 Asian Americans or Pacific Islanders, 2 Hispanic Americans), 1 international. Average age 31. 49 applicants, 67% accepted, 27 enrolled. In 2006, 89 master's, 4 other advanced degrees awarded. *Degree requirements:* For master's, thesis optional. *Entrance requirements:* For master's, GRE General Test. Additional exam requirements/recommendations for international students: Required—TOEFL (minimum score 555 paper-based; 213 computer-based; 79 iBT). *Application deadline:* For fall admission, 8/1 priority date for domestic students, 4/1 for international students; for spring admission, 12/1 for domestic students, 9/1 for international students. Applications are processed on a rolling basis. Application fee: $35. *Expenses:* Tuition, state resident: full-time $6,520; part-time $226 per hour. Tuition, nonresident: full-time $7,140; part-time $357 per hour. International tuition: $15,820 full-time. *Financial support:* In 2006–07, 1 research assistantship with partial tuition reimbursement (averaging $8,000 per year) was awarded; Federal Work-Study, institutionally sponsored loans, and service awards also available. Financial award application deadline: 4/1; financial award applicants required to submit FAFSA. *Faculty research:* Counselor education, research for residential workers. *Unit head:* Dr. Aaron W Hughey, Department Head, 270-745-4953, E-mail: aaron.hughey@wku.edu.

Western Kentucky University, Graduate Studies, College of Education and Behavioral Sciences, Department of Curriculum and Instruction, Bowling Green, KY 42101. Offers business and marketing education (MAE); elementary education (MAE, Ed S); middle grades education (MAE); secondary education (MAE, Ed S). *Faculty:* 10 full-time (7 women), 1 (woman) part-time/adjunct. *Students:* 7 full-time (3 women), 133 part-time (109 women); includes 2 minority (1 African American, 1 Hispanic American), 1 international. Average age 31. 30 applicants, 63% accepted, 14 enrolled. In 2006, 56 degrees awarded. *Degree requirements:* For master's, comprehensive exam; for Ed S, thesis. *Entrance requirements:* For master's, GRE. Additional exam requirements/recommendations for international students: Required—TOEFL (minimum score 555 paper-based; 213 computer-based; 79 iBT). *Application deadline:* For fall admission, 7/1 priority date for domestic students, 5/15 for international students; for spring admission, 11/1 for domestic students, 9/15 for international students. Applications are processed on a rolling basis. Application fee: $35. *Expenses:* Tuition, state resident: full-time $6,520; part-time $226 per hour. Tuition, nonresident: full-time $7,140; part-time $357 per hour. International tuition: $15,820 full-time. *Financial support:* In 2006–07, 1 research assistantship with partial tuition reimbursement (averaging $7,200 per year) was awarded. Total annual research expenditures: $17,998. *Unit head:* Dr. Tabitha Daniel, Head, 270-745-2157, E-mail: tabitha.daniel@wku.edu.

Western Michigan University, Graduate College, College of Education, Department of Teaching, Learning, and Leadership, Program in Middle School Education, Kalamazoo, MI 49008-5202. Offers MA. *Accreditation:* NCATE.

Widener University, School of Human Service Professions, Center for Education, Chester, PA 19013-5792. Offers adult education (M Ed); counseling in higher education (M Ed); counselor education (M Ed); early childhood education (M Ed); educational foundations (M Ed); educational leadership (M Ed); educational psychology (M Ed); elementary education (M Ed); English and language arts (M Ed); health education (M Ed); higher education leadership (Ed D); home and school visitor (M Ed); human sexuality (M Ed); mathematics education (M Ed); middle school education (M Ed); principalship (M Ed); reading and language arts (Ed D); reading education (M Ed); school administration (Ed D); science education (M Ed); social studies education (M Ed); special education (M Ed); technology education (M Ed). Part-time and evening/weekend programs available. Terminal master's awarded for partial completion of doctoral program. *Degree requirements:* For doctorate, thesis/dissertation. *Entrance requirements:* For master's, minimum GPA of 2.5; for doctorate, GRE or MAT, minimum GPA of 2.0 (undergraduate), 3.5 (graduate). Electronic applications accepted. Expenses: Contact institution. *Faculty research:* Reading and cognition, adult education, technology education, educational leadership, special education.

Winthrop University, College of Education, Program in Middle Level Education, Rock Hill, SC 29733. Offers M Ed. *Students:* 1 (woman) full-time, 29 part-time (24 women); includes 7 minority (all African Americans) Average age 29. In 2006, 13 degrees awarded. *Entrance requirements:* For master's, minimum GPA of 3.0, South Carolina Class III Teaching Certificate. *Application deadline:* For fall admission, 7/15 priority date for domestic students; for spring admission, 12/1 for domestic students. Applications are processed on a rolling basis. Application fee: $35 ($50 for international students). Electronic applications accepted. *Expenses:* Tuition, state resident: full-time $9,148; part-time $383 per hour. Tuition, nonresident: full-time $16,864; part-time $704 per hour. *Financial support:* Application deadline: 2/1; *Unit head:* Dr. Barbara Blackburn, Graduate Program Advisor, 803-323-4728, Fax: 803-323-2585, E-mail: blackburnb@winthrop.edu. *Application contact:* 800-411-7041, Fax: 803-323-2292, E-mail: graduatestu@winthrop.edu.

Worcester State College, Graduate Studies, Department of Education, Concentration in Middle School Education, Worcester, MA 01602-2597. Offers M Ed. Part-time programs available. *Students:* Average age 35. 17 applicants, 100% accepted, 0 enrolled. In 2006, 5 degrees awarded. *Degree requirements:* For master's, thesis optional. *Entrance requirements:* For master's, GRE General Test or MAT. Additional exam requirements/recommendations for international students: Required—TOEFL (minimum score 550 paper-based; 213 computer-based). *Application deadline:* Applications are processed on a rolling basis. Application fee: $30. *Expenses:* Tuition, state resident: full-time $4,518; part-time $251 per credit hour. Tuition, nonresident: full-time $4,518; part-time $251 per credit hour. *Financial support:* Career-related internships or fieldwork, Federal Work-Study, scholarships/grants, and unspecified assistantships available. Support available to part-time students. Financial award application deadline: 3/1; financial award applicants required to submit FAFSA. *Unit head:* Dr. O. Joshua Aisiku, Coordinator, 508-929-8668, Fax: 508-929-8164, E-mail: oaisiku@worcester.edu. *Application contact:* Nicole Brown, Assistant Dean of Graduate and Continuing Education, 508-929-8787, Fax: 508-929-8100, E-mail: nbrown@worcester.edu.

Wright State University, School of Graduate Studies, College of Education and Human Services, Department of Teacher Education, Dayton, OH 45435. Offers adolescent young adult (M Ed, MA); classroom teacher education (M Ed, MA); early childhood education (M Ed, MA); intervention specialist (M Ed, MA), including gifted educational needs, mild to moderate educational needs, moderate to intensive educational needs; middle childhood (M Ed); middle childhood education (MA); multi-age (M Ed, MA); workforce education (M Ed, MA), including career, technology and vocational education, computer/technology education, library/media, vocational education. *Accreditation:* NCATE. *Students:* 74 full-time (55 women), 137 part-time (120 women); includes 12 minority (9 African Americans, 2 Asian Americans or Pacific Islanders, 1 Hispanic American), 1 international. Average age 34. 68 applicants, 97% accepted. In 2006, 119 degrees awarded. *Entrance requirements:* For master's, GRE General Test, MAT, PRAXIS II. Additional exam requirements/recommendations for international students: Required—TOEFL. Application fee: $25. *Financial support:* Available to part-time students. Applicants required to submit FAFSA. *Faculty research:* Reading recovery, early kindergarten birthdays, international children's literature, discipline models, university and public schools cooperation. *Unit head:* Dr. Colleen A. Finegan, Chair, 937-775-2332, Fax: 937-775-3308, E-mail: colleen.finegan@wright.edu. *Application contact:* John Kimble, Associate Director of Graduate Admissions and Records, 937-775-2957, Fax: 937-775-2453, E-mail: john.kimble@wright.edu.

Youngstown State University, Graduate School, College of Education, Department of Teacher Education, Program in Early and Middle Childhood Education, Youngstown, OH 44555-0001. Offers teaching—elementary education (MS Ed); teaching—secondary reading (MS Ed). *Accreditation:* NCATE. Part-time and evening/weekend programs available. *Degree requirements:* For master's, comprehensive exam. *Entrance requirements:* For master's, GRE, MAT, or teaching certificate; minimum GPA of 2.7. Additional exam requirements/recommendations for international students: Required—TOEFL.

Secondary Education

Adelphi University, School of Education, Program in Adolescent Education, Garden City, NY 11530-0701. Offers MA. Part-time and evening/weekend programs available. *Students:* 64 full-time (48 women), 120 part-time (75 women); includes 26 minority (13 African Americans, 8 Asian Americans or Pacific Islanders, 5 Hispanic Americans). Average age 28. In 2006, 98 degrees awarded. *Entrance requirements:* For master's, 2 letters of recommendation, resumé. Additional exam requirements/recommendations for international students: Required—TOEFL (minimum score 550 paper-based; 213 computer-based). *Application deadline:* For fall admission, 4/1 priority date for domestic students; for spring admission, 11/1 priority date for domestic students. Applications are processed on a rolling basis. Application fee: $50. Electronic applications accepted. *Financial support:* Fellowships, research assistantships with partial tuition reimbursements, teaching assistantships, career-related internships or fieldwork, Federal Work-Study, institutionally sponsored loans, tuition waivers (full), and unspecified assistantships available. Support available to part-time students. Financial award application deadline: 2/15; financial award applicants required to submit FAFSA. *Faculty research:* Methods to enhance the development of teaching dispositions, ethical and moral issues in education. *Application contact:* Christine Murphy, Director of Admissions, 516-877-3050, Fax: 516-877-3039, E-mail: graduateadmissions@adelphi.edu.

Alabama Agricultural and Mechanical University, School of Graduate Studies, School of Education, Department of Curriculum and Instruction, Area in Secondary Education, Huntsville, AL 35811. Offers education (M Ed, Ed S); higher administration (MS). *Accreditation:* NCATE. Evening/weekend programs available. *Faculty:* 8 full-time (3 women), 2 part-time/adjunct (0 women). *Students:* 50 full-time (36 women), 124 part-time (82 women); includes 128 minority (122 African Americans, 3 Asian Americans or Pacific Islanders, 3 Hispanic Americans), 4 international. In 2006, 47 degrees awarded. *Degree requirements:* For master's, comprehensive exam; for Ed S, thesis. *Entrance requirements:* For master's, GRE General Test. *Application deadline:* For fall admission, 5/1 for domestic students. Applications are processed on a rolling basis. Application fee: $25. Electronic applications accepted. *Financial support:* In 2006–07, 2 research assistantships (averaging $5,300 per year) were awarded; career-related internships or fieldwork, Federal Work-Study, institutionally sponsored loans, and traineeships also available. Financial award application deadline: 4/1. *Faculty research:* World peace through education, computer-assisted instruction. *Unit head:* Dr. Bruce Crawford, Chairperson, 256-372-5520, Fax: 256-372-5526.

Alabama State University, School of Graduate Studies, College of Education, Department of Curriculum and Instruction, Program in Secondary Education, Montgomery, AL 36101-0271. Offers biology education (M Ed, Ed S); English/language arts (M Ed); history education (M Ed, Ed S); mathematics education (M Ed); secondary education (Ed S); social studies (Ed S). Part-time programs available. *Students:* 31 full-time (23 women), 123 part-time (81 women); includes 114 minority (111 African Americans, 2 Asian Americans or Pacific Islanders, 1 Hispanic American), 1 international. In 2006, 27 degrees awarded. *Degree requirements:* For master's, comprehensive exam; for Ed S, thesis, comprehensive exam. *Entrance requirements:* For master's, GRE General Test, MAT, graduate writing competency test; for Ed S, graduate writing competency test, GRE, MAT. Additional exam requirements/recommendations for international students: Required—TOEFL (minimum score 500 paper-based; 173 computer-based). *Application deadline:* For fall admission, 7/15 for domestic students; for spring admission, 12/15 for domestic students. Applications are processed on a rolling basis. Application fee: $10. *Expenses:* Tuition, state resident: full-time $1,728; part-time $192 per hour. Tuition, nonresident: full-time $3,456; part-time $334 per hour. *Financial support:* In 2006–07, research assistantships (averaging $9,450 per year).

Alcorn State University, School of Graduate Studies, School of Psychology and Education, Alcorn State, MS 39096-7500. Offers agricultural education (MS Ed); elementary education (MS Ed, Ed S); guidance and counseling (MS Ed); industrial education (MS Ed); secondary education (MS Ed), including health and physical education; special education (MS Ed). *Accreditation:* NCATE. *Faculty:* 14 full-time (9 women), 21 part-time/adjunct (13 women). *Students:* 76 full-time (44 women), 271 part-time (226 women); includes 333 minority (all African Americans) In 2006, 119 degrees awarded. *Degree requirements:* For master's, thesis optional. *Application deadline:* For fall admission, 7/15 priority date for domestic students; for spring admission, 11/25 for domestic students. Applications are processed on a rolling basis. Application fee: $0 ($10 for international students). *Financial support:* Career-related internships or fieldwork available. Support available to part-time students. *Unit head:* Dr. Josephine M. Posey, Dean, 601-877-6141, Fax: 601-877-3867.

American International College, School of Psychology and Education, Department of Education, Springfield, MA 01109-3189. Offers administration (M Ed, CAGS); child development (MA, Ed D), including educational psychology; elementary education (M Ed, CAGS); reading

Secondary Education

American International College (continued)
(M Ed, CAGS); secondary education (M Ed, CAGS); special education (M Ed, CAGS); teaching (MAT). Part-time and evening/weekend programs available. *Faculty:* 5 full-time (3 women), 15 part-time/adjunct (9 women). *Students:* 31 full-time (27 women), 268 part-time (217 women); includes 25 minority (13 African Americans, 4 Asian Americans or Pacific Islanders, 8 Hispanic Americans), 2 international. Average age 39. In 2006, 38 master's, 2 doctorates, 5 other advanced degrees awarded. Terminal master's awarded for partial completion of doctoral program. *Degree requirements:* For master's, thesis (for some programs), practicum, comprehensive exam (for some programs), registration; for doctorate, thesis/dissertation, comprehensive exam (for some programs), registration; for CAGS, practicum. *Entrance requirements:* For master's, minimum B- average in undergraduate course work; for doctorate, GRE General Test, interview. Additional exam requirements/recommendations for international students: Required—TOEFL. *Application deadline:* For fall admission, 7/1 priority date for domestic and international students; for spring admission, 12/1 priority date for domestic and international students. Applications are processed on a rolling basis. Application fee: $50. *Expenses:* Tuition: Part-time $585 per semester hour. Required fees: $100 per year. Full-time tuition and fees vary according to program. *Financial support:* Career-related internships or fieldwork and institutionally sponsored loans available. Financial award applicants required to submit FAFSA. *Unit head:* Dr. Barbara Dautrich, Chair, 413-205-3407, Fax: 413-205-3943, E-mail: barbara.dautrich@aic.edu. *Application contact:* Keshawn Dodds, Associate Director of Graduate Admissions, 413-205-3549, Fax: 413-205-3911, E-mail: keshawn.dodds@aic.edu.

American University, College of Arts and Sciences, School of Education, Teaching, and Health, Program in Secondary Teaching, Washington, DC 20016-8001. Offers MAT, Certificate. *Students:* 6 full-time (all women), 155 part-time (101 women); includes 36 minority (26 African Americans, 6 Asian Americans or Pacific Islanders, 4 Hispanic Americans). Average age 28. In 2006, 17 master's, 6 other advanced degrees awarded. *Degree requirements:* For master's, PRAXIS II. *Entrance requirements:* For master's, GRE General Test or MAT, minimum GPA of 3.0. *Application deadline:* For fall admission, 2/1 priority date for domestic students; for spring admission, 10/1 priority date for domestic students. Applications are processed on a rolling basis. Application fee: $50. *Expenses:* Tuition: Full-time $18,864; part-time $1,048 per credit. Required fees: $380. Tuition and fees vary according to program. *Financial support:* Research assistantships with partial tuition reimbursements available. Financial award application deadline: 2/1.

Andrews University, School of Graduate Studies, School of Education, Department of Teaching, Learning, and Curriculum, Berrien Springs, MI 49104. Offers curriculum and instruction (MA, Ed D, PhD, Ed S); elementary education (MAT); reading (MA); secondary education (MAT), including biology, education, English, English as a second language, French, history, physics; special education/learning disabilities (MS); teacher education (MAT). *Entrance requirements:* For master's, GRE Subject Test.

Appalachian State University, Cratis D. Williams Graduate School, College of Education, Department of Curriculum and Instruction, Boone, NC 28608. Offers curriculum specialist (MA); educational media (MA); elementary education (MA); secondary education (MA). *Accreditation:* NCATE. Part-time and evening/weekend programs available. Postbaccalaureate distance learning degree programs offered (minimal on-campus study). *Faculty:* 32 full-time (21 women). *Students:* 7 full-time (5 women), 206 part-time (172 women); includes 2 minority (both African Americans), 2 international. 100 applicants, 97% accepted, 95 enrolled. In 2006, 96 degrees awarded. *Degree requirements:* For master's, thesis or alternative, comprehensive exam, registration. *Entrance requirements:* For master's, GRE General Test or MAT. Additional exam requirements/recommendations for international students: Required—TOEFL (minimum score 570 paper-based; 230 computer-based). *Application deadline:* For fall admission, 7/1 priority date for domestic students, 1/1 for international students; for spring admission, 11/1 for domestic students, 6/1 for international students. Application fee: $50. *Expenses:* Tuition, state resident: full-time $2,600; part-time $127 per hour. Tuition, nonresident: full-time $13,200; part-time $597 per hour. Required fees: $2,000; $546 per term. *Financial support:* In 2006–07, 6 teaching assistantships (averaging $7,000 per year) were awarded; fellowships, research assistantships, career-related internships or fieldwork, Federal Work-Study, scholarships/grants, and unspecified assistantships also available. Support available to part-time students. Financial award application deadline: 7/1; financial award applicants required to submit FAFSA. Total annual research expenditures: $366,043. *Unit head:* Dr. Michael Jacobson, Chairperson, 828-262-2224.

Arcadia University, Graduate Studies, Department of Education, Glenside, PA 19038-3295. Offers art education (M Ed, MA Ed); biology education (MA Ed); chemistry education (MA Ed); child development (CAS); computer education (M Ed, CAS); computer education 7–12 (MA Ed); early childhood education (M Ed, CAS), including individualized (M Ed), master teacher (M Ed), research in child development (M Ed); educational leadership (M Ed, CAS); educational psychology (CAS); elementary education (M Ed, CAS); English education (MA Ed); environmental education (MA Ed, CAS); history education (MA Ed); language arts (M Ed, CAS); mathematics education (M Ed, MA Ed, CAS); music education (MA Ed); psychology (MA Ed); pupil personnel services (CAS); reading (M Ed, CAS); school library science (M Ed); science education (M Ed, CAS); secondary education (M Ed, CAS); special education (M Ed, Ed D, CAS); theater arts (MA Ed); written communication (MA Ed). *Accreditation:* NASAD. Part-time and evening/weekend programs available. Postbaccalaureate distance learning degree programs offered (minimal on-campus study). *Faculty:* 12 full-time (8 women), 38 part-time/adjunct (26 women). *Students:* 60 full-time (56 women), 419 part-time (324 women); includes 70 minority (57 African Americans, 1 American Indian/Alaska Native, 6 Asian Americans or Pacific Islanders, 6 Hispanic Americans), 1 international. In 2006, 257 master's, 4 doctorates awarded. *Application deadline:* Applications are processed on a rolling basis. Application fee: $35. Electronic applications accepted. *Financial support:* Career-related internships or fieldwork, tuition waivers (partial), and unspecified assistantships available. *Unit head:* Dr. Steven P. Gulkus, Chair, 215-572-2120. *Application contact:* 215-572-2925, Fax: 215-572-2126, E-mail: grad@arcadia.edu.

Argosy University, Atlanta Campus, College of Education, Atlanta, GA 30328. Offers educational leadership (MAEd, Ed D, Ed S), including higher education administration (Ed D), k-12 administration (Ed D); instructional leadership (MAEd, Ed D, Ed S), including higher education (Ed D), K-12 education (Ed D). Evening/weekend programs available. *Students:* 459 full-time (377 women), 324 part-time (255 women); includes 388 minority (335 African Americans, 10 American Indian/Alaska Native, 14 Asian Americans or Pacific Islanders, 29 Hispanic Americans). *Entrance requirements:* For master's and doctorate, 3 letters of recommendation, minimum GPA of 3.0, resumé. Additional exam requirements/recommendations for international students: Required—TOEFL (minimum score 550 paper-based; 213 computer-based). *Application deadline:* For fall admission, 8/1 for domestic students; for spring admission, 10/1 for domestic students. Application fee: $50. *Financial support:* Teaching assistantships, Federal Work-Study available. *Unit head:* Jacqueline Jenkins, Department Chair, 770-407-1067, Fax: 770-671-0476, E-mail: jbeard@argosy.edu. *Application contact:* Christa Holton, Director of Admissions, 770-671-1200, Fax: 770-671-9050, E-mail: inquiry@argosy.edu.

See Close-Up on page 1101.

Argosy University, Chicago Campus, College of Education, Chicago, IL 60603. Offers community college executive leadership (Ed D); educational leadership (MA Ed, Ed D, Ed S), including administrative certification (MA Ed), district leadership (Ed D), higher education administration (Ed D), K-12 education (Ed D), principal/general (MA Ed), superintendent certification (Ed S); instructional leadership (MA Ed, Ed D, Ed S), including higher education (Ed D), K-12 education (Ed D). Part-time and evening/weekend programs available. *Faculty:* 3 full-time (1 woman), 7 part-time/adjunct (0 women). *Students:* 116 full-time (96 women), 42 part-time (32 women); includes 112 minority (108 African Americans, 1 Asian American or Pacific Islander, 3 Hispanic Americans). Average age 45. 56 applicants, 84% accepted, 45 enrolled. In 2006, 4 master's, 10 doctorates awarded. *Entrance requirements:* For master's and doctorate, minimum GPA of 3.0. Additional exam requirements/recommendations for international students: Required—TOEFL (minimum score 550 paper-based; 213 computer-based). *Application deadline:* For fall admission, 2/28 for domestic and international students; for spring admission, 10/30 for domestic and international students. Applications are processed on a rolling basis. Application fee: $50. Electronic applications accepted. *Financial support:* In 2006–07, 35 students received support. Scholarships/grants available. Financial award application deadline: 4/1. *Unit head:* Dr. Paul Busceni, Head, 800-626-4123, Fax: 312-777-7750, E-mail: pbusceni@argosy.edu. *Application contact:* Ashley Delaney, Director of Admissions, 800-626-4123, Fax: 312-777-7750, E-mail: argosyadmissions@argosy.edu.

See Close-Up on page 825.

Argosy University, Hawai'i Campus, College of Education, Honolulu, HI 96813. Offers educational leadership (MAEd, Ed D), including higher education administration (Ed D), K-12 education (Ed D); instructional leadership (MAEd, Ed D), including higher education (Ed D), K-12 education (Ed D). *Faculty:* 9 part-time/adjunct (4 women). *Students:* 26 full-time (18 women), 4 part-time (all women); includes 16 minority (13 Asian Americans or Pacific Islanders, 3 Hispanic Americans). 17 applicants, 94% accepted, 14 enrolled. *Degree requirements:* For doctorate, thesis/dissertation. *Entrance requirements:* Additional exam requirements/recommendations for international students: Required—TOEFL (minimum score 550 paper-based; 214 computer-based). *Application deadline:* For fall admission, 1/15 priority date for domestic students; for spring admission, 10/15 for domestic students. Applications are processed on a rolling basis. Application fee: $50. Electronic applications accepted. *Unit head:* Dr. Kristine Lesperance, Chair, 888-323-2777, Fax: 808-536-5505, E-mail: klesperance@argosy.edu. *Application contact:* Cherie Andrade, Director of Admissions, 888-323-2777, Fax: 808-536-5505, E-mail: candrade@argosy.edu.

See Close-Up on page 831.

Argosy University, Inland Empire Campus, College of Education, San Bernardino, CA 92408. Offers community college executive leadership (Ed D); educational leadership (MA Ed, Ed D), including higher education administration (Ed D), K-12 education (Ed D); instructional leadership (MA Ed, Ed D), including higher education (Ed D), K-12 education (Ed D), multiple subject teacher credential preparation (MA Ed), multiple subject teacher credntial preparation with BCLAD (MA Ed), single subject teacher credential preparation (MA Ed), single subject teacher credential preparation with BCLAD (MA Ed).

See Close-Up on page 1103.

Argosy University, Nashville Campus, College of Education, Program in Educational Leadership, Franklin, TN 37067-7226. Offers educational leadership (MA Ed); higher education administration (Ed D); K-12 education (Ed D).

See Close-Up on page 1105.

Argosy University, Nashville Campus, College of Education, Program in Instructional Leadership, Franklin, TN 37067-7226. Offers higher education administration (Ed D); instructional leadership (MA Ed); K-12 education (Ed D).

Argosy University, Orange County Campus, College of Education, Santa Ana, CA 92704. Offers community college executive leadership (Ed D); educational leadership (MA Ed, Ed D), including higher education administration (Ed D), K-12 education (Ed D); instructional leadership (MA Ed, Ed D), including educational technology (Ed D), higher education (Ed D), K-12 education (Ed D), multiple subject teacher credential preparation (MA Ed), multiple subject teacher credential preparation with BCLAD (MA Ed), single subject teacher credential preparation (MA Ed), single subject teacher credential preparation with BCLAD (MA Ed). Part-time and evening/weekend programs available. *Faculty:* 3 full-time (2 women), 33 part-time/adjunct (15 women). *Students:* 185 full-time (112 women), 49 part-time (28 women). Average age 37. 91 applicants, 76 enrolled. In 2006, 58 master's, 17 doctorates awarded. Terminal master's awarded for partial completion of doctoral program. *Degree requirements:* For master's, comprehensive exam; for doctorate, thesis/dissertation, preliminary and final dissertation defense, comprehensive exam. *Entrance requirements:* For master's, minimum GPA of 3.0 in final 2 years of course work, 3 letters of recommendation, resumé; for doctorate, minimum GPA of 3.0 in graduate study, 3 letters of recommendation, resumé. Additional exam requirements/recommendations for international students: Required—TOEFL. *Application deadline:* Applications are processed on a rolling basis. Application fee: $50. Electronic applications accepted. *Financial support:* Federal Work-Study and scholarships/grants available. Support available to part-time students. Financial award applicants required to submit FAFSA. *Faculty research:* Educational leadership, higher education, qualitative research, K-12 education, multicultural education. *Unit head:* Dr. Christine Zeppos, Dean, 800-7196-9598, Fax: 714-437-1287, E-mail: czeppos@argosy.edu. *Application contact:* Mark Betz, Director of Admissions, 800-716-9598, Fax: 714-437-1697, E-mail: mbetz@argosy.edu.

See Close-Up on page 833.

Argosy University, Phoenix Campus, College of Education, Phoenix, AZ 85021. Offers community college executive leadership (Ed D); educational leadership (MA Ed, Ed D, Ed S), including higher education administration (Ed D), K-12 education (Ed D); instructional leadership (MA Ed, Ed D, Ed S), including higher education (Ed D), K-12 education (Ed D). Part-time and evening/weekend programs available. *Faculty:* 13 part-time/adjunct (4 women). *Students:* 26 full-time (17 women), 2 part-time (1 woman); includes 3 minority (2 African Americans, 1 Hispanic American). Average age 44. 10 applicants, 100% accepted, 9 enrolled. *Entrance requirements:* For doctorate, minimum GPA of 3.0, master's degree. Additional exam requirements/recommendations for international students: Required—TOEFL (minimum score 550 paper-based; 213 computer-based). *Application deadline:* Applications are processed on a rolling basis. Application fee: $50. Electronic applications accepted. *Financial support:* Federal Work-Study available. Financial award applicants required to submit FAFSA. *Unit head:* Dr. Gayle Schou, Director, 866-216-2777, E-mail: argosyadmissions@argosy.edu. *Application contact:* Andy Hughes, Director of Admissions, 866-216-2777, Fax: 602-216-2601, E-mail: ahughes@argosy.edu.

See Close-Up on page 835.

Argosy University, San Diego Campus, College of Education, San Diego, CA 92108. Offers community college executive leadership (Ed D); educational leadership (MA Ed, Ed D), including higher education administration (Ed D), K-12 education (Ed D); instructional leadership (MA Ed, Ed D), including higher education (Ed D), K-12 education (Ed D), multiple subject teacher credential preparation (MA Ed), multiple subject teacher credential preparation with BCLAD (MA Ed), single subject teacher credential preparation (MA Ed), single subject teacher credential preparation with BCLAD (MA Ed).

See Close-Up on page 837.

Argosy University, San Francisco Bay Area Campus, College of Education, Point Richmond, CA 94804-3547. Offers community college executive leadership (Ed D); educational leadership (MA Ed, Ed D), including higher education administration (Ed D), K–12 education (Ed D); instructional leadership (MA Ed, Ed D), including higher education (Ed D), K–12 education (Ed D), multiple subject teacher credential preparation (MA Ed), multiple subject teacher credential preparation with BCLAD (MA Ed), single subject teacher credential preparation (MA Ed), single subject teacher credential preparation with BCLAD (MA Ed). Part-time and evening/weekend programs available. Postbaccalaureate distance learning degree programs offered (minimal on-campus study). *Faculty:* 1 (woman) full-time, 14 part-time/adjunct. *Students:* 59 full-time (41 women), 30 part-time (14 women); includes 26 minority (11 African Americans, 11 Asian Americans or Pacific Islanders, 4 Hispanic Americans), 1 international. 34 applicants, 82% accepted, 20 enrolled. In 2006, 7 degrees awarded. *Degree requirements:* For master's, capstone project; for doctorate, thesis/dissertation, comprehensive exam, registration. *Entrance* *requirements:* For master's and doctorate, minimum GPA of 3.0. Additional exam requirements/recommendations for international students: Required—TOEFL (minimum score 550 paper-based; 213 computer-based). *Application deadline:* For fall admission, 7/1 priority date for domestic students, 7/1 for international students; for winter admission, 11/1 priority date for domestic and international students; for spring admission, 4/1 priority date for domestic and international students. Applications are processed on a rolling basis. Application fee: $50. Electronic applications accepted. *Financial support:* Career-related internships or fieldwork, Federal Work-Study, and scholarships/grants available. Support available to part-time students. Financial award application deadline: 4/20; financial award applicants required to submit FAFSA. *Unit head:* Dr. Keyes Kelly, 510-837-3740, E-mail: kkelly@argosy.edu. *Application contact:* John Vincent Stofan, Director, Admissions, 510-215-0277, Fax: 510-215-0299, E-mail: jstofan@argosy.edu.

See Close-Up on page 839.

Argosy University, Santa Monica Campus, College of Education, Santa Monica, CA 90405. Offers community college executive leadership (Ed D); educational leadership (MA Ed, Ed D), including higher education administration (Ed D), K-12 education (Ed D); instructional leadership (MA Ed, Ed D), including higher education (Ed D), K-12 education (Ed D), multiple subject teacher credential preparation (MA Ed), multiple subject teacher credential preparation with BCLAD (MA Ed), single subject teacher credential preparation (MA Ed), single subject teacher credential preparation with BCLAD (MA Ed).

See Close-Up on page 841.

Argosy University, Sarasota Campus, College of Education, Sarasota, FL 34235-8246. Offers community college educational leadership (Ed D); educational leadership (MA Ed, Ed D, Ed S), including higher education administration (Ed D), K-12 education (Ed D); instructional leadership (MA Ed, Ed D, Ed S), including education technology (Ed D), higher education (Ed D), K-12 education (Ed D). Part-time and evening/weekend programs available. Postbaccalaureate distance learning degree programs offered (minimal on-campus study). *Faculty:* 15 full-time (8 women), 49 part-time/adjunct (21 women). *Students:* 149 applicants, 96% accepted, 121 enrolled. In 2006, 9 master's, 141 doctorates awarded. *Degree requirements:* For doctorate, thesis/dissertation, comprehensive exam. *Entrance requirements:* For doctorate, minimum undergraduate GPA of 3.0. Additional exam requirements/recommendations for international students: Required—TOEFL. *Application deadline:* Applications are processed on a rolling basis. Application fee: $50. Electronic applications accepted. *Expenses:* Contact institution. *Financial support:* Federal Work-Study available. Support available to part-time students. Financial award application deadline: 4/1; financial award applicants required to submit FAFSA. *Unit head:* Dr. Chuck Mlynarczyk, Dean, 800-331-5995, Fax: 941-371-9464, E-mail: cmlynarczyk@argosy.edu. *Application contact:* Admissions Representative, 800-331-5995 Ext. 221, Fax: 941-371-8910.

See Close-Up on page 843.

Argosy University, Schaumburg Campus, College of Education, Schaumburg, IL 60173-5403. Offers community college executive leadership (Ed D); educational leadership (MA Ed, Ed D, Ed S), including administrative certification (MA Ed), higher education administration (Ed D), K-12 education (Ed D), principal/general (MA Ed), superintendent certification (Ed S); instructional leadership (MA Ed, Ed D, Ed S), including higher education (Ed D), K-12 education (Ed D). Part-time and evening/weekend programs available. *Faculty:* 1 (woman) full-time, 7 part-time/adjunct (3 women). *Students:* 19 full-time, 19 part-time. 15 applicants, 80% accepted, 10 enrolled. In 2006, 1 master's, 3 doctorates, 2 other advanced degrees awarded. *Degree requirements:* For doctorate, thesis/dissertation, comprehensive exam. *Entrance requirements:* For master's and doctorate, minimum GPA of 3.0. Additional exam requirements/recommendations for international students: Required—TOEFL. *Application deadline:* For fall admission, 3/15 priority date for domestic and international students; for spring admission, 10/15 priority date for domestic and international students. Applications are processed on a rolling basis. Application fee: $50. Electronic applications accepted. *Expenses:* Contact institution. *Financial support:* Federal Work-Study and scholarships/grants available. *Unit head:* Dr. Narjis Hyder, Program Chair, 866-290-7400, Fax: 847-598-6158, E-mail: nhyder@argosy.edu. *Application contact:* Jamal Scott, Application Contact, 866-290-7400, Fax: 630-598-6191, E-mail: jscott@argosy.edu.

See Close-Up on page 845.

Argosy University, Seattle Campus, College of Education, Seattle, WA 98121. Offers community college executive leadership (Ed D); education (MA Ed); educational leadership (MA Ed, Ed D), including higher education administration (Ed D), K-12 education (Ed D); instructional leadership (MA Ed, Ed D), including education technology (Ed D), higher education (Ed D), K-12 education (Ed D). Part-time and evening/weekend programs available. *Students:* 29 full-time, 15 part-time. *Degree requirements:* For master's, thesis or alternative, capstone project; for doctorate, thesis/dissertation, comprehensive exam, registration. *Entrance requirements:* For master's, minimum GPA of 3.0 in last 60 hours of course work or minimum cumulative GPA of 2.7; for doctorate, minimum GPA of 3.0. Additional exam requirements/recommendations for international students: Required—TOEFL (minimum score 550 paper-based; 213 computer-based). *Application deadline:* For fall admission, 4/15 priority date for domestic students, 4/15 for international students. Application fee: $50. *Expenses:* Contact institution. *Financial support:* Teaching assistantships with partial tuition reimbursements, Federal Work-Study, scholarships/grants, and unspecified assistantships available. Support available to part-time students. Financial award application deadline: 4/19; financial award applicants required to submit FAFSA. *Unit head:* Dr. Leslie Aune Oja, Chair of Education, 206-393-3570, Fax: 206-283-5777, E-mail: ioja@argosy.edu. *Application contact:* Josh Pond, Director of Admissions, 206-283-4500, Fax: 206-283-5777, E-mail: jpond@argosyu.edu.

See Close-Up on page 847.

Argosy University, Tampa Campus, College of Education, Tampa, FL 33614. Offers community college executive leadership (Ed D); educational leadership (MA Ed, Ed D, Ed S), including higher education administration (Ed D), K-12 education (Ed D); instructional leadership (MA Ed, Ed D, Ed S), including higher education (Ed D), K-12 education (Ed D). *Faculty:* 1 (woman) full-time, 8 part-time/adjunct (3 women). *Degree requirements:* For master's, capstone project; for doctorate, thesis/dissertation. *Entrance requirements:* For master's, minimum GPA of 3.0 in last 2 years of undergraduate course work, resumé, 3 letters of recommendation; for doctorate, minimum GPA of 3.0, 3 letters of recommendation, resumé. Additional exam requirements/recommendations for international students: Required—TOEFL (minimum score 550 paper-based; 213 computer-based). *Application deadline:* Applications are processed on a rolling basis. Application fee: $50. Electronic applications accepted. *Faculty research:* Reading methods, elementary education, educational leadership, instructional design and instructional technology. *Unit head:* Dr. Patty O'Grady, Head, 813-246-4419, Fax: 813-246-4045, E-mail: pogrady@argosy.edu.

See Close-Up on page 849.

Argosy University, Twin Cities Campus, College of Education, Eagan, MN 55121. Offers educational leadership (MA Ed, Ed D, Ed S), including higher education administration (Ed D), K-12 education (Ed D); instructional leadership (MA Ed, Ed D, Ed S), including education technology (Ed D), higher education (Ed D), K-12 education (Ed D). Part-time and evening/weekend programs available. *Faculty:* 1 full-time (0 women), 10 part-time/adjunct (4 women). *Students:* 30 full-time (22 women), 12 part-time (9 women); includes 3 minority (1 African American, 1 American Indian/Alaska Native, 1 Asian American or Pacific Islander). Average age 45. 35 applicants, 86% accepted, 12 enrolled. In 2006, 1 master's, 6 doctorates awarded. *Degree requirements:* For doctorate, thesis/dissertation, comprehensive exam. *Entrance requirements:* For master's, 3 letters of recommendation, minimum undergraduate GPA of 3.0, resumé; for doctorate, 3 letters of recommendation, master's degree, minimum GPA of 3.0, resumé. Additional exam requirements/recommendations for international students: Required—TOEFL (minimum score 550 paper-based; 213 computer-based). *Application deadline:* For fall admission, 5/15 priority date for domestic students, 5/15 for international students; for spring admission, 10/15 priority date for domestic students, 10/15 for international students. Applications are processed on a rolling basis. Application fee: $50. Electronic applications accepted. *Financial support:* In 2006–07, 12 fellowships with partial tuition reimbursements, 3 teaching assistantships with partial tuition reimbursements were awarded; Federal Work-Study and scholarships/grants also available. Financial award applicants required to submit FAFSA. *Unit head:* Dr. David Lange, Program Chair, 888-844-2004. *Application contact:* Jennifer Radke, 2nd Director of Graduate Admissions, 651-846-3300, Fax: 651-994-7954, E-mail: tcadmissions@argosy.edu.

See Close-Up on page 851.

Argosy University, Washington DC Campus, College of Education, Arlington, VA 22209. Offers educational leadership (MA Ed, Ed D, Ed S), including higher education administration (Ed D), K-12 education (Ed D); instructional leadership (MA Ed, Ed D, Ed S), including higher education (Ed D), K-12 education (Ed D). Part-time and evening/weekend programs available. *Faculty:* 2 full-time (1 woman), 2 part-time/adjunct (0 women). *Students:* 22 full-time (16 women), 11 part-time (6 women); includes 24 minority (all African Americans) Average age 45. 16 applicants, 69% accepted, 9 enrolled. In 2006, 1 degree awarded. *Degree requirements:* For master's, thesis (for some programs), comprehensive exam (for some programs); for doctorate, thesis/dissertation, comprehensive exam. *Entrance requirements:* For master's and doctorate, minimum GPA of 3.0. Additional exam requirements/recommendations for international students: Required—TOEFL (minimum score 550 paper-based; 213 computer-based). *Application deadline:* For fall admission, 6/15 priority date for domestic and international students; for spring admission, 10/15 priority date for domestic and international students. Applications are processed on a rolling basis. Application fee: $50. Electronic applications accepted. *Financial support:* Federal Work-Study and scholarships/grants available. Financial award applicants required to submit FAFSA. *Unit head:* Dr. Colleen Logan, Academic Affairs Officer, 866-703-2777, Fax: 703-521-5850, E-mail: dcadmissions@argosy.edu. *Application contact:* Emily Peck, Director of Admissions, 866-703-2777 Ext. 5851, Fax: 703-526-5850, E-mail: dcadmissions@argosy.edu.

See Close-Up on page 853.

Arizona State University at the West campus, College of Teacher Education and Leadership, Phoenix, AZ 85069-7100. Offers educational administration and supervision (M Ed); elementary education (M Ed, Certificate); leadership/innovation (administration) (Ed D); leadership/innovation (teaching) (Ed D); secondary education (M Ed, Certificate); special education (M Ed). Part-time and evening/weekend programs available. *Faculty:* 25 full-time (18 women), 27 part-time/adjunct (21 women). *Students:* 169 full-time (133 women), 245 part-time (200 women); includes 76 minority (16 African Americans, 8 American Indian/Alaska Native, 7 Asian Americans or Pacific Islanders, 45 Hispanic Americans), 3 international. Average age 35. 308 applicants, 63% accepted, 171 enrolled. In 2006, 84 degrees awarded. *Degree requirements:* For master's, applied project or comprehensive exams; for doctorate, thesis/dissertation, comprehensive exam. *Entrance requirements:* For master's, 3 letters of recommendation; for doctorate, master's degree in education or related field, 3 professional references, resumé. Additional exam requirements/recommendations for international students: Required—TOEFL (minimum score 550 paper-based; 213 computer-based; 83 iBT), IELTS (minimum score 7). *Application deadline:* Applications are processed on a rolling basis. Application fee: $50. Electronic applications accepted. *Expenses:* Tuition, state resident: full-time $5,930. Tuition, nonresident: full-time $16,516. Tuition and fees vary according to course load. *Financial support:* In 2006–07, 2 research assistantships with partial tuition reimbursements (averaging $16,413 per year) were awarded; fellowships with tuition reimbursements, career-related internships or fieldwork, institutionally sponsored loans, scholarships/grants, tuition waivers (full and partial), and unspecified assistantships also available. Support available to part-time students. Financial award application deadline: 4/1; financial award applicants required to submit FAFSA. *Faculty research:* Self-regulated learning in students, collaboration and consultation skills for educators, school reform and restructuring, hands-on science and mathematics programs, educational technology. *Unit head:* Dr. Mari Koerner, Dean, 602-543-6352, Fax: 602-543-6350, E-mail: mari.koerner@asu.edu. *Application contact:* Marie Wright, Administrative Assistant, 602-543-3634, Fax: 602-543-6350, E-mail: marie.wright@asu.edu or ctelgrad@asu.edu.

Arkansas Tech University, Graduate School, School of Education, Russellville, AR 72801. Offers college student personnel (MSE); educational leadership (M Ed, Ed S); English education (M Ed); gifted education (MSE); instructional improvement (M Ed); secondary education (M Ed); teaching, learning and leadership (M Ed). *Accreditation:* NCATE. Part-time programs available. *Students:* 44 full-time (33 women), 244 part-time (181 women); includes 20 minority (14 African Americans, 1 American Indian/Alaska Native, 3 Asian Americans or Pacific Islanders, 2 Hispanic Americans), 18 international. Average age 34. In 2006, 72 master's, 4 other advanced degrees awarded. *Degree requirements:* For master's, action research project, thesis optional. *Entrance requirements:* For master's, GRE General Test or MAT. Additional exam requirements/recommendations for international students: Required—TOEFL (minimum score 500 paper-based; 173 computer-based). *Application deadline:* For fall admission, 3/1 priority date for domestic students, 5/1 priority date for international students; for winter admission, 10/1 priority date for international students; for spring admission, 10/1 priority date for domestic and international students. Applications are processed on a rolling basis. Application fee: $0 ($30 for international students). Electronic applications accepted. *Expenses:* Tuition, state resident: full-time $3,060; part-time $170 per hour. Tuition, nonresident: full-time $6,120; part-time $340 per hour. Required fees: $312; $4 per hour. $84 per term. Part-time tuition and fees vary according to course load. *Financial support:* In 2006–07, teaching assistantships with full tuition reimbursements (averaging $4,000 per year); career-related internships or fieldwork, Federal Work-Study, scholarships/grants, health care benefits, and unspecified assistantships also available. Support available to part-time students. Financial award application deadline: 4/15; financial award applicants required to submit FAFSA. *Unit head:* Dr. C. Glenn Sheets, Dean, 479-968-0350, Fax: 479-968-0350, E-mail: glenn.sheets@atu.edu. *Application contact:* Dr. Eldon G. Clary, Dean of Graduate School, 479-968-0398, Fax: 479-964-0542, E-mail: graduate.school@atu.edu.

Armstrong Atlantic State University, School of Graduate Studies, Program in Education, Savannah, GA 31419-1997. Offers adult education (M Ed); early childhood education (M Ed); education (M Ed); elementary education (M Ed); middle grades education (M Ed); secondary education (M Ed), including business education, English education, mathematics education, science education, social science education; special education (M Ed), including behavioral disorders, curriculum and instruction, learning disabilities, speech-language pathology. *Accreditation:* NCATE. Part-time and evening/weekend programs available. Postbaccalaureate distance learning degree programs offered (minimal on-campus study). *Faculty:* 11 full-time (9 women), 13 part-time/adjunct (10 women). *Students:* 50 full-time (42 women), 219 part-time (175 women); includes 71 minority (67 African Americans, 3 Asian Americans or Pacific Islanders, 1 Hispanic American), 6 international. Average age 35. In 2006, 151 degrees awarded. *Degree requirements:* For master's, portfolio. *Entrance requirements:* For master's, GRE General Test or MAT, minimum GPA of 2.5, letters of recommendation. Additional exam requirements/recommendations for international students: Required—TOEFL (minimum score 523 paper-based; 193 computer-based). *Application deadline:* For fall admission, 7/1 priority date for domestic and international students; for spring admission, 11/15 priority date for domestic and international students. Applications are processed on a rolling basis. Application fee: $25. Electronic applications accepted. *Expenses:* Tuition, state resident: full-time $2,286; part-time $127 per credit. Tuition, nonresident: full-time $9,144; part-time $508 per credit. One-time fee: $257. *Financial support:* In 2006–07, research assistantships with partial tuition reimbursements (averaging $2,500 per year); career-related internships or fieldwork, Federal Work-Study, scholarships/grants, and unspecified assistantships also available. Support available to part-time students. Financial award applicants required to submit FAFSA. *Unit*

Secondary Education

Armstrong Atlantic State University (continued)
head: Dr. Jane McHaney, College of Education Dean, 912-927-5398, Fax: 912-921-7425, E-mail: mchaneia@mail.armstrong.edu.

Auburn University, Graduate School, College of Education, Department of Curriculum and Teaching, Auburn University, AL 36849. Offers business education (M Ed, MS, PhD); early childhood education (M Ed, MS, PhD, Ed S); elementary education (M Ed, MS, PhD, Ed S); foreign languages (M Ed, MS); music education (M Ed, MS, PhD, Ed S); postsecondary education (PhD); reading education (PhD, Ed S); secondary education (M Ed, MS, PhD, Ed S), including English language arts, mathematics, science, social studies. *Accreditation:* NASM (one or more programs are accredited); NCATE. Part-time programs available. *Faculty:* 26 full-time (19 women). *Students:* 51 full-time (36 women), 116 part-time (86 women); includes 24 minority (23 African Americans, 1 Asian American or Pacific Islander). Average age 33. 181 applicants, 56% accepted, 68 enrolled. In 2006, 63 master's, 12 doctorates, 14 other advanced degrees awarded. *Degree requirements:* For master's, thesis (for some programs); for doctorate, thesis/dissertation; for Ed S, field project. *Entrance requirements:* For master's, doctorate, and Ed S, GRE General Test. *Application deadline:* For fall admission, 7/7 for domestic students; for spring admission, 11/24 for domestic students. Applications are processed on a rolling basis. Application fee: $25 ($50 for international students). Electronic applications accepted. *Expenses:* Tuition, state resident: full-time $5,000. Tuition, nonresident: full-time $15,000. Required fees: $416. Tuition and fees vary according to program. *Financial support:* Fellowships, teaching assistantships, career-related internships or fieldwork and Federal Work-Study available. Support available to part-time students. Financial award application deadline: 3/15. *Faculty research:* Emerging literacy, reading attitudes, music for at-risk youth, portfolio assessment. *Unit head:* Dr. Andrew M. Weaver, Head, 334-844-4434, E-mail: weaveam@mail.auburn.edu. *Application contact:* Dr. Joe Pittman, Interim Dean of the Graduate School, 334-844-4700.

Auburn University Montgomery, School of Education, Department of Foundations, Secondary, and Physical Education, Montgomery, AL 36124-4023. Offers physical education (M Ed); secondary education (M Ed, Ed S). *Accreditation:* NCATE. Part-time and evening/weekend programs available. *Faculty:* 9 full-time (5 women), 1 (woman) part-time/adjunct. *Students:* 22 full-time (13 women), 59 part-time (50 women); includes 29 minority (27 African Americans, 2 Hispanic Americans). Average age 33. In 2006, 27 master's, 4 other advanced degrees awarded. *Degree requirements:* For master's and Ed S, thesis optional. *Entrance requirements:* For master's, GRE General Test or MAT, certification, BS in teaching; for Ed S, GRE General Test or MAT, certification. *Application deadline:* Applications are processed on a rolling basis. Application fee: $25. Electronic applications accepted. *Financial support:* In 2006–07, 3 teaching assistantships were awarded; career-related internships or fieldwork and scholarships/grants also available. Support available to part-time students. Financial award application deadline: 3/1; financial award applicants required to submit FAFSA. *Unit head:* Dr. Henry N. Williford, Head, 334-244-3548, Fax: 334-244-3547, E-mail: hwilliford@mail.aum.edu.

Augustana College, Department of Education, Program in Education, Sioux Falls, SD 57197. Offers elementary (MA); secondary (MA). *Accreditation:* NCATE. Part-time programs available. *Degree requirements:* For master's, oral exam, paper, synthesis portfolio. *Entrance requirements:* For master's, appropriate bachelor's degree, minimum GPA of 3.0, teaching certificate. Additional exam requirements/recommendations for international students: Required—TOEFL.

Augusta State University, Graduate Studies, College of Education, Program in Secondary Education, Augusta, GA 30904-2200. Offers M Ed, Ed S. *Accreditation:* NCATE. Part-time and evening/weekend programs available. *Faculty:* 1 full-time (0 women), 1 (woman) part-time/adjunct. *Students:* 8 full-time (7 women), 23 part-time (19 women); includes 6 minority (5 African Americans, 1 American Indian/Alaska Native). Average age 35. 2 applicants, 100% accepted, 2 enrolled. In 2006, 1 master's, 2 other advanced degrees awarded. *Degree requirements:* For Ed S, thesis. *Entrance requirements:* For master's, GRE, MAT, minimum GPA of 2.5; for Ed S, GRE, MAT. *Application deadline:* For fall admission, 8/1 priority date for domestic students. Applications are processed on a rolling basis. Application fee: $20. *Expenses:* Tuition, state resident: full-time $3,044; part-time $127 per credit hour. Tuition, nonresident: full-time $12,172; part-time $508 per credit hour. *Financial support:* Career-related internships or fieldwork, Federal Work-Study, and institutionally sponsored loans available. Support available to part-time students. Financial award application deadline: 4/15; financial award applicants required to submit FAFSA. *Faculty research:* Effective teaching practices. *Unit head:* Dr. J. Gordon Eisenman, Chair, 706-737-1496, Fax: 706-667-4706, E-mail: geisenman@aug.edu. *Application contact:* Andrea M. Scott, Secretary to the Dean, 706-737-1499, Fax: 706-667-4706, E-mail: ascott1@aug.edu.

Austin College, Program in Education, Sherman, TX 75090-4400. Offers art education (MA); elementary education (MA); middle school education (MA); music education (MA); physical education and coaching (MA); secondary education (MA). Applicants must meet Austin College's undergraduate curriculum requirements. Part-time programs available. *Faculty:* 5 full-time (3 women), 1 (woman) part-time/adjunct. *Students:* 33 full-time (26 women); includes 3 minority (2 Asian Americans or Pacific Islanders, 1 Hispanic American). Average age 25. In 2006, 24 degrees awarded. *Degree requirements:* For master's, one foreign language, thesis or alternative. *Entrance requirements:* For master's, Texas Academic Skills Program Test. *Application deadline:* For fall admission, 5/1 priority date for domestic students; for spring admission, 1/15 priority date for domestic students. Applications are processed on a rolling basis. Application fee: $35. Electronic applications accepted. *Expenses:* Tuition: Full-time $27,385. Required fees: $160. *Financial support:* In 2006–07, 27 students received support. Career-related internships or fieldwork, Federal Work-Study, scholarships/grants, and unspecified assistantships available. Support available to part-time students. Financial award application deadline: 4/1; financial award applicants required to submit FAFSA. *Unit head:* Dr. Barbara Sylvester, Director of Teaching Program, 903-813-2498, Fax: 903-813-2326, E-mail: bsylvester@austincollege.edu.

Ball State University, Graduate School, Teachers College, Department of Educational Studies, Program in Secondary Education, Muncie, IN 47306-1099. Offers MA. *Accreditation:* NCATE. *Students:* 16 full-time (8 women), 19 part-time (11 women); includes 3 minority (all African Americans) Average age 30. 11 applicants, 100% accepted, 7 enrolled. In 2006, 24 degrees awarded. Application fee: $25 ($35 for international students). *Financial support:* Application deadline: 3/1. *Unit head:* Barbara Graham, Head, 785-285-5460, Fax: 785-285-5489.

Belhaven College, School of Education, Jackson, MS 39202-1789. Offers elementary education (M Ed, MAT); secondary education (M Ed, MAT). *Degree requirements:* For master's, portfolio. *Entrance requirements:* For master's, PRAXIS I, PRAXIS II, minimum GPA of 2.8.

Bellarmine University, Annsley Frazier Thornton School of Education, Louisville, KY 40205-0671. Offers early elementary education (MA, MAT); instructional leadership and school administration/school principal (MA); learning and behavior disorders (MA); middle school education (MA, MAT); reading and writing endorsement (MA); secondary school education (MAT); Waldorf inspired curriculum (MA);). *Accreditation:* NCATE. Part-time and evening/weekend programs available. *Faculty:* 10 full-time (8 women), 5 part-time/adjunct (all women). *Students:* 92 full-time (68 women), 140 part-time (104 women); includes 16 minority (11 African Americans, 1 Asian American or Pacific Islander, 4 Hispanic Americans). Average age 32. In 2006, 98 degrees awarded. *Degree requirements:* For master's, thesis (for some programs), comprehensive exam. *Entrance requirements:* For master's, minimum overall GPA of 2.75, 3.0 in major; letters of recommendation; valid Kentucky provisional or professional certificate. Additional exam requirements/recommendations for international students: Required—TOEFL (minimum score 550 paper-based; 213 computer-based; 80 iBT), GRE. *Application deadline:* Applications are processed on a rolling basis. Application fee: $25. Electronic applications accepted. *Expenses: Contact institution.* Tuition and fees vary according to program. *Faculty research:* Social justice, service learning dispositions, educational technology, special education. *Unit head:* Dr. Milton Brown, Dean (Interim), 502-452-8486, Fax: 502-452-8189, E-mail: mbrown@bellarmine.edu. *Application contact:* Theresa Klapheke, Director of Graduate Programs, 502-452-8033, Fax: 502-452-8189, E-mail: tklapheke@bellarmine.edu.

Belmont University, College of Arts and Sciences, School of Education, Nashville, TN 37212-3757. Offers education (MAT); elementary education (M Ed), including early childhood education, elementary education, gifted education, language arts education; English (M Ed); history (M Ed); mathematics (M Ed); middle grade education (M Ed); science (M Ed); secondary education (M Ed), including gifted education; sports administration (MSA); technology (M Ed). *Accreditation:* NCATE. Part-time and evening/weekend programs available. *Faculty:* 9 full-time (7 women), 20 part-time/adjunct (15 women). *Students:* 50 full-time (36 women), 116 part-time (76 women); includes 23 minority (20 African Americans, 1 Asian American or Pacific Islander, 2 Hispanic Americans), 1 international. Average age 30. 55 applicants, 60% accepted, 30 enrolled. In 2006, 82 degrees awarded. *Degree requirements:* For master's, thesis, comprehensive exam. *Entrance requirements:* For master's, MAT or GRE, minimum GPA of 2.75. Additional exam requirements/recommendations for international students: Required—TOEFL. *Application deadline:* For fall admission, 8/1 priority date for domestic students, 5/1 for international students; for spring admission, 12/1 priority date for domestic students, 9/1 for international students. Applications are processed on a rolling basis. Application fee: $50. *Expenses: Contact institution. Financial support:* In 2006–07, 25 students received support; fellowships with partial tuition reimbursements available, institutionally sponsored loans and tuition waivers (partial) available. Financial award application deadline: 4/15; financial award applicants required to submit FAFSA. *Faculty research:* Technology grant, professional development schools. Total annual research expenditures: $6,500. *Unit head:* Dr. Trevor F. Hutchins, Associate Dean, 615-460-6232, Fax: 615-460-6414, E-mail: hutchinst@mail.belmont.edu. *Application contact:* Julie Hullett, Admission/Licensure Officer, 615-460-6879, Fax: 615-460-5556, E-mail: hullettj@email.belmont.edu.

Benedictine University, Graduate Programs, Program in Education, Lisle, IL 60532-0900. Offers curriculum and instruction and collaborative teaching (M Ed); elementary education (MA Ed); leadership and administration (M Ed); reading and literacy (M Ed); secondary education (MA Ed); special education (MA Ed). Part-time and evening/weekend programs available. *Faculty:* 4 full-time (2 women), 52 part-time/adjunct (30 women). *Students:* 257 (196 women); includes 22 minority (4 African Americans, 1 American Indian/Alaska Native, 3 Asian Americans or Pacific Islanders, 14 Hispanic Americans) 2 international. Average age 33. 130 applicants, 93% accepted, 13 enrolled. In 2006, 181 degrees awarded. *Degree requirements:* For master's, thesis (for some programs), comprehensive exam. *Entrance requirements:* For master's, GRE or MAT. Additional exam requirements/recommendations for international students: Required—TOEFL (minimum score 550 paper-based; 213 computer-based). *Application deadline:* For fall admission, 9/1 for domestic students; for winter admission, 12/1 for domestic students; for spring admission, 2/15 for domestic students. Applications are processed on a rolling basis. Application fee: $40. Electronic applications accepted. *Expenses: Contact institution. Financial support:* Career-related internships or fieldwork and health care benefits available. Support available to part-time students. *Unit head:* Dr. Richard Campbell, Director, 630-829-6242, Fax: 630-960-1126, E-mail: rcampbell@ben.edu. *Application contact:* Kari Gibbons, Director, Admissions, 630-829-6200, Fax: 630-829-6584, E-mail: kgibbons@ben.edu.

Bennington College, Graduate Programs, Program in Teaching, Bennington, VT 05201. Offers art education (MAT); early childhood (MAT); elementary education (MAT); English education (MAT); foreign language education (MAT); mathematics education (MAT); music education (MAT); science education (MAT); secondary education (MAT); social science education (MAT). *Faculty:* 4 part-time/adjunct (3 women). *Students:* 11 full-time (7 women), 1 (woman) part-time; includes 2 minority (both Hispanic Americans) Average age 31. 12 applicants, 75% accepted, 3 enrolled. In 2006, 13 degrees awarded. *Degree requirements:* For master's, 1 year teaching practicum, professional portfolio. *Entrance requirements:* For master's, interview. *Application deadline:* For fall admission, 3/1 for domestic students. Application fee: $60. *Expenses: Contact institution.* One-time fee: $75 full-time. Tuition and fees vary according to program. *Financial support:* In 2006–07, 10 students received support, including 4 fellowships (averaging $6,875 per year); scholarships/grants and unspecified assistantships also available. Financial award application deadline: 4/1; financial award applicants required to submit FAFSA. *Unit head:* George Kamberelis, Director of Center for Creative Teaching, 802-440-4863, E-mail: gkamberelis@bennington.edu. *Application contact:* Ken Himmelman, Dean of Admissions, 802-440-4312, Fax: 802-440-4320, E-mail: admissions@bennington.edu.

See Close-Up on page 861.

Berry College, Graduate Programs, Graduate Programs in Education, Program in Secondary Education, Mount Berry, GA 30149-0159. Offers M Ed. *Faculty:* 5 part-time/adjunct (1 woman). *Students:* 2 full-time (both women), 19 part-time (14 women), 1 international. Average age 29. In 2006, 8 degrees awarded. *Degree requirements:* For master's, oral exams, thesis optional. *Entrance requirements:* For master's, GRE General Test, MAT, or NTE, minimum GPA of 2.5. Additional exam requirements/recommendations for international students: Required—TOEFL (minimum score 550 paper-based; 213 computer-based). *Application deadline:* For fall admission, 5/1 for domestic students; for spring admission, 10/1 for domestic students. Applications are processed on a rolling basis. Application fee: $25 ($30 for international students). *Expenses: Contact institution. Financial support:* In 2006–07, 10 students received support, including 1 research assistantship with full tuition reimbursement available (averaging $3,500 per year); scholarships/grants and unspecified assistantships also available. Support available to part-time students. Financial award application deadline: 4/1. *Faculty research:* Curriculum development, teacher training, pedagogy. *Application contact:* Richard D. Paul, Dean of Admissions and Financial Aid, 706-236-2215, Fax: 706-290-2178, E-mail: dpaul@berry.edu.

Bethel University, Graduate School, Department of Education, St. Paul, MN 55112-6999. Offers education K-12 (MA); educational administration (Ed D); literacy (Certificate); literacy education (MA); secondary education (MA); special education (M Ed). Evening/weekend programs available. *Faculty:* 20 full-time (10 women), 34 part-time/adjunct (18 women). *Students:* 192 full-time (119 women), 110 part-time (71 women); includes 16 minority (6 African Americans, 5 Asian Americans or Pacific Islanders, 5 Hispanic Americans). Average age 35. In 2006, 58 master's, 9 other advanced degrees awarded. *Degree requirements:* For master's, thesis, practicum; for doctorate, thesis/dissertation, registration. *Entrance requirements:* For master's, interview, current teaching license, minimum GPA of 3.0, teaching experience (if applicable), letters of reference; for doctorate, MAT or GRE, minimum GPA of 3.5, letters of reference, master's degree. Additional exam requirements/recommendations for international students: Required—TOEFL (minimum score 550 paper-based; 213 computer-based). *Application deadline:* For fall admission, 8/1 priority date for domestic students; for winter admission, 12/10 priority date for domestic students; for spring admission, 5/1 priority date for domestic students. Applications are processed on a rolling basis. Application fee: $25. Electronic applications accepted. *Expenses: Contact institution.* Tuition and fees vary according to program. *Financial support:* Institutionally sponsored loans and scholarships/grants available. Financial award applicants required to submit FAFSA. *Unit head:* Dr. Jay B. Rasmussen, Director, 651-638-6237, Fax: 651-638-8004, E-mail: jay-rasmussen@bethel.edu. *Application contact:* Michael Price, Director of Admissions, 651-635-8000 Ext. 8017, Fax: 651-635-8004, E-mail: m_price@bethel.edu.

Bob Jones University, Graduate Programs, Greenville, SC 29614. Offers accountancy (MS); Bible (MA); Bible translation (MA); Biblical studies (Certificate); broadcast management (MS); business administration (MBA); church history (MA, PhD); church ministries (MA); church music (MM); cinema and video production (MA); counseling (MS); curriculum and instruction (Ed D); divinity (M Div); dramatic production (MA); educational leadership (MS, Ed D, Ed S); elementary education (M Ed, MAT); English (M Ed, MA, MAT); fine arts (MA); graphic design (MA); history (M Ed, MA); illustration (MA); interpretative speech (MA); mathematics (M Ed, MAT); medical missions (Certificate); ministry (MM, D Min); multi-categorical special education

(M Ed, MAT); music (M Ed); New Testament interpretation (PhD); Old Testament interpretation (PhD); orchestral instrument performance (MM); organ performance (MM); pastoral studies (MA); personnel services (MS, Ed S); piano pedagogy (MM); piano performance (MM); platform arts (MA); radio and television broadcasting (MS); rhetoric and public address (MA); secondary education (M Ed); studio art (MA); teaching Bible (MA); theology (MA, PhD); voice performance (MM); youth ministries (MA); M Div/MM.

Boston College, Lynch Graduate School of Education, Department of Teacher Education/ Special Education and Curriculum and Instruction, Program in Secondary Education, Chestnut Hill, MA 02467-3800. Offers biology (MST); chemistry (MST); English (MAT); French (MAT); geology (MST); history (MAT); Latin and classical humanities (MAT); mathematics (MST); physics (MST); secondary teaching (M Ed), including biology, chemistry, English, French, geology, history, Latin and classical humanities, mathematics, physics, Spanish; Spanish (MAT). *Students:* 70 full-time (46 women), 28 part-time (15 women); includes 8 minority (4 African Americans, 1 American Indian/Alaska Native, 3 Asian Americans or Pacific Islanders), 2 international. 217 applicants, 72% accepted, 64 enrolled. In 2006, 48 degrees awarded. *Degree requirements:* For master's, comprehensive exam. *Entrance requirements:* For master's, GRE General Test or MAT. Additional exam requirements/recommendations for international students: Required—TOEFL. *Application deadline:* For fall admission, 1/1 priority date for domestic students. Application fee: $60. *Financial support:* Fellowships with full and partial tuition reimbursements, research assistantships with full and partial tuition reimbursements, teaching assistantships with full and partial tuition reimbursements, career-related internships or fieldwork, Federal Work-Study, scholarships/grants, traineeships, tuition waivers (full and partial), and unspecified assistantships available. Support available to part-time students. Financial award applicants required to submit FAFSA. *Faculty research:* Curriculum theory and practice, teacher preparation, learning styles, teacher research. *Application contact:* Timothy P. Blackman, Director, Graduate Admission and Financial Aid, 617-552-4214, Fax: 617-552-0398, E-mail: timothy.blackman.1@bc.edu.

Bowie State University, Graduate Programs, Program in Secondary Education, Bowie, MD 20715-9465. Offers M Ed. *Accreditation:* NCATE. Part-time and evening/weekend programs available. *Faculty:* 1 full-time (0 women). *Students:* 1 full-time (0 women), 8 part-time (5 women); includes 6 minority (all African Americans) Average age 37. 3 applicants, 100% accepted, 2 enrolled. In 2006, 6 degrees awarded. *Degree requirements:* For master's, research paper, thesis optional. *Entrance requirements:* For master's, minimum undergraduate GPA of 3.0, bachelor's degree in education, teaching certificate, teaching experience. *Application deadline:* For fall admission, 4/1 priority date for domestic and international students; for spring admission, 11/1 priority date for domestic and international students. Applications are processed on a rolling basis. Application fee: $40. Electronic applications accepted. *Expenses:* Tuition, state resident: full-time $7,344; part-time $306 per credit. Tuition, nonresident: full-time $14,304; part-time $396 per credit. Required fees: $1,078; $77 per credit. $539 per term. One-time fee: $40. *Financial support:* Application deadline: 4/1. *Unit head:* Dr. Bruce Crim, Coordinator, 301-860-3127, E-mail: bcrim@bowiestate.edu. *Application contact:* Angela Issac, Information Contact.

Brandeis University, Graduate School of Arts and Sciences, Program in Elementary Education, Waltham, MA 02454-9110. Offers Jewish day school (MAT); public education elementary (MAT); secondary education (English, history, biology, Bible) (MAT). *Faculty:* 6 full-time (2 women), 9 part-time/adjunct (all women). *Students:* 7 full-time (5 women); includes 1 African American. Average age 27. In 2006, 9 degrees awarded. *Degree requirements:* For master's, research program MTEL. *Application deadline:* For fall admission, 1/15 priority date for domestic students, 1/15 for international students. Applications are processed on a rolling basis. Application fee: $55. Electronic applications accepted. *Financial support:* In 2006–07, 7 students received support, including 7 fellowships with tuition reimbursements available; scholarships/grants also available. Financial award applicants required to submit CSS PROFILE. *Faculty research:* Teacher education, induction, philosophy, education, democracy education. *Unit head:* Dr. Dirck Roosevelt, Director, MAT Program, 781-736-2020, Fax: 781-736-5020, E-mail: drooseve@brandeis.edu. *Application contact:* Marlene Mihalsky, Department Coordinator, 781-736-2022, Fax: 781-736-5020.

Bridgewater State College, School of Graduate Studies, School of Education and Allied Science, Department of Secondary Education and Professional Programs, Program in Secondary Education, Bridgewater, MA 02325-0001. Offers MAT. *Accreditation:* NCATE. Part-time and evening/weekend programs available. *Entrance requirements:* For master's, GRE General Test. *Application deadline:* For fall admission, 3/1 priority date for domestic students; for spring admission, 10/1 priority date for domestic students. Application fee: $50. *Financial support:* Career-related internships or fieldwork, health care benefits, and unspecified assistantships available. Support available to part-time students.

Brooklyn College of the City University of New York, Division of Graduate Studies, School of Education, Program in Adolescence Education and Special Subjects, Brooklyn, NY 11210-2889. Offers art teacher (MA); biology teacher (MA); chemistry teacher (MA); English teacher (MA); French teacher (MA); health and nutrition sciences: health teacher (MS Ed); mathematics teacher (MA); music education (CAS); music teacher (MA); physical education teacher (MS Ed); physics teacher (MA); social studies teacher (MA); Spanish teacher (MA). Part-time and evening/weekend programs available. *Students:* 30 full-time (22 women), 450 part-time (257 women); includes 167 minority (101 African Americans, 21 Asian Americans or Pacific Islanders, 45 Hispanic Americans), 21 international. 277 applicants, 84% accepted, 113 enrolled. In 2006, 172 master's, 6 other advanced degrees awarded. *Degree requirements:* For master's, comprehensive exam (for some programs). *Entrance requirements:* For master's, LAST, previous course work in education, resumé, 2 letters of recommendation, essay. Additional exam requirements/recommendations for international students: Required—TOEFL. *Application deadline:* For fall admission, 3/1 priority date for domestic students, 2/1 priority date for international students; for spring admission, 11/1 priority date for domestic students, 10/1 priority date for international students. Applications are processed on a rolling basis. Application fee: $125. Electronic applications accepted. *Expenses:* Tuition, state resident: full-time $6,400; part-time $270 per credit. Tuition, nonresident: full-time $12,000; part-time $500 per credit. Required fees: $118 per semester. *Financial support:* Career-related internships or fieldwork, Federal Work-Study, institutionally sponsored loans, and scholarships/grants available. Support available to part-time students. Financial award application deadline: 5/1; financial award applicants required to submit FAFSA. *Faculty research:* Interdisciplinary education, semiotics, discourse analysis, autobiography, teacher identity. *Unit head:* Prof. Stephen Phillips, Program Facilitator, 718-951-5214, E-mail: phillips@brooklyn.cuny.edu. *Application contact:* Karen Alleyne-Pierre, Director of Admissions Services and Enrollment Communications, 718-951-5902, Fax: 718-951-4506, E-mail: grads@brooklyn.cuny.edu.

Brown University, Graduate School, Department of Education, Providence, RI 02912. Offers elementary education 1-6 (MAT); secondary biology (MAT); secondary English (MAT); secondary social studies/history (MAT). *Faculty:* 4 full-time (2 women), 7 part-time/adjunct (all women). *Students:* 28 full-time (23 women); includes 5 minority (2 African Americans, 1 Asian American or Pacific Islander, 2 Hispanic Americans). Average age 25. 89 applicants, 61% accepted, 28 enrolled. In 2006, 35 degrees awarded. *Degree requirements:* For master's, student teaching, portfolio. *Entrance requirements:* For master's, GRE General Test (secondary only), PRAXIS II (elementary), letters of recommendation, interview. *Application deadline:* For winter admission, 1/3 for domestic students. Application fee: $70. Electronic applications accepted. *Financial support:* In 2006–07, 23 students received support, including 2 fellowships (averaging $7,000 per year); Federal Work-Study, institutionally sponsored loans, scholarships/grants, tuition waivers (partial), and proctorships also available. Financial award application deadline: 2/1; financial award applicants required to submit FAFSA. *Faculty research:* Literacy, performance-based assessment, teaching English as a foreign language. *Unit head:* Lawrence Wakeford, Chairman, 401-863-3428, Fax: 401-863-1276, E-mail: lawrence_wakeford@brown.edu. *Application contact:* Carin Algava, Assistant Director, 401-863-3364, Fax: 401-863-1276, E-mail: carin_algava@brown.edu.

Butler University, College of Education, Indianapolis, IN 46208-3485. Offers administration (MS); elementary education (MS); reading (MS); school counseling (MS); secondary education (MS); special education (MS). *Accreditation:* ACA; NCATE. Part-time and evening/weekend programs available. *Faculty:* 12 full-time (6 women), 11 part-time/adjunct (8 women). *Students:* 18 full-time (10 women), 156 part-time (125 women); includes 21 minority (16 African Americans, 2 Asian Americans or Pacific Islanders, 3 Hispanic Americans), 7 international. Average age 31. 56 applicants, 57% accepted, 29 enrolled. In 2006, 72 degrees awarded. *Entrance requirements:* For master's, GRE General Test, MAT, interview. *Application deadline:* For fall admission, 8/15 priority date for domestic students. Applications are processed on a rolling basis. Application fee: $35. Electronic applications accepted. *Expenses:* Tuition: Full-time $6,030; part-time $335 per credit. Tuition and fees vary according to program. *Financial support:* Institutionally sponsored loans available. Support available to part-time students. Financial award application deadline: 7/15; financial award applicants required to submit FAFSA. *Faculty research:* Ethics in cybercounseling, history of sports for disabled effect of fetal alcohol syndrome on perceptual learning, Reading Recovery's theoretical framework in teacher education. *Unit head:* Dr. Ena Shelley, Dean, 317-940-9752, Fax: 317-940-6481. *Application contact:* Karen Farrell, Department Secretary, 317-940-9220, E-mail: kfarrell@butler.edu.

California State University, Bakersfield, Division of Graduate Studies and Research, School of Natural Sciences and Mathematics, Program in Secondary School Mathematics Teaching, Bakersfield, CA 93311-1022. Offers MA.

California State University, Fullerton, Graduate Studies, College of Education, Department of Secondary Education, Fullerton, CA 92834-9480. Offers middle school mathematics (MS); secondary education (MS); teacher induction (MS). *Students:* 2 full-time (both women), 30 part-time (20 women); includes 12 minority (7 Asian Americans or Pacific Islanders, 5 Hispanic Americans). Average age 31. 43 applicants, 70% accepted, 25 enrolled. In 2006, 28 degrees awarded. *Expenses:* Tuition, nonresident: part-time $339 per unit. Required fees: $1,155 per semester. *Unit head:* Dr. Victoria Costa, Head, 714-278-7037.

California State University, Los Angeles, Graduate Studies, Charter College of Education, Division of Curriculum and Instruction, Los Angeles, CA 90032-8530. Offers elementary teaching (MA); reading (MA); secondary teaching (MA). Part-time and evening/weekend programs available. *Faculty:* 13 full-time (8 women), 8 part-time/adjunct (all women). *Students:* 269 full-time (184 women), 572 part-time (406 women); includes 528 minority (48 African Americans, 1 American Indian/Alaska Native, 142 Asian Americans or Pacific Islanders, 337 Hispanic Americans), 20 international. In 2006, 134 degrees awarded. *Entrance requirements:* For master's, minimum GPA of 2.75 in last 90 units of course work, teaching certificate. Additional exam requirements/recommendations for international students: Required—TOEFL. *Application deadline:* For fall admission, 6/30 for domestic students; for spring admission, 2/1 for domestic students. Applications are processed on a rolling basis. Application fee: $55. *Expenses:* Tuition, nonresident: part-time $226 per unit. *Financial support:* Federal Work-Study available. Support available to part-time students. Financial award application deadline: 3/1. *Faculty research:* Media, language arts, mathematics, computers, drug-free schools. *Unit head:* Dr. Andrea Maxie, Chair, 323-343-4350, Fax: 323-343-5458.

California State University, Northridge, Graduate Studies, College of Education, Department of Secondary Education, Northridge, CA 91330. Offers MA. *Accreditation:* NCATE. Part-time programs available. *Faculty:* 15 full-time (8 women), 56 part-time/adjunct (32 women). *Students:* 12 full-time (3 women), 104 part-time (42 women); includes 42 minority (4 African Americans, 1 American Indian/Alaska Native, 15 Asian Americans or Pacific Islanders, 22 Hispanic Americans), 3 international. Average age 36. 63 applicants, 46% accepted, 27 enrolled. In 2006, 49 degrees awarded. *Degree requirements:* For master's, thesis optional. *Entrance requirements:* For master's, GRE General Test, MAT, or minimum GPA of 3.0. Additional exam requirements/recommendations for international students: Required—TOEFL. *Application deadline:* For fall admission, 11/30 for domestic students. Application fee: $55. *Expenses:* Tuition, nonresident: full-time $8,136; part-time $4,068 per year. Required fees: $3,624; $1,161 per term. *Financial support:* Application deadline: 3/1. *Unit head:* Dr. Bonnie Ericson, Chair, 818-677-2580. *Application contact:* Suzanne Hendley, Administrative Support Assistant, 818-677-2581.

California State University, San Bernardino, Graduate Studies, College of Education, Program in Secondary Education, San Bernardino, CA 92407-2397. Offers MA. *Accreditation:* NCATE. Part-time and evening/weekend programs available. *Degree requirements:* For master's, thesis or alternative. *Entrance requirements:* For master's, GRE General Test, minimum GPA of 3.0 in education. *Application deadline:* For fall admission, 8/31 priority date for domestic students. Application fee: $55. *Financial support:* Career-related internships or fieldwork and Federal Work-Study available. Support available to part-time students. *Unit head:* Dr. Corinne Martinez, Director, 909-537-7625, Fax: 909-537-7510, E-mail: corinnem@csusb.edu.

California State University, Stanislaus, Graduate School, College of Education, Department of Teacher Education, Turlock, CA 95382. Offers curriculum and instruction (MA Ed), including elementary education, multilingual education, reading education, secondary education. Part-time and evening/weekend programs available. *Degree requirements:* For master's, thesis. *Entrance requirements:* For master's, MAT or GRE, minimum GPA of 3.0. Additional exam requirements/recommendations for international students: Required—TOEFL (minimum score 550 paper-based; 213 computer-based).

California University of Pennsylvania, School of Graduate Studies and Research, School of Education, Department of Secondary Education, California, PA 15419-1394. Offers MAT. Part-time and evening/weekend programs available. Postbaccalaureate distance learning degree programs offered (no on-campus study). *Faculty:* 4 full-time (1 woman). *Students:* 31 full-time (17 women), 48 part-time (33 women). Average age 31. 52 applicants, 79% accepted, 40 enrolled. In 2006, 21 degrees awarded. *Median time to degree:* Master's–2 years full-time, 3.25 years part-time. *Degree requirements:* For master's, thesis, comprehensive exam. *Entrance requirements:* For master's, PRAXIS, minimum GPA of 3.0, clearances. Additional exam requirements/recommendations for international students: Required—TOEFL (minimum score 550 paper-based; 213 computer-based; 80 iBT). *Application deadline:* For fall admission, 8/1 priority date for domestic and international students; for winter admission, 12/1 priority date for domestic and international students; for spring admission, 5/1 priority date for domestic and international students. Applications are processed on a rolling basis. Application fee: $25. Electronic applications accepted. *Expenses:* Tuition, state resident: full-time $6,048; part-time $336 per credit. Tuition, nonresident: full-time $9,678; part-time $538 per credit. Required fees: $1,854; $263 per credit. Full-time tuition and fees vary according to course load, campus/location and program. *Financial support:* Career-related internships or fieldwork, scholarships/grants, traineeships, and unspecified assistantships available. Financial award applicants required to submit FAFSA. *Faculty research:* The effectiveness of online instruction, student-centered instruction strategies in secondary education, computer technology in education, environmental education, multi-media in education. Total annual research expenditures: $11,000. *Unit head:* Dr. Joseph Zisk, Coordinator, 724-938-4487, Fax: 724-938-1590, E-mail: zisk@cup.edu.

Campbell University, Graduate and Professional Programs, School of Education, Buies Creek, NC 27506. Offers administration (MSA); community counseling (MA); elementary education (M Ed); English education (M Ed); interdisciplinary studies (M Ed); mathematics education (M Ed); middle grades education (M Ed); physical education (M Ed); school counseling (M Ed); secondary education (M Ed); social science education (M Ed). *Accreditation:* NCATE. Part-time and evening/weekend programs available. *Faculty:* 14 full-time (9 women), 12 part-time/adjunct (7 women). *Students:* 27 full-time (25 women), 183 part-time (146 women); includes 30 minority (24 African Americans, 3 American Indian/Alaska Native, 3 Hispanic Americans), 1 international. Average age 31. 112 applicants, 74% accepted, 74 enrolled. In 2006, 65 degrees awarded. *Degree requirements:* For master's, comprehensive exam. *Entrance requirements:* For master's, GRE General Test, minimum GPA of 2.7. *Application deadline:* For fall admission, 8/1 priority date for domestic students; for spring admission, 1/2 priority date for

Secondary Education

Campbell University (continued)

domestic students. Applications are processed on a rolling basis. Application fee: $65. *Expenses:* Tuition: Part-time $380 per semester hour. *Financial support:* In 2006–07, 67 students received support. Career-related internships or fieldwork and Federal Work-Study available. Financial award application deadline: 4/15; financial award applicants required to submit FAFSA. *Faculty research:* Spiritual values and wellness issues in counseling, stress and professional burnout among counselors, thinking strategies, leadership, adaptive technology. *Unit head:* Dr. Karen P. Nery, Dean, 910-893-1630, Fax: 910-893-1999, E-mail: nery@campbell.edu. *Application contact:* James S. Farthing, Director of Graduate Admissions for Business and Education, 910-893-1200 Ext. 1318, Fax: 910-814-4718, E-mail: farthing@campbell.edu.

Canisius College, Graduate Division, School of Education and Human Services, Department of Graduate Education, Buffalo, NY 14208-1098. Offers business education (MS); childhood education (MS); college student personnel (MS); differentiated instruction (MS Ed); early childhood education (MS); education administration (MS); education of the deaf and hard of hearing (MS); general education (MS Ed); literacy education (MS Ed); reading education (MS Ed); secondary education (MS); special education (MS). *Accreditation:* NCATE. Part-time and evening/weekend programs available. *Faculty:* 13 full-time (12 women), 74 part-time/adjunct (44 women). *Students:* 377 full-time (267 women), 303 part-time (219 women); includes 43 minority (27 African Americans, 2 American Indian/Alaska Native, 6 Asian Americans or Pacific Islanders, 8 Hispanic Americans), 187 international. Average age 30. In 2006, 296 degrees awarded. Application fee: $25. *Expenses:* Tuition: Part-time $645 per credit hour. Required fees: $19 per credit hour. Tuition and fees vary according to program. *Financial support:* Research assistantships with full tuition reimbursements, career-related internships or fieldwork, institutionally sponsored loans, scholarships/grants, health care benefits, tuition waivers (full and partial), and unspecified assistantships available. *Faculty research:* Autism, Asperger's disease, private higher education, reading strategies. *Unit head:* Rev. Paul Nochelski, Chair of Graduate Education and Leadership, 716-888-3297, Fax: 716-888-3299. *Application contact:* James D. Bagwell, Director of Graduate Recruitment and Admissions, 716-888-2544, Fax: 716-888-3290, E-mail: bagwellj@canisius.edu.

Carlow University, School of Education, Program in Education, Pittsburgh, PA 15213-3165. Offers elementary education (M Ed); instructional technology specialist (M Ed); secondary education (M Ed); special education (M Ed). Part-time and evening/weekend programs available. *Entrance requirements:* For master's, resumé, 3 letters of recommendation, minimum GPA of 3.0, interview. Electronic applications accepted.

Carson-Newman College, Graduate Program in Education, Jefferson City, TN 37760. Offers curriculum and instruction (M Ed); elementary education (MAT); school counseling (M Ed); secondary education (MAT); teaching English as a second language (MATESL). *Accreditation:* NCATE. Part-time and evening/weekend programs available. *Faculty:* 5 full-time (2 women), 10 part-time/adjunct (3 women). *Students:* 77 full-time (60 women), 41 part-time (29 women); includes 2 minority (both African Americans), 27 international. Average age 32. 65 applicants, 97% accepted. In 2006, 64 degrees awarded. *Degree requirements:* For master's, thesis or alternative. *Entrance requirements:* For master's, NTE, minimum GPA of 3.0 in major, 2.5 overall. *Application deadline:* For fall admission, 7/15 priority date for domestic students. Applications are processed on a rolling basis. Application fee: $25 ($50 for international students). *Expenses:* Tuition: Part-time $270 per credit hour. *Financial support:* In 2006–07, 86 students received support. Federal Work-Study and unspecified assistantships available. Financial award application deadline: 4/1; financial award applicants required to submit FAFSA. *Unit head:* Dr. Jean Love, Chair, 865-471-3461. *Application contact:* Graduate Admissions and Services Adviser, 865-471-3460, Fax: 865-471-3875.

Centenary College of Louisiana, Graduate Programs, Department of Education, Shreveport, LA 71104. Offers administration (M Ed); elementary education (MAT); secondary education (MAT); supervision of instruction (M Ed). Part-time and evening/weekend programs available. *Degree requirements:* For master's, comprehensive exam. *Entrance requirements:* For master's, GRE General Test (M Ed), PRAXIS I and PRAXIS II (MAT), teacher certification (M Ed), minimum GPA of 2.5. Expenses: Contact institution. *Faculty research:* Teachers as advocates for teachers, portfolio assessment, disabled readers.

Central Connecticut State University, School of Graduate Studies, School of Education and Professional Studies, Department of Teacher Education, Program in Educational Foundations Policy/Secondary Education, New Britain, CT 06050-4010. Offers MS. Part-time and evening/weekend programs available. *Students:* 2 full-time (both women), 22 part-time (15 women); includes 2 minority (1 African American, 1 Hispanic American). 13 applicants, 54% accepted, 5 enrolled. In 2006, 12 degrees awarded. *Degree requirements:* For master's, thesis or alternative, comprehensive exam. *Entrance requirements:* For master's, minimum GPA of 2.7. Additional exam requirements/recommendations for international students: Required—TOEFL. *Application deadline:* For fall admission, 7/1 for domestic students; for spring admission, 12/1 for domestic students. Applications are processed on a rolling basis. Application fee: $50. Electronic applications accepted. *Expenses:* Tuition, area resident: Full-time $3,970; part-time $380 per credit. Tuition, state resident: full-time $5,955; part-time $380 per credit. Tuition, nonresident: full-time $11,061; part-time $380 per credit. Required fees: $3,189. One-time fee: $62 part-time. Tuition and fees vary according to degree level and program.

Central Michigan University, College of Graduate Studies, College of Education and Human Services, Department of Teacher Education and Professional Development, Mount Pleasant, MI 48859. Offers educational technology (MA); elementary education (MA), including classroom teaching, early childhood education, reading in the elementary school; library, media, and technology (MA), including library media, media and technology; middle level education (MA); reading improvement (MA); secondary education (MA); teaching senior high (MA). *Accreditation:* NCATE. *Degree requirements:* For master's, thesis or alternative, registration. *Faculty research:* Reading instruction and reading disabilities, teaching and learning styles, school and business partnerships, school restructuring and improvement, mathematics learning and instruction.

Chadron State College, School of Professional and Graduate Studies, Department of Education, Chadron, NE 69337. Offers business (MA Ed); community counseling (MA Ed); educational administration (MS Ed, Sp Ed); elementary education (MS Ed); history (MA Ed); language and literature (MA Ed); secondary administration (MS Ed); secondary education (MS Ed). *Accreditation:* NCATE. Part-time and evening/weekend programs available. Postbaccalaureate distance learning degree programs offered. *Degree requirements:* For master's, thesis optional. *Entrance requirements:* For master's, GRE General Test, GRE Writing Test, minimum GPA of 2.75 or 12 graduate hours at CSC with minimum GPA of 3.25. Additional exam requirements/recommendations for international students: Required—TOEFL. Electronic applications accepted. *Faculty research:* Rural education, technology, mental health.

Chapman University, Graduate Studies, School of Education, Program in Teaching: Secondary Education, Orange, CA 92866. Offers MA. Part-time and evening/weekend programs available. *Faculty:* 16 full-time (11 women), 25 part-time/adjunct (14 women). *Students:* 35 full-time (22 women), 27 part-time (19 women); includes 18 minority (1 African American, 1 American Indian/Alaska Native, 6 Asian Americans or Pacific Islanders, 10 Hispanic Americans). Average age 28. 24 applicants, 67% accepted, 12 enrolled. In 2006, 15 degrees awarded. *Degree requirements:* For master's, thesis, registration. *Entrance requirements:* For master's, GRE General Test, MAT, or California Subject Examinations for Teachers, minimum GPA of 2.75. Additional exam requirements/recommendations for international students: Required—TOEFL (minimum score 550 paper-based). *Application deadline:* Applications are processed on a rolling basis. Application fee: $55. Electronic applications accepted. *Expenses: Contact institution. Financial support:* In 2006–07, 62 students received support, including 4 fellowships (averaging $1,750 per year); Federal Work-Study also available. Financial award application deadline: 6/30; financial award applicants required to submit FAFSA. *Unit head:* Dr. Jan Osborn, Coordinator, 714-628-7221, E-mail: josborn@chapman.edu. *Application contact:* Rika Judd, Graduate Admission Counselor, 714-997-6786, Fax: 714-997-6713, E-mail: rjudd@chapman.edu.

Charleston Southern University, Programs in Education, Charleston, SC 29423-8087. Offers administration and supervision (M Ed), including elementary, secondary; elementary education (M Ed); English (MAT); science (MAT); secondary education (M Ed); social studies (MAT). *Accreditation:* NCATE. Part-time and evening/weekend programs available. *Degree requirements:* For master's, thesis optional. *Entrance requirements:* For master's, GRE or MAT. Expenses: Contact institution. *Faculty research:* Economic education, multicultural education, restructuring teacher education, participation in mathematics and science by minorities and women, at-risk children.

Chatham University, Program in Education, Pittsburgh, PA 15232-2826. Offers early childhood education (MAT); elementary education (MAT); English—secondary (MAT); environmental education (K-12) (MAT); secondary art (MAT); secondary biology education (MAT); secondary chemistry education (MAT); secondary English education (MAT); secondary math education (MAT); secondary physics education (MAT); secondary social studies education (MAT); special education (MAT). *Students:* 60 full-time (43 women), 23 part-time (22 women). Average age 29. 48 applicants, 77% accepted, 32 enrolled. In 2006, 59 degrees awarded. *Degree requirements:* For master's, thesis, teaching experience. *Entrance requirements:* For master's, PRAXIS I, minimum GPA of 3.0, sample of written work, recommendation letters. Additional exam requirements/recommendations for international students: Required—TOEFL (minimum score 600 paper-based; 250 computer-based; 100 iBT); Recommended—IELTS (minimum score 7), TWE (minimum score 5). *Application deadline:* For fall admission, 5/1 priority date for domestic and international students; for winter admission, 10/1 priority date for domestic and international students. Applications are processed on a rolling basis. Application fee: $45. Electronic applications accepted. *Financial support:* Career-related internships or fieldwork available. Financial award applicants required to submit FAFSA. *Faculty research:* Gifted education, environmental education, technology in education, writing as learning, class size and achievement. *Unit head:* Dr. Wendy Weiner, Director, 412-365-1146, Fax: 412-365-1505, E-mail: wweiner@chatham.edu. *Application contact:* 412-365-1825, Fax: 412-365-1609, E-mail: admissions@chatham.edu.

Chestnut Hill College, School of Graduate Studies, Department of Education, Program in Secondary Education, Philadelphia, PA 19118-2693. Offers M Ed. *Students:* Average age 30. *Expenses:* Tuition: Part-time $470 per credit hour. Required fees: $30 per semester. Tuition and fees vary according to degree level. *Application contact:* Jayne Mashett, Director of Graduate Admissions, 215-248-7020, Fax: 215-248-7161, E-mail: mashettj@chc.edu.

Chicago State University, School of Graduate and Professional Studies, College of Education, Department of Technology and Education, Chicago, IL 60628. Offers secondary education (MAT); technology and education (MS Ed). Postbaccalaureate distance learning degree programs offered. *Degree requirements:* For master's, thesis optional. *Entrance requirements:* For master's, minimum GPA of 2.75.

The Citadel, The Military College of South Carolina, College of Graduate and Professional Studies, School of Education, Program in Secondary Education, Charleston, SC 29409. Offers MAT. *Accreditation:* NCATE. Part-time and evening/weekend programs available. *Students:* 39 full-time (27 women), 95 part-time (56 women); includes 22 minority (20 African Americans, 2 Asian Americans or Pacific Islanders), 2 international. Average age 29. In 2006, 28 degrees awarded. *Entrance requirements:* For master's, GRE General Test, MAT, or 12 hours of graduate course work with a minimum GPA of 3.5. Additional exam requirements/recommendations for international students: Required—TOEFL (minimum score 550 paper-based; 213 computer-based). *Application deadline:* Applications are processed on a rolling basis. Application fee: $30. *Expenses:* Tuition, state resident: part-time $259 per credit hour. Tuition, nonresident: part-time $482 per credit hour. *Financial support:* Application deadline: 7/1; *Unit head:* Dr. Kathryn Richardson-Jones, Head, 843-953-3163, E-mail: kathryn.jones@citadel.edu. *Application contact:* Dean, College of Graduate and Professional Studies, 843-953-5089, Fax: 843-953-7630.

City College of the City University of New York, Graduate School, School of Education, Department of Secondary Education, New York, NY 10031-9198. Offers adolescent mathematics education (MA, AC); English education (MA); middle school mathematics education (MS); science education (MA); social studies education (AC). *Accreditation:* NCATE. *Students:* 286 applicants, 94% accepted, 219 enrolled. *Entrance requirements:* For master's, Liberal Arts and Sciences Test (LAST), Content Specialty Test (CST). Additional exam requirements/recommendations for international students: Required—TOEFL. *Application deadline:* For fall admission, 3/15 for domestic students; for spring admission, 10/15 for domestic students. Application fee: $125. *Unit head:* Susan Semel, Chair, 212-650-7262, E-mail: ssemel@ccny.cuny.edu. *Application contact:* Stacia Pusey, Graduate Admissions Adviser-Education, 212-650-5345, E-mail: spusey@ccny.cuny.edu.

Clemson University, Graduate School, College of Health, Education, and Human Development, School of Education, Program in Secondary Education, Clemson, SC 29634. Offers English (M Ed); mathematics (M Ed); natural sciences (M Ed). *Accreditation:* NCATE. *Students:* 5 full-time (2 women), 9 part-time (8 women); includes 1 minority (American Indian/Alaska Native). 11 applicants, 45% accepted, 2 enrolled. In 2006, 9 degrees awarded. *Entrance requirements:* For master's, teaching certificate. Additional exam requirements/recommendations for international students: Required—TOEFL. *Application deadline:* For fall admission, 6/1 for domestic students. Application fee: $50. *Expenses:* Tuition, state resident: full-time $8,812; part-time $450 per hour. Tuition, nonresident: full-time $18,036; part-time $760 per hour. Required fees: $474; $5 per term. *Financial support:* Application deadline: 6/1; *Unit head:* Dr. William Fisk, Graduate Coordinator, 864-656-5119, Fax: 864-656-1322, E-mail: bill252@clemson.edu.

See Close-Up on page 1273.

Coastal Carolina University, College of Education, Conway, SC 29528-6054. Offers early childhood education (M Ed); education (MAT); elementary education (M Ed); secondary education (M Ed). *Accreditation:* NCATE. Part-time and evening/weekend programs available. *Faculty:* 8 full-time (4 women), 16 part-time/adjunct (10 women). *Students:* 48 full-time (31 women), 45 part-time (33 women); includes 8 minority (6 African Americans, 2 Asian Americans or Pacific Islanders). Average age 30. In 2006, 70 degrees awarded. *Degree requirements:* For master's, comprehensive exam. *Entrance requirements:* For master's, GRE General Test, MAT, 2 letters of recommendation, copy of teaching credential. Additional exam requirements/recommendations for international students: Required—TOEFL. *Application deadline:* For fall admission, 8/15 priority date for domestic students. Applications are processed on a rolling basis. Application fee: $45. Electronic applications accepted. *Expenses:* Tuition, state resident: full-time $7,920; part-time $330 per credit hour. Tuition, nonresident: full-time $9,600; part-time $400 per credit hour. Required fees: $80; $40 per term. *Financial support:* Fellowships, research assistantships, unspecified assistantships available. Support available to part-time students. Financial award application deadline: 4/1; financial award applicants required to submit FAFSA. *Unit head:* Dr. Gilbert H. Hunt, Dean, 843-349-2607, Fax: 843-349-2332, E-mail: hunt@coastal.edu. *Application contact:* Dr. Judy W. Vogt, Vice President, Enrollment Services, 843-349-2037, Fax: 843-349-2127, E-mail: jvogt@coastal.edu.

Colgate University, Graduate Programs, Department of Educational Studies, Hamilton, NY 13346-1386. Offers secondary education (MAT). Part-time programs available. *Faculty:* 10 full-time (5 women). *Students:* 5 full-time (2 women), 1 part-time; includes 2 minority (both African Americans) Average age 23. 7 applicants, 57% accepted, 4 enrolled. In 2006, 3 degrees awarded. *Median time to degree:* Master's–1.2 years full-time. *Degree requirements:* For master's, special project or thesis. *Entrance requirements:* For master's, GRE General Test. *Application deadline:* For fall admission, 3/15 priority date for domestic students; for spring admission, 9/1 for domestic students. Applications are processed on a rolling basis. Application fee: $50. *Expenses:* Tuition: Part-time $3,866 per course. *Financial support:* In 2006–07, 3 students received support; research assistantships, institutionally sponsored loans and unspecified assistantships available. Support available to part-time students. Financial award applicants required to submit FAFSA. *Faculty research:* Multicultural education, moral problem solving, China, Native Americans, gender achievement in mathematics and science. *Unit head:* Dr. D. Kay Johnston, Chair, 315-228-7256. *Application contact:* Joan Thompson, Administrative Assistant, 315-228-7256, Fax: 315-228-7857, E-mail: jthompson@mail.colgate.edu.

College of Mount St. Joseph, Graduate Education Program, Cincinnati, OH 45233-1670. Offers adolescent young adult education (MA); art (MA); inclusive early childhood education (MA); instructional leadership (MA); middle childhood education (MA); multicultural special education (MA); music (MA); reading (MA). *Accreditation:* Teacher Education Accreditation Council. Part-time and evening/weekend programs available. Postbaccalaureate distance learning degree programs offered (minimal on-campus study). *Faculty:* 22 full-time (14 women), 11 part-time/adjunct (6 women). *Students:* 68 full-time (54 women), 115 part-time (96 women); includes 21 minority (16 African Americans, 2 American Indian/Alaska Native, 1 Asian American or Pacific Islander, 2 Hispanic Americans). Average age 34. 91 applicants, 98% accepted, 62 enrolled. In 2006, 61 degrees awarded. *Degree requirements:* For master's, research project. *Entrance requirements:* For master's, GRE, PRAXIS II in teaching content area (math or science), 2 letters of recommendation, interview, resumé, prerequisite courses in communications, behavioral sciences and mathematics. Additional exam requirements/recommendations for international students: Required—TOEFL (minimum score 560 paper-based; 220 computer-based). *Application deadline:* Applications are processed on a rolling basis. Application fee: $50. Electronic applications accepted. *Expenses:* Contact institution. *Financial support:* In 2006–07, 3 students received support. Career-related internships or fieldwork and scholarships/grants available. Support available to part-time students. Financial award application deadline: 6/1; financial award applicants required to submit FAFSA. *Faculty research:* Foreign and second language learning problems/reading disabilities/hyperlexia, multicultural/bilingual special education, alternative educator licensure, science education, pedagogical content knowledge. *Unit head:* Dr. Mifrando Obach, Chair, 513-244-3263, Fax: 513-244-4867, E-mail: mifrando_obach@mail.msj.edu. *Application contact:* Marilyn Hoskins, Assistant Director of Admissions for Graduate Recruitment, 513-244-4723, Fax: 513-244-4629, E-mail: marilyn_hoskins@mail.msg.edu.

The College of New Jersey, Graduate Division, School of Education, Department of Educational Administration and Secondary Education, Program in Secondary Education, Ewing, NJ 08628. Offers MAT. *Students:* 24 full-time (9 women), 16 part-time (12 women); includes 3 minority (all Asian Americans or Pacific Islanders) 60 applicants, 75% accepted. In 2006, 35 degrees awarded. *Degree requirements:* For master's, comprehensive exam. *Entrance requirements:* For master's, GRE, minimum GPA of 3.0 in field or 2.75 overall. Additional exam requirements/recommendations for international students: Required—TOEFL. *Application deadline:* For fall admission, 4/15 for domestic students; for spring admission, 10/15 for domestic students. Application fee: $60. Electronic applications accepted. *Financial support:* Unspecified assistantships available. *Unit head:* Dr. Stuart Carroll, Coordinator, 609-771-2586. *Application contact:* Susan L. Hydro, Office of Graduate Studies, Assistant Dean, 609-771-2300, Fax: 609-637-5105, E-mail: graduate@tcnj.edu.

College of St. Joseph, Graduate Program, Division of Education, Program in Secondary Education, Rutland, VT 05701-3899. Offers English (M Ed); mathematics (M Ed); social studies (M Ed). Part-time and evening/weekend programs available. *Faculty:* 2 full-time (1 woman), 8 part-time/adjunct (5 women). *Students:* 4 full-time, 4 part-time. Average age 32. 7 applicants, 100% accepted, 6 enrolled. In 2006, 4 degrees awarded. *Entrance requirements:* For master's, PRAXIS I, 2 letters of recommendation, minimum GPA of 3.0, interview. *Application deadline:* Applications are processed on a rolling basis. Application fee: $35. *Expenses:* Tuition: Full-time $10,990; part-time $300 per credit. Part-time tuition and fees vary according to program. *Financial support:* Career-related internships or fieldwork, Federal Work-Study, and unspecified assistantships available. Support available to part-time students. Financial award application deadline: 3/1. *Unit head:* Dr. David Balfour, Director, 802-773-5900 Ext. 3230, Fax: 802-776-5258, E-mail: dbalfour@csj.edu. *Application contact:* Tracy Gallipo, Director of Admissions, 802-773-5900 Ext. 3262, Fax: 802-773-5900, E-mail: tracygallipo@csj.edu.

The College of Saint Rose, Graduate Studies, School of Education, Teacher Education Department, Albany, NY 12203-1419. Offers business and marketing (MS Ed); childhood education (MS Ed); early childhood education (MS Ed); elementary education (K-6) (MS Ed); secondary education (MS Ed, Certificate); teacher education (MS Ed, Certificate), including bilingual pupil personnel services (Certificate). Part-time and evening/weekend programs available. *Entrance requirements:* For master's, minimum undergraduate GPA of 3.0. Additional exam requirements/recommendations for international students: Required—TOEFL (minimum score 550 paper-based; 213 computer-based). Electronic applications accepted.

College of Staten Island of the City University of New York, Graduate Programs, Department of Education, Program in Adolescence Education, Staten Island, NY 10314-6600. Offers MS Ed. Part-time and evening/weekend programs available. *Faculty:* 6 full-time (4 women), 2 part-time/adjunct (0 women). *Students:* 10 full-time (7 women), 173 part-time (109 women); includes 29 minority (12 African Americans, 7 Asian Americans or Pacific Islanders, 10 Hispanic Americans), 3 international. Average age 31. 70 applicants, 87% accepted, 48 enrolled. In 2006, 47 degrees awarded. *Degree requirements:* For master's, research project. *Entrance requirements:* For master's, minimum GPA of 2.75, 2 letters of recommendation. Additional exam requirements/recommendations for international students: Required—TOEFL (minimum score 550 paper-based; 213 computer-based; 79 iBT). *Application deadline:* For fall admission, 4/28 priority date for domestic and international students; for spring admission, 11/19 priority date for domestic and international students. Applications are processed on a rolling basis. Application fee: $125. *Expenses:* Tuition, state resident: full-time $6,400; part-time $270 per credit. Tuition, nonresident: part-time $500 per credit. Required fees: $53 per semester. *Financial support:* Federal Work-Study available. Financial award applicants required to submit FAFSA. *Unit head:* Dr. Kenneth Gold, Coordinator, 718-982-3737, Fax: 718-982-3743, E-mail: gold@mail.csi.cuny.edu. *Application contact:* Emmanuel Esperance, Deputy Director of Office of Recruitment and Admissions, 718-982-2190, Fax: 718-982-2500, E-mail: admissions@mail.csi.cuny.edu.

The College of William and Mary, School of Education, Program in Curriculum and Instruction, Williamsburg, VA 23187-8795. Offers elementary education (MA Ed); gifted education (MA Ed); reading education (MA Ed); secondary education (MA Ed), including English education, mathematics education, modern foreign languages education, science education, social studies education; special education (MA Ed), including emotionally disturbed, learning disabled, mental retardation, resource collaborating teaching. *Accreditation:* NCATE. Part-time programs available. *Faculty:* 15 full-time (6 women), 13 part-time/adjunct (10 women). *Students:* 51 full-time (39 women), 51 part-time (45 women); includes 6 minority (all African Americans) Average age 29. 161 applicants, 68% accepted, 61 enrolled. In 2006, 68 degrees awarded. *Degree requirements:* For master's, master's project. *Entrance requirements:* For master's, GRE or MAT, minimum GPA of 2.5. Additional exam requirements/recommendations for international students: Required—TOEFL. *Application deadline:* For fall admission, 2/1 for domestic and international students; for spring admission, 10/1 for domestic and international students. Application fee: $30. *Expenses:* Tuition, state resident: full-time $6,100; part-time $260 per credit. Tuition, nonresident: full-time $18,790; part-time $725 per credit. Required fees: $3,314. Tuition and fees vary according to program. *Financial support:* In 2006–07, 10 research assistantships with full and partial tuition reimbursements (averaging $5,000 per year) were awarded; career-related internships or fieldwork, Federal Work-Study, institutionally sponsored loans, scholarships/grants, and unspecified assistantships also available. Financial award application deadline: 2/1; financial award applicants required to submit FAFSA. *Faculty research:* National Council of Teachers of Mathematics Standards, counseling, self-concept and self-esteem, special education, curriculum development. *Unit head:* Dr. John Moore, Area Coordinator, 757-221-2333, E-mail: jnmoor@wm.edu. *Application contact:* Dorothy Osborne, Director of Admissions, 757-221-2317, E-mail: dsosbo@wm.edu.

The Colorado College, Department of Education, Program in Secondary Education, Colorado Springs, CO 80903-3294. Offers art teaching (MAT); English teaching (MAT); foreign language teaching (MAT); mathematics teaching (MAT); music teaching (MAT); science teaching (MAT); social studies teaching (MAT). *Faculty:* 2 full-time (1 woman), 10 part-time/adjunct (7 women). *Students:* 18 full-time (12 women); includes 2 minority (1 African American, 1 Asian American or Pacific Islander). Average age 27. 30 applicants, 90% accepted, 18 enrolled. In 2006, 16 degrees awarded. *Degree requirements:* For master's, thesis, internship. *Entrance requirements:* For master's, PRAXIS II or PLACE. *Application deadline:* For fall admission, 2/1 for domestic and international students. Application fee: $50. *Expenses:* Tuition: Full-time $23,567. One-time fee: $1,485 full-time. *Financial support:* In 2006–07, 15 teaching assistantships (averaging $16,000 per year) were awarded; career-related internships or fieldwork, institutionally sponsored loans, health care benefits, and tuition waivers (partial) also available. Financial award application deadline: 2/15; financial award applicants required to submit FAFSA. *Unit head:* Mike Taber, Director, 719-389-6026, Fax: 719-389-6473, E-mail: pveronesi@coloradocollege.edu. *Application contact:* Marsha E. Unruh, Director of Education Career Services, 719-389-6472, Fax: 719-389-6473, E-mail: munruh@coloradocollege.edu.

The Colorado College, Programs for Experienced Teachers, Colorado Springs, CO 80903-3294. Offers American Southwest studies for all teachers (MAT); arts and humanities for secondary school teachers and administrators (MAT); integrated natural science for all teachers (MAT); liberal arts for elementary school teachers and administrators (MAT). Programs offered during summer only. Part-time programs available. *Faculty:* 18 part-time/adjunct (8 women). *Students:* 78; includes 2 minority (both Hispanic Americans) Average age 31. In 2006, 28 degrees awarded. *Degree requirements:* For master's, thesis, oral exam, 50 page paper. *Application deadline:* Applications are processed on a rolling basis. Application fee: $50. *Expenses:* Contact institution. One-time fee: $1,485 full-time. *Financial support:* Institutionally sponsored loans and half-tuition waivers to teachers with a contract available. *Unit head:* Dr. Libby Rittenberg, Dean of Summer Programs, 719-389-6657, Fax: 719-389-6955. *Application contact:* Ann H. Van Horn, Assistant Dean of Summer Session, 719-389-6656, Fax: 719-389-6955, E-mail: avanhorn@coloradocollege.edu.

Columbus State University, Graduate Studies, College of Education, Department of Teacher Education, Columbus, GA 31907-5645. Offers early childhood education (M Ed, Ed S); instructional technology (MS); middle grades education (M Ed, Ed S); physical education (M Ed); secondary education (M Ed, Ed S), including English/language arts, general science (M Ed), mathematics, science (Ed S), social science; special education (Ed S), including behavior disorders, learning disabilities, mental retardation. *Accreditation:* NCATE. Part-time and evening/weekend programs available. Postbaccalaureate distance learning degree programs offered (minimal on-campus study). *Faculty:* 16 full-time (8 women), 2 part-time/adjunct (1 woman). *Students:* 61 full-time (45 women), 128 part-time (89 women); includes 44 minority (36 African Americans, 3 Asian Americans or Pacific Islanders, 5 Hispanic Americans), 1 international. Average age 36. 77 applicants, 49% accepted, 26 enrolled. In 2006, 66 master's, 13 other advanced degrees awarded. *Degree requirements:* For master's, thesis, exit exam; for Ed S, thesis or alternative. *Entrance requirements:* For master's, GRE General Test, minimum GPA of 2.75; for Ed S, GRE General Test. Additional exam requirements/recommendations for international students: Required—TOEFL (minimum score 550 paper-based; 213 computer-based). *Application deadline:* For fall admission, 5/1 priority date for domestic students, 5/1 for international students; for spring admission, 11/1 for domestic and international students. Applications are processed on a rolling basis. Application fee: $25. Electronic applications accepted. *Expenses:* Tuition, state resident: part-time $127 per semester hour. Tuition, nonresident: part-time $508 per semester hour. Required fees: $264 per semester. Tuition and fees vary according to course load. *Financial support:* In 2006–07, 118 students received support, including 21 research assistantships with partial tuition reimbursements available (averaging $3,000 per year); career-related internships or fieldwork, Federal Work-Study, institutionally sponsored loans, scholarships/grants, tuition waivers (partial), and unspecified assistantships also available. Support available to part-time students. Financial award application deadline: 5/1; financial award applicants required to submit FAFSA. *Unit head:* Dr. Deborah Gober, Acting Chair, 706-568-2255, Fax: 706-568-3134, E-mail: gober_deborah@colstate.edu. *Application contact:* Katie Thornton, Graduate Admissions Specialist, 706-568-2035, Fax: 706-568-2462, E-mail: thornton_katie@colstate.edu.

Concordia University, College of Education, Portland, OR 97211-6099. Offers curriculum and instruction (elementary) (M Ed); educational administration (M Ed); elementary education (MAT); secondary education (MAT). Part-time programs available. Postbaccalaureate distance learning degree programs offered (no on-campus study). *Degree requirements:* For master's, work samples/portfolio. *Entrance requirements:* For master's, California Basic Educational Skills Test or PRAXIS I, minimum undergraduate GPA of 2.8, graduate 3.0; 2 letters of recommendation. Additional exam requirements/recommendations for international students: Required—TOEFL (minimum score 525 paper-based; 195 computer-based). Electronic applications accepted. *Faculty research:* Learner centered classroom, brain-based learning future of on-line learning.

Connecticut College, Graduate School, Programs in Education, Program in Secondary Education, New London, CT 06320-4196. Offers MAT. Part-time programs available. *Entrance requirements:* For master's, MAT.

Converse College, School of Education and Graduate Studies, Program in Secondary Education, Spartanburg, SC 29302-0006. Offers biology (MAT); chemistry (MAT); English (M Ed, MAT); mathematics (M Ed, MAT); natural sciences (M Ed); social sciences (M Ed, MAT). Part-time programs available. *Students:* Average age 35. In 2006, 40 degrees awarded. *Degree requirements:* For master's, capstone paper. *Entrance requirements:* For master's, NTE or PRAXIS II (M Ed), minimum GPA of 2.75, 2 recommendations. *Application deadline:* For fall admission, 8/1 for domestic and international students; for winter admission, 11/15 for domestic and international students; for spring admission, 1/15 for domestic and international students. Applications are processed on a rolling basis. Application fee: $40. Electronic applications accepted. *Expenses:* Tuition: Part-time $305 per credit hour. Required fees: $20 per term. *Financial support:* Available to part-time students. Applicants required to submit FAFSA.

Delta State University, Graduate Programs, College of Education, Thad Cochran Center for Rural School Leadership and Research, Program in Administration and Supervision, Cleveland, MS 38733-0001. Offers educational administration and supervision (Ed S); educational leadership (M Ed); elementary education (Ed S); secondary education (Ed S). *Accreditation:* NCATE. Part-time and evening/weekend programs available. *Degree requirements:* For master's, thesis optional. *Entrance requirements:* For master's, GRE General Test or MAT; for Ed S, master's degree, teaching certificate. *Application deadline:* For fall admission, 8/1 priority date for domestic students; for spring admission, 12/1 priority date for domestic students. Applications are processed on a rolling basis. Application fee: $0. *Financial support:* Research assistantships, career-related internships or fieldwork, Federal Work-Study, and institutionally sponsored loans available. Support available to part-time students. Financial award application deadline: 6/1.

DePaul University, School of Education, Chicago, IL 60604-2287. Offers bilingual and bicultural education (M Ed, MA); curriculum studies (M Ed, MA); education (Ed D), including curriculum studies, educational leadership; educational leadership (M Ed, MA), including administration and supervision, Catholic school leadership, physical education; human development and learning (MA); human services and counseling (M Ed, MA), including agencies, family concerns, and higher education, elementary schools, human services management, secondary schools; reading and learning disabilities (M Ed, MA); social culture studies in education and development (M Ed, MA), including curriculum studies/development; teaching and learning (early childhood, elementary and secondary) (M Ed), including elementary education (M Ed, MA), secondary education (M Ed, MA); teaching and learning (early childhood, elementary, and

Secondary Education

DePaul University (continued)

secondary) (MA), including elementary education (M Ed, MA), secondary education (M Ed, MA). *Accreditation:* NCATE. Part-time and evening/weekend programs available. *Faculty:* 61 full-time (40 women), 76 part-time/adjunct (46 women). *Students:* 1,371 full-time (1,103 women), 474 part-time (362 women); includes 435 minority (144 African Americans, 7 American Indian/Alaska Native, 89 Asian Americans or Pacific Islanders, 195 Hispanic Americans), 11 international. Average age 30. 993 applicants, 80% accepted, 617 enrolled. In 2006, 324 master's, 7 doctorates awarded. *Degree requirements:* For doctorate, thesis/dissertation. *Entrance requirements:* For master's, interview, minimum GPA of 2.75, 2 letters of recommendation; for doctorate, interview, master's degree, 2 years of work experience (recommended), writing sample, 3 letters of recommendation. Application fee: $25. Electronic applications accepted. *Financial support:* In 2006–07, 16 research assistantships with tuition reimbursements (averaging $4,370 per year), 1 teaching assistantship (averaging $6,000 per year) were awarded; career-related internships or fieldwork also available. *Faculty research:* Reflective teaching, children at risk, loss, ethnicity, urban education. Total annual research expenditures: $556,194. *Unit head:* Dr. Clara Jennings, Dean, 773-325-7581, Fax: 773-325-7728, E-mail: cjennings@depaul.edu. *Application contact:* Dr. John Bollwark, Data Project Manager, 773-325-7582, Fax: 773-325-7713, E-mail: jbollwar@depaul.edu.

Dowling College, Graduate Programs in Education, Oakdale, NY 11769-1999. Offers educational administration (Ed D, PD), including computers in education (PD), educational administration (Ed D), school administration and supervision (PD), school district administration (PD); human development and learning (MS Ed); literacy (MS Ed); literacy/special education (MS Ed); secondary education (MS Ed); special education (MS Ed). *Accreditation:* NCATE. Part-time and evening/weekend programs available. Postbaccalaureate distance learning degree programs offered. *Faculty:* 29 full-time (13 women), 91 part-time/adjunct (60 women). *Students:* 496 full-time (364 women), 1,083 part-time (827 women); includes 119 minority (37 African Americans, 20 Asian Americans or Pacific Islanders, 62 Hispanic Americans), 2 international. Average age 38. 618 applicants, 86% accepted, 300 enrolled. In 2006, 641 master's, 25 doctorates awarded. *Degree requirements:* For master's and PD, comprehensive exam; for doctorate, thesis/dissertation. *Entrance requirements:* For master's, minimum GPA of 3.0; for doctorate, GRE, master's degree; for PD, teaching certificate. Additional exam requirements/recommendations for international students: Required—TOEFL (minimum score 550 paper-based). *Application deadline:* For fall admission, 9/1 priority date for domestic students; for winter admission, 1/1 priority date for domestic students; for spring admission, 2/1 priority date for domestic students. Applications are processed on a rolling basis. Application fee: $25. Electronic applications accepted. *Expenses:* Tuition: Full-time $16,008; part-time $667 per credit. Tuition and fees vary according to course load. *Financial support:* In 2006–07, 358 students received support, including 20 research assistantships with tuition reimbursements available (averaging $3,150 per year); career-related internships or fieldwork, Federal Work-Study, scholarships/grants, tuition waivers (partial), and unspecified assistantships also available. Support available to part-time students. Financial award application deadline: 6/30; financial award applicants required to submit FAFSA. *Faculty research:* Natural readers, Korean styles and learning strategies, mothers of children with disabilities, computers in instruction, cultural background and organizational roadblocks to problem solving. *Unit head:* Dr. Clyde Payne, Associate Provost, 631-244-3404, Fax: 631-589-6644, E-mail: paynec@dowling.edu. *Application contact:* Franks S. Pizzardi, Director of Admissions Operations, 631-244-3227, Fax: 631-244-1059, E-mail: pizzardf@dowling.edu.

Drake University, School of Education, Department of Leadership, Counseling and Adult Development, Program in Counseling, Des Moines, IA 50311-4516. Offers community agency counseling (MSE); guidance counseling (MSE), including elementary, secondary. *Accreditation:* CORE. Part-time and evening/weekend programs available. *Faculty:* 10 full-time (3 women), 28 part-time/adjunct (16 women). *Students:* 137 applicants, 61% accepted. In 2006, 41 degrees awarded. *Degree requirements:* For master's, comprehensive exam. *Entrance requirements:* For master's, GRE General Test, MAT, or Drake Writing Assessment, resumé, 2 letters of recommendation. Additional exam requirements/recommendations for international students: Required—TOEFL (minimum score 550 paper-based; 213 computer-based). *Application deadline:* For fall admission, 7/1 priority date for domestic students, 6/1 priority date for international students; for spring admission, 11/1 priority date for domestic students, 10/1 priority date for international students. Applications are processed on a rolling basis. Application fee: $25. Electronic applications accepted. *Financial support:* Career-related internships or fieldwork and unspecified assistantships available. Support available to part-time students. *Faculty research:* Counseling and rehabilitation, behavioral supports, inquiry-based science methods, teacher quality enhancements. Total annual research expenditures: $1.5 million. *Unit head:* Dr. Matt Bruinekool, Director, 515-271-4507, E-mail: matt.bruinekool@drake.edu. *Application contact:* Ann J. Martin, Graduate Coordinator, 515-271-2034, Fax: 515-271-2831, E-mail: ann.martin@drake.edu.

Drake University, School of Education, Department of Teaching and Learning, Program in Secondary Education, Des Moines, IA 50311-4516. Offers art (MAT); biology (MAT); business (MAT); chemistry (MAT); English (MAT); general science (MAT); history-American (MAT); history-world (MAT); journalism (MAT); mathematics (MAT); physical science (MAT); physics (MAT); sociology (MAT); speech (MAT); speech communication (MAT); theatre (MAT). Part-time programs available. *Faculty:* 10 full-time (3 women), 28 part-time/adjunct (16 women). *Students:* 13 full-time (7 women), 33 part-time (20 women). 41 applicants, 56% accepted. In 2006, 12 degrees awarded. *Degree requirements:* For master's, thesis (for some programs), internships (s), comprehensive exam, registration. *Entrance requirements:* For master's, GRE General Test, MAT, or Drake Writing Assessment, resumé, 2 letters of recommendation. Additional exam requirements/recommendations for international students: Required—TOEFL (minimum score 550 paper-based; 213 computer-based). *Application deadline:* For fall admission, 7/1 priority date for domestic students, 6/1 priority date for international students; for spring admission, 11/1 priority date for domestic students, 10/1 priority date for international students. Applications are processed on a rolling basis. Application fee: $25. Electronic applications accepted. *Financial support:* Career-related internships or fieldwork and unspecified assistantships available. Support available to part-time students. *Faculty research:* Counseling and rehabilitation, behavioral supports, inquiry-based science methods, teacher quality enhancement. Total annual research expenditures: $1.5 million. *Unit head:* Dr. Linda Espey, Head, 515-271-1954, E-mail: linda.espey@drake.edu. *Application contact:* Ann J. Martin, Graduate Coordinator, 515-271-2034, Fax: 515-271-2831, E-mail: ann.martin@drake.edu.

Drury University, Graduate Programs in Education, Program in Secondary Education, Springfield, MO 65802. Offers M Ed. *Accreditation:* NCATE. Part-time and evening/weekend programs available. *Degree requirements:* For master's, thesis. *Entrance requirements:* For master's, GRE or MAT, minimum GPA of 2.75. *Faculty research:* International baccalaureate, block school scheduling.

Duquesne University, School of Education, Department of Instruction and Leadership, Program in Secondary Education, Pittsburgh, PA 15282-0001. Offers MS Ed. Part-time and evening/weekend programs available. *Faculty:* 4 full-time (1 woman), 1 part-time/adjunct (0 women). *Students:* 112. Average age 29. 50 applicants, 84% accepted, 40 enrolled. In 2006, 62 degrees awarded. *Degree requirements:* For master's, thesis optional. *Entrance requirements:* For master's, MAT, minimum GPA of 3.0. Additional exam requirements/recommendations for international students: Required—TOEFL. *Application deadline:* For fall admission, 8/1 for domestic students; for spring admission, 12/1 for domestic students. Applications are processed on a rolling basis. Application fee: $50. *Expenses:* Tuition: Part-time $723 per credit. Required fees: $71 per credit. Tuition and fees vary according to degree level and program. *Financial support:* In 2006–07, 1 research assistantship with full and partial tuition reimbursement (averaging $5,200 per year) was awarded; Federal Work-Study also available. Support available to part-time students.

D'Youville College, Department of Education, Buffalo, NY 14201-1084. Offers elementary education (MS Ed, Teaching Certificate); secondary education (MS Ed, Teaching Certificate); special education (MS Ed). Part-time and evening/weekend programs available. *Faculty:* 31 full-time (18 women), 38 part-time/adjunct (25 women). *Students:* 613 full-time (434 women), 303 part-time (223 women); includes 26 minority (14 African Americans, 1 American Indian/Alaska Native, 2 Asian Americans or Pacific Islanders, 9 Hispanic Americans), 727 international. Average age 28. 1,092 applicants. In 2006, 328 master's, 401 other advanced degrees awarded. *Degree requirements:* For master's, project or thesis. *Entrance requirements:* For master's, minimum GPA of 3.0. Additional exam requirements/recommendations for international students: Required—TOEFL (minimum score 500 paper-based; 173 computer-based). *Application deadline:* For fall admission, 5/1 priority date for international students; for spring admission, 9/1 priority date for international students. Applications are processed on a rolling basis. Application fee: $25. Electronic applications accepted. *Financial support:* In 2006–07, 1 research assistantship with partial tuition reimbursement (averaging $3,000 per year) was awarded; career-related internships or fieldwork and scholarships/grants also available. Support available to part-time students. Financial award application deadline: 3/1; financial award applicants required to submit FAFSA. *Faculty research:* Developmentally disabled, multiculturalism, early childhood education. *Unit head:* Dr. David Gorlewski, Chair, 716-829-8140, Fax: 716-829-7660. *Application contact:* Linda Fisher, Graduate Admissions Director, 716-829-8400, Fax: 716-829-7900, E-mail: graduateadmissions@dyc.edu.

Eastern Connecticut State University, School of Education and Professional Studies/Graduate Division, Program in Secondary Education, Willimantic, CT 06226-2295. Offers MS. *Accreditation:* NCATE. Part-time and evening/weekend programs available. *Faculty:* 5 full-time (3 women), 3 part-time/adjunct (1 woman). *Students:* 25 full-time (11 women), 27 part-time (15 women); includes 2 minority (1 African American, 1 Hispanic American). Average age 29. 8 applicants, 25% accepted, 1 enrolled. In 2006, 11 degrees awarded. *Degree requirements:* For master's, comprehensive exam or thesis. *Entrance requirements:* For master's, PRAXIS I and II, minimum GPA of 2.7. Additional exam requirements/recommendations for international students: Required—TOEFL (minimum score 550 paper-based; 213 computer-based). *Application deadline:* For fall admission, 7/6 priority date for domestic and international students; for spring admission, 11/3 priority date for domestic and international students. Application fee: $50. *Expenses:* Tuition, state resident: full-time $3,970. Tuition, nonresident: full-time $11,061; part-time $336 per credit. Required fees: $35 per credit. *Financial support:* Teaching assistantships, career-related internships or fieldwork, scholarships/grants, and unspecified assistantships available. Support available to part-time students. Financial award application deadline: 3/15. *Unit head:* Dr. Jeanelle Bland, Advisor, 860-465-4532, Fax: 860-465-5099, E-mail: blandj@easternct.edu. *Application contact:* Dr. Tuesday L. Cooper, Associate Dean, 860-465-4543, Fax: 860-465-4538, E-mail: coopert@easternct.edu.

Eastern Kentucky University, The Graduate School, College of Education, Department of Curriculum and Instruction, Program in Secondary and Higher Education, Richmond, KY 40475-3102. Offers agricultural education (MA Ed); allied health sciences education (MA Ed); art education (MA Ed); biological sciences education (MA Ed); business education (MA Ed); chemistry education (MA Ed); earth science education (MA Ed); English education (MA Ed); general science education (MA Ed); geography education (MA Ed); history education (MA Ed); home economics education (MA Ed); industrial education (MA Ed); mathematical sciences education (MA Ed); physical education (MA Ed); physics education (MA Ed); political science education (MA Ed); psychology education (MA Ed); reading (MA Ed); school health education (MA Ed); sociology education (MA Ed). *Accreditation:* NCATE. Part-time programs available. *Students:* 16 full-time (8 women), 63 part-time (43 women); includes 5 minority (2 African Americans, 2 American Indian/Alaska Native, 1 Asian American or Pacific Islander). Average age 32. *Entrance requirements:* For master's, GRE General Test, minimum GPA of 2.5. Application fee: $30. *Expenses:* Tuition, state resident: full-time $5,610. Tuition, nonresident: full-time $15,910. *Financial support:* Research assistantships, teaching assistantships, Federal Work-Study available. Support available to part-time students. *Unit head:* Dr. Michael Martin, Chair, Department of Curriculum and Instruction, 859-622-2154, Fax: 859-622-2004.

Eastern Michigan University, Graduate School, College of Education, Department of Teacher Education, Program in Secondary School Teaching, Ypsilanti, MI 48197. Offers MA. *Accreditation:* NCATE. Part-time and evening/weekend programs available. Postbaccalaureate distance learning degree programs offered (minimal on-campus study). *Students:* Average age 31. In 2006, 7 degrees awarded. *Entrance requirements:* For master's, GRE. Additional exam requirements/recommendations for international students: Required—TOEFL. *Application deadline:* For fall admission, 5/15 priority date for domestic students, 5/1 priority date for international students; for winter admission, 10/15 priority date for domestic students, 10/1 priority date for international students; for spring admission, 3/15 priority date for domestic students, 3/1 priority date for international students. Applications are processed on a rolling basis. Application fee: $35. *Expenses:* Tuition, state resident: part-time $341 per credit hour. Tuition, nonresident: full-time $16,104; part-time $671 per credit hour. Required fees: $816; $34 per credit hour. $40 per term. One-time fee: $82 full-time. Tuition and fees vary according to course level, course load, degree level and reciprocity agreements. *Financial support:* Fellowships, research assistantships with full tuition reimbursements, teaching assistantships with full tuition reimbursements, career-related internships or fieldwork, Federal Work-Study, institutionally sponsored loans, scholarships/grants, tuition waivers (partial), and unspecified assistantships available. Support available to part-time students. Financial award applicants required to submit FAFSA.

Eastern Nazarene College, Adult and Graduate Studies, Division of Education, Quincy, MA 02170-2999. Offers early childhood education (M Ed, Certificate); elementary education (M Ed, Certificate); English as a second language (M Ed, Certificate); instructional enrichment and development (M Ed, Certificate); middle school education (M Ed, Certificate); moderate special needs education (M Ed, Certificate); principal (Certificate); program development and supervision (M Ed, Certificate); secondary education (M Ed, Certificate); special education administrator (Certificate); supervisor (Certificate); teacher of reading (M Ed, Certificate). M Ed and Certificate also available through weekend program for administration, special needs, and reading only. Part-time and evening/weekend programs available. *Faculty:* 9 full-time (5 women), 11 part-time/adjunct (5 women). *Students:* 135. Average age 35. 20 applicants, 100% accepted. In 2006, 2 degrees awarded. *Entrance requirements:* Additional exam requirements/recommendations for international students: Required—TOEFL (minimum score 550 paper-based). *Application deadline:* Applications are processed on a rolling basis. Application fee: $35. *Financial support:* Career-related internships or fieldwork available. Support available to part-time students. Financial award applicants required to submit FAFSA. *Unit head:* Dr. Lorne Ranstrom, Chair, 617-745-3528, E-mail: randstrol@enc.edu. *Application contact:* Christine Galbraith, Graduate Studies Recruiter, 617-774-6703, Fax: 617-984-4901, E-mail: christine.galbraith@enc.edu.

Eastern Oregon University, School of Education and Business, Program in Secondary Education, La Grande, OR 97850-2899. Offers MTE. Part-time programs available. Postbaccalaureate distance learning degree programs offered (minimal on-campus study). *Degree requirements:* For master's, thesis. *Entrance requirements:* For master's, NTE.

East Stroudsburg University of Pennsylvania, Graduate School, School of Professional Studies, Department of Professional and Secondary Education, East Stroudsburg, PA 18301-2999. Offers M Ed. *Accreditation:* NCATE. Part-time and evening/weekend programs available. *Faculty:* 7 full-time (3 women). *Students:* 48 full-time (30 women), 100 part-time (66 women). Average age 34. In 2006, 32 degrees awarded. *Degree requirements:* For master's, comprehensive exam. *Entrance requirements:* For master's, PRAXIS/teacher certification, letter of recommendation, Pennsylvania Department of Education requirements. Additional exam requirements/recommendations for international students: Required—TOEFL (minimum score 560 paper-based; 220 computer-based; 83 iBT). *Application deadline:* For fall admission, 7/31 priority date for domestic students, 5/1 priority date for international students; for spring admission, 11/30 for domestic students, 10/1 for international students. Applications are processed on a rolling basis. Application fee: $50. *Expenses:* Tuition, state resident: full-time $6,048; part-time $336 per credit. Tuition, nonresident: full-time $9,678; part-time $538 per credit. Required fees: $1,353; $67 per credit. One-time fee: $37 part-time. *Financial support:* In 2006–07, 13 research assistantships with full and partial tuition reimbursements were awarded; career-related internships or fieldwork, Federal Work-Study, and institutionally sponsored loans also available. Financial award application deadline: 3/1; financial award applicants required to submit FAFSA. *Unit head:* Dr. Kathleen Foster, Graduate Coordinator, 570-422-3373, Fax: 570-422-3506, E-mail: kfoster@po-box.esu.edu.

East Tennessee State University, School of Graduate Studies, College of Education, Department of Curriculum and Instruction, Johnson City, TN 37614. Offers 7-12 (MAT); classroom technology (M Ed); educational communication (M Ed); educational media/educational technology (M Ed); elementary education (M Ed, MAT); K-12 (MAT); reading and storytelling (M Ed, MA); reading education (M Ed, MA); school library media (M Ed); secondary education (M Ed, MAT). *Accreditation:* NCATE. Part-time and evening/weekend programs available. *Degree requirements:* For master's, thesis (for some programs). *Entrance requirements:* For master's, GRE, minimum GPA of 3.0. Additional exam requirements/recommendations for international students: Required—TOEFL (minimum score 550 paper-based; 213 computer-based). *Faculty research:* Critical thinking, curriculum development, cultural diversity, cognitive processes, effective teaching strategies.

Edinboro University of Pennsylvania, Graduate Studies and Research, School of Education, Department of Secondary Education, Edinboro, PA 16444. Offers M Ed. Part-time and evening/weekend programs available. *Faculty:* 6 full-time (3 women). *Students:* 54 full-time (29 women), 28 part-time (20 women); includes 1 minority (Hispanic American) Average age 30. In 2006, 19 degrees awarded. *Degree requirements:* For master's, thesis or alternative, competency exam, portfolio, oral presentation, comprehensive exam. *Entrance requirements:* For master's, GRE or MAT, minimum QPA of 2.5. *Application deadline:* Applications are processed on a rolling basis. Application fee: $30. Electronic applications accepted. *Expenses:* Tuition, state resident: full-time $6,048; part-time $336 per credit. Tuition, nonresident: full-time $9,678; part-time $538 per credit. Required fees: $1,849; $42 per credit. *Financial support:* In 2006–07, 15 research assistantships with full and partial tuition reimbursements (averaging $3,850 per year) were awarded; Federal Work-Study, scholarships/grants, and unspecified assistantships also available. Support available to part-time students. Financial award application deadline: 2/15; financial award applicants required to submit FAFSA. *Unit head:* Dr. Kathleen Benson, Chairperson, 814-732-2788, E-mail: kbenson@edinboro.edu. *Application contact:* Dr. R. Scott Baldwin, Dean, 814-732-2752, Fax: 814-732-2268, E-mail: sbaldwin@edinboro.edu.

Elms College, Division of Education, Chicopee, MA 01013-2839. Offers early childhood education (MAT); education (M Ed, CAGS); elementary education (MAT); English as a second language (MAT); reading (MAT); secondary education (MAT), including biology education, English education, Spanish education; special education (MAT). Part-time and evening/weekend programs available. *Faculty:* 9 full-time (6 women), 4 part-time/adjunct (2 women). *Students:* 8 full-time (6 women), 97 part-time (89 women); includes 4 minority (2 Asian Americans or Pacific Islanders, 2 Hispanic Americans). Average age 36. 48 applicants, 90% accepted, 40 enrolled. In 2006, 37 master's, 8 other advanced degrees awarded. *Degree requirements:* For master's, thesis (for some programs). *Entrance requirements:* For master's, Massachusetts Educators Certification Test, minimum GPA of 3.0; for CAGS, master's degree in education. Additional exam requirements/recommendations for international students: Required—TOEFL. *Application deadline:* For fall admission, 7/1 priority date for domestic students; for spring admission, 11/1 priority date for domestic students. Applications are processed on a rolling basis. Application fee: $30. *Expenses:* Tuition: Full-time $9,180; part-time $510 per credit. Tuition and fees vary according to course load. *Financial support:* In 2006–07, 3 teaching assistantships with partial tuition reimbursements were awarded; tuition waivers (partial) also available. Support available to part-time students. Financial award application deadline: 4/15; financial award applicants required to submit FAFSA. *Unit head:* Dr. Mary Janeczek, Director, 413-594-2761, Fax: 413-592-4871, E-mail: janeczeke@elms.edu.

Emmanuel College, Graduate Programs, Programs in Education, Boston, MA 02115. Offers educational leadership (CAGS); elementary education (MAT); school administration (M Ed); secondary education (MAT). Part-time and evening/weekend programs available. *Faculty:* 4 full-time (all women), 8 part-time/adjunct (4 women). *Students:* 5 full-time (all women), 34 part-time (24 women); includes 6 minority (3 African Americans, 1 Asian American or Pacific Islander, 2 Hispanic Americans). Average age 29. 44 applicants, 23% accepted, 10 enrolled. In 2006, 21 master's, 3 other advanced degrees awarded. *Entrance requirements:* For master's, interview, resumé, 2 letters of recommendation; for CAGS, interview, leadership statement, resumé, 2 letters of recommendation. Additional exam requirements/recommendations for international students: Required—TOEFL (minimum score 600 paper-based; 250 computer-based). *Application deadline:* For fall admission, 8/15 priority date for domestic students; for spring admission, 12/8 priority date for domestic students. Applications are processed on a rolling basis. Application fee: $50. Electronic applications accepted. *Expenses:* Tuition: Full-time $5,256. *Faculty research:* Literature/reading, history of education, multicultural education, special education. *Unit head:* Brian Minchello, Associate Director, Graduate and Professional Programs, 617-735-9928, Fax: 617-735-9708, E-mail: gpp@emmanuel.edu. *Application contact:* Kristin Balutis, Enrollment Counselor, 617-735-9859, Fax: 617-735-9708, E-mail: balutkr@emmanuel.edu.

Emory University, Graduate School of Arts and Sciences, Division of Educational Studies, Atlanta, GA 30322-1100. Offers educational studies (MA, PhD, DAST); middle grades teaching (M Ed, MAT); secondary teaching (M Ed, MAT). *Accreditation:* NCATE. Terminal master's awarded for partial completion of doctoral program. *Degree requirements:* For master's, thesis/dissertation, registration; for doctorate, thesis/dissertation, comprehensive exam, registration. *Entrance requirements:* For master's and doctorate, GRE General Test, minimum GPA of 3.0. Additional exam requirements/recommendations for international students: Required—TOEFL. Electronic applications accepted. *Expenses:* Tuition: Full-time $30,246. *Faculty research:* Educational policy, educational measurement, urban and multicultural education, mathematics and science education, comparative education.

Emporia State University, School of Graduate Studies, The Teachers College, Department of Early Childhood/Elementary Teacher Education, Program in Master Teacher, Emporia, KS 66801-5087. Offers master teacher (MS), including elementary subject matter, English as a second language, reading, secondary subject matter. *Accreditation:* NCATE. Part-time programs available. *Students:* 1 (woman) full-time, 83 part-time (82 women); includes 2 minority (1 American Indian/Alaska Native, 1 Hispanic American). 14 applicants, 93% accepted, 13 enrolled. In 2006, 23 degrees awarded. *Degree requirements:* For master's, comprehensive exam or thesis, practicum. *Entrance requirements:* For master's, GRE General Test or MAT, graduate essay exam, appropriate bachelor's degree, letters of recommendation. Additional exam requirements/recommendations for international students: Required—TOEFL. *Application deadline:* For fall admission, 8/15 priority date for domestic students. Applications are processed on a rolling basis. Application fee: $30 ($75 for international students). Electronic applications accepted. *Expenses:* Tuition, state resident: full-time $3,438; part-time $143 per credit hour. Tuition, nonresident: full-time $10,398; part-time $433 per credit hour. Required fees: $724; $44 per credit hour. *Financial support:* Federal Work-Study, institutionally sponsored loans, health care benefits, and unspecified assistantships available. Financial award application deadline: 3/15; financial award applicants required to submit FAFSA. *Unit head:* Dr. Jean Morrow, Chair, Department of Early Childhood/Elementary Teacher Education, 620-341-5766, E-mail: jmorrow@emporia.edu.

Evangel University, Department of Education, Springfield, MO 65802-2191. Offers educational leadership (M Ed); reading education (M Ed); secondary teaching (M Ed); teaching (MA). Part-time and evening/weekend programs available. *Faculty:* 4 full-time (2 women), 6 part-time/adjunct (5 women). *Students:* 2 full-time (both women), 17 part-time (14 women); includes 2 minority (1 Asian American or Pacific Islander, 1 Hispanic American). Average age 26. 10 applicants, 100% accepted, 10 enrolled. In 2006, 13 degrees awarded. *Degree requirements:* For master's, thesis optional. *Entrance requirements:* For master's, PRAXIS II (preferred), GRE (accepted). Additional exam requirements/recommendations for international students: Required—TOEFL (minimum score 550 paper-based; 213 computer-based). *Application deadline:* For fall admission, 7/15 priority date for domestic students; for spring admission, 11/15 priority date for domestic students. Applications are processed on a rolling basis. Application fee: $25. *Financial support:* In 2006–07, 6 students received support. Career-related internships or fieldwork, institutionally sponsored loans, and scholarships/grants available. Support available to part-time students. Financial award application deadline: 3/1; financial award applicants required to submit FAFSA. *Unit head:* Dr. Jeff Hittenberger, Chair, 417-865-2815 Ext. 8559, E-mail: hittenbergerj@evangel.edu. *Application contact:* Charity H. Fahlstrom, Director of Graduate and Professional Studies Admissions, 417-865-2811 Ext. 1227, Fax: 417-575-5484.

Fairfield University, Graduate School of Education and Allied Professions, Department of Curriculum and Instruction, Fairfield, CT 06824-5195. Offers elementary education (MA); secondary education (MA); teaching and foundations (MA, CAS). Part-time and evening/weekend programs available. *Faculty:* 5 full-time (4 women), 5 part-time/adjunct (3 women). *Students:* 58 full-time (43 women), 98 part-time (81 women). Average age 28. 49 applicants, 55% accepted, 20 enrolled. In 2006, 45 master's, 1 other advanced degree awarded. *Degree requirements:* For master's, thesis or alternative, educational technology course, comprehensive exam. *Entrance requirements:* For master's, PRAXIS I (PPST), minimum QPA of 2.67, 2 recommendations, resumè. Additional exam requirements/recommendations for international students: Required—TOEFL (minimum score 550 paper-based; 213 computer-based). *Application deadline:* For fall admission, 3/1 for domestic students; for spring admission, 10/15 for domestic students. Applications are processed on a rolling basis. Application fee: $55. Electronic applications accepted. *Financial support:* Tuition waivers (partial) and unspecified assistantships available. Support available to part-time students. Financial award applicants required to submit FAFSA. *Faculty research:* Participatory action research, adolescent homosexuality, assessment of student teachers, supervision and staff development, writing process, Piaget. *Unit head:* Dr. Wendy R. Kohli, Chair, 203-254-4000 Ext. 2286, Fax: 203-254-4047, E-mail: wkohli@mail.fairfield.edu. *Application contact:* Marianne Gumpper, Director of Graduate and Continuing Studies Admissions, 203-254-4184, Fax: 203-254-4073, E-mail: gradadmis@mail.fairfield.edu.

Fayetteville State University, Graduate School, Program in Middle Grades, Secondary and Special Education, Fayetteville, NC 28301-4298. Offers biology (MA Ed); history (MA Ed); mathematics (MA Ed); middle grades (MA Ed); political science (MA Ed); reading (MA Ed); sociology (MA Ed); special education (MA Ed), including behavioral-emotional handicaps, mentally handicapped, specific training disability. *Accreditation:* NCATE. Part-time and evening/weekend programs available. *Faculty:* 19 full-time (12 women), 3 part-time/adjunct (2 women). *Students:* 14 full-time (10 women), 48 part-time (40 women); includes 44 minority (40 African Americans, 2 American Indian/Alaska Native, 1 Asian American or Pacific Islander, 1 Hispanic American). Average age 39. 16 applicants, 100% accepted, 16 enrolled. In 2006, 33 degrees awarded. *Degree requirements:* For master's, internship. *Application deadline:* For fall admission, 7/1 for domestic students; for spring admission, 12/1 for domestic students. Applications are processed on a rolling basis. Application fee: $25. Electronic applications accepted. *Expenses:* Tuition, state resident: full-time $2,118. Tuition, nonresident: full-time $11,708. Required fees: $1,099. Tuition and fees vary according to course load. *Unit head:* Dr. Charletta Barringer-Brown, Interim Chair, 910-672-1182, E-mail: cbarringerbrown@uncfsu.edu.

Fitchburg State College, Division of Graduate and Continuing Education, Program in Secondary Education, Fitchburg, MA 01420-2697. Offers M Ed. *Accreditation:* NCATE. Part-time and evening/weekend programs available. *Students:* Average age 33. 5 applicants, 100% accepted, 4 enrolled. In 2006, 8 degrees awarded. *Entrance requirements:* For master's, GRE General Test or MAT, teaching certificate, letters of recommendation, resumé. Additional exam requirements/recommendations for international students: Required—TOEFL (minimum score 550 paper-based; 213 computer-based; 79 iBT). *Application deadline:* Applications are processed on a rolling basis. Application fee: $25 ($50 for international students). *Expenses:* Tuition, state resident: part-time $150 per credit. Tuition, nonresident: part-time $150 per credit. Required fees: $90 per credit. *Financial support:* In 2006–07, research assistantships with partial tuition reimbursements (averaging $5,500 per year); Federal Work-Study, scholarships/grants, and unspecified assistantships also available. Support available to part-time students. Financial award application deadline: 3/1; financial award applicants required to submit FAFSA. *Unit head:* Dr. Nancy Kelly, Chair, 978-665-3447, Fax: 978-665-3658, E-mail: gce@fsc.edu. *Application contact:* Director of Admissions, 978-665-3144, Fax: 978-665-4540, E-mail: admissions@fsc.edu.

Florida Agricultural and Mechanical University, Division of Graduate Studies, Research, and Continuing Education, College of Education, Program in Secondary Education and Foundation, Tallahassee, FL 32307-3200. Offers biology (M Ed); chemistry (MS Ed); English (MS Ed); history (MS Ed); math (MS Ed); physics (MS Ed). *Accreditation:* NCATE. *Degree requirements:* For master's, thesis (for some programs). *Entrance requirements:* For master's, GRE General Test, minimum GPA of 3.0. Additional exam requirements/recommendations for international students: Required—TOEFL.

Florida Gulf Coast University, College of Education, Program in Secondary Education, Fort Myers, FL 33965-6565. Offers biology (MAT); English (MAT); mathematics (MAT); social sciences (MAT). Part-time and evening/weekend programs available. *Faculty:* 31 full-time (21 women), 30 part-time/adjunct (24 women). *Entrance requirements:* For master's, GRE General Test, MAT, minimum GPA of 3.0. Additional exam requirements/recommendations for international students: Required—TOEFL (minimum score 550 paper-based; 213 computer-based). *Application deadline:* For fall admission, 7/1 priority date for domestic students; for spring admission, 10/15 for domestic students. Applications are processed on a rolling basis. Application fee: $30. Electronic applications accepted. *Expenses:* Tuition, state resident: full-time $4,326. Tuition, nonresident: full-time $18,523. Required fees: $1,211. One-time fee: $5 full-time. *Faculty research:* Integration of technology in the classroom, year-round schools, school choice, virtual high schools. *Unit head:* Dr. Pat Wachholz, Associate Dean, 239-590-7808, Fax: 239-590-7801, E-mail: wachhol@fgcu.edu.

Fordham University, Graduate School of Education, Division of Curriculum and Teaching, New York, NY 10023. Offers adult education (MS, MSE); bilingual teacher education (MSE); curriculum and teaching (MSE); early childhood education (MSE); elementary education (MST); language, literacy, and learning (PhD); reading education (MSE, Adv C); secondary education (MAT, MSE); special education (MSE, Adv C); teaching English as a second language (MSE). *Accreditation:* NCATE. *Faculty:* 22 full-time (18 women), 38 part-time/adjunct (28 women). *Students:* 68 full-time (51 women), 663 part-time (612 women); includes 200 minority (74 African Americans, 1 American Indian/Alaska Native, 37 Asian Americans or Pacific Islanders, 88 Hispanic Americans), 3 international. Average age 32. 636 applicants, 86% accepted, 322 enrolled. In 2006, 351 master's, 8 doctorates awarded. *Degree requirements:* For doctorate and Adv C, thesis/dissertation. *Entrance requirements:* For doctorate, MAT, GRE General Test. Application fee: $65. *Financial support:* Applicants required to submit FAFSA. *Unit head:* Dr. Terry Osborn, Chairperson, 212-636-6450.

Fort Hays State University, Graduate School, College of Education and Technology, Department of Teacher Education, Program in Secondary Education, Hays, KS 67601-4099. Offers MS. *Accreditation:* NCATE. *Faculty:* 8 full-time (6 women). *Students:* Average age 35. In 2006, 5 degrees awarded. *Degree requirements:* For master's, comprehensive exam. *Entrance requirements:* Additional exam requirements/recommendations for international students: Required—TOEFL (minimum score 550 paper-based; 213 computer-based). *Application deadline:* For fall admission, 7/1 priority date for domestic students. Applications are processed on a rolling basis. Application fee: $35. Electronic applications accepted. *Financial support:* Research assistantships, teaching assistantships available. *Faculty research:* Special education, testing out secondary gifted, effect of parent attitudes on student performances, severe

Secondary Education

Fort Hays State University (continued)
behavior disorders (treatments), consulting. *Unit head:* Dr. Germaine Taggart, Interim Dean, Department of Teacher Education, 785-628-4204, E-mail: gtaggart@fhsu.edu.

Francis Marion University, Graduate Programs, School of Education, Florence, SC 29501-0547. Offers early childhood education (M Ed); elementary education (M Ed); learning disabilities (M Ed, MAT); remedial education (M Ed); secondary education (M Ed). *Accreditation:* NCATE. Part-time programs available. *Faculty:* 19 full-time (11 women), 1 part-time/adjunct (0 women). *Students:* 11 full-time (8 women), 158 part-time (141 women); includes 54 minority (all African Americans), 1 international. Average age 34. 248 applicants, 100% accepted. In 2006, 91 degrees awarded. *Degree requirements:* For master's, comprehensive exam. *Entrance requirements:* For master's, GRE General Test, MAT, NTE, or PRAXIS II. *Application deadline:* For fall admission, 4/15 priority date for domestic students; for spring admission, 10/15 priority date for domestic students. Applications are processed on a rolling basis. Application fee: $30. *Expenses:* Tuition, state resident: full-time $6,527; part-time $326 per credit hour. Tuition, nonresident: full-time $13,054; part-time $653 per credit hour. Required fees: $185; $5 per credit hour. $45 per term. *Financial support:* In 2006–07, 3 research assistantships (averaging $6,000 per year) were awarded; unspecified assistantships also available. Support available to part-time students. Financial award application deadline: 3/1; financial award applicants required to submit FAFSA. *Faculty research:* Identification and alternate assessment of at-risk students. *Unit head:* Dr. James R. Faulkenberry, Dean, 843-661-1460, Fax: 843-661-4647.

Friends University, Graduate School, Division of Science, Arts, and Education, Program in Teaching, Wichita, KS 67213. Offers elementary education (MAT); secondary education (MAT). *Accreditation:* NCATE. Evening/weekend programs available. Postbaccalaureate distance learning degree programs offered (minimal on-campus study). *Faculty:* 1 (woman) full-time, 5 part-time/adjunct (2 women). *Students:* 79 full-time. In 2006, 32 degrees awarded. *Entrance requirements:* Additional exam requirements/recommendations for international students: Required—TOEFL (minimum score 560 paper-based; 220 computer-based). *Application deadline:* For fall admission, 3/15 priority date for domestic and international students; for spring admission, 12/15 priority date for domestic and international students. Applications are processed on a rolling basis. Application fee: $45 ($65 for international students). Electronic applications accepted. *Unit head:* Dr. Dona Gibson, Director, 800-794-6945 Ext. 5826. *Application contact:* Craig Davis, Executive Director of Recruitment-Adult and Graduate Studies, 800-794-6945 Ext. 5573, Fax: 316-295-5050, E-mail: cdavis@friends.edu.

Frostburg State University, Graduate School, College of Education, Department of Educational Professions, Program in Curriculum and Instruction, Frostburg, MD 21532-1099. Offers educational technology (M Ed); elementary education (M Ed); secondary education (M Ed). Part-time and evening/weekend programs available. *Degree requirements:* For master's, thesis or alternative. *Entrance requirements:* For master's, teaching certificate. Electronic applications accepted.

Frostburg State University, Graduate School, College of Education, Department of Educational Professions, Program in Secondary Teaching, Frostburg, MD 21532-1099. Offers MAT. *Entrance requirements:* For master's, PRAXIS I, entry portfolio.

Gallaudet University, The Graduate School, School of Education and Human Services, Department of Education, Washington, DC 20002-3625. Offers early childhood education (MA, Ed S); education of deaf and hard of hearing students and multihandicapped deaf and hard of hearing students (MA, Ed S); elementary education (MA, Ed S); individualized program of study (PhD); parent/infant specialty (MA, Ed S); secondary education (MA, Ed S). *Accreditation:* NCATE. *Degree requirements:* For master's, thesis optional; for doctorate, thesis/dissertation. *Entrance requirements:* For master's, GRE General Test or MAT; for doctorate, GRE General Test or MAT, interview.

George Mason University, Graduate School of Education, Programs in Curriculum and Instruction, Fairfax, VA 22030. Offers bilingual/multicultural/English as a second language education (M Ed); early childhood education (M Ed); instructional technology (M Ed); middle education (M Ed); reading (M Ed); secondary education (M Ed); special education (M Ed). Part-time and evening/weekend programs available. *Faculty:* 108 full-time (70 women), 193 part-time/adjunct (140 women). *Students:* 185 full-time (144 women), 816 part-time (683 women); includes 148 minority (46 African Americans, 2 American Indian/Alaska Native, 44 Asian Americans or Pacific Islanders, 56 Hispanic Americans), 28 international. Average age 34. 822 applicants, 72% accepted, 473 enrolled. In 2006, 606 master's awarded. *Entrance requirements:* For master's, minimum GPA of 3.0 in last 60 hours. *Application deadline:* For fall admission, 5/1 for domestic students; for spring admission, 11/1 for domestic students. Application fee: $60 ($75 for international students). Electronic applications accepted. *Expenses:* Tuition, state resident: full-time $5,724; part-time $238 per credit. Tuition, nonresident: full-time $16,896; part-time $704 per credit. Required fees: $1,656; $69 per credit. *Financial support:* Career-related internships or fieldwork available. Support available to part-time students. Financial award application deadline: 3/1; financial award applicants required to submit FAFSA. *Unit head:* Martin E. Ford, Senior Associate Dean, 703-993-2008.

The George Washington University, Graduate School of Education and Human Development, Department of Teacher Preparation and Special Education, Program in Secondary Education, Washington, DC 20052. Offers M Ed. *Accreditation:* NCATE. *Degree requirements:* For master's, comprehensive exam. *Entrance requirements:* For master's, GRE General Test or MAT, interview, minimum GPA of 2.75.

Georgia College & State University, Graduate School, School of Education, Department of Foundations and Secondary Education, Milledgeville, GA 31061. Offers English education (M Ed); instructional technology (M Ed); mathematics education (M Ed); natural science education (M Ed, Ed S); secondary education (MAT); social science education (M Ed, Ed S). *Accreditation:* NCATE. *Students:* 49 full-time (33 women), 66 part-time (47 women); includes 13 minority (11 African Americans, 2 Hispanic Americans), 2 international. Average age 32. 75 applicants, 27% accepted, 9 enrolled. In 2006, 83 master's awarded. *Degree requirements:* For master's and Ed S, comprehensive exam. *Entrance requirements:* For master's, GRE General Test or MAT, 2 letters of recommendation; for Ed S, GRE General Test or MAT, master's degree, 2 letters of recommendation, 2 years teaching experience. Additional exam requirements/recommendations for international students: Required—TOEFL. *Application deadline:* For fall admission, 7/1 priority date for domestic students. Applications are processed on a rolling basis. Application fee: $25. Electronic applications accepted. *Expenses:* Tuition, state resident: full-time $3,222; part-time $179 per credit hour. Tuition, nonresident: full-time $12,870; part-time $715 per credit hour. Required fees: $391 per semester. Tuition and fees vary according to course load. *Financial support:* In 2006–07, 10 research assistantships (averaging $3,800 per year) were awarded; career-related internships or fieldwork and Federal Work-Study also available. Support available to part-time students. Financial award application deadline: 3/15. *Unit head:* Dr. Cynthia Alby, Chair/MAT Cohort Leader, 478-445-2513, Fax: 478-445-7362, E-mail: cynthia.alby@gcsu.edu.

Georgia Southwestern State University, Graduate Studies, School of Education, Americus, GA 31709-4693. Offers early childhood education (M Ed, Ed S); health and physical education (M Ed); middle grades education (M Ed, Ed S); reading (M Ed); secondary education (M Ed); special education (M Ed). *Accreditation:* NCATE. *Degree requirements:* For master's, comprehensive exam. *Entrance requirements:* For master's, GRE General Test or MAT, minimum GPA of 2.5; for Ed S, GRE General Test or MAT, minimum graduate GPA of 3.25, M Ed from accredited college or university, 3 years teaching experience. Electronic applications accepted.

Grand Canyon University, College of Education, Phoenix, AZ 85017-1097. Offers elementary education (M Ed, MA); reading education (MA); secondary education (M Ed); teaching (MAT); teaching English as a second language (MA). Part-time and evening/weekend programs available. Postbaccalaureate distance learning degree programs offered (no on-campus study). *Degree requirements:* For master's, publishable research paper (M Ed). *Entrance requirements:* For master's, MAT, GRE or minimum GPA of 3.0.

See Close-Up on page 885.

Greenville College, Program in Education, Greenville, IL 62246-0159. Offers education (MAT); elementary education (MAE); secondary education (MAE). *Degree requirements:* For master's, thesis (for some programs). *Entrance requirements:* For master's, GRE, Illinois Basic Skills Test, teacher certification. Electronic applications accepted.

Harding University, College of Education, Searcy, AR 72149-0001. Offers advanced studies in teaching and learning (M Ed); art (MSE); behavioral science (MSE); Bible and religion (MSE); counseling (MS, Ed S); early childhood education (M Ed); early childhood special education (M Ed, MSE); education (MSE); educational leadership (M Ed, Ed S); elementary education (M Ed); English (MSE); family and consumer science (MSE); French (MSE); history/social science (MSE); kinesiology (MSE); math (MSE); physical science (MSE); reading (M Ed); secondary education (M Ed); Spanish (MSE); special education licensure (M Ed); teaching (MAT). *Accreditation:* NCATE. Part-time programs available. *Faculty:* 8 full-time (2 women), 45 part-time/adjunct (30 women). *Students:* 153 full-time (123 women), 469 part-time (341 women); includes 72 minority (63 African Americans, 4 American Indian/Alaska Native, 1 Asian American or Pacific Islander, 4 Hispanic Americans), 9 international. Average age 35. 175 applicants, 90% accepted, 147 enrolled. In 2006, 241 degrees awarded. *Degree requirements:* For master's, portfolio(s), thesis optional; for Ed S, portfolio, specialist project. *Entrance requirements:* For master's, GRE, MAT, PRAXIS; for Ed S, MAT or GRE. Additional exam requirements/recommendations for international students: Required—TOEFL (minimum score 550 paper-based). *Application deadline:* For fall admission, 8/1 for domestic and international students; for spring admission, 1/1 for domestic and international students. Applications are processed on a rolling basis. Application fee: $35. *Expenses:* Tuition: Part-time $455 per semester hour. Required fees: $20 per semester hour. Tuition and fees vary according to course load. *Financial support:* Scholarships/grants and unspecified assistantships available. Support available to part-time students. *Faculty research:* Reading, comprehension, school violence, educational technology, behavior, college choice, differentiated instruction, brain based teaching. *Unit head:* Pat Bashaw, Chair, 501-279-4183, Fax: 501-279-4051, E-mail: pbashaw@harding.edu.

Hawai'i Pacific University, Program in Secondary Education, Honolulu, HI 96813. Offers M Ed. *Faculty:* 12 full-time (6 women). *Students:* 24 full-time (13 women), 28 part-time (13 women); includes 25 minority (1 American Indian/Alaska Native, 22 Asian Americans or Pacific Islanders, 2 Hispanic Americans), 1 international. Average age 28. 46 applicants, 65% accepted, 22 enrolled. *Degree requirements:* For master's, thesis. *Entrance requirements:* For master's, PRAXIS I and II. Additional exam requirements/recommendations for international students: Recommended—TOEFL (minimum score 550 paper-based; 213 computer-based), TWE (minimum score 5). *Application deadline:* For fall admission, 2/15 priority date for domestic students; for spring admission, 10/15 priority date for domestic students. Applications are processed on a rolling basis. Application fee: $50. Electronic applications accepted. *Expenses:* Tuition: Full-time $10,080; part-time $560 per credit. *Financial support:* In 2006–07, 31 students received support. Career-related internships or fieldwork, Federal Work-Study, scholarships/grants, and unspecified assistantships available. Support available to part-time students. Financial award application deadline: 3/1. *Unit head:* Dr. Valentina Abordonado, Director, Teacher Education Program, 808-544-1143, Fax: 808-544-0841, E-mail: vabordonado@hpu.edu. *Application contact:* Danny Lam, Assistant Director of Graduate Admissions, 808-544-1135, Fax: 808-544-0280, E-mail: graduate@hpu.edu.

See Close-Up on page 1277.

Hofstra University, School of Education and Allied Human Services, Department of Counseling, Research, Special Education and Rehabilitation, Program in Special Education, Hempstead, NY 11549. Offers early childhood special education (MS Ed, Advanced Certificate); gifted education (Advanced Certificate); inclusive early childhood special education (MS Ed); inclusive elementary special education (MS Ed); inclusive secondary special education (MS Ed); literacy studies and special education (MS Ed); special education (MA, MS Ed, PD); special education assessment and diagnosis (Advanced Certificate); teaching students with severe/multiple disabilities (Advanced Certificate). *Accreditation:* NCATE. Part-time and evening/weekend programs available. Postbaccalaureate distance learning degree programs offered. *Students:* 87 full-time (82 women), 116 part-time (110 women); includes 21 minority (8 African Americans, 4 Asian Americans or Pacific Islanders, 9 Hispanic Americans). Average age 28. 110 applicants, 79% accepted, 61 enrolled. In 2006, 74 master's, 7 other advanced degrees awarded. *Degree requirements:* For master's, thesis (for some programs), seminars, student teaching, comprehensive exam (for some programs), registration; for other advanced degree, fieldwork. *Entrance requirements:* For master's, interview, 3 letters of reference, resumé, minimum GPA of 3.0; for other advanced degree, interview, 3 letters of recommendation, resumé. Additional exam requirements/recommendations for international students: Required—TOEFL (minimum score 550 paper-based; 213 computer-based). *Application deadline:* Applications are processed on a rolling basis. Application fee: $60. Electronic applications accepted. *Expenses:* Tuition: Full-time $13,320; part-time $740 per credit. Required fees: $930; $155 per term. *Financial support:* In 2006–07, 64 students received support, including 6 fellowships with tuition reimbursements available (averaging $2,552 per year), 4 research assistantships with full and partial tuition reimbursements available (averaging $4,378 per year); Federal Work-Study, scholarships/grants, tuition waivers (full and partial), and unspecified assistantships also available. Support available to part-time students. Financial award applicants required to submit FAFSA. *Faculty research:* Inclusive schooling, autism spectrum disorders related services, parent participation in the special education process, co-teaching student teaching. *Unit head:* Dr. George Guiliani, Director, 516-463-5778, Fax: 516-463-6184, E-mail: cprdcs@hofstra.edu. *Application contact:* Carol Drummer, Dean of Graduate Admissions, 516-463-4876, Fax: 516-463-4664, E-mail: gradstudent@hofstra.edu.

Holy Family University, Graduate School, School of Education, Philadelphia, PA 19114-2094. Offers education (M Ed); elementary education (M Ed); reading specialist (M Ed); secondary education (M Ed). Part-time and evening/weekend programs available. *Degree requirements:* For master's, thesis optional. *Entrance requirements:* For master's, GRE or MAT, interview. *Faculty research:* Cognition, developmental issues, sociological issues in education.

Hood College, Graduate School, Department of Education, Frederick, MD 21701-8575. Offers curriculum and instruction (MS), including early childhood education, elementary education, elementary school science and mathematics, secondary education, special education; educational leadership (MS); reading specialization (MS); teaching the struggling reader (Certificate). Part-time and evening/weekend programs available. *Faculty:* 4 full-time (3 women), 32 part-time/adjunct (16 women). *Students:* 5 full-time (3 women), 371 part-time (313 women); includes 30 minority (23 African Americans, 4 Asian Americans or Pacific Islanders, 3 Hispanic Americans). Average age 32. 71 applicants, 99% accepted, 59 enrolled. In 2006, 67 degrees awarded. *Degree requirements:* For master's, action research project, portfolio (reading). *Entrance requirements:* For master's, minimum GPA of 2.5, teaching certification. *Application deadline:* Applications are processed on a rolling basis. Application fee: $35. *Expenses:* Tuition: Part-time $350 per credit. Required fees: $20 per semester. *Financial support:* Applicants required to submit FAFSA. *Faculty research:* Leadership, action research, brain research, learning styles. *Unit head:* Dr. John George, Chairperson, 301-696-3471, Fax: 301-696-3597, E-mail: george@hood.edu. *Application contact:* Dr. Kathleen C. Bands, Associate Dean of Graduate School, 301-696-3811, Fax: 301-696-3597, E-mail: gofurther@hood.edu.

Howard University, School of Education, Department of Curriculum and Instruction, Program in Secondary Education, Washington, DC 20059-0002. Offers M Ed, MA, MAT, CAGS. MA offered through the Graduate School of Arts and Sciences. *Accreditation:* NCATE. *Faculty:* 3 full-time (2 women). *Students:* 4 full-time (2 women), 22 part-time (17 women); includes 22 minority (19 African Americans, 2 Asian Americans or Pacific Islanders, 1 Hispanic American). Average age 26. 54 applicants, 50% accepted, 17 enrolled. In 2006, 2 degrees awarded. *Degree requirements:* For master's, thesis (for some programs), expository writing exam, internships, practicum, comprehensive exam. *Entrance requirements:* For master's, GRE General Test (MA), minimum GPA of 2.7. *Application deadline:* For fall admission, 4/1 priority date for domestic students; for spring admission, 11/1 for domestic students. Applications are processed on a rolling basis. Application fee: $45. *Financial support:* Fellowships, research assistantships, teaching assistantships, career-related internships or fieldwork, Federal Work-Study, institutionally sponsored loans, scholarships/grants, and unspecified assistantships available. Financial award application deadline: 4/1. *Unit head:* Dr. Gerunda B. Hughes, Associate Professor/Coordinator, 202-806-6501, Fax: 202-806-5297, E-mail: ghughes@howard.edu.

Hunter College of the City University of New York, Graduate School, School of Arts and Sciences, Department of Mathematics and Statistics, New York, NY 10021-5085. Offers applied mathematics (MA); mathematics for secondary education (MA); pure mathematics (MA). Part-time and evening/weekend programs available. *Faculty:* 1 full-time (0 women), 19 part-time/adjunct (9 women). *Students:* 5 full-time (3 women), 24 part-time (10 women); includes 12 minority (1 African American, 8 Asian Americans or Pacific Islanders, 3 Hispanic Americans). Average age 34. 46 applicants, 50% accepted, 16 enrolled. In 2006, 17 degrees awarded. *Degree requirements:* For master's, one foreign language, thesis (for some programs), comprehensive exam. *Entrance requirements:* For master's, GRE General Test, 24 credits in mathematics. Additional exam requirements/recommendations for international students: Required—TOEFL. *Application deadline:* For fall admission, 4/1 for domestic students, 2/1 for international students; for spring admission, 11/1 for domestic students, 9/1 for international students. Application fee: $125. *Expenses:* Tuition, state resident: full-time $3,200; part-time $270 per credit. Tuition, nonresident: part-time $500 per credit. Required fees: $45 per semester. *Financial support:* Federal Work-Study, institutionally sponsored loans, scholarships/grants, and tuition waivers (partial) available. Support available to part-time students. *Faculty research:* Data analysis, dynamical systems, computer graphics, topology, statistical decision theory. *Unit head:* Ada Peluso, Chairperson, 212-772-5300, Fax: 212-772-4858, E-mail: peluso@math.hunter.cuny.edu. *Application contact:* William Zlata, Director for Graduate Admissions, 212-772-4482, Fax: 212-650-3336, E-mail: admissions@hunter.cuny.edu.

Hunter College of the City University of New York, Graduate School, School of Education, Programs in Secondary Education, New York, NY 10021-5085. Offers biology education (MA); chemistry education (MA); earth science (MA); English education (MA); French education (MA); Italian education (MA); mathematics education (MA); physics education (MA); social studies education (MA); Spanish education (MA). *Accreditation:* NCATE. *Students:* 11 full-time (9 women), 269 part-time (177 women); includes 65 minority (13 African Americans, 9 Asian Americans or Pacific Islanders, 43 Hispanic Americans). Average age 33. 183 applicants, 43% accepted, 49 enrolled. In 2006, 39 degrees awarded. *Degree requirements:* For master's, thesis. *Application deadline:* For fall admission, 4/1 for domestic students, 2/1 for international students; for spring admission, 11/1 for domestic students, 9/1 for international students. Applications are processed on a rolling basis. Application fee: $125. *Expenses:* Tuition, state resident: full-time $3,200; part-time $270 per credit. Tuition, nonresident: part-time $500 per credit. Required fees: $45 per semester. *Financial support:* Fellowships, tuition waivers (full and partial) available. Support available to part-time students. *Unit head:* Dr. Kate Garret, Coordinator, 212-772-5049, E-mail: kgarret@hunter.cuny.edu. *Application contact:* William Zlata, Director for Graduate Admissions, 212-772-4482, Fax: 212-650-3336, E-mail: admissions@hunter.cuny.edu.

Idaho State University, Office of Graduate Studies, College of Education, Department of Educational Foundations, Pocatello, ID 83209. Offers child and family studies (M Ed); curriculum leadership (M Ed); education (M Ed); educational administration (M Ed); educational foundations (5th Year Certificate); elementary education (M Ed), including K-12 education, literacy, secondary education. Part-time and evening/weekend programs available. Postbaccalaureate distance learning degree programs offered (no on-campus study). *Faculty:* 12 full-time (8 women). *Students:* 16 full-time (11 women), 161 part-time (102 women); includes 2 minority (1 Asian American or Pacific Islander, 1 Hispanic American), 2 international. Average age 40. In 2006, 15 degrees awarded. *Degree requirements:* For master's, oral exam, written exam, thesis optional; for 5th Year Certificate, thesis (for some programs), oral exam, written exam, comprehensive exam, registration (for some programs). *Entrance requirements:* For master's, GRE General Test or MAT, minimum undergraduate GPA of 3.0; for 5th Year Certificate, GRE General Test, minimum undergraduate GPA of 3.0, master's degree. Additional exam requirements/recommendations for international students: Required—TOEFL (minimum score 550 paper-based; 213 computer-based; 80 iBT). *Application deadline:* For fall admission, 7/1 for domestic students, 6/1 for international students; for spring admission, 12/1 for domestic students, 11/1 for international students. Applications are processed on a rolling basis. Application fee: $55. *Expenses:* Tuition, state resident: part-time $251 per credit. Tuition, nonresident: part-time $366 per credit. Tuition and fees vary according to degree level, program and reciprocity agreements. *Financial support:* Career-related internships or fieldwork, Federal Work-Study, institutionally sponsored loans, scholarships/grants, tuition waivers, and unspecified assistantships available. Support available to part-time students. Financial award application deadline: 1/1. *Faculty research:* Child and families studies; business education; special education; math, science, and technology education. *Unit head:* Dr. Jack Newsome, Chair, 208-282-4838, E-mail: newsjack@isu.edu. *Application contact:* Dr. Peter Denner, Assistant Dean, 208-282-3807, Fax: 208-282-4697, E-mail: dennpete@isu.edu.

Immaculata University, College of Graduate Studies, Program in Educational Leadership and Administration, Immaculata, PA 19345. Offers educational leadership and administration (MA, Ed D); elementary education (Certificate); intermediate unit director (Certificate); school principal (Certificate); school superintendent (Certificate); secondary education (Certificate); special education (Certificate). Part-time and evening/weekend programs available. *Students:* 27 full-time (15 women), 510 part-time (353 women). Average age 33. 86 applicants, 74% accepted, 53 enrolled. In 2006, 47 master's, 27 doctorates awarded. *Degree requirements:* For master's, thesis optional; for doctorate, thesis/dissertation, comprehensive exam. *Entrance requirements:* For master's, GRE or MAT, minimum GPA of 3.0; for doctorate, GRE General Test, minimum GPA of 3.5. Additional exam requirements/recommendations for international students: Required—TOEFL. Application fee: $35. *Financial support:* Application deadline:5/1. *Faculty research:* Cooperative learning, school-based management, whole language, performance assessment. *Unit head:* Sr. Carol Anne Couchara, Chair, 610-647-4400 Ext. 3280, E-mail: ccouchara@immaculata.edu. *Application contact:* 610-647-4400 Ext. 3211, Fax: 610-993-8550, E-mail: graduate@immaculata.edu.

Indiana University Bloomington, School of Education, Department of Curriculum and Instruction, Bloomington, IN 47405-7000. Offers art education (MS, Ed D, PhD); curriculum studies (Ed D, PhD); elementary education (MS, Ed D, PhD, Ed S); mathematics education (MS, Ed D, PhD); science education (MS, Ed D, PhD); secondary education (MS, Ed D, PhD); social studies education (MS, PhD); special education (MS, Ed D, PhD, Ed S). PhD offered through the University Graduate School. *Accreditation:* NCATE. Part-time and evening/weekend programs available. *Students:* 39 full-time (28 women), 82 part-time (54 women); includes 15 minority (5 African Americans, 1 American Indian/Alaska Native, 6 Asian Americans or Pacific Islanders, 3 Hispanic Americans), 33 international. Average age 37. In 2006, 1 degree awarded. Terminal master's awarded for partial completion of doctoral program. *Degree requirements:* For doctorate, thesis/dissertation; for Ed S, comprehensive exam or project. *Entrance requirements:* For master's, doctorate, and Ed S, GRE General Test. *Application deadline:* For fall admission, 6/1 priority date for domestic students, 3/1 for international students; for winter admission, 11/1 priority date for domestic students; for spring admission, 9/1 for international students. Applications are processed on a rolling basis. Application fee: $50 ($60 for international students). Electronic applications accepted. *Expenses:* Tuition, state resident: full-time $5,791; part-time $241 per credit hour. Tuition, nonresident: full-time $16,866; part-time $703 per credit hour. *Financial support:* Fellowships with full and partial tuition reimbursements, research assistantships with full and partial tuition reimbursements, teaching assistantships with full and partial tuition reimbursements, career-related internships or fieldwork, Federal Work-Study, institutionally sponsored loans, and tuition waivers (partial) available. Support available to part-time students. *Unit head:* Cary Buzzelli, Chairperson, 812-856-8100. *Application contact:* Bobbie Partenheimer, Admissions Services Coordinator, 812-856-8127, Fax: 812-856-8333, E-mail: partenhe@indiana.edu.

Indiana University Kokomo, Division of Education, Kokomo, IN 46904-9003. Offers elementary education (MS); secondary education (MS). *Accreditation:* NCATE. Part-time and evening/weekend programs available. *Faculty:* 1 full-time (0 women). *Students:* Average age 32. In 2006, 3 degrees awarded. *Degree requirements:* For master's, research project, thesis optional. *Entrance requirements:* For master's, GRE General Test, minimum GPA of 2.5. *Application deadline:* For fall admission, 8/1 for domestic students; for spring admission, 12/1 for domestic students. Applications are processed on a rolling basis. Application fee: $40 ($50 for international students). *Expenses:* Tuition, state resident: full-time $4,391; part-time $183 per hour. Tuition, nonresident: full-time $10,043; part-time $418 per hour. Tuition and fees vary according to course load, campus/location and program. *Financial support:* Minority teacher scholarships available. *Faculty research:* Reading, teaching effectiveness, portfolio, curriculum development. *Unit head:* D. Antonio Cantu, Dean, 765-455-9287, Fax: 765-455-9503. *Application contact:* Charlotte Miller, Coordinator Educational/Student Resources, 765-455-9367, Fax: 765-455-9503, E-mail: cmiller@iuk.edu.

Indiana University Northwest, School of Education, Gary, IN 46408-1197. Offers elementary education (MS Ed); secondary education (MS Ed). *Accreditation:* NCATE. Part-time and evening/weekend programs available. *Faculty:* 5 full-time (2 women). *Students:* 3 full-time (all women), 64 part-time (49 women); includes 26 minority (23 African Americans, 3 Hispanic Americans). Average age 40. In 2006, 36 degrees awarded. *Degree requirements:* For master's, registration. *Entrance requirements:* For master's, GRE General Test or MAT, minimum GPA of 3.0. *Application deadline:* For fall admission, 7/15 priority date for domestic students; for spring admission, 11/15 for domestic students. Application fee: $25. *Expenses:* Tuition, state resident: full-time $4,332; part-time $181 per credit hour. Tuition, nonresident: full-time $10,081; part-time $420 per credit hour. Tuition and fees vary according to course load, campus/location and program. *Unit head:* Dr. Stanley E. Wigle, Dean, 219-980-6510, Fax: 219-981-4208, E-mail: amsanche@iun.edu.

Indiana University–Purdue University Fort Wayne, School of Education, Department of Educational Studies, Fort Wayne, IN 46805-1499. Offers elementary education (MS Ed); secondary education (MS Ed). *Accreditation:* NCATE. Part-time programs available. *Faculty:* 14 full-time (10 women). *Students:* 5 full-time (4 women), 117 part-time (93 women); includes 8 minority (5 African Americans, 3 Hispanic Americans), 1 international. Average age 40. 66 applicants, 100% accepted, 59 enrolled. In 2006, 37 degrees awarded. *Entrance requirements:* For master's, minimum GPA of 2.5. Additional exam requirements/recommendations for international students: Required—TOEFL (minimum score 600 paper-based; 260 computer-based). *Application deadline:* For fall admission, 7/1 priority date for domestic students; for spring admission, 12/1 for domestic students. Applications are processed on a rolling basis. Application fee: $30. *Expenses:* Tuition, state resident: full-time $4,039; part-time $224 per credit. Tuition, nonresident: full-time $9,220; part-time $512 per credit. Required fees: $429; $24 per credit. Tuition and fees vary according to course load. *Financial support:* Teaching assistantships with partial tuition reimbursements, scholarships/grants available. Support available to part-time students. Financial award application deadline: 3/1; financial award applicants required to submit FAFSA. *Unit head:* Dr. Joe Nichols, Chair, 260-481-6445, E-mail: nicholsj@ipfw.edu. *Application contact:* Vicky L. Schmidt, Graduate Recorder, 260-481-6450, Fax: 260-481-5408, E-mail: schmidt@ipfw.edu.

Indiana University South Bend, School of Education, South Bend, IN 46634-7111. Offers counseling and human services (MS Ed); elementary education (MS Ed); secondary education (MS Ed); special education (MS Ed). *Accreditation:* NCATE. Part-time and evening/weekend programs available. *Faculty:* 21 full-time (11 women), 9 part-time/adjunct (3 women). *Students:* 58 full-time (38 women), 237 part-time (186 women); includes 33 minority (22 African Americans, 1 American Indian/Alaska Native, 6 Asian Americans or Pacific Islanders, 4 Hispanic Americans), 5 international. Average age 35. 127 applicants, 100% accepted, 61 enrolled. In 2006, 141 degrees awarded. *Degree requirements:* For master's, thesis or alternative, exit project. *Entrance requirements:* For master's, letters of recommendation, GRE or minimum GPA of 3.0. Additional exam requirements/recommendations for international students: Required—TOEFL. *Application deadline:* For fall admission, 7/1 for domestic students; for spring admission, 11/1 for domestic students. Applications are processed on a rolling basis. Application fee: $45. Electronic applications accepted. *Expenses:* Tuition, state resident: full-time $4,450; part-time $185 per credit hour. Tuition, nonresident: full-time $10,954; part-time $456 per credit hour. Tuition and fees vary according to course load, campus/location and program. *Financial support:* Career-related internships or fieldwork available. Support available to part-time students. Financial award application deadline: 3/1; financial award applicants required to submit FAFSA. *Faculty research:* Professional dispositions, early childhood literacy, online learning, program assessments, problem-based learning. *Unit head:* Dr. Michael Horvath, Professor and Dean, School of Education, 574-520-4339, Fax: 574-520-4550. *Application contact:* Gil L. Martin, Graduate Admissions and Recruitment Officer, 574-520-4585, Fax: 574-520-5549, E-mail: marting@iusb.edu.

Indiana University Southeast, School of Education, New Albany, IN 47150-6405. Offers counselor education (MS Ed); elementary education (MS Ed); secondary education (MS Ed). *Accreditation:* NCATE. Part-time and evening/weekend programs available. *Students:* 5 full-time (4 women), 339 part-time (275 women); includes 19 minority (17 African Americans, 1 Asian American or Pacific Islander, 1 Hispanic American). Average age 32. In 2006, 176 degrees awarded. *Degree requirements:* For master's, registration. *Entrance requirements:* For master's, minimum undergraduate GPA of 2.5, graduate 3.0. *Application deadline:* Applications are processed on a rolling basis. Application fee: $30. *Expenses:* Tuition, state resident: full-time $4,458; part-time $186 per credit hour. Tuition, nonresident: full-time $10,196; part-time $425 per credit hour. Tuition and fees vary according to course load, campus/location and program. *Financial support:* In 2006–07, 29 students received support. Career-related internships or fieldwork, Federal Work-Study, and institutionally sponsored loans available. Support available to part-time students. Financial award applicants required to submit FAFSA. *Faculty research:* Learning styles, technology, constructivism, group process, innovative math strategies. *Unit head:* Dr. Gloria Murray, Dean, 812-941-2385, Fax: 812-941-2667, E-mail: soeinfo@ius.edu.

Iona College, School of Arts and Science, Program in Adolescence Education, New Rochelle, NY 10801-1890. Offers biology education (MS Ed, MST); English education (MS Ed, MST); mathematics education (MS Ed, MST); social studies education (MS Ed, MST); Spanish education (MS Ed, MST). *Accreditation:* NCATE. Part-time and evening/weekend programs available. *Faculty:* 11 full-time (6 women), 21 part-time/adjunct (13 women). *Students:* 15 full-time (9 women), 68 part-time (52 women); includes 6 minority (1 African American, 1 Asian American or Pacific Islander, 4 Hispanic Americans). Average age 28. 42 applicants, 57% accepted, 11 enrolled. In 2006, 29 degrees awarded. *Degree requirements:* For master's, thesis or alternative. *Entrance requirements:* For master's, minimum GPA of 2.5 (MST), New York teaching certificate (MS Ed). Additional exam requirements/recommendations for international students: Required—TOEFL (minimum score 550 paper-based; 213 computer-based). *Application deadline:* Applications are processed on a rolling basis. Application fee: $50. Electronic applications accepted. *Expenses:* Tuition: Part-time $665 per credit. Required fees: $150 per term. *Financial support:* Unspecified assistantships available. Support available to part-time students. *Faculty research:* Reading/writing, educational technology, administration, early literacy assessment, literacy development. *Unit head:* Dr. Patricia Antonacci, Chair, 914-633-2080, Fax: 914-633-2608, E-mail: pantonacci@iona.edu. *Application contact:* Veronica Jarek-Prinz, Graduate Admissions, 914-633-2289, Fax: 914-633-2012, E-mail: vjarekprinz@iona.edu.

Secondary Education

Ithaca College, Graduate Studies, School of Humanities and Sciences, Program in Adolescent Education, Ithaca, NY 14850-7020. Offers biology 7-12 (MAT); chemistry 7-12 (MAT); English 7-12 (MAT); French 7-12 (MAT); math 7-12 (MAT); physics 7-12 (MAT); social studies 7-12 (MAT); Spanish (MAT). *Faculty:* 14 full-time (5 women), 1 (woman) part-time/adjunct. *Students:* 8 full-time (2 women), 2 part-time (both women); includes 1 minority (Hispanic American) Average age 28. 12 applicants, 92% accepted, 10 enrolled. *Entrance requirements:* For master's, minimum GPA of 3.0. *Application deadline:* For fall admission, 5/15 for domestic students; for spring admission, 12/1 for domestic students. Application fee: $40. *Expenses: Contact institution. Financial support:* In 2006-07, 10 students received support, including 8 teaching assistantships (averaging $5,820 per year). Financial award application deadline:3/1. *Unit head:* Linda Hanrahan, Chairperson, 607-274-3147, E-mail: lhanrahan@ithaca.edu.

Jackson State University, Graduate School, School of Education, Department of Educational Foundations and Leadership, Jackson, MS 39217. Offers education administration (Ed S); educational administration (MS Ed, PhD); secondary education (MS Ed, Ed S), including educational technology (MS Ed). *Accreditation:* NCATE. Part-time and evening/weekend programs available. *Faculty:* 21 full-time (10 women), 5 part-time/adjunct (1 woman). *Students:* 43 full-time (24 women), 58 part-time (34 women); includes 82 minority (all African Americans), 2 international. In 2006, 38 master's, 5 doctorates, 5 other advanced degrees awarded. *Degree requirements:* For master's, thesis or alternative, comprehensive exam; for doctorate and Ed S, thesis/dissertation, comprehensive exam. *Entrance requirements:* For master's, GRE General Test; for doctorate, MAT, GRE, teaching experience. Additional exam requirements/recommendations for international students: Required—TOEFL. *Application deadline:* For fall admission, 3/1 priority date for domestic students; for spring admission, 10/1 for domestic students. Applications are processed on a rolling basis. Application fee: $20. *Financial support:* In 2006-07, 33 students received support. Career-related internships or fieldwork, Federal Work-Study, scholarships/grants, and unspecified assistantships available. Support available to part-time students. Financial award application deadline: 3/1; financial award applicants required to submit FAFSA. *Unit head:* Dr. Carrine Bishop, Interim Chair, 601-968-2351, Fax: 601-968-2213, E-mail: carrine.h.bishop@jsums.edu. *Application contact:* Curtis Gore, Director of Graduate Admissions, 601-979-2455, Fax: 601-974-4325, E-mail: cgore@ccaix.jsums.edu.

Jacksonville State University, College of Graduate Studies and Continuing Education, College of Education and Professional Studies, Program in Secondary Education, Jacksonville, AL 36265-1602. Offers MS Ed. *Accreditation:* NCATE. *Faculty:* 3 full-time (2 women), 1 part-time/adjunct (0 women). *Students:* 46 full-time (34 women), 107 part-time (74 women); includes 28 minority (26 African Americans, 1 Asian American or Pacific Islander, 1 Hispanic American), 1 international. In 2006, 25 degrees awarded. *Entrance requirements:* For master's, GRE General Test or MAT. *Application deadline:* Applications are processed on a rolling basis. Application fee: $20. *Expenses:* Tuition, state resident: full-time $5,400; part-time $225 per credit hour. Tuition, nonresident: full-time $10,800; part-time $450 per credit hour. One-time fee: $20 full-time. *Financial support:* In 2006-07, 1 research assistantship was awarded; teaching assistantships. Support available to part-time students. Financial award application deadline: 4/1. *Unit head:* Dr. Jan Wilson, Head, 256-782-5852. *Application contact:* 256-782-5329.

James Madison University, College of Graduate and Outreach Programs, College of Education, Middle, Secondary, and Mathematics Education Department, Program in Secondary Education, Harrisonburg, VA 22807. Offers MAT. *Accreditation:* NCATE. Part-time and evening/weekend programs available. *Students:* Average age 27. *Entrance requirements:* For master's, GRE General Test. Additional exam requirements/recommendations for international students: Required—TOEFL. *Application deadline:* For fall admission, 5/1 priority date for domestic students; for spring admission, 9/1 priority date for domestic students. Applications are processed on a rolling basis. Application fee: $55. Electronic applications accepted. *Expenses:* Tuition, state resident: full-time $6,336; part-time $264 per credit hour. Tuition, nonresident: full-time $17,832; part-time $743 per credit hour. *Financial support:* Federal Work-Study and unspecified assistantships available. Financial award application deadline: 3/1; financial award applicants required to submit FAFSA. *Unit head:* Dr. Lou Ann Lovin, Academic Unit Head, 540-568-6701.

John Carroll University, Graduate School, Department of Education and Allied Studies, Program in School Based Adolescent-Young Adult Education, University Heights, OH 44118-4581. Offers M Ed. *Faculty:* 1 (woman) full-time, 3 part-time/adjunct (1 woman). *Students:* 13 full-time (4 women). Average age 29. 28 applicants, 46% accepted, 13 enrolled. In 2006, 13 degrees awarded. *Degree requirements:* For master's, comprehensive exam. *Entrance requirements:* For master's, GRE General Test or MAT, minimum GPA of 2.75. *Application deadline:* For spring admission, 5/15 for domestic students. Applications are processed on a rolling basis. Application fee: $25 ($35 for international students). *Expenses:* Tuition: Full-time $9,675; part-time $645 per credit hour. Tuition and fees vary according to program. *Financial support:* Application deadline: 3/1; *Unit head:* Dr. Barbara Garson, Coordinator, Teacher Education, 216-397-4689, Fax: 216-397-3045, E-mail: bgarson@jcu.edu.

The Johns Hopkins University, School of Professional Studies in Business and Education, School of Education, Department of Teacher Preparation, Baltimore, MD 21218-2699. Offers elementary education (MAT); English for speakers of other languages (MAT); secondary education (MAT). Part-time and evening/weekend programs available. *Students:* 234 full-time (173 women), 240 part-time (172 women); includes 87 minority (61 African Americans, 19 Asian Americans or Pacific Islanders, 7 Hispanic Americans), 4 international. Average age 27. 360 applicants, 71% accepted, 243 enrolled. In 2006, 218 degrees awarded. *Degree requirements:* For master's, portfolio. *Entrance requirements:* For master's, PRAXIS I, minimum GPA of 3.0, interview, resumé, letter of recommendation. Additional exam requirements/recommendations for international students: Required—TOEFL (minimum score 600 paper-based; 250 computer-based; 100 iBT). *Application deadline:* For fall admission, 4/1 priority date for domestic students, 4/1 for international students; for winter admission, 10/1 priority date for domestic students; for spring admission, 10/1 priority date for domestic students, 10/1 for international students. Applications are processed on a rolling basis. Application fee: $60. *Expenses:* Tuition: Full-time $32,976. Tuition and fees vary according to degree level and program. *Financial support:* Scholarships/grants available. Support available to part-time students. Financial award application deadline: 6/1; financial award applicants required to submit FAFSA. *Faculty research:* Professional development schools, data-informed instruction, alternative certification, dispositions. *Unit head:* Dr. Elaine Stotko, Chair, 410-309-1289, Fax: 410-290-0467, E-mail: matjhu@jhu.edu. *Application contact:* Carol Herrman, Admissions Coordinator, 410-872-1234, Fax: 410-872-1251, E-mail: onestop.admissions@jhu.edu.

Johnson State College, Graduate Program in Education, Program in Secondary Education, Johnson, VT 05656-9405. Offers teaching all secondary students (MA Ed, CAGS). *Faculty:* 1 (woman) full-time, 4 part-time/adjunct (2 women). *Entrance requirements:* Additional exam requirements/recommendations for international students: Required—TOEFL. *Application deadline:* For fall admission, 4/1 priority date for domestic students, 4/15 priority date for international students; for spring admission, 11/1 priority date for domestic students, 8/15 priority date for international students. Applications are processed on a rolling basis. Application fee: $35. *Application contact:* Catherine H. Higley, Administrative Assistant for Graduate Programs, 800-635-2356 Ext. 1244, Fax: 802-635-1248, E-mail: higleyc@jsc.vsc.edu.

Jones International University, Graduate School of Education, Centennial, CO 80112. Offers adult education (M Ed); corporate training and knowledge management (M Ed); curriculum and instruction (M Ed), including elementary teacher licensure, secondary teacher licensure; e-learning technology and design (M Ed); educational leadership and administration (M Ed); educational leadership and administration: principal and administrator licensure (M Ed); elementary curriculum instruction and assessment (M Ed); higher education leadership and administration (M Ed); K-12 instructional technology (M Ed); K-12 instructional technology: teacher licensure (M Ed); secondary curriculum instruction and assessment (M Ed); technology and design (M Ed). Part-time and evening/weekend programs available. Postbaccalaureate distance learning degree programs offered (no on-campus study). *Entrance requirements:* For

master's, minimum cumulative GPA of 2.5. Additional exam requirements/recommendations for international students: Recommended—TOEFL (minimum score 550 paper-based; 213 computer-based). Electronic applications accepted.

Kansas State University, Graduate School, College of Education, Department of Secondary Education, Manhattan, KS 66506. Offers curriculum and instruction (MS, Ed D, PhD). *Faculty:* 15 full-time (6 women), 1 part-time/adjunct (0 women). *Application deadline:* For fall admission, 3/1 priority date for domestic students, 2/1 priority date for international students; for spring admission, 10/1 priority date for domestic students, 8/1 priority date for international students. Application fee: $30 ($55 for international students). *Expenses:* Tuition, state resident: full-time $6,352; part-time $240 per credit hour. Tuition, nonresident: full-time $14,296; part-time $571 per credit hour. Required fees: $585. *Financial support:* In 2006-07, 2 research assistantships (averaging $12,227 per year), 5 teaching assistantships (averaging $11,411 per year) were awarded. *Faculty research:* Curriculum development, gender issues in teaching and learning, instructional improvement, nature of science and instructional role of scientific theories, discourse communities. Total annual research expenditures: $450,541. *Unit head:* Lawrence Scharmann, Head, 785-532-5904, Fax: 785-532-7304, E-mail: lscharm@ksu.edu. *Application contact:* Linda Thurston, Director, 785-532-5595, Fax: 785-532-7304, E-mail: coegrads@ksu.edu.

Kent State University, Graduate School of Education, Health, and Human Services, Department of Teaching, Leadership, and Curriculum Studies, Program in Secondary Education, Kent, OH 44242-0001. Offers MAT. *Accreditation:* NCATE. *Faculty:* 10 full-time (6 women), 1 part-time/adjunct (0 women). *Students:* 37 full-time (19 women), 4 part-time (3 women); includes 5 minority (3 African Americans, 1 Asian American or Pacific Islander, 1 Hispanic American). 52 applicants, 75% accepted. In 2006, 34 degrees awarded. *Degree requirements:* For master's, thesis (for some programs), registration. *Entrance requirements:* For master's, GRE General Test. Additional exam requirements/recommendations for international students: Required—TOEFL. *Application deadline:* For spring admission, 2/1 for domestic students. Application fee: $30. Electronic applications accepted. *Financial support:* In 2006-07, fellowships with full tuition reimbursements (averaging $7,210 per year); research assistantships with full tuition reimbursements, teaching assistantships with full tuition reimbursements, career-related internships or fieldwork, Federal Work-Study, institutionally sponsored loans, scholarships/grants, health care benefits, and unspecified assistantships also available. Support available to part-time students. Financial award application deadline: 4/1; financial award applicants required to submit FAFSA. *Faculty research:* Creativity in science, women in science, teaching of writing, curriculum theory, mathematical reasoning. *Unit head:* Dr. Judith Mellzlo, Coordinator, 330-672-2580, E-mail: jmellzlo@kent.edu. *Application contact:* Nancy Miller, Academic Program Coordinator, Office of Graduate Student Services, 330-672-2576, Fax: 330-672-9162, E-mail: ogs@kent.edu.

Kutztown University of Pennsylvania, College of Graduate Studies and Extended Learning, College of Education, Program in Secondary Education, Kutztown, PA 19530-0730. Offers biology (M Ed); curriculum and instruction (M Ed); English (M Ed); mathematics (M Ed); secondary education (Certificate); social studies (M Ed). *Accreditation:* NCATE. Part-time and evening/weekend programs available. *Faculty:* 5 full-time (2 women). *Students:* 69 full-time (32 women), 80 part-time (44 women); includes 5 minority (1 African American, 1 American Indian/Alaska Native, 2 Asian Americans or Pacific Islanders, 1 Hispanic American), 3 international. Average age 32. 80 applicants, 88% accepted, 34 enrolled. In 2006, 26 degrees awarded. *Degree requirements:* For master's, thesis optional. *Entrance requirements:* For master's, GRE General Test. Additional exam requirements/recommendations for international students: Required—TOEFL. *Application deadline:* Applications are processed on a rolling basis. Application fee: $35. Electronic applications accepted. *Expenses:* Tuition, state resident: full-time $6,048; part-time $336 per credit. Tuition, nonresident: full-time $9,678; part-time $538 per credit. *Financial support:* In 2006-07, research assistantships with full tuition reimbursements (averaging $5,000 per year); career-related internships or fieldwork, Federal Work-Study, and unspecified assistantships also available. Financial award application deadline: 3/15; financial award applicants required to submit FAFSA. *Unit head:* Dr. Kathleen Dolgos, Chairperson, 610-683-4279, Fax: 610-683-1338, E-mail: dolgos@kutztown.edu.

LaGrange College, Graduate Programs, Department of Education, LaGrange, GA 30240-2999. Offers art education (MAT); curriculum and instruction (M Ed); music education (MAT); secondary education (MAT). Part-time and evening/weekend programs available. *Degree requirements:* For master's, comprehensive exam. *Entrance requirements:* For master's, GRE, MAT, or NTE, minimum GPA of 2.5. Additional exam requirements/recommendations for international students: Required—TOEFL (minimum score 550 paper-based).

Lee University, Program in Education, Cleveland, TN 37320-3450. Offers classroom teaching (M Ed); educational leadership (M Ed); elementary/secondary education (MAT); special education (elementary) (M Ed); special education (secondary) (M Ed, MAT); special education (severe disabilities) (M Ed). *Faculty:* 25 full-time (11 women). *Students:* 103 full-time (66 women), 22 part-time (15 women); includes 43 minority (5 African Americans, 36 American Indian/Alaska Native, 2 Hispanic Americans), 3 international. 49 applicants, 100% accepted, 28 enrolled. In 2006, 75 degrees awarded. *Degree requirements:* For master's, variable foreign language requirement, thesis, internship, comprehensive exam. *Entrance requirements:* For master's, MAT or GRE General Test, minimum GPA of 2.75, 3 letters of recommendation, interview, writing sample. Additional exam requirements/recommendations for international students: Required—TOEFL. *Application deadline:* For fall admission, 4/1 for domestic students; for spring admission, 10/1 for domestic students. Applications are processed on a rolling basis. Application fee: $25. *Expenses:* Tuition: Part-time $412 per credit. Required fees: $10 per semester. Tuition and fees vary according to course load. *Financial support:* Career-related internships or fieldwork, Federal Work-Study, and institutionally sponsored loans available. *Unit head:* Dr. Gary Riggins, Director, 423-614-8193. *Application contact:* Vicki Glasscock, Graduate Admissions Director, 423-614-8059, E-mail: vglasscock@leeuniversity.edu.

Lehigh University, College of Education, Department of Education and Human Services, Program in Technology–Based Teacher Education, Bethlehem, PA 18015-3094. Offers elementary education (M Ed); learning sciences and technology (PhD); secondary education (M Ed, MA). Part-time and evening/weekend programs available. *Faculty:* 29 full-time (16 women), 17 part-time/adjunct (9 women). *Students:* 36 full-time (30 women), 34 part-time (22 women); includes 2 minority (both Asian Americans or Pacific Islanders), 2 international. 27 applicants, 85% accepted, 10 enrolled. In 2006, 53 master's, 1 doctorate awarded. *Entrance requirements:* For master's, minimum GPA of 3.0; for doctorate, GRE General Test, minimum GPA of 3.0. Additional exam requirements/recommendations for international students: Required—TOEFL (minimum score 600 paper-based; 250 computer-based). *Application deadline:* Applications are processed on a rolling basis. Application fee: $60. Electronic applications accepted. *Financial support:* Career-related internships or fieldwork, Federal Work-Study, institutionally sponsored loans, scholarships/grants, and tuition waivers (full and partial) available. Financial award application deadline: 1/31. *Unit head:* Dr. H. Lynn Columba, Head, 610-758-3230, Fax: 610-758-3243, E-mail: hlc0@lehigh.edu.

Lewis & Clark College, Graduate School of Education and Counseling, Department of Education, Program in Middle Level/High School Education, Portland, OR 97219-7899. Offers MAT. *Accreditation:* NCATE. *Faculty:* 8 full-time (4 women), 5 part-time/adjunct (2 women). *Students:* 62 full-time (42 women), 3 part-time (all women); includes 7 minority (2 American Indian/Alaska Native, 2 Asian Americans or Pacific Islanders, 3 Hispanic Americans), 2 international. Average age 28. 99 applicants, 92% accepted, 61 enrolled. In 2006, 55 master's awarded. *Degree requirements:* For master's, thesis optional. *Entrance requirements:* For master's, minimum GPA of 2.75. Additional exam requirements/recommendations for international students: Required—TOEFL (minimum score 575 paper-based; 233 computer-based). *Application deadline:* For fall admission, 1/2 priority date for domestic and international students. Application fee: $50. Electronic applications accepted. *Expenses:* Tuition: Part-time

$610 per semester hour. *Financial support:* In 2006–07, 52 students received support. Career-related internships or fieldwork, Federal Work-Study, institutionally sponsored loans, scholarships/grants, health care benefits, and tuition waivers (partial) available. Support available to part-time students. Financial award applicants required to submit FAFSA. *Faculty research:* Classroom management, classroom assessment, science education, classroom ethnography, moral development. *Unit head:* Dr. Kimberly Campbell, Coordinator, 503-768-6108, Fax: 503-768-7715, E-mail: lcteach@lclark.edu. *Application contact:* Becky Haas, Director of Admissions, 503-768-6200, Fax: 503-768-6205, E-mail: gseadmit@lclark.edu.

Liberty University, School of Education, Lynchburg, VA 24502. Offers administration and supervision (M Ed); curriculum and instruction (M Ed); early childhood education (M Ed); education specialist (Ed S); educational leadership (Ed D); elementary education (M Ed); gifted education (M Ed); reading specialist (M Ed); school counseling (M Ed); secondary education (M Ed); special education (M Ed). *Accreditation:* NCATE. Part-time programs available. Postbaccalaureate distance learning degree programs offered (minimal on-campus study). *Faculty:* 8 full-time (3 women), 7 part-time/adjunct (3 women). *Students:* 33 full-time (22 women), 308 part-time (180 women); includes 22 minority (12 African Americans, 2 American Indian/Alaska Native, 2 Asian Americans or Pacific Islanders, 6 Hispanic Americans), 5 international. Average age 39. 434 applicants, 77% accepted, 111 enrolled. In 2006, 39 master's, 12 doctorates, 16 other advanced degrees awarded. *Degree requirements:* For doctorate, thesis/dissertation, comprehensive exam. *Entrance requirements:* For master's, GRE General Test or MAT (if taken on or before 1999), 2 letters of recommendation, minimum undergraduate GPA of 3.0, curriculum vitae, graduate status record; for doctorate, GRE General Test or MAT (if taken before 1999), minimum master's GPA of 3.0, 3 years of teacher experience; for Ed S, GRE General Test or MAT (if taken before 1999), minimum master's GPA of 3.0, 3 years of teaching experience. Additional exam requirements/recommendations for international students: Required—TOEFL (minimum score 600 paper-based; 250 computer-based). *Application deadline:* For fall admission, 6/1 priority date for domestic students; for spring admission, 11/1 for domestic students. Applications are processed on a rolling basis. Application fee: $35. Electronic applications accepted. *Expenses:* Contact institution. *Financial support:* In 2006–07, 226 students received support. Federal Work-Study and tuition waivers (partial) available. *Faculty research:* Self-determination, character education, bibliotherapy, learning styles, distance education. *Unit head:* Dr. Karen L. Parker, Dean, 434-582-2195, Fax: 434-582-2468, E-mail: kparker@liberty.edu. *Application contact:* Kyle A Falce, Director of Graduate Admissions, 800-424-9596, Fax: 800-628-7977, E-mail: gradadmissions@liberty.edu.

Lincoln University, School of Graduate Studies and Continuing Education, College of Liberal Arts, Education and Journalism, Department of Education, Jefferson City, MO 65102. Offers educational leadership (Ed S), including elementary leadership, secondary leadership, superintendency; guidance and counseling (M Ed), including community/agency counseling, elementary school, secondary school; school administration and supervision (M Ed), including elementary school administration, secondary school administration, special education administration; school teaching (M Ed), including elementary school teaching, secondary school teaching. *Accreditation:* NCATE. Part-time and evening/weekend programs available. *Faculty:* 1 (woman) full-time, 10 part-time/adjunct (5 women). *Students:* 24 full-time (21 women), 62 part-time (51 women); includes 10 minority (8 African Americans, 2 Asian Americans or Pacific Islanders), 4 international. Average age 35. 13 applicants, 100% accepted, 10 enrolled. In 2006, 25 master's, 3 other advanced degrees awarded. *Degree requirements:* For master's and Ed S, portfolio. *Entrance requirements:* For master's, GRE or MAT, teaching certificate (school administration and supervision); background check; interview (elementary and secondary school teaching); for Ed S, GRE or MAT, principal certificate. Additional exam requirements/recommendations for international students: Required—TOEFL (minimum score 500 paper-based; 173 computer-based; 61 iBT). *Application deadline:* For fall admission, 7/1 priority date for domestic and international students; for spring admission, 12/1 priority date for domestic and international students. Applications are processed on a rolling basis. Application fee: $17. *Expenses:* Tuition, state resident: part-time $189 per credit hour. Tuition, nonresident: part-time $351 per credit hour. Required fees: $15 per credit hour. $20 per semester. *Financial support:* Federal Work-Study and scholarships/grants available. Financial award application deadline: 4/1; financial award applicants required to submit FAFSA. *Unit head:* Dr. Cynthia Chapel, Department Head, 573-681-5250, Fax: 573-681-5257, E-mail: chapelc@lincolnu.edu.

Long Island University, C.W. Post Campus, College of Liberal Arts and Sciences, Department of English, Brookville, NY 11548-1300. Offers English (MA); English for adolescence education (MS). Part-time and evening/weekend programs available. *Degree requirements:* For master's, thesis (for some programs), comprehensive exam (for some programs). *Entrance requirements:* For master's, minimum GPA of 3.5 in major, 3.0 overall; 21 credits of English. Electronic applications accepted. *Faculty research:* English Renaissance, Sinclair Lewis: The Early Years, puppetry archives, Irish-American Experiences: literature of memory, Henry James's anxiety of Poe's influence.

Long Island University, Westchester Graduate Campus, Programs in Education-Teaching, Program in Special Education and Secondary Education, Purchase, NY 10577. Offers MS Ed. Part-time and evening/weekend programs available. *Faculty:* 1 (woman) full-time, 14 part-time/adjunct (12 women). *Students:* 25 applicants, 96% accepted, 21 enrolled. In 2006, 12 degrees awarded. *Application deadline:* Applications are processed on a rolling basis. *Expenses:* Tuition: Part-time $790 per credit. *Financial support:* In 2006–07, 35 students received support. Scholarships/grants, tuition waivers (partial), and unspecified assistantships available. *Unit head:* Dr. Janet Simon, Director, 914-831-2715, Fax: 914-251-5959, E-mail: janet.simon@liu.edu. *Application contact:* Ellen Brief, Coordinator of Admissions, Marketing, Student Services and Public Relations, 914-831-2701, Fax: 914-251-5959, E-mail: ellen.brief@liu.edu.

Longwood University, Office of Graduate Studies, College of Education and Human Services, Farmville, VA 23909. Offers communication sciences and disorders (MS); community and college counseling (MS); curriculum and instruction specialist-elementary (MS), including mild disabilities, modern languages; curriculum and instruction specialist-secondary (MS), including English, mild disabilities, modern languages; educational leadership (MS); guidance and counseling (MS); literacy and culture (MS); school library media (MS). *Accreditation:* NCATE. Part-time and evening/weekend programs available. *Degree requirements:* For master's, thesis optional. *Entrance requirements:* For master's, GRE (communication sciences and disorders), minimum GPA of 2.75. Additional exam requirements/recommendations for international students: Required—TOEFL (minimum score 550 paper-based; 213 computer-based).

Louisiana State University and Agricultural and Mechanical College, Graduate School, College of Education, Department of Educational Theory, Policy and Practice, Baton Rouge, LA 70803. Offers counseling (M Ed, MA, Ed S); educational administration (M Ed, MA, PhD, Ed S); educational technology (MA); elementary education (M Ed); higher education (PhD); research methodology (PhD); secondary education (M Ed). *Accreditation:* ACA (one or more programs are accredited); NCATE. Part-time and evening/weekend programs available. *Faculty:* 39 full-time (24 women). *Students:* 147 full-time (115 women), 183 part-time (143 women); includes 63 minority (51 African Americans, 3 American Indian/Alaska Native, 3 Asian Americans or Pacific Islanders, 6 Hispanic Americans), 14 international. Average age 35. 110 applicants, 58% accepted, 15 enrolled. In 2006, 93 master's, 24 doctorates awarded. Terminal master's awarded for partial completion of doctoral program. *Degree requirements:* For doctorate, thesis/dissertation; for Ed S, thesis optional. *Entrance requirements:* For master's and doctorate, GRE General Test, minimum GPA of 3.0. Additional exam requirements/recommendations for international students: Required—TOEFL (minimum score 550 paper-based; 213 computer-based; 79 iBT). *Application deadline:* For fall admission, 1/25 priority date for domestic students, 5/15 for international students; for spring admission, 10/15 for international students. Applications are processed on a rolling basis. Application fee: $25. Electronic applications accepted. *Financial support:* In 2006–07, 82 students received support, including 6 fellowships with full tuition reimbursements available (averaging $26,273 per year), 24 research assistantships with full and partial tuition reimbursements available (averaging $9,812 per year), teaching assistantships with full and partial tuition reimbursements available (averaging $11,693 per year); career-related internships or fieldwork, Federal Work-Study, institutionally sponsored loans, and unspecified assistantships also available. Support available to part-time students. Financial award applicants required to submit FAFSA. *Faculty research:* Literacy, curriculum studies, science education, K-12 leadership, higher education. Total annual research expenditures: $335,618. *Unit head:* Dr. Earl Cheek, Chair, 225-578-6897, Fax: 225-578-1045, E-mail: echeek@lsu.edu.

Louisiana Tech University, Graduate School, College of Education, Department of Curriculum, Instruction and Leadership, Ruston, LA 71272. Offers curriculum and instruction (MS, Ed D); educational leadership (Ed D); secondary education (M Ed), including business education, English education, foreign language education, health and physical education, mathematics education, science education, social studies education, speech education. *Accreditation:* NCATE. Part-time programs available. *Degree requirements:* For doctorate, thesis/dissertation. *Entrance requirements:* For master's and doctorate, GRE General Test.

Loyola Marymount University, Graduate Division, School of Education, Program in Secondary Education, Los Angeles, CA 90045-2659. Offers MA. Part-time and evening/weekend programs available. *Students:* 241 full-time (152 women), 26 part-time (17 women); includes 118 minority (26 African Americans, 1 American Indian/Alaska Native, 36 Asian Americans or Pacific Islanders, 55 Hispanic Americans), 3 international. In 2006, 96 degrees awarded. *Degree requirements:* For master's, comprehensive exam. *Entrance requirements:* For master's, GRE General Test, interview. Additional exam requirements/recommendations for international students: Required—TOEFL (minimum score 600 paper-based; 250 computer-based). *Application deadline:* For fall admission, 7/15 for domestic students; for spring admission, 11/15 for domestic students. Application fee: $50. Electronic applications accepted. *Financial support:* In 2006–07, 208 students received support; research assistantships, Federal Work-Study and scholarships/grants available. Support available to part-time students. Financial award application deadline: 6/1; financial award applicants required to submit FAFSA. *Unit head:* Dr. Ermundo Litton, Coordinator, 310-338-2863, E-mail: elitton@lmu.edu.

Loyola University Chicago, School of Education, Program in Initial Teacher Preparation, Chicago, IL 60611-2196. Offers elementary education (M Ed); reading specialist (M Ed); school technology (M Ed); science education (M Ed); secondary education (M Ed); special education (M Ed). *Accreditation:* NCATE. *Faculty:* 11 full-time (9 women), 6 part-time/adjunct (4 women). *Students:* 138. Average age 28. 95 applicants, 65% accepted, 39 enrolled. In 2006, 84 degrees awarded. *Degree requirements:* For master's, comprehensive exam. *Entrance requirements:* For master's, Illinois Basic Skills Test, 3 letters of recommendation, minimum GPA of 3.0, resumé. Additional exam requirements/recommendations for international students: Required—TOEFL (minimum score 550 paper-based; 213 computer-based; 79 iBT). *Application deadline:* For fall admission, 7/1 priority date for domestic and international students; for spring admission, 11/1 priority date for domestic and international students. Applications are processed on a rolling basis. Application fee: $50. Electronic applications accepted. *Financial support:* In 2006–07, 2 research assistantships with full tuition reimbursements (averaging $8,500 per year), 1 teaching assistantship were awarded. Financial award application deadline: 2/15. *Faculty research:* Positive behavior support, school reform, school improvement. *Unit head:* Dr. Dorothy Giroux, Director, 312-915-7027, E-mail: dgiroux@luc.edu. *Application contact:* Marie Rosin-Dittmar, Information Contact, 312-915-6800, E-mail: schleduc@luc.edu.

Loyola University New Orleans, College of Arts and Sciences, Department of Education and Counseling, Program in Secondary Education, New Orleans, LA 70118-6195. Offers MS. Part-time and evening/weekend programs available. *Degree requirements:* For master's, comprehensive exam. *Entrance requirements:* For master's, GRE or MAT (preferred), interview, letters of recommendation, writing sample. Additional exam requirements/recommendations for international students: Required—TOEFL (minimum score 550 paper-based; 213 computer-based). Electronic applications accepted. *Faculty research:* Moral development, curriculum, gifted education, literature and education.

Maharishi University of Management, Graduate Studies, Department of Education, Fairfield, IA 52557. Offers teaching elementary education (MA); teaching secondary education (MA). *Degree requirements:* For master's, thesis or alternative. *Entrance requirements:* For master's, GRE, minimum GPA of 3.0. Additional exam requirements/recommendations for international students: Required—TOEFL. *Faculty research:* Unified field-based approach to education, moral climate, scientific study of teaching.

Manhattanville College, Graduate Programs, School of Education, Program in Middle Childhood/Adolescence Education (Grades 5-12), Purchase, NY 10577-2132. Offers biology (MAT); biology and special education (MPS); chemistry (MAT); chemistry and special education (MPS); English (MAT); English and special education (MPS); literacy (MPS), including reading and writing, writing; literacy and special education (MPS); math (MAT); math and special education (MPS); second language (MAT), including French, Italian, Latin, Spanish; social studies (MAT); social studies and special education (MPS); special education (MPS). Part-time and evening/weekend programs available. *Students:* 76 full-time (53 women), 109 part-time (68 women); includes 8 African Americans, 1 Asian American or Pacific Islander, 10 Hispanic Americans, 1 international. In 2006, 165 degrees awarded. *Degree requirements:* For master's, comprehensive exam or research project, field experience. *Entrance requirements:* For master's, minimum undergraduate GPA of 3.0, 2 letters of recommendation. *Application deadline:* Applications are processed on a rolling basis. Application fee: $55. *Financial support:* Career-related internships or fieldwork and institutionally sponsored loans available. Support available to part-time students. *Application contact:* Alyce Ware Poli, Director of Admissions, 914-323-5142, Fax: 914-694-1732, E-mail: edschool@mville.edu.

Mansfield University of Pennsylvania, Graduate Studies, Department of Education and Special Education, Mansfield, PA 16933. Offers elementary education (M Ed); secondary education (MS). *Accreditation:* NCATE (one or more programs are accredited). Part-time and evening/weekend programs available. Postbaccalaureate distance learning degree programs offered (no on-campus study). *Faculty:* 13 full-time (9 women), 1 (woman) part-time/adjunct. *Students:* 50 full-time (44 women), 72 part-time (52 women); includes 8 minority (4 African Americans, 1 Asian American or Pacific Islander, 3 Hispanic Americans). Average age 31. 130 applicants, 80% accepted, 34 enrolled. In 2006, 47 degrees awarded. *Degree requirements:* For master's, thesis optional. *Entrance requirements:* For master's, minimum GPA of 3.0. Additional exam requirements/recommendations for international students: Required—TOEFL (minimum score 550 paper-based; 220 computer-based). *Application deadline:* For fall admission, 8/1 priority date for domestic students, 8/1 for international students; for spring admission, 11/1 priority date for domestic students, 9/1 for international students. Applications are processed on a rolling basis. Application fee: $25. Electronic applications accepted. *Expenses:* Tuition, state resident: part-time $336 per credit. Tuition, nonresident: part-time $538 per credit. Tuition and fees vary according to course load and reciprocity agreements. *Financial support:* Career-related internships or fieldwork and unspecified assistantships available. Support available to part-time students. Financial award application deadline: 5/1; financial award applicants required to submit FAFSA. *Unit head:* Dr. Celeste Burns, Chairperson, 570-662-4563, E-mail: cburns@mnsfld.edu. *Application contact:* Judi Brayer, Assistant Director of Enrollment Management/Graduate Admissions, 570-662-4818, Fax: 570-662-4121, E-mail: jbrayer@mansfield.edu.

Marshall University, Academic Affairs Division, College of Education and Human Services, Graduate School of Education and Professional Development, Program in Secondary Education, Huntington, WV 25755. Offers MA. *Accreditation:* NCATE. Part-time and evening/weekend programs available. *Faculty:* 8 full-time (5 women). *Students:* 26 full-time (17 women), 70 part-time (50 women); includes 6 minority (2 African Americans, 1 American Indian/Alaska Native, 1 Asian American or Pacific Islander, 2 Hispanic Americans), 2 international. Average age 35. In 2006, 14 degrees awarded. *Degree requirements:* For master's, comprehensive or

Secondary Education

Marshall University (continued)
oral assessment, thesis optional. *Entrance requirements:* For master's, GRE General Test or MAT. Application fee: $40. *Financial support:* Federal Work-Study, tuition waivers (full), and unspecified assistantships available. Support available to part-time students. Financial award applicants required to submit FAFSA. *Unit head:* Dr. Calvin Meyer, Director, 304-746-1936, E-mail: meyer@marshall.edu. *Application contact:* Information Contact, 304-746-1900, Fax: 304-746-1902, E-mail: services@marshall.edu.

Marygrove College, Graduate Division, Education Unit, Program in Sage, Detroit, MI 48221-2599. Offers M Ed. *Entrance requirements:* For master's, Michigan Teacher Test for Certification.

Marymount University, School of Arts and Sciences, Program in Humanities, Arlington, VA 22207-4299. Offers humanities (MA); humanities: teaching licensure in secondary English (MA). Part-time and evening/weekend programs available. *Students:* 3 full-time (all women), 6 part-time (5 women); includes 3 minority (all African Americans), 1 international. Average age 28. 4 applicants, 100% accepted, 3 enrolled. In 2006, 3 degrees awarded. *Degree requirements:* For master's, thesis or alternative. *Entrance requirements:* For master's, GRE; GRE or MAT and Praxis I or SAT/ACT (for teaching licensure), interview, writing sample, 2 letters of recommendation. Additional exam requirements/recommendations for international students: Required—TOEFL (minimum score 600 paper-based; 250 computer-based). *Application deadline:* Applications are processed on a rolling basis. Application fee: $40. Electronic applications accepted. *Expenses:* Tuition: Full-time $11,160; part-time $620 per credit. Required fees: $113; $630 per credit. *Financial support:* Research assistantships with full tuition reimbursements, career-related internships or fieldwork, scholarships/grants, and unspecified assistantships available. Support available to part-time students. Financial award applicants required to submit FAFSA.

Marymount University, School of Education and Human Services, Program in Education, Arlington, VA 22207-4299. Offers alternative teacher licensure (Certificate); elementary education (M Ed); English as a second language (M Ed); learning disabilities (M Ed); professional studies (M Ed); secondary education (M Ed). *Accreditation:* NCATE. Part-time and evening/weekend programs available. Postbaccalaureate distance learning degree programs offered (minimal on-campus study). *Faculty:* 10 full-time (8 women), 5 part-time/adjunct (2 women). *Students:* 75 full-time (65 women), 95 part-time (82 women); includes 25 minority (13 African Americans, 2 American Indian/Alaska Native, 6 Asian Americans or Pacific Islanders, 4 Hispanic Americans), 6 international. Average age 32. 58 applicants, 100% accepted, 45 enrolled. In 2006, 113 degrees awarded. *Degree requirements:* For master's, thesis or alternative. *Entrance requirements:* For master's, GRE General Test or MAT, PRAXIS I or SAT/ACT, interview, 2 letters of recommendation. Additional exam requirements/recommendations for international students: Required—TOEFL (minimum score 600 paper-based; 250 computer-based). *Application deadline:* Applications are processed on a rolling basis. Application fee: $40. Electronic applications accepted. *Expenses:* Tuition: Full-time $11,160; part-time $620 per credit. Required fees: $113; $630 per credit. *Financial support:* Research assistantships with full tuition reimbursements, career-related internships or fieldwork, scholarships/grants, and unspecified assistantships available. Support available to part-time students. Financial award applicants required to submit FAFSA. *Unit head:* Dr. Shelly Haser, Chair, 703-284-6955, Fax: 703-284-1631, E-mail: shelly.haser@marymount.edu.

Maryville University of Saint Louis, School of Education, St. Louis, MO 63141-7299. Offers art education (MA Ed); early childhood education (MA Ed); education (Ed D); elementary education (MA Ed); elementary education/English (MA Ed); environmental education (MA Ed); gifted education (MA Ed); middle grades education (MA Ed); reading specialist (MA Ed); secondary education (MA Ed), including educational leadership, secondary teaching and inquiry. *Accreditation:* NASAD; NCATE. Part-time and evening/weekend programs available. *Students:* 17 full-time (14 women), 168 part-time (129 women); includes 20 African Americans, 2 Asian Americans or Pacific Islanders, 1 Hispanic American, 2 international. Average age 37. 39 applicants, 95% accepted, 24 enrolled. In 2006, 37 degrees awarded. *Degree requirements:* For master's, thesis, project. *Entrance requirements:* For master's and doctorate, minimum GPA of 3.0, 3 professional recommendations. Additional exam requirements/recommendations for international students: Required—TOEFL (minimum score 550 paper-based). *Application deadline:* Applications are processed on a rolling basis. Application fee: $35 ($50 for international students). Electronic applications accepted. *Expenses:* Tuition: Full-time $17,800; part-time $555 per credit. Required fees: $55 per semester. Tuition and fees vary according to degree level and program. *Financial support:* Career-related internships or fieldwork, Federal Work-Study, tuition waivers (partial), and professional educator discounts available. Financial award application deadline: 7/31; financial award applicants required to submit FAFSA. *Faculty research:* Collaboration with public schools, preservice program development, mathematics, diversity, literacy. *Unit head:* Dr. Sam Hausfather, Dean, 314-529-9466, Fax: 314-529-9921, E-mail: shausfather@maryville.edu. *Application contact:* Dr. Lillian Curtis, Graduate Admissions Coordinator, 314-529-9542, Fax: 314-529-9921, E-mail: teachered@maryville.edu.

Marywood University, Academic Affairs, College of Education and Human Development, Department of Education, Program in Secondary Education, Scranton, PA 18509-1598. Offers MAT. *Expenses:* Tuition: Part-time $672 per credit. Tuition and fees vary according to degree level, campus/location and program. *Application contact:* Dr. Deborah M. Flynn, Coordinator of Graduate Advising (Enrollment Management), 570-348-6211, E-mail: flynn@ac.marywood.edu.

McDaniel College, Graduate and Professional Studies, Program in Elementary and Secondary Education, Westminster, MD 21157-4390. Offers elementary education (MS); secondary education (MS). *Accreditation:* NCATE. Part-time and evening/weekend programs available. *Degree requirements:* For master's, thesis optional. *Entrance requirements:* For master's, GRE General Test, MAT, or NTE/PRAXIS I, letters of reference (3). Additional exam requirements/recommendations for international students: Required—TOEFL (minimum score 213 computer-based).

McNeese State University, Graduate School, College of Education, Department of Teacher Education, Program in Curriculum and Instruction, Lake Charles, LA 70609. Offers early childhood education (M Ed); elementary education (M Ed); secondary education (M Ed). Evening/weekend programs available. *Faculty:* 12 full-time (8 women), 2 part-time/adjunct (1 woman). *Students:* 7 full-time (6 women), 40 part-time (37 women); includes 20 minority (19 African Americans, 1 American Indian/Alaska Native). In 2006, 22 degrees awarded. *Entrance requirements:* For master's, GRE, teaching certificate. *Application deadline:* For fall admission, 5/15 priority date for domestic students. Applications are processed on a rolling basis. Application fee: $20 ($30 for international students). *Expenses:* Tuition, area resident: Full-time $2,226; part-time $193 per hour. Required fees: $919; $106 per hour. *Financial support:* Application deadline: 5/1. *Unit head:* Dr. Wayne R Fetter, Dean, College of Education, 337-475-5432, Fax: 337-475-5467, E-mail: wfetter@mcneese.edu.

McNeese State University, Graduate School, College of Education, Department of Teacher Education, Program in Teaching, Lake Charles, LA 70609. Offers elementary education (MAT); secondary education (MAT); special education (mild/moderate) (MAT). Evening/weekend programs available. *Faculty:* 12 full-time (8 women), 2 part-time/adjunct (1 woman). *Students:* 37 full-time (30 women), 168 part-time (146 women); includes 53 minority (47 African Americans, 2 Asian Americans or Pacific Islanders, 4 Hispanic Americans), 2 international. In 2006, 26 degrees awarded. *Entrance requirements:* For master's, GRE, PRAXIS. *Application deadline:* For fall admission, 5/15 priority date for domestic students. Applications are processed on a rolling basis. Application fee: $20 ($30 for international students). *Expenses:* Tuition, area resident: Full-time $2,226; part-time $193 per hour. Required fees: $919; $106 per hour. *Financial support:* Application deadline: 5/1. *Unit head:* Dr. Wayne R Fetter, Dean, College of Education, 337-475-5432, Fax: 337-475-5467, E-mail: wfetter@mcneese.edu.

Mercer University, Graduate Studies, Cecil B. Day Campus, Tift College of Education, Macon, GA 31207-0003. Offers early childhood education (M Ed, MAT); educational leadership (M Ed, PhD); middle grades education (M Ed, MAT); reading education (M Ed); secondary education (M Ed, MAT); teacher leadership (Ed S). Part-time and evening/weekend programs available. *Faculty:* 13 full-time (6 women), 7 part-time/adjunct (3 women). *Students:* 31 full-time (23 women), 211 part-time (174 women); includes 111 minority (101 African Americans, 2 American Indian/Alaska Native, 6 Asian Americans or Pacific Islanders, 2 Hispanic Americans), 2 international. Average age 33. In 2006, 57 master's, 4 other advanced degrees awarded. *Degree requirements:* For master's and Ed S, research project; for doctorate, thesis/dissertation. *Entrance requirements:* For master's, GRE or MAT, minimum undergraduate GPA of 2.75; for doctorate, GRE; for Ed S, GRE or MAT, minimum GPA of 3.25, 3 years of teaching experience. *Application deadline:* For fall admission, 8/1 for domestic and international students; for spring admission, 12/1 for domestic and international students. Applications are processed on a rolling basis. Application fee: $25. *Expenses: Contact institution. Financial support:* Federal Work-Study available. Support available to part-time students. Financial award application deadline: 5/1. *Faculty research:* Educational computing, content area reading, concept learning, importance of play for young children, multicultural literature. *Unit head:* Dr. Carl R. Martray, Dean, 478-301-5397, Fax: 478-301-2280, E-mail: martray_cr@mercer.edu. *Application contact:* Dr. Allison Gilmore, Associate Dean for Graduate Teacher Education, 678-547-6330, Fax: 678-547-6055, E-mail: gilmore_a@mercer.edu.

Mercy College, Division of Education, Dobbs Ferry, NY 10522-1189. Offers adolescence education: grades 7-12 (MS); applied behavior analysis (MS); bilingual education (MS); childhood education: grades 1-6 (MS); early childhood education: birth—grade 2 (MS); education (MS); elementary education (MS); learning technology (MS); middle childhood education: grades 5-9 (MS); reading (MS); school administration and supervision (MS); school building leadership (MS); school business administration (MS); secondary education (MS); special education (MS); students with disabilities: grades 5-9 (MS); students with disabilities: grades 7-12 (MS); teaching English to speakers of other languages (MS); teaching literacy: birth—grade 6 (MS); teaching literacy: grades 5-12 (MS); urban education (MS). *Students:* 572 full-time (467 women), 1,719 part-time (1,287 women); includes 943 minority (470 African Americans, 7 American Indian/Alaska Native, 48 Asian Americans or Pacific Islanders, 418 Hispanic Americans), 6 international. Average age 33. In 2006, 1090 degrees awarded. *Entrance requirements:* For master's, teaching certificate. *Application deadline:* For fall admission, 2/1 for domestic students. Applications are processed on a rolling basis. Application fee: $37. *Expenses: Contact institution.* Tuition and fees vary according to program. *Financial support:* Institutionally sponsored loans, scholarships/grants, and unspecified assistantships available. Support available to part-time students. *Faculty research:* Distance learning, literacy, assessment, community schools, impact of staff development. *Unit head:* Dr. William Prattella, Chairperson, 914-674-7555, Fax: 914-674-7352, E-mail: wprattella@mercy.edu. *Application contact:* Kathleen Jackson, Director of Admissions, 800-Mercy-NY, Fax: 914-674-7382, E-mail: admissions@mercy.edu.

Miami University, Graduate School, School of Education and Allied Professions, Department of Teacher Education, Program in Secondary Education, Oxford, OH 45056. Offers adolescent education (MAT), including integrated English, integrated mathematics, integrated social studies, language arts; elementary mathematics education (M Ed); secondary education (M Ed, MAT). *Accreditation:* NCATE. Part-time programs available. *Degree requirements:* For master's, thesis (for some programs), final exam. *Entrance requirements:* For master's, MAT, minimum undergraduate GPA of 3.0 during previous 2 years or 2.75 overall. *Faculty research:* Teacher effectiveness, collaboration models.

Mills College, Graduate Studies, Education Department, Oakland, CA 94613-1000. Offers administration (Ed D); child life in health care settings (MA); early childhood education (MA); education (MA), including curriculum and instruction, elementary education, English education, mathematics education, science education, secondary education, social sciences education, teaching. Part-time and evening/weekend programs available. *Faculty:* 10 full-time (7 women), 15 part-time/adjunct (12 women). *Students:* 192 full-time (153 women), 41 part-time (36 women); includes 62 minority (28 African Americans, 13 Asian Americans or Pacific Islanders, 21 Hispanic Americans), 2 international. Average age 34. 160 applicants, 74% accepted, 73 enrolled. In 2006, 52 master's, 1 doctorate awarded. Terminal master's awarded for partial completion of doctoral program. *Degree requirements:* For master's, comprehensive exam. *Entrance requirements:* For doctorate, GRE General Test. Additional exam requirements/recommendations for international students: Required—TOEFL. *Application deadline:* For fall admission, 2/1 for domestic and international students; for spring admission, 11/1 for domestic and international students. Applications are processed on a rolling basis. Application fee: $50. Electronic applications accepted. *Financial support:* In 2006–07, 56 fellowships with tuition reimbursements (averaging $2,700 per year), 15 teaching assistantships (averaging $6,350 per year) were awarded; career-related internships or fieldwork, institutionally sponsored loans, scholarships/grants, and residence awards also available. Support available to part-time students. Financial award application deadline: 2/1; financial award applicants required to submit CSS PROFILE or FAFSA. *Faculty research:* Child development, gender and education, public policy, cross-cultural development, development of literacy. *Unit head:* Joseph Kahne, Chairperson, 510-430-3190, Fax: 510-430-3314, E-mail: grad-studies@mills.edu. *Application contact:* Randy McGlauthing, Director of Graduate Admissions, 510-430-2355, Fax: 510-430-2159, E-mail: rmglaut@mills.edu.

Mississippi College, Graduate School, School of Education, Department of Teacher Education and Leadership, Clinton, MS 39058. Offers art (M Ed); biological science (M Ed); business education (M Ed); computer science (M Ed); dyslexia therapy (M Ed); educational leadership (M Ed, Ed S); elementary education (M Ed, Ed S); English (M Ed); higher education administration (MS); mathematics (M Ed); secondary education (M Ed); social studies (history) (M Ed); teaching arts (M Ed). Part-time programs available. *Faculty:* 9 full-time (5 women), 14 part-time/adjunct (10 women). *Students:* 52 full-time (36 women), 286 part-time (247 women); includes 173 minority (171 African Americans, 1 American Indian/Alaska Native, 1 Hispanic American), 1 international. Average age 32. In 2006, 131 degrees awarded. *Degree requirements:* For master's, thesis optional. *Entrance requirements:* For master's, NTE. Additional exam requirements/recommendations for international students: Recommended—IELTS. *Application deadline:* Applications are processed on a rolling basis. Application fee: $25. Electronic applications accepted. *Expenses:* Tuition: Full-time $7,290; part-time $405 per hour. Required fees: $150 per term. Tuition and fees vary according to campus/location and program. *Financial support:* Teaching assistantships, career-related internships or fieldwork, Federal Work-Study, scholarships/grants, and unspecified assistantships available. Support available to part-time students. Financial award applicants required to submit FAFSA. *Unit head:* Dr. Tom Williams, Chair, 601-925-3844, E-mail: twilliams@mc.edu.

Mississippi State University, College of Education, Department of Curriculum and Instruction, Mississippi State, MS 39762. Offers curriculum and instruction (PhD); elementary education (MS, Ed D, PhD, Ed S); secondary education (MS, Ed D, PhD, Ed S). *Accreditation:* NCATE. Part-time and evening/weekend programs available. *Faculty:* 23 full-time (20 women), 13 part-time/adjunct (9 women). *Students:* 15 full-time (8 women), 85 part-time (67 women); includes 23 minority (22 African Americans, 1 American Indian/Alaska Native). Average age 31. 10 applicants, 60% accepted, 4 enrolled. In 2006, 48 master's, 14 doctorates awarded. *Degree requirements:* For master's, comprehensive exam; for doctorate, thesis/dissertation; for Ed S, thesis or alternative, comprehensive exam. *Entrance requirements:* For master's, GRE, minimum GPA of 2.75 in junior and senior year, eligibility for initial teacher certification; for doctorate, GRE, minimum graduate GPA of 3.4; for Ed S, GRE, minimum graduate GPA of 3.2. *Application deadline:* For fall admission, 3/1 priority date for domestic students; for spring admission, 9/1 priority date for domestic students. Applications are processed on a rolling basis. Application fee: $30. Electronic applications accepted. *Expenses:* Tuition, state resident: full-time $4,550; part-time $253 per hour. Tuition, nonresident: full-time $10,552; part-time $584 per hour. International tuition: $10,882 full-time. Tuition and fees vary according to course load. *Financial support:* In 2006–07, 30 students received support; research assistantships with tuition reimbursements available, teaching assistantships with tuition reimbursements available, Federal Work-Study, institutionally sponsored loans, scholarships/grants, unspecified assistantships, and work on faculty secured grants available. Financial award applicants required to submit FAFSA. *Faculty research:* Early childhood education, reading, rural schools, multicultural education, use of technology in instruction. *Unit head:* Dr. Unda T. Coats, Interim Head, 662-325-3747, Fax: 662-325-7857, E-mail: ltc1@ra.msstate.edu. *Application contact:* Dr. Phil Bonfanti, Director of Admissions, 662-325-4104, Fax: 662-325-8872, E-mail: admit@msstate.edu.

Missouri State University, Graduate College, College of Arts and Letters, Department of Art and Design, Springfield, MO 65804-0094. Offers secondary education (MS Ed), including art. *Faculty:* 7 full-time (3 women). *Students:* 2 full-time (both women), 3 part-time (2 women). Average age 49. In 2006, 2 degrees awarded. *Entrance requirements:* For master's, minimum GPA of 3.0, 9-12 certification. Additional exam requirements/recommendations for international students: Required—TOEFL (minimum score 550 paper-based; 213 computer-based; 79 iBT). *Application deadline:* For fall admission, 7/20 priority date for domestic students; for spring admission, 12/20 priority date for domestic students. Application fee: $35. *Expenses:* Tuition, state resident: full-time $3,582; part-time $199 per credit hour. Tuition, nonresident: full-time $6,984; part-time $199 per credit hour. Required fees: $548. Full-time tuition and fees vary according to course level, course load, program and reciprocity agreements. *Financial support:* Applicants required to submit FAFSA. *Unit head:* Dr. Andrew Cohen, Head, 407-836-6055, E-mail: artanddesign@missouristate.edu. *Application contact:* Judith Fowler, Graduate Program Director, E-mail: judyfowler@missouristate.edu.

Missouri State University, Graduate College, College of Arts and Letters, Department of English, Springfield, MO 65804-0094. Offers English and writing (MA); secondary education (MS Ed), including English. Part-time and evening/weekend programs available. *Faculty:* 24 full-time (13 women). *Students:* 59 full-time (39 women), 31 part-time (18 women); includes 4 minority (1 African American, 3 Asian Americans or Pacific Islanders), 3 international. Average age 30. 29 applicants, 59% accepted, 16 enrolled. In 2006, 19 degrees awarded. *Degree requirements:* For master's, one foreign language, thesis or alternative, comprehensive exam. *Entrance requirements:* For master's, GRE (MA), minimum GPA of 3.0 (MA), 9-12 teacher certification (MS Ed). Additional exam requirements/recommendations for international students: Required—TOEFL (minimum score 550 paper-based; 213 computer-based; 79 iBT). *Application deadline:* For fall admission, 7/20 for domestic students; for spring admission, 12/20 for domestic students. Applications are processed on a rolling basis. Application fee: $35. Electronic applications accepted. *Expenses:* Tuition, state resident: full-time $3,582; part-time $199 per credit hour. Tuition, nonresident: full-time $6,984; part-time $199 per credit hour. Required fees: $548. Full-time tuition and fees vary according to course level, course load, program and reciprocity agreements. *Financial support:* In 2006–07, research assistantships with full tuition reimbursements (averaging $8,750 per year), 25 teaching assistantships with full tuition reimbursements (averaging $6,780 per year) were awarded; Federal Work-Study, institutionally sponsored loans, scholarships/grants, tuition waivers (partial), and unspecified assistantships also available. Support available to part-time students. Financial award application deadline: 3/31; financial award applicants required to submit FAFSA. *Unit head:* Dr. W. D. Blackmon, Head, 417-836-5107, Fax: 417-836-6940, E-mail: wdblackon@missouristate.edu.

Missouri State University, Graduate College, College of Arts and Letters, Department of Modern and Classical Languages, Springfield, MO 65804-0094. Offers secondary education (MS Ed), including French, German, Spanish. *Faculty:* 5 full-time (2 women). *Students:* 2 full-time (both women), 2 part-time (both women); includes 1 minority (Hispanic American) Average age 33. 2 applicants, 50% accepted, 1 enrolled. In 2006, 1 degree awarded. *Entrance requirements:* For master's, grades 9–12 teaching certification. Additional exam requirements/recommendations for international students: Required—TOEFL (minimum score 550 paper-based; 213 computer-based; 79 iBT), IELTS (minimum score 6). *Application deadline:* For fall admission, 7/20 priority date for domestic students; for spring admission, 12/20 priority date for domestic students. Application fee: $35. *Expenses:* Tuition, state resident: full-time $3,582; part-time $199 per credit hour. Tuition, nonresident: full-time $6,984; part-time $199 per credit hour. Required fees: $548. Full-time tuition and fees vary according to course level, course load, program and reciprocity agreements. *Financial support:* Teaching assistantships with full tuition reimbursements available. Financial award applicants required to submit FAFSA. *Unit head:* Dr. Madeleine Kernen, Head, 417-836-7626, E-mail: mcl@missouristate.edu.

Missouri State University, Graduate College, College of Arts and Letters, Department of Music, Springfield, MO 65804-0094. Offers music (MM); secondary education (MS Ed), including music. *Accreditation:* NASM. Part-time and evening/weekend programs available. *Faculty:* 21 full-time (8 women). *Students:* 11 full-time (4 women), 16 part-time (9 women); includes 2 minority (1 Asian American or Pacific Islander, 1 Hispanic American), 1 international. Average age 26. 16 applicants, 56% accepted, 5 enrolled. In 2006, 18 degrees awarded. *Degree requirements:* For master's, thesis or alternative, comprehensive exam. *Entrance requirements:* For master's, GRE, 9-12 teaching certification (MS Ed). Additional exam requirements/recommendations for international students: Required—TOEFL (minimum score 550 paper-based; 213 computer-based; 79 iBT). *Application deadline:* For fall admission, 7/20 for domestic students; for spring admission, 12/20 for domestic students. Applications are processed on a rolling basis. Application fee: $35. Electronic applications accepted. *Expenses:* Tuition, state resident: full-time $3,582; part-time $199 per credit hour. Tuition, nonresident: full-time $6,984; part-time $199 per credit hour. Required fees: $548. Full-time tuition and fees vary according to course level, course load, program and reciprocity agreements. *Financial support:* In 2006–07, 10 teaching assistantships with full tuition reimbursements (averaging $6,780 per year) were awarded; research assistantships with full tuition reimbursements, Federal Work-Study, institutionally sponsored loans, scholarships/grants, tuition waivers (partial), and unspecified assistantships also available. Financial award application deadline: 3/31; financial award applicants required to submit FAFSA. *Unit head:* Dr. Roger Stoner, Head, 417-836-4122, Fax: 417-836-7665, E-mail: music@missouristate.edu.

Missouri State University, Graduate College, College of Arts and Letters, Department of Theatre and Dance, Springfield, MO 65804-0094. Offers secondary education (MS Ed), including speech and theatre; theatre (MA). *Accreditation:* NAST. Part-time programs available. *Faculty:* 8 full-time (4 women). *Students:* 3 full-time (0 women), 3 part-time (1 woman); includes 2 minority (both African Americans) Average age 33. 9 applicants, 44% accepted, 2 enrolled. In 2006, 6 degrees awarded. *Degree requirements:* For master's, thesis or alternative, comprehensive exam. *Entrance requirements:* For master's, minimum GPA of 3.0 (MA), 9-12 teaching certification (MS Ed). Additional exam requirements/recommendations for international students: Required—TOEFL (minimum score 550 paper-based; 213 computer-based; 79 iBT). *Application deadline:* For fall admission, 7/20 for domestic students; for spring admission, 12/20 for domestic students. Applications are processed on a rolling basis. Application fee: $35. Electronic applications accepted. *Expenses:* Tuition, state resident: full-time $3,582; part-time $199 per credit hour. Tuition, nonresident: full-time $6,984; part-time $199 per credit hour. Required fees: $548. Full-time tuition and fees vary according to course level, course load, program and reciprocity agreements. *Financial support:* In 2006–07, 4 teaching assistantships with tuition reimbursements (averaging $6,780 per year) were awarded; research assistantships with full tuition reimbursements, Federal Work-Study, institutionally sponsored loans, scholarships/grants, and unspecified assistantships also available. Financial award application deadline: 3/31; financial award applicants required to submit FAFSA. *Unit head:* Wade S. Thompson, Acting Head, 417-836-4400, Fax: 417-836-4234, E-mail: wadethompson@missouristate.edu.

Missouri State University, Graduate College, College of Business Administration, Department of Computer Information Systems, Springfield, MO 65804-0094. Offers computer information systems (MS); secondary education (MS Ed), including business. Part-time and evening/weekend programs available. *Faculty:* 13 full-time (4 women). *Students:* 30 full-time (8 women), 9 part-time (7 women); includes 2 minority (1 African American, 1 Hispanic American), 2 international. Average age 35. 30 applicants, 40% accepted, 12 enrolled. In 2006, 11 degrees awarded. *Degree requirements:* For master's, thesis optional. *Entrance requirements:* For master's, GMAT, 3 years of work experience in computer information systems, minimum GPA of 2.75 (MS), 9-12 teaching certification (MS Ed). Additional exam requirements/recommendations for international students: Required—TOEFL (minimum score 550 paper-based; 213 computer-based; 79 iBT), IELTS (minimum score 6). *Application deadline:* For fall admission, 7/20 priority date for domestic students; for spring admission, 12/20 priority date for domestic students. Applications are processed on a rolling basis. Application fee: $35. *Expenses:* Contact institution. Full-time tuition and fees vary according to course level, course load, program and reciprocity agreements. *Financial support:* Teaching assistantships with full tuition reimbursements, career-related internships or fieldwork, institutionally sponsored loans, scholarships/grants, tuition waivers (partial), and unspecified assistantships available. Support available to part-time students. Financial award application deadline: 3/31; financial award applicants required to submit FAFSA. *Unit head:* Dr. Jerry Chin, Head, 417-836-4131, Fax: 417-836-6907, E-mail: jerrychin@missouristate.edu.

Missouri State University, Graduate College, College of Education, Department of Educational Administration, Springfield, MO 65804-0094. Offers director of special education (Ed S); educational administration (MS Ed, Ed S); elementary education (MS Ed); elementary principal (Ed S); secondary education (MS Ed); secondary principal (Ed S); special education (MS Ed); superintendent (Ed S). Part-time and evening/weekend programs available. *Faculty:* 6 full-time (1 woman), 3 part-time/adjunct (0 women). *Students:* 10 full-time (8 women), 143 part-time (94 women); includes 1 minority (African American), 1 international. Average age 37. 13 applicants, 92% accepted, 10 enrolled. In 2006, 33 master's, 17 other advanced degrees awarded. *Degree requirements:* For master's and Ed S, thesis or alternative, comprehensive exam. *Entrance requirements:* For master's, minimum GPA of 2.75; for Ed S, GRE General Test, MAT, minimum GPA of 2.75. Additional exam requirements/recommendations for international students: Required—TOEFL (minimum score 550 paper-based; 213 computer-based; 79 iBT). *Application deadline:* For fall admission, 7/20 priority date for domestic students; for spring admission, 12/20 priority date for domestic students. Applications are processed on a rolling basis. Application fee: $35. Electronic applications accepted. *Expenses:* Tuition, state resident: full-time $3,582; part-time $199 per credit hour. Tuition, nonresident: full-time $6,984; part-time $199 per credit hour. Required fees: $548. Full-time tuition and fees vary according to course level, course load, program and reciprocity agreements. *Financial support:* In 2006–07, 1 teaching assistantship with full tuition reimbursement (averaging $6,780 per year) was awarded; career-related internships or fieldwork, Federal Work-Study, scholarships/grants, and unspecified assistantships also available. Financial award application deadline: 3/31; financial award applicants required to submit FAFSA. *Unit head:* Dr. Charles Barke, Acting Head, 417-836-5392, Fax: 417-836-6905, E-mail: edadmin@missouristate.edu.

Missouri State University, Graduate College, College of Health and Human Services, Department of Health, Physical Education, and Recreation, Springfield, MO 65804-0094. Offers health promotion and wellness management (MS); public health (MPH); secondary education (MS Ed), including physical education. Part-time programs available. *Faculty:* 12 full-time (4 women). *Students:* 43 full-time (11 women), 36 part-time (18 women); includes 1 minority (Hispanic American), 45 international. Average age 27. 126 applicants, 73% accepted, 37 enrolled. In 2006, 15 degrees awarded. *Degree requirements:* For master's, thesis or alternative, comprehensive exam. *Entrance requirements:* For master's, GRE (MS, MPH), minimum GPA of 2.8 (MS), minimum GPA of 3.0 (MPH), 9-12 teaching certification (MS Ed). Additional exam requirements/recommendations for international students: Required—TOEFL (minimum score 550 paper-based; 213 computer-based; 79 iBT). *Application deadline:* For fall admission, 7/20 priority date for domestic students; for spring admission, 12/20 priority date for domestic students. Applications are processed on a rolling basis. Application fee: $35. Electronic applications accepted. *Expenses:* Tuition, state resident: full-time $3,582; part-time $199 per credit hour. Tuition, nonresident: full-time $6,984; part-time $199 per credit hour. Required fees: $548. Full-time tuition and fees vary according to course level, course load, program and reciprocity agreements. *Financial support:* In 2006–07, 6 teaching assistantships with full tuition reimbursements (averaging $6,780 per year) were awarded; research assistantships with full tuition reimbursements, Federal Work-Study, scholarships/grants, and unspecified assistantships also available. Financial award application deadline: 3/31; financial award applicants required to submit FAFSA. *Unit head:* Dr. Sarah McCallister, Acting Head, 417-836-6582, Fax: 417-836-5371, E-mail: sarahmccallister@missouristate.edu. *Application contact:* Dr. Sarah McCallister, Acting Head, 417-836-6582, Fax: 417-836-5371, E-mail: sarahmccallister@missouristate.edu.

Missouri State University, Graduate College, College of Humanities and Public Affairs, Department of History, Springfield, MO 65804-0094. Offers history (MA); secondary education (MS Ed), including history, social science. Part-time programs available. *Faculty:* 16 full-time (1 woman). *Students:* 12 full-time (5 women), 58 part-time (24 women); includes 2 minority (1 American Indian/Alaska Native, 1 Hispanic American). Average age 34. 23 applicants, 83% accepted, 12 enrolled. In 2006, 9 degrees awarded. *Degree requirements:* For master's, thesis or alternative, comprehensive exam. *Entrance requirements:* For master's, minimum GPA of 2.75, 24 hours of undergraduate course work in history (MA), 9-12 teaching certification (MS Ed). Additional exam requirements/recommendations for international students: Required—TOEFL (minimum score 550 paper-based; 213 computer-based; 79 iBT), IELTS (minimum score 6). *Application deadline:* For fall admission, 7/20 priority date for domestic students; for spring admission, 12/20 priority date for domestic students. Applications are processed on a rolling basis. Application fee: $35. Electronic applications accepted. *Expenses:* Tuition, state resident: full-time $3,582; part-time $199 per credit hour. Tuition, nonresident: full-time $6,984; part-time $199 per credit hour. Required fees: $548. Full-time tuition and fees vary according to course level, course load, program and reciprocity agreements. *Financial support:* In 2006–07, 2 research assistantships with full tuition reimbursements (averaging $9,000 per year), 2 teaching assistantships with full tuition reimbursements (averaging $9,000 per year) were awarded; Federal Work-Study, scholarships/grants, and unspecified assistantships also available. Support available to part-time students. Financial award application deadline: 3/31; financial award applicants required to submit FAFSA. *Faculty research:* Recent U.S. history, Native American history, legal history, women's history, ancient Near East. *Unit head:* Michael Sheng, Head, 417-836-5511, Fax: 417-836-5523, E-mail: history@missouristate.edu.

Missouri State University, Graduate College, College of Natural and Applied Sciences, Department of Agriculture, Springfield, MO 65804-0094. Offers agriculture (MNAS); fruit science (MNAS); plant science (MS); secondary education (MS Ed), including agriculture. *Faculty:* 15 full-time (2 women), 1 (woman) part-time/adjunct. *Students:* 16 full-time (10 women), 10 part-time (5 women); includes 1 minority (Asian American or Pacific Islander), 3 international. Average age 29. 17 applicants, 76% accepted, 12 enrolled. In 2006, 7 degrees awarded. *Degree requirements:* For master's, thesis or alternative, comprehensive exam. *Entrance requirements:* For master's, GRE (MS plant science, MNAS), 9–12 teacher certification (MS Ed), minimum GPA of 3.0 (MS plant science, MNAS). Additional exam requirements/recommendations for international students: Required—TOEFL (minimum score 550 paper-based; 213 computer-based; 79 iBT). *Application deadline:* For fall admission, 7/20 priority date for domestic students; for spring admission, 12/20 priority date for domestic students. Applications are processed on a rolling basis. Application fee: $35. Electronic applications accepted. *Expenses:* Tuition, state resident: full-time $3,582; part-time $199 per credit hour. Tuition, nonresident: full-time $6,984; part-time $199 per credit hour. Required fees: $548. Full-time tuition and fees vary according to course level, course load, program and reciprocity agreements. *Financial support:* In 2006–07, 4 research assistantships (averaging $9,000 per year), 7 teaching assistantships (averaging $9,000 per year) were awarded. Financial award application deadline: 3/31; financial award applicants required to submit FAFSA. *Unit head:* Dr. W. Anson Elliott, Head, 417-836-5638, E-mail: ansonelliot@missouristate.edu. *Application contact:* Dr. W. Anson Elliott, Head, 417-836-5638, E-mail: ansonelliot@missouristate.edu.

Missouri State University, Graduate College, College of Natural and Applied Sciences, Department of Applied Consumer Sciences, Springfield, MO 65804-0094. Offers consumer sciences (MNAS); secondary education (MS Ed), including consumer sciences. *Faculty:* 2

Secondary Education

Missouri State University (continued)
full-time (both women). *Students:* Average age 26. 1 applicant, 100% accepted, 1 enrolled. In 2006, 2 degrees awarded. *Degree requirements:* For master's, thesis or alternative, comprehensive exam. *Entrance requirements:* For master's, GRE (MNAS), 9–12 teaching certification (MS Ed), minimum GPA of 3.0 (MNAS). Additional exam requirements/recommendations for international students: Required—TOEFL (minimum score 550 paper-based; 213 computer-based; 79 iBT). *Application deadline:* For fall admission, 7/20 priority date for domestic students; for spring admission, 12/20 priority date for domestic students. Application fee: $35. *Expenses:* Tuition, state resident: full-time $3,582; part-time $199 per credit hour. Tuition, nonresident: full-time $6,984; part-time $199 per credit hour. Required fees: $548. Full-time tuition and fees vary according to course level, course load, program and reciprocity agreements. *Financial support:* In 2006–07, 1 research assistantship (averaging $9,000 per year) was awarded; teaching assistantships with full tuition reimbursements, career-related internships or fieldwork, Federal Work-Study, scholarships/grants, and unspecified assistantships also available. Financial award application deadline: 3/31; financial award applicants required to submit FAFSA. *Faculty research:* Clothing design, merchandising, hospitality and restaurant management, interior design. *Unit head:* Dr. Michele Granger, Head, 417-836-5175, Fax: 417-836-4341, E-mail: michelegranger@missouristate.edu. *Application contact:* Dr. Michele Granger, Head, 417-836-5175, Fax: 417-836-4341, E-mail: michelegranger@missouristate.edu.

Missouri State University, Graduate College, College of Natural and Applied Sciences, Department of Biology, Springfield, MO 65804-0094. Offers biology (MNAS, MS); secondary education (MS Ed), including biology. *Faculty:* 19 full-time (4 women), 5 part-time/adjunct (1 woman). *Students:* 20 full-time (5 women), 25 part-time (9 women); includes 2 minority (both American Indian/Alaska Native), 3 international. Average age 25. 26 applicants, 65% accepted, 14 enrolled. In 2006, 17 degrees awarded. *Degree requirements:* For master's, thesis or alternative, comprehensive exam. *Entrance requirements:* For master's, GRE (MS and MNAS), 24 hours of course work in biology, minimum GPA of 3.0 (MS), 9-12 teacher certification (MS Ed), 3.0 GPA (MNAS). Additional exam requirements/recommendations for international students: Required—TOEFL (minimum score 550 paper-based; 213 computer-based; 79 iBT). *Application deadline:* For fall admission, 7/20 priority date for domestic students; for spring admission, 12/20 priority date for domestic students. Applications are processed on a rolling basis. Application fee: $35. Electronic applications accepted. *Expenses:* Tuition, state resident: full-time $3,582; part-time $199 per credit hour. Tuition, nonresident: full-time $6,984; part-time $199 per credit hour. Required fees: $548. Full-time tuition and fees vary according to course level, course load, program and reciprocity agreements. *Financial support:* In 2006–07, 2 research assistantships with full tuition reimbursements (averaging $9,000 per year), 6 teaching assistantships with full tuition reimbursements (averaging $9,000 per year) were awarded; Federal Work-Study, scholarships/grants, and unspecified assistantships also available. Financial award application deadline: 3/31; financial award applicants required to submit FAFSA. *Faculty research:* Field biology, organismal biology, microbiology. *Unit head:* Dr. S. Alicia Mathis, Head, 417-836-5126, Fax: 417-836-6934, E-mail: biology@missouristate.edu. *Application contact:* Dr. Thomas Tomasi, Graduate Director, 417-836-5169, Fax: 417-836-6934, E-mail: tomtomasi@missouristate.edu.

Missouri State University, Graduate College, College of Natural and Applied Sciences, Department of Chemistry, Springfield, MO 65804-0094. Offers chemistry (MNAS, MS); secondary education (MS Ed), including chemistry. Part-time programs available. *Faculty:* 14 full-time (1 woman), 1 part-time/adjunct (0 women). *Students:* 7 full-time (3 women), 8 part-time (2 women), 3 international. Average age 26. 18 applicants, 17% accepted, 2 enrolled. In 2006, 4 degrees awarded. *Degree requirements:* For master's, thesis, comprehensive exam. *Entrance requirements:* For master's, GRE General Test (MS, MNAS), minimum undergraduate GPA of 3.0 (MS and MNAS), 9-12 teacher certification (MS Ed). Additional exam requirements/recommendations for international students: Required—TOEFL (minimum score 550 paper-based; 213 computer-based; 79 iBT). *Application deadline:* For fall admission, 7/20 priority date for domestic students; for spring admission, 12/20 priority date for domestic students. Applications are processed on a rolling basis. Application fee: $35. Electronic applications accepted. *Expenses:* Tuition, state resident: full-time $3,582; part-time $199 per credit hour. Tuition, nonresident: full-time $6,984; part-time $199 per credit hour. Required fees: $548. Full-time tuition and fees vary according to course level, course load, program and reciprocity agreements. *Financial support:* In 2006–07, 1 research assistantship with full tuition reimbursement (averaging $9,000 per year) was awarded; teaching assistantships with full tuition reimbursements, Federal Work-Study, scholarships/grants, and unspecified assistantships also available. Financial award application deadline: 3/31; financial award applicants required to submit FAFSA. *Faculty research:* Chemistry of environmental systems, mechanisms of organic and organometallic reactions, enzymatic activity in lipid and protein reactions, computational chemistry, polymer properties. Total annual research expenditures: $80,000. *Unit head:* Dr. Paul Toom, Acting Head, 417-836-5506, Fax: 417-836-6934, E-mail: chemistry@missouristate.edu.

Missouri State University, Graduate College, College of Natural and Applied Sciences, Department of Geography, Geology, and Planning, Springfield, MO 65804-0094. Offers geography, geology and planning (MNAS); geospatial sciences (MS); secondary education (MS Ed), including earth science, geography. *Accreditation:* ACSP. Part-time and evening/weekend programs available. *Faculty:* 19 full-time (3 women). *Students:* 9 full-time (4 women), 20 part-time (7 women), 4 international. Average age 32. 15 applicants, 93% accepted, 8 enrolled. In 2006, 8 degrees awarded. *Degree requirements:* For master's, thesis (for some programs), comprehensive exam. *Entrance requirements:* For master's, GRE General Test (MS, MNAS), minimum undergraduate GPA of 3.0 (MS, MNAS), 9-12 teacher certification (MS Ed). Additional exam requirements/recommendations for international students: Required—TOEFL (minimum score 550 paper-based; 213 computer-based; 79 iBT). *Application deadline:* For fall admission, 7/20 priority date for domestic students; for spring admission, 12/20 priority date for domestic students. Applications are processed on a rolling basis. Application fee: $35. Electronic applications accepted. *Expenses:* Tuition, state resident: full-time $3,582; part-time $199 per credit hour. Tuition, nonresident: full-time $6,984; part-time $199 per credit hour. Required fees: $548. Full-time tuition and fees vary according to course level, course load, program and reciprocity agreements. *Financial support:* In 2006–07, 2 research assistantships with full tuition reimbursements (averaging $9,000 per year), 6 teaching assistantships with full tuition reimbursements (averaging $6,780 per year) were awarded; career-related internships or fieldwork, Federal Work-Study, scholarships/grants, and unspecified assistantships also available. Financial award application deadline: 3/31; financial award applicants required to submit FAFSA. *Faculty research:* Water resources, small town planning, recreation and open space planning. *Unit head:* Dr. Tom Plymate, Acting Head, 417-836-5800, Fax: 417-836-6934, E-mail: tomplymate@missouristate.edu. *Application contact:* Dr. Robert T. Pavlowsky, Graduate Adviser, 417-836-8473, Fax: 417-836-6006, E-mail: bobpavlowsky@missouristate.edu.

Missouri State University, Graduate College, College of Natural and Applied Sciences, Department of Mathematics, Springfield, MO 65804-0094. Offers mathematics (MS); secondary education (MS Ed), including mathematics. Part-time programs available. *Faculty:* 21 full-time (4 women). *Students:* 10 full-time (3 women), 12 part-time (6 women); includes 1 minority (Asian American or Pacific Islander) Average age 26. 11 applicants, 91% accepted, 9 enrolled. In 2006, 9 degrees awarded. *Degree requirements:* For master's, thesis or alternative, comprehensive exam. *Entrance requirements:* For master's, GRE (MS, MNAS), minimum undergraduate GPA of 3.0 (MS, MNAS), 9-12 teacher certification (MS Ed). Additional exam requirements/recommendations for international students: Required—TOEFL (minimum score 550 paper-based; 213 computer-based; 79 iBT). *Application deadline:* For fall admission, 7/20 priority date for domestic students; for spring admission, 12/20 priority date for domestic students. Applications are processed on a rolling basis. Application fee: $35. Electronic applications accepted. *Expenses:* Tuition, state resident: full-time $3,582; part-time $199 per credit hour. Tuition, nonresident: full-time $6,984; part-time $199 per credit hour. Required fees: $548. Full-time tuition and fees vary according to course level, course load, program and reciprocity agreements. *Financial support:* In 2006–07, 6 teaching assistantships with full tuition reimbursements (averaging $9,000 per year) were awarded; research assistantships with full tuition reimbursements, Federal Work-Study, scholarships/grants, and unspecified assistantships also available. Financial award application deadline: 3/31; financial award applicants required to submit FAFSA. *Faculty research:* Harmonic analysis, commutative algebra, number theory, K-theory, probability. *Unit head:* Dr. Yungchen Cheng, Head, 417-836-5112, Fax: 417-836-6966, E-mail: yungchencheng@missouristate.edu.

Missouri State University, Graduate College, College of Natural and Applied Sciences, Department of Physics, Astronomy, and Materials Science, Springfield, MO 65804-0094. Offers materials science (MS); physics, astronomy, and materials science (MNAS); secondary education (MS Ed), including physics. Part-time programs available. *Faculty:* 11 full-time (0 women). *Students:* 11 full-time (2 women), 3 part-time; includes 1 minority (Hispanic American), 7 international. Average age 26. 12 applicants, 42% accepted, 1 enrolled. In 2006, 5 degrees awarded. *Degree requirements:* For master's, thesis, comprehensive exam. *Entrance requirements:* For master's, GRE (MS, MNAS), minimum undergraduate GPA of 3.0 (MS and MNAS), 9-12 teaching certification (MS Ed). Additional exam requirements/recommendations for international students: Required—TOEFL (minimum score 550 paper-based; 213 computer-based; 79 iBT). *Application deadline:* For fall admission, 7/20 priority date for domestic students; for spring admission, 12/20 priority date for domestic students. Applications are processed on a rolling basis. Application fee: $35. Electronic applications accepted. *Expenses:* Tuition, state resident: full-time $3,582; part-time $199 per credit hour. Tuition, nonresident: full-time $6,984; part-time $199 per credit hour. Required fees: $548. Full-time tuition and fees vary according to course level, course load, program and reciprocity agreements. *Financial support:* In 2006–07, 8 research assistantships with full tuition reimbursements (averaging $9,000 per year), 1 teaching assistantship with full tuition reimbursement (averaging $9,000 per year) were awarded; Federal Work-Study, scholarships/grants, and unspecified assistantships also available. Financial award application deadline: 3/31; financial award applicants required to submit FAFSA. *Faculty research:* Nanocomposites, ferroelectricity, infrared focal plane array sensors, biosensors. *Unit head:* Dr. Pawan Kahol, Head, 417-836-5131, Fax: 417-836-6226, E-mail: materialsscience@missouristate.edu.

Montana State University–Billings, College of Education and Human Services, Department of Educational Theory and Practice, Option in Secondary Education, Billings, MT 59101-0298. Offers M Ed. *Accreditation:* NCATE. Part-time programs available. *Students:* 59. 7 applicants, 100% accepted, 7 enrolled. In 2006, 18 degrees awarded. *Degree requirements:* For master's, professional paper or thesis, thesis optional. *Entrance requirements:* For master's, GRE General Test or MAT, minimum GPA of 3.0 (undergraduate), 3.25 (graduate). *Application deadline:* Applications are processed on a rolling basis. Application fee: $40. *Expenses:* Tuition, state resident: full-time $4,599. Tuition, nonresident: full-time $10,786. *Financial support:* Teaching assistantships, career-related internships or fieldwork, Federal Work-Study, institutionally sponsored loans, scholarships/grants, tuition waivers (partial), and unspecified assistantships available. Support available to part-time students. Financial award application deadline: 5/1; financial award applicants required to submit FAFSA. *Application contact:* David M. Sullivan, Graduate Studies Counselor, 406-657-2053, Fax: 406-657-2299, E-mail: dsullivan@msubillings.edu.

Morehead State University, Graduate Programs, College of Education, Department of Curriculum and Instruction, Program in Secondary Education, Morehead, KY 40351. Offers MA Ed, MAT. *Accreditation:* NCATE. Part-time and evening/weekend programs available. *Students:* 59 full-time (39 women), 97 part-time (59 women); includes 5 minority (1 African American, 1 American Indian/Alaska Native, 3 Hispanic Americans), 2 international. Average age 32. In 2006, 65 degrees awarded. *Degree requirements:* For master's, oral and/or written comprehensive exams, thesis optional. *Entrance requirements:* For master's, GRE General Test, minimum GPA of 2.5, teaching certificate. Additional exam requirements/recommendations for international students: Required—TOEFL (minimum score 500 paper-based; 173 computer-based). *Application deadline:* For fall admission, 8/1 priority date for domestic and international students; for spring admission, 12/1 priority date for domestic and international students. Applications are processed on a rolling basis. Application fee: $0. Electronic applications accepted. *Financial support:* In 2006–07, 2 teaching assistantships (averaging $6,000 per year) were awarded; career-related internships or fieldwork and Federal Work-Study also available. Financial award application deadline: 4/1; financial award applicants required to submit FAFSA. *Faculty research:* Critical thinking techniques, student ability concepts, instructional applications of microcomputers, dropout prevention. *Application contact:* Michelle Barber, Graduate Admissions Counselor, 606-783-2039, Fax: 606-783-5061, E-mail: m.barber@moreheadstate.edu.

Morgan State University, School of Graduate Studies, School of Education and Urban Studies, MAT Program, Baltimore, MD 21251. Offers elementary education (MAT); high school education (MAT); middle school education (MAT). Part-time programs available. *Students:* 1. Average age 30. In 2006, 4 degrees awarded. *Degree requirements:* For master's, comprehensive exam. *Entrance requirements:* For master's, GRE General Test or MAT. *Application deadline:* For fall admission, 2/1 priority date for domestic students; for spring admission, 10/1 priority date for domestic students. Applications are processed on a rolling basis. Application fee: $0. *Expenses:* Tuition, state resident: part-time $272 per credit. Tuition, nonresident: part-time $478 per credit. Required fees: $38 per credit. *Financial support:* Fellowships available. Financial award application deadline: 4/1. *Faculty research:* Multicultural education, cooperative learning, psychology of cognition. *Unit head:* Dr. Marlene Greer-Chase, Graduate Coordinator, 443-885-1984, Fax: 443-885-8240. *Application contact:* Dr. Maurice C. Taylor, Dean, 443-885-3185, Fax: 443-885-8226, E-mail: mctaylor@moac.morgan.edu.

Mount Saint Mary College, Division of Education, Newburgh, NY 12550-3494. Offers adolescence and special education (MS Ed); adolescence education (MS Ed); childhood and special education (MS Ed); childhood education (MS Ed); literacy and special education (MS Ed); literacy/childhood (MS Ed); middle school (5-6) (MS Ed); middle school (7-9) (MS Ed); special education (1-6) (MS Ed); special education (7-12) (MS Ed). *Accreditation:* NCATE. Part-time and evening/weekend programs available. *Faculty:* 11 full-time (8 women), 21 part-time/adjunct (18 women). *Students:* 87 full-time (74 women), 368 part-time (303 women); includes 38 minority (12 African Americans, 2 American Indian/Alaska Native, 5 Asian Americans or Pacific Islanders, 19 Hispanic Americans). Average age 31. 164 applicants, 45% accepted, 58 enrolled. In 2006, 131 degrees awarded. *Application deadline:* Applications are processed on a rolling basis. Application fee: $35. *Expenses:* Tuition: Full-time $11,880; part-time $660 per credit. *Financial support:* In 2006–07, 30 students received support. Unspecified assistantships available. Financial award application deadline: 3/15. *Faculty research:* Learning and teaching styles, computers in special education, language development. *Unit head:* Theresa Lewis, Coordinator, 845-569-3149, Fax: 845-569-3535, E-mail: tlewis@msmc.edu.

Mount St. Mary's College, Graduate Division, Department of Education, Specialization in Secondary Education, Los Angeles, CA 90049-1599. Offers MS. *Students:* 29 full-time (17 women), 31 part-time (23 women); includes 6 African Americans, 6 Asian Americans or Pacific Islanders, 14 Hispanic Americans. Average age 33. *Degree requirements:* For master's, thesis, research project. *Entrance requirements:* For master's, MAT, minimum GPA of 3.0. Application fee: $50 ($75 for international students). *Expenses:* Tuition: Part-time $630 per unit. *Financial support:* Application deadline: 3/15; *Unit head:* Dr. Robin Gordon, Director, 213-477-2623. *Application contact:* Tom Hoener, Director, Graduate Recruitment, 213-477-2800, Fax: 213-477-2519, E-mail: thoener@msmc.la.edu.

Murray State University, College of Education, Department of Adolescent, Career and Special Education, Program in Secondary Education, Murray, KY 42071. Offers MA Ed, Ed S. *Accreditation:* NCATE. Part-time programs available. *Students:* 58. 5 applicants, 100% accepted. *Degree requirements:* For master's, thesis optional. *Entrance requirements:* Additional exam requirements/recommendations for international students: Required—TOEFL. *Application deadline:* Applications are processed on a rolling basis. Application fee: $25. *Financial support:*

Research assistantships, teaching assistantships, Federal Work-Study available. Financial award application deadline: 4/1. *Unit head:* Dr. Ginny Richerson, Chair, 270-809-4257, Fax: 270-809-2540, E-mail: ginny.richerson@murraystate.edu.

National-Louis University, National College of Education, Program in Secondary Education, Chicago, IL 60603. Offers MAT. *Students:* 197 full-time (111 women), 368 part-time (196 women); includes 66 minority (21 African Americans, 27 Asian Americans or Pacific Islanders, 18 Hispanic Americans). Average age 32. 58 applicants, 100% accepted. *Degree requirements:* For master's, student teaching experience. *Entrance requirements:* For master's, GRE, minimum GPA of 3.0. *Application deadline:* Applications are processed on a rolling basis. Application fee: $25. *Expenses:* Tuition: Full-time $17,685. One-time fee: $40 full-time. *Financial support:* Fellowships, career-related internships or fieldwork, Federal Work-Study, institutionally sponsored loans, and scholarships/grants available. Support available to part-time students. Financial award applicants required to submit FAFSA. *Unit head:* Dr. Carol Porter, Coordinator, 827-475-1100 Ext. 5180. *Application contact:* David McCulloch, Vice President for University Services, 800-443-5522 Ext. 5127, Fax: 847-465-0593, E-mail: dmcc@wheeling1.nl.edu.

New Jersey City University, Graduate and Continuing Education, College of Education, Department of Elementary and Secondary Education, Jersey City, NJ 07305-1597. Offers elementary education (MAT); secondary education (MAT). Part-time and evening/weekend programs available. *Faculty:* 11. *Students:* 1 (woman) full-time, 81 part-time (57 women); includes 13 minority (2 African Americans, 4 Asian Americans or Pacific Islanders, 7 Hispanic Americans). Average age 34. In 2006, 19 degrees awarded. *Application deadline:* For fall admission, 8/1 priority date for domestic students; for spring admission, 12/1 for domestic students. Applications are processed on a rolling basis. Application fee: $0. *Expenses:* Tuition, state resident: full-time $7,038; part-time $391 per credit. Tuition, nonresident: full-time $12,510; part-time $695 per credit. Required fees: $65 per credit. *Financial support:* Teaching assistantships, career-related internships or fieldwork and unspecified assistantships available. *Unit head:* Dr. Althea Hall, Coordinator, 201-200-2101.

Niagara University, Graduate Division of Education, Concentration in Teacher Education, Niagara Falls, Niagara University, NY 14109. Offers elementary education (MS Ed); secondary education (MS Ed). *Accreditation:* NCATE. *Faculty:* 4 full-time (1 woman), 6 part-time/adjunct (4 women). *Students:* 344 full-time (234 women), 3 part-time (all women); includes 14 minority (10 African Americans, 3 American Indian/Alaska Native, 1 Hispanic American), 259 international. Average age 25. In 2006, 206 degrees awarded. *Entrance requirements:* For master's, GRE General Test or MAT. *Application deadline:* For fall admission, 8/1 for domestic students. Applications are processed on a rolling basis. Application fee: $30. *Expenses:* Contact institution. *Financial support:* Career-related internships or fieldwork, Federal Work-Study, and scholarships/grants available. Financial award application deadline: 3/15. *Unit head:* Dr. Chandra Foote, Chair, 716-286-8549. *Application contact:* Dr. Debra A. Colley, Dean of Education, 716-286-8560, Fax: 716-286-8561, E-mail: dcolley@niagara.edu.

Norfolk State University, School of Graduate Studies, School of Education, Department of Secondary Education and School Leadership, Norfolk, VA 23504. Offers principal preparation (MA); secondary education (MAT); urban education/administration (MA), including teaching. *Accreditation:* NCATE. Part-time programs available. *Entrance requirements:* For master's, GRE General Test, PRAXIS I, minimum GPA of 3.0 in major, 2.5 overall. Additional exam requirements/recommendations for international students: Required—TOEFL (minimum score 500 paper-based).

Northern Arizona University, Graduate College, College of Education, Program in Secondary Education, Flagstaff, AZ 86011. Offers M Ed. *Degree requirements:* For master's, thesis optional. *Faculty research:* Early adolescent stress, vocational education, portfolio assessment, school-to-work, gender issues.

Northern Illinois University, Graduate School, College of Education, Department of Teaching and Learning, De Kalb, IL 60115-2854. Offers curriculum and instruction (MS Ed, Ed D), including curriculum leadership (Ed D), elementary education (Ed D), secondary education (Ed D); early childhood education (MS Ed); elementary education (MS Ed); special education (MS Ed). Part-time and evening/weekend programs available. *Faculty:* 22 full-time (14 women), 2 part-time/adjunct (both women). *Students:* 81 full-time (64 women), 534 part-time (417 women); includes 122 minority (21 African Americans, 12 Asian Americans or Pacific Islanders, 89 Hispanic Americans), 11 international. Average age 36. 92 applicants, 57% accepted, 43 enrolled. In 2006, 256 master's, 12 doctorates awarded. *Degree requirements:* For master's, thesis optional; for doctorate, thesis/dissertation, candidacy exam, dissertation defense. *Entrance requirements:* For master's, GRE General Test or MAT, minimum undergraduate GPA of 2.75; for doctorate, GRE General Test or MAT, minimum undergraduate GPA of 2.75, graduate 3.2. Additional exam requirements/recommendations for international students: Required—TOEFL (minimum score 550 paper-based; 213 computer-based). *Application deadline:* For fall admission, 6/1 for domestic students, 5/1 for international students; for spring admission, 11/1 for domestic students, 10/1 for international students. Applications are processed on a rolling basis. Application fee: $30. Electronic applications accepted. *Financial support:* In 2006–07, 27 research assistantships with full tuition reimbursements, 1 teaching assistantship with full tuition reimbursement were awarded; fellowships with full tuition reimbursements, career-related internships or fieldwork, Federal Work-Study, scholarships/grants, tuition waivers (full), and unspecified assistantships also available. Support available to part-time students. Financial award applicants required to submit FAFSA. *Faculty research:* Teacher certification, stress reduction during student teaching, teaching history, portfolios in student teaching. *Unit head:* Dr. Pamela Jackson, Acting Chair, 815-753-8452, E-mail: p30ngd1@wpo.cso.niu.edu.

Northern Michigan University, College of Graduate Studies, College of Professional Studies, School of Education, Program in Secondary Education, Marquette, MI 49855-5301. Offers MA Ed. *Accreditation:* NCATE. Part-time programs available. *Degree requirements:* For master's, thesis or alternative. *Entrance requirements:* For master's, minimum GPA of 3.0. *Faculty research:* Supervision and improvement of instruction.

Northern State University, Division of Graduate Studies in Education, Program in Teaching and Learning, Aberdeen, SD 57401-7198. Offers educational studies (MS Ed); elementary classroom teaching (MS Ed); health, physical education, and coaching (MS Ed); language and literacy (MS Ed); secondary classroom teaching (MS Ed); special education (MS Ed). *Accreditation:* NCATE. Part-time and evening/weekend programs available. *Faculty:* 69 full-time (19 women). *Students:* 5 full-time (3 women), 70 part-time (51 women); includes 3 minority (1 African American, 1 American Indian/Alaska Native, 1 Asian American or Pacific Islander). Average age 32. In 2006, 23 degrees awarded. *Degree requirements:* For master's, thesis optional. *Entrance requirements:* For master's, minimum GPA of 2.75. Additional exam requirements/recommendations for international students: Required—TOEFL (minimum score 550 paper-based; 213 computer-based). *Application deadline:* For fall admission, 8/15 priority date for domestic students; for spring admission, 12/15 for domestic students. Applications are processed on a rolling basis. Application fee: $35. Electronic applications accepted. *Expenses:* Tuition, state resident: full-time $3,373; part-time $120 per credit. Tuition, nonresident: full-time $9,943; part-time $355 per credit. International tuition: $13,000 full-time. Required fees: $86 per credit. One-time fee: $35 full-time. Tuition and fees vary according to course load, degree level and reciprocity agreements. *Financial support:* In 2006–07, 17 teaching assistantships with partial tuition reimbursements (averaging $4,812 per year) were awarded; career-related internships or fieldwork, Federal Work-Study, institutionally sponsored loans, scholarships/grants, and unspecified assistantships also available. Support available to part-time students. Financial award application deadline: 3/1; financial award applicants required to submit FAFSA. *Application contact:* Tammy K. Griffith, Senior Secretary, 605-626-2558, Fax: 605-626-2542, E-mail: griffith@northern.edu.

North Georgia College & State University, Graduate Studies, Program in Teacher Education, Dahlonega, GA 30597. Offers early childhood education (M Ed); educational leadership (Ed S); middle grades education (M Ed); secondary education (M Ed), including art education, biology education, chemistry education, English education, history education, mathematics education, physical education, science education; special education (M Ed), including inter-related special education, learning disabilities. *Accreditation:* NCATE. Part-time and evening/weekend programs available. Postbaccalaureate distance learning degree programs offered (minimal on-campus study). *Faculty:* 35 full-time (18 women), 9 part-time/adjunct (6 women). *Students:* 260. Average age 32. 120 applicants, 63% accepted. In 2006, 134 degrees awarded. *Degree requirements:* For master's, thesis optional. *Entrance requirements:* For master's, GRE General Test or MAT, minimum GPA of 2.75; for Ed S, GRE General Test or MAT, 3 years of teaching experience, master's degree, minimum graduate GPA of 3.25. *Application deadline:* For fall admission, 7/1 priority date for domestic students; for spring admission, 12/10 priority date for domestic students. Applications are processed on a rolling basis. Application fee: $25. Electronic applications accepted. *Expenses:* Tuition, state resident: full-time $3,044; part-time $127 per credit hour. Tuition, nonresident: full-time $12,172; part-time $508 per credit hour. Required fees: $892; $458 per semester. *Financial support:* Teaching assistantships, career-related internships or fieldwork and scholarships/grants available. Support available to part-time students. Financial award application deadline: 5/1. *Faculty research:* Computers and teachers' attitudes, rural versus urban teacher attitudes, teacher leadership roles, minority recruitment in teaching force. *Unit head:* Dr. Bob Michael, Dean, School of Education, 706-864-1998, Fax: 706-867-2850, E-mail: bmichael@ngcsu.edu. *Application contact:* Dr. Donna A. Gessell, Director of Graduate Studies and External Programs, 706-864-1528, Fax: 706-867-2795, E-mail: dgessell@ngcsu.edu.

Northwestern Oklahoma State University, School of Professional Studies, Program in Secondary Education, Alva, OK 73717-2799. Offers M Ed. *Accreditation:* NCATE. Part-time programs available. *Faculty:* 7 full-time (4 women). In 2006, 11 degrees awarded. *Degree requirements:* For master's, portfolio, thesis optional. *Entrance requirements:* For master's, GRE General Test or MAT, minimum GPA of 2.75. *Application deadline:* Applications are processed on a rolling basis. Application fee: $15. *Expenses:* Tuition, state resident: part-time $700 per year. Tuition, nonresident: part-time $1,715 per year. *Financial support:* Federal Work-Study available. Support available to part-time students. Financial award application deadline: 5/1. *Faculty research:* Teacher education, professional school models of pedagogy, competency exams for teachers, teacher accreditation/certification. *Unit head:* Dr. James Bowen, Dean of the School of Professional Studies, 580-327-8455.

Northwestern State University of Louisiana, Graduate Studies and Research, College of Education, Program in Secondary Education, Natchitoches, LA 71497. Offers MAT. *Students:* 2 full-time (0 women), 28 part-time (21 women); includes 7 minority (4 African Americans, 3 Hispanic Americans). Average age 31. *Degree requirements:* For master's, thesis or alternative, comprehensive exam, registration. *Entrance requirements:* For master's, GRE General Test, minimum undergraduate GPA of 2.5. *Application contact:* Dr. Steven G. Horton, Associate Provost/Dean, Graduate Studies, Research, and Information Systems, 318-357-5851, Fax: 318-357-5019, E-mail: grad_school@nsula.edu.

Northwestern State University of Louisiana, Graduate Studies and Research, College of Education, Programs in Education, Natchitoches, LA 71497. Offers business and distributive education (M Ed); counseling (M Ed); early childhood education (M Ed); education (M Ed); education leadership (M Ed); educational technology (M Ed); elementary teaching (M Ed); English education (M Ed); home economics education (M Ed); mathematics education (M Ed); reading (M Ed); science education (M Ed); secondary teaching (M Ed); social sciences education (M Ed). *Students:* 49 full-time (41 women), 245 part-time (206 women); includes 78 minority (70 African Americans, 5 American Indian/Alaska Native, 2 Asian Americans or Pacific Islanders, 1 Hispanic American). Average age 35. In 2006, 158 degrees awarded. *Degree requirements:* For master's, thesis or alternative, comprehensive exam, registration. *Entrance requirements:* For master's, GRE General Test, minimum undergraduate GPA of 2.5. *Application contact:* Dr. Steven G. Horton, Associate Provost/Dean, Graduate Studies, Research, and Information Systems, 318-357-5851, Fax: 318-357-5019, E-mail: grad_school@nsula.edu.

Northwestern State University of Louisiana, Graduate Studies and Research, College of Education, Programs in Educational Leadership and Instruction, Natchitoches, LA 71497. Offers counseling (Ed S); educational leadership (Ed S); educational technology (Ed S); elementary teaching (Ed S); reading (Ed S); secondary teaching (Ed S); special education (Ed S). *Students:* 17 full-time (15 women), 114 part-time (87 women); includes 55 minority (51 African Americans, 1 Asian American or Pacific Islander, 3 Hispanic Americans). Average age 39. In 2006, 11 degrees awarded. *Entrance requirements:* For degree, GRE General Test. *Application contact:* Dr. Steven G. Horton, Associate Provost/Dean, Graduate Studies, Research, and Information Systems, 318-357-5851, Fax: 318-357-5019, E-mail: grad_school@nsula.edu.

Northwestern University, The Graduate School, School of Education and Social Policy, Master of Science in Education Program, Evanston, IL 60208. Offers advanced teaching (MS); elementary education and policy (MS); higher education administration (MS); secondary teaching (MS). Part-time and evening/weekend programs available. *Faculty:* 4 full-time (2 women), 33 part-time/adjunct (17 women). *Students:* 64 full-time (40 women), 90 part-time (66 women); includes 21 minority (3 African Americans, 13 Asian Americans or Pacific Islanders, 5 Hispanic Americans), 1 international. Average age 25. 88 applicants, 65% accepted, 36 enrolled. In 2006, 82 degrees awarded. *Degree requirements:* For master's, project. *Entrance requirements:* For master's, GRE General Test, State of Illinois Basic Skills Exam (secondary and elementary). *Application deadline:* For fall admission, 7/1 priority date for domestic students; for winter admission, 11/5 priority date for domestic students; for spring admission, 1/21 priority date for domestic students. Applications are processed on a rolling basis. Application fee: $45. *Financial support:* In 2006–07, 6 students received support. Career-related internships or fieldwork, Federal Work-Study, institutionally sponsored loans, scholarships/grants, tuition waivers (partial), and unspecified assistantships available. Financial award application deadline: 1/7; financial award applicants required to submit FAFSA. *Faculty research:* Discussion/questioning. *Unit head:* Dr. Sophie Haroutunian-Gordon, Director, 847-467-1458, Fax: 847-467-2495, E-mail: shg@northwestern.edu. *Application contact:* Patricia Rodriguez, Assistant Director, 847-491-7526, Fax: 847-467-2495.

Northwest Missouri State University, Graduate School, College of Education and Human Services, Department of Curriculum and Instruction, Maryville, MO 64468-6001. Offers reading (MS Ed); special education (MS Ed); teaching: early childhood (MS Ed); teaching: elementary self contained (MS Ed); teaching: middle school (MS Ed); teaching: secondary (MS Ed). *Accreditation:* NCATE. Part-time programs available. *Faculty:* 10 full-time (all women). *Students:* 4 full-time (all women), 62 part-time (59 women); includes 2 minority (both Hispanic Americans) 26 applicants, 85% accepted, 12 enrolled. In 2006, 12 degrees awarded. *Degree requirements:* For master's, comprehensive exam. *Entrance requirements:* For master's, GRE General Test, minimum undergraduate GPA of 2.75, teaching certificate, writing sample. Additional exam requirements/recommendations for international students: Required—TOEFL (minimum score 550 paper-based; 213 computer-based). *Application deadline:* For fall admission, 7/1 for domestic and international students; for spring admission, 11/15 for domestic and international students. Applications are processed on a rolling basis. Application fee: $0 ($50 for international students). Electronic applications accepted. *Financial support:* In 2006–07, 14 students received support, including 3 research assistantships with full tuition reimbursements available (averaging $6,000 per year), 1 teaching assistantship with full tuition reimbursement available (averaging $6,000 per year); unspecified assistantships also available. Financial award application deadline: 3/1; financial award applicants required to submit FAFSA. *Unit head:* Dr. Barbara Crossland, Head, 660-562-1776, E-mail: barbara@mail.nwmissouri.edu. *Application contact:* Dr. Frances Shipley, Dean of Graduate School, 660-562-1145, Fax: 660-562-1096, E-mail: gradsch@nwmissouri.edu.

Northwest Missouri State University, Graduate School, College of Education and Human Services, Department of Educational Leadership, Program in Educational Leadership, Maryville,

Secondary Education

Northwest Missouri State University (continued)
MO 64468-6001. Offers educational leadership: elementary (MS Ed); educational leadership: secondary (MS Ed); elementary principalship (Ed S); secondary principalship (Ed S); superintendency (Ed S). *Accreditation:* NCATE. Part-time programs available. *Faculty:* 12 full-time (4 women). *Students:* 13 full-time (7 women), 87 part-time (56 women); includes 5 minority (4 African Americans, 1 Asian American or Pacific Islander). 29 applicants, 93% accepted, 20 enrolled. In 2006, 42 master's, 17 other advanced degrees awarded. *Degree requirements:* For master's, comprehensive exam; for Ed S, thesis, comprehensive exam. *Entrance requirements:* For master's, GRE General Test, minimum undergraduate GPA of 2.75, teaching certificate, writing sample; for Ed S, minimum graduate GPA of 3.25. Additional exam requirements/recommendations for international students: Required—TOEFL (minimum score 550 paper-based; 213 computer-based). *Application deadline:* For fall admission, 7/1 for domestic and international students; for spring admission, 11/15 for domestic and international students. Application fee: $0 ($50 for international students). *Financial support:* In 2006–07, 3 research assistantships with full tuition reimbursements (averaging $6,000 per year), 2 teaching assistantships with full tuition reimbursements (averaging $6,000 per year) were awarded; unspecified assistantships also available. Financial award application deadline: 3/1; financial award applicants required to submit FAFSA. *Application contact:* Dr. Frances Shipley, Dean of Graduate School, 660-562-1145, Fax: 660-562-1096, E-mail: gradsch@nwmissouri.edu.

Northwest Missouri State University, Graduate School, College of Education and Human Services, Department of Educational Leadership, Program in Secondary Individualized Prescribed Programs, Maryville, MO 64468-6001. Offers teaching secondary (MS Ed). *Faculty:* 13 full-time (4 women). *Entrance requirements:* Additional exam requirements/recommendations for international students: Required—TOEFL (minimum score 550 paper-based; 213 computer-based). *Application deadline:* For fall admission, 7/1 for domestic and international students; for spring admission, 11/15 for domestic and international students. Application fee: $0 ($50 for international students). *Unit head:* Dr. Cheryl Malm, Director, 660-562-1206. *Application contact:* Dr. Frances Shipley, Dean of Graduate School, 660-562-1145, Fax: 660-562-1096, E-mail: gradsch@nwmissouri.edu.

Nova Southeastern University, Fischler School of Education and Human Services, Graduate Teacher Education Program, Fort Lauderdale, FL 33314-7796. Offers athletic administration (MS); cognitive and behavioral disabilities (MS); computer science education (Ed S); computer science education (K-12) (MS); curriculum and teaching (Ed S); curriculum, instruction and technology (MS); curriculum, instruction, management and administration (Ed S); early childhood special education (MS); early literacy and reading (Ed S); early literacy education (MS); education technology (MS); educational leadership (administration K–12) (MS, Ed S); educational media (Ed S); educational media (K-12) (MS); elementary education (MS, Ed S), including ESOL endorsement (MS); English (MS, Ed S); exceptional student education (MS), including ESOL endorsement; gifted education (MS, Ed S); interdisciplinary arts education (MS); management and administration of educational programs (MS); mathematics (MS, Ed S); multicultural early intervention (MS); pre-kindergarten/primary (MS); preschool education (MS); reading (MS, Ed S); science (MS, Ed S); secondary education (MS); social studies (MS, Ed S); Spanish language (MS); teaching and learning (MA, MS), including curriculum and instruction (MA), elementary mathematics (MA), elementary reading (MA), K-12 technology integration (MA); teaching English to speakers of other languages (MS, Ed S); technology management and administration (Ed S); urban studies education (MS); varying exceptionalities (Ed S). Part-time and evening/weekend programs available. Postbaccalaureate distance learning degree programs offered. *Faculty:* 131 full-time (78 women), 548 part-time/adjunct (342 women). *Students:* 1,418 full-time (1,139 women), 3,464 part-time (2,877 women); includes 2,462 minority (1,732 African Americans, 13 American Indian/Alaska Native, 44 Asian Americans or Pacific Islanders, 673 Hispanic Americans), 77 international. Average age 38. 1,771 applicants, 80% accepted, 1419 enrolled. In 2006, 2,078 master's, 425 other advanced degrees awarded. *Degree requirements:* For master's and Ed S, thesis, practicum, internship. *Entrance requirements:* For master's, MAT, GRE, CLAST, CBEST, PRAXIS I, GKT, minimum GPA of 2.5; for Ed S, MAT or GRE, master's degree, teaching certificate, minimum GPA of 3.0. Additional exam requirements/recommendations for international students: Recommended—TOEFL (minimum score 550 paper-based; 213 computer-based), IELTS (minimum score 6). *Application deadline:* For fall admission, 8/11 priority date for domestic and international students; for winter admission, 12/28 priority date for domestic and international students; for spring admission, 4/22 priority date for domestic and international students. Applications are processed on a rolling basis. Application fee: $50. Electronic applications accepted. *Financial support:* Federal Work-Study available. Support available to part-time students. Financial award application deadline: 1/7. *Faculty research:* School effectiveness, critical thinking, leadership skills acquisition, child education, multicultural education. *Unit head:* Dr. Meline Kevorkian, Associate Dean of Master's and Educational Programs, 954-262-8500, Fax: 954-262-3606, E-mail: melinek@nova.edu. *Application contact:* Jennifer Quiñones Nottingham, Dean of Student Affairs, 800-986-3223 Ext. 8624, Fax: 954-262-3911, E-mail: jlquinon@nova.edu.

Oakland University, Graduate Study and Lifelong Learning, School of Education and Human Services, Department of Teacher Development and Educational Studies, Rochester, MI 48309-4401. Offers education studies (M Ed); secondary education (MAT). *Accreditation:* NCATE. *Faculty:* 6 full-time (5 women), 2 part-time/adjunct (both women). *Students:* 190 full-time (158 women), 170 part-time (130 women); includes 24 minority (13 African Americans, 1 American Indian/Alaska Native, 8 Asian Americans or Pacific Islanders, 2 Hispanic Americans). Average age 32. 146 applicants, 97% accepted, 125 enrolled. In 2006, 57 degrees awarded. *Entrance requirements:* For master's, minimum GPA of 3.0 for unconditional admission. *Application deadline:* For fall admission, 3/1 for domestic students. Application fee: $35. Electronic applications accepted. *Expenses:* Tuition, state resident: full-time $9,936; part-time $414 per credit. Tuition, nonresident: full-time $17,202; part-time $716 per credit. *Financial support:* Federal Work-Study, institutionally sponsored loans, and tuition waivers (full) available. Financial award application deadline: 3/1; financial award applicants required to submit FAFSA. *Faculty research:* Earth science for middle and high school teachers through real world connections, learning communities, content enrichment. *Unit head:* Dr. Dyanne M Tracy, Chair, 248-370-3064, Fax: 248-370-4605, E-mail: dtracy@oakland.edu.

Occidental College, Graduate Studies, Department of Education, Program in Secondary Education, Los Angeles, CA 90041-3314. Offers English and comparative literary studies (MAT); history (MAT); life science (MAT); mathematics (MAT); physical science (MAT); social science (MAT); Spanish (MAT). Part-time programs available. *Faculty:* 3 full-time (2 women), 2 part-time/adjunct (both women). *Students:* 4 full-time (all women), 3 part-time (1 woman); includes 5 minority (1 Asian American or Pacific Islander, 4 Hispanic Americans). Average age 25. 4 applicants, 100% accepted, 4 enrolled. In 2006, 4 degrees awarded. *Degree requirements:* For master's, final exam, graduate synthesis paper. *Entrance requirements:* For master's, GRE General Test, minimum GPA of 3.0. Additional exam requirements/recommendations for international students: Required—TOEFL (minimum score 625 paper-based). *Application deadline:* For fall admission, 3/1 for domestic and international students; for spring admission, 10/1 for domestic and international students. Applications are processed on a rolling basis. Application fee: $50. *Expenses: Contact institution. Financial support:* Fellowships, Federal Work-Study, institutionally sponsored loans, and scholarships/grants available. Support available to part-time students. Financial award application deadline: 3/1; financial award applicants required to submit FAFSA. *Unit head:* Chair, 323-259-2781, E-mail: edudept@oxy.edu. *Application contact:* Angela Allen, Credential Analyst/Department Services Coordinator, 323-259-2781, E-mail: edudept@oxy.edu.

Ohio University, Graduate Studies, College of Education, Department of Teacher Education, Athens, OH 45701-2979. Offers adolescent to young adult education (M Ed); curriculum and instruction (M Ed, PhD); mathematics education (PhD); middle child education (M Ed); reading and language arts (PhD); reading education (M Ed); social studies education (PhD); special education (M Ed, PhD). Part-time and evening/weekend programs available. *Faculty:* 21 full-time (13 women), 7 part-time/adjunct (all women). *Students:* 57 full-time (44 women), 61 part-time (46 women); includes 4 minority (2 African Americans, 1 Asian American or Pacific Islander, 1 Hispanic American), 36 international. 93 applicants, 61% accepted, 37 enrolled. *Median time to degree:* Of those who began their doctoral program in fall 1998, 92% received their degree in 8 years or less. *Degree requirements:* For master's, thesis or alternative, registration; for doctorate, thesis/dissertation, comprehensive exam, registration. *Entrance requirements:* For master's, GRE General Test or MAT if GPA is less than 2.9; for doctorate, GRE General Test, minimum GPA of 3.4, work experience. Additional exam requirements/recommendations for international students: Required—TOEFL (minimum score 550 paper-based; 213 computer-based). *Application deadline:* For fall admission, 4/1 priority date for domestic and international students. Applications are processed on a rolling basis. Application fee: $45. Electronic applications accepted. *Financial support:* In 2006–07, 52 students received support, including 31 research assistantships with full tuition reimbursements available (averaging $6,500 per year), teaching assistantships with full tuition reimbursements available (averaging $7,200 per year); Federal Work-Study, institutionally sponsored loans, tuition waivers (full), and unspecified assistantships also available. Financial award application deadline: 3/15. *Faculty research:* Cognition literacy, character education, teacher's education reform, disabilities. Total annual research expenditures: $605,070. *Unit head:* Dr. William Earl Smith, Chair, 740-593-4483, Fax: 740-593-0477, E-mail: smithw@ohio.edu. *Application contact:* Floyd J. Doney, Director of Student Affairs, 740-593-4400, Fax: 740-593-9310, E-mail: doney@ohio.edu.

Old Dominion University, Darden College of Education, Programs in Occupational and Technical Studies, Norfolk, VA 23529. Offers business and industry training (MS); career and technical education (PhD); community college teaching (MS); human resources training (PhD); middle and secondary teaching (MS); technology education (PhD). *Accreditation:* NCATE (one or more programs are accredited). Part-time and evening/weekend programs available. Postbaccalaureate distance learning degree programs offered (minimal on-campus study). *Faculty:* 7 full-time (1 woman), 5 part-time/adjunct (2 women). *Students:* 15 full-time (11 women), 68 part-time (39 women); includes 13 minority (9 African Americans, 2 American Indian/Alaska Native, 2 Asian Americans or Pacific Islanders), 1 international. Average age 39. 44 applicants, 95% accepted, 37 enrolled. In 2006, 29 degrees awarded. *Degree requirements:* For master's, writing exam, candidacy exam, thesis optional; for doctorate, thesis/dissertation, writing exam, candidacy exam, comprehensive exam, registration. *Entrance requirements:* For master's, GRE General Test or MAT, minimum GPA of 2.8; for doctorate, GRE, minimum GPA of 3.0, 3 letters of reference. Additional exam requirements/recommendations for international students: Required—TOEFL. *Application deadline:* For fall admission, 6/1 priority date for domestic students, 6/1 for international students; for winter admission, 11/1 priority date for domestic students, 11/1 for international students; for spring admission, 3/1 priority date for domestic students, 3/1 for international students. Applications are processed on a rolling basis. Application fee: $40. Electronic applications accepted. *Expenses:* Tuition, area resident: Part-time $285 per credit hour. Tuition, nonresident: part-time $715 per credit hour. Required fees: $94 per semester. *Financial support:* In 2006–07, 19 students received support, including 1 fellowship with full tuition reimbursement available (averaging $15,000 per year), 2 research assistantships with partial tuition reimbursements available (averaging $9,000 per year), 5 teaching assistantships with partial tuition reimbursements available (averaging $12,600 per year); career-related internships or fieldwork, scholarships/grants, tuition waivers (partial), and unspecified assistantships also available. Support available to part-time students. Financial award application deadline: 2/15; financial award applicants required to submit FAFSA. *Faculty research:* Training and development, marketing, technology, special populations, support of academic subjects. Total annual research expenditures: $799,773. *Unit head:* Dr. John M. Ritz, Graduate Program Director, 757-683-4305, Fax: 757-683-5227, E-mail: otsgpd@odu.edu.

Old Dominion University, Darden College of Education, Programs in Secondary Education, Norfolk, VA 23529. Offers biology (MS Ed); chemistry (MS Ed); English (MS Ed); instructional technology (MS Ed); library science (MS Ed); secondary education (MS Ed). *Accreditation:* NCATE. Part-time and evening/weekend programs available. Postbaccalaureate distance learning degree programs offered (minimal on-campus study). *Faculty:* 28 full-time (11 women). *Students:* 61 full-time (45 women), 119 part-time (72 women); includes 21 minority (13 African Americans, 4 Asian Americans or Pacific Islanders, 4 Hispanic Americans), 1 international. Average age 35. 47 applicants, 87% accepted. In 2006, 119 degrees awarded. *Degree requirements:* For master's, thesis optional. *Entrance requirements:* For master's, GRE General Test, or MAT, PRAXIS I for master's with licensure, minimum GPA of 2.8, teaching certificate. Additional exam requirements/recommendations for international students: Required—TOEFL. *Application deadline:* Applications are processed on a rolling basis. Application fee: $40. Electronic applications accepted. *Expenses:* Tuition, area resident: Part-time $285 per credit hour. Tuition, nonresident: part-time $715 per credit hour. Required fees: $94 per semester. *Financial support:* In 2006–07, 58 students received support, including 2 research assistantships with tuition reimbursements available (averaging $6,777 per year), 3 teaching assistantships with tuition reimbursements available (averaging $5,333 per year); fellowships, career-related internships or fieldwork, Federal Work-Study, institutionally sponsored loans, scholarships/grants, and tuition waivers (partial) also available. Support available to part-time students. Financial award application deadline: 2/15; financial award applicants required to submit FAFSA. *Faculty research:* Mathematics retraining, writing project for teachers, geography teaching, reading. *Unit head:* Dr. Robert Lucking, Graduate Program Director, 757-683-5545, Fax: 757-683-5862, E-mail: rlucking@odu.edu.

Olivet Nazarene University, Graduate School, Division of Education, Program in Secondary Education, Bourbonnais, IL 60914-2271. Offers MAT. *Accreditation:* NCATE. Evening/weekend programs available. *Degree requirements:* For master's, thesis or alternative.

Pacific University, College of Education, Forest Grove, OR 97116-1797. Offers early childhood education (MAT); education (MAE); elementary education (MAT); high school education (MAT); middle school education (MAT); special education (MAT); visual function in learning (M Ed). Part-time and evening/weekend programs available. *Faculty:* 20 full-time (12 women), 40 part-time/adjunct (21 women). *Students:* 222 full-time (151 women), 115 part-time (90 women); includes 30 minority (3 African Americans, 5 American Indian/Alaska Native, 12 Asian Americans or Pacific Islanders, 10 Hispanic Americans). Average age 32. 92 applicants, 83% accepted, 69 enrolled. In 2006, 257 degrees awarded. *Degree requirements:* For master's, research project. *Entrance requirements:* For master's, California Basic Educational Skills Test, Praxis I, minimum undergraduate GPA of 2.75, 3.0 graduate. Additional exam requirements/recommendations for international students: Required—TOEFL. *Application deadline:* For fall admission, 6/15 priority date for domestic students; for spring admission, 10/15 for domestic students. Applications are processed on a rolling basis. Application fee: $35. Electronic applications accepted. *Expenses: Contact institution. Financial support:* In 2006–07, 287 students received support; fellowships, research assistantships, teaching assistantships, career-related internships or fieldwork, institutionally sponsored loans, and scholarships/grants available. Support available to part-time students. Financial award application deadline: 5/1; financial award applicants required to submit FAFSA. *Faculty research:* Defining a culturally competent classroom, technology in the k-12 classroom, Socratic seminars, social studies education. *Unit head:* Dr. Mark Ankeny, Acting Dean, 503-352-2102, E-mail: mankeny@pacificu.edu. *Application contact:* Diana Watkins, Assistant Director Graduate and Professional Admissions, 503-352-2958, Fax: 503-352-2907, E-mail: teach@pacificu.edu.

Park University, College of Graduate and Professional Studies, Kansas City, MO 54105. Offers adult education (M Ed); at-risk students (M Ed); disaster and emergency management (MPA); educational administration (M Ed); entrepreneurship (MBA); general business (MBA); general education (M Ed); government/business relations (MPA); healthcare/services management (MBA, MPA); international business (MBA); K-12 certification (MAT); management information systems (MBA); management of information systems (MPA); middle school certification (MAT); multi-cultural education (M Ed); nonprofit management (MPA); public management (MPA); school law (M Ed); secondary school certification (MAT); special education (M Ed). Part-time and evening/weekend programs available. Postbaccalaureate distance learning degree programs offered (no on-campus study). *Degree requirements:* For master's, thesis (for some programs), comprehensive exam, registration. *Entrance requirements:* For master's, GRE, GMAT, teacher certification (M Ed). Additional exam requirements/recommendations for international students: Required—TOEFL (minimum score 550 paper-based). Electronic applications accepted. *Faculty research:* Literacy, leadership, brain based research, multicultural education, diversity.

Piedmont College, School of Education, Demorest, GA 30535-0010. Offers early childhood education (MA, MAT); instruction (Ed S); secondary education (MA, MAT). Part-time and evening/weekend programs available. *Faculty:* 20 full-time (17 women), 22 part-time/adjunct (5 women). *Students:* 210 full-time (158 women), 846 part-time (734 women); includes 95 minority (72 African Americans, 2 American Indian/Alaska Native, 10 Asian Americans or Pacific Islanders, 11 Hispanic Americans), 7 international. 327 applicants, 92% accepted, 235 enrolled. In 2006, 422 master's, 203 other advanced degrees awarded. *Degree requirements:* For master's, thesis, field experience in the teaching classroom. *Entrance requirements:* For master's, GRE General Test, MAT, minimum undergraduate GPA of 2.5; for Ed S, minimum graduate GPA of 3.5, valid teaching certificate. Additional exam requirements/recommendations for international students: Required—TOEFL (minimum score 550 paper-based; 213 computer-based). *Application deadline:* For fall admission, 7/15 for domestic students; for spring admission, 12/1 for domestic students. Application fee: $30. *Expenses:* Tuition: Part-time $310 per credit hour. *Financial support:* Career-related internships or fieldwork, Federal Work-Study, institutionally sponsored loans, and unspecified assistantships available. Support available to part-time students. Financial award applicants required to submit FAFSA. *Unit head:* Dr. Jane McFerrin, Dean, 706-778-3000 Ext. 1201, Fax: 706-776-9608, E-mail: jmcferrin@piedmont.edu. *Application contact:* Carol E. Kokesh, Director of Graduate Studies, 706-778-8500 Ext. 1181, Fax: 706-776-6635, E-mail: ckokesh@piedmont.edu.

Pittsburg State University, Graduate School, College of Education, Department of Curriculum and Instruction, Pittsburg, KS 66762. Offers classroom reading teacher (MS); early childhood education (MS); elementary education (MS); reading (MS); reading specialist (MS); secondary education (MS); teaching (MAT). *Accreditation:* NCATE. *Students:* 141. *Degree requirements:* For master's, thesis or alternative. *Entrance requirements:* For master's, GRE or MAT. Application fee: $35 ($60 for international students). *Expenses:* Tuition, state resident: full-time $2,144; part-time $181 per credit hour. Tuition, nonresident: full-time $5,273; part-time $442 per credit hour. Tuition and fees vary according to course load and campus/location. *Financial support:* In 2006–07, teaching assistantships (averaging $5,000 per year); career-related internships or fieldwork, Federal Work-Study, and unspecified assistantships also available. *Unit head:* Dr. V. June Taylor, Chairperson, 620-235-4508. *Application contact:* Jamie Vanderbeck, Assistant Director, 620-235-4223, Fax: 620-235-4219, E-mail: jvanderb@pittstate.edu.

Plymouth State University, College of Graduate Studies, Graduate Studies in Education, Program in K-12 Education, Plymouth, NH 03264-1595. Offers M Ed. *Accreditation:* NCATE. Part-time and evening/weekend programs available. *Students:* 1 (woman) full-time, 222 part-time (168 women); includes 7 minority (2 African Americans, 3 Asian Americans or Pacific Islanders, 2 Hispanic Americans). Average age 39. 48 applicants, 100% accepted, 48 enrolled. In 2006, 59 degrees awarded. *Degree requirements:* For master's, PRAXIS. *Entrance requirements:* For master's, MAT, minimum GPA of 3.0. *Application deadline:* Applications are processed on a rolling basis. Application fee: $75. *Expenses:* Tuition, state resident: part-time $369 per credit. Tuition, nonresident: part-time $407 per credit. Tuition and fees vary according to course level. *Financial support:* Career-related internships or fieldwork, scholarships/grants, and unspecified assistantships available. Support available to part-time students. Financial award applicants required to submit FAFSA. *Unit head:* Dr. Kathleen Norris, Director of Graduate Admissions, Programs and Certification, 603-535-3023, Fax: 603-535-2572, E-mail: knorris@plymouth.edu.

Plymouth State University, College of Graduate Studies, Graduate Studies in Education, Program in Secondary Education, Plymouth, NH 03264-1595. Offers M Ed. Part-time and evening/weekend programs available. *Students:* Average age 39. 50 applicants, 100% accepted, 50 enrolled. In 2006, 47 degrees awarded. *Entrance requirements:* For master's, MAT. Application fee: $75. *Expenses:* Tuition, state resident: part-time $369 per credit. Tuition, nonresident: part-time $407 per credit. Tuition and fees vary according to course level. *Unit head:* Dr. Kathleen Norris, Director of Graduate Admissions, Programs and Certification, 603-535-3023, Fax: 603-535-2572, E-mail: knorris@plymouth.edu.

Portland State University, Graduate Studies, School of Education, Department of Curriculum and Instruction, Portland, OR 97207-0751. Offers early childhood education (MA, MS); education (M Ed, MA, MS); educational leadership: curriculum and instruction (Ed D); educational media/school librarianship (MA, MS); elementary education (M Ed, MAT, MST); reading (MA, MS); secondary education (M Ed, MAT, MST). *Accreditation:* NCATE. Part-time programs available. *Faculty:* 20 full-time (14 women), 18 part-time/adjunct (9 women). *Students:* 185 full-time (135 women), 209 part-time (160 women); includes 53 minority (7 African Americans, 4 American Indian/Alaska Native, 13 Asian Americans or Pacific Islanders, 29 Hispanic Americans), 13 international. Average age 32. 372 applicants, 87% accepted, 171 enrolled. In 2006, 352 master's, 4 doctorates awarded. *Degree requirements:* For master's, special project or thesis, written exam; for doctorate, thesis/dissertation. *Entrance requirements:* For master's, California Basic Educational Skills Test, minimum GPA of 3.0 in upper-division course work or 2.75 overall. Additional exam requirements/recommendations for international students: Required—TOEFL (minimum score 550 paper-based; 213 computer-based). *Application deadline:* For fall admission, 4/1 for domestic and international students; for winter admission, 9/1 for domestic and international students; for spring admission, 11/1 for domestic and international students. Applications are processed on a rolling basis. Application fee: $50. *Expenses:* Tuition, state resident: full-time $6,426; part-time $238 per credit. Tuition, nonresident: full-time $11,016; part-time $408 per credit. Tuition and fees vary according to course load. *Financial support:* In 2006–07, 5 research assistantships with full tuition reimbursements (averaging $5,508 per year) were awarded; teaching assistantships with full tuition reimbursements, career-related internships or fieldwork, Federal Work-Study, and institutionally sponsored loans also available. Support available to part-time students. Financial award application deadline: 3/1; financial award applicants required to submit FAFSA. *Faculty research:* Early literacy, characteristics of successful teachers of at-risk students, participation of women/minorities in technology courses, selection of cooperating teachers. Total annual research expenditures: $308,420. *Unit head:* Steven Lee, Head, 503-725-4689, Fax: 503-725-8475. *Application contact:* Majken Elek, Department Secretary, 503-725-4756, Fax: 503-725-8475, E-mail: majkene@pdx.edu.

Purdue University Calumet, Graduate School, School of Education, Program in Secondary Education, Hammond, IN 46323-2094. Offers MS Ed. *Accreditation:* NCATE. *Entrance requirements:* Additional exam requirements/recommendations for international students: Required—TOEFL.

Queens College of the City University of New York, Division of Graduate Studies, Division of Education, Department of Secondary Education, Flushing, NY 11367-1597. Offers art (MS Ed); biology (MS Ed, AC); chemistry (MS Ed, AC); earth sciences (MS Ed, AC); English (MS Ed, AC); French (MS Ed, AC); Italian (MS Ed, AC); mathematics (MS Ed, AC); music (MS Ed, AC); physics (MS Ed, AC); social studies (MS Ed, AC); Spanish (MS Ed, AC). Part-time and evening/weekend programs available. *Faculty:* 22 full-time (14 women). *Students:* 50 full-time (28 women), 974 part-time (627 women). 633 applicants, 82% accepted, 407 enrolled. In 2006, 227 degrees awarded. *Degree requirements:* For master's, research project; for AC, thesis optional. *Entrance requirements:* For master's, minimum GPA of 3.0. Additional exam requirements/recommendations for international students: Required—TOEFL. *Application deadline:* For fall admission, 4/1 for domestic students; for spring admission, 11/1 for domestic students. Applications are processed on a rolling basis. Application fee: $125. *Financial support:* Career-related internships or fieldwork, Federal Work-Study, institutionally sponsored loans, and tuition waivers (partial) available. Support available to part-time students. Financial award application deadline: 4/1; financial award applicants required to submit FAFSA. *Unit head:* Dr. Eleanor Armour-Thomas, Chairperson, 718-997-5150, E-mail: armourthomas@yahoo.com. *Application contact:* Mario Caruso, Director of Graduate Admissions, 718-997-5200, Fax: 718-997-5193, E-mail: graduate_admissions@qc.edu.

Quinnipiac University, Division of Education, Program in Secondary Education, Hamden, CT 06518-1940. Offers biology (MAT); chemistry (MAT); English (MAT); French (MAT); history/social studies (MAT); mathematics (MAT); physics (MAT); Spanish (MAT). *Faculty:* 7 full-time (5 women), 23 part-time/adjunct (14 women). *Students:* 64 full-time (41 women); includes 5 minority (1 African American, 4 Hispanic Americans). Average age 26. 63 applicants, 87% accepted, 42 enrolled. In 2006, 37 degrees awarded. *Entrance requirements:* For master's, PRAXIS I, minimum GPA of 2.67, interview. Additional exam requirements/recommendations for international students: Required—TOEFL (minimum score 575 paper-based; 233 computer-based; 90 iBT), IELTS (minimum score 7). *Application deadline:* For fall admission, 3/15 priority date for domestic students. Applications are processed on a rolling basis. Application fee: $45. Electronic applications accepted. *Expenses:* Tuition: Part-time $675 per credit. Required fees: $30 per credit. *Financial support:* Career-related internships or fieldwork and tuition waivers (partial) available. Financial award application deadline: 4/15; financial award applicants required to submit FAFSA. *Faculty research:* Multicultural and urban education, role of technology in education, challenges of teaching divers learners, socio-cultural nature of learning. *Unit head:* Dr. Bernadine Krawczyk, Assistant Dean, Division of Education, 203-582-3510, Fax: 203-582-3473, E-mail: bernadine.krawczyk@quinnipiac.edu. *Application contact:* 800-462-1944, Fax: 203-582-3443, E-mail: graduate@quinnipiac.edu.

See Close-Up on page 911.

Regis University, School for Professional Studies, Program in Teacher Education, Denver, CO 80221-1099. Offers adult learning, training, and development (M Ed); curriculum, instruction, and assessment (M Ed); early childhood (M Ed); educational technology (Certificate); elementary (M Ed); ESL (M Ed); fine arts (M Ed), including arts, music; instructional technology (M Ed); professional leadership (M Ed); reading (M Ed); secondary (M Ed); self-designed (M Ed); space studies (M Ed); special education (M Ed); teacher licensure (M Ed). Program also offered in Henderson and Las Vegas (Summerlin), NV. Postbaccalaureate distance learning degree programs offered. *Unit head:* Dr. Suzie Perry, Dean, 303-458-4302. *Application contact:* Partick Lowenthal, Assistant Director, 303-458-4300 Ext. 4314, E-mail: masters@regis.edu.

Rhode Island College, School of Graduate Studies, Feinstein School of Education and Human Development, Department of Educational Studies, Providence, RI 02908-1991. Offers bilingual/bicultural education (M Ed); educational administration (CAGS); English (MAT); French (MAT); history (MAT); math (MAT); secondary education (M Ed); Spanish (MAT); teaching English as a second language (M Ed, MAT); technology education (M Ed). *Accreditation:* NCATE. Part-time and evening/weekend programs available. *Faculty:* 12 full-time (5 women), 4 part-time/adjunct (all women). *Students:* 10 full-time (7 women), 27 part-time (23 women); includes 1 minority (Hispanic American) Average age 32. In 2006, 22 degrees awarded. *Entrance requirements:* For master's, BA in English, French, history, math or Spanish; evaluation of content area knowledge; 3 letters of recommendation; interview. *Application deadline:* For fall admission, 3/15 for domestic students; for spring admission, 11/1 for domestic students. Applications are processed on a rolling basis. Application fee: $50. *Expenses:* Tuition, state resident: part-time $244 per credit. Tuition, nonresident: part-time $512 per credit. Required fees: $12 per credit. $66 per term. Tuition and fees vary according to degree level, program and reciprocity agreements. *Financial support:* Teaching assistantships with full tuition reimbursements, career-related internships or fieldwork, Federal Work-Study, scholarships/grants, health care benefits, and unspecified assistantships available. Support available to part-time students. Financial award application deadline: 5/15; financial award applicants required to submit FAFSA. *Faculty research:* School administration, school/college articulation. *Unit head:* Dr. Charles McLaughlin, Chair, 401-456-8170.

Roberts Wesleyan College, Division of Teacher Education, Rochester, NY 14624-1997. Offers adolescence education (M Ed); childhood and special education (M Ed); literacy education (M Ed); urban education (M Ed). Part-time and evening/weekend programs available. *Faculty:* 17 part-time/adjunct (7 women). *Students:* 1 (woman) full-time, 66 part-time (47 women). Average age 33. 52 applicants, 63% accepted. In 2006, 20 degrees awarded. *Degree requirements:* For master's, thesis. *Application deadline:* For fall admission, 8/1 priority date for domestic students; for spring admission, 12/1 for domestic students. Applications are processed on a rolling basis. Application fee: $35. *Financial support:* In 2006–07, 7 students received support. Career-related internships or fieldwork available. Financial award application deadline: 9/1; financial award applicants required to submit FAFSA. *Unit head:* Dr. Richard Mace, Chair, 585-594-6934. *Application contact:* Paula Finch, Graduate Admissions Coordinator, 585-594-6683, E-mail: finch_paula@roberts.edu.

Rochester Institute of Technology, Graduate Enrollment Services, National Technical Institute for the Deaf, Department of Graduate Secondary Education, Rochester, NY 14623-5603. Offers MS. *Accreditation:* Teacher Education Accreditation Council. *Students:* 49 full-time (37 women), 5 part-time (all women); includes 50 minority (7 African Americans, 43 Hispanic Americans), 2 international. 34 applicants, 88% accepted, 26 enrolled. In 2006, 25 degrees awarded. *Entrance requirements:* For master's, minimum GPA of 3.0. Additional exam requirements/recommendations for international students: Required—TOEFL (minimum score 550 paper-based; 213 computer-based; 88 iBT). *Application deadline:* For fall admission, 3/1 priority date for domestic students. Applications are processed on a rolling basis. Application fee: $50. Electronic applications accepted. *Expenses:* Tuition: Full-time $28,491; part-time $800 per credit. Required fees: $201. *Unit head:* Gerald Bateman, Director, 585-475-6480, E-mail: gcbnmp@rit.edu.

Rockford College, Graduate Studies, Department of Education, Program in Secondary Education, Rockford, IL 61108-2393. Offers art education (MAT); English (MAT); history (MAT); political science (MAT); secondary education (MAT); social sciences (MAT). Part-time and evening/weekend programs available. *Degree requirements:* For master's, thesis optional. *Entrance requirements:* For master's, GRE General Test.

Rollins College, Hamilton Holt School, Program in Education, Winter Park, FL 32789-4499. Offers elementary education (M Ed, MAT); secondary education (MAT), including English, mathematics, music. Part-time and evening/weekend programs available. *Students:* 14 full-time (12 women), 36 part-time (32 women); includes 5 minority (2 African Americans, 1 Asian American or Pacific Islander, 2 Hispanic Americans), 1 international. Average age 35. In 2006, 14 degrees awarded. *Degree requirements:* For master's, comprehensive exam. *Entrance requirements:* For master's, GRE or MAT, interview. Additional exam requirements/recommendations for international students: Required—TOEFL. *Application deadline:* For fall admission, 7/16 for domestic students; for winter admission, 12/3 for domestic students; for spring admission, 4/22 for domestic students. Applications are processed on a rolling basis. Application fee: $50. Electronic applications accepted. *Expenses: Contact institution. Financial support:* Teaching assistantships, scholarships/grants available. Support available to part-time students. *Unit head:* Dr. J. Scott Hewit, Director, 407-646-2300, E-mail: jhewit@rollins.edu. *Application contact:* Rebecca Cordray, Coordinator of Records and Registration, 407-646-1568, Fax: 407-975-6430, E-mail: rcordray@rollins.edu.

Roosevelt University, Graduate Division, College of Education, Program in Secondary Education, Chicago, IL 60605-1394. Offers MA. *Students:* 38 full-time (22 women), 130 part-time (71 women); includes 25 minority (19 African Americans, 2 Asian Americans or Pacific Islanders, 4 Hispanic Americans). Average age 33. 111 applicants, 64% accepted, 65 enrolled. In 2006, 159 degrees awarded. *Unit head:* Dr. Linda Pincham, Chair, 312-341-2439. *Application contact:* Joanne Canyon-Heller, Coordinator of Graduate Admission, 877-APPLY RU, Fax: 312-281-3356, E-mail: applyru@roosevelt.edu.

Secondary Education

Rowan University, Graduate School, College of Education, Department of Foundations of Education, Program in Teaching-Secondary, Glassboro, NJ 08028-1701. Offers MST. *Accreditation:* NCATE. Part-time and evening/weekend programs available. *Students:* 5 full-time (2 women). Average age 26. In 2006, 1 degree awarded. *Degree requirements:* For master's, thesis, comprehensive exam. *Entrance requirements:* For master's, GRE General Test, minimum GPA of 2.8. Additional exam requirements/recommendations for international students: Required—TOEFL. *Application deadline:* For spring admission, 4/1 for domestic students. Application fee: $50. Electronic applications accepted. *Expenses:* Tuition, state resident: full-time $9,882; part-time $549 per credit. Tuition, nonresident: full-time $9,882; part-time $549 per credit. Tuition and fees vary according to degree level. *Financial support:* Career-related internships or fieldwork, Federal Work-Study, and unspecified assistantships available. Support available to part-time students.

Sacred Heart University, Graduate Studies, College of Education and Health Professions, Department of Education, Fairfield, CT 06825-1000. Offers administration (CAS); educational technology (MAT); elementary education (MAT); reading (CAS); secondary education (MAT); teaching (CAS). Part-time and evening/weekend programs available. Postbaccalaureate distance learning degree programs offered (minimal on-campus study). *Faculty:* 23 full-time (10 women). *Students:* 360 full-time (285 women), 710 part-time (520 women); includes 39 minority (15 African Americans, 4 American Indian/Alaska Native, 5 Asian Americans or Pacific Islanders, 15 Hispanic Americans), 4 international. Average age 34. 335 applicants, 87% accepted, 270 enrolled. In 2006, 312 master's, 59 other advanced degrees awarded. *Degree requirements:* For master's, thesis or alternative. *Entrance requirements:* For master's, PRAXIS (teacher certification/MAT); for CAS, PRAXIS I. Additional exam requirements/recommendations for international students: Required—TOEFL (minimum score 550 paper-based; 213 computer-based). *Application deadline:* Applications are processed on a rolling basis. Application fee: $50 ($100 for international students). Electronic applications accepted. *Expenses: Contact institution.* Full-time tuition and fees vary according to degree level and program. *Financial support:* Teaching assistantships with partial tuition reimbursements, career-related internships or fieldwork, institutionally sponsored loans, traineeships, tuition waivers (partial), and unspecified assistantships available. Support available to part-time students. Financial award applicants required to submit FAFSA. *Faculty research:* Reading education, learning theory, teacher preparation, education of underachievers. *Unit head:* Dr. Edward Malin, Director, 203-371-7800, Fax: 203-365-7513. *Application contact:* Alexis Haakonsen, Dean of Graduate Admissions, 203-365-7619, Fax: 203-365-4732, E-mail: haakonsena@sacredheart.edu.

Saginaw Valley State University, College of Education, Program in Natural Science Teaching, University Center, MI 48710. Offers elementary (MAT); middle school (MAT); secondary school (MAT). *Accreditation:* NCATE. Part-time and evening/weekend programs available. *Students:* 1 (woman) full-time, 22 part-time (16 women). Average age 36. 3 applicants, 100% accepted, 3 enrolled. In 2006, 15 degrees awarded. *Degree requirements:* For master's, capstone course. *Entrance requirements:* For master's, minimum GPA of 3.0, teaching certificate. *Application deadline:* Applications are processed on a rolling basis. Application fee: $25. Electronic applications accepted. *Expenses:* Tuition, state resident: full-time $7,225; part-time $301 per credit hour. Tuition, nonresident: full-time $13,888; part-time $579 per credit hour. Required fees: $330; $14 per credit hour. Tuition and fees vary according to course load. *Financial support:* Applicants required to submit FAFSA. *Application contact:* Jeanne Chipman, Certification Officer, 989-964-4083, Fax: 989-964-4385, E-mail: jdc@svsu.edu.

Saginaw Valley State University, College of Education, Program in Secondary Classroom Teaching, University Center, MI 48710. Offers MAT. *Accreditation:* NCATE. Part-time and evening/weekend programs available. *Students:* 7 full-time (all women), 49 part-time (31 women); includes 2 minority (1 American Indian/Alaska Native, 1 Asian American or Pacific Islander). Average age 33. 18 applicants, 100% accepted, 12 enrolled. In 2006, 16 degrees awarded. *Degree requirements:* For master's, capstone course. *Entrance requirements:* For master's, minimum GPA of 3.0, teaching certificate. *Application deadline:* Applications are processed on a rolling basis. Application fee: $25. Electronic applications accepted. *Expenses:* Tuition, state resident: full-time $7,225; part-time $301 per credit hour. Tuition, nonresident: full-time $13,888; part-time $579 per credit hour. Required fees: $330; $14 per credit hour. Tuition and fees vary according to course load. *Financial support:* Applicants required to submit FAFSA. *Application contact:* Jeanne Chipman, Certification Officer, 989-964-4083, Fax: 989-964-4385, E-mail: jdc@svsu.edu.

St. John's University, The School of Education, Division of Early Childhood, Childhood and Adolescent Education, Program in Adolescent Education, Queens, NY 11439. Offers MS Ed. Part-time and evening/weekend programs available. *Students:* 23 full-time (14 women), 298 part-time (183 women); includes 99 minority (41 African Americans, 1 American Indian/Alaska Native, 31 Asian Americans or Pacific Islanders, 26 Hispanic Americans), 4 international. Average age 29. 193 applicants, 89% accepted, 121 enrolled. In 2006, 96 degrees awarded. *Degree requirements:* For master's, variable foreign language requirement, comprehensive exam, internship. *Entrance requirements:* For master's, minimum GPA of 3.0. Additional exam requirements/recommendations for international students: Required—TOEFL (minimum score 500 paper-based; 173 computer-based). *Application deadline:* For fall admission, 4/15 for domestic students, 5/1 priority date for international students; for spring admission, 11/1 priority date for international students. Applications are processed on a rolling basis. Application fee: $40. Electronic applications accepted. *Expenses:* Tuition: Full-time $18,480; part-time $770 per credit. Required fees: $125 per semester. Tuition and fees vary according to program. *Financial support:* Research assistantships, career-related internships or fieldwork and scholarships/grants available. Support available to part-time students. Financial award application deadline: 3/1; financial award applicants required to submit FAFSA. *Faculty research:* Investigating self-efficacy in literacy learning. *Application contact:* Kelly Ronayne, Assistant Dean, 718-990-2303, Fax: 718-990-6069, E-mail: graded@stjohns.edu.

Saint Joseph's University, College of Arts and Sciences, Department of Education, Philadelphia, PA 19131-1395. Offers educational leadership (Ed D); elementary education (MS); instructional technology (MS); professional education (MS); reading (MS); secondary education (MS); special education (MS); training and organizational development (MS, Certificate). Part-time and evening/weekend programs available. *Faculty:* 18 full-time (9 women), 67 part-time/adjunct (34 women). *Students:* 77 full-time (63 women), 551 part-time (417 women); includes 115 minority (94 African Americans, 2 American Indian/Alaska Native, 8 Asian Americans or Pacific Islanders, 11 Hispanic Americans), 12 international. In 2006, 286 master's, 5 doctorates awarded. *Entrance requirements:* For master's, 2 letters of recommendation, minimum GPA of 3.0; for doctorate, GRE/MAT, 2 letters of recommendation, resumé. Additional exam requirements/recommendations for international students: Required—TOEFL. *Application deadline:* For fall admission, 7/15 for domestic students. Application fee: $35. *Expenses: Contact institution. Financial support:* Fellowships, research assistantships, career-related internships or fieldwork and Federal Work-Study available. Support available to part-time students. *Unit head:* Dr. Encarnacion Rodriguez, Director of Graduate Education, 610-660-3348.

Saint Mary's University of Minnesota, School of Graduate and Professional Programs, Program in Instruction, Winona, MN 55987-1399. Offers MA, Certificate. *Unit head:* Rebecca Hopkins, Director, 507-457-6620, E-mail: rhopkins@smumn.edu.

St. Thomas Aquinas College, Division of Teacher Education, Sparkill, NY 10976. Offers adolescence education (MST); childhood and special education (MST); childhood education (MST); reading (MS Ed, PMC); special education (MS Ed, PMC); teaching (MS Ed), including elementary education, middle school education, secondary education. *Accreditation:* NCATE. Part-time and evening/weekend programs available. *Degree requirements:* For master's, comprehensive professional portfolio; for PMC, action research project. *Entrance requirements:* For master's, New York State Qualifying Exam, GRE General Test or minimum GPA of 3.0, teaching certificate; for PMC, GRE General Test or minimum GPA of 3.0. Electronic applications accepted. *Faculty research:* Computer applications in education, adolescent special education students, literacy development, inclusive practices for special education students.

See Close-Up on page 917.

Saint Xavier University, Graduate Studies, School of Education, Chicago, IL 60655-3105. Offers counseling (MA); counselor education (MA); curriculum and instruction (MA); early childhood education (MA); education (CAS); educational administration (MA); elementary education (MA); field-based education (MA); general educational studies (MA); individualized program (MA); learning disabilities (MA); reading (MA); secondary education (MA). *Accreditation:* NCATE. Part-time and evening/weekend programs available. *Faculty:* 92. *Students:* 45 full-time (35 women), 1,529 part-time (1,309 women). In 2006, 474 degrees awarded. *Degree requirements:* For master's, thesis or project. *Entrance requirements:* For master's, minimum GPA of 3.0. *Application deadline:* For fall admission, 8/15 priority date for domestic students. Applications are processed on a rolling basis. Application fee: $35. *Expenses: Contact institution. Financial support:* Career-related internships or fieldwork available. Support available to part-time students. Financial award applicants required to submit FAFSA. *Unit head:* Dr. Beverly Gulley, Dean, 773-298-3221, Fax: 773-779-9061, E-mail: gulley@sxu.edu. *Application contact:* Beth Gierach, Managing Director of Admission, 773-298-3053, Fax: 773-298-3076, E-mail: gierach@sxu.edu.

Salem College, Department of Education, Winston-Salem, NC 27108-0548. Offers early education and leadership (MAT); elementary education (MAT); English as a second language (MAT); language and literacy (M Ed); middle school education (MAT); secondary education (MAT); special education (MAT). *Accreditation:* NCATE. Part-time and evening/weekend programs available. *Faculty:* 8 full-time (6 women), 5 part-time/adjunct (all women). *Students:* 8 full-time (all women), 250 part-time (238 women); includes 19 minority (16 African Americans, 1 Asian American or Pacific Islander, 2 Hispanic Americans). Average age 33. 110 applicants, 65% accepted, 68 enrolled. In 2006, 34 degrees awarded. *Degree requirements:* For master's, practicum (MAT), project (M Ed), oral and written comprehensive exams. *Entrance requirements:* For master's, GRE, minimum GPA of 2.5. *Application deadline:* Applications are processed on a rolling basis. Application fee: $30. *Financial support:* In 2006–07, 152 students received support. Federal Work-Study and scholarships/grants available. Support available to part-time students. Financial award applicants required to submit FAFSA. *Faculty research:* Content area reading strategies, literacy development, brain compatible instruction. *Unit head:* Dr. Paula Grubbs, Director of Teacher Education, 336-721-2610, Fax: 336-721-2683, E-mail: grubbs@salem.edu.

Salem State College, Graduate School, Professional Studies—Physical Education 5-12, Salem, MA 01970-5353. Offers M Ed. Part-time and evening/weekend programs available. *Students:* Average age 32. In 2006, 2 degrees awarded. *Application deadline:* Applications are processed on a rolling basis. Application fee: $35. *Unit head:* MaryLou Breitborde, Associate Dean of Education, 978-542-6262, E-mail: mbreitborde@salemstate.edu.

Salem State College, Graduate School, Professional Studies: Program in Secondary Education, Salem, MA 01970-5353. Offers M Ed. Part-time and evening/weekend programs available. *Students:* 4 full-time (all women), 36 part-time (24 women); includes 2 Hispanic Americans. Average age 33. In 2006, 39 degrees awarded. *Entrance requirements:* For master's, GRE, MAT. *Application deadline:* Applications are processed on a rolling basis. Application fee: $35. *Unit head:* Dr. A. Thomas Billings, Assistant Professor, 978-542-7215, Fax: 978-542-7023, E-mail: tbillings@salemstate.edu.

Salem State College, Graduate School, Program in Spanish, Salem, MA 01970-5353. Offers MAT. Part-time and evening/weekend programs available. *Students:* Average age 33. In 2006, 1 degree awarded. Application fee: $35. *Unit head:* Dr. Nicole Sherf, Coordinator, 978-542-6468, E-mail: nsherf@salemstate.edu.

Salisbury University, Graduate Division, Department of Education, Salisbury, MD 21801-6837. Offers art (MAT); biology (MAT); business education (MAT); chemistry (MAT); early childhood education (M Ed); educational administration (M Ed); elementary education (M Ed); English (M Ed, MAT); French (MAT); geography (MAT); history (MAT); mathematics (MAT); media and technology (MAT); music (MAT); psychology (MAT); reading education (MAT); science (MAT); secondary education (MAT); social studies (MAT); Spanish (MAT). *Accreditation:* NCATE. Part-time and evening/weekend programs available. *Faculty:* 12 full-time (6 women), 10 part-time/adjunct (8 women). *Students:* 17 full-time (9 women), 84 part-time (72 women); includes 6 minority (5 African Americans, 1 Hispanic American). Average age 30. 15 applicants, 73% accepted, 11 enrolled. In 2006, 63 degrees awarded. *Degree requirements:* For master's, comprehensive exam (for some programs). *Entrance requirements:* For master's, PRAXIS, minimum GPA of 2.75. Additional exam requirements/recommendations for international students: Required—TOEFL (minimum score 550 paper-based; 213 computer-based). *Application deadline:* For fall admission, 8/1 priority date for domestic students; for spring admission, 1/1 for domestic students. Applications are processed on a rolling basis. Application fee: $45. *Expenses:* Tuition, state resident: part-time $260 per credit hour. Tuition, nonresident: part-time $546 per credit hour. Required fees: $52 per credit hour. *Financial support:* In 2006–07, 3 teaching assistantships with full tuition reimbursements were awarded; career-related internships or fieldwork and scholarships/grants also available. Support available to part-time students. Financial award applicants required to submit FAFSA. *Faculty research:* Middle-level education, student outcomes. *Unit head:* Dr. Edward C. Robeck, Program Coordinator, 410-543-6292, Fax: 410-548-2593, E-mail: ecrobeck@salisbury.edu. *Application contact:* Debra J. Clark, Administrative Assistant I, 410-543-6281, Fax: 410-548-2593, E-mail: djclark@salisbury.edu.

Sam Houston State University, College of Education and Applied Science, Department of Curriculum and Instruction, Huntsville, TX 77341. Offers elementary education (M Ed, MA); secondary education (M Ed, MA). *Accreditation:* NCATE. Part-time and evening/weekend programs available. *Faculty:* 4 full-time (3 women). *Students:* 26 full-time (21 women), 86 part-time (61 women); includes 19 minority (11 African Americans, 1 American Indian/Alaska Native, 2 Asian Americans or Pacific Islanders, 5 Hispanic Americans), 3 international. Average age 32. In 2006, 35 degrees awarded. *Entrance requirements:* For master's, GRE General Test. *Application deadline:* For fall admission, 8/1 for domestic students; for spring admission, 12/1 for domestic students. Application fee: $20. *Expenses:* Tuition, state resident: full-time $5,904; part-time $164 per semester hour. Tuition, nonresident: full-time $15,804; part-time $439 per semester hour. Required fees: $1,374; $462 per semester. *Financial support:* Teaching assistantships, institutionally sponsored loans available. Financial award application deadline: 5/31; financial award applicants required to submit FAFSA. *Unit head:* Dr. Charlene Crocker, Chair, 936-294-1136, Fax: 936-294-1056, E-mail: csc001@shsu.edu. *Application contact:* Dr. Eren Johnson, Advisor, 936-294-1140, E-mail: edu_mej@shsu.edu.

San Diego State University, Graduate and Research Affairs, College of Education, School of Teacher Education, Program in Secondary Curriculum and Instruction, San Diego, CA 92182. Offers MA. *Accreditation:* NCATE. *Students:* 3 full-time (all women), 27 part-time (17 women); includes 8 minority (1 African American, 4 Asian Americans or Pacific Islanders, 3 Hispanic Americans). Average age 29. 26 applicants, 62% accepted, 0 enrolled. In 2006, 47 degrees awarded. *Entrance requirements:* For master's, GRE General Test, letters of reference. Additional exam requirements/recommendations for international students: Required—TOEFL. *Application deadline:* For fall admission, 5/1 for domestic and international students; for spring admission, 11/1 for domestic students, 10/1 for international students. Applications are processed on a rolling basis. Application fee: $55. Electronic applications accepted. *Financial support:* Applicants required to submit FAFSA. *Unit head:* Dr. Valerie Pang, Graduate Advisor, 619-594-6286, Fax: 619-594-7828.

San Francisco State University, Division of Graduate Studies, College of Education, Department of Secondary Education, San Francisco, CA 94132-1722. Offers MA Ed. *Accreditation:* NCATE. Part-time and evening/weekend programs available. *Faculty:* 12 full-time (6 women),

7 part-time/adjunct (5 women). *Students:* 27 (14 women). Average age 28. In 2006, 12 degrees awarded. *Entrance requirements:* For master's, minimum GPA of 2.5 in last 60 units. *Application deadline:* For fall admission, 11/30 priority date for domestic students; for spring admission, 3/15 for domestic students. Applications are processed on a rolling basis. Application fee: $55. *Financial support:* Application deadline: 3/1. *Faculty research:* Science education, substance abuse, impact of television on adolescents, middle schools. *Unit head:* Dr. Nathan Avani, Chair, 415-338-6442, E-mail: natalio@sfsu.edu. *Application contact:* Linda Petsche, Admissions Coordinator for Credentials, 415-338-7038, E-mail: lpetsche@sfsu.edu.

San Jose State University, Graduate Studies and Research, College of Education, Department of Secondary Education, San Jose, CA 95192-0001. Offers Certificate. *Accreditation:* NCATE. Evening/weekend programs available. *Students:* 188 full-time (113 women), 67 part-time (47 women); includes 86 minority (2 American Indian/Alaska Native, 52 Asian Americans or Pacific Islanders, 32 Hispanic Americans), 4 international. Average age 35. 204 applicants, 61% accepted, 112 enrolled. *Application deadline:* For fall admission, 6/29 for domestic students; for spring admission, 11/30 for domestic students. Applications are processed on a rolling basis. Application fee: $59. Electronic applications accepted. *Financial support:* Career-related internships or fieldwork available. Financial award applicants required to submit FAFSA. *Unit head:* Dr. Cathy Buell, Chair, 408-924-3732, Fax: 408-924-3755.

San Jose State University, Graduate Studies and Research, College of Humanities and the Arts, Department of English and Comparative Literature, San Jose, CA 95192-0001. Offers creative writing (MFA); English (MA); secondary English education (Certificate). *Students:* 31 full-time (22 women), 59 part-time (45 women); includes 16 minority (3 African Americans, 1 American Indian/Alaska Native, 6 Asian Americans or Pacific Islanders, 6 Hispanic Americans), 2 international. Average age 34. 94 applicants, 73% accepted, 36 enrolled. In 2006, 37 degrees awarded. *Degree requirements:* For master's, one foreign language, thesis or alternative. *Entrance requirements:* For master's, GRE. Additional exam requirements/recommendations for international students: Required—TOEFL. *Application deadline:* For fall admission, 6/29 for domestic students; for spring admission, 11/30 for domestic students. Applications are processed on a rolling basis. Application fee: $59. Electronic applications accepted. *Financial support:* Applicants required to submit FAFSA. *Unit head:* John Engell, Chair, 408-924-4499, Fax: 408-924-4580, E-mail: jfengell@email.sjsu.edu. *Application contact:* Dr. Noelle Brada-Williams, Graduate Coordinator, 408-924-4435.

Seattle Pacific University, Graduate School, School of Education, Program in Secondary Teaching, Seattle, WA 98119-1997. Offers MAT. *Accreditation:* NCATE. Part-time and evening/weekend programs available. *Students:* 47 full-time (38 women), 74 part-time (46 women); includes 9 minority (1 African American, 1 American Indian/Alaska Native, 5 Asian Americans or Pacific Islanders, 2 Hispanic Americans), 1 international. 132 applicants, 69% accepted, 80 enrolled. In 2006, 54 degrees awarded. *Entrance requirements:* For master's, GRE General Test or MAT, minimum GPA of 3.0. *Application deadline:* For fall admission, 9/24 for domestic students; for spring admission, 4/15 for domestic students. Application fee: $50. *Expenses:* Contact institution. *Financial support:* Applicants required to submit FAFSA. *Unit head:* Dr. Sharon Hartnett, Chair, Secondary Education, 206-281-2216, Fax: 206-281-2756, E-mail: shartnett@spu.edu. *Application contact:* Allan Blomquist, Graduate Programs Manager, 206-281-2378, Fax: 206-281-2756, E-mail: blomqa@spu.edu.

Shenandoah University, College of Arts and Sciences, Winchester, VA 22601-5195. Offers administrative leadership (D Ed); advanced professional teaching English to speakers of other languages (Certificate); education (MSE); elementary education (Certificate); middle school education (Certificate); professional studies (Certificate); professional teaching English to speakers of other languages (Certificate); public management (Certificate); secondary education (Certificate); women's studies (Certificate). Part-time and evening/weekend programs available. Postbaccalaureate distance learning degree programs offered (minimal on-campus study). *Faculty:* 14 full-time (9 women), 7 part-time/adjunct (4 women). *Students:* 28 full-time (16 women), 283 part-time (208 women); includes 8 minority (3 African Americans, 1 American Indian/Alaska Native, 3 Asian Americans or Pacific Islanders, 1 Hispanic American), 26 international. Average age 40. 182 applicants, 68% accepted, 98 enrolled. In 2006, 96 master's, 6 doctorates, 22 other advanced degrees awarded. *Degree requirements:* For master's, thesis (for some programs), internship, comprehensive exam (for some programs); for doctorate, thesis/dissertation, comprehensive exam. *Entrance requirements:* For master's, minimum GPA of 3.0 or satisfactory GRE, 3 letters of recommendation, valid teaching license; for doctorate, minimum GPA of 3.5 in master's, 3 years of teaching experience, 3 letters of recommendation, writing samples. Additional exam requirements/recommendations for international students: Required—TOEFL (minimum score 527 paper-based; 197 computer-based; 71 iBT). *Application deadline:* For fall admission, 7/15 for domestic students; for spring admission, 10/15 for domestic students. Applications are processed on a rolling basis. Application fee: $30. Electronic applications accepted. *Expenses:* Tuition: Full-time $12,200; part-time $610 per credit. Required fees: $150. Full-time tuition and fees vary according to course load and program. *Financial support:* In 2006–07, fellowships with partial tuition reimbursements (averaging $2,581 per year); career-related internships or fieldwork, institutionally sponsored loans, and unspecified assistantships also available. Support available to part-time students. Financial award application deadline: 3/15; financial award applicants required to submit FAFSA. *Faculty research:* Nanotechnology, writing pedagogy and writing centers, violence in schools, Virginia/Shenandoah Valley history and culture, stress in children. *Unit head:* Dr. Calvin Allen, Dean, 540-665-4587, Fax: 540-665-4644, E-mail: callen@su.edu. *Application contact:* David Anthony, Dean of Admissions, 540-665-4581, Fax: 540-665-4627, E-mail: admit@su.edu.

See Close-Up on page 919.

Siena Heights University, Graduate College, Program in Teacher Education, Concentration in Secondary Education, Adrian, MI 49221-1796. Offers secondary education/reading (MA). Part-time programs available. *Degree requirements:* For master's, thesis, presentation. *Entrance requirements:* For master's, minimum GPA of 3.0, interview.

Sierra Nevada College, Teacher Education Program, Incline Village, NV 89451. Offers elementary education (MAT); secondary education (MAT). Part-time and evening/weekend programs available. *Faculty:* 2 full-time (both women), 26 part-time/adjunct (16 women). *Students:* 179 full-time (136 women), 85 part-time (58 women); includes 21 minority (6 African Americans, 1 American Indian/Alaska Native, 2 Asian Americans or Pacific Islanders, 12 Hispanic Americans). Average age 35. In 2006, 29 degrees awarded. *Median time to degree:* Master's–2.5 years full-time, 3.5 years part-time. *Degree requirements:* For master's, thesis, PRAXIS I and II, comprehensive exam, registration. *Entrance requirements:* For master's, 2 letters of recommendation, minimum GPA of 3.0. *Application deadline:* For fall admission, 8/16 priority date for domestic students; for winter admission, 1/10 priority date for domestic students; for spring admission, 5/25 priority date for domestic students. Applications are processed on a rolling basis. Application fee: $50. *Expenses:* Tuition: Full-time $3,590; part-time $350 per credit. *Financial support:* In 2006–07, 230 students received support. Federal Work-Study available. Support available to part-time students. Financial award application deadline: 8/16; financial award applicants required to submit FAFSA. *Unit head:* Dr. Francesca Bero, Statewide Director, 775-831-1314, Fax: 775-832-1686, E-mail: fbero@sierranevada.edu. *Application contact:* Katrina Midgley, Teacher Education Admissions Counselor, 775-831-1314 Ext. 7517, Fax: 775-832-1694, E-mail: kmidgley@sierranevada.edu.

Simmons College, Graduate School, College of Arts and Sciences Graduate Studies, Department of Education, Program in Teacher Preparation, Boston, MA 02115. Offers educational leadership (MS Ed, CAGS); elementary education (MAT, CAGS); general education (CAGS); general purposes (MS); middle school education (MAT, CAGS); professional license (CAGS); professional license: elementary (MS Ed); professional license: middle/high (MS Ed); secondary education (MAT, CAGS); urban education (MS Ed, CAGS). *Faculty:* 4 full-time (3 women), 22 part-time/adjunct (13 women). *Students:* 61 full-time (53 women), 141 part-time (128 women); includes 33 minority (13 African Americans, 10 Asian Americans or Pacific Islanders, 10 Hispanic Americans), 1 international. Average age 24. 86 applicants, 77% accepted, 39 enrolled. In 2006, 128 master's, 12 other advanced degrees awarded. *Degree requirements:* For master's, student teaching experience or internship. *Entrance requirements:* For master's, GRE General Test, MAT or Massachusetts Tests for Educator Licensure (MTEL). Additional exam requirements/recommendations for international students: Required—TOEFL (minimum score 600 paper-based; 250 computer-based; 100 iBT). *Application deadline:* For fall admission, 8/1 priority date for domestic and international students; for spring admission, 12/15 priority date for domestic and international students. Applications are processed on a rolling basis. Application fee: $35. Electronic applications accepted. *Expenses:* Contact institution. *Financial support:* Teaching assistantships, career-related internships or fieldwork, Federal Work-Study, institutionally sponsored loans, scholarships/grants, and tuition waivers (partial) available. Support available to part-time students. Financial award application deadline: 3/1; financial award applicants required to submit FAFSA. *Faculty research:* Putting standards/frameworks into practice, restructuring middle and high schools, interactive teaching and learning developing curriculum for Third World countries. Total annual research expenditures: $110,000. *Unit head:* Lynda Johnson, Assistant Dean, 617-521-2576, Fax: 617-521-3133, E-mail: gsa@simmons.edu. *Application contact:* Kristen Haack, Director, Graduate Studies Admission, 617-521-2915, Fax: 617-521-3058, E-mail: gsa@simmons.edu.

Slippery Rock University of Pennsylvania, Graduate Studies (Recruitment), College of Education, Department of Secondary Education/Foundations of Education, Slippery Rock, PA 16057-1383. Offers secondary education in math/science (M Ed). *Accreditation:* NCATE. *Degree requirements:* For master's, thesis (for some programs), comprehensive exam (for some programs). *Entrance requirements:* For master's, GRE General Test, MAT, minimum GPA of 2.75 (minimum GPA of 3.0 for initial certification programs). Additional exam requirements/recommendations for international students: Required—TOEFL (minimum score 550 paper-based; 213 computer-based). *Application deadline:* For fall admission, 7/1 priority date for domestic and international students; for spring admission, 11/1 priority date for domestic and international students. Applications are processed on a rolling basis. Application fee: $25. Electronic applications accepted. *Expenses:* Tuition, state resident: part-time $336 per credit. Tuition, nonresident: part-time $538 per credit. Required fees: $84 per credit. $37 per semester. *Financial support:* Career-related internships or fieldwork, Federal Work-Study, scholarships/grants, and unspecified assistantships available. Support available to part-time students. Financial award application deadline: 5/1; financial award applicants required to submit FAFSA. *Unit head:* Graduate Coordinator, 724-738-2041, Fax: 724-738-2880. *Application contact:* April Longwell, Interim Director of Graduate Studies, 724-738-2051 Ext. 2116, Fax: 724-738-2146, E-mail: graduate.studies@sru.edu.

Smith College, Graduate Programs, Department of Education and Child Study, Program in Secondary Education, Northampton, MA 01063. Offers biological sciences education (MAT); chemistry education (MAT); English education (MAT); French education (MAT); geology education (MAT); government education (MAT); history education (MAT); mathematics education (MAT); physics education (MAT); Spanish education (MAT). Part-time programs available. *Faculty:* 6 full-time (4 women), 3 part-time/adjunct (2 women). *Students:* 4 full-time (2 women). Average age 36. 12 applicants, 67% accepted, 3 enrolled. In 2006, 5 master's awarded. *Entrance requirements:* For master's, GRE General Test. Additional exam requirements/recommendations for international students: Required—TOEFL. *Application deadline:* For fall admission, 4/1 for domestic students, 1/15 for international students; for spring admission, 12/1 for domestic students. Application fee: $60. *Expenses:* Tuition: Full-time $32,320; part-time $1,010 per credit. Tuition and fees vary according to course load. *Financial support:* In 2006–07, 3 students received support. Career-related internships or fieldwork, institutionally sponsored loans, and scholarships/grants available. Support available to part-time students. Financial award application deadline: 1/15; financial award applicants required to submit CSS PROFILE or FAFSA. *Unit head:* Rosetta Cohen, Graduate Student Advisor, 413-585-3266.

South Carolina State University, School of Graduate Studies, Department of Education, Orangeburg, SC 29117-0001. Offers early childhood and special education (M Ed); early childhood education (MAT); elementary education (M Ed, MAT); engineering (MAT); general science (MAT); mathematics (MAT); secondary education (M Ed), including biology education, business education, counselor education, English education, home economics education, industrial education, mathematics education, science education, social studies education; special education (M Ed), including emotionally handicapped, learning disabilities, mentally handicapped. *Accreditation:* NCATE. Part-time and evening/weekend programs available. *Faculty:* 21 full-time (10 women), 4 part-time/adjunct (0 women). *Students:* 34 full-time (28 women), 33 part-time (25 women); includes 63 minority (61 African Americans, 1 American Indian/Alaska Native, 1 Asian American or Pacific Islander). Average age 35. 46 applicants, 67% accepted, 19 enrolled. In 2006, 28 degrees awarded. *Degree requirements:* For master's, departmental qualifying exam, thesis optional. *Entrance requirements:* For master's, GRE General Test, NTE, interview, teaching certificate. *Application deadline:* For fall admission, 6/15 priority date for domestic students, 6/15 for international students; for spring admission, 11/1 for domestic and international students. Applications are processed on a rolling basis. Application fee: $25. Electronic applications accepted. *Expenses:* Tuition, state resident: full-time $7,278. Tuition, nonresident: full-time $14,322. *Financial support:* Fellowships, research assistantships, career-related internships or fieldwork, Federal Work-Study, and institutionally sponsored loans available. Financial award application deadline: 6/1. *Faculty research:* Critical thinking, child abuse, stress, test-taking skills, conflict resolution, mainstreaming. *Unit head:* Dr. Gail Joyner-Fleming, Interim Chair, 803-533-3769, Fax: 803-536-8492, E-mail: zf-gfleming@scsu.edu. *Application contact:* Annette Hazzard-Jones, Program Coordinator II, 803-536-8809, Fax: 803-536-8812, E-mail: zs_ahazzard@scsu.edu.

Southeastern Louisiana University, College of Education and Human Development, Department of Teaching and Learning, Hammond, LA 70402. Offers curriculum and instruction (M Ed); elementary education (MAT); secondary education (MAT); special education (M Ed, MAT). *Accreditation:* NCATE. Part-time programs available. *Faculty:* 23 full-time (18 women), 1 (woman) part-time/adjunct. *Students:* 31 full-time (27 women), 300 part-time (269 women); includes 50 minority (39 African Americans, 2 Asian Americans or Pacific Islanders, 9 Hispanic Americans), 3 international. Average age 33. 47 applicants, 100% accepted, 31 enrolled. In 2006, 101 degrees awarded. *Degree requirements:* For master's, comprehensive exam (for some programs). *Entrance requirements:* For master's, GRE, PRAXIS (MAT), minimum GPA of 2.5. Additional exam requirements/recommendations for international students: Required—TOEFL (minimum score 500 paper-based; 173 computer-based). *Application deadline:* For fall admission, 7/15 priority date for domestic students, 6/1 priority date for international students; for spring admission, 12/1 priority date for domestic students, 10/1 priority date for international students. Applications are processed on a rolling basis. Application fee: $20 ($30 for international students). Electronic applications accepted. *Expenses:* Tuition, state resident: full-time $2,216; part-time $123 per credit. Tuition, nonresident: full-time $6,212; part-time $345 per credit. Required fees: $986; $55 per credit. Part-time tuition and fees vary according to course load. *Financial support:* Federal Work-Study, institutionally sponsored loans, unspecified assistantships, and administrative assistantship available. Support available to part-time students. Financial award application deadline: 5/1; financial award applicants required to submit FAFSA. *Faculty research:* Reading, instructional methodology, science education, math education, early childhood. *Unit head:* Dr. Shirley Jacob, Department Head, 985-549-2221, Fax: 985-549-5009, E-mail: sjacob@selu.edu. *Application contact:* Sandra Meyers, Graduate Admissions Analyst, 985-549-2066, Fax: 985-549-5632, E-mail: admissions@selu.edu.

Southeastern Oklahoma State University, Graduate School, School of Education, Durant, OK 74701-0609. Offers educational administration (M Ed); educational instruction and leadership (M Ed); educational technology (M Ed); elementary education (M Ed); school counseling (M Ed); secondary education (M Ed). *Accreditation:* NCATE. Part-time and evening/weekend programs available. *Degree requirements:* For master's, portfolio (M Ed), thesis optional. *Entrance requirements:* For master's, GRE General Test (MBS), minimum GPA of 3.0 in last 60 hours or 2.75 overall. Additional exam requirements/recommendations for international

Secondary Education

Southeastern Oklahoma State University (continued)
students: Required—TOEFL (minimum score 550 paper-based; 213 computer-based). Electronic applications accepted.

Southeast Missouri State University, School of Graduate Studies, Department of Middle and Secondary Education, Cape Girardeau, MO 63701-4799. Offers educational studies (MA); middle level education (MA). *Accreditation:* NCATE. Part-time and evening/weekend programs available. *Faculty:* 3 full-time (all women). *Students:* Average age 35. 16 applicants, 88% accepted. In 2006, 6 degrees awarded. *Degree requirements:* For master's, thesis or alternative. *Entrance requirements:* For master's, GRE General Test, MAT, PRAXIS II, minimum GPA of 2.75. Additional exam requirements/recommendations for international students: Required—TOEFL (minimum score 550 paper-based; 213 computer-based). *Application deadline:* For fall admission, 8/1 for domestic students, 4/1 for international students; for spring admission, 11/21 for domestic students, 10/1 for international students. Applications are processed on a rolling basis. Application fee: $20 ($100 for international students). Electronic applications accepted. *Financial support:* In 2006–07, 6 students received support. Applicants required to submit FAFSA. *Unit head:* Dr. Simin Cwick, Interim Chair, 573-651-2008, Fax: 573-651-6141, E-mail: scwick@semo.edu. *Application contact:* Marsha L. Arant, Senior Administrative Assistant, Office of Graduate Studies, 573-651-2192, Fax: 573-651-2001, E-mail: marant@semo.edu.

Southern Arkansas University–Magnolia, Graduate Programs, Magnolia, AR 71753. Offers computer and information sciences (MS); counseling (MS); education (M Ed), including counseling and development, educational administration and supervision, elementary education, secondary education; kinesiology (MS); library media and information specialist (M Ed); school counseling (M Ed); teaching (MAT). *Accreditation:* NCATE. Part-time and evening/weekend programs available. *Degree requirements:* For master's, thesis optional. *Entrance requirements:* For master's, GRE or MAT, minimum GPA of 2.75. *Faculty research:* Alternative certification for teachers, supervision of instruction, instructional leadership, counseling.

Southern Illinois University Edwardsville, Graduate Studies and Research, School of Education, Department of Curriculum and Instruction, Program in Secondary Education, Edwardsville, IL 62026-0001. Offers art (MS Ed); biology (MS Ed); chemistry (MS Ed); English (MS Ed); foreign languages (MS Ed); history (MS Ed); mathematics (MS Ed); physics (MS Ed); reading (MS Ed); science (MS Ed). *Accreditation:* NCATE. Part-time and evening/weekend programs available. *Students:* 2 full-time (both women), 23 part-time (14 women); includes 2 minority (both African Americans) Average age 33. 12 applicants, 42% accepted. In 2006, 10 degrees awarded. *Degree requirements:* For master's, thesis or alternative, final exam. *Entrance requirements:* For master's, MAT. Additional exam requirements/recommendations for international students: Required—TOEFL. *Application deadline:* For fall admission, 7/20 for domestic students, 6/1 for international students; for spring admission, 12/14 for domestic students, 10/1 for international students. Application fee: $30. Electronic applications accepted. *Financial support:* Fellowships, research assistantships, teaching assistantships, Federal Work-Study, institutionally sponsored loans, and unspecified assistantships available. Support available to part-time students. Financial award application deadline: 3/1; financial award applicants required to submit FAFSA. *Unit head:* Dr. David DeWeese, Director, 618-650-3432, E-mail: ddewees@siue.edu.

Southern New Hampshire University, School of Education, Manchester, NH 03106-1045. Offers business education (MS); child development (M Ed); computer technology education (Certificate); curriculum and instruction (M Ed); education (M Ed, CAS); elementary education (M Ed); general special education (Certificate); school business administrator (Certificate); school counseling (M Ed); school psychology (M Ed); secondary education (M Ed); training and development (Certificate). Part-time and evening/weekend programs available. Postbaccalaureate distance learning degree programs offered. *Faculty:* 6 full-time (3 women), 9 part-time/adjunct (7 women). *Students:* Average age 35. In 2006, 52 degrees awarded. *Degree requirements:* For master's, thesis or alternative, comprehensive exam (for some programs). *Entrance requirements:* For master's, GRE General Test or MAT, minimum GPA of 3.0. Additional exam requirements/recommendations for international students: Required—TOEFL (minimum score 550 paper-based; 213 computer-based). *Application deadline:* Applications are processed on a rolling basis. Application fee: $25. Electronic applications accepted. *Expenses:* Contact institution. *Financial support:* Institutionally sponsored loans available. Financial award applicants required to submit FAFSA. *Unit head:* Dr. Patrick J. Hartwick, Dean, 603-668-2211 Ext. 4698, Fax: 603-629-4673, E-mail: p.hartwick@snhu.edu. *Application contact:* Scott Durand, Director of Graduate Enrollment Services, 603-644-3102 Ext. 3338, Fax: 603-644-3144, E-mail: s.durand@snhu.edu.

Southern Oregon University, Graduate Studies, School of Social Sciences, Department of Education, Ashland, OR 97520. Offers elementary education (MA Ed, MS Ed), including classroom teacher, early childhood, handicapped learner, reading, supervision; secondary education (MA Ed, MS Ed), including classroom teacher, handicapped learner, reading, supervision; teaching (MAT). *Degree requirements:* For master's, thesis optional. *Entrance requirements:* For master's, GRE General Test, minimum GPA of 3.0. Electronic applications accepted.

Southern University and Agricultural and Mechanical College, Graduate School, College of Education, Department of Curriculum and Instruction, Baton Rouge, LA 70813. Offers elementary education (M Ed); media (M Ed); secondary education (M Ed). *Degree requirements:* For master's, thesis optional. *Entrance requirements:* For master's, GMAT or GRE General Test. Additional exam requirements/recommendations for international students: Required—TOEFL (minimum score 525 paper-based; 193 computer-based).

Southwestern Oklahoma State University, College of Professional and Graduate Studies, School of Behavioral Sciences and Education, Weatherford, OK 73096-3098. Offers community counseling (M Ed); early childhood education (M Ed); educational administration (M Ed); elementary education (M Ed); health sciences and microbiology (M Ed); kinesiology (M Ed); parks and recreation management (M Ed); school counseling (M Ed); school psychology (MS); school psychometry (M Ed); secondary education (M Ed); special education (M Ed). *Accreditation:* NCATE. Part-time and evening/weekend programs available. Postbaccalaureate distance learning degree programs offered (minimal on-campus study). *Degree requirements:* For master's, exam. *Entrance requirements:* For master's, GRE General Test or minimum undergraduate GPA of 3.0. Additional exam requirements/recommendations for international students: Required—TOEFL.

Spalding University, Graduate Studies, College of Education, Programs in Education, Louisville, KY 40203-2188. Offers elementary school education (MAT); general education (MA); high school education (MAT); middle school education (MAT); school administration (MA); special education (learning and behavioral disorders) (MAT). MAT degree programs offered for first teaching certificate/license students. *Accreditation:* NCATE. Part-time and evening/weekend programs available. *Degree requirements:* For master's, portfolio, final project, clinical experience. *Entrance requirements:* For master's, GRE General Test or MAT, interview, recommendations, resumé. Additional exam requirements/recommendations for international students: Required—TOEFL. Electronic applications accepted. *Faculty research:* Instructional technology, achievement gap, classroom management, assessment.

Springfield College, Graduate Programs, Program in Education, Springfield, MA 01109-3797. Offers counseling and secondary education (M Ed, MS); education (M Ed, MS). Part-time and evening/weekend programs available. *Faculty:* 9 full-time (6 women), 2 part-time/adjunct (both women). *Students:* 52; includes 4 minority (3 African Americans, 1 Hispanic American). Average age 30. 36 applicants, 78% accepted, 21 enrolled. In 2006, 10 master's awarded. *Degree requirements:* For master's, comprehensive exam. *Entrance requirements:* Additional exam requirements/recommendations for international students: Required—TOEFL (minimum score 550 paper-based; 213 computer-based). *Application deadline:* For fall admission, 1/15 for domestic students; for winter admission, 11/1 for domestic students; for spring admission, 12/1 for domestic students. Applications are processed on a rolling basis. Application fee: $50. Electronic applications accepted. *Expenses:* Tuition: Full-time $12,222; part-time $679 per credit. Required fees: $25; $25 per year. One-time fee: $25 full-time. *Financial support:* In 2006–07, 2 teaching assistantships with partial tuition reimbursements were awarded; fellowships with partial tuition reimbursements, career-related internships or fieldwork, Federal Work-Study, institutionally sponsored loans, and tuition waivers (full and partial) also available. Financial award application deadline: 3/1. *Faculty research:* Varied educational research. Total annual research expenditures: $50,000. *Unit head:* Dr. Gerard Thibodeau, Director, 413-748-3312, E-mail: gthibodeau@spfldcol.edu. *Application contact:* Donald James Shaw, Director of Graduate Admissions, 413-748-3060, Fax: 413-748-3069, E-mail: donald_shaw_jr@spfldcol.edu.

Spring Hill College, Graduate Programs, Program in Education, Mobile, AL 36608-1791. Offers early childhood education (MAT, MS Ed); elementary education (MAT, MS Ed); secondary education (MAT, MS Ed). Part-time and evening/weekend programs available. *Faculty:* 2 full-time (both women), 7 part-time/adjunct (5 women). *Students:* 11 full-time (10 women), 44 part-time (34 women); includes 19 minority (all African Americans) Average age 33. In 2006, 21 degrees awarded. *Degree requirements:* For master's, comprehensive exam. *Entrance requirements:* For master's, GRE, MAT, NTE, or PRAXIS, minimum undergraduate GPA of 3.0. Additional exam requirements/recommendations for international students: Required—TOEFL (minimum score 550 paper-based; 213 computer-based). *Application deadline:* For fall admission, 8/1 priority date for domestic students, 6/1 priority date for international students; for spring admission, 12/1 priority date for domestic students, 11/1 priority date for international students. Applications are processed on a rolling basis. Application fee: $25 ($35 for international students). Electronic applications accepted. *Expenses:* Contact institution. *Financial support:* In 2006–07, 49 students received support. Career-related internships or fieldwork and scholarships/grants available. Support available to part-time students. Financial award applicants required to submit FAFSA. *Unit head:* Dr. Ann A. Adams, Chair of Teacher Education, 251-380-3479, Fax: 251-460-2184, E-mail: aadams@shc.edu. *Application contact:* Joyce Genz, Dean of Life Long Learning and Director of Graduate Programs, 251-380-3094, Fax: 251-460-2190, E-mail: grad@shc.edu.

State University of New York at Binghamton, Graduate School, School of Education, Program in Secondary Education, Binghamton, NY 13902-6000. Offers biology education (MAT, MS Ed, MST); earth science education (MAT, MS Ed, MST); English education (MAT, MS Ed, MST); French education (MAT, MST); mathematical sciences education (MAT, MS Ed, MST); physics (MAT, MS Ed, MST); social studies (MAT, MS Ed, MST); Spanish education (MAT, MST). *Accreditation:* Teacher Education Accreditation Council. Part-time and evening/weekend programs available. *Students:* 89 full-time (50 women), 47 part-time (32 women); includes 6 minority (1 African American, 3 Asian Americans or Pacific Islanders, 2 Hispanic Americans). Average age 29. 72 applicants, 72% accepted, 23 enrolled. In 2006, 44 degrees awarded. *Entrance requirements:* For master's, GRE General Test. Additional exam requirements/recommendations for international students: Required—TOEFL. *Application deadline:* For fall admission, 4/15 priority date for domestic students, 1/15 priority date for international students; for spring admission, 11/1 for domestic students, 10/1 priority date for international students. Applications are processed on a rolling basis. Application fee: $60. Electronic applications accepted. *Financial support:* In 2006–07, 25 students received support, including 2 fellowships with partial tuition reimbursements available (averaging $2,350 per year), 4 research assistantships with full and partial tuition reimbursements available (averaging $6,638 per year), 13 teaching assistantships with full tuition reimbursements available (averaging $5,944 per year); career-related internships or fieldwork, Federal Work-Study, institutionally sponsored loans, tuition waivers (full and partial), and unspecified assistantships also available. Support available to part-time students. Financial award application deadline: 2/15. *Unit head:* Dr. Thomas O'Brien, Coordinator, 607-777-7329, E-mail: tobrien@binghamton.edu.

State University of New York at Fredonia, Graduate Studies, College of Education, Program in Secondary Education, Fredonia, NY 14063-1136. Offers MS Ed. *Accreditation:* NCATE. Part-time and evening/weekend programs available. *Faculty:* 3 full-time (1 woman). *Students:* 10 full-time (7 women), 17 part-time (13 women). Average age 27. In 2006, 26 degrees awarded. *Degree requirements:* For master's, thesis optional. *Application deadline:* For fall admission, 8/5 for domestic students; for spring admission, 12/1 for domestic students. Application fee: $50. *Expenses:* Tuition, state resident: full-time $6,900; part-time $288 per credit hour. Tuition, nonresident: full-time $10,920; part-time $455 per credit hour. Required fees: $1,132; $47 per credit hour. *Financial support:* In 2006–07, 4 teaching assistantships (averaging $6,500 per year) were awarded; research assistantships, career-related internships or fieldwork and tuition waivers (full and partial) also available. Support available to part-time students. Financial award application deadline: 3/15. *Unit head:* Dr. Christine Givner, Dean, College of Education, 716-673-3311, E-mail: christine.givner@fredonia.edu.

State University of New York at New Paltz, Graduate School, Faculty of Education, Department of Secondary Education, New Paltz, NY 12561. Offers MAT, MS Ed. *Accreditation:* NCATE. Part-time and evening/weekend programs available. *Faculty:* 10 full-time (7 women), 37 part-time/adjunct (23 women). *Students:* 88 full-time (65 women), 127 part-time (78 women); includes 21 minority (2 African Americans, 2 American Indian/Alaska Native, 4 Asian Americans or Pacific Islanders, 13 Hispanic Americans), 6 international. Average age 31. 171 applicants. In 2006, 76 degrees awarded. *Degree requirements:* For master's, portfolio. *Entrance requirements:* For master's, minimum GPA of 3.0, teaching certificate (MS Ed). Additional exam requirements/recommendations for international students: Required—TOEFL (minimum score 550 paper-based; 213 computer-based; 80 iBT). *Application deadline:* For fall admission, 3/1 for domestic and international students; for spring admission, 10/1 for domestic and international students. Application fee: $50. Electronic applications accepted. *Expenses:* Tuition, state resident: full-time $6,900; part-time $288 per credit hour. Tuition, nonresident: full-time $10,920; part-time $455 per credit hour. *Financial support:* Federal Work-Study and institutionally sponsored loans available. *Unit head:* Dr. Devon Duhaney, Chair, 845-257-2850, E-mail: duhaneyd@newpaltz.edu.

State University of New York at New Paltz, Graduate School, Faculty of Education, Department of Special Education, New Paltz, NY 12561. Offers adolescence (7-12) (MS Ed); childhood (1-6) (MS Ed). *Accreditation:* NCATE. Part-time and evening/weekend programs available. *Faculty:* 11 full-time (9 women), 21 part-time/adjunct (15 women). *Students:* 40 full-time (38 women), 59 part-time (49 women); includes 5 minority (1 African American, 2 Asian Americans or Pacific Islanders, 2 Hispanic Americans), 1 international. Average age 29. 63 applicants. In 2006, 56 degrees awarded. *Degree requirements:* For master's, portfolio. *Entrance requirements:* For master's, minimum GPA of 3.0, teaching certificate. Additional exam requirements/recommendations for international students: Required—TOEFL (minimum score 550 paper-based; 213 computer-based; 80 iBT). *Application deadline:* For fall admission, 5/1 priority date for domestic students, 5/1 for international students; for spring admission, 11/15 for domestic and international students. Application fee: $50. Electronic applications accepted. *Expenses:* Tuition, state resident: full-time $6,900; part-time $288 per credit hour. Tuition, nonresident: full-time $10,920; part-time $455 per credit hour. *Financial support:* Career-related internships or fieldwork, Federal Work-Study, and institutionally sponsored loans available. *Unit head:* Dr. Spencer Salend, Coordinator, 845-257-2846, E-mail: salends@newpaltz.edu.

State University of New York at Oswego, Graduate Studies, School of Education, Department of Curriculum and Instruction, Oswego, NY 13126. Offers art education (MAT); elementary education (MS Ed); literacy education (MS Ed); secondary education (MS Ed); special education (MS Ed). Part-time and evening/weekend programs available. *Faculty:* 23 full-time, 45 part-time/adjunct. *Students:* 184 full-time (139 women), 220 part-time (185 women); includes 12 minority (5 African Americans, 1 American Indian/Alaska Native, 1 Asian American or Pacific Islander, 5 Hispanic Americans), 1 international. Average age 33. 266 applicants, 89% accepted. In 2006, 255 degrees awarded. *Degree requirements:* For master's, thesis optional. *Entrance requirements:* For master's, GRE General Test, minimum GPA of 2.7, provisional teaching certificate. Additional exam requirements/recommendations for international students:

Required—TOEFL (minimum score 560 paper-based; 220 computer-based). *Application deadline:* For fall admission, 3/1 for domestic students; for spring admission, 10/1 for domestic students. Application fee: $50. *Expenses:* Tuition, state resident: part-time $288 per credit. Tuition, nonresident: part-time $455 per credit. Tuition and fees vary according to program. *Financial support:* In 2006–07, 9 students received support, including 3 fellowships, 6 teaching assistantships with full tuition reimbursements available; career-related internships or fieldwork, Federal Work-Study, institutionally sponsored loans, scholarships/grants, and unspecified assistantships also available. Support available to part-time students. Financial award application deadline: 4/1; financial award applicants required to submit FAFSA. *Faculty research:* Classroom applications for microcomputers; classroom questioning, wait-time, and achievement; values clarification and academic achievement. *Unit head:* Dr. Pamela Michel, Chair, 315-312-4052. *Application contact:* Dr. Joyce Smith, Coordinator, Graduate Education, 315-312-4052.

State University of New York at Plattsburgh, Division of Education, Health, and Human Services, Department of Adolescence Education/Health, Plattsburgh, NY 12901-2681. Offers adolescence education (MST); biology 7-12 (MST); chemistry 7-12 (MST); earth science 7-12 (MST); English 7-12 (MST); French 7-12 (MST); mathematics 7-12 (MST); physics 7-12 (MST); social studies 7-12 (MST); Spanish 7-12 (MST). *Faculty:* 4 full-time (3 women), 2 part-time/adjunct (0 women). *Students:* 58 full-time (38 women), 14 part-time (10 women); includes 5 minority (1 African American, 4 Hispanic Americans). Average age 30. 49 applicants, 78% accepted, 32 enrolled. In 2006, 30 degrees awarded. *Degree requirements:* For master's, comprehensive exam or research project. *Entrance requirements:* For master's, GRE General Test or MAT, minimum GPA of 2.5. *Application deadline:* For fall admission, 2/15 priority date for domestic students; for spring admission, 10/15 priority date for domestic students. Applications are processed on a rolling basis. Application fee: $50. *Expenses:* Tuition, state resident: full-time $6,900; part-time $288 per credit hour. Tuition, nonresident: full-time $10,920; part-time $455 per credit hour. *Financial support:* Application deadline: 4/15; *Unit head:* Dr. Lois Beach, Chair, 578-564-5750, E-mail: lois.beach@plattsburgh.edu. *Application contact:* Sharon Derr, Assistant Director, Graduate Admission, 518-564-4723, Fax: 518-564-4722, E-mail: derrsl@plattsburgh.edu.

State University of New York College at Cortland, Graduate Studies, School of Arts and Sciences, Programs in Adolescence Education, Cortland, NY 13045. Offers biology (MAT, MS Ed); chemistry (MAT, MS Ed); earth science (MAT, MS Ed); English (MS Ed); French (MS Ed); mathematics (MAT, MS Ed); physics (MAT, MS Ed); social studies (MS Ed); Spanish (MS Ed). *Accreditation:* NCATE. Part-time and evening/weekend programs available. *Degree requirements:* For master's, one foreign language, thesis (for some programs), comprehensive exam (for some programs). *Entrance requirements:* For master's, GRE General Test.

State University of New York College at Geneseo, Graduate Studies, School of Education, Program in Secondary Education, Geneseo, NY 14454-1401. Offers MS Ed. Part-time and evening/weekend programs available. *Faculty:* 12 full-time (6 women). *Students:* 12 full-time (9 women), 20 part-time (12 women); includes 2 minority (1 Asian American or Pacific Islander, 1 Hispanic American). Average age 24. 18 applicants, 94% accepted, 12 enrolled. In 2006, 17 degrees awarded. *Degree requirements:* For master's, thesis optional. *Entrance requirements:* For master's, GRE General Test. *Application deadline:* For fall admission, 6/1 priority date for domestic students; for spring admission, 10/1 for domestic students. Application fee: $50. *Financial support:* In 2006–07, 1 student received support; teaching assistantships with tuition reimbursements available, career-related internships or fieldwork, Federal Work-Study, and institutionally sponsored loans available. Financial award application deadline: 4/1; financial award applicants required to submit FAFSA. *Unit head:* Dr. Osman Alawiye, Chairperson, School of Education, 585-245-5560, Fax: 585-245-5220.

State University of New York College at Oneonta, Graduate Studies, Division of Education, Department of Adolescence Education, Oneonta, NY 13820-4015. Offers adolescence education (MS Ed); family and consumer science education (MS Ed). *Accreditation:* NCATE. Part-time and evening/weekend programs available. *Entrance requirements:* For master's, GRE General Test.

State University of New York College at Potsdam, School of Education, Program in Secondary Education, Potsdam, NY 13676. Offers MS Ed, MST. *Accreditation:* NCATE. Part-time programs available. *Faculty:* 8 full-time (2 women), 5 part-time/adjunct (2 women). *Students:* 47 full-time (30 women), 12 part-time (7 women); includes 1 minority (American Indian/Alaska Native), 7 international. In 2006, 47 degrees awarded. *Degree requirements:* For master's, variable foreign language requirement, culminating experience, thesis optional. *Entrance requirements:* For master's, minimum GPA of 2.75 in last 60 hours of course work, 3.0 for English program. Additional exam requirements/recommendations for international students: Required—TOEFL (minimum score 550 paper-based; 213 computer-based). *Application deadline:* Applications are processed on a rolling basis. Application fee: $50. *Financial support:* Fellowships, teaching assistantships, career-related internships or fieldwork, Federal Work-Study, and scholarships/grants available. Support available to part-time students. Financial award application deadline: 3/1. *Unit head:* Dr. Peter Brouwer, Chairperson, 315-267-3018, Fax: 315-267-4802, E-mail: brouweps@potsdam.edu. *Application contact:* Peter Cutler, Graduate Admissions Counselor, 315-267-3154, Fax: 315-267-4802, E-mail: cutlerpj@potsdam.edu.

Stephen F. Austin State University, Graduate School, College of Education, Department of Secondary Education and Educational Leadership, Nacogdoches, TX 75962. Offers educational leadership (Ed D); secondary education (M Ed). *Accreditation:* NCATE. *Degree requirements:* For master's, comprehensive exam; for doctorate, thesis/dissertation. *Entrance requirements:* For master's, GRE General Test; for doctorate, GRE General Test, interview, writing sample. Additional exam requirements/recommendations for international students: Required—TOEFL. Electronic applications accepted.

Suffolk University, College of Arts and Sciences, Department of Education and Human Services, Program in Secondary School Teaching, Boston, MA 02108-2770. Offers MS. Part-time and evening/weekend programs available. *Entrance requirements:* For master's, GRE General Test or MAT. *Application deadline:* For fall admission, 6/15 priority date for domestic students, 6/15 for international students; for spring admission, 11/15 priority date for domestic students, 11/15 for international students. Applications are processed on a rolling basis. Application fee: $35. *Financial support:* Fellowships, career-related internships or fieldwork, Federal Work-Study, and institutionally sponsored loans available. Support available to part-time students. Financial award application deadline: 4/1; financial award applicants required to submit FAFSA. *Faculty research:* Assessment systems, reflection, teamwork, learning environment. *Unit head:* Dr. Sarah M. Carroll, Graduate Program Director, 617-573-8261, Fax: 617-722-9440, E-mail: scarroll@suffolk.edu. *Application contact:* Judith Reynolds, Director of Graduate Admissions, 617-573-8302, Fax: 617-523-0116, E-mail: grad.admission@suffolk.edu.

Sul Ross State University, Rio Grande College of Sul Ross State University, Alpine, TX 79832. Offers business administration (MBA); teacher education (M Ed), including bilingual education, counseling, educational diagnostics, elementary education, general education, reading, school administration, secondary education. Part-time and evening/weekend programs available. *Degree requirements:* For master's, thesis optional. *Entrance requirements:* For master's, GMAT or GRE General Test, minimum GPA of 2.5 in last 60 hours of undergraduate work. *Faculty research:* Drug and substance abuse counseling, U.S.-Mexico border economic development.

Sul Ross State University, School of Professional Studies, Department of Teacher Education, Program in Secondary Education, Alpine, TX 79832. Offers M Ed. Part-time and evening/weekend programs available. *Degree requirements:* For master's, thesis optional. *Entrance requirements:* For master's, GMAT or GRE General Test, minimum GPA of 2.5 in last 60 hours of undergraduate work.

Tarleton State University, College of Graduate Studies, College of Education, Department of Educational Administration, Counseling, and Psychology, Stephenville, TX 76402. Offers counseling and psychology (M Ed), including counseling, counseling psychology, educational psychology; educational administration (M Ed, Certificate); educational leadership (Ed D); secondary education (Certificate); special education (Certificate). Part-time and evening/weekend programs available. Postbaccalaureate distance learning degree programs offered (minimal on-campus study). *Faculty:* 45 full-time (23 women), 37 part-time/adjunct (9 women). *Students:* 210 full-time (124 women), 613 part-time (464 women); includes 82 minority (11 Asian Americans or Pacific Islanders, 71 Hispanic Americans), 1 international. Average age 35. In 2006, 203 degrees awarded. *Degree requirements:* For master's, thesis optional. *Entrance requirements:* For master's, GRE General Test, minimum GPA of 3.0. Additional exam requirements/recommendations for international students: Required—TOEFL (minimum score 550 paper-based; 220 computer-based). *Application deadline:* For fall admission, 8/5 priority date for domestic students; for spring admission, 12/1 for domestic students. Applications are processed on a rolling basis. Application fee: $25 ($75 for international students). *Financial support:* In 2006–07, 3 research assistantships (averaging $12,000 per year), 12 teaching assistantships (averaging $12,000 per year) were awarded; career-related internships or fieldwork, Federal Work-Study, institutionally sponsored loans, and tuition waivers (partial) also available. Support available to part-time students. Financial award application deadline: 5/1; financial award applicants required to submit FAFSA. *Unit head:* Dr. Robert Newby, Head, 254-968-9945.

Tennessee Technological University, Graduate School, College of Education, Department of Curriculum and Instruction, Program in Secondary Education, Cookeville, TN 38505. Offers MA, Ed S. *Accreditation:* NCATE. Part-time and evening/weekend programs available. *Faculty:* 7 full-time (0 women). *Students:* 22 full-time (13 women), 22 part-time (12 women); includes 2 minority (both Hispanic Americans) Average age 27. 25 applicants, 84% accepted, 9 enrolled. In 2006, 11 degrees awarded. *Degree requirements:* For Ed S, thesis or alternative. *Entrance requirements:* For master's, MAT; for Ed S, MAT, NTE. Additional exam requirements/recommendations for international students: Required—TOEFL. *Application deadline:* For fall admission, 3/1 priority date for domestic students; for spring admission, 8/1 for domestic students. Application fee: $25 ($30 for international students). *Expenses:* Tuition, state resident: full-time $8,748; part-time $319 per hour. Tuition, nonresident: full-time $23,524; part-time $740 per hour. *Financial support:* In 2006–07, 1 fellowship (averaging $8,000 per year), 1 research assistantship (averaging $4,000 per year), 1 teaching assistantship (averaging $4,000 per year) were awarded; career-related internships or fieldwork also available. Financial award application deadline: 4/1. *Application contact:* Dr. Francis O. Otuonye, Associate Vice President for Research and Graduate Studies, 931-372-3233, Fax: 931-372-3497, E-mail: fotuonye@tntech.edu.

Texas A&M University–Commerce, Graduate School, College of Education and Human Services, Department of Secondary and Higher Education, Commerce, TX 75429-3011. Offers higher education (MS), including administration, teaching; learning technology and information systems (M Ed, MS), including educational computing, library and information science, media and technology; secondary education (M Ed, MS); supervision, curriculum, and instruction (Ed D); training and development (MS). Part-time programs available. Terminal master's awarded for partial completion of doctoral program. *Degree requirements:* For master's, thesis (for some programs), comprehensive exam; for doctorate, thesis/dissertation, departmental qualifying exam. *Entrance requirements:* For master's and doctorate, GRE General Test. Electronic applications accepted. *Faculty research:* Deviance, migration.

Texas A&M University–Corpus Christi, Graduate Studies and Research, College of Education, Program in Secondary Education, Corpus Christi, TX 78412-5503. Offers MS. Part-time and evening/weekend programs available. *Degree requirements:* For master's, thesis (for some programs), comprehensive exam, registration. *Entrance requirements:* For master's, GRE General Test. Additional exam requirements/recommendations for international students: Required—TOEFL. Electronic applications accepted.

Texas A&M University–Kingsville, College of Graduate Studies, College of Education, Department of Education, Program in Secondary Education, Kingsville, TX 78363. Offers MA, MS. Part-time and evening/weekend programs available. *Degree requirements:* For master's, thesis or alternative, research report, comprehensive exam. *Entrance requirements:* For master's, GRE General Test, MAT, minimum GPA of 3.0. *Faculty research:* Professional development/technology, interdisciplinary teaming, educational restructuring.

Texas Southern University, Graduate School, College of Education, Area of Curriculum and Instruction, Houston, TX 77004-4584. Offers bilingual education (M Ed); curriculum, instruction, and urban education (Ed D); early childhood education (M Ed); elementary education (M Ed); reading education (M Ed); secondary education (M Ed); special education (M Ed). Part-time and evening/weekend programs available. *Faculty:* 8 full-time (6 women), 1 part-time/adjunct (0 women). *Students:* 41 full-time (36 women), 43 part-time (38 women); includes 82 minority (77 African Americans, 2 Asian Americans or Pacific Islanders, 3 Hispanic Americans). Average age 36. 34 applicants, 82% accepted, 24 enrolled. In 2006, 6 master's, 13 doctorates awarded. *Degree requirements:* For master's, comprehensive exam; for doctorate, thesis/dissertation, comprehensive exam. *Entrance requirements:* For master's, GRE General Test, minimum GPA of 2.5; for doctorate, GRE General Test or MAT, master's degree, minimum B+ average. Additional exam requirements/recommendations for international students: Required—TOEFL. *Application deadline:* For fall admission, 7/15 priority date for domestic students. Applications are processed on a rolling basis. Application fee: $50 ($75 for international students). *Financial support:* Federal Work-Study and institutionally sponsored loans available. Financial award application deadline: 5/1. *Unit head:* Dr. Cherry Gooden, Chair, 713-313-7496, Fax: 713-313-7496, E-mail: gooden_cr@tsu.edu.

Texas State University-San Marcos, Graduate School, College of Education, Department of Curriculum and Instruction, Program in Secondary Education, San Marcos, TX 78666. Offers M Ed, MA. Part-time and evening/weekend programs available. *Faculty:* 14 full-time (10 women), 4 part-time/adjunct (2 women). *Students:* 40 full-time (27 women), 67 part-time (47 women); includes 15 minority (3 African Americans, 12 Hispanic Americans), 2 international. Average age 32. 30 applicants, 100% accepted, 26 enrolled. In 2006, 32 degrees awarded. *Degree requirements:* For master's, thesis (for some programs), comprehensive exam. *Entrance requirements:* For master's, GRE General Test, minimum GPA of 2.75 in last 60 hours of course work, teaching experience. Additional exam requirements/recommendations for international students: Required—TOEFL. *Application deadline:* For fall admission, 6/15 priority date for domestic students; for spring admission, 10/15 priority date for domestic students. Applications are processed on a rolling basis. Application fee: $40 ($90 for international students). *Financial support:* In 2006–07, 85 students received support, including 1 research assistantship (averaging $11,165 per year), 5 teaching assistantships (averaging $4,315 per year); career-related internships or fieldwork, Federal Work-Study, and institutionally sponsored loans also available. Support available to part-time students. Financial award application deadline: 4/1; financial award applicants required to submit FAFSA. *Faculty research:* Gifted and talented education, general secondary education, induction of first-year teachers. *Unit head:* Dr. Gene Martin, Graduate Advisor, 512-245-3908, Fax: 512-245-7911, E-mail: gm01@txstate.edu.

Texas Tech University, Graduate School, College of Education, Division of Curriculum and Instruction, Lubbock, TX 79409. Offers bilingual education (M Ed); curriculum and instruction (M Ed, PhD); elementary education (M Ed); language and literacy education (M Ed); secondary education (M Ed). *Accreditation:* NCATE. Part-time programs available. *Students:* 68 full-time (48 women), 99 part-time (82 women); includes 35 minority (6 African Americans, 1 Asian American or Pacific Islander, 28 Hispanic Americans), 10 international. Average age 34. 165 applicants, 59% accepted, 10 enrolled. In 2006, 61 master's, 7 doctorates awarded. *Degree requirements:* For master's, thesis optional; for doctorate, thesis/dissertation. *Entrance requirements:* For master's and doctorate, GRE General Test. Additional exam requirements/recommendations for international students: Required—TOEFL (minimum score 550 paper-

Secondary Education

Texas Tech University (continued)
based; 213 computer-based). *Application deadline:* For fall admission, 3/1 priority date for international students; for spring admission, 11/1 priority date for international students. Applications are processed on a rolling basis. Application fee: $50 ($60 for international students). Electronic applications accepted. *Expenses:* Tuition, state resident: full-time $4,440. Tuition, nonresident: full-time $11,040. Required fees: $2,136. *Financial support:* In 2006–07, 100 students received support; research assistantships with partial tuition reimbursements available, teaching assistantships with partial tuition reimbursements available, career-related internships or fieldwork, Federal Work-Study, and institutionally sponsored loans available. Support available to part-time students. Financial award application deadline: 4/15; financial award applicants required to submit FAFSA. *Faculty research:* Multicultural foundations of education, teacher education, instruction and pedagogy in subject areas, curriculum theory, language and literary. *Unit head:* Dr. Peggy Johnson, Associate Dean, 806-742-1988 Ext. 437, Fax: 806-742-2179, E-mail: peggy.johnson@ttu.edu.

Towson University, Graduate School, Program in Secondary Education, Towson, MD 21252-0001. Offers M Ed. *Accreditation:* NCATE. Part-time and evening/weekend programs available. *Faculty:* 6 full-time (3 women). *Students:* 2 full-time (1 woman), 85 part-time (66 women); includes 9 minority (8 African Americans, 1 Hispanic American), 44 international. 10 applicants, 50% accepted, 3 enrolled. In 2006, 52 degrees awarded. *Degree requirements:* For master's, thesis optional. *Entrance requirements:* For master's, Maryland teaching certification or permission of program director, minimum GPA of 3.0. *Application deadline:* Applications are processed on a rolling basis. Application fee: $50. Electronic applications accepted. *Expenses:* Tuition, state resident: part-time $275 per unit. Tuition, nonresident: part-time $577 per unit. Required fees: $72 per unit. *Financial support:* Federal Work-Study and unspecified assistantships available. Financial award application deadline: 4/1; financial award applicants required to submit FAFSA. *Faculty research:* Assessment, learning disabilities. *Unit head:* Cynthia Hartzler-Miller, Graduate Program Director, 410-704-4957, E-mail: chartzlermiller@towson.edu. *Application contact:* 410-704-2501, Fax: 410-704-4675, E-mail: grads@towson.edu.

Trevecca Nazarene University, Graduate Division, School of Education, Major in Teaching, Nashville, TN 37210-2877. Offers teaching 7-12 (MAT); teaching K-6 (MAT). Part-time and evening/weekend programs available. *Students:* 185 full-time (153 women), 37 part-time (24 women); includes 64 minority (59 African Americans, 1 American Indian/Alaska Native, 2 Asian Americans or Pacific Islanders, 2 Hispanic Americans), 2 international. In 2006, 63 degrees awarded. *Degree requirements:* For master's, exit assessment, student teaching. *Entrance requirements:* For master's, GRE General Test, MAT, Praxis I: Pre-Professional Skills Test, minimum GPA of 2.7, 2 letters of reference. Additional exam requirements/recommendations for international students: Required—TOEFL (minimum score 500 paper-based; 173 computer-based). *Application deadline:* Applications are processed on a rolling basis. Application fee: $25. *Expenses: Contact institution.* Tuition and fees vary according to degree level and program. *Financial support:* Applicants required to submit FAFSA. *Application contact:* Admissions Office, 615-248-1201, Fax: 615-248-1597, E-mail: admissions_ged@trevecca.edu.

Trinity (Washington) University, School of Education, Washington, DC 20017-1094. Offers democracy, diversity, and social justice (M Ed); early childhood (MAT); educational administration (MSA); elementary education (MAT); English as a second language (M Ed, MAT); literacy and reading education (M Ed); school counseling (MA); secondary education (MAT), including English, math, science, social studies; special education (MAT). *Accreditation:* NCATE. Part-time and evening/weekend programs available. *Degree requirements:* For master's, thesis (for some programs), capstone project(s). *Entrance requirements:* For master's, PRAXIS I, minimum GPA of 2.8. Additional exam requirements/recommendations for international students: Required—TOEFL (minimum score 550 paper-based; 213 computer-based). *Faculty research:* Technology, literacy, special education, organizations, inclusion models.

Troy University, Graduate School, College of Education, Program in Secondary Education, Troy, AL 36082. Offers MS, Ed S. *Accreditation:* NCATE. Part-time and evening/weekend programs available. *Students:* 9 full-time (all women), 32 part-time (22 women); includes 9 minority (7 African Americans, 1 American Indian/Alaska Native, 1 Hispanic American). Average age 29. In 2006, 16 degrees awarded. *Degree requirements:* For master's, thesis, comprehensive exam, registration. *Entrance requirements:* For master's, minimum GPA of 2.5; for Ed S, GRE General Test or MAT, Alabama Class A certificate or equivalent, minimum graduate GPA of 3.0. Additional exam requirements/recommendations for international students: Required—TOEFL (minimum score 523 paper-based; 200 computer-based). *Application deadline:* Applications are processed on a rolling basis. Application fee: $50. Electronic applications accepted. *Expenses:* Tuition, state resident: full-time $4,368; part-time $182 per hour. Tuition, nonresident: full-time $8,736; part-time $364 per hour. Required fees: $50 per term. *Financial support:* Career-related internships or fieldwork available. Support available to part-time students. Financial award applicants required to submit FAFSA. *Unit head:* Dr. Marian Parker, Coordinator, 334-670-5661, Fax: 334-670-3548, E-mail: mjparker@troy.edu. *Application contact:* Brenda K. Campbell, Director of Graduate Admissions, 334-670-3178, Fax: 334-670-3733, E-mail: bcamp@troy.edu.

Tufts University, Graduate School of Arts and Sciences, Department of Education, Program in Education, Medford, MA 02155. Offers education (MS, PhD); elementary education (MAT); middle and secondary education (MA, MAT); secondary education (MA). *Faculty:* 13 full-time, 9 part-time/adjunct. *Students:* 114 (77 women); includes 22 minority (9 African Americans, 4 Asian Americans or Pacific Islanders, 9 Hispanic Americans) 7 international. 199 applicants, 79% accepted, 75 enrolled. In 2006, 72 degrees awarded. *Degree requirements:* For master's, thesis optional; for doctorate, thesis/dissertation. *Entrance requirements:* For master's, GRE General Test. Additional exam requirements/recommendations for international students: Required—TOEFL (minimum score 550 paper-based; 213 computer-based; 80 iBT). *Application deadline:* For fall admission, 2/1 for domestic students, 12/30 for international students; for spring admission, 10/15 for domestic students, 9/15 for international students. Applications are processed on a rolling basis. Application fee: $70. Electronic applications accepted. *Expenses:* Tuition: Full-time $33,672. Tuition and fees vary according to degree level and program. *Financial support:* Teaching assistantships with full and partial tuition reimbursements, Federal Work-Study, scholarships/grants, and tuition waivers (full and partial) available. Financial award application deadline: 2/1. *Unit head:* Analucia Schliemann, Chair, Department of Education, 617-627-3244, Fax: 617-627-3901.

Union College, Graduate Programs, Department of Education, Program in Secondary Education, Barbourville, KY 40906-1499. Offers MA. *Degree requirements:* For master's, thesis optional. *Entrance requirements:* For master's, GRE General Test, NTE.

The University of Akron, Graduate School, College of Education, Department of Curricular and Instructional Studies, Program in Secondary Education, Akron, OH 44325. Offers secondary education (MA, PhD); secondary education with licensure (MS). *Accreditation:* NCATE. *Students:* 121 full-time (85 women), 127 part-time (89 women); includes 29 minority (20 African Americans, 2 American Indian/Alaska Native, 3 Asian Americans or Pacific Islanders, 4 Hispanic Americans), 3 international. Average age 35. 36 applicants, 53% accepted, 15 enrolled. In 2006, 58 master's, 6 doctorates awarded. *Degree requirements:* For master's, portfolio; for doctorate, one foreign language, thesis/dissertation, written and oral exams, other language alternatives, comprehensive exam. *Entrance requirements:* For master's, minimum GPA of 2.75; for doctorate, MAT or GRE, interview, minimum GPA of 3.5, writing sample, letters of reference. Additional exam requirements/recommendations for international students: Required—TOEFL (minimum score 550 paper-based; 213 computer-based; 79 iBT). *Application deadline:* For fall admission, 3/1 for domestic students. Applications are processed on a rolling basis. Application fee: $30 ($40 for international students). Electronic applications accepted. *Expenses:* Tuition, state resident: full-time $6,164; part-time $342 per credit. Tuition, nonresident: full-time $10,575; part-time $588 per credit. Required fees: $806; $43 per credit. $12 per term. Tuition and fees vary according to course load, degree level and program.

The University of Alabama at Birmingham, School of Education, Department of Curriculum and Instruction, Program in High School Education, Birmingham, AL 35294. Offers MA Ed. *Accreditation:* NCATE. *Students:* 44 full-time (25 women), 71 part-time (42 women); includes 16 minority (14 African Americans, 1 Asian American or Pacific Islander, 1 Hispanic American), 1 international. 35 applicants, 86% accepted. In 2006, 67 degrees awarded. *Degree requirements:* For master's, thesis optional. *Entrance requirements:* For master's, GRE General Test, MAT, or NTE, minimum GPA of 3.0. *Application deadline:* Applications are processed on a rolling basis. Application fee: $35 ($60 for international students). Electronic applications accepted. *Expenses:* Tuition, state resident: part-time $170 per credit hour. Tuition, nonresident: part-time $425 per credit hour. Required fees: $15 per credit hour. $122 per term. Tuition and fees vary according to program. *Faculty research:* Soviet education, religious education, cultural pluralism. *Unit head:* Dr. Charles Calhoun, Chair, Department of Curriculum and Instruction, 205-934-5371, Fax: 205-934-4792.

University of Alaska Southeast, Graduate Programs, Program in Education, Juneau, AK 99801. Offers early childhood education (M Ed, MAT); educational technology (M Ed); elementary education (MAT); reading (M Ed); secondary education (MAT). *Accreditation:* NCATE. Part-time and evening/weekend programs available. Postbaccalaureate distance learning degree programs offered (minimal on-campus study). *Faculty:* 12 full-time (7 women), 6 part-time/adjunct (5 women). *Students:* 81 full-time (49 women), 109 part-time (88 women); includes 24 minority (3 African Americans, 11 American Indian/Alaska Native, 5 Asian Americans or Pacific Islanders, 5 Hispanic Americans), 6 international. Average age 34. In 2006, 84 degrees awarded. *Degree requirements:* For master's, comprehensive exam or project, portfolio. *Entrance requirements:* For master's, PRAXIS, minimum GPA of 3.0, writing sample, letters of recommendation. *Application deadline:* For fall admission, 3/8 for domestic students. Applications are processed on a rolling basis. Application fee: $50. Electronic applications accepted. *Financial support:* Federal Work-Study, scholarships/grants, and tuition waivers (full and partial) available. Support available to part-time students. Financial award applicants required to submit FAFSA. *Faculty research:* Applied classroom research, culturally responsive practices, action research, teaching effectiveness. *Unit head:* Dr. Larry Harris, Dean, 907-796-6551, Fax: 907-796-6550, E-mail: larry.harris@uas.alaska.edu. *Application contact:* Susan A. Stuck, Administrative Assistant, 866-465-6424, Fax: 866-465-5159, E-mail: jnsas@uas.alaska.edu.

University of Alberta, Faculty of Graduate Studies and Research, Department of Secondary Education, Edmonton, AB T6G 2E1, Canada. Offers M Ed, Ed D, PhD. Part-time programs available. *Faculty:* 17 full-time (7 women). *Students:* 32 full-time (21 women), 47 part-time (22 women). 34 applicants, 88% accepted. In 2006, 5 master's, 6 doctorates awarded. *Degree requirements:* For master's, thesis or alternative, 1 year of residency; for doctorate, thesis/dissertation, 2 years of residency (PhD), 1 year of residency (Ed D). *Entrance requirements:* For master's, teaching certificate, 2 years of teaching experience; for doctorate, master's degree. *Application deadline:* For fall admission, 4/1 priority date for domestic students; for spring admission, 10/1 for domestic students. Application fee: $60. *Financial support:* In 2006–07, 32 students received support, including 2 fellowships, 10 research assistantships, 20 teaching assistantships; scholarships/grants and graduate teaching awards also available. Financial award application deadline: 6/1. *Faculty research:* Curriculum studies, teacher education, subject area specializations. Total annual research expenditures: $100,000. *Unit head:* Dr. D. Sumara, Graduate Coordinator, 780-492-2688, Fax: 403-492-9402, E-mail: educ.sec@ualberta.ca. *Application contact:* Barb Keppy, Graduate Secretary, 403-492-2688, Fax: 403-492-9402.

The University of Arizona, Graduate College, College of Education, Department of Teaching and Teacher Education, Concentration in Secondary Education, Tucson, AZ 85721. Offers M Ed, Ed D. *Degree requirements:* For doctorate, one foreign language, thesis/dissertation. *Entrance requirements:* For master's, GRE General Test, minimum GPA of 3.0, 5 units of education course work; for doctorate, GRE General Test, minimum graduate GPA of 3.0, 15 units of education course work, 2 years of teaching experience. Additional exam requirements/recommendations for international students: Required—TOEFL. *Faculty research:* Teacher effectiveness, experimental curriculum design, middle schools.

University of Arkansas, Graduate School, College of Education and Health Professions, Department of Curriculum and Instruction, Program in Secondary Education, Fayetteville, AR 72701-1201. Offers M Ed, MAT, Ed S. *Accreditation:* NCATE. *Students:* 58 full-time (31 women), 5 part-time (all women); includes 2 minority (1 African American, 1 Asian American or Pacific Islander), 5 international. 29 applicants, 34% accepted. In 2006, 56 degrees awarded. Application fee: $40 ($50 for international students). *Financial support:* In 2006–07, 2 teaching assistantships were awarded; fellowships with tuition reimbursements, research assistantships, career-related internships or fieldwork and Federal Work-Study also available. Support available to part-time students. Financial award application deadline: 4/1; financial award applicants required to submit FAFSA. *Faculty research:* Mathematics. *Unit head:* Unit Head, 479-575-4209.

University of Arkansas at Little Rock, Graduate School, College of Education, Department of Teacher Education, Program in Secondary Education, Little Rock, AR 72204-1099. Offers M Ed. *Accreditation:* NCATE. Part-time programs available. *Degree requirements:* For master's, comprehensive exam. *Entrance requirements:* For master's, interview, minimum GPA of 2.75, GRE General Test or teaching certificate.

University of Arkansas at Pine Bluff, Program in Education, Pine Bluff, AR 71601-2799. Offers elementary education (M Ed); secondary education (M Ed), including English, general science, mathematics, physical education, social studies. Part-time and evening/weekend programs available. *Degree requirements:* For master's, comprehensive exam. *Entrance requirements:* For master's, GRE, minimum GPA of 2.75, NTE or Standard Arkansas Teaching Certificate. *Faculty research:* Teacher certification, accreditation, assessment, standards, portfolio development, rehabilitation, technology.

University of Bridgeport, School of Education and Human Resources, Division of Education, Program in Secondary Education, Bridgeport, CT 06604. Offers computer specialist (Diploma); international education (Diploma); reading specialist (MS, Diploma); secondary education (MS, Diploma). Part-time and evening/weekend programs available. *Faculty:* 12 full-time (5 women), 72 part-time/adjunct (44 women). *Students:* 1 full-time (0 women), 5 part-time (all women). Average age 37. 8 applicants, 63% accepted, 1 enrolled. In 2006, 4 degrees awarded. *Degree requirements:* For master's, final exam, final project, or thesis; for Diploma, thesis or alternative, final project. *Entrance requirements:* For master's, GRE General Test, MAT, minimum undergraduate QPA of 2.5; for Diploma, GRE General Test or MAT, minimum graduate QPA of 3.0. *Application deadline:* For fall admission, 8/1 priority date for domestic students; for spring admission, 12/1 priority date for domestic students. Applications are processed on a rolling basis. Application fee: $25 ($35 for international students). Electronic applications accepted. *Financial support:* Career-related internships or fieldwork, Federal Work-Study, and institutionally sponsored loans available. Support available to part-time students. Financial award application deadline: 6/1; financial award applicants required to submit FAFSA. *Faculty research:* Self-concept, internship assessment, stress and situational development, follow-up of graduation, trend analysis. *Unit head:* Dr. Allen P. Cook, Associate Dean, Division of Education, 203-576-4206, Fax: 203-576-4200, E-mail: acook@bridgeport.edu.

University of California, Irvine, Office of Graduate Studies, Department of Education, Irvine, CA 92697. Offers educational administration (Ed D); educational administration and leadership (Ed D); elementary and secondary education (MAT). Part-time and evening/weekend programs available. *Students:* 138 full-time (95 women), 3 part-time (all women); includes 61 minority (14 African Americans, 1 American Indian/Alaska Native, 26 Asian Americans or Pacific Islanders, 20 Hispanic Americans). Average age 34. In 2006, 67 master's, 8 doctorates awarded. *Degree requirements:* For doctorate, thesis/dissertation. *Entrance requirements:* For master's, GRE, minimum GPA of 3.0; for doctorate, GRE General Test, minimum GPA of 3.0. Additional exam requirements/recommendations for international students: Required—TOEFL (minimum score 550 paper-based; 213 computer-based). *Application deadline:* For fall admission, 4/1 priority date for domestic students. Application fee: $60. Electronic applications accepted. *Financial support:* Fellowships, research assistantships with full tuition reimbursements, institutionally sponsored loans, traineeships, health care benefits, and unspecified assistantships available. Financial award application deadline: 3/1; financial award applicants required to submit FAFSA. *Faculty research:* Education technology, learning theory, social theory, cultural diversity, postmodernism. *Unit head:* David Brant, Interim Chair, 949-824-7840, E-mail: dbrant@uci.edu. *Application contact:* Sarah K. Singh, Student Affairs Officer, 949-824-7832, Fax: 949-824-2965. E-mail: sksingh@uci.edu.

University of Central Missouri, The Graduate School, College of Education, Department of Curriculum and Instruction, Warrensburg, MO 64093. Offers curriculum and instruction (Ed S); elementary education (MSE); K–12 education (MSE); literacy education (MSE); secondary education (MSE). *Accreditation:* NCATE. Part-time programs available. *Faculty:* 22 full-time (14 women). *Students:* 43 full-time (33 women), 309 part-time (237 women); includes 27 minority (23 African Americans, 1 Asian American or Pacific Islander, 3 Hispanic Americans), 3 international. Average age 33. 81 applicants, 81% accepted, 65 enrolled. In 2006, 70 master's, 1 other advanced degree awarded. *Degree requirements:* For master's, comprehensive exam or thesis; for Ed S, thesis, comprehensive exam. *Entrance requirements:* For master's, GRE General Test, minimum GPA of 2.75, teaching certificate; for Ed S, GRE General Test, minimum GPA of 3.25, teaching certificate. Additional exam requirements/recommendations for international students: Required—TOEFL (minimum score 500 paper-based; 173 computer-based). *Application deadline:* For fall admission, 6/1 priority date for domestic students, 5/1 priority date for international students; for spring admission, 10/1 priority date for domestic students, 10/1 for international students. Applications are processed on a rolling basis. Application fee: $30 ($50 for international students). *Expenses:* Tuition, state resident: full-time $5,448; part-time $227 per credit hour. Tuition, nonresident: full-time $10,896; part-time $454 per credit hour. Required fees: $336; $14 per credit hour. *Financial support:* In 2006–07, 4 students received support. Federal Work-Study, scholarships/grants, unspecified assistantships, and administrative and laboratory assistantships available. Support available to part-time students. Financial award application deadline: 3/1; financial award applicants required to submit FAFSA. *Faculty research:* Reading maturity, student and faculty evaluation, online teaching and learning, video documentation, teacher candidates' assessment of student thinking and learning. *Unit head:* Dr. Sharon Lamson, Chair, 660-543-4235, Fax: 660-543-4167, E-mail: lamson@ucmo.edu.

University of Central Oklahoma, College of Graduate Studies and Research, College of Education, Department of Professional Teacher Education, Program in Secondary Education, Edmond, OK 73034-5209. Offers M Ed. *Accreditation:* NCATE. Part-time programs available. *Entrance requirements:* For master's, GRE General Test. Additional exam requirements/recommendations for international students: Required—TOEFL (minimum score 550 paper-based; 213 computer-based). Electronic applications accepted.

University of Cincinnati, Division of Research and Advanced Studies, College of Education, Criminal Justice, and Human Services, Division of Teacher Education, Program in Secondary Education, Cincinnati, OH 45221. Offers M Ed. *Accreditation:* NCATE. Part-time programs available. *Students:* 75. *Degree requirements:* For master's, thesis or alternative. *Entrance requirements:* For master's, GRE General Test. Additional exam requirements/recommendations for international students: Required—TOEFL (minimum score 550 paper-based), TWE (minimum score 4.5), OEPT. *Application deadline:* For fall admission, 2/1 for domestic students. Application fee: $40. Electronic applications accepted. *Financial support:* Fellowships, tuition waivers (partial) and unspecified assistantships available. *Application contact:* Chester Laine, Chair, 513-556-3588, Fax: 513-556-1001, E-mail: chester.laine@uc.edu.

University of Connecticut, Graduate School, Neag School of Education, Department of Curriculum and Instruction, Storrs, CT 06269. Offers curriculum and instruction (MA, PhD), including agriculture education, bilingual and bicultural education, elementary education, English education, history and social sciences education, mathematics education, reading education, science education, secondary education, world languages education. *Accreditation:* NCATE. *Faculty:* 28 full-time (12 women). *Students:* 158 full-time (120 women), 54 part-time (44 women); includes 24 minority (3 African Americans, 1 American Indian/Alaska Native, 3 Asian Americans or Pacific Islanders, 17 Hispanic Americans), 2 international. Average age 27. 268 applicants, 76% accepted, 203 enrolled. In 2006, 181 master's, 4 doctorates awarded. Terminal master's awarded for partial completion of doctoral program. *Degree requirements:* For master's, thesis or alternative, comprehensive exam; for doctorate, thesis/dissertation. *Entrance requirements:* For doctorate, GRE General Test. Additional exam requirements/recommendations for international students: Required—TOEFL (minimum score 550 paper-based; 213 computer-based). *Application deadline:* For fall admission, 2/1 priority date for domestic and international students; for spring admission, 11/1 for domestic students, 10/1 for international students. Applications are processed on a rolling basis. Application fee: $55. Electronic applications accepted. *Financial support:* In 2006–07, 14 research assistantships with full tuition reimbursements, 4 teaching assistantships with full tuition reimbursements were awarded; fellowships, Federal Work-Study, scholarships/grants, health care benefits, and unspecified assistantships also available. Financial award application deadline: 2/1; financial award applicants required to submit FAFSA. *Unit head:* Mary Anne Doyle, Head, 860-486-2433, Fax: 860-486-0280. *Application contact:* Lisa Rasicot, Graduate Coordinator, 860-486-3065, Fax: 860-486-0210, E-mail: soeadm02@uconnvm.uconn.edu.

University of Connecticut, Graduate School, Neag School of Education, Department of Curriculum and Instruction, Field of Curriculum and Instruction, Program in Secondary Education, Storrs, CT 06269. Offers MA, PhD. *Accreditation:* NCATE. *Faculty:* 22 full-time (10 women). *Students:* Average age 46. 3 applicants, 67% accepted, 2 enrolled. In 2006, 4 master's, 1 doctorate awarded. Terminal master's awarded for partial completion of doctoral program. *Degree requirements:* For master's, thesis or alternative, comprehensive exam; for doctorate, thesis/dissertation. *Entrance requirements:* For doctorate, GRE General Test. Additional exam requirements/recommendations for international students: Required—TOEFL (minimum score 550 paper-based; 213 computer-based). *Application deadline:* For fall admission, 2/1 priority date for domestic and international students; for spring admission, 11/1 for domestic students, 10/1 for international students. Applications are processed on a rolling basis. Application fee: $55. Electronic applications accepted. *Financial support:* Fellowships, research assistantships with full tuition reimbursements, teaching assistantships with full tuition reimbursements, Federal Work-Study, scholarships/grants, health care benefits, and unspecified assistantships available. Financial award application deadline: 2/1; financial award applicants required to submit FAFSA. *Application contact:* Lisa Rasicot, Graduate Coordinator, 860-486-3065, Fax: 860-486-0210, E-mail: soeadm02@uconnvm.uconn.edu.

University of Dayton, Graduate School, School of Education and Allied Professions, Department of Teacher Education, Dayton, OH 45469-1300. Offers adolescent/young adult (MS Ed); art education (MS Ed); early childhood education (MS Ed); inclusive early childhood (MS Ed); interdisciplinary education (MS Ed); intervention specialist education, mild/moderate (MS Ed); literacy (MS Ed); middle childhood (MS Ed); multi-age education (MS Ed); music education (MS Ed); teacher as leader (MS Ed); technology in education (MS Ed). Part-time and evening/weekend programs available. *Faculty:* 13 full-time (9 women), 33 part-time/adjunct (25 women). *Students:* 149 full-time (120 women), 284 part-time (241 women); includes 37 minority (31 African Americans, 3 Asian Americans or Pacific Islanders, 3 Hispanic Americans), 3 international. Average age 33. 201 applicants, 58% accepted, 31 enrolled. In 2006, 150 degrees awarded. *Degree requirements:* For master's, thesis, capstone research project. *Entrance requirements:* For master's, GRE General Test, minimum GPA of 2.75. Additional exam requirements/recommendations for international students: Required—TOEFL (minimum score 550 paper-based; 213 computer-based). *Application deadline:* For fall admission, 3/15 priority date for domestic students, 3/1 priority date for international students. Applications are processed on a rolling basis. Application fee: $0. Electronic applications accepted. *Expenses:* Contact institution. *Financial support:* In 2006–07, 8 teaching assistantships with partial tuition reimbursements (averaging $7,600 per year) were awarded; career-related internships or fieldwork, institutionally sponsored loans, health care benefits, and unspecified assistantships also available.

Financial award applicants required to submit FAFSA. *Faculty research:* Diversity, literacy, art representation by young children, preservice teacher preparation. Total annual research expenditures: $330,000. *Unit head:* Dr. Katie A. Kinnucan-Welsch, Chair, 937-229-3346. *Application contact:* Erika Eavers, Graduate Admission Processor, 937-229-3065, Fax: 937-229-4729, E-mail: erika.eavers@notes.udayton.edu.

University of Guam, Graduate School and Research, College of Education, Program in Secondary Education, Mangilao, GU 96923. Offers M Ed. *Degree requirements:* For master's, thesis, comprehensive oral and written exams. *Entrance requirements:* For master's, GRE General Test. Additional exam requirements/recommendations for international students: Required—TOEFL.

University of Houston, College of Education, Department of Curriculum and Instruction, Houston, TX 77204. Offers art education (M Ed); bilingual education (M Ed); curriculum and instruction (Ed D); early childhood education (M Ed); education of the gifted (M Ed); elementary education (M Ed); mathematics education (M Ed); reading and language arts education (M Ed); science education (M Ed); second language education (M Ed); secondary education (M Ed); social studies education (M Ed); teaching (M Ed). *Accreditation:* NCATE. Part-time and evening/weekend programs available. *Faculty:* 24 full-time (11 women), 16 part-time/adjunct (14 women). *Students:* 134 full-time (102 women), 327 part-time (256 women); includes 142 minority (49 African Americans, 1 American Indian/Alaska Native, 29 Asian Americans or Pacific Islanders, 63 Hispanic Americans), 19 international. Average age 37. 113 applicants, 72% accepted, 61 enrolled. In 2006, 106 master's, 32 doctorates awarded. *Degree requirements:* For master's, comprehensive exam or thesis; for doctorate, thesis/dissertation, comprehensive exam. *Entrance requirements:* For master's, GRE General Test or MAT; for doctorate, GRE General Test, interview. *Application deadline:* For fall admission, 7/3 priority date for domestic students. Applications are processed on a rolling basis. Application fee: $35 ($75 for international students). *Expenses:* Tuition, state resident: full-time $5,429; part-time $226 per credit. Tuition, nonresident: full-time $12,029; part-time $501 per credit. Required fees: $2,454. *Financial support:* In 2006–07, 2 fellowships with full tuition reimbursements (averaging $9,500 per year), 6 research assistantships with full tuition reimbursements (averaging $8,800 per year), 25 teaching assistantships with full tuition reimbursements (averaging $8,800 per year) were awarded; career-related internships or fieldwork, Federal Work-Study, institutionally sponsored loans, scholarships/grants, health care benefits, and unspecified assistantships also available. Support available to part-time students. Financial award application deadline: 3/10. *Faculty research:* Teaching-learning process, instructional technology in schools, teacher education, classroom management, at-risk students. *Unit head:* Dr. Juanita Copley, Chairperson, 713-743-4950, Fax: 713-743-4990, E-mail: ncopley@aol.com.

University of Illinois at Chicago, Graduate College, College of Education, Department of Curriculum and Instruction, Chicago, IL 60607-7128. Offers curriculum and instruction (PhD); educational psychology (PhD); instructional leadership (M Ed), including elementary education, reading, secondary education; leadership and administration (M Ed); policy and administration (PhD); policy studies in urban education (PhD). Part-time and evening/weekend programs available. *Degree requirements:* For doctorate, thesis/dissertation. *Entrance requirements:* For master's, minimum GPA of 2.75; for doctorate, GRE General Test, minimum GPA of 2.75. Additional exam requirements/recommendations for international students: Required—TOEFL. Electronic applications accepted. *Faculty research:* Curriculum theory, curriculum development, research on teaching, curriculum and context, reading/literacy.

University of Indianapolis, Graduate Programs, School of Education, Indianapolis, IN 46227-3697. Offers art education (MAT); biology (MAT); chemistry (MAT); curriculum and instruction (MA); earth sciences (MAT); education (MA, MAT); educational leadership (MA); elementary education (MA); English (MAT); French (MAT); math (MAT); physical education (MAT); physics (MAT); secondary education (MA), including art education, education, English education, social studies education; social studies (MAT); Spanish (MAT). *Accreditation:* NCATE. Part-time and evening/weekend programs available. *Faculty:* 4 full-time (2 women), 6 part-time/adjunct (2 women). *Students:* 32 full-time (16 women), 70 part-time (42 women); includes 2 minority (1 African American, 1 Hispanic American). Average age 31. In 2006, 51 degrees awarded. *Entrance requirements:* For master's, GRE Subject Test, minimum GPA of 2.5, 3 letters of recommendation, interview, Praxis I, writing exercise, be within 9 hours of completing content requirements. Additional exam requirements/recommendations for international students: Required—TOEFL (minimum score 550 paper-based; 213 computer-based). *Application deadline:* Applications are processed on a rolling basis. Application fee: $50. *Financial support:* Federal Work-Study available. Financial award application deadline: 5/1; financial award applicants required to submit FAFSA. *Faculty research:* Assessment of teacher education, perceptions of prospective teachers by parents. *Unit head:* Dr. E. Lynne Weisenbach, Dean, 317-788-3446, Fax: 317-788-3300, E-mail: weisenbach@uindy.edu.

The University of Iowa, Graduate College, College of Education, Department of Teaching and Learning, Program in Secondary Education, Iowa City, IA 52242-1316. Offers art education (MA, PhD); curriculum and supervision (PhD); curriculum supervision (MA); developmental reading (MA); English education (MA, MAT, PhD); foreign language education (MA, MAT); foreign language/ESL education (PhD); language, literature and culture (PhD); math education (PhD); mathematics education (MA); music education (MA, PhD); social studies (MA, PhD). *Faculty:* 11 full-time. *Students:* 53 full-time (33 women), 53 part-time (41 women); includes 5 minority (1 African American, 1 American Indian/Alaska Native, 2 Asian Americans or Pacific Islanders, 1 Hispanic American), 19 international. 66 applicants, 47% accepted, 17 enrolled. In 2006, 22 master's, 14 doctorates awarded. *Degree requirements:* For master's, exam, thesis optional; for doctorate, thesis/dissertation, comprehensive exam, registration. *Entrance requirements:* For master's and doctorate, GRE General Test, minimum GPA of 3.0. Additional exam requirements/recommendations for international students: Required—TOEFL (minimum score 550 paper-based; 213 computer-based; 81 iBT). Application fee: $60 ($85 for international students). Electronic applications accepted. *Financial support:* In 2006–07, 1 fellowship, 12 research assistantships with partial tuition reimbursements, 31 teaching assistantships with partial tuition reimbursements were awarded. Financial award applicants required to submit FAFSA. *Unit head:* Gary Sasso, Chair, 319-335-5324, Fax: 319-335-5608.

University of Louisiana at Monroe, Graduate Studies and Research, College of Education and Human Development, Department of Curriculum and Instruction, Program in Secondary Education, Monroe, LA 71209-0001. Offers M Ed, MAT. *Accreditation:* NCATE. Part-time and evening/weekend programs available. *Students:* 3 full-time (2 women), 21 part-time (14 women); includes 6 minority (all African Americans) Average age 31. In 2006, 10 degrees awarded. *Entrance requirements:* For master's, GRE General Test, minimum GPA of 2.5. *Application deadline:* For fall admission, 6/1 priority date for domestic students; for spring admission, 11/1 for domestic students. Applications are processed on a rolling basis. Application fee: $20 ($30 for international students). *Expenses:* Tuition, state resident: part-time $124 per credit hour. Tuition, nonresident: part-time $124 per credit hour. *Financial support:* Research assistantships, teaching assistantships available. Financial award application deadline: 7/1. *Unit head:* Dr. Gary Stringer, Head, Department of Curriculum and Instruction, 318-342-1266, Fax: 318-342-1240, E-mail: stringer@ulm.edu.

University of Louisville, Graduate School, College of Education and Human Development, Department of Teaching and Learning, Program in Secondary Education, Louisville, KY 40292-0001. Offers M Ed, MAT. *Accreditation:* NCATE. *Students:* 73 full-time (41 women), 76 part-time (42 women); includes 18 minority (12 African Americans, 1 American Indian/Alaska Native, 1 Asian American or Pacific Islander, 4 Hispanic Americans), 4 international. Average age 32. In 2006, 62 degrees awarded. *Entrance requirements:* For master's, GRE General Test. *Application deadline:* Applications are processed on a rolling basis. Application fee: $50. Electronic applications accepted. *Financial support:* Fellowships, research assistantships, teaching assistantships, Federal Work-Study and scholarships/grants available. *Unit head:* Dr. Randall L. Wells, Head, 502-852-0598, Fax: 502-852-1497, E-mail: randy.wells@louisville.edu.

Secondary Education

University of Maine, Graduate School, College of Education and Human Development, Program in Secondary Education, Orono, ME 04469. Offers M Ed, MA, MAT, MS, CAS. *Accreditation:* NCATE. Part-time and evening/weekend programs available. *Students:* 12 full-time (9 women), 1 part-time; includes 1 minority (American Indian/Alaska Native). Average age 29. In 2006, 20 degrees awarded. *Degree requirements:* For master's, thesis or alternative. *Entrance requirements:* For master's, MAT; for CAS, MAT, MA, M Ed, or MS. Additional exam requirements/recommendations for international students: Required—TOEFL. *Application deadline:* For fall admission, 2/1 priority date for domestic students. Applications are processed on a rolling basis. Application fee: $50. Electronic applications accepted. *Financial support:* In 2006–07, teaching assistantships with tuition reimbursements (averaging $9,010 per year); career-related internships or fieldwork, Federal Work-Study, tuition waivers (full and partial), and unspecified assistantships also available. Support available to part-time students. Financial award application deadline: 3/1. *Unit head:* Dr. Dorothy Breen, Coordinator, 207-581-2444, Fax: 207-581-2423. *Application contact:* Scott G. Delcourt, Associate Dean of the Graduate School, 207-581-3219, Fax: 207-581-3232, E-mail: graduate@maine.edu.

University of Maryland, Baltimore County, Graduate School, College of Arts, Humanities and Social Sciences, Department of Education, Program in Education, Baltimore, MD 21250. Offers early childhood education (MAT); elementary education (MAT); secondary education (MAT). Part-time and evening/weekend programs available. *Faculty:* 17 full-time (15 women), 3 part-time/adjunct (all women). *Students:* 49 full-time (43 women), 89 part-time (69 women); includes 11 minority (8 African Americans, 2 Asian Americans or Pacific Islanders, 1 Hispanic American). Average age 30. In 2006, 21 master's awarded. *Median time to degree:* Of those who began their doctoral program in fall 1998, 95% received their degree in 8 years or less. *Degree requirements:* For master's, thesis (for some programs), comprehensive exam, registration. *Entrance requirements:* For master's, PRAXIS I and II, minimum GPA of 3.0. *Application deadline:* Applications are processed on a rolling basis. Application fee: $50. Electronic applications accepted. *Expenses:* Tuition, state resident: part-time $412 per credit hour. Tuition, nonresident: part-time $681 per credit hour. Required fees: $91 per credit hour. One-time fee: $75 part-time. *Financial support:* In 2006–07, 6 students received support, including research assistantships with full tuition reimbursements available (averaging $12,000 per year); career-related internships or fieldwork, Federal Work-Study, scholarships/grants, tuition waivers, and unspecified assistantships also available. Financial award application deadline: 3/1. *Faculty research:* STEM teacher education, culturally sensitive pedagogy. Total annual research expenditures: $1.3 million. *Unit head:* Dr. Susan M. Blunck, Director, 410-455-2869, Fax: 410-455-3986, E-mail: blunck@umbc.edu. *Application contact:* Dr. Susan M. Blunck, Director, 410-455-2869, Fax: 410-455-3986, E-mail: blunck@umbc.edu.

University of Maryland, College Park, Graduate Studies, College of Education, Department of Curriculum and Instruction, College Park, MD 20742. Offers reading (M Ed, MA, PhD, CAGS); secondary education (M Ed, MA, Ed D, PhD, CAGS); teaching English to speakers of other languages (M Ed). *Accreditation:* NCATE. Part-time and evening/weekend programs available. Postbaccalaureate distance learning degree programs offered (no on-campus study). *Faculty:* 52 full-time (32 women), 33 part-time/adjunct (30 women). *Students:* 200 full-time (159 women), 189 part-time (155 women); includes 101 minority (48 African Americans, 30 Asian Americans or Pacific Islanders, 23 Hispanic Americans), 33 international. 258 applicants, 62% accepted, 101 enrolled. In 2006, 118 master's, 14 doctorates awarded. *Median time to degree:* Of those who began their doctoral program in fall 1998, 38% received their degree in 8 years or less. *Degree requirements:* For master's, seminar paper; for doctorate, thesis/dissertation, published paper, oral exam, comprehensive exam. *Entrance requirements:* For master's, GRE General Test or MAT, minimum GPA of 3.0, 3 letters of recommendation; for doctorate, GRE General Test or MAT, minimum undergraduate GPA of 3.0, graduate 3.5; 3 letters of recommendation. *Application deadline:* For fall admission, 1/15 for domestic students, 2/1 for international students; for spring admission, 9/1 for domestic students, 6/1 for international students. Applications are processed on a rolling basis. Application fee: $60. Electronic applications accepted. *Financial support:* In 2006–07, 3 fellowships with full tuition reimbursements (averaging $5,677 per year), 25 research assistantships with tuition reimbursements (averaging $16,943 per year), 53 teaching assistantships with tuition reimbursements (averaging $14,810 per year) were awarded; Federal Work-Study and scholarships/grants also available. Support available to part-time students. Financial award applicants required to submit FAFSA. *Faculty research:* Teacher preparation, curriculum study, in-service education. Total annual research expenditures: $3.3 million. *Unit head:* Dr. Stephen M. Koziol, Chairman, 301-405-3117, Fax: 301-314-9055, E-mail: skoziol@umd.edu. *Application contact:* Dean of Graduate School, 301-405-0358, Fax: 301-314-9305.

University of Massachusetts Amherst, Graduate School, School of Education, Program in Education, Amherst, MA 01003. Offers cultural diversity and curriculum reform (M Ed, Ed D, CAGS); early childhood education and development (M Ed, Ed D, CAGS); educational administration (M Ed, Ed D, CAGS); elementary teacher education (M Ed, Ed D, CAGS); higher education (M Ed, Ed D, CAGS); international education (M Ed, Ed D, CAGS); mathematics, science, and instructional technology (M Ed, Ed D, CAGS); physical education teacher education (M Ed, Ed D, CAGS); reading and writing (M Ed, Ed D, CAGS); research and evaluation methods (M Ed, Ed D, CAGS); school psychology and school counseling (M Ed, Ed D, CAGS); secondary teacher education (M Ed, Ed D, CAGS); social justice education (M Ed, Ed D, CAGS); special education (M Ed, Ed D, CAGS). *Accreditation:* NCATE. *Students:* 418 full-time (286 women), 447 part-time (319 women); includes 147 minority (70 African Americans, 4 American Indian/Alaska Native, 28 Asian Americans or Pacific Islanders, 45 Hispanic Americans), 81 international. Average age 36. In 2006, 260 master's, 30 doctorates awarded. *Degree requirements:* For doctorate, thesis/dissertation. *Entrance requirements:* For master's and doctorate, GRE General Test. Additional exam requirements/recommendations for international students: Required—TOEFL (minimum score 530 paper-based; 197 computer-based). *Application deadline:* For fall admission, 1/15 for domestic and international students; for spring admission, 10/1 for domestic and international students. Applications are processed on a rolling basis. Application fee: $40 ($65 for international students). Electronic applications accepted. *Expenses:* Tuition, state resident: full-time $2,640; part-time $110 per credit. Tuition, nonresident: full-time $9,936; part-time $414 per credit. Required fees: $8,969; $3,129 per term. One-time fee: $257 full-time. Tuition and fees vary according to class time, course load, campus/location and reciprocity agreements. *Financial support:* Fellowships with full tuition reimbursements, research assistantships with full tuition reimbursements, teaching assistantships with full tuition reimbursements, career-related internships or fieldwork, Federal Work-Study, scholarships/grants, traineeships, and unspecified assistantships available. Support available to part-time students. Financial award application deadline: 1/15. *Unit head:* Linda L. Griffin, Professor, 413-545-6984.

University of Massachusetts Boston, Office of Graduate Studies, Graduate College of Education, School Organization, Curriculum and Instruction Department, Boston, MA 02125-3393. Offers education (M Ed, Ed D), including elementary and secondary education/certification (M Ed), higher education administration (Ed D), teacher certification (M Ed), urban school leadership (Ed D); educational administration (M Ed, CAGS); special education (M Ed). *Students:* 141 full-time (103 women), 403 part-time (291 women); includes 81 minority (44 African Americans, 1 American Indian/Alaska Native, 13 Asian Americans or Pacific Islanders, 23 Hispanic Americans), 7 international. Average age 37. 381 applicants, 72% accepted, 178 enrolled. In 2006, 117 master's, 18 doctorates, 10 other advanced degrees awarded. *Degree requirements:* For master's and CAGS, comprehensive exam; for doctorate, thesis/dissertation, comprehensive exam. *Entrance requirements:* For master's, GRE General Test or MAT; for doctorate, GRE General Test or MAT, minimum GPA of 2.75; for CAGS, minimum GPA of 2.75. *Application deadline:* For fall admission, 3/1 for domestic students. Application fee: $25 ($35 for international students). *Expenses:* Tuition, state resident: full-time $2,590; part-time $301 per credit. Tuition, nonresident: full-time $9,758; part-time $427 per credit. One-time fee: $495 full-time. *Financial support:* In 2006–07, 37 research assistantships with full tuition reimbursements (averaging $2,000 per year), teaching assistantships with full tuition reimbursements (averaging $2,000 per year) were awarded; unspecified assistantships also available. Financial award application deadline: 3/1; financial award applicants required to submit FAFSA. *Unit head:* Dr. Lisa Coonsalves, Director, 617-287-7642, E-mail: lisa.gonsalves@umb.edu. *Application contact:* Peggy Roldan, Graduate Admissions Coordinator, 617-287-6400, Fax: 617-287-6236, E-mail: bos.gadm@dpc.umassp.edu.

University of Massachusetts Boston, Office of Graduate Studies, Graduate College of Education, School Organization, Curriculum and Instruction Department, Program in Education, Track in Elementary and Secondary Education/Certification, Boston, MA 02125-3393. Offers M Ed. *Accreditation:* NCATE. Part-time and evening/weekend programs available. *Students:* 113 full-time (86 women), 241 part-time (182 women); includes 38 minority (21 African Americans, 7 Asian Americans or Pacific Islanders, 10 Hispanic Americans), 2 international. Average age 31. 259 applicants, 80% accepted, 124 enrolled. In 2006, 98 degrees awarded. *Degree requirements:* For master's, practicum, thesis optional. *Entrance requirements:* For master's, GRE General Test or MAT, minimum GPA of 3.0, 2 years of teaching experience. *Application deadline:* For fall admission, 3/1 priority date for domestic students; for spring admission, 11/1 for domestic students. Application fee: $25 ($40 for international students). *Expenses:* Tuition, state resident: full-time $2,590; part-time $301 per credit. Tuition, nonresident: full-time $9,758; part-time $427 per credit. One-time fee: $495 full-time. *Financial support:* In 2006–07, 30 research assistantships with full tuition reimbursements (averaging $4,000 per year), teaching assistantships with full tuition reimbursements (averaging $4,000 per year) were awarded; career-related internships or fieldwork, Federal Work-Study, and unspecified assistantships also available. Support available to part-time students. Financial award application deadline: 3/1; financial award applicants required to submit FAFSA. *Faculty research:* Anti-bias education, inclusionary curriculum and instruction, creativity and learning, science, technology and society, teaching of reading. *Unit head:* Dr. Joseph Check, Director, 617-287-7655, E-mail: joseph.check@umb.edu. *Application contact:* Peggy Roldan, Graduate Admissions Coordinator, 617-287-6400, Fax: 617-287-6236, E-mail: bos.gadm@dpc.umassp.edu.

University of Memphis, Graduate School, College of Education, Department of Instruction and Curriculum Leadership, Memphis, TN 38152. Offers early childhood education (MAT, MS, Ed D); elementary education (MAT); instruction and curriculum (MS, Ed D); instruction design and technology (MS, Ed D); reading (MS, Ed D); secondary education (MAT); special education (MAT, MS, Ed D). *Accreditation:* NCATE (one or more programs are accredited). Part-time programs available. Terminal master's awarded for partial completion of doctoral program. *Degree requirements:* For master's, thesis or alternative, comprehensive exam; for doctorate, thesis/dissertation, comprehensive exam. *Entrance requirements:* For master's, GRE General Test, minimum GPA of 2.5; for doctorate, GRE General Test, GRE Subject Test, 2 years of teaching experience. Electronic applications accepted. *Faculty research:* Effective urban teachers, preparation and retention of urban teachers, technology utilization in schools, field-based preparation teacher preparation programs, effective use of online instruction.

University of Michigan, Horace H. Rackham School of Graduate Studies, School of Education, Programs in Educational Studies, Ann Arbor, MI 48109. Offers curriculum development (MA); early childhood education (MA, PhD); educational administration and policy (MA, PhD); educational foundation, administration, policy, and research methods (MA); educational foundations and policy (MA, PhD); elementary education (MA-Certification); English education (MA); English language learning in school settings (MA); learning technologies (MA, PhD); literacy, language, and culture (MA, PhD); mathematics education (MA, PhD); research methods (MA); science education (MA, PhD); secondary education (MA-Certification); social studies education (MA); special education (PhD); teaching and teacher education (PhD); MA-Certification; MBA/MA; PhD/MA. Terminal master's awarded for partial completion of doctoral program. *Degree requirements:* For master's, thesis (for some programs); for doctorate, thesis/dissertation, comprehensive exam. *Entrance requirements:* For master's and doctorate, GRE General Test. Additional exam requirements/recommendations for international students: Required—TOEFL (minimum score 600 paper-based; 250 computer-based). *Application deadline:* For fall admission, 12/1 priority date for domestic students, 12/1 for international students. Application fee: $60 ($75 for international students). Electronic applications accepted. *Financial support:* Applicants required to submit FAFSA. *Unit head:* Dr. Addison Stone, Chairperson, 734-763-7500, Fax: 734-615-1290, E-mail: addison@umich.edu. *Application contact:* Roberta Perry, Office of Student Services, 734-764-7563, Fax: 734-763-1495, E-mail: ed.grad.admit@umich.edu.

University of Mississippi, Graduate School, School of Education, Department of Curriculum and Instruction, Oxford, University, MS 38677. Offers curriculum and instruction (M Ed, Ed D, Ed S); education (PhD); secondary education (MA). *Accreditation:* NCATE. *Faculty:* 30 full-time (24 women), 6 part-time/adjunct (5 women). *Students:* 69 full-time (59 women), 268 part-time (227 women); includes 106 minority (94 African Americans, 10 Asian Americans or Pacific Islanders, 2 Hispanic Americans), 6 international. In 2006, 162 master's, 8 doctorates, 11 other advanced degrees awarded. *Degree requirements:* For master's, thesis (for some programs); for doctorate, one foreign language, thesis/dissertation. *Entrance requirements:* For master's, GRE General Test, minimum GPA of 3.0; for doctorate, GRE General Test. Additional exam requirements/recommendations for international students: Required—TOEFL. *Application deadline:* For fall admission, 7/1 for domestic students; for spring admission, 10/1 for domestic students. Applications are processed on a rolling basis. Application fee: $25. *Expenses:* Tuition, state resident: full-time $4,602; part-time $256 per credit hour. Tuition, nonresident: full-time $10,566; part-time $587 per credit hour. *Financial support:* Scholarships/grants available. Financial award application deadline: 3/1; financial award applicants required to submit FAFSA. *Unit head:* Dr. Fannye Love, Chair, 662-915-7530, E-mail: flove@olemiss.edu.

University of Missouri–St. Louis, College of Education, Division of Teaching and Learning, St. Louis, MO 63121. Offers elementary education (M Ed), including reading; secondary education (M Ed), including curriculum and instruction, middle school, reading; special education (M Ed), including behavioral disorders, early childhood special education, learning disabilities, mentally retardation; teaching-learning processes (Ed D, PhD). *Faculty:* 20 full-time (13 women), 5 part-time/adjunct (4 women). *Students:* 118 full-time (84 women), 353 part-time (311 women); includes 90 minority (75 African Americans, 1 American Indian/Alaska Native, 3 Asian Americans or Pacific Islanders, 11 Hispanic Americans), 4 international. Average age 36. In 2006, 136 master's, 3 doctorates awarded. *Entrance requirements:* For doctorate, GRE General Test, 3 letters of recommendation. *Application deadline:* For fall admission, 7/15 for domestic students; for spring admission, 12/15 for domestic students. *Expenses:* Tuition, state resident: part-time $332 per credit hour. Tuition, nonresident: part-time $770 per credit hour. *Financial support:* In 2006–07, 9 teaching assistantships (averaging $14,250 per year) were awarded; research assistantships. *Unit head:* Dr. Gayle Wilkinson, Chair, 314-516-5791. *Application contact:* 314-516-5458, Fax: 314-516-6996, E-mail: gadadm@umsl.edu.

University of Montevallo, College of Education, Program in Secondary Education, Montevallo, AL 35115. Offers M Ed. *Accreditation:* NCATE. *Degree requirements:* For master's, comprehensive exam. *Entrance requirements:* For master's, GRE General Test, MAT, minimum undergraduate GPA of 2.5. Additional exam requirements/recommendations for international students: Required—TOEFL (minimum score 550 paper-based).

University of Nebraska at Omaha, Graduate Studies and Research, College of Education, Department of Teacher Education, Program in Secondary Education, Omaha, NE 68182. Offers MA, MS. *Accreditation:* NCATE. Part-time and evening/weekend programs available. *Faculty:* 10 full-time (5 women). *Students:* 27 full-time (22 women), 100 part-time (68 women); includes 9 minority (5 African Americans, 1 Asian American or Pacific Islander, 3 Hispanic Americans), 1 international. Average age 34. 25 applicants, 88% accepted, 16 enrolled. In 2006, 36 degrees awarded. *Degree requirements:* For master's, thesis (for some programs), comprehensive exam. *Entrance requirements:* For master's, minimum GPA of 3.0. Additional exam requirements/recommendations for international students: Required—TOEFL (minimum score 550 paper-based; 213 computer-based; 80 iBT). *Application deadline:* For fall admission, 7/1 priority date for domestic students; for spring admission, 12/1 priority date for domestic students. Applications are processed on a rolling basis. Application fee: $45. Electronic applications accepted. *Financial support:* In 2006–07, 58 students received support; fellowships, teaching assistantships with tuition reimbursements available, Federal Work-Study, institutionally sponsored loans, scholarships/grants, tuition waivers (full), and unspecified assistantships available. Support available to part-time students. Financial award application deadline: 3/1.

University of Nevada, Las Vegas, Graduate College, College of Education, Department of Curriculum and Instruction, Las Vegas, NV 89154-9900. Offers curriculum and instruction (Ed D, PhD, Ed S); elementary education (M Ed, MS); English education (M Ed, MS); library science (M Ed, MS); literacy education (M Ed, MS); mathematics education (M Ed, MS); multicultural education (M Ed, MS); reading specialist (M Ed, MS); secondary education (M Ed, MS); teacher leadership (M Ed, MS); teaching English as a second language (M Ed, MS); technology integration and leadership (M Ed, MS). *Accreditation:* NCATE. Part-time and evening/weekend programs available. *Faculty:* 40 full-time (19 women), 21 part-time/adjunct (14 women). *Students:* 257 full-time (189 women), 387 part-time (296 women); includes 114 minority (28 African Americans, 5 American Indian/Alaska Native, 34 Asian Americans or Pacific Islanders, 47 Hispanic Americans), 7 international. 261 applicants, 70% accepted, 168 enrolled. In 2006, 231 master's, 5 doctorates awarded. *Degree requirements:* For master's, thesis (for some programs), comprehensive exam (for some programs); for doctorate, thesis/dissertation, oral exam. *Entrance requirements:* For master's, minimum GPA of 3.0; for doctorate, GRE General Test, minimum graduate GPA of 3.0. Additional exam requirements/recommendations for international students: Required—TOEFL (minimum score 550 paper-based; 213 computer-based; 80 iBT). *Application deadline:* For fall admission, 2/15 for domestic and international students; for spring admission, 9/30 for domestic and international students. Application fee: $60 ($75 for international students). Electronic applications accepted. *Financial support:* In 2006–07, 30 research assistantships with partial tuition reimbursements (averaging $10,000 per year), 7 teaching assistantships with partial tuition reimbursements (averaging $12,000 per year) were awarded; career-related internships or fieldwork, Federal Work-Study, institutionally sponsored loans, scholarships/grants, health care benefits, and unspecified assistantships also available. Support available to part-time students. Financial award application deadline: 3/1. *Unit head:* Dr. Greg Levitt, Chair, 702-895-3241. *Application contact:* Graduate College Admissions Evaluator, 702-895-3320, E-mail: gradcollege@unlv.edu.

University of Nevada, Reno, Graduate School, College of Education, Department of Curriculum, Teaching and Learning, Reno, NV 89557. Offers curriculum, teaching and learning (Ed D, PhD); elementary education (M Ed, MA, Ed S); secondary education (M Ed, MA, MS, Ed S); special education and disability studies (PhD). *Students:* 82 full-time (65 women), 74 part-time (58 women); includes 12 minority (1 African American, 3 American Indian/Alaska Native, 5 Asian Americans or Pacific Islanders, 3 Hispanic Americans), 2 international. Average age 35. 66 applicants, 85% accepted, 0 enrolled. In 2006, 51 degrees awarded. *Degree requirements:* For master's, thesis optional. *Entrance requirements:* For master's, GRE General Test, minimum GPA of 2.75. Additional exam requirements/recommendations for international students: Required—TOEFL (minimum score 500 paper-based; 173 computer-based). *Application deadline:* For fall admission, 3/1 priority date for domestic students; for spring admission, 10/1 for domestic students. Applications are processed on a rolling basis. Application fee: $60 ($95 for international students). Electronic applications accepted. *Unit head:* Dr. Margaret Ferrara, Program Director, 775-682-7530, E-mail: ferrara@unr.edu.

University of New Hampshire, Graduate School, College of Liberal Arts, Department of Education, Program in Secondary Education, Durham, NH 03824. Offers M Ed, MAT. Part-time programs available. *Faculty:* 32 full-time. *Students:* 71 full-time (51 women), 59 part-time (34 women); includes 1 minority (Asian American or Pacific Islander), 1 international. Average age 28. 49 applicants, 92% accepted, 30 enrolled. In 2006, 77 degrees awarded. *Degree requirements:* For master's, thesis or alternative. *Entrance requirements:* For master's, GRE General Test. Additional exam requirements/recommendations for international students: Required—TOEFL (minimum score 550 paper-based; 213 computer-based). *Application deadline:* For fall admission, 4/1 priority date for domestic students, 4/1 for international students; for winter admission, 12/1 for domestic students. Applications are processed on a rolling basis. Application fee: $60. Electronic applications accepted. *Expenses:* Tuition, state resident: full-time $8,540; part-time $474 per credit hour. Tuition, nonresident: full-time $20,990; part-time $862 per credit hour. Required fees: $1,343; $356 per term. Tuition and fees vary according to course load, program and reciprocity agreements. *Financial support:* In 2006–07, 5 fellowships, 2 teaching assistantships were awarded; research assistantships, career-related internships or fieldwork, Federal Work-Study, scholarships/grants, and tuition waivers (full and partial) also available. Support available to part-time students. Financial award application deadline: 2/15. *Faculty research:* Pre-service teacher education. *Unit head:* Dr. Michael D. Andrew, Coordinator, 603-862-2371, E-mail: education.department@unh.edu.

University of New Mexico, Graduate School, College of Education, Department of Teacher Education, Program in Secondary Education, Albuquerque, NM 87131-2039. Offers MA, EDSPC. Part-time and evening/weekend programs available. *Students:* 65 full-time (29 women), 72 part-time (50 women); includes 39 minority (5 African Americans, 6 American Indian/Alaska Native, 2 Asian Americans or Pacific Islanders, 26 Hispanic Americans), 2 international. Average age 35. 78 applicants, 63% accepted, 38 enrolled. In 2006, 49 degrees awarded. *Degree requirements:* For master's, thesis optional. *Entrance requirements:* For master's, overall GPA of 3.0, some experience working with students, 3 letters of reference, 1 letter of intent, International students: Above information plus I-20; for EDSPC, master's degree required, overall GPA of 3.0, experience working with students, 3 letters of reference, 1 letter of intent, International students: Above information plus I-20. Additional exam requirements/recommendations for international students: Required—TOEFL (minimum score 550 paper-based; 213 computer-based). *Application deadline:* For fall admission, 3/1 priority date for domestic students; for spring admission, 10/1 priority date for domestic students. Application fee: $50. Electronic applications accepted. *Financial support:* In 2006–07, 2 teaching assistantships with partial tuition reimbursements (averaging $11,641 per year) were awarded. *Unit head:* Dr. Rosalita Mitchell, Chair, 505-277-9611, Fax: 505-277-0455, E-mail: rosalita@unm.edu. *Application contact:* Tamora Trujillo, Administrative Assistant, 505-277-0513, Fax: 505-277-1169, E-mail: tctrujil@unm.edu.

University of North Alabama, College of Education, Department of Secondary Education, Program in Secondary Education, Florence, AL 35632-0001. Offers MA Ed. *Accreditation:* NCATE. Part-time and evening/weekend programs available. *Faculty:* 1 (woman) full-time, 26 part-time/adjunct (11 women). *Students:* 53 full-time (34 women), 71 part-time (47 women); includes 12 minority (8 African Americans, 3 American Indian/Alaska Native, 1 Asian American or Pacific Islander). Average age 32. In 2006, 46 degrees awarded. *Degree requirements:* For master's, comprehensive exam. *Entrance requirements:* For master's, GRE, MAT, or NTE, minimum GPA of 2.5, Alabama Class B Certificate or equivalent, teaching experience. *Application deadline:* For fall admission, 7/1 priority date for domestic students; for spring admission, 12/1 for domestic students. Applications are processed on a rolling basis. Application fee: $25. Electronic applications accepted. *Expenses:* Tuition, state resident: full-time $4,080. Tuition, nonresident: full-time $8,160. Required fees: $764. *Financial support:* Federal Work-Study available. Support available to part-time students. Financial award application deadline: 4/1. *Application contact:* Dr. Sue Wilson, Dean of Enrollment Management, 256-765-4316, Fax: 256-765-4349, E-mail: sjwilson@una.edu.

The University of North Carolina at Chapel Hill, Graduate School, School of Education, Program in Secondary Education, Chapel Hill, NC 27599. Offers English (Grades 9-12) (MAT); French (Grades K-12) (MAT); German (Grades K-12) (MAT); Japanese (Grades K-12) (MAT); Latin (Grades 9-12) (MAT); mathematics (Grades 9-12) (MAT); music (Grades K-12) (MAT); science (Grades 9-12) (MAT); social studies/social science (Grades 9-12) (MAT); Spanish (Grades K-12) (MAT). *Accreditation:* NCATE. In 2006, 72 degrees awarded. *Degree requirements:* For master's, comprehensive exam. *Entrance requirements:* For master's, GRE General Test, minimum GPA of 3.0 during last 2 years of undergraduate course work. Additional exam requirements/recommendations for international students: Required—TOEFL (minimum score 550 paper-based; 213 computer-based), ACTFL oral proficiency interview. *Application deadline:* For fall admission, 1/1 priority date for domestic and international students. Applications are processed on a rolling basis. Application fee: $60. Electronic applications accepted. *Financial support:* Federal Work-Study available. Support available to part-time students. Financial award application deadline: 3/1; financial award applicants required to submit FAFSA. *Faculty research:* Curriculum and instruction, teacher education per subject. *Unit head:* Dr. James Trier, Coordinator, 919-843-4627. *Application contact:* Janet Carroll, Registrar, 919-962-8690, Fax: 919-962-1533, E-mail: jscarrol@email.unc.edu.

The University of North Carolina at Charlotte, Graduate School, College of Education, Department of Middle, Secondary and K-12 Education, Charlotte, NC 28223-0001. Offers middle grades and secondary education (M Ed); teaching English as a second language (M Ed). *Faculty:* 16 full-time (10 women), 6 part-time/adjunct (all women). *Students:* 7 full-time (all women), 79 part-time (67 women); includes 12 minority (6 African Americans, 2 Asian Americans or Pacific Islanders, 4 Hispanic Americans), 3 international. Average age 32. 19 applicants, 89% accepted, 16 enrolled. In 2006, 16 degrees awarded. *Entrance requirements:* For master's, GRE or MAT. Additional exam requirements/recommendations for international students: Required—TOEFL (minimum score 557 paper-based; 220 computer-based). *Application deadline:* For fall admission, 7/1 for domestic students, 5/1 for international students; for spring admission, 11/1 for domestic students, 10/1 for international students. Applications are processed on a rolling basis. Application fee: $55. Electronic applications accepted. *Expenses:* Tuition, state resident: full-time $2,719; part-time $170 per credit. Tuition, nonresident: full-time $12,926; part-time $808 per credit. Required fees: $1,555. *Financial support:* In 2006–07, 7 teaching assistantships (averaging $8,475 per year) were awarded; fellowships, research assistantships, career-related internships or fieldwork, Federal Work-Study, institutionally sponsored loans, scholarships/grants, and unspecified assistantships also available. Support available to part-time students. Financial award application deadline: 4/1; financial award applicants required to submit FAFSA. *Unit head:* Melba Spooner, Chair, 704-687-8704, Fax: 704-687-6430. *Application contact:* Kathy B. Giddings, Director of Graduate Admissions, 704-687-3366, Fax: 704-687-3279, E-mail: gradadm@email.uncc.edu.

The University of North Carolina at Charlotte, Graduate School, College of Education, Program in Teacher Education, Charlotte, NC 28223-0001. Offers art education (K-12) (MAT); dance education (K-12) (MAT); elementary education (K-6) (MAT); English as a second language (K-12) (MAT); foreign language education (K-12) (MAT); general teacher education (MAT); middle grades education (6-9) (MAT); music education (K-12) (MAT); secondary education (9-12) (MAT); special education (K-12) (MAT); theatre education (K-12) (MAT). *Students:* 16 full-time (12 women), 200 part-time (170 women); includes 30 minority (22 African Americans, 2 American Indian/Alaska Native, 2 Asian Americans or Pacific Islanders, 4 Hispanic Americans), 2 international. Average age 33. 74 applicants, 85% accepted, 49 enrolled. In 2006, 43 degrees awarded. *Entrance requirements:* For master's, GRE or MAT. Additional exam requirements/recommendations for international students: Required—TOEFL (minimum score 557 paper-based; 220 computer-based). *Application deadline:* For fall admission, 7/1 for domestic students, 5/1 for international students; for spring admission, 11/1 for domestic students, 10/1 for international students. Applications are processed on a rolling basis. Application fee: $55. Electronic applications accepted. *Expenses:* Tuition, state resident: full-time $2,719; part-time $170 per credit. Tuition, nonresident: full-time $12,926; part-time $808 per credit. Required fees: $1,555. *Financial support:* Fellowships, research assistantships, teaching assistantships, career-related internships or fieldwork, Federal Work-Study, institutionally sponsored loans, scholarships/grants, and unspecified assistantships available. Support available to part-time students. Financial award application deadline: 4/1; financial award applicants required to submit FAFSA. *Unit head:* Dr. Kimberly J. Hartman, Coordinator, 704-687-8883, Fax: 704-687-6430, E-mail: khartman@email.uncc.edu. *Application contact:* Kathy B. Giddings, Director of Graduate Admissions, 704-687-3366, Fax: 704-687-3279, E-mail: gradadm@email.uncc.edu.

The University of North Carolina Wilmington, School of Education, Department of Instructional Technology, Foundations and Secondary Education, Program in Secondary Education, Wilmington, NC 28403-3297. Offers M Ed. *Students:* 4 full-time (3 women), 16 part-time (13 women); includes 1 minority (Hispanic American) 129 applicants, 5% accepted, 5 enrolled. In 2006, 5 degrees awarded. *Degree requirements:* For master's, comprehensive exam. *Application deadline:* For fall admission, 6/1 for domestic students. Applications are processed on a rolling basis. Application fee: $45. *Financial support:* Application deadline: 3/15. *Unit head:* Dr. Robert Smith, Coordinator, 910-962-4076. *Application contact:* Dr. Robert D. Roer, Dean, Graduate School, 910-962-4117, Fax: 910-962-3787, E-mail: roer@uncw.edu.

University of North Dakota, Graduate School, College of Education and Human Development, Teaching and Learning Program, Grand Forks, ND 58202. Offers elementary education (Ed D, PhD); measurement and statistics (Ed D, PhD); secondary education (Ed D, PhD); special education (Ed D, PhD). *Accreditation:* NCATE. *Faculty:* 19 full-time (16 women), 2 part-time/adjunct (1 woman). *Students:* 9 applicants, 0% accepted. In 2006, 18 degrees awarded. *Degree requirements:* For doctorate, thesis/dissertation, final exam, comprehensive exam. *Entrance requirements:* For doctorate, minimum GPA of 3.5. Additional exam requirements/recommendations for international students: Required—TOEFL (minimum score 550 paper-based; 213 computer-based; 79 iBT), IELTS (minimum score 6). *Application deadline:* For fall admission, 2/15 priority date for domestic and international students; for spring admission, 10/15 priority date for domestic and international students. Application fee: $35. Electronic applications accepted. *Expenses:* Tuition, state resident: full-time $5,650; part-time $214 per credit. Tuition, nonresident: full-time $14,248; part-time $572 per credit. Required fees: $1,008; $42 per credit. Tuition and fees vary according to reciprocity agreements. *Financial support:* In 2006–07, 17 students received support, including 1 research assistantship with full tuition reimbursement available (averaging $4,877 per year), 4 teaching assistantships with full tuition reimbursements available (averaging $7,609 per year); fellowships, career-related internships or fieldwork, Federal Work-Study, institutionally sponsored loans, scholarships/grants, tuition waivers (full and partial), and unspecified assistantships also available. Support available to part-time students. Financial award application deadline: 3/15; financial award applicants required to submit FAFSA. *Application contact:* Linda M. Baeza, Admissions Officer, 701-777-2945, Fax: 701-777-3619, E-mail: gradschool@mail.und.nodak.edu.

University of North Florida, College of Education and Human Services, Division of Curriculum and Instruction, Program in Secondary Education, Jacksonville, FL 32224-2645. Offers M Ed. *Accreditation:* NCATE. Part-time and evening/weekend programs available. *Faculty:* 31 full-time (17 women). *Students:* 9 full-time (5 women), 38 part-time (29 women); includes 14 minority (9 African Americans, 1 Asian American or Pacific Islander, 4 Hispanic Americans), 3 international. Average age 36. 24 applicants, 46% accepted, 8 enrolled. In 2006, 24 degrees awarded. *Entrance requirements:* For master's, GRE General Test, minimum GPA of 3.0 in last 60 hours, interview, 3 letters of recommendation. Additional exam requirements/recommendations for international students: Required—TOEFL (minimum score 500 paper-based; 173 computer-based). *Application deadline:* For fall admission, 7/1 priority date for domestic students, 5/1 for international students; for spring admission, 11/1 priority date for domestic students, 10/1 for international students. Applications are processed on a rolling basis. Application fee: $30. Electronic applications accepted. *Expenses:* Tuition, state resident: full-time $4,948; part-time $206 per semester hour. Tuition, nonresident: full-time $19,140; part-time $408 per semester hour. *Financial support:* In 2006–07, 17 students received support, including 1 teaching assistantship (averaging $4,000 per year); career-related internships or fieldwork, Federal Work-Study, and tuition waivers (partial) also available. Support available to part-time students. Financial award application deadline: 4/1; financial award applicants required to submit FAFSA. *Faculty research:* Using children's literature to enhance metalinguistic awareness, education, oral language diagnosis of middle-schoolers, science inquiry teaching and learning.

Secondary Education

University of North Texas, Robert B. Toulouse School of Graduate Studies, College of Education, Department of Teacher Education and Administration, Program in Secondary Education, Denton, TX 76203. Offers M Ed, MS. *Accreditation:* NCATE. *Students:* 10 full-time (6 women), 54 part-time (42 women); includes 10 minority (2 American Indian/Alaska Native, 2 Asian Americans or Pacific Islanders, 6 Hispanic Americans). Average age 31. 25 applicants, 68% accepted, 9 enrolled. In 2006, 31 degrees awarded. *Entrance requirements:* For master's, GRE General Test. Additional exam requirements/recommendations for international students: Recommended—TOEFL (minimum score 550 paper-based; 213 computer-based). *Application deadline:* For fall admission, 7/15 for domestic students. Application fee: $50 ($75 for international students). *Expenses:* Tuition, state resident: full-time $3,573; part-time $198 per credit. Tuition, nonresident: full-time $8,577; part-time $476 per credit. Required fees: $1,258; $126 per credit. One-time fee: $150 full-time. Tuition and fees vary according to course load. *Financial support:* Fellowships, research assistantships, teaching assistantships, career-related internships or fieldwork, Federal Work-Study, and institutionally sponsored loans available. Financial award application deadline: 4/1. *Application contact:* Dr. Scott Forney, Graduate Adviser, 940-565-4447, Fax: 940-565-4952, E-mail: forney@coe.unt.edu.

University of Oklahoma, Graduate College, College of Education, Department of Instructional Leadership and Academic Curriculum, Norman, OK 73019-0390. Offers education (Certificate); instructional leadership and academic curriculum (M Ed, PhD), including bilingual education, early childhood education, elementary education, English education, math education, reading education, science education, secondary education, social studies education. *Accreditation:* NCATE. Part-time and evening/weekend programs available. *Faculty:* 20 full-time (11 women), 6 part-time/adjunct (all women). *Students:* 76 full-time (63 women), 115 part-time (89 women); includes 25 minority (8 African Americans, 12 American Indian/Alaska Native, 4 Asian Americans or Pacific Islanders, 1 Hispanic American), 12 international. 72 applicants, 96% accepted, 56 enrolled. In 2006, 11 master's, 10 doctorates awarded. *Degree requirements:* For doctorate, thesis/dissertation. *Entrance requirements:* For master's, 12 hours of course work in education; for doctorate, GRE General Test, master's degree, minimum graduate GPA of 3.0. Additional exam requirements/recommendations for international students: Required—TOEFL (minimum score 550 paper-based; 213 computer-based). *Application deadline:* For fall admission, 6/1 priority date for domestic students, 4/1 for international students; for spring admission, 11/1 for domestic students, 9/1 for international students. Applications are processed on a rolling basis. Application fee: $40 ($90 for international students). *Expenses:* Tuition, state resident: full-time $3,180; part-time $133 per credit hour. Tuition, nonresident: full-time $11,347; part-time $473 per credit hour. Required fees: $1,729; $62 per credit hour. $117 per semester. Tuition and fees vary according to course load and program. *Financial support:* In 2006–07, 76 students received support, including 5 research assistantships with partial tuition reimbursements available (averaging $9,773 per year), 7 teaching assistantships with partial tuition reimbursements available (averaging $10,403 per year); scholarships/grants and unspecified assistantships also available. Financial award applicants required to submit FAFSA. *Faculty research:* Early literacy, learning cycle, social justice, teacher education. Total annual research expenditures: $119,917. *Unit head:* Dr. Priscilla Griffith, Chair and Graduate Liaison, 405-325-1498, Fax: 405-325-4061, E-mail: pgriffith@ou.edu.

University of Pennsylvania, Graduate School of Education, Division of Foundations and Practices in Education, Programs in Secondary Education, Philadelphia, PA 19104. Offers MS Ed. *Degree requirements:* For master's, comprehensive exam or portfolio. *Entrance requirements:* For master's, GRE, MAT. Electronic applications accepted. Expenses: Contact institution.

University of Phoenix–Central Florida Campus, The Artemis School, College of Education, Maitland, FL 32751-7057. Offers administration and supervision (MA Ed); curriculum and instruction (MA Ed); elementary teacher education (MA Ed); secondary teacher education (MA Ed). Evening/weekend programs available. *Faculty:* 10 full-time (9 women), 16 part-time/adjunct (6 women). *Students:* 20 full-time (18 women); includes 5 minority (3 African Americans, 2 Hispanic Americans), 1 international. Average age 38. In 2006, 7 degrees awarded. *Degree requirements:* For master's, thesis (for some programs), registration. *Entrance requirements:* For master's, 3 years of work experience, minimum undergraduate GPA of 2.5. Additional exam requirements/recommendations for international students: Required—TOEFL (minimum score 550 paper-based; 213 computer-based; 79 iBT). *Application deadline:* Applications are processed on a rolling basis. Application fee: $45. Electronic applications accepted. *Expenses:* Tuition: Full-time $9,450. Required fees: $760. *Financial support:* Institutionally sponsored loans and scholarships/grants available. Financial award applicants required to submit FAFSA. *Unit head:* Dr. Marla LaRue, Dean/Executive Director, 480-557-1218. *Application contact:* Chair, 407-667-0555, Fax: 407-667-0560.

University of Phoenix–Central Valley Campus, College of Education, Fresno, CA 93720. Offers curriculum and instruction (MA Ed); elementary teacher education (MA Ed); secondary teacher education (MA Ed).

University of Phoenix–Denver Campus, The Artemis School, College of Education, Lone Tree, CO 80124-5453. Offers administration and supervision (MAEd); curriculum instruction (MAEd); elementary teacher education (MAEd); school counseling (MSC); secondary teacher education (MAEd). Evening/weekend programs available. *Faculty:* 19 full-time (14 women), 141 part-time/adjunct (84 women). *Students:* 738 full-time (513 women); includes 72 minority (27 African Americans, 4 American Indian/Alaska Native, 9 Asian Americans or Pacific Islanders, 32 Hispanic Americans), 66 international. Average age 37. In 2006, 435 master's awarded. *Degree requirements:* For master's, thesis (for some programs), registration. *Entrance requirements:* For master's, minimum undergraduate GPA of 2.5, 3 years work experience. Additional exam requirements/recommendations for international students: Required—TOEFL (minimum score 550 paper-based; 213 computer-based; 79 iBT). *Application deadline:* Applications are processed on a rolling basis. Application fee: $45. Electronic applications accepted. *Expenses:* Tuition: Full-time $10,032. Required fees: $760. *Financial support:* Institutionally sponsored loans and scholarships/grants available. Financial award applicants required to submit FAFSA. *Unit head:* Dr. Marla LaRue, Dean/Executive Director, 480-557-1218, E-mail: marla.larue@phoenix.edu. *Application contact:* Chair, 303-694-9093, Fax: 303-662-0911.

University of Phoenix–Fort Lauderdale Campus, The Artemis School, College of Education, Fort Lauderdale, FL 33309. Offers administration and supervision (MA Ed); computer education (MA Ed); curriculum and instruction (MA Ed); elementary teacher education (MA Ed); secondary teacher education (MA Ed). Evening/weekend programs available. *Faculty:* 10 full-time (5 women), 17 part-time/adjunct (7 women). *Students:* 132 full-time (114 women); includes 60 minority (52 African Americans, 1 Asian American or Pacific Islander, 7 Hispanic Americans), 5 international. Average age 39. In 2006, 25 degrees awarded. *Degree requirements:* For master's, thesis (for some programs), registration. *Entrance requirements:* For master's, 3 years of work experience, minimum undergraduate GPA of 2.5. Additional exam requirements/recommendations for international students: Required—TOEFL (minimum score 550 paper-based; 213 computer-based; 79 iBT). *Application deadline:* Applications are processed on a rolling basis. Application fee: $45. Electronic applications accepted. *Expenses:* Tuition: Full-time $9,450. Required fees: $760. *Financial support:* Institutionally sponsored loans and scholarships/grants available. Financial award applicants required to submit FAFSA. *Unit head:* Dr. Marla LaRue, Dean/Executive Director, 480-557-1218. *Application contact:* Chair, 954-382-5303, Fax: 954-382-5304.

University of Phoenix–Hawaii Campus, The Artemis School, College of Education, Honolulu, HI 96813-4317. Offers administration and supervision (MA Ed); curriculum and instruction (MA Ed); elementary education (MA Ed); secondary education (MA Ed); teacher education for elementary licensure (MA Ed). Evening/weekend programs available. *Faculty:* 10 full-time (7 women), 58 part-time/adjunct (34 women). *Students:* 261 full-time (176 women); includes 61 minority (1 African American, 1 American Indian/Alaska Native, 53 Asian Americans or Pacific Islanders, 6 Hispanic Americans), 106 international. Average age 36. In 2006, 151 degrees awarded. *Degree requirements:* For master's, thesis (for some programs), registration. *Entrance requirements:* For master's, minimum undergraduate GPA of 2.5, 3 years of work experience. Additional exam requirements/recommendations for international students: Required—TOEFL (minimum score 550 paper-based; 213 computer-based; 79 iBT). *Application deadline:* Applications are processed on a rolling basis. Application fee: $45. Electronic applications accepted. *Expenses:* Tuition: Full-time $11,520. Required fees: $760. *Financial support:* Institutionally sponsored loans and scholarships/grants available. Financial award applicants required to submit FAFSA. *Unit head:* Dr. Marla LaRue, Dean/Executive Director, 480-557-1309, E-mail: marla.larue@phoenix.edu. *Application contact:* Chair, 580-536-2686, Fax: 808-536-3848.

University of Phoenix–Nashville Campus, The Artemis School, College of Education, Nashville, TN 37214-5048. Offers administration and supervision (MA Ed); curriculum and instruction (MA Ed); elementary teacher education (MA Ed); secondary teacher education (MA Ed). Evening/weekend programs available. *Degree requirements:* For master's, thesis (for some programs), registration. *Entrance requirements:* For master's, minimum undergraduate GPA of 2.5, 3 years work experience. Additional exam requirements/recommendations for international students: Required—TOEFL (minimum score 500 paper-based; 213 computer-based; 79 iBT). *Application deadline:* Applications are processed on a rolling basis. Application fee: $45. Electronic applications accepted. *Expenses:* Tuition: Full-time $10,104. Required fees: $760. *Financial support:* Institutionally sponsored loans and scholarships/grants available. Financial award applicants required to submit FAFSA. *Unit head:* Dr. Marla LaRue, Dean/Executive Director, 480-557-1218, E-mail: marla.larue@phoenix.edu. *Application contact:* Chair, 615-872-0188.

University of Phoenix–New Mexico Campus, The Artemis School, College of Education, Albuquerque, NM 87109-4645. Offers administration (MAEd); curriculum and instruction (MAEd); teacher education (MAEd), including elementary, secondary. Evening/weekend programs available. *Faculty:* 9 full-time (5 women), 62 part-time/adjunct (40 women). *Students:* 234 full-time (181 women); includes 116 minority (5 African Americans, 1 Asian American or Pacific Islander, 110 Hispanic Americans), 10 international. Average age 39. In 2006, 131 degrees awarded. *Degree requirements:* For master's, thesis (for some programs), registration. *Entrance requirements:* For master's, minimum undergraduate GPA of 2.5, 3 years of work experience. Additional exam requirements/recommendations for international students: Required—TOEFL (minimum score 550 paper-based; 213 computer-based; 79 iBT). *Application deadline:* Applications are processed on a rolling basis. Application fee: $45. Electronic applications accepted. *Expenses:* Tuition: Full-time $9,005. Required fees: $760. *Financial support:* Institutionally sponsored loans and scholarships/grants available. Financial award applicants required to submit FAFSA. *Unit head:* Dr. Marla LaRue, Dean/Executive Director, 480-557-1218, E-mail: marla.larue@phoenix.edu. *Application contact:* Chair, 505-821-4800, Fax: 505-821-5551.

University of Phoenix–North Florida Campus, The Artemis School, College of Education, Jacksonville, FL 32216-0959. Offers administration (MA Ed); curriculum and instruction (MA Ed); curriculum and instruction—computer education (MA Ed); elementary teacher education (MA Ed); secondary teacher education (MA Ed). Evening/weekend programs available. *Faculty:* 9 full-time (5 women), 10 part-time/adjunct (4 women). *Students:* 98 full-time (78 women); includes 41 minority (37 African Americans, 4 Hispanic Americans), 1 international. Average age 37. In 2006, 22 master's awarded. *Degree requirements:* For master's, thesis (for some programs), registration. *Entrance requirements:* For master's, 3 years of work experience, minimum undergraduate GPA of 2.5. Additional exam requirements/recommendations for international students: Required—TOEFL (minimum score 550 paper-based; 213 computer-based; 49 iBT). *Application deadline:* Applications are processed on a rolling basis. Application fee: $45. Electronic applications accepted. *Financial support:* Institutionally sponsored loans and scholarships/grants available. Financial award applicants required to submit FAFSA. *Unit head:* Dr. Marla LaRue, Dean, 480-557-1218, E-mail: marla.larue@phoenix.edu. *Application contact:* Chair, 904-636-6645, Fax: 904-636-0998.

University of Phoenix–Omaha Campus, College of Education, Omaha, NE 68154-5240. Offers administration and supervision (MA Ed); curriculum and instruction (MA Ed); curriculum and instruction—English and language arts education (MA Ed); curriculum and instruction—adult education (MA Ed); curriculum and instruction—computer education (MA Ed); curriculum and instruction—English as a second language (MA Ed); curriculum and instruction—mathematics education (MA Ed); elementary teacher education (MA Ed); secondary teacher education (MA Ed); special education (MA Ed).

University of Phoenix Online Campus, The Artemis School, College of Education, Phoenix, AZ 85034-7209. Offers administration and supervision (MAEd); adult education and training (MAEd); curriculum and instruction-adult education (MAEd); curriculum and instruction-English and language arts education (MAEd); curriculum and instruction-mathematics education (MAEd); curriculum education (MAEd); curriculum instruction (MAEd); early childhood (MAEd); English as a second language (MAEd); teacher education elementary (MAEd); teacher education secondary (MAEd). Evening/weekend programs available. Postbaccalaureate distance learning degree programs offered (no on-campus study). *Faculty:* 12 full-time (5 women), 8,196 part-time/adjunct (6,937 women). *Students:* 11,937 full-time (9,375 women); includes 2,972 minority (2,210 African Americans, 74 American Indian/Alaska Native, 205 Asian Americans or Pacific Islanders, 483 Hispanic Americans), 906 international. Average age 36. *Degree requirements:* For master's, thesis (for some programs), registration. *Entrance requirements:* For master's, 3 years of work experience, minimum GPA of 2.5. Additional exam requirements/recommendations for international students: Required—TOEFL (minimum score 550 paper-based; 213 computer-based; 79 iBT). *Application deadline:* Applications are processed on a rolling basis. Application fee: $45. Electronic applications accepted. *Expenses:* Tuition: Full-time $12,664. Required fees: $760. *Financial support:* Institutionally sponsored loans and scholarships/grants available. Financial award applicants required to submit FAFSA. *Unit head:* Dr. Marla LaRue, Dean/Executive Director, 480-557-1218, E-mail: marla.larue@phoenix.edu. *Application contact:* Dr. Marla LaRue, Dean/Executive Director, 480-557-1218, E-mail: marla.larue@phoenix.edu.

University of Phoenix–Oregon Campus, The Artemis School, College of Education, Tigard, OR 97223. Offers early childhood and elementary education (MA Ed); secondary education (MA Ed). Evening/weekend programs available. *Faculty:* 3 full-time (2 women), 33 part-time/adjunct (14 women). *Students:* 90 full-time (59 women); includes 7 minority (4 African Americans, 1 American Indian/Alaska Native, 2 Hispanic Americans), 14 international. Average age 36. In 2006, 12 degrees awarded. *Degree requirements:* For master's, thesis (for some programs), registration. *Entrance requirements:* For master's, minimum undergraduate GPA of 2.5, 3 years work experience. Additional exam requirements/recommendations for international students: Required—TOEFL (minimum score 550 paper-based; 213 computer-based; 79 iBT). *Application deadline:* Applications are processed on a rolling basis. Application fee: $45. Electronic applications accepted. *Expenses:* Tuition: Full-time $10,200. Required fees: $760. *Financial support:* Institutionally sponsored loans and scholarships/grants available. Financial award applicants required to submit FAFSA. *Unit head:* Dr. Marla LaRue, Dean/Executive Director, 480-557-1218, E-mail: marla.larue@phoenix.edu. *Application contact:* Chair, 503-403-2500, Fax: 503-670-0614.

University of Phoenix–Phoenix Campus, The Artemis School, College of Education, Phoenix, AZ 85040-1958. Offers administration and supervision (MA Ed); curriculum and instruction (MA Ed); elementary licensure (MA Ed); secondary licensure (MA Ed). Evening/weekend programs available. *Faculty:* 39 full-time (23 women), 422 part-time/adjunct (255 women). *Students:* 850 full-time (614 women); includes 135 minority (45 African Americans, 7 American Indian/Alaska Native, 20 Asian Americans or Pacific Islanders, 63 Hispanic Americans), 15 international. Average age 35. In 2006, 500 degrees awarded. *Degree requirements:* For master's, thesis (for some programs), registration. *Entrance requirements:* For master's, 3 years of work experience, minimum undergraduate GPA of 2.5. Additional exam requirements/recommendations for international students: Required—TOEFL (minimum score 550 paper-based; 213 computer-based; 79 iBT). *Application deadline:* Applications are processed on a rolling basis. Application fee: $45. Electronic applications accepted. *Financial support:* Institutionally sponsored loans and scholarships/grants available. Financial award applicants required to submit FAFSA. *Unit head:* Dr. Marla LaRue, Dean/Executive Director, 480-557-1218, E-mail: marla.larue@phoenix.edu. *Application contact:* College Chair, 480-804-7400, Fax: 480-557-2320.

University of Phoenix–Sacramento Valley Campus, The Artemis School, College of Education, Sacramento, CA 95833-3632. Offers adult education (MA Ed); curriculum instruction (MA Ed); elementary education (MA Ed); secondary education (MA Ed); teacher education (Certificate). Evening/weekend programs available. *Faculty:* 9 full-time (5 women), 95 part-time/adjunct (41 women). *Students:* 234 full-time (161 women); includes 51 minority (20 African Americans, 2 American Indian/Alaska Native, 9 Asian Americans or Pacific Islanders, 20 Hispanic Americans), 15 international. Average age 36. In 2006, 80 degrees awarded. *Degree requirements:* For master's, thesis (for some programs), registration. *Entrance requirements:* For master's, 3 years of work experience, minimum undergraduate GPA of 2.5. Additional exam requirements/recommendations for international students: Required—TOEFL (minimum score 550 paper-based; 213 computer-based; 79 iBT). *Application deadline:* Applications are processed on a rolling basis. Application fee: $45. Electronic applications accepted. *Expenses:* Tuition: Full-time $12,024. Required fees: $760. *Financial support:* Institutionally sponsored loans and scholarships/grants available. Financial award applicants required to submit FAFSA. *Unit head:* Dr. Marla LaRue, Dean, 480-557-1218, E-mail: marla.larue@phoenix.edu. *Application contact:* Campus College Chair, 916-923-2107, Fax: 916-923-3914.

University of Phoenix–San Diego Campus, The Artemis School, College of Education, San Diego, CA 92123. Offers curriculum and instruction (MA Ed); elementary education (MA Ed); secondary education (MA Ed). Evening/weekend programs available. *Faculty:* 6 full-time (3 women), 69 part-time/adjunct (36 women). *Students:* 165 full-time (110 women); includes 42 minority (9 African Americans, 8 Asian Americans or Pacific Islanders, 25 Hispanic Americans), 12 international. Average age 34. In 2006, 81 degrees awarded. *Degree requirements:* For master's, thesis (for some programs), registration. *Entrance requirements:* For master's, 3 years of work experience, minimum undergraduate GPA of 3.0. Additional exam requirements/recommendations for international students: Required—TOEFL (minimum score 550 paper-based; 213 computer-based; 79 iBT). *Application deadline:* Applications are processed on a rolling basis. Application fee: $45. Electronic applications accepted. *Expenses:* Tuition: Full-time $11,419. Required fees: $760. *Financial support:* Institutionally sponsored loans and scholarships/grants available. Financial award applicants required to submit FAFSA. *Unit head:* Dr. Marla LaRue, Dean/Executive Director, 480-557-1218, E-mail: marla.larue@phoenix.edu. *Application contact:* Campus College Chair, 888-UOP-INFO, Fax: 858-509-4399.

University of Phoenix–Southern Arizona Campus, The Artemis School, College of Education, Tucson, AZ 85712-2732. Offers curriculum instruction (MA Ed); educational counseling (MA Ed); elementary licensure (MA Ed); school counseling (MSC); secondary licensure (MA Ed); special education (Certificate). Evening/weekend programs available. *Faculty:* 101. *Students:* 75 full-time (55 women); includes 16 minority (2 African Americans, 1 American Indian/Alaska Native, 1 Asian American or Pacific Islander, 12 Hispanic Americans), 2 international. Average age 38. In 2006, 113 degrees awarded. *Degree requirements:* For master's, thesis (for some programs), registration. *Entrance requirements:* For master's, minimum undergraduate GPA of 2.5, 3 years of work experience. Additional exam requirements/recommendations for international students: Required—TOEFL (minimum score 550 paper-based; 213 computer-based; 79 iBT). *Application deadline:* Applications are processed on a rolling basis. Application fee: $45. Electronic applications accepted. *Expenses:* Tuition: Full-time $8,669. Required fees: $760. *Financial support:* Institutionally sponsored loans and scholarships/grants available. Financial award applicants required to submit FAFSA. *Unit head:* Dr. Marla LaRue, Dean/Executive Director, 480-557-1218, E-mail: marla.larue@phoenix.edu. *Application contact:* Campus College Chair, 520-881-6512, Fax: 520-795-6177.

University of Phoenix–Southern California Campus, The Artemis School, College of Education, Costa Mesa, CA 92626. Offers curriculum and instruction (MA Ed); elementary education (MA Ed); secondary education (MA Ed). Evening/weekend programs available. *Faculty:* 22 full-time (9 women), 195 part-time/adjunct (108 women). *Students:* 1,152 full-time (858 women); includes 420 minority (135 African Americans, 7 American Indian/Alaska Native, 59 Asian Americans or Pacific Islanders, 219 Hispanic Americans), 78 international. Average age 34. In 2006, 359 degrees awarded. *Degree requirements:* For master's, thesis (for some programs), registration. *Entrance requirements:* For master's, minimum undergraduate GPA of 2.5, 3 years work experience. Additional exam requirements/recommendations for international students: Required—TOEFL (minimum score 550 paper-based; 213 computer-based; 79 iBT). *Application deadline:* Applications are processed on a rolling basis. Application fee: $45. Electronic applications accepted. *Expenses:* Tuition: Full-time $13,512. Required fees: $760. *Financial support:* Institutionally sponsored loans and scholarships/grants available. Financial award applicants required to submit FAFSA. *Unit head:* Dr. Marla LaRue, Dean/Executive Director, 480-557-1218, E-mail: marla.larue@phoenix.edu. *Application contact:* Campus College Chair, 714-378-1878, Fax: 714-378-5875.

University of Phoenix–Southern Colorado Campus, The Artemis School, College of Education, Colorado Springs, CO 80919-2335. Offers administration and supervision (MA Ed); curriculum and instruction (MA Ed); elementary licensure (MA Ed); principal licensure certification (Certificate); school counseling (MSC); secondary licensure (MA Ed). Evening/weekend programs available. *Faculty:* 7 full-time (3 women), 90 part-time/adjunct (53 women). *Students:* 220 full-time (162 women); includes 22 minority (7 African Americans, 1 American Indian/Alaska Native, 4 Asian Americans or Pacific Islanders, 10 Hispanic Americans), 15 international. Average age 37. In 2006, 122 degrees awarded. *Degree requirements:* For master's, thesis (for some programs), registration. *Entrance requirements:* For master's, minimum undergraduate GPA of 2.5, 3 years of work experience. Additional exam requirements/recommendations for international students: Required—TOEFL (minimum score 550 paper-based; 213 computer-based; 79 iBT). *Application deadline:* Applications are processed on a rolling basis. Application fee: $45. Electronic applications accepted. *Expenses:* Tuition: Full-time $10,291. Required fees: $760. *Financial support:* Institutionally sponsored loans and scholarships/grants available. Financial award applicants required to submit FAFSA. *Unit head:* Dr. Marla LaRue, Dean/Executive Director, 480-557-1218, E-mail: marla.larue@phoenix.edu. *Application contact:* Chair, 719-599-5282, Fax: 719-599-7973.

University of Phoenix–Utah Campus, The Artemis School, College of Education, Salt Lake City, UT 84123-4617. Offers administration and supervision (MA Ed); curriculum and instruction (MA Ed); elementary education (MA Ed); school counseling (MSC); secondary education (MA Ed). Evening/weekend programs available. *Faculty:* 14 full-time (8 women), 78 part-time/adjunct (39 women). *Students:* 395 full-time (246 women); includes 20 minority (2 African Americans, 1 American Indian/Alaska Native, 8 Asian Americans or Pacific Islanders, 9 Hispanic Americans), 4 international. Average age 37. In 2006, 233 degrees awarded. *Degree requirements:* For master's, thesis (for some programs), registration. *Entrance requirements:* For master's, minimum undergraduate GPA of 2.5, 3 years work experience. Additional exam requirements/recommendations for international students: Required—TOEFL (minimum score 550 paper-based; 213 computer-based; 79 iBT). *Application deadline:* Applications are processed on a rolling basis. Application fee: $45. Electronic applications accepted. *Expenses:* Tuition: Full-time $9,104. Required fees: $760. *Financial support:* Institutionally sponsored loans and scholarships/grants available. Financial award applicants required to submit FAFSA. *Unit head:* Dr. Marla LaRue, Dean/Executive Director, 480-557-1218, E-mail: marla.larue@phoenix.edu. *Application contact:* Chair, 801-263-1444, Fax: 801-269-9766.

University of Phoenix–West Florida Campus, The Artemis School, College of Education, Temple Terrace, FL 33637. Offers administration and supervision (MA Ed); curriculum and instruction (MA Ed); curriculum and technology (MA Ed); elementary teacher education (MA Ed); secondary teacher education (MA Ed). Evening/weekend programs available. *Faculty:* 10 full-time (8 women), 15 part-time/adjunct (7 women). *Students:* 67 full-time (61 women); includes 24 minority (20 African Americans, 1 American Indian/Alaska Native, 3 Hispanic Americans), 3 international. Average age 40. In 2006, 8 degrees awarded. *Degree requirements:* For master's, thesis (for some programs), registration. *Entrance requirements:* For master's, 3 years of work experience, minimum undergraduate GPA of 2.5. Additional exam requirements/recommendations for international students: Required—TOEFL (minimum score 550 paper-based; 213 computer-based; 79 iBT). Application fee: $45. *Expenses:* Tuition: Full-time $9,450. Required fees: $760. *Financial support:* Institutionally sponsored loans and scholarships/grants available. Financial award applicants required to submit FAFSA. *Unit head:* Dr. Marla LaRue, Dean, 480-557-1218, E-mail: marla.larue@phoenix.edu. *Application contact:* Chair, 813-626-7911, Fax: 813-977-1449.

University of Pittsburgh, School of Education, Department of Instruction and Learning, Program in Secondary Education, Pittsburgh, PA 15260. Offers English/communications education (M Ed, MAT, Ed D, PhD); foreign languages education (M Ed, MAT, Ed D, PhD); mathematics education (M Ed, MAT, Ed D); reading education (PhD); science education (M Ed, MAT, MS, Ed D); social studies education (M Ed, MAT, Ed D, PhD). Part-time and evening/weekend programs available. *Students:* 157 full-time (111 women), 84 part-time (61 women); includes 18 minority (7 African Americans, 5 Asian Americans or Pacific Islanders, 6 Hispanic Americans), 13 international. 163 applicants, 74% accepted, 86 enrolled. In 2006, 114 master's, 7 doctorates awarded. *Degree requirements:* For master's and doctorate, thesis/dissertation. *Entrance requirements:* For master's, PRAXIS I; for doctorate, GRE General Test. Additional exam requirements/recommendations for international students: Required—TOEFL. *Application deadline:* For fall admission, 2/1 priority date for domestic students; for spring admission, 11/15 priority date for domestic students. Applications are processed on a rolling basis. Application fee: $50. Electronic applications accepted. *Financial support:* Fellowships, teaching assistantships, career-related internships or fieldwork, Federal Work-Study, tuition waivers (partial), and unspecified assistantships available. Support available to part-time students. Financial award application deadline: 3/15; financial award applicants required to submit FAFSA. *Application contact:* Joan M. Cutone, Director, School of Education Student Service Center, 412-648-2230, Fax: 412-648-1899, E-mail: soeinfo@pitt.edu.

University of Portland, Graduate School, School of Education, Program in Secondary Education, Portland, OR 97203-5798. Offers M Ed, MA, MAT. Part-time and evening/weekend programs available. *Degree requirements:* For master's, thesis optional. *Entrance requirements:* For master's, GRE General Test (MA); California Basic Educational Skills Test, PRAXIS, Oregon Educator Licensure Assessment (MAT); GRE General Test or MAT (M Ed), minimum GPA of 3.0, teaching certificate, letters of recommendation, resumé. Additional exam requirements/recommendations for international students: Required—TOEFL (minimum score 550 paper-based; 80 iBT). *Application deadline:* For fall admission, 8/1 priority date for domestic students; for spring admission, 12/1 for domestic students. Applications are processed on a rolling basis. Application fee: $50. *Expenses:* Tuition: Part-time $728 per semester hour. Required fees: $5 per semester hour. Tuition and fees vary according to program. *Financial support:* Federal Work-Study and scholarships/grants available. Financial award application deadline: 3/1; financial award applicants required to submit FAFSA. *Application contact:* Dr. Thomas G. Greene, Associate Dean, 503-943-7135, Fax: 503-943-7315, E-mail: greene@up.edu.

University of Puerto Rico, Río Piedras, College of Education, Program in Curriculum and Teaching, San Juan, PR 00931-3300. Offers biology education (M Ed); chemistry education (M Ed); curriculum and teaching (Ed D); English education (M Ed); history education (M Ed); mathematics education (M Ed); physics education (M Ed); secondary education (M Ed); Spanish education (M Ed). Part-time programs available. *Students:* 64 full-time (42 women), 123 part-time (91 women); all minorities (all Hispanic Americans) In 2006, 8 master's, 19 doctorates awarded. *Degree requirements:* For master's, thesis; for doctorate, thesis/dissertation, internship. *Entrance requirements:* For master's, PAEG or GRE, minimum GPA of 3.0, letter of recommendation; for doctorate, GRE or PAEG, master's degree, minimum GPA of 3.0, letter of recommendation (2), interview. *Application deadline:* For fall admission, 2/1 for domestic and international students. Application fee: $17. *Expenses:* Tuition, state resident: part-time $100 per credit. Tuition, nonresident: part-time $291 per credit. Required fees: $72 per semester. *Financial support:* Fellowships, research assistantships, teaching assistantships, career-related internships or fieldwork, Federal Work-Study, institutionally sponsored loans, and tuition waivers (partial) available. Financial award application deadline: 5/31. *Faculty research:* Science curriculum, administration management. *Unit head:* Dr. Loyda Martinez, Coordinator, 787-764-0000 Ext. 4361, Fax: 787-763-4130. *Application contact:* Information Contact, 787-764-0000 Ext. 4368, Fax: 787-763-4130.

University of Puget Sound, Graduate Studies, School of Education, Program in Teaching, Tacoma, WA 98416. Offers elementary education (MAT); middle school education (MAT); secondary education (MAT). *Accreditation:* NASM; NCATE. *Faculty:* 10 full-time (6 women), 2 part-time/adjunct (both women). *Students:* 53 full-time (35 women), 1 (woman) part-time; includes 7 minority (2 African Americans, 2 American Indian/Alaska Native, 3 Asian Americans or Pacific Islanders), 1 international. Average age 26. 96 applicants, 88% accepted, 51 enrolled. In 2006, 41 degrees awarded. *Median time to degree:* Master's–1 year full-time. *Entrance requirements:* For master's, GRE General Test, West-B for WA residents, PRAXIS I, minimum GPA of 3.0. Additional exam requirements/recommendations for international students: Required—TOEFL (minimum score 550 paper-based; 213 computer-based; 80 iBT). *Application deadline:* For fall admission, 3/1 priority date for domestic and international students. Applications are processed on a rolling basis. Application fee: $65. Electronic applications accepted. *Expenses:* Tuition: Full-time $26,390. Tuition and fees vary according to course load. *Financial support:* In 2006–07, 24 students received support, including 16 fellowships (averaging $7,575 per year); career-related internships or fieldwork and scholarships/grants also available. Support available to part-time students. Financial award application deadline: 3/31; financial award applicants required to submit FAFSA. *Faculty research:* Economic support for schools, teacher thinking/student understanding, self-reflection in teacher education, civics and decision making. Total annual research expenditures: $11,005. *Application contact:* Dr. George H. Mills, Vice President for Enrollment, 253-879-3211, Fax: 253-879-3993, E-mail: admission@ups.edu.

University of Rhode Island, Graduate School, College of Human Science and Services, School of Education, Program in Secondary Education, Kingston, RI 02881. Offers MA. *Accreditation:* NCATE. Evening/weekend programs available. *Entrance requirements:* For master's, GRE or MAT. Additional exam requirements/recommendations for international students: Required—TOEFL. *Application deadline:* For fall admission, 4/15 priority date for domestic students; for spring admission, 11/15 for domestic students. Applications are processed on a rolling basis. Application fee: $35. *Expenses:* Tuition, state resident: full-time $6,032; part-time $335 per credit. Tuition, nonresident: full-time $17,288; part-time $960 per credit. Required fees: $65 per credit. $30 per semester. One-time fee: $80 part-time. *Financial support:* Career-related internships or fieldwork available.

University of St. Francis, College of Education, Joliet, IL 60435-6169. Offers curriculum and instruction (MS); educational leadership (MS), including reading, special education; elementary education certification (M Ed); secondary education certification (M Ed), including English education, math education, science education, social studies education; special education (M Ed); teaching and learning (MS). Part-time and evening/weekend programs available. *Faculty:* 11 full-time (10 women), 25 part-time/adjunct (12 women). *Students:* 52 full-time (38 women), 381 part-time (293 women); includes 38 minority (21 African Americans, 1 American Indian/Alaska Native, 4 Asian Americans or Pacific Islanders, 12 Hispanic Americans). Average age 33. 194 applicants, 80% accepted, 117 enrolled. In 2006, 165 degrees awarded. *Degree requirements:* For master's, comprehensive exam (for some programs), registration. *Entrance requirements:* For master's, minimum undergraduate GPA of 2.75, 2 letters of recommendation, computer competency. Additional exam requirements/recommendations for international students: Required—TOEFL (minimum score 550 paper-based; 213 computer-based). *Application deadline:* Applications are processed on a rolling basis. Application fee: $30. Electronic applications accepted. *Expenses: Contact institution.* Part-time tuition and fees

Secondary Education

University of St. Francis (continued)

vary according to campus/location and program. *Financial support:* In 2006–07, 272 students received support. Scholarships/grants, tuition waivers (partial), and unspecified assistantships available. Support available to part-time students. Financial award applicants required to submit FAFSA. *Unit head:* Dr. John Gambro, Dean, 815-740-3456, Fax: 815-740-2264, E-mail: jgambro@stfrancis.edu. *Application contact:* Sandra Sloka, Director of Admissions for Graduate and Degree Completion Programs, 800-735-7500, Fax: 815-740-5032, E-mail: ssloka@stfrancis.edu.

The University of Scranton, Graduate School, Department of Education, Program in Secondary Education, Scranton, PA 18510. Offers MS. *Accreditation:* NCATE. Part-time and evening/weekend programs available. *Students:* 18 full-time (10 women), 9 part-time (5 women). Average age 28. 19 applicants, 100% accepted. In 2006, 7 degrees awarded. *Degree requirements:* For master's, capstone experience. *Entrance requirements:* For master's, minimum GPA of 2.75. Additional exam requirements/recommendations for international students: Required—TOEFL (minimum score 500 paper-based; 173 computer-based), IELTS (minimum score 6). *Application deadline:* Applications are processed on a rolling basis. Application fee: $50. *Expenses:* Tuition: Part-time $684 per credit. Required fees: $25 per term. *Financial support:* Teaching assistantships, career-related internships or fieldwork, Federal Work-Study, and unspecified assistantships available. Support available to part-time students. Financial award application deadline: 3/1. *Unit head:* Dr. Derry Stufft, Director, 570-941-7421, Fax: 570-941-7401, E-mail: stufftda@scranton.edu.

University of South Alabama, Graduate School, College of Education, Department of Leadership and Teacher Education, Mobile, AL 36688-0002. Offers early childhood education (M Ed); educational administration (Ed S); educational leadership (M Ed); elementary education (M Ed); reading education (M Ed); science education (M Ed); secondary education (M Ed); special education (M Ed, Ed S). *Accreditation:* NCATE. Part-time programs available. *Faculty:* 22 full-time (13 women). *Students:* 287 full-time (251 women), 229 part-time (194 women); includes 137 minority (125 African Americans, 8 American Indian/Alaska Native, 3 Asian Americans or Pacific Islanders, 1 Hispanic American), 4 international. 43 applicants, 84% accepted, 20 enrolled. In 2006, 169 master's, 12 other advanced degrees awarded. *Degree requirements:* For master's, comprehensive exam. *Entrance requirements:* For master's, GRE General Test or MAT, minimum GPA of 3.0. *Application deadline:* For fall admission, 9/1 priority date for domestic students. Applications are processed on a rolling basis. Application fee: $25. *Financial support:* In 2006–07, 6 research assistantships were awarded; career-related internships or fieldwork also available. Support available to part-time students. Financial award application deadline: 4/1. *Unit head:* Dr. David L. Gray, Chair, 251-380-2894.

University of South Carolina, The Graduate School, College of Education, Department of Instruction and Teacher Education, Program in Secondary Education, Columbia, SC 29208. Offers art education (IMA, MAT); business education (IMA, MAT); English (MAT); foreign language (MAT); health education (MAT); mathematics (IMA, MAT); science (IMA, MAT); secondary education (M Ed, MA, MT, PhD); social studies (IMA, MAT); theatre and speech (IMA, MAT). IMA and MT offered jointly with the subject areas. *Accreditation:* NCATE. *Degree requirements:* For master's, thesis (for some programs), foreign language (MA), comprehensive exam; for doctorate, one foreign language, thesis/dissertation, comprehensive exam. *Entrance requirements:* For master's, GRE General Test or MAT, teaching certificate (IMA, M Ed), interview; for doctorate, GRE General Test or MAT, interview. *Faculty research:* Middle school programs, professional development, school collaboration.

The University of South Dakota, Graduate School, School of Education, Division of Curriculum and Instruction, Program in Secondary Education, Vermillion, SD 57069-2390. Offers MA. *Accreditation:* NCATE. Part-time programs available. Postbaccalaureate distance learning degree programs offered. *Students:* 14 (8 women). In 2006, 12 degrees awarded. *Degree requirements:* For master's, thesis or alternative, comprehensive exam. *Entrance requirements:* For master's, GRE General Test, MAT, minimum GPA of 2.7. Additional exam requirements/recommendations for international students: Required—TOEFL (minimum score 550 paper-based; 213 computer-based; 79 iBT). *Application deadline:* Applications are processed on a rolling basis. Application fee: $35. Electronic applications accepted. *Expenses:* Tuition, state resident: part-time $120 per credit hour. Tuition, nonresident: part-time $355 per credit hour. Required fees: $90 per credit hour. *Financial support:* In 2006–07, research assistantships with partial tuition reimbursements (averaging $4,626 per year), teaching assistantships with partial tuition reimbursements (averaging $4,626 per year) were awarded; career-related internships or fieldwork, Federal Work-Study, and unspecified assistantships also available. Financial award applicants required to submit FAFSA.

University of Southern Indiana, Graduate Studies, College of Education and Human Services, Department of Teacher Education, Program in Secondary Education, Evansville, IN 47712-3590. Offers MS. *Accreditation:* NCATE. Part-time and evening/weekend programs available. *Faculty:* 13 full-time (5 women), 4 part-time/adjunct (1 woman). *Students:* 5 full-time (4 women), 58 part-time (37 women); includes 2 minority (1 Asian American or Pacific Islander, 1 Hispanic American), 3 international. Average age 34. 27 applicants, 100% accepted, 16 enrolled. In 2006, 21 degrees awarded. *Entrance requirements:* For master's, GRE General Test, NTE or Praxis I, minimum GPA of 3.0, teaching license. Additional exam requirements/recommendations for international students: Required—TOEFL (minimum score 500 paper-based; 173 computer-based). *Application deadline:* For fall admission, 7/1 priority date for domestic students, 1/1 priority date for international students. Applications are processed on a rolling basis. Application fee: $25. *Expenses:* Tuition, state resident: full-time $3,888; part-time $216 per credit hour. Tuition, nonresident: full-time $7,688; part-time $426 per credit hour. Required fees: $220; $23 per term. Tuition and fees vary according to course load and reciprocity agreements. *Financial support:* In 2006–07, 16 students received support. Federal Work-Study, institutionally sponsored loans, scholarships/grants, tuition waivers (full and partial), and unspecified assistantships available. Financial award application deadline: 3/1; financial award applicants required to submit FAFSA. *Unit head:* Dr. Michael L. Slavkin, Coordinator, 812-465-1858, E-mail: mslavkin@usi.edu.

University of Southern Mississippi, Graduate School, College of Education and Psychology, Department of Curriculum, Instruction, and Special Education, Hattiesburg, MS 39406-0001. Offers alternative secondary teacher education (MAT); early childhood education (M Ed, Ed S); education of the gifted (M Ed, Ed D, PhD, Ed S); elementary education (M Ed, Ed D, PhD, Ed S); reading (M Ed, MS, Ed S); secondary education (M Ed, MS, Ed D, PhD, Ed S); special education (M Ed, Ed D, PhD, Ed S). *Faculty:* 16 full-time (11 women). *Students:* 31 full-time (28 women), 54 part-time (51 women); includes 5 minority (4 African Americans, 1 Hispanic American), 1 international. Average age 35. 59 applicants, 27% accepted, 11 enrolled. In 2006, 43 master's, 3 doctorates, 4 other advanced degrees awarded. *Degree requirements:* For master's, thesis (for some programs), comprehensive exam, registration; for doctorate and Ed S, thesis/dissertation, comprehensive exam, registration. *Entrance requirements:* For master's, GRE General Test, MAT, minimum GPA of 3.0; for doctorate, GRE General Test, minimum GPA of 3.5; for Ed S, GRE General Test, MAT, minimum GPA of 3.25. Additional exam requirements/recommendations for international students: Required—TOEFL. *Application deadline:* For fall admission, 3/1 priority date for domestic students, 3/1 for international students. Applications are processed on a rolling basis. Application fee: $25 ($30 for international students). *Financial support:* In 2006–07, 10 research assistantships with full tuition reimbursements (averaging $22,333 per year), 2 teaching assistantships with full tuition reimbursements (averaging $22,333 per year) were awarded; Federal Work-Study, institutionally sponsored loans, and tuition waivers (partial) also available. Financial award application deadline: 3/15. *Faculty research:* Mathematical problem solving, integrative curriculum, writing process, teacher education models. Total annual research expenditures: $100,000. *Unit head:* Dr. Dana Thames, Chair, 601-266-4547, Fax: 601-266-4175. *Application contact:* B.J. Davis, Administrative Assistant, 601-266-6987, Fax: 601-266-4548.

University of South Florida, Graduate School, College of Education, Department of Secondary Education, Tampa, FL 33620-9951. Offers English education (M Ed, MA, PhD); foreign language education (M Ed, MA); instructional technology (M Ed); mathematics education (M Ed, MA, PhD, Ed S); middle school education (M Ed); science education (M Ed, MA, MAT, PhD); second language acquisition/instructional technology (PhD); secondary education (PhD); social science education (M Ed, MA). *Accreditation:* NCATE. Part-time and evening/weekend programs available. *Faculty:* 29 full-time (16 women), 15 part-time/adjunct (8 women). *Students:* 136 full-time (95 women), 279 part-time (188 women); includes 85 minority (35 African Americans, 1 American Indian/Alaska Native, 13 Asian Americans or Pacific Islanders, 36 Hispanic Americans), 19 international. 212 applicants, 71% accepted, 96 enrolled. In 2006, 87 master's, 12 doctorates awarded. *Entrance requirements:* For master's and doctorate, GRE General Test, minimum GPA of 3.5; for Ed S, GRE General Test. *Application deadline:* For fall admission, 6/1 for domestic students; for spring admission, 10/15 for domestic students. Application fee: $30. Electronic applications accepted. *Financial support:* Scholarships/grants and unspecified assistantships available. Total annual research expenditures: $477,202. *Unit head:* Dr. Jane H. Applegate, Interim Chairperson, 813-974-3533, Fax: 813-974-3837, E-mail: applegat@tempest.coedu.usf.edu.

The University of Tennessee, Graduate School, College of Education, Health and Human Sciences, Program in Education, Knoxville, TN 37996. Offers art education (MS); counseling education (PhD); cultural studies in education (PhD); curriculum (MS, Ed S); curriculum, educational research and evaluation (Ed D, PhD); early childhood education (PhD); early childhood special education (MS); education of deaf and hard of hearing (MS); educational administration and policy studies (Ed D, PhD); educational administration and supervision (Ed S); educational psychology (Ed D, PhD); elementary education (MS, Ed S); elementary teaching (MS); English education (MS, Ed S); exercise science (PhD); foreign language/ESL education (MS, Ed S); instructional technology (MS, Ed D, PhD, Ed S); literacy, language and ESL education (PhD); literacy, language education, and ESL education (Ed D); mathematics education (MS, Ed S); modified and comprehensive special education (MS); reading education (MS, Ed S); school counseling (Ed S); school psychology (PhD, Ed S); science education (MS, Ed S); secondary teaching (MS); social foundations (MS); social science education (MS, Ed S); socio-cultural foundations of sports and education (PhD); special education (Ed S); teacher education (Ed D, PhD). *Accreditation:* NCATE. Part-time and evening/weekend programs available. *Students:* 529 (401 women); includes 39 minority (23 African Americans, 2 American Indian/Alaska Native, 9 Asian Americans or Pacific Islanders, 5 Hispanic Americans) 34 international. 420 applicants, 50% accepted. In 2006, 258 master's, 28 doctorates awarded. *Degree requirements:* For master's and Ed S, thesis optional; for doctorate, variable foreign language requirement, thesis/dissertation. *Entrance requirements:* For master's, minimum GPA of 2.7; for doctorate and Ed S, GRE General Test, minimum GPA of 2.7. Additional exam requirements/recommendations for international students: Required—TOEFL. *Application deadline:* For fall admission, 2/1 priority date for domestic students. Applications are processed on a rolling basis. Application fee: $35. Electronic applications accepted. *Expenses:* Tuition, state resident: full-time $5,574. Tuition, nonresident: full-time $16,840. Required fees: $792. *Financial support:* In 2006–07, 4 fellowships, 9 teaching assistantships were awarded; career-related internships or fieldwork, Federal Work-Study, institutionally sponsored loans, and unspecified assistantships also available. Financial award application deadline: 2/1; financial award applicants required to submit FAFSA. *Unit head:* Dr. Lester Knight, Head, 865-974-0907, Fax: 865-974-8718, E-mail: lknight@utk.edu.

The University of Tennessee at Chattanooga, Graduate School, College of Health, Education and Professional Studies, Graduate Studies Division of Education, Chattanooga, TN 37403-2598. Offers counseling (M Ed); educational leadership (Ed D); educational specialist (Ed S), including educational technology, school psychology; elementary education (M Ed); school leadership (M Ed); secondary education (M Ed); special education (M Ed). *Accreditation:* ACA; NCATE. Part-time and evening/weekend programs available. *Faculty:* 28 full-time (18 women), 7 part-time/adjunct (3 women). *Students:* 166 full-time (123 women), 309 part-time (238 women); includes 57 minority (46 African Americans, 2 American Indian/Alaska Native, 7 Asian Americans or Pacific Islanders, 2 Hispanic Americans). Average age 33. 138 applicants, 95% accepted, 66 enrolled. In 2006, 133 master's, 25 other advanced degrees awarded. *Degree requirements:* For master's, thesis optional; for doctorate, thesis/dissertation, comprehensive exam. *Entrance requirements:* For master's, GRE General Test or MAT, teaching certificate. *Application deadline:* For fall admission, 8/1 for domestic students; for spring admission, 12/1 for domestic students. Applications are processed on a rolling basis. Application fee: $30. *Expenses:* Tuition, state resident: full-time $5,434; part-time $339 per hour. Tuition, nonresident: full-time $14,830; part-time $861 per hour. Required fees: $940; $178 per hour. *Financial support:* Fellowships, research assistantships, Federal Work-Study and institutionally sponsored loans available. Support available to part-time students. Financial award application deadline: 4/1; financial award applicants required to submit FAFSA. *Faculty research:* School counseling, community counseling, elementary and secondary education, school leadership and administration. Total annual research expenditures: $258,901. *Unit head:* Dr. Anthony Lease, Head, 423-425-4211, Fax: 423-425-5380, E-mail: tony-lease@utc.edu. *Application contact:* Dr. Deborah E. Arfken, Dean of Graduate Studies, 423-425-4666, Fax: 423-425-5223, E-mail: deborah-arfken@utc.edu.

The University of Tennessee at Martin, Graduate Programs, College of Education and Behavioral Sciences, Program in Teaching, Martin, TN 38238-1000. Offers advanced elementary (MS Ed); advanced secondary (MS Ed); initial licensure comprehensive (MS Ed); initial licensure elementary (MS Ed); initial licensure secondary (MS Ed). Part-time programs available. *Students:* 176 (129 women); includes 28 African Americans. 69 applicants, 71% accepted, 34 enrolled. In 2006, 46 degrees awarded. *Degree requirements:* For master's, comprehensive exam. *Entrance requirements:* For master's, GRE General Test, minimum GPA of 2.5. Additional exam requirements/recommendations for international students: Required—TOEFL (minimum score 525 paper-based; 197 computer-based). *Application deadline:* For fall admission, 8/1 priority date for domestic students, 8/1 for international students; for spring admission, 1/1 priority date for domestic students, 1/1 for international students. Applications are processed on a rolling basis. Application fee: $30 ($50 for international students). Electronic applications accepted. *Expenses:* Tuition, state resident: part-time $303 per credit hour. Tuition, nonresident: part-time $829 per credit hour. *Financial support:* Research assistantships with full tuition reimbursements, teaching assistantships with full tuition reimbursements, career-related internships or fieldwork, scholarships/grants, tuition waivers (partial), and unspecified assistantships available. Financial award application deadline: 3/1. *Faculty research:* Special education, science/math/technology, school reform, reading. *Unit head:* Dr. Suzanne Maniss, Coordinator, 731-881-7163, Fax: 731-881-7975, E-mail: smaniss@utm.edu.

The University of Texas at Tyler, College of Education and Psychology, Department of Curriculum and Instruction, Tyler, TX 75799-0001. Offers curriculum and instruction (M Ed); secondary teaching (MAT), including art, biology, computer science, English, history, journalism, mathematics, music, political science, sociology, speech, theatre. Part-time programs available. *Faculty:* 10 full-time (6 women), 2 part-time/adjunct (1 woman). *Students:* 3 full-time (2 women), 7 part-time (6 women); includes 1 minority (African American) Average age 32. 1 applicant, 100% accepted, 1 enrolled. In 2006, 6 degrees awarded. *Degree requirements:* For master's, research project (M Ed). *Entrance requirements:* For master's, GRE or MAT. Application fee: $0 ($50 for international students). Electronic applications accepted. *Expenses:* Tuition, state resident: part-time $50 per credit hour. Tuition, nonresident: part-time $328 per credit hour. Required fees: $107 per credit hour. $426 per term. *Financial support:* Scholarships/grants available. *Unit head:* Dr. Robert Stevens, Chair/Professor of Education, 903-566-7315, E-mail: rstevens@uttyler.edu. *Application contact:* Bonnie Purser, Office of Graduate Studies, 903-566-7142, Fax: 903-566-7068, E-mail: bpurser@uttyler.edu.

The University of Texas–Pan American, College of Education, Department of Curriculum and Instruction: Elementary and Secondary, Edinburg, TX 78541-2999. Offers bilingual education (M Ed); early childhood education (M Ed); elementary education (M Ed); reading (M Ed); secondary education (M Ed). Part-time programs available. *Degree requirements:* For master's, thesis optional. *Entrance requirements:* For master's, GRE. Additional exam requirements/recommendations for international students: Required—TOEFL, IELTS. *Expenses:* Tuition, state resident: full-time $2,577; part-time $143 per credit hour. Tuition, nonresident: full-time $7,527; part-time $418 per credit hour. Required fees: $561. *Faculty research:* Dual language instruction, literacy and technology, teacher education in diverse populations, mathematics and science education.

University of the Cumberlands, Graduate Programs in Education, Program in Elementary/Secondary Teaching, Williamsburg, KY 40769-1372. Offers MA Ed, MAT, Certificate. *Entrance requirements:* For degree, master's degree, 3 years of teaching experience.

University of the Cumberlands, Graduate Programs in Education, Program in Secondary General Education, Williamsburg, KY 40769-1372. Offers MA Ed, MAT. *Degree requirements:* For master's, comprehensive exam. *Entrance requirements:* For master's, GRE or NTE, Kentucky teaching certificate.

University of the Incarnate Word, School of Graduate Studies and Research, Dreeben School of Education, Program in Teaching, San Antonio, TX 78209-6397. Offers elementary teaching (MAT); secondary teaching (MAT). *Students:* 11 full-time (9 women), 90 part-time (64 women); includes 57 minority (8 African Americans, 2 Asian Americans or Pacific Islanders, 47 Hispanic Americans), 2 international. Average age 35. In 2006, 15 degrees awarded. Application fee: $20. *Expenses:* Tuition: Part-time $570 per credit hour. Required fees: $54 per credit hour. One-time fee: $195 part-time. Tuition and fees vary according to degree level. *Financial support:* Federal Work-Study and scholarships/grants available. *Unit head:* Dr. Elda Martinez, Director of Teacher Education, 210-832-3297, Fax: 210-829-3134, E-mail: eemartin@uiwtx.edu. *Application contact:* Andrea Cyterski-Acosta, Dean of Enrollment, 210-829-6005, Fax: 210-829-3921, E-mail: cyterski@uiwtx.edu.

The University of Toledo, College of Graduate Studies, College of Education, Department of Curriculum and Instruction, Program in Secondary Education, Toledo, OH 43606-3390. Offers ME, DE, PhD, Ed S. *Students:* 23 full-time (13 women), 18 part-time (11 women); includes 8 minority (4 African Americans, 1 Asian American or Pacific Islander, 3 Hispanic Americans). Average age 36. 12 applicants, 92% accepted, 6 enrolled. In 2006, 16 degrees awarded.

University of Utah, The Graduate School, College of Education, Department of Teaching and Learning, Salt Lake City, UT 84112-1107. Offers elementary education (MAT); secondary education (MAT); teaching and learning (M Ed, M Phil, MA, MS, PhD). Part-time and evening/weekend programs available. *Faculty:* 10 full-time (8 women). *Students:* 71 full-time (59 women), 109 part-time (88 women); includes 9 minority (1 American Indian/Alaska Native, 4 Asian Americans or Pacific Islanders, 4 Hispanic Americans), 1 international. Average age 35. 50 applicants, 62% accepted, 26 enrolled. In 2006, 100 master's, 3 doctorates awarded. *Degree requirements:* For master's, thesis optional; for doctorate, thesis/dissertation. *Entrance requirements:* For master's, GRE General Test or MAT, GRE Subject Test, minimum GPA of 3.0; for doctorate, GRE General Test, minimum graduate GPA of 3.5, minimum undergraduate GPA of 3.0. Additional exam requirements/recommendations for international students: Required—TOEFL (minimum score 500 paper-based; 173 computer-based). *Application deadline:* For fall admission, 3/1 for domestic students, 4/1 for international students; for spring admission, 10/15 for domestic students, 11/1 for international students. Applications are processed on a rolling basis. Application fee: $45 ($65 for international students). *Expenses:* Tuition, state resident: full-time $3,208. Tuition, nonresident: full-time $11,326. Required fees: $608. Tuition and fees vary according to class time and program. *Financial support:* Fellowships, research assistantships with full and partial tuition reimbursements, teaching assistantships with full and partial tuition reimbursements, career-related internships or fieldwork and tuition waivers (partial) available. Financial award application deadline: 2/1; financial award applicants required to submit FAFSA. *Faculty research:* Teacher development, teacher education, reading instruction, math instruction, technology. Total annual research expenditures: $1,111. *Unit head:* Lynne Schrum, Department Chair, 801-587-7800, Fax: 801-581-3609, E-mail: lynne.schrum@ed.utah.edu. *Application contact:* Becky Owen, Graduate Academic Program Specialist, 801-581-7158, Fax: 801-581-3609, E-mail: becky.owen@ed.utah.edu.

The University of West Alabama, School of Graduate Studies, College of Education, Department of Teacher Education, Program in Secondary Education, Livingston, AL 35470. Offers MAT. Part-time programs available. *Faculty:* 3 full-time (2 women), 13 part-time/adjunct (10 women). *Students:* 19 full-time (14 women), 20 part-time (15 women); includes 15 minority (14 African Americans, 1 American Indian/Alaska Native). In 2006, 29 degrees awarded. *Entrance requirements:* For master's, GRE General Test, MAT, minimum GPA of 2.75. *Application deadline:* For fall admission, 9/10 priority date for domestic students; for spring admission, 3/24 for domestic students. Applications are processed on a rolling basis. Application fee: $20 ($50 for international students). *Financial support:* Career-related internships or fieldwork, Federal Work-Study, scholarships/grants, and unspecified assistantships available. Support available to part-time students. *Faculty research:* Integrated arts into the curriculum, moral development of children.

University of West Florida, College of Professional Studies, Division of Teacher Education, Master's Program in Curriculum and Instruction, Specialization in Middle and Secondary Level Education, Pensacola, FL 32514-5750. Offers M Ed. *Accreditation:* NCATE. Part-time and evening/weekend programs available. *Students:* 39 full-time (29 women), 35 part-time (25 women); includes 29 minority (12 African Americans, 4 Asian Americans or Pacific Islanders, 13 Hispanic Americans). Average age 38. 27 applicants, 100% accepted, 27 enrolled. In 2006, 39 degrees awarded. *Degree requirements:* For master's, thesis or alternative. *Entrance requirements:* For master's, GRE General Test or minimum GPA of 3.0. Additional exam requirements/recommendations for international students: Required—TOEFL (minimum score 550 paper-based; 213 computer-based). *Application deadline:* For fall admission, 6/1 for domestic students, 5/15 for international students; for spring admission, 11/1 for domestic students, 10/1 for international students. Applications are processed on a rolling basis. Application fee: $30. *Expenses:* Tuition, state resident: full-time $5,871; part-time $245 per credit hour. Tuition, nonresident: full-time $21,241; part-time $885 per credit hour. *Financial support:* Fellowships, Federal Work-Study, scholarships/grants, and unspecified assistantships available.

University of West Georgia, Graduate School, College of Education, Department of Curriculum and Instruction, Program in Secondary Education—English, Carrollton, GA 30118. Offers M Ed, Ed S. *Accreditation:* NCATE. Part-time and evening/weekend programs available. *Students:* 1 (woman) full-time, 9 part-time (7 women); includes 1 minority (African American) Average age 34. In 2006, 2 master's, 4 other advanced degrees awarded. *Degree requirements:* For master's, comprehensive exam; for Ed S, research project. *Entrance requirements:* For master's, GRE General Test or MAT, minimum GPA of 2.7; for Ed S, GRE General Test or MAT, master's degree, minimum graduate GPA of 3.0. *Application deadline:* For fall admission, 8/1 for domestic students. Applications are processed on a rolling basis. Application fee: $20. *Expenses:* Tuition, state resident: full-time $2,286; part-time $127 per credit. Tuition, nonresident: full-time $9,144; part-time $508 per credit. Required fees: $494; $27 per credit. $121 per semester. *Financial support:* In 2006–07, research assistantships with full tuition reimbursements (averaging $3,000 per year); career-related internships or fieldwork, scholarships/grants, and unspecified assistantships also available. Support available to part-time students. Financial award applicants required to submit FAFSA. *Application contact:* Dr. Charles W. Clark, Chair, 678-839-6508, E-mail: cclark@westga.edu.

University of West Georgia, Graduate School, College of Education, Department of Curriculum and Instruction, Program in Secondary Education—Mathematics, Carrollton, GA 30118. Offers M Ed, Ed S. Part-time and evening/weekend programs available. *Students:* 4 full-time (2 women), 12 part-time (9 women). Average age 26. In 2006, 5 master's, 1 other advanced degree awarded. *Degree requirements:* For master's, comprehensive exam; for Ed S, research project. *Entrance requirements:* For master's and Ed S, GRE or MAT. *Application deadline:* For fall admission, 8/1 for domestic students. Applications are processed on a rolling basis. Application fee: $20. *Expenses:* Tuition, state resident: full-time $2,286; part-time $127 per credit. Tuition, nonresident: full-time $9,144; part-time $508 per credit. Required fees: $494; $27 per credit. $121 per semester. *Financial support:* In 2006–07, research assistantships with full tuition reimbursements (averaging $3,000 per year). Financial award applicants required to submit FAFSA. *Application contact:* Dr. Charles W. Clark, Chair, 678-839-6508, E-mail: cclark@westga.edu.

University of West Georgia, Graduate School, College of Education, Department of Curriculum and Instruction, Program in Secondary Education—Science, Carrollton, GA 30118. Offers M Ed, Ed S. Part-time and evening/weekend programs available. *Students:* 2 full-time (both women), 7 part-time (6 women); includes 1 minority (African American) Average age 33. In 2006, 3 master's, 2 other advanced degrees awarded. *Degree requirements:* For master's, comprehensive exam; for Ed S, research project. *Entrance requirements:* For master's and Ed S, GRE or MAT. *Application deadline:* For fall admission, 8/1 for domestic students. Applications are processed on a rolling basis. Application fee: $20. *Expenses:* Tuition, state resident: full-time $2,286; part-time $127 per credit. Tuition, nonresident: full-time $9,144; part-time $508 per credit. Required fees: $494; $27 per credit. $121 per semester. *Financial support:* In 2006–07, research assistantships with full tuition reimbursements (averaging $3,000 per year). Financial award applicants required to submit FAFSA. *Application contact:* Dr. Charles W. Clark, Chair, 678-839-6508, E-mail: cclark@westga.edu.

University of West Georgia, Graduate School, College of Education, Department of Curriculum and Instruction, Program in Secondary Education—Social Studies, Carrollton, GA 30118. Offers M Ed, Ed S. Part-time and evening/weekend programs available. *Students:* 1 full-time (0 women), 5 part-time (2 women); includes 1 minority (African American) Average age 20. In 2006, 3 master's, 1 other advanced degree awarded. *Degree requirements:* For master's, comprehensive exam; for Ed S, research project. *Entrance requirements:* For master's and Ed S, GRE or MAT. *Application deadline:* For fall admission, 8/1 for domestic students. Applications are processed on a rolling basis. Application fee: $20. *Expenses:* Tuition, state resident: full-time $2,286; part-time $127 per credit. Tuition, nonresident: full-time $9,144; part-time $508 per credit. Required fees: $494; $27 per credit. $121 per semester. *Financial support:* In 2006–07, research assistantships with full tuition reimbursements (averaging $3,000 per year). Financial award applicants required to submit FAFSA. *Application contact:* Dr. Charles W. Clark, Chair, 678-839-6508, E-mail: cclark@westga.edu.

University of Wisconsin–Eau Claire, College of Education and Human Sciences, Program in Secondary Education, Eau Claire, WI 54702-4004. Offers biology (MAT, MST); education and professional development (MEPD); English (MAT, MST); history (MAT, MST); mathematics (MAT, MST). *Faculty:* 9 full-time (6 women). *Students:* 10 full-time (7 women), 23 part-time (20 women), 1 international. Average age 33. 21 applicants, 57% accepted, 4 enrolled. In 2006, 22 degrees awarded. *Degree requirements:* For master's, thesis optional. *Entrance requirements:* For master's, 2 years of teaching experience or the equivalent. *Application deadline:* For fall admission, 7/1 for domestic students; for spring admission, 12/1 for domestic students. Applications are processed on a rolling basis. Application fee: $45. *Expenses:* Tuition, state resident: full-time $6,533; part-time $363 per credit. Tuition, nonresident: full-time $17,143; part-time $952 per credit. Tuition and fees vary according to program and reciprocity agreements. *Financial support:* In 2006–07, 17 students received support, including 2 teaching assistantships (averaging $5,200 per year); Federal Work-Study also available. Financial award application deadline: 3/1; financial award applicants required to submit FAFSA. *Unit head:* Dr. Tamara Lindsey, Chair, 715-836-4737, Fax: 715-836-4868, E-mail: lindsetp@uwec.edu.

University of Wisconsin–La Crosse, Office of University Graduate Studies, College of Liberal Studies, Department of Educational Studies, Program in Professional Development, La Crosse, WI 54601-3742. Offers elementary education (MEPD), including grades 1 through 6, grades 1 through 9; K–12 (MEPD); professional development (MEPD); secondary education (MEPD), including grades 6 through 12. Part-time programs available. *Students:* 26 full-time (18 women), 691 part-time (498 women); includes 20 minority (5 African Americans, 1 American Indian/Alaska Native, 10 Asian Americans or Pacific Islanders, 4 Hispanic Americans). Average age 32. 219 applicants, 93% accepted, 189 enrolled. In 2006, 221 degrees awarded. *Degree requirements:* For master's, thesis optional. *Entrance requirements:* For master's, PPST, minimum GPA of 2.85; minimum cumulative GPA of 3.0 in subject area. Additional exam requirements/recommendations for international students: Required—TOEFL (minimum score 550 paper-based; 213 computer-based). *Application deadline:* Applications are processed on a rolling basis. Application fee: $45. Electronic applications accepted. *Financial support:* In 2006–07, 9 research assistantships with partial tuition reimbursements (averaging $8,109 per year) were awarded; career-related internships or fieldwork, Federal Work-Study, health care benefits, unspecified assistantships, and grant-funded positions also available. Support available to part-time students. Financial award application deadline: 3/15; financial award applicants required to submit FAFSA. *Faculty research:* Professional development, adult learning theory, transformative learning, learning in community, teacher leadership. *Unit head:* Dr. Teri Staloch, Director, 608-785-8146, Fax: 608-785-6560, E-mail: staloch.teri@uwlax.edu. *Application contact:* Kathryn Kiefer, Associate Director of Admissions, 608-785-8939, E-mail: admissions@uwlax.edu.

University of Wisconsin–Milwaukee, Graduate School, School of Education, Department of Curriculum and Instruction, Milwaukee, WI 53201-0413. Offers curriculum planning and instruction improvement (MS); early childhood education (MS); elementary education (MS); junior high/middle school education (MS); reading education (MS); secondary education (MS); teaching in an urban setting (MS). Part-time programs available. *Faculty:* 27 full-time (17 women). *Students:* 21 full-time (17 women), 67 part-time (54 women); includes 15 minority (8 African Americans, 3 Asian Americans or Pacific Islanders, 4 Hispanic Americans), 3 international. 44 applicants, 43% accepted, 19 enrolled. In 2006, 38 degrees awarded. *Degree requirements:* For master's, thesis or alternative. *Application deadline:* For fall admission, 1/1 priority date for domestic students; for spring admission, 9/1 for domestic students. Applications are processed on a rolling basis. Application fee: $45 ($75 for international students). *Expenses:* Tuition, state resident: part-time $510 per credit. Tuition, nonresident: part-time $1,408 per credit. Tuition and fees vary according to program. *Financial support:* Fellowships, research assistantships, teaching assistantships, career-related internships or fieldwork and unspecified assistantships available. Support available to part-time students. Financial award application deadline: 4/15. *Unit head:* Linda Post, Chair, 414-229-4884, Fax: 414-229-5571, E-mail: lpost@uwm.edu.

University of Wisconsin–Platteville, School of Graduate Studies, College of Liberal Arts and Education, School of Education, Platteville, WI 53818-3099. Offers adult education (MSE); elementary education (MSE); middle school education (MSE); secondary education (MSE); vocational and technical education (MSE). *Accreditation:* NCATE. Part-time programs available. *Faculty:* 8 part-time/adjunct (3 women). *Students:* 48 full-time (37 women), 103 part-time (72 women); includes 33 minority (27 African Americans, 1 Asian American or Pacific Islander, 5 Hispanic Americans), 39 international. 39 applicants, 72% accepted. In 2006, 55 degrees awarded. *Degree requirements:* For master's, thesis or alternative, comprehensive exam, registration. *Entrance requirements:* Additional exam requirements/recommendations for international students: Required—TOEFL (minimum score 500 paper-based; 173 computer-based). *Application deadline:* For fall admission, 7/1 priority date for domestic students; for spring admission, 11/1 for domestic students. Applications are processed on a rolling basis. Application fee: $45. Electronic applications accepted. *Expenses:* Tuition, state resident: part-time $365 per credit. Tuition, nonresident: part-time $955 per credit. *Financial support:* Research assistantships with partial tuition reimbursements, career-related internships or fieldwork, Federal Work-Study, institutionally sponsored loans, scholarships/grants, and unspecified assistantships available. Support available to part-time students. *Unit head:* Dr. Michael Anderson, Director, 608-342-1131, Fax: 608-342-1133, E-mail: andersonmi@uwplatt.edu. *Application contact:* Kristal Prohaska, Admissions and Enrollment Management, 608-342-1125, Fax: 608-342-1122, E-mail: admit@uwplatt.edu.

Secondary Education

University of Wisconsin–Whitewater, School of Graduate Studies, College of Business and Economics, Department of Business Education, Whitewater, WI 53190-1790. Offers general business education (MS); post-secondary business education (MS); secondary business education (MS). *Accreditation:* NCATE. Part-time and evening/weekend programs available. Post-baccalaureate distance learning degree programs offered (no on-campus study). *Students:* 5 full-time (1 woman), 14 part-time (10 women); includes 1 minority (African American) Average age 33. 8 applicants, 75% accepted, 4 enrolled. In 2006, 11 degrees awarded. *Degree requirements:* For master's, thesis or alternative. *Entrance requirements:* For master's, interview, teaching license. Additional exam requirements/recommendations for international students: Required—TOEFL (minimum score 550 paper-based; 213 computer-based). *Application deadline:* For fall admission, 7/15 priority date for domestic and international students; for spring admission, 12/1 priority date for domestic and international students. Applications are processed on a rolling basis. Application fee: $45. Electronic applications accepted. *Expenses:* Tuition, state resident: full-time $3,311. Tuition, nonresident: full-time $8,616. Required fees: $368 per credit. *Financial support:* In 2006–07, 2 research assistantships (averaging $7,385 per year) were awarded; Federal Work-Study, unspecified assistantships, and out of state fee waiver also available. Support available to part-time students. Financial award application deadline: 3/15; financial award applicants required to submit FAFSA. *Faculty research:* Active learning and performance strategies, technology-enhanced formative assessment, computer-supported cooperative work, privacy surveillance. *Unit head:* Dr. Lila Waldman, Coordinator, 262-472-5475. *Application contact:* Sally A. Lange, School of Graduate Studies, 262-472-1006, Fax: 262-472-5027, E-mail: gradschl@uww.edu.

Utah State University, School of Graduate Studies, College of Education and Human Services, Department of Secondary Education, Logan, UT 84322. Offers M Ed, MA, MS. *Accreditation:* NCATE. Part-time and evening/weekend programs available. *Faculty:* 9 full-time (7 women). *Students:* 17 full-time (11 women), 16 part-time (10 women), 2 international. Average age 33. 57 applicants, 68% accepted, 30 enrolled. In 2006, 10 degrees awarded. *Degree requirements:* For master's, thesis (for some programs). *Entrance requirements:* For master's, GRE General Test or MAT, minimum GPA of 3.0, 1 year teaching, teaching license, transcripts, letters of recommendation. Additional exam requirements/recommendations for international students: Required—TOEFL. *Application deadline:* Applications are processed on a rolling basis. Application fee: $50 ($60 for international students). Electronic applications accepted. *Financial support:* In 2006–07, fellowships with partial tuition reimbursements (averaging $12,000 per year), 2 teaching assistantships with partial tuition reimbursements (averaging $12,000 per year) were awarded; research assistantships with partial tuition reimbursements, career-related internships or fieldwork and tuition waivers (partial) also available. Financial award application deadline: 4/15. *Faculty research:* Character education, science education, reading/writing skills, mathematics education, pre-service teacher education. Total annual research expenditures: $153,162. *Unit head:* Dr. Martha T. Deever, Head, 435-797-2225, Fax: 435-797-1441, E-mail: martha.deever@usu.edu.

Valdosta State University, Graduate School, College of Education, Department of Middle Grades and Secondary Education, Valdosta, GA 31698. Offers middle grades education (M Ed, Ed S); secondary education (M Ed, Ed S). *Accreditation:* NCATE. Part-time and evening/weekend programs available. *Degree requirements:* For master's, thesis (for some programs), comprehensive written and/or oral exams; for Ed S, thesis. *Entrance requirements:* For master's, GRE General Test or MAT, minimum GPA of 2.5; for Ed S, GRE General Test or MAT, minimum GPA of 3.0. Additional exam requirements/recommendations for international students: Required—TOEFL (minimum score 523 paper-based; 193 computer-based). Electronic applications accepted. *Faculty research:* Distance education, learning styles, alternative assessment methods, interactive teaching strategies, learning styles of pre-service teachers.

Vanderbilt University, Peabody College, Department of Teaching and Learning, Nashville, TN 37240-1001. Offers curriculum and instructional leadership (M Ed); early childhood education (M Ed); early childhood leadership (Ed D); elementary education (M Ed); English education (M Ed); English language learners (M Ed); mathematics education (M Ed); reading education (M Ed); science education (M Ed); secondary education (M Ed). *Accreditation:* NCATE. *Faculty:* 23 full-time (13 women), 28 part-time/adjunct (19 women). *Students:* 71 full-time (62 women), 21 part-time (15 women); includes 9 minority (8 African Americans, 1 Hispanic American), 2 international. Average age 27. 102 applicants, 60% accepted, 27 enrolled. In 2006, 53 master's, 3 doctorates awarded. *Degree requirements:* For master's, thesis optional. *Entrance requirements:* For master's, GRE General Test, MAT. Additional exam requirements/recommendations for international students: Required—TOEFL (minimum score 550 paper-based; 213 computer-based). *Application deadline:* For fall admission, 12/31 priority date for domestic and international students; for spring admission, 11/1 priority date for domestic and international students. Applications are processed on a rolling basis. Application fee: $0. Electronic applications accepted. *Expenses:* Tuition: Full-time $24,462. Required fees: $2,515. One-time fee: $30 full-time. Full-time tuition and fees vary according to course load, degree level and program. *Financial support:* In 2006–07, 62 students received support, including 36 fellowships with full and partial tuition reimbursements available, 13 research assistantships with full and partial tuition reimbursements available, 13 teaching assistantships with full and partial tuition reimbursements available; Federal Work-Study, institutionally sponsored loans, scholarships/grants, tuition waivers (partial), and unspecified assistantships also available. Support available to part-time students. Financial award application deadline: 2/1; financial award applicants required to submit FAFSA. *Faculty research:* Teaching and learning; development of subject matter knowledge; learning and policy; development students' mathematical and scientific knowledge, development of literacy. *Unit head:* Leona Schauble, Chair, 615-322-8100, Fax: 615-322-8999, E-mail: leona.schauble@vanderbilt.edu. *Application contact:* Angela Saylor, Educational Coordinator, 615-322-8092, Fax: 615-322-8999.

Villanova University, Graduate School of Liberal Arts and Sciences, Department of Education and Human Services, Program in Secondary Teacher Education, Villanova, PA 19085-1699. Offers MA. Part-time and evening/weekend programs available. *Students:* 2 full-time (both women), 31 part-time (23 women); includes 1 minority (Hispanic American) Average age 28. In 2006, 22 degrees awarded. *Degree requirements:* For master's, comprehensive exam. *Entrance requirements:* For master's, GRE or MAT, minimum GPA of 3.0. *Application deadline:* For fall admission, 8/1 priority date for domestic students; for spring admission, 12/1 for domestic students. Applications are processed on a rolling basis. Application fee: $50. Electronic applications accepted. *Expenses:* Tuition: Part-time $565 per credit. *Financial support:* Career-related internships or fieldwork and Federal Work-Study available. Financial award applicants required to submit FAFSA. *Unit head:* Fr. Robert Murray, Coordinator, 610-519-4620.

Virginia Commonwealth University, Graduate School, School of Education, Program in Teaching and Learning, Richmond, VA 23284-9005. Offers early education (MT); middle education (MT); secondary education (MT, Certificate); special education (MT). *Accreditation:* NCATE. Part-time programs available. *Faculty:* 22 full-time (12 women). *Students:* 152 full-time (130 women), 126 part-time (111 women); includes 42 minority (35 African Americans, 2 American Indian/Alaska Native, 4 Asian Americans or Pacific Islanders, 1 Hispanic American), 4 international. 551 applicants, 74% accepted. In 2006, 77 degrees awarded. *Entrance requirements:* For master's, GRE General Test or MAT. *Application deadline:* For fall admission, 5/15 for domestic students; for spring admission, 11/15 for domestic students. Applications are processed on a rolling basis. Application fee: $50. *Financial support:* Application deadline: 3/1. *Unit head:* Dr. Michael D. Davis, Director, Graduate Studies, 804-828-6530, Fax: 804-827-0676, E-mail: mddavis@vcu.edu. *Application contact:* Dr. Michael D. Davis, Director, Graduate Studies, 804-828-6530, Fax: 804-827-0676, E-mail: mddavis@vcu.edu.

See Close-Up on page 1137.

Wagner College, Division of Graduate Studies, Department of Education, Program in Adolescent Education, Staten Island, NY 10301-4495. Offers MS Ed. Part-time and evening/weekend programs available. *Students:* 17 full-time (3 women), 4 part-time (2 women); includes 1 Asian American or Pacific Islander. 11 applicants, 100% accepted, 9 enrolled. In 2006, 11 degrees awarded. *Entrance requirements:* For master's, Liberal Arts and Sciences Test (LAST), New York State Teacher Certification Examinations (NYSTCE), minimum GPA of 2.75. Additional exam requirements/recommendations for international students: Required—TOEFL (minimum score 550 paper-based; 217 computer-based). *Application deadline:* For fall admission, 8/1 priority date for domestic students, 6/30 priority date for international students; for spring admission, 12/10 for domestic students, 11/15 for international students. Applications are processed on a rolling basis. Application fee: $50 ($85 for international students). *Expenses:* Tuition: Full-time $15,120; part-time $840 per credit. *Financial support:* Fellowships, tuition waivers (partial) and unspecified assistantships available. *Application contact:* Susan Rosenberg, Office of Graduate Studies, 718-390-3106, Fax: 718-390-3456, E-mail: graduate@wagner.edu.

Wake Forest University, Graduate School, Department of Education, Winston-Salem, NC 27109. Offers secondary education (MA Ed). *Accreditation:* ACA; NCATE. Part-time programs available. *Faculty:* 6 full-time (3 women), 5 part-time/adjunct (2 women). *Students:* 27 full-time (21 women), 15 part-time (12 women); includes 15 minority (7 African Americans, 1 Asian American or Pacific Islander, 7 Hispanic Americans). Average age 28. 76 applicants, 46% accepted, 35 enrolled. In 2006, 35 degrees awarded. *Degree requirements:* For master's, thesis optional. *Entrance requirements:* For master's, GRE General Test. Additional exam requirements/recommendations for international students: Required—TOEFL (minimum score 550 paper-based; 213 computer-based). *Application deadline:* For fall admission, 1/15 for domestic students, 1/15 priority date for international students. Application fee: $45 ($55 for international students). Electronic applications accepted. *Expenses:* Contact institution. *Financial support:* In 2006–07, 26 students received support, including 22 fellowships with full tuition reimbursements available (averaging $6,000 per year), 4 teaching assistantships with full tuition reimbursements available (averaging $7,000 per year); scholarships/grants and tuition waivers (full) also available. Support available to part-time students. Financial award application deadline: 2/15. *Faculty research:* Cognitive development, teacher performance appraisal, reading styles, teaching assessment and epistemology, reading achievement with heterogeneous classes. Total annual research expenditures: $37,603. *Unit head:* Dr. MaryLynn Redmond, Chairperson, 336-758-5341, Fax: 336-758-4591, E-mail: redmond@wfu.edu. *Application contact:* Linda Dunlap, Certification Officer, 336-758-5990, Fax: 336-758-4591, E-mail: dunlaplb@wfu.edu.

Washington State University, Graduate School, College of Education, Department of Teaching and Learning, Pullman, WA 99164. Offers curriculum and instruction (Ed D, PhD); diverse languages (M Ed, MA); elementary education (M Ed, MA, MIT); exercise science (MS); literacy education (M Ed, MA, PhD); math education (PhD); secondary education (M Ed, MA). *Accreditation:* NCATE. *Faculty:* 27. *Students:* 54 full-time (43 women), 20 part-time (14 women); includes 13 minority (4 African Americans, 2 American Indian/Alaska Native, 2 Asian Americans or Pacific Islanders, 5 Hispanic Americans), 5 international. Average age 34. 244 applicants, 16% accepted, 11 enrolled. In 2006, 20 master's, 3 doctorates awarded. *Degree requirements:* For master's, thesis (for some programs), oral or written exam, comprehensive exam (for some programs); for doctorate, thesis/dissertation, oral, written exam, comprehensive exam. *Entrance requirements:* For master's and doctorate, GRE General Test, minimum GPA of 3.0, 3 letters of recommendation. Additional exam requirements/recommendations for international students: Required—TOEFL. *Application deadline:* For fall admission, 2/1 for domestic students, 3/1 for international students; for spring admission, 9/1 for domestic students, 7/1 for international students. Applications are processed on a rolling basis. Application fee: $50. *Expenses:* Tuition, state resident: full-time $7,066. Tuition, nonresident: full-time $17,204. *Financial support:* In 2006–07, 13 research assistantships with partial tuition reimbursements (averaging $13,917 per year), 22 teaching assistantships with partial tuition reimbursements (averaging $13,056 per year) were awarded; career-related internships or fieldwork, Federal Work-Study, institutionally sponsored loans, tuition waivers (partial), unspecified assistantships, and staff assistantships, teaching associateships also available. Financial award application deadline: 4/1. *Faculty research:* Evolution of middle school education issues in special education, computer-assisted language learning. Total annual research expenditures: $1.1 million. *Unit head:* Dr. Corinne Mantle-Bromley, Chair, 509-335-5027. *Application contact:* Graduate School Admissions, 800-GRADWSU, Fax: 509-335-1949, E-mail: gradsch@wsu.edu.

Washington State University Tri-Cities, Graduate Programs, Program in Education, Richland, WA 99352-1671. Offers counseling (Ed M); educational leadership (Ed M, Ed D); literacy (Ed M); secondary certification (Ed M); teaching (MIT). Part-time programs available. *Faculty:* 23. *Students:* 27 full-time (20 women), 82 part-time (68 women); includes 11 minority (all Hispanic Americans) Average age 36. 77 applicants, 71% accepted, 34 enrolled. *Degree requirements:* For master's, thesis or alternative, comprehensive exam, registration; for doctorate, thesis/dissertation, comprehensive exam. *Entrance requirements:* For master's, GRE, minimum GPA of 3.0, Working with Youth form, Character and Fitness form, 3 letters of recommendation. Additional exam requirements/recommendations for international students: Required—TOEFL. *Application deadline:* For fall admission, 2/1 priority date for domestic students, 3/1 for international students; for spring admission, 9/1 priority date for domestic students, 7/1 for international students. Applications are processed on a rolling basis. Application fee: $50. Electronic applications accepted. *Expenses:* Tuition, state resident: full-time $7,066. Tuition, nonresident: full-time $17,204. *Financial support:* In 2006–07, 59 students received support, including 1 fellowship (averaging $7,950 per year), teaching assistantships (averaging $13,056 per year); Federal Work-Study, scholarships/grants, and unspecified assistantships also available. *Faculty research:* Multicultural counseling, socio-cultural influences in schools, diverse learners, teacher education, K-12 educational leadership. *Unit head:* Dr. Nancy Kyle, Director, 509-372-7396.

Washington University in St. Louis, Graduate School of Arts and Sciences, Department of Education, Program in Secondary Education, St. Louis, MO 63130-4899. Offers MA Ed, MAT. *Degree requirements:* For master's, thesis or alternative. *Entrance requirements:* For master's, GRE General Test or MAT. Electronic applications accepted.

Wayne State University, College of Education, Division of Administrative and Organizational Studies, Detroit, MI 48202. Offers administration and supervision-secondary (Ed S); college and university teaching (Certificate); curriculum and instruction (PhD); educational leadership (M Ed, Ed S); educational leadership and policy studies (Ed D, PhD); elementary education curriculum and instruction (MA, Ed S); general administration and supervision (Ed D, PhD, Ed S); higher education (Ed D, PhD); instructional technology (M Ed, Ed D, PhD, Ed S); secondary curriculum and instruction (M Ed, Ed S). *Faculty:* 24 full-time (13 women), 1 (woman) part-time/adjunct. *Students:* 153 full-time (103 women), 389 part-time (266 women); includes 252 minority (223 African Americans, 6 American Indian/Alaska Native, 8 Asian Americans or Pacific Islanders, 15 Hispanic Americans), 19 international. Average age 38. 138 applicants, 79% accepted, 74 enrolled. In 2006, 116 master's, 30 doctorates, 64 other advanced degrees awarded. *Degree requirements:* For doctorate, thesis/dissertation. *Entrance requirements:* For doctorate, interview, minimum GPA of 3.0. Additional exam requirements/recommendations for international students: Required—TOEFL (minimum score 550 paper-based; 213 computer-based), TWE (minimum score 6). *Application deadline:* For fall admission, 7/1 for domestic students, 6/1 for international students; for winter admission, 10/1 for international students; for spring admission, 2/1 for international students. Application fee: $30 ($50 for international students). Electronic applications accepted. *Financial support:* In 2006–07, 4 research assistantships (averaging $12,797 per year) were awarded; career-related internships or fieldwork, Federal Work-Study, and institutionally sponsored loans also available. Support available to part-time students. *Faculty research:* Total quality management, participatory management, administering educational technology, school improvement, principalship. Total annual research expenditures: $344,504. *Unit head:* Dr. JoAnne Holbert, Assistant Dean, 313-577-1721, E-mail: jholbert@wayne.edu.

Wayne State University, College of Education, Division of Teacher Education, Detroit, MI 48202. Offers adult and continuing education (M Ed); art education (M Ed); bilingual/bicultural education (M Ed, MAT); business education (M Ed, MAT); career and technical education (M Ed, Ed D, PhD, Ed S); curriculum and instruction (Ed D, PhD, Ed S); distributive education (M Ed, MAT); early childhood education (M Ed); elementary education (M Ed, MAT, Ed D, PhD, Ed S); elementary education curriculum and instruction (M Ed); English education (M Ed); English education-secondary (M Ed, Ed S); foreign language education (M Ed); general education (Ed D, Ed S); health occupations education (M Ed); industrial education (M Ed); mathematics education (M Ed, Ed S); pre-school and parent education (M Ed); reading (M Ed, Ed D, Ed S); reading, languages and literature (Ed D); school music-vocal (M Ed); science education (M Ed, MAT, Ed S); secondary education (MAT); secondary school reading (M Ed); social studies education (M Ed, Ed S), including education-secondary (M Ed); special education (M Ed, Ed D, PhD, Ed S); teacher education (MAT, Ed D, PhD). *Faculty:* 41 full-time (22 women), 2 part-time/adjunct (both women). *Students:* 401 full-time (295 women), 1,021 part-time (784 women); includes 527 minority (452 African Americans, 6 American Indian/Alaska Native, 32 Asian Americans or Pacific Islanders, 37 Hispanic Americans), 18 international. Average age 36. 296 applicants, 81% accepted, 132 enrolled. In 2006, 386 master's, 1 doctorate awarded. *Degree requirements:* For doctorate, thesis/dissertation. *Entrance requirements:* For master's, minimum GPA of 2.6; for doctorate, minimum undergraduate GPA of 3.0, graduate 3.5; interview. Additional exam requirements/recommendations for international students: Required—TOEFL (minimum score 550 paper-based; 213 computer-based), TWE (minimum score 6). *Application deadline:* For fall admission, 7/1 for domestic students, 6/1 for international students; for winter admission, 10/1 for international students; for spring admission, 2/1 for international students. Application fee: $30 ($50 for international students). Electronic applications accepted. *Financial support:* In 2006–07, 1 fellowship (averaging $34,919 per year) was awarded; research assistantships. *Faculty research:* Reading and writing literacy and literature. Total annual research expenditures: $209,400. *Unit head:* Dr. Joann Snyder, Academic Director, 313-577-1644, E-mail: joanne.snyder@wayne.edu. *Application contact:* Sharon Elliott, Assistant Dean, 313-577-0902, E-mail: sharon.elliott@wayne.edu.

West Chester University of Pennsylvania, Graduate Studies, School of Education, Department of Professional and Secondary Education, West Chester, PA 19383. Offers educational research (MS); secondary education (M Ed). Part-time and evening/weekend programs available. *Students:* 23 full-time (17 women), 50 part-time (30 women); includes 2 Asian Americans or Pacific Islanders. Average age 31. 55 applicants, 93% accepted, 28 enrolled. In 2006, 14 degrees awarded. *Degree requirements:* For master's, thesis (for some programs), comprehensive exam. *Entrance requirements:* For master's, GRE or MAT, teaching certificate. *Application deadline:* For fall admission, 4/15 priority date for domestic students; for spring admission, 10/15 priority date for domestic students. Applications are processed on a rolling basis. Application fee: $35. *Financial support:* In 2006–07, 1 research assistantship with full tuition reimbursement (averaging $5,000 per year) was awarded; unspecified assistantships also available. Support available to part-time students. Financial award application deadline: 2/15; financial award applicants required to submit FAFSA. *Faculty research:* Technology integration: preparing our teachers for the 21st century. *Unit head:* Dr. Lesley Welsh, Chair, 610-436-2958, E-mail: lwelsh@wcupa.edu. *Application contact:* Dr. Cynthia Haggard, Graduate Coordinator, 610-436-6934, E-mail: chaggard@wcupa.edu.

Western Carolina University, Graduate School, College of Education and Allied Professions, Department of Educational Leadership and Foundations, Programs in Secondary Education, Cullowhee, NC 28723. Offers art education (MAT); biology (MAT); chemistry (MAT); comprehensive education (MA Ed), including art, biology, English, mathematics, music, physical education, reading, social sciences; English (MAT); family and consumer sciences (MAT); mathematics (MAT); physical education (MAT); reading (MAT); social sciences (MAT). *Accreditation:* NCATE (one or more programs are accredited). Part-time and evening/weekend programs available. *Degree requirements:* For master's, comprehensive exam. *Entrance requirements:* For master's, GRE General Test, portfolio. Additional exam requirements/recommendations for international students: Required—TOEFL (minimum score 550 paper-based; 213 computer-based).

Western Illinois University, School of Graduate Studies, College of Education and Human Services, Department of Educational and Interdisciplinary Studies, Program in Secondary Education, Macomb, IL 61455-1390. Offers MAT. Part-time programs available. *Students:* 7 full-time (3 women), 3 part-time. Average age 24. 3 applicants, 67% accepted. In 2006, 7 degrees awarded. *Degree requirements:* For master's, thesis or alternative. *Entrance requirements:* For master's, Illinois certification basic skills and content area exam, interview, minimum GPA of 3.0. Additional exam requirements/recommendations for international students: Required—TOEFL (minimum score 550 paper-based; 213 computer-based; 80 iBT). *Application deadline:* Applications are processed on a rolling basis. Application fee: $30. Electronic applications accepted. *Expenses:* Tuition, state resident: part-time $200 per credit hour. Tuition, nonresident: part-time $400 per credit hour. *Financial support:* In 2006–07, 5 students received support, including 5 research assistantships with full tuition reimbursements available (averaging $6,568 per year). Financial award applicants required to submit FAFSA. *Unit head:* Dr. Reinhard W Lindner, Graduate Advisor, 309-298-1183. *Application contact:* Dr. Barbara Baily, Director of Graduate Studies/Associate Provost, 309-298-1806, Fax: 309-298-2345, E-mail: grad-office@wiu.edu.

Western Kentucky University, Graduate Studies, College of Education and Behavioral Sciences, Department of Counseling and Student Affairs, Bowling Green, KY 42101. Offers business and marketing education (MA Ed); counseling (MA Ed); counselor education (Ed S); education and behavioral science (MA Ed); elementary education (MA Ed, Ed S); middle years education (MA Ed); secondary education (MA Ed, Ed S); student affairs (MA Ed). *Accreditation:* ACA; NCATE. Part-time and evening/weekend programs available. *Faculty:* 11 full-time (5 women), 9 part-time/adjunct (3 women). *Students:* 59 full-time (47 women), 157 part-time (126 women); includes 18 minority (13 African Americans, 1 American Indian/Alaska Native, 2 Asian Americans or Pacific Islanders, 2 Hispanic Americans), 1 international. Average age 31. 49 applicants, 67% accepted, 27 enrolled. In 2006, 89 master's, 4 other advanced degrees awarded. *Degree requirements:* For master's, thesis optional. *Entrance requirements:* For master's, GRE General Test. Additional exam requirements/recommendations for international students: Required—TOEFL (minimum score 555 paper-based; 213 computer-based; 79 iBT). *Application deadline:* For fall admission, 8/1 priority date for domestic students, 4/1 for international students; for spring admission, 12/1 for domestic students, 9/1 for international students. Applications are processed on a rolling basis. Application fee: $35. *Expenses:* Tuition, state resident: full-time $6,520; part-time $226 per hour. Tuition, nonresident: full-time $7,140; part-time $357 per hour. International tuition: $15,820 full-time. *Financial support:* In 2006–07, 1 research assistantship with partial tuition reimbursement (averaging $8,000 per year) was awarded; Federal Work-Study, institutionally sponsored loans, and service awards also available. Financial award application deadline: 4/1; financial award applicants required to submit FAFSA. *Faculty research:* Counselor education, research for residential workers. *Unit head:* Dr. Aaron W Hughey, Department Head, 270-745-4953, E-mail: aaron.hughey@wku.edu.

Western Kentucky University, Graduate Studies, College of Education and Behavioral Sciences, Department of Curriculum and Instruction, Bowling Green, KY 42101. Offers business and marketing education (MAE); elementary education (MAE, Ed S); middle grades education (MAE); secondary education (MAE, Ed S). *Faculty:* 10 full-time (7 women), 1 (woman) part-time/adjunct. *Students:* 7 full-time (3 women), 133 part-time (109 women); includes 2 minority (1 African American, 1 Hispanic American), 1 international. Average age 31. 30 applicants, 63% accepted, 14 enrolled. In 2006, 56 degrees awarded. *Degree requirements:* For master's, comprehensive exam; for Ed S, thesis. *Entrance requirements:* For master's, GRE. Additional exam requirements/recommendations for international students: Required—TOEFL (minimum score 555 paper-based; 213 computer-based; 79 iBT). *Application deadline:* For fall admission, 7/1 priority date for domestic students, 5/15 for international students; for spring admission, 11/1 for domestic students, 9/15 for international students. Applications are processed on a rolling basis. Application fee: $35. *Expenses:* Tuition, state resident: full-time $6,520; part-time $226 per hour. Tuition, nonresident: full-time $7,140; part-time $357 per hour. International tuition: $15,820 full-time. *Financial support:* In 2006–07, 1 research assistantship with partial tuition reimbursement (averaging $7,200 per year) was awarded. Total annual research expenditures: $17,998. *Unit head:* Dr. Tabitha Daniel, Head, 270-745-2157, E-mail: tabitha.daniel@wku.edu.

Western New Mexico University, Graduate Division, School of Education, Silver City, NM 88062-0680. Offers counselor education (MA); elementary education (MAT); reading education (MAT); school administration (MA); secondary education (MAT); special education (MAT). *Accreditation:* NCATE. *Degree requirements:* For master's, comprehensive exam. *Entrance requirements:* For master's, GRE General Test, GRE Subject Test, minimum GPA of 3.2 in last 64 hours of undergraduate study. Additional exam requirements/recommendations for international students: Required—TOEFL (minimum score 550 paper-based; 213 computer-based). Electronic applications accepted. *Expenses:* Tuition, state resident: full-time $1,329. Tuition, nonresident: full-time $4,779.

Western Oregon University, Graduate Programs, College of Education, Division of Teacher Education, Program in Secondary Education, Monmouth, OR 97361-1394. Offers bilingual education (MS Ed); health (MS Ed); humanities (MAT, MS Ed); initial licensure (MAT); mathematics (MAT, MS Ed); science (MAT, MS Ed); social science (MAT, MS Ed). *Accreditation:* NCATE. Part-time and evening/weekend programs available. *Faculty:* 7 full-time (4 women), 15 part-time/adjunct (7 women). *Students:* 12 full-time (4 women), 21 part-time (10 women). Average age 32. In 2006, 31 degrees awarded. *Degree requirements:* For master's, written exam, thesis optional. *Entrance requirements:* For master's, minimum GPA of 3.0, teaching license. *Application deadline:* Applications are processed on a rolling basis. Application fee: $50. *Expenses:* Tuition, state resident: full-time $8,250; part-time $250 per credit. Tuition, nonresident: full-time $14,025; part-time $250 per credit. Required fees: $1,173. *Financial support:* In 2006–07, 16 teaching assistantships with full tuition reimbursements (averaging $706 per year) were awarded; research assistantships with full tuition reimbursements, career-related internships or fieldwork, Federal Work-Study, and tuition waivers (full and partial) also available. Support available to part-time students. Financial award application deadline: 3/1; financial award applicants required to submit FAFSA. *Faculty research:* Literacy, science in primary grades, geography education, retention, teacher burnout. *Unit head:* Dr. Mary Bucy, Unit Head, 503-838-8794, Fax: 503-838-8228. *Application contact:* Dr. David McDonald, Dean of Admissions, Retention and Enrollment Management, 503-838-8919, Fax: 503-838-8067, E-mail: mcdonald@wou.edu.

Western Washington University, Graduate School, Woodring College of Education, Department of Secondary Education, Bellingham, WA 98225-5996. Offers MIT. *Accreditation:* NCATE. Part-time programs available. *Faculty:* 8. *Students:* 112 full-time (68 women), 4 part-time (2 women); includes 7 minority (1 African American, 6 Asian Americans or Pacific Islanders). 57 applicants, 44% accepted, 23 enrolled. In 2006, 66 degrees awarded. *Degree requirements:* For master's, thesis optional. *Entrance requirements:* For master's, GRE General Test or MAT, minimum GPA of 3.0 in last 60 semester hours or last 90 quarter hours, secondary teaching certification. Additional exam requirements/recommendations for international students: Required—TOEFL (minimum score 567 paper-based; 227 computer-based). *Application deadline:* For fall admission, 4/1 priority date for domestic students; for winter admission, 10/1 for domestic students; for spring admission, 2/1 for domestic students. Application fee: $50. *Expenses:* Tuition, state resident: full-time $6,609; part-time $199 per credit. Tuition, nonresident: full-time $16,845; part-time $540 per credit. *Financial support:* In 2006–07, 3 teaching assistantships with partial tuition reimbursements (averaging $9,339 per year) were awarded; career-related internships or fieldwork, Federal Work-Study, institutionally sponsored loans, scholarships/grants, tuition waivers (partial), and unspecified assistantships also available. Support available to part-time students. Financial award application deadline: 2/15; financial award applicants required to submit FAFSA. *Unit head:* Dr. Ray Walpow, Chair, 360-650-3337. *Application contact:* Patricia Roberts, Program Manager, 360-650-3327, E-mail: patricia.roberts@wwu.edu.

Westfield State College, Division of Graduate and Continuing Education, Department of Education, Program in Secondary Education, Westfield, MA 01086. Offers M Ed. *Accreditation:* NCATE. Part-time and evening/weekend programs available. *Degree requirements:* For master's, practicum. *Entrance requirements:* For master's, GRE General Test or MAT, minimum undergraduate GPA of 2.7.

West Virginia University, College of Human Resources and Education, Department of Curriculum and Instruction-Literacy, Program in Secondary Education, Morgantown, WV 26506. Offers higher education curriculum and teaching (MA); secondary education (MA). Students enter program as undergraduates. *Accreditation:* NCATE. Part-time programs available. *Students:* 134 full-time (84 women), 28 part-time (19 women); includes 14 minority (6 African Americans, 2 Asian Americans or Pacific Islanders, 6 Hispanic Americans), 9 international. Average age 29. 88 applicants, 90% accepted, 50 enrolled. In 2006, 80 degrees awarded. *Degree requirements:* For master's, content exams, thesis optional. *Entrance requirements:* For master's, minimum GPA of 2.75. Additional exam requirements/recommendations for international students: Required—TOEFL. *Application deadline:* Applications are processed on a rolling basis. Application fee: $50. Electronic applications accepted. *Expenses:* Tuition, state resident: full-time $4,926; part-time $276 per credit hour. Tuition, nonresident: full-time $14,278; part-time $796 per credit hour. Tuition and fees vary according to program. *Financial support:* In 2006–07, 117 students received support, including 2 teaching assistantships with full tuition reimbursements available (averaging $8,264 per year); research assistantships, career-related internships or fieldwork, Federal Work-Study, institutionally sponsored loans, and tuition waivers (full and partial) also available. Financial award application deadline: 2/1; financial award applicants required to submit FAFSA. *Faculty research:* Teacher education, school reform, curriculum development, education technology. *Application contact:* Dr. Elizabeth A. Dooley, Chair, 304-293-3441, Fax: 304-293-3802, E-mail: elizabeth.dooley@mail.wvu.edu.

West Virginia University, Eberly College of Arts and Sciences, Department of Mathematics, Morgantown, WV 26506. Offers applied mathematics (MS, PhD); discrete mathematics (PhD); interdisciplinary mathematics (MS); mathematics for secondary education (MS); pure mathematics (MS). Part-time programs available. *Faculty:* 26 full-time (3 women), 19 part-time/adjunct (11 women). *Students:* 40 full-time (17 women), 3 part-time (1 woman), 23 international. Average age 29. 44 applicants, 91% accepted, 17 enrolled. In 2006, 10 master's, 4 doctorates awarded. Terminal master's awarded for partial completion of doctoral program. *Degree requirements:* For master's, thesis optional; for doctorate, one foreign language, thesis/dissertation, comprehensive exam. *Entrance requirements:* For master's, minimum GPA of 2.5; for doctorate, master's degree in mathematics. Additional exam requirements/recommendations for international students: Required—TOEFL (paper-based 550; computer-based 213) or IELTS (paper-based 6). *Application deadline:* For fall admission, 2/15 priority date for domestic and international students. Applications are processed on a rolling basis. Application fee: $50. *Expenses:* Tuition, state resident: full-time $4,926; part-time $276 per credit hour. Tuition, nonresident: full-time $14,278; part-time $796 per credit hour. Tuition and fees vary according to program. *Financial support:* In 2006–07, 41 students received support, including 6 research assistantships with full tuition reimbursements available (averaging $12,000 per year), 18 teaching assistantships with full tuition reimbursements available (averaging $10,000 per year); Federal Work-Study, institutionally sponsored loans, and tuition waivers (full and partial) also available. Financial award application deadline: 2/15; financial award applicants required to submit FAFSA. *Faculty research:* Combinatorics and graph theory, topology, differential equations, applied and computational mathematics. Total annual research expenditures: $578,444. *Unit head:* Dr. Sherman D. Riemenschneider, Chair, 304-293-2011 Ext. 2322, Fax: 304-293-3982, E-mail: sherm.riemenschneider@mail.wvu.edu. *Application contact:* Dr. Harvey R. Diamond, Director of Graduate Studies, 304-293-2011 Ext. 2347, Fax: 304-293-3982, E-mail: harvey.diamond@mail.wvu.edu.

Wheaton College, Graduate School, Department of Education, Wheaton, IL 60187-5593. Offers elementary level (MAT); secondary level (MAT). *Accreditation:* NCATE. *Students:* 9. 10

Secondary Education

Wheaton College *(continued)*
applicants, 80% accepted, 4 enrolled. *Degree requirements:* For master's, thesis or alternative. *Entrance requirements:* For master's, GRE General Test. *Application deadline:* For fall admission, 3/1 priority date for domestic students; for spring admission, 11/1 for domestic students. Applications are processed on a rolling basis. Application fee: $30. *Financial support:* Career-related internships or fieldwork and Federal Work-Study available. Financial award application deadline: 3/1; financial award applicants required to submit FAFSA. *Unit head:* Dr. Andrew Brulle, Chair, 630-752-5763, E-mail: andrew.brulle@wheaton.edu. *Application contact:* Julie A. Huebner, Director of Graduate Admissions, 630-752-5195, Fax: 630-752-5935, E-mail: gradadm@wheaton.edu.

Whittier College, Graduate Programs, Department of Education and Child Development, Program in Secondary Education, Whittier, CA 90608-0634. Offers MA Ed. Part-time and evening/weekend programs available. *Degree requirements:* For master's, thesis, registration. *Entrance requirements:* For master's, GRE General Test, MAT.

Whitworth University, School of Education, Graduate Studies in Education, Spokane, WA 99251-0001. Offers administration (M Ed); counseling (M Ed), including school counselors, social agency/church setting; elementary education (M Ed); gifted and talented (MAT); secondary education (M Ed); special education (MAT); teaching (MIT). *Accreditation:* NCATE. Part-time and evening/weekend programs available. *Faculty:* 2 full-time (both women), 25 part-time/adjunct (15 women). *Degree requirements:* For master's, thesis (for some programs), comprehensive exam. *Entrance requirements:* For master's, GRE General Test, MAT. Additional exam requirements/recommendations for international students: Required—TOEFL. *Application deadline:* For fall admission, 9/1 priority date for domestic students; for spring admission, 2/1 priority date for domestic students. Applications are processed on a rolling basis. Application fee: $35. *Financial support:* Fellowships with partial tuition reimbursements, career-related internships or fieldwork, institutionally sponsored loans, and scholarships/grants available. Financial award application deadline: 2/1. *Faculty research:* Rural program development, mainstreaming, special needs learners. *Unit head:* Dr. Sharon Mowry, Director, 509-777-4393, Fax: 509-777-3785, E-mail: smowry@whitworth.edu. *Application contact:* Pat Bailey, Program Assistant, 509-777-3228, Fax: 509-777-4753, E-mail: gse@whitworth.edu.

Wilkes University, Graduate Studies and Continued Learning, College of Arts, Humanities and Social Sciences, Program in Teacher Education, Wilkes-Barre, PA 18766-0002. Offers classroom technology (MS Ed); educational computing (MS Ed); educational development and strategies (MS Ed); educational leadership (MS Ed); elementary education (MS Ed); instructional technology (MS Ed); school business leadership (MS Ed); secondary education (MS Ed), including biology, chemistry, English, history; special education (MS Ed). Part-time and evening/weekend programs available. Postbaccalaureate distance learning degree programs offered (minimal on-campus study). *Students:* 32 full-time (21 women), 1,588 part-time (1,106 women); includes 29 minority (6 African Americans, 2 American Indian/Alaska Native, 4 Asian Americans or Pacific Islanders, 17 Hispanic Americans). Average age 33. In 2006, 754 degrees awarded. *Entrance requirements:* Additional exam requirements/recommendations for international students: Required—TOEFL (minimum score 500 paper-based; 173 computer-based). *Application deadline:* Applications are processed on a rolling basis. Application fee: $40. *Expenses:* Contact institution. *Financial support:* Federal Work-Study and unspecified assistantships available. Financial award application deadline: 3/1; financial award applicants required to submit FAFSA. *Unit head:* Dr. Michael Speziale, Interim Dean, 570-408-4679, Fax: 570-408-4905, E-mail: michael.speziale@wilkes.edu. *Application contact:* Kathleen Houlihan, Director of Graduate Studies, 570-408-3235, Fax: 570-408-7846, E-mail: kathleen.houlihan@wilkes.edu.

William Carey University, Graduate Studies, School of Education, Hattiesburg, MS 39401-5499. Offers art education (M Ed); art of teaching (M Ed); elementary education (M Ed, Ed S); English education (M Ed); gifted education (M Ed); history and social science (M Ed); mild/moderate disabilities (M Ed); secondary education (M Ed). Part-time programs available. *Faculty:* 19 full-time (12 women), 25 part-time/adjunct (17 women). *Students:* 142 full-time (111 women), 412 part-time (343 women); includes 123 minority (121 African Americans, 1 Asian American or Pacific Islander, 1 Hispanic American). In 2006, 305 master's, 2 other advanced degrees awarded. *Degree requirements:* For master's, comprehensive exam. *Entrance requirements:* For master's, GRE, MAT, minimum GPA of 2.5, Class A teacher's license. Additional exam requirements/recommendations for international students: Required—TOEFL (minimum score 550 paper-based; 213 computer-based). *Application deadline:* For fall admission, 8/7 for domestic and international students; for winter admission, 10/30 for domestic and international students; for spring admission, 2/12 for domestic and international students. Application fee: $25. *Expenses:* Tuition: Full-time $5,040; part-time $240 per credit hour. Tuition and fees vary according to course load. *Financial support:* In 2006–07, 371 students received support. Federal Work-Study and scholarships/grants available. Support available to part-time students. *Unit head:* Dr. Patty Ward, Dean, 601-318-6139, Fax: 601-318-6185, E-mail: patty.ward@wmcarey.edu. *Application contact:* Jason Douglas, Clerical Assistant, Graduate Admissions, 601-318-6774, Fax: 601-318-6765, E-mail: jason.douglas@wmcarey.edu.

Wilmington College, Division of Education, New Castle, DE 19720-6491. Offers applied education technology (M Ed); career and technical education (M Ed); elementary and secondary school counseling (M Ed); elementary special education (M Ed); elementary studies (M Ed); instruction: gifted and talented (M Ed); instruction: teaching and learning (M Ed); literacy (M Ed); reading (M Ed); school leadership (M Ed); secondary teaching (MAT). Part-time and evening/weekend programs available. *Faculty:* 7 full-time (4 women). *Students:* 609 full-time (447 women), 1,350 part-time (1,013 women); includes 144 minority (131 African

Americans, 3 American Indian/Alaska Native, 1 Asian American or Pacific Islander, 9 Hispanic Americans). Average age 34. 818 applicants, 100% accepted, 599 enrolled. In 2006, 737 degrees awarded. *Entrance requirements:* For master's, 2 letters of recommendation, interview. Additional exam requirements/recommendations for international students: Required—TOEFL (minimum score 500 paper-based; 173 computer-based). *Application deadline:* For fall admission, 4/30 for domestic students. Applications are processed on a rolling basis. Application fee: $25. *Financial support:* Applicants required to submit FAFSA. *Unit head:* Dr. Richard Gochnauer, Chair, 302-328-6795 Ext. 163, Fax: 302-328-7081. *Application contact:* Chris Ferguson, Director of Admissions and Financial Aid, 302-328-9407 Ext. 256, Fax: 302-328-5164, E-mail: inquire@wilmcoll.edu.

Winthrop University, College of Education, Program in Secondary Education, Rock Hill, SC 29733. Offers M Ed, MAT. *Accreditation:* NCATE. Part-time programs available. *Students:* 31 full-time (14 women), 13 part-time (9 women); includes 6 minority (5 African Americans, 1 Asian American or Pacific Islander). Average age 28. In 2006, 12 degrees awarded. *Entrance requirements:* For master's, PRAXIS, minimum GPA of 3.0, South Carolina Class III Teaching Certificate. *Application deadline:* For fall admission, 7/15 priority date for domestic students; for spring admission, 12/1 for domestic students. Applications are processed on a rolling basis. Application fee: $35. Electronic applications accepted. *Expenses:* Tuition, state resident: full-time $9,148; part-time $383 per hour. Tuition, nonresident: full-time $16,864; part-time $704 per hour. *Financial support:* Career-related internships or fieldwork, Federal Work-Study, scholarships/grants, and unspecified assistantships available. Support available to part-time students. Financial award application deadline: 2/1; financial award applicants required to submit FAFSA. *Unit head:* Dr. Sue Peck, Acting Chair, 803-323-4725, E-mail: pecks@winthrop.edu. *Application contact:* 800-411-7041, Fax: 803-323-2292, E-mail: graduatestu@winthrop.edu.

Worcester State College, Graduate Studies, Department of Education, Concentration in Secondary Education, Worcester, MA 01602-2597. Offers M Ed. Part-time programs available. *Students:* Average age 34. 31 applicants, 52% accepted, 5 enrolled. In 2006, 13 degrees awarded. *Degree requirements:* For master's, thesis optional. *Entrance requirements:* For master's, GRE General Test or MAT. Additional exam requirements/recommendations for international students: Required—TOEFL (minimum score 550 paper-based; 213 computer-based). *Application deadline:* Applications are processed on a rolling basis. Application fee: $30. *Expenses:* Tuition, state resident: full-time $4,518; part-time $251 per credit hour. Tuition, nonresident: full-time $4,518; part-time $251 per credit hour. *Financial support:* Career-related internships or fieldwork, Federal Work-Study, institutionally sponsored loans, scholarships/grants, and unspecified assistantships available. Support available to part-time students. Financial award application deadline: 3/1; financial award applicants required to submit FAFSA. *Unit head:* Dr. O. Joshua Aisiku, Coordinator, 508-929-8668, Fax: 508-929-8164, E-mail: oaisiku@worcester.edu. *Application contact:* Nicole Brown, Assistant Dean of Continuing Education, 508-929-8787, Fax: 508-929-8100, E-mail: nbrown@worcester.edu.

Wright State University, School of Graduate Studies, College of Education and Human Services, Department of Teacher Education, Programs in Classroom Teacher Education, Dayton, OH 45435. Offers M Ed, MA. *Accreditation:* NCATE. *Students:* 51 full-time (36 women), 54 part-time (47 women); includes 8 minority (7 African Americans, 1 Hispanic American). Average age 34. 30 applicants, 97% accepted. In 2006, 59 degrees awarded. *Degree requirements:* For master's, thesis (for some programs). *Entrance requirements:* For master's, GRE General Test, MAT, PRAXIS II. Additional exam requirements/recommendations for international students: Required—TOEFL. Application fee: $25. *Financial support:* Available to part-time students. Applicants required to submit FAFSA. *Application contact:* John Kimble, Associate Director of Graduate Admissions and Records, 937-775-2957, Fax: 937-775-2453, E-mail: john.kimble@wright.edu.

Xavier University, College of Social Sciences, Health and Education, School of Education, Program in Secondary Education, Cincinnati, OH 45207. Offers M Ed. Part-time programs available. *Faculty:* 7 full-time (2 women), 4 part-time/adjunct (0 women). *Students:* 82 full-time (47 women), 133 part-time (68 women); includes 22 minority (18 African Americans, 2 Asian Americans or Pacific Islanders, 2 Hispanic Americans). Average age 32. 83 applicants, 64% accepted, 49 enrolled. In 2006, 76 degrees awarded. *Degree requirements:* For master's, research paper. *Entrance requirements:* For master's, GRE or MAT, minimum GPA of 2.7. Additional exam requirements/recommendations for international students: Required—TOEFL (minimum score 550 paper-based; 213 computer-based). *Application deadline:* For fall admission, 8/15 priority date for domestic students. Applications are processed on a rolling basis. Application fee: $35. Electronic applications accepted. *Expenses:* Tuition: Part-time $462 per credit hour. Part-time tuition and fees vary according to degree level, campus/location and program. *Financial support:* Scholarships/grants and unspecified assistantships available. Support available to part-time students. Financial award applicants required to submit FAFSA. *Faculty research:* Ethics, school violence, teaching methods, educational technology. *Unit head:* Dr. Michael Flick, Director, 513-745-2984, Fax: 513-745-1052, E-mail: flick@xavier.edu. *Application contact:* Roger Bosse, Interim Director of Graduate Studies, 513-745-3357, Fax: 513-745-1048, E-mail: bosse@xavier.edu.

Youngstown State University, Graduate School, College of Education, Department of Teacher Education, Program in Secondary Education, Youngstown, OH 44555-0001. Offers MS Ed. *Accreditation:* NCATE. Part-time and evening/weekend programs available. *Degree requirements:* For master's, thesis optional. *Entrance requirements:* For master's, GRE, MAT, or teaching certificate; minimum GPA of 2.7. Additional exam requirements/recommendations for international students: Required—TOEFL. *Faculty research:* Critical reflectivity, gender issues in classroom instruction, collaborative research and analysis, literacy methodology.

CLEMSON UNIVERSITY

Elementary Education

Program of Study
The Master of Education (M.Ed.) degree in elementary education at Clemson University includes course work in psychological and sociological foundations, curriculum development and teaching methods, specialized content, and research. The program is intended to strengthen and enhance teaching skills, promote research and reflection on innovative teaching strategies, and expand content knowledge. By examining and reflecting on best practices, students have the opportunity to improve the qualities that make them effective teachers who can respond to the emotional, motivational, cognitive, and cultural needs of all students.

Students follow the approved program of study for the degree. Before enrolling in any graduate course, the student should arrange a conference with the coordinator of elementary education. Courses taken prior to this conference may or may not be acceptable for the degree. Professional development courses are not counted toward the degree. Exceptions to the program of study must be approved by the student's advisory committee, which consists of the major adviser and 2 faculty members from the department in which the student has taken course work.

The degree requires 36 semester hours. When the student has successfully completed 27 credit hours toward the degree, the student may take the comprehensive examination. The examination is written and arranged at a specified time each semester. Upon the student's receipt of a passing grade, the advisory committee recommends that the degree be granted.

Research Facilities
For more information about the Eugene T. Moore School of Education's centers and collaborations, prospective students should visit the Web site at http://www.hehd.clemson.edu/schoolofed/centers.htm.

Financial Aid
A small number of graduate assistantships are available for students enrolled in Clemson's teacher education programs.

Cost of Study
Tuition for 2007–08 is $3641 per semester for in-state students and $7285 per semester for nonresidents. Off-campus rates are $330 per hour for in-state students and $660 per hour for nonresidents. Graduate assistants pay a flat fee of $950 per semester. Graduate fellows pay South Carolina resident fees.

Living and Housing Costs
On-campus housing is available. For information, students should visit http://www.housing.clemson.edu. The cost of living in Clemson is quite low compared to the national average. Students who choose to live off the campus typically spend $300–$400 per month for rent, depending on location, amenities, roommates, etc.

Student Group
Students in the M.Ed. degree program are usually teachers who want to stay in their chosen profession. However, many are seeking leadership positions within the teaching profession. They typically become department chairs, curriculum specialists, or instructional coaches. There are approximately 10 students in the program; 100 percent are women, 80 percent attend on a part-time basis, and all of the students are from the United States.

Location
Clemson is a small, beautiful college town near the Blue Ridge Mountains and Lake Hartwell in upstate South Carolina. The Upstate is one of the country's fastest-growing areas and is the midpoint of the Charlotte-to-Atlanta I-85 corridor, a multistate area along Interstate 85 that runs from metro Atlanta to Richmond, Virginia, and encompasses Charlotte, North Carolina, and North Carolina's Research Triangle. Atlanta and Charlotte are each a 2-hour's drive away. Many financial institutions and other industries have national headquarters for a major presence in the Upstate, including Wachovia, Bank of America, BMW, Bon Secours St. Francis Health System, Bosch North America, Bowater, Charter Communications, Ernst and Young, Fluor Corporation, IBM, Microsoft, Michelin of North America, and many others.

The University
Clemson is classified by the Carnegie Foundation as an RU/H: Research University (high research activity), a category comprising just 10 percent of all graduate degree-granting universities in America. The University's mission is to fulfill the covenant between its founder and the people of South Carolina to establish a "high seminary of learning" through its responsibilities of teaching, research, and extended public service. The University has identified eight areas of academic emphasis that create collaborations that, in turn, help fulfill the University's mission.

Applying
Applicants may apply on the Web at http://www.grad.clemson.edu/p_apply.html. Applications with a $50 nonrefundable fee should be received no later than five weeks prior to registration. Every required item in support of the application must be on file by that date. Students are advised to contact the department for the deadlines of the program of proposed study.

Correspondence and Information
David S. Fleming, Ph.D.
Graduate Coordinator
Eugene T. Moore School of Education
G-01 Tillman Hall
Clemson University
Clemson, South Carolina 29634-0702
Phone: 864-656-1881
Fax: 864-656-0311
E-mail: dflemin@clemson.edu
Web site: http://www.hehd.clemson.edu/schoolofed/

Clemson University

THE FACULTY AND THEIR RESEARCH

Beatrice Naff Bailey, Professor; Ed.D., Virginia Tech. Curriculum and instruction.
David E. Barrett, Professor; Ph.D., USC. Education psychology.
Rhonda W. Buford, Assistant Professor; Ph.D., Southern Mississippi. Special education.
Gail C. Delicio, Associate Professor; Ph.D., Florida State. Education psychology.
Pamela J. Dunston, Associate Professor; Ph.D., Georgia. Reading education.
Lienne C. Federico, Assistant Professor; Ph.D., East Carolina. Educational leadership/English education.
William R. Fisk, Professor and Department Chair; Ph.D., Florida State. School psychology.
Susan King Fullerton, Associate Professor; Ph.D., Maryland. Curriculum and instruction.
Robert P. Green Jr., Alumni Professor; Ed.D., Virginia. Curriculum and instruction.
Kathy Neal Headley, Professor; Ed.D., Auburn. Reading.
Martha J. Hodge, Associate Professor; Ph.D., Vanderbilt. Special education.
Robert M. Horton, Associate Professor; Ed.D., Cincinnati. Curriculum and instruction.
Antonis Katsiyannis, Professor; Ed.D., William and Mary. Education administration, special education–behavior disorders.
Cheryl Olivia Lane, Assistant Professor; Ph.D., Clemson. Curriculum and instruction.
William H. Leonard, Professor; Ph.D., Berkeley. Science education.
Charles C. Linnell, Associate Professor; Ed.D., North Carolina State. Industrial arts education.
Jonda Cecole McNair, Assistant Professor; Ph.D., Ohio State. Language, literacy, and culture.
Emma M. Owens, Associate Professor; Ed.D., Clemson. Vocational and technical education.
Susan J. Pass, Assistant Professor; Ed.D., Houston. Social studies.
Chris L. Peters, Associate Professor; Ed.D., Georgia. Instructional technology.
David Paul Reinking, Named Professor; Ph.D., Minnesota, Twin Cities. Reading education.
Paul J. Riccomini, Assistant Professor; Ph.D., Penn State. Special education.
Victoria G. Ridgeway, Associate Professor; Ph.D., Georgia. Reading education.
Suzanne N. Rosenblith, Assistant Professor; Ph.D., Wisconsin–Madison. Educational policy studies.
Dorothy J. Sluss, Associate Professor; Ph.D., Virginia Tech. Family and child development.
Deborah A. Smith, Associate Professor; Ed.D., Tennessee. Physical education.
Pamela M. Stecker, Associate Professor; Ph.D., Vanderbilt. Education and human development.
Dolores A. Stegelin, Associate Professor; Ph.D., Florida. Early childhood development and interdisciplinary research.
Deborah M. Switzer, Professor; Ph.D., Illinois; Educational psychology.
Carol G. Weatherford, Associate Professor; Ed.D., North Carolina State. Occupational education.
Elaine Mumbauer Wiegert, Assistant Professor; Ph.D., Clemson. Curriculum and instruction.
Dalun Zhang, Assistant Professor; Ph.D., New Orleans. Special education.

CLEMSON UNIVERSITY

Middle Grades Education

Program of Study

The Master of Arts in Teaching (M.A.T.) degree in middle grades education at Clemson University is a 36-hour field-based program that is housed at the University Center of Greenville. Students can graduate in as little as one year of full-time study (from May to May). Many students take an extra semester or attend summer semester to graduate. This program provides initial certification in grades 5–8 in the four content areas: English/language arts, math, science, and social studies. Candidates may qualify for up to two content areas. Graduates are qualified to become middle school teachers in South Carolina and forty-seven other states. Most research conducted by M.A.T. students is considered action research and involves data collection in the public schools. There are presentation and publication opportunities available.

Research Facilities

The Greenville University Center has extensive computer facilities and an interlibrary loan program with its six other member institutions. In addition, Clemson has a Middle Grades Curriculum Center on site.

Financial Aid

A small number of graduate assistantships are available for students enrolled in Clemson's teacher education programs. There are two to three graduate assistantships available through the M.A.T. program. These are usually offered in the spring only and for students who begin the program in January, before they are in the school full-time. Some aid may also be possible through faculty grant projects, particularly in math.

Cost of Study

Tuition for 2007–08 is $3641 per semester for in-state students and $7285 per semester for nonresidents. Off-campus rates are $330 per hour for in-state students and $660 per hour for nonresidents. Graduate assistants pay a flat fee of $950 per semester and $315 per summer session. Graduate fellows pay South Carolina resident fees.

Living and Housing Costs

On-campus housing is available. For information, students should visit http://www.housing.clemson.edu. The cost of living in Clemson is quite low compared to the national average. Students who choose to live off the campus typically spend $300–$400 per month for rent, depending on location, amenities, roommates, etc.

Student Group

Each incoming class (cohort) is limited to 40 students. Admission is dealt with on a case-by-case basis involving transcript evaluation and interview. Approximately 60 percent of the students in the program are women, 98 percent attend on a full-time basis, and all of the students are from the United States.

Student Outcomes

The M.A.T. program has a 100 percent hire rate.

Location

Clemson is a small, beautiful college town near the Blue Ridge Mountains and Lake Hartwell in upstate South Carolina. The Upstate is one of the country's fastest-growing areas and is the midpoint of the Charlotte-to-Atlanta I-85 corridor, a multistate area along Interstate 85 that runs from metro Atlanta to Richmond, Virginia, and encompasses Charlotte, North Carolina, and North Carolina's Research Triangle. Atlanta and Charlotte are each a 2-hour's drive away. Many financial institutions and other industries have national headquarters for a major presence in the Upstate, including Wachovia, Bank of America, BMW, Bon Secours St. Francis Health System, Bosch North America, Bowater, Charter Communications, Ernst and Young, Fluor Corporation, IBM, Microsoft, Michelin of North America, and many others.

The University

Clemson is classified by the Carnegie Foundation as an RU/H: Research University (high research activity), a category comprising just 10 percent of all graduate degree-granting universities in America. The University's mission is to fulfill the covenant between its founder and the people of South Carolina to establish a "high seminary of learning" through its responsibilities of teaching, research, and extended public service. The University has identified eight areas of academic emphasis that create collaborations that, in turn, help fulfill the University's mission.

Applying

Applicants may apply on the Web at http://www.grad.clemson.edu/p_apply.html. Applications with a $50 nonrefundable fee should be received no later than five weeks prior to registration. Every required item in support of the application must be on file by that date. Students are advised to contact the department for the deadlines of the program of proposed study.

Correspondence and Information

David S. Fleming, Ph.D.
Graduate Coordinator
Eugene T. Moore School of Education
G-01 Tillman Hall
Clemson University
Clemson, South Carolina 29634-0702
Phone: 864-656-1881
Fax: 864-656-0311
E-mail: dflemin@clemson.edu
Web site: http://www.hehd.clemson.edu/schoolofed/g-mat_po.htm

Clemson University

THE FACULTY AND THEIR RESEARCH

Beatrice Naff Bailey, Professor; Ed.D., Virginia Tech. Curriculum and instruction.
David E. Barrett, Professor; Ph.D., USC. Education psychology.
Rhonda W. Buford, Assistant Professor; Ph.D., Southern Mississippi. Special education.
Gail C. Delicio, Associate Professor; Ph.D., Florida State. Education psychology.
Pamela J. Dunston, Associate Professor; Ph.D., Georgia. Reading education.
Lienne C. Federico, Assistant Professor; Ph.D., East Carolina. Educational leadership/English education.
William R. Fisk, Professor and Department Chair; Ph.D., Florida State. School psychology.
Susan King Fullerton, Associate Professor; Ph.D., Maryland. Curriculum and instruction.
Robert P. Green Jr., Alumni Professor; Ed.D., Virginia. Curriculum and instruction.
Kathy Neal Headley, Professor; Ed.D., Auburn. Reading.
Martha J. Hodge, Associate Professor; Ph.D., Vanderbilt. Special education.
Robert M. Horton, Associate Professor; Ed.D., Cincinnati. Curriculum and instruction.
Antonis Katsiyannis, Professor; Ed.D., William and Mary. Education administration, special education–behavior disorders.
Cheryl Olivia Lane, Assistant Professor; Ph.D., Clemson. Curriculum and instruction.
William H. Leonard, Professor; Ph.D., Berkeley. Science education.
Charles C. Linnell, Associate Professor; Ed.D., North Carolina State. Industrial arts education.
Jonda Cecole McNair, Assistant Professor; Ph.D., Ohio State. Language, literacy, and culture.
Emma M. Owens, Associate Professor; Ed.D., Clemson. Vocational and technical education.
Susan J. Pass, Assistant Professor; Ed.D., Houston. Social studies.
Chris L. Peters, Associate Professor; Ed.D., Georgia. Instructional technology.
David Paul Reinking, Named Professor; Ph.D., Minnesota, Twin Cities. Reading education.
Paul J. Riccomini, Assistant Professor; Ph.D., Penn State. Special education.
Victoria G. Ridgeway, Associate Professor; Ph.D., Georgia. Reading education.
Suzanne N. Rosenblith, Assistant Professor; Ph.D., Wisconsin–Madison. Educational policy studies.
Dorothy J. Sluss, Associate Professor; Ph.D., Virginia Tech. Family and child development.
Deborah A. Smith, Associate Professor; Ed.D., Tennessee. Physical education.
Pamela M. Stecker, Associate Professor; Ph.D., Vanderbilt. Education and human development.
Dolores A. Stegelin, Associate Professor; Ph.D., Florida. Early childhood development and interdisciplinary research.
Deborah M. Switzer, Professor; Ph.D., Illinois; Educational psychology.
Carol G. Weatherford, Associate Professor; Ed.D., North Carolina State. Occupational education.
Elaine Mumbauer Wiegert, Assistant Professor; Ph.D., Clemson. Curriculum and instruction.
Dalun Zhang, Assistant Professor; Ph.D., New Orleans. Special education.

CLEMSON UNIVERSITY

Master of Education in Secondary Education

Program of Study

The purpose of the Master of Education (M.Ed.) in secondary education program is to assist secondary teachers in increasing competency in both subject content and instruction. Therefore, the program has practical and theoretical work in education as well as appropriate content in the selected content area. There are four possible areas of concentration: English, mathematics, natural sciences, and social studies. Although a thesis is not required, one course requires a classroom action research project.

The degree requirements are a minimum of 36 semester hours in graduate courses with a GPR of at least 3.0, of which at least 18 hours must be from 700-level or higher numbered courses; a minimum of 15 semester hours in graduate courses in professional education or substitute courses approved by the major adviser in the College of Education; a minimum of 18 semester hours of graduate courses in the selected content area or in related areas approved by the major adviser and a representative from the content department; and a comprehensive examination.

All course work to be credited must have been enrolled in and completed within six calendar years prior to the date on which the degree is to be awarded. This includes up to 12 hours of approved graduate work that may be transferred from another institution. Before enrolling for any graduate course, the student should arrange a conference with the major adviser. Courses taken prior to this conference may or may not be acceptable for the degree. The advisory committee consists of the major adviser, a faculty member chosen from the appropriate content teaching area department from whom the student has taken course work, and a third member at-large (typically one from whom courses are taken). Upon successful completion of the examination, the committee recommends whether the degree should be granted. The examination is written and arranged at a specified time each semester.

Research Facilities

For more information about the School of Education's centers and collaboratives, students should visit http://www.hehd.clemson.edu/schoolofed/centers.htm.

Financial Aid

A small number of graduate assistantships are available in teacher education.

Cost of Study

Tuition for 2007–08 is $3641 per semester for in-state students and $7285 per semester for nonresidents. Off-campus rates are $330 per hour for in-state students and $660 per hour for nonresidents. Graduate assistants pay a flat fee of $950 per semester and $315 per summer session. Graduate fellows pay South Carolina resident fees.

Living and Housing Costs

On-campus housing is available; for information, students should visit http://www.housing.clemson.edu. The cost of living in Clemson is quite low compared to the national average; students who choose to live off campus typically spend $300–$400 per month for rent, depending on location, amenities, roommates, etc.

Student Group

The program has approximately 27 students. Sixty-nine percent are women and 36 percent are full-time students.

Location

Clemson is a small, beautiful college town near the Blue Ridge Mountains and Lake Hartwell in Upstate South Carolina. The Upstate is one of the country's fastest-growing areas and is an important part of the I-85 corridor, a multistate area along Interstate 85 that runs from metro Atlanta to Richmond, Virginia, and encompasses Charlotte, North Carolina, and North Carolina's Research Triangle. Atlanta and Charlotte are each a 2-hour drive away. Many financial institutions and other industries have national headquarters for a major presence in the Upstate, including Wachovia, Bank of America, BMW, Bon Secours St. Francis Health System, Bosch North America, Bowater, Charter Communications, Ernst & Young, Fluor Corporation, IBM, Microsoft, Michelin of North America, and many others.

The University

Clemson is classified by the Carnegie Foundation as an RU/H: Research University (high research activity), a category comprising just 10 percent of all graduate degree–granting universities in America. The University's mission is to fulfill the covenant between its founder and the people of South Carolina to establish a "high seminary of learning" through its responsibilities of teaching, research, and extended public service. The University has identified eight areas of academic emphasis that create collaborations that, in turn, help fulfill the University's mission.

Applying

Students in these programs are expected to be of high integrity, motivated, and committed to implementing evidence-based instructional and behavioral interventions. Applicants may apply on the Web at http://www.grad.clemson.edu/p_apply.html. Applications with a $50 nonrefundable fee should be received no later than five weeks prior to registration. Every required item in support of the application must be on file by that date. Students are advised to contact the department for the deadlines of the program of proposed study.

Correspondence and Information

David S. Fleming, Ph.D.
Graduate Coordinator
Eugene T. Moore School of Education
G-01 Tillman Hall
Clemson University
Clemson, South Carolina 29634-0702
Phone: 864-656-1881
Fax: 864-656-0311
E-mail: dflemin@clemson.edu
Web site: http://www.hehd.clemson.edu/schoolofed/g-sec-ed_po.htm

Clemson University

THE FACULTY AND THEIR RESEARCH

Beatrice Naff Bailey, Professor; Ed.D., Virginia Tech. Curriculum and instruction.
David E. Barrett, Professor; Ph.D., USC. Education psychology.
Wanda Calvert, Clinical Faculty; Ph.D., South Carolina. Elementary education.
Chrystal Dean, Assistant Professor; Ph.D., Vanderbilt. Teaching and learning, math education.
Gail C. Delicio, Associate Professor; Ph.D., Florida State. Education psychology.
Pamela J. Dunston, Associate Professor; Ph.D., Georgia. Reading education.
Elizabeth Edmondson, Assistant Professor; Ph.D., Clemson. Curriculum and instruction.
Lienne C. Federico, Assistant Professor; Ph.D., East Carolina. Educational leadership/English education.
William R. Fisk, Professor and Department Chair; Ph.D., Florida State. School psychology.
Susan King Fullerton, Associate Professor; Ph.D., Maryland. Curriculum and instruction, reading.
Linda Gambrell, Full Professor; Ph.D., Maryland. Curriculum and instruction, reading.
Robert P. Green Jr., Alumni Professor; Ed.D., Virginia. Curriculum and instruction.
Kathy Neal Headley, Professor; Ed.D., Auburn. Reading.
Martha J. Hodge, Associate Professor; Ph.D., Vanderbilt. Special education.
Robert M. Horton, Associate Professor; Ed.D., Cincinnati. Curriculum and instruction.
Larry Brent Igo, Assistant Professor; Ph.D., Nebraska–Lincoln. Educational psychology.
Rebecca Kaminski, Clinical Faculty; Ed.D., Pittsburgh. Instruction and learning.
Antonis Katsiyannis, Professor; Ed.D., William and Mary. Education administration, special education–behavior disorders.
Cheryl Olivia Lane, Assistant Professor; Ph.D., Clemson. Curriculum and instruction.
Charles C. Linnell, Associate Professor; Ed.D., North Carolina State. Industrial arts education.
Jonda Cecole McNair, Assistant Professor; Ph.D., Ohio State. Language, literacy, and culture.
William Paige, Professor; Ph.D., Ohio State. Industrial technology education.
Susan J. Pass, Assistant Professor; Ed.D., Houston. Social studies.
Chris L. Peters, Associate Professor; Ed.D., Georgia. Instructional technology.
Cheryl Poston, Associate Professor; Ed.D., Georgia. Vocational education.
David Paul Reinking, Named Professor; Ph.D., Minnesota, Twin Cities. Reading education.
Paul J. Riccomini, Assistant Professor; Ph.D., Penn State. Special education.
Victoria G. Ridgeway, Associate Professor; Ph.D., Georgia. Reading education.
Suzanne N. Rosenblith, Assistant Professor; Ph.D., Wisconsin–Madison. Educational policy studies.
Joseph Ryan, Assistant Professor; Ph.D., Nebraska–Lincoln. Special education.
Deborah A. Smith, Associate Professor; Ed.D., Tennessee. Physical education.
Pamela M. Stecker, Associate Professor; Ph.D., Vanderbilt. Education and human development.
Dolores A. Stegelin, Professor; Ph.D., Florida. Early childhood development and interdisciplinary research.
Deborah M. Switzer, Professor; Ph.D., Illinois. Educational psychology.
Carol G. Weatherford, Associate Professor; Ed.D., North Carolina State. Occupational education.
Elaine Mumbauer Wiegert, Assistant Professor; Ph.D., Clemson. Curriculum and instruction.
Seal Wilson, Clinical Faculty; Ph.D., Southern Mississippi. Special education.

ERIKSON INSTITUTE

Early Childhood Education

Programs of Study

Erikson Institute offers the Master of Science (M.S.) in Early Childhood Education program with opportunities for specialization. All programs have a strong focus on teaching in diverse and inclusive settings and reflect Erikson's extensive partnerships with the Chicago Public Schools.

The 38-credit-hour M.S. in Early Childhood Education program is designed for certified teachers who want to strengthen their understanding of child development and carry their teaching to the next level. Candidates for the program should have a bachelor's degree and Type 04 certification or Type 03 certification and experience in an early childhood classroom.

Core courses provide a comprehensive, interdisciplinary understanding of child development as well as advanced assessment and teaching methods to enhance classroom skills. A special internship, a methods seminar, and a tutorial sequence focus on preparing teachers to meet the requirements for national board certification as an early childhood/generalist. Those who are not interested in national board certification take the same course work but devote their internship and tutorial to a special project or research topic of their own choosing. Students receive advanced instruction in critical subject areas and participate in a supervised internship in their own classrooms.

The M.S. in Early Childhood Education program with Type 04 teacher certification requires 42 credit hours and is a comprehensive and integrated curriculum for prospective teachers of young children from birth through third grade. Students work toward early childhood teacher certification (Type 04) from the Illinois State Board of Education together with the degree.

The 44-credit-hour M.S. in Early Childhood Education program with specialization in Bilingual/English as a Second Language prepares students for early childhood bilingual or ESL approval by the Illinois State Board of Education. Intended for teachers who have Type 03 or Type 04 certification, the program offers specialized courses in language development, assessment, literacy, and methods to prepare students to work with new language learners.

Research Facilities

The Edward Neisser Library and Learning Center combines a print and electronic library, state-of-the-art media center, and hands-on curriculum resource center for teachers. Among the services that the facility provides for students and faculty members is FirstSearch, a growing collection of information resources, many with full-text articles linked to bibliographic citations. It also offers special collections, featuring curriculum resources for the classroom as well as books on children's literature, infant studies, and the developing brain.

In 2005, Erikson Institute established a new research center to inform, support, and encourage effective early-childhood policy in the Great Lakes region. The Herr Research Center for Children and Social Policy is designed to foster the production of original applied research and analysis to help shape public policies that support the healthy development of young children (from birth to age 8) and their families. This new knowledge will be useful to state and local legislators, advocates, foundation officials, and other participants in the policy process. Initially, the Center plans to study policy issues in Illinois, Wisconsin, and Michigan, collaborating with organizations already working on these issues in those states. Unique in its regional approach, the Center plans to provide important comparisons of policies across the states to determine which work best and why. The Center will help address important unanswered questions about the optimal organization, funding, assessment, and replication of high-quality early-childhood programs and services.

Financial Aid

Need-based grants as well as competitive fellowships and scholarships are awarded annually to international and domestic students enrolled in Erikson's master's degree and certificate programs. To be considered for a scholarship, students must submit the Free Application for Federal Student Aid (FAFSA) and the Erikson Financial Aid Application, even if they are not requesting student loans. International students do not submit the FAFSA. Grant awards are based primarily on need, are limited by the availability of funds, and are awarded on a first-come, first-served basis. The highly selective scholarships and fellowships offer partial or full tuition awards and, in the case of fellowships, include a living stipend for two years (three years for Ph.D. students). Direct loans and other federal aid are also available to U.S. citizens and permanent residents.

Cost of Study

Erikson master's degree students are charged by the credit hour. Tuition was $625 for the 2006–07 academic year. Fees totaled about $210.

Living and Housing Costs

Erikson does not provide housing for its students, but the Institute's central location in the downtown River North neighborhood makes it an easy commute from anywhere in the city or suburbs. A list of resources for finding an apartment is available online.

Student Group

In 2006–07, 96 percent of the students in the program were women, and 33 percent were members of minority groups. About 20 percent had advanced degrees. The average age was 31.

Location

The Institute occupies three floors (38,000 square feet) of renovated office and classroom space in Chicago's River North district. The third-largest city in the United States, Chicago is home to an ethnically and economically diverse population. Social service and government agencies, advocacy groups, public and private day-care centers and elementary schools, research institutions, children's hospitals, and even children's museums have responded with a wide variety of early care and education programs. Nearly all provide Erikson students and alumni with opportunities for research, internships, employment, and community service and engagement. One of the nation's most livable cities, Chicago has neighborhoods that cater to every demographic and a public transportation system that is convenient, extensive, and reasonably priced. A wealth of cultural and recreational attractions, as well as architectural and natural beauty, make the city a vibrant and unique place to call home.

The Institute

Erikson Institute is one of the nation's leading graduate schools in child development and early childhood education. The Institute works to improve the care and education of young children (birth through age eight) nationwide in three ways: comprehensive graduate degree and professional development programs, research that can be directly applied to programs and policies, and community service and engagement. The Institute offers master's degrees in child development and early childhood education; a dual degree (Master of Science in child development/Master of Social Work with Loyola University Chicago); a doctorate in child development (with Loyola); and graduate certificate programs in infant studies, infant mental health, administration, and bilingual/ESL education. On- and off-campus professional development programming includes a variety of short courses for parents, teachers, social workers, day-care providers, and other early childhood practitioners.

Applying

Master's degree applicants must demonstrate prior academic competency, practical experience in one of the human services, and professional and leadership potential in the field. To be considered, candidates must hold a bachelor's degree from an accredited institution of higher education, with a minimum grade point average of 2.75 on a 4.0 scale. Applicants must complete an application for admission and the applicant self-disclosure form, pay the $40 application fee, write several short essays in response to questions, provide three letters of recommendation, and submit official transcripts from all colleges and universities attended. Scores of the GRE are not required. Applicants whose native language is not English and/or whose previous education was conducted in a language other than English may be required to take the Test of English as a Foreign Language (TOEFL). All candidates are interviewed by a faculty member.

Erikson makes admissions decisions on a rolling basis. The priority application deadline is April 1. However, candidates for the teacher certification program, which begins in the summer session, are encouraged to apply by March 1. Applications are accepted after these deadlines if space is available.

Correspondence and Information

Valerie Williams, Associate Director, Admissions and Multicultural Student Affairs
Erikson Institute
420 North Wabash Avenue
Chicago, Illinois 60611-5627
Phone: 312-893-7142
E-mail: vwilliams@erikson.edu
Web site: http://www.erikson.edu

Erikson Institute

THE FACULTY AND THEIR RESEARCH

Samuel J. Meisels, President; Ed.D., Harvard. Developmental assessment of young children, effect of standardized tests on children, impact of state and federal policies on the families of children with disabilities, development of alternative assessment strategies, developmental consequences of high-risk birth.

Frances Stott, Vice President and Dean of Academic Affairs; Ph.D., Northwestern. Parent-child relationships, social-emotional development of young children, children and families at risk.

Zachariah Boukydis, Associate Professor; Ph.D., Penn State. Infant mental health, including crying and sleep disturbances; support services for at-risk infants and families; NICU neurobehavioral scale; effects of substance abuse on maternal-infant attachment.

Barbara Bowman, Professor; M.A., Chicago. Head Start; teacher training, salary equity, and uniform standards; education of and educational equity for low-income and minority students.

Jie-Qi Chen, Associate Professor; Ph.D., Tufts. Cognitive development and early education, implications and applications of multiple intelligences theory, assessment of children's learning, technology and learning, cultural variation in child development.

Molly Fuller Collins, Assistant Professor; Ed.D., Boston University. Emergent writing, early literacy and language acquisition, preschool curricula and instruction.

Linda Gilkerson, Professor; Ph.D., Illinois. Early intervention with infants and families, with special emphasis on high-risk children in hospital settings; applications of neuroscience research findings on early infancy to childhood care and education; infant mental health and early-intervention services.

Robert Halpern, Professor; Ph.D., Florida State. After-school programs and youth services/community-development initiatives; history of youth and family services; program evaluation and public policy, design, management, and evaluation of parent support and education programs; literacy in nonschool settings; implications of youth programs, including decreased physical activity; prevention of abuse and neglect.

Patty Horsch, Clinical Assistant Professor; Ph.D., Erikson Institute/Loyola Chicago. Teacher education and professional development, curriculum and methods of teaching, home and school community partnerships.

Jon Korfmacher, Associate Professor; Ph.D., Minnesota. Treatment processes in early-childhood interventions, infant mental health, emotional development, child abuse and neglect, structure and benefits of doula programs for young mothers.

Gillian D. McNamee, Professor; Ph.D., Northwestern. Language development, educational programs for preschool and school-aged children, after-school programs, learning-disabled children, early literacy development, family literacy, role of the arts in early education, teacher professional development, assessment of teaching and children's learning across the curriculum.

Aisha Ray, Associate Professor; M.Ed., Erikson Institute/Loyola Chicago; Ph.D., Michigan. Development of children in multigenerational caregiving families in urban communities; role of father in African-American families; development of parenting roles in unmarried, low-income couples; socialization of women and girls in urban communities; effects of a multicultural society on teaching and learning.

Sharon Syc, Clinical Assistant Professor; Ph.D., Chicago. Infant development, early intervention, special education, developmental psychology.

Senior Instructors
Colette Davison, Ph.D., Northwestern.
Mary Hynes-Berry, Ph.D., Wisconsin–Madison.
Rebeca Itzkowich, M.A., NYU.

Instructors
Barbara Abel, Ph.D., Erikson Institute/Loyola Chicago.
Theresa Atchley, M.Ed., Boston College.
Judith Bertacchi, M.Ed., Erikson Institute/Loyola Chicago.
JoAnn Burnside, M.Ed., Erikson Institute/Loyola Chicago.
Stephanie Bynum, M.S., Erikson Institute.
Charles Chang, M.A., Chicago.
Bonnie Fields, M.S.W., Illinois.
Sonja Hall, M.Ed., Erikson Institute/Loyola Chicago.
Carey Halsey, M.S., Wheelock.
Deborah Hampton, M.Ed., Erikson Institute/Loyola Chicago.
Megan Hillegass, M.S., Erikson Institute.
Patricia Husband, M.A., Northeastern Illinois.
Laurie Kabb, M.S.W., Smith.
Mary Marovich, M.Ed., Erikson Institute/Loyola Chicago.
Ann Masur, Ph.D., Erikson Institute/Loyola Chicago.
Luisiana Melendez, M.Ed., Erikson Institute/Loyola Chicago.
Rebecca Mermelstein, Ph.D., Illinois at Chicago.
Margret Nickels, Ph.D., Northwestern.
Eleanor Nicholson, Ph.D., Loyola Chicago.
Anna Perry, M.Ed., Harvard.
Nancy Segall, M.A., Chicago.
Priya Shimpi, M.S., Chicago.
Char Slezak, Psy.D.
Deborah Weatherston, Ph.D., Wayne State.

HAWAI'I PACIFIC UNIVERSITY

Master of Education in Secondary Education

Programs of Study

The Master of Education in Secondary Education degree program at Hawai'i Pacific University develops professional educators who are reflective practitioners dedicated to the scholarship of teaching and school renewal. The program is based on an innovative, standards-driven, field-based curriculum that employs cutting-edge educational technology to integrate content and pedagogy. Upon completing the program, each teacher candidate is able to demonstrate knowledge of his or her content area, the ability to develop and modify instruction plans to meet learner needs, a commitment to the education profession by engaging in appropriate professional practices, and the desire to collaborate with colleagues, families, and community members. The program is accredited by the Accrediting Commission for Senior Colleges and Universities of the Western Association of Schools and Colleges.

Students may choose to pursue a Professional Certificate in Secondary Education, which prepares candidates for licensure in secondary education. The certificate requires 32 credit hours: four core courses in secondary education; one content area concentration course in computer science, English curriculum, ESL, mathematics, science, or social studies; and a teaching internship and seminar. Each course is accompanied by relevant field experience. In order to complete the masters' degree program, students must complete an additional 9 credit hours in one research methods course and two professional papers courses. Those students who obtain licensure are qualified to teach in forty-four states.

Research Facilities

Meader Library occupies three separate floors in the Bishop Street Building in downtown Honolulu. The second floor contains specialized and general reference and information services, interlibrary loan, and online database searching services. The third floor collection is primarily devoted to business, social sciences, and computer sciences. There is also a collection of books to support the University's English Foundations Program. Online access to the libraries' holdings is available through HPU Pipeline via the HPU Libraries' Public Access Catalog (PAC). eBooks can be accessed and checked out from off-campus locations through the PAC. The fifth floor contains a periodical collection that includes academic journals and a broad selection of local, national, and international newspapers. A specially designated room contains the various volumes of books that, because of their uniqueness and presentation of information, require special consideration and handling. A major collection of books on Hawai'i and the Pacific area includes materials that document the social, historical, educational, scientific, and economic events of this area and its people.

Financial Aid

The Trustees' Scholar Program awards a 50 percent tuition waiver for two semesters to qualified full-time students. The Deans' Scholarship Program awards a 20 percent tuition waiver for one semester. Graduate assistants work 10 hours per week in exchange for a 50 percent tuition waiver. Under the Federal Stafford Loan program, students may borrow up to $8500 per academic year in subsidized loans or $18,500 in unsubsidized loans. However, loan forgiveness is an option for those who teach full-time at low-income elementary or secondary schools for 5 years. Most teachers are forgiven $5000, while math, science, and special education teachers are forgiven up to $17,500.

Cost of Study

In 2007–08, graduate tuition is $560 per credit; full-time students pay $13,440 per academic year. Other costs include health insurance for $880 per academic year and approximately $1680 for books, supplies, and transportation.

Living and Housing Costs

The University has residence halls, off-campus housing for graduate students, and an apartment referral service. For the 2007–08 academic year, housing expenses are approximately $9840. For off-campus housing, students can expect to pay $700–$1000 per month for a studio, $900–$1500 for a one-bedroom, or $1300–$2000 for a two-bedroom apartment. For further graduate housing information, students should call HPU's Center for Off-Campus Housing at 808-544-1430 or contact Hawaiian Island Student Suites directly: http://www.campushousing.com/hawaii/.

Student Group

Students come from a wide variety of academic and social backgrounds. As the largest private university in Hawai'i, HPU students come from every state in the U.S. and more than other 100 countries. The diversity of the student body stimulates learning about other cultures firsthand, both in and out of the classroom. There is no majority population at HPU. Students are encouraged to examine the values, customs, traditions, and principles of others to gain a clearer understanding of their own perspectives. HPU students develop friendships with students throughout the United States and the world and establish important connections for success in the global economy of the twenty-first century.

Location

With three campuses linked by shuttle, Hawai'i Pacific combines the excitement of an urban, downtown campus with the serenity of the windward side of the island. The main campus is located in downtown Honolulu, the business and financial center of the Pacific, within walking distance of shopping and dining. Iolani Palace, the only palace in the U.S., is a few blocks away, as are the State Capitol, City Hall, and the Blaisdell Concert Hall. The Honolulu Academy of Arts, Museum of Contemporary Art, Waikiki Aquarium, Honolulu Zoo, and many other cultural attractions are located nearby.

The Hawai'i Loa campus is 8 miles away in Kaneohe, at the base of the Ko'olau Mountains; it is the site of the School of Nursing, the marine science program, and a variety of other course offerings. The third campus, Oceanic Institute, is an applied aquaculture research facility located on a 56-acre site at Makapu'u Point on the windward coast.

The University

Hawai'i Pacific University, a coeducational, nonsectarian, career-oriented university founded in 1965, is the largest private institution for higher learning in Hawai'i, offering more than sixty degree programs to more than 9,000 students. HPU's innovative programs anticipate the changing needs of the community and prepare graduates to live and work as active members of a global society. Students come from all fifty states and from more than 100 countries, making HPU one of the most culturally diverse universities in the world.

Applying

Applicants are required to submit a signed and completed application form, official transcripts from all previously attended colleges and universities, two letters of recommendation, a personal statement and essay, official GRE scores, official PRAXIS I Pre-Professional Skills test scores of 171 or higher, and a $50 nonrefundable application fee. Applicants may also schedule an interview with a faculty member. Applications are accepted throughout the year for entry in the summer or fall semesters.

Correspondence and Information

Graduate Admissions
Hawai'i Pacific University
1164 Bishop Street, #911
Honolulu, Hawai'i 96813
Phone: 808-544-1135
        866-GRAD-HPU (toll-free)
Fax: 808-544-0280
E-mail: graduate@hpu.edu
Web site: http://www.hpu.edu/med

Hawai'i Pacific University

THE FACULTY

Valentina M. Abordonado, Associate Professor of English and Director of Teacher Education Program; Ph.D., Arizona.
Eric Brewe, Assistant Professor of Physics; Ph.D., Arizona State.
Kathleen J. Cassity, Assistant Professor of English; Ph.D., Hawaii.
Jean Coffman, Associate Professor of TESL; M.A., Columbia Teachers College.
Leslie Correa, Dean, College of Liberal Arts; Ed.D., Hawaii.
Jon Davidann, Associate Professor of History; Ph.D., Minnesota.
Dorothy Douthit, Visiting Assistant Professor of Education; Ph.D., Texas at Austin.
John Hawkins Jr., Adjunct Faculty, Education; M.Ed., Hawaii at Manoa.
Gordon L. Jones, Professor of Computer Science and Information Systems; Ph.D., New Mexico.
Evelyn Pua'a, Instructor of Mathematics; M.Ed., USC.
Mitchell Robertson, Associate Professor of Chemistry; Ph.D., Iowa State.
Kenneth Rossi, Assistant Professor of Information Systems; Ed.D., USC.
Edwin Van Gorder, Associate Professor of Management and Mathematics; Ph.D., Stanford.
Linda Wheeler, Assistant Professor of Education and TEP Field Coordinator; Ed.D., Hawaii at Manoa.

VIRGINIA COMMONWEALTH UNIVERSITY

M.Ed. in Adult Learning Program

Program of Study	The School of Education at Virginia Commonwealth University (VCU) offers an M.Ed. in Adult Learning Program, a 39-credit-hour program of study that prepares individuals for a broad range of positions related to the education of adult learners. The M.Ed. in Adult Learning Program provides a three-course foundation in educational research, evaluation, and adult development. A strong core of seven courses related to the design, development, and delivery of adult-learning programs and activities composes the major portion of the curriculum. The emphasis is on equipping an educator of adults with the requisite knowledge, skills, and dispositions to work with a broad array of adult learners in business and industry, government, education, nonprofit, and community and human service agencies.
	In the last year of the program, students select one of three specialization tracks for a three-course concentration—adult literacy, human resource development, or adults with disabilities. The last course in the program, a capstone seminar in action learning, reunites students from all three specialty tracks for a comprehensive synthesis of learning as they work in action learning teams to solve a real problem of strategic importance to an organization in the community.
	A unique feature of the program is an e-portfolio assessment, which, in combination with the capstone seminar, replaces a comprehensive examination requirement. For the e-portfolio, students are required to write a reflective essay at the end of each core and specialty track course taken, evaluating their learning experiences and how they intend to apply what has been learned. The reflective essay, along with a copy of the student's best work from each course, is placed in the e-portfolio, to be reviewed at the end of the program by the student and his or her adviser. The e-portfolio serves as a demonstration of the graduate's abilities to a prospective employer.
Research Facilities	VCU libraries provide a combined capacity of more than 1.7 million volumes and 10,200 periodical titles and an online bibliographic search service accessing hundreds of databases. In addition, the Virginia State and Richmond Public Libraries are within walking distance of both VCU campuses. Academic Computing provides a variety of microcomputer, minicomputer, and mainframe computing services to support the research and instructional endeavors of the faculty and students, including consultation, instruction, and computer acquisition.
	The School of Education sponsors a variety of centers and institutes that connect students and faculty members to the field of practice, including the Center for School Community Collaboration, the Center for Teacher Leadership, the Child Development Center, the Commonwealth Educational Policy Institute (CEPI), the Metropolitan Educational Research Consortium (MERC), the Partnership for People with Disabilities, the Virginia Department of Education's (VDOE) Training & Technical Assistance Center (T/TAC), the Rehabilitation Research and Training Center, the Virginia Adult Learning Resource Center, the Virginia Center for Teaching International Studies, and the Metropolitan Educational Training Alliance (META).
Financial Aid	Students may apply for need-based assistance with the University's Financial Aid Office. Current information on financial aid programs, policies, and procedures is available at http://www.vcu.edu/enroll/finaid.
Cost of Study	For full-time study (9–15 credits) in 2007–08, Virginia residents pay tuition and fees of $4452 per semester; nonresidents, $8876 per semester. For part-time study, Virginia residents pay tuition and fees of $465 per hour; nonresidents, $954 per hour. Some programs require additional fees. On the Medical College of Virginia (MCV) campus, tuition, fees, and other expenses vary in the medicine, pharmacy, nurse anesthesia, dentistry, and School of Allied Health programs.
Living and Housing Costs	Graduate student housing is available on both the MCV campus and the academic campus of Virginia Commonwealth University. Many graduate students live in off-campus housing, which is reasonably priced and readily available in a variety of styles and settings in nearby residential areas or within easy commuting distance. On- and off-campus housing information is available on the Web at http://www.housing.vcu.edu/.
Student Group	VCU enrolls 30,452 students, 7,611 of whom are graduate students. More than 200 clubs and organizations reflect the diverse social, recreational, educational, political, and religious interests of the student body.
Location	Richmond is Virginia's capital and a major East Coast financial and manufacturing center that offers students a wide range of cultural, educational, and recreational activities. Richmond is located in central Virginia at the intersection of Interstates 95 and 64, 2 hours south of Washington, D.C., and nestled between the Blue Ridge Mountains and the Atlantic coast. The Richmond region is easily accessible by plane, car, and train. With nearly 1 million residents, the historic city of Richmond combines big-city offerings with small-town hospitality. Applicants are encouraged to explore http://www.visit.richmond.com/ for more information on the city.
The University	VCU is a state-supported coeducational university with a graduate school, a major teaching hospital, and twelve academic and professional units that offer fifty-two undergraduate, twenty-two postbaccalaureate certificate, sixty-five master's, six post-master's certificate, and twenty-nine Ph.D. programs. VCU also offers M.D., D.D.S., D.P.T., and Pharm.D. programs as well as cooperative degree programs with other major Virginia colleges and universities. VCU has one of the largest evening colleges in the United States. The academic campus is located in Richmond's historic Fan District. The health sciences campus and hospital are located 2 miles east in the downtown business district. A University bus service provides free intercampus transportation for faculty members and students.
	With more than $211 million in annual research funding, Virginia Commonwealth University is classified as one of the nation's top research universities by the Carnegie Foundation for the Advancement of Teaching. More than 29,000 undergraduate, certificate, graduate, post-master's, professional, and doctoral students are enrolled in 162 academic programs, forty of which are unique in the commonwealth of Virginia. The faculty members represent the finest American and international graduate institutions and enhance the University's position among the important institutions of higher learning in the United States and the world via their work in the classroom, laboratory, studio, and clinic and in their scholarly publications.
Applying	Admission procedures and program requirements are detailed in the *Graduate Bulletin* and on the School of Education's Web site (http://www.soe.vcu.edu). Application deadlines and materials, including the application and the *Graduate Bulletin*, are available online at the Graduate School Web site at http://www.graduate.vcu.edu. Virginia Commonwealth University is an equal opportunity/affirmative action institution providing access to education and employment without regard to age, race, color, national origin, gender, religion, sexual orientation, veteran's status, political affiliation, or disability.
Correspondence and Information	Teresa J. Carter School of Education Virginia Commonwealth University 1015 West Main Street Richmond, Virginia 23284-2020 Phone: 804-828-2628 Fax: 804-828-1326 E-mail: tjcarter@vcu.edu Web site: http://www.soe.vcu.edu/departments/tl/MEd_AdultLearning.htm

Virginia Commonwealth University

THE FACULTY AND THEIR RESEARCH

Nora Alder, Associate Professor; Ed.D., Nevada. Caring student/teacher relationships and urban schooling, teacher education.

Teresa J. Carter, Assistant Professor; Ed.D., George Washington. Transformative learning among professionals in the workplace; learning through developmental relationships, including mentoring.

Seonhee Cho, Assistant Professor; Ph.D., Tennessee. ESL/international students' academic socialization issues, including relationships with peers and teachers, group work, institutional support, and access to academic resources.

Leila Christenbury, Professor; Ed.D., Virginia Tech. Classroom interaction strategies, specifically questioning; all aspects of young adult literature; the teaching of writing to secondary school students; approaches to teaching and learning in the secondary English classroom.

Michael Davis, Professor and Chair; Ph.D., Illinois. School change and teacher preparation.

Terry Dozier, Associate Professor and Director of the Center for Teacher Leadership, Ed.D. Promoting and supporting teacher leadership that enhances the quality of teaching and the teaching profession.

Ena Gross, Associate Professor; Ph.D., Georgia State. Math education.

Jacqueline McDonnough, Assistant Professor; Ph.D., Virginia. Assessing how preservice teachers K–12 science experiences interact with their self-efficacy as future teachers of science.

Tammy Milby, Instructor; M.Ed., Radford. Struggling readers and writers, teacher quality/professional development practices, low-performing schools.

William Muth, Assistant Professor; Ph.D., George Mason. Thirdspace and Reading Components theories, especially as these apply to prison-based family literacy programs and children of incarcerated parents.

Gabriel Reich, Assistant Professor, Ph.D. Social studies teaching and learning, assessment, curriculum.

Joan Rhodes, Assistant Professor; Ph.D., Virginia Commonwealth. Early literacy development, using hypertext for increasing comprehension, Instant Messaging and social networking, electronic study skills, emerging and new literacies, assessment and instructional strategies for remediating reading difficulties.

Valerie Robnolt, Assistant Professor; Ph.D., Virginia. Assessment and instruction of reading comprehension, vocabulary, and fluency; the most effective methods of providing professional development to elementary teachers.

Gary Sarkozi, Assistant Professor; Ph.D., Virginia Commonwealth. Collecting, analyzing, and evaluating data on activities related to technological integration in the many facets of today's global environment.

Loraine Stewart, Associate Professor; Ed.D., North Carolina at Greensboro. Examining strategies used by classroom teachers to integrate African American children's literature into the elementary curriculum and the impact this literature has on student achievement.

Doris White, Associate Professor; Ed.D., Illinois. Multicultural education, urban education, testing and achievement outcomes.

Section 25
Special Focus

This section contains a directory of institutions offering graduate work in special focus, followed by in-depth entries submitted by institutions that chose to prepare detailed program descriptions. Additional information about programs listed in the directory but not augmented by an in-depth entry may be obtained by writing directly to the dean of a graduate school or chair of a department at the address given in the directory.

For programs offering related work, see also in this book Administration, Instruction, and Theory; Education; Health-Related Professions; Instructional Levels; Leisure Studies and Recreation; Physical Education and Kinesiology; and Subject Areas; and in Book 2, Psychology and Counseling (School Psychology) and Public, Regional, and Industrial Affairs (Urban Studies)

CONTENTS

Education of the Gifted

Arkansas State University, Graduate School, College of Education, Department of Educational Leadership, Curriculum, and Special Education, Jonesboro, State University, AR 72467. Offers community college administration education (SCCT); education theory and practice (MSE); educational leadership (MSE, Ed D, Ed S), including curriculum and instruction (Ed S), elementary curriculum and instruction (MSE), elementary principalship (Ed S), secondary principalship (Ed S), superintendency (Ed S); special education (MSE), including emotionally disturbed, gifted, talented and creative, instructional specialist 4-12, instructional specialist P-4; special education program administration (Ed S). *Accreditation:* NCATE. Part-time programs available. *Faculty:* 14 full-time (7 women), 5 part-time/adjunct (2 women). *Students:* 28 full-time (21 women), 328 part-time (233 women); includes 63 minority (58 African Americans, 3 American Indian/Alaska Native, 1 Asian American or Pacific Islander, 1 Hispanic American), 2 international. Average age 36. 181 applicants, 78% accepted, 70 enrolled. In 2006, 70 master's, 13 doctorates, 14 other advanced degrees awarded. *Degree requirements:* For master's, thesis or alternative, comprehensive exam; for doctorate, thesis/dissertation, comprehensive exam. *Entrance requirements:* For master's, GRE General Test or MAT, appropriate bachelor's degree, letters of reference, interview, official transcript; for doctorate and other advanced degree, GRE General Test or MAT, interview, master's degree, letters of reference, official transcript. Additional exam requirements/recommendations for international students: Required—TOEFL (minimum score 213 computer-based). *Application deadline:* Applications are processed on a rolling basis. Application fee: $30 ($40 for international students). Electronic applications accepted. *Expenses:* Tuition, state resident: full-time $3,393; part-time $189 per hour. Tuition, nonresident: full-time $8,577; part-time $477 per hour. Required fees: $752; $39 per hour. $25 per semester. *Financial support:* Teaching assistantships, career-related internships or fieldwork, scholarships/grants, and unspecified assistantships available. Financial award application deadline: 7/1; financial award applicants required to submit FAFSA. *Unit head:* Dr. Mitchell Holifield, Chair, 870-972-3062, Fax: 870-680-8130, E-mail: hfield@astate.edu.

Arkansas Tech University, Graduate School, School of Education, Russellville, AR 72801. Offers college student personnel (MSE); educational leadership (M Ed, Ed S); English education (M Ed); gifted education (MSE); instructional improvement (M Ed); secondary education (M Ed); teaching, learning and leadership (M Ed). *Accreditation:* NCATE. Part-time programs available. *Students:* 44 full-time (33 women), 244 part-time (181 women); includes 20 minority (14 African Americans, 1 American Indian/Alaska Native, 3 Asian Americans or Pacific Islanders, 2 Hispanic Americans), 18 international. Average age 34. In 2006, 72 master's, 4 other advanced degrees awarded. *Degree requirements:* For master's, action research project, thesis optional. *Entrance requirements:* For master's, GRE General Test or MAT. Additional exam requirements/recommendations for international students: Required—TOEFL (minimum score 500 paper-based; 173 computer-based). *Application deadline:* For fall admission, 3/1 priority date for domestic students, 5/1 priority date for international students; for winter admission, 10/1 priority date for international students; for spring admission, 10/1 priority date for domestic and international students. Applications are processed on a rolling basis. Application fee: $0 ($30 for international students). Electronic applications accepted. *Expenses:* Tuition, state resident: full-time $3,060; part-time $170 per hour. Tuition, nonresident: full-time $6,120; part-time $340 per hour. Required fees: $312; $4 per hour. $84 per term. Part-time tuition and fees vary according to course load. *Financial support:* In 2006–07, teaching assistantships with full tuition reimbursements (averaging $4,000 per year); career-related internships or fieldwork, Federal Work-Study, scholarships/grants, health care benefits, and unspecified assistantships also available. Support available to part-time students. Financial award application deadline: 4/15; financial award applicants required to submit FAFSA. *Unit head:* Dr. C. Glenn Sheets, Dean, 479-968-0350, Fax: 479-968-0350, E-mail: glenn.sheets@atu.edu. *Application contact:* Dr. Eldon G. Clary, Dean of Graduate School, 479-968-0398, Fax: 479-964-0542, E-mail: graduate.school@atu.edu.

Ashland University, College of Education, Graduate Studies in Education, Department of Curriculum and Instruction, Ashland, OH 44805-3702. Offers educational technology (M Ed); intervention specialist-mild/moderate (M Ed); intervention specialist-moderate/intensive (M Ed); middle school education (M Ed); talent development (M Ed). *Accreditation:* NCATE. Part-time and evening/weekend programs available. *Faculty:* 11 full-time (7 women), 93 part-time/adjunct (54 women). *Students:* 188 full-time (161 women), 354 part-time (314 women); includes 25 minority (19 African Americans, 3 Asian Americans or Pacific Islanders, 3 Hispanic Americans), 1 international. Average age 32. In 2006, 220 degrees awarded. *Degree requirements:* For master's, thesis or alternative, internship, practicum, seminar. *Entrance requirements:* For master's, GRE General Test or MAT, teaching certificate, minimum GPA of 2.75 (or 2.5 with 2.75 in education or major subject field). Additional exam requirements/recommendations for international students: Required—TOEFL. *Application deadline:* For fall admission, 8/27 for domestic students; for spring admission, 1/14 for domestic students. Applications are processed on a rolling basis. Application fee: $30. *Expenses:* Tuition: Part-time $403 per credit. Tuition and fees vary according to degree level and program. *Financial support:* In 2006–07, 189 students received support. Institutionally sponsored loans and scholarships/grants available. Financial award application deadline: 4/15. *Faculty research:* Gender equity, postmodern children's and young adult literature, outdoor/experimental education, re-examining literature study in middle grades, morality and giftedness. *Unit head:* Dr. James P. Van Keuren, Chair, 419-289-5377, Fax: 419-207-4949, E-mail: jvankeu1@ashland.edu.

Barry University, School of Education, Program in Curriculum and Instruction, Miami Shores, FL 33161-6695. Offers accomplished teacher (Ed S); culture, language and literacy (TESOL) (PhD); curriculum evaluation and research (PhD); early childhood (Ed S); early childhood education (PhD); elementary (Ed S); elementary education (PhD); ESOL (Ed S); gifted (Ed S); Montessori (Ed S); PKP/elementary (Ed S); reading (Ed S); reading, language and cognition (PhD). *Students:* 2 full-time (both women), 36 part-time (27 women); includes 21 minority (12 African Americans, 9 Hispanic Americans), 6 international. 45 applicants, 33% accepted, 4 enrolled. In 2006, 4 degrees awarded. *Entrance requirements:* For doctorate, GRE, minimum GPA of 3.25. Application fee: $30. *Unit head:* Dr. Jill Farrell, Director, 305-899-3198, Fax: 305-899-4708, E-mail: jfarrell@mail.barry.edu. *Application contact:* Dave Fletcher, Director of Graduate Admissions, 305-899-3113, Fax: 305-899-2971, E-mail: dfletcher@mail.barry.edu.

Barry University, School of Education, Program in Exceptional Student Education, Miami Shores, FL 33161-6695. Offers exceptional student education (MS, Ed S). Part-time and evening/weekend programs available. *Students:* 78 full-time (70 women), 27 part-time (24 women); includes 74 minority (45 African Americans, 1 Asian American or Pacific Islander, 28 Hispanic Americans), 1 international. 37 applicants, 84% accepted, 23 enrolled. In 2006, 45 master's, 1 other advanced degree awarded. *Degree requirements:* For master's, comprehensive exam; for Ed S, practicum. *Entrance requirements:* For master's, GRE General Test or MAT, minimum GPA of 3.0; for Ed S, GRE General Test, minimum GPA of 3.0. *Application deadline:* For fall admission, 5/1 priority date for domestic students. Applications are processed on a rolling basis. Application fee: $30. Electronic applications accepted. *Unit head:* Dr. Judy Harris-Looby, Director, 305-899-3709, Fax: 305-899-4708, E-mail: jhlooby@mail.barry.edu. *Application contact:* Dave Fletcher, Director of Graduate Admissions, 305-899-3113, Fax: 305-899-2971, E-mail: dfletcher@mail.barry.edu.

Barry University, School of Education, Program in Leadership and Education, Miami Shores, FL 33161-6695. Offers educational technology (PhD); exceptional student education (PhD); higher education administration (PhD); human resource development (PhD); leadership (PhD). Part-time and evening/weekend programs available. *Students:* 15 full-time (7 women), 233 part-time (147 women); includes 97 minority (52 African Americans, 45 Hispanic Americans), 7 international. 58 applicants, 34% accepted, 18 enrolled. In 2006, 23 degrees awarded. *Degree requirements:* For doctorate, thesis/dissertation. *Entrance requirements:* For doctorate, GRE General Test, minimum GPA of 3.25. *Application deadline:* For fall admission, 5/1 priority date for domestic students. Applications are processed on a rolling basis. Application fee: $30. Electronic applications accepted. *Unit head:* Dr. Carmen McCrink, Director, 305-899-3702, Fax: 305-899-4708, E-mail: cmccrink@mail.barry.edu. *Application contact:* Dave Fletcher, Director of Graduate Admissions, 305-899-3113, Fax: 305-899-2971, E-mail: dfletcher@mail.barry.edu.

Belmont University, College of Arts and Sciences, School of Education, Nashville, TN 37212-3757. Offers education (MAT); elementary education (M Ed), including early childhood education, elementary education, gifted education, language arts education; English (M Ed); history (M Ed); mathematics (M Ed); middle grade education (M Ed); science (M Ed); secondary education (M Ed), including gifted education; sports administration (MSA); technology (M Ed). *Accreditation:* NCATE. Part-time and evening/weekend programs available. *Faculty:* 9 full-time (7 women), 20 part-time/adjunct (15 women). *Students:* 50 full-time (36 women), 116 part-time (76 women); includes 23 minority (20 African Americans, 1 Asian American or Pacific Islander, 2 Hispanic Americans), 1 international. Average age 30. 55 applicants, 60% accepted, 30 enrolled. In 2006, 82 degrees awarded. *Degree requirements:* For master's, thesis, comprehensive exam. *Entrance requirements:* For master's, MAT or GRE, minimum GPA of 2.75. Additional exam requirements/recommendations for international students: Required—TOEFL. *Application deadline:* For fall admission, 8/1 priority date for domestic students, 5/1 for international students; for spring admission, 12/1 priority date for domestic students, 9/1 for international students. Applications are processed on a rolling basis. Application fee: $50. *Expenses:* Contact institution. *Financial support:* In 2006–07, 25 students received support; fellowships with partial tuition reimbursements available, institutionally sponsored loans and tuition waivers (partial) available. Financial award application deadline: 4/15; financial award applicants required to submit FAFSA. *Faculty research:* Technology grant, professional development schools. Total annual research expenditures: $6,500. *Unit head:* Dr. Trevor F. Hutchins, Associate Dean, 615-460-6232, Fax: 615-460-6414, E-mail: hutchinst@mail.belmont.edu. *Application contact:* Julie Hullett, Admission/Licensure Officer, 615-460-6879, Fax: 615-460-5556, E-mail: hullettj@email.belmont.edu.

Bowling Green State University, Graduate College, College of Education and Human Development, School of Education and Intervention Services, Intervention Services Division, Program in Special Education, Bowling Green, OH 43403. Offers assistive technology (M Ed); early childhood intervention (M Ed); gifted education (M Ed); hearing impaired intervention (M Ed); mild/moderate intervention (M Ed); moderate/intensive intervention (M Ed). *Accreditation:* NCATE. Part-time programs available. *Students:* 26 full-time (21 women), 84 part-time (78 women); includes 4 minority (all African Americans) Average age 35. 39 applicants, 87% accepted, 12 enrolled. In 2006, 47 degrees awarded. *Degree requirements:* For master's, thesis or alternative. *Entrance requirements:* For master's, GRE General Test. Additional exam requirements/recommendations for international students: Required—TOEFL. *Application deadline:* For fall admission, 3/1 priority date for domestic students. Applications are processed on a rolling basis. Application fee: $30. Electronic applications accepted. *Expenses:* Tuition, state resident: part-time $535 per hour. Tuition, nonresident: part-time $884 per hour. *Financial support:* In 2006–07, 16 research assistantships with full tuition reimbursements (averaging $5,202 per year) were awarded; teaching assistantships with full tuition reimbursements, Federal Work-Study and unspecified assistantships also available. Financial award applicants required to submit FAFSA. *Faculty research:* Reading and special populations, deafness, early childhood, gifted and talented, behavior disorders. *Application contact:* Dr. Lessie Cochran, Graduate Coordinator, 419-372-7298.

Carlos Albizu University, Miami Campus, Graduate Programs, Miami, FL 33172-2209. Offers clinical psychology (Psy D); entrepreneurship (MBA); exceptional student education (MS); industrial/organizational psychology (MS); marriage and family therapy (MS); mental health counseling (MS); nonprofit management (MBA); organizational management (MBA); psychology (MS); school counseling (MS); teaching English as a second language (MS). *Accreditation:* APA. Part-time and evening/weekend programs available. Terminal master's awarded for partial completion of doctoral program. *Degree requirements:* For master's, one foreign language, comprehensive exam, integrative project (MBA), research project (MSESE); for doctorate, one foreign language, comprehensive exam, internship, doctoral project. *Entrance requirements:* For master's, 3 letters of recommendation, interview, minimum GPA of 3.0, resumé; for doctorate, 3 letters of recommendation, minimum GPA of 3.0, resumé, interview. *Faculty research:* Psychotherapy, forensic psychology, neuropsychology, marketing strategy, entrepreneurship.

Carthage College, Division of Teacher Education, Kenosha, WI 53140. Offers classroom guidance and counseling (M Ed); creative arts (M Ed); gifted and talented children (M Ed); language arts (M Ed); modern language (M Ed); natural sciences (M Ed); reading (M Ed, Certificate); social sciences (M Ed); teacher leadership (M Ed). Part-time and evening/weekend programs available. *Degree requirements:* For master's, thesis optional. *Entrance requirements:* For master's, MAT, minimum B average, letters of reference.

Clark Atlanta University, School of Education, Department of Exceptional Student Education, Atlanta, GA 30314. Offers MA, Ed S. *Degree requirements:* For master's, one foreign language, thesis; for Ed S, thesis. *Entrance requirements:* For master's, GRE General Test, minimum undergraduate GPA of 2.5; for Ed S, GRE General Test, minimum graduate GPA of 3.0.

The College of New Rochelle, Graduate School, Division of Education, Program in Creative Teaching and Learning, New Rochelle, NY 10805-2308. Offers MS Ed, Certificate. Part-time programs available. *Faculty:* 1 (woman) full-time, 1 (woman) part-time/adjunct. *Students:* Average age 25. In 2006, 5 degrees awarded. *Degree requirements:* For master's, practicum. *Entrance requirements:* For master's, interview, minimum GPA of 3.0 in field, 2.7 overall. *Application deadline:* For fall admission, 8/1 priority date for domestic students; for spring admission, 4/6 for domestic students. Applications are processed on a rolling basis. Application fee: $35. *Expenses:* Tuition: Part-time $575 per credit. Required fees: $90 per term. *Financial support:* In 2006–07, 2 research assistantships with tuition reimbursements were awarded; career-related internships or fieldwork, scholarships/grants, and unspecified assistantships also available. Support available to part-time students. *Unit head:* Dr. Marie Ribarich, Acting Division Head, Division of Education, 914-654-5333, Fax: 914-654-5593, E-mail: mribarich@cnr.edu.

The College of William and Mary, School of Education, Program in Curriculum and Instruction, Williamsburg, VA 23187-8795. Offers elementary education (MA Ed); gifted education (MA Ed); reading education (MA Ed); secondary education (MA Ed), including English education, mathematics education, modern foreign languages education, science education, social studies education; special education (MA Ed), including emotionally disturbed, learning disabled, mental retardation, resource collaborating teaching. *Accreditation:* NCATE. Part-time programs available. *Faculty:* 15 full-time (6 women), 13 part-time/adjunct (10 women). *Students:* 51 full-time (39 women), 51 part-time (45 women); includes 6 minority (all African Americans) Average age 29. 161 applicants, 68% accepted, 61 enrolled. In 2006, 68 degrees awarded. *Degree requirements:* For master's, master's project. *Entrance requirements:* For master's, GRE or MAT, minimum GPA of 2.5. Additional exam requirements/recommendations for international students: Required—TOEFL. *Application deadline:* For fall admission, 2/1 for domestic and international students; for spring admission, 10/1 for domestic and international students. Application fee: $30. *Expenses:* Tuition, state resident: full-time $6,100; part-time $260 per credit. Tuition, nonresident: full-time $18,790; part-time $725 per credit. Required fees: $3,314. Tuition and fees vary according to program. *Financial support:* In 2006–07, 10 research assistantships with full and partial tuition reimbursements (averaging $5,000 per year) were awarded; career-related internships or fieldwork, Federal Work-Study, institutionally sponsored loans, scholarships/grants, and unspecified assistantships also available. Financial award application deadline: 2/1; financial award applicants required to submit FAFSA. *Faculty research:* National Council of Teachers of Mathematics Standards, counseling, self-concept and self-esteem, special education, curriculum development. *Unit head:* Dr. John Moore, Area Coordinator, 757-221-2333, E-mail: jnmoor@wm.edu. *Application contact:* Dorothy Osborne, Director of Admissions, 757-221-2317, E-mail: dsosbo@wm.edu.

Converse College, School of Education and Graduate Studies, Program in Gifted Education, Spartanburg, SC 29302-0006. Offers M Ed. Part-time programs available. *Faculty:* 1 full-time, 2 part-time/adjunct. *Students:* Average age 35. In 2006, 8 degrees awarded. *Degree requirements:* For master's, capstone paper. *Entrance requirements:* For master's, NTE or PRAXIS II, minimum GPA of 2.75, teaching certificate, 2 recommendations. *Application deadline:* For fall admission, 8/1 for domestic and international students; for winter admission, 11/15 for domestic and international students; for spring admission, 1/15 for domestic and international students. Applications are processed on a rolling basis. Application fee: $40. Electronic applications accepted. *Expenses:* Tuition: Part-time $305 per credit hour. Required fees: $20 per term. *Financial support:* Career-related internships or fieldwork available. Support available to part-time students. Financial award applicants required to submit FAFSA. *Faculty research:* Identification of gifted minorities, arts in gifted education. Total annual research expenditures: $50,000. *Unit head:* Dr. Nancy Breard, Director of Gifted Education Program, 864-596-9732, Fax: 864-596-9221, E-mail: nancy.breard@converse.edu.

Drury University, Graduate Programs in Education, Program in Gifted Education, Springfield, MO 65802. Offers M Ed. *Accreditation:* NCATE. Part-time and evening/weekend programs available. *Degree requirements:* For master's, thesis. *Entrance requirements:* For master's, GRE or MAT, minimum GPA of 2.75. *Faculty research:* Affective needs of gifted, gender equity academic enrichment programs.

Elon University, Program in Education, Elon, NC 27244-2010. Offers elementary education (M Ed); gifted education (M Ed); special education (M Ed). *Accreditation:* NCATE. Part-time programs available. *Faculty:* 11 full-time (8 women), 5 part-time/adjunct (all women). *Students:* Average age 31. 62 applicants, 69% accepted, 30 enrolled. In 2006, 30 degrees awarded. *Entrance requirements:* For master's, GRE, MAT. Additional exam requirements/recommendations for international students: Required—TOEFL (minimum score 550 paper-based; 213 computer-based; 79 iBT). *Application deadline:* For winter admission, 6/1 priority date for domestic students. Applications are processed on a rolling basis. Application fee: $50. Electronic applications accepted. *Expenses: Contact institution. Financial support:* In 2006–07, 2 students received support, including 2 fellowships (averaging $2,635 per year); Federal Work-Study and scholarships/grants also available. Support available to part-time students. Financial award application deadline: 6/1; financial award applicants required to submit FAFSA. *Faculty research:* Teaching reading to low-achieving second and third graders; pre-and post-student teaching attitudes toward teaching; children's writing; whole language methodology; critical creative thinking. *Unit head:* Dr. Judith B. Howard, Director, 336-278-5885, Fax: 336-278-5919, E-mail: howardj@elon.edu. *Application contact:* Art Fadde, Director of Graduate Admissions, 800-334-8448 Ext. 3, Fax: 336-278-7699, E-mail: afadde@elon.edu.

Emporia State University, School of Graduate Studies, The Teachers College, Department of Psychology and Special Education, Program in Special Education, Emporia, KS 66801-5087. Offers behavior disorders (MS); gifted, talented, and creative (MS); interrelated special education (MS); learning disabilities (MS); mental retardation (MS). *Accreditation:* NCATE. Part-time programs available. *Students:* 31 applicants, 81% accepted, 23 enrolled. In 2006, 38 degrees awarded. *Degree requirements:* For master's, comprehensive exam or thesis, practicum. *Entrance requirements:* For master's, GRE General Test or MAT, graduate essay exam, appropriate bachelor's degree, teacher certification, letters of recommendation. Additional exam requirements/recommendations for international students: Required—TOEFL. *Application deadline:* For fall admission, 8/15 priority date for domestic students. Applications are processed on a rolling basis. Application fee: $30 ($75 for international students). Electronic applications accepted. *Expenses:* Tuition, state resident: full-time $3,438; part-time $143 per credit hour. Tuition, nonresident: full-time $10,398; part-time $433 per credit hour. Required fees: $724; $44 per credit hour. *Financial support:* Federal Work-Study, institutionally sponsored loans, health care benefits, and unspecified assistantships available. Financial award application deadline: 3/15; financial award applicants required to submit FAFSA. *Unit head:* Dr. Kenneth A. Weaver, Chair, Department of Psychology and Special Education, 620-341-5317, E-mail: kweaver@emporia.edu.

Grand Valley State University, College of Education, Programs in General Education, Allendale, MI 49401-9403. Offers adult and higher education (M Ed); early childhood education (M Ed); education of the gifted and talented (M Ed); educational leadership (M Ed); educational technology (M Ed); elementary education (M Ed); middle and high school education (M Ed); teaching English to speakers of other languages (M Ed). Part-time and evening/weekend programs available. Postbaccalaureate distance learning degree programs offered (minimal on-campus study). *Faculty:* 82 full-time (42 women), 43 part-time/adjunct (25 women). *Students:* 136 full-time (97 women), 828 part-time (565 women); includes 55 minority (26 African Americans, 7 American Indian/Alaska Native, 5 Asian Americans or Pacific Islanders, 17 Hispanic Americans). Average age 33. 280 applicants, 94% accepted, 188 enrolled. In 2006, 322 degrees awarded. *Degree requirements:* For master's, thesis. *Entrance requirements:* For master's, GRE General Test or minimum GPA of 3.0. Additional exam requirements/recommendations for international students: Required—TOEFL. *Application deadline:* Applications are processed on a rolling basis. Application fee: $30. Electronic applications accepted. *Expenses:* Tuition, state resident: full-time $5,850; part-time $325 per credit. Tuition, nonresident: full-time $10,800; part-time $600 per credit. Tuition and fees vary according to course load. *Financial support:* In 2006–07, 2 research assistantships with full and partial tuition reimbursements (averaging $8,000 per year) were awarded; career-related internships or fieldwork, Federal Work-Study, scholarships/grants, and unspecified assistantships also available. *Faculty research:* Effectiveness of technology in education, parental involvement, effective teaching, effective schools research. *Unit head:* Dr. Linda McCrea, Director, 616-331-2080, E-mail: mccreal@gvsu.edu. *Application contact:* Dr. Douglas Busman, Director, Student Information and Services, 616-331-6831, Fax: 616-331-6217, E-mail: busmando@gvsu.edu.

Hardin-Simmons University, Graduate School, Irvin School of Education, Department of Education, Program in Gifted Education, Abilene, TX 79698-0001. Offers M Ed. Part-time programs available. *Faculty:* 1 (woman) full-time. *Students:* Average age 39. 12 applicants, 100% accepted, 9 enrolled. In 2006, 12 degrees awarded. *Degree requirements:* For master's, comprehensive exam. *Entrance requirements:* For master's, minimum undergraduate GPA of 3.0 in major, 2.7 overall. Additional exam requirements/recommendations for international students: Required—TOEFL (minimum score 550 paper-based; 213 computer-based). *Application deadline:* For fall admission, 8/15 priority date for domestic students; for spring admission, 1/5 priority date for domestic students. Applications are processed on a rolling basis. Application fee: $50 ($100 for international students). *Expenses:* Tuition: Full-time $9,090; part-time $505 per hour. Required fees: $490; $66 per semester. One-time fee: $50. Tuition and fees vary according to course load and degree level. *Financial support:* In 2006–07, 6 students received support, including 4 fellowships (averaging $1,200 per year); scholarships/grants also available. Support available to part-time students. Financial award application deadline: 6/30; financial award applicants required to submit FAFSA. *Faculty research:* Experiences of gifted learners in college, use of authentic assessment, brain research and how it works in learning, theories of multiple intelligence beyond Gardner. *Unit head:* Dr. Lori Copeland, Director, 325-670-1348, E-mail: lcope@hsutx.edu. *Application contact:* Dr. Gary Stanlake, Dean of Graduate Studies, 325-670-1298, Fax: 325-670-1564, E-mail: gradoff@hsutx.edu.

Hofstra University, School of Education and Allied Human Services, Department of Counseling, Research, Special Education and Rehabilitation, Program in Special Education, Hempstead, NY 11549. Offers early childhood special education (MS Ed, Advanced Certificate); gifted education (Advanced Certificate); inclusive early childhood special education (MS Ed); inclusive elementary special education (MS Ed); inclusive secondary special education (MS Ed); literacy studies and special education (MS Ed); special education (MA, MS Ed, PD); special education assessment and diagnosis (Advanced Certificate); teaching students with severe/multiple disabilities (Advanced Certificate). *Accreditation:* NCATE. Part-time and evening/weekend programs available. Postbaccalaureate distance learning degree programs offered. *Students:* 87 full-time (82 women), 116 part-time (110 women); includes 21 minority (8 African Americans, 4 Asian Americans or Pacific Islanders, 9 Hispanic Americans). Average age 28. 110 applicants, 79% accepted, 61 enrolled. In 2006, 74 master's, 7 other advanced degrees awarded. *Degree requirements:* For master's, thesis (for some programs), seminars, student teaching, comprehensive exam (for some programs), registration; for other advanced degree, fieldwork. *Entrance requirements:* For master's, interview, 3 letters of reference, resumé, minimum GPA of 3.0; for other advanced degree, interview, 3 letters of recommendation, resumé. Additional exam requirements/recommendations for international students: Required—TOEFL (minimum score 550 paper-based; 213 computer-based). *Application deadline:* Applications are processed on a rolling basis. Application fee: $60. Electronic applications accepted. *Expenses:* Tuition: Full-time $13,320; part-time $740 per credit. Required fees: $930; $155 per term. *Financial support:* In 2006–07, 64 students received support, including 6 fellowships with tuition reimbursements available (averaging $2,552 per year), 4 research assistantships with full and partial tuition reimbursements available (averaging $4,378 per year); Federal Work-Study, scholarships/grants, tuition waivers (full and partial), and unspecified assistantships also available. Support available to part-time students. Financial award applicants required to submit FAFSA. *Faculty research:* Inclusive schooling, autism spectrum disorders related services, parent participation in the special education process, co-teaching student teaching. *Unit head:* Dr. George Guiliani, Director, 516-463-5778, Fax: 516-463-6184, E-mail: cprdcs@hofstra.edu. *Application contact:* Carol Drummer, Dean of Graduate Admissions, 516-463-4876, Fax: 516-463-4664, E-mail: gradstudent@hofstra.edu.

The Johns Hopkins University, School of Professional Studies in Business and Education, School of Education, Department of Teacher Development and Leadership, Baltimore, MD 21218-2699. Offers adult learning (Certificate); business leadership for independent schools (Certificate); earth/space science (Certificate); educational leadership for independent schools (Certificate); educational studies (MS); effective teaching of reading (Certificate); ESL instruction (Certificate); gifted education (Certificate); leadership for school, family and community collaboration (Certificate); reading (MS); school administration and supervision (MS, Certificate); teacher development and leadership (Ed D); teacher leadership (Certificate); technology for educators (MS); urban education (Certificate). Part-time and evening/weekend programs available. Postbaccalaureate distance learning degree programs offered (minimal on-campus study). *Students:* 19 full-time (18 women), 535 part-time (413 women); includes 98 minority (76 African Americans, 1 American Indian/Alaska Native, 18 Asian Americans or Pacific Islanders, 3 Hispanic Americans), 2 international. Average age 31. 544 applicants, 79% accepted, 374 enrolled. In 2006, 151 master's, 180 other advanced degrees awarded. *Degree requirements:* For master's and Certificate, portfolio; for doctorate, thesis/dissertation, comprehensive exam, registration. *Entrance requirements:* For master's and Certificate, minimum GPA of 3.0; for doctorate, GRE, interview, master's degree, minimum GPA of 3.0, resumé, letters of recommendation. Additional exam requirements/recommendations for international students: Required—TOEFL (minimum score 600 paper-based; 250 computer-based; 100 iBT). *Application deadline:* For fall admission, 5/1 for international students; for spring admission, 10/15 for international students. Applications are processed on a rolling basis. Application fee: $60. *Expenses:* Tuition: Full-time $32,976. Tuition and fees vary according to degree level and program. *Financial support:* Scholarships/grants available. Support available to part-time students. Financial award application deadline: 6/1; financial award applicants required to submit FAFSA. *Unit head:* Dr. Edward Pajak, Chair, 410-309-1265, Fax: 410-290-0467. *Application contact:* Carol Herrman, Admissions Coordinator, 410-872-1234, Fax: 410-872-1251, E-mail: onestop.admissions@jhu.edu.

Johnson State College, Graduate Program in Education, Program in Education of the Gifted, Johnson, VT 05656-9405. Offers MA Ed. Part-time programs available. *Faculty:* 1 (woman) part-time/adjunct. *Degree requirements:* For master's, thesis or alternative, comprehensive exam. *Entrance requirements:* For master's, interview. Additional exam requirements/recommendations for international students: Required—TOEFL. *Application deadline:* For fall admission, 7/15 priority date for domestic students, 4/15 priority date for international students; for spring admission, 11/1 priority date for domestic students, 8/15 priority date for international students. Applications are processed on a rolling basis. Application fee: $35. *Financial support:* Career-related internships or fieldwork, Federal Work-Study, and institutionally sponsored loans available. Support available to part-time students. Financial award application deadline: 3/1; financial award applicants required to submit FAFSA. *Application contact:* Catherine H. Higley, Administrative Assistant for Graduate Programs, 800-635-2356 Ext. 1244, Fax: 802-635-1248, E-mail: higleyc@jsc.vsc.edu.

Kent State University, Graduate School of Education, Health, and Human Services, Department of Educational Foundations and Special Services, Program in Intervention Specialist, Kent, OH 44242-0001. Offers deaf education (M Ed, MA); early childhood education (M Ed, MA); educational interpreter (M Ed, MA); general special education (M Ed, MA); gifted (M Ed, MA); mild/moderate (M Ed, MA); moderate/intensive (M Ed, MA); transition to work (M Ed, MA). *Faculty:* 13 full-time (9 women), 15 part-time/adjunct (13 women). *Students:* 41 full-time (37 women), 103 part-time (91 women); includes 2 minority (1 African American, 1 American Indian/Alaska Native), 1 international. 30 applicants, 80% accepted. In 2006, 53 degrees awarded. *Entrance requirements:* For master's, GRE. Application fee: $30. *Financial support:* In 2006–07, fellowships with tuition reimbursements (averaging $7,210 per year); research assistantships with tuition reimbursements, teaching assistantships with tuition reimbursements, career-related internships or fieldwork, Federal Work-Study, institutionally sponsored loans, scholarships/grants, health care benefits, and unspecified assistantships also available. Support available to part-time students. *Unit head:* Dr. Penny Griffith, Coordinator, 330-672-2477, E-mail: pgriffith@kent.edu. *Application contact:* Nancy Miller, Academic Program Coordinator, Office of Graduate Student Services, 330-672-2576, Fax: 330-672-9162, E-mail: ogs@kent.edu.

Liberty University, School of Education, Lynchburg, VA 24502. Offers administration and supervision (M Ed); curriculum and instruction (M Ed); early childhood education (M Ed); education specialist (Ed S); educational leadership (Ed D); elementary education (M Ed); gifted education (M Ed); reading specialist (M Ed); school counseling (M Ed); secondary education (M Ed); special education (M Ed). *Accreditation:* NCATE. Part-time programs available. Postbaccalaureate distance learning degree programs offered (minimal on-campus study). *Faculty:* 8 full-time (3 women), 7 part-time/adjunct (3 women). *Students:* 33 full-time (22 women), 308 part-time (180 women); includes 22 minority (12 African Americans, 2 American Indian/Alaska Native, 2 Asian Americans or Pacific Islanders, 6 Hispanic Americans), 5 international. Average age 39. 434 applicants, 77% accepted, 111 enrolled. In 2006, 39 master's, 12 doctorates, 16 other advanced degrees awarded. *Degree requirements:* For doctorate, thesis/dissertation, comprehensive exam. *Entrance requirements:* For master's, GRE General Test or MAT (if taken on or before 1999), 2 letters of recommendation, minimum undergraduate GPA of 3.0, curriculum vitae, graduate status record; for doctorate, GRE General Test or MAT (if taken before 1999), minimum master's GPA of 3.0, 3 years of teacher experience; for Ed S, GRE General Test or MAT (if taken before 1999), minimum master's GPA of 3.0, 3 years of teaching experience. Additional exam requirements/recommendations for international students: Required—TOEFL (minimum score 600 paper-based; 250 computer-based). *Application deadline:* For fall admission, 6/1 priority date for domestic students; for spring admission, 11/1 for domestic students. Applications are processed on a rolling basis. Application fee: $35. Electronic applications accepted. *Expenses: Contact institution. Financial support:* In 2006–07, 226 students received support. Federal Work-Study and tuition waivers (partial) available. *Faculty research:* Self-determination, character education, bibliotherapy, learning styles, distance education. *Unit head:* Dr. Karen L. Parker, Dean, 434-582-2195, Fax: 434-582-2468, E-mail: kparker@liberty.edu. *Application contact:* Kyle A Falce, Director of Graduate Admissions, 800-424-9596, Fax: 800-628-7977, E-mail: gradadmissions@liberty.edu.

Lynn University, Donald and Helen Ross College of Education, Boca Raton, FL 33431-5598. Offers exceptional student education (M Ed); global leadership (PhD). Part-time and evening/

Education of the Gifted

Lynn University (continued)

weekend programs available. *Faculty:* 5 full-time (3 women), 8 part-time/adjunct (4 women). *Students:* 29 full-time (22 women), 88 part-time (61 women); includes 30 minority (18 African Americans, 1 Asian American or Pacific Islander, 11 Hispanic Americans), 10 international. Average age 36. 48 applicants, 79% accepted, 33 enrolled. In 2006, 69 master's, 6 doctorates awarded. *Degree requirements:* For master's, thesis (for some programs); for doctorate, thesis/dissertation, qualifying paper. *Entrance requirements:* For master's, GRE, minimum undergraduate GPA of 3.0, resumé, 2 letters of recommendation; for doctorate, GRE or GMAT, minimum GPA of 3.25, resumé, 2 letters of recommendation. Additional exam requirements/recommendations for international students: Required—TOEFL (minimum score 550 paper-based; 213 computer-based). *Application deadline:* Applications are processed on a rolling basis. Application fee: $50. Electronic applications accepted. *Expenses:* Tuition: Full-time $26,200. Required fees: $1,500. Tuition and fees vary according to class time, course load and degree level. *Financial support:* Career-related internships or fieldwork, Federal Work-Study, institutionally sponsored loans, scholarships/grants, tuition waivers (partial), and unspecified assistantships available. Support available to part-time students. Financial award application deadline: 8/1; financial award applicants required to submit FAFSA. *Faculty research:* Non-traditional education, innovative curricula, multicultural education, simulation games. *Unit head:* Dr. Patrick Hartwick, Dean, 561-237-7441, Fax: 561-237-7792, E-mail: phartwick@lynn.edu. *Application contact:* Dr. Larissa Baia, Assistant Director of Graduate Admissions, 561-237-7916, Fax: 561-237-7100, E-mail: lbaia@lynn.edu.

Maryville University of Saint Louis, School of Education, St. Louis, MO 63141-7299. Offers art education (MA Ed); early childhood education (MA Ed); education (Ed D); elementary education (MA Ed); elementary education/English (MA Ed); environmental education (MA Ed); gifted education (MA Ed); middle grades education (MA Ed); reading specialist (MA Ed); secondary education (MA Ed), including educational leadership, secondary teaching and inquiry. *Accreditation:* NASAD; NCATE. Part-time and evening/weekend programs available. *Students:* 17 full-time (14 women), 168 part-time (129 women); includes 20 African Americans, 2 Asian Americans or Pacific Islanders, 1 Hispanic American, 2 international. Average age 37. 39 applicants, 95% accepted, 24 enrolled. In 2006, 37 degrees awarded. *Degree requirements:* For master's, thesis, project. *Entrance requirements:* For master's and doctorate, minimum GPA of 3.0, 3 professional recommendations. Additional exam requirements/recommendations for international students: Required—TOEFL (minimum score 550 paper-based). *Application deadline:* Applications are processed on a rolling basis. Application fee: $35 ($50 for international students). Electronic applications accepted. *Expenses:* Tuition: Full-time $17,800; part-time $555 per credit. Required fees: $55 per semester. Tuition and fees vary according to degree level and program. *Financial support:* Career-related internships or fieldwork, Federal Work-Study, tuition waivers (partial), and professional educator discounts available. Financial award application deadline: 7/31; financial award applicants required to submit FAFSA. *Faculty research:* Collaboration with public schools, preservice program development, mathematics, diversity, literacy. *Unit head:* Dr. Sam Hausfather, Dean, 314-529-9466, Fax: 314-529-9921, E-mail: shausfather@maryville.edu. *Application contact:* Dr. Lillian Curtis, Graduate Admissions Coordinator, 314-529-9542, Fax: 314-529-9921, E-mail: teachered@maryville.edu.

Minnesota State University Mankato, College of Graduate Studies, College of Education, Department of Educational Studies: Special Populations, Program in Talent Development and Gifted Education, Mankato, MN 56001. Offers MS, Certificate, SP. *Accreditation:* NCATE. In 2006, 4 degrees awarded. *Degree requirements:* For master's, thesis or alternative, comprehensive exam. *Entrance requirements:* For master's, GRE General Test or MAT, minimum GPA of 3.0 during previous 2 years. Additional exam requirements/recommendations for international students: Required—TOEFL. *Application deadline:* For fall admission, 7/1 priority date for domestic students; for spring admission, 11/1 for domestic students. Applications are processed on a rolling basis. Application fee: $40. Electronic applications accepted. *Financial support:* Research assistantships, teaching assistantships available. Financial award application deadline: 3/15. *Unit head:* Dr. Nancy Sprengeler, Director, 507-389-5175. *Application contact:* 507-389-2321, E-mail: grad@mnsu.edu.

Mississippi University for Women, Graduate School, Division of Education and Human Sciences, Columbus, MS 39701-9998. Offers gifted studies (M Ed); instructional management (M Ed); speech/language pathology (MS). *Accreditation:* ASHA; NCATE. Part-time programs available. *Degree requirements:* For master's, thesis optional. *Entrance requirements:* For master's, GRE General Test or NTE (M Ed in gifted education or MS in speech/language pathology), MAT (M Ed in instructional management), minimum QPA of 3.0.

Northeastern Illinois University, Graduate College, College of Education, Department of Special Education, Program in Gifted Education, Chicago, IL 60625-4699. Offers MA. Part-time and evening/weekend programs available. *Faculty:* 18 full-time (11 women), 2 part-time/adjunct (both women). *Students:* 2 full-time (both women), 31 part-time (28 women); includes 4 minority (1 African American, 3 Hispanic Americans), 2 international. Average age 37. 4 applicants, 100% accepted. In 2006, 5 degrees awarded. *Degree requirements:* For master's, thesis or alternative, comprehensive exam. *Entrance requirements:* For master's, teaching certificate or previous course work in history or philosophy of education, minimum GPA of 2.75. *Application deadline:* For fall admission, 4/1 priority date for domestic students; for spring admission, 8/15 for domestic students. Applications are processed on a rolling basis. Application fee: $25. *Financial support:* In 2006–07, 6 students received support, including research assistantships with full tuition reimbursements available (averaging $6,600 per year); career-related internships or fieldwork, Federal Work-Study, institutionally sponsored loans, and tuition waivers (full and partial) also available. Support available to part-time students. *Faculty research:* Effect of inclusion in public school gifted programs, social and emotional needs of gifted children, problem-based learning strategies.

Nova Southeastern University, Fischler School of Education and Human Services, Graduate Teacher Education Program, Fort Lauderdale, FL 33314-7796. Offers athletic administration (MS); cognitive and behavioral disabilities (MS); computer science education (Ed S); computer science education (K-12) (MS); curriculum and teaching (Ed S); curriculum, instruction and technology (MS); curriculum, instruction, management and administration (Ed S); early childhood special education (MS); early literacy and reading (Ed S); early literacy education (MS); education technology (MS); educational leadership (administration K–12) (MS, Ed S); educational media (Ed S); educational media (K-12) (MS); elementary education (MS, Ed S), including ESOL endorsement (MS); English (MS, Ed S); exceptional student education (MS), including ESOL endorsement; gifted education (MS, Ed S); interdisciplinary arts education (MS); management and administration of educational programs (MS); mathematics (MS, Ed S); multicultural early intervention (MS); pre-kindergarten/primary (MS); preschool education (MS); reading (MS, Ed S); science (MS, Ed S); secondary education (MS); social studies (MS, Ed S); Spanish language (MS); teaching and learning (MA, MS), including curriculum and instruction (MA), elementary mathematics (MA), elementary reading (MA), K-12 technology integration (MA); teaching English to speakers of other languages (MS, Ed S); technology management and administration (Ed S); urban studies education (MS); varying exceptionalities (Ed S). Part-time and evening/weekend programs available. Postbaccalaureate distance learning degree programs offered. *Faculty:* 131 full-time (78 women), 548 part-time/adjunct (342 women). *Students:* 1,418 full-time (1,139 women), 3,464 part-time (2,877 women); includes 2,462 minority (1,732 African Americans, 13 American Indian/Alaska Native, 44 Asian Americans or Pacific Islanders, 673 Hispanic Americans), 77 international. Average age 38. 1,771 applicants, 80% accepted, 1419 enrolled. In 2006, 2,078 master's, 425 other advanced degrees awarded. *Degree requirements:* For master's and Ed S, thesis, practicum, internship. *Entrance requirements:* For master's, MAT, GRE, CLAST, CBEST, PRAXIS I, GKT, minimum GPA of 2.5; for Ed S, MAT or GRE, master's degree, teaching certificate, minimum GPA of 3.0. Additional exam requirements/recommendations for international students: Recommended—TOEFL (minimum score 550 paper-based; 213 computer-based), IELTS (minimum score 6). *Application deadline:* For fall admission, 8/11 priority date for domestic and international students; for winter admission, 12/28 priority date for domestic and international students; for spring admission, 4/22 priority date for domestic and international students. Applications are processed on a rolling basis. Application fee: $50. Electronic applications accepted. *Financial support:* Federal Work-Study available. Support available to part-time students. Financial award application deadline: 1/7. *Faculty research:* School effectiveness, critical thinking, leadership skills acquisition, child education, multicultural education. *Unit head:* Dr. Meline Kevorkian, Associate Dean of Master's and Educational Programs, 954-262-8500, Fax: 954-262-3606, E-mail: melinek@nova.edu. *Application contact:* Jennifer Quiñones Nottingham, Dean of Student Affairs, 800-986-3223 Ext. 8624, Fax: 954-262-3911, E-mail: jlquinon@nova.edu.

Purdue University, Graduate School, School of Education, Department of Educational Studies, West Lafayette, IN 47907. Offers administration (MS Ed, PhD, Ed S); counseling and development (MS Ed, PhD); education of the gifted (MS Ed); educational psychology (MS Ed, PhD); foundations of education (MS Ed, PhD); higher education administration (MS Ed, PhD); special education (MS Ed, PhD). *Accreditation:* ACA (one or more programs are accredited); NCATE (one or more programs are accredited). Part-time and evening/weekend programs available. *Faculty:* 28 full-time (18 women). *Students:* 100 full-time (71 women), 126 part-time (77 women); includes 32 minority (19 African Americans, 2 American Indian/Alaska Native, 6 Asian Americans or Pacific Islanders, 5 Hispanic Americans), 33 international. Average age 36. 152 applicants, 62% accepted, 56 enrolled. In 2006, 51 master's, 17 doctorates awarded. *Degree requirements:* For master's, thesis optional; for doctorate, thesis/dissertation, oral and written exams; for Ed S, oral presentation, project. *Entrance requirements:* For master's, GRE General Test, minimum undergraduate GPA of 3.0; for doctorate, GRE General Test; for Ed S, GRE, minimum B average. Additional exam requirements/recommendations for international students: Required—TOEFL. *Application deadline:* For fall admission, 1/15 for domestic students; for spring admission, 9/15 for domestic students. Applications are processed on a rolling basis. Application fee: $55. Electronic applications accepted. *Financial support:* In 2006–07, 6 fellowships with full tuition reimbursements (averaging $13,300 per year), 23 research assistantships with full tuition reimbursements (averaging $11,500 per year), 33 teaching assistantships with full tuition reimbursements (averaging $10,800 per year) were awarded; career-related internships or fieldwork and tuition waivers (full) also available. Support available to part-time students. Financial award application deadline: 3/1; financial award applicants required to submit FAFSA. *Faculty research:* Motivation, learning disabilities, school learning, group processes, cognitive development. *Unit head:* Dr. Kevin R Kelly, Head, 765-494-9170, Fax: 765-496-1228. *Application contact:* Patricia Mason, Coordinator of Graduate Studies, 765-494-2346, Fax: 765-494-5832, E-mail: gradoffice@soe.purdue.edu.

Saint Leo University, Graduate Studies in Education, Saint Leo, FL 33574-6665. Offers education (MAT); educational leadership (M Ed); exceptional student education (M Ed); instructional leadership (M Ed); reading (M Ed). Part-time and evening/weekend programs available. Postbaccalaureate distance learning degree programs offered (minimal on-campus study). *Faculty:* 8 full-time (5 women), 10 part-time/adjunct (all women). *Students:* 96 full-time (77 women), 169 part-time (143 women); includes 22 minority (16 African Americans, 6 Hispanic Americans), 2 international. Average age 35. 365 applicants, 54% accepted, 116 enrolled. In 2006, 39 degrees awarded. *Degree requirements:* For master's, comprehensive exam or passing FELE scores. *Entrance requirements:* For master's, GRE General Test or MAT, 2 letters of recommendation, minimum undergraduate GPA of 3.0 or GRE or MAT, professional teaching certificate, resumé. Additional exam requirements/recommendations for international students: Required—TOEFL (minimum score 550 paper-based; 213 computer-based). *Application deadline:* For fall admission, 7/1 priority date for domestic students; for spring admission, 11/12 priority date for domestic students. Applications are processed on a rolling basis. Application fee: $45. Electronic applications accepted. *Financial support:* In 2006–07, 242 students received support. Career-related internships or fieldwork, Federal Work-Study, and scholarships/grants available. Support available to part-time students. Financial award application deadline: 3/1; financial award applicants required to submit FAFSA. *Faculty research:* The role of the school leader in (1) data analysis of student achievement (2) teacher recruitment (3) teacher effectiveness. *Unit head:* Dr. John Smith, Director, 352-588-8309, Fax: 352-588-8861, E-mail: med@saintleo.edu. *Application contact:* Scott Cathcart, Vice President of Enrollment, 800-707-8846, Fax: 352-588-7873, E-mail: grad.admission@saintleo.edu.

Samford University, School of Education, Birmingham, AL 35229-0002. Offers early childhood education (Ed S); early childhood/elementary education (MS Ed); educational administration (Ed S); educational leadership (Ed D); elementary education (Ed S); gifted education (MS Ed); M Div/MS Ed. *Accreditation:* NCATE. Part-time programs available. *Faculty:* 12 full-time (7 women), 8 part-time/adjunct (4 women). *Students:* 16 full-time (14 women), 160 part-time (124 women); includes 25 minority (all African Americans) Average age 38. 45 applicants, 100% accepted, 17 enrolled. In 2006, 15 master's, 20 doctorates, 20 other advanced degrees awarded. *Entrance requirements:* For master's, GRE or MAT, minimum GPA of 3.0; for doctorate, minimum GPA of 3.7; for Ed S, GRE, master's degree, teaching certificate, minimum GPA of 3.25. Additional exam requirements/recommendations for international students: Required—TOEFL (minimum score 550 paper-based; 213 computer-based). *Application deadline:* Applications are processed on a rolling basis. Application fee: $25. *Expenses:* Tuition: Part-time $500 per credit. One-time fee: $25 part-time. Full-time tuition and fees vary according to program and student level. *Financial support:* In 2006–07, 54 students received support; research assistantships, career-related internships or fieldwork, Federal Work-Study, scholarships/grants, and tuition waivers (partial) available. Support available to part-time students. Financial award applicants required to submit FAFSA. *Faculty research:* School law, the characteristics of beginning teachers, the nature of school reform, school culture, quality improvement in education, K-12 student achievement. *Unit head:* Dr. Jean Ann Box, Dean, 205-726-2559, E-mail: jabox@samford.edu. *Application contact:* Dr. Maurice Persall, Director, Graduate Office, 205-726-2019, E-mail: jmpersal@samford.edu.

Teachers College Columbia University, Graduate Faculty of Education, Department of Curriculum and Teaching, Program in Giftedness, New York, NY 10027-6696. Offers MA, Ed D. Part-time programs available. *Faculty:* 1 full-time (0 women), 2 part-time/adjunct. *Students:* 7 full-time (6 women), 24 part-time (20 women); includes 6 minority (all African Americans), 5 international. Average age 41. 10 applicants, 80% accepted, 6 enrolled. In 2006, 8 master's, 2 doctorates awarded. Terminal master's awarded for partial completion of doctoral program. *Degree requirements:* For master's, thesis or alternative; for doctorate, thesis/dissertation. *Entrance requirements:* For doctorate, GRE General Test or MAT. *Application deadline:* For fall admission, 5/15 for domestic students; for spring admission, 12/1 for domestic students. Application fee: $50. *Expenses:* Tuition: Full-time $23,400; part-time $975 per credit. Required fees: $320 per term. *Financial support:* Research assistantships, career-related internships or fieldwork, Federal Work-Study, institutionally sponsored loans, and tuition waivers (full and partial) available. Support available to part-time students. Financial award application deadline: 2/1. *Faculty research:* Urban and economically disadvantaged gifted children, identification issues with regard to gifted and early childhood giftedness. *Application contact:* Peter Shon, Assistant Director of Admission, 212-678-3305, Fax: 212-678-4171, E-mail: shon@exchange.tc.columbia.edu.

See Close-Up on page 1127.

Tennessee Technological University, Graduate School, College of Education, Department of Curriculum and Instruction, Program in Exceptional Learning, Cookeville, TN 38505. Offers PhD. *Students:* 22 full-time (13 women), 20 part-time (17 women); includes 14 minority (10 African Americans, 4 Asian Americans or Pacific Islanders). 19 applicants, 21% accepted, 3 enrolled. In 2006, 6 degrees awarded. *Degree requirements:* For doctorate, one foreign language, thesis/dissertation. *Entrance requirements:* For doctorate, GRE, minimum GPA of 3.0. Additional exam requirements/recommendations for international students: Required—TOEFL. *Application deadline:* For fall admission, 6/1 priority date for domestic students, 3/1 priority date for international students; for spring admission, 11/1 priority date for domestic students, 8/1 priority date for international students. Application fee: $25 ($30 for international students). Electronic applications accepted. *Expenses:* Tuition, state resident: full-time $8,748; part-time $319 per hour. Tuition, nonresident: full-time $23,524; part-time $740 per hour. *Financial support:* In 2006–07, 4 fellowships (averaging $8,000 per year), 10 research assistantships (averaging $12,000 per year), 1 teaching assistantship (averaging $12,000 per year) were awarded. *Unit head:* Dr. John J. Wheeler, Director, Doctoral Studies, 931-372-3078, Fax: 931-372-3517. *Application contact:* Dr. Francis O. Otuonye, Associate Vice President for Research and Graduate Studies, 931-372-3233, Fax: 931-372-3497, E-mail: fotuonye@tntech.edu.

Texas A&M University, College of Education and Human Development, Department of Educational Psychology, College Station, TX 77843. Offers counseling psychology (PhD); educational psychology (PhD); educational technology (M Ed); gifted and talented education (M Ed, MS); Hispanic bilingual education (M Ed, PhD); human learning and development (MS); intelligence, creativity, and giftedness (PhD); learning, development, and instruction (PhD); research, measurement and statistics (MS); research, measurement, and statistics (PhD); school counseling (M Ed); school psychology (PhD); special education (M Ed, PhD). *Accreditation:* APA (one or more programs are accredited); NCATE. Part-time and evening/weekend programs available. Postbaccalaureate distance learning degree programs offered (no on-campus study). *Faculty:* 25 full-time (11 women), 5 part-time/adjunct (2 women). *Students:* 156 full-time (123 women), 109 part-time (89 women); includes 66 minority (20 African Americans, 1 American Indian/Alaska Native, 7 Asian Americans or Pacific Islanders, 38 Hispanic Americans), 36 international. 159 applicants, 52% accepted, 51 enrolled. In 2006, 59 master's, 21 doctorates awarded. *Median time to degree:* Of those who began their doctoral program in fall 1998, 89% received their degree in 8 years or less. *Degree requirements:* For master's, thesis optional; for doctorate, thesis/dissertation. *Entrance requirements:* For master's and doctorate, GRE General Test. Additional exam requirements/recommendations for international students: Required—TOEFL. Application fee: $50 ($75 for international students). Electronic applications accepted. *Expenses:* Tuition, state resident: full-time $4,697. Tuition, nonresident: full-time $11,297. Required fees: $2,272. *Financial support:* In 2006–07, fellowships (averaging $12,000 per year), research assistantships (averaging $9,000 per year), teaching assistantships (averaging $9,000 per year) were awarded; career-related internships or fieldwork, institutionally sponsored loans, scholarships/grants, and unspecified assistantships also available. Financial award applicants required to submit FAFSA. *Unit head:* Dr. Michael R. Benz, Head, 979-845-1394, Fax: 979-862-1256, E-mail: mbanz@tamu.edu. *Application contact:* Carol A. Wagner, Director of Advising, 979-845-1833, Fax: 979-862-1256, E-mail: c-wagner@tamu.edu.

The University of Alabama, Graduate School, College of Education, Department of Special Education and Multiple Abilities, Tuscaloosa, AL 35487. Offers collaborative teacher program (M Ed, Ed S); early intervention (M Ed, Ed S); gifted education (M Ed, Ed S); multiple abilities program (M Ed); special education (Ed D, PhD). Part-time and evening/weekend programs available. *Faculty:* 10 full-time (8 women). *Students:* 14 full-time (all women), 25 part-time (23 women); includes 2 minority (1 African American, 1 American Indian/Alaska Native). Average age 34. 24 applicants, 54% accepted, 10 enrolled. In 2006, 14 master's, 2 doctorates, 4 Ed Ss awarded. Terminal master's awarded for partial completion of doctoral program. *Degree requirements:* For master's, thesis optional; for doctorate, one foreign language, thesis/dissertation, comprehensive exam, registration. *Entrance requirements:* For master's, GRE or MAT, minimum undergraduate GPA of 3.0, teaching certificate, 3 letters of recommendation; for doctorate, GRE or MAT, 3 years of teaching experience, minimum undergraduate GPA of 3.25. Additional exam requirements/recommendations for international students: Required—TOEFL. *Application deadline:* For fall admission, 7/1 for domestic students; for spring admission, 11/1 for domestic students. Applications are processed on a rolling basis. Application fee: $25. Electronic applications accepted. *Financial support:* In 2006–07, 8 students received support, including 4 research assistantships with tuition reimbursements available (averaging $9,000 per year), 4 teaching assistantships with tuition reimbursements available (averaging $9,000 per year); health care benefits and unspecified assistantships also available. Financial award application deadline: 7/1; financial award applicants required to submit FAFSA. *Faculty research:* Gifted education; mild disabilities, early intervention, severe disabilities. *Unit head:* James A. Siders, Associate Professor and Head, 205-348-5577, Fax: 205-348-6782, E-mail: jsiders@bama.ua.edu. *Application contact:* April Zark, Office Support, 205-348-6093, Fax: 205-348-6782, E-mail: azark@bamaed.ua.edu.

University of Arkansas at Little Rock, Graduate School, College of Education, Department of Teacher Education, Program in Teaching the Gifted and Talented, Little Rock, AR 72204-1099. Offers M Ed. *Accreditation:* NCATE. Part-time and evening/weekend programs available. *Degree requirements:* For master's, comprehensive exam. *Entrance requirements:* For master's, interview, minimum GPA of 2.75, GRE General Test or teaching certificate.

University of Calgary, Faculty of Graduate Studies, Faculty of Education, Graduate Division of Educational Research, Calgary, AB T2N 1N4, Canada. Offers community rehabilitation and disability studies (M Ed, M Sc, Ed D, PhD, Graduate Certificate, Graduate Diploma); curriculum, teaching and learning (M Ed, M Sc, MA, Ed D, PhD, Graduate Certificate, Graduate Diploma); educational contexts (M Ed, MA, Ed D, PhD, Graduate Certificate, Graduate Diploma); educational leadership (M Ed, MA, Ed D, PhD, Graduate Certificate, Graduate Diploma); educational technology (M Ed, M Sc, MA, Ed D, PhD, Graduate Certificate, Graduate Diploma); gifted education (M Sc, MA, Ed D, PhD, Graduate Certificate, Graduate Diploma); higher education administration (Ed D); interpretive studies in education (M Ed, M Sc, MA, Ed D, PhD, Graduate Certificate, Graduate Diploma); second language teaching (M Ed, Ed D, PhD, Graduate Certificate, Graduate Diploma); teaching English as a second language (M Ed, M Sc, MA, Ed D, PhD, Graduate Certificate, Graduate Diploma); workplace and adult learning (M Ed, MA, Ed D, PhD, Graduate Certificate, Graduate Diploma). Ed D in both higher education administration and educational leadership offered via distance delivery. Part-time and evening/weekend programs available. Postbaccalaureate distance learning degree programs offered (minimal on-campus study). *Faculty:* 44 full-time, 52 part-time/adjunct. *Students:* 488 full-time, 550 part-time. 400 applicants, 50% accepted. In 2006, 102 master's, 18 doctorates awarded. *Degree requirements:* For master's, thesis (for some programs); for doctorate, thesis/dissertation, candidacy exam. *Entrance requirements:* For master's, minimum GPA of 3.0, 3 letters of reference; for doctorate, minimum GPA of 3.5, 3 letters of reference; for other advanced degree, minimum GPA of 3.0. Additional exam requirements/recommendations for international students: Required—TOEFL, IELTS. *Application deadline:* For fall admission, 2/15 for domestic students, 2/5 for international students; for winter admission, 6/15 for domestic and international students. Application fee: $100. Electronic applications accepted. *Financial support:* In 2006–07, research assistantships (averaging $3,920 per year); teaching assistantships, career-related internships or fieldwork, scholarships/grants, and unspecified assistantships also available. Financial award application deadline: 2/1. *Faculty research:* Curriculum, leadership, technology, contexts, gifted, second language teaching, work place and adult learning. *Unit head:* Dr. Charles F. Webber, Associate Dean, 403-220-5675, Fax: 403-282-3005, E-mail: cwebber@ucalgary.ca. *Application contact:* Patricia A. Brown, Program Officer, Graduate Division of Educational Research, 403-220-3178, Fax: 403-282-3005, E-mail: brownp@ucalgary.ca.

University of Connecticut, Graduate School, Neag School of Education, Department of Educational Psychology, Storrs, CT 06269. Offers educational psychology (MA, PhD), including cognition and instruction, counseling psychology, gifted and talented education, learning technology, measurement, evaluation, and assessment, school psychology, special education. *Faculty:* 34 full-time (16 women). *Students:* 154 full-time (127 women), 147 part-time (114 women); includes 35 minority (15 African Americans, 2 American Indian/Alaska Native, 7 Asian Americans or Pacific Islanders, 11 Hispanic Americans), 20 international. Average age 34. 331 applicants, 48% accepted, 139 enrolled. In 2006, 115 master's, 20 doctorates awarded. *Degree requirements:* For master's, comprehensive exam; for doctorate, thesis/dissertation. *Entrance requirements:* For doctorate, GRE General Test. Additional exam requirements/recommendations for international students: Required—TOEFL (minimum score 550 paper-based; 213 computer-based). *Application deadline:* For fall admission, 2/1 priority date for domestic and international students; for spring admission, 11/1 for domestic students, 10/1 for international students. Applications are processed on a rolling basis. Application fee: $55. Electronic applications accepted. *Financial support:* In 2006–07, 87 research assistantships with full tuition reimbursements, 1 teaching assistantship with full tuition reimbursement were awarded; fellowships, Federal Work-Study, scholarships/grants, health care benefits, and unspecified assistantships also available. Financial award application deadline: 2/1; financial award applicants required to submit FAFSA. *Unit head:* Sally Reis, Head, 860-486-4031, Fax: 860-486-0210. *Application contact:* Lisa Rasicot, Graduate Coordinator, 860-486-3065, Fax: 860-486-0210, E-mail: soeadm02@uconnvm.uconn.edu.

University of Connecticut, Graduate School, Neag School of Education, Department of Educational Psychology, Field of Educational Psychology, Program in Gifted and Talented Education, Storrs, CT 06269. Offers MA, PhD. *Accreditation:* NCATE. *Faculty:* 10 full-time (6 women). *Students:* 24 full-time (21 women), 65 part-time (59 women); includes 9 minority (3 African Americans, 1 American Indian/Alaska Native, 2 Asian Americans or Pacific Islanders, 3 Hispanic Americans), 8 international. Average age 38. 55 applicants, 73% accepted, 40 enrolled. In 2006, 31 master's, 5 doctorates awarded. Terminal master's awarded for partial completion of doctoral program. *Degree requirements:* For master's, thesis or alternative, comprehensive exam; for doctorate, thesis/dissertation. *Entrance requirements:* For master's and doctorate, GRE General Test. Additional exam requirements/recommendations for international students: Required—TOEFL (minimum score 550 paper-based; 213 computer-based). *Application deadline:* For fall admission, 2/1 priority date for domestic and international students; for spring admission, 11/1 for domestic students, 10/1 for international students. Applications are processed on a rolling basis. Application fee: $55. Electronic applications accepted. *Financial support:* In 2006–07, 17 research assistantships with full tuition reimbursements were awarded; fellowships, teaching assistantships with full tuition reimbursements, Federal Work-Study, scholarships/grants, health care benefits, and unspecified assistantships also available. Financial award application deadline: 2/1; financial award applicants required to submit FAFSA. *Application contact:* Lisa Rasicot, Graduate Coordinator, 860-486-3065, Fax: 860-486-0210, E-mail: soeadm02@uconnvm.uconn.edu.

University of Houston, College of Education, Department of Curriculum and Instruction, Houston, TX 77204. Offers art education (M Ed); bilingual education (M Ed); curriculum and instruction (Ed D); early childhood education (M Ed); education of the gifted (M Ed); elementary education (M Ed); mathematics education (M Ed); reading and language arts education (M Ed); science education (M Ed); second language education (M Ed); secondary education (M Ed); social studies education (M Ed); teaching (M Ed). *Accreditation:* NCATE. Part-time and evening/weekend programs available. *Faculty:* 24 full-time (11 women), 16 part-time/adjunct (14 women). *Students:* 134 full-time (102 women), 327 part-time (256 women); includes 142 minority (49 African Americans, 1 American Indian/Alaska Native, 29 Asian Americans or Pacific Islanders, 63 Hispanic Americans), 19 international. Average age 37. 113 applicants, 72% accepted, 61 enrolled. In 2006, 106 master's, 32 doctorates awarded. *Degree requirements:* For master's, comprehensive exam or thesis; for doctorate, thesis/dissertation, comprehensive exam. *Entrance requirements:* For master's, GRE General Test or MAT; for doctorate, GRE General Test, interview. *Application deadline:* For fall admission, 7/3 priority date for domestic students. Applications are processed on a rolling basis. Application fee: $35 ($75 for international students). *Expenses:* Tuition, state resident: full-time $5,429; part-time $226 per credit. Tuition, nonresident: full-time $12,029; part-time $501 per credit. Required fees: $2,454. *Financial support:* In 2006–07, 2 fellowships with full tuition reimbursements (averaging $9,500 per year), 6 research assistantships with full tuition reimbursements (averaging $8,800 per year), 25 teaching assistantships with full tuition reimbursements (averaging $8,800 per year) were awarded; career-related internships or fieldwork, Federal Work-Study, institutionally sponsored loans, scholarships/grants, health care benefits, and unspecified assistantships also available. Support available to part-time students. Financial award application deadline: 3/10. *Faculty research:* Teaching-learning process, instructional technology in schools, teacher education, classroom management, at-risk students. *Unit head:* Dr. Juanita Copley, Chairperson, 713-743-4950, Fax: 713-743-4990, E-mail: ncopley@aol.com.

University of Louisiana at Lafayette, Graduate School, College of Education, Graduate Studies and Research in Education, Program in Education of the Gifted, Lafayette, LA 70504. Offers M Ed. *Accreditation:* NCATE. *Faculty:* 3 full-time (2 women). *Students:* 3 full-time (all women), 13 part-time (12 women); includes 1 minority (African American), 1 international. Average age 33. 6 applicants, 17% accepted, 0 enrolled. In 2006, 4 degrees awarded. *Degree requirements:* For master's, thesis or alternative. *Entrance requirements:* For master's, GRE General Test, teaching certificate. Additional exam requirements/recommendations for international students: Required—TOEFL (minimum score 550 paper-based; 213 computer-based). *Application deadline:* For fall admission, 5/15 for domestic and international students; for spring admission, 10/1 for domestic and international students. Applications are processed on a rolling basis. Application fee: $25 ($30 for international students). Electronic applications accepted. *Expenses:* Tuition, state resident: full-time $3,247; part-time $93 per credit hour. Tuition, nonresident: full-time $9,427; part-time $350 per credit hour. *Financial support:* Federal Work-Study available. Financial award application deadline: 5/1. *Unit head:* Dr. Sally Dobyns, Director, 337-482-6701, Fax: 337-482-5842, E-mail: dobyns@louisiana.edu. *Application contact:* Dr. Nathan Roberts, Coordinator, 337-482-6747, Fax: 337-482-5842, E-mail: nmr0713@louisiana.edu.

University of Minnesota, Twin Cities Campus, Graduate School, College of Education and Human Development, Department of Educational Psychology, Minneapolis, MN 55455-0213. Offers counseling and student personnel psychology (MA, PhD, Ed S); early childhood education (M Ed, MA, PhD); educational psychology (PhD); psychological foundations of education (MA, PhD, Ed S); school psychology (MA, PhD, Ed S); special education (M Ed, MA, PhD, Ed S); talent development and gifted education (Certificate). *Accreditation:* APA (one or more programs are accredited). *Faculty:* 33 full-time (11 women). *Students:* 323 full-time (260 women), 118 part-time (95 women); includes 39 minority (15 African Americans, 4 American Indian/Alaska Native, 14 Asian Americans or Pacific Islanders, 6 Hispanic Americans), 56 international. Average age 32. 334 applicants, 53% accepted, 122 enrolled. In 2006, 112 master's, 20 doctorates, 10 other advanced degrees awarded. *Expenses:* Tuition, state resident: full-time $9,302; part-time $775 per credit. Tuition, nonresident: full-time $16,400; part-time $1,367 per credit. Full-time tuition and fees vary according to class time, course load, program, reciprocity agreements and student level. *Financial support:* In 2006–07, 8 fellowships (averaging $24,775 per year), 72 research assistantships (averaging $24,775 per year), 40 teaching assistantships (averaging $24,775 per year) were awarded. *Faculty research:* Social psychology and development in education, multicultural education and counseling, international psychology, learning and readiness processes, measurement and statistical processes. Total annual research expenditures: $2.5 million. *Unit head:* Dr. John Romano, Chair, 612-624-1099, Fax: 612-624-8241, E-mail: roman001@umn.edu. *Application contact:* Dr. Mary Bents, Associate Dean, 612-625-6501, Fax: 612-626-1580, E-mail: mbents@tc.umn.edu.

University of Missouri–Columbia, Graduate School, College of Education, Department of Special Education, Columbia, MO 65211. Offers administration and supervision of special education (PhD); behavior disorders (M Ed, PhD); curriculum development of exceptional students (M Ed, PhD); early childhood special education (M Ed, PhD); general special education (M Ed, MA, PhD); learning and instruction (M Ed); learning disabilities (M Ed, PhD); mental retardation (M Ed, PhD). *Accreditation:* NCATE. Part-time and evening/weekend programs available. Postbaccalaureate distance learning degree programs offered (no on-campus study). *Faculty:* 8 full-time (6 women). *Students:* 27 full-time (26 women), 28 part-time (24 women); includes 2 minority (both Asian Americans or Pacific Islanders), 5 international. 22 applicants, 77% accepted, 14 enrolled. In 2006, 12 master's, 3 doctorates awarded. *Degree requirements:* For master's, thesis or alternative, comprehensive exam; for doctorate, thesis/dissertation, comprehensive exam. *Entrance requirements:* For master's and doctorate, GRE General Test, letters of recommendation. Additional exam requirements/recommendations for international students: Required—TOEFL (minimum score 500 paper-based; 173 computer-based). *Application deadline:* For fall admission, 7/1 priority date for domestic and international students; for winter admission, 11/1 priority date for domestic and international students; for spring admission, 4/1 priority date for domestic and international

Education of the Gifted

University of Missouri–Columbia (continued)

students. Application fee: $45 ($60 for international students). Electronic applications accepted. *Financial support:* Fellowships with full and partial tuition reimbursements, research assistantships with full and partial tuition reimbursements, teaching assistantships with full and partial tuition reimbursements, career-related internships or fieldwork, scholarships/grants, health care benefits, and unspecified assistantships available. *Faculty research:* Positive behavior support, applied behavior analysis, attention deficit disorder, pre-linguistic development, school discipline. Total annual research expenditures: $1.4 million. *Unit head:* Dr. Melissa Stormont, Director of Graduate Studies, 573-882-7383, E-mail: stormontm@missouri.edu. *Application contact:* Fran Colley, Office Support Staff III, 573-882-6462, Fax: 573-884-2917, E-mail: cigrad@coe.missouri.edu.

University of Nevada, Las Vegas, Graduate College, College of Education, Department of Special Education, Las Vegas, NV 89154-9900. Offers assistive technology (Ed S); emotional disturbance (Ed D); general special education (Ed D); gifted and talented education (Ed D); learning disabilities (Ed D); mental retardation (Ed D); special education (M Ed, MS, PhD, Ed S). *Accreditation:* NCATE. Part-time and evening/weekend programs available. *Faculty:* 21 full-time (15 women), 23 part-time/adjunct (20 women). *Students:* 161 full-time (119 women), 119 part-time (105 women); includes 44 minority (18 African Americans, 2 American Indian/Alaska Native, 11 Asian Americans or Pacific Islanders, 13 Hispanic Americans), 4 international. 187 applicants, 70% accepted, 117 enrolled. In 2006, 129 master's, 9 doctorates awarded. *Degree requirements:* For master's, thesis (for some programs), oral exam, comprehensive exam (for some programs); for doctorate, thesis/dissertation, oral exam, comprehensive exam. *Entrance requirements:* For master's, minimum GPA of 3.0; for doctorate, GRE General Test, minimum graduate GPA of 3.0; for Ed S, GRE General Test or MAT, minimum graduate GPA of 3.0. Additional exam requirements/recommendations for international students: Required—TOEFL (minimum score 550 paper-based; 213 computer-based; 80 iBT). *Application deadline:* For fall admission, 2/12 for domestic and international students; for spring admission, 11/15 for domestic students, 10/1 for international students. Application fee: $60 ($75 for international students). Electronic applications accepted. *Financial support:* In 2006–07, 14 research assistantships with partial tuition reimbursements (averaging $10,000 per year), 3 teaching assistantships with partial tuition reimbursements (averaging $12,000 per year) were awarded; career-related internships or fieldwork, Federal Work-Study, institutionally sponsored loans, scholarships/grants, health care benefits, and unspecified assistantships also available. Support available to part-time students. Financial award application deadline: 3/1. *Unit head:* Dr. Tom Pierce, Chair, 702-895-3205. *Application contact:* Graduate College Admissions Evaluator, 702-895-3320, Fax: 702-895-4180, E-mail: gradcollege@unlv.edu.

The University of North Carolina at Charlotte, Graduate School, College of Education, Department of Special Education and Child Development, Charlotte, NC 28223-0001. Offers special education (M Ed, PhD), including academically gifted (M Ed), behavioral—emotional handicaps (M Ed), cross-categorical disabilities (M Ed), learning disabilities (M Ed), mental handicaps (M Ed), severe and profound handicaps (M Ed). Part-time programs available. *Faculty:* 25 full-time (19 women), 7 part-time/adjunct (all women). *Students:* 9 full-time (8 women), 41 part-time (38 women); includes 1 minority (African American), 1 international. Average age 34. 27 applicants, 41% accepted, 9 enrolled. In 2006, 3 master's, 4 doctorates awarded. *Degree requirements:* For doctorate, dissertation, portfolio, qualifying exam. *Entrance requirements:* For master's, GRE or MAT; for doctorate, GRE or MAT, 3 letters of reference, resumé or curriculum vitae, minimum GPA of 3.5, master's degree in special education or related field, 3 years of teaching experience. Additional exam requirements/recommendations for international students: Required—TOEFL (paper-based 550; computer-based 220) or Michigan English Language Assessment Battery. *Application deadline:* For fall admission, 7/15 for domestic students, 5/1 for international students; for spring admission, 11/15 for domestic students, 10/1 for international students. Application fee: $55. *Expenses:* Tuition, state resident: full-time $2,719; part-time $170 per credit. Tuition, nonresident: full-time $12,926; part-time $808 per credit. Required fees: $1,555. *Financial support:* In 2006–07, 13 research assistantships (averaging $12,615 per year), 6 teaching assistantships (averaging $8,000 per year) were awarded. Financial award application deadline: 4/1; financial award applicants required to submit FAFSA. *Faculty research:* Transition to adulthood and self-determination, teaching reading and other academic skills to students with disabilities, alternate assessment, early intervention, preschool education. *Unit head:* David Gilmore, Unit Head, 704-687-8186, Fax: 704-687-2916. *Application contact:* Kathy B. Giddings, Director of Graduate Admissions, 704-687-3366, Fax: 704-687-3279, E-mail: gradadm@email.uncc.edu.

University of St. Thomas, Graduate Studies, School of Education, Department of Curriculum and Instruction, St. Paul, MN 55105-1096. Offers critical pedagogy (Ed D); curriculum and instruction (MA, Ed S), including elementary (MA), K-12 (MA), secondary (MA); gifted, creative, and talented education (MA, Certificate); learning technology (MA, Certificate); reading (MA). Part-time and evening/weekend programs available. Postbaccalaureate distance learning degree programs offered (minimal on-campus study). *Students:* 5 full-time (all women), 109 part-time (91 women); includes 12 minority (7 African Americans, 1 American Indian/Alaska Native, 2 Asian Americans or Pacific Islanders, 2 Hispanic Americans), 2 international. Average age 35. 103 applicants, 91% accepted, 89 enrolled. In 2006, 13 master's, 7 doctorates, 11 other advanced degrees awarded. *Degree requirements:* For master's, thesis (for some programs), registration; for doctorate and other advanced degree, thesis/dissertation, registration. *Entrance requirements:* For master's, minimum GPA of 2.75 or MAT; for doctorate, minimum 3 years of experience as an educator; master's degree; minimum graduate GPA of 2.75, interview, writing sample; for other advanced degree, MAT, minimum graduate GPA of 2.75. Additional exam requirements/recommendations for international students: Required—TOEFL (minimum score 550 paper-based; 213 computer-based). *Application deadline:* For fall admission, 6/1 priority date for domestic students; for spring admission, 11/1 priority date for domestic students. Applications are processed on a rolling basis. Application fee: $50. *Financial support:* In 2006–07, 59 students received support; fellowships, research assistantships, institutionally sponsored loans and scholarships/grants available. Support available to part-time students. *Faculty research:* Multicultural education for gifted children, education plans for gifted children, globalization and adult learning, best gifted practices in Minnesota, exploring cultural tools. *Unit head:* Dr. Karen L. Westberg, Department Chair, 651-962-4985, Fax: 651-962-4169, E-mail: klwestberg@stthomas.edu. *Application contact:* Daniel Vevang, Department Assistant, 651-962-4460, Fax: 651-962-4169, E-mail: dvevang@stthomas.edu.

University of Southern Mississippi, Graduate School, College of Education and Psychology, Department of Curriculum, Instruction, and Special Education, Hattiesburg, MS 39406-0001. Offers alternative secondary teacher education (MAT); early childhood education (M Ed, Ed S); education of the gifted (M Ed, Ed D, PhD, Ed S); elementary education (M Ed, Ed D, PhD, Ed S); reading (M Ed, MS, Ed S); secondary education (M Ed, MS, Ed D, PhD, Ed S); special education (M Ed, Ed D, PhD, Ed S). *Faculty:* 16 full-time (11 women). *Students:* 31 full-time (28 women), 54 part-time (51 women); includes 5 minority (4 African Americans, 1 Hispanic American), 1 international. Average age 35. 59 applicants, 27% accepted, 11 enrolled. In 2006, 43 master's, 3 doctorates, 4 other advanced degrees awarded. *Degree requirements:* For master's, thesis (for some programs), comprehensive exam, registration; for doctorate and Ed S, thesis/dissertation, comprehensive exam, registration. *Entrance requirements:* For master's, GRE General Test, MAT, minimum GPA of 3.0; for doctorate, GRE General Test, minimum GPA of 3.5; for Ed S, GRE General Test, MAT, minimum GPA of 3.25. Additional exam requirements/recommendations for international students: Required—TOEFL. *Application deadline:* For fall admission, 3/1 priority date for domestic students, 3/1 for international students. Applications are processed on a rolling basis. Application fee: $25 ($30 for international students). *Financial support:* In 2006–07, 10 research assistantships with tuition reimbursements (averaging $22,333 per year), 2 teaching assistantships with full tuition reimbursements (averaging $22,333 per year) were awarded; Federal Work-Study, institutionally sponsored loans, and tuition waivers (partial) also available. Financial award application deadline: 3/15. *Faculty research:* Mathematical problem solving, integrative curriculum, writing process, teacher education models. Total annual research expenditures: $100,000. *Unit head:* Dr. Dana Thames, Chair, 601-266-4547, Fax: 601-266-4175. *Application contact:* B.J. Davis, Administrative Assistant, 601-266-6987, Fax: 601-266-4548.

University of South Florida, Graduate School, College of Education, Department of Special Education, Tampa, FL 33620-9951. Offers education of the mentally handicapped (MA); gifted education (online) (MA); learning disabilities (MA); varying exceptionalities (MA, MAT). *Accreditation:* NCATE. Part-time and evening/weekend programs available. *Faculty:* 17 full-time (11 women), 3 part-time/adjunct (all women). *Students:* 56 full-time (51 women), 85 part-time (78 women); includes 32 minority (17 African Americans, 1 American Indian/Alaska Native, 5 Asian Americans or Pacific Islanders, 9 Hispanic Americans), 4 international. 63 applicants, 76% accepted, 38 enrolled. In 2006, 48 master's awarded. *Entrance requirements:* For master's, GRE General Test, minimum GPA of 3.5 in last 60 hours. *Application deadline:* For fall admission, 6/1 for domestic students, 1/2 for international students; for spring admission, 10/15 for domestic students, 7/1 for international students. Application fee: $30. Electronic applications accepted. *Financial support:* Career-related internships or fieldwork, scholarships/grants, tuition waivers (partial), and unspecified assistantships available. Financial award application deadline: 6/1; financial award applicants required to submit FAFSA. *Faculty research:* Ethics, teaching cases, early intervention, systems and program evaluation, school restructuring. Total annual research expenditures: $3.4 million. *Unit head:* Dr. Daphene Thomas, Chairperson, 813-974-1383, Fax: 813-974-5542, E-mail: dthomas@tempest.coedu.usf.edu. *Application contact:* Dr. James L. Paul, Doctoral Program Coordinator, 813-974-4166, Fax: 813-974-5542, E-mail: jpaul@tempest.coedu.usf.edu.

The University of Texas–Pan American, College of Education, Department of Educational Psychology, Edinburg, TX 78541-2999. Offers counseling (M Ed); educational diagnostician (M Ed); gifted education (M Ed); school psychology (MA); special education (M Ed). Part-time and evening/weekend programs available. *Degree requirements:* For master's, thesis (for some programs), comprehensive exam (for some programs). *Entrance requirements:* For master's, GRE General Test, interview. *Expenses:* Tuition, state resident: full-time $2,577; part-time $143 per credit hour. Tuition, nonresident: full-time $7,527; part-time $418 per credit hour. Required fees: $561. *Faculty research:* Reading instruction, assessment practice, behavior interventions consultation, mental retardation.

The University of Toledo, College of Graduate Studies, College of Education, Department of Early Childhood, Physical and Special Education, Program in Gifted and Talented, Toledo, OH 43606-3390. Offers Ed S. *Students:* 2 full-time (both women). Average age 29. 1 applicant, 0% accepted. *Unit head:* Dr. Laurie Dinnebeil, Chair, Department of Early Childhood, Physical and Special Education, 419-530-4330.

Western Washington University, Graduate School, Woodring College of Education, Department of Special Education, Bellingham, WA 98225-5996. Offers M Ed. *Accreditation:* NCATE. Part-time programs available. *Faculty:* 9. *Students:* 3 full-time (all women), 1 international. 3 applicants, 100% accepted, 3 enrolled. In 2006, 2 degrees awarded. *Degree requirements:* For master's, thesis optional. *Entrance requirements:* For master's, GRE General Test or MAT, minimum GPA of 3.0 in last 60 semester hours or last 90 quarter hours. Additional exam requirements/recommendations for international students: Required—TOEFL (minimum score 567 paper-based; 227 computer-based). *Application deadline:* For fall admission, 6/1 for domestic students; for winter admission, 10/1 for domestic students; for spring admission, 2/1 for domestic students. Applications are processed on a rolling basis. Application fee: $50. *Expenses:* Tuition, state resident: full-time $6,609; part-time $199 per credit. Tuition, nonresident: full-time $16,845; part-time $540 per credit. *Financial support:* In 2006–07, 1 teaching assistantship with partial tuition reimbursement (averaging $9,339 per year) was awarded; Federal Work-Study, institutionally sponsored loans, scholarships/grants, tuition waivers (partial), and unspecified assistantships also available. Support available to part-time students. Financial award application deadline: 2/15; financial award applicants required to submit FAFSA. *Faculty research:* Educational issues and trends in Kenyan preschool and primary school, curriculum based assessment/evaluation, curriculum based assessment in early childhood special education, inclusive education, culturally responsive teaching. *Unit head:* Dr. Kristine Slentz, Chair, 360-650-3724. *Application contact:* Pam Clark Hamilton, Department Manager, 360-650-3981.

West Virginia University, College of Human Resources and Education, Department of Special Education, Morgantown, WV 26506. Offers autism spectrum disorder (5-adult) (Ed D); autism spectrum disorder (K-6) (Ed D); early intervention (preschool) (MA); early intervention/early childhood special education (MA); gifted education (1-12) (MA); multicategorical special education (5-adult) (Ed D); multicategorical special education (K-6) (Ed D); severe/multiple disabilities (K-adult) (MA); special education (Ed D); vision impairments (PreK-adult) (Ed D). *Accreditation:* NCATE. Part-time and evening/weekend programs available. Postbaccalaureate distance learning degree programs offered (no on-campus study). *Faculty:* 5 full-time (4 women), 2 part-time/adjunct (both women). *Students:* 57 full-time (43 women), 193 part-time (159 women); includes 14 minority (8 African Americans, 1 American Indian/Alaska Native, 1 Asian American or Pacific Islander, 4 Hispanic Americans), 1 international. Average age 36. 119 applicants, 68% accepted, 44 enrolled. In 2006, 100 master's, 2 doctorates awarded. *Degree requirements:* For master's, thesis optional; for doctorate, thesis/dissertation, comprehensive exam, registration. *Entrance requirements:* For master's, minimum GPA of 2.75; for doctorate, GRE General Test or MAT. Additional exam requirements/recommendations for international students: Required—TOEFL. *Application deadline:* Applications are processed on a rolling basis. Application fee: $50. *Expenses:* Tuition, state resident: full-time $4,926; part-time $276 per credit hour. Tuition, nonresident: full-time $14,278; part-time $796 per credit hour. Tuition and fees vary according to program. *Financial support:* In 2006–07, 91 students received support, including 1 research assistantship with full tuition reimbursement available; teaching assistantships, career-related internships or fieldwork, Federal Work-Study, institutionally sponsored loans, tuition waivers (partial), and graduate resident hall assistantships also available. Financial award application deadline: 2/1; financial award applicants required to submit FAFSA. *Unit head:* Dr. Barbara Ludlow, Professor, 304-293-3450 Ext. 1127, Fax: 304-293-6834, E-mail: barbara.ludlow@mail.wvu.edu. *Application contact:* Sherilyn A. Bunner, Program Coordinator, 304-293-7143, Fax: 304-293-6834, E-mail: sherry.bunner@mail.wvu.edu.

Whitworth University, School of Education, Graduate Studies in Education, Program in Gifted and Talented, Spokane, WA 99251-0001. Offers MAT. *Accreditation:* NCATE. Part-time and evening/weekend programs available. *Degree requirements:* For master's, thesis (for some programs), comprehensive exam. *Entrance requirements:* For master's, GRE General Test, MAT. *Application deadline:* For fall admission, 9/1 priority date for domestic students; for spring admission, 2/1 for domestic students. Applications are processed on a rolling basis. Application fee: $35. *Financial support:* Application deadline: 2/1. *Unit head:* Margo Long, Chair, Center for Gifted Education, 509-777-3226, Fax: 509-777-4753, E-mail: mlong@whitworth.edu. *Application contact:* Chris Huss, Department Secretary, 509-777-3226, Fax: 509-777-4753, E-mail: chuss@whitworth.edu.

William Carey University, Graduate Studies, School of Education, Hattiesburg, MS 39401-5499. Offers art education (M Ed); art of teaching (M Ed); elementary education (M Ed, Ed S); English education (M Ed); gifted education (M Ed); history and social science (M Ed); mild/moderate disabilities (M Ed); secondary education (M Ed). Part-time programs available. *Faculty:* 19 full-time (12 women), 25 part-time/adjunct (17 women). *Students:* 142 full-time (111 women), 412 part-time (343 women); includes 123 minority (121 African Americans, 1 Asian American or Pacific Islander, 1 Hispanic American). In 2006, 305 master's, 2 other advanced degrees awarded. *Degree requirements:* For master's, comprehensive exam. *Entrance requirements:* For master's, GRE, MAT, minimum GPA of 2.5, Class A teacher's license. Additional exam requirements/recommendations for international students: Required—TOEFL (minimum score 550 paper-based; 213 computer-based). *Application deadline:* For fall admission, 8/7 for domestic and international students; for winter admission, 10/30 for domestic and international students; for spring admission, 2/12 for domestic and international students. Application fee: $25. *Expenses:* Tuition: Full-time $5,040; part-time $240 per credit hour.

Tuition and fees vary according to course load. *Financial support:* In 2006–07, 371 students received support. Federal Work-Study and scholarships/grants available. Support available to part-time students. *Unit head:* Dr. Patty Ward, Dean, 601-318-6139, Fax: 601-318-6185, E-mail: patty.ward@wmcarey.edu. *Application contact:* Jason Douglas, Clerical Assistant, Graduate Admissions, 601-318-6774, Fax: 601-318-6765, E-mail: jason.douglas@wmcarey.edu.

Wilmington College, Division of Education, New Castle, DE 19720-6491. Offers applied education technology (M Ed); career and technical education (M Ed); elementary and secondary school counseling (M Ed); elementary special education (M Ed); elementary studies (M Ed); instruction: gifted and talented (M Ed); instruction: teaching and learning (M Ed); literacy (M Ed); reading (M Ed); school leadership (M Ed); secondary teaching (MAT). Part-time and evening/weekend programs available. *Faculty:* 7 full-time (4 women). *Students:* 609 full-time (447 women), 1,350 part-time (1,013 women); includes 144 minority (131 African Americans, 3 American Indian/Alaska Native, 1 Asian American or Pacific Islander, 9 Hispanic Americans). Average age 34. 818 applicants, 100% accepted, 599 enrolled. In 2006, 737 degrees awarded. *Entrance requirements:* For master's, 2 letters of recommendation, interview. Additional exam requirements/recommendations for international students: Required—TOEFL (minimum score 500 paper-based; 173 computer-based). *Application deadline:* For fall admission, 4/30 for domestic students. Applications are processed on a rolling basis. Application fee: $25. *Financial support:* Applicants required to submit FAFSA. *Unit head:* Dr. Richard Gochnauer, Chair, 302-328-6795 Ext. 163, Fax: 302-328-7081. *Application contact:* Chris Ferguson, Director of Admissions and Financial Aid, 302-328-9407 Ext. 256, Fax: 302-328-5164, E-mail: inquire@wilmcoll.edu.

Wright State University, School of Graduate Studies, College of Education and Human Services, Department of Teacher Education, Programs in Intervention Specialist, Dayton, OH 45435. Offers gifted educational needs (M Ed, MA); mild to moderate educational needs (M Ed, MA); moderate to intensive educational needs (M Ed, MA). *Accreditation:* NCATE. *Students:* 18 full-time (16 women), 52 part-time (45 women); includes 2 minority (both African Americans) Average age 34. 13 applicants, 100% accepted. In 2006, 32 degrees awarded. *Degree requirements:* For master's, thesis (for some programs). *Entrance requirements:* For master's, GRE General Test, MAT. Additional exam requirements/recommendations for international students: Required—TOEFL. Application fee: $25. *Financial support:* Available to part-time students. Applicants required to submit FAFSA. *Unit head:* Dr. Patricia R. Renick, Program Advisor, 937-775-2677, Fax: 937-775-3308, E-mail: patricia.renick@wright.edu. *Application contact:* John Kimble, Associate Director of Graduate Admissions and Records, 937-775-2957, Fax: 937-775-2453, E-mail: john.kimble@wright.edu.

Youngstown State University, Graduate School, College of Education, Department of Teacher Education, Program in Special Education, Youngstown, OH 44555-0001. Offers gifted and talented education (MS Ed); special education (MS Ed). *Accreditation:* NCATE. Part-time and evening/weekend programs available. *Degree requirements:* For master's, comprehensive exam. *Entrance requirements:* For master's, GRE, MAT, or teaching certificate; interview; minimum GPA of 2.7. Additional exam requirements/recommendations for international students: Required—TOEFL. *Faculty research:* Learning disabilities, learning styles, developing self-esteem and social skills of severe behaviorally handicapped students, inclusion.

Education of the Multiply Handicapped

Cleveland State University, College of Graduate Studies, College of Education and Human Services, Department of Teacher Education, Cleveland, OH 44115. Offers art education (M Ed); early childhood education (M Ed); foreign language education (M Ed); mathematics and science education (M Ed); middle childhood education (M Ed); special education (M Ed), including mild/moderate disabilities, moderate/intensive disabilities; teaching English to speakers of other languages (M Ed). Part-time and evening/weekend programs available. *Faculty:* 14 full-time (8 women), 5 part-time/adjunct (4 women). *Students:* 120 full-time (96 women), 592 part-time (485 women); includes 145 minority (123 African Americans, 7 Asian Americans or Pacific Islanders, 15 Hispanic Americans), 7 international. Average age 34. 526 applicants, 41% accepted, 144 enrolled. In 2006, 324 degrees awarded. *Degree requirements:* For master's, thesis or alternative, comprehensive exam (for some programs). *Entrance requirements:* For master's, GRE General Test or MAT, minimum GPA of 2.75. Additional exam requirements/recommendations for international students: Required—TOEFL (minimum score 525 paper-based; 197 computer-based), IELTS (minimum score 6). *Application deadline:* For fall admission, 7/15 priority date for domestic students. Applications are processed on a rolling basis. Application fee: $30. *Financial support:* In 2006–07, 12 research assistantships with full tuition reimbursements (averaging $3,480 per year) were awarded; tuition waivers (partial) and unspecified assistantships also available. *Faculty research:* Early literacy, professional development in reading, reading recovery, dual language, induction programs. Total annual research expenditures: $6.2 million. *Unit head:* Dr. Clifford T. Bennett, Chairperson, 216-523-7105, Fax: 216-687-5379, E-mail: c.t.bennett@csuohio.edu.

Fresno Pacific University, Graduate Programs, Programs in Education, Division of Special Education, Fresno, CA 93702-4709. Offers mild/moderate (MA Ed); moderate/severe (MA Ed); physical and health impairments (MA Ed). Part-time and evening/weekend programs available. *Faculty:* 3 full-time (1 woman), 5 part-time/adjunct (3 women). *Students:* 11 full-time (9 women), 87 part-time (74 women); includes 23 minority (2 African Americans, 4 American Indian/Alaska Native, 1 Asian American or Pacific Islander, 16 Hispanic Americans), 1 international. Average age 41. 21 applicants, 71% accepted, 1 enrolled. In 2006, 1 degree awarded. *Degree requirements:* For master's, thesis or alternative, registration. *Entrance requirements:* Additional exam requirements/recommendations for international students: Required—TOEFL (minimum score 550 paper-based; 213 computer-based). *Application deadline:* For fall admission, 7/15 for domestic and international students; for spring admission, 11/15 for domestic and international students. Applications are processed on a rolling basis. Application fee: $90. *Expenses:* Tuition: Full-time $7,470; part-time $415 per credit. *Financial support:* In 2006–07, 53 students received support. Career-related internships or fieldwork, scholarships/grants, and tuition waivers (full and partial) available. Support available to part-time students. Financial award applicants required to submit FAFSA. *Unit head:* Dr. Peter G. Kopriva, Head, 559-453-2202, Fax: 559-453-2001, E-mail: pgkopriv@fresno.edu.

Gallaudet University, The Graduate School, School of Education and Human Services, Department of Education, Washington, DC 20002-3625. Offers early childhood education (MA, Ed S); education of deaf and hard of hearing students and multihandicapped deaf and hard of hearing students (MA, Ed S); elementary education (MA, Ed S); individualized program of study (PhD); parent/infant specialty (MA, Ed S); secondary education (MA, Ed S). *Accreditation:* NCATE. *Degree requirements:* For master's, thesis optional; for doctorate, thesis/dissertation. *Entrance requirements:* For master's, GRE General Test or MAT; for doctorate, GRE General Test or MAT, interview.

Georgia State University, College of Education, Department of Educational Psychology and Special Education, Program in Multiple and Severe Disabilities, Atlanta, GA 30303-3083. Offers M Ed. *Accreditation:* NCATE. *Students:* 11 full-time (10 women), 41 part-time (39 women); includes 2 minority (both African Americans), 1 international. Average age 30. 14 applicants, 86% accepted. In 2006, 16 degrees awarded. *Degree requirements:* For master's, comprehensive exam. *Entrance requirements:* For master's, GRE General Test, minimum GPA of 2.5. *Application deadline:* For fall admission, 5/1 for domestic students; for spring admission, 10/1 for domestic students. Application fee: $25. *Financial support:* Research assistantships available. *Faculty research:* Cognition, discipline, curriculum development, social maladjustment. *Unit head:* Dr. Ron P. Colarusso, Dean, College of Education, 404-651-2310.

Hunter College of the City University of New York, Graduate School, School of Education, Department of Special Education, New York, NY 10021-5085. Offers blind or visually impaired (MS Ed); deaf or hard of hearing (MS Ed); severe/multiple disabilities (MS Ed); special education (MS Ed). *Accreditation:* NCATE. *Faculty:* 10 full-time (8 women), 31 part-time/adjunct (26 women). *Students:* 46 full-time (44 women), 354 part-time (321 women); includes 74 minority (21 African Americans, 25 Asian Americans or Pacific Islanders, 28 Hispanic Americans). Average age 30. 74 applicants. In 2006, 119 degrees awarded. *Degree requirements:* For master's, thesis, student teaching practica and clinical teaching lab courses, New York State Teacher Certification exams, comprehensive exam. *Entrance requirements:* For master's, minimum GPA of 2.8. Additional exam requirements/recommendations for international students: Required—TOEFL, TWE. *Application deadline:* For fall admission, 4/1 for domestic students, 2/1 for international students; for spring admission, 11/1 for domestic students, 9/1 for international students. Applications are processed on a rolling basis. Application fee: $50. *Expenses:* Tuition, state resident: part-time $270 per credit. Tuition, nonresident: part-time $500 per credit. Required fees: $45 per semester. *Financial support:* Career-related internships or fieldwork, Federal Work-Study, institutionally sponsored loans, and tuition waivers (partial) available. Support available to part-time students. *Faculty research:* Mathematics learning disabilities; street behavior; assessment; bilingual special education; families, diversity, and disabilities. *Unit head:* Dr. Kate Garnett, Chairperson, 212-772-4701, E-mail: kgarnett@hunter.cuny.edu. *Application contact:* William Zlata, Director for Graduate Admissions, 212-772-4482, Fax: 212-650-3336, E-mail: admissions@hunter.cuny.edu.

Minot State University, Graduate School, Program in Special Education, Minot, ND 58707-0002. Offers education of the deaf (MS); learning disabilities (MS); special education strategist (MS), including early childhood special education, severe multiple handicaps. *Accreditation:* NCATE. *Faculty:* 11 full-time (7 women). *Students:* 68. In 2006, 15 degrees awarded. *Degree requirements:* For master's, thesis (for some programs), comprehensive exam (for some programs). *Entrance requirements:* For master's, GRE General Test or minimum GPA of 3.0. Application fee: $35. *Financial support:* Research assistantships with partial tuition reimbursements, teaching assistantships with partial tuition reimbursements, career-related internships or fieldwork, institutionally sponsored loans, scholarships/grants, traineeships, tuition waivers (partial), and unspecified assistantships available. Support available to part-time students. Financial award application deadline: 4/1. *Faculty research:* Special education team diagnostic unit; individual diagnostic assessments of mentally retarded, learning-disabled, hearing-impaired, and speech-impaired youth; educational programming for the hearing impaired. *Unit head:* Dr. Lori Garnes, Chairperson, 701-858-3139. *Application contact:* Brenda Anderson, Administrative Assistant, 701-858-3250, Fax: 701-858-4286, E-mail: brenda.anderson@minotstateu.edu.

Montclair State University, The Graduate School, College of Education and Human Services, Department of Curriculum and Teaching, Montclair, NJ 07043-1624. Offers education (M Ed); educational technology (M Ed); school library media specialist (Certificate); teaching (MAT, Certificate), including art (MAT), biological science (MAT), early childhood education (P-3) (MAT), earth science (MAT), elementary education (K-8) (MAT), English (MAT), French (MAT), health and physical education (MAT), health education (MAT), home economics (MAT), mathematics (MAT), music (MAT), physical education (MAT), physical science (MAT), social studies (MAT), Spanish (MAT), teacher of ESL (MAT), teacher of students with disabilities (MAT). Part-time and evening/weekend programs available. *Faculty:* 16 full-time (12 women), 13 part-time/adjunct (8 women). *Students:* 147 full-time (113 women), 230 part-time (188 women); includes 58 minority (33 African Americans, 1 American Indian/Alaska Native, 12 Asian Americans or Pacific Islanders, 12 Hispanic Americans), 4 international. Average age 33. 118 applicants, 38% accepted, 37 enrolled. In 2006, 166 master's, 11 other advanced degrees awarded. *Degree requirements:* For master's, field experience. *Entrance requirements:* For master's, PRAXIS II, minimum GPA of 2.67, 2 letters of recommendation. Additional exam requirements/recommendations for international students: Required—TOEFL (minimum score 83 computer-based). *Application deadline:* For fall admission, 2/15 for domestic and international students; for spring admission, 9/15 for domestic and international students. Applications are processed on a rolling basis. Application fee: $60. Electronic applications accepted. *Expenses:* Tuition, state resident: part-time $450 per credit. Tuition, nonresident: part-time $682 per credit. Tuition and fees vary according to degree level and program. *Financial support:* In 2006–07, 7 research assistantships with full tuition reimbursements (averaging $7,000 per year) were awarded; Federal Work-Study, scholarships/grants, and unspecified assistantships also available. Support available to part-time students. Financial award application deadline: 3/1; financial award applicants required to submit FAFSA. *Unit head:* Dr. Deborah Eldridge, Chairperson, 973-655-5187.

Norfolk State University, School of Graduate Studies, School of Education, Department of Special Education, Program in Severe Disabilities, Norfolk, VA 23504. Offers MA. *Accreditation:* NCATE. Part-time programs available. *Degree requirements:* For master's, thesis or alternative. *Entrance requirements:* For master's, GRE, minimum GPA of 3.0 in major, 2.5 overall.

University of Arkansas at Little Rock, Graduate School, College of Education, Department of Teacher Education, Program in Special Education, Little Rock, AR 72204-1099. Offers early childhood special education (M Ed); teaching deaf and hard of hearing (M Ed); teaching of the mildly disabled student (M Ed); teaching persons with severe disabilities (M Ed); teaching the visually impaired (M Ed). *Accreditation:* NCATE. Part-time and evening/weekend programs available. *Degree requirements:* For master's, portfolio or thesis. *Entrance requirements:* For master's, interview, minimum GPA of 2.75, GRE General Test or teaching certificate.

University of Illinois at Urbana–Champaign, Graduate College, College of Education, Department of Special Education, Champaign, IL 61820. Offers Ed M, MA, MS, PhD, CAS. Part-time programs available. *Faculty:* 11 full-time (8 women), 3 part-time/adjunct (all women). *Students:* 57 full-time (50 women), 50 part-time (41 women); includes 12 minority (7 African Americans, 5 Asian Americans or Pacific Islanders), 16 international. 82 applicants, 56% accepted, 18 enrolled. In 2006, 21 master's, 4 doctorates awarded. *Degree requirements:* For master's and doctorate, thesis/dissertation. *Entrance requirements:* For master's and doctorate, GRE General Test or MAT, minimum GPA of 3.0. *Application deadline:* Applications are processed on a rolling basis. Application fee: $50 ($60 for international students). Electronic applications accepted. *Financial support:* In 2006–07, 41 fellowships, 18 research assistantships, 21 teaching assistantships were awarded; tuition waivers (full and partial) also available. Financial award application deadline: 2/15. *Unit head:* Adelle Renzaglia, Head, 217-333-0260, Fax: 217-333-6555, E-mail: renzag@uiuc.edu. *Application contact:* Mary Walle, Administrative Secretary, 217-333-0260, Fax: 217-333-6555, E-mail: mwalle@uiuc.edu.

Western Oregon University, Graduate Programs, College of Education, Division of Teacher Education, Division of Special Education, Monmouth, OR 97361-1394. Offers deaf education (MS Ed); learning disabilities (MS Ed); multihandicapped education (MS Ed); rehabilitation counseling (MS). *Accreditation:* NCATE. Part-time and evening/weekend programs available.

Education of the Multiply Handicapped

Western Oregon University (continued)
Faculty: 6 full-time (4 women). *Students:* 32 full-time (28 women), 12 part-time (10 women); includes 1 minority (Hispanic American) Average age 36. 30 applicants, 80% accepted. In 2006, 43 degrees awarded. *Degree requirements:* For master's, oral exam, portfolio, written exam, thesis optional. *Entrance requirements:* For master's, California Basic Educational Skills Test or PRAXIS, GRE General Test or MAT, interview, minimum GPA of 3.0, teaching license. *Application deadline:* Applications are processed on a rolling basis. Application fee: $50. *Expenses:* Tuition, state resident: full-time $8,250; part-time $250 per credit. Tuition, nonresident: full-time $14,025; part-time $250 per credit. Required fees: $1,173. *Financial support:* Research assistantships with full tuition reimbursements, teaching assistantships with full tuition reimbursements, career-related internships or fieldwork, Federal Work-Study, and tuition waivers (full and partial) available. Support available to part-time students. Financial award application deadline: 3/1; financial award applicants required to submit FAFSA. *Faculty research:* Interpreter teacher training, hearing disabilities, mental retardation. *Unit head:* Henri Bersani, Unit Head, 503-838-8687, Fax: 503-838-8228. *Application contact:* Dr. David McDonald, Dean of Admissions, Retention and Enrollment Management, 503-838-8919, Fax: 503-838-8067, E-mail: mcdonald@wou.edu.

West Virginia University, College of Human Resources and Education, Department of Special Education, Morgantown, WV 26506. Offers autism spectrum disorder (5-adult) (Ed D); autism spectrum disorder (K-6) (Ed D); early intervention (preschool) (MA); early intervention/early childhood special education (MA); gifted education (1-12) (MA); multicategorical special education (5-adult) (Ed D); multicategorical special education (K-6) (Ed D); severe/multiple disabilities (K-adult) (MA); special education (Ed D); vision impairments (PreK-adult) (Ed D). *Accreditation:* NCATE. Part-time and evening/weekend programs available. Postbaccalaureate distance learning degree programs offered (no on-campus study). *Faculty:* 5 full-time (4 women), 2 part-time/adjunct (both women). *Students:* 57 full-time (43 women), 193 part-time (159 women); includes 14 minority (8 African Americans, 1 American Indian/Alaska Native, 1 Asian American or Pacific Islander, 4 Hispanic Americans), 1 international. Average age 36. 119 applicants, 68% accepted, 44 enrolled. In 2006, 100 master's, 2 doctorates awarded. *Degree requirements:* For master's, thesis optional; for doctorate, thesis/dissertation, comprehensive exam, registration. *Entrance requirements:* For master's, minimum GPA of 2.75; for doctorate, GRE General Test or MAT. Additional exam requirements/recommendations for international students: Required—TOEFL. *Application deadline:* Applications are processed on a rolling basis. Application fee: $50. *Expenses:* Tuition, state resident: full-time $4,926; part-time $276 per credit hour. Tuition, nonresident: full-time $14,278; part-time $796 per credit hour. Tuition and fees vary according to program. *Financial support:* In 2006–07, 91 students received support, including 1 research assistantship with full tuition reimbursement available; teaching assistantships, career-related internships or fieldwork, Federal Work-Study, institutionally sponsored loans, tuition waivers (partial), and graduate resident hall assistantships also available. Financial award application deadline: 2/1; financial award applicants required to submit FAFSA. *Unit head:* Dr. Barbara Ludlow, Professor, 304-293-3450 Ext. 1127, Fax: 304-293-6834, E-mail: barbara.ludlow@mail.wvu.edu. *Application contact:* Sherilyn A. Bunner, Program Coordinator, 304-293-7143, Fax: 304-293-6834, E-mail: sherry.bunner@mail.wvu.edu.

English as a Second Language

Adelphi University, School of Education, Program in Teaching English to Speakers of Other Languages, Garden City, NY 11530-0701. Offers MA, Certificate. Part-time and evening/weekend programs available. *Students:* 7 full-time (all women), 68 part-time (58 women); includes 29 minority (4 African Americans, 4 Asian Americans or Pacific Islanders, 21 Hispanic Americans), 3 international. Average age 36. In 2006, 28 master's, 2 other advanced degrees awarded. *Entrance requirements:* For master's, 2 letters of recommendation, resumé. Additional exam requirements/recommendations for international students: Required—TOEFL (minimum score 550 paper-based; 213 computer-based). *Application deadline:* For fall admission, 4/1 priority date for domestic students; for spring admission, 11/1 priority date for domestic students. Applications are processed on a rolling basis. Application fee: $50. Electronic applications accepted. *Financial support:* Fellowships, research assistantships with partial tuition reimbursements, teaching assistantships, career-related internships or fieldwork, Federal Work-Study, institutionally sponsored loans, tuition waivers (full), and unspecified assistantships available. Support available to part-time students. Financial award application deadline: 2/15; financial award applicants required to submit FAFSA. *Faculty research:* Theories of language acquisition, English as a second language in the content areas, apprenticeship in English as a second language instruction. *Unit head:* Eva Roca, Director, 516-877-4072, E-mail: rocaz@adelphi.edu. *Application contact:* Christine Murphy, Director of Admissions, 516-877-3050, Fax: 516-877-3039, E-mail: graduateadmissions@adelphi.edu.

Albright College, Department of Education—Graduate Division, Reading, PA 19612-5234. Offers early childhood education (MS); elementary education (MS); English as a second language (MA); general education (MA); special education (MS). Part-time and evening/weekend programs available. *Degree requirements:* For master's, thesis. *Entrance requirements:* For master's, GRE General Test or MAT, minimum undergraduate GPA of 3.0, 2 letters of recommendation, interview. Additional exam requirements/recommendations for international students: Recommended—TOEFL (minimum score 525 paper-based; 197 computer-based). Electronic applications accepted.

Alliant International University–Fresno, Graduate School of Education, Program in Teaching English to Speakers of Other Languages, Fresno, CA 93727. Offers MA, Ed D, Certificate. Part-time programs available. *Students:* 7. Average age 26. 4 applicants, 100% accepted, 3 enrolled. In 2006, 5 degrees awarded. *Degree requirements:* For doctorate, thesis/dissertation. *Entrance requirements:* For master's and doctorate, minimum GPA of 3.0, letters of recommendation. Additional exam requirements/recommendations for international students: Required—TOEFL (minimum score 550 paper-based; 213 computer-based), TWE. *Application deadline:* For fall admission, 7/1 priority date for domestic and international students; for spring admission, 12/1 priority date for domestic and international students. Applications are processed on a rolling basis. Application fee: $55. Electronic applications accepted. *Financial support:* Federal Work-Study, institutionally sponsored loans, and scholarships/grants available. Financial award application deadline: 2/15; financial award applicants required to submit FAFSA. *Faculty research:* Technology and second language instruction, curriculum design, sociolinguistics, TESOL teaching training, bilingualism. *Unit head:* Dr. Mary Ellen Butler-Pascoe, Systemwide Program Director for International Teacher Education, 858-635-4507, Fax: 559-253-2267, E-mail: admissions@alliant.edu. *Application contact:* Alliant International University Central Contact Center, 866-U-ALLIANT, Fax: 858-635-4555, E-mail: admissions@alliant.edu.

See Close-Up on page 1363.

Alliant International University–Irvine, Graduate School of Education, Program in Teaching English to Speakers of Other Languages, Irvine, CA 92612. Offers MA, Ed D. Part-time programs available. *Students:* 7. In 2006, 4 master's, 1 doctorate awarded. *Degree requirements:* For doctorate, thesis/dissertation. *Entrance requirements:* For master's and doctorate, minimum GPA of 3.0, letters of recommendation. Additional exam requirements/recommendations for international students: Required—TOEFL (minimum score 550 paper-based; 213 computer-based), TWE. *Application deadline:* For fall admission, 7/1 priority date for domestic and international students; for spring admission, 12/1 priority date for domestic and international students. Applications are processed on a rolling basis. Application fee: $70. Electronic applications accepted. *Financial support:* Federal Work-Study, institutionally sponsored loans, and scholarships/grants available. Financial award applicants required to submit FAFSA. *Unit head:* Dr. Ellen Butler-Pascoe, Systemwide Program Director for International Teacher Education, 866-825-5426, Fax: 949-833-3507, E-mail: admissions@alliant.edu. *Application contact:* Alliant International University Central Contact Center, 866-U-ALLIANT, Fax: 858-635-4555, E-mail: admissions@alliant.edu.

See Close-Up on page 1363.

Alliant International University–San Diego, Graduate School of Education, Program in Teaching English to Speakers of Other Languages, San Diego, CA 92131-1799. Offers MA, Ed D, Certificate. Part-time programs available. *Faculty:* 3 full-time (all women), 7 part-time/adjunct (6 women). *Students:* 31 full-time (25 women), 31 part-time (21 women); includes 15 minority (2 African Americans, 8 Asian Americans or Pacific Islanders, 5 Hispanic Americans), 28 international. Average age 39. 50 applicants, 52% accepted, 17 enrolled. In 2006, 15 master's, 3 doctorates awarded. *Median time to degree:* Of those who began their doctoral program in fall 1998, 50% received their degree in 8 years or less. *Degree requirements:* For doctorate, thesis/dissertation. *Entrance requirements:* For master's and doctorate, minimum GPA of 3.0, letters of recommendation. Additional exam requirements/recommendations for international students: Required—TOEFL (minimum score 550 paper-based; 213 computer-based), TWE. *Application deadline:* For fall admission, 7/1 priority date for domestic and international students; for spring admission, 12/1 priority date for domestic and international students. Applications are processed on a rolling basis. Application fee: $55. Electronic applications accepted. *Expenses:* Tuition: Part-time $825 per unit. Tuition and fees vary according to course load, degree level and program. *Financial support:* In 2006–07, 35 students received support. Federal Work-Study, institutionally sponsored loans, and scholarships/grants available. Financial award applicants required to submit FAFSA. *Unit head:* Dr. Mary Ellen Butler-Pascoe, Systemwide Program Director for International Teacher Education, 866-825-5426, Fax: 858-635-4739, E-mail: admissions@alliant.edu. *Application contact:* Alliant International University Central Contact Center, 866-U-ALLIANT, Fax: 858-635-4555, E-mail: admissions@alliant.edu.

See Close-Up on page 1363.

American University, College of Arts and Sciences, Department of Language and Foreign Studies, Program in Teaching English to Speakers of Other Languages, Washington, DC 20016-8001. Offers MA, Certificate. *Students:* 15 full-time (14 women), 15 part-time (10 women); includes 2 minority (1 African American, 1 Hispanic American), 9 international. Average age 33. In 2006, 17 master's, 21 other advanced degrees awarded. *Degree requirements:* For master's, one foreign language, thesis or alternative, portfolio, comprehensive exam. *Entrance requirements:* For master's, GRE. Additional exam requirements/recommendations for international students: Required—TOEFL. *Application deadline:* For fall admission, 2/1 for domestic students; for spring admission, 10/1 for domestic students. Application fee: $50. *Expenses:* Tuition: Full-time $18,864; part-time $1,048 per credit. Required fees: $380. Tuition and fees vary according to program. *Financial support:* Fellowships with full and partial tuition reimbursements available. Financial award application deadline: 2/1. *Faculty research:* Language, acquisition, written language, e-mail. *Unit head:* Brock Brady, Coordinator, 202-885-1146, Fax: 202-885-1076, E-mail: bbrady@american.edu.

American University, College of Arts and Sciences, School of Education, Teaching, and Health, Program in English for Speakers of Other Languages, Washington, DC 20016-8001. Offers MAT, Certificate. *Students:* 3 full-time (all women), 27 part-time (19 women); includes 8 minority (2 African Americans, 2 Asian Americans or Pacific Islanders, 4 Hispanic Americans). Average age 31. In 2006, 12 degrees awarded. *Degree requirements:* For master's, PRAXIS II. *Entrance requirements:* For master's, GRE General Test or MAT, minimum GPA of 3.0. *Application deadline:* For fall admission, 2/1 priority date for domestic students; for spring admission, 10/1 priority date for domestic students. Application fee: $50. *Expenses:* Tuition: Full-time $18,864; part-time $1,048 per credit. Required fees: $380. Tuition and fees vary according to program. *Financial support:* Research assistantships with partial tuition reimbursements available. Financial award application deadline: 2/1.

The American University in Cairo, Graduate Studies and Research, School of Humanities and Social Sciences, English Language Institute, Cairo, Egypt. Offers teaching English as a foreign language (MA, Diploma). Part-time programs available. *Degree requirements:* For master's, one foreign language, thesis optional. *Entrance requirements:* Additional exam requirements/recommendations for international students: Required—English entrance exam and/or TOEFL. Electronic applications accepted. *Faculty research:* Teacher education, social linguistics, teaching methodology pragmatics.

Andrews University, School of Graduate Studies, School of Education, Department of Teaching, Learning, and Curriculum, Berrien Springs, MI 49104. Offers curriculum and instruction (MA, Ed D, PhD, Ed S); elementary education (MAT); reading (MA); secondary education (MAT), including biology, education, English, English as a second language, French, history, physics; special education/learning disabilities (MS); teacher education (MAT). *Entrance requirements:* For master's, GRE Subject Test.

Arizona State University, Division of Graduate Studies, College of Liberal Arts and Sciences, Division of Humanities, Department of English, Tempe, AZ 85287. Offers English (MA, PhD), including comparative literature (MA), linguistics (MA), literature (PhD), literature and language (MA), rhetoric and composition (MA), rhetoric/composition and linguistics (PhD); teaching English as a second language (MTESL). *Degree requirements:* For doctorate, thesis/dissertation. *Entrance requirements:* For master's and doctorate, GRE.

Arkansas Tech University, Graduate School, School of Liberal and Fine Arts, Russellville, AR 72801. Offers communication (MLA); English (M Ed, MA); fine arts (MLA); history (MA); multi-media journalism (MA); social science (MLA); social studies (M Ed); Spanish (MA, MLA); teaching English as a second language (MA, MLA). Part-time programs available. *Students:* 47 full-time (36 women), 102 part-time (82 women); includes 9 minority (2 African Americans, 1 American Indian/Alaska Native, 1 Asian American or Pacific Islander, 5 Hispanic Americans), 20 international. Average age 33. In 2006, 20 degrees awarded. *Degree requirements:* For master's, project. *Entrance requirements:* For master's, GRE General Test or MAT. Additional exam requirements/recommendations for international students: Required—TOEFL (minimum score 500 paper-based; 173 computer-based). *Application deadline:* For fall admission, 3/1 priority date for domestic students, 5/1 priority date for international students; for winter admission, 10/1 priority date for international students; for spring admission, 10/1 priority date for domestic and international students. Applications are processed on a rolling basis. Application fee: $0 ($30 for international students). Electronic applications accepted. *Expenses:* Tuition, state resident: full-time $3,060; part-time $170 per hour. Tuition, nonresident: full-time $6,120; part-time $340 per hour. Required fees: $312; $4 per hour. $84 per term. Part-time tuition and fees vary according to course load. *Financial support:* In 2006–07, teaching assistantships with full tuition reimbursements (averaging $4,000 per year); career-related internships or fieldwork, Federal Work-Study, scholarships/grants, health care benefits, and unspecified assistantships also available. Support available to part-time students. Financial award application deadline: 4/15; financial award applicants required to submit FAFSA. *Unit head:* Dr. Georgena Duncan, Dean, 479-968-0266, Fax: 479-968-0275, E-mail: georgena.duncan@atu.edu. *Application contact:* Dr. Eldon G. Clary, Dean of Graduate School, 479-968-0398, Fax: 479-964-0542, E-mail: graduate.school@atu.edu.

Asbury College, Graduate Programs, Wilmore, KY 40390-1198. Offers biology: alternative certificate (MA Ed); chemistry: alternative certificate (MA Ed); English (Certificate); English as a second language (MA Ed); ESL (Certificate); French (Certificate); mathematics: alternative certificate (MA Ed); reading / writing (MA Ed); social studies (Certificate); Spanish (Certificate); special education (MA Ed); special education: alternative certificate (MA Ed). *Accreditation:* NCATE. Part-time programs available. *Faculty:* 8 full-time (7 women), 9 part-time/adjunct (4 women). *Students:* Average age 36. 14 applicants, 100% accepted, 10 enrolled. In 2006, 17 degrees awarded. *Median time to degree:* Master's–2.5 years part-time. *Degree requirements:* For master's, action research project, portfolio. *Entrance requirements:* For master's, PRAXIS/NTE or GRE, minimum GPA of 2.75, letters of recommendation. Additional exam requirements/recommendations for international students: Recommended—TOEFL (minimum score 550 paper-based). *Application deadline:* Applications are processed on a rolling basis. Application fee: $25. *Expenses:* Tuition: Part-time $335 per credit hour. *Financial support:* Scholarships/grants and traineeships available. Financial award applicants required to submit FAFSA. *Unit head:* Dr. Bonnie J. Banker, Director, 859-858-3511 Ext. 2221, Fax: 859-858-3921, E-mail: bonnie.banker@asbury.edu. *Application contact:* Melanie S. Kinnell, Graduate Program Assistant and Certification Specialist, 859-858-3511 Ext. 2304, Fax: 859-858-3921, E-mail: graded@asbury.edu.

Avila University, School of Education, Kansas City, MO 64145-1698. Offers education (MA); English for speakers of other languages (Advanced Certificate); special reading (Advanced Certificate). Part-time and evening/weekend programs available. *Faculty:* 7 full-time (5 women), 17 part-time/adjunct (13 women). *Students:* 144 full-time (112 women), 42 part-time (24 women); includes 17 minority (15 African Americans, 2 Hispanic Americans). Average age 37. 72 applicants, 42% accepted, 14 enrolled. In 2006, 34 degrees awarded. *Entrance requirements:* For master's, minimum GPA of 3.0. *Application deadline:* Applications are processed on a rolling basis. Application fee: $0. Electronic applications accepted. *Expenses:* Tuition: Full-time $7,470; part-time $415 per credit. *Financial support:* In 2006–07, 1 research assistantship was awarded; career-related internships or fieldwork also available. Support available to part-time students. Financial award applicants required to submit FAFSA. *Unit head:* Dr. Laura Sloan, Dean, 816-501-3663, Fax: 816-501-2455, E-mail: laura.sloan@avila.edu. *Application contact:* Deana Angotti, Director of Graduate Education, 816-501-2446, Fax: 816-501-2915, E-mail: deana.augotti@avila.edu.

Azusa Pacific University, College of Liberal Arts and Sciences, Program in Teaching English to Speakers of Other Languages, Azusa, CA 91702-7000. Offers MA. *Students:* 12 full-time (all women), 83 part-time (63 women); includes 12 minority (1 American Indian/Alaska Native, 10 Asian Americans or Pacific Islanders, 1 Hispanic American), 12 international. Average age 30. In 2006, 28 degrees awarded. Application fee: $45 ($65 for international students). *Expenses:* Tuition: Part-time $475 per credit. *Unit head:* Richard Robinson, Chair and Professor, E-mail: rrobinson@apu.edu.

Azusa Pacific University, School of Education, Department of Education, Program in Language Development, Azusa, CA 91702-7000. Offers MA. *Accreditation:* NCATE. *Degree requirements:* For master's, comprehensive exam or thesis, core exams, oral presentation. *Entrance requirements:* For master's, 12 units of course work in education, minimum GPA of 3.0. Application fee: $45 ($65 for international students). *Expenses:* Tuition: Part-time $475 per credit. *Faculty research:* Biliteracy development, home-school connections, integrated curriculum. *Unit head:* Dr. Don Dorr, Director, 626-815-3483. *Application contact:* Dr. Dan Doorn, Director, 626-815-5371.

Ball State University, Graduate School, College of Sciences and Humanities, Department of English, Muncie, IN 47306-1099. Offers English (MA, PhD), including composition, creative writing (MA), general (MA), literature; linguistics (MA, PhD), including applied linguistics (PhD); linguistics and teaching English to speakers of other languages (MA); teaching English to speakers of other languages (MA). *Faculty:* 38. *Students:* 47 full-time (31 women), 26 part-time (14 women); includes 3 minority (1 American Indian/Alaska Native, 2 Hispanic Americans), 15 international. Average age 27. 51 applicants, 57% accepted, 12 enrolled. In 2006, 23 master's, 6 doctorates awarded. *Degree requirements:* For doctorate, variable foreign language requirement, thesis/dissertation. *Entrance requirements:* For master's, GRE General Test, writing sample; for doctorate, GRE General Test, GRE Subject Test, minimum graduate GPA of 3.2, writing sample. Application fee: $25 ($35 for international students). *Financial support:* In 2006–07, 3 fellowships with full tuition reimbursements (averaging $12,000 per year), 44 teaching assistantships with full tuition reimbursements (averaging $8,768 per year) were awarded; research assistantships with full tuition reimbursements, career-related internships or fieldwork and unspecified assistantships also available. Financial award application deadline: 3/1. *Faculty research:* American literature; literary editing; Medieval, Renaissance, and eighteenth century British literature; rhetoric. *Unit head:* Dr. Bruce Hozeski, Chairperson, 765-285-8535, Fax: 765-285-3765, E-mail: bhozeski@bsu.edu.

Barry University, School of Education, Program in Curriculum and Instruction, Miami Shores, FL 33161-6695. Offers accomplished teacher (Ed S); culture, language and literacy (TESOL) (PhD); curriculum evaluation and research (PhD); early childhood (Ed S); early childhood education (PhD); elementary (Ed S); elementary education (PhD); ESOL (Ed S); gifted (Ed S); Montessori (Ed S); PKP/elementary (Ed S); reading (Ed S); reading, language and cognition (PhD). *Students:* 2 full-time (both women), 36 part-time (27 women); includes 21 minority (12 African Americans, 9 Hispanic Americans), 6 international. 45 applicants, 33% accepted, 4 enrolled. In 2006, 4 degrees awarded. *Entrance requirements:* For doctorate, GRE, minimum GPA of 3.25. Application fee: $30. *Unit head:* Dr. Jill Farrell, Director, 305-899-3198, Fax: 305-899-4708, E-mail: jfarrell@mail.barry.edu. *Application contact:* Dave Fletcher, Director of Graduate Admissions, 305-899-3113, Fax: 305-899-2971, E-mail: dfletcher@mail.barry.edu.

Barry University, School of Education, Program in Technology and TESOL, Miami Shores, FL 33161-6695. Offers MS, Ed S. *Unit head:* Dr. Rita Oates, Director, 305-899-3740, Fax: 305-899-4708, E-mail: roates@mail.barry.edu. *Application contact:* Dave Fletcher, Director of Graduate Admissions, 305-899-3113, Fax: 305-899-2971, E-mail: dfletcher@mail.barry.edu.

Barry University, School of Education, Program in TESOL, Miami Shores, FL 33161-6695. Offers TESOL (MS); TESOL international (MS). *Students:* 17 applicants, 18% accepted, 2 enrolled. In 2006, 26 degrees awarded. *Entrance requirements:* For master's, GRE or MAT. Application fee: $30. *Application contact:* Dave Fletcher, Director of Graduate Admissions, 305-899-3113, Fax: 305-899-2971, E-mail: dfletcher@mail.barry.edu.

Biola University, School of Intercultural Studies, La Mirada, CA 90639-0001. Offers applied linguistics (MA); intercultural education (PhD); intercultural studies (MAICS); missiology (D Miss); missions (MA); teaching English to speakers of other languages (MA, Certificate). Part-time and evening/weekend programs available. Terminal master's awarded for partial completion of doctoral program. *Degree requirements:* For master's, one foreign language, comprehensive exam; for doctorate, one foreign language, thesis/dissertation, comprehensive exam. *Entrance requirements:* For master's, minimum undergraduate GPA of 3.0; for doctorate, MA, 3 years of ministry experience, minimum graduate GPA of 3.3. Additional exam requirements/recommendations for international students: Required—TOEFL (minimum score 550 paper-based; 213 computer-based). Electronic applications accepted.

Bishop's University, School of Education, Sherbrooke, QC J1M 0C8, Canada. Offers advanced studies in education (Diploma); education (M Ed, MA); teaching English as a second language (Certificate). Part-time programs available. Postbaccalaureate distance learning degree programs offered (minimal on-campus study). *Degree requirements:* For master's, thesis (for some programs). *Entrance requirements:* For master's, teaching license, 2 years of teaching experience. *Faculty research:* Integration of special needs students, multigrade classes/small schools, leadership in organizational development, second language acquisition.

Boston University, School of Education, Department of Literacy and Language, Counseling and Development, Teaching of English to Speakers of Other Languages Program, Boston, MA 02215. Offers Ed M, CAGS. *Students:* 20 full-time (18 women), 23 part-time (21 women); includes 2 minority (1 Asian American or Pacific Islander, 1 Hispanic American), 17 international. Average age 29. 107 applicants, 71% accepted. In 2006, 17 degrees awarded. *Degree requirements:* For CAGS, comprehensive exam. *Entrance requirements:* For master's and CAGS, GRE General Test or MAT. Additional exam requirements/recommendations for international students: Required—TOEFL. *Application deadline:* For fall admission, 2/15 priority date for domestic students; for winter admission, 11/1 priority date for domestic students. Applications are processed on a rolling basis. Application fee: $65. Electronic applications accepted. *Expenses:* Tuition: Full-time $33,330; part-time $1,042 per credit. Required fees: $462; $40. *Financial support:* Application deadline: 2/15. *Faculty research:* Second language acquisition, innovative approaches to language teaching. *Unit head:* Dr. Marnie Reed, Coordinator, 617-353-1811, E-mail: tesol@bu.edu. *Application contact:* 617-353-4237, Fax: 617-353-8937, E-mail: sedgrad@bu.edu.

Brigham Young University, Graduate Studies, College of Humanities, Department of Linguistics and English Language, Provo, UT 84602. Offers general linguistics (MA); teaching English as a second language (MA, Certificate). Part-time programs available. *Faculty:* 19 full-time (2 women). *Students:* 63 full-time (41 women), 19 international. Average age 28. 66 applicants, 73% accepted, 40 enrolled. In 2006, 12 master's, 23 other advanced degrees awarded. *Degree requirements:* For master's, one foreign language, thesis. *Entrance requirements:* For master's, GRE General Test, minimum GPA of 3.6 in last 60 hours of course work. Additional exam requirements/recommendations for international students: Required—TOEFL (minimum score 580 paper-based; 237 computer-based; 90 iBT), TWE. *Application deadline:* 1/15 for domestic and international students. Application fee: $50. Electronic applications accepted. *Financial support:* In 2006–07, 51 students received support, including 1 fellowship with partial tuition reimbursement available (averaging $8,000 per year), 8 research assistantships with partial tuition reimbursements available (averaging $5,344 per year), 9 teaching assistantships with partial tuition reimbursements available (averaging $5,720 per year); career-related internships or fieldwork, institutionally sponsored loans, scholarships/grants, tuition waivers (partial), unspecified assistantships, and student instructorships also available. Support available to part-time students. Financial award application deadline: 4/1. *Faculty research:* Mayan languages, second language acquisition, computational linguistics, semiotics and semantics, computer-assisted language instruction. Total annual research expenditures: $250,000. *Unit head:* Dr. William G. Eggington, Chair, 801-422-2937, Fax: 801-422-0906, E-mail: bill_eggington@byu.edu. *Application contact:* Phyllis Ann Daniel, Secretary, 801-422-2937, Fax: 801-422-0906, E-mail: phyllis_daniel@byu.edu.

Brock University, Faculty of Graduate Studies, Faculty of Humanities, Program in Applied Linguistics, St. Catharines, ON L2S 3A1, Canada. Offers MA. Part-time programs available. *Faculty:* 5 full-time (2 women). *Students:* 13 full-time (9 women), 2 part-time. 29 applicants, 62% accepted, 12 enrolled. In 2006, 9 degrees awarded. *Degree requirements:* For master's, thesis optional. *Entrance requirements:* For master's, honours degree with a background in English, English literature, teaching English as a second language, or a comparable field. Additional exam requirements/recommendations for international students: Required—TOEFL (minimum score 550 paper-based; 213 computer-based; 80 iBT), IELTS (minimum score 7), TWE (minimum score 4). *Application deadline:* For fall admission, 3/1 for domestic students; for spring admission, 12/1 for international students. Application fee: $75. Electronic applications accepted. *Expenses:* Contact institution. *Financial support:* Fellowships, research assistantships, teaching assistantships, scholarships/grants, unspecified assistantships, and bursaries available. *Faculty research:* Metalinguistic ability in subsequent language learning, language teaching methodology, forensic linguistics, philosophy of education, culturally appropriate pedagogy. *Unit head:* Dr. David Hayes, Gradute Program Director, 905-688-5550 Ext. 5359, Fax: 905-688-2360, E-mail: david.hayes@brocku.ca.

California State University, Dominguez Hills, College of Liberal Arts, Department of English, Carson, CA 90747-0001. Offers English (MA); rhetoric and composition (Certificate); teaching English as a second language (Certificate). Part-time and evening/weekend programs available. *Faculty:* 17 full-time (9 women). *Students:* 22 full-time (15 women), 57 part-time (44 women); includes 35 minority (11 African Americans, 1 American Indian/Alaska Native, 9 Asian Americans or Pacific Islanders, 14 Hispanic Americans), 11 international. Average age 35. 42 applicants, 90% accepted, 21 enrolled. In 2006, 14 degrees awarded. *Degree requirements:* For master's, thesis (for some programs), comprehensive exam (for some programs). *Entrance requirements:* For master's, minimum GPA of 3.0 in last 60 units. Additional exam requirements/recommendations for international students: Required—TOEFL (minimum score 550 paper-based; 213 computer-based). *Application deadline:* Applications are processed on a rolling basis. Application fee: $55. Electronic applications accepted. *Expenses:* Tuition, nonresident: part-time $339 per unit. Required fees: $1,148 per term. Tuition and fees vary according to program. *Faculty research:* Gender studies, transnationalism, discourse analysis, visual culture, Shakespeare. *Unit head:* Dr. Cyril Zoerner, Chair, 310-243-3322. *Application contact:* 310-243-3600.

California State University, Fresno, Division of Graduate Studies, College of Arts and Humanities, Department of Linguistics, Fresno, CA 93740-8027. Offers linguistics (MA), including Teaching English as a second language. Part-time and evening/weekend programs available. *Degree requirements:* For master's, comprehensive exam. *Entrance requirements:* For master's, GRE General Test, minimum GPA of 3.0. Additional exam requirements/recommendations for international students: Required—TOEFL. Electronic applications accepted. *Faculty research:* Communication systems, bilingual education, animal communication, conflict resolution, literacy programs.

California State University, Fullerton, Graduate Studies, College of Humanities and Social Sciences, Department of Modern Languages and Literatures, Fullerton, CA 92834-9480. Offers French (MA); German (MA); Spanish (MA); teaching English to speakers of other languages (MS). Part-time programs available. *Students:* 51 full-time (39 women), 77 part-time (61 women); includes 58 minority (23 Asian Americans or Pacific Islanders, 35 Hispanic Americans), 22 international. Average age 34. 109 applicants, 67% accepted, 42 enrolled. In 2006, 34 degrees awarded. *Degree requirements:* For master's, thesis or alternative, comprehensive exam. *Entrance requirements:* For master's, minimum GPA of 2.5 in last 60 hours of course work, undergraduate major in a language. Application fee: $55. *Expenses:* Tuition, nonresident: part-time $339 per unit. Required fees: $1,155 per semester. *Financial support:* Federal Work-Study, institutionally sponsored loans, and scholarships/grants available. Support available to part-time students. Financial award application deadline: 3/1. *Unit head:* Dr. Janet Eyring, Chair, 714-278-3534.

California State University, Los Angeles, Graduate Studies, Charter College of Education, Division of Applied and Advanced Studies in Education, Major in Teaching English to Speakers of Other Languages, Los Angeles, CA 90032-8530. Offers MA. *Accreditation:* NCATE. *Students:* 9 full-time (7 women), 53 part-time (33 women); includes 28 minority (1 African American, 17 Asian Americans or Pacific Islanders, 10 Hispanic Americans), 10 international. In 2006, 41 degrees awarded. *Entrance requirements:* For master's, minimum GPA of 2.75 in last 90 units of course work, teaching certificate. Additional exam requirements/recommendations for international students: Required—TOEFL. *Application deadline:* For fall admission, 6/30 for domestic students; for spring admission, 2/1 for domestic students. Applications are processed on a rolling basis. Application fee: $55. *Expenses:* Tuition, nonresident: part-time $226 per unit.

English as a Second Language

California State University, Los Angeles (continued)
Financial support: Application deadline: 3/1. *Unit head:* Dr. Chogollah Maroufi, Chair, Division of Applied and Advanced Studies in Education, 323-343-4330, Fax: 323-343-5336.

California State University, Sacramento, Graduate Studies, College of Arts and Letters, Department of English, Sacramento, CA 95819-6048. Offers creative writing (MA); teaching English to speakers of other languages (MA). Part-time programs available. *Students:* 85 full-time (60 women), 112 part-time (74 women); includes 37 minority (7 African Americans, 2 American Indian/Alaska Native, 12 Asian Americans or Pacific Islanders, 16 Hispanic Americans), 6 international. Average age 33. 112 applicants, 79% accepted, 51 enrolled. *Degree requirements:* For master's, thesis, project, or comprehensive exam; writing proficiency exam. *Entrance requirements:* For master's, portfolio (creative writing); minimum GPA of 3.0 in English, 2.75 overall during previous 2 years. Additional exam requirements/recommendations for international students: Required—TOEFL. *Application deadline:* Applications are processed on a rolling basis. Application fee: $55. Electronic applications accepted. *Financial support:* Research assistantships, teaching assistantships, career-related internships or fieldwork and Federal Work-Study available. Support available to part-time students. Financial award application deadline: 3/1. *Faculty research:* Teaching composition, remedial writing. *Unit head:* Dr. Sheree Meyer, Chairman, 916-278-6586, Fax: 916-278-4588.

California State University, San Bernardino, Graduate Studies, College of Education, San Bernardino, CA 92407-2397. Offers bilingual/cross-cultural education (MA); curriculum and instruction (MA); educational administration (MA); educational psychology and counseling (MA, MS), including counseling and guidance (MS), rehabilitation counseling (MA); elementary education (MA); English as a second language (MA); environmental education (MA); history and English for secondary teachers (MA); instructional technology (MA); reading (MA); secondary education (MA); special education and rehabilitation counseling (MA), including rehabilitation counseling, special education; teaching of science (MA); vocational and career education (MA). *Accreditation:* NCATE. Part-time and evening/weekend programs available. *Faculty:* 69 full-time, 145 part-time/adjunct. *Students:* 692 full-time (515 women), 345 part-time (245 women); includes 479 minority (145 African Americans, 12 American Indian/Alaska Native, 45 Asian Americans or Pacific Islanders, 277 Hispanic Americans), 17 international. Average age 33. 450 applicants, 82% accepted, 147 enrolled. In 2006, 349 degrees awarded. *Entrance requirements:* For master's, minimum GPA of 3.0 in education. *Application deadline:* For fall admission, 8/31 priority date for domestic students. Application fee: $55. *Financial support:* Career-related internships or fieldwork and Federal Work-Study available. Support available to part-time students. *Faculty research:* Multicultural education, brain-based learning, science education, social studies/global education. *Unit head:* Dr. Patricia Arlin, Dean, 909-537-5600, Fax: 909-537-7011, E-mail: parlin@csusb.edu.

Carlos Albizu University, Miami Campus, Graduate Programs, Miami, FL 33172-2209. Offers clinical psychology (Psy D); entrepreneurship (MBA); exceptional student education (MS); industrial/organizational psychology (MS); marriage and family therapy (MS); mental health counseling (MS); nonprofit management (MBA); organizational management (MBA); psychology (MS); school counseling (MS); teaching English as a second language (MS). *Accreditation:* APA. Part-time and evening/weekend programs available. Terminal master's awarded for partial completion of doctoral program. *Degree requirements:* For master's, one foreign language, comprehensive exam, integrative project (MBA), research project (MSESE); for doctorate, one foreign language, comprehensive exam, internship, doctoral project. *Entrance requirements:* For master's, 3 letters of recommendation, interview, minimum GPA of 3.0, resumé; for doctorate, 3 letters of recommendation, minimum GPA of 3.0, resumé, interview. *Faculty research:* Psychotherapy, forensic psychology, neuropsychology, marketing strategy, entrepreneurship.

Carson-Newman College, Graduate Program in Education, Jefferson City, TN 37760. Offers curriculum and instruction (M Ed); elementary education (MAT); school counseling (M Ed); secondary education (MAT); teaching English as a second language (MATESL). *Accreditation:* NCATE. Part-time and evening/weekend programs available. *Faculty:* 5 full-time (2 women), 10 part-time/adjunct (3 women). *Students:* 77 full-time (60 women), 41 part-time (29 women); includes 2 minority (both African Americans), 27 international. Average age 32. 65 applicants, 97% accepted. In 2006, 64 degrees awarded. *Degree requirements:* For master's, thesis or alternative. *Entrance requirements:* For master's, NTE, minimum GPA of 3.0 in major, 2.5 overall. *Application deadline:* For fall admission, 7/15 priority date for domestic students. Applications are processed on a rolling basis. Application fee: $25 ($50 for international students). *Expenses:* Tuition: Part-time $270 per credit hour. *Financial support:* In 2006–07, 86 students received support. Federal Work-Study and unspecified assistantships available. Financial award application deadline: 4/1; financial award applicants required to submit FAFSA. *Unit head:* Dr. Jean Love, Chair, 865-471-3461. *Application contact:* Graduate Admissions and Services Adviser, 865-471-3460, Fax: 865-471-3875.

The Catholic University of America, School of Arts and Sciences, Department of Education, Washington, DC 20064. Offers administration, curriculum, and policy studies (MA); Catholic school leadership (MA); counselor education (MA); educational administration (PhD); educational psychology (PhD); English as a second language (MA); learning and instruction (MA); policy studies (PhD); teacher education (MA). *Accreditation:* NCATE. Part-time programs available. *Faculty:* 11 full-time (8 women), 3 part-time/adjunct (2 women). *Students:* 11 full-time (8 women), 52 part-time (34 women); includes 13 minority (9 African Americans, 1 Asian American or Pacific Islander, 3 Hispanic Americans), 2 international. Average age 35. 67 applicants, 55% accepted, 13 enrolled. In 2006, 19 master's, 2 doctorates awarded. *Degree requirements:* For master's, thesis or alternative, comprehensive exam; for doctorate, thesis/dissertation, comprehensive exam. *Entrance requirements:* For master's and doctorate, GRE General Test or MAT, 3 letters of recommendation. Additional exam requirements/recommendations for international students: Required—TOEFL (minimum score 580 paper-based; 237 computer-based). *Application deadline:* For fall admission, 2/1 priority date for domestic students; for spring admission, 11/15 priority date for domestic students. Applications are processed on a rolling basis. Application fee: $55. Electronic applications accepted. *Expenses:* Tuition: Full-time $27,700; part-time $1,045 per credit hour. Required fees: $1,290. Part-time tuition and fees vary according to campus/location and program. *Financial support:* Research assistantships, teaching assistantships, career-related internships or fieldwork, Federal Work-Study, scholarships/grants, tuition waivers (full and partial), and unspecified assistantships available. Support available to part-time students. Financial award application deadline: 2/1; financial award applicants required to submit FAFSA. *Faculty research:* Catholic school issues, reflective teaching, cognitive psychology, urban education. *Unit head:* Dr. Merylann Schuttloffel, Chair, 202-319-5805, Fax: 202-319-5815, E-mail: schuttloffel@cua.edu.

Central Connecticut State University, School of Graduate Studies, School of Arts and Sciences, Department of English, Program in Teaching English to Speakers of Other Languages, New Britain, CT 06050-4010. Offers Certificate. Part-time and evening/weekend programs available. *Students:* 10 full-time (9 women), 21 part-time (17 women); includes 5 minority (1 African American, 4 Hispanic Americans), 7 international. 27 applicants, 63% accepted, 8 enrolled. In 2006, 8 degrees awarded. *Entrance requirements:* Additional exam requirements/recommendations for international students: Required—TOEFL. *Application deadline:* For fall admission, 7/1 for domestic students; for spring admission, 12/1 for domestic students. Applications are processed on a rolling basis. Application fee: $50. Electronic applications accepted. *Expenses:* Tuition, area resident: Full-time $3,970; part-time $380 per credit. Tuition, state resident: full-time $5,955; part-time $380 per credit. Tuition, nonresident: full-time $11,061; part-time $380 per credit. Required fees: $3,189. One-time fee: $62 part-time. Tuition and fees vary according to degree level and program. *Faculty research:* Phonology, general linguistics, second language writing, East Asian languages, English language structure. *Unit head:* Dr. Leyla Zidani-Eroglu, Coordinator: Department of English, TESOL, 860-832-2795.

Central Michigan University, College of Graduate Studies, College of Humanities and Social and Behavioral Sciences, Department of English Language and Literature, Mount Pleasant, MI 48859. Offers composition and communication (MA); creative writing (MA); English language and literature (MA); teaching English to speakers of other languages (MA). *Degree requirements:* For master's, thesis or alternative, registration. *Entrance requirements:* For master's, minimum GPA of 2.7, portfolio. Additional exam requirements/recommendations for international students: Required—TOEFL, Michigan English Language Assessment Battery. *Faculty research:* Composition theory, science fiction history and bibliography, medieval studies, nineteenth century American literature, applied linguistics.

Central Washington University, Graduate Studies, Research and Continuing Education, College of Arts and Humanities, Department of English, Ellensburg, WA 98926. Offers English (MA); teaching English as a second language (MA). Part-time programs available. *Faculty:* 20 full-time (10 women). *Students:* 22 full-time (12 women), 11 part-time (5 women); includes 5 minority (1 African American, 2 American Indian/Alaska Native, 1 Asian American or Pacific Islander, 1 Hispanic American). 28 applicants, 71% accepted, 20 enrolled. In 2006, 20 degrees awarded. *Degree requirements:* For master's, thesis or alternative. *Entrance requirements:* For master's, GRE General Test, minimum GPA of 3.0, writing sample. Additional exam requirements/recommendations for international students: Required—TOEFL (minimum score 550 paper-based; 213 computer-based; 79 iBT). *Application deadline:* For fall admission, 4/1 priority date for domestic students; for winter admission, 10/1 for domestic students; for spring admission, 1/1 for domestic students. Applications are processed on a rolling basis. Application fee: $50. Electronic applications accepted. *Expenses:* Tuition, state resident: full-time $6,312. Tuition, nonresident: full-time $14,112. Tuition and fees vary according to course load and degree level. *Financial support:* In 2006–07, 15 teaching assistantships with partial tuition reimbursements (averaging $8,100 per year) were awarded; research assistantships with partial tuition reimbursements, Federal Work-Study, health care benefits, and unspecified assistantships also available. Financial award application deadline: 3/1; financial award applicants required to submit FAFSA. *Unit head:* Joseph Powell, Chair, 509-963-1546, Fax: 509-963-1561, E-mail: powellj@cwu.edu. *Application contact:* Justine Eason, Admissions Program Coordinator, 509-963-3103, Fax: 509-963-1799, E-mail: masters@cwu.edu.

City University, Graduate Division, Gordon Albright School of Education, Bellevue, WA 98005. Offers curriculum and instruction (M Ed); educational leadership (M Ed); educational leadership: principal certification (M Ed, Certificate); educational leadership: principal/program administrator certification (Certificate); educational leadership: program administrator certification (M Ed, Certificate); guidance and counseling (M Ed, Certificate); integrated arts and performance learning (M Ed); professional certification-teachers (Certificate); reading (Certificate); reading and literacy (M Ed); reading. literacy, and ESL/ELL (M Ed); teacher certification (MIT); technology, curriculum and instruction (M Ed). Part-time and evening/weekend programs available. Postbaccalaureate distance learning degree programs offered (no on-campus study). *Entrance requirements:* Additional exam requirements/recommendations for international students: Required—TOEFL (minimum score 540 paper-based; 207 computer-based); Recommended—IELTS. Electronic applications accepted.

Cleveland State University, College of Graduate Studies, College of Education and Human Services, Department of Teacher Education, Cleveland, OH 44115. Offers art education (M Ed); early childhood education (M Ed); foreign language education (M Ed); mathematics and science education (M Ed); middle childhood education (M Ed); special education (M Ed), including mild/moderate disabilities, moderate/intensive disabilities; teaching English to speakers of other languages (M Ed). Part-time and evening/weekend programs available. *Faculty:* 14 full-time (8 women), 5 part-time/adjunct (4 women). *Students:* 120 full-time (96 women), 592 part-time (485 women); includes 145 minority (123 African Americans, 7 Asian Americans or Pacific Islanders, 15 Hispanic Americans), 7 international. Average age 34. 526 applicants, 41% accepted, 144 enrolled. In 2006, 324 degrees awarded. *Degree requirements:* For master's, thesis or alternative, comprehensive exam (for some programs). *Entrance requirements:* For master's, GRE General Test or MAT, minimum GPA of 2.75. Additional exam requirements/recommendations for international students: Required—TOEFL (minimum score 525 paper-based; 197 computer-based), IELTS (minimum score 6). *Application deadline:* For fall admission, 7/15 priority date for domestic students. Applications are processed on a rolling basis. Application fee: $30. *Financial support:* In 2006–07, 12 research assistantships with full tuition reimbursements (averaging $3,480 per year) were awarded; tuition waivers (partial) and unspecified assistantships also available. *Faculty research:* Early literacy, professional development in reading, reading recovery, dual language, induction programs. Total annual research expenditures: $6.2 million. *Unit head:* Dr. Clifford T. Bennett, Chairperson, 216-523-7105, Fax: 216-687-5379, E-mail: c.t.bennett@csuohio.edu.

College of Charleston, Graduate School, School of Education, Program in English to Speakers of Other Languages, Charleston, SC 29424-0001. Offers Certificate. Electronic applications accepted.

The College of New Jersey, Graduate Division, School of Education, Department of Special Education, Language and Literacy, Program in Teaching English as a Second Language, Ewing, NJ 08628. Offers English as a second language (M Ed); teaching English as a second language (Certificate). *Accreditation:* NCATE. *Students:* 1 full-time (0 women), 48 part-time (44 women); includes 13 minority (5 Asian Americans or Pacific Islanders, 8 Hispanic Americans). 12 applicants, 100% accepted. In 2006, 31 master's, 3 other advanced degrees awarded. *Degree requirements:* For master's, comprehensive exam. *Entrance requirements:* For master's, GRE General Test, minimum GPA of 3.0 in field or 2.75 overall. Additional exam requirements/recommendations for international students: Required—TOEFL. *Application deadline:* For fall admission, 4/15 for domestic students; for spring admission, 10/15 for domestic students. Application fee: $60. Electronic applications accepted. *Financial support:* Application deadline: 5/1; *Unit head:* Dr. Yiqiang Wu, Coordinator, 609-771-2808, E-mail: wuyiqian@tcnj.edu. *Application contact:* Susan L. Hydro, Office of Graduate Studies, Assistant Dean, 609-771-2300, Fax: 609-637-5105, E-mail: graduate@tcnj.edu.

The College of New Rochelle, Graduate School, Division of Education, Program in Teaching English as a Second Language and Multilingual/Multicultural Education, New Rochelle, NY 10805-2308. Offers bilingual education (Certificate); teaching English as a second language (MS Ed). Part-time and evening/weekend programs available. *Faculty:* 1 full-time (0 women), 4 part-time/adjunct (3 women). *Students:* 12 full-time (10 women), 37 part-time (25 women); includes 16 minority (2 African Americans, 1 American Indian/Alaska Native, 3 Asian Americans or Pacific Islanders, 10 Hispanic Americans). Average age 38. In 2006, 52 degrees awarded. *Degree requirements:* For master's, practicum. *Entrance requirements:* For master's, interview, minimum GPA of 3.0 in field, 2.7 overall. *Application deadline:* For fall admission, 8/1 priority date for domestic students; for spring admission, 4/6 for domestic students. Applications are processed on a rolling basis. Application fee: $35. *Expenses:* Tuition: Part-time $575 per credit. Required fees: $90 per term. *Financial support:* Scholarships/grants available. *Unit head:* Dr. Marie Ribarich, Acting Division Head, Division of Education, 914-654-5333, Fax: 914-654-5593, E-mail: mribarich@cnr.edu.

College of Notre Dame of Maryland, Graduate Studies, Program in Teaching English to Speakers of Other Languages, Baltimore, MD 21210-2476. Offers MA. *Accreditation:* NCATE. Part-time and evening/weekend programs available. *Students:* 3 full-time (2 women), 28 part-time (24 women). *Entrance requirements:* Additional exam requirements/recommendations for international students: Required—TOEFL (minimum score 500 paper-based; 173 computer-based; 61 iBT). *Application deadline:* For fall admission, 7/5 for domestic students; for winter admission, 11/5 for domestic students; for spring admission, 12/5 for domestic students. Applications are processed on a rolling basis. Application fee: $40. Electronic applications accepted. *Financial support:* Application deadline: 6/30; *Unit head:* Sr. Sharon Slear, Head, 410-532-3169, Fax: 410-532-5333, E-mail: sslear@ndm.edu. *Application contact:* Kathy Benzinger, Education Office Manager, 410-532-5349, Fax: 410-532-5333, E-mail: kbenzinger@ndm.edu.

Columbia International University, Columbia Graduate School, Columbia, SC 29230-3122. Offers Bible teaching (MABT); Christian higher education leadership (Ed D); Christian school educational leadership (Ed D); counseling (MACN); curriculum and instruction (M Ed), including Christian school guidance, English as a second language, learning disabilities, school technology; early childhood and elementary education (MAT); educational administration (M Ed); teaching English as a foreign language (Certificate); teaching English as a foreign language and intercultural studies (MATF). Part-time and evening/weekend programs available. *Faculty:* 11 full-time (4 women), 7 part-time/adjunct (5 women). *Students:* 52 full-time (44 women), 93 part-time (59 women); includes 17 minority (11 African Americans, 2 Asian Americans or Pacific Islanders, 4 Hispanic Americans), 10 international. Average age 35. 107 applicants, 56% accepted, 41 enrolled. In 2006, 62 degrees awarded. *Degree requirements:* For master's, internships, professional project. *Entrance requirements:* For master's, Minnesota Multiphasic Personality Inventory, MAT, minimum GPA of 2.7. Additional exam requirements/recommendations for international students: Required—TOEFL. *Application deadline:* For fall admission, 8/1 priority date for domestic and international students; for winter admission, 12/15 priority date for domestic and international students; for spring admission, 1/15 priority date for domestic and international students. Applications are processed on a rolling basis. Application fee: $45. Electronic applications accepted. *Expenses:* Tuition: Part-time $400 per semester hour. Tuition and fees vary according to course load and program. *Financial support:* In 2006–07, 35 students received support. Career-related internships or fieldwork, Federal Work-Study, institutionally sponsored loans, and scholarships/grants available. Financial award application deadline: 3/17; financial award applicants required to submit FAFSA. *Unit head:* Dr. Milton Uecker, Dean, 803-807-5319, Fax: 803-786-4209, E-mail: muecker@ciu.edu. *Application contact:* Michelle MacGregor, Director of Admissions, 800-777-2227 Ext. 5335, Fax: 803-786-4209, E-mail: yescbs@ciu.edu.

Concordia University, School of Graduate Studies, Faculty of Arts and Science, Department of Education, Program in Applied Linguistics, Montréal, QC H3G 1M8, Canada. Offers applied linguistics (MA); teaching English as a second language (Certificate). *Students:* 20 full-time (16 women), 70 part-time (57 women). 99 applicants, 76% accepted, 45 enrolled. In 2006, 10 degrees awarded. Application fee: $50. *Unit head:* Dr. Laura Collins, Director, 514-848-2424 Ext. 2445. *Application contact:* Dr. Joanna White, Associate Professor, 514-848-2455 Ext. 2041.

Dallas Baptist University, College of Adult Education, Liberal Arts Program, Dallas, TX 75211-9299. Offers arts (MLA); Christian ministry (MLA); English (MLA); English as a second language (MLA); fine arts (MLA); history (MLA); missions (MLA); political science (MLA). Part-time and evening/weekend programs available. *Faculty:* 49 full-time (21 women), 112 part-time/adjunct (46 women). *Students:* 10 full-time, 33 part-time. 36 applicants, 44% accepted, 15 enrolled. In 2006, 12 degrees awarded. *Entrance requirements:* For master's, minimum GPA of 3.0. Additional exam requirements/recommendations for international students: Required—TOEFL. *Application deadline:* Applications are processed on a rolling basis. Application fee: $25. Electronic applications accepted. *Expenses:* Tuition: Full-time $8,370; part-time $465 per credit hour. Required fees: $465 per credit hour. *Financial support:* Federal Work-Study, institutionally sponsored loans, scholarships/grants, and tuition waivers (full and partial) available. Support available to part-time students. *Faculty research:* Milton and seventeenth century Puritans, inter-Biblical years, nineteenth century literature, Latin American and Texas history. *Unit head:* Lynda Jackson, Director, 214-333-6830, Fax: 214-333-5558, E-mail: graduate@dbu.edu. *Application contact:* Kit P. Montgomery, Director of Graduate Programs, 214-333-5242, Fax: 214-333-5579, E-mail: graduate@dbu.edu.

Dallas Baptist University, College of Adult Education, Professional Development Program, Dallas, TX 75211-9299. Offers accounting (MA); business (MA); church leadership (MA); corporate management (MA); counseling (MA); criminal justice (MA); English as a second language (MA); finance (MA); higher education (MA); leadership studies (MA); management (MA); management information systems (MA); marketing (MA); missions (MA). Part-time and evening/weekend programs available. *Faculty:* 49 full-time (21 women), 112 part-time/adjunct (46 women). *Students:* 31 full-time, 65 part-time. 51 applicants, 49% accepted, 15 enrolled. In 2006, 41 degrees awarded. Application fee: $25. *Expenses:* Tuition: Full-time $8,370; part-time $465 per credit hour. Required fees: $465 per credit hour. *Financial support:* Tuition waivers (full and partial) available. *Unit head:* Lynda Jackson, Director, 214-333-6830, Fax: 214-333-5558, E-mail: graduate@dbu.edu. *Application contact:* Kit P. Montgomery, Director of Graduate Programs, 214-333-5242, Fax: 214-333-5579, E-mail: graduate@dbu.edu.

Dallas Baptist University, Dorothy M. Bush College of Education, Program in Education in Reading and ESL, Dallas, TX 75211-9299. Offers M Ed. *Faculty:* 49 full-time (21 women), 112 part-time/adjunct (46 women). Application fee: $25. *Expenses:* Tuition: Full-time $8,370; part-time $465 per credit hour. Required fees: $465 per credit hour. *Unit head:* Amie Sarker, Director, 214-333-5413, E-mail: graduate@dbu.edu. *Application contact:* Kit P. Montgomery, Director of Graduate Programs, 214-333-5242, Fax: 214-333-5579, E-mail: graduate@dbu.edu.

DeSales University, Graduate Division, Program in Education, Center Valley, PA 18034-9568. Offers academic standards and information (Certificate); bilingual/ESL studies (Certificate); biology (M Ed); chemistry (M Ed); computers in education (K-12) (M Ed); computers in education (K-8) (M Ed); English (M Ed); instructional technology specialist (Certificate); mathematics (M Ed); special education (M Ed, Certificate); TESOL (M Ed). Part-time and evening/weekend programs available. Postbaccalaureate distance learning degree programs offered (minimal on-campus study). *Students:* 34 full-time, 190 part-time. In 2006, 30 degrees awarded. *Degree requirements:* For master's, thesis project. *Entrance requirements:* For master's, teaching certificate. *Application deadline:* Applications are processed on a rolling basis. Application fee: $35. Electronic applications accepted. *Expenses:* Contact institution. *Financial support:* Unspecified assistantships available. Support available to part-time students. Financial award application deadline: 5/1. *Faculty research:* Effective teaching, computer interfacing in chemistry labs, computer applications to teaching, history of philosophy, aesthetics multidrug-resistant cancer. *Unit head:* Dr. Lujean Baab, Director of M.Ed. Program, 610-282-1100 Ext. 1739, Fax: 610-282-3734, E-mail: lujean.baab@desales.edu. *Application contact:* Donna L. Cressman, Program Secretary, 610-282-1100 Ext. 1461, Fax: 610-282-3734, E-mail: med@desales.edu.

Drexel University, School of Education, Philadelphia, PA 19104-2875. Offers educational administration and collaborative learning (MS); educational leadership and learning technology (PhD); global and international education (MS); graduate intern teaching (Certificate); higher education (MS); instructional technology (Spt); post-bachelor's teaching (Certificate); school principal (Certificate); school superintendent (Certificate); science of instruction (MS); teaching English as a second language (Certificate); teaching, learning and curriculum (MS). Part-time and evening/weekend programs available. Postbaccalaureate distance learning degree programs offered. *Degree requirements:* For doctorate, thesis/dissertation. Electronic applications accepted. Expenses: Contact institution.

See Close-Up on page 871.

Duquesne University, School of Education, Department of Instruction and Leadership, Pittsburgh, PA 15282-0001. Offers early childhood education (MS Ed); elementary education (MS Ed); English as a second language (MS Ed); instructional leadership excellence (Ed D); instructional technology (MS Ed, Ed D); reading and language arts (MS Ed); secondary education (MS Ed). Part-time and evening/weekend programs available. *Faculty:* 21 full-time (11 women), 17 part-time/adjunct (8 women). *Students:* 369. 128 applicants, 92% accepted, 102 enrolled. In 2006, 142 master's, 7 doctorates awarded. *Degree requirements:* For doctorate, thesis/dissertation. *Entrance requirements:* For master's, MAT, minimum GPA of 3.0; for doctorate, GRE General Test, MAT, interview, minimum GPA of 3.25. *Application deadline:* For fall admission, 8/1 priority date for domestic students; for spring admission, 12/1 priority date for domestic students. Applications are processed on a rolling basis. *Expenses:* Tuition: Part-time $723 per credit. Required fees: $71 per credit. Tuition and fees vary according to degree level and program. *Financial support:* In 2006–07, 3 research assistantships with full and partial tuition reimbursements (averaging $5,200 per year), 6 teaching assistantships with

full and partial tuition reimbursements were awarded; career-related internships or fieldwork, Federal Work-Study, and institutionally sponsored loans also available. Support available to part-time students. Total annual research expenditures: $10,000. *Unit head:* Dr. Barbara Manner, Chair, 412-396-6106, Fax: 412-396-5388, E-mail: manner@duq.edu.

Eastern Michigan University, Graduate School, College of Arts and Sciences, Department of Foreign Languages and Bilingual Studies, Program in Teaching English to Speakers of Other Languages, Ypsilanti, MI 48197. Offers MA. Part-time and evening/weekend programs available. Postbaccalaureate distance learning degree programs offered (minimal on-campus study). *Students:* 12 full-time (10 women), 27 part-time (20 women); includes 3 minority (2 Asian Americans or Pacific Islanders, 1 Hispanic American), 7 international. Average age 32. In 2006, 28 degrees awarded. *Degree requirements:* For master's, one foreign language. *Entrance requirements:* Additional exam requirements/recommendations for international students: Required—TOEFL. *Application deadline:* For fall admission, 5/15 priority date for domestic students, 5/1 priority date for international students; for winter admission, 10/15 priority date for domestic students, 10/1 priority date for international students; for spring admission, 3/15 priority date for domestic students, 3/1 priority date for international students. Applications are processed on a rolling basis. Application fee: $35. *Expenses:* Tuition, state resident: part-time $341 per credit hour. Tuition, nonresident: full-time $16,104; part-time $671 per credit hour. Required fees: $816; $34 per credit hour. $40 per term. One-time fee: $82 full-time. Tuition and fees vary according to course level, course load, degree level and reciprocity agreements. *Financial support:* Fellowships, research assistantships with full tuition reimbursements, teaching assistantships with full tuition reimbursements, career-related internships or fieldwork, Federal Work-Study, institutionally sponsored loans, scholarships/grants, tuition waivers (partial), and unspecified assistantships available. Support available to part-time students. Financial award applicants required to submit FAFSA. *Application contact:* Dr. Wendy Wang, Program Advisor, 734-487-1995, E-mail: wwang@emich.edu.

Eastern Nazarene College, Adult and Graduate Studies, Division of Education, Quincy, MA 02170-2999. Offers early childhood education (M Ed, Certificate); elementary education (M Ed, Certificate); English as a second language (M Ed, Certificate); instructional enrichment and development (M Ed, Certificate); middle school education (M Ed, Certificate); moderate special needs education (M Ed, Certificate); principal (Certificate); program development and supervision (M Ed, Certificate); secondary education (M Ed, Certificate); special education administrator (Certificate); supervisor (Certificate); teacher of reading (M Ed, Certificate). M Ed and Certificate also available through weekend program for administration, special needs, and reading only. Part-time and evening/weekend programs available. *Faculty:* 9 full-time (5 women), 11 part-time/adjunct (5 women). *Students:* 135. Average age 35. 20 applicants, 100% accepted. In 2006, 2 degrees awarded. *Entrance requirements:* Additional exam requirements/recommendations for international students: Required—TOEFL (minimum score 550 paper-based). *Application deadline:* Applications are processed on a rolling basis. Application fee: $35. *Financial support:* Career-related internships or fieldwork available. Support available to part-time students. Financial award applicants required to submit FAFSA. *Unit head:* Dr. Lorne Ranstrom, Chair, 617-745-3528, E-mail: randstrol@enc.edu. *Application contact:* Christine Galbraith, Graduate Studies Recruiter, 617-774-6703, Fax: 617-984-4901, E-mail: christine.galbraith@enc.edu.

Eastern University, Graduate Education Programs, Program in English as a Second or Foreign Language, St. Davids, PA 19087-3696. Offers Certificate.

Elms College, Division of Education, Chicopee, MA 01013-2839. Offers early childhood education (MAT); education (M Ed, CAGS); elementary education (MAT); English as a second language (MAT); reading (MAT); secondary education (MAT), including biology education, English education, Spanish education; special education (MAT). Part-time and evening/weekend programs available. *Faculty:* 9 full-time (6 women), 4 part-time/adjunct (2 women). *Students:* 8 full-time (6 women), 97 part-time (89 women); includes 4 minority (2 Asian Americans or Pacific Islanders, 2 Hispanic Americans). Average age 36. 48 applicants, 90% accepted, 40 enrolled. In 2006, 37 master's, 8 other advanced degrees awarded. *Degree requirements:* For master's, thesis (for some programs). *Entrance requirements:* For master's, Massachusetts Educators Certification Test, minimum GPA of 3.0; for CAGS, master's degree in education. Additional exam requirements/recommendations for international students: Required—TOEFL. *Application deadline:* For fall admission, 7/1 priority date for domestic students; for spring admission, 11/1 priority date for domestic students. Applications are processed on a rolling basis. Application fee: $30. *Expenses:* Tuition: Full-time $9,180; part-time $510 per credit. Tuition and fees vary according to course load. *Financial support:* In 2006–07, 3 teaching assistantships with partial tuition reimbursements were awarded; tuition waivers (partial) also available. Support available to part-time students. Financial award application deadline: 4/15; financial award applicants required to submit FAFSA. *Unit head:* Dr. Mary Janeczek, Director, 413-594-2761, Fax: 413-592-4871, E-mail: janeczeke@elms.edu.

Emporia State University, School of Graduate Studies, College of Liberal Arts and Sciences, Department of Modern Languages and Literatures, Program in Teaching English to Speakers of Other Languages, Emporia, KS 66801-5087. Offers MA. Part-time programs available. *Faculty:* 13 full-time (8 women), 3 part-time/adjunct (all women). *Students:* 6 full-time (3 women), 2 part-time (both women); includes 2 minority (1 Asian American or Pacific Islander, 1 Hispanic American), 4 international. 7 applicants, 86% accepted, 5 enrolled. *Degree requirements:* For master's, thesis optional. *Entrance requirements:* For master's, minimum undergraduate GPA of 2.75 over last 60 hours. Additional exam requirements/recommendations for international students: Required—TOEFL (minimum score 550 paper-based; 133 computer-based). *Application deadline:* For fall admission, 8/15 priority date for domestic students. Applications are processed on a rolling basis. Application fee: $30 ($75 for international students). Electronic applications accepted. *Expenses:* Tuition, state resident: full-time $3,438; part-time $143 per credit hour. Tuition, nonresident: full-time $10,398; part-time $433 per credit hour. Required fees: $724; $44 per credit hour. *Financial support:* In 2006–07, 2 research assistantships (averaging $6,752 per year) were awarded; Federal Work-Study, institutionally sponsored loans, health care benefits, and unspecified assistantships also available. Financial award application deadline: 2/15. *Unit head:* Dr. Abdelilah Salim Sehlaoui, Unit Head, 620-341-5237, E-mail: asehlaou@emporia.edu.

Emporia State University, School of Graduate Studies, The Teachers College, Department of Early Childhood/Elementary Teacher Education, Program in Master Teacher, Emporia, KS 66801-5087. Offers master teacher (MS), including elementary subject matter, English as a second language, reading, secondary subject matter. *Accreditation:* NCATE. Part-time programs available. *Students:* 1 (woman) full-time, 83 part-time (82 women); includes 2 minority (1 American Indian/Alaska Native, 1 Hispanic American). 14 applicants, 93% accepted, 13 enrolled. In 2006, 23 degrees awarded. *Degree requirements:* For master's, comprehensive exam or thesis, practicum. *Entrance requirements:* For master's, GRE General Test or MAT, graduate essay exam, appropriate bachelor's degree, letters of recommendation. Additional exam requirements/recommendations for international students: Required—TOEFL. *Application deadline:* For fall admission, 8/15 priority date for domestic students. Applications are processed on a rolling basis. Application fee: $30 ($75 for international students). Electronic applications accepted. *Expenses:* Tuition, state resident: full-time $3,438; part-time $143 per credit hour. Tuition, nonresident: full-time $10,398; part-time $433 per credit hour. Required fees: $724; $44 per credit hour. *Financial support:* Federal Work-Study, institutionally sponsored loans, health care benefits, and unspecified assistantships available. Financial award application deadline: 3/15; financial award applicants required to submit FAFSA. *Unit head:* Dr. Jean Morrow, Chair, Department of Early Childhood/Elementary Teacher Education, 620-341-5766, E-mail: jmorrow@emporia.edu.

Erikson Institute, Academic Programs, Chicago, IL 60611-5627. Offers administration (Certificate); bilingual/ESL (Certificate); child development (MS); early childhood education (MS); infant mental health (Certificate); infant studies (Certificate); MS/MSW. Part-time and evening/weekend programs available. *Degree requirements:* For master's, internship; for

English as a Second Language

Erikson Institute (continued)

Certificate, internship. *Entrance requirements:* For master's and Certificate, minimum GPA of 2.75. Additional exam requirements/recommendations for international students: Required—TOEFL. *Faculty research:* Assessment strategies from early childhood through elementary years; language, literacy, and the arts in children's development; inclusive special education; parent-child relationships; cognitive development.

Fairfield University, Graduate School of Education and Allied Professions, Department of TESOL, Foreign Language and Bilingual/Multicultural Education, Fairfield, CT 06824-5195. Offers MA, CAS. Part-time and evening/weekend programs available. *Faculty:* 1 (woman) full-time, 2 part-time/adjunct (both women). *Students:* 9 full-time (7 women), 39 part-time (31 women). Average age 34. 14 applicants, 57% accepted, 7 enrolled. In 2006, 11 master's, 5 other advanced degrees awarded. *Degree requirements:* For master's, educational technology course, thesis optional. *Entrance requirements:* For master's, PRAXIS I (PPST), minimum QPA of 2.67, 2 recommendations, resumè. Additional exam requirements/recommendations for international students: Required—TOEFL (minimum score 550 paper-based; 213 computer-based; 79 iBT). *Application deadline:* Applications are processed on a rolling basis. Application fee: $55. Electronic applications accepted. *Financial support:* Scholarships/grants, tuition waivers (partial), and unspecified assistantships available. Financial award applicants required to submit FAFSA. *Faculty research:* Teacher education. *Unit head:* Sr. Julianna Poole, SSND, Chair, 203-254-4000 Ext. 2873, Fax: 203-254-4047, E-mail: jpoole@mail.fairfield.edu. *Application contact:* Marianne Gumpper, Director of Graduate and Continuing Studies Admissions, 203-254-4184, Fax: 203-254-4073, E-mail: gradadmis@mail.fairfield.edu.

Florida International University, College of Education, Department of Curriculum and Instruction, Miami, FL 33199. Offers art education (MAT, MS, Ed D); curriculum and instruction (Ed S); curriculum development (MS); curriculum studies (PhD); early childhood education (MS, Ed D); elementary education (MS, Ed D); English education (MAT, MS, Ed D); foreign language education—teaching English to speakers of other languages (TESOL) (Certificate), including foreign language education; foreign language education- teaching English to speakers of other languages (TESOL) (MS), including teaching English; French education—initial teacher preparation (MAT); international and intercultural development education (Ed D); international and intercultural developmental education (MS); language, literacy and culture (PhD); learning technologies (MS, Ed D, PhD); mathematics education (MAT, MS, Ed D, PhD); modern language education/bilingual education (MS, Ed D); physical education (MS); reading education (MS, Ed D); science education (MAT, MS, Ed D, PhD); social studies education (MAT, MS, Ed D); Spanish education—initial teacher preparation (MAT); special education (MS). Part-time and evening/weekend programs available. *Faculty:* 19 full-time (11 women). *Students:* 89 full-time (66 women), 258 part-time (221 women); includes 99 minority (72 African Americans, 10 Asian Americans or Pacific Islanders, 17 Hispanic Americans). Average age 35. 167 applicants, 50% accepted, 81 enrolled. In 2006, 141 master's, 8 doctorates, 1 other advanced degree awarded. *Degree requirements:* For doctorate, thesis/dissertation, comprehensive exam, registration. *Entrance requirements:* For master's, GRE General Test, Florida General Knowledge Test or Florida College Level Academic Skills Test; for doctorate and other advanced degree, GRE General Test. Additional exam requirements/recommendations for international students: Required—TOEFL (minimum score 550 paper-based; 213 computer-based; 80 iBT), IELTS (minimum score 6). *Application deadline:* For fall admission, 6/1 priority date for domestic students, 4/1 for international students; for winter admission, 10/1 priority date for domestic students, 9/1 for international students; for spring admission, 3/1 priority date for domestic students, 2/1 for international students. Applications are processed on a rolling basis. Application fee: $30. Electronic applications accepted. *Expenses:* Tuition, state resident: part-time $249 per credit hour. Tuition, nonresident: part-time $753 per credit hour. Tuition and fees vary according to program. *Financial support:* Research assistantships with full and partial tuition reimbursements, teaching assistantships with full and partial tuition reimbursements available. *Unit head:* Dr. Lisbeth Dixon-Krauss, Interim Chairperson, 305-348-3609, Fax: 305-348-2086, E-mail: kraussl@fiu.edu. *Application contact:* Marisa Salazar, Student Recruiter, 305-348-3002, Fax: 305-348-3227, E-mail: marisa.salazar@fiu.edu.

Fordham University, Graduate School of Education, Division of Curriculum and Teaching, New York, NY 10023. Offers adult education (MS, MSE); bilingual teacher education (MSE); curriculum and teaching (MSE); early childhood education (MSE); elementary education (MST); language, literacy, and learning (PhD); reading education (MSE, Adv C); secondary education (MAT, MSE); special education (MSE, Adv C); teaching English as a second language (MSE). *Accreditation:* NCATE. *Faculty:* 22 full-time (18 women), 38 part-time/adjunct (28 women). *Students:* 68 full-time (51 women), 663 part-time (612 women); includes 200 minority (74 African Americans, 1 American Indian/Alaska Native, 37 Asian Americans or Pacific Islanders, 88 Hispanic Americans), 3 international. Average age 32. 636 applicants, 86% accepted, 322 enrolled. In 2006, 351 master's, 8 doctorates awarded. *Degree requirements:* For doctorate and Adv C, thesis/dissertation. *Entrance requirements:* For doctorate, MAT, GRE General Test. Application fee: $65. *Financial support:* Applicants required to submit FAFSA. *Unit head:* Dr. Terry Osborn, Chairperson, 212-636-6450.

Framingham State College, Division of Graduate and Continuing Education, Program in the Teaching of English as a Second Language, Framingham, MA 01701-9101. Offers M Ed. *Students:* 24. In 2006, 27 degrees awarded. *Unit head:* Margot Mahler, Coordinator, 508-626-4676, Fax: 508-626-4030, E-mail: mmahler@frc.mass.edu. *Application contact:* 508-626-4550, Fax: 508-626-4030, E-mail: dgce@frc.mass.edu.

Fresno Pacific University, Graduate Programs, Program in Teaching English to Speakers of Other Languages, Fresno, CA 93702-4709. Offers MA. Part-time and evening/weekend programs available. *Students:* 1 full-time (0 women), 7 part-time (all women); includes 4 minority (1 African American, 3 Hispanic Americans), 2 international. Average age 39. 2 applicants, 100% accepted, 0 enrolled. In 2006, 2 degrees awarded. *Degree requirements:* For master's, thesis, registration. *Entrance requirements:* For master's, GMAT, MAT, GRE, interview, 2 writing samples. Additional exam requirements/recommendations for international students: Required—TOEFL (minimum score 550 paper-based; 213 computer-based). *Application deadline:* For fall admission, 7/15 for domestic and international students; for spring admission, 11/15 for domestic and international students. Applications are processed on a rolling basis. Application fee: $90. Electronic applications accepted. *Expenses:* Tuition: Full-time $7,470; part-time $415 per credit. *Financial support:* In 2006–07, 4 students received support. Scholarships/grants and tuition waivers (full and partial) available. Support available to part-time students. Financial award applicants required to submit FAFSA. *Unit head:* Sandra Mercuri, Director, 559-453-7100, Fax: 559-453-2001, E-mail: smercuri@fresno.edu.

Fresno Pacific University, Graduate Programs, Programs in Education, Division of Language, Literacy, and Culture, Program in Reading, Fresno, CA 93702-4709. Offers reading/English as a second language (MA Ed); reading/language arts (MA Ed). Part-time and evening/weekend programs available. *Students:* 1 (woman) full-time, 27 part-time (26 women); includes 12 minority (2 Asian Americans or Pacific Islanders, 10 Hispanic Americans). Average age 41. 3 applicants, 100% accepted, 1 enrolled. In 2006, 3 degrees awarded. *Degree requirements:* For master's, thesis or alternative, registration. *Entrance requirements:* Additional exam requirements/recommendations for international students: Required—TOEFL (minimum score 550 paper-based; 213 computer-based). *Application deadline:* For fall admission, 7/15 for domestic and international students; for spring admission, 11/15 for domestic and international students. Applications are processed on a rolling basis. Application fee: $90. Electronic applications accepted. *Expenses:* Tuition: Full-time $7,470; part-time $415 per credit. *Financial support:* In 2006–07, 9 students received support. Scholarships/grants and tuition waivers (full and partial) available. Support available to part-time students. Financial award applicants required to submit FAFSA.

Furman University, Graduate Division, Department of Education, Greenville, SC 29613. Offers early childhood education (MA); elementary education (MA); English as a second language (MA); middle school education (MA); reading (MA); school administration (MA); special education (MA). *Accreditation:* NCATE. Part-time and evening/weekend programs available. *Faculty:* 17 full-time (12 women), 19 part-time/adjunct (15 women). *Students:* 114 full-time (89 women), 72 part-time (59 women); includes 27 minority (23 African Americans, 4 Hispanic Americans). Average age 32. 36 applicants, 100% accepted, 36 enrolled. In 2006, 111 degrees awarded. *Degree requirements:* For master's, thesis (for some programs), comprehensive exam. *Entrance requirements:* For master's, GRE General Test or PRAXIS. *Application deadline:* For fall admission, 8/1 priority date for domestic and international students; for winter admission, 12/1 priority date for domestic and international students; for spring admission, 2/1 priority date for domestic and international students. Applications are processed on a rolling basis. Application fee: $50. *Expenses:* Tuition: Part-time $347 per credit. *Financial support:* In 2006–07, 97 students received support; fellowships, scholarships/grants and unspecified assistantships available. Financial award application deadline: 1/15; financial award applicants required to submit FAFSA. *Unit head:* Dr. Nelly Hecker, Head, 864-294-3385.

Gannon University, School of Graduate Studies, College of Humanities, Business, and Education, School of Education, Program in English as a Second Language, Erie, PA 16541-0001. Offers Certificate. Part-time and evening/weekend programs available. *Entrance requirements:* Additional exam requirements/recommendations for international students: Required—TOEFL (minimum score 500 paper-based; 173 computer-based). Application fee: $25. *Expenses:* Tuition: Full-time $12,240; part-time $680 per credit. Required fees: $496; $16 per credit. Tuition and fees vary according to course load, degree level, campus/location and program. *Financial support:* Available to part-time students. Application deadline: 7/1; *Application contact:* Debra Meszaros, Director of Graduate Recruitment, 814-871-5819, Fax: 814-871-5827, E-mail: cfal@gannon.edu.

George Mason University, Graduate School of Education, Programs in Curriculum and Instruction, Fairfax, VA 22030. Offers bilingual/multicultural/English as a second language education (M Ed); early childhood education (M Ed); instructional technology (M Ed); middle education (M Ed); reading (M Ed); secondary education (M Ed); special education (M Ed). Part-time and evening/weekend programs available. *Faculty:* 108 full-time (70 women), 193 part-time/adjunct (140 women). *Students:* 185 full-time (144 women), 816 part-time (683 women); includes 148 minority (46 African Americans, 2 American Indian/Alaska Native, 44 Asian Americans or Pacific Islanders, 56 Hispanic Americans), 28 international. Average age 34. 822 applicants, 72% accepted, 473 enrolled. In 2006, 606 master's awarded. *Entrance requirements:* For master's, minimum GPA of 3.0 in last 60 hours. *Application deadline:* For fall admission, 5/1 for domestic students; for spring admission, 11/1 for domestic students. Application fee: $60 ($75 for international students). Electronic applications accepted. *Expenses:* Tuition, state resident: full-time $5,724; part-time $238 per credit. Tuition, nonresident: full-time $16,896; part-time $704 per credit. Required fees: $1,656; $69 per credit. *Financial support:* Career-related internships or fieldwork available. Support available to part-time students. Financial award application deadline: 3/1; financial award applicants required to submit FAFSA. *Unit head:* Martin E. Ford, Senior Associate Dean, 703-993-2008.

Georgetown University, Graduate School of Arts and Sciences, Department of Linguistics, Washington, DC 20057. Offers bilingual education (Certificate); linguistics (MS, PhD); teaching English as a second language (MAT, Certificate); teaching English as a second language and bilingual education (MAT). Terminal master's awarded for partial completion of doctoral program. *Degree requirements:* For master's, one foreign language, comprehensive exam, optional research project; for doctorate, 2 foreign languages, thesis/dissertation, comprehensive exam. *Entrance requirements:* For master's and doctorate, 18 undergraduate credits in a foreign language. Additional exam requirements/recommendations for international students: Required—TOEFL.

Georgia State University, College of Education, Department of Middle-Secondary Education and Instructional Technology, Program in Reading Instruction, Atlanta, GA 30303-3083. Offers reading, language and literacy (M Ed); reading, language, and literacy (PhD, Ed S); teaching English as a second language (M Ed). *Accreditation:* NCATE. Part-time and evening/weekend programs available. *Students:* 6 full-time (all women), 24 part-time (20 women); includes 4 minority (3 African Americans, 1 Asian American or Pacific Islander), 1 international. Average age 29. 14 applicants, 71% accepted. In 2006, 11 degrees awarded. *Degree requirements:* For master's, comprehensive exam; for Ed S, project/exam. *Entrance requirements:* For master's, GRE General Test, minimum GPA of 2.5; for Ed S, GRE General Test or MAT, minimum graduate GPA of 3.25. *Application deadline:* For fall admission, 7/15 for domestic students; for spring admission, 1/15 for domestic students. Application fee: $25. *Financial support:* Career-related internships or fieldwork, Federal Work-Study, and institutionally sponsored loans available. *Faculty research:* Language development, attribution theory, linguistics. *Unit head:* Dr. Ruth Hough, Acting Chair, Department of Middle-Secondary Education and Instructional Technology, 404-651-2510.

Gonzaga University, Program in Teaching English as a Second Language, Spokane, WA 99258. Offers MATESL. *Students:* 2 full-time (1 woman), 12 part-time (11 women); includes 1 minority (Asian American or Pacific Islander), 5 international. Average age 35. 12 applicants, 83% accepted. In 2006, 9 degrees awarded. *Application deadline:* Applications are processed on a rolling basis. Application fee: $40. Electronic applications accepted. *Expenses:* Tuition: Full-time $10,620; part-time $590 per credit. *Unit head:* Dr. Mary Jeannot, Chairperson, 509-324-6559.

Grand Canyon University, College of Education, Phoenix, AZ 85017-1097. Offers elementary education (M Ed, MA); reading education (MA); secondary education (M Ed); teaching (MAT); teaching English as a second language (MA). Part-time and evening/weekend programs available. Postbaccalaureate distance learning degree programs offered (no on-campus study). *Degree requirements:* For master's, publishable research paper (M Ed). *Entrance requirements:* For master's, MAT, GRE or minimum GPA of 3.0.

See Close-Up on page 885.

Grand Valley State University, College of Education, Programs in General Education, Allendale, MI 49401-9403. Offers adult and higher education (M Ed); early childhood education (M Ed); education of the gifted and talented (M Ed); educational leadership (M Ed); educational technology (M Ed); elementary education (M Ed); middle and high school education (M Ed); teaching English to speakers of other languages (M Ed). Part-time and evening/weekend programs available. Postbaccalaureate distance learning degree programs offered (minimal on-campus study). *Faculty:* 82 full-time (42 women), 43 part-time/adjunct (25 women). *Students:* 136 full-time (97 women), 828 part-time (565 women); includes 55 minority (26 African Americans, 7 American Indian/Alaska Native, 5 Asian Americans or Pacific Islanders, 17 Hispanic Americans). Average age 33. 280 applicants, 94% accepted, 188 enrolled. In 2006, 322 degrees awarded. *Degree requirements:* For master's, thesis. *Entrance requirements:* For master's, GRE General Test or minimum GPA of 3.0. Additional exam requirements/recommendations for international students: Required—TOEFL. *Application deadline:* Applications are processed on a rolling basis. Application fee: $30. Electronic applications accepted. *Expenses:* Tuition, state resident: full-time $5,850; part-time $325 per credit. Tuition, nonresident: full-time $10,800; part-time $600 per credit. Tuition and fees vary according to course load. *Financial support:* In 2006–07, 2 research assistantships with full and partial tuition reimbursements (averaging $8,000 per year) were awarded; career-related internships or fieldwork, Federal Work-Study, scholarships/grants, and unspecified assistantships also available. *Faculty research:* Effectiveness of technology in education, parental involvement, effective teaching, effective schools research. *Unit head:* Dr. Linda McCrea, Director, 616-331-2080, E-mail: mccreal@gvsu.edu. *Application contact:* Dr. Douglas Busman, Director, Student Information and Services, 616-331-6831, Fax: 616-331-6217, E-mail: busmando@gvsu.edu.

Greensboro College, Program in Teaching English to Speakers of Other Languages, Greensboro, NC 27401-1875. Offers MA. *Accreditation:* NCATE. Part-time and evening/weekend programs available. *Faculty:* 3 full-time (2 women). *Students:* Average age 35. 4 applicants, 75% accepted, 2 enrolled. In 2006, 14 degrees awarded. *Degree requirements:*

For master's, thesis, portfolio. *Entrance requirements:* For master's, GRE or MAT, 2 letters of reference. Additional exam requirements/recommendations for international students: Required—TOEFL (minimum score 550 paper-based; 213 computer-based). *Application deadline:* For fall admission, 3/15 for domestic students. Applications are processed on a rolling basis. Application fee: $35. Electronic applications accepted. *Expenses:* Tuition: Part-time $275 per credit hour. Required fees: $30 per semester. *Financial support:* In 2006–07, 11 students received support. Scholarships/grants available. Support available to part-time students. Financial award applicants required to submit FAFSA. *Unit head:* Dr. Rebecca Blomgren, Graduate and Professional Studies, 336-272-7102, Fax: 336-271-6634, E-mail: blomgrenc@gborocollege.edu. *Application contact:* Office of Graduate and Professional Studies, 336-272-7102, E-mail: adults@gborocollege.edu.

Hawai'i Pacific University, College of International Studies, Honolulu, HI 96813. Offers teaching English as a second language (MA). Part-time and evening/weekend programs available. *Faculty:* 6 full-time (4 women), 2 part-time/adjunct (both women). *Students:* 41 full-time (25 women), 19 part-time (13 women); includes 18 minority (3 African Americans, 15 Asian Americans or Pacific Islanders), 29 international. Average age 32. 31 applicants, 55% accepted, 15 enrolled. In 2006, 26 degrees awarded. *Entrance requirements:* Additional exam requirements/recommendations for international students: Recommended—TOEFL (minimum score 550 paper-based; 213 computer-based), TWE (minimum score 5). *Application deadline:* For fall admission, 2/15 priority date for domestic students; for spring admission, 10/15 priority date for domestic students. Applications are processed on a rolling basis. Application fee: $50. Electronic applications accepted. *Expenses:* Tuition: Full-time $10,080; part-time $560 per credit. *Financial support:* In 2006–07, 16 students received support. Career-related internships or fieldwork, Federal Work-Study, scholarships/grants, and unspecified assistantships available. Support available to part-time students. Financial award application deadline: 3/1; financial award applicants required to submit FAFSA. *Unit head:* Dr. Carlos Juarez, Dean, 808-566-2493, Fax: 808-544-0834, E-mail: cjuarez@hpu.edu. *Application contact:* Danny Lam, Assistant Director of Graduate Admissions, 808-544-1135, Fax: 808-544-0280, E-mail: graduate@hpu.edu.

See Close-Up on page 1367.

Henderson State University, Graduate Studies, School of Education, Department of Curriculum, Instruction and Leadership, Arkadelphia, AR 71999-0001. Offers early childhood (P-4) (MSE); English (MSE); English as a second language (MSE, CP); math (MSE); middle school (MSE); reading (MSE); social science (MSE). *Accreditation:* NCATE. Part-time programs available. *Faculty:* 19 full-time (6 women), 4 part-time/adjunct (2 women). *Students:* 38 full-time (36 women), 49 part-time (47 women); includes 6 minority (5 African Americans, 1 Hispanic American), 16 international. Average age 37. In 2006, 31 degrees awarded. *Entrance requirements:* For master's, GRE General Test or MAT, minimum GPA of 2.7, teacher certification. *Application deadline:* For fall admission, 5/1 priority date for domestic students, 5/1 for international students; for winter admission, 10/1 for international students; for spring admission, 12/1 priority date for domestic students, 4/1 for international students. Applications are processed on a rolling basis. Application fee: $0 ($30 for international students). *Expenses:* Tuition, state resident: full-time $3,294; part-time $183 per credit hour. Tuition, nonresident: full-time $6,588; part-time $366 per credit hour. Required fees: $176 per term. *Financial support:* In 2006–07, 1 teaching assistantship with full tuition reimbursement (averaging $4,000 per year) was awarded; research assistantships, Federal Work-Study and institutionally sponsored loans also available. Support available to part-time students. Financial award application deadline: 7/31. *Unit head:* Dr. Kenneth Harris, Chairperson, 870-230-5203, Fax: 870-230-5455, E-mail: harris@hsu.edu. *Application contact:* Dr. Marck L. Beggs, Graduate Dean, 870-230-5126, Fax: 870-230-5479, E-mail: beggsm@hsu.edu.

Heritage University, Graduate Programs in Education, Program in Professional Studies, Toppenish, WA 98948-9599. Offers bilingual education/ESL (M Ed); biology (M Ed); English and literature (M Ed); reading/literacy (M Ed); special education (M Ed). Part-time and evening/weekend programs available. *Students:* 174 (125 women); includes 52 minority (1 African American, 4 American Indian/Alaska Native, 6 Asian Americans or Pacific Islanders, 41 Hispanic Americans). Average age 37. In 2006, 84 degrees awarded. *Degree requirements:* For master's, thesis (for some programs), comprehensive exam (for some programs), registration. *Application deadline:* Applications are processed on a rolling basis. Application fee: $50 ($100 for international students). *Financial support:* Career-related internships or fieldwork, Federal Work-Study, institutionally sponsored loans, and tuition waivers (partial) available. Support available to part-time students. *Unit head:* Dr. Jack McPherson, Head, 509-865-8626, E-mail: mcpherson_j@heritage.edu. *Application contact:* Kathy Otto, Coordinator of Administrative Services, 509-865-8635, Fax: 509-865-8629, E-mail: otto_k@heritage.edu.

Hofstra University, School of Education and Allied Human Services, Department of Curriculum and Teaching, Programs in TESL/Bilingual Education, Hempstead, NY 11549. Offers bilingual education (MA); bilingual extension education (CAS); TESOL (MS Ed, CAS). *Accreditation:* NCATE. Part-time programs available. *Students:* 28 full-time (23 women), 29 part-time (28 women); includes 17 minority (3 African Americans, 1 Asian American or Pacific Islander, 13 Hispanic Americans), 1 international. Average age 31. 33 applicants, 67% accepted, 13 enrolled. In 2006, 15 degrees awarded. *Degree requirements:* For master's, one foreign language, thesis or alternative, completion of electronic portfolio. *Entrance requirements:* For master's, interview, 2 letters of recommendation, teaching certificate, essay, proficiency in language; for CAS, 2 letters of recommendation, interview, teaching certificate, essay, proficiency in language. Additional exam requirements/recommendations for international students: Required—TOEFL (minimum score 550 paper-based; 213 computer-based). *Application deadline:* Applications are processed on a rolling basis. Application fee: $60. Electronic applications accepted. *Expenses:* Tuition: Full-time $13,320; part-time $740 per credit. Required fees: $930; $155 per term. *Financial support:* In 2006–07, 16 students received support, including 4 fellowships with tuition reimbursements available (averaging $2,533 per year); research assistantships with full and partial tuition reimbursements available, career-related internships or fieldwork, scholarships/grants, tuition waivers (full and partial), and unspecified assistantships also available. Support available to part-time students. Financial award applicants required to submit FAFSA. *Faculty research:* Linking TESOL theory and practice, content-based ESL instruction, cognitively stimulating ESL instruction. *Unit head:* Dr. Tatiana Gordon, Director, 516-463-5170, Fax: 516-463-6196, E-mail: cattzg@hofstra.edu. *Application contact:* Carol Drummer, Dean of Graduate Admissions, 516-463-4876, Fax: 516-463-4664, E-mail: gradstudent@hofstra.edu.

Holy Names University, Graduate Division, Department of Education, Oakland, CA 94619-1699. Offers advanced curriculum studies (M Ed); educational therapy (M Ed); mild/moderate disabilities (Ed S); multiple subject credential (M Ed); single subject credential (M Ed); special education (M Ed); teaching English as a second language (M Ed, Certificate); urban education (M Ed). Part-time programs available. *Faculty:* 6 full-time (all women), 9 part-time/adjunct (all women). *Students:* 17 full-time (14 women), 131 part-time (90 women); includes 58 minority (36 African Americans, 1 American Indian/Alaska Native, 11 Asian Americans or Pacific Islanders, 10 Hispanic Americans). Average age 40. 75 applicants, 80% accepted, 49 enrolled. In 2006, 11 master's, 29 Certificates awarded. *Degree requirements:* For master's, research paper, thesis or project. *Entrance requirements:* For master's, minimum undergraduate GPA of 2.6 overall, 3.0 in major. Additional exam requirements/recommendations for international students: Required—TOEFL. *Application deadline:* For fall admission, 8/1 priority date for domestic students; for spring admission, 12/1 priority date for domestic students. Applications are processed on a rolling basis. Application fee: $50. *Expenses:* Tuition: Full-time $10,800; part-time $600 per unit. Required fees: $240; $120 per term. *Financial support:* In 2006–07, 67 students received support. Scholarships/grants available. Support available to part-time students. Financial award application deadline: 3/2; financial award applicants required to submit FAFSA. *Faculty research:* Cognitive development, language development, learning handicaps. *Unit head:* Dr. Zaida McCall-Perez, Chairperson, 510-436-1288, E-mail: mccall-perez@hnu.edu. *Application contact:* 800-430-1351, Fax: 510-436-1325, E-mail: admissions@hnu.edu.

Houston Baptist University, College of Education and Behavioral Sciences, Programs in Education, Houston, TX 77074-3298. Offers bilingual education (M Ed); counselor education (M Ed); curriculum and instruction (M Ed); educational administration (M Ed); educational diagnostician (M Ed); reading education (M Ed). Part-time programs available. *Degree requirements:* For master's, registration. *Entrance requirements:* For master's, GRE General Test or MAT. Additional exam requirements/recommendations for international students: Required—TOEFL (minimum score 550 paper-based; 213 computer-based).

Hunter College of the City University of New York, Graduate School, School of Education, Department of Curriculum and Teaching, Program in Teaching English as a Second Language, New York, NY 10021-5085. Offers MA. *Accreditation:* NCATE. *Faculty:* 2 full-time (0 women), 6 part-time/adjunct (4 women). *Students:* 13 full-time (11 women), 150 part-time (117 women); includes 34 minority (4 African Americans, 13 Asian Americans or Pacific Islanders, 17 Hispanic Americans). Average age 35. 78 applicants, 59% accepted, 30 enrolled. In 2006, 19 degrees awarded. *Degree requirements:* For master's, one foreign language, thesis, comprehensive exam or master's essay, New York state teacher certification exams. *Entrance requirements:* For master's, minimum GPA of 2.8, 2 letters of recommendation, interview. Additional exam requirements/recommendations for international students: Required—TOEFL (minimum score 600 paper-based), TWE (minimum score 5). *Application deadline:* For fall admission, 4/1 for domestic students, 2/1 for international students; for spring admission, 11/1 for domestic students, 9/1 for international students. Applications are processed on a rolling basis. Application fee: $125. *Expenses:* Tuition, state resident: part-time $270 per credit. Tuition, nonresident: part-time $500 per credit. Required fees: $45 per semester. *Financial support:* Federal Work-Study, scholarships/grants, and tuition waivers (partial) available. Support available to part-time students. *Unit head:* Dr. Anne M. Ediger, Head, 212-777-4763, E-mail: anne.ediger@hunter.cuny.edu. *Application contact:* William Zlata, Director for Graduate Admissions, 212-772-4482, Fax: 212-650-3336, E-mail: admissions@hunter.cuny.edu.

Indiana State University, School of Graduate Studies, College of Arts and Sciences, Department of Languages, Literatures, and Linguistics, Terre Haute, IN 47809-1401. Offers French (MA, MS); linguistics/teaching English as a second language (MA, MS); Spanish (MA, MS); TESL/TEFL (CAS). *Faculty:* 7 full-time (4 women), 2 part-time/adjunct (1 woman). *Students:* 26 full-time (16 women), 16 part-time (12 women); includes 4 minority (2 Asian Americans or Pacific Islanders, 2 Hispanic Americans), 25 international. Average age 31. 50 applicants, 92% accepted, 13 enrolled. In 2006, 18 degrees awarded. *Degree requirements:* For master's, comprehensive exam. *Application deadline:* For fall admission, 7/1 priority date for domestic students; for spring admission, 11/1 priority date for domestic students. Applications are processed on a rolling basis. Application fee: $35. Electronic applications accepted. *Expenses:* Tuition, state resident: part-time $278 per credit. Tuition, nonresident: part-time $552 per credit. *Financial support:* In 2006–07, 9 teaching assistantships (averaging $6,300 per year) were awarded; research assistantships with partial tuition reimbursements, tuition waivers (partial) also available. Financial award application deadline: 3/1; financial award applicants required to submit FAFSA. *Unit head:* Dr. Ronald W. Dunbar, Chairperson, 812-237-2368. *Application contact:* Information Contact, 812-237-2366.

Indiana University of Pennsylvania, School of Graduate Studies and Research, College of Humanities and Social Sciences, Department of English, Program in Composition and Teaching English to Speakers of Other Languages, Indiana, PA 15705-1087. Offers composition and teaching English to speakers of other languages (PhD); teaching English (MAT); teaching English to speakers of other languages (MA). *Faculty:* 39 full-time (20 women). *Students:* 169 full-time (95 women), 8 part-time (4 women); includes 12 minority (9 African Americans, 1 Asian American or Pacific Islander, 2 Hispanic Americans), 68 international. Average age 36. 208 applicants, 52% accepted. In 2006, 23 master's, 24 doctorates awarded. *Degree requirements:* For master's, thesis optional; for doctorate, one foreign language, thesis/dissertation, comprehensive exam. *Entrance requirements:* For master's and doctorate, 2 letters of recommendation. Additional exam requirements/recommendations for international students: Required—TOEFL. *Application deadline:* For fall admission, 7/1 priority date for domestic students; for spring admission, 11/1 for domestic students. Applications are processed on a rolling basis. Application fee: $30. *Expenses:* Tuition, state resident: full-time $6,048; part-time $336 per credit. Tuition, nonresident: full-time $9,678; part-time $538 per credit. Required fees: $1,069; $148 per year. *Financial support:* In 2006–07, 2 fellowships (averaging $5,000 per year), 18 research assistantships with full and partial tuition reimbursements (averaging $6,170 per year), 8 teaching assistantships with partial tuition reimbursements (averaging $17,001 per year) were awarded. Financial award application deadline: 3/15; financial award applicants required to submit FAFSA. *Unit head:* Dr. Ben Rafoth, Graduate Coordinator, 724-357-2272.

Indiana University–Purdue University Fort Wayne, College of Arts and Sciences, Department of English and Linguistics, Fort Wayne, IN 46805-1499. Offers English (MA, MAT); TENL (teaching English as a new language) (Certificate). Part-time programs available. *Faculty:* 28 full-time (17 women). *Students:* 7 full-time (4 women), 23 part-time (19 women); includes 2 minority (1 African American, 1 Hispanic American), 1 international. Average age 31. 12 applicants, 83% accepted, 10 enrolled. In 2006, 10 master's, 3 other advanced degrees awarded. *Degree requirements:* For master's, one foreign language, thesis (for some programs), teaching certificate (MAT). *Entrance requirements:* For master's, GRE General Test, minimum GPA of 3.0, major or minor in English, 3 letters of recommendation. Additional exam requirements/recommendations for international students: Required—TOEFL (minimum score 600 paper-based; 260 computer-based). *Application deadline:* For fall admission, 8/1 for domestic students; for spring admission, 10/15 for domestic students. Applications are processed on a rolling basis. Application fee: $30. *Expenses:* Tuition, state resident: full-time $4,039; part-time $224 per credit. Tuition, nonresident: full-time $9,220; part-time $512 per credit. Required fees: $429; $24 per credit. Tuition and fees vary according to course load. *Financial support:* In 2006–07, 9 teaching assistantships with partial tuition reimbursements (averaging $11,950 per year) were awarded; career-related internships or fieldwork, scholarships/grants, and unspecified assistantships also available. Support available to part-time students. Financial award application deadline: 3/1; financial award applicants required to submit FAFSA. *Faculty research:* Colloquial American English, parthenogenesis, Octoavio Paz and Theory of Static. Total annual research expenditures: $49,403. *Unit head:* Dr. Richard M. Ramsey, Chairperson, 260-481-6841, Fax: 260-481-6985, E-mail: ramseyr@ipfw.edu.

Inter American University of Puerto Rico, Metropolitan Campus, Faculty of Liberal Arts, Program in Teaching English as a Second Language, San Juan, PR 00919-1293. Offers MA. Part-time and evening/weekend programs available. *Degree requirements:* For master's, thesis or alternative, comprehensive exam. *Entrance requirements:* For master's, GRE General Test or EXADEP, interview, minimum GPA of 2.5. Electronic applications accepted.

Inter American University of Puerto Rico, Ponce Campus, Graduate School, Mercedita, PR 00715-1602. Offers accounting (MBA); biology (M Ed); chemistry (M Ed); criminal justice (MA); elementary education (M Ed); English as a Second Language (M Ed); finance (MBA); history (M Ed); human resources (MBA); mathematics (M Ed); Spanish (M Ed); trade (MBA). *Entrance requirements:* For master's, minimum GPA of 2.5.

Inter American University of Puerto Rico, San Germán Campus, Graduate Studies Center, Graduate Program in Teaching English as a Second Language, San Germán, PR 00683-5008. Offers MA. Part-time and evening/weekend programs available. *Faculty:* 6 full-time, 1 part-time/adjunct. *Students:* 79. Average age 39. In 2006, 49 degrees awarded. *Degree requirements:* For master's, comprehensive exam. *Entrance requirements:* For master's, GRE General Test or EXADEP, minimum GPA of 3.0. *Application deadline:* For fall admission, 4/30 priority date for domestic students; for spring admission, 11/15 for domestic students. Applications are processed on a rolling basis. Application fee: $31. *Expenses:* Tuition: Part-time $175 per

English as a Second Language

Inter American University of Puerto Rico, San Germán Campus (continued)
credit. Required fees: $238 per semester. Tuition and fees vary according to degree level. *Financial support:* Teaching assistantships available. *Application contact:* Dr. Aurora Melendez, Graduate Coordinator, 787-264-1912 Ext. 7540, Fax: 787-892-6350, E-mail: a_melendez@sg.inter.edu.

The Johns Hopkins University, School of Professional Studies in Business and Education, School of Education, Department of Teacher Preparation, Baltimore, MD 21218-2699. Offers elementary education (MAT); English for speakers of other languages (MAT); secondary education (MAT). Part-time and evening/weekend programs available. *Students:* 234 full-time (173 women), 240 part-time (172 women); includes 87 minority (61 African Americans, 19 Asian Americans or Pacific Islanders, 7 Hispanic Americans), 4 international. Average age 27. 360 applicants, 71% accepted, 243 enrolled. In 2006, 218 degrees awarded. *Degree requirements:* For master's, portfolio. *Entrance requirements:* For master's, PRAXIS I, minimum GPA of 3.0, interview, resumé, letter of recommendation. Additional exam requirements/recommendations for international students: Required—TOEFL (minimum score 600 paper-based; 250 computer-based; 100 iBT). *Application deadline:* For fall admission, 4/1 priority date for domestic students, 4/1 for international students; for winter admission, 10/1 priority date for domestic students; for spring admission, 10/1 priority date for domestic students, 10/1 for international students. Applications are processed on a rolling basis. Application fee: $60. *Expenses:* Tuition: Full-time $32,976. Tuition and fees vary according to degree level and program. *Financial support:* Scholarships/grants available. Support available to part-time students. Financial award application deadline: 6/1; financial award applicants required to submit FAFSA. *Faculty research:* Professional development schools, data-informed instruction, alternative certification, dispositions. *Unit head:* Dr. Elaine Stotko, Chair, 410-309-1289, Fax: 410-290-0467, E-mail: matjhu@jhu.edu. *Application contact:* Carol Herrman, Admissions Coordinator, 410-872-1234, Fax: 410-872-1251, E-mail: onestop.admissions@jhu.edu.

Kean University, College of Education, Program in Classroom Instruction and Curriculum, Union, NJ 07083. Offers bilingual/bicultural education (MA); classroom instruction (MA); earth science (MA); educational technology (MA); elementary education (MA); mathematics/science/computer education (MA); teaching (MA); teaching English as a second language (MA). *Accreditation:* NCATE. Part-time and evening/weekend programs available. *Faculty:* 19 full-time (10 women). *Students:* 34 full-time (29 women), 174 part-time (139 women); includes 73 minority (9 African Americans, 7 Asian Americans or Pacific Islanders, 57 Hispanic Americans), 4 international. Average age 34. 103 applicants, 93% accepted, 67 enrolled. In 2006, 82 degrees awarded. *Degree requirements:* For master's, 2 foreign languages, thesis, comprehensive exam. *Entrance requirements:* For master's, GRE General Test or MAT, PRAXIS, minimum GPA of 2.75, 2 letters of recommendation, interview. *Application deadline:* For fall admission, 5/1 for domestic students; for spring admission, 11/1 for domestic students. Application fee: $60 ($150 for international students). Electronic applications accepted. *Expenses:* Tuition, state resident: full-time $8,856; part-time $369 per credit. Tuition, nonresident: full-time $11,256; part-time $469 per credit. *Financial support:* In 2006–07, 2 research assistantships with full tuition reimbursements (averaging $3,217 per year) were awarded; unspecified assistantships also available. *Unit head:* Dr. Frank H. Osborn, Program Coordinator, 908-737-4289, E-mail: fosborne@kean.edu. *Application contact:* Joanne Morris, Director of Graduate Admissions, 908-737-3355, Fax: 908-737-3354, E-mail: grad-adm@kean.edu.

Kent State University, College of Arts and Sciences, Department of English, Kent, OH 44242-0001. Offers comparative literature (MA); creative writing (MFA); English for teachers (MA); literature (PhD); literature and writing (MA); rhetoric and composition (PhD); teaching English as a second language (MA). Part-time programs available. Terminal master's awarded for partial completion of doctoral program. *Degree requirements:* For master's, one foreign language, thesis optional; for doctorate, one foreign language, thesis/dissertation, qualifying exams. *Entrance requirements:* For master's and doctorate, GRE General Test, writing sample, letters of recommendation. Additional exam requirements/recommendations for international students: Required—TOEFL (minimum score 600 paper-based). Electronic applications accepted. *Faculty research:* British and American literature, textual editing, rhetoric and composition, cultural studies, linguistic and critical theories.

Langston University, School of Education and Behavioral Sciences, Langston, OK 73050-0907. Offers bilingual/multicultural (M Ed); elementary education (M Ed); English as a second language (M Ed); rehabilitation counseling (M Sc); urban education (M Ed). *Accreditation:* CORE; NCATE (one or more programs are accredited). Part-time programs available. *Degree requirements:* For master's, thesis optional. *Entrance requirements:* For master's, GRE, writing skills test, minimum GPA of 2.5, 3 letters of recommendation. Additional exam requirements/recommendations for international students: Required—TOEFL, TWE. *Faculty research:* Bilingual/multicultural education, financing post-secondary education.

Lehman College of the City University of New York, Division of Education, Department of Middle and High School Education, Program in Teaching English to Speakers of Other Languages, Bronx, NY 10468-1589. Offers MS Ed. *Accreditation:* NCATE. *Degree requirements:* For master's, thesis. *Entrance requirements:* For master's, minimum GPA of 3.0.

Long Island University, Brooklyn Campus, School of Education, Department of Teaching and Learning, Program in Teaching English to Speakers of Other Languages, Brooklyn, NY 11201-8423. Offers MS Ed. Part-time and evening/weekend programs available. *Degree requirements:* For master's, thesis optional. *Entrance requirements:* For master's, 2 letters of recommendation. Additional exam requirements/recommendations for international students: Required—TOEFL (minimum score 500 paper-based; 173 computer-based). Electronic applications accepted.

Long Island University, C.W. Post Campus, School of Education, Department of Curriculum and Instruction, Brookville, NY 11548-1300. Offers adolescence education (MS); adolescence education: biology (MS); adolescence education: earth science (MS); adolescence education: English (MS); adolescence education: mathematics (MS); adolescence education: social studies (MS); adolescence education: Spanish (MS); art education (MS); bilingual education (MS); childhood education (MS); early childhood education (MS); middle childhood education (MS); music education (MS); teaching English to speakers of other languages (MS). Part-time and evening/weekend programs available. *Degree requirements:* For master's, comprehensive exam or thesis, student teaching. *Entrance requirements:* For master's, minimum GPA of 2.75 in major, 2.5 overall. Electronic applications accepted. *Faculty research:* Ethics and education, teaching strategies.

Long Island University, Westchester Graduate Campus, Programs in Education-Teaching, Program in Second Language, TESOL, Bilingual Education, Purchase, NY 10577. Offers MS Ed. Part-time and evening/weekend programs available. *Faculty:* 1 (woman) full-time, 5 part-time/adjunct (4 women). *Students:* 4 applicants, 100% accepted, 4 enrolled. In 2006, 3 degrees awarded. *Application deadline:* Applications are processed on a rolling basis. *Expenses:* Tuition: Part-time $790 per credit. *Financial support:* Scholarships/grants, tuition waivers (partial), and unspecified assistantships available. *Unit head:* Dr. Helaine Marshall, Director, 914-831-2713, Fax: 914-251-5959, E-mail: helaine.marshall@liu.edu. *Application contact:* Ellen Brief, Coordinator of Admissions, Marketing, Student Services and Public Relations, 914-831-2701, Fax: 914-251-5959, E-mail: ellen.brief@liu.edu.

Madonna University, Department of English, Livonia, MI 48150-1173. Offers teaching English to speakers of other languages (MATESOL). Part-time and evening/weekend programs available. *Faculty:* 3 full-time (2 women), 1 (woman) part-time/adjunct. *Students:* 21 full-time (19 women); includes 8 minority (2 African Americans, 2 American Indian/Alaska Native, 2 Asian Americans or Pacific Islanders, 2 Hispanic Americans), 2 international. Average age 38. 16 applicants, 56% accepted. In 2006, 13 degrees awarded. *Degree requirements:* For master's, one foreign language, thesis or alternative. *Application deadline:* For fall admission, 8/1 priority date for domestic students; for winter admission, 12/1 priority date for domestic students; for spring admission, 4/1 priority date for domestic students. Applications are processed on a rolling basis. Application fee: $25 ($200 for international students). Electronic applications accepted. *Financial support:* Institutionally sponsored loans available. Support available to part-time students. Financial award application deadline: 3/1; financial award applicants required to submit FAFSA. *Unit head:* Dr. Andrew Domzalski, Director, 734-432-5420, E-mail: adomzalski@madonna.edu. *Application contact:* Sandra Kellums, Coordinator of Graduate Admissions and Records, 734-432-5667, Fax: 734-432-5862, E-mail: skellum@madonna.edu.

Manhattanville College, Graduate Programs, School of Education, Program in English as a Second Language, Purchase, NY 10577-2132. Offers teaching English as a second language (MPS). Part-time and evening/weekend programs available. *Students:* 5 full-time (all women), 25 part-time (23 women); includes 5 minority (all Hispanic Americans), 1 international. In 2006, 10 degrees awarded. *Degree requirements:* For master's, comprehensive exam or research project, field experience. *Entrance requirements:* For master's, minimum undergraduate GPA of 3.0. *Application deadline:* Applications are processed on a rolling basis. Application fee: $55. *Financial support:* Career-related internships or fieldwork and institutionally sponsored loans available. Support available to part-time students. *Application contact:* Alyce Ware Poli, Director of Admissions, 914-323-5142, Fax: 914-694-1732, E-mail: edschool@mville.edu.

Marymount University, School of Education and Human Services, Program in Education, Arlington, VA 22207-4299. Offers alternative teacher licensure (Certificate); elementary education (M Ed); English as a second language (M Ed); learning disabilities (M Ed); professional studies (M Ed); secondary education (M Ed). *Accreditation:* NCATE. Part-time and evening/weekend programs available. Postbaccalaureate distance learning degree programs offered (minimal on-campus study). *Faculty:* 10 full-time (8 women), 5 part-time/adjunct (2 women). *Students:* 75 full-time (65 women), 95 part-time (82 women); includes 25 minority (13 African Americans, 2 American Indian/Alaska Native, 6 Asian Americans or Pacific Islanders, 4 Hispanic Americans), 6 international. Average age 32. 58 applicants, 100% accepted, 45 enrolled. In 2006, 113 degrees awarded. *Degree requirements:* For master's, thesis or alternative. *Entrance requirements:* For master's, GRE General Test or MAT, PRAXIS I or SAT/ACT, interview, 2 letters of recommendation. Additional exam requirements/recommendations for international students: Required—TOEFL (minimum score 600 paper-based; 250 computer-based). *Application deadline:* Applications are processed on a rolling basis. Application fee: $40. Electronic applications accepted. *Expenses:* Tuition: Full-time $11,160; part-time $620 per credit. Required fees: $113; $630 per credit. *Financial support:* Research assistantships with full tuition reimbursements, career-related internships or fieldwork, scholarships/grants, and unspecified assistantships available. Support available to part-time students. Financial award applicants required to submit FAFSA. *Unit head:* Dr. Shelly Haser, Chair, 703-284-6955, Fax: 703-284-1631, E-mail: shelly.haser@marymount.edu.

Mercy College, Division of Education, Dobbs Ferry, NY 10522-1189. Offers adolescence education: grades 7-12 (MS); applied behavior analysis (MS); bilingual education (MS); childhood education: grades 1-6 (MS); early childhood education: birth—grade 2 (MS); education (MS); elementary education (MS); learning technology (MS); middle childhood education: grades 5-9 (MS); reading (MS); school administration and supervision (MS); school building leadership (MS); school business administration (MS); secondary education (MS); special education (MS); students with disabilities: grades 5-9 (MS); students with disabilities: grades 7-12 (MS); teaching English to speakers of other languages (MS); teaching literacy: birth—grade 6 (MS); teaching literacy: grades 5-12 (MS); urban education (MS). *Students:* 572 full-time (467 women), 1,719 part-time (1,287 women); includes 943 minority (470 African Americans, 7 American Indian/Alaska Native, 48 Asian Americans or Pacific Islanders, 418 Hispanic Americans), 6 international. Average age 33. In 2006, 1090 degrees awarded. *Entrance requirements:* For master's, teaching certificate. *Application deadline:* For fall admission, 2/1 for domestic students. Applications are processed on a rolling basis. Application fee: $37. *Expenses: Contact institution.* Tuition and fees vary according to program. *Financial support:* Institutionally sponsored loans, scholarships/grants, and unspecified assistantships available. Support available to part-time students. *Faculty research:* Distance learning, literacy, assessment, community schools, impact of staff development. *Unit head:* Dr. William Prattella, Chairperson, 914-674-7555, Fax: 914-674-7352, E-mail: wprattella@mercy.edu. *Application contact:* Kathleen Jackson, Director of Admissions, 800-Mercy-NY, Fax: 914-674-7382, E-mail: admissions@mercy.edu.

Michigan State University, The Graduate School, College of Arts and Letters, Department of Linguistics and Germanic, Slavic, Asian, and African Languages, East Lansing, MI 48824. Offers German studies (MA, PhD); linguistics (MA, PhD); teaching English to speakers of other languages (MA). Part-time and evening/weekend programs available. *Faculty:* 27 full-time (15 women). *Students:* 84 full-time (56 women), 15 part-time (10 women); includes 3 minority (1 African American, 1 American Indian/Alaska Native, 1 Asian American or Pacific Islander), 46 international. Average age 30. 121 applicants, 55% accepted. In 2006, 20 master's, 7 doctorates awarded. *Entrance requirements:* For master's, GRE General Test, minimum GPA of 3.2 in last 2 undergraduate years, 2 years of college-level foreign language, 3 letters of recommendation, portfolio (German studies); for doctorate, GRE General Test, minimum graduate GPA of 3.5, 3 letters of recommendation, master's degree or sufficient graduate course work in linguistics or language of study, master's thesis or major research paper. Additional exam requirements/recommendations for international students: Required—TOEFL. Electronic applications accepted. *Expenses:* Tuition, state resident: part-time $346 per credit hour. Tuition, nonresident: part-time $730 per credit hour. Tuition and fees vary according to program. *Financial support:* In 2006–07, 23 fellowships with tuition reimbursements, 14 research assistantships with tuition reimbursements (averaging $12,278 per year), 30 teaching assistantships with tuition reimbursements (averaging $12,198 per year) were awarded. Total annual research expenditures: $488,667. *Unit head:* Dr. David K. Prestel, Chairperson, 517-353-0740, Fax: 517-432-2736, E-mail: prestel@msu.edu. *Application contact:* Julie Delgado, Graduate Studies Secretary, 517-353-0740, Fax: 517-432-2736, E-mail: delgadof@msu.edu.

Middle Tennessee State University, College of Graduate Studies, College of Education and Behavioral Science, Department of Educational Leadership, Major in Curriculum and Instruction, Murfreesboro, TN 37132. Offers curriculum and instruction (M Ed, Ed S); English as a second language (M Ed). *Accreditation:* NCATE. Part-time and evening/weekend programs available. Postbaccalaureate distance learning degree programs offered. *Students:* 9 full-time (8 women), 140 part-time (118 women); includes 11 minority (4 African Americans, 1 American Indian/Alaska Native, 1 Asian American or Pacific Islander, 5 Hispanic Americans). 42 applicants, 100% accepted. In 2006, 66 degrees awarded. *Degree requirements:* For master's, comprehensive exam. *Entrance requirements:* For master's and Ed S, GRE or MAT. Additional exam requirements/recommendations for international students: Required—TOEFL (minimum score 525 paper-based; 195 computer-based). *Application deadline:* For fall admission, 8/1 priority date for domestic students. Applications are processed on a rolling basis. Application fee: $25. Electronic applications accepted. *Financial support:* Application deadline: 5/1. *Unit head:* Dr. James Huffman, Chair, Department of Educational Leadership, 615-898-2855, Fax: 615-898-2859.

Mississippi College, Graduate School, College of Arts and Sciences, School of Humanities and Social Sciences, Department of Foreign Languages, Clinton, MS 39058. Offers teaching English to speakers of other languages (MA, MS). Part-time programs available. *Faculty:* 2 full-time (both women). *Students:* 5 full-time (all women), 4 part-time (all women); includes 3 minority (all African Americans), 4 international. Average age 27. *Degree requirements:* For master's, thesis (for some programs), registration. *Entrance requirements:* For master's, GRE or NTE. Additional exam requirements/recommendations for international students: Recommended—IELTS. *Application deadline:* Applications are processed on a rolling basis. Application fee: $25. Electronic applications accepted. *Expenses:* Tuition: Full-time $7,290; part-time $405 per hour. Required fees: $150 per term. Tuition and fees vary according to campus/location and program. *Financial support:* Career-related internships or fieldwork, Federal Work-Study, and unspecified assistantships available. Support available to part-time students.

Financial award applicants required to submit FAFSA. *Unit head:* Dr. Deborah Pierce, Chair, 601-925-3216, E-mail: pierce@mc.edu.

Montclair State University, The Graduate School, College of Education and Human Services, Department of Curriculum and Teaching, Montclair, NJ 07043-1624. Offers education (M Ed); educational technology (M Ed); school library media specialist (Certificate); teaching (MAT, Certificate), including art (MAT), biological science (MAT), early childhood education (P-3) (MAT), earth science (MAT), elementary education (K-8) (MAT), English (MAT), French (MAT), health and physical education (MAT), health education (MAT), home economics (MAT), mathematics (MAT), music (MAT), physical education (MAT), physical science (MAT), social studies (MAT), Spanish (MAT), teacher of ESL (MAT), teacher of students with disabilities (MAT). Part-time and evening/weekend programs available. *Faculty:* 16 full-time (12 women), 13 part-time/adjunct (8 women). *Students:* 147 full-time (113 women), 230 part-time (188 women); includes 58 minority (33 African Americans, 1 American Indian/Alaska Native, 12 Asian Americans or Pacific Islanders, 12 Hispanic Americans), 4 international. Average age 33. 118 applicants, 38% accepted, 37 enrolled. In 2006, 166 master's, 11 other advanced degrees awarded. *Degree requirements:* For master's, field experience. *Entrance requirements:* For master's, PRAXIS II, minimum GPA of 2.67, 2 letters of recommendation. Additional exam requirements/recommendations for international students: Required—TOEFL (minimum score 83 computer-based). *Application deadline:* For fall admission, 2/15 for domestic and international students; for spring admission, 9/15 for domestic and international students. Applications are processed on a rolling basis. Application fee: $60. Electronic applications accepted. *Expenses:* Tuition, state resident: part-time $450 per credit. Tuition, nonresident: part-time $682 per credit. Tuition and fees vary according to degree level and program. *Financial support:* In 2006–07, 7 research assistantships with full tuition reimbursements (averaging $7,000 per year) were awarded; Federal Work-Study, scholarships/grants, and unspecified assistantships also available. Support available to part-time students. Financial award application deadline: 3/1; financial award applicants required to submit FAFSA. *Unit head:* Dr. Deborah Eldridge, Chairperson, 973-655-5187.

Montclair State University, The Graduate School, College of Humanities and Social Sciences, Department of Linguistics, Montclair, NJ 07043-1624. Offers applied linguistics (MA); teaching English to speakers of other languages (MA). Part-time and evening/weekend programs available. *Faculty:* 6 full-time (5 women), 10 part-time/adjunct (all women). *Students:* 14 full-time (12 women), 89 part-time (71 women); includes 18 minority (7 African Americans, 4 Asian Americans or Pacific Islanders, 7 Hispanic Americans), 5 international. 28 applicants, 54% accepted, 12 enrolled. In 2006, 1 degree awarded. *Degree requirements:* For master's, comprehensive exam. *Entrance requirements:* For master's, GRE General Test, 2 letters of recommendation. Additional exam requirements/recommendations for international students: Required—TOEFL (minimum score 83 computer-based). *Application deadline:* For fall admission, 6/1 for international students; for spring admission, 10/1 for international students. Applications are processed on a rolling basis. Application fee: $60. Electronic applications accepted. *Expenses:* Tuition, state resident: part-time $450 per credit. Tuition, nonresident: part-time $682 per credit. Tuition and fees vary according to degree level and program. *Financial support:* In 2006–07, 1 research assistantship with full tuition reimbursement (averaging $7,000 per year) was awarded; Federal Work-Study, scholarships/grants, and unspecified assistantships also available. Support available to part-time students. Financial award application deadline: 3/1; financial award applicants required to submit FAFSA. *Unit head:* Dr. Eileen Fitzpatrick, Chairperson, 973-655-4480. *Application contact:* Dr. Steve Seegmiller, Adviser, 973-655-7500, E-mail: seegmillerm@mail.montclair.edu.

Monterey Institute of International Studies, Graduate School of Language and Educational Linguistics, Program in Teaching English to Speakers of Other Languages, Monterey, CA 93940-2691. Offers MATESOL. *Students:* 37 full-time (30 women), 18 part-time (17 women); includes 2 minority (both Asian Americans or Pacific Islanders), 16 international. Average age 28. 65 applicants, 94% accepted, 26 enrolled. In 2006, 29 degrees awarded. *Degree requirements:* For master's, portfolio and oral defense. *Entrance requirements:* For master's, minimum GPA of 3.0. Additional exam requirements/recommendations for international students: Required—TOEFL. *Application deadline:* For fall admission, 3/15 priority date for domestic students; for spring admission, 10/1 priority date for domestic students. Applications are processed on a rolling basis. Application fee: $50. Electronic applications accepted. *Expenses:* Tuition: Full-time $26,500; part-time $1,200 per credit. Required fees: $200. *Financial support:* Federal Work-Study and institutionally sponsored loans available. Support available to part-time students. Financial award application deadline: 3/15; financial award applicants required to submit FAFSA. *Unit head:* Dr. Renee Jourdenais, Head, 831-647-6570, E-mail: gslel@miis.edu. *Application contact:* 831-647-4123, Fax: 831-647-6405, E-mail: admit@miis.edu.

See Close-Up on page 1369.

Moody Bible Institute, Graduate School, Chicago, IL 60610-3284. Offers biblical studies (MABS, Certificate); intercultural studies (MAIS); ministry (M Div, MA Min, MAUM); spiritual formation (MASF); teaching English to speakers of other languages (Certificate); urban ministry (MAUM). Part-time programs available. *Degree requirements:* For master's, 2 foreign languages. *Entrance requirements:* For master's, 30 hours in Bible/theology, 2 years of ministry experience (MA Min).

Mount Saint Vincent University, Graduate Programs, Faculty of Education, Program in Curriculum Studies, Halifax, NS B3M 2J6, Canada. Offers education of young adolescents (M Ed, MA Ed, MA-R); general studies (M Ed, MA Ed, MA-R); teaching English as a second language (M Ed, MA Ed, MA-R). Part-time and evening/weekend programs available. Postbaccalaureate distance learning degree programs offered (minimal on-campus study). *Degree requirements:* For master's, thesis (for some programs). *Entrance requirements:* For master's, bachelor's degree in related field, minimum B average, 1 year of teaching experience. Electronic applications accepted. *Faculty research:* Science education, cultural studies, international education, curriculum development.

Murray State University, College of Humanities and Fine Arts, Department of English and Philosophy, Program in Teaching English to Speakers of Other Languages, Murray, KY 42071. Offers MA. Part-time programs available. Postbaccalaureate distance learning degree programs offered (no on-campus study). *Faculty:* 4 full-time (3 women). *Students:* 53; includes 3 minority (1 African American, 1 Asian American or Pacific Islander, 1 Hispanic American), 16 international. 10 applicants, 100% accepted. In 2006, 16 degrees awarded. *Degree requirements:* For master's, one foreign language, comprehensive exam, registration, 12 hours for portfolio. *Entrance requirements:* For master's, minimum GPA of 2.25. Additional exam requirements/recommendations for international students: Required—TOEFL (minimum score 525 paper-based), IELTS (minimum score 6). *Application deadline:* Applications are processed on a rolling basis. Application fee: $25. *Financial support:* In 2006–07, 1 research assistantship (averaging $3,600 per year), 2 teaching assistantships (averaging $3,600 per year) were awarded. Financial award application deadline: 4/1. *Faculty research:* Methods, integrated skills, intercultural communication, assessment. *Unit head:* Dr. Sue Sroda, Graduate Coordinator, 270-809-4715, Fax: 270-809-4545, E-mail: sue.sroda@murraystate.edu.

Nazareth College of Rochester, Graduate Studies, Department of Education, Program in Teaching English to Speakers of Other Languages, Rochester, NY 14618-3790. Offers MS Ed. Accreditation: Teacher Education Accreditation Council. *Faculty:* 1 (woman) full-time, 1 (woman) part-time/adjunct. *Students:* 13 full-time (12 women), 41 part-time (36 women); includes 11 minority (1 Asian American or Pacific Islander, 10 Hispanic Americans), 1 international. Average age 30. 18 applicants, 100% accepted, 12 enrolled. In 2006, 28 degrees awarded. *Entrance requirements:* For master's, minimum GPA of 3.0. *Application deadline:* For fall admission, 4/1 priority date for domestic students; for spring admission, 10/1 for domestic students. Application fee: $40. *Financial support:* Research assistantships with partial tuition reimbursements available. Financial award application deadline: 3/1; financial award applicants required to submit FAFSA. *Unit head:* Dr. Cynthia McPhail, Director, 585-389-2607, Fax:

585-389-2452, E-mail: cmcphai2@naz.edu. *Application contact:* Judith G. Baker, Director, Graduate Admissions, 585-389-2050, Fax: 585-389-2817, E-mail: gradstudies@naz.edu.

New Jersey City University, Graduate and Continuing Education, College of Education, Department of Educational Leadership, Jersey City, NJ 07305-1597. Offers basics and urban studies (MA); bilingual/bicultural education and English as a second language (MA); educational administration and supervision (MA). Evening/weekend programs available. *Students:* 4 full-time (3 women), 237 part-time (149 women); includes 52 minority (11 African Americans, 4 Asian Americans or Pacific Islanders, 37 Hispanic Americans), 26 international. Average age 35. In 2006, 162 degrees awarded. *Entrance requirements:* For master's, GRE General Test or MAT. Additional exam requirements/recommendations for international students: Required—TOEFL. *Application deadline:* For fall admission, 8/1 priority date for domestic students; for spring admission, 12/1 for domestic students. Applications are processed on a rolling basis. Application fee: $0. *Expenses:* Tuition, state resident: full-time $7,038; part-time $391 per credit. Tuition, nonresident: full-time $12,510; part-time $695 per credit. Required fees: $65 per credit. *Financial support:* Fellowships, teaching assistantships, career-related internships or fieldwork and unspecified assistantships available. *Unit head:* Dr. Carrie Robinson, Chairperson, 201-200-3400, E-mail: crobinson@njcu.edu.

Newman University, School of Education, Wichita, KS 67213-2097. Offers building leadership (MS Ed); curriculum and instruction (MS Ed), including accountability, English as a second language. Part-time programs available. Postbaccalaureate distance learning degree programs offered (no on-campus study). *Faculty:* 3 full-time (0 women), 4 part-time/adjunct (all women). *Students:* 2 full-time (both women), 41 part-time (24 women); includes 3 minority (2 African Americans, 1 American Indian/Alaska Native), 3 international. Average age 35. 25 applicants, 92% accepted, 17 enrolled. In 2006, 35 degrees awarded. *Degree requirements:* For master's, thesis optional. *Entrance requirements:* For master's, GRE General Test or MAT, interview, minimum GPA of 3.0, writing sample, 3 letters of recommendation. Additional exam requirements/recommendations for international students: Required—TOEFL (minimum score 600 paper-based; 250 computer-based). *Application deadline:* For fall admission, 8/15 priority date for domestic students; for spring admission, 1/10 priority date for domestic students. Applications are processed on a rolling basis. Application fee: $25 ($40 for international students). Electronic applications accepted. *Financial support:* In 2006–07, 8 students received support. Federal Work-Study and tuition waivers (full) available. Financial award application deadline: 8/15; financial award applicants required to submit FAFSA. *Unit head:* Dr. Guy Glidden, Director, 316-942-4291 Ext. 2331, Fax: 316-942-4483, E-mail: gliddeng@newmanu.edu. *Application contact:* Linda Kay Sabala, Director of Graduate Admissions, 316-942-4291 Ext. 2230, Fax: 316-942-4483, E-mail: sabalal@newmanu.edu.

The New School: A University, The New School for General Studies, Program in Teaching English to Speakers of Other Languages, New York, NY 10011. Offers MA. *Entrance requirements:* Additional exam requirements/recommendations for international students: Required—TOEFL (minimum score 600 paper-based; 250 computer-based; 100 iBT), IELTS (minimum score 7), TWE. *Application deadline:* For fall admission, 3/15 for domestic students. Application fee: $50. Electronic applications accepted. *Unit head:* Marjorie Vai, Chair, English Language Studies, and Director, MATESOL Program, 212-229-5630, E-mail: vaim@newschool.edu.

New York University, Steinhardt School of Culture, Education and Human Development, Department of Teaching and Learning, Program in Multilingual/Multicultural Studies, New York, NY 10012-1019. Offers bilingual education (MA, PhD, Advanced Certificate); foreign language education (MA, Advanced Certificate); foreign language education/TESOL (MA); teaching English to speakers of other languages (MA, PhD, Advanced Certificate). *Accreditation:* Teacher Education Accreditation Council. Part-time and evening/weekend programs available. *Faculty:* 3 full-time (2 women). *Students:* 121 full-time (105 women), 103 part-time (89 women); includes 38 minority (3 African Americans, 19 Asian Americans or Pacific Islanders, 16 Hispanic Americans), 95 international. 272 applicants, 75% accepted, 87 enrolled. In 2006, 103 master's, 5 doctorates, 6 other advanced degrees awarded. Terminal master's awarded for partial completion of doctoral program. *Degree requirements:* For master's, thesis (for some programs); for doctorate, thesis/dissertation. *Entrance requirements:* For doctorate, GRE General Test, interview; for Advanced Certificate, master's degree. Additional exam requirements/recommendations for international students: Required—TOEFL. *Application deadline:* For fall admission, 12/15 priority date for domestic and international students; for spring admission, 11/1 for domestic and international students. Applications are processed on a rolling basis. Application fee: $50. *Expenses:* Tuition: Part-time $1,080 per unit. Required fees: $56 per unit. $329 per term. Tuition and fees vary according to program. *Financial support:* Fellowships with full and partial tuition reimbursements, career-related internships or fieldwork, Federal Work-Study, institutionally sponsored loans, scholarships/grants, and tuition waivers (partial) available. Support available to part-time students. Financial award application deadline: 2/1; financial award applicants required to submit FAFSA. *Faculty research:* Second language acquisition, cross-cultural communication, technology-enhanced language learning, language variation, action learning. *Unit head:* Dr. Miriam Eisenstein Ebsworth, Director, 212-998-5460, Fax: 212-995-4049. *Application contact:* 212-998-5030, Fax: 212-995-4328, E-mail: steinhardt.gradadmissions@nyu.edu.

Northern Arizona University, Graduate College, College of Arts and Letters, Department of English, Program in Teaching English as a Second Language/Applied Linguistics, Flagstaff, AZ 86011. Offers applied linguistics (PhD); teaching English as a second language (MA); teaching English as a second language/English as a second language (Certificate). *Degree requirements:* For master's, departmental qualifying exam; for doctorate, thesis/dissertation. *Entrance requirements:* For master's and doctorate, GRE General Test.

Northern Arizona University, Graduate College, College of Education, Program in Bilingual/Multicultural Education, Flagstaff, AZ 86011. Offers bilingual multicultural education (M Ed); English as a Second Language/Teaching English as a second language (Certificate). Part-time and evening/weekend programs available. *Entrance requirements:* For master's, GRE General Test or minimum GPA of 3.0. *Faculty research:* Second language literacy; biliteracy and metalinguistic awareness; language shift, maintenance, and revitalization; American Indian education; minority student retention.

Notre Dame de Namur University, Division of Academic Affairs, School of Arts and Humanities, Department of English, Belmont, CA 94002-1908. Offers English (MA); teaching English to speakers of other languages (Certificate). Part-time and evening/weekend programs available. *Faculty:* 5 full-time (2 women), 5 part-time/adjunct (3 women). *Students:* 4 full-time (2 women), 17 part-time (12 women); includes 7 minority (1 African American, 1 American Indian/Alaska Native, 1 Asian American or Pacific Islander, 4 Hispanic Americans), 1 international. Average age 41. 10 applicants, 100% accepted, 8 enrolled. In 2006, 11 degrees awarded. *Degree requirements:* For master's, exam, thesis optional. *Entrance requirements:* For master's, minimum GPA of 2.5, writing sample. Additional exam requirements/recommendations for international students: Required—TOEFL. *Application deadline:* For fall admission, 8/1 priority date for domestic students; for spring admission, 12/1 priority date for domestic students. Applications are processed on a rolling basis. Application fee: $50 ($500 for international students). Electronic applications accepted. *Expenses:* Tuition: Part-time $655 per credit. *Financial support:* Career-related internships or fieldwork available. Support available to part-time students. Financial award applicants required to submit FAFSA. *Unit head:* Jacqueline Berger, Director, 650-508-3730. *Application contact:* Helen Valine, Director of Graduate Admissions, 650-508-3534, Fax: 650-508-3426, E-mail: grad.admit@ndnu.edu.

Nova Southeastern University, Fischler School of Education and Human Services, Graduate Teacher Education Program, Fort Lauderdale, FL 33314-7796. Offers athletic administration (MS); cognitive and behavioral disabilities (MS); computer science education (Ed S); computer science education (K-12) (MS); curriculum and teaching (Ed S); curriculum, instruction and technology (MS); curriculum, instruction, management and administration (Ed S); early childhood special education (MS); early literacy and reading (Ed S); early literacy education (MS);

English as a Second Language

Nova Southeastern University (continued)
education technology (MS); educational leadership (administration K–12) (MS, Ed S); educational media (Ed S); educational media (K-12) (MS); elementary education (MS, Ed S), including ESOL endorsement (MS); English (MS, Ed S); exceptional student education (MS), including ESOL endorsement; gifted education (MS, Ed S); interdisciplinary arts education (MS); management and administration of educational programs (MS); mathematics (MS, Ed S); multicultural early intervention (MS); pre-kindergarten/primary (MS); preschool education (MS); reading (MS, Ed S); science (MS, Ed S); secondary education (MS); social studies (MS, Ed S); Spanish language (MS); teaching and learning (MA, MS), including curriculum and instruction (MA), elementary mathematics (MA), elementary reading (MA), K-12 technology integration (MA); teaching English to speakers of other languages (MS, Ed S); technology management and administration (Ed S); urban studies education (MS); varying exceptionalities (Ed S). Part-time and evening/weekend programs available. Postbaccalaureate distance learning degree programs offered. *Faculty:* 131 full-time (78 women), 548 part-time/adjunct (342 women). *Students:* 1,418 full-time (1,139 women), 3,464 part-time (2,877 women); includes 2,462 minority (1,732 African Americans, 13 American Indian/Alaska Native, 44 Asian Americans or Pacific Islanders, 673 Hispanic Americans), 77 international. Average age 38. 1,771 applicants, 80% accepted, 1419 enrolled. In 2006, 2,078 master's, 425 other advanced degrees awarded. *Degree requirements:* For master's and Ed S, thesis, practicum, internship. *Entrance requirements:* For master's, MAT, GRE, CLAST, CBEST, PRAXIS I, GKT, minimum GPA of 2.5; for Ed S, MAT or GRE, master's degree, teaching certificate, minimum GPA of 3.0. Additional exam requirements/recommendations for international students: Recommended—TOEFL (minimum score 550 paper-based; 213 computer-based), IELTS (minimum score 6). *Application deadline:* For fall admission, 8/11 priority date for domestic and international students; for winter admission, 12/28 priority date for domestic and international students; for spring admission, 4/22 priority date for domestic and international students. Applications are processed on a rolling basis. Application fee: $50. Electronic applications accepted. *Financial support:* Federal Work-Study available. Support available to part-time students. Financial award application deadline: 1/7. *Faculty research:* School effectiveness, critical thinking, leadership skills acquisition, child education, multicultural education. *Unit head:* Dr. Meline Kevorkian, Associate Dean of Master's and Educational Programs, 954-262-8500, Fax: 954-262-3606, E-mail: melinek@nova.edu. *Application contact:* Jennifer Quiñones Nottingham, Dean of Student Affairs, 800-986-3223 Ext. 8624, Fax: 954-262-3911, E-mail: jlquinon@nova.edu.

Oakland University, Graduate Study and Lifelong Learning, College of Arts and Sciences, Department of Linguistics, Rochester, MI 48309-4401. Offers linguistics (MA); teaching English as a second language (Certificate). Part-time and evening/weekend programs available. *Faculty:* 5 full-time (2 women), 1 (woman) part-time/adjunct. *Students:* 9 full-time (7 women), 5 part-time (4 women). Average age 41. 21 applicants, 90% accepted, 14 enrolled. In 2006, 3 master's, 1 other advanced degree awarded. *Entrance requirements:* For master's, minimum GPA of 3.0 for unconditional admission. Additional exam requirements/recommendations for international students: Required—TOEFL (minimum score 550 paper-based; 213 computer-based). *Application deadline:* For fall admission, 7/15 priority date for domestic students, 5/1 for international students; for winter admission, 12/1 priority date for domestic students, 9/1 for international students; for spring admission, 3/15 priority date for domestic students. Application fee: $35. *Expenses:* Tuition, state resident: full-time $9,936; part-time $414 per credit. Tuition, nonresident: full-time $17,202; part-time $716 per credit. *Financial support:* Federal Work-Study, institutionally sponsored loans, and tuition waivers (full) available. Financial award application deadline: 3/1; financial award applicants required to submit FAFSA. *Unit head:* Dr. Peter J. Binkert, Chair, 248-370-2175, Fax: 248-370-3144.

Ohio Dominican University, Graduate Programs, TESOL Program, Columbus, OH 43219-2099. Offers MA. Part-time and evening/weekend programs available. *Students:* 28 full-time (24 women), 12 part-time (9 women); includes 6 minority (5 African Americans, 1 Asian American or Pacific Islander). Average age 32. *Degree requirements:* For master's, thesis, registration. *Entrance requirements:* For master's, minimum undergraduate GPA of 3.0, 3 letters of recommendation, interview. Additional exam requirements/recommendations for international students: Required—TOEFL (minimum score 550 paper-based; 213 computer-based). *Application deadline:* For fall admission, 8/15 priority date for domestic and international students; for spring admission, 1/13 priority date for domestic and international students. Applications are processed on a rolling basis. Application fee: $25. *Expenses:* Tuition: Part-time $450 per credit. Required fees: $10 per semester. *Financial support:* Applicants required to submit FAFSA. *Unit head:* Dr. Timothy Micek, Director, MA in TESOL, 614-251-4675, E-mail: micekt@ohiodominican.edu. *Application contact:* Jill M. Westerfeld, Graduate Admissions Recruiter, 614-251-4725, Fax: 614-251-4634, E-mail: westerfj@ohiodominican.edu.

Ohio University, Graduate Studies, College of Arts and Sciences, Department of Linguistics, Athens, OH 45701-2979. Offers applied linguistics/TESOL (MA). Part-time programs available. *Faculty:* 11 full-time (4 women), 5 part-time/adjunct (3 women). *Students:* 32 full-time (24 women), 22 international. Average age 26. 42 applicants, 67% accepted, 15 enrolled. In 2006, 22 degrees awarded. *Degree requirements:* For master's, one foreign language, thesis or alternative, registration. *Entrance requirements:* For master's, minimum GPA of 3.0. Additional exam requirements/recommendations for international students: Required—TOEFL (minimum score 600 paper-based; 250 computer-based); Recommended—TWE (minimum score 5). *Application deadline:* For fall admission, 2/15 priority date for domestic and international students. Applications are processed on a rolling basis. Application fee: $45. Electronic applications accepted. *Financial support:* In 2006–07, 2 fellowships with tuition reimbursements, 5 research assistantships with tuition reimbursements (averaging $7,000 per year), 24 teaching assistantships with tuition reimbursements (averaging $10,000 per year) were awarded; institutionally sponsored loans, tuition waivers (full and partial), and unspecified assistantships also available. Financial award application deadline: 3/15. *Faculty research:* Syntax, language learning, language teaching, computers for teaching, sociolinguistics. Total annual research expenditures: $250,000. *Unit head:* Dr. Scott Jarvis, Chair, 740-593-4564, Fax: 740-593-2967, E-mail: jarvis@ohio.edu. *Application contact:* Dr. Hiroyuki Oshita, Graduate Chair, 740-593-4570, Fax: 740-593-2967, E-mail: oshita@ohio.edu.

Oklahoma City University, Petree College of Arts and Sciences, Division of Education and Kinesiology Exercise Studies, Program in Teaching English to Speakers of Other Languages, Oklahoma City, OK 73106-1402. Offers MA. Part-time and evening/weekend programs available. *Faculty:* 1 full-time (0 women), 1 (woman) part-time/adjunct. *Students:* 51 full-time (39 women), 11 part-time (8 women); includes 1 minority (Asian American or Pacific Islander), 54 international. Average age 35. 5 applicants, 80% accepted. In 2006, 38 degrees awarded. *Degree requirements:* For master's, thesis optional. *Entrance requirements:* For master's, minimum GPA of 3.0. Additional exam requirements/recommendations for international students: Required—TOEFL. *Application deadline:* For fall admission, 8/22 for domestic students; for spring admission, 1/15 for domestic students. Applications are processed on a rolling basis. Application fee: $35 ($70 for international students). *Expenses:* Tuition: Full-time $12,780; part-time $710 per hour. Required fees: $89 per hour. *Financial support:* Fellowships, career-related internships or fieldwork, Federal Work-Study, institutionally sponsored loans, and tuition waivers (partial) available. Support available to part-time students. Financial award application deadline: 8/1. *Faculty research:* L2 language acquisition, L2 writing language. *Unit head:* Dr. Robert Griffin, Acting Director, 405-208-5941, Fax: 405-208-5447, E-mail: rgriffin@okcu.edu. *Application contact:* Leslie McKenzie, Director, Graduate Admissions, 800-633-7242, Fax: 405-208-5356, E-mail: gadmissions@okcu.edu.

Oral Roberts University, School of Education, Tulsa, OK 74171-0001. Offers Christian school administration (MA Ed, Ed D); Christian school administration (K-12) (MA Ed, Ed D); Christian school curriculum development (MA Ed); college and higher education administration (MA Ed, Ed D); public school administration (K-12) (MA Ed, Ed D); public school teaching (MA Ed); teaching English as a second language (MA Ed). *Accreditation:* NCATE. Part-time programs available. Postbaccalaureate distance learning degree programs offered (minimal on-campus study). *Faculty:* 9 full-time (2 women), 9 part-time/adjunct (4 women). *Students:* 331 full-time (217 women); includes 118 minority (96 African Americans, 7 American Indian/Alaska Native, 10 Asian Americans or Pacific Islanders, 5 Hispanic Americans). 125 applicants, 96% accepted, 116 enrolled. In 2006, 25 master's, 10 doctorates awarded. *Degree requirements:* For master's, thesis (for some programs), comprehensive exam; for doctorate, thesis/dissertation, comprehensive exam. *Entrance requirements:* For master's, GRE General Test or MAT, minimum GPA of 3.0; for doctorate, minimum GPA of 3.0. Additional exam requirements/recommendations for international students: Required—TOEFL (minimum score 500 paper-based; 173 computer-based). *Application deadline:* For fall admission, 7/1 priority date for domestic students, 5/1 priority date for international students; for spring admission, 12/1 priority date for domestic students, 10/1 priority date for international students. Applications are processed on a rolling basis. Application fee: $35. *Expenses:* Contact institution. *Financial support:* In 2006–07, 4 research assistantships (averaging $5,000 per year) were awarded; scholarships/grants and unspecified assistantships also available. Financial award application deadline: 6/1; financial award applicants required to submit FAFSA. *Faculty research:* Teacher effectiveness, college success in high achieving, African-Americans, professional development practices. *Unit head:* Dr. David Hand, Dean, 918-495-7084, Fax: 918-495-6050, E-mail: dhand@oru.edu. *Application contact:* Kim Schmeisser, Graduate Admissions, 918-495-6058, Fax: 918-495-6222, E-mail: gradeducation@oru.edu.

Pontifical Catholic University of Puerto Rico, College of Education, Ponce, PR 00717-0777. Offers commercial education (MRE); curriculum instruction (M Ed); education (PhD); education-general (MRE); English as a second language (MRE); religious education (MA Ed); scholar psychology (MRE). Part-time and evening/weekend programs available. *Degree requirements:* For master's, thesis (for some programs), comprehensive exam. *Entrance requirements:* For master's, GRE, 2 letters of recommendation, interview, minimum GPA of 2.75; for doctorate, EXADEP, GRE or MAT, 3 letters of recommendation. *Faculty research:* Teaching English as a second language, learning styles, leadership styles.

Portland State University, Graduate Studies, College of Liberal Arts and Sciences, Department of Applied Linguistics, Portland, OR 97207-0751. Offers teaching English to speakers of other languages (MA). Part-time programs available. *Faculty:* 11 full-time (5 women), 5 part-time/adjunct (3 women). *Students:* 34 full-time (23 women), 47 part-time (38 women); includes 6 minority (1 American Indian/Alaska Native, 3 Asian Americans or Pacific Islanders, 2 Hispanic Americans), 19 international. Average age 33. 62 applicants, 74% accepted, 20 enrolled. In 2006, 32 degrees awarded. *Degree requirements:* For master's, one foreign language, thesis, comprehensive exam. *Entrance requirements:* For master's, minimum GPA of 3.0 in upper-division course work or 2.75 overall, proficiency in at least 1 foreign language. Additional exam requirements/recommendations for international students: Required—TOEFL (minimum score 600 paper-based; 250 computer-based). *Application deadline:* For fall admission, 2/1 priority date for domestic students, 2/1 for international students; for spring admission, 11/1 for domestic students. Applications are processed on a rolling basis. Application fee: $50. *Expenses:* Tuition, state resident: full-time $6,426; part-time $238 per credit. Tuition, nonresident: full-time $11,016; part-time $408 per credit. Tuition and fees vary according to course load. *Financial support:* In 2006–07, 3 research assistantships with full tuition reimbursements (averaging $6,540 per year), 4 teaching assistantships with full tuition reimbursements (averaging $5,400 per year) were awarded; career-related internships or fieldwork, Federal Work-Study, scholarships/grants, tuition waivers (partial), and unspecified assistantships also available. Support available to part-time students. Financial award application deadline: 3/1; financial award applicants required to submit FAFSA. *Faculty research:* Sociolinguistics, linguistics and cognitive science, language proficiency testing, lexical phrases and language teaching, teaching English as a second language methodology. Total annual research expenditures: $1 million. *Unit head:* Dr. Steve Reder, Chair, 503-725-4088, Fax: 503-725-4139, E-mail: reders@pdx.edu. *Application contact:* Karin Tittelbach, Office Coordinator, 503-725-4098, Fax: 503-725-4139, E-mail: tittelk@pdx.edu.

Prescott College, Graduate Programs, Program in Education, Prescott, AZ 86301. Offers bilingual education (MA), including English as a second language, Native American bilingual teacher education; education (MA, PhD); multicultural education (MA). Part-time programs available. Postbaccalaureate distance learning degree programs offered (minimal on-campus study). *Faculty:* 1 (woman) full-time, 26 part-time/adjunct (18 women). *Students:* 44 full-time (24 women), 23 part-time (15 women); includes 8 minority (1 African American, 3 American Indian/Alaska Native, 1 Asian American or Pacific Islander, 3 Hispanic Americans), 2 international. Average age 40. In 2006, 17 degrees awarded. *Degree requirements:* For master's, thesis, fieldwork or internship, practicum; for doctorate, thesis/dissertation. *Entrance requirements:* For master's and doctorate, 2 letters of recommendation, resumé. *Application deadline:* For fall admission, 5/1 priority date for domestic students; for spring admission, 11/1 priority date for domestic students. Applications are processed on a rolling basis. Application fee: $40. Electronic applications accepted. *Expenses:* Tuition: Full-time $12,408; part-time $517 per credit. One-time fee: $130. *Financial support:* Career-related internships or fieldwork and Federal Work-Study available. Financial award applicants required to submit FAFSA. *Unit head:* Noël Caniglia, Head, 928-358-3201, Fax: 928-776-5151, E-mail: ncaniglia@prescott.edu. *Application contact:* Kerstin Alicki, Admissions Counselor, 877-350-2100 Ext. 2102, Fax: 928-776-5242, E-mail: admissions@prescott.edu.

Providence College and Theological Seminary, Theological Seminary, Otterburne, MB R0A 1G0, Canada. Offers children's ministry (Certificate); Christian studies (MA, Certificate); counseling (MA); cross-cultural discipleship (Certificate); divinity (M Div); educational studies (MA), including counseling psychology, educational ministries, student development, teaching English to speakers of other languages, training teachers of English to speakers of other languages; global studies (MA); lay counseling (Diploma); ministry (D Min); teaching English to speakers of other languages (Certificate); theological studies (MA); training teacher of English to speakers of other languages (Certificate); youth ministry (Certificate). *Accreditation:* ATS. Part-time programs available. *Degree requirements:* For M Div, 2 foreign languages, thesis (for some programs), comprehensive exam; for master's, variable foreign language requirement, thesis (for some programs); for doctorate, thesis/dissertation. *Entrance requirements:* Additional exam requirements/recommendations for international students: Recommended—TOEFL (minimum score 550 paper-based; 213 computer-based). *Faculty research:* Studies in Isaiah, theology of sin.

Queens College of the City University of New York, Division of Graduate Studies, Arts and Humanities Division, Department of Linguistics and Communication Disorders, Program in Teaching English to Speakers of Other Languages, Flushing, NY 11367-1597. Offers MS Ed. Part-time and evening/weekend programs available. *Faculty:* 8 full-time (5 women). *Students:* 4 full-time (all women), 45 part-time (42 women). 56 applicants, 84% accepted, 34 enrolled. In 2006, 10 degrees awarded. *Degree requirements:* For master's, thesis optional. *Entrance requirements:* For master's, minimum GPA of 3.0. Additional exam requirements/recommendations for international students: Required—TOEFL. *Application deadline:* For fall admission, 4/1 for domestic students; for spring admission, 11/1 for domestic students. Applications are processed on a rolling basis. Application fee: $125. *Financial support:* Career-related internships or fieldwork, Federal Work-Study, institutionally sponsored loans, and tuition waivers (partial) available. Support available to part-time students. Financial award application deadline: 4/1; financial award applicants required to submit FAFSA. *Application contact:* Mario Caruso, Director of Graduate Admissions, 718-997-5200, Fax: 718-997-5193, E-mail: graduate_admissions@qc.edu.

Regent University, Graduate School, School of Education, Virginia Beach, VA 23464-9800. Offers Christian school program (M Ed); cross-categorical special education (M Ed); education (M Ed, Ed D); educational leadership (M Ed); elementary education (M Ed); individual degree plan (M Ed); master teacher (M Ed); special education leadership (Ed S); TESOL (M Ed). Part-time and evening/weekend programs available. Postbaccalaureate distance learning degree programs offered (minimal on-campus study). *Faculty:* 25 full-time (11 women), 132 part-time/adjunct (90 women). *Students:* 220 full-time (176 women), 501 part-time (374 women); includes 264 minority (229 African Americans, 9 Asian Americans or Pacific Islanders, 26 Hispanic

Americans), 13 international. Average age 38. 472 applicants, 79% accepted, 256 enrolled. In 2006, 185 master's, 5 doctorates awarded. *Degree requirements:* For master's, thesis or alternative; for doctorate, thesis/dissertation, comprehensive exam. *Entrance requirements:* For master's, MAT, minimum undergraduate GPA of 2.75, writing sample, resumé; for doctorate, GRE, writing sample, 3 years of relevant professional experience, master's-level paper, copies of published work. Additional exam requirements/recommendations for international students: Required—TOEFL (minimum score 577 paper-based; 233 computer-based). *Application deadline:* For fall admission, 4/1 priority date for domestic students; for spring admission, 10/15 priority date for domestic students. Applications are processed on a rolling basis. Application fee: $50. Electronic applications accepted. *Expenses:* Contact institution. *Financial support:* In 2006–07, 721 students received support; fellowships, career-related internships or fieldwork, scholarships/grants, tuition waivers (full and partial), and unspecified assistantships available. Support available to part-time students. Financial award application deadline: 4/1; financial award applicants required to submit FAFSA. *Faculty research:* Character development and discipline for children, education leadership development, diversity in schools, classroom management, technology in education settings. *Unit head:* Dr. Alan A. Arroyo, Dean, 757-226-4261, Fax: 757-226-4318, E-mail: alanarr@regent.edu. *Application contact:* Althea Bishard, Registrar and Executive Director of Enrollment and Academic Services, 800-373-5504, Fax: 757-226-4381, E-mail: admissions@regent.edu.

Regis University, School for Professional Studies, Program in Teacher Education, Denver, CO 80221-1099. Offers adult learning, training, and development (M Ed); curriculum, instruction, and assessment (M Ed); early childhood (M Ed); educational technology (Certificate); elementary (M Ed); ESL (M Ed); fine arts (M Ed), including arts, music; instructional technology (M Ed); professional leadership (M Ed); reading (M Ed); secondary (M Ed); self-designed (M Ed); space studies (M Ed); special education (M Ed); teacher licensure (M Ed). Program also offered in Henderson and Las Vegas (Summerlin), NV. Postbaccalaureate distance learning degree programs offered. *Unit head:* Dr. Suzie Perry, Dean, 303-458-4302. *Application contact:* Partick Lowenthal, Assistant Director, 303-458-4300 Ext. 4314, E-mail: masters@regis.edu.

Rhode Island College, School of Graduate Studies, Feinstein School of Education and Human Development, Department of Educational Studies, Providence, RI 02908-1991. Offers bilingual/bicultural education (M Ed); educational administration (CAGS); English (MAT); French (MAT); history (MAT); math (MAT); secondary education (M Ed); Spanish (MAT); teaching English as a second language (M Ed, MAT); technology education (M Ed). *Accreditation:* NCATE. Part-time and evening/weekend programs available. *Faculty:* 12 full-time (5 women), 4 part-time/adjunct (all women). *Students:* 10 full-time (7 women), 27 part-time (23 women); includes 1 minority (Hispanic American). Average age 32. In 2006, 22 degrees awarded. *Entrance requirements:* For master's, BA in English, French, history, math or Spanish; evaluation of content area knowledge; 3 letters of recommendation; interview. *Application deadline:* For fall admission, 3/15 for domestic students; for spring admission, 11/1 for domestic students. Applications are processed on a rolling basis. Application fee: $50. *Expenses:* Tuition, state resident: part-time $244 per credit. Tuition, nonresident: part-time $512 per credit. Required fees: $12 per credit. $66 per term. Tuition and fees vary according to degree level, program and reciprocity agreements. *Financial support:* Teaching assistantships with full tuition reimbursements, career-related internships or fieldwork, Federal Work-Study, scholarships/grants, health care benefits, and unspecified assistantships available. Support available to part-time students. Financial award application deadline: 5/15; financial award applicants required to submit FAFSA. *Faculty research:* School administration, school/college articulation. *Unit head:* Dr. Charles McLaughlin, Chair, 401-456-8170.

Rider University, Department of Graduate Education, Leadership and Counseling, Lawrenceville, NJ 08648-3001. Offers counseling services (MA, Ed S); curriculum, instruction and supervision (MA); director of school counseling services (Certificate); educational administration (MA); organizational leadership (MA); principal (Certificate); reading/language arts (MA, Certificate, including reading specialist (Certificate), reading/language arts (MA); school business administrator (Certificate); school counseling services (Certificate); school psychology (Ed S); special education (MA); supervisor (Certificate); teacher certification (Certificate), including business education, elementary education, English as a second language, English education, mathematics education, preschool to grade 3, science education, social studies education, world languages; teaching (MA). *Accreditation:* NCATE. Part-time and evening/weekend programs available. *Faculty:* 24 full-time (12 women), 30 part-time/adjunct (15 women). *Students:* 90 full-time (75 women), 457 part-time (369 women); includes 73 minority (50 African Americans, 2 American Indian/Alaska Native, 6 Asian Americans or Pacific Islanders, 15 Hispanic Americans), 1 international. Average age 32. 314 applicants, 61% accepted, 138 enrolled. In 2006, 116 master's, 19 other advanced degrees awarded. *Degree requirements:* For master's, thesis or alternative, internship, portfolios, comprehensive exam (for some programs); for other advanced degree, internship, professional portfolio. *Entrance requirements:* For master's, GRE (counseling, school psychology), MAT, interview, resumé, letters of recommendation; for other advanced degree, PRAXIS. Additional exam requirements/recommendations for international students: Required—TOEFL (minimum score 550 paper-based; 213 computer-based). *Application deadline:* For fall admission, 5/1 priority date for domestic students, 6/1 priority date for international students; for spring admission, 11/1 priority date for domestic and international students. Applications are processed on a rolling basis. Application fee: $50. Electronic applications accepted. *Expenses:* Tuition: Part-time $525 per credit. Required fees: $35 per course. $30 per semester. *Financial support:* In 2006–07, 271 students received support. Career-related internships or fieldwork, Federal Work-Study, institutionally sponsored loans, and unspecified assistantships available. Support available to part-time students. Financial award applicants required to submit FAFSA. *Faculty research:* Gifted students, self-esteem, hope and mental health, conflicts in group work, cultural diversity and counseling assessment of special needs in children. *Unit head:* Dr. Dennis C. Buss, Chair, 609-895-5353, Fax: 609-896-5362, E-mail: dbuss@rider.edu. *Application contact:* Jamie L Mitchell, Director of Graduate Admissions, 609-896-5036, Fax: 609-895-5680, E-mail: jmitchell@rider.edu.

See Close-Up on page 913.

Rutgers, The State University of New Jersey, New Brunswick, Graduate School of Education, Department of Learning and Teaching, Program in Language Education, New Brunswick, NJ 08901-1281. Offers English as a second language education (Ed M); language education (Ed M, Ed D). Part-time programs available. *Faculty:* 3 full-time (2 women). *Students:* 34 full-time (31 women), 25 part-time (19 women). 92 applicants, 53% accepted, 29 enrolled. In 2006, 22 master's awarded. Terminal master's awarded for partial completion of doctoral program. *Degree requirements:* For master's, comprehensive exam; for doctorate, thesis/dissertation, concept paper, qualifying exam. *Entrance requirements:* For master's, GRE General Test, minimum GPA of 3.0; for doctorate, GRE General Test, minimum GPA of 3.5. Additional exam requirements/recommendations for international students: Required—TOEFL. *Application deadline:* For fall admission, 2/1 for domestic and international students. Application fee: $60. Electronic applications accepted. *Financial support:* Application deadline: 3/15; *Faculty research:* Linguistics, sociolinguistics, cross-cultural/international communication. *Unit head:* Dr. Mary Curran, Coordinator, 732-932-7496 Ext. 8101, Fax: 732-932-7552, E-mail: mcurran@rci.rutgers.edu.

St. Cloud State University, School of Graduate Studies, College of Fine Arts and Humanities, Department of English, St. Cloud, MN 56301-4498. Offers English (MA, MS), teaching English as a second language (MA). Part-time programs available. *Faculty:* 35 full-time (16 women). *Students:* 44 full-time (30 women), 27 part-time (21 women); includes 2 minority (both Hispanic Americans), 10 international. 27 applicants, 100% accepted. In 2006, 24 degrees awarded. *Degree requirements:* For master's, thesis or alternative. *Entrance requirements:* For master's, GRE General Test, minimum GPA of 2.75. Additional exam requirements/recommendations for international students: Required—MELAB; Recommended—TOEFL (minimum score 550 paper-based; 213 computer-based), IELTS (minimum score 7). *Application deadline:* For fall admission, 6/1 priority date for domestic students, 4/1 for international students; for spring admission, 10/1 priority date for domestic students, 8/1 for international students. Applications are processed on a rolling basis. Application fee: $35. Electronic applications accepted. *Financial support:* Federal Work-Study, scholarships/grants, and unspecified assistantships available. Financial award application deadline: 3/1. *Unit head:* Dr. Robert Inkster, Chairperson, 320-308-3061, Fax: 320-308-5524. *Application contact:* Linda Lou Krueger, School of Graduate Studies, 320-308-2113, Fax: 320-308-5371, E-mail: lekrueger@stcloudstate.edu.

St. John's University, The School of Education, Division of Human Services and Counseling, Program in Bilingual/Multicultural Education/Teaching English to Speakers of Other Languages, Queens, NY 11439. Offers MS Ed. Part-time and evening/weekend programs available. *Students:* 8 full-time (7 women), 104 part-time (88 women); includes 23 minority (4 African Americans, 8 Asian Americans or Pacific Islanders, 11 Hispanic Americans), 8 international. Average age 31. 59 applicants, 93% accepted, 27 enrolled. In 2006, 43 degrees awarded. *Degree requirements:* For master's, internship. *Entrance requirements:* For master's, minimum GPA of 3.0, New York teaching certificate. Additional exam requirements/recommendations for international students: Required—TOEFL (minimum score 500 paper-based; 173 computer-based). *Application deadline:* For fall admission, 4/1 for domestic students, 5/1 priority date for international students; for spring admission, 11/1 for domestic students, 11/1 priority date for international students. Applications are processed on a rolling basis. Application fee: $40. Electronic applications accepted. *Expenses:* Tuition: Full-time $18,480; part-time $770 per credit. Required fees: $125 per semester. Tuition and fees vary according to program. *Financial support:* Research assistantships, career-related internships or fieldwork and scholarships/grants available. Support available to part-time students. Financial award application deadline: 3/1; financial award applicants required to submit FAFSA. *Faculty research:* Literacy development for second language, learners and investigating Caribbean and Creole language and culture. *Application contact:* Kelly Ronayne, Assistant Dean, 718-990-2303, Fax: 718-990-6069, E-mail: graded@stjohns.edu.

Saint Martin's University, Graduate Programs, Department of Education, Lacey, WA 98503-1297. Offers administration (M Ed); English as a second language (M Ed); guidance and counseling (M Ed); reading (M Ed); special education (M Ed); teaching (MIT); technology in education (M Ed). Part-time and evening/weekend programs available. *Degree requirements:* For master's, thesis or alternative, project or comprehensives, comprehensive exam (for some programs). *Entrance requirements:* For master's, GRE General Test or MAT, resumé. Additional exam requirements/recommendations for international students: Required—TOEFL (minimum score 560 paper-based). *Faculty research:* Reader's theatre and reader/writer workshops, curriculum and assessment integration, gender and equity, classroom evaluations, organizational leadership.

Saint Michael's College, Graduate Programs, Program in Teaching English as a Second Language, Colchester, VT 05439. Offers MATESL, Certificate. Part-time and evening/weekend programs available. *Faculty:* 8 full-time (5 women), 10 part-time/adjunct (7 women). *Students:* 21 full-time (16 women), 24 part-time (18 women); includes 2 minority (1 Asian American or Pacific Islander, 1 Hispanic American), 10 international. Average age 32. 29 applicants, 79% accepted, 13 enrolled. In 2006, 32 degrees awarded. *Degree requirements:* For master's, one foreign language, thesis or alternative, comprehensive exam. *Entrance requirements:* For master's, minimum GPA of 3.0. Additional exam requirements/recommendations for international students: Required—TOEFL (minimum score 550 paper-based; 213 computer-based). *Application deadline:* For fall admission, 6/1 priority date for domestic students. Applications are processed on a rolling basis. Application fee: $35. *Financial support:* Research assistantships, career-related internships or fieldwork, Federal Work-Study, institutionally sponsored loans, and scholarships/grants available. Financial award applicants required to submit FAFSA. *Faculty research:* Language teaching methodology, discourse analysis, second language acquisition, language assessment, sociolinguistics, K–12 English as a second language for children. *Unit head:* Dr. Susan Jenkins, Director, 802-654-2801, Fax: 802-654-2595, E-mail: sjenkins@smcvt.edu.

Salem College, Department of Education, Winston-Salem, NC 27108-0548. Offers early education and leadership (MAT); elementary education (MAT); English as a second language (MAT); language and literacy (M Ed); middle school education (MAT); secondary education (MAT); special education (MAT). *Accreditation:* NCATE. Part-time and evening/weekend programs available. *Faculty:* 8 full-time (6 women), 5 part-time/adjunct (all women). *Students:* 8 full-time (all women), 250 part-time (238 women); includes 19 minority (16 African Americans, 1 Asian American or Pacific Islander, 2 Hispanic Americans). Average age 33. 110 applicants, 65% accepted, 68 enrolled. In 2006, 34 degrees awarded. *Degree requirements:* For master's, practicum (MAT), project (M Ed), oral and written comprehensive exams. *Entrance requirements:* For master's, GRE, minimum GPA of 2.5. *Application deadline:* Applications are processed on a rolling basis. Application fee: $30. *Financial support:* In 2006–07, 152 students received support. Federal Work-Study and scholarships/grants available. Support available to part-time students. Financial award applicants required to submit FAFSA. *Faculty research:* Content area reading strategies, literacy development, brain compatible instruction. *Unit head:* Dr. Paula Grubbs, Director of Teacher Education, 336-721-2610, Fax: 336-721-2683, E-mail: grubbs@salem.edu.

Salem International University, School of Education, Salem, WV 26426-0500. Offers curriculum and instruction (M Ed), including curriculum and instruction, educational technology leadership, physical education/health, teaching English as a second language; educational administration (M Ed). Part-time and evening/weekend programs available. Postbaccalaureate distance learning degree programs offered. *Faculty:* 5 full-time (4 women), 17 part-time/adjunct (8 women). *Students:* 74 full-time (45 women), 154 part-time (75 women); includes 7 minority (2 African Americans, 5 Asian Americans or Pacific Islanders), 28 international. Average age 41. 200 applicants, 75% accepted, 130 enrolled. In 2006, 18 degrees awarded. *Degree requirements:* For master's, thesis (for some programs), comprehensive exam (for some programs), registration. *Entrance requirements:* For master's, GRE, MAT, NTE, 3 letters of recommendation. Additional exam requirements/recommendations for international students: Required—TOEFL (minimum score 550 paper-based; 213 computer-based). *Application deadline:* Applications are processed on a rolling basis. Application fee: $25. Electronic applications accepted. *Expenses:* Contact institution. One-time fee: $25 part-time. Tuition and fees vary according to program. *Financial support:* Application deadline: 4/15; *Faculty research:* Improved classroom effectiveness. *Unit head:* Dean, School of Education, 304-326-1253, Fax: 304-326-1246. *Application contact:* Thomas White, Director of Admissions, 304-326-1549, Fax: 304-326-1246, E-mail: admission@salemiu.edu.

Salem State College, Graduate School, Program in English, Salem, MA 01970-5353. Offers English (MA, MAT, MA/MAT); English as a second language (MAT); MA/MAT. Part-time and evening/weekend programs available. *Faculty:* 3 part-time/adjunct (1 woman). *Students:* 13 full-time (8 women), 49 part-time (34 women); includes 1 minority (Asian American or Pacific Islander), 1 international. Average age 32. In 2006, 20 degrees awarded. *Degree requirements:* For master's, one foreign language. *Entrance requirements:* For master's, GRE General Test, MAT. *Application deadline:* Applications are processed on a rolling basis. Application fee: $35. *Unit head:* Nancy Schultz, Coordinator, 978-542-6105, E-mail: nschultz@salemstate.edu.

Salem State College, Graduate School, Program in Teaching English as a Second Language, Salem, MA 01970-5353. Offers MAT. Part-time and evening/weekend programs available. *Students:* 3 full-time (all women), 14 part-time (13 women); includes 3 Hispanic Americans, 4 international. Average age 41. In 2006, 10 degrees awarded. Application fee: $35. *Unit head:* Ellen Rintell, Coordinator, 978-542-6321, E-mail: erintell@salemstate.edu.

Salisbury University, Graduate Division, Program in English, Salisbury, MD 21801-6837. Offers composition, language and rhetoric (MA); literature (MA); teaching English to speakers of other languages (MA). Part-time programs available. *Faculty:* 13 full-time (5 women). *Students:* 5 full-time (3 women), 26 part-time (22 women); includes 2 minority (1 African American, 1 Hispanic American). Average age 31. 26 applicants, 46% accepted, 12 enrolled.

English as a Second Language

Salisbury University (continued)

In 2006, 20 degrees awarded. *Degree requirements:* For master's, thesis optional. *Entrance requirements:* For master's, GRE General Test, MAT or PRAXIS, minimum GPA of 3.0, 2 letters of recommendation. Additional exam requirements/recommendations for international students: Required—TOEFL (minimum score 550 paper-based; 213 computer-based). *Application deadline:* For fall admission, 8/1 for domestic students; for spring admission, 1/1 for domestic students. Applications are processed on a rolling basis. Application fee: $45. Electronic applications accepted. *Expenses:* Tuition, state resident: part-time $260 per credit hour. Tuition, nonresident: part-time $546 per credit hour. Required fees: $52 per credit hour. *Financial support:* Teaching assistantships with full tuition reimbursements, career-related internships or fieldwork and scholarships/grants available. Support available to part-time students. Financial award applicants required to submit FAFSA. *Faculty research:* Shakespeare, Keats, J. D. Salinger, feminist theory, film, folklore. *Unit head:* Dr. Elizabeth H. Curtin, Director, 410-548-5594, Fax: 410-548-2142, E-mail: ehcurtin@salisbury.edu.

San Diego State University, Graduate and Research Affairs, College of Arts and Letters, Department of Linguistics and Oriental Languages, San Diego, CA 92182. Offers applied linguistics and English as a second language (CAL); computational linguistics (MA); English as a second language/applied linguistics (MA); general linguistics (MA). *Students:* 24 full-time (17 women), 27 part-time (18 women); includes 8 minority (4 Asian Americans or Pacific Islanders, 4 Hispanic Americans), 11 international. Average age 30. 31 applicants, 61% accepted, 1 enrolled. In 2006, 6 degrees awarded. *Degree requirements:* For master's, one foreign language, comprehensive exam. *Entrance requirements:* For master's, GRE General Test, 2 letters of recommendation. Additional exam requirements/recommendations for international students: Required—TOEFL (minimum score 570 paper-based). *Application deadline:* For fall admission, 5/1 for domestic and international students; for spring admission, 11/1 for domestic students, 10/1 for international students. Applications are processed on a rolling basis. Application fee: $55. Electronic applications accepted. *Financial support:* In 2006–07, 16 teaching assistantships were awarded; fellowships, career-related internships or fieldwork also available. Financial award applicants required to submit FAFSA. *Faculty research:* Cross-cultural linguistic studies of semantics. Total annual research expenditures: $256,582. *Unit head:* Jeffrey Kaplan, Chair, 619-594-5268, Fax: 619-594-4877, E-mail: jkaplan@mail.sdsu.edu. *Application contact:* Dr. Soonja Choi, Adviser, 619-594-5885, E-mail: schoi@mail.sdsu.edu.

San Francisco State University, Division of Graduate Studies, College of Humanities, Department of English Language and Literature, Program in Teaching English to Speakers of Other Languages, San Francisco, CA 94132-1722. Offers MA. Part-time programs available. *Faculty:* 12 full-time (7 women). *Students:* 215. 207 applicants, 83% accepted, 75 enrolled. In 2006, 54 degrees awarded. *Degree requirements:* For master's, thesis (for some programs), comprehensive exam (for some programs). *Entrance requirements:* For master's, minimum GPA of 3.0 in last 60 units. Additional exam requirements/recommendations for international students: Required—TOEFL (minimum score 570 paper-based; 230 computer-based). *Application deadline:* For fall admission, 4/1 priority date for domestic and international students; for spring admission, 10/1 priority date for domestic students, 10/1 for international students. Applications are processed on a rolling basis. Application fee: $55. Electronic applications accepted. *Financial support:* Application deadline: 3/1. *Faculty research:* Second language acquisition, sociolinguistics, ESL teaching methods, curriculum and materials, classroom research. *Application contact:* Dr. May Shih, Graduate Coordinator, 415-338-1586, E-mail: mshih@sfsu.edu.

San Jose State University, Graduate Studies and Research, College of Humanities and the Arts, Department of Linguistics and Language Development, San Jose, CA 95192-0001. Offers computational linguistics (Certificate); linguistics (MA, Certificate); teaching English to speakers of other languages (MA, Certificate). *Students:* 56 full-time (42 women), 44 part-time (36 women); includes 20 minority (14 Asian Americans or Pacific Islanders, 6 Hispanic Americans), 27 international. Average age 34. 95 applicants, 74% accepted, 41 enrolled. In 2006, 30 degrees awarded. *Entrance requirements:* Additional exam requirements/recommendations for international students: Required—TOEFL (minimum score 570 paper-based; 230 computer-based). *Application deadline:* For fall admission, 6/29 for domestic students; for spring admission, 11/30 for domestic students. Applications are processed on a rolling basis. Application fee: $59. Electronic applications accepted. *Financial support:* Applicants required to submit FAFSA. *Unit head:* Thom Huebner, Chair, 408-924-3742, Fax: 408-924-4703.

School for International Training, Graduate Programs, Programs in Language Teacher Education, Brattleboro, VT 05302-0676. Offers English for speakers of other languages (MAT); French (MAT); Spanish (MAT). *Students:* 55 full-time (45 women), 85 part-time (61 women); includes 15 minority (6 African Americans, 2 American Indian/Alaska Native, 1 Asian American or Pacific Islander, 6 Hispanic Americans), 33 international. Average age 32. 186 applicants, 81% accepted, 85 enrolled. In 2006, 61 degrees awarded. *Degree requirements:* For master's, one foreign language, thesis, practice teaching. *Entrance requirements:* For master's, 4 letters of reference. Additional exam requirements/recommendations for international students: Required—TOEFL. *Application deadline:* Applications are processed on a rolling basis. Application fee: $50. *Expenses:* Tuition: Full-time $27,355; part-time $638 per credit hour. Required fees: $1,092. *Financial support:* Career-related internships or fieldwork, Federal Work-Study, institutionally sponsored loans, and scholarships/grants available. Financial award application deadline: 3/1; financial award applicants required to submit FAFSA. *Unit head:* Marla Solomon, Graduate Dean, 802-258-3325, Fax: 802-258-3241, E-mail: marla.solomon@sit.edu. *Application contact:* Information Contact, 800-336-1616, Fax: 802-258-3500, E-mail: admissions@sit.edu.

Seattle Pacific University, Graduate School, College of Arts and Sciences, Program in Teaching English as a Second Language, Seattle, WA 98119-1997. Offers MA. Part-time programs available. *Students:* 10 full-time (8 women), 18 part-time (14 women); includes 8 minority (1 African American, 2 American Indian/Alaska Native, 5 Asian Americans or Pacific Islanders), 6 international. 9 applicants, 56% accepted, 3 enrolled. In 2006, 6 degrees awarded. *Degree requirements:* For master's, one foreign language. *Entrance requirements:* For master's, GRE General Test, minimum GPA of 3.0. Additional exam requirements/recommendations for international students: Required—TOEFL. *Application deadline:* For fall admission, 8/11 priority date for domestic students; for spring admission, 3/11 for domestic students. Applications are processed on a rolling basis. Application fee: $50. *Expenses: Contact institution. Financial support:* In 2006–07, 1 research assistantship was awarded; career-related internships or fieldwork also available. Financial award applicants required to submit FAFSA. *Faculty research:* Second language acquisition. *Unit head:* Dr. Kathryn Bartholomew, Chair, 206-281-2670, Fax: 206-281-2500.

Seattle University, College of Education, Program in Teaching English to Speakers of Other Languages, Seattle, WA 98122-1090. Offers M Ed, MA, Certificate. *Accreditation:* NCATE. Part-time programs available. *Students:* 7 full-time (4 women), 36 part-time (26 women); includes 4 minority (2 Asian Americans or Pacific Islanders, 2 Hispanic Americans), 8 international. Average age 34. 37 applicants, 73% accepted, 15 enrolled. In 2006, 21 master's, 1 other advanced degree awarded. *Degree requirements:* For master's, thesis, internship, comprehensive exam. *Entrance requirements:* For master's, GRE, MAT, or minimum GPA of 3.0. Additional exam requirements/recommendations for international students: Required—TOEFL. *Application deadline:* For fall admission, 8/20 priority date for domestic students; for winter admission, 11/20 for domestic students; for spring admission, 2/20 for domestic students. Applications are processed on a rolling basis. Application fee: $55. *Financial support:* Career-related internships or fieldwork and Federal Work-Study available. Support available to part-time students. Financial award applicants required to submit FAFSA. *Unit head:* Dr. Jian Yang, Coordinator, 209-296-5908. *Application contact:* Janet Shandley, Associate Dean of Graduate Admissions, 206-296-5900, Fax: 206-298-5656, E-mail: grad_admissions@seattleu.edu.

Shenandoah University, College of Arts and Sciences, Winchester, VA 22601-5195. Offers administrative leadership (D Ed); advanced professional teaching English to speakers of other languages (Certificate); education (MSE); elementary education (Certificate); middle school education (Certificate); professional studies (Certificate); professional teaching English to speakers of other languages (Certificate); public management (Certificate); secondary education (Certificate); women's studies (Certificate). Part-time and evening/weekend programs available. Postbaccalaureate distance learning degree programs offered (minimal on-campus study). *Faculty:* 14 full-time (9 women), 7 part-time/adjunct (4 women). *Students:* 28 full-time (16 women), 283 part-time (208 women); includes 8 minority (3 African Americans, 1 American Indian/Alaska Native, 3 Asian Americans or Pacific Islanders, 1 Hispanic American), 26 international. Average age 40. 182 applicants, 68% accepted, 98 enrolled. In 2006, 96 master's, 6 doctorates, 22 other advanced degrees awarded. *Degree requirements:* For master's, thesis (for some programs), internship, comprehensive exam (for some programs); for doctorate, thesis/dissertation, comprehensive exam. *Entrance requirements:* For master's, minimum GPA of 3.0 or satisfactory GRE, 3 letters of recommendation, valid teaching license; for doctorate, minimum GPA of 3.5 in master's, 3 years of teaching experience, 3 letters of recommendation, writing samples. Additional exam requirements/recommendations for international students: Required—TOEFL (minimum score 527 paper-based; 197 computer-based; 71 iBT). *Application deadline:* For fall admission, 7/15 for domestic students; for spring admission, 10/15 for domestic students. Applications are processed on a rolling basis. Application fee: $30. Electronic applications accepted. *Expenses:* Tuition: Full-time $12,200; part-time $610 per credit. Required fees: $150. Full-time tuition and fees vary according to course load and program. *Financial support:* In 2006–07, fellowships with partial tuition reimbursements (averaging $2,581 per year); career-related internships or fieldwork, institutionally sponsored loans, and unspecified assistantships also available. Support available to part-time students. Financial award application deadline: 3/15; financial award applicants required to submit FAFSA. *Faculty research:* Nanotechnology, writing pedagogy and writing centers, violence in schools, Virginia/Shenandoah Valley history and culture, stress in children. *Unit head:* Dr. Calvin Allen, Dean, 540-665-4587, Fax: 540-665-4644, E-mail: callen@su.edu. *Application contact:* David Anthony, Dean of Admissions, 540-665-4581, Fax: 540-665-4627, E-mail: admit@su.edu.

See Close-Up on page 919.

Simmons College, Graduate School, College of Arts and Sciences Graduate Studies, Program in Teaching English as a Second Language, Boston, MA 02115. Offers MAT. *Faculty:* 2 full-time (1 woman), 2 part-time/adjunct (both women). *Students:* 4 full-time (all women), 12 part-time (all women); includes 1 minority (Hispanic American) Average age 33. 13 applicants, 77% accepted. In 2006, 9 degrees awarded. *Degree requirements:* For master's, one foreign language. *Entrance requirements:* For master's, GRE General Test, MAT, or Massachusetts Test for Education Licensure in Communication and Literacy, intermediate proficiency in a second language. Additional exam requirements/recommendations for international students: Required—TOEFL (minimum score 600 paper-based; 250 computer-based; 100 iBT). *Application deadline:* For fall admission, 8/1 priority date for domestic students; for spring admission, 12/15 priority date for domestic students. Applications are processed on a rolling basis. Application fee: $35. Electronic applications accepted. *Expenses: Contact institution. Financial support:* In 2006–07, teaching assistantships (averaging $2,000 per year); career-related internships or fieldwork, Federal Work-Study, institutionally sponsored loans, and scholarships/grants also available. Support available to part-time students. Financial award application deadline: 3/1; financial award applicants required to submit FAFSA. *Faculty research:* Teacher learning, writing theory and practice, reading theory and practice. *Unit head:* Dr. Paul Abraham, Director, 617-521-2579, Fax: 617-521-3133, E-mail: paul.abraham@simmons.edu. *Application contact:* Kristen Haack, Director, Graduate Studies Admission, 617-521-2915, Fax: 617-521-3058, E-mail: gsa@simmons.edu.

Southeast Missouri State University, School of Graduate Studies, Department of English, Cape Girardeau, MO 63701-4799. Offers English (MA); teaching English to speakers of other languages (MA). Part-time and evening/weekend programs available. *Faculty:* 16 full-time (8 women). *Students:* 19 full-time (14 women), 78 part-time (66 women); includes 9 minority (3 African Americans, 3 Asian Americans or Pacific Islanders, 3 Hispanic Americans), 10 international. Average age 34. 37 applicants, 92% accepted. In 2006, 15 degrees awarded. *Degree requirements:* For master's, thesis or alternative, comprehensive exam (for some programs). *Entrance requirements:* For master's, minimum GPA of 2.5. Additional exam requirements/recommendations for international students: Required—TOEFL (minimum score 550 paper-based; 213 computer-based). *Application deadline:* For fall admission, 8/1 for domestic students, 4/1 for international students; for spring admission, 11/21 for domestic students, 10/1 for international students. Applications are processed on a rolling basis. Application fee: $20 ($100 for international students). Electronic applications accepted. *Financial support:* In 2006–07, 43 students received support, including 9 research assistantships with full tuition reimbursements available (averaging $7,100 per year), 16 teaching assistantships with full tuition reimbursements available (averaging $7,100 per year); unspecified assistantships also available. Financial award applicants required to submit FAFSA. *Faculty research:* Hawthorne, Mark Twain, Faulkner. *Unit head:* Dr. Carol Scates, Chairperson, 573-651-2156, E-mail: cscates@semo.edu. *Application contact:* Marsha L. Arant, Senior Administrative Assistant, Office of Graduate Studies, 573-651-2192, Fax: 573-651-2001, E-mail: marant@semo.edu.

Southern Connecticut State University, School of Graduate Studies, School of Arts and Sciences, Department of Foreign Languages, New Haven, CT 06515-1355. Offers French (MA); multicultural-bilingual education/teaching English to speakers of other languages (MS); Romance languages (MA); Spanish (MA); MLS/MS. Part-time and evening/weekend programs available. *Faculty:* 6 full-time. *Students:* 16 full-time (9 women), 25 part-time (22 women); includes 7 minority (1 Asian American or Pacific Islander, 6 Hispanic Americans). 36 applicants, 83% accepted, 12 enrolled. In 2006, 24 degrees awarded. *Degree requirements:* For master's, one foreign language, thesis or alternative. *Entrance requirements:* For master's, interview, minimum undergraduate GPA of 2.7. *Application deadline:* For fall admission, 7/15 priority date for domestic students. Applications are processed on a rolling basis. Application fee: $50. Electronic applications accepted. *Financial support:* Application deadline: 4/15. *Unit head:* Dr. Carlos Arboleda, Chairperson, 203-392-6754, Fax: 203-392-6136, E-mail: arboledac1@southernct.edu.

Southern Illinois University Carbondale, Graduate School, College of Liberal Arts, Department of Applied Linguistics, Carbondale, IL 62901-4701. Offers applied linguistics (MA); teaching English to speakers of other languages (MA). *Faculty:* 9 full-time (6 women), 1 part-time/adjunct (0 women). *Students:* 7 full-time (5 women), 10 part-time (6 women); includes 3 minority (1 African American, 2 Hispanic Americans), 5 international. Average age 27. 16 applicants, 44% accepted, 4 enrolled. In 2006, 4 degrees awarded. *Degree requirements:* For master's, one foreign language, thesis. *Entrance requirements:* For master's, minimum GPA of 3.0. Additional exam requirements/recommendations for international students: Required—TOEFL. *Application deadline:* For fall admission, 4/1 priority date for domestic students. Applications are processed on a rolling basis. Application fee: $20. *Financial support:* Fellowships with full tuition reimbursements, research assistantships with full tuition reimbursements, teaching assistantships with full tuition reimbursements, career-related internships or fieldwork, Federal Work-Study, institutionally sponsored loans, and tuition waivers (full) available. Support available to part-time students. Financial award application deadline: 4/1. *Faculty research:* Theory and methods, second language acquisition, pidgin and Creole languages, cognitive grammar. *Unit head:* Dr. John E. Dotson, Chair, 618-536-3385, Fax: 618-453-6527, E-mail: jdotson@siu.edu. *Application contact:* Diane Korando, Departmental Secretary, 618-536-3385, Fax: 618-453-6527, E-mail: ling@siu.edu.

Southern Illinois University Carbondale, Graduate School, College of Liberal Arts, Program in Teaching English to Speakers of Other Languages, Carbondale, IL 62901-4701. Offers MA. *Students:* 32 full-time (22 women), 15 part-time (3 women); includes 5 minority (1 African American, 1 Asian American or Pacific Islander, 3 Hispanic Americans), 24 international. 63 applicants, 49% accepted, 11 enrolled. In 2006, 20 degrees awarded. *Unit head:* Dr. John E. Dotson, Chair, 618-536-3385, E-mail: jdotson@siu.edu. *Application contact:* Diane Korando, Office Specialist, 618-536-3385, E-mail: ling@siu.edu.

Southern Illinois University Edwardsville, Graduate Studies and Research, College of Arts and Sciences, Department of English Language and Literature, Program in Teaching English as a Second Language, Edwardsville, IL 62026-0001. Offers MA, Postbaccalaureate Certificate. Part-time and evening/weekend programs available. *Students:* 5 full-time (3 women), 20 part-time (16 women); includes 3 minority (1 Asian American or Pacific Islander, 2 Hispanic Americans), 4 international. Average age 33. 21 applicants, 67% accepted. In 2006, 9 degrees awarded. *Degree requirements:* For master's, one foreign language, thesis or alternative, final exam. *Entrance requirements:* Additional exam requirements/recommendations for international students: Required—TOEFL. *Application deadline:* For fall admission, 7/20 for domestic students, 6/1 for international students; for spring admission, 12/14 for domestic students, 10/1 for international students. Application fee: $30. Electronic applications accepted. *Financial support:* Fellowships with full tuition reimbursements, research assistantships with full tuition reimbursements, teaching assistantships with full tuition reimbursements, institutionally sponsored loans available. Support available to part-time students. Financial award application deadline: 3/1. *Unit head:* Dr. Jack Voller, Director, 618-650-2460, E-mail: jvoller@siue.edu.

Southern New Hampshire University, School of Liberal Arts, Manchester, NH 03106-1045. Offers clinical services for adults psychiatric disabilities (Certificate); clinical services for children and adolescents with psychiatric disabilities (Certificate); clinical services for persons with co-occurring substance abuse and psychiatric disabilities (Certificate); community mental health (MS); fiction writing (MFA); non-fiction writing (MFA); teaching English as a foreign language (MS). Part-time and evening/weekend programs available. *Faculty:* 18 full-time. *Students:* 187 full-time, 12 part-time. Average age 35. In 2006, 35 degrees awarded. *Degree requirements:* For master's, one foreign language, thesis, registration (for some programs). *Entrance requirements:* For master's, minimum GPA of 2.75: MS-TEFL, 3.0: MFA. Additional exam requirements/recommendations for international students: Required—TOEFL (minimum score 550 paper-based; 213 computer-based; 79 iBT), IELTS (minimum score 7), TWE (minimum score 5). *Application deadline:* For fall admission, 7/1 priority date for domestic students; for winter admission, 11/1 priority date for domestic students; for spring admission, 6/1 priority date for domestic students. Applications are processed on a rolling basis. Application fee: $40. Electronic applications accepted. *Expenses: Contact institution. Financial support:* In 2006–07, 4 research assistantships were awarded; career-related internships or fieldwork and scholarships/grants also available. Financial award applicants required to submit FAFSA. *Faculty research:* Action research, state of the art practice in behavioral health services, wraparound approaches to working with youth, learning styles. *Unit head:* Dr. Karen Erickson, Dean, 603-668-2211, E-mail: k.erickson@shnu.edu. *Application contact:* Scott Durand, Director of Graduate Enrollment Services, 603-644-3102 Ext. 3338, Fax: 603-644-3144, E-mail: s.durand@snhu.edu.

State University of New York at Fredonia, Graduate Studies, College of Education, Program in Teaching English to Speakers of Other Languages, Fredonia, NY 14063-1136. Offers MS Ed. *Faculty:* 4 full-time (3 women). *Students:* 9 full-time (all women), 13 part-time (11 women); includes 4 minority (1 American Indian/Alaska Native, 3 Hispanic Americans). In 2006, 15 degrees awarded. *Expenses:* Tuition, state resident: full-time $6,900; part-time $288 per credit hour. Tuition, nonresident: full-time $10,920; part-time $455 per credit hour. Required fees: $1,132; $47 per credit hour. *Unit head:* Dr. Christine Givner, Dean, College of Education, 716-673-3311, E-mail: christine.givner@fredonia.edu.

State University of New York at New Paltz, Graduate School, Faculty of Education, Program in Second Language Education, New Paltz, NY 12561. Offers English as a second language (MS Ed). *Accreditation:* NCATE. Part-time and evening/weekend programs available. *Students:* 61 applicants. In 2006, 15 degrees awarded. *Degree requirements:* For master's, practicum. *Entrance requirements:* For master's, minimum GPA of 3.0, 12 credits of a foreign language. Additional exam requirements/recommendations for international students: Required—TOEFL (minimum score 575 paper-based; 233 computer-based; 80 iBT). *Application deadline:* For fall admission, 4/15 for domestic and international students. Application fee: $50. Electronic applications accepted. *Expenses:* Tuition, state resident: full-time $6,900; part-time $288 per credit hour. Tuition, nonresident: full-time $10,920; part-time $455 per credit hour. *Unit head:* Prof. Vern Todd, Coordinator, 845-257-2818, E-mail: toddv@newpaltz.edu.

State University of New York College at Cortland, Graduate Studies, School of Arts and Sciences, Department of Second Language Education, Cortland, NY 13045. Offers MS Ed. *Accreditation:* NCATE.

Stony Brook University, State University of New York, Graduate School, College of Arts and Sciences, Department of Linguistics, Program in Teaching English to Speakers of Other Languages, Stony Brook, NY 11794. Offers foreign languages (DA), including teaching English to speakers of other languages; teaching English to speakers of other languages (MA). *Accreditation:* NCATE. *Students:* 19 full-time (all women), 28 part-time (25 women); includes 7 minority (2 Asian Americans or Pacific Islanders, 5 Hispanic Americans), 1 international. Average age 30. 48 applicants, 71% accepted. In 2006, 18 degrees awarded. *Application deadline:* For fall admission, 1/15 for domestic students. Application fee: $60. *Expenses:* Tuition, state resident: full-time $6,900; part-time $288 per credit. Tuition, nonresident: full-time $10,920; part-time $455 per credit. *Financial support:* Fellowships, research assistantships, teaching assistantships available. *Application contact:* Dr. Frank Anshen, Director, 631-632-7776, Fax: 631-632-9789, E-mail: fank.anshen@stonybrook.edu.

Teachers College Columbia University, Graduate Faculty of Education, Department of Arts and Humanities, Program in Teaching English to Speakers of Other Languages, New York, NY 10027-6696. Offers Ed M, MA, Ed D. *Accreditation:* NCATE. Part-time programs available. *Faculty:* 16 part-time/adjunct. *Students:* 23 full-time (17 women), 177 part-time (139 women); includes 41 minority (4 African Americans, 32 Asian Americans or Pacific Islanders, 5 Hispanic Americans), 48 international. Average age 30. 180 applicants, 49% accepted, 38 enrolled. In 2006, 65 degrees awarded. *Degree requirements:* For doctorate, thesis/dissertation. *Entrance requirements:* For doctorate, MA in teaching English to speakers of other languages. Additional exam requirements/recommendations for international students: Required—TOEFL. *Application deadline:* For fall admission, 2/1 priority date for domestic students. Application fee: $65. *Expenses:* Tuition: Full-time $23,400; part-time $975 per credit. Required fees: $320 per term. *Financial support:* Career-related internships or fieldwork, Federal Work-Study, institutionally sponsored loans, and tuition waivers (full and partial) available. Support available to part-time students. Financial award application deadline: 2/1. *Faculty research:* Classroom-centered research, electronic media, K–12 English as a second language, second language acquisition. *Application contact:* Mark E. Stearns, Associate Director of Admission, 212-678-3710, Fax: 212-678-4171.

Temple University, Graduate School, College of Education, Department of Curriculum, Instruction, and Technology in Education, Philadelphia, PA 19122-6096. Offers applied behavioral analysis (MS Ed); career and technical education (MS Ed); early childhood education and elementary education (MS Ed); English education (MS Ed); language arts education (Ed D); math/science education (Ed D); mathematics education (MS Ed); science education (MS Ed); second and foreign language education (MS Ed); special education (MS Ed); teaching English as a second language (MS Ed). Part-time and evening/weekend programs available. *Faculty:* 31 full-time (14 women). *Students:* 96 full-time (71 women), 482 part-time (336 women); includes 109 minority (67 African Americans, 3 American Indian/Alaska Native, 23 Asian Americans or Pacific Islanders, 16 Hispanic Americans), 28 international. 308 applicants, 64% accepted, 116 enrolled. In 2006, 225 master's, 21 doctorates awarded. Terminal master's awarded for partial completion of doctoral program. *Degree requirements:* For master's, thesis or alternative; for doctorate, thesis/dissertation. *Entrance requirements:* For master's and doctorate, GRE General Test or MAT, minimum GPA of 3.0. Additional exam requirements/recommendations for international students: Required—TOEFL (minimum score 550 paper-based; 213 computer-based; 79 iBT). *Application deadline:* For fall admission, 4/1 for domestic students, 12/15 for international students; for spring admission, 10/1 for domestic students, 8/1 for international students. Application fee: $50. Electronic applications accepted. *Expenses:* Tuition, state resident: full-time $12,264; part-time $511 per credit. Tuition, nonresident: full-time $17,904; part-time $746 per credit. Required fees: $84 per course. Tuition and fees vary according to program. *Financial support:* Fellowships, research assistantships with full tuition reimbursements, teaching assistantships with full tuition reimbursements available. Financial award application deadline: 1/15; financial award applicants required to submit FAFSA. *Faculty research:* School improvement, problem solving, literacy, language development. *Unit head:* Dr. Thomas Walker, Chair, 215-204-2117, Fax: 215-204-1414, E-mail: tjwalker@temple.edu.

Texas A&M University–Kingsville, College of Graduate Studies, College of Education, Department of Education, Program in English as a Second Language, Kingsville, TX 78363. Offers M Ed. *Degree requirements:* For master's, comprehensive exam. *Entrance requirements:* For master's, GRE General Test, MAT, minimum GPA of 3.0.

Trevecca Nazarene University, Graduate Division, School of Education, Major in English Language Learners (PreK-12), Nashville, TN 37210-2877. Offers M Ed. Part-time and evening/weekend programs available. *Students:* 15 full-time (11 women); includes 3 minority (1 African American, 2 Hispanic Americans). In 2006, 4 degrees awarded. *Degree requirements:* For master's, exit assessment. *Entrance requirements:* For master's, GRE General Test, MAT, minimum GPA of 2.7, 2 reference forms. Additional exam requirements/recommendations for international students: Required—TOEFL (minimum score 500 paper-based; 173 computer-based). *Application deadline:* Applications are processed on a rolling basis. Application fee: $25. *Expenses: Contact institution.* Tuition and fees vary according to degree level and program. *Financial support:* Applicants required to submit FAFSA. *Application contact:* Admissions Office, 615-248-1201, Fax: 615-248-1597, E-mail: admissions_ged@trevecca.edu.

Trinity (Washington) University, School of Education, Washington, DC 20017-1094. Offers democracy, diversity, and social justice (M Ed); early childhood (MAT); educational administration (MSA); elementary education (MAT); English as a second language (M Ed, MAT); literacy and reading education (M Ed); school counseling (MA); secondary education (MAT), including English, math, science, social studies; special education (MAT). *Accreditation:* NCATE. Part-time and evening/weekend programs available. *Degree requirements:* For master's, thesis (for some programs), capstone project(s). *Entrance requirements:* For master's, PRAXIS I, minimum GPA of 2.8. Additional exam requirements/recommendations for international students: Required—TOEFL (minimum score 550 paper-based; 213 computer-based). *Faculty research:* Technology, literacy, special education, organizations, inclusion models.

Trinity Western University, Program in Teaching English as a Second or Other Language (TESOL), Langley, BC V2Y 1Y1, Canada. Offers MA. *Degree requirements:* For master's, project. *Entrance requirements:* For master's, minimum GPA of 3.0. Additional exam requirements/recommendations for international students: Required—TOEFL (minimum score 600 paper-based; 250 computer-based).

Universidad del Este, Graduate School, Carolina, PR 00983. Offers accounting (MBA); administration (M Ed); criminal justice and criminology (MA); education (M Ed); elementary education (M Ed); human resources (MBA); management (MBA); social work (MA); teaching English (M Ed); teaching Spanish (M Ed).

Universidad del Turabo, Graduate Programs, Programs in Education, Program in Teaching English as a Second Language, Gurabo, PR 00778-3030. Offers MA. *Entrance requirements:* For master's, GRE, EXADEP, interview.

University at Buffalo, the State University of New York, Graduate School, Graduate School of Education, Department of Learning and Instruction, Buffalo, NY 14260. Offers adolescence education (Certificate); biology (Ed M); chemistry (Ed M); childhood education (Ed M); early childhood and childhood education with bilingual extension (Ed M); early childhood education (Ed M); earth science (Ed M); elementary education (Ed D, PhD); English (Ed M); English education (PhD); English for speakers of other languages (Ed M); foreign and second language education (PhD); French (Ed M); general education (Ed M); German (Ed M); Italian (Ed M); Japanese (Ed M); Latin (Ed M); literary specialist (Ed M); mathematics (Ed M); mathematics education (PhD); mentoring teachers (Certificate); music education (Ed M, Certificate); physics (Ed M); reading education (PhD); Russian (Ed M); school administrator and supervisor (Certificate); science education (PhD); social studies (Ed M); Spanish (Ed M); special education (PhD); teaching and leading for diversity (Certificate); teaching English to speakers of other languages (Ed M). Part-time and evening/weekend programs available. Postbaccalaureate distance learning degree programs offered (no on-campus study). *Faculty:* 30 full-time (20 women), 53 part-time/adjunct (38 women). *Students:* 368 full-time (269 women), 297 part-time (226 women); includes 50 minority (15 African Americans, 2 American Indian/Alaska Native, 14 Asian Americans or Pacific Islanders, 19 Hispanic Americans), 66 international. Average age 31. 638 applicants, 75% accepted, 298 enrolled. In 2006, 248 master's, 18 doctorates, 48 other advanced degrees awarded. Terminal master's awarded for partial completion of doctoral program. *Degree requirements:* For master's, comprehensive exam, registration; for doctorate, thesis/dissertation, research analysis exam, research experience component. *Entrance requirements:* For doctorate, GRE General Test or MAT, interview, writing sample, letters of recommendation. Additional exam requirements/recommendations for international students: Required—TOEFL (minimum score 600 paper-based; 250 computer-based). *Application deadline:* For fall admission, 2/1 priority date for domestic and international students; for spring admission, 11/15 priority date for domestic students, 10/1 for international students. Applications are processed on a rolling basis. Application fee: $50. Electronic applications accepted. *Financial support:* In 2006–07, 70 students received support, including 6 fellowships with full tuition reimbursements available (averaging $10,000 per year), 16 research assistantships with full tuition reimbursements available (averaging $9,000 per year), teaching assistantships with full tuition reimbursements available (averaging $9,000 per year); career-related internships or fieldwork, Federal Work-Study, institutionally sponsored loans, scholarships/grants, tuition waivers (partial), and unspecified assistantships also available. Financial award application deadline: 2/28; financial award applicants required to submit FAFSA. *Faculty research:* Science assessment, state-level testing, early learning, literacy, second language acquisition. Total annual research expenditures: $432,366. *Unit head:* Dr. Maria E. Runfola, Chair, 716-645-2455, Fax: 716-645-3161. *Application contact:* Barbara Belz, Admissions Secretary, 716-645-2110 Ext. 1159, Fax: 716-645-3161, E-mail: belz@buffalo.edu.

The University of Alabama, Graduate School, College of Arts and Sciences, Department of English, Tuscaloosa, AL 35487. Offers composition and rhetoric (PhD); creative writing (MFA), including fiction, poetry; literature (MA, PhD); rhetoric and composition (MA); teaching English as a second language (MATESOL). *Faculty:* 25 full-time (10 women). *Students:* 53 full-time (31 women), 78 part-time (44 women); includes 14 minority (10 African Americans, 2 American Indian/Alaska Native, 1 Asian American or Pacific Islander, 1 Hispanic American), 4 international. Average age 28. 242 applicants, 25% accepted, 43 enrolled. In 2006, 32 master's, 8 doctorates awarded. *Median time to degree:* Of those who began their doctoral program in fall 1998, 100% received their degree in 8 years or less. *Degree requirements:* For master's, one foreign language, thesis (for some programs), comprehensive exam, registration; for doctorate, 2 foreign languages, thesis/dissertation, comprehensive exam, registration; for degree. *Entrance requirements:* For master's and doctorate, GRE, minimum GPA of 3.0, critical writing sample. Additional exam requirements/recommendations for international students: Required—TOEFL. *Application deadline:* For fall admission, 1/1 priority date for domestic students, 2/1 for international students. Electronic applications accepted. *Financial support:* In 2006–07, 6 fellowships with full tuition reimbursements (averaging $15,000 per year), 106 teaching assistantships with full tuition reimbursements (averaging $11,090 per year) were awarded; career-related internships or fieldwork, scholarships/grants, health care benefits, and unspecified assistantships also available. Financial award application deadline: 1/15. *Faculty research:* Critical theory; modern, Renaissance, and African-American literature. *Unit head:* Dr. Catherine E. Davies, Director of Graduate Studies, 205-348-8499, E-mail: cdavies@bama.ua.edu.

English as a Second Language

The University of Alabama in Huntsville, School of Graduate Studies, College of Liberal Arts, Department of English, Huntsville, AL 35899. Offers English (MA); teaching of English to speakers of other languages (Certificate); technical communications (Certificate). Part-time and evening/weekend programs available. *Faculty:* 12 full-time (5 women), 1 (woman) part-time/adjunct. *Students:* 18 full-time (17 women), 38 part-time (27 women); includes 4 minority (all African Americans), 1 international. Average age 34. 20 applicants, 100% accepted, 18 enrolled. In 2006, 23 master's, 17 other advanced degrees awarded. *Degree requirements:* For master's, one foreign language, thesis or alternative, oral and written exams, comprehensive exam, registration. *Entrance requirements:* For master's, GRE General Test, minimum GPA of 3.0. Additional exam requirements/recommendations for international students: Required—TOEFL (minimum score 500 paper-based; 173 computer-based). *Application deadline:* For fall admission, 5/30 priority date for domestic students, 2/28 priority date for international students; for spring admission, 10/10 priority date for domestic students, 7/10 priority date for international students. Applications are processed on a rolling basis. Application fee: $40. *Expenses:* Tuition, state resident: full-time $6,072; part-time $253 per credit hour. Tuition, nonresident: full-time $12,476; part-time $519 per credit hour. *Financial support:* In 2006–07, 7 students received support, including 4 teaching assistantships with full and partial tuition reimbursements available (averaging $8,460 per year); fellowships with full and partial tuition reimbursements available, research assistantships with full and partial tuition reimbursements available, career-related internships or fieldwork, Federal Work-Study, institutionally sponsored loans, scholarships/grants, health care benefits, and unspecified assistantships also available. Support available to part-time students. Financial award application deadline: 4/1; financial award applicants required to submit FAFSA. *Faculty research:* American and British literature, linguistics, technical writing, women's studies, rhetoric. *Unit head:* Dr. Rose Norman, Chair, 256-824-6320, Fax: 256-824-6949.

University of Alberta, Faculty of Graduate Studies and Research, Department of Educational Psychology, Edmonton, AB T6G 2E1, Canada. Offers counseling psychology (M Ed, PhD); educational psychology (M Ed, PhD); instructional technology (M Ed); school counseling (M Ed); school psychology (M Ed, PhD); special education (M Ed, PhD); special education-deafness studies (M Ed); teaching English as a second language (M Ed). Part-time programs available. *Faculty:* 34 full-time (14 women), 12 part-time/adjunct (6 women). *Students:* 117 full-time (93 women), 173 part-time (121 women), 15 international. Average age 36. 252 applicants, 34% accepted. In 2006, 30 master's, 10 doctorates awarded. *Degree requirements:* For master's, thesis optional; for doctorate, thesis/dissertation, comprehensive exam. *Entrance requirements:* For master's and doctorate, minimum GPA of 3.0. Additional exam requirements/recommendations for international students: Required—TOEFL. *Application deadline:* For fall admission, 2/1 priority date for domestic and international students. Applications are processed on a rolling basis. *Financial support:* In 2006–07, 10 fellowships with full tuition reimbursements (averaging $16,120 per year), 36 research assistantships with full tuition reimbursements (averaging $12,614 per year), 46 teaching assistantships with full tuition reimbursements (averaging $5,462 per year) were awarded; career-related internships or fieldwork and scholarships/grants also available. *Faculty research:* Human learning, development and assessment. *Unit head:* Dr. Linda M. McDonald, Chair, 780-492-1149, Fax: 780-492-1318, E-mail: linda.mcdonald@ualberta.ca. *Application contact:* Judy Maynes, Information Contact, 780-492-1149, Fax: 780-492-1318, E-mail: edpygrad@ualberta.ca.

The University of Arizona, Graduate College, College of Humanities, Department of English, English Language/Linguistics Program, Tucson, AZ 85721. Offers ESL (MA). Part-time programs available. *Degree requirements:* For master's, one foreign language, comprehensive exam. *Entrance requirements:* For master's, GRE General Test, foreign language, sample of written work, teaching experience. Additional exam requirements/recommendations for international students: Required—TOEFL (minimum score 600 paper-based; 250 computer-based). *Faculty research:* First and second language acquisition, writing in ESL, sociolinguistics of second language learning, linguistic universals.

The University of Arizona, Graduate College, Graduate Interdisciplinary Programs, Graduate Interdisciplinary Program in Second Language Acquisition and Teaching, Tucson, AZ 85721. Offers PhD. *Degree requirements:* For doctorate, one foreign language, thesis/dissertation, comprehensive exam, registration. *Entrance requirements:* For doctorate, GRE, master's degree. Additional exam requirements/recommendations for international students: Required—TOEFL; Recommended—TWE.

The University of British Columbia, Faculty of Graduate Studies, Faculty of Education, Program in Language and Literacy Education, Vancouver, BC V6T 1Z1, Canada. Offers library education (M Ed, MA, PhD); literacy education (M Ed, MA, PhD); modern language education (M Ed, MA, PhD); teaching English as a second language (M Ed, MA, PhD). Part-time and evening/weekend programs available. *Faculty:* 27 full-time (14 women). *Students:* 127 (102 women). 80 applicants, 73% accepted, 42 enrolled. In 2006, 28 master's, 2 doctorates awarded. *Degree requirements:* For master's, thesis (MA); for doctorate, thesis/dissertation. *Entrance requirements:* For master's and doctorate, minimum B+ average in last 2 years with minimum 2 courses at A standing. Additional exam requirements/recommendations for international students: Required—TOEFL (minimum score 550 paper-based; 213 computer-based), TWE (minimum score 4.5). *Application deadline:* For fall admission, 2/1 priority date for domestic students, 12/15 for international students; for spring admission, 8/1 for domestic students. Applications are processed on a rolling basis. Application fee: $90 Canadian dollars ($150 Canadian dollars for international students). Electronic applications accepted. *Financial support:* In 2006–07, fellowships with partial tuition reimbursements (averaging $16,000 per year), research assistantships (averaging $4,000 per year), teaching assistantships (averaging $5,344 per year) were awarded; institutionally sponsored loans, scholarships/grants, tuition waivers (full and partial), and unspecified assistantships also available. *Faculty research:* Language and literacy development, second language acquisition, Asia Pacific language curriculum, children's literature, whole language instruction. Total annual research expenditures: $500,000. *Unit head:* Dr. Geoff Williams, Head, 604-827-5785, Fax: 604-822-3154, E-mail: lled.educ@ubc.ca. *Application contact:* Graduate Secretary, 604-822-8259, Fax: 604-822-3154, E-mail: lled.educ@ubc.ca.

University of Calgary, Faculty of Graduate Studies, Faculty of Education, Graduate Division of Educational Research, Calgary, AB T2N 1N4, Canada. Offers community rehabilitation and disability studies (M Ed, M Sc, Ed D, PhD, Graduate Certificate, Graduate Diploma); curriculum, teaching and learning (M Ed, M Sc, MA, Ed D, PhD, Graduate Certificate, Graduate Diploma); educational contexts (M Ed, MA, Ed D, PhD, Graduate Certificate, Graduate Diploma); educational leadership (M Ed, MA, Ed D, PhD, Graduate Certificate, Graduate Diploma); educational technology (M Ed, M Sc, MA, Ed D, PhD, Graduate Certificate, Graduate Diploma); gifted education (M Sc, MA, Ed D, PhD, Graduate Certificate, Graduate Diploma); higher education administration (Ed D); interpretive studies in education (M Ed, M Sc, MA, Ed D, PhD, Graduate Certificate, Graduate Diploma); second language teaching (M Ed, Ed D, PhD, Graduate Certificate, Graduate Diploma); teaching English as a second language (M Ed, M Sc, MA, Ed D, PhD, Graduate Certificate, Graduate Diploma); workplace and adult learning (M Ed, MA, Ed D, PhD, Graduate Certificate, Graduate Diploma). Ed D in both higher education administration and educational leadership offered via distance delivery. Part-time and evening/weekend programs available. Postbaccalaureate distance learning degree programs offered (minimal on-campus study). *Faculty:* 44 full-time, 52 part-time/adjunct. *Students:* 488 full-time, 550 part-time. 400 applicants, 50% accepted. In 2006, 102 master's, 18 doctorates awarded. *Degree requirements:* For master's, thesis (for some programs); for doctorate, thesis/dissertation, candidacy exam. *Entrance requirements:* For master's, minimum GPA of 3.0, 3 letters of reference; for doctorate, minimum GPA of 3.5, 3 letters of reference; for other advanced degree, minimum GPA of 3.0. Additional exam requirements/recommendations for international students: Required—TOEFL, IELTS. *Application deadline:* For fall admission, 2/15 for domestic students, 2/5 for international students; for winter admission, 6/15 for domestic and international students. Application fee: $100. Electronic applications accepted. *Financial support:* In 2006–07, research assistantships (averaging $3,920 per year); teaching assistantships, career-related internships or fieldwork, scholarships/grants, and unspecified assistantships also available. Financial award application deadline: 2/1. *Faculty research:* Curriculum, leadership, technology, contexts, gifted, second language teaching, work place and adult learning. *Unit head:* Dr. Charles F. Webber, Associate Dean, 403-220-5675, Fax: 403-282-3005, E-mail: cwebber@ucalgary.ca. *Application contact:* Patricia A. Brown, Program Officer, Graduate Division of Educational Research, 403-220-3178, Fax: 403-282-3005, E-mail: brownp@ucalgary.ca.

University of California, Los Angeles, Graduate Division, College of Letters and Science, Department of Applied Linguistics and Teaching English as a Second Language, Los Angeles, CA 90095. Offers MA. *Degree requirements:* For master's, thesis. *Entrance requirements:* For master's, GRE General Test, minimum GPA of 3.0, sample of research writing. Electronic applications accepted.

University of Central Florida, College of Arts and Humanities, Department of Modern Languages and Literatures, Program in Teaching English to Speakers of Other Languages, Orlando, FL 32816. Offers MA, Certificate. *Accreditation:* NCATE. Part-time and evening/weekend programs available. *Students:* 16 full-time (14 women), 27 part-time (22 women); includes 14 minority (1 African American, 2 Asian Americans or Pacific Islanders, 11 Hispanic Americans), 7 international. Average age 38. In 2006, 31 master's, 11 other advanced degrees awarded. *Degree requirements:* For master's, thesis or alternative, comprehensive exam. *Entrance requirements:* For master's, GRE General Test, minimum GPA of 3.0 in last 60 hours. Additional exam requirements/recommendations for international students: Required—TOEFL. *Application deadline:* For fall admission, 6/15 for domestic students; for spring admission, 11/1 for domestic students. Application fee: $30. Electronic applications accepted. *Expenses:* Tuition, state resident: full-time $6,167; part-time $257 per credit hour. Tuition, nonresident: full-time $22,790; part-time $950 per credit hour. *Financial support:* In 2006–07, 1 fellowship with partial tuition reimbursement (averaging $5,000 per year), 2 research assistantships with partial tuition reimbursements (averaging $4,500 per year), 1 teaching assistantship with partial tuition reimbursement (averaging $6,000 per year) were awarded; career-related internships or fieldwork, Federal Work-Study, institutionally sponsored loans, tuition waivers (partial), and unspecified assistantships also available. Financial award application deadline: 3/1; financial award applicants required to submit FAFSA. *Unit head:* Dr. Keith Folse, Coordinator, 407-823-4555, E-mail: kfolse@mail.ucf.edu.

University of Central Missouri, The Graduate School, College of Arts, Humanities and Social Sciences, Department of English and Philosophy, Warrensburg, MO 64093. Offers English (MA); teaching English as a second language (MA). Part-time programs available. *Faculty:* 24 full-time (8 women). *Students:* 10 full-time (7 women), 40 part-time (32 women); includes 4 minority (all Asian Americans or Pacific Islanders), 7 international. Average age 31. 18 applicants, 83% accepted, 11 enrolled. In 2006, 16 degrees awarded. *Degree requirements:* For master's, comprehensive exam. *Entrance requirements:* For master's, minimum GPA of 2.75 overall and in major, 18 hours of course work in English. Additional exam requirements/recommendations for international students: Required—TOEFL (minimum score 500 paper-based; 173 computer-based). *Application deadline:* For fall admission, 6/1 priority date for domestic students, 5/1 priority date for international students; for spring admission, 10/1 priority date for domestic students, 10/1 for international students. Applications are processed on a rolling basis. Application fee: $30 ($50 for international students). *Expenses:* Tuition, state resident: full-time $5,448; part-time $227 per credit hour. Tuition, nonresident: full-time $10,896; part-time $454 per credit hour. Required fees: $336; $14 per credit hour. *Financial support:* In 2006–07, 12 students received support; teaching assistantships with full and partial tuition reimbursements available, Federal Work-Study, scholarships/grants, unspecified assistantships, and administrative and laboratory assistantships available. Support available to part-time students. Financial award application deadline: 3/1; financial award applicants required to submit FAFSA. *Faculty research:* Use of virtual environments as distance learning sites; culture studies: Jane Austin's world, original poetry and fiction; literary analysis: Shakespeare's plays, application of descriptive linguistics to teaching English language learners. *Unit head:* Dr. Cheryl Eason, Chair, 660-543-4425, Fax: 660-543-8544, E-mail: eason@ucmo.edu.

University of Central Oklahoma, College of Graduate Studies and Research, College of Liberal Arts, Department of English, Edmond, OK 73034-5209. Offers composition skills (MA); contemporary literature (MA); creative writing (MA); teaching English as a second language (MA); traditional studies (MA). Part-time programs available. *Degree requirements:* For master's, one foreign language. *Entrance requirements:* For master's, 24 hours of course work in English language and literature. Additional exam requirements/recommendations for international students: Required—TOEFL (minimum score 550 paper-based; 213 computer-based). Electronic applications accepted. *Faculty research:* John Milton, Harriet Beecher Stowe.

University of Cincinnati, Division of Research and Advanced Studies, College of Education, Criminal Justice, and Human Services, Division of Teacher Education, Program in Teaching English as a Second Language, Cincinnati, OH 45221. Offers M Ed, Ed D, Certificate. *Entrance requirements:* For master's and doctorate, GRE General Test. Additional exam requirements/recommendations for international students: Required—TOEFL (minimum score 550 paper-based; 213 computer-based), TWE (minimum score 5), Test of Spoken English 50. Application fee: $40. *Financial support:* Scholarships/grants and unspecified assistantships available. Support available to part-time students. *Application contact:* Dr. Gulbahar Beckett, Chair, 513-556-3590, Fax: 513-556-1581, E-mail: gulbahar.beckett@uc.edu.

University of Colorado at Denver and Health Sciences Center, College of Liberal Arts and Sciences, Department of English, Denver, CO 80217-3364. Offers applied linguistics (MA); English studies (MA); literature (MA); teaching English to speakers of other languages (Certificate); teaching of writing (MA). Part-time and evening/weekend programs available. *Faculty:* 31 full-time (20 women). *Students:* 3 full-time (1 woman), 60 part-time (40 women); includes 7 minority (4 Asian Americans or Pacific Islanders, 3 Hispanic Americans), 1 international. Average age 32. 33 applicants, 61% accepted, 14 enrolled. In 2006, 22 degrees awarded. *Degree requirements:* For master's, thesis optional. *Entrance requirements:* For master's, GRE General Test, minimum GPA of 3.0. Additional exam requirements/recommendations for international students: Required—TOEFL (minimum score 550 paper-based). *Application deadline:* For fall admission, 5/25 for domestic students; for spring admission, 10/25 for domestic students. Applications are processed on a rolling basis. Application fee: $50 ($75 for international students). Electronic applications accepted. *Financial support:* Research assistantships, teaching assistantships, Federal Work-Study available. Financial award application deadline: 4/1; financial award applicants required to submit FAFSA. *Unit head:* Prof. Nancy Ciccone, Chair, 303-556-8395, Fax: 303-556-2959, E-mail: nancy.ciccone@cudenver.edu. *Application contact:* Prof. Ian Ying, Program Advisor, 303-556-6728, Fax: 303-556-2959, E-mail: hongguang.ying@cudenver.edu.

University of Delaware, College of Human Services, Education and Public Policy, School of Education, Newark, DE 19716. Offers curriculum and instruction (M Ed); education (PhD); educational leadership (M Ed, Ed D); exceptional children and youth (M Ed); instruction (MI); school counseling (M Ed); school psychology (MA); teaching English as a second language (TESL) (MA). *Accreditation:* NCATE. Part-time and evening/weekend programs available. Terminal master's awarded for partial completion of doctoral program. *Degree requirements:* For master's, thesis (for some programs), comprehensive exam (for some programs), registration; for doctorate, thesis/dissertation, comprehensive exam (for some programs), registration. *Entrance requirements:* For master's and doctorate, GRE, 3 letters of recommendation. Additional exam requirements/recommendations for international students: Required—TOEFL (minimum score 600 paper-based; 250 computer-based). Electronic applications accepted. *Faculty research:* Teacher education; education policy; educational assessment, measurement, and evaluation; curriculum theory and development; community based education models.

The University of Findlay, Graduate and Professional Studies, College of Liberal Arts, Intensive English Language Program, Findlay, OH 45840-3653. Offers bilingual and multicultural education (MA); teaching English to speakers of other languages (MA). Part-time and evening/weekend programs available. *Faculty:* 3 full-time. *Students:* 25 full-time (24 women),

17 part-time (16 women); includes 1 minority (Asian American or Pacific Islander), 28 international. Average age 35. 19 applicants, 95% accepted, 17 enrolled. In 2006, 14 degrees awarded. *Degree requirements:* For master's, cumulative project. *Entrance requirements:* For master's, minimum undergraduate GPA of 3.0 in last 60 hours of course work, 3 letters of recommendation. Additional exam requirements/recommendations for international students: Required—TOEFL (minimum score 550 paper-based). *Application deadline:* Applications are processed on a rolling basis. Application fee: $25. Electronic applications accepted. *Expenses:* Contact institution. *Financial support:* In 2006–07, 1 student received support, including 1 teaching assistantship with full tuition reimbursement available (averaging $6,000 per year). Financial award application deadline: 4/1; financial award applicants required to submit FAFSA. *Unit head:* Dr. Michael C. Reed, Graduate Director, 419-434-4679, Fax: 419-434-4822, E-mail: reed@findlay.edu. *Application contact:* Heather Riffle, Director, Graduate and Special Programs, 419-434-4640, Fax: 419-434-5517, E-mail: riffle@findlay.edu.

University of Florida, Graduate School, College of Liberal Arts and Sciences, Program in Linguistics, Gainesville, FL 32611. Offers linguistics (MA, PhD); teaching English as a second language (Certificate). *Faculty:* 11 full-time (8 women). *Students:* 46 (33 women); includes 1 minority (Hispanic American) 21 international. In 2006, 8 master's, 6 doctorates awarded. *Degree requirements:* For master's, one foreign language, comprehensive exam; for doctorate, 2 foreign languages, thesis/dissertation, qualifying exam. *Entrance requirements:* For master's and doctorate, GRE General Test, minimum GPA of 3.0. Additional exam requirements/recommendations for international students: Required—TOEFL (minimum score 550 paper-based; 213 computer-based). *Application deadline:* For fall admission, 6/1 priority date for domestic students. Applications are processed on a rolling basis. Application fee: $30. Electronic applications accepted. *Expenses:* Tuition, state resident: full-time $6,827. Tuition, nonresident: full-time $21,951. Required fees: $999. *Financial support:* In 2006–07, 4 research assistantships (averaging $11,797 per year), 8 teaching assistantships with tuition reimbursements (averaging $12,159 per year) were awarded; fellowships with tuition reimbursements, institutionally sponsored loans and unspecified assistantships also available. Financial award application deadline: 1/7. *Faculty research:* Theoretical, applied, and descriptive linguistics. *Unit head:* Dr. Caroline Wiltshire, Interim Director, 352-392-0639 Ext. 224, Fax: 352-392-8480, E-mail: wiltshir@lin.ufl.edu. *Application contact:* Dr. Caroline Wiltshire, Interim Director, 352-392-0639 Ext. 224, Fax: 352-392-8480, E-mail: wiltshir@lin.ufl.edu.

University of Guam, Graduate School and Research, College of Education, Program in Teaching English to Speakers of Other Languages, Mangilao, GU 96923. Offers M Ed. *Degree requirements:* For master's, comprehensive oral and written exams, special project or thesis. *Entrance requirements:* For master's, GRE General Test. Additional exam requirements/recommendations for international students: Required—TOEFL.

University of Hawaii at Manoa, Graduate Division, Colleges of Arts and Sciences, College of Language, Linguistics and Literature, Department of Second Language Studies, Honolulu, HI 96822. Offers English as a second language (MA, Graduate Certificate); second language acquisition (PhD). *Faculty:* 94 full-time (31 women), 1 part-time/adjunct (0 women). *Students:* 112 full-time (79 women), 26 part-time (11 women); includes 8 minority (6 Asian Americans or Pacific Islanders, 2 Hispanic Americans), 21 international. Average age 33. 96 applicants, 58% accepted, 37 enrolled. In 2006, 40 master's, 5 other advanced degrees awarded. *Degree requirements:* For master's, 2 foreign languages, thesis/dissertation; for doctorate, 2 foreign languages, thesis/dissertation, comprehensive exam. *Entrance requirements:* For master's, GRE General Test, minimum GPA of 3.0; for doctorate, GRE General Test, MA, scholarly publications. Additional exam requirements/recommendations for international students: Required—TOEFL (minimum score 600 paper-based; 250 computer-based; 100 iBT). *Application deadline:* For fall admission, 1/15 for domestic and international students; for spring admission, 9/1 for domestic and international students. Applications are processed on a rolling basis. Application fee: $50. *Financial support:* In 2006–07, 48 students received support, including 18 research assistantships (averaging $16,541 per year), 30 teaching assistantships (averaging $13,930 per year); fellowships, career-related internships or fieldwork, Federal Work-Study, institutionally sponsored loans, scholarships/grants, and tuition waivers (full and partial) also available. Financial award application deadline: 2/1; financial award applicants required to submit FAFSA. *Faculty research:* Second language use, second language analysis, second language pedagogy and testing, second language learning, qualitative and quantitative research methods for second languages. Total annual research expenditures: $339,700. *Application contact:* Thomas Hudson, Information Contact, 808-956-6131, Fax: 808-956-2802.

University of Houston, College of Education, Department of Curriculum and Instruction, Houston, TX 77204. Offers art education (M Ed); bilingual education (M Ed); curriculum and instruction (Ed D); early childhood education (M Ed); education of the gifted (M Ed); elementary education (M Ed); mathematics education (M Ed); reading and language arts education (M Ed); science education (M Ed); second language education (M Ed); secondary education (M Ed); social studies education (M Ed); teaching (M Ed). *Accreditation:* NCATE. Part-time and evening/weekend programs available. *Faculty:* 24 full-time (11 women), 16 part-time/adjunct (14 women). *Students:* 134 full-time (102 women), 327 part-time (256 women); includes 142 minority (49 African Americans, 1 American Indian/Alaska Native, 29 Asian Americans or Pacific Islanders, 63 Hispanic Americans), 19 international. Average age 37. 113 applicants, 72% accepted, 61 enrolled. In 2006, 106 master's, 32 doctorates awarded. *Degree requirements:* For master's, comprehensive exam or thesis; for doctorate, thesis/dissertation, comprehensive exam. *Entrance requirements:* For master's, GRE General Test or MAT; for doctorate, GRE General Test, interview. *Application deadline:* For fall admission, 7/3 priority date for domestic students. Applications are processed on a rolling basis. Application fee: $35 ($75 for international students). *Expenses:* Tuition, state resident: full-time $5,429; part-time $226 per credit. Tuition, nonresident: full-time $12,029; part-time $501 per credit. Required fees: $2,454. *Financial support:* In 2006–07, 2 fellowships with full tuition reimbursements (averaging $9,500 per year), 6 research assistantships with full tuition reimbursements (averaging $8,800 per year), 25 teaching assistantships with full tuition reimbursements (averaging $8,800 per year) were awarded; career-related internships or fieldwork, Federal Work-Study, institutionally sponsored loans, scholarships/grants, health care benefits, and unspecified assistantships also available. Support available to part-time students. Financial award application deadline: 3/10. *Faculty research:* Teaching-learning process, instructional technology in schools, teacher education, classroom management, at-risk students. *Unit head:* Dr. Juanita Copley, Chairperson, 713-743-4950, Fax: 713-743-4990, E-mail: ncopley@aol.com.

University of Idaho, College of Graduate Studies, College of Letters, Arts and Social Sciences, Department of English, Program in Teaching English as a Second Language, Moscow, ID 83844-2282. Offers MA. *Students:* 18 (13 women). Average age 29. In 2006, 9 degrees awarded. *Entrance requirements:* For master's, minimum GPA of 2.8. *Application deadline:* For fall admission, 8/1 for domestic students; for spring admission, 12/15 for domestic students. Application fee: $55 ($60 for international students). *Expenses:* Tuition, nonresident: full-time $9,600; part-time $140 per credit. Required fees: $4,740; $227 per credit. *Financial support:* Application deadline: 2/15. *Unit head:* Kurt Olsson, Chair, Department of English, 208-883-6156.

University of Illinois at Chicago, Graduate College, College of Liberal Arts and Sciences, Department of English, Program in Linguistics, Chicago, IL 60607-7128. Offers applied linguistics (teaching English as a second language) (MA). Part-time programs available. *Degree requirements:* For master's, one foreign language, thesis (for some programs), comprehensive exam. *Entrance requirements:* For master's, minimum GPA of 3.0. Additional exam requirements/recommendations for international students: Required—TOEFL. Electronic applications accepted. *Faculty research:* Second language acquisition, methodology of second language teaching, lexicography, language, sex and gender.

University of Illinois at Urbana–Champaign, Graduate College, College of Liberal Arts and Sciences, Division of English as an International Language, Champaign, IL 61820. Offers MA. *Faculty:* 5 full-time (1 woman), 1 part-time/adjunct (0 women). *Students:* 30 full-time (23 women), 24 part-time (19 women); includes 2 minority (both Asian Americans or Pacific Islanders), 31 international. 112 applicants, 51% accepted, 22 enrolled. In 2006, 14 degrees awarded. *Entrance requirements:* For master's, minimum GPA of 3.0. Additional exam requirements/recommendations for international students: Required—TOEFL. *Application deadline:* For fall admission, 1/16 for domestic students. Applications are processed on a rolling basis. Application fee: $50 ($60 for international students). Electronic applications accepted. *Financial support:* In 2006–07, 5 fellowships, 1 research assistantship, 36 teaching assistantships were awarded; tuition waivers (full and partial) also available. Financial award application deadline: 2/15. *Unit head:* Douglas Kibbee, Director, 217-333-1506, Fax: 217-244-3050, E-mail: dkibbee@uiuc.edu. *Application contact:* Lynn Stanke, Secretary, 217-333-1506, Fax: 217-244-3050, E-mail: stanke@uiuc.edu.

University of Manitoba, Faculty of Graduate Studies, Faculty of Education, Department of Curriculum, Teaching and Learning, Winnipeg, MB R3T 2N2, Canada. Offers general curriculum (M Ed); language and literacy (M Ed); post-secondary studies (M Ed); teaching English as a second language (M Ed). *Degree requirements:* For master's, thesis or alternative.

University of Maryland, College Park, Graduate Studies, College of Education, Department of Curriculum and Instruction, College Park, MD 20742. Offers reading (M Ed, MA, PhD, CAGS); secondary education (M Ed, MA, Ed D, PhD, CAGS); teaching English to speakers of other languages (M Ed). *Accreditation:* NCATE. Part-time and evening/weekend programs available. Postbaccalaureate distance learning degree programs offered (no on-campus study). *Faculty:* 52 full-time (32 women), 33 part-time/adjunct (30 women). *Students:* 200 full-time (159 women), 189 part-time (155 women); includes 101 minority (48 African Americans, 30 Asian Americans or Pacific Islanders, 23 Hispanic Americans), 33 international. 258 applicants, 62% accepted, 101 enrolled. In 2006, 118 master's, 14 doctorates awarded. *Median time to degree:* Of those who began their doctoral program in fall 1998, 38% received their degree in 8 years or less. *Degree requirements:* For master's, seminar paper; for doctorate, thesis/dissertation, published paper, oral exam, comprehensive exam. *Entrance requirements:* For master's, GRE General Test or MAT, minimum GPA of 3.0, 3 letters of recommendation; for doctorate, GRE General Test or MAT, minimum undergraduate GPA of 3.0, graduate 3.5; 3 letters of recommendation. *Application deadline:* For fall admission, 1/15 for domestic students, 2/1 for international students; for spring admission, 9/1 for domestic students, 6/1 for international students. Applications are processed on a rolling basis. Application fee: $60. Electronic applications accepted. *Financial support:* In 2006–07, 3 fellowships with full tuition reimbursements (averaging $5,677 per year), 25 research assistantships with tuition reimbursements (averaging $16,943 per year), 53 teaching assistantships with tuition reimbursements (averaging $14,810 per year) were awarded; Federal Work-Study and scholarships/grants also available. Support available to part-time students. Financial award applicants required to submit FAFSA. *Faculty research:* Teacher preparation, curriculum study, in-service education. Total annual research expenditures: $3.3 million. *Unit head:* Dr. Stephen M. Koziol, Chairman, 301-405-3117, Fax: 301-314-9055, E-mail: skoziol@umd.edu. *Application contact:* Dean of Graduate School, 301-405-0358, Fax: 301-314-9305.

University of Massachusetts Boston, Office of Graduate Studies, College of Liberal Arts, Program in Applied Linguistics, Boston, MA 02125-3393. Offers bilingual education (MA); English as a second language (MA); foreign language pedagogy (MA). Part-time and evening/weekend programs available. *Students:* 21 full-time (16 women), 76 part-time (56 women); includes 23 minority (8 African Americans, 4 Asian Americans or Pacific Islanders, 11 Hispanic Americans), 12 international. Average age 36. 57 applicants, 79% accepted, 22 enrolled. In 2006, 44 degrees awarded. *Median time to degree:* Master's–4 years full-time. *Degree requirements:* For master's, one foreign language, comprehensive exam. *Entrance requirements:* For master's, minimum GPA of 2.75. *Application deadline:* For fall admission, 2/1 priority date for domestic students; for spring admission, 10/15 for domestic students. Application fee: $25 ($40 for international students). *Expenses:* Tuition, state resident: full-time $2,590; part-time $301 per credit. Tuition, nonresident: full-time $9,758; part-time $427 per credit. One-time fee: $495 full-time. *Financial support:* In 2006–07, 8 research assistantships with full tuition reimbursements (averaging $13,000 per year), 6 teaching assistantships with full tuition reimbursements (averaging $13,000 per year) were awarded; career-related internships or fieldwork, Federal Work-Study, and unspecified assistantships also available. Support available to part-time students. Financial award application deadline: 3/1; financial award applicants required to submit FAFSA. *Faculty research:* Multicultural theory and curriculum development, foreign language pedagogy, language and culture, applied psycholinguistics, bilingual education. *Unit head:* Dr. Donaldo Macedo, Director, 617-287-5760, E-mail: donalde.macedo@umb.edu. *Application contact:* Peggy Roldan, Graduate Admissions Coordinator, 617-287-6400, Fax: 617-287-6236, E-mail: bos.gadm@dpc.umassp.edu.

University of Miami, Graduate School, School of Education, Department of Teaching and Learning, Program in Elementary Education/TESOL, Coral Gables, FL 33124. Offers MS Ed. *Accreditation:* NCATE. Part-time and evening/weekend programs available. *Students:* 10 full-time (9 women), 8 part-time (all women); includes 3 minority (all Hispanic Americans), 2 international. 9 applicants, 56% accepted, 4 enrolled. In 2006, 7 degrees awarded. *Degree requirements:* For master's, electronic portfolio review. *Entrance requirements:* For master's, GRE General Test. Additional exam requirements/recommendations for international students: Required—TOEFL (minimum score 550 paper-based; 212 computer-based). *Application deadline:* Applications are processed on a rolling basis. Application fee: $50. Electronic applications accepted. *Financial support:* In 2006–07, 12 students received support. Federal Work-Study and tuition waivers (partial) available. Financial award application deadline: 3/1; financial award applicants required to submit FAFSA. *Faculty research:* Mathematics, technology. *Unit head:* Dr. Cory Buxton, Advisor, 305-284-5946, Fax: 305-284-4439, E-mail: cbuxton@miami.edu.

University of Miami, Graduate School, School of Education, Department of Teaching and Learning, Program in Teaching and Learning, Coral Gables, FL 33124. Offers exceptional student education (PhD); mathematics and science education (PhD); reading (PhD); teaching English to speakers of other languages (PhD). Part-time and evening/weekend programs available. *Students:* 25 full-time (20 women), 6 part-time (5 women); includes 11 minority (2 African Americans, 9 Hispanic Americans), 5 international. Average age 38. 23 applicants, 61% accepted, 4 enrolled. In 2006, 3 doctorates awarded. *Median time to degree:* Of those who began their doctoral program in fall 1998, 100% received their degree in 8 years or less. *Degree requirements:* For doctorate, thesis/dissertation. *Entrance requirements:* For doctorate, GRE General Test, GRE Subject Test. Additional exam requirements/recommendations for international students: Required—TOEFL (minimum score 550 paper-based; 212 computer-based). Application fee: $50. Electronic applications accepted. *Financial support:* In 2006–07, 16 research assistantships with full tuition reimbursements (averaging $13,000 per year), 3 teaching assistantships with full tuition reimbursements (averaging $13,000 per year) were awarded; fellowships, tuition waivers (partial) also available. Financial award application deadline: 3/1; financial award applicants required to submit FAFSA. *Faculty research:* Teacher education, multicultural education, technology, second language acquisition.

University of Michigan, Horace H. Rackham School of Graduate Studies, School of Education, Programs in Educational Studies, Ann Arbor, MI 48109. Offers curriculum development (MA); early childhood education (MA, PhD); educational administration and policy (MA, PhD); educational foundation, administration, policy, and research methods (MA); educational foundations and policy (MA, PhD); elementary education (MA-Certification); English education (MA); English language learning in school settings (MA); learning technologies (MA, PhD); literacy, language, and culture (MA, PhD); mathematics education (MA, PhD); research methods (MA); science education (MA, PhD); secondary education (MA-Certification); social studies education (MA); special education (PhD); teaching and teacher education (PhD); MA-Certification; MBA/MA; PhD/MA. Terminal master's awarded for partial completion of doctoral program. *Degree requirements:* For master's, thesis (for some programs); for doctorate, thesis/dissertation, comprehensive exam. *Entrance requirements:* For master's and doctorate, GRE General Test. Additional exam requirements/recommendations for international students:

English as a Second Language

University of Michigan (continued)

Required—TOEFL (minimum score 600 paper-based; 250 computer-based). *Application deadline:* For fall admission, 12/1 priority date for domestic students, 12/1 for international students. Application fee: $60 ($75 for international students). Electronic applications accepted. *Financial support:* Applicants required to submit FAFSA. *Unit head:* Dr. Addison Stone, Chairperson, 734-763-7500, Fax: 734-615-1290, E-mail: addison@umich.edu. *Application contact:* Roberta Perry, Office of Student Services, 734-764-7563, Fax: 734-763-1495, E-mail: ed.grad.admit@umich.edu.

University of Minnesota, Twin Cities Campus, Graduate School, College of Education and Human Development, Department of Curriculum and Instruction, Program in Teaching, Minneapolis, MN 55455-0213. Offers Chinese (M Ed); earth science (M Ed); elementary special education (M Ed); English (M Ed); English as a second language (M Ed); French (M Ed); German (M Ed); Hebrew (M Ed); Japanese (M Ed); life sciences (M Ed); mathematics (M Ed); middle school science (M Ed); science (M Ed); second languages and cultures (M Ed); social studies (M Ed); Spanish (M Ed). *Students:* 324 full-time (230 women), 132 part-time (86 women); includes 44 minority (5 African Americans, 2 American Indian/Alaska Native, 27 Asian Americans or Pacific Islanders, 10 Hispanic Americans), 4 international. Average age 27. 499 applicants, 74% accepted, 327 enrolled. In 2006, 545 degrees awarded. *Expenses:* Tuition, state resident: full-time $9,302; part-time $775 per credit. Tuition, nonresident: full-time $16,400; part-time $1,367 per credit. Full-time tuition and fees vary according to class time, course load, program, reciprocity agreements and student level. *Application contact:* Dr. Mary Bents, Associate Dean, 612-625-6501, Fax: 612-626-1580, E-mail: mbents@tc.umn.edu.

University of Minnesota, Twin Cities Campus, Graduate School, College of Liberal Arts, Institute of Linguistics, English as a Second Language, and Slavic Languages and Literatures (ILES), English as a Second Language Program, Minneapolis, MN 55455-0213. Offers MA. *Faculty:* 3 full-time (1 woman), 5 part-time/adjunct (all women). *Students:* 16 full-time (11 women), 8 part-time (7 women); includes 1 minority (Asian American or Pacific Islander) Average age 34. 25 applicants, 28% accepted, 7 enrolled. In 2006, 9 degrees awarded. *Median time to degree:* Master's–2.6 years full-time. *Degree requirements:* For master's, one foreign language, thesis, comprehensive exam, registration. *Entrance requirements:* For master's, GRE, 3 letters of recommendation. Additional exam requirements/recommendations for international students: Required—TOEFL (minimum score 600 paper-based; 250 computer-based). *Application deadline:* For fall admission, 3/1 for domestic and international students. Application fee: $55 ($75 for international students). Electronic applications accepted. *Expenses:* Tuition, state resident: full-time $9,302; part-time $775 per credit. Tuition, nonresident: full-time $16,400; part-time $1,367 per credit. Full-time tuition and fees vary according to class time, course load, program, reciprocity agreements and student level. *Financial support:* In 2006–07, 5 students received support, including 5 teaching assistantships with partial tuition reimbursements available (averaging $6,000 per year); fellowships, Federal Work-Study, scholarships/grants, health care benefits, and unspecified assistantships also available. Financial award application deadline: 1/15. *Faculty research:* Second language acquisitions, communication strategies, English for specific purposes, literacy, speech act, proymatics in general, language assessment, discourse analysis, research methods. *Unit head:* Dr. Andrew D. Cohen, Professor, 612-624-3806, Fax: 612-624-4579, E-mail: adcohen@umn.edu. *Application contact:* Dr. Anne Lazaraton, Professor, 612-626-9372, Fax: 612-624-4579, E-mail: lazaratn@umn.edu.

University of Nebraska at Omaha, Graduate Studies and Research, College of Arts and Sciences, Department of English, Omaha, NE 68182. Offers advanced writing (Certificate); English (MA); teaching English to speakers of other languages (Certificate); technical communication (Certificate). Part-time and evening/weekend programs available. *Faculty:* 25 full-time (15 women). *Students:* 8 full-time (5 women), 48 part-time (33 women); includes 3 minority (2 African Americans, 1 Hispanic American), 1 international. Average age 33. 31 applicants, 61% accepted, 12 enrolled. In 2006, 12 master's, 16 other advanced degrees awarded. *Degree requirements:* For master's, thesis (for some programs), comprehensive exam. *Entrance requirements:* For master's, minimum GPA of 3.0, statement of purpose, 3 letters of recommendation, writing sample. Additional exam requirements/recommendations for international students: Required—TOEFL (minimum score 600 paper-based; 250 computer-based; 100 iBT). *Application deadline:* For fall admission, 8/1 priority date for domestic students; for spring admission, 12/1 priority date for domestic students. Applications are processed on a rolling basis. Application fee: $45. Electronic applications accepted. *Financial support:* In 2006–07, 34 students received support; fellowships, teaching assistantships with tuition reimbursements available, Federal Work-Study, institutionally sponsored loans, scholarships/grants, tuition waivers (partial), and unspecified assistantships available. Support available to part-time students. Financial award application deadline: 3/1; financial award applicants required to submit FAFSA. *Unit head:* Dr. Susan Maher, Chairperson, 402-554-3636. *Application contact:* Dr. Joan Latchaw, Student Contact, 402-554-3636.

University of Nevada, Las Vegas, Graduate College, College of Education, Department of Curriculum and Instruction, Las Vegas, NV 89154-9900. Offers curriculum and instruction (Ed D, PhD, Ed S); elementary education (M Ed, MS); English education (M Ed, MS); library science (M Ed, MS); literacy education (M Ed, MS); mathematics education (M Ed, MS); multicultural education (M Ed, MS); reading specialist (M Ed, MS); secondary education (M Ed, MS); teacher leadership (M Ed, MS); teaching English as a second language (M Ed, MS); technology integration and leadership (M Ed, MS). *Accreditation:* NCATE. Part-time and evening/weekend programs available. *Faculty:* 40 full-time (19 women), 21 part-time/adjunct (14 women). *Students:* 257 full-time (189 women), 387 part-time (296 women); includes 114 minority (28 African Americans, 5 American Indian/Alaska Native, 34 Asian Americans or Pacific Islanders, 47 Hispanic Americans), 7 international. 261 applicants, 70% accepted, 168 enrolled. In 2006, 231 master's, 5 doctorates awarded. *Degree requirements:* For master's, thesis (for some programs), comprehensive exam (for some programs); for doctorate, thesis/dissertation, oral exam. *Entrance requirements:* For master's, minimum GPA of 3.0; for doctorate, GRE General Test, minimum graduate GPA of 3.0. Additional exam requirements/recommendations for international students: Required—TOEFL (minimum score 550 paper-based; 213 computer-based; 80 iBT). *Application deadline:* For fall admission, 2/15 for domestic and international students; for spring admission, 9/30 for domestic and international students. Application fee: $60 ($75 for international students). Electronic applications accepted. *Financial support:* In 2006–07, 30 research assistantships with partial tuition reimbursements (averaging $10,000 per year), 7 teaching assistantships with partial tuition reimbursements (averaging $12,000 per year) were awarded; career-related internships or fieldwork, Federal Work-Study, institutionally sponsored loans, scholarships/grants, health care benefits, and unspecified assistantships also available. Support available to part-time students. Financial award application deadline: 3/1. *Unit head:* Dr. Greg Levitt, Chair, 702-895-3241. *Application contact:* Graduate College Admissions Evaluator, 702-895-3320, E-mail: gradcollege@unlv.edu.

University of Nevada, Reno, Graduate School, College of Education, Department of Educational Specialties, Reno, NV 89557. Offers educational specialties (MA, MS, PhD, Ed S); literacy studies (M Ed, MA, Ed D, PhD); special education (M Ed); teaching English as a second language (MA). *Students:* 75 full-time (58 women), 188 part-time (161 women); includes 29 minority (2 African Americans, 1 American Indian/Alaska Native, 10 Asian Americans or Pacific Islanders, 16 Hispanic Americans), 20 international. Average age 38. 123 applicants, 82% accepted, 50 enrolled. In 2006, 50 master's, 1 doctorate awarded. *Degree requirements:* For master's, thesis optional; for doctorate, thesis/dissertation, comprehensive exam. *Entrance requirements:* For master's, minimum GPA of 2.75; for doctorate, GRE. Additional exam requirements/recommendations for international students: Required—TOEFL (minimum score 500 paper-based; 173 computer-based). *Application deadline:* For fall admission, 3/1 priority date for domestic students; for spring admission, 10/1 for domestic students. Applications are processed on a rolling basis. Application fee: $60 ($95 for international students). Electronic applications accepted. *Unit head:* Dr. Chris Cheney, Head, 775-784-7853.

The University of North Carolina at Charlotte, Graduate School, College of Education, Program in Teacher Education, Charlotte, NC 28223-0001. Offers art education (K-12) (MAT); dance education (K-12) (MAT); elementary education (K-6) (MAT); English as a second language (K-12) (MAT); foreign language education (K-12) (MAT); general teacher education (MAT); middle grades education (6-9) (MAT); music education (K-12) (MAT); secondary education (9-12) (MAT); special education (K-12) (MAT); theatre education (K-12) (MAT). *Students:* 16 full-time (12 women), 200 part-time (170 women); includes 30 minority (22 African Americans, 2 American Indian/Alaska Native, 2 Asian Americans or Pacific Islanders, 4 Hispanic Americans), 2 international. Average age 33. 74 applicants, 85% accepted, 49 enrolled. In 2006, 43 degrees awarded. *Entrance requirements:* For master's, GRE or MAT. Additional exam requirements/recommendations for international students: Required—TOEFL (minimum score 557 paper-based; 220 computer-based). *Application deadline:* For fall admission, 7/1 for domestic students, 5/1 for international students; for spring admission, 11/1 for domestic students, 10/1 for international students. Applications are processed on a rolling basis. Application fee: $55. Electronic applications accepted. *Expenses:* Tuition, state resident: full-time $2,719; part-time $170 per credit. Tuition, nonresident: full-time $12,926; part-time $808 per credit. Required fees: $1,555. *Financial support:* Fellowships, research assistantships, teaching assistantships, career-related internships or fieldwork, Federal Work-Study, institutionally sponsored loans, scholarships/grants, and unspecified assistantships available. Support available to part-time students. Financial award application deadline: 4/1; financial award applicants required to submit FAFSA. *Unit head:* Dr. Kimberly J. Hartman, Coordinator, 704-687-8883, Fax: 704-687-6430, E-mail: khartman@email.uncc.edu. *Application contact:* Kathy B. Giddings, Director of Graduate Admissions, 704-687-3366, Fax: 704-687-3279, E-mail: gradadm@email.uncc.edu.

The University of North Carolina at Greensboro, Graduate School, School of Education, Department of Curriculum and Instruction, Greensboro, NC 27412-5001. Offers college teaching and adult learning (Certificate); curriculum and instruction (M Ed), including chemistry education, elementary education, English as a second language, French education, instructional technology, mathematics education, middle grades education, reading education, science education, social studies education, Spanish education; curriculum and teaching (PhD), including higher education, teacher education and development; English as a second language (Certificate); higher education (M Ed); supervision (M Ed). *Accreditation:* NCATE. Part-time programs available. *Faculty:* 27 full-time (18 women), 8 part-time/adjunct (3 women). *Students:* 137 full-time (114 women), 231 part-time (195 women); includes 63 minority (52 African Americans, 2 American Indian/Alaska Native, 5 Asian Americans or Pacific Islanders, 4 Hispanic Americans). 146 applicants, 32% accepted. *Degree requirements:* For doctorate, thesis/dissertation. *Entrance requirements:* For master's and doctorate, GRE General Test. Additional exam requirements/recommendations for international students: Required—TOEFL. Application fee: $45. Electronic applications accepted. *Expenses:* Tuition, state resident: full-time $2,692. Tuition, nonresident: full-time $13,742. *Financial support:* Fellowships, research assistantships with full tuition reimbursements, teaching assistantships with full tuition reimbursements, career-related internships or fieldwork, Federal Work-Study, scholarships/grants, traineeships, and unspecified assistantships available. Support available to part-time students. *Faculty research:* Community college literacy program, middle school mathematics/computer mathematics. *Unit head:* Dr. Sam Miller, Chair, 336-334-3445, Fax: 336-334-4120, E-mail: sdmille2@uncg.edu. *Application contact:* Michelle Harkleroad, Director of Graduate Admissions, 336-334-4884, Fax: 336-334-4424, E-mail: mbharkle@uncg.edu.

University of Northern Iowa, Graduate College, College of Humanities and Fine Arts, Department of English Language and Literature, Cedar Falls, IA 50614. Offers English (MA); teaching English to speakers of other languages (MA). Part-time and evening/weekend programs available. *Faculty:* 28 full-time (11 women). *Students:* 40 full-time (27 women), 18 part-time (16 women); includes 5 minority (3 African Americans, 2 Asian Americans or Pacific Islanders), 18 international. 38 applicants, 79% accepted, 11 enrolled. In 2006, 26 degrees awarded. *Degree requirements:* For master's, one foreign language, comprehensive exam. *Entrance requirements:* Additional exam requirements/recommendations for international students: Required—TOEFL (minimum score 600 paper-based; 250 computer-based; 100 iBT). *Application deadline:* For fall admission, 8/1 priority date for domestic students. Applications are processed on a rolling basis. Application fee: $30 ($50 for international students). Electronic applications accepted. *Expenses:* Tuition, state resident: full-time $5,936. Tuition, nonresident: full-time $14,074. *Financial support:* Career-related internships or fieldwork, Federal Work-Study, scholarships/grants, and tuition waivers (full and partial) available. Support available to part-time students. Financial award application deadline: 2/1. *Unit head:* Dr. Jeffrey S. Copeland, Head, 319-273-3855, Fax: 319-273-5807, E-mail: jeffrey.copeland@uni.edu.

University of Northern Iowa, Graduate College, College of Humanities and Fine Arts, Department of Modern Languages, Program in French, Cedar Falls, IA 50614. Offers French (MA); teaching English to speakers of other languages/French (MA). Part-time and evening/weekend programs available. *Students:* 4 full-time (2 women), 7 part-time (all women), 4 international. 3 applicants, 100% accepted, 1 enrolled. In 2006, 6 degrees awarded. *Degree requirements:* For master's, one foreign language, thesis or alternative, comprehensive exam. *Entrance requirements:* Additional exam requirements/recommendations for international students: Required—TOEFL (minimum score 500 paper-based; 180 computer-based; 61 iBT). *Application deadline:* For fall admission, 8/1 priority date for domestic students. Applications are processed on a rolling basis. Application fee: $30 ($50 for international students). Electronic applications accepted. *Expenses:* Tuition, state resident: full-time $5,936. Tuition, nonresident: full-time $14,074. *Financial support:* Career-related internships or fieldwork, Federal Work-Study, and tuition waivers (full and partial) available. Support available to part-time students. Financial award application deadline: 2/1. *Unit head:* Dr. Anne Lair, Coordinator, 319-273-2183, Fax: 319-273-2848, E-mail: anne.lair@uni.edu.

University of Northern Iowa, Graduate College, College of Humanities and Fine Arts, Department of Modern Languages, Program in German, Cedar Falls, IA 50614. Offers German (MA); teaching English to speakers of other languages/German (MA). Part-time and evening/weekend programs available. *Students:* 6 full-time (all women), 1 part-time, 6 international. 1 applicant, 100% accepted, 1 enrolled. In 2006, 4 degrees awarded. *Degree requirements:* For master's, one foreign language, thesis or alternative, comprehensive exam. *Entrance requirements:* Additional exam requirements/recommendations for international students: Required—TOEFL (minimum score 500 paper-based; 180 computer-based; 61 iBT). *Application deadline:* For fall admission, 8/1 priority date for domestic students. Applications are processed on a rolling basis. Application fee: $30 ($50 for international students). *Expenses:* Tuition, state resident: full-time $5,936. Tuition, nonresident: full-time $14,074. *Financial support:* Career-related internships or fieldwork, Federal Work-Study, and tuition waivers (full and partial) available. Support available to part-time students. Financial award application deadline: 2/1.

University of Northern Iowa, Graduate College, College of Humanities and Fine Arts, Department of Modern Languages, Program in Spanish, Cedar Falls, IA 50614. Offers Spanish (MA); teaching English to speakers of other languages/Spanish (MA). Part-time and evening/weekend programs available. *Students:* 12 full-time (8 women), 7 part-time (all women); includes 2 minority (1 African American, 1 Hispanic American), 5 international. 10 applicants, 100% accepted, 6 enrolled. In 2006, 18 degrees awarded. *Degree requirements:* For master's, one foreign language, thesis or alternative, comprehensive exam. *Entrance requirements:* Additional exam requirements/recommendations for international students: Required—TOEFL (minimum score 500 paper-based; 180 computer-based; 61 iBT). *Application deadline:* For fall admission, 8/1 priority date for domestic students. Applications are processed on a rolling basis. Application fee: $30 ($50 for international students). Electronic applications accepted. *Expenses:* Tuition, state resident: full-time $5,936. Tuition, nonresident: full-time $14,074. *Financial support:* Career-related internships or fieldwork, Federal Work-Study, and tuition waivers (full and partial) available. Support available to part-time students. Financial award application deadline: 2/1. *Unit head:* Dr. Juan Carlos, Coordinator, 319-273-2200, Fax: 319-273-2848.

University of Northern Virginia, Graduate Programs, Manassas, VA 20109. Offers accountancy (MS); accounting (MBA); business administration (DBA); computer science (MS); counseling education (M Ed); early childhood education (M Ed); educational communication and instructional technology (M Ed); educational leadership (M Ed); finance (MBA); information systems technology (MS); management (MBA); marketing (MBA); project management (MBA); public administration (MPA); teaching English to speakers of other languages (M Ed). Part-time and evening/weekend programs available. Postbaccalaureate distance learning degree programs offered (no on-campus study). *Degree requirements:* For doctorate, thesis/dissertation, comprehensive exam, registration. *Entrance requirements:* Additional exam requirements/recommendations for international students: Required—TOEFL (minimum score 550 paper-based; 230 computer-based), IELTS (minimum score 6). Electronic applications accepted.

University of Pennsylvania, Graduate School of Education, Division of Language in Education, Programs in Teaching English to Speakers of Other Languages and Intercultural Communication, Philadelphia, PA 19104. Offers educational linguistics (PhD); intercultural communication (MS Ed); teaching English to speakers of other languages (MS Ed). Part-time programs available. Postbaccalaureate distance learning degree programs offered (minimal on-campus study). Terminal master's awarded for partial completion of doctoral program. *Degree requirements:* For master's, thesis (for some programs), comprehensive exam; for doctorate, one foreign language, thesis/dissertation, preliminary exam. *Entrance requirements:* For master's and doctorate, GRE General Test or MAT. Additional exam requirements/recommendations for international students: Required—TOEFL. Electronic applications accepted. Expenses: Contact institution. *Faculty research:* Second language acquisition, social linguistics, English as a second language.

University of Phoenix–Omaha Campus, College of Education, Omaha, NE 68154-5240. Offers administration and supervision (MA Ed); curriculum and instruction (MA Ed); curriculum and instruction—English and language arts education (MA Ed); curriculum and instruction—adult education (MA Ed); curriculum and instruction—computer education (MA Ed); curriculum and instruction—English as a second language (MA Ed); curriculum and instruction—mathematics education (MA Ed); elementary teacher education (MA Ed); secondary teacher education (MA Ed); special education (MA Ed).

University of Phoenix Online Campus, The Artemis School, College of Education, Phoenix, AZ 85034-7209. Offers administration and supervision (MAEd); adult education and training (MAEd); curriculum and instruction-adult education (MAEd); curriculum and instruction-English and language arts education (MAEd); curriculum and instruction-mathematics education (MAEd); curriculum education (MAEd); curriculum instruction (MAEd); early childhood (MAEd); English as a second language (MAEd); teacher education elementary (MAEd); teacher education secondary (MAEd). Evening/weekend programs available. Postbaccalaureate distance learning degree programs offered (no on-campus study). *Faculty:* 12 full-time (5 women), 8,196 part-time/adjunct (6,937 women). *Students:* 11,937 full-time (9,375 women); includes 2,972 minority (2,210 African Americans, 74 American Indian/Alaska Native, 205 Asian Americans or Pacific Islanders, 483 Hispanic Americans), 906 international. Average age 36. *Degree requirements:* For master's, thesis (for some programs), registration. *Entrance requirements:* For master's, 3 years of work experience, minimum GPA of 2.5. Additional exam requirements/recommendations for international students: Required—TOEFL (minimum score 550 paper-based; 213 computer-based; 79 iBT). *Application deadline:* Applications are processed on a rolling basis. Application fee: $45. Electronic applications accepted. *Expenses:* Tuition: Full-time $12,664. Required fees: $760. *Financial support:* Institutionally sponsored loans and scholarships/grants available. Financial award applicants required to submit FAFSA. *Unit head:* Dr. Marla LaRue, Dean/Executive Director, 480-557-1218, E-mail: marla.larue@phoenix.edu. *Application contact:* Dr. Marla LaRue, Dean/Executive Director, 480-557-1218, E-mail: marla.larue@phoenix.edu.

University of Phoenix–Springfield Campus, College of Education, Springfield, MO 65804-7211. Offers administration and supervision (MA Ed); curriculum and instruction (MA Ed); curriculum and instruction/adult education (MA Ed); curriculum and instruction/computer education (MA Ed); curriculum and instruction/English as a second language (MA Ed); English and language arts education (MA Ed); mathematics education (MA Ed).

University of Pittsburgh, School of Arts and Sciences, TESOL Certificate Program, Pittsburgh, PA 15260. Offers Certificate. Part-time programs available. *Faculty:* 10 full-time (4 women). *Students:* 12 full-time (10 women), 12 part-time (9 women); includes 1 minority (Hispanic American), 5 international. Average age 30. 12 applicants, 67% accepted. In 2006, 6 degrees awarded. *Entrance requirements:* Additional exam requirements/recommendations for international students: Required—TOEFL (minimum score 600 paper-based; 250 computer-based). *Application deadline:* Applications are processed on a rolling basis. Application fee: $50. Electronic applications accepted. *Faculty research:* Language contact, second language acquisition, applied linguistics, sociolinguistics. *Unit head:* Dr. Scott Kiesling, Chair, 412-624-5900, Fax: 412-624-6130, E-mail: kiesling@pitt.edu. *Application contact:* Patricia C Cochran, Graduate Secretary, 412-624-5900, Fax: 412-624-6130, E-mail: lingpitt@pitt.edu.

University of Puerto Rico, Río Piedras, College of Education, Program in Teaching English as a Second Language, San Juan, PR 00931-3300. Offers M Ed. Part-time programs available. *Students:* 16 full-time (14 women), 8 part-time (6 women); all minorities (all Hispanic Americans) In 2006, 3 degrees awarded. *Degree requirements:* For master's, thesis. *Entrance requirements:* For master's, PAEG or GRE, minimum GPA of 3.0, letter of recommendation. *Application deadline:* For fall admission, 2/1 for domestic and international students. Application fee: $17. *Expenses:* Tuition, state resident: part-time $100 per credit. Tuition, nonresident: part-time $291 per credit. Required fees: $72 per semester. *Financial support:* Fellowships, research assistantships, teaching assistantships, career-related internships or fieldwork, Federal Work-Study, institutionally sponsored loans, and tuition waivers (partial) available. Financial award application deadline: 5/31. *Faculty research:* Second language acquisition, bilingual education. *Unit head:* Dr. Loyda Martinez, Coordinator, 787-764-0000 Ext. 4361, Fax: 787-763-4130. *Application contact:* Information Contact, 787-764-0000 Ext. 4368, Fax: 787-763-4130.

University of San Francisco, School of Education, Department of International and Multicultural Education, San Francisco, CA 94117-1080. Offers international and multicultural education (MA, Ed D); multicultural literature for children and young adults (MA); teaching English as a second language (MA). *Faculty:* 6 full-time (4 women), 8 part-time/adjunct (6 women). *Students:* 102 full-time (80 women), 71 part-time (64 women); includes 74 minority (16 African Americans, 24 Asian Americans or Pacific Islanders, 34 Hispanic Americans), 37 international. Average age 34. 163 applicants, 88% accepted, 50 enrolled. In 2006, 37 master's, 11 doctorates awarded. *Degree requirements:* For doctorate, thesis/dissertation. Application fee: $55 ($65 for international students). *Expenses:* Tuition: Full-time $17,370; part-time $965 per unit. Tuition and fees vary according to degree level, campus/location and program. *Financial support:* In 2006–07, 93 students received support; fellowships, research assistantships, teaching assistantships available. Financial award application deadline: 3/2; financial award applicants required to submit FAFSA. *Unit head:* Dr. Rosita Galang, Chair, 415-422-6878.

The University of Scranton, Graduate School, Department of Education, Program in English as a Second Language, Scranton, PA 18510. Offers MS. Part-time and evening/weekend programs available. *Students:* 2 full-time (1 woman), 5 part-time (all women), 3 international. Average age 26. 8 applicants, 100% accepted. *Degree requirements:* For master's, capstone experience. *Entrance requirements:* For master's, minimum GPA of 2.75. Additional exam requirements/recommendations for international students: Required—TOEFL (minimum score 500 paper-based; 173 computer-based), IELTS (minimum score 6). *Application deadline:* Applications are processed on a rolling basis. Application fee: $50. *Expenses:* Tuition: Part-time $684 per credit. Required fees: $25 per term. *Financial support:* Application deadline: 3/1. *Unit head:* Dr. Derry Stufft, Director, 570-941-7421, Fax: 570-941-7401, E-mail: stufftda@scranton.edu.

University of South Carolina, The Graduate School, College of Arts and Sciences, Linguistics Program, Columbia, SC 29208. Offers linguistics (MA, PhD); teaching English to speakers of other languages (Certificate). Part-time programs available. Terminal master's awarded for partial completion of doctoral program. *Degree requirements:* For master's, one foreign language, comprehensive exam; for doctorate, 3 foreign languages, thesis/dissertation, comprehensive exam. *Entrance requirements:* For master's and Certificate, GRE General Test, minimum GPA of 3.0; for doctorate, GRE General Test, minimum GPA of 3.5. Additional exam requirements/recommendations for international students: Required—TOEFL. Electronic applications accepted. *Faculty research:* Second language acquisition, sociolinguistics, syntax, historical linguistics and phonology.

University of Southern Maine, College of Education and Human Development, Program in Literacy Education, Portland, ME 04104-9300. Offers applied literacy (MS Ed); English as a second language (MS Ed, CAS); literacy education (MS Ed, CAS, Certificate). *Accreditation:* NCATE. Part-time and evening/weekend programs available. *Faculty:* 4 full-time (3 women), 3 part-time/adjunct (0 women). *Students:* 2 full-time (both women), 51 part-time (47 women); includes 1 minority (Asian American or Pacific Islander) 18 applicants, 89% accepted, 13 enrolled. In 2006, 28 degrees awarded. *Degree requirements:* For master's, thesis or alternative, comprehensive exam; for other advanced degree, thesis or alternative. *Entrance requirements:* For master's, GRE General Test or MAT; for other advanced degree, master's degree. *Application deadline:* For fall admission, 2/1 for domestic students; for spring admission, 9/15 for domestic students. Application fee: $50. Electronic applications accepted. *Expenses:* Tuition, state resident: full-time $4,860; part-time $270 per credit hour. Tuition, nonresident: full-time $13,572; part-time $754 per credit hour. Required fees: $222 per semester. Tuition and fees vary according to course load. *Financial support:* In 2006–07, 4 students received support, including 1 research assistantship with tuition reimbursement available (averaging $4,500 per year); career-related internships or fieldwork, Federal Work-Study, institutionally sponsored loans, scholarships/grants, and unspecified assistantships also available. Support available to part-time students. Financial award application deadline: 3/1; financial award applicants required to submit FAFSA. *Unit head:* Dr. James Curry, Chair, Professional Education Department, 207-780-5400, Fax: 207-780-8277, E-mail: jcurry@usm.maine.edu. *Application contact:* Robin Audesse, Associate Director of Graduate Admissions, 207-780-5306, Fax: 207-780-5193, E-mail: raudesse@usm.maine.edu.

The University of Tennessee, Graduate School, College of Education, Health and Human Sciences, Program in Education, Knoxville, TN 37996. Offers art education (MS); counseling education (PhD); cultural studies in education (PhD); curriculum (MS, Ed S); curriculum, educational research and evaluation (Ed D, PhD); early childhood education (PhD); early childhood special education (MS); education of deaf and hard of hearing (MS); educational administration and policy studies (Ed D, PhD); educational administration and supervision (Ed S); educational psychology (Ed D, PhD); elementary education (MS, Ed S); elementary teaching (MS); English education (MS, Ed S); exercise science (PhD); foreign language/ESL education (MS, Ed S); instructional technology (MS, Ed D, PhD, Ed S); literacy, language and ESL education (PhD); literacy, language education, and ESL education (Ed D); mathematics education (MS, Ed S); modified and comprehensive special education (MS); reading education (MS, Ed S); school counseling (Ed S); school psychology (PhD, Ed S); science education (MS, Ed S); secondary teaching (MS); social foundations (MS); social science education (MS, Ed S); socio-cultural foundations of sports and education (PhD); special education (Ed S); teacher education (Ed D, PhD). *Accreditation:* NCATE. Part-time and evening/weekend programs available. *Students:* 529 (401 women); includes 39 minority (23 African Americans, 2 American Indian/Alaska Native, 9 Asian Americans or Pacific Islanders, 5 Hispanic Americans) 34 international. 420 applicants, 50% accepted. In 2006, 258 master's, 28 doctorates awarded. *Degree requirements:* For master's and Ed S, thesis optional; for doctorate, variable foreign language requirement, thesis/dissertation. *Entrance requirements:* For master's, minimum GPA of 2.7; for doctorate and Ed S, GRE General Test, minimum GPA of 2.7. Additional exam requirements/recommendations for international students: Required—TOEFL. *Application deadline:* For fall admission, 2/1 priority date for domestic students. Applications are processed on a rolling basis. Application fee: $35. Electronic applications accepted. *Expenses:* Tuition, state resident: full-time $5,574. Tuition, nonresident: full-time $16,840. Required fees: $792. *Financial support:* In 2006–07, 4 fellowships, 9 teaching assistantships were awarded; career-related internships or fieldwork, Federal Work-Study, institutionally sponsored loans, and unspecified assistantships also available. Financial award application deadline: 2/1; financial award applicants required to submit FAFSA. *Unit head:* Dr. Lester Knight, Head, 865-974-0907, Fax: 865-974-8718, E-mail: lknight@utk.edu.

The University of Texas at Arlington, Graduate School, College of Liberal Arts, Department of Linguistics and TESOL, Program in Teaching English to Speakers of Other Languages, Arlington, TX 76019. Offers MA. *Accreditation:* NCATE. *Students:* 4 full-time (all women), 19 part-time (15 women); includes 2 minority (both Asian Americans or Pacific Islanders), 4 international. In 2006, 6 degrees awarded. *Degree requirements:* For master's, thesis optional. *Entrance requirements:* For master's, GRE General Test, minimum undergraduate GPA of 3.0, 6 credits of undergraduate foundation courses, the equivalent of 2 years of university level foreign language study. Additional exam requirements/recommendations for international students: Required—TOEFL (minimum score 550 paper-based; 213 computer-based). Application fee: $35 ($50 for international students). *Expenses:* Tuition, state resident: full-time $5,528. Tuition, nonresident: full-time $10,478. International tuition: $10,608 full-time. *Financial support:* In 2006–07, 3 fellowships (averaging $1,000 per year), 1 teaching assistantship were awarded. *Application contact:* Dr. Laurel Stvan, Graduate Advisor, 817-272-3133, Fax: 817-272-2731.

The University of Texas at Brownsville, Graduate Studies, School of Education, Brownsville, TX 78520-4991. Offers bilingual education (M Ed); counseling and guidance (M Ed); curriculum and instruction (M Ed); early childhood education (M Ed); educational administration (M Ed); educational technology (M Ed); English as a second language (M Ed); reading specialist (M Ed); special education/educational diagnostician (M Ed). Part-time and evening/weekend programs available. Postbaccalaureate distance learning degree programs offered (minimal on-campus study). *Degree requirements:* For master's, thesis optional. *Entrance requirements:* For master's, GRE General Test. Additional exam requirements/recommendations for international students: Required—TOEFL.

The University of Texas at San Antonio, College of Education and Human Development, Division of Bicultural-Bilingual Studies, San Antonio, TX 78249-0617. Offers bicultural studies (MA); bicultural-bilingual studies (MA); culture, literacy, and language (PhD); teaching English as a second language (MA). Part-time and evening/weekend programs available. *Faculty:* 12 full-time (9 women). *Students:* 50 full-time (38 women), 95 part-time (75 women); includes 102 minority (5 African Americans, 1 American Indian/Alaska Native, 3 Asian Americans or Pacific Islanders, 93 Hispanic Americans), 12 international. Average age 35. 63 applicants, 75% accepted, 44 enrolled. In 2006, 41 master's, 4 doctorates awarded. *Degree requirements:* For master's, one foreign language, comprehensive exam, registration; for doctorate, one foreign language, thesis/dissertation, comprehensive exam, registration. *Entrance requirements:* For master's and doctorate, GRE General Test. Additional exam requirements/recommendations for international students: Required—TOEFL (minimum score 500 paper-based; 173 computer-based). *Application deadline:* For fall admission, 7/1 for domestic students, 4/1 for international students; for spring admission, 11/1 for domestic students, 9/1 for international students. Applications are processed on a rolling basis. Application fee: $45 ($80 for international students). Electronic applications accepted. *Expenses:* Tuition, state resident: full-time $1,730; part-time $192 per credit hour. Tuition, nonresident: full-time $6,680; part-time $742 per credit hour. Required fees: $733; $308,359 per credit hour. *Financial support:* In 2006–07, 1 fellowship (averaging $45,000 per year), 4 research assistantships (averaging $24,563 per year), 13 teaching assistantships (averaging $17,354 per year) were awarded; career-related internships or fieldwork and Federal Work-Study also available. Support available to part-time students. *Faculty research:* Spanish-English bilingualism, cultural transmission in bilingual communities, literacy in bilingual settings, content-based ESL, second language acquisition in classroom contexts. Total annual research expenditures: $78,604. *Unit head:* Dr. Robert D. Milk, Director, 210-458-4426, Fax: 210-458-5962, E-mail: rmilk@utsa.edu.

The University of Texas of the Permian Basin, Office of Graduate Studies, School of Education, Program in Bilingual/English as a second language Education, Odessa, TX 79762-

English as a Second Language

The University of Texas of the Permian Basin (continued)
0001. Offers MA. *Degree requirements:* For master's, thesis (for some programs), comprehensive exam (for some programs), registration. *Entrance requirements:* For master's, GRE General Test. Additional exam requirements/recommendations for international students: Required—TOEFL (minimum score 550 paper-based; 213 computer-based).

The University of Texas–Pan American, College of Arts and Humanities, Department of English, Program in English as a Second Language, Edinburg, TX 78541-2999. Offers MA. Part-time and evening/weekend programs available. *Degree requirements:* For master's, thesis optional. *Entrance requirements:* For master's, GRE General Test, minimum GPA of 3.0. *Expenses:* Tuition, state resident: full-time $2,577; part-time $143 per credit hour. Tuition, nonresident: full-time $7,527; part-time $418 per credit hour. Required fees: $561. *Faculty research:* Oral versus literary culture discourse analysis, language shift among Hispanics.

The University of Toledo, College of Graduate Studies, College of Arts and Sciences, Department of English Language and Literature, Toledo, OH 43606-3390. Offers English as a second language (MA); literature (MA); teaching of writing (Certificate). Part-time programs available. *Faculty:* 14 full-time (5 women), 4 part-time/adjunct (2 women). *Students:* 35 full-time (24 women), 11 part-time (8 women); includes 5 minority (all African Americans), 1 international. Average age 28. 39 applicants, 87% accepted, 24 enrolled. In 2006, 18 degrees awarded. *Degree requirements:* For master's, one foreign language. *Entrance requirements:* For master's, minimum GPA of 2.7. *Application deadline:* For fall admission, 8/1 priority date for domestic students. Applications are processed on a rolling basis. Application fee: $45. Electronic applications accepted. *Financial support:* In 2006–07, 35 teaching assistantships with full tuition reimbursements (averaging $8,200 per year) were awarded; research assistantships, Federal Work-Study, institutionally sponsored loans, and tuition waivers (full) also available. Support available to part-time students. Financial award application deadline: 4/1; financial award applicants required to submit FAFSA. *Faculty research:* Literary criticism, linguistics, creative writing, folklore and cultural studies. *Unit head:* Dr. Sara Lundquist, Interim Chair, 419-530-2506, Fax: 419-530-2590, E-mail: sara.lundquist@utoledo.edu.

The University of Toledo, College of Graduate Studies, College of Education, Department of Curriculum and Instruction, Program in English as a Second Language, Toledo, OH 43606-3390. Offers MAE. *Students:* 1 (woman) full-time, 1 (woman) part-time. 4 applicants, 50% accepted, 1 enrolled.

University of Washington, Graduate School, College of Arts and Sciences, Department of English, Seattle, WA 98195. Offers English (MA, MAT, MFA, PhD); English as a second language (MAT). Part-time programs available. Terminal master's awarded for partial completion of doctoral program. *Degree requirements:* For master's, one foreign language, thesis (for some programs); for doctorate, one foreign language, thesis/dissertation. *Entrance requirements:* For master's, GRE General Test, GRE Subject Test (for English (MA, MAT) only), minimum GPA of 3.0; for doctorate, GRE General Test, GRE Subject Test. Additional exam requirements/recommendations for international students: Required—TOEFL. Electronic applications accepted. *Faculty research:* English and American literature, critical theory, creative writing, language theory.

Wayne State College, School of Education and Counseling, Department of Educational Foundations and Leadership, Program in Curriculum and Instruction, Wayne, NE 68787. Offers alternative education (MSE); business education (MSE); communication arts education (MSE); curriculum and instruction (MSE); early childhood education (MSE); elementary education (MSE); English as a second language (MSE); English education (MSE); family consumer science of education (MSE); industrial technology education (MSE); learning communities (MSE); mathematics education (MSE); music education (MSE); science education (MSE); social science education (MSE). *Accreditation:* NCATE. Part-time and evening/weekend programs available. *Faculty:* 17 part-time/adjunct (11 women). *Students:* 17 full-time (10 women), 307 part-time (248 women); includes 6 minority (2 African Americans, 1 American Indian/Alaska Native, 2 Asian Americans or Pacific Islanders, 1 Hispanic American), 1 international. Average age 35. In 2006, 167 degrees awarded. *Degree requirements:* For master's, thesis optional. *Entrance requirements:* For master's, GRE General Test. Additional exam requirements/recommendations for international students: Required—TOEFL (minimum score 550 paper-based; 213 computer-based). *Application deadline:* Applications are processed on a rolling basis. Application fee: $30. *Expenses:* Tuition, state resident: full-time $3,114; part-time $130 per credit hour. Tuition, nonresident: full-time $6,228; part-time $260 per credit hour. Required fees: $894; $37 per credit hour. Tuition and fees vary according to course load. *Financial support:* Applicants required to submit FAFSA.

Webster University, School of Education, Department of Communication Arts, Reading and Early Childhood, St. Louis, MO 63119-3194. Offers communications (MAT); early childhood education (MAT). *Students:* 47 full-time (44 women), 166 part-time (154 women); includes 35 minority (30 African Americans, 1 American Indian/Alaska Native, 3 Asian Americans or Pacific Islanders, 1 Hispanic American), 5 international. Average age 33. *Entrance requirements:* For master's, minimum GPA of 2.5. *Application deadline:* Applications are processed on a rolling basis. Application fee: $25 ($50 for international students). *Expenses:* Tuition: Full-time $8,820; part-time $490 per credit hour. Tuition and fees vary according to degree level, campus/location and program. *Financial support:* Federal Work-Study available. Support available to part-time students. Financial award application deadline: 4/1; financial award applicants required to submit FAFSA. *Unit head:* Phyllis Wilkinson, Chair, 314-968-7096, Fax: 314-968-7118. *Application contact:* Director of Graduate and Evening Student Admissions, Fax: 314-968-7116, E-mail: gadmit@webster.edu.

West Chester University of Pennsylvania, Graduate Studies, College of Arts and Sciences, Program in Teaching English as a Second Language, West Chester, PA 19383. Offers MA. Part-time and evening/weekend programs available. *Students:* 11 full-time (9 women), 28 part-time (26 women); includes 1 Hispanic American, 5 international. Average age 36. 24 applicants, 100% accepted, 13 enrolled. In 2006, 35 degrees awarded. *Degree requirements:* For master's, one foreign language, comprehensive exam. *Entrance requirements:* For master's, GRE or MAT. *Application deadline:* For fall admission, 4/15 priority date for domestic students; for spring admission, 10/15 for domestic students. Applications are processed on a rolling basis. Application fee: $35. *Financial support:* In 2006–07, research assistantships with full tuition reimbursements (averaging $5,000 per year); unspecified assistantships also available. Support available to part-time students. Financial award application deadline: 2/15; financial award applicants required to submit FAFSA. *Unit head:* Dr. Garrett Molholt, Head, 610-436-2425, E-mail: gmolholt@wcupa.edu. *Application contact:* Charles Grove, Graduate Coordinator, 610-436-2752, E-mail: cgrove@wcupa.edu.

Western Kentucky University, Graduate Studies, Potter College of Arts and Letters, Department of English, Bowling Green, KY 42101. Offers education (MA); English (MA Ed); literature (MA), including American literature, British literature, literary theory, women writers, world literature; teaching English as a second language (MA); writing (MA). Part-time and evening/weekend programs available. *Faculty:* 16 full-time (11 women), 1 part-time/adjunct (0 women). *Students:* 16 full-time (9 women), 20 part-time (16 women); includes 4 minority (3 African Americans, 1 Hispanic American). Average age 29. 13 applicants, 62% accepted, 4 enrolled. In 2006, 17 master's awarded. *Degree requirements:* For master's, final exam, thesis optional. *Entrance requirements:* For master's, GRE General Test, minimum GPA of 2.75. Additional exam requirements/recommendations for international students: Required—TOEFL (minimum score 555 paper-based; 213 computer-based; 79 iBT). *Application deadline:* For fall admission, 7/1 priority date for domestic students, 4/1 for international students; for spring admission, 11/1 for domestic students, 9/1 for international students. Applications are processed on a rolling basis. Application fee: $35. *Expenses:* Tuition, state resident: full-time $6,520; part-time $226 per hour. Tuition, nonresident: full-time $7,140; part-time $357 per hour. International tuition: $15,820 full-time. *Financial support:* In 2006–07, 12 students received support, including 2 research assistantships with partial tuition reimbursements available (averaging $9,400 per year), 9 teaching assistantships with partial tuition reimbursements available (averaging $9,400 per year); Federal Work-Study, institutionally sponsored loans, tuition waivers (partial), and service awards also available. Support available to part-time students. Financial award application deadline: 4/1; financial award applicants required to submit FAFSA. *Faculty research:* Improving writing, linking teacher knowledge and performance, Victorian women writers, Kentucky women writers, Kentucky poets. Total annual research expenditures: $2,800. *Unit head:* Dr. Karen L Schneider, Head, 270-745-3046, Fax: 270-745-2533, E-mail: karen.scheider@wku.edu.

West Virginia University, Eberly College of Arts and Sciences, Department of Foreign Languages, Morgantown, WV 26506. Offers comparative literature (MA); French (MA); German (MA); linguistics (MA); Spanish (MA); teaching English to speakers of other languages (MA). Part-time programs available. *Faculty:* 19 full-time (12 women), 22 part-time/adjunct (16 women). *Students:* 65 full-time (47 women), 5 part-time (3 women); includes 6 minority (all Hispanic Americans), 31 international. Average age 29. 61 applicants, 80% accepted, 31 enrolled. In 2006, 27 degrees awarded. *Degree requirements:* For master's, variable foreign language requirement, comprehensive exam (for some programs). *Entrance requirements:* For master's, minimum GPA of 3.0. Additional exam requirements/recommendations for international students: Required—TOEFL. *Application deadline:* For fall admission, 2/1 priority date for domestic and international students; for spring admission, 10/1 for domestic and international students. Applications are processed on a rolling basis. Application fee: $50. Electronic applications accepted. *Expenses:* Tuition, state resident: full-time $4,926; part-time $276 per credit hour. Tuition, nonresident: full-time $14,278; part-time $796 per credit hour. Tuition and fees vary according to program. *Financial support:* In 2006–07, 66 students received support, including 62 teaching assistantships with full tuition reimbursements available (averaging $8,264 per year); research assistantships, Federal Work-Study, institutionally sponsored loans, and tuition waivers (full and partial) also available. Financial award application deadline: 2/1; financial award applicants required to submit FAFSA. *Faculty research:* French, German, and Spanish literature; foreign language pedagogy; English as a second language; cultural studies; linguistics. Total annual research expenditures: $26,458. *Unit head:* Dr. Donald E. Hall, Chair, 304-293-3107 Ext. 33435, Fax: 304-293-7655, E-mail: donald.hall@mail.wvu.edu. *Application contact:* Dr. Susan Braidi, Director of Graduate Studies, 304-293-5121, Fax: 304-293-7655, E-mail: susan.braidi@mail.wvu.edu.

Wheaton College, Graduate School, Department of Intercultural Studies, Wheaton, IL 60187-5593. Offers evangelism (MA); intercultural studies (MA); intercultural studies/teaching English as a second language (MA); missions (MA); teaching English as a second language (Certificate). Part-time programs available. *Faculty:* 5 full-time (2 women), 4 part-time/adjunct (2 women). *Students:* 115. 54 applicants, 98% accepted, 41 enrolled. In 2006, 29 degrees awarded. *Degree requirements:* For master's, thesis or alternative. *Entrance requirements:* For master's, GRE General Test, MAT. *Application deadline:* For fall admission, 3/1 priority date for domestic students; for spring admission, 11/1 for domestic students. Applications are processed on a rolling basis. Application fee: $30. *Financial support:* Career-related internships or fieldwork, scholarships/grants, and unspecified assistantships available. Financial award application deadline: 3/1; financial award applicants required to submit FAFSA. *Unit head:* Dr. Evvy Campbell, Chair, 630-752-5258. *Application contact:* Julie A. Huebner, Director of Graduate Admissions, 630-752-5195, Fax: 630-752-5935, E-mail: gradadm@wheaton.edu.

Wright State University, School of Graduate Studies, College of Liberal Arts, Department of English Language and Literatures, Dayton, OH 45435. Offers composition and rhetoric (MA); English (MA); literature (MA); teaching English to speakers of other languages (MA). *Students:* 30 full-time (22 women), 16 part-time (12 women); includes 4 minority (3 African Americans, 1 American Indian/Alaska Native), 2 international. Average age 35. 25 applicants, 88% accepted. In 2006, 20 degrees awarded. *Degree requirements:* For master's, portfolio, thesis optional. *Entrance requirements:* For master's, 20 hours in upper-level English. Additional exam requirements/recommendations for international students: Required—TOEFL. *Application deadline:* Applications are processed on a rolling basis. Application fee: $25. *Financial support:* Fellowships, research assistantships, teaching assistantships, unspecified assistantships available. Support available to part-time students. Financial award applicants required to submit FAFSA. *Faculty research:* American literature, world literature in English, applied linguistics, writing theory and pedagogy. *Unit head:* Dr. Henry S. Limouze, Chair, 937-775-3136, Fax: 937-775-2707, E-mail: henry.limouze@wright.edu. *Application contact:* Dr. Chris Hall, Director, 937-775-2268, Fax: 937-775-2707, E-mail: chris.hall@wright.edu.

Multilingual and Multicultural Education

Alliant International University–Irvine, Graduate School of Education, Teacher Education Programs, Irvine, CA 92612. Offers auditory oral education (Certificate); CLAD (Certificate); preliminary multiple subject (Credential); preliminary multiple subject with BCLAD (Credential); preliminary single subject (Credential); professional clear multiple subject (Credential); professional clear single subject (Credential); teaching (MA, Credential); technology and learning (MA). Part-time and evening/weekend programs available. *Students:* 4. In 2006, 6 degrees awarded. *Entrance requirements:* For degree, California Basic Educational Skills Test, minimum GPA of 2.5. Additional exam requirements/recommendations for international students: Required—TOEFL (minimum score 550 paper-based; 213 computer-based), TWE. *Application deadline:* For fall admission, 7/1 priority date for domestic and international students; for spring admission, 12/1 priority date for domestic and international students. Applications are processed on a rolling basis. Application fee: $55. Electronic applications accepted. *Financial support:* Career-related internships or fieldwork, Federal Work-Study, institutionally sponsored loans, and scholarships/grants available. Financial award applicants required to submit FAFSA. *Unit head:* Dr. Trudy Day, Assistant Dean, 866-825-5426, Fax: 949-833-3507, E-mail: admissions@alliant.edu. *Application contact:* Alliant International University Central Contact Center, 866-U-ALLIANT, Fax: 858-635-4555, E-mail: admissions@alliant.edu.

Alliant International University–San Francisco, Graduate School of Education, Teacher Education Programs, San Francisco, CA 94133-1221. Offers auditory oral education (Certificate); CLAD (Certificate); preliminary multiple subject (Credential); preliminary multiple subject with BCLAD (Credential); preliminary single subject (Credential); professional clear multiple subject (Credential); professional clear single subject (Credential); teaching (MA). Part-time and evening/weekend programs available. *Faculty:* 2 full-time (1 woman), 7 part-time/adjunct (4 women). *Students:* 16 full-time (11 women), 73 part-time (45 women); includes 25 minority (8 African Americans, 10 Asian Americans or Pacific Islanders, 7 Hispanic Americans), 1 international. Average age 28. 91 applicants, 81% accepted, 65 enrolled. In 2006, 9 degrees awarded. *Entrance requirements:* For degree, California Basic Educational Skills Test, minimum GPA of

2.5. Additional exam requirements/recommendations for international students: Required—TOEFL (minimum score 550 paper-based; 213 computer-based), TWE. *Application deadline:* For fall admission, 7/1 priority date for domestic and international students; for spring admission, 12/1 priority date for domestic and international students. Application fee: $45. *Expenses:* Tuition: Part-time $825 per unit. Tuition and fees vary according to course load, degree level and program. *Financial support:* Career-related internships or fieldwork, Federal Work-Study, institutionally sponsored loans, and scholarships/grants available. Financial award application deadline: 2/15; financial award applicants required to submit FAFSA. *Unit head:* Dr. Trudy Day, Assistant Dean, 866-825-5426, Fax: 415-955-2179, E-mail: admissions@alliant.edu. *Application contact:* Alliant International University Central Contact Center, 866-U-ALLIANT, Fax: 858-635-4555, E-mail: admissions@alliant.edu.

See Close-Up on page 819.

Azusa Pacific University, School of Education, Department of Advanced Studies, Program in Curriculum and Instruction in a Multicultural Setting, Azusa, CA 91702-7000. Offers MA. *Accreditation:* NCATE. Part-time and evening/weekend programs available. In 2006, 42 degrees awarded. *Degree requirements:* For master's, core exams, oral presentation. *Entrance requirements:* For master's, 12 units of course work in education, minimum GPA of 3.0. Application fee: $45 ($65 for international students). *Expenses:* Tuition: Part-time $475 per credit. *Faculty research:* Diversity in teacher education programs, teacher morale, student perception of school, case study instruction. *Unit head:* Dr. Susan Warren, Director, 626-815-5416, E-mail: swarren@apu.edu.

Azusa Pacific University, School of Education, Department of Education, Program in Language Development, Azusa, CA 91702-7000. Offers MA. *Accreditation:* NCATE. *Degree requirements:* For master's, comprehensive exam or thesis, core exams, oral presentation. *Entrance requirements:* For master's, 12 units of course work in education, minimum GPA of 3.0. Application fee: $45 ($65 for international students). *Expenses:* Tuition: Part-time $475 per credit. *Faculty research:* Biliteracy development, home-school connections, integrated curriculum. *Unit head:* Dr. Don Dorr, Director, 626-815-3483. *Application contact:* Dr. Dan Doorn, Director, 626-815-5371.

Bank Street College of Education, Graduate School, Department of Curriculum and Instruction, Program in Bilingual Education, New York, NY 10025. Offers bilingual childhood special education (Ed M, MS Ed); bilingual early childhood education (MS Ed); bilingual early childhood special and general education (MS Ed); bilingual early childhood special education (Ed M, MS Ed); bilingual elementary/childhood general education (MS Ed); bilingual elementary/childhood special and general education (MS Ed); bilingual middle school general education (MS Ed); bilingual middle school special and general education (Ed M, MS Ed); bilingual middle school special education (MS Ed). *Accreditation:* NCATE. *Faculty:* 2 full-time (both women), 5 part-time/adjunct (all women). *Students:* 8 full-time (7 women), 22 part-time (19 women); includes 21 minority (2 African Americans, 2 Asian Americans or Pacific Islanders, 17 Hispanic Americans). Average age 27. 19 applicants, 68% accepted, 10 enrolled. In 2006, 8 degrees awarded. *Degree requirements:* For master's, thesis, registration. *Entrance requirements:* For master's, interview. Additional exam requirements/recommendations for international students: Required—TOEFL (minimum score 600 paper-based; 250 computer-based). *Application deadline:* For fall admission, 3/1 priority date for domestic students; for spring admission, 11/1 priority date for domestic students. Applications are processed on a rolling basis. Application fee: $50. *Expenses:* Tuition: Part-time $940 per credit. Required fees: $100 per term. *Financial support:* Career-related internships or fieldwork, Federal Work-Study, scholarships/grants, and unspecified assistantships available. Support available to part-time students. Financial award application deadline: 4/15; financial award applicants required to submit FAFSA. *Faculty research:* Dual language education, language immersion, bilingual education in the urban classroom, community and school partnerships. Total annual research expenditures: $58,717. *Unit head:* Dr. Olga Romero, Director, 212-875-4468, Fax: 212-875-4753, E-mail: olgar@bankstreet.edu. *Application contact:* Ann Morgan, Director of Graduate Admissions, 212-875-4403, Fax: 212-875-4678, E-mail: amorgan@bankstreet.edu.

Belhaven College, School of Education, Jackson, MS 39202-1789. Offers elementary education (M Ed, MAT); secondary education (M Ed, MAT). *Degree requirements:* For master's, portfolio. *Entrance requirements:* For master's, PRAXIS I, PRAXIS II, minimum GPA of 2.8.

Bennington College, Graduate Programs, Program in Teaching a Second Language, Bennington, VT 05201. Offers education (MATSL); foreign language education (MATSL); French (MATSL); Spanish (MATSL). Part-time programs available. *Faculty:* 2 full-time (0 women), 5 part-time/adjunct (3 women). *Students:* Average age 40. 8 applicants, 75% accepted, 5 enrolled. In 2006, 5 degrees awarded. *Degree requirements:* For master's, one foreign language. *Entrance requirements:* For master's, oral proficiency interview (OPI). Additional exam requirements/recommendations for international students: Required—TOEFL (minimum score 577 paper-based; 233 computer-based). *Application deadline:* For spring admission, 4/1 priority date for domestic and international students. Applications are processed on a rolling basis. Application fee: $60. *Expenses: Contact institution.* One-time fee: $75 full-time. Tuition and fees vary according to program. *Financial support:* In 2006–07, 1 student received support. Scholarships/grants available. Financial award application deadline: 4/1; financial award applicants required to submit FAFSA. *Faculty research:* Acquisition, evaluation, assessment, conceptual teaching and learning content-driven communication, applied linguistics. *Unit head:* Carol Meyer, Director of Isabelle Kaplan Center for Languages and Cultures, 802-440-4710, Fax: 802-447-4269, E-mail: matsl@bennington.edu. *Application contact:* Nancy Pearlman, Assistant Director, 802-440-4710, Fax: 802-447-4269, E-mail: matsl@benington.edu.

Boston University, School of Education, Department of Literacy and Language, Counseling and Development, Program in Bilingual Education, Boston, MA 02215. Offers Ed M, CAGS. Part-time programs available. *Students:* 1 (woman) full-time, 2 part-time (both women); includes 2 minority (both Hispanic Americans) Average age 27. 10 applicants, 90% accepted. In 2006, 3 degrees awarded. *Degree requirements:* For CAGS, comprehensive exam. *Entrance requirements:* For master's and CAGS, GRE General Test or MAT. Additional exam requirements/recommendations for international students: Required—TOEFL. *Application deadline:* For fall admission, 2/15 priority date for domestic students; for winter admission, 10/1 priority date for domestic students. Applications are processed on a rolling basis. Application fee: $70. Electronic applications accepted. *Expenses:* Tuition: Full-time $33,330; part-time $1,042 per credit. Required fees: $462; $40. *Financial support:* Application deadline: 2/15. *Faculty research:* Use of computers in second language acquisition, cross-cultural communication, reading and language development. *Unit head:* Dr. Julie Coppola, Head, 617-353-3260. *Application contact:* 617-353-4237, Fax: 617-353-8937, E-mail: sedgrad@bu.edu.

Brooklyn College of the City University of New York, Division of Graduate Studies, School of Education, Program in Childhood Education, Brooklyn, NY 11210-2889. Offers bilingual education (MS Ed); liberal arts (MS Ed); mathematics (MS Ed); science/environmental education (MS Ed). Part-time and evening/weekend programs available. *Students:* 10 full-time (9 women), 275 part-time (233 women); includes 130 minority (84 African Americans, 12 Asian Americans or Pacific Islanders, 34 Hispanic Americans), 11 international. 154 applicants, 81% accepted, 80 enrolled. In 2006, 214 degrees awarded. *Entrance requirements:* For master's, LAST, interview, previous course work in education, writing sample, resumé, 2 letters of recommendation. Additional exam requirements/recommendations for international students: Required—TOEFL. *Application deadline:* For fall admission, 3/1 priority date for domestic students, 2/1 priority date for international students; for spring admission, 11/1 priority date for domestic students, 10/1 priority date for international students. Applications are processed on a rolling basis. Application fee: $125. Electronic applications accepted. *Expenses:* Tuition, state resident: full-time $6,400; part-time $270 per credit. Tuition, nonresident: full-time $12,000; part-time $500 per credit. Required fees: $118 per semester. *Financial support:* Career-related internships or fieldwork, Federal Work-Study, institutionally sponsored loans, and scholarships/grants available. Support available to part-time students. Financial award application deadline: 5/1; financial award applicants required to submit FAFSA. *Faculty research:* Emotional intelligence, multiculturalism, arts immersion, the Holocaust. *Unit head:* Dr. Sharon O'Connor-Petruso, Program Head, 718-951-5214. *Application contact:* Karen Alleyne-Pierre, Director of Admissions Services and Enrollment Communications, 718-951-5902, Fax: 718-951-4506, E-mail: grads@brooklyn.cuny.edu.

Brooklyn College of the City University of New York, Division of Graduate Studies, School of Education, Program in Special Education, Brooklyn, NY 11210-2889. Offers bilingual special education (MS Ed); children with emotional handicaps (MS Ed); children with neuropsychological learning disabilities (MS Ed); children with retarded mental development (MS Ed); teacher of students with disabilities (MS Ed), including birth-grade 2, grades 1-6, grades 5-9. Part-time programs available. *Students:* 172 applicants, 83% accepted, 125 enrolled. In 2006, 80 degrees awarded. *Degree requirements:* For master's, practicum. *Entrance requirements:* For master's, LAST, interview; previous course work in education and psychology; minimum GPA of 3.0 in education, 2.8 overall; resumé, 2 letters of recommendation; essay. Additional exam requirements/recommendations for international students: Required—TOEFL. *Application deadline:* For fall admission, 3/1 priority date for domestic students, 2/1 priority date for international students; for spring admission, 11/1 priority date for domestic students, 10/1 priority date for international students. Applications are processed on a rolling basis. Application fee: $125. Electronic applications accepted. *Expenses:* Tuition, state resident: full-time $6,400; part-time $270 per credit. Tuition, nonresident: full-time $12,000; part-time $500 per credit. Required fees: $118 per semester. *Financial support:* Federal Work-Study, institutionally sponsored loans, and scholarships/grants available. Support available to part-time students. Financial award application deadline: 5/1; financial award applicants required to submit FAFSA. *Faculty research:* School reform, conflict resolution, curriculum for inclusive settings, urban issues in special education. *Unit head:* Prof. Lynda Sarnoff, Facilitator, 718-951-5214, Fax: 718-951-4816, E-mail: lsarnoff@brooklyn.cuny.edu. *Application contact:* Karen Alleyne-Pierre, Director of Admissions Services and Enrollment Communications, 718-951-5902, Fax: 718-951-4506, E-mail: grads@brooklyn.cuny.edu.

Brown University, Graduate School, Center for Portuguese and Brazilian Studies, Providence, RI 02912. Offers Brazilian studies (AM); Luso-Brazilian studies (PhD); Portuguese studies and bilingual education (AM). *Degree requirements:* For doctorate, thesis/dissertation.

Buffalo State College, State University of New York, Graduate Studies and Research, Faculty of Applied Science and Education, Department of Exceptional Education, Program in Teaching Bilingual Exceptional Individuals, Buffalo, NY 14222-1095. Offers MS Ed. *Accreditation:* NCATE. Part-time and evening/weekend programs available. *Degree requirements:* For master's, project. *Entrance requirements:* For master's, minimum GPA of 2.5. Additional exam requirements/recommendations for international students: Required—TOEFL (minimum score 550 paper-based; 213 computer-based).

California Baptist University, Program in Education, Riverside, CA 92504-3206. Offers cross-cultural language and academic development (MA Ed); educational leadership (MS Ed); educational technology (MS Ed); instructional computer applications (MS Ed); reading (MS Ed); special education (MS Ed); teaching (MS Ed). Part-time programs available. *Faculty:* 16 full-time (10 women), 16 part-time/adjunct (13 women). *Students:* 77 full-time (64 women), 408 part-time (342 women); includes 157 minority (41 African Americans, 12 American Indian/Alaska Native, 18 Asian Americans or Pacific Islanders, 86 Hispanic Americans), 2 international. 282 applicants, 70% accepted, 171 enrolled. In 2006, 63 degrees awarded. *Degree requirements:* For master's, thesis optional. *Entrance requirements:* For master's, minimum undergraduate GPA of 2.75, 12 semester hours of course work in education. Additional exam requirements/recommendations for international students: Required—TOEFL (minimum score 575 paper-based; 230 computer-based), IELTS (minimum score 7). *Application deadline:* For fall admission, 9/1 for domestic students, 7/15 priority date for international students; for spring admission, 1/3 for domestic students, 11/1 priority date for international students. Applications are processed on a rolling basis. Application fee: $45. Electronic applications accepted. *Expenses:* Tuition: Full-time $7,812; part-time $434 per unit. Required fees: $120 per semester. Tuition and fees vary according to program. *Financial support:* In 2006–07, 19 students received support. Career-related internships or fieldwork, Federal Work-Study, and scholarships/grants available. Support available to part-time students. Financial award applicants required to submit FAFSA. *Unit head:* Dr. Mary Crist, Dean, School of Education, 951-343-4313, Fax: 951-343-4516, E-mail: mcrist@calbaptist.edu. *Application contact:* Gail Ronveaux, Dean of Graduate Enrollment, 951-343-5045, Fax: 951-343-5095, E-mail: graduateadmissions@calbaptist.edu.

California State University, Bakersfield, Division of Graduate Studies and Research, School of Education, Program in Bilingual/Bicultural Education, Bakersfield, CA 93311-1022. Offers MA.

California State University, Chico, Graduate School, College of Communication and Education, Department of Education, Program in Education, Chico, CA 95929-0722. Offers curriculum and instruction (MA); educational administration (MA); linguistically and culturally diverse learners (MA); reading/language arts (MA); special education (MA). *Students:* 23 full-time (14 women), 58 part-time (45 women); includes 10 minority (2 African Americans, 1 American Indian/Alaska Native, 1 Asian American or Pacific Islander, 6 Hispanic Americans), 1 international. Average age 37. 39 applicants, 100% accepted, 32 enrolled. In 2006, 37 degrees awarded. *Unit head:* Dr. Michael Kotar, Graduate Coordinator, 530-898-6610.

California State University, Dominguez Hills, College of Education, Division of Graduate Education, Program in Multicultural Education, Carson, CA 90747-0001. Offers MA. Part-time and evening/weekend programs available. *Faculty:* 3 full-time (2 women), 3 part-time/adjunct (all women). *Students:* 22 full-time (17 women), 72 part-time (60 women); includes 73 minority (19 African Americans, 6 Asian Americans or Pacific Islanders, 48 Hispanic Americans). Average age 37. 36 applicants, 92% accepted, 9 enrolled. In 2006, 41 degrees awarded. *Degree requirements:* For master's, comprehensive exam, registration. *Entrance requirements:* For master's, minimum GPA of 2.75. *Application deadline:* For fall admission, 8/1 for domestic students; for spring admission, 10/1 for domestic students. Applications are processed on a rolling basis. Application fee: $55. *Expenses:* Tuition, nonresident: part-time $339 per unit. Required fees: $1,148 per term. Tuition and fees vary according to program. *Faculty research:* English learning, intercultural communications. *Unit head:* Dr. Maximilian Contreras, Chairperson, 310-343-3918 Ext. 3524, E-mail: mcontreras@csudh.edu. *Application contact:* Admissions Office, 310-243-3530.

California State University, Fullerton, Graduate Studies, College of Education, Department of Elementary and Bilingual Education, Fullerton, CA 92834-9480. Offers bilingual/bicultural education (MS); elementary curriculum and instruction (MS). *Accreditation:* NCATE. Part-time programs available. *Students:* 17 full-time (all women), 214 part-time (198 women); includes 95 minority (1 African American, 25 Asian Americans or Pacific Islanders, 69 Hispanic Americans), 2 international. Average age 31. 178 applicants, 90% accepted, 100 enrolled. In 2006, 70 degrees awarded. *Degree requirements:* For master's, project or thesis. *Entrance requirements:* For master's, minimum GPA of 2.5, teaching certificate. Application fee: $55. *Expenses:* Tuition, nonresident: part-time $339 per unit. Required fees: $1,155 per semester. *Financial support:* Teaching assistantships, career-related internships or fieldwork, Federal Work-Study, institutionally sponsored loans, and scholarships/grants available. Support available to part-time students. Financial award application deadline: 3/1. *Faculty research:* Teacher training and tracking, model for improvement of teaching. *Unit head:* Dr. Karen Ivers, Chair, 714-278-2470. *Application contact:* Dr. Ruth Yopp-Edwards, Co-Chair, 714-278-3411.

California State University, Sacramento, Graduate Studies, College of Education, Department of Bilingual/Cross-Cultural Education, Sacramento, CA 95819-6048. Offers MA. Part-time programs available. *Students:* 8 full-time (5 women), 32 part-time (24 women); includes 22 minority (7 African Americans, 1 American Indian/Alaska Native, 5 Asian Americans or Pacific Islanders, 9 Hispanic Americans), 2 international. Average age 34. 17 applicants, 76% accepted, 11 enrolled. *Degree requirements:* For master's, thesis or alternative, writing proficiency exam. *Entrance requirements:* For master's, minimum GPA of 2.5. Additional exam requirements/recommendations for international students: Required—TOEFL. *Application*

Multilingual and Multicultural Education

California State University, Sacramento (continued)
deadline: For fall admission, 4/1 for domestic students; for spring admission, 10/1 for domestic students. Applications are processed on a rolling basis. Application fee: $55. Electronic applications accepted. *Financial support:* Career-related internships or fieldwork and Federal Work-Study available. Support available to part-time students. Financial award application deadline: 3/1. *Unit head:* Nadeen Ruiz, Chair, 916-278-5942, Fax: 916-278-5993.

California State University, San Bernardino, Graduate Studies, College of Education, Program in Bilingual/Cross-Cultural Education, San Bernardino, CA 92407-2397. Offers MA. *Accreditation:* NCATE. *Students:* 8 full-time (6 women), 16 part-time (13 women); includes 21 minority (all Hispanic Americans) Average age 30. 4 applicants, 50% accepted, 1 enrolled. In 2006, 5 degrees awarded. *Unit head:* Dr. Mary Jo Skillings, Chair, 909-537-5639, Fax: 909-537-5992, E-mail: maryjosk@csusb.edu.

California State University, Stanislaus, Graduate School, College of Education, Department of Teacher Education, Turlock, CA 95382. Offers curriculum and instruction (MA Ed), including elementary education, multilingual education, reading education, secondary education. Part-time and evening/weekend programs available. *Degree requirements:* For master's, thesis. *Entrance requirements:* For master's, MAT or GRE, minimum GPA of 3.0. Additional exam requirements/recommendations for international students: Required—TOEFL (minimum score 550 paper-based; 213 computer-based).

Capella University, School of Human Services, Minneapolis, MN 55402. Offers addictions counseling (Certificate); counseling studies (MS, PhD); criminal justice (MS, PhD, Certificate); diversity studies (Certificate); general human services (MS, PhD); health care administration (MS, PhD, Certificate); management of nonprofit agencies (MS, PhD, Certificate); marital, couple and family counseling/therapy (MS); marriage and family services (Certificate); mental health counseling (MS); professional counseling (Certificate); social and community services (MS, PhD, Certificate). Part-time and evening/weekend programs available. Postbaccalaureate distance learning degree programs offered (minimal on-campus study). Terminal master's awarded for partial completion of doctoral program. *Degree requirements:* For master's, integrative project, thesis optional; for doctorate, thesis/dissertation, comprehensive exam, registration. *Entrance requirements:* Additional exam requirements/recommendations for international students: Required—TOEFL (minimum score 550 paper-based; 213 computer-based), TWE (minimum score 4). Electronic applications accepted. *Faculty research:* Compulsive and addictive behaviors, substance abuse, assessment of psychopathology and neuropsychology.

Chicago State University, School of Graduate and Professional Studies, College of Education, Department of Special Education, Early Childhood Education and Bilingual Education, Program in Bilingual Education, Chicago, IL 60628. Offers M Ed. *Accreditation:* NCATE. *Degree requirements:* For master's, thesis optional. *Entrance requirements:* For master's, minimum GPA of 2.75.

City College of the City University of New York, Graduate School, School of Education, Program in Bilingual Education, New York, NY 10031-9198. Offers MS. *Accreditation:* NCATE. Part-time programs available. *Students:* 149. 63 applicants, 89% accepted, 56 enrolled. *Degree requirements:* For master's, thesis. *Entrance requirements:* For master's, Liberal Arts and Sciences Test (LAST), Content Specialty Test (CST). Additional exam requirements/recommendations for international students: Required—TOEFL. *Application deadline:* For fall admission, 3/15 for domestic students; for spring admission, 10/15 for domestic students. Application fee: $125. *Financial support:* Career-related internships or fieldwork available. *Unit head:* Joseph Davis, Head, 212-650-6420, E-mail: jdavis@ccny.cuny.edu. *Application contact:* Stacia Pusey, Graduate Admissions Adviser-Education, 212-650-5345, E-mail: spusey@ccny.cuny.edu.

College of Mount St. Joseph, Graduate Education Program, Cincinnati, OH 45233-1670. Offers adolescent young adult education (MA); art (MA); inclusive early childhood education (MA); instructional leadership (MA); middle childhood education (MA); multicultural special education (MA); music (MA); reading (MA). *Accreditation:* Teacher Education Accreditation Council. Part-time and evening/weekend programs available. Postbaccalaureate distance learning degree programs offered (minimal on-campus study). *Faculty:* 22 full-time (14 women), 11 part-time/adjunct (6 women). *Students:* 68 full-time (54 women), 115 part-time (96 women); includes 21 minority (16 African Americans, 2 American Indian/Alaska Native, 1 Asian American or Pacific Islander, 2 Hispanic Americans). Average age 34. 91 applicants, 98% accepted, 62 enrolled. In 2006, 61 degrees awarded. *Degree requirements:* For master's, research project. *Entrance requirements:* For master's, GRE, PRAXIS II in teaching content area (math or science), 2 letters of recommendation, interview, resumé, prerequisite courses in communications, behavioral sciences and mathematics. Additional exam requirements/recommendations for international students: Required—TOEFL (minimum score 560 paper-based; 220 computer-based). *Application deadline:* Applications are processed on a rolling basis. Application fee: $50. Electronic applications accepted. *Expenses:* Contact institution. *Financial support:* In 2006–07, 3 students received support. Career-related internships or fieldwork and scholarships/grants available. Support available to part-time students. Financial award application deadline: 6/1; financial award applicants required to submit FAFSA. *Faculty research:* Foreign and second language learning problems/reading disabilities/hyperlexia, multicultural/bilingual special education, alternative educator licensure, science education, pedagogical content knowledge. *Unit head:* Dr. Mifrando Obach, Chair, 513-244-3263, Fax: 513-244-4867, E-mail: mifrando_obach@mail.msj.edu. *Application contact:* Marilyn Hoskins, Assistant Director of Admissions for Graduate Recruitment, 513-244-4723, Fax: 513-244-4629, E-mail: marilyn_hoskins@mail.msg.edu.

College of Mount Saint Vincent, School of Professional and Continuing Studies, Department of Teacher Education, Riverdale, NY 10471-1093. Offers instructional technology and global perspectives (Certificate); middle level education (Certificate); multicultural studies (Certificate); urban and multicultural education (MS Ed). *Accreditation:* Teacher Education Accreditation Council. Part-time programs available. *Faculty:* 1 full-time (0 women), 18 part-time/adjunct (12 women). *Students:* 20 full-time (13 women), 239 part-time (172 women); includes 101 minority (50 African Americans, 11 Asian Americans or Pacific Islanders, 40 Hispanic Americans). Average age 38. 35 applicants, 57% accepted. In 2006, 124 degrees awarded. *Degree requirements:* For master's, comprehensive exam, registration. *Entrance requirements:* For master's, interview, New York teaching certificate. Additional exam requirements/recommendations for international students: Required—TOEFL. *Application deadline:* For fall admission, 9/1 priority date for domestic students, 7/1 priority date for international students; for winter admission, 11/1 priority date for domestic students, 10/1 priority date for international students; for spring admission, 12/1 priority date for domestic students, 11/1 priority date for international students. Applications are processed on a rolling basis. Application fee: $50. *Financial support:* Career-related internships or fieldwork available. Financial award applicants required to submit FAFSA. *Unit head:* Mary Ellen Sullivan, Chair, 718-405-3281, Fax: 718-601-6392. *Application contact:* Beigica Collado, Executive Assistant, 718-405-3322, Fax: 718-405-3764, E-mail: beigica.collado@mountsaintvincent.edu.

The College of New Rochelle, Graduate School, Division of Education, Program in Teaching English as a Second Language and Multilingual/Multicultural Education, New Rochelle, NY 10805-2308. Offers bilingual education (Certificate); teaching English as a second language (MS Ed). Part-time and evening/weekend programs available. *Faculty:* 1 full-time (0 women), 4 part-time/adjunct (3 women). *Students:* 12 full-time (10 women), 37 part-time (25 women); includes 16 minority (2 African Americans, 1 American Indian/Alaska Native, 3 Asian Americans or Pacific Islanders, 10 Hispanic Americans). Average age 38. In 2006, 52 degrees awarded. *Degree requirements:* For master's, practicum. *Entrance requirements:* For master's, interview, minimum GPA of 3.0 in field, 2.7 overall. *Application deadline:* For fall admission, 8/1 priority date for domestic students; for spring admission, 4/6 for domestic students. Applications are processed on a rolling basis. Application fee: $35. *Expenses:* Tuition: Part-time $575 per credit. Required fees: $90 per term. *Financial support:* Scholarships/grants available. *Unit head:* Dr. Marie Ribarich, Acting Division Head, Division of Education, 914-654-5333, Fax: 914-654-5593, E-mail: mribarich@cnr.edu.

The College of Saint Rose, Graduate Studies, School of Education, Teacher Education Department, Program in Teacher Education, Albany, NY 12203-1419. Offers bilingual pupil personnel services (Certificate); teacher education (MS Ed). Part-time and evening/weekend programs available. *Degree requirements:* For master's, comprehensive exam or thesis. *Entrance requirements:* For master's, minimum undergraduate GPA of 3.0, provisional or initial certification in a teaching area. Additional exam requirements/recommendations for international students: Required—TOEFL (minimum score 550 paper-based; 213 computer-based). Electronic applications accepted.

College of Santa Fe, Department of Education, Santa Fe, NM 87505-7634. Offers at-risk youth (MA), including bilingual/multicultural education, classroom teaching, community counseling, educational administration, leadership, school counseling, self-designed program, TESOL/Multicultural; curriculum and instruction (MA); multicultural special education (MA). Part-time and evening/weekend programs available. *Entrance requirements:* For master's, minimum GPA of 3.0. *Faculty research:* Integrated curriculum, child development, brain research, learning styles, systemic issues in education.

Columbia College Chicago, Graduate School, Department of Educational Studies, Chicago, IL 60605-1996. Offers elementary (MAT); English (MAT); interdisciplinary arts (MAT); multicultural education (MA); urban teaching (MA). Part-time and evening/weekend programs available. *Degree requirements:* For master's, thesis, student teaching experience, 100 pre-clinical hours. *Entrance requirements:* For master's, NTE, minimum GPA of 3.0, portfolio. Additional exam requirements/recommendations for international students: Required—TOEFL (minimum score 550 paper-based; 213 computer-based). Electronic applications accepted.

Columbia International University, Columbia Graduate School, Columbia, SC 29230-3122. Offers Bible teaching (MABT); Christian higher education leadership (Ed D); Christian school educational leadership (Ed D); counseling (MACN); curriculum and instruction (M Ed), including Christian school guidance, English as a second language, learning disabilities, school technology; early childhood and elementary education (MAT); educational administration (M Ed); teaching English as a foreign language (Certificate); teaching English as a foreign language and intercultural studies (MATF). Part-time and evening/weekend programs available. *Faculty:* 11 full-time (4 women), 7 part-time/adjunct (5 women). *Students:* 52 full-time (44 women), 93 part-time (59 women); includes 17 minority (11 African Americans, 2 Asian Americans or Pacific Islanders, 4 Hispanic Americans), 10 international. Average age 35. 107 applicants, 56% accepted, 41 enrolled. In 2006, 62 degrees awarded. *Degree requirements:* For master's, internships, professional project. *Entrance requirements:* For master's, Minnesota Multiphasic Personality Inventory, MAT, minimum GPA of 2.7. Additional exam requirements/recommendations for international students: Required—TOEFL. *Application deadline:* For fall admission, 8/1 priority date for domestic and international students; for winter admission, 12/15 priority date for domestic and international students; for spring admission, 1/15 priority date for domestic and international students. Applications are processed on a rolling basis. Application fee: $45. Electronic applications accepted. *Expenses:* Tuition: Part-time $400 per semester hour. Tuition and fees vary according to course load and program. *Financial support:* In 2006–07, 35 students received support. Career-related internships or fieldwork, Federal Work-Study, institutionally sponsored loans, and scholarships/grants available. Financial award application deadline: 3/17; financial award applicants required to submit FAFSA. *Unit head:* Dr. Milton Uecker, Dean, 803-807-5319, Fax: 803-786-4209, E-mail: muecker@ciu.edu. *Application contact:* Michelle MacGregor, Director of Admissions, 800-777-2227 Ext. 5335, Fax: 803-786-4209, E-mail: yescbs@ciu.edu.

DePaul University, School of Education, Chicago, IL 60604-2287. Offers bilingual and bicultural education (M Ed, MA); curriculum studies (M Ed, MA); education (Ed D), including curriculum studies, educational leadership; educational leadership (M Ed, MA), including administration and supervision, Catholic school leadership, physical education; human development and learning (MA); human services and counseling (M Ed, MA), including agencies, family concerns, and higher education, elementary schools, human services management, secondary schools; reading and learning disabilities (M Ed, MA); social culture studies in education and development (M Ed, MA), including curriculum studies/development; teaching and learning (early childhood, elementary and secondary) (M Ed), including elementary education (M Ed, MA), secondary education (M Ed, MA); teaching and learning (early childhood, elementary, and secondary) (MA), including elementary education (M Ed, MA), secondary education (M Ed, MA). *Accreditation:* NCATE. Part-time and evening/weekend programs available. *Faculty:* 61 full-time (40 women), 76 part-time/adjunct (46 women). *Students:* 1,371 full-time (1,103 women), 474 part-time (362 women); includes 435 minority (144 African Americans, 7 American Indian/Alaska Native, 89 Asian Americans or Pacific Islanders, 195 Hispanic Americans), 11 international. Average age 30. 993 applicants, 80% accepted, 617 enrolled. In 2006, 324 master's, 7 doctorates awarded. *Degree requirements:* For doctorate, thesis/dissertation. *Entrance requirements:* For master's, interview, minimum GPA of 2.75, 2 letters of recommendation; for doctorate, interview, master's degree, 2 years of work experience (recommended), writing sample, 3 letters of recommendation. Application fee: $25. Electronic applications accepted. *Financial support:* In 2006–07, 16 research assistantships with tuition reimbursements (averaging $4,370 per year), 1 teaching assistantship (averaging $6,000 per year) were awarded; career-related internships or fieldwork also available. *Faculty research:* Reflective teaching, children at risk, loss, ethnicity, urban education. Total annual research expenditures: $556,194. *Unit head:* Dr. Clara Jennings, Dean, 773-325-7581, Fax: 773-325-7728, E-mail: cjennings@depaul.edu. *Application contact:* Dr. John Bollwark, Data Project Manager, 773-325-7582, Fax: 773-325-7713, E-mail: jbollwar@depaul.edu.

DeSales University, Graduate Division, Program in Education, Center Valley, PA 18034-9568. Offers academic standards and information (Certificate); bilingual/ESL studies (Certificate); biology (M Ed); chemistry (M Ed); computers in education (K-12) (M Ed); computers in education (K-8) (M Ed); English (M Ed); instructional technology specialist (Certificate); mathematics (M Ed); special education (M Ed, Certificate); TESOL (M Ed). Part-time and evening/weekend programs available. Postbaccalaureate distance learning degree programs offered (minimal on-campus study). *Students:* 34 full-time, 190 part-time. In 2006, 30 degrees awarded. *Degree requirements:* For master's, thesis project. *Entrance requirements:* For master's, teaching certificate. *Application deadline:* Applications are processed on a rolling basis. Application fee: $35. Electronic applications accepted. *Expenses:* Contact institution. *Financial support:* Unspecified assistantships available. Support available to part-time students. Financial award application deadline: 5/1. *Faculty research:* Effective teaching, computer interfacing in chemistry labs, computer applications to teaching, history of philosophy, aesthetics multidrug-resistant cancer. *Unit head:* Dr. Lujean Baab, Director of M.Ed. Program, 610-282-1100 Ext. 1739, Fax: 610-282-3734, E-mail: lujean.baab@desales.edu. *Application contact:* Donna L. Cressman, Program Secretary, 610-282-1100 Ext. 1461, Fax: 610-282-3734, E-mail: med@desales.edu.

Eastern Michigan University, Graduate School, College of Arts and Sciences, Department of Foreign Languages and Bilingual Studies, Program in Spanish (Bilingual-Bicultural Education), Ypsilanti, MI 48197. Offers MA. Part-time and evening/weekend programs available. Postbaccalaureate distance learning degree programs offered (minimal on-campus study). In 2006, 2 degrees awarded. *Degree requirements:* For master's, one foreign language. *Entrance requirements:* Additional exam requirements/recommendations for international students: Required—TOEFL. *Application deadline:* For fall admission, 5/15 priority date for domestic students, 5/1 priority date for international students; for winter admission, 10/15 priority date for domestic students, 10/1 priority date for international students; for spring admission, 3/15 priority date for domestic students, 3/1 priority date for international students. Applications are processed on a rolling basis. Application fee: $35. *Expenses:* Tuition, state resident: part-time $341 per credit hour. Tuition, nonresident: full-time $16,104; part-time $671 per credit hour. Required fees: $816; $34 per credit hour. $40 per term. One-time fee: $82 full-time. Tuition and fees vary according to course level, course load, degree level and reciprocity agreements. *Financial support:* Fellowships, research assistantships with full tuition reimbursements, teaching assistantships with full tuition reimbursements available. Support available to part-time students. Financial award applicants required to submit FAFSA. *Unit head:* Dr. Ronald Cere, Coordinator, 734-487-0433.

Eastern Michigan University, Graduate School, College of Education, Department of Teacher Education, Program in Teaching for Diversity, Ypsilanti, MI 48197. Offers MA. Part-time and evening/weekend programs available. Postbaccalaureate distance learning degree programs offered (minimal on-campus study). *Students:* Average age 32. In 2006, 1 degree awarded. *Entrance requirements:* Additional exam requirements/recommendations for international students: Required—TOEFL. *Application deadline:* For fall admission, 5/15 priority date for domestic students, 5/1 priority date for international students; for winter admission, 10/15 priority date for domestic students, 10/1 priority date for international students; for spring admission, 3/15 priority date for domestic students, 3/1 priority date for international students. Application fee: $35. *Expenses:* Tuition, state resident: part-time $341 per credit hour. Tuition, nonresident: full-time $16,104; part-time $671 per credit hour. Required fees: $816; $34 per credit hour. $40 per term. One-time fee: $82 full-time. Tuition and fees vary according to course level, course load, degree level and reciprocity agreements. *Financial support:* Fellowships, research assistantships with full tuition reimbursements, teaching assistantships with full tuition reimbursements, career-related internships or fieldwork, Federal Work-Study, institutionally sponsored loans, scholarships/grants, tuition waivers (partial), and unspecified assistantships available. Support available to part-time students. Financial award applicants required to submit FAFSA.

Eastern University, Graduate Education Programs, Program in Multicultural Education, St. Davids, PA 19087-3696. Offers M Ed. *Entrance requirements:* For master's, minimum GPA of 2.5. Additional exam requirements/recommendations for international students: Required—TOEFL.

Fairfield University, Graduate School of Education and Allied Professions, Department of TESOL, Foreign Language and Bilingual/Multicultural Education, Fairfield, CT 06824-5195. Offers MA, CAS. Part-time and evening/weekend programs available. *Faculty:* 1 (woman) full-time, 2 part-time/adjunct (both women). *Students:* 9 full-time (7 women), 39 part-time (31 women). Average age 34. 14 applicants, 57% accepted, 7 enrolled. In 2006, 11 master's, 5 other advanced degrees awarded. *Degree requirements:* For master's, educational technology course, thesis optional. *Entrance requirements:* For master's, PRAXIS I (PPST), minimum QPA of 2.67, 2 recommendations, resumè. Additional exam requirements/recommendations for international students: Required—TOEFL (minimum score 550 paper-based; 213 computer-based; 79 iBT). *Application deadline:* Applications are processed on a rolling basis. Application fee: $55. Electronic applications accepted. *Financial support:* Scholarships/grants, tuition waivers (partial), and unspecified assistantships available. Financial award applicants required to submit FAFSA. *Faculty research:* Teacher education. *Unit head:* Sr. Julianna Poole, SSND, Chair, 203-254-4000 Ext. 2873, Fax: 203-254-4047, E-mail: jpoole@mail.fairfield.edu. *Application contact:* Marianne Gumpper, Director of Graduate and Continuing Studies Admissions, 203-254-4184, Fax: 203-254-4073, E-mail: gradadmis@mail.fairfield.edu.

Fairleigh Dickinson University, Metropolitan Campus, University College: Arts, Sciences, and Professional Studies, Peter Sammartino School of Education, Program in Multilingual Education, Teaneck, NJ 07666-1914. Offers MA. *Students:* 14 full-time (11 women), 1 (woman) part-time, 14 international. Average age 31. 11 applicants, 91% accepted, 6 enrolled. In 2006, 8 degrees awarded. *Application deadline:* Applications are processed on a rolling basis. Application fee: $40.

Florida Atlantic University, College of Education, Department of Teacher Education, Boca Raton, FL 33431-0991. Offers art teacher education (M Ed); curriculum and instruction (M Ed, Ed D, Ed S); educational psychology (MSF); elementary education (M Ed); foundations of education (M Ed); multicultural education (MSF); reading teacher education (M Ed). *Accreditation:* NCATE. Part-time and evening/weekend programs available. *Faculty:* 29 full-time (23 women), 75 part-time/adjunct (50 women). *Students:* 78 full-time (65 women), 176 part-time (159 women); includes 50 minority (20 African Americans, 1 American Indian/Alaska Native, 6 Asian Americans or Pacific Islanders, 23 Hispanic Americans), 1 international. Average age 35. 132 applicants, 64% accepted, 62 enrolled. In 2006, 95 master's, 2 doctorates awarded. *Degree requirements:* For master's, registration; for doctorate, thesis/dissertation, departmental qualifying exam, comprehensive exam, registration; for Ed S, departmental qualifying exam. *Entrance requirements:* For master's, GRE General Test, minimum GPA of 3.0 in last 2 years of undergraduate course work; for doctorate, GRE General Test, GRE Subject Test, minimum graduate GPA of 3.2, 3.0 in last 2 years of undergraduate course work; for Ed S, GRE General Test. Additional exam requirements/recommendations for international students: Required—TOEFL. *Application deadline:* Applications are processed on a rolling basis. Application fee: $30. *Expenses:* Tuition, area resident: Full-time $4,394. Tuition, nonresident: full-time $16,441. *Financial support:* In 2006–07, 4 research assistantships with partial tuition reimbursements (averaging $8,000 per year), 3 teaching assistantships with partial tuition reimbursements (averaging $8,000 per year) were awarded; fellowships with partial tuition reimbursements, career-related internships or fieldwork, scholarships/grants, and unspecified assistantships also available. *Faculty research:* Technology, teaching English to speakers of other languages, math teaching, electronic portfolio assessment, global perspectives through social studies. *Unit head:* Dr. Penelope Fritzer, Chairperson, 561-297-3584.

Florida State University, Graduate Studies, College of Education, Department of Middle and Secondary Education, Program in Multilingual-Multicultural Education, Tallahassee, FL 32306. Offers MS, PhD, Ed S. Part-time programs available. *Faculty:* 1 (woman) full-time, 3 part-time/adjunct (1 woman). *Students:* 16 full-time (11 women), 6 part-time (3 women); includes 11 minority (1 African American, 8 Asian Americans or Pacific Islanders, 2 Hispanic Americans). 21 applicants, 52% accepted, 3 enrolled. In 2006, 2 master's, 3 doctorates awarded. *Degree requirements:* For master's and Ed S, thesis optional; for doctorate, thesis/dissertation, comprehensive exam. *Entrance requirements:* For master's, doctorate, and Ed S, GRE General Test, minimum GPA of 3.0. *Application deadline:* For fall admission, 7/1 priority date for domestic students; for spring admission, 11/1 for domestic students. Applications are processed on a rolling basis. Application fee: $30. *Expenses:* Tuition, state resident: full-time $5,822; part-time $243 per credit hour. Tuition, nonresident: full-time $20,976; part-time $874 per credit hour. Tuition and fees vary according to program. *Financial support:* Fellowships, research assistantships, teaching assistantships, career-related internships or fieldwork available. Financial award applicants required to submit FAFSA. *Unit head:* Dr. Deborah Hasson, Head, 850-644-6553, Fax: 850-644-1880, E-mail: hasson@coe.fsu.edu. *Application contact:* Christina Crotty, Office Manager, 850-644-7810, Fax: 850-644-1880, E-mail: crotty@mailer.fsu.edu.

Fordham University, Graduate School of Education, Division of Curriculum and Teaching, New York, NY 10023. Offers adult education (MS, MSE); bilingual teacher education (MSE); curriculum and teaching (MSE); early childhood education (MSE); elementary education (MST); language, literacy, and learning (PhD); reading education (MSE, Adv C); secondary education (MAT, MSE); special education (MSE, Adv C); teaching English as a second language (MSE). *Accreditation:* NCATE. *Faculty:* 22 full-time (18 women), 38 part-time/adjunct (28 women). *Students:* 68 full-time (51 women), 663 part-time (612 women); includes 200 minority (74 African Americans, 1 American Indian/Alaska Native, 37 Asian Americans or Pacific Islanders, 88 Hispanic Americans), 3 international. Average age 32. 636 applicants, 86% accepted, 322 enrolled. In 2006, 351 master's, 8 doctorates awarded. *Degree requirements:* For doctorate and Adv C, thesis/dissertation. *Entrance requirements:* For doctorate, MAT, GRE General Test. Application fee: $65. *Financial support:* Applicants required to submit FAFSA. *Unit head:* Dr. Terry Osborn, Chairperson, 212-636-6450.

Fresno Pacific University, Graduate Programs, Programs in Education, Fresno, CA 93702-4709. Offers administration (MA Ed), including administrative services; foundations, curriculum and teaching (MA Ed), including curriculum and teaching, school library and information technology; language, literacy, and culture (MA Ed), including bilingual/cross-cultural education, language development, multilingual contexts, reading; mathematics/science/computer education (MA Ed), including educational technology, integrated mathematics/science education, mathematics education; pupil personnel services (MA Ed), including school counseling, school psychology; special education (MA Ed), including mild/moderate, moderate/severe, physical and health impairments. Part-time and evening/weekend programs available. *Faculty:* 12 full-time (5 women), 19 part-time/adjunct (9 women). *Students:* 73 full-time (59 women), 399 part-time (295 women); includes 136 minority (9 African Americans, 5 American Indian/Alaska Native, 12 Asian Americans or Pacific Islanders, 110 Hispanic Americans), 2 international. Average age 39. 124 applicants, 73% accepted, 10 enrolled. In 2006, 128 degrees awarded. *Degree requirements:* For master's, thesis (for some programs), registration. *Entrance requirements:* For master's, interview; GMAT, GRE, MAT, or 6 units of course work with a faculty recommendation. Additional exam requirements/recommendations for international students: Required—TOEFL (minimum score 550 paper-based; 213 computer-based). *Application deadline:* For fall admission, 7/15 for domestic and international students; for spring admission, 11/15 for domestic and international students. Applications are processed on a rolling basis. Application fee: $90. Electronic applications accepted. *Expenses:* Tuition: Full-time $7,470; part-time $415 per credit. *Financial support:* In 2006–07, 260 students received support. Career-related internships or fieldwork, scholarships/grants, and tuition waivers (full and partial) available. Support available to part-time students. Financial award applicants required to submit FAFSA.

Fresno Pacific University, Graduate Programs, Programs in Education, Division of Language, Literacy, and Culture, Program in Bilingual/Cross-Cultural Education, Fresno, CA 93702-4709. Offers MA Ed. Part-time and evening/weekend programs available. *Students:* 1 (woman) full-time, 8 part-time (all women); includes 7 minority (all Hispanic Americans), 1 international. Average age 37. 2 applicants, 50% accepted, 1 enrolled. In 2006, 1 degree awarded. *Degree requirements:* For master's, thesis or alternative, registration. *Entrance requirements:* Additional exam requirements/recommendations for international students: Required—TOEFL (minimum score 550 paper-based; 213 computer-based). *Application deadline:* For fall admission, 7/15 for domestic and international students; for spring admission, 11/15 for domestic and international students. Applications are processed on a rolling basis. Application fee: $90. Electronic applications accepted. *Expenses:* Tuition: Full-time $7,470; part-time $415 per credit. *Financial support:* In 2006–07, 5 students received support. Scholarships/grants and tuition waivers (full and partial) available. Support available to part-time students. Financial award applicants required to submit FAFSA.

Fresno Pacific University, Graduate Programs, Programs in Education, Division of Language, Literacy, and Culture, Program in Multilingual Contexts, Fresno, CA 93702-4709. Offers MA Ed. Part-time and evening/weekend programs available. *Students:* Average age 41. 1 applicant, 100% accepted, 0 enrolled. *Degree requirements:* For master's, thesis or alternative, registration. *Entrance requirements:* Additional exam requirements/recommendations for international students: Required—TOEFL (minimum score 550 paper-based; 213 computer-based). *Application deadline:* For fall admission, 7/15 for domestic and international students; for spring admission, 11/15 for domestic and international students. Applications are processed on a rolling basis. Application fee: $90. Electronic applications accepted. *Expenses:* Tuition: Full-time $7,470; part-time $415 per credit. *Financial support:* In 2006–07, 2 students received support. Scholarships/grants and tuition waivers (full and partial) available. Support available to part-time students. Financial award applicants required to submit FAFSA.

George Mason University, Graduate School of Education, Programs in Curriculum and Instruction, Fairfax, VA 22030. Offers bilingual/multicultural/English as a second language education (M Ed); early childhood education (M Ed); instructional technology (M Ed); middle education (M Ed); reading (M Ed); secondary education (M Ed); special education (M Ed). Part-time and evening/weekend programs available. *Faculty:* 108 full-time (70 women), 193 part-time/adjunct (140 women). *Students:* 185 full-time (144 women), 816 part-time (683 women); includes 148 minority (46 African Americans, 2 American Indian/Alaska Native, 44 Asian Americans or Pacific Islanders, 56 Hispanic Americans), 28 international. Average age 34. 822 applicants, 72% accepted, 473 enrolled. In 2006, 606 master's awarded. *Entrance requirements:* For master's, minimum GPA of 3.0 in last 60 hours. *Application deadline:* For fall admission, 5/1 for domestic students; for spring admission, 11/1 for domestic students. Application fee: $60 ($75 for international students). Electronic applications accepted. *Expenses:* Tuition, state resident: full-time $5,724; part-time $238 per credit. Tuition, nonresident: full-time $16,896; part-time $704 per credit. Required fees: $1,656; $69 per credit. *Financial support:* Career-related internships or fieldwork available. Support available to part-time students. Financial award application deadline: 3/1; financial award applicants required to submit FAFSA. *Unit head:* Martin E. Ford, Senior Associate Dean, 703-993-2006.

Georgetown University, Graduate School of Arts and Sciences, Department of Linguistics, Washington, DC 20057. Offers bilingual education (Certificate); linguistics (MS, PhD); teaching English as a second language (MAT, Certificate); teaching English as a second language and bilingual education (MAT). Terminal master's awarded for partial completion of doctoral program. *Degree requirements:* For master's, one foreign language, comprehensive exam, optional research project; for doctorate, 2 foreign languages, thesis/dissertation, comprehensive exam. *Entrance requirements:* For master's and doctorate, 18 undergraduate credits in a foreign language. Additional exam requirements/recommendations for international students: Required—TOEFL.

Graduate Institute of Applied Linguistics, Graduate Programs, Dallas, TX 75236. Offers applied linguistics (MA, Certificate); language development (MA). Part-time programs available. *Students:* 41 full-time (19 women), 54 part-time (30 women); includes 6 minority (4 Asian Americans or Pacific Islanders, 2 Hispanic Americans). Average age 32. 56 applicants, 98% accepted. In 2006, 20 degrees awarded. *Degree requirements:* For master's, one foreign language, thesis (for some programs), comprehensive exam (for some programs), registration. *Entrance requirements:* For master's, GRE. Additional exam requirements/recommendations for international students: Required—TOEFL. *Application deadline:* Applications are processed on a rolling basis. Application fee: $20. Electronic applications accepted. *Expenses:* Tuition: Part-time $340 per credit. Full-time tuition and fees vary according to program. *Financial support:* In 2006–07, 51 students received support. Scholarships/grants and tuition waivers (partial) available. Financial award application deadline: 11/20. *Faculty research:* Minority languages. *Application contact:* Grace M. Fuqua, Admissions Officer, 972-708-7343, Fax: 972-708-7396, E-mail: admissions@gial.edu.

Harvard University, Graduate School of Education, Doctoral Program in Education, Cambridge, MA 02138. Offers culture, communities and education (Ed D); education policy (Ed D); education policy, leadership and instructional practice (Ed D); higher education (Ed D); human development and education (Ed D); quantitative policy analysis in education (Ed D); urban superintendency (Ed D). Part-time programs available. *Faculty:* 58 full-time (25 women), 40 part-time/adjunct (22 women). *Students:* 306 full-time (216 women), 35 part-time (26 women); includes 95 minority (38 African Americans, 4 American Indian/Alaska Native, 35 Asian Americans or Pacific Islanders, 18 Hispanic Americans), 46 international. Average age 35. 494 applicants, 12% accepted, 48 enrolled. In 2006, 70 degrees awarded. Terminal master's awarded for partial completion of doctoral program. *Degree requirements:* For doctorate, thesis/dissertation. *Entrance requirements:* For doctorate, GRE General Test, 3 letters of recommendation, official transcripts, statement of purpose. Additional exam requirements/recommendations for international students: Required—TOEFL (minimum score 600 paper-based; 250 computer-based; 100 iBT), TWE (minimum score 5). *Application deadline:* For fall admission, 12/14 for domestic and international students. Application fee: $85. Electronic applications accepted. *Expenses:* *Contact institution.* *Financial support:* In 2006–07, 171 fellowships with full and partial tuition reimbursements (averaging $11,489 per year), 47 research assistantships (averaging $9,340 per year), 153 teaching assistantships (averaging $7,710 per year) were awarded; career-related internships or fieldwork, Federal Work-Study, institutionally sponsored loans, scholarships/grants, health care benefits, tuition waivers (full

Multilingual and Multicultural Education

Harvard University (continued)

and partial), and unspecified assistantships also available. Support available to part-time students. Financial award application deadline: 2/2; financial award applicants required to submit FAFSA. *Faculty research:* Learning and development; educational leadership and organizations; education policy analysis. Total annual research expenditures: $4.8 million. *Unit head:* Dr. James Stiles, Associate Dean for Degree Programs. *Application contact:* Information Contact, 617-495-3414, Fax: 617-496-3577, E-mail: gseadmissions@harvard.edu.

Heritage University, Graduate Programs in Education, Program in Professional Studies, Toppenish, WA 98948-9599. Offers bilingual education/ESL (M Ed); biology (M Ed); English and literature (M Ed); reading/literacy (M Ed); special education (M Ed). Part-time and evening/weekend programs available. *Students:* 174 (125 women); includes 52 minority (1 African American, 4 American Indian/Alaska Native, 6 Asian Americans or Pacific Islanders, 41 Hispanic Americans). Average age 37. In 2006, 84 degrees awarded. *Degree requirements:* For master's, thesis (for some programs), comprehensive exam (for some programs), registration. *Application deadline:* Applications are processed on a rolling basis. Application fee: $50 ($100 for international students). *Financial support:* Career-related internships or fieldwork, Federal Work-Study, institutionally sponsored loans, and tuition waivers (partial) available. Support available to part-time students. *Unit head:* Dr. Jack McPherson, Head, 509-865-8626, E-mail: mcpherson_j@heritage.edu. *Application contact:* Kathy Otto, Coordinator of Administrative Services, 509-865-8635, Fax: 509-865-8629, E-mail: otto_k@heritage.edu.

Hofstra University, School of Education and Allied Human Services, Department of Counseling, Research, Special Education and Rehabilitation, Program in Counseling, Hempstead, NY 11549. Offers counseling (PD); mental health counseling (MA); school counselor (MS Ed); school counselor-bilingual extension (Advanced Certificate). *Accreditation:* NCATE. Part-time programs available. *Students:* 39 full-time (32 women), 33 part-time (22 women); includes 11 minority (3 African Americans, 8 Hispanic Americans), 1 international. Average age 26. 68 applicants, 56% accepted, 23 enrolled. In 2006, 27 master's, 2 other advanced degrees awarded. *Degree requirements:* For master's, comprehensive exam, registration (for some programs); for other advanced degree, one foreign language. *Entrance requirements:* For master's, GRE General Test, interview, 3 letters of recommendation, essay; for other advanced degree, GRE, interview, 3 letters of recommendation, essay. Additional exam requirements/recommendations for international students: Required—TOEFL (minimum score 550 paper-based; 213 computer-based). *Application deadline:* Applications are processed on a rolling basis. Application fee: $60. Electronic applications accepted. *Expenses:* Tuition: Full-time $13,320; part-time $740 per credit. Required fees: $930; $155 per term. *Financial support:* In 2006–07, 43 students received support, including 3 fellowships with tuition reimbursements available (averaging $2,587 per year), 10 research assistantships with full and partial tuition reimbursements available (averaging $5,947 per year); institutionally sponsored loans, scholarships/grants, tuition waivers (full and partial), and unspecified assistantships also available. Support available to part-time students. Financial award applicants required to submit FAFSA. *Faculty research:* Multicultural counseling; bereavement, loss and trauma counseling; GLBT issues in counseling; college student development; conflict and peace education. *Unit head:* Dr. Laurie Johnson, Director, 516-463-5754, Fax: 516-463-6184, E-mail: cprlzj@hofstra.edu. *Application contact:* Carol Drummer, Dean of Graduate Admissions, 516-463-4876, Fax: 516-463-4664, E-mail: gradstudent@hofstra.edu.

Hofstra University, School of Education and Allied Human Services, Department of Curriculum and Teaching, Programs in TESL/Bilingual Education, Hempstead, NY 11549. Offers bilingual education (MA); bilingual extension education (CAS); TESOL (MS Ed, CAS). *Accreditation:* NCATE. Part-time programs available. *Students:* 28 full-time (23 women), 29 part-time (28 women); includes 17 minority (3 African Americans, 1 Asian American or Pacific Islander, 13 Hispanic Americans), 1 international. Average age 31. 33 applicants, 67% accepted, 13 enrolled. In 2006, 15 degrees awarded. *Degree requirements:* For master's, one foreign language, thesis or alternative, completion of electronic portfolio. *Entrance requirements:* For master's, interview, 2 letters of recommendation, teaching certificate, essay, proficiency in language; for CAS, 2 letters of recommendation, interview, teaching certificate, essay, proficiency in language. Additional exam requirements/recommendations for international students: Required—TOEFL (minimum score 550 paper-based; 213 computer-based). *Application deadline:* Applications are processed on a rolling basis. Application fee: $60. Electronic applications accepted. *Expenses:* Tuition: Full-time $13,320; part-time $740 per credit. Required fees: $930; $155 per term. *Financial support:* In 2006–07, 16 students received support, including 4 fellowships with tuition reimbursements available (averaging $2,533 per year); research assistantships with full and partial tuition reimbursements available, career-related internships or fieldwork, scholarships/grants, tuition waivers (full and partial), and unspecified assistantships also available. Support available to part-time students. Financial award applicants required to submit FAFSA. *Faculty research:* Linking TESOL theory and practice, content-based ESL instruction, cognitively stimulating ESL instruction. *Unit head:* Dr. Tatiana Gordon, Director, 516-463-5170, Fax: 516-463-6196, E-mail: cattzg@hofstra.edu. *Application contact:* Carol Drummer, Dean of Graduate Admissions, 516-463-4876, Fax: 516-463-4664, E-mail: gradstudent@hofstra.edu.

Howard University, School of Communications, Department of Communication and Culture, Washington, DC 20059-0002. Offers intercultural communication (MA, PhD); organizational communication (MA, PhD). Offered through the Graduate School of Arts and Sciences. Part-time programs available. Terminal master's awarded for partial completion of doctoral program. *Degree requirements:* For master's, comprehensive exam or thesis; for doctorate, one foreign language, thesis/dissertation, comprehensive exam. *Entrance requirements:* For master's, English proficiency exam, GRE General Test, minimum GPA of 3.0; for doctorate, English proficiency exam, GRE General Test, master's degree in related field, minimum GPA of 3.5. Additional exam requirements/recommendations for international students: Required—TOEFL. *Faculty research:* Media effects, black discourse, development communication, African-American organizations.

Hunter College of the City University of New York, Graduate School, School of Education, Department of Curriculum and Teaching, Program in Bilingual Education, New York, NY 10021-5085. Offers MS. *Accreditation:* NCATE. *Faculty:* 2 full-time (both women), 3 part-time/adjunct (2 women). *Students:* Average age 32. 15 applicants, 33% accepted, 5 enrolled. In 2006, 15 degrees awarded. *Degree requirements:* For master's, one foreign language, thesis, research seminar, student teaching experience or practicum, New York State Teacher Certification Exams. *Entrance requirements:* For master's, interview, minimum GPA of 2.8, writing sample in English and Spanish. Additional exam requirements/recommendations for international students: Required—TOEFL, TWE. *Application deadline:* For fall admission, 4/1 for domestic students, 2/1 for international students; for spring admission, 11/1 for domestic students, 9/1 for international students. Applications are processed on a rolling basis. Application fee: $125. *Expenses:* Tuition, state resident: part-time $270 per credit. Tuition, nonresident: part-time $500 per credit. Required fees: $45 per semester. *Financial support:* Federal Work-Study, scholarships/grants, and tuition waivers (partial) available. Support available to part-time students. *Faculty research:* Teacher effectiveness, language development, Spanish language and linguistics and multicultural education. *Unit head:* Yvonne DeGaetano, Coordinator, 212-772-4683, E-mail: ydegaetano@hunter.cuny.edu. *Application contact:* William Zlata, Director for Graduate Admissions, 212-772-4482, Fax: 212-650-3336, E-mail: admissions@hunter.cuny.edu.

Hunter College of the City University of New York, Graduate School, School of Education, Department of Educational Foundations and Counseling Programs, Programs in School Counselor, New York, NY 10021-5085. Offers school counseling (MS Ed); school counseling with bilingual extension (MS Ed). *Accreditation:* NCATE. *Faculty:* 18 full-time (15 women), 14 part-time/adjunct (8 women). *Students:* 38 full-time (32 women), 90 part-time (71 women); includes 22 minority (10 African Americans, 3 Asian Americans or Pacific Islanders, 9 Hispanic Americans). Average age 30. 268 applicants, 21% accepted, 32 enrolled. In 2006, 29 degrees awarded. *Degree requirements:* For master's, thesis, internship, practicum, research seminar. *Entrance requirements:* For master's, interview, minimum GPA of 2.7. Additional exam requirements/recommendations for international students: Required—TOEFL, TWE. *Application deadline:* For fall admission, 4/1 for domestic students, 2/1 for international students; for spring admission, 11/1 for domestic students, 9/1 for international students. Applications are processed on a rolling basis. Application fee: $125. *Expenses:* Tuition, state resident: part-time $270 per credit. Tuition, nonresident: part-time $500 per credit. Required fees: $45 per semester. *Financial support:* Federal Work-Study and tuition waivers (partial) available. Support available to part-time students. *Unit head:* Dr. John O'Neill, Coordinator, 212-772-5188, E-mail: joneil@hunter.cuny.edu. *Application contact:* William Zlata, Director for Graduate Admissions, 212-772-4482, Fax: 212-650-3336, E-mail: admissions@hunter.cuny.edu.

Immaculata University, College of Graduate Studies, Program in Cultural and Linguistic Diversity, Immaculata, PA 19345. Offers MA. Part-time and evening/weekend programs available. *Students:* Average age 31. 3 applicants, 100% accepted, 2 enrolled. In 2006, 1 degree awarded. *Degree requirements:* For master's, one foreign language, comprehensive exam, professional experience, thesis optional. *Entrance requirements:* For master's, GRE or MAT, proficiency in Spanish or Asian language, minimum GPA of 3.0. *Application deadline:* Applications are processed on a rolling basis. Application fee: $35. Electronic applications accepted. *Financial support:* Application deadline: 5/1. *Faculty research:* Cognitive learning, Caribbean literature and culture, English as a second language, teaching English to speakers of other languages. *Unit head:* Dr. Margaret Van Naerrsen, Coordinator, 610-647-4400 Ext. 3282, E-mail: mvannaerssen@immaculata.edu. *Application contact:* 610-647-4400 Ext. 3211, Fax: 610-993-8550, E-mail: graduate@immaculata.edu.

Indiana State University, School of Graduate Studies, College of Arts and Sciences, Department of Languages, Literatures, and Linguistics, Terre Haute, IN 47809-1401. Offers French (MA, MS); linguistics/teaching English as a second language (MA, MS); Spanish (MA, MS); TESL/TEFL (CAS). *Faculty:* 7 full-time (4 women), 2 part-time/adjunct (1 woman). *Students:* 26 full-time (16 women), 16 part-time (12 women); includes 4 minority (2 Asian Americans or Pacific Islanders, 2 Hispanic Americans), 25 international. Average age 31. 50 applicants, 92% accepted, 13 enrolled. In 2006, 18 degrees awarded. *Degree requirements:* For master's, comprehensive exam. *Application deadline:* For fall admission, 7/1 priority date for domestic students; for spring admission, 11/1 priority date for domestic students. Applications are processed on a rolling basis. Application fee: $35. Electronic applications accepted. *Expenses:* Tuition, state resident: part-time $278 per credit. Tuition, nonresident: part-time $552 per credit. *Financial support:* In 2006–07, 9 teaching assistantships (averaging $6,300 per year) were awarded; research assistantships with partial tuition reimbursements, tuition waivers (partial) also available. Financial award application deadline: 3/1; financial award applicants required to submit FAFSA. *Unit head:* Dr. Ronald W. Dunbar, Chairperson, 812-237-2368. *Application contact:* Information Contact, 812-237-2366.

Iona College, School of Arts and Science, Program in Multicultural Education, New Rochelle, NY 10801-1890. Offers MS Ed. *Accreditation:* NCATE. Part-time and evening/weekend programs available. *Faculty:* 11 full-time (6 women), 21 part-time/adjunct (13 women). *Students:* 1 (woman) full-time, 6 part-time (5 women); includes 2 minority (1 African American, 1 Hispanic American). Average age 29. 3 applicants, 100% accepted, 3 enrolled. In 2006, 8 degrees awarded. *Entrance requirements:* For master's, New York teaching certificate, minimum undergraduate GPA of 2.75. Additional exam requirements/recommendations for international students: Required—TOEFL (minimum score 550 paper-based; 213 computer-based). *Application deadline:* Applications are processed on a rolling basis. Application fee: $50. Electronic applications accepted. *Expenses:* Tuition: Part-time $665 per credit. Required fees: $150 per term. *Financial support:* Career-related internships or fieldwork, tuition waivers (partial), and unspecified assistantships available. Support available to part-time students. *Faculty research:* Early literacy assessment, literacy development, cultural approaches in teaching and learning of mathematics, middle school assessment strategies, critical thinking and questioning strategies. *Unit head:* Dr. Patricia Antonacci, Chair, 914-633-2080, Fax: 914-633-2608, E-mail: pantonacci@iona.edu. *Application contact:* Veronica Jarek-Prinz, Graduate Admissions, 914-633-2289, Fax: 914-633-2012, E-mail: vjarekprinz@iona.edu.

Kean University, College of Education, Program in Classroom Instruction and Curriculum, Union, NJ 07083. Offers bilingual/bicultural education (MA); classroom instruction (MA); earth science (MA); educational technology (MA); elementary education (MA); mathematics/science/computer education (MA); teaching (MA); teaching English as a second language (MA). *Accreditation:* NCATE. Part-time and evening/weekend programs available. *Faculty:* 19 full-time (10 women). *Students:* 34 full-time (29 women), 174 part-time (139 women); includes 73 minority (9 African Americans, 7 Asian Americans or Pacific Islanders, 57 Hispanic Americans), 4 international. Average age 34. 103 applicants, 93% accepted, 67 enrolled. In 2006, 82 degrees awarded. *Degree requirements:* For master's, 2 foreign languages, thesis, comprehensive exam. *Entrance requirements:* For master's, GRE General Test or MAT, PRAXIS, minimum GPA of 2.75, 2 letters of recommendation, interview. *Application deadline:* For fall admission, 5/1 for domestic students; for spring admission, 11/1 for domestic students. Application fee: $60 ($150 for international students). Electronic applications accepted. *Expenses:* Tuition, state resident: full-time $8,856; part-time $369 per credit. Tuition, nonresident: full-time $11,256; part-time $469 per credit. *Financial support:* In 2006–07, 2 research assistantships with full tuition reimbursements (averaging $3,217 per year) were awarded; unspecified assistantships also available. *Unit head:* Dr. Frank H. Osborn, Program Coordinator, 908-737-4289, E-mail: fosborne@kean.edu. *Application contact:* Joanne Morris, Director of Graduate Admissions, 908-737-3355, Fax: 908-737-3354, E-mail: grad-adm@kean.edu.

Langston University, School of Education and Behavioral Sciences, Langston, OK 73050-0907. Offers bilingual/multicultural (M Ed); elementary education (M Ed); English as a second language (M Ed); rehabilitation counseling (M Sc); urban education (M Ed). *Accreditation:* CORE; NCATE (one or more programs are accredited). Part-time programs available. *Degree requirements:* For master's, thesis optional. *Entrance requirements:* For master's, GRE, writing skills test, minimum GPA of 2.5, 3 letters of recommendation. Additional exam requirements/recommendations for international students: Required—TOEFL, TWE. *Faculty research:* Bilingual/multicultural education, financing post-secondary education.

Lehman College of the City University of New York, Division of Education, Department of Specialized Services in Education, Bronx, NY 10468-1589. Offers guidance and counseling (MS Ed); reading teacher (MS Ed); teachers of special education (MS Ed), including bilingual special education, early special education, emotional handicaps, learning disabilities, mental retardation. Part-time and evening/weekend programs available. *Faculty research:* Battered women, whole language classrooms, parent education, mainstreaming.

Lehman College of the City University of New York, Division of Education, Department of Specialized Services in Education, Teachers of Special Education Program, Option in Bilingual Special Education, Bronx, NY 10468-1589. Offers MS Ed. *Accreditation:* NCATE. *Entrance requirements:* For master's, minimum GPA of 3.0.

Long Island University, Brooklyn Campus, School of Education, Department of Teaching and Learning, Program in Bilingual Education, Brooklyn, NY 11201-8423. Offers MS Ed. Part-time and evening/weekend programs available. *Degree requirements:* For master's, one foreign language, thesis optional. *Entrance requirements:* For master's, 2 letters of recommendation. Additional exam requirements/recommendations for international students: Required—TOEFL (minimum score 500 paper-based; 173 computer-based). Electronic applications accepted.

Long Island University, C.W. Post Campus, School of Education, Department of Curriculum and Instruction, Brookville, NY 11548-1300. Offers adolescence education (MS); adolescence education: biology (MS); adolescence education: earth science (MS); adolescence education: English (MS); adolescence education: mathematics (MS); adolescence education: social studies (MS); adolescence education: Spanish (MS); art education (MS); bilingual education (MS); childhood education (MS); early childhood education (MS); middle childhood education (MS); music education (MS); teaching English to speakers of other languages (MS). Part-time and evening/weekend programs available. *Degree requirements:* For master's, comprehensive exam or thesis, student teaching. *Entrance requirements:* For master's, minimum GPA of 2.75 in major, 2.5 overall. Electronic applications accepted. *Faculty research:* Ethics and education, teaching strategies.

Long Island University, Westchester Graduate Campus, Programs in Education-Teaching, Program in Second Language, TESOL, Bilingual Education, Purchase, NY 10577. Offers MS Ed. Part-time and evening/weekend programs available. *Faculty:* 1 (woman) full-time, 5 part-time/adjunct (4 women). *Students:* 4 applicants, 100% accepted, 4 enrolled. In 2006, 3 degrees awarded. *Application deadline:* Applications are processed on a rolling basis. *Expenses:* Tuition: Part-time $790 per credit. *Financial support:* Scholarships/grants, tuition waivers (partial), and unspecified assistantships available. *Unit head:* Dr. Helaine Marshall, Director, 914-831-2713, Fax: 914-251-5959, E-mail: helaine.marshall@liu.edu. *Application contact:* Ellen Brief, Coordinator of Admissions, Marketing, Student Services and Public Relations, 914-831-2701, Fax: 914-251-5959, E-mail: ellen.brief@liu.edu.

Loyola Marymount University, Graduate Division, School of Education, Program in Bilingual and Bicultural Education, Los Angeles, CA 90045-2659. Offers MA. Part-time and evening/weekend programs available. *Students:* 3 full-time (1 woman), 1 (woman) part-time; all minorities (all Hispanic Americans) In 2006, 6 degrees awarded. *Degree requirements:* For master's, comprehensive exam. *Entrance requirements:* For master's, GRE General Test, competency in Spanish, interview, minimum undergraduate GPA of 2.7, minimum graduate GPA of 3.0. Additional exam requirements/recommendations for international students: Required—TOEFL (minimum score 600 paper-based; 250 computer-based). *Application deadline:* For fall admission, 7/15 for domestic students; for spring admission, 11/15 for domestic students. Application fee: $50. Electronic applications accepted. *Financial support:* Federal Work-Study and scholarships/grants available. Support available to part-time students. Financial award application deadline: 6/1; financial award applicants required to submit FAFSA. *Unit head:* Dr. Martha Baltodano, Coordinator, 310-338-2924, E-mail: mbaltoda@lmu.edu.

McNeese State University, Graduate School, College of Education, Department of Teacher Education, Program in Teaching, Lake Charles, LA 70609. Offers elementary education (MAT); secondary education (MAT); special education (mild/moderate) (MAT). Evening/weekend programs available. *Faculty:* 12 full-time (8 women), 2 part-time/adjunct (1 woman). *Students:* 37 full-time (30 women), 168 part-time (146 women); includes 53 minority (47 African Americans, 2 Asian Americans or Pacific Islanders, 4 Hispanic Americans), 2 international. In 2006, 26 degrees awarded. *Entrance requirements:* For master's, GRE, PRAXIS. *Application deadline:* For fall admission, 5/15 priority date for domestic students. Applications are processed on a rolling basis. Application fee: $20 ($30 for international students). *Expenses:* Tuition, area resident: Full-time $2,226; part-time $193 per hour. Required fees: $919; $106 per hour. *Financial support:* Application deadline: 5/1. *Unit head:* Dr. Wayne R Fetter, Dean, College of Education, 337-475-5432, Fax: 337-475-5467, E-mail: wfetter@mcneese.edu.

Mercy College, Division of Education, Dobbs Ferry, NY 10522-1189. Offers adolescence education: grades 7-12 (MS); applied behavior analysis (MS); bilingual education (MS); childhood education: grades 1-6 (MS); early childhood education: birth—grade 2 (MS); education (MS); elementary education (MS); learning technology (MS); middle childhood education: grades 5-9 (MS); reading (MS); school administration and supervision (MS); school building leadership (MS); school business administration (MS); secondary education (MS); special education (MS); students with disabilities: grades 5-9 (MS); students with disabilities: grades 7-12 (MS); teaching English to speakers of other languages (MS); teaching literacy: birth—grade 6 (MS); teaching literacy: grades 5-12 (MS); urban education (MS). *Students:* 572 full-time (467 women), 1,719 part-time (1,287 women); includes 943 minority (470 African Americans, 7 American Indian/Alaska Native, 48 Asian Americans or Pacific Islanders, 418 Hispanic Americans), 6 international. Average age 33. In 2006, 1090 degrees awarded. *Entrance requirements:* For master's, teaching certificate. *Application deadline:* For fall admission, 2/1 for domestic students. Applications are processed on a rolling basis. Application fee: $37. *Expenses: Contact institution.* Tuition and fees vary according to program. *Financial support:* Institutionally sponsored loans, scholarships/grants, and unspecified assistantships available. Support available to part-time students. *Faculty research:* Distance learning, literacy, assessment, community schools, impact of staff development. *Unit head:* Dr. William Prattella, Chairperson, 914-674-7555, Fax: 914-674-7352, E-mail: wprattella@mercy.edu. *Application contact:* Kathleen Jackson, Director of Admissions, 800-Mercy-NY, Fax: 914-674-7382, E-mail: admissions@mercy.edu.

Mercy College, Division of Social and Behavioral Sciences, Dobbs Ferry, NY 10522-1189. Offers counseling (MS, AC), including alcohol and substance abuse counseling (AC), counseling (MS), family counseling (AC), retirement counseling (AC); health services management (MPA, MS, AC, Certificate); marriage and family therapy (MS); mental health counseling (MS); psychology (MS), including psychology, school psychology; school psychology (MS), including bilingual extension. *Students:* 168 full-time (139 women), 280 part-time (237 women); includes 287 minority (131 African Americans, 1 American Indian/Alaska Native, 9 Asian Americans or Pacific Islanders, 146 Hispanic Americans), 1 international. Average age 34. In 2006, 97 degrees awarded. Application fee: $37. *Expenses:* Tuition: Part-time $595 per credit. Required fees: $9 per credit. Tuition and fees vary according to program. *Unit head:* Diana Juettner, Chair, 914-674-7338. *Application contact:* Kathleen Jackson, Director of Admissions, 800-Mercy-NY, Fax: 914-674-7382, E-mail: admissions@mercy.edu.

Mercyhurst College, Graduate Program, Program in Special Education, Erie, PA 16546. Offers bilingual/bicultural special education (MS); educational leadership (Certificate); special education (MS). Part-time and evening/weekend programs available. *Degree requirements:* For master's, thesis optional. *Entrance requirements:* For master's, GRE General Test, MAT, or minimum GPA of 3.0, interview. Additional exam requirements/recommendations for international students: Required—TOEFL. Electronic applications accepted. *Faculty research:* College age learning disabled program, teacher preparation/collaboration, applied behavior analysis, special education policy issues.

Minnesota State University Mankato, College of Graduate Studies, College of Social and Behavioral Sciences, Department of Ethnic and Multicultural Studies, Mankato, MN 56001. Offers MS. *Students:* 8 full-time (4 women), 8 part-time (3 women). *Unit head:* Dr. Wayne Allen, Graduate Coordinator, 507-389-5013.

National University, Academic Affairs, School of Education, Department of Teacher Education, La Jolla, CA 92037-1011. Offers best practices (MA); cross-cultural teaching (M Ed); teaching (MA). Part-time and evening/weekend programs available. Postbaccalaureate distance learning degree programs offered (no on-campus study). *Faculty:* 44 full-time (27 women), 900 part-time/adjunct (537 women). *Students:* 3,258 full-time (2,269 women), 5,303 part-time (3,400 women); includes 2,266 minority (501 African Americans, 49 American Indian/Alaska Native, 443 Asian Americans or Pacific Islanders, 1,273 Hispanic Americans), 18 international. Average age 35. 4,932 applicants, 4475 enrolled. In 2006, 1702 degrees awarded. *Degree requirements:* For master's, thesis. *Entrance requirements:* For master's, interview, minimum GPA of 2.5. Additional exam requirements/recommendations for international students: Required—TOEFL (minimum score 550 paper-based; 213 computer-based; 80 iBT), IELTS (minimum score 6). *Application deadline:* Applications are processed on a rolling basis. Application fee: $60 ($65 for international students). Electronic applications accepted. *Expenses:* Tuition: Full-time $7,722; part-time $286 per unit. One-time fee: $60. *Financial support:* Career-related internships or fieldwork, institutionally sponsored loans, scholarships/grants, and tuition waivers (partial) available. Support available to part-time students. Financial award application deadline: 6/30; financial award applicants required to submit FAFSA. *Unit head:* Dr. Carl Beyer, Chair, 858-642-8320, Fax: 858-642-8724, E-mail: cbeyer@nu.edu. *Application contact:* Dominick Giovanniello, Associate Regional Dean—San Diego, 800-NAT-UNIV, Fax: 858-642-8709, E-mail: dgiovann@nu.edu.

New Jersey City University, Graduate and Continuing Education, College of Education, Department of Educational Leadership, Jersey City, NJ 07305-1597. Offers basics and urban studies (MA); bilingual/bicultural education and English as a second language (MA); educational administration and supervision (MA). Evening/weekend programs available. *Students:* 4 full-time (3 women), 237 part-time (149 women); includes 52 minority (11 African Americans, 4 Asian Americans or Pacific Islanders, 37 Hispanic Americans), 26 international. Average age 35. In 2006, 162 degrees awarded. *Entrance requirements:* For master's, GRE General Test or MAT. Additional exam requirements/recommendations for international students: Required—TOEFL. *Application deadline:* For fall admission, 8/1 priority date for domestic students; for spring admission, 12/1 for domestic students. Applications are processed on a rolling basis. Application fee: $0. *Expenses:* Tuition, state resident: full-time $7,038; part-time $391 per credit. Tuition, nonresident: full-time $12,510; part-time $695 per credit. Required fees: $65 per credit. *Financial support:* Fellowships, teaching assistantships, career-related internships or fieldwork and unspecified assistantships available. *Unit head:* Dr. Carrie Robinson, Chairperson, 201-200-3400, E-mail: crobinson@njcu.edu.

New York University, Steinhardt School of Culture, Education and Human Development, Department of Humanities and Social Sciences in the Professions, Program in Sociology of Education, New York, NY 10012-1019. Offers education policy (MA); social and cultural studies of education (MA); sociology of education (PhD). Part-time and evening/weekend programs available. *Faculty:* 5 full-time (2 women). *Students:* 21 full-time (19 women), 9 part-time (6 women); includes 11 minority (2 African Americans, 2 Asian Americans or Pacific Islanders, 7 Hispanic Americans), 1 international. 65 applicants, 71% accepted, 15 enrolled. In 2006, 6 master's, 2 doctorates awarded. Terminal master's awarded for partial completion of doctoral program. *Degree requirements:* For master's, thesis (for some programs); for doctorate, thesis/dissertation. *Entrance requirements:* For master's, letters of recommendation; for doctorate, GRE General Test, interview. Additional exam requirements/recommendations for international students: Required—TOEFL. *Application deadline:* For fall admission, 12/15 priority date for domestic and international students; for spring admission, 11/1 for domestic and international students. Applications are processed on a rolling basis. Application fee: $50. *Expenses:* Tuition: Part-time $1,080 per unit. Required fees: $56 per unit. $329 per term. Tuition and fees vary according to program. *Financial support:* Fellowships with full and partial tuition reimbursements, Federal Work-Study, institutionally sponsored loans, scholarships/grants, and tuition waivers (partial) available. Support available to part-time students. Financial award application deadline: 2/1; financial award applicants required to submit FAFSA. *Faculty research:* Legal and institutional environments of schools; social inequality; high school reform and achievement; education's link with occupations, professions and inequality. *Unit head:* Dr. Floyd M. Hammack, Program Director, 212-992-9475, Fax: 212-995-4832, E-mail: fmhl@nyu.edu. *Application contact:* 212-998-5030, Fax: 212-995-4328, E-mail: steinhardt.gradadmissions@nyu.edu.

New York University, Steinhardt School of Culture, Education and Human Development, Department of Teaching and Learning, Program in Multilingual/Multicultural Studies, New York, NY 10012-1019. Offers bilingual education (MA, PhD, Advanced Certificate); foreign language education (MA, Advanced Certificate); foreign language education/TESOL (MA); teaching English to speakers of other languages (MA, PhD, Advanced Certificate). *Accreditation:* Teacher Education Accreditation Council. Part-time and evening/weekend programs available. *Faculty:* 3 full-time (2 women). *Students:* 121 full-time (105 women), 103 part-time (89 women); includes 38 minority (3 African Americans, 19 Asian Americans or Pacific Islanders, 16 Hispanic Americans), 95 international. 272 applicants, 75% accepted, 87 enrolled. In 2006, 103 master's, 5 doctorates, 6 other advanced degrees awarded. Terminal master's awarded for partial completion of doctoral program. *Degree requirements:* For master's, thesis (for some programs); for doctorate, thesis/dissertation. *Entrance requirements:* For doctorate, GRE General Test, interview; for Advanced Certificate, master's degree. Additional exam requirements/recommendations for international students: Required—TOEFL. *Application deadline:* For fall admission, 12/15 priority date for domestic and international students; for spring admission, 11/1 for domestic and international students. Applications are processed on a rolling basis. Application fee: $50. *Expenses:* Tuition: Part-time $1,080 per unit. Required fees: $56 per unit. $329 per term. Tuition and fees vary according to program. *Financial support:* Fellowships with full and partial tuition reimbursements, career-related internships or fieldwork, Federal Work-Study, institutionally sponsored loans, scholarships/grants, and tuition waivers (partial) available. Support available to part-time students. Financial award application deadline: 2/1; financial award applicants required to submit FAFSA. *Faculty research:* Second language acquisition, cross-cultural communication, technology-enhanced language learning, language variation, action learning. *Unit head:* Dr. Miriam Eisenstein Ebsworth, Director, 212-998-5460, Fax: 212-995-4049. *Application contact:* 212-998-5030, Fax: 212-995-4328, E-mail: steinhardt.gradadmissions@nyu.edu.

Northeastern Illinois University, Graduate College, College of Education, School of Teacher Education, Program in Bilingual/Bicultural Education, Chicago, IL 60625-4699. Offers MAT, MSI. *Faculty:* 30 full-time (20 women), 39 part-time/adjunct (29 women). *Students:* 8 full-time (6 women), 43 part-time (34 women); includes 36 minority (1 African American, 3 Asian Americans or Pacific Islanders, 32 Hispanic Americans), 1 international. 11 applicants, 100% accepted. In 2006, 8 degrees awarded. *Entrance requirements:* For master's, minimum GPA of 2.75. *Application deadline:* For fall admission, 4/1 priority date for domestic students; for spring admission, 8/15 for domestic students. Applications are processed on a rolling basis. Application fee: $25. *Financial support:* In 2006–07, research assistantships with full tuition reimbursements (averaging $6,600 per year). *Faculty research:* Bilingual teacher preparation, linguistics and phonetics, Middle Eastern languages and cultures, TOEFL. *Unit head:* Dr. Joaquin Villegas, Coordinator, 773-442-5381, Fax: 773-442-5360, E-mail: j-villegas1@neiu.edu.

Northern Arizona University, Graduate College, College of Education, Program in Bilingual/Multicultural Education, Flagstaff, AZ 86011. Offers bilingual multicultural education (M Ed); English as a Second Language/Teaching English as a second language (Certificate). Part-time and evening/weekend programs available. *Entrance requirements:* For master's, GRE General Test or minimum GPA of 3.0. *Faculty research:* Second language literacy; biliteracy and metalinguistic awareness; language shift, maintenance, and revitalization; American Indian education; minority student retention.

Nova Southeastern University, Fischler School of Education and Human Services, Graduate Teacher Education Program, Fort Lauderdale, FL 33314-7796. Offers athletic administration (MS); cognitive and behavioral disabilities (MS); computer science education (Ed S); computer science education (K-12) (MS); curriculum and teaching (Ed S); curriculum, instruction and technology (MS); curriculum, instruction, management and administration (Ed S); early childhood special education (MS); early literacy and reading (Ed S); early literacy education (MS); education technology (MS); educational leadership (administration K–12) (MS, Ed S); educational media (Ed S); educational media (K-12) (MS); elementary education (MS, Ed S), including ESOL endorsement (MS); English (MS, Ed S); exceptional student education (MS), including ESOL endorsement; gifted education (MS, Ed S); interdisciplinary arts education (MS); management and administration of educational programs (MS); mathematics (MS, Ed S); multicultural early intervention (MS); pre-kindergarten/primary (MS); preschool education (MS); reading (MS, Ed S); science (MS, Ed S); secondary education (MS); social studies (MS, Ed S); Spanish language (MS); teaching and learning (MA, MS), including curriculum and instruction (MA), elementary mathematics (MA), elementary reading (MA), K-12 technology integration (MA); teaching English to speakers of other languages (MS, Ed S); technology management and administration (Ed S); urban studies education (MS); varying exceptionalities (Ed S). Part-time and evening/weekend programs available. Postbaccalaureate distance learning degree programs offered. *Faculty:* 131 full-time (78 women), 548 part-time/adjunct (342 women). *Students:* 1,418 full-time (1,139 women), 3,464 part-time (2,877 women); includes 2,462 minority (1,732 African Americans, 13 American Indian/Alaska Native, 44 Asian Americans or

Multilingual and Multicultural Education

Nova Southeastern University (continued)

Pacific Islanders, 673 Hispanic Americans), 77 international. Average age 38. 1,771 applicants, 80% accepted, 1419 enrolled. In 2006, 2,078 master's, 425 other advanced degrees awarded. *Degree requirements:* For master's and Ed S, thesis, practicum, internship. *Entrance requirements:* For master's, MAT, GRE, CLAST, CBEST, PRAXIS I, GKT, minimum GPA of 2.5; for Ed S, MAT or GRE, master's degree, teaching certificate, minimum GPA of 3.0. Additional exam requirements/recommendations for international students: Recommended—TOEFL (minimum score 550 paper-based; 213 computer-based), IELTS (minimum score 6). *Application deadline:* For fall admission, 8/11 priority date for domestic and international students; for winter admission, 12/28 priority date for domestic and international students; for spring admission, 4/22 priority date for domestic and international students. Applications are processed on a rolling basis. Application fee: $50. Electronic applications accepted. *Financial support:* Federal Work-Study available. Support available to part-time students. Financial award application deadline: 1/7. *Faculty research:* School effectiveness, critical thinking, leadership skills acquisition, child education, multicultural education. *Unit head:* Dr. Meline Kevorkian, Associate Dean of Master's and Educational Programs, 954-262-8500, Fax: 954-262-3606, E-mail: melinek@nova.edu. *Application contact:* Jennifer Quiñones Nottingham, Dean of Student Affairs, 800-986-3223 Ext. 8624, Fax: 954-262-3911, E-mail: jlquinon@nova.edu.

Park University, College of Graduate and Professional Studies, Kansas City, MO 54105. Offers adult education (M Ed); at-risk students (M Ed); disaster and emergency management (MPA); educational administration (M Ed); entrepreneurship (MBA); general business (MBA); general education (M Ed); government/business relations (MPA); healthcare/services management (MBA, MPA); international business (MBA); K-12 certification (MAT); management information systems (MBA); management of information systems (MPA); middle school certification (MAT); multi-cultural education (M Ed); nonprofit management (MPA); public management (MPA); school law (M Ed); secondary school certification (MAT); special education (M Ed). Part-time and evening/weekend programs available. Postbaccalaureate distance learning degree programs offered (no on-campus study). *Degree requirements:* For master's, thesis (for some programs), comprehensive exam, registration. *Entrance requirements:* For master's, GRE, GMAT, teacher certification (M Ed). Additional exam requirements/recommendations for international students: Required—TOEFL (minimum score 550 paper-based). Electronic applications accepted. *Faculty research:* Literacy, leadership, brain based research, multicultural education, diversity.

Penn State University Park, Graduate School, College of Education, Department of Curriculum and Instruction, State College, University Park, PA 16802-1503. Offers bilingual education (M Ed, MS, PhD); early childhood education (M Ed, MS, PhD); elementary education (M Ed, MS, PhD); instructional systems (M Ed, MS, PhD); language arts and reading (M Ed, MS, PhD); science education (M Ed, MS, PhD); social studies education (MS, PhD); supervisor and curriculum development (M Ed, MS, PhD). *Accreditation:* NCATE. *Unit head:* Dr. Murry R. Nelson, Head, 814-865-6321, Fax: 814-863-7602, E-mail: mrn2@psu.edu. *Application contact:* Judy Nastase, Graduate Staff Assistant, 814-865-2168, E-mail: jcn3@psu.edu.

Prescott College, Graduate Programs, Program in Education, Prescott, AZ 86301. Offers bilingual education (MA), including English as a second language, Native American bilingual teacher education; education (MA, PhD); multicultural education (MA). Part-time programs available. Postbaccalaureate distance learning degree programs offered (minimal on-campus study). *Faculty:* 1 (woman) full-time, 26 part-time/adjunct (18 women). *Students:* 44 full-time (24 women), 23 part-time (15 women); includes 8 minority (1 African American, 3 American Indian/Alaska Native, 1 Asian American or Pacific Islander, 3 Hispanic Americans), 2 international. Average age 40. In 2006, 17 degrees awarded. *Degree requirements:* For master's, thesis, fieldwork or internship, practicum; for doctorate, thesis/dissertation. *Entrance requirements:* For master's and doctorate, 2 letters of recommendation, resumé. *Application deadline:* For fall admission, 5/1 priority date for domestic students; for spring admission, 11/1 priority date for domestic students. Applications are processed on a rolling basis. Application fee: $40. Electronic applications accepted. *Expenses:* Tuition: Full-time $12,408; part-time $517 per credit. One-time fee: $130. *Financial support:* Career-related internships or fieldwork and Federal Work-Study available. Financial award applicants required to submit FAFSA. *Unit head:* Noël Caniglia, Head, 928-358-3201, Fax: 928-776-5151, E-mail: ncaniglia@prescott.edu. *Application contact:* Kerstin Alicki, Admissions Counselor, 877-350-2100 Ext. 2102, Fax: 928-776-5242, E-mail: admissions@prescott.edu.

Queens College of the City University of New York, Division of Graduate Studies, Division of Education, Department of Elementary and Early Childhood Education, Flushing, NY 11367-1597. Offers bilingual education (MS Ed); childhood education (MA); early childhood education (MA); elementary education (MS Ed, AC); literacy (MS Ed). Part-time and evening/weekend programs available. *Faculty:* 31 full-time (25 women). *Students:* 87 full-time (80 women), 505 part-time (454 women). In 2006, 338 degrees awarded. *Degree requirements:* For master's, research project; for AC, thesis optional. *Entrance requirements:* For master's, minimum GPA of 3.0. Additional exam requirements/recommendations for international students: Required—TOEFL. *Application deadline:* For fall admission, 4/1 for domestic students; for spring admission, 11/1 for domestic students. Applications are processed on a rolling basis. Application fee: $125. *Financial support:* Career-related internships or fieldwork, Federal Work-Study, institutionally sponsored loans, and tuition waivers (partial) available. Support available to part-time students. Financial award application deadline: 4/1; financial award applicants required to submit FAFSA. *Unit head:* Dr. Myra Zarnowski, Chairperson, 718-997-5328.

Rhode Island College, School of Graduate Studies, Feinstein School of Education and Human Development, Department of Educational Studies, Providence, RI 02908-1991. Offers bilingual/bicultural education (M Ed); educational administration (CAGS); English (MAT); French (MAT); history (MAT); math (MAT); secondary education (M Ed); Spanish (MAT); teaching English as a second language (M Ed, MAT); technology education (M Ed). *Accreditation:* NCATE. Part-time and evening/weekend programs available. *Faculty:* 12 full-time (5 women), 4 part-time/adjunct (all women). *Students:* 10 full-time (7 women), 27 part-time (23 women); includes 1 minority (Hispanic American) Average age 32. In 2006, 22 degrees awarded. *Entrance requirements:* For master's, BA in English, French, history, math or Spanish; evaluation of content area knowledge; 3 letters of recommendation; interview. *Application deadline:* For fall admission, 3/15 for domestic students; for spring admission, 11/1 for domestic students. Applications are processed on a rolling basis. Application fee: $50. *Expenses:* Tuition, state resident: part-time $244 per credit. Tuition, nonresident: part-time $512 per credit. Required fees: $12 per credit. $66 per term. Tuition and fees vary according to degree level, program and reciprocity agreements. *Financial support:* Teaching assistantships with full tuition reimbursements, career-related internships or fieldwork, Federal Work-Study, scholarships/grants, health care benefits, and unspecified assistantships available. Support available to part-time students. Financial award application deadline: 5/15; financial award applicants required to submit FAFSA. *Faculty research:* School administration, school/college articulation. *Unit head:* Dr. Charles McLaughlin, Chair, 401-456-8170.

St. John's University, The School of Education, Division of Human Services and Counseling, Program in Bilingual/Multicultural Education/Teaching English to Speakers of Other Languages, Queens, NY 11439. Offers MS Ed. Part-time and evening/weekend programs available. *Students:* 8 full-time (7 women), 104 part-time (88 women); includes 23 minority (4 African Americans, 8 Asian Americans or Pacific Islanders, 11 Hispanic Americans), 8 international. Average age 31. 59 applicants, 93% accepted, 27 enrolled. In 2006, 43 degrees awarded. *Degree requirements:* For master's, internship. *Entrance requirements:* For master's, minimum GPA of 3.0, New York teaching certificate. Additional exam requirements/recommendations for international students: Required—TOEFL (minimum score 500 paper-based; 173 computer-based). *Application deadline:* For fall admission, 4/1 for domestic students, 5/1 priority date for international students; for spring admission, 11/1 for domestic students, 11/1 priority date for international students. Applications are processed on a rolling basis. Application fee: $40. Electronic applications accepted. *Expenses:* Tuition: Full-time $18,480; part-time $770 per credit. Required fees: $125 per semester. Tuition and fees vary according to program. *Financial support:* Research assistantships, career-related internships or fieldwork and scholarships/grants available. Support available to part-time students. Financial award application deadline: 3/1; financial award applicants required to submit FAFSA. *Faculty research:* Literacy development for second language, learners and investigating Caribbean and Creole language and culture. *Application contact:* Kelly Ronayne, Assistant Dean, 718-990-2303, Fax: 718-990-6069, E-mail: graded@stjohns.edu.

Salem State College, Graduate School, Program in Bilingual Education, Salem, MA 01970-5353. Offers M Ed. Part-time and evening/weekend programs available. *Students:* Average age 54. *Entrance requirements:* For master's, GRE General Test, MAT. *Application deadline:* Applications are processed on a rolling basis. Application fee: $35. *Unit head:* Dr. Ellen H. Rintell, Assistant Professor, 978-542-6473, Fax: 978-542-7023, E-mail: ellen.rintell@salemstate.edu.

San Diego State University, Graduate and Research Affairs, College of Education, Department of Policy Studies in Language and Cross Cultural Education, San Diego, CA 92182. Offers multi-cultural emphasis (PhD); policy studies in language and cross cultural education (MA). *Accreditation:* NCATE. *Students:* 6 full-time (4 women), 36 part-time (28 women); includes 27 minority (1 African American, 2 Asian Americans or Pacific Islanders, 24 Hispanic Americans). 18 applicants, 72% accepted, 1 enrolled. In 2006, 7 degrees awarded. *Entrance requirements:* For master's, GRE General Test, letters of reference; for doctorate, GRE General Test, 3 letters of reference, resumé. Additional exam requirements/recommendations for international students: Required—TOEFL. *Application deadline:* For fall admission, 5/1 for domestic and international students; for spring admission, 11/1 for domestic students, 10/1 for international students. Applications are processed on a rolling basis. Application fee: $55. Electronic applications accepted. *Financial support:* Applicants required to submit FAFSA. Total annual research expenditures: $1.8 million. *Unit head:* Ruben Espinosa, Chair, 619-594-5155, Fax: 619-594-1183. *Application contact:* Karen Cadiero-Kaplan, Graduate Advisor, 619-594-4994, Fax: 619-594-1183, E-mail: kcadiero@mail.sdsu.edu.

Seton Hall University, College of Education and Human Services, Department of Educational Studies, Program in Bilingual Education, South Orange, NJ 07079-2697. Offers Ed S. *Accreditation:* NCATE. Part-time and evening/weekend programs available. *Faculty:* 2 full-time (0 women). *Students:* 1 (woman) full-time, 7 part-time (6 women); includes 1 Hispanic American. Average age 42. *Entrance requirements:* For degree, GRE or MAT minimum GPA of 2.75. *Application deadline:* For fall admission, 5/1 for domestic students; for spring admission, 10/1 for domestic students. Applications are processed on a rolling basis Application fee: $50. *Financial support:* Fellowships with full tuition reimbursements, unspecified assistantships available. Financial award application deadline: 2/1. *Faculty research:* Spanish, Mandarin and Cantonese Chinese, Japanese, Korean, school administration and supervision. *Unit head:* Dr. Juan Cobarrubias, Director, 973-761-9617, E-mail: cobarrju@shu.edu. *Application contact:* 973-761-9617.

Southern Connecticut State University, School of Graduate Studies, School of Arts and Sciences, Department of Foreign Languages, New Haven, CT 06515-1355. Offers French (MA); multicultural-bilingual education/teaching English to speakers of other languages (MS); Romance languages (MA); Spanish (MA); MLS/MS. Part-time and evening/weekend programs available. *Faculty:* 6 full-time. *Students:* 16 full-time (9 women), 25 part-time (22 women); includes 7 minority (1 Asian American or Pacific Islander, 6 Hispanic Americans). 36 applicants, 83% accepted, 12 enrolled. In 2006, 24 degrees awarded. *Degree requirements:* For master's, one foreign language, thesis or alternative. *Entrance requirements:* For master's, interview, minimum undergraduate GPA of 2.7. *Application deadline:* For fall admission, 7/15 priority date for domestic students. Applications are processed on a rolling basis. Application fee: $50. Electronic applications accepted. *Financial support:* Application deadline: 4/15; *Unit head:* Dr. Carlos Arboleda, Chairperson, 203-392-6754, Fax: 203-392-6136, E-mail: arboledac1@southernct.edu.

Southern Methodist University, School of Education and Human Development, Department of Literacy and Language Acquisition, Dallas, TX 75275. Offers MBE. Part-time and evening/weekend programs available. *Degree requirements:* For master's, one foreign language. *Entrance requirements:* For master's, minimum GPA of 3.0. Additional exam requirements/recommendations for international students: Required—TOEFL, TASP. Electronic applications accepted.

State University of New York at New Paltz, Graduate School, Faculty of Education, Department of Educational Studies, Program in Humanistic/Multicultural Education, New Paltz, NY 12561. Offers MPS. *Accreditation:* NCATE. Part-time and evening/weekend programs available. *Students:* 23 applicants. *Degree requirements:* For master's, portfolio. *Entrance requirements:* For master's, minimum GPA of 3.0. Additional exam requirements/recommendations for international students: Required—TOEFL (minimum score 550 paper-based; 213 computer-based; 80 iBT). *Application deadline:* For fall admission, 3/15 priority date for domestic students, 3/15 for international students; for spring admission, 10/15 for domestic and international students. Application fee: $50. Electronic applications accepted. *Expenses:* Tuition, state resident: full-time $6,900; part-time $288 per credit hour. Tuition, nonresident: full-time $10,920; part-time $455 per credit hour. *Unit head:* Dr. Nancy Schniedewind, Coordinator, 845-257-2827, E-mail: schniedn@newpaltz.edu.

State University of New York College at Brockport, School of Professions, Department of Education and Human Development, Program in Bilingual Education, Brockport, NY 14420-2997. Offers MS Ed. *Accreditation:* NCATE. Part-time programs available. *Students:* 3 full-time (2 women), 6 part-time (all women); includes 3 minority (all Hispanic Americans) 3 applicants, 100% accepted, 3 enrolled. In 2006, 3 degrees awarded. *Degree requirements:* For master's, thesis or alternative. *Entrance requirements:* For master's, minimum GPA of 3.0, letters of recommendation. Additional exam requirements/recommendations for international students: Required—TOEFL (minimum score 550 paper-based; 213 computer-based; 80 iBT). *Application deadline:* For fall admission, 2/15 for domestic and international students; for spring admission, 9/15 for domestic and international students. Application fee: $50. *Expenses:* Tuition, state resident: full-time $6,900; part-time $288 per credit. Tuition, nonresident: full-time $10,920; part-time $455 per credit. *Financial support:* Career-related internships or fieldwork Federal Work-Study, scholarships/grants, and unspecified assistantships available. Financial award application deadline: 3/15; financial award applicants required to submit FAFSA.

Sul Ross State University, Rio Grande College of Sul Ross State University, Alpine, TX 79832. Offers business administration (MBA); teacher education (M Ed), including bilingual education, counseling, educational diagnostics, elementary education, general education, reading, school administration, secondary education. Part-time and evening/weekend programs available. *Degree requirements:* For master's, thesis optional. *Entrance requirements:* For master's, GMAT or GRE General Test, minimum GPA of 2.5 in last 60 hours of undergraduate work. *Faculty research:* Drug and substance abuse counseling, U.S.-Mexico border economic development.

Sul Ross State University, School of Professional Studies, Department of Teacher Education, Program in Bilingual Education, Alpine, TX 79832. Offers M Ed. Part-time and evening/weekend programs available. *Degree requirements:* For master's, thesis optional. *Entrance requirements:* For master's, GMAT or GRE General Test, minimum GPA of 2.5 in last 60 hours of undergraduate work.

Teachers College Columbia University, Graduate Faculty of Education, Department of International and Transcultural Studies, Program in Bilingual and Bicultural Education, New York, NY 10027-6696. Offers MA. *Accreditation:* NCATE. Part-time programs available. *Faculty:* 2 full-time (both women), 2 part-time/adjunct (both women). *Students:* 7 full-time (all women), 46 part-time (42 women); includes 19 minority (2 African Americans, 5 Asian Americans or Pacific Islanders, 12 Hispanic Americans), 12 international. Average age 28. 34 applicants,

94% accepted, 19 enrolled. In 2006, 19 degrees awarded. *Degree requirements:* For master's, one foreign language. *Application deadline:* For fall admission, 5/15 for domestic students. Application fee: $65. *Expenses:* Tuition: Full-time $23,400; part-time $975 per credit. Required fees: $320 per term. *Financial support:* Research assistantships, career-related internships or fieldwork, Federal Work-Study, institutionally sponsored loans, scholarships/grants, and tuition waivers (full and partial) available. Support available to part-time students. Financial award application deadline: 2/1. *Faculty research:* Cross-cultural research in bilingual and bicultural school settings, diversity and teacher education. *Application contact:* Deanna Ghozati, Assistant Director of Admission, 212-678-4018, Fax: 212-678-4171, E-mail: ghozati@tc.edu.

Texas A&M International University, Office of Graduate Studies and Research, College of Education, Department of Curriculum and Instruction, Laredo, TX 78041-1900. Offers bilingual education (PhD); curriculum and instruction (MS, PhD); early childhood education (PhD); reading (MS). *Expenses:* Tuition, state resident: full-time $1,580. Tuition, nonresident: full-time $5,432. Required fees: $3,808. *Unit head:* Dr. Barbara Greybeck, Interim Chair, 956-326-2678, E-mail: bgreybeck@tamiu.edu. *Application contact:* Rosie Dickinson, Director of Admissions, 956-326-2200.

Texas A&M University, College of Education and Human Development, Department of Teaching, Learning, and Culture, College Station, TX 77843. Offers curriculum and instruction (M Ed, MS, PhD); mathematics education (M Ed, MS, PhD); multicultural/urban/ESL/international education (M Ed, MS, PhD); reading/language arts (M Ed, MS, PhD); science education (M Ed, MS, PhD); social studies education (M Ed, MS, PhD). *Accreditation:* NCATE. Part-time programs available. *Faculty:* 25 full-time (9 women), 2 part-time/adjunct (both women). *Students:* 156 full-time (115 women), 226 part-time (191 women); includes 95 minority (43 African Americans, 1 American Indian/Alaska Native, 9 Asian Americans or Pacific Islanders, 42 Hispanic Americans), 36 international. Average age 36. 137 applicants, 83% accepted, 80 enrolled. In 2006, 69 master's, 15 doctorates awarded. *Median time to degree:* Of those who began their doctoral program in fall 1998, 77% received their degree in 8 years or less. *Degree requirements:* For master's, thesis (for some programs), comprehensive exam; for doctorate, thesis/dissertation, comprehensive exam. *Entrance requirements:* For master's, GRE General Test, minimum GPA of 3.0; for doctorate, GRE General Test, 3 years of teaching experience. Additional exam requirements/recommendations for international students: Required—TOEFL (minimum score 550 paper-based; 213 computer-based). *Application deadline:* For fall admission, 1/15 priority date for domestic and international students; for spring admission, 9/15 priority date for domestic and international students. Applications are processed on a rolling basis. Application fee: $50 ($75 for international students). Electronic applications accepted. *Expenses:* Tuition, state resident: full-time $4,697. Tuition, nonresident: full-time $11,297. Required fees: $2,272. *Financial support:* In 2006–07, fellowships with partial tuition reimbursements (averaging $3,000 per year), teaching assistantships with partial tuition reimbursements (averaging $7,200 per year) were awarded; research assistantships with partial tuition reimbursements, career-related internships or fieldwork, Federal Work-Study, institutionally sponsored loans, scholarships/grants, tuition waivers (partial), and unspecified assistantships also available. Support available to part-time students. Financial award application deadline: 4/1; financial award applicants required to submit FAFSA. *Unit head:* Dr. Dennie Smith, Head, 979-845-8384, Fax: 979-845-9663. *Application contact:* Graduate Admissions Supervisor, 979-845-8382, Fax: 979-845-9663.

Texas A&M University–Kingsville, College of Graduate Studies, College of Education, Department of Bilingual Education, Kingsville, TX 78363. Offers MA, MS, Ed D. *Degree requirements:* For master's, one foreign language, thesis or alternative, comprehensive exam; for doctorate, one foreign language, thesis/dissertation, comprehensive exam. *Entrance requirements:* For master's, GRE General Test, minimum GPA of 3.0; for doctorate, GRE General Test, MAT, minimum GPA of 3.25. *Faculty research:* Language acquisition, acculturation in minority communities, English as a second language strategies.

Texas Southern University, Graduate School, College of Education, Area of Curriculum and Instruction, Houston, TX 77004-4584. Offers bilingual education (M Ed); curriculum, instruction, and urban education (Ed D); early childhood education (M Ed); elementary education (M Ed); reading education (M Ed); secondary education (M Ed); special education (M Ed). Part-time and evening/weekend programs available. *Faculty:* 8 full-time (6 women), 1 part-time/adjunct (0 women). *Students:* 41 full-time (36 women), 43 part-time (38 women); includes 82 minority (77 African Americans, 2 Asian Americans or Pacific Islanders, 3 Hispanic Americans). Average age 36. 34 applicants, 82% accepted, 24 enrolled. In 2006, 6 master's, 13 doctorates awarded. *Degree requirements:* For master's, comprehensive exam; for doctorate, thesis/dissertation, comprehensive exam. *Entrance requirements:* For master's, GRE General Test, minimum GPA of 2.5; for doctorate, GRE General Test or MAT, master's degree, minimum B+ average. Additional exam requirements/recommendations for international students: Required—TOEFL. *Application deadline:* For fall admission, 7/15 priority date for domestic students. Applications are processed on a rolling basis. Application fee: $50 ($75 for international students). *Financial support:* Federal Work-Study and institutionally sponsored loans available. Financial award application deadline: 5/1. *Unit head:* Dr. Cherry Gooden, Chair, 713-313-7496, Fax: 713-313-7496, E-mail: gooden_cr@tsu.edu.

Texas State University-San Marcos, Graduate School, College of Education, Department of Curriculum and Instruction, Program in Elementary Education-Bilingual/Bicultural, San Marcos, TX 78666. Offers M Ed, MA. *Faculty:* 1 (woman) part-time/adjunct. *Students:* 2 full-time (1 woman), 5 part-time (all women); includes 5 minority (all Hispanic Americans), 1 international. Average age 33. 3 applicants, 100% accepted, 2 enrolled. In 2006, 10 degrees awarded. *Degree requirements:* For master's, comprehensive exam. *Entrance requirements:* For master's, GRE General Test, minimum GPA of 2.75 in last 60 hours of course work, teaching experience. Additional exam requirements/recommendations for international students: Required—TOEFL. *Application deadline:* For fall admission, 6/15 priority date for domestic students; for spring admission, 10/15 priority date for domestic students. Applications are processed on a rolling basis. Application fee: $40 ($90 for international students). *Financial support:* In 2006–07, 7 students received support. *Unit head:* Carolyn McCall, Graduate Advisor, 512-245-2041, Fax: 512-245-7911, E-mail: cm06@txstate.edu.

Texas Tech University, Graduate School, College of Education, Division of Curriculum and Instruction, Lubbock, TX 79409. Offers bilingual education (M Ed); curriculum and instruction (M Ed, PhD); elementary education (M Ed); language and literacy education (M Ed); secondary education (M Ed). *Accreditation:* NCATE. Part-time programs available. *Students:* 68 full-time (48 women), 99 part-time (82 women); includes 35 minority (6 African Americans, 1 Asian American or Pacific Islander, 28 Hispanic Americans), 10 international. Average age 34. 165 applicants, 59% accepted, 10 enrolled. In 2006, 61 master's, 7 doctorates awarded. *Degree requirements:* For master's, thesis optional; for doctorate, thesis/dissertation. *Entrance requirements:* For master's and doctorate, GRE General Test. Additional exam requirements/recommendations for international students: Required—TOEFL (minimum score 550 paper-based; 213 computer-based). *Application deadline:* For fall admission, 3/1 priority date for international students; for spring admission, 11/1 priority date for international students. Applications are processed on a rolling basis. Application fee: $50 ($60 for international students). Electronic applications accepted. *Expenses:* Tuition, state resident: full-time $4,440. Tuition, nonresident: full-time $11,040. Required fees: $2,136. *Financial support:* In 2006–07, 100 students received support; research assistantships with partial tuition reimbursements available, teaching assistantships with partial tuition reimbursements available, career-related internships or fieldwork, Federal Work-Study, and institutionally sponsored loans available. Support available to part-time students. Financial award application deadline: 4/15; financial award applicants required to submit FAFSA. *Faculty research:* Multicultural foundations of education, teacher education, instruction and pedagogy in subject areas, curriculum theory, language and literary. *Unit head:* Dr. Peggy Johnson, Associate Dean, 806-742-1988 Ext. 437, Fax: 806-742-2179, E-mail: peggy.johnson@ttu.edu.

Universidad del Turabo, Graduate Programs, Programs in Education, Program in Bilingual Education, Gurabo, PR 00778-3030. Offers MA. *Entrance requirements:* For master's, GRE, EXADEP, interview.

University at Buffalo, the State University of New York, Graduate School, Graduate School of Education, Department of Learning and Instruction, Buffalo, NY 14260. Offers adolescence education (Certificate); biology (Ed M); chemistry (Ed M); childhood education (Ed M); early childhood and childhood education with bilingual extension (Ed M); early childhood education (Ed M); earth science (Ed M); elementary education (Ed D, PhD); English (Ed M); English education (PhD); English for speakers of other languages (Ed M); foreign and second language education (PhD); French (Ed M); general education (Ed M); German (Ed M); Italian (Ed M); Japanese (Ed M); Latin (Ed M); literary specialist (Ed M); mathematics (Ed M); mathematics education (PhD); mentoring teachers (Certificate); music education (Ed M, Certificate); physics (Ed M); reading education (PhD); Russian (Ed M); school administrator and supervisor (Certificate); science education (PhD); social studies (Ed M); Spanish (Ed M); special education (PhD); teaching and leading for diversity (Certificate); teaching English to speakers of other languages (Ed M). Part-time and evening/weekend programs available. Postbaccalaureate distance learning degree programs offered (no on-campus study). *Faculty:* 30 full-time (20 women), 53 part-time/adjunct (38 women). *Students:* 368 full-time (269 women), 297 part-time (226 women); includes 50 minority (15 African Americans, 2 American Indian/Alaska Native, 14 Asian Americans or Pacific Islanders, 19 Hispanic Americans), 66 international. Average age 31. 638 applicants, 75% accepted, 298 enrolled. In 2006, 248 master's, 18 doctorates, 48 other advanced degrees awarded. Terminal master's awarded for partial completion of doctoral program. *Degree requirements:* For master's, comprehensive exam, registration; for doctorate, thesis/dissertation, research analysis exam, research experience component. *Entrance requirements:* For doctorate, GRE General Test or MAT, interview, writing sample, letters of recommendation. Additional exam requirements/recommendations for international students: Required—TOEFL (minimum score 600 paper-based; 250 computer-based). *Application deadline:* For fall admission, 2/1 priority date for domestic and international students; for spring admission, 11/15 priority date for domestic students, 10/1 for international students. Applications are processed on a rolling basis. Application fee: $50. Electronic applications accepted. *Financial support:* In 2006–07, 70 students received support, including 6 fellowships with full tuition reimbursements available (averaging $10,000 per year), 16 research assistantships with full tuition reimbursements available (averaging $9,000 per year), teaching assistantships with full tuition reimbursements available (averaging $9,000 per year); career-related internships or fieldwork, Federal Work-Study, institutionally sponsored loans, scholarships/grants, tuition waivers (partial), and unspecified assistantships also available. Financial award application deadline: 2/28; financial award applicants required to submit FAFSA. *Faculty research:* Science assessment, state-level testing, early learning, literacy, second language acquisition. Total annual research expenditures: $432,366. *Unit head:* Dr. Maria E. Runfola, Chair, 716-645-2455, Fax: 716-645-3161. *Application contact:* Barbara Belz, Admissions Secretary, 716-645-2110 Ext. 1159, Fax: 716-645-3161, E-mail: belz@buffalo.edu.

University of Alaska Fairbanks, College of Liberal Arts, Department of Alaska Native Studies, Fairbanks, AK 99775-7520. Offers cross cultural studies (MA). *Faculty:* 13 full-time (4 women). *Students:* 8 (5 women); includes 2 minority (both American Indian/Alaska Native). Average age 42. 7 applicants, 86% accepted, 3 enrolled. *Degree requirements:* For master's, thesis or alternative, comprehensive exam, registration. *Entrance requirements:* For master's, GRE General Test. Additional exam requirements/recommendations for international students: Required—TOEFL (minimum score 550 paper-based; 213 computer-based). *Application deadline:* For fall admission, 6/1 for domestic students, 3/1 for international students; for spring admission, 10/15 for domestic students, 9/1 for international students. *Financial support:* Fellowships with tuition reimbursements, teaching assistantships with tuition reimbursements, Federal Work-Study, scholarships/grants, and unspecified assistantships available. Financial award applicants required to submit FAFSA. *Faculty research:* Alaska native literature, oral traditions, history, law and policy; Alaska native cultures, art, native American religion and philosophy. *Unit head:* Dr. James K. Ruppert, Chair, 907-474-7181, Fax: 907-474-5666, E-mail: fngdb@uaf.edu.

University of Alaska Fairbanks, School of Education, Fairbanks, AK 99775-7520. Offers cross cultural education (M Ed); curriculum instruction (M Ed); education (M Ed); guidance and counseling (M Ed); k-12 reading (M Ed); language and literacy (M Ed). *Accreditation:* NCATE. Part-time programs available. Postbaccalaureate distance learning degree programs offered. *Faculty:* 18 full-time (10 women), 3 part-time/adjunct (all women). *Students:* 56 full-time (40 women), 89 part-time (72 women); includes 31 minority (4 African Americans, 21 American Indian/Alaska Native, 2 Asian Americans or Pacific Islanders, 4 Hispanic Americans), 1 international. Average age 37. 69 applicants, 67% accepted, 42 enrolled. In 2006, 33 degrees awarded. *Degree requirements:* For master's, thesis or alternative, student teaching, comprehensive exam, registration. *Entrance requirements:* For master's, GRE General Test, PRAXIS I. Additional exam requirements/recommendations for international students: Required—TOEFL (minimum score 550 paper-based; 213 computer-based). *Application deadline:* For fall admission, 3/1 for domestic and international students; for spring admission, 10/1 for domestic students, 9/1 for international students. Application fee: $50. Electronic applications accepted. *Financial support:* In 2006–07, 2 research assistantships with tuition reimbursements (averaging $6,510 per year), 4 teaching assistantships with tuition reimbursements (averaging $10,441 per year) were awarded; fellowships with tuition reimbursements, career-related internships or fieldwork, Federal Work-Study, and scholarships/grants also available. Financial award applicants required to submit FAFSA. *Faculty research:* Native ways of knowing, classroom research in methods of literacy instruction, multiple intelligence theory, geometry concept development, mathematics and science curriculum development. *Unit head:* Dr. Eric C. Madsen, Dean, 907-474-7341, Fax: 907-474-5451, E-mail: fysoed@uaf.edu.

University of Alberta, Faculty of Graduate Studies and Research, Faculté Saint Jean, Edmonton, AB T6G 2E1, Canada. Offers M Ed. Part-time and evening/weekend programs available. Postbaccalaureate distance learning degree programs offered (minimal on-campus study). *Faculty:* 9 full-time (7 women). *Students:* 4 full-time (2 women), 64 part-time (50 women). Average age 30. 25 applicants, 92% accepted. In 2006, 9 degrees awarded. *Degree requirements:* For master's, thesis (for some programs). *Entrance requirements:* For master's, proficiency in French, 2 years of teaching experience. *Application deadline:* Applications are processed on a rolling basis. Application fee: $0. *Financial support:* In 2006–07, 3 fellowships (averaging $9,000 per year), 1 research assistantship with tuition reimbursement were awarded; teaching assistantships, scholarships/grants also available. *Faculty research:* First and second language acquisition, first and second language learning through subject matter, cultural transmission. *Unit head:* Dr. M. Cavanagh, Graduate Coordinator, 780-465-8770, Fax: 403-465-8760. *Application contact:* Lise Desbiens, Department Office, 403-465-8703, Fax: 403-465-8760, E-mail: medu@ualberta.ca.

The University of Arizona, Graduate College, College of Education, Department of Language, Reading, and Culture, Tucson, AZ 85721. Offers bilingual education (M Ed); bilingual/multicultural education (MA); language, reading and culture (MA, Ed D, PhD, Ed S). Part-time programs available. *Faculty:* 9 full-time (6 women), 12 part-time/adjunct (9 women). *Students:* 81 full-time (62 women), 89 part-time (71 women); includes 54 minority (4 African Americans, 13 American Indian/Alaska Native, 5 Asian Americans or Pacific Islanders, 32 Hispanic Americans), 20 international. Average age 40. 56 applicants, 75% accepted, 37 enrolled. In 2006, 28 master's, 13 doctorates awarded. Terminal master's awarded for partial completion of doctoral program. *Degree requirements:* For master's, thesis (MA), thesis optional; for doctorate, thesis/dissertation, comprehensive exam, registration; for Ed S, thesis optional. *Entrance requirements:* For doctorate and Ed S, GRE, MAT. Additional exam requirements/recommendations for international students: Required—TOEFL. *Application deadline:* For fall admission, 2/1 for domestic students; for spring admission, 10/1 for domestic students. Application fee: $50. *Financial support:* In 2006–07, 12 fellowships with full and partial tuition reimbursements (averaging $1,333 per year), 6 research assistantships with full and partial tuition reimbursements (averaging $5,200 per year), 5 teaching assistantships with full and partial tuition reimbursements (averaging $5,500 per year) were awarded; career-related internships or fieldwork, scholarships/grants, health care benefits, tuition waivers (full and partial), and unspecified assistantships also available. Financial award application deadline: 3/7; financial

Multilingual and Multicultural Education

The University of Arizona (continued)
award applicants required to submit FAFSA. *Faculty research:* Reading, Native American education, language policy, children's literature, bilingual/bicultural literacy. Total annual research expenditures: $500,000. *Unit head:* Dr. Patricia L. Anders, Head, 520-621-1311, Fax: 520-621-1853. *Application contact:* Maria Fierro, Graduate Coordinator, 520-621-1311, Fax: 520-621-1853.

University of California, Berkeley, Graduate Division, School of Education, Division of Language and Literacy, Society and Culture, Berkeley, CA 94720-1500. Offers education and single subject credential: English (MA); language, literacy, and culture (MA, Ed D, PhD), including athletes and academic achievement (MA), language, literacy, and culture (MA); social and cultural studies in education (MA, PhD); PhD/MA. *Degree requirements:* For master's, exam or thesis; for doctorate, thesis/dissertation, oral qualifying exam (PhD). *Entrance requirements:* For master's and doctorate, GRE General Test, minimum GPA of 3.0 during last 2 years of undergraduate course work. *Application deadline:* For fall admission, 12/1 for domestic students. Application fee: $60 ($80 for international students). Electronic applications accepted. *Financial support:* Fellowships, research assistantships, teaching assistantships, unspecified assistantships available. *Faculty research:* Literature, English education, reading education, second language teaching and learning, teacher education. *Application contact:* Admissions Office, 510-642-0841, Fax: 510-642-4808, E-mail: gse_info@uclink.berkeley.edu.

University of Colorado at Boulder, Graduate School, School of Education, Division of Social Multicultural and Bilingual Foundations, Boulder, CO 80309. Offers MA, PhD. *Accreditation:* NCATE. Part-time programs available. *Students:* 56 full-time (43 women), 94 part-time (79 women); includes 33 minority (4 African Americans, 1 American Indian/Alaska Native, 4 Asian Americans or Pacific Islanders, 24 Hispanic Americans), 1 international. Average age 34. 47 applicants, 85% accepted. In 2006, 75 master's, 3 doctorates awarded. *Degree requirements:* For master's, thesis or alternative, comprehensive exam; for doctorate, one foreign language, thesis/dissertation, comprehensive exam. *Entrance requirements:* For master's, GRE General Test or MAT, minimum undergraduate GPA of 2.75; for doctorate, GRE General Test. *Application deadline:* For fall admission, 2/1 priority date for domestic students, 12/1 for international students; for spring admission, 9/1 for domestic students, 12/1 for international students. Application fee: $50 ($60 for international students). *Financial support:* In 2006–07, 15 fellowships (averaging $5,479 per year), 12 research assistantships (averaging $8,376 per year), 8 teaching assistantships (averaging $10,811 per year) were awarded. Financial award application deadline: 2/1. *Faculty research:* Bilingual education, inclusion. *Unit head:* Ruben Donato, Program Chair, 303-492-7946, Fax: 303-492-7090, E-mail: ruben.donato@colorado.edu. *Application contact:* 303-492-6555, Fax: 303-492-5839, E-mail: edadvise@colorado.edu.

University of Connecticut, Graduate School, Neag School of Education, Department of Curriculum and Instruction, Storrs, CT 06269. Offers curriculum and instruction (MA, PhD), including agriculture education, bilingual and bicultural education, elementary education, English education, history and social sciences education, mathematics education, reading education, science education, secondary education, world languages education. *Accreditation:* NCATE. *Faculty:* 28 full-time (12 women). *Students:* 158 full-time (120 women), 54 part-time (44 women); includes 24 minority (3 African Americans, 1 American Indian/Alaska Native, 3 Asian Americans or Pacific Islanders, 17 Hispanic Americans), 2 international. Average age 27. 268 applicants, 76% accepted, 203 enrolled. In 2006, 181 master's, 4 doctorates awarded. Terminal master's awarded for partial completion of doctoral program. *Degree requirements:* For master's, thesis or alternative, comprehensive exam; for doctorate, thesis/dissertation. *Entrance requirements:* For doctorate, GRE General Test. Additional exam requirements/recommendations for international students: Required—TOEFL (minimum score 550 paper-based; 213 computer-based). *Application deadline:* For fall admission, 2/1 priority date for domestic and international students; for spring admission, 11/1 for domestic students, 10/1 for international students. Applications are processed on a rolling basis. Application fee: $55. Electronic applications accepted. *Financial support:* In 2006–07, 14 research assistantships with full tuition reimbursements, 4 teaching assistantships with full tuition reimbursements were awarded; fellowships, Federal Work-Study, scholarships/grants, health care benefits, and unspecified assistantships also available. Financial award application deadline: 2/1; financial award applicants required to submit FAFSA. *Unit head:* Mary Anne Doyle, Head, 860-486-2433, Fax: 860-486-0280. *Application contact:* Lisa Rasicot, Graduate Coordinator, 860-486-3065, Fax: 860-486-0210, E-mail: soeadm02@uconnvm.uconn.edu.

University of Connecticut, Graduate School, Neag School of Education, Department of Curriculum and Instruction, Field of Curriculum and Instruction, Program in Bilingual and Bicultural Education, Storrs, CT 06269. Offers MA, PhD. *Accreditation:* NCATE. *Faculty:* 11 full-time (9 women). *Students:* 4 full-time (all women), 11 part-time (7 women); includes 8 minority (all Hispanic Americans) Average age 36. 11 applicants, 36% accepted, 4 enrolled. In 2006, 11 master's, 1 doctorate awarded. Terminal master's awarded for partial completion of doctoral program. *Degree requirements:* For master's, comprehensive exam; for doctorate, thesis/dissertation. *Entrance requirements:* For doctorate, GRE General Test. Additional exam requirements/recommendations for international students: Required—TOEFL (minimum score 550 paper-based; 213 computer-based). *Application deadline:* For fall admission, 2/1 priority date for domestic and international students; for spring admission, 11/1 for domestic students, 10/1 for international students. Applications are processed on a rolling basis. Application fee: $55. Electronic applications accepted. *Financial support:* In 2006–07, 1 research assistantship with full tuition reimbursement was awarded; fellowships, teaching assistantships with full tuition reimbursements, Federal Work-Study, scholarships/grants, health care benefits, and unspecified assistantships also available. Financial award application deadline: 2/1; financial award applicants required to submit FAFSA. *Application contact:* Lisa Rasicot, Graduate Coordinator, 860-486-3065, Fax: 860-486-0210, E-mail: soeadm02@uconnvm.uconn.edu.

University of Delaware, College of Human Services, Education and Public Policy, School of Education, Newark, DE 19716. Offers curriculum and instruction (M Ed); education (PhD); educational leadership (M Ed, Ed D); exceptional children and youth (M Ed); instruction (MI); school counseling (M Ed); school psychology (MA); teaching English as a second language (TESL) (MA). *Accreditation:* NCATE. Part-time and evening/weekend programs available. Terminal master's awarded for partial completion of doctoral program. *Degree requirements:* For master's, thesis (for some programs), comprehensive exam (for some programs), registration; for doctorate, thesis/dissertation, comprehensive exam (for some programs), registration. *Entrance requirements:* For master's and doctorate, GRE, 3 letters of recommendation. Additional exam requirements/recommendations for international students: Required—TOEFL (minimum score 600 paper-based; 250 computer-based). Electronic applications accepted. *Faculty research:* Teacher education; education policy; educational assessment, measurement, and evaluation; curriculum theory and development; community based education models.

The University of Findlay, Graduate and Professional Studies, College of Liberal Arts, Intensive English Language Program, Findlay, OH 45840-3653. Offers bilingual and multicultural education (MA); teaching English to speakers of other languages (MA). Part-time and evening/weekend programs available. *Faculty:* 3 full-time. *Students:* 25 full-time (24 women), 17 part-time (16 women); includes 1 minority (Asian American or Pacific Islander), 28 international. Average age 35. 19 applicants, 95% accepted, 17 enrolled. In 2006, 14 degrees awarded. *Degree requirements:* For master's, cumulative project. *Entrance requirements:* For master's, minimum undergraduate GPA of 3.0 in last 60 hours of course work, 3 letters of recommendation. Additional exam requirements/recommendations for international students: Required—TOEFL (minimum score 550 paper-based). *Application deadline:* Applications are processed on a rolling basis. Application fee: $25. Electronic applications accepted. *Expenses:* Contact institution. *Financial support:* In 2006–07, 1 student received support, including 1 teaching assistantship with full tuition reimbursement available (averaging $6,000 per year). Financial award application deadline: 4/1; financial award applicants required to submit FAFSA. *Unit head:* Dr. Michael C. Reed, Graduate Director, 419-434-4679, Fax: 419-434-4822, E-mail: reed@findlay.edu. *Application contact:* Heather Riffle, Director, Graduate and Special Programs, 419-434-4640, Fax: 419-434-5517, E-mail: riffle@findlay.edu.

University of Florida, Graduate School, College of Education, School of Teaching and Learning, Gainesville, FL 32611. Offers bilingual/ESOL education (M Ed, MAE, Ed D, PhD, Ed S); curriculum and instruction (M Ed, MAE, Ed D, PhD, Ed S); early childhood education (Ed D, PhD, Ed S); elementary education (M Ed, MAE); English education (M Ed, MAE); mathematics education (M Ed, MAE); reading education (M Ed, MAE); science education (M Ed, MAE); social foundations (M Ed, MAE, Ed D, PhD); social studies education (M Ed, MAE). *Accreditation:* NCATE. *Faculty:* 29 full-time (20 women). *Students:* 506 (406 women); includes 87 minority (20 African Americans, 3 American Indian/Alaska Native, 13 Asian Americans or Pacific Islanders, 51 Hispanic Americans) 34 international. In 2006, 278 master's, 8 doctorates awarded. *Degree requirements:* For master's, thesis optional; for doctorate, variable foreign language requirement, thesis/dissertation. *Entrance requirements:* For master's and doctorate, GRE General Test, minimum GPA of 3.0; for Ed S, GRE General Test. Additional exam requirements/recommendations for international students: Required—TOEFL (minimum score 550 paper-based; 213 computer-based). *Application deadline:* For fall admission 6/1 for domestic students. Applications are processed on a rolling basis. Application fee: $30. Electronic applications accepted. *Expenses:* Tuition, state resident: full-time $6,827. Tuition, nonresident: full-time $21,951. Required fees: $999. *Financial support:* In 2006–07, 5 research assistantships (averaging $11,947 per year), 22 teaching assistantships (averaging $9,709 per year) were awarded; fellowships, career-related internships or fieldwork and unspecified assistantships also available. *Faculty research:* Teacher education, inclusive education, classroom processes, curriculum and technology. *Unit head:* Dr. Tom Dana, Director, 352-392-9191 Ext. 200, Fax: 352-392-9193, E-mail: tdana@coe.ufl.edu. *Application contact:* Dr. Linda C. Jones, Coordinator, 352-392-0761 Ext. 267, Fax: 352-392-9193, E-mail: lcjones@coe.ufl.edu.

University of Houston, College of Education, Department of Curriculum and Instruction, Houston, TX 77204. Offers art education (M Ed); bilingual education (M Ed); curriculum and instruction (Ed D); early childhood education (M Ed); education of the gifted (M Ed); elementary education (M Ed); mathematics education (M Ed); reading and language arts education (M Ed); science education (M Ed); second language education (M Ed); secondary education (M Ed); social studies education (M Ed); teaching (M Ed). *Accreditation:* NCATE. Part-time and evening/weekend programs available. *Faculty:* 24 full-time (11 women), 16 part-time/adjunct (14 women). *Students:* 134 full-time (102 women), 327 part-time (256 women); includes 142 minority (49 African Americans, 1 American Indian/Alaska Native, 29 Asian Americans or Pacific Islanders, 63 Hispanic Americans), 19 international. Average age 37. 113 applicants, 72% accepted, 61 enrolled. In 2006, 106 master's, 32 doctorates awarded. *Degree requirements:* For master's, comprehensive exam or thesis; for doctorate, thesis/dissertation, comprehensive exam. *Entrance requirements:* For master's, GRE General Test or MAT; for doctorate, GRE General Test, interview. *Application deadline:* For fall admission, 7/3 priority date for domestic students. Applications are processed on a rolling basis. Application fee: $35 ($75 for international students). *Expenses:* Tuition, state resident: full-time $5,429; part-time $226 per credit. Tuition, nonresident: full-time $12,029; part-time $501 per credit. Required fees: $2,454. *Financial support:* In 2006–07, 2 fellowships with full tuition reimbursements (averaging $9,500 per year), 6 research assistantships with full tuition reimbursements (averaging $8,800 per year), 25 teaching assistantships with full tuition reimbursements (averaging $8,800 per year) were awarded; career-related internships or fieldwork, Federal Work-Study, institutionally sponsored loans, scholarships/grants, health care benefits, and unspecified assistantships also available. Support available to part-time students. Financial award application deadline: 3/10. *Faculty research:* Teaching-learning process, instructional technology in schools, teacher education, classroom management, at-risk students. *Unit head:* Dr. Juanita Copley, Chairperson, 713-743-4950, Fax: 713-743-4990, E-mail: ncopley@aol.com.

University of Houston–Clear Lake, School of Education, Program in Foundations and Professional Studies, Houston, TX 77058-1098. Offers counseling (MS); instructional technology (MS); multicultural studies (MS). Part-time and evening/weekend programs available. *Faculty:* 15 full-time (11 women), 11 part-time/adjunct (6 women). *Students:* 35 full-time (29 women), 283 part-time (239 women); includes 111 minority (58 African Americans, 1 American Indian/Alaska Native, 10 Asian Americans or Pacific Islanders, 42 Hispanic Americans), 10 international. Average age 35. In 2006, 86 degrees awarded. *Degree requirements:* For master's, thesis optional. *Entrance requirements:* For master's, GRE or minimum GPA of 3.0 in last 60 hours. Additional exam requirements/recommendations for international students: Required—TOEFL (minimum score 550 paper-based; 213 computer-based). *Application deadline:* For fall admission, 7/1 for domestic students, 6/1 for international students; for spring admission, 10/1 for domestic and international students. Applications are processed on a rolling basis. Application fee: $35 ($75 for international students). Electronic applications accepted. *Financial support:* Career-related internships or fieldwork, Federal Work-Study, institutionally sponsored loans, and scholarships/grants available. Support available to part-time students. Financial award application deadline: 5/1; financial award applicants required to submit FAFSA. *Unit head:* Dr. Judy Marquez, Chair, 281-283-3580, E-mail: marquez@uhcl.edu. *Application contact:* Janis S. Bigelow, Assistant Director of Admissions, Recruitment and Communications, 281-283-2540, Fax: 281-283-2530, E-mail: bigelow@uhcl.edu.

University of La Verne, Regional Campus Administration, Graduate Credential Program in Education, California Statewide Campus, La Verne, CA 91750-4443. Offers cross cultural language and academic development (Credential); multiple subject (Credential); single subject (Credential). *Faculty:* 1 part-time/adjunct (0 women). *Students:* 113 full-time (95 women), 41 part-time (27 women); includes 49 minority (8 African Americans, 1 American Indian/Alaska Native, 40 Hispanic Americans). Average age 33. *Entrance requirements:* For degree, California Basic Educational Skills Test, minimum undergraduate GPA of 2.75, 3 letters of recommendation, interview. *Application deadline:* Applications are processed on a rolling basis. Application fee: $50. *Expenses:* Contact institution. *Financial support:* Institutionally sponsored loans available. Financial award application deadline: 3/2; financial award applicants required to submit FAFSA. *Unit head:* Juline Behrens, Director, 909-985-0944, Fax: 909-981-8695, E-mail: behrensj@ulv.edu.

University of Maryland, Baltimore County, Graduate School, College of Arts, Humanities and Social Sciences, Department of Education, Program in Instructional Systems Development, Baltimore, MD 21250. Offers ESOL/bilingual education (Postbaccalaureate Certificate); ESOL/bilingual training systems (MA). Part-time and evening/weekend programs available. *Faculty:* 3 full-time (2 women), 3 part-time/adjunct (all women). *Students:* 39 full-time (34 women), 149 part-time (119 women); includes 39 minority (25 African Americans, 10 Asian Americans or Pacific Islanders, 4 Hispanic Americans), 12 international. Average age 37. *Degree requirements:* For master's, thesis (for some programs), comprehensive exam, registration. *Entrance requirements:* Additional exam requirements/recommendations for international students: Required—TOEFL. *Application deadline:* Applications are processed on a rolling basis. Application fee: $50. Electronic applications accepted. *Expenses:* Tuition, state resident: part-time $412 per credit hour. Tuition, nonresident: part-time $681 per credit hour. Required fees: $91 per credit hour. One-time fee: $75 part-time. *Financial support:* Research assistantships, career-related internships or fieldwork, Federal Work-Study, scholarships/grants, tuition waivers, and unspecified assistantships available. Financial award application deadline: 3/1. *Faculty research:* Cross-cultural communication, culturally sensitive pedagogy. *Unit head:* Dr. John Nelson, Coordinator, 410-455-3056.

University of Maryland, Baltimore County, Graduate School, College of Arts, Humanities and Social Sciences, Department of Modern Languages and Linguistics, Program in Intercultural Communication, Baltimore, MD 21250. Offers French (MA); German (MA); Russian (MA); Spanish (MA). Part-time and evening/weekend programs available. *Degree requirements:* For master's, one foreign language, thesis (for some programs), comprehensive or oral exam. *Entrance requirements:* For master's, GRE General Test, minimum GPA of 3.0. Additional exam requirements/recommendations for international students: Required—TOEFL. *Expenses:*

Tuition, state resident: part-time $412 per credit hour. Tuition, nonresident: part-time $681 per credit hour. Required fees: $91 per credit hour. One-time fee: $75 part-time.

University of Maryland, Baltimore County, Graduate School, College of Arts, Humanities and Social Sciences, Program in Language, Literacy, and Culture, Baltimore, MD 21250. Offers PhD. Part-time and evening/weekend programs available. *Faculty:* 65 full-time (33 women), 9 part-time/adjunct (6 women). *Students:* 12 full-time (8 women), 35 part-time (26 women); includes 16 minority (10 African Americans, 1 American Indian/Alaska Native, 4 Asian Americans or Pacific Islanders, 1 Hispanic American), 10 international. Average age 47. 64 applicants, 17% accepted, 10 enrolled. In 2006, 7 degrees awarded. *Median time to degree:* Of those who began their doctoral program in fall 1998, 38% received their degree in 8 years or less. *Degree requirements:* For doctorate, thesis/dissertation, comprehensive exam. *Entrance requirements:* For doctorate, research writing sample, resumé, or curriculum vitae, master's degree. Additional exam requirements/recommendations for international students: Required—TOEFL. *Application deadline:* For fall admission, 2/1 for domestic and international students. Application fee: $50. Electronic applications accepted. *Expenses:* Tuition, state resident: part-time $412 per credit hour. Tuition, nonresident: part-time $681 per credit hour. Required fees: $91 per credit hour. One-time fee: $75 part-time. *Financial support:* In 2006–07, 2 research assistantships with full and partial tuition reimbursements (averaging $14,800 per year), 5 teaching assistantships with full and partial tuition reimbursements (averaging $14,800 per year) were awarded; fellowships, career-related internships or fieldwork, Federal Work-Study, scholarships/grants, and tuition waivers (partial) also available. Support available to part-time students. Financial award application deadline: 3/1; financial award applicants required to submit FAFSA. *Faculty research:* Public policy, educational equity, identity, intercultural communication, technology and communication. *Unit head:* Dr. Jo Ann Crandall, Director, 410-455-2313, Fax: 410-455-8947, E-mail: crandall@umbc.edu. *Application contact:* Pam Gimmell, Administrative Assistant, 410-455-2376, Fax: 410-455-8947, E-mail: llc@umbc.edu.

University of Massachusetts Amherst, Graduate School, School of Education, Program in Education, Amherst, MA 01003. Offers cultural diversity and curriculum reform (M Ed, Ed D, CAGS); early childhood education and development (M Ed, Ed D, CAGS); educational administration (M Ed, Ed D, CAGS); elementary teacher education (M Ed, Ed D, CAGS); higher education (M Ed, Ed D, CAGS); international education (M Ed, Ed D, CAGS); mathematics, science, and instructional technology (M Ed, Ed D, CAGS); physical education teacher education (M Ed, Ed D, CAGS); reading and writing (M Ed, Ed D, CAGS); research and evaluation methods (M Ed, Ed D, CAGS); school psychology and school counseling (M Ed, Ed D, CAGS); secondary teacher education (M Ed, Ed D, CAGS); social justice education (M Ed, Ed D, CAGS); special education (M Ed, Ed D, CAGS). *Accreditation:* NCATE. *Students:* 418 full-time (286 women), 447 part-time (319 women); includes 147 minority (70 African Americans, 4 American Indian/Alaska Native, 28 Asian Americans or Pacific Islanders, 45 Hispanic Americans), 81 international. Average age 36. In 2006, 260 master's, 30 doctorates awarded. *Degree requirements:* For doctorate, thesis/dissertation. *Entrance requirements:* For master's and doctorate, GRE General Test. Additional exam requirements/recommendations for international students: Required—TOEFL (minimum score 530 paper-based; 197 computer-based). *Application deadline:* For fall admission, 1/15 for domestic and international students; for spring admission, 10/1 for domestic and international students. Applications are processed on a rolling basis. Application fee: $40 ($65 for international students). Electronic applications accepted. *Expenses:* Tuition, state resident: full-time $2,640; part-time $110 per credit. Tuition, nonresident: full-time $9,936; part-time $414 per credit. Required fees: $8,969; $3,129 per term. One-time fee: $257 full-time. Tuition and fees vary according to class time, course load, campus/location and reciprocity agreements. *Financial support:* Fellowships with full tuition reimbursements, research assistantships with full tuition reimbursements, teaching assistantships with full tuition reimbursements, career-related internships or fieldwork, Federal Work-Study, scholarships/grants, traineeships, and unspecified assistantships available. Support available to part-time students. Financial award application deadline: 1/15. *Unit head:* Linda L. Griffin, Professor, 413-545-6984.

University of Massachusetts Boston, Office of Graduate Studies, College of Liberal Arts, Program in Applied Linguistics, Boston, MA 02125-3393. Offers bilingual education (MA); English as a second language (MA); foreign language pedagogy (MA). Part-time and evening/weekend programs available. *Students:* 21 full-time (16 women), 76 part-time (56 women); includes 23 minority (8 African Americans, 4 Asian Americans or Pacific Islanders, 11 Hispanic Americans), 12 international. Average age 36. 57 applicants, 79% accepted, 22 enrolled. In 2006, 44 degrees awarded. *Median time to degree:* Master's–4 years full-time. *Degree requirements:* For master's, one foreign language, comprehensive exam. *Entrance requirements:* For master's, minimum GPA of 2.75. *Application deadline:* For fall admission, 2/1 priority date for domestic students; for spring admission, 10/15 for domestic students. Application fee: $25 ($40 for international students). *Expenses:* Tuition, state resident: full-time $2,590; part-time $301 per credit. Tuition, nonresident: full-time $9,758; part-time $427 per credit. One-time fee: $495 full-time. *Financial support:* In 2006–07, 8 research assistantships with full tuition reimbursements (averaging $13,000 per year), 6 teaching assistantships with full tuition reimbursements (averaging $13,000 per year) were awarded; career-related internships or fieldwork, Federal Work-Study, and unspecified assistantships also available. Support available to part-time students. Financial award application deadline: 3/1; financial award applicants required to submit FAFSA. *Faculty research:* Multicultural theory and curriculum development, foreign language pedagogy, language and culture, applied psycholinguistics, bilingual education. *Unit head:* Dr. Donaldo Macedo, Director, 617-287-5760, E-mail: donalde.macedo@umb.edu. *Application contact:* Peggy Roldan, Graduate Admissions Coordinator, 617-287-6400, Fax: 617-287-6236, E-mail: bos.gadm@dpc.umassp.edu.

University of Michigan, Horace H. Rackham School of Graduate Studies, School of Education, Programs in Educational Studies, Ann Arbor, MI 48109. Offers curriculum development (MA); early childhood education (MA, PhD); educational administration and policy (MA, PhD); educational foundation, administration, policy, and research methods (MA); educational foundations and policy (MA, PhD); elementary education (MA-Certification); English education (MA); English language learning in school settings (MA); learning technologies (MA, PhD); literacy, language, and culture (MA, PhD); mathematics education (MA, PhD); research methods (MA); science education (MA, PhD); secondary education (MA-Certification); social studies education (MA); special education (PhD); teaching and teacher education (PhD); MA-Certification; MBA/MA; PhD/MA. Terminal master's awarded for partial completion of doctoral program. *Degree requirements:* For master's, thesis (for some programs); for doctorate, thesis/dissertation, comprehensive exam. *Entrance requirements:* For master's and doctorate, GRE General Test. Additional exam requirements/recommendations for international students: Required—TOEFL (minimum score 600 paper-based; 250 computer-based). *Application deadline:* For fall admission, 12/1 priority date for domestic students, 12/1 for international students. Application fee: $60 ($75 for international students). Electronic applications accepted. *Financial support:* Applicants required to submit FAFSA. *Unit head:* Dr. Addison Stone, Chairperson, 734-763-7500, Fax: 734-615-1290, E-mail: addison@umich.edu. *Application contact:* Roberta Perry, Office of Student Services, 734-764-7563, Fax: 734-763-1495, E-mail: ed.grad.admit@umich.edu.

University of Michigan–Flint, School of Education and Human Services, Department of Education, Flint, MI 48502-1950. Offers early childhood education (MA Ed); education (MA Ed); elementary education with teaching certificate (MA Ed); literacy (K-12) (MA Ed); special education (MA Ed); urban and multicultural education (MA Ed). Part-time programs available. *Faculty:* 19 full-time (15 women), 9 part-time/adjunct (6 women). *Students:* 20 full-time (18 women), 193 part-time (167 women); includes 15 minority (12 African Americans, 1 American Indian/Alaska Native, 2 Hispanic Americans), 2 international. 109 applicants, 80% accepted, 65 enrolled. In 2006, 54 degrees awarded. *Entrance requirements:* Additional exam requirements/recommendations for international students: Required—TOEFL (minimum score 550 paper-based; 220 computer-based), IELTS (minimum score 7). *Application deadline:* For fall admission, 8/1 priority date for domestic students, 3/1 priority date for international students; for winter admission, 11/15 priority date for domestic students, 7/15 priority date for international students; for spring admission, 3/15 priority date for domestic students, 11/15 priority date for international students. Application fee: $55. *Expenses:* Contact institution. *Unit head:* Dr. Beverly Schumer, Director, 810-424-5215, E-mail: bschumer@umflint.edu. *Application contact:* Beulah Alexander, Executive Secretary, 810-766-6879, Fax: 810-766-6891, E-mail: beulaha@umflint.edu.

University of Minnesota, Twin Cities Campus, Graduate School, College of Education and Human Development, Department of Curriculum and Instruction, Program in Teaching, Minneapolis, MN 55455-0213. Offers Chinese (M Ed); earth science (M Ed); elementary special education (M Ed); English (M Ed); English as a second language (M Ed); French (M Ed); German (M Ed); Hebrew (M Ed); Japanese (M Ed); life sciences (M Ed); mathematics (M Ed); middle school science (M Ed); science (M Ed); second languages and cultures (M Ed); social studies (M Ed); Spanish (M Ed). *Students:* 324 full-time (230 women), 132 part-time (86 women); includes 44 minority (5 African Americans, 2 American Indian/Alaska Native, 27 Asian Americans or Pacific Islanders, 10 Hispanic Americans), 4 international. Average age 27. 499 applicants, 74% accepted, 327 enrolled. In 2006, 545 degrees awarded. *Expenses:* Tuition, state resident: full-time $9,302; part-time $775 per credit. Tuition, nonresident: full-time $16,400; part-time $1,367 per credit. Full-time tuition and fees vary according to class time, course load, program, reciprocity agreements and student level. *Application contact:* Dr. Mary Bents, Associate Dean, 612-625-6501, Fax: 612-626-1580, E-mail: mbents@tc.umn.edu.

University of Nevada, Las Vegas, Graduate College, College of Education, Department of Curriculum and Instruction, Las Vegas, NV 89154-9900. Offers curriculum and instruction (Ed D, PhD, Ed S); elementary education (M Ed, MS); English education (M Ed, MS); library science (M Ed, MS); literacy education (M Ed, MS); mathematics education (M Ed, MS); multicultural education (M Ed, MS); reading specialist (M Ed, MS); secondary education (M Ed, MS); teacher leadership (M Ed, MS); teaching English as a second language (M Ed, MS); technology integration and leadership (M Ed, MS). *Accreditation:* NCATE. Part-time and evening/weekend programs available. *Faculty:* 40 full-time (19 women), 21 part-time/adjunct (14 women). *Students:* 257 full-time (189 women), 387 part-time (296 women); includes 114 minority (28 African Americans, 5 American Indian/Alaska Native, 34 Asian Americans or Pacific Islanders, 47 Hispanic Americans), 7 international. 261 applicants, 70% accepted, 168 enrolled. In 2006, 231 master's, 5 doctorates awarded. *Degree requirements:* For master's, thesis (for some programs), comprehensive exam (for some programs); for doctorate, thesis/dissertation, oral exam. *Entrance requirements:* For master's, minimum GPA of 3.0; for doctorate, GRE General Test, minimum graduate GPA of 3.0. Additional exam requirements/recommendations for international students: Required—TOEFL (minimum score 550 paper-based; 213 computer-based; 80 iBT). *Application deadline:* For fall admission, 2/15 for domestic and international students; for spring admission, 9/30 for domestic and international students. Application fee: $60 ($75 for international students). Electronic applications accepted. *Financial support:* In 2006–07, 30 research assistantships with partial tuition reimbursements (averaging $10,000 per year), 7 teaching assistantships with partial tuition reimbursements (averaging $12,000 per year) were awarded; career-related internships or fieldwork, Federal Work-Study, institutionally sponsored loans, scholarships/grants, health care benefits, and unspecified assistantships also available. Support available to part-time students. Financial award application deadline: 3/1. *Unit head:* Dr. Greg Levitt, Chair, 702-895-3241. *Application contact:* Graduate College Admissions Evaluator, 702-895-3320, E-mail: gradcollege@unlv.edu.

University of New Mexico, Graduate School, College of Education, Department of Educational Specialties, Program in Multicultural Teacher and Childhood Education, Albuquerque, NM 87131-2039. Offers Ed D, PhD, EDSPC. *Accreditation:* NCATE. Part-time and evening/weekend programs available. *Students:* 3 full-time (2 women), 11 part-time (8 women); includes 5 minority (2 American Indian/Alaska Native, 3 Hispanic Americans). Average age 53. 4 applicants. *Degree requirements:* For doctorate, thesis/dissertation. *Entrance requirements:* For doctorate, master's degree, 3.0 GPA, 3 years teaching experience, 3-5 letters of reference, 1 letter of intent. Additional exam requirements/recommendations for international students: Required—TOEFL (minimum score 550 paper-based; 213 computer-based). *Application deadline:* For fall admission, 3/1 priority date for domestic students; for spring admission, 10/1 for domestic students. Application fee: $50. Electronic applications accepted. *Financial support:* In 2006–07, 2 teaching assistantships with partial tuition reimbursements (averaging $12,805 per year) were awarded; fellowships, career-related internships or fieldwork, scholarships/grants, and unspecified assistantships also available. Financial award application deadline: 4/15; financial award applicants required to submit FAFSA. *Faculty research:* Mathematics/science/technology education. *Unit head:* Dr. Rosalita Mitchell, Chair, 505-277-9611, Fax: 505-277-0455, E-mail: rosalita@unm.edu. *Application contact:* Mary Francis, Program Office, 505-277-6510, Fax: 505-277-6929, E-mail: mfrancis@unm.edu.

The University of North Carolina at Greensboro, Graduate School, School of Education, Department of Educational Leadership and Cultural Foundations, Greensboro, NC 27412-5001. Offers curriculum and teaching (PhD), including cultural studies; educational leadership (Ed D, Ed S); school administration (MSA). *Accreditation:* NCATE. *Faculty:* 12 full-time (7 women), 1 part-time/adjunct (0 women). *Students:* 100 full-time (71 women), 113 part-time (79 women); includes 74 minority (70 African Americans, 1 American Indian/Alaska Native, 1 Asian American or Pacific Islander, 2 Hispanic Americans). 124 applicants, 35% accepted. *Degree requirements:* For doctorate, thesis/dissertation. *Entrance requirements:* For master's, doctorate, and Ed S, GRE General Test. Additional exam requirements/recommendations for international students: Required—TOEFL. *Application deadline:* For fall admission, 1/1 priority date for domestic students; for spring admission, 11/1 for domestic students. Applications are processed on a rolling basis. Application fee: $45. Electronic applications accepted. *Expenses:* Tuition, state resident: full-time $2,692. Tuition, nonresident: full-time $13,742. *Financial support:* Fellowships with full tuition reimbursements, research assistantships with full tuition reimbursements, teaching assistantships with full tuition reimbursements, career-related internships or fieldwork, Federal Work-Study, scholarships/grants, and traineeships available. Support available to part-time students. *Unit head:* Dr. Ulrich Reitzug, Chair, 336-334-3490, Fax: 336-334-4120, E-mail: ucreitzu@uncg.edu. *Application contact:* Michelle Harkleroad, Director of Graduate Admissions, 336-334-4884, Fax: 336-334-4424, E-mail: mbharkle@uncg.edu.

University of Oklahoma, Graduate College, College of Education, Department of Instructional Leadership and Academic Curriculum, Norman, OK 73019-0390. Offers education (Certificate); instructional leadership and academic curriculum (M Ed, PhD), including bilingual education, early childhood education, elementary education, English education, math education, reading education, science education, secondary education, social studies education. *Accreditation:* NCATE. Part-time and evening/weekend programs available. *Faculty:* 20 full-time (11 women), 6 part-time/adjunct (all women). *Students:* 76 full-time (63 women), 115 part-time (89 women); includes 25 minority (8 African Americans, 12 American Indian/Alaska Native, 4 Asian Americans or Pacific Islanders, 1 Hispanic American), 12 international. 72 applicants, 96% accepted, 56 enrolled. In 2006, 11 master's, 10 doctorates awarded. *Degree requirements:* For doctorate, thesis/dissertation. *Entrance requirements:* For master's, 12 hours of course work in education; for doctorate, GRE General Test, master's degree, minimum graduate GPA of 3.0. Additional exam requirements/recommendations for international students: Required—TOEFL (minimum score 550 paper-based; 213 computer-based). *Application deadline:* For fall admission, 6/1 priority date for domestic students, 4/1 for international students; for spring admission, 11/1 for domestic students, 9/1 for international students. Applications are processed on a rolling basis. Application fee: $40 ($90 for international students). *Expenses:* Tuition, state resident: full-time $3,180; part-time $133 per credit hour. Tuition, nonresident: full-time $11,347; part-time $473 per credit hour. Required fees: $1,729; $62 per credit hour. $117 per semester. Tuition and fees vary according to course load and program. *Financial support:* In 2006–07, 76 students received support, including 5 research assistantships with partial tuition reimbursements available (averaging $9,773 per year), 7 teaching assistantships with partial tuition reimbursements available (averaging $10,403 per year); scholarships/grants and unspecified assistantships also available. Financial award applicants required to submit FAFSA. *Faculty research:* Early literacy, learning cycle, social justice, teacher education. Total annual research

Multilingual and Multicultural Education

University of Oklahoma (continued)
expenditures: $119,917. *Unit head:* Dr. Priscilla Griffith, Chair and Graduate Liaison, 405-325-1498, Fax: 405-325-4061, E-mail: pgriffith@ou.edu.

University of Pennsylvania, Graduate School of Education, Division of Language in Education, Program in Intercultural Communication, Philadelphia, PA 19104. Offers MS Ed, Ed D, PhD. Part-time programs available. *Degree requirements:* For master's, thesis, comprehensive exam; for doctorate, thesis/dissertation, oral exams, comprehensive exam. *Entrance requirements:* For master's, GRE General Test or MAT; for doctorate, GRE General Test. Electronic applications accepted. Expenses: Contact institution. *Faculty research:* Anthropology of education, history of education, bicultural education, identity and gender education.

University of Pennsylvania, Graduate School of Education, Division of Language in Education, Programs in Teaching English to Speakers of Other Languages and Intercultural Communication, Philadelphia, PA 19104. Offers educational linguistics (PhD); intercultural communication (MS Ed); teaching English to speakers of other languages (MS Ed). Part-time programs available. Postbaccalaureate distance learning degree programs offered (minimal on-campus study). Terminal master's awarded for partial completion of doctoral program. *Degree requirements:* For master's, thesis (for some programs), comprehensive exam; for doctorate, one foreign language, thesis/dissertation, preliminary exam. *Entrance requirements:* For master's and doctorate, GRE General Test or MAT. Additional exam requirements/recommendations for international students: Required—TOEFL. Electronic applications accepted. Expenses: Contact institution. *Faculty research:* Second language acquisition, social linguistics, English as a second language.

University of San Francisco, School of Education, Department of International and Multicultural Education, San Francisco, CA 94117-1080. Offers international and multicultural education (MA, Ed D); multicultural literature for children and young adults (MA); teaching English as a second language (MA). *Faculty:* 6 full-time (4 women), 8 part-time/adjunct (6 women). *Students:* 102 full-time (80 women), 71 part-time (64 women); includes 74 minority (16 African Americans, 24 Asian Americans or Pacific Islanders, 34 Hispanic Americans), 37 international. Average age 34. 163 applicants, 88% accepted, 50 enrolled. In 2006, 37 master's, 11 doctorates awarded. *Degree requirements:* For doctorate, thesis/dissertation. Application fee: $55 ($65 for international students). *Expenses:* Tuition: Full-time $17,370; part-time $965 per unit. Tuition and fees vary according to degree level, campus/location and program. *Financial support:* In 2006–07, 93 students received support; fellowships, research assistantships, teaching assistantships available. Financial award application deadline: 3/2; financial award applicants required to submit FAFSA. *Unit head:* Dr. Rosita Galang, Chair, 415-422-6878.

The University of Tennessee, Graduate School, College of Education, Health and Human Sciences, Program in Education, Knoxville, TN 37996. Offers art education (MS); counseling education (PhD); cultural studies in education (PhD); curriculum (MS, Ed S); curriculum, educational research and evaluation (Ed D, PhD); early childhood education (PhD); early childhood special education (MS); education of deaf and hard of hearing (MS); educational administration and policy studies (Ed D, PhD); educational administration and supervision (Ed S); educational psychology (Ed D, PhD); elementary education (MS, Ed S); elementary teaching (MS); English education (MS, Ed S); exercise science (PhD); foreign language/ESL education (MS, Ed S); instructional technology (MS, Ed D, PhD, Ed S); literacy, language and ESL education (PhD); literacy, language education, and ESL education (Ed D); mathematics education (MS, Ed S); modified and comprehensive special education (MS); reading education (MS, Ed S); school counseling (Ed S); school psychology (PhD, Ed S); science education (MS, Ed S); secondary teaching (MS); social foundations (MS); social science education (MS, Ed S); socio-cultural foundations of sports and education (PhD); special education (Ed S); teacher education (Ed D, PhD). *Accreditation:* NCATE. Part-time and evening/weekend programs available. *Students:* 529 (401 women); includes 39 minority (23 African Americans, 2 American Indian/Alaska Native, 9 Asian Americans or Pacific Islanders, 5 Hispanic Americans) 34 international. 420 applicants, 50% accepted. In 2006, 258 master's, 28 doctorates awarded. *Degree requirements:* For master's and Ed S, thesis optional; for doctorate, variable foreign language requirement, thesis/dissertation. *Entrance requirements:* For master's, minimum GPA of 2.7; for doctorate and Ed S, GRE General Test, minimum GPA of 2.7. Additional exam requirements/recommendations for international students: Required—TOEFL. *Application deadline:* For fall admission, 2/1 priority date for domestic students. Applications are processed on a rolling basis. Application fee: $35. Electronic applications accepted. *Expenses:* Tuition, state resident: full-time $5,574. Tuition, nonresident: full-time $16,840. Required fees: $792. *Financial support:* In 2006–07, 4 fellowships, 9 teaching assistantships were awarded; career-related internships or fieldwork, Federal Work-Study, institutionally sponsored loans, and unspecified assistantships also available. Financial award application deadline: 2/1; financial award applicants required to submit FAFSA. *Unit head:* Dr. Lester Knight, Head, 865-974-0907, Fax: 865-974-8718, E-mail: lknight@utk.edu.

The University of Texas at Brownsville, Graduate Studies, School of Education, Brownsville, TX 78520-4991. Offers bilingual education (M Ed); counseling and guidance (M Ed); curriculum and instruction (M Ed); early childhood education (M Ed); educational administration (M Ed); educational technology (M Ed); English as a second language (M Ed); reading specialist (M Ed); special education/educational diagnostician (M Ed). Part-time and evening/weekend programs available. Postbaccalaureate distance learning degree programs offered (minimal on-campus study). *Degree requirements:* For master's, thesis optional. *Entrance requirements:* For master's, GRE General Test. Additional exam requirements/recommendations for international students: Required—TOEFL.

The University of Texas at San Antonio, College of Education and Human Development, Division of Bicultural-Bilingual Studies, San Antonio, TX 78249-0617. Offers bicultural studies (MA); bicultural-bilingual studies (MA); culture, literacy, and language (PhD); teaching English as a second language (MA). Part-time and evening/weekend programs available. *Faculty:* 12 full-time (9 women). *Students:* 50 full-time (38 women), 95 part-time (75 women); includes 102 minority (5 African Americans, 1 American Indian/Alaska Native, 3 Asian Americans or Pacific Islanders, 93 Hispanic Americans), 12 international. Average age 35. 63 applicants, 75% accepted, 44 enrolled. In 2006, 41 master's, 4 doctorates awarded. *Degree requirements:* For master's, one foreign language, comprehensive exam, registration; for doctorate, one foreign language, thesis/dissertation, comprehensive exam, registration. *Entrance requirements:* For master's and doctorate, GRE General Test. Additional exam requirements/recommendations for international students: Required—TOEFL (minimum score 500 paper-based; 173 computer-based). *Application deadline:* For fall admission, 7/1 for domestic students, 4/1 for international students; for spring admission, 11/1 for domestic students, 9/1 for international students. Applications are processed on a rolling basis. Application fee: $45 ($80 for international students). Electronic applications accepted. *Expenses:* Tuition, state resident: full-time $1,730; part-time $192 per credit hour. Tuition, nonresident: full-time $6,680; part-time $742 per credit hour. Required fees: $733; $308,359 per credit hour. *Financial support:* In 2006–07, 1 fellowship (averaging $45,000 per year), 4 research assistantships (averaging $24,563 per year), 13 teaching assistantships (averaging $17,354 per year) were awarded; career-related internships or fieldwork and Federal Work-Study also available. Support available to part-time students. *Faculty research:* Spanish-English bilingualism, cultural transmission in bilingual communities, literacy in bilingual settings, content-based ESL, second language acquisition in classroom contexts. Total annual research expenditures: $78,604. *Unit head:* Dr. Robert D. Milk, Director, 210-458-4426, Fax: 210-458-5962, E-mail: rmilk@utsa.edu.

The University of Texas–Pan American, College of Education, Department of Curriculum and Instruction: Elementary and Secondary, Edinburg, TX 78541-2999. Offers bilingual education (M Ed); early childhood education (M Ed); elementary education (M Ed); reading (M Ed); secondary education (M Ed). Part-time programs available. *Degree requirements:* For master's, thesis optional. *Entrance requirements:* For master's, GRE. Additional exam requirements/recommendations for international students: Required—TOEFL, IELTS. *Expenses:* Tuition, state resident: full-time $2,577; part-time $143 per credit hour. Tuition, nonresident: full-time $7,527; part-time $418 per credit hour. Required fees: $561. *Faculty research:* Dual language instruction, literacy and technology, teacher education in diverse populations, mathematics and science education.

University of Washington, Graduate School, College of Education, Seattle, WA 98195. Offers curriculum and instruction (M Ed, Ed D, PhD), including educational technology, general curriculum (Ed D, PhD), language, literacy, and culture, mathematics education, multicultural education, reading and language arts education (Ed D), science education, social studies education, teaching and curriculum (M Ed); educational leadership and policy studies (M Ed, Ed D, PhD), including administration, educational organization and policy, higher education, school district leadership (Ed D), social/cultural foundations; educational psychology (M Ed, PhD), including human development and cognition, measurement and research, school counseling (M Ed), school psychology; special education (M Ed, Ed D, PhD), *including early childhood* education, elementary special education, emotional and behavioral disabilities (M Ed), general special education, severe disabilities; teacher education (MIT). *Accreditation:* APA. Part-time and evening/weekend programs available. *Degree requirements:* For master's, thesis optional; for doctorate, thesis/dissertation. *Entrance requirements:* For master's and doctorate, GRE General Test, minimum GPA of 3.0. Additional exam requirements/recommendations for international students: Required—TOEFL. Electronic applications accepted. *Faculty research:* School restructuring/effective schools, special education interventions, literacy and writing, technology, school partnerships, teacher preparation.

Utah State University, School of Graduate Studies, College of Humanities, Arts and Social Sciences, Department of Languages, Philosophy, and Speech Communication, Logan, UT 84322. Offers second language teaching (MSLT). *Faculty:* 2 full-time (1 woman), 1 (woman) part-time/adjunct. *Students:* Average age 29. 22 applicants, 82% accepted. In 2006, 16 degrees awarded. *Entrance requirements:* For master's, GRE General Test or MAT, minimum GPA of 3.0. Additional exam requirements/recommendations for international students: Required—TOEFL. *Application deadline:* For fall admission, 2/15 priority date for domestic students, 2/15 for international students; for spring admission, 10/15 priority date for domestic students, 10/15 for international students. Applications are processed on a rolling basis. Application fee: $50 ($60 for international students). *Financial support:* In 2006–07, 1 research assistantship with partial tuition reimbursement (averaging $3,000 per year), 6 teaching assistantships with partial tuition reimbursements (averaging $6,000 per year) were awarded; fellowships with partial tuition reimbursements also available. Financial award application deadline: 2/1. *Unit head:* Dr. Charlie Huenemann, Head, 435-797-1209, Fax: 435-797-1329. *Application contact:* Dr. Karin de Jonge-Kannan, Information Contact, 435-797-8318, Fax: 435-797-1329, E-mail: dejongek@cc.usu.edu.

Vanderbilt University, Graduate School, Program in Learning, Teaching and Diversity, Nashville, TN 37240-1001. Offers MS, PhD. *Faculty:* 29 full-time (17 women). *Students:* 39 full-time (24 women); includes 4 minority (3 African Americans, 1 Asian American or Pacific Islander), 9 international. 68 applicants, 13% accepted, 7 enrolled. In 2006, 1 degree awarded. *Application deadline:* For fall admission, 1/15 for domestic and international students. Application fee: $0. Electronic applications accepted. *Expenses:* Tuition: Full-time $24,462. Required fees: $2,515. One-time fee: $30 full-time. Full-time tuition and fees vary according to course load, degree level and program. *Financial support:* Fellowships with tuition reimbursements, research assistantships with full tuition reimbursements, teaching assistantships with full tuition reimbursements, Federal Work-Study, institutionally sponsored loans, and traineeships available. Financial award application deadline: 1/15. *Unit head:* Leona Schauble, Chair, 615-322-8100, Fax: 615-322-8999, E-mail: leona.schauble@vanderbilt.edu. *Application contact:* Dr. Clifford A. Hofwolt, Director of Graduate Studies, 615-322-8100, Fax: 615-322-8999, E-mail: clifford.hofwolt@vanderbilt.edu.

Washington State University, Graduate School, College of Education, Department of Teaching and Learning, Pullman, WA 99164. Offers curriculum and instruction (Ed D, PhD); diverse languages (M Ed, MA); elementary education (M Ed, MA, MIT); exercise science (MS); literacy education (M Ed, MA, PhD); math education (PhD); secondary education (M Ed, MA). *Accreditation:* NCATE. *Faculty:* 27. *Students:* 54 full-time (43 women), 20 part-time (14 women); includes 13 minority (4 African Americans, 2 American Indian/Alaska Native, 2 Asian Americans or Pacific Islanders, 5 Hispanic Americans), 5 international. Average age 34. 244 applicants, 16% accepted, 11 enrolled. In 2006, 20 master's, 3 doctorates awarded. *Degree requirements:* For master's, thesis (for some programs), oral or written exam, comprehensive exam (for some programs); for doctorate, thesis/dissertation, oral, written exam, comprehensive exam. *Entrance requirements:* For master's and doctorate, GRE General Test, minimum GPA of 3.0, 3 letters of recommendation. Additional exam requirements/recommendations for international students: Required—TOEFL. *Application deadline:* For fall admission, 2/1 for domestic students, 3/1 for international students; for spring admission, 9/1 for domestic students, 7/1 for international students. Applications are processed on a rolling basis. Application fee: $50. *Expenses:* Tuition, state resident: full-time $7,066. Tuition, nonresident: full-time $17,204. *Financial support:* In 2006–07, 13 research assistantships with partial tuition reimbursements (averaging $13,917 per year), 22 teaching assistantships with partial tuition reimbursements (averaging $13,056 per year) were awarded; career-related internships or fieldwork, Federal Work-Study, institutionally sponsored loans, tuition waivers (partial), unspecified assistantships, and staff assistantships, teaching associateships also available. Financial award application deadline: 4/1. *Faculty research:* Evolution of middle school education issues in special education, computer-assisted language learning. Total annual research expenditures: $1.1 million. *Unit head:* Dr. Corinne Mantle-Bromley, Chair, 509-335-5027. *Application contact:* Graduate School Admissions, 800-GRADWSU Fax: 509-335-1949, E-mail: gradsch@wsu.edu.

Wayne State University, College of Education, Division of Teacher Education, Detroit, MI 48202. Offers adult and continuing education (M Ed); art education (M Ed); bilingual/bicultural education (M Ed, MAT); business education (M Ed, MAT); career and technical education (M Ed, Ed D, PhD, Ed S); curriculum and instruction (Ed D, PhD, Ed S); distributive education (M Ed, MAT); early childhood education (M Ed); elementary education (M Ed, MAT, Ed D, PhD, Ed S); elementary education curriculum and instruction (M Ed); English education (M Ed); English education-secondary (M Ed, Ed S); foreign language education (M Ed); general education (Ed D, Ed S); health occupations education (M Ed); industrial education (M Ed); mathematics education (M Ed, Ed S); pre-school and parent education (M Ed); reading (M Ed, Ed D, Ed S); reading, languages and literature (Ed D); school music-vocal (M Ed); science education (M Ed, MAT, Ed S); secondary education (MAT); secondary school reading (M Ed); social studies education (M Ed, Ed S), including education-secondary (M Ed); special education (M Ed, Ed D, PhD, Ed S); teacher education (MAT, Ed D, PhD). *Faculty:* 41 full-time (22 women), 2 part-time/adjunct (both women). *Students:* 401 full-time (295 women), 1,021 part-time (784 women); includes 527 minority (452 African Americans, 6 American Indian/Alaska Native, 32 Asian Americans or Pacific Islanders, 37 Hispanic Americans), 18 international. Average age 36. 296 applicants, 81% accepted, 132 enrolled. In 2006, 386 master's, 1 doctorate awarded. *Degree requirements:* For doctorate, thesis/dissertation. *Entrance requirements:* For master's, minimum GPA of 2.6; for doctorate, minimum undergraduate GPA of 3.0, graduate 3.5; interview. Additional exam requirements/recommendations for international students: Required—TOEFL (minimum score 550 paper-based; 213 computer-based), TWE (minimum score 6). *Application deadline:* For fall admission, 7/1 for domestic students, 6/1 for international students; for winter admission, 10/1 for international students; for spring admission, 2/1 for international students. Application fee: $30 ($50 for international students). Electronic applications accepted. *Financial support:* In 2006–07, 1 fellowship (averaging $34,919 per year) was awarded; research assistantships. *Faculty research:* Reading and writing literacy and literature. Total annual research expenditures: $209,400. *Unit head:* Dr. Joann Snyder, Academic Director, 313-577-1644, E-mail: joanne.snyder@wayne.edu. *Application contact:* Sharon Elliott, Assistant Dean, 313-577-0902, E-mail: sharon.elliott@wayne.edu.

Western Oregon University, Graduate Programs, College of Education, Division of Teacher Education, Program in Secondary Education, Monmouth, OR 97361-1394. Offers bilingual education (MS Ed); health (MS Ed); humanities (MAT, MS Ed); initial licensure (MAT); mathematics (MAT, MS Ed); science (MAT, MS Ed); social science (MAT, MS Ed). *Accreditation:* NCATE. Part-time and evening/weekend programs available. *Faculty:* 7 full-time (4 women), 15 part-time/adjunct (7 women). *Students:* 12 full-time (4 women), 21 part-time (10 women). Average age 32. In 2006, 31 degrees awarded. *Degree requirements:* For master's, written exam, thesis optional. *Entrance requirements:* For master's, minimum GPA of 3.0, teaching license. *Application deadline:* Applications are processed on a rolling basis. Application fee: $50. *Expenses:* Tuition, state resident: full-time $8,250; part-time $250 per credit. Tuition, nonresident: full-time $14,025; part-time $250 per credit. Required fees: $1,173. *Financial support:* In 2006–07, 16 teaching assistantships with full tuition reimbursements (averaging $706 per year) were awarded; research assistantships with full tuition reimbursements, career-related internships or fieldwork, Federal Work-Study, and tuition waivers (full and partial) also available. Support available to part-time students. Financial award application deadline: 3/1; financial award applicants required to submit FAFSA. *Faculty research:* Literacy, science in primary grades, geography education, retention, teacher burnout. *Unit head:* Dr. Mary Bucy, Unit Head, 503-838-8794; Fax: 503-838-8228. *Application contact:* Dr. David McDonald, Dean of Admissions, Retention and Enrollment Management, 503-838-8919, Fax: 503-838-8067, E-mail: mcdonald@wou.edu.

Xavier University, College of Social Sciences, Health and Education, School of Education, Program in Multicultural Literature for Children, Cincinnati, OH 45207. Offers M Ed. Part-time and evening/weekend programs available. *Faculty:* 2 full-time (1 woman), 4 part-time/adjunct (0 women). *Students:* 1 (woman) full-time, 8 part-time (all women); includes 1 minority (African American) Average age 35. 2 applicants, 100% accepted, 2 enrolled. In 2006, 7 degrees awarded. *Degree requirements:* For master's, research project. *Entrance requirements:* For master's, GRE or MAT, minimum GPA of 2.8. Additional exam requirements/recommendations for international students: Required—TOEFL. *Application deadline:* For fall admission, 8/15 priority date for domestic students. Applications are processed on a rolling basis. Application fee: $35. *Expenses:* Tuition: Part-time $462 per credit hour. Part-time tuition and fees vary according to degree level, campus/location and program. *Financial support:* Scholarships/grants and unspecified assistantships available. Support available to part-time students. Financial award applicants required to submit FAFSA. *Faculty research:* Analysis of Canadian children's literature, adolescent literature, gender issues in literature for children. *Unit head:* Dr. Leslie Prosak-Beres, Director, 513-745-3652, Fax: 513-745-1052, E-mail: prosak@xavier.edu. *Application contact:* Roger Bosse, Interim Director of Graduate Studies, 513-745-3357, Fax: 513-745-1048, E-mail: bosse@xavier.edu.

Special Education

Acadia University, Faculty of Professional Studies, School of Education, Program in Special Education, Wolfville, NS B4P 2R6, Canada. Offers M Ed. Part-time and evening/weekend programs available. *Faculty:* 2 full-time (both women). *Students:* 2 full-time (0 women), 45 part-time (39 women). In 2006, 28 degrees awarded. *Degree requirements:* For master's, thesis optional. *Entrance requirements:* For master's, bachelor's degree in education, minimum B average in undergraduate course work, course work in special education. Additional exam requirements/recommendations for international students: Required—TOEFL (minimum score 580 paper-based; 237 computer-based). *Application deadline:* For fall admission, 3/15 priority date for domestic and international students. Application fee: $50. Electronic applications accepted. *Financial support:* In 2006–07, teaching assistantships (averaging $4,000 per year). Financial award application deadline: 2/1. *Faculty research:* Technology and human interaction, inclusive education and community, accommodating diversity, program evaluation. *Application contact:* Sheila Langille, Secretary, 902-585-1229, Fax: 902-585-1071, E-mail: sheila.langille@acadiau.ca.

Adams State College, The Graduate School, Department of Teacher Education, Program in Special Education, Alamosa, CO 81102. Offers MA. *Accreditation:* Teacher Education Accreditation Council. Part-time programs available. Postbaccalaureate distance learning degree programs offered. *Degree requirements:* For master's, practicum, qualifying exam. *Entrance requirements:* For master's, GRE General Test or MAT, minimum undergraduate GPA of 3.0.

Adelphi University, School of Education, Program in Childhood Special Education, Garden City, NY 11530-0701. Offers childhood special education (Certificate); childhood special education studies (MS); grades 1-6 (MS); inclusive setting, grades 1-6 preservice or in-service track (MS). Part-time and evening/weekend programs available. *Students:* 31 full-time (29 women), 88 part-time (79 women); includes 26 minority (5 African Americans, 1 Asian American or Pacific Islander, 20 Hispanic Americans). Average age 33. In 2006, 57 degrees awarded. *Entrance requirements:* For master's, 2 letters of recommendation, resumé detailing paid/volunteer experience and organizational membership. Additional exam requirements/recommendations for international students: Required—TOEFL (minimum score 550 paper-based; 213 computer-based). *Application deadline:* For fall admission, 4/1 priority date for domestic students; for spring admission, 11/1 priority date for domestic students. Applications are processed on a rolling basis. Application fee: $50. Electronic applications accepted. *Financial support:* Fellowships, research assistantships with partial tuition reimbursements, teaching assistantships, career-related internships or fieldwork, Federal Work-Study, institutionally sponsored loans, tuition waivers (full), and unspecified assistantships available. Support available to part-time students. Financial award application deadline: 2/15; financial award applicants required to submit FAFSA. *Unit head:* Anne Mungai, Director, 516-877-4096, E-mail: mungai@adelphi.edu. *Application contact:* Christine Murphy, Director of Admissions, 516-877-3050, Fax: 516-877-3039, E-mail: graduateadmissions@adelphi.edu.

Adelphi University, School of Education, Program in Early Childhood Special Education, Garden City, NY 11530-0701. Offers birth through grade 2 (Certificate); in-service (MS); preservice (MS). *Students:* 12 full-time (all women), 45 part-time (44 women); includes 4 minority (1 African American, 3 Hispanic Americans). Average age 31. In 2006, 4 degrees awarded. *Entrance requirements:* For master's, 2 letters of recommendation, resumé, detailing paid/volunteer experience and organizational membership. Additional exam requirements/recommendations for international students: Required—TOEFL (minimum score 550 paper-based; 213 computer-based). *Application deadline:* For fall admission, 4/1 for domestic students; for spring admission, 11/1 for domestic students. Application fee: $50. *Faculty research:* Personnel preparation for: early intervention, early childhood special education teachers preparing to be interventionists for infants and young children with disabilities. *Unit head:* Dr. Crystal Kaiser, Director, 516-877-4064, E-mail: kaiser@adelphi.edu. *Application contact:* Christine Murphy, Director of Admissions, 516-877-3050, Fax: 516-877-3039, E-mail: graduateadmissions@adelphi.edu.

Alabama Agricultural and Mechanical University, School of Graduate Studies, School of Education, Department of Counseling and Special Education, Huntsville, AL 35811. Offers communicative disorders (M Ed, MS); psychology and counseling (MS, Ed S), including clinical psychology (MS), counseling and guidance, counseling psychology (MS), personnel management (MS), psychometry (MS), school psychology (MS); special education (M Ed, MS). *Accreditation:* CORE; NCATE. Part-time and evening/weekend programs available. *Faculty:* 4 full-time (3 women), 3 part-time/adjunct (1 woman). *Students:* 62 full-time (50 women), 121 part-time (93 women); includes 121 minority (113 African Americans, 2 American Indian/Alaska Native, 6 Hispanic Americans), 12 international. In 2006, 55 master's, 2 other advanced degrees awarded. *Degree requirements:* For master's, comprehensive exam. *Entrance requirements:* For master's, GRE General Test. *Application deadline:* For fall admission, 5/1 for domestic students. Application fee: $15 ($20 for international students). *Financial support:* Career-related internships or fieldwork available. Support available to part-time students. Financial award application deadline: 4/1. *Faculty research:* Increasing numbers of minorities in special education and speech-language pathology. Total annual research expenditures: $300,000. *Unit head:* Dr. Terry L. Douglas, Chair, 256-372-5533.

Alabama State University, School of Graduate Studies, College of Education, Department of Curriculum and Instruction, Program in Special Education, Montgomery, AL 36101-0271. Offers M Ed. Part-time programs available. *Students:* 20 full-time (16 women), 60 part-time (47 women); includes 68 minority (all African Americans), 1 international. In 2006, 31 degrees awarded. *Degree requirements:* For master's, comprehensive exam. *Entrance requirements:* For master's, GRE General Test, MAT, graduate writing competency test. Additional exam requirements/recommendations for international students: Required—TOEFL (minimum score 500 paper-based; 173 computer-based). *Application deadline:* For fall admission, 7/15 for domestic students; for spring admission, 12/15 for domestic students. Applications are processed on a rolling basis. Application fee: $10. *Expenses:* Tuition, state resident: full-time $1,728; part-time

$192 per hour. Tuition, nonresident: full-time $3,456; part-time $334 per hour. *Financial support:* In 2006–07, research assistantships (averaging $9,450 per year).

Albany State University, College of Education, Program in Special Education, Albany, GA 31705-2717. Offers M Ed. *Accreditation:* NCATE. Part-time programs available. *Degree requirements:* For master's, comprehensive exam. *Entrance requirements:* For master's, GRE General Test, MAT or NTE. Electronic applications accepted.

Albright College, Department of Education—Graduate Division, Reading, PA 19612-5234. Offers early childhood education (MS); elementary education (MS); English as a second language (MA); general education (MA); special education (MS). Part-time and evening/weekend programs available. *Degree requirements:* For master's, thesis. *Entrance requirements:* For master's, GRE General Test or MAT, minimum undergraduate GPA of 3.0, 2 letters of recommendation, interview. Additional exam requirements/recommendations for international students: Recommended—TOEFL (minimum score 525 paper-based; 197 computer-based). Electronic applications accepted.

Alcorn State University, School of Graduate Studies, School of Psychology and Education, Alcorn State, MS 39096-7500. Offers agricultural education (MS Ed); elementary education (MS Ed, Ed S); guidance and counseling (MS Ed); industrial education (MS Ed); secondary education (MS Ed), including health and physical education; special education (MS Ed). *Accreditation:* NCATE. *Faculty:* 14 full-time (9 women), 21 part-time/adjunct (13 women). *Students:* 76 full-time (44 women), 271 part-time (226 women); includes 333 minority (all African Americans) In 2006, 119 degrees awarded. *Degree requirements:* For master's, thesis optional. *Application deadline:* For fall admission, 7/15 priority date for domestic students; for spring admission, 11/25 for domestic students. Applications are processed on a rolling basis. Application fee: $0 ($10 for international students). *Financial support:* Career-related internships or fieldwork available. Support available to part-time students. *Unit head:* Dr. Josephine M. Posey, Dean, 601-877-6141, Fax: 601-877-3867.

Alliant International University–Irvine, Graduate School of Education, Teacher Education Programs, Irvine, CA 92612. Offers auditory oral education (Certificate); CLAD (Certificate); preliminary multiple subject (Credential); preliminary multiple subject with BCLAD (Credential); preliminary single subject (Credential); professional clear multiple subject (Credential); professional clear single subject (Credential); teaching (MA, Credential); technology and learning (MA). Part-time and evening/weekend programs available. *Students:* 4. In 2006, 6 degrees awarded. *Entrance requirements:* For degree, California Basic Educational Skills Test, minimum GPA of 2.5. Additional exam requirements/recommendations for international students: Required—TOEFL (minimum score 550 paper-based; 213 computer-based), TWE. *Application deadline:* For fall admission, 7/1 priority date for domestic and international students; for spring admission, 12/1 priority date for domestic and international students. Applications are processed on a rolling basis. Application fee: $55. Electronic applications accepted. *Financial support:* Career-related internships or fieldwork, Federal Work-Study, institutionally sponsored loans, and scholarships/grants available. Financial award applicants required to submit FAFSA. *Unit head:* Dr. Trudy Day, Assistant Dean, 866-825-5426, Fax: 949-833-3507, E-mail: admissions@alliant.edu. *Application contact:* Alliant International University Central Contact Center, 866-U-ALLIANT, Fax: 858-635-4555, E-mail: admissions@alliant.edu.

Alliant International University–San Francisco, Graduate School of Education, Teacher Education Programs, San Francisco, CA 94133-1221. Offers auditory oral education (Certificate); CLAD (Certificate); preliminary multiple subject (Credential); preliminary multiple subject with BCLAD (Credential); preliminary single subject (Credential); professional clear multiple subject (Credential); professional clear single subject (Credential); teaching (MA). Part-time and evening/weekend programs available. *Faculty:* 2 full-time (1 woman), 7 part-time/adjunct (4 women). *Students:* 16 full-time (11 women), 73 part-time (45 women); includes 25 minority (8 African Americans, 10 Asian Americans or Pacific Islanders, 7 Hispanic Americans), 1 international. Average age 28. 91 applicants, 81% accepted, 65 enrolled. In 2006, 9 degrees awarded. *Entrance requirements:* For degree, California Basic Educational Skills Test, minimum GPA of 2.5. Additional exam requirements/recommendations for international students: Required—TOEFL (minimum score 550 paper-based; 213 computer-based), TWE. *Application deadline:* For fall admission, 7/1 priority date for domestic and international students; for spring admission, 12/1 priority date for domestic and international students. Application fee: $45. *Expenses:* Tuition: Part-time $825 per unit. Tuition and fees vary according to course load, degree level and program. *Financial support:* Career-related internships or fieldwork, Federal Work-Study, institutionally sponsored loans, and scholarships/grants available. Financial award application deadline: 2/15; financial award applicants required to submit FAFSA. *Unit head:* Dr. Trudy Day, Assistant Dean, 866-825-5426, Fax: 415-955-2179, E-mail: admissions@alliant.edu. *Application contact:* Alliant International University Central Contact Center, 866-U-ALLIANT, Fax: 858-635-4555, E-mail: admissions@alliant.edu.

See Close-Up on page 819.

American International College, School of Psychology and Education, Department of Education, Springfield, MA 01109-3189. Offers administration (M Ed, CAGS); child development (MA, Ed D), including educational psychology; elementary education (M Ed, CAGS); reading (M Ed, CAGS); secondary education (M Ed, CAGS); special education (M Ed, CAGS); teaching (MAT). Part-time and evening/weekend programs available. *Faculty:* 5 full-time (3 women), 15 part-time/adjunct (9 women). *Students:* 31 full-time (27 women), 268 part-time (217 women); includes 25 minority (13 African Americans, 4 Asian Americans or Pacific Islanders, 8 Hispanic Americans), 2 international. Average age 39. In 2006, 38 master's, 2 doctorates, 5 other advanced degrees awarded. Terminal master's awarded for partial completion of doctoral program. *Degree requirements:* For master's, thesis (for some programs), practicum, comprehensive exam (for some programs), registration; for doctorate, thesis/dissertation, comprehensive exam (for some programs), registration; for CAGS, practicum.

Special Education

American International College (continued)
Entrance requirements: For master's, minimum B- average in undergraduate course work; for doctorate, GRE General Test, interview. Additional exam requirements/recommendations for international students: Required—TOEFL. *Application deadline:* For fall admission, 7/1 priority date for domestic and international students; for spring admission, 12/1 priority date for domestic and international students. Applications are processed on a rolling basis. Application fee: $50. *Expenses:* Tuition: Part-time $585 per semester hour. Required fees: $100 per year. Full-time tuition and fees vary according to program. *Financial support:* Career-related internships or fieldwork and institutionally sponsored loans available. Financial award applicants required to submit FAFSA. *Unit head:* Dr. Barbara Dautrich, Chair, 413-205-3407, Fax: 413-205-3943, E-mail: barbara.dautrich@aic.edu. *Application contact:* Keshawn Dodds, Associate Director of Graduate Admissions, 413-205-3549, Fax: 413-205-3911, E-mail: keshawn.dodds@aic.edu.

American University, College of Arts and Sciences, School of Education, Teaching, and Health, Programs in Special Education, Washington, DC 20016-8001. Offers learning disabilities (MA). Part-time and evening/weekend programs available. *Students:* 14 full-time (13 women), 31 part-time (27 women); includes 7 minority (2 African Americans, 2 Asian Americans or Pacific Islanders, 3 Hispanic Americans), 3 international. Average age 28. In 2006, 16 degrees awarded. *Degree requirements:* For master's, PRAXIS II. *Entrance requirements:* For master's, GRE General Test or MAT, minimum GPA of 3.0. *Application deadline:* For fall admission, 2/1 priority date for domestic students; for spring admission, 10/1 priority date for domestic students. Applications are processed on a rolling basis. Application fee: $50. *Expenses:* Tuition: Full-time $18,864; part-time $1,048 per credit. Required fees: $380. Tuition and fees vary according to program. *Financial support:* Fellowships with full tuition reimbursements, research assistantships, teaching assistantships, career-related internships or fieldwork, Federal Work-Study, and institutionally sponsored loans available. Support available to part-time students. Financial award application deadline: 2/1.

American University of Puerto Rico, Program in Education, Bayamón, PR 00960-2037. Offers art history (M Ed); elementary education (4-6) (M Ed); elementary education (k-3) (M Ed); general science education (M Ed); physical education (k-12) (M Ed); special education at secondary level (transition) (M Ed). *Entrance requirements:* For master's, EXADEP or GRE or MAT, 2 letters of recommendation, minimum GPA of 2.5.

Andrews University, School of Graduate Studies, School of Education, Department of Teaching, Learning, and Curriculum, Berrien Springs, MI 49104. Offers curriculum and instruction (MA, Ed D, PhD, Ed S); elementary education (MAT); reading (MA); secondary education (MAT), including biology, education, English, English as a second language, French, history, physics; special education/learning disabilities (MS); teacher education (MAT). *Entrance requirements:* For master's, GRE Subject Test.

Andrews University, School of Graduate Studies, School of Education, Program in Special Education, Berrien Springs, MI 49104. Offers MS.

Appalachian State University, Cratis D. Williams Graduate School, College of Education, Department of Language, Reading, and Exceptionalities, Program in Special Education, Boone, NC 28608. Offers MA. *Students:* 13 full-time (10 women), 39 part-time (29 women); includes 4 minority (all African Americans), 2 international. 10 applicants, 100% accepted, 9 enrolled. In 2006, 17 degrees awarded. *Degree requirements:* For master's, thesis optional. *Entrance requirements:* For master's, GRE General Test or MAT, minimum GPA of 2.7 in last 60 hours of course work. *Application deadline:* For fall admission, 7/1 priority date for domestic students; for spring admission, 11/1 priority date for domestic students. Applications are processed on a rolling basis. Application fee: $50. *Expenses:* Tuition, state resident: full-time $2,600; part-time $127 per hour. Tuition, nonresident: full-time $13,200; part-time $597 per hour. Required fees: $2,000; $546 per term. *Financial support:* Research assistantships, teaching assistantships available. Financial award application deadline: 7/1. *Faculty research:* Learning disabilities, mental retardation, behavior disorders, teaching assistants, advocacy. Total annual research expenditures: $108,000. *Unit head:* Dr. Monica Lambert, Director, 828-262-6072, E-mail: lambertm@appstate.edu.

Arcadia University, Graduate Studies, Department of Education, Glenside, PA 19038-3295. Offers art education (M Ed, MA Ed); biology education (MA Ed); chemistry education (MA Ed); child development (CAS); computer education (M Ed, CAS); computer education 7–12 (MA Ed); early childhood education (M Ed, CAS), including individualized (M Ed), master teacher (M Ed), research in child development (M Ed); educational leadership (M Ed, CAS); educational psychology (CAS); elementary education (M Ed, CAS); English education (MA Ed); environmental education (MA Ed, CAS); history education (MA Ed); language arts (M Ed, CAS); mathematics education (M Ed, MA Ed, CAS); music education (MA Ed); psychology (MA Ed); pupil personnel services (CAS); reading (M Ed, CAS); school library science (M Ed); science education (M Ed, CAS); secondary education (M Ed, CAS); special education (M Ed, Ed D, CAS); theater arts (MA Ed); written communication (MA Ed). *Accreditation:* NASAD. Part-time and evening/weekend programs available. Postbaccalaureate distance learning degree programs offered (minimal on-campus study). *Faculty:* 12 full-time (8 women), 38 part-time/adjunct (26 women). *Students:* 60 full-time (56 women), 419 part-time (324 women); includes 70 minority (57 African Americans, 1 American Indian/Alaska Native, 6 Asian Americans or Pacific Islanders, 6 Hispanic Americans), 1 international. In 2006, 257 master's, 4 doctorates awarded. *Application deadline:* Applications are processed on a rolling basis. Application fee: $35. Electronic applications accepted. *Financial support:* Career-related internships or fieldwork, tuition waivers (partial), and unspecified assistantships available. *Unit head:* Dr. Steven P. Gulkus, Chair, 215-572-2120. *Application contact:* 215-572-2925, Fax: 215-572-2126, E-mail: grad@arcadia.edu.

Arizona State University, Division of Graduate Studies, College of Education, Division of Curriculum and Instruction, Academic Program of Special Education, Tempe, AZ 85287. Offers M Ed, MA. *Degree requirements:* For master's, thesis or alternative. *Entrance requirements:* For master's, GRE General Test or MAT.

Arizona State University at the West campus, College of Teacher Education and Leadership, Phoenix, AZ 85069-7100. Offers educational administration and supervision (M Ed); elementary education (M Ed, Certificate); leadership/innovation (administration) (Ed D); leadership/innovation (teaching) (Ed D); secondary education (M Ed, Certificate); special education (M Ed). Part-time and evening/weekend programs available. *Faculty:* 25 full-time (18 women), 27 part-time/adjunct (21 women). *Students:* 169 full-time (133 women), 245 part-time (200 women); includes 76 minority (16 African Americans, 8 American Indian/Alaska Native, 7 Asian Americans or Pacific Islanders, 45 Hispanic Americans), 3 international. Average age 35. 308 applicants, 63% accepted, 171 enrolled. In 2006, 84 degrees awarded. *Degree requirements:* For master's, applied project or comprehensive exams; for doctorate, thesis/dissertation, comprehensive exam. *Entrance requirements:* For master's, 3 letters of recommendation; for doctorate, master's degree in education or related field, 3 professional references, resumé. Additional exam requirements/recommendations for international students: Required—TOEFL (minimum score 550 paper-based; 213 computer-based; 83 iBT), IELTS (minimum score 7). *Application deadline:* Applications are processed on a rolling basis. Application fee: $50. Electronic applications accepted. *Expenses:* Tuition, state resident: full-time $5,930. Tuition, nonresident: full-time $16,516. Tuition and fees vary according to course load. *Financial support:* In 2006–07, 2 research assistantships with partial tuition reimbursements (averaging $16,413 per year) were awarded; fellowships with tuition reimbursements, career-related internships or fieldwork, institutionally sponsored loans, scholarships/grants, tuition waivers (full and partial), and unspecified assistantships also available. Support available to part-time students. Financial award application deadline: 4/1; financial award applicants required to submit FAFSA. *Faculty research:* Self-regulated learning in students, collaboration and consultation skills for educators, school reform and restructuring, hands-on science and mathematics programs, educational technology. *Unit head:* Dr. Mari Koerner, Dean, 602-543-6352, Fax: 602-543-6350, E-mail: mari.koerner@asu.edu. *Application contact:* Marie Wright, Administrative Assistant, 602-543-3634, Fax: 602-543-6350, E-mail: marie.wright@asu.edu or ctelgrad@asu.edu.

Arkansas State University, Graduate School, College of Education, Department of Educational Leadership, Curriculum, and Special Education, Jonesboro, State University, AR 72467. Offers community college administration education (SCCT); education theory and practice (MSE); educational leadership (MSE, Ed D, Ed S), including curriculum and instruction (Ed S), elementary curriculum and instruction (MSE), elementary principalship (Ed S), secondary principalship (Ed S), superintendency (Ed S); special education (MSE), including emotionally disturbed, gifted, talented and creative, instructional specialist 4-12, instructional specialist P-4; special education program administration (Ed S). *Accreditation:* NCATE. Part-time programs available. *Faculty:* 14 full-time (7 women), 5 part-time/adjunct (2 women). *Students:* 28 full-time (21 women), 328 part-time (233 women); includes 63 minority (58 African Americans, 3 American Indian/Alaska Native, 1 Asian American or Pacific Islander, 1 Hispanic American), 2 international. Average age 36. 181 applicants, 78% accepted, 70 enrolled. In 2006, 70 master's, 13 doctorates, 14 other advanced degrees awarded. *Degree requirements:* For master's, thesis or alternative, comprehensive exam; for doctorate, thesis/dissertation, comprehensive exam. *Entrance requirements:* For master's, GRE General Test or MAT, appropriate bachelor's degree, letters of reference, interview, official transcript; for doctorate and other advanced degree, GRE General Test or MAT, interview, master's degree, letters of reference, official transcript. Additional exam requirements/recommendations for international students: Required—TOEFL (minimum score 213 computer-based). *Application deadline:* Applications are processed on a rolling basis. Application fee: $30 ($40 for international students). Electronic applications accepted. *Expenses:* Tuition, state resident: full-time $3,393; part-time $189 per hour. Tuition, nonresident: full-time $8,577; part-time $477 per hour. Required fees: $752; $39 per hour. $25 per semester. *Financial support:* Teaching assistantships, career-related internships or fieldwork, scholarships/grants, and unspecified assistantships available. Financial award application deadline: 7/1; financial award applicants required to submit FAFSA. *Unit head:* Dr. Mitchell Holifield, Chair, 870-972-3062, Fax: 870-680-8130, E-mail: hfield@astate.edu.

Armstrong Atlantic State University, School of Graduate Studies, Program in Education, Savannah, GA 31419-1997. Offers adult education (M Ed); early childhood education (M Ed); education (M Ed); elementary education (M Ed); middle grades education (M Ed); secondary education (M Ed), including business education, English education, mathematics education, science education, social science education; special education (M Ed), including behavioral disorders, curriculum and instruction, learning disabilities, speech-language pathology. *Accreditation:* NCATE. Part-time and evening/weekend programs available. Postbaccalaureate distance learning degree programs offered (minimal on-campus study). *Faculty:* 11 full-time (9 women), 13 part-time/adjunct (10 women). *Students:* 50 full-time (42 women), 219 part-time (175 women); includes 71 minority (67 African Americans, 3 Asian Americans or Pacific Islanders, 1 Hispanic American), 6 international. Average age 35. In 2006, 151 degrees awarded. *Degree requirements:* For master's, portfolio. *Entrance requirements:* For master's, GRE General Test or MAT, minimum GPA of 2.5, letters of recommendation. Additional exam requirements/recommendations for international students: Required—TOEFL (minimum score 523 paper-based; 193 computer-based). *Application deadline:* For fall admission, 7/1 priority date for domestic and international students; for spring admission, 11/15 priority date for domestic and international students. Applications are processed on a rolling basis. Application fee: $25. Electronic applications accepted. *Expenses:* Tuition, state resident: full-time $2,286; part-time $127 per credit. Tuition, nonresident: full-time $9,144; part-time $508 per credit. One-time fee: $257. *Financial support:* In 2006–07, research assistantships with partial tuition reimbursements (averaging $2,500 per year); career-related internships or fieldwork, Federal Work-Study, scholarships/grants, and unspecified assistantships also available. Support available to part-time students. Financial award applicants required to submit FAFSA. *Unit head:* Dr. Jane McHaney, College of Education Dean, 912-927-5398, Fax: 912-921-7425, E-mail: mchaneia@mail.armstrong.edu.

Asbury College, Graduate Programs, Wilmore, KY 40390-1198. Offers biology: alternative certificate (MA Ed); chemistry: alternative certificate (MA Ed); English (Certificate); English as a second language (MA Ed); ESL (Certificate); French (Certificate); mathematics: alternative certificate (MA Ed); reading / writing (MA Ed); social studies (Certificate); Spanish (Certificate); special education (MA Ed); special education: alternative certificate (MA Ed). *Accreditation:* NCATE. Part-time programs available. *Faculty:* 8 full-time (7 women), 9 part-time/adjunct (4 women). *Students:* Average age 36. 14 applicants, 100% accepted, 10 enrolled. In 2006, 17 degrees awarded. *Median time to degree:* Master's–2.5 years part-time. *Degree requirements:* For master's, action research project, portfolio. *Entrance requirements:* For master's, PRAXIS NTE or GRE, minimum GPA of 2.75, letters of recommendation. Additional exam requirements/recommendations for international students: Recommended—TOEFL (minimum score 550 paper-based). *Application deadline:* Applications are processed on a rolling basis. Application fee: $25. *Expenses:* Tuition: Part-time $335 per credit hour. *Financial support:* Scholarships/grants and traineeships available. Financial award applicants required to submit FAFSA. *Unit head:* Dr. Bonnie J. Banker, Director, 859-858-3511 Ext. 2221, Fax: 859-858-3921, E-mail: bonnie.banker@asbury.edu. *Application contact:* Melanie S. Kinnell, Graduate Program Assistant and Certification Specialist, 859-858-3511 Ext. 2304, Fax: 859-858-3921, E-mail: graded@asbury.edu.

Ashland University, College of Education, Graduate Studies in Education, Department of Curriculum and Instruction, Ashland, OH 44805-3702. Offers educational technology (M Ed); intervention specialist-mild/moderate (M Ed); intervention specialist-moderate/intensive (M Ed); middle school education (M Ed); talent development (M Ed). *Accreditation:* NCATE. Part-time and evening/weekend programs available. *Faculty:* 11 full-time (7 women), 93 part-time/adjunct (54 women). *Students:* 188 full-time (161 women), 354 part-time (314 women); includes 25 minority (19 African Americans, 3 Asian Americans or Pacific Islanders, 3 Hispanic Americans), 1 international. Average age 32. In 2006, 220 degrees awarded. *Degree requirements:* For master's, thesis or alternative, internship, practicum, seminar. *Entrance requirements:* For master's, GRE General Test or MAT, teaching certificate, minimum GPA of 2.75 (or 2.5 with 2.75 in education or major subject field). Additional exam requirements/recommendations for international students: Required—TOEFL. *Application deadline:* For fall admission, 8/27 for domestic students; for spring admission, 1/14 for domestic students. Applications are processed on a rolling basis. Application fee: $30. *Expenses:* Tuition: Part-time $403 per credit. Tuition and fees vary according to degree level and program. *Financial support:* In 2006–07, 189 students received support. Institutionally sponsored loans and scholarships/grants available. Financial award application deadline: 4/15. *Faculty research:* Gender equity, postmodern children's and young adult literature, outdoor/experimental education, re-examining literature study in middle grades, morality and giftedness. *Unit head:* Dr. James P. Van Keuren, Chair, 419-289-5377, Fax: 419-207-4949, E-mail: jvankeu1@ashland.edu.

Ashland University, College of Education, Graduate Studies in Education, Program in Early Childhood Education, Ashland, OH 44805-3702. Offers early childhood education (M Ed); early childhood intervention (M Ed). Part-time and evening/weekend programs available. *Faculty:* 4 full-time (3 women), 52 part-time/adjunct (45 women). *Students:* 6 full-time (all women), 17 part-time (all women). Average age 30. In 2006, 9 degrees awarded. *Degree requirements:* For master's, thesis or alternative. *Entrance requirements:* For master's, GRE General Test or MAT, teaching certificate, minimum GPA of 2.75. Additional exam requirements/recommendations for international students: Required—TOEFL. Application fee: $30. *Expenses:* Tuition: Part-time $403 per credit. Tuition and fees vary according to degree level and program. *Financial support:* In 2006–07, 11 students received support. Application deadline: 4/15. *Faculty research:* Child behavior, literary technology, teacher licensure exams. *Unit head:* Dr. Linda Billman, Chair, 419-289-5369, Fax: 419-207-6702, E-mail: lbillman@ashland.edu.

Assumption College, Graduate School, Special Education Program, Worcester, MA 01609-1296. Offers MA. Part-time and evening/weekend programs available. *Faculty:* 4 part-time/

adjunct (1 woman). *Students:* 9 full-time (all women), 30 part-time (27 women); includes 1 minority (Hispanic American) Average age 29. 34 applicants, 97% accepted. In 2006, 20 degrees awarded. *Degree requirements:* For master's, internship, practicum. *Entrance requirements:* For master's, 3 letters of recommendation, resumé, essay. Additional exam requirements/recommendations for international students: Required—TOEFL, IELTS. *Application deadline:* For fall admission, 6/1 priority date for domestic students, 5/1 priority date for international students; for spring admission, 11/1 priority date for domestic students, 10/1 priority date for international students. Applications are processed on a rolling basis. Application fee: $30. Electronic applications accepted. *Financial support:* In 2006–07, 21 students received support; teaching assistantships with partial tuition reimbursements available, institutional discounts available. Financial award application deadline: 6/1; financial award applicants required to submit FAFSA. *Unit head:* Dr. Nanho Vander Hart, Director, 508-767-7380, Fax: 508-767-7263, E-mail: nvanderh@assumption.edu. *Application contact:* Adrian O. Dumas, Director of Graduate Enrollment Management and Services, 508-767-7365, Fax: 508-767-7030, E-mail: adumas@assumption.edu.

Auburn University, Graduate School, College of Education, Department of Rehabilitation and Special Education, Auburn University, AL 36849. Offers collaborative teacher special education (M Ed, MS); early childhood special education (M Ed, MS); rehabilitation counseling (M Ed, MS, PhD). *Accreditation:* CORE; NCATE. Part-time programs available. *Faculty:* 12 full-time (6 women). *Students:* 85 full-time (68 women), 45 part-time (36 women); includes 30 minority (24 African Americans, 3 American Indian/Alaska Native, 2 Asian Americans or Pacific Islanders, 1 Hispanic American). Average age 32. 69 applicants, 77% accepted, 41 enrolled. In 2006, 64 master's, 1 doctorate awarded. *Degree requirements:* For master's, thesis (for some programs); for doctorate, thesis/dissertation. *Entrance requirements:* For master's, GRE General Test; for doctorate, GRE General Test, interview. *Application deadline:* For fall admission, 7/17 for domestic students; for spring admission, 11/24 for domestic students. Applications are processed on a rolling basis. Application fee: $25 ($50 for international students). Electronic applications accepted. *Expenses:* Tuition, state resident: full-time $5,000. Tuition, nonresident: full-time $15,000. Required fees: $416. Tuition and fees vary according to program. *Financial support:* Research assistantships, teaching assistantships, Federal Work-Study available. Support available to part-time students. Financial award application deadline: 3/15. *Faculty research:* Emotional conflict/behavior disorders, gifted and talented, learning disabilities, mental retardation, multi-handicapped. *Unit head:* Dr. Philip L. Browning, Head, 334-844-5943. *Application contact:* Dr. Joe Pittman, Interim Dean of the Graduate School, 334-844-4700.

Auburn University Montgomery, School of Education, Department of Counselor Leadership and Special Education, Montgomery, AL 36124-4023. Offers counseling (M Ed, Ed S); education administration (M Ed, Ed S); special education (M Ed, Ed S). *Accreditation:* NCATE. Part-time and evening/weekend programs available. *Faculty:* 8 full-time (4 women), 1 part-time/adjunct (0 women). *Students:* 34 full-time (28 women), 91 part-time (66 women); includes 75 minority (72 African Americans, 1 American Indian/Alaska Native, 1 Asian American or Pacific Islander, 1 Hispanic American). Average age 35. In 2006, 12 master's, 3 other advanced degrees awarded. *Degree requirements:* For master's and Ed S, comprehensive exam. *Entrance requirements:* For master's, GRE General Test or MAT, certification, BS in teaching; for Ed S, GRE General Test or MAT, certification. *Application deadline:* Applications are processed on a rolling basis. Application fee: $25. Electronic applications accepted. *Financial support:* In 2006–07, 1 teaching assistantship was awarded; career-related internships or fieldwork and scholarships/grants also available. Support available to part-time students. Financial award application deadline: 3/1; financial award applicants required to submit FAFSA. *Unit head:* Dr. James V. Wright, Head, 334-244-3457, Fax: 334-344-3102, E-mail: jwright@mail.aum.edu.

Augusta State University, Graduate Studies, College of Education, Program in Special Education, Augusta, GA 30904-2200. Offers M Ed, Ed S. *Accreditation:* NCATE. Part-time and evening/weekend programs available. *Faculty:* 4 full-time (3 women), 3 part-time/adjunct (all women). *Students:* 9 full-time (6 women), 60 part-time (49 women); includes 21 minority (18 African Americans, 1 American Indian/Alaska Native, 1 Asian American or Pacific Islander, 1 Hispanic American). Average age 36. 14 applicants, 100% accepted, 10 enrolled. *Degree requirements:* For master's, thesis, portfolio. *Entrance requirements:* For master's, GRE, MAT, minimum GPA of 2.5; for Ed S, GRE, MAT. *Application deadline:* For fall admission, 8/1 priority date for domestic students. Applications are processed on a rolling basis. Application fee: $20. *Expenses:* Tuition, state resident: full-time $3,044; part-time $127 per credit hour. Tuition, nonresident: full-time $12,172; part-time $508 per credit hour. *Financial support:* Career-related internships or fieldwork, Federal Work-Study, institutionally sponsored loans, and unspecified assistantships available. Support available to part-time students. Financial award application deadline: 4/15; financial award applicants required to submit FAFSA. *Faculty research:* Behavior disorders, gifted programs. *Unit head:* Dr. Samuel B Hardy, Acting Chair, 706-737-1497, Fax: 706-667-4706, E-mail: shardy@aug.edu. *Application contact:* Andrea M. Scott, Secretary to the Dean, 706-737-1499, Fax: 706-667-4706, E-mail: ascott1@aug.edu.

Averett University, Graduate Studies in Education, Danville, VA 24541-3692. Offers art education (M Ed); biology (M Ed); chemistry (M Ed); curriculum and instruction (M Ed); elementary education (M Ed); English (M Ed); health and physical education (M Ed); history and social studies (M Ed); mathematics education (M Ed); physical science (M Ed); reading (M Ed); special education (learning disabilities specialization PK-12) (M Ed). Part-time and evening/weekend programs available. *Faculty:* 10 full-time (4 women), 7 part-time/adjunct (6 women). *Students:* 14 full-time (10 women), 85 part-time (67 women); includes 20 minority (18 African Americans, 2 Asian Americans or Pacific Islanders). Average age 33. 52 applicants, 100% accepted, 40 enrolled. In 2006, 48 degrees awarded. *Degree requirements:* For master's, thesis optional. *Entrance requirements:* For master's, PRAXIS, GRE General Test, MAT or NTE, writing proficiency exam, 3 letters of recommendation, current teacher's licensure or eligibility for licensure, minimum undergraduate GPA of 3.0 in previous 2 years. Additional exam requirements/recommendations for international students: Required—TOEFL (minimum score 600 paper-based; 200 computer-based). *Application deadline:* Applications are processed on a rolling basis. Application fee: $20. *Expenses:* Contact institution. *Financial support:* In 2006–07, 23 students received support. Federal Work-Study and scholarships/grants available. Financial award application deadline: 4/1; financial award applicants required to submit FAFSA. *Faculty research:* Literary assessment-PreK-6, handwriting instruction and assessment-PreK-6, written language instruction and assessment-PreK-6 and special needs students learning styles, curriculum and instruction processes. *Unit head:* Dr. Lynn H. Wolf, Chair, 434-793-3995, Fax: 434-791-4392, E-mail: lynn.wolf@averett.edu.

Azusa Pacific University, School of Education, Program in Special Education, Azusa, CA 91702-7000. Offers MA. *Accreditation:* NCATE. Part-time and evening/weekend programs available. *Students:* 10 full-time (0 women), 340 part-time (93 women); includes 126 minority (34 African Americans, 5 American Indian/Alaska Native, 15 Asian Americans or Pacific Islanders, 72 Hispanic Americans), 3 international. In 2006, 139 degrees awarded. *Degree requirements:* For master's, core exams, oral presentations. *Entrance requirements:* For master's, 12 units of course work in education, minimum GPA of 3.0. Application fee: $45 ($65 for international students). *Expenses:* Tuition: Part-time $475 per credit. *Unit head:* Dr. David Colachico, Head, 626-815-5425, E-mail: dcolachico@apu.edu.

Baldwin-Wallace College, Graduate Programs, Division of Education, Specialization in Mild/Moderate Educational Needs, Berea, OH 44017-2088. Offers MA Ed. *Accreditation:* NCATE. Part-time and evening/weekend programs available. *Students:* 17 full-time (13 women), 34 part-time (all women); includes 6 minority (4 African Americans, 1 Asian American or Pacific Islander, 1 Hispanic American), 1 international. Average age 34. 33 applicants, 79% accepted, 16 enrolled. In 2006, 33 degrees awarded. *Degree requirements:* For master's, comprehensive exam. *Entrance requirements:* For master's, bachelor's degree in field, MAT or minimum GPA of 2.75. *Application deadline:* For fall admission, 8/15 priority date for domestic students; for spring admission, 12/15 priority date for domestic students. Applications are processed on a rolling basis. Application fee: $25. Electronic applications accepted. *Expenses:* Tuition: Part-time $760 per credit hour. Tuition and fees vary according to program. *Financial support:* Career-related internships or fieldwork available. Financial award applicants required to submit FAFSA. *Application contact:* Winifred W. Gerhardt, Director of Admission for the Evening and Weekend College, 440-826-2222, Fax: 440-826-3830, E-mail: admission@bw.edu.

Ball State University, Graduate School, Teachers College, Department of Special Education, Muncie, IN 47306-1099. Offers MA, MAE, Ed D, Ed S. *Accreditation:* NCATE. *Faculty:* 12. *Students:* 12 full-time (9 women), 115 part-time (102 women); includes 6 minority (3 African Americans, 1 Asian American or Pacific Islander, 2 Hispanic Americans), 3 international. Average age 33. 29 applicants, 90% accepted, 18 enrolled. In 2006, 58 master's, 11 doctorates awarded. *Degree requirements:* For doctorate and Ed S, thesis/dissertation. *Entrance requirements:* For doctorate, GRE General Test, interview, minimum graduate GPA of 3.2; for Ed S, GRE General Test. Application fee: $25 ($35 for international students). *Financial support:* In 2006–07, 15 teaching assistantships (averaging $8,165 per year) were awarded; research assistantships with full tuition reimbursements, career-related internships or fieldwork also available. Financial award application deadline: 3/1. *Faculty research:* Language development and utilization in the handicapped (preschool through adult). *Unit head:* John Merbler, Chairperson, 765-285-5700, Fax: 765-285-4280, E-mail: jmerbler@bsu.edu.

Bank Street College of Education, Graduate School, Department of Curriculum and Instruction, Program in Bilingual Education, New York, NY 10025. Offers bilingual childhood special education (Ed M, MS Ed); bilingual early childhood education (MS Ed); bilingual early childhood special and general education (MS Ed); bilingual early childhood special education (Ed M, MS Ed); bilingual elementary/childhood general education (MS Ed); bilingual elementary/childhood special and general education (MS Ed); bilingual middle school general education (MS Ed); bilingual middle school special and general education (Ed M, MS Ed); bilingual middle school special education (MS Ed). *Accreditation:* NCATE. *Faculty:* 2 full-time (both women), 5 part-time/adjunct (all women). *Students:* 8 full-time (7 women), 22 part-time (19 women); includes 21 minority (2 African Americans, 2 Asian Americans or Pacific Islanders, 17 Hispanic Americans). Average age 27. 19 applicants, 68% accepted, 10 enrolled. In 2006, 8 degrees awarded. *Degree requirements:* For master's, thesis, registration. *Entrance requirements:* For master's, interview. Additional exam requirements/recommendations for international students: Required—TOEFL (minimum score 600 paper-based; 250 computer-based). *Application deadline:* For fall admission, 3/1 priority date for domestic students; for spring admission, 11/1 priority date for domestic students. Applications are processed on a rolling basis. Application fee: $50. *Expenses:* Tuition: Part-time $940 per credit. Required fees: $100 per term. *Financial support:* Career-related internships or fieldwork, Federal Work-Study, scholarships/grants, and unspecified assistantships available. Support available to part-time students. Financial award application deadline: 4/15; financial award applicants required to submit FAFSA. *Faculty research:* Dual language education, language immersion, bilingual education in the urban classroom, community and school partnerships. Total annual research expenditures: $58,717. *Unit head:* Dr. Olga Romero, Director, 212-875-4468, Fax: 212-875-4753, E-mail: olgar@bankstreet.edu. *Application contact:* Ann Morgan, Director of Graduate Admissions, 212-875-4403, Fax: 212-875-4678, E-mail: amorgan@bankstreet.edu.

Bank Street College of Education, Graduate School, Department of Curriculum and Instruction, Program in Infant and Parent Development and Early Intervention, New York, NY 10025. Offers infant and parent development and early intervention (MS Ed); infant and parent development and early intervention/early childhood special and general education (MS Ed); infant and parent development and early intervention/early childhood special education (Ed M). *Accreditation:* NCATE. *Students:* 14 full-time (all women), 29 part-time (27 women); includes 10 minority (3 African Americans, 7 Hispanic Americans). Average age 31. 27 applicants, 63% accepted, 12 enrolled. In 2006, 7 degrees awarded. *Degree requirements:* For master's, thesis, registration. *Entrance requirements:* For master's, interview. Additional exam requirements/recommendations for international students: Required—TOEFL (minimum score 600 paper-based; 250 computer-based). *Application deadline:* For fall admission, 3/1 priority date for domestic students; for spring admission, 11/1 priority date for domestic students. Applications are processed on a rolling basis. Application fee: $50. *Expenses:* Tuition: Part-time $940 per credit. Required fees: $100 per term. *Financial support:* Career-related internships or fieldwork, Federal Work-Study, scholarships/grants, and unspecified assistantships available. Support available to part-time students. Financial award application deadline: 4/15; financial award applicants required to submit FAFSA. *Faculty research:* Early intervention, early attachment practice in infant and toddler childcare, parenting skills in adolescents. *Unit head:* Carla Poole, Director, 212-875-4523, Fax: 212-875-4753, E-mail: @bankstreet.edu. *Application contact:* Ann Morgan, Director of Graduate Admissions, 212-875-4403, Fax: 212-875-4678, E-mail: amorgan@bankstreet.edu.

Bank Street College of Education, Graduate School, Department of Curriculum and Instruction, Program in Special Education, New York, NY 10025. Offers early childhood special and general education (MS Ed); early childhood special education (Ed M, MS Ed); elementary/childhood special and general education (MS Ed); elementary/childhood special education (MS Ed); elementary/childhood special education certification (Ed M); middle school special and general education (MS Ed); middle school special education (Ed M). *Students:* 98 full-time (86 women), 167 part-time (162 women); includes 57 minority (17 African Americans, 10 Asian Americans or Pacific Islanders, 30 Hispanic Americans), 1 international. Average age 31. 147 applicants, 78% accepted, 80 enrolled. In 2006, 68 degrees awarded. *Degree requirements:* For master's, thesis, registration. *Entrance requirements:* For master's, interview. Additional exam requirements/recommendations for international students: Required—TOEFL (minimum score 600 paper-based; 250 computer-based). *Application deadline:* For fall admission, 3/1 priority date for domestic students; for spring admission, 11/1 priority date for domestic students. Applications are processed on a rolling basis. Application fee: $50. *Expenses:* Tuition: Part-time $940 per credit. Required fees: $100 per term. *Financial support:* Career-related internships or fieldwork available. Financial award application deadline: 3/1; financial award applicants required to submit FAFSA. *Faculty research:* Inclusion, observation and assessment, early intervention, neurodevelopmental assessment. *Unit head:* Dr. Andrea (Penny) Spencer, Chairperson, 212-875-4602, Fax: 212-875-4753, E-mail: aspencer@bankstreet.edu. *Application contact:* Ann Morgan, Director of Graduate Admissions, 212-875-4403, Fax: 212-875-4678, E-mail: amorgan@bankstreet.edu.

See Close-Up on page 857.

Barry University, School of Education, Program in Education for Teachers of Students with Hearing Impairments, Miami Shores, FL 33161-6695. Offers MS. *Unit head:* Dr. Judy Harris-Looby, Director, 305-899-3709, Fax: 305-899-4708, E-mail: jhlooby@mail.barry.edu. *Application contact:* Dave Fletcher, Director of Graduate Admissions, 305-899-3113, Fax: 305-899-2971, E-mail: dfletcher@mail.barry.edu.

Barry University, School of Education, Program in Exceptional Student Education, Miami Shores, FL 33161-6695. Offers exceptional student education (MS, Ed S). Part-time and evening/weekend programs available. *Students:* 78 full-time (70 women), 27 part-time (24 women); includes 74 minority (45 African Americans, 1 Asian American or Pacific Islander, 28 Hispanic Americans), 1 international. 37 applicants, 84% accepted, 23 enrolled. In 2006, 45 master's, 1 other advanced degree awarded. *Degree requirements:* For master's, comprehensive exam; for Ed S, practicum. *Entrance requirements:* For master's, GRE General Test or MAT, minimum GPA of 3.0; for Ed S, GRE General Test, minimum GPA of 3.0. *Application deadline:* For fall admission, 5/1 priority date for domestic students. Applications are processed on a rolling basis. Application fee: $30. Electronic applications accepted. *Unit head:* Dr. Judy Harris-Looby, Director, 305-899-3709, Fax: 305-899-4708, E-mail: jhlooby@mail.barry.edu. *Application contact:* Dave Fletcher, Director of Graduate Admissions, 305-899-3113, Fax: 305-899-2971, E-mail: dfletcher@mail.barry.edu.

Barry University, School of Education, Program in Leadership and Education, Miami Shores, FL 33161-6695. Offers educational technology (PhD); exceptional student education (PhD);

Special Education

Barry University (continued)

higher education administration (PhD); human resource development (PhD); leadership (PhD). Part-time and evening/weekend programs available. *Students:* 15 full-time (7 women), 233 part-time (147 women); includes 97 minority (52 African Americans, 45 Hispanic Americans), 7 international. 58 applicants, 34% accepted, 18 enrolled. In 2006, 23 degrees awarded. *Degree requirements:* For doctorate, thesis/dissertation. *Entrance requirements:* For doctorate, GRE General Test, minimum GPA of 3.25. *Application deadline:* For fall admission, 5/1 priority date for domestic students. Applications are processed on a rolling basis. Application fee: $30. Electronic applications accepted. *Unit head:* Dr. Carmen McCrink, Director, 305-899-3702, Fax: 305-899-4708, E-mail: cmccrink@mail.barry.edu. *Application contact:* Dave Fletcher, Director of Graduate Admissions, 305-899-3113, Fax: 305-899-2971, E-mail: dfletcher@mail.barry.edu.

Bayamón Central University, Graduate Programs, Program in Education, Bayamón, PR 00960-1725. Offers administration and supervision (MA Ed); commercial education (MA Ed); education of the autistic (MA Ed); elementary education (K–3) (MA Ed); elementary education (K–6) (MA Ed); elementary physical education (MA Ed); guidance and counseling (MA Ed); pre-elementary teacher (MA Ed); special education (MA Ed), including attention deficit disorder, learning disabilities. Part-time and evening/weekend programs available. *Degree requirements:* For master's, comprehensive exam. *Entrance requirements:* For master's, EXADEP, bachelor's degree in education or related field.

Bellarmine University, Annsley Frazier Thornton School of Education, Louisville, KY 40205-0671. Offers early elementary education (MA, MAT); instructional leadership and school administration/school principal (MA); learning and behavior disorders (MA); middle school education (MA, MAT); reading and writing endorsement (MA); secondary school education (MAT); Waldorf inspired curriculum (MA);). *Accreditation:* NCATE. Part-time and evening/weekend programs available. *Faculty:* 10 full-time (8 women), 5 part-time/adjunct (all women). *Students:* 92 full-time (68 women), 140 part-time (104 women); includes 16 minority (11 African Americans, 1 Asian American or Pacific Islander, 4 Hispanic Americans). Average age 32. In 2006, 98 degrees awarded. *Degree requirements:* For master's, thesis (for some programs), comprehensive exam. *Entrance requirements:* For master's, minimum overall GPA of 2.75, 3.0 in major; letters of recommendation; valid Kentucky provisional or professional certificate. Additional exam requirements/recommendations for international students: Required—TOEFL (minimum score 550 paper-based; 213 computer-based; 80 iBT), GRE. *Application deadline:* Applications are processed on a rolling basis. Application fee: $25. Electronic applications accepted. *Expenses: Contact institution.* Tuition and fees vary according to program. *Faculty research:* Social justice, service learning dispositions, educational technology, special education. *Unit head:* Dr. Milton Brown, Dean (Interim), 502-452-8486, Fax: 502-452-8189, E-mail: mbrown@bellarmine.edu. *Application contact:* Theresa Klapheke, Director of Graduate Programs, 502-452-8033, Fax: 502-452-8189, E-mail: tklapheke@bellarmine.edu.

Bemidji State University, School of Graduate Studies, College of Professional Studies, Program in Special Education, Bemidji, MN 56601-2699. Offers M Sp Ed, MS. Part-time programs available. *Faculty:* 4 full-time (3 women). *Students:* 10 full-time (all women), 39 part-time (33 women); includes 1 minority (Asian American or Pacific Islander) Average age 42. 20 applicants, 100% accepted. In 2006, 10 degrees awarded. *Degree requirements:* For master's, thesis. *Entrance requirements:* Additional exam requirements/recommendations for international students: Required—TOEFL. *Application deadline:* For fall admission, 5/1 for domestic students. Applications are processed on a rolling basis. Application fee: $20. Electronic applications accepted. *Expenses:* Tuition, nonresident: part-time $284 per credit. Required fees: $86 per credit. *Financial support:* In 2006–07, 1 research assistantship with partial tuition reimbursement (averaging $8,250 per year), teaching assistantships with partial tuition reimbursements (averaging $8,250 per year) were awarded; career-related internships or fieldwork, Federal Work-Study, scholarships/grants, and unspecified assistantships also available. Support available to part-time students. Financial award application deadline: 5/1. *Unit head:* Dr. Judy Olson, Coordinator, 218-755-3749, Fax: 218-755-3787, E-mail: jolson@bemidjistate.edu.

Benedictine University, Graduate Programs, Program in Education, Lisle, IL 60532-0900. Offers curriculum and instruction and collaborative teaching (M Ed); elementary education (MA Ed); leadership and administration (M Ed); reading and literacy (M Ed); secondary education (MA Ed); special education (MA Ed). Part-time and evening/weekend programs available. *Faculty:* 4 full-time (2 women), 52 part-time/adjunct (30 women). *Students:* 257 (196 women); includes 22 minority (4 African Americans, 1 American Indian/Alaska Native, 3 Asian Americans or Pacific Islanders, 14 Hispanic Americans) 2 international. Average age 33. 130 applicants, 93% accepted, 13 enrolled. In 2006, 181 degrees awarded. *Degree requirements:* For master's, thesis (for some programs), comprehensive exam. *Entrance requirements:* For master's, GRE or MAT. Additional exam requirements/recommendations for international students: Required—TOEFL (minimum score 550 paper-based; 213 computer-based). *Application deadline:* For fall admission, 9/1 for domestic students; for winter admission, 12/1 for domestic students; for spring admission, 2/15 for domestic students. Applications are processed on a rolling basis. Application fee: $40. Electronic applications accepted. *Expenses: Contact institution. Financial support:* Career-related internships or fieldwork and health care benefits available. Support available to part-time students. *Unit head:* Dr. Richard Campbell, Director, 630-829-6242, Fax: 630-960-1126, E-mail: rcampbell@ben.edu. *Application contact:* Kari Gibbons, Director, Admissions, 630-829-6200, Fax: 630-829-6584, E-mail: kgibbons@ben.edu.

Bethel College, Program in Education, McKenzie, TN 38201. Offers administration and supervision (MA Ed); biology education K8-12 (MAT); elementary education (MAT); English education K8-12 (MAT); history education K8-12 (MAT); physical education K8-12 (MAT); special education K8-12 (MAT). Part-time and evening/weekend programs available. *Degree requirements:* For master's, thesis (for some programs). *Entrance requirements:* For master's, GRE General Test or MAT, minimum undergraduate GPA of 2.5.

Bethel University, Graduate School, Department of Education, St. Paul, MN 55112-6999. Offers education K-12 (MA); educational administration (Ed D); literacy (Certificate); literacy education (MA); secondary education (MA); special education (M Ed). Evening/weekend programs available. *Faculty:* 20 full-time (10 women), 34 part-time/adjunct (18 women). *Students:* 192 full-time (119 women), 110 part-time (71 women); includes 16 minority (6 African Americans, 5 Asian Americans or Pacific Islanders, 5 Hispanic Americans). Average age 35. In 2006, 58 master's, 9 other advanced degrees awarded. *Degree requirements:* For master's, thesis, practicum; for doctorate, thesis/dissertation, registration. *Entrance requirements:* For master's, interview, current teaching license, minimum GPA of 3.0, teaching experience (if applicable), letters of reference; for doctorate, MAT or GRE, minimum GPA of 3.5, letters of reference, master's degree. Additional exam requirements/recommendations for international students: Required—TOEFL (minimum score 550 paper-based; 213 computer-based). *Application deadline:* For fall admission, 8/1 priority date for domestic students; for winter admission, 12/10 priority date for domestic students; for spring admission, 5/1 priority date for domestic students. Applications are processed on a rolling basis. Application fee: $25. Electronic applications accepted. *Expenses: Contact institution.* Tuition and fees vary according to program. *Financial support:* Institutionally sponsored loans and scholarships/grants available. Financial award applicants required to submit FAFSA. *Unit head:* Dr. Jay B. Rasmussen, Director, 651-638-6237, Fax: 651-638-8004, E-mail: jay-rasmussen@bethel.edu. *Application contact:* Michael Price, Director of Admissions, 651-635-8000 Ext. 8017, Fax: 651-635-8004, E-mail: m_price@bethel.edu.

Bloomsburg University of Pennsylvania, School of Graduate Studies, College of Professional Studies, School of Education, Department of Exceptionality Programs, Program in Special Education, Bloomsburg, PA 17815-1301. Offers exceptionality programs (MS). *Accreditation:* NCATE. *Faculty:* 7 full-time (3 women). *Students:* 42 full-time (36 women), 38 part-time (32 women), 1 international. Average age 32. 35 applicants, 100% accepted, 23 enrolled. In 2006, 32 degrees awarded. *Degree requirements:* For master's, thesis or alternative. *Entrance requirements:* For master's, teaching certificate, minimum QPA of 3.0. Additional exam requirements/recommendations for international students: Required—TOEFL (minimum score 550 paper-based; 213 computer-based; 79 iBT). *Application deadline:* Applications are processed on a rolling basis. Application fee: $30. Electronic applications accepted. *Expenses:* Tuition, state resident: full-time $6,048; part-time $336 per credit. Tuition, nonresident: full-time $9,678; part-time $538 per credit. Required fees: $1,415. *Financial support:* Unspecified assistantships available. *Faculty research:* Exceptionalities, learning disabilities, behavior disorders, gifted, early childhood. *Unit head:* Dr. Sheila Dove Jones, Chair, 570-389-4815, Fax: 570-389-3980, E-mail: sjones@bloomu.edu.

Bob Jones University, Graduate Programs, Greenville, SC 29614. Offers accountancy (MS); Bible (MA); Bible translation (MA); Biblical studies (Certificate); broadcast management (MS); business administration (MBA); church history (MA, PhD); church ministries (MA); church music (MM); cinema and video production (MA); counseling (MS); curriculum and instruction (Ed D); divinity (M Div); dramatic production (MA); educational leadership (MS, Ed D, Ed S); elementary education (M Ed, MAT); English (M Ed, MA, MAT); fine arts (MA); graphic design (MA); history (M Ed, MA); illustration (MA); interpretative speech (MA); mathematics (M Ed, MAT); medical missions (Certificate); ministry (MM, D Min); multi-categorical special education (M Ed, MAT); music (M Ed); New Testament interpretation (PhD); Old Testament interpretation (PhD); orchestral instrument performance (MM); organ performance (MM); pastoral studies (MA); personnel services (MS, Ed S); piano pedagogy (MM); piano performance (MM); platform arts (MA); radio and television broadcasting (MS); rhetoric and public address (MA); secondary education (M Ed); studio art (MA); teaching Bible (MA); theology (MA, PhD); voice performance (MM); youth ministries (MA); M Div/MM.

Boise State University, Graduate College, College of Education, Programs in Teacher Education, Program in Special Education, Boise, ID 83725-0399. Offers M Ed, MA. *Accreditation:* NCATE. *Faculty:* 16 full-time (9 women), 4 part-time/adjunct (all women). *Students:* 2 full-time (both women), 15 part-time (14 women). Average age 39. 7 applicants, 100% accepted, 3 enrolled. In 2006, 3 degrees awarded. *Degree requirements:* For master's, thesis optional. *Entrance requirements:* For master's, minimum GPA of 3.0. *Application deadline:* For fall admission, 7/1 priority date for domestic students; for spring admission, 11/15 priority date for domestic students. Applications are processed on a rolling basis. Application fee: $0. Electronic applications accepted. *Financial support:* Career-related internships or fieldwork, Federal Work-Study, institutionally sponsored loans, and unspecified assistantships available. Support available to part-time students. Financial award application deadline: 3/1. *Unit head:* Dr. Melinda Lindsey, Head, 208-426-1548, Fax: 208-426-4365, E-mail: mlindse@boisestate.edu.

Boston College, Lynch Graduate School of Education, Department of Teacher Education/Special Education and Curriculum and Instruction, Program in Special Needs: Moderate Disabilities, Chestnut Hill, MA 02467-3800. Offers M Ed, CAES. *Students:* 30 full-time (27 women), 9 part-time (6 women); includes 5 minority (3 African Americans, 1 American Indian/Alaska Native, 1 Hispanic American), 3 international. 61 applicants, 62% accepted, 30 enrolled. In 2006, 36 degrees awarded. *Degree requirements:* For master's and CAES, comprehensive exam. *Entrance requirements:* For master's and CAES, GRE General Test or MAT. Additional exam requirements/recommendations for international students: Required—TOEFL. *Application deadline:* For fall admission, 1/1 priority date for domestic students. Application fee: $60. *Financial support:* Fellowships with full and partial tuition reimbursements, research assistantships with full and partial tuition reimbursements, teaching assistantships with full and partia tuition reimbursements, career-related internships or fieldwork, Federal Work-Study, scholarships/grants, traineeships, and unspecified assistantships available. Support available to part-time students. Financial award applicants required to submit FAFSA. *Faculty research:* Applicatior of cognitive and metacognitive learning strategies within regular curriculum, strategies fo supporting learning-disabled college students. *Application contact:* Timothy P. Blackman, Director, Graduate Admission and Financial Aid, 617-552-4214, Fax: 617-552-0398, E-mail: timothy blackman.1@bc.edu.

Boston College, Lynch Graduate School of Education, Department of Teacher Education Special Education and Curriculum and Instruction, Program in Special Needs: Severe Dis abilities, Chestnut Hill, MA 02467-3800. Offers M Ed. *Students:* 16 full-time (all women), 12 part-time (11 women); includes 6 minority (2 African Americans, 3 Asian Americans or Pacifi Islanders, 1 Hispanic American), 1 international. 20 applicants, 75% accepted, 12 enrolled. I 2006, 19 degrees awarded. *Degree requirements:* For master's, comprehensive exam. *Entranc requirements:* For master's, GRE General Test or MAT. Additional exam requirements recommendations for international students: Required—TOEFL. *Application deadline:* For fa admission, 1/1 priority date for domestic students. Application fee: $60. *Financial suppor* Fellowships with full and partial tuition reimbursements, research assistantships with full an partial tuition reimbursements, teaching assistantships with full and partial tuition reimburse ments, career-related internships or fieldwork, Federal Work-Study, scholarships/grants, trainee ships, tuition waivers (full and partial), and unspecified assistantships available. Suppo available to part-time students. Financial award applicants required to submit FAFSA. *Facult research:* Delivery of education and support services for children with severe special needs *Application contact:* Timothy P. Blackman, Director, Graduate Admission and Financial Aid 617-552-4214, Fax: 617-552-0398, E-mail: timothy.blackman.1@bc.edu.

Boston University, School of Education, Department of Curriculum and Teaching, Program Special Education, Boston, MA 02215. Offers special education (Ed M, Ed D, CAGS), inclu- ing alternative community settings (Ed D), learning and behavioral disabilities (Ed D, CAG), severe disabilities (Ed D, CAGS), therapeutic recreation (Ed D), young children with spe a needs (Ed D, CAGS); MSW/Ed D; MSW/Ed M. *Students:* 19 full-time (17 women), 29 part- ne (24 women); includes 3 minority (all Asian Americans or Pacific Islanders), 6 internatio al. Average age 30. 51 applicants, 78% accepted. In 2006, 19 master's, 1 doctorate, 3 e her advanced degrees awarded. *Degree requirements:* For master's, thesis optional; for do torate, thesis/dissertation, comprehensive exam. *Entrance requirements:* For master's, d ctorate, and CAGS, GRE General Test or MAT. Additional exam requirements/recommend tions for international students: Required—TOEFL. *Application deadline:* For fall admissio 2/15 priority date for domestic students; for winter admission, 10/1 priority date for do nestic students. Applications are processed on a rolling basis. Application fee: $70. Electronic pplications accepted. *Expenses:* Tuition: Full-time $33,330; part-time $1,042 per credit. R equired fees: $462; $40. *Financial support:* Application deadline: 2/15. *Unit head:* Dr. Don a Lehr Head, 617-353-3240, E-mail: dlehr@bu.edu. *Application contact:* 617-353-4237, Fax: 617-353 8937, E-mail: sedgrad@bu.edu.

Boston University, School of Education, Department of Literacy and Language, Counseling and Development, Program in Education of the Deaf, Boston, MA 02215. Offers Ed M, CAGS. Part-time programs available. *Students:* 9 full-time (all women), 6 part-time (5 women); includes 2 minority (both Hispanic Americans), 2 international. Average age 25. 21 applicants, 71 % accepted. In 2006, 11 degrees awarded. *Degree requirements:* For CAGS, comprehensive exam. *Entrance requirements:* For master's and CAGS, GRE General Test or MAT. Additional exam requirements/recommendations for international students: Required—TOEFL. *Application deadline:* For fall admission, 2/15 priority date for domestic students; for winter admission, 10/1 priority date for domestic students. Applications are processed on a rolling basis. Application fee: $70. Electronic applications accepted. *Expenses:* Tuition: Full-time $33,330; part-time $1,042 per credit. Required fees: $462; $40. *Financial support:* Application deadline: 2/1 5. *Faculty research:* Structure of American Sign Language, acquisition of American Sign Language, problems in educating the deaf, impact of legislation on the deaf, relations between hearing parents and deaf children. *Unit head:* Dr. Robert Hoffmeister, Coordinator, 617-353-320 5, E-mail: rhoff@bu.edu. *Application contact:* 617-353-4237, Fax: 617-353-8937, E-mail: sedgrad @bu.edu.

Bowie State University, Graduate Programs, Program in Special Education, Bowie, MD 2071 5-9465. Offers M Ed. *Accreditation:* NCATE. Part-time and evening/weekend programs avail- able. *Faculty:* 3 full-time (1 woman), 1 part-time/adjunct (0 women). *Students:* 10 full-time (7 women), 59 part-time (44 women); includes 59 minority (57 African Americans, 1 Americ an

Indian/Alaska Native, 1 Asian American or Pacific Islander), 1 international. Average age 36. 15 applicants, 100% accepted, 15 enrolled. In 2006, 15 degrees awarded. *Degree requirements:* For master's, research paper, thesis optional. *Entrance requirements:* For master's, teaching experience, typed 2-3 page essay on Philosophy Teaching diverse learners, 3 professional letters of recommendation. *Application deadline:* For fall admission, 4/1 priority date for domestic and international students; for spring admission, 11/1 priority date for domestic and international students. Applications are processed on a rolling basis. Application fee: $40. Electronic applications accepted. *Expenses:* Tuition, state resident: full-time $7,344; part-time $306 per credit. Tuition, nonresident: full-time $14,304; part-time $396 per credit. Required fees: $1,078; $77 per credit. $539 per term. One-time fee: $40. *Financial support:* Institutionally sponsored loans available. Support available to part-time students. Financial award application deadline: 4/1. *Unit head:* Dr. Thelon Byrd, Coordinator, 301-860-3137, E-mail: tbyrd@bowiestate.edu. *Application contact:* Angela Issac, Information Contact.

Bowling Green State University, Graduate College, College of Education and Human Development, School of Education and Intervention Services, Intervention Services Division, Program in Special Education, Bowling Green, OH 43403. Offers assistive technology (M Ed); early childhood intervention (M Ed); gifted education (M Ed); hearing impaired intervention (M Ed); mild/moderate intervention (M Ed); moderate/intensive intervention (M Ed). *Accreditation:* NCATE. Part-time programs available. *Students:* 26 full-time (21 women), 84 part-time (78 women); includes 4 minority (all African Americans) Average age 35. 39 applicants, 87% accepted, 12 enrolled. In 2006, 47 degrees awarded. *Degree requirements:* For master's, thesis or alternative. *Entrance requirements:* For master's, GRE General Test. Additional exam requirements/recommendations for international students: Required—TOEFL. *Application deadline:* For fall admission, 3/1 priority date for domestic students. Applications are processed on a rolling basis. Application fee: $30. Electronic applications accepted. *Expenses:* Tuition, state resident: part-time $535 per hour. Tuition, nonresident: part-time $884 per hour. *Financial support:* In 2006–07, 16 research assistantships with full tuition reimbursements (averaging $5,202 per year) were awarded; teaching assistantships with full tuition reimbursements, Federal Work-Study and unspecified assistantships also available. Financial award applicants required to submit FAFSA. *Faculty research:* Reading and special populations, deafness, early childhood, gifted and talented, behavior disorders. *Application contact:* Dr. Lessie Cochran, Graduate Coordinator, 419-372-7298.

Brandon University, Faculty of Education, Brandon, MB R7A 6A9, Canada. Offers curriculum (Diploma); curriculum studies (M Ed); education administration (M Ed, Diploma); guidance and counseling (M Ed, Diploma); special education (M Ed, Diploma). *Degree requirements:* For master's, thesis. *Entrance requirements:* For master's, minimum GPA of 3.0, teaching certificate or equivalent. Additional exam requirements/recommendations for international students: Required—TOEFL. *Faculty research:* Comparative education, environmental studies, parent/school council.

Brenau University, Graduate Programs, School of Education, Gainesville, GA 30501. Offers early childhood education (M Ed, Ed S), including behavior disorders (M Ed); learning disabilities (M Ed), including special education; middle grades education (M Ed, Ed S). *Accreditation:* NCATE. Part-time and evening/weekend programs available. *Faculty:* 12 full-time (9 women), 17 part-time/adjunct (9 women). *Students:* 104 full-time (89 women), 160 part-time (140 women); includes 34 minority (28 African Americans, 3 Asian Americans or Pacific Islanders, 3 Hispanic Americans), 2 international. Average age 37. 187 applicants. In 2006, 92 master's, 24 other advanced degrees awarded. *Degree requirements:* For master's, comprehensive exam or applied research project, effective portfolio, thesis optional; for Ed S, applied research project. *Entrance requirements:* For master's, GRE, MAT, interview, minimum GPA of 3.0, teaching certificate, 3 references, writing samples; for Ed S, GRE, MAT, master's degree, minimum GPA of 3.0, writing sample, letters of reference. Additional exam requirements/recommendations for international students: Required—TOEFL (minimum score 550 paper-based). *Application deadline:* Applications are processed on a rolling basis. Application fee: $30. *Expenses:* Contact institution. *Financial support:* Career-related internships or fieldwork available. Financial award application deadline: 7/15; financial award applicants required to submit FAFSA. *Faculty research:* Environmental science literacy and awareness, curriculum integration for improved student success, teaching dispositions, impact of parent involvement on student success, grade inflation in higher education. *Unit head:* Dr. William B. Ware, Dean, 770-534-6220, Fax: 770-534-6221, E-mail: bware@brenau.edu. *Application contact:* Nathan Goss, Admissions Coordinator, 770-534-6162, Fax: 770-538-4701, E-mail: ngoss@brenau.edu.

Bridgewater State College, School of Graduate Studies, School of Education and Allied Science, Department of Special Education, Bridgewater, MA 02325-0001. Offers M Ed. *Accreditation:* NCATE. Part-time and evening/weekend programs available. *Entrance requirements:* For master's, GRE General Test or Massachusetts Test for Educator Licensure. *Application deadline:* For fall admission, 3/1 priority date for domestic students; for spring admission, 10/1 priority date for domestic students. Application fee: $50. *Financial support:* Career-related internships or fieldwork, health care benefits, and unspecified assistantships available. Support available to part-time students.

Brigham Young University, Graduate Studies, David O. McKay School of Education, Department of Counseling Psychology and Special Education, Provo, UT 84602-1001. Offers counseling psychology (PhD); school psychology (Ed S); special education (MS). *Accreditation:* ACA; NCATE. Part-time programs available. *Faculty:* 13 full-time (8 women), 10 part-time/adjunct (2 women). *Students:* 63 full-time (41 women), 13 part-time (10 women); includes 14 minority (1 African American, 3 American Indian/Alaska Native, 7 Asian Americans or Pacific Islanders, 3 Hispanic Americans), 4 international. Average age 30. 66 applicants, 36% accepted, 17 enrolled. In 2006, 16 master's, 5 doctorates, 19 other advanced degrees awarded. *Median time to degree:* Master's–3 years full-time; doctorate–5 years full-time. *Degree requirements:* For master's and doctorate, thesis/dissertation, comprehensive exam. *Entrance requirements:* For master's and doctorate, GRE General Test, minimum GPA of 3.0 in last 60 hours of course work. Additional exam requirements/recommendations for international students: Required—TOEFL (minimum score 580 paper-based; 237 computer-based), IELTS (minimum score 7). *Application deadline:* For fall admission, 1/15 for domestic and international students. Application fee: $50. Electronic applications accepted. *Financial support:* In 2006–07, 55 students received support, including 36 research assistantships with partial tuition reimbursements available (averaging $5,120 per year), 5 teaching assistantships with partial tuition reimbursements available (averaging $4,500 per year); career-related internships or fieldwork, institutionally sponsored loans, and tuition waivers (partial) also available. *Faculty research:* Gender issues in education, psychotherapy progress and outcome, and behavior disorders and ABA. Total annual research expenditures: $253,211. *Unit head:* Dr. Mary Anne Prater, Chair, 801-422-3857, Fax: 801-422-0198, E-mail: prater@byu.edu. *Application contact:* Diane E. Hancock, Department Secretary, 801-422-3859, Fax: 801-422-0198, E-mail: diane_hancock@byu.edu.

Brooklyn College of the City University of New York, Division of Graduate Studies, School of Education, Program in Special Education, Brooklyn, NY 11210-2889. Offers bilingual special education (MS Ed); children with emotional handicaps (MS Ed); children with neuropsychological learning disabilities (MS Ed); children with retarded mental development (MS Ed); teacher of students with disabilities (MS Ed), including birth-grade 2, grades 1-6, grades 5-9. Part-time programs available. *Students:* 172 applicants, 83% accepted, 125 enrolled. In 2006, 80 degrees awarded. *Degree requirements:* For master's, practicum. *Entrance requirements:* For master's, LAST, interview; previous course work in education and psychology; minimum GPA of 3.0 in education, 2.8 overall; resumé, 2 letters of recommendation; essay. Additional exam requirements/recommendations for international students: Required—TOEFL. *Application deadline:* For fall admission, 3/1 priority date for domestic students, 2/1 priority date for international students; for spring admission, 11/1 priority date for domestic students, 10/1 priority date for international students. Applications are processed on a rolling basis. Application fee: $125. Electronic applications accepted. *Expenses:* Tuition, state resident: full-time $6,400; part-time $270 per credit. Tuition, nonresident: full-time $12,000; part-time $500 per credit. Required fees: $118 per semester. *Financial support:* Federal Work-Study, institutionally sponsored loans, and scholarships/grants available. Support available to part-time students. Financial award application deadline: 5/1; financial award applicants required to submit FAFSA. *Faculty research:* School reform, conflict resolution, curriculum for inclusive settings, urban issues in special education. *Unit head:* Prof. Lynda Sarnoff, Facilitator, 718-951-5214, Fax: 718-951-4816, E-mail: lsarnoff@brooklyn.cuny.edu. *Application contact:* Karen Alleyne-Pierre, Director of Admissions Services and Enrollment Communications, 718-951-5902, Fax: 718-951-4506, E-mail: grads@brooklyn.cuny.edu.

Buffalo State College, State University of New York, Graduate Studies and Research, Faculty of Applied Science and Education, Department of Exceptional Education, Programs in Special Education, Buffalo, NY 14222-1095. Offers special education (MS Ed); special education: adolescents (MS Ed); special education: childhood (MS Ed); special education: early childhood (MS Ed). *Accreditation:* NCATE. Part-time and evening/weekend programs available. *Degree requirements:* For master's, thesis or project. *Entrance requirements:* For master's, minimum GPA of 2.5. Additional exam requirements/recommendations for international students: Required—TOEFL (minimum score 550 paper-based; 213 computer-based).

Butler University, College of Education, Indianapolis, IN 46208-3485. Offers administration (MS); elementary education (MS); reading (MS); school counseling (MS); secondary education (MS); special education (MS). *Accreditation:* ACA; NCATE. Part-time and evening/weekend programs available. *Faculty:* 12 full-time (6 women), 11 part-time/adjunct (8 women). *Students:* 18 full-time (10 women), 156 part-time (125 women); includes 21 minority (16 African Americans, 2 Asian Americans or Pacific Islanders, 3 Hispanic Americans), 7 international. Average age 31. 56 applicants, 57% accepted, 29 enrolled. In 2006, 72 degrees awarded. *Entrance requirements:* For master's, GRE General Test, MAT, interview. *Application deadline:* For fall admission, 8/15 priority date for domestic students. Applications are processed on a rolling basis. Application fee: $35. Electronic applications accepted. *Expenses:* Tuition: Full-time $6,030; part-time $335 per credit. Tuition and fees vary according to program. *Financial support:* Institutionally sponsored loans available. Support available to part-time students. Financial award application deadline: 7/15; financial award applicants required to submit FAFSA. *Faculty research:* Ethics in cybercounseling, history of sports for disabled effect of fetal alcohol syndrome on perceptual learning, Reading Recovery's theoretical framework in teacher education. *Unit head:* Dr. Ena Shelley, Dean, 317-940-9752, Fax: 317-940-6481. *Application contact:* Karen Farrell, Department Secretary, 317-940-9220, E-mail: kfarrell@butler.edu.

Caldwell College, Graduate Studies, Program in Special Education, Caldwell, NJ 07006-6195. Offers MA. *Degree requirements:* For master's, thesis. *Entrance requirements:* For master's, GRE General Test or MAT, minimum GPA of 3.0, writing sample. Additional exam requirements/recommendations for international students: Required—TOEFL (minimum score 580 paper-based; 237 computer-based). Electronic applications accepted.

California Baptist University, Program in Education, Riverside, CA 92504-3206. Offers cross-cultural language and academic development (MA Ed); educational leadership (MS Ed); educational technology (MS Ed); instructional computer applications (MS Ed); reading (MS Ed); special education (MS Ed); teaching (MS Ed). Part-time programs available. *Faculty:* 16 full-time (10 women), 16 part-time/adjunct (13 women). *Students:* 77 full-time (64 women), 408 part-time (342 women); includes 157 minority (41 African Americans, 12 American Indian/Alaska Native, 18 Asian Americans or Pacific Islanders, 86 Hispanic Americans), 2 international. 282 applicants, 70% accepted, 171 enrolled. In 2006, 63 degrees awarded. *Degree requirements:* For master's, thesis optional. *Entrance requirements:* For master's, minimum undergraduate GPA of 2.75, 12 semester hours of course work in education. Additional exam requirements/recommendations for international students: Required—TOEFL (minimum score 575 paper-based; 230 computer-based), IELTS (minimum score 7). *Application deadline:* For fall admission, 9/1 for domestic students, 7/15 priority date for international students; for spring admission, 1/3 for domestic students, 11/1 priority date for international students. Applications are processed on a rolling basis. Application fee: $45. Electronic applications accepted. *Expenses:* Tuition: Full-time $7,812; part-time $434 per unit. Required fees: $120 per semester. Tuition and fees vary according to program. *Financial support:* In 2006–07, 19 students received support. Career-related internships or fieldwork, Federal Work-Study, and scholarships/grants available. Support available to part-time students. Financial award applicants required to submit FAFSA. *Unit head:* Dr. Mary Crist, Dean, School of Education, 951-343-4313, Fax: 951-343-4516, E-mail: mcrist@calbaptist.edu. *Application contact:* Gail Ronveaux, Dean of Graduate Enrollment, 951-343-5045, Fax: 951-343-5095, E-mail: graduateadmissions@calbaptist.edu.

California Lutheran University, Graduate Studies, School of Education, Emphasis in Special Education, Thousand Oaks, CA 91360-2787. Offers MS. *Accreditation:* NCATE. Evening/weekend programs available. *Degree requirements:* For master's, thesis or comprehensive exam. *Entrance requirements:* For master's, GRE General Test, interview, minimum GPA of 3.0.

California State University, Bakersfield, Division of Graduate Studies and Research, School of Education, Program in Special Education, Bakersfield, CA 93311-1022. Offers MA. *Accreditation:* NCATE. *Degree requirements:* For master's, thesis or alternative, culminating projects.

California State University, Chico, Graduate School, College of Communication and Education, Department of Education, Program in Education, Chico, CA 95929-0722. Offers curriculum and instruction (MA); educational administration (MA); linguistically and culturally diverse learners (MA); reading/language arts (MA); special education (MA). *Students:* 23 full-time (14 women), 58 part-time (45 women); includes 10 minority (2 African Americans, 1 American Indian/Alaska Native, 1 Asian American or Pacific Islander, 6 Hispanic Americans), 1 international. Average age 37. 39 applicants, 100% accepted, 32 enrolled. In 2006, 37 degrees awarded. *Unit head:* Dr. Michael Kotar, Graduate Coordinator, 530-898-6610.

California State University, Dominguez Hills, College of Education, Division of Graduate Education, Program in Special Education, Carson, CA 90747-0001. Offers early childhood (MA); mild/moderate (MA); moderate/severe (MA). Part-time and evening/weekend programs available. *Faculty:* 7 full-time (6 women), 13 part-time/adjunct (10 women). *Students:* 163 full-time (124 women), 269 part-time (194 women); includes 233 minority (104 African Americans, 2 American Indian/Alaska Native, 34 Asian Americans or Pacific Islanders, 93 Hispanic Americans), 1 international. Average age 38. 102 applicants, 94% accepted, 61 enrolled. In 2006, 77 degrees awarded. *Degree requirements:* For master's, thesis or alternative, registration. *Entrance requirements:* For master's, minimum GPA of 2.75 in last 60 units, 3 letters of recommendation. *Application deadline:* For fall admission, 6/1 for domestic students. Applications are processed on a rolling basis. Application fee: $55. *Expenses:* Tuition, nonresident: part-time $339 per unit. Required fees: $1,148 per term. Tuition and fees vary according to program. Total annual research expenditures: $4 million. *Unit head:* Dr. Dawn Berlin, Coordinator, 310-243-3496, E-mail: dberlin@csudh.edu. *Application contact:* Admissions Office, 310-243-3530.

California State University, East Bay, Academic Programs and Graduate Studies, College of Education and Allied Studies, Department of Educational Psychology, Hayward, CA 94542-3000. Offers counseling (MS); special education (MS). Part-time programs available. *Faculty:* 9 full-time (4 women), 1 part-time/adjunct (0 women). *Students:* 115 full-time (90 women); includes 36 minority (9 African Americans, 14 Asian Americans or Pacific Islanders, 13 Hispanic Americans). Average age 31. 128 applicants, 34% accepted, 40 enrolled. In 2006, 44 degrees awarded. *Entrance requirements:* For master's, GRE or MAT, interview, minimum GPA of 2.5 during previous 2 years of course work. Additional exam requirements/recommendations for international students: Required—TOEFL (minimum score 550 paper-based; 213 computer-based). *Application deadline:* For fall admission, 4/15 for domestic students, 4/30 for international students; for winter admission, 9/30 for domestic and international students; for spring admission, 12/31 for domestic students, 11/30 for international students. Application fee: $55. Electronic applications accepted. *Financial support:* Career-related internships or fieldwork, Federal Work-Study, and institutionally sponsored loans available. Support available to part-time students. Financial award application deadline: 3/2. *Unit head:*

Special Education

California State University, East Bay (continued)
Dr. Jack Davis, Chair, 510-885-3052, E-mail: jack.davis@csueastbay.edu. *Application contact:* My Huynh, Graduate Prospect Specialist, 510-885-2989, Fax: 510-885-4059, E-mail: my.huynh@csueastbay.edu.

California State University, East Bay, Academic Programs and Graduate Studies, College of Education and Allied Studies, Unit of Special Education, Hayward, CA 94542-3000. Offers special education (MS), including moderate, moderate/severe. *Accreditation:* NCATE. *Faculty:* 4 full-time (3 women), 1 (woman) part-time/adjunct. *Students:* 45 full-time (35 women), 24 part-time (22 women); includes 19 minority (1 African American, 1 American Indian/Alaska Native, 9 Asian Americans or Pacific Islanders, 8 Hispanic Americans), 4 international. Average age 36. 9 applicants, 78% accepted, 7 enrolled. In 2006, 7 degrees awarded. *Degree requirements:* For master's, project or thesis. *Entrance requirements:* For master's, GRE or MAT, interview, minimum GPA of 2.5 during previous 2 years of course work. Additional exam requirements/recommendations for international students: Required—TOEFL (minimum score 550 paper-based; 213 computer-based). *Application deadline:* For fall admission, 5/31 for domestic students, 4/30 for international students; for winter admission, 9/30 for domestic and international students; for spring admission, 12/31 for domestic students, 11/30 for international students. Application fee: $55. Electronic applications accepted. *Financial support:* Career-related internships or fieldwork, Federal Work-Study, and institutionally sponsored loans available. Support available to part-time students. Financial award application deadline: 3/2. *Unit head:* Dr. Jack Davis, Chair, 510-885-3052, E-mail: jack.davis@csueastbay.edu. *Application contact:* My Huynh, Graduate Prospect Specialist, 510-885-2989, Fax: 510-885-4059, E-mail: my.huynh@csueastbay.edu.

California State University, Fresno, Division of Graduate Studies, School of Education and Human Development, Department of Counseling and Special Education, Program in Special Education, Fresno, CA 93740-8027. Offers MA. *Accreditation:* NCATE. Part-time and evening/weekend programs available. *Degree requirements:* For master's, thesis or alternative. *Entrance requirements:* For master's, GRE General Test, MAT, minimum GPA of 3.0. Additional exam requirements/recommendations for international students: Required—TOEFL. Electronic applications accepted.

California State University, Fullerton, Graduate Studies, College of Education, Department of Special Education, Fullerton, CA 92834-9480. Offers MS. *Accreditation:* NCATE. Part-time programs available. *Students:* 85 full-time (78 women), 192 part-time (164 women); includes 76 minority (3 African Americans, 2 American Indian/Alaska Native, 25 Asian Americans or Pacific Islanders, 46 Hispanic Americans), 1 international. Average age 36. 206 applicants, 52% accepted, 57 enrolled. In 2006, 50 degrees awarded. *Degree requirements:* For master's, project or thesis. *Entrance requirements:* For master's, minimum GPA of 2.75. Application fee: $55. *Expenses:* Tuition, nonresident: part-time $339 per unit. Required fees: $1,155 per semester. *Financial support:* Teaching assistantships, career-related internships or fieldwork, Federal Work-Study, institutionally sponsored loans, and scholarships/grants available. Support available to part-time students. Financial award application deadline: 3/1. *Unit head:* Dr. Barbara Glaeser, Chair, 714-278-4711.

California State University, Long Beach, Graduate Studies, College of Education, Department of Educational Psychology, Administration, and Counseling, Program in Special Education, Long Beach, CA 90840. Offers MS. *Accreditation:* NCATE. *Students:* 4 full-time (3 women), 30 part-time (28 women); includes 12 minority (2 African Americans, 4 Asian Americans or Pacific Islanders, 6 Hispanic Americans), 1 international. Average age 33. 29 applicants, 28% accepted, 1 enrolled. In 2006, 7 degrees awarded. *Degree requirements:* For master's, comprehensive exam or thesis. *Entrance requirements:* For master's, GRE General Test, minimum GPA of 2.75. *Application deadline:* For fall admission, 7/1 for domestic students; for spring admission, 12/1 for domestic students. Applications are processed on a rolling basis. Application fee: $55. Electronic applications accepted. *Financial support:* Federal Work-Study, institutionally sponsored loans, and scholarships/grants available. Financial award application deadline: 3/2. *Unit head:* Dr. Jennifer Coots, Coordinator, 562-985-8354, Fax: 562-985-4534, E-mail: jcoots@csulb.edu.

California State University, Los Angeles, Graduate Studies, Charter College of Education, Division of Special Education and Counseling, Major in Special Education, Los Angeles, CA 90032-8530. Offers MA. *Accreditation:* NCATE. Part-time and evening/weekend programs available. *Students:* 86 full-time (63 women), 299 part-time (233 women); includes 201 minority (27 African Americans, 5 American Indian/Alaska Native, 41 Asian Americans or Pacific Islanders, 128 Hispanic Americans), 23 international. In 2006, 248 degrees awarded. *Degree requirements:* For master's, comprehensive exam. *Entrance requirements:* For master's, minimum GPA of 2.75 in last 90 units of course work, teaching certificate. Additional exam requirements/recommendations for international students: Required—TOEFL. *Application deadline:* For fall admission, 6/30 for domestic students; for spring admission, 2/1 for domestic students. Applications are processed on a rolling basis. Application fee: $55. *Expenses:* Tuition, nonresident: part-time $226 per unit. *Financial support:* Federal Work-Study available. Support available to part-time students. Financial award application deadline: 3/1. *Faculty research:* Drug-free schools. *Unit head:* Dr. Diane Fazzi, Chair, Division of Special Education and Counseling, 323-343-4400, Fax: 323-343-5605.

California State University, Northridge, Graduate Studies, College of Education, Department of Special Education, Northridge, CA 91330. Offers early childhood special education (MA); education of the deaf and hard of hearing (MA); educational therapy (MA); genetic counseling (MS); mild/moderate disabilities (MA); moderate/severe disabilities (MA). *Accreditation:* NCATE. *Faculty:* 17 full-time (14 women), 50 part-time/adjunct (40 women). *Students:* 96 full-time (13 women), 312 part-time (58 women); includes 121 minority (24 African Americans, 4 American Indian/Alaska Native, 34 Asian Americans or Pacific Islanders, 59 Hispanic Americans), 7 international. Average age 36. 77 applicants, 77% accepted, 46 enrolled. In 2006, 55 degrees awarded. *Entrance requirements:* For master's, GRE General Test. Additional exam requirements/recommendations for international students: Required—TOEFL. *Application deadline:* For fall admission, 11/30 for domestic students. Application fee: $55. *Expenses:* Tuition, nonresident: full-time $8,136; part-time $4,068 per year. Required fees: $3,624; $1,161 per term. *Financial support:* Application deadline: 3/1. *Faculty research:* Teacher training, classroom aide training. *Unit head:* Dr. Nancy Burstein, Chair, 818-677-2596. *Application contact:* Dr. Ellen Schneiderman, Graduate Studies Coordinator, 818-677-2649.

California State University, Sacramento, Graduate Studies, College of Education, Department of Special Education, Rehabilitation, and School Psychology, Sacramento, CA 95819-6048. Offers school psychology (MS); special education (MA); vocational rehabilitation (MS). *Accreditation:* CORE. Part-time programs available. *Students:* 130 full-time (112 women), 71 part-time (57 women); includes 48 minority (16 African Americans, 1 American Indian/Alaska Native, 10 Asian Americans or Pacific Islanders, 21 Hispanic Americans), 3 international. Average age 33. 103 applicants, 69% accepted, 45 enrolled. *Degree requirements:* For master's, thesis or alternative, writing proficiency exam. *Entrance requirements:* For master's, minimum GPA of 2.5. Additional exam requirements/recommendations for international students: Required—TOEFL. *Application deadline:* Applications are processed on a rolling basis. Application fee: $55. Electronic applications accepted. *Financial support:* Career-related internships or fieldwork and Federal Work-Study available. Support available to part-time students. Financial award application deadline: 3/1. *Unit head:* Bernice Bassde Martinez, Chair, 916-278-6622, Fax: 916-278-3498.

California State University, San Bernardino, Graduate Studies, College of Education, Programs in Special Education and Rehabilitation Counseling, San Bernardino, CA 92407-2397. Offers rehabilitation counseling (MA); special education (MA). *Accreditation:* CORE; NCATE. Part-time and evening/weekend programs available. *Students:* 259 full-time (198 women), 95 part-time (66 women); includes 160 minority (59 African Americans, 5 American Indian/Alaska Native, 15 Asian Americans or Pacific Islanders, 81 Hispanic Americans), 2 international. Average age 36. 122 applicants, 88% accepted, 60 enrolled. In 2006, 62 degrees awarded. *Degree requirements:* For master's, thesis or alternative. *Entrance requirements:* For master's, minimum GPA of 3.0 in education. *Application deadline:* For fall admission, 8/31 priority date for domestic students. Application fee: $55. *Financial support:* Career-related internships or fieldwork and Federal Work-Study available. Support available to part-time students. *Unit head:* Dr. Ruth Ann Sandlin, Chair, 909-537-5641, Fax: 909-537-7040, E-mail: rsandlin@csusb.edu.

California University of Pennsylvania, School of Graduate Studies and Research, School of Education, Department of Special Education, California, PA 15419-1394. Offers mentally and/or physically handicapped education (M Ed). *Accreditation:* NCATE. Part-time and evening/weekend programs available. *Faculty:* 6 full-time (3 women). *Students:* 23 full-time (18 women), 46 part-time (34 women). Average age 32. 32 applicants, 91% accepted, 27 enrolled. In 2006, 27 degrees awarded. *Median time to degree:* Master's–1.5 years full-time, 2 years part-time. *Degree requirements:* For master's, thesis optional. *Entrance requirements:* For master's, MAT, PRAXIS. Additional exam requirements/recommendations for international students: Required—TOEFL (minimum score 550 paper-based; 213 computer-based; 80 iBT). *Application deadline:* For fall admission, 8/1 priority date for domestic and international students; for winter admission, 12/1 priority date for domestic and international students; for spring admission, 5/1 priority date for domestic and international students. Applications are processed on a rolling basis. Application fee: $25. Electronic applications accepted. *Expenses:* Tuition, state resident: full-time $6,048; part-time $336 per credit. Tuition, nonresident: full-time $9,678; part-time $538 per credit. Required fees: $1,854; $263 per credit. Full-time tuition and fees vary according to course load, campus/location and program. *Financial support:* Career-related internships or fieldwork, scholarships/grants, traineeships, and unspecified assistantships available. Financial award applicants required to submit FAFSA. *Faculty research:* Case-based instruction, electronic performance support tools, students with disabilities, teacher preparation, No Child Left Behind. Total annual research expenditures: $300,000. *Unit head:* Dr. Katherine Mitchem, Coordinator, 724-938-6039, Fax: 724-938-1527, E-mail: mitchem_k@cup.edu.

Calvin College, Graduate Programs in Education, Grand Rapids, MI 49546-4388. Offers curriculum and instruction (M Ed); educational leadership (M Ed); learning disabilities (M Ed); literacy (M Ed). *Accreditation:* NCATE. Part-time programs available. *Faculty:* 2 full-time (both women), 6 part-time/adjunct (2 women). *Students:* 6 full-time (5 women), 87 part-time (66 women); includes 9 minority (3 African Americans, 1 American Indian/Alaska Native, 4 Asian Americans or Pacific Islanders, 1 Hispanic American). Average age 29. 26 applicants, 100% accepted. In 2006, 14 degrees awarded. *Degree requirements:* For master's, thesis or seminar; for degree. *Entrance requirements:* For master's, teaching certificate. Additional exam requirements/recommendations for international students: Required—TOEFL (minimum score 550 paper-based; 213 computer-based). *Application deadline:* For fall admission, 8/1 priority date for domestic students, 5/1 priority date for international students; for spring admission, 1/1 priority date for domestic students, 11/1 priority date for international students. Applications are processed on a rolling basis. Application fee: $0. Electronic applications accepted. *Expenses:* Tuition: Part-time $420 per credit hour. *Financial support:* In 2006–07, 19 students received support. Federal Work-Study, scholarships/grants, and tuition waivers (full and partial) available. Support available to part-time students. Financial award application deadline: 4/3. *Faculty research:* Literacy, racialized gender and gendered identity, teacher learning, learning disabilities identification. *Unit head:* Dr. Susan S. Hasseler, Associate Dean for Teacher Education, 616-526-6597, Fax: 616-526-6505, E-mail: shassele@calvin.edu. *Application contact:* Deb Abbott, Administrative Assistant, 616-526-6105, Fax: 616-526-6505, E-mail: dka2@calvin.edu.

Campbellsville University, School of Education, Campbellsville, KY 42718-2799. Offer curriculum and instruction (MAE); special education (MASE). *Accreditation:* NCATE. Part-time and evening/weekend programs available. Postbaccalaureate distance learning degree program offered (minimal on-campus study). *Faculty:* 5 full-time (2 women), 12 part-time/adjunct (women). *Students:* 365 full-time (230 women); includes 20 minority (14 African Americans, Asian American or Pacific Islander, 5 Hispanic Americans), 1 international. Average age 31. 8 applicants, 99% accepted, 76 enrolled. In 2006, 110 degrees awarded. *Degree requirement* For master's, thesis, research paper. *Entrance requirements:* For master's, GRE or PRAXIS minimum undergraduate GPA of 2.75, teaching certificate, professional growth plan, letters o recommendation, disposition assessment, entrance interview. *Application deadline:* For fal admission, 6/1 priority date for domestic students, 5/1 priority date for international student for spring admission, 11/1 priority date for domestic students, 10/1 priority date for internationa students. Applications are processed on a rolling basis. Application fee: $0. Electronic applica tions accepted. *Expenses:* Tuition: Full-time $6,570; part-time $365 per hour. Tuition and fee vary according to program. *Financial support:* In 2006–07, 250 students received suppor Institutionally sponsored loans, scholarships/grants, and unspecified assistantships available Support available to part-time students. Financial award application deadline: 6/1; financia award applicants required to submit FAFSA. *Faculty research:* Professional development curriculum development, school governance, assessment, special education. *Unit head:* D Brenda A. Priddy, Dean, 270-789-5344, Fax: 270-789-5206, E-mail: bapriddy@campbellsville edu. *Application contact:* Karla Deaton, Assistant Director of Admissions, 270-789-5078, Fax 270-789-5071, E-mail: redeaton@campbellsville.edu.

Canisius College, Graduate Division, School of Education and Human Services, Departmen of Graduate Education, Buffalo, NY 14208-1098. Offers business education (MS); childhoo education (MS); college student personnel (MS); differentiated instruction (MS Ed); ear childhood education (MS); education administration (MS); education of the deaf and hard of hearing (MS); general education (MS Ed); literacy education (MS Ed); reading educatio (MS Ed); secondary education (MS); special education (MS). *Accreditation:* NCATE. Part-time and evening/weekend programs available. *Faculty:* 13 full-time (12 women), 74 part-time/ adjunct (44 women). *Students:* 377 full-time (267 women), 303 part-time (219 women); includes 43 minority (27 African Americans, 2 American Indian/Alaska Native, 6 Asian Americans or Pacific Islanders, 8 Hispanic Americans), 187 international. Average age 30. In 2006, 29 degrees awarded. Application fee: $25. *Expenses:* Tuition: Part-time $645 per credit hou Required fees: $19 per credit hour. Tuition and fees vary according to program. *Financia support:* Research assistantships with full tuition reimbursements, career-related internship or fieldwork, institutionally sponsored loans, scholarships/grants, health care benefits, tuitio waivers (full and partial), and unspecified assistantships available. *Faculty research:* Autism Asperger's disease, private higher education, reading strategies. *Unit head:* Rev. Paul Nochelsk Chair of Graduate Education and Leadership, 716-888-3297, Fax: 716-888-3299. *Applicatio contact:* James D. Bagwell, Director of Graduate Recruitment and Admissions, 716-888-254 Fax: 716-888-3290, E-mail: bagwellj@canisius.edu.

Cardinal Stritch University, College of Education, Department of Reading/Language Art Reading/Learning Disability, Milwaukee, WI 53217-3985. Offers reading/language arts (MA reading/learning disability (MA). *Accreditation:* NCATE. Part-time and evening/weeken programs available. *Degree requirements:* For master's, thesis, faculty recommendatio research project, comprehensive exam. *Entrance requirements:* For master's, letters of recon mendation (2), minimum GPA of 2.75.

Cardinal Stritch University, College of Education, Department of Special Education, Milwauke WI 53217-3985. Offers MA. *Accreditation:* NCATE. Part-time and evening/weekend programs ava able. *Degree requirements:* For master's, thesis, practica, comprehensive exam. *Entran requirements:* For master's, letters of recommendation (2), minimum GPA of 2.75.

Caribbean University, Graduate School, Bayamón, PR 00960-0493. Offers accounting (MB administration and supervision (MA Ed); criminal justice (MA); curriculum and instructi (MA Ed); education (PhD); gerontology (MSN); human resources (MBA); museology, archivi and art history (MA Ed); neonatal pediatrics (MSN); physical education (MA Ed); spec education (MA Ed). *Entrance requirements:* For master's, interview, minimum GPA of 2.5.

Carlos Albizu University, Miami Campus, Graduate Programs, Miami, FL 33172-2209. Offers clinical psychology (Psy D); entrepreneurship (MBA); exceptional student education (MS); industrial/organizational psychology (MS); marriage and family therapy (MS); mental health counseling (MS); nonprofit management (MBA); organizational management (MBA); psychology (MS); school counseling (MS); teaching English as a second language (MS). *Accreditation:* APA. Part-time and evening/weekend programs available. Terminal master's awarded for partial completion of doctoral program. *Degree requirements:* For master's, one foreign language, comprehensive exam, integrative project (MBA), research project (MSESE); for doctorate, one foreign language, comprehensive exam, internship, doctoral project. *Entrance requirements:* For master's, 3 letters of recommendation, interview, minimum GPA of 3.0, resumé; for doctorate, 3 letters of recommendation, minimum GPA of 3.0, resumé, interview. *Faculty research:* Psychotherapy, forensic psychology, neuropsychology, marketing strategy, entrepreneurship.

Carlow University, School of Education, Program in Education, Pittsburgh, PA 15213-3165. Offers elementary education (M Ed); instructional technology specialist (M Ed); secondary education (M Ed); special education (M Ed). Part-time and evening/weekend programs available. *Entrance requirements:* For master's, resumé, 3 letters of recommendation, minimum GPA of 3.0, interview. Electronic applications accepted.

Castleton State College, Division of Graduate Studies, Department of Education, Program in Special Education, Castleton, VT 05735. Offers MA Ed, CAGS. Part-time and evening/weekend programs available. *Degree requirements:* For master's, thesis or alternative; for CAGS, publishable paper. *Entrance requirements:* For master's, GRE General Test, MAT, interview, minimum undergraduate GPA of 3.0; for CAGS, educational research, master's degree, minimum undergraduate GPA of 3.0.

Centenary College, Program in Education, Hackettstown, NJ 07840-2100. Offers instructional leadership (MA); special education (MA). Part-time and evening/weekend programs available. Postbaccalaureate distance learning degree programs offered (minimal on-campus study). *Degree requirements:* For master's, thesis. *Entrance requirements:* For master's. interview, minimum undergraduate GPA of 2.8.

Central Connecticut State University, School of Graduate Studies, School of Education and Professional Studies, Department of Special Education, New Britain, CT 06050-4010. Offers special education for special educators (MS); special education for teachers certified in areas other than education (MS). Part-time and evening/weekend programs available. *Faculty:* 5 full-time (2 women), 7 part-time/adjunct (5 women). *Students:* 25 full-time (20 women), 114 part-time (95 women); includes 6 minority (2 African Americans, 1 American Indian/Alaska Native, 3 Hispanic Americans), 2 international. Average age 33. 55 applicants, 73% accepted, 27 enrolled. In 2006, 43 degrees awarded. *Degree requirements:* For master's, thesis or alternative, comprehensive exam. *Entrance requirements:* For master's, minimum GPA of 2.7. Additional exam requirements/recommendations for international students: Required—TOEFL. *Application deadline:* For fall admission, 7/1 for domestic students; for spring admission, 12/1 for domestic students. Applications are processed on a rolling basis. Application fee: $50. Electronic applications accepted. *Expenses:* Tuition, area resident: Full-time $3,970; part-time $380 per credit. Tuition, state resident: full-time $5,955; part-time $380 per credit. Tuition, nonresident: full-time $11,061; part-time $380 per credit. Required fees: $3,189. One-time fee: $62 part-time. Tuition and fees vary according to degree level and program. *Financial support:* In 2006–07, 3 students received support; research assistantships, career-related internships or fieldwork, Federal Work-Study, scholarships/grants, and unspecified assistantships available. Support available to part-time students. Financial award application deadline: 3/1; financial award applicants required to submit FAFSA. *Faculty research:* Learning disabilities/language development, consulting teacher practice, occupational/special education, teaching emotionally disturbed students. *Unit head:* Dr. Mitchell Beck, Chair, 860-832-2400.

Central Michigan University, College of Graduate Studies, College of Education and Human Services, Department of Counseling and Special Education, Program in Special Education, Mount Pleasant, MI 48859. Offers MA. *Accreditation:* NCATE. *Degree requirements:* For master's, thesis or alternative, registration. *Entrance requirements:* For master's, MAT, minimum undergraduate GPA of 2.75, teaching certificate. *Faculty research:* Mainstreaming, learning disabled, attention and organization disorders.

Central Washington University, Graduate Studies, Research and Continuing Education, College of Education and Professional Studies, Department of Education, Program in Special Education, Ellensburg, WA 98926. Offers M Ed. Part-time programs available. *Faculty:* 21 full-time (10 women). *Students:* 1 (woman) full-time, 1 part-time. 3 applicants, 100% accepted, 2 enrolled. In 2006, 3 degrees awarded. *Degree requirements:* For master's, thesis or alternative. *Entrance requirements:* For master's, minimum GPA of 3.0. Additional exam requirements/recommendations for international students: Required—TOEFL (minimum score 550 paper-based; 213 computer-based; 79 iBT). *Application deadline:* For fall admission, 4/1 priority date for domestic students; for winter admission, 10/1 for domestic students; for spring admission, 1/1 for domestic students. Applications are processed on a rolling basis. Application fee: $50. *Expenses:* Tuition, state resident: full-time $6,312. Tuition, nonresident: full-time $14,112. Tuition and fees vary according to course load and degree level. *Financial support:* Research assistantships with partial tuition reimbursements, teaching assistantships, Federal Work-Study, health care benefits, and unspecified assistantships available. Financial award application deadline: 3/1; financial award applicants required to submit FAFSA. *Application contact:* Justine Eason, Admissions Program Coordinator, 509-963-3103, Fax: 509-963-1799, E-mail: masters@cwu.edu.

Chapman University, Graduate Studies, School of Education, Program in Special Education, Orange, CA 92866. Offers MA. Part-time and evening/weekend programs available. *Faculty:* 16 full-time (11 women), 25 part-time/adjunct (14 women). *Students:* 15 full-time (13 women), 47 part-time (38 women); includes 12 minority (3 Asian Americans or Pacific Islanders, 9 Hispanic Americans). Average age 33. 26 applicants, 73% accepted, 16 enrolled. In 2006, 19 degrees awarded. *Degree requirements:* For master's, thesis optional. *Entrance requirements:* For master's, GRE General Test, MAT, or California Subject Examinations for Teachers, minimum undergraduate GPA of 2.5. Additional exam requirements/recommendations for international students: Required—TOEFL (minimum score 550 paper-based). *Application deadline:* Applications are processed on a rolling basis. Application fee: $55. Electronic applications accepted. *Expenses: Contact institution. Financial support:* In 2006–07, 57 students received support, including 1 fellowship (averaging $2,000 per year); Federal Work-Study also available. Financial award application deadline: 6/30; financial award applicants required to submit FAFSA. *Unit head:* Dr. Dawn Hunter, Coordinator, 714-997-6781. *Application contact:* Rika Judd, Information Contact, 714-997-6786, Fax: 714-997-6713, E-mail: rjudd@chapman.edu.

Chatham University, Program in Education, Pittsburgh, PA 15232-2826. Offers early childhood education (MAT); elementary education (MAT); English—secondary (MAT); environmental education (K-12) (MAT); secondary art (MAT); secondary biology education (MAT); secondary chemistry education (MAT); secondary English education (MAT); secondary math education (MAT); secondary physics education (MAT); secondary social studies education (MAT); special education (MAT). *Students:* 60 full-time (43 women), 23 part-time (22 women). Average age 29. 48 applicants, 77% accepted, 32 enrolled. In 2006, 59 degrees awarded. *Degree requirements:* For master's, thesis, teaching experience. *Entrance requirements:* For master's, PRAXIS I, minimum GPA of 3.0, sample of written work, recommendation letters. Additional exam requirements/recommendations for international students: Required—TOEFL (minimum score 600 paper-based; 250 computer-based; 100 iBT). Recommended—IELTS (minimum score 7), TWE (minimum score 5). *Application deadline:* For fall admission, 5/1 priority date for domestic and international students; for winter admission, 10/1 priority date for domestic and international students. Applications are processed on a rolling basis. Application fee: $45. Electronic applications accepted. *Financial support:* Career-related internships or fieldwork available. Financial award applicants required to submit FAFSA. *Faculty research:*

Gifted education, environmental education, technology in education, writing as learning, class size and achievement. *Unit head:* Dr. Wendy Weiner, Director, 412-365-1146, Fax: 412-365-1505, E-mail: wweiner@chatham.edu. *Application contact:* 412-365-1825, Fax: 412-365-1609, E-mail: admissions@chatham.edu.

Cheyney University of Pennsylvania, School of Education, Program in Special Education, Cheyney, PA 19319-0200. Offers M Ed. MS. *Accreditation:* NCATE. Part-time and evening/weekend programs available. *Degree requirements:* For master's, thesis or alternative. *Entrance requirements:* For master's, GRE General Test, MAT, minimum GPA of 2.75. Electronic applications accepted.

Chicago State University, School of Graduate and Professional Studies, College of Education, Department of Special Education, Early Childhood Education and Bilingual Education, Program in Special Education, Chicago, IL 60628. Offers M Ed. *Accreditation:* NCATE. *Degree requirements:* For master's, thesis optional. *Entrance requirements:* For master's, minimum GPA of 2.75. *Faculty research:* Assistive technology, teacher efficiency.

City College of the City University of New York, Graduate School, School of Education, Program in Teaching Students with Disabilities, New York, NY 10031-9198. Offers MA. *Accreditation:* NCATE. *Students:* 9 full-time (6 women), 238 part-time (154 women); includes 200 minority (79 African Americans, 39 Asian Americans or Pacific Islanders, 82 Hispanic Americans), 9 international. 104 applicants, 98% accepted, 57 enrolled. In 2006, 106 degrees awarded. *Degree requirements:* For master's, thesis. *Entrance requirements:* For master's, Liberal Arts and Sciences Test (LAST), Content Specialty Test (CST). Additional exam requirements/recommendations for international students: Required—TOEFL. *Application deadline:* For fall admission, 3/15 for domestic students; for spring admission, 10/15 for domestic students. Application fee: $125. *Financial support:* Application deadline: 5/1. *Unit head:* Joseph Jiggetts, Head, 212-650-7986, E-mail: jjiggetts@ccny.cuny.edu. *Application contact:* Stacia Pusey, Graduate Admissions Adviser-Education, 212-650-5345, E-mail: spusey@ccny.cuny.edu.

Clarion University of Pennsylvania, Office of Research and Graduate Studies, College of Education and Human Services, Department of Special Education and Rehabilitative Sciences, Clarion, PA 16214. Offers rehabilitative sciences (MS); special education (MS). *Accreditation:* NCATE. Part-time programs available. *Faculty:* 11 full-time (5 women). *Students:* 2 applicants, 100% accepted. In 2006, 2 degrees awarded. *Degree requirements:* For master's, thesis or alternative. *Entrance requirements:* For master's, GRE General Test or MAT, minimum QPA of 3.0. Additional exam requirements/recommendations for international students: Required—TOEFL (minimum score 550 paper-based; 213 computer-based; 80 iBT). *Application deadline:* For fall admission, 8/1 priority date for domestic students, 4/15 priority date for international students; for spring admission, 12/1 priority date for domestic students, 9/15 priority date for international students. Applications are processed on a rolling basis. Application fee: $30. *Expenses:* Tuition, state resident: part-time $336 per credit. Tuition, nonresident: part-time $538 per credit. *Financial support:* In 2006–07, 2 research assistantships with full and partial tuition reimbursements (averaging $2,001 per year) were awarded. Support available to part-time students. Financial award application deadline: 3/1. *Unit head:* Dr. James Krouse, Chair, 814-393-2325, Fax: 814-393-1951, E-mail: jkrouse@clarion.edu. *Application contact:* Dr. Lorie Taylor, Graduate Program Coordinator, 814-393-2480, Fax: 814-393-1951, E-mail: ltaylor@clarion.edu.

Clarke College, Program in Education, Dubuque, IA 52001-3198. Offers early childhood/special education (MA); educational administration: elementary and secondary (MA); educational media: elementary and secondary (MA); multi-categorical resource K–12 (MA); multidisciplinary studies (MA); reading: elementary (MA); technology in education (MA). Part-time and evening/weekend programs available. Postbaccalaureate distance learning degree programs offered (minimal on-campus study). *Degree requirements:* For master's, thesis optional. *Entrance requirements:* For master's, GRE General Test or MAT, minimum GPA of 2.75. Electronic applications accepted.

Clemson University, Graduate School, College of Health, Education, and Human Development, School of Education, Program in Special Education, Clemson, SC 29634. Offers M Ed. *Accreditation:* NCATE. Part-time and evening/weekend programs available. *Students:* 2 full-time (both women), 24 part-time (23 women); includes 1 minority (Hispanic American) 6 applicants, 50% accepted, 3 enrolled. In 2006, 5 degrees awarded. *Entrance requirements:* For master's, GRE or minimum GPA of 3.0, teaching certificate. Additional exam requirements/recommendations for international students: Required—TOEFL. *Application deadline:* For fall admission, 6/1 for domestic students. Application fee: $50. *Expenses:* Tuition, state resident: full-time $8,812; part-time $450 per hour. Tuition, nonresident: full-time $18,036; part-time $760 per hour. Required fees: $474; $5 per term. *Financial support:* Research assistantships, teaching assistantships, career-related internships or fieldwork, Federal Work-Study, tuition waivers (full), and stipends available. Support available to part-time students. Financial award application deadline: 6/1; financial award applicants required to submit FAFSA. *Faculty research:* Field-based teacher training transition, assessment, national policy outcome. Total annual research expenditures: $250,000. *Unit head:* Dr. Antonis Katsiyammis, Graduate Coordinator, 864-656-5119.

See Close-Up on page 1365.

Cleveland State University, College of Graduate Studies, College of Education and Human Services, Department of Teacher Education, Cleveland, OH 44115. Offers art education (M Ed); early childhood education (M Ed); foreign language education (M Ed); mathematics and science education (M Ed); middle childhood education (M Ed); special education (M Ed), including mild/moderate disabilities, moderate/intensive disabilities; teaching English to speakers of other languages (M Ed). Part-time and evening/weekend programs available. *Faculty:* 14 full-time (8 women), 5 part-time/adjunct (4 women). *Students:* 120 full-time (96 women), 592 part-time (485 women); includes 145 minority (123 African Americans, 7 Asian Americans or Pacific Islanders, 15 Hispanic Americans), 7 international. Average age 34. 526 applicants, 41% accepted, 144 enrolled. In 2006, 324 degrees awarded. *Degree requirements:* For master's, thesis or alternative, comprehensive exam (for some programs). *Entrance requirements:* For master's, GRE General Test or MAT, minimum GPA of 2.75. Additional exam requirements/recommendations for international students: Required—TOEFL (minimum score 525 paper-based; 197 computer-based), IELTS (minimum score 6). *Application deadline:* For fall admission, 7/15 priority date for domestic students. Applications are processed on a rolling basis. Application fee: $30. *Financial support:* In 2006–07, 12 research assistantships with full tuition reimbursements (averaging $3,480 per year) were awarded; tuition waivers (partial) and unspecified assistantships also available. *Faculty research:* Early literacy, professional development in reading, reading recovery, dual language, induction programs. Total annual research expenditures: $6.2 million. *Unit head:* Dr. Clifford T. Bennett, Chairperson, 216-523-7105, Fax: 216-687-5379, E-mail: c.t.bennett@csuohio.edu.

College of Charleston, Graduate School, School of Education, Department of Foundations, Secondary, and Special Education, Program in Special Education, Charleston, SC 29424-0001. Offers M Ed. *Entrance requirements:* For master's, GRE. Additional exam requirements/recommendations for international students: Required—TOEFL. Electronic applications accepted.

The College of New Jersey, Graduate Division, School of Education, Department of Special Education, Language and Literacy, Program in Special Education, Ewing, NJ 08628. Offers M Ed, MAT. *Accreditation:* NCATE. *Students:* 19 full-time (16 women), 74 part-time (66 women); includes 12 minority (6 African Americans, 4 Asian Americans or Pacific Islanders, 2 Hispanic Americans). 34 applicants, 91% accepted. In 2006, 29 degrees awarded. *Degree requirements:* For master's, comprehensive exam. *Entrance requirements:* For master's, GRE General Test, minimum GPA of 3.0 in field or 2.75 overall. Additional exam requirements/recommendations for international students: Required—TOEFL. *Application deadline:* For fall admission, 4/15 for domestic students; for spring admission, 10/15 for domestic students.

Special Education

The College of New Jersey (continued)

Application fee: $60. Electronic applications accepted. *Financial support:* Unspecified assistantships available. Financial award application deadline: 5/1; financial award applicants required to submit FAFSA. *Unit head:* Dr. Shndevi Rao, Coordinator, 609-771-2308. *Application contact:* Susan L. Hydro, Office of Graduate Studies, Assistant Dean, 609-771-2300, Fax: 609-637-5105, E-mail: graduate@tcnj.edu.

The College of New Jersey, Graduate Division, School of Education, Department of Special Education, Language and Literacy, Program in Special Education with Learning Disabilities, Ewing, NJ 08628. Offers Certificate. *Accreditation:* NCATE. *Students:* 10 applicants, 100% accepted. In 2006, 7 degrees awarded. *Entrance requirements:* Additional exam requirements/recommendations for international students: Required—TOEFL. *Application deadline:* For fall admission, 4/15 for domestic students; for spring admission, 10/15 for domestic students. Application fee: $60. Electronic applications accepted. *Financial support:* Application deadline: 5/1; *Unit head:* Dr. Shndevi Rao, Coordinator, 609-771-2308. *Application contact:* Susan L. Hydro, Office of Graduate Studies, Assistant Dean, 609-771-2300, Fax: 609-637-5105, E-mail: graduate@tcnj.edu.

The College of New Rochelle, Graduate School, Division of Education, Program in Special Education, New Rochelle, NY 10805-2308. Offers MS Ed. Part-time programs available. *Faculty:* 3 full-time (2 women), 8 part-time/adjunct (6 women). *Students:* 31 full-time (29 women), 140 part-time (130 women); includes 26 minority (18 African Americans, 2 American Indian/Alaska Native, 2 Asian Americans or Pacific Islanders, 4 Hispanic Americans), 1 international. Average age 31. In 2006, 22 degrees awarded. *Degree requirements:* For master's, practicum. *Entrance requirements:* For master's, interview, minimum GPA of 3.0 in field, 2.7 overall. *Application deadline:* For fall admission, 8/1 priority date for domestic students; for spring admission, 4/6 for domestic students. Applications are processed on a rolling basis. Application fee: $35. *Expenses:* Tuition: Part-time $575 per credit. Required fees: $90 per term. *Financial support:* Scholarships/grants and unspecified assistantships available. *Unit head:* Dr. Marie Ribarich, Acting Division Head, Division of Education, 914-654-5333, Fax: 914-654-5593, E-mail: mribarich@cnr.edu.

College of St. Joseph, Graduate Program, Division of Education, Program in Special Education, Rutland, VT 05701-3899. Offers M Ed. Part-time and evening/weekend programs available. *Faculty:* 3 full-time (2 women), 8 part-time/adjunct (5 women). *Students:* 16. Average age 33. 8 applicants, 75% accepted, 5 enrolled. In 2006, 15 degrees awarded. *Degree requirements:* For master's, comprehensive exam, registration. *Entrance requirements:* For master's, PRAXIS I (for initial licensure), interview, 2 letters of reference, minimum GPA of 3.0 (initial licensure) or 2.7 (nonlicensure). *Application deadline:* Applications are processed on a rolling basis. Application fee: $35. *Expenses:* Tuition: Full-time $10,990; part-time $300 per credit. Part-time tuition and fees vary according to program. *Financial support:* Career-related internships or fieldwork, Federal Work-Study, and unspecified assistantships available. Support available to part-time students. Financial award application deadline: 3/1. *Application contact:* Tracy Gallipo, Director of Admissions, 802-773-5900 Ext. 3262, Fax: 802-773-5900, E-mail: tracygallipo@csj.edu.

The College of Saint Rose, Graduate Studies, School of Education, Reading/Special Education Department, Albany, NY 12203-1419. Offers literacy: birth-grade 6 (MS Ed); literacy: grades 5-12 (MS Ed); reading (Certificate), including literacy: birth—grade 6, literacy: grades 5-12; special education (MS Ed), including adolescent education, childhood education, special education advanced study. Part-time and evening/weekend programs available. *Entrance requirements:* For master's, minimum undergraduate GPA of 3.0. Additional exam requirements/recommendations for international students: Required—TOEFL (minimum score 550 paper-based; 213 computer-based). Electronic applications accepted.

College of Santa Fe, Department of Education, Santa Fe, NM 87505-7634. Offers at-risk youth (MA), including bilingual/multicultural education, classroom teaching, community counseling, educational administration, leadership, school counseling, self-designed program, TESOL/Multicultural; curriculum and instruction (MA); multicultural special education (MA). Part-time and evening/weekend programs available. *Entrance requirements:* For master's, minimum GPA of 3.0. *Faculty research:* Integrated curriculum, child development, brain research, learning styles, systemic issues in education.

College of Staten Island of the City University of New York, Graduate Programs, Department of Education, Program in Special Education, Staten Island, NY 10314-6600. Offers MS Ed. Evening/weekend programs available. *Faculty:* 3 full-time (all women), 4 part-time/adjunct (all women). *Students:* 7 full-time (5 women), 90 part-time (86 women); includes 9 minority (1 African American, 1 American Indian/Alaska Native, 1 Asian American or Pacific Islander, 6 Hispanic Americans). Average age 31. 45 applicants, 91% accepted, 33 enrolled. In 2006, 67 degrees awarded. *Degree requirements:* For master's, research project. *Entrance requirements:* For master's, minimum GPA of 3.0, 2 letters of recommendation. Additional exam requirements/recommendations for international students: Required—TOEFL (minimum score 550 paper-based; 213 computer-based; 79 iBT). *Application deadline:* For fall admission, 4/28 priority date for domestic and international students; for spring admission, 11/19 priority date for domestic and international students. Applications are processed on a rolling basis. Application fee: $125. *Expenses:* Tuition, state resident: full-time $6,400; part-time $270 per credit. Tuition, nonresident: part-time $500 per credit. Required fees: $53 per semester. *Financial support:* Career-related internships or fieldwork, Federal Work-Study, and scholarships/grants available. Financial award applicants required to submit FAFSA. *Unit head:* Dr. Effie Simmonds, Coordinator, 718-982-3742, Fax: 718-982-3743, E-mail: simmonds@mail.csi.cuny.edu. *Application contact:* Emmanuel Esperance, Deputy Director of Office of Recruitment and Admissions, 718-982-2190, Fax: 718-982-2500, E-mail: admissions@mail.csi.cuny.edu.

The College of William and Mary, School of Education, Program in Curriculum and Instruction, Williamsburg, VA 23187-8795. Offers elementary education (MA Ed); gifted education (MA Ed); reading education (MA Ed); secondary education (MA Ed), including English education, mathematics education, modern foreign languages education, science education, social studies education; special education (MA Ed), including emotionally disturbed, learning disabled, mental retardation, resource collaborating teaching. *Accreditation:* NCATE. Part-time programs available. *Faculty:* 15 full-time (6 women), 13 part-time/adjunct (10 women). *Students:* 51 full-time (39 women), 51 part-time (45 women); includes 6 minority (all African Americans) Average age 29. 161 applicants, 68% accepted, 61 enrolled. In 2006, 68 degrees awarded. *Degree requirements:* For master's, master's project. *Entrance requirements:* For master's, GRE or MAT, minimum GPA of 2.5. Additional exam requirements/recommendations for international students: Required—TOEFL. *Application deadline:* For fall admission, 2/1 for domestic and international students; for spring admission, 10/1 for domestic and international students. Application fee: $30. *Expenses:* Tuition, state resident: full-time $6,100; part-time $260 per credit. Tuition, nonresident: full-time $18,790; part-time $725 per credit. Required fees: $3,314. Tuition and fees vary according to program. *Financial support:* In 2006–07, 10 research assistantships with full and partial tuition reimbursements (averaging $5,000 per year) were awarded; career-related internships or fieldwork, Federal Work-Study, institutionally sponsored loans, scholarships/grants, and unspecified assistantships also available. Financial award application deadline: 2/1; financial award applicants required to submit FAFSA. *Faculty research:* National Council of Teachers of Mathematics Standards, counseling, self-concept and self-esteem, special education, curriculum development. *Unit head:* Dr. John Moore, Area Coordinator, 757-221-2333, E-mail: jnmoor@wm.edu. *Application contact:* Dorothy Osborne, Director of Admissions, 757-221-2317, E-mail: dsosbo@wm.edu.

Columbia International University, Columbia Graduate School, Columbia, SC 29230-3122. Offers Bible teaching (MABT); Christian higher education leadership (Ed D); Christian school educational leadership (Ed D); counseling (MACN); curriculum and instruction (M Ed), including Christian school guidance, English as a second language, learning disabilities, school technology; early childhood and elementary education (MAT); educational administration (M Ed); teaching English as a foreign language (Certificate); teaching English as a foreign language and intercultural studies (MATF). Part-time and evening/weekend programs available. *Faculty:* 11 full-time (4 women), 7 part-time/adjunct (5 women). *Students:* 52 full-time (44 women), 93 part-time (59 women); includes 17 minority (11 African Americans, 2 Asian Americans or Pacific Islanders, 4 Hispanic Americans), 10 international. Average age 35. 107 applicants, 56% accepted, 41 enrolled. In 2006, 62 degrees awarded. *Degree requirements:* For master's, internships, professional project. *Entrance requirements:* For master's, Minnesota Multiphasic Personality Inventory, MAT, minimum GPA of 2.7. Additional exam requirements/recommendations for international students: Required—TOEFL. *Application deadline:* For fall admission, 8/1 priority date for domestic and international students; for winter admission, 12/15 priority date for domestic and international students; for spring admission, 1/15 priority date for domestic and international students. Applications are processed on a rolling basis. Application fee: $45. Electronic applications accepted. *Expenses:* Tuition: Part-time $400 per semester hour. Tuition and fees vary according to course load and program. *Financial support:* In 2006–07, 35 students received support. Career-related internships or fieldwork, Federal Work-Study, institutionally sponsored loans, and scholarships/grants available. Financial award application deadline: 3/17; financial award applicants required to submit FAFSA. *Unit head:* Dr. Milton Uecker, Dean, 803-807-5319, Fax: 803-786-4209, E-mail: muecker@ciu.edu. *Application contact:* Michelle MacGregor, Director of Admissions, 800-777-2227 Ext. 5335, Fax: 803-786-4209, E-mail: yescbs@ciu.edu.

Columbus State University, Graduate Studies, College of Education, Department of Teacher Education, Columbus, GA 31907-5645. Offers early childhood education (M Ed, Ed S); instructional technology (MS); middle grades education (M Ed, Ed S); physical education (M Ed); secondary education (M Ed, Ed S), including English/language arts, general science (M Ed), mathematics, science (Ed S), social science; special education (Ed S), including behavior disorders, learning disabilities, mental retardation. *Accreditation:* NCATE. Part-time and evening/weekend programs available. Postbaccalaureate distance learning degree programs offered (minimal on-campus study). *Faculty:* 16 full-time (8 women), 2 part-time/adjunct (1 woman). *Students:* 61 full-time (45 women), 128 part-time (89 women); includes 44 minority (36 African Americans, 3 Asian Americans or Pacific Islanders, 5 Hispanic Americans), 1 international. Average age 36. 77 applicants, 49% accepted, 26 enrolled. In 2006, 66 master's, 13 other advanced degrees awarded. *Degree requirements:* For master's, thesis, exit exam; for Ed S, thesis or alternative. *Entrance requirements:* For master's, GRE General Test, minimum GPA of 2.75; for Ed S, GRE General Test. Additional exam requirements/recommendations for international students: Required—TOEFL (minimum score 550 paper-based; 213 computer-based). *Application deadline:* For fall admission, 5/1 priority date for domestic students, 5/1 for international students; for spring admission, 11/1 for domestic and international students. Applications are processed on a rolling basis. Application fee: $25. Electronic applications accepted. *Expenses:* Tuition, state resident: part-time $127 per semester hour. Tuition, nonresident: part-time $508 per semester hour. Required fees: $264 per semester. Tuition and fees vary according to course load. *Financial support:* In 2006–07, 118 students received support, including 21 research assistantships with partial tuition reimbursements available (averaging $3,000 per year); career-related internships or fieldwork, Federal Work-Study, institutionally sponsored loans, scholarships/grants, tuition waivers (partial), and unspecified assistantships also available. Support available to part-time students. Financial award application deadline: 5/1; financial award applicants required to submit FAFSA. *Unit head:* Dr. Deborah Gober, Acting Chair, 706-568-2255, Fax: 706-568-3134, E-mail: gober_deborah@colstate.edu. *Application contact:* Katie Thornton, Graduate Admissions Specialist, 706-568-2035, Fax: 706-568-2462, E-mail: thornton_katie@colstate.edu.

Concordia University, St. Paul, College of Education, St. Paul, MN 55104-5494. Offers differentiated instruction (MA Ed); early childhood (MA Ed); family life education (MAHS); special education (Certificate). *Accreditation:* NCATE. Evening/weekend programs available. Postbaccalaureate distance learning degree programs offered (minimal on-campus study). *Faculty:* 8 full-time (7 women), 12 part-time/adjunct (7 women). *Students:* 101 full-time (95 women), 10 part-time (9 women); includes 29 minority (21 African Americans, 1 American Indian/Alaska Native, 6 Asian Americans or Pacific Islanders, 1 Hispanic American). Average age 34. In 2006, 59 master's, 8 other advanced degrees awarded. *Entrance requirements:* Additional exam requirements/recommendations for international students: Required—TOEFL. *Application deadline:* Applications are processed on a rolling basis. Application fee: $50. Electronic applications accepted. *Unit head:* Prof. Lonn Maly, Dean, 651-641-8278, Fax: 651-641-8807, E-mail: maly@csp.edu. *Application contact:* Kimberly Craig, Director of Graduate and Cohort Admission, 651-603-6223, Fax: 651-603-6320, E-mail: craig@csp.edu.

Concordia University Wisconsin, Graduate Programs, Department of Education, Mequon, WI 53097-2402. Offers art education (MS Ed); curriculum and instruction (MS Ed); early childhood (MS Ed); educational administration (MS Ed); environmental education (MS Ed); family studies (MS Ed); reading (MS Ed); school counseling (MS Ed); special education (MS Ed). Part-time and evening/weekend programs available. Postbaccalaureate distance learning degree programs offered (minimal on-campus study). *Faculty:* 30. *Students:* 396 (284 women). In 2006, 51 degrees awarded. *Degree requirements:* For master's, thesis or alternative, comprehensive exam. *Entrance requirements:* For master's, minimum GPA of 3.0, teaching license. Additional exam requirements/recommendations for international students: Required—TOEFL. Application fee: $35. *Financial support:* Career-related internships or fieldwork and tuition waivers (partial) available. Financial award application deadline: 8/1. *Faculty research:* Motivation, developmental learning, learning styles. *Unit head:* Dr. James Juergensen, Director, 262-243-4214, E-mail: james.juergensen@cuw.edu. *Application contact:* Graduate Admissions, 262-243-4248, Fax: 262-243-4428.

Converse College, School of Education and Graduate Studies, Program in Special Education, Spartanburg, SC 29302-0006. Offers learning disabilities (MAT); mental disabilities (MAT); special education (M Ed). Part-time programs available. *Faculty:* 3 full-time, 2 part-time/adjunct. *Students:* Average age 35. In 2006, 20 degrees awarded. *Degree requirements:* For master's, capstone paper. *Entrance requirements:* For master's, NTE or PRAXIS II (M Ed), minimum GPA of 2.75, 2 recommendations. *Application deadline:* For fall admission, 8/1 for domestic and international students; for winter admission, 11/15 for domestic and international students; for spring admission, 1/15 for domestic and international students. Applications are processed on a rolling basis. Application fee: $40. Electronic applications accepted. *Expenses:* Tuition: Part-time $305 per credit hour. Required fees: $20 per term. *Financial support:* Available to part-time students. Applicants required to submit FAFSA. *Unit head:* Dr. Ansley H. Boggs, Director of Special Education Program, 864-596-9084, E-mail: ansley.boggs@converse.edu. *Application contact:* Thomas M. Faulkenberry, Dean of the School of Education and Graduate Studies, 864-596-9082, Fax: 864-596-9221, E-mail: tom.faulkenberry@converse.edu.

Coppin State University, Division of Graduate Studies, Division of Education, Department o Special Education, Baltimore, MD 21216-3698. Offers M Ed. Part-time and evening/weekenc programs available. *Faculty:* 7 full-time (3 women). *Students:* 16 full-time (10 women), 35 part-time (26 women); includes 45 minority (all African Americans), 2 international. Average age 38. 22 applicants, 86% accepted, 18 enrolled. In 2006, 6 degrees awarded. *Degree requirements:* For master's, exit portfolio. *Entrance requirements:* For master's, PRAXIS I minimum GPA of 3.0, interview, writing sample, resumé, references. *Application deadline:* Fo fall admission, 8/15 priority date for domestic students; for spring admission, 12/15 priority date for domestic students. Applications are processed on a rolling basis. Application fee: $45 *Financial support:* Career-related internships or fieldwork, Federal Work-Study, institutionally sponsored loans, and scholarships/grants available. Support available to part-time students Financial award application deadline: 6/30; financial award applicants required to submit FAFSA *Faculty research:* Survey of colleges and universities in Maryland with programs for the learning disabled. *Unit head:* Dr. Thaddeus Phillips, Chair, 410-951-3023, Fax: 410-951-3544 E-mail: tphillips@coppin.edu.

Creighton University, Graduate School, College of Arts and Sciences, Department of Educa tion, Program in Special Populations in Education, Omaha, NE 68178-0001. Offers MS

Part-time and evening/weekend programs available. *Students:* 1 applicant, 100% accepted, 1 enrolled. *Entrance requirements:* For master's, GRE, 3 letters of recommendation. Additional exam requirements/recommendations for international students: Required—TOEFL (minimum score 550 paper-based; 213 computer-based; 80 iBT). *Application deadline:* For fall admission, 7/1 priority date for domestic and international students; for winter admission, 12/1 priority date for domestic and international students; for spring admission, 4/1 priority date for domestic and international students. Applications are processed on a rolling basis. Application fee: $40. Electronic applications accepted. *Expenses:* Tuition: Part-time $595 per credit hour. Required fees: $38 per semester. *Financial support:* Tuition waivers (partial) available. Financial award applicants required to submit FAFSA. *Unit head:* Dr. Sharon Ishii-Jordan, Director, 402-280-2553, E-mail: sharonishii-jordan@creighton.edu. *Application contact:* LuAnn M. Schwery, Coordinator of Graduate Programs, 402-280-2870, Fax: 402-280-5762, E-mail: lschwery@creighton.edu.

Curry College, Division of Continuing Education and Graduate Studies, Program in Education, Milton, MA 02186-9984. Offers adult education (Certificate); educational administration (M Ed); educational therapy (Certificate); elementary education (M Ed); foundations (non-license) (M Ed); learning disabilities across the lifespan (Certificate); reading (M Ed, Certificate); special education (M Ed). Part-time and evening/weekend programs available. *Faculty:* 6 full-time (4 women), 11 part-time/adjunct (7 women). *Degree requirements:* For master's, research project. *Entrance requirements:* For master's, MAT, interview, recommendations, resumé. Additional exam requirements/recommendations for international students: Required—TOEFL (minimum score 550 paper-based). *Application deadline:* For fall admission, 8/1 priority date for domestic students; for spring admission, 1/1 for domestic students. Applications are processed on a rolling basis. Application fee: $50. *Expenses: Contact institution. Financial support:* Career-related internships or fieldwork and tuition waivers (partial) available. *Faculty research:* Classroom trauma, therapeutic writing, inclusionary practices. *Unit head:* Dr. Donald Gratz, Director and Associate Professor, 617-333-2243, E-mail: dgratz0703@curry.edu. *Application contact:* John Bresnahan, Director of Graduate Enrollment and Student Services, 617-333-2243, Fax: 617-333-2045, E-mail: jbresnah0104@curry.edu.

Daemen College, Education Department, Amherst, NY 14226-3592. Offers adolescence education (MS); childhood education (MS); childhood special education (MS). Part-time programs available. *Faculty:* 5 full-time (4 women), 53 part-time/adjunct (45 women). *Students:* 263 full-time (224 women), 238 part-time (202 women); includes 1 minority (African American), 192 international. Average age 33. 314 applicants, 71% accepted, 184 enrolled. In 2006, 284 degrees awarded. *Degree requirements:* For master's, thesis, registration. *Entrance requirements:* For master's, GRE, minimum GPA of 3.0, 3 letters of recommendation, proof of initial certification for licensure. Additional exam requirements/recommendations for international students: Required—TOEFL (minimum score 500 paper-based; 173 computer-based). *Application deadline:* For fall admission, 3/1 priority date for domestic and international students; for spring admission, 10/1 priority date for domestic and international students. Applications are processed on a rolling basis. Application fee: $25. Electronic applications accepted. *Expenses:* Tuition: Full-time $11,700; part-time $650 per credit hour. Required fees: $15 per credit hour. Tuition and fees vary according to course load. *Financial support:* In 2006–07, 48 students received support. Federal Work-Study, institutionally sponsored loans, traineeships, and tuition waivers (partial) available. Support available to part-time students. Financial award application deadline: 2/15; financial award applicants required to submit FAFSA. *Faculty research:* Transition for students with disabilities, early childhood special education, traumatic brain injury (TBI), reading assessment. *Unit head:* Dr. Mary H. Fox, Chair, 716-839-8530, Fax: 716-839-8516, E-mail: mfox@daemen.edu. *Application contact:* Karl Shallowhorn, Associate Director of Graduate Admissions, 716-839-8225, Fax: 716-839-8229, E-mail: kshallow@daemen.edu.

Delaware State University, Graduate Programs, Department of Education, Program in Special Education, Dover, DE 19901-2277. Offers MA. Part-time and evening/weekend programs available. *Degree requirements:* For master's, thesis optional. *Entrance requirements:* For master's, GRE General Test, minimum GPA of 3.0 in field, 2.75 overall. Electronic applications accepted. *Faculty research:* Curriculum and instruction, distributive education.

Delta State University, Graduate Programs, College of Education, Division of Teacher Education, Program in Special Education, Cleveland, MS 38733-0001. Offers M Ed. *Accreditation:* NCATE. Part-time and evening/weekend programs available. *Degree requirements:* For master's, practicum, thesis optional. *Application deadline:* For fall admission, 8/1 priority date for domestic students; for spring admission, 12/1 priority date for domestic students. Applications are processed on a rolling basis. Application fee: $0. *Financial support:* Research assistantships, career-related internships or fieldwork, Federal Work-Study, and institutionally sponsored loans available. Support available to part-time students. Financial award application deadline: 6/1.

DePaul University, School of Education, Chicago, IL 60604-2287. Offers bilingual and bicultural education (M Ed, MA); curriculum studies (M Ed, MA); education (Ed D), including curriculum studies, educational leadership; educational leadership (M Ed, MA), including administration and supervision, Catholic school leadership, physical education; human development and learning (MA); human services and counseling (M Ed, MA), including agencies, family concerns, and higher education, elementary schools, human services management, secondary schools; reading and learning disabilities (M Ed, MA); social culture studies in education and development (M Ed, MA), including curriculum studies/development; teaching and learning (early childhood, elementary and secondary) (M Ed), including elementary education (M Ed, MA), secondary education (M Ed, MA); teaching and learning (early childhood, elementary, and secondary) (MA), including elementary education (M Ed, MA), secondary education (M Ed, MA). *Accreditation:* NCATE. Part-time and evening/weekend programs available. *Faculty:* 61 full-time (40 women), 76 part-time/adjunct (46 women). *Students:* 1,371 full-time (1,103 women), 474 part-time (362 women); includes 435 minority (144 African Americans, 7 American Indian/Alaska Native, 89 Asian Americans or Pacific Islanders, 195 Hispanic Americans), 11 international. Average age 30. 993 applicants, 80% accepted, 617 enrolled. In 2006, 324 master's, 7 doctorates awarded. *Degree requirements:* For doctorate, thesis/dissertation. *Entrance requirements:* For master's, interview, minimum GPA of 2.75, 2 letters of recommendation; for doctorate, interview, master's degree, 2 years of work experience (recommended), writing sample, 3 letters of recommendation. Application fee: $25. Electronic applications accepted. *Financial support:* In 2006–07, 16 research assistantships with tuition reimbursements (averaging $4,370 per year), 1 teaching assistantship (averaging $6,000 per year) were awarded; career-related internships or fieldwork also available. *Faculty research:* Reflective teaching, children at risk, loss, ethnicity, urban education. Total annual research expenditures: $556,194. *Unit head:* Dr. Clara Jennings, Dean, 773-325-7581, Fax: 773-325-7728, E-mail: cjennings@depaul.edu. *Application contact:* Dr. John Bollwark, Data Project Manager, 773-325-7582, Fax: 773-325-7713, E-mail: jbollwar@depaul.edu.

DeSales University, Graduate Division, Program in Education, Center Valley, PA 18034-9568. Offers academic standards and information (Certificate); bilingual/ESL studies (Certificate); biology (M Ed); chemistry (M Ed); computers in education (K-12) (M Ed); computers in education (K-8) (M Ed); English (M Ed); instructional technology specialist (Certificate); mathematics (M Ed); special education (M Ed, Certificate); TESOL (M Ed). Part-time and evening/weekend programs available. Postbaccalaureate distance learning degree programs offered (minimal on-campus study). *Students:* 34 full-time, 190 part-time. In 2006, 30 degrees awarded. *Degree requirements:* For master's, thesis project. *Entrance requirements:* For master's, teaching certificate. *Application deadline:* Applications are processed on a rolling basis. Application fee: $35. Electronic applications accepted. *Expenses: Contact institution. Financial support:* Unspecified assistantships available. Support available to part-time students. Financial award application deadline: 5/1. *Faculty research:* Effective teaching, computer interfacing in chemistry labs, computer applications to teaching, history of philosophy, aesthetics multidrug-resistant cancer. *Unit head:* Dr. Lujean Baab, Director of M.Ed. Program, 610-282-1100 Ext. 1739, Fax: 610-282-3734, E-mail: lujean.baab@desales.edu. *Application contact:* Donna L. Cressman, Program Secretary, 610-282-1100 Ext. 1461, Fax: 610-282-3734, E-mail: med@desales.edu.

Dominican College, Division of Teacher Education, Department of Teacher Education, Orangeburg, NY 10962-1210. Offers teacher of students with disabilities (MS Ed); teacher of visually impaired (MS Ed). Part-time and evening/weekend programs available. Postbaccalaureate distance learning degree programs offered (minimal on-campus study). *Faculty:* 2 full-time (both women), 6 part-time/adjunct (all women). *Students:* 1 (woman) full-time, 59 part-time (48 women); includes 10 minority (2 African Americans, 2 Asian Americans or Pacific Islanders, 6 Hispanic Americans). Average age 41. In 2006, 10 degrees awarded. *Degree requirements:* For master's, practicum, research project. *Entrance requirements:* For master's, interview, 3 letters of recommendation, minimum undergraduate GPA of 3.0. Additional exam requirements/recommendations for international students: Required—TOEFL (minimum score 550 paper-based; 213 computer-based). *Application deadline:* Applications are processed on a rolling basis. Application fee: $50. *Financial support:* Applicants required to submit FAFSA. *Unit head:* Dr. Rona Shaw, Program Director, 845-848-4081, Fax: 845-359-7802, E-mail: rona.shaw@dc.edu. *Application contact:* Director of Admissions, 845-848-7900, Fax: 845-365-3150, E-mail: admissions@dc.edu.

Dominican University, School of Education, River Forest, IL 60305-1099. Offers curriculum and instruction (MA Ed); early childhood education (MS); education (MAT); educational administration (MA); literacy (MS); special education (MS). Part-time and evening/weekend programs available. *Faculty:* 17 full-time (14 women), 37 part-time/adjunct (24 women). *Students:* 65 full-time (46 women), 514 part-time (425 women); includes 78 minority (23 African Americans, 16 Asian Americans or Pacific Islanders, 39 Hispanic Americans), 2 international. Average age 34. 130 applicants, 89% accepted, 100 enrolled. In 2006, 203 degrees awarded. *Entrance requirements:* For master's, Illinois certification test of basic skills. Additional exam requirements/recommendations for international students: Required—TOEFL (minimum score 550 paper-based; 213 computer-based). *Application deadline:* Applications are processed on a rolling basis. Application fee: $25. *Expenses: Contact institution.* Tuition and fees vary according to campus/location and program. *Financial support:* In 2006–07, 63 students received support. Career-related internships or fieldwork, scholarships/grants, and tuition waivers (partial) available. Support available to part-time students. Financial award application deadline: 8/15; financial award applicants required to submit FAFSA. *Faculty research:* Governance of private education institutions, reading and language arts, inclusion, organizational planning, leadership and vision. *Unit head:* Sr. Colleen McNicholas, Dean, 708-524-6830, Fax: 708-524-6665, E-mail: educate@dom.edu. *Application contact:* Keven Hansen, Coordinator of Admissions and Recruitment, 708-524-6921, Fax: 708-524-6665, E-mail: educate@dom.edu.

Dominican University of California, Graduate Programs, School of Business, Education and Leadership, Division of Education, Special Education Credential Program, San Rafael, CA 94901-2298. Offers Credential. *Entrance requirements:* Additional exam requirements/recommendations for international students: Required—TOEFL (minimum score 550 paper-based; 213 computer-based). Electronic applications accepted.

Dowling College, Graduate Programs in Education, Oakdale, NY 11769-1999. Offers educational administration (Ed D, PD), including computers in education (PD), educational administration (Ed D), school administration and supervision (PD), school district administration (PD); human development and learning (MS Ed); literacy (MS Ed); literacy/special education (MS Ed); secondary education (MS Ed); special education (MS Ed). *Accreditation:* NCATE. Part-time and evening/weekend programs available. Postbaccalaureate distance learning degree programs offered. *Faculty:* 29 full-time (13 women), 91 part-time/adjunct (60 women). *Students:* 496 full-time (364 women), 1,083 part-time (827 women); includes 119 minority (37 African Americans, 20 Asian Americans or Pacific Islanders, 62 Hispanic Americans), 2 international. Average age 38. 618 applicants, 86% accepted, 300 enrolled. In 2006, 641 master's, 25 doctorates awarded. *Degree requirements:* For master's and PD, comprehensive exam; for doctorate, thesis/dissertation. *Entrance requirements:* For master's, minimum GPA of 3.0; for doctorate, GRE, master's degree; for PD, teaching certificate. Additional exam requirements/recommendations for international students: Required—TOEFL (minimum score 550 paper-based). *Application deadline:* For fall admission, 9/1 priority date for domestic students; for winter admission, 1/1 priority date for domestic students; for spring admission, 2/1 priority date for domestic students. Applications are processed on a rolling basis. Application fee: $25. Electronic applications accepted. *Expenses:* Tuition: Full-time $16,008; part-time $667 per credit. Tuition and fees vary according to course load. *Financial support:* In 2006–07, 358 students received support, including 20 research assistantships with tuition reimbursements available (averaging $3,150 per year); career-related internships or fieldwork, Federal Work-Study, scholarships/grants, tuition waivers (partial), and unspecified assistantships also available. Support available to part-time students. Financial award application deadline: 6/30; financial award applicants required to submit FAFSA. *Faculty research:* Natural readers, Korean styles and learning strategies, mothers of children with disabilities, computers in instruction, cultural background and organizational roadblocks to problem solving. *Unit head:* Dr. Clyde Payne, Associate Provost, 631-244-3404, Fax: 631-589-6644, E-mail: paynec@dowling.edu. *Application contact:* Franks S. Pizzardi, Director of Admissions Operations, 631-244-3227, Fax: 631-244-1059, E-mail: pizzardf@dowling.edu.

Drake University, School of Education, Department of Teaching and Learning, Program in Special Education, Des Moines, IA 50311-4516. Offers MSE. Part-time programs available. *Faculty:* 10 full-time (3 women), 28 part-time/adjunct (16 women). *Students:* 25 applicants, 76% accepted. In 2006, 18 degrees awarded. *Degree requirements:* For master's, thesis (for some programs), internships (s), comprehensive exam, registration. *Entrance requirements:* For master's, GRE General Test, MAT, or Drake Writing Assessment, resumé, 2 letters of recommendation. Additional exam requirements/recommendations for international students: Required—TOEFL (minimum score 550 paper-based; 213 computer-based). *Application deadline:* For fall admission, 7/1 priority date for domestic students, 6/1 priority date for international students; for spring admission, 11/1 priority date for domestic students, 10/1 priority date for international students. Applications are processed on a rolling basis. Application fee: $25. Electronic applications accepted. *Financial support:* Career-related internships or fieldwork and unspecified assistantships available. Support available to part-time students. *Faculty research:* Counseling and rehabilitation, behavioral supports, inquiry-based science methods, teacher quality enhancement. Total annual research expenditures: $1.5 million. *Unit head:* Dr. Kathy Fejes, Advisor, 515-271-2168, E-mail: kathy.fejes@drake.edu. *Application contact:* Ann J. Martin, Graduate Coordinator, 515-271-2034, Fax: 515-271-2831, E-mail: ann.martin@drake.edu.

Duquesne University, School of Education, Department of Counseling, Psychology, and Special Education, Program in Special Education, Pittsburgh, PA 15282-0001. Offers MS Ed. Part-time and evening/weekend programs available. *Faculty:* 6 full-time (all women). *Students:* 27. Average age 31. 23 applicants, 39% accepted, 9 enrolled. In 2006, 24 degrees awarded. *Degree requirements:* For master's, thesis optional. *Entrance requirements:* For master's, MAT, minimum GPA of 3.0. Additional exam requirements/recommendations for international students: Required—TOEFL. *Application deadline:* For fall admission, 8/1 for domestic students; for spring admission, 12/1 for domestic students. Applications are processed on a rolling basis. Application fee: $50. *Expenses:* Tuition: Part-time $723 per credit. Required fees: $71 per credit. Tuition and fees vary according to degree level and program. *Financial support:* In 2006–07, 1 research assistantship with full and partial tuition reimbursement (averaging $5,200 per year) was awarded. Support available to part-time students. *Unit head:* Dr. Susan Munson, Director, 412-396-6097, E-mail: munson@duq.edu.

D'Youville College, Department of Education, Buffalo, NY 14201-1084. Offers elementary education (MS Ed, Teaching Certificate); secondary education (MS Ed, Teaching Certificate); special education (MS Ed). Part-time and evening/weekend programs available. *Faculty:* 31 full-time (18 women), 38 part-time/adjunct (25 women). *Students:* 613 full-time (434 women), 303 part-time (223 women); includes 26 minority (14 African Americans, 1 American Indian/

Special Education

D'Youville College (continued)
Alaska Native, 2 Asian Americans or Pacific Islanders, 9 Hispanic Americans), 727 international. Average age 28. 1,092 applicants. In 2006, 328 master's, 401 other advanced degrees awarded. *Degree requirements:* For master's, project or thesis. *Entrance requirements:* For master's, minimum GPA of 3.0. Additional exam requirements/recommendations for international students: Required—TOEFL (minimum score 500 paper-based; 173 computer-based). *Application deadline:* For fall admission, 5/1 priority date for international students; for spring admission, 9/1 priority date for international students. Applications are processed on a rolling basis. Application fee: $25. Electronic applications accepted. *Financial support:* In 2006–07, 1 research assistantship with partial tuition reimbursement (averaging $3,000 per year) was awarded; career-related internships or fieldwork and scholarships/grants also available. Support available to part-time students. Financial award application deadline: 3/1; financial award applicants required to submit FAFSA. *Faculty research:* Developmentally disabled, multiculturalism, early childhood education. *Unit head:* Dr. David Gorlewski, Chair, 716-829-8140, Fax: 716-829-7660. *Application contact:* Linda Fisher, Graduate Admissions Director, 716-829-8400, Fax: 716-829-7900, E-mail: graduateadmissions@dyc.edu.

East Carolina University, Graduate School, College of Education, Department of Curriculum and Instruction, Greenville, NC 27858-4353. Offers behavior/emotional disabilities (MA Ed); elementary education (MA Ed); English education (MA Ed); learning disabilities (MA Ed); low incidence disabilities (MA Ed); mental retardation (MA Ed); middle grade education (MA Ed); reading education (MA Ed); social studies education (MA Ed). Part-time programs available. Postbaccalaureate distance learning degree programs offered. *Students:* 92 full-time (85 women), 233 part-time (211 women); includes 42 minority (39 African Americans, 1 American Indian/Alaska Native, 1 Asian American or Pacific Islander, 1 Hispanic American). Average age 30. 25 applicants, 100% accepted, 25 enrolled. In 2006, 195 degrees awarded. *Degree requirements:* For master's, thesis optional. *Entrance requirements:* For master's, GRE General Test or MAT, interview, bachelor's degree in related field, minimum GPA of 2.5, teaching license. Additional exam requirements/recommendations for international students: Required—TOEFL. *Application deadline:* For fall admission, 6/1 priority date for domestic students. Applications are processed on a rolling basis. Application fee: $50. *Financial support:* Research assistantships, teaching assistantships, Federal Work-Study available. Support available to part-time students. Financial award application deadline: 6/1; financial award applicants required to submit FAFSA. *Unit head:* Dr. Sandra H. Warren, Interim Chair, 252-328-2699, E-mail: warrens@ecu.edu. *Application contact:* Dean of Graduate School, 252-328-6012, Fax: 252-328-6071, E-mail: gradschool@ecu.edu.

Eastern Illinois University, Graduate School, College of Education and Professional Studies, Department of Special Education, Charleston, IL 61920-3099. Offers MS Ed. *Accreditation:* NCATE. Part-time programs available. *Faculty:* 4 full-time (all women). In 2006, 4 degrees awarded. *Degree requirements:* For master's, comprehensive exam. *Entrance requirements:* For master's, GRE General Test or MAT. *Application deadline:* For fall admission, 7/31 priority date for domestic students. Applications are processed on a rolling basis. Application fee: $30. *Expenses:* Tuition, state resident: part-time $169 per semester hour. Tuition, nonresident: part-time $508 per semester hour. Required fees: $60 per semester hour. *Financial support:* In 2006–07, research assistantships with tuition reimbursements (averaging $7,200 per year), 3 teaching assistantships with tuition reimbursements (averaging $7,200 per year) were awarded. *Unit head:* Dr. Kathlene Shank, Chairperson, 217-581-5315, E-mail: ksshank@eiu.edu.

Eastern Kentucky University, The Graduate School, College of Education, Department of Special Education, Richmond, KY 40475-3102. Offers MA Ed. *Accreditation:* NCATE. Part-time programs available. *Faculty:* 14 full-time (12 women), 3 part-time/adjunct (all women). *Students:* 36 full-time (35 women), 73 part-time (61 women); includes 5 minority (3 African Americans, 2 Hispanic Americans). Average age 30. 135 applicants, 34% accepted, 31 enrolled. In 2006, 39 degrees awarded. *Entrance requirements:* For master's, GRE General Test, minimum GPA of 2.5. Application fee: $35. *Expenses:* Tuition, state resident: full-time $5,610. Tuition, nonresident: full-time $15,910. *Financial support:* In 2006–07, research assistantships (averaging $6,500 per year), teaching assistantships (averaging $6,500 per year) were awarded; fellowships, Federal Work-Study also available. Support available to part-time students. *Faculty research:* Personnel needs in communication disorders, education needs of people who stutter, variables importing on interpreting for the deaf. *Unit head:* Dr. Justin Cooper, Chair, 859-622-4442, Fax: 859-622-4443.

Eastern Michigan University, Graduate School, College of Education, Department of Special Education, Programs in Special Education, Ypsilanti, MI 48197. Offers MA, SPA. *Accreditation:* NCATE. Part-time and evening/weekend programs available. Postbaccalaureate distance learning degree programs offered (minimal on-campus study). *Students:* 68 full-time (56 women), 231 part-time (183 women); includes 24 minority (12 African Americans, 3 American Indian/Alaska Native, 3 Asian Americans or Pacific Islanders, 6 Hispanic Americans), 1 international. Average age 36. In 2006, 48 master's awarded. *Entrance requirements:* For master's, GRE General Test. Additional exam requirements/recommendations for international students: Required—TOEFL. *Application deadline:* For fall admission, 5/15 priority date for domestic students, 5/1 priority date for international students; for winter admission, 10/15 priority date for domestic students, 10/1 priority date for international students; for spring admission, 3/15 priority date for domestic students, 3/1 priority date for international students. Applications are processed on a rolling basis. Application fee: $35. *Expenses:* Tuition, state resident: part-time $341 per credit hour. Tuition, nonresident: full-time $16,104; part-time $671 per credit hour. Required fees: $816; $34 per credit hour. $40 per term. One-time fee: $82 full-time. Tuition and fees vary according to course level, course load, degree level and reciprocity agreements. *Financial support:* Fellowships, research assistantships with full tuition reimbursements, teaching assistantships with full tuition reimbursements, career-related internships or fieldwork, Federal Work-Study, institutionally sponsored loans, scholarships/grants, tuition waivers (partial), and unspecified assistantships available. Support available to part-time students. Financial award applicants required to submit FAFSA.

Eastern Nazarene College, Adult and Graduate Studies, Division of Education, Quincy, MA 02170-2999. Offers early childhood education (M Ed, Certificate); elementary education (M Ed, Certificate); English as a second language (M Ed, Certificate); instructional enrichment and development (M Ed, Certificate); middle school education (M Ed, Certificate); moderate special needs education (M Ed, Certificate); principal (Certificate); program development and supervision (M Ed, Certificate); secondary education (M Ed, Certificate); special education administrator (Certificate); supervisor (Certificate); teacher of reading (M Ed, Certificate). M Ed and Certificate also available through weekend program for administration, special needs, and reading only. Part-time and evening/weekend programs available. *Faculty:* 9 full-time (5 women), 11 part-time/adjunct (5 women). *Students:* 135. Average age 35. 20 applicants, 100% accepted. In 2006, 2 degrees awarded. *Entrance requirements:* Additional exam requirements/recommendations for international students: Required—TOEFL (minimum score 550 paper-based). *Application deadline:* Applications are processed on a rolling basis. Application fee: $35. *Financial support:* Career-related internships or fieldwork available. Support available to part-time students. Financial award applicants required to submit FAFSA. *Unit head:* Dr. Lorne Ranstrom, Chair, 617-745-3528, E-mail: randstrol@enc.edu. *Application contact:* Christine Galbraith, Graduate Studies Recruiter, 617-774-6703, Fax: 617-984-4901, E-mail: christine.galbraith@enc.edu.

Eastern New Mexico University, Graduate School, College of Education and Technology, Department of Educational Studies, Program in Special Education, Portales, NM 88130. Offers M Ed, M Sp Ed. Part-time programs available. *Faculty:* 3 full-time (2 women). *Students:* Average age 38. 6 applicants, 100% accepted. In 2006, 3 degrees awarded. *Degree requirements:* For master's, thesis optional. *Entrance requirements:* For master's, minimum GPA of 2.5. *Application deadline:* For fall admission, 8/20 priority date for domestic students. Applications are processed on a rolling basis. Application fee: $0. Electronic applications accepted. *Expenses:* Tuition, state resident: full-time $2,478; part-time $103 per credit hour. Tuition, nonresident: full-time $8,034; part-time $335 per credit hour. Required fees: $35 per credit hour. *Financial support:* Research assistantships, teaching assistantships, career-related internships or fieldwork and Federal Work-Study available. Support available to part-time students. Financial award application deadline: 3/1.

Eastern Washington University, Graduate Studies, College of Education and Human Development, Department of Counseling, Educational, and Developmental Psychology, Program in Special Education, Cheney, WA 99004-2431. Offers M Ed. *Degree requirements:* For master's, thesis or alternative, comprehensive exam. *Entrance requirements:* For master's, GRE General Test, minimum GPA of 3.0.

East Stroudsburg University of Pennsylvania, Graduate School, School of Professional Studies, Department of Special Education, East Stroudsburg, PA 18301-2999. Offers M Ed. Part-time and evening/weekend programs available. *Faculty:* 6 full-time (4 women), 1 (woman) part-time/adjunct. *Students:* 25 full-time (16 women), 93 part-time (82 women); includes 9 minority (3 African Americans, 1 American Indian/Alaska Native, 1 Asian American or Pacific Islander, 4 Hispanic Americans). Average age 34. In 2006, 43 degrees awarded. *Degree requirements:* For master's, comprehensive exam. *Entrance requirements:* For master's, PRAXIS/teacher certification, letter of recommendation, Pennsylvania Department of Education requirements. Additional exam requirements/recommendations for international students: Required—TOEFL (minimum score 560 paper-based; 220 computer-based; 83 iBT). *Application deadline:* For fall admission, 7/31 priority date for domestic students, 5/1 priority date for international students; for spring admission, 11/30 for domestic students, 10/1 for international students. Applications are processed on a rolling basis. Application fee: $50. *Expenses:* Tuition, state resident: full-time $6,048; part-time $336 per credit. Tuition, nonresident: full-time $9,678; part-time $538 per credit. Required fees: $1,353; $67 per credit. One-time fee: $37 part-time. *Financial support:* In 2006–07, 5 research assistantships with full and partial tuition reimbursements were awarded; career-related internships or fieldwork, Federal Work-Study, and institutionally sponsored loans also available. Financial award application deadline: 3/1; financial award applicants required to submit FAFSA. *Unit head:* Dr. Teri Burcroff, Graduate Coordinator, 570-422-3558, Fax: 570-422-3506, E-mail: tburcroff@po-box.esu.edu.

East Tennessee State University, School of Graduate Studies, College of Education, Department of Human Development and Learning, Johnson City, TN 37614. Offers advanced practitioner (M Ed); community agency counseling (M Ed, MA); comprehensive concentration (M Ed); counseling (M Ed, MA); early childhood education (M Ed, MA); early childhood general (M Ed); early childhood special education (M Ed); early childhood teaching (M Ed); elementary and secondary (school counseling) (M Ed, MA); marriage and family therapy (M Ed, MA); modified concentration (M Ed). *Accreditation:* ACA; NCATE. Part-time programs available. *Degree requirements:* For master's, thesis (for some programs), comprehensive exam. *Entrance requirements:* For master's, GRE General Test, minimum GPA of 3.0. Additional exam requirements/recommendations for international students: Required—TOEFL (minimum score 550 paper-based; 213 computer-based). *Faculty research:* Drug and alcohol abuse, marriage and family counseling, severe mental retardation, parenting of children with disabilities.

East Tennessee State University, School of Graduate Studies, College of Public and Allied Health, Department of Communicative Disorders, Johnson City, TN 37614. Offers audiology (MS, Au D); communicative disorders (MS); special education audiology pre-K-12 (MS); special education speech pathology pre-K-12 (MS); speech pathology (MS). *Accreditation:* ASHA (one or more programs are accredited). Part-time and evening/weekend programs available. *Degree requirements:* For master's, thesis or alternative, comprehensive exam. *Entrance requirements:* For master's, GRE General Test, minimum GPA of 3.0; for doctorate, GRE. Additional exam requirements/recommendations for international students: Required—TOEFL (minimum score 550 paper-based; 213 computer-based). *Faculty research:* Treatment efficacy, hearing aid trials, language development of cleft palate children, phonological processes, neurogenic disorders.

Edgewood College, Program in Education, Madison, WI 53711-1997. Offers director of instruction (Certificate); director of special education and pupil services (Certificate); education (MA Ed); educational administration (MA); educational leadership (Ed D); emotional disturbances (MA, Certificate); learning disabilities (MA, Certificate); learning disabilities and emotional disturbances (MA, Certificate); school business administration (Certificate); school principalship K-12 (Certificate). *Accreditation:* NCATE (one or more programs are accredited). Part-time and evening/weekend programs available. *Students:* 30 full-time (21 women), 180 part-time (117 women); includes 7 minority (5 African Americans, 2 Asian Americans or Pacific Islanders), 2 international. Average age 38. In 2006, 25 master's, 20 doctorates awarded. *Degree requirements:* For master's, practicum, research project. *Entrance requirements:* For master's, minimum GPA of 2.75, 2 letters of recommendation. Additional exam requirements/recommendations for international students: Required—TOEFL. *Application deadline:* For fall admission, 8/24 for domestic students, 8/1 for international students; for spring admission, 1/10 for domestic students, 1/1 for international students. Applications are processed on a rolling basis. Application fee: $25. Electronic applications accepted. *Unit head:* Dr. Joseph Schmiedicke, Chair, 608-663-2293, Fax: 608-663-3291, E-mail: schmied@edgewood.edu. *Application contact:* Paula O'Malley, Graduate Student Admissions Counselor, 608-663-2282, Fax: 608-663-3291, E-mail: gradprograms@edgewood.edu.

Edinboro University of Pennsylvania, Graduate Studies and Research, School of Education, Department of Special Education and School Psychology, Program in Special Education, Edinboro, PA 16444. Offers M Ed. Part-time and evening/weekend programs available. Postbaccalaureate distance learning degree programs offered. *Students:* 25 full-time (21 women), 50 part-time (39 women); includes 1 minority (American Indian/Alaska Native). Average age 31. In 2006, 23 degrees awarded. *Degree requirements:* For master's, thesis or alternative, competency exam. *Entrance requirements:* For master's, GRE or MAT, minimum QPA of 2.5. *Application deadline:* Applications are processed on a rolling basis. Application fee: $30. *Expenses:* Tuition, state resident: full-time $6,048; part-time $336 per credit. Tuition, nonresident: full-time $9,678; part-time $538 per credit. Required fees: $1,849; $42 per credit. *Financial support:* In 2006–07, 3 research assistantships with full and partial tuition reimbursements (averaging $3,850 per year) were awarded; career-related internships or fieldwork, Federal Work-Study, scholarships/grants, and unspecified assistantships also available. Support available to part-time students. Financial award application deadline: 2/15; financial award applicants required to submit FAFSA. *Unit head:* Dr. Susan Criswell, Interim Head, 814-732-2590, Fax: 814-732-2268, E-mail: scriswell@edinboro.edu. *Application contact:* Dr. R. Scott Baldwin, Dean, 814-732-2752, Fax: 814-732-2268, E-mail: sbaldwin@edinboro.edu.

Elmhurst College, Graduate Programs, Program in Early Childhood Special Education, Elmhurst, IL 60126-3296. Offers M Ed. *Accreditation:* NCATE. Part-time and evening/weekend programs available. *Faculty:* 3 full-time (2 women), 3 part-time/adjunct (all women). *Students:* Average age 35. 20 applicants, 90% accepted, 14 enrolled. In 2006, 7 degrees awarded. *Median time to degree:* Master's–2 years part-time. *Entrance requirements:* For master's, 3 recommendations. Additional exam requirements/recommendations for international students: Required—TOEFL (minimum score 550 paper-based; 213 computer-based). *Application deadline:* Applications are processed on a rolling basis. Application fee: $25. Electronic applications accepted. *Expenses:* Tuition: Part-time $781 per hour. Required fees: $75 per hour. Part-time tuition and fees vary according to course load and student level. *Financial support:* In 2006–07, 21 students received support. Federal Work-Study and scholarships/grants available. Support available to part-time students. Financial award application deadline: 6/1; financial award applicants required to submit FAFSA. *Application contact:* Elizabeth D. Kuebler, Director of Adult and Graduate Admission, 630-617-3069, Fax: 630-617-5501, E-mail: betsyk@elmhurst.edu.

Elms College, Division of Education, Chicopee, MA 01013-2839. Offers early childhood education (MAT); education (M Ed, CAGS); elementary education (MAT); English as a second language (MAT); reading (MAT); secondary education (MAT), including biology education, English education, Spanish education; special education (MAT). Part-time and evening weekend programs available. *Faculty:* 9 full-time (6 women), 4 part-time/adjunct (2 women). *Students:* 8 full-time (6 women), 97 part-time (89 women); includes 4 minority (2 Asian Americans or Pacific Islanders, 2 Hispanic Americans). Average age 36. 48 applicants, 90% accepted, 40 enrolled. In 2006, 37 master's, 8 other advanced degrees awarded. *Degree requirements:* For master's, thesis (for some programs). *Entrance requirements:* For master's, Massachusetts Educators Certification Test, minimum GPA of 3.0; for CAGS, master's degree in education. Additional exam requirements/recommendations for international students: Required—TOEFL. *Application deadline:* For fall admission, 7/1 priority date for domestic students; for spring admission, 11/1 priority date for domestic students. Applications are processed on a rolling basis. Application fee: $30. *Expenses:* Tuition: Full-time $9,180; part-time $510 per credit. Tuition and fees vary according to course load. *Financial support:* In 2006–07, 3 teaching assistantships with partial tuition reimbursements were awarded; tuition waivers (partial) also available. Support available to part-time students. Financial award application deadline: 4/15; financial award applicants required to submit FAFSA. *Unit head:* Dr. Mary Janeczek, Director, 413-594-2761, Fax: 413-592-4871, E-mail: janeczeke@elms.edu.

Elon University, Program in Education, Elon, NC 27244-2010. Offers elementary education (M Ed); gifted education (M Ed); special education (M Ed). *Accreditation:* NCATE. Part-time programs available. *Faculty:* 11 full-time (8 women), 5 part-time/adjunct (all women). *Students:* Average age 31. 62 applicants, 69% accepted, 30 enrolled. In 2006, 30 degrees awarded. *Entrance requirements:* For master's, GRE, MAT. Additional exam requirements/recommendations for international students: Required—TOEFL (minimum score 550 paper-based; 213 computer-based; 79 iBT). *Application deadline:* For winter admission, 6/1 priority date for domestic students. Applications are processed on a rolling basis. Application fee: $50. Electronic applications accepted. *Expenses: Contact institution. Financial support:* In 2006–07, 2 students received support, including 2 fellowships (averaging $2,635 per year); Federal Work-Study and scholarships/grants also available. Support available to part-time students. Financial award application deadline: 6/1; financial award applicants required to submit FAFSA. *Faculty research:* Teaching reading to low-achieving second and third graders; pre-and post-student teaching attitudes toward teaching; children's writing; whole language methodology; critical creative thinking. *Unit head:* Dr. Judith B. Howard, Director, 336-278-5885, Fax: 336-278-5919, E-mail: howardj@elon.edu. *Application contact:* Art Fadde, Director of Graduate Admissions, 800-334-8448 Ext. 3, Fax: 336-278-7699, E-mail: afadde@elon.edu.

Emporia State University, School of Graduate Studies, The Teachers College, Department of Early Childhood/Elementary Teacher Education, Program in Early Childhood Education, Emporia, KS 66801-5087. Offers early childhood education (MS), including early childhood curriculum, early childhood special education. *Accreditation:* NCATE. *Students:* 5 full-time (all women), 42 part-time (41 women); includes 3 minority (2 African Americans, 1 Hispanic American), 2 international. 8 applicants, 75% accepted, 4 enrolled. In 2006, 9 degrees awarded. *Degree requirements:* For master's, comprehensive exam or thesis, practicum. *Entrance requirements:* For master's, GRE General Test or MAT, graduate essay exam, appropriate bachelor's degree, letters of recommendation. Additional exam requirements/recommendations for international students: Required—TOEFL. *Application deadline:* For fall admission, 8/15 priority date for domestic students. Applications are processed on a rolling basis. Application fee: $30 ($75 for international students). Electronic applications accepted. *Expenses:* Tuition, state resident: full-time $3,438; part-time $143 per credit hour. Tuition, nonresident: full-time $10,398; part-time $433 per credit hour. Required fees: $724; $44 per credit hour. *Financial support:* Federal Work-Study, institutionally sponsored loans, health care benefits, and unspecified assistantships available. Financial award application deadline: 3/15; financial award applicants required to submit FAFSA. *Unit head:* Dr. Jean Morrow, Chair, Department of Early Childhood/Elementary Teacher Education, 620-341-5766, E-mail: jmorrow@emporia.edu.

Emporia State University, School of Graduate Studies, The Teachers College, Department of Psychology and Special Education, Program in Special Education, Emporia, KS 66801-5087. Offers behavior disorders (MS); gifted, talented, and creative (MS); interrelated special education (MS); learning disabilities (MS); mental retardation (MS). *Accreditation:* NCATE. Part-time programs available. *Students:* 31 applicants, 81% accepted, 23 enrolled. In 2006, 38 degrees awarded. *Degree requirements:* For master's, comprehensive exam or thesis, practicum. *Entrance requirements:* For master's, GRE General Test or MAT, graduate essay exam, appropriate bachelor's degree, teacher certification, letters of recommendation. Additional exam requirements/recommendations for international students: Required—TOEFL. *Application deadline:* For fall admission, 8/15 priority date for domestic students. Applications are processed on a rolling basis. Application fee: $30 ($75 for international students). Electronic applications accepted. *Expenses:* Tuition, state resident: full-time $3,438; part-time $143 per credit hour. Tuition, nonresident: full-time $10,398; part-time $433 per credit hour. Required fees: $724; $44 per credit hour. *Financial support:* Federal Work-Study, institutionally sponsored loans, health care benefits, and unspecified assistantships available. Financial award application deadline: 3/15; financial award applicants required to submit FAFSA. *Unit head:* Dr. Kenneth A. Weaver, Chair, Department of Psychology and Special Education, 620-341-5317, E-mail: kweaver@emporia.edu.

Endicott College, Van Loan School of Graduate and Professional Studies, Program in Special Education, Beverly, MA 01915-2096. Offers initial and professional licensure (M Ed). Part-time and evening/weekend programs available. *Faculty:* 19 part-time/adjunct (6 women). *Students:* Average age 30. In 2006, 19 degrees awarded. *Degree requirements:* For master's, comprehensive exam, registration. *Entrance requirements:* For master's, MAT or GRE, Massachusetts teaching certificate, letters of recommendation. *Application deadline:* Applications are processed on a rolling basis. Application fee: $50. *Expenses:* Tuition: Part-time $279 per credit. Tuition and fees vary according to program. *Financial support:* Career-related internships or fieldwork, Federal Work-Study, and institutionally sponsored loans available. *Faculty research:* Literacy, parent education, inclusion, school reform, technology in education. *Unit head:* Dr. John D. MacLean, Director of Licensure Programs, 978-232-2408, E-mail: jmaclean@endicott.edu.

Fairfield University, Graduate School of Education and Allied Professions, Department of Psychology and Special Education, Fairfield, CT 06824-5195. Offers applied psychology (MA); school psychology (MA, CAS); special education (MA, CAS). Part-time and evening/weekend programs available. *Faculty:* 5 full-time (3 women), 7 part-time/adjunct (4 women). *Students:* 52 full-time (40 women), 109 part-time (92 women). Average age 28. 95 applicants, 38% accepted, 25 enrolled. In 2006, 31 master's, 17 other advanced degrees awarded. *Degree requirements:* For master's, educational technology course, thesis optional. *Entrance requirements:* For master's, PRAXIS I (PPST), minimum QPA of 2.67, 2 recommendations, resumè. Additional exam requirements/recommendations for international students: Required—TOEFL (minimum score 550 paper-based; 213 computer-based; 79 iBT). *Application deadline:* For fall admission, 2/15 for domestic students; for spring admission, 10/15 for domestic students. Applications are processed on a rolling basis. Application fee: $55. Electronic applications accepted. *Financial support:* Scholarships/grants, tuition waivers (partial), and unspecified assistantships available. Financial award applicants required to submit FAFSA. *Faculty research:* School university collaboration, special education consultation, child neuropsychology, disabilities, effect of pretreatment orientation on treatment. *Unit head:* Dr. Daniel Geller, Chair, 203-254-4000 Ext. 2324, Fax: 203-254-4047, E-mail: dgeller@mail.fairfield.edu. *Application contact:* Marianne Gumpper, Director of Graduate and Continuing Studies Admissions, 203-254-4184, Fax: 203-254-4073, E-mail: gradadmis@mail.fairfield.edu.

Fairleigh Dickinson University, Metropolitan Campus, University College: Arts, Sciences, and Professional Studies, Peter Sammartino School of Education, Program in Learning Disabilities, Teaneck, NJ 07666-1914. Offers MA. *Students:* 1 (woman) full-time, 20 part-time (19 women). Average age 41. 4 applicants, 50% accepted, 1 enrolled. In 2006, 11 degrees awarded. *Application deadline:* Applications are processed on a rolling basis. Application fee: $40.

Felician College, Program in Education, Lodi, NJ 07644-2117. Offers elementary education (MA); supervisory (MA); teacher for students with disabilities (MA). Part-time and evening/weekend programs available. *Students:* 18 applicants, 50% accepted, 9 enrolled. *Degree requirements:* For master's, project. *Entrance requirements:* For master's, MAT, minimum GPA of 3.0, 3 letters of recommendation. Additional exam requirements/recommendations for international students: Recommended—TOEFL (minimum score 550 paper-based; 213 computer-based). *Application deadline:* Applications are processed on a rolling basis. Application fee: $40. *Expenses:* Tuition: Part-time $675 per credit. Tuition and fees vary according to program. *Financial support:* Federal Work-Study available. *Unit head:* Dr. Julie Goods, Associate Dean, 201-559-3529, E-mail: goodj@felician.edu. *Application contact:* Wendy Lin-Cook, Director of Adult and Graduate Admission, 201-559-6077, Fax: 201-559-6138, E-mail: adultandgraduate@felician.edu.

See Close-Up on page 879.

Ferris State University, College of Education and Human Services, School of Education, Big Rapids, MI 49307. Offers administration (MSCTE); curriculum and instruction (M Ed), including administration, elementary education, philanthropic education, reading, secondary education, special education, subject matter option; education technology (MSCTE); instructor (MSCTE); post-secondary administration (MSCTE); training and development (MSCTE). Part-time and evening/weekend programs available. Postbaccalaureate distance learning degree programs offered (no on-campus study). *Faculty:* 13 full-time (9 women), 26 part-time/adjunct (19 women). *Students:* 38 full-time (27 women), 254 part-time (164 women); includes 30 minority (22 African Americans, 1 American Indian/Alaska Native, 2 Asian Americans or Pacific Islanders, 5 Hispanic Americans), 1 international. Average age 37. 171 applicants, 99% accepted. In 2006, 92 degrees awarded. *Degree requirements:* For master's, thesis, research paper. *Entrance requirements:* For master's, 2 years of work experience, minimum GPA of 3.0. *Application deadline:* For fall admission, 6/1 priority date for domestic students; for winter admission, 12/10 priority date for domestic students. Applications are processed on a rolling basis. Application fee: $30. *Expenses:* Tuition, state resident: part-time $355 per credit hour. Tuition, nonresident: part-time $687 per credit hour. *Financial support:* Career-related internships or fieldwork and tuition waivers (full and partial) available. Support available to part-time students. Financial award applicants required to submit FAFSA. *Faculty research:* Suicide prevention, reading, women in education, special needs, administration. *Unit head:* Interim Director, 231-591-5362, Fax: 231-591-2041. *Application contact:* Sigrid Robertson, Secretary, 231-591-3511, Fax: 231-591-2041, E-mail: robertss@ferris.edu.

Fitchburg State College, Division of Graduate and Continuing Education, Program in Special Education, Fitchburg, MA 01420-2697. Offers guided studies (M Ed); reading specialist (M Ed); teaching students with moderate disabilities (M Ed); teaching students with severe disabilities (M Ed). *Accreditation:* NCATE. Part-time and evening/weekend programs available. *Students:* 28 full-time (23 women), 143 part-time (126 women); includes 1 Hispanic American, 3 international. Average age 35. 63 applicants, 95% accepted, 43 enrolled. In 2006, 84 degrees awarded. *Degree requirements:* For master's, internship. *Entrance requirements:* For master's, GRE General Test or MAT, letters of recommendation, resumé. Additional exam requirements/recommendations for international students: Required—TOEFL (minimum score 550 paper-based; 213 computer-based; 79 iBT). *Application deadline:* Applications are processed on a rolling basis. Application fee: $25 ($50 for international students). *Expenses:* Tuition, state resident: part-time $150 per credit. Tuition, nonresident: part-time $150 per credit. Required fees: $90 per credit. *Financial support:* In 2006–07, research assistantships with partial tuition reimbursements (averaging $5,500 per year); Federal Work-Study, scholarships/grants, and unspecified assistantships also available. Support available to part-time students. Financial award application deadline: 3/1; financial award applicants required to submit FAFSA. *Unit head:* Dr. Anne Howard, Chair, 978-665-3309, Fax: 978-665-3658, E-mail: gce@fsc.edu. *Application contact:* Director of Admissions, 978-665-3144, Fax: 978-665-4540, E-mail: admissions@fsc.edu.

Florida Atlantic University, College of Education, Department of Exceptional Student Education, Boca Raton, FL 33431-0991. Offers emotional handicaps (M Ed); exceptional student education (M Ed, Ed D); learning disabilities (M Ed); mental retardation (M Ed); special education (Ed D); varying exceptionalities (M Ed). *Accreditation:* NCATE. Part-time and evening/weekend programs available. *Faculty:* 13 full-time (8 women), 12 part-time/adjunct (8 women). *Students:* 14 full-time (13 women), 30 part-time (26 women); includes 9 minority (6 African Americans, 1 Asian American or Pacific Islander, 2 Hispanic Americans), 1 international. Average age 36. 21 applicants, 38% accepted, 7 enrolled. In 2006, 14 master's, 1 doctorate awarded. *Degree requirements:* For master's, internship, thesis optional; for doctorate, thesis/dissertation, internship, comprehensive exam, registration. *Entrance requirements:* For master's, GRE General Test, minimum GPA of 3.0 during previous 2 years; for doctorate, GRE General Test, 3 years teaching experience, interview. *Application deadline:* Applications are processed on a rolling basis. Application fee: $30. Electronic applications accepted. *Expenses:* Tuition, area resident: Full-time $4,394. Tuition, nonresident: full-time $16,441. *Financial support:* In 2006–07, 7 students received support, including 1 fellowship with tuition reimbursement available (averaging $10,000 per year), research assistantships with tuition reimbursements available (averaging $7,500 per year), 2 teaching assistantships with partial tuition reimbursements available (averaging $7,500 per year); career-related internships or fieldwork, Federal Work-Study, scholarships/grants, tuition waivers (partial), and unspecified assistantships also available. Support available to part-time students. Financial award applicants required to submit FAFSA. *Faculty research:* Instructional design, assessment, educational reform, behavioral research, social integration. Total annual research expenditures: $725,000. *Unit head:* Dr. Michael P. Brady, Chairperson, 561-297-3280, Fax: 561-297-2507, E-mail: mbrady@fau.edu.

Florida Atlantic University, Jupiter Campus, College of Education, Jupiter, FL 33458. Offers exceptional student education (M Ed); reading (M Ed).

Florida Gulf Coast University, College of Education, Program in Special Education, Fort Myers, FL 33965-6565. Offers behavior disorders (MA); mental retardation (MA); specific learning disabilities (MA); varying exceptionalities (MA). Part-time and evening/weekend programs available. *Faculty:* 31 full-time (21 women), 30 part-time/adjunct (24 women). *Students:* 28 full-time (24 women), 4 part-time (all women); includes 4 minority (all Hispanic Americans) Average age 38. 13 applicants, 77% accepted, 10 enrolled. In 2006, 8 degrees awarded. *Degree requirements:* For master's, thesis or alternative. *Entrance requirements:* For master's, GRE General Test, MAT, minimum GPA of 3.0. Additional exam requirements/recommendations for international students: Required—TOEFL (minimum score 550 paper-based; 213 computer-based). *Application deadline:* For fall admission, 7/1 priority date for domestic students; for spring admission, 10/15 for domestic students. Applications are processed on a rolling basis. Application fee: $30. Electronic applications accepted. *Expenses:* Tuition, state resident: full-time $4,326. Tuition, nonresident: full-time $18,523. Required fees: $1,211. One-time fee: $5 full-time. *Faculty research:* Inclusion, interacting with families, alternative certification. *Unit head:* Dr. Patricia Wachholz, Head, 239-590-7808, Fax: 239-590-7801, E-mail: pwachhol@fgcu.edu.

Florida International University, College of Education, Department of Curriculum and Instruction, Miami, FL 33199. Offers art education (MAT, MS, Ed D); curriculum and instruction (Ed S); curriculum development (MS); curriculum studies (PhD); early childhood education (MS, Ed D); elementary education (MS, Ed D); English education (MAT, MS, Ed D); foreign language education—teaching English to speakers of other languages (TESOL) (Certificate), including foreign language education; foreign language education- teaching English to speakers of other languages (TESOL) (MS), including teaching English; French education—initial teacher preparation (MAT); international and intercultural development education (Ed D); international and intercultural developmental education (MS); language, literacy and culture (PhD); learning technologies (MS, Ed D, PhD); mathematics education (MAT, MS, Ed D, PhD); modern language education/bilingual education (MS, Ed D); physical education (MS); reading education (MS, Ed D); science education (MAT, MS, Ed D, PhD); social studies education (MAT, MS, Ed D); Spanish education—initial teacher preparation (MAT); special educa-

Special Education

Florida International University (continued)

tion (MS). Part-time and evening/weekend programs available. *Faculty:* 19 full-time (11 women). *Students:* 89 full-time (66 women), 258 part-time (221 women); includes 99 minority (72 African Americans, 10 Asian Americans or Pacific Islanders, 17 Hispanic Americans). Average age 35. 167 applicants, 50% accepted, 81 enrolled. In 2006, 141 master's, 8 doctorates, 1 other advanced degree awarded. *Degree requirements:* For doctorate, thesis/dissertation, comprehensive exam, registration. *Entrance requirements:* For master's, GRE General Test, Florida General Knowledge Test or Florida College Level Academic Skills Test; for doctorate and other advanced degree, GRE General Test. Additional exam requirements/recommendations for international students: Required—TOEFL (minimum score 550 paper-based; 213 computer-based; 80 iBT), IELTS (minimum score 6). *Application deadline:* For fall admission, 6/1 priority date for domestic students, 4/1 for international students; for winter admission, 10/1 priority date for domestic students, 9/1 for international students; for spring admission, 3/1 priority date for domestic students, 2/1 for international students. Applications are processed on a rolling basis. Application fee: $30. Electronic applications accepted. *Expenses:* Tuition, state resident: part-time $249 per credit hour. Tuition, nonresident: part-time $753 per credit hour. Tuition and fees vary according to program. *Financial support:* Research assistantships with full and partial tuition reimbursements, teaching assistantships with full and partial tuition reimbursements available. *Unit head:* Dr. Lisbeth Dixon-Krauss, Interim Chairperson, 305-348-3609, Fax: 305-348-2086, E-mail: kraussl@fiu.edu. *Application contact:* Marisa Salazar, Student Recruiter, 305-348-3002, Fax: 305-348-3227, E-mail: marisa.salazar@fiu.edu.

Florida International University, College of Education, Department of Educational and Psychological Studies, Program in Exceptional Student Education, Miami, FL 33199. Offers MS, Ed D. *Accreditation:* NCATE. Part-time and evening/weekend programs available. *Faculty:* 8 full-time (7 women). *Students:* 6 full-time (5 women), 29 part-time (23 women); includes 28 minority (10 African Americans, 18 Hispanic Americans). 5 applicants, 60% accepted, 3 enrolled. In 2006, 2 master's, 1 doctorate awarded. *Degree requirements:* For doctorate, thesis/dissertation, qualifying exams, comprehensive exam. *Entrance requirements:* For doctorate, GRE General Test, interview. Additional exam requirements/recommendations for international students: Required—TOEFL (minimum score 550 paper-based; 213 computer-based; 80 iBT), IELTS (minimum score 6). *Application deadline:* For fall admission, 6/1 priority date for domestic students, 4/1 for international students; for winter admission, 10/1 priority date for domestic students, 9/1 for international students; for spring admission, 3/1 for domestic students, 2/1 for international students. Applications are processed on a rolling basis. Application fee: $30. Electronic applications accepted. *Expenses:* Tuition, state resident: part-time $249 per credit hour. Tuition, nonresident: part-time $753 per credit hour. Tuition and fees vary according to program. *Faculty research:* Handicapped adolescents and young adults, learning disabilities, mild disabilities, autism. *Unit head:* Dr. Patricia Barbetta, Program Leader, 305-348-3002, E-mail: barbetta@fiu.edu. *Application contact:* Marisa Salazar, Student Recruiter, 305-348-3002, Fax: 305-348-3227, E-mail: marisa.salazar@fiu.edu.

Florida International University, College of Education, Department of Educational and Psychological Studies, Program in Special Education, Miami, FL 33199. Offers MS. *Accreditation:* NCATE. Part-time and evening/weekend programs available. *Students:* 6 full-time (all women), 29 part-time (24 women); includes 22 minority (5 African Americans, 2 Asian Americans or Pacific Islanders, 15 Hispanic Americans). Average age 35. 13 applicants, 62% accepted, 5 enrolled. In 2006, 3 degrees awarded. *Entrance requirements:* For master's, minimum GPA of 3.0, interview. Additional exam requirements/recommendations for international students: Required—TOEFL (minimum score 550 paper-based; 213 computer-based; 80 iBT), IELTS (minimum score 6). *Application deadline:* For fall admission, 6/1 priority date for domestic students, 4/1 for international students; for winter admission, 10/1 priority date for domestic students, 9/1 for international students; for spring admission, 3/1 priority date for domestic students, 2/1 for international students. Applications are processed on a rolling basis. Application fee: $30. Electronic applications accepted. *Expenses:* Tuition, state resident: part-time $249 per credit hour. Tuition, nonresident: part-time $753 per credit hour. Tuition and fees vary according to program. *Faculty research:* Reading, brain disorders, language arts. *Unit head:* Dr. Patricia Barbetta, Program Leader, 305-348-3002, E-mail: barbetta@fiu.edu. *Application contact:* Marisa Salazar, Student Recruiter, 305-348-3002, Fax: 305-348-3227, E-mail: marisa.salazar@fiu.edu.

Florida State University, Graduate Studies, College of Education, Department of Childhood Education, Reading, and Disability Services, Tallahassee, FL 32306. Offers early childhood education (MS, Ed D, PhD, Ed S); elementary education (MS, Ed D, PhD, Ed S); reading education/language arts (MS, Ed D, PhD, Ed S); special education (MS, PhD, Ed S), including emotional disturbance/learning disabilities (MS), mental retardation (MS), rehabilitation counseling, special education (PhD, Ed S), visual disabilities (MS). Part-time programs available. *Faculty:* 24 full-time (19 women), 3 part-time/adjunct (all women). *Students:* 85 full-time (73 women), 205 part-time (189 women); includes 60 minority (36 African Americans, 2 American Indian/Alaska Native, 13 Asian Americans or Pacific Islanders, 9 Hispanic Americans). 189 applicants, 61% accepted, 71 enrolled. In 2006, 76 master's, 7 doctorates, 5 other advanced degrees awarded. *Degree requirements:* For master's and Ed S, thesis optional; for doctorate, thesis/dissertation, comprehensive exam. *Entrance requirements:* For master's, doctorate, and Ed S, GRE General Test, minimum GPA of 3.0. *Application deadline:* For fall admission, 7/1 priority date for domestic students; for spring admission, 11/1 for domestic students. Applications are processed on a rolling basis. Application fee: $30. *Expenses:* Tuition, state resident: full-time $5,822; part-time $243 per credit hour. Tuition, nonresident: full-time $20,976; part-time $874 per credit hour. Tuition and fees vary according to program. *Financial support:* In 2006–07, 2 fellowships, 4 research assistantships, 12 teaching assistantships were awarded; career-related internships or fieldwork also available. Financial award applicants required to submit FAFSA. *Unit head:* Dr. Mary Frances Hanline, Chair, 850-644-5458, Fax: 850-644-7736, E-mail: mhanline@coe.fsu.edu. *Application contact:* Timolin Lynette Bodison-Baker, Program Assistant, 850-644-5458, Fax: 850-644-7736, E-mail: bodison@coe.fsu.edu.

Fontbonne University, Graduate Programs, Department of Communication Disorders and Deaf Education, Studies in Early Intervention in Deaf Education, St. Louis, MO 63105-3098. Offers MA. *Faculty:* 3 full-time (all women), 1 (woman) part-time/adjunct. *Students:* 8 full-time (all women), 2 part-time (both women); includes 1 minority (American Indian/Alaska Native). Average age 26. 30 applicants, 33% accepted. In 2006, 11 degrees awarded. *Entrance requirements:* For master's, minimum GPA of 3.0. *Application deadline:* For fall admission, 2/1 for domestic students. Application fee: $25. *Expenses:* Tuition: Full-time $4,890; part-time $489 per credit. Required fees: $160; $76 per credit. Full-time tuition and fees vary according to course load and program. *Financial support:* Application deadline: 4/1; *Unit head:* Dr. Gale Rice, Chair, 314-889-1407, Fax: 314-719-8016, E-mail: grice@fontbonne.edu. *Application contact:* Dr. Susan Lenihan, Director, 314-889-1461, Fax: 314-719-8016, E-mail: slenihan@fontbonne.edu.

Fordham University, Graduate School of Education, Division of Curriculum and Teaching, New York, NY 10023. Offers adult education (MS, MSE); bilingual teacher education (MSE); curriculum and teaching (MSE); early childhood education (MSE); elementary education (MST); language, literacy, and learning (PhD); reading education (MSE, Adv C); secondary education (MAT, MSE); special education (MSE, Adv C); teaching English as a second language (MSE). *Accreditation:* NCATE. *Faculty:* 22 full-time (18 women), 38 part-time/adjunct (28 women). *Students:* 68 full-time (51 women), 663 part-time (612 women); includes 200 minority (74 African Americans, 1 American Indian/Alaska Native, 37 Asian Americans or Pacific Islanders, 88 Hispanic Americans), 3 international. Average age 32. 636 applicants, 86% accepted, 322 enrolled. In 2006, 351 master's, 8 doctorates awarded. *Degree requirements:* For doctorate and Adv C, thesis/dissertation. *Entrance requirements:* For doctorate, MAT, GRE General Test. Application fee: $65. *Financial support:* Applicants required to submit FAFSA. *Unit head:* Dr. Terry Osborn, Chairperson, 212-636-6450.

Fort Hays State University, Graduate School, College of Education and Technology, Department of Special Education, Hays, KS 67601-4099. Offers MS. *Accreditation:* NCATE. *Faculty:* 3 full-time (0 women). *Students:* 2 full-time (both women), 65 part-time (54 women). Average age 36. 36 applicants, 78% accepted. In 2006, 15 degrees awarded. *Degree requirements:* For master's, thesis optional. *Entrance requirements:* Additional exam requirements/recommendations for international students: Required—TOEFL (minimum score 550 paper-based; 213 computer-based). *Application deadline:* For fall admission, 7/1 priority date for domestic students. Applications are processed on a rolling basis. Application fee: $35. Electronic applications accepted. *Financial support:* Research assistantships, teaching assistantships available. *Faculty research:* Severe behavior disorders, early childhood language, multicultural speech. *Unit head:* Dr. Dorothy Fulton, Chair, 785-628-4212.

Framingham State College, Division of Graduate and Continuing Education, Program in Special Education, Framingham, MA 01701-9101. Offers M Ed. Part-time and evening/weekend programs available. *Faculty:* 2 part-time/adjunct. *Students:* 120. In 2006, 40 degrees awarded. *Entrance requirements:* For master's, MAT, interview. *Unit head:* Dr. Katherine Hibbard, Coordinator, 508-626-4830, Fax: 508-626-4030, E-mail: khibbard@frc.mass.edu. *Application contact:* Graduate Office, 508-626-4550, Fax: 508-626-4030, E-mail: dgce@frc.mass.edu.

Francis Marion University, Graduate Programs, School of Education, Florence, SC 29501-0547. Offers early childhood education (M Ed); elementary education (M Ed); learning disabilities (M Ed, MAT); remedial education (M Ed); secondary education (M Ed). *Accreditation:* NCATE. Part-time programs available. *Faculty:* 19 full-time (11 women), 1 part-time/adjunct (0 women). *Students:* 11 full-time (8 women), 158 part-time (141 women); includes 54 minority (all African Americans), 1 international. Average age 34. 248 applicants, 100% accepted. In 2006, 91 degrees awarded. *Degree requirements:* For master's, comprehensive exam. *Entrance requirements:* For master's, GRE General Test, MAT, NTE, or PRAXIS II. *Application deadline:* For fall admission, 4/15 priority date for domestic students; for spring admission, 10/15 priority date for domestic students. Applications are processed on a rolling basis. Application fee: $30. *Expenses:* Tuition, state resident: full-time $6,527; part-time $326 per credit hour. Tuition, nonresident: full-time $13,054; part-time $653 per credit hour. Required fees: $185; $5 per credit hour. $45 per term. *Financial support:* In 2006–07, 3 research assistantships (averaging $6,000 per year) were awarded; unspecified assistantships also available. Support available to part-time students. Financial award application deadline: 3/1; financial award applicants required to submit FAFSA. *Faculty research:* Identification and alternate assessment of at-risk students. *Unit head:* Dr. James R. Faulkenberry, Dean, 843-661-1460, Fax: 843-661-4647.

Fresno Pacific University, Graduate Programs, Programs in Education, Division of Special Education, Fresno, CA 93702-4709. Offers mild/moderate (MA Ed); moderate/severe (MA Ed); physical and health impairments (MA Ed). Part-time and evening/weekend programs available. *Faculty:* 3 full-time (1 woman), 5 part-time/adjunct (3 women). *Students:* 11 full-time (9 women), 87 part-time (74 women); includes 23 minority (2 African Americans, 4 American Indian/Alaska Native, 1 Asian American or Pacific Islander, 16 Hispanic Americans), 1 international. Average age 41. 21 applicants, 71% accepted, 1 enrolled. In 2006, 1 degree awarded. *Degree requirements:* For master's, thesis or alternative, registration. *Entrance requirements:* Additional exam requirements/recommendations for international students: Required—TOEFL (minimum score 550 paper-based; 213 computer-based). *Application deadline:* For fall admission, 7/15 for domestic and international students; for spring admission, 11/15 for domestic and international students. Applications are processed on a rolling basis. Application fee: $90. *Expenses:* Tuition: Full-time $7,470; part-time $415 per credit. *Financial support:* In 2006–07, 53 students received support. Career-related internships or fieldwork, scholarships/grants, and tuition waivers (full and partial) available. Support available to part-time students. Financial award applicants required to submit FAFSA. *Unit head:* Dr. Peter G. Kopriva, Head, 559-453-2202, Fax: 559-453-2001, E-mail: pgkopriv@fresno.edu.

Frostburg State University, Graduate School, College of Education, Department of Educational Professions, Program in Special Education, Frostburg, MD 21532-1099. Offers M Ed. *Accreditation:* NCATE. Part-time and evening/weekend programs available. *Degree requirements:* For master's, thesis or alternative, PRAXIS II special education section. *Entrance requirements:* For master's, teaching certificate. Electronic applications accepted.

Furman University, Graduate Division, Department of Education, Greenville, SC 29613. Offers early childhood education (MA); elementary education (MA); English as a second language (MA); middle school education (MA); reading (MA); school administration (MA); special education (MA). *Accreditation:* NCATE. Part-time and evening/weekend programs available. *Faculty:* 17 full-time (12 women), 19 part-time/adjunct (15 women). *Students:* 114 full-time (89 women), 72 part-time (59 women); includes 27 minority (23 African Americans, 4 Hispanic Americans). Average age 32. 36 applicants, 100% accepted, 36 enrolled. In 2006, 111 degrees awarded. *Degree requirements:* For master's, thesis (for some programs), comprehensive exam. *Entrance requirements:* For master's, GRE General Test or PRAXIS. *Application deadline:* For fall admission, 8/1 priority date for domestic and international students; for winter admission, 12/1 priority date for domestic and international students; for spring admission, 2/1 priority date for domestic and international students. Applications are processed on a rolling basis. Application fee: $50. *Expenses:* Tuition: Part-time $347 per credit. *Financial support:* In 2006–07, 97 students received support; fellowships, scholarships/grants and unspecified assistantships available. Financial award application deadline: 1/15; financial award applicants required to submit FAFSA. *Unit head:* Dr. Nelly Hecker, Head, 864-294-3385.

Gallaudet University, The Graduate School, School of Education and Human Services, Department of Administration and Supervision, Washington, DC 20002-3625. Offers administration (MS); administration and supervision (PhD, Ed S); instructional supervision (Ed S); leadership training (MS); special education administration (PhD). *Degree requirements:* For master's, thesis optional; for doctorate, 2 foreign languages, thesis/dissertation; for Ed S, 2 foreign languages, thesis (for some programs). *Entrance requirements:* For master's, GRE Genera Test or MAT; for doctorate, GRE General Test or MAT, interview.

Gallaudet University, The Graduate School, School of Education and Human Services, Department of Education, Washington, DC 20002-3625. Offers early childhood education (MA, Ed S); education of deaf and hard of hearing students and multihandicapped deaf and hard of hearing students (MA, Ed S); elementary education (MA, Ed S); individualized program of study (PhD); parent/infant specialty (MA, Ed S); secondary education (MA, Ed S). *Accreditation* NCATE. *Degree requirements:* For master's, thesis optional; for doctorate, thesis/dissertation *Entrance requirements:* For master's, GRE General Test or MAT; for doctorate, GRE Genera Test or MAT, interview.

Geneva College, Program in Special Education, Beaver Falls, PA 15010-3599. Offers M Ed Part-time and evening/weekend programs available. *Entrance requirements:* For master's letters of recommendation, proof of certification. Additional exam requirements/recommendation for international students: Required—TOEFL. Electronic applications accepted.

George Mason University, Graduate School of Education, Programs in Curriculum and Instruction, Fairfax, VA 22030. Offers bilingual/multicultural/English as a second languag education (M Ed); early childhood education (M Ed); instructional technology (M Ed); middl education (M Ed); reading (M Ed); secondary education (M Ed); special education (M Ed Part-time and evening/weekend programs available. *Faculty:* 108 full-time (70 women), 19 part-time/adjunct (140 women). *Students:* 185 full-time (144 women), 816 part-time (68 women); includes 148 minority (46 African Americans, 2 American Indian/Alaska Native, 4 Asian Americans or Pacific Islanders, 56 Hispanic Americans), 28 international. Average ag 34. 822 applicants, 72% accepted, 473 enrolled. In 2006, 606 master's awarded. *Entranc requirements:* For master's, minimum GPA of 3.0 in last 60 hours. *Application deadline:* For fa admission, 5/1 for domestic students; for spring admission, 11/1 for domestic students. Applica tion fee: $60 ($75 for international students). Electronic applications accepted. *Expenses* Tuition, state resident: full-time $5,724; part-time $238 per credit. Tuition, nonresident: full-tim $16,896; part-time $704 per credit. Required fees: $1,656; $69 per credit. *Financial suppor* Career-related internships or fieldwork available. Support available to part-time students

Financial award application deadline: 3/1; financial award applicants required to submit FAFSA. *Unit head:* Martin E. Ford, Senior Associate Dean, 703-993-2008.

The George Washington University, Graduate School of Education and Human Development, Department of Teacher Preparation and Special Education, Program in Early Childhood Special Education, Washington, DC 20052. Offers MA Ed. *Accreditation:* NCATE. *Degree requirements:* For master's, comprehensive exam. *Entrance requirements:* For master's, GRE General Test or MAT, minimum GPA of 2.75. *Faculty research:* Computer-assisted instruction and learning, disabled learner assessment of preschool, handicapped children.

The George Washington University, Graduate School of Education and Human Development, Department of Teacher Preparation and Special Education, Program in Infant Special Education, Washington, DC 20052. Offers MA Ed. *Accreditation:* NCATE. *Degree requirements:* For master's, comprehensive exam. *Entrance requirements:* For master's, GRE General Test or MAT, minimum GPA of 2.75. *Faculty research:* Assessment, early intervention.

The George Washington University, Graduate School of Education and Human Development, Department of Teacher Preparation and Special Education, Program in Special Education, Washington, DC 20052. Offers Ed D, Ed S. *Accreditation:* NCATE. *Degree requirements:* For doctorate, thesis/dissertation, comprehensive exam. *Entrance requirements:* For doctorate and Ed S, GRE General Test or MAT, interview, minimum GPA of 3.3.

The George Washington University, Graduate School of Education and Human Development, Department of Teacher Preparation and Special Education, Program in Special Education of Seriously Emotionally Disturbed Students, Washington, DC 20052. Offers MA Ed. *Accreditation:* NCATE. *Degree requirements:* For master's, comprehensive exam. *Entrance requirements:* For master's, GRE General Test or MAT, interview, minimum GPA of 2.75. *Faculty research:* Action research on the act of teaching emotionally disturbed students, teacher training.

The George Washington University, Graduate School of Education and Human Development, Department of Teacher Preparation and Special Education, Program in Transitional Special Education, Washington, DC 20052. Offers MA Ed, Certificate. *Accreditation:* NCATE. Evening/weekend programs available. *Degree requirements:* For master's, comprehensive exam. *Entrance requirements:* For master's, GRE General Test or MAT, interview, minimum GPA of 2.75. *Faculty research:* Computer applications for transition, transition follow-up research, curriculum-based vocational assessment, traumatic brain injury.

Georgia College & State University, Graduate School, School of Education, Department of Special Education and Administration, Program in Special Education, Milledgeville, GA 31061. Offers behavior disorders (M Ed); interrelated teaching (M Ed); learning disabilities (M Ed); mental retardation (M Ed). *Accreditation:* NCATE. *Students:* 24 full-time (22 women), 1 (woman) part-time; includes 10 minority (all African Americans) Average age 28. 32 applicants, 66% accepted, 13 enrolled. In 2006, 50 degrees awarded. *Degree requirements:* For master's, comprehensive exam. *Entrance requirements:* For master's, GRE General Test or MAT. Additional exam requirements/recommendations for international students: Required—TOEFL. *Application deadline:* For fall admission, 7/15 priority date for domestic students. Applications are processed on a rolling basis. Application fee: $25. Electronic applications accepted. *Expenses:* Tuition, state resident: full-time $3,222; part-time $179 per credit hour. Tuition, nonresident: full-time $12,870; part-time $715 per credit hour. Required fees: $391 per semester. Tuition and fees vary according to course load. *Financial support:* Career-related internships or fieldwork, Federal Work-Study, and unspecified assistantships available. Support available to part-time students. Financial award application deadline: 3/1; financial award applicants required to submit FAFSA. *Unit head:* Dr. Craig Smith, Chair, Department of Special Education and Administration, 478-445-4577, E-mail: craig.smith@gcsu.edu.

Georgian Court University, School of Education, Lakewood, NJ 08701-2697. Offers administration, supervision, and curriculum planning (MA); early intervention studies (Certificate); education (MA); instructional technology (MA, Certificate); special education (MA); substance awareness coordinator (Certificate). Part-time and evening/weekend programs available. *Faculty:* 25 full-time (14 women), 41 part-time/adjunct (23 women). *Students:* 128 full-time (110 women), 594 part-time (495 women); includes 56 minority (17 African Americans, 8 Asian Americans or Pacific Islanders, 31 Hispanic Americans), 1 international. Average age 34. 676 applicants, 80% accepted, 312 enrolled. In 2006, 130 master's, 4 other advanced degrees awarded. *Degree requirements:* For master's, thesis (for some programs), comprehensive exam (for some programs). *Entrance requirements:* For master's, GRE, MAT or NTE/PRAXIS, 3 letters of recommendation. Additional exam requirements/recommendations for international students: Required—TOEFL (minimum score 550 paper-based; 213 computer-based). *Application deadline:* For fall admission, 8/1 priority date for domestic students, 4/1 for international students; for spring admission, 1/1 priority date for domestic students, 7/1 for international students. Applications are processed on a rolling basis. Application fee: $40. Electronic applications accepted. *Financial support:* In 2006–07, 183 students received support. Scholarships/grants, health care benefits, and unspecified assistantships available. Financial award application deadline: 4/15; financial award applicants required to submit FAFSA. *Unit head:* Sr. Mary Gurley, OSF, Dean, 732-987-2525, E-mail: garleym@gergian.edu. *Application contact:* Eugene Soltys, Director of Graduate Admissions, 732-987-2760 Ext. 2760, Fax: 732-987-2000, E-mail: admissions@georgian.edu.

Georgia Southern University, Jack N. Averitt College of Graduate Studies, College of Education, Department of Teaching and Learning, Program in Special Education, Statesboro, GA 30460. Offers M Ed, MAT. *Accreditation:* NCATE. Part-time and evening/weekend programs available. *Students:* 12 full-time (11 women), 15 part-time (13 women); includes 9 minority (all African Americans) Average age 33. 13 applicants, 92% accepted, 6 enrolled. In 2006, 15 master's awarded. *Degree requirements:* For master's, electronic portfolio. *Entrance requirements:* For master's, GRE General Test or MAT, minimum GPA of 2.5. Additional exam requirements/recommendations for international students: Required—TOEFL (minimum score 550 paper-based; 213 computer-based; 80 iBT). *Application deadline:* For fall admission, 3/1 priority date for domestic students, 3/1 for international students; for spring admission, 10/1 priority date for domestic students, 10/1 for international students. Applications are processed on a rolling basis. Application fee: $50. Electronic applications accepted. *Financial support:* In 2006–07, 21 students received support, including research assistantships with partial tuition reimbursements available (averaging $5,500 per year), teaching assistantships with partial tuition reimbursements available (averaging $5,500 per year); career-related internships or fieldwork, Federal Work-Study, scholarships/grants, tuition waivers (partial), and unspecified assistantships also available. Support available to part-time students. Financial award application deadline: 4/15; financial award applicants required to submit FAFSA. *Faculty research:* Learning disorders, behavior disorders, education of the mentally retarded. *Unit head:* Dr. Margaret Lamontagne, Coordinator/Assistant Professor, 912-681-0353, Fax: 912-486-7104, E-mail: lamontag@georgiasouthern.edu. *Application contact:* 912-681-5384, Fax: 912-681-0740, E-mail: gradadmissions@georgiasouthern.edu.

Georgia Southwestern State University, Graduate Studies, School of Education, Americus, GA 31709-4693. Offers early childhood education (M Ed, Ed S); health and physical education (M Ed); middle grades education (M Ed, Ed S); reading (M Ed); secondary education (M Ed); special education (M Ed). *Accreditation:* NCATE. *Degree requirements:* For master's, comprehensive exam. *Entrance requirements:* For master's, GRE General Test or MAT, minimum GPA of 2.5; for Ed S, GRE General Test or MAT, minimum graduate GPA of 3.25, M Ed from accredited college or university, 3 years teaching experience. Electronic applications accepted.

Georgia State University, College of Education, Department of Educational Psychology and Special Education, Program in Behavior and Learning Disabilities, Atlanta, GA 30303-3083. Offers M Ed. *Accreditation:* NCATE. *Students:* 9 full-time (7 women), 81 part-time (74 women); includes 11 minority (8 African Americans, 3 American Indian/Alaska Native), 1 international. Average age 34. 20 applicants, 65% accepted. In 2006, 26 degrees awarded. *Entrance requirements:* For master's, GRE General Test, minimum GPA of 2.5. *Application deadline:* For fall admission, 5/1 for domestic students; for spring admission, 10/1 for domestic students. Application fee: $25. *Financial support:* Research assistantships available. *Faculty research:* Inclusion, behavior management, basic teaching strategies. *Unit head:* Dr. Ron P. Colarusso, Dean, College of Education, 404-651-2310.

Georgia State University, College of Education, Department of Educational Psychology and Special Education, Program in Communication Disorders, Atlanta, GA 30303-3083. Offers M Ed. *Accreditation:* ASHA; NCATE. *Students:* 46 full-time (44 women), 1 (woman) part-time; includes 5 minority (2 African Americans, 3 Asian Americans or Pacific Islanders), 1 international. Average age 26. 57 applicants, 32% accepted. In 2006, 19 degrees awarded. *Degree requirements:* For master's, comprehensive exam. *Entrance requirements:* For master's, GRE General Test, minimum GPA of 2.5. *Application deadline:* For fall admission, 2/15 for domestic students. Application fee: $25. *Financial support:* Research assistantships available. *Faculty research:* Language development, minority students, adult language disorders. *Unit head:* Dr. Ron P. Colarusso, Dean, College of Education, 404-651-2310.

Georgia State University, College of Education, Department of Educational Psychology and Special Education, Program in Education of Students with Exceptionalities, Atlanta, GA 30303-3083. Offers PhD. *Accreditation:* NCATE. *Students:* 6 full-time (all women), 22 part-time (19 women); includes 6 minority (all African Americans) Average age 39. 12 applicants, 83% accepted. In 2006, 2 degrees awarded. *Degree requirements:* For doctorate, thesis/dissertation, comprehensive exam. *Entrance requirements:* For doctorate, GRE General Test, minimum GPA of 3.3. *Application deadline:* For fall admission, 3/1 for domestic students. Application fee: $25. *Unit head:* Dr. Ron P. Colarusso, Dean, College of Education, 404-651-2310.

Gonzaga University, School of Education, Program in Special Education, Spokane, WA 99258. Offers MES. *Accreditation:* NCATE. *Faculty:* 5 full-time (1 woman), 4 part-time/adjunct (1 woman). *Students:* 6 full-time (5 women), 15 part-time (13 women); includes 3 minority (2 African Americans, 1 Hispanic American). Average age 31. In 2006, 10 degrees awarded. *Degree requirements:* For master's, comprehensive exam. *Entrance requirements:* For master's, GRE General Test or MAT, minimum B average in undergraduate course work. Additional exam requirements/recommendations for international students: Required—TOEFL. *Application deadline:* For fall admission, 7/20 priority date for domestic students; for spring admission, 11/1 for domestic students. Applications are processed on a rolling basis. Application fee: $40. *Expenses:* Tuition: Full-time $10,620; part-time $590 per credit. *Financial support:* Teaching assistantships available. Support available to part-time students. Financial award application deadline: 3/1. *Unit head:* Dr. Thomas F. McLaughlin, Chairman, 509-328-4220 Ext. 3508.

Governors State University, College of Education, Program in Multi-Categorical Special Education, University Park, IL 60466-0975. Offers MA. *Accreditation:* NCATE. Part-time and evening/weekend programs available. *Students:* 1 full-time, 152 part-time. Average age 33. *Degree requirements:* For master's, practicum. *Entrance requirements:* For master's, minimum GPA of 2.75 in last 60 hours of undergraduate course work, minimum graduate GPA of 3.0. *Application deadline:* For fall admission, 7/15 priority date for domestic students; for spring admission, 11/10 for domestic students. Applications are processed on a rolling basis. Application fee: $25. *Expenses:* Tuition, state resident: full-time $4,104; part-time $171 per hour. Tuition, nonresident: part-time $513 per hour. *Financial support:* Career-related internships or fieldwork, Federal Work-Study, institutionally sponsored loans, and tuition waivers (full and partial) available. Support available to part-time students. Financial award application deadline: 5/1.

Grambling State University, School of Graduate Studies and Research, College of Education, Department of Educational Leadership, Grambling, LA 71245. Offers curriculum and instruction (Ed D); developmental education (Ed D); educational leadership (M Ed, Ed D); special education (M Ed). Part-time and evening/weekend programs available. Post-baccalaureate distance learning degree programs offered (minimal on-campus study). *Faculty:* 8 full-time (1 woman), 2 part-time/adjunct (0 women). *Students:* 19 full-time (17 women), 63 part-time (49 women); includes 59 minority (58 African Americans, 1 Asian American or Pacific Islander), 2 international. Average age 41. In 2006, 5 master's, 4 doctorates awarded. *Degree requirements:* For master's, thesis (for some programs), comprehensive exam; for doctorate, thesis/dissertation, comprehensive exam. *Entrance requirements:* For master's, GRE, TOEFL, minimum GPA of 2.5 on last degree; for doctorate, GRE, master's degree, minimum 1000 on GRE, minimum GPA of 3.0 on last degree, minimum 500 on GRE Verbal. *Application deadline:* For fall admission, 7/1 for domestic students; for spring admission, 12/1 for domestic students. Application fee: $20 ($30 for international students). *Expenses:* Tuition, state resident: full-time $2,232; part-time $124 per credit hour. Tuition, nonresident: full-time $7,582; part-time $124 per credit hour. Required fees: $1,127. *Financial support:* In 2006–07, 59 students received support, including 7 research assistantships (averaging $5,786 per year); institutionally sponsored loans and unspecified assistantships also available. Financial award application deadline: 5/31; financial award applicants required to submit FAFSA. *Unit head:* Dr. Olatunde Ogunyemi, Director, 318-274-6105, Fax: 318-274-2799, E-mail: ogunymio@gram.edu.

Grand Valley State University, College of Education, Program in Special Education, Allendale, MI 49401-9403. Offers early childhood developmental delay (M Ed); emotional impairment (M Ed); learning disabilities (M Ed); special education endorsements (M Ed). *Accreditation:* NCATE. Part-time and evening/weekend programs available. *Faculty:* 10 full-time (6 women), 6 part-time/adjunct (3 women). *Students:* 37 full-time (33 women), 289 part-time (252 women); includes 14 minority (8 African Americans, 3 American Indian/Alaska Native, 3 Hispanic Americans). Average age 36. 46 applicants, 93% accepted, 31 enrolled. In 2006, 77 degrees awarded. *Degree requirements:* For master's, thesis. *Entrance requirements:* For master's, GRE General Test or minimum GPA of 3.0. Additional exam requirements/recommendations for international students: Required—TOEFL. *Application deadline:* Applications are processed on a rolling basis. Application fee: $30. Electronic applications accepted. *Expenses:* Tuition, state resident: full-time $5,850; part-time $325 per credit. Tuition, nonresident: full-time $10,800; part-time $600 per credit. Tuition and fees vary according to course load. *Financial support:* In 2006–07, research assistantships with full and partial tuition reimbursements (averaging $8,000 per year); career-related internships or fieldwork, Federal Work-Study, scholarships/grants, and unspecified assistantships also available. *Faculty research:* Evaluation of special education program effects, adaptive behavior assessment, language development, writing disorders, comparative effects of presentation methods. *Unit head:* Dr. Sandy Miller, Director, 616-3344. *Application contact:* Dr. Douglas Busman, Director, Student Information and Services, 616-331-6831, Fax: 616-331-6217, E-mail: busmando@gvsu.edu.

Greensboro College, Program in Education, Greensboro, NC 27401-1875. Offers elementary education (M Ed); special education (M Ed). Part-time and evening/weekend programs available. *Faculty:* 4 full-time (3 women). *Students:* 2 full-time (both women), 16 part-time (all women); includes 2 minority (1 African American, 1 Hispanic American). 5 applicants, 40% accepted, 2 enrolled. In 2006, 12 degrees awarded. *Degree requirements:* For master's, thesis. *Entrance requirements:* For master's, GRE, teacher license, 2 years of teaching experience, 2 letters of recommendation. Additional exam requirements/recommendations for international students: Required—TOEFL (minimum score 550 paper-based; 213 computer-based). *Application deadline:* For fall admission, 3/15 for domestic students. Applications are processed on a rolling basis. Application fee: $35. Electronic applications accepted. *Expenses:* Tuition: Part-time $275 per credit hour. Required fees: $30 per semester. *Financial support:* In 2006–07, 12 students received support. Scholarships/grants available. Support available to part-time students. *Unit head:* Dr. Rebecca Blomgren, Dean of Graduate and Professional Studies, 336-272-7102, Fax: 336-271-6634, E-mail: blomgrenr@gborocollege.edu.

Gwynedd-Mercy College, School of Education, Gwynedd Valley, PA 19437-0901. Offers educational administration (MS); master teacher (MS); reading (MS); school counseling (MS); special education (MS). Part-time and evening/weekend programs available. *Faculty:* 9 full-time (5 women), 37 part-time/adjunct (17 women). *Students:* 92 full-time (66 women), 464

Special Education

Gwynedd-Mercy College (continued)
part-time (374 women); includes 52 minority (49 African Americans, 3 Hispanic Americans), 1 international. Average age 34. In 2006, 160 degrees awarded. *Degree requirements:* For master's, thesis, internship, practicum. *Entrance requirements:* For master's, GRE or MAT; PPST Praxis Test, minimum GPA of 3.0. *Application deadline:* Applications are processed on a rolling basis. *Application fee:* $25. *Expenses:* Tuition: Part-time $525 per credit hour. *Financial support:* In 2006–07, 2 research assistantships were awarded; career-related internships or fieldwork, Federal Work-Study, tuition waivers (full and partial), and unspecified assistantships also available. Financial award applicants required to submit FAFSA. *Faculty research:* Learning and the brain, reading literacy, ethics and moral judgment, leadership, teaching and multicultural education. *Unit head:* Dr. Lorraine Cavaliere, EdD, Dean, 215-641-5549, Fax: 215-542-4695, E-mail: cavaliere.l@gmc.edu. *Application contact:* Marian Watkins, Graduate Program Coordinator, 215-641-5561, Fax: 215-542-4695, E-mail: watkins.m@gmc.edu.

Hampton University, Graduate College, Department of Education, Program in Special Education, Hampton, VA 23668. Offers MA. *Accreditation:* NCATE. Part-time and evening/weekend programs available. *Entrance requirements:* For master's, GRE General Test.

Harding University, College of Education, Searcy, AR 72149-0001. Offers advanced studies in teaching and learning (M Ed); art (MSE); behavioral science (MSE); Bible and religion (MSE); counseling (MS, Ed S); early childhood education (M Ed); early childhood special education (M Ed, MSE); education (MSE); educational leadership (M Ed, Ed S); elementary education (M Ed); English (MSE); family and consumer science (MSE); French (MSE); history/social science (MSE); kinesiology (MSE); math (MSE); physical science (MSE); reading (M Ed); secondary education (M Ed); Spanish (MSE); special education licensure (M Ed); teaching (MAT). *Accreditation:* NCATE. Part-time programs available. *Faculty:* 8 full-time (2 women), 45 part-time/adjunct (30 women). *Students:* 153 full-time (123 women), 469 part-time (341 women); includes 72 minority (63 African Americans, 4 American Indian/Alaska Native, 1 Asian American or Pacific Islander, 4 Hispanic Americans), 9 international. Average age 35. 175 applicants, 90% accepted, 147 enrolled. In 2006, 241 degrees awarded. *Degree requirements:* For master's, portfolio(s), thesis optional; for Ed S, portfolio, specialist project. *Entrance requirements:* For master's, GRE, MAT, PRAXIS; for Ed S, MAT or GRE. Additional exam requirements/recommendations for international students: Required—TOEFL (minimum score 550 paper-based). *Application deadline:* For fall admission, 8/1 for domestic and international students; for spring admission, 1/1 for domestic and international students. Applications are processed on a rolling basis. *Application fee:* $35. *Expenses:* Tuition: Part-time $455 per semester hour. Required fees: $20 per semester hour. Tuition and fees vary according to course load. *Financial support:* Scholarships/grants and unspecified assistantships available. Support available to part-time students. *Faculty research:* Reading, comprehension, school violence, educational technology, behavior, college choice, differentiated instruction, brain based teaching. *Unit head:* Pat Bashaw, Chair, 501-279-4183, Fax: 501-279-4051, E-mail: pbashaw@harding.edu.

Hebrew College, Shoolman Graduate School of Education, Newton Centre, MA 02459. Offers early childhood Jewish education (Certificate); Jewish day school education (Certificate); Jewish education (MJ Ed); Jewish family education (Certificate); Jewish special education (Certificate); Jewish youth education, informal education and camping (Certificate). Part-time and evening/weekend programs available. Postbaccalaureate distance learning degree programs offered. *Faculty:* 6 full-time (1 woman), 19 part-time/adjunct (7 women). *Students:* 51 (42 women). Average age 37. 33 applicants, 79% accepted, 19 enrolled. In 2006, 5 degrees awarded. *Degree requirements:* For master's, one foreign language. *Entrance requirements:* For master's, GRE, interview. Additional exam requirements/recommendations for international students: Required—TOEFL. *Application deadline:* For fall admission, 12/15 priority date for domestic and international students; for winter admission, 2/15 priority date for domestic and international students; for spring admission, 5/30 priority date for domestic and international students. *Application fee:* $50. *Financial support:* Fellowships, career-related internships or fieldwork and tuition waivers (partial) available. Support available to part-time students. Financial award application deadline: 4/15; financial award applicants required to submit FAFSA. *Unit head:* Dr. Barry Mesch, Provost, 617-559-8600, Fax: 617-559-8601, E-mail: bmesch@hebrewcollege.edu. *Application contact:* Kate Nachman, Director of Admissions, 617-559-8610, Fax: 617-559-8601, E-mail: admissions@hebrewcollege.edu.

Henderson State University, Graduate Studies, School of Education, Department of Educational Leadership and Special Education, Arkadelphia, AR 71999-0001. Offers early childhood special education (MSE); education (MAT); educational leadership (Ed S); instructional specialist (MSE); school administration (MSE). *Faculty:* 7 full-time (4 women), 3 part-time/adjunct (2 women). *Students:* 6 full-time (3 women), 144 part-time (113 women); includes 14 minority (all African Americans) Average age 35. In 2006, 18 degrees awarded. *Expenses:* Tuition, state resident: full-time $3,294; part-time $183 per credit hour. Tuition, nonresident: full-time $6,588; part-time $366 per credit hour. Required fees: $176 per term. *Unit head:* Dr. Bruce Smith, Chairperson, 870-230-5282. *Application contact:* Dr. Marck L. Beggs, Graduate Dean, 870-230-5126, Fax: 870-230-5479, E-mail: beggsm@hsu.edu.

Heritage University, Graduate Programs in Education, Program in Professional Studies, Toppenish, WA 98948-9599. Offers bilingual education/ESL (M Ed); biology (M Ed); English and literature (M Ed); reading/literacy (M Ed); special education (M Ed). Part-time and evening/weekend programs available. *Students:* 174 (125 women); includes 52 minority (1 African American, 4 American Indian/Alaska Native, 6 Asian Americans or Pacific Islanders, 41 Hispanic Americans). Average age 37. In 2006, 84 degrees awarded. *Degree requirements:* For master's, thesis (for some programs), comprehensive exam (for some programs), registration. *Application deadline:* Applications are processed on a rolling basis. *Application fee:* $50 ($100 for international students). *Financial support:* Career-related internships or fieldwork, Federal Work-Study, institutionally sponsored loans, and tuition waivers (partial) available. Support available to part-time students. *Unit head:* Dr. Jack McPherson, Head, 509-865-8626, E-mail: mcpherson_j@heritage.edu. *Application contact:* Kathy Otto, Coordinator of Administrative Services, 509-865-8635, Fax: 509-865-8629, E-mail: otto_k@heritage.edu.

High Point University, Norcross Graduate School, High Point, NC 27262-3598. Offers business administration (MBA); educational leadership (M Ed); elementary education (M Ed); history (MA); nonprofit organizations (MPA); special education (M Ed); sport studies (MS). *Accreditation:* ACBSP; NCATE. Part-time and evening/weekend programs available. *Faculty:* 31 full-time (11 women), 1 part-time/adjunct (0 women). *Students:* 49 full-time (29 women), 202 part-time (130 women); includes 72 minority (66 African Americans, 1 American Indian/Alaska Native, 2 Asian Americans or Pacific Islanders, 3 Hispanic Americans), 11 international. Average age 33. 171 applicants, 71% accepted, 94 enrolled. In 2006, 95 degrees awarded. *Degree requirements:* For master's, thesis (for some programs), comprehensive exam (for some programs), registration. *Entrance requirements:* For master's, GMAT (MBA), GRE, MAT, minimum GPA of 3.0. Additional exam requirements/recommendations for international students: Required—TOEFL (minimum score 550 paper-based). *Application deadline:* For fall admission, 4/15 priority date for domestic and international students; for spring admission, 10/15 priority date for domestic and international students. Applications are processed on a rolling basis. *Application fee:* $50. Electronic applications accepted. *Expenses:* Tuition: Full-time $9,270; part-time $1,545 per course. *Financial support:* In 2006–07, 190 students received support. Federal Work-Study, scholarships/grants, and unspecified assistantships available. Support available to part-time students. Financial award application deadline: 3/1; financial award applicants required to submit FAFSA. *Application contact:* Dr. Alberta Haynes Herron, Dean of Norcross Graduate School, 336-841-9198, Fax: 336-888-6378, E-mail: aherron@highpoint.edu.

Hofstra University, School of Education and Allied Human Services, Department of Counseling, Research, Special Education and Rehabilitation, Program in Creative Arts Therapy, Hempstead, NY 11549. Offers creative arts therapy (MA); creative arts therapy and special

---

education (birth-grade 2) (MS Ed); creative arts therapy and special education (grades 1-12) (MS Ed). Part-time programs available. *Students:* 45 full-time (44 women), 16 part-time (15 women); includes 6 minority (1 African American, 2 Asian Americans or Pacific Islanders, 3 Hispanic Americans), 7 international. Average age 29. 62 applicants, 87% accepted, 29 enrolled. In 2006, 22 degrees awarded. *Degree requirements:* For master's, thesis optional. *Entrance requirements:* For master's, interview, portfolio, 3 letters of recommendation, 12 hours of course work in psychology, 18 hours of course work in studio art, certificate, minimum GPA of 2.75. Additional exam requirements/recommendations for international students: Required—TOEFL (minimum score 550 paper-based; 213 computer-based). *Application deadline:* Applications are processed on a rolling basis. *Application fee:* $60. Electronic applications accepted. *Expenses:* Tuition: Full-time $13,320; part-time $740 per credit. Required fees: $930; $155 per term. *Financial support:* In 2006–07, 29 students received support, including 2 fellowships with tuition reimbursements available (averaging $3,000 per year), 3 research assistantships with full and partial tuition reimbursements available (averaging $5,387 per year); career-related internships or fieldwork, scholarships/grants, and tuition waivers (full and partial) also available. Financial award applicants required to submit FAFSA. *Faculty research:* Creativity for non-artists, medical art therapy, play therapy, community art therapy. *Unit head:* Dr. Joan S. Bloomgarden, Director, 516-463-5300, Fax: 516-463-6184, E-mail: cprjsb@hofstra.edu. *Application contact:* Carol Drummer, Dean of Graduate Admissions, 516-463-4876, Fax: 516-463-4664, E-mail: gradstudent@hofstra.edu.

Hofstra University, School of Education and Allied Human Services, Department of Counseling, Research, Special Education and Rehabilitation, Program in Special Education, Hempstead, NY 11549. Offers early childhood special education (MS Ed, Advanced Certificate); gifted education (Advanced Certificate); inclusive early childhood special education (MS Ed); inclusive elementary special education (MS Ed); inclusive secondary special education (MS Ed); literacy studies and special education (MS Ed); special education (MA, MS Ed, PD); special education assessment and diagnosis (Advanced Certificate); teaching students with severe/multiple disabilities (Advanced Certificate). *Accreditation:* NCATE. Part-time and evening/weekend programs available. Postbaccalaureate distance learning degree programs offered. *Students:* 87 full-time (82 women), 116 part-time (110 women); includes 21 minority (8 African Americans, 4 Asian Americans or Pacific Islanders, 9 Hispanic Americans). Average age 28. 110 applicants, 79% accepted, 61 enrolled. In 2006, 74 master's, 7 other advanced degrees awarded. *Degree requirements:* For master's, thesis (for some programs), seminars, student teaching, comprehensive exam (for some programs), registration; for other advanced degree, fieldwork. *Entrance requirements:* For master's, interview, 3 letters of reference, resumé, minimum GPA of 3.0; for other advanced degree, interview, 3 letters of recommendation, resumé. Additional exam requirements/recommendations for international students: Required—TOEFL (minimum score 550 paper-based; 213 computer-based). *Application deadline:* Applications are processed on a rolling basis. *Application fee:* $60. Electronic applications accepted. *Expenses:* Tuition: Full-time $13,320; part-time $740 per credit. Required fees: $930; $155 per term. *Financial support:* In 2006–07, 64 students received support, including 6 fellowships with tuition reimbursements available (averaging $2,552 per year), 4 research assistantships with full and partial tuition reimbursements available (averaging $4,378 per year); Federal Work-Study, scholarships/grants, tuition waivers (full and partial), and unspecified assistantships also available. Support available to part-time students. Financial award applicants required to submit FAFSA. *Faculty research:* Inclusive schooling, autism spectrum disorders related services, parent participation in the special education process, co-teaching student teaching. *Unit head:* Dr. George Guiliani, Director, 516-463-5778, Fax: 516-463-6184, E-mail: cprdcs@hofstra.edu. *Application contact:* Carol Drummer, Dean of Graduate Admissions, 516-463-4876, Fax: 516-463-4664, E-mail: gradstudent@hofstra.edu.

Holy Names University, Graduate Division, Department of Education, Oakland, CA 94619-1699. Offers advanced curriculum studies (M Ed); educational therapy (M Ed); mild/moderate disabilities (Ed S); multiple subject credential (M Ed); single subject credential (M Ed); special education (M Ed); teaching English as a second language (M Ed, Certificate); urban education (M Ed). Part-time programs available. *Faculty:* 6 full-time (all women), 9 part-time/adjunct (all women). *Students:* 17 full-time (14 women), 131 part-time (90 women); includes 58 minority (36 African Americans, 1 American Indian/Alaska Native, 11 Asian Americans or Pacific Islanders, 10 Hispanic Americans). Average age 40. 75 applicants, 80% accepted, 49 enrolled. In 2006, 11 master's, 29 Certificates awarded. *Degree requirements:* For master's, research paper, thesis or project. *Entrance requirements:* For master's, minimum undergraduate GPA of 2.6 overall, 3.0 in major. Additional exam requirements/recommendations for international students: Required—TOEFL. *Application deadline:* For fall admission, 8/1 priority date for domestic students; for spring admission, 12/1 priority date for domestic students. Applications are processed on a rolling basis. *Application fee:* $50. *Expenses:* Tuition: Full-time $10,800; part-time $600 per unit. Required fees: $240; $120 per term. *Financial support:* In 2006–07, 67 students received support. Scholarships/grants available. Support available to part-time students. Financial award application deadline: 3/2; financial award applicants required to submit FAFSA. *Faculty research:* Cognitive development, language development, learning handicaps. *Unit head:* Dr. Zaida McCall-Perez, Chairperson, 510-436-1288, E-mail: mccallperez@hnu.edu. *Application contact:* 800-430-1351, Fax: 510-436-1325, E-mail: admissions@hnu.edu.

Hood College, Graduate School, Department of Education, Frederick, MD 21701-8575. Offers curriculum and instruction (MS), including early childhood education, elementary education, elementary school science and mathematics, secondary education, special education; educational leadership (MS); reading specialization (MS); teaching the struggling reader (Certificate). Part-time and evening/weekend programs available. *Faculty:* 4 full-time (3 women), 32 part-time/adjunct (16 women). *Students:* 5 full-time (3 women), 371 part-time (313 women); includes 30 minority (23 African Americans, 4 Asian Americans or Pacific Islanders, 3 Hispanic Americans). Average age 32. 71 applicants, 99% accepted, 59 enrolled. In 2006, 67 degrees awarded. *Degree requirements:* For master's, action research project, portfolio (reading). *Entrance requirements:* For master's, minimum GPA of 2.5, teaching certification. *Application deadline:* Applications are processed on a rolling basis. *Application fee:* $35. *Expenses:* Tuition: Part-time $350 per credit. Required fees: $20 per semester. *Financial support:* Applicants required to submit FAFSA. *Faculty research:* Leadership, action research, brain research, learning styles. *Unit head:* Dr. John George, Chairperson, 301-696-3471, Fax: 301-696-3597, E-mail: george@hood.edu. *Application contact:* Dr. Kathleen C. Bands, Associate Dean of Graduate School, 301-696-3811, Fax: 301-696-3597, E-mail: gofurther@hood.edu.

Howard University, School of Education, Department of Curriculum and Instruction, Program in Special Education, Washington, DC 20059-0002. Offers M Ed, MA, CAGS. MA offered through the Graduate School of Arts and Sciences. *Accreditation:* NCATE. Part-time programs available. *Faculty:* 2 full-time (1 woman). *Students:* 3 full-time (2 women), 6 part-time (3 women); includes 8 minority (all African Americans), 1 international. Average age 32. 9 applicants, 33% accepted, 1 enrolled. In 2006, 6 degrees awarded. *Degree requirements:* For master's, thesis (for some programs), expository writing exam, internships, practicum, comprehensive exam. *Entrance requirements:* For master's, GRE General Test (MA), minimum GPA of 2.7. *Application deadline:* For fall admission, 4/1 priority date for domestic students; for spring admission, 11/1 for domestic students. Applications are processed on a rolling basis. *Application fee:* $45. *Financial support:* Fellowships, research assistantships, teaching assistantships, career-related internships or fieldwork, Federal Work-Study, institutionally sponsored loans, scholarships/grants, and unspecified assistantships available. Financial award application deadline: 4/1. *Unit head:* Dr. Wilfred A. Johnson, Associate Professor/Coordinator, 202-806-7339, Fax: 202-806-5297, E-mail: wajohnson@howard.edu.

Hunter College of the City University of New York, Graduate School, School of Education, Department of Special Education, New York, NY 10021-5085. Offers blind or visually impaired (MS Ed); deaf or hard of hearing (MS Ed); severe/multiple disabilities (MS Ed); special education (MS Ed). *Accreditation:* NCATE. *Faculty:* 10 full-time (8 women), 31 part-time/adjunct (26 women). *Students:* 46 full-time (44 women), 354 part-time (321 women); includes 74 minority (21 African Americans, 25 Asian Americans or Pacific Islanders, 28 Hispanic Americans).

Average age 30. 74 applicants. In 2006, 119 degrees awarded. *Degree requirements:* For master's, thesis, student teaching practica and clinical teaching lab courses, New York State Teacher Certification exams, comprehensive exam. *Entrance requirements:* For master's, minimum GPA of 2.8. Additional exam requirements/recommendations for international students: Required—TOEFL, TWE. *Application deadline:* For fall admission, 4/1 for domestic students, 2/1 for international students; for spring admission, 11/1 for domestic students, 9/1 for international students. Applications are processed on a rolling basis. Application fee: $50. *Expenses:* Tuition, state resident: part-time $270 per credit. Tuition, nonresident: part-time $500 per credit. Required fees: $45 per semester. *Financial support:* Career-related internships or fieldwork, Federal Work-Study, institutionally sponsored loans, and tuition waivers (partial) available. Support available to part-time students. *Faculty research:* Mathematics learning disabilities; street behavior; assessment; bilingual special education; families, diversity, and disabilities. *Unit head:* Dr. Kate Garnett, Chairperson, 212-772-4701, E-mail: kgarnett@hunter.cuny.edu. *Application contact:* William Zlata, Director for Graduate Admissions, 212-772-4482, Fax: 212-650-3336, E-mail: admissions@hunter.cuny.edu.

Hunter College of the City University of New York, Graduate School, Schools of the Health Professions, Communication Sciences Program, New York, NY 10021-5085. Offers audiology (MS); speech language pathology (MS); teacher of speech and hearing handicapped (MS). *Accreditation:* ASHA. Part-time programs available. *Faculty:* 14 full-time (13 women), 3 part-time/adjunct (2 women). *Students:* 49 full-time (47 women), 2 part-time (1 woman); includes 5 minority (3 African Americans, 2 Hispanic Americans). Average age 28. 360 applicants, 28% accepted, 45 enrolled. In 2006, 46 degrees awarded. *Degree requirements:* For master's, National Teacher Exam, research project. *Entrance requirements:* For master's, GRE, letters of reference. Additional exam requirements/recommendations for international students: Required—TOEFL. *Application deadline:* For fall admission, 4/1 for domestic students, 2/1 for international students; for spring admission, 11/1 for domestic students, 9/1 for international students. Application fee: $125. *Expenses:* Tuition, state resident: part-time $270 per credit. Tuition, nonresident: part-time $500 per credit. Required fees: $45 per semester. *Financial support:* In 2006–07, 12 students received support, including 3 fellowships with partial tuition reimbursements available (averaging $1,000 per year), 6 research assistantships; career-related internships or fieldwork, Federal Work-Study, institutionally sponsored loans, scholarships/grants, and tuition waivers (full and partial) also available. Support available to part-time students. Financial award application deadline: 3/1. *Faculty research:* Aging and communication disorders, fluency, speech science, diagnostic audiology, amplification. Total annual research expenditures: $600,000. *Unit head:* Dr. Dava Waltzman, Director, 212-481-4339, Fax: 212-481-4467, E-mail: dwaltzma@hejira.hunter.cuny.edu. *Application contact:* William Zlata, Director for Graduate Admissions, 212-772-4482, Fax: 212-650-3336, E-mail: admissions@hunter.cuny.edu.

Idaho State University, Office of Graduate Studies, College of Education, Department of Educational Learning and Development, Pocatello, ID 83209. Offers human exceptionality (M Ed); school psychology (Ed S); special education (Ed S). Part-time programs available. *Faculty:* 3 full-time (1 woman). *Students:* 24 full-time (19 women), 26 part-time (20 women); includes 2 minority (both Hispanic Americans), 4 international. Average age 41. In 2006, 12 master's, 1 other advanced degree awarded. *Degree requirements:* For master's, thesis (for some programs), comprehensive exam, registration (for some programs); for Ed S, thesis (for some programs), oral exam, comprehensive exam, registration. *Entrance requirements:* For master's, GRE or MAT, minimum undergraduate GPA of 3.0; for Ed S, master's degree. Additional exam requirements/recommendations for international students: Required—TOEFL (minimum score 550 paper-based; 213 computer-based; 80 iBT). *Application deadline:* For fall admission, 7/1 for domestic students, 6/1 for international students; for spring admission, 12/1 for domestic students, 11/1 for international students. Applications are processed on a rolling basis. Application fee: $55. *Expenses:* Tuition, state resident: part-time $251 per credit. Tuition, nonresident: part-time $366 per credit. Tuition and fees vary according to degree level, program and reciprocity agreements. *Unit head:* Dr. Lloyd Peterson, Chairman, 208-282-6058, Fax: 208-282-4697, E-mail: petelloy@isu.edu. *Application contact:* Dr. Peter Denner, Assistant Dean, 208-282-3807, Fax: 208-282-4697, E-mail: dennpete@isu.edu.

Idaho State University, Office of Graduate Studies, Kasiska College of Health Professions, Department of Communication Sciences and Disorders and Education of the Deaf, Pocatello, ID 83209. Offers audiology (MS, Au D); deaf education (MS); speech language pathology (MS). *Accreditation:* ASHA (one or more programs are accredited). Part-time programs available. Postbaccalaureate distance learning degree programs offered (minimal on-campus study). *Faculty:* 5 full-time (1 woman), 1 (woman) part-time/adjunct. *Students:* 95 full-time (72 women), 16 part-time (13 women); includes 5 minority (4 Asian Americans or Pacific Islanders, 1 Hispanic American), 1 international. Average age 35. In 2006, 35 degrees awarded. *Degree requirements:* For master's and doctorate, externship, thesis optional. *Entrance requirements:* For master's, GRE General Test, minimum GPA of 3.0, 3 letters of recommendation; for doctorate, GRE General Test, minimum GPA of 3.0, 3 letters or recommendation. Additional exam requirements/recommendations for international students: Required—TOEFL (minimum score 600 paper-based; 250 computer-based). *Application deadline:* For fall admission, 7/1 for domestic students, 6/1 for international students; for spring admission, 12/1 for domestic students, 11/1 for international students. Applications are processed on a rolling basis. Application fee: $55. *Financial support:* In 2006–07, 5 teaching assistantships with full and partial tuition reimbursements (averaging $8,694 per year) were awarded; career-related internships or fieldwork, Federal Work-Study, institutionally sponsored loans, scholarships/grants, and unspecified assistantships also available. Financial award application deadline: 1/1. *Faculty research:* Clinical efficacy, voice disorders, closed head injury, phonology, assistive technology. Total annual research expenditures: $497,331. *Unit head:* Joni Loftin, Chairman, 208-282-4196, Fax: 208-282-4571, E-mail: loftjoni@isu.edu. *Application contact:* Ellen Combs, Graduate School Technical Records Specialist, 208-282-2150, Fax: 208-282-4847.

Illinois State University, Graduate School, College of Education, Department of Special Education, Normal, IL 61790-2200. Offers guidance and counseling (MS, MS Ed); special education (MS, MS Ed, Ed D). *Accreditation:* NCATE. *Faculty:* 14 full-time (9 women). *Students:* 7 full-time (all women), 112 part-time (104 women); includes 3 minority (2 African Americans, 1 Asian American or Pacific Islander), 1 international. 23 applicants, 78% accepted. In 2006, 23 master's, 1 doctorate awarded. *Degree requirements:* For doctorate, thesis/dissertation, 2 terms of residency. *Entrance requirements:* For master's, GRE General Test, minimum GPA of 3.0 in last 60 hours; for doctorate, GRE General Test. *Application deadline:* Applications are processed on a rolling basis. Application fee: $40. *Expenses:* Tuition, state resident: full-time $3,330; part-time $185 per credit hour. Tuition, nonresident: full-time $6,948; part-time $438 per credit hour. Required fees: $1,259; $52 per credit hour. *Financial support:* In 2006–07, 6 research assistantships (averaging $4,950 per year) were awarded; tuition waivers (full and partial) and unspecified assistantships also available. Financial award application deadline: 4/1. *Faculty research:* Center for adult learning leadership, promoting a learning community, autism/spectrum professional development and technical assistance project, early intervention for children who are deaf and hard of hearing in Illinois. Total annual research expenditures: $1.1 million. *Unit head:* Dr. James Thompson, Chairperson, 309-438-5419.

Immaculata University, College of Graduate Studies, Program in Educational Leadership and Administration, Immaculata, PA 19345. Offers educational leadership and administration (MA, Ed D); elementary education (Certificate); intermediate unit director (Certificate); school principal (Certificate); school superintendent (Certificate); secondary education (Certificate); special education (Certificate). Part-time and evening/weekend programs available. *Students:* 27 full-time (15 women), 510 part-time (353 women). Average age 33. 86 applicants, 74% accepted, 53 enrolled. In 2006, 47 master's, 27 doctorates awarded. *Degree requirements:* For master's, thesis optional; for doctorate, thesis/dissertation, comprehensive exam. *Entrance requirements:* For master's, GRE or MAT, minimum GPA of 3.0; for doctorate, GRE General Test, minimum GPA of 3.5. Additional exam requirements/recommendations for international students: Required—TOEFL. Application fee: $35. *Financial support:* Application deadline:5/1. *Faculty research:* Cooperative learning, school-based management, whole language, performance assessment. *Unit head:* Sr. Carol Anne Couchara, Chair, 610-647-4400 Ext. 3280, E-mail: ccouchara@immaculata.edu. *Application contact:* 610-647-4400 Ext. 3211, Fax: 610-993-8550, E-mail: graduate@immaculata.edu.

Indiana University Bloomington, School of Education, Department of Curriculum and Instruction, Bloomington, IN 47405-7000. Offers art education (MS, Ed D, PhD); curriculum studies (Ed D, PhD); elementary education (MS, Ed D, PhD, Ed S); mathematics education (MS, Ed D, PhD); science education (MS, Ed D, PhD); secondary education (MS, Ed D, PhD); social studies education (MS, PhD); special education (MS, Ed D, PhD, Ed S). PhD offered through the University Graduate School. *Accreditation:* NCATE. Part-time and evening/weekend programs available. *Students:* 39 full-time (28 women), 82 part-time (54 women); includes 15 minority (5 African Americans, 1 American Indian/Alaska Native, 6 Asian Americans or Pacific Islanders, 3 Hispanic Americans), 33 international. Average age 37. In 2006, 1 degree awarded. Terminal master's awarded for partial completion of doctoral program. *Degree requirements:* For doctorate, thesis/dissertation; for Ed S, comprehensive exam or project. *Entrance requirements:* For master's, doctorate, and Ed S, GRE General Test. *Application deadline:* For fall admission, 6/1 priority date for domestic students, 3/1 for international students; for winter admission, 11/1 priority date for domestic students; for spring admission, 9/1 for international students. Applications are processed on a rolling basis. Application fee: $50 ($60 for international students). Electronic applications accepted. *Expenses:* Tuition, state resident: full-time $5,791; part-time $241 per credit hour. Tuition, nonresident: full-time $16,866; part-time $703 per credit hour. *Financial support:* Fellowships with full and partial tuition reimbursements, research assistantships with full and partial tuition reimbursements, teaching assistantships with full and partial tuition reimbursements, career-related internships or fieldwork, Federal Work-Study, institutionally sponsored loans, and tuition waivers (partial) available. Support available to part-time students. *Unit head:* Cary Buzzelli, Chairperson, 812-856-8100. *Application contact:* Bobbie Partenheimer, Admissions Services Coordinator, 812-856-8127, Fax: 812-856-8333, E-mail: partenhe@indiana.edu.

Indiana University of Pennsylvania, School of Graduate Studies and Research, College of Education and Educational Technology, Department of Special Education and Clinical Services, Program in Education of Exceptional Persons, Indiana, PA 15705-1087. Offers M Ed. *Accreditation:* NCATE. *Faculty:* 9 full-time (8 women), 1 (woman) part-time/adjunct. *Students:* 5 full-time (3 women), 28 part-time (25 women), 1 international. Average age 30. 21 applicants, 57% accepted. In 2006, 10 degrees awarded. *Degree requirements:* For master's, thesis optional. *Entrance requirements:* For master's, 2 letters of recommendation. Additional exam requirements/recommendations for international students: Required—TOEFL. *Application deadline:* For fall admission, 3/1 priority date for domestic students; for spring admission, 7/1 for domestic students. Applications are processed on a rolling basis. Application fee: $30. *Expenses:* Tuition, state resident: full-time $6,048; part-time $336 per credit. Tuition, nonresident: full-time $9,678; part-time $538 per credit. Required fees: $1,069; $148 per year. *Financial support:* In 2006–07, 2 research assistantships with full and partial tuition reimbursements (averaging $4,990 per year) were awarded; career-related internships or fieldwork and Federal Work-Study also available. Support available to part-time students. Financial award application deadline: 3/15; financial award applicants required to submit FAFSA. *Unit head:* Dr. Janice Baker, Graduate Coordinator, 724-357-5680, E-mail: jmbaker@iup.edu.

Indiana University South Bend, School of Education, South Bend, IN 46634-7111. Offers counseling and human services (MS Ed); elementary education (MS Ed); secondary education (MS Ed); special education (MS Ed). *Accreditation:* NCATE. Part-time and evening/weekend programs available. *Faculty:* 21 full-time (11 women), 9 part-time/adjunct (3 women). *Students:* 58 full-time (38 women), 237 part-time (186 women); includes 33 minority (22 African Americans, 1 American Indian/Alaska Native, 6 Asian Americans or Pacific Islanders, 4 Hispanic Americans), 5 international. Average age 35. 127 applicants, 100% accepted, 61 enrolled. In 2006, 141 degrees awarded. *Degree requirements:* For master's, thesis or alternative, exit project. *Entrance requirements:* For master's, letters of recommendation, GRE or minimum GPA of 3.0. Additional exam requirements/recommendations for international students: Required—TOEFL. *Application deadline:* For fall admission, 7/1 for domestic students; for spring admission, 11/1 for domestic students. Applications are processed on a rolling basis. Application fee: $45. Electronic applications accepted. *Expenses:* Tuition, state resident: full-time $4,450; part-time $185 per credit hour. Tuition, nonresident: full-time $10,954; part-time $456 per credit hour. Tuition and fees vary according to course load, campus/location and program. *Financial support:* Career-related internships or fieldwork available. Support available to part-time students. Financial award application deadline: 3/1; financial award applicants required to submit FAFSA. *Faculty research:* Professional dispositions, early childhood literacy, online learning, program assessments, problem-based learning. *Unit head:* Dr. Michael Horvath, Professor and Dean, School of Education, 574-520-4339, Fax: 574-520-4550. *Application contact:* Gil L. Martin, Graduate Admissions and Recruitment Officer, 574-520-4585, Fax: 574-520-5549, E-mail: marting@iusb.edu.

Inter American University of Puerto Rico, Metropolitan Campus, Faculty of Education, Program in Special Education, San Juan, PR 00919-1293. Offers MA Ed. *Degree requirements:* For master's, comprehensive exam. *Entrance requirements:* For master's, GRE or EXADEP, interview. Electronic applications accepted.

Inter American University of Puerto Rico, San Germán Campus, Graduate Studies Center, Graduate Program in Special Education, San Germán, PR 00683-5008. Offers MA. Part-time and evening/weekend programs available. *Faculty:* 8 full-time, 11 part-time/adjunct. *Students:* 43. Average age 33. In 2006, 7 degrees awarded. *Degree requirements:* For master's, comprehensive exam. *Entrance requirements:* For master's, GRE General Test or EXADEP, minimum GPA of 3.0. *Application deadline:* For fall admission, 4/30 priority date for domestic students; for spring admission, 11/15 for domestic students. Applications are processed on a rolling basis. Application fee: $31. *Expenses:* Tuition: Part-time $175 per credit. Required fees: $238 per semester. Tuition and fees vary according to degree level. *Financial support:* Teaching assistantships available. *Application contact:* Dr. Aurora Graniela, Graduate Coordinator, 787-264-1912 Ext. 7355, Fax: 787-892-7510, E-mail: aurora@sg.inter.edu.

Iowa State University of Science and Technology, Graduate College, College of Human Sciences, Department of Curriculum and Instruction, Ames, IA 50011. Offers curriculum and instructional technology (M Ed, MS, PhD); elementary education (M Ed, MS); historical, philosophical, and comparative studies in education (M Ed, MS); special education (M Ed, MS). *Faculty:* 28 full-time, 3 part-time/adjunct. *Students:* 54 full-time (40 women), 78 part-time (54 women); includes 11 minority (3 African Americans, 4 Asian Americans or Pacific Islanders, 4 Hispanic Americans), 26 international. 64 applicants, 69% accepted, 32 enrolled. In 2006, 31 master's, 10 doctorates awarded. *Degree requirements:* For master's, thesis or alternative; for doctorate, thesis/dissertation. *Entrance requirements:* For doctorate, GRE General Test. Additional exam requirements/recommendations for international students: Required—TOEFL (paper-based 560; computer-based 220; iBT 83) or IELTS (6.5). *Application deadline:* For fall admission, 1/1 priority date for domestic and international students; for spring admission, 9/1 for domestic and international students. Application fee: $30 ($70 for international students). Electronic applications accepted. *Expenses:* Tuition, state resident: full-time $5,936; part-time $330 per credit. Tuition, nonresident: full-time $16,350; part-time $330 per credit. *Financial support:* In 2006–07, 22 research assistantships with full and partial tuition reimbursements (averaging $17,457 per year), 17 teaching assistantships with full and partial tuition reimbursements (averaging $17,788 per year) were awarded; fellowships, scholarships/grants, health care benefits, and unspecified assistantships also available. *Unit head:* Dr. Carl Smith, Chair, 515-294-7021, E-mail: cigrad@iastate.edu. *Application contact:* Dr. Patricia Leigh, Director of Graduate Education, 515-294-7021, E-mail: cigrad@iastate.edu.

Jackson State University, Graduate School, School of Education, Department of Special Education and Rehabilitative Services, Jackson, MS 39217. Offers rehabilitative counseling service (MS Ed); special education (MS Ed, Ed S). *Accreditation:* NCATE. Evening/weekend programs available. *Faculty:* 9 full-time (7 women), 3 part-time/adjunct (1 woman). *Students:* 3

Special Education

Jackson State University *(continued)*
full-time (1 woman), 9 part-time (3 women); includes 11 minority (all African Americans) In 2006, 7 master's, 2 other advanced degrees awarded. *Degree requirements:* For master's, thesis or alternative, comprehensive exam. *Entrance requirements:* For master's, GRE General Test. Additional exam requirements/recommendations for international students: Required—TOEFL. *Application deadline:* For fall admission, 3/1 priority date for domestic students; for spring admission, 10/1 for domestic students. Applications are processed on a rolling basis. Application fee: $20. *Financial support:* In 2006–07, 6 students received support. Career-related internships or fieldwork, Federal Work-Study, scholarships/grants, and unspecified assistantships available. Support available to part-time students. Financial award application deadline: 3/1; financial award applicants required to submit FAFSA. *Unit head:* Dr. Gladys Johnson, Chair, 601-979-2370, Fax: 601-979-2213, E-mail: gladys.johnson@jsums.edu. *Application contact:* Curtis Gore, Director of Graduate Admissions, 601-979-2455, Fax: 601-974-4325, E-mail: cgore@ccaix.jsums.edu.

Jacksonville State University, College of Graduate Studies and Continuing Education, College of Education and Professional Studies, Program in Special Education, Jacksonville, AL 36265-1602. Offers MS Ed. *Accreditation:* NCATE. *Faculty:* 4 full-time (2 women), 1 (woman) part-time/adjunct. *Students:* 16 full-time (14 women), 41 part-time (34 women); includes 6 minority (all African Americans) In 2006, 37 degrees awarded. *Entrance requirements:* For master's, GRE General Test or MAT. *Application deadline:* Applications are processed on a rolling basis. Application fee: $20. *Expenses:* Tuition, state resident: full-time $5,400; part-time $225 per credit hour. Tuition, nonresident: full-time $10,800; part-time $450 per credit hour. One-time fee: $20 full-time. *Financial support:* In 2006–07, 1 research assistantship was awarded; teaching assistantships. Support available to part-time students. Financial award application deadline: 4/1. *Unit head:* Dr. Steve Armstrong, Head, 256-782-5842. *Application contact:* 256-782-5329.

James Madison University, College of Graduate and Outreach Programs, College of Education, Exceptional Education Department, Program in Exceptional Education, Harrisonburg, VA 22807. Offers M Ed. *Accreditation:* NCATE. Part-time programs available. *Students:* 50 full-time (all women), 6 part-time (4 women). Average age 27. In 2006, 49 degrees awarded. *Entrance requirements:* For master's, GRE General Test. Additional exam requirements/recommendations for international students: Required—TOEFL. *Application deadline:* For fall admission, 5/1 priority date for domestic students; for spring admission, 9/1 priority date for domestic students. Applications are processed on a rolling basis. Application fee: $55. Electronic applications accepted. *Expenses:* Tuition, state resident: full-time $6,336; part-time $264 per credit hour. Tuition, nonresident: full-time $17,832; part-time $743 per credit hour. *Financial support:* In 2006–07, 9 students received support. Federal Work-Study and unspecified assistantships available. Financial award application deadline: 3/1; financial award applicants required to submit FAFSA. *Unit head:* Dr. Maggie Kyger, Academic Unit Head, 540-568-6137.

The Johns Hopkins University, School of Professional Studies in Business and Education, School of Education, Department of Special Education, Baltimore, MD 21218-2699. Offers advanced methods for differential instruction and inclusive education (Certificate); assistive technology for communication and social interaction (Certificate); early intervention/preschool special education specialist (Certificate); education of students with autism and other pervasive developmental disorders (Certificate); special education (MS, Ed D, CAGS). *Accreditation:* NCATE. Part-time and evening/weekend programs available. *Students:* 33 full-time (31 women), 269 part-time (234 women); includes 41 minority (30 African Americans, 5 Asian Americans or Pacific Islanders, 6 Hispanic Americans), 3 international. Average age 29. 233 applicants, 76% accepted, 167 enrolled. In 2006, 69 master's, 1 doctorate, 14 other advanced degrees awarded. *Degree requirements:* For master's, registration; for doctorate, thesis/dissertation, comprehensive exam, registration. *Entrance requirements:* For master's, minimum GPA of 3.0, interview; for doctorate, GRE, interview, minimum GPA of 3.0, letters of recommendation, professional experience, resumé; for other advanced degree, master's or doctoral degree, interview, minimum GPA of 3.0. Additional exam requirements/recommendations for international students: Required—TOEFL (minimum score 600 paper-based; 250 computer-based; 100 iBT). *Application deadline:* For fall admission, 5/1 for international students; for spring admission, 10/15 for international students. Applications are processed on a rolling basis. Application fee: $60. *Expenses:* Tuition: Full-time $32,976. Tuition and fees vary according to degree level and program. *Financial support:* Scholarships/grants available. Support available to part-time students. Financial award application deadline: 6/1; financial award applicants required to submit FAFSA. *Unit head:* Dr. Gloria Lane, Chair, 410-516-8275. *Application contact:* Carol Herrman, Admissions Coordinator, 410-872-1234, Fax: 410-872-1251, E-mail: onestop. admissions@jhu.edu.

Johnson State College, Graduate Program in Education, Programs in Special Education, Johnson, VT 05656-9405. Offers MA Ed. Part-time programs available. *Degree requirements:* For master's, thesis or alternative, comprehensive exam. *Entrance requirements:* For master's, interview. Additional exam requirements/recommendations for international students: Required—TOEFL. *Application deadline:* For fall admission, 7/15 priority date for domestic students, 4/15 priority date for international students; for spring admission, 11/1 priority date for domestic students, 8/15 priority date for international students. Applications are processed on a rolling basis. Application fee: $35. *Financial support:* Career-related internships or fieldwork, Federal Work-Study, and institutionally sponsored loans available. Support available to part-time students. Financial award application deadline: 3/1; financial award applicants required to submit FAFSA. *Application contact:* Catherine H. Higley, Administrative Assistant for Graduate Programs, 800-635-2356 Ext. 1244, Fax: 802-635-1248, E-mail: higleyc@jsc.vsc.edu.

Kansas State University, Graduate School, College of Education, Department of Special Education, Manhattan, KS 66506. Offers MS, Ed D. *Accreditation:* NCATE. Part-time programs available. *Faculty:* 3 full-time (2 women), 1 (woman) part-time/adjunct. *Students:* 13 full-time (12 women), 23 part-time (20 women); includes 3 minority (all African Americans) Average age 30. 7 applicants, 71% accepted, 2 enrolled. In 2006, 11 master's, 3 doctorates awarded. *Degree requirements:* For master's, thesis or alternative, final written exam. *Entrance requirements:* For master's, GRE General Test or MAT, teaching experience, BS in education with minimum B average. Additional exam requirements/recommendations for international students: Required—TOEFL. *Application deadline:* For fall admission, 3/1 priority date for domestic students, 2/1 priority date for international students; for spring admission, 10/1 priority date for domestic students, 8/1 priority date for international students. Applications are processed on a rolling basis. Application fee: $30 ($55 for international students). Electronic applications accepted. *Expenses:* Tuition, state resident: full-time $6,352; part-time $240 per credit hour. Tuition, nonresident: full-time $14,296; part-time $571 per credit hour. Required fees: $585. *Financial support:* Research assistantships, teaching assistantships, career-related internships or fieldwork, Federal Work-Study, institutionally sponsored loans, and scholarships/grants available. Support available to part-time students. Financial award application deadline: 3/1; financial award applicants required to submit FAFSA. *Faculty research:* Application of principles of universal design for learning, on-line applications for supervision of practicum students, interpretation of facial expressions by students with EBD and ASD, school-wide screening techniques for behavioral concerns, field-based observation technique refinements. Total annual research expenditures: $29,725. *Unit head:* Stephen Benton, Head, 785-532-5784, Fax: 785-532-7304, E-mail: leroy@ksu.edu. *Application contact:* Linda Thurston, Director, 785-532-5595, Fax: 785-532-7304, E-mail: coegrads@ksu.edu.

Kean University, College of Education, Program in Special Education, Union, NJ 07083. Offers developmental disabilities (MA); emotionally disturbed and socially maladjusted (MA); learning disabilities (MA); pre-school handicapped (MA). *Accreditation:* NCATE. Part-time and evening/weekend programs available. *Faculty:* 9 full-time (8 women). *Students:* 9 full-time (6 women), 268 part-time (231 women); includes 56 minority (29 African Americans, 5 Asian Americans or Pacific Islanders, 22 Hispanic Americans). Average age 35. 123 applicants, 100% accepted, 97 enrolled. In 2006, 56 degrees awarded. *Degree requirements:* For master's,

thesis, portfolio, comprehensive exam. *Entrance requirements:* For master's, GRE General Test or MAT, teaching certificate, 2 letters of recommendation, interview. *Application deadline:* For fall admission, 5/1 for domestic students; for spring admission, 11/1 for domestic students. Application fee: $60 ($150 for international students). Electronic applications accepted. *Expenses:* Tuition, state resident: full-time $8,856; part-time $369 per credit. Tuition, nonresident: full-time $11,256; part-time $469 per credit. *Financial support:* Research assistantships with full tuition reimbursements, career-related internships or fieldwork and unspecified assistantships available. *Unit head:* Dr. Beverly Kling, Program Coordinator, 908-737-3845, E-mail: bkling@kean. edu. *Application contact:* Joanne Morris, Director of Graduate Admissions, 908-737-3355, Fax: 908-737-3354, E-mail: grad-adm@kean.edu.

Keene State College, Division of Graduate and Professional Studies, Program in Special Education, Keene, NH 03435. Offers M Ed, PMC. Part-time and evening/weekend programs available. *Entrance requirements:* For master's, MAT or GRE, PRAXIS I, resumé, special education certification, teaching experience. *Application deadline:* For fall admission, 6/15 for domestic students; for spring admission, 10/15 for domestic students. Applications are processed on a rolling basis. Application fee: $25 ($35 for international students). *Expenses:* Tuition, area resident: Part-time $265 per credit. Tuition, state resident: full-time $5,780; part-time $290 per credit. Tuition, nonresident: full-time $13,050. Required fees: $80 per credit. Part-time tuition and fees vary according to course load. *Financial support:* Application deadline: 3/1. *Application contact:* Peggy Richmond, Director of Admissions, 603-358-2276, Fax: 603-358-2767, E-mail: admissions@keene.edu.

Kennesaw State University, Leland and Clarice C. Bagwell College of Education, Program in Graduate Education, Kennesaw, GA 30144-5591. Offers adolescent education (M Ed); early childhood education (M Ed); educational leadership (M Ed); special education (M Ed). *Accreditation:* NCATE. Part-time programs available. *Faculty:* 60 full-time (38 women), 12 part-time/adjunct (4 women). *Students:* 150 full-time (143 women), 489 part-time (371 women); includes 95 minority (85 African Americans, 1 American Indian/Alaska Native, 1 Asian American or Pacific Islander, 8 Hispanic Americans), 21 international. Average age 35. 165 applicants, 97% accepted, 142 enrolled. In 2006, 283 degrees awarded. *Degree requirements:* For master's, thesis or alternative. *Entrance requirements:* For master's, GRE General Test, T-4 state certification, minimum GPA of 2.75. Additional exam requirements/recommendations for international students: Required—TOEFL (minimum score 550 paper-based; 213 computer-based; 80 iBT), IELTS (minimum score 6). *Application deadline:* For fall admission, 7/15 priority date for domestic students; for spring admission, 10/15 priority date for domestic students. Application fee: $50. Electronic applications accepted. *Expenses:* Tuition, state resident: full-time $3,044; part-time $127 per semester hour. Tuition, nonresident: full-time $12,172; part-time $508 per semester hour. Required fees: $353 per semester. Full-time tuition and fees vary according to campus/location and program. *Financial support:* Federal Work-Study and unspecified assistantships available. Support available to part-time students. Financial award application deadline: 6/15; financial award applicants required to submit FAFSA. *Application contact:* Alisha O'Brien, Administrative Coordinator, 770-423-6043, Fax: 770-420-4435, E-mail: aobrien@kennesaw.edu.

Kent State University, Graduate School of Education, Health, and Human Services, Department of Educational Foundations and Special Services, Program in Intervention Specialist, Kent, OH 44242-0001. Offers deaf education (M Ed, MA); early childhood education (M Ed, MA); educational interpreter (M Ed, MA); general special education (M Ed, MA); gifted (M Ed, MA); mild/moderate (M Ed, MA); moderate/intensive (M Ed, MA); transition to work (M Ed, MA). *Faculty:* 13 full-time (9 women), 15 part-time/adjunct (13 women). *Students:* 41 full-time (37 women), 103 part-time (91 women); includes 2 minority (1 African American, 1 American Indian/Alaska Native), 1 international. 30 applicants, 80% accepted. In 2006, 53 degrees awarded. *Entrance requirements:* For master's, GRE. Application fee: $30. *Financial support:* In 2006–07, fellowships with tuition reimbursements (averaging $7,210 per year); research assistantships with tuition reimbursements, teaching assistantships with tuition reimbursements, career-related internships or fieldwork, Federal Work-Study, institutionally sponsored loans, scholarships/grants, health care benefits, and unspecified assistantships also available. Support available to part-time students. *Unit head:* Dr. Penny Griffith, Coordinator, 330-672-2477, E-mail: pgriffith@kent.edu. *Application contact:* Nancy Miller, Academic Program Coordinator, Office of Graduate Student Services, 330-672-2576, Fax: 330-672-9162, E-mail: ogs@kent.edu.

Kent State University, Graduate School of Education, Health, and Human Services, Department of Educational Foundations and Special Services, Program in Special Education, Kent, OH 44242-0001. Offers PhD, Ed S. *Accreditation:* NCATE. *Faculty:* 13 full-time (9 women), 15 part-time/adjunct (13 women). *Students:* 21 full-time (16 women), 3 part-time (all women), 1 international. 4 applicants, 50% accepted. In 2006, 7 doctorates, 1 Ed S awarded. *Degree requirements:* For doctorate, thesis/dissertation, comprehensive exam, registration. *Entrance requirements:* For doctorate and Ed S, GRE General Test. Additional exam requirements/recommendations for international students: Required—TOEFL. *Application deadline:* Applications are processed on a rolling basis. Application fee: $30. Electronic applications accepted. *Financial support:* In 2006–07, fellowships with full tuition reimbursements (averaging $8,497 per year); research assistantships with full tuition reimbursements, teaching assistantships with full tuition reimbursements, career-related internships or fieldwork, Federal Work-Study, institutionally sponsored loans, scholarships/grants, health care benefits, and unspecified assistantships also available. Support available to part-time students. Financial award application deadline: 4/1; financial award applicants required to submit FAFSA. *Faculty research:* Social/emotional needs of gifted, inclusion transition services, early intervention/ecobehavioral assessments, applied behavioral analysis. *Unit head:* Dr. Penny Griffith, Coordinator, 330-672-2477, E-mail: pgriffith@kent.edu. *Application contact:* Nancy Miller, Academic Program Coordinator, Office of Graduate Student Services, 330-672-2576, Fax: 330-672-9162, E-mail: ogs@kent.edu.

Kentucky State University, College of Professional Studies, Frankfort, KY 40601. Offers business (MBA); public administration (MPA); special education (MA). Part-time and evening/weekend programs available. *Faculty:* 11 full-time (2 women). *Students:* 44 full-time (26 women), 69 part-time (40 women); includes 67 minority (64 African Americans, 1 Asian American or Pacific Islander, 2 Hispanic Americans), 1 international. Average age 32. 70 applicants, 74% accepted, 41 enrolled. In 2006, 26 degrees awarded. *Degree requirements:* For master's, thesis optional. *Entrance requirements:* For master's, GMAT. Additional exam requirements/recommendations for international students: Required—TOEFL. *Application deadline:* For fall admission, 7/1 priority date for domestic students, 4/1 priority date for international students; for spring admission, 11/15 priority date for domestic students, 8/15 priority date for international students. Applications are processed on a rolling basis. Application fee: $30 ($100 for international students). Electronic applications accepted. *Expenses:* Tuition, state resident: part-time $285 per credit. Tuition, nonresident: part-time $685 per credit. Required fees: $35 per credit. *Financial support:* In 2006–07, 4 research assistantships (averaging $613 per year) were awarded. Financial award application deadline: 4/15; financial award applicants required to submit FAFSA. *Unit head:* Dr. Gashaw Lake, Dean, E-mail: gashaw.lake@kysu.edu. *Application contact:* James Burrell, Director of Admission, 502-597-6322, Fax: 502-597-5814, E-mail: james.burrell@kysu.edu.

Kutztown University of Pennsylvania, College of Graduate Studies and Extended Learning, College of Education, Program in Elementary Education, Kutztown, PA 19530-0730. Offers early childhood education (Certificate); elementary education (M Ed, Certificate); special education (Certificate). *Accreditation:* NCATE. Part-time and evening/weekend programs available. *Faculty:* 8 full-time (6 women), 1 (woman) part-time/adjunct. *Students:* 38 full-time (27 women), 64 part-time (54 women); includes 2 minority (both Hispanic Americans) Average age 29. 66 applicants, 85% accepted, 42 enrolled. In 2006, 15 degrees awarded. *Degree requirements:* For master's, comprehensive project, thesis optional. *Entrance requirements:* For master's, GRE General Test. Additional exam requirements/recommendations for international students: Required—TOEFL. *Application deadline:* Applications are processed on a rolling basis. Application fee: $35. Electronic applications accepted. *Expenses:* Tuition, state resident: full-time

$6,048; part-time $336 per credit. Tuition, nonresident: full-time $9,678; part-time $538 per credit. *Financial support:* In 2006–07, research assistantships with full tuition reimbursements (averaging $5,000 per year); career-related internships or fieldwork, Federal Work-Study, and unspecified assistantships also available. Financial award application deadline: 3/15; financial award applicants required to submit FAFSA. *Faculty research:* Whole language, middle schools, cooperative learning discussion techniques, oral reading techniques, hemisphericity. *Unit head:* Dr. Elsa Geskus, Chairperson, 610-683-4262, Fax: 610-683-1327, E-mail: geskus@kutztown.edu.

Lamar University, College of Graduate Studies, College of Fine Arts and Communication, Department of Deaf Studies/Deaf Education, Beaumont, TX 77710. Offers MS, Ed D. *Accreditation:* ASHA. Part-time and evening/weekend programs available. *Faculty:* 5 full-time (4 women). *Students:* 34 full-time (27 women), 25 part-time (16 women); includes 16 minority (8 African Americans, 1 American Indian/Alaska Native, 1 Asian American or Pacific Islander, 6 Hispanic Americans), 1 international. Average age 35. 558 applicants, 2% accepted, 12 enrolled. In 2006, 21 master's, 1 doctorate awarded. *Degree requirements:* For master's, thesis optional; for doctorate, thesis/dissertation. *Entrance requirements:* For master's, GRE General Test, minimum GPA of 2.5, performance IQ score of 115 required for deaf students; for doctorate, GRE General Test, performance IQ score of 115 required for deaf students. Additional exam requirements/recommendations for international students: Required—TOEFL. *Application deadline:* For fall admission, 8/1 priority date for domestic students; for spring admission, 12/1 for domestic students. Applications are processed on a rolling basis. Application fee: $25 ($50 for international students). *Expenses:* Tuition, nonresident: part-time $33 per hour. Required fees: $43 per hour. $110 per semester. *Financial support:* In 2006–07, 43 fellowships were awarded; research assistantships. Financial award application deadline: 4/1. *Faculty research:* Multicultural and deaf teacher training, central auditory processing, BSER, voice sign language. *Unit head:* Dr. Gabriel A. Martin, Chair, 409-880-8175, Fax: 409-880-2265.

Lancaster Bible College, Graduate School, Lancaster, PA 17608-3403. Offers Bible (MA); consulting resource teacher (M Ed); counseling (MA); ministry (MA); school counseling (M Ed). Part-time and evening/weekend programs available. *Faculty:* 8 full-time (1 woman), 5 part-time/adjunct (1 woman). *Students:* 55 full-time (28 women), 117 part-time (55 women); includes 21 minority (15 African Americans, 5 Asian Americans or Pacific Islanders, 1 Hispanic American). Average age 36. In 2006, 16 degrees awarded. *Degree requirements:* For master's, thesis (for some programs), comprehensive exam (for some programs). *Entrance requirements:* For master's, bachelor's degree with a minimum of 30 credits of course work in Bible, minimum undergraduate GPA of 3.0, interview. Additional exam requirements/recommendations for international students: Required—TOEFL. *Application deadline:* Applications are processed on a rolling basis. Application fee: $25. *Expenses:* Tuition: Full-time $4,620; part-time $385 per credit. *Financial support:* In 2006–07, 31 students received support, including 2 teaching assistantships (averaging $1,800 per year); scholarships/grants and unspecified assistantships also available. Support available to part-time students. Financial award application deadline: 6/1; financial award applicants required to submit FAFSA. *Unit head:* Dr. Ray A. Naugle, Dean of Graduate Education, 717-560-8297, Fax: 717-560-8236, E-mail: rnaugle@lbc.edu. *Application contact:* Emily Higgins, Student Application Contact, 717-560-8297, E-mail: ehiggins@lbc.edu.

La Sierra University, School of Education, Department of Curriculum and Instruction, Riverside, CA 92515. Offers curriculum and instruction (MA, Ed D, Ed S); special education (MA). Part-time and evening/weekend programs available. *Degree requirements:* For doctorate, thesis/dissertation; for Ed S, thesis optional. *Entrance requirements:* For master's, minimum GPA of 3.0; for doctorate, GRE General Test, GRE Subject Test, minimum GPA of 3.3; for Ed S, minimum GPA of 3.3. *Faculty research:* New teacher success, politics of knowledge, computer-assisted instruction, diversity issues.

Lee University, Program in Education, Cleveland, TN 37320-3450. Offers classroom teaching (M Ed); educational leadership (M Ed); elementary/secondary education (MAT); special education (elementary) (M Ed); special education (secondary) (M Ed, MAT); special education (severe disabilities) (M Ed). *Faculty:* 25 full-time (11 women). *Students:* 103 full-time (66 women), 22 part-time (15 women); includes 43 minority (5 African Americans, 36 American Indian/Alaska Native, 2 Hispanic Americans), 3 international. 49 applicants, 100% accepted, 28 enrolled. In 2006, 75 degrees awarded. *Degree requirements:* For master's, variable foreign language requirement, thesis, internship, comprehensive exam. *Entrance requirements:* For master's, MAT or GRE General Test, minimum GPA of 2.75, 3 letters of recommendation, interview, writing sample. Additional exam requirements/recommendations for international students: Required—TOEFL. *Application deadline:* For fall admission, 4/1 for domestic students; for spring admission, 10/1 for domestic students. Applications are processed on a rolling basis. Application fee: $25. *Expenses:* Tuition: Part-time $412 per credit. Required fees: $10 per semester. Tuition and fees vary according to course load. *Financial support:* Career-related internships or fieldwork, Federal Work-Study, and institutionally sponsored loans available. *Unit head:* Dr. Gary Riggins, Director, 423-614-8193. *Application contact:* Vicki Glasscock, Graduate Admissions Director, 423-614-8059, E-mail: vglasscock@leeuniversity.edu.

Lehigh University, College of Education, Department of Education and Human Services, Program in Special Education, Bethlehem, PA 18015-3094. Offers academic intervention (M Ed); special education (M Ed, PhD, Certificate). Part-time and evening/weekend programs available. *Faculty:* 29 full-time (16 women), 17 part-time/adjunct (9 women). *Students:* 10 full-time (all women), 72 part-time (60 women); includes 5 minority (all African Americans), 7 international. 33 applicants, 61% accepted, 17 enrolled. In 2006, 25 master's, 1 doctorate awarded. *Median time to degree:* Of those who began their doctoral program in fall 1998, 100% received their degree in 8 years or less. *Degree requirements:* For doctorate, thesis/dissertation. *Entrance requirements:* For master's and Certificate, minimum GPA of 3.0; for doctorate, GRE General Test, minimum GPA of 3.5. Additional exam requirements/recommendations for international students: Required—TOEFL (minimum score 600 paper-based; 250 computer-based). Application fee: $60. Electronic applications accepted. *Financial support:* Research assistantships, career-related internships or fieldwork, Federal Work-Study, institutionally sponsored loans, scholarships/grants, tuition waivers (full and partial), and field-based positions available. Financial award application deadline: 1/31. *Unit head:* Dr. Lee Kern, 610-758-3267, Fax: 610-758-6223, E-mail: lek6@lehigh.edu.

Lehman College of the City University of New York, Division of Education, Department of Specialized Services in Education, Bronx, NY 10468-1589. Offers guidance and counseling (MS Ed); reading teacher (MS Ed); teachers of special education (MS Ed), including bilingual special education, early special education, emotional handicaps, learning disabilities, mental retardation. Part-time and evening/weekend programs available. *Faculty research:* Battered women, whole language classrooms, parent education, mainstreaming.

Lehman College of the City University of New York, Division of Education, Department of Specialized Services in Education, Teachers of Special Education Program, Option in Bilingual Special Education, Bronx, NY 10468-1589. Offers MS Ed. *Accreditation:* NCATE. *Entrance requirements:* For master's, minimum GPA of 3.0.

Lehman College of the City University of New York, Division of Education, Department of Specialized Services in Education, Teachers of Special Education Program, Option in Early Special Education, Bronx, NY 10468-1589. Offers MS Ed. *Accreditation:* NCATE. *Entrance requirements:* For master's, minimum GPA of 3.0.

Lehman College of the City University of New York, Division of Education, Department of Specialized Services in Education, Teachers of Special Education Program, Option in Emotional Handicaps, Bronx, NY 10468-1589. Offers MS Ed. *Accreditation:* NCATE. Part-time and evening/weekend programs available. *Entrance requirements:* For master's, minimum GPA of 2.7. *Faculty research:* Behavioral disorders, self-evaluation, applied behavior analysis.

Lehman College of the City University of New York, Division of Education, Department of Specialized Services in Education, Teachers of Special Education Program, Option in Learning Disabilities, Bronx, NY 10468-1589. Offers MS Ed. *Accreditation:* NCATE. Part-time and evening/weekend programs available. *Entrance requirements:* For master's, interview, minimum GPA of 2.7. *Faculty research:* Emergent literacy, language-based classrooms, primary and secondary social contexts of language and literacy, innovative in-service education models, adult literacy.

Lehman College of the City University of New York, Division of Education, Department of Specialized Services in Education, Teachers of Special Education Program, Option in Mental Retardation, Bronx, NY 10468-1589. Offers MS Ed. *Accreditation:* NCATE. Part-time and evening/weekend programs available. *Entrance requirements:* For master's, minimum GPA of 2.7. *Faculty research:* Conductive education, homeless infants and their families, infant stimulation, hospitalizing infants with AIDS, legislation PL99-457.

Lesley University, School of Education, Cambridge, MA 02138-2790. Offers curriculum and instruction (M Ed, CAGS); early childhood education (M Ed); educational studies (PhD); elementary education (M Ed); individually designed (M Ed); middle school education (M Ed); moderate special needs (M Ed); reading (M Ed, CAGS); science in education (M Ed); severe special needs (M Ed); special needs (CAGS); technology in education (M Ed, CAGS). Part-time and evening/weekend programs available. Postbaccalaureate distance learning degree programs offered (no on-campus study). *Faculty:* 47 full-time (39 women), 208 part-time/adjunct (135 women). *Students:* 242 full-time (222 women), 2,903 part-time (2,495 women); includes 279 minority (179 African Americans, 7 American Indian/Alaska Native, 25 Asian Americans or Pacific Islanders, 68 Hispanic Americans), 10 international. Average age 36. 1,186 applicants, 96% accepted, 792 enrolled. In 2006, 1,724 master's, 6 doctorates, 17 other advanced degrees awarded. *Degree requirements:* For master's, practicum; for doctorate, thesis/dissertation. *Entrance requirements:* For doctorate, GRE General Test or MAT, interview, master's degree, resumé; for CAGS, interview, master's degree. Additional exam requirements/recommendations for international students: Required—TOEFL (minimum score 550 paper-based; 213 computer-based; 80 iBT). *Application deadline:* Applications are processed on a rolling basis. Application fee: $50. Electronic applications accepted. *Financial support:* In 2006–07, 26 students received support, including research assistantships (averaging $3,400 per year), teaching assistantships (averaging $3,400 per year); career-related internships or fieldwork, Federal Work-Study, scholarships/grants, and unspecified assistantships also available. Support available to part-time students. Financial award application deadline: 4/15; financial award applicants required to submit FAFSA. *Faculty research:* Assessment in literacy, mathematics and science; autism spectrum disorders; instructional technology and online learning; multicultural education and ELL. *Unit head:* Dr. Mario Borunda, Dean, 617-349-8375, Fax: 617-349-8607, E-mail: mborunda@lesley.edu. *Application contact:* Kristen Card, Associate Director of On-Campus Admissions, 617-349-8734, Fax: 617-349-8313, E-mail: kmcard@lesley.edu.

See Close-Up on page 893.

Lewis & Clark College, Graduate School of Education and Counseling, Department of Education, Program in Special Education, Portland, OR 97219-7899. Offers M Ed. *Accreditation:* NCATE. Part-time and evening/weekend programs available. *Faculty:* 2 full-time (1 woman), 1 (woman) part-time/adjunct. *Students:* Average age 42. 8 applicants, 100% accepted, 4 enrolled. In 2006, 7 degrees awarded. *Entrance requirements:* For master's, minimum GPA of 2.75. Additional exam requirements/recommendations for international students: Required—TOEFL (minimum score 575 paper-based; 233 computer-based). Application fee: $50. Electronic applications accepted. *Expenses:* Tuition: Part-time $610 per semester hour. *Financial support:* In 2006–07, 7 students received support. Career-related internships or fieldwork, Federal Work-Study, institutionally sponsored loans, scholarships/grants, and tuition waivers (partial) available. Support available to part-time students. Financial award applicants required to submit FAFSA. *Unit head:* Christine Moore, Program Coordinator, 503-768-6128, E-mail: cmoore@lclark.edu. *Application contact:* Becky Haas, Director of Admissions, 503-768-6200, Fax: 503-768-6205, E-mail: gseadmit@lclark.edu.

Lewis University, College of Arts and Sciences, Graduate Programs in Education, Program in Special Education, Romeoville, IL 60446. Offers MA.

Liberty University, School of Education, Lynchburg, VA 24502. Offers administration and supervision (M Ed); curriculum and instruction (M Ed); early childhood education (M Ed); education specialist (Ed S); educational leadership (Ed D); elementary education (M Ed); gifted education (M Ed); reading specialist (M Ed); school counseling (M Ed); secondary education (M Ed); special education (M Ed). *Accreditation:* NCATE. Part-time programs available. Postbaccalaureate distance learning degree programs offered (minimal on-campus study). *Faculty:* 8 full-time (3 women), 7 part-time/adjunct (3 women). *Students:* 33 full-time (22 women), 308 part-time (180 women); includes 22 minority (12 African Americans, 2 American Indian/Alaska Native, 2 Asian Americans or Pacific Islanders, 6 Hispanic Americans), 5 international. Average age 39. 434 applicants, 77% accepted, 111 enrolled. In 2006, 39 master's, 12 doctorates, 16 other advanced degrees awarded. *Degree requirements:* For doctorate, thesis/dissertation, comprehensive exam. *Entrance requirements:* For master's, GRE General Test or MAT (if taken on or before 1999), 2 letters of recommendation, minimum undergraduate GPA of 3.0, curriculum vitae, graduate status record; for doctorate, GRE General Test or MAT (if taken before 1999), minimum master's GPA of 3.0, 3 years of teacher experience; for Ed S, GRE General Test or MAT (if taken before 1999), minimum master's GPA of 3.0, 3 years of teaching experience. Additional exam requirements/recommendations for international students: Required—TOEFL (minimum score 600 paper-based; 250 computer-based). *Application deadline:* For fall admission, 6/1 priority date for domestic students; for spring admission, 11/1 for domestic students. Applications are processed on a rolling basis. Application fee: $35. Electronic applications accepted. *Expenses: Contact institution. Financial support:* In 2006–07, 226 students received support. Federal Work-Study and tuition waivers (partial) available. *Faculty research:* Self-determination, character education, bibliotherapy, learning styles, distance education. *Unit head:* Dr. Karen L. Parker, Dean, 434-582-2195, Fax: 434-582-2468, E-mail: kparker@liberty.edu. *Application contact:* Kyle A Falce, Director of Graduate Admissions, 800-424-9596, Fax: 800-628-7977, E-mail: gradadmissions@liberty.edu.

Lincoln University, School of Graduate Studies and Continuing Education, College of Liberal Arts, Education and Journalism, Department of Education, Jefferson City, MO 65102. Offers educational leadership (Ed S), including elementary leadership, secondary leadership, superintendency; guidance and counseling (M Ed), including community/agency counseling, elementary school, secondary school; school administration and supervision (M Ed), including elementary school administration, secondary school administration, special education administration; school teaching (M Ed), including elementary school teaching, secondary school teaching. *Accreditation:* NCATE. Part-time and evening/weekend programs available. *Faculty:* 1 (woman) full-time, 10 part-time/adjunct (5 women). *Students:* 24 full-time (21 women), 62 part-time (51 women); includes 10 minority (8 African Americans, 2 Asian Americans or Pacific Islanders), 4 international. Average age 35. 13 applicants, 100% accepted, 10 enrolled. In 2006, 25 master's, 3 other advanced degrees awarded. *Degree requirements:* For master's and Ed S, portfolio. *Entrance requirements:* For master's, GRE or MAT, teaching certificate (school administration and supervision); background check; interview (elementary and secondary school teaching); for Ed S, GRE or MAT, principal certificate. Additional exam requirements/recommendations for international students: Required—TOEFL (minimum score 500 paper-based; 173 computer-based; 61 iBT). *Application deadline:* For fall admission, 7/1 priority date for domestic and international students; for spring admission, 12/1 priority date for domestic and international students. Applications are processed on a rolling basis. Application fee: $17. *Expenses:* Tuition, state resident: part-time $189 per credit hour. Tuition, nonresident: part-time $351 per credit hour. Required fees: $15 per credit hour. $20 per semester. *Financial support:* Federal Work-Study and scholarships/grants available. Financial award application

Special Education

Lincoln University (continued)

deadline: 4/1; financial award applicants required to submit FAFSA. *Unit head:* Dr. Cynthia Chapel, Department Head, 573-681-5250, Fax: 573-681-5257, E-mail: chapelc@lincolnu.edu.

Lipscomb University, Program in Education, Nashville, TN 37204-3951. Offers instructional leadership (M Ed); learning and teaching (MALT); school administration and supervision (M Ed); special education instruction, K-12 (MASE). *Accreditation:* NCATE. Part-time and evening/weekend programs available. *Faculty:* 3 full-time (1 woman), 9 part-time/adjunct (6 women). *Students:* 95 full-time (59 women), 30 part-time (22 women); includes 14 minority (13 African Americans, 1 Asian American or Pacific Islander). Average age 32. In 2006, 25 degrees awarded. *Degree requirements:* For master's, registration. *Entrance requirements:* For master's, MAT or GRE General Test, 2 reference letters. Additional exam requirements/recommendations for international students: Required—TOEFL (minimum score 570 paper-based; 230 computer-based). *Application deadline:* For fall admission, 8/29 priority date for domestic students; for spring admission, 1/16 priority date for domestic students. Applications are processed on a rolling basis. Application fee: $60. *Expenses:* Tuition: Part-time $560 per semester hour. Tuition and fees vary according to program. *Financial support:* In 2006–07, 67 students received support. Federal Work-Study, tuition waivers (full), and unspecified assistantships available. Support available to part-time students. Financial award applicants required to submit FAFSA. *Faculty research:* Facilitative learning styles, leadership, student assessment, interactive multimedia inclusion. *Unit head:* Dr. Junior High, Director, 615-966-1000 Ext. 6067, Fax: 615-966-7628, E-mail: junior.high@lipscomb.edu. *Application contact:* Jackie Sanders, Administrative Assistant, 615-966-1000 Ext. 6081, Fax: 615-966-7628, E-mail: jackie.sanders@lipscomb.edu.

Long Island University, Brentwood Campus, School of Education, Brentwood, NY 11717. Offers elementary education (MS); reading (MS); school counseling (MS); school district administration and supervision (MS); special education (MS). Part-time and evening/weekend programs available.

Long Island University, Brooklyn Campus, School of Education, Department of Teaching and Learning, Program in Special Education, Brooklyn, NY 11201-8423. Offers MS Ed. Part-time and evening/weekend programs available. *Degree requirements:* For master's, thesis optional. *Entrance requirements:* For master's, 2 letters of recommendation. Additional exam requirements/recommendations for international students: Required—TOEFL (minimum score 500 paper-based; 173 computer-based). Electronic applications accepted.

Long Island University, C.W. Post Campus, School of Education, Department of Special Education and Literacy, Brookville, NY 11548-1300. Offers childhood education/literacy (MS); childhood education/special education (MS); literacy (MS Ed); special education (MS Ed). Part-time and evening/weekend programs available. *Degree requirements:* For master's, research project, comprehensive exam or thesis. *Entrance requirements:* For master's, interview; minimum GPA of 2.75 in major, 2.5 overall. Electronic applications accepted. *Faculty research:* Autism, mainstreaming, robotics and microcomputers in special education, transition from school to work.

Long Island University, Rockland Graduate Campus, Graduate School, Programs in Special Education and Literacy, Orangeburg, NY 10962. Offers childhood literacy (MS); childhood special education (MS); literacy (MS Ed); special education (MS Ed).

Long Island University, Southampton Graduate Campus, Education Division, Program in Teaching Students with Disabilities, Southampton, NY 11968-4198. Offers MS Ed. *Students:* Average age 31. 31 applicants, 97% accepted, 26 enrolled. In 2006, 1 degree awarded. *Degree requirements:* For master's, thesis. *Entrance requirements:* For master's, minimum GPA of 2.75, New York state teacher certification. Additional exam requirements/recommendations for international students: Required—TOEFL (minimum score 550 paper-based; 250 computer-based). *Application deadline:* For fall admission, 4/15 priority date for domestic and international students; for spring admission, 11/30 priority date for domestic and international students. Applications are processed on a rolling basis. Application fee: $30. Electronic applications accepted. *Expenses:* Tuition: Part-time $790 per credit. Required fees: $220 per semester. *Financial support:* In 2006–07, 21 students received support, including 1 research assistantship with full tuition reimbursement available. Financial award applicants required to submit FAFSA. *Unit head:* Dr. Sanja Cale, Unit Head, 631-287-8010, Fax: 631-287-8130, E-mail: sanja.cale@liu.edu. *Application contact:* Joyce Tuttle, Director of Graduate Admissions and Program Administration, 631-287-8010, Fax: 631-287-8253, E-mail: joyce.tuttle@liu.edu.

Long Island University, Westchester Graduate Campus, Programs in Education-Teaching, Program in Special Education and Secondary Education, Purchase, NY 10577. Offers MS Ed. Part-time and evening/weekend programs available. *Faculty:* 1 (woman) full-time, 14 part-time/adjunct (12 women). *Students:* 25 applicants, 96% accepted, 21 enrolled. In 2006, 12 degrees awarded. *Application deadline:* Applications are processed on a rolling basis. *Expenses:* Tuition: Part-time $790 per credit. *Financial support:* In 2006–07, 35 students received support. Scholarships/grants, tuition waivers (partial), and unspecified assistantships available. *Unit head:* Dr. Janet Simon, Director, 914-831-2715, Fax: 914-251-5959, E-mail: janet.simon@liu.edu. *Application contact:* Ellen Brief, Coordinator of Admissions, Marketing, Student Services and Public Relations, 914-831-2701, Fax: 914-251-5959, E-mail: ellen.brief@liu.edu.

Longwood University, Office of Graduate Studies, College of Education and Human Services, Farmville, VA 23909. Offers communication sciences and disorders (MS); community and college counseling (MS); curriculum and instruction specialist-elementary (MS), including mild disabilities, modern languages; curriculum and instruction specialist-secondary (MS), including English, mild disabilities, modern languages; educational leadership (MS); guidance and counseling (MS); literacy and culture (MS); school library media (MS). *Accreditation:* NCATE. Part-time and evening/weekend programs available. *Degree requirements:* For master's, thesis optional. *Entrance requirements:* For master's, GRE (communication sciences and disorders), minimum GPA of 2.75. Additional exam requirements/recommendations for international students: Required—TOEFL (minimum score 550 paper-based; 213 computer-based).

Loras College, Graduate Division, Program in Education with an Emphasis in Special Education, Dubuque, IA 52004-0178. Offers instructional strategist I K-6 and 7-12 (MA). Part-time and evening/weekend programs available. *Faculty:* 1 (woman) part-time/adjunct. *Students:* Average age 29. 8 applicants, 100% accepted, 4 enrolled. In 2006, 7 degrees awarded. *Degree requirements:* For master's, thesis optional. *Entrance requirements:* For master's, minimum cumulative undergraduate GPA of 3.0. *Application deadline:* Applications are processed on a rolling basis. Application fee: $25. *Expenses:* Tuition: Full-time $7,650; part-time $425 per credit. *Financial support:* Applicants required to submit FAFSA. *Unit head:* Dr. David Salyer, Graduate Coordinator, 563-588-7836, E-mail: david.salyer@loras.edu. *Application contact:* Michelle Rice, Graduate Admissions Counselor, 563-588-7166, E-mail: michelle.rice@loras.edu.

Louisiana Tech University, Graduate School, College of Education, Department of Behavioral Sciences and Psychology, Ruston, LA 71272. Offers counseling (MA); counseling psychology (PhD); industrial/organizational psychology (MA); special education (MA). *Accreditation:* APA (one or more programs are accredited). Part-time programs available. *Degree requirements:* For master's, thesis or alternative; for doctorate, thesis/dissertation. *Entrance requirements:* For master's and doctorate, GRE General Test.

Loyola College in Maryland, Graduate Programs, College of Arts and Sciences, Department of Education, Program in Special Education, Baltimore, MD 21210-2699. Offers M Ed, CAS. *Accreditation:* NCATE. Part-time and evening/weekend programs available. *Students:* 9 full-time (all women), 53 part-time (49 women); includes 4 minority (2 African Americans, 2 Hispanic Americans). Average age 31. 47 applicants, 85% accepted, 32 enrolled. In 2006, 8

master's, 1 other advanced degree awarded. *Entrance requirements:* For master's and CAS, GRE General Test, GRE Subject Test (recommended). Additional exam requirements/recommendations for international students: Required—TOEFL (minimum score 550 paper-based; 213 computer-based). *Application deadline:* For fall admission, 7/1 priority date for domestic students; for spring admission, 10/1 priority date for domestic students. Applications are processed on a rolling basis. Application fee: $50. *Financial support:* Career-related internships or fieldwork available. Financial award applicants required to submit FAFSA. *Unit head:* Dr. Elana Rock, Director, 410-617-2000 Ext. 5177, E-mail: erock@loyola.edu.

Loyola Marymount University, Graduate Division, School of Education, Program in Special Education, Los Angeles, CA 90045-2659. Offers MA. *Students:* 49 full-time (40 women), 11 part-time (10 women); includes 29 minority (8 African Americans, 1 American Indian/Alaska Native, 7 Asian Americans or Pacific Islanders, 13 Hispanic Americans), 2 international. Average age 26. In 2006, 40 degrees awarded. *Degree requirements:* For master's, comprehensive exam. *Application deadline:* For fall admission, 7/15 for domestic students; for spring admission, 11/15 for domestic students. Application fee: $60. Electronic applications accepted. *Financial support:* In 2006–07, 46 students received support. Application deadline: 6/1; *Unit head:* Dr. Victoria L. Graf, Head, 310-338-7305, E-mail: vgraf@lmu.edu.

Loyola Marymount University, Graduate Division, School of Education, Program in Special Education Specialist in Mild and Moderate Disabilities, Los Angeles, CA 90045-2659. Offers MA. Part-time and evening/weekend programs available. *Students:* 6 full-time (all women), 5 part-time (1 woman); includes 6 minority (all Hispanic Americans) *Degree requirements:* For master's, comprehensive exam. *Entrance requirements:* For master's, GRE General Test, interview. Additional exam requirements/recommendations for international students: Required—TOEFL (minimum score 600 paper-based; 250 computer-based). *Application deadline:* For fall admission, 7/15 for domestic students; for spring admission, 11/15 for domestic students. Application fee: $50. Electronic applications accepted. *Financial support:* In 2006–07, 2 students received support; research assistantships, Federal Work-Study and scholarships/grants available. Support available to part-time students. Financial award application deadline: 6/1; financial award applicants required to submit FAFSA. *Unit head:* Dr. Victoria L. Graf, Head, 310-338-7305, E-mail: vgraf@lmu.edu.

Loyola University Chicago, School of Education, Program in Initial Teacher Preparation, Chicago, IL 60611-2196. Offers elementary education (M Ed); reading specialist (M Ed); school technology (M Ed); science education (M Ed); secondary education (M Ed); special education (M Ed). *Accreditation:* NCATE. *Faculty:* 11 full-time (9 women), 6 part-time/adjunct (4 women). *Students:* 138. Average age 28. 95 applicants, 65% accepted, 39 enrolled. In 2006, 84 degrees awarded. *Degree requirements:* For master's, comprehensive exam. *Entrance requirements:* For master's, Illinois Basic Skills Test, 3 letters of recommendation, minimum GPA of 3.0, resumé. Additional exam requirements/recommendations for international students: Required—TOEFL (minimum score 550 paper-based; 213 computer-based; 79 iBT). *Application deadline:* For fall admission, 7/1 priority date for domestic and international students; for spring admission, 11/1 priority date for domestic and international students. Applications are processed on a rolling basis. Application fee: $50. Electronic applications accepted. *Financial support:* In 2006–07, 2 research assistantships with full tuition reimbursements (averaging $8,500 per year), 1 teaching assistantship were awarded. Financial award application deadline: 2/15. *Faculty research:* Positive behavior support, school reform, school improvement. *Unit head:* Dr. Dorothy Giroux, Director, 312-915-7027, E-mail: dgiroux@luc.edu. *Application contact:* Marie Rosin-Dittmar, Information Contact, 312-915-6800, E-mail: schleduc@luc.edu.

Lynchburg College, Graduate Studies, School of Education and Human Development, Program in Special Education, Lynchburg, VA 24501-3199. Offers early childhood special education (M Ed); mental retardation (M Ed); severely/profoundly handicapped education (M Ed); teaching children with learning disabilities (M Ed); teaching the emotionally disturbed (M Ed). *Faculty:* 4 full-time (3 women), 2 part-time/adjunct (0 women). *Students:* 14 full-time (13 women), 30 part-time (25 women); includes 2 African Americans, 2 Hispanic Americans. In 2006, 21 degrees awarded. *Entrance requirements:* For master's, minimum undergraduate GPA of 3.0. *Expenses:* Tuition: Full-time $6,300; part-time $350 per credit. Required fees: $100. *Financial support:* Fellowships, teaching assistantships, career-related internships or fieldwork, scholarships/grants, and unspecified assistantships available. *Unit head:* Dr. Glenn Buck, Program Coordinator, 434-544-8689.

Lyndon State College, Graduate Programs in Education, Department of Education, Lyndonville, VT 05851-0919. Offers curriculum and instruction (M Ed); reading specialist (M Ed); special education (M Ed); teaching and counseling (M Ed). Part-time and evening/weekend programs available. *Degree requirements:* For master's, exam or major field project. *Entrance requirements:* Additional exam requirements/recommendations for international students: Recommended—TOEFL (minimum score 500 paper-based; 173 computer-based).

Lynn University, Donald and Helen Ross College of Education, Boca Raton, FL 33431-5598. Offers exceptional student education (M Ed); global leadership (PhD). Part-time and evening/weekend programs available. *Faculty:* 5 full-time (3 women), 8 part-time/adjunct (4 women). *Students:* 29 full-time (22 women), 88 part-time (61 women); includes 30 minority (18 African Americans, 1 Asian American or Pacific Islander, 11 Hispanic Americans), 10 international. Average age 36. 48 applicants, 79% accepted, 33 enrolled. In 2006, 69 master's, 6 doctorates awarded. *Degree requirements:* For master's, thesis (for some programs); for doctorate, thesis/dissertation, qualifying paper. *Entrance requirements:* For master's, GRE, minimum undergraduate GPA of 3.0, resumé, 2 letters of recommendation; for doctorate, GRE or GMAT, minimum GPA of 3.25, resumé, 2 letters of recommendation. Additional exam requirements/recommendations for international students: Required—TOEFL (minimum score 550 paper-based; 213 computer-based). *Application deadline:* Applications are processed on a rolling basis. Application fee: $50. Electronic applications accepted. *Expenses:* Tuition: Full-time $26,200. Required fees: $1,500. Tuition and fees vary according to class time, course load and degree level. *Financial support:* Career-related internships or fieldwork, Federal Work-Study, institutionally sponsored loans, scholarships/grants, tuition waivers (partial), and unspecified assistantships available. Support available to part-time students. Financial award application deadline: 8/1; financial award applicants required to submit FAFSA. *Faculty research:* Non-traditional education, innovative curricula, multicultural education, simulation games. *Unit head:* Dr. Patrick Hartwick, Dean, 561-237-7441, Fax: 561-237-7792, E-mail: phartwick@lynn.edu. *Application contact:* Dr. Larissa Baia, Assistant Director of Graduate Admissions, 561-237-7916, Fax: 561-237-7100, E-mail: lbaia@lynn.edu.

Madonna University, Programs in Education, Livonia, MI 48150-1173. Offers Catholic school leadership (MSA); educational leadership (MSA); learning disabilities (MAT); literacy education (MAT); teaching and learning (MAT). *Accreditation:* NCATE. Part-time and evening/weekend programs available. *Faculty:* 11 full-time (7 women), 8 part-time/adjunct (2 women). *Students:* 2 full-time (both women), 154 part-time (134 women); includes 10 minority (6 African Americans, 1 Asian American or Pacific Islander, 3 Hispanic Americans), 2 international. Average age 36. 20 applicants, 85% accepted. In 2006, 133 degrees awarded. *Degree requirements:* For master's, thesis or alternative. *Application deadline:* For fall admission, 8/1 priority date for domestic students; for winter admission, 12/1 priority date for domestic students; for spring admission, 4/1 priority date for domestic students. Applications are processed on a rolling basis. Application fee: $25 ($200 for international students). Electronic applications accepted. *Financial support:* Career-related internships or fieldwork, Federal Work-Study, institutionally sponsored loans, and scholarships/grants available. Support available to part-time students. *Unit head:* Dr. Robert Kimball, Dean, 734-432-5652, E-mail: rkimball@madonna.edu. *Application contact:* Sandra Kellums, Coordinator of Graduate Admissions and Records, 734-432-5667, Fax: 734-432-5862, E-mail: skellum@madonna.edu.

Malone College, School of Education, Graduate Program in Education, Canton, OH 44709-3897. Offers curriculum and instruction (MA); curriculum, instruction, and professional development (MA); instructional technology (MA); intervention specialist (MA); reading (MA). Part-time and evening/weekend programs available. *Faculty:* 11 full-time (4 women), 12 part-time/adjunct (9 women). *Students:* 4 full-time (2 women), 96 part-time (78 women); includes 5 minority (1 African American, 2 Asian Americans or Pacific Islanders, 2 Hispanic Americans). Average age 33. In 2006, 26 degrees awarded. *Degree requirements:* For master's, research project. *Entrance requirements:* For master's, minimum GPA of 3.0, teaching license. *Application deadline:* Applications are processed on a rolling basis. Application fee: $25. *Expenses:* Tuition: Part-time $399 per credit hour. *Financial support:* Tuition waivers (partial) available. Support available to part-time students. Financial award application deadline: 6/30. *Faculty research:* The Bible as children's literature, special needs students and literacy development, middle level education, school/university partnerships and professional development, child/adolescent literature and popular culture. *Unit head:* Dr. Donald Williams, Director, 330-471-8509, Fax: 330-471-8563, E-mail: dwilliams@malone.edu. *Application contact:* Dr. David Kleffman, Recruiter, 330-471-8447, Fax: 330-471-8343, E-mail: dkleffman@malone.edu.

Manhattan College, Graduate Division, School of Education, Program in Special Education, Riverdale, NY 10471. Offers 5 year dual childhood/special education (MS Ed); dual childhood/special education (MS Ed); special education (MS Ed). Part-time and evening/weekend programs available. *Faculty:* 6 full-time (4 women), 9 part-time/adjunct (7 women). *Students:* 17 full-time (all women), 57 part-time (53 women). Average age 25. 39 applicants, 92% accepted, 35 enrolled. In 2006, 24 degrees awarded. *Degree requirements:* For master's, thesis, internship. *Entrance requirements:* For master's, minimum GPA of 3.0, NYSTE Last Test. Additional exam requirements/recommendations for international students: Required—TOEFL (minimum score 550 paper-based). *Application deadline:* For fall admission, 8/10 priority date for domestic students; for spring admission, 1/7 priority date for domestic students. Applications are processed on a rolling basis. Application fee: $50. *Expenses: Contact institution. Financial support:* Federal Work-Study, scholarships/grants, unspecified assistantships, and TOC/TLQP Grants—partial tuition available. Financial award application deadline: 2/1. *Faculty research:* Adapted physical education. *Unit head:* Dr. Elizabeth Mary Kosky, Director of Graduate Special Education Programs, 718-862-7969, Fax: 718-862-7816, E-mail: elizabeth.kosky@manhattan.edu. *Application contact:* Weldon Jackson.

Manhattanville College, Graduate Programs, School of Education, Program in Childhood Education, Purchase, NY 10577-2132. Offers childhood and special education (MPS); childhood education (MAT); special education childhood (MPS). Part-time and evening/weekend programs available. *Students:* 67 full-time (62 women), 150 part-time (120 women); includes 6 African Americans, 3 Asian Americans or Pacific Islanders, 10 Hispanic Americans, 2 international. In 2006, 65 degrees awarded. *Degree requirements:* For master's, comprehensive exam or research project, field experience. *Entrance requirements:* For master's, minimum undergraduate GPA of 3.0, 2 letters of recommendation. *Application deadline:* Applications are processed on a rolling basis. Application fee: $55. *Financial support:* Career-related internships or fieldwork and institutionally sponsored loans available. Support available to part-time students. *Application contact:* Alyce Ware Poli, Director of Admissions, 914-323-5142, Fax: 914-694-1732, E-mail: edschool@mville.edu.

Manhattanville College, Graduate Programs, School of Education, Program in Early Childhood Education, Purchase, NY 10577-2132. Offers childhood and early childhood education (MAT); early childhood education (birth-grade 2) (MAT); literacy (birth-grade 6) (MPS), including reading, writing; literacy (birth-grade 6) and special education (grades 1-6) (MPS); special education (birth-grade 2) (MPS); special education (birth-grade 6) (MPS). Part-time and evening/weekend programs available. *Students:* 43 full-time (42 women), 62 part-time (59 women); includes 1 African American, 1 Asian American or Pacific Islander, 7 Hispanic Americans. In 2006, 5 degrees awarded. *Degree requirements:* For master's, comprehensive exam or research project, field experience. *Entrance requirements:* For master's, minimum undergraduate GPA of 3.0, 2 letters of recommendation. *Application deadline:* Applications are processed on a rolling basis. Application fee: $55. *Financial support:* Career-related internships or fieldwork and institutionally sponsored loans available. Support available to part-time students. *Application contact:* Alyce Ware Poli, Director of Admissions, 914-323-5142, Fax: 914-694-1732, E-mail: edschool@mville.edu.

Manhattanville College, Graduate Programs, School of Education, Program in Middle Childhood/Adolescence Education (Grades 5-12), Purchase, NY 10577-2132. Offers biology (MAT); biology and special education (MPS); chemistry (MAT); chemistry and special education (MPS); English (MAT); English and special education (MPS); literacy (MPS), including reading and writing, writing; literacy and special education (MPS); math (MAT); math and special education (MPS); second language (MAT), including French, Italian, Latin, Spanish; social studies (MAT); social studies and special education (MPS); special education (MPS). Part-time and evening/weekend programs available. *Students:* 76 full-time (53 women), 109 part-time (68 women); includes 8 African Americans, 1 Asian American or Pacific Islander, 10 Hispanic Americans, 1 international. In 2006, 165 degrees awarded. *Degree requirements:* For master's, comprehensive exam or research project, field experience. *Entrance requirements:* For master's, minimum undergraduate GPA of 3.0, 2 letters of recommendation. *Application deadline:* Applications are processed on a rolling basis. Application fee: $55. *Financial support:* Career-related internships or fieldwork and institutionally sponsored loans available. Support available to part-time students. *Application contact:* Alyce Ware Poli, Director of Admissions, 914-323-5142, Fax: 914-694-1732, E-mail: edschool@mville.edu.

Marshall University, Academic Affairs Division, College of Education and Human Services, Graduate School of Education and Professional Development, Program in Special Education, Huntington, WV 25755. Offers MA. *Accreditation:* NCATE. Part-time and evening/weekend programs available. *Faculty:* 4 full-time (2 women), 18 part-time/adjunct (16 women). *Students:* 83 full-time (65 women), 345 part-time (279 women); includes 9 minority (4 African Americans, 3 American Indian/Alaska Native, 1 Asian American or Pacific Islander, 1 Hispanic American), 3 international. Average age 37. In 2006, 71 degrees awarded. *Degree requirements:* For master's, comprehensive or oral assessment, research project, thesis optional. *Entrance requirements:* For master's, GRE General Test or MAT, minimum GPA of 3.0. Application fee: $40. *Financial support:* Federal Work-Study, tuition waivers (full), and unspecified assistantships available. Support available to part-time students. Financial award applicants required to submit FAFSA. *Faculty research:* Teaching the severely handicapped, career/vocational education, education of the gifted. *Unit head:* Dr. Mike Sullivan, Director, 304-746-2076, E-mail: msullivan@marshall.edu. *Application contact:* Information Contact, 304-746-1900, Fax: 304-746-1902, E-mail: services@marshall.edu.

Marymount University, School of Education and Human Services, Program in Education, Arlington, VA 22207-4299. Offers alternative teacher licensure (Certificate); elementary education (M Ed); English as a second language (M Ed); learning disabilities (M Ed); professional studies (M Ed); secondary education (M Ed). *Accreditation:* NCATE. Part-time and evening/weekend programs available. Postbaccalaureate distance learning degree programs offered (minimal on-campus study). *Faculty:* 10 full-time (8 women), 5 part-time/adjunct (2 women). *Students:* 75 full-time (65 women), 95 part-time (82 women); includes 25 minority (13 African Americans, 2 American Indian/Alaska Native, 6 Asian Americans or Pacific Islanders, 4 Hispanic Americans), 6 international. Average age 32. 58 applicants, 100% accepted, 45 enrolled. In 2006, 113 degrees awarded. *Degree requirements:* For master's, thesis or alternative. *Entrance requirements:* For master's, GRE General Test or MAT, PRAXIS I or SAT/ACT, interview, 2 letters of recommendation. Additional exam requirements/recommendations for international students: Required—TOEFL (minimum score 600 paper-based; 250 computer-based). *Application deadline:* Applications are processed on a rolling basis. Application fee: $40. Electronic applications accepted. *Expenses:* Tuition: Full-time $11,160; part-time $620 per credit. Required fees: $113; $630 per credit. *Financial support:* Research assistantships with full tuition reimbursements, career-related internships or fieldwork, scholarships/grants, and unspecified assistantships available. Support available to part-time students. Financial award applicants required to submit FAFSA. *Unit head:* Dr. Shelly Haser, Chair, 703-284-6955, Fax: 703-284-1631, E-mail: shelly.haser@marymount.edu.

Marywood University, Academic Affairs, College of Education and Human Development, Department of Special Education, Program in Special Education, Scranton, PA 18509-1598. Offers MS. *Accreditation:* NCATE. Evening/weekend programs available. *Students:* 3 full-time (all women), 36 part-time (31 women); includes 1 minority (Hispanic American) Average age 34. In 2006, 16 degrees awarded. *Degree requirements:* For master's, thesis or alternative. *Entrance requirements:* For master's, MAT. Additional exam requirements/recommendations for international students: Required—TOEFL (minimum score 550 paper-based; 213 computer-based). *Application deadline:* For fall admission, 4/15 priority date for domestic and international students; for spring admission, 11/15 priority date for domestic and international students. Applications are processed on a rolling basis. Application fee: $30. Electronic applications accepted. *Expenses:* Tuition: Part-time $672 per credit. Tuition and fees vary according to degree level, campus/location and program. *Financial support:* Research assistantships with tuition reimbursements, career-related internships or fieldwork, scholarships/grants, tuition waivers (partial), and unspecified assistantships available. Support available to part-time students. Financial award application deadline: 2/15; financial award applicants required to submit FAFSA. *Application contact:* Dr. Deborah M. Flynn, Coordinator of Graduate Advising (Enrollment Management), 570-348-6211, E-mail: flynn@ac.marywood.edu.

Marywood University, Academic Affairs, College of Education and Human Development, Department of Special Education, Program in Special Education Administration and Supervision, Scranton, PA 18509-1598. Offers MS. *Accreditation:* NCATE. Evening/weekend programs available. *Students:* Average age 31. In 2006, 1 degree awarded. *Degree requirements:* For master's, thesis or alternative. *Entrance requirements:* For master's, MAT. Additional exam requirements/recommendations for international students: Required—TOEFL (minimum score 550 paper-based; 213 computer-based). *Application deadline:* For fall admission, 4/15 priority date for domestic and international students; for spring admission, 11/15 priority date for domestic and international students. Applications are processed on a rolling basis. Application fee: $30. Electronic applications accepted. *Expenses:* Tuition: Part-time $672 per credit. Tuition and fees vary according to degree level, campus/location and program. *Financial support:* Research assistantships with tuition reimbursements, career-related internships or fieldwork, scholarships/grants, tuition waivers (partial), and unspecified assistantships available. Support available to part-time students. Financial award application deadline: 2/15; financial award applicants required to submit FAFSA. *Application contact:* Dr. Deborah M. Flynn, Coordinator of Graduate Advising (Enrollment Management), 570-348-6211, E-mail: flynn@ac.marywood.edu.

Massachusetts College of Liberal Arts, Program in Education, North Adams, MA 01247-4100. Offers curriculum and instruction (M Ed); educational administration (M Ed); reading (M Ed); special education (M Ed). Part-time and evening/weekend programs available. *Degree requirements:* For master's, thesis. *Entrance requirements:* For master's, writing sample. *Faculty research:* Anxiety, methodology, mainstreaming.

McDaniel College, Graduate and Professional Studies, Program in Education of the Deaf, Westminster, MD 21157-4390. Offers MS. *Accreditation:* NCATE. Part-time programs available. *Degree requirements:* For master's, thesis optional. *Entrance requirements:* For master's, ASLPI (American Sign Language Proficiency Interview). Additional exam requirements/recommendations for international students: Required—TOEFL (minimum score 213 computer-based), English Proficiency Essay. *Faculty research:* Mainstreaming of multihandicapped children.

McDaniel College, Graduate and Professional Studies, Program in Human Service Management in Special Education, Westminster, MD 21157-4390. Offers MS. *Accreditation:* NCATE. Evening/weekend programs available. *Degree requirements:* For master's, internship. *Entrance requirements:* For master's, letters of reference (3). Additional exam requirements/recommendations for international students: Required—TOEFL (minimum score 213 computer-based).

McDaniel College, Graduate and Professional Studies, Program in Special Education, Westminster, MD 21157-4390. Offers MS. *Accreditation:* NCATE. Part-time and evening/weekend programs available. *Degree requirements:* For master's, thesis optional. *Entrance requirements:* For master's, GRE General Test, MAT, or NTE/PRAXIS I, letters of reference (3). Additional exam requirements/recommendations for international students: Required—TOEFL (minimum score 213 computer-based).

Medaille College, Program in Education, Buffalo, NY 14214-2695. Offers curriculum and instruction (MS Ed); education preparation (MS Ed); literacy (MS Ed); special education (MS). Part-time and evening/weekend programs available. *Faculty:* 30 full-time (20 women), 28 part-time/adjunct (18 women). *Students:* 516 full-time (417 women), 334 part-time (276 women); includes 16 minority (13 African Americans, 2 Asian Americans or Pacific Islanders, 1 Hispanic American), 654 international. Average age 27. 725 applicants, 97% accepted, 655 enrolled. In 2006, 229 degrees awarded. *Degree requirements:* For master's, thesis or alternative. *Entrance requirements:* For master's, minimum undergraduate GPA of 2.7. Additional exam requirements/recommendations for international students: Required—TOEFL (minimum score 550 paper-based; 213 computer-based). *Application deadline:* For fall admission, 8/15 priority date for domestic students; for spring admission, 1/15 priority date for domestic students. Applications are processed on a rolling basis. Application fee: $35. Electronic applications accepted. *Expenses:* Tuition: Part-time $580 per credit hour. Full-time tuition and fees vary according to program. *Financial support:* In 2006–07, 390 students received support. Federal Work-Study available. Financial award applicants required to submit FAFSA. *Faculty research:* Curriculum planning, truancy, tracking minority students, curriculum design, mentoring students. *Unit head:* Dr. Robert DiSibio, Director of Graduate Programs, 716-635-5033 Ext. 2017, Fax: 716-634-2232, E-mail: rdisibio@medaille.edu. *Application contact:* Susan Greenwald, Executive Director of Admissions, 716-635-5033 Ext. 2011, Fax: 716-631-1380, E-mail: sgreenwald@medaille.edu.

Mercy College, Division of Education, Dobbs Ferry, NY 10522-1189. Offers adolescence education: grades 7-12 (MS); applied behavior analysis (MS); bilingual education (MS); childhood education: grades 1-6 (MS); early childhood education: birth—grade 2 (MS); education (MS); elementary education (MS); learning technology (MS); middle childhood education: grades 5-9 (MS); reading (MS); school administration and supervision (MS); school building leadership (MS); school business administration (MS); secondary education (MS); special education (MS); students with disabilities: grades 5-9 (MS); students with disabilities: grades 7-12 (MS); teaching English to speakers of other languages (MS); teaching literacy: birth—grade 6 (MS); teaching literacy: grades 5-12 (MS); urban education (MS). *Students:* 572 full-time (467 women), 1,719 part-time (1,287 women); includes 943 minority (470 African Americans, 7 American Indian/Alaska Native, 48 Asian Americans or Pacific Islanders, 418 Hispanic Americans), 6 international. Average age 33. In 2006, 1090 degrees awarded. *Entrance requirements:* For master's, teaching certificate. *Application deadline:* For fall admission, 2/1 for domestic students. Applications are processed on a rolling basis. Application fee: $37. *Expenses: Contact institution.* Tuition and fees vary according to program. *Financial support:* Institutionally sponsored loans, scholarships/grants, and unspecified assistantships available. Support available to part-time students. *Faculty research:* Distance learning, literacy, assessment, community schools, impact of staff development. *Unit head:* Dr. William Prattella, Chairperson, 914-674-7555, Fax: 914-674-7352, E-mail: wprattella@mercy.edu. *Application contact:* Kathleen Jackson, Director of Admissions, 800-Mercy-NY, Fax: 914-674-7382, E-mail: admissions@mercy.edu.

Mercyhurst College, Graduate Program, Program in Special Education, Erie, PA 16546. Offers bilingual/bicultural special education (MS); educational leadership (Certificate); special education (MS). Part-time and evening/weekend programs available. *Degree requirements:* For master's, thesis optional. *Entrance requirements:* For master's, GRE General Test, MAT, or minimum GPA of 3.0, interview. Additional exam requirements/recommendations for international students: Required—TOEFL. Electronic applications accepted. *Faculty research:* College age learning disabled program, teacher preparation/collaboration, applied behavior analysis, special education policy issues.

Special Education

Miami University, Graduate School, School of Education and Allied Professions, Department of Educational Psychology, Program in Special Education, Oxford, OH 45056. Offers M Ed. *Accreditation:* NCATE. *Degree requirements:* For master's, thesis or alternative, oral or written final exam. *Entrance requirements:* For master's, GRE General Test or MAT, minimum undergraduate GPA of 3.0 during previous 2 years or 2.75 overall. *Faculty research:* Language development, teacher effectiveness, intervention.

Michigan State University, The Graduate School, College of Education, Department of Counseling, Educational Psychology and Special Education, East Lansing, MI 48824. Offers counseling (MA); educational psychology and educational technology (PhD); educational technology (MA); measurement and quantitative methods (PhD); rehabilitation counseling (MA); rehabilitation counselor education (PhD); school psychology (MA, PhD, Ed S); special education (MA, PhD). *Accreditation:* APA (one or more programs are accredited); CORE (one or more programs are accredited). Part-time programs available. *Faculty:* 36 full-time (13 women). *Students:* 218 full-time (149 women), 75 part-time (60 women); includes 38 minority (31 African Americans, 4 Asian Americans or Pacific Islanders, 3 Hispanic Americans), 63 international. Average age 31. 243 applicants, 44% accepted. In 2006, 136 master's, 34 doctorates awarded. *Entrance requirements:* Additional exam requirements/recommendations for international students: Required—TOEFL. Electronic applications accepted. *Expenses:* Tuition, state resident: part-time $346 per credit hour. Tuition, nonresident: part-time $730 per credit hour. Tuition and fees vary according to program. *Financial support:* In 2006–07, 125 fellowships with tuition reimbursements, 87 research assistantships with tuition reimbursements (averaging $13,854 per year), 67 teaching assistantships with tuition reimbursements (averaging $13,722 per year) were awarded. Total annual research expenditures: $3.4 million. *Unit head:* Dr. Richard S. Prawat, Chairperson, 517-353-6417, E-mail: rsprawat@msu.edu. *Application contact:* Kathy Dimoff, Admissions Coordinator, 517-355-6683, E-mail: dimoff@msu.edu.

MidAmerica Nazarene University, Graduate Studies in Education, Olathe, KS 66062-1899. Offers curriculum and instruction (M Ed); educational technology (MET); special education (MA). *Accreditation:* NCATE. Evening/weekend programs available. *Degree requirements:* For master's, thesis or alternative, creative project, technology leadership practicum. *Entrance requirements:* For master's, minimum undergraduate GPA of 2.8, 2 years of teaching experience. Expenses: Contact institution.

Middle Tennessee State University, College of Graduate Studies, College of Education and Behavioral Science, Department of Dyslexic Studies, Murfreesboro, TN 37132. Offers Graduate Certificate. Part-time and evening/weekend programs available. Postbaccalaureate distance learning degree programs offered. *Entrance requirements:* Additional exam requirements/recommendations for international students: Required—TOEFL (minimum score 525 paper-based; 195 computer-based). *Financial support:* Application deadline: 5/1. *Unit head:* Dr. Diane Sawyer, Chair, 615-898-5642.

Middle Tennessee State University, College of Graduate Studies, College of Education and Behavioral Science, Department of Elementary and Special Education, Major in Special Education, Murfreesboro, TN 37132. Offers M Ed. *Accreditation:* NCATE. Part-time and evening/weekend programs available. Postbaccalaureate distance learning degree programs offered. *Students:* 2 full-time (both women), 27 part-time (24 women); includes 3 minority (1 African American, 1 Asian American or Pacific Islander, 1 Hispanic American). 10 applicants, 80% accepted. In 2006, 23 degrees awarded. *Degree requirements:* For master's, comprehensive exam. *Entrance requirements:* For master's, GRE or MAT. Additional exam requirements/recommendations for international students: Required—TOEFL (minimum score 525 paper-based; 195 computer-based). *Application deadline:* For fall admission, 8/1 priority date for domestic students. Applications are processed on a rolling basis. Application fee: $25. Electronic applications accepted. *Financial support:* Application deadline: 5/1. *Unit head:* Dr. Connie Jones, Chair, Department of Elementary and Special Education, 615-898-2680, Fax: 615-898-5309, E-mail: cojones@mtsu.edu.

Midwestern State University, Graduate Studies, College of Education, Program in Special Education, Wichita Falls, TX 76308. Offers M Ed. Part-time and evening/weekend programs available. *Faculty:* 8 full-time (6 women), 3 part-time/adjunct (all women). *Students:* 1 (woman) full-time, 11 part-time (9 women). Average age 39. 1 applicant, 100% accepted, 0 enrolled. In 2006, 6 degrees awarded. *Degree requirements:* For master's, comprehensive exam. *Entrance requirements:* For master's, GRE General Test, MAT, or GMAT, Texas teacher certificate or equivalent GPA of 3.0 in previous education courses . Additional exam requirements/recommendations for international students: Required—TOEFL (minimum score 550 paper-based; 213 computer-based). *Application deadline:* For fall admission, 7/1 for domestic students, 4/1 for international students; for spring admission, 11/1 for domestic students, 8/1 for international students. Applications are processed on a rolling basis. Application fee: $35 ($50 for international students). Electronic applications accepted. *Financial support:* In 2006–07, 8 students received support, including 1 teaching assistantship with partial tuition reimbursement available (averaging $8,218 per year); career-related internships or fieldwork, Federal Work-Study, institutionally sponsored loans, scholarships/grants, tuition waivers (partial), and unspecified assistantships also available. Support available to part-time students. Financial award application deadline: 5/1; financial award applicants required to submit FAFSA. *Faculty research:* Fragile-X syndrome, phenylketonuria and other causes of handicapping conditions. *Unit head:* Dr. Michaelle Kitchen, Chair, 940-397-4141, Fax: 940-397-4694, E-mail: michaelle.kitchen@mwsu.edu. *Application contact:* Dr. Millie Gore, Admissions Office, 940-397-4269, Fax: 940-397-4694, E-mail: millie.gore@mwsu.edu.

Millersville University of Pennsylvania, Graduate School, School of Education, Department of Special Education, Millersville, PA 17551-0302. Offers M Ed. *Accreditation:* NCATE. Part-time and evening/weekend programs available. *Faculty:* 8 full-time (7 women), 5 part-time/adjunct (3 women). *Students:* 2 full-time (both women), 30 part-time (22 women). Average age 34. 3 applicants, 100% accepted, 3 enrolled. In 2006, 9 degrees awarded. *Degree requirements:* For master's, departmental exam, thesis optional. *Entrance requirements:* For master's, GRE General Test, MAT, minimum undergraduate GPA of 2.75. Additional exam requirements/recommendations for international students: Required—TOEFL (minimum score 500 paper-based; 183 computer-based). *Application deadline:* For fall admission, 3/1 for domestic students; for spring admission, 10/1 for domestic students. Applications are processed on a rolling basis. Application fee: $35. *Expenses:* Tuition, state resident: full-time $6,048; part-time $336 per credit. Tuition, nonresident: full-time $9,678; part-time $538 per credit. Required fees: $1,244. Tuition and fees vary according to course load. *Financial support:* Research assistantships with full tuition reimbursements, career-related internships or fieldwork, Federal Work-Study, institutionally sponsored loans, and unspecified assistantships available. Support available to part-time students. Financial award application deadline: 3/15; financial award applicants required to submit FAFSA. *Unit head:* Dr. Barbara A. Beakley, Chair, 717-872-3147, Fax: 717-871-5754, E-mail: barbara.beakley@millersville.edu. *Application contact:* Dr. Victor S. DeSantis, Dean of Graduate Studies, 717-872-3099, Fax: 717-871-2022, E-mail: victor.desantis@millersville.edu.

Minnesota State University Mankato, College of Graduate Studies, College of Education, Department of Educational Studies: Special Populations, Mankato, MN 56001. Offers early education for exceptional children (MS); emotional/behavioral disorders (MS, Certificate); learning disabilities (MS, Certificate); talent development and gifted education (MS, Certificate, SP). *Accreditation:* NCATE. Part-time programs available. *Students:* 10 full-time (7 women), 179 part-time (134 women). Average age 36. In 2006, 24 degrees awarded. *Degree requirements:* For master's, thesis or alternative, comprehensive exam. *Entrance requirements:* For master's, Council for Exceptional Children pre-program assessment, minimum GPA of 3.2 during previous 2 years. *Application deadline:* For fall admission, 7/1 priority date for domestic students; for spring admission, 11/1 for domestic students. Applications are processed on a rolling basis. Application fee: $40. Electronic applications accepted. *Financial support:* Research assistantships, teaching assistantships with full tuition reimbursements, career-related internships or fieldwork, Federal Work-Study, and institutionally sponsored loans available. Support available to part-time students. Financial award application deadline: 3/15; financial award applicants required to submit FAFSA. *Unit head:* Dr. Gail Zahn, Graduate Coordinator, 507-389-5650. *Application contact:* 507-389-2321, E-mail: grad@mnsu.edu.

Minnesota State University Moorhead, Graduate Studies, College of Education and Human Services, Program in Special Education, Moorhead, MN 56563-0002. Offers MS. *Accreditation:* NCATE. Part-time and evening/weekend programs available. *Faculty:* 5 full-time (4 women). *Students:* 4 full-time (all women), 18 part-time (15 women). 11 applicants, 100% accepted. In 2006, 19 degrees awarded. *Degree requirements:* For master's, final oral exam, project or thesis. *Entrance requirements:* For master's, MAT, 1 year teaching experience or bachelor's degree in education, minimum GPA of 3.0. Additional exam requirements/recommendations for international students: Required—TOEFL (minimum score 550 paper-based; 213 computer-based). *Application deadline:* For fall admission, 4/15 priority date for domestic students, 3/15 for international students; for spring admission, 11/1 priority date for domestic students. Applications are processed on a rolling basis. Application fee: $20. Electronic applications accepted. *Financial support:* In 2006–07, 5 research assistantships (averaging $2,000 per year) were awarded; career-related internships or fieldwork, Federal Work-Study, and unspecified assistantships also available. Financial award application deadline: 7/15; financial award applicants required to submit FAFSA. *Unit head:* Dr. Linda Svobodny, Coordinator, 218-477-2005, E-mail: svobodny@mnstate.edu.

Minot State University, Graduate School, Program in Special Education, Minot, ND 58707-0002. Offers education of the deaf (MS); learning disabilities (MS); special education strategist (MS), including early childhood special education, severe multiple handicaps. *Accreditation:* NCATE. *Faculty:* 11 full-time (7 women). *Students:* 68. In 2006, 15 degrees awarded. *Degree requirements:* For master's, thesis (for some programs), comprehensive exam (for some programs). *Entrance requirements:* For master's, GRE General Test or minimum GPA of 3.0. Application fee: $35. *Financial support:* Research assistantships with partial tuition reimbursements, teaching assistantships with partial tuition reimbursements, career-related internships or fieldwork, institutionally sponsored loans, scholarships/grants, traineeships, tuition waivers (partial), and unspecified assistantships available. Support available to part-time students. Financial award application deadline: 4/1. *Faculty research:* Special education team diagnostic unit; individual diagnostic assessments of mentally retarded, learning-disabled, hearing-impaired, and speech-impaired youth; educational programming for the hearing impaired. *Unit head:* Dr. Lori Garnes, Chairperson, 701-858-3139. *Application contact:* Brenda Anderson, Administrative Assistant, 701-858-3250, Fax: 701-858-4286, E-mail: brenda.anderson@minotstateu.edu.

Mississippi College, Graduate School, School of Education, Department of Teacher Education and Leadership, Clinton, MS 39058. Offers art (M Ed); biological science (M Ed); business education (M Ed); computer science (M Ed); dyslexia therapy (M Ed); educational leadership (M Ed, Ed S); elementary education (M Ed, Ed S); English (M Ed); higher education administration (MS); mathematics (M Ed); secondary education (M Ed); social studies (history) (M Ed); teaching arts (M Ed). Part-time programs available. *Faculty:* 9 full-time (5 women), 14 part-time/adjunct (10 women). *Students:* 52 full-time (36 women), 286 part-time (247 women); includes 173 minority (171 African Americans, 1 American Indian/Alaska Native, 1 Hispanic American), 1 international. Average age 32. In 2006, 131 degrees awarded. *Degree requirements:* For master's, thesis optional. *Entrance requirements:* For master's, NTE. Additional exam requirements/recommendations for international students: Recommended—IELTS. *Application deadline:* Applications are processed on a rolling basis. Application fee: $25. Electronic applications accepted. *Expenses:* Tuition: Full-time $7,290; part-time $405 per hour. Required fees: $150 per term. Tuition and fees vary according to campus/location and program. *Financial support:* Teaching assistantships, career-related internships or fieldwork, Federal Work-Study, scholarships/grants, and unspecified assistantships available. Support available to part-time students. Financial award applicants required to submit FAFSA. *Unit head:* Dr. Tom Williams, Chair, 601-925-3844, E-mail: twilliams@mc.edu.

Mississippi State University, College of Education, Department of Counseling, Educational Psychology, and Special Education, Mississippi State, MS 39762. Offers counselor education (MS, PhD, Ed S); educational psychology (MS, PhD, Ed S); special education (MS, Ed S). *Accreditation:* ACA (one or more programs are accredited); APA; CORE (one or more programs are accredited); NCATE. Part-time programs available. Postbaccalaureate distance learning degree programs offered (minimal on-campus study). *Faculty:* 24 full-time (13 women), 10 part-time/adjunct (8 women). *Students:* 120 full-time (94 women), 72 part-time (62 women); includes 68 minority (66 African Americans, 2 Asian Americans or Pacific Islanders), 4 international. Average age 29. 61 applicants, 72% accepted, 32 enrolled. In 2006, 73 master's, 2 doctorates awarded. Terminal master's awarded for partial completion of doctoral program. *Degree requirements:* For master's, thesis optional; for doctorate, thesis/dissertation, comprehensive oral and written exam. *Entrance requirements:* For master's, GRE, minimum QPA of 3.0; for doctorate, GRE, interview, minimum GPA of 3.4. Additional exam requirements/recommendations for international students: Required—TOEFL. *Application deadline:* For fall admission, 3/15 for domestic students. Application fee: $30. *Expenses:* Tuition, state resident: full-time $4,550; part-time $253 per hour. Tuition, nonresident: full-time $10,552; part-time $584 per hour. International tuition: $10,882 full-time. Tuition and fees vary according to course load. *Financial support:* In 2006–07, 30 students received support, including 6 teaching assistantships with full tuition reimbursements available (averaging $7,554 per year); research assistantships with full tuition reimbursements available, career-related internships or fieldwork, Federal Work-Study, institutionally sponsored loans, and unspecified assistantships also available. Financial award application deadline: 2/1; financial award applicants required to submit FAFSA. *Faculty research:* HIV-AIDS in college population, substance abuse in youth and college students, ADHD and conduct disorders in youth, assessment and identification of early childhood disabilities, assessment and vocational transition of the disabled. *Unit head:* Dr. Thomas W. Hosie, Head, 662-325-3426, Fax: 662-325-3263, E-mail: hosie@colled.msstate.edu. *Application contact:* Dr. Phil Bonfanti, Director of Admissions, 662-325-4104, Fax: 662-325-8872, E-mail: admit@msstate.edu.

Missouri State University, Graduate College, College of Education, Department of Educational Administration, Springfield, MO 65804-0094. Offers director of special education (Ed S); educational administration (MS Ed, Ed S); elementary education (MS Ed); elementary principal (Ed S); secondary education (MS Ed); secondary principal (Ed S); special education (MS Ed); superintendent (Ed S). Part-time and evening/weekend programs available. *Faculty:* 6 full-time (1 woman), 3 part-time/adjunct (0 women). *Students:* 10 full-time (8 women), 143 part-time (94 women); includes 1 minority (African American), 1 international. Average age 37. 13 applicants, 92% accepted, 10 enrolled. In 2006, 33 master's, 17 other advanced degrees awarded. *Degree requirements:* For master's and Ed S, thesis or alternative, comprehensive exam. *Entrance requirements:* For master's, minimum GPA of 2.75; for Ed S, GRE General Test, MAT, minimum GPA of 2.75. Additional exam requirements/recommendations for international students: Required—TOEFL (minimum score 550 paper-based; 213 computer-based; 79 iBT). *Application deadline:* For fall admission, 7/20 priority date for domestic students; for spring admission, 12/20 priority date for domestic students. Applications are processed on a rolling basis. Application fee: $35. Electronic applications accepted. *Expenses:* Tuition, state resident: full-time $3,582; part-time $199 per credit hour. Tuition, nonresident: full-time $6,984; part-time $199 per credit hour. Required fees: $548. Full-time tuition and fees vary according to course level, course load, program and reciprocity agreements. *Financial support:* In 2006–07, 1 teaching assistantship with full tuition reimbursement (averaging $6,780 per year) was awarded; career-related internships or fieldwork, Federal Work-Study, scholarships/grants, and unspecified assistantships also available. Financial award application deadline: 3/31; financial award applicants required to submit FAFSA. *Unit head:* Dr. Charles Barke, Acting Head, 417-836-5392, Fax: 417-836-6905, E-mail: edadmin@missouristate.edu.

Missouri State University, Graduate College, College of Education, School of Teacher Education, Program in Special Education, Springfield, MO 65804-0094. Offers MS Ed. Part-time and evening/weekend programs available. *Students:* 1 (woman) full-time, 88 part-time (70 women); includes 6 minority (2 African Americans, 2 American Indian/Alaska Native, 1 Asian American or Pacific Islander, 1 Hispanic American). Average age 36. 14 applicants, 71% accepted, 9 enrolled. In 2006, 9 degrees awarded. *Degree requirements:* For master's, thesis or alternative, comprehensive exam. *Entrance requirements:* For master's, GRE or minimum GPA of 3.0, teaching certificate. Additional exam requirements/recommendations for international students: Required—TOEFL (minimum score 550 paper-based; 213 computer-based; 79 iBT). *Application deadline:* For fall admission, 7/20 for domestic students; for spring admission, 12/20 for domestic students. Application fee: $35. *Expenses:* Tuition, state resident: full-time $3,582; part-time $199 per credit hour. Tuition, nonresident: full-time $6,984; part-time $199 per credit hour. Required fees: $548. Full-time tuition and fees vary according to course level, course load, program and reciprocity agreements. *Financial support:* Teaching assistantships with full tuition reimbursements, Federal Work-Study available. Financial award application deadline: 3/31; financial award applicants required to submit FAFSA. *Unit head:* Dr. Paris DePaepe, Graduate Program Director, 417-836-4761, Fax: 417-836-6252, E-mail: parisdepaepe@missouristate.edu. *Application contact:* Dr. Paris DePaepe, Graduate Director, 417-836-4761, Fax: 417-836-6252, E-mail: parisdepaepe@missouristate.edu.

Monmouth University, Graduate School, School of Education, West Long Branch, NJ 07764-1898. Offers educational counseling (MS Ed); elementary education (MAT), including certified teachers, non-certified teachers; learning disabilities-teacher consultant (Certificate); principal studies (MS Ed); reading specialist (MS Ed, Certificate); special education (MS Ed); supervisor (Certificate); teacher of the handicapped (Certificate). Part-time and evening/weekend programs available. *Faculty:* 24 full-time (15 women), 25 part-time/adjunct (17 women). *Students:* 169 full-time (133 women), 426 part-time (374 women); includes 45 minority (21 African Americans, 2 American Indian/Alaska Native, 2 Asian Americans or Pacific Islanders, 20 Hispanic Americans). Average age 31. 355 applicants, 96% accepted, 138 enrolled. In 2006, 209 degrees awarded. *Entrance requirements:* For master's, minimum GPA of 3.0 in major, 2.75 overall. Additional exam requirements/recommendations for international students: Required—TOEFL (minimum score 550 paper-based; 213 computer-based; 79 iBT), IELTS (minimum score 5), MELAB 77, Cambridge A, B, C. *Application deadline:* For fall admission, 7/15 priority date for domestic students; for spring admission, 11/15 priority date for domestic students. Applications are processed on a rolling basis. Application fee: $50. Electronic applications accepted. *Expenses:* Tuition: Full-time $12,780; part-time $710 per credit. Required fees: $628; $314 per term. *Financial support:* In 2006–07, 221 fellowships (averaging $2,053 per year), 17 research assistantships (averaging $6,527 per year) were awarded; career-related internships or fieldwork, scholarships/grants, tuition waivers (partial), and unspecified assistantships also available. Support available to part-time students. Financial award application deadline: 3/1; financial award applicants required to submit FAFSA. *Faculty research:* Multicultural literacy, science and mathematics teaching strategies, teacher as reflective practitioner, children with disabilities, varied contexts of learning. *Unit head:* Dr. Lynn Romeo, Program Director, 732-571-4484, Fax: 732-263-5277, E-mail: lromeo@monmouth.edu. *Application contact:* Kevin Roane, Director, Office of Graduate Admission, 732-571-3452, Fax: 732-263-5123, E-mail: gradadm@monmouth.edu.

Montana State University–Billings, College of Education and Human Services, Department of Special Education, Counseling, Reading and Early Childhood, Program in Special Education, Billings, MT 59101-0298. Offers advanced studies (MS Sp Ed); special education generalist (MS Sp Ed). *Accreditation:* NCATE. Part-time programs available. *Students:* 40. 29 applicants, 100% accepted, 29 enrolled. In 2006, 13 degrees awarded. *Degree requirements:* For master's, thesis or professional paper and/or field experience, thesis optional. *Entrance requirements:* For master's, GRE General Test or MAT, minimum GPA of 3.0 (undergraduate), 3.25 (graduate). *Application deadline:* Applications are processed on a rolling basis. Application fee: $40. *Expenses:* Tuition, state resident: full-time $4,599. Tuition, nonresident: full-time $10,786. *Financial support:* Teaching assistantships, career-related internships or fieldwork, Federal Work-Study, institutionally sponsored loans, scholarships/grants, tuition waivers (partial), and unspecified assistantships available. Support available to part-time students. Financial award application deadline: 5/1; financial award applicants required to submit FAFSA. *Application contact:* David M. Sullivan, Graduate Studies Counselor, 406-657-2053, Fax: 406-657-2299, E-mail: dsullivan@msubillings.edu.

Montclair State University, The Graduate School, College of Education and Human Services, Department of Early Childhood, Elementary and Literacy Education, Montclair, NJ 07043-1624. Offers early childhood /elementary education (M Ed); early childhood education and teaching students in disabilities (MAT); early childhood special education (M Ed, Certificate); elementary education with disabilities (MAT); elementary school teacher (Certificate); learning disabilities (Certificate); reading (MA, Certificate); reading specialist (Certificate). Part-time and evening/weekend programs available. *Faculty:* 15 full-time (13 women), 65 part-time/adjunct (52 women). *Students:* 27 full-time (24 women), 189 part-time (179 women); includes 24 minority (12 African Americans, 3 Asian Americans or Pacific Islanders, 9 Hispanic Americans), 1 international. 116 applicants, 47% accepted, 35 enrolled. In 2006, 40 master's, 53 other advanced degrees awarded. *Degree requirements:* For master's, clinical experience, portfolio. *Entrance requirements:* For master's, GRE, PRAXIS II, 2 letters of recommendation. Additional exam requirements/recommendations for international students: Required—TOEFL (minimum score 83 computer-based). *Application deadline:* For fall admission, 6/1 for international students; for spring admission, 10/1 for international students. Applications are processed on a rolling basis. Application fee: $60. Electronic applications accepted. *Expenses:* Tuition, state resident: part-time $450 per credit. Tuition, nonresident: part-time $682 per credit. Tuition and fees vary according to degree level and program. *Financial support:* In 2006–07, 15 research assistantships with full tuition reimbursements (averaging $7,000 per year) were awarded; Federal Work-Study, scholarships/grants, and unspecified assistantships also available. Support available to part-time students. Financial award application deadline: 3/1; financial award applicants required to submit FAFSA. *Unit head:* Dr. Nancy Lauter, Chairperson, 973-655-5407, E-mail: lautern@mail.montclair.edu. *Application contact:* Dr. Linda Luise, Adviser, 973-655-4247, E-mail: wisel@mail.montclair.edu.

Morehead State University, Graduate Programs, College of Education, Department of Curriculum and Instruction, Program in Special Education, Morehead, KY 40351. Offers MA Ed, MAT. *Accreditation:* NCATE. Part-time programs available. *Students:* 26 full-time (22 women), 34 part-time (29 women); includes 1 minority (American Indian/Alaska Native). Average age 32. In 2006, 36 degrees awarded. *Degree requirements:* For master's, thesis optional. *Entrance requirements:* For master's, GRE General Test, minimum GPA of 2.75, teaching certificate in special education. Additional exam requirements/recommendations for international students: Required—TOEFL (minimum score 500 paper-based; 173 computer-based). *Application deadline:* For fall admission, 8/1 priority date for domestic and international students; for spring admission, 12/1 priority date for domestic and international students. Applications are processed on a rolling basis. Application fee: $0 ($55 for international students). Electronic applications accepted. *Financial support:* Career-related internships or fieldwork, Federal Work-Study, and unspecified assistantships available. Financial award application deadline: 4/1; financial award applicants required to submit FAFSA. *Faculty research:* Communicative competence of learning-disabled students, study skills. *Application contact:* Michelle Barber, Graduate Admissions Counselor, 606-783-2039, Fax: 606-783-5061, E-mail: m.barber@moreheadstate.edu.

Morningside College, Graduate Division, Department of Education, Program in Special Education, Sioux City, IA 51106. Offers MAT. Part-time and evening/weekend programs available. *Entrance requirements:* For master's, MAT, writing sample.

Mount Saint Mary College, Division of Education, Newburgh, NY 12550-3494. Offers adolescence and special education (MS Ed); adolescence education (MS Ed); childhood and special education (MS Ed); childhood education (MS Ed); literacy and special education (MS Ed); literacy/childhood (MS Ed); middle school (5-6) (MS Ed); middle school (7-9) (MS Ed); special education (1-6) (MS Ed); special education (7-12) (MS Ed). *Accreditation:* NCATE. Part-time and evening/weekend programs available. *Faculty:* 11 full-time (8 women), 21 part-time/adjunct (18 women). *Students:* 87 full-time (74 women), 368 part-time (303 women); includes 38 minority (12 African Americans, 2 American Indian/Alaska Native, 5 Asian Americans or Pacific Islanders, 19 Hispanic Americans). Average age 31. 164 applicants, 45% accepted, 58 enrolled. In 2006, 131 degrees awarded. *Application deadline:* Applications are processed on a rolling basis. Application fee: $35. *Expenses:* Tuition: Full-time $11,880; part-time $660 per credit. *Financial support:* In 2006–07, 30 students received support. Unspecified assistantships available. Financial award application deadline: 3/15. *Faculty research:* Learning and teaching styles, computers in special education, language development. *Unit head:* Theresa Lewis, Coordinator, 845-569-3149, Fax: 845-569-3535, E-mail: tlewis@msmc.edu.

Mount St. Mary's College, Graduate Division, Department of Education, Specialization in Special Education, Los Angeles, CA 90049-1599. Offers MS. Part-time and evening/weekend programs available. *Students:* 6 full-time (5 women), 16 part-time (all women); includes 5 minority (all Hispanic Americans) Average age 35. In 2006, 5 degrees awarded. *Degree requirements:* For master's, thesis, research project. *Entrance requirements:* For master's, MAT, minimum GPA of 3.0. Application fee: $50 ($75 for international students). *Expenses:* Tuition: Part-time $630 per unit. *Financial support:* Institutionally sponsored loans and tuition waivers (partial) available. Support available to part-time students. Financial award application deadline: 3/15; financial award applicants required to submit FAFSA. *Unit head:* Dr. Anne Wilcoxen, Chair, 213-477-2622. *Application contact:* Tom Hoener, Director, Graduate Recruitment, 213-477-2800, Fax: 213-477-2519, E-mail: thoener@msmc.la.edu.

Mount Saint Vincent University, Graduate Programs, Faculty of Education, Program in Educational Psychology, Halifax, NS B3M 2J6, Canada. Offers education of the blind or visually impaired (M Ed, MA Ed); education of the deaf or hard of hearing (M Ed, MA Ed); educational psychology (MA-R); human relations (M Ed, MA Ed). Part-time and evening/weekend programs available. Postbaccalaureate distance learning degree programs offered (minimal on-campus study). *Degree requirements:* For master's, thesis (for some programs). *Entrance requirements:* For master's, bachelor's degree in related field, 1 year of teaching experience. Electronic applications accepted. *Faculty research:* Personality measurement, values reasoning, aggression and sexuality, power and control, quantitative and qualitative research methodologies.

Murray State University, College of Education, Department of Adolescent, Career and Special Education, Program in Special Education, Murray, KY 42071. Offers advanced learning behavior disorders (MA Ed); learning disabilities (MA Ed); moderate/severe disorders (MA Ed). *Accreditation:* NCATE. Part-time and evening/weekend programs available. *Faculty:* 3 full-time (2 women). *Students:* 1 (woman) full-time, 238 part-time (179 women); includes 5 minority (all Hispanic Americans) 59 applicants, 97% accepted, 55 enrolled. In 2006, 31 degrees awarded. *Degree requirements:* For master's, portfolio, thesis optional. *Entrance requirements:* For master's, GRE General Test or MAT, teacher certification. Additional exam requirements/recommendations for international students: Required—TOEFL. *Application deadline:* For fall admission, 8/1 for domestic students; for spring admission, 1/13 for domestic students. Applications are processed on a rolling basis. Application fee: $30. *Financial support:* Research assistantships, teaching assistantships, Federal Work-Study available. Financial award application deadline: 4/1. *Faculty research:* Attention Deficit Hyperactivity Disorder, assistive technology. *Unit head:* Dr. Arlene Hall, Graduate Coordinator, 270-809-6847, Fax: 270-809-2540, E-mail: arlene.hall@coe.murraystate.edu.

National-Louis University, National College of Education, Programs in Special Education, Chicago, IL 60603. Offers general special education (M Ed, MAT, CAS); learning disabilities (M Ed, CAS); learning disabilities/behavior disorders (M Ed, MAT, CAS). Part-time and evening/weekend programs available. *Students:* 70 full-time (52 women), 183 part-time (134 women); includes 19 minority (9 African Americans, 4 Asian Americans or Pacific Islanders, 6 Hispanic Americans). Average age 34. 26 applicants, 100% accepted. In 2006, 40 master's, 2 other advanced degrees awarded. *Degree requirements:* For master's, thesis (for some programs), practicum; for CAS, practicum. *Entrance requirements:* For master's, MAT or GRE, minimum GPA of 3.0; for CAS, master's degree, teaching certificate. *Application deadline:* Applications are processed on a rolling basis. Application fee: $25. *Expenses:* Tuition: Full-time $17,685. One-time fee: $40 full-time. *Financial support:* Fellowships, Federal Work-Study, institutionally sponsored loans, and scholarships/grants available. Support available to part-time students. Financial award applicants required to submit FAFSA. *Unit head:* Dr. Patrick Schwarz, Coordinator, 847-475-1100 Ext. 5379. *Application contact:* David McCulloch, Vice President for University Services, 800-443-5522 Ext. 5127, Fax: 847-465-0593, E-mail: dmcc@wheeling1.nl.edu.

National University, Academic Affairs, School of Education, Department of Special Education and Technology, La Jolla, CA 92037-1011. Offers deaf and hard of hearing education (MS); educational technology (MS); exceptional student education (MS); special education (MS). Part-time and evening/weekend programs available. Postbaccalaureate distance learning degree programs offered (no on-campus study). *Faculty:* 15 full-time (12 women), 389 part-time/adjunct (232 women). *Students:* 1,039 full-time (706 women), 2,426 part-time (1,549 women); includes 997 minority (337 African Americans, 27 American Indian/Alaska Native, 179 Asian Americans or Pacific Islanders, 454 Hispanic Americans), 19 international. Average age 38. 1,579 applicants, 1481 enrolled. In 2006, 215 degrees awarded. *Degree requirements:* For master's, thesis (for some programs). *Entrance requirements:* For master's, interview, minimum GPA of 2.5. Additional exam requirements/recommendations for international students: Required—TOEFL (minimum score 550 paper-based; 213 computer-based; 80 iBT), IELTS (minimum score 6). *Application deadline:* Applications are processed on a rolling basis. Application fee: $60 ($65 for international students). Electronic applications accepted. *Expenses:* Tuition: Full-time $7,722; part-time $286 per unit. One-time fee: $60. *Financial support:* Career-related internships or fieldwork, institutionally sponsored loans, scholarships/grants, and tuition waivers (partial) available. Support available to part-time students. Financial award application deadline: 6/30; financial award applicants required to submit FAFSA. *Unit head:* Dr. Jane Duckett, Chair, 858-642-8346, Fax: 858-642-8724, E-mail: jduckett@nu.edu. *Application contact:* Dominick Giovanniello, Associate Regional Dean—San Diego, 800-NAT-UNIV, Fax: 858-642-8709, E-mail: dgiovann@nu.edu.

New England College, Program in Education, Henniker, NH 03242-3293. Offers literacy and language arts (M Ed); meeting the needs of all learners/special education (M Ed); teacher leadership/school reform (M Ed). Part-time and evening/weekend programs available.

New Jersey City University, Graduate and Continuing Education, College of Education, Department of Special Education, Jersey City, NJ 07305-1597. Offers MA. Evening/weekend programs available. *Faculty:* 36. *Students:* 7 full-time (5 women), 134 part-time (100 women); includes 18 minority (10 African Americans, 1 Asian American or Pacific Islander, 7 Hispanic Americans), 8 international. Average age 36. In 2006, 208 degrees awarded. *Entrance requirements:* For master's, GRE General Test or MAT. Additional exam requirements/recommendations for international students: Required—TOEFL. *Application deadline:* For fall admission, 8/1 priority date for domestic students; for spring admission, 12/1 for domestic students. Applications are processed on a rolling basis. Application fee: $0. *Expenses:* Tuition, state resident: full-time $7,038; part-time $391 per credit. Tuition, nonresident: full-time $12,510; part-time $695 per credit. Required fees: $65 per credit. *Financial support:* Unspecified assistantships available. *Faculty research:* Mainstreaming the handicapped child and the autistic child. *Unit head:* Dr. Carol Fleres, Chairperson, 201-200-3023.

New Mexico Highlands University, Graduate Studies, School of Education, Las Vegas, NM 87701. Offers education (MA), including curriculum and instruction; educational leadership (MA); exercise and sport sciences (MA), including human performance and sport, sports administration, teacher education; guidance and counseling (MA), including professional counseling, rehabilitation counseling, school counseling; special education (MA), including). *Accreditation:* NCATE. Part-time programs available. *Faculty:* 14 full-time (6 women), 11 part-time/adjunct (9 women). *Students:* 171 full-time (117 women), 413 part-time (286 women); includes 305 minority (17 African Americans, 30 American Indian/Alaska Native, 4 Asian

Special Education

New Mexico Highlands University (continued)
Americans or Pacific Islanders, 254 Hispanic Americans), 3 international. Average age 40. 111 applicants, 84% accepted, 63 enrolled. In 2006, 111 degrees awarded. *Degree requirements:* For master's, thesis or alternative, comprehensive exam, registration. *Entrance requirements:* For master's, minimum undergraduate GPA of 3.0. Additional exam requirements/ recommendations for international students: Required—TOEFL (minimum score 540 paper-based; 190 computer-based). *Application deadline:* For fall admission, 8/1 priority date for domestic students. Applications are processed on a rolling basis. Application fee: $15. *Expenses:* Tuition, state resident: part-time $101 per credit hour. Tuition, nonresident: part-time $101 per credit hour. *Financial support:* In 2006–07, 205 students received support, including 16 teaching assistantships with full and partial tuition reimbursements available (averaging $6,500 per year); career-related internships or fieldwork, Federal Work-Study, institutionally sponsored loans, scholarships/grants, traineeships, tuition waivers (partial), and unspecified assistantships also available. Support available to part-time students. Financial award application deadline: 3/1; financial award applicants required to submit FAFSA. *Unit head:* Dr. Francisco Hidalgo, Dean, 505-454-3357, Fax: 505-454-3384, E-mail: fhidalgo@nmhu.edu. *Application contact:* Diane Trujillo, Administrative Assistant Graduate Studies, 505-454-3266, Fax: 505-454-3558, E-mail: dtrujillo@nmhu.edu.

New Mexico State University, Graduate School, College of Education, Department of Special Education and Communication Disorders, Las Cruces, NM 88003-8001. Offers special education (MA, Ed D, PhD). *Accreditation:* ASHA (one or more programs are accredited); NCATE. Part-time and evening/weekend programs available. Postbaccalaureate distance learning degree programs offered. *Faculty:* 11 full-time (9 women), 1 (woman) part-time/adjunct. *Students:* 43 full-time (38 women), 106 part-time (82 women); includes 61 minority (3 African Americans, 3 American Indian/Alaska Native, 55 Hispanic Americans), 2 international. Average age 37. 42 applicants, 69% accepted. *Degree requirements:* For master's, thesis or alternative. *Entrance requirements:* For master's, GRE General Test or MAT. *Application deadline:* For fall admission, 3/1 priority date for domestic students. Applications are processed on a rolling basis. Application fee: $30 ($50 for international students). Electronic applications accepted. *Financial support:* In 2006–07, 11 teaching assistantships were awarded; fellowships, research assistantships, career-related internships or fieldwork, Federal Work-Study, and health care benefits also available. Support available to part-time students. Financial award application deadline: 3/1. *Faculty research:* Multicultural special education, multicultural communication disorders, mild disability, school psychology, deaf education, early childhood, bilingual special education. *Unit head:* Dr. Robert Rhodes, Head, 505-646-2402, Fax: 505-646-4234, E-mail: rorhodes@nmsu.edu.

New York University, Steinhardt School of Culture, Education and Human Development, Department of Teaching and Learning, Program in Special Education, New York, NY 10012-1019. Offers childhood special education (MA); early childhood special education (MA). *Accreditation:* Teacher Education Accreditation Council. Part-time and evening/weekend programs available. *Faculty:* 5 full-time (3 women). *Students:* 66 full-time (61 women), 16 part-time (15 women); includes 28 minority (11 African Americans, 11 Asian Americans or Pacific Islanders, 6 Hispanic Americans), 7 international. 93 applicants, 77% accepted, 34 enrolled. In 2006, 66 degrees awarded. *Degree requirements:* For master's, thesis (for some programs). *Entrance requirements:* Additional exam requirements/recommendations for international students: Required—TOEFL. *Application deadline:* For fall admission, 12/15 priority date for domestic and international students; for spring admission, 11/1 priority date for domestic and international students. Applications are processed on a rolling basis. Application fee: $50. *Expenses:* Tuition: Part-time $1,080 per unit. Required fees: $56 per unit. $329 per term. Tuition and fees vary according to program. *Financial support:* Career-related internships or fieldwork, Federal Work-Study, institutionally sponsored loans, scholarships/grants, and tuition waivers (partial) available. Support available to part-time students. Financial award application deadline: 2/1; financial award applicants required to submit FAFSA. *Faculty research:* Special education referrals, attention deficit disorders in children, mainstreaming, curriculum-based assessment and program implementation, special education policy. *Unit head:* Dr. Lisa Fleisher, Director, 212-998-5460, Fax: 212-995-4049. *Application contact:* 212-998-5030, Fax: 212-995-4328, E-mail: steinhardt.gradadmissions@nyu.edu.

Niagara University, Graduate Division of Education, Concentration in Inclusive Education, Niagara Falls, Niagara University, NY 14109. Offers MS Ed. *Students:* 11 full-time (all women), 2 part-time (both women); includes 1 minority (American Indian/Alaska Native), 1 international. In 2006, 4 degrees awarded. *Application deadline:* For fall admission, 8/1 for domestic students. Applications are processed on a rolling basis. Application fee: $30. *Financial support:* Application deadline: 3/15. *Unit head:* Dr. Chandra Foote, Chair, 716-286-8549.

Norfolk State University, School of Graduate Studies, School of Education, Department of Special Education, Norfolk, VA 23504. Offers severe disabilities (MA). *Accreditation:* NCATE. Part-time programs available. *Degree requirements:* For master's, thesis or alternative. *Entrance requirements:* For master's, minimum GPA of 3.0 in major, 2.5 overall.

North Carolina Central University, Division of Academic Affairs, School of Education, Special Education Program, Durham, NC 27707-3129. Offers education of the emotionally handicapped (M Ed); education of the mentally handicapped (M Ed). *Accreditation:* NCATE. Part-time and evening/weekend programs available. *Degree requirements:* For master's, thesis or alternative, comprehensive exam. *Entrance requirements:* For master's, GRE, minimum GPA of 3.0 in major, 2.5 overall. Additional exam requirements/recommendations for international students: Required—TOEFL. *Faculty research:* Vocational programs for special needs learners.

North Carolina State University, Graduate School, College of Education, Department of Curriculum and Instruction, Program in Special Education, Raleigh, NC 27695. Offers M Ed, MS. *Accreditation:* NCATE. *Degree requirements:* For master's, thesis optional. *Entrance requirements:* For master's, GRE General Test and MAT, minimum GPA of 3.0 in major. Electronic applications accepted. *Faculty research:* Nature of disabilities, intervention research.

Northeastern Illinois University, Graduate College, College of Education, Department of Special Education, Program in Special Education, Chicago, IL 60625-4699. Offers early childhood special education (MA); educating children with behavior disorders (MA); educating individuals with mental retardation (MA); teaching children with learning disabilities (MA). Part-time and evening/weekend programs available. *Faculty:* 18 full-time (11 women), 2 part-time/adjunct (both women). *Students:* Average age 34. *Degree requirements:* For master's, project, thesis optional. *Entrance requirements:* For master's, minimum GPA of 2.75; previous course work in history or philosophy of education or teaching certificate. *Financial support:* In 2006–07, 62 students received support, including 5 research assistantships with full tuition reimbursements available (averaging $6,600 per year); career-related internships or fieldwork, Federal Work-Study, institutionally sponsored loans, and tuition waivers (full and partial) also available. Support available to part-time students. *Faculty research:* Bilingual special education, use of technology in the classroom, teachers' attitudes toward inclusion, standards for special education teachers.

Northeastern University, Bouvé College of Health Sciences Graduate School, Department of Counseling and Applied Educational Psychology, Boston, MA 02115-5096. Offers applied behavior analysis (MS); applied educational psychology (MS), including school counseling, school psychology; college student development and counseling (MS); counseling psychology (MS, PhD, CAGS); school psychology (PhD, CAGS); special needs and intensive special needs (MS Ed). *Accreditation:* APA (one or more programs are accredited). Part-time and evening/weekend programs available. *Faculty:* 18 full-time (11 women), 24 part-time/adjunct. *Students:* 353 full-time (308 women), 51 part-time (42 women). Average age 27. 452 applicants, 24% accepted. In 2006, 95 master's, 10 doctorates, 25 other advanced degrees awarded. *Degree requirements:* For doctorate, thesis/dissertation, qualifying exams, comprehensive exam. *Entrance requirements:* For master's and CAGS, GRE General Test or MAT; for doctorate, GRE General Test. Additional exam requirements/recommendations for international students:

Required—TOEFL. *Application deadline:* Applications are processed on a rolling basis. Application fee: $50. *Financial support:* In 2006–07, 2 teaching assistantships with full tuition reimbursements (averaging $13,832 per year) were awarded; research assistantships, career-related internships or fieldwork, Federal Work-Study, tuition waivers (partial), and unspecified assistantships also available. Support available to part-time students. Financial award application deadline: 3/1; financial award applicants required to submit FAFSA. *Faculty research:* Early intervention, career development and choice, crisis intervention, family systems, bilingual education in special education. *Unit head:* Dr. William Sanchez, Chair, 617-373-2404, Fax: 617-373-8892. *Application contact:* Margaret Schnabel, Director of Graduate Admissions, 617-373-2708, Fax: 617-373-4704, E-mail: bouvegrad@neu.edu.

Northern Arizona University, Graduate College, College of Education, Program in Special Education, Flagstaff, AZ 86011. Offers M Ed. Part-time programs available. *Degree requirements:* For master's, thesis optional. *Faculty research:* Special education teacher training, mainstreaming, assessing and teaching mildly disabled, emotional disturbance, parent involvement.

Northern Illinois University, Graduate School, College of Education, Department of Teaching and Learning, De Kalb, IL 60115-2854. Offers curriculum and instruction (MS Ed, Ed D), including curriculum leadership (Ed D); elementary education (Ed D); secondary education (Ed D); early childhood education (MS Ed); elementary education (MS Ed); special education (MS Ed). Part-time and evening/weekend programs available. *Faculty:* 22 full-time (14 women), 2 part-time/adjunct (both women). *Students:* 81 full-time (64 women), 534 part-time (417 women); includes 122 minority (21 African Americans, 12 Asian Americans or Pacific Islanders, 89 Hispanic Americans), 11 international. Average age 36. 92 applicants, 57% accepted, 43 enrolled. In 2006, 256 master's, 12 doctorates awarded. *Degree requirements:* For master's, thesis optional; for doctorate, thesis/dissertation, candidacy exam, dissertation defense. *Entrance requirements:* For master's, GRE General Test or MAT, minimum undergraduate GPA of 2.75; for doctorate, GRE General Test or MAT, minimum undergraduate GPA of 2.75, graduate 3.2. Additional exam requirements/recommendations for international students: Required—TOEFL (minimum score 550 paper-based; 213 computer-based). *Application deadline:* For fall admission, 6/1 for domestic students, 5/1 for international students; for spring admission, 11/1 for domestic students, 10/1 for international students. Applications are processed on a rolling basis. Application fee: $30. Electronic applications accepted. *Financial support:* In 2006–07, 27 research assistantships with full tuition reimbursements, 1 teaching assistantship with full tuition reimbursement were awarded; fellowships with full tuition reimbursements, career-related internships or fieldwork, Federal Work-Study, scholarships/grants, tuition waivers (full), and unspecified assistantships also available. Support available to part-time students. Financial award applicants required to submit FAFSA. *Faculty research:* Teacher certification, stress reduction during student teaching, teaching history, portfolios in student teaching. *Unit head:* Dr. Pamela Jackson, Acting Chair, 815-753-8452, E-mail: p30ngd1@wpo.cso.niu.edu.

Northern Kentucky University, Office of Graduate Programs, College of Education and Human Services, Program in Alternative Certification in Special Education, Highland Heights, KY 41099. Offers Certificate. Program offered only in summer. *Entrance requirements:* For degree, GRE, PRAXIS II. Additional exam requirements/recommendations for international students: Required—TOEFL. *Expenses:* Tuition, state resident: full-time $5,274; part-time $293 per hour. Tuition, nonresident: full-time $10,314; part-time $573 per hour. Tuition and fees vary according to course load, program and reciprocity agreements. *Unit head:* Dr. Paul J. Wirtz, Associate Dean/Director of Graduate Studies, 859-572-6068, Fax: 859-572-6623, E-mail: wirtzp1@nku.edu. *Application contact:* Dr. Peg Griffin, Director of Graduate Programs, 859-572-1555, Fax: 859-572-6670, E-mail: gradprog@nku.edu.

Northern Michigan University, College of Graduate Studies, College of Professional Studies, School of Education, Program in Special Education, Marquette, MI 49855-5301. Offers MA Ed. *Accreditation:* NCATE. Part-time programs available. *Degree requirements:* For master's, thesis or alternative. *Entrance requirements:* For master's, GRE General Test, minimum GPA of 3.0. *Faculty research:* Interdisciplinary approaches to learning disabilities, neurological bases for cognitive processing of information.

Northern State University, Division of Graduate Studies in Education, Program in Teaching and Learning, Aberdeen, SD 57401-7198. Offers educational studies (MS Ed); elementary classroom teaching (MS Ed); health, physical education, and coaching (MS Ed); language and literacy (MS Ed); secondary classroom teaching (MS Ed); special education (MS Ed). *Accreditation:* NCATE. Part-time and evening/weekend programs available. *Faculty:* 69 full-time (19 women). *Students:* 5 full-time (3 women), 70 part-time (51 women); includes 3 minority (1 African American, 1 American Indian/Alaska Native, 1 Asian American or Pacific Islander). Average age 32. In 2006, 23 degrees awarded. *Degree requirements:* For master's, thesis optional. *Entrance requirements:* For master's, minimum GPA of 2.75. Additional exam requirements/recommendations for international students: Required—TOEFL (minimum score 550 paper-based; 213 computer-based). *Application deadline:* For fall admission, 8/15 priority date for domestic students; for spring admission, 12/15 for domestic students. Applications are processed on a rolling basis. Application fee: $35. Electronic applications accepted. *Expenses:* Tuition, state resident: full-time $3,373; part-time $120 per credit. Tuition, nonresident: full-time $9,943; part-time $355 per credit. International tuition: $13,000 full-time. Required fees: $86 per credit. One-time fee: $35 full-time. Tuition and fees vary according to course load, degree level and reciprocity agreements. *Financial support:* In 2006–07, 17 teaching assistantships with partial tuition reimbursements (averaging $4,812 per year) were awarded; career-related internships or fieldwork, Federal Work-Study, institutionally sponsored loans, scholarships/grants, and unspecified assistantships also available. Support available to part-time students. Financial award application deadline: 3/1; financial award applicants required to submit FAFSA. *Application contact:* Tammy K. Griffith, Senior Secretary, 605-626-2558, Fax: 605-626-2542, E-mail: griffith@northern.edu.

North Georgia College & State University, Graduate Studies, Program in Teacher Education, Dahlonega, GA 30597. Offers early childhood education (M Ed); educational leadership (Ed S); middle grades education (M Ed); secondary education (M Ed), including art education, biology education, chemistry education, English education, history education, mathematics education, physical education, science education; special education (M Ed), including inter-related special education, learning disabilities. *Accreditation:* NCATE. Part-time and evening/weekend programs available. Postbaccalaureate distance learning degree programs offered (minimal on-campus study). *Faculty:* 35 full-time (18 women), 9 part-time/adjunct (6 women). *Students:* 260. Average age 32. 120 applicants, 63% accepted. In 2006, 134 degrees awarded. *Degree requirements:* For master's, thesis optional. *Entrance requirements:* For master's, GRE General Test or MAT, minimum GPA of 2.75; for Ed S, GRE General Test or MAT, 3 years of teaching experience, master's degree, minimum graduate GPA of 3.25. *Application deadline:* For fall admission, 7/1 priority date for domestic students; for spring admission, 12/10 priority date for domestic students. Applications are processed on a rolling basis. Application fee: $25. Electronic applications accepted. *Expenses:* Tuition, state resident: full-time $3,044; part-time $127 per credit hour. Tuition, nonresident: full-time $12,172; part-time $508 per credit hour. Required fees: $892; $458 per semester. *Financial support:* Teaching assistantships, career-related internships or fieldwork and scholarships/grants available. Support available to part-time students. Financial award application deadline: 5/1. *Faculty research:* Computers and teachers' attitudes, rural versus urban teacher attitudes, teacher leadership roles, minority recruitment in teaching force. *Unit head:* Dr. Bob Michael, Dean, School of Education, 706-864-1998, Fax: 706-867-2850, E-mail: bmichael@ngcsu.edu. *Application contact:* Dr. Donna A. Gessell, Director of Graduate Studies and External Programs, 706-864-1528, Fax: 706-867-2795, E-mail: dgessell@ngcsu.edu.

Northwestern State University of Louisiana, Graduate Studies and Research, College of Education, Program in Student Personnel Services, Natchitoches, LA 71497. Offers counseling and guidance (M Ed, Ed S); special education (M Ed, Ed S); student personnel services (MA). *Accreditation:* NCATE (one or more programs are accredited). *Faculty:* 3 full-time (2 women),

2 part-time/adjunct (1 woman). *Students:* 39 full-time (31 women), 12 part-time (all women); includes 29 minority (27 African Americans, 2 American Indian/Alaska Native). Average age 29. In 2006, 13 degrees awarded. *Degree requirements:* For master's, thesis or alternative, comprehensive exam, registration. *Entrance requirements:* For master's, GRE General Test, GRE Subject Test, minimum undergraduate GPA of 2.5. *Application deadline:* For fall admission, 8/1 priority date for domestic students; for spring admission, 1/10 for domestic students. Applications are processed on a rolling basis. Application fee: $20 ($30 for international students). *Financial support:* Application deadline: 7/15. *Application contact:* Dr. Steven G. Horton, Associate Provost/Dean, Graduate Studies, Research, and Information Systems, 318-357-5851, Fax: 318-357-5019, E-mail: grad_school@nsula.edu.

Northwestern State University of Louisiana, Graduate Studies and Research, College of Education, Programs in Educational Leadership and Instruction, Natchitoches, LA 71497. Offers counseling (Ed S); educational leadership (Ed S); educational technology (Ed S); elementary teaching (Ed S); reading (Ed S); secondary teaching (Ed S); special education (Ed S). *Students:* 17 full-time (15 women), 114 part-time (87 women); includes 55 minority (51 African Americans, 1 Asian American or Pacific Islander, 3 Hispanic Americans). Average age 39. In 2006, 11 degrees awarded. *Entrance requirements:* For degree, GRE General Test. *Application contact:* Dr. Steven G. Horton, Associate Provost/Dean, Graduate Studies, Research, and Information Systems, 318-357-5851, Fax: 318-357-5019, E-mail: grad_school@nsula.edu.

Northwestern University, The Graduate School, School of Communication, The Roxelyn and Richard Pepper Department of Communication Sciences and Disorders, Program in Learning Disabilities, Evanston, IL 60208. Offers MA, PhD. Admissions and degrees offered through The Graduate School. Part-time programs available. Terminal master's awarded for partial completion of doctoral program. *Degree requirements:* For master's, thesis optional; for doctorate, pre-dissertation research project, qualifying exam. *Entrance requirements:* For master's and doctorate, GRE General Test, letters of recommendation. Additional exam requirements/recommendations for international students: Required—TOEFL. *Faculty research:* Reading and writing disabilities, inter-relations of oral and written language, social context of atypical development, attention deficit disorder, neuroscience of learning disorders.

See Close-Up on page 1717.

Northwestern University, The Graduate School, School of Communication, The Roxelyn and Richard Pepper Department of Communication Sciences and Disorders, Program in Speech and Language Pathology and Learning Disabilities, Evanston, IL 60208. Offers MA. Admissions and degree offered through The Graduate School. *Accreditation:* ASHA. *Degree requirements:* For master's, seminar paper, thesis optional. *Entrance requirements:* For master's, GRE General Test, letters of recommendation. Additional exam requirements/recommendations for international students: Required—TOEFL. *Faculty research:* Language and cognitive development, phonological and reading development.

See Close-Up on page 1717.

Northwest Missouri State University, Graduate School, College of Education and Human Services, Department of Curriculum and Instruction, Program in Special Education, Maryville, MO 64468-6001. Offers MS Ed. *Faculty:* 10 full-time (all women). *Students:* 1 (woman) full-time, 8 part-time (all women). 7 applicants, 86% accepted, 4 enrolled. In 2006, 3 degrees awarded. *Entrance requirements:* For master's, GRE General Test, minimum GPA of 2.75, teaching certificate. Additional exam requirements/recommendations for international students: Required—TOEFL (minimum score 550 paper-based; 213 computer-based). *Application deadline:* For fall admission, 7/1 for domestic and international students; for spring admission, 11/15 for domestic and international students. Application fee: $0 ($50 for international students). *Unit head:* Dr. Shirley Steffens, Head, 660-562-1443. *Application contact:* Dr. Frances Shipley, Dean of Graduate School, 660-562-1145, Fax: 660-562-1096, E-mail: gradsch@nwmissouri.edu.

Northwest Nazarene University, Graduate Studies, Program in Teacher Education, Nampa, ID 83686-5897. Offers curriculum and instruction (M Ed); educational leadership (M Ed); exceptional child (M Ed); reading education (M Ed); school counseling (M Ed). *Accreditation:* ACA; NCATE. Part-time programs available. *Faculty:* 11 full-time (4 women), 10 part-time/adjunct (6 women). *Students:* 113 full-time (79 women), 20 part-time (18 women); includes 4 minority (2 Asian Americans or Pacific Islanders, 2 Hispanic Americans). Average age 34. In 2006, 35 degrees awarded. *Degree requirements:* For master's, action research project. *Entrance requirements:* For master's, minimum undergraduate GPA of 2.8 overall or 3.0 during final 30 semester credits. *Application deadline:* For fall admission, 9/1 for domestic students. Applications are processed on a rolling basis. Application fee: $25. *Faculty research:* Action research, cooperative learning, accountability, institutional accreditation. *Unit head:* Dr. Karen Blacklock, Chair, 208-467-8399, Fax: 208-467-8562.

Notre Dame College, Graduate Studies, South Euclid, OH 44121-4293. Offers accounting (Certificate); creative critical thinking (M Ed); financial services management (Certificate); information systems (Certificate); learning disabilities (M Ed); management (Certificate); paralegal (Certificate); pastoral ministry (Certificate); reading (M Ed); teacher education (Certificate). Part-time and evening/weekend programs available. *Degree requirements:* For master's, thesis. *Entrance requirements:* For master's, GRE General Test, MAT, minimum GPA of 2.75, valid teaching certificate. *Faculty research:* Cognitive psychology, teaching critical thinking in the classroom.

Notre Dame de Namur University, Division of Academic Affairs, School of Education and Leadership, Program in Special Education, Belmont, CA 94002-1908. Offers MA, Certificate. *Degree requirements:* For master's, thesis. *Entrance requirements:* For master's, interview, minimum GPA of 2.5. Additional exam requirements/recommendations for international students: Required—TOEFL. *Application deadline:* For fall admission, 8/1 priority date for domestic students; for spring admission, 12/1 priority date for domestic students. Applications are processed on a rolling basis. Electronic applications accepted. *Expenses:* Tuition: Part-time $655 per credit. *Financial support:* Applicants required to submit FAFSA. *Unit head:* Dr. Barbara Kammerlohr, Director, 650-508-3627. *Application contact:* Helen Valine, Director of Graduate Admissions, 650-508-3534, Fax: 650-508-3426, E-mail: grad.admit@ndnu.edu.

Nova Southeastern University, Fischler School of Education and Human Services, Graduate Teacher Education Program, Fort Lauderdale, FL 33314-7796. Offers athletic administration (MS); cognitive and behavioral disabilities (MS); computer science education (Ed S); computer science education (K-12) (MS); curriculum and teaching (Ed S); curriculum, instruction and technology (MS); curriculum, instruction, management and administration (Ed S); early childhood special education (MS); early literacy and reading (Ed S); early literacy education (MS); education technology (MS); educational leadership (administration K–12) (MS, Ed S); educational media (Ed S); educational media (K-12) (MS); elementary education (MS, Ed S), including ESOL endorsement (MS); English (MS, Ed S); exceptional student education (MS), including ESOL endorsement; gifted education (MS, Ed S); interdisciplinary arts education (MS); management and administration of educational programs (MS); mathematics (MS, Ed S); multicultural early intervention (MS); pre-kindergarten/primary (MS); preschool education (MS); reading (MS, Ed S); science (MS, Ed S); secondary education (MS); social studies (MS, Ed S); Spanish language (MS); teaching and learning (MA, MS), including curriculum and instruction (MA), elementary mathematics (MA), elementary reading (MA), K-12 technology integration (MA); teaching English to speakers of other languages (MS, Ed S); technology management and administration (Ed S); urban studies education (MS); varying exceptionalities (Ed S). Part-time and evening/weekend programs available. Postbaccalaureate distance learning degree programs offered. *Faculty:* 131 full-time (78 women), 548 part-time/adjunct (342 women). *Students:* 1,418 full-time (1,139 women), 3,464 part-time (2,877 women); includes 2,462 minority (1,732 African Americans, 13 American Indian/Alaska Native, 44 Asian Americans or Pacific Islanders, 673 Hispanic Americans), 77 international. Average age 38. 1,771 applicants, 80% accepted, 1419 enrolled. In 2006, 2,078 master's, 425 other advanced degrees awarded. *Degree requirements:* For master's and Ed S, thesis, practicum, internship. *Entrance requirements:* For master's, MAT, GRE, CLAST, CBEST, PRAXIS I, GKT, minimum GPA of 2.5; for Ed S, MAT or GRE, master's degree, teaching certificate, minimum GPA of 3.0. Additional exam requirements/recommendations for international students: Recommended—TOEFL (minimum score 550 paper-based; 213 computer-based), IELTS (minimum score 6). *Application deadline:* For fall admission, 8/11 priority date for domestic and international students; for winter admission, 12/28 priority date for domestic and international students; for spring admission, 4/22 priority date for domestic and international students. Applications are processed on a rolling basis. Application fee: $50. Electronic applications accepted. *Financial support:* Federal Work-Study available. Support available to part-time students. Financial award application deadline: 1/7. *Faculty research:* School effectiveness, critical thinking, leadership skills acquisition, child education, multicultural education. *Unit head:* Dr. Meline Kevorkian, Associate Dean of Master's and Educational Programs, 954-262-8500, Fax: 954-262-3606, E-mail: melinek@nova.edu. *Application contact:* Jennifer Quiñones Nottingham, Dean of Student Affairs, 800-986-3223 Ext. 8624, Fax: 954-262-3911, E-mail: jlquinon@nova.edu.

Nova Southeastern University, Fischler School of Education and Human Services, Program in Education, Fort Lauderdale, FL 33314-7796. Offers educational leadership (Ed D); health care education (Ed D); higher education (Ed D); human serviced administration (Ed D); instructional leadership (Ed D); instructional technology distance education (Ed D); organizational leadership (Ed D); special education (Ed D); speech language pathology (Ed D). *Students:* 619 full-time (452 women), 615 part-time (473 women); includes 737 minority (616 African Americans, 2 American Indian/Alaska Native, 14 Asian Americans or Pacific Islanders, 105 Hispanic Americans), 8 international. Average age 38. 480 applicants, 83% accepted, 398 enrolled. *Degree requirements:* For doctorate, thesis/dissertation. *Entrance requirements:* For doctorate, MAT or GRE, master's degree, 2 letters of recommendation, work experience. Additional exam requirements/recommendations for international students: Required—TSE (recommended) with a minimum score of 50; Recommended—TOEFL (minimum score 550 paper-based; 213 computer-based), IELTS (minimum score 6). *Application deadline:* For fall admission, 8/11 priority date for domestic and international students; for winter admission, 12/28 priority date for domestic and international students; for spring admission, 4/22 priority date for domestic and international students. Applications are processed on a rolling basis. Application fee: $50. Electronic applications accepted. *Financial support:* In 2006–07, 2 fellowships (averaging $9,375 per year) were awarded; scholarships/grants and tuition waivers (full) also available. Support available to part-time students. Financial award application deadline: 1/7; financial award applicants required to submit FAFSA. *Unit head:* Dr. Karen D. Bowser, Associate Dean of Doctoral Programs, 954-262-8500, Fax: 954-262-3912, E-mail: bowserk@nova.edu. *Application contact:* Jennifer Quiñones Nottingham, Dean of Student Affairs, 800-986-3223 Ext. 8624, Fax: 954-262-3911, E-mail: jlquinon@nova.edu.

Oakland University, Graduate Study and Lifelong Learning, School of Education and Human Services, Department of Human Development and Child Studies, Program in Special Education, Rochester, MI 48309-4401. Offers M Ed, Certificate. *Students:* 78 full-time (74 women), 180 part-time (165 women); includes 11 minority (5 African Americans, 1 American Indian/Alaska Native, 5 Asian Americans or Pacific Islanders), 1 international. Average age 33. 37 applicants, 97% accepted, 8 enrolled. In 2006, 56 degrees awarded. *Entrance requirements:* For master's, minimum GPA of 3.0 for unconditional admission, interview. Additional exam requirements/recommendations for international students: Required—TOEFL (minimum score 550 paper-based; 213 computer-based). *Application deadline:* For fall admission, 7/1 for domestic students, 5/1 for international students; for winter admission, 11/1 for domestic students, 9/1 for international students; for spring admission, 3/1 for domestic students. Applications are processed on a rolling basis. Application fee: $35. Electronic applications accepted. *Expenses:* Tuition, state resident: full-time $9,936; part-time $414 per credit. Tuition, nonresident: full-time $17,202; part-time $716 per credit. *Financial support:* Career-related internships or fieldwork, Federal Work-Study, institutionally sponsored loans, and tuition waivers (full) available. Financial award application deadline: 3/1; financial award applicants required to submit FAFSA. *Unit head:* Dr. Sherri Oden, Coordinator, 248-370-3027, E-mail: oden@oakland.edu. *Application contact:* Information Contact, 248-370-3077.

Ohio University, Graduate Studies, College of Education, Department of Teacher Education, Athens, OH 45701-2979. Offers adolescent to young adult education (M Ed); curriculum and instruction (M Ed, PhD); mathematics education (PhD); middle child education (M Ed); reading and language arts (PhD); reading education (M Ed); social studies education (PhD); special education (M Ed, PhD). Part-time and evening/weekend programs available. *Faculty:* 21 full-time (13 women), 7 part-time/adjunct (all women). *Students:* 57 full-time (44 women), 61 part-time (46 women); includes 4 minority (2 African Americans, 1 Asian American or Pacific Islander, 1 Hispanic American), 36 international. 93 applicants, 61% accepted, 37 enrolled. *Median time to degree:* Of those who began their doctoral program in fall 1998, 92% received their degree in 8 years or less. *Degree requirements:* For master's, thesis or alternative, registration; for doctorate, thesis/dissertation, comprehensive exam, registration. *Entrance requirements:* For master's, GRE General Test or MAT if GPA is less than 2.9; for doctorate, GRE General Test, minimum GPA of 3.4, work experience. Additional exam requirements/recommendations for international students: Required—TOEFL (minimum score 550 paper-based; 213 computer-based). *Application deadline:* For fall admission, 4/1 priority date for domestic and international students. Applications are processed on a rolling basis. Application fee: $45. Electronic applications accepted. *Financial support:* In 2006–07, 52 students received support, including 31 research assistantships with full tuition reimbursements available (averaging $6,500 per year), teaching assistantships with full tuition reimbursements available (averaging $7,200 per year); Federal Work-Study, institutionally sponsored loans, tuition waivers (full), and unspecified assistantships also available. Financial award application deadline: 3/15. *Faculty research:* Cognition literacy, character education, teacher's education reform, disabilities. Total annual research expenditures: $605,070. *Unit head:* Dr. William Earl Smith, Chair, 740-593-4483, Fax: 740-593-0477, E-mail: smithw@ohio.edu. *Application contact:* Floyd J. Doney, Director of Student Affairs, 740-593-4400, Fax: 740-593-9310, E-mail: doney@ohio.edu.

Old Dominion University, Darden College of Education, Program in Special Education, Norfolk, VA 23529. Offers MS Ed, PhD. *Accreditation:* NCATE. Part-time and evening/weekend programs available. Postbaccalaureate distance learning degree programs offered (no on-campus study). *Faculty:* 9 full-time (6 women), 15 part-time/adjunct (10 women). *Students:* 32 full-time (30 women), 158 part-time (136 women); includes 23 minority (19 African Americans, 2 Asian Americans or Pacific Islanders, 2 Hispanic Americans). Average age 35. 141 applicants, 74% accepted, 89 enrolled. In 2006, 92 degrees awarded. *Degree requirements:* For master's and doctorate, comprehensive exam. *Entrance requirements:* For master's, GRE General Test or MAT, PRAXIS I, minimum GPA of 2.8; for doctorate, GRE. Additional exam requirements/recommendations for international students: Recommended—TOEFL (minimum score 550 paper-based; 213 computer-based). *Application deadline:* For fall admission, 6/1 priority date for domestic students; for winter admission, 11/1 priority date for domestic students; for spring admission, 3/1 priority date for domestic students. Applications are processed on a rolling basis. Application fee: $40. Electronic applications accepted. *Expenses:* Tuition, area resident: Part-time $285 per credit hour. Tuition, nonresident: part-time $715 per credit hour. Required fees: $94 per semester. *Financial support:* In 2006–07, 70 students received support, including 1 research assistantship with tuition reimbursement available (averaging $9,000 per year), 5 teaching assistantships with tuition reimbursements available (averaging $7,500 per year); fellowships, career-related internships or fieldwork, scholarships/grants, tuition waivers (partial), and unspecified assistantships also available. Financial award application deadline: 2/15; financial award applicants required to submit FAFSA. *Faculty research:* Inclusion, clinical practice, infant and preschool handicapped, distance learning. Total annual research expenditures: $1 million. *Unit head:* Dr. Cheryl S. Baker, Graduate Program Director, 757-683-3226, Fax: 757-683-4129, E-mail: essegpd@odu.edu.

Ottawa University, Graduate Studies-Arizona, Program in Education, Ottawa, KS 66067-3399. Offers community college counseling (MA); curriculum and instruction (MA); early

Special Education

Ottawa University (continued)
childhood (MA); education intervention (MA); education leadership (MA); education technology (MA); Montessori early childhood education (MA); Montessori elementary education (MA); professional development (MA); school guidance counseling (MA); special education—cross categorical (MA). Programs offered in Mesa, Phoenix, Tempe and West Valley, AZ. *Accreditation:* NCATE. Part-time programs available. *Faculty:* 7 full-time (3 women), 24 part-time/adjunct (11 women). *Students:* 14 full-time (9 women), 162 part-time (128 women); includes 31 minority (13 African Americans, 2 American Indian/Alaska Native, 1 Asian American or Pacific Islander, 15 Hispanic Americans), 1 international. Average age 38. In 2006, 56 degrees awarded. *Degree requirements:* For master's, thesis or alternative, registration. *Entrance requirements:* For master's, minimum undergraduate GPA of 3.0, copy of current state certification or teaching license. Additional exam requirements/recommendations for international students: Required—TOEFL (minimum score 550 paper-based; 213 computer-based). *Application deadline:* For fall admission, 7/1 priority date for domestic students; for winter admission, 11/1 priority date for domestic students; for spring admission, 2/1 priority date for domestic students. Applications are processed on a rolling basis. Application fee: $50. Electronic applications accepted. *Expenses: Contact institution. Application contact:* Bunny Simpson, Secretary, 602-371-1188, Fax: 602-371-0035, E-mail: bunny.simpson@ottawa.edu.

Our Lady of the Lake University of San Antonio, School of Education and Clinical Studies, Program in Special Education, San Antonio, TX 78207-4689. Offers MA. Part-time and evening/weekend programs available. *Degree requirements:* For master's, examination for the Certification of Education in Texas, thesis optional. *Entrance requirements:* For master's, GRE General Test or MAT, interview. Additional exam requirements/recommendations for international students: Required—TOEFL. Electronic applications accepted.

Pacific University, College of Education, Forest Grove, OR 97116-1797. Offers early childhood education (MAT); education (MAE); elementary education (MAT); high school education (MAT); middle school education (MAT); special education (MAT); visual function in learning (M Ed). Part-time and evening/weekend programs available. *Faculty:* 20 full-time (12 women), 40 part-time/adjunct (21 women). *Students:* 222 full-time (151 women), 115 part-time (90 women); includes 30 minority (3 African Americans, 5 American Indian/Alaska Native, 12 Asian Americans or Pacific Islanders, 10 Hispanic Americans). Average age 32. 92 applicants, 83% accepted, 69 enrolled. In 2006, 257 degrees awarded. *Degree requirements:* For master's, research project. *Entrance requirements:* For master's, California Basic Educational Skills Test, Praxis I, minimum undergraduate GPA of 2.75, 3.0 graduate. Additional exam requirements/recommendations for international students: Required—TOEFL. *Application deadline:* For fall admission, 6/15 priority date for domestic students; for spring admission, 10/15 for domestic students. Applications are processed on a rolling basis. Application fee: $35. Electronic applications accepted. *Expenses: Contact institution. Financial support:* In 2006–07, 287 students received support; fellowships, research assistantships, teaching assistantships, career-related internships or fieldwork, institutionally sponsored loans, and scholarships/grants available. Support available to part-time students. Financial award application deadline: 5/1; financial award applicants required to submit FAFSA. *Faculty research:* Defining a culturally competent classroom, technology in the k-12 classroom, Socratic seminars, social studies education. *Unit head:* Dr. Mark Ankeny, Acting Dean, 503-352-2102, E-mail: mankeny@pacificu.edu. *Application contact:* Diana Watkins, Assistant Director Graduate and Professional Admissions, 503-352-2958, Fax: 503-352-2907, E-mail: teach@pacificu.edu.

Park University, College of Graduate and Professional Studies, Kansas City, MO 54105. Offers adult education (M Ed); at-risk students (M Ed); disaster and emergency management (MPA); educational administration (M Ed); entrepreneurship (MBA); general business (MBA); general education (M Ed); government/business relations (MPA); healthcare/services management (MBA, MPA); international business (MBA); K-12 certification (MAT); management information systems (MBA); management of information systems (MPA); middle school certification (MAT); multi-cultural education (M Ed); nonprofit management (MPA); public management (MPA); school law (M Ed); secondary school certification (MAT); special education (M Ed). Part-time and evening/weekend programs available. Postbaccalaureate distance learning degree programs offered (no on-campus study). *Degree requirements:* For master's, thesis (for some programs), comprehensive exam, registration. *Entrance requirements:* For master's, GRE, GMAT, teacher certification (M Ed). Additional exam requirements/recommendations for international students: Required—TOEFL (minimum score 550 paper-based). Electronic applications accepted. *Faculty research:* Literacy, leadership, brain based research, multicultural education, diversity.

Penn State Great Valley, Graduate Studies, Education Division, Malvern, PA 19355-1488. Offers curriculum and instruction (M Ed); instructional systems (M Ed, MS); special education (M Ed, MS). *Unit head:* Dr. Arlene Mitchell, Academic Division Head, 610-648-3355, E-mail: ahm13@psu.edu. *Application contact:* Dr. Arlene Mitchell, Academic Division Head, 610-648-3355, E-mail: ahm13@psu.edu.

Penn State University Park, Graduate School, College of Education, Department of Educational and School Psychology and Special Education, State College, University Park, PA 16802-1503. Offers educational psychology (MS, PhD); school psychology (M Ed, MS, PhD); special education (M Ed, MS, PhD). *Unit head:* Dr. Kathy L. Ruhl, Head, 814-865-6072, Fax: 814-865-7066, E-mail: klr3@psu.edu. *Application contact:* Bobbi Jo Robison, Department Head Secretary, 814-863-4450, E-mail: bjb9@psu.edu.

Pennsylvania College of Optometry, Graduate Studies in Vision Impairment and Audiology, Elkins Park, PA 19027-1598. Offers audiology (Au D); education of children and youth with visual and multiple impairments (M Ed, Certificate); low vision rehabilitation (MS, Certificate); orientation and mobility therapy (MS, Certificate); rehabilitation teaching (MS, Certificate); OD/MS. *Accreditation:* ASHA. Part-time programs available. *Entrance requirements:* For master's, GRE or MAT, letters of reference (3), interviews (2). Additional exam requirements/recommendations for international students: Required—TOEFL, TWE. Expenses: Contact institution. *Faculty research:* Knowledge utilization, technology transfer.

Pittsburg State University, Graduate School, College of Education, Department of Special Services and Leadership Studies, Program in Special Education Teaching, Pittsburg, KS 66762. Offers behavioral disorders (MS); learning disabilities (MS); mentally retarded (MS). *Accreditation:* NCATE. *Students:* 59. *Degree requirements:* For master's, thesis or alternative. *Entrance requirements:* For master's, GRE General Test or MAT. Application fee: $35 ($60 for international students). *Expenses:* Tuition, state resident: full-time $2,144; part-time $181 per credit hour. Tuition, nonresident: full-time $5,273; part-time $442 per credit hour. Tuition and fees vary according to course load and campus/location. *Financial support:* In 2006–07, teaching assistantships (averaging $5,000 per year); career-related internships or fieldwork, Federal Work-Study, and unspecified assistantships also available. *Application contact:* Jamie Vanderbeck, Assistant Director, 620-235-4223, Fax: 620-235-4219, E-mail: jvanderb@pittstate.edu.

Plymouth State University, College of Graduate Studies, Graduate Studies in Education, Plymouth, NH 03264-1595. Offers athletic training (M Ed, MS); counselor education (M Ed); education (CAGS); educational leadership (M Ed); elementary education (M Ed); English education (M Ed); health education (M Ed); k-12 education (M Ed); mathematics education (M Ed); reading and writing specialist (M Ed); science (MS), including applied meteorology, environmental science and policy, science education; secondary education (M Ed); special education administration (M Ed); special education k-12 (M Ed); teaching (MAT). *Accreditation:* NCATE (one or more programs are accredited). Part-time and evening/weekend programs available. Postbaccalaureate distance learning degree programs offered (minimal on-campus study). *Faculty:* 52 full-time (29 women), 91 part-time/adjunct (53 women). *Students:* 20 full-time (18 women), 1,278 part-time (959 women); includes 26 minority (9 African Americans, 11 Asian Americans or Pacific Islanders, 6 Hispanic Americans). Average age 39. 358 applicants, 100% accepted, 357 enrolled. In 2006, 264 master's, 32 other advanced degrees awarded. *Degree requirements:* For master's, registration. *Entrance requirements:* For master's, MAT or other standardized exam, minimum GPA of 3.0. Additional exam requirements/recommendations for international students: Required—TOEFL (minimum score 550 paper-based). *Application deadline:* For fall admission, 5/15 for international students; for winter admission, 5/15 for international students; for spring admission, 10/15 for international students. Applications are processed on a rolling basis. Application fee: $75. *Expenses: Contact institution.* Tuition and fees vary according to course level. *Financial support:* In 2006–07, fellowships with partial tuition reimbursements (averaging $10,000 per year), teaching assistantships with full tuition reimbursements (averaging $4,000 per year) were awarded; career-related internships or fieldwork, institutionally sponsored loans, scholarships/grants, and unspecified assistantships also available. Support available to part-time students. Financial award application deadline: 4/15; financial award applicants required to submit FAFSA. *Faculty research:* Special education, technology, math and science methodology. *Application contact:* Cheryl B. Baker, Director of Recruitment and Outreach, 603-535-2737, Fax: 603-535-2572, E-mail: cbaker@plymouth.edu.

Portland State University, Graduate Studies, School of Education, Department of Special Education and Counselor Education, Portland, OR 97207-0751. Offers counselor education (MA, MS); special and counselor education (Ed D); special education (MA, MS). *Accreditation:* ACA (one or more programs are accredited). Part-time and evening/weekend programs available. *Faculty:* 19 full-time (10 women), 20 part-time/adjunct (16 women). *Students:* 125 full-time (102 women), 198 part-time (143 women); includes 25 minority (7 African Americans, 2 American Indian/Alaska Native, 7 Asian Americans or Pacific Islanders, 9 Hispanic Americans), 2 international. Average age 37. 240 applicants, 75% accepted, 129 enrolled. In 2006, 111 degrees awarded. *Degree requirements:* For master's, thesis or alternative. *Entrance requirements:* For master's, California Basic Educational Skills Test, minimum GPA of 3.0 in upper-division course work or 2.75 overall. Additional exam requirements/recommendations for international students: Required—TOEFL (minimum score 550 paper-based; 213 computer-based). *Application deadline:* For fall admission, 3/1 for domestic and international students. Application fee: $50. *Expenses:* Tuition, state resident: full-time $6,426; part-time $238 per credit. Tuition, nonresident: full-time $11,016; part-time $408 per credit. Tuition and fees vary according to course load. *Financial support:* In 2006–07, 3 research assistantships with full tuition reimbursements (averaging $6,540 per year) were awarded; teaching assistantships with full tuition reimbursements, career-related internships or fieldwork, Federal Work-Study, and institutionally sponsored loans also available. Support available to part-time students. Financial award application deadline: 3/1; financial award applicants required to submit FAFSA. *Faculty research:* Transition of students with disabilities, functional curriculum, supported/inclusive education, leisure/recreation, autism. Total annual research expenditures: $867,731. *Unit head:* Dr. Ann Fullerton, Head, 503-725-4632, Fax: 503-725-5599. *Application contact:* Kris Smith, Admission Secretary, 503-725-4632, Fax: 503-725-5599, E-mail: kmsmith@pdx.edu.

Prairie View A&M University, Graduate School, College of Education, Department of Curriculum and Instruction, Prairie View, TX 77446-0519. Offers curriculum and instruction (M Ed, MA Ed, MS Ed); special education (M Ed, MS Ed). *Accreditation:* NCATE. Part-time and evening/weekend programs available. *Faculty:* 10 full-time (5 women), 7 part-time/adjunct (all women). *Students:* 11 full-time (7 women), 162 part-time (128 women); includes 156 minority (155 African Americans, 1 Hispanic American), 5 international. Average age 37. 173 applicants, 98% accepted, 167 enrolled. In 2006, 57 degrees awarded. *Median time to degree:* Master's–1.5 years full-time, 2 years part-time. *Entrance requirements:* For master's, GRE General Test. *Application deadline:* For fall admission, 10/2 priority date for domestic students; for spring admission, 2/19 priority date for domestic students. Applications are processed on a rolling basis. Application fee: $50. *Financial support:* In 2006–07, 160 students received support, including 1 research assistantship with tuition reimbursement available (averaging $15,000 per year); fellowships with tuition reimbursements available, teaching assistantships, career-related internships or fieldwork, Federal Work-Study, institutionally sponsored loans, and tuition waivers (full and partial) also available. Support available to part-time students. Financial award application deadline: 4/1. *Faculty research:* Metacognitive strategies, emotionally disturbed, language arts, teachers recruit, diversity. Total annual research expenditures: $25,000. *Unit head:* Dr. Edward Mason, Head, 936-261-3403, Fax: 936-857-4414, E-mail: elmason@pvamu.edu.

Pratt Institute, School of Art and Design, Programs in Creative Arts Therapy, Brooklyn, NY 11205-3899. Offers art therapy and creativity development (MPS); art therapy-special education (MPS); dance/movement therapy (MS). *Accreditation:* NASAD (one or more programs are accredited). Part-time programs available. *Faculty:* 3 full-time (all women), 19 part-time/adjunct (16 women). *Students:* 90 full-time (all women), 3 part-time (all women); includes 20 minority (8 African Americans, 1 American Indian/Alaska Native, 6 Asian Americans or Pacific Islanders, 5 Hispanic Americans), 4 international. Average age 31. 150 applicants, 33% accepted, 27 enrolled. In 2006, 22 degrees awarded. *Degree requirements:* For master's, thesis. *Entrance requirements:* Additional exam requirements/recommendations for international students: Required—TOEFL (minimum score 600 paper-based; 250 computer-based). *Application deadline:* For fall admission, 2/1 for domestic students; for spring admission, 10/1 for domestic students. Applications are processed on a rolling basis. Application fee: $40 ($90 for international students). Electronic applications accepted. *Expenses:* Tuition: Full-time $24,240. Tuition and fees vary according to course load and program. *Financial support:* In 2006–07, 41 students received support, including 5 fellowships (averaging $2,000 per year); career-related internships or fieldwork, Federal Work-Study, institutionally sponsored loans, scholarships/grants, tuition waivers (full), and unspecified assistantships also available. Support available to part-time students. Financial award application deadline: 2/1; financial award applicants required to submit FAFSA. *Faculty research:* Psychology and aesthetic interaction, art therapy and AIDS, art therapy and autism, art diagnosis. *Unit head:* Laurel Thompson, Chairperson, 718-636-4532, Fax: 718-636-3597, E-mail: lthompso@pratt.edu. *Application contact:* Young Hah, Director of Graduate Admissions, 718-636-3683, Fax: 718-399-4242, E-mail: yhah@pratt.edu.

Providence College, Graduate Studies, Department of Education, Program in Special Education, Providence, RI 02918. Offers M Ed. Part-time and evening/weekend programs available. *Faculty:* 6 full-time (5 women), 45 part-time/adjunct (25 women). *Students:* 13 full-time (12 women), 54 part-time (42 women); includes 2 minority (1 African American, 1 Hispanic American), 2 international. Average age 32. 19 applicants, 95% accepted. In 2006, 32 degrees awarded. *Degree requirements:* For master's, comprehensive exam. *Entrance requirements:* For master's, GRE General Test. Additional exam requirements/recommendations for international students: Required—TOEFL (minimum score 550 paper-based; 213 computer-based). *Application deadline:* For fall admission, 8/1 for domestic students; for spring admission, 12/1 for domestic students. Applications are processed on a rolling basis. Application fee: $55. *Expenses:* Tuition: Full-time $6,573; part-time $939 per unit. *Financial support:* In 2006–07, 4 research assistantships with full tuition reimbursements (averaging $8,400 per year) were awarded; career-related internships or fieldwork and unspecified assistantships also available. Support available to part-time students. Financial award application deadline: 8/1; financial award applicants required to submit FAFSA. *Unit head:* Dr. Thomas Flaherty, Dean, Graduate Studies, Department of Education, 401-865-2247, E-mail: tflahert@providence.edu.

Purdue University, Graduate School, School of Education, Department of Educational Studies, West Lafayette, IN 47907. Offers administration (MS Ed, PhD, Ed S); counseling and development (MS Ed, PhD); education of the gifted (MS Ed); educational psychology (MS Ed, PhD); foundations of education (MS Ed, PhD); higher education administration (MS Ed, PhD); special education (MS Ed, PhD). *Accreditation:* ACA (one or more programs are accredited); NCATE (one or more programs are accredited). Part-time and evening/weekend programs available. *Faculty:* 28 full-time (18 women). *Students:* 100 full-time (71 women), 126 part-time (77 women); includes 32 minority (19 African Americans, 2 American Indian/Alaska Native, 6 Asian Americans or Pacific Islanders, 5 Hispanic Americans), 33 international. Average age 36. 152 applicants, 62% accepted, 56 enrolled. In 2006, 51 master's, 17 doctorates awarded. *Degree* *requirements:* For master's, thesis optional; for doctorate, thesis/dissertation, oral and written exams; for Ed S, oral presentation, project. *Entrance requirements:* For master's, GRE General Test, minimum undergraduate GPA of 3.0; for doctorate, GRE General Test; for Ed S, GRE, minimum B average. Additional exam requirements/recommendations for international students: Required—TOEFL. *Application deadline:* For fall admission, 1/15 for domestic students; for spring admission, 9/15 for domestic students. Applications are processed on a rolling basis. Application fee: $55. Electronic applications accepted. *Financial support:* In 2006–07, 6 fellowships with full tuition reimbursements (averaging $13,300 per year), 23 research assistantships with full tuition reimbursements (averaging $11,500 per year), 33 teaching assistantships with full tuition reimbursements (averaging $10,800 per year) were awarded; career-related internships or fieldwork and tuition waivers (full) also available. Support available to part-time students. Financial award application deadline: 3/1; financial award applicants required to submit FAFSA. *Faculty research:* Motivation, learning disabilities, school learning, group processes, cognitive development. *Unit head:* Dr. Kevin R Kelly, Head, 765-494-9170, Fax: 765-496-1228. *Application contact:* Patricia Mason, Coordinator of Graduate Studies, 765-494-2346, Fax: 765-494-5832, E-mail: gradoffice@soe.purdue.edu.

Queens College of the City University of New York, Division of Graduate Studies, Division of Education, Department of Educational and Community Programs, Program in Special Education, Flushing, NY 11367-1597. Offers MS Ed. Part-time programs available. *Faculty:* 5 full-time (3 women). *Students:* 238 applicants, 99% accepted, 202 enrolled. In 2006, 59 degrees awarded. *Degree requirements:* For master's, research project. *Entrance requirements:* For master's, minimum GPA of 3.0. Additional exam requirements/recommendations for international students: Required—TOEFL. *Application deadline:* For fall admission, 4/1 for domestic students; for spring admission, 11/1 for domestic students. Applications are processed on a rolling basis. Application fee: $125. *Financial support:* Career-related internships or fieldwork, Federal Work-Study, institutionally sponsored loans, and tuition waivers (partial) available. Support available to part-time students. Financial award application deadline: 4/1; financial award applicants required to submit FAFSA. *Unit head:* Dr. Craig Michaels, Coordinator/ Graduate Adviser, 718-997-5266. *Application contact:* Mario Caruso, Director of Graduate Admissions, 718-997-5200, Fax: 718-997-5193, E-mail: graduate_admissions@qc.edu.

Radford University, Graduate College, College of Education and Human Development, School of Teacher and Educational Leadership, Program in Special Education, Radford, VA 24142. Offers deaf and hard of hearing (MS); early childhood special education (MS); high incidence disability (MS); severe disability (MS). *Accreditation:* NCATE. Part-time and evening/ weekend programs available. Postbaccalaureate distance learning degree programs offered (minimal on-campus study). *Faculty:* 8 full-time (6 women), 4 part-time/adjunct (all women). *Students:* 17 full-time (14 women), 49 part-time (42 women); includes 7 minority (4 African Americans, 1 Asian American or Pacific Islander, 2 Hispanic Americans). Average age 34. 9 applicants, 100% accepted, 7 enrolled. In 2006, 24 degrees awarded. *Degree requirements:* For master's, comprehensive exam. *Entrance requirements:* For master's, Virginia Communication and Literacy Assessment (VCLA). Additional exam requirements/recommendations for international students: Required—TOEFL. *Application deadline:* For fall admission, 3/1 priority date for domestic students, 4/1 for international students; for spring admission, 10/1 for domestic students, 8/1 for international students. Applications are processed on a rolling basis. Application fee: $40. Electronic applications accepted. *Expenses:* Tuition, state resident: full-time $4,680; part-time $260 per credit hour. Tuition, nonresident: full-time $8,604; part-time $478 per credit hour. *Financial support:* In 2006–07, 10 students received support, including 3 research assistantships with partial tuition reimbursements available (averaging $8,000 per year), teaching assistantships with partial tuition reimbursements available (averaging $8,700 per year); career-related internships or fieldwork, Federal Work-Study, institutionally sponsored loans, scholarships/grants, and unspecified assistantships also available. Financial award application deadline: 3/1; financial award applicants required to submit FAFSA. *Unit head:* Dr. Debora Bays, Coordinator, 540-831-5190, Fax: 540-831-5059.

Regent University, Graduate School, School of Education, Virginia Beach, VA 23464-9800. Offers Christian school program (M Ed); cross-categorical special education (M Ed); education (M Ed, Ed D); educational leadership (M Ed); elementary education (M Ed); individual degree plan (M Ed); master teacher (M Ed); special education leadership (Ed S); TESOL (M Ed). Part-time and evening/weekend programs available. Postbaccalaureate distance learning degree programs offered (minimal on-campus study). *Faculty:* 25 full-time (11 women), 132 part-time/ adjunct (90 women). *Students:* 220 full-time (176 women), 501 part-time (374 women); includes 264 minority (229 African Americans, 9 Asian Americans or Pacific Islanders, 26 Hispanic Americans), 13 international. Average age 38. 472 applicants, 79% accepted, 256 enrolled. In 2006, 185 master's, 5 doctorates awarded. *Degree requirements:* For master's, thesis or alternative; for doctorate, thesis/dissertation, comprehensive exam. *Entrance requirements:* For master's, MAT, minimum undergraduate GPA of 2.75, writing sample, resumé; for doctorate, GRE, writing sample, 3 years of relevant professional experience, master's-level paper, copies of published work. Additional exam requirements/recommendations for international students: Required—TOEFL (minimum score 577 paper-based; 233 computer-based). *Application deadline:* For fall admission, 4/1 priority date for domestic students; for spring admission, 10/15 priority date for domestic students. Applications are processed on a rolling basis. Application fee: $50. Electronic applications accepted. *Expenses: Contact institution. Financial support:* In 2006–07, 721 students received support; fellowships, career-related internships or fieldwork, scholarships/grants, tuition waivers (full and partial), and unspecified assistantships available. Support available to part-time students. Financial award application deadline: 4/1; financial award applicants required to submit FAFSA. *Faculty research:* Character development and discipline for children, education leadership development, diversity in schools, classroom management, technology in education settings. *Unit head:* Dr. Alan A. Arroyo, Dean, 757-226-4261, Fax: 757-226-4318, E-mail: alanarr@regent.edu. *Application contact:* Althea Bishard, Registrar and Executive Director of Enrollment and Academic Services, 800-373-5504, Fax: 757-226-4381, E-mail: admissions@regent.edu.

Regis University, School for Professional Studies, Program in Teacher Education, Denver, CO 80221-1099. Offers adult learning, training, and development (M Ed); curriculum, instruction, and assessment (M Ed); early childhood (M Ed); educational technology (Certificate); elementary (M Ed); ESL (M Ed); fine arts (M Ed), including arts, music; instructional technology (M Ed); professional leadership (M Ed); reading (M Ed); secondary (M Ed); self-designed (M Ed); space studies (M Ed); special education (M Ed); teacher licensure (M Ed). Program also offered in Henderson and Las Vegas (Summerlin), NV. Postbaccalaureate distance learning degree programs offered. *Unit head:* Dr. Suzie Perry, Dean, 303-458-4302. *Application contact:* Partick Lowenthal, Assistant Director, 303-458-4300 Ext. 4314, E-mail: masters@regis.edu.

Rhode Island College, School of Graduate Studies, Feinstein School of Education and Human Development, Department of Special Education, Providence, RI 02908-1991. Offers M Ed, CAGS. *Accreditation:* NCATE. Part-time and evening/weekend programs available. *Faculty:* 7 full-time (2 women), 4 part-time/adjunct (2 women). *Students:* 6 full-time (all women), 50 part-time (41 women); includes 1 minority (African American) Average age 34. In 2006, 35 degrees awarded. *Entrance requirements:* For master's, GRE General Test or MAT, 3 letters of recommendation, interview; for CAGS, GRE or MAT, master's degree or equivalent, teaching certificate, 3 letters of recommendation, interview. *Application deadline:* For fall admission, 3/15 for domestic students; for spring admission, 11/1 for domestic students. Applications are processed on a rolling basis. Application fee: $50. *Expenses:* Tuition, state resident: part-time $244 per credit. Tuition, nonresident: part-time $512 per credit. Required fees: $12 per credit. $66 per term. Tuition and fees vary according to degree level, program and reciprocity agreements. *Financial support:* Teaching assistantships with full tuition reimbursements, career-related internships or fieldwork, Federal Work-Study, scholarships/grants, health care benefits, and unspecified assistantships available. Support available to part-time students. Financial award application deadline: 5/15; financial award applicants required to submit FAFSA. *Faculty research:* Early detection, handicapped infants. *Unit head:* Dr. Susan Dell, Chair, 401-456-8557.

Rider University, Department of Graduate Education, Leadership and Counseling, Lawrenceville, NJ 08648-3001. Offers counseling services (MA, Ed S); curriculum, instruction and supervision (MA); director of school counseling services (Certificate); educational administration (MA); organizational leadership (MA); principal (Certificate); reading/language arts (MA, Certificate), including reading specialist (Certificate), reading/language arts (MA); school business administrator (Certificate); school counseling services (Certificate); school psychology (Ed S); special education (MA); supervisor (Certificate); teacher certification (Certificate), including business education, elementary education, English as a second language, English education, mathematics education, preschool to grade 3, science education, social studies education, world languages; teaching (MA). *Accreditation:* NCATE. Part-time and evening/ weekend programs available. *Faculty:* 24 full-time (12 women), 30 part-time/adjunct (15 women). *Students:* 90 full-time (75 women), 457 part-time (369 women); includes 73 minority (50 African Americans, 2 American Indian/Alaska Native, 6 Asian Americans or Pacific Islanders, 15 Hispanic Americans), 1 international. Average age 32. 314 applicants, 61% accepted, 138 enrolled. In 2006, 116 master's, 19 other advanced degrees awarded. *Degree requirements:* For master's, thesis or alternative, internship, portfolios, comprehensive exam (for some programs); for other advanced degree, internship, professional portfolio. *Entrance requirements:* For master's, GRE (counseling, school psychology), MAT, interview, resumé, letters of recommendation; for other advanced degree, PRAXIS. Additional exam requirements/ recommendations for international students: Required—TOEFL (minimum score 550 paper-based; 213 computer-based). *Application deadline:* For fall admission, 5/1 priority date for domestic students, 6/1 priority date for international students; for spring admission, 11/1 priority date for domestic and international students. Applications are processed on a rolling basis. Application fee: $50. Electronic applications accepted. *Expenses:* Tuition: Part-time $525 per credit. Required fees: $35 per course. $30 per semester. *Financial support:* In 2006–07, 271 students received support. Career-related internships or fieldwork, Federal Work-Study, institutionally sponsored loans, and unspecified assistantships available. Support available to part-time students. Financial award applicants required to submit FAFSA. *Faculty research:* Gifted students, self-esteem, hope and mental health, conflicts in group work, cultural diversity and counseling assessment of special needs in children. *Unit head:* Dr. Dennis C. Buss, Chair, 609-895-5353, Fax: 609-896-5362, E-mail: dbuss@rider.edu. *Application contact:* Jamie L Mitchell, Director of Graduate Admissions, 609-896-5036, Fax: 609-895-5680, E-mail: jmitchell@rider.edu.

See Close-Up on page 913.

Rivier College, School of Graduate Studies, Department of Education, Nashua, NH 03060-5086. Offers curriculum and instruction (M Ed); early childhood education (M Ed); educational administration (M Ed); educational studies (M Ed); elementary education (M Ed); elementary education and general special education (M Ed); emotional and behavioral disorders (M Ed); general social education (M Ed); leadership and learning (CAGS); learning disabilities (M Ed); learning disabilities and reading (M Ed); mental health counseling (MA); reading (M Ed); school counseling (M Ed). Part-time and evening/weekend programs available. *Faculty:* 11 full-time (7 women), 40 part-time/adjunct (29 women). *Students:* 41 full-time (33 women), 221 part-time (192 women); includes 4 minority (2 African Americans, 2 Hispanic Americans). Average age 37. In 2006, 134 degrees awarded. *Degree requirements:* For master's, internships. *Entrance requirements:* For master's, GRE General Test or MAT. *Application deadline:* Applications are processed on a rolling basis. Application fee: $25. *Financial support:* Available to part-time students. Application deadline: 2/1; *Unit head:* Dr. Charles L. Mitsakos, Chairman, 603-888-1311 Ext. 8582. *Application contact:* Diane Monahan, Director of Graduate Admissions, 603-897-8129, Fax: 603-897-8810, E-mail: gradadm@rivier.edu.

Roberts Wesleyan College, Division of Teacher Education, Rochester, NY 14624-1997. Offers adolescence education (M Ed); childhood and special education (M Ed); literacy education (M Ed); urban education (M Ed). Part-time and evening/weekend programs available. *Faculty:* 17 part-time/adjunct (7 women). *Students:* 1 (woman) full-time, 66 part-time (47 women). Average age 33. 52 applicants, 63% accepted. In 2006, 20 degrees awarded. *Degree requirements:* For master's, thesis. *Application deadline:* For fall admission, 8/1 priority date for domestic students; for spring admission, 12/1 for domestic students. Applications are processed on a rolling basis. Application fee: $35. *Financial support:* In 2006–07, 7 students received support. Career-related internships or fieldwork available. Financial award application deadline: 9/1; financial award applicants required to submit FAFSA. *Unit head:* Dr. Richard Mace, Chair, 585-594-6934. *Application contact:* Paula Finch, Graduate Admissions Coordinator, 585-594-6683, E-mail: finch_paula@roberts.edu.

Rochester Institute of Technology, Graduate Enrollment Services, National Technical Institute for the Deaf, Department of Graduate Secondary Education, Rochester, NY 14623-5603. Offers MS. *Accreditation:* Teacher Education Accreditation Council. *Students:* 49 full-time (37 women), 5 part-time (all women); includes 50 minority (7 African Americans, 43 Hispanic Americans), 2 international. 34 applicants, 88% accepted, 26 enrolled. In 2006, 25 degrees awarded. *Entrance requirements:* For master's, minimum GPA of 3.0. Additional exam requirements/recommendations for international students: Required—TOEFL (minimum score 550 paper-based; 213 computer-based; 88 iBT). *Application deadline:* For fall admission, 3/1 priority date for domestic students. Applications are processed on a rolling basis. Application fee: $50. Electronic applications accepted. *Expenses:* Tuition: Full-time $28,491; part-time $800 per credit. Required fees: $201. *Unit head:* Gerald Bateman, Director, 585-475-6480, E-mail: gcbnmp@rit.edu.

Rockford College, Graduate Studies, Department of Education, Program in Learning Disabilities, Rockford, IL 61108-2393. Offers MAT. Part-time and evening/weekend programs available. *Degree requirements:* For master's, thesis optional. *Entrance requirements:* For master's, GRE General Test.

Roosevelt University, Graduate Division, College of Education, Program in Special Education, Chicago, IL 60605-1394. Offers MA. *Students:* 30 full-time (23 women), 79 part-time (61 women); includes 48 minority (38 African Americans, 4 Asian Americans or Pacific Islanders, 6 Hispanic Americans). Average age 33. 47 applicants, 77% accepted, 32 enrolled. In 2006, 49 degrees awarded. *Unit head:* Dr. Sharon Grant, Chair, 847-619-8831. *Application contact:* Joanne Canyon-Heller, Coordinator of Graduate Admission, 877-APPLY RU, Fax: 312-281-3356, E-mail: applyru@roosevelt.edu.

Rowan University, Graduate School, College of Education, Department of Special Educational Services/Instruction, Program in Learning Disabilities, Glassboro, NJ 08028-1701. Offers MA. *Accreditation:* NCATE. Part-time and evening/weekend programs available. *Students:* 1 (woman) full-time, 41 part-time (39 women). Average age 37. 3 applicants, 100% accepted, 3 enrolled. In 2006, 12 degrees awarded. *Degree requirements:* For master's, thesis, comprehensive exam. *Entrance requirements:* For master's, GRE General Test, minimum GPA of 2.8, 1 year of teaching experience. Additional exam requirements/recommendations for international students: Required—TOEFL. *Application deadline:* For winter admission, 12/1 priority date for domestic students; for spring admission, 4/1 priority date for domestic students. Applications are processed on a rolling basis. Application fee: $50. Electronic applications accepted. *Expenses:* Tuition, state resident: full-time $9,882; part-time $549 per credit. Tuition, nonresident: full-time $9,882; part-time $549 per credit. Tuition and fees vary according to degree level. *Financial support:* Career-related internships or fieldwork, Federal Work-Study, and unspecified assistantships available. Support available to part-time students. *Unit head:* Dr. Sharon Davis-Bianco, Adviser, 856-256-4500 Ext. 3796.

Rowan University, Graduate School, College of Education, Department of Special Educational Services/Instruction, Program in Special Education, Glassboro, NJ 08028-1701. Offers MA. *Accreditation:* NCATE. Part-time and evening/weekend programs available. *Students:* 1 (woman) full-time, 17 part-time (15 women). Average age 35. 1 applicant, 100% accepted, 1 enrolled. In 2006, 7 degrees awarded. *Degree requirements:* For master's, thesis, comprehensive exam. *Entrance requirements:* For master's, GRE General Test, minimum GPA of 2.8. Additional exam requirements/recommendations for international students: Required—TOEFL. *Applica-*

Special Education

Rowan University (continued)

tion deadline: Applications are processed on a rolling basis. Application fee: $50. Electronic applications accepted. *Expenses:* Tuition, state resident: full-time $9,882; part-time $549 per credit. Tuition, nonresident: full-time $9,882; part-time $549 per credit. Tuition and fees vary according to degree level. *Financial support:* Career-related internships or fieldwork, Federal Work-Study, and unspecified assistantships available. Support available to part-time students. *Unit head:* Dr. Joy Xin, MA Adviser, 856-256-4734.

Rutgers, The State University of New Jersey, New Brunswick, Graduate School of Education, Department of Educational Psychology, Program in Special Education, New Brunswick, NJ 08901-1281. Offers Ed M, Ed D. Part-time and evening/weekend programs available. *Faculty:* 2 full-time (0 women). *Students:* 23 full-time (22 women), 42 part-time (38 women). 52 applicants, 69% accepted, 31 enrolled. In 2006, 40 master's, 1 doctorate awarded. *Degree requirements:* For doctorate, thesis/dissertation, residency. *Entrance requirements:* For master's, GRE General Test, 3 letters of recommendation; for doctorate, GRE General Test, 3 letters of recommendation, masters degree. Additional exam requirements/recommendations for international students: Required—TOEFL (minimum score 550 paper-based; 233 computer-based; 83 iBT). *Application deadline:* For fall admission, 2/1 for domestic and international students; for spring admission, 11/1 for domestic and international students. Application fee: $60. Electronic applications accepted. *Financial support:* Application deadline: 3/15; *Faculty research:* Pre- and in-service teacher education, teacher development, inclusion, early identification and intervention of reading disabilities, special education law and social policy. *Unit head:* Dr. Stanley J. Vitello, Chairperson, 732-932-7496 Ext. 8326, Fax: 732-932-6829, E-mail: vitello@rutgers.edu.

Sage Graduate School, Graduate School, Division of Education, Program in Childhood Special Education, Troy, NY 12180-4115. Offers MS Ed. *Accreditation:* NCATE. Part-time and evening/weekend programs available. *Faculty:* 11 full-time (8 women), 20 part-time/adjunct (15 women). *Students:* 7 full-time (all women), 31 part-time (all women); includes 2 minority (1 African American, 1 Asian American or Pacific Islander). Average age 29. 16 applicants, 69% accepted, 7 enrolled. In 2006, 17 degrees awarded. *Degree requirements:* For master's, thesis optional. *Entrance requirements:* For master's, minimum GPA of 2.75. Additional exam requirements/recommendations for international students: Required—TOEFL (minimum score 550 paper-based; 213 computer-based). *Application deadline:* Applications are processed on a rolling basis. Application fee: $40. *Expenses:* Tuition: Full-time $9,270; part-time $515 per credit hour. *Financial support:* Career-related internships or fieldwork, scholarships/grants, and unspecified assistantships available. Support available to part-time students. Financial award application deadline: 3/1; financial award applicants required to submit FAFSA. *Faculty research:* Effective behavioral strategies for classroom instruction. *Application contact:* Shannon K. Easton, Director of Graduate and Adult Admission, 518-244-2443, Fax: 518-244-6880, E-mail: sgsadm@sage.edu.

Sage Graduate School, Graduate School, Division of Education, Program in Literacy/Childhood Special Education, Troy, NY 12180-4115. Offers MS Ed. *Accreditation:* NCATE.Part-time and evening/weekend programs available. *Faculty:* 11 full-time (8 women), 20 part-time/adjunct (15 women). *Students:* 8 full-time (all women), 12 part-time (all women); includes 2 minority (both African Americans) Average age 27. 8 applicants, 63% accepted, 3 enrolled. In 2006, 6 degrees awarded. *Entrance requirements:* For master's, minimum GPA of 2.75. Additional exam requirements/recommendations for international students: Required—TOEFL (minimum score 550 paper-based; 213 computer-based). *Application deadline:* Applications are processed on a rolling basis. Application fee: $40. *Expenses:* Tuition: Full-time $9,270; part-time $515 per credit hour. *Financial support:* Career-related internships or fieldwork, scholarships/grants, and unspecified assistantships available. Support available to part-time students. Financial award application deadline: 3/1; financial award applicants required to submit FAFSA. *Faculty research:* Commonalities in the roles of reading specialists and resource/consultant teachers. *Application contact:* Shannon K. Easton, Director of Graduate and Adult Admission, 518-244-2443, Fax: 518-244-6880, E-mail: sgsadm@sage.edu.

Saginaw Valley State University, College of Education, Program in Learning and Behavioral Disorders, University Center, MI 48710. Offers MAT. *Accreditation:* NCATE. *Students:* 5 full-time (all women), 125 part-time (101 women); includes 4 minority (3 African Americans, 1 Hispanic American). Average age 37. In 2006, 74 degrees awarded. *Degree requirements:* For master's, practicum. *Entrance requirements:* For master's, minimum GPA of 3.0, teaching certificate. *Application deadline:* Applications are processed on a rolling basis. Application fee: $25. Electronic applications accepted. *Expenses:* Tuition, state resident: full-time $7,225; part-time $301 per credit hour. Tuition, nonresident: full-time $13,888; part-time $579 per credit hour. Required fees: $330; $14 per credit hour. Tuition and fees vary according to course load. *Financial support:* Applicants required to submit FAFSA. *Application contact:* Jeanne Chipman, Certification Officer, 989-964-4083, Fax: 989-964-4385, E-mail: jdc@svsu.edu.

Saginaw Valley State University, College of Education, Program in Special Education, University Center, MI 48710. Offers MAT. Part-time and evening/weekend programs available. *Students:* 21 full-time (15 women), 242 part-time (200 women); includes 2 minority (both Hispanic Americans) Average age 35. 63 applicants, 100% accepted, 47 enrolled. In 2006, 11 degrees awarded. *Degree requirements:* For master's, capstone course. *Entrance requirements:* For master's, minimum GPA of 3.0. *Application deadline:* Applications are processed on a rolling basis. Application fee: $25. Electronic applications accepted. *Expenses:* Tuition, state resident: full-time $7,225; part-time $301 per credit hour. Tuition, nonresident: full-time $13,888; part-time $579 per credit hour. Required fees: $330; $14 per credit hour. Tuition and fees vary according to course load. *Financial support:* Applicants required to submit FAFSA. *Unit head:* Jeanne Chipman, Certification Officer, 989-964-4083, Fax: 989-964-4385, E-mail: jolc@svsu.edu.

St. Ambrose University, College of Education and Health Sciences, Program in Education, Davenport, IA 52803-2898. Offers special education (M Ed); teaching (M Ed). Part-time and evening/weekend programs available. Postbaccalaureate distance learning degree programs offered (no on-campus study). *Faculty:* 3 full-time (0 women), 3 part-time/adjunct (2 women). *Students:* 5 full-time (all women), 67 part-time (61 women); includes 2 minority (both Hispanic Americans) Average age 39. 24 applicants, 92% accepted, 22 enrolled. In 2006, 5 degrees awarded. *Degree requirements:* For master's, comprehensive exam. *Entrance requirements:* For master's, GRE General Test or MAT, minimum GPA of 2.75. Additional exam requirements/recommendations for international students: Required—TOEFL. *Application deadline:* For fall admission, 8/15 priority date for domestic students; for spring admission, 11/1 for domestic students. Applications are processed on a rolling basis. Application fee: $25. Electronic applications accepted. *Financial support:* In 2006–07, 13 students received support, including 2 research assistantships with partial tuition reimbursements available (averaging $3,600 per year); career-related internships or fieldwork, tuition waivers (full and partial), and unspecified assistantships also available. Support available to part-time students. Financial award application deadline: 3/15; financial award applicants required to submit FAFSA. *Faculty research:* Disabilities and postsecondary career avenues, self-determination. *Unit head:* Dr. William Hitchings, Head, 563-333-6113, Fax: 563-333-6297. *Application contact:* Elizabeth Berridge, Director of Graduate Student Recruitment, 563-333-6271, Fax: 563-333-6268, E-mail: berridgeelizabethb@sau.edu.

St. Cloud State University, School of Graduate Studies, College of Education, Department of Special Education, St. Cloud, MN 56301-4498. Offers educable mentally handicapped (MS); emotionally disturbed (MS); gifted and talented (MS); learning disabled (MS); special education (MS); trainable mentally retarded (MS). *Accreditation:* NCATE. *Faculty:* 11 full-time (6 women), 5 part-time/adjunct (4 women). *Students:* 21 full-time (16 women), 99 part-time (79 women); includes 1 minority (Hispanic American), 1 international. 64 applicants, 98% accepted. In 2006, 35 degrees awarded. *Degree requirements:* For master's, thesis or alternative. *Entrance requirements:* For master's, GRE General Test, minimum GPA of 2.75. Additional exam requirements/recommendations for international students: Required—MELAB; Recommended—TOEFL (minimum score 550 paper-based; 213 computer-based), IELTS (minimum score 7). *Application deadline:* For fall admission, 6/1 priority date for domestic students, 4/1 for international students; for spring admission, 10/1 priority date for domestic students, 8/1 for international students. Applications are processed on a rolling basis. Application fee: $35. Electronic applications accepted. *Financial support:* Federal Work-Study, scholarships/grants, and unspecified assistantships available. Financial award application deadline: 3/1. *Unit head:* Dr. Mary Beth Noll, Chairperson, 320-308-2041, E-mail: mbknoll@stcloudstate.edu. *Application contact:* Linda Lou Krueger, School of Graduate Studies, 320-308-2113, Fax: 320-308-5371, E-mail: lekrueger@stcloudstate.edu.

St. John Fisher College, Office of the Provost, Ralph C. Wilson Jr. School of Education, Special Education Program, Rochester, NY 14618-3597. Offers MS, Certificate. Part-time programs available. *Faculty:* 4 full-time (3 women), 10 part-time/adjunct (8 women). *Students:* 57 full-time (42 women), 80 part-time (65 women); includes 14 minority (8 African Americans, 1 American Indian/Alaska Native, 3 Asian Americans or Pacific Islanders, 2 Hispanic Americans). Average age 30. 102 applicants, 82% accepted, 48 enrolled. In 2006, 55 degrees awarded. *Degree requirements:* For master's, project, practicum or student teaching; for Certificate, practicum. *Entrance requirements:* For master's and Certificate, minimum GPA of 3.0, letters of reference, personal statement. Additional exam requirements/recommendations for international students: Required—TOEFL (minimum score 575 paper-based; 233 computer-based; 80 iBT). *Application deadline:* For fall admission, 4/1 for domestic students; for spring admission, 10/30 for domestic students. Applications are processed on a rolling basis. Application fee: $30. *Expenses:* Tuition: Part-time $615 per credit. Tuition and fees vary according to program. *Financial support:* Federal Work-Study and scholarships/grants available. Financial award application deadline: 2/15; financial award applicants required to submit FAFSA. *Faculty research:* Inclusion, assistive technology, inquiry-based learning, gifted students, equity in education. *Unit head:* Dr. Michael Wischnowski, Director, 585-385-5265, E-mail: mwischnowski@sjfc.edu. *Application contact:* Shannon Cleverley, Director of Graduate Admissions, 585-385-8161, Fax: 585-385-8344, E-mail: scleverley@sjfc.edu.

St. John's University, The School of Education, Division of Human Services and Counseling, Program in Teaching Children with Disabilities, Queens, NY 11439. Offers MS Ed. *Students:* 4 full-time (3 women), 38 part-time (28 women); includes 11 minority (4 African Americans, 2 Asian Americans or Pacific Islanders, 5 Hispanic Americans), 2 international. Average age 28. 15 applicants, 100% accepted, 8 enrolled. In 2006, 52 degrees awarded. *Degree requirements:* For master's, comprehensive exam. *Entrance requirements:* Additional exam requirements/recommendations for international students: Required—TOEFL (minimum score 500 paper-based; 173 computer-based). *Application deadline:* For fall admission, 4/1 for domestic students, 5/1 priority date for international students; for spring admission, 11/1 for domestic students, 11/1 priority date for international students. Applications are processed on a rolling basis. Application fee: $40. Electronic applications accepted. *Expenses:* Tuition: Full-time $18,480; part-time $770 per credit. Required fees: $125 per semester. Tuition and fees vary according to program. *Financial support:* Research assistantships available. *Application contact:* Kelly Ronayne, Assistant Dean, 718-990-2303, Fax: 718-990-6069, E-mail: graded@stjohns.edu.

Saint Joseph College, Graduate Division, Department of Education, West Hartford, CT 06117-2700. Offers early childhood education (MA); education (MA), including self-designed specializations; special education (MA). Part-time and evening/weekend programs available. *Degree requirements:* For master's, thesis or alternative, comprehensive exam. *Entrance requirements:* For master's, 2 letters of recommendation. Electronic applications accepted.

St. Joseph's College, New York, Graduate Programs, Program in Education, Field of Infant/Toddler Early Childhood Special Education, Brooklyn, NY 11205-3688. Offers MA.

See Close-Up on page 915.

St. Joseph's College, New York, Graduate Programs, Program in Education, Field of Special Education, Brooklyn, NY 11205-3688. Offers severe and multiple disabilities (MA).

See Close-Up on page 915.

St. Joseph's College, Suffolk Campus, Program in Infant/Toddler Early Childhood Special Education, Patchogue, NY 11772-2399. Offers MA. Part-time and evening/weekend programs available. *Degree requirements:* For master's, thesis, full-time practicum experience. *Entrance requirements:* For master's, 1 course in child development, 2 courses in special education, minimum undergraduate GPA of 3.0, New York state teaching certificate, writing sample, interview. Additional exam requirements/recommendations for international students: Required—TOEFL (minimum score 550 paper-based; 213 computer-based).

Saint Joseph's University, College of Arts and Sciences, Department of Education, Philadelphia, PA 19131-1395. Offers educational leadership (Ed D); elementary education (MS); instructional technology (MS); professional education (MS); reading (MS); secondary education (MS); special education (MS); training and organizational development (MS, Certificate). Part-time and evening/weekend programs available. *Faculty:* 18 full-time (9 women), 67 part-time/adjunct (34 women). *Students:* 77 full-time (63 women), 551 part-time (417 women); includes 115 minority (94 African Americans, 2 American Indian/Alaska Native, 8 Asian Americans or Pacific Islanders, 11 Hispanic Americans), 12 international. In 2006, 286 master's, 5 doctorates awarded. *Entrance requirements:* For master's, 2 letters of recommendation, minimum GPA of 3.0; for doctorate, GRE/MAT, 2 letters of recommendation, resumé. Additional exam requirements/recommendations for international students: Required—TOEFL. *Application deadline:* For fall admission, 7/15 for domestic students. Application fee: $35. *Expenses:* Contact institution. *Financial support:* Fellowships, research assistantships, career-related internships or fieldwork and Federal Work-Study available. Support available to part-time students. *Unit head:* Dr. Encarnacion Rodriguez, Director of Graduate Education, 610-660-3348.

Saint Louis University, Graduate School, College of Public Service and Graduate School, Department of Educational Studies, St. Louis, MO 63103-2097. Offers curriculum and instruction (MA, Ed D, PhD); educational foundations (MA, Ed D, PhD); special education (MA); teaching (MAT). *Accreditation:* NCATE. Part-time programs available. *Faculty:* 12 full-time (8 women), 18 part-time/adjunct (12 women). *Students:* 15 full-time (10 women), 53 part-time (42 women); includes 3 minority (1 African American, 2 Asian Americans or Pacific Islanders), 4 international. Average age 36. 25 applicants, 80% accepted, 14 enrolled. In 2006, 2 master's, 5 doctorates awarded. *Degree requirements:* For master's, comprehensive exam, registration; for doctorate, thesis/dissertation, preliminary oral and written exams, comprehensive exam, registration. *Entrance requirements:* For master's, GRE General Test or MAT, letters of recommendation, resumé; for doctorate, GRE General Test, letters of recommendation, resumé. Additional exam requirements/recommendations for international students: Required—TOEFL (minimum score 525 paper-based; 194 computer-based). *Application deadline:* For fall admission, 7/1 for domestic and international students; for spring admission, 11/1 for domestic and international students. Applications are processed on a rolling basis. Application fee: $40. *Expenses:* Tuition: Part-time $800 per credit hour. Required fees: $105 per semester. *Financial support:* In 2006–07, 24 students received support, including 4 teaching assistantships with full tuition reimbursements available (averaging $11,000 per year); Federal Work-Study, scholarships/grants, traineeships, health care benefits, and unspecified assistantships also available. Support available to part-time students. Financial award application deadline: 6/1; financial award applicants required to submit FAFSA. *Faculty research:* Teacher preparation, multicultural issues, children with special needs, qualitative research in education, inclusion. *Unit head:* Dr. Mary Chittooran, Interim Chairperson, 314-977-4062, Fax: 314-977-3214, E-mail: chittomm@slu.edu. *Application contact:* Gary Behrman, Associate Dean of the Graduate School, 314-977-3827, E-mail: behrmang@slu.edu.

Saint Martin's University, Graduate Programs, Department of Education, Lacey, WA 98503-1297. Offers administration (M Ed); English as a second language (M Ed); guidance and counseling (M Ed); reading (M Ed); special education (M Ed); teaching (MIT); technology in education (M Ed). Part-time and evening/weekend programs available. *Degree requirements:* For master's, thesis or alternative, project or comprehensives, comprehensive exam (for some programs). *Entrance requirements:* For master's, GRE General Test or MAT, resumé. Additional exam requirements/recommendations for international students: Required—TOEFL (minimum score 560 paper-based). *Faculty research:* Reader's theatre and reader/writer workshops, curriculum and assessment integration, gender and equity, classroom evaluations, organizational leadership.

Saint Mary's College of California, School of Education, Program in Special Education, Moraga, CA 94575. Offers M Ed, MA. Part-time programs available. *Faculty:* 1 full-time (0 women), 1 (woman) part-time/adjunct. *Students:* 9 full-time (8 women), 33 part-time (30 women); includes 6 minority (2 African Americans, 1 American Indian/Alaska Native, 3 Hispanic Americans), 2 international. Average age 37. 12 applicants, 100% accepted, 12 enrolled. *Degree requirements:* For master's, thesis or alternative. *Entrance requirements:* For master's, writing proficiency exam, interview, minimum GPA of 3.0, teaching experience. *Application deadline:* Applications are processed on a rolling basis. Application fee: $50. *Financial support:* Scholarships/grants and tuition waivers (partial) available. Support available to part-time students. Financial award application deadline: 2/15. *Faculty research:* Consultation model, impact of gifted model on special education. *Unit head:* Dr. David Krapf, Director, 925-631-8177, Fax: 925-376-8379, E-mail: dkrapf@stmarys-ca.edu.

Saint Michael's College, Graduate Programs, Program in Education, Colchester, VT 05439. Offers administration (M Ed, CAGS); arts in education (CAGS); curriculum and instruction (M Ed, CAGS); information technology (CAGS); reading (M Ed); special education (M Ed, CAGS); technology (M Ed). Part-time and evening/weekend programs available. *Faculty:* 5 full-time (3 women), 35 part-time/adjunct (29 women). *Students:* 26 full-time (18 women), 114 part-time (86 women), 2 international. Average age 34. 48 applicants, 81% accepted, 36 enrolled. In 2006, 46 degrees awarded. *Degree requirements:* For master's, thesis. *Entrance requirements:* For master's, minimum GPA of 3.0. *Application deadline:* Applications are processed on a rolling basis. Application fee: $35. Electronic applications accepted. *Financial support:* Fellowships, scholarships/grants available. Support available to part-time students. Financial award applicants required to submit FAFSA. *Faculty research:* Integrative curriculum, moral and spiritual dimensions of education, learning styles, multiple intelligences, integrating technology into the curriculum. *Unit head:* Dr. Anne P. Judson, Director, 802-654-2649, Fax: 802-654-2664, E-mail: ajudson@smcvt.edu.

St. Thomas Aquinas College, Division of Teacher Education, Sparkill, NY 10976. Offers adolescence education (MST); childhood and special education (MST); childhood education (MST); reading (MS Ed, PMC); special education (MS Ed, PMC); teaching (MS Ed), including elementary education, middle school education, secondary education. *Accreditation:* NCATE. Part-time and evening/weekend programs available. *Degree requirements:* For master's, comprehensive professional portfolio; for PMC, action research project. *Entrance requirements:* For master's, New York State Qualifying Exam, GRE General Test or minimum GPA of 3.0, teaching certificate; for PMC, GRE General Test or minimum GPA of 3.0. Electronic applications accepted. *Faculty research:* Computer applications in education, adolescent special education students, literacy development, inclusive practices for special education students.

See Close-Up on page 917.

St. Thomas University, School of Graduate Studies, Department of Education, Miami Gardens, FL 33054-6459. Offers educational administration (MS, Certificate); educational leadership (Ed D); elementary education (MS); reading (MS); special education (MS). Part-time and evening/weekend programs available. *Degree requirements:* For master's, comprehensive exam; for doctorate, thesis/dissertation, comprehensive exam. *Entrance requirements:* For master's, interview, minimum GPA of 3.0 or GRE; for doctorate, GRE or MAT. Additional exam requirements/recommendations for international students: Required—TOEFL. Electronic applications accepted.

Saint Vincent College, Program in Education, Latrobe, PA 15650-2690. Offers curriculum and instruction (MS); environmental education (MS); library media management (MS); school administration (MS); special education (MS). Part-time and evening/weekend programs available. *Degree requirements:* For master's, comprehensive exam. *Entrance requirements:* For master's, GRE (if undergraduate GPA is below 3.0). Additional exam requirements/recommendations for international students: Required—TOEFL (minimum score 550 paper-based; 213 computer-based). *Faculty research:* Assessment and instructional technology

Saint Xavier University, Graduate Studies, School of Education, Chicago, IL 60655-3105. Offers counseling (MA); counselor education (MA); curriculum and instruction (MA); early childhood education (MA); education (CAS); educational administration (MA); elementary education (MA); field-based education (MA); general educational studies (MA); individualized program (MA); learning disabilities (MA); reading (MA); secondary education (MA). *Accreditation:* NCATE. Part-time and evening/weekend programs available. *Faculty:* 92. *Students:* 45 full-time (35 women), 1,529 part-time (1,309 women). In 2006, 474 degrees awarded. *Degree requirements:* For master's, thesis or project. *Entrance requirements:* For master's, minimum GPA of 3.0. *Application deadline:* For fall admission, 8/15 priority date for domestic students. Applications are processed on a rolling basis. Application fee: $35. *Expenses:* Contact institution. *Financial support:* Career-related internships or fieldwork available. Support available to part-time students. Financial award applicants required to submit FAFSA. *Unit head:* Dr. Beverly Gulley, Dean, 773-298-3221, Fax: 773-779-9061, E-mail: gulley@sxu.edu. *Application contact:* Beth Gierach, Managing Director of Admission, 773-298-3053, Fax: 773-298-3076, E-mail: gierach@sxu.edu.

Salem College, Department of Education, Winston-Salem, NC 27108-0548. Offers early education and leadership (MAT); elementary education (MAT); English as a second language (MAT); language and literacy (M Ed); middle school education (MAT); secondary education (MAT); special education (MAT). *Accreditation:* NCATE. Part-time and evening/weekend programs available. *Faculty:* 8 full-time (6 women), 5 part-time/adjunct (all women). *Students:* 8 full-time (all women), 250 part-time (238 women); includes 19 minority (16 African Americans, 1 Asian American or Pacific Islander, 2 Hispanic Americans). Average age 33. 110 applicants, 65% accepted, 68 enrolled. In 2006, 34 degrees awarded. *Degree requirements:* For master's, practicum (MAT), project (M Ed), oral and written comprehensive exams. *Entrance requirements:* For master's, GRE, minimum GPA of 2.5. *Application deadline:* Applications are processed on a rolling basis. Application fee: $30. *Financial support:* In 2006–07, 152 students received support. Federal Work-Study and scholarships/grants available. Support available to part-time students. Financial award applicants required to submit FAFSA. *Faculty research:* Content area reading strategies, literacy development, brain compatible instruction. *Unit head:* Dr. Paula Grubbs, Director of Teacher Education, 336-721-2610, Fax: 336-721-2683, E-mail: grubbs@salem.edu.

Salem State College, Graduate School, Program in Special Education, Salem, MA 01970-5353. Offers M Ed, MAT. *Accreditation:* NCATE. Part-time and evening/weekend programs available. *Faculty:* 4 part-time/adjunct (2 women). *Students:* 7 full-time (all women), 126 part-time (104 women); includes 4 minority (1 American Indian/Alaska Native, 3 Hispanic Americans), 1 international. Average age 36. In 2006, 70 degrees awarded. *Entrance requirements:* For master's, GRE General Test or MAT. *Application deadline:* Applications are processed on a rolling basis. Application fee: $35. *Unit head:* Dr. Vicki Gallagher, Coordinator, 978-542-6382, Fax: 978-542-7215, E-mail: vgallagher@salemstate.edu.

Sam Houston State University, College of Education and Applied Science, Department of Language, Literacy, and Special Populations, Huntsville, TX 77341. Offers early childhood education (M Ed); reading (M Ed, MA); special education (M Ed, MA). Part-time and evening/weekend programs available. *Faculty:* 6 full-time (4 women). *Students:* 2 full-time (both women), 104 part-time (100 women); includes 18 minority (6 African Americans, 1 American Indian/Alaska Native, 11 Hispanic Americans), 2 international. Average age 37. In 2006, 26 degrees awarded. *Entrance requirements:* For master's, GRE General Test, minimum GPA of 2.5. *Application deadline:* For fall admission, 8/1 for domestic students; for spring admission, 12/1 for domestic students. Application fee: $20. *Expenses:* Tuition, state resident: full-time $5,904; part-time $164 per semester hour. Tuition, nonresident: full-time $15,804; part-time $439 per semester hour. Required fees: $1,374; $462 per semester. *Financial support:* Teaching assistantships available. Financial award application deadline: 5/31; financial award applicants required to submit FAFSA. *Unit head:* Dr. Mary Robbins, Chair, 936-294-3890, Fax: 936-294-1131, E-mail: edu_mer@shsu.edu. *Application contact:* Molly Doughtie, Advisor, 936-294-1105, E-mail: edu_mxd@shsu.edu.

San Diego State University, Graduate and Research Affairs, College of Education, Department of Administration, Rehabilitation and Post-Secondary Education, San Diego, CA 92182. Offers educational leadership in post-secondary education (MA); rehabilitation counseling (MS), including deafness. Evening/weekend programs available. Postbaccalaureate distance learning degree programs offered. *Students:* 56 full-time (41 women), 4 part-time (1 woman); includes 21 minority (7 African Americans, 1 American Indian/Alaska Native, 4 Asian Americans or Pacific Islanders, 9 Hispanic Americans), 1 international. 50 applicants, 72% accepted, 11 enrolled. In 2006, 41 degrees awarded. *Degree requirements:* For master's, thesis (for some programs), comprehensive exam (for some programs). *Entrance requirements:* For master's, GRE General Test, letters of reference. Additional exam requirements/recommendations for international students: Required—TOEFL. *Application deadline:* For fall admission, 5/1 for domestic and international students; for spring admission, 11/1 for domestic students, 10/1 for international students. Applications are processed on a rolling basis. Application fee: $55. Electronic applications accepted. *Financial support:* Career-related internships or fieldwork available. Financial award applicants required to submit FAFSA. *Faculty research:* Rehabilitation in cultural diversity, distance learning technology. Total annual research expenditures: $3.3 million. *Unit head:* Fred McFarlane, Chair, 619-594-6115, Fax: 619-594-4208, E-mail: fmcfarla@mail.sdsu.edu.

San Diego State University, Graduate and Research Affairs, College of Education, Department of Special Education, San Diego, CA 92182. Offers MA. *Accreditation:* NCATE. Evening/weekend programs available. *Students:* 11 full-time (10 women), 42 part-time (38 women); includes 12 minority (1 African American, 5 Asian Americans or Pacific Islanders, 6 Hispanic Americans), 3 international. Average age 29. 71 applicants, 14% accepted, 1 enrolled. In 2006, 19 degrees awarded. *Entrance requirements:* For master's, GRE General Test, letters of reference. Additional exam requirements/recommendations for international students: Required—TOEFL. *Application deadline:* For fall admission, 5/1 for domestic and international students; for spring admission, 11/1 for domestic students, 10/1 for international students. Applications are processed on a rolling basis. Application fee: $55. Electronic applications accepted. *Financial support:* In 2006–07, 2 teaching assistantships were awarded; fellowships, career-related internships or fieldwork also available. Financial award applicants required to submit FAFSA. Total annual research expenditures: $1.2 million. *Unit head:* Anne Graves, Chair, 619-594-6616, Fax: 619-594-6628. *Application contact:* Jose Luis Alvarado, Graduate Advisor, 619-594-2748, Fax: 619-594-6628, E-mail: alvarado@mail.sdsu.edu.

San Francisco State University, Division of Graduate Studies, College of Education, Department of Special Education, Program in Special Education, San Francisco, CA 94132-1722. Offers MA, Ed D, PhD, AC. *Accreditation:* NCATE. Part-time programs available. *Students:* 157 (121 women). *Degree requirements:* For doctorate, thesis/dissertation. *Entrance requirements:* For master's, minimum GPA of 2.5 in last 60 units; for doctorate, GRE General Test. *Application deadline:* For fall admission, 11/30 priority date for domestic students. Applications are processed on a rolling basis. Application fee: $55. *Financial support:* Application deadline: 3/1. *Application contact:* Louise Guy, Office Coordinator, 415-338-2501, E-mail: lguy@sfsu.edu.

San Jose State University, Graduate Studies and Research, College of Education, Department of Special Education, San Jose, CA 95192-0001. Offers MA, Certificate. *Accreditation:* NCATE. Evening/weekend programs available. *Students:* 85 full-time (74 women), 177 part-time (131 women); includes 62 minority (10 African Americans, 26 Asian Americans or Pacific Islanders, 26 Hispanic Americans), 10 international. Average age 38. 117 applicants, 70% accepted, 66 enrolled. In 2006, 34 degrees awarded. *Application deadline:* For fall admission, 6/29 for domestic students; for spring admission, 11/30 for domestic students. Applications are processed on a rolling basis. Application fee: $59. Electronic applications accepted. *Financial support:* Career-related internships or fieldwork available. Financial award applicants required to submit FAFSA. *Unit head:* Elba Maldonado-Colon, Chair, 408-924-3786, Fax: 408-924-3713.

Santa Clara University, School of Education, Counseling Psychology, and Pastoral Ministries, Department of Education, Program in Special Education, Santa Clara, CA 95053. Offers MA, Certificate. Part-time and evening/weekend programs available. *Students:* 4 full-time (all women), 34 part-time (33 women); includes 9 minority (2 African Americans, 5 Asian Americans or Pacific Islanders, 2 Hispanic Americans), 1 international. Average age 39. 18 applicants, 67% accepted, 9 enrolled. In 2006, 20 master's, 8 other advanced degrees awarded. *Degree requirements:* For master's, comprehensive exam. *Entrance requirements:* For master's, GRE or MAT, minimum GPA of 3.0. Additional exam requirements/recommendations for international students: Required—TOEFL. *Application deadline:* Applications are processed on a rolling basis. *Expenses:* Tuition: Part-time $627 per unit. Tuition and fees vary according to program. *Financial support:* Fellowships, teaching assistantships, career-related internships or fieldwork, Federal Work-Study, institutionally sponsored loans, and scholarships/grants available. Support available to part-time students. Financial award application deadline: 3/1; financial award applicants required to submit FAFSA. *Unit head:* Dr. Ruth E. Cook, Director, 408-554-4119.

Seattle University, College of Education, Program in Special Education, Seattle, WA 98122-1090. Offers M Ed, MA, Certificate. *Students:* Average age 37. 5 applicants, 80% accepted, 3 enrolled. *Entrance requirements:* For master's, GRE, MAT or minimum GPA of 3.0, 1 year K-12 teaching experience; for Certificate, master's degree, minimum GPA of 3.0, 1 year K-12 teaching experience. *Application deadline:* For fall admission, 8/20 priority date for domestic students; for winter admission, 11/20 priority date for domestic students; for spring admission, 2/20 priority date for domestic students. *Unit head:* Dr. Katherine Schlick Noe, Director, 206-296-5768, E-mail: kschlnoe@seattleu.edu.

Seton Hill University, Program in Special Education, Greensburg, PA 15601. Offers MA, Teaching Certificate. Part-time and evening/weekend programs available. *Faculty:* 7 full-time (5 women), 4 part-time/adjunct (2 women). *Students:* 10 full-time (7 women), 28 part-time (26 women). Average age 31. 16 applicants, 88% accepted, 14 enrolled. In 2006, 20 master's awarded. *Degree requirements:* For master's, thesis optional. *Entrance requirements:* For master's, minimum GPA of 3.0. Additional exam requirements/recommendations for international students: Required—TOEFL (minimum score 600 paper-based; 250 computer-based). *Application deadline:* For fall admission, 8/15 priority date for domestic students; for spring admission, 12/15 for domestic students. Applications are processed on a rolling basis. Application fee: $35. Electronic applications accepted. *Expenses:* Tuition: Part-time $620 per credit. Required fees: $100 per semester. *Financial support:* In 2006–07, 38 students received support. Scholarships/grants, tuition waivers (partial), and unspecified assistantships available. Support available to part-time students. Financial award application deadline: 8/15; financial award applicants required to submit FAFSA. *Faculty research:* Experiential learning environments, instructional technologies, reading methods. *Unit head:* Dr. Sondra Lettrich, Director, 724-830-1010, Fax: 724-830-1294, E-mail: lettrich@setonhill.edu. *Application contact:* Dane Zimmer, Advisor, 724-838-4209, Fax: 724-830-1891, E-mail: zimmer@setonhill.edu.

Special Education

Shippensburg University of Pennsylvania, School of Graduate Studies, College of Education and Human Services, Department of Teacher Education, Shippensburg, PA 17257-2299. Offers curriculum and instruction (M Ed); reading (M Ed); special education (M Ed). *Accreditation:* NCATE. Part-time and evening/weekend programs available. *Faculty:* 16 full-time (11 women), 3 part-time/adjunct (all women). *Students:* 14 full-time (9 women), 201 part-time (181 women); includes 4 minority (3 African Americans, 1 Hispanic American). Average age 30. 66 applicants, 52% accepted, 28 enrolled. In 2006, 75 degrees awarded. *Degree requirements:* For master's, practicum or internship required for some programs. *Entrance requirements:* For master's, MAT (if GPA is below 2.75), interview, letters of recommendation, writing sample, resumé. Additional exam requirements/recommendations for international students: Required—TOEFL (minimum score 560 paper-based; 220 computer-based). *Application deadline:* For fall admission, 6/1 priority date for domestic students, 3/1 for international students; for spring admission, 9/1 priority date for domestic students, 7/1 for international students. Applications are processed on a rolling basis. Application fee: $30. Electronic applications accepted. *Expenses:* Tuition, state resident: part-time $336 per credit. Tuition, nonresident: part-time $538 per credit. *Financial support:* In 2006–07, 10 research assistantships with full tuition reimbursements (averaging $3,125 per year) were awarded; career-related internships or fieldwork, scholarships/grants, and unspecified assistantships also available. Support available to part-time students. Financial award application deadline: 3/1; financial award applicants required to submit FAFSA. *Unit head:* Dr. Elizabeth Vaughan, Chairperson, 717-477-1688, Fax: 717-477-4046, E-mail: ejvaug@ship.edu. *Application contact:* Renee Payne, Associate Dean of Graduate Admissions, 717-477-1231, Fax: 717-477-4016, E-mail: rmpayn@ship.edu.

Silver Lake College, Division of Graduate Studies, Program in Special Education, Manitowoc, WI 54220-9319. Offers MA. *Faculty:* 2 full-time (both women), 1 (woman) part-time/adjunct. *Students:* 7 applicants, 71% accepted, 2 enrolled.Application fee: $35. *Expenses:* Tuition: Full-time $6,120; part-time $340 per credit. *Financial support:* Federal Work-Study and scholarships/grants available. Support available to part-time students. Financial award applicants required to submit FAFSA. *Unit head:* Sr. Mary Karen Oudeans, OSF, Director- Special Education, 920-686-6157.

Simmons College, Graduate School, College of Arts and Sciences Graduate Studies, Department of Education, Program in Special Education, Boston, MA 02115. Offers applied behavior analysis (PhD); assistive technology (MS Ed, Ed S); behavioral education (MS Ed, Ed S); health professions education (PhD); language and literacy (MS Ed, Ed S); moderate disabilities (Ed S); moderate special needs (MS Ed); severe disabilities (Ed S); severe special needs (MS Ed); special education administration (MS Ed, PhD, Ed S). Part-time and evening/weekend programs available. *Faculty:* 9 full-time (7 women), 34 part-time/adjunct (23 women). *Students:* 51 full-time (46 women), 405 part-time (339 women); includes 31 minority (13 African Americans, 2 American Indian/Alaska Native, 7 Asian Americans or Pacific Islanders, 9 Hispanic Americans), 2 international. Average age 28. 155 applicants, 91% accepted, 121 enrolled. In 2006, 122 master's, 27 other advanced degrees awarded. *Degree requirements:* For master's, practicum; for doctorate, thesis/dissertation. *Entrance requirements:* For doctorate, GRE, research proposal interview. Additional exam requirements/recommendations for international students: Required—TOEFL (minimum score 600 paper-based; 250 computer-based; 100 iBT). *Application deadline:* For fall admission, 8/1 priority date for domestic students; for spring admission, 12/1 priority date for domestic students. Applications are processed on a rolling basis. Application fee: $35. Electronic applications accepted. *Expenses:* Contact institution. *Financial support:* Career-related internships or fieldwork, Federal Work-Study, institutionally sponsored loans, scholarships/grants, and tuition waivers (partial) available. Support available to part-time students. Financial award application deadline: 3/1; financial award applicants required to submit FAFSA. *Faculty research:* Classroom-based research, inclusion strategies, beginning teacher development. *Unit head:* Dr. Cathryn Mercier, Associate Dean, 617-521-2091. *Application contact:* Kristen Haack, Director, Graduate Studies Admission, 617-521-2915, Fax: 617-521-3058, E-mail: gsa@simmons.edu.

Slippery Rock University of Pennsylvania, Graduate Studies (Recruitment), College of Education, Department of Special Education, Slippery Rock, PA 16057-1383. Offers master teacher (M Ed); supervision (M Ed). *Accreditation:* NCATE. Part-time and evening/weekend programs available. *Degree requirements:* For master's, thesis (for some programs), portfolio presentation, comprehensive exam (for some programs). *Entrance requirements:* For master's, GRE General Test, MAT, minimum GPA of 2.75 (minimum GPA of 3.0 for initial certification). Additional exam requirements/recommendations for international students: Required—TOEFL (minimum score 550 paper-based; 213 computer-based). *Application deadline:* For fall admission, 7/1 priority date for domestic and international students; for spring admission, 11/1 priority date for domestic and international students. Applications are processed on a rolling basis. Application fee: $25. Electronic applications accepted. *Expenses:* Tuition, state resident: part-time $336 per credit. Tuition, nonresident: part-time $538 per credit. Required fees: $84 per credit. $37 per semester. *Financial support:* Career-related internships or fieldwork, Federal Work-Study, scholarships/grants, and unspecified assistantships available. Support available to part-time students. Financial award application deadline: 5/1. *Faculty research:* In-service teacher education, contemporary issues in special education, education for developmentally disabled, educational assessment. *Unit head:* Dr. Dennis Fair, Graduate Coordinator, 724-738-2085, Fax: 724-738-4395, E-mail: dennis.fair@sru.edu. *Application contact:* April Longwell, Interim Director of Graduate Studies, 724-738-2051 Ext. 2116, Fax: 724-738-2146, E-mail: graduate.studies@sru.edu.

Smith College, Graduate Programs, Department of Education and Child Study, Program in the Education of the Deaf, Northampton, MA 01063. Offers MED. Part-time programs available. *Students:* 11 full-time (all women), 1 (woman) part-time, 1 international. Average age 31. 19 applicants, 63% accepted, 11 enrolled. In 2006, 12 degrees awarded. *Entrance requirements:* For master's, GRE General Test or MAT. Additional exam requirements/recommendations for international students: Required—TOEFL. *Application deadline:* For fall admission, 4/1 for domestic students, 1/15 for international students. Application fee: $60. *Expenses:* Tuition: Full-time $32,320; part-time $1,010 per credit. Tuition and fees vary according to course load. *Financial support:* In 2006–07, 12 students received support. Career-related internships or fieldwork, institutionally sponsored loans, and scholarships/grants available. Support available to part-time students. Financial award application deadline: 1/15; financial award applicants required to submit CSS PROFILE or FAFSA. *Unit head:* Alan L. Marvelli, Director, 413-585-3255, Fax: 413-585-3268, E-mail: amarvell@smith.edu.

Sonoma State University, School of Education, Department of Educational Leadership and Special Education, Rohnert Park, CA 94928-3609. Offers educational leadership (MA); special education (MA). Part-time and evening/weekend programs available. *Faculty:* 7 full-time (0 women). *Degree requirements:* For master's, thesis or alternative. *Entrance requirements:* For master's, GRE General Test, minimum GPA of 2.5. Application fee: $55. *Expenses:* Tuition, nonresident: part-time $339 per unit. Required fees: $1,464 per term. *Financial support:* Application deadline: 3/2.

South Carolina State University, School of Graduate Studies, Department of Education, Orangeburg, SC 29117-0001. Offers early childhood and special education (M Ed); early childhood education (MAT); elementary education (M Ed, MAT); engineering (MAT); general science (MAT); mathematics (MAT); secondary education (M Ed), including biology education, business education, counselor education, English education, home economics education, industrial education, mathematics education, science education, social studies education; special education (M Ed), including emotionally handicapped, learning disabilities, mentally handicapped. *Accreditation:* NCATE. Part-time and evening/weekend programs available. *Faculty:* 21 full-time (10 women), 4 part-time/adjunct (0 women). *Students:* 34 full-time (28 women), 33 part-time (25 women); includes 63 minority (61 African Americans, 1 American Indian/Alaska Native, 1 Asian American or Pacific Islander). Average age 35. 46 applicants, 67% accepted, 19 enrolled. In 2006, 28 degrees awarded. *Degree requirements:* For master's, departmental qualifying exam, thesis optional. *Entrance requirements:* For master's, GRE General Test, NTE, interview, teaching certificate. *Application deadline:* For fall admission, 6/15 priority date for domestic students, 6/15 for international students; for spring admission, 11/1 for domestic and international students. Applications are processed on a rolling basis. Application fee: $25. Electronic applications accepted. *Expenses:* Tuition, state resident: full-time $7,278. Tuition, nonresident: full-time $14,322. *Financial support:* Fellowships, research assistantships, career-related internships or fieldwork, Federal Work-Study, and institutionally sponsored loans available. Financial award application deadline: 6/1. *Faculty research:* Critical thinking, child abuse, stress, test-taking skills, conflict resolution, mainstreaming. *Unit head:* Dr. Gail Joyner-Fleming, Interim Chair, 803-533-3769, Fax: 803-536-8492, E-mail: zf-gfleming@scsu.edu. *Application contact:* Annette Hazzard-Jones, Program Coordinator II, 803-536-8809, Fax: 803-536-8812, E-mail: zs_ahazzard@scsu.edu.

Southeastern Louisiana University, College of Education and Human Development, Department of Teaching and Learning, Hammond, LA 70402. Offers curriculum and instruction (M Ed); elementary education (MAT); secondary education (MAT); special education (M Ed, MAT). *Accreditation:* NCATE. Part-time programs available. *Faculty:* 23 full-time (18 women), 1 (woman) part-time/adjunct. *Students:* 31 full-time (27 women), 300 part-time (269 women); includes 50 minority (39 African Americans, 2 Asian Americans or Pacific Islanders, 9 Hispanic Americans), 3 international. Average age 33. 47 applicants, 100% accepted, 31 enrolled. In 2006, 101 degrees awarded. *Degree requirements:* For master's, comprehensive exam (for some programs). *Entrance requirements:* For master's, GRE, PRAXIS (MAT), minimum GPA of 2.5. Additional exam requirements/recommendations for international students: Required—TOEFL (minimum score 500 paper-based; 173 computer-based). *Application deadline:* For fall admission, 7/15 priority date for domestic students, 6/1 priority date for international students; for spring admission, 12/1 priority date for domestic students, 10/1 priority date for international students. Applications are processed on a rolling basis. Application fee: $20 ($30 for international students). Electronic applications accepted. *Expenses:* Tuition, state resident: full-time $2,216; part-time $123 per credit. Tuition, nonresident: full-time $6,212; part-time $345 per credit. Required fees: $986; $55 per credit. Part-time tuition and fees vary according to course load. *Financial support:* Federal Work-Study, institutionally sponsored loans, unspecified assistantships, and administrative assistantship available. Support available to part-time students. Financial award application deadline: 5/1; financial award applicants required to submit FAFSA. *Faculty research:* Reading, instructional methodology, science education, math education, early childhood. *Unit head:* Dr. Shirley Jacob, Department Head, 985-549-2221, Fax: 985-549-5009, E-mail: sjacob@selu.edu. *Application contact:* Sandra Meyers, Graduate Admissions Analyst, 985-549-2066, Fax: 985-549-5632, E-mail: admissions@selu.edu.

Southeastern Louisiana University, College of Nursing and Health Sciences, Department of Communication Sciences and Disorders, Hammond, LA 70402. Offers MS. *Accreditation:* ASHA; NCATE. *Faculty:* 5 full-time (4 women). *Students:* 37 full-time (35 women), 28 part-time (27 women); includes 4 minority (all African Americans), 1 international. Average age 28. 27 applicants, 100% accepted, 19 enrolled. In 2006, 32 degrees awarded. *Degree requirements:* For master's, thesis optional. *Entrance requirements:* For master's, GRE General Test, 3 letters of reference, minimum GPA of 2.5. Additional exam requirements/recommendations for international students: Required—TOEFL (minimum score 500 paper-based; 173 computer-based). *Application deadline:* For fall admission, 7/15 priority date for domestic students, 6/1 priority date for international students; for spring admission, 12/1 priority date for domestic students, 10/1 priority date for international students. Applications are processed on a rolling basis. Application fee: $20 ($30 for international students). Electronic applications accepted. *Expenses:* Tuition, state resident: full-time $2,216; part-time $123 per credit. Tuition, nonresident: full-time $6,212; part-time $345 per credit. Required fees: $986; $55 per credit. Part-time tuition and fees vary according to course load. *Financial support:* Federal Work-Study, institutionally sponsored loans, scholarships/grants, unspecified assistantships, and administrative assistantships available. Support available to part-time students. Financial award application deadline: 5/1; financial award applicants required to submit FAFSA. *Faculty research:* Conversation in standard and communication disordered, autism, language disorders and literacy, acoustic characteristics of American English, educational needs of children with cochlear implants. *Unit head:* Dr. Paula Currie, Department Head, 985-549-2214, Fax: 985-549-5030, E-mail: pcurrie@selu.edu. *Application contact:* Sandra Meyers, Graduate Admissions Analyst, 985-549-2066, Fax: 985-549-5632, E-mail: admissions@selu.edu.

Southeast Missouri State University, School of Graduate Studies, Department of Elementary and Special Education, Program in Exceptional Child Education, Cape Girardeau, MO 63701-4799. Offers MA. *Accreditation:* NCATE. Part-time and evening/weekend programs available. *Faculty:* 1 (woman) full-time. *Students:* 2 full-time (both women), 7 part-time (all women). Average age 37. 1 applicant, 100% accepted. In 2006, 3 degrees awarded. *Degree requirements:* For master's, thesis or alternative. *Entrance requirements:* For master's, GRE General Test, MAT, minimum GPA of 2.75. Additional exam requirements/recommendations for international students: Required—TOEFL (minimum score 550 paper-based; 213 computer-based). *Application deadline:* For fall admission, 8/1 for domestic students, 4/1 for international students; for spring admission, 11/21 for domestic students, 10/1 for international students. Applications are processed on a rolling basis. Application fee: $20 ($100 for international students). Electronic applications accepted. *Financial support:* In 2006–07, 4 students received support. Career-related internships or fieldwork available. Financial award applicants required to submit FAFSA. *Application contact:* Marsha L. Arant, Senior Administrative Assistant, Office of Graduate Studies, 573-651-2192, Fax: 573-651-2001, E-mail: marant@semo.edu.

Southern Connecticut State University, School of Graduate Studies, School of Education, Program in Special Education, New Haven, CT 06515-1355. Offers MS Ed, Diploma. Part-time and evening/weekend programs available. *Faculty:* 12 full-time, 9 part-time/adjunct. *Students:* 64 full-time (47 women), 260 part-time (225 women); includes 22 minority (13 African Americans, 2 Asian Americans or Pacific Islanders, 7 Hispanic Americans). 89 applicants, 93% accepted, 68 enrolled. In 2006, 110 master's, 5 other advanced degrees awarded. *Degree requirements:* For master's, thesis or alternative. *Entrance requirements:* For master's, interview; for Diploma, 3 years of teaching experience, master's degree, teacher certification, interview. *Application deadline:* For fall admission, 7/15 for domestic students. Application fee: $50. Electronic applications accepted. *Financial support:* Career-related internships or fieldwork available. Financial award application deadline: 4/15; financial award applicants required to submit FAFSA. *Unit head:* Dr. Pamela Brucker, Chairperson, 203-392-5925, Fax: 203-392-5927, E-mail: bruckerp1@southernct.edu. *Application contact:* Dr. Patricia Major, Graduate Coordinator, 203-392-5952, Fax: 203-392-5927, E-mail: majorp1@southernct.edu.

Southern Illinois University Carbondale, Graduate School, College of Education, Department of Educational Psychology and Special Education, Program in Special Education, Carbondale, IL 62901-4701. Offers MS Ed. *Accreditation:* NCATE. Part-time programs available. *Faculty:* 19 full-time (9 women), 7 part-time/adjunct (2 women). *Students:* 3 full-time (all women), 39 part-time (31 women); includes 2 minority (1 African American, 1 Hispanic American), 2 international. Average age 28. 12 applicants, 50% accepted, 1 enrolled. In 2006, 5 degrees awarded. *Degree requirements:* For master's, thesis. *Entrance requirements:* For master's, GRE General Test, minimum GPA of 2.7. Additional exam requirements/recommendations for international students: Required—TOEFL. *Application deadline:* Applications are processed on a rolling basis. Application fee: $20. *Financial support:* In 2006–07, 3 students received support; fellowships with full tuition reimbursements available, research assistantships with full tuition reimbursements available, teaching assistantships with full tuition reimbursements available, career-related internships or fieldwork, Federal Work-Study, institutionally sponsored loans, tuition waivers (full), and unspecified assistantships available. Support available to part-time students. *Faculty research:* Applied and action research; scientific methods used to evaluate effectiveness of products and programs for the handicapped; scientific methods used to develop generalizations about instructional, motivational, and learning processes of the handicapped. *Application contact:* Cathy Earnhart, Administrative Clerk, 618-453-6932, E-mail: pern@siu.edu.

Southern Illinois University Edwardsville, Graduate Studies and Research, School of Education, Department of Special Education and Communication Disorders, Program in Special

Education, Edwardsville, IL 62026-0001. Offers MS Ed. Part-time and evening/weekend programs available. *Students:* 4 full-time (3 women), 53 part-time (46 women); includes 1 minority (African American) 22 applicants, 68% accepted. In 2006, 13 degrees awarded. *Degree requirements:* For master's, thesis or alternative, final exam. *Entrance requirements:* For master's, MAT. Additional exam requirements/recommendations for international students: Required—TOEFL. *Application deadline:* For fall admission, 7/20 for domestic students, 6/1 for international students; for spring admission, 12/14 for domestic students, 10/1 for international students. Application fee: $30. Electronic applications accepted. *Financial support:* Fellowships, research assistantships, teaching assistantships available. *Unit head:* Dr. Vicki Scott, Director, 618-650-3491.

Southern New Hampshire University, School of Education, Manchester, NH 03106-1045. Offers business education (MS); child development (M Ed); computer technology education (Certificate); curriculum and instruction (M Ed); education (M Ed, CAS); elementary education (M Ed); general special education (Certificate); school business administrator (Certificate); school counseling (M Ed); school psychology (M Ed); secondary education (M Ed); training and development (Certificate). Part-time and evening/weekend programs available. Postbaccalaureate distance learning degree programs offered. *Faculty:* 6 full-time (3 women), 9 part-time/adjunct (7 women). *Students:* Average age 35. In 2006, 52 degrees awarded. *Degree requirements:* For master's, thesis or alternative, comprehensive exam (for some programs). *Entrance requirements:* For master's, GRE General Test or MAT, minimum GPA of 3.0. Additional exam requirements/recommendations for international students: Required—TOEFL (minimum score 550 paper-based; 213 computer-based). *Application deadline:* Applications are processed on a rolling basis. Application fee: $25. Electronic applications accepted. *Expenses:* Contact institution. *Financial support:* Institutionally sponsored loans available. Financial award applicants required to submit FAFSA. *Unit head:* Dr. Patrick J. Hartwick, Dean, 603-668-2211 Ext. 4698, Fax: 603-629-4673, E-mail: p.hartwick@snhu.edu. *Application contact:* Scott Durand, Director of Graduate Enrollment Services, 603-644-3102 Ext. 3338, Fax: 603-644-3144, E-mail: s.durand@snhu.edu.

Southern Oregon University, Graduate Studies, School of Social Sciences, Department of Education, Ashland, OR 97520. Offers elementary education (MA Ed, MS Ed), including classroom teacher, early childhood, handicapped learner, reading, supervision; secondary education (MA Ed, MS Ed), including classroom teacher, handicapped learner, reading, supervision; teaching (MAT). *Degree requirements:* For master's, thesis optional. *Entrance requirements:* For master's, GRE General Test, minimum GPA of 3.0. Electronic applications accepted.

Southern University and Agricultural and Mechanical College, Graduate School and College of Education, Department of Special Education, Baton Rouge, LA 70813. Offers M Ed, PhD. *Accreditation:* NCATE. Part-time and evening/weekend programs available. *Degree requirements:* For master's, thesis optional; for doctorate, thesis/dissertation, comprehensive qualifying exam, oral defense of dissertation. *Entrance requirements:* For master's, GMAT or GRE General Test, PRAXIS; for doctorate, GRE General Test, PRAXIS, letters of recommendation, 2 years experience (individuals with disabilities). Additional exam requirements/recommendations for international students: Required—TOEFL. *Faculty research:* Classroom discipline/management, minority students in gifted/special education, learning styles/brain hemisphericity, school violence and prevention, certifications for special education teachers.

Southwestern College, Center for Teaching Excellence, Winfield, KS 67156-2499. Offers special education (M Ed). *Accreditation:* NCATE. Part-time and evening/weekend programs available. Postbaccalaureate distance learning degree programs offered (minimal on-campus study). *Degree requirements:* For master's, thesis, practicum, comprehensive exam, registration. Electronic applications accepted.

Southwestern Oklahoma State University, College of Professional and Graduate Studies, School of Behavioral Sciences and Education, Specialization in Special Education, Weatherford, OK 73096-3098. Offers M Ed. M Ed distance learning degree program offered to Oklahoma residents only. *Accreditation:* NCATE. Part-time and evening/weekend programs available. *Degree requirements:* For master's, exam. *Entrance requirements:* For master's, GRE General Test or minimum undergraduate GPA of 3.0. Additional exam requirements/recommendations for international students: Required—TOEFL.

Southwest Minnesota State University, Department of Education, Marshall, MN 56258. Offers education (MS); education development and leadership (MS); special education (MS). *Faculty:* 8 full-time (4 women), 3 part-time/adjunct (2 women). *Students:* 119 full-time (89 women), 245 part-time (195 women); includes 5 minority (1 Asian American or Pacific Islander, 4 Hispanic Americans), 1 international. 148 applicants. In 2006, 172 degrees awarded. *Application deadline:* Applications are processed on a rolling basis. Application fee: $20. *Expenses:* Tuition, area resident: Full-time $4,835. Tuition, state resident: full-time $4,835; part-time $269 per credit. Tuition, nonresident: part-time $269 per credit. Required fees: $589; $33 per credit. Tuition and fees vary according to course load and reciprocity agreements. *Unit head:* Donna Burgraff, Dean, 507-537-6218, E-mail: burgraff@southwestmsu.edu. *Application contact:* Rich Shearer, Director of Enrollment Management, 507-537-6286, E-mail: shearerr@southwestmsu.edu.

Spalding University, Graduate Studies, College of Education, Programs in Education, Louisville, KY 40203-2188. Offers elementary school education (MAT); general education (MA); high school education (MAT); middle school education (MAT); school administration (MA); special education (learning and behavioral disorders) (MAT). MAT degree programs offered for first teaching certificate/license students. *Accreditation:* NCATE. Part-time and evening/weekend programs available. *Degree requirements:* For master's, portfolio, final project, clinical experience. *Entrance requirements:* For master's, GRE General Test or MAT, interview, recommendations, resumé. Additional exam requirements/recommendations for international students: Required—TOEFL. Electronic applications accepted. *Faculty research:* Instructional technology, achievement gap, classroom management, assessment.

State University of New York at Binghamton, Graduate School, School of Education, Program in Special Education, Binghamton, NY 13902-6000. Offers MS Ed. *Accreditation:* Teacher Education Accreditation Council. Part-time and evening/weekend programs available. *Students:* 3 full-time (all women), 29 part-time (23 women). Average age 35. 18 applicants, 72% accepted. In 2006, 12 degrees awarded. *Entrance requirements:* For master's, GRE General Test. Additional exam requirements/recommendations for international students: Required—TOEFL. *Application deadline:* For fall admission, 4/15 priority date for domestic students, 1/15 priority date for international students; for spring admission, 11/1 for domestic students, 10/1 priority date for international students. Applications are processed on a rolling basis. Application fee: $60. Electronic applications accepted. *Financial support:* Fellowships, research assistantships, teaching assistantships with full tuition reimbursements, career-related internships or fieldwork, Federal Work-Study, institutionally sponsored loans, and unspecified assistantships available. Support available to part-time students. Financial award application deadline: 2/15. *Unit head:* Dr. Beverly Rainforth, Coordinator, 607-777-2277.

State University of New York at New Paltz, Graduate School, Faculty of Education, Department of Educational Studies, New Paltz, NY 12561. Offers humanistic/multicultural education (MPS); special education (MS Ed). Part-time and evening/weekend programs available. *Faculty:* 11 full-time (9 women), 21 part-time/adjunct (15 women). *Students:* 6 full-time (4 women), 64 part-time (51 women); includes 16 minority (7 African Americans, 1 Asian American or Pacific Islander, 8 Hispanic Americans). Average age 36. 86 applicants. *Degree requirements:* For master's, portfolio. *Entrance requirements:* For master's, minimum GPA of 3.0, teaching certificate (MS Ed). Additional exam requirements/recommendations for international students: Required—TOEFL (minimum score 550 paper-based; 213 computer-based; 80 iBT). *Application deadline:* For fall admission, 3/15 priority date for domestic students, 3/15 for international students; for spring admission, 10/15 for domestic and international students. Application fee: $50. Electronic applications accepted. *Expenses:* Tuition, state resident: full-time $6,900; part-time $288 per credit hour. Tuition, nonresident: full-time $10,920; part-time $455 per credit hour. *Financial support:* Career-related internships or fieldwork, Federal Work-Study, and institutionally sponsored loans available. *Unit head:* Dr. Gowri Parameswaran, Chair, 845-257-2834.

State University of New York at New Paltz, Graduate School, Faculty of Education, Department of Special Education, New Paltz, NY 12561. Offers adolescence (7-12) (MS Ed); childhood (1-6) (MS Ed). *Accreditation:* NCATE. Part-time and evening/weekend programs available. *Faculty:* 11 full-time (9 women), 21 part-time/adjunct (15 women). *Students:* 40 full-time (38 women), 59 part-time (49 women); includes 5 minority (1 African American, 2 Asian Americans or Pacific Islanders, 2 Hispanic Americans), 1 international. Average age 29. 63 applicants. In 2006, 56 degrees awarded. *Degree requirements:* For master's, portfolio. *Entrance requirements:* For master's, minimum GPA of 3.0, teaching certificate. Additional exam requirements/recommendations for international students: Required—TOEFL (minimum score 550 paper-based; 213 computer-based; 80 iBT). *Application deadline:* For fall admission, 5/1 priority date for domestic students, 5/1 for international students; for spring admission, 11/15 for domestic and international students. Application fee: $50. Electronic applications accepted. *Expenses:* Tuition, state resident: full-time $6,900; part-time $288 per credit hour. Tuition, nonresident: full-time $10,920; part-time $455 per credit hour. *Financial support:* Career-related internships or fieldwork, Federal Work-Study, and institutionally sponsored loans available. *Unit head:* Dr. Spencer Salend, Coordinator, 845-257-2846, E-mail: salends@newpaltz.edu.

State University of New York at Oswego, Graduate Studies, School of Education, Department of Curriculum and Instruction, Oswego, NY 13126. Offers art education (MAT); elementary education (MS Ed); literacy education (MS Ed); secondary education (MS Ed); special education (MS Ed). Part-time and evening/weekend programs available. *Faculty:* 23 full-time, 45 part-time/adjunct. *Students:* 184 full-time (139 women), 220 part-time (185 women); includes 12 minority (5 African Americans, 1 American Indian/Alaska Native, 1 Asian American or Pacific Islander, 5 Hispanic Americans), 1 international. Average age 33. 266 applicants, 89% accepted. In 2006, 255 degrees awarded. *Degree requirements:* For master's, thesis optional. *Entrance requirements:* For master's, GRE General Test, minimum GPA of 2.7, provisional teaching certificate. Additional exam requirements/recommendations for international students: Required—TOEFL (minimum score 560 paper-based; 220 computer-based). *Application deadline:* For fall admission, 3/1 for domestic students; for spring admission, 10/1 for domestic students. Application fee: $50. *Expenses:* Tuition, state resident: part-time $288 per credit. Tuition, nonresident: part-time $455 per credit. Tuition and fees vary according to program. *Financial support:* In 2006–07, 9 students received support, including 3 fellowships, 6 teaching assistantships with full tuition reimbursements available; career-related internships or fieldwork, Federal Work-Study, institutionally sponsored loans, scholarships/grants, and unspecified assistantships also available. Support available to part-time students. Financial award application deadline: 4/1; financial award applicants required to submit FAFSA. *Faculty research:* Classroom applications for microcomputers; classroom questioning, wait-time, and achievement; values clarification and academic achievement. *Unit head:* Dr. Pamela Michel, Chair, 315-312-4052. *Application contact:* Dr. Joyce Smith, Coordinator, Graduate Education, 315-312-4052.

State University of New York at Plattsburgh, Division of Education, Health, and Human Services, Program in Special Education, Plattsburgh, NY 12901-2681. Offers birth to grade 2 (MS Ed); grades 1 to 6 (MS Ed); grades 7 to 12 (MS Ed). Part-time and evening/weekend programs available. *Faculty:* 6 full-time (3 women), 3 part-time/adjunct (2 women). *Students:* 24 full-time (20 women), 16 part-time (14 women); includes 3 minority (2 Asian Americans or Pacific Islanders, 1 Hispanic American). Average age 28. 14 applicants, 100% accepted, 14 enrolled. In 2006, 17 degrees awarded. *Degree requirements:* For master's, comprehensive exam or research project, thesis optional. *Entrance requirements:* For master's, GRE General Test or MAT, minimum GPA of 2.5. *Application deadline:* Applications are processed on a rolling basis. Application fee: $50. *Expenses:* Tuition, state resident: full-time $6,900; part-time $288 per credit hour. Tuition, nonresident: full-time $10,920; part-time $455 per credit hour. *Financial support:* In 2006–07, 11 students received support. Federal Work-Study available. Support available to part-time students. Financial award application deadline: 4/15; financial award applicants required to submit FAFSA. *Faculty research:* Inclusion behavior management technology, applied behavior analysis. *Unit head:* Dr. Kathleen S. Whittier, Chair, 518-564-5129, Fax: 518-564-2149, E-mail: whittiks@splava.cc.plattsburgh.edu.

State University of New York College at Cortland, Graduate Studies, School of Education, Programs in Teaching Students with Disabilities, Cortland, NY 13045. Offers MS Ed. *Accreditation:* NCATE. Part-time and evening/weekend programs available. *Degree requirements:* For master's, one foreign language, thesis (for some programs), comprehensive exam. *Entrance requirements:* For master's, provisional certification. Additional exam requirements/recommendations for international students: Required—TOEFL.

State University of New York College at Potsdam, School of Education, Program in Special Education, Potsdam, NY 13676. Offers MS Ed. *Accreditation:* NCATE. Part-time and evening/weekend programs available. *Faculty:* 3 full-time (2 women), 1 part-time/adjunct (0 women). *Students:* 23 full-time (21 women), 10 part-time (all women); includes 1 minority (American Indian/Alaska Native). In 2006, 30 degrees awarded. *Degree requirements:* For master's, culminating experience, thesis optional. *Entrance requirements:* For master's, minimum GPA of 2.75 in last 60 hours of course work. Additional exam requirements/recommendations for international students: Required—TOEFL (minimum score 550 paper-based; 213 computer-based). *Application deadline:* Applications are processed on a rolling basis. Application fee: $50. *Financial support:* Application deadline: 3/1. *Unit head:* Dr. Anjali Misra, Chairperson, 315-267-2764, Fax: 315-267-4802, E-mail: misraa@potsdam.edu. *Application contact:* Peter Cutler, Graduate Admissions Counselor, 315-267-3154, Fax: 315-267-4802, E-mail: cutlerpj@potsdam.edu.

Stephen F. Austin State University, Graduate School, College of Education, Department of Human Services, Nacogdoches, TX 75962. Offers counseling (MA); school psychology (MA); special education (M Ed); speech pathology (MS). *Accreditation:* ACA (one or more programs are accredited); ASHA (one or more programs are accredited); CORE; NCATE. *Degree requirements:* For master's, thesis (for some programs), comprehensive exam. *Entrance requirements:* For master's, GRE General Test, minimum GPA of 2.8. Additional exam requirements/recommendations for international students: Required—TOEFL.

Stetson University, College of Arts and Sciences, Division of Education, Department of Teacher Education, Program in Exceptional Student Education, DeLand, FL 32723. Offers M Ed. *Accreditation:* NCATE. *Students:* Average age 28. In 2006, 6 degrees awarded. *Entrance requirements:* For master's, GRE General Test or MAT. *Application deadline:* For fall admission, 3/1 priority date for domestic students; for spring admission, 11/1 for domestic students. Applications are processed on a rolling basis. Application fee: $25. *Unit head:* Dr. Kathy Piechura-Couture, Coordinator, 386-822-7075. *Application contact:* Midge McDaniel, Office of Graduate Studies, 386-822-7075, Fax: 386-822-7388, E-mail: mmcdanie@stetson.edu.

Syracuse University, Graduate School, School of Education, Department of Teaching and Leadership, Program in Early Childhood Special Education, Syracuse, NY 13244. Offers MS. *Students:* 13 full-time (11 women), 20 part-time (19 women); includes 2 African Americans, 1 Asian American or Pacific Islander, 1 international. *Entrance requirements:* For master's, interview. *Application deadline:* For fall admission, 2/1 for domestic students. *Expenses:* Tuition: Full-time $16,920; part-time $940 per credit hour. Required fees: $930; $930 per year. *Unit head:* Dr. Gail Ensher, Progarm Director, 315-443-9650. *Application contact:* Liza Rochelson, Graduate Admission Recruiter, 315-443-2505, Fax: 315-443-2258, E-mail: gradcrt@gwmail.syr.edu.

Syracuse University, Graduate School, School of Education, Department of Teaching and Leadership, Program in Inclusive Special Education (grades 1-6), Syracuse, NY 13244. Offers MS. Part-time and evening/weekend programs available. *Students:* 4 full-time (2 women), 5 part-time (4 women); includes 1 minority (Hispanic American) 6 applicants, 83% accepted, 2 enrolled. *Degree requirements:* For master's, thesis or alternative. *Entrance requirements:* For

Special Education

Syracuse University (continued)
master's, interview. Additional exam requirements/recommendations for international students: Required—TOEFL. *Application deadline:* For fall admission, 2/1 for domestic students. Applications are processed on a rolling basis. Application fee: $65. Electronic applications accepted. *Expenses:* Tuition: Full-time $16,920; part-time $940 per credit hour. Required fees: $930; $930 per year. *Financial support:* Fellowships with tuition reimbursements, teaching assistantships with tuition reimbursements available. *Unit head:* Dr. Corinne Smith, Graduate Chair, 315-443-2684. *Application contact:* Liza Rochelson, Graduate Admission Recruiter, 315-443-2505, Fax: 315-443-2258, E-mail: gradcrt@gwmail.syr.edu.

Syracuse University, Graduate School, School of Education, Department of Teaching and Leadership, Program in Inclusive Special Education (grades 7-12), Syracuse, NY 13244. Offers MS. Part-time and evening/weekend programs available. *Students:* 1 (woman) full-time, 1 (woman) part-time. 3 applicants, 100% accepted, 2 enrolled. *Degree requirements:* For master's, thesis or alternative. *Entrance requirements:* Additional exam requirements/recommendations for international students: Required—TOEFL. *Application deadline:* For fall admission, 2/1 priority date for domestic students. Applications are processed on a rolling basis. Application fee: $65. Electronic applications accepted. *Expenses:* Tuition: Full-time $16,920; part-time $940 per credit hour. Required fees: $930; $930 per year. *Unit head:* Dr. Beth Ferri, Program Director, 315-443-1465. *Application contact:* Liza Rochelson, Graduate Admission Recruiter, 315-443-2505, Fax: 315-443-2258, E-mail: gradcrt@gwmail.syr.edu.

Syracuse University, Graduate School, School of Education, Department of Teaching and Leadership, Program in Special Education, Syracuse, NY 13244. Offers PhD. Part-time and evening/weekend programs available. *Students:* 8 full-time (all women), 11 part-time (10 women); includes 2 minority (1 African American, 1 American Indian/Alaska Native), 5 international. 2 applicants, 100% accepted, 1 enrolled. *Degree requirements:* For doctorate, thesis/dissertation. *Entrance requirements:* For doctorate, GRE General Test, interview. Additional exam requirements/recommendations for international students: Required—TOEFL. *Application deadline:* For fall admission, 2/1 priority date for domestic students. Applications are processed on a rolling basis. Application fee: $65. Electronic applications accepted. *Expenses:* Tuition: Full-time $16,920; part-time $940 per credit hour. Required fees: $930; $930 per year. *Financial support:* Fellowships, research assistantships, teaching assistantships, institutionally sponsored loans and health care benefits available. *Faculty research:* Aggression, inclusive education, autistic children, validation of social skills, cooperative learning in the heterogeneous classroom. *Unit head:* Dr. Beth Ferri, Program Director, 315-443-1465. *Application contact:* Liza Rochelson, Graduate Admission Recruiter, 315-443-2505, Fax: 315-443-2258, E-mail: gradcrt@gwmail.syr.edu.

Tarleton State University, College of Graduate Studies, College of Education, Department of Educational Administration, Counseling, and Psychology, Stephenville, TX 76402. Offers counseling and psychology (M Ed), including counseling, counseling psychology, educational psychology; educational administration (M Ed, Certificate); educational leadership (Ed D); secondary education (Certificate); special education (Certificate). Part-time and evening/weekend programs available. Postbaccalaureate distance learning degree programs offered (minimal on-campus study). *Faculty:* 45 full-time (23 women), 37 part-time/adjunct (9 women). *Students:* 210 full-time (124 women), 613 part-time (464 women); includes 82 minority (11 Asian Americans or Pacific Islanders, 71 Hispanic Americans), 1 international. Average age 35. In 2006, 203 degrees awarded. *Degree requirements:* For master's, thesis optional. *Entrance requirements:* For master's, GRE General Test, minimum GPA of 3.0. Additional exam requirements/recommendations for international students: Required—TOEFL (minimum score 550 paper-based; 220 computer-based). *Application deadline:* For fall admission, 8/5 priority date for domestic students; for spring admission, 12/1 for domestic students. Applications are processed on a rolling basis. Application fee: $25 ($75 for international students). *Financial support:* In 2006–07, 3 research assistantships (averaging $12,000 per year), 12 teaching assistantships (averaging $12,000 per year) were awarded; career-related internships or fieldwork, Federal Work-Study, institutionally sponsored loans, and tuition waivers (partial) also available. Support available to part-time students. Financial award application deadline: 5/1; financial award applicants required to submit FAFSA. *Unit head:* Dr. Robert Newby, Head, 254-968-9945.

Teachers College Columbia University, Graduate Faculty of Education, Department of Curriculum and Teaching, Program in Dual Certificate Childhood/Disabilities, New York, NY 10027-6696. Offers Certificate. *Students:* 5 full-time (3 women), 29 part-time (26 women); includes 5 minority (2 African Americans, 1 Asian American or Pacific Islander, 2 Hispanic Americans). Average age 26. 42 applicants, 33% accepted, 13 enrolled. Application fee: $65. *Expenses:* Tuition: Full-time $23,400; part-time $975 per credit. Required fees: $320 per term. *Application contact:* Peter Shon, Assistant Director of Admission, 212-678-3305, Fax: 212-678-4171, E-mail: shon@exchange.tc.columbia.edu.

Teachers College Columbia University, Graduate Faculty of Education, Department of Curriculum and Teaching, Program in Early Childhood Special Education, New York, NY 10027-6696. Offers Ed M, MA. *Accreditation:* NCATE. Evening/weekend programs available. *Faculty:* 1 (woman) full-time, 1 part-time/adjunct. *Students:* 13 full-time (all women), 35 part-time (all women); includes 18 minority (13 Asian Americans or Pacific Islanders, 5 Hispanic Americans), 6 international. Average age 30. 53 applicants, 53% accepted, 14 enrolled. In 2006, 23 degrees awarded. *Application deadline:* For fall admission, 5/15 for domestic students; for spring admission, 12/1 for domestic students. Application fee: $65. *Expenses:* Tuition: Full-time $23,400; part-time $975 per credit. Required fees: $320 per term. *Financial support:* Research assistantships, teaching assistantships, career-related internships or fieldwork, Federal Work-Study, institutionally sponsored loans, and tuition waivers (full and partial) available. Support available to part-time students. Financial award application deadline: 2/1. *Faculty research:* Curriculum development, infants, urban education, visually impaired infants. *Application contact:* Peter Shon, Assistant Director of Admission, 212-678-3305, Fax: 212-678-4171, E-mail: shon@exchange.tc.columbia.edu.

See Close-Up on page 1127.

Teachers College Columbia University, Graduate Faculty of Education, Department of Curriculum and Teaching, Program in Learning Disabilities, New York, NY 10027-6696. Offers Ed M, MA, Ed D. *Accreditation:* NCATE. *Faculty:* 1 (woman) full-time, 2 part-time/adjunct. *Students:* 4 full-time (3 women), 12 part-time (11 women); includes 2 minority (1 African American, 1 Hispanic American), 1 international. Average age 38. 8 applicants, 25% accepted, 1 enrolled. In 2006, 29 master's, 1 doctorate awarded. *Degree requirements:* For doctorate, thesis/dissertation. *Entrance requirements:* For doctorate, GRE General Test or MAT. *Application deadline:* For fall admission, 5/15 for domestic students; for spring admission, 12/1 for domestic students. Application fee: $50. *Expenses:* Tuition: Full-time $23,400; part-time $975 per credit. Required fees: $320 per term. *Financial support:* Fellowships, teaching assistantships, career-related internships or fieldwork, Federal Work-Study, institutionally sponsored loans, and tuition waivers (full and partial) available. Support available to part-time students. Financial award application deadline: 2/1. *Faculty research:* Reading and mathematics disorders in students with learning disabilities, special education curriculum development. *Application contact:* Peter Shon, Assistant Director of Admission, 212-678-3305, Fax: 212-678-4171, E-mail: shon@exchange.tc.columbia.edu.

See Close-Up on page 1127.

Teachers College Columbia University, Graduate Faculty of Education, Department of Health and Behavioral Studies, Program in Behavioral Disorders, New York, NY 10027-6696. Offers MA, Ed D, PhD. Part-time programs available. *Faculty:* 2 full-time (1 woman), 3 part-time/adjunct. *Students:* 5 full-time (4 women), 59 part-time (56 women); includes 12 minority (1 African American, 6 Asian Americans or Pacific Islanders, 5 Hispanic Americans), 10 international. Average age 36. 48 applicants, 71% accepted, 21 enrolled. In 2006, 19 master's, 6 doctorates awarded. Terminal master's awarded for partial completion of doctoral program. *Degree requirements:* For doctorate, thesis/dissertation. *Application deadline:* For fall admission, 5/15 for domestic students; for spring admission, 12/1 for domestic students. Application fee: $65. *Expenses:* Tuition: Full-time $23,400; part-time $975 per credit. Required fees: $320 per term. *Financial support:* Fellowships, research assistantships, career-related internships or fieldwork, Federal Work-Study, institutionally sponsored loans, and tuition waivers (full and partial) available. Support available to part-time students. Financial award application deadline: 2/1. *Faculty research:* Functional analysis of behavior, comprehensive analysis, comprehensive application of behavior analysis to schooling. *Application contact:* Peter Shon, Assistant Director of Admission, 212-678-3305, Fax: 212-678-4171, E-mail: shon@exchange.tc.columbia.edu.

See Close-Up on page 1129.

Teachers College Columbia University, Graduate Faculty of Education, Department of Health and Behavioral Studies, Program in Blind and Visual Impairment, New York, NY 10027-6696. Offers MA, Ed D. *Students:* 2 full-time (both women), 3 part-time (all women); includes 1 minority (Asian American or Pacific Islander), 2 international. Average age 31. 6 applicants, 50% accepted, 3 enrolled. In 2006, 2 degrees awarded. *Degree requirements:* For doctorate, thesis/dissertation. *Application deadline:* For fall admission, 5/15 for domestic students; for spring admission, 12/1 for domestic students. Application fee: $50. *Expenses:* Tuition: Full-time $23,400; part-time $975 per credit. Required fees: $320 per term. *Financial support:* Career-related internships or fieldwork, Federal Work-Study, institutionally sponsored loans, and tuition waivers (full and partial) available. Support available to part-time students. Financial award application deadline: 2/1. *Faculty research:* Cross-modality transfer, issues in early childhood. *Application contact:* Peter Shon, Assistant Director of Admission, 212-678-3305, Fax: 212-678-4171, E-mail: shon@exchange.tc.columbia.edu.

See Close-Up on page 1129.

Teachers College Columbia University, Graduate Faculty of Education, Department of Health and Behavioral Studies, Program in Hearing Impairment, New York, NY 10027-6696. Offers MA, Ed D. *Faculty:* 1 full-time (0 women), 2 part-time/adjunct. *Students:* 20 full-time (all women), 20 part-time (16 women); includes 7 minority (1 African American, 1 American Indian/Alaska Native, 4 Asian Americans or Pacific Islanders, 1 Hispanic American), 1 international. Average age 26. 21 applicants, 90% accepted, 12 enrolled. In 2006, 16 degrees awarded. *Degree requirements:* For doctorate, thesis/dissertation. *Application deadline:* For fall admission, 5/15 for domestic students; for spring admission, 12/1 for domestic students. Application fee: $65. *Expenses:* Tuition: Full-time $23,400; part-time $975 per credit. Required fees: $320 per term. *Financial support:* Fellowships, career-related internships or fieldwork, Federal Work-Study, institutionally sponsored loans, and tuition waivers (full and partial) available. Support available to part-time students. Financial award application deadline: 2/1. *Faculty research:* Language development, reading/writing, cognitive abilities, text analysis, auditory streaming. *Application contact:* Peter Shon, Assistant Director of Admission, 212-678-3305, Fax: 212-678-4171, E-mail: shon@exchange.tc.columbia.edu.

See Close-Up on page 1129.

Teachers College Columbia University, Graduate Faculty of Education, Department of Health and Behavioral Studies, Program in Mental Retardation, New York, NY 10027-6696. Offers MA, Ed D, PhD. Part-time programs available. *Faculty:* 1 (woman) full-time, 2 part-time/adjunct. *Students:* 9 full-time (all women), 31 part-time (28 women); includes 8 minority (2 African Americans, 4 Asian Americans or Pacific Islanders, 2 Hispanic Americans), 4 international. Average age 30. 31 applicants, 71% accepted, 8 enrolled. In 2006, 11 master's, 4 doctorates awarded. Terminal master's awarded for partial completion of doctoral program. *Degree requirements:* For doctorate, thesis/dissertation. *Application deadline:* For fall admission, 5/15 for domestic students; for spring admission, 12/1 for domestic students. Application fee: $65. *Expenses:* Tuition: Full-time $23,400; part-time $975 per credit. Required fees: $320 per term. *Financial support:* Fellowships, research assistantships, teaching assistantships, career-related internships or fieldwork, Federal Work-Study, institutionally sponsored loans, and tuition waivers (full and partial) available. Support available to part-time students. Financial award application deadline: 2/1. *Faculty research:* Information processing, memory comprehension and problem-solving issues related to mental retardation, transition issues, cognition and comprehension. *Application contact:* Peter Shon, Assistant Director of Admission, 212-678-3305, Fax: 212-678-4171, E-mail: shon@exchange.tc.columbia.edu.

See Close-Up on page 1129.

Teachers College Columbia University, Graduate Faculty of Education, Department of Health and Behavioral Studies, Program in Physical Disabilities, New York, NY 10027-6696. Offers MA, Ed D, PhD. Part-time and evening/weekend programs available. *Students:* Average age 35. 3 applicants, 67% accepted, 0 enrolled. *Degree requirements:* For doctorate, variable foreign language requirement, thesis/dissertation. *Entrance requirements:* For doctorate, GRE General Test or MAT. *Application deadline:* For fall admission, 5/15 priority date for domestic students; for spring admission, 12/1 for domestic students. Applications are processed on a rolling basis. Application fee: $65. *Expenses:* Tuition: Full-time $23,400; part-time $975 per credit. Required fees: $320 per term. *Financial support:* Fellowships, teaching assistantships, career-related internships or fieldwork, Federal Work-Study, institutionally sponsored loans, and tuition waivers (full and partial) available. Support available to part-time students. Financial award application deadline: 2/1. *Faculty research:* Students with traumatic brain injury, health impairments, learning disabilities. *Application contact:* Peter Shon, Assistant Director of Admission, 212-678-3305, Fax: 212-678-4171, E-mail: shon@exchange.tc.columbia.edu.

See Close-Up on page 1129.

Teachers College Columbia University, Graduate Faculty of Education, Department of Health and Behavioral Studies, Program in Research in Special Education, New York, NY 10027-6696. Offers Ed D. *Accreditation:* NCATE. *Students:* Average age 34. *Degree requirements:* For doctorate, thesis/dissertation. *Application deadline:* For fall admission, 5/15 for domestic students. Application fee: $65. *Expenses:* Tuition: Full-time $23,400; part-time $975 per credit. Required fees: $320 per term. *Financial support:* Career-related internships or fieldwork, Federal Work-Study, institutionally sponsored loans, and tuition waivers (full and partial) available. Support available to part-time students. Financial award application deadline: 2/1. *Application contact:* Peter Shon, Assistant Director of Admission, 212-678-3305, Fax: 212-678-4171, E-mail: shon@exchange.tc.columbia.edu.

See Close-Up on page 1129.

Teachers College Columbia University, Graduate Faculty of Education, Department of Health and Behavioral Studies, Program in Special Education, New York, NY 10027-6696. Offers Ed M, MA, Ed D. *Accreditation:* NCATE. Part-time and evening/weekend programs available. *Faculty:* 1 full-time (0 women), 3 part-time/adjunct. *Students:* 3 full-time (all women), 23 part-time (16 women); includes 6 minority (4 African Americans, 1 Asian American or Pacific Islander, 1 Hispanic American), 2 international. Average age 34. 18 applicants, 56% accepted, 5 enrolled. In 2006, 6 degrees awarded. Terminal master's awarded for partial completion of doctoral program. *Application deadline:* For fall admission, 5/15 for domestic students; for spring admission, 12/1 for domestic students. Application fee: $50. *Expenses:* Tuition: Full-time $23,400; part-time $975 per credit. Required fees: $320 per term. *Financial support:* Career-related internships or fieldwork, Federal Work-Study, institutionally sponsored loans, and tuition waivers (full and partial) available. Support available to part-time students. Financial award application deadline: 2/1. *Application contact:* Peter Shon, Assistant Director of Admission, 212-678-3305, Fax: 212-678-4171, E-mail: shon@exchange.tc.columbia.edu.

See Close-Up on page 1129.

Teachers College Columbia University, Graduate Faculty of Education, Department of Health and Behavioral Studies, Program in Teaching of Sign Language, New York, NY 10027-6696. Offers MA. *Accreditation:* NCATE. *Students:* 5 full-time (4 women), 17 part-time (14 women); includes 3 minority (2 African Americans, 1 Asian American or Pacific Islander).

Average age 33. 17 applicants, 65% accepted, 9 enrolled. In 2006, 6 degrees awarded. Application fee: $65. *Expenses:* Tuition: Full-time $23,400; part-time $975 per credit. Required fees: $320 per term. *Application contact:* Peter Shon, Assistant Director of Admission, 212-678-3305, Fax: 212-678-4171, E-mail: shon@exchange.tc.columbia.edu.

See Close-Up on page 1129.

Teachers College Columbia University, Graduate Faculty of Education, Program in Administration and Supervision in Special Education, New York, NY 10027-6696. Offers Ed M, MA, Ed D, PhD. *Accreditation:* NCATE. *Students:* 3 full-time (2 women), 20 part-time (13 women); includes 6 minority (4 African Americans, 1 Asian American or Pacific Islander, 1 Hispanic American), 2 international. Average age 35. In 2006, 1 degree awarded. *Degree requirements:* For doctorate, thesis/dissertation. *Application deadline:* For fall admission, 5/15 for domestic students. Application fee: $65. *Expenses:* Tuition: Full-time $23,400; part-time $975 per credit. Required fees: $320 per term. *Financial support:* Career-related internships or fieldwork, Federal Work-Study, institutionally sponsored loans, and tuition waivers (full and partial) available. Support available to part-time students. Financial award application deadline: 2/1. *Faculty research:* Cognition and comprehension, disability studies, self-determination, literacy development. *Application contact:* Ursula Felton, Office of Admissions, 212-678-3710, Fax: 212-678-4171.

See Close-Up on page 1127.

Teachers College Columbia University, Graduate Faculty of Education, Program in Reading/Learning Disability, New York, NY 10027-6696. Offers Ed M. *Application deadline:* For fall admission, 5/15 for domestic students. Application fee: $50. *Expenses:* Tuition: Full-time $23,400; part-time $975 per credit. Required fees: $320 per term. *Financial support:* Career-related internships or fieldwork, Federal Work-Study, institutionally sponsored loans, and tuition waivers (partial) available. Support available to part-time students. Financial award application deadline: 2/1. *Faculty research:* Reading and spelling disorders, workplace literacy, reading and writing among children and adults. *Application contact:* Director of Admissions, 212-678-3083, Fax: 212-678-4171.

Temple University, Graduate School, College of Education, Department of Curriculum, Instruction, and Technology in Education, Philadelphia, PA 19122-6096. Offers applied behavioral analysis (MS Ed); career and technical education (MS Ed); early childhood education and elementary education (MS Ed); English education (MS Ed); language arts education (Ed D); math/science education (Ed D); mathematics education (MS Ed); science education (MS Ed); second and foreign language education (MS Ed); special education (MS Ed); teaching English as a second language (MS Ed). Part-time and evening/weekend programs available. *Faculty:* 31 full-time (14 women). *Students:* 96 full-time (71 women), 482 part-time (336 women); includes 109 minority (67 African Americans, 3 American Indian/Alaska Native, 23 Asian Americans or Pacific Islanders, 16 Hispanic Americans), 28 international. 308 applicants, 64% accepted, 116 enrolled. In 2006, 225 master's, 21 doctorates awarded. Terminal master's awarded for partial completion of doctoral program. *Degree requirements:* For master's, thesis or alternative; for doctorate, thesis/dissertation. *Entrance requirements:* For master's and doctorate, GRE General Test or MAT, minimum GPA of 3.0. Additional exam requirements/recommendations for international students: Required—TOEFL (minimum score 550 paper-based; 213 computer-based; 79 iBT). *Application deadline:* For fall admission, 4/1 for domestic students, 12/15 for international students; for spring admission, 10/1 for domestic students, 8/1 for international students. Application fee: $50. Electronic applications accepted. *Expenses:* Tuition, state resident: full-time $12,264; part-time $511 per credit. Tuition, nonresident: full-time $17,904; part-time $746 per credit. Required fees: $84 per course. Tuition and fees vary according to program. *Financial support:* Fellowships, research assistantships with full tuition reimbursements, teaching assistantships with full tuition reimbursements available. Financial award application deadline: 1/15; financial award applicants required to submit FAFSA. *Faculty research:* School improvement, problem solving, literacy, language development. *Unit head:* Dr. Thomas Walker, Chair, 215-204-2117, Fax: 215-204-1414, E-mail: tjwalker@temple.edu.

Tennessee State University, The School of Graduate Studies and Research, College of Education, Department of Teaching and Learning, Program in Special Education, Nashville, TN 37209-1561. Offers M Ed, MA Ed, Ed D. *Accreditation:* NCATE. *Students:* 45 applicants. *Degree requirements:* For master's, comprehensive exam (M Ed), thesis (MA Ed); for doctorate, thesis/dissertation. *Entrance requirements:* For master's, GRE General Test, GRE Subject Test, or MAT, minimum GPA of 2.5; for doctorate, GRE General Test, GRE Subject Test, or MAT, minimum GPA of 3.25. *Application deadline:* Applications are processed on a rolling basis. *Financial support:* Application deadline: 5/1. *Application contact:* Dr. Helen Barrett, Dean, 615-963-5139, Fax: 615-963-5963, E-mail: hbarrett@tnstate.edu.

Tennessee Technological University, Graduate School, College of Education, Department of Curriculum and Instruction, Program in Special Education, Cookeville, TN 38505. Offers MA, Ed S. *Accreditation:* NCATE. Part-time programs available. *Faculty:* 6 full-time (3 women). *Students:* 13 full-time (9 women), 47 part-time (39 women); includes 4 minority (2 African Americans, 1 American Indian/Alaska Native, 1 Asian American or Pacific Islander). Average age 27. 11 applicants, 100% accepted, 11 enrolled. In 2006, 12 degrees awarded. *Degree requirements:* For Ed S, thesis or alternative. *Entrance requirements:* For master's, MAT; for Ed S, MAT, NTE. Additional exam requirements/recommendations for international students: Required—TOEFL. *Application deadline:* For fall admission, 3/1 priority date for domestic students; for spring admission, 8/1 for domestic students. Application fee: $25 ($30 for international students). *Expenses:* Tuition, state resident: full-time $8,748; part-time $319 per hour. Tuition, nonresident: full-time $23,524; part-time $740 per hour. *Financial support:* In 2006–07, fellowships (averaging $8,000 per year), research assistantships (averaging $5,000 per year), 2 teaching assistantships (averaging $4,000 per year) were awarded; career-related internships or fieldwork also available. Financial award application deadline: 4/1. *Application contact:* Dr. Francis O. Otuonye, Associate Vice President for Research and Graduate Studies, 931-372-3233, Fax: 931-372-3497, E-mail: fotuonye@tntech.edu.

Texas A&M International University, Office of Graduate Studies and Research, Department of Professional Programs, Laredo, TX 78041-1900. Offers educational administration (MS Ed); generic special education (MS Ed); school counseling (MS). *Expenses:* Tuition, state resident: full-time $1,580. Tuition, nonresident: full-time $5,432. Required fees: $3,808. *Application contact:* Rosie Dickinson, Director of Admissions, 956-326-2200.

Texas A&M University, College of Education and Human Development, Department of Educational Psychology, College Station, TX 77843. Offers counseling psychology (PhD); educational psychology (PhD); educational technology (M Ed); gifted and talented education (M Ed, MS); Hispanic bilingual education (M Ed, PhD); human learning and development (MS); intelligence, creativity, and giftedness (PhD); learning, development, and instruction (PhD); research, measurement and statistics (MS); research, measurement, and statistics (PhD); school counseling (M Ed); school psychology (PhD); special education (M Ed, PhD). *Accreditation:* APA (one or more programs are accredited); NCATE. Part-time and evening/weekend programs available. Postbaccalaureate distance learning degree programs offered (no on-campus study). *Faculty:* 25 full-time (11 women), 5 part-time/adjunct (2 women). *Students:* 156 full-time (123 women), 109 part-time (89 women); includes 66 minority (20 African Americans, 1 American Indian/Alaska Native, 7 Asian Americans or Pacific Islanders, 38 Hispanic Americans), 36 international. 159 applicants, 52% accepted, 51 enrolled. In 2006, 59 master's, 21 doctorates awarded. *Median time to degree:* Of those who began their doctoral program in fall 1998, 89% received their degree in 8 years or less. *Degree requirements:* For master's, thesis optional; for doctorate, thesis/dissertation. *Entrance requirements:* For master's and doctorate, GRE General Test. Additional exam requirements/recommendations for international students: Required—TOEFL. Application fee: $50 ($75 for international students). Electronic applications accepted. *Expenses:* Tuition, state resident: full-time $4,697. Tuition, nonresident: full-time $11,297. Required fees: $2,272. *Financial support:* In 2006–07, fellowships (averaging $12,000 per year), research assistantships (averaging $9,000 per year), teaching assistantships (averaging $9,000 per year) were awarded; career-related internships or fieldwork, institutionally sponsored loans, scholarships/grants, and unspecified assistantships also available. Financial award applicants required to submit FAFSA. *Unit head:* Dr. Michael R. Benz, Head, 979-845-1394, Fax: 979-862-1256, E-mail: mbanz@tamu.edu. *Application contact:* Carol A. Wagner, Director of Advising, 979-845-1833, Fax: 979-862-1256, E-mail: c-wagner@tamu.edu.

Texas A&M University–Commerce, Graduate School, College of Education and Human Services, Department of Psychology and Special Education, Commerce, TX 75429-3011. Offers educational psychology (PhD); psychology (MA, MS); special education (M Ed, MA, MS). Part-time programs available. Terminal master's awarded for partial completion of doctoral program. *Degree requirements:* For master's, thesis (for some programs), comprehensive exam; for doctorate, thesis/dissertation, departmental qualifying exam. *Entrance requirements:* For master's, GRE General Test; for doctorate, GRE General Test, 3 letters of recommendation. Electronic applications accepted. *Faculty research:* Human learning, study skills, multicultural bilingual, diversity and special education, educationally handicapped.

Texas A&M University–Corpus Christi, Graduate Studies and Research, College of Education, Program in Special Education, Corpus Christi, TX 78412-5503. Offers MS. Part-time and evening/weekend programs available. *Degree requirements:* For master's, thesis (for some programs), comprehensive exam, registration. *Entrance requirements:* For master's, GRE General Test. Additional exam requirements/recommendations for international students: Required—TOEFL. Electronic applications accepted.

Texas A&M University–Kingsville, College of Graduate Studies, College of Education, Department of Education, Program in Special Education, Kingsville, TX 78363. Offers M Ed. Part-time and evening/weekend programs available. *Degree requirements:* For master's, mini-thesis. *Entrance requirements:* For master's, GRE General Test, MAT, minimum GPA of 3.0. *Faculty research:* Training for trainers of the disabled.

Texas A&M University–Texarkana, Graduate Studies and Research, College of Arts and Sciences and Education, Texarkana, TX 75505-5518. Offers adult education (MS); curriculum and instruction (MS); education (MS); educational administration (M Ed); English (MA); history (MS); instructional technology (MS); interdisciplinary studies (MA, MS); special education (M Ed, MS). Part-time and evening/weekend programs available. *Students:* 285. Average age 32. 41 applicants, 76% accepted. In 2006, 51 degrees awarded. *Degree requirements:* For master's, thesis optional. *Entrance requirements:* For master's, minimum GPA of 2.5 on last 60 hours of bachelor's degree. Additional exam requirements/recommendations for international students: Required—TOEFL. *Application deadline:* For fall admission, 7/15 priority date for domestic students; for spring admission, 12/1 priority date for domestic students. Applications are processed on a rolling basis. Application fee: $0 ($25 for international students). Electronic applications accepted. *Expenses:* Tuition, state resident: part-time $112 per credit hour. Tuition, nonresident: part-time $387 per credit hour. Required fees: $8 per credit hour. $8 per term. *Financial support:* Career-related internships or fieldwork and scholarships/grants available. Financial award applicants required to submit FAFSA. *Unit head:* Dr. Rosannce Stripling, Dean, 903-223-3073, E-mail: rosanne.stripling@tamut.edu. *Application contact:* Patricia E. Black, Director of Admissions and Registrar, 903-223-3068, Fax: 903-223-3140, E-mail: pat.black@tamut.edu.

Texas Christian University, School of Education, Program in Special Education, Fort Worth, TX 76129-0002. Offers M Ed. Part-time and evening/weekend programs available. *Degree requirements:* For master's, thesis optional. *Entrance requirements:* Additional exam requirements/recommendations for international students: Required—TOEFL. *Application deadline:* For fall admission, 3/1 for domestic students; for spring admission, 12/1 for domestic students. Applications are processed on a rolling basis. Application fee: $0. *Expenses:* Tuition: Part-time $800 per credit hour. *Financial support:* Career-related internships or fieldwork and unspecified assistantships available. Financial award application deadline: 3/1. *Application contact:* Dr. Sherrie Reynolds, Director of Graduate Studies, 817-257-7664, E-mail: s.reynolds@tcu.edu.

Texas Southern University, Graduate School, College of Education, Area of Curriculum and Instruction, Houston, TX 77004-4584. Offers bilingual education (M Ed); curriculum, instruction, and urban education (Ed D); early childhood education (M Ed); elementary education (M Ed); reading education (M Ed); secondary education (M Ed); special education (M Ed). Part-time and evening/weekend programs available. *Faculty:* 8 full-time (6 women), 1 part-time/adjunct (0 women). *Students:* 41 full-time (36 women), 43 part-time (38 women); includes 82 minority (77 African Americans, 2 Asian Americans or Pacific Islanders, 3 Hispanic Americans). Average age 36. 34 applicants, 82% accepted, 24 enrolled. In 2006, 6 master's, 13 doctorates awarded. *Degree requirements:* For master's, comprehensive exam; for doctorate, thesis/dissertation, comprehensive exam. *Entrance requirements:* For master's, GRE General Test, minimum GPA of 2.5; for doctorate, GRE General Test or MAT, master's degree, minimum B+ average. Additional exam requirements/recommendations for international students: Required—TOEFL. *Application deadline:* For fall admission, 7/15 priority date for domestic students. Applications are processed on a rolling basis. Application fee: $50 ($75 for international students). *Financial support:* Federal Work-Study and institutionally sponsored loans available. Financial award application deadline: 5/1. *Unit head:* Dr. Cherry Gooden, Chair, 713-313-7496, Fax: 713-313-7496, E-mail: gooden_cr@tsu.edu.

Texas State University-San Marcos, Graduate School, College of Education, Department of Curriculum and Instruction, Program in Special Education, San Marcos, TX 78666. Offers M Ed. Part-time programs available. *Faculty:* 3 full-time (2 women), 3 part-time/adjunct (all women). *Students:* 14 full-time (13 women), 48 part-time (42 women); includes 10 minority (5 African Americans, 1 American Indian/Alaska Native, 4 Hispanic Americans), 2 international. Average age 34. 6 applicants, 100% accepted, 0 enrolled. In 2006, 26 degrees awarded. *Degree requirements:* For master's, comprehensive exam. *Entrance requirements:* For master's, GRE General Test, minimum GPA of 2.75 in last 60 hour of course work, teaching experience. Additional exam requirements/recommendations for international students: Required—TOEFL. *Application deadline:* For fall admission, 6/15 priority date for domestic students; for spring admission, 10/15 priority date for domestic students. Applications are processed on a rolling basis. Application fee: $40 ($90 for international students). *Financial support:* In 2006–07, 40 students received support, including 1 research assistantship (averaging $6,768 per year); fellowships, teaching assistantships, career-related internships or fieldwork, Federal Work-Study, and institutionally sponsored loans also available. Support available to part-time students. Financial award application deadline: 4/1; financial award applicants required to submit FAFSA. *Faculty research:* Educational diagnostics; generic, severely handicapped, emotionally disturbed, and autistic education. *Unit head:* Dr. Larry J. Wheeler, Graduate Adviser, 512-245-2037, Fax: 512-245-7911, E-mail: lw06@txstate.edu.

Texas Tech University, Graduate School, College of Education, Department of Educational Psychology and Leadership, Lubbock, TX 79409. Offers counselor (Certificate); counselor education (M Ed, PhD); education diagnostician (Certificate); educational leadership (M Ed, Ed D); educational psychology (M Ed, PhD); gifted and talented (Certificate); higher education (M Ed, Ed D, PhD); information processing technologist (Certificate); instructional technology (M Ed, Ed D); principal (Certificate); special education (M Ed, Ed D); special education counselor (Certificate); superintendent (Certificate); visually handicapped (Certificate). *Accreditation:* ACA; NCATE. Part-time programs available. *Students:* 128 full-time (88 women), 321 part-time (233 women); includes 67 minority (23 African Americans, 1 American Indian/Alaska Native, 5 Asian Americans or Pacific Islanders, 38 Hispanic Americans), 22 international. Average age 38. 347 applicants, 49% accepted, 61 enrolled. In 2006, 110 master's, 16 doctorates awarded. *Degree requirements:* For master's, thesis optional; for doctorate, thesis/dissertation. *Entrance requirements:* For master's and doctorate, GRE General Test. Additional exam requirements/recommendations for international students: Required—TOEFL (minimum score 550 paper-based; 213 computer-based). *Application deadline:* For fall admission, 3/1 priority date for international students; for spring admission, 11/1 priority date for international

Special Education

Texas Tech University (continued)
students. Applications are processed on a rolling basis. Application fee: $50 ($60 for international students). Electronic applications accepted. *Expenses:* Tuition, state resident: full-time $4,440. Tuition, nonresident: full-time $11,040. Required fees: $2,136. *Financial support:* In 2006–07, 242 students received support; research assistantships with partial tuition reimbursements available, teaching assistantships with partial tuition reimbursements available, career-related internships or fieldwork, Federal Work-Study, and institutionally sponsored loans available. Support available to part-time students. Financial award application deadline: 4/15; financial award applicants required to submit FAFSA. *Faculty research:* Psychological processes of teaching and learning, teaching populations with special needs, instructional technology, educational administration in education, theories and practice in counseling and counselor education K-12 and higher. *Unit head:* Dr. Fred Hartmeister, Chair, 806-742-1998 Ext. 436, Fax: 806-742-2179, E-mail: fred.hartmeister@ttu.edu. *Application contact:* Graduate Adviser, 806-742-1998, Fax: 806-742-2179.

Texas Woman's University, Graduate School, College of Professional Education, Department of Teacher Education, Denton, TX 76201. Offers education administration (M Ed, MA); elementary education (M Ed, MA); special education (M Ed, MA, PhD), including educational diagnostician (M Ed, MA), mental retardation (M Ed, MA), physically handicapped (M Ed, MA); teaching (MAT). Part-time programs available. *Students:* 45 full-time (30 women), 226 part-time (194 women); includes 95 minority (53 African Americans, 1 American Indian/Alaska Native, 5 Asian Americans or Pacific Islanders, 36 Hispanic Americans), 11 international. Average age 37. In 2006, 106 master's, 6 doctorates awarded. Terminal master's awarded for partial completion of doctoral program. *Degree requirements:* For master's, professional paper (M Ed); for doctorate, thesis/dissertation, comprehensive exam. *Entrance requirements:* For master's, 3 letters of reference, curriculum vitae, copy of certifications, Teacher Service Record; for doctorate, minimum graduate GPA of 3.5, 3 reference letters, resumé, copy of certifications, Teacher Service Record. Additional exam requirements/recommendations for international students: Required—TOEFL (minimum score 550 paper-based; 213 computer-based; 79 iBT). *Application deadline:* For fall admission, 4/1 for international students; for spring admission, 8/1 for international students. Applications are processed on a rolling basis. Application fee: $30 ($50 for international students). Electronic applications accepted. *Expenses:* Tuition, area resident: Part-time $168 per unit. Tuition, state resident: full-time $4,369. Tuition, nonresident: full-time $9,373; part-time $443 per unit. Required fees: $20 per unit. $177 per term. *Financial support:* In 2006–07, 3 research assistantships (averaging $10,206 per year), teaching assistantships (averaging $10,206 per year) were awarded; career-related internships or fieldwork, Federal Work-Study, institutionally sponsored loans, scholarships/grants, traineeships, health care benefits, tuition waivers (partial), and unspecified assistantships also available. Support available to part-time students. Financial award application deadline: 3/1; financial award applicants required to submit FAFSA. *Faculty research:* Classroom management, learning disabilities, staff and professional development, leadership assessment. *Application contact:* Samuel Wheeler, Coordinator of Graduate Admissions, 940-898-3188, Fax: 940-898-3081, E-mail: wheelersr@twu.edu.

Towson University, Graduate School, Program in Special Education, Towson, MD 21252-0001. Offers special education certification (M Ed); special education leadership (M Ed). *Accreditation:* NCATE. Part-time and evening/weekend programs available. *Faculty:* 1 (woman) full-time, 8 part-time/adjunct (6 women). *Students:* 8 full-time (7 women), 84 part-time (70 women); includes 7 minority (5 African Americans, 1 Asian American or Pacific Islander, 1 Hispanic American), 2 international. 36 applicants, 61% accepted, 18 enrolled. In 2006, 8 degrees awarded. *Degree requirements:* For master's, thesis optional. *Entrance requirements:* For master's, letter of recommendation, professional teacher certification, minimum GPA of 3.0. Additional exam requirements/recommendations for international students: Required—TOEFL (minimum score 550 paper-based). *Application deadline:* For fall admission, 2/15 priority date for domestic and international students; for spring admission, 10/15 priority date for domestic and international students. Applications are processed on a rolling basis. Application fee: $50. Electronic applications accepted. *Expenses:* Tuition, state resident: part-time $275 per unit. Tuition, nonresident: part-time $577 per unit. Required fees: $72 per unit. *Financial support:* Career-related internships or fieldwork available. *Faculty research:* Parent involvement, transition to adulthood, cultural diversity in special education. *Unit head:* Dr. Claudia Carlson, Graduate Program Director, 410-704-6001, Fax: 410-704-2733, E-mail: ccarlson@towson.edu. *Application contact:* 410-704-2501, Fax: 410-704-4675, E-mail: grads@towson.edu.

Trinity Baptist College, Graduate Programs, Jacksonville, FL 32221. Offers Bible (M Ed); Christian school administration (M Ed); classroom practices (M Ed); ministry (M Min); special education (M Ed). Postbaccalaureate distance learning degree programs offered. *Faculty:* 10. *Entrance requirements:* For master's, GRE (M Ed), 2 letters of recommendation; minimum GPA of 2.5 (M Min) or 3.0 (M Ed); computer proficiency.

Trinity (Washington) University, School of Education, Washington, DC 20017-1094. Offers democracy, diversity, and social justice (M Ed); early childhood (MAT); educational administration (MSA); elementary education (MAT); English as a second language (M Ed, MAT); literacy and reading education (M Ed); school counseling (MA); secondary education (MAT), including English, math, science, social studies; special education (MAT). *Accreditation:* NCATE. Part-time and evening/weekend programs available. *Degree requirements:* For master's, thesis (for some programs), capstone project(s). *Entrance requirements:* For master's, PRAXIS I, minimum GPA of 2.8. Additional exam requirements/recommendations for international students: Required—TOEFL (minimum score 550 paper-based; 213 computer-based). *Faculty research:* Technology, literacy, special education, organizations, inclusion models.

Union College, Graduate Programs, Department of Education, Program in Special Education, Barbourville, KY 40906-1499. Offers MA. *Degree requirements:* For master's, thesis optional. *Entrance requirements:* For master's, GRE General Test, NTE.

Universidad del Turabo, Graduate Programs, Programs in Education, Program in Special Education, Gurabo, PR 00778-3030. Offers MA. *Entrance requirements:* For master's, GRE, EXADEP, interview.

Universidad Metropolitana, Graduate Programs in Education, Program in Special Education, San Juan, PR 00928-1150. Offers MA. *Degree requirements:* For master's, thesis or alternative. Electronic applications accepted.

Université de Sherbrooke, Faculty of Education, Program in Special Education, Sherbrooke, QC J1K 2R1, Canada. Offers M Ed, Diploma. Part-time and evening/weekend programs available. *Degree requirements:* For master's, thesis.

University at Albany, State University of New York, School of Education, Department of Educational and Counseling Psychology, Program in Special Education, Albany, NY 12222-0001. Offers MS. *Entrance requirements:* Additional exam requirements/recommendations for international students: Required—TOEFL (minimum score 550 paper-based; 213 computer-based). *Application deadline:* For fall admission, 3/1 for domestic students, 5/1 for international students. Applications are processed on a rolling basis. Application fee: $75. Electronic applications accepted. *Expenses:* Tuition, state resident: full-time $6,900; part-time $288 per credit. Tuition, nonresident: full-time $10,920; part-time $455 per credit. Required fees: $1,139. *Financial support:* Fellowships, career-related internships or fieldwork available. *Unit head:* Deborah May, Program Director, 516-442-5074.

University at Buffalo, the State University of New York, Graduate School, Graduate School of Education, Department of Learning and Instruction, Buffalo, NY 14260. Offers adolescence education (Certificate); biology (Ed M); chemistry (Ed M); childhood education (Ed M); early childhood and childhood education with bilingual extension (Ed M); early childhood education (Ed M); earth science (Ed M); elementary education (Ed D, PhD); English (Ed M); English education (PhD); English for speakers of other languages (Ed M); foreign and second language education (PhD); French (Ed M); general education (Ed M); German (Ed M); Italian (Ed M); Japanese (Ed M); Latin (Ed M); literary specialist (Ed M); mathematics (Ed M); mathematics education (PhD); mentoring teachers (Certificate); music education (Ed M, Certificate); physics (Ed M); reading education (PhD); Russian (Ed M); school administrator and supervisor (Certificate); science education (PhD); social studies (Ed M); Spanish (Ed M); special education (PhD); teaching and leading for diversity (Certificate); teaching English to speakers of other languages (Ed M). Part-time and evening/weekend programs available. Postbaccalaureate distance learning degree programs offered (no on-campus study). *Faculty:* 30 full-time (20 women), 53 part-time/adjunct (38 women). *Students:* 368 full-time (269 women), 297 part-time (226 women); includes 50 minority (15 African Americans, 2 American Indian/Alaska Native, 14 Asian Americans or Pacific Islanders, 19 Hispanic Americans), 66 international. Average age 31. 638 applicants, 75% accepted, 298 enrolled. In 2006, 248 master's, 18 doctorates, 48 other advanced degrees awarded. Terminal master's awarded for partial completion of doctoral program. *Degree requirements:* For master's, comprehensive exam, registration; for doctorate, thesis/dissertation, research analysis exam, research experience component. *Entrance requirements:* For doctorate, GRE General Test or MAT, interview, writing sample, letters of recommendation. Additional exam requirements/recommendations for international students: Required—TOEFL (minimum score 600 paper-based; 250 computer-based). *Application deadline:* For fall admission, 2/1 priority date for domestic and international students; for spring admission, 11/15 priority date for domestic students, 10/1 for international students. Applications are processed on a rolling basis. Application fee: $50. Electronic applications accepted. *Financial support:* In 2006–07, 70 students received support, including 6 fellowships with full tuition reimbursements available (averaging $10,000 per year), 16 research assistantships with full tuition reimbursements available (averaging $9,000 per year), teaching assistantships with full tuition reimbursements available (averaging $9,000 per year); career-related internships or fieldwork, Federal Work-Study, institutionally sponsored loans, scholarships/grants, tuition waivers (partial), and unspecified assistantships also available. Financial award application deadline: 2/28; financial award applicants required to submit FAFSA. *Faculty research:* Science assessment, state-level testing, early learning, literacy, second language acquisition. Total annual research expenditures: $432,366. *Unit head:* Dr. Maria E. Runfola, Chair, 716-645-2455, Fax: 716-645-3161. *Application contact:* Barbara Belz, Admissions Secretary, 716-645-2110 Ext. 1159, Fax: 716-645-3161, E-mail: belz@buffalo.edu.

The University of Akron, Graduate School, College of Education, Department of Curricular and Instructional Studies, Program in Special Education, Akron, OH 44325. Offers MA, MS. *Accreditation:* NCATE. *Students:* 6 full-time (5 women), 35 part-time (30 women); includes 1 minority (African American) Average age 28. 52 applicants, 56% accepted, 23 enrolled. In 2006, 3 degrees awarded. *Degree requirements:* For master's, comprehensive exam. *Entrance requirements:* For master's, minimum GPA of 2.75, letters of recommendation. Additional exam requirements/recommendations for international students: Required—TOEFL (minimum score 550 paper-based; 213 computer-based; 79 iBT). *Application deadline:* For fall admission, 8/15 for domestic students. Applications are processed on a rolling basis. Application fee: $30 ($40 for international students). Electronic applications accepted. *Expenses:* Tuition, state resident: full-time $6,164; part-time $342 per credit. Tuition, nonresident: full-time $10,575; part-time $588 per credit. Required fees: $806; $43 per credit. $12 per term. Tuition and fees vary according to course load, degree level and program. *Financial support:* Fellowships, research assistantships, teaching assistantships, career-related internships or fieldwork and unspecified assistantships available.

The University of Alabama, Graduate School, College of Education, Department of Special Education and Multiple Abilities, Tuscaloosa, AL 35487. Offers collaborative teacher program (M Ed, Ed S); early intervention (M Ed, Ed S); gifted education (M Ed, Ed S); multiple abilities program (M Ed); special education (Ed D, PhD). Part-time and evening/weekend programs available. *Faculty:* 10 full-time (8 women). *Students:* 14 full-time (all women), 25 part-time (23 women); includes 2 minority (1 African American, 1 American Indian/Alaska Native). Average age 34. 24 applicants, 54% accepted, 10 enrolled. In 2006, 14 master's, 2 doctorates, 4 Ed Ss awarded. Terminal master's awarded for partial completion of doctoral program. *Degree requirements:* For master's, thesis optional; for doctorate, one foreign language, thesis/dissertation, comprehensive exam, registration. *Entrance requirements:* For master's, GRE or MAT, minimum undergraduate GPA of 3.0, teaching certificate, 3 letters of recommendation; for doctorate, GRE or MAT, 3 years of teaching experience, minimum undergraduate GPA of 3.25. Additional exam requirements/recommendations for international students: Required—TOEFL. *Application deadline:* For fall admission, 7/1 for domestic students; for spring admission, 11/1 for domestic students. Applications are processed on a rolling basis. Application fee: $25. Electronic applications accepted. *Financial support:* In 2006–07, 8 students received support, including 4 research assistantships with tuition reimbursements available (averaging $9,000 per year), 4 teaching assistantships with tuition reimbursements available (averaging $9,000 per year); health care benefits and unspecified assistantships also available. Financial award application deadline: 7/1; financial award applicants required to submit FAFSA. *Faculty research:* Gifted education; mild disabilities, early intervention, severe disabilities. *Unit head:* James A. Siders, Associate Professor and Head, 205-348-5577, Fax: 205-348-6782, E-mail: jsiders@bama.ua.edu. *Application contact:* April Zark, Office Support, 205-348-6093, Fax: 205-348-6782, E-mail: azark@bamaed.ua.edu.

The University of Alabama at Birmingham, School of Education, Department of Leadership, Special Education and Foundations, Program in Special Education, Birmingham, AL 35294. Offers MA Ed. *Accreditation:* NCATE. *Students:* 12 full-time (11 women), 50 part-time (37 women); includes 13 minority (12 African Americans, 1 American Indian/Alaska Native), 1 international. 12 applicants, 92% accepted. In 2006, 25 degrees awarded. *Degree requirements:* For master's, thesis optional. *Entrance requirements:* For master's, GRE General Test or NTE, minimum GPA of 3.0. *Application deadline:* Applications are processed on a rolling basis. Application fee: $35 ($60 for international students). Electronic applications accepted. *Expenses:* Tuition, state resident: part-time $170 per credit hour. Tuition, nonresident: part-time $425 per credit hour. Required fees: $15 per credit hour. $122 per term. Tuition and fees vary according to program. *Unit head:* Dr. William Boyd Rogan, Chair, Department of Leadership, Special Education and Foundations, 205-934-4892, Fax: 205-934-2317, E-mail: nrogan@uab.edu.

University of Alaska Anchorage, College of Education, Program in Special Education, Anchorage, AK 99508-8060. Offers early childhood special education (M Ed); special education (M Ed, Certificate). Part-time programs available. *Students:* 6 full-time (5 women), 26 part-time (24 women); includes 4 minority (2 American Indian/Alaska Native, 2 Asian Americans or Pacific Islanders), 1 international. 9 applicants, 56% accepted. In 2006, 16 degrees awarded. *Degree requirements:* For master's, thesis or alternative, comprehensive exam (for some programs), registration. *Entrance requirements:* For master's, GRE or MAT, interview, minimum GPA of 2.75. Additional exam requirements/recommendations for international students: Required—TOEFL (minimum score 550 paper-based; 213 computer-based). *Application deadline:* For fall admission, 3/15 for domestic students; for spring admission, 10/15 for domestic students. Application fee: $45. *Expenses:* Tuition, state resident: part-time $268 per credit. Tuition, nonresident: part-time $547 per credit. Required fees: $124 per semester. Tuition and fees vary according to reciprocity agreements and student level. *Financial support:* Career-related internships or fieldwork and Federal Work-Study available. Support available to part-time students. Financial award application deadline: 4/1; financial award applicants required to submit FAFSA. *Faculty research:* Mild disabilities, substance abuse issues for educators, partnerships to improve at-risk youth, analysis of planning models for teachers in special education. *Unit head:* Dr. Dean Konopasek, Chair, 907-786-4439, Fax: 907-786-4445, E-mail: dkonopasek@uaa.alaska.edu. *Application contact:* Jane Jordan, Graduate Programs Assistant, 907-786-4401, Fax: 907-786-4445, E-mail: anjmj@uaa.alaska.edu.

University of Alberta, Faculty of Graduate Studies and Research, Department of Educational Psychology, Edmonton, AB T6G 2E1, Canada. Offers counseling psychology (M Ed, PhD); educational psychology (M Ed, PhD); instructional technology (M Ed); school counseling (M Ed); school psychology (M Ed, PhD); special education (M Ed, PhD); special education-deafness studies (M Ed); teaching English as a second language (M Ed). Part-time programs available. *Faculty:* 34 full-time (14 women), 12 part-time/adjunct (6 women). *Students:* 117 full-time (93 women), 173 part-time (121 women), 15 international. Average age 36. 252 applicants, 34% accepted. In 2006, 30 master's, 10 doctorates awarded. *Degree requirements:* For master's, thesis optional; for doctorate, thesis/dissertation, comprehensive exam. *Entrance requirements:* For master's and doctorate, minimum GPA of 3.0. Additional exam requirements/recommendations for international students: Required—TOEFL. *Application deadline:* For fall admission, 2/1 priority date for domestic and international students. Applications are processed on a rolling basis. *Financial support:* In 2006–07, 10 fellowships with full tuition reimbursements (averaging $16,120 per year), 36 research assistantships with full tuition reimbursements (averaging $12,614 per year), 46 teaching assistantships with full tuition reimbursements (averaging $5,462 per year) were awarded; career-related internships or fieldwork and scholarships/grants also available. *Faculty research:* Human learning, development and assessment. *Unit head:* Dr. Linda M. McDonald, Chair, 780-492-1149, Fax: 780-492-1318, E-mail: linda.mcdonald@ualberta.ca. *Application contact:* Judy Maynes, Information Contact, 780-492-1149, Fax: 780-492-1318, E-mail: edpygrad@ualberta.ca.

The University of Arizona, Graduate College, College of Education, Department of Special Education, Rehabilitation and School Psychology, Tucson, AZ 85721. Offers M Ed, MA, MS, Ed D, PhD, Ed S. *Accreditation:* CORE. Part-time programs available. *Faculty:* 17 full-time (7 women), 19 part-time/adjunct (14 women). *Students:* 166 full-time (131 women), 119 part-time (98 women); includes 72 minority (10 African Americans, 13 American Indian/Alaska Native, 5 Asian Americans or Pacific Islanders, 44 Hispanic Americans), 16 international. Average age 37. 109 applicants, 59% accepted, 56 enrolled. In 2006, 82 master's, 10 doctorates, 12 other advanced degrees awarded. Terminal master's awarded for partial completion of doctoral program. *Degree requirements:* For master's, thesis optional; for doctorate, thesis/dissertation, comprehensive exam, registration. *Entrance requirements:* For doctorate, GRE General Test or MAT. Additional exam requirements/recommendations for international students: Required—TOEFL (minimum score 550 paper-based; 213 computer-based). *Application deadline:* For fall admission, 2/15 for domestic students, 2/1 for international students; for spring admission, 9/1 priority date for domestic students, 10/1 for international students. Applications are processed on a rolling basis. Application fee: $50. *Financial support:* In 2006–07, 83 students received support, including 11 fellowships with partial tuition reimbursements available (averaging $2,379 per year), 2 teaching assistantships with partial tuition reimbursements available (averaging $9,414 per year); research assistantships, career-related internships or fieldwork, institutionally sponsored loans, and tuition waivers (full) also available. Financial award applicants required to submit FAFSA. *Faculty research:* Teacher assistant teams, self-advocacy, language development in preschool, the deaf, comprehension of the learning disabled. *Unit head:* Dr. Lawrence M. Aleamoni, Head, 520-621-7822, Fax: 520-621-3821. *Application contact:* Cecilia Carlon, Coordinator, 520-621-7822, Fax: 520-621-3821, E-mail: sergrad@mail.ed.arizona.edu.

University of Arkansas, Graduate School, College of Education and Health Professions, Department of Curriculum and Instruction, Program in Special Education, Fayetteville, AR 72701-1201. Offers M Ed, MAT. *Accreditation:* NCATE. Part-time and evening/weekend programs available. Postbaccalaureate distance learning degree programs offered (no on-campus study). *Students:* 10 full-time (all women), 41 part-time (39 women); includes 8 minority (all African Americans) 17 applicants, 82% accepted. In 2006, 12 degrees awarded. *Entrance requirements:* For master's, GRE General Test or MAT. Application fee: $40 ($50 for international students). *Financial support:* In 2006–07, 1 fellowship was awarded; research assistantships, teaching assistantships, career-related internships or fieldwork and Federal Work-Study also available. Support available to part-time students. Financial award application deadline: 4/1; financial award applicants required to submit FAFSA. *Unit head:* Unit Head, 479-575-3548.

University of Arkansas at Little Rock, Graduate School, College of Education, Department of Counseling and Rehabilitation Education, Little Rock, AR 72204-1099. Offers adult education (M Ed); counseling rehabilitation (MA); counselor education (M Ed), including school counseling; rehabilitation of the blind (MA), including orientation and mobility, rehabilitation teaching. *Accreditation:* CORE; NCATE. Part-time programs available. *Entrance requirements:* For master's, interview, minimum GPA of 2.75. *Faculty research:* Low vision, orientation and mobility instruction.

University of Arkansas at Little Rock, Graduate School, College of Education, Department of Teacher Education, Program in Special Education, Little Rock, AR 72204-1099. Offers early childhood special education (M Ed); teaching deaf and hard of hearing (M Ed); teaching of the mildly disabled student (M Ed); teaching persons with severe disabilities (M Ed); teaching the visually impaired (M Ed). *Accreditation:* NCATE. Part-time and evening/weekend programs available. *Degree requirements:* For master's, portfolio or thesis. *Entrance requirements:* For master's, interview, minimum GPA of 2.75, GRE General Test or teaching certificate.

The University of British Columbia, Faculty of Graduate Studies, Faculty of Education, Department of Educational and Counseling Psychology, and Special Education, Vancouver, BC V6T 1Z1, Canada. Offers counseling psychology (M Ed, MA, PhD); development, learning and culture (MA, PhD); guidance studies (Diploma); measurement and evaluation and research methodology (M Ed); measurement, evaluation and research methodology (MA); measurement, evaluation, and research methodology (PhD); school psychology (M Ed, MA, PhD); special education (M Ed, MA, PhD, Diploma). Part-time programs available. *Faculty:* 39 full-time (26 women). *Students:* 304 full-time (247 women), 82 part-time (77 women). 266 applicants, 39% accepted. In 2006, 100 master's, 10 doctorates awarded. *Median time to degree:* Of those who began their doctoral program in fall 1998, 95% received their degree in 8 years or less. *Degree requirements:* For master's, thesis (for some programs), registration; for doctorate, thesis/dissertation, comprehensive exam, registration. *Entrance requirements:* For master's, GRE General Test (counseling psychology MA); for doctorate, GRE General Test. Additional exam requirements/recommendations for international students: Required—TOEFL. *Application deadline:* For fall admission, 12/1 for domestic and international students. Application fee: $90 Canadian dollars ($150 Canadian dollars for international students). Electronic applications accepted. *Financial support:* In 2006–07, 20 fellowships (averaging $19,000 per year), 50 research assistantships (averaging $12,000 per year), 30 teaching assistantships (averaging $5,000 per year) were awarded; career-related internships or fieldwork, Federal Work-Study, institutionally sponsored loans, scholarships/grants, health care benefits, tuition waivers (full and partial), and unspecified assistantships also available. *Faculty research:* Women, family, social problems, career transition, stress and coping problems. *Unit head:* Dr. Sandra Mathison, Head, 604-822-6352, Fax: 604-822-3302, E-mail: sandra.mathison@ubc.ca. *Application contact:* Lynda McDicken, Graduate Admissions, 604-822-5351, Fax: 604-822-3302, E-mail: lynda.mcdicken@ubc.ca.

University of Calgary, Faculty of Graduate Studies, Faculty of Education, Division of Applied Psychology, Calgary, AB T2N 1N4, Canada. Offers counseling psychology (M Ed, M Sc, PhD); human development and learning (M Ed, M Sc, PhD); school psychology (M Ed, M Sc, PhD); special education (M Ed, M Sc, PhD). Part-time programs available. *Faculty:* 16 full-time, 25 part-time/adjunct. *Students:* 130 full-time, 29 part-time. Average age 36. 117 applicants, 19% accepted. In 2006, 35 master's, 13 doctorates awarded. *Degree requirements:* For master's, thesis (for some programs), final oral exam; for doctorate, thesis/dissertation, candidacy exam, final oral exam. *Entrance requirements:* For master's, minimum GPA of 3.0, 3 letters of reference; for doctorate, minimum GPA of 3.5, 3 letters of reference. *Application deadline:* For winter admission, 2/1 for domestic students. Application fee: $60. *Financial support:* In 2006–07, research assistantships (averaging $3,920 per year), teaching assistantships (averaging $5,651 per year) were awarded; fellowships, scholarships/grants also available. Financial award application deadline: 2/1. *Faculty research:* Counselor education, family life studies, learning and cognition. *Unit head:* Dr. Vicki Schean, Associate Dean, 403-220-5651. *Application contact:* Dr. John Mueller, Graduate Coordinator, 403-220-5664, Fax: 403-282-9244, E-mail: mueller@ucalgary.ca.

University of California, Berkeley, Graduate Division, School of Education, Division of Cognition and Development, Program in Special Education, Berkeley, CA 94720-1500. Offers PhD. Applicants must apply to both the University of California, Berkeley and San Francisco State University. *Degree requirements:* For doctorate, thesis/dissertation, oral qualifying exam. *Entrance requirements:* For doctorate, GRE General Test, minimum undergraduate GPA of 3.0 during last 2 years. *Application deadline:* For fall admission, 12/1 for domestic students. Application fee: $60 ($80 for international students). Electronic applications accepted. *Financial support:* Fellowships, unspecified assistantships available. *Unit head:* Dr. P. David Pearson, Coordinator, 510-643-7974, E-mail: ppearson@socrates.berkeley.edu. *Application contact:* Admissions Office, 510-642-0841, Fax: 510-642-4808, E-mail: gse_info@berkeley.edu.

University of California, Los Angeles, Graduate Division, Graduate School of Education and Information Studies, Program in Special Education, Los Angeles, CA 90095. Offers PhD. *Degree requirements:* For doctorate, thesis/dissertation, oral and written qualifying exams. *Entrance requirements:* For doctorate, GRE General Test, MAT, or Doppelt Mathematical Reasoning Test, minimum undergraduate GPA of 3.0. Electronic applications accepted.

University of California, Santa Barbara, Graduate Division, Gevirtz Graduate School of Education, Santa Barbara, CA 93106. Offers counseling, clinical and school psychology (PhD), including clinical psychology, counseling psychology; education (M Ed, MA, PhD), including child and adolescent development (MA, PhD), cultural perspectives and comparative education (MA, PhD), educational leadership and organizations (MA, PhD), research methodology (MA, PhD), special education disabilities and risk studies (MA), special education, disabilities and risk studies (PhD), teaching and learning (MA, PhD); educational leadership (Ed D). *Accreditation:* APA (one or more programs are accredited). Postbaccalaureate distance learning degree programs offered (minimal on-campus study). *Faculty:* 39 full-time (18 women). *Students:* 375 full-time (285 women); includes 111 minority (13 African Americans, 2 American Indian/Alaska Native, 33 Asian Americans or Pacific Islanders, 63 Hispanic Americans), 14 international. Average age 29. 777 applicants, 36% accepted, 154 enrolled. In 2006, 151 master's, 31 doctorates awarded. Terminal master's awarded for partial completion of doctoral program. *Median time to degree:* Master's–1.5 years full-time; doctorate–5.5 years full-time. *Degree requirements:* For master's, thesis optional; for doctorate, thesis/dissertation, qualifying exam, comprehensive exam (for some programs), registration; for degree. *Entrance requirements:* For master's, GRE, MAT (M Ed); for doctorate, GRE. Additional exam requirements/recommendations for international students: Required—TOEFL (minimum score 550 paper-based; 213 computer-based; 80 iBT). *Application deadline:* For fall admission, 12/15 for domestic and international students. Application fee: $60. Electronic applications accepted. *Financial support:* In 2006–07, 181 fellowships with full and partial tuition reimbursements (averaging $4,200 per year), 64 research assistantships with full and partial tuition reimbursements (averaging $6,200 per year), 75 teaching assistantships with partial tuition reimbursements (averaging $7,500 per year) were awarded; career-related internships or fieldwork, Federal Work-Study, institutionally sponsored loans, scholarships/grants, traineeships, health care benefits, and unspecified assistantships also available. Support available to part-time students. Financial award application deadline: 12/15; financial award applicants required to submit FAFSA. Total annual research expenditures: $4 million. *Unit head:* Dr. Jane Conoley, Chair, 805-893-3917, E-mail: jane_conoley@education.ucsb.edu. *Application contact:* Student Affairs Office, 805-893-2137, E-mail: sao@education.ucsb.edu.

University of Central Arkansas, Graduate School, College of Education, Department of Early Childhood and Special Education, Program in Special Education, Conway, AR 72035-0001. Offers collaborative instructional specialist (ages 0–8) (MSE); collaborative instructional specialist (grades 4–12) (MSE). *Accreditation:* NCATE. *Students:* 3 full-time (all women), 64 part-time (59 women); includes 2 minority (1 African American, 1 Hispanic American). 36 applicants, 97% accepted, 35 enrolled. In 2006, 9 degrees awarded. *Degree requirements:* For master's, thesis optional. *Entrance requirements:* For master's, GRE General Test, minimum GPA of 2.7. Additional exam requirements/recommendations for international students: Required—TOEFL (minimum score 550 paper-based; 213 computer-based). *Application deadline:* For fall admission, 3/1 priority date for domestic and international students; for spring admission, 10/1 priority date for domestic and international students. Applications are processed on a rolling basis. Application fee: $25 ($40 for international students). *Expenses:* Tuition, state resident: full-time $4,194; part-time $233 per semester. Tuition, nonresident: full-time $5,963; part-time $429 per semester. International tuition: $6,162 full-time. Required fees: $65; $23 per semester. One-time fee: $65 part-time. *Financial support:* Federal Work-Study, scholarships/grants, tuition waivers (partial), and unspecified assistantships available. Financial award application deadline: 2/15; financial award applicants required to submit FAFSA. *Unit head:* Dr. David Naylor, Coordinator, 501-450-3171, Fax: 501-450-5457, E-mail: davidn@uca.edu. *Application contact:* Brenda Herring, Admissions Assistant, 501-450-5065, Fax: 501-450-5678, E-mail: bherring@uca.edu.

University of Central Florida, College of Education, Department of Child, Family and Community Sciences, Program in Exceptional Education, Orlando, FL 32816. Offers M Ed, MA. *Accreditation:* NCATE. Part-time and evening/weekend programs available. *Students:* 16 full-time (all women), 174 part-time (166 women); includes 36 minority (16 African Americans, 4 American Indian/Alaska Native, 5 Asian Americans or Pacific Islanders, 11 Hispanic Americans), 2 international. Average age 36. 57 applicants, 88% accepted, 38 enrolled. In 2006, 74 master's awarded. *Degree requirements:* For master's, thesis or alternative, research project. *Entrance requirements:* For master's, GRE General Test. Additional exam requirements/recommendations for international students: Required—TOEFL. *Application deadline:* For fall admission, 7/15 for domestic students; for spring admission, 12/1 for domestic students. Application fee: $30. Electronic applications accepted. *Expenses:* Tuition, state resident: full-time $6,167; part-time $257 per credit hour. Tuition, nonresident: full-time $22,790; part-time $950 per credit hour. *Financial support:* In 2006–07, 2 research assistantships with partial tuition reimbursements (averaging $4,200 per year) were awarded; fellowships with partial tuition reimbursements, teaching assistantships with partial tuition reimbursements, career-related internships or fieldwork, Federal Work-Study, institutionally sponsored loans, tuition waivers (partial), and unspecified assistantships also available. Financial award application deadline: 3/1; financial award applicants required to submit FAFSA. *Unit head:* Dr. Lee Cross, Coordinator, 407-823-5477, E-mail: lcross@mail.ucf.edu.

University of Central Florida, College of Education, Doctoral Program in Education, Orlando, FL 32816. Offers communication sciences and disorders (PhD); counselor education (PhD); curriculum and instruction (PhD); elementary education (PhD); exceptional education (PhD); hospitality education (PhD); instructional technology (PhD); mathematics education (PhD). *Students:* 86 full-time (63 women), 9 part-time (4 women); includes 21 minority (15 African Americans, 2 Asian Americans or Pacific Islanders, 4 Hispanic Americans), 19 international. Average age 39. In 2006, 16 degrees awarded. Application fee: $30. Electronic applications accepted. *Expenses:* Tuition, state resident: full-time $6,167; part-time $257 per credit hour. Tuition, nonresident: full-time $22,790; part-time $950 per credit hour. *Financial support:* In 2006–07, 44 fellowships with partial tuition reimbursements (averaging $3,700 per year), 54 research assistantships with partial tuition reimbursements (averaging $7,000 per year), 9 teaching assistantships with partial tuition reimbursements (averaging $7,000 per year) were awarded.

University of Central Missouri, The Graduate School, College of Education, Department of Educational Leadership and Human Development, Program in Special Education, Warrensburg, MO 64093. Offers special education (MSE); special education/human services (Ed S). *Accreditation:* NCATE. Part-time programs available. *Students:* 1 (woman) full-time, 38 part-time (35 women); includes 3 minority (all African Americans) Average age 41. 3 applicants, 33% accepted, 1 enrolled. In 2006, 8 degrees awarded. *Degree requirements:* For master's, thesis (for some programs), internship; for Ed S, thesis or alternative, internship. *Entrance requirements:* For master's, GRE General Test, written test, minimum GPA of 2.75, teaching certificate, professional evaluations; for Ed S, GRE General Test, master's or bachelor's degree in education, minimum GPA of 3.25. Additional exam requirements/recommendations for international students: Required—TOEFL (minimum score 500 paper-based; 173 computer-based). *Application*

Special Education

University of Central Missouri (continued)
deadline: For fall admission, 6/1 priority date for domestic students, 5/1 priority date for international students; for spring admission, 10/1 priority date for domestic students, 10/1 for international students. Applications are processed on a rolling basis. Application fee: $30 ($50 for international students). *Expenses:* Tuition, state resident: full-time $5,448; part-time $227 per credit hour. Tuition, nonresident: full-time $10,896; part-time $454 per credit hour. Required fees: $336; $14 per credit hour. *Financial support:* Career-related internships or fieldwork, Federal Work-Study, and scholarships/grants available. Support available to part-time students. Financial award application deadline: 3/1; financial award applicants required to submit FAFSA. *Faculty research:* Assistive technology; best practices in special education diagnosis/evaluation; autism; assessment of P-12 learning in public schools; teacher education assessments (portfolios). *Unit head:* Dr. Jerry Neal, Coordinator, 660-543-8497, Fax: 660-543-4164, E-mail: jwneal@ucmo.edu.

University of Central Oklahoma, College of Graduate Studies and Research, College of Education, Department of Curriculum and Instruction, Program in Special Education, Edmond, OK 73034-5209. Offers M Ed. *Accreditation:* NCATE. Part-time programs available. *Entrance requirements:* For master's, GRE General Test. Additional exam requirements/recommendations for international students: Required—TOEFL (minimum score 550 paper-based; 213 computer-based). Electronic applications accepted.

University of Cincinnati, Division of Research and Advanced Studies, College of Education, Criminal Justice, and Human Services, Division of Teacher Education, Program in Special Education, Cincinnati, OH 45221. Offers M Ed, Ed D. *Accreditation:* NCATE. Part-time programs available. *Students:* 57. *Degree requirements:* For master's, thesis or alternative; for doctorate, thesis/dissertation. *Entrance requirements:* For master's, GRE General Test; for doctorate, GRE General Test, GRE Subject Test. Additional exam requirements/recommendations for international students: Required—TOEFL (minimum score 550 paper-based; 213 computer-based), TWE (minimum score 4.5), OEPT. *Application deadline:* For fall admission, 2/1 for domestic students. Application fee: $40. Electronic applications accepted. *Financial support:* Fellowships, tuition waivers (partial) and unspecified assistantships available. *Application contact:* Dorothyann Feldis, Student Contact, 513-556-1104, Fax: 513-556-1001, E-mail: dorothyann.feldis@uc.edu.

University of Colorado at Colorado Springs, Graduate School, College of Education, Colorado Springs, CO 80933-7150. Offers counseling and human services (MA); curriculum and instruction (MA); educational administration (MA); educational leadership (MA, PhD); special education (MA). *Accreditation:* ACA; NCATE. Part-time and evening/weekend programs available. *Faculty:* 22 full-time (15 women), 29 part-time/adjunct (17 women). *Students:* 331 full-time (246 women), 173 part-time (135 women); includes 85 minority (26 African Americans, 4 American Indian/Alaska Native, 13 Asian Americans or Pacific Islanders, 42 Hispanic Americans). Average age 35. 107 applicants, 93% accepted, 49 enrolled. In 2006, 234 degrees awarded. *Degree requirements:* For master's, thesis or alternative, microcomputer proficiency, comprehensive exam; for doctorate, doctoral research lab requirement. *Entrance requirements:* For master's, GRE General Test, MAT. *Application deadline:* For fall admission, 6/15 for domestic students; for spring admission, 10/15 for domestic students. Applications are processed on a rolling basis. Application fee: $60 ($75 for international students). *Expenses:* Tuition, state resident: part-time $303 per credit hour. Tuition, nonresident: part-time $840 per credit hour. Tuition and fees vary according to course load, campus/location and program. *Financial support:* Fellowships, career-related internships or fieldwork and Federal Work-Study available. *Faculty research:* Job training for special populations, materials development for classroom. Total annual research expenditures: $961,803. *Unit head:* Dr. LaVonne Neal, Dean, 719-262-4111, Fax: 719-262-4110, E-mail: lneal@uccs.edu. *Application contact:* Connie Wroten, Professional Assistant, 719-262-4102, Fax: 719-262-4110, E-mail: cwroten@uccs.edu.

University of Connecticut, Graduate School, Neag School of Education, Department of Educational Psychology, Storrs, CT 06269. Offers educational psychology (MA, PhD), including cognition and instruction, counseling psychology, gifted and talented education, learning technology, measurement, evaluation, and assessment, school psychology, special education. *Faculty:* 34 full-time (16 women). *Students:* 154 full-time (127 women), 147 part-time (114 women); includes 35 minority (15 African Americans, 2 American Indian/Alaska Native, 7 Asian Americans or Pacific Islanders, 11 Hispanic Americans), 20 international. Average age 34. 331 applicants, 48% accepted, 139 enrolled. In 2006, 115 master's, 20 doctorates awarded. *Degree requirements:* For master's, comprehensive exam; for doctorate, thesis/dissertation. *Entrance requirements:* For doctorate, GRE General Test. Additional exam requirements/recommendations for international students: Required—TOEFL (minimum score 550 paper-based; 213 computer-based). *Application deadline:* For fall admission, 2/1 priority date for domestic and international students; for spring admission, 11/1 for domestic students, 10/1 for international students. Applications are processed on a rolling basis. Application fee: $55. Electronic applications accepted. *Financial support:* In 2006–07, 87 research assistantships with full tuition reimbursements, 1 teaching assistantship with full tuition reimbursement were awarded; fellowships, Federal Work-Study, scholarships/grants, health care benefits, and unspecified assistantships also available. Financial award application deadline: 2/1; financial award applicants required to submit FAFSA. *Unit head:* Sally Reis, Head, 860-486-4031, Fax: 860-486-0210. *Application contact:* Lisa Rasicot, Graduate Coordinator, 860-486-3065, Fax: 860-486-0210, E-mail: soeadm02@uconnvm.uconn.edu.

University of Connecticut, Graduate School, Neag School of Education, Department of Educational Psychology, Field of Educational Psychology, Program in Special Education, Storrs, CT 06269. Offers MA, PhD. *Accreditation:* NCATE. *Faculty:* 16 full-time (7 women). *Students:* 29 full-time (26 women), 17 part-time (12 women); includes 6 minority (4 African Americans, 1 American Indian/Alaska Native, 1 Asian American or Pacific Islander), 1 international. Average age 33. 39 applicants, 69% accepted, 24 enrolled. In 2006, 28 master's, 5 doctorates awarded. Terminal master's awarded for partial completion of doctoral program. *Degree requirements:* For master's, thesis or alternative, comprehensive exam; for doctorate, thesis/dissertation. *Entrance requirements:* For doctorate, GRE General Test. Additional exam requirements/recommendations for international students: Required—TOEFL (minimum score 550 paper-based; 213 computer-based). *Application deadline:* For fall admission, 2/1 priority date for domestic and international students; for spring admission, 11/1 for domestic students, 10/1 for international students. Applications are processed on a rolling basis. Application fee: $55. Electronic applications accepted. *Financial support:* Fellowships, research assistantships with full tuition reimbursements, teaching assistantships with full tuition reimbursements, Federal Work-Study, scholarships/grants, health care benefits, and unspecified assistantships available. Financial award application deadline: 2/1; financial award applicants required to submit FAFSA. *Application contact:* Lisa Rasicot, Graduate Coordinator, 860-486-3065, Fax: 860-486-0210, E-mail: soeadm02@uconnvm.uconn.edu.

University of Dayton, Graduate School, School of Education and Allied Professions, Department of Teacher Education, Dayton, OH 45469-1300. Offers adolescent/young adult (MS Ed); art education (MS Ed); early childhood education (MS Ed); inclusive early childhood (MS Ed); interdisciplinary education (MS Ed); intervention specialist education, mild/moderate (MS Ed); literacy (MS Ed); middle childhood (MS Ed); multi-age education (MS Ed); music education (MS Ed); teacher as leader (MS Ed); technology in education (MS Ed). Part-time and evening/weekend programs available. *Faculty:* 13 full-time (9 women), 33 part-time/adjunct (25 women). *Students:* 149 full-time (120 women), 284 part-time (241 women); includes 37 minority (31 African Americans, 3 Asian Americans or Pacific Islanders, 3 Hispanic Americans), 3 international. Average age 33. 201 applicants, 58% accepted, 31 enrolled. In 2006, 150 degrees awarded. *Degree requirements:* For master's, thesis, capstone research project. *Entrance requirements:* For master's, GRE General Test, minimum GPA of 2.75. Additional exam requirements/recommendations for international students: Required—TOEFL (minimum score 550 paper-based; 213 computer-based). *Application deadline:* For fall admission, 3/15 priority date for domestic students, 3/1 priority date for international students. Applications are processed on a rolling basis. Application fee: $0. Electronic applications accepted. *Expenses: Contact institution. Financial support:* In 2006–07, 8 teaching assistantships with partial tuition reimbursements (averaging $7,600 per year) were awarded; career-related internships or fieldwork, institutionally sponsored loans, health care benefits, and unspecified assistantships also available. Financial award applicants required to submit FAFSA. *Faculty research:* Diversity, literacy, art representation by young children, preservice teacher preparation. Total annual research expenditures: $330,000. *Unit head:* Dr. Katie A. Kinnucan-Welsch, Chair, 937-229-3346. *Application contact:* Erika Eavers, Graduate Admission Processor, 937-229-3065, Fax: 937-229-4729, E-mail: erika.eavers@notes.udayton.edu.

University of Delaware, College of Human Services, Education and Public Policy, School of Education, Newark, DE 19716. Offers curriculum and instruction (M Ed); education (PhD); educational leadership (M Ed, Ed D); exceptional children and youth (M Ed); instruction (MI); school counseling (M Ed); school psychology (MA); teaching English as a second language (TESL) (MA). *Accreditation:* NCATE. Part-time and evening/weekend programs available. Terminal master's awarded for partial completion of doctoral program. *Degree requirements:* For master's, thesis (for some programs), comprehensive exam (for some programs), registration; for doctorate, thesis/dissertation, comprehensive exam (for some programs), registration. *Entrance requirements:* For master's and doctorate, GRE, 3 letters of recommendation. Additional exam requirements/recommendations for international students: Required—TOEFL (minimum score 600 paper-based; 250 computer-based). Electronic applications accepted. *Faculty research:* Teacher education; education policy; educational assessment, measurement, and evaluation; curriculum theory and development; community based education models.

University of Detroit Mercy, College of Liberal Arts and Education, Department of Education, Program in Special Education, Detroit, MI 48221. Offers emotionally impaired (MA); learning disabilities (MA). Part-time programs available. *Degree requirements:* For master's, thesis or alternative, practicum. *Entrance requirements:* For master's, minimum GPA of 2.75. *Expenses:* Tuition: Full-time $15,750; part-time $875 per credit hour. Required fees: $570. *Faculty research:* Emerging roles of special education, inclusionary education, high potential underachievers in secondary schools.

The University of Findlay, Graduate and Professional Studies, College of Education, Findlay, OH 45840-3653. Offers administration (MA Ed); early childhood (MA Ed); elementary education (MA Ed); human resource development (MA Ed); leadership (MA Ed); special education (MA Ed); technology (MA Ed); web instruction (MA Ed). *Accreditation:* NCATE. Part-time and evening/weekend programs available. *Faculty:* 12 full-time, 6 part-time/adjunct. *Students:* 84 full-time (65 women), 223 part-time (169 women); includes 11 minority (3 African Americans, 2 American Indian/Alaska Native, 1 Asian American or Pacific Islander, 5 Hispanic Americans), 13 international. Average age 35. 91 applicants, 97% accepted, 76 enrolled. In 2006, 146 degrees awarded. *Degree requirements:* For master's, thesis, cumulative project. *Entrance requirements:* For master's, minimum undergraduate GPA of 3.0 in last 60 hours of course work. Additional exam requirements/recommendations for international students: Required—TOEFL. *Application deadline:* Applications are processed on a rolling basis. Application fee: $25. Electronic applications accepted. *Expenses: Contact institution. Financial support:* In 2006–07, 6 students received support, including 6 teaching assistantships with full tuition reimbursements available (averaging $6,000 per year); unspecified assistantships also available. Financial award application deadline: 4/1; financial award applicants required to submit FAFSA. *Faculty research:* Children's literature, books and artwork, educational technology, professional development. *Unit head:* Dr. Melissa A. Cain, Dean, 419-434-4840, Fax: 419-434-4822. *Application contact:* Heather Riffle, Director, Graduate and Special Programs, 419-434-4642, Fax: 419-434-5517, E-mail: riffle@findlay.edu.

University of Florida, Graduate School, College of Education, Department of Special Education, Gainesville, FL 32611. Offers M Ed, MAE, Ed D, PhD, Ed S. *Accreditation:* NCATE. *Faculty:* 17 full-time (15 women). *Students:* 117 (101 women); includes 19 minority (10 African Americans, 1 American Indian/Alaska Native, 3 Asian Americans or Pacific Islanders, 5 Hispanic Americans) 3 international. In 2006, 32 master's, 2 doctorates awarded. *Degree requirements:* For master's, thesis (MAE); for doctorate, variable foreign language requirement, thesis/dissertation. *Entrance requirements:* For master's and doctorate, GRE General Test, minimum GPA of 3.0; for Ed S, GRE General Test. Additional exam requirements/recommendations for international students: Required—TOEFL (minimum score 550 paper-based; 213 computer-based). *Application deadline:* For fall admission, 6/1 priority date for domestic students. Applications are processed on a rolling basis. Application fee: $30. Electronic applications accepted. *Expenses:* Tuition, state resident: full-time $6,827. Tuition, nonresident: full-time $21,951. Required fees: $999. *Financial support:* In 2006–07, 21 research assistantships (averaging $12,305 per year), 5 teaching assistantships (averaging $12,233 per year) were awarded; fellowships, career-related internships or fieldwork and unspecified assistantships also available. *Faculty research:* Teacher attrition, school restructuring, Latino families. *Unit head:* James McLeskey, Chair, 352-392-0701 Ext. 278, Fax: 352-392-2655, E-mail: mcleskey@coe.ufl.edu. *Application contact:* Dr. Penny R. Cox, Coordinator, 352-392-0701 Ext. 251, Fax: 352-392-2655, E-mail: pcox@coe.ufl.edu.

University of Georgia, Graduate School, College of Education, Department of Communication Sciences and Special Education, Athens, GA 30602. Offers M Ed, MA, Ed D, PhD, Ed S. *Accreditation:* ASHA (one or more programs are accredited). *Faculty:* 17 full-time (6 women). *Students:* 88 full-time (82 women), 73 part-time (65 women); includes 15 minority (8 African Americans, 4 Asian Americans or Pacific Islanders, 3 Hispanic Americans), 7 international. Average age 24. 191 applicants, 51% accepted, 47 enrolled. In 2006, 45 master's, 4 doctorates, 5 other advanced degrees awarded. Terminal master's awarded for partial completion of doctoral program. *Degree requirements:* For master's, thesis (for some programs), comprehensive exam (for some programs); for doctorate, thesis/dissertation. *Entrance requirements:* For master's, doctorate, and Ed S, GRE General Test. Additional exam requirements/recommendations for international students: Required—TOEFL. *Application deadline:* For fall admission, 7/1 priority date for domestic students; for spring admission, 11/15 for domestic students. Application fee: $50. Electronic applications accepted. *Financial support:* Fellowships, research assistantships, teaching assistantships, unspecified assistantships available. *Unit head:* Dr. Anne C. Bothe, Head, 706-542-0436, Fax: 706-542-5348, E-mail: abothe@uga.edu. *Application contact:* Dr. Anne C. Bothe, Graduate Coordinator, 706-542-0436, Fax: 706-542-5348, E-mail: abothe@coe.uga.edu.

University of Guam, Graduate School and Research, College of Education, Program in Special Education, Mangilao, GU 96923. Offers M Ed. *Degree requirements:* For master's, comprehensive oral and written exams, special project or thesis. *Entrance requirements:* For master's, GRE General Test. Additional exam requirements/recommendations for international students: Required—TOEFL. *Faculty research:* Mainstreaming, multiculturalism.

University of Hawaii at Manoa, Graduate Division, College of Education, Department of Special Education, Honolulu, HI 96822. Offers M Ed. *Accreditation:* NCATE. Part-time and evening/weekend programs available. *Faculty:* 13 full-time (8 women). *Students:* 39 full-time (27 women), 28 part-time (20 women); includes 17 minority (2 African Americans, 12 Asian Americans or Pacific Islanders, 3 Hispanic Americans), 1 international. Average age 37. 46 applicants, 65% accepted, 15 enrolled. In 2006, 33 degrees awarded. *Degree requirements:* For master's, thesis optional. *Entrance requirements:* For master's, GRE General Test, interview, minimum GPA of 3.0. Additional exam requirements/recommendations for international students: Required—TOEFL (minimum score 580 paper-based; 237 computer-based; 92 iBT). *Application deadline:* For fall admission, 3/1 for domestic and international students; for spring admission, 10/1 for domestic and international students. Application fee: $50. *Financial support:* In 2006–07, 1 research assistantship (averaging $16,176 per year) was awarded; teaching assistantships, career-related internships or fieldwork, institutionally sponsored loans, and tuition waivers (full and partial) also available. Support available to part-time students. Financial award application deadline: 3/1. *Faculty research:* Mild/moderate/severe disabilities, early childhood interventions, inclusion, transition. Total annual research expenditures: $2 million. *Application contact:* Amelia Jenkins, Chair, 808-956-8450, Fax: 808-956-4345, E-mail: amelia@hawaii.edu.

University of Hawaii at Manoa, Graduate Division, College of Education, Education Program, Honolulu, HI 96822. Offers curriculum and instruction (PhD); educational administration (PhD); educational foundations (PhD); educational policy studies (PhD); exceptionalities (PhD). Evening/weekend programs available. *Faculty:* 78 full-time (44 women), 1 part-time/adjunct (0 women). *Students:* 54 full-time (37 women), 97 part-time (66 women); includes 28 minority (6 African Americans, 1 American Indian/Alaska Native, 19 Asian Americans or Pacific Islanders, 2 Hispanic Americans), 3 international. Average age 45. 63 applicants, 52% accepted, 24 enrolled. In 2006, 17 degrees awarded. *Median time to degree:* Of those who began their doctoral program in fall 1998, 35% received their degree in 8 years or less. *Degree requirements:* For doctorate, thesis/dissertation. *Entrance requirements:* For doctorate, GRE General Test, sample of written work. Additional exam requirements/recommendations for international students: Required—TOEFL (minimum score 600 paper-based; 250 computer-based; 100 iBT). *Application deadline:* For fall admission, 2/1 for domestic students, 1/15 for international students. Application fee: $50. *Financial support:* In 2006–07, 12 research assistantships (averaging $16,565 per year), 5 teaching assistantships (averaging $13,964 per year) were awarded; career-related internships or fieldwork, Federal Work-Study, and tuition waivers (full and partial) also available. *Application contact:* Dr. Helen Slaughter, Chairperson, 808-956-7913, Fax: 808-956-9100, E-mail: slaughte@hawaii.edu.

University of Houston, College of Education, Department of Educational Psychology, Houston, TX 77204. Offers counseling psychology (M Ed, PhD); educational psychology (M Ed); educational psychology and individual differences (PhD); special education (M Ed, Ed D). *Accreditation:* NCATE. Part-time and evening/weekend programs available. *Faculty:* 17 full-time (9 women), 9 part-time/adjunct (6 women). *Students:* 104 full-time (95 women), 119 part-time (107 women); includes 66 minority (24 African Americans, 1 American Indian/Alaska Native, 15 Asian Americans or Pacific Islanders, 26 Hispanic Americans), 4 international. Average age 33. 107 applicants, 39% accepted, 27 enrolled. In 2006, 47 master's, 11 doctorates awarded. *Degree requirements:* For master's, comprehensive exam or thesis; for doctorate, thesis/dissertation, comprehensive exam. *Entrance requirements:* For master's, GRE General Test or MAT, interview (counseling psychology); for doctorate, GRE General Test, interview. *Application deadline:* For fall admission, 2/1 for domestic students. Application fee: $35 ($75 for international students). *Expenses:* Tuition, state resident: full-time $5,429; part-time $226 per credit. Tuition, nonresident: full-time $12,029; part-time $501 per credit. Required fees: $2,454. *Financial support:* In 2006–07, 1 fellowship with full tuition reimbursement (averaging $9,500 per year), 3 research assistantships with full tuition reimbursements (averaging $10,225 per year), 35 teaching assistantships with full tuition reimbursements (averaging $10,225 per year) were awarded; career-related internships or fieldwork, Federal Work-Study, institutionally sponsored loans, scholarships/grants, health care benefits, and unspecified assistantships also available. Support available to part-time students. Financial award application deadline: 3/10. *Faculty research:* Cross-cultural assessment and counseling, cognitive and psychosocial development, learning and emotional disturbances. *Unit head:* Dr. Jacqueline Hawkins, Chairperson, 713-743-9827, Fax: 713-743-4996, E-mail: jhawkins@uh.edu. *Application contact:* Graduate Adviser, 713-743-5019, Fax: 713-743-4996, E-mail: epsy@uh.edu.

University of Idaho, College of Graduate Studies, College of Education, Department of Counseling and School Psychology, Special Education, and Educational Leadership, Program in Special Education, Moscow, ID 83844-2282. Offers M Ed, MS, Ed S. *Accreditation:* NCATE. *Students:* 24. Average age 41. In 2006, 16 degrees awarded. *Entrance requirements:* For master's, minimum GPA of 2.8. *Application deadline:* For fall admission, 8/1 for domestic students; for spring admission, 12/15 for domestic students. Application fee: $55 ($60 for international students). *Expenses:* Tuition, nonresident: full-time $9,600; part-time $140 per credit. Required fees: $4,740; $227 per credit. *Financial support:* Research assistantships, teaching assistantships available. Financial award application deadline: 2/15. *Unit head:* Dr. Jeanne S. Christiansen, Unit Head, 208-885-7537.

University of Illinois at Chicago, Graduate College, College of Education, Program in Special Education, Chicago, IL 60607-7128. Offers M Ed, PhD. Part-time programs available. Terminal master's awarded for partial completion of doctoral program. *Degree requirements:* For doctorate, thesis/dissertation. *Entrance requirements:* For master's, minimum GPA of 2.75; for doctorate, GRE General Test, minimum GPA of 2.75. Additional exam requirements/recommendations for international students: Required—TOEFL. Electronic applications accepted. *Faculty research:* Teaching and learning for special learners, individual differences.

University of Illinois at Urbana–Champaign, Graduate College, College of Education, Department of Special Education, Champaign, IL 61820. Offers Ed M, MA, MS, PhD, CAS. Part-time programs available. *Faculty:* 11 full-time (8 women), 3 part-time/adjunct (all women). *Students:* 57 full-time (50 women), 50 part-time (41 women); includes 12 minority (7 African Americans, 5 Asian Americans or Pacific Islanders), 16 international. 82 applicants, 56% accepted, 18 enrolled. In 2006, 21 master's, 4 doctorates awarded. *Degree requirements:* For master's and doctorate, thesis/dissertation. *Entrance requirements:* For master's and doctorate, GRE General Test or MAT, minimum GPA of 3.0. *Application deadline:* Applications are processed on a rolling basis. Application fee: $50 ($60 for international students). Electronic applications accepted. *Financial support:* In 2006–07, 41 fellowships, 18 research assistantships, 21 teaching assistantships were awarded; tuition waivers (full and partial) also available. Financial award application deadline: 2/15. *Unit head:* Adelle Renzaglia, Head, 217-333-0260, Fax: 217-333-6555, E-mail: renzag@uiuc.edu. *Application contact:* Mary Walle, Administrative Secretary, 217-333-0260, Fax: 217-333-6555, E-mail: mwalle@uiuc.edu.

The University of Iowa, Graduate College, College of Education, Department of Teaching and Learning, Program in Special Education, Iowa City, IA 52242-1316. Offers MA, PhD. *Faculty:* 4 full-time. *Students:* 17 full-time (14 women), 19 part-time (14 women); includes 2 minority (both Asian Americans or Pacific Islanders), 5 international. 22 applicants, 45% accepted, 8 enrolled. In 2006, 18 master's, 2 doctorates awarded. *Degree requirements:* For master's, exam, thesis optional; for doctorate, thesis/dissertation, comprehensive exam, registration. *Entrance requirements:* For master's and doctorate, GRE General Test, minimum GPA of 3.0. Additional exam requirements/recommendations for international students: Required—TOEFL (minimum score 550 paper-based; 213 computer-based; 81 iBT). *Application deadline:* Applications are processed on a rolling basis. Application fee: $60 ($85 for international students). Electronic applications accepted. *Financial support:* In 2006–07, 4 research assistantships with partial tuition reimbursements, 5 teaching assistantships with partial tuition reimbursements were awarded; fellowships also available. Financial award applicants required to submit FAFSA. *Unit head:* Gary Sasso, Chair, 319-335-5324, Fax: 319-335-5608.

University of Kansas, Graduate Studies, School of Education, Department of Special Education, Lawrence, KS 66045. Offers MS Ed, Ed D, PhD. Offered jointly with the Kansas City campus. *Accreditation:* NCATE. Part-time programs available. *Faculty:* 21 full-time (9 women), 8 part-time/adjunct (all women). *Students:* 93 full-time (88 women), 154 part-time (131 women); includes 19 minority (8 African Americans, 3 American Indian/Alaska Native, 8 Hispanic Americans), 31 international. Average age 34. 94 applicants, 80% accepted. In 2006, 89 master's, 17 doctorates awarded. *Degree requirements:* For doctorate, variable foreign language requirement, thesis/dissertation. *Entrance requirements:* For master's, minimum GPA of 3.0; for doctorate, GRE General Test. Additional exam requirements/recommendations for international students: Required—TOEFL. *Application deadline:* For fall admission, 3/15 for domestic and international students; for spring admission, 10/15 for domestic and international students. Applications are processed on a rolling basis. Application fee: $55 ($60 for international students). Electronic applications accepted. *Expenses:* Tuition, area resident: Part-time $227 per credit. Tuition, state resident: part-time $543 per credit. Tuition and fees vary

according to course load, campus/location, program and reciprocity agreements. *Financial support:* Fellowships, research assistantships with partial tuition reimbursements, teaching assistantships with full and partial tuition reimbursements, Federal Work-Study, scholarships/grants, and unspecified assistantships available. *Faculty research:* Autism spectrum disorders, LD research, leadership development, qualitative research and evaluation. *Unit head:* Chriss Walther-Thomas, Chair, 785-864-4954, Fax: 785-864-4149, E-mail: chrisswt@ku.edu. *Application contact:* Sherrie Saathoff, Admissions and Recruitment, 785-864-0556, Fax: 785-864-4149, E-mail: ssaathoff@ku.edu.

University of Kentucky, Graduate School, College of Education, Program in Special Education, Lexington, KY 40506-0032. Offers early childhood special education (MS Ed); rehabilitation counseling (MRC); special education (MS Ed); special education leadership personnel preparation (Ed D). *Accreditation:* CORE; NCATE. *Faculty:* 38 full-time (24 women), 5 part-time/adjunct (4 women). *Students:* 108 full-time (76 women), 74 part-time (70 women); includes 28 minority (23 African Americans, 1 American Indian/Alaska Native, 3 Asian Americans or Pacific Islanders, 1 Hispanic American). Average age 37. 57 applicants, 65% accepted, 32 enrolled. In 2006, 48 master's, 2 doctorates awarded. Terminal master's awarded for partial completion of doctoral program. *Median time to degree:* Of those who began their doctoral program in fall 1998, 90% received their degree in 8 years or less. *Degree requirements:* For master's, thesis optional; for doctorate, thesis/dissertation, comprehensive exam. *Entrance requirements:* For master's, GRE General Test, minimum undergraduate GPA of 2.75; for doctorate, GRE General Test, minimum graduate GPA of 3.0. Additional exam requirements/recommendations for international students: Required—TOEFL (minimum score 550 paper-based; 213 computer-based). *Application deadline:* For fall admission, 7/17 priority date for domestic students, 2/1 priority date for international students; for spring admission, 12/13 priority date for domestic students, 6/15 priority date for international students. Application fee: $40 ($55 for international students). Electronic applications accepted. *Expenses:* Tuition, state resident: full-time $7,670; part-time $401 per credit hour. Tuition, nonresident: full-time $16,158; part-time $873 per credit hour. *Financial support:* In 2006–07, 10 fellowships with full tuition reimbursements (averaging $2,600 per year), 2 research assistantships with full tuition reimbursements (averaging $8,400 per year), 1 teaching assistantship with full tuition reimbursement (averaging $10,500 per year) were awarded; career-related internships or fieldwork, Federal Work-Study, institutionally sponsored loans, scholarships/grants, traineeships, health care benefits, tuition waivers (partial), and unspecified assistantships also available. Support available to part-time students. Financial award application deadline: 3/15. *Faculty research:* Applied behavior analysis applications in special education, single subject research design in classroom settings, transition research across life span, rural special education personnel. Total annual research expenditures: $1.6 million. *Unit head:* Dr. John Schuster, Director of Graduate Studies, 859-257-8594, Fax: 859-257-1325. *Application contact:* Dr. Brian Jackson, Senior Associate Dean, 859-257-4667, Fax: 859-257-4676, E-mail: brian.jackson@uky.edu.

University of La Verne, College of Education and Organizational Leadership, Department of Education, Master's Program in Education, La Verne, CA 91750-4443. Offers advanced teaching skills (M Ed); education (special emphasis) (M Ed). Part-time programs available. *Faculty:* 18 full-time (13 women), 7 part-time/adjunct (all women). *Students:* 78 full-time (66 women), 212 part-time (157 women); includes 121 minority (17 African Americans, 8 Asian Americans or Pacific Islanders, 96 Hispanic Americans), 2 international. Average age 32. In 2006, 161 degrees awarded. *Degree requirements:* For master's, thesis optional. *Entrance requirements:* For master's, California Basic Educational Skills Test, interview, writing sample, minimum GPA of 3.0, 3 letters of recommendation. Additional exam requirements/recommendations for international students: Required—TOEFL (minimum score 550 paper-based; 213 computer-based). *Application deadline:* Applications are processed on a rolling basis. Application fee: $50. *Expenses:* Contact institution. *Financial support:* Institutionally sponsored loans and unspecified assistantships available. Financial award application deadline: 3/2; financial award applicants required to submit FAFSA. *Unit head:* Valerie Beltran, Chair, 909-593-3511 Ext. 4659, E-mail: beltranv@ulv.edu. *Application contact:* Jo Nell Baker, Director, Graduate Admissions and Academic Services, 909-593-3511 Ext. 4244, Fax: 909-392-2761, E-mail: gradadmt@ulv.edu.

University of Louisiana at Monroe, Graduate Studies and Research, College of Education and Human Development, Department of Curriculum and Instruction, Program in Special Education, Monroe, LA 71209-0001. Offers M Ed, MAT. *Accreditation:* NCATE. Part-time and evening/weekend programs available. *Students:* 3 full-time (all women), 36 part-time (31 women); includes 11 minority (all African Americans). Average age 36. In 2006, 34 degrees awarded. *Entrance requirements:* For master's, GRE General Test, minimum GPA of 2.5. *Application deadline:* For fall admission, 6/1 priority date for domestic students; for spring admission, 11/1 for domestic students. Applications are processed on a rolling basis. Application fee: $20 ($30 for international students). *Expenses:* Tuition, state resident: part-time $124 per credit hour. Tuition, nonresident: part-time $124 per credit hour. *Financial support:* Research assistantships, teaching assistantships, unspecified assistantships available. Financial award application deadline: 7/1. *Unit head:* Dr. Gary Stringer, Head, Department of Curriculum and Instruction, 318-342-1266, Fax: 318-342-1240, E-mail: stringer@ulm.edu.

University of Louisville, Graduate School, College of Education and Human Development, Department of Teaching and Learning, Program in Special Education, Louisville, KY 40292-0001. Offers M Ed, PhD. *Accreditation:* NCATE. *Students:* 37 full-time (26 women), 181 part-time (149 women); includes 15 minority (12 African Americans, 3 Asian Americans or Pacific Islanders), 3 international. Average age 37. In 2006, 61 degrees awarded. *Degree requirements:* For master's, thesis. *Entrance requirements:* For master's, GRE General Test. *Application deadline:* Applications are processed on a rolling basis. Application fee: $50. Electronic applications accepted. *Financial support:* Fellowships, research assistantships, teaching assistantships, Federal Work-Study and scholarships/grants available. *Unit head:* Dr. Tom Simmons, Chair, 502-852-6434, Fax: 502-852-1419, E-mail: tsimmons@louisville.edu.

University of Maine, Graduate School, College of Education and Human Development, Program in Special Education, Orono, ME 04469. Offers M Ed, CAS. *Accreditation:* NCATE. Part-time and evening/weekend programs available. *Students:* 17 full-time (15 women), 54 part-time (48 women); includes 1 minority (African American). Average age 41. 21 applicants, 67% accepted, 11 enrolled. In 2006, 38 master's, 3 other advanced degrees awarded. *Degree requirements:* For master's, thesis or alternative. *Entrance requirements:* For master's, MAT; for CAS, MA, M Ed, or MS. Additional exam requirements/recommendations for international students: Required—TOEFL. *Application deadline:* For fall admission, 2/1 priority date for domestic students. Applications are processed on a rolling basis. Application fee: $50. Electronic applications accepted. *Financial support:* Research assistantships, teaching assistantships with tuition reimbursements, career-related internships or fieldwork and tuition waivers (full and partial) available. Support available to part-time students. Financial award application deadline: 3/1. *Unit head:* Dr. Dorothy Breen, Coordinator, 207-581-2444, Fax: 207-581-2423. *Application contact:* Scott G. Delcourt, Associate Dean of the Graduate School, 207-581-3219, Fax: 207-581-3232, E-mail: graduate@maine.edu.

University of Manitoba, Faculty of Graduate Studies, Faculty of Education, Department of Educational Administration, Foundations and Psychology, Winnipeg, MB R3T 2N2, Canada. Offers adult education (M Ed); educational administration (M Ed); guidance and counseling (M Ed); inclusive special education (M Ed); special foundations education (M Ed). *Degree requirements:* For master's, thesis or alternative.

University of Mary, Program in Education, Bismarck, ND 58504-9652. Offers college teaching (MS Ed); curriculum and instruction (MS Ed); early childhood education (MS Ed); early childhood special education (MS Ed); elementary education administration (MS Ed); reading (MS Ed); secondary education administration (MS Ed); special education (MS Ed). Part-time programs available. *Faculty:* 8 full-time (4 women), 12 part-time/adjunct (7 women). *Students:* 2 full-time (1 woman), 34 part-time (25 women), 2 international. Average age 35. In 2006, 17 degrees awarded. *Degree requirements:* For master's, portfolio or thesis. *Entrance requirements:*

Special Education

University of Mary (continued)

For master's, interview, letters of reference. *Application deadline:* Applications are processed on a rolling basis. Application fee: $40. *Financial support:* In 2006–07, 1 teaching assistantship with full tuition reimbursement was awarded; career-related internships or fieldwork also available. Support available to part-time students. Financial award application deadline: 8/1; financial award applicants required to submit FAFSA. *Faculty research:* Innovative pedagogy in higher education, technology in education, content standards, children of poverty, children with diverse learning needs. *Unit head:* Dr. Rebecca Yunker Salveson, Director, 701-355-8186, E-mail: rysalves@umary.edu. *Application contact:* Leona Friedig, Administrative Secretary, 701-355-8058, E-mail: lfriedig@umary.edu.

University of Maryland, College Park, Graduate Studies, College of Education, Department of Special Education, College Park, MD 20742. Offers M Ed, MA, PhD, CAGS. *Accreditation:* NCATE. Part-time and evening/weekend programs available. *Faculty:* 24 full-time (19 women), 15 part-time/adjunct (all women). *Students:* 77 full-time (70 women), 47 part-time (42 women); includes 29 minority (17 African Americans, 1 American Indian/Alaska Native, 5 Asian Americans or Pacific Islanders, 6 Hispanic Americans), 5 international. 98 applicants, 76% accepted, 56 enrolled. In 2006, 58 master's, 9 doctorates awarded. *Median time to degree:* Of those who began their doctoral program in fall 1998, 33% received their degree in 8 years or less. *Degree requirements:* For master's, thesis (for some programs); for doctorate, thesis/dissertation, 1 year residency. *Entrance requirements:* For master's, GRE General Test or MAT, minimum GPA of 3.0, 3 letters of recommendation; for doctorate, GRE General Test or MAT, minimum undergraduate GPA of 3.0, graduate 3.5; 3 letters of recommendation. *Application deadline:* For fall admission, 3/1 for domestic students, 2/1 for international students; for spring admission, 9/1 for domestic students, 6/1 for international students. Applications are processed on a rolling basis. Application fee: $60. Electronic applications accepted. *Financial support:* In 2006–07, 40 fellowships with full tuition reimbursements (averaging $12,991 per year), 12 research assistantships with tuition reimbursements (averaging $14,174 per year), 5 teaching assistantships with tuition reimbursements (averaging $15,648 per year) were awarded; career-related internships or fieldwork, Federal Work-Study, and scholarships/grants also available. Support available to part-time students. Financial award applicants required to submit FAFSA. *Faculty research:* Educational diagnosis and prescription, mental retardation, severely/profoundly handicapped. Total annual research expenditures: $3.7 million. *Unit head:* Dr. Philip J. Burke, Chairman, 301-405-6514, Fax: 301-314-9158, E-mail: pjburke@umd.edu. *Application contact:* Dean of Graduate School, 301-405-0358, Fax: 301-314-9305.

University of Maryland Eastern Shore, Graduate Programs, Department of Education, Program in Special Education, Princess Anne, MD 21853-1299. Offers M Ed. *Accreditation:* NCATE. *Faculty:* 2 full-time (1 woman). *Students:* 5 full-time (3 women), 3 part-time (all women); includes 2 minority (both African Americans) Average age 30. 2 applicants, 50% accepted, 1 enrolled. In 2006, 3 degrees awarded. *Degree requirements:* For master's, seminar paper, internship. *Entrance requirements:* For master's, PRAXIS I, interview, minimum GPA of 3.0. Additional exam requirements/recommendations for international students: Required—TOEFL (minimum score 213 computer-based). *Application deadline:* For fall admission, 5/1 priority date for domestic and international students; for spring admission, 11/1 priority date for domestic and international students. Applications are processed on a rolling basis. Application fee: $30. Electronic applications accepted. *Financial support:* In 2006–07, 3 students received support, including 2 research assistantships with partial tuition reimbursements available (averaging $10,378 per year); career-related internships or fieldwork, scholarships/grants, and unspecified assistantships also available. Financial award application deadline: 3/1; financial award applicants required to submit FAFSA.

University of Massachusetts Amherst, Graduate School, School of Education, Program in Education, Amherst, MA 01003. Offers cultural diversity and curriculum reform (M Ed, Ed D, CAGS); early childhood education and development (M Ed, Ed D, CAGS); educational administration (M Ed, Ed D, CAGS); elementary teacher education (M Ed, Ed D, CAGS); higher education (M Ed, Ed D, CAGS); international education (M Ed, Ed D, CAGS); mathematics, science, and instructional technology (M Ed, Ed D, CAGS); physical education teacher education (M Ed, Ed D, CAGS); reading and writing (M Ed, Ed D, CAGS); research and evaluation methods (M Ed, Ed D, CAGS); school psychology and school counseling (M Ed, Ed D, CAGS); secondary teacher education (M Ed, Ed D, CAGS); social justice education (M Ed, Ed D, CAGS); special education (M Ed, Ed D, CAGS). *Accreditation:* NCATE. *Students:* 418 full-time (286 women), 447 part-time (319 women); includes 147 minority (70 African Americans, 4 American Indian/Alaska Native, 28 Asian Americans or Pacific Islanders, 45 Hispanic Americans), 81 international. Average age 36. In 2006, 260 master's, 30 doctorates awarded. *Degree requirements:* For doctorate, thesis/dissertation. *Entrance requirements:* For master's and doctorate, GRE General Test. Additional exam requirements/recommendations for international students: Required—TOEFL (minimum score 530 paper-based; 197 computer-based). *Application deadline:* For fall admission, 1/15 for domestic and international students; for spring admission, 10/1 for domestic and international students. Applications are processed on a rolling basis. Application fee: $40 ($65 for international students). Electronic applications accepted. *Expenses:* Tuition, state resident: full-time $2,640; part-time $110 per credit. Tuition, nonresident: full-time $9,936; part-time $414 per credit. Required fees: $8,969; $3,129 per term. One-time fee: $257 full-time. Tuition and fees vary according to class time, course load, campus/location and reciprocity agreements. *Financial support:* Fellowships with full tuition reimbursements, research assistantships with full tuition reimbursements, teaching assistantships with full tuition reimbursements, career-related internships or fieldwork, Federal Work-Study, scholarships/grants, traineeships, and unspecified assistantships available. Support available to part-time students. Financial award application deadline: 1/15. *Unit head:* Linda L. Griffin, Professor, 413-545-6984.

University of Massachusetts Boston, Office of Graduate Studies, Graduate College of Education, School Organization, Curriculum and Instruction Department, Program in Special Education, Boston, MA 02125-3393. Offers M Ed. *Accreditation:* NCATE. Part-time and evening/weekend programs available. *Students:* 12 full-time (8 women), 135 part-time (108 women); includes 15 minority (6 African Americans, 1 American Indian/Alaska Native, 4 Asian Americans or Pacific Islanders, 4 Hispanic Americans), 1 international. Average age 30. 39 applicants, 67% accepted, 18 enrolled. In 2006, 36 degrees awarded. *Median time to degree:* Master's–3 years full-time. *Degree requirements:* For master's, practicum. *Entrance requirements:* For master's, GRE General Test or MAT, minimum GPA of 2.75. *Application deadline:* For fall admission, 3/1 priority date for domestic students; for spring admission, 11/1 for domestic students. Application fee: $25 ($40 for international students). *Expenses:* Tuition, state resident: full-time $2,590; part-time $301 per credit. Tuition, nonresident: full-time $9,758; part-time $427 per credit. One-time fee: $495 full-time. *Financial support:* In 2006–07, 2 research assistantships with full tuition reimbursements (averaging $13,000 per year), 1 teaching assistantship with full tuition reimbursement (averaging $4,000 per year) were awarded; career-related internships or fieldwork, Federal Work-Study, and unspecified assistantships also available. Support available to part-time students. Financial award application deadline: 3/1; financial award applicants required to submit FAFSA. *Faculty research:* Inclusionary learning, cross-cultural special needs, special education restructuring. *Unit head:* Dr. Elizabeth Glenn Mitchell, Director, 617-287-7620, E-mail: glen.mitchell@umb.edu. *Application contact:* Peggy Roldan, Graduate Admissions Coordinator, 617-287-6400, Fax: 617-287-6236, E-mail: bos.gadm@dpc.umassp.edu.

University of Memphis, Graduate School, College of Education, Department of Instruction and Curriculum Leadership, Memphis, TN 38152. Offers early childhood education (MAT, MS, Ed D); elementary education (MAT); instruction and curriculum (MS, Ed D); instruction design and technology (MS, Ed D); reading (MS, Ed D); secondary education (MAT); special education (MAT, MS, Ed D). *Accreditation:* NCATE (one or more programs are accredited). Part-time programs available. Terminal master's awarded for partial completion of doctoral program. *Degree requirements:* For master's, thesis or alternative, comprehensive exam; for doctorate, thesis/dissertation, comprehensive exam. *Entrance requirements:* For master's, GRE General Test, minimum GPA of 2.5; for doctorate, GRE General Test, GRE Subject Test, 2 years of teaching experience. Electronic applications accepted. *Faculty research:* Effective urban teachers, preparation and retention of urban teachers, technology utilization in schools, field-based preparation teacher preparation programs, effective use of online instruction.

University of Miami, Graduate School, School of Education, Department of Teaching and Learning, Program in Exceptional Student Education, Pre–K Disabilities and ESOL, Coral Gables, FL 33124. Offers MS Ed, Ed S. *Accreditation:* NCATE. Part-time and evening/weekend programs available. *Students:* 9 full-time (all women), 17 part-time (16 women); includes 9 minority (4 African Americans, 5 Hispanic Americans). 15 applicants, 67% accepted, 6 enrolled. In 2006, 9 degrees awarded. *Degree requirements:* For master's, electronic portfolio review; for Ed S, thesis optional. *Entrance requirements:* For master's and Ed S, GRE General Test. Additional exam requirements/recommendations for international students: Required—TOEFL (minimum score 550 paper-based; 212 computer-based). *Application deadline:* Applications are processed on a rolling basis. Application fee: $50. Electronic applications accepted. *Financial support:* In 2006–07, 25 students received support; teaching assistantships with tuition reimbursements available, Federal Work-Study available. Financial award application deadline: 3/1; financial award applicants required to submit FAFSA. *Faculty research:* Technology, social skills, inclusion, plan, evaluation. *Unit head:* Dr. Batya Elbaum, Advisor, 305-284-4218, Fax: 305-284-4439, E-mail: elbaum@miami.edu.

University of Miami, Graduate School, School of Education, Department of Teaching and Learning, Program in Exceptional Education, Reading and ESOL, Coral Gables, FL 33124. Offers MS Ed, Ed S. Part-time and evening/weekend programs available. *Students:* 11 full-time (all women), 37 part-time (31 women); includes 32 minority (11 African Americans, 21 Hispanic Americans), 1 international. 24 applicants, 75% accepted, 15 enrolled. In 2006, 72 degrees awarded. *Degree requirements:* For master's, electronic portfolio review; for Ed S, thesis optional. *Entrance requirements:* For master's and Ed S, GRE General Test. Additional exam requirements/recommendations for international students: Required—TOEFL (minimum score 550 paper-based; 212 computer-based). *Application deadline:* Applications are processed on a rolling basis. Electronic applications accepted. *Financial support:* Tuition waivers (full and partial) available. Financial award application deadline: 3/1; financial award applicants required to submit FAFSA. *Faculty research:* Inclusion, behavior disorders, emotional disorders, learning disabilities, math problem solving and special education. *Unit head:* Dr. Marjorie Montague, Coordinator, 305-284-2902, Fax: 305-284-3003, E-mail: mmontague@miami.edu.

University of Miami, Graduate School, School of Education, Department of Teaching and Learning, Program in Teaching and Learning, Coral Gables, FL 33124. Offers exceptional student education (PhD); mathematics and science education (PhD); reading (PhD); teaching English to speakers of other languages (PhD). Part-time and evening/weekend programs available. *Students:* 25 full-time (20 women), 6 part-time (5 women); includes 11 minority (2 African Americans, 9 Hispanic Americans), 5 international. Average age 38. 23 applicants, 61% accepted, 4 enrolled. In 2006, 3 doctorates awarded. *Median time to degree:* Of those who began their doctoral program in fall 1998, 100% received their degree in 8 years or less. *Degree requirements:* For doctorate, thesis/dissertation. *Entrance requirements:* For doctorate, GRE General Test, GRE Subject Test. Additional exam requirements/recommendations for international students: Required—TOEFL (minimum score 550 paper-based; 212 computer-based). Application fee: $50. Electronic applications accepted. *Financial support:* In 2006–07, 16 research assistantships with full tuition reimbursements (averaging $13,000 per year), 3 teaching assistantships with full tuition reimbursements (averaging $13,000 per year) were awarded; fellowships, tuition waivers (partial) also available. Financial award application deadline: 3/1; financial award applicants required to submit FAFSA. *Faculty research:* Teacher education, multicultural education, technology, second language acquisition.

University of Michigan, Horace H. Rackham School of Graduate Studies, School of Education, Programs in Educational Studies, Ann Arbor, MI 48109. Offers curriculum development (MA); early childhood education (MA, PhD); educational administration and policy (MA, PhD); educational foundation, administration, policy, and research methods (MA); educational foundations and policy (MA, PhD); elementary education (MA-Certification); English education (MA); English language learning in school settings (MA); learning technologies (MA, PhD); literacy, language, and culture (MA, PhD); mathematics education (MA, PhD); research methods (MA); science education (MA, PhD); secondary education (MA-Certification); social studies education (MA); special education (PhD); teaching and teacher education (PhD); MA-Certification; MBA/MA; PhD/MA. Terminal master's awarded for partial completion of doctoral program. *Degree requirements:* For master's, thesis (for some programs); for doctorate, thesis/dissertation, comprehensive exam. *Entrance requirements:* For master's and doctorate, GRE General Test. Additional exam requirements/recommendations for international students: Required—TOEFL (minimum score 600 paper-based; 250 computer-based). *Application deadline:* For fall admission, 12/1 priority date for domestic students, 12/1 for international students. Application fee: $60 ($75 for international students). Electronic applications accepted. *Financial support:* Applicants required to submit FAFSA. *Unit head:* Dr. Addison Stone, Chairperson, 734-763-7500, Fax: 734-615-1290, E-mail: addison@umich.edu. *Application contact:* Roberta Perry, Office of Student Services, 734-764-7563, Fax: 734-763-1495, E-mail: ed.grad.admit@umich.edu.

University of Michigan–Dearborn, School of Education, Division of Special Education, Dearborn, MI 48128-1491. Offers emotional impairments endorsement (M Ed); inclusion specialist (M Ed); learning disabilities endorsement (M Ed). Part-time and evening/weekend programs available. *Entrance requirements:* For master's, minimum GPA of 3.0.

University of Michigan–Flint, School of Education and Human Services, Department of Education, Flint, MI 48502-1950. Offers early childhood education (MA Ed); education (MA Ed); elementary education with teaching certificate (MA Ed); literacy (K-12) (MA Ed); special education (MA Ed); urban and multicultural education (MA Ed). Part-time programs available. *Faculty:* 19 full-time (15 women), 9 part-time/adjunct (6 women). *Students:* 20 full-time (18 women), 193 part-time (167 women); includes 15 minority (12 African Americans, 1 American Indian/Alaska Native, 2 Hispanic Americans), 2 international. 109 applicants, 80% accepted, 65 enrolled. In 2006, 54 degrees awarded. *Entrance requirements:* Additional exam requirements/recommendations for international students: Required—TOEFL (minimum score 550 paper-based; 220 computer-based), IELTS (minimum score 7). *Application deadline:* For fall admission, 8/1 priority date for domestic students, 3/1 priority date for international students; for winter admission, 11/15 priority date for domestic students, 7/15 priority date for international students; for spring admission, 3/15 priority date for domestic students, 11/15 priority date for international students. Application fee: $55. *Expenses:* Contact institution. *Unit head:* Dr. Beverly Schumer, Director, 810-424-5215, E-mail: bschumer@umflint.edu. *Application contact:* Beulah Alexander, Executive Secretary, 810-766-6879, Fax: 810-766-6891, E-mail: beulaha@umflint.edu.

University of Minnesota, Twin Cities Campus, Graduate School, College of Education and Human Development, Department of Curriculum and Instruction, Program in Teaching, Minneapolis, MN 55455-0213. Offers Chinese (M Ed); earth science (M Ed); elementary special education (M Ed); English (M Ed); English as a second language (M Ed); French (M Ed); German (M Ed); Hebrew (M Ed); Japanese (M Ed); life sciences (M Ed); mathematics (M Ed); middle school science (M Ed); science (M Ed); second languages and cultures (M Ed); social studies (M Ed); Spanish (M Ed). *Students:* 324 full-time (230 women), 132 part-time (86 women); includes 44 minority (5 African Americans, 2 American Indian/Alaska Native, 27 Asian Americans or Pacific Islanders, 10 Hispanic Americans), 4 international. Average age 27. 499 applicants, 74% accepted, 327 enrolled. In 2006, 545 degrees awarded. *Expenses:* Tuition, state resident: full-time $9,302; part-time $775 per credit. Tuition, nonresident: full-time $16,400; part-time $1,367 per credit. Full-time tuition and fees vary according to class time, course load, program, reciprocity agreements and student level. *Application contact:* Dr. Mary Bents, Associate Dean, 612-625-6501, Fax: 612-626-1580, E-mail: mbents@tc.umn.edu.

University of Minnesota, Twin Cities Campus, Graduate School, College of Education and Human Development, Department of Educational Psychology, Program in Special Education, Minneapolis, MN 55455-0213. Offers M Ed, MA, PhD, Ed S. *Students:* 115 full-time (95 women), 60 part-time (50 women); includes 10 minority (4 African Americans, 1 American Indian/Alaska Native, 3 Asian Americans or Pacific Islanders, 2 Hispanic Americans), 16 international. Average age 33. 114 applicants, 64% accepted, 60 enrolled. In 2006, 55 master's, 3 doctorates, 2 other advanced degrees awarded. *Expenses:* Tuition, state resident: full-time $9,302; part-time $775 per credit. Tuition, nonresident: full-time $16,400; part-time $1,367 per credit. Full-time tuition and fees vary according to class time, course load, program, reciprocity agreements and student level. *Application contact:* Dr. Mary Bents, Associate Dean, 612-625-6501, Fax: 612-626-1580, E-mail: mbents@tc.umn.edu.

University of Missouri–Columbia, Graduate School, College of Education, Department of Special Education, Columbia, MO 65211. Offers administration and supervision of special education (PhD); behavior disorders (M Ed, PhD); curriculum development of exceptional students (M Ed, PhD); early childhood special education (M Ed, PhD); general special education (M Ed, MA, PhD); learning and instruction (M Ed); learning disabilities (M Ed, PhD); mental retardation (M Ed, PhD). *Accreditation:* NCATE. Part-time and evening/weekend programs available. Postbaccalaureate distance learning degree programs offered (no on-campus study). *Faculty:* 8 full-time (6 women). *Students:* 27 full-time (26 women), 28 part-time (24 women); includes 2 minority (both Asian Americans or Pacific Islanders), 5 international. 22 applicants, 77% accepted, 14 enrolled. In 2006, 12 master's, 3 doctorates awarded. *Degree requirements:* For master's, thesis or alternative, comprehensive exam; for doctorate, thesis/dissertation, comprehensive exam. *Entrance requirements:* For master's and doctorate, GRE General Test, letters of recommendation. Additional exam requirements/recommendations for international students: Required—TOEFL (minimum score 500 paper-based; 173 computer-based). *Application deadline:* For fall admission, 7/1 priority date for domestic and international students; for winter admission, 11/1 priority date for domestic and international students; for spring admission, 4/1 priority date for domestic and international students. Application fee: $45 ($60 for international students). Electronic applications accepted. *Financial support:* Fellowships with full and partial tuition reimbursements, research assistantships with full and partial tuition reimbursements, teaching assistantships with full and partial tuition reimbursements, career-related internships or fieldwork, scholarships/grants, health care benefits, and unspecified assistantships available. *Faculty research:* Positive behavior support, applied behavior analysis, attention deficit disorder, pre-linguistic development, school discipline. Total annual research expenditures: $1.4 million. *Unit head:* Dr. Melissa Stormont, Director of Graduate Studies, 573-882-7383, E-mail: stormontm@missouri.edu. *Application contact:* Fran Colley, Office Support Staff III, 573-882-6462, Fax: 573-884-2917, E-mail: cigrad@coe.missouri.edu.

University of Missouri–Kansas City, School of Education, Kansas City, MO 64110-2499. Offers administration (Ed D); counseling and guidance (MA, Ed S); counseling psychology (PhD); curriculum and instruction (MA, Ed S); education (PhD); educational administration (Ed S); reading education (MA, Ed S); special education (MA). *Accreditation:* NCATE. Part-time and evening/weekend programs available. *Faculty:* 59 full-time (46 women), 39 part-time/adjunct (29 women). *Students:* 182 full-time (151 women), 470 part-time (344 women); includes 148 minority (117 African Americans, 5 American Indian/Alaska Native, 8 Asian Americans or Pacific Islanders, 18 Hispanic Americans), 9 international. Average age 34. 560 applicants, 79% accepted, 253 enrolled. In 2006, 196 master's, 4 doctorates, 41 other advanced degrees awarded. *Degree requirements:* For doctorate, thesis/dissertation, internship, practicum. *Entrance requirements:* For master's, GRE, minimum GPA of 2.75, 2 letters of references, a written statement of purpose; for doctorate, GRE, minimum GPA of 3.0; for Ed S, minimum GPA of 3.0. Additional exam requirements/recommendations for international students: Required—TOEFL (minimum score 550 paper-based; 213 computer-based). *Application deadline:* For fall admission, 4/1 priority date for domestic students, 4/1 for international students; for winter admission, 10/1 priority date for domestic students, 10/1 for international students; for spring admission, 10/1 priority date for domestic students, 10/1 for international students. Applications are processed on a rolling basis. Application fee: $35 ($50 for international students). *Expenses:* Tuition, state resident: full-time $4,975; part-time $276 per credit. Tuition, nonresident: full-time $12,847; part-time $713 per credit. Required fees: $595; $595 per year. *Financial support:* In 2006–07, 361 students received support, including 13 research assistantships with partial tuition reimbursements available (averaging $10,560 per year); fellowships with full tuition reimbursements available, teaching assistantships, career-related internships or fieldwork, Federal Work-Study, institutionally sponsored loans, and tuition waivers (full and partial) also available. Support available to part-time students. Financial award application deadline: 3/1. *Faculty research:* Urban education, inquiry-based field study, theories of counseling and psychotherapy, school literacy, educational technology. Total annual research expenditures: $94,515. *Unit head:* Dr. Linda Edwards, Dean, 816-235-2236, Fax: 816-235-5270, E-mail: edwardsli@umkc.edu. *Application contact:* Dr. Lori Reesor, Assistant Dean, 816-235-1473, Fax: 816-235-5270, E-mail: reesorl@umkc.edu.

University of Missouri–St. Louis, College of Education, Division of Teaching and Learning, St. Louis, MO 63121. Offers elementary education (M Ed), including reading; secondary education (M Ed), including curriculum and instruction, middle school, reading; special education (M Ed), including behavioral disorders, early childhood special education, learning disabilities, mentally retardation; teaching-learning processes (Ed D, PhD). *Faculty:* 20 full-time (13 women), 5 part-time/adjunct (4 women). *Students:* 118 full-time (84 women), 353 part-time (311 women); includes 90 minority (75 African Americans, 1 American Indian/Alaska Native, 3 Asian Americans or Pacific Islanders, 11 Hispanic Americans), 4 international. Average age 36. In 2006, 136 master's, 3 doctorates awarded. *Entrance requirements:* For doctorate, GRE General Test, 3 letters of recommendation. *Application deadline:* For fall admission, 7/15 for domestic students; for spring admission, 12/15 for domestic students. *Expenses:* Tuition, state resident: part-time $332 per credit hour. Tuition, nonresident: part-time $770 per credit hour. *Financial support:* In 2006–07, 9 teaching assistantships (averaging $14,250 per year) were awarded; research assistantships. *Unit head:* Dr. Gayle Wilkinson, Chair, 314-516-5791. *Application contact:* 314-516-5458, Fax: 314-516-6996, E-mail: gadadm@umsl.edu.

University of Nebraska at Kearney, College of Graduate Study, College of Education, Department of Teacher Education, Kearney, NE 68849-0001. Offers curriculum and instruction (MS Ed); instructional technology (MS Ed); reading education (MA Ed); special education (MA Ed). Part-time and evening/weekend programs available. *Faculty:* 9 full-time (5 women). *Students:* 15 full-time (10 women), 226 part-time (173 women); includes 5 minority (1 African American, 1 Asian American or Pacific Islander, 3 Hispanic Americans), 4 international. 46 applicants, 78% accepted. In 2006, 66 degrees awarded. *Degree requirements:* For master's, thesis optional. *Entrance requirements:* For master's, portfolio or GRE. Additional exam requirements/recommendations for international students: Required—TOEFL (minimum score 550 paper-based; 213 computer-based). *Application deadline:* For fall admission, 5/1 for domestic and international students; for spring admission, 8/15 for domestic students, 8/1 for international students. Applications are processed on a rolling basis. Application fee: $45. Electronic applications accepted. *Expenses:* Tuition, state resident: part-time $161 per hour. Tuition, nonresident: part-time $332 per hour. Required fees: $57 per hour. *Financial support:* In 2006–07, 8 research assistantships with full tuition reimbursements (averaging $8,200 per year) were awarded; career-related internships or fieldwork, scholarships/grants, and unspecified assistantships also available. Support available to part-time students. *Unit head:* Dr. Dennis Pottnoff, Chair, 308-865-8513, E-mail: pottnoffd@unk.edu.

University of Nebraska at Omaha, Graduate Studies and Research, College of Education, Department of Special Education and Communication Disorders, Omaha, NE 68182. Offers special education (MS); speech-language pathology (MA, MS). *Accreditation:* ASHA (one or more programs are accredited); NCATE. Part-time and evening/weekend programs available. *Faculty:* 9 full-time (7 women). *Students:* 20 full-time (all women), 67 part-time (57 women); includes 2 minority (1 African American, 1 Asian American or Pacific Islander). Average age 30. 63 applicants, 70% accepted, 18 enrolled. In 2006, 41 degrees awarded. *Degree requirements:* For master's, thesis (for some programs), comprehensive exam. *Entrance requirements:* For master's, GRE General Test or MAT, minimum GPA of 3.0. Additional exam requirements/recommendations for international students: Required—TOEFL (minimum score 500 paper-based; 173 computer-based; 61 iBT). *Application deadline:* For fall admission, 2/1 for domestic students; for spring admission, 9/1 for domestic students. Applications are processed on a rolling basis. Application fee: $45. Electronic applications accepted. *Financial support:* In 2006–07, 69 students received support; fellowships, research assistantships with tuition reimbursements available, career-related internships or fieldwork, Federal Work-Study, institutionally sponsored loans, scholarships/grants, tuition waivers (partial), and unspecified assistantships available. Support available to part-time students. Financial award application deadline: 3/1; financial award applicants required to submit FAFSA. *Unit head:* Dr. Mary Friehe, Chairperson, 402-554-2201.

University of Nebraska–Lincoln, Graduate College, College of Education and Human Services, Department of Special Education and Communication Disorders, Program in Special Education, Lincoln, NE 68588. Offers M Ed, MA. *Accreditation:* NCATE. *Degree requirements:* For master's, thesis optional. *Entrance requirements:* For master's, GRE. Additional exam requirements/recommendations for international students: Required—TOEFL (minimum score 500 paper-based; 173 computer-based). Electronic applications accepted.

University of Nevada, Las Vegas, Graduate College, College of Education, Department of Special Education, Las Vegas, NV 89154-9900. Offers assistive technology (Ed S); emotional disturbance (Ed D); general special education (Ed D); gifted and talented education (Ed D); learning disabilities (Ed D); mental retardation (Ed D); special education (M Ed, MS, PhD, Ed S). *Accreditation:* NCATE. Part-time and evening/weekend programs available. *Faculty:* 21 full-time (15 women), 23 part-time/adjunct (20 women). *Students:* 161 full-time (119 women), 119 part-time (105 women); includes 44 minority (18 African Americans, 2 American Indian/Alaska Native, 11 Asian Americans or Pacific Islanders, 13 Hispanic Americans), 4 international. 187 applicants, 70% accepted, 117 enrolled. In 2006, 129 master's, 9 doctorates awarded. *Degree requirements:* For master's, thesis (for some programs), oral exam, comprehensive exam (for some programs); for doctorate, thesis/dissertation, oral exam, comprehensive exam. *Entrance requirements:* For master's, minimum GPA of 3.0; for doctorate, GRE General Test, minimum graduate GPA of 3.0; for Ed S, GRE General Test or MAT, minimum graduate GPA of 3.0. Additional exam requirements/recommendations for international students: Required—TOEFL (minimum score 550 paper-based; 213 computer-based; 80 iBT). *Application deadline:* For fall admission, 2/12 for domestic and international students; for spring admission, 11/15 for domestic students, 10/1 for international students. Application fee: $60 ($75 for international students). Electronic applications accepted. *Financial support:* In 2006–07, 14 research assistantships with partial tuition reimbursements (averaging $10,000 per year), 3 teaching assistantships with partial tuition reimbursements (averaging $12,000 per year) were awarded; career-related internships or fieldwork, Federal Work-Study, institutionally sponsored loans, scholarships/grants, health care benefits, and unspecified assistantships also available. Support available to part-time students. Financial award application deadline: 3/1. *Unit head:* Dr. Tom Pierce, Chair, 702-895-3205. *Application contact:* Graduate College Admissions Evaluator, 702-895-3320, Fax: 702-895-4180, E-mail: gradcollege@unlv.edu.

University of Nevada, Reno, Graduate School, College of Education, Department of Curriculum, Teaching and Learning, Reno, NV 89557. Offers curriculum, teaching and learning (Ed D, PhD); elementary education (M Ed, MA, Ed S); secondary education (M Ed, MA, MS, Ed S); special education and disability studies (PhD). *Students:* 82 full-time (65 women), 74 part-time (58 women); includes 12 minority (1 African American, 3 American Indian/Alaska Native, 5 Asian Americans or Pacific Islanders, 3 Hispanic Americans), 2 international. Average age 35. 66 applicants, 85% accepted, 0 enrolled. In 2006, 51 degrees awarded. *Degree requirements:* For master's, thesis optional. *Entrance requirements:* For master's, GRE General Test, minimum GPA of 2.75. Additional exam requirements/recommendations for international students: Required—TOEFL (minimum score 500 paper-based; 173 computer-based). *Application deadline:* For fall admission, 3/1 priority date for domestic students; for spring admission, 10/1 for domestic students. Applications are processed on a rolling basis. Application fee: $60 ($95 for international students). Electronic applications accepted. *Unit head:* Dr. Margaret Ferrara, Program Director, 775-682-7530, E-mail: ferrara@unr.edu.

University of Nevada, Reno, Graduate School, College of Education, Department of Educational Specialties, Reno, NV 89557. Offers educational specialties (MA, MS, PhD, Ed S); literacy studies (M Ed, MA, Ed D, PhD); special education (M Ed); teaching English as a second language (MA). *Students:* 75 full-time (58 women), 188 part-time (161 women); includes 29 minority (2 African Americans, 1 American Indian/Alaska Native, 10 Asian Americans or Pacific Islanders, 16 Hispanic Americans), 20 international. Average age 38. 123 applicants, 82% accepted, 50 enrolled. In 2006, 50 master's, 1 doctorate awarded. *Degree requirements:* For master's, thesis optional; for doctorate, thesis/dissertation, comprehensive exam. *Entrance requirements:* For master's, minimum GPA of 2.75; for doctorate, GRE. Additional exam requirements/recommendations for international students: Required—TOEFL (minimum score 500 paper-based; 173 computer-based). *Application deadline:* For fall admission, 3/1 priority date for domestic students; for spring admission, 10/1 for domestic students. Applications are processed on a rolling basis. Application fee: $60 ($95 for international students). Electronic applications accepted. *Unit head:* Dr. Chris Cheney, Head, 775-784-7853.

University of New Hampshire, Graduate School, College of Liberal Arts, Department of Education, Program in Early Childhood Education, Durham, NH 03824. Offers early childhood education (M Ed); special needs (M Ed). Part-time programs available. *Faculty:* 32 full-time. *Students:* 3 full-time (all women), 13 part-time (11 women); includes 1 minority (African American) Average age 31. 6 applicants, 100% accepted, 6 enrolled. In 2006, 10 degrees awarded. *Degree requirements:* For master's, thesis or alternative. *Entrance requirements:* For master's, GRE General Test. Additional exam requirements/recommendations for international students: Required—TOEFL (minimum score 550 paper-based; 213 computer-based). *Application deadline:* For fall admission, 4/1 priority date for domestic students, 4/1 for international students; for winter admission, 12/1 for domestic students. Applications are processed on a rolling basis. Application fee: $60. Electronic applications accepted. *Expenses:* Tuition, state resident: full-time $8,540; part-time $474 per credit hour. Tuition, nonresident: full-time $20,990; part-time $862 per credit hour. Required fees: $1,343; $356 per term. Tuition and fees vary according to course load, program and reciprocity agreements. *Financial support:* In 2006–07, 1 fellowship, 1 teaching assistantship were awarded; research assistantships, career-related internships or fieldwork, Federal Work-Study, scholarships/grants, and tuition waivers (full and partial) also available. Support available to part-time students. Financial award application deadline: 2/15. *Faculty research:* Young children with special needs. *Unit head:* Dr. John Hornstein, Coordinator, 603-862-2310, E-mail: education.department@unh.edu.

University of New Hampshire, Graduate School, College of Liberal Arts, Department of Education, Program in Special Education, Durham, NH 03824. Offers M Ed. Part-time programs available. *Faculty:* 32 full-time. *Students:* 5 full-time (all women), 28 part-time (23 women); includes 1 minority (Asian American or Pacific Islander) Average age 33. 6 applicants, 67% accepted, 4 enrolled. In 2006, 8 degrees awarded. *Degree requirements:* For master's, thesis or alternative. *Entrance requirements:* For master's, GRE General Test. Additional exam requirements/recommendations for international students: Required—TOEFL (minimum score 550 paper-based; 213 computer-based). *Application deadline:* For fall admission, 4/1 priority date for domestic students, 4/1 for international students; for winter admission, 12/1 for domestic students. Applications are processed on a rolling basis. Application fee: $60. Electronic applications accepted. *Expenses:* Tuition, state resident: full-time $8,540; part-time $474 per credit hour. Tuition, nonresident: full-time $20,990; part-time $862 per credit hour. Required fees: $1,343; $356 per term. Tuition and fees vary according to course load, program and reciprocity agreements. *Financial support:* In 2006–07, 1 teaching assistantship was awarded; fellowships, research assistantships, career-related internships or fieldwork, Federal Work-Study, scholarships/grants, and tuition waivers (full and partial) also available. Support avail-

Special Education

University of New Hampshire (continued)
able to part-time students. Financial award application deadline: 2/15. *Unit head:* Dr. Georgia Kerns, Coordinator, 603-862-3446, E-mail: education.department@unh.edu.

University of New Mexico, Graduate School, College of Education, Department of Educational Specialties, Program in Special Education, Albuquerque, NM 87131-2039. Offers MA, Ed D, PhD, EDSPC. *Accreditation:* NCATE. Part-time and evening/weekend programs available. *Students:* 48 full-time (32 women), 172 part-time (116 women); includes 68 minority (6 African Americans, 10 American Indian/Alaska Native, 7 Asian Americans or Pacific Islanders, 45 Hispanic Americans), 9 international. Average age 40. 30 applicants, 80% accepted, 22 enrolled. In 2006, 67 master's, 9 doctorates, 1 other advanced degree awarded. *Degree requirements:* For master's, thesis optional; for doctorate, thesis/dissertation, screening, proposal hearing, comprehensive exam. *Entrance requirements:* For master's, minimum GPA of 3.2; for doctorate, minimum GPA of 3.2, 2 years of relevant experience; for EDSPC, special education degree, 2 years of teaching experience with the disabled, writing sample, minimum GPA of 3.2. *Application deadline:* For fall admission, 3/31 priority date for domestic students; for spring admission, 9/30 priority date for domestic students. Application fee: $40. Electronic applications accepted. *Financial support:* In 2006–07, 64 students received support, including 12 fellowships (averaging $17,250 per year), 4 teaching assistantships with tuition reimbursements available (averaging $4,060 per year); research assistantships with tuition reimbursements available, career-related internships or fieldwork, Federal Work-Study, scholarships/grants, health care benefits, unspecified assistantships, and stipends also available. Support available to part-time students. Financial award application deadline: 3/1; financial award applicants required to submit FAFSA. *Faculty research:* Mathematics instruction, bilingual special education, inclusive education, autism, reading instruction for students with cognitive disabilities, alternative assessment, human rights and disability. *Unit head:* Prof. Ruth Luckasson, Chair, 505-277-6510, Fax: 505-277-6929, E-mail: luckasson@unm.edu. *Application contact:* Jo Sanchez, Information Contact, 505-277-5018, Fax: 505-277-8679, E-mail: jsanchez@unm.edu.

University of New Orleans, Graduate School, College of Education and Human Development, Department of Special Education, New Orleans, LA 70148. Offers M Ed, PhD, GCE. *Accreditation:* NCATE. Evening/weekend programs available. *Students:* 36 (31 women). Average age 36. In 2006, 29 master's, 1 doctorate awarded. *Degree requirements:* For doctorate, variable foreign language requirement, thesis/dissertation. *Entrance requirements:* For master's, GRE General Test; for doctorate, GRE General Test, GRE Subject Test. Additional exam requirements/recommendations for international students: Required—TOEFL (minimum score 550 paper-based; 213 computer-based). *Application deadline:* For fall admission, 7/1 priority date for domestic students, 6/1 for international students; for spring admission, 11/15 priority date for domestic students, 10/1 for international students. Applications are processed on a rolling basis. Application fee: $40. Electronic applications accepted. *Expenses:* Tuition, state resident: full-time $3,292. Tuition, nonresident: full-time $10,336. Required fees: $158. *Financial support:* Research assistantships, teaching assistantships, career-related internships or fieldwork, scholarships/grants, and tuition waivers (partial) available. Financial award application deadline: 3/15; financial award applicants required to submit FAFSA. *Faculty research:* Inclusion, transition, early childhood, mild/moderate, severe/profound. *Unit head:* Dr. Randall Scott, Chairperson, 504-280-7162, Fax: 504-280-5588, E-mail: rlscott@uno.edu. *Application contact:* Dr. Linda Flynn, Graduate Coordinator, 504-280-7063, Fax: 504-280-5588, E-mail: lflynnwi@uno.edu.

University of North Alabama, College of Education, Department of Elementary Education, Programs in Special Education, Florence, AL 35632-0001. Offers learning disabilities (MA Ed); mentally retarded (MA Ed); mild learning handicapped (MA Ed). *Accreditation:* NCATE. Part-time and evening/weekend programs available. *Faculty:* 2 part-time/adjunct (both women). *Students:* Average age 33. In 2006, 9 degrees awarded. *Degree requirements:* For master's, comprehensive exam. *Entrance requirements:* For master's, GRE, MAT, or NTE, minimum GPA of 2.5, Alabama Class B Certificate or equivalent, teaching experience. *Application deadline:* For fall admission, 7/1 priority date for domestic students; for spring admission, 12/1 for domestic students. Applications are processed on a rolling basis. Application fee: $25. Electronic applications accepted. *Expenses:* Tuition, state resident: full-time $4,080. Tuition, nonresident: full-time $8,160. Required fees: $764. *Financial support:* Federal Work-Study available. Support available to part-time students. Financial award application deadline: 4/1. *Application contact:* Dr. Sue Wilson, Dean of Enrollment Management, 256-765-4316, Fax: 256-765-4349, E-mail: sjwilson@una.edu.

The University of North Carolina at Charlotte, Graduate School, College of Education, Department of Special Education and Child Development, Charlotte, NC 28223-0001. Offers special education (M Ed, PhD), including academically gifted (M Ed), behavioral—emotional handicaps (M Ed), cross-categorical disabilities (M Ed), learning disabilities (M Ed), mental handicaps (M Ed), severe and profound handicaps (M Ed). Part-time programs available. *Faculty:* 25 full-time (19 women), 7 part-time/adjunct (all women). *Students:* 9 full-time (8 women), 41 part-time (38 women); includes 1 minority (African American), 1 international. Average age 34. 27 applicants, 41% accepted, 9 enrolled. In 2006, 3 master's, 4 doctorates awarded. *Degree requirements:* For doctorate, dissertation, portfolio, qualifying exam. *Entrance requirements:* For master's, GRE or MAT; for doctorate, GRE or MAT, 3 letters of reference, resumé or curriculum vitae, minimum GPA of 3.5, master's degree in special education or related field, 3 years of teaching experience. Additional exam requirements/recommendations for international students: Required—TOEFL (paper-based 550; computer-based 220) or Michigan English Language Assessment Battery. *Application deadline:* For fall admission, 7/15 for domestic students, 5/1 for international students; for spring admission, 11/15 for domestic students, 10/1 for international students. Application fee: $55. *Expenses:* Tuition, state resident: full-time $2,719; part-time $170 per credit. Tuition, nonresident: full-time $12,926; part-time $808 per credit. Required fees: $1,555. *Financial support:* In 2006–07, 13 research assistantships (averaging $12,615 per year), 6 teaching assistantships (averaging $8,000 per year) were awarded. Financial award application deadline: 4/1; financial award applicants required to submit FAFSA. *Faculty research:* Transition to adulthood and self-determination, teaching reading and other academic skills to students with disabilities, alternate assessment, early intervention, preschool education. *Unit head:* David Gilmore, Unit Head, 704-687-8186, Fax: 704-687-2916. *Application contact:* Kathy B. Giddings, Director of Graduate Admissions, 704-687-3366, Fax: 704-687-3279, E-mail: gradadm@email.uncc.edu.

The University of North Carolina at Charlotte, Graduate School, College of Education, Program in Teacher Education, Charlotte, NC 28223-0001. Offers art education (K-12) (MAT); dance education (K-12) (MAT); elementary education (K-6) (MAT); English as a second language (K-12) (MAT); foreign language education (K-12) (MAT); general teacher education (MAT); middle grades education (6-9) (MAT); music education (K-12) (MAT); secondary education (9-12) (MAT); special education (K-12) (MAT); theatre education (K-12) (MAT). *Students:* 16 full-time (12 women), 200 part-time (170 women); includes 30 minority (22 African Americans, 2 American Indian/Alaska Native, 2 Asian Americans or Pacific Islanders, 4 Hispanic Americans), 2 international. Average age 33. 74 applicants, 85% accepted, 49 enrolled. In 2006, 43 degrees awarded. *Entrance requirements:* For master's, GRE or MAT. Additional exam requirements/recommendations for international students: Required—TOEFL (minimum score 557 paper-based; 220 computer-based). *Application deadline:* For fall admission, 7/1 for domestic students, 5/1 for international students; for spring admission, 11/1 for domestic students, 10/1 for international students. Applications are processed on a rolling basis. Application fee: $55. Electronic applications accepted. *Expenses:* Tuition, state resident: full-time $2,719; part-time $170 per credit. Tuition, nonresident: full-time $12,926; part-time $808 per credit. Required fees: $1,555. *Financial support:* Fellowships, research assistantships, teaching assistantships, career-related internships or fieldwork, Federal Work-Study, institutionally sponsored loans, scholarships/grants, and unspecified assistantships available. Support available to part-time students. Financial award application deadline: 4/1; financial award applicants required to submit FAFSA. *Unit head:* Dr. Kimberly J. Hartman, Coordinator, 704-687-8883, Fax: 704-687-6430, E-mail: khartman@email.uncc.edu. *Application contact:* Kathy B. Giddings, Director of Graduate Admissions, 704-687-3366, Fax: 704-687-3279, E-mail: gradadm@email.uncc.edu.

The University of North Carolina at Greensboro, Graduate School, School of Education, Department of Specialized Education Services, Greensboro, NC 27412-5001. Offers cross-categorical special education (M Ed); interdisciplinary studies in special education (M Ed); leadership early care and education (Certificate); special education (M Ed, PhD). *Faculty:* 10 full-time (7 women), 1 (woman) part-time/adjunct. *Students:* 41 full-time (36 women), 36 part-time (33 women); includes 21 minority (18 African Americans, 3 Asian Americans or Pacific Islanders). 29 applicants, 45% accepted. *Degree requirements:* For master's, thesis or alternative. *Entrance requirements:* For master's, GRE General Test. Additional exam requirements/recommendations for international students: Required—TOEFL. Application fee: $45. Electronic applications accepted. *Expenses:* Tuition, state resident: full-time $2,692. Tuition, nonresident: full-time $13,742. *Financial support:* Fellowships, research assistantships with full tuition reimbursements, career-related internships or fieldwork, Federal Work-Study, scholarships/grants, and traineeships available. Support available to part-time students. *Unit head:* Dr. Marilyn Friend, Chair, 336-256-0153, E-mail: m_friend@uncg.edu. *Application contact:* Michelle Harkleroad, Director of Graduate Admissions, 336-334-4884, Fax: 336-334-4424, E-mail: mbharkle@uncg.edu.

The University of North Carolina Wilmington, School of Education, Department of Early Childhood and Special Education, Program in Special Education, Wilmington, NC 28403-3297. Offers M Ed. *Accreditation:* NCATE. Part-time and evening/weekend programs available. In 2006, 1 degree awarded. *Degree requirements:* For master's, thesis, comprehensive exam. *Entrance requirements:* For master's, GRE General Test, MAT, minimum B average in upper-division undergraduate course work, bachelor's degree in special education. *Application deadline:* For fall admission, 6/1 for domestic students. Applications are processed on a rolling basis. Application fee: $45. *Financial support:* Application deadline: 3/15. *Application contact:* Dr. Robert D. Roer, Dean, Graduate School, 910-962-4117, Fax: 910-962-3787, E-mail: roer@uncw.edu.

University of North Dakota, Graduate School, College of Education and Human Development, Program in Special Education, Grand Forks, ND 58202. Offers M Ed, MS. *Accreditation:* NCATE. Part-time programs available. Postbaccalaureate distance learning degree programs offered (minimal on-campus study). *Faculty:* 1 (woman) full-time. *Students:* 33 applicants, 67% accepted, 22 enrolled. In 2006, 49 degrees awarded. *Degree requirements:* For master's, thesis or alternative, comprehensive exam. *Entrance requirements:* For master's, minimum GPA of 3.0. Additional exam requirements/recommendations for international students: Required—TOEFL (minimum score 550 paper-based; 213 computer-based; 79 iBT), IELTS (minimum score 6). *Application deadline:* For fall admission, 3/15 for domestic and international students; for spring admission, 8/15 for domestic and international students. Application fee: $35. Electronic applications accepted. *Expenses:* Tuition, state resident: full-time $5,650; part-time $214 per credit. Tuition, nonresident: full-time $14,248; part-time $572 per credit. Required fees: $1,008; $42 per credit. Tuition and fees vary according to reciprocity agreements. *Financial support:* In 2006–07, 21 students received support, including 21 teaching assistantships with full tuition reimbursements available (averaging $8,517 per year); fellowships, research assistantships, career-related internships or fieldwork, Federal Work-Study, institutionally sponsored loans, scholarships/grants, tuition waivers (full and partial), and unspecified assistantships also available. Support available to part-time students. Financial award application deadline: 3/15; financial award applicants required to submit FAFSA. *Faculty research:* Visual, emotional, and mental disabilities; early childhood. *Unit head:* Dr. Lynne Chalmers, Director, 701-777-3187, Fax: 701-777-4393, E-mail: lynne.chalmers@mail.und.nodak.edu. *Application contact:* Linda M. Baeza, Admissions Officer, 701-777-2945, Fax: 701-777-3619, E-mail: gradschool@mail.und.nodak.edu.

University of North Dakota, Graduate School, College of Education and Human Development, Teaching and Learning Program, Grand Forks, ND 58202. Offers elementary education (Ed D, PhD); measurement and statistics (Ed D, PhD); secondary education (Ed D, PhD); special education (Ed D, PhD). *Accreditation:* NCATE. *Faculty:* 19 full-time (16 women), 2 part-time/adjunct (1 woman). *Students:* 9 applicants, 0% accepted. In 2006, 18 degrees awarded. *Degree requirements:* For doctorate, thesis/dissertation, final exam, comprehensive exam. *Entrance requirements:* For doctorate, minimum GPA of 3.5. Additional exam requirements/recommendations for international students: Required—TOEFL (minimum score 550 paper-based; 213 computer-based; 79 iBT), IELTS (minimum score 6). *Application deadline:* For fall admission, 2/15 priority date for domestic and international students; for spring admission, 10/15 priority date for domestic and international students. Application fee: $35. Electronic applications accepted. *Expenses:* Tuition, state resident: full-time $5,650; part-time $214 per credit. Tuition, nonresident: full-time $14,248; part-time $572 per credit. Required fees: $1,008; $42 per credit. Tuition and fees vary according to reciprocity agreements. *Financial support:* In 2006–07, 17 students received support, including 1 research assistantship with full tuition reimbursement available (averaging $4,877 per year), 4 teaching assistantships with full tuition reimbursements available (averaging $7,609 per year); fellowships, career-related internships or fieldwork, Federal Work-Study, institutionally sponsored loans, scholarships/grants, tuition waivers (full and partial), and unspecified assistantships also available. Support available to part-time students. Financial award application deadline: 3/15; financial award applicants required to submit FAFSA. *Application contact:* Linda M. Baeza, Admissions Officer, 701-777-2945, Fax: 701-777-3619, E-mail: gradschool@mail.und.nodak.edu.

University of Northern Colorado, Graduate School, College of Education and Behavioral Sciences, School of Special Education, Program in Special Education, Greeley, CO 80639. Offers MA, Ed D. *Accreditation:* NCATE. Part-time and evening/weekend programs available. Postbaccalaureate distance learning degree programs offered (no on-campus study). *Faculty:* 11 full-time (6 women). *Students:* 144 full-time (114 women), 57 part-time (44 women); includes 15 minority (2 African Americans, 2 American Indian/Alaska Native, 1 Asian American or Pacific Islander, 10 Hispanic Americans), 2 international. Average age 35. 80 applicants, 94% accepted, 33 enrolled. In 2006, 146 master's, 4 doctorates awarded. *Degree requirements:* For master's, thesis or alternative, comprehensive exam; for doctorate, thesis/dissertation, comprehensive exam. *Entrance requirements:* For master's, letters of recommendation, interview; for doctorate, GRE General Test, resumé. *Application deadline:* Applications are processed on a rolling basis. Application fee: $50 ($60 for international students). Electronic applications accepted. *Expenses:* Tuition, state resident: full-time $5,118; part-time $213 per credit hour. Tuition, nonresident: full-time $14,832; part-time $618 per credit hour. Required fees: $674; $34 per credit hour. *Financial support:* In 2006–07, 173 students received support, including 6 fellowships (averaging $1,458 per year), 7 research assistantships (averaging $8,792 per year), 5 teaching assistantships (averaging $10,516 per year); unspecified assistantships also available. Financial award application deadline: 3/1; financial award applicants required to submit FAFSA. *Unit head:* Dr. Harvey Rude, Director, School of Special Education, 970-351-2691, Fax: 970-351-1061.

University of Northern Iowa, Graduate College, College of Education, Department of Special Education, Cedar Falls, IA 50614. Offers MAE, Ed D. Part-time and evening/weekend programs available. *Faculty:* 8 full-time (5 women). *Students:* 9 full-time (8 women), 65 part-time (60 women), 1 international. 11 applicants, 64% accepted, 5 enrolled. In 2006, 14 degrees awarded. *Degree requirements:* For master's, thesis or alternative, comprehensive exam (for some programs); for doctorate, thesis/dissertation. *Entrance requirements:* For master's, 3 years of educational experience, minimum GPA of 3.5. Additional exam requirements/recommendations for international students: Required—TOEFL (minimum score 500 paper-based; 180 computer-based; 61 iBT). *Application deadline:* For fall admission, 8/1 priority date for domestic students. Applications are processed on a rolling basis. Application fee: $30 ($50 for international students). Electronic applications accepted. *Expenses:* Tuition, state resident: full-time $5,936. Tuition, nonresident: full-time $14,074. *Financial support:* Career-related internships or fieldwork, Federal Work-Study, scholarships/grants, and tuition waivers (full and partial) available. Support available to part-time students. Financial award application deadline: 2/1. *Unit head:* Dr. Sandra Alper, Interim Head, 319-273-6061, Fax: 319-273-7852, E-mail: sandra.alper@uni.edu.

University of North Florida, College of Education and Human Services, Department of Special Education, Jacksonville, FL 32224-2645. Offers deaf education (M Ed); disability services (M Ed); exceptional student education (M Ed). *Accreditation:* NCATE. Part-time and evening/weekend programs available. *Faculty:* 11 full-time (6 women). *Students:* 28 full-time (26 women), 25 part-time (24 women); includes 12 minority (10 African Americans, 1 Asian American or Pacific Islander, 1 Hispanic American), 2 international. Average age 31. 25 applicants, 56% accepted, 12 enrolled. In 2006, 16 degrees awarded. *Entrance requirements:* For master's, GRE General Test, minimum GPA of 3.0 in last 60 hours, interview, 3 letters of recommendation. Additional exam requirements/recommendations for international students: Required—TOEFL (minimum score 500 paper-based; 173 computer-based). *Application deadline:* For fall admission, 7/1 priority date for domestic students, 5/1 for international students; for spring admission, 11/1 priority date for domestic students, 10/1 for international students. Applications are processed on a rolling basis. Application fee: $30. Electronic applications accepted. *Expenses:* Tuition, state resident: full-time $4,948; part-time $206 per semester hour. Tuition, nonresident: full-time $19,140; part-time $408 per semester hour. *Financial support:* In 2006–07, 32 students received support, including 1 teaching assistantship (averaging $1,152 per year); research assistantships, career-related internships or fieldwork, Federal Work-Study, and tuition waivers (partial) also available. Support available to part-time students. Financial award application deadline: 4/1; financial award applicants required to submit FAFSA. *Faculty research:* Transition, integrating technology into teacher education, written language development, professional school development, learning strategies. Total annual research expenditures: $335,511. *Unit head:* Dr. Janice J. Seabrooks, Chair, 904-620-2930, E-mail: jseabroo@unf.edu.

University of North Texas, Robert B. Toulouse School of Graduate Studies, College of Education, Department of Technology and Cognition, Program in Special Education, Denton, TX 76203. Offers M Ed, MS, PhD. *Accreditation:* NCATE. *Students:* 33 full-time (28 women), 72 part-time (64 women); includes 18 minority (11 African Americans, 3 American Indian/Alaska Native, 1 Asian American or Pacific Islander, 3 Hispanic Americans), 6 international. Average age 33. 54 applicants, 61% accepted, 21 enrolled. In 2006, 45 master's, 4 doctorates awarded. *Degree requirements:* For doctorate, one foreign language, thesis/dissertation, internship. *Entrance requirements:* For master's, GRE General Test; for doctorate, GRE General Test, admissions exam. Additional exam requirements/recommendations for international students: Recommended—TOEFL (minimum score 550 paper-based; 213 computer-based). *Application deadline:* For fall admission, 7/15 for domestic students. Application fee: $50 ($75 for international students). *Expenses:* Tuition, state resident: full-time $3,573; part-time $198 per credit. Tuition, nonresident: full-time $8,577; part-time $476 per credit. Required fees: $1,258; $126 per credit. One-time fee: $150 full-time. Tuition and fees vary according to course load. *Financial support:* Fellowships, research assistantships, teaching assistantships, career-related internships or fieldwork, Federal Work-Study, and institutionally sponsored loans available. Financial award application deadline: 4/1. *Unit head:* Dr. Bertina Combes, Coordinator, 940-565-2628, Fax: 940-565-2185, E-mail: combes@unt.edu. *Application contact:* Jeanie McMahan, Graduate Adviser, 940-565-2628, Fax: 940-565-2185, E-mail: mcmahan@unt.edu.

University of Oklahoma, Graduate College, College of Education, Department of Educational Psychology, Program in Special Education, Norman, OK 73019-0390. Offers M Ed, PhD. *Accreditation:* NCATE. Part-time and evening/weekend programs available. *Students:* 28 full-time (20 women), 23 part-time (20 women); includes 16 minority (9 African Americans, 6 American Indian/Alaska Native, 1 Hispanic American), 9 international. 23 applicants, 52% accepted, 11 enrolled. In 2006, 5 degrees awarded. *Degree requirements:* For master's, thesis optional; for doctorate, variable foreign language requirement, thesis/dissertation. *Entrance requirements:* For master's, minimum GPA of 3.0; for doctorate, GRE General Test, master's degree, minimum graduate GPA of 3.0. Additional exam requirements/recommendations for international students: Required—TOEFL (minimum score 550 paper-based; 213 computer-based). *Application deadline:* For fall admission, 4/1 for domestic and international students; for spring admission, 11/1 for domestic students, 9/1 for international students. Applications are processed on a rolling basis. Application fee: $40 ($90 for international students). *Expenses:* Tuition, state resident: full-time $3,180; part-time $133 per credit hour. Tuition, nonresident: full-time $11,347; part-time $473 per credit hour. Required fees: $1,729; $62 per credit hour. $117 per semester. Tuition and fees vary according to course load and program. *Financial support:* In 2006–07, 30 students received support; research assistantships with partial tuition reimbursements available, teaching assistantships with partial tuition reimbursements available, institutionally sponsored loans, scholarships/grants, health care benefits, tuition waivers (full), and unspecified assistantships available. Financial award applicants required to submit FAFSA. *Faculty research:* Mental retardation, learning disabilities, early intervention and transition, law and education policy. *Unit head:* Dr. David Lovett, Associate Professor, 405-325-1507, E-mail: dlovett@ou.edu. *Application contact:* Graduate Programs Officer, 405-325-4525, Fax: 405-325-6655, E-mail: gpoedpsych@ou.edu.

University of Oklahoma Health Sciences Center, Graduate College, College of Allied Health, Department of Communication Sciences and Disorders, Oklahoma City, OK 73190. Offers audiology (MS, Au D, PhD); communication sciences and disorders (Certificate); education of the deaf (MS); speech-language pathology (MS, PhD). *Accreditation:* ASHA (one or more programs are accredited). Part-time programs available. Terminal master's awarded for partial completion of doctoral program. *Degree requirements:* For master's, thesis optional; for doctorate, one foreign language, thesis/dissertation, comprehensive exam. *Entrance requirements:* For master's and doctorate, GRE General Test, 3 letters of recommendation. Additional exam requirements/recommendations for international students: Required—TOEFL (minimum score 550 paper-based). *Faculty research:* Event-related potentials, cleft palate, fluency disorders, language disorders, hearing and speech science.

University of Phoenix–Metro Detroit Campus, The Artemis School, College of Education, Troy, MI 48098-2623. Offers administration and supervision (MA Ed); adult education and distance learning (MA Ed); curriculum and development (MA Ed); special education (MA Ed); teacher education elementary (MA Ed). Evening/weekend programs available. *Faculty:* 8 full-time (3 women), 27 part-time/adjunct (21 women). *Students:* 102 full-time (75 women); includes 59 minority (57 African Americans, 1 American Indian/Alaska Native, 1 Asian American or Pacific Islander), 1 international. Average age 40. In 2006, 30 master's awarded. *Degree requirements:* For master's, thesis (for some programs), registration. *Entrance requirements:* For master's, 3 years of work experience, minimum undergraduate GPA of 2.5. Additional exam requirements/recommendations for international students: Required—TOEFL (minimum score 550 paper-based; 213 computer-based; 79 iBT). *Application deadline:* Applications are processed on a rolling basis. Application fee: $45. Electronic applications accepted. *Expenses:* Tuition: Full-time $12,168. Required fees: $760. *Financial support:* Institutionally sponsored loans and scholarships/grants available. Financial award applicants required to submit FAFSA. *Unit head:* Dr. Marla LaRue, Dean/Executive Director, 480-557-1218. *Application contact:* Chair, 800-834-2438, Fax: 248-267-0147.

University of Phoenix–Omaha Campus, College of Education, Omaha, NE 68154-5240. Offers administration and supervision (MA Ed); curriculum and instruction (MA Ed); curriculum and instruction—English and language arts education (MA Ed); curriculum and instruction—adult education (MA Ed); curriculum and instruction—computer education (MA Ed); curriculum and instruction—English as a second language (MA Ed); curriculum and instruction—mathematics education (MA Ed); elementary teacher education (MA Ed); secondary teacher education (MA Ed); special education (MA Ed).

University of Phoenix–Southern Arizona Campus, The Artemis School, College of Education, Tucson, AZ 85712-2732. Offers curriculum instruction (MA Ed); educational counseling (MA Ed); elementary licensure (MA Ed); school counseling (MSC); secondary licensure (MA Ed); special education (Certificate). Evening/weekend programs available. *Faculty:* 101. *Students:* 75 full-time (55 women); includes 16 minority (2 African Americans, 1 American Indian/Alaska Native, 1 Asian American or Pacific Islander, 12 Hispanic Americans), 2 international. Average age 38. In 2006, 113 degrees awarded. *Degree requirements:* For master's, thesis (for some programs), registration. *Entrance requirements:* For master's, minimum undergraduate GPA of 2.5, 3 years of work experience. Additional exam requirements/recommendations for international students: Required—TOEFL (minimum score 550 paper-based; 213 computer-based; 79 iBT). *Application deadline:* Applications are processed on a rolling basis. Application fee: $45. Electronic applications accepted. *Expenses:* Tuition: Full-time $8,669. Required fees: $760. *Financial support:* Institutionally sponsored loans and scholarships/grants available. Financial award applicants required to submit FAFSA. *Unit head:* Dr. Marla LaRue, Dean/Executive Director, 480-557-1218, E-mail: marla.larue@phoenix.edu. *Application contact:* Campus College Chair, 520-881-6512, Fax: 520-795-6177.

University of Pittsburgh, School of Education, Department of Instruction and Learning, Program in Special Education, Pittsburgh, PA 15260. Offers deaf and hard of hearing (M Ed); early education of disabled students (M Ed); education of students with mental and physical disabilities (M Ed); education of the visually impaired (M Ed); general special education (M Ed); special education (Ed D, PhD). Part-time and evening/weekend programs available. *Students:* 41 full-time (33 women), 105 part-time (96 women); includes 10 minority (8 African Americans, 1 Asian American or Pacific Islander, 1 Hispanic American), 3 international. 56 applicants, 80% accepted, 41 enrolled. In 2006, 28 master's, 4 doctorates awarded. *Degree requirements:* For master's and doctorate, thesis/dissertation. *Entrance requirements:* For master's, PRAXIS I; for doctorate, GRE General Test. Additional exam requirements/recommendations for international students: Required—TOEFL. *Application deadline:* For fall admission, 2/1 priority date for domestic students; for spring admission, 11/1 priority date for domestic students. Applications are processed on a rolling basis. Application fee: $50. *Financial support:* Research assistantships, teaching assistantships, career-related internships or fieldwork, Federal Work-Study, and tuition waivers (partial) available. Support available to part-time students. Financial award application deadline: 3/15; financial award applicants required to submit FAFSA. *Application contact:* Joan M. Cutone, Director, School of Education Student Service Center, 412-648-2230, Fax: 412-648-1899, E-mail: soeinfo@pitt.edu.

University of Portland, Graduate School, School of Education, Program in Special Education, Portland, OR 97203-5798. Offers M Ed. Part-time and evening/weekend programs available. *Degree requirements:* For master's, thesis optional. *Entrance requirements:* For master's, GRE General Test or MAT, minimum GPA of 3.0, teaching certificate, letters of recommendation, resumé. Additional exam requirements/recommendations for international students: Required—TOEFL (minimum score 550 paper-based; 80 iBT). *Application deadline:* For fall admission, 8/1 priority date for domestic students; for spring admission, 12/1 for domestic students. Applications are processed on a rolling basis. Application fee: $50. *Expenses:* Tuition: Part-time $728 per semester hour. Required fees: $5 per semester hour. Tuition and fees vary according to program. *Financial support:* Federal Work-Study and scholarships/grants available. Financial award application deadline: 3/1; financial award applicants required to submit FAFSA. *Application contact:* Dr. Thomas G. Greene, Associate Dean, 503-943-7135, Fax: 503-943-7315, E-mail: greene@up.edu.

University of Puerto Rico, Medical Sciences Campus, Graduate School of Public Health, Department of Human Development, Program in Developmental Disabilities-Early Intervention, San Juan, PR 00936-5067. Offers Certificate. Part-time and evening/weekend programs available. *Students:* 11 (10 women). *Application deadline:* For fall admission, 3/15 for domestic students. Application fee: $20. *Financial support:* Application deadline: 4/30. *Unit head:* Dr. Annie Alonso, Coordinator, 787-758-2525 Ext. 1447, Fax: 787-759-6719, E-mail: tainno@yahoo.com. *Application contact:* Prof. Mayra E. Santiago-Vargas, Counselor, 787-756-5244, Fax: 787-759-6719, E-mail: msantiago@rcm.upr.edu.

University of Puerto Rico, Río Piedras, College of Education, Graduate Program in Special Education, San Juan, PR 00931-3300. Offers M Ed. *Students:* 16 full-time (all women), 5 part-time (all women); all minorities (all Hispanic Americans) Average age 23. In 2006, 4 degrees awarded. *Degree requirements:* For master's, thesis. *Entrance requirements:* For master's, GRE or PAEG, interview, minimum GPA of 3.0, letter of recommendation. *Application deadline:* For fall admission, 2/1 for domestic and international students. Application fee: $17. *Expenses:* Tuition, state resident: part-time $100 per credit. Tuition, nonresident: part-time $291 per credit. Required fees: $72 per semester. *Financial support:* Application deadline: 5/31. *Faculty research:* Hearing impaired education. *Unit head:* Dr. Loyda Martinez, Coordinator, 787-764-0000 Ext. 4361, Fax: 787-763-4130.

University of Rio Grande, Graduate School, Rio Grande, OH 45674. Offers classroom teaching (M Ed), including fine arts, learning disabilities, mathematics, reading education. Part-time and evening/weekend programs available. *Degree requirements:* For master's, final research project, portfolio. *Entrance requirements:* For master's, minimum GPA of 2.7 in major, 2.5 overall. *Faculty research:* Interagency collaboration, reading and mathematics, learning styles, college access, literacy.

University of St. Francis, College of Education, Joliet, IL 60435-6169. Offers curriculum and instruction (MS); educational leadership (MS), including reading, special education; elementary education certification (M Ed); secondary education certification (M Ed), including English education, math education, science education, social studies education; special education (M Ed); teaching and learning (MS). Part-time and evening/weekend programs available. *Faculty:* 11 full-time (10 women), 25 part-time/adjunct (12 women). *Students:* 52 full-time (38 women), 381 part-time (293 women); includes 38 minority (21 African Americans, 1 American Indian/Alaska Native, 4 Asian Americans or Pacific Islanders, 12 Hispanic Americans). Average age 33. 194 applicants, 80% accepted, 117 enrolled. In 2006, 165 degrees awarded. *Degree requirements:* For master's, comprehensive exam (for some programs), registration. *Entrance requirements:* For master's, minimum undergraduate GPA of 2.75, 2 letters of recommendation, computer competency. Additional exam requirements/recommendations for international students: Required—TOEFL (minimum score 550 paper-based; 213 computer-based). *Application deadline:* Applications are processed on a rolling basis. Application fee: $30. Electronic applications accepted. *Expenses: Contact institution.* Part-time tuition and fees vary according to campus/location and program. *Financial support:* In 2006–07, 272 students received support. Scholarships/grants, tuition waivers (partial), and unspecified assistantships available. Support available to part-time students. Financial award applicants required to submit FAFSA. *Unit head:* Dr. John Gambro, Dean, 815-740-3456, Fax: 815-740-2264, E-mail: jgambro@stfrancis.edu. *Application contact:* Sandra Sloka, Director of Admissions for Graduate and Degree Completion Programs, 800-735-7500, Fax: 815-740-5032, E-mail: ssloka@stfrancis.edu.

University of Saint Francis, Graduate School, Department of Education, Fort Wayne, IN 46808-3994. Offers special education (MS Ed). *Accreditation:* NCATE. Part-time and evening/weekend programs available. *Faculty:* 3 full-time (all women), 4 part-time/adjunct (all women). *Students:* 4 full-time (3 women), 17 part-time (13 women); includes 1 minority (African American) Average age 42. 2 applicants, 100% accepted. In 2006, 9 degrees awarded. *Entrance requirements:* For master's, MAT, minimum GPA of 2.5. *Application deadline:* For fall admission, 7/1 priority date for domestic students; for spring admission, 11/1 for domestic students. Applications are processed on a rolling basis. Application fee: $20. *Financial support:* In 2006–07, 21 students received support. Federal Work-Study and unspecified assistantships available. Support available to part-time students. Financial award applicants required to submit FAFSA. *Unit head:* Dr. Rolf Daniel, Dean, 260-399-7700 Ext. 8403, Fax: 260-399-8170, E-mail: rdaniel@sf.edu. *Application contact:* Michelle Kuhlhorst, Admissions Counselor, 260-434-7748, Fax: 260-434-7590, E-mail: mkuhlhorst@st.edu.

University of Saint Mary, Graduate Programs, Program in Special Education, Leavenworth, KS 66048-5082. Offers MA. Part-time and evening/weekend programs available.

Special Education

University of St. Thomas, Graduate Studies, School of Education, Department of Special Education, St. Paul, MN 55105-1096. Offers autism spectrum disorders (Certificate); director of special education (Ed S); Orton-Gillingham reading (Certificate); special education (MA). *Accreditation:* NCATE. Part-time and evening/weekend programs available. *Faculty:* 5 full-time (all women), 26 part-time/adjunct (24 women). *Students:* 22 full-time (19 women), 226 part-time (197 women); includes 14 minority (4 African Americans, 3 American Indian/Alaska Native, 3 Asian Americans or Pacific Islanders, 4 Hispanic Americans), 4 international. Average age 34. 241 applicants, 83% accepted, 193 enrolled. In 2006, 48 master's, 39 other advanced degrees awarded. *Degree requirements:* For master's, thesis, registration; for other advanced degree, professional portfolio. *Entrance requirements:* For master's, minimum GPA of 2.75 or MAT; for other advanced degree, MAT or minimum GPA of 2.75. Additional exam requirements/recommendations for international students: Required—TOEFL (minimum score 550 paper-based; 213 computer-based). *Application deadline:* For fall admission, 6/1 priority date for domestic students; for spring admission, 11/1 priority date for domestic students. Applications are processed on a rolling basis. Application fee: $50. *Financial support:* In 2006–07, 118 students received support; fellowships, research assistantships, institutionally sponsored loans and scholarships/grants available. Support available to part-time students. Financial award applicants required to submit FAFSA. *Faculty research:* Reading and math fluency; inclusion curriculum for developmental disorders; parent involvement in positive behavior supports; children's friendships; preschool inclusion. Total annual research expenditures: $700,000. *Unit head:* Dr. Ann G. Ryan, Chair, 651-962-4388, Fax: 651-962-4169, E-mail: agryan@stthomas.edu. *Application contact:* Patricia L. Helland, Department Assistant, 651-962-4980, Fax: 651-962-4169, E-mail: plhelland@stthomas.edu.

University of Saskatchewan, College of Graduate Studies and Research, College of Education, Department of Educational Psychology and Special Education, Saskatoon, SK S7N 5A2, Canada. Offers M Ed, PhD, Diploma. *Degree requirements:* For master's, thesis (for some programs), registration; for doctorate, thesis/dissertation, registration. *Entrance requirements:* Additional exam requirements/recommendations for international students: Required—TOEFL.

The University of Scranton, Graduate School, Department of Education, Program in Special Education, Scranton, PA 18510. Offers MS. Part-time and evening/weekend programs available. *Students:* 14 full-time (all women), 1 (woman) part-time; includes 1 minority (Hispanic American) Average age 23. 13 applicants, 100% accepted. In 2006, 15 degrees awarded. *Degree requirements:* For master's, capstone experience. *Entrance requirements:* For master's, minimum GPA of 2.75. Additional exam requirements/recommendations for international students: Required—TOEFL (minimum score 500 paper-based; 173 computer-based), IELTS (minimum score 6). Application fee: $50. *Expenses:* Tuition: Part-time $684 per credit. Required fees: $25 per term. *Financial support:* Unspecified assistantships available. *Unit head:* Dr. Derry Stufft, Director, 570-941-7421, Fax: 570-941-7401, E-mail: stufftda@scranton.edu.

University of South Alabama, Graduate School, College of Education, Department of Leadership and Teacher Education, Mobile, AL 36688-0002. Offers early childhood education (M Ed); educational administration (Ed S); educational leadership (M Ed); elementary education (M Ed); reading education (M Ed); science education (M Ed); secondary education (M Ed); special education (M Ed, Ed S). *Accreditation:* NCATE. Part-time programs available. *Faculty:* 22 full-time (13 women). *Students:* 287 full-time (251 women), 229 part-time (194 women); includes 137 minority (125 African Americans, 8 American Indian/Alaska Native, 3 Asian Americans or Pacific Islanders, 1 Hispanic American), 4 international. 43 applicants, 84% accepted, 20 enrolled. In 2006, 169 master's, 12 other advanced degrees awarded. *Degree requirements:* For master's, comprehensive exam. *Entrance requirements:* For master's, GRE General Test or MAT, minimum GPA of 3.0. *Application deadline:* For fall admission, 9/1 priority date for domestic students. Applications are processed on a rolling basis. Application fee: $25. *Financial support:* In 2006–07, 6 research assistantships were awarded; career-related internships or fieldwork also available. Support available to part-time students. Financial award application deadline: 4/1. *Unit head:* Dr. David L. Gray, Chair, 251-380-2894.

University of South Carolina, The Graduate School, College of Education, Department of Educational Studies, Program in Special Education, Columbia, SC 29208. Offers M Ed, MAT, PhD. *Accreditation:* NCATE. *Degree requirements:* For master's, comprehensive exam; for doctorate, one foreign language, thesis/dissertation, comprehensive exam. *Entrance requirements:* For master's, GRE General Test, MAT, interview, sample of written work; for doctorate, GRE General Test or MAT, interview, sample of written work. *Faculty research:* Strategy training, transition, technology, rural special education, behavior management.

University of South Carolina Upstate, Graduate Programs, Spartanburg, SC 29303-4999. Offers early childhood education (M Ed); elementary education (M Ed); special education: visual impairment (M Ed). *Accreditation:* NCATE. Part-time and evening/weekend programs available. *Faculty:* 9 full-time (7 women). *Students:* 5 full-time (4 women), 29 part-time (26 women); includes 3 minority (all African Americans) Average age 34. 15 applicants, 100% accepted, 9 enrolled. In 2006, 9 degrees awarded. *Degree requirements:* For master's, graduate professional portfolio. *Entrance requirements:* For master's, GRE General Test, MAT, interview, minimum GPA of 2.5, teaching certificate. *Application deadline:* Applications are processed on a rolling basis. Application fee: $40. *Expenses:* Tuition, state resident: full-time $6,890; part-time $342 per semester hour. Tuition, nonresident: full-time $14,920; part-time $727 per semester hour. *Financial support:* Institutionally sponsored loans and institutional work-study available. Financial award application deadline: 7/15; financial award applicants required to submit FAFSA. *Faculty research:* Rough and tumble play, social justice education, American Indian literatures and cultures, diversity and multicultural education, science teaching strategy. *Unit head:* Dr. Rebecca L. Stevens, Director, 864-503-5521, Fax: 864-503-5574, E-mail: ystevens@uscupstate.edu. *Application contact:* Donette Stewart, Associate Vice Chancellor for Enrollment Services, 864-503-5280, E-mail: dstewart@uscupstate.edu.

The University of South Dakota, Graduate School, School of Education, Division of Curriculum and Instruction, Program in Special Education, Vermillion, SD 57069-2390. Offers MA. *Accreditation:* NCATE. Part-time programs available. Postbaccalaureate distance learning degree programs offered. *Students:* 21 (17 women). In 2006, 19 degrees awarded. *Degree requirements:* For master's, thesis or alternative, comprehensive exam. *Entrance requirements:* For master's, GRE General Test, MAT, minimum GPA of 2.7. Additional exam requirements/recommendations for international students: Required—TOEFL (minimum score 550 paper-based; 213 computer-based; 79 iBT). *Application deadline:* Applications are processed on a rolling basis. Application fee: $35. Electronic applications accepted. *Expenses:* Tuition, state resident: part-time $120 per credit hour. Tuition, nonresident: part-time $355 per credit hour. Required fees: $90 per credit hour. *Financial support:* In 2006–07, research assistantships with partial tuition reimbursements (averaging $4,626 per year), teaching assistantships with partial tuition reimbursements (averaging $4,626 per year) were awarded; career-related internships or fieldwork, Federal Work-Study, and unspecified assistantships also available. Financial award applicants required to submit FAFSA.

University of Southern Maine, College of Education and Human Development, Program in Special Education, Portland, ME 04104-9300. Offers MS. *Accreditation:* NCATE. Part-time and evening/weekend programs available. *Faculty:* 2 full-time (1 woman), 3 part-time/adjunct (0 women). *Students:* 4 full-time (3 women), 69 part-time (52 women); includes 2 minority (1 American Indian/Alaska Native, 1 Hispanic American). 15 applicants, 87% accepted, 10 enrolled. In 2006, 48 degrees awarded. *Degree requirements:* For master's, thesis or alternative, portfolio. *Entrance requirements:* For master's, GRE General Test or MAT. *Application deadline:* For fall admission, 2/1 for domestic students; for spring admission, 9/15 for domestic students. Application fee: $50. Electronic applications accepted. *Expenses:* Tuition, state resident: full-time $4,860; part-time $270 per credit hour. Tuition, nonresident: full-time $13,572; part-time $754 per credit hour. Required fees: $222 per semester. Tuition and fees vary according to course load. *Financial support:* In 2006–07, 1 student received support; research assistantships, career-related internships or fieldwork, Federal Work-Study, institutionally sponsored loans, scholarships/grants, and unspecified assistantships available. Support available to part-time students. Financial award application deadline: 3/1; financial award applicants required to submit FAFSA. *Unit head:* Dr. James Curry, Chair, Professional Education Department, 207-780-5400, Fax: 207-228-8277, E-mail: jcurry@usm.maine.edu. *Application contact:* Robin Audesse, Associate Director of Graduate Admissions, 207-780-5306, Fax: 207-780-5193, E-mail: raudesse@usm.maine.edu.

University of Southern Mississippi, Graduate School, College of Education and Psychology, Department of Curriculum, Instruction, and Special Education, Hattiesburg, MS 39406-0001. Offers alternative secondary teacher education (MAT); early childhood education (M Ed, Ed S); education of the gifted (M Ed, Ed D, PhD, Ed S); elementary education (M Ed, Ed D, PhD, Ed S); reading (M Ed, MS, Ed S); secondary education (M Ed, MS, Ed D, PhD, Ed S); special education (M Ed, Ed D, PhD, Ed S). *Faculty:* 16 full-time (11 women). *Students:* 31 full-time (28 women), 54 part-time (51 women); includes 5 minority (4 African Americans, 1 Hispanic American), 1 international. Average age 35. 59 applicants, 27% accepted, 11 enrolled. In 2006, 43 master's, 3 doctorates, 4 other advanced degrees awarded. *Degree requirements:* For master's, thesis (for some programs), comprehensive exam, registration; for doctorate and Ed S, thesis/dissertation, comprehensive exam, registration. *Entrance requirements:* For master's, GRE General Test, MAT, minimum GPA of 3.0; for doctorate, GRE General Test, minimum GPA of 3.5; for Ed S, GRE General Test, MAT, minimum GPA of 3.25. Additional exam requirements/recommendations for international students: Required—TOEFL. *Application deadline:* For fall admission, 3/1 priority date for domestic students, 3/1 for international students. Applications are processed on a rolling basis. Application fee: $25 ($30 for international students). *Financial support:* In 2006–07, 10 research assistantships with tuition reimbursements (averaging $22,333 per year), 2 teaching assistantships with full tuition reimbursements (averaging $22,333 per year) were awarded; Federal Work-Study, institutionally sponsored loans, and tuition waivers (partial) also available. Financial award application deadline: 3/15. *Faculty research:* Mathematical problem solving, integrative curriculum, writing process, teacher education models. Total annual research expenditures: $100,000. *Unit head:* Dr. Dana Thames, Chair, 601-266-4547, Fax: 601-266-4175. *Application contact:* B.J. Davis, Administrative Assistant, 601-266-6987, Fax: 601-266-4548.

University of South Florida, Graduate School, College of Education, Department of Special Education, Tampa, FL 33620-9951. Offers education of the mentally handicapped (MA); gifted education (online) (MA); learning disabilities (MA); varying exceptionalities (MA, MAT). *Accreditation:* NCATE. Part-time and evening/weekend programs available. *Faculty:* 17 full-time (11 women), 3 part-time/adjunct (all women). *Students:* 56 full-time (51 women), 85 part-time (78 women); includes 32 minority (17 African Americans, 1 American Indian/Alaska Native, 5 Asian Americans or Pacific Islanders, 9 Hispanic Americans), 4 international. 63 applicants, 76% accepted, 38 enrolled. In 2006, 48 master's awarded. *Entrance requirements:* For master's, GRE General Test, minimum GPA of 3.5 in last 60 hours. *Application deadline:* For fall admission, 6/1 for domestic students, 1/2 for international students; for spring admission, 10/15 for domestic students, 7/1 for international students. Application fee: $30. Electronic applications accepted. *Financial support:* Career-related internships or fieldwork, scholarships/grants, tuition waivers (partial), and unspecified assistantships available. Financial award application deadline: 6/1; financial award applicants required to submit FAFSA. *Faculty research:* Ethics, teaching cases, early intervention, systems and program evaluation, school restructuring. Total annual research expenditures: $3.4 million. *Unit head:* Dr. Daphene Thomas, Chairperson, 813-974-1383, Fax: 813-974-5542, E-mail: dthomas@tempest.coedu.usf.edu. *Application contact:* Dr. James L. Paul, Doctoral Program Coordinator, 813-974-4166, Fax: 813-974-5542, E-mail: jpaul@tempest.coedu.usf.edu.

The University of Tennessee, Graduate School, College of Education, Health and Human Sciences, Program in Education, Knoxville, TN 37996. Offers art education (MS); counseling education (PhD); cultural studies in education (PhD); curriculum (MS, Ed S); curriculum, educational research and evaluation (Ed D, PhD); early childhood education (PhD); early childhood special education (MS); education of deaf and hard of hearing (MS); educational administration and policy studies (Ed D, PhD); educational administration and supervision (Ed S); educational psychology (Ed D, PhD); elementary education (MS, Ed S); elementary teaching (MS); English education (MS, Ed S); exercise science (PhD); foreign language/ESL education (MS, Ed S); instructional technology (MS, Ed D, PhD, Ed S); literacy, language and ESL education (PhD); literacy, language education, and ESL education (Ed D); mathematics education (MS, Ed S); modified and comprehensive special education (MS); reading education (MS, Ed S); school counseling (Ed S); school psychology (PhD, Ed S); science education (MS, Ed S); secondary teaching (MS); social foundations (MS); social science education (MS, Ed S); socio-cultural foundations of sports and education (PhD); special education (Ed S); teacher education (Ed D, PhD). *Accreditation:* NCATE. Part-time and evening/weekend programs available. *Students:* 529 (401 women); includes 39 minority (23 African Americans, 2 American Indian/Alaska Native, 9 Asian Americans or Pacific Islanders, 5 Hispanic Americans) 34 international. 420 applicants, 50% accepted. In 2006, 258 master's, 28 doctorates awarded. *Degree requirements:* For master's and Ed S, thesis optional; for doctorate, variable foreign language requirement, thesis/dissertation. *Entrance requirements:* For master's, minimum GPA of 2.7; for doctorate and Ed S, GRE General Test, minimum GPA of 2.7. Additional exam requirements/recommendations for international students: Required—TOEFL. *Application deadline:* For fall admission, 2/1 priority date for domestic students. Applications are processed on a rolling basis. Application fee: $35. Electronic applications accepted. *Expenses:* Tuition, state resident: full-time $5,574. Tuition, nonresident: full-time $16,840. Required fees: $792. *Financial support:* In 2006–07, 4 fellowships, 9 teaching assistantships were awarded; career-related internships or fieldwork, Federal Work-Study, institutionally sponsored loans, and unspecified assistantships also available. Financial award application deadline: 2/1; financial award applicants required to submit FAFSA. *Unit head:* Dr. Lester Knight, Head, 865-974-0907, Fax: 865-974-8718, E-mail: lknight@utk.edu.

The University of Tennessee at Chattanooga, Graduate School, College of Health, Education and Professional Studies, Graduate Studies Division of Education, Chattanooga, TN 37403-2598. Offers counseling (M Ed); educational leadership (Ed D); educational specialist (Ed S), including educational technology, school psychology; elementary education (M Ed); school leadership (M Ed); secondary education (M Ed); special education (M Ed). *Accreditation:* ACA; NCATE. Part-time and evening/weekend programs available. *Faculty:* 28 full-time (18 women), 7 part-time/adjunct (3 women). *Students:* 166 full-time (123 women), 309 part-time (238 women); includes 57 minority (46 African Americans, 2 American Indian/Alaska Native, 7 Asian Americans or Pacific Islanders, 2 Hispanic Americans). Average age 33. 138 applicants, 95% accepted, 66 enrolled. In 2006, 133 master's, 25 other advanced degrees awarded. *Degree requirements:* For master's, thesis optional; for doctorate, thesis/dissertation, comprehensive exam. *Entrance requirements:* For master's, GRE General Test or MAT, teaching certificate. *Application deadline:* For fall admission, 8/1 for domestic students; for spring admission, 12/1 for domestic students. Applications are processed on a rolling basis. Application fee: $30. *Expenses:* Tuition, state resident: full-time $5,434; part-time $339 per hour. Tuition, nonresident: full-time $14,830; part-time $861 per hour. Required fees: $940; $178 per hour. *Financial support:* Fellowships, research assistantships, Federal Work-Study and institutionally sponsored loans available. Support available to part-time students. Financial award application deadline: 4/1; financial award applicants required to submit FAFSA. *Faculty research:* School counseling, community counseling, elementary and secondary education, school leadership and administration. Total annual research expenditures: $258,901. *Unit head:* Dr. Anthony Lease, Head, 423-425-4211, Fax: 423-425-5380, E-mail: tony-lease@utc.edu. *Application contact:* Dr. Deborah E. Arfken, Dean of Graduate Studies, 423-425-4666, Fax: 423-425-5223, E-mail: deborah-arfken@utc.edu.

The University of Texas at Austin, Graduate School, College of Education, Department of Special Education, Austin, TX 78712-1111. Offers M Ed, MA, Ed D, PhD. *Accreditation:* CORE. Part-time and evening/weekend programs available. Postbaccalaureate distance learning degree programs offered (no on-campus study). *Degree requirements:* For master's, thesis or alternative; for doctorate, thesis/dissertation. *Entrance requirements:* For master's and doctorate, GRE General Test. *Faculty research:* Anchored instruction, reading disabilities, multicultural/bilingual.

The University of Texas at Brownsville, Graduate Studies, School of Education, Brownsville, TX 78520-4991. Offers bilingual education (M Ed); counseling and guidance (M Ed); curriculum and instruction (M Ed); early childhood education (M Ed); educational administration (M Ed); educational technology (M Ed); English as a second language (M Ed); reading specialist (M Ed); special education/educational diagnostician (M Ed). Part-time and evening/weekend programs available. Postbaccalaureate distance learning degree programs offered (minimal on-campus study). *Degree requirements:* For master's, thesis optional. *Entrance requirements:* For master's, GRE General Test. Additional exam requirements/recommendations for international students: Required—TOEFL.

The University of Texas at San Antonio, College of Education and Human Development, Department of Interdisciplinary Learning and Teaching, San Antonio, TX 78249-0617. Offers curriculum and instruction (MA); early childhood and elementary education (MA); educational psychology/special education (MA); instructional technology (MA); reading and literacy (MA). Part-time and evening/weekend programs available. *Faculty:* 26 full-time (all women), 1 part-time/adjunct (0 women). *Students:* 40 full-time (32 women), 240 part-time (207 women); includes 155 minority (20 African Americans, 1 American Indian/Alaska Native, 6 Asian Americans or Pacific Islanders, 128 Hispanic Americans), 3 international. Average age 35. 94 applicants, 100% accepted, 94 enrolled. In 2006, 61 degrees awarded. *Degree requirements:* For master's, thesis optional. *Entrance requirements:* For master's, GRE General Test. Additional exam requirements/recommendations for international students: Required—TOEFL (minimum score 500 paper-based; 173 computer-based). *Application deadline:* For fall admission, 7/1 for domestic students, 4/1 for international students; for spring admission, 11/1 for domestic students, 9/1 for international students. Applications are processed on a rolling basis. Application fee: $45 ($80 for international students). Electronic applications accepted. *Expenses:* Tuition, state resident: full-time $1,730; part-time $192 per credit hour. Tuition, nonresident: full-time $6,680; part-time $742 per credit hour. Required fees: $733; $308,359 per credit hour. *Financial support:* In 2006–07, 3 research assistantships (averaging $28,891 per year) were awarded; career-related internships or fieldwork, Federal Work-Study, scholarships/grants, and unspecified assistantships also available. *Faculty research:* Early childhood, reading, special education, foundations, curriculum and instruction. Total annual research expenditures: $570,791. *Unit head:* Dr. Belinda B. Flores, Chair, 210-458-5969, Fax: 210-458-7281, E-mail: belinda.flores@utsa.edu.

The University of Texas at Tyler, College of Education and Psychology, Department of Early Childhood Education, Reading and Special Education, Tyler, TX 75799-0001. Offers early childhood education (M Ed, MA); reading (M Ed, MA); special education (M Ed, MA). Part-time and evening/weekend programs available. *Faculty:* 13 full-time (11 women), 3 part-time/adjunct (2 women). *Students:* 9 full-time (8 women), 46 part-time (42 women); includes 8 minority (6 African Americans, 2 Hispanic Americans), 2 international. Average age 36. 5 applicants, 4 enrolled. In 2006, 16 degrees awarded. *Degree requirements:* For master's, thesis (for some programs), research project, comprehensive exam. *Entrance requirements:* For master's, GRE General Test. *Application deadline:* For fall admission, 11/1 for domestic students. Applications are processed on a rolling basis. Application fee: $0 ($50 for international students). Electronic applications accepted. *Expenses:* Tuition, state resident: part-time $50 per credit hour. Tuition, nonresident: part-time $328 per credit hour. Required fees: $107 per credit hour. $426 per term. *Financial support:* In 2006–07, 2 research assistantships (averaging $12,000 per year) were awarded; scholarships/grants also available. Financial award application deadline: 7/1. *Faculty research:* Improving quality in childcare settings, play and creativity, teacher interactions, effects of modeling on early childhood teachers, biofeedback, literacy instruction. *Unit head:* Dr. Brenda Gilliam, Head, 903-566-7087, Fax: 903-565-5527, E-mail: bgilliam@mail.uttyl.edu. *Application contact:* Bonnie Purser, Office of Graduate Studies, 903-566-7142, Fax: 903-566-7068, E-mail: bpurser@uttyler.edu.

The University of Texas of the Permian Basin, Office of Graduate Studies, School of Education, Program in Special Education, Odessa, TX 79762-0001. Offers MA. *Degree requirements:* For master's, thesis (for some programs), comprehensive exam (for some programs), registration. *Entrance requirements:* For master's, GRE General Test. Additional exam requirements/recommendations for international students: Required—TOEFL (minimum score 550 paper-based; 213 computer-based).

The University of Texas–Pan American, College of Education, Department of Educational Psychology, Edinburg, TX 78541-2999. Offers counseling (M Ed); educational diagnostician (M Ed); gifted education (M Ed); school psychology (MA); special education (M Ed). Part-time and evening/weekend programs available. *Degree requirements:* For master's, thesis (for some programs), comprehensive exam (for some programs). *Entrance requirements:* For master's, GRE General Test, interview. *Expenses:* Tuition, state resident: full-time $2,577; part-time $143 per credit hour. Tuition, nonresident: full-time $7,527; part-time $418 per credit hour. Required fees: $561. *Faculty research:* Reading instruction, assessment practice, behavior interventions consultation, mental retardation.

University of the Cumberlands, Graduate Programs in Education, Program in Special Education, Williamsburg, KY 40769-1372. Offers MA Ed, MAT. Evening/weekend programs available. *Degree requirements:* For master's, comprehensive exam. *Entrance requirements:* For master's, GRE or NTE, Kentucky teaching certificate.

University of the District of Columbia, College of Arts and Sciences, Department of Education, Program in Special Education, Washington, DC 20008-1175. Offers MA. *Accreditation:* NCATE. Part-time programs available. *Students:* 1 full-time (0 women), 1 part-time; includes 1 minority (African American) 16 applicants, 75% accepted. *Application deadline:* For fall admission, 6/15 priority date for domestic students; for spring admission, 11/1 for domestic students. Applications are processed on a rolling basis. Application fee: $20. *Financial support:* Fellowships, research assistantships available. *Application contact:* LaVerne Hill Flannigan, Director of Admission, 202-274-6069.

University of the Incarnate Word, School of Graduate Studies and Research, Dreeben School of Education, Programs in Education, San Antonio, TX 78209-6397. Offers adult education (M Ed, MA); diversity education (M Ed, MA); early childhood education (M Ed, MA); instructional technology (M Ed, MA); international education and entrepreneurship (PhD); kinesiology (M Ed, MA); mathematics education (PhD); organizational leadership (PhD); organizational learning (M Ed, MA); reading (M Ed, MA); special education (M Ed, MA). *Students:* 15 full-time (8 women), 179 part-time (117 women); includes 70 minority (20 African Americans, 1 American Indian/Alaska Native, 1 Asian American or Pacific Islander, 48 Hispanic Americans), 54 international. Average age 39. In 2006, 15 degrees awarded. Application fee: $20. *Expenses:* Tuition: Part-time $570 per credit hour. Required fees: $54 per credit hour. One-time fee: $195 part-time. Tuition and fees vary according to degree level. *Financial support:* Federal Work-Study and scholarships/grants available. *Unit head:* Dr. Richard Gray, Director, 210-829-3138, Fax: 210-829-3134, E-mail: gray@uiwtx.edu. *Application contact:* Andrea Cyterski-Acosta, Dean of Enrollment, 210-829-6005, Fax: 210-829-3921, E-mail: cyterski@uiwtx.edu.

University of the Pacific, School of Education, Department of Curriculum and Instruction, Stockton, CA 95211-0197. Offers curriculum and instruction (M Ed, MA, Ed D); education (M Ed); special education (MA). *Accreditation:* NCATE. *Faculty:* 11 full-time (7 women), 5 part-time/adjunct (2 women). *Students:* 20 full-time (19 women), 21 part-time (16 women); includes 15 minority (2 African Americans, 5 Asian Americans or Pacific Islanders, 8 Hispanic Americans), 1 international. Average age 33. 42 applicants, 69% accepted, 24 enrolled. In 2006, 34 master's, 4 doctorates awarded. *Degree requirements:* For master's, thesis (for some programs). *Entrance requirements:* For master's, GRE General Test. Additional exam requirements/recommendations for international students: Required—TOEFL (minimum score 475 paper-based; 150 computer-based). *Application deadline:* For fall admission, 3/1 priority date for domestic students; for spring admission, 10/1 priority date for domestic students. Applications are processed on a rolling basis. Application fee: $75. *Expenses:* Tuition: Full-time $26,920. Required fees: $430. Tuition and fees vary according to course load. *Financial support:* In 2006–07, 7 teaching assistantships were awarded. Financial award application deadline: 3/1; financial award applicants required to submit FAFSA. *Unit head:* Dr. Marilyn Draheim, Chairperson, 209-946-2685, E-mail: mdraheim@pacific.edu.

The University of Toledo, College of Graduate Studies, College of Education, Department of Early Childhood, Physical and Special Education, Program in Special Education, Toledo, OH 43606-3390. Offers ME, DE, PhD, Ed S. *Students:* 45 full-time (36 women), 83 part-time (77 women); includes 17 minority (13 African Americans, 1 Asian American or Pacific Islander, 3 Hispanic Americans). Average age 32. 51 applicants, 92% accepted, 39 enrolled. In 2006, 35 degrees awarded. *Unit head:* Dr. Laurie Dinnebeil, Chair, Department of Early Childhood, Physical and Special Education, 419-530-4330.

University of Utah, The Graduate School, College of Education, Department of Special Education, Salt Lake City, UT 84112-1107. Offers M Ed, M Phil, MS, PhD. Part-time and evening/weekend programs available. *Faculty:* 14 full-time (8 women), 2 part-time/adjunct (1 woman). *Students:* 40 full-time (37 women), 25 part-time (18 women); includes 8 minority (5 American Indian/Alaska Native, 1 Asian American or Pacific Islander, 2 Hispanic Americans), 1 international. Average age 34. 21 applicants, 33% accepted, 6 enrolled. In 2006, 32 master's, 3 doctorates awarded. *Degree requirements:* For master's, thesis (for some programs); for doctorate, thesis/dissertation. *Entrance requirements:* For master's and doctorate, GRE General Test, minimum GPA of 3.0. Additional exam requirements/recommendations for international students: Required—TOEFL (minimum score 600 paper-based; 250 computer-based). *Application deadline:* For fall admission, 3/15 for domestic and international students; for spring admission, 10/15 for domestic and international students. Applications are processed on a rolling basis. Application fee: $45 ($65 for international students). *Expenses:* Tuition, state resident: full-time $3,208. Tuition, nonresident: full-time $11,326. Required fees: $608. Tuition and fees vary according to class time and program. *Financial support:* In 2006–07, 40 students received support, including 35 fellowships with tuition reimbursements available (averaging $8,571 per year); teaching assistantships with full tuition reimbursements available, career-related internships or fieldwork and scholarships/grants also available. Financial award application deadline: 3/1; financial award applicants required to submit FAFSA. *Faculty research:* Inclusive education, early childhood/special education sensory impairments, behavior. Total annual research expenditures: $13,938. *Unit head:* Michael Hardman, Chair, 801-581-8121, Fax: 801-585-6476, E-mail: michael.hardman@ed.utah.edu. *Application contact:* Patty Davis, Academic Advisor, 801-581-4764, Fax: 801-585-6476, E-mail: patty.davis@ed.utah.edu.

University of Vermont, Graduate College, College of Education and Social Services, Department of Education, Program in Special Education, Burlington, VT 05405. Offers M Ed. *Accreditation:* NCATE. *Students:* 35 (28 women). 30 applicants, 70% accepted, 16 enrolled. In 2006, 24 degrees awarded. *Degree requirements:* For master's, thesis or alternative. *Entrance requirements:* Additional exam requirements/recommendations for international students: Required—TOEFL (minimum score 550 paper-based; 213 computer-based). *Application deadline:* For fall admission, 3/15 priority date for domestic students. Applications are processed on a rolling basis. Application fee: $40. *Expenses:* Tuition, state resident: part-time $434 per credit. Tuition, nonresident: part-time $1,096 per credit. *Financial support:* Research assistantships, teaching assistantships, career-related internships or fieldwork available. Financial award application deadline: 3/1. *Unit head:* W. Williams, Chairperson, 802-656-2936.

University of Victoria, Faculty of Graduate Studies, Faculty of Education, Department of Educational Psychology and Leadership Studies, Victoria, BC V8W 2Y2, Canada. Offers counseling (M Ed, MA); educational psychology (M Ed, MA, PhD), including counseling psychology (M Ed, MA), learning and development (PhD), learning development (MA), measurement and evaluation (PhD), measurement evaluation (M Ed, MA), special education (M Ed, MA); leadership studies (M Ed, MA). Part-time programs available. *Degree requirements:* For master's, thesis (for some programs), comprehensive exam (M Ed); for doctorate, thesis/dissertation, candidacy exam, comprehensive exam, registration. *Entrance requirements:* For master's, 2 years of work experience in a relevant field, minimum B average; for doctorate, GRE, 2 years of work experience in a relevant field, minimum B average. Additional exam requirements/recommendations for international students: Required—TOEFL (minimum score 575 paper-based; 233 computer-based), IELTS (minimum score 7). *Faculty research:* Learning and development (child, adolescent and adult), special education and exceptional children, evaluation and measurement.

University of Virginia, Curry School of Education, Department of Curriculum, Instruction, and Special Education, Program in Special Education, Charlottesville, VA 22903. Offers M Ed, Ed D, Ed S. *Accreditation:* Teacher Education Accreditation Council. *Students:* 7 full-time (6 women), 6 part-time (5 women), 1 international. Average age 32. 6 applicants, 67% accepted, 4 enrolled. In 2006, 24 degrees awarded. *Degree requirements:* For master's, thesis (for some programs), comprehensive exam (for some programs); for doctorate, thesis/dissertation, comprehensive exam (for some programs). *Entrance requirements:* For master's, doctorate, and Ed S, GRE General Test. Additional exam requirements/recommendations for international students: Required—TOEFL (minimum score 600 paper-based; 250 computer-based). *Application deadline:* Applications are processed on a rolling basis. Application fee: $60. *Financial support:* Applicants required to submit FAFSA. *Application contact:* Martha E. Snell, Coordinator, 434-924-0768.

University of Washington, Graduate School, College of Education, Program in Special Education, Seattle, WA 98195. Offers early childhood education (M Ed, Ed D, PhD); elementary special education (M Ed, Ed D, PhD); emotional and behavioral disabilities (M Ed); general special education (M Ed, Ed D, PhD); severe disabilities (M Ed, Ed D, PhD). *Degree requirements:* For master's, thesis optional; for doctorate, thesis/dissertation. *Entrance requirements:* For master's and doctorate, GRE General Test, minimum GPA of 3.0. Additional exam requirements/recommendations for international students: Required—TOEFL.

The University of West Alabama, School of Graduate Studies, College of Education, Department of Teacher Education, Program in Special Education, Livingston, AL 35470. Offers M Ed. *Accreditation:* NCATE. Part-time programs available. *Faculty:* 1 (woman) full-time, 2 part-time/adjunct (both women). *Students:* 15 full-time (12 women), 35 part-time (31 women); includes 34 minority (33 African Americans, 1 Asian American or Pacific Islander). In 2006, 11 degrees awarded. *Entrance requirements:* For master's, GRE General Test, MAT, minimum GPA of 2.75. *Application deadline:* For fall admission, 9/10 priority date for domestic students; for spring admission, 3/24 for domestic students. Applications are processed on a rolling basis. Application fee: $20 ($50 for international students). *Financial support:* Career-related internships or fieldwork, Federal Work-Study, scholarships/grants, and unspecified assistantships available. Support available to part-time students. *Faculty research:* Learning strategies/reading; imagine, discuss, and decide; transition; at-risk students. *Unit head:* Dr. Marion Madison, Coordinator, 205-652-3436.

The University of Western Ontario, Faculty of Graduate Studies, Social Sciences Division, Faculty of Education, Program in Educational Studies, London, ON N6A 5B8, Canada. Offers curriculum studies (M Ed); educational policy studies (M Ed); educational psychology/special education (M Ed). Part-time programs available. *Application deadline:* For fall admission, 2/1 for domestic students. Application fee: $50. *Financial support:* Research assistantships, teaching assistantships available. Financial award application deadline: 4/1. *Faculty research:* Reflective practice, gender and schooling, feminist pedagogy, narrative inquiry, second language, multiculturalism in Canada, education and law. *Unit head:* Allan Pitman, Graduate Chair, 519-661-2111 Ext. 88870, Fax: 519-661-3833, E-mail: pitman@uwo.ca. *Application contact:* L. Kulak, Graduate Supervisor, 519-661-2099, Fax: 519-661-3833, E-mail: kulak@edu.uwo.ca.

University of West Florida, College of Professional Studies, Division of Teacher Education, Program in Special Education-Clinical Teaching, Pensacola, FL 32514-5750. Offers clinical teaching (MA), including emotionally handicapped, learning disabled, mentally handicapped;

Special Education

University of West Florida (continued)
habilitative science (MA). *Accreditation:* NCATE. Part-time and evening/weekend programs available. *Students:* 15 full-time (12 women), 34 part-time (all women); includes 13 minority (11 African Americans, 2 Hispanic Americans). Average age 33. 18 applicants, 89% accepted, 16 enrolled. In 2006, 20 degrees awarded. *Entrance requirements:* For master's, GRE General Test or minimum GPA of 3.0, 1 year of teaching experience. Additional exam requirements/recommendations for international students: Required—TOEFL (minimum score 550 paper-based; 213 computer-based). *Application deadline:* For fall admission, 6/1 for domestic students, 5/15 for international students; for spring admission, 11/1 for domestic students, 10/1 for international students. Applications are processed on a rolling basis. Application fee: $30. *Expenses:* Tuition, state resident: full-time $5,871; part-time $245 per credit hour. Tuition, nonresident: full-time $21,241; part-time $885 per credit hour. *Financial support:* Fellowships, career-related internships or fieldwork, Federal Work-Study, scholarships/grants, and unspecified assistantships available. Financial award application deadline: 4/15; financial award applicants required to submit FAFSA. *Faculty research:* Memory, semantic structure, remedial programming. *Unit head:* Dr. Joseph M. Peters, Chairperson and Associate Dean, Division of Teacher Education, 850-474-2768.

University of West Georgia, Graduate School, College of Education, Department of Special Education and Speech-Language Pathology, Program in Learning Disabled, Carrollton, GA 30118. Offers Ed S. *Expenses:* Tuition, state resident: full-time $2,286; part-time $127 per credit. Tuition, nonresident: full-time $9,144; part-time $508 per credit. Required fees: $494; $27 per credit. $121 per semester.

University of West Georgia, Graduate School, College of Education, Department of Special Education and Speech-Language Pathology, Program in Special Education-Behavior Disorders, Carrollton, GA 30118. Offers M Ed. In 2006, 1 degree awarded. *Expenses:* Tuition, state resident: full-time $2,286; part-time $127 per credit. Tuition, nonresident: full-time $9,144; part-time $508 per credit. Required fees: $494; $27 per credit. $121 per semester. *Application contact:* Dr. Charles W. Clark, Chair, 678-839-6508, E-mail: cclark@westga.edu.

University of West Georgia, Graduate School, College of Education, Department of Special Education and Speech-Language Pathology, Program in Special Education-General, Carrollton, GA 30118. Offers curriculum and instruction (Ed S); leadership (Ed S). Part-time and evening/weekend programs available. *Students:* Average age 39. In 2006, 6 degrees awarded. *Degree requirements:* For Ed S, research project. *Application deadline:* For fall admission, 8/1 for domestic students. Applications are processed on a rolling basis. Application fee: $20. Electronic applications accepted. *Expenses:* Tuition, state resident: full-time $2,286; part-time $127 per credit. Tuition, nonresident: full-time $9,144; part-time $508 per credit. Required fees: $494; $27 per credit. $121 per semester. *Financial support:* Applicants required to submit FAFSA. *Application contact:* Dr. Charles W. Clark, Chair, 678-839-6508, E-mail: cclark@westga.edu.

University of West Georgia, Graduate School, College of Education, Department of Special Education and Speech-Language Pathology, Program in Special Education-Interrelated, Carrollton, GA 30118. Offers M Ed. Part-time and evening/weekend programs available. *Students:* 5 full-time (3 women), 76 part-time (67 women); includes 16 minority (14 African Americans, 1 Asian American or Pacific Islander, 1 Hispanic American). Average age 30. In 2006, 36 master's awarded. *Entrance requirements:* For master's, GRE, minimum GPA of 2.7, 3 letters of recommendation. *Application deadline:* For fall admission, 8/1 priority date for domestic students; for spring admission, 12/18 for domestic students. Application fee: $20. Electronic applications accepted. *Expenses:* Tuition, state resident: full-time $2,286; part-time $127 per credit. Tuition, nonresident: full-time $9,144; part-time $508 per credit. Required fees: $494; $27 per credit. $121 per semester. *Financial support:* Applicants required to submit FAFSA. *Application contact:* Dr. Charles W. Clark, Chair, 678-839-6508, E-mail: cclark@westga.edu.

University of Wisconsin–Eau Claire, College of Education and Human Sciences, Program in Special Education, Eau Claire, WI 54702-4004. Offers MSE. *Faculty:* 5 full-time (2 women). *Students:* 3 full-time (2 women), 13 part-time (11 women). Average age 34. 8 applicants, 50% accepted, 4 enrolled. In 2006, 10 degrees awarded. *Degree requirements:* For master's, thesis optional. *Application deadline:* For fall admission, 7/1 for domestic students; for spring admission, 12/1 for domestic students. Applications are processed on a rolling basis. Application fee: $45. *Expenses:* Tuition, state resident: full-time $6,533; part-time $363 per credit. Tuition, nonresident: full-time $17,143; part-time $952 per credit. Tuition and fees vary according to program and reciprocity agreements. *Financial support:* In 2006–07, 4 students received support, including 2 teaching assistantships (averaging $5,200 per year); Federal Work-Study also available. Financial award application deadline: 3/1; financial award applicants required to submit FAFSA. *Unit head:* Dr. J. Todd Stephens, Chair, 715-836-4328, Fax: 715-836-3162, E-mail: stephej@uwec.edu.

University of Wisconsin–La Crosse, Office of University Graduate Studies, College of Liberal Studies, Department of Educational Studies, Program in Special Education, La Crosse, WI 54601-3742. Offers emotional disturbance (MS Ed); learning disabilities (MS Ed). Part-time programs available. *Students:* 8 full-time (6 women), 14 part-time (11 women). Average age 34. 13 applicants, 62% accepted, 7 enrolled. In 2006, 8 degrees awarded. *Degree requirements:* For master's, thesis optional. *Entrance requirements:* For master's, GRE General Test, minimum undergraduate GPA of 3.0, 3 letters of recommendation. Additional exam requirements/recommendations for international students: Required—TOEFL (minimum score 550 paper-based; 213 computer-based). *Application deadline:* For fall admission, 5/1 priority date for domestic students; for spring admission, 11/1 priority date for domestic students. Applications are processed on a rolling basis. Application fee: $45. Electronic applications accepted. *Financial support:* In 2006–07, 3 students received support, including 1 research assistantship (averaging $6,323 per year); career-related internships or fieldwork, health care benefits, and unspecified assistantships also available. Financial award application deadline: 3/15; financial award applicants required to submit FAFSA. *Faculty research:* Inclusion, self-determination, teacher education, transition, early reading instruction. *Unit head:* Dr. Jeanne E. Danneker, Director, 608-785-8147, E-mail: danneker.jean@uwlax.edu. *Application contact:* Kathryn Kiefer, Associate Director of Admissions, 608-785-8939, E-mail: admissions@uwlax.edu.

University of Wisconsin–La Crosse, Office of University Graduate Studies, College of Science and Health, Department of Exercise and Sport Science, La Crosse, WI 54601-3742. Offers clinical exercise physiology (MS); human performance (MS), including athletic training, human performance; physical education teaching (MS); special/adapted physical education (MS); sport administration (MS). Part-time and evening/weekend programs available. *Faculty:* 18 full-time (5 women), 6 part-time/adjunct (1 woman). *Students:* 82 full-time (38 women), 57 part-time (18 women); includes 6 minority (3 African Americans, 2 American Indian/Alaska Native, 1 Hispanic American), 5 international. Average age 27. 126 applicants, 69% accepted, 47 enrolled. In 2006, 115 degrees awarded. *Entrance requirements:* For master's, minimum GPA of 3.0 during previous 2 years, 2.85 overall. Additional exam requirements/recommendations for international students: Required—TOEFL (minimum score 550 paper-based; 213 computer-based). *Application deadline:* Applications are processed on a rolling basis. Application fee: $45. Electronic applications accepted. *Financial support:* In 2006–07, 24 students received support; research assistantships, career-related internships or fieldwork, Federal Work-Study, institutionally sponsored loans, scholarships/grants, traineeships, health care benefits, tuition waivers (full and partial), unspecified assistantships, and grant-funded positions, external contracts available. Support available to part-time students. Financial award application deadline: 3/15; financial award applicants required to submit FAFSA. *Faculty research:* Exercise physiology, motor development of the disabled, energy metabolism, muscle physiology, biomechanics and motor learning. Total annual research expenditures: $200,000. *Unit head:* Dr. Patrick DiRocco, Chair, 608-785-8173, Fax: 608-785-6520, E-mail: dirocco.patr@uwlax.edu. *Application contact:* Kathryn Kiefer, Associate Director of Admissions, 608-785-8939, E-mail: admissions@uwlax.edu.

University of Wisconsin–Madison, Graduate School, School of Education, Department of Rehabilitation Psychology and Special Education, Program in Special Education, Madison, WI 53706-1380. Offers MA, MS, PhD. *Degree requirements:* For doctorate, thesis/dissertation. *Application deadline:* For fall admission, 3/15 for domestic and international students; for spring admission, 10/15 for domestic and international students. Application fee: $45. Electronic applications accepted. *Financial support:* Fellowships with full tuition reimbursements, research assistantships with full tuition reimbursements, teaching assistantships with full tuition reimbursements, project assistantships available. *Unit head:* Dr. Cheryl Hanley-Maxwell, Chair, Department of Rehabilitation Psychology and Special Education, 608-262-5860.

University of Wisconsin–Milwaukee, Graduate School, School of Education, Department of Exceptional Education, Milwaukee, WI 53201-0413. Offers MS. Part-time programs available. *Faculty:* 12 full-time (10 women). *Students:* 33 full-time (27 women), 46 part-time (39 women); includes 12 minority (11 African Americans, 1 American Indian/Alaska Native), 1 international. 18 applicants, 39% accepted. In 2006, 22 degrees awarded. *Degree requirements:* For master's, thesis. *Application deadline:* For fall admission, 1/1 priority date for domestic students; for spring admission, 9/1 for domestic students. Applications are processed on a rolling basis. Application fee: $45 ($75 for international students). *Expenses:* Tuition, state resident: part-time $510 per credit. Tuition, nonresident: part-time $1,408 per credit. Tuition and fees vary according to program. *Financial support:* Fellowships, research assistantships, teaching assistantships, career-related internships or fieldwork and unspecified assistantships available. Support available to part-time students. Financial award application deadline: 4/15. *Faculty research:* Emotional disturbance, hearing impairment, learning disabilities, mental retardation. *Unit head:* Festus Obiakor, Chair, 414-229-4666, Fax: 414-229-5500.

University of Wisconsin–Oshkosh, The School of Graduate Studies, College of Education and Human Services, Department of Special Education, Oshkosh, WI 54901. Offers cross-categorical (MSE); early childhood: exceptional education needs (MSE); non-licensure (MSE). *Accreditation:* NCATE. Part-time and evening/weekend programs available. *Degree requirements:* For master's, thesis or alternative, field report, comprehensive exam (for some programs), registration. *Entrance requirements:* For master's, interview, minimum GPA of 3.0, teaching license, letters of recommendation. Additional exam requirements/recommendations for international students: Required—TOEFL (minimum score 550 paper-based; 213 computer-based). Electronic applications accepted. *Faculty research:* Private agency contributions to the disabled, graduation requirements for exceptional education needs students, direct instruction in spelling for learning disabled, effects of behavioral parent training, secondary education programming issues.

University of Wisconsin–Stevens Point, College of Professional Studies, School of Education, Program in Education—General/Special, Stevens Point, WI 54481-3897. Offers MSE. Part-time programs available. *Faculty:* 13 full-time (11 women). *Degree requirements:* For master's, thesis or alternative, comprehensive exam. *Entrance requirements:* For master's, minimum undergraduate GPA of 3.0, 2 years teaching experience, letters of recommendation, teacher certification. *Application deadline:* For fall admission, 5/1 priority date for domestic students. Applications are processed on a rolling basis. Application fee: $45. *Expenses:* Tuition, state resident: full-time $5,910; part-time $328 per credit. Tuition, nonresident: full-time $16,520; part-time $918 per credit. Required fees: $756; $73 per credit. *Financial support:* In 2006–07, 4 research assistantships with partial tuition reimbursements (averaging $9,807 per year) were awarded; Federal Work-Study also available. Support available to part-time students. Financial award application deadline: 5/1; financial award applicants required to submit FAFSA. *Faculty research:* Curriculum and instruction, early childhood special education, standards-based education. *Application contact:* Dr. Patricia Caro, Director, 715-346-4403, Fax: 715-346-4846, E-mail: pcaro@uwsp.edu.

University of Wisconsin–Superior, Graduate Division, Department of Teacher Education, Program in Special Education, Superior, WI 54880-4500. Offers emotional/behavior disabilities (MSE); learning disabilities (MSE). Part-time and evening/weekend programs available. Postbaccalaureate distance learning degree programs offered (minimal on-campus study). *Degree requirements:* For master's, research project. *Entrance requirements:* For master's, minimum GPA of 2.75, teaching certificate.

University of Wisconsin–Whitewater, School of Graduate Studies, College of Education, Department of Special Education, Whitewater, WI 53190-1790. Offers MS Ed. *Accreditation:* NCATE. Part-time and evening/weekend programs available. Postbaccalaureate distance learning degree programs offered (no on-campus study). *Students:* 14 full-time (9 women), 58 part-time (54 women); includes 4 minority (all African Americans) Average age 42. 21 applicants, 90% accepted, 3 enrolled. In 2006, 22 degrees awarded. *Degree requirements:* For master's, thesis or alternative. *Entrance requirements:* Additional exam requirements/recommendations for international students: Required—TOEFL (minimum score 550 paper-based; 213 computer-based). *Application deadline:* For fall admission, 7/15 priority date for domestic students; for spring admission, 12/1 priority date for domestic students. Applications are processed on a rolling basis. Application fee: $45. Electronic applications accepted. *Expenses:* Tuition, state resident: full-time $3,311. Tuition, nonresident: full-time $8,616. Required fees: $368 per credit. *Financial support:* In 2006–07, 5 research assistantships (averaging $4,938 per year) were awarded; Federal Work-Study, unspecified assistantships, and out of state fee waiver also available. Support available to part-time students. Financial award application deadline: 3/15; financial award applicants required to submit FAFSA. *Faculty research:* Language ability, cultural interaction with disability, juvenile corrections, early childhood programming and childcare issues. *Unit head:* Dr. Shannon Stuart, Coordinator, 262-472-4877, Fax: 262-472-2843. *Application contact:* Sally A. Lange, School of Graduate Studies, 262-472-1006, Fax: 262-472-5027, E-mail: gradschl@uww.edu.

University of Wyoming, Graduate School, College of Education, Department of Special Education, Laramie, WY 82070. Offers MA, Ed S. *Faculty:* 5 full-time (3 women). *Students:* 7 full-time (6 women), 44 part-time (38 women); includes 2 minority (1 American Indian/Alaska Native, 1 Hispanic American). Average age 37. 5 applicants, 80% accepted, 4 enrolled. In 2006, 1 degree awarded. *Degree requirements:* For master's, thesis, comprehensive exam, registration. *Entrance requirements:* For master's, GRE, 2 years teaching experience, 3 letters of recommendation, writing sample. Application fee: $50. *Unit head:* Dr. Martin Agran, Head, 307-766-2082, Fax: 307-766-2018, E-mail: magran@uwyo.edu. *Application contact:* Connie Turner, Office Associate, 307-766-6325, E-mail: cturner@uwyo.edu.

Utah State University, School of Graduate Studies, College of Education and Human Services, Department of Special Education and Rehabilitation, Logan, UT 84322. Offers disability disciplines (PhD); rehabilitation counselor education (MRC); special education (M Ed, MS, Ed S). *Accreditation:* NCATE (one or more programs are accredited). Part-time programs available. Postbaccalaureate distance learning degree programs offered (minimal on-campus study). *Faculty:* 15 full-time (7 women), 2 part-time/adjunct (both women). *Students:* 75 full-time (42 women), 22 part-time (19 women); includes 5 minority (1 African American, 1 American Indian/Alaska Native, 1 Asian American or Pacific Islander, 2 Hispanic Americans), 22 international. Average age 30. 146 applicants, 87% accepted, 11 enrolled. In 2006, 13 master's, 2 doctorates awarded. *Degree requirements:* For master's, thesis (for some programs), internships (for some programs); for doctorate, thesis/dissertation, comprehensive exam, registration. *Entrance requirements:* For master's and doctorate, GRE General Test, minimum GPA of 3.0. Additional exam requirements/recommendations for international students: Required—TOEFL (minimum score 550 paper-based; 213 computer-based). *Application deadline:* For fall admission, 3/15 priority date for domestic students, 3/15 for international students; for winter admission, 6/15 priority date for domestic students, 6/15 for international students; for spring admission, 10/15 priority date for domestic students, 10/15 for international students. Application fee: $50 ($60 for international students). Electronic applications accepted. *Financial support:* In 2006–07, 9 students received support, including 8 research assistantships with full and partial tuition reimbursements available, 1 teaching assistantship with full and partial tuition reimbursement available; fellowships with full and partial tuition reimbursements available, career-related internships or fieldwork, Federal Work-Study, institutionally sponsored loans, traineeships, tuition waivers (partial), and unspecified assistantships also available. *Faculty research:* Applied behavior analysis, effective instructional practices, early childhood teacher training research, distance education, multicultural rehabilitation. Total annual research expenditures: $3.5 million. *Unit head:* Dr. Ben Lignugaris-Kraft, Head, 435-797-2382, Fax: 435-797-3572, E-mail: lig@cc.usu.edu. *Application contact:* Kristine Wengreen, Staff Assistant, 435-797-3246, Fax: 435-797-3572, E-mail: kris2@cc.usu.edu.

Valdosta State University, Graduate School, College of Education, Department of Special Education and Communication Disorders, Valdosta, GA 31698. Offers communication disorders (M Ed); special education (M Ed, Ed S). *Accreditation:* ASHA (one or more programs are accredited); NCATE. Part-time and evening/weekend programs available. *Degree requirements:* For master's, thesis (for some programs), comprehensive written and/or oral exams; for Ed S, thesis. *Entrance requirements:* For master's, GRE General Test or MAT, minimum GPA of 2.5; for Ed S, GRE General Test or MAT, minimum GPA of 3.0. Additional exam requirements/recommendations for international students: Required—TOEFL (minimum score 523 paper-based; 193 computer-based). Electronic applications accepted.

Vanderbilt University, Graduate School, Department of Special Education, Nashville, TN 37240-1001. Offers MS, PhD. *Faculty:* 28 full-time (18 women), 1 (woman) part-time/adjunct. *Students:* 44 full-time (36 women); includes 3 minority (2 African Americans, 1 American Indian/Alaska Native). 38 applicants, 39% accepted, 14 enrolled. In 2006, 2 master's, 8 doctorates awarded. *Application deadline:* For fall admission, 1/15 for domestic and international students. Application fee: $0. Electronic applications accepted. *Expenses:* Tuition: Full-time $24,462. Required fees: $2,515. One-time fee: $30 full-time. Full-time tuition and fees vary according to course load, degree level and program. *Financial support:* Fellowships with tuition reimbursements, research assistantships with full tuition reimbursements, teaching assistantships with full tuition reimbursements, Federal Work-Study, institutionally sponsored loans, and traineeships available. Financial award application deadline: 1/15. *Unit head:* Craig Kennedy, Chair, 615-322-8150, Fax: 615-343-1570, E-mail: craig.kennedy@vanderbilt.edu. *Application contact:* Dr. Mark Wolery, Director of Graduate Studies, 615-322-8120, Fax: 615-343-1570, E-mail: mark.wolery@vanderbilt.edu.

Vanderbilt University, Peabody College, Department of Special Education, Nashville, TN 37240-1001. Offers M Ed. *Accreditation:* NCATE. *Faculty:* 25 full-time (13 women), 5 part-time/adjunct (3 women). *Students:* 76 full-time (72 women), 23 part-time (22 women); includes 7 minority (2 African Americans, 3 Asian Americans or Pacific Islanders, 2 Hispanic Americans), 4 international. Average age 27. 60 applicants, 75% accepted, 34 enrolled. In 2006, 51 master's awarded. *Degree requirements:* For master's, thesis optional. *Entrance requirements:* For master's, GRE General Test, MAT. Additional exam requirements/recommendations for international students: Required—TOEFL (minimum score 550 paper-based; 213 computer-based). *Application deadline:* For fall admission, 12/31 priority date for domestic and international students; for spring admission, 11/1 priority date for domestic and international students. Applications are processed on a rolling basis. Application fee: $0. Electronic applications accepted. *Expenses:* Tuition: Full-time $24,462. Required fees: $2,515. One-time fee: $30 full-time. Full-time tuition and fees vary according to course load, degree level and program. *Financial support:* In 2006–07, 99 students received support, including 14 fellowships with full and partial tuition reimbursements available, 85 research assistantships with full and partial tuition reimbursements available; teaching assistantships with full and partial tuition reimbursements available, Federal Work-Study, institutionally sponsored loans, scholarships/grants, traineeships, tuition waivers (partial), and unspecified assistantships also available. Support available to part-time students. Financial award application deadline: 2/1. *Faculty research:* Learning disabilities, autism, behavioral disorders; at risk students; visual impairments. *Unit head:* Craig Kennedy, Chair, 615-322-8150, Fax: 615-343-1570, E-mail: craig.kennedy@vanderbilt.edu. *Application contact:* Lynda F. Wyatt, Administrative Assistant, 615-322-8195, Fax: 615-343-1570, E-mail: lynda.wyatt@vanderbilt.edu.

Vanderbilt University, School of Medicine, Department of Hearing and Speech Sciences, Nashville, TN 37240-1001. Offers audiology (Au D, PhD); education of the deaf (MED); hearing and speech sciences (MS); speech-language-pathology (MS). *Faculty:* 25 full-time (10 women), 7 part-time/adjunct (5 women). *Students:* 98 full-time (85 women); includes 7 minority (1 African American, 4 Asian Americans or Pacific Islanders, 2 Hispanic Americans). Average age 28. 224 applicants, 25% accepted, 35 enrolled. In 2006, 15 master's, 10 doctorates awarded. *Median time to degree:* Master's–2 years full-time; doctorate–4 years full-time. *Degree requirements:* For master's, thesis optional; for doctorate, thesis/dissertation, final and qualifying exams. *Entrance requirements:* For master's and doctorate, GRE General Test. Additional exam requirements/recommendations for international students: Required—TOEFL. *Application deadline:* For fall admission, 1/15 for domestic and international students. Electronic applications accepted. *Expenses:* Tuition: Full-time $24,462. Required fees: $2,515. One-time fee: $30 full-time. Full-time tuition and fees vary according to course load, degree level and program. *Financial support:* In 2006–07, fellowships with full tuition reimbursements (averaging $12,000 per year), research assistantships with full tuition reimbursements (averaging $12,000 per year) were awarded; career-related internships or fieldwork, institutionally sponsored loans, and tuition waivers (full and partial) also available. Financial award application deadline: 1/15. *Faculty research:* Audiology, speech-language pathology, child language. *Unit head:* Dr. Fred H. Bess, Chair, 615-936-5000, Fax: 615-936-5014, E-mail: fred.h.bess@vanderbilt.edu. *Application contact:* Edward G. Conture, Director of Graduate Studies, 615-936-5103, Fax: 615-936-5013, E-mail: edward.g.conture@vanderbilt.edu.

Virginia Commonwealth University, Graduate School, School of Education, Program in Adult and Organizational Learning, Richmond, VA 23284-9005. Offers adult literacy (M Ed); adults with disabilities (M Ed); human resource development (M Ed). *Accreditation:* NCATE. Part-time programs available. *Students:* 1 applicant, 0% accepted. In 2006, 14 degrees awarded. *Entrance requirements:* For master's, GRE General Test or MAT. *Application deadline:* For fall admission, 5/15 for domestic students; for spring admission, 11/15 for domestic students. Applications are processed on a rolling basis. Application fee: $50. *Financial support:* Career-related internships or fieldwork and Federal Work-Study available. Financial award application deadline: 3/1. *Faculty research:* Adult development and learning, program planning and evaluation. *Unit head:* James McMillan, Division Head, 804-828-1305. *Application contact:* Dr. Michael D. Davis, Director, Graduate Studies, 804-828-6530, Fax: 804-827-0676, E-mail: mddavis@vcu.edu.

See Close-Up on page 1279.

Virginia Commonwealth University, Graduate School, School of Education, Program in Special Education, Richmond, VA 23284-9005. Offers early childhood (M Ed); emotionally disturbed (M Ed, MT); learning disabilities (M Ed); mentally retarded (M Ed, MT); severely/profoundly handicapped (M Ed). *Accreditation:* NCATE. *Faculty:* 7 full-time (3 women). *Students:* 14 full-time (10 women), 78 part-time (71 women); includes 21 minority (19 African Americans, 2 American Indian/Alaska Native), 1 international. 21 applicants, 100% accepted. In 2006, 29 degrees awarded. *Degree requirements:* For master's, comprehensive exam. *Entrance requirements:* For master's, GRE General Test or MAT. *Application deadline:* For fall admission, 5/15 for domestic students; for spring admission, 11/15 for domestic students. Applications are processed on a rolling basis. Application fee: $50. *Financial support:* Tuition waivers (partial) available. Financial award application deadline: 3/1. *Unit head:* Dr. John Kregel, Division Head, 804-828-1305. *Application contact:* Dr. Michael D. Davis, Director, Graduate Studies, 804-828-6530, Fax: 804-827-0676, E-mail: mddavis@vcu.edu.

See Close-Up on page 1371.

Virginia Polytechnic Institute and State University, Graduate School, College of Liberal Arts and Human Sciences, School of Education, Department of Educational Leadership and Policy Studies, Program in Administration and Supervision of Special Education, Blacksburg, VA 24061. Offers Ed D, PhD, Ed S. *Accreditation:* NCATE. Postbaccalaureate distance learning degree programs offered (minimal on-campus study). *Degree requirements:* For doctorate, thesis/dissertation, internship. *Entrance requirements:* For doctorate and Ed S, GRE General Test, teaching experience. Additional exam requirements/recommendations for international students: Required—TOEFL. *Application deadline:* Applications are processed on a rolling basis. Application fee: $45. Electronic applications accepted. *Expenses:* Tuition, state resident: full-time $7,017; part-time $390 per credit hour. Tuition, nonresident: full-time $12,414; part-time $690 per credit hour. International tuition: $11,296 full-time. Required fees: $1,523; $256 per term. *Financial support:* In 2006–07, research assistantships with full tuition reimbursements (averaging $11,250 per year); career-related internships or fieldwork and unspecified assistantships also available. Financial award application deadline: 4/1. *Unit head:* Jean B. Crockett, Program Area Leader and Associate Professor, 540-231-4546, Fax: 540-231-7845, E-mail: crocketj@vt.edu.

Walla Walla College, Graduate School, School of Education and Psychology, Specialization in Students at Risk, College Place, WA 99324-1198. Offers M Ed, MA, MAT. *Faculty:* 8 full-time (3 women), 3 part-time/adjunct (1 woman). *Degree requirements:* For master's, thesis (for some programs). *Entrance requirements:* For master's, GRE General Test, minimum GPA of 2.75. *Application deadline:* For fall admission, 4/1 priority date for domestic students. Applications are processed on a rolling basis. Application fee: $50. Electronic applications accepted. *Expenses:* Tuition: Full-time $20,124; part-time $516 per quarter hour. *Financial support:* Teaching assistantships with partial tuition reimbursements available. Financial award application deadline: 4/1; financial award applicants required to submit FAFSA. *Application contact:* Dr. Joe G. Galusha, Dean of Graduate Studies, 509-527-2421, Fax: 509-527-2237, E-mail: galujo@wwc.edu.

Washburn University, College of Arts and Sciences, Department of Education, Program in Special Education, Topeka, KS 66621. Offers M Ed. *Accreditation:* NCATE. *Degree requirements:* For master's, portfolio. *Entrance requirements:* For master's, GRE General Test, MAT, minimum GPA of 3.0 during previous 2 years. *Expenses:* Tuition, state resident: full-time $4,338; part-time $241 per credit hour. Tuition, nonresident: full-time $8,820; part-time $490 per credit hour. Required fees: $62; $31 per semester. *Application contact:* Tara Porter, Licensure Officer, 785-670-1434, Fax: 785-670-1046, E-mail: tara.porter@washburn.edu.

Washington University in St. Louis, School of Medicine, Program in Audiology and Communication Sciences, St Louis, MO 63110. Offers audiology (Au D); deaf education (MS); speech and hearing sciences (PhD). *Accreditation:* ASHA (one or more programs are accredited). *Faculty:* 22 full-time (12 women), 18 part-time/adjunct (12 women). *Students:* 64 full-time (all women), 7 part-time (6 women); includes 5 minority (2 African Americans, 2 Asian Americans or Pacific Islanders, 1 Hispanic American), 1 international. Average age 24. 111 applicants, 23% accepted, 26 enrolled. In 2006, 12 master's, 8 doctorates awarded. Terminal master's awarded for partial completion of doctoral program. *Median time to degree:* Master's–2 years full-time; doctorate–4 years full-time. Of those who began their doctoral program in fall 1998, 100% received their degree in 8 years or less. *Degree requirements:* For master's, thesis, independent study project, oral exam, comprehensive exam, registration; for doctorate, thesis/dissertation, capstone project, oral exam, comprehensive exam, registration. *Entrance requirements:* For master's, GRE General Test, minimum B average in undergraduate course work; for doctorate, GRE General Test, minimum B average. Additional exam requirements/recommendations for international students: Required—TOEFL (minimum score 600 paper-based; 250 computer-based). *Application deadline:* For fall admission, 2/15 for domestic and international students. Application fee: $50 ($75 for international students). *Expenses:* Contact institution. *Financial support:* In 2006–07, 64 students received support, including 64 fellowships (averaging $15,000 per year); career-related internships or fieldwork, institutionally sponsored loans, scholarships/grants, health care benefits, tuition waivers (partial), and unspecified assistantships also available. Support available to part-time students. Financial award application deadline: 2/15; financial award applicants required to submit FAFSA. *Faculty research:* Sensory aids, noise, speech perception, biological deafness, audiology. *Unit head:* Dr. William W. Clark, Program Director, 314-747-0104, Fax: 314-747-0105, E-mail: clarkw@wustl.edu. *Application contact:* Elizabeth A. Elliott, Graduate Program Coordinator, 314-747-0104, Fax: 314-747-0105, E-mail: elliottb@wustl.edu.

Wayne State College, School of Education and Counseling, Department of Counseling and Special Education, Program in Special Education, Wayne, NE 68787. Offers MSE. *Accreditation:* NCATE. Part-time and evening/weekend programs available. *Faculty:* 4 full-time (3 women), 4 part-time/adjunct (3 women). *Students:* Average age 37. In 2006, 1 degree awarded. *Degree requirements:* For master's, thesis, comprehensive exam. *Entrance requirements:* For master's, GRE General Test, minimum GPA of 3.0. Additional exam requirements/recommendations for international students: Required—TOEFL (minimum score 550 paper-based; 213 computer-based). *Application deadline:* Applications are processed on a rolling basis. Application fee: $30. Electronic applications accepted. *Expenses:* Tuition, state resident: full-time $3,114; part-time $130 per credit hour. Tuition, nonresident: full-time $6,228; part-time $260 per credit hour. Required fees: $894; $37 per credit hour. Tuition and fees vary according to course load. *Financial support:* Teaching assistantships available. Financial award applicants required to submit FAFSA.

Wayne State University, College of Education, Division of Teacher Education, Detroit, MI 48202. Offers adult and continuing education (M Ed); art education (M Ed); bilingual/bicultural education (M Ed, MAT); business education (M Ed, MAT); career and technical education (M Ed, Ed D, PhD, Ed S); curriculum and instruction (Ed D, PhD, Ed S); distributive education (M Ed, MAT); early childhood education (M Ed); elementary education (M Ed, MAT, Ed D, PhD, Ed S); elementary education curriculum and instruction (M Ed); English education (M Ed); English education-secondary (M Ed, Ed S); foreign language education (M Ed); general education (Ed D, Ed S); health occupations education (M Ed); industrial education (M Ed); mathematics education (M Ed, Ed S); pre-school and parent education (M Ed); reading (M Ed, Ed D, Ed S); reading, languages and literature (Ed D); school music-vocal (M Ed); science education (M Ed, MAT, Ed S); secondary education (MAT); secondary school reading (M Ed); social studies education (M Ed, Ed S), including education-secondary (M Ed); special education (M Ed, Ed D, PhD, Ed S); teacher education (MAT, Ed D, PhD). *Faculty:* 41 full-time (22 women), 2 part-time/adjunct (both women). *Students:* 401 full-time (295 women), 1,021 part-time (784 women); includes 527 minority (452 African Americans, 6 American Indian/Alaska Native, 32 Asian Americans or Pacific Islanders, 37 Hispanic Americans), 18 international. Average age 36. 296 applicants, 81% accepted, 132 enrolled. In 2006, 386 master's, 1 doctorate awarded. *Degree requirements:* For doctorate, thesis/dissertation. *Entrance requirements:* For master's, minimum GPA of 2.6; for doctorate, minimum undergraduate GPA of 3.0, graduate 3.5; interview. Additional exam requirements/recommendations for international students: Required—TOEFL (minimum score 550 paper-based; 213 computer-based), TWE (minimum score 6). *Application deadline:* For fall admission, 7/1 for domestic students, 6/1 for international students; for winter admission, 10/1 for international students; for spring admission, 2/1 for international students. Application fee: $30 ($50 for international students). Electronic applications accepted. *Financial support:* In 2006–07, 1 fellowship (averaging $34,919 per year) was awarded; research assistantships. *Faculty research:* Reading and writing literacy and literature. Total annual research expenditures: $209,400. *Unit head:* Dr. Joann Snyder, Academic Director, 313-577-1644, E-mail: joanne.snyder@wayne.edu. *Application contact:* Sharon Elliott, Assistant Dean, 313-577-0902, E-mail: sharon.elliott@wayne.edu.

Webster University, School of Education, Department of Multidisciplinary Studies, St. Louis, MO 63119-3194. Offers administrative leadership (Ed S); education leadership (Ed S); educational technology (MAT); mathematics (MAT); multidisciplinary studies (MAT); school systems, superintendency and leadership (Ed S); social science (MAT); special education (MAT). Part-time programs available. *Students:* 97 full-time (83 women), 687 part-time (573 women); includes 173 minority (142 African Americans, 2 American Indian/Alaska Native, 13 Asian Americans or Pacific Islanders, 16 Hispanic Americans), 6 international. Average age 34. In 2006, 14 degrees awarded. *Entrance requirements:* For master's, minimum GPA of 2.5.

Special Education

Webster University (continued)
Application deadline: Applications are processed on a rolling basis. Application fee: $25 ($50 for international students). *Expenses:* Tuition: Full-time $8,820; part-time $490 per credit. Tuition and fees vary according to degree level, campus/location and program. *Financial support:* Federal Work-Study available. Support available to part-time students. Financial award application deadline: 4/1; financial award applicants required to submit FAFSA. *Unit head:* Dr. Donna Campbell, Chair, 314-961-2660 Ext. 7042, Fax: 314-968-7118. *Application contact:* Director of Graduate and Evening Student Admissions, Fax: 314-968-7116, E-mail: gadmit@webster.edu.

West Chester University of Pennsylvania, Graduate Studies, School of Education, Department of Early Childhood and Special Education, West Chester, PA 19383. Offers special education (M Ed). *Accreditation:* NCATE. Part-time and evening/weekend programs available. *Students:* 20 full-time (17 women), 59 part-time (54 women); includes 3 African Americans, 2 Hispanic Americans. Average age 28. 38 applicants, 97% accepted, 15 enrolled. In 2006, 26 degrees awarded. *Degree requirements:* For master's, thesis optional. *Entrance requirements:* For master's, MAT, interview, teaching certificate. *Application deadline:* For fall admission, 4/15 priority date for domestic students; for spring admission, 10/15 for domestic students. Applications are processed on a rolling basis. Application fee: $35. *Financial support:* Research assistantships with full tuition reimbursements, unspecified assistantships available. Support available to part-time students. Financial award application deadline: 2/15; financial award applicants required to submit FAFSA. *Faculty research:* Developing online instruction for children with disabilities. *Unit head:* Dr. Vicki McGinley, Chair, 610-436-2579, E-mail: vmcginley@wcupa.edu. *Application contact:* Dr. George Drake, Graduate Coordinator, E-mail: gdrake@wcupa.edu.

Western Carolina University, Graduate School, College of Education and Allied Professions, Department of Human Services, Programs in General Special Education, Cullowhee, NC 28723. Offers behavioral disorders (MA Ed); comprehensive education-special education (MA Ed); learning disabilities (MA Ed); mental retardation (MA Ed); special education-learning disabilities (MAT). *Accreditation:* NCATE. Part-time and evening/weekend programs available. *Degree requirements:* For master's, comprehensive exam. *Entrance requirements:* For master's, GRE General Test. Additional exam requirements/recommendations for international students: Required—TOEFL (minimum score 550 paper-based; 213 computer-based).

Western Connecticut State University, Division of Graduate Studies, School of Professional Studies, Department of Education and Educational Psychology, Special Education Option, Danbury, CT 06810-6885. Offers MS. Part-time and evening/weekend programs available. *Students:* 1 (woman) full-time, 29 part-time (24 women); includes 1 minority (Hispanic American). Average age 29. In 2006, 17 degrees awarded. *Degree requirements:* For master's, thesis or research project. *Entrance requirements:* For master's, minimum GPA of 2.8, teaching certificate. *Application deadline:* For fall admission, 8/1 priority date for domestic students. Applications are processed on a rolling basis. Application fee: $40. *Financial support:* Fellowships, career-related internships or fieldwork available. Support available to part-time students. Financial award application deadline: 5/1; financial award applicants required to submit FAFSA. *Application contact:* Chris Shankle, Associate Director of Graduate Admissions, 203-837-8244, Fax: 203-837-8338, E-mail: shanklec@wcsu.edu.

Western Illinois University, School of Graduate Studies, College of Education and Human Services, Department of Special Education, Macomb, IL 61455-1390. Offers MS Ed. *Accreditation:* NCATE. Part-time programs available. *Students:* 6 full-time (4 women), 40 part-time (36 women); includes 2 minority (1 African American, 1 Hispanic American). Average age 34. 12 applicants, 75% accepted. In 2006, 6 degrees awarded. *Degree requirements:* For master's, thesis or alternative, comprehensive exam. *Entrance requirements:* For master's, teacher certification. Additional exam requirements/recommendations for international students: Required—TOEFL (minimum score 550 paper-based; 213 computer-based; 80 iBT). *Application deadline:* Applications are processed on a rolling basis. Application fee: $30. Electronic applications accepted. *Expenses:* Tuition, state resident: part-time $200 per credit hour. Tuition, nonresident: part-time $400 per credit hour. *Financial support:* In 2006–07, 1 student received support, including 1 research assistantship with full tuition reimbursement available (averaging $6,568 per year). Financial award applicants required to submit FAFSA. *Unit head:* Dr. Rori Carson, Chairperson, 309-298-1909. *Application contact:* Dr. Barbara Baily, Director of Graduate Studies/Associate Provost, 309-298-1806, Fax: 309-298-2345, E-mail: grad-office@wiu.edu.

Western Kentucky University, Graduate Studies, College of Education and Behavioral Sciences, Department of Special Instructional Programs, Bowling Green, KY 42101. Offers exceptional child education (MAE); interdisciplinary early child education (MAE); library media education (MS); literacy (MAE). Part-time and evening/weekend programs available. Post-baccalaureate distance learning degree programs offered (minimal on-campus study). *Faculty:* 15 full-time (12 women), 1 (woman) part-time/adjunct. *Students:* 38 full-time (35 women), 347 part-time (296 women); includes 18 minority (8 African Americans, 2 American Indian/Alaska Native, 1 Asian American or Pacific Islander, 7 Hispanic Americans), 2 international. Average age 33. 131 applicants, 66% accepted, 57 enrolled. In 2006, 146 degrees awarded. *Degree requirements:* For master's, comprehensive exam. *Entrance requirements:* For master's, GRE General Test. Additional exam requirements/recommendations for international students: Required—TOEFL (minimum score 555 paper-based; 213 computer-based; 79 iBT). *Application deadline:* For fall admission, 7/1 for domestic students, 4/1 for international students; for spring admission, 11/1 for domestic students, 9/1 for international students. Application fee: $35. *Expenses:* Tuition, state resident: full-time $6,520; part-time $226 per hour. Tuition, nonresident: full-time $7,140; part-time $357 per hour. International tuition: $15,820 full-time. *Financial support:* In 2006–07, 2 research assistantships with partial tuition reimbursements (averaging $8,000 per year) were awarded; tuition waivers (partial) and unspecified assistantships also available. *Faculty research:* Teacher preparation in moderate/severe disabilities. Total annual research expenditures: $125,538. *Unit head:* Dr. Sherry Powers, Department Head, 270-745-4607, Fax: 270-745-3441, E-mail: sherry.powers@wku.edu.

Western Michigan University, Graduate College, College of Education, Department of Educational Studies, Kalamazoo, MI 49008-5202. Offers educational studies (MA, Ed D); evaluation, measurement, and research (MA, PhD). *Accreditation:* NCATE. *Degree requirements:* For master's, written exams; for doctorate, thesis/dissertation, internships. *Entrance requirements:* For doctorate, GRE General Test.

Western Michigan University, Graduate College, College of Education, Department of Health, Physical Education and Recreation, Kalamazoo, MI 49008-5202. Offers administration (MA); athletic training (MA); coaching and sports studies (MA); exercise science (MA); motor development (MA); physical education (MA); special education for handicapped children (MA).

Western New Mexico University, Graduate Division, School of Education, Silver City, NM 88062-0680. Offers counselor education (MA); elementary education (MAT); reading education (MAT); school administration (MA); secondary education (MAT); special education (MAT). *Accreditation:* NCATE. *Degree requirements:* For master's, comprehensive exam. *Entrance requirements:* For master's, GRE General Test, GRE Subject Test, minimum GPA of 3.2 in last 64 hours of undergraduate study. Additional exam requirements/recommendations for international students: Required—TOEFL (minimum score 550 paper-based; 213 computer-based). Electronic applications accepted. *Expenses:* Tuition, state resident: full-time $1,329. Tuition, nonresident: full-time $4,779.

Western Oregon University, Graduate Programs, College of Education, Division of Teacher Education, Division of Special Education, Monmouth, OR 97361-1394. Offers deaf education (MS Ed); learning disabilities (MS Ed); multihandicapped education (MS Ed); rehabilitation counseling (MS). *Accreditation:* NCATE. Part-time and evening/weekend programs available. *Faculty:* 6 full-time (4 women). *Students:* 32 full-time (28 women), 12 part-time (10 women);

includes 1 minority (Hispanic American). Average age 36. 30 applicants, 80% accepted. In 2006, 43 degrees awarded. *Degree requirements:* For master's, oral exam, portfolio, written exam, thesis optional. *Entrance requirements:* For master's, California Basic Educational Skills Test or PRAXIS, GRE General Test or MAT, interview, minimum GPA of 3.0, teaching license. *Application deadline:* Applications are processed on a rolling basis. Application fee: $50. *Expenses:* Tuition, state resident: full-time $8,250; part-time $250 per credit. Tuition, nonresident: full-time $14,025; part-time $250 per credit. Required fees: $1,173. *Financial support:* Research assistantships with full tuition reimbursements, teaching assistantships with full tuition reimbursements, career-related internships or fieldwork, Federal Work-Study, and tuition waivers (full and partial) available. Support available to part-time students. Financial award application deadline: 3/1; financial award applicants required to submit FAFSA. *Faculty research:* Interpreter teacher training, hearing disabilities, mental retardation. *Unit head:* Henri Bersani, Unit Head, 503-838-8687, Fax: 503-838-8228. *Application contact:* Dr. David McDonald, Dean of Admissions, Retention and Enrollment Management, 503-838-8919, Fax: 503-838-8067, E-mail: mcdonald@wou.edu.

Westfield State College, Division of Graduate and Continuing Education, Department of Education, Program in Special Education, Westfield, MA 01086. Offers M Ed. *Accreditation:* NCATE. Part-time and evening/weekend programs available. *Degree requirements:* For master's, practicum. *Entrance requirements:* For master's, GRE General Test or MAT, minimum undergraduate GPA of 2.7.

West Texas A&M University, College of Education and Social Sciences, Division of Education, Program in Special Education, Canyon, TX 79016-0001. Offers M Ed. *Degree requirements:* For master's, thesis optional. *Entrance requirements:* For master's, GRE, standard classroom teaching certificate. Additional exam requirements/recommendations for international students: Required—TOEFL.

West Virginia University, College of Human Resources and Education, Department of Curriculum and Instruction-Literacy, Morgantown, WV 26506. Offers curriculum and instruction (Ed D); elementary education (MA); reading (MA); secondary education (MA), including higher education curriculum and teaching, secondary education; special education (Ed D), including special education. *Accreditation:* NCATE. Part-time and evening/weekend programs available. *Faculty:* 18 full-time (13 women), 4 part-time/adjunct (3 women). *Students:* 314 full-time (238 women), 187 part-time (163 women); includes 27 minority (15 African Americans, 1 American Indian/Alaska Native, 2 Asian Americans or Pacific Islanders, 9 Hispanic Americans), 26 international. Average age 31. 239 applicants, 86% accepted, 135 enrolled. In 2006, 242 master's, 8 doctorates awarded. *Degree requirements:* For doctorate, thesis/dissertation, comprehensive exam. *Entrance requirements:* For master's, minimum GPA of 2.75; for doctorate, GRE General Test or MAT, 3 letters of recommendation, curriculum vitae. Additional exam requirements/recommendations for international students: Required—TOEFL. *Application deadline:* Applications are processed on a rolling basis. Application fee: $50. *Expenses:* Tuition, state resident: full-time $4,926; part-time $276 per credit hour. Tuition, nonresident: full-time $14,278; part-time $796 per credit hour. Tuition and fees vary according to program. *Financial support:* In 2006–07, 313 students received support, including 1 research assistantship with full tuition reimbursement available (averaging $8,264 per year), 5 teaching assistantships with full tuition reimbursements available (averaging $8,264 per year); fellowships, career-related internships or fieldwork, Federal Work-Study, institutionally sponsored loans, tuition waivers (full and partial), and graduate administrative assistantships also available. Financial award application deadline: 2/1; financial award applicants required to submit FAFSA. *Faculty research:* Teacher education, curriculum development, educational technology, curriculum assessment. Total annual research expenditures: $440,189. *Unit head:* Dr. Elizabeth A. Dooley, Chair, 304-293-3441, Fax: 304-293-3802, E-mail: elizabeth.dooley@mail.wvu.edu.

West Virginia University, College of Human Resources and Education, Department of Special Education, Morgantown, WV 26506. Offers autism spectrum disorder (5-adult) (Ed D); autism spectrum disorder (K-6) (Ed D); early intervention (preschool) (MA); early intervention/early childhood special education (MA); gifted education (1-12) (MA); multicategorical special education (5-adult) (Ed D); multicategorical special education (K-6) (Ed D); severe/multiple disabilities (K-adult) (MA); special education (Ed D); vision impairments (PreK-adult) (Ed D). *Accreditation:* NCATE. Part-time and evening/weekend programs available. Postbaccalaureate distance learning degree programs offered (no on-campus study). *Faculty:* 5 full-time (4 women), 2 part-time/adjunct (both women). *Students:* 57 full-time (43 women), 193 part-time (159 women); includes 14 minority (8 African Americans, 1 American Indian/Alaska Native, 1 Asian American or Pacific Islander, 4 Hispanic Americans), 1 international. Average age 36. 119 applicants, 68% accepted, 44 enrolled. In 2006, 100 master's, 2 doctorates awarded. *Degree requirements:* For master's, thesis optional; for doctorate, thesis/dissertation, comprehensive exam, registration. *Entrance requirements:* For master's, minimum GPA of 2.75; for doctorate, GRE General Test or MAT. Additional exam requirements/recommendations for international students: Required—TOEFL. *Application deadline:* Applications are processed on a rolling basis. Application fee: $50. *Expenses:* Tuition, state resident: full-time $4,926; part-time $276 per credit hour. Tuition, nonresident: full-time $14,278; part-time $796 per credit hour. Tuition and fees vary according to program. *Financial support:* In 2006–07, 91 students received support, including 1 research assistantship with full tuition reimbursement available; teaching assistantships, career-related internships or fieldwork, Federal Work-Study, institutionally sponsored loans, tuition waivers (partial), and graduate resident hall assistantships also available. Financial award application deadline: 2/1; financial award applicants required to submit FAFSA. *Unit head:* Dr. Barbara Ludlow, Professor, 304-293-3450 Ext. 1127, Fax: 304-293-6834, E-mail: barbara.ludlow@mail.wvu.edu. *Application contact:* Sherilyn A. Bunner, Program Coordinator, 304-293-7143, Fax: 304-293-6834, E-mail: sherry.bunner@mail.wvu.edu.

West Virginia University, School of Physical Education, Morgantown, WV 26506. Offers athletic coaching (MS); athletic training (MS); exercise physiology (Ed D); physical education/teacher education (MS, Ed D), including administration of physical education (Ed D), curriculum and instruction (Ed D), motor development (Ed D), special physical education (Ed D); sport management (MS); sport psychology (MS, Ed D). *Degree requirements:* For doctorate, thesis/dissertation, oral exam, comprehensive exam. *Entrance requirements:* For master's, GRE or MAT, minimum GPA of 3.0; for doctorate, GRE General Test or MAT, minimum GPA of 3.5. Additional exam requirements/recommendations for international students: Required—TOEFL (minimum score 550 paper-based; 213 computer-based). Electronic applications accepted. *Expenses:* Tuition, state resident: full-time $4,926; part-time $276 per credit hour. Tuition, nonresident: full-time $14,278; part-time $796 per credit hour. Tuition and fees vary according to program. *Faculty research:* Sport psychosociology, teacher education, exercise psychology, counseling.

Wheelock College, Graduate Programs, Division of Education, Boston, MA 02215-4176. Offers early childhood education (MS); education leadership (MS); elementary education (MS); language, literacy, and reading (MS); teaching students with moderate disabilities (MS). *Accreditation:* NCATE. Postbaccalaureate distance learning degree programs offered (minimal on-campus study). *Degree requirements:* For master's, comprehensive exam. *Entrance requirements:* Additional exam requirements/recommendations for international students: Required—TOEFL. Electronic applications accepted. *Faculty research:* Symbolic learning, emergent literacy, diversity inclusion, beginning reading language and culture, math education.

Whitworth University, School of Education, Graduate Studies in Education, Program in Special Education, Spokane, WA 99251-0001. Offers MAT. *Accreditation:* NCATE. Part-time and evening/weekend programs available. *Degree requirements:* For master's, internship, practicum, research project, or thesis. *Entrance requirements:* For master's, GRE General Test, MAT. Additional exam requirements/recommendations for international students: Required—TOEFL. *Application deadline:* For fall admission, 9/1 priority date for domestic students; for spring admission, 2/1 for domestic students. Applications are processed on a rolling basis. Application fee: $35. *Financial support:* Application deadline: 2/1. *Unit head:* Dr. Betty Fry

Williams, Chair, 509-777-4688, Fax: 509-777-4753, E-mail: bwilliams@whitworth.edu. *Application contact:* Pat Bailey, Program Assistant, 509-777-3228, Fax: 509-777-4753, E-mail: gse@whitworth.edu.

Wichita State University, Graduate School, College of Education, Department of Curriculum and Instruction, Wichita, KS 67260. Offers curriculum and instruction (M Ed); special education (M Ed). *Accreditation:* NCATE. Part-time and evening/weekend programs available. *Degree requirements:* For master's, portfolio, thesis optional. *Entrance requirements:* For master's, MAT, minimum GPA of 2.75. Additional exam requirements/recommendations for international students: Required—TOEFL. Electronic applications accepted.

Widener University, School of Human Service Professions, Center for Education, Chester, PA 19013-5792. Offers adult education (M Ed); counseling in higher education (M Ed); counselor education (M Ed); early childhood education (M Ed); educational foundations (M Ed); educational leadership (M Ed); educational psychology (M Ed); elementary education (M Ed); English and language arts (M Ed); health education (M Ed); higher education leadership (Ed D); home and school visitor (M Ed); human sexuality (M Ed); mathematics education (M Ed); middle school education (M Ed); principalship (M Ed); reading and language arts (Ed D); reading education (M Ed); school administration (Ed D); science education (M Ed); social studies education (M Ed); special education (M Ed); technology education (M Ed). Part-time and evening/weekend programs available. Terminal master's awarded for partial completion of doctoral program. *Degree requirements:* For doctorate, thesis/dissertation. *Entrance requirements:* For master's, minimum GPA of 2.5; for doctorate, GRE or MAT, minimum GPA of 2.0 (undergraduate), 3.5 (graduate). Electronic applications accepted. Expenses: Contact institution. *Faculty research:* Reading and cognition, adult education, technology education, educational leadership, special education.

Wilkes University, Graduate Studies and Continued Learning, College of Arts, Humanities and Social Sciences, Program in Teacher Education, Wilkes-Barre, PA 18766-0002. Offers classroom technology (MS Ed); educational computing (MS Ed); educational development and strategies (MS Ed); educational leadership (MS Ed); elementary education (MS Ed); instructional technology (MS Ed); school business leadership (MS Ed); secondary education (MS Ed), including biology, chemistry, English, history; special education (MS Ed). Part-time and evening/weekend programs available. Postbaccalaureate distance learning degree programs offered (minimal on-campus study). *Students:* 32 full-time (21 women), 1,588 part-time (1,106 women); includes 29 minority (6 African Americans, 2 American Indian/Alaska Native, 4 Asian Americans or Pacific Islanders, 17 Hispanic Americans). Average age 33. In 2006, 754 degrees awarded. *Entrance requirements:* Additional exam requirements/recommendations for international students: Required—TOEFL (minimum score 500 paper-based; 173 computer-based). *Application deadline:* Applications are processed on a rolling basis. Application fee: $40. *Expenses:* Contact institution. *Financial support:* Federal Work-Study and unspecified assistantships available. Financial award application deadline: 3/1; financial award applicants required to submit FAFSA. *Unit head:* Dr. Michael Speziale, Interim Dean, 570-408-4679, Fax: 570-408-4905, E-mail: michael.speziale@wilkes.edu. *Application contact:* Kathleen Houlihan, Director of Graduate Studies, 570-408-3235, Fax: 570-408-7846, E-mail: kathleen.houlihan@wilkes.edu.

William Carey University, Graduate Studies, School of Education, Hattiesburg, MS 39401-5499. Offers art education (M Ed); art of teaching (M Ed); elementary education (M Ed, Ed S); English education (M Ed); gifted education (M Ed); history and social science (M Ed); mild/moderate disabilities (M Ed); secondary education (M Ed). Part-time programs available. *Faculty:* 19 full-time (12 women), 25 part-time/adjunct (17 women). *Students:* 142 full-time (111 women), 412 part-time (343 women); includes 123 minority (121 African Americans, 1 Asian American or Pacific Islander, 1 Hispanic American). In 2006, 305 master's, 2 other advanced degrees awarded. *Degree requirements:* For master's, comprehensive exam. *Entrance requirements:* For master's, GRE, MAT, minimum GPA of 2.5, Class A teacher's license. Additional exam requirements/recommendations for international students: Required—TOEFL (minimum score 550 paper-based; 213 computer-based). *Application deadline:* For fall admission, 8/7 for domestic and international students; for winter admission, 10/30 for domestic and international students; for spring admission, 2/12 for domestic and international students. Application fee: $25. *Expenses:* Tuition: Full-time $5,040; part-time $240 per credit hour. Tuition and fees vary according to course load. *Financial support:* In 2006–07, 371 students received support. Federal Work-Study and scholarships/grants available. Support available to part-time students. *Unit head:* Dr. Patty Ward, Dean, 601-318-6139, Fax: 601-318-6185, E-mail: patty.ward@wmcarey.edu. *Application contact:* Jason Douglas, Clerical Assistant, Graduate Admissions, 601-318-6774, Fax: 601-318-6765, E-mail: jason.douglas@wmcarey.edu.

William Paterson University of New Jersey, College of Education, Department of Special Education and Counseling Services, Program in Special Education, Wayne, NJ 07470-8420. Offers M Ed. *Accreditation:* NCATE. *Degree requirements:* For master's, thesis, comprehensive exam. *Entrance requirements:* For master's, GRE General Test, MAT, minimum GPA of 2.75, teaching certificate. *Application deadline:* Applications are processed on a rolling basis. Application fee: $50. Electronic applications accepted. *Financial support:* In 2006–07, 9 students received support; research assistantships with full tuition reimbursements available available. Financial award application deadline: 4/1. *Unit head:* Chris Mulrin, Coordinator, 973-720-3123, E-mail: danzingerp@wpunj.edu. *Application contact:* Danielle Liautaud, Director, 973-720-3579, Fax: 973-720-2035, E-mail: liautaudd@wpunj.edu.

Wilmington College, Department of Education, Wilmington, OH 45177. Offers reading (M Ed); special education (M Ed). Part-time programs available. *Degree requirements:* For master's, comprehensive exam. *Entrance requirements:* For master's, GRE or MAT, minimum GPA of 3.0, 2 letters of recommendation. Additional exam requirements/recommendations for international students: Required—TOEFL. *Faculty research:* Reading instruction, special education practices, conflict resolution in the schools, models of higher education for teachers.

Wilmington College, Division of Education, New Castle, DE 19720-6491. Offers applied education technology (M Ed); career and technical education (M Ed); elementary and secondary school counseling (M Ed); elementary special education (M Ed); elementary studies (M Ed); instruction: gifted and talented (M Ed); instruction: teaching and learning (M Ed); literacy (M Ed); reading (M Ed); school leadership (M Ed); secondary teaching (MAT). Part-time and evening/weekend programs available. *Faculty:* 7 full-time (4 women). *Students:* 609 full-time (447 women), 1,350 part-time (1,013 women); includes 144 minority (131 African Americans, 3 American Indian/Alaska Native, 1 Asian American or Pacific Islander, 9 Hispanic Americans). Average age 34. 818 applicants, 100% accepted, 599 enrolled. In 2006, 737 degrees awarded. *Entrance requirements:* For master's, 2 letters of recommendation, interview. Additional exam requirements/recommendations for international students: Required—TOEFL (minimum score 500 paper-based; 173 computer-based). *Application deadline:* For fall admission, 4/30 for domestic students. Applications are processed on a rolling basis. Application fee: $25. *Financial support:* Applicants required to submit FAFSA. *Unit head:* Dr. Richard Gochnauer, Chair, 302-328-6795 Ext. 163, Fax: 302-328-7081. *Application contact:* Chris Ferguson, Director of Admissions and Financial Aid, 302-328-9407 Ext. 256, Fax: 302-328-5164, E-mail: inquire@wilmcoll.edu.

Winona State University, Graduate Studies, College of Education, Department of Special Education, Winona, MN 55987-5838. Offers special education (MS), including developmental disabilities, learning disabilities. *Students:* 6 applicants, 100% accepted, 2 enrolled. In 2006, 3 degrees awarded. *Unit head:* Dr. Barbara Boseker, Chair, 507-457-5364, Fax: 507-457-2483, E-mail: bboseker@winona.edu.

Winthrop University, College of Education, Program in Special Education, Rock Hill, SC 29733. Offers M Ed. *Accreditation:* NCATE. Part-time programs available. *Students:* 2 full-time (both women), 19 part-time (18 women); includes 2 minority (both African Americans) Average age 30. In 2006, 10 degrees awarded. *Entrance requirements:* For master's, PRAXIS, South Carolina Class III Teaching Certificate, sample of written work. *Application deadline:* For fall admission, 7/15 priority date for domestic students; for spring admission, 12/1 for domestic students. Applications are processed on a rolling basis. Application fee: $35. Electronic applications accepted. *Expenses:* Tuition, state resident: full-time $9,148; part-time $383 per hour. Tuition, nonresident: full-time $16,864; part-time $704 per hour. *Financial support:* Career-related internships or fieldwork, Federal Work-Study, scholarships/grants, and unspecified assistantships available. Support available to part-time students. Financial award application deadline: 2/1; financial award applicants required to submit FAFSA. *Unit head:* Dr. Brad Witzel, Graduate Program Advisor, 803-323-2453, E-mail: witzelb@winthrop.edu. *Application contact:* 800-411-7041, Fax: 803-323-2292, E-mail: graduatestu@winthrop.edu.

Worcester State College, Graduate Studies, Department of Education, Concentration in Moderate Special Needs, Worcester, MA 01602-2597. Offers M Ed. Part-time and evening/weekend programs available. *Students:* Average age 30. 5 applicants, 40% accepted, 1 enrolled. *Degree requirements:* For master's, thesis optional. *Entrance requirements:* For master's, GRE General Test or MAT, teaching certificate. Additional exam requirements/recommendations for international students: Required—TOEFL (minimum score 550 paper-based; 213 computer-based). *Application deadline:* Applications are processed on a rolling basis. Application fee: $30. *Expenses:* Tuition, state resident: full-time $4,518; part-time $251 per credit hour. Tuition, nonresident: full-time $4,518; part-time $251 per credit hour. *Financial support:* Career-related internships or fieldwork, Federal Work-Study, institutionally sponsored loans, scholarships/grants, and unspecified assistantships available. Support available to part-time students. Financial award application deadline: 3/1; financial award applicants required to submit FAFSA. *Unit head:* Dr. Carol Donnelly, Coordinator, 508-929-8667, Fax: 508-929-8164, E-mail: cdonnelly@worcester.edu. *Application contact:* Nicole Brown, Assistant Dean of Graduate and Continuing Education, 508-929-8787, Fax: 508-929-8100, E-mail: nbrown@worcester.edu.

Wright State University, School of Graduate Studies, College of Education and Human Services, Department of Teacher Education, Programs in Intervention Specialist, Dayton, OH 45435. Offers gifted educational needs (M Ed, MA); mild to moderate educational needs (M Ed, MA); moderate to intensive educational needs (M Ed, MA). *Accreditation:* NCATE. *Students:* 18 full-time (16 women), 52 part-time (45 women); includes 2 minority (both African Americans) Average age 34. 13 applicants, 100% accepted. In 2006, 32 degrees awarded. *Degree requirements:* For master's, thesis (for some programs). *Entrance requirements:* For master's, GRE General Test, MAT. Additional exam requirements/recommendations for international students: Required—TOEFL. Application fee: $25. *Financial support:* Available to part-time students. Applicants required to submit FAFSA. *Unit head:* Dr. Patricia R. Renick, Program Advisor, 937-775-2677, Fax: 937-775-3308, E-mail: patricia.renick@wright.edu. *Application contact:* John Kimble, Associate Director of Graduate Admissions and Records, 937-775-2957, Fax: 937-775-2453, E-mail: john.kimble@wright.edu.

Xavier University, College of Social Sciences, Health and Education, School of Education, Program in Special Education, Cincinnati, OH 45207. Offers M Ed. Part-time and evening/weekend programs available. *Faculty:* 3 full-time (all women), 16 part-time/adjunct (10 women). *Students:* 31 full-time (25 women), 116 part-time (103 women); includes 18 minority (16 African Americans, 2 Hispanic Americans). Average age 35. 106 applicants, 53% accepted, 55 enrolled. In 2006, 41 degrees awarded. *Degree requirements:* For master's, research project. *Entrance requirements:* For master's, MAT, minimum GPA of 2.7, interview. Additional exam requirements/recommendations for international students: Required—TOEFL (minimum score 550 paper-based; 217 computer-based). *Application deadline:* For fall admission, 8/15 priority date for domestic students. Applications are processed on a rolling basis. Application fee: $35. Electronic applications accepted. *Expenses:* Tuition: Part-time $462 per credit hour. Part-time tuition and fees vary according to degree level, campus/location and program. *Financial support:* Scholarships/grants and unspecified assistantships available. Support available to part-time students. Financial award applicants required to submit FAFSA. *Faculty research:* School and community relationship, professional development, inclusion, tutoring, student teaching field experiences. *Unit head:* Dr. Sharon A. Merrill, Director, Special Education Programs, 513-745-3655, Fax: 513-745-2920, E-mail: merrill@xavier.edu. *Application contact:* Roger Bosse, Interim Director of Graduate Studies, 513-745-3357, Fax: 513-745-1048, E-mail: bosse@xavier.edu.

Youngstown State University, Graduate School, College of Education, Department of Teacher Education, Program in Special Education, Youngstown, OH 44555-0001. Offers gifted and talented education (MS Ed); special education (MS Ed). *Accreditation:* NCATE. Part-time and evening/weekend programs available. *Degree requirements:* For master's, comprehensive exam. *Entrance requirements:* For master's, GRE, MAT, or teaching certificate; interview; minimum GPA of 2.7. Additional exam requirements/recommendations for international students: Required—TOEFL. *Faculty research:* Learning disabilities, learning styles, developing self-esteem and social skills of severe behaviorally handicapped students, inclusion.

Urban Education

Claremont Graduate University, Graduate Programs, School of Educational Studies, Claremont, CA 91711-6160. Offers Africana education (Certificate); education policy issues (MA, PhD); higher education (PhD); higher education administration (MA); human development (MA, PhD); public school administration (MA, PhD); teacher education (MA, PhD); teaching and learning (MA, PhD); urban education administration (MA, PhD); MBA/PhD. Part-time programs available. *Faculty:* 15 full-time (9 women), 11 part-time/adjunct (9 women). *Students:* 236 full-time (155 women), 168 part-time (117 women); includes 177 minority (34 African Americans, 2 American Indian/Alaska Native, 43 Asian Americans or Pacific Islanders, 98 Hispanic Americans), 7 international. Average age 38. In 2006, 90 master's, 20 doctorates awarded. Terminal master's awarded for partial completion of doctoral program. *Degree requirements:* For master's, thesis or alternative, comprehensive exam (for some programs); for doctorate, thesis/dissertation, comprehensive exam. *Entrance requirements:* For master's and doctorate, GRE General Test. *Application deadline:* For fall admission, 2/15 priority date for domestic students. Applications are processed on a rolling basis. Electronic applications accepted. *Financial support:* Fellowships, research assistantships, Federal Work-Study and institutionally sponsored loans available. Support available to part-time students. Financial award application deadline: 2/15; financial award applicants required to submit FAFSA. *Faculty research:* Education administration, K–12 and higher education, multicultural education, education policy, diversity in higher education, faculty issues. *Unit head:* Philip H. Dreyer, Dean,

Urban Education

Claremont Graduate University (continued)

909-621-8075, Fax: 909-621-8734, E-mail: philip.dreyer@cgu.edu. *Application contact:* Cece Gaddy, Administrative Director, 909-621-8317, Fax: 909-621-8734, E-mail: cece.gaddy@cgu.edu.

Cleveland State University, College of Graduate Studies, College of Education and Human Services, Program in Urban Education, Cleveland, OH 44115. Offers counseling (PhD); counseling psychology (PhD); leadership and lifelong learning (PhD); learning and development (PhD); policy studies (PhD); school administration (PhD). Part-time programs available. *Faculty:* 14 full-time (9 women), 4 part-time/adjunct (2 women). *Students:* 16 full-time (11 women), 78 part-time (47 women); includes 22 minority (20 African Americans, 2 Asian Americans or Pacific Islanders), 5 international. Average age 43. 29 applicants, 24% accepted, 4 enrolled. In 2006, 9 degrees awarded. *Degree requirements:* For doctorate, one foreign language, thesis/dissertation, comprehensive exam, registration. *Entrance requirements:* For doctorate, GRE General Test, minimum graduate GPA of 3.25. Additional exam requirements/recommendations for international students: Required—TOEFL (minimum score 525 paper-based; 197 computer-based), IELTS (minimum score 6). *Application deadline:* For fall admission, 2/5 for domestic students. Application fee: $30. *Financial support:* In 2006–07, 7 students received support, including 4 research assistantships with full and partial tuition reimbursements available (averaging $7,800 per year), 3 teaching assistantships with full and partial tuition reimbursements available (averaging $7,800 per year); tuition waivers (full) and unspecified assistantships also available. Financial award applicants required to submit FAFSA. *Faculty research:* Equity issues (race, ethnicity, and gender), education development consequences for special needs of urban populations, urban education programming, counseling the violent or aggressive adolescent. Total annual research expenditures: $5,662. *Unit head:* Dr. Joshua Bagakas, Director, 216-687-4591, Fax: 216-875-9697, E-mail: j.bagakas@csuohio.edu. *Application contact:* Wanda Butler, Administrative Assistant, 216-687-4697, Fax: 216-875-9697, E-mail: w.pruett-butler@csuohio.edu.

College of Mount Saint Vincent, School of Professional and Continuing Studies, Department of Teacher Education, Riverdale, NY 10471-1093. Offers instructional technology and global perspectives (Certificate); middle level education (Certificate); multicultural studies (Certificate); urban and multicultural education (MS Ed). *Accreditation:* Teacher Education Accreditation Council. Part-time programs available. *Faculty:* 1 full-time (0 women), 18 part-time/adjunct (12 women). *Students:* 20 full-time (13 women), 239 part-time (172 women); includes 101 minority (50 African Americans, 11 Asian Americans or Pacific Islanders, 40 Hispanic Americans). Average age 38. 35 applicants, 57% accepted. In 2006, 124 degrees awarded. *Degree requirements:* For master's, comprehensive exam, registration. *Entrance requirements:* For master's, interview, New York teaching certificate. Additional exam requirements/recommendations for international students: Required—TOEFL. *Application deadline:* For fall admission, 9/1 priority date for domestic students, 7/1 priority date for international students; for winter admission, 11/1 priority date for domestic students, 10/1 priority date for international students; for spring admission, 12/1 priority date for domestic students, 11/1 priority date for international students. Applications are processed on a rolling basis. Application fee: $50. *Financial support:* Career-related internships or fieldwork available. Financial award applicants required to submit FAFSA. *Unit head:* Mary Ellen Sullivan, Chair, 718-405-3281, Fax: 718-601-6392. *Application contact:* Beigica Collado, Executive Assistant, 718-405-3322, Fax: 718-405-3764, E-mail: beigica.collado@mountsaintvincent.edu.

Columbia College Chicago, Graduate School, Department of Educational Studies, Chicago, IL 60605-1996. Offers elementary (MAT); English (MAT); interdisciplinary arts (MAT); multicultural education (MA); urban teaching (MA). Part-time and evening/weekend programs available. *Degree requirements:* For master's, thesis, student teaching experience, 100 preclinical hours. *Entrance requirements:* For master's, NTE, minimum GPA of 3.0, portfolio. Additional exam requirements/recommendations for international students: Required—TOEFL (minimum score 550 paper-based; 213 computer-based). Electronic applications accepted.

Concordia University, College of Education, Program in Urban Teaching, River Forest, IL 60305-1499. Offers MA. *Entrance requirements:* For master's, minimum GPA of 2.9. Additional exam requirements/recommendations for international students: Required—TOEFL (minimum score 550 paper-based; 195 computer-based). Electronic applications accepted.

DePaul University, School of Education, Chicago, IL 60604-2287. Offers bilingual and bicultural education (M Ed, MA); curriculum studies (M Ed, MA); education (Ed D), including curriculum studies, educational leadership; educational leadership (M Ed, MA), including administration and supervision, Catholic school leadership, physical education; human development and learning (MA); human services and counseling (M Ed, MA), including agencies, family concerns, and higher education, elementary schools, human services management, secondary schools; reading and learning disabilities (M Ed, MA); social culture studies in education and development (M Ed, MA), including curriculum studies/development; teaching and learning (early childhood, elementary and secondary) (M Ed), including elementary education (M Ed, MA), secondary education (M Ed, MA); teaching and learning (early childhood, elementary, and secondary) (MA), including elementary education (M Ed, MA), secondary education (M Ed, MA). *Accreditation:* NCATE. Part-time and evening/weekend programs available. *Faculty:* 61 full-time (40 women), 76 part-time/adjunct (46 women). *Students:* 1,371 full-time (1,103 women), 474 part-time (362 women); includes 435 minority (144 African Americans, 7 American Indian/Alaska Native, 89 Asian Americans or Pacific Islanders, 195 Hispanic Americans), 11 international. Average age 30. 993 applicants, 80% accepted, 617 enrolled. In 2006, 324 master's, 7 doctorates awarded. *Degree requirements:* For doctorate, thesis/dissertation. *Entrance requirements:* For master's, interview, minimum GPA of 2.75, 2 letters of recommendation; for doctorate, interview, master's degree, 2 years of work experience (recommended), writing sample, 3 letters of recommendation. Application fee: $25. Electronic applications accepted. *Financial support:* In 2006–07, 16 research assistantships with tuition reimbursements (averaging $4,370 per year), 1 teaching assistantship (averaging $6,000 per year) were awarded; career-related internships or fieldwork also available. *Faculty research:* Reflective teaching, children at risk, loss, ethnicity, urban education. Total annual research expenditures: $556,194. *Unit head:* Dr. Clara Jennings, Dean, 773-325-7581, Fax: 773-325-7728, E-mail: cjennings@depaul.edu. *Application contact:* Dr. John Bollwark, Data Project Manager, 773-325-7582, Fax: 773-325-7713, E-mail: jbollwar@depaul.edu.

Florida International University, College of Education, Department of Educational Leadership and Policy Studies, Program in Urban Education, Miami, FL 33199. Offers MS. *Accreditation:* NCATE. Part-time and evening/weekend programs available. *Faculty:* 4 full-time (3 women). *Students:* 1 full-time (0 women), 7 part-time (3 women); includes 5 minority (1 African American, 4 Hispanic Americans). Average age 37. 5 applicants, 80% accepted, 4 enrolled. In 2006, 15 degrees awarded. *Entrance requirements:* For master's, minimum undergraduate GPA of 3.0 in last 60 credits. Additional exam requirements/recommendations for international students: Required—TOEFL (minimum score 550 paper-based; 213 computer-based; 80 iBT), IELTS (minimum score 6). *Application deadline:* For fall admission, 6/1 priority date for domestic students, 4/1 for international students; for winter admission, 10/1 priority date for domestic students, 9/1 for international students; for spring admission, 3/1 priority date for domestic students, 2/1 for international students. Applications are processed on a rolling basis. Application fee: $30. Electronic applications accepted. *Expenses:* Tuition, state resident: part-time $249 per credit hour. Tuition, nonresident: part-time $753 per credit hour. Tuition and fees vary according to program. *Financial support:* Fellowships available. *Faculty research:* Urban education, literacy. *Unit head:* Dr. Delia Garcia, Chairperson, 305-348-3418, Fax: 305-348-3825, E-mail: delia.garcia@fiu.edu. *Application contact:* Marisa Salazar, Student Recruiter, 305-348-3002, Fax: 305-348-3227, E-mail: marisa.salazar@fiu.edu.

Graduate School and University Center of the City University of New York, Graduate Studies, Program in Urban Education, New York, NY 10016-4039. Offers PhD. *Students:* 87 full-time (57 women), 14 part-time (6 women); includes 42 minority (23 African Americans, 1 American Indian/Alaska Native, 4 Asian Americans or Pacific Islanders, 14 Hispanic Americans), 4 international. Average age 39. 83 applicants, 39% accepted, 16 enrolled. In 2006, 9 degrees awarded. *Entrance requirements:* For doctorate, GRE General Test. Additional exam requirements/recommendations for international students: Required—TOEFL. *Application deadline:* For fall admission, 2/1 for domestic students. Application fee: $125. Electronic applications accepted. *Financial support:* In 2006–07, 57 fellowships, 1 teaching assistantship were awarded. *Unit head:* Dr. Philip Anderson, Executive Officer, 212-817-8281, Fax: 212-817-1515, E-mail: panderson@gc.cuny.edu.

Harvard University, Graduate School of Education, Doctoral Program in Education, Cambridge, MA 02138. Offers culture, communities and education (Ed D); education policy (Ed D); education policy, leadership and instructional practice (Ed D); higher education (Ed D); human development and education (Ed D); quantitative policy analysis in education (Ed D); urban superintendency (Ed D). Part-time programs available. *Faculty:* 58 full-time (25 women), 40 part-time/adjunct (22 women). *Students:* 306 full-time (216 women), 35 part-time (26 women); includes 95 minority (38 African Americans, 4 American Indian/Alaska Native, 35 Asian Americans or Pacific Islanders, 18 Hispanic Americans), 46 international. Average age 35. 494 applicants, 12% accepted, 48 enrolled. In 2006, 70 degrees awarded. Terminal master's awarded for partial completion of doctoral program. *Degree requirements:* For doctorate, thesis/dissertation. *Entrance requirements:* For doctorate, GRE General Test, 3 letters of recommendation, official transcripts, statement of purpose. Additional exam requirements/recommendations for international students: Required—TOEFL (minimum score 600 paper-based; 250 computer-based; 100 iBT), TWE (minimum score 5). *Application deadline:* For fall admission, 12/14 for domestic and international students. Application fee: $85. Electronic applications accepted. *Expenses: Contact institution. Financial support:* In 2006–07, 171 fellowships with full and partial tuition reimbursements (averaging $11,489 per year), 47 research assistantships (averaging $9,340 per year), 153 teaching assistantships (averaging $7,710 per year) were awarded; career-related internships or fieldwork, Federal Work-Study, institutionally sponsored loans, scholarships/grants, health care benefits, tuition waivers (full and partial), and unspecified assistantships also available. Support available to part-time students. Financial award application deadline: 2/2; financial award applicants required to submit FAFSA. *Faculty research:* Learning and development; educational leadership and organizations; education policy analysis. Total annual research expenditures: $4.8 million. *Unit head:* Dr. James Stiles, Associate Dean for Degree Programs. *Application contact:* Information Contact, 617-495-3414, Fax: 617-496-3577, E-mail: gseadmissions@harvard.edu.

Holy Names University, Graduate Division, Department of Education, Oakland, CA 94619-1699. Offers advanced curriculum studies (M Ed); educational therapy (M Ed); mild/moderate disabilities (Ed S); multiple subject credential (M Ed); single subject credential (M Ed); special education (M Ed); teaching English as a second language (M Ed, Certificate); urban education (M Ed). Part-time programs available. *Faculty:* 6 full-time (all women), 9 part-time/adjunct (all women). *Students:* 17 full-time (14 women), 131 part-time (90 women); includes 58 minority (36 African Americans, 1 American Indian/Alaska Native, 11 Asian Americans or Pacific Islanders, 10 Hispanic Americans). Average age 40. 75 applicants, 80% accepted, 49 enrolled. In 2006, 11 master's, 29 Certificates awarded. *Degree requirements:* For master's, research paper, thesis or project. *Entrance requirements:* For master's, minimum undergraduate GPA of 2.6 overall, 3.0 in major. Additional exam requirements/recommendations for international students: Required—TOEFL. *Application deadline:* For fall admission, 8/1 priority date for domestic students; for spring admission, 12/1 priority date for domestic students. Applications are processed on a rolling basis. Application fee: $50. *Expenses:* Tuition: Full-time $10,800; part-time $600 per unit. Required fees: $240; $120 per term. *Financial support:* In 2006–07, 67 students received support. Scholarships/grants available. Support available to part-time students. Financial award application deadline: 3/2; financial award applicants required to submit FAFSA. *Faculty research:* Cognitive development, language development, learning handicaps. *Unit head:* Dr. Zaida McCall-Perez, Chairperson, 510-436-1288, E-mail: mccall-perez@hnu.edu. *Application contact:* 800-430-1351, Fax: 510-436-1325, E-mail: admissions@hnu.edu.

The Johns Hopkins University, School of Professional Studies in Business and Education, School of Education, Department of Teacher Development and Leadership, Baltimore, MD 21218-2699. Offers adult learning (Certificate); business leadership for independent schools (Certificate); earth/space science (Certificate); educational leadership for independent schools (Certificate); educational studies (MS); effective teaching of reading (Certificate); ESL instruction (Certificate); gifted education (Certificate); leadership for school, family and community collaboration (Certificate); reading (MS); school administration and supervision (MS, Certificate); teacher development and leadership (Ed D); teacher leadership (Certificate); technology for educators (MS); urban education (Certificate). Part-time and evening/weekend programs available. Postbaccalaureate distance learning degree programs offered (minimal on-campus study). *Students:* 19 full-time (18 women), 535 part-time (413 women); includes 98 minority (76 African Americans, 1 American Indian/Alaska Native, 18 Asian Americans or Pacific Islanders, 3 Hispanic Americans), 2 international. Average age 31. 544 applicants, 79% accepted, 374 enrolled. In 2006, 151 master's, 180 other advanced degrees awarded. *Degree requirements:* For master's and Certificate, portfolio; for doctorate, thesis/dissertation, comprehensive exam, registration. *Entrance requirements:* For master's and Certificate, minimum GPA of 3.0; for doctorate, GRE, interview, master's degree, minimum GPA of 3.0, resumé, letters of recommendation. Additional exam requirements/recommendations for international students: Required—TOEFL (minimum score 600 paper-based; 250 computer-based; 100 iBT). *Application deadline:* For fall admission, 5/1 for international students; for spring admission, 10/15 for international students. Applications are processed on a rolling basis. Application fee: $60. *Expenses:* Tuition: Full-time $32,976. Tuition and fees vary according to degree level and program. *Financial support:* Scholarships/grants available. Support available to part-time students. Financial award application deadline: 6/1; financial award applicants required to submit FAFSA. *Unit head:* Dr. Edward Pajak, Chair, 410-309-1265, Fax: 410-290-0467. *Application contact:* Carol Herrman, Admissions Coordinator, 410-872-1234, Fax: 410-872-1251, E-mail: onestop.admissions@jhu.edu.

Langston University, School of Education and Behavioral Sciences, Langston, OK 73050-0907. Offers bilingual/multicultural (M Ed); elementary education (M Ed); English as a second language (M Ed); rehabilitation counseling (M Sc); urban education (M Ed). *Accreditation:* CORE; NCATE (one or more programs are accredited). Part-time programs available. *Degree requirements:* For master's, thesis optional. *Entrance requirements:* For master's, GRE, writing skills test, minimum GPA of 2.5, 3 letters of recommendation. Additional exam requirements/recommendations for international students: Required—TOEFL, TWE. *Faculty research:* Bilingual/multicultural education, financing post-secondary education.

Marygrove College, Graduate Division, Education Unit, Griot Program, Detroit, MI 48221-2599. Offers M Ed.

Mercy College, Division of Education, Dobbs Ferry, NY 10522-1189. Offers adolescence education: grades 7-12 (MS); applied behavior analysis (MS); bilingual education (MS); childhood education: grades 1-6 (MS); early childhood education: birth—grade 2 (MS); education (MS); elementary education (MS); learning technology (MS); middle childhood education: grades 5-9 (MS); reading (MS); school administration and supervision (MS); school building leadership (MS); school business administration (MS); secondary education (MS); special education (MS); students with disabilities: grades 5-9 (MS); students with disabilities: grades 7-12 (MS); teaching English to speakers of other languages (MS); teaching literacy: birth—grade 6 (MS); teaching literacy: grades 5-12 (MS); urban education (MS). *Students:* 572 full-time (467 women), 1,719 part-time (1,287 women); includes 943 minority (470 African Americans, 7 American Indian/Alaska Native, 48 Asian Americans or Pacific Islanders, 418 Hispanic Americans), 6 international. Average age 33. In 2006, 1090 degrees awarded. *Entrance requirements:* For master's, teaching certificate. *Application deadline:* For fall admission, 2/1 for domestic students. Applications are processed on a rolling basis. Application fee: $37. *Expenses: Contact institution.* Tuition and fees vary according to program. *Financial support:* Institutionally sponsored loans, scholarships/grants, and unspecified assistantships available. Support available to part-time students. *Faculty research:* Distance learning, literacy, assessment, community schools, impact of staff development. *Unit head:* Dr. William Prattella, Chairperson, 914-674-7555, Fax: 914-674-7352, E-mail: wprattella@mercy.edu. *Application contact:* Kathleen Jackson, Director of Admissions, 800-Mercy-NY, Fax: 914-674-7382, E-mail: admissions@mercy.edu.

New Jersey City University, Graduate and Continuing Education, College of Education, Department of Educational Leadership, Jersey City, NJ 07305-1597. Offers basics and urban studies (MA); bilingual/bicultural education and English as a second language (MA); educational administration and supervision (MA). Evening/weekend programs available. *Students:* 4 full-time (3 women), 237 part-time (149 women); includes 52 minority (11 African Americans, 4 Asian Americans or Pacific Islanders, 37 Hispanic Americans), 26 international. Average age 35. In 2006, 162 degrees awarded. *Entrance requirements:* For master's, GRE General Test or MAT. Additional exam requirements/recommendations for international students: Required—TOEFL. *Application deadline:* For fall admission, 8/1 priority date for domestic students; for spring admission, 12/1 for domestic students. Applications are processed on a rolling basis. Application fee: $0. *Expenses:* Tuition, state resident: full-time $7,038; part-time $391 per credit. Tuition, nonresident: full-time $12,510; part-time $695 per credit. Required fees: $65 per credit. *Financial support:* Fellowships, teaching assistantships, career-related internships or fieldwork and unspecified assistantships available. *Unit head:* Dr. Carrie Robinson, Chairperson, 201-200-3400, E-mail: crobinson@njcu.edu.

Norfolk State University, School of Graduate Studies, School of Education, Department of Secondary Education and School Leadership, Program in Urban Education/Administration, Norfolk, VA 23504. Offers teaching (MA). *Accreditation:* NCATE. Part-time programs available. *Entrance requirements:* For master's, GRE General Test, PRAXIS I, minimum GPA of 3.0 in major, 2.5 overall.

Northeastern Illinois University, Graduate College, College of Education, Department of Educational Leadership and Development, Program in Inner City Studies, Chicago, IL 60625-4699. Offers MA. Part-time and evening/weekend programs available. *Faculty:* 1 (woman) part-time/adjunct. *Students:* 12 full-time (9 women), 34 part-time (27 women); includes 44 minority (43 African Americans, 1 Hispanic American). Average age 40. 11 applicants, 91% accepted. In 2006, 3 degrees awarded. *Degree requirements:* For master's, thesis or alternative, comprehensive exam. *Entrance requirements:* For master's, minimum GPA of 2.75. *Application deadline:* For fall admission, 4/1 priority date for domestic students; for spring admission, 8/15 for domestic students. Applications are processed on a rolling basis. Application fee: $25. *Financial support:* In 2006–07, 12 students received support, including research assistantships with full tuition reimbursements available (averaging $6,600 per year); career-related internships or fieldwork, Federal Work-Study, institutionally sponsored loans, and tuition waivers (full and partial) also available. Support available to part-time students. *Unit head:* Dr. Conrad Worrill, Coordinator, 773-268-7500 Ext. 144, Fax: 773-256-2030, E-mail: c-worrill@neiu.edu.

Nova Southeastern University, Fischler School of Education and Human Services, Graduate Teacher Education Program, Fort Lauderdale, FL 33314-7796. Offers athletic administration (MS); cognitive and behavioral disabilities (MS); computer science education (Ed S); computer science education (K-12) (MS); curriculum and teaching (Ed S); curriculum, instruction and technology (MS); curriculum, instruction, management and administration (Ed S); early childhood special education (MS); early literacy and reading (Ed S); early literacy education (MS); education technology (MS); educational leadership (administration K–12) (MS, Ed S); educational media (Ed S); educational media (K-12) (MS); elementary education (MS, Ed S), including ESOL endorsement (MS); English (MS, Ed S); exceptional student education (MS), including ESOL endorsement; gifted education (MS, Ed S); interdisciplinary arts education (MS); management and administration of educational programs (MS); mathematics (MS, Ed S); multicultural early intervention (MS); pre-kindergarten/primary (MS); preschool education (MS); reading (MS, Ed S); science (MS, Ed S); secondary education (MS); social studies (MS, Ed S); Spanish language (MS); teaching and learning (MA, MS), including curriculum and instruction (MA), elementary mathematics (MA), elementary reading (MA), K-12 technology integration (MA); teaching English to speakers of other languages (MS, Ed S); technology management and administration (Ed S); urban studies education (MS); varying exceptionalities (Ed S). Part-time and evening/weekend programs available. Postbaccalaureate distance learning degree programs offered. *Faculty:* 131 full-time (78 women), 548 part-time/adjunct (342 women). *Students:* 1,418 full-time (1,139 women), 3,464 part-time (2,877 women); includes 2,462 minority (1,732 African Americans, 13 American Indian/Alaska Native, 44 Asian Americans or Pacific Islanders, 673 Hispanic Americans), 77 international. Average age 38. 1,771 applicants, 80% accepted, 1419 enrolled. In 2006, 2,078 master's, 425 other advanced degrees awarded. *Degree requirements:* For master's and Ed S, thesis, practicum, internship. *Entrance requirements:* For master's, MAT, GRE, CLAST, CBEST, PRAXIS I, GKT, minimum GPA of 2.5; for Ed S, MAT or GRE, master's degree, teaching certificate, minimum GPA of 3.0. Additional exam requirements/recommendations for international students: Recommended—TOEFL (minimum score 550 paper-based; 213 computer-based), IELTS (minimum score 6). *Application deadline:* For fall admission, 8/11 priority date for domestic and international students; for winter admission, 12/28 priority date for domestic and international students; for spring admission, 4/22 priority date for domestic and international students. Applications are processed on a rolling basis. Application fee: $50. Electronic applications accepted. *Financial support:* Federal Work-Study available. Support available to part-time students. Financial award application deadline: 1/7. *Faculty research:* School effectiveness, critical thinking, leadership skills acquisition, child education, multicultural education. *Unit head:* Dr. Meline Kevorkian, Associate Dean of Master's and Educational Programs, 954-262-8500, Fax: 954-262-3606, E-mail: melinek@nova.edu. *Application contact:* Jennifer Quiñones Nottingham, Dean of Student Affairs, 800-986-3223 Ext. 8624, Fax: 954-262-3911, E-mail: jlquinon@nova.edu.

Roberts Wesleyan College, Division of Teacher Education, Rochester, NY 14624-1997. Offers adolescence education (M Ed); childhood and special education (M Ed); literacy education (M Ed); urban education (M Ed). Part-time and evening/weekend programs available. *Faculty:* 17 part-time/adjunct (7 women). *Students:* 1 (woman) full-time, 66 part-time (47 women). Average age 33. 52 applicants, 63% accepted. In 2006, 20 degrees awarded. *Degree requirements:* For master's, thesis. *Application deadline:* For fall admission, 8/1 priority date for domestic students; for spring admission, 12/1 for domestic students. Applications are processed on a rolling basis. Application fee: $35. *Financial support:* In 2006–07, 7 students received support. Career-related internships or fieldwork available. Financial award application deadline: 9/1; financial award applicants required to submit FAFSA. *Unit head:* Dr. Richard Mace, Chair, 585-594-6934. *Application contact:* Paula Finch, Graduate Admissions Coordinator, 585-594-6683, E-mail: finch_paula@roberts.edu.

Saint Peter's College, Graduate Programs in Education, Program in Urban Education, Jersey City, NJ 07306-5997. Offers MA. Part-time and evening/weekend programs available. *Degree requirements:* For master's, departmental qualifying exam. *Entrance requirements:* For master's, GRE or MAT.

Simmons College, Graduate School, College of Arts and Sciences Graduate Studies, Department of Education, Program in Teacher Preparation, Boston, MA 02115. Offers educational leadership (MS Ed, CAGS); elementary education (MAT, CAGS); general education (CAGS); general purposes (MS); middle school education (MAT, CAGS); professional license (CAGS); professional license: elementary (MS Ed); professional license: middle/high (MS Ed); secondary education (MAT, CAGS); urban education (MS Ed, CAGS). *Faculty:* 4 full-time (3 women), 22 part-time/adjunct (13 women). *Students:* 61 full-time (53 women), 141 part-time (128 women); includes 33 minority (13 African Americans, 10 Asian Americans or Pacific Islanders, 10 Hispanic Americans), 1 international. Average age 24. 86 applicants, 77% accepted, 39 enrolled. In 2006, 128 master's, 12 other advanced degrees awarded. *Degree requirements:* For master's, student teaching experience or internship. *Entrance requirements:* For master's, GRE General Test, MAT or Massachusetts Tests for Educator Licensure (MTEL). Additional exam requirements/recommendations for international students: Required—TOEFL (minimum score 600 paper-based; 250 computer-based; 100 iBT). *Application deadline:* For fall admission, 8/1 priority date for domestic and international students; for spring admission, 12/15 priority date for domestic and international students. Applications are processed on a rolling basis. Application fee: $35. Electronic applications accepted. *Expenses: Contact institution. Financial support:* Teaching assistantships, career-related internships or fieldwork, Federal Work-Study, institutionally sponsored loans, scholarships/grants, and tuition waivers (partial) available. Support available to part-time students. Financial award application deadline: 3/1; financial award applicants required to submit FAFSA. *Faculty research:* Putting standards/frameworks into practice, restructuring middle and high schools, interactive teaching and learning developing curriculum for Third World countries. Total annual research expenditures: $110,000. *Unit head:* Lynda Johnson, Assistant Dean, 617-521-2576, Fax: 617-521-3133, E-mail: gsa@simmons.edu. *Application contact:* Kristen Haack, Director, Graduate Studies Admission, 617-521-2915, Fax: 617-521-3058, E-mail: gsa@simmons.edu.

Sojourner-Douglass College, Graduate Program, Baltimore, MD 21205-1814. Offers human services (MASS); public administration (MASS); urban education (reading) (MASS).

Temple University, Graduate School, College of Education, Department of Educational Leadership and Policy Studies, Philadelphia, PA 19122-6096. Offers educational administration (Ed M, Ed D); urban education (Ed M, Ed D). Part-time and evening/weekend programs available. *Faculty:* 12 full-time (6 women). *Students:* 40 full-time (28 women), 128 part-time (79 women); includes 41 minority (34 African Americans, 2 American Indian/Alaska Native, 1 Asian American or Pacific Islander, 4 Hispanic Americans), 3 international. 134 applicants, 46% accepted, 31 enrolled. In 2006, 48 master's, 14 doctorates awarded. Terminal master's awarded for partial completion of doctoral program. *Degree requirements:* For master's, thesis or alternative, comprehensive exam; for doctorate, thesis/dissertation, preliminary exam. *Entrance requirements:* For master's and doctorate, GRE General Test or MAT, minimum GPA of 3.0. Additional exam requirements/recommendations for international students: Required—TOEFL (minimum score 550 paper-based; 213 computer-based; 79 iBT). *Application deadline:* For fall admission, 12/15 for international students; for spring admission, 8/1 for international students. Application fee: $50. Electronic applications accepted. *Expenses:* Tuition, state resident: full-time $12,264; part-time $511 per credit. Tuition, nonresident: full-time $17,904; part-time $746 per credit. Required fees: $84 per course. Tuition and fees vary according to program. *Financial support:* Fellowships, research assistantships with full tuition reimbursements, teaching assistantships with full tuition reimbursements, career-related internships or fieldwork and Federal Work-Study available. Financial award application deadline: 1/15; financial award applicants required to submit FAFSA. *Faculty research:* Women in education, school effectiveness, financial policy, school improvement in city schools, nongraded schools. *Unit head:* Dr. Erin McNamara Horvat, Chair, 215-204-8061, E-mail: horvat@temple.edu.

Texas A&M University, College of Education and Human Development, Department of Teaching, Learning, and Culture, College Station, TX 77843. Offers curriculum and instruction (M Ed, MS, PhD); mathematics education (M Ed, MS, PhD); multicultural/urban/ESL/international education (M Ed, MS, PhD); reading/language arts (M Ed, MS, PhD); science education (M Ed, MS, PhD); social studies education (M Ed, MS, PhD). *Accreditation:* NCATE. Part-time programs available. *Faculty:* 25 full-time (9 women), 2 part-time/adjunct (both women). *Students:* 156 full-time (115 women), 226 part-time (191 women); includes 95 minority (43 African Americans, 1 American Indian/Alaska Native, 9 Asian Americans or Pacific Islanders, 42 Hispanic Americans), 36 international. Average age 36. 137 applicants, 83% accepted, 80 enrolled. In 2006, 69 master's, 15 doctorates awarded. *Median time to degree:* Of those who began their doctoral program in fall 1998, 77% received their degree in 8 years or less. *Degree requirements:* For master's, thesis (for some programs), comprehensive exam; for doctorate, thesis/dissertation, comprehensive exam. *Entrance requirements:* For master's, GRE General Test, minimum GPA of 3.0; for doctorate, GRE General Test, 3 years of teaching experience. Additional exam requirements/recommendations for international students: Required—TOEFL (minimum score 550 paper-based; 213 computer-based). *Application deadline:* For fall admission, 1/15 priority date for domestic and international students; for spring admission, 9/15 priority date for domestic and international students. Applications are processed on a rolling basis. Application fee: $50 ($75 for international students). Electronic applications accepted. *Expenses:* Tuition, state resident: full-time $4,697. Tuition, nonresident: full-time $11,297. Required fees: $2,272. *Financial support:* In 2006–07, fellowships with partial tuition reimbursements (averaging $3,000 per year), teaching assistantships with partial tuition reimbursements (averaging $7,200 per year) were awarded; research assistantships with partial tuition reimbursements, career-related internships or fieldwork, Federal Work-Study, institutionally sponsored loans, scholarships/grants, tuition waivers (partial), and unspecified assistantships also available. Support available to part-time students. Financial award application deadline: 4/1; financial award applicants required to submit FAFSA. *Unit head:* Dr. Dennie Smith, Head, 979-845-8384, Fax: 979-845-9663. *Application contact:* Graduate Admissions Supervisor, 979-845-8382, Fax: 979-845-9663.

Texas Southern University, Graduate School, College of Education, Area of Curriculum and Instruction, Houston, TX 77004-4584. Offers bilingual education (M Ed); curriculum, instruction, and urban education (Ed D); early childhood education (M Ed); elementary education (M Ed); reading education (M Ed); secondary education (M Ed); special education (M Ed). Part-time and evening/weekend programs available. *Faculty:* 8 full-time (6 women), 1 part-time/adjunct (0 women). *Students:* 41 full-time (36 women), 43 part-time (38 women); includes 82 minority (77 African Americans, 2 Asian Americans or Pacific Islanders, 3 Hispanic Americans). Average age 36. 34 applicants, 82% accepted, 24 enrolled. In 2006, 6 master's, 13 doctorates awarded. *Degree requirements:* For master's, comprehensive exam; for doctorate, thesis/dissertation, comprehensive exam. *Entrance requirements:* For master's, GRE General Test, minimum GPA of 2.5; for doctorate, GRE General Test or MAT, master's degree, minimum B+ average. Additional exam requirements/recommendations for international students: Required—TOEFL. *Application deadline:* For fall admission, 7/15 priority date for domestic students. Applications are processed on a rolling basis. Application fee: $50 ($75 for international students). *Financial support:* Federal Work-Study and institutionally sponsored loans available. Financial award application deadline: 5/1. *Unit head:* Dr. Cherry Gooden, Chair, 713-313-7496, Fax: 713-313-7496, E-mail: gooden_cr@tsu.edu.

University of Houston–Downtown, Graduate Programs, Houston, TX 77002-1001. Offers criminal justice (MS); professional writing and technical communication (MS); urban education (MAT). *Entrance requirements:* For master's, GRE, MAT or GMAT, 3 letters of reference. Application fee: $35. *Financial support:* Scholarships/grants available. Financial award application deadline: 4/1. *Unit head:* Yolanda Salinas, Coordinator of Graduate Admissions, 713-221-8522.

University of Illinois at Chicago, Graduate College, College of Education, Department of Curriculum and Instruction, Chicago, IL 60607-7128. Offers curriculum and instruction (PhD); educational psychology (PhD); instructional leadership (M Ed), including elementary education, reading, secondary education; leadership and administration (M Ed); policy and administration (PhD); policy studies in urban education (PhD). Part-time and evening/weekend programs available. *Degree requirements:* For doctorate, thesis/dissertation. *Entrance requirements:* For master's, minimum GPA of 2.75; for doctorate, GRE General Test, minimum GPA of 2.75. Additional exam requirements/recommendations for international students: Required—TOEFL. Electronic applications accepted. *Faculty research:* Curriculum theory, curriculum development, research on teaching, curriculum and context, reading/literacy.

University of Massachusetts Boston, Office of Graduate Studies, Graduate College of Education, School Organization, Curriculum and Instruction Department, Boston, MA 02125-3393. Offers education (M Ed, Ed D), including elementary and secondary education/certification (M Ed), higher education administration (Ed D), teacher certification (M Ed), urban school leadership (Ed D); educational administration (M Ed, CAGS); special education (M Ed). *Students:* 141 full-time (103 women), 403 part-time (291 women); includes 81 minority (44

Urban Education

University of Massachusetts Boston (continued)
African Americans, 1 American Indian/Alaska Native, 13 Asian Americans or Pacific Islanders, 23 Hispanic Americans), 7 international. Average age 37. 381 applicants, 72% accepted, 178 enrolled. In 2006, 117 master's, 18 doctorates, 10 other advanced degrees awarded. *Degree requirements:* For master's and CAGS, comprehensive exam; for doctorate, thesis/dissertation, comprehensive exam. *Entrance requirements:* For master's, GRE General Test or MAT; for doctorate, GRE General Test or MAT, minimum GPA of 2.75; for CAGS, minimum GPA of 2.75. *Application deadline:* For fall admission, 3/1 for domestic students. Application fee: $25 ($35 for international students). *Expenses:* Tuition, state resident: full-time $2,590; part-time $301 per credit. Tuition, nonresident: full-time $9,758; part-time $427 per credit. One-time fee: $495 full-time. *Financial support:* In 2006–07, 37 research assistantships with full tuition reimbursements (averaging $2,000 per year), teaching assistantships with full tuition reimbursements (averaging $2,000 per year) were awarded; unspecified assistantships also available. Financial award application deadline: 3/1; financial award applicants required to submit FAFSA. *Unit head:* Dr. Lisa Coonsalves, Director, 617-287-7642, E-mail: lisa.gonsalves@umb.edu. *Application contact:* Peggy Roldan, Graduate Admissions Coordinator, 617-287-6400, Fax: 617-287-6236, E-mail: bos.gadm@dpc.umassp.edu.

University of Massachusetts Boston, Office of Graduate Studies, Graduate College of Education, School Organization, Curriculum and Instruction Department, Program in Education, Track in Urban School Leadership, Boston, MA 02125-3393. Offers Ed D. *Accreditation:* NCATE. Part-time and evening/weekend programs available. *Students:* 2 full-time (both women), 46 part-time (32 women); includes 22 minority (12 African Americans, 1 American Indian/Alaska Native, 3 Asian Americans or Pacific Islanders, 6 Hispanic Americans), 1 international. Average age 41. 26 applicants, 46% accepted, 8 enrolled. In 2006, 5 degrees awarded. *Median time to degree:* Doctorate–8 years full-time. *Degree requirements:* For doctorate, thesis/dissertation, comprehensive exam. *Entrance requirements:* For doctorate, GRE General Test or MAT, minimum GPA of 2.75. *Application deadline:* For fall admission, 3/1 for domestic students. Application fee: $25 ($40 for international students). *Expenses:* Tuition, state resident: full-time $2,590; part-time $301 per credit. Tuition, nonresident: full-time $9,758; part-time $427 per credit. One-time fee: $495 full-time. *Financial support:* In 2006–07, 4 research assistantships with full tuition reimbursements (averaging $13,000 per year) were awarded; teaching assistantships with full tuition reimbursements, career-related internships or fieldwork, Federal Work-Study, and unspecified assistantships also available. Support available to part-time students. Financial award application deadline: 3/1; financial award applicants required to submit FAFSA. *Faculty research:* School reform, race and culture in schools, race and higher education, language, literacy and writing. *Unit head:* Dr. Joseph Check, Director, 617-287-7655, E-mail: joseph.check@umb.edu. *Application contact:* Peggy Roldan, Graduate Admissions Coordinator, 617-287-6400, Fax: 617-287-6236, E-mail: bos.gadm@dpc.umassp.edu.

University of Michigan–Flint, School of Education and Human Services, Department of Education, Flint, MI 48502-1950. Offers early childhood education (MA Ed); education (MA Ed); elementary education with teaching certificate (MA Ed); literacy (K-12) (MA Ed); special education (MA Ed); urban and multicultural education (MA Ed). Part-time programs available. *Faculty:* 19 full-time (15 women), 9 part-time/adjunct (6 women). *Students:* 20 full-time (18 women), 193 part-time (167 women); includes 15 minority (12 African Americans, 1 American Indian/Alaska Native, 2 Hispanic Americans), 2 international. 109 applicants, 80% accepted, 65 enrolled. In 2006, 54 degrees awarded. *Entrance requirements:* Additional exam requirements/recommendations for international students: Required—TOEFL (minimum score 550 paper-based; 220 computer-based), IELTS (minimum score 7). *Application deadline:* For fall admission, 8/1 priority date for domestic students, 3/1 priority date for international students; for winter admission, 11/15 priority date for domestic students, 7/15 priority date for international students; for spring admission, 3/15 priority date for domestic students, 11/15 priority date for international students. Application fee: $55. *Expenses: Contact institution. Unit head:* Dr. Beverly Schumer, Director, 810-424-5215, E-mail: bschumer@umflint.edu. *Application contact:* Beulah Alexander, Executive Secretary, 810-766-6879, Fax: 810-766-6891, E-mail: beulah@umflint.edu.

University of Nebraska at Omaha, Graduate Studies and Research, College of Education, Department of Teacher Education, Omaha, NE 68182. Offers elementary education (MA, MS); instruction in urban schools (Certificate); instructional technology (Certificate); reading education (MS); secondary education (MA, MS). Part-time and evening/weekend programs available. *Faculty:* 24 full-time (15 women). *Students:* 33 full-time (28 women), 277 part-time (236 women); includes 18 minority (11 African Americans, 2 Asian Americans or Pacific Islanders, 5 Hispanic Americans), 1 international. Average age 32. 85 applicants, 84% accepted, 46 enrolled. In 2006, 101 master's, 5 other advanced degrees awarded. *Degree requirements:* For master's, thesis, (for some programs), comprehensive exam. *Entrance requirements:* For master's, minimum GPA of 3.0. Additional exam requirements/recommendations for international students: Required—TOEFL (minimum score 550 paper-based; 213 computer-based; 80 iBT). *Application deadline:* For fall admission, 7/1 priority date for domestic students; for spring admission, 12/1 priority date for domestic students. Applications are processed on a rolling basis. Application fee: $45. Electronic applications accepted. *Financial support:* In 2006–07, 116 students received support; fellowships, teaching assistantships with tuition reimbursements available, Federal Work-Study, institutionally sponsored loans, scholarships/grants, tuition waivers (partial), and unspecified assistantships available. Support available to part-time students. Financial award application deadline: 3/1; financial award applicants required to submit FAFSA. *Unit head:* Dr. Lana Danielson, Advisor, 402-554-2212. *Application contact:* Dr. Wilma Kuhlman, Student Contact, 402-554-2212.

University of Wisconsin–Milwaukee, Graduate School, School of Education, Department of Curriculum and Instruction, Milwaukee, WI 53201-0413. Offers curriculum planning and instruction improvement (MS); early childhood education (MS); elementary education (MS); junior high/middle school education (MS); reading education (MS); secondary education (MS); teaching in an urban setting (MS). Part-time programs available. *Faculty:* 27 full-time (17 women). *Students:* 21 full-time (17 women), 67 part-time (54 women); includes 15 minority (8 African Americans, 3 Asian Americans or Pacific Islanders, 4 Hispanic Americans), 3 international. 44 applicants, 43% accepted, 19 enrolled. In 2006, 38 degrees awarded. *Degree requirements:* For master's, thesis or alternative. *Application deadline:* For fall admission, 1/1 priority date for domestic students; for spring admission, 9/1 for domestic students. Applications are processed on a rolling basis. Application fee: $45 ($75 for international students). *Expenses:* Tuition, state resident: part-time $510 per credit. Tuition, nonresident: part-time $1,408 per credit. Tuition and fees vary according to program. *Financial support:* Fellowships, research assistantships, teaching assistantships, career-related internships or fieldwork and unspecified assistantships available. Support available to part-time students. Financial award application deadline: 4/15. *Unit head:* Linda Post, Chair, 414-229-4884, Fax: 414-229-5571, E-mail: lpost@uwm.edu.

University of Wisconsin–Milwaukee, Graduate School, School of Education, Program in Urban Education, Milwaukee, WI 53201-0413. Offers PhD. *Students:* 113 full-time (81 women), 72 part-time (48 women); includes 49 minority (27 African Americans, 3 American Indian/Alaska Native, 9 Asian Americans or Pacific Islanders, 10 Hispanic Americans), 10 international. 100 applicants, 44% accepted, 27 enrolled. In 2006, 16 degrees awarded. *Degree requirements:* For doctorate, thesis/dissertation. *Entrance requirements:* For doctorate, GRE General Test. *Application deadline:* For fall admission, 1/1 priority date for domestic students; for spring admission, 9/1 for domestic students. Applications are processed on a rolling basis. Application fee: $45 ($75 for international students). *Expenses:* Tuition, state resident: part-time $510 per credit. Tuition, nonresident: part-time $1,408 per credit. Tuition and fees vary according to program. *Financial support:* Fellowships, research assistantships, teaching assistantships, career-related internships or fieldwork and unspecified assistantships available. Support available to part-time students. Financial award application deadline: 3/1. *Unit head:* Larry Martin, Representative, 414-229-4729, Fax: 414-229-2920, E-mail: lmartin@uwm.edu.

Virginia Commonwealth University, Graduate School, School of Education, Doctoral Program in Education, Richmond, VA 23284-9005. Offers educational leadership (PhD); instructional leadership (PhD); research and evaluation (PhD); urban services leadership (PhD). *Accreditation:* NCATE. Part-time programs available. *Students:* 53 full-time (44 women), 112 part-time (77 women); includes 38 minority (35 African Americans, 1 American Indian/Alaska Native, 2 Hispanic Americans), 5 international. 39 applicants, 67% accepted, 22 enrolled. In 2006, 13 degrees awarded. *Degree requirements:* For doctorate, thesis/dissertation. *Entrance requirements:* For doctorate, GRE, interview, master's degree, writing sample. *Application deadline:* For fall admission, 3/15 for domestic students. Application fee: $50. *Financial support:* Fellowships, research assistantships, career-related internships or fieldwork, Federal Work-Study, and institutionally sponsored loans available. Financial award application deadline: 3/1. *Unit head:* Dr. Henry Clark, Director, Graduate Studies, 804-828-3382. *Application contact:* Patricia Willard, Administrative Assistant, 804-828-6530, E-mail: pawillar@vcu.edu.

See Close-Up on page 1135.

ALLIANT INTERNATIONAL UNIVERSITY

Graduate School of Education
Teaching English to Speakers of Other Languages Programs

Programs of Study

The Graduate School of Education (GSOE) at Alliant International University offers a certificate, master's, and doctoral program in teaching English to speakers of other languages (TESOL).

The 15-unit TESOL graduate certificate program—offered on Alliant's Fresno, Irvine, and San Diego campuses—provides students with the knowledge and skills needed to effectively teach English in a variety of English as a second language (ESL) and English as a foreign language (EFL) settings. Students who enroll in this program include not only teachers and other educators but also professionals from airlines, travel, and business who want to gain the skills needed to communicate with and teach speakers of other languages. The certificate can be completed in nine to twelve months.

The master's degree program offers a balance between theory and practice through a combination of TESOL methodology, linguistics, and education courses. Students gain firsthand experience in classrooms through the School's Partners for Success program by collaborating with local schools and community college districts. The program is designed for both prospective and experienced ESL and EFL educators. The adult-education-emphasis TESOL master's program is offered on the Fresno, Irvine, and San Diego campuses. The master's program meets the course work requirements for the TESOL graduate certificate.

The doctoral program produces scholar practitioners with expertise in seven key areas—TESOL theory and methodology; teacher training; design, implementation, evaluation, and administration of second-language programs; curriculum and materials development; cultural, sociolinguistic, and psycholinguistic factors of second-language acquisition; applied research; and the integration of technology in second-language teaching. Graduates begin careers as professors at the college or university level or as directors of teacher-training programs in the United States and abroad. They administer regional, state, and national programs focused on the needs of English language learners and work in administrative positions in international organization that address national and international language policies. Students may perform field work and conduct research in the ESL program at the San Diego or Mexico City campus.

The master's degree is also available as an online program with a three-course residency requirement. The Cross-Cultural Language and Academic Development (CLAD) Certificate is also offered at the Fresno, Irvine, and San Diego campuses.

Research Facilities

Alliant International offers excellent research facilities throughout the system. The Alliant libraries maintain a diverse available collection of more than 160,000 books, 1,150 current print journal subscriptions, 12 electronic database subscriptions, approximately 995 psychological test titles, 1,700 audiotapes, and more than 1,200 videotapes. Each campus library is a resource for a variety of research topics and works in cooperation with several other four-year institutions in the immediate area. Each academic school or college has research clusters, labs, and/or other resources to support original scholarly and applied research. The Computer Lab and Learning Center has a number of computers available for student use. The computers are loaded with current versions of word processing, statistical, and other software programs and are connected to laser printers. Further, Alliant maintains partnerships with area university libraries that allow students to access material.

Financial Aid

Most students interested in school-based financial aid pursue college work-study. Students work as teaching or research assistants to core faculty members. In addition, students can work on campus in a number of departments, including admissions and field placement. Stipends generally average about $1000 per assistantship per semester. For complete information, students should contact the Financial Aid Office.

Cost of Study

Master's programs are $500 per semester unit; doctoral programs cost $900 per semester unit. Fees are additional.

Living and Housing Costs

On-campus housing is not available on the Fresno and Irvine campuses. Most Alliant students live in communities adjacent to the campuses. The estimated cost of living for a graduate student (including housing and food, transportation, and personal expenses) for the nine-month academic year is $17,262. Room and board on the San Diego campus cost $9820 for the academic year for a private room and $7430 for double occupancy. Students can expect to pay between $700 and $1000 per month plus utilities (gas and electricity) for an off-campus unfurnished, one-bedroom apartment. The estimated cost for books and supplies is $1500 per year.

Student Group

Alliant ranked first in international students in *U.S. News & World Report*'s 2007 nationwide survey. *Diverse* magazine ranked Alliant sixth for awarding doctorates to minority women and fourteenth for doctorates to minorities (all disciplines combined). Alliant International University has students from almost every state plus 407 international students from sixty-nine countries, including Botswana, Cameroon, Greece, Iceland, Portugal, and Turkey.

Location

The ambience on the Fresno campus is friendly and warm, a reflection of its Central Valley location. Blessed with abundant sunshine and mild temperatures, the region brims with orchards and blossoms. Conveniently located adjacent to Fresno's Yosemite International Airport, Alliant's Fresno campus serves one of the fastest growing cities in California. The Irvine campus is a friendly, conveniently-located center that caters to the needs of working adults, with evening classes and free on-site parking. Small class sizes offer personalized learning, and quiet classrooms, computer labs, and a comfortable student lounge provide a conductive learning environment. An hour south of Los Angeles and conveniently accessible to two major freeways and the John Wayne Airport, Irvine is within easy driving distance of beautiful Corona Del Mar and the sun drenched sand of Laguna Beach and Newport Beach. Even closer at hand is an extensive system nature preserves, wilderness parks and trails that offers get-aways to hikers, bicyclists, equestrians, and photographers. The San Diego campus is located in what is often called "America's Finest City." San Diego is a dynamic, multicultural location in which to study. A vibrant, metropolitan city with a laid-back, small-town feel, the area is filled with an incredible selection of activities and attractions. There are many cultural and historic attractions, shopping centers, fine dining establishments, and places to relax and reenergize. From the beautiful beaches to the inland mountains, the views are spectacular, and San Diego has a climate unmatched for mildness nationwide.

The University and The School

Alliant International University focuses on preparing students for professional careers. Alliant International University was officially formed in 2001 by the combination of the California School of Professional Psychology (CSPP), founded in 1969, and United States International University (USIU), founded in 1967. But their history goes back more than the forty plus years since USIU's founding. USIU was the successor to two other institutions: California Western University, founded in 1952, and Balboa College, founded in 1924.

The Graduate School of Education trains professionals who make a difference in the lives of others through teaching, counseling, leadership, advocacy, administration, management, and community work. GSOE infuses its curricula with multicultural content and emphasizes student achievement, instructional technology, assessment, neuropsychology, mentoring of diverse populations, and comprehensive community service. At the core of its professional practitioner model is the cohort structure, which supports learning while students are enrolled in advanced studies and provides a professional support system of colleagues throughout their career.

Applying

Master's and certificate applicants must possess a bachelor's degree or higher and have a minimum GPA of 2.5. In general, applicants should submit the completed application, the application fee ($55 for the master's and certificate programs, $70 for the doctoral program), all official transcripts, a personal essay, and letters of recommendation (two for certificate and master's students, three for doctoral). Doctoral students must have a master's degree and must submit a resume; MAT or GRE scores are optional. International students must also submit TOEFL scores.

Correspondence and Information

Alliant Admissions
Alliant International University
10455 Pomerado Road
San Diego, California 92131

Phone: 866-U-ALLIANT (toll-free)
E-mail: admissions@alliant.edu
Web site: http://alliant.edu/gsoe

Alliant International University

THE FACULTY AND THEIR RESEARCH

Core and Noncore Faculty

Joseph Adwere-Boamah, Assistant Professor and Program Coordinator, Educational Leadership (San Diego); Ph.D., Berkeley, 1970.

Hassana Alidou, Professor and Program Coordinator, TESOL (San Diego and Irvine); Ph.D., Illinois at Urbana–Champaign, 1997. Sociolinguistics, teacher training in TESOL.

Frederick Ansoff, Assistant Professor, Educational Leadership and Management (San Diego); Ph.D., Georgetown, 1998. Statistical analyses.

Shirley Baker, Instructor, TESOL (Fresno) and Director, International Language and Cultural Center; M.A., Kentucky, 1987; M.A., US International, 1999. TESOL program description, TESOL teacher preparation.

Suzanne Borman, Professor (San Diego); Ed.D., Columbia Teachers College, 1983. Curriculum and instructional planning.

Mary Ellen Butler-Pascoe, Professor and Systemwide Program Director, TESOL (San Diego); Ph.D., US International, 1990. ESL/EFL teacher training, integration of technology and second-language instruction, program and curriculum design.

Ana Guisela Chupina, Assistant Professor, Teacher Education, Higher Education (San Francisco); Ph.D., Iowa State, 2004. Immigrant women as adult learners, first-generation and culturally diverse students in higher education, methodological issues in cross-cultural research.

Geoffrey M. Cox, Professor of Higher Education (San Francisco) and President, Alliant International University; Ph.D., Chicago, 1987. Social and political philosophy, leadership in higher education.

Trudy Day, Assistant Professor, Teacher Education, Higher Education (San Francisco); Systemwide Assistant Dean, Graduate School of Education; and Systemwide Director, TeachersCHOICE; Ed.D., Louisville, 1996. Leadership and crisis, first-year teachers, shared governance, instructional strategies for the university professor.

Steven Fisher, Assistant Professor and Program Director, School and Educational Psychology (San Diego); Ph.D., US International, 1998. Clinical psychology.

Xuanning Fu, Assistant Professor and Program Coordinator, Educational Leadership and Management (Fresno); Ph.D., Brigham Young, 1993. Program analysis and evaluation.

James F. Hiramoto, Principal Lecturer and Program Coordinator, School and Educational Psychology (San Francisco); Ph.D., Berkeley, 2004. Effects of sightedness on areas of knowledge, social skills, and perceptions of self; ADHD.

Kenneth Kelch, Assistant Professor of TESOL and Director, International Languages and Cultural Center (San Diego); Ed.D., Alliant International, 2005. TESOL pedagogy.

Jerry Kill, Assistant Professor and Coordinator, Educational Leadership and Management (Irvine); Ed.D., California Coast, 2005. Educational leadership, school administration.

Yury Kostin, Assistant Professor (Fresno); Ed.D., California State, Fresno, 2003. Technological applications.

Robert D. Kreger, Associate Professor (San Francisco); Ph.D., Michigan, 1980. Teacher preparation, child development and disorder issues in education, special education.

Irving Leung, Assistant Professor and Field Services Coordinator, Teacher Education–Early Completion Option (San Francisco); Ed.D., San Francisco, 1998. Bilingual education, special education.

Estela C. Matriano, Professor and Secretary, World Council for Curriculum and Instruction (San Diego); Ed.D., Indiana, 1968. Global education.

Jerold D. Miller, Professor; Program Director, Teacher Education; and Director, Partners for Success Tech and Media Center (San Diego); Ed.D., US International, 1985. Technology planning and curriculum development.

Beverly J. Palley, Field Services Coordinator, Teacher Education; Ed.D., Fielding Graduate University, 2003. Teacher-training programs, improving alternative certification approaches in teacher internship programs.

Carlton Parks, Professor and Campus Program Director, Educational Psychology (Los Angeles); Ph.D., Minnesota, 1986. Interpersonal relations, interpersonal violence, sexual and ethnic minorities, psychosocial aspects of HIV infection/AIDS, feminist studies, spirituality and mental health.

Connell Persico, University Professor and Systemwide Program Director, Educational Leadership, Educational Administration; Ph.D., Stanford, 1974. Education leadership, higher education organization, politics of education.

Debra Reeves-Gutierrez, Assistant Professor, Teacher Education–Early Completion Option (San Francisco); Ed.D., University of the Pacific, 2005. Pedagogy.

Robert Reyes, Assistant Professor and Program Coordinator, Educational Leadership and Management (Los Angeles); Ph.D., Berne, 2001. English language development, educational leadership, global education.

Karen Schuster Webb, Professor of Higher Education and TESOL and Systemwide Dean, Graduate School of Education (San Francisco); Ph.D., Indiana–Bloomington, 1980. Language and cognition, discourse pragmatics, inclusive pedagogy.

Ed Shenk, Associate Professor and Program Director, Educational Leadership and Management, Higher Education (San Francisco); Ed.D., Oregon, 1981. Student services, student discipline, leadership, organizational structures.

George Stamos, Associate Professor; Ed.D., Northern Arizona, 1996. Teacher education reform.

Barbara Stein-Stover, Assistant Professor and Program Director, Teacher Education–Early Completion Option (Los Angeles and San Diego); Ed.D., Alliant International, 2006. Adolescent mental health issues, pedagogy.

Holly Wilson, Associate Professor (San Diego); Ph.D., New Mexico, 1999. Second-language-learner errors, grammar instruction, proposed use of covert grammar.

Donald Wofford, Assistant Professor and Interim Systemwide Director, Educational and School Psychology (Irvine); Psy.D., California School of Professional Psychology, 2002. School-based mental health.

Adjunct Faculty

Christine Alexander (San Diego); Ed.D., US International, 2001.

Remijio Alvarez, Lecturer (Irvine); M.A., Pepperdine, 1976.

Robert Appenzeller (San Diego); M.A., US International, 1987.

Theresa M. Ashby (Los Angeles); Ph.D., Alliant International, 2002.

Tomiko Lynn Bobo (Los Angeles), PPS Credential in School Counseling, National.

Celeste Cusumano, Senior Lecturer (Fresno); Ed.D., University of the Pacific, 1984.

Diane DeBoer (Los Angeles); Ph.D., US International, 1997.

Greg Dhuyvetter, Lecturer (Irvine); M.A., US International, 2002.

Diane di Bari (San Francisco); M.S., California State, Fresno, 1976.

Richard G. Duke (Fresno); Ed.D., Brigham Young, 1981.

Krystel Edmonds-Biglow (Los Angeles); Psy.D., Alliant International, 2001.

Joe Fox (Irvine); M.A., Northern Colorado, 1966.

La Faune Yvette Gordon (Los Angeles); Ph.D., California School of Professional Psychology, 1993.

Michelyn Gould (Los Angeles); Psy.D., California School of Professional Psychology, 1999.

Mary Lou Hamaker, Lecturer (Irvine); Ph.D., USC, 1986.

Leanne Harmon-Doyle (Los Angeles); Psy.D., Alliant International, 2003.

Christine A. Hoffman (Irvine); Ed.D., Northern Arizona, 1997.

Erica L. Holmes (Los Angeles); Psy.D., US International, 2001.

Elena M. Ingrao (San Diego); M.S., National, 1993.

Adi´na Janzen (Fresno); J.D., San Joaquin College of Law, 1985.

Vallarie Johnson (Los Angeles); Psy.D., Alliant International, 2004.

Dan Kettlehake (San Diego); Ph.D., Bowling Green State, 1997.

Lori Lambertson, Lecturer (San Francisco); M.A., San Francisco State, 1993.

Susan Lees (Los Angeles); Psy.D., Alliant International, 2003.

Bill Madigan (San Diego); M.A., San Diego State, 1990.

Sally Madruga (San Diego); M.A., San Diego State, 1981.

N. Bert McIntosh Jr. (San Diego); M.A., San Diego State, 1969.

Erv Metzgar (San Diego); M.A., San Diego State.

Susan Moore (San Diego); Ed.D., Alliant International, 2005.

Emil Nolte, Lecturer (Irvine).

Romelia Orozco (San Diego); Ed.D., Alliant International, 2002.

Cyndi Paik, Lecturer (Irvine); M.A., US International, 2002.

Walter T. Parry (San Diego); M.A., Stanford, 1964.

Ernest Proud (Los Angeles); Ph.D., California School of Professional Psychology.

Thomas Ryerson (Los Angeles); Psy.D., Alliant International, 2004.

Jerry Salazar, Lecturer (Irvine); M.A., California State, Long Beach, 1972.

Marilyn Shepherd (Fresno); Ed.D., California, Davis, 1996.

Erlinda Teisinger (Fresno); Ed.D., USC, 2000.

Marvin Warner (San Diego); M.A., Azusa Pacific, 1978.

Gary E. Warren (Los Angeles); Ed.D., US International, 1987.

Lori Williams (Los Angeles); Psy.D., Alliant International, 2004.

CLEMSON UNIVERSITY

Special Education Programs

Programs of Study	The Master of Education (M.Ed.) degree in special education is designed to ensure that students are knowledgeable in the field of special education. The degree program prepares students in at least one of the following areas: learning disabilities (LD), emotional/behavioral disorders (E/BD), and mental retardation (MR). The program of study enables students to identify important legal and policy issues in special education, demonstrate knowledge of the research processes within the field of special education, demonstrate knowledge of specific characteristics of individuals with mild disabilities, and implement scientifically based interventions for students with disabilities in a variety of settings. Successful graduates will evaluate critically special education literature, recognize and evaluate current issues and problems in special education, and identify potential solutions for these problems.
	The doctoral program in special education is designed to provide intensive and rigorous preparation for participants in teacher education, research methodology, policy/advocacy, home/community services, and evidence-based practices to improve outcomes for students with disabilities in high-needs schools. Graduates of this program are poised to take leadership roles in the field of special education and are equipped with specific knowledge and skills related to staffing high-needs schools and addressing the academic and social needs of students in those schools. Program graduates will be highly competitive for special education faculty positions in institutions of higher education (IHEs). Program graduates contribute to the field of special education by conducting research to enhance current knowledge of effective practices related to students with disabilities and in high-needs schools.
	Research opportunities are varied as faculty members bring expertise in applied behavior analysis, elementary and secondary instructional methodologies, mathematics instruction, early literacy, transition, direct instruction, peer tutoring, curriculum-based measurement, social skills instruction, functional behavioral assessment, legal and policy issues, crisis prevention and intervention, delinquency, and instructional technology.
Research Facilities	Centers and collaboratives include the South Carolina Center for Excellence in Instructional Technology, America Reads, the Houston Center for the Study of the Black Experience in Education, and the National Drop Out Prevention Center. For more information, students should visit http://www.hehd.clemson.edu/schoolofed/centers.htm.
Financial Aid	Several half-time graduate assistantships are available through the School of Education. Each of these assistantships is for a calendar year and requires a minimum of 20 hours work per week. Duties for graduate assistants vary with the assignment but can range from assisting in the teaching of courses to assisting with research projects. Duty assignments are usually made by the department administration in consultation with Unit Coordinators and are based on the student's academic preparation, any relevant experience, and, when possible, interviews.
Cost of Study	Tuition for 2007–08 is $3641 per semester for in-state students and $7285 per semester for nonresidents. Off-campus rates are $330 per hour for in-state students and $660 per hour for nonresidents. Graduate assistants pay a flat fee of $950 per semester. Graduate fellows pay South Carolina resident fees.
Living and Housing Costs	On-campus housing is available. For information, students should visit http://www.housing.clemson.edu. The cost of living in Clemson is quite low compared to the national average. Students who choose to live off the campus typically spend $300–$400 per month for rent, depending on location, amenities, roommates, and other factors.
Student Group	The program has approximately 27 students. Eighty-five percent are women, and 22 percent are full-time students.
Student Outcomes	Graduates are prepared for instructional and leadership positions in public schools, state agencies, and institutions of higher education.
Location	Clemson is a small, beautiful college town near the Blue Ridge Mountains and Lake Hartwell in upstate South Carolina. The Upstate is one of the country's fastest-growing areas and is an important part of the I-85 corridor, a multi-state area along Interstate 85 that runs from metro Atlanta to Richmond, Virginia, and encompasses Charlotte, North Carolina, and North Carolina's Research Triangle. Atlanta and Charlotte are each a two-hour drive away. Many financial institutions and other industries have a national headquarters or a major presence in the Upstate, including Wachovia, Bank of America, BMW, Bon Secours St. Francis Health System, Bosch North America, Bowater, Charter Communications, Ernst and Young, Fluor Corporation, IBM, Microsoft, Michelin of North America, and many others.
The University	Clemson is classified by the Carnegie Foundation as an RU/H: Research University (high research activity), a category comprising just 10 percent of all graduate degree-granting universities in America. The University's mission is to fulfill the covenant between its founder and the people of South Carolina to establish a "high seminary of learning" through its responsibilities of teaching, research, and extended public service. The University has identified eight areas of academic emphasis that create collaborations that, in turn, help fulfill the University's mission.
Applying	Students in these programs are expected to be of high integrity, motivated, and committed to implementing evidence-based instructional and behavioral interventions. Applicants may apply on the Web at http://www.grad.clemson.edu/p_apply.html. Applications with a $50 nonrefundable fee should be received no later than five weeks prior to registration. Every required item in support of the application must be on file by that date. Students are advised to contact the department for the deadlines of the program of proposed study.
Correspondence and Information	David S. Fleming, Ph.D. Graduate Coordinator Eugene T. Moore School of Education G-01 Tillman Hall Clemson University Clemson, South Carolina 29634 Phone: 864-656-1881 Fax: 864-656-0311 E-mail: dflemin@clemson.edu Web site: http://www.hehd.clemson.edu/schoolofed/g-special-ed_po.htm

Clemson University

THE FACULTY AND THEIR RESEARCH

Vivian I. Correa, Distinguished Professor of Early Childhood and Special Education; Ph.D., Vanderbilt (Peabody). Early childhood special education, family involvement, multicultural education, teacher education.

Robin E. Fish, Clinical Faculty; M.Ed., Clemson. Teacher training.

Janie Hodge, Associate Professor; Ph.D., Vanderbilt. LD, effective instruction, literacy.

Antonis Katsiyannis, Professor; Ed.D., William and Mary. Legal and policy issues in special education, delinquency, outcomes for students with E/BD.

Kimberly A. McDuffie, Assistant Professor; Ph.D., George Mason. Co-teaching and collaboration, secondary instructional strategies for effective inclusive instruction, co-teaching, and teacher education.

Paul J. Riccomini, Associate Professor; Ph.D., Pennsylvania State. Effective mathematics instruction, instructional technology, dropout prevention for students with disabilities, implementation of school-wide early reading assessment models.

Joe Ryan, Assistant Professor; Ph.D., Nebraska. Classroom management, policy related to use of restraint and timeout in schools, special education law, psychotropic treatments for students with behavioral disorders, therapeutic recreation.

Pamela M. Stecker, Professor; Ph.D., Vanderbilt. Progress monitoring and academic interventions in literacy and mathematics for students who are low achieving or have mild disabilities.

HAWAI'I PACIFIC UNIVERSITY

Teaching English as a Second Language

Programs of Study

Hawai'i Pacific University's Master of Arts in Teaching English as a Second Language (M.A.T.E.S.L.) focuses on practical, hands-on education that teaches graduates the essential skills they need to become successful educators. By learning about the current theories, methods, and materials, M.A.T.E.S.L. graduates are prepared and ready to teach English as a second language in the classroom.

The M.A.T.E.S.L. features a solid curriculum in three types of courses. Linguistic theory courses taught from an applied viewpoint help the M.A.T.E.S.L. student better understand languages in general and English in particular. The second type is pedagogy courses, which present a range of current approaches, designs, and procedures for teaching language in a wide variety of contexts. In these classes, teaching demonstrations and videotaped peer practice sessions are used extensively. The third type, two practicum courses, allows future teachers to observe master teachers, serve with them in the classroom as assistants, and assume full class responsibility as practice teachers. The capstone activity synthesizes several semesters of classroom study and practicum training. Students have three options for this completion requirement: a portfolio, a comprehensive exam, or an extensive in-service project.

Research Facilities

To support graduate studies, University libraries, with a collection exceeding 153,000 volumes, add an average of 2,500 volumes annually. Periodical titles number more than 1,700; 205,000 pieces of microfiche and 5,300 rolls of microfilm are maintained.

Libraries are electronically linked to the catalogs and databases of Hawai'i's major publicly supported library systems, other specialized libraries on Oahu, and remote-site libraries. Hawai'i Pacific University (HPU) students are provided with e-mail, Internet access, and online access to state-of-the-art research databases. Students are encouraged to prepare papers for publication in the *TESL Working Paper Series,* an in-house journal, which showcases the best scholarly work from the University's student body.

Financial Aid

The University participates in all federal financial aid programs designated for graduate students. These programs provide aid in the form of subsidized (need-based) and unsubsidized (non-need-based) Federal Stafford Student Loans. Through these loans, funds may be available to cover the student's entire cost of education. To apply for aid, students must submit the Free Application for Federal Student Aid (FAFSA) after January 1. Mailing of student award letters usually begins by the end of March. The University also offers several institutional scholarships and assistantships.

Cost of Study

For the 2007–08 academic year, graduate tuition is $560 per credit hour, and books cost approximately $1500 for the entire program.

Living and Housing Costs

The University has both residence halls and an apartment referral service. Including tuition, books, housing, food, health insurance, and miscellaneous expenses, the cost of living for a typical single student for two semesters (nine months) is approximately $25,840.

Student Group

University enrollment currently stands at nearly 9,000, including more than 1,200 graduate students. All fifty states and more than 100 countries are represented.

Location

The University has three campuses linked by shuttle. Hawai'i Pacific combines the excitement of an urban, downtown campus with the serenity of the windward side of the island. The main campus is located in downtown Honolulu, the business and financial center of the Pacific, and it is the location where all M.A.T.E.S.L. classes are held. The Hawai'i Loa campus is 8 miles away situated in Kaneohe at the base of the Ko'olau Mountains; it is the site of the School of Nursing, the marine science program, and a variety of other course offerings. The third campus, Oceanic Institute, is an applied aquaculture research facility located on a 56-acre site at Makapu'u Point on the windward coast.

The University

HPU is the largest private postsecondary institution in the state of Hawai'i. The University is coeducational, with a faculty of more than 300 members, a student-faculty ratio of 18:1, and an average class size of 20, although M.A.T.E.S.L. classes are generally smaller. A wide range of counseling and student support services are available. There are more than ninety student organizations, including the Graduate Student Organization. M.A.T.E.S.L. students usually join the student club called Intercultural Teachers Organization (ITO), which sponsors many professional and social events throughout the year.

Applying

Hawai'i Pacific University seeks students with academic promise, outstanding career potential, and high motivation. Applicants should complete and forward a graduate admissions application form, have official transcripts sent from all colleges or universities, submit two original and current letters of recommendation, and submit two essays. International students should submit results of the TOEFL. Admissions decisions are made on a rolling basis, and applicants are notified between one and two weeks after all documents have been submitted. Applicants to Hawai'i Pacific University's graduate program are encouraged to submit applications online at http://www.hpu.edu/matesl.

Correspondence and Information

Graduate Admissions
Hawai'i Pacific University
1164 Bishop Street, #911
Honolulu, Hawai'i 96813
Phone: 808-544-1135
        866-GRAD-HPU (toll-free)
Fax: 808-544-0280
E-mail: graduate@hpu.edu
Web site: http://www.hpu.edu/grad

Hawai'i Pacific University

THE FACULTY

Edward F. Klein, Professor of Applied Linguistics and Program Chair, TESL Programs; Ph.D., Hawai'i at Manoa.
Jean Coffman, Associate Professor of English (ESL); M.A., Columbia Teachers College.
Kenneth Cook, Professor of Linguistics; Ph.D., California, San Diego.
Irene Gordon, Instructor of Arabic; M.A., Wayne State.
Barbara Hannum, Assistant Professor of ESL and Program Chair, Center for English Language Programs; M.A., Hawai'i at Manoa.
Jean Kirschenmann, Assistant Professor of English (ESL) and Coordinator, Proficiency in English Program (PEP); M.A., Hawai'i at Manoa.
Teresa Lane, Assistant Professor of Spanish; M.A., Hawai'i at Manoa; M.A.T.L., Southern Mississippi.
Candise Lee, Assistant Professor of English (ESL); Ed.D., USC.
Hanh T. Nguyen, Assistant Professor of Applied Linguistics; Ph.D., Wisconsin–Madison.
Carol Perrin, Assistant Professor of English (ESL) and Director, Tutoring and Placement Testing Services; M.A., Hawai'i at Manoa.
Catherine Sajna, Assistant Professor of English (ESL); M.A., Hawai'i at Manoa.

MONTEREY INSTITUTE OF INTERNATIONAL STUDIES

Graduate School of Language and Educational Linguistics

Programs of Study

The Master of Arts (M.A.) degrees in teaching English to speakers of other languages (TESOL) and the teaching a foreign language (TFL) combine strong academic preparation with practical training in language pedagogy. These M.A. programs offer courses in applied linguistics, pedagogical theory and practice, sociolinguistics, and second language acquisition as well as research design for behavioral scientists.

The Master's International (M.I.) program provides two semesters of intensive on-campus study toward an M.A. in TESOL before two years in the Peace Corps in a related overseas assignment. After successful completion of Peace Corps service, volunteers return to the Institute and receive partial scholarships for the final semester of study in the M.A. in TESOL program.

The Graduate School also offers several professional certificate programs; 17-credit certificates in TESOL or TFL are available for those who wish to focus solely on practical courses. A 17-credit certificate in Language Program Administration (LPA) prepares graduates to administer language programs and may be completed in combination with the M.A. in TESOL or TFL. The Computer Assisted Language Learning (CALL) certificate includes 12 credits of course work and enables graduates to manage and develop curriculum for language-learning programs utilizing computer technology. This certificate may be combined with the TESOL or TFL degrees. CALL online courses can be completed by qualified teachers from anywhere in the world.

The Monterey Institute offers specialized language programs in foreign languages and English as a second language. For detailed information about the foreign language programs, students should send an e-mail to silp@miis.edu. Information about the English language programs can be received by sending an e-mail to english@miis.edu.

Research Facilities

Innovative and challenging curricula at the Institute require appropriate facilities and cutting-edge technology. The classrooms vary in size—from large halls where plenary sessions with simultaneous interpretation can be held to smaller classrooms and labs befitting seminar-style classes for no more than 15 students.

The Max Kade Language and Technology Center is a fully equipped language-learning center. It provides multimedia classrooms and conference rooms with state-of-the-art technology.

In addition to numerous computer labs, the campus is fully networked, utilizing 802.11 wireless standards. Every student is encouraged, for flexibility, to have a personal laptop computer adapted for wireless connectivity.

The Institute's specialized international library has a collection of more than 10,000 volumes and maintains 500 periodicals, 400 online journals, and thirty-five daily and weekly newspapers.

Financial Aid

Candidates with a minimum grade point average of 3.3 on a 4.0 scale (or equivalent) are considered for scholarships of up to $14,000 per year. Scholarships are renewable for a second year depending on the recipient's program and academic performance.

Numerous part-time jobs are available on campus, and some faculty members employ research assistants. Some of these opportunities are awarded with scholarships, and others are available when students enroll.

U.S. citizens and permanent residents may apply for need-based financial aid programs, including low-interest loans.

Cost of Study

Tuition for 2005–06 was $25,500. The cost of fees, books, and supplies was estimated to be $900.

Living and Housing Costs

Housing, transportation, and living expenses for the academic year was estimated at $10,500.

Student Group

Institute enrollment is approximately 750. About one third of the students are from more than fifty countries other than the U.S. More than 90 percent of the American students have worked or studied abroad. More than fifty languages are spoken by students on campus. Language classes are offered in English, Spanish, Arabic, French, Russian, Japanese, Chinese (Mandarin), and German.

Student Outcomes

Graduates work all over the U.S. and in more than sixty-five countries. They teach in colleges, public schools, community programs, and corporate or government-sponsored educational programs. They take leadership roles in assessment, program administration, and teacher education. Prominent employers include Concordia Language Villages; Fairfax County Public Schools; Englishtown.com; Time Warner; Defense Language Institute; and Georgetown, Rice, Keio, and Zayed Universities. Students have interned in Bolivia, China, Japan, Mexico, the United States, and Vietnam.

A dedicated career staff works closely with students to develop internships and assist in seeking employment opportunities in the U.S. and other countries. The needs and interests of students are met through individual academic and career advising throughout the program.

Location

The Monterey Institute is situated in one of the most spectacular natural environments in the world. The Monterey Peninsula is 130 miles south of San Francisco on California's central coast surrounded by ocean and mountains; it has a population of 100,000. The area combines a variety of rich cultural resources and agricultural activities.

The Institute

Opened in 1955 with summer classes in language and culture, the Monterey Institute of Foreign Studies was the first institute dedicated to the then-revolutionary concept that a living language should be taught as such: French in French, German in German, etc. Full-year degree programs began in 1961. By 1979, the Institute had grown to international distinction and was renamed the Monterey Institute of International Studies.

Applying

Applicants to the master's programs in the Graduate School of Language and Educational Linguistics must have a U.S. bachelor's degree or the equivalent. Application may be made at any time, provided it is received at least one month prior to the applicant's proposed semester of enrollment or three months in advance for international students residing in their home countries.

Students should visit the Web site (http://www.miis.edu) for complete information on admission requirements and the deadlines for scholarship and financial aid.

Correspondence and Information

Admissions Office
Monterey Institute of International Studies
460 Pierce Street
Monterey, California 93940
Phone: 831-647-4123
        800-824-7235 (toll-free in the United States)
Fax: 831-647-6405
E-mail: admit@miis.edu
Web site: http://www.miis.edu

Monterey Institute of International Studies

THE FACULTY AND THEIR RESEARCH

TESOL/TFL Faculty

The TESOL/TFL staff is made up of 7 full-time members who bring to the Institute a combination of superior academic credentials and professional experience in their respective fields. Although the primary emphasis is placed on teaching, faculty members are expected and encouraged to maintain research agendas and to publish or consult in their fields. The full-time members of the TESOL/TFL faculty and their current research interests are listed below.

Ruth Larimer, Professor and Dean; Ph.D., Berkeley. Teaching methodology, curriculum design, the development of authentic materials.

Kathleen M. Bailey, Professor and Language Program Administration Advisor; Ph.D., UCLA. Educational research, assessment, teacher education, language program administration.

Lynn M. Goldstein, Professor; Ed.D., Columbia Teachers College. Sociolinguistics, English discourse and grammar, applied linguistics research, composition, second language acquisition, writing for publication.

John Hedgcock, Professor; Ph.D., USC. Language analysis, second language acquisition, methodology, teaching practicum, composition.

Renee Jourdenais, Associate Professor; Ph.D., Georgetown. Second language acquisition, teacher education, sociolinguistics, educational research, language assessment.

Peter Shaw, Professor; Ph.D., USC. Methodology, curriculum design, practicum, portfolios, authentic assessment, discourse analysis.

Jean Turner, Professor; Ph.D., UCLA. Language testing, program evaluation, research design and statistics, second language acquisition.

Leo van Lier, Professor and Computer-Assisted Language Learning Advisor; Ph.D., Lancaster (England). Educational linguistics, second language acquisition, contrastive studies, computer-assisted language learning and instruction, discourse analysis, bilingual education.

Language Studies Program Heads

Language Studies faculty members combine their diverse international experiences and professional expertise to teach language courses to students in all Monterey Institute graduate programs, with advanced instruction in seven languages. With extensive backgrounds in linguistics, business language, political science, and environmental issues, the language faculty members offer unique perspectives and develop practical exercises for advancing foreign language acquisition.

Ovidio Casado-Fuente, Professor and Hispanic Studies Program Head; Ph.D., Pontifical Gregorian University (Rome).

David Colclasure, Assistant Professor and German Program Head; Ph.D., Washington (St. Louis).

Michel Gueldry, Associate Professor and French Program Head; Ph.D., Toulouse.

Robert Kohls, Assistant Professor and English Program Head; M.A., Monterey Institute.

Naoko Matsuo, Assistant Professor and Japanese Program Head; M.A., Monterey Institute.

Anna Vassilieva, Associate Professor and Russian Program Head; Ph.D., Russian Diplomatic Academy.

VIRGINIA COMMONWEALTH UNIVERSITY

Program in Special Education

Program of Study

Virginia Commonwealth University (VCU) offers the Master of Education in special education, which prepares graduates for work in one of five areas—early childhood special education, emotional disturbance, learning disabilities, mental retardation, or severe disabilities.

The early-childhood track is a sequentially planned series of courses and clinical experiences designed to prepare individuals to work with young children, from birth through age five, with developmental disabilities and their families. Successful completion of the degree program qualifies students for teacher licensure with endorsement in early-childhood special education by the Virginia Department of Education.

The concentration in emotional disturbance provides teachers the professional knowledge and skills needed to work in a variety of settings—general education classrooms (where children with special needs are being included), resource rooms, self-contained classrooms, and residential programs. In developing teacher competencies, the program focuses on specific skills and strategies for diagnosing and remediating behavior and learning problems of students with emotional disturbance.

The specialization in learning disabilities develops and refines the competencies needed for work with persons with learning disabilities in collaborative resource and self-contained settings at all levels, as well as in a variety of cultural environments. Course work encompasses broad concepts of education, research, development, related disciplines, and special education to build a foundation of professional knowledge and understanding. Specialized courses develop the intensive diagnostic, remedial, decision-making, and consultative skills and understandings required of a professional in learning disabilities.

Graduates of the mental retardation track may fill roles as resource room, modified resource room, or self-contained classroom teachers in varied urban, suburban, or rural areas. Some graduates are employed in residential programs for individuals with mental retardation or in programs in community or state department settings.

The severe disabilities program is designed to prepare teachers to work with students, ages five to twenty-one, in public school settings. Throughout the program, emphasis is placed on person-centered planning, school and community inclusion, transdisciplinary teamwork, and the role of the family.

Research Facilities

VCU libraries provide a combined capacity of more than 1.7 million volumes and 10,200 periodical titles and an online bibliographic search service accessing hundreds of databases. In addition, the Virginia State and Richmond Public libraries are within walking distance of both VCU campuses. Academic Computing provides a variety of microcomputer, minicomputer, and mainframe computing services to support the research and instructional endeavors of its faculty and students, including consultation, instruction, and computer acquisition.

The School of Education sponsors a variety of centers and institutes that connect students and faculty to the field of practice, including the Center for School Community Collaboration, the Center for Teacher Leadership, the Child Development Center, the Commonwealth Educational Policy Institute (CEPI), the Metropolitan Educational Research Consortium (MERC), the Partnership for People with Disabilities, the Virginia Department of Education's (VDOE) Training & Technical Assistance Center (T/TAC), the Rehabilitation Research and Training Center, the Virginia Adult Learning Resource Center, the Virginia Center for Teaching International Studies, and the Metropolitan Educational Training Alliance (META).

Financial Aid

Students may apply for need-based assistance through the University's Financial Aid Office. Current information on financial aid programs, policies, and procedures is available at http://www.vcu.edu/enroll/finaid.

Cost of Study

For full-time study (9–15 credits) in 2007–08, Virginia residents pay tuition and fees of $4452 per semester; nonresidents, $8876 per semester. For part-time study, Virginia residents pay tuition and fees of $465 per hour; nonresidents, $954 per hour. Some programs require additional fees. On the Medical College of Virginia (MCV) campus, tuition, fees, and other expenses vary in the medicine, pharmacy, nurse anesthesia, dentistry, and School of Allied Health programs.

Living and Housing Costs

Graduate student housing is available on both the MCV campus and the academic campus of Virginia Commonwealth University. Many graduate students live in off-campus housing, which is reasonably priced and readily available in a variety of styles and settings in nearby residential areas or within easy commuting distance. On- and off-campus housing information is available on the Web at http://www.housing.vcu.edu/.

Student Group

VCU enrolls 30,452 students, 7,611 of whom are graduate students. More than 200 clubs and organizations reflect the diverse social, recreational, educational, political, and religious interests of the student body.

Location

Richmond is Virginia's capital and a major East Coast financial and manufacturing center that offers students a wide range of cultural, educational, and recreational activities. Richmond is located in central Virginia at the intersection of Interstates 95 and 64, 2 hours south of Washington, D.C., and nestled between the Blue Ridge Mountains and the Atlantic coast. The Richmond region is easily accessible by plane, car, and train. With nearly 1 million residents, the historic city of Richmond combines big-city offerings with small-town hospitality. Applicants are encouraged to explore http://www.visit.richmond.com/ for more information on the city.

The University

VCU is a state-supported coeducational university with a graduate school, a major teaching hospital, and twelve academic and professional units that offer fifty-two undergraduate, twenty-two postbaccalaureate certificate, sixty-five master's, six post-master's certificate, and twenty-nine Ph.D. programs. VCU also offers M.D., D.D.S., D.P.T., and Pharm.D. programs as well as cooperative degree programs with other major Virginia colleges and universities. VCU has one of the largest evening colleges in the United States. The academic campus is located in Richmond's historic Fan District. The health sciences campus and hospital are located 2 miles east in the downtown business district. A University bus service provides free intercampus transportation for faculty members and students.

With more than $211 million in annual research funding, Virginia Commonwealth University is classified as one of the nation's top research universities by the Carnegie Foundation for the Advancement of Teaching. More than 29,000 undergraduate, certificate, graduate, post-master's, professional, and doctoral students are enrolled in 162 academic programs, forty of which are unique in the commonwealth of Virginia. The faculty members represent the finest American and international graduate institutions and enhance the University's position among the important institutions of higher learning in the United States and the world via their work in the classroom, laboratory, studio, and clinic and in their scholarly publications.

Applying

Admission procedures and program requirements are detailed in the *Graduate Bulletin*. Application deadlines and materials, including the application and the *Graduate Bulletin*, are available online at the Graduate School Web site at http://www.graduate.vcu.edu. Virginia Commonwealth University is an equal opportunity/affirmative action institution providing access to education and employment without regard to age, race, color, national origin, gender, religion, sexual orientation, veteran's status, political affiliation, or disability.

Correspondence and Information

John J. Kregel, Chair
Department of Special Education and Disability Policy
School of Education
1015 West Main Street
Virginia Commonwealth University
Richmond, Virginia 23284-2020
Phone: 804-828-1872
Fax: 804-828-1323
E-mail: jkregel @vcu.edu
Web site: http://www.soe.vcu.edu/

Virginia Commonwealth University

THE FACULTY AND THEIR RESEARCH

Maureen Conroy, Professor; Ph.D., Vanderbilt, 1986. Functional assessment and analysis of behavioral problems, assessment and intervention of social skills, antecedent intervention.

Paul Gerber, Professor; Ph.D., Michigan, 1978. Adults with learning disabilities, post-school, and lifespan issues.

John Kregel, Professor and Chair; Ed.D., Georgia, 1983. Identifying and eliminating barriers to employment and economic self-sufficiency for people with disabilities.

Fred Orelove, Professor; Ph.D., Illinois, 1978. Learners with severe disabilities.

Evelyn Reed-Victor, Associate Professor; Ph.D., William and Mary, 1998. Infants and young children with developmental delays or disabilities and their families, children and families living in poverty, particularly those experiencing homelessness.

Diane Simon, Associate Professor; Ph.D., NYU, 1981. Recruitment and retention in higher education, engaging at-risk middle school students.

Kevin Sutherland, Assistant Professor; Ph.D., Vanderbilt, 2000. Effective practices for students with emotional and behavioral disorders (EBD), teacher/student interactions in classrooms for students with EBD, the teacher's role in systems of care.

Colleen Thoma, Associate Professor; Ph.D., Indiana, 1997. Self-determination in transition planning, transition assessment, transition from school to post-secondary education, universal design for instruction, positive behavior supports, preparing special educators to facilitate self-determined transition planning for students with disabilities.

Paul Wehman, Professor; Ph.D., Wisconsin, 1976. Transition from school to adulthood, special education as it relates for young adulthood.

Yaoying Xu, Assistant Professor; Ph.D., Nevada, Las Vegas. Culturally appropriate learning contexts for young English-language learners, impact of social interactions of young children on their school performance, empowering culturally diverse families of young children with disabilities, linking assessment and intervention for infants and young children who are at risk for disabilities/delays.

Section 26
Subject Areas

This section contains a directory of institutions offering graduate work in subject areas, followed by in-depth entries submitted by institutions that chose to prepare detailed program descriptions. Additional information about programs listed in the directory but not augmented by an in-depth entry may be obtained by writing directly to the dean of a graduate school or chair of a department at the address given in the directory.

For programs offering related work, see also in this book Administration, Instruction, and Theory; Business Administration and Management; Education; Health-Related Professions; Instructional Levels; Leisure Studies and Recreation; Physical Education and Kinesiology; and Special Focus. In Book 2, see Art and Art History; Family and Consumer Sciences; Language and Literature; Performing Arts; Psychology and Counseling (School Psychology); Public, Regional, and Industrial Affairs (Urban Studies); Religious Studies; and Social Sciences; in Book 4, see Mathematical Sciences; and in Book 5, see Computer Science and Information Technology.

CONTENTS

Agricultural Education

Alcorn State University, School of Graduate Studies, School of Psychology and Education, Alcorn State, MS 39096-7500. Offers agricultural education (MS Ed); elementary education (MS Ed, Ed S); guidance and counseling (MS Ed); industrial education (MS Ed); secondary education (MS Ed), including health and physical education; special education (MS Ed). *Accreditation:* NCATE. *Faculty:* 14 full-time (9 women), 21 part-time/adjunct (13 women). *Students:* 76 full-time (44 women), 271 part-time (226 women); includes 333 minority (all African Americans) In 2006, 119 degrees awarded. *Degree requirements:* For master's, thesis optional. *Application deadline:* For fall admission, 7/15 priority date for domestic students; for spring admission, 11/25 for domestic students. Applications are processed on a rolling basis. Application fee: $0 ($10 for international students). *Financial support:* Career-related internships or fieldwork available. Support available to part-time students. *Unit head:* Dr. Josephine M. Posey, Dean, 601-877-6141, Fax: 601-877-3867.

Arkansas State University, Graduate School, College of Agriculture, Jonesboro, State University, AR 72467. Offers agricultural education (MSA, SCCT); agriculture (MSA); vocational-technical administration (MS, SCCT). Part-time programs available. *Faculty:* 10 full-time (1 woman), 3 part-time/adjunct (1 woman). *Students:* 7 full-time (0 women), 19 part-time (11 women); includes 1 minority (African American) Average age 30. 13 applicants, 77% accepted, 7 enrolled. In 2006, 17 degrees awarded. *Degree requirements:* For master's, thesis or alternative, comprehensive exam. *Entrance requirements:* For master's, GRE General Test or MAT, appropriate bachelor's degree, official transcript; for SCCT, GRE General Test or MAT, interview, master's degree, official transcript. Additional exam requirements/recommendations for international students: Required—TOEFL (minimum score 213 computer-based). *Application deadline:* Applications are processed on a rolling basis. Application fee: $30 ($40 for international students). Electronic applications accepted. *Expenses:* Tuition, state resident: full-time $3,393; part-time $189 per hour. Tuition, nonresident: full-time $8,577; part-time $477 per hour. Required fees: $752; $39 per hour. $25 per semester. *Financial support:* Teaching assistantships, scholarships/grants and unspecified assistantships available. Financial award application deadline: 7/1; financial award applicants required to submit FAFSA. *Unit head:* Dr. Gregory Phillips, Dean, 870-972-2085, Fax: 870-972-3885, E-mail: gphillips@astate.edu.

Clemson University, Graduate School, College of Agriculture, Forestry and Life Sciences, Department of Agricultural and Biological Engineering, Program in Agricultural Education, Clemson, SC 29634. Offers M Ag Ed. *Accreditation:* NCATE. Part-time programs available. *Students:* 10 full-time (7 women), 2 part-time. Average age 28. 7 applicants, 57% accepted, 3 enrolled. In 2006, 10 degrees awarded. *Entrance requirements:* For master's, GRE General Test. Additional exam requirements/recommendations for international students: Required—TOEFL. *Application deadline:* For fall admission, 6/1 for domestic students. Application fee: $50. *Expenses:* Tuition, state resident: full-time $8,812; part-time $450 per hour. Tuition, nonresident: full-time $18,036; part-time $760 per hour. Required fees: $474; $5 per term. *Financial support:* Teaching assistantships, career-related internships or fieldwork, Federal Work-Study, institutionally sponsored loans, and scholarships/grants available. Financial award application deadline: 4/1; financial award applicants required to submit FAFSA. *Faculty research:* Adaptation and change, curriculum assessment and innovation, career development, adult and extension education, technology transfer. *Unit head:* Dr. Harold Allen, Chair, 864-656-4039, Fax: 864-656-0338, E-mail: whallen@clemson.edu. *Application contact:* Dr. Tom Dobbins, Coordinator, 864-656-3834, Fax: 864-656-5675, E-mail: tdbbns@clemson.edu.

See Close-Up on page 1601.

Cornell University, Graduate School, Graduate Fields of Agriculture and Life Sciences, Field of Education, Ithaca, NY 14853-0001. Offers agricultural education (MAT); biology (7-12) (MAT); chemistry (7-12) (MAT); curriculum and instruction (MPS, MS, PhD); earth science (7-12) (MAT); extension, and adult education (MPS, MS, PhD); mathematics (7-12) (MAT); physics (7-12) (MAT). *Faculty:* 26 full-time (9 women). *Students:* 56 full-time (33 women); includes 10 minority (1 African American, 5 Asian Americans or Pacific Islanders, 4 Hispanic Americans), 4 international. Average age 31. 96 applicants, 40% accepted, 18 enrolled. In 2006, 22 master's, 8 doctorates awarded. Terminal master's awarded for partial completion of doctoral program. *Degree requirements:* For master's, thesis (MS); for doctorate, thesis/dissertation, comprehensive exam. *Entrance requirements:* For master's and doctorate, GRE General Test, sample of written work (recommended), 2 letters of recommendation. Additional exam requirements/recommendations for international students: Required—TOEFL (minimum score 550 paper-based; 213 computer-based). *Application deadline:* For fall admission, 2/15 for domestic students. Application fee: $60. Electronic applications accepted. *Expenses:* Tuition: Full-time $32,800. Full-time tuition and fees vary according to program. *Financial support:* In 2006–07, 31 students received support, including 4 fellowships with full tuition reimbursements available, 7 research assistantships with full tuition reimbursements available, 20 teaching assistantships with full tuition reimbursements available; institutionally sponsored loans, scholarships/grants, health care benefits, tuition waivers (full and partial), and unspecified assistantships also available. Financial award applicants required to submit FAFSA. *Faculty research:* Moral development and professional ethics; public issues education and community development; socio/political issues in public education; teacher education and curriculum in agricultural science, and mathematics; extension research. *Unit head:* Director of Graduate Studies, 607-255-4278, Fax: 607-255-7905. *Application contact:* Graduate Field Assistant, 607-255-4278, Fax: 607-255-7905, E-mail: rh22@cornell.edu.

Eastern Kentucky University, The Graduate School, College of Education, Department of Curriculum and Instruction, Program in Secondary and Higher Education, Richmond, KY 40475-3102. Offers agricultural education (MA Ed); allied health sciences education (MA Ed); art education (MA Ed); biological sciences education (MA Ed); business education (MA Ed); chemistry education (MA Ed); earth science education (MA Ed); English education (MA Ed); general science education (MA Ed); geography education (MA Ed); history education (MA Ed); home economics education (MA Ed); industrial education (MA Ed); mathematical sciences education (MA Ed); physical education (MA Ed); physics education (MA Ed); political science education (MA Ed); psychology education (MA Ed); reading (MA Ed); school health education (MA Ed); sociology education (MA Ed). *Accreditation:* NCATE. Part-time programs available. *Students:* 16 full-time (8 women), 63 part-time (43 women); includes 5 minority (2 African Americans, 2 American Indian/Alaska Native, 1 Asian American or Pacific Islander). Average age 32. *Entrance requirements:* For master's, GRE General Test, minimum GPA of 2.5. Application fee: $30. *Expenses:* Tuition, state resident: full-time $5,610. Tuition, nonresident: full-time $15,910. *Financial support:* Research assistantships, teaching assistantships, Federal Work-Study available. Support available to part-time students. *Unit head:* Dr. Michael Martin, Chair, Department of Curriculum and Instruction, 859-622-2154, Fax: 859-622-2004.

Iowa State University of Science and Technology, Graduate College, College of Agriculture, Department of Agricultural Education and Studies, Ames, IA 50011. Offers MS, PhD. Postbaccalaureate distance learning degree programs offered (minimal on-campus study). *Faculty:* 11 full-time. *Students:* 16 full-time (9 women), 18 part-time (9 women); includes 2 minority (1 African American, 1 Hispanic American), 7 international. 23 applicants, 61% accepted, 11 enrolled. In 2006, 8 master's, 2 doctorates awarded. *Degree requirements:* For master's, thesis or alternative; for doctorate, thesis/dissertation. *Entrance requirements:* For master's and doctorate, resumé. Additional exam requirements/recommendations for international students: Required—TOEFL (paper-based 550; computer-based 213; iBT 79) or IELTS (6.5). *Application deadline:* For fall admission, 3/15 priority date for domestic and international students; for spring admission, 10/15 priority date for domestic and international students. Applications are processed on a rolling basis. Application fee: $30 ($70 for international students). Electronic applications accepted. *Expenses:* Tuition, state resident: full-time $5,936; part-time $330 per credit. Tuition, nonresident: full-time $16,350; part-time $330 per credit. *Financial support:* In 2006–07, 13 research assistantships with full and partial tuition reimbursements (averaging $15,000 per year) were awarded; fellowships, teaching assistantships with full and partial tuition reimbursements, scholarships/grants, health care benefits, and unspecified assistantships also available. *Faculty research:* Agricultural extension education, teaching, learning processes, distance education, international education, adult education. *Unit head:* Dr. Robert A. Martin, Head, 515-294-5872, E-mail: agedsinfo@iastate.edu. *Application contact:* Dr. Greg Miller, Director of Graduate Education, 515-294-2583, E-mail: agedsinfo@iastate.edu.

Louisiana State University and Agricultural and Mechanical College, Graduate School, College of Agriculture, School of Human Resource Education and Workforce Development, Baton Rouge, LA 70803. Offers comprehensive vocational education (MS, PhD); extension and international education (MS, PhD); industrial education (MS); vocational agriculture education (MS, PhD); vocational business education (MS); vocational home economics education (MS). *Accreditation:* NCATE. Part-time programs available. *Faculty:* 13 full-time (6 women). *Students:* 39 full-time (24 women), 68 part-time (42 women); includes 12 African Americans, 3 Hispanic Americans, 9 international. Average age 38. 20 applicants, 60% accepted, 3 enrolled. In 2006, 18 master's, 33 doctorates awarded. Terminal master's awarded for partial completion of doctoral program. *Degree requirements:* For master's, thesis (for some programs); for doctorate, thesis/dissertation. *Entrance requirements:* For master's and doctorate, GRE General Test, minimum GPA of 3.0. Additional exam requirements/recommendations for international students: Required—TOEFL (minimum score 550 paper-based; 213 computer-based; 79 iBT). *Application deadline:* For fall admission, 1/25 priority date for domestic students, 5/15 for international students; for spring admission, 10/15 for international students. Applications are processed on a rolling basis. Application fee: $25. Electronic applications accepted. *Financial support:* In 2006–07, 23 students received support, including 1 fellowship with full and partial tuition reimbursement available (averaging $23,678 per year), 10 research assistantships with full and partial tuition reimbursements available (averaging $11,750 per year), 5 teaching assistantships with partial tuition reimbursements available (averaging $10,210 per year); career-related internships or fieldwork, institutionally sponsored loans, tuition waivers (full and partial), and unspecified assistantships also available. Financial award application deadline: 3/1; financial award applicants required to submit FAFSA. *Faculty research:* Adult education, history and philosophy of vocational education, curriculum and instruction, career decision making. *Unit head:* Dr. Michael F. Burnett, Director, 225-578-5748, Fax: 225-578-2526, E-mail: vocbur@lsu.edu.

Mississippi State University, College of Agriculture and Life Sciences, Department of Agricultural Information Science and Education, Mississippi State, MS 39762. Offers agriculture and extension education (MS). *Accreditation:* NCATE. Part-time programs available. *Faculty:* 4 full-time (1 woman), 1 part-time/adjunct (0 women). *Students:* 5 full-time (2 women), 12 part-time (10 women); includes 6 minority (all African Americans) Average age 32. 6 applicants, 83% accepted, 4 enrolled. In 2006, 6 master's awarded. *Degree requirements:* For master's, comprehensive oral or written exam, thesis optional. *Entrance requirements:* For master's, minimum GPA of 2.75 in last 4 semesters of course work. Additional exam requirements/recommendations for international students: Required—TOEFL. *Application deadline:* For fall admission, 7/1 for domestic students; for spring admission, 11/1 for domestic students. Applications are processed on a rolling basis. Application fee: $30. *Expenses:* Tuition, state resident: full-time $4,550; part-time $253 per hour. Tuition, nonresident: full-time $10,552; part-time $584 per hour. International tuition: $10,882 full-time. Tuition and fees vary according to course load. *Financial support:* Teaching assistantships with full tuition reimbursements, Federal Work-Study, institutionally sponsored loans, and unspecified assistantships available. Financial award application deadline: 4/1; financial award applicants required to submit FAFSA. *Faculty research:* Animal welfare, agroscience, information technology, learning styles, problem solving. *Unit head:* Dr. Walter N. Taylor, Head, 662-325-3326, Fax: 662-325-7832, E-mail: wntaylor@ais.msstate.edu. *Application contact:* Dr. Phil Bonfanti, Director of Admissions, 662-325-4104, Fax: 662-325-8872, E-mail: admit@msstate.edu.

Missouri State University, Graduate College, College of Natural and Applied Sciences, Department of Agriculture, Springfield, MO 65804-0094. Offers agriculture (MNAS); fruit science (MNAS); plant science (MS); secondary education (MS Ed), including agriculture. *Faculty:* 15 full-time (2 women), 1 (woman) part-time/adjunct. *Students:* 16 full-time (10 women), 10 part-time (5 women); includes 1 minority (Asian American or Pacific Islander), 3 international. Average age 29. 17 applicants, 76% accepted, 12 enrolled. In 2006, 7 degrees awarded. *Degree requirements:* For master's, thesis or alternative, comprehensive exam. *Entrance requirements:* For master's, GRE (MS plant science, MNAS), 9–12 teacher certification (MS Ed), minimum GPA of 3.0 (MS plant science, MNAS). Additional exam requirements/recommendations for international students: Required—TOEFL (minimum score 550 paper-based; 213 computer-based; 79 iBT). *Application deadline:* For fall admission, 7/20 priority date for domestic students; for spring admission, 12/20 priority date for domestic students. Applications are processed on a rolling basis. Application fee: $35. Electronic applications accepted. *Expenses:* Tuition, state resident: full-time $3,582; part-time $199 per credit hour. Tuition, nonresident: full-time $6,984; part-time $199 per credit hour. Required fees: $548. Full-time tuition and fees vary according to course level, course load, program and reciprocity agreements. *Financial support:* In 2006–07, 4 research assistantships (averaging $9,000 per year), 7 teaching assistantships (averaging $9,000 per year) were awarded. Financial award application deadline: 3/31; financial award applicants required to submit FAFSA. *Unit head:* Dr. W. Anson Elliott, Head, 417-836-5638, E-mail: ansonelliot@missouristate.edu. *Application contact:* Dr. W. Anson Elliott, Head, 417-836-5638, E-mail: ansonelliot@missouristate.edu.

Murray State University, School of Agriculture, Murray, KY 42071. Offers agriculture (MS); agriculture education (MS). Evening/weekend programs available. Postbaccalaureate distance learning degree programs offered (minimal on-campus study). *Faculty:* 10 full-time (0 women). *Students:* 37 full-time (17 women), 22 part-time (8 women); includes 1 minority (African American), 1 international. Average age 25. 18 applicants, 83% accepted. *Degree requirements:* For master's, thesis (for some programs), comprehensive exam, registration. *Entrance requirements:* Additional exam requirements/recommendations for international students: Required—TOEFL. *Application deadline:* Applications are processed on a rolling basis. Application fee: $25. *Financial support:* Research assistantships, teaching assistantships, Federal Work-Study available. Financial award application deadline: 4/1. *Faculty research:* Ultrasound in beef, corn and soybean research, tobacco research. *Unit head:* Dr. Tony L. Brannon, Dean, 270-809-6423, Fax: 270-809-5454, E-mail: tony.brannon@murraystate.edu. *Application contact:* Dr. Jay A. Morgan, Graduate Coordinator, 270-809-6924, Fax: 270-809-5454, E-mail: jay.morgan@murraystate.edu.

New Mexico State University, Graduate School, College of Agriculture and Home Economics, Department of Agriculture and Extension Education, Las Cruces, NM 88003-8001. Offers MA. *Accreditation:* NCATE. Part-time and evening/weekend programs available. Postbaccalaureate distance learning degree programs offered (minimal on-campus study). *Faculty:* 4 full-time (2 women), 4 part-time/adjunct (2 women). *Students:* 8 full-time (3 women), 15 part-time (6 women); includes 7 minority (1 American Indian/Alaska Native, 6 Hispanic Americans). Average age 34. 9 applicants, 89% accepted. In 2006, 16 degrees awarded. *Degree requirements:* For master's, thesis or creative component. *Entrance requirements:* For master's, 3 letters of recommendation. Additional exam requirements/recommendations for international students: Required—TOEFL, Language Proficiency Exam. *Application deadline:* For fall admission, 7/1 priority date for domestic and international students; for spring admission, 11/1 priority date for domestic and international students. Applications are processed on a rolling basis. Application fee: $30 ($50 for international students). Electronic applications accepted. *Financial support:* In 2006–07, 2 teaching assistantships were awarded; research assistantships, career-related internships or fieldwork, Federal Work-Study, institutionally sponsored loans, scholarships/grants, health care benefits, and unspecified assistantships also available. Financial award application deadline: 3/1. *Faculty research:* Secondary agricultural education programs, teaching and learning, agricultural technology and safety, volunteer programs, youth leadership development. *Unit head:* Dr. Thomas J. Dormody, Head, 505-646-4511, Fax: 505-646-4082, E-mail: tdormody@nmsu.edu. *Application contact:* Dr. Brenda S. Seevers, Professor, 505-646-4511, Fax: 505-646-4082, E-mail: bseevers@nmsu.edu.

North Carolina Agricultural and Technical State University, Graduate School, School of Agriculture and Environmental and Allied Sciences, Department of Agribusiness, Applied Economics, and Agriscience Education, Greensboro, NC 27411. Offers agricultural economics (MS); agricultural education (MS). *Accreditation:* NCATE. Part-time and evening/weekend programs available. *Degree requirements:* For master's, thesis or alternative, qualifying exam, comprehensive exam. *Entrance requirements:* For master's, GRE General Test, minimum GPA of 3.0. *Faculty research:* Aid for small farmers, agricultural technology resources, labor force mobility, agrology.

North Carolina State University, Graduate School, College of Agriculture and Life Sciences, Department of Agricultural and Extension Education, Program in Agricultural Education, Raleigh, NC 27695. Offers MAEE, MS. *Degree requirements:* For master's, thesis optional. *Entrance requirements:* For master's, GRE or MAT. Electronic applications accepted. *Faculty research:* Instructional methodology, distance education, leadership development, foundations, curriculum development.

North Dakota State University, The Graduate School, College of Human Development and Education, School of Education, Program in Agricultural Education, Fargo, ND 58105. Offers agricultural education (M Ed, MS); agricultural extension education (MS). *Accreditation:* NCATE. Part-time programs available. *Faculty:* 2 part-time/adjunct (1 woman). *Students:* Average age 32. In 2006, 2 degrees awarded. *Degree requirements:* For master's, thesis or alternative, comprehensive exam. *Entrance requirements:* Additional exam requirements/recommendations for international students: Required—TOEFL. *Application deadline:* Applications are processed on a rolling basis. Application fee: $45 ($60 for international students). *Financial support:* Research assistantships, career-related internships or fieldwork, Federal Work-Study, institutionally sponsored loans, and tuition waivers (full) available. Financial award application deadline: 4/15. *Faculty research:* Vocational and cooperative extension education, rural leadership, rural education, international extension. *Application contact:* Dr. Brent Young, Assistant Professor, 701-231-7439, Fax: 701-231-9685, E-mail: brent.young@ndsu.edu.

Northwest Missouri State University, Graduate School, Melvin and Valorie Booth College of Business and Professional Studies, Department of Agriculture, Maryville, MO 64468-6001. Offers agricultural economics (MBA); agriculture (MS); teaching agriculture (MS Ed). Part-time programs available. *Faculty:* 5 full-time (1 woman). *Students:* 4 full-time (1 woman), 1 (woman) part-time, 2 international. 8 applicants, 75% accepted, 2 enrolled. In 2006, 3 degrees awarded. *Degree requirements:* For master's, thesis (for some programs), comprehensive exam. *Entrance requirements:* For master's, GRE General Test, minimum undergraduate GPA of 2.5, writing sample. Additional exam requirements/recommendations for international students: Required—TOEFL (minimum score 550 paper-based; 213 computer-based). *Application deadline:* For fall admission, 7/1 for domestic and international students; for spring admission, 11/15 for domestic and international students. Applications are processed on a rolling basis. Application fee: $0 ($50 for international students). *Financial support:* In 2006–07, 3 research assistantships with full tuition reimbursements (averaging $6,000 per year), 2 teaching assistantships with full tuition reimbursements (averaging $6,000 per year) were awarded; unspecified assistantships also available. Financial award application deadline: 3/1; financial award applicants required to submit FAFSA. *Unit head:* Dr. Arley Larson, Chairperson, 660-562-1161. *Application contact:* Dr. Frances Shipley, Dean of Graduate School, 660-562-1145, Fax: 660-562-1096, E-mail: gradsch@nwmissouri.edu.

The Ohio State University, Graduate School, College of Food, Agricultural, and Environmental Sciences, Department of Human and Community Resource Development, Columbus, OH 43210. Offers M Ed, MS, PhD. *Faculty:* 23. *Students:* 11 full-time (6 women), 9 part-time (5 women); includes 1 minority (Hispanic American) Average age 32. 9 applicants, 100% accepted, 4 enrolled. In 2006, 4 master's, 7 doctorates awarded. *Degree requirements:* For master's, thesis optional; for doctorate, thesis/dissertation. *Entrance requirements:* For master's and doctorate, GRE General Test or GMAT. Additional exam requirements/recommendations for international students: Required—TOEFL (paper-based 550; computer-based 213) or IELTS (7) or Michigan English Language Assessment Battery (87). *Application deadline:* For fall admission, 8/15 priority date for domestic students, 7/1 priority date for international students; for winter admission, 12/1 priority date for domestic students, 11/1 priority date for international students; for spring admission, 3/1 priority date for domestic students, 2/1 priority date for international students. Applications are processed on a rolling basis. Application fee: $40 ($50 for international students). Electronic applications accepted. *Expenses:* Tuition, state resident: full-time $9,438. Tuition, nonresident: full-time $22,791. Tuition and fees vary according to course load, campus/location and program. *Financial support:* Fellowships, research assistantships, teaching assistantships, Federal Work-Study, institutionally sponsored loans, and unspecified assistantships available. Support available to part-time students. *Unit head:* Jamie M. Cano, Graduate Studies Committee Chair, 614-292-6321, Fax: 614-292-7007, E-mail: cano.1@osu.edu. *Application contact:* Graduate Admissions, 614-292-9444, Fax: 614-292-3895, E-mail: domestic.grad@osu.edu.

Oklahoma State University, College of Agricultural Science and Natural Resources, Department of Agricultural Education, Communications and 4H Youth Development, Stillwater, OK 74078. Offers M Ag, MS, PhD. *Faculty:* 11 full-time (5 women), 1 part-time/adjunct (0 women). *Students:* 28 full-time (20 women), 36 part-time (27 women); includes 8 minority (1 African American, 6 American Indian/Alaska Native, 1 Hispanic American), 1 international. Average age 30. 40 applicants, 53% accepted, 15 enrolled. In 2006, 4 master's, 3 doctorates awarded. *Degree requirements:* For master's, thesis or report; for doctorate, thesis/dissertation. *Entrance requirements:* For master's and doctorate, GRE. Additional exam requirements/recommendations for international students: Required—TOEFL. *Application deadline:* For fall admission, 7/1 priority date for domestic students, 3/1 priority date for international students; for spring admission, 8/1 priority date for international students. Applications are processed on a rolling basis. Application fee: $40 ($75 for international students). Electronic applications accepted. *Expenses:* Tuition, state resident: part-time $146 per credit hour. Tuition, nonresident: part-time $516 per credit hour. Required fees: $44 per credit hour. Tuition and fees vary according to program. *Financial support:* In 2006–07, 6 research assistantships (averaging $17,174 per year), 3 teaching assistantships (averaging $13,200 per year) were awarded; career-related internships or fieldwork, Federal Work-Study, scholarships/grants, health care benefits, tuition waivers (partial), and unspecified assistantships also available. Support available to part-time students. Financial award application deadline: 3/1. *Faculty research:* Teaching and learning about and in agriculture, agriculture teacher evaluation, evaluation of information dissemination delivery methods, agricultural literacy curriculum model development, distance education delivery methods. *Unit head:* Dr. James Leising, Head, 405-744-5129, Fax: 405-744-5176, E-mail: james.leising@okstate.edu.

Oregon State University, Graduate School, College of Agricultural Sciences, Department of Agricultural Education, Corvallis, OR 97331. Offers M Agr, MAIS, MAT, MS. Part-time programs available. *Faculty:* 1 full-time (0 women), 3 part-time/adjunct (0 women). *Students:* 7 full-time (2 women). In 2006, 10 degrees awarded. *Degree requirements:* For master's, thesis (for some programs). *Entrance requirements:* For master's, GRE General Test, minimum GPA of 3.0 in last 90 hours of course work. Additional exam requirements/recommendations for international students: Required—TOEFL. *Application deadline:* Applications are processed on a rolling basis. Application fee: $50. *Financial support:* Fellowships, research assistantships, teaching assistantships, career-related internships or fieldwork, Federal Work-Study, and institutionally sponsored loans available. Support available to part-time students. Financial award application deadline: 2/1. *Faculty research:* Curriculum development and vocational education program evaluation, agricultural extension education. *Unit head:* Dr. Greg Thompson, Interim Head, 541-737-1337, Fax: 541-737-3178.

Penn State University Park, Graduate School, College of Agricultural Sciences, Department of Agricultural and Extension Education, State College, University Park, PA 16802-1503. Offers agricultural and extension education (M Ed, MS, D Ed, PhD); youth and family education (M Ed). *Unit head:* Dr. Tracy S. Hoover, Head, 814-865-1688, Fax: 814-863-4753, E-mail: tsh102@psu.edu. *Application contact:* Dr. Joan S. Thomson, Graduate Program Officer, 814-863-3825, Fax: 814-863-4753, E-mail: jthomson@psu.edu.

Purdue University, Graduate School, College of Agriculture, Department of Youth Development and Agricultural Education, West Lafayette, IN 47907. Offers MA, PhD. *Faculty:* 10 full-time (4 women), 1 (woman) part-time/adjunct. *Students:* 5 full-time (4 women), 11 part-time (5 women); includes 2 African Americans. 11 applicants, 73% accepted, 6 enrolled. In 2006, 5 degrees awarded. *Entrance requirements:* For master's, writing sample; for doctorate, GRE, writing sample. Additional exam requirements/recommendations for international students: Required—TOEFL, GRE; Recommended—TWE. *Application deadline:* For fall admission, 1/15 priority date for domestic students, 1/15 for international students; for spring admission, 9/15 priority date for domestic students, 9/15 for international students. Applications are processed on a rolling basis. Application fee: $55. Electronic applications accepted. *Unit head:* Roger L Tormoehlen, Head, 765-494-8422. *Application contact:* Terry A. Saunders, Student Contact, 765-494-8439, E-mail: tasaunde@purdue.edu.

Purdue University, Graduate School, School of Education, Department of Curriculum and Instruction, West Lafayette, IN 47907. Offers agricultural and extension education (PhD, Ed S); agriculture and extension education (MS, MS Ed); art education (PhD); consumer and family sciences and extension education (MS Ed, PhD, Ed S); curriculum studies (MS Ed, PhD, Ed S); educational technology (MS Ed, PhD, Ed S); elementary education (MS Ed); foreign language education (MS Ed, PhD, Ed S); industrial technology (PhD, Ed S); language arts (MS Ed, PhD, Ed S); literacy (MS Ed, PhD, Ed S); mathematics/science education (MS, MS Ed, PhD, Ed S); social studies (MS Ed, PhD); social studies education (Ed S); vocational/industrial education (MS Ed, PhD, Ed S); vocational/technical education (MS Ed, PhD, Ed S). *Accreditation:* NCATE. Part-time and evening/weekend programs available. *Faculty:* 26 full-time (13 women), 3 part-time/adjunct (all women). *Students:* 59 full-time (37 women), 112 part-time (70 women); includes 24 minority (13 African Americans, 3 American Indian/Alaska Native, 4 Asian Americans or Pacific Islanders, 4 Hispanic Americans), 38 international. Average age 35. 92 applicants, 68% accepted, 38 enrolled. In 2006, 52 master's, 23 doctorates awarded. *Degree requirements:* For master's, thesis optional; for doctorate, thesis/dissertation, oral and written exams; for Ed S, oral presentation, project. *Entrance requirements:* For master's, GRE General Test, minimum B average; for doctorate, GRE General Test; for Ed S, GRE, minimum B average. Additional exam requirements/recommendations for international students: Required—TOEFL. *Application deadline:* For fall admission, 1/15 priority date for domestic students, 1/15 for international students; for spring admission, 9/15 for domestic and international students. Applications are processed on a rolling basis. Application fee: $55. Electronic applications accepted. *Financial support:* In 2006–07, 3 fellowships with full tuition reimbursements (averaging $10,500 per year), 11 research assistantships with full tuition reimbursements (averaging $11,500 per year), 43 teaching assistantships with full tuition reimbursements (averaging $10,800 per year) were awarded; career-related internships or fieldwork and tuition waivers (full) also available. Support available to part-time students. Financial award application deadline: 3/1; financial award applicants required to submit FAFSA. *Faculty research:* Literacy acquisition and development, teacher beliefs and knowledge, recruitment and retention of underrepresented students, economic education, literacy discourse. *Unit head:* Dr. James D Lehman, Head, 765-494-7935, Fax: 765-496-1622. *Application contact:* Patricia Mason, Coordinator of Graduate Studies, 765-494-2345, Fax: 765-494-5832, E-mail: gradoffice@soe.purdue.edu.

State University of New York at Oswego, Graduate Studies, School of Education, Department of Vocational Teacher Preparation, Oswego, NY 13126. Offers agriculture (MS Ed); business and marketing (MS Ed); family and consumer sciences (MS Ed); health careers (MS Ed); technical education (MS Ed); trade education (MS Ed). *Accreditation:* NCATE. Part-time and evening/weekend programs available. *Faculty:* 3 full-time, 8 part-time/adjunct. *Students:* 24 full-time (10 women), 52 part-time (23 women); includes 4 minority (3 African Americans, 1 Hispanic American). Average age 40. 50 applicants, 100% accepted. In 2006, 31 degrees awarded. *Degree requirements:* For master's, thesis or alternative. *Entrance requirements:* Additional exam requirements/recommendations for international students: Required—TOEFL (minimum score 560 paper-based; 220 computer-based). *Application deadline:* For fall admission, 4/1 for domestic students; for spring admission, 10/1 for domestic students. Applications are processed on a rolling basis. Application fee: $50. *Expenses:* Tuition, state resident: part-time $288 per credit. Tuition, nonresident: part-time $455 per credit. Tuition and fees vary according to program. *Financial support:* In 2006–07, 3 students received support, including 2 fellowships, 1 teaching assistantship; career-related internships or fieldwork, Federal Work-Study, institutionally sponsored loans, health care benefits, and unspecified assistantships also available. Support available to part-time students. Financial award application deadline: 4/1; financial award applicants required to submit FAFSA. *Unit head:* Dr. Margaret Martin, Chair, 315-312-2480.

Stephen F. Austin State University, Graduate School, College of Forestry and Agriculture, Department of Agriculture, Nacogdoches, TX 75962. Offers MS. *Accreditation:* NCATE. *Degree requirements:* For master's, thesis (for some programs), comprehensive exam. *Entrance requirements:* For master's, GRE General Test, minimum GPA of 2.8 in last half of major, 2.5 overall. Additional exam requirements/recommendations for international students: Required—TOEFL (minimum score 550 paper-based; 213 computer-based). *Faculty research:* Asian vegetables, soil fertility, animal breeding, animal nutrition.

Tarleton State University, College of Graduate Studies, College of Agriculture and Human Sciences, Department of Agricultural Services and Development, Stephenville, TX 76402. Offers agriculture education (MS). Part-time and evening/weekend programs available. Postbaccalaureate distance learning degree programs offered. *Faculty:* 19 full-time (1 woman), 1 part-time/adjunct (0 women). *Students:* 14 full-time (6 women), 15 part-time (3 women); includes 1 minority (Hispanic American) Average age 29. In 2006, 6 degrees awarded. *Entrance requirements:* For master's, GRE General Test, minimum GPA of 3.0. Additional exam requirements/recommendations for international students: Required—TOEFL. *Application deadline:* For fall admission, 8/5 priority date for domestic students; for spring admission, 12/1 priority date for domestic students. Application fee: $25 ($100 for international students). Electronic applications accepted. *Financial support:* Federal Work-Study, institutionally sponsored loans, scholarships/grants, and unspecified assistantships available. *Unit head:* Dr. David Drueckhammer, Head, 254-968-9200, Fax: 254-968-9199, E-mail: drueckh@tarleton.edu.

Texas A&M University, College of Agriculture and Life Sciences, Department of Agricultural Leadership, Education and Communications, College Station, TX 77843. Offers agricultural education (M Ed, MS, Ed D, PhD); agriculture (M Agr). *Accreditation:* NCATE. Part-time programs available. Postbaccalaureate distance learning degree programs offered (no on-campus study). *Faculty:* 16 full-time (7 women), 3 part-time/adjunct (0 women). *Students:* 75 full-time (49 women), 62 part-time (23 women); includes 19 minority (9 African Americans, 1 Asian American or Pacific Islander, 9 Hispanic Americans), 5 international. Average age 27. 80 applicants, 80% accepted, 54 enrolled. In 2006, 34 master's, 6 doctorates awarded. Terminal master's awarded for partial completion of doctoral program. *Degree requirements:* For master's, thesis (for some programs), comprehensive exam, registration; for doctorate, thesis/dissertation, comprehensive exam, registration. *Entrance requirements:* For master's, GRE General Test, letters of reference, curriculum vitae; for doctorate, GRE General Test, 3 years of professional experience, letters of reference, curriculum vitae. Additional exam requirements/recommendations for international students: Required—TOEFL. *Application deadline:* For fall admission, 3/15 priority date for domestic students; for spring admission, 10/15 for domestic students. Application fee: $50 ($75 for international students). Electronic applications accepted. *Expenses:* Tuition, state resident: full-time $4,697. Tuition, nonresident: full-time $11,297. Required fees: $2,272. *Financial support:* In 2006–07, fellowships with

Agricultural Education

Texas A&M University (continued)
partial tuition reimbursements (averaging $12,000 per year), research assistantships with partial tuition reimbursements (averaging $12,000 per year), teaching assistantships with partial tuition reimbursements (averaging $12,000 per year) were awarded; career-related internships or fieldwork, institutionally sponsored loans, scholarships/grants, tuition waivers (partial), and unspecified assistantships also available. Financial award application deadline: 3/15; financial award applicants required to submit FAFSA. *Faculty research:* Planning and needs assessment, instructional design, delivery strategies, evaluation and accountability, distance education. *Unit head:* Glen C. Shinn, Head, 979-862-3012, Fax: 979-845-6296, E-mail: g-shinn@tamu.edu. *Application contact:* Diann Dillingham, Graduate Program Coordinator, 979-845-2952, Fax: 979-845-6296, E-mail: dillingham@tamu.edu.

Texas A&M University–Commerce, Graduate School, College of Arts and Sciences, Department of Agriculture, Commerce, TX 75429-3011. Offers agricultural education (M Ed, MS); agricultural sciences (M Ed, MS). Part-time programs available. *Degree requirements:* For master's, thesis (for some programs), comprehensive exam. *Entrance requirements:* For master's, GRE General Test. Electronic applications accepted. *Faculty research:* Soil conservation, retention.

Texas A&M University–Kingsville, College of Graduate Studies, College of Agriculture and Home Economics, Program in Agricultural Education, Kingsville, TX 78363. Offers MS. *Degree requirements:* For master's, thesis or alternative, comprehensive exam. *Entrance requirements:* For master's, GRE General Test, minimum GPA of 3.0. Additional exam requirements/recommendations for international students: Required—TOEFL.

Texas State University-San Marcos, Graduate School, College of Applied Arts, Department of Agriculture, San Marcos, TX 78666. Offers M Ed. Part-time and evening/weekend programs available. *Faculty:* 1 (woman) full-time. *Students:* 1 (woman) full-time, 6 part-time (5 women); includes 1 Hispanic American. Average age 28. 2 applicants, 100% accepted, 2 enrolled. In 2006, 2 degrees awarded. *Degree requirements:* For master's, comprehensive exam. *Entrance requirements:* For master's, GRE General Test, minimum GPA of 2.75 in last 60 hours of course work. Additional exam requirements/recommendations for international students: Required—TOEFL. *Application deadline:* For fall admission, 6/15 priority date for domestic students; for spring admission, 10/15 priority date for domestic students. Applications are processed on a rolling basis. Application fee: $40 ($90 for international students). *Financial support:* In 2006–07, 7 students received support; research assistantships, career-related internships or fieldwork, Federal Work-Study, and institutionally sponsored loans available. Support available to part-time students. Financial award application deadline: 4/1; financial award applicants required to submit FAFSA. *Faculty research:* Computerized monitoring of tractor fuel efficiency, safety research, technical preparation program integration, internationalization of secondary curriculum, e-mail networking of secondary teachers. *Unit head:* Dr. C.Reed Richardson, Chair, 512-245-3324, Fax: 512-245-3320, E-mail: cr36@txstate.edu. *Application contact:* Dr. Tina Cade, Graduate Adviser, 512-245-3324, Fax: 512-245-3320, E-mail: tc10@txstate.edu.

Texas Tech University, Graduate School, College of Agricultural Sciences and Natural Resources, Department of Agricultural Education and Communications, Lubbock, TX 79409. Offers agricultural education (MS, Ed D). Part-time programs available. *Faculty:* 9 full-time (1 woman). *Students:* 29 full-time (17 women), 43 part-time (16 women); includes 7 minority (3 African Americans, 4 Hispanic Americans), 2 international. Average age 33. 55 applicants, 78% accepted, 31 enrolled. In 2006, 17 master's, 4 doctorates awarded. *Entrance requirements:* For master's, GRE General Test. Additional exam requirements/recommendations for international students: Required—TOEFL (minimum score 550 paper-based; 213 computer-based). *Application deadline:* For fall admission, 3/1 priority date for international students; for spring admission, 11/1 priority date for international students. Applications are processed on a rolling basis. Application fee: $50 ($60 for international students). Electronic applications accepted. *Expenses:* Tuition, state resident: full-time $4,440. Tuition, nonresident: full-time $11,040. Required fees: $2,136. *Financial support:* In 2006–07, 21 students received support, including 14 research assistantships with partial tuition reimbursements available (averaging $8,807 per year), 2 teaching assistantships with partial tuition reimbursements available (averaging $11,025 per year); Federal Work-Study and institutionally sponsored loans also available. Support available to part-time students. Financial award application deadline: 4/15; financial award applicants required to submit FAFSA. *Faculty research:* Planning needs assessment, learner-centered instructional design, program delivery, evaluation accountability, research measurement and analysis. Total annual research expenditures: $130,087. *Unit head:* Dr. Matt Baker, Chairman, 806-742-2816, Fax: 806-742-2880, E-mail: matt.baker@ttu.edu. *Application contact:* Dr. David Doerfert, Graduate Adviser, 806-742-2816, Fax: 806-742-2880, E-mail: david.doerfert@ttu.edu.

The University of Arizona, Graduate College, College of Agriculture and Life Sciences, Department of Agricultural Education, Tucson, AZ 85721. Offers M Ag Ed, MS. *Faculty:* 5 full-time (1 woman), 1 part-time/adjunct (0 women). *Students:* 12 full-time, 6 part-time; includes 2 minority (both Hispanic Americans) Average age 25. 4 applicants, 100% accepted, 4 enrolled. In 2006, 10 degrees awarded. *Degree requirements:* For master's, thesis. *Entrance requirements:* For master's, teaching/extension experience or equivalent. Additional exam requirements/recommendations for international students: Required—TOEFL. *Application deadline:* For fall admission, 4/15 for domestic students. Applications are processed on a rolling basis. Application fee: $50. *Financial support:* In 2006–07, 5 students received support, including 3 teaching assistantships (averaging $13,986 per year); fellowships, research assistantships, career-related internships or fieldwork, scholarships/grants, and tuition waivers (full) also available. *Faculty research:* Career placement, learning styles, noise impact on learning, computer technology, vocational education. *Unit head:* Dr. Jack F. Elliot, Head, 520-621-7173, Fax: 520-621-9889, E-mail: elliot@ag.arizona.edu. *Application contact:* Susan M. Scalero, Administrative Associate, 520-621-1523, Fax: 520-621-9889, E-mail: sscalero@ag.arizona.edu.

University of Arkansas, Graduate School, Dale Bumpers College of Agricultural, Food and Life Sciences, Department of Agricultural and Extension Education, Program in Agricultural and Extension Education, Fayetteville, AR 72701-1201. Offers MS. Part-time programs available. Postbaccalaureate distance learning degree programs offered (minimal on-campus study). *Students:* 6 full-time (4 women), 3 part-time (all women). 12 applicants, 33% accepted. In 2006, 10 degrees awarded. *Degree requirements:* For master's, thesis optional. Application fee: $40 ($50 for international students). *Financial support:* In 2006–07, 1 research assistantship, 2 teaching assistantships were awarded; fellowships also available. Financial award application deadline: 4/1. *Application contact:* Dr. George Wardlow, Graduate Coordinator, 479-575-2035, E-mail: wardlow@uark.edu.

University of Connecticut, Graduate School, Neag School of Education, Department of Curriculum and Instruction, Field of Curriculum and Instruction, Storrs, CT 06269. Offers agriculture education (MA, PhD); bilingual and bicultural education (MA, PhD); elementary education (MA, PhD); English education (MA, PhD); history and social sciences education (MA, PhD); mathematics education (MA, PhD); reading education (MA, PhD); science education (MA, PhD); secondary education (MA, PhD); world languages education (MA, PhD). *Faculty:* 25 full-time (12 women). *Students:* 158 full-time (120 women), 54 part-time (44 women); includes 24 minority (3 African Americans, 1 American Indian/Alaska Native, 3 Asian Americans or Pacific Islanders, 17 Hispanic Americans), 2 international. Average age 27. 268 applicants, 76% accepted, 203 enrolled. In 2006, 181 master's, 4 doctorates awarded. *Degree requirements:* For master's, comprehensive exam; for doctorate, thesis/dissertation. *Entrance requirements:* For doctorate, GRE General Test. Additional exam requirements/recommendations for international students: Required—TOEFL (minimum score 550 paper-based; 213 computer-based). *Application deadline:* For fall admission, 2/1 priority date for domestic and international students; for spring admission, 11/1 for domestic students, 10/1 for international students. Applications are processed on a rolling basis. Application fee: $55. Electronic applications accepted. *Financial support:* In 2006–07, 14 research assistantships with full tuition reimbursements, 4 teaching assistantships with full tuition reimbursements were awarded; fellowships, Federal Work-Study, scholarships/grants, health care benefits, and unspecified assistantships also available. Financial award application deadline: 2/1; financial award applicants required to submit FAFSA. *Application contact:* Lisa Rasicot, Graduate Coordinator, 860-486-3065, Fax: 860-486-0210, E-mail: soeadm02@uconnvm.uconn.edu.

University of Florida, Graduate School, College of Agricultural and Life Sciences, Department of Agricultural Education and Communication, Gainesville, FL 32611. Offers M Ag, MS, PhD. *Faculty:* 9 full-time (2 women). *Students:* 77 (50 women); includes 2 minority (both African Americans) 6 international. In 2006, 12 master's, 3 doctorates awarded. *Degree requirements:* For master's, thesis optional. *Entrance requirements:* For master's, GRE General Test, minimum GPA of 3.0; for doctorate, GRE General Test. Additional exam requirements/recommendations for international students: Required—TOEFL. *Application deadline:* For fall admission, 6/1 priority date for domestic students. Applications are processed on a rolling basis. Application fee: $20. Electronic applications accepted. *Expenses:* Tuition, state resident: full-time $6,827. Tuition, nonresident: full-time $21,951. Required fees: $999. *Financial support:* In 2006–07, 6 research assistantships (averaging $11,959 per year), 13 teaching assistantships (averaging $11,466 per year) were awarded; fellowships, unspecified assistantships also available. *Faculty research:* Cooperative extension service, including home economics, agriculture, 4-H, foods, housing, and nutrition. *Unit head:* Dr. Edward W. Osborne, Chair, 352-392-0502 Ext. 231, Fax: 352-392-9585, E-mail: ewo@ufl.edu. *Application contact:* Dr. Nick Place, Coordinator, 352-392-0502 Ext. 227, Fax: 352-392-9585, E-mail: nplace@ifas.ufl.edu.

University of Georgia, Graduate School, College of Agricultural and Environmental Sciences, Department of Agricultural Leadership, Education, and Communication, Athens, GA 30602. Offers MA Ext, MAL. *Faculty:* 8 full-time (2 women). *Students:* 13 full-time (9 women), 27 part-time (12 women); includes 3 minority (all African Americans) Average age 25. 15 applicants, 80% accepted, 10 enrolled. In 2006, 9 degrees awarded. *Degree requirements:* For master's, thesis optional. *Entrance requirements:* For master's, GRE General Test. *Application deadline:* For fall admission, 7/1 priority date for domestic students; for spring admission, 11/15 for domestic students. Application fee: $50. Electronic applications accepted. *Financial support:* In 2006–07, 2 teaching assistantships were awarded; fellowships, research assistantships, unspecified assistantships also available. *Unit head:* Dr. Ray V. Herren, Head, 706-542-3898, Fax: 706-542-0262, E-mail: rherren@uga.edu. *Application contact:* Dr. Richard Rohs, Coordinator, 706-542-8913, E-mail: frohs@uga.edu.

University of Idaho, College of Graduate Studies, College of Agricultural and Life Sciences, Department of Agricultural and Extension Education, Moscow, ID 83844-2282. Offers agricultural education (MS); education (PhD). *Accreditation:* NCATE. *Students:* 6. Average age 31. In 2006, 2 degrees awarded. *Entrance requirements:* For master's, minimum GPA of 2.8. *Application deadline:* For fall admission, 8/1 for domestic students; for spring admission, 12/15 for domestic students. Application fee: $55 ($60 for international students). *Expenses:* Tuition, nonresident: full-time $9,600; part-time $140 per credit. Required fees: $4,740; $227 per credit. *Financial support:* Application deadline: 2/15. *Unit head:* Dr. Louis E. Riesenberg, Head, 208-885-6358.

University of Illinois at Urbana–Champaign, Graduate College, College of Agricultural, Consumer and Environmental Sciences, Department of Human and Community Development, Champaign, IL 61820. Offers extension education (MS); human and community development (MS, PhD). *Faculty:* 21 full-time (12 women), 1 part-time/adjunct (0 women). *Students:* 31 full-time (24 women), 11 part-time (8 women); includes 7 minority (3 African Americans, 3 Asian Americans or Pacific Islanders, 1 Hispanic American), 8 international. 61 applicants, 49% accepted, 17 enrolled. In 2006, 13 master's, 3 doctorates awarded. *Degree requirements:* For doctorate, thesis/dissertation. *Entrance requirements:* For master's, GRE, minimum GPA of 3.0. *Application deadline:* For fall admission, 1/16 for domestic students; for spring admission, 12/1 for domestic students. Applications are processed on a rolling basis. Application fee: $50 ($60 for international students). Electronic applications accepted. *Financial support:* In 2006–07, 12 fellowships, 18 research assistantships, 18 teaching assistantships were awarded; tuition waivers (full and partial) also available. Financial award application deadline: 2/15. *Unit head:* Robert Hughes, Head, 217-333-3790, Fax: 217-244-7877, E-mail: hughesro@uiuc.edu. *Application contact:* Leann Topol, Clerk, 217-333-3869, Fax: 217-244-7877, E-mail: ltopol@uiuc.edu.

University of Minnesota, Twin Cities Campus, Graduate School, College of Education and Human Development, Department of Work and Human Resource Education, Program in Agricultural, Food and Environmental Education, Minneapolis, MN 55455-0213. Offers M Ed, MA, Ed D, PhD. *Students:* 5 full-time (4 women), 12 part-time (4 women). Average age 29. 9 applicants, 89% accepted, 7 enrolled. In 2006, 16 degrees awarded. *Expenses:* Tuition, state resident: full-time $9,302; part-time $775 per credit. Tuition, nonresident: full-time $16,400; part-time $1,367 per credit. Full-time tuition and fees vary according to class time, course load, program, reciprocity agreements and student level. *Application contact:* Dr. Mary Bents, Associate Dean, 612-625-6501, Fax: 612-626-1580, E-mail: mbents@tc.umn.edu.

University of Missouri–Columbia, Graduate School, College of Agriculture, Food and Natural Resources, Department of Agricultural Education, Columbia, MO 65211. Offers MS, PhD. *Faculty:* 3 full-time (0 women). *Students:* 6 full-time (3 women), 15 part-time (5 women); includes 1 minority (African American), 1 international. In 2006, 16 master's, 2 doctorates awarded. *Entrance requirements:* For doctorate, minimum GPA of 3.5 on prior graduate coursework. Application fee: $45 ($60 for international students). *Unit head:* Dr. Bryan L. Garton, Director of Graduate Studies, 573-882-9599, E-mail: gartonb@missouri.edu.

University of Missouri–Columbia, Graduate School, College of Education, Department of Curriculum and Instruction, Columbia, MO 65211. Offers agricultural education (M Ed, PhD, Ed S); art education (M Ed, PhD, Ed S); business and office education (M Ed, PhD, Ed S); early childhood education (M Ed, PhD, Ed S); elementary education (M Ed, PhD, Ed S); English education (M Ed, PhD, Ed S); foreign language education (M Ed, PhD, Ed S); health education and promotion (M Ed, PhD); learning and instruction (M Ed); marketing education (M Ed, PhD, Ed S); mathematics education (M Ed, PhD, Ed S); music education (M Ed, PhD, Ed S); reading education (M Ed, PhD, Ed S); science education (M Ed, PhD, Ed S); social studies education (M Ed, PhD, Ed S); vocational education (M Ed, PhD, Ed S). Part-time programs available. *Faculty:* 24 full-time (12 women). *Students:* 195 full-time (148 women), 260 part-time (214 women); includes 27 minority (8 African Americans, 1 American Indian/Alaska Native, 10 Asian Americans or Pacific Islanders, 8 Hispanic Americans), 19 international. In 2006, 186 master's, 12 doctorates awarded. Terminal master's awarded for partial completion of doctoral program. *Degree requirements:* For doctorate, thesis/dissertation. *Entrance requirements:* For master's and Ed S, GRE General Test or MAT, minimum GPA of 3.0; for doctorate, GRE General Test, minimum GPA of 3.0. *Application deadline:* Applications are processed on a rolling basis. Application fee: $45 ($60 for international students). *Financial support:* Fellowships, research assistantships, teaching assistantships, institutionally sponsored loans available. *Unit head:* Dr. Lloyd H. Barrow, Director of Graduate Studies, 573-882-8247, E-mail: robinsonr@missouri.edu.

University of Nebraska–Lincoln, Graduate College, College of Agricultural Sciences and Natural Resources, Department of Agricultural Leadership, Education and Communication, Lincoln, NE 68588. Offers MS. *Degree requirements:* For master's, thesis optional. *Entrance requirements:* For master's, resumé. Additional exam requirements/recommendations for international students: Required—TOEFL (minimum score 550 paper-based; 213 computer-based). Electronic applications accepted. *Faculty research:* Teaching and instruction, extension education, leadership and human resource development, international agricultural education.

University of Puerto Rico, Mayagüez Campus, Graduate Studies, College of Agricultural Sciences, Department of Agricultural Education, Mayagüez, PR 00681-9000. Offers agricultural education (MS); agricultural extension (MS). Part-time programs available. *Faculty:* 5 full-time (2 women). *Students:* 6 full-time (4 women), 35 part-time (22 women); includes 39 minority (all Hispanic Americans), 2 international. 7 applicants, 100% accepted, 7 enrolled. In 2006, 3 degrees awarded. *Degree requirements:* For master's, thesis, comprehensive exam. *Entrance requirements:* For master's, BA in home economics; BS in agricultural education, agriculture, home economics, or equivalent. *Application deadline:* For fall admission, 2/15 for domestic and international students; for spring admission, 9/15 for domestic and international students. Applications are processed on a rolling basis. Application fee: $25. *Expenses:* Tuition, nonresident: full-time $4,655. Required fees: $210. One-time fee: $77 full-time. Part-time tuition and fees vary according to course load and reciprocity agreements. *Financial support:* In 2006–07, fellowships (averaging $12,000 per year), research assistantships with tuition reimbursements (averaging $15,000 per year), teaching assistantships with tuition reimbursements (averaging $8,500 per year) were awarded. *Faculty research:* Curricular development and supervision, youth education, rural sociology. *Unit head:* Dr. David Padilla, Director, 787-832-4040 Ext. 3855, Fax: 787-265-3814, E-mail: dpadilla@uprm.edu. *Application contact:* Nydia Sánchez, Secretary, 787-832-4040 Ext. 3120, Fax: 787-265-3814, E-mail: nsanchez@uprm.edu.

The University of Tennessee, Graduate School, College of Agricultural Sciences and Natural Resources, Department of Agricultural Economics, Knoxville, TN 37996. Offers agricultural education (MS); agricultural extension education (MS). *Accreditation:* NCATE. Part-time programs available. Postbaccalaureate distance learning degree programs offered (minimal on-campus study). In 2006, 6 degrees awarded. *Degree requirements:* For master's, thesis or alternative. *Entrance requirements:* For master's, minimum GPA of 2.7. Additional exam requirements/recommendations for international students: Required—TOEFL. *Application deadline:* For fall admission, 2/1 priority date for domestic students. Applications are processed on a rolling basis. Application fee: $35. Electronic applications accepted. *Expenses:* Tuition, state resident: full-time $5,574. Tuition, nonresident: full-time $16,840. Required fees: $792. *Financial support:* In 2006–07, 2 research assistantships were awarded; career-related internships or fieldwork, Federal Work-Study, institutionally sponsored loans, and unspecified assistantships also available. Financial award application deadline: 2/1; financial award applicants required to submit FAFSA. *Unit head:* Dr. Richard Poling, Head, 865-974-7371, Fax: 865-974-7448.

University of Wisconsin–River Falls, Outreach and Graduate Studies, College of Agriculture, Food, and Environmental Sciences, Department of Agricultural Education, River Falls, WI 54022-5001. Offers MS. *Accreditation:* NCATE. Part-time programs available. *Degree requirements:* For master's, thesis (for some programs), comprehensive exam, registration. *Entrance requirements:* For master's, minimum GPA of 2.75. Electronic applications accepted.

Utah State University, School of Graduate Studies, College of Agriculture, Department of Agricultural Systems Technology and Education, Logan, UT 84322. Offers agricultural systems technology (MS), including agricultural extension education, agricultural mechanization, international agricultural extension, secondary and postsecondary agricultural education; family and consumer sciences education (MS). Part-time programs available. Postbaccalaureate distance learning degree programs offered (minimal on-campus study). *Faculty:* 11 full-time (4 women), 2 part-time/adjunct (1 woman). *Students:* 14 full-time (7 women), 6 part-time (4 women); includes 1 minority (Hispanic American) Average age 30. 20 applicants, 100% accepted, 15 enrolled. In 2006, 14 degrees awarded. *Degree requirements:* For master's, thesis (for some programs), comprehensive exam (for some programs), registration. *Entrance requirements:* For master's, GRE General Test, MAT, BS in agricultural education, agricultural extension, or related agricultural or science discipline; minimum GPA of 3.0. Additional exam requirements/recommendations for international students: Required—TOEFL. *Application deadline:* For fall admission, 7/1 priority date for domestic and international students; for spring admission, 11/1 priority date for domestic and international students. Applications are processed on a rolling basis. Application fee: $50 ($60 for international students). *Financial support:* In 2006–07, 3 research assistantships (averaging $10,000 per year) were awarded; career-related internships or fieldwork, Federal Work-Study, institutionally sponsored loans, and tuition waivers (partial) also available. Support available to part-time students. Financial award application deadline: 2/1. *Faculty research:* Extension and adult education; structures and environment; low-input agriculture; farm safety, systems, and mechanizations. Total annual research expenditures: $310,000. *Unit head:* Dr. Bruce E. Miller, Head, 435-797-2232, Fax: 435-797-4002, E-mail: bruce.miller@usu.edu. *Application contact:* Lazell W. Allen, Staff Assistant II, 435-797-2230, Fax: 435-797-4002, E-mail: lazella@cc.usu.edu.

West Virginia University, Davis College of Agriculture, Forestry and Consumer Sciences, Division of Resource Management and Sustainable Development, Program in Agricultural and Extension Education, Morgantown, WV 26506. Offers agricultural extension education (MS); teaching vocational-agriculture (MS). *Accreditation:* NCATE. Part-time programs available. *Students:* 5 full-time (4 women), 3 part-time (2 women). Average age 29. 6 applicants, 100% accepted, 3 enrolled. In 2006, 4 degrees awarded. *Degree requirements:* For master's, thesis, registration. *Entrance requirements:* For master's, GRE General Test, minimum GPA of 2.75. Additional exam requirements/recommendations for international students: Required—TOEFL. *Application deadline:* For fall admission, 7/1 priority date for domestic students. Applications are processed on a rolling basis. Application fee: $50. *Expenses:* Tuition, state resident: full-time $4,926; part-time $276 per credit hour. Tuition, nonresident: full-time $14,278; part-time $796 per credit hour. Tuition and fees vary according to program. *Financial support:* In 2006–07, 5 students received support, including 1 teaching assistantship with full tuition reimbursement available (averaging $8,100 per year); Federal Work-Study, institutionally sponsored loans, and tuition waivers (partial) also available. Financial award application deadline: 2/1; financial award applicants required to submit FAFSA. *Faculty research:* Program development in vocational agriculture, agricultural extension, supervised experience programs, leadership development. *Unit head:* Dr. Stacy A. Gartin, Chair, 304-293-3431 Ext. 4480, Fax: 304-293-3752, E-mail: stacy.gartin@mail.wvu.edu.

Art Education

American University of Puerto Rico, Program in Education, Bayamón, PR 00960-2037. Offers art history (M Ed); elementary education (4-6) (M Ed); elementary education (k-3) (M Ed); general science education (M Ed); physical education (k-12) (M Ed); special education at secondary level (transition) (M Ed). *Entrance requirements:* For master's, EXADEP or GRE or MAT, 2 letters of recommendation, minimum GPA of 2.5.

Arcadia University, Graduate Studies, Department of Education, Glenside, PA 19038-3295. Offers art education (M Ed, MA Ed); biology education (MA Ed); chemistry education (MA Ed); child development (CAS); computer education (M Ed, CAS); computer education 7–12 (MA Ed); early childhood education (M Ed, CAS), including individualized (M Ed), master teacher (M Ed), research in child development (M Ed); educational leadership (M Ed, CAS); educational psychology (CAS); elementary education (M Ed, CAS); English education (MA Ed); environmental education (MA Ed, CAS); history education (MA Ed); language arts (M Ed, CAS); mathematics education (M Ed, MA Ed, CAS); music education (MA Ed); psychology (MA Ed); pupil personnel services (CAS); reading (M Ed, CAS); school library science (M Ed); science education (M Ed, CAS); secondary education (M Ed, CAS); special education (M Ed, Ed D, CAS); theater arts (MA Ed); written communication (MA Ed). *Accreditation:* NASAD. Part-time and evening/weekend programs available. Postbaccalaureate distance learning degree programs offered (minimal on-campus study). *Faculty:* 12 full-time (8 women), 38 part-time/adjunct (26 women). *Students:* 60 full-time (56 women), 419 part-time (324 women); includes 70 minority (57 African Americans, 1 American Indian/Alaska Native, 6 Asian Americans or Pacific Islanders, 6 Hispanic Americans), 1 international. In 2006, 257 master's, 4 doctorates awarded. *Application deadline:* Applications are processed on a rolling basis. Application fee: $35. Electronic applications accepted. *Financial support:* Career-related internships or fieldwork, tuition waivers (partial), and unspecified assistantships available. *Unit head:* Dr. Steven P. Gulkus, Chair, 215-572-2120. *Application contact:* 215-572-2925, Fax: 215-572-2126, E-mail: grad@arcadia.edu.

Art Academy of Cincinnati, Program in Art Education, Cincinnati, OH 45202. Offers MA. Offered during summer only. *Accreditation:* NASAD. Part-time programs available. *Faculty:* 3 full-time (1 woman), 6 part-time/adjunct (5 women). *Students:* 12 full-time (6 women), 1 (woman) part-time. Average age 36. 5 applicants, 80% accepted, 4 enrolled. In 2006, 2 degrees awarded. *Degree requirements:* For master's, thesis, portfolio/exhibit. *Entrance requirements:* For master's, portfolio, 1 letter of recommendation. Additional exam requirements/recommendations for international students: Required—TOEFL. *Application deadline:* For fall admission, 5/1 priority date for domestic students. Applications are processed on a rolling basis. Application fee: $25. Electronic applications accepted. *Expenses:* Tuition: Full-time $9,240; part-time $840 per hour. *Financial support:* In 2006–07, 9 students received support. Institutionally sponsored loans and scholarships/grants available. Support available to part-time students. Financial award applicants required to submit FAFSA. *Unit head:* Keith Benjamin, Chair, 513-562-6262, E-mail: kbenjamin@artacademy.edu. *Application contact:* John J. Wadell, Director of Admissions, 513-562-8744, Fax: 513-562-8778, E-mail: jwadell@artacademy.edu.

Austin College, Program in Education, Sherman, TX 75090-4400. Offers art education (MA); elementary education (MA); middle school education (MA); music education (MA); physical education and coaching (MA); secondary education (MA). Applicants must meet Austin College's undergraduate curriculum requirements. Part-time programs available. *Faculty:* 5 full-time (3 women), 1 (woman) part-time/adjunct. *Students:* 33 full-time (26 women); includes 3 minority (2 Asian Americans or Pacific Islanders, 1 Hispanic American). Average age 25. In 2006, 24 degrees awarded. *Degree requirements:* For master's, one foreign language, thesis or alternative. *Entrance requirements:* For master's, Texas Academic Skills Program Test. *Application deadline:* For fall admission, 5/1 priority date for domestic students; for spring admission, 1/15 priority date for domestic students. Applications are processed on a rolling basis. Application fee: $35. Electronic applications accepted. *Expenses:* Tuition: Full-time $27,385. Required fees: $160. *Financial support:* In 2006–07, 27 students received support. Career-related internships or fieldwork, Federal Work-Study, scholarships/grants, and unspecified assistantships available. Support available to part-time students. Financial award application deadline: 4/1; financial award applicants required to submit FAFSA. *Unit head:* Dr. Barbara Sylvester, Director of Teaching Program, 903-813-2498, Fax: 903-813-2326, E-mail: bsylvester@austincollege.edu.

Averett University, Graduate Studies in Education, Danville, VA 24541-3692. Offers art education (M Ed); biology (M Ed); chemistry (M Ed); curriculum and instruction (M Ed); elementary education (M Ed); English (M Ed); health and physical education (M Ed); history and social studies (M Ed); mathematics education (M Ed); physical science (M Ed); reading (M Ed); special education (learning disabilities specialization PK-12) (M Ed). Part-time and evening/weekend programs available. *Faculty:* 10 full-time (4 women), 7 part-time/adjunct (6 women). *Students:* 14 full-time (10 women), 85 part-time (67 women); includes 20 minority (18 African Americans, 2 Asian Americans or Pacific Islanders). Average age 33. 52 applicants, 100% accepted, 40 enrolled. In 2006, 48 degrees awarded. *Degree requirements:* For master's, thesis optional. *Entrance requirements:* For master's, PRAXIS, GRE General Test, MAT or NTE, writing proficiency exam, 3 letters of recommendation, current teacher's licensure or eligibility for licensure, minimum undergraduate GPA of 3.0 in previous 2 years. Additional exam requirements/recommendations for international students: Required—TOEFL (minimum score 600 paper-based; 200 computer-based). *Application deadline:* Applications are processed on a rolling basis. Application fee: $20. *Expenses:* Contact institution. *Financial support:* In 2006–07, 23 students received support. Federal Work-Study and scholarships/grants available. Financial award application deadline: 4/1; financial award applicants required to submit FAFSA. *Faculty research:* Literary assessment-PreK-6, handwriting instruction and assessment-PreK-6, written language instruction and assessment-PreK-6 and special needs students learning styles, curriculum and instruction processes. *Unit head:* Dr. Lynn H. Wolf, Chair, 434-793-3995, Fax: 434-791-4392, E-mail: lynn.wolf@averett.edu.

Ball State University, Graduate School, College of Fine Arts, Department of Art, Muncie, IN 47306-1099. Offers art (MA); art education (MA, MAE). *Accreditation:* NASAD. *Faculty:* 18. *Students:* 9 full-time (4 women), 6 part-time (4 women), 1 international. Average age 27. 15 applicants, 73% accepted, 8 enrolled. In 2006, 7 degrees awarded. Application fee: $25 ($35 for international students). *Financial support:* In 2006–07, research assistantships with full tuition reimbursements (averaging $7,000 per year), 6 teaching assistantships with full tuition reimbursements (averaging $7,000 per year) were awarded. Financial award application deadline: 3/1. *Unit head:* David Jackson, Head, 765-285-5838, Fax: 765-285-5275. *Application contact:* Kenton Hall, Director, 765-285-5838, Fax: 765-285-5275, E-mail: khall@bsu.edu.

Bennington College, Graduate Programs, Program in Teaching, Bennington, VT 05201. Offers art education (MAT); early childhood (MAT); elementary education (MAT); English education (MAT); foreign language education (MAT); mathematics education (MAT); music education (MAT); science education (MAT); secondary education (MAT); social science education (MAT). *Faculty:* 4 part-time/adjunct (3 women). *Students:* 11 full-time (7 women), 1 (woman) part-time; includes 2 minority (both Hispanic Americans) Average age 31. 12 applicants, 75% accepted, 3 enrolled. In 2006, 13 degrees awarded. *Degree requirements:* For master's, 1 year teaching practicum, professional portfolio. *Entrance requirements:* For master's, interview. *Application deadline:* For fall admission, 3/1 for domestic students. Application fee: $60. *Expenses:* Contact institution. One-time fee: $75 full-time. Tuition and fees vary according to program. *Financial support:* In 2006–07, 10 students received support, including 4 fellowships (averaging $6,875 per year); scholarships/grants and unspecified assistantships also available. Financial award application deadline: 4/1; financial award applicants required to submit FAFSA. *Unit head:* George Kamberelis, Director of Center for Creative Teaching, 802-440-4863, E-mail: gkamberelis@bennington.edu. *Application contact:* Ken Himmelman, Dean of Admissions, 802-440-4312, Fax: 802-440-4320, E-mail: admissions@bennington.edu.

See Close-Up on page 861.

Boise State University, Graduate College, College of Arts and Sciences, Department of Art, Program in Art Education, Boise, ID 83725-0399. Offers MA. *Accreditation:* NASAD; NCATE. Part-time programs available. *Students:* Average age 41. 1 applicant, 100% accepted, 1 enrolled. In 2006, 2 degrees awarded. *Degree requirements:* For master's, thesis optional. *Entrance requirements:* For master's, minimum GPA of 3.0, portfolio. Additional exam requirements/recommendations for international students: Required—TOEFL (minimum score 587 paper-based; 240 computer-based). *Application deadline:* For fall admission, 7/17 priority date for domestic students; for spring admission, 12/5 priority date for domestic students. Applications are processed on a rolling basis. Application fee: $0. Electronic applica-

Art Education

Boise State University *(continued)* tions accepted. *Financial support:* Career-related internships or fieldwork, Federal Work-Study, institutionally sponsored loans, and unspecified assistantships available. Support available to part-time students. Financial award application deadline: 3/1. *Unit head:* Cheryl K. Shurtleff-Young, Director, 208-426-3450, Fax: 208-426-1243, E-mail: cshurtle@boisestate.edu.

Boston University, College of Fine Arts, School of Visual Arts, Program in Art Education, Boston, MA 02215. Offers MFA. *Students:* 6 full-time (5 women), 2 part-time (1 woman), 2 international. Average age 27. 14 applicants, 79% accepted, 4 enrolled. In 2006, 7 degrees awarded. *Entrance requirements:* For master's, portfolio. Additional exam requirements/recommendations for international students: Required—TOEFL. *Application deadline:* For fall admission, 2/15 priority date for domestic students, 2/1 for international students. Applications are processed on a rolling basis. Application fee: $65. *Expenses:* Tuition: Full-time $33,330; part-time $1,042 per credit. Required fees: $462; $40. *Financial support:* Fellowships, teaching assistantships available. Financial award application deadline: 2/15. *Application contact:* Mark Krone, Manager, Graduate Admissions, 617-353-3350, E-mail: arts@bu.edu.

Boston University, College of Fine Arts, School of Visual Arts, Program in Studio Teaching, Boston, MA 02215. Offers MFA. *Students:* 11 full-time; includes 2 minority (both Asian Americans or Pacific Islanders) Average age 25. 16 applicants, 63% accepted, 7 enrolled. *Entrance requirements:* For master's, portfolio. Additional exam requirements/recommendations for international students: Required—TOEFL. *Application deadline:* For fall admission, 2/15 priority date for domestic and international students. Applications are processed on a rolling basis. Application fee: $65. *Expenses:* Tuition: Full-time $33,330; part-time $1,042 per credit. Required fees: $462; $40. *Financial support:* Fellowships, teaching assistantships available. Financial award application deadline: 2/15. *Application contact:* Mark Krone, Manager, Graduate Admissions, 617-353-3350, E-mail: arts@bu.edu.

Bowling Green State University, Graduate College, College of Arts and Sciences, School of Art, Bowling Green, OH 43403. Offers 2-D studio art (MA, MFA); 3-D studio art (MA, MFA); art education (MA); art history (MA); computer art (MA, MFA); design (MFA); graphics (MFA). *Accreditation:* NASAD. Part-time programs available. *Faculty:* 26 full-time (14 women), 11 part-time/adjunct (3 women). *Students:* 24 full-time (11 women), 5 part-time (3 women); includes 2 minority (both Asian Americans or Pacific Islanders), 3 international. Average age 34. 77 applicants, 23% accepted, 10 enrolled. In 2006, 18 degrees awarded. *Degree requirements:* For master's, thesis or alternative, final exhibit (MFA). *Entrance requirements:* For master's, GRE General Test, slide portfolio (15-20 slides). Additional exam requirements/recommendations for international students: Required—TOEFL. *Application deadline:* For fall admission, 2/15 for domestic students. Application fee: $30. Electronic applications accepted. *Expenses:* Tuition, state resident: part-time $535 per hour. Tuition, nonresident: part-time $884 per hour. *Financial support:* In 2006–07, 14 research assistantships with full and partial tuition reimbursements (averaging $7,176 per year), 8 teaching assistantships with full and partial tuition reimbursements (averaging $8,110 per year) were awarded; career-related internships or fieldwork, institutionally sponsored loans, and unspecified assistantships also available. Support available to part-time students. Financial award applicants required to submit FAFSA. *Faculty research:* Computer animation and virtual reality, Spanish still-life painting from 1600 to 1800, art and psychotherapy, Japanese wood-firing techniques in ceramics, non-toxic printmaking technologies. *Unit head:* Dr. Katerina Rüedi Ray, Director, 419-372-8575. *Application contact:* Gregory Little, Graduate Coordinator, 419-372-2293.

Bridgewater State College, School of Graduate Studies, School of Arts and Sciences, Department of Art, Bridgewater, MA 02325-0001. Offers MAT. Part-time and evening/weekend programs available. *Degree requirements:* For master's, comprehensive exam. *Entrance requirements:* For master's, GRE General Test. *Application deadline:* For fall admission, 3/1 priority date for domestic students; for spring admission, 10/1 priority date for domestic students. Application fee: $50. *Financial support:* Career-related internships or fieldwork, health care benefits, and unspecified assistantships available. Support available to part-time students.

Brigham Young University, Graduate Studies, College of Fine Arts and Communications, Department of Visual Arts, Provo, UT 84602-1001. Offers art education (MA); art history (MA); studio art (MFA). Art education applications accepted biennially. *Accreditation:* NASAD. *Faculty:* 27 full-time (7 women), 2 part-time/adjunct (1 woman). *Students:* 35 full-time (20 women); includes 3 minority (all Asian Americans or Pacific Islanders) Average age 26. 21 applicants, 48% accepted, 10 enrolled. In 2006, 15 degrees awarded. *Degree requirements:* For master's, 2 foreign languages. *Entrance requirements:* For master's, GRE (art history), minimum GPA of 3.0 (MFA, MA in art education), 3.3 (MA in art history), portfolio in slide form (MFA), writing samples (MA in art education, art history). Additional exam requirements/recommendations for international students: Required—TOEFL (minimum score 500 paper-based). *Application deadline:* For fall admission, 2/1 for domestic and international students. Application fee: $50. Electronic applications accepted. *Financial support:* In 2006–07, 31 students received support, including 29 teaching assistantships with partial tuition reimbursements available; research assistantships, scholarships/grants and tuition waivers (partial) also available. Financial award application deadline: 2/1. *Faculty research:* Methodology-standards-assessment, Medieval architecture, classical/Islamic eighteenth- and nineteenth-century art, Netherlandish art, contemporary art. Total annual research expenditures: $83,932. *Unit head:* Linda A. Sullivan, Chair, 801-422-4429, Fax: 801-422-0695, E-mail: sullivan@byu.edu. *Application contact:* Sharon Lyn Heelis, Secretary, 801-422-4429, Fax: 801-422-0695, E-mail: sharon_heelis@byu.edu.

Brooklyn College of the City University of New York, Division of Graduate Studies, School of Education, Program in Adolescence Education and Special Subjects, Brooklyn, NY 11210-2889. Offers art teacher (MA); biology teacher (MA); chemistry teacher (MA); English teacher (MA); French teacher (MA); health and nutrition sciences: health teacher (MS Ed); mathematics teacher (MA); music education (CAS); music teacher (MA); physical education teacher (MS Ed); physics teacher (MA); social studies teacher (MA); Spanish teacher (MA). Part-time and evening/weekend programs available. *Students:* 30 full-time (22 women), 450 part-time (257 women); includes 167 minority (101 African Americans, 21 Asian Americans or Pacific Islanders, 45 Hispanic Americans), 21 international. 277 applicants, 84% accepted, 113 enrolled. In 2006, 172 master's, 6 other advanced degrees awarded. *Degree requirements:* For master's, comprehensive exam (for some programs). *Entrance requirements:* For master's, LAST, previous course work in education, resumé, 2 letters of recommendation, essay. Additional exam requirements/recommendations for international students: Required—TOEFL. *Application deadline:* For fall admission, 3/1 priority date for domestic students, 2/1 priority date for international students; for spring admission, 11/1 priority date for domestic students, 10/1 priority date for international students. Applications are processed on a rolling basis. Application fee: $125. Electronic applications accepted. *Expenses:* Tuition, state resident: full-time $6,400; part-time $270 per credit. Tuition, nonresident: full-time $12,000; part-time $500 per credit. Required fees: $118 per semester. *Financial support:* Career-related internships or fieldwork, Federal Work-Study, institutionally sponsored loans, and scholarships/grants available. Support available to part-time students. Financial award application deadline: 5/1; financial award applicants required to submit FAFSA. *Faculty research:* Interdisciplinary education, semiotics, discourse analysis, autobiography, teacher identity. *Unit head:* Prof. Stephen Phillips, Program Facilitator, 718-951-5214, E-mail: phillips@brooklyn.cuny.edu. *Application contact:* Karen Alleyne-Pierre, Director of Admissions Services and Enrollment Communications, 718-951-5902, Fax: 718-951-4506, E-mail: grads@brooklyn.cuny.edu.

Buffalo State College, State University of New York, Graduate Studies and Research, Faculty of Arts and Humanities, Department of Art Education, Buffalo, NY 14222-1095. Offers MS Ed. *Accreditation:* NASAD; NCATE. Part-time and evening/weekend programs available. *Degree requirements:* For master's, thesis or alternative, project. *Entrance requirements:* For master's, New York teaching certificate, interview, minimum GPA of 3.0. Additional exam

requirements/recommendations for international students: Required—TOEFL (minimum score 550 paper-based; 213 computer-based).

California State University, Los Angeles, Graduate Studies, College of Arts and Letters, Department of Art, Los Angeles, CA 90032-8530. Offers art (MA), including art education, art history, art therapy, ceramics, metals, and textiles, design (MA, MFA), painting, sculpture, and graphic arts, photography; fine arts (MFA), including crafts, design (MA, MFA), studio arts. *Accreditation:* NASAD (one or more programs are accredited). Part-time and evening/weekend programs available. *Faculty:* 8 full-time (3 women). *Students:* 24 full-time (15 women), 80 part-time (51 women); includes 35 minority (5 African Americans, 10 Asian Americans or Pacific Islanders, 20 Hispanic Americans), 7 international. In 2006, 12 degrees awarded. *Degree requirements:* For master's, project or thesis. *Entrance requirements:* For master's, portfolio. Additional exam requirements/recommendations for international students: Required—TOEFL. *Application deadline:* For fall admission, 6/30 for domestic students; for spring admission, 2/1 for domestic students. Applications are processed on a rolling basis. Application fee: $55. *Expenses:* Tuition, nonresident: part-time $226 per unit. *Financial support:* Federal Work-Study available. Support available to part-time students. Financial award application deadline: 3/1. *Faculty research:* The artist and the book, conceptual art, ceramic processes, computer graphics, architectural graphics. *Unit head:* Dr. Robert Martin, Chair, 323-343-4010, Fax: 323-343-4045.

California State University, Northridge, Graduate Studies, College of Arts, Media, and Communication, Department of Art, Northridge, CA 91330. Offers art education (MA); art history (MA); studio art (MA, MFA); visual communication (MA, MFA). *Accreditation:* NASAD. *Faculty:* 25 full-time (12 women), 54 part-time/adjunct (35 women). *Students:* 26 full-time (7 women), 44 part-time (10 women); includes 14 minority (1 African American, 2 American Indian/Alaska Native, 4 Asian Americans or Pacific Islanders, 7 Hispanic Americans), 5 international. Average age 40. 40 applicants, 35% accepted, 11 enrolled. In 2006, 12 degrees awarded. *Application deadline:* For fall admission, 11/30 for domestic students. Application fee: $55. *Expenses:* Tuition, nonresident: full-time $8,136; part-time $4,068 per year. Required fees: $3,624; $1,161 per term. *Financial support:* Application deadline: 3/1. *Unit head:* Prof. Edward Alfano, Acting Chair, 818-677-2242, E-mail: art.dept@csun.edu.

Cape Breton University, School of Education, Health, and Wellness, Sydney, NS B1P 6L2, Canada. Offers educational counseling (Diploma); educational studies-arts education (Certificate); educational technology (Diploma). Part-time and evening/weekend programs available. Postbaccalaureate distance learning degree programs offered (no on-campus study). Electronic applications accepted.

Carlow University, School of Education, Program in Art Education, Pittsburgh, PA 15213-3165. Offers M Ed. Part-time and evening/weekend programs available. *Degree requirements:* For master's, thesis or alternative. *Entrance requirements:* For master's, interview, minimum GPA of 3.0, resumé, 1 year professional experience, portfolio, 3 letters of recommendation. Additional exam requirements/recommendations for international students: Required—TOEFL (minimum score 550 paper-based; 213 computer-based). Electronic applications accepted.

Carthage College, Division of Teacher Education, Kenosha, WI 53140. Offers classroom guidance and counseling (M Ed); creative arts (M Ed); gifted and talented children (M Ed); language arts (M Ed); modern language (M Ed); natural sciences (M Ed); reading (M Ed, Certificate); social sciences (M Ed); teacher leadership (M Ed). Part-time and evening/weekend programs available. *Degree requirements:* For master's, thesis optional. *Entrance requirements:* For master's, MAT, minimum B average, letters of reference.

Case Western Reserve University, School of Graduate Studies, Department of Art History and Art, Program in Art Education, Cleveland, OH 44106. Offers MA. Part-time programs available. *Faculty:* 1 full-time (0 women), 4 part-time/adjunct (2 women). *Students:* 5 full-time (all women). Average age 29. In 2006, 4 degrees awarded. *Degree requirements:* For master's, thesis (for some programs), art exhibit. *Entrance requirements:* For master's, NTE, interview, portfolio. Additional exam requirements/recommendations for international students: Required—TOEFL. *Application deadline:* For fall admission, 7/10 for domestic students. Applications are processed on a rolling basis. Application fee: $50. *Financial support:* Career-related internships or fieldwork, Federal Work-Study, and tuition waivers (partial) available. Financial award application deadline: 7/10. *Faculty research:* Visual and aesthetic education, ethnographic arts, multiculturalism. *Unit head:* Dr. Tim Shuckerow, Director, 216-368-2714, Fax: 216-368-2715, E-mail: txs10@po.cwru.edu.

Central Connecticut State University, School of Graduate Studies, School of Arts and Sciences, Department of Art, New Britain, CT 06050-4010. Offers art education (MS, Certificate). Part-time and evening/weekend programs available. *Faculty:* 12 full-time (6 women), 22 part-time/adjunct (11 women). *Students:* 1 (woman) full-time, 26 part-time (22 women), 1 international. Average age 36. 28 applicants, 50% accepted, 9 enrolled. In 2006, 8 master's, 3 other advanced degrees awarded. *Degree requirements:* For master's, thesis or alternative, exhibit or special project. *Entrance requirements:* For master's, minimum GPA of 2.7. Additional exam requirements/recommendations for international students: Required—TOEFL. *Application deadline:* For fall admission, 7/1 for domestic students; for spring admission, 12/1 for domestic students. Applications are processed on a rolling basis. Application fee: $50. Electronic applications accepted. *Expenses:* Tuition, area resident: full-time $3,970; part-time $380 per credit. Tuition, state resident: full-time $5,955; part-time $380 per credit. Tuition, nonresident: full-time $11,061; part-time $380 per credit. Required fees: $3,189. One-time fee: $62 part-time. Tuition and fees vary according to degree level and program. *Financial support:* In 2006–07, 5 students received support, including 1 research assistantship; career-related internships or fieldwork, Federal Work-Study, scholarships/grants, and unspecified assistantships also available. Support available to part-time students. Financial award application deadline: 3/1; financial award applicants required to submit FAFSA. *Faculty research:* Visual arts. *Unit head:* Dr. Cora Marshall, Chair, 860-832-2620.

Chatham University, Program in Education, Pittsburgh, PA 15232-2826. Offers early childhood education (MAT); elementary education (MAT); English—secondary (MAT); environmental education (K-12) (MAT); secondary art (MAT); secondary biology education (MAT); secondary chemistry education (MAT); secondary English education (MAT); secondary math education (MAT); secondary physics education (MAT); secondary social studies education (MAT); special education (MAT). *Students:* 60 full-time (43 women), 23 part-time (22 women). Average age 29. 48 applicants, 77% accepted, 32 enrolled. In 2006, 59 degrees awarded. *Degree requirements:* For master's, thesis, teaching experience. *Entrance requirements:* For master's, PRAXIS I, minimum GPA of 3.0, sample of written work, recommendation letters. Additional exam requirements/recommendations for international students: Required—TOEFL (minimum score 600 paper-based; 250 computer-based; 100 iBT); Recommended—IELTS (minimum score 7), TWE (minimum score 5). *Application deadline:* For fall admission, 5/1 priority date for domestic and international students; for winter admission, 10/1 priority date for domestic and international students. Applications are processed on a rolling basis. Application fee: $45. Electronic applications accepted. *Financial support:* Career-related internships or fieldwork available. Financial award applicants required to submit FAFSA. *Faculty research:* Gifted education, environmental education, technology in education, writing as learning, class size and achievement. *Unit head:* Dr. Wendy Weiner, Director, 412-365-1146, Fax: 412-365-1505, E-mail: wweiner@chatham.edu. *Application contact:* 412-365-1825, Fax: 412-365-1609, E-mail: admissions@chatham.edu.

Christopher Newport University, Graduate Studies, Department of Teacher Preparation, Newport News, VA 23606-2998. Offers art (PK-12) (MAT); biology (6-12) (MAT); computer science (6-12) (MAT); elementary (PK-6) (MAT); English (6-12) (MAT); French (PK-12) (MAT); history (6-12) (MAT); history and social science (MAT); mathematics (6-12) (MAT); music (PK-12) (MAT), including choral, instrumental; physics (6-12) (MAT); Spanish (PK-12) (MAT); theater (PK-12) (MAT). Part-time and evening/weekend programs available. *Degree requirements:* For master's, thesis or alternative, comprehensive exam. *Entrance requirements:* For master's,

PRAXIS I, minimum GPA of 3.0. Electronic applications accepted. *Faculty research:* Early literacy development, instructional innovations, professional teaching standards, multicultural issues, aesthetic education.

City University, Graduate Division, Gordon Albright School of Education, Bellevue, WA 98005. Offers curriculum and instruction (M Ed); educational leadership (M Ed); educational leadership: principal certification (M Ed, Certificate); educational leadership: principal/program administrator certification (Certificate); educational leadership: program administrator certification (M Ed, Certificate); guidance and counseling (M Ed, Certificate); integrated arts and performance learning (M Ed); professional certification-teachers (Certificate); reading (Certificate); reading and literacy (M Ed); reading. literacy, and ESL/ELL (M Ed); teacher certification (MIT); technology, curriculum and instruction (M Ed). Part-time and evening/weekend programs available. Postbaccalaureate distance learning degree programs offered (no on-campus study). *Entrance requirements:* Additional exam requirements/recommendations for international students: Required—TOEFL (minimum score 540 paper-based; 207 computer-based); Recommended—IELTS. Electronic applications accepted.

Cleveland State University, College of Graduate Studies, College of Education and Human Services, Department of Teacher Education, Cleveland, OH 44115. Offers art education (M Ed); early childhood education (M Ed); foreign language education (M Ed); mathematics and science education (M Ed); middle childhood education (M Ed); special education (M Ed), including mild/moderate disabilities, moderate/intensive disabilities; teaching English to speakers of other languages (M Ed). Part-time and evening/weekend programs available. *Faculty:* 14 full-time (8 women), 5 part-time/adjunct (4 women). *Students:* 120 full-time (96 women), 592 part-time (485 women); includes 145 minority (123 African Americans, 7 Asian Americans or Pacific Islanders, 15 Hispanic Americans), 7 international. Average age 34. 526 applicants, 41% accepted, 144 enrolled. In 2006, 324 degrees awarded. *Degree requirements:* For master's, thesis or alternative, comprehensive exam (for some programs). *Entrance requirements:* For master's, GRE General Test or MAT, minimum GPA of 2.75. Additional exam requirements/recommendations for international students: Required—TOEFL (minimum score 525 paper-based; 197 computer-based), IELTS (minimum score 6). *Application deadline.* For fall admission, 7/15 priority date for domestic students. Applications are processed on a rolling basis. Application fee: $30. *Financial support:* In 2006–07, 12 research assistantships with full tuition reimbursements (averaging $3,480 per year) were awarded; tuition waivers (partial) and unspecified assistantships also available. *Faculty research:* Early literacy, professional development in reading, reading recovery, dual language, induction programs. Total annual research expenditures: $6.2 million. *Unit head:* Dr. Clifford T. Bennett, Chairperson, 216-523-7105, Fax: 216-687-5379, E-mail: c.t.bennett@csuohio.edu.

Cleveland State University, College of Graduate Studies, College of Liberal Arts and Social Sciences, Department of Art, Cleveland, OH 44115. Offers art education (M Ed); art history (MA). *Students:* 1 (woman) full-time, 4 part-time (all women). In 2006, 2 degrees awarded. *Unit head:* Howie Smith, Chair, 212-523-7546, E-mail: art.chair@csuohio.edu.

College of Mount St. Joseph, Graduate Education Program, Cincinnati, OH 45233-1670. Offers adolescent young adult education (MA); art (MA); inclusive early childhood education (MA); instructional leadership (MA); middle childhood education (MA); multicultural special education (MA); music (MA); reading (MA). *Accreditation:* Teacher Education Accreditation Council. Part-time and evening/weekend programs available. Postbaccalaureate distance learning degree programs offered (minimal on-campus study). *Faculty:* 22 full-time (14 women), 11 part-time/adjunct (6 women). *Students:* 68 full-time (54 women), 115 part-time (96 women); includes 21 minority (16 African Americans, 2 American Indian/Alaska Native, 1 Asian American or Pacific Islander, 2 Hispanic Americans). Average age 34. 91 applicants, 98% accepted, 62 enrolled. In 2006, 61 degrees awarded. *Degree requirements:* For master's, research project. *Entrance requirements:* For master's, GRE, PRAXIS II in teaching content area (math or science), 2 letters of recommendation, interview, resumé, prerequisite courses in communications, behavioral sciences and mathematics. Additional exam requirements/recommendations for international students: Required—TOEFL (minimum score 560 paper-based; 220 computer-based). *Application deadline:* Applications are processed on a rolling basis. Application fee: $50. Electronic applications accepted. *Expenses:* Contact institution. *Financial support:* In 2006–07, 3 students received support. Career-related internships or fieldwork and scholarships/grants available. Support available to part-time students. Financial award application deadline: 6/1; financial award applicants required to submit FAFSA. *Faculty research:* Foreign and second language learning problems/reading disabilities/hyperlexia, multicultural/bilingual special education, alternative educator licensure, science education, pedagogical content knowledge. *Unit head:* Dr. Mifrando Obach, Chair, 513-244-3263, Fax: 513-244-4867, E-mail: mifrando_obach@mail.msj.edu. *Application contact:* Marilyn Hoskins, Assistant Director of Admissions for Graduate Recruitment, 513-244-4723, Fax: 513-244-4629, E-mail: marilyn_hoskins@mail.msg.edu.

The College of New Rochelle, Graduate School, Division of Art and Communication Studies, Program in Art Education, New Rochelle, NY 10805-2308. Offers MA. Part-time and evening/weekend programs available. *Faculty:* 1 (woman) full-time, 6 part-time/adjunct (all women). *Students:* 11 full-time (all women), 20 part-time (18 women); includes 1 minority (African American) Average age 32. In 2006, 19 degrees awarded. *Degree requirements:* For master's, thesis, registration. *Entrance requirements:* For master's, interview, minimum GPA of 3.0 in field, 2.7 overall, portfolio, 36 credits of course work in studio art. *Application deadline:* For fall admission, 8/1 priority date for domestic students. Applications are processed on a rolling basis. Application fee: $35. *Expenses:* Tuition: Part-time $575 per credit. Required fees: $90 per term. *Financial support:* Career-related internships or fieldwork, scholarships/grants, tuition waivers (partial), and unspecified assistantships available. Support available to part-time students. *Faculty research:* Developmental stages in art, assessment and evaluation, curriculum development, multicultural education, art museum education. *Unit head:* Dr. John Patton, Head, Division of Art and Communication Studies, 914-654-5208, Fax: 914-654-5593.

The College of Saint Rose, Graduate Studies, School of Arts and Humanities, Program in Art Education, Albany, NY 12203-1419. Offers MS Ed, Certificate. *Accreditation:* NASAD; NCATE. Part-time and evening/weekend programs available. *Degree requirements:* For master's, final project. *Entrance requirements:* For master's, minimum undergraduate GPA of 3.0, art portfolio, undergraduate art degree; for Certificate, minimum undergraduate GPA of 3.0, slide portfolio. Additional exam requirements/recommendations for international students: Required—TOEFL (minimum score 550 paper-based; 213 computer-based). Electronic applications accepted.

The Colorado College, Department of Education, Program in Secondary Education, Colorado Springs, CO 80903-3294. Offers art teaching (MAT); English teaching (MAT); foreign language teaching (MAT); mathematics teaching (MAT); music teaching (MAT); science teaching (MAT); social studies teaching (MAT). *Faculty:* 2 full-time (1 woman), 10 part-time/adjunct (7 women). *Students:* 18 full-time (12 women); includes 2 minority (1 African American, 1 Asian American or Pacific Islander). Average age 27. 30 applicants, 90% accepted, 18 enrolled. In 2006, 16 degrees awarded. *Degree requirements:* For master's, thesis, internship. *Entrance requirements:* For master's, PRAXIS II or PLACE. *Application deadline:* For fall admission, 2/1 for domestic and international students. Application fee: $50. *Expenses:* Tuition: Full-time $23,567. One-time fee: $1,485 full-time. *Financial support:* In 2006–07, 15 teaching assistantships (averaging $16,000 per year) were awarded; career-related internships or fieldwork, institutionally sponsored loans, health care benefits, and tuition waivers (partial) also available. Financial award application deadline: 2/15; financial award applicants required to submit FAFSA. *Unit head:* Mike Taber, Director, 719-389-6026, Fax: 719-389-6473, E-mail: pveronesi@coloradocollege.edu. *Application contact:* Marsha E. Unruh, Director of Education Career Services, 719-389-6472, Fax: 719-389-6473, E-mail: munruh@coloradocollege.edu.

Columbus State University, Graduate Studies, College of Arts and Letters, Program in Art Education, Columbus, GA 31907-5645. Offers M Ed. *Accreditation:* NASAD; NCATE. Part-time and evening/weekend programs available. *Faculty:* 1 full-time (0 women). *Students:* 4 full-time (all women), 4 part-time (2 women); includes 1 minority (African American) Average age 36. 6 applicants, 33% accepted, 2 enrolled. In 2006, 1 degree awarded. *Degree requirements:* For master's, exhibit. *Entrance requirements:* For master's, GRE General Test, minimum GPA of 2.75. Additional exam requirements/recommendations for international students: Required—TOEFL (minimum score 550 paper-based; 213 computer-based). *Application deadline:* For fall admission, 5/1 priority date for domestic students, 5/1 for international students; for spring admission, 11/1 for domestic and international students. Applications are processed on a rolling basis. Application fee: $25. Electronic applications accepted. *Expenses:* Tuition, state resident: part-time $127 per semester hour. Tuition, nonresident: part-time $508 per semester hour. Required fees: $264 per semester. Tuition and fees vary according to course load. *Financial support:* In 2006–07, 4 students received support; research assistantships, career-related internships or fieldwork, Federal Work-Study, institutionally sponsored loans, scholarships/grants, tuition waivers (partial), and unspecified assistantships available. Support available to part-time students. Financial award application deadline: 5/1; financial award applicants required to submit FAFSA. *Unit head:* Prof. Mara Scrupe, Acting Chair, 706-507-8300, E-mail: scrupe_mara@colstate.edu. *Application contact:* Katie Thornton, Graduate Admissions Specialist, 706-568-2035, Fax: 706-568-2462, E-mail: thornton_katie@colstate.edu.

Concordia University, School of Graduate Studies, Faculty of Fine Arts, Department of Art Education, Montréal, QC H3G 1M8, Canada. Offers art education (MA, PhD), including art in education (MA). *Students:* 28 full-time (23 women), 24 part-time (22 women). 40 applicants, 70% accepted, 18 enrolled. In 2006, 13 master's, 2 doctorates awarded. *Degree requirements:* For master's, thesis (for some programs), practicum; for doctorate, thesis/dissertation, comprehensive exam. *Entrance requirements:* For master's, teaching experience; for doctorate, teaching or related professional experience. *Application deadline:* For fall admission, 1/15 for domestic students. Application fee: $50. *Financial support:* Fellowships available. Financial award application deadline: 2/1. *Faculty research:* Vernacular culture, museum education, psychotic art, adults and families. *Unit head:* Dr. Richard Lachapelle, Chair, 514-848-2424 Ext. 4783, Fax: 514-848-8627. *Application contact:* Paul Langdon, Director, 514-848-2424 Ext. 4645, Fax: 514-848-8627.

Concordia University Wisconsin, Graduate Programs, Department of Education, Mequon, WI 53097-2402. Offers art education (MS Ed); curriculum and instruction (MS Ed); early childhood (MS Ed); educational administration (MS Ed); environmental education (MS Ed); family studies (MS Ed); reading (MS Ed); school counseling (MS Ed); special education (MS Ed). Part-time and evening/weekend programs available. Postbaccalaureate distance learning degree programs offered (minimal on-campus study). *Faculty:* 30. *Students:* 396 (284 women). In 2006, 51 degrees awarded. *Degree requirements:* For master's, thesis or alternative, comprehensive exam. *Entrance requirements:* For master's, minimum GPA of 3.0, teaching license. Additional exam requirements/recommendations for international students: Required—TOEFL. Application fee: $35. *Financial support:* Career-related internships or fieldwork and tuition waivers (partial) available. Financial award application deadline: 8/1. *Faculty research:* Motivation, developmental learning, learning styles. *Unit head:* Dr. James Juergensen, Director, 262-243-4214, E-mail: james.juergensen@cuw.edu. *Application contact:* Graduate Admissions, 262-243-4248, Fax: 262-243-4428.

Converse College, School of Education and Graduate Studies, Spartanburg, SC 29302-0006. Offers art education (M Ed); early childhood education (MAT); education (Ed S), including administration and supervision, curriculum and instruction, marriage and family therapy; elementary education (M Ed, MAT); gifted education (M Ed); leadership (M Ed); liberal arts (MLA), including English (M Ed, MAT, MLA), history, political science; secondary education (M Ed, MAT), including biology (MAT), chemistry (MAT), English (M Ed, MAT, MLA), mathematics, natural sciences (M Ed), social sciences; special education (M Ed, MAT), including learning disabilities (MAT), mental disabilities (MAT), special education (M Ed). Part-time and evening/weekend programs available. *Faculty:* 13 full-time (8 women), 23 part-time/adjunct (16 women). *Students:* 156 full-time (136 women), 1,069 part-time (847 women). Average age 35. 115 applicants, 88% accepted. In 2006, 186 master's, 26 other advanced degrees awarded. *Entrance requirements:* For master's, PRAXIS II (M Ed), minimum GPA of 2.75; for Ed S, GRE or MAT, minimum GPA of 3.0. *Application deadline:* For fall admission, 8/1 for domestic and international students; for winter admission, 11/15 for domestic and international students; for spring admission, 1/15 for domestic and international students. Applications are processed on a rolling basis. Application fee: $40. Electronic applications accepted. *Expenses:* Tuition: Part-time $305 per credit hour. Required fees: $20 per term. *Financial support:* In 2006–07, 500 students received support; research assistantships, career-related internships or fieldwork and scholarships/grants available. Support available to part-time students. Financial award applicants required to submit FAFSA. *Faculty research:* Motivation, classroom management, predictors of success in classroom teaching, sex equity in public education, gifted research. Total annual research expenditures: $50,000. *Unit head:* Thomas M. Faulkenberry, Dean of the School of Education and Graduate Studies, 864-596-9082, Fax: 864-596-9221, E-mail: tom.faulkenberry@converse.edu.

Corcoran College of Art and Design, Graduate Programs, Washington, DC 20006-4804. Offers art education (MAT); history of decorative arts (MA); interior design (MA). *Accreditation:* NASAD. Part-time programs available. *Students:* 77 full-time (72 women), 48 part-time (44 women); includes 11 minority (7 African Americans, 2 Asian Americans or Pacific Islanders, 2 Hispanic Americans), 10 international. Average age 31. 103 applicants, 78% accepted, 49 enrolled. In 2006, 2 degrees awarded. *Entrance requirements:* Additional exam requirements/recommendations for international students: Required—TOEFL. *Application deadline:* For fall and spring admission, 3/15 priority date for domestic and international students. Applications are processed on a rolling basis. Application fee: $75. *Financial support:* In 2006–07, 10 fellowships (averaging $3,000 per year) were awarded; career-related internships or fieldwork and Federal Work-Study also available. Financial award applicants required to submit FAFSA.

Eastern Illinois University, Graduate School, College of Arts and Humanities, Department of Art, Charleston, IL 61920-3099. Offers art (MA); art education (MA). *Accreditation:* NASAD. *Faculty:* 18 full-time (7 women). *Students:* 11 applicants, 64% accepted. In 2006, 7 degrees awarded. *Degree requirements:* For master's, thesis or alternative, portfolio. *Application deadline:* For fall admission, 7/31 priority date for domestic students. Applications are processed on a rolling basis. Application fee: $30. *Expenses:* Tuition, state resident: part-time $169 per semester hour. Tuition, nonresident: part-time $508 per semester hour. Required fees: $60 per semester hour. *Financial support:* In 2006–07, research assistantships with tuition reimbursements (averaging $7,200 per year), 6 teaching assistantships with tuition reimbursements (averaging $7,200 per year) were awarded. *Unit head:* Glenn Hild, Chairperson, 217-581-3410. *Application contact:* Chris Kahler, Coordinator, 217-581-6259, E-mail: cbkahler@eiu.edu.

Eastern Kentucky University, The Graduate School, College of Education, Department of Curriculum and Instruction, Program in Secondary and Higher Education, Richmond, KY 40475-3102. Offers agricultural education (MA Ed); allied health sciences education (MA Ed); art education (MA Ed); biological sciences education (MA Ed); business education (MA Ed); chemistry education (MA Ed); earth science education (MA Ed); English education (MA Ed); general science education (MA Ed); geography education (MA Ed); history education (MA Ed); home economics education (MA Ed); industrial education (MA Ed); mathematical sciences education (MA Ed); physical education (MA Ed); physics education (MA Ed); political science education (MA Ed); psychology education (MA Ed); reading (MA Ed); school health education (MA Ed); sociology education (MA Ed). *Accreditation:* NCATE. Part-time programs available. *Students:* 16 full-time (8 women), 63 part-time (43 women); includes 5 minority (2 African Americans, 2 American Indian/Alaska Native, 1 Asian American or Pacific Islander). Average age 32. *Entrance requirements:* For master's, GRE General Test, minimum GPA of 2.5. Application fee: $30. *Expenses:* Tuition, state resident: full-time $5,610. Tuition, nonresident: full-time $15,910. *Financial support:* Research assistantships, teaching assistantships, Federal Work-Study available. Support available to part-time students. *Unit head:* Dr. Michael Martin, Chair, Department of Curriculum and Instruction, 859-622-2154, Fax: 859-622-2004.

Art Education

Eastern Michigan University, Graduate School, College of Arts and Sciences, Department of Art, Program in Art Education, Ypsilanti, MI 48197. Offers MA. *Accreditation:* NCATE. Part-time and evening/weekend programs available. Postbaccalaureate distance learning degree programs offered (minimal on-campus study). *Students:* Average age 29. In 2006, 10 degrees awarded. *Entrance requirements:* Additional exam requirements/recommendations for international students: Required—TOEFL. *Application deadline:* For fall admission, 5/15 priority date for domestic students, 5/1 priority date for international students; for winter admission, 10/15 priority date for domestic students, 10/1 priority date for international students; for spring admission, 3/15 priority date for domestic students, 3/1 priority date for international students. Applications are processed on a rolling basis. Application fee: $35. *Expenses:* Tuition, state resident: part-time $341 per credit hour. Tuition, nonresident: full-time $16,104; part-time $671 per credit hour. Required fees: $816; $34 per credit hour. $40 per term. One-time fee: $82 full-time. Tuition and fees vary according to course level, course load, degree level and reciprocity agreements. *Financial support:* Fellowships, research assistantships with full tuition reimbursements, teaching assistantships with full tuition reimbursements, career-related internships or fieldwork, Federal Work-Study, institutionally sponsored loans, scholarships/grants, and unspecified assistantships available. Support available to part-time students. Financial award applicants required to submit FAFSA. *Application contact:* Prof. Christopher Bocklage, Graduate Advisor, 734-487-1268, E-mail: christopher.bocklage@emich.edu.

East Tennessee State University, School of Graduate Studies, College of Arts and Sciences, Department of Art and Design, Johnson City, TN 37614. Offers art education (MA); art history (MA); studio art (MA, MFA). *Accreditation:* NASAD. *Degree requirements:* For master's, thesis, exhibit, oral exam (MFA). *Entrance requirements:* For master's, GRE General Test, portfolio (MFA), bachelor's degree in art, minimum GPA of 3.0. Additional exam requirements/recommendations for international students: Required—TOEFL (minimum score 550 paper-based; 213 computer-based). *Faculty research:* History of sculpture, art and senior citizens, encaustic paintings, digital media in art history.

Endicott College, Van Loan School of Graduate and Professional Studies, Program in Arts and Learning, Beverly, MA 01915-2096. Offers M Ed. Part-time and evening/weekend programs available. Postbaccalaureate distance learning degree programs offered (minimal on-campus study). *Faculty:* 12 part-time/adjunct (7 women). *Students:* Average age 35. 14 applicants, 100% accepted, 14 enrolled. In 2006, 7 degrees awarded. *Degree requirements:* For master's, portfolio, written integrative paper, major presentation. *Entrance requirements:* For master's, MAT or GRE. *Application deadline:* Applications are processed on a rolling basis. Application fee: $50. *Expenses:* Tuition: Part-time $279 per credit. Tuition and fees vary according to program. *Financial support:* Available to part-time students. *Faculty research:* Linkage of creative processes to effective teaching and learning. *Unit head:* Enid E. Larsen, Assistant Dean of Academic Programs, 978-232-2198, Fax: 978-232-3000, E-mail: elarsen@endicott.edu. *Application contact:* Enid E. Larsen, Assistant Dean of Academic Programs, 978-232-2198, Fax: 978-232-3000, E-mail: elarsen@endicott.edu.

Fitchburg State College, Division of Graduate and Continuing Education, Program in Arts Education, Fitchburg, MA 01420-2697. Offers arts education (M Ed); fine arts director (Certificate). *Accreditation:* NCATE. Part-time and evening/weekend programs available. *Students:* Average age 45. 3 applicants, 100% accepted, 2 enrolled. In 2006, 9 degrees awarded. *Entrance requirements:* For master's, GRE General Test or MAT, letters of recommendation, resumé. Additional exam requirements/recommendations for international students: Required—TOEFL (minimum score 550 paper-based; 213 computer-based; 79 iBT). *Application deadline:* Applications are processed on a rolling basis. Application fee: $25 ($50 for international students). *Expenses:* Tuition, state resident: part-time $150 per credit. Tuition, nonresident: part-time $150 per credit. Required fees: $90 per credit. *Financial support:* In 2006–07, research assistantships with partial tuition reimbursements (averaging $5,500 per year); Federal Work-Study, scholarships/grants, and unspecified assistantships also available. Support available to part-time students. Financial award application deadline: 3/1; financial award applicants required to submit FAFSA. *Unit head:* Dr. Harry Semerjian, Chair, 978-665-3279, Fax: 978-665-3658, E-mail: gce@fsc.edu. *Application contact:* Director of Admissions, 978-665-3144, Fax: 978-665-4540, E-mail: admissions@fsc.edu.

Florida Atlantic University, College of Education, Department of Teacher Education, Boca Raton, FL 33431-0991. Offers art teacher education (M Ed); curriculum and instruction (M Ed, Ed D, Ed S); educational psychology (MSF); elementary education (M Ed); foundations of education (M Ed); multicultural education (MSF); reading teacher education (M Ed). *Accreditation:* NCATE. Part-time and evening/weekend programs available. *Faculty:* 29 full-time (23 women), 75 part-time/adjunct (50 women). *Students:* 78 full-time (65 women), 176 part-time (159 women); includes 50 minority (20 African Americans, 1 American Indian/Alaska Native, 6 Asian Americans or Pacific Islanders, 23 Hispanic Americans), 1 international. Average age 35. 132 applicants, 64% accepted, 62 enrolled. In 2006, 95 master's, 2 doctorates awarded. *Degree requirements:* For master's, registration; for doctorate, thesis/dissertation, departmental qualifying exam, comprehensive exam, registration; for Ed S, departmental qualifying exam. *Entrance requirements:* For master's, GRE General Test, minimum GPA of 3.0 in last 2 years of undergraduate course work; for doctorate, GRE General Test, GRE Subject Test, minimum graduate GPA of 3.2, 3.0 in last 2 years of undergraduate course work; for Ed S, GRE General Test. Additional exam requirements/recommendations for international students: Required—TOEFL. *Application deadline:* Applications are processed on a rolling basis. Application fee: $30. *Expenses:* Tuition, area resident: Full-time $4,394. Tuition, nonresident: full-time $16,441. *Financial support:* In 2006–07, 4 research assistantships with partial tuition reimbursements (averaging $8,000 per year), 3 teaching assistantships with partial tuition reimbursements (averaging $8,000 per year) were awarded; fellowships with partial tuition reimbursements, career-related internships or fieldwork, scholarships/grants, and unspecified assistantships also available. *Faculty research:* Technology, teaching English to speakers of other languages, math teaching, electronic portfolio assessment, global perspectives through social studies. *Unit head:* Dr. Penelope Fritzer, Chairperson, 561-297-3584.

Florida Atlantic University, Dorothy F. Schmidt College of Arts and Letters, Department of Art, Boca Raton, FL 33431-0991. Offers art education (MAT); ceramics (MFA); painting (MFA). *Faculty:* 16 full-time (6 women). *Students:* 21 full-time (13 women), 5 part-time (1 woman); includes 5 minority (all Hispanic Americans), 2 international. Average age 34. 34 applicants, 32% accepted, 10 enrolled. In 2006, 12 degrees awarded. *Degree requirements:* For master's, one foreign language. *Entrance requirements:* For master's, GRE General Test, minimum GPA of 3.0 during last 60 hours of course work, slide portfolio. *Application deadline:* For spring admission, 3/1 for domestic students. Application fee: $30. Electronic applications accepted. *Expenses:* Tuition, area resident: Full-time $4,394. Tuition, nonresident: full-time $16,441. *Financial support:* In 2006–07, 5 students received support, including 2 research assistantships with full tuition reimbursements available (averaging $7,200 per year), 3 teaching assistantships with full tuition reimbursements available (averaging $7,200 per year); career-related internships or fieldwork, Federal Work-Study, and institutionally sponsored loans also available. Financial award applicants required to submit FAFSA. *Faculty research:* Painting, ceramics (traditional and non-traditional), installation, video and interactive sculpture. *Unit head:* Michaela Angela Di Cosola, Chair, 561-297-3871, Fax: 561-297-3078, E-mail: mdicosol@fau.edu. *Application contact:* James A Novak, Associate Professor/Graduate Coordinator/Advisor, 561-297-2430, Fax: 561-297-3078, E-mail: jnovak@fau.edu.

Florida International University, College of Education, Department of Curriculum and Instruction, Program in Art Education, Miami, FL 33199. Offers MAT, MS, Ed D. *Accreditation:* NCATE. Part-time and evening/weekend programs available. *Faculty:* 2 full-time (0 women). *Students:* 2 full-time (1 woman), 22 part-time (17 women); includes 17 minority (1 African American, 16 Hispanic Americans). 7 applicants, 43% accepted, 3 enrolled. In 2006, 10 degrees awarded. *Entrance requirements:* Additional exam requirements/recommendations for international students: Required—TOEFL (minimum score 550 paper-based; 213 computer-based; 80 iBT), IELTS (minimum score 6). *Application deadline:* For fall admission, 6/1 priority date for domestic students, 4/1 for international students; for winter admission, 10/1 priority date for domestic students, 9/1 for international students; for spring admission, 3/1 priority date for domestic students, 2/1 for international students. Applications are processed on a rolling basis. Application fee: $25. Electronic applications accepted. *Expenses:* Tuition, state resident: part-time $249 per credit hour. Tuition, nonresident: part-time $753 per credit hour. Tuition and fees vary according to program. *Faculty research:* Elementary art, macramé, stained glass works, watercolors. *Unit head:* Dr. David Change, Professor, 305-348-3393, E-mail: changd@fiu.edu. *Application contact:* Marisa Salazar, Student Recruiter, 305-348-3002, Fax: 305-348-3227, E-mail: marisa.salazar@fiu.edu.

Florida State University, Graduate Studies, College of Visual Arts, Theatre and Dance, Department of Art Education, Tallahassee, FL 32306. Offers MA, MS, Ed D, PhD, Ed S. *Accreditation:* NASAD (one or more programs are accredited). Part-time programs available. *Faculty:* 7 full-time (5 women), 4 part-time/adjunct (all women). *Students:* 69 full-time (61 women), 19 part-time (12 women); includes 33 minority (13 African Americans, 1 American Indian/Alaska Native, 16 Asian Americans or Pacific Islanders, 3 Hispanic Americans). Average age 33. 56 applicants, 75% accepted, 27 enrolled. In 2006, 14 master's, 11 doctorates awarded. *Degree requirements:* For master's, thesis (for some programs); for doctorate, thesis/dissertation. *Entrance requirements:* For master's, GRE General Test or minimum GPA of 3.0 in last 2 years; for doctorate, GRE General Test or minimum GPA of 3.5. Additional exam requirements/recommendations for international students: Required—TOEFL (minimum score 550 paper-based; 213 computer-based; 80 iBT). *Application deadline:* For fall admission, 4/17 priority date for domestic and international students; for spring admission, 10/17 priority date for domestic and international students. Applications are processed on a rolling basis. Application fee: $30. Electronic applications accepted. *Expenses:* Tuition, state resident: full-time $5,822; part-time $243 per credit hour. Tuition, nonresident: full-time $20,976; part-time $874 per credit hour. Tuition and fees vary according to program. *Financial support:* In 2006–07, 19 research assistantships with full tuition reimbursements (averaging $3,200 per year), 8 teaching assistantships with full tuition reimbursements (averaging $3,200 per year) were awarded; fellowships, career-related internships or fieldwork, Federal Work-Study, and scholarships/grants also available. Financial award applicants required to submit FAFSA. *Faculty research:* Teaching and learning in art, museum education, art therapy, arts administration, discipline-based art education. Total annual research expenditures: $110,000. *Unit head:* Dr. Marcia L. Rosal, Chairman, 850-664-2926, Fax: 850-644-5067, E-mail: mrosal@mailer.fsu.edu. *Application contact:* Susan Messersmith, Program Assistant, 850-644-5473, Fax: 850-644-5067, E-mail: smessersmith@fsu.edu.

Georgia Southern University, Jack N. Averitt College of Graduate Studies, College of Education, Department of Teaching and Learning, Program in Art Education, Statesboro, GA 30460. Offers M Ed, MAT. *Accreditation:* NASAD (one or more programs are accredited); NCATE (one or more programs are accredited). Part-time and evening/weekend programs available. *Students:* 1 (woman) full-time, 5 part-time (all women); includes 1 minority (African American) Average age 32. 1 applicant, 100% accepted, 1 enrolled. In 2006, 1 degree awarded. *Degree requirements:* For master's, exit assessment. *Entrance requirements:* For master's, GRE General Test or MAT, minimum GPA of 2.5. Additional exam requirements/recommendations for international students: Required—TOEFL (minimum score 550 paper-based; 213 computer-based; 80 iBT). *Application deadline:* For fall admission, 3/1 priority date for domestic students, 3/1 for international students; for spring admission, 10/1 priority date for domestic students, 10/1 for international students. Applications are processed on a rolling basis. Application fee: $50. Electronic applications accepted. *Financial support:* In 2006–07, 2 students received support, including research assistantships with partial tuition reimbursements available (averaging $5,500 per year), teaching assistantships with partial tuition reimbursements available (averaging $5,500 per year); career-related internships or fieldwork, Federal Work-Study, scholarships/grants, tuition waivers (partial), and unspecified assistantships also available. Support available to part-time students. Financial award application deadline: 4/15; financial award applicants required to submit FAFSA. *Unit head:* Patricia Carter, Coordinator, 912-681-5172, Fax: 912-681-9926, E-mail: pwcarter@georgiasouthern.edu. *Application contact:* 912-681-5384, Fax: 912-681-0740, E-mail: gradadmissions@georgiasouthern.edu.

Georgia State University, College of Arts and Sciences, Ernest G. Welch School of Art and Design, Program in Art Education, Atlanta, GA 30303-3083. Offers MA Ed. *Accreditation:* NASAD. Part-time programs available. *Faculty:* 3 full-time (all women). *Students:* 4 full-time (all women), 30 part-time (27 women); includes 5 minority (3 African Americans, 2 Asian Americans or Pacific Islanders). Average age 30. 6 applicants, 50% accepted, 2 enrolled. In 2006, 5 degrees awarded. *Degree requirements:* For master's, thesis. *Entrance requirements:* For master's, GRE General Test or MAT, portfolio. Additional exam requirements/recommendations for international students: Required—TOEFL (minimum score 550 paper-based; 213 computer-based). *Application deadline:* For fall admission, 1/6 for domestic and international students; for spring admission, 9/15 for domestic and international students. Application fee: $50. Electronic applications accepted. *Financial support:* In 2006–07, 4 students received support, including 4 research assistantships with full tuition reimbursements available (averaging $4,800 per year); career-related internships or fieldwork, Federal Work-Study, institutionally sponsored loans, scholarships/grants, health care benefits, and unspecified assistantships also available. Financial award application deadline: 1/6; financial award applicants required to submit FAFSA. *Faculty research:* Art–maturing adults, computer instruction in art, intercultural thematic art education. *Application contact:* Prof. Nancy Floyd, Director of Graduate Studies, 404-651-0488, Fax: 404-651-1779, E-mail: artgrad@gsu.edu.

Georgia State University, College of Education, Department of Middle-Secondary Education and Instructional Technology, Programs in Secondary Education, Atlanta, GA 30303-3083. Offers art education (Ed S); English education (M Ed, Ed S); mathematics education (M Ed, PhD, Ed S); music education (PhD); science education (M Ed, PhD, Ed S); social studies education (M Ed, PhD, Ed S). *Accreditation:* NASM (one or more programs are accredited); NCATE. Part-time and evening/weekend programs available. *Students:* 103 full-time (71 women), 140 part-time (92 women); includes 53 minority (48 African Americans, 2 Asian Americans or Pacific Islanders, 3 Hispanic Americans), 12 international. Average age 35. 36 applicants, 86% accepted. In 2006, 87 master's, 12 doctorates, 12 other advanced degrees awarded. *Degree requirements:* For master's, comprehensive exam; for doctorate, thesis/dissertation, comprehensive exam; for Ed S, project/exam. *Entrance requirements:* For master's, GRE General Test, minimum GPA of 2.5; for doctorate, GRE General Test or MAT, minimum GPA of 3.3; for Ed S, GRE General Test or MAT, minimum graduate GPA of 3.25. Application fee: $25. *Financial support:* Career-related internships or fieldwork, Federal Work-Study, and institutionally sponsored loans available. *Faculty research:* Women and science, problem solving in mathematics, dialects, economic education. *Unit head:* Dr. Ruth Hough, Acting Chair, Department of Middle-Secondary Education and Instructional Technology, 404-651-2510.

Harding University, College of Education, Searcy, AR 72149-0001. Offers advanced studies in teaching and learning (M Ed); art (MSE); behavioral science (MSE); Bible and religion (MSE); counseling (MS, Ed S); early childhood education (M Ed); early childhood special education (M Ed, MSE); education (MSE); educational leadership (M Ed, Ed S); elementary education (M Ed); English (MSE); family and consumer science (MSE); French (MSE); history/social science (MSE); kinesiology (MSE); math (MSE); physical science (MSE); reading (M Ed); secondary education (M Ed); Spanish (MSE); special education licensure (M Ed); teaching (MAT). *Accreditation:* NCATE. Part-time programs available. *Faculty:* 8 full-time (2 women), 45 part-time/adjunct (30 women). *Students:* 153 full-time (123 women), 469 part-time (341 women); includes 72 minority (63 African Americans, 4 American Indian/Alaska Native, 1 Asian American or Pacific Islander, 4 Hispanic Americans), 9 international. Average age 35. 175 applicants, 90% accepted, 147 enrolled. In 2006, 241 degrees awarded. *Degree requirements:* For master's, portfolio(s), thesis optional; for Ed S, portfolio, specialist project. *Entrance requirements:* For master's, GRE, MAT, PRAXIS; for Ed S, MAT or GRE. Additional exam requirements/recommendations for international students: Required—TOEFL (minimum score 550 paper-based). *Application deadline:* For fall admission, 8/1 for domestic and international students; for spring admission, 1/1 for domestic and international students. Applications are processed on a rolling basis. Application fee: $35. *Expenses:* Tuition: Part-time $455 per semester hour. Required fees: $20 per semester hour. Tuition and fees vary according to course load. *Financial support:* Scholarships/grants and unspecified assistantships available. Support available to part-time students. *Faculty research:* Reading, comprehension, school violence, educational technology, behavior, college choice, differentiated instruction, brain based teaching. *Unit head:* Pat Bashaw, Chair, 501-279-4183, Fax: 501-279-4051, E-mail: pbashaw@harding.edu.

Harvard University, Graduate School of Education, Master's Programs in Education, Cambridge, MA 02138. Offers arts in education (Ed M); education policy and management (Ed M); higher education (Ed M); human development and psychology (Ed M); international education policy (Ed M); language and literacy (Ed M); learning and teaching (Ed M); mid-career mathematics and science (teaching certificate) (Ed M); mind brain and education (Ed M); risk and prevention (Ed M); school leadership (Ed M); special studies (Ed M); teaching and curriculum (teaching certificate) (Ed M); technology innovation and education (Ed M). Part-time programs available. *Faculty:* 58 full-time (25 women), 40 part-time/adjunct (22 women). *Students:* 540 full-time (412 women), 90 part-time (70 women); includes 137 minority (49 African Americans, 2 American Indian/Alaska Native, 61 Asian Americans or Pacific Islanders, 25 Hispanic Americans), 70 international. Average age 29. 1,211 applicants, 61% accepted, 585 enrolled. In 2006, 591 degrees awarded. *Entrance requirements:* For master's, GRE General Test, 3 letters of recommendation, official transcripts, statement of purpose. Additional exam requirements/recommendations for international students: Required—TOEFL (minimum score 600 paper-based; 250 computer-based; 100 iBT), TWE (minimum score 5). *Application deadline:* For fall admission, 1/2 for domestic and international students. Application fee: $85. Electronic applications accepted. *Expenses: Contact institution. Financial support:* In 2006–07, 392 students received support, including 23 fellowships (averaging $15,870 per year); career-related internships or fieldwork, Federal Work-Study, institutionally sponsored loans, scholarships/grants, health care benefits, tuition waivers (full and partial), and unspecified assistantships also available. Support available to part-time students. Financial award application deadline: 2/2; financial award applicants required to submit FAFSA. *Faculty research:* Learning and development; educational leadership and organizations; educational policy analysis. Total annual research expenditures: $14.8 million. *Unit head:* Dr. James Stiles, Associate Dean for Degree Programs. *Application contact:* Information Contact, 617-495-3414, Fax: 617-496-3577, E-mail: gseadmissions@harvard.edu.

Hofstra University, School of Education and Allied Human Services, Department of Curriculum and Teaching, Program in Fine Arts Education, Hempstead, NY 11549. Offers MA, MS Ed. *Students:* 20 full-time (16 women), 12 part-time (7 women); includes 1 minority (Asian American or Pacific Islander) Average age 28. 18 applicants, 78% accepted, 10 enrolled. In 2006, 19 degrees awarded. *Degree requirements:* For master's, thesis. *Entrance requirements:* For master's, 2 letters of recommendation, portfolio, teacher certification (MA), essay. Additional exam requirements/recommendations for international students: Required—TOEFL (minimum score 550 paper-based; 213 computer-based). *Application deadline:* Applications are processed on a rolling basis. Application fee: $60. Electronic applications accepted. *Expenses:* Tuition: Full-time $13,320; part-time $740 per credit. Required fees: $930; $155 per term. *Financial support:* In 2006–07, 22 students received support, including 2 fellowships with tuition reimbursements available (averaging $2,667 per year); research assistantships with full and partial tuition reimbursements available, scholarships/grants, tuition waivers (full and partial), and unspecified assistantships also available. Financial award applicants required to submit FAFSA. *Faculty research:* Artistic teacher model, interdisciplinary art education. *Unit head:* Dr. Susan G. Zwirn, Director, 516-463-4976, Fax: 516-463-6196, E-mail: catsgz@hofstra.edu. *Application contact:* Carol Drummer, Dean of Graduate Admissions, 516-463-4876, Fax: 516-463-4664, E-mail: gradstudent@hofstra.edu.

Indiana University Bloomington, School of Education, Department of Curriculum and Instruction, Bloomington, IN 47405-7000. Offers art education (MS, Ed D, PhD); curriculum studies (Ed D, PhD); elementary education (MS, Ed D, PhD, Ed S); mathematics education (MS, Ed D, PhD); science education (MS, Ed D, PhD); secondary education (MS, Ed D, PhD); social studies education (MS, PhD); special education (MS, Ed D, PhD, Ed S). PhD offered through the University Graduate School. *Accreditation:* NCATE. Part-time and evening/weekend programs available. *Students:* 39 full-time (28 women), 82 part-time (54 women); includes 15 minority (5 African Americans, 1 American Indian/Alaska Native, 6 Asian Americans or Pacific Islanders, 3 Hispanic Americans), 33 international. Average age 37. In 2006, 1 degree awarded. Terminal master's awarded for partial completion of doctoral program. *Degree requirements:* For doctorate, thesis/dissertation; for Ed S, comprehensive exam or project. *Entrance requirements:* For master's, doctorate, and Ed S, GRE General Test. *Application deadline:* For fall admission, 6/1 priority date for domestic students, 3/1 for international students; for winter admission, 11/1 priority date for domestic students; for spring admission, 9/1 for international students. Applications are processed on a rolling basis. Application fee: $50 ($60 for international students). Electronic applications accepted. *Expenses:* Tuition, state resident: full-time $5,791; part-time $241 per credit hour. Tuition, nonresident: full-time $16,866; part-time $703 per credit hour. *Financial support:* Fellowships with full and partial tuition reimbursements, research assistantships with full and partial tuition reimbursements, teaching assistantships with full and partial tuition reimbursements, career-related internships or fieldwork, Federal Work-Study, institutionally sponsored loans, and tuition waivers (partial) available. Support available to part-time students. *Unit head:* Cary Buzzelli, Chairperson, 812-856-8100. *Application contact:* Bobbie Partenheimer, Admissions Services Coordinator, 812-856-8127, Fax: 812-856-8333, E-mail: partenhe@indiana.edu.

Indiana University–Purdue University Indianapolis, Herron School of Art and Design, Indianapolis, IN 46202-2896. Offers art education (MAE); furniture design (MFA); printmaking (MFA); sculpture (MFA); visual communication (MFA). *Accreditation:* NASAD. Part-time and evening/weekend programs available. *Faculty:* 2 full-time (both women). *Students:* 2 full-time (both women), 11 part-time (7 women); includes 1 minority (Hispanic American) Average age 37. In 2006, 1 degree awarded. *Entrance requirements:* For master's, portfolio, 44 hours of course work in art history and studio art. *Application deadline:* For fall admission, 6/1 priority date for domestic students, 3/15 priority date for international students; for spring admission, 11/1 priority date for domestic students, 10/15 priority date for international students. Applications are processed on a rolling basis. Application fee: $50 ($60 for international students). Electronic applications accepted. *Expenses:* Tuition, state resident: full-time $5,437; part-time $227 per credit hour. Tuition, nonresident: full-time $15,694; part-time $654 per credit hour. Required fees: $620. Tuition and fees vary according to course load, campus/location and program. *Financial support:* Career-related internships or fieldwork, Federal Work-Study, institutionally sponsored loans, scholarships/grants, and tuition waivers (partial) available. Support available to part-time students. Total annual research expenditures: $6,097. *Unit head:* Valerie Eickmeier, Dean, 317-278-9470, Fax: 317-278-9471, E-mail: herron@iupui.edu. *Application contact:* Herron Student Services Office, 317-378-9400, E-mail: herrart@iupui.edu.

Iowa State University of Science and Technology, Graduate College, College of Design, Department of Art and Design, Ames, IA 50011. Offers art and design (MA); art education (MA); graphic design (MFA); integrated visual arts (MFA); interior design (MFA). Part-time programs available. *Faculty:* 35 full-time. *Students:* 36 full-time (22 women), 10 part-time (7 women); includes 4 minority (1 African American, 3 Asian Americans or Pacific Islanders), 13 international. 35 applicants, 60% accepted, 12 enrolled. In 2006, 20 degrees awarded. *Degree requirements:* For master's, thesis (for some programs). *Entrance requirements:* For master's, portfolio, resumé. Additional exam requirements/recommendations for international students: Required—TOEFL (paper-based 550; computer-based 213) or IELTS (score 6.5). *Application deadline:* For fall admission, 5/1 priority date for domestic and international students. Applications are processed on a rolling basis. Application fee: $30 ($70 for international students). Electronic applications accepted. *Expenses:* Tuition, state resident: full-time $5,936; part-time $330 per credit. Tuition, nonresident: full-time $16,350; part-time $330 per credit. *Financial support:* In 2006–07, 18 research assistantships with full and partial tuition reimbursements (averaging $17,760 per year), 6 teaching assistantships with full and partial tuition reimbursements (averaging $17,760 per year) were awarded; career-related internships or fieldwork, Federal Work-Study, institutionally sponsored loans, and tuition waivers (partial) also available. Support available to part-time students. Financial award application deadline: 2/15; financial award applicants required to submit FAFSA. *Faculty research:* Computer applications, fire safety, human factors in design, art and design education, fine arts, craft design. *Unit head:* Roger Baer, Chair, 515-294-6724, Fax: 515-294-2725, E-mail: artdn@iastate.edu.

James Madison University, College of Graduate and Outreach Programs, College of Visual and Performing Arts, School of Art and Art History, Harrisonburg, VA 22807. Offers art education (MA); art history (MA); ceramics (MFA); drawing/painting (MFA); metal/jewelry (MFA); photography (MFA); printmaking (MFA); sculpture (MFA); studio art (MA); weaving/fibers (MFA). *Accreditation:* NASAD. Part-time programs available. *Faculty:* 6 full-time (3 women), 2 part-time/adjunct (1 woman). *Students:* 8 full-time (2 women), 8 part-time (6 women); includes 1 minority (Asian American or Pacific Islander) Average age 27. In 2006, 7 degrees awarded. *Degree requirements:* For master's, thesis (for some programs). *Entrance requirements:* For master's, GRE General Test, language exam in French or German, portfolio, 3 letters of recommendation, research paper. Additional exam requirements/recommendations for international students: Required—TOEFL. *Application deadline:* For fall admission, 2/15 priority date for domestic students; for spring admission, 10/15 priority date for domestic students. Applications are processed on a rolling basis. Application fee: $55. Electronic applications accepted. *Expenses:* Tuition, state resident: full-time $6,336; part-time $264 per credit hour. Tuition, nonresident: full-time $17,832; part-time $743 per credit hour. *Financial support:* In 2006–07, 7 students received support, including 3 teaching assistantships with full tuition reimbursements available (averaging $8,167 per year); Federal Work-Study and unspecified assistantships also available. Financial award application deadline: 3/1; financial award applicants required to submit FAFSA. *Unit head:* Leslie M. Bellavance, Academic Unit Head, 540-568-6216.

Kean University, School of Visual and Performing Arts, Program in Fine Arts Education, Union, NJ 07083. Offers certification (MA); studio/research (MA); supervision (MA). *Accreditation:* NASAD. Part-time and evening/weekend programs available. *Faculty:* 16 full-time (5 women). *Students:* 20 full-time (16 women), 32 part-time (21 women); includes 11 minority (3 African Americans, 2 Asian Americans or Pacific Islanders, 6 Hispanic Americans). Average age 35. 20 applicants, 85% accepted, 11 enrolled. In 2006, 16 degrees awarded. *Degree requirements:* For master's, thesis or alternative, PRAXIS, exhibition, 3 years of teaching experience. *Entrance requirements:* For master's, GRE General Test or MAT, portfolio, minimum 2.75 GPA (fine arts education), undergraduate prerequisites, interview, 2 letters of recommendation. *Application deadline:* For fall admission, 5/1 for domestic students; for spring admission, 11/1 for domestic students. Application fee: $60 ($150 for international students). *Expenses:* Tuition, state resident: full-time $8,856; part-time $369 per credit. Tuition, nonresident: full-time $11,256; part-time $469 per credit. *Financial support:* In 2006–07, 2 research assistantships with full tuition reimbursements (averaging $3,217 per year) were awarded; unspecified assistantships also available. *Unit head:* Prof. J. King E. Black, Program Coordinator, 908-737-4411, E-mail: jblack@kean.edu. *Application contact:* Joanne Morris, Director of Graduate Admissions, 908-737-3355, Fax: 908-737-3354, E-mail: grad-adm@kean.edu.

Kent State University, College of Fine and Professional Arts, School of Art, Kent, OH 44242-0001. Offers art education (MA); art history (MA); crafts (MA, MFA), including ceramics (MA), glass, jewelry/metals, textiles/art; fine arts (MA, MFA), including drawing/painting, printmaking, sculpture. *Accreditation:* NASAD (one or more programs are accredited). *Degree requirements:* For master's, one foreign language, thesis. *Entrance requirements:* For master's, undergraduate degree in proposed area of study (for fine arts and crafts programs); minimum overall GPA of 2.75 (3.0 for art major); 3 letters of recommendation; portfolio (15-20 slides for MA, 20-25 for MFA), brief autobiographical statement (MFA). Additional exam requirements/recommendations for international students: Required—TOEFL. Electronic applications accepted.

Kutztown University of Pennsylvania, College of Graduate Studies and Extended Learning, College of Visual and Performing Arts, Program in Art Education, Kutztown, PA 19530-0730. Offers M Ed, Certificate. *Accreditation:* NASAD; NCATE. Part-time programs available. *Faculty:* 7 full-time (4 women), 2 part-time/adjunct (both women). *Students:* 26 full-time (19 women), 36 part-time (33 women). Average age 29. 34 applicants, 79% accepted, 16 enrolled. In 2006, 13 degrees awarded. *Degree requirements:* For master's, thesis optional. *Entrance requirements:* For master's, GRE, teacher certification. Additional exam requirements/recommendations for international students: Required—TOEFL. *Application deadline:* Applications are processed on a rolling basis. Application fee: $35. Electronic applications accepted. *Expenses:* Tuition, state resident: full-time $6,048; part-time $336 per credit. Tuition, nonresident: full-time $9,678; part-time $538 per credit. *Financial support:* In 2006–07, research assistantships with full tuition reimbursements (averaging $5,000 per year); career-related internships or fieldwork, Federal Work-Study, and unspecified assistantships also available. Financial award application deadline: 3/15; financial award applicants required to submit FAFSA. *Faculty research:* Teaching of art history, child development in art, aesthetics and criticism curriculum, multi-cultural education, assessment in art. *Unit head:* Dr. John White, Chairperson, 610-683-4520, E-mail: white@kutztown.edu.

LaGrange College, Graduate Programs, Department of Education, LaGrange, GA 30240-2999. Offers art education (MAT); curriculum and instruction (M Ed); music education (MAT); secondary education (MAT). Part-time and evening/weekend programs available. *Degree requirements:* For master's, comprehensive exam. *Entrance requirements:* For master's, GRE, MAT, or NTE, minimum GPA of 2.5. Additional exam requirements/recommendations for international students: Required—TOEFL (minimum score 550 paper-based).

Lesley University, Graduate School of Arts and Social Sciences, Cambridge, MA 02138-2790. Offers clinical mental health counseling (MA), including expressive therapies counseling, holistic counseling, school and community counseling; counseling psychology (MA, CAGS), including professional counseling (MA), school counseling (MA); creative arts in learning (CAGS); creative writing (MFA); ecological teaching and learning (MS); environmental education (MS); expressive therapies (MA, PhD, CAGS), including art (MA), dance (MA), expressive therapies, music (MA); independent studies (CAGS); independent study (MA); intercultural relations (MA, CAGS); interdisciplinary studies (MA), including individualized studies, integrative holistic health, women's studies; visual arts (MFA). Part-time and evening/weekend programs available. Postbaccalaureate distance learning degree programs offered (minimal on-campus study). *Faculty:* 49 full-time (41 women), 185 part-time/adjunct (137 women). *Students:* 721 full-time (648 women), 2,074 part-time (1,897 women); includes 182 minority (104 African Americans, 12 American Indian/Alaska Native, 14 Asian Americans or Pacific Islanders, 52 Hispanic Americans), 66 international. Average age 37. 1,005 applicants, 92% accepted, 717 enrolled. In 2006, 1,179 master's, 2 doctorates, 1 other advanced degree awarded. *Degree requirements:* For master's, internship, practicum, thesis (expressive therapies); for doctorate and CAGS, thesis/dissertation, arts apprenticeship, field placement; for CAGS, thesis, internship (counseling psychology, expressive therapies). *Entrance requirements:* For master's, MAT (counseling psychology), interview, writing samples, art portfolio; for doctorate, GRE or MAT; for CAGS, interview, master's degree. Additional exam requirements/recommendations for international students: Required—TOEFL (minimum score 550 paper-based; 213 computer-based; 80 iBT). *Application deadline:* Applications are processed on a rolling basis. Application fee: $50. Electronic applications accepted. *Financial support:* In 2006–07, 64 students received support, including research assistantships (averaging $3,400 per year), 1 teaching assistantship (averaging $7,298 per year); career-related internships or fieldwork, Federal Work-Study, scholarships/grants, and unspecified assistantships also available. Support available to part-time students. Financial award application deadline: 4/15; financial award applicants required to submit FAFSA. *Faculty research:* Psychotherapy and culture; psychotherapy and psychological trauma; women's issues in art, teaching and psychotherapy; community based art, psycho-spiritual inquiry. *Unit head:* Dr. Julia Halevy, Dean, 617-349-8317, Fax: 617-349-8366, E-mail: jhalevy@lesley.edu. *Application contact:* Christina Murray, Senior Assistant Director, On-Campus Admissions, 617-349-8827, Fax: 617-349-8313, E-mail: cmurray3@lesley.edu.

Art Education

Long Island University, C.W. Post Campus, School of Education, Department of Curriculum and Instruction, Brookville, NY 11548-1300. Offers adolescence education (MS); adolescence education: biology (MS); adolescence education: earth science (MS); adolescence education: English (MS); adolescence education: mathematics (MS); adolescence education: social studies (MS); adolescence education: Spanish (MS); art education (MS); bilingual education (MS); childhood education (MS); early childhood education (MS); middle childhood education (MS); music education (MS); teaching English to speakers of other languages (MS). Part-time and evening/weekend programs available. *Degree requirements:* For master's, comprehensive exam or thesis, student teaching. *Entrance requirements:* For master's, minimum GPA of 2.75 in major, 2.5 overall. Electronic applications accepted. *Faculty research:* Ethics and education, teaching strategies.

Long Island University, C.W. Post Campus, School of Visual and Performing Arts, Department of Art, Brookville, NY 11548-1300. Offers art (MA); art education (MS); clinical art therapy (MA); fine art and design (MFA). Part-time and evening/weekend programs available. *Degree requirements:* For master's, thesis. Electronic applications accepted. *Faculty research:* Painting, sculpture, installation, computers, video.

Manhattanville College, Graduate Programs, School of Education, Program in Visual Arts Education, Purchase, NY 10577-2132. Offers MAT. *Students:* 32 (28 women); includes 4 minority (1 African American, 1 American Indian/Alaska Native, 2 Hispanic Americans). In 2006, 17 degrees awarded. Application fee: $55. *Unit head:* Alyce Ware Poli, Director of Admissions, 914-323-5941, Fax: 914-694-1732, E-mail: edschool@mville.edu. *Application contact:* Alyce Ware Poli, Director of Admissions, 914-323-5142, Fax: 914-694-1732, E-mail: edschool@mville.edu.

Mansfield University of Pennsylvania, Graduate Studies, Department of Art, Mansfield, PA 16933. Offers art education (M Ed). Part-time programs available. *Faculty:* 2 full-time (1 woman), 2 part-time/adjunct (1 woman). *Students:* 7 full-time (6 women), 13 part-time (10 women). Average age 35. 10 applicants, 50% accepted, 5 enrolled. In 2006, 5 degrees awarded. *Degree requirements:* For master's, thesis optional. *Entrance requirements:* For master's, minimum GPA of 3.0, portfolio. Additional exam requirements/recommendations for international students: Required—TOEFL (minimum score 550 paper-based; 230 computer-based). *Application deadline:* For fall admission, 8/1 priority date for domestic students, 6/1 for international students. Applications are processed on a rolling basis. Application fee: $25. Electronic applications accepted. *Expenses:* Tuition, state resident: part-time $336 per credit. Tuition, nonresident: part-time $538 per credit. Tuition and fees vary according to course load and reciprocity agreements. *Financial support:* Unspecified assistantships available. Support available to part-time students. Financial award application deadline: 5/1; financial award applicants required to submit FAFSA. *Unit head:* Dr. Lee Wright, Chairperson, 570-662-4787, E-mail: lwright@mnsfld.edu. *Application contact:* Judi Brayer, Assistant Director of Enrollment Management/Graduate Admissions, 570-662-4818, Fax: 570-662-4121, E-mail: jbrayer@mansfield.edu.

Maryland Institute College of Art, Graduate Studies, Program in Art Education, Baltimore, MD 21217. Offers MA, MAT. MA program offered in summer only. *Accreditation:* NASAD. Part-time programs available. *Faculty:* 8 full-time (7 women), 7 part-time/adjunct (all women). *Students:* 31 full-time (28 women), 18 part-time (15 women); includes 5 minority (2 African Americans, 2 Asian Americans or Pacific Islanders, 1 Hispanic American). Average age 28. In 2006, 25 degrees awarded. *Degree requirements:* For master's, thesis, seminar. *Entrance requirements:* For master's, portfolio, professional certification (BFA), 40 studio credits, 6 credits in art history. Additional exam requirements/recommendations for international students: Required—TOEFL (minimum score 550 paper-based; 213 computer-based). *Application deadline:* For fall admission, 2/15 for domestic and international students; for spring admission, 10/1 for domestic and international students. Application fee: $50. *Expenses:* Tuition: Full-time $27,840; part-time $1,160 per credit. Required fees: $830; $415 per term. *Financial support:* In 2006–07, 38 students received support, including 1 fellowship (averaging $13,920 per year), 6 teaching assistantships (averaging $1,800 per year); career-related internships or fieldwork and scholarships/grants also available. Financial award application deadline: 3/1; financial award applicants required to submit FAFSA. *Unit head:* Dr. Karen Carroll, Director, 410-225-2297, Fax: 410-225-2257. *Application contact:* Scott G. Kelly, Associate Dean of Graduate Admission, 410-225-2256, Fax: 410-225-2408, E-mail: graduate@mica.edu.

Maryville University of Saint Louis, School of Education, St. Louis, MO 63141-7299. Offers art education (MA Ed); early childhood education (MA Ed); education (Ed D); elementary education (MA Ed); elementary education/English (MA Ed); environmental education (MA Ed); gifted education (MA Ed); middle grades education (MA Ed); reading specialist (MA Ed); secondary education (MA Ed), including educational leadership, secondary teaching and inquiry. *Accreditation:* NASAD; NCATE. Part-time and evening/weekend programs available. *Students:* 17 full-time (14 women), 168 part-time (129 women); includes 20 African Americans, 2 Asian Americans or Pacific Islanders, 1 Hispanic American, 2 international. Average age 37. 39 applicants, 95% accepted, 24 enrolled. In 2006, 37 degrees awarded. *Degree requirements:* For master's, thesis, project. *Entrance requirements:* For master's and doctorate, minimum GPA of 3.0, 3 professional recommendations. Additional exam requirements/recommendations for international students: Required—TOEFL (minimum score 550 paper-based). *Application deadline:* Applications are processed on a rolling basis. Application fee: $35 ($50 for international students). Electronic applications accepted. *Expenses:* Tuition: Full-time $17,800; part-time $555 per credit. Required fees: $55 per semester. Tuition and fees vary according to degree level and program. *Financial support:* Career-related internships or fieldwork, Federal Work-Study, tuition waivers (partial), and professional educator discounts available. Financial award application deadline: 7/31; financial award applicants required to submit FAFSA. *Faculty research:* Collaboration with public schools, preservice program development, mathematics, diversity, literacy. *Unit head:* Dr. Sam Hausfather, Dean, 314-529-9466, Fax: 314-529-9921, E-mail: shausfather@maryville.edu. *Application contact:* Dr. Lillian Curtis, Graduate Admissions Coordinator, 314-529-9542, Fax: 314-529-9921, E-mail: teachered@maryville.edu.

Marywood University, Academic Affairs, Insalaco College of Creative Arts and Management, Art Department, Program in Art Education, Scranton, PA 18509-1598. Offers MA. *Accreditation:* NASAD; NCATE. Part-time and evening/weekend programs available. *Students:* 2 full-time (both women), 1 (woman) part-time. Average age 35. In 2006, 3 degrees awarded. *Degree requirements:* For master's, thesis or alternative, comprehensive exam. *Entrance requirements:* For master's, portfolio. Additional exam requirements/recommendations for international students: Required—TOEFL (minimum score 550 paper-based; 213 computer-based). *Application deadline:* For fall admission, 4/15 priority date for domestic and international students; for spring admission, 11/15 priority date for domestic and international students. Applications are processed on a rolling basis. Application fee: $30. Electronic applications accepted. *Expenses:* Tuition: Part-time $672 per credit. Tuition and fees vary according to degree level, campus/location and program. *Financial support:* Research assistantships with tuition reimbursements, scholarships/grants, tuition waivers (partial), and unspecified assistantships available. Support available to part-time students. Financial award application deadline: 2/15; financial award applicants required to submit FAFSA. *Faculty research:* Current trends in art education, color theories, research in Mariology. *Application contact:* Dr. Deborah M. Flynn, Coordinator of Graduate Advising (Enrollment Management), 570-348-6211, E-mail: flynn@ac.marywood.edu.

Massachusetts College of Art, Graduate Programs, Program in Art Education, Boston, MA 02115-5882. Offers MSAE. *Accreditation:* NASAD. Part-time programs available. *Faculty:* 3 full-time (1 woman), 4 part-time/adjunct (2 women). *Students:* 4 full-time (2 women), 30 part-time (23 women); includes 5 minority (2 African Americans, 3 Asian Americans or Pacific Islanders), 2 international. Average age 37. 20 applicants, 35% accepted, 7 enrolled. In 2006, 9 degrees awarded. *Degree requirements:* For master's, thesis (for some programs), comprehensive exam. *Entrance requirements:* For master's, portfolio, resumé, writing sample. *Application deadline:* For fall admission, 3/15 for domestic students; for spring admission, 11/1 for domestic students. Application fee: $75. *Expenses:* Tuition, nonresident: full-time $15,500; part-time $1,550 per unit. Required fees: $1,330. *Financial support:* In 2006–07, 5 research assistantships (averaging $1,000 per year), 1 teaching assistantship (averaging $1,000 per year) were awarded; career-related internships or fieldwork, Federal Work-Study, unspecified assistantships, and clerical/technical assistantships also available. Support available to part-time students. Financial award application deadline: 5/1. *Faculty research:* Museum education, history of visual arts education, teaching studio art K–12. *Unit head:* Maureen Kelly, Chairperson, 617-879-7525. *Application contact:* George Creamer, Director, 617-879-7163, Fax: 617-879-7171, E-mail: creamer@massart.edu.

Memphis College of Art, Graduate Programs, Program in Art Education, Memphis, TN 38104-2764. Offers MA, MAT. *Faculty:* 4 full-time (2 women), 1 (woman) part-time/adjunct. *Students:* Average age 28. 9 applicants, 89% accepted, 8 enrolled. *Degree requirements:* For master's, thesis. *Entrance requirements:* For master's, portfolio, resumé, interview. Additional exam requirements/recommendations for international students: Required—TOEFL (minimum score 525 paper-based; 195 computer-based). *Application deadline:* For fall admission, 3/1 priority date for domestic and international students; for spring admission, 11/1 priority date for domestic and international students. Application fee: $50. *Expenses:* Tuition: Full-time $21,000; part-time $875 per hour. Required fees: $560. Tuition and fees vary according to program. *Financial support:* In 2006–07, 2 students received support, including research assistantships (averaging $1,000 per year); career-related internships or fieldwork, Federal Work-Study, scholarships/grants, tuition waivers (partial), and unspecified assistantships also available. *Unit head:* Dr. Cathy Wilson, Director, 901-272-5100, Fax: 901-272-5134, E-mail: cwilson@mca.edu. *Application contact:* Annette James Moore, Director of Admissions, 800-727-1088, Fax: 901-272-5158, E-mail: info@mca.edu.

Miami University, Graduate School, School of Fine Arts, Department of Art, Program in Art Education, Oxford, OH 45056. Offers MA. *Accreditation:* NASAD; NCATE. *Degree requirements:* For master's, thesis or alternative, exhibit, speech, article, or oral exam. *Entrance requirements:* For master's, minimum undergraduate GPA of 3.0 during previous 2 years or 2.75 overall. Additional exam requirements/recommendations for international students: Required—TOEFL, TWE.

Millersville University of Pennsylvania, Graduate School, School of Humanities and Social Sciences, Department of Art, Millersville, PA 17551-0302. Offers art education (M Ed). *Accreditation:* NASAD; NCATE. Part-time and evening/weekend programs available. *Faculty:* 15 full-time (9 women), 4 part-time/adjunct (1 woman). *Students:* 1 full-time (0 women), 11 part-time (8 women). Average age 34. 2 applicants, 50% accepted, 1 enrolled. In 2006, 2 degrees awarded. *Degree requirements:* For master's, thesis, departmental exam. *Entrance requirements:* For master's, GRE or MAT, minimum GPA of 3.25 in art, 2.75 overall; portfolio; PA instructional certification in art education; interview, letters of recommendation. *Application deadline:* For fall admission, 3/1 priority date for domestic students. Applications are processed on a rolling basis. Application fee: $35. *Expenses:* Tuition, state resident: full-time $6,048; part-time $336 per credit. Tuition, nonresident: full-time $9,678; part-time $538 per credit. Required fees: $1,244. Tuition and fees vary according to course load. *Financial support:* In 2006–07, 1 student received support, including 1 research assistantship with full tuition reimbursement available (averaging $4,250 per year); Federal Work-Study, institutionally sponsored loans, and unspecified assistantships also available. Support available to part-time students. Financial award application deadline: 3/15; financial award applicants required to submit FAFSA. *Unit head:* Prof. Jeri L. Robinson, Chair, 717-871-2194, Fax: 717-871-2004, E-mail: jeri.robinson@millersville.edu. *Application contact:* Dr. Victor S. DeSantis, Dean of Graduate Studies, 717-872-3099, Fax: 717-871-2022, E-mail: victor.desantis@millersville.edu.

Minnesota State University Mankato, College of Graduate Studies, College of Arts and Humanities, Department of Art, Mankato, MN 56001. Offers art education (MS); studio art (MA); teaching art (MAT, MT). *Accreditation:* NASAD (one or more programs are accredited). Part-time programs available. *Students:* 6 full-time (2 women), 14 part-time (8 women). Average age 31. In 2006, 4 degrees awarded. *Degree requirements:* For master's, one foreign language, thesis or alternative, comprehensive exam. *Entrance requirements:* For master's, minimum GPA of 3.0 during previous 2 years, portfolio (MA). Additional exam requirements/recommendations for international students: Required—TOEFL. *Application deadline:* For fall admission, 7/1 priority date for domestic students; for spring admission, 11/1 for domestic students. Applications are processed on a rolling basis. Application fee: $40. Electronic applications accepted. *Financial support:* Research assistantships, teaching assistantships with full tuition reimbursements, unspecified assistantships available. Financial award application deadline: 3/15; financial award applicants required to submit FAFSA. *Faculty research:* Photographic documentation. *Unit head:* James Johnson, Chairperson, 507-389-6412. *Application contact:* 507-389-2321, E-mail: grad@mnsu.edu.

Mississippi College, Graduate School, School of Education, Department of Teacher Education and Leadership, Clinton, MS 39058. Offers art (M Ed); biological science (M Ed); business education (M Ed); computer science (M Ed); dyslexia therapy (M Ed); educational leadership (M Ed, Ed S); elementary education (M Ed, Ed S); English (M Ed); higher education administration (MS); mathematics (M Ed); secondary education (M Ed); social studies (history) (M Ed); teaching arts (M Ed). Part-time programs available. *Faculty:* 9 full-time (5 women), 14 part-time/adjunct (10 women). *Students:* 52 full-time (36 women), 286 part-time (247 women); includes 173 minority (171 African Americans, 1 American Indian/Alaska Native, 1 Hispanic American), 1 international. Average age 32. In 2006, 131 degrees awarded. *Degree requirements:* For master's, thesis optional. *Entrance requirements:* For master's, NTE. Additional exam requirements/recommendations for international students: Recommended—IELTS. *Application deadline:* Applications are processed on a rolling basis. Application fee: $25. Electronic applications accepted. *Expenses:* Tuition: Full-time $7,290; part-time $405 per hour. Required fees: $150 per term. Tuition and fees vary according to campus/location and program. *Financial support:* Teaching assistantships, career-related internships or fieldwork, Federal Work-Study, scholarships/grants, and unspecified assistantships available. Support available to part-time students. Financial award applicants required to submit FAFSA. *Unit head:* Dr. Tom Williams, Chair, 601-925-3844, E-mail: twilliams@mc.edu.

Missouri State University, Graduate College, College of Arts and Letters, Department of Art and Design, Springfield, MO 65804-0094. Offers secondary education (MS Ed), including art. *Faculty:* 7 full-time (3 women). *Students:* 2 full-time (both women), 3 part-time (2 women). Average age 49. In 2006, 2 degrees awarded. *Entrance requirements:* For master's, minimum GPA of 3.0, 9-12 certification. Additional exam requirements/recommendations for international students: Required—TOEFL (minimum score 550 paper-based; 213 computer-based; 79 iBT). *Application deadline:* For fall admission, 7/20 priority date for domestic students; for spring admission, 12/20 priority date for domestic students. Application fee: $35. *Expenses:* Tuition, state resident: full-time $3,582; part-time $199 per credit hour. Tuition, nonresident: full-time $6,984; part-time $199 per credit hour. Required fees: $548. Full-time tuition and fees vary according to course level, course load, program and reciprocity agreements. *Financial support:* Applicants required to submit FAFSA. *Unit head:* Dr. Andrew Cohen, Head, 407-836-6055, E-mail: artanddesign@missouristate.edu. *Application contact:* Judith Fowler, Graduate Program Director, E-mail: judyfowler@missouristate.edu.

Montclair State University, The Graduate School, College of Education and Human Services, Department of Curriculum and Teaching, Montclair, NJ 07043-1624. Offers education (M Ed); educational technology (M Ed); school library media specialist (Certificate); teaching (MAT, Certificate), including art (MAT), biological science (MAT), early childhood education (P-3) (MAT), earth science (MAT), elementary education (K-8) (MAT), English (MAT), French (MAT), health and physical education (MAT), health education (MAT), home economics (MAT), mathematics (MAT), music (MAT), physical education (MAT), physical science (MAT), social studies (MAT), Spanish (MAT), teacher of ESL (MAT), teacher of students with disabilities (MAT). Part-time and evening/weekend programs available. *Faculty:* 16 full-time (12 women), 13 part-time/adjunct (8 women). *Students:* 147 full-time (113 women), 230 part-time (188 women); includes 58 minority (33 African Americans, 1 American Indian/Alaska Native, 12 Asian Americans or Pacific Islanders, 12 Hispanic Americans), 4 international. Average age 33. 118 applicants, 38% accepted, 37 enrolled. In 2006, 166 master's, 11 other advanced degrees awarded. *Degree requirements:* For master's, field experience. *Entrance requirements:* For master's, PRAXIS II, minimum GPA of 2.67, 2 letters of recommendation. Additional exam requirements/recommendations for international students: Required—TOEFL (minimum score 83 computer-based). *Application deadline:* For fall admission, 2/15 for domestic and international students; for spring admission, 9/15 for domestic and international students. Applications are processed on a rolling basis. Application fee: $60. Electronic applications accepted. *Expenses:* Tuition, state resident: part-time $450 per credit. Tuition, nonresident: part-time $682 per credit. Tuition and fees vary according to degree level and program. *Financial support:* In 2006–07, 7 research assistantships with full tuition reimbursements (averaging $7,000 per year) were awarded; Federal Work-Study, scholarships/grants, and unspecified assistantships also available. Support available to part-time students. Financial award application deadline: 3/1; financial award applicants required to submit FAFSA. *Unit head:* Dr. Deborah Eldridge, Chairperson, 973-655-5187.

Montclair State University, The Graduate School, School of the Arts, Department of Art and Design, Montclair, NJ 07043-1624. Offers art education (MA); art history (MA); studio arts (MA, MFA). *Accreditation:* NASAD (one or more programs are accredited). Part-time and evening/weekend programs available. *Faculty:* 24 full-time (10 women), 46 part-time/adjunct (30 women). *Students:* 35 full-time (23 women), 38 part-time (31 women); includes 6 minority (4 Asian Americans or Pacific Islanders, 2 Hispanic Americans), 2 international. 59 applicants, 47% accepted, 15 enrolled. In 2006, 17 degrees awarded. *Degree requirements:* For master's, project. *Entrance requirements:* For master's, GRE General Test or MAT (MA), portfolio, undergraduate degree in fine arts or equivalent, 2 letters of recommendation, teaching certificate (art education). Additional exam requirements/recommendations for international students: Required—TOEFL (minimum score 83 computer-based). *Application deadline:* For fall admission, 2/1 for domestic and international students. Applications are processed on a rolling basis. Application fee: $60. Electronic applications accepted. *Expenses:* Tuition, state resident: part-time $450 per credit. Tuition, nonresident: part-time $682 per credit. Tuition and fees vary according to degree level and program. *Financial support:* In 2006–07, 3 research assistantships with full tuition reimbursements (averaging $7,000 per year) were awarded; Federal Work-Study, scholarships/grants, and unspecified assistantships also available. Support available to part-time students. Financial award application deadline: 3/1; financial award applicants required to submit FAFSA. *Unit head:* Daryl Moore, Chairperson, 973-655-7295, E-mail: moored@mail.montclair.edu. *Application contact:* Dr. Dorothy Heard, Adviser, 973-655-7295, E-mail: heardd@mail.montclair.edu.

Morehead State University, Graduate Programs, Caudill College of Humanities, Department of Art, Morehead, KY 40351. Offers art education (MA); studio art (MA). Part-time and evening/weekend programs available. *Faculty:* 12 full-time (4 women), 3 part-time/adjunct (all women). *Students:* 7 full-time (4 women), 5 part-time (3 women). Average age 32. In 2006, 4 degrees awarded. *Degree requirements:* For master's, thesis (for some programs), oral exam, comprehensive exam, registration. *Entrance requirements:* For master's, GRE General Test, minimum GPA of 3.0 in major, 2.5 overall; portfolio; bachelor's degree in art. Additional exam requirements/recommendations for international students: Required—TOEFL (minimum score 500 paper-based; 173 computer-based). *Application deadline:* For fall admission, 8/1 priority date for domestic and international students; for spring admission, 12/1 priority date for domestic and international students. Applications are processed on a rolling basis. Application fee: $0 ($55 for international students). Electronic applications accepted. *Financial support:* In 2006–07, 6 teaching assistantships (averaging $6,000 per year) were awarded; career-related internships or fieldwork, Federal Work-Study, and unspecified assistantships also available. Financial award application deadline: 4/1; financial award applicants required to submit FAFSA. *Faculty research:* Computer art, painting, drawing, ceramics, photography. *Unit head:* Robert Franzini, Chair, 606-783-2193, Fax: 606-783-5048, E-mail: r.franzi@moreheadstate.edu. *Application contact:* Michelle Barber, Graduate Admissions Counselor, 606-783-2039, Fax: 606-783-5061, E-mail: m.barber@moreheadstate.edu.

Nazareth College of Rochester, Graduate Studies, Department of Art, Program in Art Education, Rochester, NY 14618-3790. Offers MS Ed. *Accreditation:* Teacher Education Accreditation Council. Part-time and evening/weekend programs available. *Faculty:* 3 full-time (2 women), 1 (woman) part-time/adjunct. *Students:* 25 full-time (19 women), 37 part-time (28 women). Average age 30. 22 applicants, 77% accepted, 13 enrolled. In 2006, 30 degrees awarded. *Entrance requirements:* For master's, minimum GPA of 3.0, portfolio review. *Application deadline:* For fall admission, 4/1 for domestic students; for spring admission, 10/1 for domestic students. Application fee: $40. *Financial support:* Research assistantships with partial tuition reimbursements available. Financial award application deadline: 3/1; financial award applicants required to submit FAFSA. *Unit head:* Dr. Karen Trickey, Director, 585-389-2537, Fax: 585-586-2452, E-mail: kbtricke3@naz.edu. *Application contact:* Judith G. Baker, Director, Graduate Admissions, 585-389-2050, Fax: 585-389-2817, E-mail: gradstudies@naz.edu.

New Jersey City University, Graduate and Continuing Education, College of Arts and Sciences, Department of Art, Jersey City, NJ 07305-1597. Offers art (MFA); art education (MA); studio art (MFA). *Accreditation:* NASAD. Evening/weekend programs available. *Faculty:* 11. *Students:* 3 full-time (all women), 5 part-time (4 women); includes 1 minority (Hispanic American) Average age 36. In 2006, 2 degrees awarded. *Degree requirements:* For master's, thesis or alternative, exhibit. *Entrance requirements:* For master's, GRE General Test or MAT, portfolio. Additional exam requirements/recommendations for international students: Required—TOEFL. *Application deadline:* For fall admission, 8/1 priority date for domestic students; for spring admission, 12/1 for domestic students. Applications are processed on a rolling basis. Application fee: $0. *Expenses:* Tuition, state resident: full-time $7,038; part-time $391 per credit. Tuition, nonresident: full-time $12,510; part-time $695 per credit. Required fees: $65 per credit. *Financial support:* Unspecified assistantships available. *Unit head:* Dr. Herbert Rosenberg, Chairperson, 201-200-2367.

New York University, Steinhardt School of Culture, Education and Human Development, Department of Art and Art Professions, Program in Art Education, New York, NY 10012-1019. Offers MA, PhD. *Accreditation:* Teacher Education Accreditation Council. Part-time and evening/weekend programs available. *Faculty:* 2 full-time (1 woman). *Students:* 24 full-time (23 women), 32 part-time (28 women); includes 10 minority (3 African Americans, 1 American Indian/Alaska Native, 5 Asian Americans or Pacific Islanders, 1 Hispanic American), 8 international. 48 applicants, 83% accepted, 17 enrolled. In 2006, 20 master's, 3 doctorates awarded. Terminal master's awarded for partial completion of doctoral program. *Degree requirements:* For master's, thesis (for some programs); for doctorate, thesis/dissertation. *Entrance requirements:* For master's, portfolio; for doctorate, GRE General Test, interview. Additional exam requirements/recommendations for international students: Required—TOEFL. *Application deadline:* For fall admission, 12/15 priority date for domestic and international students; for spring admission, 11/1 for domestic and international students. Applications are processed on a rolling basis. Application fee: $50. *Expenses:* Tuition: Part-time $1,080 per unit. Required fees: $56 per unit. $329 per term. Tuition and fees vary according to program. *Financial support:* Fellowships with full and partial tuition reimbursements, career-related internships or fieldwork, Federal Work-Study, institutionally sponsored loans, and tuition waivers (partial) available. Support available to part-time students. Financial award application deadline: 2/1; financial award applicants required to submit FAFSA. *Faculty research:* Multicultural aesthetic inquiry, urban art education, feminism, equity and social justice. *Unit head:* Dr. Dipti Desai, Director, 212-998-5700, Fax: 212-995-4320, E-mail: dd25@nyu.edu. *Application contact:* 212-998-5030, Fax: 212-995-4328, E-mail: steinhardt.gradadmissions@nyu.edu.

North Carolina Agricultural and Technical State University, Graduate School, College of Arts and Sciences, Department of Visual and Theatre Arts, Greensboro, NC 27411. Offers art education (MS). *Accreditation:* NCATE. Part-time and evening/weekend programs available. *Degree requirements:* For master's, thesis or alternative, qualifying exam, comprehensive exam. *Entrance requirements:* For master's, GRE General Test, minimum GPA of 2.6.

North Georgia College & State University, Graduate Studies, Program in Teacher Education, Dahlonega, GA 30597. Offers early childhood education (M Ed); educational leadership (Ed S); middle grades education (M Ed); secondary education (M Ed), including art education, biology education, chemistry education, English education, history education, mathematics education, physical education, science education; special education (M Ed), including interrelated special education, learning disabilities. *Accreditation:* NCATE. Part-time and evening/weekend programs available. Postbaccalaureate distance learning degree programs offered (minimal on-campus study). *Faculty:* 35 full-time (18 women), 9 part-time/adjunct (6 women). *Students:* 260. Average age 32. 120 applicants, 63% accepted. In 2006, 134 degrees awarded. *Degree requirements:* For master's, thesis optional. *Entrance requirements:* For master's, GRE General Test or MAT, minimum GPA of 2.75; for Ed S, GRE General Test or MAT, 3 years of teaching experience, master's degree, minimum graduate GPA of 3.25. *Application deadline:* For fall admission, 7/1 priority date for domestic students; for spring admission, 12/10 priority date for domestic students. Applications are processed on a rolling basis. Application fee: $25. Electronic applications accepted. *Expenses:* Tuition, state resident: full-time $3,044; part-time $127 per credit hour. Tuition, nonresident: full-time $12,172; part-time $508 per credit hour. Required fees: $892; $458 per semester. *Financial support:* Teaching assistantships, career-related internships or fieldwork and scholarships/grants available. Support available to part-time students. Financial award application deadline: 5/1. *Faculty research:* Computers and teachers' attitudes, rural versus urban teacher attitudes, teacher leadership roles, minority recruitment in teaching force. *Unit head:* Dr. Bob Michael, Dean, School of Education, 706-864-1998, Fax: 706-867-2850, E-mail: bmichael@ngcsu.edu. *Application contact:* Dr. Donna A. Gessell, Director of Graduate Studies and External Programs, 706-864-1528, Fax: 706-867-2795, E-mail: dgessell@ngcsu.edu.

Nova Southeastern University, Fischler School of Education and Human Services, Graduate Teacher Education Program, Fort Lauderdale, FL 33314-7796. Offers athletic administration (MS); cognitive and behavioral disabilities (MS); computer science education (Ed S); computer science education (K-12) (MS); curriculum and teaching (Ed S); curriculum, instruction and technology (MS); curriculum, instruction, management and administration (Ed S); early childhood special education (MS); early literacy and reading (Ed S); early literacy education (MS); education technology (MS); educational leadership (administration K–12) (MS, Ed S); educational media (Ed S); educational media (K-12) (MS); elementary education (MS, Ed S), including ESOL endorsement (MS); English (MS, Ed S); exceptional student education (MS), including ESOL endorsement; gifted education (MS, Ed S); interdisciplinary arts education (MS); management and administration of educational programs (MS); mathematics (MS, Ed S); multicultural early intervention (MS); pre-kindergarten/primary (MS); preschool education (MS); reading (MS, Ed S); science (MS, Ed S); secondary education (MS); social studies (MS, Ed S); Spanish language (MS); teaching and learning (MA, MS), including curriculum and instruction (MA), elementary mathematics (MA), elementary reading (MA), K-12 technology integration (MA); teaching English to speakers of other languages (MS, Ed S); technology management and administration (Ed S); urban studies education (MS); varying exceptionalities (Ed S). Part-time and evening/weekend programs available. Postbaccalaureate distance learning degree programs offered. *Faculty:* 131 full-time (78 women), 548 part-time/adjunct (342 women). *Students:* 1,418 full-time (1,139 women), 3,464 part-time (2,877 women); includes 2,462 minority (1,732 African Americans, 13 American Indian/Alaska Native, 44 Asian Americans or Pacific Islanders, 673 Hispanic Americans), 77 international. Average age 38. 1,771 applicants, 80% accepted, 1419 enrolled. In 2006, 2,078 master's, 425 other advanced degrees awarded. *Degree requirements:* For master's and Ed S, thesis, practicum, internship. *Entrance requirements:* For master's, MAT, GRE, CLAST, CBEST, PRAXIS I, GKT, minimum GPA of 2.5; for Ed S, MAT or GRE, master's degree, teaching certificate, minimum GPA of 3.0. Additional exam requirements/recommendations for international students: Recommended—TOEFL (minimum score 550 paper-based; 213 computer-based), IELTS (minimum score 6). *Application deadline:* For fall admission, 8/11 priority date for domestic and international students; for winter admission, 12/28 priority date for domestic and international students; for spring admission, 4/22 priority date for domestic and international students. Applications are processed on a rolling basis. Application fee: $50. Electronic applications accepted. *Financial support:* Federal Work-Study available. Support available to part-time students. Financial award application deadline: 1/7. *Faculty research:* School effectiveness, critical thinking, leadership skills acquisition, child education, multicultural education. *Unit head:* Dr. Meline Kevorkian, Associate Dean of Master's and Educational Programs, 954-262-8500, Fax: 954-262-3606, E-mail: melinek@nova.edu. *Application contact:* Jennifer Quiñones Nottingham, Dean of Student Affairs, 800-986-3223 Ext. 8624, Fax: 954-262-3911, E-mail: jlquinon@nova.edu.

The Ohio State University, Graduate School, College of the Arts, Department of Art Education, Columbus, OH 43210. Offers art education (MA, PhD); arts policy and administration (MA). *Accreditation:* NASAD; NCATE. *Faculty:* 20. *Students:* 74 full-time (58 women), 80 part-time (63 women); includes 13 minority (7 African Americans, 3 American Indian/Alaska Native, 2 Asian Americans or Pacific Islanders, 1 Hispanic American), 25 international. Average age 34. 67 applicants, 91% accepted, 9 enrolled. In 2006, 17 master's, 4 doctorates awarded. *Degree requirements:* For master's and doctorate, thesis/dissertation. *Entrance requirements:* For master's and doctorate, GRE General Test. Additional exam requirements/recommendations for international students: Recommended—TOEFL (minimum score 600 paper-based; 250 computer-based). *Application deadline:* For fall admission, 8/15 priority date for domestic students, 7/1 priority date for international students; for winter admission, 12/1 priority date for domestic students, 11/1 priority date for international students; for spring admission, 3/1 priority date for domestic students, 2/1 priority date for international students. Applications are processed on a rolling basis. Application fee: $40 ($50 for international students). Electronic applications accepted. *Expenses:* Tuition, state resident: full-time $9,438. Tuition, nonresident: full-time $22,791. Tuition and fees vary according to course load, campus/location and program. *Financial support:* Fellowships, research assistantships, teaching assistantships, career-related internships or fieldwork, Federal Work-Study, institutionally sponsored loans, and unspecified assistantships available. Support available to part-time students. Financial award applicants required to submit FAFSA. *Unit head:* Candace Stout, Graduate Studies Committee Chair, 614-292-7183, Fax: 614-688-4483, E-mail: stout.127@osu.edu. *Application contact:* 614-292-9444, Fax: 614-688-3895, E-mail: domestic.grad@osu.edu.

Ohio University, Graduate Studies, College of Fine Arts, School of Art, Athens, OH 45701-2979. Offers art education (MA); art history (MA); art history/studio (MFA); ceramics (MFA); painting (MFA); photography (MFA); printmaking (MFA); sculpture (MFA). Part-time programs available. *Faculty:* 30 full-time (16 women), 7 part-time/adjunct (3 women). *Students:* 53 full-time (34 women), 11 part-time (7 women); includes 1 minority (Hispanic American), 7 international. Average age 27. 174 applicants, 22% accepted, 32 enrolled. In 2006, 18 degrees awarded. *Degree requirements:* For master's, thesis. *Entrance requirements:* For master's, portfolio. Additional exam requirements/recommendations for international students: Required—TOEFL. *Application deadline:* For fall admission, 2/1 for domestic students. Application fee: $45. *Financial support:* In 2006–07, 57 students received support, including 35 teaching assistantships with full and partial tuition reimbursements available (averaging $9,198 per year); career-related internships or fieldwork, Federal Work-Study, institutionally sponsored loans, scholarships/grants, tuition waivers (full), unspecified assistantships, and associateships also available. Financial award application deadline: 2/1. *Faculty research:* Vapor fired ceramics, video installation, art theory, digital photography, mixed and interdisciplinary media work. *Unit head:* Robert Lazuka, Director, 740-593-4290, Fax: 740-593-0457, E-mail: lazuka@ohio.edu. *Application contact:* Carolyn Cardenas, Associate Director and Chair, Graduate Programs, 740-597-1425, Fax: 740-593-0457, E-mail: cardenas@ohiou.edu.

Penn State University Park, Graduate School, College of Arts and Architecture, School of Visual Arts, State College, University Park, PA 16802-1503. Offers art (MFA), including ceramics, drawing/painting, photography, printmaking, sculpture; art education (M Ed, MS, PhD).

Art Education

Penn State University Park (continued)

Accreditation: NASAD. *Unit head:* Dr. Charles R. Garoian, Director, 814-865-0444, Fax: 814-865-1158, E-mail: crg2@psu.edu. *Application contact:* Dr. Charles R. Garoian, Director, 814-865-0444, Fax: 814-865-1158, E-mail: crg2@psu.edu.

Pittsburg State University, Graduate School, College of Arts and Sciences, Department of Art, Pittsburg, KS 66762-7512. Offers art education (MA); studio art (MA). *Students:* 5. *Degree requirements:* For master's, thesis or alternative. Application fee: $35 ($60 for international students). *Expenses:* Tuition, state resident: full-time $2,144; part-time $181 per credit hour. Tuition, nonresident: full-time $5,273; part-time $442 per credit hour. Tuition and fees vary according to course load and campus/location. *Financial support:* In 2006–07, teaching assistantships (averaging $5,000 per year); career-related internships or fieldwork, Federal Work-Study, and unspecified assistantships also available. *Unit head:* Dr. Larrie Moody, Chairperson, 620-235-4304. *Application contact:* Jamie Vanderbeck, Assistant Director, 620-235-4223, Fax: 620-235-4219, E-mail: jvanderb@pittstate.edu.

Pratt Institute, School of Art and Design, Program in Art and Design Education, Brooklyn, NY 11205-3899. Offers MS. *Accreditation:* NASAD. *Faculty:* 1 (woman) full-time, 15 part-time/adjunct (13 women). *Students:* 17 full-time (15 women), 8 part-time (6 women); includes 4 minority (2 African Americans, 2 Hispanic Americans), 1 international. Average age 29. 19 applicants, 58% accepted, 7 enrolled. In 2006, 13 degrees awarded. *Degree requirements:* For master's, thesis. *Entrance requirements:* Additional exam requirements/recommendations for international students: Required—TOEFL (minimum score 550 paper-based; 213 computer-based). *Application deadline:* For fall admission, 2/1 for domestic students; for spring admission, 10/1 for domestic students. Application fee: $40 ($90 for international students). *Expenses:* Tuition: Full-time $24,240. Tuition and fees vary according to course load and program. *Financial support:* In 2006–07, 3 fellowships (averaging $2,000 per year) were awarded; career-related internships or fieldwork, Federal Work-Study, institutionally sponsored loans, scholarships/grants, and unspecified assistantships also available. Support available to part-time students. Financial award application deadline: 2/1; financial award applicants required to submit FAFSA. *Unit head:* Dr. Amy Brook Snider, Chairperson, 718-636-3637, E-mail: absnider@pratt.edu. *Application contact:* Young Hah, Director of Graduate Admissions, 718-636-3683, Fax: 718-399-4242, E-mail: yhah@pratt.edu.

Purdue University, Graduate School, School of Education, Department of Curriculum and Instruction, West Lafayette, IN 47907. Offers agricultural and extension education (PhD, Ed S); agriculture and extension education (MS, MS Ed); art education (PhD); consumer and family sciences and extension education (MS Ed, PhD, Ed S); curriculum studies (MS Ed, PhD, Ed S); educational technology (MS Ed, PhD, Ed S); elementary education (MS Ed); foreign language education (MS Ed, PhD, Ed S); industrial technology (PhD, Ed S); language arts (MS Ed, PhD, Ed S); literacy (MS Ed, PhD, Ed S); mathematics/science education (MS, MS Ed, PhD, Ed S); social studies (MS Ed, PhD); social studies education (Ed S); vocational/industrial education (MS Ed, PhD, Ed S); vocational/technical education (MS Ed, PhD, Ed S). *Accreditation:* NCATE. Part-time and evening/weekend programs available. *Faculty:* 26 full-time (13 women), 3 part-time/adjunct (all women). *Students:* 59 full-time (37 women), 112 part-time (70 women); includes 24 minority (13 African Americans, 3 American Indian/Alaska Native, 4 Asian Americans or Pacific Islanders, 4 Hispanic Americans), 38 international. Average age 35. 92 applicants, 68% accepted, 38 enrolled. In 2006, 52 master's, 23 doctorates awarded. *Degree requirements:* For master's, thesis optional; for doctorate, thesis/dissertation, oral and written exams; for Ed S, oral presentation, project. *Entrance requirements:* For master's, GRE General Test, minimum B average; for doctorate, GRE General Test; for Ed S, GRE, minimum B average. Additional exam requirements/recommendations for international students: Required—TOEFL. *Application deadline:* For fall admission, 1/15 priority date for domestic students, 1/15 for international students; for spring admission, 9/15 for domestic and international students. Applications are processed on a rolling basis. Application fee: $55. Electronic applications accepted. *Financial support:* In 2006–07, 3 fellowships with full tuition reimbursements (averaging $10,500 per year), 11 research assistantships with full tuition reimbursements (averaging $11,500 per year), 43 teaching assistantships with full tuition reimbursements (averaging $10,800 per year) were awarded; career-related internships or fieldwork and tuition waivers (full) also available. Support available to part-time students. Financial award application deadline: 3/1; financial award applicants required to submit FAFSA. *Faculty research:* Literacy acquisition and development, teacher beliefs and knowledge, recruitment and retention of underrepresented students, economic education, literacy discourse. *Unit head:* Dr. James D Lehman, Head, 765-494-7935, Fax: 765-496-1622. *Application contact:* Patricia Mason, Coordinator of Graduate Studies, 765-494-2345, Fax: 765-494-5832, E-mail: gradoffice@soe.purdue.edu.

Queens College of the City University of New York, Division of Graduate Studies, Division of Education, Department of Secondary Education, Flushing, NY 11367-1597. Offers art (MS Ed); biology (MS Ed, AC); chemistry (MS Ed, AC); earth sciences (MS Ed, AC); English (MS Ed, AC); French (MS Ed, AC); Italian (MS Ed, AC); mathematics (MS Ed, AC); music (MS Ed, AC); physics (MS Ed, AC); social studies (MS Ed, AC); Spanish (MS Ed, AC). Part-time and evening/weekend programs available. *Faculty:* 22 full-time (14 women). *Students:* 50 full-time (28 women), 974 part-time (627 women). 633 applicants, 82% accepted, 407 enrolled. In 2006, 227 degrees awarded. *Degree requirements:* For master's, research project; for AC, thesis optional. *Entrance requirements:* For master's, minimum GPA of 3.0. Additional exam requirements/recommendations for international students: Required—TOEFL. *Application deadline:* For fall admission, 4/1 for domestic students; for spring admission, 11/1 for domestic students. Applications are processed on a rolling basis. Application fee: $125. *Financial support:* Career-related internships or fieldwork, Federal Work-Study, institutionally sponsored loans, and tuition waivers (partial) available. Support available to part-time students. Financial award application deadline: 4/1; financial award applicants required to submit FAFSA. *Unit head:* Dr. Eleanor Armour-Thomas, Chairperson, 718-997-5150, E-mail: armourthomas@yahoo.com. *Application contact:* Mario Caruso, Director of Graduate Admissions, 718-997-5200, Fax: 718-997-5193, E-mail: graduate_admissions@qc.edu.

Rhode Island College, School of Graduate Studies, Faculty of Arts and Sciences, Department of Art, Providence, RI 02908-1991. Offers art (MA); art education (MAT); media studies (MA). *Accreditation:* NASAD (one or more programs are accredited). Part-time and evening/weekend programs available. *Faculty:* 7 full-time (4 women), 1 part-time/adjunct (0 women). *Students:* 6 full-time (3 women), 16 part-time (8 women); includes 2 minority (both Asian Americans or Pacific Islanders) Average age 34. In 2006, 7 degrees awarded. *Degree requirements:* For master's, thesis. *Entrance requirements:* For master's, GRE General Test or MAT, portfolio (MA), 3 letters of recommendation, interview. *Application deadline:* For fall admission, 4/1 for domestic students; for spring admission, 11/1 for domestic students. Applications are processed on a rolling basis. Application fee: $50. *Expenses:* Tuition, state resident: part-time $244 per credit. Tuition, nonresident: part-time $512 per credit. Required fees: $12 per credit. $66 per term. Tuition and fees vary according to degree level, program and reciprocity agreements. *Financial support:* Teaching assistantships with full tuition reimbursements, career-related internships or fieldwork, Federal Work-Study, scholarships/grants, health care benefits, and unspecified assistantships available. Support available to part-time students. Financial award application deadline: 5/15; financial award applicants required to submit FAFSA. *Unit head:* Heemong Kim, Chair, 401-456-8054.

Rhode Island School of Design, Graduate Studies, Program in Art Education, Providence, RI 02903-2784. Offers MA, MAT. *Accreditation:* NASAD. *Degree requirements:* For master's, thesis, exhibit. *Entrance requirements:* For master's, portfolio, letters of recommendation. Additional exam requirements/recommendations for international students: Required—TOEFL (minimum score 580 paper-based; 237 computer-based), IELTS (minimum score 7).

Rochester Institute of Technology, Graduate Enrollment Services, College of Imaging Arts and Sciences, School of Art, Program in Art Education, Rochester, NY 14623-5603. Offers MST. *Accreditation:* NASAD; Teacher Education Accreditation Council. *Students:* 15 full-time (14 women); includes 1 minority (Asian American or Pacific Islander) 31 applicants, 61% accepted, 15 enrolled. In 2006, 15 degrees awarded. *Entrance requirements:* For master's, portfolio, minimum GPA of 3.0. Additional exam requirements/recommendations for international students: Required—TOEFL (minimum score 550 paper-based; 230 computer-based; 79 iBT). *Application deadline:* For fall admission, 3/1 priority date for domestic students. Applications are processed on a rolling basis. Application fee: $50. *Expenses:* Tuition: Full-time $28,491; part-time $800 per credit. Required fees: $201. *Unit head:* Carol Woodlock, Chairperson, 585-475-7556, E-mail: cmwfaa@rit.edu.

Rockford College, Graduate Studies, Department of Education, Program in Secondary Education, Rockford, IL 61108-2393. Offers art education (MAT); English (MAT); history (MAT); political science (MAT); secondary education (MAT); social sciences (MAT). Part-time and evening/weekend programs available. *Degree requirements:* For master's, thesis optional. *Entrance requirements:* For master's, GRE General Test.

Sage Graduate School, Graduate School, Division of Education, Program in Teaching, Troy, NY 12180-4115. Offers art education (MAT); biology (MAT); English (MAT); mathematics (MAT); social studies (MAT). Part-time and evening/weekend programs available. *Faculty:* 11 full-time (8 women), 20 part-time/adjunct (15 women). *Students:* 34 full-time (28 women), 41 part-time (29 women); includes 3 minority (1 African American, 1 Asian American or Pacific Islander, 1 Hispanic American). Average age 27. 72 applicants, 64% accepted, 33 enrolled. In 2006, 31 degrees awarded. *Entrance requirements:* For master's, minimum undergraduate GPA of 2.75 overall, minimum undergraduate GPA of 3.0 in content area. Additional exam requirements/recommendations for international students: Required—TOEFL (minimum score 550 paper-based; 213 computer-based). *Application deadline:* For fall admission, 8/1 for domestic students. Applications are processed on a rolling basis. Application fee: $40. *Expenses:* Tuition: Full-time $9,270; part-time $515 per credit hour. *Financial support:* Career-related internships or fieldwork, scholarships/grants, and unspecified assistantships available. Support available to part-time students. Financial award application deadline: 3/1; financial award applicants required to submit FAFSA. *Unit head:* Peter McDermott, Director, 518-244-2493, E-mail: mcderp@sage.edu. *Application contact:* Shannon K. Easton, Director of Graduate and Adult Admission, 518-244-2443, Fax: 518-244-6880, E-mail: sgsadm@sage.edu.

Saint Michael's College, Graduate Programs, Program in Education, Colchester, VT 05439. Offers administration (M Ed, CAGS); arts in education (CAGS); curriculum and instruction (M Ed, CAGS); information technology (CAGS); reading (M Ed); special education (M Ed, CAGS); technology (M Ed). Part-time and evening/weekend programs available. *Faculty:* 5 full-time (3 women), 35 part-time/adjunct (29 women). *Students:* 26 full-time (18 women), 114 part-time (86 women), 2 international. Average age 34. 48 applicants, 81% accepted, 36 enrolled. In 2006, 46 degrees awarded. *Degree requirements:* For master's, thesis. *Entrance requirements:* For master's, minimum GPA of 3.0. *Application deadline:* Applications are processed on a rolling basis. Application fee: $35. Electronic applications accepted. *Financial support:* Fellowships, scholarships/grants available. Support available to part-time students. Financial award applicants required to submit FAFSA. *Faculty research:* Integrative curriculum, moral and spiritual dimensions of education, learning styles, multiple intelligences, integrating technology into the curriculum. *Unit head:* Dr. Anne P. Judson, Director, 802-654-2649, Fax: 802-654-2664, E-mail: ajudson@smcvt.edu.

Salem State College, Graduate School, Program in Art, Salem, MA 01970-5353. Offers MAT. *Accreditation:* NASAD. *Students:* 1 (woman) full-time, 17 part-time (16 women). Average age 38. In 2006, 3 degrees awarded. *Application deadline:* Applications are processed on a rolling basis. Application fee: $35. *Unit head:* Maureen Creegon-Quinquis, Visiting Associate Professor, 978-542-6321, E-mail: mcreeganquinqu@salemstate.edu.

Salisbury University, Graduate Division, Department of Education, Salisbury, MD 21801-6837. Offers art (MAT); biology (MAT); business education (MAT); chemistry (MAT); early childhood education (M Ed); educational administration (M Ed); elementary education (M Ed); English (M Ed, MAT); French (MAT); geography (MAT); history (MAT); mathematics (MAT); media and technology (MAT); music (MAT); psychology (MAT); reading education (MAT); science (MAT); secondary education (MAT); social studies (MAT); Spanish (MAT). *Accreditation:* NCATE. Part-time and evening/weekend programs available. *Faculty:* 12 full-time (6 women), 10 part-time/adjunct (8 women). *Students:* 17 full-time (9 women), 84 part-time (72 women); includes 6 minority (5 African Americans, 1 Hispanic American). Average age 30. 15 applicants, 73% accepted, 11 enrolled. In 2006, 63 degrees awarded. *Degree requirements:* For master's, comprehensive exam (for some programs). *Entrance requirements:* For master's, PRAXIS, minimum GPA of 2.75. Additional exam requirements/recommendations for international students: Required—TOEFL (minimum score 550 paper-based; 213 computer-based). *Application deadline:* For fall admission, 8/1 priority date for domestic students; for spring admission, 1/1 for domestic students. Applications are processed on a rolling basis. Application fee: $45. *Expenses:* Tuition, state resident: part-time $260 per credit hour. Tuition, nonresident: part-time $546 per credit hour. Required fees: $52 per credit hour. *Financial support:* In 2006–07, 3 teaching assistantships with full tuition reimbursements were awarded; career-related internships or fieldwork and scholarships/grants also available. Support available to part-time students. Financial award applicants required to submit FAFSA. *Faculty research:* Middle-level education, student outcomes. *Unit head:* Dr. Edward C. Robeck, Program Coordinator, 410-543-6292, Fax: 410-548-2593, E-mail: ecrobeck@salisbury.edu. *Application contact:* Debra J. Clark, Administrative Assistant I, 410-543-6281, Fax: 410-548-2593, E-mail: djclark@salisbury.edu.

School of the Art Institute of Chicago, Graduate Division, Program in Art Education, Chicago, IL 60603-3103. Offers MAAE, Certificate. *Accreditation:* NASAD. *Entrance requirements:* Additional exam requirements/recommendations for international students: Required—TOEFL.

School of Visual Arts, Graduate Programs, Program in Art Criticism and Writing, New York, NY 10010-3994. Offers MFA. *Faculty:* 10 full-time (3 women). *Students:* 16 full-time (13 women), 4 part-time (2 women); includes 3 minority (1 African American, 2 Hispanic Americans), 4 international. Average age 31. 24 applicants, 79% accepted, 10 enrolled. *Degree requirements:* For master's, thesis. *Entrance requirements:* Additional exam requirements/recommendations for international students: Required—TOEFL (minimum score 550 paper-based; 213 computer-based; 79 iBT). *Application deadline:* For fall admission, 2/1 for domestic students. Application fee: $70 ($80 for international students). *Expenses:* Tuition: Full-time $22,400. Full-time tuition and fees vary according to program. *Financial support:* Application deadline: 2/1. *Unit head:* Thomas McEvilley, Chair, 212-592-2409, Fax: 212-989-3516, E-mail: tmcevilley@sva.edu.

School of Visual Arts, Graduate Programs, Program in Art Education, New York, NY 10010-3994. Offers MAT. *Faculty:* 3 full-time (2 women), 9 part-time/adjunct (6 women). *Students:* 27 full-time (24 women); includes 5 minority (1 African American, 1 Asian American or Pacific Islander, 3 Hispanic Americans), 1 international. Average age 33. 57 applicants, 75% accepted, 27 enrolled. In 2006, 27 degrees awarded. *Entrance requirements:* For master's, portfolio. Additional exam requirements/recommendations for international students: Required—TOEFL (minimum score 550 paper-based; 213 computer-based; 79 iBT). *Application deadline:* For fall admission, 2/1 for domestic students. Application fee: $70 ($80 for international students). *Expenses:* Tuition: Full-time $22,400. Full-time tuition and fees vary according to program. *Financial support:* In 2006–07, 8 students received support. Application deadline: 2/1; *Unit head:* Dr. Rose Viggiano, Chair, 212-592-2560, E-mail: rviggiano@sva.edu. *Application contact:* Information Contact, 646-592-2560, Fax: 646-336-7702, E-mail: matarted@sva.edu.

Southern Connecticut State University, School of Graduate Studies, School of Arts and Sciences, Department of Art, New Haven, CT 06515-1355. Offers art education (MS). Part-time and evening/weekend programs available. *Faculty:* 5 full-time, 5 part-time/adjunct. *Students:* 22 full-time (20 women), 50 part-time (44 women); includes 1 minority (Asian American or Pacific Islander) 40 applicants, 43% accepted, 14 enrolled. In 2006, 14 degrees awarded. *Degree requirements:* For master's, thesis or alternative. *Entrance requirements:* For master's, interview. *Application deadline:* For fall admission, 5/1 priority date for domestic students; for spring admission, 12/1 priority date for domestic students. Applications are processed on a rolling basis. Application fee: $50. Electronic applications accepted. *Financial support:* Application deadline: 4/15; *Unit head:* Mitchell Bills, Chairperson, 203-392-6649, Fax: 203-392-6658, E-mail: billsm1@southernct.edu. *Application contact:* Dr. Jessie Whitehead, Graduate Coordinator, 203-392-8913, Fax: 203-392-6658, E-mail: whiteheadj3@southernct.edu.

Southern Illinois University Edwardsville, Graduate Studies and Research, School of Education, Department of Curriculum and Instruction, Program in Secondary Education, Edwardsville, IL 62026-0001. Offers art (MS Ed); biology (MS Ed); chemistry (MS Ed); English (MS Ed); foreign languages (MS Ed); history (MS Ed); mathematics (MS Ed); physics (MS Ed); reading (MS Ed); science (MS Ed). *Accreditation:* NCATE. Part-time and evening/weekend programs available. *Students:* 2 full-time (both women), 23 part-time (14 women); includes 2 minority (both African Americans) Average age 33. 12 applicants, 42% accepted. In 2006, 10 degrees awarded. *Degree requirements:* For master's, thesis or alternative, final exam. *Entrance requirements:* For master's, MAT. Additional exam requirements/recommendations for international students: Required—TOEFL. *Application deadline:* For fall admission, 7/20 for domestic students, 6/1 for international students; for spring admission, 12/14 for domestic students, 10/1 for international students. Application fee: $30. Electronic applications accepted. *Financial support:* Fellowships, research assistantships, teaching assistantships, Federal Work-Study, institutionally sponsored loans, and unspecified assistantships available. Support available to part-time students. Financial award application deadline: 3/1; financial award applicants required to submit FAFSA. *Unit head:* Dr. David DeWeese, Director, 618-650-3432, E-mail: ddewees@siue.edu.

Southwestern Oklahoma State University, College of Arts and Sciences, Department of Art, Weatherford, OK 73096-3098. Offers art education (M Ed). Part-time programs available. *Degree requirements:* For master's, exam. *Entrance requirements:* For master's, GRE General Test or minimum undergraduate GPA of 3.0. Additional exam requirements/recommendations for international students: Required—TOEFL.

Stanford University, School of Education, Program in Curriculum Studies and Teacher Education, Stanford, CA 94305-9991. Offers art education (MA, PhD); dance education (MA); English education (MA, PhD); general curriculum studies (MA, PhD); mathematics education (MA, PhD); science education (MA, PhD); social studies education (PhD); teacher education (MA, PhD). *Degree requirements:* For master's, thesis (for some programs); for doctorate, thesis/dissertation. *Entrance requirements:* For master's and doctorate, GRE General Test. Electronic applications accepted.

State University of New York at New Paltz, Graduate School, Faculty of Fine and Performing Arts, Department of Art Education, New Paltz, NY 12561. Offers visual arts education (MS Ed). *Accreditation:* NASAD. Part-time and evening/weekend programs available. *Students:* Average age 32. 4 applicants. In 2006, 10 degrees awarded. *Degree requirements:* For master's, thesis, portfolio. *Entrance requirements:* For master's, art education certificate, minimum GPA of 3.0. Additional exam requirements/recommendations for international students: Required—TOEFL (minimum score 550 paper-based; 213 computer-based; 80 iBT). *Application deadline:* For fall admission, 4/15 for domestic and international students; for spring admission, 11/1 for domestic and international students. Application fee: $50. Electronic applications accepted. *Expenses:* Tuition, state resident: full-time $6,900; part-time $288 per credit hour. Tuition, nonresident: full-time $10,920; part-time $455 per credit hour. *Financial support:* In 2006–07, 2 students received support, including 2 research assistantships with partial tuition reimbursements available (averaging $5,000 per year). *Unit head:* Prof. Patricia Phillips, Chair, 845-257-3833, E-mail: phillipp@newpaltz.edu. *Application contact:* Dr. Margaret Johnson, Coordinator, 845-257-3851, E-mail: johnsonm@newpaltz.edu.

State University of New York at Oswego, Graduate Studies, School of Education, Department of Curriculum and Instruction, Oswego, NY 13126. Offers art education (MAT); elementary education (MS Ed); literacy education (MS Ed); secondary education (MS Ed); special education (MS Ed). Part-time and evening/weekend programs available. *Faculty:* 23 full-time, 45 part-time/adjunct. *Students:* 184 full-time (139 women), 220 part-time (185 women); includes 12 minority (5 African Americans, 1 American Indian/Alaska Native, 1 Asian American or Pacific Islander, 5 Hispanic Americans), 1 international. Average age 33. 266 applicants, 89% accepted. In 2006, 255 degrees awarded. *Degree requirements:* For master's, thesis optional. *Entrance requirements:* For master's, GRE General Test, minimum GPA of 2.7, provisional teaching certificate. Additional exam requirements/recommendations for international students: Required—TOEFL (minimum score 560 paper-based; 220 computer-based). *Application deadline:* For fall admission, 3/1 for domestic students; for spring admission, 10/1 for domestic students. Application fee: $50. *Expenses:* Tuition, state resident: part-time $288 per credit. Tuition, nonresident: part-time $455 per credit. Tuition and fees vary according to program. *Financial support:* In 2006–07, 9 students received support, including 3 fellowships, 6 teaching assistantships with full tuition reimbursements available; career-related internships or fieldwork, Federal Work-Study, institutionally sponsored loans, scholarships/grants, and unspecified assistantships also available. Support available to part-time students. Financial award application deadline: 4/1; financial award applicants required to submit FAFSA. *Faculty research:* Classroom applications for microcomputers; classroom questioning, wait-time, and achievement; values clarification and academic achievement. *Unit head:* Dr. Pamela Michel, Chair, 315-312-4052. *Application contact:* Dr. Joyce Smith, Coordinator, Graduate Education, 315-312-4052.

Sul Ross State University, School of Arts and Sciences, Department of Fine Arts and Communication, Alpine, TX 79832. Offers art education (M Ed); art history (M Ed); studio art (M Ed), including ceramics, design, drawing, jewelry, painting, printmaking, sculpture, weaving. Part-time programs available. *Degree requirements:* For master's, oral or written exam. *Entrance requirements:* For master's, GRE General Test, minimum GPA of 2.5 in last 60 hours of undergraduate work. *Faculty research:* Ceramic sculpture, watercolor, wood sculpture, rock art.

Syracuse University, Graduate School, College of Visual and Performing Arts, School of Art and Design, Syracuse, NY 13244. Offers art (MFA), including ceramics, metalsmithing, painting, printmaking, sculpture; arts education (MS); museum studies (MA); transmedia (MFA), including art photography, art video, computer art, film. *Accreditation:* NASAD (one or more programs are accredited). Part-time programs available. Postbaccalaureate distance learning degree programs offered (no on-campus study). *Students:* 94 full-time (56 women), 12 part-time (4 women); includes 10 minority (4 African Americans, 1 American Indian/Alaska Native, 4 Asian Americans or Pacific Islanders, 1 Hispanic American), 16 international. 233 applicants, 30% accepted, 37 enrolled. *Degree requirements:* For master's, thesis or alternative. *Entrance requirements:* For master's, portfolio. Additional exam requirements/recommendations for international students: Required—TOEFL. *Application deadline:* For fall admission, 1/1 priority date for domestic students; for spring admission, 3/1 priority date for domestic students. Applications are processed on a rolling basis. Application fee: $65. Electronic applications accepted. *Expenses:* Tuition: Full-time $16,920; part-time $940 per credit hour. Required fees: $930; $930 per year. *Financial support:* Fellowships with full tuition reimbursements, research assistantships with full and partial tuition reimbursements, teaching assistantships with full and partial tuition reimbursements, Federal Work-Study and tuition waivers (partial) available. *Application contact:* Harriett Conti, Associate Director, Graduate Student Services, 315-443-3089, E-mail: hmconti@syr.edu.

Syracuse University, Graduate School, School of Education, Department of Teaching and Leadership, Program in Art Education, Syracuse, NY 13244. Offers art education (CAS); art education/professional certification (MS); art education: preparation (MS). Part-time and evening/weekend programs available. *Students:* 13 full-time (11 women), 8 part-time (5 women), 1 international. 12 applicants, 92% accepted, 6 enrolled. *Degree requirements:* For master's, thesis or alternative; for CAS, thesis. *Entrance requirements:* For master's and CAS, GRE. Additional exam requirements/recommendations for international students: Required—TOEFL. *Application deadline:* For fall admission, 2/1 priority date for domestic students. Applications are processed on a rolling basis. Application fee: $65. Electronic applications accepted. *Expenses:* Tuition: Full-time $16,920; part-time $940 per credit hour. Required fees: $930; $930 per year. *Unit head:* Dr. Hope Irvine, Chair, 315-443-2355. *Application contact:* Liza Rochelson, Graduate Admission Recruiter, 315-443-2505, Fax: 315-443-2258, E-mail: gradcrt@gwmail.syr.edu.

Teachers College Columbia University, Graduate Faculty of Education, Department of Arts and Humanities, Program in Art and Art Education, New York, NY 10027-6696. Offers Ed M, MA, Ed D, Ed DCT. *Accreditation:* NCATE. Part-time and evening/weekend programs available. *Faculty:* 4 full-time (2 women). *Students:* 15 full-time (13 women), 151 part-time (114 women); includes 31 minority (6 African Americans, 1 American Indian/Alaska Native, 18 Asian Americans or Pacific Islanders, 6 Hispanic Americans), 20 international. Average age 36. 79 applicants, 80% accepted, 44 enrolled. In 2006, 26 master's, 5 doctorates awarded. Terminal master's awarded for partial completion of doctoral program. *Degree requirements:* For doctorate, variable foreign language requirement, thesis/dissertation. *Entrance requirements:* For doctorate, portfolio. *Application deadline:* For fall admission, 5/15 for domestic students; for spring admission, 12/1 for domestic students. Application fee: $65. *Expenses:* Tuition: Full-time $23,400; part-time $975 per credit. Required fees: $320 per term. *Financial support:* Research assistantships, teaching assistantships, career-related internships or fieldwork, Federal Work-Study, institutionally sponsored loans, and tuition waivers (full and partial) available. Support available to part-time students. Financial award application deadline: 2/1. *Faculty research:* Technology and creativity with respect to pedagogy and curriculum, artistic-aesthetic development in children and adolescents. *Application contact:* Mark E. Stearns, Associate Director of Admission, 212-678-3710, Fax: 212-678-4171.

Temple University, Graduate School, Tyler School of Art, Department of Art and Art Education, Philadelphia, PA 19122-6096. Offers Ed M. *Accreditation:* NASAD. *Faculty:* 3 full-time (2 women). *Students:* 6 full-time (all women), 11 part-time (8 women). 8 applicants, 75% accepted. In 2006, 3 degrees awarded. *Degree requirements:* For master's, paper, portfolio review. *Entrance requirements:* For master's, GRE or MAT, minimum GPA of 3.0, slide portfolio, 40 credits in studio art, 9 credits in art history. Additional exam requirements/recommendations for international students: Required—TOEFL (minimum score 550 paper-based; 213 computer-based; 79 iBT). *Application deadline:* For fall admission, 4/1 for domestic students, 12/15 for international students; for spring admission, 11/1 for domestic students, 8/1 for international students. Application fee: $50. Electronic applications accepted. *Expenses:* Tuition, state resident: full-time $12,264; part-time $511 per credit. Tuition, nonresident: full-time $17,904; part-time $746 per credit. Required fees: $84 per course. Tuition and fees vary according to program. *Financial support:* Research assistantships with full tuition reimbursements, teaching assistantships, Federal Work-Study available. Support available to part-time students. Financial award application deadline: 1/15; financial award applicants required to submit FAFSA. *Unit head:* Dr. Jo-Anna J. Moore, Chair, 215-782-7191, Fax: 215-204-1869, E-mail: jmoore06@temple.edu. *Application contact:* Carmina Cianciulli, Assistant Dean for Admissions, 215-782-2875, Fax: 215-782-2711, E-mail: tylerart@temple.edu.

Texas Tech University, Graduate School, College of Visual and Performing Arts, School of Art, Lubbock, TX 79409. Offers art (MFA); art education (MAE). *Accreditation:* NASAD (one or more programs are accredited). Part-time programs available. *Faculty:* 20 full-time (10 women). *Students:* 35 full-time (19 women), 16 part-time (12 women); includes 7 minority (1 American Indian/Alaska Native, 6 Hispanic Americans), 1 international. Average age 35. 49 applicants, 59% accepted, 9 enrolled. In 2006, 10 degrees awarded. *Degree requirements:* For master's, thesis (for some programs). *Entrance requirements:* For master's, GRE General Test. Additional exam requirements/recommendations for international students: Required—TOEFL (minimum score 550 paper-based; 213 computer-based). *Application deadline:* For fall admission, 3/1 priority date for international students; for spring admission, 11/1 priority date for international students. Applications are processed on a rolling basis. Application fee: $50 ($60 for international students). Electronic applications accepted. *Expenses:* Tuition, state resident: full-time $4,440. Tuition, nonresident: full-time $11,040. Required fees: $2,136. *Financial support:* In 2006–07, 42 students received support, including 33 teaching assistantships with partial tuition reimbursements available (averaging $7,590 per year); research assistantships with partial tuition reimbursements available, career-related internships or fieldwork, Federal Work-Study, and institutionally sponsored loans also available. Support available to part-time students. Financial award application deadline: 4/15; financial award applicants required to submit FAFSA. *Faculty research:* Studio, art history, art education. *Unit head:* Dr. Tina Fuentes, Interim Director, 806-742-3825 Ext. 255, Fax: 806-742-1971, E-mail: tina.fuentes@ttu.edu. *Application contact:* Andrew Martin, Graduate Advisor, 806-742-3825 Ext. 228, Fax: 806-742-1971, E-mail: andrew.martin@ttu.edu.

Towson University, Graduate School, Program in Art Education, Towson, MD 21252-0001. Offers M Ed. *Accreditation:* NCATE. Part-time and evening/weekend programs available. *Faculty:* 13 full-time (3 women), 2 part-time/adjunct (1 woman). *Students:* 11 applicants, 45% accepted, 2 enrolled. In 2006, 3 degrees awarded. *Degree requirements:* For master's, research project, thesis optional. *Entrance requirements:* For master's, bachelor's degree/certification in art education, minimum GPA of 3.0. *Application deadline:* Applications are processed on a rolling basis. Application fee: $50. Electronic applications accepted. *Expenses:* Tuition, state resident: part-time $275 per unit. Tuition, nonresident: part-time $577 per unit. Required fees: $72 per unit. *Financial support:* Federal Work-Study and unspecified assistantships available. Financial award application deadline: 4/1; financial award applicants required to submit FAFSA. *Unit head:* Jane Bates, Graduate Program Director, 410-704-2797, Fax: 410-704-2810, E-mail: jbates@towson.edu. *Application contact:* 410-704-2501, Fax: 410-704-4675, E-mail: grads@towson.edu.

The University of Alabama at Birmingham, School of Education, Department of Curriculum and Instruction, Program in Arts Education, Birmingham, AL 35294. Offers MA Ed. *Accreditation:* NCATE. *Students:* 18 full-time (14 women), 78 part-time (67 women); includes 16 minority (11 African Americans, 1 Asian American or Pacific Islander, 4 Hispanic Americans). 26 applicants, 88% accepted. In 2006, 25 degrees awarded. *Degree requirements:* For master's, thesis optional. *Entrance requirements:* For master's, GRE General Test, MAT, or NTE, minimum GPA of 3.0. *Application deadline:* Applications are processed on a rolling basis. Application fee: $35 ($60 for international students). Electronic applications accepted. *Expenses:* Tuition, state resident: part-time $170 per credit hour. Tuition, nonresident: part-time $425 per credit hour. Required fees: $15 per credit hour. $122 per term. Tuition and fees vary according to program. *Unit head:* Dr. Charles Calhoun, Chair, Department of Curriculum and Instruction, 205-934-5371, Fax: 205-934-4792.

The University of Arizona, Graduate College, College of Fine Arts, School of Art, Program in Art Education, Tucson, AZ 85721. Offers MA. *Accreditation:* NASAD. *Degree requirements:* For master's, thesis. *Entrance requirements:* For master's, minimum GPA of 3.0, teaching certificate. Additional exam requirements/recommendations for international students: Required—TOEFL. *Faculty research:* Artistic styles, visual perception, integration of arts into elementary curricula, aesthetics of the vanishing roadsides of America.

University of Arkansas at Little Rock, Graduate School, College of Arts, Humanities, and Social Science, Department of Art, Little Rock, AR 72204-1099. Offers art education (MA); art history (MA); studio art (MA). *Accreditation:* NASAD. Part-time programs available. *Degree requirements:* For master's, 4 foreign languages. *Entrance requirements:* For master's, portfolio review or term paper evaluation, minimum GPA of 2.7.

The University of British Columbia, Faculty of Graduate Studies, Faculty of Education, Department of Curriculum Studies, Vancouver, BC V6T 1Z1, Canada. Offers art education (M Ed, MA); curriculum studies (M Ed, MA, PhD); home economics education (M Ed, MA); math education (M Ed, MA); music education (M Ed, MA); physical education (M Ed, MA); science education (M Ed, MA); social studies education (M Ed, MA); technical studies educa-

Art Education

The University of British Columbia (continued)
tion (M Ed, MA). Part-time programs available. *Faculty:* 31 full-time (17 women), 1 (woman) part-time/adjunct. *Students:* 153 full-time (102 women), 101 part-time (67 women), 25 international. Average age 40. 118 applicants, 64% accepted, 62 enrolled. In 2006, 46 master's, 4 doctorates awarded. *Degree requirements:* For master's, thesis (MA); for doctorate, thesis/dissertation, comprehensive exam, registration. *Entrance requirements:* Additional exam requirements/recommendations for international students: Required—TOEFL (minimum score 580 paper-based; 237 computer-based). *Application deadline:* For fall admission, 2/1 for domestic students, 1/1 for international students; for spring admission, 10/1 for domestic students, 9/1 for international students. Application fee: $90 ($150 for international students). Electronic applications accepted. *Expenses:* Contact institution. *Financial support:* In 2006–07, 10 fellowships with partial tuition reimbursements (averaging $16,000 per year), 11 research assistantships with partial tuition reimbursements (averaging $14,000 per year), 27 teaching assistantships with partial tuition reimbursements (averaging $14,000 per year) were awarded; tuition waivers (partial) also available. *Faculty research:* School subjects, teaching and learning. *Unit head:* Dr. Linda Peterat, Interim Head, 604-822-5422, Fax: 604-822-4714. *Application contact:* Basia Zurek, Graduate Secretary, 604-822-5367, Fax: 604-822-4714, E-mail: cust.grad@ubc.ca.

University of Central Florida, College of Education, Department of Teaching and Learning Principles, Program in Art Education, Orlando, FL 32816. Offers M Ed, MA. *Accreditation:* NCATE. Part-time and evening/weekend programs available. *Students:* 2 full-time (both women), 10 part-time (9 women); includes 3 minority (1 African American, 1 Asian American or Pacific Islander, 1 Hispanic American). Average age 34. In 2006, 5 degrees awarded. *Degree requirements:* For master's, thesis or alternative, research report, internship (MA). *Entrance requirements:* Additional exam requirements/recommendations for international students: Required—TOEFL. *Application deadline:* For fall admission, 7/15 for domestic students; for spring admission, 12/1 for domestic students. Application fee: $30. Electronic applications accepted. *Expenses:* Tuition, state resident: full-time $6,167; part-time $257 per credit hour. Tuition, nonresident: full-time $22,790; part-time $950 per credit hour. *Financial support:* In 2006–07, 1 research assistantship with tuition reimbursement (averaging $10,000 per year) was awarded; fellowships with partial tuition reimbursements, teaching assistantships with partial tuition reimbursements, career-related internships or fieldwork, Federal Work-Study, institutionally sponsored loans, tuition waivers (partial), and unspecified assistantships also available. Financial award application deadline: 3/1; financial award applicants required to submit FAFSA. *Unit head:* Dr. Thomas Brewer, Coordinator, 407-823-3550.

University of Cincinnati, Division of Research and Advanced Studies, College of Design, Architecture, Art, and Planning, School of Art, Program in Art Education, Cincinnati, OH 45221. Offers MA. *Accreditation:* NASAD; NCATE. *Entrance requirements:* For master's, MAT. Electronic applications accepted.

University of Dayton, Graduate School, School of Education and Allied Professions, Department of Teacher Education, Dayton, OH 45469-1300. Offers adolescent/young adult (MS Ed); art education (MS Ed); early childhood education (MS Ed); inclusive early childhood (MS Ed); interdisciplinary education (MS Ed); intervention specialist education, mild/moderate (MS Ed); literacy (MS Ed); middle childhood (MS Ed); multi-age education (MS Ed); music education (MS Ed); teacher as leader (MS Ed); technology in education (MS Ed). Part-time and evening/weekend programs available. *Faculty:* 13 full-time (9 women), 33 part-time/adjunct (25 women). *Students:* 149 full-time (120 women), 284 part-time (241 women); includes 37 minority (31 African Americans, 3 Asian Americans or Pacific Islanders, 3 Hispanic Americans), 3 international. Average age 33. 201 applicants, 58% accepted, 31 enrolled. In 2006, 150 degrees awarded. *Degree requirements:* For master's, thesis, capstone research project. *Entrance requirements:* For master's, GRE General Test, minimum GPA of 2.75. Additional exam requirements/recommendations for international students: Required—TOEFL (minimum score 550 paper-based; 213 computer-based). *Application deadline:* For fall admission, 3/15 priority date for domestic students, 3/1 priority date for international students. Applications are processed on a rolling basis. Application fee: $0. Electronic applications accepted. *Expenses:* Contact institution. *Financial support:* In 2006–07, 8 teaching assistantships with partial tuition reimbursements (averaging $7,600 per year) were awarded; career-related internships or fieldwork, institutionally sponsored loans, health care benefits, and unspecified assistantships also available. Financial award applicants required to submit FAFSA. *Faculty research:* Diversity, literacy, art representation by young children, preservice teacher preparation. Total annual research expenditures: $330,000. *Unit head:* Dr. Katie A. Kinnucan-Welsch, Chair, 937-229-3346. *Application contact:* Erika Eavers, Graduate Admission Processor, 937-229-3065, Fax: 937-229-4729, E-mail: erika.eavers@notes.udayton.edu.

University of Florida, Graduate School, College of Fine Arts, School of Art and Art History, Gainesville, FL 32611. Offers art (MFA), including ceramics, creative photography, drawing, electronic intermedia, graphic design, painting, printmaking, sculpture; art education (MA); art history (MA, PhD); digital arts and sciences (MA); museology (museum studies) (MA). *Accreditation:* NASAD. *Faculty:* 28 full-time (12 women), 2 part-time/adjunct (1 woman). *Students:* 80 (45 women); includes 8 minority (2 Asian Americans or Pacific Islanders, 6 Hispanic Americans) 2 international. In 2006, 26 degrees awarded. *Entrance requirements:* For master's, portfolio (MFA), writing sample (MA), GRE General Test or minimum GPA of 3.0. Additional exam requirements/recommendations for international students: Required—TOEFL (minimum score 550 paper-based; 213 computer-based). *Application deadline:* For fall admission, 1/15 priority date for domestic students. Applications are processed on a rolling basis. Application fee: $30. Electronic applications accepted. *Expenses:* Tuition, state resident: full-time $6,827. Tuition, nonresident: full-time $21,951. Required fees: $999. *Financial support:* In 2006–07, 57 teaching assistantships with tuition reimbursements (averaging $8,610 per year) were awarded; fellowships, research assistantships with tuition reimbursements, Federal Work-Study, institutionally sponsored loans, and unspecified assistantships also available. Financial award applicants required to submit FAFSA. *Faculty research:* Studio production, art historical studies of style context. *Unit head:* Glenn Willumson, Program Director, 352-392-0201 Ext. 234. *Application contact:* Prof. Richard Heipp, Coordinator, 352-392-0201 Ext. 239, Fax: 352-392-8453, E-mail: heipp@ufl.edu.

University of Georgia, Graduate School, College of Arts and Sciences, Lamar Dodd School of Art and College of Education, Program in Art Education, Athens, GA 30602. Offers MA Ed, Ed D, Ed S. *Accreditation:* NASAD; NCATE. *Students:* 6 full-time, 14 part-time; includes 1 minority (Asian American or Pacific Islander) 14 applicants, 71% accepted, 4 enrolled. In 2006, 2 degrees awarded. *Degree requirements:* For doctorate, thesis/dissertation. *Entrance requirements:* For master's, GRE General Test, MAT; for doctorate, GRE General Test; for Ed S, GRE General Test or MAT. *Application deadline:* For fall admission, 7/1 priority date for domestic students; for spring admission, 11/15 for domestic students. Application fee: $50. Electronic applications accepted. *Financial support:* Fellowships, research assistantships, teaching assistantships, unspecified assistantships available.

University of Houston, College of Education, Department of Curriculum and Instruction, Houston, TX 77204. Offers art education (M Ed); bilingual education (M Ed); curriculum and instruction (Ed D); early childhood education (M Ed); education of the gifted (M Ed); elementary education (M Ed); mathematics education (M Ed); reading and language arts education (M Ed); science education (M Ed); second language education (M Ed); secondary education (M Ed); social studies education (M Ed); teaching (M Ed). *Accreditation:* NCATE. Part-time and evening/weekend programs available. *Faculty:* 24 full-time (11 women), 16 part-time/adjunct (14 women). *Students:* 134 full-time (102 women), 327 part-time (256 women); includes 142 minority (49 African Americans, 1 American Indian/Alaska Native, 29 Asian Americans or Pacific Islanders, 63 Hispanic Americans), 19 international. Average age 37. 113 applicants, 72% accepted, 61 enrolled. In 2006, 106 master's, 32 doctorates awarded. *Degree requirements:* For master's, comprehensive exam or thesis; for doctorate, thesis/dissertation, comprehensive exam. *Entrance requirements:* For master's, GRE General Test or MAT; for doctorate, GRE General Test, interview. *Application deadline:* For fall admission, 7/3 priority date for domestic students. Applications are processed on a rolling basis. Application fee: $35 ($75 for international students). *Expenses:* Tuition, state resident: full-time $5,429; part-time $226 per credit. Tuition, nonresident: full-time $12,029; part-time $501 per credit. Required fees: $2,454. *Financial support:* In 2006–07, 2 fellowships with full tuition reimbursements (averaging $9,500 per year), 6 research assistantships with full tuition reimbursements (averaging $8,800 per year), 25 teaching assistantships with full tuition reimbursements (averaging $8,800 per year) were awarded; career-related internships or fieldwork, Federal Work-Study, institutionally sponsored loans, scholarships/grants, health care benefits, and unspecified assistantships also available. Support available to part-time students. Financial award application deadline: 3/10. *Faculty research:* Teaching-learning process, instructional technology in schools, teacher education, classroom management, at-risk students. *Unit head:* Dr. Juanita Copley, Chairperson, 713-743-4950, Fax: 713-743-4990, E-mail: ncopley@aol.com.

University of Idaho, College of Graduate Studies, College of Art and Architecture, Department of Art and Design, Moscow, ID 83844-2282. Offers art (MFA); art education (MAT). *Accreditation:* NASAD. *Students:* 15 (10 women). Average age 31. In 2006, 10 degrees awarded. *Degree requirements:* For master's, thesis (for some programs). *Entrance requirements:* For master's, minimum GPA of 2.8. *Application deadline:* For fall admission, 8/1 for domestic students; for spring admission, 12/15 for domestic students. Application fee: $55 ($60 for international students). *Expenses:* Tuition, nonresident: full-time $9,600; part-time $140 per credit. Required fees: $4,740; $227 per credit. *Financial support:* Research assistantships, teaching assistantships available. Financial award application deadline: 2/15. *Unit head:* Jill Dacey, Chair, 208-885-6750.

University of Illinois at Urbana–Champaign, Graduate College, College of Fine and Applied Arts, School of Art and Design, Program in Art Education, Champaign, IL 61820. Offers MA, Ed D. *Accreditation:* NASAD. *Students:* 27 full-time (20 women), 2 part-time (both women); includes 3 minority (all Asian Americans or Pacific Islanders), 9 international. 17 applicants, 53% accepted, 6 enrolled. In 2006, 12 master's, 1 doctorate awarded. *Degree requirements:* For doctorate, thesis/dissertation. *Entrance requirements:* For master's, minimum GPA of 3.0, portfolio. *Application deadline:* Applications are processed on a rolling basis. Application fee: $50 ($60 for international students). Electronic applications accepted. *Financial support:* Application deadline: 2/15. *Unit head:* Paul Duncum, Chairman, 217-333-4841, Fax: 217-244-7688, E-mail: pduncum@uiuc.edu.

University of Indianapolis, Graduate Programs, School of Education, Indianapolis, IN 46227-3697. Offers art education (MAT); biology (MAT); chemistry (MAT); curriculum and instruction (MA); earth sciences (MAT); education (MA, MAT); educational leadership (MA); elementary education (MA); English (MAT); French (MAT); math (MAT); physical education (MAT); physics (MAT); secondary education (MA), including art education, education, English education, social studies education; social studies (MAT); Spanish (MAT). *Accreditation:* NCATE. Part-time and evening/weekend programs available. *Faculty:* 4 full-time (2 women), 6 part-time/adjunct (2 women). *Students:* 32 full-time (16 women), 70 part-time (42 women); includes 2 minority (1 African American, 1 Hispanic American). Average age 31. In 2006, 51 degrees awarded. *Entrance requirements:* For master's, GRE Subject Test, minimum GPA of 2.5, 3 letters of recommendation, interview, Praxis I, writing exercise, be within 9 hours of completing content requirements. Additional exam requirements/recommendations for international students: Required—TOEFL (minimum score 550 paper-based; 213 computer-based). *Application deadline:* Applications are processed on a rolling basis. Application fee: $50. *Financial support:* Federal Work-Study available. Financial award application deadline: 5/1; financial award applicants required to submit FAFSA. *Faculty research:* Assessment of teacher education, perceptions of prospective teachers by parents. *Unit head:* Dr. E. Lynne Weisenbach, Dean, 317-788-3446, Fax: 317-788-3300, E-mail: weisenbach@uindy.edu.

The University of Iowa, Graduate College, College of Education, Department of Teaching and Learning, Program in Secondary Education, Iowa City, IA 52242-1316. Offers art education (MA, PhD); curriculum and supervision (PhD); curriculum supervision (MA); developmental reading (MA); English education (MA, MAT, PhD); foreign language education (MA, MAT); foreign language/ESL education (PhD); language, literature and culture (PhD); math education (PhD); mathematics education (MA); music education (MA, PhD); social studies (MA, PhD). *Faculty:* 11 full-time. *Students:* 53 full-time (33 women), 53 part-time (41 women); includes 5 minority (1 African American, 1 American Indian/Alaska Native, 2 Asian Americans or Pacific Islanders, 1 Hispanic American), 19 international. 66 applicants, 47% accepted, 17 enrolled. In 2006, 22 master's, 14 doctorates awarded. *Degree requirements:* For master's, exam, thesis optional; for doctorate, thesis/dissertation, comprehensive exam, registration. *Entrance requirements:* For master's and doctorate, GRE General Test, minimum GPA of 3.0. Additional exam requirements/recommendations for international students: Required—TOEFL (minimum score 550 paper-based; 213 computer-based; 81 iBT). Application fee: $60 ($85 for international students). Electronic applications accepted. *Financial support:* In 2006–07, 1 fellowship, 12 research assistantships with partial tuition reimbursements, 31 teaching assistantships with partial tuition reimbursements were awarded. Financial award applicants required to submit FAFSA. *Unit head:* Gary Sasso, Chair, 319-335-5324, Fax: 319-335-5608.

University of Kansas, Graduate Studies, School of Fine Arts, Department of Design, Lawrence, KS 66045. Offers design (MA, MFA), including design (MFA), special studies (MA); visual arts education (MA). *Accreditation:* NASAD (one or more programs are accredited). *Faculty:* 32. *Students:* 31 full-time (21 women), 7 part-time (4 women); includes 1 minority (Asian American or Pacific Islander), 1 international. Average age 29. 50 applicants, 48% accepted. In 2006, 13 degrees awarded. *Degree requirements:* For master's, thesis. *Entrance requirements:* For master's, portfolio, 3 letters of recommendation, minimum GPA of 3.0. Additional exam requirements/recommendations for international students: Required—TOEFL, IELTS. *Application deadline:* For fall admission, 2/1 for domestic students; for spring admission, 10/15 for domestic students. Application fee: $55 ($60 for international students). Electronic applications accepted. *Expenses:* Tuition, area resident: Part-time $227 per credit. Tuition, state resident: part-time $543 per credit. Tuition and fees vary according to course load, campus/location, program and reciprocity agreements. *Financial support:* Fellowships, teaching assistantships with full and partial tuition reimbursements, Federal Work-Study, scholarships/grants, and unspecified assistantships available. Financial award application deadline: 2/1; financial award applicants required to submit FAFSA. *Faculty research:* Crafts, industrial design, textiles/fiber, ceramics, metals/jewelry, visual art education. *Unit head:* Prof. Gregory Thomas, Chairperson, 785-864-4401. *Application contact:* Gina Westergard, Director, 785-864-4401, Fax: 785-864-4404, E-mail: ginaw@ku.edu.

University of Kentucky, Graduate School, College of Fine Arts, Program in Art Education, Lexington, KY 40506-0032. Offers MA. *Faculty:* 18 full-time (7 women). *Students:* 2 full-time (both women), 1 (woman) part-time. Average age 36. 2 applicants, 50% accepted, 1 enrolled. In 2006, 4 degrees awarded. *Degree requirements:* For master's, thesis optional. *Entrance requirements:* For master's, GRE General Test, minimum undergraduate GPA of 2.75. Additional exam requirements/recommendations for international students: Required—TOEFL (minimum score 550 paper-based; 213 computer-based). *Application deadline:* For fall admission, 7/17 priority date for domestic students, 2/1 priority date for international students; for spring admission, 12/13 priority date for domestic students, 6/15 priority date for international students. Application fee: $40 ($55 for international students). Electronic applications accepted. *Expenses:* Tuition, state resident: full-time $7,670; part-time $401 per credit hour. Tuition, nonresident: full-time $16,158; part-time $873 per credit hour. *Financial support:* In 2006–07, 1 student received support, including 1 teaching assistantship with full tuition reimbursement available (averaging $9,494 per year); fellowships with full tuition reimbursements available, research assistantships with full tuition reimbursements available, Federal Work-Study, scholarships/grants, traineeships, health care benefits, tuition waivers (partial), and unspecified assistantships also available. Support available to part-time students. Financial award application deadline: 3/15. *Faculty research:* Multicultural art education, women's issues in art education, lifelong learning in the arts, the artist-teacher, art teaching as a form of art, place and art, children's home art and creativity as a basis for school art instruction. *Unit head:* Dr. Dennis Carpenter, Director of Graduate Studies, 859-257-6041, Fax: 859-257-3042. *Application contact:* Dr. Brian Jackson, Senior Associate Dean, 859-257-4667, Fax: 859-257-4676, E-mail: brian.jackson@uky.edu.

University of Louisville, Graduate School, College of Education and Human Development, Department of Teaching and Learning, Program in Art Education, Louisville, KY 40292-0001. Offers MAT. *Accreditation:* NCATE. *Students:* 12 full-time (9 women), 2 part-time (1 woman); includes 1 minority (African American) Average age 30. In 2006, 12 degrees awarded. *Entrance requirements:* For master's, GRE General Test. *Application deadline:* Applications are processed on a rolling basis. Application fee: $50. Electronic applications accepted. *Financial support:* Fellowships, research assistantships, teaching assistantships, Federal Work-Study and scholarships/grants available. *Unit head:* Prof. Barbara Hanger, Head, 502-852-0879, Fax: 502-852-6791, E-mail: hanger@louisville.edu.

University of Massachusetts Dartmouth, Graduate School, College of Visual and Performing Arts, Program in Art Education, North Dartmouth, MA 02747-2300. Offers MAE. *Accreditation:* NASAD. Part-time programs available. *Faculty:* 2 full-time (both women), 2 part-time/adjunct (both women). *Students:* 7 full-time (5 women), 27 part-time (24 women), 1 international. Average age 34. 9 applicants, 89% accepted, 7 enrolled. In 2006, 5 degrees awarded. *Degree requirements:* For master's, thesis or alternative. *Entrance requirements:* For master's, Massachusetts Tests for Educator Licensure (MTEL), interview, portfolio, minimum GPA of 2.75. Additional exam requirements/recommendations for international students: Required—TOEFL (minimum score 500 paper-based). *Application deadline:* For fall admission, 3/15 priority date for domestic students, 1/15 priority date for international students; for spring admission, 11/15 priority date for domestic students, 9/15 priority date for international students. Applications are processed on a rolling basis. Application fee: $40 ($60 for international students). Electronic applications accepted. *Expenses:* Tuition, state resident: full-time $2,071; part-time $86 per credit. Tuition, nonresident: full-time $8,099; part-time $337 per credit. *Financial support:* Research assistantships with full tuition reimbursements, teaching assistantships with full tuition reimbursements, Federal Work-Study and unspecified assistantships available. Financial award application deadline: 3/1; financial award applicants required to submit FAFSA. *Faculty research:* Integrative models of technology in art classrooms. Total annual research expenditures: $7,025. *Unit head:* Dr. Kathy Miraglia, Director, 508-910-6936, Fax: 508-999-8901, E-mail: kmiraglia@umassd.edu. *Application contact:* Carol Novo, Graduate Admissions Officer, 508-999-8604, Fax: 508-999-8183, E-mail: graduate@umassd.edu.

University of Minnesota, Twin Cities Campus, Graduate School, College of Education and Human Development, Department of Curriculum and Instruction, Minneapolis, MN 55455-0213. Offers art education (M Ed, MA, PhD); children's literature (M Ed, MA, PhD); curriculum and instruction (MA, PhD); early childhood education (M Ed, PhD); elementary education (M Ed, MA, PhD); English education (MA, PhD); environmental education (M Ed); family education (M Ed, MA, Ed D, PhD); instructional systems and technology (M Ed, MA, PhD); language arts (MA, PhD); language immersion education (Certificate); literacy education (MA); mathematics education (MA, PhD); reading education (MA, PhD); science education (MA, PhD); second languages and cultures education (MA, PhD); social studies education (MA, PhD); teaching (M Ed), including Chinese, earth science, elementary special education, English, English as a second language, French, German, Hebrew, Japanese, life sciences, mathematics, middle school science, science, second languages and cultures, social studies, Spanish; technology enhanced learning (Certificate); writing education (M Ed, MA, PhD). *Faculty:* 30 full-time (18 women). *Students:* 496 full-time (363 women), 338 part-time (235 women); includes 89 minority (26 African Americans, 4 American Indian/Alaska Native, 42 Asian Americans or Pacific Islanders, 17 Hispanic Americans), 33 international. Average age 29. 734 applicants, 66% accepted, 425 enrolled. In 2006, 644 master's, 18 doctorates, 11 other advanced degrees awarded. *Expenses:* Tuition, state resident: full-time $9,302; part-time $775 per credit. Tuition, nonresident: full-time $16,400; part-time $1,367 per credit. Full-time tuition and fees vary according to class time, course load, program, reciprocity agreements and student level. *Financial support:* In 2006–07, 7 fellowships (averaging $24,775 per year), 22 research assistantships with full tuition reimbursements (averaging $24,775 per year), 52 teaching assistantships with full tuition reimbursements (averaging $24,775 per year) were awarded. *Faculty research:* Educational practice for a democratic and just society; curriculum history and development/assessment; teacher preparation/induction/mentoring/development; cultural, linguistic, social, political, technological, and economic factors that influence teaching and learning. Total annual research expenditures: $1.2 million. *Unit head:* Dr. Ruth Thomas, Chair, 612-624-4772, Fax: 612-624-8277, E-mail: thoma006@umn.edu. *Application contact:* Dr. Mary Bents, Associate Dean, 612-625-6501, Fax: 612-626-1580, E-mail: mbents@tc.umn.edu.

University of Mississippi, Graduate School, College of Liberal Arts, Department of Art, Oxford, University, MS 38677. Offers art education (MA); art history (MA); fine arts (MFA). *Accreditation:* NASAD (one or more programs are accredited). Part-time programs available. *Faculty:* 11 full-time (7 women), 9 part-time/adjunct (6 women). *Students:* 12 full-time (6 women), 1 (woman) part-time; includes 2 minority (both African Americans), 2 international. 17 applicants, 41% accepted, 5 enrolled. In 2006, 4 degrees awarded. *Degree requirements:* For master's, thesis (for some programs). *Entrance requirements:* For master's, GRE General Test, minimum GPA of 3.0. Additional exam requirements/recommendations for international students: Required—TOEFL. *Application deadline:* For fall admission, 3/1 for domestic students; for spring admission, 10/1 for domestic students. Applications are processed on a rolling basis. Application fee: $25. Electronic applications accepted. *Expenses:* Tuition, state resident: full-time $4,602; part-time $256 per credit hour. Tuition, nonresident: full-time $10,566; part-time $587 per credit hour. *Financial support:* Fellowships, scholarships/grants and unspecified assistantships available. Financial award application deadline: 3/1; financial award applicants required to submit FAFSA. *Unit head:* Dr. Nancy Wicker, Chair, 662-915-7193, Fax: 662-915-5013, E-mail: nwicker@olemiss.edu.

University of Missouri–Columbia, Graduate School, College of Education, Department of Curriculum and Instruction, Columbia, MO 65211. Offers agricultural education (M Ed, PhD, Ed S); art education (M Ed, PhD, Ed S); business and office education (M Ed, PhD, Ed S); early childhood education (M Ed, PhD, Ed S); elementary education (M Ed, PhD, Ed S); English education (M Ed, PhD, Ed S); foreign language education (M Ed, PhD, Ed S); health education and promotion (M Ed, PhD); learning and instruction (M Ed); marketing education (M Ed, PhD, Ed S); mathematics education (M Ed, PhD, Ed S); music education (M Ed, PhD, Ed S); reading education (M Ed, PhD, Ed S); science education (M Ed, PhD, Ed S); social studies education (M Ed, PhD, Ed S); vocational education (M Ed, PhD, Ed S). Part-time programs available. *Faculty:* 24 full-time (12 women). *Students:* 195 full-time (148 women), 260 part-time (214 women); includes 27 minority (8 African Americans, 1 American Indian/Alaska Native, 10 Asian Americans or Pacific Islanders, 8 Hispanic Americans), 19 international. In 2006, 186 master's, 12 doctorates awarded. Terminal master's awarded for partial completion of doctoral program. *Degree requirements:* For doctorate, thesis/dissertation. *Entrance requirements:* For master's and Ed S, GRE General Test or MAT, minimum GPA of 3.0; for doctorate, GRE General Test, minimum GPA of 3.0. *Application deadline:* Applications are processed on a rolling basis. Application fee: $45 ($60 for international students). *Financial support:* Fellowships, research assistantships, teaching assistantships, institutionally sponsored loans available. *Unit head:* Dr. Lloyd H. Barrow, Director of Graduate Studies, 573-882-8247, E-mail: robinsonr@missouri.edu.

University of Nebraska at Kearney, College of Graduate Study, College of Fine Arts and Humanities, Department of Art, Kearney, NE 68849-0001. Offers art education (MA Ed). *Accreditation:* NCATE. Part-time and evening/weekend programs available. *Faculty:* 5 full-time (2 women). *Degree requirements:* For master's, thesis optional. *Entrance requirements:* For master's, slide portfolio. Additional exam requirements/recommendations for international students: Required—TOEFL (minimum score 550 paper-based; 213 computer-based). *Application deadline:* For fall admission, 5/1 for domestic and international students; for spring admission, 8/15 for domestic students, 8/1 for international students. Application fee: $45. Electronic applications accepted. *Expenses:* Tuition, state resident: part-time $161 per hour. Tuition, nonresident: part-time $332 per hour. Required fees: $57 per hour. *Financial support:* In 2006–07, 1 teaching assistantship with full tuition reimbursement (averaging $8,200 per year) was awarded; research assistantships, career-related internships or fieldwork, scholarships/grants, and unspecified assistantships also available. Support available to part-time students. Financial award application deadline: 3/1; financial award applicants required to submit FAFSA. *Faculty research:* Fibers, art education, kiln design construction and low-fire glaze. *Unit head:* Mark Hartman, Chair, 308-865-8353, E-mail: hartmanmd@unk.edu.

University of New Mexico, Graduate School, College of Education, Department of Educational Specialties, Program in Art Education, Albuquerque, NM 87131-2039. Offers MA. *Accreditation:* NCATE. *Students:* 24 full-time (18 women), 23 part-time (18 women); includes 7 minority (4 American Indian/Alaska Native, 3 Hispanic Americans), 3 international. Average age 39. 21 applicants, 67% accepted, 10 enrolled. In 2006, 19 degrees awarded. *Degree requirements:* For master's, participation in art exhibit, thesis optional. *Entrance requirements:* Additional exam requirements/recommendations for international students: Required—TOEFL. *Application deadline:* For fall admission, 3/30 for domestic students; for spring admission, 10/30 for domestic students. Application fee: $50. Electronic applications accepted. *Financial support:* In 2006–07, 30 students received support, including 1 research assistantship (averaging $5,150 per year), 1 teaching assistantship (averaging $5,150 per year); Federal Work-Study, institutionally sponsored loans, scholarships/grants, and unspecified assistantships also available. Financial award application deadline: 3/1; financial award applicants required to submit FAFSA. *Faculty research:* Studio in art education, visual culture, curricular issues regarding gender and sexual identity, archetypal thought in art education. *Unit head:* Prof. Ruth Luckasson, Chair, 505-277-6510, Fax: 505-277-6929, E-mail: luckasson@unm.edu. *Application contact:* Dolores Mendoza, Information Contact, 505-277-4112, Fax: 505-277-0576, E-mail: arted@unm.edu.

The University of North Carolina at Charlotte, Graduate School, College of Education, Program in Teacher Education, Charlotte, NC 28223-0001. Offers art education (K-12) (MAT); dance education (K-12) (MAT); elementary education (K-6) (MAT); English as a second language (K-12) (MAT); foreign language education (K-12) (MAT); general teacher education (MAT); middle grades education (6-9) (MAT); music education (K-12) (MAT); secondary education (9-12) (MAT); special education (K-12) (MAT); theatre education (K-12) (MAT). *Students:* 16 full-time (12 women), 200 part-time (170 women); includes 30 minority (22 African Americans, 2 American Indian/Alaska Native, 2 Asian Americans or Pacific Islanders, 4 Hispanic Americans), 2 international. Average age 33. 74 applicants, 85% accepted, 49 enrolled. In 2006, 43 degrees awarded. *Entrance requirements:* For master's, GRE or MAT. Additional exam requirements/recommendations for international students: Required—TOEFL (minimum score 557 paper-based; 220 computer-based). *Application deadline:* For fall admission, 7/1 for domestic students, 5/1 for international students; for spring admission, 11/1 for domestic students, 10/1 for international students. Applications are processed on a rolling basis. Application fee: $55. Electronic applications accepted. *Expenses:* Tuition, state resident: full-time $2,719; part-time $170 per credit. Tuition, nonresident: full-time $12,926; part-time $808 per credit. Required fees: $1,555. *Financial support:* Fellowships, research assistantships, teaching assistantships, career-related internships or fieldwork, Federal Work-Study, institutionally sponsored loans, scholarships/grants, and unspecified assistantships available. Support available to part-time students. Financial award application deadline: 4/1; financial award applicants required to submit FAFSA. *Unit head:* Dr. Kimberly J. Hartman, Coordinator, 704-687-8883, Fax: 704-687-6430, E-mail: khartman@email.uncc.edu. *Application contact:* Kathy B. Giddings, Director of Graduate Admissions, 704-687-3366, Fax: 704-687-3279, E-mail: gradadm@email.uncc.edu.

The University of North Carolina at Pembroke, Graduate Studies, Department of Art, Pembroke, NC 28372-1510. Offers art education (MA, MAT). Part-time and evening/weekend programs available. *Faculty:* 2 full-time (both women). *Students:* Average age 34. 17 applicants, 100% accepted, 17 enrolled. In 2006, 3 degrees awarded. *Degree requirements:* For master's, capstone show. *Entrance requirements:* For master's, GRE or MAT, minimum GPA of 3.0 in major or 2.5 overall. Additional exam requirements/recommendations for international students: Required—TOEFL. *Application deadline:* For fall admission, 7/15 priority date for domestic and international students; for spring admission, 12/1 priority date for domestic and international students. Applications are processed on a rolling basis. Application fee: $40. *Expenses:* Contact institution. Tuition and fees vary according to class time, course load, degree level and campus/location. *Financial support:* In 2006–07, 1 research assistantship with full tuition reimbursement (averaging $6,000 per year) was awarded; unspecified assistantships also available. Support available to part-time students. Financial award application deadline: 4/15; financial award applicants required to submit FAFSA. *Unit head:* Dr. Doris Ann Horton-Lopez, Director, 910-521-6407, Fax: 910-521-6164, E-mail: ann.horton@uncp.edu. *Application contact:* Dr. Kathleen C. Hilton, Dean of Graduate Studies, 910-521-6271, Fax: 910-521-6751, E-mail: grad@uncp.edu.

University of Northern Iowa, Graduate College, College of Humanities and Fine Arts, Department of Art, Cedar Falls, IA 50614. Offers art (MA); art education (MA). *Accreditation:* NASAD. Part-time and evening/weekend programs available. *Faculty:* 18 full-time (6 women). *Students:* 2 full-time (both women), 1 (woman) part-time. 4 applicants, 25% accepted, 1 enrolled. In 2006, 7 degrees awarded. *Degree requirements:* For master's, comprehensive exam (for some programs). *Entrance requirements:* Additional exam requirements/recommendations for international students: Required—TOEFL (minimum score 500 paper-based; 180 computer-based; 61 iBT). *Application deadline:* For fall admission, 8/1 priority date for domestic students. Applications are processed on a rolling basis. Application fee: $30 ($50 for international students). Electronic applications accepted. *Expenses:* Tuition, state resident: full-time $5,936. Tuition, nonresident: full-time $14,074. *Financial support:* Career-related internships or fieldwork, Federal Work-Study, scholarships/grants, and tuition waivers (full and partial) available. Support available to part-time students. Financial award application deadline: 2/1. *Unit head:* Dr. Jeffery Byrd, Acting Head, 319-273-2077, Fax: 319-273-7333, E-mail: jeffery.byrd@uni.edu.

University of North Texas, Robert B. Toulouse School of Graduate Studies, School of Visual Arts, Denton, TX 76203. Offers art (PhD); art education (MA, MFA, PhD); art history (MA, MFA); ceramics (MFA); communication design (MFA); fashion design (MFA); fibers (MFA); interior design (MFA); metalsmithing and jewelry (MFA); painting and drawing (MFA); photography (MFA); printmaking (MFA); sculpture (MFA). Part-time programs available. *Faculty:* 50 full-time (26 women). *Students:* 83 full-time (63 women), 72 part-time (53 women); includes 23 minority (4 African Americans, 1 American Indian/Alaska Native, 5 Asian Americans or Pacific Islanders, 13 Hispanic Americans), 14 international. Average age 31. 133 applicants, 56% accepted, 37 enrolled. In 2006, 46 master's, 3 doctorates awarded. *Degree requirements:* For master's, variable foreign language requirement, thesis (for some programs); for doctorate, thesis/dissertation. *Entrance requirements:* For master's and doctorate, GRE General Test, portfolio. Additional exam requirements/recommendations for international students: Recommended—TOEFL (minimum score 550 paper-based; 213 computer-based). *Application deadline:* For fall admission, 7/15 priority date for domestic students; for spring admission, 10/1 for domestic students. Applications are processed on a rolling basis. Application fee: $50 ($75 for international students). *Expenses:* Tuition, state resident: full-time $3,573; part-time $198 per credit. Tuition, nonresident: full-time $8,577; part-time $476 per credit. Required fees: $1,258; $126 per credit. One-time fee: $150 full-time. Tuition and fees vary according to course load. *Financial support:* Fellowships, teaching assistantships, career-related internships or fieldwork, Federal Work-Study, and institutionally sponsored loans available. Support available to part-time students. Financial award application deadline: 4/1. *Faculty research:* Large-scale watercolors, enameling, serigraphy, clay bodies, discipline-based art education. Total annual research expenditures: $363,000. *Unit head:* Dr. Robert Milnes, Dean, 940-565-4003, Fax: 940-565-4717, E-mail: milnes@unt.edu.

University of Rio Grande, Graduate School, Rio Grande, OH 45674. Offers classroom teaching (M Ed), including fine arts, learning disabilities, mathematics, reading education.

Art Education

University of Rio Grande (continued)
Part-time and evening/weekend programs available. *Degree requirements:* For master's, final research project, portfolio. *Entrance requirements:* For master's, minimum GPA of 2.7 in major, 2.5 overall. *Faculty research:* Interagency collaboration, reading and mathematics, learning styles, college access, literacy.

University of South Carolina, The Graduate School, College of Arts and Sciences, Department of Art, Program in Art Education, Columbia, SC 29208. Offers IMA, MA, MAT. IMA and MAT offered in cooperation with the College of Education. *Accreditation:* NCATE. *Degree requirements:* For master's, thesis (for some programs), comprehensive exam, registration. *Entrance requirements:* For master's, GRE General Test or MAT, portfolio. Additional exam requirements/recommendations for international students: Required—TOEFL. Electronic applications accepted. *Faculty research:* Teaching art at the primary and secondary levels of education.

University of South Carolina, The Graduate School, College of Education, Department of Instruction and Teacher Education, Program in Secondary Education, Columbia, SC 29208. Offers art education (IMA, MAT); business education (IMA, MAT); English (MAT); foreign language (MAT); health education (MAT); mathematics (MAT); science (IMA, MAT); secondary education (M Ed, MA, MT, PhD); social studies (IMA, MAT); theatre and speech (IMA, MAT). IMA and MT offered jointly with the subject areas. *Accreditation:* NCATE. *Degree requirements:* For master's, thesis (for some programs), foreign language (MA), comprehensive exam; for doctorate, one foreign language, thesis/dissertation, comprehensive exam. *Entrance requirements:* For master's, GRE General Test or MAT, teaching certificate (IMA, M Ed), interview; for doctorate, GRE General Test or MAT, interview. *Faculty research:* Middle school programs, professional development, school collaboration.

University of Southern Mississippi, Graduate School, College of Arts and Letters, Department of Art and Design, Hattiesburg, MS 39406-0001. Offers art education (MAE). *Accreditation:* NASAD. *Faculty:* 11 full-time (7 women). *Students:* 2 full-time (both women). Average age 29. 1 applicant, 0% accepted. In 2006, 2 degrees awarded. *Degree requirements:* For master's, project. *Entrance requirements:* For master's, GRE General Test, BFA, minimum GPA of 3.0, portfolio. Additional exam requirements/recommendations for international students: Required—TOEFL. *Application deadline:* For fall admission, 3/1 priority date for domestic students, 3/1 for international students. Applications are processed on a rolling basis. Application fee: $25 ($30 for international students). *Financial support:* In 2006–07, 2 teaching assistantships with full tuition reimbursements (averaging $5,500 per year) were awarded; research assistantships, career-related internships or fieldwork, Federal Work-Study, scholarships/grants, and unspecified assistantships also available. Financial award application deadline: 3/15. *Unit head:* Susan Fitzsimmons, Chair, 601-266-4972, Fax: 601-266-6379, E-mail: graduate.studies@usm.edu.

The University of Tennessee, Graduate School, College of Education, Health and Human Sciences, Program in Education, Knoxville, TN 37996. Offers art education (MS); counseling education (PhD); cultural studies in education (PhD); curriculum (MS, Ed S); curriculum, educational research and evaluation (Ed D, PhD); early childhood education (PhD); early childhood special education (MS); education of deaf and hard of hearing (MS); educational administration and policy studies (Ed D, PhD); educational administration and supervision (Ed S); educational psychology (Ed D, PhD); elementary education (MS, Ed S); elementary teaching (MS); English education (MS, Ed S); exercise science (PhD); foreign language/ESL education (MS, Ed S); instructional technology (MS, Ed D, PhD, Ed S); literacy, language and ESL education (PhD); literacy, language education, and ESL education (Ed D); mathematics education (MS, Ed S); modified and comprehensive special education (MS); reading education (MS, Ed S); school counseling (Ed S); school psychology (PhD, Ed S); science education (MS, Ed S); secondary teaching (MS); social foundations (MS); social science education (MS, Ed S); socio-cultural foundations of sports and education (PhD); special education (Ed S); teacher education (Ed D, PhD). *Accreditation:* NCATE. Part-time and evening/weekend programs available. *Students:* 529 (401 women); includes 39 minority (23 African Americans, 2 American Indian/Alaska Native, 9 Asian Americans or Pacific Islanders, 5 Hispanic Americans) 34 international. 420 applicants, 50% accepted. In 2006, 258 master's, 28 doctorates awarded. *Degree requirements:* For master's and Ed S, thesis optional; for doctorate, variable foreign language requirement, thesis/dissertation. *Entrance requirements:* For master's, minimum GPA of 2.7; for doctorate and Ed S, GRE General Test, minimum GPA of 2.7. Additional exam requirements/recommendations for international students: Required—TOEFL. *Application deadline:* For fall admission, 2/1 priority date for domestic students. Applications are processed on a rolling basis. Application fee: $35. Electronic applications accepted. *Expenses:* Tuition, state resident: full-time $5,574. Tuition, nonresident: full-time $16,840. Required fees: $792. *Financial support:* In 2006–07, 4 fellowships, 9 teaching assistantships were awarded; career-related internships or fieldwork, Federal Work-Study, institutionally sponsored loans, and unspecified assistantships also available. Financial award application deadline: 2/1; financial award applicants required to submit FAFSA. *Unit head:* Dr. Lester Knight, Head, 865-974-0907, Fax: 865-974-8718, E-mail: lknight@utk.edu.

The University of Texas at Austin, Graduate School, College of Fine Arts, Department of Art and Art History, Program in Art Education, Austin, TX 78712-1111. Offers MA. *Accreditation:* NASAD. Part-time programs available. *Degree requirements:* For master's, thesis, oral and written exam. *Entrance requirements:* For master's, GRE General Test, 2 samples of written work, 10 slides of art work. Electronic applications accepted. *Faculty research:* Museum education; community-based, environmental, and multicultural art education; interdisciplinary art education, elementary and secondary art education.

The University of Texas at Tyler, College of Education and Psychology, Department of Curriculum and Instruction, Tyler, TX 75799-0001. Offers curriculum and instruction (M Ed); secondary teaching (MAT), including art, biology, computer science, English, history, journalism, mathematics, music, political science, sociology, speech, theatre. Part-time programs available. *Faculty:* 10 full-time (6 women), 2 part-time/adjunct (1 woman). *Students:* 3 full-time (2 women), 7 part-time (6 women); includes 1 minority (African American) Average age 32. 1 applicant, 100% accepted, 1 enrolled. In 2006, 6 degrees awarded. *Degree requirements:* For master's, research project (M Ed). *Entrance requirements:* For master's, GRE or MAT. Application fee: $0 ($50 for international students). Electronic applications accepted. *Expenses:* Tuition, state resident: part-time $50 per credit hour. Tuition, nonresident: part-time $328 per credit hour. Required fees: $107 per credit hour. $426 per term. *Financial support:* Scholarships/grants available. *Unit head:* Dr. Robert Stevens, Chair/Professor of Education, 903-566-7315, E-mail: rstevens@uttyler.edu. *Application contact:* Bonnie Purser, Office of Graduate Studies, 903-566-7142, Fax: 903-566-7068, E-mail: bpurser@uttyler.edu.

The University of the Arts, College of Art and Design, Department of Art Education, Philadelphia, PA 19102-4944. Offers art education (MA); visual arts (MAT). *Accreditation:* NASAD (one or more programs are accredited). Part-time programs available. *Degree requirements:* For master's, thesis (for some programs), student teaching experience (MAT). *Entrance requirements:* For master's, portfolio, 45 credits of studio work (MAT), 12 credits of art history (MAT), BFA or BA in art. Additional exam requirements/recommendations for international students: Required—TOEFL (minimum score 550 paper-based; 213 computer-based). *Faculty research:* Using technology and visual arts concepts to develop critical and creative thinking skills.

The University of Toledo, College of Graduate Studies, College of Education, Department of Curriculum and Instruction, Program in Art Education, Toledo, OH 43606-3390. Offers ME. *Students:* 8 full-time (7 women), 13 part-time (10 women); includes 4 minority (3 African Americans, 1 Asian American or Pacific Islander). Average age 32. 8 applicants, 100% accepted, 6 enrolled. In 2006, 7 degrees awarded. Application fee: $45.

University of Utah, The Graduate School, College of Fine Arts, Department of Art and Art History, Salt Lake City, UT 84112-1107. Offers art history (MA); ceramics (MFA); community-based art education (MFA); drawing (MFA); graphic design (MFA); illustration (MFA); painting (MFA); photography/digital imaging (MFA); printmaking (MFA); sculpture/intermedia (MFA). *Faculty:* 18 full-time (6 women). *Students:* 17 full-time (7 women), 5 part-time (3 women); includes 1 minority (American Indian/Alaska Native). Average age 31. 40 applicants, 18% accepted, 6 enrolled. In 2006, 7 degrees awarded. *Entrance requirements:* For master's, GRE General Test or GMAT (MA), slide portfolio (MFA). Additional exam requirements/recommendations for international students: Required—TOEFL (minimum score 600 paper-based; 173 computer-based). *Application deadline:* For fall admission, 2/1 priority date for domestic and international students. Application fee: $45 ($65 for international students). *Expenses:* Tuition, state resident: full-time $3,208. Tuition, nonresident: full-time $11,326. Required fees: $608. Tuition and fees vary according to class time and program. *Financial support:* Fellowships, teaching assistantships with tuition reimbursements, Federal Work-Study, institutionally sponsored loans, scholarships/grants, tuition waivers (partial), and unspecified assistantships available. Financial award application deadline: 2/1; financial award applicants required to submit FAFSA. *Faculty research:* Intermedia, digital arts, installation, traditional media, Asian art, medieval arts. Total annual research expenditures: $27,305. *Unit head:* Dr. Elizabeth A. Peterson, Chair/Art History Program Director, 801-581-7012, Fax: 801-585-6171, E-mail: elizabeth.peterson@art.utah.edu. *Application contact:* Prof. Brian Snapp, Director of Graduate Studies, 801-581-8677, Fax: 801-585-6171, E-mail: fireart@xmission.com.

University of Victoria, Faculty of Graduate Studies, Faculty of Education, Department of Curriculum and Instruction, Victoria, BC V8W 2Y2, Canada. Offers art (M Ed, MA, PhD); curriculum studies (M Ed, MA, PhD); early childhood (M Ed, MA, PhD); language and literacy (M Ed, MA, PhD); mathematics (M Ed, MA, PhD); music (M Ed, MA); music education (PhD); science (M Ed, MA, PhD); social studies (M Ed, MA); social, cultural and foundational studies (PhD); technology and environmental education (PhD). Part-time programs available. *Degree requirements:* For master's, thesis, project (M Ed); for doctorate, thesis/dissertation, comprehensive exam, registration. *Entrance requirements:* For master's, minimum B average. Additional exam requirements/recommendations for international students: Required—TOEFL (minimum score 575 paper-based; 233 computer-based), IELTS (minimum score 7). Electronic applications accepted. *Faculty research:* Elementary and secondary English, language arts, curriculum theory and practice, educational media and technology, educational administration and leadership, history and philosophy of education.

University of West Georgia, Graduate School, College of Education, Department of Curriculum and Instruction, Program in Art Education, Carrollton, GA 30118. Offers M Ed. *Accreditation:* NASAD. Part-time programs available. *Faculty:* 11 full-time (5 women), 7 part-time/adjunct (5 women). *Students:* Average age 32. In 2006, 5 degrees awarded. *Degree requirements:* For master's, thesis. *Entrance requirements:* For master's, GRE General Test or GMAT, minimum GPA of 2.5, portfolio. *Application deadline:* For fall admission, 8/1 for domestic students; for spring admission, 12/18 for domestic students. Application fee: $20. Electronic applications accepted. *Expenses:* Tuition, state resident: full-time $2,286; part-time $127 per credit. Tuition, nonresident: full-time $9,144; part-time $508 per credit. Required fees: $494; $27 per credit. $121 per semester. *Financial support:* In 2006–07, 1 student received support, including 1 research assistantship with full tuition reimbursement available (averaging $6,200 per year); career-related internships or fieldwork, scholarships/grants, tuition waivers (partial), and unspecified assistantships also available. Support available to part-time students. Financial award applicants required to submit FAFSA. *Faculty research:* Iron casting, painting, digital imaging technology, zinc crystalline glazes, medieval art history. *Unit head:* Kevin Shunn, Interim Chair, 678-839-4959, Fax: 678-839-4961, E-mail: kshunn@westga.edu. *Application contact:* Dr. Charles W. Clark, Chair, 678-839-6508, E-mail: cclark@westga.edu.

University of Wisconsin–Madison, Graduate School, School of Education, Department of Art and Department of Curriculum and Instruction, Program in Art Education, Madison, WI 53706-1380. Offers MA. *Accreditation:* NASAD. *Application deadline:* For fall admission, 1/10 for domestic students; for spring admission, 11/15 for domestic students. Application fee: $45. *Financial support:* Fellowships with full tuition reimbursements, research assistantships with full tuition reimbursements, teaching assistantships with full tuition reimbursements, project assistantships available. *Unit head:* Elaine Scheer, Chair, Department of Art, 608-262-1662.

University of Wisconsin–Madison, Graduate School, School of Education, Department of Curriculum and Instruction, Madison, WI 53706-1380. Offers art education (MA); curriculum and instruction (MS, PhD); education and mathematics (MA); French education (MA); German education (MA); music education (MS); science education (MS); Spanish education (MA). *Accreditation:* NASM (one or more programs are accredited). *Degree requirements:* For doctorate, thesis/dissertation. Application fee: $45. *Financial support:* Project assistantships available. *Unit head:* Dr. Alan Lockwood, Chair, 608-262-4000.

University of Wisconsin–Milwaukee, Graduate School, Peck School of the Arts, Department of Art, Milwaukee, WI 53201-0413. Offers art (MA, MFA); art education (MA, MFA, MS). Part-time programs available. *Faculty:* 24 full-time (14 women). *Students:* 17 full-time (11 women), 7 part-time (2 women); includes 2 minority (1 American Indian/Alaska Native, 1 Hispanic American), 2 international. 58 applicants, 14% accepted, 7 enrolled. In 2006, 7 degrees awarded. *Degree requirements:* For master's, thesis or alternative. *Application deadline:* For fall admission, 1/1 priority date for domestic students; for spring admission, 9/1 for domestic students. Applications are processed on a rolling basis. Application fee: $45 ($75 for international students). *Expenses:* Tuition, state resident: part-time $510 per credit. Tuition, nonresident: part-time $1,408 per credit. Tuition and fees vary according to program. *Financial support:* In 2006–07, 5 teaching assistantships were awarded; fellowships, research assistantships, career-related internships or fieldwork and unspecified assistantships also available. Support available to part-time students. Financial award application deadline: 4/15. *Unit head:* Lane Hall, Representative, 414-229-6053.

University of Wisconsin–Superior, Graduate Division, Department of Visual Arts, Superior, WI 54880-4500. Offers art education (MA); art history (MA); art therapy (MA); studio arts (MA). Part-time programs available. *Degree requirements:* For master's, exhibit. *Entrance requirements:* For master's, minimum GPA of 2.75, portfolio.

Virginia Commonwealth University, Graduate School, School of the Arts, Department of Art Education, Richmond, VA 23284-9005. Offers MAE. *Accreditation:* NASAD. *Faculty:* 6 full-time (4 women). *Students:* 9 full-time (8 women), 11 part-time (9 women); includes 1 minority (Hispanic American), 2 international. 10 applicants, 60% accepted, 2 enrolled. In 2006, 7 degrees awarded. *Degree requirements:* For master's, thesis optional. *Entrance requirements:* For master's, portfolio. *Application deadline:* For fall admission, 3/1 for domestic students; for spring admission, 11/1 for domestic students. Application fee: $50. *Financial support:* Fellowships, career-related internships or fieldwork, Federal Work-Study, and institutionally sponsored loans available. Financial award application deadline: 3/15. *Faculty research:* Teaching methods. *Unit head:* Dr. Charles F. Bleick, Chair, 804-828-1995, Fax: 804-828-6469, E-mail: cfbleick@vcu.edu.

See Close-Up on page 1619.

Wayne State University, College of Education, Division of Teacher Education, Detroit, MI 48202. Offers adult and continuing education (M Ed); art education (M Ed); bilingual/bicultural education (M Ed, MAT); business education (M Ed, MAT); career and technical education (M Ed, Ed D, PhD, Ed S); curriculum and instruction (Ed D, PhD, Ed S); distributive education (M Ed, MAT); early childhood education (M Ed); elementary education (M Ed, MAT, Ed D, PhD, Ed S); elementary education curriculum and instruction (M Ed); English education (M Ed); English education-secondary (M Ed, Ed S); foreign language education (M Ed); general education (Ed D, Ed S); health occupations education (M Ed); industrial education (M Ed); mathematics education (M Ed, Ed S); pre-school and parent education (M Ed); reading (M Ed, Ed D, Ed S); reading, languages and literature (Ed D); school music-vocal (M Ed); science education (M Ed, MAT, Ed S); secondary education (MAT); secondary school reading (M Ed); social studies education (M Ed, Ed S), including education-secondary (M Ed); special education (M Ed, Ed D, PhD, Ed S); teacher education (MAT, Ed D, PhD). *Faculty:* 41 full-time (22 women), 2 part-time/adjunct (both women). *Students:* 401 full-time (295 women), 1,021 part-time (784 women); includes 527 minority (452 African Americans, 6 American Indian/Alaska Native, 32 Asian Americans or Pacific Islanders, 37 Hispanic Americans), 18 international. Average age 36. 296 applicants, 81% accepted, 132 enrolled. In 2006, 386 master's, 1 doctorate awarded. *Degree requirements:* For doctorate, thesis/dissertation. *Entrance requirements:* For master's, minimum GPA of 2.6; for doctorate, minimum undergraduate GPA of 3.0, graduate 3.5; interview. Additional exam requirements/recommendations for international students: Required—TOEFL (minimum score 550 paper-based; 213 computer-based), TWE (minimum score 6). *Application deadline:* For fall admission, 7/1 for domestic students, 6/1 for international students; for winter admission, 10/1 for international students; for spring admission, 2/1 for international students. Application fee: $30 ($50 for international students). Electronic applications accepted. *Financial support:* In 2006–07, 1 fellowship (averaging $34,919 per year) was awarded; research assistantships. *Faculty research:* Reading and writing literacy and literature. Total annual research expenditures: $209,400. *Unit head:* Dr. Joann Snyder, Academic Director, 313-577-1644, E-mail: joanne.snyder@wayne.edu. *Application contact:* Sharon Elliott, Assistant Dean, 313-577-0902, E-mail: sharon.elliott@wayne.edu.

Western Carolina University, Graduate School, College of Arts and Sciences, Department of Art, Program in Art Education, Cullowhee, NC 28723. Offers art education (MAT); comprehensive education—art (MA Ed). *Accreditation:* NCATE. Part-time and evening/weekend programs available. *Degree requirements:* For master's, thesis, exhibit, comprehensive exam. *Entrance requirements:* For master's, GRE General Test, portfolio. Additional exam requirements/recommendations for international students: Required—TOEFL (minimum score 550 paper-based; 213 computer-based).

Western Carolina University, Graduate School, College of Education and Allied Professions, Department of Educational Leadership and Foundations, Programs in Secondary Education, Cullowhee, NC 28723. Offers art education (MAT); biology (MAT); chemistry (MAT); comprehensive education (MA Ed), including art, biology, English, mathematics, music, physical education, reading, social sciences; English (MAT); family and consumer sciences (MAT); mathematics (MAT); physical education (MAT); reading (MAT); social sciences (MAT). *Accreditation:* NCATE (one or more programs are accredited). Part-time and evening/weekend programs available. *Degree requirements:* For master's, comprehensive exam. *Entrance requirements:* For master's, GRE General Test, portfolio. Additional exam requirements/recommendations for international students: Required—TOEFL (minimum score 550 paper-based; 213 computer-based).

Western Kentucky University, Graduate Studies, Potter College of Arts and Letters, Department of Art, Bowling Green, KY 42101. Offers art education (MA Ed). *Accreditation:* NASAD; NCATE. Part-time and evening/weekend programs available. *Faculty:* 1 full-time (0 women). *Students:* Average age 38. In 2006, 2 degrees awarded. *Degree requirements:* For master's, final exam. *Entrance requirements:* For master's, GRE General Test, minimum GPA of 2.75. Additional exam requirements/recommendations for international students: Required—TOEFL (minimum score 555 paper-based; 213 computer-based; 79 iBT). *Application deadline:* For fall admission, 7/1 priority date for domestic students, 4/1 for international students; for spring admission, 11/1 for domestic students, 9/1 for international students. Applications are processed on a rolling basis. Application fee: $35. *Expenses:* Tuition, state resident: full-time $6,520; part-time $226 per hour. Tuition, nonresident: full-time $7,140; part-time $357 per hour. International tuition: $15,820 full-time. *Financial support:* Federal Work-Study, institutionally sponsored loans, and service awards available. Support available to part-time students. Financial award application deadline: 4/1; financial award applicants required to submit FAFSA. *Faculty research:* Nineteenth century Kentucky women artists. *Unit head:* James K Chalmers, Head, 270-745-3944, Fax: 270-745-5932, E-mail: james.chalmers@wku.edu.

West Virginia University, College of Creative Arts, Division of Art, Morgantown, WV 26506. Offers art education (MA); art history (MA); ceramics (MFA); graphic design (MFA); painting (MFA); printmaking (MFA); sculpture (MFA); studio art (MA). *Accreditation:* NASAD. *Faculty:* 17 full-time (9 women), 8 part-time/adjunct (4 women). *Students:* 23 full-time (15 women), 1 (woman) part-time, 6 international. Average age 28. 55 applicants, 40% accepted, 11 enrolled. In 2006, 7 degrees awarded. *Degree requirements:* For master's, thesis, exhibit. *Entrance requirements:* For master's, minimum GPA of 2.75, portfolio. Additional exam requirements/recommendations for international students: Required—TOEFL. *Application deadline:* For fall admission, 3/1 for domestic students, 2/15 for international students; for spring admission, 10/15 for domestic and international students. Application fee: $45. *Expenses:* Contact institution. Tuition and fees vary according to program. *Financial support:* In 2006–07, 22 students received support, including 11 teaching assistantships with full tuition reimbursements available; research assistantships with full tuition reimbursements available, Federal Work-Study, institutionally sponsored loans, tuition waivers (full and partial), and graduate administrative assistantships also available. Financial award application deadline: 3/15; financial award applicants required to submit FAFSA. *Faculty research:* Medieval art history. *Unit head:* Allison Helm, Interim Chair, 304-293-4841 Ext. 3140, Fax: 304-293-3136, E-mail: allison.helm@wvu.edu.

Wichita State University, Graduate School, College of Fine Arts, School of Art and Design, Wichita, KS 67260. Offers art education (MA); studio arts (MFA). *Degree requirements:* For master's, project. *Entrance requirements:* For master's, GRE, BAE or BFA, portfolio. Additional exam requirements/recommendations for international students: Required—TOEFL. Electronic applications accepted.

William Carey University, Graduate Studies, School of Education, Hattiesburg, MS 39401-5499. Offers art education (M Ed); art of teaching (M Ed); elementary education (M Ed, Ed S); English education (M Ed); gifted education (M Ed); history and social science (M Ed); mild/moderate disabilities (M Ed); secondary education (M Ed). Part-time programs available. *Faculty:* 19 full-time (12 women), 25 part-time/adjunct (17 women). *Students:* 142 full-time (111 women), 412 part-time (343 women); includes 123 minority (121 African Americans, 1 Asian American or Pacific Islander, 1 Hispanic American). In 2006, 305 master's, 2 other advanced degrees awarded. *Degree requirements:* For master's, comprehensive exam. *Entrance requirements:* For master's, GRE, MAT, minimum GPA of 2.5, Class A teacher's license. Additional exam requirements/recommendations for international students: Required—TOEFL (minimum score 550 paper-based; 213 computer-based). *Application deadline:* For fall admission, 8/7 for domestic and international students; for winter admission, 10/30 for domestic and international students; for spring admission, 2/12 for domestic and international students. Application fee: $25. *Expenses:* Tuition: Full-time $5,040; part-time $240 per credit hour. Tuition and fees vary according to course load. *Financial support:* In 2006–07, 371 students received support. Federal Work-Study and scholarships/grants available. Support available to part-time students. *Unit head:* Dr. Patty Ward, Dean, 601-318-6139, Fax: 601-318-6185, E-mail: patty.ward@wmcarey.edu. *Application contact:* Jason Douglas, Clerical Assistant, Graduate Admissions, 601-318-6774, Fax: 601-318-6765, E-mail: jason.douglas@wmcarey.edu.

Winthrop University, College of Visual and Performing Arts, Department of Art and Design, Rock Hill, SC 29733. Offers art (MFA); art administration (MA); art education (MA). *Accreditation:* NASAD. Part-time programs available. *Faculty:* 11 full-time (4 women), 4 part-time/adjunct (3 women). *Students:* 4 full-time (all women), 32 part-time (23 women); includes 4 minority (2 African Americans, 2 American Indian/Alaska Native), 1 international. Average age 38. In 2006, 10 degrees awarded. *Degree requirements:* For master's, thesis, documented exhibit, oral exam. *Entrance requirements:* For master's, GRE General Test or MAT, PRAXIS (MA), minimum GPA of 3.0, resumé, slide portfolio, teaching certificate (MA). *Application deadline:* For fall admission, 3/1 priority date for domestic students; for spring admission, 9/1 for domestic students. Applications are processed on a rolling basis. Application fee: $35 ($50 for international students). Electronic applications accepted. *Expenses:* Tuition, state resident: full-time $9,148; part-time $383 per hour. Tuition, nonresident: full-time $16,864; part-time $704 per hour. *Financial support:* Federal Work-Study, scholarships/grants, and unspecified assistantships available. Support available to part-time students. Financial award application deadline: 2/1; financial award applicants required to submit FAFSA. *Unit head:* Dr. Alice Burmeister, Chair, 803-323-2653, E-mail: burmeistera@winthrop.edu. *Application contact:* 800-411-7041, Fax: 803-323-2292, E-mail: graduatestu@winthrop.edu.

Business Education

Albany State University, College of Education, Program in Business Education, Albany, GA 31705-2717. Offers M Ed. *Accreditation:* NCATE. Part-time programs available. *Degree requirements:* For master's, comprehensive exam. *Entrance requirements:* For master's, GRE General Test, MAT or NTE. Electronic applications accepted.

Arkansas State University, Graduate School, College of Business, Department of Computer and Information Technology, Jonesboro, State University, AR 72467. Offers business education (SCCT); business technology education (MSE); information systems and e-commerce (MS). Part-time programs available. *Faculty:* 6 full-time (1 woman), 1 part-time/adjunct (0 women). *Students:* 8 full-time (4 women), 17 part-time (13 women); includes 8 minority (all African Americans), 1 international. Average age 33. 13 applicants, 100% accepted, 13 enrolled. In 2006, 9 degrees awarded. *Degree requirements:* For master's and SCCT, thesis or alternative, comprehensive exam. *Entrance requirements:* For master's, GRE General Test or MAT, appropriate bachelor's degree, official transcript. Additional exam requirements/recommendations for international students: Required—TOEFL (minimum score 213 computer-based). *Application deadline:* Applications are processed on a rolling basis. Application fee: $30 ($40 for international students). Electronic applications accepted. *Expenses:* Contact institution. *Financial support:* Teaching assistantships, career-related internships or fieldwork and unspecified assistantships available. Financial award application deadline: 7/1; financial award applicants required to submit FAFSA. *Unit head:* Dr. John Seydel, Chair, 870-972-3416, Fax: 870-972-3417, E-mail: jseydel@astate.edu.

Arkansas State University, Graduate School, College of Business, Department of Management and Marketing, Jonesboro, State University, AR 72467. Offers business administration (SCCT); business education (SCCT). *Accreditation:* NCATE. Part-time programs available. *Faculty:* 7 full-time (2 women). *Students:* 14 applicants, 86% accepted, 0 enrolled. In 2006, 1 degree awarded. *Degree requirements:* For SCCT, comprehensive exam. *Entrance requirements:* For degree, GRE General Test or MAT, interview, master's degree, official transcript. Additional exam requirements/recommendations for international students: Required—TOEFL (minimum score 213 computer-based). *Application deadline:* Applications are processed on a rolling basis. Application fee: $30 ($40 for international students). Electronic applications accepted. *Expenses:* Contact institution. *Financial support:* Career-related internships or fieldwork, scholarships/grants, and unspecified assistantships available. Financial award application deadline: 7/1; financial award applicants required to submit FAFSA. *Unit head:* Dr. Gail Hudson, Chair, 870-972-3430, Fax: 870-972-3833, E-mail: ghud@astate.edu.

Armstrong Atlantic State University, School of Graduate Studies, Program in Education, Savannah, GA 31419-1997. Offers adult education (M Ed); early childhood education (M Ed); education (M Ed); elementary education (M Ed); middle grades education (M Ed); secondary education (M Ed), including business education, English education, mathematics education, science education, social science education; special education (M Ed), including behavioral disorders, curriculum and instruction, learning disabilities, speech-language pathology. *Accreditation:* NCATE. Part-time and evening/weekend programs available. Postbaccalaureate distance learning degree programs offered (minimal on-campus study). *Faculty:* 11 full-time (9 women), 13 part-time/adjunct (10 women). *Students:* 50 full-time (42 women), 219 part-time (175 women); includes 71 minority (67 African Americans, 3 Asian Americans or Pacific Islanders, 1 Hispanic American), 6 international. Average age 35. In 2006, 151 degrees awarded. *Degree requirements:* For master's, portfolio. *Entrance requirements:* For master's, GRE General Test or MAT, minimum GPA of 2.5, letters of recommendation. Additional exam requirements/recommendations for international students: Required—TOEFL (minimum score 523 paper-based; 193 computer-based). *Application deadline:* For fall admission, 7/1 priority date for domestic and international students; for spring admission, 11/15 priority date for domestic and international students. Applications are processed on a rolling basis. Application fee: $25. Electronic applications accepted. *Expenses:* Tuition, state resident: full-time $2,286; part-time $127 per credit. Tuition, nonresident: full-time $9,144; part-time $508 per credit. One-time fee: $257. *Financial support:* In 2006–07, research assistantships with partial tuition reimbursements (averaging $2,500 per year); career-related internships or fieldwork, Federal Work-Study, scholarships/grants, and unspecified assistantships also available. Support available to part-time students. Financial award applicants required to submit FAFSA. *Unit head:* Dr. Jane McHaney, College of Education Dean, 912-927-5398, Fax: 912-921-7425, E-mail: mchaneia@mail.armstrong.edu.

Auburn University, Graduate School, College of Education, Department of Curriculum and Teaching, Auburn University, AL 36849. Offers business education (M Ed, MS, PhD); early childhood education (M Ed, MS, PhD, Ed S); elementary education (M Ed, MS, PhD, Ed S); foreign languages (M Ed, MS); music education (M Ed, MS, PhD, Ed S); postsecondary education (PhD); reading education (PhD, Ed S); secondary education (M Ed, MS, PhD, Ed S), including English language arts, mathematics, science, social studies. *Accreditation:* NASM (one or more programs are accredited); NCATE. Part-time programs available. *Faculty:* 26 full-time (19 women). *Students:* 51 full-time (36 women), 116 part-time (86 women); includes 24 minority (23 African Americans, 1 Asian American or Pacific Islander). Average age 33. 181 applicants, 56% accepted, 68 enrolled. In 2006, 63 master's, 12 doctorates, 14 other advanced degrees awarded. *Degree requirements:* For master's, thesis (for some programs); for doctorate, thesis/dissertation; for Ed S, field project. *Entrance requirements:* For master's, doctorate, and Ed S, GRE General Test. *Application deadline:* For fall admission, 7/7 for domestic students; for spring admission, 11/24 for domestic students. Applications are processed on a rolling basis. Application fee: $25 ($50 for international students). Electronic applications accepted. *Expenses:* Tuition, state resident: full-time $5,000. Tuition, nonresident: full-time $15,000. Required fees: $416. Tuition and fees vary according to program. *Financial support:* Fellowships, teaching assistantships, career-related internships or fieldwork and Federal Work-Study available. Support available to part-time students. Financial award application deadline: 3/15. *Faculty research:* Emerging literacy, reading attitudes, music for at-risk youth, portfolio assessment. *Unit head:* Dr. Andrew M. Weaver, Head, 334-844-4434, E-mail:

Business Education

Auburn University (continued)

weaveam@mail.auburn.edu. *Application contact:* Dr. Joe Pittman, Interim Dean of the Graduate School, 334-844-4700.

Ball State University, Graduate School, Miller College of Business, Department of Information Systems and Operations Management, Muncie, IN 47306-1099. Offers MAE. *Accreditation:* NCATE. *Faculty:* 4. *Students:* 1 full-time (0 women), 9 part-time (7 women). 4 applicants, 100% accepted, 2 enrolled. In 2006, 2 degrees awarded. *Entrance requirements:* For master's, GMAT. *Application fee:* $25 ($35 for international students). *Financial support:* In 2006–07, 8 teaching assistantships with full tuition reimbursements (averaging $8,356 per year) were awarded. Financial award application deadline: 3/1. *Unit head:* Dr. Thomas Harris, Chair, 765-285-5227, Fax: 765-285-8024.

Bloomsburg University of Pennsylvania, School of Graduate Studies, College of Business, Department of Business Education and Business Information Systems, Program in Business Education, Bloomsburg, PA 17815-1301. Offers M Ed. *Faculty:* 3 full-time (0 women). *Students:* 8 full-time (6 women), 13 part-time (3 women). Average age 31. 10 applicants, 100% accepted, 5 enrolled. In 2006, 19 degrees awarded. *Degree requirements:* For master's, thesis optional. *Entrance requirements:* For master's, GRE General Test, minimum QPA of 3.0, 2 letters of recommendation. Additional exam requirements/recommendations for international students: Required—TOEFL. *Application deadline:* Applications are processed on a rolling basis. Application fee: $30. Electronic applications accepted. *Expenses:* Tuition, state resident: full-time $6,048; part-time $336 per credit. Tuition, nonresident: full-time $9,678; part-time $538 per credit. Required fees: $1,415. *Financial support:* Unspecified assistantships available. *Faculty research:* Records and information management, training and development, ergonomics, office technology, telecommunications.

Bowling Green State University, Graduate College, College of Education and Human Development, School of Education and Intervention Services, Teacher and Learning Division, Department of Business Education, Bowling Green, OH 43403. Offers M Ed. *Accreditation:* NCATE. Part-time programs available. *Students:* 15 full-time (4 women), 3 part-time (1 woman); includes 2 minority (both African Americans), 1 international. Average age 29. 9 applicants, 78% accepted, 2 enrolled. In 2006, 18 degrees awarded. *Degree requirements:* For master's, thesis or alternative. *Entrance requirements:* For master's, GRE General Test. Additional exam requirements/recommendations for international students: Required—TOEFL. *Application deadline:* Applications are processed on a rolling basis. Application fee: $30. Electronic applications accepted. *Expenses:* Tuition, state resident: part-time $535 per hour. Tuition, nonresident: part-time $884 per hour. *Financial support:* In 2006–07, 6 research assistantships with full tuition reimbursements (averaging $6,090 per year), 6 teaching assistantships with full tuition reimbursements (averaging $5,413 per year) were awarded; career-related internships or fieldwork, Federal Work-Study, and unspecified assistantships also available. Financial award applicants required to submit FAFSA. *Faculty research:* School to work, workforce education, marketing education, contextual teaching and learning. *Unit head:* Dr. Leigh Chiarelott, Director, 419-372-7352. *Application contact:* Dr. Bob Berns, Graduate Coordinator, 419-372-2904.

Buffalo State College, State University of New York, Graduate Studies and Research, Faculty of Applied Science and Education, Department of Business Studies, Buffalo, NY 14222-1095. Offers business and marketing education (MS Ed). Part-time and evening/weekend programs available. *Degree requirements:* For master's, thesis or alternative, project. *Entrance requirements:* For master's, minimum GPA of 2.5, New York teaching certificate.

Canisius College, Graduate Division, School of Education and Human Services, Department of Graduate Education, Buffalo, NY 14208-1098. Offers business education (MS); childhood education (MS); college student personnel (MS); differentiated instruction (MS Ed); early childhood education (MS); education administration (MS); education of the deaf and hard of hearing (MS); general education (MS Ed); literacy education (MS Ed); reading education (MS Ed); secondary education (MS); special education (MS). *Accreditation:* NCATE. Part-time and evening/weekend programs available. *Faculty:* 13 full-time (12 women), 74 part-time/adjunct (44 women). *Students:* 377 full-time (267 women), 303 part-time (219 women); includes 43 minority (27 African Americans, 2 American Indian/Alaska Native, 6 Asian Americans or Pacific Islanders, 8 Hispanic Americans), 187 international. Average age 30. In 2006, 296 degrees awarded. *Application fee:* $25. *Expenses:* Tuition: Part-time $645 per credit hour. Required fees: $19 per credit hour. Tuition and fees vary according to program. *Financial support:* Research assistantships with full tuition reimbursements, career-related internships or fieldwork, institutionally sponsored loans, scholarships/grants, health care benefits, tuition waivers (full and partial), and unspecified assistantships available. *Faculty research:* Autism, Asperger's disease, private higher education, reading strategies. *Unit head:* Rev. Paul Nochelski, Chair of Graduate Education and Leadership, 716-888-3297, Fax: 716-888-3299. *Application contact:* James D. Bagwell, Director of Graduate Recruitment and Admissions, 716-888-2544, Fax: 716-888-3290, E-mail: bagwellj@canisius.edu.

Central Connecticut State University, School of Graduate Studies, School of Business, Program in Business Education, New Britain, CT 06050-4010. Offers MS, Certificate. Part-time and evening/weekend programs available. *Students:* 8 full-time (7 women), 4 part-time (all women). 3 applicants, 67% accepted, 0 enrolled. In 2006, 2 master's, 1 other advanced degree awarded. *Degree requirements:* For master's, thesis or alternative, comprehensive exam. *Entrance requirements:* For master's, bachelor's degree in business or equivalent, minimum GPA of 2.7. Additional exam requirements/recommendations for international students: Required—TOEFL. *Application deadline:* For fall admission, 7/1 for domestic students; for spring admission, 12/1 for domestic students. Applications are processed on a rolling basis. Application fee: $50. Electronic applications accepted. *Expenses:* Tuition, area resident: Full-time $3,970; part-time $380 per credit. Tuition, state resident: full-time $5,955; part-time $380 per credit. Tuition, nonresident: full-time $11,061; part-time $380 per credit. Required fees: $3,189. One-time fee: $62 part-time. Tuition and fees vary according to degree level and program. *Financial support:* In 2006–07, 1 student received support, including 1 research assistantship; Federal Work-Study and scholarships/grants also available. Financial award application deadline: 3/1; financial award applicants required to submit FAFSA. *Faculty research:* Marketing education, office systems education, accounting education for secondary schools. *Unit head:* Dr. George Claffey, Coordinator, 860-832-2509.

Central Michigan University, College of Graduate Studies, College of Business Administration, Department of Business Information Systems, Mount Pleasant, MI 48859. Offers business education (MBE); information systems (MS). *Degree requirements:* For master's, thesis or alternative, registration. *Entrance requirements:* For master's, GMAT or GRE (MBE). *Faculty research:* Business teacher education, office systems, management information systems, decision support systems.

See Close-Up on page 611.

Chadron State College, School of Professional and Graduate Studies, Department of Education, Chadron, NE 69337. Offers business (MA Ed); community counseling (MA Ed); educational administration (MS Ed, Sp Ed); elementary education (MS Ed); history (MA Ed); language and literature (MA Ed); secondary administration (MS Ed); secondary education (MS Ed). *Accreditation:* NCATE. Part-time and evening/weekend programs available. Postbaccalaureate distance learning degree programs offered. *Degree requirements:* For master's, thesis optional. *Entrance requirements:* For master's, GRE General Test, GRE Writing Test, minimum GPA of 2.75 or 12 graduate hours at CSC with minimum GPA of 3.25. Additional exam requirements/recommendations for international students: Required—TOEFL. Electronic applications accepted. *Faculty research:* Rural education, technology, mental health.

The College of Saint Rose, Graduate Studies, School of Education, Teacher Education Department, Albany, NY 12203-1419. Offers business and marketing (MS Ed); childhood education (MS Ed); early childhood education (MS Ed); elementary education (K-6) (MS Ed);

secondary education (MS Ed, Certificate); teacher education (MS Ed, Certificate), including bilingual pupil personnel services (Certificate). Part-time and evening/weekend programs available. *Entrance requirements:* For master's, minimum undergraduate GPA of 3.0. Additional exam requirements/recommendations for international students: Required—TOEFL (minimum score 550 paper-based; 213 computer-based). Electronic applications accepted.

Drake University, School of Education, Department of Teaching and Learning, Program in Secondary Education, Des Moines, IA 50311-4516. Offers art (MAT); biology (MAT); business (MAT); chemistry (MAT); English (MAT); general science (MAT); history-American (MAT); history-world (MAT); journalism (MAT); mathematics (MAT); physical science (MAT); physics (MAT); sociology (MAT); speech (MAT); speech communication (MAT); theatre (MAT). Part-time programs available. *Faculty:* 10 full-time (3 women), 28 part-time/adjunct (16 women). *Students:* 13 full-time (7 women), 33 part-time (20 women). 41 applicants, 56% accepted. In 2006, 12 degrees awarded. *Degree requirements:* For master's, thesis (for some programs), internships (s), comprehensive exam, registration. *Entrance requirements:* For master's, GRE General Test, MAT, or Drake Writing Assessment, resumé, 2 letters of recommendation. Additional exam requirements/recommendations for international students: Required—TOEFL (minimum score 550 paper-based; 213 computer-based). *Application deadline:* For fall admission, 7/1 priority date for domestic students, 6/1 priority date for international students; for spring admission, 11/1 priority date for domestic students, 10/1 priority date for international students. Applications are processed on a rolling basis. Application fee: $25. Electronic applications accepted. *Financial support:* Career-related internships or fieldwork and unspecified assistantships available. Support available to part-time students. *Faculty research:* Counseling and rehabilitation, behavioral supports, inquiry-based science methods, teacher quality enhancement. Total annual research expenditures: $1.5 million. *Unit head:* Dr. Linda Espey, Head, 515-271-1954, E-mail: linda.espey@drake.edu. *Application contact:* Ann J. Martin, Graduate Coordinator, 515-271-2034, Fax: 515-271-2831, E-mail: ann.martin@drake.edu.

Eastern Kentucky University, The Graduate School, College of Education, Department of Curriculum and Instruction, Program in Secondary and Higher Education, Richmond, KY 40475-3102. Offers agricultural education (MA Ed); allied health sciences education (MA Ed); art education (MA Ed); biological sciences education (MA Ed); business education (MA Ed); chemistry education (MA Ed); earth science education (MA Ed); English education (MA Ed); general science education (MA Ed); geography education (MA Ed); history education (MA Ed); home economics education (MA Ed); industrial education (MA Ed); mathematical sciences education (MA Ed); physical education (MA Ed); physics education (MA Ed); political science education (MA Ed); psychology education (MA Ed); reading (MA Ed); school health education (MA Ed); sociology education (MA Ed). *Accreditation:* NCATE. Part-time programs available. *Students:* 16 full-time (8 women), 63 part-time (43 women); includes 5 minority (2 African Americans, 2 American Indian/Alaska Native, 1 Asian American or Pacific Islander). Average age 32. *Entrance requirements:* For master's, GRE General Test, minimum GPA of 2.5. Application fee: $30. *Expenses:* Tuition, state resident: full-time $5,610. Tuition, nonresident: full-time $15,910. *Financial support:* Research assistantships, teaching assistantships, Federal Work-Study available. Support available to part-time students. *Unit head:* Dr. Michael Martin, Chair, Department of Curriculum and Instruction, 859-622-2154, Fax: 859-622-2004.

Emporia State University, School of Graduate Studies, School of Business, Department of Business Administration and Education, Program in Business Education, Emporia, KS 66801-5087. Offers MSBE. Part-time and evening/weekend programs available. Postbaccalaureate distance learning degree programs offered (no on-campus study). *Students:* 2 full-time (0 women), 25 part-time (21 women); includes 1 minority (African American) 3 applicants, 100% accepted, 2 enrolled. In 2006, 22 degrees awarded. *Entrance requirements:* For master's, GRE, 15 undergraduate credits in business; minimum undergraduate GPA of 2.7 over last 60 hours. Additional exam requirements/recommendations for international students: Required—TOEFL (minimum score 550 paper-based). *Application deadline:* For fall admission, 8/15 priority date for domestic students. Applications are processed on a rolling basis. Application fee: $30 ($75 for international students). Electronic applications accepted. *Expenses:* Tuition, state resident: full-time $3,438; part-time $143 per credit hour. Tuition, nonresident: full-time $10,398; part-time $433 per credit hour. Required fees: $724; $44 per credit hour. *Financial support:* Career-related internships or fieldwork, institutionally sponsored loans, health care benefits, and unspecified assistantships available. Financial award application deadline: 3/15; financial award applicants required to submit FAFSA. *Application contact:* Dr. Nancy Hite, Information Contact, 620-341-5345, Fax: 620-341-6345, E-mail: nhite@emporia.edu.

Florida Agricultural and Mechanical University, Division of Graduate Studies, Research, and Continuing Education, College of Education, Department of Vocational Education, Tallahassee, FL 32307-3200. Offers business education (MBE); industrial education (M Ed, MS Ed). *Accreditation:* NCATE. *Degree requirements:* For master's, thesis (for some programs). *Entrance requirements:* For master's, GRE General Test, minimum GPA of 3.0. Additional exam requirements/recommendations for international students: Required—TOEFL.

Georgia Southern University, Jack N. Averitt College of Graduate Studies, College of Education, Department of Teaching and Learning, Program in Business Education, Statesboro, GA 30460. Offers M Ed, MAT. *Accreditation:* NCATE. Part-time and evening/weekend programs available. *Students:* 6 full-time (5 women), 2 part-time (both women); includes 1 minority (African American) Average age 34. 4 applicants, 75% accepted, 0 enrolled. In 2006, 1 degree awarded. *Degree requirements:* For master's, exit assessment. *Entrance requirements:* For master's, GRE General Test or MAT, minimum GPA of 2.5. Additional exam requirements/recommendations for international students: Required—TOEFL (minimum score 550 paper-based; 213 computer-based; 80 iBT). *Application deadline:* For fall admission, 3/1 priority date for domestic students, 3/1 for international students; for spring admission, 10/1 priority date for domestic students, 10/1 for international students. Applications are processed on a rolling basis. Application fee: $50. Electronic applications accepted. *Financial support:* In 2006–07, 5 students received support, including research assistantships with partial tuition reimbursements available (averaging $5,500 per year), teaching assistantships with partial tuition reimbursements available (averaging $5,500 per year); Federal Work-Study, scholarships/grants, tuition waivers (partial), and unspecified assistantships also available. Support available to part-time students. Financial award application deadline: 4/15; financial award applicants required to submit FAFSA. *Faculty research:* Technology applications. *Unit head:* Dr. Mary Bennett, Assistant Professor, 912-681-0356, Fax: 912-681-0026, E-mail: mbennett@georgiasouthern.edu. *Application contact:* 912-681-5384, Fax: 912-681-0740, E-mail: gradadmissions@georgiasouthern.edu.

Hofstra University, School of Education and Allied Human Services, Department of Curriculum and Teaching, Program in Business Education, Hempstead, NY 11549. Offers MS Ed. Part-time programs available. *Students:* 15 full-time (10 women), 15 part-time (9 women); includes 6 minority (3 African Americans, 1 Asian American or Pacific Islander, 2 Hispanic Americans). Average age 29. 26 applicants, 100% accepted, 14 enrolled. In 2006, 9 degrees awarded. *Degree requirements:* For master's, one foreign language, registration. *Entrance requirements:* For master's, 2 letters of recommendation, teacher certification (MA), BBA degree, essay. Additional exam requirements/recommendations for international students: Required—TOEFL (minimum score 550 paper-based; 213 computer-based). *Application deadline:* Applications are processed on a rolling basis. Application fee: $60. Electronic applications accepted. *Expenses:* Tuition: Full-time $13,320; part-time $740 per credit. Required fees: $930; $155 per term. *Financial support:* In 2006–07, 5 students received support; fellowships with tuition reimbursements available, research assistantships with full and partial tuition reimbursements available, institutionally sponsored loans, scholarships/grants, tuition waivers (full and partial), and unspecified assistantships available. Support available to part-time students. Financial award applicants required to submit FAFSA. *Unit head:* Dr. Sandra L. Stacki, Director, 516-463-5783, Fax: 516-463-6196, E-mail: catsls@hofstra.edu. *Application contact:* Carol Drummer, Dean of Graduate Admissions, 516-463-4876, Fax: 516-463-4664, E-mail: gradstudent@hofstra.edu.

Inter American University of Puerto Rico, Metropolitan Campus, Graduate Programs, Faculty of Economics and Administrative Sciences, Program in Business Education, San

Juan, PR 00919-1293. Offers MA. *Degree requirements:* For master's, comprehensive exam. *Entrance requirements:* For master's, GRE or EXADEP, interview. Electronic applications accepted.

Inter American University of Puerto Rico, San Germán Campus, Graduate Studies Center, Graduate Program in Business Education, San Germán, PR 00683-5008. Offers MA. Part-time and evening/weekend programs available. *Faculty:* 12 full-time, 4 part-time/adjunct. *Students:* 22. Average age 30. In 2006, 6 degrees awarded. *Degree requirements:* For master's, comprehensive exam. *Entrance requirements:* For master's, GRE General Test or EXADEP, minimum GPA of 3.0. *Application deadline:* For fall admission, 4/30 priority date for domestic students; for spring admission, 11/15 for domestic students. Applications are processed on a rolling basis. Application fee: $31. *Expenses:* Tuition: Part-time $175 per credit. Required fees: $238 per semester. Tuition and fees vary according to degree level. *Financial support:* Teaching assistantships, Federal Work-Study and unspecified assistantships available. *Application contact:* Prof. Duay Rivera, Graduate Coordinator, 787-264-1912 Ext. 7218, Fax: 787-892-7510, E-mail: durivera@sg.inter.edu.

International College of the Cayman Islands, Graduate Program in Management, Newlands, Cayman Islands. Offers business administration (MBA); management (MS), including education, human resources. Part-time and evening/weekend programs available. *Degree requirements:* For master's, comprehensive exam. *Faculty research:* International human resources administration.

Lehman College of the City University of New York, Division of Education, Department of Middle and High School Education, Program in Business Education, Bronx, NY 10468-1589. Offers MS Ed. *Accreditation:* NCATE. Part-time and evening/weekend programs available. *Degree requirements:* For master's, thesis. *Entrance requirements:* For master's, minimum GPA of 2.7.

Louisiana State University and Agricultural and Mechanical College, Graduate School, College of Agriculture, School of Human Resource Education and Workforce Development, Baton Rouge, LA 70803. Offers comprehensive vocational education (MS, PhD); extension and international education (MS, PhD); industrial education (MS); vocational agriculture education (MS, PhD); vocational business education (MS); vocational home economics education (MS). *Accreditation:* NCATE. Part-time programs available. *Faculty:* 13 full-time (6 women). *Students:* 39 full-time (24 women), 68 part-time (42 women); includes 12 African Americans, 3 Hispanic Americans, 9 international. Average age 38. 20 applicants, 60% accepted, 3 enrolled. In 2006, 18 master's, 33 doctorates awarded. Terminal master's awarded for partial completion of doctoral program. *Degree requirements:* For master's, thesis (for some programs); for doctorate, thesis/dissertation. *Entrance requirements:* For master's and doctorate, GRE General Test, minimum GPA of 3.0. Additional exam requirements/recommendations for international students: Required—TOEFL (minimum score 550 paper-based; 213 computer-based; 79 iBT). *Application deadline:* For fall admission, 1/25 priority date for domestic students, 5/15 for international students; for spring admission, 10/15 for international students. Applications are processed on a rolling basis. Application fee: $25. Electronic applications accepted. *Financial support:* In 2006–07, 23 students received support, including 1 fellowship with full and partial tuition reimbursement available (averaging $23,678 per year), 10 research assistantships with full and partial tuition reimbursements available (averaging $11,750 per year), 5 teaching assistantships with partial tuition reimbursements available (averaging $10,210 per year); career-related internships or fieldwork, institutionally sponsored loans, tuition waivers (full and partial), and unspecified assistantships also available. Financial award application deadline: 3/1; financial award applicants required to submit FAFSA. *Faculty research:* Adult education, history and philosophy of vocational education, curriculum and instruction, career decision making. *Unit head:* Dr. Michael F. Burnett, Director, 225-578-5748, Fax: 225-578-2526, E-mail: vocbur@lsu.edu.

Louisiana Tech University, Graduate School, College of Education, Department of Curriculum, Instruction and Leadership, Ruston, LA 71272. Offers curriculum and instruction (MS, Ed D); educational leadership (Ed D); secondary education (M Ed), including business education, English education, foreign language education, health and physical education, mathematics education, science education, social studies education, speech education. *Accreditation:* NCATE. Part-time programs available. *Degree requirements:* For doctorate, thesis/dissertation. *Entrance requirements:* For master's and doctorate, GRE General Test.

Maryville University of Saint Louis, The John E. Simon School of Business, St. Louis, MO 63141-7299. Offers accounting (MBA, PGC); business studies (PGC); e-business (MBA, PGC); management (MBA, PGC); marketing (MBA, PGC). *Accreditation:* ACBSP. Part-time and evening/weekend programs available. *Students:* 34 full-time (23 women), 162 part-time (101 women); includes 9 African Americans, 8 Asian Americans or Pacific Islanders, 2 international. Average age 31. 56 applicants, 96% accepted, 38 enrolled. In 2006, 89 degrees awarded. *Entrance requirements:* For master's, GMAT (unless applicant possesses a graduate degree or an undergaduate degree in business with a minimum GPA of 3.0), minimum AACSB index of 950. Additional exam requirements/recommendations for international students: Required—TOEFL (minimum score 550 paper-based). *Application deadline:* Applications are processed on a rolling basis. Application fee: $35 ($50 for international students). Electronic applications accepted. *Expenses:* Tuition: Full-time $17,800; part-time $555 per credit. Required fees: $55 per semester. Tuition and fees vary according to degree level and program. *Financial support:* Career-related internships or fieldwork, Federal Work-Study, tuition waivers (partial), and campus employment available. Financial award application deadline: 7/31; financial award applicants required to submit FAFSA. *Faculty research:* International business, e-business, strategic planning, interpersonal management skills, financial analysis. *Unit head:* Dr. Pamela Horwitz, Dean, 314-529-9418, Fax: 314-529-9975, E-mail: horwitz@maryville.edu. *Application contact:* Kathy Dougherty, Director of MBA Admissions and Enrollment, 314-529-9382, Fax: 314-529-9975, E-mail: business@marville.edu.

Middle Tennessee State University, College of Graduate Studies, College of Business, Department of Business Communication and Entrepreneurship, Murfreesboro, TN 37132. Offers business education (MBE). Part-time and evening/weekend programs available. Postbaccalaureate distance learning degree programs offered. *Faculty:* 6 full-time (3 women). *Students:* 8 full-time (5 women), 31 part-time (21 women); includes 10 minority (all African Americans) Average age 29. 9 applicants, 100% accepted. In 2006, 17 degrees awarded. *Degree requirements:* For master's, comprehensive exam. *Entrance requirements:* For master's, GRE or MAT. Additional exam requirements/recommendations for international students: Required—TOEFL (minimum score 525 paper-based; 195 computer-based). *Application deadline:* For fall admission, 8/1 priority date for domestic students. Applications are processed on a rolling basis. Application fee: $25. Electronic applications accepted. *Financial support:* In 2006–07, 4 students received support. Institutionally sponsored loans available. Support available to part-time students. Financial award application deadline: 5/1. *Faculty research:* Entrepreneurship, business and organizational communication, corporate training and development, teaching and assessment methods, administrative support personality. *Unit head:* Dr. Stephen D. Lewis, Coordinator, 615-898-2902, Fax: 615-898-5439.

Mississippi College, Graduate School, School of Business, Clinton, MS 39058. Offers accounting (Certificate); business administration (MBA), including accounting; business education (M Ed); JD/MBA. *Accreditation:* ACBSP. Part-time and evening/weekend programs available. *Faculty:* 12 full-time (2 women), 1 part-time/adjunct (0 women). *Students:* 55 full-time (28 women), 111 part-time (58 women); includes 41 minority (35 African Americans, 6 Asian Americans or Pacific Islanders), 32 international. Average age 29. In 2006, 45 master's, 5 other advanced degrees awarded. *Degree requirements:* For master's, thesis optional. *Entrance requirements:* For master's, GMAT, minimum GPA of 2.5, 24 hours of undergraduate course work in business. Additional exam requirements/recommendations for international students: Recommended—IELTS. *Application deadline:* For fall admission, 8/15 priority date for domestic students. Applications are processed on a rolling basis. Application fee: $25. Electronic applications accepted. *Expenses:* Tuition: Full-time $7,290; part-time $405 per hour. Required fees: $150 per term. Tuition and fees vary according to campus/location and program. *Financial support:* Federal Work-Study and unspecified assistantships available. Support available to part-time students. Financial award application deadline: 4/1; financial award applicants required to submit FAFSA. *Unit head:* Dr. Marcelo Eduardo, Dean, 601-925-3420, E-mail: eduardo@mc.edu.

Mississippi College, Graduate School, School of Education, Department of Teacher Education and Leadership, Clinton, MS 39058. Offers art (M Ed); biological science (M Ed); business education (M Ed); computer science (M Ed); dyslexia therapy (M Ed); educational leadership (M Ed, Ed S); elementary education (M Ed, Ed S); English (M Ed); higher education administration (MS); mathematics (M Ed); secondary education (M Ed); social studies (history) (M Ed); teaching arts (M Ed). Part-time programs available. *Faculty:* 9 full-time (5 women), 14 part-time/adjunct (10 women). *Students:* 52 full-time (36 women), 286 part-time (247 women); includes 173 minority (171 African Americans, 1 American Indian/Alaska Native, 1 Hispanic American), 1 international. Average age 32. In 2006, 131 degrees awarded. *Degree requirements:* For master's, thesis optional. *Entrance requirements:* For master's, NTE. Additional exam requirements/recommendations for international students: Recommended—IELTS. *Application deadline:* Applications are processed on a rolling basis. Application fee: $25. Electronic applications accepted. *Expenses:* Tuition: Full-time $7,290; part-time $405 per hour. Required fees: $150 per term. Tuition and fees vary according to campus/location and program. *Financial support:* Teaching assistantships, career-related internships or fieldwork, Federal Work-Study, scholarships/grants, and unspecified assistantships available. Support available to part-time students. Financial award applicants required to submit FAFSA. *Unit head:* Dr. Tom Williams, Chair, 601-925-3844, E-mail: twilliams@mc.edu.

Nazareth College of Rochester, Graduate Studies, Department of Business, Program in Business Education, Rochester, NY 14618-3790. Offers MS Ed. Part-time and evening/weekend programs available. *Faculty:* 1 full-time (0 women), 1 part-time/adjunct (0 women). *Students:* 12 full-time (5 women), 12 part-time (9 women); includes 3 minority (1 African American, 2 Asian Americans or Pacific Islanders). 15 applicants, 100% accepted, 11 enrolled. In 2006, 13 degrees awarded. *Entrance requirements:* For master's, minimum GPA of 3.0. *Application deadline:* For fall admission, 4/1 for domestic students; for spring admission, 10/1 for domestic students. Application fee: $40. *Financial support:* Research assistantships with partial tuition reimbursements available. Financial award application deadline: 3/1; financial award applicants required to submit FAFSA. *Unit head:* Dr. Robert C. Marino, Director, 585-389-2604, Fax: 585-586-2452, E-mail: rmarino9@naz.edu. *Application contact:* Judith G. Baker, Director, Graduate Admissions, 585-389-2050, Fax: 585-389-2817, E-mail: gradstudies@naz.edu.

New York University, Steinhardt School of Culture, Education and Human Development, Department of Administration, Leadership, and Technology, Program in Business Education, New York, NY 10012-1019. Offers business education (Advanced Certificate); business education in higher education (MA); workplace learning (Advanced Certificate). *Accreditation:* Teacher Education Accreditation Council. Part-time and evening/weekend programs available. *Faculty:* 2 full-time (1 woman). *Students:* 5 full-time (3 women), 24 part-time (15 women); includes 9 minority (1 African American, 1 American Indian/Alaska Native, 6 Asian Americans or Pacific Islanders, 1 Hispanic American), 2 international. 16 applicants, 94% accepted, 3 enrolled. In 2006, 5 master's, 1 other advanced degree awarded. *Degree requirements:* For master's, thesis (for some programs). *Entrance requirements:* For degree, master's degree. Additional exam requirements/recommendations for international students: Required—TOEFL. *Application deadline:* For fall admission, 12/15 priority date for domestic and international students; for spring admission, 11/1 for domestic and international students. Applications are processed on a rolling basis. Application fee: $50. *Expenses:* Tuition: Part-time $1,080 per unit. Required fees: $56 per unit. $329 per term. Tuition and fees vary according to program. *Financial support:* Fellowships with full and partial tuition reimbursements, career-related internships or fieldwork, Federal Work-Study, institutionally sponsored loans, scholarships/grants, tuition waivers (partial), and unspecified assistantships available. Support available to part-time students. Financial award application deadline: 2/1; financial award applicants required to submit FAFSA. *Faculty research:* Applications of technology to instruction, end user information systems. *Unit head:* Dr. Bridget N. O'Connor, Director, 212-998-5488, Fax: 212-995-4041, E-mail: bridget.oconnor@nyu.edu. *Application contact:* 212-998-5030, Fax: 212-995-4328, E-mail: steinhardt.gradadmissions@nyu.edu.

Northwestern State University of Louisiana, Graduate Studies and Research, College of Education, Programs in Education, Natchitoches, LA 71497. Offers business and distributive education (M Ed); counseling (M Ed); early childhood education (M Ed); education (M Ed); education leadership (M Ed); educational technology (M Ed); elementary teaching (M Ed); English education (M Ed); home economics education (M Ed); mathematics education (M Ed); reading (M Ed); science education (M Ed); secondary teaching (M Ed); social sciences education (M Ed). *Students:* 49 full-time (41 women), 245 part-time (206 women); includes 78 minority (70 African Americans, 5 American Indian/Alaska Native, 2 Asian Americans or Pacific Islanders, 1 Hispanic American). Average age 35. In 2006, 158 degrees awarded. *Degree requirements:* For master's, thesis or alternative, comprehensive exam, registration. *Entrance requirements:* For master's, GRE General Test, minimum undergraduate GPA of 2.5. *Application contact:* Dr. Steven G. Horton, Associate Provost/Dean, Graduate Studies, Research, and Information Systems, 318-357-5851, Fax: 318-357-5019, E-mail: grad_school@nsula.edu.

Old Dominion University, Darden College of Education, Programs in Occupational and Technical Studies, Norfolk, VA 23529. Offers business and industry training (MS); career and technical education (PhD); community college teaching (MS); human resources training (PhD); middle and secondary teaching (MS); technology education (PhD). *Accreditation:* NCATE (one or more programs are accredited). Part-time and evening/weekend programs available. Postbaccalaureate distance learning degree programs offered (minimal on-campus study). *Faculty:* 7 full-time (1 woman), 5 part-time/adjunct (2 women). *Students:* 15 full-time (11 women), 68 part-time (39 women); includes 13 minority (9 African Americans, 2 American Indian/Alaska Native, 2 Asian Americans or Pacific Islanders), 1 international. Average age 39. 44 applicants, 95% accepted, 37 enrolled. In 2006, 29 degrees awarded. *Degree requirements:* For master's, writing exam, candidacy exam, thesis optional; for doctorate, thesis/dissertation, writing exam, candidacy exam, comprehensive exam, registration. *Entrance requirements:* For master's, GRE General Test or MAT, minimum GPA of 2.8; for doctorate, GRE, minimum GPA of 3.0, 3 letters of reference. Additional exam requirements/recommendations for international students: Required—TOEFL. *Application deadline:* For fall admission, 6/1 priority date for domestic students, 6/1 for international students; for winter admission, 11/1 priority date for domestic students, 11/1 for international students; for spring admission, 3/1 priority date for domestic students, 3/1 for international students. Applications are processed on a rolling basis. Application fee: $40. Electronic applications accepted. *Expenses:* Tuition, area resident: Part-time $285 per credit hour. Tuition, nonresident: part-time $715 per credit hour. Required fees: $94 per semester. *Financial support:* In 2006–07, 19 students received support, including 1 fellowship with full tuition reimbursement available (averaging $15,000 per year), 2 research assistantships with partial tuition reimbursements available (averaging $9,000 per year), 5 teaching assistantships with partial tuition reimbursements available (averaging $12,600 per year); career-related internships or fieldwork, scholarships/grants, tuition waivers (partial), and unspecified assistantships also available. Support available to part-time students. Financial award application deadline: 2/15; financial award applicants required to submit FAFSA. *Faculty research:* Training and development, marketing, technology, special populations, support of academic subjects. Total annual research expenditures: $799,773. *Unit head:* Dr. John M. Ritz, Graduate Program Director, 757-683-4305, Fax: 757-683-5227, E-mail: otsgpd@odu.edu.

Penn State Harrisburg, Graduate School, School of Behavioral Sciences and Education, Middletown, PA 17057-4898. Offers adult education (D Ed); applied behavior analysis (MA); applied clinical psychology (MA); applied psychological research (MA); community psychology and social change (MA); health education (M Ed); teaching and curriculum (M Ed); training and development (M Ed). Part-time and evening/weekend programs available. *Expenses:* Tuition,

Business Education

Penn State Harrisburg (continued)
state resident: full-time $13,224; part-time $551 per credit. Tuition, nonresident: full-time $18,652; part-time $777 per credit. Required fees: $84 per semester. *Financial support:* Career-related internships or fieldwork available. *Unit head:* Dr. William D. Milheim, Director, 717-948-6205, Fax: 717-948-6209, E-mail: wdm2@psu.edu.

Rider University, Department of Graduate Education, Leadership and Counseling, Lawrenceville, NJ 08648-3001. Offers counseling services (MA, Ed S); curriculum, instruction and supervision (MA); director of school counseling services (Certificate); educational administration (MA); organizational leadership (MA); principal (Certificate); reading/language arts (MA, Certificate), including reading specialist (Certificate), reading/language arts (MA); school business administrator (Certificate); school counseling services (Certificate); school psychology (Ed S); special education (MA); supervisor (Certificate); teacher certification (Certificate), including business education, elementary education, English as a second language, English education, mathematics education, preschool to grade 3, science education, social studies education, world languages; teaching (MA). *Accreditation:* NCATE. Part-time and evening/weekend programs available. *Faculty:* 24 full-time (12 women), 30 part-time/adjunct (15 women). *Students:* 90 full-time (75 women), 457 part-time (369 women); includes 73 minority (50 African Americans, 2 American Indian/Alaska Native, 6 Asian Americans or Pacific Islanders, 15 Hispanic Americans), 1 international. Average age 32. 314 applicants, 61% accepted, 138 enrolled. In 2006, 116 master's, 19 other advanced degrees awarded. *Degree requirements:* For master's, thesis or alternative, internship, portfolios, comprehensive exam (for some programs); for other advanced degree, internship, professional portfolio. *Entrance requirements:* For master's, GRE (counseling, school psychology), MAT, interview, resumé, letters of recommendation; for other advanced degree, PRAXIS. Additional exam requirements/recommendations for international students: Required—TOEFL (minimum score 550 paper-based; 213 computer-based). *Application deadline:* For fall admission, 5/1 priority date for domestic students, 6/1 priority date for international students; for spring admission, 11/1 priority date for domestic and international students. Applications are processed on a rolling basis. Application fee: $50. Electronic applications accepted. *Expenses:* Tuition: Part-time $525 per credit. Required fees: $35 per course. $30 per semester. *Financial support:* In 2006–07, 271 students received support. Career-related internships or fieldwork, Federal Work-Study, institutionally sponsored loans, and unspecified assistantships available. Support available to part-time students. Financial award applicants required to submit FAFSA. *Faculty research:* Gifted students, self-esteem, hope and mental health, conflicts in group work, cultural diversity and counseling assessment of special needs in children. *Unit head:* Dr. Dennis C. Buss, Chair, 609-895-5353, Fax: 609-896-5362, E-mail: dbuss@rider.edu. *Application contact:* Jamie L Mitchell, Director of Graduate Admissions, 609-896-5036, Fax: 609-895-5680, E-mail: jmitchell@rider.edu.

See Close-Up on page 913.

Salisbury University, Graduate Division, Department of Education, Salisbury, MD 21801-6837. Offers art (MAT); biology (MAT); business education (MAT); chemistry (MAT); early childhood education (M Ed); educational administration (M Ed); elementary education (M Ed); English (M Ed, MAT); French (MAT); geography (MAT); history (MAT); mathematics (MAT); media and technology (MAT); music (MAT); psychology (MAT); reading education (MAT); science (MAT); secondary education (MAT); social studies (MAT); Spanish (MAT). *Accreditation:* NCATE. Part-time and evening/weekend programs available. *Faculty:* 12 full-time (6 women), 10 part-time/adjunct (8 women). *Students:* 17 full-time (9 women), 84 part-time (72 women); includes 6 minority (5 African Americans, 1 Hispanic American). Average age 30. 15 applicants, 73% accepted, 11 enrolled. In 2006, 63 degrees awarded. *Degree requirements:* For master's, comprehensive exam (for some programs). *Entrance requirements:* For master's, PRAXIS, minimum GPA of 2.75. Additional exam requirements/recommendations for international students: Required—TOEFL (minimum score 550 paper-based; 213 computer-based). *Application deadline:* For fall admission, 8/1 priority date for domestic students; for spring admission, 1/1 for domestic students. Applications are processed on a rolling basis. Application fee: $45. *Expenses:* Tuition, state resident: part-time $260 per credit hour. Tuition, nonresident: part-time $546 per credit hour. Required fees: $52 per credit hour. *Financial support:* In 2006–07, 3 teaching assistantships with full tuition reimbursements were awarded; career-related internships or fieldwork and scholarships/grants also available. Support available to part-time students. Financial award applicants required to submit FAFSA. *Faculty research:* Middle-level education, student outcomes. *Unit head:* Dr. Edward C. Robeck, Program Coordinator, 410-543-6292, Fax: 410-548-2593, E-mail: ecrobeck@salisbury.edu. *Application contact:* Debra J. Clark, Administrative Assistant I, 410-543-6281, Fax: 410-548-2593, E-mail: djclark@salisbury.edu.

South Carolina State University, School of Graduate Studies, Department of Education, Orangeburg, SC 29117-0001. Offers early childhood and special education (M Ed); early childhood education (MAT); elementary education (M Ed, MAT); engineering (MAT); general science (MAT); mathematics (MAT); secondary education (M Ed), including biology education, business education, counselor education, English education, home economics education, industrial education, mathematics education, science education, social studies education; special education (M Ed), including emotionally handicapped, learning disabilities, mentally handicapped. *Accreditation:* NCATE. Part-time and evening/weekend programs available. *Faculty:* 21 full-time (10 women), 4 part-time/adjunct (0 women). *Students:* 34 full-time (28 women), 33 part-time (25 women); includes 63 minority (61 African Americans, 1 American Indian/Alaska Native, 1 Asian American or Pacific Islander). Average age 35. 46 applicants, 67% accepted, 19 enrolled. In 2006, 28 degrees awarded. *Degree requirements:* For master's, departmental qualifying exam, thesis optional. *Entrance requirements:* For master's, GRE General Test, NTE, interview, teaching certificate. *Application deadline:* For fall admission, 6/15 priority date for domestic students, 6/15 for international students; for spring admission, 11/1 for domestic and international students. Applications are processed on a rolling basis. Application fee: $25. Electronic applications accepted. *Expenses:* Tuition, state resident: full-time $7,278. Tuition, nonresident: full-time $14,322. *Financial support:* Fellowships, research assistantships, career-related internships or fieldwork, Federal Work-Study, and institutionally sponsored loans available. Financial award application deadline: 6/1. *Faculty research:* Critical thinking, child abuse, stress, test-taking skills, conflict resolution, mainstreaming. *Unit head:* Dr. Gail Joyner-Fleming, Interim Chair, 803-533-3769, Fax: 803-536-8492, E-mail: zf-gfleming@scsu.edu. *Application contact:* Annette Hazzard-Jones, Program Coordinator II, 803-536-8809, Fax: 803-536-8812, E-mail: zs_ahazzard@scsu.edu.

Southern New Hampshire University, School of Education, Manchester, NH 03106-1045. Offers business education (MS); child development (M Ed); computer technology education (Certificate); curriculum and instruction (M Ed); education (M Ed, CAS); elementary education (M Ed); general special education (Certificate); school business administrator (Certificate); school counseling (M Ed); school psychology (M Ed); secondary education (M Ed); training and development (Certificate). Part-time and evening/weekend programs available. Post-baccalaureate distance learning degree programs offered. *Faculty:* 6 full-time (3 women), 9 part-time/adjunct (7 women). *Students:* Average age 35. In 2006, 52 degrees awarded. *Degree requirements:* For master's, thesis or alternative, comprehensive exam (for some programs). *Entrance requirements:* For master's, GRE General Test or MAT, minimum GPA of 3.0. Additional exam requirements/recommendations for international students: Required—TOEFL (minimum score 550 paper-based; 213 computer-based). *Application deadline:* Applications are processed on a rolling basis. Application fee: $25. Electronic applications accepted. *Expenses:* Contact institution. *Financial support:* Institutionally sponsored loans available. Financial award applicants required to submit FAFSA. *Unit head:* Dr. Patrick J. Hartwick, Dean, 603-668-2211 Ext. 4698, Fax: 603-629-4673, E-mail: p.hartwick@snhu.edu. *Application contact:* Scott Durand, Director of Graduate Enrollment Services, 603-644-3102 Ext. 3338, Fax: 603-644-3144, E-mail: s.durand@snhu.edu.

State University of New York at Oswego, Graduate Studies, School of Education, Department of Vocational Teacher Preparation, Oswego, NY 13126. Offers agriculture (MS Ed); business and marketing (MS Ed); family and consumer sciences (MS Ed); health careers (MS Ed); technical education (MS Ed); trade education (MS Ed). *Accreditation:* NCATE. Part-time and evening/weekend programs available. *Faculty:* 3 full-time, 8 part-time/adjunct. *Students:* 24 full-time (10 women), 52 part-time (23 women); includes 4 minority (3 African Americans, 1 Hispanic American). Average age 40. 50 applicants, 100% accepted. In 2006, 31 degrees awarded. *Degree requirements:* For master's, thesis or alternative. *Entrance requirements:* Additional exam requirements/recommendations for international students: Required—TOEFL (minimum score 560 paper-based; 220 computer-based). *Application deadline:* For fall admission, 4/1 for domestic students; for spring admission, 10/1 for domestic students. Applications are processed on a rolling basis. Application fee: $50. *Expenses:* Tuition, state resident: part-time $288 per credit. Tuition, nonresident: part-time $455 per credit. Tuition and fees vary according to program. *Financial support:* In 2006–07, 3 students received support, including 2 fellowships, 1 teaching assistantship; career-related internships or fieldwork, Federal Work-Study, institutionally sponsored loans, health care benefits, and unspecified assistantships also available. Support available to part-time students. Financial award application deadline: 4/1; financial award applicants required to submit FAFSA. *Unit head:* Dr. Margaret Martin, Chair, 315-312-2480.

Thomas College, Graduate School, Programs in Business, Waterville, ME 04901-5097. Offers business (MBA); computer technology education (MS); education (MS); human resource management (MBA). Part-time and evening/weekend programs available. *Entrance requirements:* For master's, GMAT or minimum GPA of 3.3 in first 3 graduate-level courses, GRE or minimum GPA of 3.3 in first 3 graduate-level courses, MAT or minimum GPA of 3.3 in first 3 graduate-level courses.

University of Delaware, Alfred Lerner College of Business and Economics, Department of Economics, Newark, DE 19716. Offers economics (MA, MS, PhD); economics for entrepreneurship and educators (MA); MA/MBA. Part-time programs available. *Degree requirements:* For master's, thesis (for some programs), mathematics review exam, research project, comprehensive exam; for doctorate, thesis/dissertation, field exam, comprehensive exam. *Entrance requirements:* For master's, GMAT or GRE General Test, minimum GPA of 2.5; for doctorate, GRE General Test, minimum GPA of 3.5 in graduate economics course work. Additional exam requirements/recommendations for international students: Required—TOEFL (minimum score 550 paper-based; 225 computer-based). Electronic applications accepted. *Faculty research:* Applied quantitative economics, industrial organization, resource economics, monetary economics, labor economics.

University of Minnesota, Twin Cities Campus, Graduate School, College of Education and Human Development, Department of Work and Human Resource Education, Program in Business and Industry Education, Minneapolis, MN 55455-0213. Offers M Ed, MA, Ed D, PhD. *Students:* 18 full-time (6 women), 15 part-time (9 women); includes 3 minority (2 African Americans, 1 Hispanic American). Average age 35. 22 applicants, 73% accepted, 15 enrolled. In 2006, 20 degrees awarded. *Expenses:* Tuition, state resident: full-time $9,302; part-time $775 per credit. Tuition, nonresident: full-time $16,400; part-time $1,367 per credit. Full-time tuition and fees vary according to class time, course load, program, reciprocity agreements and student level. *Application contact:* Dr. Mary Bents, Associate Dean, 612-625-6501, Fax: 612-626-1580, E-mail: mbents@tc.umn.edu.

University of Missouri–Columbia, Graduate School, College of Education, Department of Curriculum and Instruction, Columbia, MO 65211. Offers agricultural education (M Ed, PhD, Ed S); art education (M Ed, PhD, Ed S); business and office education (M Ed, PhD, Ed S); early childhood education (M Ed, PhD, Ed S); elementary education (M Ed, PhD, Ed S); English education (M Ed, PhD, Ed S); foreign language education (M Ed, PhD, Ed S); health education and promotion (M Ed, PhD); learning and instruction (M Ed); marketing education (M Ed, PhD, Ed S); mathematics education (M Ed, PhD, Ed S); music education (M Ed, PhD, Ed S); reading education (M Ed, PhD, Ed S); science education (M Ed, PhD, Ed S); social studies education (M Ed, PhD, Ed S); vocational education (M Ed, PhD, Ed S). Part-time programs available. *Faculty:* 24 full-time (12 women). *Students:* 195 full-time (148 women), 260 part-time (214 women); includes 27 minority (8 African Americans, 1 American Indian/Alaska Native, 10 Asian Americans or Pacific Islanders, 8 Hispanic Americans), 19 international. In 2006, 186 master's, 12 doctorates awarded. Terminal master's awarded for partial completion of doctoral program. *Degree requirements:* For doctorate, thesis/dissertation. *Entrance requirements:* For master's and Ed S, GRE General Test or MAT, minimum GPA of 3.0; for doctorate, GRE General Test, minimum GPA of 3.0. *Application deadline:* Applications are processed on a rolling basis. Application fee: $45 ($60 for international students). *Financial support:* Fellowships, research assistantships, teaching assistantships, institutionally sponsored loans available. *Unit head:* Dr. Lloyd H. Barrow, Director of Graduate Studies, 573-882-8247, E-mail: robinsonr@missouri.edu.

University of South Carolina, The Graduate School, College of Education, Department of Instruction and Teacher Education, Program in Secondary Education, Columbia, SC 29208. Offers art education (IMA, MAT); business education (IMA, MAT); English (MAT); foreign language (MAT); health education (MAT); mathematics (MAT); science (IMA, MAT); secondary education (M Ed, MA, MT, PhD); social studies (IMA, MAT); theatre and speech (IMA, MAT). IMA and MT offered jointly with the subject areas. *Accreditation:* NCATE. *Degree requirements:* For master's, thesis (for some programs), foreign language (MA), comprehensive exam; for doctorate, one foreign language, thesis/dissertation, comprehensive exam. *Entrance requirements:* For master's, GRE General Test or MAT, teaching certificate (IMA, M Ed), interview; for doctorate, GRE General Test or MAT, interview. *Faculty research:* Middle school programs, professional development, school collaboration.

The University of Toledo, College of Graduate Studies, College of Education, Department of Curriculum and Instruction, Program in Education and Economics, Toledo, OH 43606-3390. Offers MAE.

University of Washington, Graduate School, Business School, Seattle, WA 98195-3200. Offers auditing and assurance (MP Acc); business (PhD); evening part-time (MBA); executive (MBA); full time (MBA); global (MBA); global executive (MBA); taxation (MP Acc); technology management (MBA); JD/MBA; MBA/MAIS; MBA/MHA. *Accreditation:* AACSB. Part-time and evening/weekend programs available. *Degree requirements:* For master's, registration; for doctorate, thesis/dissertation, comprehensive exam, registration. *Entrance requirements:* For master's, GMAT; for doctorate, GMAT, GRE. Additional exam requirements/recommendations for international students: Required—TOEFL (minimum score 600 paper-based; 250 computer-based). Electronic applications accepted. Expenses: Contact institution.

University of West Georgia, Graduate School, College of Education, Department of Curriculum and Instruction, Program in Business Education, Carrollton, GA 30118. Offers M Ed, Ed S. Part-time and evening/weekend programs available. *Students:* 26 full-time (19 women), 55 part-time (37 women); includes 29 minority (27 African Americans, 1 Asian American or Pacific Islander, 1 Hispanic American). Average age 26. In 2006, 31 master's, 5 other advanced degrees awarded. *Degree requirements:* For master's, research paper; for Ed S, research project. *Entrance requirements:* For master's, PRAXIS I, GRE, minimum GPA of 2.5; for Ed S, GRE, minimum GPA of 2.5. *Application deadline:* For fall admission, 8/1 for domestic students; for spring admission, 12/1 for domestic students. Applications are processed on a rolling basis. Application fee: $20. Electronic applications accepted. *Expenses:* Tuition, state resident: full-time $2,286; part-time $127 per credit. Tuition, nonresident: full-time $9,144; part-time $508 per credit. Required fees: $494; $27 per credit. $121 per semester. *Financial support:* In 2006–07, 2 research assistantships with full tuition reimbursements (averaging $4,000 per year) were awarded; scholarships/grants also available. Financial award applicants required to submit FAFSA. *Faculty research:* Instructional technology, online learning, scans reports, assessment. *Unit head:* Dr. Jorge Gaytan, Director, 678-839-4839, Fax: 678-839-5040, E-mail: jgaytan@westga.edu. *Application contact:* Dr. Charles W. Clark, Chair, 678-839-6508, E-mail: cclark@westga.edu.

University of Wisconsin–Whitewater, School of Graduate Studies, College of Business and Economics, Department of Business Education, Whitewater, WI 53190-1790. Offers general business education (MS); post-secondary business education (MS); secondary business education (MS). *Accreditation:* NCATE. Part-time and evening/weekend programs available. Postbaccalaureate distance learning degree programs offered (no on-campus study). *Students:* 5 full-time (1 woman), 14 part-time (10 women); includes 1 minority (African American) Average age 33. 8 applicants, 75% accepted, 4 enrolled. In 2006, 11 degrees awarded. *Degree requirements:* For master's, thesis or alternative. *Entrance requirements:* For master's, interview, teaching license. Additional exam requirements/recommendations for international students: Required—TOEFL (minimum score 550 paper-based; 213 computer-based). *Application deadline:* For fall admission, 7/15 priority date for domestic and international students; for spring admission, 12/1 priority date for domestic and international students. Applications are processed on a rolling basis. Application fee: $45. Electronic applications accepted. *Expenses:* Tuition, state resident: full-time $3,311. Tuition, nonresident: full-time $8,616. Required fees: $368 per credit. *Financial support:* In 2006–07, 2 research assistantships (averaging $7,385 per year) were awarded; Federal Work-Study, unspecified assistantships, and out of state fee waiver also available. Support available to part-time students. Financial award application deadline: 3/15; financial award applicants required to submit FAFSA. *Faculty research:* Active learning and performance strategies, technology-enhanced formative assessment, computer-supported cooperative work, privacy surveillance. *Unit head:* Dr. Lila Waldman, Coordinator, 262-472-5475. *Application contact:* Sally A. Lange, School of Graduate Studies, 262-472-1006, Fax: 262-472-5027, E-mail: gradschl@uww.edu.

Utah State University, School of Graduate Studies, College of Business, Department of Business Information Systems, Logan, UT 84322. Offers business education (MS); business information systems (MS); business information systems and education (Ed D); education (PhD). Part-time programs available. *Faculty:* 11 full-time (2 women). *Students:* 29 full-time (4 women), 10 part-time (2 women); includes 1 minority (Hispanic American), 7 international. Average age 30. 37 applicants, 59% accepted, 19 enrolled. In 2006, 19 degrees awarded. Terminal master's awarded for partial completion of doctoral program. *Degree requirements:* For master's, thesis optional; for doctorate, thesis/dissertation. *Entrance requirements:* For master's, GMAT, minimum GPA of 3.2; for doctorate, GRE General Test, minimum GPA of 3.0. Additional exam requirements/recommendations for international students: Required—TOEFL. *Application deadline:* For fall admission, 6/6 priority date for domestic students, 6/1 for international students; for winter admission, 3/1 for domestic and international students; for spring admission, 10/1 for domestic and international students. Applications are processed on a rolling basis. Application fee: $50 ($60 for international students). *Financial support:* In 2006–07, 2 research assistantships with partial tuition reimbursements, 9 teaching assistantships with partial tuition reimbursements were awarded; fellowships with partial tuition reimbursements, career-related internships or fieldwork and Federal Work-Study also available. Financial award application deadline: 3/1. *Faculty research:* Oral and written communication, methods of teaching, CASE tools, object-oriented programming, decision support systems. Total annual research expenditures: $10,000. *Unit head:* Dr. Karen Forcht, Head, 435-797-2341, Fax: 435-797-2351. *Application contact:* Janet Bringhurst, Graduate Director, 435-797-2344, Fax: 435-797-2351, E-mail: janet.bringhurst@usu.edu.

Utah State University, School of Graduate Studies, College of Education and Human Services, Doctoral Program in Education, Logan, UT 84322. Offers business information systems (Ed D, PhD); curriculum and instruction (Ed D, PhD); research and evaluation (PhD). *Accreditation:* NCATE. *Faculty:* 61 full-time (19 women). *Students:* 107 full-time (75 women), 100 part-time (60 women); includes 6 minority (3 African Americans, 3 Hispanic Americans), 18 international. Average age 36. 43 applicants, 49% accepted, 12 enrolled. In 2006, 14 degrees awarded. *Degree requirements:* For doctorate, thesis/dissertation, comprehensive exam, registration. *Entrance requirements:* For doctorate, GRE General Test, minimum GPA of 3.0, master's degree. Additional exam requirements/recommendations for international students: Required—TOEFL. *Application deadline:* For fall admission, 6/15 priority date for domestic and international students; for spring admission, 10/15 priority date for domestic and international students. Applications are processed on a rolling basis. Application fee: $50 ($60 for international students). Electronic applications accepted. *Financial support:* In 2006–07, 7 fellowships were awarded; research assistantships with partial tuition reimbursements, teaching assistantships with partial tuition reimbursements, career-related internships or fieldwork, Federal Work-Study, and institutionally sponsored loans also available. Financial award application deadline: 2/1. *Faculty research:* Language and literacy development, math and science education, instructional technology, hearing problems/deafness, domestic violence and animal abuse. Total annual research expenditures: $30.6 million. *Application contact:* Shannon Johnson, Staff Assistant, 435-797-1470, Fax: 435-797-3939, E-mail: shannon.johnson@usu.edu.

Valdosta State University, Graduate School, College of Education, Department of Adult and Career Education, Valdosta, GA 31698. Offers adult and career education (M Ed, Ed D); business education (M Ed). *Accreditation:* NCATE. Evening/weekend programs available. *Degree requirements:* For master's, portfolio; for doctorate, thesis/dissertation, comprehensive written and/or oral exams. *Entrance requirements:* For master's, GRE General Test or MAT, minimum GPA of 2.5; for doctorate, GRE General Test, minimum GPA of 3.5, 3 years of experience. Additional exam requirements/recommendations for international students: Required—TOEFL (minimum score 523 paper-based; 193 computer-based). Electronic applications accepted.

Wayne State College, School of Education and Counseling, Department of Educational Foundations and Leadership, Program in Curriculum and Instruction, Wayne, NE 68787. Offers alternative education (MSE); business education (MSE); communication arts education (MSE); curriculum and instruction (MSE); early childhood education (MSE); elementary education (MSE); English as a second language (MSE); English education (MSE); family consumer science of education (MSE); industrial technology education (MSE); learning communities (MSE); mathematics education (MSE); music education (MSE); science education (MSE); social science education (MSE). *Accreditation:* NCATE. Part-time and evening/weekend programs available. *Faculty:* 17 part-time/adjunct (11 women). *Students:* 17 full-time (10 women), 307 part-time (248 women); includes 6 minority (2 African Americans, 1 American Indian/Alaska Native, 2 Asian Americans or Pacific Islanders, 1 Hispanic American), 1 international. Average age 35. In 2006, 167 degrees awarded. *Degree requirements:* For master's, thesis optional. *Entrance requirements:* For master's, GRE General Test. Additional exam requirements/recommendations for international students: Required—TOEFL (minimum score 550 paper-based; 213 computer-based). *Application deadline:* Applications are processed on a rolling basis. Application fee: $30. *Expenses:* Tuition, state resident: full-time $3,114; part-time $130 per credit hour. Tuition, nonresident: full-time $6,228; part-time $260 per credit hour. Required fees: $894; $37 per credit hour. Tuition and fees vary according to course load. *Financial support:* Applicants required to submit FAFSA.

Wayne State University, College of Education, Division of Teacher Education, Detroit, MI 48202. Offers adult and continuing education (M Ed); art education (M Ed); bilingual/bicultural education (M Ed, MAT); business education (M Ed, MAT); career and technical education (M Ed, Ed D, PhD, Ed S); curriculum and instruction (Ed D, PhD, Ed S); distributive education (M Ed, MAT); early childhood education (M Ed); elementary education (M Ed, MAT, Ed D, PhD, Ed S); elementary education curriculum and instruction (M Ed); English education (M Ed); English education-secondary (M Ed, Ed S); foreign language education (M Ed); general education (Ed D, Ed S); health occupations education (M Ed); industrial education (M Ed); mathematics education (M Ed, Ed S); pre-school and parent education (M Ed); reading (M Ed, Ed D, Ed S); reading, languages and literature (Ed D); school music-vocal (M Ed); science education (M Ed, MAT, Ed S); secondary education (MAT); secondary school reading (M Ed); social studies education (M Ed, Ed S), including education-secondary (M Ed); special education (M Ed, Ed D, PhD, Ed S); teacher education (MAT, Ed D, PhD). *Faculty:* 41 full-time (22 women), 2 part-time/adjunct (both women). *Students:* 401 full-time (295 women), 1,021 part-time (784 women); includes 527 minority (452 African Americans, 6 American Indian/Alaska Native, 32 Asian Americans or Pacific Islanders, 37 Hispanic Americans), 18 international. Average age 36. 296 applicants, 81% accepted, 132 enrolled. In 2006, 386 master's, 1 doctorate awarded. *Degree requirements:* For doctorate, thesis/dissertation. *Entrance requirements:* For master's, minimum GPA of 2.6; for doctorate, minimum undergraduate GPA of 3.0, graduate 3.5; interview. Additional exam requirements/recommendations for international students: Required—TOEFL (minimum score 550 paper-based; 213 computer-based), TWE (minimum score 6). *Application deadline:* For fall admission, 7/1 for domestic students, 6/1 for international students; for winter admission, 10/1 for international students; for spring admission, 2/1 for international students. Application fee: $30 ($50 for international students). Electronic applications accepted. *Financial support:* In 2006–07, 1 fellowship (averaging $34,919 per year) was awarded; research assistantships. *Faculty research:* Reading and writing literacy and literature. Total annual research expenditures: $209,400. *Unit head:* Dr. Joann Snyder, Academic Director, 313-577-1644, E-mail: joanne.snyder@wayne.edu. *Application contact:* Sharon Elliott, Assistant Dean, 313-577-0902, E-mail: sharon.elliott@wayne.edu.

Western Kentucky University, Graduate Studies, College of Education and Behavioral Sciences, Department of Counseling and Student Affairs, Bowling Green, KY 42101. Offers business and marketing education (MA Ed); counseling (MA Ed); counselor education (Ed S); education and behavioral science (MA Ed); elementary education (MA Ed, Ed S); middle years education (MA Ed); secondary education (MA Ed, Ed S); student affairs (MA Ed). *Accreditation:* ACA; NCATE. Part-time and evening/weekend programs available. *Faculty:* 11 full-time (5 women), 9 part-time/adjunct (3 women). *Students:* 59 full-time (47 women), 157 part-time (126 women); includes 18 minority (13 African Americans, 1 American Indian/Alaska Native, 2 Asian Americans or Pacific Islanders, 2 Hispanic Americans), 1 international. Average age 31. 49 applicants, 67% accepted, 27 enrolled. In 2006, 89 master's, 4 other advanced degrees awarded. *Degree requirements:* For master's, thesis optional. *Entrance requirements:* For master's, GRE General Test. Additional exam requirements/recommendations for international students: Required—TOEFL (minimum score 555 paper-based; 213 computer-based; 79 iBT). *Application deadline:* For fall admission, 8/1 priority date for domestic students, 4/1 for international students; for spring admission, 12/1 for domestic students, 9/1 for international students. Applications are processed on a rolling basis. Application fee: $35. *Expenses:* Tuition, state resident: full-time $6,520; part-time $226 per hour. Tuition, nonresident: full-time $7,140; part-time $357 per hour. International tuition: $15,820 full-time. *Financial support:* In 2006–07, 1 research assistantship with partial tuition reimbursement (averaging $8,000 per year) was awarded; Federal Work-Study, institutionally sponsored loans, and service awards also available. Financial award application deadline: 4/1 financial award applicants required to submit FAFSA. *Faculty research:* Counselor education, research for residential workers. *Unit head:* Dr. Aaron W Hughey, Department Head, 270-745-4953, E-mail: aaron.hughey@wku.edu.

Western Kentucky University, Graduate Studies, College of Education and Behavioral Sciences, Department of Curriculum and Instruction, Bowling Green, KY 42101. Offers business and marketing education (MAE); elementary education (MAE, Ed S); middle grades education (MAE); secondary education (MAE, Ed S). *Faculty:* 10 full-time (7 women), 1 (woman) part-time/adjunct. *Students:* 7 full-time (3 women), 133 part-time (109 women); includes 2 minority (1 African American, 1 Hispanic American), 1 international. Average age 31. 30 applicants, 63% accepted, 14 enrolled. In 2006, 56 degrees awarded. *Degree requirements:* For master's, comprehensive exam; for Ed S, thesis. *Entrance requirements:* For master's, GRE. Additional exam requirements/recommendations for international students: Required—TOEFL (minimum score 555 paper-based; 213 computer-based; 79 iBT). *Application deadline:* For fall admission, 7/1 priority date for domestic students, 5/15 for international students; for spring admission, 11/1 for domestic students, 9/15 for international students. Applications are processed on a rolling basis. Application fee: $35. *Expenses:* Tuition, state resident: full-time $6,520; part-time $226 per hour. Tuition, nonresident: full-time $7,140; part-time $357 per hour. International tuition: $15,820 full-time. *Financial support:* In 2006–07, 1 research assistantship with partial tuition reimbursement (averaging $7,200 per year) was awarded. Total annual research expenditures: $17,998. *Unit head:* Dr. Tabitha Daniel, Head, 270-745-2157, E-mail: tabitha.daniel@wku.edu.

Wright State University, School of Graduate Studies, College of Education and Human Services, Department of Teacher Education, Programs in Workforce Education, Dayton, OH 45435. Offers career, technology and vocational education (M Ed, MA); computer/technology education (M Ed, MA); library/media (M Ed MA); vocational education (M Ed, MA). *Accreditation:* NCATE. *Students:* 5 full-time (3 women), 30 part-time (27 women), 1 international. 17 applicants, 94% accepted. In 2006, 14 degrees awarded. *Degree requirements:* For master's, thesis (for some programs). *Entrance requirements:* For master's, GRE General Test, MAT. Additional exam requirements/recommendations for international students: Required—TOEFL. Application fee: $25. *Financial support:* Available to part-time students. Applicants required to submit FAFSA. *Unit head:* Dr. Stephanie Davis, Associate Dean and Program Advisor, 937-775-2880, Fax: 937-775-3308, E-mail: stephanie.davis@wright.edu. *Application contact:* John Kimble, Associate Director of Graduate Admissions and Records, 937-775-2957, Fax: 937-775-2453, E-mail: john.kimble@wright.edu.

Computer Education

Arcadia University, Graduate Studies, Department of Education, Glenside, PA 19038-3295. Offers art education (M Ed, MA Ed); biology education (MA Ed); chemistry education (MA Ed); child development (CAS); computer education (M Ed, CAS); computer education 7–12 (MA Ed); early childhood education (M Ed, CAS), including individualized (M Ed), master teacher (M Ed), research in child development (M Ed); educational leadership (M Ed, CAS); educational psychology (CAS); elementary education (M Ed, CAS); English education (MA Ed); environmental education (MA Ed, CAS); history education (MA Ed); language arts (M Ed, CAS); mathematics education (M Ed, MA Ed, CAS); music education (MA Ed); psychology (MA Ed); pupil personnel services (CAS); reading (M Ed, CAS); school library science (M Ed); science education (M Ed, CAS); secondary education (M Ed, CAS); special education (M Ed, Ed D, CAS); theater arts (MA Ed); written communication (MA Ed). *Accreditation:* NASAD. Part-time and evening/weekend programs available. Postbaccalaureate distance learning degree programs offered (minimal on-campus study). *Faculty:* 12 full-time (8 women), 38 part-time/adjunct (26 women). *Students:* 60 full-time (56 women), 419 part-time (324 women); includes 70 minority (57 African Americans, 1 American Indian/Alaska Native, 6 Asian Americans or Pacific Islanders, 6 Hispanic Americans), 1 international. In 2006, 257 master's, 4 doctorates awarded. *Application deadline:* Applications are processed on a rolling basis. Application fee: $35. Electronic applications accepted. *Financial support:* Career-related internships or fieldwork,

Computer Education

Arcadia University *(continued)*
tuition waivers (partial), and unspecified assistantships available. *Unit head:* Dr. Steven P. Gulkus, Chair, 215-572-2120. *Application contact:* 215-572-2925, Fax: 215-572-2126, E-mail: grad@arcadia.edu.

California State University, Dominguez Hills, College of Education, Division of Graduate Education, Program in Technology-Based Education, Carson, CA 90747-0001. Offers MA, Certificate. Part-time and evening/weekend programs available. *Faculty:* 2 full-time (1 woman). *Students:* 21 full-time (10 women), 32 part-time (20 women); includes 31 minority (11 African Americans, 1 American Indian/Alaska Native, 6 Asian Americans or Pacific Islanders, 13 Hispanic Americans), 1 international. Average age 39. 16 applicants, 100% accepted, 8 enrolled. In 2006, 10 degrees awarded. *Degree requirements:* For master's, thesis or alternative, comprehensive exam, registration. *Entrance requirements:* For master's, minimum GPA of 2.75. *Application deadline:* For fall admission, 6/1 for domestic students. Application fee: $55. *Expenses:* Tuition, nonresident: part-time $339 per unit. Required fees: $1,148 per term. Tuition and fees vary according to program. *Faculty research:* Media literacy, assistive technology. *Unit head:* Dr. Peter Desberg, Unit Head, E-mail: pdesberg@csudh.edu. *Application contact:* Admissions Office, 310-243-3530.

California State University, Los Angeles, Graduate Studies, Charter College of Education, Division of Applied and Advanced Studies in Education, Major in Computer Education, Los Angeles, CA 90032-8530. Offers MA. *Accreditation:* NCATE. *Students:* 4 full-time (1 woman), 21 part-time (10 women); includes 14 minority (6 Asian Americans or Pacific Islanders, 8 Hispanic Americans), 3 international. *Entrance requirements:* For master's, minimum GPA of 2.75 in last 90 units of course work, teaching certificate. Additional exam requirements/recommendations for international students: Required—TOEFL. *Application deadline:* For fall admission, 6/30 for domestic students; for spring admission, 2/1 for domestic students. Applications are processed on a rolling basis. Application fee: $55. *Expenses:* Tuition, nonresident: part-time $226 per unit. *Financial support:* Application deadline: 3/1. *Unit head:* Dr. Chogollah Maroufi, Chair, Division of Applied and Advanced Studies in Education, 323-343-4330, Fax: 323-343-5336.

Canadian Southern Baptist Seminary, Graduate Programs, Cochrane, AB T4C 2G1, Canada. Offers ministry (M Div); religious education (MRE). *Accreditation:* ATS. Part-time programs available. *Faculty:* 8 full-time (0 women), 3 part-time/adjunct (1 woman). *Students:* 26 full-time (3 women), 18 part-time (8 women); includes 12 minority (1 American Indian/Alaska Native, 10 Asian Americans or Pacific Islanders, 1 Hispanic American), 12 international. Average age 30. 11 applicants, 100% accepted, 10 enrolled. In 2006, 13 degrees awarded. *Median time to degree:* Master's–3 years full-time. *Entrance requirements:* Additional exam requirements/recommendations for international students: Required—TOEFL (minimum score 560 paper-based; 220 computer-based), IELTS (minimum score 7). *Application deadline:* For fall admission, 7/1 priority date for domestic and international students; for winter admission, 11/15 priority date for domestic and international students. Applications are processed on a rolling basis. Application fee: $50. *Expenses:* Tuition: Full-time $4,760; part-time $170 per credit hour. *Application contact:* Kathleen McNaughton, Registrar, E-mail: registrar@csbs.ca.

Cardinal Stritch University, College of Education, Department of Educational Computing, Milwaukee, WI 53217-3985. Offers computer science education (MS); educational computing (ME). Part-time and evening/weekend programs available. *Degree requirements:* For master's, thesis, faculty recommendation, comprehensive exam. *Entrance requirements:* For master's, letters of recommendation (2), minimum GPA of 2.75.

Christopher Newport University, Graduate Studies, Department of Teacher Preparation, Newport News, VA 23606-2998. Offers art (PK-12) (MAT); biology (6-12) (MAT); computer science (6-12) (MAT); elementary (PK-6) (MAT); English (6-12) (MAT); French (PK-12) (MAT); history (6-12) (MAT); history and social science (MAT); mathematics (6-12) (MAT); music (PK-12) (MAT), including choral, instrumental; physics (6-12) (MAT); Spanish (PK-12) (MAT); theater (PK-12) (MAT). Part-time and evening/weekend programs available. *Degree requirements:* For master's, thesis or alternative, comprehensive exam. *Entrance requirements:* For master's, PRAXIS I, minimum GPA of 3.0. Electronic applications accepted. *Faculty research:* Early literacy development, instructional innovations, professional teaching standards, multicultural issues, aesthetic education.

Dalhousie University, Faculty of Graduate Studies, Henson College of Public Affairs and Continuing Education, Halifax, NS B3H 4R2, Canada. Offers information technology education (MITE).

DeSales University, Graduate Division, Program in Education, Center Valley, PA 18034-9568. Offers academic standards and information (Certificate); bilingual/ESL studies (Certificate); biology (M Ed); chemistry (M Ed); computers in education (K-12) (M Ed); computers in education (K-8) (M Ed); English (M Ed); instructional technology specialist (Certificate); mathematics (M Ed); special education (M Ed, Certificate); TESOL (M Ed). Part-time and evening/weekend programs available. Postbaccalaureate distance learning degree programs offered (minimal on-campus study). *Students:* 34 full-time, 190 part-time. In 2006, 30 degrees awarded. *Degree requirements:* For master's, thesis project. *Entrance requirements:* For master's, teaching certificate. *Application deadline:* Applications are processed on a rolling basis. Application fee: $35. Electronic applications accepted. *Expenses:* Contact institution. *Financial support:* Unspecified assistantships available. Support available to part-time students. Financial award application deadline: 5/1. *Faculty research:* Effective teaching, computer interfacing in chemistry labs, computer applications to teaching, history of philosophy, aesthetics multidrug-resistant cancer. *Unit head:* Dr. Lujean Baab, Director of M.Ed. Program, 610-282-1100 Ext. 1739, Fax: 610-282-3734, E-mail: lujean.baab@desales.edu. *Application contact:* Donna L. Cressman, Program Secretary, 610-282-1100 Ext. 1461, Fax: 610-282-3734, E-mail: med@desales.edu.

Eastern Washington University, Graduate Studies, College of Science, Mathematics and Technology, Department of Computer Science, Cheney, WA 99004-2431. Offers M Ed, MS. *Accreditation:* NCATE. Part-time programs available. *Degree requirements:* For master's, thesis or alternative, comprehensive exam. *Entrance requirements:* For master's, minimum GPA of 3.0.

Florida Institute of Technology, Graduate Programs, College of Science, Department of Science and Mathematics Education, Melbourne, FL 32901-6975. Offers computer education (MS); elementary science education (M Ed); environmental education (MS); mathematics education (MS, Ed D, PhD, Ed S); science and mathematics education (MAT); science education (MS, Ed D, PhD, Ed S). Part-time and evening/weekend programs available. *Faculty:* 4 full-time (1 woman), 2 part-time/adjunct (1 woman). *Students:* 11 full-time (6 women), 21 part-time (14 women); includes 2 minority (1 African American, 1 American Indian/Alaska Native), 7 international. Average age 38. 40 applicants, 58% accepted, 5 enrolled. In 2006, 7 master's, 2 doctorates, 1 other advanced degree awarded. Terminal master's awarded for partial completion of doctoral program. *Degree requirements:* For master's, thesis (for some programs), comprehensive exam (for some programs), registration; for doctorate, thesis/dissertation, oral defense of dissertation, comprehensive exam, registration. *Entrance requirements:* For master's, minimum GPA of 3.0, resumé, 3 letters of recommendation (elementary science education); for doctorate, minimum GPA of 3.2, resumé, 3 letters of recommendation; for Ed S, minimum GPA of 3.0, resumé, 3 letters of recommendation. Additional exam requirements/recommendations for international students: Required—TOEFL (minimum score 550 paper-based; 213 computer-based). *Application deadline:* Applications are processed on a rolling basis. Application fee: $50. Electronic applications accepted. *Expenses:* Tuition: Part-time $900 per credit. *Financial support:* In 2006–07, 1 student received support, including 1 research assistantship with full and partial tuition reimbursement available (averaging $5,346 per year); career-related internships or fieldwork and tuition remissions also available. Support available to part-time students. Financial award application deadline: 3/1;

financial award applicants required to submit FAFSA. *Faculty research:* Measurement and evaluation, computers in education, educational technology. Total annual research expenditures: $6,000. *Unit head:* Dr. David E. Cook, Department Head, 321-674-8126, Fax: 321-674-7598, E-mail: dcook@fit.edu. *Application contact:* Carolyn P. Farrior, Director of Graduate Admissions, 321-674-7118, Fax: 321-723-9468, E-mail: cfarrior@fit.edu.

Fontbonne University, Graduate Programs, Department of Mathematics and Computer Science, St. Louis, MO 63105-3098. Offers computer education (MS). Part-time and evening/weekend programs available. *Faculty:* 1 (woman) full-time, 8 part-time/adjunct (4 women). *Students:* 5 full-time (4 women), 23 part-time (17 women); includes 13 minority (all African Americans) Average age 40. 18 applicants, 94% accepted. In 2006, 16 degrees awarded. *Degree requirements:* For master's, thesis optional. *Entrance requirements:* For master's, minimum GPA of 3.0. *Application deadline:* For fall admission, 8/1 priority date for domestic students; for spring admission, 12/15 for domestic students. Applications are processed on a rolling basis. Application fee: $25. *Expenses:* Tuition: Full-time $4,890; part-time $489 per credit. Required fees: $160; $76 per credit. Full-time tuition and fees vary according to course load and program. *Financial support:* Available to part-time students. Application deadline: 4/1; *Unit head:* Dr. Elizabeth Newton, Chairperson, 314-719-8096, Fax: 314-889-1401, E-mail: bnewton@fontbonne.edu. *Application contact:* Dr. Mary Abkemeier, Director, 314-889-1497, Fax: 314-889-1451, E-mail: mabkemei@fontbonne.edu.

Jacksonville University, College of Arts and Sciences, School of Education, Program in Computer Sciences, Jacksonville, FL 32211-3394. Offers MAT. Part-time and evening/weekend programs available. *Degree requirements:* For master's, comprehensive exam. *Entrance requirements:* For master's, GRE General Test, minimum GPA of 3.0. Additional exam requirements/recommendations for international students: Required—TOEFL.

Kean University, College of Natural, Applied and Health Sciences, Program in Mathematics Education, Union, NJ 07083. Offers computer applications (MA); supervision of math education (MA); teaching of math (MA). Part-time and evening/weekend programs available. *Faculty:* 24 full-time (6 women). *Students:* 2 full-time (1 woman), 11 part-time (2 women); includes 6 minority (2 African Americans, 2 Asian Americans or Pacific Islanders, 2 Hispanic Americans), 1 international. Average age 40. 4 applicants, 100% accepted, 1 enrolled. In 2006, 8 degrees awarded. *Degree requirements:* For master's, thesis, comprehensive exam. *Entrance requirements:* For master's, GRE General Test, undergraduate major or strong minor in math, 2 letters of recommendation, interview. *Application deadline:* For fall admission, 5/1 for domestic students; for spring admission, 11/1 for domestic students. Application fee: $60 ($150 for international students). *Expenses:* Tuition, state resident: full-time $8,856; part-time $369 per credit. Tuition, nonresident: full-time $11,256; part-time $469 per credit. *Financial support:* In 2006–07, 1 research assistantship with full tuition reimbursement (averaging $3,217 per year) was awarded. *Unit head:* Dr. Francine Abeles, Program Coordinator, 908-737-3714, E-mail: fabeles@kean.edu. *Application contact:* Joanne Morris, Director of Graduate Admissions, 908-737-3355, Fax: 908-737-3354, E-mail: grad-adm@kean.edu.

Lesley University, School of Education, Cambridge, MA 02138-2790. Offers curriculum and instruction (M Ed, CAGS); early childhood education (M Ed); educational studies (PhD); elementary education (M Ed); individually designed (M Ed); middle school education (M Ed); moderate special needs (M Ed); reading (M Ed, CAGS); science in education (M Ed); severe special needs (M Ed); special needs (CAGS); technology in education (M Ed, CAGS). Part-time and evening/weekend programs available. Postbaccalaureate distance learning degree programs offered (no on-campus study). *Faculty:* 47 full-time (39 women), 208 part-time/adjunct (135 women). *Students:* 242 full-time (222 women), 2,903 part-time (2,495 women); includes 279 minority (179 African Americans, 7 American Indian/Alaska Native, 25 Asian Americans or Pacific Islanders, 68 Hispanic Americans), 10 international. Average age 36. 1,186 applicants, 96% accepted, 792 enrolled. In 2006, 1,724 master's, 6 doctorates, 17 other advanced degrees awarded. *Degree requirements:* For master's, practicum; for doctorate, thesis/dissertation. *Entrance requirements:* For doctorate, GRE General Test or MAT, interview, master's degree, resumé; for CAGS, interview, master's degree. Additional exam requirements/recommendations for international students: Required—TOEFL (minimum score 550 paper-based; 213 computer-based; 80 iBT). *Application deadline:* Applications are processed on a rolling basis. Application fee: $50. Electronic applications accepted. *Financial support:* In 2006–07, 26 students received support, including research assistantships (averaging $3,400 per year), teaching assistantships (averaging $3,400 per year); career-related internships or fieldwork, Federal Work-Study, scholarships/grants, and unspecified assistantships also available. Support available to part-time students. Financial award application deadline: 4/15; financial award applicants required to submit FAFSA. *Faculty research:* Assessment in literacy, mathematics and science; autism spectrum disorders; instructional technology and online learning; multicultural education and ELL. *Unit head:* Dr. Mario Borunda, Dean, 617-349-8375, Fax: 617-349-8607, E-mail: mborunda@lesley.edu. *Application contact:* Kristen Card, Associate Director of On-Campus Admissions, 617-349-8734, Fax: 617-349-8313, E-mail: kmcard@lesley.edu.

See Close-Up on page 893.

Long Island University, C.W. Post Campus, College of Information and Computer Science, Department of Computer Science/Management Engineering, Brookville, NY 11548-1300. Offers information systems (MS); information technology education (MS); management engineering (MS). Part-time and evening/weekend programs available. *Degree requirements:* For master's, thesis or alternative, comprehensive exam. *Entrance requirements:* For master's, bachelor's degree in science, mathematics, or engineering; minimum GPA of 2.5. Additional exam requirements/recommendations for international students: Required—TOEFL (minimum score 500 paper-based; 173 computer-based). Electronic applications accepted. *Faculty research:* Inductive music learning, re-engineering business process, technology and ethics.

Maple Springs Baptist Bible College and Seminary, Graduate and Professional Programs, Capitol Heights, MD 20743. Offers biblical studies (MA, Certificate); Christian counseling (MA); church administration (MA); divinity (M Div); ministry (D Min); religious education (MA).

Marlboro College, Graduate Center, Program in Teaching with Internet Technologies, Marlboro, VT 05344. Offers MAT. Evening/weekend programs available. Postbaccalaureate distance learning degree programs offered (minimal on-campus study). *Faculty:* 7 part-time/adjunct (4 women). *Students:* 7 full-time (6 women), 8 part-time (4 women); includes 2 minority (both Hispanic Americans) In 2006, 7 degrees awarded. *Degree requirements:* For master's, capstone project. *Application deadline:* For fall admission, 3/1 priority date for domestic students. Applications are processed on a rolling basis. Application fee: $0. Electronic applications accepted. *Expenses:* Tuition: Full-time $18,900; part-time $630 per credit. Tuition and fees vary according to program. *Financial support:* Applicants required to submit FAFSA. *Unit head:* Kevin Bell, Academic Director, 802-258-9203, Fax: 802-258-9201, E-mail: kbell@gradcenter.marlboro.edu. *Application contact:* Bethany Catron, Director of Admissions, 802-258-9209, Fax: 802-258-9201, E-mail: bcatron@gradcenter.marlboro.edu.

Mississippi College, Graduate School, School of Education, Department of Teacher Education and Leadership, Clinton, MS 39058. Offers art (M Ed); biological science (M Ed); business education (M Ed); computer science (M Ed); dyslexia therapy (M Ed); educational leadership (M Ed, Ed S); elementary education (M Ed, Ed S); English (M Ed); higher education administration (MS); mathematics (M Ed); secondary education (M Ed); social studies (history) (M Ed); teaching arts (M Ed). Part-time programs available. *Faculty:* 9 full-time (5 women), 14 part-time/adjunct (10 women). *Students:* 52 full-time (36 women), 286 part-time (247 women); includes 173 minority (171 African Americans, 1 American Indian/Alaska Native, 1 Hispanic American), 1 international. Average age 32. In 2006, 131 degrees awarded. *Degree requirements:* For master's, thesis optional. *Entrance requirements:* For master's, NTE. Additional exam requirements/recommendations for international students: Recommended—IELTS. *Application deadline:* Applications are processed on a rolling basis. Application fee: $25. Electronic applications accepted. *Expenses:* Tuition: Full-time $7,290; part-time $405 per hour.

Required fees: $150 per term. Tuition and fees vary according to campus/location and program. *Financial support:* Teaching assistantships, career-related internships or fieldwork, Federal Work-Study, scholarships/grants, and unspecified assistantships available. Support available to part-time students. Financial award applicants required to submit FAFSA. *Unit head:* Dr. Tom Williams, Chair, 601-925-3844, E-mail: twilliams@mc.edu.

Morningside College, Graduate Division, Department of Education, Program in Technology Based Learning, Sioux City, IA 51106. Offers MAT. Part-time and evening/weekend programs available. *Entrance requirements:* For master's, MAT, writing sample.

Nova Southeastern University, Fischler School of Education and Human Services, Graduate Teacher Education Program, Fort Lauderdale, FL 33314-7796. Offers athletic administration (MS); cognitive and behavioral disabilities (MS); computer science education (Ed S); computer science education (K-12) (MS); curriculum and teaching (Ed S); curriculum, instruction and technology (MS); curriculum, instruction, management and administration (Ed S); early childhood special education (MS); early literacy and reading (Ed S); early literacy education (MS); education technology (MS); educational leadership (administration K–12) (MS, Ed S); educational media (Ed S); educational media (K-12) (MS); elementary education (MS, Ed S), including ESOL endorsement (MS); English (MS, Ed S); exceptional student education (MS), including ESOL endorsement; gifted education (MS, Ed S); interdisciplinary arts education (MS); management and administration of educational programs (MS); mathematics (MS, Ed S); multicultural early intervention (MS); pre-kindergarten/primary (MS); preschool education (MS); reading (MS, Ed S); science (MS, Ed S); secondary education (MS); social studies (MS, Ed S); Spanish language (MS); teaching and learning (MA, MS), including curriculum and instruction (MA), elementary mathematics (MA), elementary reading (MA), K-12 technology integration (MA); teaching English to speakers of other languages (MS, Ed S); technology management and administration (Ed S); urban studies education (MS); varying exceptionalities (Ed S). Part-time and evening/weekend programs available. Postbaccalaureate distance learning degree programs offered. *Faculty:* 131 full-time (78 women), 548 part-time/adjunct (342 women). *Students:* 1,418 full-time (1,139 women), 3,464 part-time (2,877 women); includes 2,462 minority (1,732 African Americans, 13 American Indian/Alaska Native, 44 Asian Americans or Pacific Islanders, 673 Hispanic Americans), 77 international. Average age 38. 1,771 applicants, 80% accepted, 1419 enrolled. In 2006, 2,078 master's, 425 other advanced degrees awarded. *Degree requirements:* For master's and Ed S, thesis, practicum, internship. *Entrance requirements:* For master's, MAT, GRE, CLAST, CBEST, PRAXIS I, GKT, minimum GPA of 2.5; for Ed S, MAT or GRE, master's degree, teaching certificate, minimum GPA of 3.0. Additional exam requirements/recommendations for international students: Recommended—TOEFL (minimum score 550 paper-based; 213 computer-based), IELTS (minimum score 6). *Application deadline:* For fall admission, 8/11 priority date for domestic and international students; for winter admission, 12/28 priority date for domestic and international students; for spring admission, 4/22 priority date for domestic and international students. Applications are processed on a rolling basis. Application fee: $50. Electronic applications accepted. *Financial support:* Federal Work-Study available. Support available to part-time students. Financial award application deadline: 1/7. *Faculty research:* School effectiveness, critical thinking, leadership skills acquisition, child education, multicultural education. *Unit head:* Dr. Meline Kevorkian, Associate Dean of Master's and Educational Programs, 954-262-8500, Fax: 954-262-3606, E-mail: melinek@nova.edu. *Application contact:* Jennifer Quiñones Nottingham, Dean of Student Affairs, 800-986-3223 Ext. 8624, Fax: 954-262-3911, E-mail: jlquinon@nova.edu.

Nova Southeastern University, Fischler School of Education and Human Services, Programs for Higher Education, Fort Lauderdale, FL 33314-7796. Offers adult education (Ed D); computing and information technology (Ed D); health care education (Ed D); higher education (Ed D); vocational, occupational and technical education (Ed D). Part-time and evening/weekend programs available. *Students:* 35 full-time (22 women), 321 part-time (222 women); includes 134 minority (116 African Americans, 1 American Indian/Alaska Native, 17 Hispanic Americans), 1 international. 4 applicants, 75% accepted, 3 enrolled. In 2006, 40 degrees awarded. *Degree requirements:* For doctorate, thesis/dissertation, practicum. *Entrance requirements:* For doctorate, MAT or GRE, master's degree, work experience in field, minimum GPA of 3.0. Additional exam requirements/recommendations for international students: Recommended—TOEFL (minimum score 550 paper-based; 213 computer-based), IELTS (minimum score 6). *Application deadline:* For fall admission, 8/11 priority date for domestic and international students; for winter admission, 12/28 priority date for domestic and international students; for spring admission, 4/22 priority date for domestic and international students. Applications are processed on a rolling basis. Application fee: $50. Electronic applications accepted. *Expenses:* Contact institution. *Financial support:* In 2006–07, 2 fellowships were awarded; career-related internships or fieldwork and tuition waivers (full) also available. Financial award application deadline: 1/7. *Unit head:* Dr. Karen D. Bowser, Associate Dean of Doctoral Programs, 954-262-8500, Fax: 954-262-3912, E-mail: bowserk@nova.edu. *Application contact:* Jennifer Quiñones Nottingham, Dean of Student Affairs, 800-986-3223 Ext. 8624, Fax: 954-262-3911, E-mail: jlquinon@nova.edu.

Ohio University, Graduate Studies, College of Education, Department of Educational Studies, Athens, OH 45701-2979. Offers computer education and technology (M Ed); educational administration (M Ed, Ed D); educational research and evaluation (M Ed, PhD); instructional technology (PhD). Part-time and evening/weekend programs available. Postbaccalaureate distance learning degree programs offered (minimal on-campus study). *Faculty:* 13 full-time (7 women), 1 (woman) part-time/adjunct. *Students:* 77 full-time (41 women), 120 part-time (55 women); includes 5 minority (3 African Americans, 1 Asian American or Pacific Islander, 1 Hispanic American), 79 international. 121 applicants, 69% accepted, 49 enrolled. In 2006, 12 master's, 14 doctorates awarded. *Median time to degree:* Of those who began their doctoral program in fall 1998, 92% received their degree in 8 years or less. *Degree requirements:* For master's, thesis or alternative, registration; for doctorate, thesis/dissertation, comprehensive exam, registration. *Entrance requirements:* For master's, GRE General Test if GPA is less than 2.8; for doctorate, GRE General Test, minimum GPA of 3.4, work experience, 3 letters of reference, autobiography. Additional exam requirements/recommendations for international students: Required—TOEFL (minimum score 550 paper-based; 213 computer-based). *Application deadline:* For fall admission, 4/1 priority date for domestic and international students. Applications are processed on a rolling basis. Application fee: $45. Electronic applications accepted. *Financial support:* In 2006–07, 26 research assistantships with full tuition reimbursements (averaging $6,500 per year), 2 teaching assistantships with full tuition reimbursements (averaging $7,200 per year) were awarded; Federal Work-Study, institutionally sponsored loans, tuition waivers (full), and unspecified assistantships also available. Financial award application deadline: 3/15. *Faculty research:* Race, class and gender; computer programs; development and organization theory; evaluation/development of instruments, leadership. Total annual research expenditures: $158,037. *Unit head:* Dr. Catherine H. Glascock, Chair, 740-593-4464, Fax: 740-593-0477, E-mail: glascock@ohio.edu. *Application contact:* Floyd J. Doney, Director of Student Affairs, 740-593-4400, Fax: 740-593-9310, E-mail: doney@ohio.edu.

Providence College, Graduate Studies, Department of Religious Studies, Providence, RI 02918. Offers biblical studies (MA); pastoral ministry (MA); religious education (MA); religious studies (MA). Part-time and evening/weekend programs available. *Faculty:* 5 full-time (0 women). *Students:* 5 full-time (0 women), 19 part-time (12 women). Average age 39. 16 applicants, 100% accepted. In 2006, 13 degrees awarded. *Degree requirements:* For master's, Greek and Hebrew (biblical studies). *Entrance requirements:* Additional exam requirements/recommendations for international students: Required—TOEFL (minimum score 550 paper-based; 213 computer-based). *Application deadline:* For fall admission, 8/1 for domestic students; for spring admission, 12/1 for domestic students. Applications are processed on a rolling basis. Application fee: $55. *Expenses:* Tuition: Full-time $6,573; part-time $939 per unit. *Financial support:* In 2006–07, 4 research assistantships with full tuition reimbursements (averaging $8,400 per year) were awarded; career-related internships or fieldwork and unspecified assistantships also available. Support available to part-time students. Financial award application deadline: 8/1; financial award applicants required to submit FAFSA. *Unit head:* Dr. Gary M. Culpepper, Director, 401-865-2863, Fax: 401-865-1449, E-mail: garyculp@providence.edu.

Southern New Hampshire University, School of Education, Manchester, NH 03106-1045. Offers business education (MS); child development (M Ed); computer technology education (Certificate); curriculum and instruction (M Ed); education (M Ed, CAS); elementary education (M Ed); general special education (Certificate); school business administrator (Certificate); school counseling (M Ed); school psychology (M Ed); secondary education (M Ed); training and development (Certificate). Part-time and evening/weekend programs available. Postbaccalaureate distance learning degree programs offered. *Faculty:* 6 full-time (3 women), 9 part-time/adjunct (7 women). *Students:* Average age 35. In 2006, 52 degrees awarded. *Degree requirements:* For master's, thesis or alternative, comprehensive exam (for some programs). *Entrance requirements:* For master's, GRE General Test or MAT, minimum GPA of 3.0. Additional exam requirements/recommendations for international students: Required—TOEFL (minimum score 550 paper-based; 213 computer-based). *Application deadline:* Applications are processed on a rolling basis. Application fee: $25. Electronic applications accepted. *Expenses:* Contact institution. *Financial support:* Institutionally sponsored loans available. Financial award applicants required to submit FAFSA. *Unit head:* Dr. Patrick J. Hartwick, Dean, 603-668-2211 Ext. 4698, Fax: 603-629-4673, E-mail: p.hartwick@snhu.edu. *Application contact:* Scott Durand, Director of Graduate Enrollment Services, 603-644-3102 Ext. 3338, Fax: 603-644-3144, E-mail: s.durand@snhu.edu.

Stanford University, School of Education, Program in Cross-Area Specializations, Stanford, CA 94305-9991. Offers learning, design, and technology (MA, PhD); symbolic systems in education (PhD). *Degree requirements:* For doctorate, thesis/dissertation. Electronic applications accepted.

Stony Brook University, State University of New York, Graduate School, College of Engineering and Applied Sciences, Department of Technology and Society, Program in Educational Technology, Stony Brook, NY 11794. Offers MS. *Accreditation:* NCATE. *Application deadline:* For fall admission, 6/1 for domestic students; for spring admission, 12/1 for domestic students. *Expenses:* Tuition, state resident: full-time $6,900; part-time $288 per credit. Tuition, nonresident: full-time $10,920; part-time $455 per credit. *Financial support:* Research assistantships, teaching assistantships available.

Announcement: The Department of Technology and Society in the College of Engineering and Applied Sciences offers a Master of Science degree in technological systems management with a concentration in educational technology. The program emphasizes use of modern technologies in colleges, schools, businesses, and other areas; research and evaluation of educational technologies; alignment with local and national educational technology standards; and ethical and other societal issues associated with the use of technology. In addition to the 30-credit master's degree, the Department of Technology and Society offers an 18-credit Advanced Graduate Certificate.

See Close-Up on page 1613.

Teachers College Columbia University, Graduate Faculty of Education, Department of Math, Science and Technology, Program in Computing in Education, New York, NY 10027-6696. Offers MA. *Accreditation:* NCATE. Part-time and evening/weekend programs available. *Faculty:* 1 full-time (0 women), 8 part-time/adjunct. *Students:* 7 full-time (6 women), 26 part-time (12 women); includes 8 minority (5 African Americans, 1 Asian American or Pacific Islander, 2 Hispanic Americans), 2 international. Average age 35. 13 applicants, 92% accepted, 6 enrolled. In 2006, 24 degrees awarded. *Application deadline:* For fall admission, 5/15 for domestic students; for spring admission, 12/1 for domestic students. Application fee: $65. *Expenses:* Tuition: Full-time $23,400; part-time $975 per credit. Required fees: $320 per term. *Financial support:* Career-related internships or fieldwork, Federal Work-Study, institutionally sponsored loans, and tuition waivers (full and partial) available. Support available to part-time students. Financial award application deadline: 2/1. *Faculty research:* Visual and interactive learning, global curriculum, cognition and learning. *Application contact:* Deanna Ghozati, Assistant Director of Admission, 212-678-4018, Fax: 212-678-4171, E-mail: ghozati@tc.edu.

See Close-Up on page 1615.

Thomas College, Graduate School, Programs in Business, Waterville, ME 04901-5097. Offers business (MBA); computer technology education (MS); education (MS); human resource management (MBA). Part-time and evening/weekend programs available. *Entrance requirements:* For master's, GMAT or minimum GPA of 3.3 in first 3 graduate-level courses, GRE or minimum GPA of 3.3 in first 3 graduate-level courses, MAT or minimum GPA of 3.3 in first 3 graduate-level courses.

University of Bridgeport, School of Education and Human Resources, Division of Education, Program in Secondary Education, Bridgeport, CT 06604. Offers computer specialist (Diploma); international education (Diploma); reading specialist (MS, Diploma); secondary education (MS, Diploma). Part-time and evening/weekend programs available. *Faculty:* 12 full-time (5 women), 72 part-time/adjunct (44 women). *Students:* 1 full-time (0 women), 5 part-time (all women). Average age 37. 8 applicants, 63% accepted, 1 enrolled. In 2006, 4 degrees awarded. *Degree requirements:* For master's, final exam, final project, or thesis; for Diploma, thesis or alternative, final project. *Entrance requirements:* For master's, GRE General Test, MAT, minimum undergraduate QPA of 2.5; for Diploma, GRE General Test or MAT, minimum graduate QPA of 3.0. *Application deadline:* For fall admission, 8/1 priority date for domestic students; for spring admission, 12/1 priority date for domestic students. Applications are processed on a rolling basis. Application fee: $25 ($35 for international students). Electronic applications accepted. *Financial support:* Career-related internships or fieldwork, Federal Work-Study, and institutionally sponsored loans available. Support available to part-time students. Financial award application deadline: 6/1; financial award applicants required to submit FAFSA. *Faculty research:* Self-concept, internship assessment, stress and situational development, follow-up of graduation, trend analysis. *Unit head:* Dr. Allen P. Cook, Associate Dean, Division of Education, 203-576-4206, Fax: 203-576-4200, E-mail: acook@bridgeport.edu.

University of Central Oklahoma, College of Graduate Studies and Research, College of Mathematics and Science, Department of Mathematics and Statistics, Edmond, OK 73034-5209. Offers applied mathematical sciences (MS), including computer science, mathematics, mathematics/computer science teaching, statistics. Part-time programs available. *Degree requirements:* For master's, thesis. *Entrance requirements:* Additional exam requirements/recommendations for international students: Required—TOEFL (minimum score 550 paper-based; 213 computer-based). Electronic applications accepted. *Faculty research:* Curvature, FAA, math education.

University of Maryland, Baltimore County, Graduate School, College of Arts, Humanities and Social Sciences, Department of Education, Baltimore, MD 21250. Offers computer/web-based instruction (Postbaccalaureate Certificate); distance education (Postbaccalaureate Certificate); early childhood education (MAT); education (MA); elementary education (MAT); instructional systems development (MA, Postbaccalaureate Certificate), including ESOL/bilingual education (Postbaccalaureate Certificate), ESOL/bilingual training systems (MA); secondary education (MA, MAT); teaching (MA). *Accreditation:* NCATE. Part-time and evening/weekend programs available. Postbaccalaureate distance learning degree programs offered (no on-campus study). *Faculty:* 17 full-time (15 women), 3 part-time/adjunct (all women). *Students:* 89 full-time (78 women), 422 part-time (340 women); includes 72 minority (41 African Americans, 19 Asian Americans or Pacific Islanders, 12 Hispanic Americans), 15 international. In 2006, 56 master's awarded. *Median time to degree:* Of those who began their doctoral program in fall 1998, 95% received their degree in 8 years or less. *Degree requirements:* For master's, thesis (for some programs), comprehensive exam, registration. *Entrance requirements:* For master's, GRE General Test, GRE Subject Test (MA), PRAXIS I (MAT), minimum GPA of 3.0. Additional exam requirements/recommendations for international students: Required—TOEFL. *Application deadline:* For fall admission, 7/1 for domestic students. Applica-

Computer Education

University of Maryland, Baltimore County *(continued)*
tions are processed on a rolling basis. Application fee: $50. Electronic applications accepted. *Expenses:* Tuition, state resident: part-time $412 per credit hour. Tuition, nonresident: part-time $681 per credit hour. Required fees: $91 per credit hour. One-time fee: $75 part-time. *Financial support:* In 2006–07, 75 students received support, including research assistantships with full tuition reimbursements available (averaging $12,000 per year); fellowships, teaching assistantships, career-related internships or fieldwork, Federal Work-Study, scholarships/grants, tuition waivers (partial), and unspecified assistantships also available. Financial award application deadline: 3/1. *Faculty research:* Teacher leadership; STEM education; ESOL/bilingual education; early childhood education; language, literacy and culture. Total annual research expenditures: $1.3 million. *Unit head:* Dr. Mary S. Rivkin, Department Chair, 410-455-2465, Fax: 410-455-3986, E-mail: rivkin@umbc.edu. *Application contact:* Dr. Susan M. Blunck, Director, 410-455-2869, Fax: 410-455-3986, E-mail: blunck@umbc.edu.

University of Michigan, Horace H. Rackham School of Graduate Studies, School of Education, Programs in Educational Studies, Ann Arbor, MI 48109. Offers curriculum development (MA); early childhood education (MA, PhD); educational administration and policy (MA, PhD); educational foundation, administration, policy, and research methods (MA); educational foundations and policy (MA, PhD); elementary education (MA-Certification); English education (MA); English language learning in school settings (MA); learning technologies (MA, PhD); literacy, language, and culture (MA, PhD); mathematics education (MA, PhD); research methods (MA); science education (MA, PhD); secondary education (MA-Certification); social studies education (MA); special education (PhD); teaching and teacher education (PhD); MA-Certification; MBA/MA; PhD/MA. Terminal master's awarded for partial completion of doctoral program. *Degree requirements:* For master's, thesis (for some programs); for doctorate, thesis/dissertation, comprehensive exam. *Entrance requirements:* For master's and doctorate, GRE General Test. Additional exam requirements/recommendations for international students: Required—TOEFL (minimum score 600 paper-based; 250 computer-based). *Application deadline:* For fall admission, 12/1 priority date for domestic students, 12/1 for international students. Application fee: $60 ($75 for international students). Electronic applications accepted. *Financial support:* Applicants required to submit FAFSA. *Unit head:* Dr. Addison Stone, Chairperson, 734-763-7500, Fax: 734-615-1290, E-mail: addison@umich.edu. *Application contact:* Roberta Perry, Office of Student Services, 734-764-7563, Fax: 734-763-1495, E-mail: ed.grad.admit@umich.edu.

University of North Texas, Robert B. Toulouse School of Graduate Studies, College of Education, Department of Technology and Cognition, Program in Computer Education and Cognitive Systems, Denton, TX 76203. Offers MS, PhD. *Accreditation:* NCATE. *Students:* 6 full-time (5 women), 61 part-time (43 women); includes 12 minority (8 African Americans, 1 Asian American or Pacific Islander, 3 Hispanic Americans), 6 international. Average age 35. 12 applicants, 75% accepted, 9 enrolled. In 2006, 61 degrees awarded. *Entrance requirements:* For master's, GRE General Test. Additional exam requirements/recommendations for international students: Required—TOEFL (minimum score 550 paper-based; 213 computer-based). *Application deadline:* For fall admission, 7/15 for domestic students. Application fee: $50 ($75 for international students). *Expenses:* Tuition, state resident: full-time $3,573; part-time $198 per credit. Tuition, nonresident: full-time $8,577; part-time $476 per credit. Required fees: $1,258; $126 per credit. One-time fee: $150 full-time. Tuition and fees vary according to course load. *Financial support:* Fellowships, research assistantships, teaching assistantships, career-related internships or fieldwork, Federal Work-Study, and institutionally sponsored loans available. Financial award application deadline: 4/1. *Unit head:* Head, 940-565-2057. *Application contact:* Dr. Mark Mortensen, Graduate Adviser, 940-565-2057, Fax: 940-565-2185, E-mail: markmort@unt.edu.

University of Phoenix–Fort Lauderdale Campus, The Artemis School, College of Education, Fort Lauderdale, FL 33309. Offers administration and supervision (MA Ed); computer education (MA Ed); curriculum and instruction (MA Ed); elementary teacher education (MA Ed); secondary teacher education (MA Ed). Evening/weekend programs available. *Faculty:* 10 full-time (5 women), 17 part-time/adjunct (7 women). *Students:* 132 full-time (114 women); includes 60 minority (52 African Americans, 1 Asian American or Pacific Islander, 7 Hispanic Americans), 5 international. Average age 39. In 2006, 25 degrees awarded. *Degree requirements:* For master's, thesis (for some programs), registration. *Entrance requirements:* For master's, 3 years of work experience, minimum undergraduate GPA of 2.5. Additional exam requirements/recommendations for international students: Required—TOEFL (minimum score 550 paper-based; 213 computer-based; 79 iBT). *Application deadline:* Applications are processed on a rolling basis. Application fee: $45. Electronic applications accepted. *Expenses:* Tuition: Full-time $9,450. Required fees: $760. *Financial support:* Institutionally sponsored loans and scholarships/grants available. Financial award applicants required to submit FAFSA. *Unit head:* Dr. Marla LaRue, Dean/Executive Director, 480-557-1218. *Application contact:* Chair, 954-382-5303, Fax: 954-382-5304.

University of Phoenix–North Florida Campus, The Artemis School, College of Education, Jacksonville, FL 32216-0959. Offers administration (MA Ed); curriculum and instruction (MA Ed); curriculum and instruction—computer education (MA Ed); elementary teacher education (MA Ed); secondary teacher education (MA Ed). Evening/weekend programs available. *Faculty:* 9 full-

time (5 women), 10 part-time/adjunct (4 women). *Students:* 98 full-time (78 women); includes 41 minority (37 African Americans, 4 Hispanic Americans), 1 international. Average age 37. In 2006, 22 master's awarded. *Degree requirements:* For master's, thesis (for some programs), registration. *Entrance requirements:* For master's, 3 years of work experience, minimum undergraduate GPA of 2.5. Additional exam requirements/recommendations for international students: Required—TOEFL (minimum score 550 paper-based; 213 computer-based; 49 iBT). *Application deadline:* Applications are processed on a rolling basis. Application fee: $45. Electronic applications accepted. *Financial support:* Institutionally sponsored loans and scholarships/grants available. Financial award applicants required to submit FAFSA. *Unit head:* Dr. Marla LaRue, Dean, 480-557-1218, E-mail: marla.larue@phoenix.edu. *Application contact:* Chair, 904-636-6645, Fax: 904-636-0998.

University of Phoenix–Omaha Campus, College of Education, Omaha, NE 68154-5240. Offers administration and supervision (MA Ed); curriculum and instruction (MA Ed); curriculum and instruction—English and language arts education (MA Ed); curriculum and instruction—adult education (MA Ed); curriculum and instruction—computer education (MA Ed); curriculum and instruction—English as a second language (MA Ed); curriculum and instruction—mathematics education (MA Ed); elementary teacher education (MA Ed); secondary teacher education (MA Ed); special education (MA Ed).

University of Phoenix–Springfield Campus, College of Education, Springfield, MO 65804-7211. Offers administration and supervision (MA Ed); curriculum and instruction (MA Ed); curriculum and instruction/adult education (MA Ed); curriculum and instruction/computer education (MA Ed); curriculum and instruction/English as a second language (MA Ed); English and language arts education (MA Ed); mathematics education (MA Ed).

The University of Texas at Tyler, College of Education and Psychology, Department of Curriculum and Instruction, Tyler, TX 75799-0001. Offers curriculum and instruction (M Ed); secondary teaching (MAT), including art, biology, computer science, English, history, journalism, mathematics, music, political science, sociology, speech, theatre. Part-time programs available. *Faculty:* 10 full-time (6 women), 2 part-time/adjunct (1 woman). *Students:* 3 full-time (2 women), 7 part-time (6 women); includes 1 minority (African American) Average age 32. 1 applicant, 100% accepted, 1 enrolled. In 2006, 6 degrees awarded. *Degree requirements:* For master's, research project (M Ed). *Entrance requirements:* For master's, GRE or MAT. Application fee: $0 ($50 for international students). Electronic applications accepted. *Expenses:* Tuition, state resident: part-time $50 per credit hour. Tuition, nonresident: part-time $328 per credit hour. Required fees: $107 per credit hour. $426 per term. *Financial support:* Scholarships/grants available. *Unit head:* Dr. Robert Stevens, Chair/Professor of Education, 903-566-7315, E-mail: rstevens@uttyler.edu. *Application contact:* Bonnie Purser, Office of Graduate Studies, 903-566-7142, Fax: 903-566-7068, E-mail: bpurser@uttyler.edu.

Wilkes University, Graduate Studies and Continued Learning, College of Arts, Humanities and Social Sciences, Program in Teacher Education, Wilkes-Barre, PA 18766-0002. Offers classroom technology (MS Ed); educational computing (MS Ed); educational development and strategies (MS Ed); educational leadership (MS Ed); elementary education (MS Ed); instructional technology (MS Ed); school business leadership (MS Ed); secondary education (MS Ed), including biology, chemistry, English, history; special education (MS Ed). Part-time and evening/weekend programs available. Postbaccalaureate distance learning degree programs offered (minimal on-campus study). *Students:* 32 full-time (21 women), 1,588 part-time (1,106 women); includes 29 minority (6 African Americans, 2 American Indian/Alaska Native, 4 Asian Americans or Pacific Islanders, 17 Hispanic Americans). Average age 33. In 2006, 754 degrees awarded. *Entrance requirements:* Additional exam requirements/recommendations for international students: Required—TOEFL (minimum score 500 paper-based; 173 computer-based). *Application deadline:* Applications are processed on a rolling basis. Application fee: $40. *Expenses:* Contact institution. *Financial support:* Federal Work-Study and unspecified assistantships available. Financial award application deadline: 3/1; financial award applicants required to submit FAFSA. *Unit head:* Dr. Michael Speziale, Interim Dean, 570-408-4679, Fax: 570-408-4905, E-mail: michael.speziale@wilkes.edu. *Application contact:* Kathleen Houlihan, Director of Graduate Studies, 570-408-3235, Fax: 570-408-7846, E-mail: kathleen.houlihan@wilkes.edu.

Wright State University, School of Graduate Studies, College of Education and Human Services, Department of Teacher Education, Programs in Workforce Education, Dayton, OH 45435. Offers career, technology and vocational education (M Ed, MA); computer/technology education (M Ed, MA); library/media (M Ed, MA); vocational education (M Ed, MA). *Accreditation:* NCATE. *Students:* 5 full-time (3 women), 30 part-time (27 women), 1 international. 17 applicants, 94% accepted. In 2006, 14 degrees awarded. *Degree requirements:* For master's, thesis (for some programs). *Entrance requirements:* For master's, GRE General Test, MAT. Additional exam requirements/recommendations for international students: Required—TOEFL. Application fee: $25. *Financial support:* Available to part-time students. Applicants required to submit FAFSA. *Unit head:* Dr. Stephanie Davis, Associate Dean and Program Advisor, 937-775-2880, Fax: 937-775-3308, E-mail: stephanie.davis@wright.edu. *Application contact:* John Kimble, Associate Director of Graduate Admissions and Records, 937-775-2957, Fax: 937-775-2453, E-mail: john.kimble@wright.edu.

Counselor Education

Acadia University, Faculty of Professional Studies, School of Education, Program in Counseling, Wolfville, NS B4P 2R6, Canada. Offers M Ed. Part-time and evening/weekend programs available. *Faculty:* 4 full-time (2 women). *Students:* 19 full-time (15 women), 39 part-time (35 women). In 2006, 25 degrees awarded. *Degree requirements:* For master's, thesis optional. *Entrance requirements:* For master's, B Ed, minimum B average in undergraduate course work, 2 years of teaching or related experience. Additional exam requirements/recommendations for international students: Required—TOEFL (minimum score 580 paper-based; 237 computer-based). *Application deadline:* For fall admission, 2/1 for domestic and international students. Application fee: $50. Electronic applications accepted. *Financial support:* Teaching assistantships available. Financial award application deadline: 2/1. *Faculty research:* Computer-assisted supervision, rural/remote school counseling, non-custodial fathers, spirituality, counseling relationships. *Application contact:* Sheila Langille, Secretary, 902-585-1229, Fax: 902-585-1071, E-mail: sheila.langille@acadiau.ca.

Adams State College, The Graduate School, Department of Counselor Education, Alamosa, CO 81102. Offers counseling (MA). *Accreditation:* ACA. Part-time programs available. *Degree requirements:* For master's, internship, qualifying exam. *Entrance requirements:* For master's, GRE General Test or MAT, minimum undergraduate GPA of 2.75.

Adler Graduate School, Program in Adlerian Studies, Richfield, MN 55423. Offers art therapy specialization (MA); clinical counseling track (MA); coaching and consulting in organizations (Certificate); management consulting and organizational leadership (MA); marriage and family track (MA); non-clinical Adlerian studies track (MA); personal and professional life coaching (Certificate); school counseling (MA). Part-time and evening/weekend programs available. *Faculty:* 4 full-time (1 woman), 36 part-time/adjunct (21 women). *Students:* Average age 37. 48 applicants, 98% accepted; 46 enrolled. In 2006, 37 degrees awarded. *Degree requirements:* For master's, thesis or alternative, 500-700 hour internship, depending on license choice. *Entrance requirements:* For master's, minimum undergraduate GPA of 3.0, 12 credits of

course work in psychology or related field. *Application deadline:* For fall admission, 10/1 priority date for domestic students; for winter admission, 1/1 priority date for domestic students; for spring admission, 4/1 priority date for domestic students. Applications are processed on a rolling basis. Application fee: $50. *Financial support:* In 2006–07, 121 students received support. Career-related internships or fieldwork and tuition waivers available. Support available to part-time students. Financial award applicants required to submit FAFSA. *Unit head:* Dr. Dennis Rislove, President, 612-861-7554 Ext. 106, Fax: 612-861-7559, E-mail: rislove@alfredadler.edu. *Application contact:* Evelyn B. Haas, Director of Student Services and Admissions, 612-861-7554 Ext. 103, Fax: 612-861-7559, E-mail: ev@alfredadler.edu.

Alabama Agricultural and Mechanical University, School of Graduate Studies, School of Education, Department of Counseling and Special Education, Huntsville, AL 35811. Offers communicative disorders (M Ed, MS); psychology and counseling (MS, Ed S), including clinical psychology (MS), counseling and guidance, counseling psychology (MS), personnel management (MS), psychometry (MS), school psychology (MS); special education (M Ed, MS). *Accreditation:* CORE; NCATE. Part-time and evening/weekend programs available. *Faculty:* 4 full-time (3 women), 3 part-time/adjunct (1 woman). *Students:* 62 full-time (50 women), 121 part-time (93 women); includes 121 minority (113 African Americans, 2 American Indian/Alaska Native, 6 Hispanic Americans), 12 international. In 2006, 55 master's, 2 other advanced degrees awarded. *Degree requirements:* For master's, comprehensive exam. *Entrance requirements:* For master's, GRE General Test. *Application deadline:* For fall admission, 5/1 for domestic students. Application fee: $15 ($20 for international students). *Financial support:* Career-related internships or fieldwork available. Support available to part-time students. Financial award application deadline: 4/1. *Faculty research:* Increasing numbers of minorities in special education and speech-language pathology. Total annual research expenditures: $300,000. *Unit head:* Dr. Terry L. Douglas, Chair, 256-372-5533.

Alabama State University, School of Graduate Studies, College of Education, Department of Instructional Support, Program in Guidance and Counseling, Montgomery, AL 36101-0271. Offers general counseling (MS, Ed S); school counseling (M Ed, Ed S). Part-time programs available. *Faculty:* 5 full-time (1 woman), 3 part-time/adjunct (1 woman). *Students:* 36 full-time (28 women), 129 part-time (100 women); includes 135 minority (134 African Americans, 1 American Indian/Alaska Native). Average age 35. In 2006, 51 master's, 1 other advanced degree awarded. *Degree requirements:* For master's, comprehensive exam; for Ed S, thesis, comprehensive exam. *Entrance requirements:* For master's, GRE General Test, MAT, graduate writing competency test; for Ed S, graduate writing competency test, GRE, MAT. Additional exam requirements/recommendations for international students: Required—TOEFL (minimum score 500 paper-based; 173 computer-based). *Application deadline:* For fall admission, 7/15 for domestic students; for spring admission, 12/15 for domestic students. Applications are processed on a rolling basis. Application fee: $10. *Expenses:* Tuition, state resident: full-time $1,728; part-time $192 per hour. Tuition, nonresident: full-time $3,456; part-time $334 per hour. *Financial support:* In 2006–07, research assistantships (averaging $9,450 per year). *Faculty research:* Enhancing self-concept, drug abuse education and training, comparison of group techniques, collaborative counseling. *Unit head:* Dr. Virginia Martin, Coordinator, 334-229-4571, E-mail: vmartin@asunet.alasu.edu.

Albany State University, College of Education, Program in School Counseling, Albany, GA 31705-2717. Offers M Ed. Part-time programs available. *Degree requirements:* For master's, comprehensive exam. *Entrance requirements:* For master's, GRE General Test, MAT. *Faculty research:* Student achievement, student motivation, preparing students for technology, students' attitude toward science, education e-courses.

Alcorn State University, School of Graduate Studies, School of Psychology and Education, Alcorn State, MS 39096-7500. Offers agricultural education (MS Ed); elementary education (MS Ed, Ed S); guidance and counseling (MS Ed); industrial education (MS Ed); secondary education (MS Ed), including health and physical education; special education (MS Ed). *Accreditation:* NCATE. *Faculty:* 14 full-time (9 women), 21 part-time/adjunct (13 women). *Students:* 76 full-time (44 women), 271 part-time (226 women); includes 333 minority (all African Americans) In 2006, 119 degrees awarded. *Degree requirements:* For master's, thesis optional. *Application deadline:* For fall admission, 7/15 priority date for domestic students; for spring admission, 11/25 for domestic students. Applications are processed on a rolling basis. Application fee: $0 ($10 for international students). *Financial support:* Career-related internships or fieldwork available. Support available to part-time students. *Unit head:* Dr. Josephine M. Posey, Dean, 601-877-6141, Fax: 601-877-3867.

Alfred University, Graduate School, Division of Education, Alfred, NY 14802-1205. Offers counseling (MS Ed, CAS); literacy teacher (MS Ed). Part-time programs available. *Students:* 12 full-time (all women), 26 part-time (18 women). Average age 24. 62 applicants, 61% accepted, 30 enrolled. In 2006, 48 master's, 19 other advanced degrees awarded. *Entrance requirements:* For master's, LAST, Assessment of Teaching Skills (written), Content Specialty Test. Additional exam requirements/recommendations for international students: Required—TOEFL (minimum score 590 paper-based; 243 computer-based; 90 iBT), IELTS (minimum score 7). *Application deadline:* Applications are processed on a rolling basis. Application fee: $50. Electronic applications accepted. *Expenses:* Tuition: Full-time $29,600; part-time $630 per credit hour. Required fees: $850; $70 per semester. Tuition and fees vary according to program. *Financial support:* In 2006–07, 12 students received support, including research assistantships (averaging $14,225 per year); tuition waivers (partial) and unspecified assistantships also available. Financial award applicants required to submit FAFSA. *Faculty research:* Whole language, ethics in counseling and psychotherapy. *Unit head:* Dr. James Curl, Chair, 607-871-2219, E-mail: fcurl@alfred.edu. *Application contact:* Valerie Stephens, Coordinator of Graduate Admissions, 607-871-2141, Fax: 607-871-2198, E-mail: gradinquiry@alfred.edu.

Angelo State University, College of Graduate Studies, College of Education, Department of Curriculum and Instruction, Program in Guidance and Counseling, San Angelo, TX 76909. Offers M Ed. Part-time and evening/weekend programs available. *Faculty:* 17 full-time (12 women). *Students:* 8 full-time (all women), 20 part-time (19 women); includes 2 minority (both Hispanic Americans) Average age 36. 9 applicants, 78% accepted, 7 enrolled. In 2006, 14 degrees awarded. *Degree requirements:* For master's, comprehensive exam. *Entrance requirements:* For master's, GRE General Test. Additional exam requirements/recommendations for international students: Required—TOEFL or IELTS. *Application deadline:* For fall admission, 7/15 priority date for domestic students, 6/15 for international students; for spring admission, 12/8 for domestic students, 11/1 for international students. Applications are processed on a rolling basis. Application fee: $40 ($50 for international students). Electronic applications accepted. *Expenses:* Tuition, state resident: full-time $2,340; part-time $130 per hour. Tuition, nonresident: full-time $7,290; part-time $405 per hour. Required fees: $906; $56 per hour. *Financial support:* In 2006–07, 19 students received support. Career-related internships or fieldwork, Federal Work-Study, scholarships/grants, and unspecified assistantships available. Support available to part-time students. Financial award application deadline: 3/1; financial award applicants required to submit FAFSA. *Application contact:* Dr. David J. Tarver, Graduate Advisor, 325-942-2052 Ext. 262, E-mail: david.tarver@angelo.edu.

Appalachian State University, Cratis D. Williams Graduate School, College of Education, Department of Human Development and Psychological Counseling, Boone, NC 28608. Offers community counseling (MA); marriage and family therapy (MA); school counseling (MA); student development (MA). *Accreditation:* AAMFT/COAMFTE; ACA; NCATE. Part-time programs available. *Faculty:* 28 full-time (15 women). *Students:* 115 full-time (91 women), 53 part-time (43 women); includes 14 minority (all African Americans), 5 international. 137 applicants, 66% accepted, 70 enrolled. In 2006, 45 degrees awarded. *Degree requirements:* For master's, internships, thesis optional. *Entrance requirements:* Additional exam requirements/recommendations for international students: Required—TOEFL (minimum score 570 paper-based; 230 computer-based). *Application deadline:* For fall admission, 2/1 priority date for domestic students, 1/1 for international students; for spring admission, 6/1 for international students. Applications are processed on a rolling basis. Application fee: $50. *Expenses:* Tuition, state resident: full-time $2,600; part-time $127 per hour. Tuition, nonresident: full-time $13,200; part-time $597 per hour. Required fees: $2,000; $546 per term. *Financial support:* In 2006–07, 1 fellowship (averaging $1,000 per year), 10 research assistantships (averaging $7,000 per year), 4 teaching assistantships (averaging $7,000 per year) were awarded; career-related internships or fieldwork, Federal Work-Study, scholarships/grants, and unspecified assistantships also available. Support available to part-time students. Financial award application deadline: 7/1; financial award applicants required to submit FAFSA. *Faculty research:* Multicultural counseling, addictions counseling, play therapy, expressive arts, child and adolescent therapy, sexual abuse counseling. *Unit head:* Dr. Lee Baruth, Chairman, 828-262-2055.

Argosy University, Atlanta Campus, College of Psychology and Behavioral Sciences, Atlanta, GA 30328. Offers clinical psychology (MA, Psy D, Postdoctoral Respecialization Certificate), including child and family psychology (Psy D), general adult clinical (Psy D), health psychology (Psy D), neuropsychology/geropsychology (Psy D); community counseling (MA), including marriage and family therapy; counselor education and supervision (Ed D); marriage and family therapy (Certificate). *Accreditation:* APA. Part-time and evening/weekend programs available. *Faculty:* 11 full-time (6 women), 16 part-time/adjunct (6 women). *Students:* 467 full-time (402 women), 223 part-time (198 women); includes 362 minority (315 African Americans, 5 American Indian/Alaska Native, 10 Asian Americans or Pacific Islanders, 32 Hispanic Americans). Average age 26. 272 applicants, 46% accepted. In 2006, 40 degrees awarded. Terminal master's awarded for partial completion of doctoral program. *Degree requirements:* For master's, comprehensive exam; for doctorate, thesis/dissertation, clinical comprehensive exam, research project, internship. *Entrance requirements:* For master's, GRE, minimum GPA of 3.0; for doctorate, GRE or MAT, minimum GPA of 3.25. *Application deadline:* For fall admission, 7/1 priority date for domestic students; for spring admission, 10/15 priority date for domestic students. Applications are processed on a rolling basis. Application fee: $50. Electronic applications accepted. *Financial support:* In 2006–07, 280 students received support, including 40 teaching assistantships (averaging $700 per year); career-related internships or fieldwork and Federal Work-Study also available. Support available to part-time students. Financial award application deadline: 6/30; financial award applicants required to submit FAFSA. *Unit head:* Dr. Edward Bouie, Vice President for the Academic Affairs, 770-671-1200 Ext. 1052, Fax: 770-671-0476, E-mail: ebouie@argosy.edu. *Application contact:* Christa Holton, Director of Admissions, 770-671-1200 Ext. 1014, Fax: 770-671-9050, E-mail: cholton@argosy.edu.

Argosy University, Chicago Campus, College of Psychology and Behavioral Sciences, Program in Counseling Psychology, Chicago, IL 60603. Offers counselor education and supervision (Ed D). *Students:* 19 full-time (10 women), 5 part-time (4 women); includes 10 African Americans, 2 Hispanic Americans. 9 applicants, 44% accepted, 4 enrolled. *Degree requirements:* For doctorate, thesis/dissertation. *Entrance requirements:* For doctorate, minimum GPA of 3.0. Additional exam requirements/recommendations for international students: Required—TOEFL (minimum score 550 paper-based; 213 computer-based). *Application deadline:* For fall admission, 2/28 for domestic students, 2/25 for international students; for spring admission, 10/30 for domestic and international students. Application fee: $50. *Financial support:* In 2006–07, 20 students received support. Federal Work-Study and scholarships/grants available. Financial award applicants required to submit FAFSA. *Unit head:* Dr. Barbara Kelly, Head, 800-626-4123, Fax: 312-777-7750, E-mail: bkelly@argosy.edu. *Application contact:* Ashley Delaney, Director of Admissions, 800-626-4123, Fax: 312-777-7750, E-mail: argosyadmissions@argosy.edu.

Argosy University, Denver Campus, College of Psychology and Behavioral Sciences, Denver, CO 80203. Offers clinical psychology (Psy D); community counseling (MA); counseling psychology (Ed D), including counselor education and supervision; counselor education and supervision (Ed D); forensic psychology (MA); organizational leadership (Ed D).

Argosy University, Nashville Campus, College of Psychology and Behavioral Sciences, Franklin, TN 37067-7226. Offers clinical psychology (MA, Psy D), including child and family psychology (Psy D), general adult psychology (Psy D), neuropsychology/geropsychology (Psy D); counselor education and supervision (Ed D); professional counseling (MA), including mental health counseling.

Argosy University, Nashville Campus, Doctoral Program in Counselor Education and Supervision, Franklin, TN 37067-7226. Offers Ed D.

Argosy University, Sarasota Campus, College of Psychology and Behavioral Sciences, Sarasota, FL 34235-8246. Offers clinical psychology (Psy D); community counseling (MA); counseling psychology (Ed D); counselor education and supervision (Ed D); forensic psychology (MA); marriage and family therapy (MA); mental health counseling (MA); organizational leadership (Ed D); pastoral community counseling (Ed D); school counseling (MA, Ed S); school psychology (MA). Part-time and evening/weekend programs available. Postbaccalaureate distance learning degree programs offered (minimal on-campus study). *Faculty:* 16 full-time (7 women), 38 part-time/adjunct (17 women). *Students:* 183 applicants, 75% accepted, 108 enrolled. In 2006, 14 master's, 24 doctorates awarded. *Degree requirements:* For master's, comprehensive exam (for some programs); for doctorate, thesis/dissertation, comprehensive exam. *Entrance requirements:* Additional exam requirements/recommendations for international students: Required—TOEFL. *Application deadline:* Applications are processed on a rolling basis. Application fee: $50. Electronic applications accepted. *Expenses: Contact institution. Financial support:* Federal Work-Study available. Support available to part-time students. Financial award application deadline: 4/1; financial award applicants required to submit FAFSA. *Unit head:* Dr. Douglas Riedmiller, Dean, 800-331-5995, Fax: 941-379-9464, E-mail: driedmiller@argosy.edu. *Application contact:* Admissions Representative, 800-331-5995 Ext. 221, Fax: 941-371-8910.

Argosy University, Schaumburg Campus, College of Psychology and Behavioral Sciences, Schaumburg, IL 60173-5403. Offers clinical health psychology (Post-Graduate Certificate); clinical psychology (MA, Psy D), including child and family psychology (Psy D), clinical health psychology (Psy D), diversity and multicultural psychology (Psy D), forensic psychology (Psy D); community counseling (MA); counseling psychology (Ed D), including counselor education and supervison; counselor education and supervision (Ed D); forensic psychology (MA, Post-Graduate Certificate); organizational leadership (Ed D); professional counseling (MA). *Accreditation:* ACA; APA. Evening/weekend programs available. *Students:* 273 full-time, 89 part-time. 220 applicants, 57% accepted, 83 enrolled. In 2006, 52 master's, 18 doctorates awarded. Terminal master's awarded for partial completion of doctoral program. *Degree requirements:* For master's, thesis, practicum; for doctorate, thesis/dissertation, internship, qualifying exam. *Entrance requirements:* For master's, 15 hours in psychology, interview, minimum GPA of 3.0; for doctorate, 15 hours in psychology, interview, minimum GPA of 3.25. Additional exam requirements/recommendations for international students: Required—TOEFL. *Application deadline:* For fall admission, 1/15 priority date for domestic and international students; for spring admission, 10/15 priority date for domestic and international students. Applications are processed on a rolling basis. Application fee: $50. Electronic applications accepted. *Financial support:* In 2006–07, 40 students received support, including 2 fellowships, 30 teaching assistantships; career-related internships or fieldwork, Federal Work-Study, and scholarships/grants also available. Support available to part-time students. *Unit head:* Dr. Jim Wasner, Dean, 866-290-2777, Fax: 847-598-6158, E-mail: argosyadmissions@argosy.edu. *Application contact:* Jamal Scott, Director of Admissions, 866-290-2777, Fax: 847-598-6191, E-mail: jscott@argosy.edu.

Argosy University, Tampa Campus, College of Psychology and Behavioral Sciences, Tampa, FL 33614. Offers clinical psychology (MA, Psy D), including child and adolescent psychology (MA), clinical psychology (Psy D), geropsychology (MA), marriage/couples and family therapy (MA), neuropsychology (MA); counselor education and supervision (Ed D); marriage and family therapy (MA); mental health counseling (MA); organizational leadership (Ed D); school counseling (MA).

Argosy University, Washington DC Campus, College of Psychology and Behavioral Sciences, Professional Programs in Psychology, Arlington, VA 22209. Offers clinical psychology (MA, Psy D, Postdoctoral Respecialization Certificate), including child and family psychology (Psy D), diversity and multicultural psychology (Psy D), forensic psychology (Psy D), health and neuropsychology (Psy D); community counseling (MA); counseling psychology (Ed D), including counselor education and supervision; forensic psychology (MA); organizational leadership (Ed D). *Accreditation:* APA. Postbaccalaureate distance learning degree programs offered (minimal on-campus study). *Faculty:* 23 full-time (15 women), 51 part-time/adjunct (34 women). *Students:* 620 full-time (521 women), 209 part-time (173 women); includes 316 minority (239 African Americans, 5 American Indian/Alaska Native, 35 Asian Americans or Pacific Islanders, 37 Hispanic Americans). Average age 34. 518 applicants, 59% accepted, 193 enrolled. In 2006, 46 master's, 67 doctorates awarded. Terminal master's awarded for partial completion of doctoral program. *Median time to degree:* Of those who began their doctoral program in fall 1998, 62% received their degree in 8 years or less. *Degree requirements:* For master's, thesis (for some programs), practicum, comprehensive exam (for some programs); for doctorate, thesis/dissertation, internship, comprehensive exam. *Entrance requirements:* For master's, clinical experience, minimum GPA of 3.0; for doctorate, clinical experience, minimum GPA of 3.25. Additional exam requirements/recommendations for international students: Required—TOEFL (minimum score 550 paper-based; 213 computer-based). *Application deadline:* For fall admission, 1/15 priority date for domestic students. Applications are processed on a rolling basis. Application fee: $50. Electronic applications accepted. *Financial support:* In 2006–07, 462 students received support, including 2 fellowships with tuition reimbursements available (averaging $3,600 per year), 50 teaching assistantships with full and partial tuition reimbursements available (averaging $2,040 per year); research assistantships, career-related internships or fieldwork, Federal Work-Study, and scholarships/grants also available. Support available to part-time students. Financial award applicants required to submit FAFSA. *Faculty research:*

Counselor Education

Argosy University, Washington DC Campus (continued)
Psychotherapy integration, minority health, forensic assessment, family violence, child maltreatment. Total annual research expenditures: $2,000. *Application contact:* Emily Peck, Director of Admissions, 866-703-2777 Ext. 5851, Fax: 703-526-5850, E-mail: dcadmissions@argosy.edu.

Arizona State University, Division of Graduate Studies, College of Education, Division of Psychology in Education, Academic Program in Counseling, Tempe, AZ 85287. Offers M Ed, MC. *Accreditation:* ACA (one or more programs are accredited). *Degree requirements:* For master's, thesis or alternative. *Entrance requirements:* For master's, GRE General Test or MAT.

Arkansas State University, Graduate School, College of Education, Department of Psychology and Counseling, Jonesboro, State University, AR 72467. Offers college student personnel services (MS); counselor education (Ed S), including college student personnel services, psychoeducational diagnosis, school counseling; rehabilitation counseling (MRC); school counseling (MSE); student affairs (Certificate). *Accreditation:* ACA (one or more programs are accredited); CORE (one or more programs are accredited); NCATE. Part-time programs available. *Faculty:* 13 full-time (6 women), 3 part-time/adjunct (1 woman). *Students:* 61 full-time (41 women), 56 part-time (43 women); includes 25 minority (22 African Americans, 3 Hispanic Americans). Average age 30. 74 applicants, 69% accepted, 40 enrolled. In 2006, 26 master's, 11 other advanced degrees awarded. *Degree requirements:* For master's and other advanced degree, thesis or alternative, comprehensive exam. *Entrance requirements:* For master's, GRE General Test or MAT (MSE), appropriate bachelor's degree, interview, letters of reference, official transcript; for other advanced degree, GRE General Test, interview, master's degree, letters of reference, official transcript. Additional exam requirements/recommendations for international students: Required—TOEFL (minimum score 213 computer-based). *Application deadline:* Applications are processed on a rolling basis. Application fee: $30 ($40 for international students). Electronic applications accepted. *Expenses:* Tuition, state resident: full-time $3,393; part-time $189 per hour. Tuition, nonresident: full-time $8,577; part-time $477 per hour. Required fees: $752; $39 per hour. $25 per semester. *Financial support:* Teaching assistantships, career-related internships or fieldwork, scholarships/grants, and unspecified assistantships available. Financial award application deadline: 7/1; financial award applicants required to submit FAFSA. *Unit head:* Dr. Loretta McGregor, Chair, 870-972-3064, Fax: 870-972-3962, E-mail: lmcgregor@astate.edu.

Auburn University, Graduate School, College of Education, Department of Counseling and Counseling Psychology, Auburn University, AL 36849. Offers community agency counseling (M Ed, MS, Ed D, PhD, Ed S); counseling psychology (PhD); counselor education (Ed D, PhD); school counseling (M Ed, MS, Ed D, PhD, Ed S); school psychometry (M Ed, MS, Ed D, PhD, Ed S). *Accreditation:* ACA (one or more programs are accredited); APA (one or more programs are accredited); NCATE. Part-time programs available. *Faculty:* 10 full-time (6 women). *Students:* 51 full-time (35 women), 41 part-time (33 women); includes 27 minority (26 African Americans, 1 Hispanic American), 5 international. Average age 31. 140 applicants, 42% accepted, 30 enrolled. In 2006, 20 master's, 9 doctorates, 4 other advanced degrees awarded. *Degree requirements:* For master's, thesis (for some programs); for doctorate, thesis/dissertation; for Ed S, thesis or alternative. *Entrance requirements:* For master's and Ed S, GRE General Test; for doctorate, GRE General Test, GRE Subject Test. *Application deadline:* For fall admission, 5/15 for domestic students. Application fee: $25 ($50 for international students). Electronic applications accepted. *Expenses:* Tuition, state resident: full-time $5,000. Tuition, nonresident: full-time $15,000. Required fees: $416. Tuition and fees vary according to program. *Financial support:* Research assistantships, Federal Work-Study and traineeships available. Support available to part-time students. Financial award application deadline: 3/15. *Faculty research:* At-risk students, substance abuse, gender roles, AIDS, professional ethics. *Unit head:* Dr. Holly Stadler, Head, 334-844-5160. *Application contact:* Dr. Joe Pittman, Interim Dean of the Graduate School, 334-844-4700.

Auburn University Montgomery, School of Education, Department of Counselor Leadership and Special Education, Montgomery, AL 36124-4023. Offers counseling (M Ed, Ed S); education administration (M Ed, Ed S); special education (M Ed, Ed S). *Accreditation:* NCATE. Part-time and evening/weekend programs available. *Faculty:* 8 full-time (4 women), 1 part-time/adjunct (0 women). *Students:* 34 full-time (28 women), 91 part-time (66 women); includes 75 minority (72 African Americans, 1 American Indian/Alaska Native, 1 Asian American or Pacific Islander, 1 Hispanic American). Average age 35. In 2006, 12 master's, 3 other advanced degrees awarded. *Degree requirements:* For master's and Ed S, comprehensive exam. *Entrance requirements:* For master's, GRE General Test or MAT, certification, BS in teaching; for Ed S, GRE General Test or MAT, certification. *Application deadline:* Applications are processed on a rolling basis. Application fee: $25. Electronic applications accepted. *Financial support:* In 2006–07, 1 teaching assistantship was awarded; career-related internships or fieldwork and scholarships/grants also available. Support available to part-time students. Financial award application deadline: 3/1; financial award applicants required to submit FAFSA. *Unit head:* Dr. James V. Wright, Head, 334-244-3457, Fax: 334-344-3102, E-mail: jwright@mail.aum.edu.

Augusta State University, Graduate Studies, College of Education, Program in Counseling/Guidance, Augusta, GA 30904-2200. Offers M Ed. *Accreditation:* ACA; NCATE. Part-time and evening/weekend programs available. *Faculty:* 4 full-time (3 women), 2 part-time/adjunct (both women). *Students:* 29 full-time (25 women), 25 part-time (23 women); includes 13 minority (12 African Americans, 1 Hispanic American). Average age 34. 13 applicants, 100% accepted, 13 enrolled. In 2006, 16 degrees awarded. *Degree requirements:* For master's, portfolio. *Entrance requirements:* For master's, GRE, MAT, minimum GPA of 2.5. *Application deadline:* For fall admission, 8/1 priority date for domestic students. Applications are processed on a rolling basis. Application fee: $20. *Expenses:* Tuition, state resident: full-time $3,044; part-time $127 per credit hour. Tuition, nonresident: full-time $12,172; part-time $508 per credit hour. *Financial support:* Federal Work-Study, institutionally sponsored loans, and unspecified assistantships available. Support available to part-time students. Financial award application deadline: 4/15; financial award applicants required to submit FAFSA. *Faculty research:* Counseling for AIDS patients, counseling for drug and alcohol abuse. *Unit head:* Dr. Samuel B Hardy, Acting Chair, 706-737-1497, Fax: 706-667-4706, E-mail: shardy@aug.edu. *Application contact:* Andrea M. Scott, Secretary to the Dean, 706-737-1499, Fax: 706-667-4706, E-mail: ascott1@aug.edu.

Austin Peay State University, College of Graduate Studies, College of Professional Programs and Social Sciences, Department of Psychology, Clarksville, TN 37044. Offers guidance and counseling (MS); psychology (MA). Part-time programs available. Postbaccalaureate distance learning degree programs offered. *Faculty:* 13 full-time (5 women), 1 (woman) part-time/adjunct. *Students:* 45 full-time (39 women), 17 part-time (15 women); includes 3 minority (all African Americans) Average age 30. In 2006, 18 degrees awarded. *Degree requirements:* For master's, thesis. *Entrance requirements:* For master's, GRE General Test, minimum GPA of 2.5. Additional exam requirements/recommendations for international students: Required—TOEFL (minimum score 500 paper-based; 173 computer-based). *Application deadline:* For fall admission, 3/31 priority date for domestic students; for spring admission, 11/1 priority date for domestic students. Applications are processed on a rolling basis. Application fee: $25. Electronic applications accepted. *Expenses:* Tuition, state resident: full-time $5,138; part-time $272 per credit hour. Tuition, nonresident: full-time $14,832; part-time $693 per credit hour. Required fees: $1,009. *Financial support:* In 2006–07, research assistantships (averaging $10,270 per year); career-related internships or fieldwork, Federal Work-Study, institutionally sponsored loans, scholarships/grants, and unspecified assistantships also available. Support available to part-time students. Financial award application deadline: 3/1; financial award applicants required to submit FAFSA. *Unit head:* Dr. Samuel Fung, Chair, 931-221-7233, Fax: 931-221-6267, E-mail: fungs@apsu.edu.

Azusa Pacific University, School of Education, Department of School Counseling and School Psychology, Program in Educational Counseling, Azusa, CA 91702-7000. Offers MA. *Students:* 19 full-time (18 women), 190 part-time (149 women); includes 90 minority (9 African Americans, 11 Asian Americans or Pacific Islanders, 70 Hispanic Americans), 2 international. In 2006, 91 degrees awarded. Application fee: $45 ($65 for international students). *Expenses:* Tuition: Part-time $475 per credit. *Unit head:* Dr. Michael Block, Director, 626-815-5436, E-mail: mblock@apu.edu.

Baptist Bible College of Pennsylvania, Graduate School, Clarks Summit, PA 18411-1297. Offers Christian school education (MS); counseling (MS). Part-time and evening/weekend programs available. *Entrance requirements:* Additional exam requirements/recommendations for international students: Required—TOEFL.

Barry University, School of Education, Program in Counseling, Miami Shores, FL 33161-6695. Offers MS, PhD, Ed S. *Accreditation:* ACA. Part-time and evening/weekend programs available. *Students:* 92 full-time (77 women), 134 part-time (102 women); includes 105 minority (57 African Americans, 1 American Indian/Alaska Native, 5 Asian Americans or Pacific Islanders, 42 Hispanic Americans), 11 international. 122 applicants, 66% accepted, 46 enrolled. In 2006, 32 master's, 3 doctorates, 4 other advanced degrees awarded. *Degree requirements:* For master's, comprehensive exam. *Entrance requirements:* For master's, GRE General Test or MAT, minimum GPA of 3.0; for doctorate, GRE, minimum GPA of 3.25; for Ed S, GRE General Test, minimum GPA of 3.0. *Application deadline:* For fall admission, 5/1 priority date for domestic students. Applications are processed on a rolling basis. Application fee: $30. *Financial support:* Application deadline: 5/1. *Unit head:* Dr. Maureen Duffy, Director, 305-899-3706, Fax: 305-899-4708, E-mail: mduffy@mail.barry.edu. *Application contact:* Dave Fletcher, Director of Graduate Admissions, 305-899-3113, Fax: 305-899-2971, E-mail: dfletcher@mail.barry.edu.

Barry University, School of Education, Program in Mental Health Counseling, Miami Shores, FL 33161-6695. Offers MS, Ed S. *Accreditation:* ACA. Part-time and evening/weekend programs available. *Degree requirements:* For master's, scholarly paper. *Entrance requirements:* For master's, GRE General Test or MAT, minimum GPA of 3.0; for Ed S, GRE General Test, minimum GPA of 3.0. *Application deadline:* For fall admission, 5/1 priority date for domestic students. Applications are processed on a rolling basis. Application fee: $30. Electronic applications accepted. *Unit head:* Dr. Jeffrey Guterman, Chair, 305-899-3862, Fax: 305-899-4708, E-mail: jguterman@mail.barry.edu. *Application contact:* Dave Fletcher, Director of Graduate Admissions, 305-899-3113, Fax: 305-899-2971, E-mail: dfletcher@mail.barry.edu.

Barry University, School of Education, Program in School Counseling, Miami Shores, FL 33161-6695. Offers MS, Ed S. *Accreditation:* ACA (one or more programs are accredited). Part-time and evening/weekend programs available. *Degree requirements:* For master's, scholarly paper. *Entrance requirements:* For master's, GRE General Test or MAT, minimum GPA of 3.0; for Ed S, GRE General Test, minimum GPA of 3.0. *Application deadline:* For fall admission, 5/1 priority date for domestic students. Applications are processed on a rolling basis. Application fee: $30. Electronic applications accepted. *Unit head:* Dr. Sylvia Fernandez, Chair, 305-899-4868, Fax: 305-899-4708, E-mail: smfernandez@mail.barry.edu. *Application contact:* Dave Fletcher, Director of Graduate Admissions, 305-899-3113, Fax: 305-899-2971, E-mail: dfletcher@mail.barry.edu.

Bayamón Central University, Graduate Programs, Program in Education, Bayamón, PR 00960-1725. Offers administration and supervision (MA Ed); commercial education (MA Ed); education of the autistic (MA Ed); elementary education (K–3) (MA Ed); elementary education (K–6) (MA Ed); elementary physical education (MA Ed); guidance and counseling (MA Ed); pre-elementary teacher (MA Ed); special education (MA Ed), including attention deficit disorder, learning disabilities. Part-time and evening/weekend programs available. *Degree requirements:* For master's, comprehensive exam. *Entrance requirements:* For master's, EXADEP, bachelor's degree in education or related field.

Bloomsburg University of Pennsylvania, School of Graduate Studies, College of Professional Studies, School of Education, Department of Educational Studies and Secondary Education, Program in Guidance Counseling and Student Affairs, Bloomsburg, PA 17815-1301. Offers M Ed. *Faculty:* 8 full-time (3 women). *Entrance requirements:* For master's, GRE, 3 letters of recommendation, resumé. *Expenses:* Tuition, state resident: full-time $6,048; part-time $336 per credit. Tuition, nonresident: full-time $9,678; part-time $538 per credit. Required fees: $1,415. *Unit head:* Dr. Robert Gates, Coordinator, Department of Educational Studies and Secondary Education, 570-389-4961, Fax: 570-389-3894, E-mail: rgates@bloomu.edu.

Bob Jones University, Graduate Programs, Greenville, SC 29614. Offers accountancy (MS); Bible (MA); Bible translation (MA); Biblical studies (Certificate); broadcast management (MS); business administration (MBA); church history (MA, PhD); church ministries (MA); church music (MM); cinema and video production (MA); counseling (MS); curriculum and instruction (Ed D); divinity (M Div); dramatic production (MA); educational leadership (MS, Ed D, Ed S); elementary education (M Ed, MAT); English (M Ed, MA, MAT); fine arts (MA); graphic design (MA); history (M Ed, MA); illustration (MA); interpretative speech (MA); mathematics (M Ed, MAT); medical missions (Certificate); ministry (MM, D Min); multi-categorical special education (M Ed, MAT); music (M Ed); New Testament interpretation (PhD); Old Testament interpretation (PhD); orchestral instrument performance (MM); organ performance (MM); pastoral studies (MA); personnel services (MS, Ed S); piano pedagogy (MM); piano performance (MM); platform arts (MA); radio and television broadcasting (MS); rhetoric and public address (MA); secondary education (M Ed); studio art (MA); teaching Bible (MA); theology (MA, PhD); voice performance (MM); youth ministries (MA); M Div/MM.

Boise State University, Graduate College, College of Education, Department of Counselor Education, Program in Counseling, Boise, ID 83725-0399. Offers MA. *Accreditation:* ACA; NCATE. *Faculty:* 7 full-time (4 women), 9 part-time/adjunct (6 women). *Students:* 17 full-time (12 women), 25 part-time (16 women); includes 4 minority (1 African American, 1 Asian American or Pacific Islander, 2 Hispanic Americans), 1 international. Average age 37. In 2006, 16 degrees awarded. *Entrance requirements:* For master's, minimum GPA of 3.0. *Application deadline:* For fall admission, 3/1 priority date for domestic students. Applications are processed on a rolling basis. Application fee: $0. Electronic applications accepted. *Financial support:* In 2006–07, 6 research assistantships with partial tuition reimbursements (averaging $4,080 per year) were awarded; Federal Work-Study, institutionally sponsored loans, and unspecified assistantships also available. Support available to part-time students. Financial award application deadline: 3/1; financial award applicants required to submit FAFSA. *Unit head:* Dr. Bobbie A. Birdsall, Coordinator, 208-426-3204, E-mail: bbirdsa@boisestate.edu.

Boston University, School of Education, Department of Literacy and Language, Counseling and Development, Program in Counseling, Boston, MA 02215. Offers Ed M, CAGS. *Students:* 49 full-time (39 women), 10 part-time (9 women). Average age 27. 155 applicants, 75% accepted. In 2006, 40 master's, 8 other advanced degrees awarded. *Degree requirements:* For master's, thesis optional. *Entrance requirements:* For master's and CAGS, GRE General Test or MAT. Additional exam requirements/recommendations for international students: Required—TOEFL. *Application deadline:* For fall admission, 2/15 priority date for domestic students; for winter admission, 10/1 priority date for domestic students. Applications are processed on a rolling basis. Application fee: $70. Electronic applications accepted. *Expenses:* Tuition: Full-time $33,330; part-time $1,042 per credit. Required fees: $462; $40. *Financial support:* Application deadline: 2/15. *Unit head:* Dr. Deborah Youngman, Coordinator, 617-353-7107, E-mail: drdjy@bu.edu. *Application contact:* 617-353-4237, Fax: 617-353-8937, E-mail: sedgrad@bu.edu.

Bowie State University, Graduate Programs, Program in Guidance and Counseling, Bowie, MD 20715-9465. Offers M Ed. Part-time and evening/weekend programs available. *Faculty:* 7 full-time (4 women), 14 part-time/adjunct (9 women). *Students:* 36 full-time (28 women), 111 part-time (97 women); includes 115 minority (110 African Americans, 1 American Indian/Alaska Native, 2 Asian Americans or Pacific Islanders, 2 Hispanic Americans), 2 international. Average age 32. 50 applicants, 92% accepted, 37 enrolled. In 2006, 16 degrees awarded. *Degree* *requirements:* For master's, research paper, thesis optional. *Entrance requirements:* For master's, teaching experience, minimum GPA of 2.5, self statement, 3 recommendations. *Application deadline:* For fall admission, 4/1 priority date for domestic and international students; for spring admission, 11/1 for domestic students, 11/1 priority date for international students. Applications are processed on a rolling basis. Application fee: $40. Electronic applications accepted. *Expenses:* Tuition, state resident: full-time $7,344; part-time $306 per credit. Tuition, nonresident: full-time $14,304; part-time $396 per credit. Required fees: $1,078; $77 per credit. $539 per term. One-time fee: $40. *Financial support:* Institutionally sponsored loans available. Support available to part-time students. Financial award application deadline: 4/1. *Unit head:* Rhonda Jeter-Tuilley, Chairperson, 301-860-3233, E-mail: rjeter@bowiestate.edu. *Application contact:* Angela Issac, Information Contact.

Bowling Green State University, Graduate College, College of Education and Human Development, School of Education and Intervention Services, Intervention Services Division, Program in Counseling, Bowling Green, OH 43403. Offers mental health counseling (MA); school counseling (M Ed). *Accreditation:* NCATE. Part-time programs available. *Students:* 44 full-time (38 women), 22 part-time (19 women); includes 10 minority (9 African Americans, 1 Hispanic American), 4 international. Average age 29. 41 applicants, 71% accepted, 16 enrolled. In 2006, 23 degrees awarded. *Degree requirements:* For master's, thesis or alternative. *Entrance requirements:* For master's, GRE General Test. Additional exam requirements/recommendations for international students: Required—TOEFL. *Application deadline:* For fall admission, 3/1 priority date for domestic students. Applications are processed on a rolling basis. Application fee: $30. Electronic applications accepted. *Expenses:* Tuition, state resident: part-time $535 per hour. Tuition, nonresident: part-time $884 per hour. *Financial support:* In 2006–07, 23 research assistantships with full tuition reimbursements (averaging $5,963 per year), 2 teaching assistantships with full tuition reimbursements (averaging $4,060 per year) were awarded; career-related internships or fieldwork and unspecified assistantships also available. Financial award applicants required to submit FAFSA. *Faculty research:* Perfectionism, multicultural counseling, suicide, ethics and legal issues related to counseling, play therapy. *Application contact:* Dr. Greg Garske, Graduate Coordinator, 415-372-7319.

Bradley University, Graduate School, College of Education and Health Sciences, Department of Educational Leadership and Human Development, Peoria, IL 61625-0002. Offers human development counseling (MA), including community and agency counseling, school counseling; leadership in educational administration (MA); leadership in human service administration (MA). *Accreditation:* ACA; NCATE. Part-time and evening/weekend programs available. *Students:* 25 full-time (23 women), 100 part-time (70 women); includes 7 minority (6 Asian Americans or Pacific Islanders, 1 Hispanic American), 1 international. 36 applicants, 78% accepted, 18 enrolled. In 2006, 41 degrees awarded. *Degree requirements:* For master's, thesis optional. *Entrance requirements:* For master's, GRE General Test or MAT, interview, 3 letters of recommendation. Additional exam requirements/recommendations for international students: Required—TOEFL (minimum score 550 paper-based; 213 computer-based; 79 iBT). *Application deadline:* For fall admission, 5/15 priority date for domestic and international students; for spring admission, 10/15 priority date for domestic and international students. Applications are processed on a rolling basis. Application fee: $40 ($50 for international students). *Financial support:* Research assistantships, scholarships/grants, tuition waivers (partial), and unspecified assistantships available. Financial award application deadline: 4/1. *Unit head:* Dr. Christopher Rybak, Chairperson, 309-677-3171, E-mail: cjr@bradley.edu.

Brandon University, Faculty of Education, Brandon, MB R7A 6A9, Canada. Offers curriculum (Diploma); curriculum studies (M Ed); education administration (M Ed, Diploma); guidance and counseling (M Ed, Diploma); special education (M Ed, Diploma). *Degree requirements:* For master's, thesis. *Entrance requirements:* For master's, minimum GPA of 3.0, teaching certificate or equivalent. Additional exam requirements/recommendations for international students: Required—TOEFL. *Faculty research:* Comparative education, environmental studies, parent/school council.

Bridgewater State College, School of Graduate Studies, School of Education and Allied Science, Department of Secondary Education and Professional Programs, Program in Counseling, Bridgewater, MA 02325-0001. Offers M Ed, CAGS. *Accreditation:* NCATE. Part-time and evening/weekend programs available. *Entrance requirements:* For master's, GRE General Test. *Application deadline:* For fall admission, 3/1 priority date for domestic students; for spring admission, 10/1 priority date for domestic students. Application fee: $50. *Financial support:* Career-related internships or fieldwork, health care benefits, and unspecified assistantships available. Support available to part-time students.

Brooklyn College of the City University of New York, Division of Graduate Studies, School of Education, Program in School Counseling, Brooklyn, NY 11210-2889. Offers guidance and counseling (CAS). Part-time programs available. *Students:* 68 full-time (54 women), 77 part-time (65 women); includes 87 minority (58 African Americans, 1 American Indian/Alaska Native, 28 Hispanic Americans), 1 international. 170 applicants, 46% accepted, 17 enrolled. In 2006, 63 master's, 38 other advanced degrees awarded. *Degree requirements:* For master's, internship. *Entrance requirements:* For master's, interview, 2 letters of recommendation, resumé, essay; for CAS, master's degree. *Application deadline:* For fall admission, 3/1 for domestic students, 2/1 for international students. Application fee: $125. Electronic applications accepted. *Expenses:* Tuition, state resident: full-time $6,400; part-time $270 per credit. Tuition, nonresident: full-time $12,000; part-time $500 per credit. Required fees: $118 per semester. *Financial support:* Career-related internships or fieldwork, Federal Work-Study, institutionally sponsored loans, and scholarships/grants available. Support available to part-time students. Financial award application deadline: 5/1; financial award applicants required to submit FAFSA. *Faculty research:* Urban school counseling, parent involvement, multicultural competence and counselor training. *Unit head:* Prof. Lynda Sarnoff, Facilitator, 718-951-5214, Fax: 718-951-4816, E-mail: lsarnoff@brooklyn.cuny.edu. *Application contact:* Karen Alleyne-Pierre, Director of Admissions Services and Enrollment Communications, 718-951-5902, Fax: 718-951-4506, E-mail: grads@brooklyn.cuny.edu.

Bucknell University, Graduate Studies, College of Arts and Sciences, Department of Education, Specialization in Elementary and Secondary Counseling, Lewisburg, PA 17837. Offers MA, MS Ed. *Degree requirements:* For master's, thesis or alternative. *Entrance requirements:* For master's, GRE General Test, minimum GPA of 2.8. Additional exam requirements/recommendations for international students: Required—TOEFL.

Buena Vista University, School of Education, Storm Lake, IA 50588. Offers school guidance and counseling (MS Ed). Offered in summer only. Part-time and evening/weekend programs available. Postbaccalaureate distance learning degree programs offered (minimal on-campus study). *Faculty:* 3 full-time (2 women), 13 part-time/adjunct (10 women). *Students:* 105 full-time (95 women). Average age 36. 38 applicants, 58% accepted, 20 enrolled. In 2006, 24 degrees awarded. *Degree requirements:* For master's, thesis, fieldwork/practicum. *Entrance requirements:* For master's, GRE Writing Test, minimum undergraduate GPA of 2.75. *Application deadline:* For spring admission, 4/15 for domestic students. Application fee: $0. Electronic applications accepted. *Financial support:* In 2006–07, teaching assistantships with full tuition reimbursements (averaging $6,000 per year); career-related internships or fieldwork also available. Financial award application deadline: 5/15; financial award applicants required to submit FAFSA. *Faculty research:* Reading, curriculum, educational psychology, special education. *Unit head:* Dr. Kline Capps, Dean, 712-749-2275, Fax: 712-749-1408, E-mail: capps@bvu.edu. *Application contact:* Rita Mckenzie, Director of Graduate Studies, 712-749-2156, Fax: 712-749-1408, E-mail: mckenzie@bvu.edu.

Butler University, College of Education, Indianapolis, IN 46208-3485. Offers administration (MS); elementary education (MS); reading (MS); school counseling (MS); secondary education (MS); special education (MS). *Accreditation:* ACA; NCATE. Part-time and evening/weekend programs available. *Faculty:* 12 full-time (6 women), 11 part-time/adjunct (8 women). *Students:* 18 full-time (10 women), 156 part-time (125 women); includes 21 minority (16 African Americans, 2 Asian Americans or Pacific Islanders, 3 Hispanic Americans), 7 international. Average age 31. 56 applicants, 57% accepted, 29 enrolled. In 2006, 72 degrees awarded. *Entrance requirements:* For master's, GRE General Test, MAT, interview. *Application deadline:* For fall admission, 8/15 priority date for domestic students. Applications are processed on a rolling basis. Application fee: $35. Electronic applications accepted. *Expenses:* Tuition: Full-time $6,030; part-time $335 per credit. Tuition and fees vary according to program. *Financial support:* Institutionally sponsored loans available. Support available to part-time students. Financial award application deadline: 7/15; financial award applicants required to submit FAFSA. *Faculty research:* Ethics in cybercounseling, history of sports for disabled effect of fetal alcohol syndrome on perceptual learning, Reading Recovery's theoretical framework in teacher education. *Unit head:* Dr. Ena Shelley, Dean, 317-940-9752, Fax: 317-940-6481. *Application contact:* Karen Farrell, Department Secretary, 317-940-9220, E-mail: kfarrell@butler.edu.

Caldwell College, Graduate Studies, Program in Counseling Psychology, Caldwell, NJ 07006-6195. Offers art therapy (MA); counseling psychology (MA); school counseling (MA). Part-time and evening/weekend programs available. *Degree requirements:* For master's, practicum. *Entrance requirements:* For master's, GRE General Test, minimum GPA of 3.0. Additional exam requirements/recommendations for international students: Required—TOEFL (minimum score 580 paper-based; 237 computer-based). Electronic applications accepted.

California Lutheran University, Graduate Studies, School of Education, Emphasis in Counseling and Guidance, Thousand Oaks, CA 91360-2787. Offers MS. Part-time and evening/weekend programs available. *Degree requirements:* For master's, thesis or comprehensive exam. *Entrance requirements:* For master's, GRE General Test, interview, minimum GPA of 3.0.

California State University, Bakersfield, Division of Graduate Studies and Research, School of Education, Program in Counseling, Bakersfield, CA 93311-1022. Offers MS. *Accreditation:* NCATE. *Students:* 32 full-time (25 women), 34 part-time (29 women); includes 37 minority (3 African Americans, 2 American Indian/Alaska Native, 4 Asian Americans or Pacific Islanders, 28 Hispanic Americans). 6 applicants, 33% accepted. In 2006, 27 degrees awarded. *Degree requirements:* For master's, thesis or alternative, culminating projects. *Application deadline:* Applications are processed on a rolling basis. Application fee: $55. *Unit head:* Dr. Nancy Bringman, Graduate Coordinator, 661-654-3087, Fax: 661-665-6916.

California State University, Dominguez Hills, College of Education, Division of Graduate Education, Program in Counseling, Carson, CA 90747-0001. Offers MA. Part-time and evening/weekend programs available. *Faculty:* 5 full-time (4 women), 4 part-time/adjunct (all women). *Students:* 75 full-time (55 women), 63 part-time (44 women); includes 87 minority (26 African Americans, 2 American Indian/Alaska Native, 17 Asian Americans or Pacific Islanders, 42 Hispanic Americans), 1 international. Average age 33. 66 applicants, 68% accepted, 24 enrolled. In 2006, 24 degrees awarded. *Degree requirements:* For master's, comprehensive exam, registration. *Entrance requirements:* For master's, minimum GPA of 3.0. *Application deadline:* For fall admission, 8/1 for domestic students; for spring admission, 10/1 for domestic students. Applications are processed on a rolling basis. Application fee: $55. *Expenses:* Tuition, nonresident: part-time $339 per unit. Required fees: $1,148 per term. Tuition and fees vary according to program. *Faculty research:* Social development. *Unit head:* Dr. Adriean Mancillas, Associate Professor, 310-243-2680, E-mail: amancillas@csudh.edu. *Application contact:* Admissions Office, 310-243-3530.

California State University, East Bay, Academic Programs and Graduate Studies, College of Education and Allied Studies, Department of Educational Psychology, Counseling Program, Hayward, CA 94542-3000. Offers MS. *Accreditation:* NCATE. *Faculty:* 9 full-time (4 women), 1 part-time/adjunct (0 women). *Students:* 115 full-time (90 women); includes 36 minority (9 African Americans, 14 Asian Americans or Pacific Islanders, 13 Hispanic Americans). Average age 31. 128 applicants, 34% accepted, 40 enrolled. In 2006, 44 degrees awarded. *Degree requirements:* For master's, project or thesis. *Entrance requirements:* For master's, GRE or MAT, interview, minimum GPA of 2.5 during previous 2 years of course work. Additional exam requirements/recommendations for international students: Required—TOEFL (minimum score 550 paper-based; 213 computer-based). *Application deadline:* For fall admission, 3/31 for domestic students, 4/30 for international students; for winter admission, 9/30 for domestic and international students; for spring admission, 12/31 for domestic students, 11/30 for international students. Application fee: $55. Electronic applications accepted. *Financial support:* Career-related internships or fieldwork, Federal Work-Study, and institutionally sponsored loans available. Support available to part-time students. Financial award application deadline: 3/2. *Unit head:* Dr. Mary Disibio, Chair, 510-885-7430, E-mail: mary.disibio@csueastlay.edu. *Application contact:* My Huynh, Graduate Prospect Specialist, 510-885-2989, Fax: 510-885-4059, E-mail: my.huynh@csueastbay.edu.

California State University, Fresno, Division of Graduate Studies, School of Education and Human Development, Department of Counseling and Special Education, Program in Counseling and Student Services, Fresno, CA 93740-8027. Offers MS. *Accreditation:* NCATE. Part-time and evening/weekend programs available. *Degree requirements:* For master's, thesis or alternative. *Entrance requirements:* For master's, GRE General Test, MAT, minimum GPA of 3.0. Additional exam requirements/recommendations for international students: Required—TOEFL. Electronic applications accepted.

California State University, Fullerton, Graduate Studies, College of Health and Human Development, Department of Counseling, Fullerton, CA 92834-9480. Offers MS. *Accreditation:* ACA; NCATE. Part-time programs available. *Students:* 112 full-time (96 women), 102 part-time (82 women); includes 82 minority (7 African Americans, 4 American Indian/Alaska Native, 26 Asian Americans or Pacific Islanders, 45 Hispanic Americans), 6 international. Average age 34. 210 applicants, 34% accepted, 56 enrolled. In 2006, 82 degrees awarded. *Degree requirements:* For master's, project or thesis. *Entrance requirements:* For master's, GRE General Test, minimum GPA of 3.0 in behavioral science, 2.5 overall. Application fee: $55. *Expenses:* Tuition, nonresident: part-time $339 per unit. Required fees: $1,155 per semester. *Financial support:* Teaching assistantships, career-related internships or fieldwork, Federal Work-Study, institutionally sponsored loans, and scholarships/grants available. Support available to part-time students. Financial award application deadline: 3/1. *Unit head:* Dr. Jeffrey Kottler, Chair, 714-278-7537.

California State University, Long Beach, Graduate Studies, College of Education, Department of Educational Psychology, Administration, and Counseling, Program in Counseling, Long Beach, CA 90840. Offers counseling-guidance (MS). *Accreditation:* NCATE. *Students:* Average age 32. 307 applicants, 27% accepted, 63 enrolled. In 2006, 70 degrees awarded. *Degree requirements:* For master's, comprehensive exam or thesis. *Entrance requirements:* For master's, GRE General Test, minimum GPA of 2.75. *Application deadline:* For fall admission, 7/1 for domestic students; for spring admission, 12/1 for domestic students. Applications are processed on a rolling basis. Application fee: $55. Electronic applications accepted. *Financial support:* Federal Work-Study, institutionally sponsored loans, and scholarships/grants available. Financial award application deadline: 3/2. *Unit head:* Dr. Rose Marie Hoffman, Coordinator, 562-985-5626, Fax: 562-985-4534, E-mail: rhoffman@csulb.edu.

California State University, Los Angeles, Graduate Studies, Charter College of Education, Division of Special Education and Counseling, Major in Counseling, Los Angeles, CA 90032-8530. Offers applied behavior analysis (MS); community college counseling (MS); rehabilitation counseling (MS); school counseling and school psychology (MS). *Accreditation:* ACA; CORE; NCATE. Part-time and evening/weekend programs available. *Students:* 99 full-time (79 women), 238 part-time (179 women); includes 236 minority (22 African Americans, 1 American Indian/Alaska Native, 47 Asian Americans or Pacific Islanders, 166 Hispanic Americans), 7 international. In 2006, 94 degrees awarded. *Degree requirements:* For master's, project or thesis. *Entrance requirements:* For master's, interview, minimum GPA of 2.75 in last 90 units of course work, teaching certificate. Additional exam requirements/recommendations for international students: Required—TOEFL. *Application deadline:* For fall admission, 6/30 for domestic students; for spring admission, 2/1 for domestic students. Applications are processed on a rolling basis. Application fee: $55. *Expenses:* Tuition, nonresident: part-time $226 per unit.

Counselor Education

California State University, Los Angeles (continued)
Financial support: Career-related internships or fieldwork and Federal Work-Study available. Support available to part-time students. Financial award application deadline: 3/1. *Unit head:* Dr. Diane Fazzi, Chair, Division of Special Education and Counseling, 323-343-4400, Fax: 323-343-5605.

California State University, Northridge, Graduate Studies, College of Education, Department of Educational Psychology and Counseling, Northridge, CA 91330. Offers counseling (MS), including career counseling, college counseling and student services, marriage and family therapy, school counseling, school psychology; educational psychology (MA Ed), including development, learning, and instruction, early childhood education; genetic counseling (MS). *Accreditation:* ACA (one or more programs are accredited); NCATE. Part-time and evening/weekend programs available. *Faculty:* 19 full-time (11 women), 57 part-time/adjunct (39 women). *Students:* 344 full-time (50 women), 135 part-time (19 women); includes 210 minority (26 African Americans, 3 American Indian/Alaska Native, 40 Asian Americans or Pacific Islanders, 141 Hispanic Americans), 11 international. Average age 32. 244 applicants, 62% accepted, 116 enrolled. In 2006, 176 degrees awarded. *Entrance requirements:* For master's, GRE General Test, MAT, or minimum GPA of 3.0. Additional exam requirements/recommendations for international students: Required—TOEFL. *Application deadline:* For fall admission, 11/30 for domestic students. Application fee: $55. *Expenses:* Tuition, nonresident: full-time $8,136; part-time $4,068 per year. Required fees: $3,624; $1,161 per term. *Financial support:* Scholarships/grants available. Support available to part-time students. Financial award application deadline: 3/1. *Unit head:* Dr. Beverly Cabello, Chair, 818-677-2599. *Application contact:* Todd Wolfe, Graduate Advisor, 818-677-5719.

California State University, Sacramento, Graduate Studies, College of Education, Department of Counselor Education, Sacramento, CA 95819-6048. Offers career counseling (MS); generic counseling (MS); guidance (MA); school counseling (MS). *Accreditation:* ACA. *Students:* 190 full-time (160 women), 103 part-time (89 women); includes 131 minority (21 African Americans, 5 American Indian/Alaska Native, 38 Asian Americans or Pacific Islanders, 67 Hispanic Americans), 5 international. Average age 32. 153 applicants, 65% accepted, 63 enrolled. *Degree requirements:* For master's, thesis or alternative, writing proficiency exam. *Entrance requirements:* For master's, minimum GPA of 2.5. Additional exam requirements/recommendations for international students: Required—TOEFL. *Application deadline:* Applications are processed on a rolling basis. Application fee: $55. Electronic applications accepted. *Financial support:* Career-related internships or fieldwork and Federal Work-Study available. Support available to part-time students. Financial award application deadline: 3/1. *Unit head:* Al Levin, Chair, 916-278-5399, Fax: 916-278-4174.

California State University, San Bernardino, Graduate Studies, College of Education, Program in Educational Psychology and Counseling, San Bernardino, CA 92407-2397. Offers counseling and guidance (MS); rehabilitation counseling (MA). *Accreditation:* NCATE. Part-time and evening/weekend programs available. *Faculty:* 19 full-time, 20 part-time/adjunct. *Students:* 112 full-time (85 women), 11 part-time (10 women); includes 87 minority (21 African Americans, 1 American Indian/Alaska Native, 6 Asian Americans or Pacific Islanders, 59 Hispanic Americans). Average age 28. 25 applicants, 60% accepted, 7 enrolled. In 2006, 4 degrees awarded. *Degree requirements:* For master's, thesis or alternative. *Entrance requirements:* For master's, minimum GPA of 3.0 in education. *Application deadline:* For fall admission, 8/31 priority date for domestic students. Application fee: $55. *Financial support:* Career-related internships or fieldwork and Federal Work-Study available. Support available to part-time students. *Unit head:* Dr. Ruth Ann Sandlin, Chair, 909-537-5641, Fax: 909-537-7040, E-mail: rsandlin@csusb.edu.

California University of Pennsylvania, School of Graduate Studies and Research, School of Education, Department of Counselor Education and Services, California, PA 15419-1394. Offers guidance and counseling (M Ed, MS). *Accreditation:* ACA; NCATE. Part-time and evening/weekend programs available. *Faculty:* 16 full-time (7 women), 5 part-time/adjunct (3 women). *Students:* 55 full-time (44 women), 49 part-time (44 women); includes 4 minority (2 African Americans, 1 American Indian/Alaska Native, 1 Hispanic American). Average age 30. 36 applicants, 31% accepted. In 2006, 39 degrees awarded. *Median time to degree:* Master's–2 years full-time, 3.5 years part-time. *Degree requirements:* For master's, thesis optional. *Entrance requirements:* For master's, MAT, minimum GPA of 3.0, resumé, letters of reference. Additional exam requirements/recommendations for international students: Required—TOEFL (minimum score 550 paper-based; 213 computer-based; 80 iBT). *Application deadline:* For fall admission, 8/1 priority date for domestic and international students. Applications are processed on a rolling basis. Application fee: $25. Electronic applications accepted. *Expenses:* Tuition, state resident: full-time $6,048; part-time $336 per credit. Tuition, nonresident: full-time $9,678; part-time $538 per credit. Required fees: $1,854; $263 per credit. Full-time tuition and fees vary according to course load, campus/location and program. *Financial support:* Career-related internships or fieldwork, scholarships/grants, traineeships, and unspecified assistantships available. Financial award applicants required to submit FAFSA. *Faculty research:* Mind-body theories and practice, grief issues, career development, supervision, sports counseling. Total annual research expenditures: $72,000. *Unit head:* Dr. Gloria Brusoski, Chairperson, 724-938-4123, Fax: 724-938-4314, E-mail: brusoski@cup.edu.

Campbell University, Graduate and Professional Programs, School of Education, Buies Creek, NC 27506. Offers administration (MSA); community counseling (MA); elementary education (M Ed); English education (M Ed); interdisciplinary studies (M Ed); mathematics education (M Ed); middle grades education (M Ed); physical education (M Ed); school counseling (M Ed); secondary education (M Ed); social science education (M Ed). *Accreditation:* NCATE. Part-time and evening/weekend programs available. *Faculty:* 14 full-time (9 women), 12 part-time/adjunct (7 women). *Students:* 27 full-time (25 women), 183 part-time (146 women); includes 30 minority (24 African Americans, 3 American Indian/Alaska Native, 3 Hispanic Americans), 1 international. Average age 31. 112 applicants, 74% accepted, 74 enrolled. In 2006, 65 degrees awarded. *Degree requirements:* For master's, comprehensive exam. *Entrance requirements:* For master's, GRE General Test, minimum GPA of 2.7. *Application deadline:* For fall admission, 8/1 priority date for domestic students; for spring admission, 1/2 priority date for domestic students. Applications are processed on a rolling basis. Application fee: $65. *Expenses:* Tuition: Part-time $380 per semester hour. *Financial support:* In 2006–07, 67 students received support. Career-related internships or fieldwork and Federal Work-Study available. Financial award application deadline: 4/15; financial award applicants required to submit FAFSA. *Faculty research:* Spiritual values and wellness issues in counseling, stress and professional burnout among counselors, thinking strategies, leadership, adaptive technology. *Unit head:* Dr. Karen P. Nery, Dean, 910-893-1630, Fax: 910-893-1999, E-mail: nery@campbell.edu. *Application contact:* James S. Farthing, Director of Graduate Admissions for Business and Education, 910-893-1200 Ext. 1318, Fax: 910-814-4718, E-mail: farthing@campbell.edu.

Canisius College, Graduate Division, School of Education and Human Services, Department of Counseling and Human Services, Buffalo, NY 14208-1098. Offers community mental health counseling (MS); counseling and human services (MS); school and agency counseling (MS). Part-time and evening/weekend programs available. *Faculty:* 5 full-time (3 women), 9 part-time/adjunct (3 women). *Students:* 70 full-time (58 women), 56 part-time (44 women); includes 17 minority (14 African Americans, 1 Asian American or Pacific Islander, 2 Hispanic Americans), 2 international. Average age 28. 82 applicants, 87% accepted, 34 enrolled. In 2006, 75 degrees awarded. *Degree requirements:* For master's, thesis, research project. *Entrance requirements:* For master's, interview, minimum GPA of 2.5. *Application deadline:* Applications are processed on a rolling basis. Application fee: $25. Electronic applications accepted. *Expenses:* Tuition: Part-time $645 per credit hour. Required fees: $19 per credit hour. Tuition and fees vary according to program. *Financial support:* In 2006–07, 2 research assistantships with partial tuition reimbursements (averaging $8,708 per year) were awarded; career-related internships or fieldwork, Federal Work-Study, institutionally sponsored loans, health care benefits, and unspecified assistantships also available. Support available to part-time students. Financial award applicants required to submit FAFSA. *Faculty research:* Positive psychology, wellness, school violence prevention, lifespan development. *Unit head:* Dr. David L. Farrugia, Chairman, 716-888-2393, Fax: 716-888-3290, E-mail: farrugia@canisius.edu. *Application contact:* James D. Bagwell, Director of Graduate Recruitment and Admissions, 716-888-2544, Fax: 716-888-3290, E-mail: bagwellj@canisius.edu.

Cape Breton University, School of Education, Health, and Wellness, Sydney, NS B1P 6L2, Canada. Offers educational counseling (Diploma); educational studies-arts education (Certificate); educational technology (Diploma). Part-time and evening/weekend programs available. Postbaccalaureate distance learning degree programs offered (no on-campus study). Electronic applications accepted.

Carson-Newman College, Graduate Program in Education, Jefferson City, TN 37760. Offers curriculum and instruction (M Ed); elementary education (MAT); school counseling (M Ed); secondary education (MAT); teaching English as a second language (MATESL). *Accreditation:* NCATE. Part-time and evening/weekend programs available. *Faculty:* 5 full-time (2 women), 10 part-time/adjunct (3 women). *Students:* 77 full-time (60 women), 41 part-time (29 women); includes 2 minority (both African Americans), 27 international. Average age 32. 65 applicants, 97% accepted. In 2006, 64 degrees awarded. *Degree requirements:* For master's, thesis or alternative. *Entrance requirements:* For master's, NTE, minimum GPA of 3.0 in major, 2.5 overall. *Application deadline:* For fall admission, 7/15 priority date for domestic students. Applications are processed on a rolling basis. Application fee: $25 ($50 for international students). *Expenses:* Tuition: Part-time $270 per credit hour. *Financial support:* In 2006–07, 86 students received support. Federal Work-Study and unspecified assistantships available. Financial award application deadline: 4/1; financial award applicants required to submit FAFSA. *Unit head:* Dr. Jean Love, Chair, 865-471-3461. *Application contact:* Graduate Admissions and Services Adviser, 865-471-3460, Fax: 865-471-3875.

Carthage College, Division of Teacher Education, Kenosha, WI 53140. Offers classroom guidance and counseling (M Ed); creative arts (M Ed); gifted and talented children (M Ed); language arts (M Ed); modern language (M Ed); natural sciences (M Ed); reading (M Ed, Certificate); social sciences (M Ed); teacher leadership (M Ed). Part-time and evening/weekend programs available. *Degree requirements:* For master's, thesis optional. *Entrance requirements:* For master's, MAT, minimum B average, letters of reference.

The Catholic University of America, School of Arts and Sciences, Department of Education, Washington, DC 20064. Offers administration, curriculum, and policy studies (MA); Catholic school leadership (MA); counselor education (MA); educational administration (PhD); educational psychology (PhD); English as a second language (MA); learning and instruction (MA); policy studies (PhD); teacher education (MA). *Accreditation:* NCATE. Part-time programs available. *Faculty:* 11 full-time (8 women), 3 part-time/adjunct (2 women). *Students:* 11 full-time (8 women), 52 part-time (34 women); includes 13 minority (9 African Americans, 1 Asian American or Pacific Islander, 3 Hispanic Americans), 2 international. Average age 35. 67 applicants, 55% accepted, 13 enrolled. In 2006, 19 master's, 2 doctorates awarded. *Degree requirements:* For master's, thesis or alternative, comprehensive exam; for doctorate, thesis/dissertation, comprehensive exam. *Entrance requirements:* For master's and doctorate, GRE General Test or MAT, 3 letters of recommendation. Additional exam requirements/recommendations for international students: Required—TOEFL (minimum score 580 paper-based; 237 computer-based). *Application deadline:* For fall admission, 2/1 priority date for domestic students; for spring admission, 11/15 priority date for domestic students. Applications are processed on a rolling basis. Application fee: $55. Electronic applications accepted. *Expenses:* Tuition: Full-time $27,700; part-time $1,045 per credit hour. Required fees: $1,290. Part-time tuition and fees vary according to campus/location and program. *Financial support:* Research assistantships, teaching assistantships, career-related internships or fieldwork, Federal Work-Study, scholarships/grants, tuition waivers (full and partial), and unspecified assistantships available. Support available to part-time students. Financial award application deadline: 2/1; financial award applicants required to submit FAFSA. *Faculty research:* Catholic school issues, reflective teaching, cognitive psychology, urban education. *Unit head:* Dr. Merylann Schuttloffel, Chair, 202-319-5805, Fax: 202-319-5815, E-mail: schuttloffel@cua.edu.

Central Connecticut State University, School of Graduate Studies, School of Education and Professional Studies, Department of Counseling and Family Therapy, New Britain, CT 06050-4010. Offers marriage and family therapy (MS); professional counseling (MS, Certificate); school counseling (MS); student development in higher education (MS). *Accreditation:* AAMFT/COAMFTE. Part-time and evening/weekend programs available. *Faculty:* 7 full-time (5 women), 9 part-time/adjunct (6 women). *Students:* 98 full-time (80 women), 197 part-time (161 women); includes 44 minority (16 African Americans, 2 American Indian/Alaska Native, 2 Asian Americans or Pacific Islanders, 24 Hispanic Americans), 4 international. Average age 33. 270 applicants, 50% accepted, 105 enrolled. In 2006, 69 master's, 8 other advanced degrees awarded. *Degree requirements:* For master's, thesis or alternative, special project. *Entrance requirements:* For master's, minimum GPA of 2.7. Additional exam requirements/recommendations for international students: Required—TOEFL. *Application deadline:* For fall admission, 7/1 for domestic students; for spring admission, 12/1 for domestic students. Applications are processed on a rolling basis. Application fee: $50. Electronic applications accepted. *Expenses:* Tuition, area resident: Full-time $3,970; part-time $380 per credit. Tuition, state resident: full-time $5,955; part-time $380 per credit. Tuition, nonresident: full-time $11,061; part-time $380 per credit. Required fees: $3,189. One-time fee: $62 part-time. Tuition and fees vary according to degree level and program. *Financial support:* In 2006–07, 13 students received support, including 11 research assistantships; career-related internships or fieldwork, Federal Work-Study, scholarships/grants, and unspecified assistantships also available. Support available to part-time students. Financial award application deadline: 3/1; financial award applicants required to submit FAFSA. *Faculty research:* Elementary/secondary school counseling, marriage/family therapy, rehabilitation counseling, counseling in higher educational settings. *Unit head:* Dr. Connie Tait, Chair, 860-832-2154.

Central Methodist University, College of Graduate and Extended Studies, Fayette, MO 65248-1198. Offers counseling (MS); education (M Ed). Part-time and evening/weekend programs available. Postbaccalaureate distance learning degree programs offered (no on-campus study). *Degree requirements:* For master's, thesis, registration. *Entrance requirements:* For master's, GRE General Test, minimum GPA of 2.75. Electronic applications accepted.

Central Michigan University, Central Michigan University Off-Campus Programs, Program in Counseling, Mount Pleasant, MI 48859. Offers MA. Part-time and evening/weekend programs available. *Entrance requirements:* For master's, MAT, minimum GPA of 2.7. Additional exam requirements/recommendations for international students: Required—TOEFL. Electronic applications accepted. *Financial support:* Scholarships/grants available. Support available to part-time students. *Unit head:* Dr. Richard Fox, Chair, 989-774-3205, E-mail: fox1r@cmich.edu. *Application contact:* 877-268-4636, E-mail: cmuoffcampus@cmich.edu.

Central Michigan University, College of Graduate Studies, College of Education and Human Services, Department of Counseling and Special Education, Program in Counseling, Mount Pleasant, MI 48859. Offers professional counseling (MA); school guidance personnel (MA). *Accreditation:* NCATE. *Degree requirements:* For master's, thesis or alternative, registration. *Entrance requirements:* For master's, MAT, teaching certificate. *Faculty research:* Stress, school counseling.

Central Washington University, Graduate Studies, Research and Continuing Education, College of the Sciences, Department of Psychology, Program in School Counseling, Ellensburg, WA 98926. Offers M Ed. *Faculty:* 22 full-time (9 women). *Students:* 8 full-time (7 women), 6 part-time (5 women); includes 3 minority (1 Asian American or Pacific Islander, 2 Hispanic Americans). In 2006, 4 degrees awarded. *Degree requirements:* For master's, thesis, internship. *Entrance requirements:* For master's, GRE General Test, minimum GPA of 3.0. Additional exam requirements/recommendations for international students: Required—TOEFL (minimum score 550 paper-based; 213 computer-based; 79 iBT). *Application deadline:*

For fall admission, 4/1 priority date for domestic students. Applications are processed on a rolling basis. Application fee: $50. Electronic applications accepted. *Expenses:* Tuition, state resident: full-time $6,312. Tuition, nonresident: full-time $14,112. Tuition and fees vary according to course load and degree level. *Financial support:* Research assistantships with partial tuition reimbursements, career-related internships or fieldwork, Federal Work-Study, health care benefits, and unspecified assistantships available. Financial award application deadline: 3/1. *Application contact:* Justine Eason, Admissions Program Coordinator, 509-963-3103, Fax: 509-963-1799, E-mail: masters@cwu.edu.

Chadron State College, School of Professional and Graduate Studies, Department of Education, Chadron, NE 69337. Offers business (MA Ed); community counseling (MA Ed); educational administration (MS Ed, Sp Ed); elementary education (MS Ed); history (MA Ed); language and literature (MA Ed); secondary administration (MS Ed); secondary education (MS Ed). *Accreditation:* NCATE. Part-time and evening/weekend programs available. Postbaccalaureate distance learning degree programs offered. *Degree requirements:* For master's, thesis optional. *Entrance requirements:* For master's, GRE General Test, GRE Writing Test, minimum GPA of 2.75 or 12 graduate hours at CSC with minimum GPA of 3.25. Additional exam requirements/recommendations for international students: Required—TOEFL. Electronic applications accepted. *Faculty research:* Rural education, technology, mental health.

Chapman University, Graduate Studies, School of Education, Program in School Counseling, Orange, CA 92866. Offers MA. Part-time and evening/weekend programs available. *Faculty:* 16 full-time (11 women), 25 part-time/adjunct (14 women). *Students:* 31 full-time (28 women), 11 part-time (7 women); includes 12 minority (1 African American, 2 Asian Americans or Pacific Islanders, 9 Hispanic Americans). Average age 27. 32 applicants, 66% accepted, 13 enrolled. In 2006, 14 degrees awarded. *Degree requirements:* For master's, comprehensive exam, registration. *Entrance requirements:* For master's, GRE General Test, MAT, or California Subject Examinations for Teachers, minimum undergraduate GPA of 2.75. Additional exam requirements/recommendations for international students: Required—TOEFL (minimum score 550 paper-based). *Application deadline:* Applications are processed on a rolling basis. Application fee: $55. Electronic applications accepted. *Expenses: Contact institution. Financial support:* In 2006–07, 32 students received support, including 10 fellowships (averaging $2,000 per year); Federal Work-Study also available. Financial award application deadline: 6/30; financial award applicants required to submit FAFSA. *Unit head:* Dr. Michael Hass, Coordinator, 714-997-6781, E-mail: hass@chapman.edu. *Application contact:* Rika Judd, Information Contact, 714-997-6786, Fax: 714-997-6713, E-mail: rjudd@chapman.edu.

The Chicago School of Professional Psychology, Graduate School, Program in Clinical Psychology, Chicago, IL 60610. Offers applied behavior analysis (MA, Certificate); clinical psychology (Psy D); counseling (MA). *Degree requirements:* For master's, thesis (for some programs); for doctorate, thesis/dissertation, comprehensive exam. *Entrance requirements:* For master's, minimum undergraduate GPA of 3.0; 1 course in psychology and 1 course in either statistics or research methods; for doctorate, GRE, 18 hours of psychology credit (including courses in statistics, normal psychology and human development). Additional exam requirements/recommendations for international students: Required—TOEFL. Electronic applications accepted.

Chicago State University, School of Graduate and Professional Studies, College of Arts and Sciences, Department of Psychology, Chicago, IL 60628. Offers counseling (MA). *Accreditation:* ACA; NCATE. *Degree requirements:* For master's, thesis optional. *Entrance requirements:* For master's, minimum GPA of 2.75.

The Citadel, The Military College of South Carolina, College of Graduate and Professional Studies, School of Education, Program in Guidance and Counseling, Charleston, SC 29409. Offers M Ed. *Accreditation:* ACA; NCATE. Part-time and evening/weekend programs available. *Students:* 12 full-time (10 women), 35 part-time (33 women); includes 6 minority (all African Americans) Average age 29. In 2006, 15 degrees awarded. *Entrance requirements:* For master's, GRE General Test, MAT, or 12 hours of graduate course work with a minimum GPA of 3.5. Additional exam requirements/recommendations for international students: Required—TOEFL (minimum score 550 paper-based; 213 computer-based). *Application deadline:* For fall admission, 6/1 for domestic students; for spring admission, 3/1 for domestic students. Applications are processed on a rolling basis. Application fee: $30. *Expenses:* Tuition, state resident: part-time $259 per credit hour. Tuition, nonresident: part-time $482 per credit hour. *Financial support:* Application deadline: 7/1; *Unit head:* Dr. George Williams, Head, 843-953-5097, E-mail: williamsg@citadel.edu. *Application contact:* Dr. Raymond S. Jones, Associate Dean, College of Graduate and Professional Studies, 843-953-5089, Fax: 843-953-7630, E-mail: ray.jones@citadel.edu.

Clark Atlanta University, School of Education, Department of Counseling and Psychological Services, Atlanta, GA 30314. Offers counseling (MA, PhD); education psychology (MA). *Degree requirements:* For master's, one foreign language, thesis; for doctorate, 2 foreign languages, thesis/dissertation. *Entrance requirements:* For master's, GRE General Test, minimum undergraduate GPA of 2.5; for doctorate, GRE General Test, minimum graduate GPA of 3.0.

Clemson University, Graduate School, College of Health, Education, and Human Development, School of Education, Program in Counselor Education, Clemson, SC 29634. Offers community counseling (M Ed); school counseling (M Ed); student affairs (M Ed). *Accreditation:* ACA; NCATE. *Students:* 120 full-time (86 women), 58 part-time (49 women); includes 22 minority (17 African Americans, 2 American Indian/Alaska Native, 3 Hispanic Americans), 2 international. 133 applicants, 41% accepted, 39 enrolled. In 2006, 61 degrees awarded. *Entrance requirements:* For master's, GRE General Test. Additional exam requirements/recommendations for international students: Required—TOEFL. *Application deadline:* For fall admission, 6/1 for domestic students. Application fee: $50. *Expenses:* Tuition, state resident: full-time $8,812; part-time $450 per hour. Tuition, nonresident: full-time $18,036; part-time $760 per hour. Required fees: $474; $5 per term. *Financial support:* Application deadline: 6/1; *Unit head:* Dr. David Scott, Coordinator, 864-656-0328.

See Close-Up on page 1603.

Cleveland State University, College of Graduate Studies, College of Education and Human Services, Department of Counseling, Administration, Supervision and Adult Learning, Cleveland, OH 44115. Offers adult learning and development (M Ed); community agency counseling (M Ed); counseling and pupil personnel administration (Ed S); educational administration (Ed S); educational administration and supervision (M Ed); school counseling (M Ed). *Accreditation:* ACA (one or more programs are accredited). Part-time programs available. *Faculty:* 15 full-time (9 women), 8 part-time/adjunct (5 women). *Students:* 43 full-time (33 women), 304 part-time (236 women); includes 91 minority (78 African Americans, 2 Asian Americans or Pacific Islanders, 11 Hispanic Americans). Average age 35. 205 applicants, 36% accepted, 54 enrolled. In 2006, 136 master's, 6 other advanced degrees awarded. *Degree requirements:* For master's, thesis optional; for Ed S, internship, thesis optional. *Entrance requirements:* For master's, GRE General Test or MAT, letter of recommendation, minimum GPA of 2.75. Additional exam requirements/recommendations for international students: Required—TOEFL (minimum score 525 paper-based; 197 computer-based), IELTS (minimum score 6). *Application deadline:* For fall admission, 6/21 for domestic students; for spring admission, 8/31 for domestic students. Application fee: $30. *Financial support:* In 2006–07, 8 students received support, including research assistantships with full and partial tuition reimbursements available (averaging $3,287 per year), teaching assistantships with full and partial tuition reimbursements available (averaging $3,480 per year); career-related internships or fieldwork, scholarships/grants, tuition waivers (full), and unspecified assistantships also available. Support available to part-time students. *Faculty research:* Education law, career development, women in school administration, psychopharmacology, counseling and spirituality. Total annual research expenditures: $478,265. *Unit head:* Dr. Rollin D. Nordgren, Interim Chairperson, 216-523-7499, Fax: 216-687-5378, E-mail: r.nordgren@csuohio.edu.

Cleveland State University, College of Graduate Studies, College of Education and Human Services, Program in Urban Education, Cleveland, OH 44115. Offers counseling (PhD); counseling psychology (PhD); leadership and lifelong learning (PhD); learning and development (PhD); policy studies (PhD); school administration (PhD). Part-time programs available. *Faculty:* 14 full-time (9 women), 4 part-time/adjunct (2 women). *Students:* 16 full-time (11 women), 78 part-time (47 women); includes 22 minority (20 African Americans, 2 Asian Americans or Pacific Islanders), 5 international. Average age 43. 29 applicants, 24% accepted, 4 enrolled. In 2006, 9 degrees awarded. *Degree requirements:* For doctorate, one foreign language, thesis/dissertation, comprehensive exam, registration. *Entrance requirements:* For doctorate, GRE General Test, minimum graduate GPA of 3.25. Additional exam requirements/recommendations for international students: Required—TOEFL (minimum score 525 paper-based; 197 computer-based), IELTS (minimum score 6). *Application deadline:* For fall admission, 2/5 for domestic students. Application fee: $30. *Financial support:* In 2006–07, 7 students received support, including 4 research assistantships with full and partial tuition reimbursements available (averaging $7,800 per year), 3 teaching assistantships with full and partial tuition reimbursements available (averaging $7,800 per year); tuition waivers (full) and unspecified assistantships also available. Financial award applicants required to submit FAFSA. *Faculty research:* Equity issues (race, ethnicity, and gender), education development consequences for special needs of urban populations, urban education programming, counseling the violent or aggressive adolescent. Total annual research expenditures: $5,662. *Unit head:* Dr. Joshua Bagakas, Director, 216-687-4591, Fax: 216-875-9697, E-mail: j.bagakas@csuohio.edu. *Application contact:* Wanda Butler, Administrative Assistant, 216-687-4697, Fax: 216-875-9697, E-mail: w.pruett-butler@csuohio.edu.

The College of New Jersey, Graduate Division, School of Education, Department of Counselor Education, Program in Community Counseling: Human Services Specialization, Ewing, NJ 08628. Offers MA. *Accreditation:* ACA. *Students:* 6 full-time (all women), 27 part-time (23 women); includes 4 minority (2 African Americans, 1 Asian American or Pacific Islander, 1 Hispanic American). 15 applicants, 60% accepted. In 2006, 8 degrees awarded. *Degree requirements:* For master's, comprehensive exam. *Entrance requirements:* For master's, GRE General Test, minimum GPA of 3.0 in field or 2.75 overall, interview. Additional exam requirements/recommendations for international students: Required—TOEFL. *Application deadline:* For fall admission, 4/15 for domestic students; for spring admission, 10/15 for domestic students. Application fee: $60. Electronic applications accepted. *Financial support:* Application deadline: 5/1; *Unit head:* Dr. Atsuko Seto, Coordinator, 609-771-2478, Fax: 609-637-5166, E-mail: seto@tcnj.edu. *Application contact:* Susan L. Hydro, Office of Graduate Studies, Assistant Dean, 609-771-2300, Fax: 609-637-5105, E-mail: graduate@tcnj.edu.

The College of New Jersey, Graduate Division, School of Education, Department of Counselor Education, Program in School Counseling, Ewing, NJ 08628. Offers MA. *Accreditation:* ACA; NCATE. *Students:* 17 full-time (16 women), 96 part-time (81 women); includes 9 minority (4 African Americans, 4 Asian Americans or Pacific Islanders, 1 Hispanic American). 46 applicants, 67% accepted. In 2006, 32 degrees awarded. *Degree requirements:* For master's, comprehensive exam. *Entrance requirements:* For master's, GRE General Test, minimum GPA of 3.0 in field or 2.75 overall, interview. Additional exam requirements/recommendations for international students: Required—TOEFL. *Application deadline:* For fall admission, 4/15 for domestic students; for spring admission, 10/15 for domestic students. Application fee: $60. Electronic applications accepted. *Financial support:* Application deadline: 5/1; *Unit head:* Dr. MaryLou Ramsey, Coordinator, 609-771-3033, Fax: 609-637-5166, E-mail: ramsey@tcnj.edu. *Application contact:* Susan L. Hydro, Office of Graduate Studies, Assistant Dean, 609-771-2300, Fax: 609-637-5105, E-mail: graduate@tcnj.edu.

College of St. Joseph, Graduate Program, Division of Psychology and Human Services, Rutland, VT 05701-3899. Offers clinical mental health counseling (MS); clinical psychology (MS); community counseling (MS); school guidance counseling (MS); substance abuse counseling (MS). Part-time and evening/weekend programs available. *Faculty:* 4 full-time (1 woman), 8 part-time/adjunct (5 women). *Students:* 20 full-time, 51 part-time, 1 international. Average age 35. 20 applicants, 90% accepted, 14 enrolled. In 2006, 11 degrees awarded. *Degree requirements:* For master's, thesis, comprehensive exam, registration. *Entrance requirements:* For master's, 2 letters of reference, interview. *Application deadline:* Applications are processed on a rolling basis. Application fee: $35. *Expenses:* Tuition: Full-time $10,990; part-time $300 per credit. Part-time tuition and fees vary according to program. *Financial support:* In 2006–07, 3 students received support, including teaching assistantships with tuition reimbursements available (averaging $3,000 per year); career-related internships or fieldwork, Federal Work-Study, and unspecified assistantships also available. Support available to part-time students. Financial award application deadline: 3/1. *Unit head:* Dr. Craig Knapp, Chair, 802-773-5900 Ext. 3219, Fax: 802-776-5258, E-mail: cknapp@csj.edu. *Application contact:* Tracy Gallipo, Director of Admissions, 802-773-5900 Ext. 3262, Fax: 802-773-5900, E-mail: tracygallipo@csj.edu.

The College of Saint Rose, Graduate Studies, School of Education, Department of Counseling and Educational Administration, Program in Counseling, Albany, NY 12203-1419. Offers college student personnel (MS Ed); community counseling (MS Ed); school counseling (MS Ed). *Accreditation:* NCATE. Part-time and evening/weekend programs available. *Degree requirements:* For master's, comprehensive exam or thesis. *Entrance requirements:* For master's, interview, minimum undergraduate GPA of 3.0, 9 hours of psychology coursework. Additional exam requirements/recommendations for international students: Required—TOEFL (minimum score 550 paper-based; 213 computer-based). Electronic applications accepted.

College of Santa Fe, Department of Education, Santa Fe, NM 87505-7634. Offers at-risk youth (MA), including bilingual/multicultural education, classroom teaching, community counseling, educational administration, leadership, school counseling, self-designed program, TESOL/Multicultural; curriculum and instruction (MA); multicultural special education (MA). Part-time and evening/weekend programs available. *Entrance requirements:* For master's, minimum GPA of 3.0. *Faculty research:* Integrated curriculum, child development, brain research, learning styles, systemic issues in education.

College of the Southwest, School of Education, Hobbs, NM 88240-9129. Offers curriculum and instruction (MS); educational administration (MS); educational counseling (MS); educational diagnostician (MS). Part-time and evening/weekend programs available. Postbaccalaureate distance learning degree programs offered. *Faculty:* 2 full-time (both women), 6 part-time/adjunct (1 woman). *Students:* 41 full-time (28 women), 43 part-time (35 women); includes 24 minority (1 African American, 1 American Indian/Alaska Native, 1 Asian American or Pacific Islander, 21 Hispanic Americans), 1 international. Average age 38. 119 applicants, 29% accepted, 34 enrolled. In 2006, 26 degrees awarded. *Degree requirements:* For master's, comprehensive exam. *Entrance requirements:* For master's, GRE General Test. Additional exam requirements/recommendations for international students: Recommended—TOEFL (minimum score 550 paper-based; 213 computer-based). *Application deadline:* For fall admission, 3/1 priority date for domestic students; for spring admission, 10/1 for domestic students. Applications are processed on a rolling basis. Application fee: $50. *Expenses:* Tuition: Part-time $375 per credit hour. *Financial support:* In 2006–07, 58 students received support, including 1 research assistantship; Federal Work-Study, scholarships/grants, and tuition waivers (partial) also available. Support available to part-time students. Financial award application deadline: 4/1; financial award applicants required to submit FAFSA. *Unit head:* Dr. Dennis Atherton, Dean, 505-392-6561 Ext. 1069, Fax: 505-392-6006, E-mail: datherton@csw.edu. *Application contact:* Kerrie Mitchell, Coordinator of Financial Aid and Admissions Operations, 505-392-6563 Ext. 1048, Fax: 505-392-6006, E-mail: kmitchell@csw.edu.

The College of William and Mary, School of Education, Program in Counselor Education, Williamsburg, VA 23187-8795. Offers community and addictions counseling (M Ed); community counseling (M Ed); educational counseling (Ed D, PhD); family counseling (M Ed); school counseling (M Ed). *Accreditation:* ACA; NCATE. Part-time and evening/weekend programs available. *Faculty:* 5 full-time (2 women), 5 part-time/adjunct (3 women). *Students:* 53 full-time (43 women), 17 part-time (15 women); includes 10 minority (5 African Americans,

Counselor Education

The College of William and Mary (continued)
2 American Indian/Alaska Native, 2 Asian Americans or Pacific Islanders, 1 Hispanic American), 3 international. Average age 32. 127 applicants, 47% accepted, 29 enrolled. In 2006, 22 master's, 9 doctorates awarded. *Degree requirements:* For doctorate, thesis/dissertation, comprehensive exam. *Entrance requirements:* For master's, GRE, minimum GPA of 2.5; for doctorate, GRE, minimum GPA of 3.5. Additional exam requirements/recommendations for international students: Required—TOEFL. *Application deadline:* For fall admission, 2/1 for domestic and international students. Application fee: $30. *Expenses:* Tuition, state resident: full-time $6,100; part-time $260 per credit. Tuition, nonresident: full-time $18,790; part-time $725 per credit. Required fees: $3,314. Tuition and fees vary according to program. *Financial support:* In 2006–07, 31 research assistantships with full tuition reimbursements (averaging $9,000 per year) were awarded; fellowships with full tuition reimbursements, career-related internships or fieldwork, Federal Work-Study, institutionally sponsored loans, scholarships/grants, and unspecified assistantships also available. Financial award application deadline: 2/1; financial award applicants required to submit FAFSA. *Faculty research:* Sexuality, multicultural education, substance abuse, transpersonal psychology. *Unit head:* Dr. Rick Gressard, Head, 757-221-2352, E-mail: cfgres@wm.edu. *Application contact:* Dorothy Osborne, Director of Admissions, 757-221-2317, E-mail: dsosbo@wm.edu.

Columbia International University, Columbia Graduate School, Columbia, SC 29230-3122. Offers Bible teaching (MABT); Christian higher education leadership (Ed D); Christian school educational leadership (Ed D); counseling (MACN); curriculum and instruction (M Ed), including Christian school guidance, English as a second language, learning disabilities, school technology; early childhood and elementary education (MAT); educational administration (M Ed); teaching English as a foreign language (Certificate); teaching English as a foreign language and intercultural studies (MATF). Part-time and evening/weekend programs available. *Faculty:* 11 full-time (4 women), 7 part-time/adjunct (5 women). *Students:* 52 full-time (44 women), 93 part-time (59 women); includes 17 minority (11 African Americans, 2 Asian Americans or Pacific Islanders, 4 Hispanic Americans), 10 international. Average age 35. 107 applicants, 56% accepted, 41 enrolled. In 2006, 62 degrees awarded. *Degree requirements:* For master's, internships, professional project. *Entrance requirements:* For master's, Minnesota Multiphasic Personality Inventory, MAT, minimum GPA of 2.7. Additional exam requirements/recommendations for international students: Required—TOEFL. *Application deadline:* For fall admission, 8/1 priority date for domestic and international students; for winter admission, 12/15 priority date for domestic and international students; for spring admission, 1/15 priority date for domestic and international students. Applications are processed on a rolling basis. Application fee: $45. Electronic applications accepted. *Expenses:* Tuition: Part-time $400 per semester hour. Tuition and fees vary according to course load and program. *Financial support:* In 2006–07, 35 students received support. Career-related internships or fieldwork, Federal Work-Study, institutionally sponsored loans, and scholarships/grants available. Financial award application deadline: 3/17; financial award applicants required to submit FAFSA. *Unit head:* Dr. Milton Uecker, Dean, 803-807-5319, Fax: 803-786-4209, E-mail: muecker@ciu.edu. *Application contact:* Michelle MacGregor, Director of Admissions, 800-777-2227 Ext. 5335, Fax: 803-786-4209, E-mail: yescbs@ciu.edu.

Columbus State University, Graduate Studies, College of Education, Department of Counseling, Educational Leadership and Professional Studies, Columbus, GA 31907-5645. Offers community counseling (MS); educational leadership (M Ed, Ed S); school counseling (M Ed, Ed S). *Accreditation:* ACA; NCATE. Part-time and evening/weekend programs available. Postbaccalaureate distance learning degree programs offered (minimal on-campus study). *Faculty:* 10 full-time (4 women), 8 part-time/adjunct (4 women). *Students:* 87 full-time (61 women), 47 part-time (38 women); includes 34 minority (33 African Americans, 1 Asian American or Pacific Islander). Average age 36. 40 applicants, 43% accepted, 13 enrolled. In 2006, 42 master's, 34 other advanced degrees awarded. *Degree requirements:* For master's, thesis, exit exam; for Ed S, thesis or alternative. *Entrance requirements:* For master's, GRE General Test, minimum GPA of 2.75; for Ed S, GRE General Test. Additional exam requirements/recommendations for international students: Required—TOEFL (minimum score 550 paper-based; 213 computer-based). *Application deadline:* For fall admission, 5/1 priority date for domestic students, 5/1 for international students; for spring admission, 11/1 for domestic and international students. Applications are processed on a rolling basis. Application fee: $25. Electronic applications accepted. *Expenses:* Tuition, state resident: part-time $127 per semester hour. Tuition, nonresident: part-time $508 per semester hour. Required fees: $264 per semester. Tuition and fees vary according to course load. *Financial support:* In 2006–07, 67 students received support, including 5 research assistantships with partial tuition reimbursements available (averaging $3,000 per year); career-related internships or fieldwork, Federal Work-Study, institutionally sponsored loans, scholarships/grants, tuition waivers (partial), and unspecified assistantships also available. Support available to part-time students. Financial award application deadline: 5/1; financial award applicants required to submit FAFSA. *Unit head:* Dr. Paul Tom Hackett, Chair, 706-568-5061, Fax: 706-569-3134, E-mail: hackett_paul@colstate.edu. *Application contact:* Katie Thornton, Graduate Admissions Specialist, 706-568-2035, Fax: 706-568-2462, E-mail: thornton_katie@colstate.edu.

Concordia University, College of Education, Program in School Counseling, River Forest, IL 60305-1499. Offers MA, CAS. *Accreditation:* ACA (one or more programs are accredited); NCATE. Part-time and evening/weekend programs available. *Degree requirements:* For master's, thesis optional; for CAS, thesis, final project. *Entrance requirements:* For master's, minimum GPA of 2.9; for CAS, master's degree. Additional exam requirements/recommendations for international students: Required—TOEFL (minimum score 550 paper-based; 195 computer-based). Electronic applications accepted. *Faculty research:* Development of comprehensive school counseling education, training of school counselors for parochial schools.

Concordia University Wisconsin, Graduate Programs, Department of Education, Mequon, WI 53097-2402. Offers art education (MS Ed); curriculum and instruction (MS Ed); early childhood (MS Ed); educational administration (MS Ed); environmental education (MS Ed); family studies (MS Ed); reading (MS Ed); school counseling (MS Ed); special education (MS Ed). Part-time and evening/weekend programs available. Postbaccalaureate distance learning degree programs offered (minimal on-campus study). *Faculty:* 30. *Students:* 396 (284 women). In 2006, 51 degrees awarded. *Degree requirements:* For master's, thesis or alternative, comprehensive exam. *Entrance requirements:* For master's, minimum GPA of 3.0, teaching license. Additional exam requirements/recommendations for international students: Required—TOEFL. Application fee: $35. *Financial support:* Career-related internships or fieldwork and tuition waivers (partial) available. Financial award application deadline: 8/1. *Faculty research:* Motivation, developmental learning, learning styles. *Unit head:* Dr. James Juergensen, Director, 262-243-4214, E-mail: james.juergensen@cuw.edu. *Application contact:* Graduate Admissions, 262-243-4248, Fax: 262-243-4428.

Creighton University, Graduate School, College of Arts and Sciences, Department of Education, Program in Guidance and Counseling, Omaha, NE 68178-0001. Offers MS. Part-time and evening/weekend programs available. *Faculty:* 4 full-time, 3 part-time/adjunct. *Students:* 10 full-time (8 women), 34 part-time (28 women); includes 6 minority (4 African Americans, 2 Hispanic Americans), 2 international. 24 applicants, 75% accepted. In 2006, 4 degrees awarded. *Entrance requirements:* For master's, GRE General Test, resumé, 3 letters of recommendation. Additional exam requirements/recommendations for international students: Required—TOEFL (minimum score 550 paper-based; 213 computer-based; 80 iBT). *Application deadline:* For fall admission, 3/1 for domestic and international students; for winter admission, 12/1 for domestic and international students; for spring admission, 4/1 for domestic students. Applications are processed on a rolling basis. Application fee: $40. Electronic applications accepted. *Expenses:* Tuition: Part-time $595 per credit hour. Required fees: $38 per semester. *Unit head:* Dr. Jeff Smith, Director, 402-280-2413, E-mail: jefsmith@creighton.edu. *Application contact:* Dr. Gail M. Jenson, Dean, 402-280-2870, Fax: 402-280-5762, E-mail: gjenson@creighton.edu.

Dallas Baptist University, Dorothy M. Bush College of Education, School Counseling Program, Dallas, TX 75211-9299. Offers M Ed. Part-time and evening/weekend programs available. *Faculty:* 49 full-time (21 women), 112 part-time/adjunct (46 women). *Students:* 12 full-time, 93 part-time. 30 applicants, 43% accepted, 13 enrolled. In 2006, 32 degrees awarded. *Entrance requirements:* For master's, GRE General Test, minimum GPA of 3.0. Additional exam requirements/recommendations for international students: Required—TOEFL. *Application deadline:* Applications are processed on a rolling basis. Application fee: $25. Electronic applications accepted. *Expenses:* Tuition: Full-time $8,370; part-time $465 per credit hour. Required fees: $465 per credit hour. *Financial support:* Federal Work-Study, institutionally sponsored loans, scholarships/grants, and tuition waivers (full and partial) available. Support available to part-time students. *Unit head:* Dr. Bonnie B. Hinkle, Director, 214-333-5413, Fax: 214-333-5551, E-mail: graduate@dbu.edu. *Application contact:* Kit P. Montgomery, Director of Graduate Programs, 214-333-5242, Fax: 214-333-5579, E-mail: graduate@dbu.edu.

Delta State University, Graduate Programs, College of Education, Division of Counselor Education and Psychology, Cleveland, MS 38733-0001. Offers counseling (M Ed). *Accreditation:* ACA; NCATE. Part-time and evening/weekend programs available. *Degree requirements:* For master's, practicum, thesis optional. *Application deadline:* For fall admission, 8/1 priority date for domestic students; for spring admission, 12/1 priority date for domestic students. Applications are processed on a rolling basis. Application fee: $0. Electronic applications accepted. *Financial support:* In 2006–07, research assistantships (averaging $4,000 per year); career-related internships or fieldwork, Federal Work-Study, and institutionally sponsored loans also available. Support available to part-time students. Financial award application deadline: 6/1. *Unit head:* Dr. Scott Hutchins, Chair, 662-846-4355, Fax: 662-846-4402.

DePaul University, School of Education, Chicago, IL 60604-2287. Offers bilingual and bicultural education (M Ed, MA); curriculum studies (M Ed, MA); education (Ed D), including curriculum studies, educational leadership; educational leadership (M Ed, MA), including administration and supervision, Catholic school leadership, physical education; human development and learning (MA); human services and counseling (M Ed, MA), including agencies, family concerns, and higher education, elementary schools, human services management, secondary schools; reading and learning disabilities (M Ed, MA); social culture studies in education and development (M Ed, MA), including curriculum studies/development; teaching and learning (early childhood, elementary and secondary) (M Ed), including elementary education (M Ed, MA), secondary education (M Ed, MA); teaching and learning (early childhood, elementary, and secondary) (MA), including elementary education (M Ed, MA), secondary education (M Ed, MA). *Accreditation:* NCATE. Part-time and evening/weekend programs available. *Faculty:* 61 full-time (40 women), 76 part-time/adjunct (46 women). *Students:* 1,371 full-time (1,103 women), 474 part-time (362 women); includes 435 minority (144 African Americans, 7 American Indian/Alaska Native, 89 Asian Americans or Pacific Islanders, 195 Hispanic Americans), 11 international. Average age 30. 993 applicants, 80% accepted, 617 enrolled. In 2006, 324 master's, 7 doctorates awarded. *Degree requirements:* For doctorate, thesis/dissertation. *Entrance requirements:* For master's, interview, minimum GPA of 2.75, 2 letters of recommendation; for doctorate, interview, master's degree, 2 years of work experience (recommended), writing sample, 3 letters of recommendation. Application fee: $25. Electronic applications accepted. *Financial support:* In 2006–07, 16 research assistantships with tuition reimbursements (averaging $4,370 per year), 1 teaching assistantship (averaging $6,000 per year) were awarded; career-related internships or fieldwork also available. *Faculty research:* Reflective teaching, children at risk, loss, ethnicity, urban education. Total annual research expenditures: $556,194. *Unit head:* Dr. Clara Jennings, Dean, 773-325-7581, Fax: 773-325-7728, E-mail: cjennings@depaul.edu. *Application contact:* Dr. John Bollwark, Data Project Manager, 773-325-7582, Fax: 773-325-7713, E-mail: jbollwar@depaul.edu.

Doane College, Program in Counseling, Crete, NE 68333-2430. Offers MAC. Evening/weekend programs available. *Degree requirements:* For master's, thesis. *Entrance requirements:* For master's, minimum GPA of 3.0. Expenses: Contact institution. *Faculty research:* Ethics.

Drake University, School of Education, Department of Leadership, Counseling and Adult Development, Program in Counseling, Des Moines, IA 50311-4516. Offers community agency counseling (MSE); guidance counseling (MSE), including elementary, secondary. *Accreditation:* CORE. Part-time and evening/weekend programs available. *Faculty:* 10 full-time (3 women), 28 part-time/adjunct (16 women). *Students:* 137 applicants, 61% accepted. In 2006, 41 degrees awarded. *Degree requirements:* For master's, comprehensive exam. *Entrance requirements:* For master's, GRE General Test, MAT, or Drake Writing Assessment, resumé, 2 letters of recommendation. Additional exam requirements/recommendations for international students: Required—TOEFL (minimum score 550 paper-based; 213 computer-based). *Application deadline:* For fall admission, 7/1 priority date for domestic students, 6/1 priority date for international students; for spring admission, 11/1 priority date for domestic students, 10/1 priority date for international students. Applications are processed on a rolling basis. Application fee: $25. Electronic applications accepted. *Financial support:* Career-related internships or fieldwork and unspecified assistantships available. Support available to part-time students. *Faculty research:* Counseling and rehabilitation, behavioral supports, inquiry-based science methods, teacher quality enhancements. Total annual research expenditures: $1.5 million. *Unit head:* Dr. Matt Bruinekool, Director, 515-271-4507, E-mail: matt.bruinekool@drake.edu. *Application contact:* Ann J. Martin, Graduate Coordinator, 515-271-2034, Fax: 515-271-2831, E-mail: ann.martin@drake.edu.

Duquesne University, School of Education, Department of Counseling, Psychology, and Special Education, Program in Counselor Education, Pittsburgh, PA 15282-0001. Offers community counseling (MS Ed); counselor education and supervision (Ed D); marriage and family therapy (MS Ed); school counseling (MS Ed). *Accreditation:* ACA (one or more programs are accredited). Part-time and evening/weekend programs available. *Faculty:* 11 full-time (4 women), 5 part-time/adjunct (3 women). *Students:* 195. Average age 31. 80 applicants, 89% accepted, 46 enrolled. In 2006, 53 master's, 4 doctorates awarded. *Degree requirements:* For master's, thesis optional; for doctorate, thesis/dissertation. *Entrance requirements:* For master's, MAT, minimum GPA of 3.0; for doctorate, GRE General Test, MAT, minimum GPA of 3.25, 5 years of professional experience. Additional exam requirements/recommendations for international students: Required—TOEFL. *Application deadline:* For fall admission, 8/1 for domestic students; for spring admission, 12/1 for domestic students. Applications are processed on a rolling basis. Application fee: $50. *Expenses:* Tuition: Part-time $723 per credit. Required fees: $71 per credit. Tuition and fees vary according to degree level and program. *Financial support:* In 2006–07, 3 research assistantships with full and partial tuition reimbursements (averaging $5,200 per year), 1 teaching assistantship with full and partial tuition reimbursement (averaging $5,200 per year) were awarded; Federal Work-Study also available. Support available to part-time students. *Faculty research:* Sexual dysfunction, multicultural assessment. *Unit head:* Dr. Maura Krushinski, Director, 412-396-4026, Fax: 412-396-5585, E-mail: krushinski@duq.edu.

East Carolina University, Graduate School, College of Education, Department of Counselor and Adult Education, Greenville, NC 27858-4353. Offers adult education (MA Ed); counselor education (MS, Ed S). *Accreditation:* NCATE. Part-time and evening/weekend programs available. *Students:* 38 full-time (35 women), 59 part-time (50 women); includes 27 minority (24 African Americans, 2 American Indian/Alaska Native, 1 Hispanic American). Average age 32. 7 applicants, 57% accepted, 4 enrolled. In 2006, 41 master's, 3 other advanced degrees awarded. *Degree requirements:* For master's, thesis optional. *Entrance requirements:* For master's, GRE General Test or MAT, interview, minimum GPA of 2.5, bachelor's degree in related field, teaching license (MA Ed). Additional exam requirements/recommendations for international students: Required—TOEFL. *Application deadline:* For fall admission, 5/15 priority date for domestic students. Applications are processed on a rolling basis. Application fee: $50. *Financial support:* Research assistantships with partial tuition reimbursements, teaching assistantships with partial tuition reimbursements, Federal Work-Study available. Support available to part-time students. Financial award application deadline: 6/1. *Unit head:* Dr. Vivian Mott, Chair, 252-328-6177, Fax: 252-328-4368, E-mail: mottv@ecu.edu. *Application contact:* Dean of Graduate School, 252-328-6012, Fax: 252-328-6071, E-mail: gradschool@ecu.edu.

East Central University, School of Graduate Studies, Department of Human Resources, Ada, OK 74820-6899. Offers administration (MSHR); counseling (MSHR); criminal justice (MSHR); rehabilitation counseling (MSHR). *Accreditation:* CORE. Part-time and evening/weekend programs available. *Faculty:* 7 part-time/adjunct (3 women). *Students:* 83 full-time (71 women), 103 part-time (73 women); includes 54 minority (11 African Americans, 38 American Indian/Alaska Native, 1 Asian American or Pacific Islander, 4 Hispanic Americans). Average age 37. 125 applicants, 90% accepted. In 2006, 60 degrees awarded. *Degree requirements:* For master's, thesis optional. *Entrance requirements:* For master's, GRE General Test, MAT, minimum GPA of 2.5. *Application deadline:* Applications are processed on a rolling basis. Application fee: $0 ($50 for international students). *Financial support:* In 2006–07, 1 teaching assistantship was awarded. *Unit head:* Dr. Steve Turner, Chairman, 580-332-8000 Ext. 481. *Application contact:* Juanita L. Pratt, Secretary, 580-310-5708, Fax: 580-282-8691, E-mail: jpratt@ecok.edu.

Eastern Illinois University, Graduate School, College of Education and Professional Studies, Department of Counseling and Student Development, Charleston, IL 61920-3099. Offers college student affairs (MS); community counseling (MS); school counseling (MS). *Accreditation:* ACA; NCATE. Part-time and evening/weekend programs available. *Faculty:* 8 full-time (2 women). In 2006, 61 degrees awarded. *Degree requirements:* For master's, comprehensive exam. *Entrance requirements:* For master's, GRE General Test or MAT. *Application deadline:* For fall admission, 7/31 priority date for domestic students. Applications are processed on a rolling basis. Application fee: $30. *Expenses:* Tuition, state resident: part-time $169 per semester hour. Tuition, nonresident: part-time $508 per semester hour. Required fees: $60 per semester hour. *Financial support:* In 2006–07, research assistantships with tuition reimbursements (averaging $7,200 per year), 4 teaching assistantships with tuition reimbursements (averaging $7,200 per year) were awarded. *Unit head:* Dr. Rick Roberts, Chairperson, 217-581-2400, Fax: 217-581-7417, E-mail: rlroberts@eiu.edu.

Eastern Kentucky University, The Graduate School, College of Education, Department of Counseling and Educational Leadership, Richmond, KY 40475-3102. Offers human services (MA); instructional leadership (MA Ed); mental health counseling (MA); school counseling (MA Ed). *Accreditation:* ACA (one or more programs are accredited); NCATE. Part-time programs available. Postbaccalaureate distance learning degree programs offered. *Students:* 73 full-time (48 women), 581 part-time (421 women); includes 22 minority (18 African Americans, 1 American Indian/Alaska Native, 3 Hispanic Americans). Average age 24. 614 applicants, 46% accepted, 199 enrolled. In 2006, 245 degrees awarded. *Entrance requirements:* For master's, GRE General Test, minimum GPA of 2.5. Application fee: $35. *Expenses:* Tuition, state resident: full-time $5,610. Tuition, nonresident: full-time $15,910. *Financial support:* In 2006–07, 2 research assistantships (averaging $6,500 per year), teaching assistantships (averaging $6,500 per year) were awarded; career-related internships or fieldwork, Federal Work-Study, and scholarships/grants also available. Support available to part-time students. *Unit head:* Dr. Kim Naugle, Chair, 859-622-1863, Fax: 859-622-1126.

Eastern Michigan University, Graduate School, College of Education, Department of Leadership and Counseling, Programs in Counseling, Ypsilanti, MI 48197. Offers college counseling (MA); community counseling (MA); school counseling (MA); school counselor (MA); school counselor licensure (Post Master's Certificate). Part-time and evening/weekend programs available. Postbaccalaureate distance learning degree programs offered (minimal on-campus study). *Students:* 21 full-time (19 women), 129 part-time (108 women); includes 38 minority (33 African Americans, 3 Asian Americans or Pacific Islanders, 2 Hispanic Americans), 1 international. Average age 31. In 2006, 34 master's, 2 other advanced degrees awarded. *Entrance requirements:* Additional exam requirements/recommendations for international students: Required—TOEFL. *Application deadline:* For fall admission, 5/15 priority date for domestic students, 5/1 priority date for international students; for winter admission, 10/15 priority date for domestic students, 10/1 priority date for international students; for spring admission, 3/15 priority date for domestic students, 3/1 priority date for international students. Applications are processed on a rolling basis. Application fee: $35. *Expenses:* Tuition, state resident: part-time $341 per credit hour. Tuition, nonresident: full-time $16,104; part-time $671 per credit hour. Required fees: $816; $34 per credit hour. $40 per term. One-time fee: $82 full-time. Tuition and fees vary according to course level, course load, degree level and reciprocity agreements. *Financial support:* Fellowships, research assistantships with full tuition reimbursements, teaching assistantships with full tuition reimbursements, career-related internships or fieldwork, Federal Work-Study, institutionally sponsored loans, scholarships/grants, tuition waivers (partial), and unspecified assistantships available. Support available to part-time students. Financial award applicants required to submit FAFSA. *Unit head:* Dr. Jaclynn Tracy, Head, Department of Leadership and Counseling, 734-487-0255, Fax: 734-487-4608, E-mail: jackie.tracy@emich.edu.

Eastern New Mexico University, Graduate School, College of Education and Technology, Department of Educational Studies, Program in Counseling, Portales, NM 88130. Offers MA. Part-time programs available. *Faculty:* 2 full-time (1 woman). *Students:* 2 full-time (1 woman), 52 part-time (40 women); includes 20 minority (3 African Americans, 2 American Indian/Alaska Native, 15 Hispanic Americans). Average age 37. 21 applicants, 76% accepted. In 2006, 10 degrees awarded. *Degree requirements:* For master's, thesis optional. *Entrance requirements:* For master's, minimum GPA of 2.5. *Application deadline:* For fall admission, 8/20 priority date for domestic students. Applications are processed on a rolling basis. Application fee: $0. Electronic applications accepted. *Expenses:* Tuition, state resident: full-time $2,478; part-time $103 per credit hour. Tuition, nonresident: full-time $8,034; part-time $335 per credit hour. Required fees: $35 per credit hour. *Financial support:* In 2006–07, 5 research assistantships (averaging $8,200 per year), teaching assistantships (averaging $8,200 per year) were awarded; Federal Work-Study also available. Support available to part-time students. Financial award application deadline: 3/1. *Unit head:* Dr. Douglas Main, Head, 505-562-2942, E-mail: douglas.main@enmu.edu.

Eastern New Mexico University, Graduate School, College of Education and Technology, Department of Educational Studies, Program in School Counseling, Portales, NM 88130. Offers M Ed. Part-time and evening/weekend programs available. *Faculty:* 2 full-time (1 woman). *Students:* Average age 32. 2 applicants, 100% accepted. In 2006, 5 degrees awarded. *Degree requirements:* For master's, thesis optional. *Entrance requirements:* For master's, minimum GPA of 2.5. *Application deadline:* For fall admission, 8/20 priority date for domestic students. Applications are processed on a rolling basis. Application fee: $0. Electronic applications accepted. *Expenses:* Tuition, state resident: full-time $2,478; part-time $103 per credit hour. Tuition, nonresident: full-time $8,034; part-time $335 per credit hour. Required fees: $35 per credit hour. *Financial support:* Federal Work-Study available. Support available to part-time students. Financial award application deadline: 3/1. *Unit head:* Dr. Douglas Main, Head, 505-562-2942, E-mail: douglas.main@enmu.edu.

Eastern University, Programs in Counseling, Program in Educational Counseling, St. Davids, PA 19087-3696. Offers school counseling (MA); school psychology (MS). *Degree requirements:* For master's, internship. *Entrance requirements:* For master's, minimum GPA of 2.5. Additional exam requirements/recommendations for international students: Required—TOEFL.

Eastern Washington University, Graduate Studies, College of Education and Human Development, Department of Counseling, Educational, and Developmental Psychology, Program in School Counseling, Cheney, WA 99004-2431. Offers counseling psychology (MS); school counseling (MS). *Accreditation:* ACA; NCATE. *Degree requirements:* For master's, thesis or alternative, comprehensive exam. *Entrance requirements:* For master's, GRE General Test, minimum GPA of 3.0.

East Tennessee State University, School of Graduate Studies, College of Education, Department of Human Development and Learning, Johnson City, TN 37614. Offers advanced practitioner (M Ed); community agency counseling (M Ed, MA); comprehensive concentration (M Ed); counseling (M Ed, MA); early childhood education (M Ed, MA); early childhood general (M Ed); early childhood special education (M Ed); early childhood teaching (M Ed); elementary and secondary (school counseling) (M Ed, MA); marriage and family therapy (M Ed, MA); modified concentration (M Ed). *Accreditation:* ACA; NCATE. Part-time programs available. *Degree requirements:* For master's, thesis (for some programs), comprehensive exam. *Entrance requirements:* For master's, GRE General Test, minimum GPA of 3.0. Additional exam requirements/recommendations for international students: Required—TOEFL (minimum score 550 paper-based; 213 computer-based). *Faculty research:* Drug and alcohol abuse, marriage and family counseling, severe mental retardation, parenting of children with disabilities.

Edinboro University of Pennsylvania, Graduate Studies and Research, School of Education, Department of Professional Studies, Program in Counseling, Edinboro, PA 16444. Offers community counseling (MA); elementary guidance (MA); rehabilitation counseling (MA); secondary guidance (MA); student personnel services (MA). *Accreditation:* ACA; CORE. Part-time and evening/weekend programs available. *Students:* 85 full-time (68 women), 43 part-time (34 women); includes 13 minority (9 African Americans, 2 Asian Americans or Pacific Islanders, 2 Hispanic Americans). Average age 29. In 2006, 64 degrees awarded. *Degree requirements:* For master's, thesis or alternative, competency exam. *Entrance requirements:* For master's, GRE or MAT, minimum QPA of 2.5. *Application deadline:* Applications are processed on a rolling basis. Application fee: $30. Electronic applications accepted. *Expenses:* Tuition, state resident: full-time $6,048; part-time $336 per credit. Tuition, nonresident: full-time $9,678; part-time $538 per credit. Required fees: $1,849; $42 per credit. *Financial support:* In 2006–07, 26 research assistantships with full and partial tuition reimbursements (averaging $3,850 per year) were awarded; career-related internships or fieldwork, Federal Work-Study, scholarships/grants, and unspecified assistantships also available. Support available to part-time students. Financial award application deadline: 2/15; financial award applicants required to submit FAFSA. *Unit head:* Dr. Susan Norton, Head, 814-732-2260, E-mail: snorton@edinboro.edu. *Application contact:* Dr. R. Scott Baldwin, Dean, 814-732-2752, Fax: 814-732-2268, E-mail: sbaldwin@edinboro.edu.

Edinboro University of Pennsylvania, Graduate Studies and Research, School of Education, Department of Special Education and School Psychology, Program in Behavior Management, Edinboro, PA 16444. Offers Certificate. Part-time and evening/weekend programs available. *Students:* 3 full-time (2 women), 6 part-time (all women). Average age 32. In 2006, 2 degrees awarded. *Degree requirements:* For Certificate, thesis or alternative. *Entrance requirements:* For degree, GRE or MAT, minimum QPA of 2.5. *Application deadline:* Applications are processed on a rolling basis. Application fee: $30. Electronic applications accepted. *Expenses:* Tuition, state resident: full-time $6,048; part-time $336 per credit. Tuition, nonresident: full-time $9,678; part-time $538 per credit. Required fees: $1,849; $42 per credit. *Financial support:* Career-related internships or fieldwork, Federal Work-Study, and scholarships/grants available. Support available to part-time students. Financial award application deadline: 2/15; financial award applicants required to submit FAFSA. *Unit head:* Dr. Donna Murphy, Coordinator, 814-732-2417, Fax: 814-732-2268, E-mail: dmurphy@edinboro.edu. *Application contact:* Dr. R. Scott Baldwin, Dean, 814-732-2752, Fax: 814-732-2268, E-mail: sbaldwin@edinboro.edu.

Emporia State University, School of Graduate Studies, The Teachers College, Department of Counselor Education and Rehabilitation Programs, Program in Counselor Education, Emporia, KS 66801-5087. Offers counselor education (MS); school counseling (MS). *Accreditation:* ACA; NCATE. Part-time programs available. *Students:* 5 full-time (all women), 65 part-time (56 women); includes 5 minority (2 African Americans, 1 Asian American or Pacific Islander, 2 Hispanic Americans), 1 international. 16 applicants, 63% accepted, 9 enrolled. In 2006, 18 degrees awarded. *Degree requirements:* For master's, comprehensive exam or thesis, practicum. *Entrance requirements:* For master's, GRE or MAT, graduate essay exam, appropriate bachelor's degree, interview, letters of recommendation. *Application deadline:* For fall admission, 8/15 priority date for domestic students. Applications are processed on a rolling basis. Application fee: $30 ($75 for international students). Electronic applications accepted. *Expenses:* Tuition, state resident: full-time $3,438; part-time $143 per credit hour. Tuition, nonresident: full-time $10,398; part-time $433 per credit hour. Required fees: $724; $44 per credit hour. *Financial support:* Career-related internships or fieldwork, Federal Work-Study, institutionally sponsored loans, health care benefits, and unspecified assistantships available. Financial award application deadline: 3/15; financial award applicants required to submit FAFSA. *Application contact:* Dr. Colleen Etzbach, Graduate Co-Coordinator, 620-341-5220, E-mail: cetzbach@emporia.edu.

Evangel University, School Counseling Program, Springfield, MO 65802-2191. Offers MS. Part-time and evening/weekend programs available. *Faculty:* 1 (woman) full-time, 1 (woman) part-time/adjunct. *Students:* 2 full-time (1 woman), 18 part-time (16 women). Average age 29. 6 applicants, 83% accepted, 5 enrolled. In 2006, 1 master's awarded. *Degree requirements:* For master's, thesis optional. *Entrance requirements:* For master's, MAT, teaching certificate. Additional exam requirements/recommendations for international students: Required—TOEFL (minimum score 550 paper-based; 213 computer-based). *Application deadline:* For fall admission, 7/15 priority date for domestic and international students; for spring admission, 11/15 priority date for domestic and international students. Application fee: $25. *Financial support:* In 2006–07, 4 students received support. Career-related internships or fieldwork, institutionally sponsored loans, scholarships/grants, and unspecified assistantships available. Support available to part-time students. Financial award application deadline: 3/1; financial award applicants required to submit FAFSA. *Unit head:* Debbie Bicket, Chair, 417-865-2815 Ext. 8618, Fax: 417-575-5484, E-mail: bicketd@evangel.edu. *Application contact:* Charity H. Fahlstrom, Director of Graduate and Professional Studies Admissions, 417-865-2811 Ext. 1227, Fax: 417-575-5484.

Fairfield University, Graduate School of Education and Allied Professions, Department of Counselor Education, Fairfield, CT 06824-5195. Offers community counseling (MA); counselor education (CAS); school counseling (MA). *Accreditation:* ACA (one or more programs are accredited). Part-time and evening/weekend programs available. *Faculty:* 3 full-time (all women), 3 part-time/adjunct (2 women). *Students:* 28 full-time (27 women), 71 part-time (63 women). Average age 30. 26 applicants, 42% accepted, 8 enrolled. In 2006, 16 master's, 1 other advanced degree awarded. *Degree requirements:* For master's, thesis or alternative, comprehensive exam. *Entrance requirements:* For master's, PRAXIS I (PPST), minimum QPA of 2.67, 2 recommendations, resumé. Additional exam requirements/recommendations for international students: Required—TOEFL (minimum score 550 paper-based; 213 computer-based; 79 iBT). *Application deadline:* For fall admission, 3/1 for domestic students; for spring admission, 11/1 for domestic students. Application fee: $55. Electronic applications accepted. *Financial support:* Career-related internships or fieldwork, tuition waivers (partial), and unspecified assistantships available. Financial award applicants required to submit FAFSA. *Unit head:* Dr. Virginia A. Kelly, Chair, 203-254-4000 Ext. 3228, Fax: 203-254-4047, E-mail: vkelly@mail.fairfield.edu. *Application contact:* Marianne Gumpper, Director of Graduate and Continuing Studies Admissions, 203-254-4184, Fax: 203-254-4073, E-mail: gradadmis@mail.fairfield.edu.

Fitchburg State College, Division of Graduate and Continuing Education, Programs in Counseling, Fitchburg, MA 01420-2697. Offers elementary school guidance counseling (MS); marriage and family therapy (Certificate); mental health counseling (MS); secondary school guidance counseling (MS). *Accreditation:* NCATE. Part-time and evening/weekend programs available. *Students:* 17 full-time (14 women), 77 part-time (64 women); includes 4 minority (1 Asian American or Pacific Islander, 3 Hispanic Americans), 4 international. Average age 32. 26 applicants, 85% accepted, 19 enrolled. In 2006, 32 degrees awarded. *Entrance requirements:* For master's, GRE General Test or MAT, letters of recommendation, resumé; for Certificate, master's degree. Additional exam requirements/recommendations for international students: Required—TOEFL (minimum score 550 paper-based; 213 computer-based; 79 iBT). *Application deadline:* Applications are processed on a rolling basis. Application fee: $25 ($50 for international students). *Expenses:* Tuition, state resident: part-time $150 per credit. Tuition, nonresident: part-time $150 per credit. Required fees: $90 per credit. *Financial support:* In 2006–07, research assistantships with partial tuition reimbursements (averaging $5,500 per year); Federal Work-Study, scholarships/grants, and unspecified assistantships also available.

Counselor Education

Fitchburg State College (continued)
Support available to part-time students. Financial award application deadline: 3/1; financial award applicants required to submit FAFSA. *Unit head:* Dr. John Hancock, Chair, 978-665-3604, Fax: 978-665-3658, E-mail: gce@fsc.edu. *Application contact:* Director of Admissions, 978-665-3144, Fax: 978-665-4540, E-mail: admissions@fsc.edu.

Florida Agricultural and Mechanical University, Division of Graduate Studies, Research, and Continuing Education, College of Education, Department of Educational Leadership and Human Services, Tallahassee, FL 32307-3200. Offers administration and supervision (M Ed, MS Ed, PhD); adult education (M Ed, MS Ed); educational leadership (PhD); guidance and counseling (M Ed, MS Ed). *Accreditation:* NCATE. *Degree requirements:* For master's, thesis (for some programs); for doctorate, thesis/dissertation. *Entrance requirements:* For master's, GRE General Test, minimum GPA of 3.0. Additional exam requirements/recommendations for international students: Required—TOEFL.

Florida Atlantic University, College of Education, Department of Counselor Education, Boca Raton, FL 33431-0991. Offers counselor education (M Ed); family counseling (Ed S); mental health counseling (M Ed, Ed S); rehabilitation counseling (M Ed); school counseling (Ed S). *Accreditation:* ACA; NCATE. Part-time and evening/weekend programs available. *Faculty:* 10 full-time (3 women), 13 part-time/adjunct (9 women). *Students:* 55 full-time (50 women), 90 part-time (76 women); includes 52 minority (21 African Americans, 5 Asian Americans or Pacific Islanders, 26 Hispanic Americans), 3 international. Average age 35. 106 applicants, 44% accepted, 39 enrolled. In 2006, 42 master's, 7 Ed Ss awarded. *Degree requirements:* For master's, registration; for Ed S, departmental qualifying exam. *Entrance requirements:* For master's, GRE General Test, minimum GPA of 3.0 during previous 2 years; for Ed S, GRE General Test, minimum graduate GPA of 3.25. Additional exam requirements/recommendations for international students: Required—TOEFL. *Application deadline:* For fall admission, 2/1 for domestic and international students; for spring admission, 7/1 for domestic and international students. Applications are processed on a rolling basis. Application fee: $30. *Expenses:* Tuition, area resident: Full-time $4,394. Tuition, nonresident: full-time $16,441. *Financial support:* In 2006–07, 6 students received support, including 2 research assistantships with partial tuition reimbursements available; teaching assistantships, career-related internships or fieldwork, scholarships/grants, and unspecified assistantships also available. *Faculty research:* Brief therapy, psychological type, marriage and family counseling, international programs, integrated services. *Unit head:* Dr. Irene Johnson, Chair, 561-297-3602, Fax: 561-297-2309. *Application contact:* Susan Foley, Senior Secretary, 561-297-3602, Fax: 561-297-2309, E-mail: cnslred@fau.edu.

Florida Gulf Coast University, College of Education, Program in Counselor Education, Fort Myers, FL 33965-6565. Offers M Ed, MA. *Accreditation:* ACA. Part-time and evening/weekend programs available. *Faculty:* 31 full-time (21 women), 30 part-time/adjunct (24 women). *Students:* 38 full-time (32 women), 16 part-time (13 women); includes 5 minority (all Hispanic Americans), 1 international. Average age 34. 36 applicants, 83% accepted, 18 enrolled. In 2006, 10 degrees awarded. *Degree requirements:* For master's, thesis or alternative. *Entrance requirements:* For master's, GRE General Test, MAT, minimum GPA of 3.0. Additional exam requirements/recommendations for international students: Required—TOEFL (minimum score 550 paper-based; 213 computer-based). *Application deadline:* For fall admission, 7/1 priority date for domestic students; for spring admission, 10/15 for domestic students. Applications are processed on a rolling basis. Application fee: $30. Electronic applications accepted. *Expenses:* Tuition, state resident: full-time $4,326. Tuition, nonresident: full-time $18,523. Required fees: $1,211. One-time fee: $5 full-time. *Faculty research:* Sexuality, confidentiality, school counselor roles, distance learning, exceptional students. *Unit head:* Dr. Pat Wachholz, Associate Dean, 239-590-7808, Fax: 239-590-7801, E-mail: wachhol@fgcu.edu.

Florida International University, College of Education, Department of Educational and Psychological Studies, Program in Counselor Education, Miami, FL 33199. Offers mental health counseling (MS); rehabilitation counseling (MS); school counseling (MS). *Accreditation:* ACA; NCATE. Part-time and evening/weekend programs available. *Faculty:* 3 full-time (2 women). *Students:* 56 full-time (53 women), 46 part-time (38 women); includes 78 minority (21 African Americans, 57 Hispanic Americans). Average age 31. 73 applicants, 40% accepted, 28 enrolled. *Entrance requirements:* For master's, General Knowledge test, College Level Academic Skills Test, GRE or PRAXIS (school counseling track), minimum GPA of 3.0, interview. Additional exam requirements/recommendations for international students: Required—TOEFL (minimum score 550 paper-based; 213 computer-based; 80 iBT), IELTS (minimum score 6). *Application deadline:* For fall admission, 6/1 priority date for domestic students, 4/1 for international students; for winter admission, 10/1 priority date for domestic students, 9/1 for international students; for spring admission, 3/1 priority date for domestic students, 2/1 for international students. Applications are processed on a rolling basis. Application fee: $30. Electronic applications accepted. *Expenses:* Tuition, state resident: part-time $249 per credit hour. Tuition, nonresident: part-time $753 per credit hour. Tuition and fees vary according to program. *Unit head:* Dr. Maureen Kenny, Program Leader, 305-348-3506, E-mail: kennym@fiu.edu. *Application contact:* Marisa Salazar, Student Recruiter, 305-348-3002, Fax: 305-348-3227, E-mail: marisa.salazar@fiu.edu.

Florida State University, Graduate Studies, College of Education, Department of Educational Psychology and Learning Systems, Tallahassee, FL 32306. Offers counseling/school psychology (PhD); educational psychology (MS, PhD), including learning and cognition, sports psychology; instructional systems (MS, PhD, Ed S), including instructional systems, open and distance learning (MS); measurement and statistics (MS, PhD); psychological services (MS, PhD, Ed S); school psychology (MS, Ed S). *Faculty:* 19 full-time (8 women), 9 part-time/adjunct (3 women). *Students:* 175 full-time (123 women), 164 part-time (102 women); includes 97 minority (35 African Americans, 42 Asian Americans or Pacific Islanders, 20 Hispanic Americans). 337 applicants, 47% accepted, 89 enrolled. In 2006, 70 master's, 16 doctorates, 29 other advanced degrees awarded. *Degree requirements:* For master's and Ed S, thesis optional; for doctorate, thesis/dissertation, comprehensive exam. *Entrance requirements:* For master's, doctorate, and Ed S, GRE General Test, minimum GPA of 3.0. *Application deadline:* For fall admission, 7/1 priority date for domestic students; for spring admission, 11/1 for domestic students. Applications are processed on a rolling basis. Application fee: $30. *Expenses:* Tuition, state resident: full-time $5,822; part-time $243 per credit hour. Tuition, nonresident: full-time $20,976; part-time $874 per credit hour. Tuition and fees vary according to program. *Financial support:* In 2006–07, 4 fellowships, 62 research assistantships, 30 teaching assistantships were awarded; career-related internships or fieldwork also available. Financial award applicants required to submit FAFSA. *Unit head:* Dr. Gary Peterson, Chair, 850-644-1781, Fax: 850-644-8776, E-mail: peterson@coe.fsu.edu. *Application contact:* Sally Gadson, Program Assistant, 850-644-8046, Fax: 850-644-5067, E-mail: gadson@coe.fsu.edu.

Fordham University, Graduate School of Education, Division of Psychological and Educational Services, New York, NY 10023. Offers counseling and personnel services (MSE, Adv C); counseling psychology (PhD); educational psychology (MSE, PhD); school psychology (PhD); urban and urban bilingual school psychology (Adv C). *Accreditation:* APA (one or more programs are accredited); NCATE. *Faculty:* 18 full-time (11 women), 23 part-time/adjunct (14 women). *Students:* 118 full-time (90 women), 272 part-time (206 women); includes 106 minority (39 African Americans, 20 Asian Americans or Pacific Islanders, 47 Hispanic Americans), 1 international. Average age 30. 503 applicants, 58% accepted, 102 enrolled. In 2006, 117 master's, 18 doctorates, 6 other advanced degrees awarded. *Degree requirements:* For doctorate, thesis/dissertation. *Entrance requirements:* For doctorate, GRE General Test. Application fee: $65. *Financial support:* Applicants required to submit FAFSA. *Unit head:* Dr. Mitch Rabinowitz, Chairman, 212-636-6461.

Fort Hays State University, Graduate School, College of Education and Technology, Department of Educational Administration and Counseling, Program in Counseling, Hays, KS 67601-4099. Offers MS. *Accreditation:* NCATE. Part-time programs available. *Faculty:* 9 full-time (2 women). *Students:* 11 full-time (8 women), 40 part-time (33 women); includes 3 minority (1 American Indian/Alaska Native, 2 Hispanic Americans). Average age 36. 12 applicants, 67% accepted. In 2006, 11 degrees awarded. *Degree requirements:* For master's, thesis or alternative, comprehensive exam. *Entrance requirements:* For master's, GRE General Test or MAT, minimum undergraduate GPA of 3.0 in last 60 hours. Additional exam requirements/recommendations for international students: Required—TOEFL (minimum score 550 paper-based; 213 computer-based). *Application deadline:* For fall admission, 7/1 priority date for domestic students. Applications are processed on a rolling basis. Application fee: $35. Electronic applications accepted. *Financial support:* In 2006–07, 2 teaching assistantships (averaging $5,000 per year) were awarded; research assistantships. *Faculty research:* Career education, evaluation and plans, counseling the disabled, marriage and family parenting, underemployment and work in the family. *Unit head:* Dr. Warren Shaffer, Coordinator, 785-628-4413, E-mail: wshaffer@fhsu.edu.

Fort Valley State University, College of Graduate Studies and Extended Education, Department of Counseling Psychology, Program in Guidance and Counseling, Fort Valley, GA 31030-4313. Offers MS, Ed S. Part-time programs available. *Degree requirements:* For master's, thesis optional. *Entrance requirements:* For master's and Ed S, GRE General Test or MAT.

Freed-Hardeman University, Program in Counseling, Henderson, TN 38340-2399. Offers MS. Part-time and evening/weekend programs available. *Faculty:* 8 full-time (2 women), 4 part-time/adjunct (3 women). *Students:* 23 full-time (17 women), 44 part-time (28 women); includes 17 minority (15 African Americans, 1 Asian American or Pacific Islander, 1 Hispanic American). Average age 31. In 2006, 25 degrees awarded. *Degree requirements:* For master's, practicum. *Entrance requirements:* For master's, GRE General Test or MAT. Additional exam requirements/recommendations for international students: Required—TOEFL (minimum score 500 paper-based; 173 computer-based). *Application deadline:* For fall admission, 8/1 priority date for domestic students; for spring admission, 12/1 for domestic students. Applications are processed on a rolling basis. Application fee: $32. *Expenses:* Tuition: Part-time $334 per credit hour. Required fees: $10 per credit hour. *Financial support:* Career-related internships or fieldwork, Federal Work-Study, tuition waivers (partial), and unspecified assistantships available. Support available to part-time students. Financial award application deadline: 8/1; financial award applicants required to submit FAFSA. *Unit head:* Dr. Mike Cravens, Graduate Director, 731-989-6666, Fax: 731-989-6065, E-mail: mcravens@fhu.edu.

Freed-Hardeman University, Program in Education, Henderson, TN 38340-2399. Offers curriculum and instruction (M Ed); school counseling (M Ed); school leadership (Ed S). *Accreditation:* NCATE. Part-time and evening/weekend programs available. *Faculty:* 9 full-time (3 women), 6 part-time/adjunct (4 women). *Students:* 51 full-time (40 women), 286 part-time (235 women); includes 203 minority (202 African Americans, 1 Asian American or Pacific Islander), 2 international. Average age 34. In 2006, 78 master's, 24 other advanced degrees awarded. *Degree requirements:* For master's, thesis optional; for Ed S, thesis. *Entrance requirements:* For master's, GRE General Test or NTE; for Ed S, 3 years of teaching experience. Additional exam requirements/recommendations for international students: Required—TOEFL (minimum score 500 paper-based; 173 computer-based). *Application deadline:* For fall admission, 8/1 for domestic students; for spring admission, 12/1 for domestic students. Applications are processed on a rolling basis. Application fee: $32. *Expenses:* Tuition: Part-time $334 per credit hour. Required fees: $10 per credit hour. *Financial support:* Career-related internships or fieldwork, Federal Work-Study, tuition waivers (partial), and unspecified assistantships available. Support available to part-time students. Financial award application deadline: 8/1; financial award applicants required to submit FAFSA. *Unit head:* Dr. Elizabeth Saunders, Graduate Director, 731-989-6082, Fax: 731-989-6065, E-mail: esaunders@fhu.edu.

Fresno Pacific University, Graduate Programs, Programs in Education, Fresno, CA 93702-4709. Offers administration (MA Ed), including administrative services; foundations, curriculum and teaching (MA Ed), including curriculum and teaching, school library and information technology; language, literacy, and culture (MA Ed), including bilingual/cross-cultural education, language development, multilingual contexts, reading; mathematics/science/computer education (MA Ed), including educational technology, integrated mathematics/science education, mathematics education; pupil personnel services (MA Ed), including school counseling, school psychology; special education (MA Ed), including mild/moderate, moderate/severe, physical and health impairments. Part-time and evening/weekend programs available. *Faculty:* 12 full-time (5 women), 19 part-time/adjunct (9 women). *Students:* 73 full-time (59 women), 399 part-time (295 women); includes 136 minority (9 African Americans, 5 American Indian/Alaska Native, 12 Asian Americans or Pacific Islanders, 110 Hispanic Americans), 2 international. Average age 39. 124 applicants, 73% accepted, 10 enrolled. In 2006, 128 degrees awarded. *Degree requirements:* For master's, thesis (for some programs), registration. *Entrance requirements:* For master's, interview; GMAT, GRE, MAT, or 6 units of course work with a faculty recommendation. Additional exam requirements/recommendations for international students: Required—TOEFL (minimum score 550 paper-based; 213 computer-based). *Application deadline:* For fall admission, 7/15 for domestic and international students; for spring admission, 11/15 for domestic and international students. Applications are processed on a rolling basis. Application fee: $90. Electronic applications accepted. *Expenses:* Tuition: Full-time $7,470; part-time $415 per credit. *Financial support:* In 2006–07, 260 students received support. Career-related internships or fieldwork, scholarships/grants, and tuition waivers (full and partial) available. Support available to part-time students. Financial award applicants required to submit FAFSA.

Fresno Pacific University, Graduate Programs, Programs in Education, Division of Pupil Personnel Services, Program in School Counseling, Fresno, CA 93702-4709. Offers MA Ed. Part-time and evening/weekend programs available. *Students:* 29 full-time (23 women), 19 part-time (12 women); includes 25 minority (3 African Americans, 2 Asian Americans or Pacific Islanders, 20 Hispanic Americans). Average age 37. 8 applicants, 50% accepted, 1 enrolled. In 2006, 5 degrees awarded. *Degree requirements:* For master's, thesis or alternative, registration. *Entrance requirements:* Additional exam requirements/recommendations for international students: Required—TOEFL (minimum score 550 paper-based; 213 computer-based). *Application deadline:* For fall admission, 7/15 for domestic and international students; for spring admission, 11/15 for domestic and international students. Applications are processed on a rolling basis. Application fee: $90. *Expenses:* Tuition: Full-time $7,470; part-time $415 per credit. *Financial support:* In 2006–07, 30 students received support. Scholarships/grants and tuition waivers (full and partial) available. Support available to part-time students. Financial award applicants required to submit FAFSA.

Frostburg State University, Graduate School, College of Education, Department of Educational Professions, Program in School Counseling, Frostburg, MD 21532-1099. Offers M Ed. *Accreditation:* NCATE. Part-time and evening/weekend programs available. *Degree requirements:* For master's, thesis or alternative, comprehensive exam. *Entrance requirements:* For master's, GRE General Test or MAT, interview. Electronic applications accepted.

Gallaudet University, The Graduate School, School of Education and Human Services, Department of Counseling, Washington, DC 20002-3625. Offers community counseling (MA); mental health counseling (MA); school counseling (MA). *Accreditation:* ACA; NCATE. *Degree requirements:* For master's, thesis optional. *Entrance requirements:* For master's, GRE General Test or MAT.

Gannon University, School of Graduate Studies, College of Humanities, Business, and Education, School of Education, Program in Advanced Counselor Studies, Erie, PA 16541-0001. Offers Certificate. Part-time and evening/weekend programs available. *Students:* Average age 35. 1 applicant, 100% accepted, 1 enrolled. *Entrance requirements:* Additional exam requirements/recommendations for international students: Required—TOEFL (minimum score 500 paper-based; 173 computer-based). *Application deadline:* Applications are processed on a rolling basis. Application fee: $25. *Expenses:* Tuition: Full-time $12,240; part-time $680 per credit. Required fees: $496; $16 per credit. Tuition and fees vary according to course load, degree level, campus/location and program. *Financial support:* Application deadline: 7/1; *Unit* *head:* Debra Meszaros, Director of Graduate Recruitment, 814-871-5819, Fax: 814-871-5827, E-mail: cfal@gannon.edu. *Application contact:* Debra Meszaros, Director of Graduate Recruitment, 814-871-5819, Fax: 814-871-5827, E-mail: cfal@gannon.edu.

Gannon University, School of Graduate Studies, College of Humanities, Business, and Education, School of Education, Program in School Counselor Preparation, Erie, PA 16541-0001. Offers Certificate. Part-time and evening/weekend programs available. *Entrance requirements:* Additional exam requirements/recommendations for international students: Required—TOEFL (minimum score 500 paper-based; 173 computer-based). *Application deadline:* Applications are processed on a rolling basis. Application fee: $25. *Expenses:* Tuition: Full-time $12,240; part-time $680 per credit. Required fees: $496; $16 per credit. Tuition and fees vary according to course load, degree level, campus/location and program. *Financial support:* Application deadline: 7/1; *Application contact:* Debra Meszaros, Director of Graduate Recruitment, 814-871-5819, Fax: 814-871-5827, E-mail: cfal@gannon.edu.

Gannon University, School of Graduate Studies, College of Humanities, Business, and Education, School of Humanities, Program in Community Counseling, Erie, PA 16541-0001. Offers MS, Certificate. Part-time and evening/weekend programs available. *Students:* 32 full-time (26 women), 25 part-time (21 women); includes 4 minority (3 African Americans, 1 Hispanic American). Average age 29. 42 applicants, 62% accepted, 19 enrolled. In 2006, 15 degrees awarded. *Degree requirements:* For master's, thesis, comprehensive exam. *Entrance requirements:* For master's, MAT, interview. Additional exam requirements/recommendations for international students: Required—TOEFL (minimum score 500 paper-based; 173 computer-based). *Application deadline:* Applications are processed on a rolling basis. Application fee: $25. *Expenses:* Tuition: Full-time $12,240; part-time $680 per credit. Required fees: $496; $16 per credit. Tuition and fees vary according to course load, degree level, campus/location and program. *Financial support:* Career-related internships or fieldwork, Federal Work-Study, and unspecified assistantships available. Support available to part-time students. Financial award application deadline: 7/1; financial award applicants required to submit FAFSA. *Unit head:* Dr. David Tobin, Director, 814-871-7537, E-mail: tobin001@gannon.edu. *Application contact:* Debra Meszaros, Director of Graduate Recruitment, 814-871-5819, Fax: 814-871-5827, E-mail: cfal@gannon.edu.

Geneva College, Program in Counseling, Beaver Falls, PA 15010-3599. Offers marriage and family (MA); mental health (MA); school counseling (MA). Part-time and evening/weekend programs available. *Degree requirements:* For master's, internship. *Entrance requirements:* For master's, GRE General Test or MAT, minimum GPA of 3.0, letters of recommendation, faith statement, 12 credits in undergraduate psychology. Additional exam requirements/recommendations for international students: Required—TOEFL. Electronic applications accepted.

George Fox University, School of Education, Graduate Department of Counseling, Newberg, OR 97132-2697. Offers counseling (MA); marriage and family therapy (MA, Certificate); school counseling (MA); school psychology (MS, Certificate); trauma (Certificate). Part-time programs available. *Faculty:* 11 full-time (5 women), 12 part-time/adjunct (9 women). *Students:* 122 full-time (93 women), 118 part-time (97 women); includes 22 minority (3 African Americans, 3 American Indian/Alaska Native, 5 Asian Americans or Pacific Islanders, 11 Hispanic Americans), 1 international. Average age 36. 91 applicants, 67% accepted, 53 enrolled. In 2006, 80 master's, 4 other advanced degrees awarded. *Degree requirements:* For master's, thesis optional. *Application deadline:* For fall admission, 7/1 for domestic students; for spring admission, 10/15 for domestic students. Applications are processed on a rolling basis. Application fee: $40. Electronic applications accepted. *Expenses:* Contact institution. *Financial support:* Career-related internships or fieldwork available. *Unit head:* Dr. Karin Jordan, Director, 503-554-6141, E-mail: kjordan@georgefox.edu. *Application contact:* Carol Namburi, Admissions Counselor, 800-631-0921, Fax: 503-554-6111, E-mail: counseling@georgefox.edu.

George Mason University, Graduate School of Education, Program in Counseling and Development, Fairfax, VA 22030. Offers M Ed. *Accreditation:* NCATE. Part-time and evening/weekend programs available. *Faculty:* 108 full-time (70 women), 193 part-time/adjunct (140 women). *Students:* 39 full-time (34 women), 122 part-time (110 women); includes 35 minority (20 African Americans, 6 Asian Americans or Pacific Islanders, 9 Hispanic Americans), 4 international. Average age 32. 97 applicants, 35% accepted, 24 enrolled. In 2006, 67 degrees awarded. *Degree requirements:* For master's, thesis (for some programs). *Entrance requirements:* For master's, interview, minimum GPA of 3.0 in last 60 hours of course work, 1 year of related work experience. *Application deadline:* For fall admission, 5/1 for domestic students; for spring admission, 11/1 for domestic students. Application fee: $60 ($75 for international students). Electronic applications accepted. *Expenses:* Tuition, state resident: full-time $5,724; part-time $238 per credit. Tuition, nonresident: full-time $16,896; part-time $704 per credit. Required fees: $1,656; $69 per credit. *Financial support:* Fellowships, research assistantships, teaching assistantships, career-related internships or fieldwork available. Support available to part-time students. Financial award application deadline: 3/1; financial award applicants required to submit FAFSA. *Unit head:* Dr. Carol Kaffenberger, Coordinator, 703-993-3161, Fax: 703-993-2013.

The George Washington University, Graduate School of Education and Human Development, Department of Counseling/Human and Organizational Studies, Program in Counseling, Washington, DC 20052. Offers PhD, Ed S. *Accreditation:* ACA (one or more programs are accredited); NCATE. Part-time and evening/weekend programs available. *Degree requirements:* For doctorate, thesis/dissertation, comprehensive exam. *Entrance requirements:* For doctorate, GRE General Test, interview, minimum GPA of 3.3; for Ed S, GRE General Test or MAT, minimum GPA of 3.3. *Faculty research:* Values in counseling, religion and counseling.

The George Washington University, Graduate School of Education and Human Development, Department of Counseling/Human and Organizational Studies, Programs in Counseling: School, Community and Rehabilitation, Washington, DC 20052. Offers MA Ed. *Accreditation:* ACA; CORE; NCATE. *Degree requirements:* For master's, comprehensive exam. *Entrance requirements:* For master's, GRE General Test or MAT, minimum GPA of 2.75. *Faculty research:* Adjustment to disability, head injury rehabilitation, cross-cultural counseling.

Georgia Southern University, Jack N. Averitt College of Graduate Studies, College of Education, Department of Leadership, Technology, and Human Development, Program in Counselor Education, Statesboro, GA 30460. Offers M Ed, Ed S. *Accreditation:* NCATE. Part-time and evening/weekend programs available. *Students:* 58 full-time (48 women), 73 part-time (69 women); includes 47 minority (45 African Americans, 2 Hispanic Americans). Average age 30. 36 applicants, 100% accepted, 27 enrolled. In 2006, 43 master's, 10 other advanced degrees awarded. *Degree requirements:* For master's, exams. *Entrance requirements:* For master's, GRE General Test or MAT, minimum GPA of 2.5, letters of recommendation, interview; for Ed S, GRE General Test or MAT, minimum graduate GPA of 3.25, letters of recommendation. Additional exam requirements/recommendations for international students: Required—TOEFL (minimum score 550 paper-based; 213 computer-based; 80 iBT). *Application deadline:* For fall admission, 3/15 priority date for domestic students, 3/1 for international students; for spring admission, 10/1 priority date for domestic students, 10/1 for international students. Applications are processed on a rolling basis. Application fee: $50. Electronic applications accepted. *Financial support:* In 2006–07, 83 students received support, including research assistantships with partial tuition reimbursements available (averaging $5,500 per year), teaching assistantships with partial tuition reimbursements available (averaging $5,500 per year); career-related internships or fieldwork, Federal Work-Study, scholarships/grants, tuition waivers (partial), and unspecified assistantships also available. Support available to part-time students. Financial award application deadline: 4/15; financial award applicants required to submit FAFSA. *Faculty research:* School counseling, test development, gender equity, career counseling. *Unit head:* Dr. Leon Spencer, Coordinator, 912-681-5917, Fax: 912-486-7104, E-mail: lespence@georgiasouthern.edu. *Application contact:* Office of Graduate Admissions, 912-681-5384, Fax: 912-681-0740, E-mail: gradadmissions@georgiasouthern.edu.

Georgia State University, College of Education, Department of Counseling and Psychological Services, Program in Professional Counseling, Atlanta, GA 30303-3083. Offers counseling psychology (PhD); counselor education and practice (PhD); professional counseling (MS, Ed S). *Accreditation:* ACA (one or more programs are accredited); APA (one or more programs are accredited). *Students:* 148 full-time (132 women), 128 part-time (105 women); includes 66 minority (52 African Americans, 4 American Indian/Alaska Native, 6 Asian Americans or Pacific Islanders, 4 Hispanic Americans), 10 international. Average age 32. 147 applicants, 67% accepted. In 2006, 63 master's, 9 doctorates, 8 other advanced degrees awarded. *Degree requirements:* For master's, comprehensive exam; for doctorate, thesis/dissertation, comprehensive exam. *Entrance requirements:* For master's, GRE General Test, minimum GPA of 2.5; for doctorate, GRE General Test, minimum GPA of 3.3; for Ed S, GRE General Test, minimum graduate GPA of 3.25. Application fee: $25. *Financial support:* Scholarships/grants available. Financial award application deadline: 4/1. *Faculty research:* Dropout prevention, school reform, school violence, lifestyle correlates, stress management. *Unit head:* Dr. Joanna White, Chairperson, Department of Counseling and Psychological Services, 404-651-3427.

Georgia State University, College of Education, Department of Counseling and Psychological Services, Program in School Counseling, Atlanta, GA 30303-3083. Offers M Ed, Ed S. *Accreditation:* ACA (one or more programs are accredited); NCATE. *Students:* 25 full-time (23 women), 63 part-time (58 women); includes 22 minority (17 African Americans, 2 American Indian/Alaska Native, 1 Asian American or Pacific Islander, 2 Hispanic Americans), 1 international. Average age 34. 85 applicants, 46% accepted. In 2006, 21 degrees awarded. *Degree requirements:* For master's, comprehensive exam. *Entrance requirements:* For master's, GRE General Test, minimum GPA of 2.5; for Ed S, GRE General Test, minimum graduate GPA of 3.25. *Application deadline:* For fall admission, 4/15 for domestic students. Application fee: $25. *Financial support:* Scholarships/grants available. Financial award application deadline: 4/1. *Faculty research:* School reform, play therapy and counseling through play, school violence, school consolation. *Unit head:* Dr. Joanna White, Chairperson, Department of Counseling and Psychological Services, 404-651-3427.

Gwynedd-Mercy College, School of Education, Gwynedd Valley, PA 19437-0901. Offers educational administration (MS); master teacher (MS); reading (MS); school counseling (MS); special education (MS). Part-time and evening/weekend programs available. *Faculty:* 9 full-time (5 women), 37 part-time/adjunct (17 women). *Students:* 92 full-time (66 women), 464 part-time (374 women); includes 52 minority (49 African Americans, 3 Hispanic Americans), 1 international. Average age 34. In 2006, 160 degrees awarded. *Degree requirements:* For master's, thesis, internship, practicum. *Entrance requirements:* For master's, GRE or MAT; PPST Praxis Test, minimum GPA of 3.0. *Application deadline:* Applications are processed on a rolling basis. Application fee: $25. *Expenses:* Tuition: Part-time $525 per credit hour. *Financial support:* In 2006–07, 2 research assistantships were awarded; career-related internships or fieldwork, Federal Work-Study, tuition waivers (full and partial), and unspecified assistantships also available. Financial award applicants required to submit FAFSA. *Faculty research:* Learning and the brain, reading literacy, ethics and moral judgment, leadership, teaching and multicultural education. *Unit head:* Dr. Lorraine Cavaliere, EdD, Dean, 215-641-5549, Fax: 215-542-4695, E-mail: cavaliere.l@gmc.edu. *Application contact:* Marian Watkins, Graduate Program Coordinator, 215-641-5561, Fax: 215-542-4695, E-mail: watkins.m@gmc.edu.

Hampton University, Graduate College, Department of Education, Program in Counseling, Hampton, VA 23668. Offers college student development (MA); community agency counseling (MA). *Accreditation:* NCATE. Part-time and evening/weekend programs available. *Entrance requirements:* For master's, GRE General Test.

Harding University, College of Education, Searcy, AR 72149-0001. Offers advanced studies in teaching and learning (M Ed); art (MSE); behavioral science (MSE); Bible and religion (MSE); counseling (MS, Ed S); early childhood education (M Ed); early childhood special education (M Ed, MSE); education (MSE); educational leadership (M Ed, Ed S); elementary education (M Ed); English (MSE); family and consumer science (MSE); French (MSE); history/social science (MSE); kinesiology (MSE); math (MSE); physical science (MSE); reading (M Ed); secondary education (M Ed); Spanish (MSE); special education licensure (M Ed); teaching (MAT). *Accreditation:* NCATE. Part-time programs available. *Faculty:* 8 full-time (2 women), 45 part-time/adjunct (30 women). *Students:* 153 full-time (123 women), 469 part-time (341 women); includes 72 minority (63 African Americans, 4 American Indian/Alaska Native, 1 Asian American or Pacific Islander, 4 Hispanic Americans), 9 international. Average age 35. 175 applicants, 90% accepted, 147 enrolled. In 2006, 241 degrees awarded. *Degree requirements:* For master's, portfolio(s), thesis optional; for Ed S, portfolio, specialist project. *Entrance requirements:* For master's, GRE, MAT, PRAXIS; for Ed S, MAT or GRE. Additional exam requirements/recommendations for international students: Required—TOEFL (minimum score 550 paper-based). *Application deadline:* For fall admission, 8/1 for domestic and international students; for spring admission, 1/1 for domestic and international students. Applications are processed on a rolling basis. Application fee: $35. *Expenses:* Tuition: Part-time $455 per semester hour. Required fees: $20 per semester hour. Tuition and fees vary according to course load. *Financial support:* Scholarships/grants and unspecified assistantships available. Support available to part-time students. *Faculty research:* Reading, comprehension, school violence, educational technology, behavior, college choice, differentiated instruction, brain based teaching. *Unit head:* Pat Bashaw, Chair, 501-279-4183, Fax: 501-279-4051, E-mail: pbashaw@harding.edu.

Hardin-Simmons University, Graduate School, Irvin School of Education, Department of Counseling and Human Development, Abilene, TX 79698-0001. Offers M Ed. Part-time programs available. *Faculty:* 2 full-time (0 women), 2 part-time/adjunct (1 woman). *Students:* 27 full-time (22 women), 29 part-time (22 women); includes 8 minority (2 African Americans, 1 Asian American or Pacific Islander, 5 Hispanic Americans). Average age 33. 21 applicants, 100% accepted, 19 enrolled. In 2006, 29 degrees awarded. *Degree requirements:* For master's, practicum. *Entrance requirements:* For master's, minimum undergraduate GPA of 3.0 in major, 2.7 overall; interview; 3 letters of recommendation; resumé. Additional exam requirements/recommendations for international students: Required—TOEFL (minimum score 550 paper-based; 213 computer-based). *Application deadline:* For fall admission, 8/15 priority date for domestic students; for spring admission, 1/5 priority date for domestic students. Applications are processed on a rolling basis. Application fee: $50 ($100 for international students). *Expenses:* Tuition: Full-time $9,090; part-time $505 per hour. Required fees: $490; $66 per semester. One-time fee: $50. Tuition and fees vary according to course load and degree level. *Financial support:* In 2006–07, 3 fellowships (averaging $1,200 per year) were awarded; career-related internships or fieldwork and scholarships/grants also available. Support available to part-time students. Financial award application deadline: 6/30; financial award applicants required to submit FAFSA. *Unit head:* Dr. Robert Barnes, Head, 325-670-1451, Fax: 325-670-5859, E-mail: rbarnes@hsutx.edu. *Application contact:* Dr. Gary Stanlake, Dean of Graduate Studies, 325-670-1298, Fax: 325-670-1564, E-mail: gradoff@hsutx.edu.

Henderson State University, Graduate Studies, School of Education, Department of Counselor Education, Arkadelphia, AR 71999-0001. Offers community counseling (MS); elementary school counseling (MSE); secondary school counseling (MSE). *Accreditation:* NCATE. Part-time programs available. *Faculty:* 5 full-time (1 woman), 2 part-time/adjunct (1 woman). *Students:* 21 full-time (14 women), 50 part-time (39 women); includes 8 minority (all African Americans) Average age 32. In 2006, 7 degrees awarded. *Entrance requirements:* For master's, GRE General Test or MAT, letters of recommendation, minimum GPA of 2.7, teacher certification. Additional exam requirements/recommendations for international students: Required—TOEFL (minimum score 550 paper-based; 213 computer-based). *Application deadline:* For fall admission, 5/1 priority date for domestic students, 5/1 for international students; for winter admission, 10/1 for international students; for spring admission, 12/1 priority date for domestic students, 4/1 for international students. Applications are processed on a rolling basis. Application fee: $0 ($30 for international students). *Expenses:* Tuition, state resident: full-time $3,294;

Counselor Education

Henderson State University (continued)
part-time $183 per credit hour. Tuition, nonresident: full-time $6,588; part-time $366 per credit hour. Required fees: $176 per term. *Financial support:* In 2006–07, 1 teaching assistantship with full tuition reimbursement (averaging $4,000 per year) was awarded; Federal Work-Study and institutionally sponsored loans also available. Support available to part-time students. Financial award application deadline: 7/31. *Unit head:* Dr. Blair Olson, Chairperson, 870-230-5395, Fax: 870-230-5455, E-mail: olsonb@hsu.edu. *Application contact:* Dr. Marck L. Beggs, Graduate Dean, 870-230-5126, Fax: 870-230-5479, E-mail: beggsm@hsu.edu.

Heritage University, Graduate Programs in Education, Program in Counseling, Toppenish, WA 98948-9599. Offers M Ed. Part-time programs available. *Faculty:* 2 full-time (1 woman), 12 part-time/adjunct (5 women). *Students:* 116 (95 women); includes 39 minority (3 African Americans, 2 American Indian/Alaska Native, 3 Asian Americans or Pacific Islanders, 31 Hispanic Americans). Average age 34. In 2006, 62 degrees awarded. *Degree requirements:* For master's, comprehensive exam, registration. *Entrance requirements:* For master's, interview, letters of recommendation, at least 9 semester-credits of behavioral sciences. *Application deadline:* Applications are processed on a rolling basis. Application fee: $50 ($100 for international students). *Unit head:* Heidi Hillmatl, Head, 509-865-8596. *Application contact:* Kathy Otto, Coordinator of Administrative Services, 509-865-8635, Fax: 509-865-8629, E-mail: otto_k@heritage.edu.

Hofstra University, School of Education and Allied Human Services, Department of Counseling, Research, Special Education and Rehabilitation, Program in Counseling, Hempstead, NY 11549. Offers counseling (PD); mental health counseling (MA); school counselor (MS Ed); school counselor-bilingual extension (Advanced Certificate). *Accreditation:* NCATE. Part-time programs available. *Students:* 39 full-time (32 women), 33 part-time (22 women); includes 11 minority (3 African Americans, 8 Hispanic Americans), 1 international. Average age 26. 68 applicants, 56% accepted, 23 enrolled. In 2006, 27 master's, 2 other advanced degrees awarded. *Degree requirements:* For master's, comprehensive exam, registration (for some programs); for other advanced degree, one foreign language. *Entrance requirements:* For master's, GRE General Test, interview, 3 letters of recommendation, essay; for other advanced degree, GRE, interview, 3 letters of recommendation, essay. Additional exam requirements/recommendations for international students: Required—TOEFL (minimum score 550 paper-based; 213 computer-based). *Application deadline:* Applications are processed on a rolling basis. Application fee: $60. Electronic applications accepted. *Expenses:* Tuition: Full-time $13,320; part-time $740 per credit. Required fees: $930; $155 per term. *Financial support:* In 2006–07, 43 students received support, including 3 fellowships with tuition reimbursements available (averaging $2,587 per year), 10 research assistantships with full and partial tuition reimbursements available (averaging $5,947 per year); institutionally sponsored loans, scholarships/grants, tuition waivers (full and partial), and unspecified assistantships also available. Support available to part-time students. Financial award applicants required to submit FAFSA. *Faculty research:* Multicultural counseling; bereavement, loss and trauma counseling; GLBT issues in counseling; college student development; conflict and peace education. *Unit head:* Dr. Laurie Johnson, Director, 516-463-5754, Fax: 516-463-6184, E-mail: cprlzj@hofstra.edu. *Application contact:* Carol Drummer, Dean of Graduate Admissions, 516-463-4876, Fax: 516-463-4664, E-mail: gradstudent@hofstra.edu.

Houston Baptist University, College of Education and Behavioral Sciences, Programs in Education, Houston, TX 77074-3298. Offers bilingual education (M Ed); counselor education (M Ed); curriculum and instruction (M Ed); educational administration (M Ed); educational diagnostician (M Ed); reading education (M Ed). Part-time programs available. *Degree requirements:* For master's, registration. *Entrance requirements:* For master's, GRE General Test or MAT. Additional exam requirements/recommendations for international students: Required—TOEFL (minimum score 550 paper-based; 213 computer-based).

Howard University, School of Education, Department of Human Development and Psychoeducational Studies, Program in Counseling and Guidance, Washington, DC 20059-0002. Offers M Ed, MA, CAGS. MA offered through the Graduate School of Arts and Sciences. *Accreditation:* NCATE. Part-time programs available. *Faculty:* 2 full-time (both women). *Students:* 9 full-time (8 women), 4 part-time (3 women); includes 10 minority (all African Americans) Average age 27. 14 applicants, 71% accepted, 5 enrolled. In 2006, 6 degrees awarded. *Entrance requirements:* For degree, GRE General Test, minimum graduate GPA of 3.0. *Application deadline:* For fall admission, 4/1 priority date for domestic students; for spring admission, 11/1 for domestic students. Applications are processed on a rolling basis. Application fee: $45. *Financial support:* In 2006–07, 1 student received support; fellowships, research assistantships, teaching assistantships, career-related internships or fieldwork, Federal Work-Study, institutionally sponsored loans, scholarships/grants, and unspecified assistantships available. Financial award application deadline: 4/1. *Faculty research:* Law and forensic evaluation, juvenile justice, ethics, clinical assessment, personality disorders, substance abuse. *Unit head:* Dr. Ann L. Carter-Obayuwana, Associate Professor/Coordinator Masters Program, 202-806-6510, Fax: 202-806-5205, E-mail: acarter-obayuwa@howard.edu.

Hunter College of the City University of New York, Graduate School, School of Education, Department of Educational Foundations and Counseling Programs, Programs in School Counselor, New York, NY 10021-5085. Offers school counseling (MS Ed); school counseling with bilingual extension (MS Ed). *Accreditation:* NCATE. *Faculty:* 18 full-time (15 women), 14 part-time/adjunct (8 women). *Students:* 38 full-time (32 women), 90 part-time (71 women); includes 22 minority (10 African Americans, 3 Asian Americans or Pacific Islanders, 9 Hispanic Americans). Average age 30. 268 applicants, 21% accepted, 32 enrolled. In 2006, 29 degrees awarded. *Degree requirements:* For master's, thesis, internship, practicum, research seminar. *Entrance requirements:* For master's, interview, minimum GPA of 2.7. Additional exam requirements/recommendations for international students: Required—TOEFL, TWE. *Application deadline:* For fall admission, 4/1 for domestic students, 2/1 for international students; for spring admission, 11/1 for domestic students, 9/1 for international students. Applications are processed on a rolling basis. Application fee: $125. *Expenses:* Tuition, state resident: part-time $270 per credit. Tuition, nonresident: part-time $500 per credit. Required fees: $45 per semester. *Financial support:* Federal Work-Study and tuition waivers (partial) available. Support available to part-time students. *Unit head:* Dr. John O'Neill, Coordinator, 212-772-5188, E-mail: joneil@hunter.cuny.edu. *Application contact:* William Zlata, Director for Graduate Admissions, 212-772-4482, Fax: 212-650-3336, E-mail: admissions@hunter.cuny.edu.

Idaho State University, Office of Graduate Studies, Kasiska College of Health Professions, Department of Counseling, Pocatello, ID 83209. Offers counseling (M Coun, Ed S, Postbaccalaureate Certificate), including family-centered practice (Postbaccalaureate Certificate), marriage and family counseling (M Coun), mental health counseling (M Coun), school counseling (M Coun), student affairs and college counseling (M Coun); counselor education and counseling (PhD). *Accreditation:* ACA (one or more programs are accredited). *Faculty:* 6 full-time (3 women). *Students:* 66 full-time (40 women), 30 part-time (20 women); includes 6 minority (1 American Indian/Alaska Native, 1 Asian American or Pacific Islander, 4 Hispanic Americans), 1 international. Average age 35. In 2006, 43 master's, 5 doctorates awarded. *Degree requirements:* For master's, thesis, comprehensive exam, registration (for some programs); for doctorate, thesis/dissertation, doctoral internship, comprehensive exam, registration; for other advanced degree, thesis, case studies, oral exam, comprehensive exam, registration (for some programs). *Entrance requirements:* For master's, GRE General Test, MAT, minimum GPA of 3.0; for doctorate, GRE General Test, MAT, minimum graduate GPA of 3.0, resumé, interview, counseling license; for other advanced degree, GRE General Test, minimum graduate GPA of 3.0, master's degree in counseling, 3 letters of recommendation, 2 years work experience. Additional exam requirements/recommendations for international students: Required—TOEFL (minimum score 600 paper-based; 213 computer-based). *Application deadline:* For fall admission, 7/1 for domestic students, 6/1 for international students; for spring admission, 12/1 for domestic students, 11/1 for international students. Applications are processed on a rolling basis. Application fee: $55. *Financial support:* In 2006–07, 14 teaching assistantships with full and partial tuition reimbursements (averaging $8,694 per year) were awarded; career-related internships or fieldwork, Federal Work-Study, scholarships/grants, and tuition waivers (full) also available. Financial award application deadline: 1/1. *Faculty research:* Group counseling, multicultural counseling, family counseling, child therapy, supervision. *Unit head:* Dr. Steve Feit, Chair, 208-282-3663, Fax: 208-282-2583, E-mail: feitstep@isu.edu. *Application contact:* Ellen Combs, Graduate School Technical Records Specialist, 208-282-2150, Fax: 208-282-4847.

Illinois State University, Graduate School, College of Education, Department of Special Education, Normal, IL 61790-2200. Offers guidance and counseling (MS, MS Ed); special education (MS, MS Ed, Ed D). *Accreditation:* NCATE. *Faculty:* 14 full-time (9 women). *Students:* 7 full-time (all women), 112 part-time (104 women); includes 3 minority (2 African Americans, 1 Asian American or Pacific Islander), 1 international. 23 applicants, 78% accepted. In 2006, 23 master's, 1 doctorate awarded. *Degree requirements:* For doctorate, thesis/dissertation, 2 terms of residency. *Entrance requirements:* For master's, GRE General Test, minimum GPA of 3.0 in last 60 hours; for doctorate, GRE General Test. *Application deadline:* Applications are processed on a rolling basis. Application fee: $40. *Expenses:* Tuition, state resident: full-time $3,330; part-time $185 per credit hour. Tuition, nonresident: full-time $6,948; part-time $438 per credit hour. Required fees: $1,259; $52 per credit hour. *Financial support:* In 2006–07, 6 research assistantships (averaging $4,950 per year) were awarded; tuition waivers (full and partial) and unspecified assistantships also available. Financial award application deadline: 4/1. *Faculty research:* Center for adult learning leadership, promoting a learning community, autism/spectrum professional development and technical assistance project, early intervention for children who are deaf and hard of hearing in Illinois. Total annual research expenditures: $1.1 million. *Unit head:* Dr. James Thompson, Chairperson, 309-438-5419.

Immaculata University, College of Graduate Studies, Department of Psychology, Immaculata, PA 19345. Offers clinical psychology (Psy D); counseling psychology (MA, Certificate), including school guidance counselor (Certificate); school psychologist (Certificate); school psychology (Psy D). *Accreditation:* APA. Part-time and evening/weekend programs available. *Students:* 64 full-time (55 women), 213 part-time (181 women). Average age 34. 173 applicants, 59% accepted, 57 enrolled. In 2006, 35 master's, 11 doctorates awarded. *Degree requirements:* For master's, thesis optional; for doctorate, thesis/dissertation, comprehensive exam. *Entrance requirements:* For master's, GRE General Test or MAT, minimum GPA of 3.0; for doctorate, GRE General Test, minimum GPA of 3.5. Additional exam requirements/recommendations for international students: Required—TOEFL. *Application deadline:* Applications are processed on a rolling basis. Application fee: $35. *Financial support:* Application deadline: 5/1. *Faculty research:* Supervision ethics, psychology of teaching, gender. *Unit head:* Dr. Jed A. Yalof, Chair, 610-647-4400 Ext. 3503, Fax: 610-993-8550, E-mail: jyalof@immaculata.edu. *Application contact:* Office of Graduate Admission, 610-647-4400 Ext. 3211, Fax: 610-993-8550, E-mail: graduate@immaculata.edu.

Indiana State University, School of Graduate Studies, College of Education, Department of Counseling, Terre Haute, IN 47809-1401. Offers counseling psychology (MS, PhD); counselor education (PhD); marriage and family counseling (MS); school counseling (M Ed); student affairs administration (PhD); student affairs and higher education (MS). *Accreditation:* ACA; NCATE. Part-time and evening/weekend programs available. *Faculty:* 4 full-time (1 woman), 5 part-time/adjunct (4 women). *Students:* 67 full-time (50 women), 87 part-time (65 women); includes 24 minority (16 African Americans, 2 American Indian/Alaska Native, 2 Asian Americans or Pacific Islanders, 4 Hispanic Americans), 3 international. Average age 30. 56 applicants, 45% accepted, 19 enrolled. In 2006, 43 master's, 7 doctorates awarded. *Degree requirements:* For master's, thesis optional; for doctorate, thesis/dissertation, research tools proficiency tests. *Entrance requirements:* For master's, GRE General Test or MAT, minimum undergraduate GPA of 2.75; for doctorate, GRE General Test, master's degree, minimum undergraduate GPA of 3.5. *Application deadline:* For fall admission, 2/15 for domestic students. Applications are processed on a rolling basis. Application fee: $35. Electronic applications accepted. *Expenses:* Tuition, state resident: part-time $278 per credit. Tuition, nonresident: part-time $552 per credit. *Financial support:* In 2006–07, 25 research assistantships with partial tuition reimbursements (averaging $5,500 per year) were awarded; teaching assistantships, career-related internships or fieldwork and tuition waivers (partial) also available. Financial award application deadline: 3/1; financial award applicants required to submit FAFSA. *Faculty research:* Vocational development supervision. *Unit head:* Dr. Michele Boyer, Chairperson, 812-237-2832.

Indiana University Bloomington, School of Education, Department of Counseling and Educational Psychology, Bloomington, IN 47405-7000. Offers counseling (MS, PhD, Ed S); counseling psychology (PhD); counselor education (MS, Ed S); educational psychology (MS, PhD); learning and developmental sciences (MS, PhD); school psychology (PhD, Ed S). PhD offered through the University Graduate School. *Accreditation:* ACA (one or more programs are accredited); APA (one or more programs are accredited); NCATE. *Students:* 96 full-time (72 women), 79 part-time (56 women); includes 16 minority (10 African Americans, 4 Asian Americans or Pacific Islanders, 2 Hispanic Americans), 38 international. Average age 29. In 2006, 50 degrees awarded. Terminal master's awarded for partial completion of doctoral program. *Degree requirements:* For master's, thesis optional; for doctorate, thesis/dissertation; for Ed S, comprehensive exam or project. *Entrance requirements:* For master's, doctorate, and Ed S, GRE General Test. *Application deadline:* For fall admission, 6/1 for domestic students, 3/1 for international students; for winter admission, 11/1 for domestic students; for spring admission, 9/1 for international students. Applications are processed on a rolling basis. Application fee: $50 ($60 for international students). Electronic applications accepted. *Expenses:* Tuition, state resident: full-time $5,791; part-time $241 per credit hour. Tuition, nonresident: full-time $16,866; part-time $703 per credit hour. *Financial support:* Fellowships with partial tuition reimbursements, research assistantships with partial tuition reimbursements, teaching assistantships with partial tuition reimbursements, career-related internships or fieldwork, Federal Work-Study, institutionally sponsored loans, tuition waivers (full and partial), and unspecified assistantships available. Support available to part-time students. *Faculty research:* Affective and maturational factors in learning complex cognitive tasks, children's strategies for representing depth, prime time evaluation, rural school psychology. *Unit head:* Dr. Joyce Alexander, Chairperson, 812-856-8300.

Indiana University of Pennsylvania, School of Graduate Studies and Research, College of Education and Educational Technology, Department of Counseling, Indiana, PA 15705-1087. Offers community counseling (MA); counselor education (M Ed). *Accreditation:* NCATE. Part-time and evening/weekend programs available. *Faculty:* 9 full-time (7 women), 7 part-time/adjunct (4 women). *Students:* 47 full-time (45 women), 189 part-time (147 women); includes 20 minority (19 African Americans, 1 Hispanic American). Average age 32. 230 applicants, 35% accepted. In 2006, 76 degrees awarded. *Degree requirements:* For master's, thesis optional. *Entrance requirements:* For master's, 2 letters of recommendation. Additional exam requirements/recommendations for international students: Required—TOEFL. *Application deadline:* For fall admission, 7/1 priority date for domestic students; for spring admission, 11/1 for domestic students. Applications are processed on a rolling basis. Application fee: $30. *Expenses:* Tuition, state resident: full-time $6,048; part-time $336 per credit. Tuition, nonresident: full-time $9,678; part-time $538 per credit. Required fees: $1,069; $148 per year. *Financial support:* In 2006–07, 2 fellowships (averaging $500 per year), 15 research assistantships with full and partial tuition reimbursements (averaging $4,990 per year) were awarded; career-related internships or fieldwork and Federal Work-Study also available. Support available to part-time students. Financial award application deadline: 3/15; financial award applicants required to submit FAFSA. *Unit head:* Dr. Claire Dandeneau, Chairperson/Graduate Coordinator, 724-357-2306, E-mail: candean@iup.edu.

Indiana University–Purdue University Fort Wayne, School of Education, Department of Professional Studies, Fort Wayne, IN 46805-1499. Offers counselor education (MS Ed); educational administration (MS Ed). Part-time programs available. *Faculty:* 10 full-time (4 women). *Students:* 2 full-time (1 woman), 151 part-time (100 women); includes 18 minority (11 African Americans, 1 Asian American or Pacific Islander, 6 Hispanic Americans). Average age 34. 65 applicants, 74% accepted, 38 enrolled. In 2006, 67 degrees awarded. *Degree requirements:* For master's, practicum, internship, portfolio. *Entrance requirements:* For master's, minimum GPA of 2.5. Additional exam requirements/recommendations for international students: Required—TOEFL (minimum score 600 paper-based; 260 computer-based). *Application deadline:* For fall admission, 7/1 priority date for domestic students; for spring admission, 12/1 for domestic students. Applications are processed on a rolling basis. Application fee: $30. *Expenses:* Tuition, state resident: full-time $4,039; part-time $224 per credit. Tuition, nonresident: full-time $9,220; part-time $512 per credit. Required fees: $429; $24 per credit. Tuition and fees vary according to course load. *Financial support:* In 2006–07, 1 teaching assistantship with partial tuition reimbursement (averaging $11,950 per year) was awarded; research assistantships with partial tuition reimbursements, scholarships/grants also available. Support available to part-time students. Financial award application deadline: 3/1; financial award applicants required to submit FAFSA. *Unit head:* Dr. James Burg, Interim Chair of Professional Studies, 260-481-4146, Fax: 260-481-5408, E-mail: burgj@ipfw.edu. *Application contact:* Vicky L. Schmidt, Graduate Recorder, 260-481-6450, Fax: 260-481-5408, E-mail: schmidt@ipfw.edu.

Indiana University South Bend, School of Education, South Bend, IN 46634-7111. Offers counseling and human services (MS Ed); elementary education (MS Ed); secondary education (MS Ed); special education (MS Ed). *Accreditation:* NCATE. Part-time and evening/weekend programs available. *Faculty:* 21 full-time (11 women), 9 part-time/adjunct (3 women). *Students:* 58 full-time (38 women), 237 part-time (186 women); includes 33 minority (22 African Americans, 1 American Indian/Alaska Native, 6 Asian Americans or Pacific Islanders, 4 Hispanic Americans), 5 international. Average age 35. 127 applicants, 100% accepted, 61 enrolled. In 2006, 141 degrees awarded. *Degree requirements:* For master's, thesis or alternative, exit project. *Entrance requirements:* For master's, letters of recommendation, GRE or minimum GPA of 3.0. Additional exam requirements/recommendations for international students: Required—TOEFL. *Application deadline:* For fall admission, 7/1 for domestic students; for spring admission, 11/1 for domestic students. Applications are processed on a rolling basis. Application fee: $45. Electronic applications accepted. *Expenses:* Tuition, state resident: full-time $4,450; part-time $185 per credit hour. Tuition, nonresident: full-time $10,954; part-time $456 per credit hour. Tuition and fees vary according to course load, campus/location and program. *Financial support:* Career-related internships or fieldwork available. Support available to part-time students. Financial award application deadline: 3/1; financial award applicants required to submit FAFSA. *Faculty research:* Professional dispositions, early childhood literacy, online learning, program assessments, problem-based learning. *Unit head:* Dr. Michael Horvath, Professor and Dean, School of Education, 574-520-4339, Fax: 574-520-4550. *Application contact:* Gil L. Martin, Graduate Admissions and Recruitment Officer, 574-520-4585, Fax: 574-520-5549, E-mail: marting@iusb.edu.

Indiana University Southeast, School of Education, New Albany, IN 47150-6405. Offers counselor education (MS Ed); elementary education (MS Ed); secondary education (MS Ed). *Accreditation:* NCATE. Part-time and evening/weekend programs available. *Students:* 5 full-time (4 women), 339 part-time (275 women); includes 19 minority (17 African Americans, 1 Asian American or Pacific Islander, 1 Hispanic American). Average age 32. In 2006, 176 degrees awarded. *Degree requirements:* For master's, registration. *Entrance requirements:* For master's, minimum undergraduate GPA of 2.5, graduate 3.0. *Application deadline:* Applications are processed on a rolling basis. Application fee: $30. *Expenses:* Tuition, state resident: full-time $4,458; part-time $186 per credit hour. Tuition, nonresident: full-time $10,196; part-time $425 per credit hour. Tuition and fees vary according to course load, campus/location and program. *Financial support:* In 2006–07, 29 students received support. Career-related internships or fieldwork, Federal Work-Study, and institutionally sponsored loans available. Support available to part-time students. Financial award applicants required to submit FAFSA. *Faculty research:* Learning styles, technology, constructivism, group process, innovative math strategies. *Unit head:* Dr. Gloria Murray, Dean, 812-941-2385, Fax: 812-941-2667, E-mail: soeinfo@ius.edu.

Indiana Wesleyan University, College of Graduate Studies, Program in Counseling, Marion, IN 46953-4974. Offers community counseling (MS); marriage and family counseling (MS); school counseling (MS). *Accreditation:* ACA. Part-time programs available. *Faculty:* 3 full-time (1 woman), 3 part-time/adjunct (2 women). *Students:* 49 full-time (33 women), 60 part-time (47 women); includes 7 minority (6 African Americans, 1 Hispanic American). Average age 32. In 2006, 22 degrees awarded. *Degree requirements:* For master's, thesis or alternative. *Entrance requirements:* For master's, GRE General Test. *Application deadline:* For fall admission, 4/1 priority date for domestic students; for spring admission, 10/1 priority date for domestic students. Application fee: $25. Electronic applications accepted. *Expenses: Contact institution.* Tuition and fees vary according to degree level, campus/location and program. *Financial support:* In 2006–07, 1 research assistantship with tuition reimbursement, 1 teaching assistantship with partial tuition reimbursement (averaging $1,000 per year) were awarded. Financial award application deadline: 3/1; financial award applicants required to submit FAFSA. *Unit head:* Dr. Jerry Davis, Director of Graduate Counseling Studies, 765-677-2995, Fax: 765-677-2504, E-mail: jerry.davis@indwes.edu. *Application contact:* David McMillan, Assistant Director of Enrollment Management, 765-677-2688, E-mail: david.mcmillan@indwes.edu.

Inter American University of Puerto Rico, Arecibo Campus, Programs in Education, Arecibo, PR 00614-4050. Offers administration and educational supervision (MA Ed); counseling and guidance (MA Ed). *Degree requirements:* For master's, thesis optional. *Entrance requirements:* For master's, GRE, EXADEP, bachelor's degree in education or teaching license (administration and supervision) or courses in education and psychology (counseling and guidance), minimum GPA of 2.5 in last 60 credits.

Inter American University of Puerto Rico, Metropolitan Campus, Faculty of Education, Program in Guidance and Counseling, San Juan, PR 00919-1293. Offers MA. *Degree requirements:* For master's, comprehensive exam. *Entrance requirements:* For master's, GRE or EXADEP, interview. Electronic applications accepted.

Inter American University of Puerto Rico, San Germán Campus, Graduate Studies Center, Graduate Program in Guidance and Counseling, San Germán, PR 00683-5008. Offers MA. Part-time and evening/weekend programs available. *Faculty:* 7 full-time, 11 part-time/adjunct. *Students:* 77. In 2006, 11 degrees awarded. *Degree requirements:* For master's, comprehensive exam. *Entrance requirements:* For master's, GRE General Test or EXADEP, minimum GPA of 3.0. *Application deadline:* For fall admission, 4/30 priority date for domestic students; for spring admission, 11/15 for domestic students. Applications are processed on a rolling basis. Application fee: $31. *Expenses:* Tuition: Part-time $175 per credit. Required fees: $238 per semester. Tuition and fees vary according to degree level. *Financial support:* Teaching assistantships, Federal Work-Study and unspecified assistantships available. *Application contact:* Dr. Aurora Graniela, Graduate Coordinator, 787-264-1912 Ext. 7355, Fax: 787-892-7510, E-mail: aurora@sg.inter.edu.

Iowa State University of Science and Technology, Graduate College, College of Human Sciences, Department of Educational Leadership and Policy Studies, Ames, IA 50011. Offers counselor education (M Ed, MS); educational administration (M Ed, MS); educational leadership (PhD); higher education (M Ed, MS); organizational learning and human resource development (M Ed, MS); research and evaluation (MS). *Faculty:* 19 full-time, 9 part-time/adjunct. *Students:* 82 full-time (53 women), 191 part-time (109 women); includes 40 minority (23 African Americans, 4 American Indian/Alaska Native, 5 Asian Americans or Pacific Islanders, 8 Hispanic Americans), 5 international. 156 applicants, 70% accepted, 76 enrolled. In 2006, 95 master's, 13 doctorates awarded. *Degree requirements:* For master's, thesis or alternative; for doctorate, thesis/dissertation. *Entrance requirements:* For doctorate, GRE General Test. Additional exam requirements/recommendations for international students: Required—TOEFL (paper-based 560; computer-based 220; iBT 79) or IELTS (6.0). *Application deadline:* For fall admission, 1/1 priority date for domestic and international students. Applications are processed on a rolling basis. Application fee: $30 ($70 for international students). Electronic applications accepted. *Expenses:* Tuition, state resident: full-time $5,936; part-time $330 per credit. Tuition, nonresident: full-time $16,350; part-time $330 per credit. *Financial support:* In 2006–07, 17 research assistantships with full and partial tuition reimbursements (averaging $16,419 per year) were awarded; fellowships, teaching assistantships with full and partial tuition reimbursements, scholarships/grants, health care benefits, and unspecified assistantships also available. *Unit head:* Dr. Laura Rendon, Chair, 515-294-7093, E-mail: lrendon@iastate.edu. *Application contact:* Dr. Daniel Robinson, Information Contact, 515-294-1241, E-mail: eldrshp@iastate.edu.

Jackson State University, Graduate School, School of Education, Department of Counseling and Human Resource Education, Jackson, MS 39217. Offers community and agency counseling (MS); guidance and counseling (MS, MS Ed, Ed S); rehabilitative counseling (MS Ed). *Accreditation:* CORE (one or more programs are accredited); NCATE. Part-time and evening/weekend programs available. *Faculty:* 5 full-time (2 women), 2 part-time/adjunct (1 woman). *Students:* 67 full-time (53 women), 60 part-time (49 women); includes 124 minority (all African Americans) In 2006, 48 master's, 2 other advanced degrees awarded. *Degree requirements:* For master's, thesis, comprehensive exam. *Entrance requirements:* For master's, GRE General Test. Additional exam requirements/recommendations for international students: Required—TOEFL. *Application deadline:* For fall admission, 3/1 priority date for domestic students; for spring admission, 10/1 for domestic students. Applications are processed on a rolling basis. Application fee: $20. *Financial support:* In 2006–07, 16 students received support. Career-related internships or fieldwork, Federal Work-Study, scholarships/grants, and unspecified assistantships available. Support available to part-time students. Financial award application deadline: 3/1; financial award applicants required to submit FAFSA. *Unit head:* Dr. Jean Farish-Jackson, Chair, 601-979-2361, Fax: 601-979-2213, E-mail: jfjackso@jsums.edu. *Application contact:* Curtis Gore, Director of Graduate Admissions, 601-979-2455, Fax: 601-974-4325, E-mail: cgore@ccaix.jsums.edu.

Jacksonville State University, College of Graduate Studies and Continuing Education, College of Education and Professional Studies, Program in Guidance and Counseling, Jacksonville, AL 36265-1602. Offers MS. *Accreditation:* NCATE. *Faculty:* 5 full-time (2 women), 4 part-time/adjunct (all women). *Students:* 68 full-time (50 women), 94 part-time (75 women); includes 79 minority (76 African Americans, 2 American Indian/Alaska Native, 1 Hispanic American). In 2006, 69 degrees awarded. *Entrance requirements:* For master's, GRE General Test or MAT. *Application deadline:* Applications are processed on a rolling basis. Application fee: $20. *Expenses:* Tuition, state resident: full-time $5,400; part-time $225 per credit hour. Tuition, nonresident: full-time $10,800; part-time $450 per credit hour. One-time fee: $20 full-time. *Financial support:* In 2006–07, 12 research assistantships were awarded. Support available to part-time students. Financial award application deadline: 4/1. *Unit head:* Dr. Jerry Kiser, Head, 256-782-5855. *Application contact:* 256-782-5329.

John Brown University, Program in Counseling, Siloam Springs, AR 72761-2121. Offers community counseling (MS); marriage and family therapy (MS); school counseling (MS). *Accreditation:* NCATE. Part-time and evening/weekend programs available. *Degree requirements:* For master's, practica or internships. *Entrance requirements:* For master's, GRE General Test, MAT, minimum GPA of 3.0. Additional exam requirements/recommendations for international students: Required—TOEFL (minimum score 550 paper-based; 173 computer-based). Electronic applications accepted.

John Carroll University, Graduate School, Department of Education and Allied Studies, Program in School Counseling, University Heights, OH 44118-4581. Offers M Ed, MA. *Accreditation:* ACA; NCATE. Part-time and evening/weekend programs available. *Faculty:* 2 full-time (1 woman), 3 part-time/adjunct (2 women). *Students:* 5 full-time (3 women), 31 part-time (29 women); includes 5 minority (all African Americans) Average age 35. 19 applicants, 79% accepted, 8 enrolled. In 2006, 8 degrees awarded. *Degree requirements:* For master's, research essay or thesis (MA only). *Entrance requirements:* For master's, GRE General Test or MAT, minimum GPA of 2.75. *Application deadline:* For fall admission, 8/15 priority date for domestic students; for spring admission, 1/3 for domestic students. Applications are processed on a rolling basis. Application fee: $25 ($35 for international students). *Expenses:* Tuition: Full-time $9,675; part-time $645 per credit hour. Tuition and fees vary according to program. *Financial support:* Scholarships/grants, tuition waivers (partial), and unspecified assistantships available. Financial award application deadline: 3/1; financial award applicants required to submit FAFSA. *Unit head:* Dr. David C. Helsel, Coordinator, 216-397-4331, Fax: 216-397-3045, E-mail: dhelsel@jcu.edu.

John Carroll University, Graduate School, Program in Community Counseling, University Heights, OH 44118-4581. Offers clinical counseling (Certificate); community counseling (MA). *Accreditation:* ACA. Part-time and evening/weekend programs available. *Faculty:* 7 full-time (4 women), 15 part-time/adjunct (10 women). *Students:* 41 full-time (35 women), 45 part-time (36 women); includes 12 minority (11 African Americans, 1 American Indian/Alaska Native). Average age 32. 18 applicants, 94% accepted. In 2006, 22 degrees awarded. *Degree requirements:* For master's, internship, practicum. *Entrance requirements:* For master's, MAT or GRE, minimum GPA of 2.75, statement of volunteer experience, interview. *Application deadline:* For fall admission, 8/15 priority date for domestic students; for spring admission, 1/3 for domestic students. Applications are processed on a rolling basis. Application fee: $25 ($35 for international students). *Expenses:* Tuition: Full-time $9,675; part-time $645 per credit hour. Tuition and fees vary according to program. *Financial support:* In 2006–07, 68 students received support, including 1 teaching assistantship with full tuition reimbursement available (averaging $8,000 per year); career-related internships or fieldwork, institutionally sponsored loans, and unspecified assistantships also available. Financial award application deadline: 3/1; financial award applicants required to submit FAFSA. *Faculty research:* Child and adolescent development, HIV, hypnosis, wellness, women's issues. *Unit head:* Dr. Christopher M. Faiver, Coordinator, 216-397-3001, Fax: 216-397-3045, E-mail: faiver@jcu.edu.

The Johns Hopkins University, School of Professional Studies in Business and Education, School of Education, Department of Counseling and Human Services, Baltimore, MD 21218-2699. Offers addictions counseling (Certificate); clinical community counseling (Certificate); counseling (MS, CAGS); counseling at-risk youth (Certificate); organizational counseling (Certificate); spiritual and existential counseling and therapy (Certificate). Part-time and evening/weekend programs available. *Students:* 59 full-time (53 women), 353 part-time (305 women); includes 85 minority (62 African Americans, 5 American Indian/Alaska Native, 12 Asian Americans or Pacific Islanders, 6 Hispanic Americans), 2 international. Average age 30. 263 applicants, 78% accepted, 173 enrolled. In 2006, 100 master's, 21 other advanced degrees awarded. *Degree requirements:* For master's and other advanced degree, registration. *Entrance requirements:* For master's, minimum GPA of 3.0, interview, resumé, letters of recommendation; for other advanced degree, master's or doctoral degree, interview, resumé, minimum GPA of 3.0, letters of recommendation. Additional exam requirements/recommendations for international students: Required—TOEFL (minimum score 600 paper-based; 250 computer-based; 100 iBT). *Application deadline:* For fall admission, 5/1 for international students; for spring admission, 10/15 for international students. Applications are processed on a rolling basis. Application fee: $60. *Expenses:* Tuition: Full-time $32,976. Tuition and fees vary according to degree level and program. *Financial support:* Scholarships/grants available. Support available to part-time students. Financial award application deadline: 6/1; financial award applicants required to submit FAFSA. *Unit head:* Dr. Mary Guindon, Chair, 301-294-7040. *Application contact:* Carol Herrman, Admissions Coordinator, 410-872-1234, Fax: 410-872-1251, E-mail: onestop.admissions@jhu.edu.

Johnson State College, Program in Counseling, Johnson, VT 05656-9405. Offers MA. Part-time programs available. *Faculty:* 5 full-time (3 women), 6 part-time/adjunct (5 women). *Students:* 54 full-time (42 women), 49 part-time (39 women). *Degree requirements:* For master's, comprehensive exam. *Entrance requirements:* For master's, interview. *Application deadline:* For fall admission, 4/1 priority date for domestic students, 4/15 priority date for

Counselor Education

Johnson State College (continued)
international students; for spring admission, 11/1 priority date for domestic students, 8/15 priority date for international students. Applications are processed on a rolling basis. Application fee: $35. *Financial support:* Career-related internships or fieldwork, Federal Work-Study, institutionally sponsored loans, and unspecified assistantships available. Support available to part-time students. Financial award application deadline: 3/1; financial award applicants required to submit FAFSA. *Application contact:* Catherine H. Higley, Administrative Assistant for Graduate Programs, 800-635-2356 Ext. 1244, Fax: 802-635-1248, E-mail: higleyc@jsc.vsc.edu.

Kansas State University, Graduate School, College of Education, Department of Counseling and Educational Psychology, Manhattan, KS 66506. Offers counseling and student development-college student personnel work (MS); counseling and student development-school counseling (MS); counselor education and supervisors (PhD); school counseling (Ed D); student affairs in higher education (PhD). *Accreditation:* ACA; NCATE. *Faculty:* 12 full-time (6 women). *Students:* 104 full-time (63 women), 30 part-time (16 women); includes 14 minority (10 African Americans, 1 American Indian/Alaska Native, 2 Asian Americans or Pacific Islanders, 1 Hispanic American), 1 international. 45 applicants, 67% accepted, 25 enrolled. In 2006, 37 master's, 3 doctorates awarded. *Degree requirements:* For master's, thesis or alternative, final written exam; for doctorate, thesis/dissertation, comprehensive exam. *Entrance requirements:* For master's, GRE General Test, MAT; for doctorate, GRE General Test. *Application deadline:* For fall admission, 3/1 priority date for domestic students, 2/1 priority date for international students; for spring admission, 10/1 priority date for domestic students, 8/1 priority date for international students. Applications are processed on a rolling basis. Application fee: $30 ($55 for international students). Electronic applications accepted. *Expenses:* Tuition, state resident: full-time $6,352; part-time $240 per credit hour. Tuition, nonresident: full-time $14,296; part-time $571 per credit hour. Required fees: $585. *Financial support:* In 2006–07, 1 research assistantship (averaging $10,868 per year), 3 teaching assistantships with full tuition reimbursements (averaging $11,568 per year) were awarded; career-related internships or fieldwork, institutionally sponsored loans, and scholarships/grants also available. Support available to part-time students. Financial award application deadline: 3/1; financial award applicants required to submit FAFSA. *Faculty research:* College student mental health, college student development, school counselor education, role of religion in student life, multicultural counseling. *Unit head:* Stephen Benton, Head, 785-532-5784, Fax: 785-532-7304, E-mail: leroy@ksu.edu. *Application contact:* Linda Thurston, Director, 785-532-5595, Fax: 785-532-7304, E-mail: coegrads@ksu.edu.

Kean University, College of Education, Program in Counselor Education, Union, NJ 07083. Offers alcohol and drug abuse counseling (MA); business and industry counseling (MA, PMC); community/agency counseling (MA); school counseling (MA). *Accreditation:* ACA; NCATE. Part-time programs available. *Faculty:* 5 full-time (3 women). *Students:* 59 full-time (47 women), 161 part-time (142 women); includes 67 minority (38 African Americans, 2 Asian Americans or Pacific Islanders, 27 Hispanic Americans). Average age 32. 123 applicants, 74% accepted, 57 enrolled. In 2006, 49 degrees awarded. *Degree requirements:* For master's, thesis, practicum, internship, comprehensive exam. *Entrance requirements:* For master's, GRE General Test or MAT, 2 letters of recommendation, interview, minimum 3.0 GPA, initial teaching certificate (school counseling). *Application deadline:* For fall admission, 5/1 for domestic students; for spring admission, 11/1 for domestic students. Application fee: $60 ($150 for international students). Electronic applications accepted. *Expenses:* Tuition, state resident: full-time $8,856; part-time $369 per credit. Tuition, nonresident: full-time $11,256; part-time $469 per credit. *Financial support:* In 2006–07, 14 research assistantships with full tuition reimbursements (averaging $3,217 per year) were awarded; career-related internships or fieldwork and unspecified assistantships also available. *Unit head:* Dr. Juneau Gary, Coordinator, 908-737-3842, E-mail: jgary@kean.edu. *Application contact:* Joanne Morris, Director of Graduate Admissions, 908-737-3355, Fax: 908-737-3354, E-mail: grad-adm@kean.edu.

Keene State College, Division of Graduate and Professional Studies, Program in Counseling and Consultation, Keene, NH 03435. Offers school counselor (M Ed, PMC). Part-time and evening/weekend programs available. *Degree requirements:* For master's, project. *Entrance requirements:* For master's, resumé. *Application deadline:* For fall admission, 6/15 for domestic students; for spring admission, 10/15 for domestic students. Applications are processed on a rolling basis. Application fee: $25 ($35 for international students). *Expenses:* Tuition, area resident: Part-time $265 per credit. Tuition, state resident: full-time $5,780; part-time $290 per credit. Tuition, nonresident: full-time $13,050. Required fees: $80 per credit. Part-time tuition and fees vary according to course load. *Financial support:* Research assistantships, career-related internships or fieldwork, Federal Work-Study, and institutionally sponsored loans available. Financial award application deadline: 3/1; financial award applicants required to submit FAFSA. *Application contact:* Peggy Richmond, Director of Admissions, 603-358-2276, Fax: 603-358-2767, E-mail: admissions@keene.edu.

Kent State University, Graduate School of Education, Health, and Human Services, Department of Adult, Counseling, Health and Vocational Education, Program in Community Counseling, Kent, OH 44242-0001. Offers M Ed, MA. *Accreditation:* ACA; NCATE. *Faculty:* 6 full-time (3 women), 7 part-time/adjunct (4 women). *Students:* 49 full-time (43 women), 81 part-time (69 women); includes 16 minority (15 African Americans, 1 Hispanic American), 3 international. 40 applicants, 70% accepted. In 2006, 27 degrees awarded. *Degree requirements:* For master's, thesis (for some programs), registration. *Entrance requirements:* Additional exam requirements/recommendations for international students: Required—TOEFL. *Application deadline:* For fall admission, 6/1 for domestic students; for spring admission, 10/1 for domestic students. Application fee: $30. Electronic applications accepted. *Financial support:* In 2006–07, fellowships with full tuition reimbursements (averaging $7,210 per year); research assistantships with full tuition reimbursements, teaching assistantships with full tuition reimbursements, career-related internships or fieldwork, Federal Work-Study, institutionally sponsored loans, scholarships/grants, health care benefits, and unspecified assistantships also available. Support available to part-time students. Financial award application deadline: 4/1; financial award applicants required to submit FAFSA. *Faculty research:* Group work, personality assessment, family/child therapy, substance abuse counseling, clinical supervision. *Unit head:* Dr. Jason McGlothlin, Coordinator, 330-672-2662, E-mail: jmcgloth@kent.edu. *Application contact:* Nancy Miller, Academic Program Coordinator, Office of Graduate Student Services, 330-672-2576, Fax: 330-672-9162, E-mail: ogs@kent.edu.

Kent State University, Graduate School of Education, Health, and Human Services, Department of Adult, Counseling, Health and Vocational Education, Program in Counseling, Kent, OH 44242-0001. Offers Ed S. *Accreditation:* ACA. *Faculty:* 9 full-time (3 women), 7 part-time/adjunct (4 women). *Students:* 2 applicants, 100% accepted. In 2006, 5 degrees awarded. *Entrance requirements:* Additional exam requirements/recommendations for international students: Required—TOEFL. *Application deadline:* Applications are processed on a rolling basis. Application fee: $30. Electronic applications accepted. *Financial support:* In 2006–07, fellowships (averaging $7,210 per year); research assistantships, teaching assistantships, career-related internships or fieldwork, Federal Work-Study, institutionally sponsored loans, scholarships/grants, health care benefits, and unspecified assistantships also available. Support available to part-time students. *Unit head:* Dr. Jason McGlothlin, Coordinator, 330-672-2662, E-mail: jmcgloth@kent.edu. *Application contact:* Nancy Miller, Academic Program Coordinator, Office of Graduate Student Services, 330-672-2576, Fax: 330-672-9162, E-mail: ogs@kent.edu.

Kent State University, Graduate School of Education, Health, and Human Services, Department of Adult, Counseling, Health and Vocational Education, Program in Counseling and Human Development Services, Kent, OH 44242-0001. Offers PhD. *Accreditation:* ACA; NCATE. *Faculty:* 9 full-time (3 women), 2 part-time/adjunct (both women). *Students:* 49 full-time (36 women), 24 part-time (17 women); includes 13 minority (11 African Americans, 1 Asian American or Pacific Islander, 1 Hispanic American), 5 international. 19 applicants, 63% accepted. In 2006, 8 degrees awarded. *Degree requirements:* For doctorate, thesis/dissertation, comprehensive exam, registration. *Entrance requirements:* For doctorate, GRE General Test. Additional exam requirements/recommendations for international students: Required—TOEFL. *Application deadline:* For fall admission, 2/15 for domestic students. Application fee: $30. Electronic applications accepted. *Financial support:* In 2006–07, fellowships with full tuition reimbursements (averaging $9,785 per year); research assistantships with full tuition reimbursements, teaching assistantships with full tuition reimbursements, career-related internships or fieldwork, Federal Work-Study, institutionally sponsored loans, scholarships/grants, health care benefits, and unspecified assistantships also available. Support available to part-time students. Financial award application deadline: 4/1; financial award applicants required to submit FAFSA. *Faculty research:* Family/child therapy, clinical supervision, group work, experiential training methods. *Unit head:* Dr. John L. West, Coordinator, 330-672-2662, E-mail: jwest@kent.edu. *Application contact:* Nancy Miller, Academic Program Coordinator, Office of Graduate Student Services, 330-672-2576, Fax: 330-672-9162, E-mail: ogs@kent.edu.

Kent State University, Graduate School of Education, Health, and Human Services, Department of Adult, Counseling, Health and Vocational Education, Program in School Counseling, Kent, OH 44242-0001. Offers M Ed, MA. *Accreditation:* ACA; NCATE. *Faculty:* 4 full-time (2 women), 5 part-time/adjunct (4 women). *Students:* 37 full-time (30 women), 90 part-time (74 women); includes 12 minority (11 African Americans, 1 American Indian/Alaska Native), 17 international. 31 applicants, 77% accepted. In 2006, 39 degrees awarded. *Degree requirements:* For master's, thesis (for some programs), registration. *Entrance requirements:* Additional exam requirements/recommendations for international students: Required—TOEFL. *Application deadline:* For fall admission, 6/1 for domestic students; for spring admission, 10/1 for domestic students. Application fee: $30. Electronic applications accepted. *Financial support:* Fellowships with full tuition reimbursements, research assistantships with full tuition reimbursements, teaching assistantships with full tuition reimbursements, career-related internships or fieldwork, Federal Work-Study, institutionally sponsored loans, scholarships/grants, health care benefits, and unspecified assistantships available. Support available to part-time students. Financial award application deadline: 4/1; financial award applicants required to submit FAFSA. *Faculty research:* Appraisal, diagnosis, group work. *Unit head:* Dr. Jason McGlothlin, Coordinator, 330-672-2662, E-mail: jmcgloth@kent.edu. *Application contact:* Nancy Miller, Academic Program Coordinator, Office of Graduate Student Services, 330-672-2576, Fax: 330-672-9162, E-mail: ogs@kent.edu.

Kutztown University of Pennsylvania, College of Graduate Studies and Extended Learning, Program in Guidance and Counseling, Kutztown, PA 19530-0730. Offers counselor education (M Ed), including elementary counseling, secondary counseling. *Accreditation:* NCATE. Part-time and evening/weekend programs available. *Faculty:* 10 full-time (5 women), 2 part-time/adjunct (0 women). *Students:* 35 full-time (29 women), 63 part-time (50 women); includes 5 minority (2 African Americans, 3 Hispanic Americans). Average age 29. 50 applicants, 52% accepted, 8 enrolled. In 2006, 24 degrees awarded. *Degree requirements:* For master's, thesis optional. *Entrance requirements:* For master's, GRE General Test, interview. Additional exam requirements/recommendations for international students: Required—TOEFL. *Application deadline:* For fall admission, 3/1 for domestic students; for spring admission, 9/1 for domestic students. Application fee: $35. Electronic applications accepted. *Expenses:* Tuition, state resident: full-time $6,048; part-time $336 per credit. Tuition, nonresident: full-time $9,678; part-time $538 per credit. *Financial support:* In 2006–07, research assistantships with full tuition reimbursements (averaging $5,000 per year); career-related internships or fieldwork, Federal Work-Study, and unspecified assistantships also available. Financial award application deadline: 3/15; financial award applicants required to submit FAFSA. *Faculty research:* Family addictions, family roles. *Unit head:* Dr. Deborah Barlieb, Chairperson, 610-683-4205, Fax: 610-683-1585, E-mail: barlieb@kutztown.edu.

Lamar University, College of Graduate Studies, College of Education and Human Development, Department of Educational Leadership, Beaumont, TX 77710. Offers counseling and development (M Ed, Certificate); education administration (M Ed); educational leadership (DE); principal (Certificate); school superintendent (Certificate); supervision (M Ed); technology application (Certificate). Part-time and evening/weekend programs available. *Faculty:* 11 full-time (5 women), 4 part-time/adjunct (1 woman). *Students:* 44 full-time (34 women), 113 part-time (86 women); includes 34 minority (27 African Americans, 2 Asian Americans or Pacific Islanders, 5 Hispanic Americans), 2 international. Average age 35. 301 applicants, 33% accepted, 32 enrolled. In 2006, 68 degrees awarded. Terminal master's awarded for partial completion of doctoral program. *Degree requirements:* For master's, thesis optional; for doctorate, thesis/dissertation, registration. *Entrance requirements:* For master's, GRE General Test, minimum GPA of 2.5; for doctorate, GRE. Additional exam requirements/recommendations for international students: Required—TOEFL. *Application deadline:* For fall admission, 8/1 priority date for domestic students; for spring admission, 12/1 priority date for domestic students. Applications are processed on a rolling basis. Application fee: $25 ($50 for international students). *Expenses:* Tuition, nonresident: part-time $33 per hour. Required fees: $43 per hour. $110 per semester. *Financial support:* In 2006–07, 3 fellowships (averaging $20,000 per year), 1 research assistantship with tuition reimbursement (averaging $6,500 per year) were awarded; teaching assistantships with tuition reimbursements, career-related internships or fieldwork and scholarships/grants also available. Support available to part-time students. Financial award application deadline: 4/1. *Faculty research:* School dropouts, suicide prevention in public school students, school climate and gifted performance, teacher evaluation. *Unit head:* Dr. Carolyn Crawford, Chair, 409-880-8689, Fax: 409-880-8685.

Lancaster Bible College, Graduate School, Lancaster, PA 17608-3403. Offers Bible (MA); consulting resource teacher (M Ed); counseling (MA); ministry (MA); school counseling (M Ed). Part-time and evening/weekend programs available. *Faculty:* 8 full-time (1 woman), 5 part-time/adjunct (1 woman). *Students:* 55 full-time (28 women), 117 part-time (55 women); includes 21 minority (15 African Americans, 5 Asian Americans or Pacific Islanders, 1 Hispanic American). Average age 36. In 2006, 16 degrees awarded. *Degree requirements:* For master's, thesis (for some programs), comprehensive exam (for some programs). *Entrance requirements:* For master's, bachelor's degree with a minimum of 30 credits of course work in Bible, minimum undergraduate GPA of 3.0, interview. Additional exam requirements/recommendations for international students: Required—TOEFL. *Application deadline:* Applications are processed on a rolling basis. Application fee: $25. *Expenses:* Tuition: Full-time $4,620; part-time $385 per credit. *Financial support:* In 2006–07, 31 students received support, including 2 teaching assistantships (averaging $1,800 per year); scholarships/grants and unspecified assistantships also available. Support available to part-time students. Financial award application deadline: 6/1; financial award applicants required to submit FAFSA. *Unit head:* Dr. Ray A. Naugle, Dean of Graduate Education, 717-560-8297, Fax: 717-560-8236, E-mail: rnaugle@lbc.edu. *Application contact:* Emily Higgins, Student Application Contact, 717-560-8297, E-mail: ehiggins@lbc.edu.

La Sierra University, School of Education, Department of Educational Psychology and Counseling, Riverside, CA 92515. Offers counseling (MA); educational psychology (Ed S); school psychology (Ed S). Part-time and evening/weekend programs available. *Degree requirements:* For master's, thesis optional; for Ed S, practicum (educational psychology). *Entrance requirements:* For master's, California Basic Educational Skills Test, NTE, minimum GPA of 3.0; for Ed S, minimum GPA of 3.3. *Faculty research:* Equivalent score scales, self perception.

Lee University, Program in Behavioral Sciences, Cleveland, TN 37320-3450. Offers mental health counseling (MS); school counseling (MS). *Faculty:* 12 full-time (3 women), 2 part-time/adjunct (0 women). *Students:* 76 full-time (63 women), 13 part-time (12 women); includes 32 minority (2 African Americans, 25 American Indian/Alaska Native, 1 Asian American or Pacific Islander, 4 Hispanic Americans), 3 international. 51 applicants, 73% accepted, 23 enrolled. In 2006, 23 degrees awarded. *Degree requirements:* For master's, variable foreign language requirement, thesis, internship, comprehensive exam. *Entrance requirements:* For master's, GRE General Test or MAT, minimum undergraduate GPA of 3.0, 3 letters of recommendation, interview. Additional exam requirements/recommendations for international students: Required—TOEFL. *Application deadline:* For fall admission, 4/1 priority date for domestic and international students; for spring admission, 10/1 for domestic and international students. Applications are processed on a rolling basis. Application fee: $25. *Expenses:* Tuition: Part-time $412 per credit. Required fees: $10 per semester. Tuition and fees vary according to course load. *Financial support:* Career-related internships or fieldwork, Federal Work-Study, and institutionally sponsored loans available. *Unit head:* Dr. Doyle Goff, Director, 423-614-8126, Fax: 423-614-8129, E-mail: drgoff@leeuniversity.edu. *Application contact:* Vicki Glasscock, Graduate Admissions Director, 423-614-8059, E-mail: vglasscock@leeuniversity.edu.

Lehigh University, College of Education, Department of Education and Human Services, Program in Counseling Psychology, Bethlehem, PA 18015-3094. Offers counseling and human services (M Ed); counseling psychology (PhD); international counseling (M Ed, Certificate); school counseling (M Ed). *Accreditation:* APA (one or more programs are accredited). Part-time and evening/weekend programs available. *Faculty:* 29 full-time (16 women), 17 part-time/adjunct (9 women). *Students:* 56 full-time (44 women), 47 part-time (43 women); includes 13 minority (5 African Americans, 1 American Indian/Alaska Native, 4 Asian Americans or Pacific Islanders, 3 Hispanic Americans), 9 international. 140 applicants, 39% accepted, 19 enrolled. In 2006, 37 master's, 2 doctorates awarded. *Degree requirements:* For doctorate, thesis/dissertation. *Entrance requirements:* For master's, GRE General Test or MAT, minimum GPA of 3.0; for doctorate, GRE General Test or MAT. Additional exam requirements/recommendations for international students: Required—TOEFL (minimum score 500 paper-based; 250 computer-based). Application fee: $60. Electronic applications accepted. *Financial support:* Fellowships with full and partial tuition reimbursements, research assistantships with full and partial tuition reimbursements, career-related internships or fieldwork, Federal Work-Study, institutionally sponsored loans, scholarships/grants, and tuition waivers (full and partial) available. Financial award application deadline: 1/31. *Faculty research:* Multicultural counseling, career development, family systems. *Unit head:* Dr. Tina Richardson, Coordinator, 610-758-3250, Fax: 610-758-3227, E-mail: tgr0@lehigh.edu.

Lehman College of the City University of New York, Division of Education, Department of Specialized Services in Education, Program in Guidance and Counseling, Bronx, NY 10468-1589. Offers MS Ed. *Accreditation:* NCATE. Part-time and evening/weekend programs available. *Degree requirements:* For master's, thesis. *Entrance requirements:* For master's, minimum GPA of 2.7. *Faculty research:* Crisis intervention, domestic violence, alcohol abuse, gender issues.

Lenoir-Rhyne College, Graduate Programs, School of Social and Behavioral Sciences, Program in Community/Agency Counseling, Hickory, NC 28603. Offers MA. Part-time and evening/weekend programs available. *Degree requirements:* For master's, thesis optional. *Entrance requirements:* For master's, GRE General Test, writing sample, minimum undergraduate GPA of 2.7, minimum graduate GPA of 3.0. Additional exam requirements/recommendations for international students: Required—TOEFL (minimum score 600 paper-based). Electronic applications accepted.

Lenoir-Rhyne College, Graduate Programs, School of Social and Behavioral Sciences, Program in School Counseling, Hickory, NC 28603. Offers MA. Part-time and evening/weekend programs available. *Degree requirements:* For master's, thesis optional. *Entrance requirements:* For master's, GRE General Test, minimum undergraduate GPA of 2.7, graduate 3.0; writing sample. Additional exam requirements/recommendations for international students: Required—TOEFL (minimum score 600 paper-based). Electronic applications accepted.

Lewis University, College of Arts and Sciences, Graduate Programs in Education, Program in School Counseling and Guidance, Romeoville, IL 60446. Offers MA. Part-time and evening/weekend programs available. *Entrance requirements:* For master's, writing exam, letters of recommendation, interview, minimum GPA of 2.75. Additional exam requirements/recommendations for international students: Required—TOEFL (minimum score 550 paper-based; 213 computer-based). Electronic applications accepted.

Liberty University, School of Education, Lynchburg, VA 24502. Offers administration and supervision (M Ed); curriculum and instruction (M Ed); early childhood education (M Ed); education specialist (Ed S); educational leadership (Ed D); elementary education (M Ed); gifted education (M Ed); reading specialist (M Ed); school counseling (M Ed); secondary education (M Ed); special education (M Ed). *Accreditation:* NCATE. Part-time programs available. Postbaccalaureate distance learning degree programs offered (minimal on-campus study). *Faculty:* 8 full-time (3 women), 7 part-time/adjunct (3 women). *Students:* 33 full-time (22 women), 308 part-time (180 women); includes 22 minority (12 African Americans, 2 American Indian/Alaska Native, 2 Asian Americans or Pacific Islanders, 6 Hispanic Americans), 5 international. Average age 39. 434 applicants, 77% accepted, 111 enrolled. In 2006, 39 master's, 12 doctorates, 16 other advanced degrees awarded. *Degree requirements:* For doctorate, thesis/dissertation, comprehensive exam. *Entrance requirements:* For master's, GRE General Test or MAT (if taken on or before 1999), 2 letters of recommendation, minimum undergraduate GPA of 3.0, curriculum vitae, graduate status record; for doctorate, GRE General Test or MAT (if taken before 1999), minimum master's GPA of 3.0, 3 years of teacher experience; for Ed S, GRE General Test or MAT (if taken before 1999), minimum master's GPA of 3.0, 3 years of teaching experience. Additional exam requirements/recommendations for international students: Required—TOEFL (minimum score 600 paper-based; 250 computer-based). *Application deadline:* For fall admission, 6/1 priority date for domestic students; for spring admission, 11/1 for domestic students. Applications are processed on a rolling basis. Application fee: $35. Electronic applications accepted. *Expenses: Contact institution. Financial support:* In 2006–07, 226 students received support. Federal Work-Study and tuition waivers (partial) available. *Faculty research:* Self-determination, character education, bibliotherapy, learning styles, distance education. *Unit head:* Dr. Karen L. Parker, Dean, 434-582-2195, Fax: 434-582-2468, E-mail: kparker@liberty.edu. *Application contact:* Kyle A Felice, Director of Graduate Admissions, 800-424-9596, Fax: 800-628-7977, E-mail: gradadmissions@liberty.edu.

Lincoln Memorial University, School of Education, Harrogate, TN 37752-1901. Offers administration and supervision (M Ed, Ed S); counseling and guidance (M Ed); curriculum and instruction (M Ed, Ed S). Part-time and evening/weekend programs available. *Faculty:* 25 full-time (13 women), 11 part-time/adjunct (6 women). *Students:* 207 full-time (159 women), 1,315 part-time (995 women); includes 106 minority (93 African Americans, 1 American Indian/Alaska Native, 1 Asian American or Pacific Islander, 11 Hispanic Americans), 2 international. 1,397 applicants, 98% accepted. In 2006, 194 master's, 778 other advanced degrees awarded. *Degree requirements:* For master's, thesis optional. *Entrance requirements:* For master's, GRE, MAT, or NTE. *Application deadline:* For fall admission, 8/10 priority date for domestic students. Application fee: $25. *Financial support:* Career-related internships or fieldwork and unspecified assistantships available. Support available to part-time students. Financial award application deadline: 4/1; financial award applicants required to submit FAFSA. *Unit head:* Dr. Fred Bedelle, Dean, School of Graduate Studies, 423-869-6223, Fax: 423-869-6261, E-mail: graduate@inetlmu.lmunet.edu. *Application contact:* Barbara McCune, Senior Assistant, Graduate Office, 423-869-6374, Fax: 423-869-6261, E-mail: graduate@lmunet.edu.

Lincoln University, School of Graduate Studies and Continuing Education, College of Liberal Arts, Education and Journalism, Department of Education, Jefferson City, MO 65102. Offers educational leadership (Ed S), including elementary leadership, secondary leadership, superintendency; guidance and counseling (M Ed), including community/agency counseling, elementary school, secondary school; school administration and supervision (M Ed), including elementary school administration, secondary school administration, special education administration; school teaching (M Ed), including elementary school teaching, secondary school teaching. *Accreditation:* NCATE. Part-time and evening/weekend programs available. *Faculty:* 1 (woman) full-time, 10 part-time/adjunct (5 women). *Students:* 24 full-time (21 women), 62 part-time (51 women); includes 10 minority (8 African Americans, 2 Asian Americans or Pacific Islanders), 4 international. Average age 35. 13 applicants, 100% accepted, 10 enrolled. In 2006, 25 master's, 3 other advanced degrees awarded. *Degree requirements:* For master's and Ed S, portfolio. *Entrance requirements:* For master's, GRE or MAT, teaching certificate (school administration and supervision); background check; interview (elementary and secondary school teaching); for Ed S, GRE or MAT, principal certificate. Additional exam requirements/recommendations for international students: Required—TOEFL (minimum score 500 paper-based; 173 computer-based; 61 iBT). *Application deadline:* For fall admission, 7/1 priority date for domestic and international students; for spring admission, 12/1 priority date for domestic and international students. Applications are processed on a rolling basis. Application fee: $17. *Expenses:* Tuition, state resident: part-time $189 per credit hour. Tuition, nonresident: part-time $351 per credit hour. Required fees: $15 per credit hour. $20 per semester. *Financial support:* Federal Work-Study and scholarships/grants available. Financial award application deadline: 4/1; financial award applicants required to submit FAFSA. *Unit head:* Dr. Cynthia Chapel, Department Head, 573-681-5250, Fax: 573-681-5257, E-mail: chapelc@lincolnu.edu.

Loma Linda University, School of Science and Technology, Department of Counseling and Family Science, Loma Linda, CA 92350. Offers MA, MS, DMFT, PhD, Certificate, MA/Certificate.

Long Island University, Brentwood Campus, School of Education, Brentwood, NY 11717. Offers elementary education (MS); reading (MS); school counseling (MS); school district administration and supervision (MS); special education (MS). Part-time and evening/weekend programs available.

Long Island University, Brooklyn Campus, School of Education, Department of Human Development and Leadership, Program in Counseling and Development, Brooklyn, NY 11201-8423. Offers MS, MS Ed, Certificate. *Degree requirements:* For master's, thesis optional. *Entrance requirements:* For master's, 2 letters of recommendation. Additional exam requirements/recommendations for international students: Required—TOEFL (minimum score 500 paper-based; 173 computer-based).

Long Island University, C.W. Post Campus, School of Education, Department of Counseling and Development, Brookville, NY 11548-1300. Offers mental health counseling (MS); school counseling (MS). *Accreditation:* ACA. Part-time and evening/weekend programs available. *Degree requirements:* For master's, comprehensive exam or thesis, internship. *Entrance requirements:* For master's, interview, minimum GPA of 3.0. Electronic applications accepted. *Faculty research:* Community prevention programs, youth gang violence, community mental health counseling.

Long Island University, Rockland Graduate Campus, Graduate School, Program in Counseling and Development, Orangeburg, NY 10962. Offers mental health counseling (MS); school counselor (MS).

Long Island University, Westchester Graduate Campus, Program in Education-School Counselor and School Psychology, Purchase, NY 10577. Offers school counselor (MS Ed); school psychologist (MS Ed). Part-time and evening/weekend programs available. *Faculty:* 2 full-time (both women), 12 part-time/adjunct (8 women). *Students:* 84 (72 women). 40 applicants, 73% accepted, 21 enrolled. In 2006, 21 degrees awarded. *Application deadline:* Applications are processed on a rolling basis. Application fee: $30. *Expenses:* Tuition: Part-time $790 per credit. *Financial support:* In 2006–07, 22 students received support. Scholarships/grants, tuition waivers (partial), and unspecified assistantships available. *Unit head:* Prof. Beth Weiner, Director, 914-831-2717, Fax: 914-251-5959, E-mail: beth.weiner@liu.edu. *Application contact:* Ellen Brief, Coordinator of Admissions, Marketing, Student Services and Public Relations, 914-831-2701, Fax: 914-251-5959, E-mail: westchester@liu.edu.

Longwood University, Office of Graduate Studies, College of Education and Human Services, Farmville, VA 23909. Offers communication sciences and disorders (MS); community and college counseling (MS); curriculum and instruction specialist-elementary (MS), including mild disabilities, modern languages; curriculum and instruction specialist-secondary (MS), including English, mild disabilities, modern languages; educational leadership (MS); guidance and counseling (MS); literacy and culture (MS); school library media (MS). *Accreditation:* NCATE. Part-time and evening/weekend programs available. *Degree requirements:* For master's, thesis optional. *Entrance requirements:* For master's, GRE (communication sciences and disorders), minimum GPA of 2.75. Additional exam requirements/recommendations for international students: Required—TOEFL (minimum score 550 paper-based; 213 computer-based).

Louisiana State University and Agricultural and Mechanical College, Graduate School, College of Education, Department of Educational Theory, Policy and Practice, Baton Rouge, LA 70803. Offers counseling (M Ed, MA, Ed S); educational administration (M Ed, MA, PhD, Ed S); educational technology (MA); elementary education (M Ed); higher education (PhD); research methodology (PhD); secondary education (M Ed). *Accreditation:* ACA (one or more programs are accredited); NCATE. Part-time and evening/weekend programs available. *Faculty:* 39 full-time (24 women). *Students:* 147 full-time (115 women), 183 part-time (143 women); includes 63 minority (51 African Americans, 3 American Indian/Alaska Native, 3 Asian Americans or Pacific Islanders, 6 Hispanic Americans), 14 international. Average age 35. 110 applicants, 58% accepted, 15 enrolled. In 2006, 93 master's, 24 doctorates awarded. Terminal master's awarded for partial completion of doctoral program. *Degree requirements:* For doctorate, thesis/dissertation; for Ed S, thesis optional. *Entrance requirements:* For master's and doctorate, GRE General Test, minimum GPA of 3.0. Additional exam requirements/recommendations for international students: Required—TOEFL (minimum score 550 paper-based; 213 computer-based; 79 iBT). *Application deadline:* For fall admission, 1/25 priority date for domestic students, 5/15 for international students; for spring admission, 10/15 for international students. Applications are processed on a rolling basis. Application fee: $25. Electronic applications accepted. *Financial support:* In 2006–07, 82 students received support, including 6 fellowships with full tuition reimbursements available (averaging $26,273 per year), 24 research assistantships with full and partial tuition reimbursements available (averaging $9,812 per year), teaching assistantships with full and partial tuition reimbursements available (averaging $11,693 per year); career-related internships or fieldwork, Federal Work-Study, institutionally sponsored loans, and unspecified assistantships also available. Support available to part-time students. Financial award applicants required to submit FAFSA. *Faculty research:* Literary, curriculum studies, science education, K-12 leadership, higher education. Total annual research expenditures: $335,618. *Unit head:* Dr. Earl Cheek, Chair, 225-578-6897, Fax: 225-578-1045, E-mail: echeek@lsu.edu.

Louisiana Tech University, Graduate School, College of Education, Department of Behavioral Sciences and Psychology, Ruston, LA 71272. Offers counseling (MA); counseling psychology (PhD); industrial/organizational psychology (MA); special education (MA). *Accreditation:* APA (one or more programs are accredited). Part-time programs available. *Degree requirements:* For master's, thesis or alternative; for doctorate, thesis/dissertation. *Entrance requirements:* For master's and doctorate, GRE General Test.

Loyola College in Maryland, Graduate Programs, College of Arts and Sciences, Department of Education, Program in Guidance and Counseling, Baltimore, MD 21210-2699. Offers M Ed, MA, CAS. *Accreditation:* ACA; NCATE. Part-time and evening/weekend programs available. *Students:* 63 full-time (55 women), 120 part-time (106 women); includes 25 minority (17 African Americans, 1 Asian American or Pacific Islander, 7 Hispanic Americans). Average age 29. 147 applicants, 75% accepted, 77 enrolled. In 2006, 60 master's, 2 other advanced degrees awarded. *Entrance requirements:* For master's and CAS, GRE General Test, GRE Subject Test (recommended). Additional exam requirements/recommendations for international students: Required—TOEFL (minimum score 550 paper-based; 213 computer-based). *Application deadline:* For fall admission, 7/1 priority date for domestic students; for spring admission, 10/1 priority date for domestic students. Applications are processed on a rolling basis. Application fee: $50. *Financial support:* Career-related internships or fieldwork available. Financial award applicants required to submit FAFSA. *Unit head:* Dr. Bradley Erford, Director of School Counseling, 410-617-2007 Ext. 1509, E-mail: berford@loyola.edu.

Loyola Marymount University, Graduate Division, School of Education, Program in Counseling, Los Angeles, CA 90045-2659. Offers MA. Part-time and evening/weekend programs avail-

Counselor Education

Loyola Marymount University (continued)

able. *Students:* 84 full-time (67 women), 22 part-time (20 women); includes 59 minority (16 African Americans, 12 Asian Americans or Pacific Islanders, 31 Hispanic Americans), 3 international. Average age 29. In 2006, 33 degrees awarded. *Degree requirements:* For master's, comprehensive exam. *Entrance requirements:* For master's, GRE General Test, interview. Additional exam requirements/recommendations for international students: Required—TOEFL (minimum score 600 paper-based; 250 computer-based). *Application deadline:* For fall admission, 7/15 for domestic students; for spring admission, 11/15 for domestic students. Application fee: $50. Electronic applications accepted. *Financial support:* In 2006–07, 38 students received support. Scholarships/grants available. Support available to part-time students. Financial award application deadline: 6/1; financial award applicants required to submit FAFSA. *Unit head:* Dr. Paul DeSena, Coordinator, 310-338-2863, E-mail: pdesena@lmu.edu.

Loyola University Chicago, School of Education, Program in Community Counseling, Chicago, IL 60611-2196. Offers M Ed, MA. MA offered through the Graduate School. Part-time programs available. *Faculty:* 5 full-time (4 women), 4 part-time/adjunct (2 women). *Students:* 35. Average age 25. 70 applicants, 49% accepted, 10 enrolled. In 2006, 15 degrees awarded. *Degree requirements:* For master's, comprehensive exam. *Entrance requirements:* For master's, GRE General Test, minimum GPA of 3.0, letters of recommendation, resumé, transcripts. Additional exam requirements/recommendations for international students: Required—TOEFL (minimum score 550 paper-based; 213 computer-based). *Application deadline:* For fall admission, 2/15 for domestic and international students. Application fee: $50. Electronic applications accepted. *Financial support:* In 2006–07, 10 students received support; fellowships with full tuition reimbursements available, research assistantships with full tuition reimbursements available, teaching assistantships with full tuition reimbursements available, career-related internships or fieldwork and Federal Work-Study available. Financial award application deadline: 2/15; financial award applicants required to submit FAFSA. *Faculty research:* Career development, prevention, group counseling, family therapy, multicultural counseling. *Unit head:* Dr. Suzette Speight, Director, 312-915-6937, E-mail: sspeigh@luc.edu. *Application contact:* Marie Rosin-Dittmar, Information Contact, 312-915-6800, E-mail: schleduc@luc.edu.

Loyola University Chicago, School of Education, Program in School Counseling, Chicago, IL 60611-2196. Offers M Ed, Certificate. *Accreditation:* NCATE. *Faculty:* 5 full-time (4 women), 4 part-time/adjunct (2 women). *Students:* 35. Average age 25. 48 applicants, 60% accepted, 8 enrolled. In 2006, 17 degrees awarded. *Degree requirements:* For master's, comprehensive exam. *Entrance requirements:* For master's, GRE General Test, minimum GPA of 3.0, transcripts, letters of recommendation, resumé. Additional exam requirements/recommendations for international students: Required—TOEFL (minimum score 550 paper-based; 213 computer-based; 79 iBT). *Application deadline:* For fall admission, 2/15 for domestic and international students. Application fee: $50. Electronic applications accepted. *Financial support:* Career-related internships or fieldwork and Federal Work-Study available. Financial award application deadline: 2/15; financial award applicants required to submit FAFSA. *Faculty research:* Career development, group counseling, family therapy, child and adolescent development, multicultural counseling. *Unit head:* Dr. Suzette Speight, Director, 312-915-6937, E-mail: sspeigh@luc.edu. *Application contact:* Marie Rosin-Dittmar, Information Contact, 312-915-6800, E-mail: schleduc@luc.edu.

Loyola University New Orleans, College of Arts and Sciences, Department of Education and Counseling, Program in Counseling, New Orleans, LA 70118-6195. Offers MS. *Accreditation:* ACA. Part-time and evening/weekend programs available. *Degree requirements:* For master's, comprehensive exam. *Entrance requirements:* For master's, GRE, MAT (recommended), interview, letters of recommendation, writing sample. Additional exam requirements/recommendations for international students: Required—TOEFL (minimum score 550 paper-based; 213 computer-based). Electronic applications accepted. Expenses: Contact institution. *Faculty research:* Counseling theory, spirituality issues, group counseling, multicultural applications.

Lynchburg College, Graduate Studies, School of Education and Human Development, Program in Counselor Education, Lynchburg, VA 24501-3199. Offers community counseling (M Ed); school counseling (M Ed). *Accreditation:* ACA. *Faculty:* 5 full-time (3 women), 1 part-time/adjunct (0 women). *Students:* 43 full-time (39 women), 22 part-time (16 women); includes 8 minority (6 African Americans, 1 Asian American or Pacific Islander, 1 Hispanic American), 1 international. In 2006, 15 degrees awarded. *Application deadline:* For fall admission, 7/31 for domestic students, 6/1 for international students; for spring admission, 11/30 for domestic students, 10/1 for international students. *Expenses:* Tuition: Full-time $6,300; part-time $350 per credit. Required fees: $100. *Financial support:* Fellowships, teaching assistantships, career-related internships or fieldwork, scholarships/grants, and unspecified assistantships available. *Unit head:* Dr. Jeanne Booth, Program Coordinator, 434-544-8551.

Lyndon State College, Graduate Programs in Education, Department of Education, Lyndonville, VT 05851-0919. Offers curriculum and instruction (M Ed); reading specialist (M Ed); special education (M Ed); teaching and counseling (M Ed). Part-time and evening/weekend programs available. *Degree requirements:* For master's, exam or major field project. *Entrance requirements:* Additional exam requirements/recommendations for international students: Recommended—TOEFL (minimum score 500 paper-based; 173 computer-based).

Malone College, School of Arts and Sciences, Graduate Program in Counselor Education, Canton, OH 44709-3897. Offers clinical counseling (MA); school counseling (MA). Part-time and evening/weekend programs available. *Faculty:* 3 full-time (2 women), 4 part-time/adjunct (3 women). *Students:* 25 full-time (21 women), 79 part-time (61 women); includes 17 minority (all African Americans) Average age 35. In 2006, 21 degrees awarded. *Entrance requirements:* For master's, minimum undergraduate GPA of 3.0. *Application deadline:* Applications are processed on a rolling basis. Application fee: $25. *Expenses:* Tuition: Part-time $399 per credit hour. *Financial support:* Tuition waivers (partial) available. Support available to part-time students. Financial award application deadline: 6/30. *Faculty research:* Understanding pathological narcissism from a theological perspective, spiritual experiences of adolescents, stages of faith development related to grief/loss, school counseling competencies, multicultural issues in counseling. *Unit head:* Dr. Brock M. Reiman, Director, 330-471-8404, Fax: 330-471-8343, E-mail: breiman@malone.edu. *Application contact:* Dr. David Kleffman, Recruiter, 330-471-8447, Fax: 330-471-8343, E-mail: dkleffman@malone.edu.

Manhattan College, Graduate Division, School of Education, Program in Counseling, Riverdale, NY 10471. Offers MA, Diploma. Part-time and evening/weekend programs available. *Faculty:* 5 full-time (3 women), 9 part-time/adjunct (6 women). *Students:* 25 full-time (20 women), 86 part-time (70 women). 83 applicants, 63% accepted, 48 enrolled. In 2006, 26 master's, 5 other advanced degrees awarded. *Degree requirements:* For master's, thesis, internship. *Entrance requirements:* For master's, minimum GPA of 3.0. *Application deadline:* For fall admission, 8/1 priority date for domestic students; for spring admission, 12/20 for domestic students. Applications are processed on a rolling basis. Application fee: $50. *Financial support:* Scholarships/grants available. Financial award application deadline: 2/1. *Faculty research:* Cognition, family counseling. *Unit head:* Dr. Corine Fitzpatrick, Director, 718-862-7497. *Application contact:* Weldon Jackson.

Marshall University, Academic Affairs Division, College of Education and Human Services, Graduate School of Education and Professional Development, Program in Counseling, Huntington, WV 25755. Offers MA, Ed S. *Accreditation:* NCATE. Part-time and evening/weekend programs available. *Faculty:* 7 full-time (4 women), 20 part-time/adjunct (9 women). *Students:* 134 full-time (110 women), 132 part-time (112 women); includes 15 minority (12 African Americans, 2 Asian Americans or Pacific Islanders, 1 Hispanic American), 1 international. Average age 32. In 2006, 61 degrees awarded. *Degree requirements:* For master's, comprehensive or oral assessment, thesis optional. *Entrance requirements:* For master's, GRE General Test, MAT. Application fee: $40. *Financial support:* Career-related internships or fieldwork, Federal Work-Study, tuition waivers (full), and unspecified assistantships available.

Support available to part-time students. Financial award applicants required to submit FAFSA. *Unit head:* Dr. Michael Burton, Director, 304-746-1928, E-mail: mburton@marshall.edu. *Application contact:* Information Contact, 304-746-1900, Fax: 304-746-1902, E-mail: services@marshall.edu.

Marymount University, School of Education and Human Services, Program in School Counseling, Arlington, VA 22207-4299. Offers MA. *Accreditation:* ACA. Part-time programs available. *Students:* 14 full-time (13 women), 19 part-time (17 women); includes 5 minority (4 Asian Americans or Pacific Islanders, 1 Hispanic American). Average age 29. 26 applicants, 85% accepted, 12 enrolled. In 2006, 20 degrees awarded. *Entrance requirements:* For master's, GRE, interview, 2 letters of recommendation, resumé. *Application deadline:* For fall admission, 2/15 for domestic students. Application fee: $40. *Expenses:* Tuition: Full-time $11,160; part-time $620 per credit. Required fees: $113; $630 per credit. *Financial support:* Research assistantships with full tuition reimbursements, career-related internships or fieldwork, scholarships/grants, and unspecified assistantships available. Support available to part-time students. Financial award applicants required to submit FAFSA. *Unit head:* Dr. Tamara Davis, Coordinator, 703-526-6822, Fax: 703-284-3859, E-mail: tamara.davis@marymount.edu.

Marywood University, Academic Affairs, College of Education and Human Development, Department of Psychology and Counseling, Program in Counseling, Scranton, PA 18509-1598. Offers Certificate. *Students:* Average age 27. *Expenses:* Tuition: Part-time $672 per credit. Tuition and fees vary according to degree level, campus/location and program. *Unit head:* Dr. John Lemoncelli, Director, 570-348-6211 Ext. 2317, E-mail: lemoncelli@marywood.edu.

Marywood University, Academic Affairs, College of Education and Human Development, Department of Psychology and Counseling, Program in Elementary School Counseling, Scranton, PA 18509-1598. Offers MS. Part-time and evening/weekend programs available. *Students:* 3 full-time (all women), 6 part-time (all women). Average age 25. In 2006, 3 degrees awarded. *Degree requirements:* For master's, internship/practicum. *Entrance requirements:* For master's, GRE or MAT. Additional exam requirements/recommendations for international students: Required—TOEFL (minimum score 550 paper-based; 213 computer-based). *Application deadline:* For fall admission, 4/15 priority date for domestic and international students; for spring admission, 11/15 priority date for domestic and international students. Applications are processed on a rolling basis. Application fee: $30. Electronic applications accepted. *Expenses:* Tuition: Part-time $672 per credit. Tuition and fees vary according to degree level, campus/location and program. *Financial support:* Research assistantships with tuition reimbursements, career-related internships or fieldwork, scholarships/grants, tuition waivers (partial), and unspecified assistantships available. Support available to part-time students. Financial award application deadline: 2/15; financial award applicants required to submit FAFSA. *Unit head:* Dr. John Lemoncelli, Director, 570-348-6211 Ext. 2317, E-mail: lemoncelli@marywood.edu. *Application contact:* Dr. Deborah M. Flynn, Coordinator of Graduate Advising (Enrollment Management), 570-348-6211, E-mail: flynn@ac.marywood.edu.

Marywood University, Academic Affairs, College of Education and Human Development, Department of Psychology and Counseling, Program in Secondary School Counseling, Scranton, PA 18509-1598. Offers MS. Part-time and evening/weekend programs available. *Students:* 9 full-time (7 women), 13 part-time (all women). Average age 29. 11 applicants, 91% accepted. In 2006, 5 degrees awarded. *Degree requirements:* For master's, internship/practicum. *Entrance requirements:* For master's, GRE or MAT. Additional exam requirements/recommendations for international students: Required—TOEFL (minimum score 550 paper-based; 213 computer-based). *Application deadline:* For fall admission, 4/15 priority date for domestic and international students; for spring admission, 11/15 priority date for domestic and international students. Applications are processed on a rolling basis. Application fee: $30. Electronic applications accepted. *Expenses:* Tuition: Part-time $672 per credit. Tuition and fees vary according to degree level, campus/location and program. *Financial support:* Research assistantships with tuition reimbursements, career-related internships or fieldwork, scholarships/grants, tuition waivers (partial), and unspecified assistantships available. Support available to part-time students. Financial award application deadline: 2/15; financial award applicants required to submit FAFSA. *Unit head:* Dr. John Lemoncelli, Director, 570-348-6211 Ext. 2317, E-mail: lemoncelli@marywood.edu. *Application contact:* Dr. Deborah M. Flynn, Coordinator of Graduate Advising (Enrollment Management), 570-348-6211, E-mail: flynn@ac.marywood.edu.

McDaniel College, Graduate and Professional Studies, Program in Guidance and Counseling, Westminster, MD 21157-4390. Offers MS. Part-time and evening/weekend programs available. *Degree requirements:* For master's, internship, thesis optional. *Entrance requirements:* For master's, GRE General Test, MAT, or NTE/PRAXIS I, letters of reference (3). Additional exam requirements/recommendations for international students: Required—TOEFL (minimum score 213 computer-based).

McNeese State University, Graduate School, College of Education, Department of Teacher Education, Program in School Counseling, Lake Charles, LA 70609. Offers M Ed. *Accreditation:* NCATE. Evening/weekend programs available. *Faculty:* 2 full-time (both women). *Students:* 4 full-time (all women), 8 part-time (all women). In 2006, 5 degrees awarded. *Entrance requirements:* For master's, GRE, teaching certificate, 18 hours in professional education. *Application deadline:* For fall admission, 5/15 priority date for domestic students. Applications are processed on a rolling basis. Application fee: $20 ($30 for international students). *Expenses:* Tuition, area resident: Full-time $2,226; part-time $193 per hour. Required fees: $919; $106 per hour. *Financial support:* Application deadline: 5/1. *Unit head:* Dr. Wayne R Fetter, Dean, College of Education, 337-475-5432, Fax: 337-475-5467, E-mail: wfetter@mcneese.edu.

Mercy College, Division of Education, Dobbs Ferry, NY 10522-1189. Offers adolescence education: grades 7-12 (MS); applied behavior analysis (MS); bilingual education (MS); childhood education: grades 1-6 (MS); early childhood education: birth—grade 2 (MS); education (MS); elementary education (MS); learning technology (MS); middle childhood education: grades 5-9 (MS); reading (MS); school administration and supervision (MS); school building leadership (MS); school business administration (MS); secondary education (MS); special education (MS); students with disabilities: grades 5-9 (MS); students with disabilities: grades 7-12 (MS); teaching English to speakers of other languages (MS); teaching literacy: birth—grade 6 (MS); teaching literacy: grades 5-12 (MS); urban education (MS). *Students:* 572 full-time (467 women), 1,719 part-time (1,287 women); includes 943 minority (470 African Americans, 7 American Indian/Alaska Native, 48 Asian Americans or Pacific Islanders, 418 Hispanic Americans), 6 international. Average age 33. In 2006, 1090 degrees awarded. *Entrance requirements:* For master's, teaching certificate. *Application deadline:* For fall admission, 2/1 for domestic students. Applications are processed on a rolling basis. Application fee: $37. *Expenses:* Contact institution. Tuition and fees vary according to program. *Financial support:* Institutionally sponsored loans, scholarships/grants, and unspecified assistantships available. Support available to part-time students. *Faculty research:* Distance learning, literacy, assessment, community schools, impact of staff development. *Unit head:* Dr. William Prattella, Chairperson, 914-674-7555, Fax: 914-674-7352, E-mail: wprattella@mercy.edu. *Application contact:* Kathleen Jackson, Director of Admissions, 800-Mercy-NY, Fax: 914-674-7382, E-mail: admissions@mercy.edu.

Michigan State University, The Graduate School, College of Education, Department of Counseling, Educational Psychology and Special Education, East Lansing, MI 48824. Offers counseling (MA); educational psychology and educational technology (PhD); educational technology (MA); measurement and quantitative methods (PhD); rehabilitation counseling (MA); rehabilitation counselor education (PhD); school psychology (MA, PhD, Ed S); special education (MA, PhD). *Accreditation:* APA (one or more programs are accredited); CORE (one or more programs are accredited). Part-time programs available. *Faculty:* 36 full-time (13 women). *Students:* 218 full-time (149 women), 75 part-time (60 women); includes 38 minority (31 African Americans, 4 Asian Americans or Pacific Islanders, 3 Hispanic Americans), 63 international. Average age 31. 243 applicants, 44% accepted. In 2006, 136 master's, 34 doctorates awarded. *Entrance requirements:* Additional exam requirements/recommendations for international students: Required—TOEFL. Electronic applications accepted. *Expenses:* Tuition, state resident: part-time $346 per credit hour. Tuition, nonresident: part-time $730 per credit hour. Tuition and fees vary according to program. *Financial support:* In 2006–07, 125 fellowships with tuition reimbursements, 87 research assistantships with tuition reimbursements (averaging $13,854 per year), 67 teaching assistantships with tuition reimbursements (averaging $13,722 per year) were awarded. Total annual research expenditures: $3.4 million. *Unit head:* Dr. Richard S. Prawat, Chairperson, 517-353-6417, E-mail: rsprawat@msu.edu. *Application contact:* Kathy Dimoff, Admissions Coordinator, 517-355-6683, E-mail: dimoff@msu.edu.

Middle Tennessee State University, College of Graduate Studies, College of Education and Behavioral Science, Department of Psychology, Program in Professional Counseling, Murfreesboro, TN 37132. Offers curriculum and instruction (Ed S), including school psychology; school counseling (M Ed). *Accreditation:* ACA; NCATE. Part-time and evening/weekend programs available. Postbaccalaureate distance learning degree programs offered. *Students:* 11 applicants, 64% accepted. In 2006, 5 degrees awarded. *Degree requirements:* For master's, comprehensive exam. *Entrance requirements:* For master's, GRE or MAT. Additional exam requirements/recommendations for international students: Required—TOEFL (minimum score 525 paper-based; 195 computer-based). *Application deadline:* For fall admission, 8/1 priority date for domestic students. Applications are processed on a rolling basis. Application fee: $25. Electronic applications accepted. *Financial support:* Career-related internships or fieldwork, institutionally sponsored loans, and scholarships/grants available. Financial award application deadline: 5/1.

Midwestern State University, Graduate Studies, College of Education, Program in Counseling, Wichita Falls, TX 76308. Offers general counseling (MA); human resource development (MA); school counseling (M Ed); training and development (MA). Part-time and evening/weekend programs available. *Faculty:* 11 full-time (7 women), 5 part-time/adjunct (4 women). *Students:* 14 full-time (12 women), 96 part-time (80 women); includes 8 minority (3 African Americans, 1 American Indian/Alaska Native, 1 Asian American or Pacific Islander, 3 Hispanic Americans), 3 international. Average age 36. 30 applicants, 73% accepted, 17 enrolled. In 2006, 29 degrees awarded. *Degree requirements:* For master's, thesis (for some programs), comprehensive exam. *Entrance requirements:* For master's, GRE General Test, MAT, or GMAT, valid teaching certificate (M Ed). Additional exam requirements/recommendations for international students: Required—TOEFL (minimum score 550 paper-based; 213 computer-based). *Application deadline:* For fall admission, 7/1 for domestic students, 4/1 for international students; for spring admission, 11/1 for domestic students, 8/1 for international students. Applications are processed on a rolling basis. Application fee: $35 ($50 for international students). Electronic applications accepted. *Financial support:* In 2006–07, 79 students received support, including 5 teaching assistantships with partial tuition reimbursements available (averaging $5,833 per year); career-related internships or fieldwork, Federal Work-Study, institutionally sponsored loans, scholarships/grants, tuition waivers (partial), and unspecified assistantships also available. Support available to part-time students. Financial award application deadline: 5/1; financial award applicants required to submit FAFSA. *Unit head:* Dr. Michaelle Kitchen, Chair, 940-397-4141, Fax: 940-397-4694, E-mail: michaelle.kitchen@mwsu.edu. *Application contact:* 800-842-1922, Fax: 940-397-4672, E-mail: admissions@mwsu.edu.

Minnesota State University Mankato, College of Graduate Studies, College of Education, Department of Counseling and Student Personnel, Mankato, MN 56001. Offers college student affairs (MS); marriage and family (Certificate); professional community counseling (MS); professional school counseling (MS). *Accreditation:* ACA (one or more programs are accredited); NCATE. *Students:* 70 full-time (59 women), 39 part-time (34 women). Average age 30. In 2006, 49 degrees awarded. *Degree requirements:* For master's, thesis or alternative, comprehensive exam. *Entrance requirements:* For master's, GRE General Test or MAT (if GPA is below 3.0 for last 2 years), minimum GPA of 3.0 during previous 2 years, 3 letters of reference. Additional exam requirements/recommendations for international students: Required—TOEFL. *Application deadline:* For fall admission, 3/15 priority date for domestic students; for spring admission, 11/20 for domestic students. Applications are processed on a rolling basis. Application fee: $40. Electronic applications accepted. *Financial support:* Research assistantships with full tuition reimbursements, teaching assistantships with full tuition reimbursements, career-related internships or fieldwork, Federal Work-Study, institutionally sponsored loans, and unspecified assistantships available. Support available to part-time students. Financial award application deadline: 3/15; financial award applicants required to submit FAFSA. *Unit head:* Dr. Richard Auger, Chairperson, 507-389-5658. *Application contact:* 507-389-2321, E-mail: grad@mnsu.edu.

Minnesota State University Moorhead, Graduate Studies, College of Education and Human Services, Program in Counseling and Student Affairs, Moorhead, MN 56563-0002. Offers MS. *Accreditation:* ACA; NCATE. Part-time and evening/weekend programs available. *Faculty:* 3 full-time (1 woman), 1 (woman) part-time/adjunct. *Students:* 8 full-time (7 women), 41 part-time (35 women); includes 1 American Indian/Alaska Native, 1 Hispanic American, 1 international. 17 applicants, 41% accepted. In 2006, 9 degrees awarded. *Degree requirements:* For master's, final oral exam, internship, project or thesis. *Entrance requirements:* For master's, GRE or MAT, interview, 3 letters of recommendation, minimum GPA of 3.0. Additional exam requirements/recommendations for international students: Required—TOEFL (minimum score 550 paper-based; 213 computer-based). *Application deadline:* For fall admission, 2/1 priority date for domestic students, 1/1 for international students; for spring admission, 9/15 priority date for domestic students, 8/15 for international students. Applications are processed on a rolling basis. Application fee: $20. Electronic applications accepted. *Financial support:* In 2006–07, 3 research assistantships (averaging $3,000 per year) were awarded; career-related internships or fieldwork, Federal Work-Study, and unspecified assistantships also available. Financial award application deadline: 7/15; financial award applicants required to submit FAFSA. *Unit head:* Dr. Wesley Erwin, Coordinator, 218-477-2009, E-mail: erwin@mnstate.edu.

Mississippi College, Graduate School, School of Education, Department of Psychology and Counseling, Clinton, MS 39058. Offers counseling (Ed S); marriage and family counseling (MS); mental health counseling (MS); school counseling (M Ed). Part-time programs available. *Faculty:* 6 full-time (2 women), 2 part-time/adjunct (0 women). *Students:* 31 full-time (27 women), 59 part-time (53 women); includes 38 minority (36 African Americans, 2 American Indian/Alaska Native), 4 international. Average age 31. In 2006, 24 degrees awarded. *Degree requirements:* For master's and Ed S, thesis optional. *Entrance requirements:* For master's, GRE or NTE. Additional exam requirements/recommendations for international students: Recommended—IELTS. *Application deadline:* Applications are processed on a rolling basis. Application fee: $25. Electronic applications accepted. *Expenses:* Tuition: Full-time $7,290; part-time $405 per hour. Required fees: $150 per term. Tuition and fees vary according to campus/location and program. *Financial support:* Career-related internships or fieldwork, Federal Work-Study, and unspecified assistantships available. Support available to part-time students. Financial award applicants required to submit FAFSA. *Unit head:* Dr. Buddy Wagner, Interim Chair, 601-925-3354, E-mail: bwagner@mc.edu.

Mississippi State University, College of Education, Department of Counseling, Educational Psychology, and Special Education, Mississippi State, MS 39762. Offers counselor education (MS, PhD, Ed S); educational psychology (MS, PhD, Ed S); special education (MS, Ed S). *Accreditation:* ACA (one or more programs are accredited); APA; CORE (one or more programs are accredited); NCATE. Part-time programs available. Postbaccalaureate distance learning degree programs offered (minimal on-campus study). *Faculty:* 24 full-time (13 women), 10 part-time/adjunct (8 women). *Students:* 120 full-time (94 women), 72 part-time (62 women); includes 68 minority (66 African Americans, 2 Asian Americans or Pacific Islanders), 4 international. Average age 29. 61 applicants, 72% accepted, 32 enrolled. In 2006, 73 master's, 2 doctorates awarded. Terminal master's awarded for partial completion of doctoral program. *Degree requirements:* For master's, thesis optional; for doctorate, thesis/dissertation, comprehensive oral and written exam. *Entrance requirements:* For master's, GRE, minimum QPA of 3.0; for doctorate, GRE, interview, minimum GPA of 3.4. Additional exam requirements/recommendations for international students: Required—TOEFL. *Application deadline:* For fall admission, 3/15 for domestic students. Application fee: $30. *Expenses:* Tuition, state resident: full-time $4,550; part-time $253 per hour. Tuition, nonresident: full-time $10,552; part-time $584 per hour. International tuition: $10,882 full-time. Tuition and fees vary according to course load. *Financial support:* In 2006–07, 30 students received support, including 6 teaching assistantships with full tuition reimbursements available (averaging $7,554 per year); research assistantships with full tuition reimbursements available, career-related internships or fieldwork, Federal Work-Study, institutionally sponsored loans, and unspecified assistantships also available. Financial award application deadline: 2/1; financial award applicants required to submit FAFSA. *Faculty research:* HIV-AIDS in college population, substance abuse in youth and college students, ADHD and conduct disorders in youth, assessment and identification of early childhood disabilities, assessment and vocational transition of the disabled. *Unit head:* Dr. Thomas W. Hosie, Head, 662-325-3426, Fax: 662-325-3263, E-mail: hosie@colled.msstate.edu. *Application contact:* Dr. Phil Bonfanti, Director of Admissions, 662-325-4104, Fax: 662-325-8872, E-mail: admit@msstate.edu.

Missouri State University, Graduate College, College of Education, Department of Counseling, Springfield, MO 65804-0094. Offers MS. Part-time and evening/weekend programs available. *Faculty:* 4 full-time (1 woman), 2 part-time/adjunct (both women). *Students:* 43 full-time (38 women), 72 part-time (64 women); includes 5 minority (4 African Americans, 1 American Indian/Alaska Native). Average age 33. 25 applicants, 64% accepted, 10 enrolled. In 2006, 47 degrees awarded. *Degree requirements:* For master's, thesis or alternative, comprehensive exam. *Entrance requirements:* For master's, GRE or MAT, minimum GPA of 2.75. Additional exam requirements/recommendations for international students: Required—TOEFL (minimum score 550 paper-based; 213 computer-based; 79 iBT). *Application deadline:* For fall admission, 2/7 for domestic students; for spring admission, 10/7 for domestic students. Applications are processed on a rolling basis. Application fee: $35. Electronic applications accepted. *Expenses:* Tuition, state resident: full-time $3,582; part-time $199 per credit hour. Tuition, nonresident: full-time $6,984; part-time $199 per credit hour. Required fees: $548. Full-time tuition and fees vary according to course level, course load, program and reciprocity agreements. *Financial support:* In 2006–07, 2 teaching assistantships with full tuition reimbursements (averaging $6,780 per year) were awarded; research assistantships with full tuition reimbursements, Federal Work-Study, institutionally sponsored loans, scholarships/grants, and unspecified assistantships also available. Financial award application deadline: 3/31; financial award applicants required to submit FAFSA. *Faculty research:* Self-esteem development, stress management, ethnic counseling, prejudices. *Unit head:* Dr. Charles Barke, Head, 417-836-5449, Fax: 417-836-6905, E-mail: crbarke@missouristate.edu.

Montana State University–Billings, College of Education and Human Services, Department of Special Education, Counseling, Reading and Early Childhood, Option in School Counseling, Billings, MT 59101-0298. Offers M Ed. *Accreditation:* NCATE. Part-time programs available. *Students:* 41. 40 applicants, 100% accepted, 40 enrolled. In 2006, 13 degrees awarded. *Degree requirements:* For master's, thesis or professional paper and/or field experience, thesis optional. *Entrance requirements:* For master's, GRE General Test or MAT, minimum GPA of 3.0 (undergraduate), 3.25 (graduate). *Application deadline:* Applications are processed on a rolling basis. Application fee: $40. *Expenses:* Tuition, state resident: full-time $4,599. Tuition, nonresident: full-time $10,786. *Financial support:* Teaching assistantships, career-related internships or fieldwork, Federal Work-Study, institutionally sponsored loans, scholarships/grants, tuition waivers (partial), and unspecified assistantships available. Support available to part-time students. Financial award application deadline: 5/1; financial award applicants required to submit FAFSA. *Application contact:* David M. Sullivan, Graduate Studies Counselor, 406-657-2053, Fax: 406-657-2299, E-mail: dsullivan@msubillings.edu.

Montana State University–Northern, College of Education and Graduate Programs, Option in Counselor Education, Havre, MT 59501-7751. Offers M Ed. *Accreditation:* NCATE. Part-time and evening/weekend programs available. *Degree requirements:* For master's, oral exams, thesis optional. *Entrance requirements:* For master's, GRE General Test or MAT, minimum GPA of 3.0. Electronic applications accepted.

Montclair State University, The Graduate School, College of Education and Human Services, Department of Counseling, Human Development, and Educational Leadership, Montclair, NJ 07043-1624. Offers administration and supervision (MA), including administration and supervision, educator/trainer; advanced counseling (Certificate); counseling and guidance (MA), including addictions counseling, community counseling, student affairs; school administrator (Certificate); school business administrator (Certificate); school counselor (Certificate); substance awareness coordinator (Certificate). *Accreditation:* NCATE. Part-time and evening/weekend programs available. *Faculty:* 14 full-time (10 women), 18 part-time/adjunct (7 women). *Students:* 144 full-time (122 women), 551 part-time (406 women); includes 142 minority (66 African Americans, 18 Asian Americans or Pacific Islanders, 58 Hispanic Americans), 5 international. Average age 33. 217 applicants, 56% accepted, 90 enrolled. In 2006, 65 master's, 10 other advanced degrees awarded. *Degree requirements:* For master's, thesis or alternative, comprehensive exam. *Entrance requirements:* For master's, GRE General Test, interview, 2 letters of recommendation. Additional exam requirements/recommendations for international students: Required—TOEFL (minimum score 83 computer-based). *Application deadline:* For fall admission, 6/1 for international students; for spring admission, 10/1 for international students. Applications are processed on a rolling basis. Application fee: $60. Electronic applications accepted. *Expenses:* Tuition, state resident: part-time $450 per credit. Tuition, nonresident: part-time $682 per credit. Tuition and fees vary according to degree level and program. *Financial support:* In 2006–07, 14 research assistantships with full tuition reimbursements (averaging $7,000 per year) were awarded; Federal Work-Study, scholarships/grants, and unspecified assistantships also available. Support available to part-time students. Financial award application deadline: 3/1; financial award applicants required to submit FAFSA. *Faculty research:* K-12 education, data collection. Total annual research expenditures: $24,000. *Unit head:* Dr. Catherine Roland, Chairperson, 973-655-7216, E-mail: rolandc@mail.montclair.edu.

Morehead State University, Graduate Programs, College of Education, Department of Professional Programs in Education, Program in Counseling, Morehead, KY 40351. Offers MA Ed, Ed S. *Accreditation:* NCATE. Part-time and evening/weekend programs available. *Students:* 12 full-time (9 women), 81 part-time (71 women); includes 2 minority (both African Americans) Average age 32. In 2006, 35 degrees awarded. *Degree requirements:* For master's, oral and/or written comprehensive exams, thesis optional; for Ed S, thesis, oral exam. *Entrance requirements:* For master's, GRE General Test, MAT, minimum GPA of 2.5, teaching certificate, 2 years of work experience; for Ed S, GRE General Test, interview, master's degree, minimum GPA of 3.5, work experience. Additional exam requirements/recommendations for international students: Required—TOEFL (minimum score 525 paper-based; 197 computer-based). *Application deadline:* For fall admission, 8/1 priority date for domestic and international students; for spring admission, 12/1 priority date for domestic and international students. Applications are processed on a rolling basis. Application fee: $0 ($55 for international students). Electronic applications accepted. *Financial support:* In 2006–07, teaching assistantships (averaging $6,000 per year); Federal Work-Study and unspecified assistantships also available. Financial award application deadline: 4/1; financial award applicants required to submit FAFSA. *Faculty research:* Child abuse and neglect, school-to-work transformation, computer use by school counselors, adult children of alcoholics. *Application contact:* Michelle Barber, Graduate Admissions Counselor, 606-783-2039, Fax: 606-783-5061, E-mail: m.barber@moreheadstate.edu.

Mount Mary College, Graduate Programs, Program in Community Counseling, Milwaukee, WI 53222-4597. Offers MS. Part-time and evening/weekend programs available. *Faculty:* 1 (woman) full-time, 6 part-time/adjunct (4 women). *Students:* 26 full-time (all women), 27 part-time (all women); includes 10 minority (9 African Americans, 1 Hispanic American). Average age 36. 41 applicants, 41% accepted, 12 enrolled. In 2006, 5 degrees awarded. *Degree requirements:* For master's, thesis or alternative, comprehensive exam. *Entrance requirements:* For master's, minimum GPA of 3.0. Additional exam requirements/recommendations for international students: Required—TOEFL (minimum score 500 paper-

Counselor Education

Mount Mary College (continued)
based; 173 computer-based). *Application deadline:* For fall admission, 8/1 priority date for domestic and international students; for spring admission, 12/1 priority date for domestic and international students. Application fee: $35 ($75 for international students). *Expenses:* Tuition: Part-time $490 per credit. Required fees: $48 per term. Tuition and fees vary according to course load and program. *Financial support:* Career-related internships or fieldwork available. Support available to part-time students. Financial award applicants required to submit FAFSA. *Faculty research:* Cognitive behavioral interventions for depression, eating disorders and compliance. *Unit head:* Dr. Amy Ridley Meyers, Director, 414-258-4810.

Murray State University, College of Education, Department of Educational Studies, Leadership and Counseling, Program in Community and Agency Counseling, Murray, KY 42071. Offers Ed S. *Accreditation:* NCATE. Part-time programs available. *Students:* 20. *Degree requirements:* For Ed S, thesis, comprehensive exam. *Entrance requirements:* For degree, GRE General Test. Additional exam requirements/recommendations for international students: Required—TOEFL. *Application deadline:* Applications are processed on a rolling basis. Application fee: $25. *Financial support:* Research assistantships, teaching assistantships, Federal Work-Study available. Financial award application deadline: 4/1.

Murray State University, College of Education, Department of Educational Studies, Leadership and Counseling, Programs in School Guidance and Counseling, Murray, KY 42071. Offers MA Ed, Ed S. *Accreditation:* NCATE. Part-time programs available. *Students:* 118. 15 applicants, 80% accepted. *Degree requirements:* For master's, thesis (for some programs), portfolio, comprehensive exam; for Ed S, portfolio. *Entrance requirements:* For master's, GRE General Test or MAT. Additional exam requirements/recommendations for international students: Required—TOEFL. *Application deadline:* Applications are processed on a rolling basis. Application fee: $25. *Financial support:* Research assistantships, teaching assistantships, Federal Work-Study available. Financial award application deadline: 4/1. *Unit head:* Dr. Thomas Holcomb, Chairman, 270-809-2795, Fax: 270-809-3799, E-mail: tom.holcomb@coe.murraystate.edu.

National-Louis University, College of Arts and Sciences, Department of Counseling and Human Services, Chicago, IL 60603. Offers addictions counseling (Certificate); addictions treatment (Certificate); career counseling and development studies (Certificate); community counseling (MS); community wellness and prevention (Certificate); counseling (Certificate); eating disorders counseling (Certificate); employee assistance programs (MS, Certificate); gerontology administration (Certificate); gerontology counseling (MS, Certificate); human services administration (MS, Certificate); long-term care administration (Certificate); school counseling (MS). Part-time programs available. *Students:* 15 full-time (11 women), 229 part-time (187 women); includes 69 minority (56 African Americans, 1 American Indian/Alaska Native, 2 Asian Americans or Pacific Islanders, 10 Hispanic Americans). Average age 38. 71 applicants, 96% accepted. In 2006, 53 master's, 6 other advanced degrees awarded. *Degree requirements:* For master's and Certificate, internship. *Entrance requirements:* For master's and Certificate, GRE, MAT, or Watson-Glaser Critical Thinking Appraisal, interview, minimum GPA of 3.0. *Application deadline:* Applications are processed on a rolling basis. Application fee: $25. *Expenses:* Tuition: Full-time $17,685. One-time fee: $40 full-time. *Financial support:* Federal Work-Study, institutionally sponsored loans, scholarships/grants, and tuition waivers available. Support available to part-time students. Financial award applicants required to submit FAFSA. *Faculty research:* Religion and aging, drug abuse prevention, hunger, homelessness, multicultural diversity. *Unit head:* Dr. Susan Thorne-Devin, Assistant Dean, 847-475-1100 Ext.4511. *Application contact:* David McCulloch, Vice President for University Services, 800-443-5522 Ext. 5127, Fax: 847-465-0593, E-mail: dmcc@wheeling1.nl.edu.

National University, Academic Affairs, School of Education, Department of School Counseling and Psychology, La Jolla, CA 92037-1011. Offers educational counseling (MS); school psychology (MS). Part-time and evening/weekend programs available. Postbaccalaureate distance learning degree programs offered (no on-campus study). *Faculty:* 9 full-time (4 women), 150 part-time/adjunct (83 women). *Students:* 312 full-time (247 women), 375 part-time (299 women); includes 269 minority (69 African Americans, 4 American Indian/Alaska Native, 32 Asian Americans or Pacific Islanders, 164 Hispanic Americans). Average age 34. 434 applicants, 395 enrolled. In 2006, 95 degrees awarded. *Degree requirements:* For master's, thesis (for some programs). *Entrance requirements:* For master's, interview, minimum GPA of 2.5. Additional exam requirements/recommendations for international students: Required—TOEFL (minimum score 550 paper-based; 213 computer-based; 80 iBT), IELTS (minimum score 6). *Application deadline:* Applications are processed on a rolling basis. Application fee: $60 ($65 for international students). Electronic applications accepted. *Expenses:* Tuition: Full-time $7,722; part-time $286 per unit. One-time fee: $60. *Financial support:* Career-related internships or fieldwork, institutionally sponsored loans, scholarships/grants, and tuition waivers (partial) available. Support available to part-time students. Financial award application deadline: 6/30; financial award applicants required to submit FAFSA. *Unit head:* Dr. Susan Eldred, Chair, 858-642-8372, Fax: 858-642-8724, E-mail: seldred@nu.edu. *Application contact:* Dominick Giovanniello, Associate Regional Dean—San Diego, 800-NAT-UNIV, Fax: 858-642-8709, E-mail: dgiovann@nu.edu.

New Mexico Highlands University, Graduate Studies, School of Education, Las Vegas, NM 87701. Offers education (MA), including curriculum and instruction; educational leadership (MA); exercise and sport sciences (MA), including human performance and sport, sports administration, teacher education; guidance and counseling (MA), including professional counseling, rehabilitation counseling, school counseling; special education (MA), including). *Accreditation:* NCATE. Part-time programs available. *Faculty:* 14 full-time (6 women), 11 part-time/adjunct (9 women). *Students:* 171 full-time (117 women), 413 part-time (286 women); includes 305 minority (17 African Americans, 30 American Indian/Alaska Native, 4 Asian Americans or Pacific Islanders, 254 Hispanic Americans), 3 international. Average age 40. 111 applicants, 84% accepted, 63 enrolled. In 2006, 111 degrees awarded. *Degree requirements:* For master's, thesis or alternative, comprehensive exam, registration. *Entrance requirements:* For master's, minimum undergraduate GPA of 3.0. Additional exam requirements/recommendations for international students: Required—TOEFL (minimum score 540 paper-based; 190 computer-based). *Application deadline:* For fall admission, 8/1 priority date for domestic students. Applications are processed on a rolling basis. Application fee: $15. *Expenses:* Tuition, state resident: part-time $101 per credit hour. Tuition, nonresident: part-time $101 per credit hour. *Financial support:* In 2006–07, 205 students received support, including 16 teaching assistantships with full and partial tuition reimbursements available (averaging $6,500 per year); career-related internships or fieldwork, Federal Work-Study, institutionally sponsored loans, scholarships/grants, traineeships, tuition waivers (partial), and unspecified assistantships also available. Support available to part-time students. Financial award application deadline: 3/1; financial award applicants required to submit FAFSA. *Unit head:* Dr. Francisco Hidalgo, Dean, 505-454-3357, Fax: 505-454-3384, E-mail: fhidalgo@nmhu.edu. *Application contact:* Diane Trujillo, Administrative Assistant Graduate Studies, 505-454-3266, Fax: 505-454-3558, E-mail: dtrujillo@nmhu.edu.

New Mexico State University, Graduate School, College of Education, Department of Counseling and Educational Psychology, Las Cruces, NM 88003-8001. Offers counseling and guidance (MA); counseling psychology (PhD); school psychology (Ed S). *Accreditation:* ACA; APA (one or more programs are accredited); NCATE. Part-time programs available. *Faculty:* 12 full-time (4 women). *Students:* 80 full-time (62 women), 15 part-time (9 women); includes 51 minority (7 African Americans, 1 American Indian/Alaska Native, 2 Asian Americans or Pacific Islanders, 41 Hispanic Americans), 2 international. Average age 33. 37 applicants, 38% accepted. In 2006, 9 master's, 3 other advanced degrees awarded. *Degree requirements:* For master's, internship, thesis optional; for doctorate, thesis/dissertation, internship; for Ed S, thesis or alternative, internship. *Entrance requirements:* For master's and Ed S, GRE General Test; for doctorate, GRE General Test, master's degree in counseling. *Application deadline:* For fall admission, 12/15 priority date for domestic students; for spring admission, 4/1 priority date for domestic students. Application fee: $30 ($50 for international students). Electronic applications accepted. *Financial support:* In 2006–07, 2 fellowships, 16 teaching assistantships were awarded; career-related internships or fieldwork, Federal Work-Study, institutionally sponsored loans, scholarships/grants, health care benefits, and unspecified assistantships also available. Support available to part-time students. Financial award application deadline: 3/1. *Faculty research:* Multicultural counseling, identity development, acculturation. *Unit head:* Dr. Luis Vazquez, Head, 505-646-2121, Fax: 505-646-8035, E-mail: lvazquez@nmsu.edu.

New York Institute of Technology, Graduate Division, School of Education and Professional Services, Program in School Counseling, Old Westbury, NY 11568-8000. Offers MS. *Students:* 2 full-time (both women), 70 part-time (56 women); includes 14 minority (9 African Americans, 1 Asian American or Pacific Islander, 4 Hispanic Americans), 3 international. Average age 32. 54 applicants, 70% accepted, 31 enrolled. In 2006, 22 degrees awarded. *Degree requirements:* For master's, internship. *Entrance requirements:* For master's, minimum GPA of 3.0, interview, 3 letters of reference. Additional exam requirements/recommendations for international students: Required—TOEFL. *Application deadline:* For fall admission, 7/1 priority date for domestic students; for spring admission, 12/1 priority date for domestic students. Applications are processed on a rolling basis. Application fee: $50. Electronic applications accepted. *Expenses:* Tuition: Full-time $16,800; part-time $700 per credit. *Financial support:* Research assistantships available. *Unit head:* Dr. Carol Dahir, Coordinator, 516-686-7616, Fax: 516-686-7655, E-mail: cdahir@nyit.edu. *Application contact:* Jacquelyn Nealon, Dean of Admissions and Financial Aid, 516-686-7925, Fax: 516-686-7613, E-mail: jnealon@nyit.edu.

New York University, Steinhardt School of Culture, Education and Human Development, Department of Applied Psychology, Program in Counselor Education, New York, NY 10012-1019. Offers counseling and guidance (MA, Advanced Certificate), including bilingual school counseling (MA), school counseling (MA); counseling for mental health and wellness (MA); counseling psychology (PhD). *Accreditation:* APA (one or more programs are accredited). Part-time and evening/weekend programs available. *Faculty:* 9 full-time (5 women). *Students:* 137 full-time (107 women), 81 part-time (67 women); includes 78 minority (34 African Americans, 19 Asian Americans or Pacific Islanders, 25 Hispanic Americans), 18 international. 463 applicants, 41% accepted, 90 enrolled. In 2006, 79 master's, 8 doctorates awarded. Terminal master's awarded for partial completion of doctoral program. *Degree requirements:* For master's, thesis (for some programs); for doctorate, thesis/dissertation. *Entrance requirements:* For doctorate, GRE General Test, interview. Additional exam requirements/recommendations for international students: Required—TOEFL. *Application deadline:* For fall admission, 1/15 priority date for domestic and international students; for spring admission, 11/1 for domestic and international students. Applications are processed on a rolling basis. Application fee: $50. *Expenses:* Tuition: Part-time $1,080 per unit. Required fees: $56 per unit. $329 per term. Tuition and fees vary according to program. *Financial support:* Fellowships with full and partial tuition reimbursements, teaching assistantships with partial tuition reimbursements, career-related internships or fieldwork, Federal Work-Study, institutionally sponsored loans, scholarships/grants, tuition waivers (partial), and unspecified assistantships available. Support available to part-time students. Financial award application deadline: 2/1; financial award applicants required to submit FAFSA. *Faculty research:* Cross-cultural counseling; group dynamics; culture, race and ethnicity; religiosity and psychological development; well-being and mental health. *Unit head:* Dr. Mary Sue Richardson, Director, 212-998-5559, Fax: 212-995-4358. *Application contact:* 212-998-5030, Fax: 212-995-4328, E-mail: steinhardt.gradadmissions@nyu.edu.

Niagara University, Graduate Division of Education, Concentration in Mental Health Counseling, Niagara Falls, Niagara University, NY 14109. Offers MS Ed, Certificate. *Faculty:* 2 full-time (1 woman), 3 part-time/adjunct (all women). *Students:* 12 full-time (all women), 14 part-time (12 women); includes 1 minority (African American), 5 international. In 2006, 4 degrees awarded. *Entrance requirements:* For master's, GRE General Test or MAT. *Application deadline:* For fall admission, 8/1 for domestic students. Applications are processed on a rolling basis. Application fee: $30. *Expenses: Contact institution. Financial support:* Fellowships, career-related internships or fieldwork and Federal Work-Study available. Financial award application deadline: 3/15. *Unit head:* Dr. Barbara Iannarelli, Chair, 716-286-8547. *Application contact:* Dr. Debra A. Colley, Dean of Education, 716-286-8560, Fax: 716-286-8561, E-mail: dcolley@niagara.edu.

Niagara University, Graduate Division of Education, Concentration in School Counseling, Niagara Falls, Niagara University, NY 14109. Offers school business administration (MS Ed, Certificate). *Accreditation:* NCATE. Part-time and evening/weekend programs available. *Faculty:* 2 full-time (1 woman), 3 part-time/adjunct (all women). *Students:* 26 full-time (18 women), 20 part-time (16 women); includes 5 minority (1 African American, 3 American Indian/Alaska Native, 1 Hispanic American), 1 international. In 2006, 17 master's, 9 other advanced degrees awarded. *Entrance requirements:* For master's, GRE General Test or MAT; for Certificate, GRE General Test, GRE Subject Test or MAT. *Application deadline:* For fall admission, 8/1 for domestic students. Applications are processed on a rolling basis. Application fee: $30. *Expenses: Contact institution. Financial support:* Career-related internships or fieldwork and Federal Work-Study available. Financial award application deadline: 3/15. *Unit head:* Dr. Barbara Iannarelli, Chair, 716-286-8547. *Application contact:* Dr. Debra A. Colley, Dean of Education, 716-286-8560, Fax: 716-286-8561, E-mail: dcolley@niagara.edu.

Nicholls State University, Graduate Studies, College of Education, Department of Teacher Education, Thibodaux, LA 70310. Offers administration and supervision (M Ed); counselor education (M Ed); curriculum and instruction (M Ed). *Accreditation:* NCATE. Part-time and evening/weekend programs available. *Faculty:* 17 full-time (13 women), 6 part-time/adjunct (4 women). *Students:* 21 full-time (17 women), 174 part-time (155 women); includes 60 minority (52 African Americans, 5 American Indian/Alaska Native, 1 Asian American or Pacific Islander, 2 Hispanic Americans). Average age 33. In 2006, 77 degrees awarded. *Degree requirements:* For master's, portfolio. *Entrance requirements:* For master's, GRE General Test, teaching license. *Application deadline:* Applications are processed on a rolling basis. Application fee: $20 ($30 for international students). Electronic applications accepted. *Expenses:* Tuition, state resident: part-time $450 per hour. Tuition, nonresident: part-time $450 per hour. *Financial support:* In 2006–07, research assistantships with tuition reimbursements (averaging $4,000 per year). Financial award application deadline: 6/17. *Unit head:* Dr. J. Lavone Landry, Head, 985-448-4314, E-mail: lavone.landry@nicholls.edu.

North Carolina Agricultural and Technical State University, Graduate School, School of Education, Department of Human Development and Services, Greensboro, NC 27411. Offers guidance and counseling (MS); human resources (MS). *Accreditation:* ACA. Part-time and evening/weekend programs available. *Degree requirements:* For master's, thesis, qualifying exam, comprehensive exam. *Entrance requirements:* For master's, GRE General Test, minimum GPA of 3.0.

North Carolina Central University, Division of Academic Affairs, School of Education, Programs in Counseling, Durham, NC 27707-3129. Offers agency counseling (MA); career counseling (MA); school counseling (MA). *Accreditation:* ACA; NCATE. Part-time and evening/weekend programs available. *Degree requirements:* For master's, thesis or alternative, comprehensive exam. *Entrance requirements:* For master's, GRE, minimum GPA of 3.0 in major, 2.5 overall. Additional exam requirements/recommendations for international students: Required—TOEFL. *Faculty research:* Becoming a leader, skill building in academia.

North Carolina State University, Graduate School, College of Education, Department of Educational Research, Leadership and Counselor Education, Program in Counselor Education, Raleigh, NC 27695. Offers M Ed, MS, PhD. *Accreditation:* ACA. *Degree requirements:* For master's, thesis (for some programs). *Entrance requirements:* For master's, GRE or MAT. Electronic applications accepted. *Faculty research:* Career development, retention of at-risk students in higher education, psycho-social development, multicultural issues, cognitive-developmental interventions.

North Dakota State University, The Graduate School, College of Human Development and Education, School of Education, Program in Counseling, Fargo, ND 58105. Offers M Ed, MS, PhD. *Accreditation:* ACA; NCATE. Part-time programs available. Postbaccalaureate distance learning degree programs offered (minimal on-campus study). *Faculty:* 5 full-time (3 women), 1 (woman) part-time/adjunct. *Students:* 23 full-time (20 women), 39 part-time (33 women); includes 5 minority (all American Indian/Alaska Native). Average age 35. 35 applicants, 54% accepted, 19 enrolled. In 2006, 18 master's, 2 doctorates awarded. *Degree requirements:* For master's, thesis or alternative, comprehensive exam; for doctorate, thesis/dissertation, comprehensive exam. *Entrance requirements:* For master's, GRE, MAT, interview. Additional exam requirements/recommendations for international students: Required—TOEFL. *Application deadline:* For fall admission, 2/15 for domestic students. Applications are processed on a rolling basis. Application fee: $45 ($60 for international students). *Financial support:* Teaching assistantships, career-related internships or fieldwork, Federal Work-Study, institutionally sponsored loans, and tuition waivers (full) available. Financial award application deadline: 4/15. *Faculty research:* Supervision, program assessment, multicultural issues. *Unit head:* Dr. Robert Nielsen, Coordinator, 701-231-7202, Fax: 701-231-7416, E-mail: robert.nielsen@ndsu.edu.

Northeastern Illinois University, Graduate College, College of Education, Department of Counselor Education, Chicago, IL 60625-4699. Offers guidance and counseling (MA), including career development, community and family counseling, elementary school counseling, secondary school counseling. *Accreditation:* ACA. Part-time and evening/weekend programs available. *Faculty:* 9 full-time (5 women), 2 part-time/adjunct (1 woman). *Students:* 44 full-time (32 women), 172 part-time (127 women); includes 41 minority (15 African Americans, 10 Asian Americans or Pacific Islanders, 16 Hispanic Americans). Average age 42. 94 applicants, 69% accepted. In 2006, 11 degrees awarded. *Degree requirements:* For master's, thesis or alternative, internship, practicum, comprehensive exam. *Entrance requirements:* For master's, GRE, minimum GPA of 2.75, workshop. *Application deadline:* For fall admission, 4/1 priority date for domestic students; for spring admission, 8/15 for domestic students. Applications are processed on a rolling basis. Application fee: $25. *Financial support:* In 2006–07, 31 students received support, including 5 research assistantships with full tuition reimbursements available (averaging $6,600 per year); career-related internships or fieldwork, Federal Work-Study, institutionally sponsored loans, and tuition waivers (full and partial) also available. Support available to part-time students. *Faculty research:* Psychological factors of the visually impaired, reclaiming self through art, ego development, multicultural counseling, family therapy.

Northeastern State University, Graduate College, College of Education, Department of Psychology and Counseling, Program in School Counseling, Tahlequah, OK 74464-2399. Offers M Ed. Part-time and evening/weekend programs available. *Students:* 31 full-time (27 women), 23 part-time (22 women); includes 16 minority (3 African Americans, 12 American Indian/Alaska Native, 1 Asian American or Pacific Islander). In 2006, 14 degrees awarded. *Degree requirements:* For master's, thesis or alternative, innovative project or research paper, written and oral exams. *Entrance requirements:* For master's, MAT or GRE, minimum GPA of 2.5. Additional exam requirements/recommendations for international students: Required—TOEFL (minimum score 213 computer-based). *Application deadline:* For fall admission, 6/1 priority date for domestic students. Applications are processed on a rolling basis. Application fee: $0 ($25 for international students). Electronic applications accepted. *Financial support:* Teaching assistantships, Federal Work-Study available. Financial award application deadline: 3/1.

Northeastern University, Bouvé College of Health Sciences Graduate School, Department of Counseling and Applied Educational Psychology, Program in Applied Educational Psychology, Boston, MA 02115-5096. Offers school counseling (MS); school psychology (MS). Part-time programs available. *Faculty:* 5 full-time (3 women), 4 part-time/adjunct (2 women). *Students:* 53 full-time (48 women), 4 part-time (all women). Average age 26. 146 applicants, 71% accepted. In 2006, 39 degrees awarded. *Entrance requirements:* For master's, GRE General Test or MAT. Additional exam requirements/recommendations for international students: Required—TOEFL. *Application deadline:* Applications are processed on a rolling basis. Application fee: $50. *Financial support:* Career-related internships or fieldwork, Federal Work-Study, tuition waivers (partial), and unspecified assistantships available. Support available to part-time students. Financial award application deadline: 3/1; financial award applicants required to submit FAFSA. *Faculty research:* Multicultural issues, assessment, early intervention, bilingual education. *Application contact:* Margaret Schnabel, Director of Graduate Admissions, 617-373-2708, Fax: 617-373-4704, E-mail: bouvegrad@neu.edu.

Northeastern University, Bouvé College of Health Sciences Graduate School, Department of Counseling and Applied Educational Psychology, Program in College Student Development and Counseling, Boston, MA 02115-5096. Offers MS. Part-time and evening/weekend programs available. *Faculty:* 1 (woman) full-time, 4 part-time/adjunct (all women). *Students:* 41 full-time (32 women), 18 part-time (15 women). Average age 27. 34 applicants, 76% accepted. In 2006, 18 degrees awarded. *Entrance requirements:* For master's, GRE General Test or MAT. Additional exam requirements/recommendations for international students: Required—TOEFL. Application fee: $50. *Financial support:* Career-related internships or fieldwork, Federal Work-Study, tuition waivers (partial), and unspecified assistantships available. Support available to part-time students. Financial award application deadline: 3/1; financial award applicants required to submit FAFSA. *Unit head:* Dr. Vanessa Johnson, Director, 617-373-5937, E-mail: v.johnson@neu.edu. *Application contact:* Margaret Schnabel, Director of Graduate Admissions, 617-373-2708, Fax: 617-373-4704, E-mail: bouvegrad@neu.edu.

Northern Arizona University, Graduate College, College of Education, Programs in Counseling, Flagstaff, AZ 86011. Offers M Ed, MA. *Accreditation:* ACA. Part-time programs available. *Degree requirements:* For master's, thesis optional. *Faculty research:* Early childhood assessment and development, cognitive psychology, multicultural issues, family functioning in abusive families, rehabilitation.

Northern Illinois University, Graduate School, College of Education, Department of Counseling, Adult and Higher Education, De Kalb, IL 60115-2854. Offers adult and higher education (MS Ed, Ed D); counseling (MS Ed, Ed D). *Accreditation:* ACA. Part-time and evening/weekend programs available. *Faculty:* 19 full-time (11 women), 2 part-time/adjunct (1 woman). *Students:* 102 full-time (73 women), 302 part-time (207 women); includes 110 minority (82 African Americans, 2 American Indian/Alaska Native, 7 Asian Americans or Pacific Islanders, 19 Hispanic Americans), 12 international. Average age 40. 124 applicants, 51% accepted, 51 enrolled. In 2006, 74 master's, 23 doctorates awarded. Terminal master's awarded for partial completion of doctoral program. *Degree requirements:* For master's, thesis optional; for doctorate, thesis/dissertation, candidacy exam, dissertation defense. *Entrance requirements:* For master's, GRE General Test or MAT, minimum undergraduate GPA of 2.75, interview (counseling); for doctorate, GRE General Test, minimum undergraduate GPA of 2.75, 3.2 graduate, interview (counseling). Additional exam requirements/recommendations for international students: Required—TOEFL (minimum score 550 paper-based; 213 computer-based). *Application deadline:* For fall admission, 6/1 for domestic students, 5/1 for international students; for spring admission, 11/1 for domestic students, 10/1 for international students. Applications are processed on a rolling basis. Application fee: $30. Electronic applications accepted. *Financial support:* In 2006–07, 14 teaching assistantships with full tuition reimbursements were awarded; fellowships with full tuition reimbursements, research assistantships with full tuition reimbursements, career-related internships or fieldwork, Federal Work-Study, scholarships/grants, tuition waivers (full), and unspecified assistantships also available. Support available to part-time students. Financial award applicants required to submit FAFSA. *Unit head:* Dr. Francesca Giordano, Chair, 815-753-9373, E-mail: watson@niu.edu.

Northern Kentucky University, Office of Graduate Programs, College of Education and Human Services, Program in School Counseling, Highland Heights, KY 41099. Offers MASC. Part-time and evening/weekend programs available. *Faculty:* 1 (woman) full-time. *Students:* 8 full-time (all women), 51 part-time (49 women); includes 3 minority (2 African Americans, 1 Hispanic American). Average age 32. 37 applicants, 65% accepted, 23 enrolled. *Degree requirements:* For master's, portfolio. *Entrance requirements:* For master's, GRE, interview, 3 letters of recommendation, minimum GPA of 2.5, criminal background check. Additional exam requirements/recommendations for international students: Required—TOEFL (minimum score 550 paper-based; 213 computer-based; 79 iBT), Michigan (must be taken at NKU). *Application deadline:* For fall admission, 8/1 priority date for domestic students, 6/1 priority date for international students; for spring admission, 12/1 priority date for domestic students, 10/1 priority date for international students. Applications are processed on a rolling basis. Application fee: $30. *Expenses:* Tuition, state resident: full-time $5,274; part-time $293 per hour. Tuition, nonresident: full-time $10,314; part-time $573 per hour. Tuition and fees vary according to course load, program and reciprocity agreements. *Financial support:* In 2006–07, 35 students received support. *Faculty research:* School counseling, guidance, counseling supervision, adolescents and mental disorders. *Unit head:* Dr. Rochelle Dunn, Program Coordinator, 859-572-1920, Fax: 859-572-6592, E-mail: dunnrl@nku.edu. *Application contact:* Dr. Peg Griffin, Director of Graduate Programs, 859-572-1555, Fax: 859-572-6670, E-mail: gradprog@nku.edu.

Northern State University, Division of Graduate Studies in Education, Program in Guidance and Counseling, Aberdeen, SD 57401-7198. Offers MS Ed. *Accreditation:* NCATE. Part-time and evening/weekend programs available. *Faculty:* 5 full-time (3 women). *Students:* 9 full-time (8 women), 42 part-time (31 women); includes 3 minority (all Asian Americans or Pacific Islanders) Average age 32. In 2006, 18 degrees awarded. *Degree requirements:* For master's, thesis optional. *Entrance requirements:* For master's, minimum GPA of 2.75. Additional exam requirements/recommendations for international students: Required—TOEFL (minimum score 550 paper-based; 213 computer-based). *Application deadline:* For fall admission, 8/15 priority date for domestic students; for spring admission, 12/15 for domestic students. Applications are processed on a rolling basis. Application fee: $35. Electronic applications accepted. *Expenses:* Tuition, state resident: full-time $3,373; part-time $120 per credit. Tuition, nonresident: full-time $9,943; part-time $355 per credit. International tuition: $13,000 full-time. Required fees: $86 per credit. One-time fee: $35 full-time. Tuition and fees vary according to course load, degree level and reciprocity agreements. *Financial support:* In 2006–07, 7 teaching assistantships with partial tuition reimbursements (averaging $4,812 per year) were awarded; career-related internships or fieldwork, Federal Work-Study, institutionally sponsored loans, scholarships/grants, and unspecified assistantships also available. Support available to part-time students. Financial award application deadline: 3/1; financial award applicants required to submit FAFSA. *Unit head:* Dr. Jill Schoen, Head, 605-626-2558, Fax: 605-626-2542, E-mail: jill.schoen@northern.edu. *Application contact:* Tammy K. Griffith, Senior Secretary, 605-626-2558, Fax: 605-626-2542, E-mail: griffith@northern.edu.

Northwest Christian College, Department of Education and Counseling, Eugene, OR 97401-3745. Offers school counseling/consulting (MA). Part-time and evening/weekend programs available. Postbaccalaureate distance learning degree programs offered (minimal on-campus study). *Entrance requirements:* For master's, MAT, interview, minimum GPA of 3.0. Electronic applications accepted. *Faculty research:* Beginning teaching/induction; increasing diversity of teacher workforce; reading and literacy; differentiating instruction.

Northwestern Oklahoma State University, School of Professional Studies, Program in Guidance and Counseling K–12, Alva, OK 73717-2799. Offers M Ed. *Accreditation:* NCATE. Part-time programs available. *Faculty:* 5 full-time (4 women). In 2006, 14 degrees awarded. *Degree requirements:* For master's, portfolio, thesis optional. *Entrance requirements:* For master's, GRE General Test or MAT, minimum GPA of 2.75. *Application deadline:* Applications are processed on a rolling basis. Application fee: $15. *Expenses:* Tuition, state resident: part-time $700 per year. Tuition, nonresident: part-time $1,715 per year. *Financial support:* Federal Work-Study available. Support available to part-time students. Financial award application deadline: 5/1. *Unit head:* Dr. Nancy Knous, Coordinator, 580-327-8443.

Northwestern State University of Louisiana, Graduate Studies and Research, College of Education, Program in Student Personnel Services, Natchitoches, LA 71497. Offers counseling and guidance (M Ed, Ed S); special education (M Ed, Ed S); student personnel services (MA). *Accreditation:* NCATE (one or more programs are accredited). *Faculty:* 3 full-time (2 women), 2 part-time/adjunct (1 woman). *Students:* 39 full-time (31 women), 12 part-time (all women); includes 29 minority (27 African Americans, 2 American Indian/Alaska Native). Average age 29. In 2006, 13 degrees awarded. *Degree requirements:* For master's, thesis or alternative, comprehensive exam, registration. *Entrance requirements:* For master's, GRE General Test, GRE Subject Test, minimum undergraduate GPA of 2.5. *Application deadline:* For fall admission, 8/1 priority date for domestic students; for spring admission, 1/10 for domestic students. Applications are processed on a rolling basis. Application fee: $20 ($30 for international students). *Financial support:* Application deadline: 7/15. *Application contact:* Dr. Steven G. Horton, Associate Provost/Dean, Graduate Studies, Research, and Information Systems, 318-357-5851, Fax: 318-357-5019, E-mail: grad_school@nsula.edu.

Northwestern State University of Louisiana, Graduate Studies and Research, College of Education, Programs in Education, Natchitoches, LA 71497. Offers business and distributive education (M Ed); counseling (M Ed); early childhood education (M Ed); education (M Ed); education leadership (M Ed); educational technology (M Ed); elementary teaching (M Ed); English education (M Ed); home economics education (M Ed); mathematics education (M Ed); reading (M Ed); science education (M Ed); secondary teaching (M Ed); social sciences education (M Ed). *Students:* 49 full-time (41 women), 245 part-time (206 women); includes 78 minority (70 African Americans, 5 American Indian/Alaska Native, 2 Asian Americans or Pacific Islanders, 1 Hispanic American). Average age 35. In 2006, 158 degrees awarded. *Degree requirements:* For master's, thesis or alternative, comprehensive exam, registration. *Entrance requirements:* For master's, GRE General Test, minimum undergraduate GPA of 2.5. *Application contact:* Dr. Steven G. Horton, Associate Provost/Dean, Graduate Studies, Research, and Information Systems, 318-357-5851, Fax: 318-357-5019, E-mail: grad_school@nsula.edu.

Northwestern State University of Louisiana, Graduate Studies and Research, College of Education, Programs in Educational Leadership and Instruction, Natchitoches, LA 71497. Offers counseling (Ed S); educational leadership (Ed S); educational technology (Ed S); elementary teaching (Ed S); reading (Ed S); secondary teaching (Ed S); special education (Ed S). *Students:* 17 full-time (15 women), 114 part-time (87 women); includes 55 minority (51 African Americans, 1 Asian American or Pacific Islander, 3 Hispanic Americans). Average age 39. In 2006, 11 degrees awarded. *Entrance requirements:* For degree, GRE General Test. *Application contact:* Dr. Steven G. Horton, Associate Provost/Dean, Graduate Studies, Research, and Information Systems, 318-357-5851, Fax: 318-357-5019, E-mail: grad_school@nsula.edu.

Northwest Missouri State University, Graduate School, College of Education and Human Services, Department of Psychology and Sociology, Program in Guidance and Counseling, Maryville, MO 64468-6001. Offers MS Ed. *Accreditation:* NCATE. *Faculty:* 9 full-time (6 women). *Students:* 7 full-time (6 women), 25 part-time (19 women); includes 1 minority (African American) 9 applicants, 22% accepted, 1 enrolled. In 2006, 5 degrees awarded. *Degree requirements:* For master's, thesis, comprehensive exam. *Entrance requirements:* For master's, GRE General Test, teaching certificate; 2 years of experience; minimum undergraduate GPA of 2.5, 3.0 in major; writing sample. Additional exam requirements/recommendations for international students: Required—TOEFL (minimum score 550 paper-based; 213 computer-based). *Application deadline:* For fall admission, 3/1 for domestic and international students. Applications are processed on a rolling basis. Application fee: $0 ($50 for international students). *Financial support:* In 2006–07, 4 research assistantships with full tuition reimbursements (averaging $6,000 per year) were awarded. Financial award application deadline: 3/1; financial award applicants required to submit FAFSA. *Unit head:* Dr. Jackie Kibler, Director, 660-562-1852. *Application contact:* Dr. Frances Shipley, Dean of Graduate School, 660-562-1145, Fax: 660-562-1096, E-mail: gradsch@nwmissouri.edu.

Northwest Nazarene University, Graduate Studies, Program in Counselor Education, Nampa, ID 83686-5897. Offers community counseling (MS); marriage and family counseling (MS); school counseling (MS). *Faculty:* 3 full-time (1 woman), 10 part-time/adjunct (6 women). *Students:* 70 full-time (53 women), 8 part-time (5 women); includes 6 minority (1 American

Counselor Education

Northwest Nazarene University (continued)
Indian/Alaska Native, 5 Hispanic Americans). In 2006, 26 degrees awarded. Application fee: $25. *Unit head:* Dr. Brenda Freeman, Chair, 208-467-8428, Fax: 208-467-8339.

Northwest Nazarene University, Graduate Studies, Program in Teacher Education, Nampa, ID 83686-5897. Offers curriculum and instruction (M Ed); educational leadership (M Ed); exceptional child (M Ed); reading education (M Ed); school counseling (M Ed). *Accreditation:* ACA; NCATE. Part-time programs available. *Faculty:* 11 full-time (4 women), 10 part-time/adjunct (6 women). *Students:* 113 full-time (79 women), 20 part-time (18 women); includes 4 minority (2 Asian Americans or Pacific Islanders, 2 Hispanic Americans). Average age 34. In 2006, 35 degrees awarded. *Degree requirements:* For master's, action research project. *Entrance requirements:* For master's, minimum undergraduate GPA of 2.8 overall or 3.0 during final 30 semester credits. *Application deadline:* For fall admission, 9/1 for domestic students. Applications are processed on a rolling basis. Application fee: $25. *Faculty research:* Action research, cooperative learning, accountability, institutional accreditation. *Unit head:* Dr. Karen Blacklock, Chair, 208-467-8399, Fax: 208-467-8562.

Ohio University, Graduate Studies, College of Education, Department of Counseling and Higher Education, Athens, OH 45701-2979. Offers college student personnel (M Ed); community/agency counseling (M Ed); counselor education (PhD); higher education (M Ed, PhD); rehabilitation counseling (M Ed); school counseling (M Ed). *Accreditation:* ACA; CORE. Part-time and evening/weekend programs available. *Faculty:* 12 full-time (5 women), 6 part-time/adjunct (0 women). *Students:* 123 full-time (89 women), 111 part-time (73 women); includes 20 minority (18 African Americans, 2 Hispanic Americans), 42 international. 209 applicants, 62% accepted, 106 enrolled. In 2006, 40 master's, 7 doctorates awarded. *Median time to degree:* Of those who began their doctoral program in fall 1998, 92% received their degree in 8 years or less. *Degree requirements:* For master's, thesis or alternative, registration; for doctorate, thesis/dissertation, comprehensive exam, registration. *Entrance requirements:* For master's, GRE General Test or MAT (if GPA below 2.9), 3 letters of reference, 5-page biography, statement of purpose; for doctorate, GRE General Test, work experience, minimum GPA of 3.4. Additional exam requirements/recommendations for international students: Required—TOEFL (minimum score 550 paper-based; 213 computer-based). *Application deadline:* For fall admission, 3/1 for domestic and international students. Applications are processed on a rolling basis. Application fee: $45. Electronic applications accepted. *Financial support:* In 2006–07, 66 students received support, including 35 research assistantships with full tuition reimbursements available (averaging $6,500 per year), 6 teaching assistantships with full tuition reimbursements available (averaging $7,200 per year); Federal Work-Study, institutionally sponsored loans, and unspecified assistantships also available. Financial award application deadline: 3/15. *Faculty research:* Youth violence, gender studies, student affairs, chemical dependency, disabilities issues. Total annual research expenditures: $527,983. *Unit head:* Dr. Jerry Olsheski, Chair, 740-593-0032, Fax: 740-593-0477, E-mail: olsheski@ohio.edu. *Application contact:* Floyd J. Doney, Director of Student Affairs, 740-593-4400, Fax: 740-593-9310, E-mail: doney@ohio.edu.

Oklahoma State University, College of Education, School of Applied Health and Educational Psychology, Stillwater, OK 74078. Offers applied behavioral studies (MS, Ed D, PhD); counseling and student personnel (MS, PhD); educational psychology (PhD); health (MS, Ed D); leisure sciences (MS, Ed D); physical education (MS, Ed D); physical education and leisure sciences (Ed D); school psychology (Ed S). *Accreditation:* APA (one or more programs are accredited). Part-time programs available. *Faculty:* 37 full-time (17 women), 12 part-time/adjunct (8 women). *Students:* 189 full-time (137 women), 180 part-time (113 women); includes 75 minority (25 African Americans, 34 American Indian/Alaska Native, 5 Asian Americans or Pacific Islanders, 11 Hispanic Americans), 27 international. Average age 33. 275 applicants, 28% accepted, 64 enrolled. In 2006, 45 master's, 21 doctorates awarded. *Degree requirements:* For master's, thesis or alternative; for doctorate, thesis/dissertation. *Entrance requirements:* For master's, GRE or MAT; for doctorate, GRE (PhD). Additional exam requirements/recommendations for international students: Required—TOEFL. *Application deadline:* For fall admission, 7/1 priority date for domestic students, 3/1 priority date for international students; for spring admission, 8/1 priority date for international students. Applications are processed on a rolling basis. Application fee: $40 ($75 for international students). Electronic applications accepted. *Expenses:* Tuition, state resident: part-time $146 per credit hour. Tuition, nonresident: part-time $516 per credit hour. Required fees: $44 per credit hour. Tuition and fees vary according to program. *Financial support:* In 2006–07, 29 research assistantships (averaging $6,452 per year), 64 teaching assistantships (averaging $8,263 per year) were awarded; career-related internships or fieldwork, Federal Work-Study, scholarships/grants, health care benefits, tuition waivers (partial), and unspecified assistantships also available. Support available to part-time students. Financial award application deadline: 3/1. *Unit head:* Dr. John Romans, Head, 405-744-6040.

Old Dominion University, Darden College of Education, Programs in Counseling, Norfolk, VA 23529. Offers MS Ed, PhD, Ed S. *Accreditation:* ACA. Part-time and evening/weekend programs available. *Faculty:* 10 full-time (4 women), 4 part-time/adjunct (2 women). *Students:* 26 full-time (23 women), 57 part-time (46 women); includes 23 minority (18 African Americans, 2 Asian Americans or Pacific Islanders, 3 Hispanic Americans). Average age 30. 75 applicants, 73% accepted, 45 enrolled. In 2006, 38 degrees awarded. *Median time to degree:* Doctorate–2 years full-time, 3 years part-time. *Degree requirements:* For master's, thesis or alternative, comprehensive exam; for doctorate, thesis/dissertation, comprehensive exam. *Entrance requirements:* For master's, GRE General Test, 2 letters of recommendation, resumé; for doctorate, GRE General Test, 3 letters of recommendation, resumé, interview. Additional exam requirements/recommendations for international students: Required—TOEFL. *Application deadline:* Applications are processed on a rolling basis. Application fee: $40. *Expenses:* Tuition, area resident: Part-time $285 per credit hour. Tuition, nonresident: part-time $715 per credit hour. Required fees: $94 per semester. *Financial support:* In 2006–07, 12 students received support, including 4 research assistantships with partial tuition reimbursements available (averaging $10,000 per year), 8 teaching assistantships with full tuition reimbursements available (averaging $22,500 per year); career-related internships or fieldwork, Federal Work-Study, institutionally sponsored loans, scholarships/grants, traineeships, and unspecified assistantships also available. Support available to part-time students. *Faculty research:* Group counseling, counselor education, career counseling, spirituality and counseling, school counseling, GLBT counseling. *Unit head:* Dr. Ted Remley, Graduate Program Director, 757-683-6695, Fax: 757-683-5756, E-mail: tremley@odu.edu.

Oregon State University, Graduate School, College of Education, Program in Counseling, Corvallis, OR 97331. Offers MS, PhD. *Accreditation:* ACA (one or more programs are accredited); NCATE. *Students:* 58 full-time (43 women), 17 part-time (13 women); includes 19 minority (2 African Americans, 3 American Indian/Alaska Native, 3 Asian Americans or Pacific Islanders, 11 Hispanic Americans), 4 international. Average age 37. In 2006, 29 master's, 4 doctorates awarded. *Degree requirements:* For master's, thesis or alternative; for doctorate, one foreign language, thesis/dissertation. *Entrance requirements:* For master's, minimum GPA of 3.0 in last 90 hours; for doctorate, GRE or MAT, master's degree, minimum GPA of 3.0 in last 90 hours of course work, 2 years of teaching experience. Additional exam requirements/recommendations for international students: Required—TOEFL. *Application deadline:* For fall admission, 2/1 for domestic students. Applications are processed on a rolling basis. Application fee: $50. *Financial support:* Teaching assistantships, career-related internships or fieldwork, Federal Work-Study, and institutionally sponsored loans available. Support available to part-time students. Financial award application deadline: 2/1. *Faculty research:* Counseling and guidance improvement in social services agencies, elementary and secondary schools. *Unit head:* Dr. Cass Dykeman, Chair, 541-737-4661.

Ottawa University, Graduate Studies-Arizona, Program in Education, Ottawa, KS 66067-3399. Offers community college counseling (MA); curriculum and instruction (MA); early childhood (MA); education intervention (MA); education leadership (MA); education technology (MA); Montessori early childhood education (MA); Montessori elementary education (MA); professional development (MA); school guidance counseling (MA); special education—cross categorical (MA). Programs offered in Mesa, Phoenix, Tempe and West Valley, AZ. *Accreditation:* NCATE. Part-time programs available. *Faculty:* 7 full-time (3 women), 24 part-time/adjunct (11 women). *Students:* 14 full-time (9 women), 162 part-time (128 women); includes 31 minority (13 African Americans, 2 American Indian/Alaska Native, 1 Asian American or Pacific Islander, 15 Hispanic Americans), 1 international. Average age 38. In 2006, 56 degrees awarded. *Degree requirements:* For master's, thesis or alternative, registration. *Entrance requirements:* For master's, minimum undergraduate GPA of 3.0, copy of current state certification or teaching license. Additional exam requirements/recommendations for international students: Required—TOEFL (minimum score 550 paper-based; 213 computer-based). *Application deadline:* For fall admission, 7/1 priority date for domestic students; for winter admission, 11/1 priority date for domestic students; for spring admission, 2/1 priority date for domestic students. Applications are processed on a rolling basis. Application fee: $50. Electronic applications accepted. *Expenses: Contact institution. Application contact:* Bunny Simpson, Secretary, 602-371-1188, Fax: 602-371-0035, E-mail: bunny.simpson@ottawa.edu.

Our Lady of Holy Cross College, Program in Education and Counseling, New Orleans, LA 70131-7399. Offers administration and supervision (M Ed); curriculum and instruction (M Ed); marriage and family counseling (MA); school counseling (M Ed, MA). *Accreditation:* ACA; NCATE. Part-time and evening/weekend programs available. *Degree requirements:* For master's, thesis. *Entrance requirements:* For master's, GRE General Test, minimum GPA of 2.7.

Our Lady of the Lake University of San Antonio, School of Education and Clinical Studies, Program in School Counseling, San Antonio, TX 78207-4689. Offers M Ed. Part-time and evening/weekend programs available. *Degree requirements:* For master's, practicum, thesis optional. *Entrance requirements:* For master's, GRE General Test or MAT, interview. Additional exam requirements/recommendations for international students: Required—TOEFL. Electronic applications accepted.

Palm Beach Atlantic University, School of Education and Behavioral Studies, West Palm Beach, FL 33416-4708. Offers counseling psychology (MSCP), including addictions/mental health, marriage and family therapy, mental health counseling, school guidance counseling; elementary education (M Ed). Part-time and evening/weekend programs available. *Faculty:* 13 full-time (3 women), 6 part-time/adjunct (5 women). *Students:* 211 full-time (169 women), 66 part-time (55 women); includes 103 minority (61 African Americans, 4 Asian Americans or Pacific Islanders, 38 Hispanic Americans), 7 international. Average age 36. 98 applicants, 71% accepted, 51 enrolled. In 2006, 49 degrees awarded. *Entrance requirements:* For master's, GRE General Test, minimum GPA of 3.0 in last 60 hours of course work. Additional exam requirements/recommendations for international students: Required—TOEFL (minimum score 550 paper-based; 213 computer-based). *Application deadline:* For fall admission, 7/15 priority date for domestic students; for spring admission, 11/15 priority date for domestic students. Applications are processed on a rolling basis. Application fee: $35. Electronic applications accepted. *Expenses:* Tuition: Full-time $10,665; part-time $395 per credit. Required fees: $90 per semester. *Financial support:* Unspecified assistantships available. Support available to part-time students. Financial award applicants required to submit FAFSA. *Unit head:* Dr. Melise Bunker, Dean, 561-803-2350, Fax: 561-803-2186, E-mail: melise_bunker@pba.edu. *Application contact:* Laura A. Leinweber, Director of Graduate and Evening Admissions, 888-468-6722, Fax: 561-803-2115, E-mail: grad@pba.edu.

Penn State University Park, Graduate School, College of Education, Department of Counselor Education, Counseling Psychology and Rehabilitation Services, State College, University Park, PA 16802-1503. Offers counseling psychology (PhD); counselor education (M Ed, MS), including elementary counseling; counselor education, counseling psychology and rehabilitation services (D Ed). *Accreditation:* ACA (one or more programs are accredited); APA (one or more programs are accredited); NCATE. *Unit head:* Dr. Spencer A. Niles, Head, 814-865-3428, Fax: 814-863-7750, E-mail: sgn3@psu.edu.

Phillips Graduate Institute, Program in Marriage and Family Therapy, Organizational Behavior and School Counseling, Encino, CA 91316-1509. Offers marital and family therapy (MA); organizational consulting (MA); school counseling (MA). Evening/weekend programs available. *Degree requirements:* For master's, thesis, comprehensive exam. *Entrance requirements:* For master's, minimum GPA of 2.5. *Faculty research:* Integration of interpersonal psychological theory, systems approach, firsthand experiential learning.

Pittsburg State University, Graduate School, College of Education, Department of Psychology and Counseling, Program in Counselor Education, Pittsburg, KS 66762. Offers counseling (MS). *Accreditation:* ACA; NCATE. *Students:* 53. *Degree requirements:* For master's, thesis or alternative. *Entrance requirements:* For master's, GRE General Test, minimum GPA of 2.8. Application fee: $35 ($60 for international students). *Expenses:* Tuition, state resident: full-time $2,144; part-time $181 per credit hour. Tuition, nonresident: full-time $5,273; part-time $442 per credit hour. Tuition and fees vary according to course load and campus/location. *Financial support:* Teaching assistantships, career-related internships or fieldwork and Federal Work-Study available. *Application contact:* Marvene Darraugh, Administrative Officer, 620-235-4220, Fax: 620-235-4219, E-mail: mdarraug@pittstate.edu.

Plymouth State University, College of Graduate Studies, Graduate Studies in Education, Program in Counselor Education, Plymouth, NH 03264-1595. Offers M Ed. *Accreditation:* ACA; NCATE. Part-time and evening/weekend programs available. *Students:* 2 full-time (both women), 114 part-time (94 women); includes 1 minority (Asian American or Pacific Islander) Average age 35. 39 applicants, 100% accepted, 39 enrolled. In 2006, 16 degrees awarded. *Degree requirements:* For master's, PRAXIS I. *Entrance requirements:* For master's, MAT, minimum GPA of 3.0. *Application deadline:* Applications are processed on a rolling basis. Application fee: $75. *Expenses:* Tuition, state resident: part-time $369 per credit. Tuition, nonresident: part-time $407 per credit. Tuition and fees vary according to course level. *Financial support:* Career-related internships or fieldwork, scholarships/grants, and unspecified assistantships available. Support available to part-time students. Financial award applicants required to submit FAFSA. *Unit head:* Dr. Gary Goodnough, Program Coordinator, 603-535-2821, E-mail: ggoodno@plymouth.edu.

Portland State University, Graduate Studies, School of Education, Department of Special Education and Counselor Education, Portland, OR 97207-0751. Offers counselor education (MA, MS); special and counselor education (Ed D); special education (MA, MS). *Accreditation:* ACA (one or more programs are accredited). Part-time and evening/weekend programs available. *Faculty:* 19 full-time (10 women), 20 part-time/adjunct (16 women). *Students:* 125 full-time (102 women), 198 part-time (143 women); includes 25 minority (7 African Americans, 2 American Indian/Alaska Native, 7 Asian Americans or Pacific Islanders, 9 Hispanic Americans), 2 international. Average age 37. 240 applicants, 75% accepted, 129 enrolled. In 2006, 111 degrees awarded. *Degree requirements:* For master's, thesis or alternative. *Entrance requirements:* For master's, California Basic Educational Skills Test, minimum GPA of 3.0 in upper-division course work or 2.75 overall. Additional exam requirements/recommendations for international students: Required—TOEFL (minimum score 550 paper-based; 213 computer-based). *Application deadline:* For fall admission, 3/1 for domestic and international students. Application fee: $50. *Expenses:* Tuition, state resident: full-time $6,426; part-time $238 per credit. Tuition, nonresident: full-time $11,016; part-time $408 per credit. Tuition and fees vary according to course load. *Financial support:* In 2006–07, 3 research assistantships with full tuition reimbursements (averaging $6,540 per year) were awarded; teaching assistantships with full tuition reimbursements, career-related internships or fieldwork, Federal Work-Study, and institutionally sponsored loans also available. Support available to part-time students. Financial award application deadline: 3/1; financial award applicants required to submit FAFSA. *Faculty research:* Transition of students with disabilities, functional curriculum, supported/inclusive education, leisure/recreation, autism. Total annual research expenditures: $867,731.

Unit head: Dr. Ann Fullerton, Head, 503-725-4632, Fax: 503-725-5599. *Application contact:* Kris Smith, Admission Secretary, 503-725-4632, Fax: 503-725-5599, E-mail: kmsmith@pdx.edu.

Prairie View A&M University, Graduate School, College of Education, Department of Educational Leadership and Counseling, Prairie View, TX 77446-0519. Offers counseling (MA, MS Ed); educational leadership (PhD); school administration (M Ed, MS Ed); school supervision (M Ed, MS Ed). *Accreditation:* NCATE. Part-time and evening/weekend programs available. *Degree requirements:* For master's, thesis optional; for doctorate, thesis/dissertation, comprehensive exam. *Entrance requirements:* For master's, GRE General Test, 3 letters of reference, minimum undergraduate GPA of 2.5; for doctorate, GRE General Test, 3 letters of reference. Additional exam requirements/recommendations for international students: Required—TOEFL (minimum score 550 paper-based). Electronic applications accepted. *Faculty research:* Mentoring, personality assessment, holistic/humanistic education.

Providence College, Graduate Studies, Department of Education, Program in Guidance and Counseling, Providence, RI 02918. Offers M Ed. Part-time and evening/weekend programs available. *Faculty:* 6 full-time (5 women), 45 part-time/adjunct (25 women). *Students:* 22 full-time (19 women), 59 part-time (49 women); includes 4 minority (2 African Americans, 2 Hispanic Americans), 2 international. Average age 31. 32 applicants, 97% accepted. In 2006, 20 degrees awarded. *Degree requirements:* For master's, comprehensive exam. *Entrance requirements:* For master's, GRE General Test. Additional exam requirements/recommendations for international students: Required—TOEFL (minimum score 550 paper-based; 213 computer-based). *Application deadline:* For fall admission, 8/1 for domestic students; for spring admission, 12/1 for domestic students. Applications are processed on a rolling basis. Application fee: $55. *Expenses:* Tuition: Full-time $6,573; part-time $939 per unit. *Financial support:* In 2006–07, 15 research assistantships with full tuition reimbursements (averaging $8,400 per year) were awarded; career-related internships or fieldwork, institutionally sponsored loans, and unspecified assistantships also available. Support available to part-time students. Financial award application deadline: 8/1; financial award applicants required to submit FAFSA. *Unit head:* Alexander Freda, Head, 401-865-2247, Fax: 401-865-1147.

Purdue University, Graduate School, School of Education, Department of Educational Studies, West Lafayette, IN 47907. Offers administration (MS Ed, PhD, Ed S); counseling and development (MS Ed, PhD); education of the gifted (MS Ed); educational psychology (MS Ed, PhD); foundations of education (MS Ed, PhD); higher education administration (MS Ed, PhD); special education (MS Ed, PhD). *Accreditation:* ACA (one or more programs are accredited); NCATE (one or more programs are accredited). Part-time and evening/weekend programs available. *Faculty:* 28 full-time (18 women). *Students:* 100 full-time (71 women), 126 part-time (77 women); includes 32 minority (19 African Americans, 2 American Indian/Alaska Native, 6 Asian Americans or Pacific Islanders, 5 Hispanic Americans), 33 international. Average age 36. 152 applicants, 62% accepted, 56 enrolled. In 2006, 51 master's, 17 doctorates awarded. *Degree requirements:* For master's, thesis optional; for doctorate, thesis/dissertation, oral and written exams; for Ed S, oral presentation, project. *Entrance requirements:* For master's, GRE General Test, minimum undergraduate GPA of 3.0; for doctorate, GRE General Test; for Ed S, GRE, minimum B average. Additional exam requirements/recommendations for international students: Required—TOEFL. *Application deadline:* For fall admission, 1/15 for domestic students; for spring admission, 9/15 for domestic students. Applications are processed on a rolling basis. Application fee: $55. Electronic applications accepted. *Financial support:* In 2006–07, 6 fellowships with full tuition reimbursements (averaging $13,300 per year), 23 research assistantships with full tuition reimbursements (averaging $11,500 per year), 33 teaching assistantships with full tuition reimbursements (averaging $10,800 per year) were awarded; career-related internships or fieldwork and tuition waivers (full) also available. Support available to part-time students. Financial award application deadline: 3/1; financial award applicants required to submit FAFSA. *Faculty research:* Motivation, learning disabilities, school learning, group processes, cognitive development. *Unit head:* Dr. Kevin R Kelly, Head, 765-494-9170, Fax: 765-496-1228. *Application contact:* Patricia Mason, Coordinator of Graduate Studies, 765-494-2346, Fax: 765-494-5832, E-mail: gradoffice@soe.purdue.edu.

Purdue University Calumet, Graduate School, School of Education, Program in Counseling and Personnel Services, Hammond, IN 46323-2094. Offers MS Ed. *Entrance requirements:* Additional exam requirements/recommendations for international students: Required—TOEFL.

Queens College of the City University of New York, Division of Graduate Studies, Division of Education, Department of Educational and Community Programs, Program in Counselor Education, Flushing, NY 11367-1597. Offers MS Ed. Part-time programs available. *Faculty:* 3 full-time (1 woman). *Students:* 39 full-time (34 women), 43 part-time (40 women). 161 applicants, 29% accepted, 44 enrolled. In 2006, 25 degrees awarded. *Degree requirements:* For master's, research project. *Entrance requirements:* For master's, minimum GPA of 3.0. Additional exam requirements/recommendations for international students: Required—TOEFL. *Application deadline:* For fall admission, 4/1 for domestic students; for spring admission, 11/1 for domestic students. Applications are processed on a rolling basis. Application fee: $125. *Financial support:* Career-related internships or fieldwork, Federal Work-Study, institutionally sponsored loans, and tuition waivers (partial) available. Support available to part-time students. Financial award application deadline: 4/1; financial award applicants required to submit FAFSA. *Unit head:* Dr. John Pellitteri, Coordinator and Graduate Adviser, 718-997-5246, E-mail: john_pellitteri@qc.edu. *Application contact:* Mario Caruso, Director of Graduate Admissions, 718-997-5200, Fax: 718-997-5193, E-mail: graduate_admissions@qc.edu.

Quincy University, Division of Education—Counseling, Quincy, IL 62301-2699. Offers counseling (MS Ed). Part-time and evening/weekend programs available. *Faculty:* 1 full-time (0 women), 3 part-time/adjunct (1 woman). *Students:* 5 full-time (all women), 58 part-time (51 women); includes 3 minority (1 African American, 2 Hispanic Americans). *Median time to degree:* Of those who began their doctoral program in fall 1998, 63% received their degree in 8 years or less. *Degree requirements:* For master's, comprehensive exam. *Entrance requirements:* For master's, MAT. Application fee: $25. *Unit head:* Dr. Duncan Sylvester, Director, Counseling Program, 217-228-5420, E-mail: sylvedu@quincy.edu. *Application contact:* Syndi Peck, Director of Admissions, 217-228-5215, Fax: 217-228-5648, E-mail: admissions@quincy.edu.

Radford University, Graduate College, College of Education and Human Development, Department of Counselor Education, Radford, VA 24142. Offers counseling and human development (MS). *Accreditation:* ACA; NCATE. Part-time and evening/weekend programs available. Postbaccalaureate distance learning degree programs offered (minimal on-campus study). *Faculty:* 9 full-time (5 women), 4 part-time/adjunct (2 women). *Students:* 65 full-time (52 women), 64 part-time (53 women); includes 15 minority (11 African Americans, 2 Asian Americans or Pacific Islanders, 2 Hispanic Americans). Average age 31. 63 applicants, 89% accepted, 32 enrolled. In 2006, 39 degrees awarded. *Degree requirements:* For master's, thesis optional. *Entrance requirements:* For master's, GRE or MAT. Additional exam requirements/recommendations for international students: Required—TOEFL. *Application deadline:* For fall admission, 3/1 priority date for domestic students, 4/1 for international students; for spring admission, 10/1 for domestic students, 8/1 for international students. Applications are processed on a rolling basis. Application fee: $40. Electronic applications accepted. *Expenses:* Tuition: state resident: full-time $4,680; part-time $260 per credit hour. Tuition, nonresident: full-time $8,604; part-time $478 per credit hour. *Financial support:* In 2006–07, 57 students received support, including 42 research assistantships with partial tuition reimbursements available (averaging $8,000 per year), teaching assistantships with partial tuition reimbursements available (averaging $8,700 per year); career-related internships or fieldwork, Federal Work-Study, institutionally sponsored loans, scholarships/grants, and unspecified assistantships also available. Financial award application deadline: 3/1; financial award applicants required to submit FAFSA. *Unit head:* Dr. Alan Forrest, Acting Dean, 540-831-5487, Fax: 540-831-6755, E-mail: aforrest@radford.edu.

Regent University, Graduate School, School of Psychology and Counseling, Virginia Beach, VA 23464-9800. Offers clinical psychology (Psy D); counseling (MA), including clinical psychology, community counseling, human services counseling, school guidance; counseling studies (CAGS); counselor education and supervision (PhD); M Div/MA; M Ed/MA; MBA/MA. PhD program offered online only. *Accreditation:* ACA; APA (one or more programs are accredited). Part-time programs available. Postbaccalaureate distance learning degree programs offered. *Faculty:* 25 full-time (13 women), 27 part-time/adjunct (13 women). *Students:* 238 full-time (181 women), 165 part-time (121 women); includes 97 minority (68 African Americans, 2 American Indian/Alaska Native, 12 Asian Americans or Pacific Islanders, 15 Hispanic Americans), 10 international. Average age 31. 434 applicants, 44% accepted, 105 enrolled. In 2006, 65 master's, 38 doctorates awarded. *Degree requirements:* For master's, thesis or alternative, internship, practicum, written competency exam; for doctorate, thesis/dissertation or alternative. *Entrance requirements:* For master's, GRE General Test including writing exam or MAT, minimum undergraduate GPA of 2.75, 3 recommendations, resumé; for doctorate, GRE General Test including writing exam, GRE Subject Test, minimum undergraduate GPA of 3.0, 3.5 (PhD), 10-15 minute VHS tape demonstrating counseling skills, 10 page writing sample, 3 recommendations, resumé. Additional exam requirements/recommendations for international students: Required—TOEFL (minimum score 577 paper-based; 233 computer-based). *Application deadline:* For fall admission, 4/1 priority date for domestic students; for spring admission, 11/1 priority date for domestic students. Applications are processed on a rolling basis. Application fee: $50. Electronic applications accepted. *Expenses:* Contact institution. *Financial support:* In 2006–07, 16 research assistantships with full and partial tuition reimbursements (averaging $3,125 per year), 11 teaching assistantships with full and partial tuition reimbursements (averaging $11,433 per year) were awarded; career-related internships or fieldwork, scholarships/grants, and tuition waivers (full and partial) also available. Support available to part-time students. Financial award application deadline: 9/1. *Faculty research:* Marriage enrichment, AIDS counseling, troubled youth. Total annual research expenditures: $12,000. *Unit head:* Dr. Rosemarie Hughes, Dean, 757-226-4269, Fax: 757-226-4282, E-mail: rosehug@regent.edu. *Application contact:* Althea Bishard, Registrar and Executive Director of Enrollment and Academic Services, 800-373-5504, Fax: 757-226-4381, E-mail: admissions@regent.edu.

Rhode Island College, School of Graduate Studies, Feinstein School of Education and Human Development, Department of Counseling, Educational Leadership, and School Psychology, Providence, RI 02908-1991. Offers counseling (MA); educational leadership (M Ed); school administration (M Ed); school counseling (CAGS). *Accreditation:* NCATE. Part-time and evening/weekend programs available. *Faculty:* 3 full-time (1 woman), 12 part-time/adjunct (5 women). *Students:* 42 full-time (39 women), 102 part-time (83 women); includes 4 minority (3 African Americans, 1 Hispanic American). Average age 33. In 2006, 52 master's, 12 other advanced degrees awarded. *Entrance requirements:* For master's, GRE General Test or MAT, 3 letters of recommendation. *Application deadline:* For fall admission, 3/15 for domestic students; for spring admission, 11/1 for domestic students. Applications are processed on a rolling basis. Application fee: $50. *Expenses:* Tuition, state resident: part-time $244 per credit. Tuition, nonresident: part-time $512 per credit. Required fees: $12 per credit. $66 per term. Tuition and fees vary according to degree level, program and reciprocity agreements. *Financial support:* Teaching assistantships with full tuition reimbursements, career-related internships or fieldwork, Federal Work-Study, scholarships/grants, health care benefits, and unspecified assistantships available. Support available to part-time students. Financial award application deadline: 5/15; financial award applicants required to submit FAFSA. *Unit head:* Dr. Monica Darcy, Chair, 401-456-8023, E-mail: mdarcy@ric.edu.

Rider University, Department of Graduate Education, Leadership and Counseling, Lawrenceville, NJ 08648-3001. Offers counseling services (MA, Ed S); curriculum, instruction and supervision (MA); director of school counseling services (Certificate); educational administration (MA); organizational leadership (MA); principal (Certificate); reading/language arts (MA, Certificate), including reading specialist (Certificate), reading/language arts (MA); school business administrator (Certificate); school counseling services (Certificate); school psychology (Ed S); special education (MA); supervisor (Certificate); teacher certification (Certificate), including business education, elementary education, English as a second language, English education, mathematics education, preschool to grade 3, science education, social studies education, world languages; teaching (MA). *Accreditation:* NCATE. Part-time and evening/weekend programs available. *Faculty:* 24 full-time (12 women), 30 part-time/adjunct (15 women). *Students:* 90 full-time (75 women), 457 part-time (369 women); includes 73 minority (50 African Americans, 2 American Indian/Alaska Native, 6 Asian Americans or Pacific Islanders, 15 Hispanic Americans), 1 international. Average age 32. 314 applicants, 61% accepted, 138 enrolled. In 2006, 116 master's, 19 other advanced degrees awarded. *Degree requirements:* For master's, thesis or alternative, internship, portfolios, comprehensive exam (for some programs); for other advanced degree, internship, professional portfolio. *Entrance requirements:* For master's, GRE (counseling, school psychology), MAT, interview, resumé, letters of recommendation; for other advanced degree, PRAXIS. Additional exam requirements/recommendations for international students: Required—TOEFL (minimum score 550 paper-based; 213 computer-based). *Application deadline:* For fall admission, 5/1 priority date for domestic students, 6/1 priority date for international students; for spring admission, 11/1 priority date for domestic and international students. Applications are processed on a rolling basis. Application fee: $50. Electronic applications accepted. *Expenses:* Tuition: Part-time $525 per credit. Required fees: $35 per course. $30 per semester. *Financial support:* In 2006–07, 271 students received support. Career-related internships or fieldwork, Federal Work-Study, institutionally sponsored loans, and unspecified assistantships available. Support available to part-time students. Financial award applicants required to submit FAFSA. *Faculty research:* Gifted students, self-esteem, hope and mental health, conflicts in group work, cultural diversity and counseling assessment of special needs in children. *Unit head:* Dr. Dennis C. Buss, Chair, 609-895-5353, Fax: 609-896-5362, E-mail: dbuss@rider.edu. *Application contact:* Jamie L Mitchell, Director of Graduate Admissions, 609-896-5036, Fax: 609-895-5680, E-mail: jmitchell@rider.edu.

See Close-Up on page 913.

Rivier College, School of Graduate Studies, Department of Education, Nashua, NH 03060-5086. Offers curriculum and instruction (M Ed); early childhood education (M Ed); educational administration (M Ed); educational studies (M Ed); elementary education (M Ed); elementary education and general special education (M Ed); emotional and behavioral disorders (M Ed); general social education (M Ed); leadership and learning (CAGS); learning disabilities (M Ed); learning disabilities and reading (M Ed); mental health counseling (MA); reading (M Ed); school counseling (M Ed). Part-time and evening/weekend programs available. *Faculty:* 11 full-time (7 women), 40 part-time/adjunct (29 women). *Students:* 41 full-time (33 women), 221 part-time (192 women); includes 4 minority (2 African Americans, 2 Hispanic Americans). Average age 37. In 2006, 134 degrees awarded. *Degree requirements:* For master's, internships. *Entrance requirements:* For master's, GRE General Test or MAT. *Application deadline:* Applications are processed on a rolling basis. Application fee: $25. *Financial support:* Available to part-time students. Application deadline: 2/1; *Unit head:* Dr. Charles L. Mitsakos, Chairman, 603-888-1311 Ext. 8582. *Application contact:* Diane Monahan, Director of Graduate Admissions, 603-897-8129, Fax: 603-897-8810, E-mail: gradadm@rivier.edu.

Roberts Wesleyan College, Division of Social Sciences, Rochester, NY 14624-1997. Offers counseling in ministry (MA); school counseling (MS); school psychology (MS). *Application contact:* Graduate Admissions Office, 585-594-6011, Fax: 585-594-6124, E-mail: gradpsychadmissions@roberts.edu.

Rollins College, Hamilton Holt School, Program in Counseling, Winter Park, FL 32789-4499. Offers mental health counseling (MA); school counseling (MA). *Accreditation:* ACA. Part-time and evening/weekend programs available. *Faculty:* 5 full-time (4 women). *Students:* 61 full-time (55 women), 49 part-time (43 women); includes 17 minority (5 African Americans, 3 Asian Americans or Pacific Islanders, 9 Hispanic Americans), 2 international. Average age 35. In 2006, 31 degrees awarded. *Degree requirements:* For master's, comprehensive exam. *Entrance*

Counselor Education

Rollins College (continued)

requirements: For master's, GRE General Test or MAT, interview. Additional exam requirements/recommendations for international students: Required—TOEFL. *Application deadline:* For fall admission, 4/1 for domestic students. Application fee: $50. Electronic applications accepted. *Expenses: Contact institution. Financial support:* In 2006–07, 2 teaching assistantships were awarded; scholarships/grants also available. Support available to part-time students. *Unit head:* Dr. Alicia Homrich, Director, 407-646-2307, E-mail: ahomrich@rollins.edu. *Application contact:* Rebecca Cordray, Coordinator of Records and Registration, 407-646-1568, Fax: 407-975-6430, E-mail: rcordray@rollins.edu.

Roosevelt University, Graduate Division, College of Education, Program in Counseling and Human Services, Chicago, IL 60605-1394. Offers MA. *Accreditation:* ACA. *Students:* 60 full-time (54 women), 119 part-time (104 women); includes 68 minority (54 African Americans, 1 American Indian/Alaska Native, 3 Asian Americans or Pacific Islanders, 10 Hispanic Americans). Average age 32. 142 applicants, 61% accepted, 54 enrolled. In 2006, 52 degrees awarded. *Unit head:* Dr. Bruce Dykeman, Interim Chair, 312-341-2424. *Application contact:* Joanne Canyon-Heller, Coordinator of Graduate Admission, 877-APPLY RU, Fax: 312-281-3356, E-mail: applyru@roosevelt.edu.

Rosemont College, Graduate School, Program in Counseling Psychology, Rosemont, PA 19010-1699. Offers human services (MA); school counseling (MA). Part-time and evening/weekend programs available. *Degree requirements:* For master's, thesis or alternative. *Entrance requirements:* For master's, GRE or MAT. Additional exam requirements/recommendations for international students: Required—TOEFL. Electronic applications accepted. Expenses: Contact institution.

Rowan University, Graduate School, College of Education, Department of Special Educational Services/Instruction, Program in Counseling in Educational Settings, Glassboro, NJ 08028-1701. Offers MA. Part-time and evening/weekend programs available. *Students:* 16 full-time (13 women), 70 part-time (62 women); includes 12 minority (9 African Americans, 1 Asian American or Pacific Islander, 2 Hispanic Americans). Average age 32. 10 applicants, 50% accepted, 5 enrolled. In 2006, 42 degrees awarded. *Degree requirements:* For master's, thesis, comprehensive exam. *Entrance requirements:* For master's, GRE General Test, minimum GPA of 2.8, 1 year of teaching experience. Additional exam requirements/recommendations for international students: Required—TOEFL. *Application deadline:* For winter admission, 12/1 priority date for domestic students; for spring admission, 4/1 priority date for domestic students. Applications are processed on a rolling basis. Application fee: $50. Electronic applications accepted. *Expenses:* Tuition, state resident: full-time $9,882; part-time $549 per credit. Tuition, nonresident: full-time $9,882; part-time $549 per credit. Tuition and fees vary according to degree level. *Financial support:* Career-related internships or fieldwork, Federal Work-Study, and unspecified assistantships available. Support available to part-time students. *Unit head:* Dr. Aertore Rios, Adviser, 856-256-4500 Ext. 3668.

Sage Graduate School, Graduate School, Division of Education, Program in Guidance and Counseling, Troy, NY 12180-4115. Offers MS, Post Master's Certificate. *Accreditation:* NCATE. Part-time and evening/weekend programs available. *Faculty:* 11 full-time (8 women), 20 part-time/adjunct (15 women). *Students:* 66 full-time (58 women), 22 part-time (21 women); includes 3 minority (1 African American, 2 Hispanic Americans). Average age 26. 69 applicants, 71% accepted, 25 enrolled. In 2006, 51 master's, 5 other advanced degrees awarded. *Entrance requirements:* For master's, minimum GPA of 2.75. Additional exam requirements/recommendations for international students: Required—TOEFL (minimum score 550 paper-based; 213 computer-based). *Application deadline:* Applications are processed on a rolling basis. Application fee: $40. *Expenses:* Tuition: Full-time $9,270; part-time $515 per credit hour. *Financial support:* Career-related internships or fieldwork, scholarships/grants, and unspecified assistantships available. Support available to part-time students. Financial award application deadline: 3/1; financial award applicants required to submit FAFSA. *Faculty research:* Roles and responsibilities of guidance personnel, projections of need for guidance counselors. *Unit head:* Dr. Laurae Wartinger, Director, 518-244-2401, Fax: 518-244-2334, E-mail: wartil@sage.edu. *Application contact:* Shannon K. Easton, Director of Graduate and Adult Admission, 518-244-2443, Fax: 518-244-6880, E-mail: sgsadm@sage.edu.

St. Bonaventure University, School of Graduate Studies, School of Education, Program in Counselor Education, St. Bonaventure, NY 14778-2284. Offers counseling education (Adv C); counseling education-agency (MS, MS Ed); counseling education-school (MS, MS Ed). *Degree requirements:* For master's, thesis optional. *Entrance requirements:* For master's, GRE, interview, writing sample. *Faculty research:* Parent education, learning disabilities, stress management.

St. Cloud State University, School of Graduate Studies, College of Education, Department of Counselor Education and Educational Psychology, Program in College Counseling and Student Development, St. Cloud, MN 56301-4498. Offers MS. *Faculty:* 12 full-time (5 women). *Students:* 11 full-time (8 women), 4 part-time (all women); includes 1 minority (Asian American or Pacific Islander) 21 applicants, 81% accepted. In 2006, 11 degrees awarded. *Degree requirements:* For master's, thesis or alternative, comprehensive exam. *Entrance requirements:* For master's, GRE General Test, minimum GPA of 2.75. Additional exam requirements/recommendations for international students: Required—MELAB; Recommended—TOEFL (minimum score 550 paper-based; 213 computer-based), IELTS (minimum score 7). *Application deadline:* For fall admission, 3/1 for domestic and international students. Application fee: $35. Electronic applications accepted. *Financial support:* Federal Work-Study, scholarships/grants, and unspecified assistantships available. Financial award application deadline: 3/1. *Unit head:* Dr. Dan Macari, Coordinator, 320-308-1044, E-mail: dpmacari@stcloudstate.edu. *Application contact:* Linda Lou Krueger, School of Graduate Studies, 320-308-2113, Fax: 320-308-5371, E-mail: lekrueger@stcloudstate.edu.

St. Cloud State University, School of Graduate Studies, College of Education, Department of Counselor Education and Educational Psychology, Program in School Counseling, St. Cloud, MN 56301-4498. Offers MS. *Accreditation:* ACA; NCATE. *Faculty:* 12 full-time (5 women). *Students:* 25 full-time (22 women), 24 part-time (21 women); includes 2 minority (1 African American, 1 Hispanic American). 20 applicants, 90% accepted. In 2006, 19 degrees awarded. *Degree requirements:* For master's, thesis or alternative, comprehensive exam (for some programs). *Entrance requirements:* For master's, GRE General Test, minimum GPA of 2.75. Additional exam requirements/recommendations for international students: Required—MELAB; Recommended—TOEFL (minimum score 550 paper-based; 213 computer-based), IELTS. *Application deadline:* For fall admission, 3/1 for domestic and international students. Application fee: $35. Electronic applications accepted. *Financial support:* Career-related internships or fieldwork, Federal Work-Study, scholarships/grants, and unspecified assistantships available. Financial award application deadline: 3/1. *Unit head:* Dr. Trae Downing, Coordinator, 320-308-3131, E-mail: tkdowning@stcloudstate.edu. *Application contact:* Linda Lou Krueger, School of Graduate Studies, 320-308-2113, Fax: 320-308-5371, E-mail: lekrueger@stcloudstate.edu.

St. John's University, The School of Education, Division of Human Services and Counseling, Program in Bilingual School Counseling, Queens, NY 11439. Offers MS Ed. Part-time and evening/weekend programs available. *Students:* 4 full-time (3 women), 11 part-time (9 women); includes 12 minority (2 African Americans, 10 Hispanic Americans). Average age 33. 11 applicants, 73% accepted, 4 enrolled. In 2006, 12 degrees awarded. *Degree requirements:* For master's, internship. *Entrance requirements:* For master's, interview, minimum GPA of 3.0, 18 credits of course work in behavioral sciences. Additional exam requirements/recommendations for international students: Required—TOEFL (minimum score 500 paper-based; 173 computer-based). *Application deadline:* For fall admission, 4/1 for domestic students, 5/1 priority date for international students; for spring admission, 11/1 for domestic students, 11/1 priority date for international students. Applications are processed on a rolling basis. Application fee: $40. Electronic applications accepted. *Expenses:* Tuition: Full-time $18,480; part-time $770 per credit. Required fees: $125 per semester. Tuition and fees vary according to program. *Financial support:* Research assistantships, career-related internships or fieldwork and scholarships/grants available. Support available to part-time students. Financial award application deadline: 3/1; financial award applicants required to submit FAFSA. *Application contact:* Kelly Ronayne, Assistant Dean, 718-990-2303, Fax: 718-990-6069, E-mail: graded@stjohns.edu.

St. John's University, The School of Education, Division of Human Services and Counseling, Program in School Counseling, Queens, NY 11439. Offers MS Ed, PD. *Accreditation:* ACA (one or more programs are accredited). Part-time and evening/weekend programs available. *Students:* 37 full-time (31 women), 51 part-time (41 women); includes 26 minority (14 African Americans, 1 Asian American or Pacific Islander, 11 Hispanic Americans), 1 international. Average age 28. 94 applicants, 59% accepted, 31 enrolled. In 2006, 40 master's, 1 other advanced degree awarded. *Degree requirements:* For master's, internship, 2 practica; for PD, internship. *Entrance requirements:* For master's, interview, minimum GPA of 3.0, 18 credits of course work in behavioral sciences; for PD, interview, minimum GPA of 3.0. Additional exam requirements/recommendations for international students: Required—TOEFL (minimum score 500 paper-based; 173 computer-based). *Application deadline:* For fall admission, 4/1 for domestic students, 5/1 priority date for international students; for spring admission, 11/1 for domestic students, 11/1 priority date for international students. Applications are processed on a rolling basis. Application fee: $40. Electronic applications accepted. *Expenses:* Tuition: Full-time $18,480; part-time $770 per credit. Required fees: $125 per semester. Tuition and fees vary according to program. *Financial support:* Research assistantships, career-related internships or fieldwork available. Support available to part-time students. Financial award application deadline: 3/1; financial award applicants required to submit FAFSA. *Faculty research:* Counseling techniques, communication skills in counseling, learning styles and counseling, computers in counseling and assisting troubled children and teens with substance abuse, truancy, and coping skills. *Application contact:* Kelly Ronayne, Assistant Dean, 718-990-2303, Fax: 718-990-6069, E-mail: graded@stjohns.edu.

Saint Joseph College, Graduate Division, Department of Counselor Education, West Hartford, CT 06117-2700. Offers community counseling (MA), including child welfare, pastoral counseling, school counseling; spirituality (Certificate). Part-time and evening/weekend programs available. *Degree requirements:* For master's, Capstone project, thesis optional. *Entrance requirements:* For master's, PRAXIS I (school counseling), 2 letters of recommendation. Electronic applications accepted.

St. Lawrence University, Department of Education, Program in Counseling and Human Development, Canton, NY 13617-1455. Offers M Ed, CAS. Part-time and evening/weekend programs available. *Entrance requirements:* For master's, GRE General Test. *Faculty research:* Defense mechanisms and mediation.

Saint Louis University, Graduate School, College of Public Service and Graduate School, Department of Counseling and Family Therapy, St. Louis, MO 63103-2097. Offers counseling and family therapy (PhD); human development counseling (MA); marriage and family therapy (Certificate); school counseling (MA, MA-R). *Accreditation:* NCATE. Part-time programs available. *Faculty:* 5 full-time (2 women), 9 part-time/adjunct (8 women). *Students:* 61 full-time (52 women), 46 part-time (37 women); includes 19 minority (13 African Americans, 1 American Indian/Alaska Native, 4 Asian Americans or Pacific Islanders, 1 Hispanic American), 2 international. Average age 33. 72 applicants, 69% accepted, 26 enrolled. In 2006, 15 degrees awarded. *Degree requirements:* For master's, thesis (for some programs), comprehensive exam, registration; for doctorate, thesis/dissertation, preliminary oral and written exams, comprehensive exam, registration. *Entrance requirements:* For master's, GRE General Test or MAT, interview, letters of recommendation, resumé; for doctorate, GRE General Test, interview, letters of recommendation, resumé. Additional exam requirements/recommendations for international students: Required—TOEFL (minimum score 550 paper-based; 213 computer-based). *Application deadline:* For fall admission, 5/1 for domestic and international students; for spring admission, 11/1 for domestic and international students. Applications are processed on a rolling basis. Application fee: $40. *Expenses:* Tuition: Part-time $800 per credit hour. Required fees: $105 per semester. *Financial support:* In 2006–07, 32 students received support, including 3 research assistantships with full tuition reimbursements available (averaging $13,000 per year), 2 teaching assistantships with full tuition reimbursements available (averaging $13,000 per year); Federal Work-Study, scholarships/grants, traineeships, health care benefits, tuition waivers (partial), and unspecified assistantships also available. Support available to part-time students. Financial award application deadline: 6/1; financial award applicants required to submit FAFSA. *Faculty research:* Medical family therapy/collaborative health care multicultural counseling, mental health needs of diverse, minority, or Immigrant/refugee populations, divorce, aging families. *Unit head:* Dr. Craig W. Smith, Chairperson, 314-977-7108, Fax: 314-977-3214, E-mail: csmith112@slu.edu. *Application contact:* Gary Behrman, Associate Dean of the Graduate School, 314-977-3827, E-mail: behrmang@slu.edu.

Saint Martin's University, Graduate Programs, Department of Education, Lacey, WA 98503-1297. Offers administration (M Ed); English as a second language (M Ed); guidance and counseling (M Ed); reading (M Ed); special education (M Ed); teaching (MIT); technology in education (M Ed). Part-time and evening/weekend programs available. *Degree requirements:* For master's, thesis or alternative, project or comprehensives, comprehensive exam (for some programs). *Entrance requirements:* For master's, GRE General Test or MAT, resumé. Additional exam requirements/recommendations for international students: Required—TOEFL (minimum score 560 paper-based). *Faculty research:* Reader's theatre and reader/writer workshops, curriculum and assessment integration, gender and equity, classroom evaluations, organizational leadership.

Saint Mary's College of California, School of Education, Program in Counseling, Moraga, CA 94575. Offers general counseling (MA); marital and family therapy (MA); school counseling (MA). Part-time and evening/weekend programs available. *Faculty:* 5 full-time (4 women), 22 part-time/adjunct (18 women). *Students:* 54 full-time (35 women), 104 part-time (74 women); includes 44 minority (11 African Americans, 12 Asian Americans or Pacific Islanders, 21 Hispanic Americans), 7 international. Average age 35. 69 applicants, 63 enrolled. In 2006, 27 degrees awarded. *Median time to degree:* Master's–2.5 years full-time. *Degree requirements:* For master's, thesis or alternative. *Entrance requirements:* For master's, interview, minimum GPA of 3.0. *Application deadline:* Applications are processed on a rolling basis. Application fee: $50. *Financial support:* In 2006–07, 5 students received support. Career-related internships or fieldwork and Federal Work-Study available. Support available to part-time students. Financial award application deadline: 2/15; financial award applicants required to submit FAFSA. *Faculty research:* Counselor training effectiveness, multicultural development, empathy, the interface of spirituality and psychotherapy, gender issues. *Unit head:* Dr. Laura Heid, Director, 925-631-4293, Fax: 925-376-8379, E-mail: lheid@stmarys.ca.edu.

St. Mary's University of San Antonio, Graduate School, Department of Counseling and Human Services, Program in Counseling Education and Supervision, San Antonio, TX 78228-8507. Offers PhD. *Accreditation:* ACA. *Faculty:* 5 full-time (1 woman), 10 part-time/adjunct (3 women). *Students:* 37; includes 19 minority (1 Asian American or Pacific Islander, 18 Hispanic Americans). Average age 36. In 2006, 6 degrees awarded. *Degree requirements:* For doctorate, thesis/dissertation, comprehensive exam, registration. *Entrance requirements:* For doctorate, GRE, master's degree, work experience, letters of recommendation. Additional exam requirements/recommendations for international students: Required—TOEFL (minimum score 550 paper-based; 213 computer-based). Application fee: $30. *Expenses:* Tuition: Full-time $10,890; part-time $605 per hour. Required fees: $500. Tuition and fees vary according to degree level. *Financial support:* Career-related internships or fieldwork, Federal Work-Study, institutionally sponsored loans, scholarships/grants, health care benefits, and unspecified assistantships available. Financial award application deadline: 3/31; financial award applicants required to submit FAFSA. *Unit head:* Dr. Ray Wooten, Director, 210-436-3226, Fax: 210-431-6886, E-mail: hrwooten@stmarytx.edu.

St. Thomas University, School of Graduate Studies, Department of Social Sciences and Counseling, Program in Guidance and Counseling, Miami Gardens, FL 33054-6459. Offers

MS, Post-Master's Certificate. Part-time and evening/weekend programs available. *Degree requirements:* For master's, comprehensive exam. *Entrance requirements:* For master's, interview, minimum GPA of 3.0 or GRE. Additional exam requirements/recommendations for international students: Required—TOEFL. Electronic applications accepted.

Saint Xavier University, Graduate Studies, School of Education, Program in Counseling, Chicago, IL 60655-3105. Offers MA. *Students:* 10 full-time (9 women), 55 part-time (50 women). Average age 35. *Degree requirements:* For master's, practicum, internship. *Entrance requirements:* For master's, 3 letters of recommendation, interview. Additional exam requirements/recommendations for international students: Required—TOEFL. Application fee: $35. Electronic applications accepted. *Financial support:* Research assistantships, teaching assistantships, institutionally sponsored loans, scholarships/grants, and unspecified assistantships available. Financial award applicants required to submit FAFSA. *Unit head:* Dr. Pamela Castellanos, Director, 773-298-3477, E-mail: castellanos@sxu.edu. *Application contact:* Office of Graduate Admission, 773-298-3053, Fax: 773-298-3951, E-mail: graduateadmission@sxu.edu.

Salem State College, Graduate School, Program in School Counseling, Salem, MA 01970-5353. Offers M Ed. *Accreditation:* NCATE. Part-time and evening/weekend programs available. *Faculty:* 8 part-time/adjunct (3 women). *Students:* 11 full-time (8 women), 41 part-time (36 women); includes 5 minority (1 African American, 1 American Indian/Alaska Native, 1 Asian American or Pacific Islander, 2 Hispanic Americans). Average age 30. In 2006, 13 degrees awarded. *Entrance requirements:* For master's, GRE General Test, MAT. *Application deadline:* Applications are processed on a rolling basis. Application fee: $35. *Unit head:* Mary Ni, Coordinator, 978-542-7076, Fax: 978-542-6596, E-mail: mni@salemstate.edu.

Sam Houston State University, College of Education and Applied Science, Department of Educational Leadership and Counseling, Huntsville, TX 77341. Offers administration (M Ed, MA); counseling (M Ed, MA); counselor education (MA, PhD); educational leadership (Ed D); instructional leadership (M Ed, MA). Part-time programs available. *Faculty:* 15 full-time (10 women). *Students:* 74 full-time (59 women), 598 part-time (458 women); includes 181 minority (74 African Americans, 3 American Indian/Alaska Native, 4 Asian Americans or Pacific Islanders, 100 Hispanic Americans), 7 international. Average age 37. In 2006, 233 master's, 20 doctorates awarded. *Entrance requirements:* For master's, GRE General Test. *Application deadline:* For fall admission, 8/1 for domestic students; for spring admission, 12/1 for domestic students. Application fee: $20. *Expenses:* Tuition, state resident: full-time $5,904; part-time $164 per semester hour. Tuition, nonresident: full-time $15,804; part-time $439 per semester hour. Required fees: $1,374; $462 per semester. *Financial support:* Career-related internships or fieldwork, Federal Work-Study, and institutionally sponsored loans available. Support available to part-time students. Financial award application deadline: 5/31; financial award applicants required to submit FAFSA. *Unit head:* Dr. Beverly Irby, Chair, 936-294-1134, Fax: 936-294-3886, E-mail: edu_bid@shsu.edu. *Application contact:* Dr. Stacey Edmondson, Advisor, 936-294-1752, E-mail: sedmonson@shsu.edu.

San Diego State University, Graduate and Research Affairs, College of Education, Department of Counseling and School Psychology, San Diego, CA 92182. Offers MS. *Accreditation:* NCATE. Evening/weekend programs available. *Students:* 123 full-time (100 women), 13 part-time (12 women). Average age 30. 260 applicants, 27% accepted, 54 enrolled. In 2006, 76 degrees awarded. *Degree requirements:* For master's, thesis (for some programs), comprehensive exam (for some programs). *Entrance requirements:* For master's, GRE General Test, interview, letters of reference. Additional exam requirements/recommendations for international students: Required—TOEFL. *Application deadline:* For fall admission, 2/1 priority date for domestic and international students; for spring admission, 11/1 for domestic students, 10/1 for international students. Applications are processed on a rolling basis. Application fee: $55. Electronic applications accepted. *Financial support:* In 2006–07, 7 teaching assistantships were awarded; career-related internships or fieldwork also available. Financial award applicants required to submit FAFSA. *Faculty research:* Multicultural and cross-cultural counseling and training, AIDS counseling. Total annual research expenditures: $626,857. *Unit head:* Carol Robinson-Zañartu, Chair, 619-594-7725, Fax: 619-594-7025, E-mail: crobinsn@mail.sdsu.edu.

San Jose State University, Graduate Studies and Research, College of Education, Department of Counselor Education, San Jose, CA 95192-0001. Offers education (counseling and student personnel) (MA). *Accreditation:* NCATE. Evening/weekend programs available. *Students:* 134 full-time (107 women), 64 part-time (52 women); includes 117 minority (22 African Americans, 2 American Indian/Alaska Native, 23 Asian Americans or Pacific Islanders, 70 Hispanic Americans), 2 international. Average age 31. 128 applicants, 78% accepted, 75 enrolled. In 2006, 62 degrees awarded. *Degree requirements:* For master's, thesis or alternative. *Application deadline:* For fall admission, 6/29 for domestic students; for spring admission, 11/30 for domestic students. Applications are processed on a rolling basis. Application fee: $59. Electronic applications accepted. *Financial support:* Career-related internships or fieldwork available. Financial award applicants required to submit FAFSA. *Unit head:* Dr. Xialou Hu, Chair, 408-924-3636, Fax: 408-924-3713.

Santa Clara University, School of Education, Counseling Psychology, and Pastoral Ministries, Department of Counseling Psychology, Program in Counseling, Santa Clara, CA 95053. Offers MA. Part-time and evening/weekend programs available. *Students:* 5 full-time (2 women), 14 part-time (10 women); includes 6 minority (1 African American, 1 Asian American or Pacific Islander, 4 Hispanic Americans), 2 international. Average age 36. 3 applicants, 100% accepted, 1 enrolled. In 2006, 15 degrees awarded. *Degree requirements:* For master's, thesis optional. *Entrance requirements:* For master's, GRE or MAT, minimum GPA of 3.0, 1 year of related experience. Additional exam requirements/recommendations for international students: Required—TOEFL. *Application deadline:* Applications are processed on a rolling basis. *Expenses:* Tuition: Part-time $627 per unit. Tuition and fees vary according to program. *Financial support:* Fellowships, teaching assistantships, career-related internships or fieldwork, Federal Work-Study, institutionally sponsored loans, and scholarships/grants available. Support available to part-time students. Financial award application deadline: 3/1; financial award applicants required to submit FAFSA.

Seattle Pacific University, Graduate School, School of Education, Program in School Counseling, Seattle, WA 98119-1997. Offers M Ed. *Accreditation:* NCATE. Part-time programs available. *Students:* 3 full-time (2 women), 47 part-time (42 women); includes 2 minority (both Asian Americans or Pacific Islanders) 32 applicants, 69% accepted, 16 enrolled. In 2006, 9 degrees awarded. *Entrance requirements:* For master's, GRE General Test or MAT, minimum GPA of 3.0. *Application deadline:* For fall admission, 7/1 priority date for domestic students; for spring admission, 3/1 priority date for domestic students. Applications are processed on a rolling basis. Application fee: $50. *Expenses:* Contact institution. *Financial support:* Applicants required to submit FAFSA. *Unit head:* Dr. Christopher Sink, Chair, 206-281-2378, Fax: 206-281-2756. *Application contact:* Allan Blomquist, Graduate Programs Manager, 206-281-2378, Fax: 206-281-2756, E-mail: blomqa@spu.edu.

Seattle University, College of Education, Program in Counseling and School Psychology, Seattle, WA 98122-1090. Offers MA, Certificate, Ed S. *Accreditation:* NCATE. Part-time and evening/weekend programs available. *Students:* 23 full-time (16 women), 115 part-time (91 women); includes 28 minority (7 African Americans, 1 American Indian/Alaska Native, 13 Asian Americans or Pacific Islanders, 7 Hispanic Americans), 1 international. Average age 32. 77 applicants, 61% accepted, 45 enrolled. In 2006, 38 master's, 10 other advanced degrees awarded. *Degree requirements:* For master's, comprehensive exam. *Entrance requirements:* For master's, interview; GRE, MAT, or minimum GPA of 3.0; related work experience. Additional exam requirements/recommendations for international students: Required—TOEFL. *Application deadline:* For fall admission, 7/1 for domestic students; for winter admission, 10/20 for domestic students; for spring admission, 1/20 for domestic students. Application fee: $55. *Unit head:* Hutch Haney, Director, 206-296-5750. *Application contact:* Janet Shandley, Associate Dean of Graduate Admissions, 206-296-5900, Fax: 206-298-5656, E-mail: grad_admissions@seattleu.edu.

Seton Hall University, College of Education and Human Services, Department of Professional Psychology and Family Therapy, Programs in Counselor Preparation, South Orange, NJ 07079-2697. Offers MA. Part-time and evening/weekend programs available. *Faculty:* 3 full-time (1 woman). *Students:* 23 full-time (16 women), 61 part-time (47 women); includes 22 minority (16 African Americans, 2 Asian Americans or Pacific Islanders, 4 Hispanic Americans), 1 international. Average age 35. 35 applicants, 100% accepted, 23 enrolled. In 2006, 15 degrees awarded. *Degree requirements:* For master's, comprehensive exam. *Entrance requirements:* For master's, GRE or MAT, interview. *Application deadline:* Applications are processed on a rolling basis. Application fee: $50. *Financial support:* Application deadline: 2/1. *Faculty research:* Vocational indecision, life skills, counseling process. *Unit head:* Dr. Jane Webber, Director, 973-275-2732, E-mail: webberja@shu.edu. *Application contact:* 973-761-9451.

Shippensburg University of Pennsylvania, School of Graduate Studies, College of Education and Human Services, Department of Counseling, Shippensburg, PA 17257-2299. Offers Adlerian studies (Certificate); advanced study in counseling (Certificate); counseling (MS); couple and family counseling (Certificate); guidance and counseling (M Ed). *Accreditation:* ACA (one or more programs are accredited); NCATE. Part-time and evening/weekend programs available. *Faculty:* 9 full-time (4 women), 3 part-time/adjunct (2 women). *Students:* 81 full-time (67 women), 94 part-time (77 women); includes 14 minority (10 African Americans, 2 Asian Americans or Pacific Islanders, 2 Hispanic Americans), 3 international. Average age 29. 135 applicants, 39% accepted, 38 enrolled. In 2006, 43 degrees awarded. *Degree requirements:* For master's, fieldwork, research project, internship, candidacy. *Entrance requirements:* For master's, minimum GPA of 2.75, interview, resumé, 3 letters of reference, 1 year relevant work experience, MAT or GRE if GPA less than 2.75. Additional exam requirements/recommendations for international students: Required—TOEFL (minimum score 560 paper-based; 220 computer-based). *Application deadline:* For fall admission, 3/1 for international students; for spring admission, 7/1 for international students. Applications are processed on a rolling basis. Application fee: $30. Electronic applications accepted. *Expenses:* Tuition, state resident: part-time $336 per credit. Tuition, nonresident: part-time $538 per credit. *Financial support:* In 2006–07, 57 research assistantships with full tuition reimbursements (averaging $3,125 per year) were awarded; career-related internships or fieldwork, scholarships/grants, and unspecified assistantships also available. Support available to part-time students. Financial award application deadline: 3/1; financial award applicants required to submit FAFSA. *Unit head:* Dr. Jan Arminio, Chairperson, 717-477-1668, Fax: 717-477-4016, E-mail: jlarmi@ship.edu. *Application contact:* Renee Payne, Associate Dean of Graduate Admissions, 717-477-1231, Fax: 717-477-4016, E-mail: rmpayn@ship.edu.

Siena Heights University, Graduate College, Program in Counselor Education, Adrian, MI 49221-1796. Offers agency counseling (MA); community counseling (Spt), including school counseling; school counseling (MA). Part-time and evening/weekend programs available. *Degree requirements:* For master's, thesis, presentation. *Entrance requirements:* For master's, minimum GPA of 3.0, interview. *Faculty research:* Consultation, special education competencies of school counselors.

Simmons College, Graduate School, College of Arts and Sciences Graduate Studies, Department of Education, Program in Special Education, Boston, MA 02115. Offers applied behavior analysis (PhD); assistive technology (MS Ed, Ed S); behavioral education (MS Ed, Ed S); health professions education (PhD); language and literacy (MS Ed, Ed S); moderate disabilities (Ed S); moderate special needs (MS Ed); severe disabilities (Ed S); severe special needs (MS Ed); special education administration (MS Ed, PhD, Ed S). Part-time and evening/weekend programs available. *Faculty:* 9 full-time (7 women), 34 part-time/adjunct (23 women). *Students:* 51 full-time (46 women), 405 part-time (339 women); includes 31 minority (13 African Americans, 2 American Indian/Alaska Native, 7 Asian Americans or Pacific Islanders, 9 Hispanic Americans), 2 international. Average age 28. 155 applicants, 91% accepted, 121 enrolled. In 2006, 122 master's, 27 other advanced degrees awarded. *Degree requirements:* For master's, practicum; for doctorate, thesis/dissertation. *Entrance requirements:* For doctorate, GRE, research proposal interview. Additional exam requirements/recommendations for international students: Required—TOEFL (minimum score 600 paper-based; 250 computer-based; 100 iBT). *Application deadline:* For fall admission, 8/1 priority date for domestic students; for spring admission, 12/1 priority date for domestic students. Applications are processed on a rolling basis. Application fee: $35. Electronic applications accepted. *Expenses:* Contact institution. *Financial support:* Career-related internships or fieldwork, Federal Work-Study, institutionally sponsored loans, scholarships/grants, and tuition waivers (partial) available. Support available to part-time students. Financial award application deadline: 3/1; financial award applicants required to submit FAFSA. *Faculty research:* Classroom-based research, inclusion strategies, beginning teacher development. *Unit head:* Dr. Cathryn Mercier, Associate Dean, 617-521-2091. *Application contact:* Kristen Haack, Director, Graduate Studies Admission, 617-521-2915, Fax: 617-521-3058, E-mail: gsa@simmons.edu.

Simon Fraser University, Graduate Studies, Faculty of Education, Program in Guidance and Counseling, Burnaby, BC V5A 1S6, Canada. Offers M Ed, MA. *Degree requirements:* For master's, project or thesis. *Entrance requirements:* For master's, minimum GPA of 3.0. Additional exam requirements/recommendations for international students: Required—TOEFL or IELTS.

Slippery Rock University of Pennsylvania, Graduate Studies (Recruitment), College of Education, Department of Counseling and Development, Slippery Rock, PA 16057-1383. Offers community counseling (MA), including addiction, adult, child and adolescent; elementary guidance and counseling (M Ed); secondary guidance and counseling (M Ed); student personnel (MA). *Accreditation:* ACA (one or more programs are accredited); NCATE. Part-time and evening/weekend programs available. *Degree requirements:* For master's, thesis (for some programs), oral comprehensive exam. *Entrance requirements:* For master's, GRE General Test, MAT, minimum GPA of 2.75. Additional exam requirements/recommendations for international students: Required—TOEFL (minimum score 550 paper-based; 213 computer-based). *Application deadline:* For fall admission, 7/1 priority date for domestic and international students; for spring admission, 11/1 priority date for domestic and international students. Applications are processed on a rolling basis. Application fee: $25. Electronic applications accepted. *Expenses:* Tuition, state resident: part-time $336 per credit. Tuition, nonresident: part-time $538 per credit. Required fees: $84 per credit. $37 per semester. *Financial support:* Career-related internships or fieldwork, Federal Work-Study, scholarships/grants, and unspecified assistantships available. Support available to part-time students. Financial award application deadline: 5/1; financial award applicants required to submit FAFSA. *Unit head:* Dr. Donald Strano, Graduate Coordinator, 724-738-2035, Fax: 724-738-2880, E-mail: donald.strano@sru.edu. *Application contact:* April Longwell, Interim Director of Graduate Studies, 724-738-2051 Ext. 2116, Fax: 724-738-2146, E-mail: graduate.studies@sru.edu.

Sonoma State University, School of Social Sciences, Department of Counseling, Rohnert Park, CA 94928-3609. Offers counseling (MA); marriage, family, and child counseling (MA); pupil personnel services (MA). *Accreditation:* ACA. Part-time programs available. *Faculty:* 6 full-time (4 women), 3 part-time/adjunct (2 women). *Students:* 45 full-time (35 women), 36 part-time (23 women); includes 12 minority (1 African American, 1 American Indian/Alaska Native, 2 Asian Americans or Pacific Islanders, 8 Hispanic Americans). Average age 33. 102 applicants, 41% accepted, 36 enrolled. In 2006, 33 degrees awarded. *Degree requirements:* For master's, internship. *Entrance requirements:* For master's, minimum GPA of 3.0. *Application deadline:* For fall admission, 11/30 for domestic students. Application fee: $55. *Expenses:* Tuition, nonresident: part-time $339 per unit. Required fees: $1,464 per term. *Financial support:* Career-related internships or fieldwork available. Support available to part-time students. Financial award application deadline: 3/2. *Faculty research:* Self-esteem, relationship of emotion and health, at-risk youth, feminist issues, supervision strategies. *Unit head:* Maureen Buckley, Chair, 707-664-2544, E-mail: maureen.buckley@sonoma.edu.

South Carolina State University, School of Graduate Studies, Department of Education, Orangeburg, SC 29117-0001. Offers early childhood and special education (M Ed); early

Counselor Education

South Carolina State University (continued)
childhood education (MAT); elementary education (M Ed, MAT); engineering (MAT); general science (MAT); mathematics (MAT); secondary education (M Ed), including biology education, business education, counselor education, English education, home economics education, industrial education, mathematics education, science education, social studies education; special education (M Ed), including emotionally handicapped, learning disabilities, mentally handicapped. *Accreditation:* NCATE. Part-time and evening/weekend programs available. *Faculty:* 21 full-time (10 women), 4 part-time/adjunct (0 women). *Students:* 34 full-time (28 women), 33 part-time (25 women); includes 63 minority (61 African Americans, 1 American Indian/Alaska Native, 1 Asian American or Pacific Islander). Average age 35. 46 applicants, 67% accepted, 19 enrolled. In 2006, 28 degrees awarded. *Degree requirements:* For master's, departmental qualifying exam, thesis optional. *Entrance requirements:* For master's, GRE General Test, NTE, interview, teaching certificate. *Application deadline:* For fall admission, 6/15 priority date for domestic students, 6/15 for international students; for spring admission, 11/1 for domestic and international students. Applications are processed on a rolling basis. Application fee: $25. Electronic applications accepted. *Expenses:* Tuition, state resident: full-time $7,278. Tuition, nonresident: full-time $14,322. *Financial support:* Fellowships, research assistantships, career-related internships or fieldwork, Federal Work-Study, and institutionally sponsored loans available. Financial award application deadline: 6/1. *Faculty research:* Critical thinking, child abuse, stress, test-taking skills, conflict resolution, mainstreaming. *Unit head:* Dr. Gail Joyner-Fleming, Interim Chair, 803-533-3769, Fax: 803-536-8492, E-mail: zf-gfleming@scsu.edu. *Application contact:* Annette Hazzard-Jones, Program Coordinator II, 803-536-8809, Fax: 803-536-8812, E-mail: zs_ahazzard@scsu.edu.

South Carolina State University, School of Graduate Studies, Department of Human Services, Orangeburg, SC 29117-0001. Offers elementary counselor education (M Ed); rehabilitation counseling (MA); secondary counselor education (M Ed). *Accreditation:* CORE. Part-time and evening/weekend programs available. *Faculty:* 9 full-time (6 women), 3 part-time/adjunct (2 women). *Students:* 106 full-time (79 women), 37 part-time (25 women); includes 137 minority (136 African Americans, 1 Asian American or Pacific Islander), 1 international. Average age 31. 76 applicants, 71% accepted, 43 enrolled. In 2006, 45 degrees awarded. *Degree requirements:* For master's, departmental qualifying exam, internship, thesis optional. *Entrance requirements:* For master's, GRE, MAT, minimum GPA of 2.7. *Application deadline:* For fall admission, 6/15 priority date for domestic students, 6/15 for international students; for spring admission, 11/1 for domestic and international students. Applications are processed on a rolling basis. Application fee: $25. Electronic applications accepted. *Expenses:* Tuition, state resident: full-time $7,278. Tuition, nonresident: full-time $14,322. *Financial support:* In 2006–07, 35 students received support; fellowships, research assistantships, career-related internships or fieldwork, institutionally sponsored loans, and unspecified assistantships available. Financial award application deadline: 6/1. *Faculty research:* Handicap, disability, rehabilitation evaluation, vocation. *Unit head:* Dr. Christine Boone, Interim Chair, 803-533-3968, Fax: 803-533-3666, E-mail: boonec@scsu.edu. *Application contact:* Annette Hazzard-Jones, Program Coordinator II, 803-536-8809, Fax: 803-536-8812, E-mail: zs_ahazzard@scsu.edu.

South Dakota State University, Graduate School, College of Education and Counseling, Department of Counseling and Human Resource Development, Brookings, SD 57007. Offers MS. *Accreditation:* ACA; NCATE. Part-time and evening/weekend programs available. *Faculty:* 8 full-time (3 women), 3 part-time/adjunct (2 women). *Students:* 133 full-time (108 women), 47 part-time (36 women); includes 17 minority (2 African Americans, 12 American Indian/Alaska Native, 3 Hispanic Americans), 1 international. 100 applicants, 65% accepted, 65 enrolled. In 2006, 48 degrees awarded. *Degree requirements:* For master's, thesis (for some programs), oral exams, comprehensive exam. *Entrance requirements:* For master's, minimum GPA of 2.75. Additional exam requirements/recommendations for international students: Required—TOEFL (minimum score 525 paper-based). *Application deadline:* For fall admission, 4/1 for domestic students; for spring admission, 10/1 for domestic students. Applications are processed on a rolling basis. Application fee: $35. *Financial support:* In 2006–07, 2 research assistantships with partial tuition reimbursements, 1 teaching assistantship with partial tuition reimbursement were awarded; career-related internships or fieldwork, scholarships/grants, and unspecified assistantships also available. *Faculty research:* Rural mental health, family issues, character education, student affairs, solution focused therapy. *Unit head:* Dr. Jay Trenhaile, Head, 605-688-4190, Fax: 605-688-5929, E-mail: jay.trenhaile@sdstate.edu.

Southeastern Louisiana University, College of Education and Human Development, Department of Counseling and Human Development, Hammond, LA 70402. Offers counselor education (M Ed). *Accreditation:* ACA; NCATE. Part-time programs available. *Faculty:* 7 full-time (5 women). *Students:* 50 full-time (42 women), 25 part-time (21 women); includes 14 minority (12 African Americans, 1 Asian American or Pacific Islander, 1 Hispanic American), 1 international. Average age 29. 30 applicants, 100% accepted, 30 enrolled. In 2006, 21 degrees awarded. *Degree requirements:* For master's, thesis optional. *Entrance requirements:* For master's, GRE General Test, 9 hours of course work in behavioral studies, 3 hours of course work in statistics, 3 letters of reference. Additional exam requirements/recommendations for international students: Required—TOEFL (minimum score 500 paper-based; 173 computer-based). *Application deadline:* For fall admission, 7/15 priority date for domestic students, 6/1 priority date for international students; for spring admission, 12/1 priority date for domestic students, 10/1 priority date for international students. Applications are processed on a rolling basis. Application fee: $20 ($30 for international students). Electronic applications accepted. *Expenses:* Tuition, state resident: full-time $2,216; part-time $123 per credit. Tuition, nonresident: full-time $6,212; part-time $345 per credit. Required fees: $986; $55 per credit. Part-time tuition and fees vary according to course load. *Financial support:* In 2006–07, 1 research assistantship with full tuition reimbursement (averaging $5,500 per year) was awarded; career-related internships or fieldwork, Federal Work-Study, institutionally sponsored loans, unspecified assistantships, and administrative assistantships also available. Support available to part-time students. Financial award application deadline: 5/1; financial award applicants required to submit FAFSA. *Faculty research:* Family of origin, substance abuse counseling, childhood and adolescent obesity, attachment disorders, counselor training issues. *Unit head:* Dr. Mary Ballard, Department Head, 985-549-2309, Fax: 985-549-3758, E-mail: mballard@selu.edu. *Application contact:* Sandra Meyers, Graduate Admissions Analyst, 985-549-2066, Fax: 985-549-5632, E-mail: admissions@selu.edu.

Southeastern Oklahoma State University, Graduate School, School of Behavioral Sciences, Durant, OK 74701-0609. Offers guidance and counseling (MBS). Part-time and evening/weekend programs available. *Degree requirements:* For master's, thesis optional. *Entrance requirements:* For master's, GRE General Test, minimum GPA of 3.0 in last 60 hours or 2.75 overall. Additional exam requirements/recommendations for international students: Required—TOEFL (minimum score 550 paper-based; 213 computer-based). Electronic applications accepted.

Southeastern Oklahoma State University, Graduate School, School of Education, Durant, OK 74701-0609. Offers educational administration (M Ed); educational instruction and leadership (M Ed); educational technology (M Ed); elementary education (M Ed); school counseling (M Ed); secondary education (M Ed). *Accreditation:* NCATE. Part-time and evening/weekend programs available. *Degree requirements:* For master's, portfolio (M Ed), thesis optional. *Entrance requirements:* For master's, GRE General Test (MBS), minimum GPA of 3.0 in last 60 hours or 2.75 overall. Additional exam requirements/recommendations for international students: Required—TOEFL (minimum score 550 paper-based; 213 computer-based). Electronic applications accepted.

Southeast Missouri State University, School of Graduate Studies, Department of Educational Leadership and Counseling, Program in Guidance and Counseling, Cape Girardeau, MO 63701-4799. Offers community counseling (MA); counseling education (Ed S); school counseling (MA), including elementary counseling, secondary counseling. *Accreditation:* ACA; NCATE. Part-time and evening/weekend programs available. *Faculty:* 4 full-time (2 women). *Students:* 20 full-time (17 women), 42 part-time (36 women); includes 4 minority (3 African Americans, 1 Asian American or Pacific Islander), 1 international. Average age 32. 26 applicants, 88% accepted. In 2006, 25 master's, 8 other advanced degrees awarded. *Degree requirements:* For master's, thesis or alternative. *Entrance requirements:* For master's, GRE General Test, MAT, minimum GPA of 3.0; for Ed S, GRE General Test, or MAT, minimum graduate GPA of 3.5. Additional exam requirements/recommendations for international students: Required—TOEFL (minimum score 550 paper-based; 213 computer-based). *Application deadline:* For fall admission, 8/1 for domestic students, 4/1 for international students; for spring admission, 11/21 for domestic students, 10/1 for international students. Applications are processed on a rolling basis. Application fee: $20 ($100 for international students). Electronic applications accepted. *Financial support:* In 2006–07, 27 students received support, including 9 research assistantships with full tuition reimbursements available (averaging $7,100 per year); career-related internships or fieldwork and unspecified assistantships also available. Financial award applicants required to submit FAFSA. *Application contact:* Marsha L. Arant, Senior Administrative Assistant, Office of Graduate Studies, 573-651-2192, Fax: 573-651-2001, E-mail: marant@semo.edu.

Southern Adventist University, School of Education and Psychology, Collegedale, TN 37315-0370. Offers curriculum and instruction (MS Ed); educational administration and supervision (MS Ed); inclusive education (MS Ed); literacy education (MS Ed); outdoor teacher education (MS Ed); professional counseling (MS); school counseling (MS). *Accreditation:* NCATE. Part-time and evening/weekend programs available. *Faculty:* 11 full-time (5 women), 1 (woman) part-time/adjunct. *Students:* 36 full-time (29 women), 7 part-time (6 women); includes 8 minority (6 African Americans, 2 Hispanic Americans). Average age 30. 15 applicants, 100% accepted, 15 enrolled. In 2006, 25 degrees awarded. *Degree requirements:* For master's, position paper (MS), portfolio (MS Ed in outdoor teacher education), thesis optional. *Entrance requirements:* For master's, GRE General Test, interview (MS); 9 semester hours of upper division course work in psychology or related field, including 1 course in psychology research or statistics; 9 semester hours of education (MS Ed). Additional exam requirements/recommendations for international students: Required—TOEFL (minimum score 600 paper-based; 250 computer-based; 100 iBT). *Application deadline:* For fall admission, 5/15 priority date for domestic and international students; for winter admission, 10/15 priority date for domestic and international students; for spring admission, 3/31 priority date for domestic and international students. Applications are processed on a rolling basis. Application fee: $25. Electronic applications accepted. *Financial support:* In 2006–07, 7 students received support, including 4 research assistantships with full tuition reimbursements available (averaging $10,000 per year); career-related internships or fieldwork, scholarships/grants, tuition waivers (partial), and unspecified assistantships also available. Support available to part-time students. Financial award application deadline: 4/1; financial award applicants required to submit FAFSA. *Unit head:* Dr. Denise Dunzweiler, Dean, 423-236-2776, Fax: 423-236-1765, E-mail: denise@southern.edu. *Application contact:* Mikhaile Spence, Information Contact, 423-236-2496, Fax: 423-236-1765, E-mail: maspence@southern.edu.

Southern Arkansas University–Magnolia, Graduate Programs, Magnolia, AR 71753. Offers computer and information sciences (MS); counseling (MS); education (M Ed), including counseling and development, educational administration and supervision, elementary education, secondary education; kinesiology (MS); library media and information specialist (M Ed); school counseling (M Ed); teaching (MAT). *Accreditation:* NCATE. Part-time and evening/weekend programs available. *Degree requirements:* For master's, thesis optional. *Entrance requirements:* For master's, GRE or MAT, minimum GPA of 2.75. *Faculty research:* Alternative certification for teachers, supervision of instruction, instructional leadership, counseling.

Southern Connecticut State University, School of Graduate Studies, School of Education, Department of Counseling and School Psychology, New Haven, CT 06515-1355. Offers community counseling (MS); counseling (Diploma); school counseling (MS); school psychology (MS, Diploma). *Accreditation:* ACA (one or more programs are accredited); NCATE. *Faculty:* 8 full-time, 10 part-time/adjunct. *Students:* 87 full-time (74 women), 77 part-time (67 women); includes 24 minority (18 African Americans, 6 Hispanic Americans), 3 international. 136 applicants, 48% accepted, 56 enrolled. In 2006, 44 master's, 12 other advanced degrees awarded. *Degree requirements:* For master's, comprehensive exam. *Entrance requirements:* For master's, interview, previous course work in behavioral sciences, minimum QPA of 2.7. *Application deadline:* For fall admission, 1/15 for domestic students; for spring admission, 10/15 for domestic students. Application fee: $50. Electronic applications accepted. *Financial support:* Teaching assistantships, career-related internships or fieldwork available. Financial award application deadline: 4/15; financial award applicants required to submit FAFSA. *Unit head:* Dr. Norris Haynes, Chairperson, 203-392-5912, E-mail: haynesn1@southernct.edu. *Application contact:* Dr. Uchenna Nwachuku, Graduate Coordinator, Community Counseling Program, 203-392-5914, E-mail: nwachuku@southernct.edu.

Southern Illinois University Carbondale, Graduate School, College of Education, Department of Educational Psychology and Special Education, Program in Educational Psychology, Carbondale, IL 62901-4701. Offers counselor education (MS Ed, PhD); educational psychology (PhD); human learning and development (MS Ed); measurement and statistics (PhD). *Accreditation:* NCATE. *Faculty:* 19 full-time (9 women), 7 part-time/adjunct (2 women). *Students:* 42 full-time (32 women), 61 part-time (46 women); includes 10 minority (7 African Americans, 1 Asian American or Pacific Islander, 2 Hispanic Americans), 12 international. Average age 36. 54 applicants, 56% accepted, 3 enrolled. In 2006, 20 master's, 5 doctorates awarded. *Degree requirements:* For master's and doctorate, thesis/dissertation. *Entrance requirements:* For master's, GRE General Test, minimum GPA of 2.7; for doctorate, minimum GPA of 3.25. Additional exam requirements/recommendations for international students: Required—TOEFL. *Application deadline:* For fall admission, 6/15 priority date for domestic students. Applications are processed on a rolling basis. Application fee: $20. *Financial support:* In 2006–07, 36 students received support, including 2 fellowships with full tuition reimbursements available, 4 research assistantships with full tuition reimbursements available; teaching assistantships with full tuition reimbursements available, career-related internships or fieldwork, Federal Work-Study, institutionally sponsored loans, and tuition waivers (full) also available. Support available to part-time students. Financial award application deadline: 5/1. *Faculty research:* Career development, problem solving, learning and instruction, cognitive development, family assessment. Total annual research expenditures: $10,000. *Application contact:* Cathy Earnhart, Administrative Clerk, 618-453-6932, E-mail: pern@siu.edu.

See Close-Up on page 1125.

Southern Oregon University, Graduate Studies, School of Social Sciences, Department of Psychology, Ashland, OR 97520. Offers applied psychology (MAP); human service-organizational training and development (MA, MS); social science (MA, MS), including professional counseling, psychology. Part-time programs available. *Degree requirements:* For master's, thesis, portfolio and oral defense. *Entrance requirements:* For master's, GRE General Test, minimum GPA of 3.0. Electronic applications accepted.

Southern University and Agricultural and Mechanical College, Graduate School, College of Education, Department of Behavioral Studies and Educational Leadership, Baton Rouge, LA 70813. Offers administration and supervision (M Ed); counselor education (MA); mental health counseling (MA). *Accreditation:* ACA; NCATE. *Degree requirements:* For master's, thesis optional. *Entrance requirements:* For master's, GRE General Test. Additional exam requirements/recommendations for international students: Required—TOEFL (minimum score 525 paper-based; 193 computer-based). *Faculty research:* Mental health, computer assisted programs, families relations, head start improvements, careers.

Southwestern Oklahoma State University, College of Professional and Graduate Studies, School of Behavioral Sciences and Education, Specialization in Community Counseling, Weatherford, OK 73096-3098. Offers M Ed. M Ed distance learning degree program offered to Oklahoma residents only. *Accreditation:* NCATE. Part-time and evening/weekend programs available. Postbaccalaureate distance learning degree programs offered (minimal on-campus study).

Degree requirements: For master's, exam. *Entrance requirements:* For master's, GRE General Test or minimum undergraduate GPA of 3.0. Additional exam requirements/recommendations for international students: Required—TOEFL.

Southwestern Oklahoma State University, College of Professional and Graduate Studies, School of Behavioral Sciences and Education, Specialization in School Counseling, Weatherford, OK 73096-3098. Offers M Ed. M Ed distance learning degree program offered to Oklahoma residents only. *Accreditation:* NCATE. Part-time and evening/weekend programs available. Postbaccalaureate distance learning degree programs offered (minimal on-campus study). *Degree requirements:* For master's, exam. *Entrance requirements:* For master's, GRE General Test or minimum undergraduate GPA of 3.0, portfolio. Additional exam requirements/recommendations for international students: Required—TOEFL.

Springfield College, Graduate Programs, Program in Education, Springfield, MA 01109-3797. Offers counseling and secondary education (M Ed, MS); education (M Ed, MS). Part-time and evening/weekend programs available. *Faculty:* 9 full-time (6 women), 2 part-time/adjunct (both women). *Students:* 52; includes 4 minority (3 African Americans, 1 Hispanic American). Average age 30. 36 applicants, 78% accepted, 21 enrolled. In 2006, 10 master's awarded. *Degree requirements:* For master's, comprehensive exam. *Entrance requirements:* Additional exam requirements/recommendations for international students: Required—TOEFL (minimum score 550 paper-based; 213 computer-based). *Application deadline:* For fall admission, 1/15 for domestic students; for winter admission, 11/1 for domestic students; for spring admission, 12/1 for domestic students. Applications are processed on a rolling basis. Application fee: $50. Electronic applications accepted. *Expenses:* Tuition: Full-time $12,222; part-time $679 per credit. Required fees: $25; $25 per year. One-time fee: $25 full-time. *Financial support:* In 2006–07, 2 teaching assistantships with partial tuition reimbursements were awarded; fellowships with partial tuition reimbursements, career-related internships or fieldwork, Federal Work-Study, institutionally sponsored loans, and tuition waivers (full and partial) also available. Financial award application deadline: 3/1. *Faculty research:* Varied educational research. Total annual research expenditures: $50,000. *Unit head:* Dr. Gerard Thibodeau, Director, 413-748-3312, E-mail: gthibodeau@spfldcol.edu. *Application contact:* Donald James Shaw, Director of Graduate Admissions, 413-748-3060, Fax: 413-748-3069, E-mail: donald_shaw_jr@spfldcol.edu.

Springfield College, Graduate Programs, Programs in Psychology and Counseling, Springfield, MA 01109-3797. Offers athletic counseling (M Ed, MS, CAS); general counseling (M Ed); industrial/organizational psychology (MS, CAS); marriage and family therapy (M Ed, MS, CAS); mental health counseling (M Ed, MS, CAS); school guidance and counseling (M Ed, MS, CAS); student personnel in higher education (M Ed, MS, CAS). Part-time and evening/weekend programs available. *Faculty:* 14 full-time (8 women), 17 part-time/adjunct (7 women). *Students:* 213. Average age 28. 161 applicants, 84% accepted, 77 enrolled. In 2006, 93 master's, 1 other advanced degree awarded. *Degree requirements:* For master's, thesis (for some programs), research project, internship, comprehensive exam. *Entrance requirements:* For master's and CAS, interview. Additional exam requirements/recommendations for international students: Required—TOEFL (minimum score 550 paper-based; 213 computer-based). *Application deadline:* For fall admission, 1/15 priority date for domestic students; for winter admission, 11/1 for domestic students; for spring admission, 12/1 for domestic students. Applications are processed on a rolling basis. Application fee: $50. Electronic applications accepted. *Expenses:* Tuition: Full-time $12,222; part-time $679 per credit. Required fees: $25; $25 per year. One-time fee: $25 full-time. *Financial support:* In 2006–07, 8 fellowships with partial tuition reimbursements (averaging $2,000 per year), 2 research assistantships (averaging $4,000 per year), 7 teaching assistantships (averaging $1,800 per year) were awarded; career-related internships or fieldwork, Federal Work-Study, institutionally sponsored loans, scholarships/grants, and tuition waivers (full and partial) also available. Financial award application deadline: 3/1. *Faculty research:* Sport psychology, leadership and emotional intelligence, violence and terrorism, performance enhancement, cognitive function. Total annual research expenditures: $715,109. *Unit head:* Dr. Anna L. Moriarty, Director, 413-748-3322, Fax: 413-748-3854, E-mail: anna_l_moriarty@spfldcol.edu. *Application contact:* Donald James Shaw, Director of Graduate Admissions, 413-748-3060, Fax: 413-748-3069, E-mail: donald_shaw_jr@spfldcol.edu.

State University of New York at Plattsburgh, Division of Education, Health, and Human Services, Department of Counselor Education, Plattsburgh, NY 12901-2681. Offers college/agency counseling (MS), including mental health counseling, student affairs professional practice; school counselor (MS Ed, CAS). *Accreditation:* ACA (one or more programs are accredited). Part-time programs available. *Faculty:* 6 full-time (2 women), 3 part-time/adjunct (2 women). *Students:* 46 full-time (36 women), 17 part-time (14 women); includes 4 minority (2 African Americans, 2 Hispanic Americans). Average age 29. 36 applicants, 61% accepted, 18 enrolled. In 2006, 25 master's, 19 CASs awarded. *Degree requirements:* For master's and CAS, thesis optional. *Entrance requirements:* For master's, GRE General Test or MAT, minimum GPA of 2.5. *Application deadline:* For fall admission, 3/1 priority date for domestic students; for spring admission, 10/15 priority date for domestic students. Applications are processed on a rolling basis. Application fee: $50. *Expenses:* Tuition, state resident: full-time $6,900; part-time $288 per credit hour. Tuition, nonresident: full-time $10,920; part-time $455 per credit hour. *Financial support:* Research assistantships, teaching assistantships, career-related internships or fieldwork, Federal Work-Study, and administrative assistantships, editorial assistantships available. Support available to part-time students. Financial award application deadline: 4/15; financial award applicants required to submit FAFSA. *Faculty research:* Campus violence, program accreditation, substance abuse, vocational assessment, group counseling, divorce. *Unit head:* Dr. Beverly Burnell, Coordinator, 518-564-4178. *Application contact:* Sharon Derr, Assistant Director, Graduate Admission, 518-564-4723, Fax: 518-564-4722, E-mail: derrsl@plattsburgh.edu.

State University of New York College at Brockport, School of Professions, Department of Counselor Education, Brockport, NY 14420-2997. Offers college counseling (MS Ed); mental health counseling (MS); school counseling (MS Ed, CAS). *Accreditation:* ACA (one or more programs are accredited). Part-time programs available. *Students:* 20 full-time (14 women), 60 part-time (47 women); includes 23 minority (16 African Americans, 2 Asian Americans or Pacific Islanders, 5 Hispanic Americans). 56 applicants, 39% accepted, 18 enrolled. In 2006, 30 master's, 2 other advanced degrees awarded. *Degree requirements:* For master's, internship, project. *Entrance requirements:* For master's, interview, letters of recommendation; for CAS, master's degree, New York state school counselor certificate. Additional exam requirements/recommendations for international students: Required—TOEFL (minimum score 550 paper-based; 213 computer-based; 80 iBT). *Application deadline:* For fall admission, 2/1 for domestic and international students; for spring admission, 9/1 for domestic and international students. Application fee: $50. *Expenses:* Tuition, state resident: full-time $6,900; part-time $288 per credit. Tuition, nonresident: full-time $10,920; part-time $455 per credit. *Financial support:* In 2006–07, 1 fellowship with tuition reimbursement (averaging $7,500 per year), 1 teaching assistantship with tuition reimbursement (averaging $6,000 per year) were awarded; career-related internships or fieldwork, Federal Work-Study, scholarships/grants, and unspecified assistantships also available. Support available to part-time students. Financial award application deadline: 3/15; financial award applicants required to submit FAFSA. *Faculty research:* Gender and diversity issues, counseling outcomes, qualitative research, qualitative counseling, mental health counseling and obesity. *Unit head:* Dr. Susan R. Seem, Chairperson, 585-395-2258, E-mail: sseem@brockport.edu.

State University of New York College at Oneonta, Graduate Studies, Division of Education, Department of Educational Psychology and Counseling, Oneonta, NY 13820-4015. Offers school counselor K-12 (MS Ed, CAS). *Accreditation:* NCATE. Part-time and evening/weekend programs available. *Degree requirements:* For master's, comprehensive exam. *Entrance requirements:* For master's, GRE General Test.

Stephen F. Austin State University, Graduate School, College of Education, Department of Human Services, Nacogdoches, TX 75962. Offers counseling (MA); school psychology (MA); special education (M Ed); speech pathology (MS). *Accreditation:* ACA (one or more programs are accredited); ASHA (one or more programs are accredited); CORE; NCATE. *Degree requirements:* For master's, thesis (for some programs), comprehensive exam. *Entrance requirements:* For master's, GRE General Test, minimum GPA of 2.8. Additional exam requirements/recommendations for international students: Required—TOEFL.

Stephens College, Division of Graduate and Continuing Studies, Program in Counseling, Columbia, MO 65215-0002. Offers M Ed. Part-time and evening/weekend programs available. *Faculty:* 2 full-time (1 woman), 1 (woman) part-time/adjunct. *Students:* 25 applicants, 80% accepted, 20 enrolled. In 2006, 8 degrees awarded. *Degree requirements:* For master's, thesis. *Entrance requirements:* For master's, GRE, minimum GPA of 3.0 in last 60 hours. Additional exam requirements/recommendations for international students: Required—TOEFL (minimum score 213 computer-based). *Application deadline:* For spring admission, 4/1 for domestic students. Applications are processed on a rolling basis. Application fee: $25. Electronic applications accepted. *Faculty research:* Counseling psychology, assessment (outcomes). *Unit head:* Dr. Linda Taylor, Program Chair, 800-388-7579. *Application contact:* Dr. Kate Getty, Associate Director, 800-388-7579, E-mail: online@stephens.edu.

Stetson University, College of Arts and Sciences, Division of Education, Department of Counselor Education, DeLand, FL 32723. Offers marriage and family therapy (MS); mental health counseling (MS); school guidance and family consultation (MS). *Accreditation:* ACA. Evening/weekend programs available. *Students:* 16 full-time (13 women), 76 part-time (66 women); includes 6 African Americans, 1 Asian American or Pacific Islander, 10 Hispanic Americans, 2 international. Average age 33. In 2006, 26 degrees awarded. *Entrance requirements:* For master's, GRE General Test. *Application deadline:* For fall admission, 3/1 priority date for domestic students; for spring admission, 11/1 for domestic students. Applications are processed on a rolling basis. Application fee: $25. *Unit head:* Dr. Lynn L. Landis-Long, Chair, 386-822-8992. *Application contact:* Midge McDaniel, Office of Graduate Studies, 386-822-7075, Fax: 386-822-7388, E-mail: mmcdanie@stetson.edu.

Suffolk University, College of Arts and Sciences, Department of Education and Human Services, Program in Counseling and Human Relations, Boston, MA 02108-2770. Offers counseling and human relations (CAGS); mental health counseling (MS); school counseling (M Ed); MPA/MS. Part-time and evening/weekend programs available. *Entrance requirements:* For master's, GRE General Test or MAT. *Application deadline:* For fall admission, 6/15 priority date for domestic students, 6/15 for international students; for spring admission, 11/15 priority date for domestic students, 11/15 for international students. Applications are processed on a rolling basis. Application fee: $35. *Financial support:* Fellowships, career-related internships or fieldwork, Federal Work-Study, and institutionally sponsored loans available. Support available to part-time students. Financial award application deadline: 4/1; financial award applicants required to submit FAFSA. *Faculty research:* School counseling, mental health counseling, human resources. *Unit head:* Dr. R. Arthur Winters, Director, 617-573-8269, Fax: 617-722-9440, E-mail: awinters@suffolk.edu. *Application contact:* Judith Reynolds, Director of Graduate Admissions, 617-573-8302, Fax: 617-523-0116, E-mail: grad.admission@suffolk.edu.

Sul Ross State University, Rio Grande College of Sul Ross State University, Alpine, TX 79832. Offers business administration (MBA); teacher education (M Ed), including bilingual education, counseling, educational diagnostics, elementary education, general education, reading, school administration, secondary education. Part-time and evening/weekend programs available. *Degree requirements:* For master's, thesis optional. *Entrance requirements:* For master's, GMAT or GRE General Test, minimum GPA of 2.5 in last 60 hours of undergraduate work. *Faculty research:* Drug and substance abuse counseling, U.S.-Mexico border economic development.

Sul Ross State University, School of Professional Studies, Department of Teacher Education, Program in Counseling, Alpine, TX 79832. Offers M Ed. Part-time and evening/weekend programs available. *Degree requirements:* For master's, thesis optional. *Entrance requirements:* For master's, GMAT or GRE General Test, minimum GPA of 2.5 in last 60 hours of undergraduate work. *Faculty research:* Input variable effects on EXCET for graduate students.

Syracuse University, Graduate School, School of Education, Counseling and Human Services Program, Program in Counselor Education, Syracuse, NY 13244. Offers PhD. *Accreditation:* ACA. Part-time programs available. *Students:* 17 full-time (13 women), 13 part-time (10 women); includes 3 minority (2 African Americans, 1 Hispanic American), 4 international. 5 applicants, 80% accepted, 4 enrolled. *Degree requirements:* For doctorate, thesis/dissertation; for degree. *Entrance requirements:* For doctorate, GRE. Additional exam requirements/recommendations for international students: Required—TOEFL. *Application deadline:* For fall admission, 2/1 priority date for domestic students; for spring admission, 10/15 priority date for domestic students. Applications are processed on a rolling basis. Application fee: $65. Electronic applications accepted. *Expenses:* Tuition: Full-time $16,920; part-time $940 per credit hour. Required fees: $930; $930 per year. *Financial support:* Fellowships with full tuition reimbursements, teaching assistantships with full tuition reimbursements available. *Unit head:* Dr. Janine Bernard, Head, 315-443-5266. *Application contact:* Liza Rochelson, Graduate Admission Recruiter, 315-443-2505, Fax: 315-443-2258, E-mail: gradcrt@gwmail.syr.edu.

Tarleton State University, College of Graduate Studies, College of Education, Department of Educational Administration, Counseling, and Psychology, Program in Counseling and Psychology, Stephenville, TX 76402. Offers counseling (M Ed); counseling psychology (M Ed); educational psychology (M Ed). Part-time programs available. *Faculty:* 45 full-time (23 women), 37 part-time/adjunct (9 women). *Students:* 58 full-time (50 women), 182 part-time (165 women); includes 49 minority (29 African Americans, 2 American Indian/Alaska Native, 2 Asian Americans or Pacific Islanders, 16 Hispanic Americans). Average age 35. 32 applicants, 94% accepted. In 2006, 78 degrees awarded. *Degree requirements:* For master's, thesis optional. *Entrance requirements:* For master's, GRE General Test, minimum GPA of 3.0. Additional exam requirements/recommendations for international students: Required—TOEFL (minimum score 550 paper-based; 220 computer-based). *Application deadline:* For fall admission, 8/5 priority date for domestic students; for spring admission, 12/1 for domestic students. Applications are processed on a rolling basis. Application fee: $25 ($75 for international students). *Financial support:* Teaching assistantships, career-related internships or fieldwork, Federal Work-Study, and institutionally sponsored loans available. Support available to part-time students. Financial award application deadline: 5/1; financial award applicants required to submit FAFSA. *Unit head:* Dr. Linda Duncan, Coordinator, 254-968-9816.

Tennessee State University, The School of Graduate Studies and Research, College of Education, Department of Psychology, Nashville, TN 37209-1561. Offers counseling and guidance (MS), including counseling, elementary school counseling, organizational counseling, secondary school counseling; counseling psychology (PhD); psychology (MS, PhD); school psychology (MS, PhD). *Accreditation:* APA. *Faculty:* 16 full-time (10 women). *Students:* 86 full-time (73 women), 113 part-time (89 women); includes 130 minority (126 African Americans, 3 Asian Americans or Pacific Islanders, 1 Hispanic American), 1 international. Average age 33. 156 applicants, 38% accepted, 43 enrolled. In 2006, 38 master's, 7 doctorates awarded. *Degree requirements:* For doctorate, thesis/dissertation (for some programs). *Entrance requirements:* For master's, GRE General Test or MAT; for doctorate, GRE General Test or MAT, minimum GPA of 3.25, work experience. Application fee: $25. *Unit head:* Dr. Linda Guthric, Head, 615-963-2920, Fax: 615-963-5140, E-mail: lguthrie@tnstate.edu.

Texas A&M International University, Office of Graduate Studies and Research, Department of Professional Programs, Laredo, TX 78041-1900. Offers educational administration (MS Ed); generic special education (MS Ed); school counseling (MS). *Expenses:* Tuition, state resident: full-time $1,580. Tuition, nonresident: full-time $5,432. Required fees: $3,808. *Application contact:* Rosie Dickinson, Director of Admissions, 956-326-2200.

Texas A&M University, College of Education and Human Development, Department of Educational Psychology, College Station, TX 77843. Offers counseling psychology (PhD);

Counselor Education

Texas A&M University (continued)
educational psychology (PhD); educational technology (M Ed); gifted and talented education (M Ed, MS); Hispanic bilingual education (M Ed, PhD); human learning and development (MS); intelligence, creativity, and giftedness (PhD); learning, development, and instruction (PhD); research, measurement and statistics (MS); research, measurement, and statistics (PhD); school counseling (M Ed); school psychology (PhD); special education (M Ed, PhD). *Accreditation:* APA (one or more programs are accredited); NCATE. Part-time and evening/weekend programs available. Postbaccalaureate distance learning degree programs offered (no on-campus study). *Faculty:* 25 full-time (11 women), 5 part-time/adjunct (2 women). *Students:* 156 full-time (123 women), 109 part-time (89 women); includes 66 minority (20 African Americans, 1 American Indian/Alaska Native, 7 Asian Americans or Pacific Islanders, 38 Hispanic Americans), 36 international. 159 applicants, 52% accepted, 51 enrolled. In 2006, 59 master's, 21 doctorates awarded. *Median time to degree:* Of those who began their doctoral program in fall 1998, 89% received their degree in 8 years or less. *Degree requirements:* For master's, thesis optional; for doctorate, thesis/dissertation. *Entrance requirements:* For master's and doctorate, GRE General Test. Additional exam requirements/recommendations for international students: Required—TOEFL. Application fee: $50 ($75 for international students). Electronic applications accepted. *Expenses:* Tuition, state resident: full-time $4,697. Tuition, nonresident: full-time $11,297. Required fees: $2,272. *Financial support:* In 2006–07, fellowships (averaging $12,000 per year), research assistantships (averaging $9,000 per year), teaching assistantships (averaging $9,000 per year) were awarded; career-related internships or fieldwork, institutionally sponsored loans, scholarships/grants, and unspecified assistantships also available. Financial award applicants required to submit FAFSA. *Unit head:* Dr. Michael R. Benz, Head, 979-845-1394, Fax: 979-862-1256, E-mail: mbanz@tamu.edu. *Application contact:* Carol A. Wagner, Director of Advising, 979-845-1833, Fax: 979-862-1256, E-mail: c-wagner@tamu.edu.

Texas A&M University–Commerce, Graduate School, College of Education and Human Services, Department of Counseling, Commerce, TX 75429-3011. Offers M Ed, MS, Ed D. *Accreditation:* ACA (one or more programs are accredited). Part-time programs available. Terminal master's awarded for partial completion of doctoral program. *Degree requirements:* For master's, thesis (for some programs), comprehensive exam; for doctorate, thesis/dissertation, departmental qualifying exam. *Entrance requirements:* For master's and doctorate, GRE General Test. *Faculty research:* Emergency responders, efficacy and effect of web-based instruction, family violence, play therapy.

Texas A&M University–Corpus Christi, Graduate Studies and Research, College of Education, Programs in Counseling, Corpus Christi, TX 78412-5503. Offers counseling (MS); counselor education (PhD). *Accreditation:* ACA. Part-time and evening/weekend programs available. *Degree requirements:* For master's, thesis (for some programs), comprehensive exam, registration. *Entrance requirements:* For master's, GRE General Test. Additional exam requirements/recommendations for international students: Required—TOEFL. Electronic applications accepted.

Texas A&M University–Kingsville, College of Graduate Studies, College of Education, Department of Education, Program in Guidance and Counseling, Kingsville, TX 78363. Offers MA, MS. Part-time and evening/weekend programs available. *Degree requirements:* For master's, mini-thesis. *Entrance requirements:* For master's, GRE General Test, MAT, minimum GPA of 3.0. *Faculty research:* Diagnostician requirements for certification, teaching methods for adult learner.

Texas Christian University, School of Education, Program in Counseling, Fort Worth, TX 76129-0002. Offers counseling (M Ed); school counseling (Certificate). Part-time and evening/weekend programs available. *Application deadline:* For fall admission, 3/1 for domestic students; for spring admission, 12/1 for domestic students. Applications are processed on a rolling basis. Application fee: $0. *Expenses:* Tuition: Part-time $800 per credit hour. *Financial support:* Application deadline: 3/1. *Application contact:* Director of Graduate Studies, 817-257-7664.

Texas Southern University, Graduate School, College of Education, Department of Counselor Education, Houston, TX 77004-4584. Offers counseling (M Ed, Ed D); counseling education (Ed D). Part-time and evening/weekend programs available. *Faculty:* 6 full-time (2 women), 1 (woman) part-time/adjunct. *Students:* 59 full-time (47 women), 94 part-time (74 women); includes 130 minority (117 African Americans, 5 Asian Americans or Pacific Islanders, 8 Hispanic Americans), 2 international. Average age 36. 60 applicants, 83% accepted, 40 enrolled. In 2006, 23 master's, 5 doctorates awarded. *Degree requirements:* For master's, one foreign language, comprehensive exam; for doctorate, thesis/dissertation, comprehensive exam. *Entrance requirements:* For master's, GRE General Test, minimum GPA of 2.5; for doctorate, GRE General Test or MAT, master's degree, minimum B+ average. Additional exam requirements/recommendations for international students: Required—TOEFL. *Application deadline:* For fall admission, 7/15 priority date for domestic students; for spring admission, 11/15 priority date for domestic students. Applications are processed on a rolling basis. Application fee: $50 ($75 for international students). *Financial support:* In 2006–07, 4 fellowships (averaging $8,000 per year), 8 teaching assistantships (averaging $8,000 per year) were awarded; career-related internships or fieldwork, Federal Work-Study, and institutionally sponsored loans also available. Financial award application deadline: 5/1. *Faculty research:* Clinical and urban psychology. *Unit head:* Dr. Joyce K Jones, Chair, 713-313-7437, Fax: 713-313-7481.

Texas State University-San Marcos, Graduate School, College of Education, Department of Educational Administration and Psychological Services, Program in Counseling and Guidance, San Marcos, TX 78666. Offers M Ed. *Accreditation:* ACA. Part-time and evening/weekend programs available. *Faculty:* 11 full-time (5 women), 12 part-time/adjunct (8 women). *Students:* 21 full-time (16 women), 56 part-time (49 women); includes 24 minority (4 African Americans, 20 Hispanic Americans), 2 international. Average age 32. 19 applicants, 84% accepted, 13 enrolled. In 2006, 17 degrees awarded. *Degree requirements:* For master's, thesis (for some programs), comprehensive exam. *Entrance requirements:* For master's, GRE General Test, minimum GPA of 3.0 in last 60 hours of course work. Additional exam requirements/recommendations for international students: Required—TOEFL. *Application deadline:* For fall admission, 4/15 for domestic students, 3/15 for international students; for spring admission, 10/1 for domestic and international students. Applications are processed on a rolling basis. Application fee: $40 ($90 for international students). *Financial support:* In 2006–07, 41 students received support, including 12 research assistantships (averaging $6,824 per year); teaching assistantships, career-related internships or fieldwork, Federal Work-Study, and institutionally sponsored loans also available. Support available to part-time students. Financial award application deadline: 4/1; financial award applicants required to submit FAFSA. *Faculty research:* Visiting teachers. *Unit head:* Dr. Linda Homeyer, Graduate Advisor, 512-245-3757, Fax: 512-245-8872, E-mail: lh10@txstate.edu.

Texas State University-San Marcos, Graduate School, College of Education, Department of Educational Administration and Psychological Services, Program in Professional Counseling, San Marcos, TX 78666. Offers MA. *Accreditation:* ACA. *Faculty:* 10 part-time/adjunct (4 women). *Students:* 74 full-time (61 women), 102 part-time (88 women); includes 35 minority (7 African Americans, 8 Asian Americans or Pacific Islanders, 20 Hispanic Americans), 1 international. Average age 30. 53 applicants, 79% accepted, 31 enrolled. In 2006, 42 degrees awarded. *Degree requirements:* For master's, internship. *Entrance requirements:* For master's, GRE General Test, minimum GPA of 3.0 in last 60 hours. *Application deadline:* For fall admission, 4/15 for domestic and international students; for spring admission, 10/1 for domestic and international students. Applications are processed on a rolling basis. Application fee: $40 ($90 for international students). *Financial support:* In 2006–07, 122 students received support, including 7 research assistantships (averaging $6,868 per year), 3 teaching assistantships (averaging $5,922 per year). Financial award application deadline: 4/1. *Unit head:* Dr. Linda Homeyer, Graduate Advisor, 512-245-3757, Fax: 512-245-8872, E-mail: lh10@txstate.edu.

Texas Tech University, Graduate School, College of Education, Department of Educational Psychology and Leadership, Lubbock, TX 79409. Offers counselor (Certificate); counselor education (M Ed, PhD); education diagnostician (Certificate); educational leadership (M Ed, Ed D); educational psychology (M Ed, PhD); gifted and talented (Certificate); higher education (M Ed, Ed D, PhD); information processing technologist (Certificate); instructional technology (M Ed, Ed D); principal (Certificate); special education (M Ed, Ed D); special education counselor (Certificate); superintendent (Certificate); visually handicapped (Certificate). *Accreditation:* ACA; NCATE. Part-time programs available. *Students:* 128 full-time (88 women), 321 part-time (233 women); includes 67 minority (23 African Americans, 1 American Indian/Alaska Native, 5 Asian Americans or Pacific Islanders, 38 Hispanic Americans), 22 international. Average age 38. 347 applicants, 49% accepted, 61 enrolled. In 2006, 110 master's, 16 doctorates awarded. *Degree requirements:* For master's, thesis optional; for doctorate, thesis/dissertation. *Entrance requirements:* For master's and doctorate, GRE General Test. Additional exam requirements/recommendations for international students: Required—TOEFL (minimum score 550 paper-based; 213 computer-based). *Application deadline:* For fall admission, 3/1 priority date for international students; for spring admission, 11/1 priority date for international students. Applications are processed on a rolling basis. Application fee: $50 ($60 for international students). Electronic applications accepted. *Expenses:* Tuition, state resident: full-time $4,440. Tuition, nonresident: full-time $11,040. Required fees: $2,136. *Financial support:* In 2006–07, 242 students received support; research assistantships with partial tuition reimbursements available, teaching assistantships with partial tuition reimbursements available, career-related internships or fieldwork, Federal Work-Study, and institutionally sponsored loans available. Support available to part-time students. Financial award application deadline: 4/15; financial award applicants required to submit FAFSA. *Faculty research:* Psychological processes of teaching and learning, teaching populations with special needs, instructional technology, educational administration in education, theories and practice in counseling and counselor education K-12 and higher. *Unit head:* Dr. Fred Hartmeister, Chair, 806-742-1998 Ext. 436, Fax: 806-742-2179, E-mail: fred.hartmeister@ttu.edu. *Application contact:* Graduate Adviser, 806-742-1998, Fax: 806-742-2179.

Texas Wesleyan University, Graduate Programs, Programs in Education, Fort Worth, TX 76105-1536. Offers education (M Ed, MAT, MS Ed); professional counseling (MA); school counseling (MS). Part-time and evening/weekend programs available. Postbaccalaureate distance learning degree programs offered (no on-campus study). *Faculty:* 9 full-time (5 women), 6 part-time/adjunct (3 women). *Students:* 44 full-time (36 women), 167 part-time (146 women); includes 74 minority (46 African Americans, 2 American Indian/Alaska Native, 4 Asian Americans or Pacific Islanders, 22 Hispanic Americans). Average age 39. In 2006, 27 degrees awarded. *Degree requirements:* For master's, thesis optional. *Entrance requirements:* For master's, GRE General Test, minimum GPA of 3.0 in final 60 hours of undergraduate course work, interview. *Application deadline:* Applications are processed on a rolling basis. Application fee: $40 ($50 for international students). Electronic applications accepted. *Expenses:* Tuition: Full-time $4,230; part-time $470 per credit hour. Required fees: $53 per credit hour. Tuition and fees vary according to program. *Financial support:* Career-related internships or fieldwork, Federal Work-Study, institutionally sponsored loans, scholarships/grants, and tuition waivers (full and partial) available. Support available to part-time students. Financial award application deadline: 3/15; financial award applicants required to submit FAFSA. *Faculty research:* Teacher effectiveness, bilingual education, analytic teaching. *Unit head:* Dr. Carlos Martinez, Dean, School of Education, 817-531-4940, Fax: 817-531-4943.

Texas Woman's University, Graduate School, College of Professional Education, Department of Family Sciences, Denton, TX 76201. Offers child development (MS, PhD); counseling and development (MS); early childhood education (M Ed, MA, MS, Ed D); family studies (MS, PhD); family therapy (MS, PhD). *Accreditation:* ACA (one or more programs are accredited). Part-time and evening/weekend programs available. *Students:* 102 full-time (96 women), 382 part-time (344 women); includes 157 minority (109 African Americans, 5 American Indian/Alaska Native, 11 Asian Americans or Pacific Islanders, 32 Hispanic Americans), 18 international. Average age 37. In 2006, 93 master's, 17 doctorates awarded. *Degree requirements:* For doctorate, thesis/dissertation, comprehensive exam. *Entrance requirements:* For master's, interview, writing sample, minimum GPA of 3.25 may be required; for doctorate, interview, writing sample may be required, GPA 3.25 last 60 hours of course work. Additional exam requirements/recommendations for international students: Required—TOEFL (minimum score 550 paper-based; 213 computer-based; 79 iBT). *Application deadline:* For fall admission, 4/1 for international students; for spring admission, 8/1 for international students. Applications are processed on a rolling basis. Application fee: $30 ($50 for international students). Electronic applications accepted. *Expenses:* Tuition, area resident: Part-time $168 per unit. Tuition, state resident: full-time $4,369. Tuition, nonresident: full-time $9,373; part-time $443 per unit. Required fees: $20 per unit. $177 per term. *Financial support:* In 2006–07, 11 research assistantships (averaging $10,494 per year), 12 teaching assistantships (averaging $10,494 per year) were awarded; career-related internships or fieldwork, Federal Work-Study, institutionally sponsored loans, scholarships/grants, traineeships, health care benefits, and unspecified assistantships also available. Support available to part-time students. Financial award application deadline: 3/1; financial award applicants required to submit FAFSA. *Faculty research:* Parenting/parent education, distance education, body image, family sexuality, diversity. *Unit head:* Dr. Larry LeFlore, Chair, 940-898-2685, Fax: 940-898-2676, E-mail: lleflore@twu.edu. *Application contact:* Samuel Wheeler, Coordinator of Graduate Admissions, 940-898-3188, Fax: 940-898-3081, E-mail: wheelersr@twu.edu.

Trevecca Nazarene University, Graduate Division, Division of Social and Behavioral Sciences, Major in Counseling, Nashville, TN 37210-2877. Offers MA. Part-time and evening/weekend programs available. *Students:* 97 full-time (74 women), 40 part-time (33 women); includes 12 minority (10 African Americans, 1 American Indian/Alaska Native, 1 Hispanic American). In 2006, 30 degrees awarded. *Degree requirements:* For master's, practicum. *Entrance requirements:* For master's, GRE General Test or MAT, minimum GPA of 2.7, 2 reference assessment forms. Additional exam requirements/recommendations for international students: Required—TOEFL (minimum score 500 paper-based; 173 computer-based). *Application deadline:* Applications are processed on a rolling basis. Application fee: $25. *Expenses: Contact institution.* Tuition and fees vary according to degree level and program. *Financial support:* Career-related internships or fieldwork available. Financial award applicants required to submit FAFSA. *Application contact:* Joyce Houk, Division of Social and Behavior Sciences, 615-248-1417, Fax: 615-248-1366, E-mail: admissions_psy@trevecca.edu.

Trinity (Washington) University, School of Education, Washington, DC 20017-1094. Offers democracy, diversity, and social justice (M Ed); early childhood (MAT); educational administration (MSA); elementary education (MAT); English as a second language (M Ed, MAT); literacy and reading education (M Ed); school counseling (MA); secondary education (MAT), including English, math, science, social studies; special education (MAT). *Accreditation:* NCATE. Part-time and evening/weekend programs available. *Degree requirements:* For master's, thesis (for some programs), capstone project(s). *Entrance requirements:* For master's, PRAXIS I, minimum GPA of 2.8. Additional exam requirements/recommendations for international students: Required—TOEFL (minimum score 550 paper-based; 213 computer-based). *Faculty research:* Technology, literacy, special education, organizations, inclusion models.

Troy University, Graduate School, College of Education, Program in Counseling and Psychology, Troy, AL 36082. Offers clinical mental health (MS); community counseling (MS); school psychology (MS); student affairs counseling (MS). *Accreditation:* ACA; NCATE. Part-time and evening/weekend programs available. *Students:* 437 full-time (377 women), 651 part-time (542 women); includes 645 minority (596 African Americans, 6 American Indian/Alaska Native, 8 Asian Americans or Pacific Islanders, 35 Hispanic Americans). Average age 34. In 2006, 279 degrees awarded. *Degree requirements:* For master's, thesis, comprehensive exam, registration. *Entrance requirements:* For master's, MAT, minimum GPA of 2.5. Additional exam requirements/recommendations for international students: Required—TOEFL (minimum score 523 paper-based; 200 computer-based). *Application deadline:* Applications are processed on a rolling basis. Application fee: $50. Electronic applications accepted. *Expenses:* Tuition, state resident:

full-time $4,368; part-time $182 per hour. Tuition, nonresident: full-time $8,736; part-time $364 per hour. Required fees: $50 per term. *Unit head:* Dr. Andrew Creamer, Chair, 334-670-3350, Fax: 334-670-32961, E-mail: drcreamer@troy.edu. *Application contact:* Brenda K. Campbell, Director of Graduate Admissions, 334-670-3178, Fax: 334-670-3733, E-mail: bcamp@troy.edu.

Troy University, Graduate School, College of Education, Program in School Counseling, Troy, AL 36082. Offers community counseling (Ed S); counselor education (MS); guidance services (MS); rehabilitation counseling (Ed S); school counseling (Ed S). *Accreditation:* ACA; NCATE. Part-time and evening/weekend programs available. *Students:* 28 full-time (all women), 83 part-time (76 women); includes 57 minority (55 African Americans, 1 American Indian/Alaska Native, 1 Hispanic American). Average age 33. In 2006, 6 master's, 19 other advanced degrees awarded. *Degree requirements:* For master's, thesis, comprehensive exam, registration. *Entrance requirements:* For master's, minimum GPA of 2.5, teaching certification, 2 years of teaching experience. Additional exam requirements/recommendations for international students: Required—TOEFL (minimum score 523 paper-based; 200 computer-based). *Application deadline:* Applications are processed on a rolling basis. Application fee: $50. Electronic applications accepted. *Expenses:* Tuition, state resident: full-time $4,368; part-time $182 per hour. Tuition, nonresident: full-time $8,736; part-time $364 per hour. Required fees: $50 per term. *Unit head:* Dr. Andrew Creamer, Chair, 334-670-3350, Fax: 334-670-32961, E-mail: drcreamer@troy.edu. *Application contact:* Brenda K. Campbell, Director of Graduate Admissions, 334-670-3178, Fax: 334-670-3733, E-mail: bcamp@troy.edu.

Université de Moncton, Faculty of Education, Graduate Studies in Education, Moncton, NB E1A 3E9, Canada. Offers educational psychology (M Ed, MA Ed); guidance (M Ed, MA Ed); school administration (M Ed, MA Ed); teaching (M Ed, MA Ed). Part-time programs available. *Degree requirements:* For master's, proficiency in English and French. *Entrance requirements:* For master's, minimum GPA of 3.0. *Faculty research:* Guidance, ethnolinguistic vitality, children's rights, ecological education, entrepreneurship.

Université Laval, Faculty of Education, Department of Foundations and Interventions in Education, Programs in Orientation Sciences, Québec, QC G1K 7P4, Canada. Offers MA, PhD. Terminal master's awarded for partial completion of doctoral program. *Degree requirements:* For master's, thesis (for some programs); for doctorate, thesis/dissertation, comprehensive exam. *Entrance requirements:* For master's, English test (comprehension of written English), knowledge of French; for doctorate, oral exam (subject of thesis), knowledge of French and English. Electronic applications accepted. *Faculty research:* Counseling psychology, psychological education, vocational guidance, growth and development.

University at Albany, State University of New York, School of Education, Department of Educational and Counseling Psychology, Albany, NY 12222-0001. Offers counseling psychology (MS, PhD, CAS); educational psychology (Ed D); educational psychology and statistics (MS); measurements and evaluation (Ed D); rehabilitation counseling (MS), including counseling psychology; school counselor (CAS); school psychology (Psy D, CAS); special education (MS); statistics and research design (Ed D). *Accreditation:* APA (one or more programs are accredited). Evening/weekend programs available. *Students:* 75 full-time (59 women), 25 part-time (21 women). Average age 28. In 2006, 33 master's, 8 doctorates, 12 other advanced degrees awarded. *Degree requirements:* For doctorate, thesis/dissertation. *Entrance requirements:* For doctorate, GRE General Test. Additional exam requirements/recommendations for international students: Required—TOEFL (minimum score 550 paper-based; 213 computer-based). Application fee: $75. Electronic applications accepted. *Expenses:* Tuition, state resident: full-time $6,900; part-time $288 per credit. Tuition, nonresident: full-time $10,920; part-time $455 per credit. Required fees: $1,139. *Financial support:* Fellowships, career-related internships or fieldwork available. *Unit head:* Deborah May, Chair, 518-442-5050.

University at Buffalo, the State University of New York, Graduate School, Graduate School of Education, Department of Counseling, School, and Educational Psychology, Buffalo, NY 14260. Offers counseling/school psychology (PhD); counselor education (PhD); educational psychology (MA, PhD); mental health counseling (MS); rehabilitation counseling (MS); school counseling (Ed M, Certificate); school psychology (MA). *Accreditation:* CORE (one or more programs are accredited). *Faculty:* 19 full-time (9 women), 11 part-time/adjunct (8 women). *Students:* 183 full-time (145 women), 63 part-time (46 women); includes 26 minority (15 African Americans, 1 American Indian/Alaska Native, 6 Asian Americans or Pacific Islanders, 4 Hispanic Americans), 20 international. Average age 25. 398 applicants, 36% accepted, 123 enrolled. In 2006, 57 master's, 20 doctorates, 12 other advanced degrees awarded. *Degree requirements:* For master's, thesis (for some programs), comprehensive exam (for some programs), registration; for doctorate, thesis/dissertation, comprehensive exam, registration. *Entrance requirements:* For master's and doctorate, GRE General Test, interview, letters of reference. Additional exam requirements/recommendations for international students: Required—TOEFL. *Application deadline:* For fall admission, 2/1 priority date for domestic students. Application fee: $50. Electronic applications accepted. *Financial support:* In 2006–07, 40 students received support, including 5 fellowships with full tuition reimbursements available (averaging $10,000 per year), 16 research assistantships with full tuition reimbursements available (averaging $9,000 per year), teaching assistantships with tuition reimbursements available (averaging $9,000 per year); career-related internships or fieldwork, Federal Work-Study, institutionally sponsored loans, and unspecified assistantships also available. Financial award application deadline: 2/1; financial award applicants required to submit FAFSA. *Faculty research:* Multicultural counseling, class size effects, quality of life, eating disorders, outcome assessment. Total annual research expenditures: $1.5 million. *Unit head:* Dr. Scott T. Meier, Chair, 716-645-2484 Ext. 1066, Fax: 716-645-6616, E-mail: stmeier@buffalo.edu. *Application contact:* Rochelle Cohen, Admissions Assistant, 716-645-2110 Ext. 1256, Fax: 716-645-7937, E-mail: recohen@buffalo.edu.

The University of Akron, Graduate School, College of Education, Department of Counseling, Program in Community Counseling, Akron, OH 44325. Offers MA, MS. *Accreditation:* ACA; NCATE. *Students:* 23 full-time (21 women), 23 part-time (19 women); includes 3 minority (1 African American, 1 American Indian/Alaska Native, 1 Asian American or Pacific Islander). Average age 31. 22 applicants, 55% accepted, 7 enrolled. In 2006, 19 degrees awarded. *Degree requirements:* For master's, comprehensive exam. *Entrance requirements:* For master's, GRE, minimum GPA of 2.75, interview, letters of recommendation. Additional exam requirements/recommendations for international students: Required—TOEFL (minimum score 550 paper-based; 213 computer-based; 79 iBT). *Application deadline:* For fall admission, 3/15 for domestic students; for spring admission, 10/1 for domestic students. Applications are processed on a rolling basis. Application fee: $30 ($40 for international students). Electronic applications accepted. *Expenses:* Tuition, state resident: full-time $6,164; part-time $342 per credit. Tuition, nonresident: full-time $10,575; part-time $588 per credit. Required fees: $806; $43 per credit. $12 per term. Tuition and fees vary according to course load, degree level and program. *Unit head:* Dr. Robert Schwartz, Coordinator, 330-972-8155, E-mail: rcs@uakron.edu.

The University of Akron, Graduate School, College of Education, Department of Counseling, Program in Counselor Education and Supervision, Akron, OH 44325. Offers PhD. *Accreditation:* ACA. *Students:* 15 full-time (13 women), 30 part-time (22 women); includes 9 minority (7 African Americans, 1 Asian American or Pacific Islander, 1 Hispanic American). Average age 38. 10 applicants, 30% accepted, 2 enrolled. In 2006, 1 degree awarded. *Degree requirements:* For doctorate, one foreign language, thesis/dissertation, written and oral exams, other language alternatives, comprehensive exam. *Entrance requirements:* For doctorate, GRE, interview, minimum GPA of 3.25, letters of recommendation. Additional exam requirements/recommendations for international students: Required—TOEFL (minimum score 550 paper-based; 213 computer-based; 79 iBT). *Application deadline:* For fall admission, 1/15 for domestic students. Applications are processed on a rolling basis. Application fee: $30 ($40 for international students). Electronic applications accepted. *Expenses:* Tuition, state resident: full-time $6,164; part-time $342 per credit. Tuition, nonresident: full-time $10,575; part-time $588 per credit. Required fees: $806; $43 per credit. $12 per term. Tuition and fees vary according to course load, degree level and program. *Financial support:* Fellowships, research assistantships, teaching assistantships, career-related internships or fieldwork and unspecified assistantships available. *Unit head:* Dr. Cynthia Reynolds, Coordinator, 330-972-6748, E-mail: creynol@uakron.edu.

The University of Akron, Graduate School, College of Education, Department of Counseling, Program in School Counseling, Akron, OH 44325. Offers MA, MS. *Accreditation:* ACA; NCATE. *Students:* 11 full-time (10 women), 36 part-time (30 women); includes 7 minority (5 African Americans, 2 Hispanic Americans). Average age 30. 13 applicants, 46% accepted, 4 enrolled. In 2006, 16 degrees awarded. *Degree requirements:* For master's, comprehensive exam. *Entrance requirements:* For master's, GRE, minimum GPA of 2.75, interview, letters of recommendation. Additional exam requirements/recommendations for international students: Required—TOEFL (minimum score 550 paper-based; 213 computer-based; 79 iBT). *Application deadline:* For fall admission, 3/15 for domestic students; for spring admission, 10/1 for domestic students. Applications are processed on a rolling basis. Application fee: $30 ($40 for international students). Electronic applications accepted. *Expenses:* Tuition, state resident: full-time $6,164; part-time $342 per credit. Tuition, nonresident: full-time $10,575; part-time $588 per credit. Required fees: $806; $43 per credit. $12 per term. Tuition and fees vary according to course load, degree level and program. *Unit head:* Dr. Cynthia Reynolds, Coordinator, 330-972-6748, E-mail: creynol@uakron.edu.

The University of Alabama, Graduate School, College of Education, Department of Educational Studies in Psychology, Research Methodology and Counseling, Tuscaloosa, AL 35487. Offers MA, Ed D, PhD, Ed S. *Accreditation:* ACA (one or more programs are accredited); CORE; NCATE. *Median time to degree:* Doctorate–4.4 years full-time, 6 years part-time. *Degree requirements:* For master's, thesis optional; for doctorate, thesis/dissertation, comprehensive exam, registration. *Entrance requirements:* For master's and doctorate, GRE General Test, MAT, or NTE, minimum GPA of 3.0; for Ed S, minimum GPA of 3.0 during previous 2 years. Additional exam requirements/recommendations for international students: Required—TOEFL (minimum score 550 paper-based; 213 computer-based), IELTS (minimum score 7). *Application deadline:* For fall admission, 7/1 for domestic students; for spring admission, 11/1 for domestic students. Applications are processed on a rolling basis. Application fee: $25. Electronic applications accepted. *Financial support:* Research assistantships with tuition reimbursements, teaching assistantships with tuition reimbursements, career-related internships or fieldwork available. Financial award application deadline: 7/14; financial award applicants required to submit FAFSA. *Unit head:* Dr. Jamie Scitcher, Interim Department Head, 205-348-1184. *Application contact:* Marie S. Marshall, Office Associate II, 205-348-8362, Fax: 205-348-0683, E-mail: mmarshal@bamaed.ua.edu.

The University of Alabama at Birmingham, School of Education, Department of Human Studies, Program in Counseling and School Psychology, Birmingham, AL 35294. Offers agency counseling (MA); marriage and family counseling (MA); rehabilitation counseling (MA); school counseling (MA); school psychology (MA Ed). *Accreditation:* CORE; NCATE. *Students:* 30 full-time (26 women), 56 part-time (47 women); includes 16 minority (all African Americans), 1 international. 26 applicants, 54% accepted. In 2006, 37 degrees awarded. *Degree requirements:* For master's, thesis optional. *Entrance requirements:* For master's, GRE General Test, MAT, or NTE, minimum GPA of 3.0. *Application deadline:* Applications are processed on a rolling basis. Application fee: $35 ($60 for international students). Electronic applications accepted. *Expenses:* Tuition, state resident: part-time $170 per credit hour. Tuition, nonresident: part-time $425 per credit hour. Required fees: $15 per credit hour. $122 per term. Tuition and fees vary according to program. *Financial support:* Career-related internships or fieldwork available. *Unit head:* Dr. David M. Macrina, Chair, Department of Human Studies, 205-934-2446, Fax: 205-975-8040, E-mail: dmacrina@uab.edu.

University of Alaska Anchorage, College of Education, Program in Counseling and Guidance, Anchorage, AK 99508-8060. Offers M Ed. Part-time programs available. *Students:* 16 full-time (15 women), 17 part-time (14 women); includes 2 minority (1 African American, 1 Asian American or Pacific Islander), 2 international. 24 applicants, 29% accepted. In 2006, 10 degrees awarded. *Entrance requirements:* For master's, GRE or MAT, interview, resumé. Additional exam requirements/recommendations for international students: Required—TOEFL (minimum score 550 paper-based; 213 computer-based). *Application deadline:* For fall admission, 5/1 for domestic and international students; for winter admission, 4/1 for domestic and international students; for spring admission, 11/1 for domestic and international students. Application fee: $45. *Expenses:* Tuition, state resident: part-time $268 per credit. Tuition, nonresident: part-time $547 per credit. Required fees: $124 per semester. Tuition and fees vary according to reciprocity agreements and student level. *Financial support:* Career-related internships or fieldwork and Federal Work-Study available. Support available to part-time students. Financial award application deadline: 4/1; financial award applicants required to submit FAFSA. *Unit head:* Dr. Carolyn Coe, Chair, 907-786-1654, Fax: 907-786-4445, E-mail: afcmc@uaa.alaska.edu. *Application contact:* Jane Jordan, Graduate Programs Assistant, 907-786-4401, Fax: 907-786-4445, E-mail: anjmj@uaa.alaska.edu.

University of Alaska Fairbanks, School of Education, Fairbanks, AK 99775-7520. Offers cross cultural education (M Ed); curriculum instruction (M Ed); education (M Ed); guidance and counseling (M Ed); k-12 reading (M Ed); language and literacy (M Ed). *Accreditation:* NCATE. Part-time programs available. Postbaccalaureate distance learning degree programs offered. *Faculty:* 18 full-time (10 women), 3 part-time/adjunct (all women). *Students:* 56 full-time (40 women), 89 part-time (72 women); includes 31 minority (4 African Americans, 21 American Indian/Alaska Native, 2 Asian Americans or Pacific Islanders, 4 Hispanic Americans), 1 international. Average age 37. 69 applicants, 67% accepted, 42 enrolled. In 2006, 33 degrees awarded. *Degree requirements:* For master's, thesis or alternative, student teaching, comprehensive exam, registration. *Entrance requirements:* For master's, GRE General Test, PRAXIS I. Additional exam requirements/recommendations for international students: Required—TOEFL (minimum score 550 paper-based; 213 computer-based). *Application deadline:* For fall admission, 3/1 for domestic and international students; for spring admission, 10/1 for domestic students, 9/1 for international students. Application fee: $50. Electronic applications accepted. *Financial support:* In 2006–07, 2 research assistantships with tuition reimbursements (averaging $6,510 per year), 4 teaching assistantships with tuition reimbursements (averaging $10,441 per year) were awarded; fellowships with tuition reimbursements, career-related internships or fieldwork, Federal Work-Study, and scholarships/grants also available. Financial award applicants required to submit FAFSA. *Faculty research:* Native ways of knowing, classroom research in methods of literacy instruction, multiple intelligence theory, geometry concept development, mathematics and science curriculum development. *Unit head:* Dr. Eric C. Madsen, Dean, 907-474-7341, Fax: 907-474-5451, E-mail: fysoed@uaf.edu.

University of Alberta, Faculty of Graduate Studies and Research, Department of Educational Psychology, Edmonton, AB T6G 2E1, Canada. Offers counseling psychology (M Ed, PhD); educational psychology (M Ed, PhD); instructional technology (M Ed); school counseling (M Ed); school psychology (M Ed, PhD); special education (M Ed, PhD); special education-deafness studies (M Ed); teaching English as a second language (M Ed). Part-time programs available. *Faculty:* 34 full-time (14 women), 12 part-time/adjunct (6 women). *Students:* 117 full-time (93 women), 173 part-time (121 women), 15 international. Average age 36. 252 applicants, 34% accepted. In 2006, 30 master's, 10 doctorates awarded. *Degree requirements:* For master's, thesis optional; for doctorate, thesis/dissertation, comprehensive exam. *Entrance requirements:* For master's and doctorate, minimum GPA of 3.0. Additional exam requirements/recommendations for international students: Required—TOEFL. *Application deadline:* For fall admission, 2/1 priority date for domestic and international students. Applications are processed on a rolling basis. *Financial support:* In 2006–07, 10 fellowships with full tuition reimbursements (averaging $16,120 per year), 36 research assistantships with full tuition reimbursements (averaging $12,614 per year), 46 teaching assistantships with full tuition reimbursements (averaging $5,462 per year) were awarded; career-related internships or fieldwork and scholarships/grants also available. *Faculty research:* Human learning, development and assessment. *Unit head:* Dr. Linda M. McDonald, Chair, 780-492-1149, Fax: 780-492-1318, E-mail:

Counselor Education

University of Alberta (continued)
linda.mcdonald@ualberta.ca. *Application contact:* Judy Maynes, Information Contact, 780-492-1149, Fax: 780-492-1318, E-mail: edpygrad@ualberta.ca.

University of Arkansas, Graduate School, College of Education and Health Professions, Department of Educational Leadership, Counseling and Foundations, Program in Counseling Education, Fayetteville, AR 72701-1201. Offers MS, PhD, Ed S. *Accreditation:* ACA; NCATE. Part-time and evening/weekend programs available. *Students:* 25 full-time (17 women), 25 part-time (23 women); includes 6 minority (2 African Americans, 1 American Indian/Alaska Native, 2 Asian Americans or Pacific Islanders, 1 Hispanic American), 1 international. 39 applicants, 33% accepted. In 2006, 11 degrees awarded. *Degree requirements:* For master's, thesis optional; for doctorate, thesis/dissertation. *Entrance requirements:* For master's, GRE General Test or MAT; for doctorate, GRE General Test. *Application deadline:* For fall admission, 3/15 for domestic students; for spring admission, 10/15 for domestic students. Application fee: $40 ($50 for international students). *Financial support:* In 2006–07, 5 fellowships with tuition reimbursements, 4 teaching assistantships were awarded; research assistantships, career-related internships or fieldwork and Federal Work-Study also available. Support available to part-time students. Financial award application deadline: 4/1; financial award applicants required to submit FAFSA. *Unit head:* Unit Head, 479-575-3509. *Application contact:* Dr. Carl Holt, Graduate Coordinator, 479-575-2207, E-mail: cholt@uark.edu.

University of Arkansas at Little Rock, Graduate School, College of Education, Department of Counseling and Rehabilitation Education, Program in Counselor Education, Little Rock, AR 72204-1099. Offers school counseling (M Ed). Part-time and evening/weekend programs available. *Degree requirements:* For master's, portfolio or thesis. *Entrance requirements:* For master's, GRE General Test, minimum GPA of 2.75, teaching certificate.

University of Central Arkansas, Graduate School, College of Health and Behavioral Sciences, Department of Counseling and Psychology, Program in School Counseling, Conway, AR 72035-0001. Offers elementary school counseling (MS); secondary school counseling (MS). *Accreditation:* NCATE. Part-time programs available. *Degree requirements:* For master's, thesis optional. *Entrance requirements:* For master's, GRE General Test, minimum GPA of 2.7. Additional exam requirements/recommendations for international students: Required—TOEFL (minimum score 550 paper-based; 213 computer-based). *Application deadline:* For fall admission, 3/1 priority date for domestic and international students; for spring admission, 10/1 priority date for domestic and international students. Applications are processed on a rolling basis. Application fee: $25 ($40 for international students). *Expenses:* Tuition, state resident: full-time $4,194; part-time $233 per semester. Tuition, nonresident: full-time $5,963; part-time $429 per semester. International tuition: $6,162 full-time. Required fees: $65; $23 per semester. One-time fee: $65 part-time. *Financial support:* Career-related internships or fieldwork, scholarships/grants, and unspecified assistantships available. Financial award application deadline: 2/15; financial award applicants required to submit FAFSA. *Unit head:* Dr. Terry Smith, Associate Professor, 501-450-3193, Fax: 501-450-5424, E-mail: terrys@uca.edu. *Application contact:* Nanette Fitzhugh, Administrative Assistant, 501-450-5063, Fax: 501-450-5678, E-mail: fitzhugh@uca.edu.

University of Central Florida, College of Education, Department of Child, Family and Community Sciences, Program in Counselor Education, Orlando, FL 32816. Offers M Ed, MA. *Accreditation:* ACA. Part-time and evening/weekend programs available. *Students:* 95 full-time (86 women), 100 part-time (86 women); includes 48 minority (18 African Americans, 2 Asian Americans or Pacific Islanders, 28 Hispanic Americans), 4 international. Average age 31. In 2006, 42 master's awarded. *Degree requirements:* For master's, thesis or alternative, comprehensive exam. *Entrance requirements:* For master's, GRE General Test, interview, minimum GPA of 3.0. Additional exam requirements/recommendations for international students: Required—TOEFL. *Application deadline:* For fall admission, 2/1 for domestic students; for spring admission, 9/1 for domestic students. Application fee: $30. Electronic applications accepted. *Expenses:* Tuition, state resident: full-time $6,167; part-time $257 per credit hour. Tuition, nonresident: full-time $22,790; part-time $950 per credit hour. *Financial support:* In 2006–07, 8 fellowships with partial tuition reimbursements (averaging $1,200 per year), 29 research assistantships with partial tuition reimbursements (averaging $6,000 per year) were awarded; teaching assistantships with partial tuition reimbursements, career-related internships or fieldwork, Federal Work-Study, institutionally sponsored loans, tuition waivers (partial), and unspecified assistantships also available. Financial award application deadline: 3/1; financial award applicants required to submit FAFSA. *Unit head:* Dr. Mike Robinson, Coordinator, 407-823-3819, E-mail: erobinso@mail.ucf.edu.

University of Central Florida, College of Education, Doctoral Program in Education, Orlando, FL 32816. Offers communication sciences and disorders (PhD); counselor education (PhD); curriculum and instruction (PhD); elementary education (PhD); exceptional education (PhD); hospitality education (PhD); instructional technology (PhD); mathematics education (PhD). *Students:* 86 full-time (63 women), 9 part-time (4 women); includes 21 minority (15 African Americans, 2 Asian Americans or Pacific Islanders, 4 Hispanic Americans), 19 international. Average age 39. In 2006, 16 degrees awarded. Application fee: $30. Electronic applications accepted. *Expenses:* Tuition, state resident: full-time $6,167; part-time $257 per credit hour. Tuition, nonresident: full-time $22,790; part-time $950 per credit hour. *Financial support:* In 2006–07, 44 fellowships with partial tuition reimbursements (averaging $3,700 per year), 54 research assistantships with partial tuition reimbursements (averaging $7,000 per year), 9 teaching assistantships with partial tuition reimbursements (averaging $7,000 per year) were awarded.

University of Central Missouri, The Graduate School, College of Education, Department of Educational Leadership and Human Development, Program in Counselor Education, Warrensburg, MO 64093. Offers counseling (MS); human service/guidance counseling (Ed S). *Students:* 6 full-time (5 women), 95 part-time (85 women); includes 6 minority (4 African Americans, 2 Hispanic Americans), 1 international. Average age 36. 20 applicants. In 2006, 17 degrees awarded. *Entrance requirements:* Additional exam requirements/recommendations for international students: Required—TOEFL (minimum score 500 paper-based; 173 computer-based). *Application deadline:* For fall admission, 6/1 priority date for domestic students, 5/1 priority date for international students; for spring admission, 10/1 priority date for domestic students, 10/1 for international students. *Expenses:* Tuition, state resident: full-time $5,448; part-time $227 per credit hour. Tuition, nonresident: full-time $10,896; part-time $454 per credit hour. Required fees: $336; $14 per credit hour. *Faculty research:* School counselor certification issues, counselor licensing issues, counselor personnel and professional development. *Unit head:* Dr. Janelle Cowles, Coordinator, 660-543-8204, E-mail: cowles@ucmo.edu.

University of Central Oklahoma, College of Graduate Studies and Research, College of Education, Department of Professional Teacher Education, Program in Guidance and Counseling, Edmond, OK 73034-5209. Offers M Ed. *Accreditation:* NCATE. Part-time programs available. *Entrance requirements:* For master's, GRE General Test. Additional exam requirements/recommendations for international students: Required—TOEFL (minimum score 550 paper-based; 213 computer-based). Electronic applications accepted.

University of Cincinnati, Division of Research and Advanced Studies, College of Education, Criminal Justice, and Human Services, Division of Human Services, Program in Counseling, Cincinnati, OH 45221. Offers counseling (Ed D); counselor education (CAGS); mental health (MA); school counseling (M Ed). *Accreditation:* ACA (one or more programs are accredited); NCATE. Part-time programs available. *Faculty:* 6 full-time (2 women), 2 part-time/adjunct (both women). *Students:* 92. Terminal master's awarded for partial completion of doctoral program. *Degree requirements:* For master's, comprehensive exam; for doctorate, thesis/dissertation, comprehensive exam. *Entrance requirements:* For master's, GRE General Test, interview; for doctorate, GRE General Test, GRE Subject Test, interview. Additional exam requirements/recommendations for international students: Required—TOEFL (minimum score 620 paper-based), OEPT. *Application deadline:* For fall admission, 1/15 priority date for domestic students. Application fee: $40. Electronic applications accepted. *Financial support:* Teaching assistantships with full tuition reimbursements, career-related internships or fieldwork, tuition waivers (full), and unspecified assistantships available. Support available to part-time students. *Faculty research:* Group work, career development, ecology, prevention, multicultural. *Unit head:* Mei Tang, Head, 513-556-3716, Fax: 513-556-2483, E-mail: mei.tang@uc.edu. *Application contact:* Linda Pelton, Student Contact, 513-556-3335, Fax: 513-556-3898, E-mail: linda.pelton@uc.edu.

University of Colorado at Colorado Springs, Graduate School, College of Education, Colorado Springs, CO 80933-7150. Offers counseling and human services (MA); curriculum and instruction (MA); educational administration (MA); educational leadership (MA, PhD); special education (MA). *Accreditation:* ACA; NCATE. Part-time and evening/weekend programs available. *Faculty:* 22 full-time (15 women), 29 part-time/adjunct (17 women). *Students:* 331 full-time (246 women), 173 part-time (135 women); includes 85 minority (26 African Americans, 4 American Indian/Alaska Native, 13 Asian Americans or Pacific Islanders, 42 Hispanic Americans). Average age 35. 107 applicants, 93% accepted, 49 enrolled. In 2006, 234 degrees awarded. *Degree requirements:* For master's, thesis or alternative, microcomputer proficiency, comprehensive exam; for doctorate, doctoral research lab requirement. *Entrance requirements:* For master's, GRE General Test, MAT. *Application deadline:* For fall admission, 6/15 for domestic students; for spring admission, 10/15 for domestic students. Applications are processed on a rolling basis. Application fee: $60 ($75 for international students). *Expenses:* Tuition, state resident: part-time $303 per credit hour. Tuition, nonresident: part-time $840 per credit hour. Tuition and fees vary according to course load, campus/location and program. *Financial support:* Fellowships, career-related internships or fieldwork and Federal Work-Study available. *Faculty research:* Job training for special populations, materials development for classroom. Total annual research expenditures: $961,803. *Unit head:* Dr. LaVonne Neal, Dean, 719-262-4111, Fax: 719-262-4110, E-mail: lneal@uccs.edu. *Application contact:* Connie Wroten, Professional Assistant, 719-262-4102, Fax: 719-262-4110, E-mail: cwroten@uccs.edu.

University of Colorado at Denver and Health Sciences Center, School of Education and Human Development, Program in Counseling Psychology and Counselor Education, Denver, CO 80217-3364. Offers counseling psychology and counselor education (MA); school psychology (Ed S). *Accreditation:* ACA (one or more programs are accredited); NCATE. Part-time and evening/weekend programs available. *Faculty:* 10 full-time (7 women). *Students:* 67 full-time (58 women), 156 part-time (133 women); includes 25 minority (7 African Americans, 3 American Indian/Alaska Native, 2 Asian Americans or Pacific Islanders, 13 Hispanic Americans). Average age 33. 130 applicants, 72% accepted, 34 enrolled. In 2006, 54 master's, 22 other advanced degrees awarded. *Degree requirements:* For master's, thesis optional. *Entrance requirements:* For master's, GRE or MAT, minimum GPA of 2.75, 4 letters of recommendation, interview, resumé. Additional exam requirements/recommendations for international students: Required—TOEFL (minimum score 525 paper-based; 197 computer-based). *Application deadline:* For fall admission, 2/15 for domestic students; for spring admission, 9/15 for domestic students. Applications are processed on a rolling basis. Application fee: $50 ($75 for international students). Electronic applications accepted. *Financial support:* Research assistantships, teaching assistantships, Federal Work-Study available. Financial award application deadline: 4/1; financial award applicants required to submit FAFSA. *Faculty research:* Spiritual issues in counseling, multicultural and diversity issues in counseling, adolescent suicide, career development. *Unit head:* Dr. Marsha Wiggins-Frame, Division Coordinator, 303-556-6032, Fax: 303-556-4479, E-mail: marsha.frame@cudenver.edu. *Application contact:* Lori Sisneros, Student Services Coordinator, 303-556-8854, Fax: 303-556-4479, E-mail: bri.sisneros@cudenver.edu.

University of Connecticut, Graduate School, Neag School of Education, Department of Educational Psychology, Field of Educational Psychology, Program in Counseling Psychology, Storrs, CT 06269. Offers counseling psychology (PhD); school counseling (MA). *Faculty:* 7 full-time (2 women). *Students:* 30 full-time (21 women), 21 part-time (18 women); includes 10 minority (5 African Americans, 5 Hispanic Americans), 2 international. Average age 31. 46 applicants, 50% accepted, 19 enrolled. In 2006, 24 master's, 2 doctorates awarded. Terminal master's awarded for partial completion of doctoral program. *Degree requirements:* For master's, thesis or alternative, comprehensive exam; for doctorate, thesis/dissertation. *Entrance requirements:* For doctorate, GRE General Test. Additional exam requirements/recommendations for international students: Required—TOEFL (minimum score 550 paper-based; 213 computer-based). *Application deadline:* For fall admission, 2/1 priority date for domestic and international students; for spring admission, 11/1 for domestic students, 10/1 for international students. Applications are processed on a rolling basis. Application fee: $55. Electronic applications accepted. *Financial support:* In 2006–07, 20 research assistantships with full tuition reimbursements, 1 teaching assistantship with full tuition reimbursement were awarded; fellowships, Federal Work-Study, scholarships/grants, health care benefits, and unspecified assistantships also available. Financial award application deadline: 2/1; financial award applicants required to submit FAFSA. *Application contact:* Lisa Rasicot, Graduate Coordinator, 860-486-3065, Fax: 860-486-0210, E-mail: soeadm02@uconnvm.uconn.edu.

University of Dayton, Graduate School, School of Education and Allied Professions, Department of Counselor Education and Human Services, Dayton, OH 45469-1300. Offers college student personnel (MS Ed); community counseling (MS Ed); higher education administration (MS Ed); human development services (MS Ed); school counseling (MS Ed); school psychology (MS Ed, Ed S); teacher as child/youth development specialist (MS Ed). *Accreditation:* NCATE. Part-time and evening/weekend programs available. *Faculty:* 11 full-time (7 women), 32 part-time/adjunct (17 women). *Students:* 271 full-time (234 women), 316 part-time (263 women); includes 85 minority (69 African Americans, 3 American Indian/Alaska Native, 13 Hispanic Americans), 1 international. Average age 32. 363 applicants, 47% accepted, 121 enrolled. In 2006, 267 degrees awarded. *Degree requirements:* For master's, exit exam, thesis optional. *Entrance requirements:* For master's, MAT or GRE (if GPA is below 2.75), interview. Additional exam requirements/recommendations for international students: Required—TOEFL (minimum score 550 paper-based; 213 computer-based). *Application deadline:* For fall admission, 2/15 priority date for domestic students, 4/10 priority date for international students; for winter admission, 9/10 priority date for international students; for spring admission, 1/10 priority date for international students. Applications are processed on a rolling basis. Application fee: $0. Electronic applications accepted. *Expenses:* Tuition: Part-time $601 per semester hour. Tuition and fees vary according to degree level and program. *Financial support:* In 2006–07, 1 research assistantship with partial tuition reimbursement (averaging $7,400 per year), 4 teaching assistantships with partial tuition reimbursements (averaging $7,600 per year) were awarded; career-related internships or fieldwork, institutionally sponsored loans, health care benefits, and unspecified assistantships also available. Financial award applicants required to submit FAFSA. *Faculty research:* Anger as part of the grief process, inclusion of children with severe disabilities, comparisons of school counselors in Bosnia and the U. S., graduate and professional student socialization, use of cohort groups in doctoral programs. *Unit head:* Dr. Thomas W. Rueth, Chairperson, 937-229-3644, Fax: 937-229-1055, E-mail: thomas.rueth@notes.udayton.edu. *Application contact:* Erika Eavers, Graduate Admission Processor, 937-229-3065, Fax: 937-229-4729, E-mail: erika.eavers@notes.udayton.edu.

University of Delaware, College of Human Services, Education and Public Policy, School of Education, Newark, DE 19716. Offers curriculum and instruction (M Ed); education (PhD); educational leadership (M Ed, Ed D); exceptional children and youth (M Ed); instruction (MI); school counseling (M Ed); school psychology (MA); teaching English as a second language (TESL) (MA). *Accreditation:* NCATE. Part-time and evening/weekend programs available. Terminal master's awarded for partial completion of doctoral program. *Degree requirements:* For master's, thesis (for some programs), comprehensive exam (for some programs), registration; for doctorate, thesis/dissertation, comprehensive exam (for some programs), registration. *Entrance requirements:* For master's and doctorate, GRE, 3 letters of recommendation. Additional exam requirements/recommendations for international students: Required—TOEFL (minimum score 600 paper-based; 250 computer-based). Electronic applications accepted. *Faculty research:* Teacher education; education policy; educational assessment, measurement, and evaluation; curriculum theory and development; community based education models.

University of Detroit Mercy, College of Liberal Arts and Education, Department of Counseling and Addiction Studies, Program in Counseling, Detroit, MI 48221. Offers addiction counseling (MA); community counseling (MA); school counseling (MA). *Accreditation:* ACA. Part-time and evening/weekend programs available. *Degree requirements:* For master's, thesis or alternative. *Entrance requirements:* For master's, minimum GPA of 2.75. *Expenses:* Tuition: Full-time $15,750; part-time $875 per credit hour. Required fees: $570.

University of Florida, Graduate School, College of Education, Department of Counselor Education, Gainesville, FL 32611. Offers marriage and family counseling (M Ed, MAE, Ed D, PhD, Ed S); mental health counseling (M Ed, MAE, Ed D, PhD, Ed S); school counseling and guidance (M Ed, MAE, Ed D, PhD, Ed S). *Accreditation:* ACA (one or more programs are accredited); NCATE. Part-time programs available. *Faculty:* 12 full-time (7 women). *Students:* 173 (135 women); includes 34 minority (14 African Americans, 1 American Indian/Alaska Native, 5 Asian Americans or Pacific Islanders, 14 Hispanic Americans) 3 international. In 2006, 86 master's, 12 doctorates awarded. Terminal master's awarded for partial completion of doctoral program. *Degree requirements:* For master's, thesis optional; for doctorate, thesis/dissertation. *Entrance requirements:* For master's and doctorate, GRE General Test, minimum GPA of 3.0 (undergraduate), 3.5 (graduate); for Ed S, GRE General Test. Additional exam requirements/recommendations for international students: Required—TOEFL (minimum score 550 paper-based; 213 computer-based). *Application deadline:* For fall admission, 2/27 priority date for domestic students. Applications are processed on a rolling basis. Application fee: $30. Electronic applications accepted. *Expenses:* Tuition, state resident: full-time $6,827. Tuition, nonresident: full-time $21,951. Required fees: $999. *Financial support:* In 2006–07, 3 research assistantships (averaging $8,971 per year), 14 teaching assistantships (averaging $9,405 per year) were awarded; fellowships, career-related internships or fieldwork and unspecified assistantships also available. *Unit head:* Dr. Harry M. Daniels, Chairman, 352-392-0731 Ext. 226, Fax: 352-846-2697, E-mail: harryd@coe.ufl.edu. *Application contact:* Dr. Peter Sherrard, Coordinator, 352-392-0731 Ext. 234, Fax: 352-846-2697, E-mail: psherrard@coe.ufl.edu.

University of Georgia, Graduate School, College of Education, Department of Counseling and Human Development Services, Athens, GA 30602. Offers M Ed, MA, Ed D, PhD, Ed S. *Accreditation:* ACA (one or more programs are accredited); APA (one or more programs are accredited); NCATE. *Faculty:* 18 full-time (10 women). *Students:* 119 full-time (76 women), 64 part-time (45 women); includes 56 minority (49 African Americans, 3 Asian Americans or Pacific Islanders, 4 Hispanic Americans), 2 international. 280 applicants, 27% accepted, 52 enrolled. In 2006, 44 master's, 16 doctorates, 21 other advanced degrees awarded. *Degree requirements:* For master's, thesis (MA); for doctorate, variable foreign language requirement, thesis/dissertation. *Entrance requirements:* For master's, GRE General Test or MAT; for doctorate, GRE General Test. *Application deadline:* For fall admission, 7/1 priority date for domestic students; for spring admission, 11/15 for domestic students. Application fee: $50. Electronic applications accepted. *Financial support:* Fellowships, research assistantships, teaching assistantships, unspecified assistantships available. *Unit head:* Dr. Rosemary E. Phelps, Head, 706-542-4128, Fax: 706-542-4130. *Application contact:* Dr. Georgia B. Calhoun, Graduate Coordinator, 706-542-1812, Fax: 706-542-4130, E-mail: chds@uga.edu.

University of Guam, Graduate School and Research, College of Education, Program in Counseling, Mangilao, GU 96923. Offers MA. *Degree requirements:* For master's, comprehensive oral and written exams, special project or thesis. *Entrance requirements:* For master's, GRE General Test. Additional exam requirements/recommendations for international students: Required—TOEFL. *Faculty research:* Drugs in the local schools, standardized teaching procedures in the elementary school, how to address the dropout problems.

University of Hartford, College of Education, Nursing, and Health Professions, Program in Counseling, West Hartford, CT 06117-1599. Offers M Ed, MS, Sixth Year Certificate. *Accreditation:* NCATE. Part-time and evening/weekend programs available. *Faculty:* 2 full-time (0 women), 2 part-time/adjunct (0 women). *Students:* 1 (woman) full-time, 26 part-time (22 women); includes 5 minority (2 African Americans, 2 Asian Americans or Pacific Islanders, 1 Hispanic American). Average age 33. 15 applicants, 80% accepted, 8 enrolled. In 2006, 7 master's, 11 other advanced degrees awarded. *Degree requirements:* For master's and Sixth Year Certificate, comprehensive exam. *Entrance requirements:* For master's, GRE General Test or MAT, PRAXIS I or waiver, interview, 2 letters of recommendation; for Sixth Year Certificate, GRE General Test or MAT, PRAXIS I or waiver, interview. Additional exam requirements/recommendations for international students: Required—TOEFL (minimum score 550 paper-based; 213 computer-based). *Application deadline:* For fall admission, 8/15 priority date for domestic students; for winter admission, 12/1 for domestic students; for spring admission, 12/1 for domestic students. Applications are processed on a rolling basis. Application fee: $40 ($55 for international students). Electronic applications accepted. *Expenses:* Tuition: Part-time $515 per credit. Required fees: $200 per term. *Financial support:* Teaching assistantships, institutionally sponsored loans and unspecified assistantships available. Financial award application deadline: 6/1; financial award applicants required to submit FAFSA. *Unit head:* Dr. Joachim Pengel, Director, 860-768-4774, E-mail: pengel@hartford.edu. *Application contact:* Susan Brown, Assistant Dean of Academic Services, 860-768-4692, Fax: 860-768-5043, E-mail: brown@hartford.edu.

University of Hawaii at Manoa, Graduate Division, College of Education, Department of Counselor Education, Program in Counseling and Guidance, Honolulu, HI 96822. Offers M Ed. *Faculty:* 6 full-time (2 women). *Students:* 31 full-time (28 women), 22 part-time (18 women); includes 6 minority (5 Asian Americans or Pacific Islanders, 1 Hispanic American). *Degree requirements:* For master's, thesis optional. *Entrance requirements:* For master's, GRE General Test. Additional exam requirements/recommendations for international students: Required—TOEFL (minimum score 600 paper-based; 250 computer-based; 100 iBT). *Application deadline:* For fall admission, 3/1 for domestic and international students. Application fee: $50. *Financial support:* In 2006–07, 4 research assistantships (averaging $16,338 per year), 1 teaching assistantship (averaging $13,296 per year) were awarded. Total annual research expenditures: $437,280. *Application contact:* Geoffrey Kucera, 808-956-7905, Fax: 808-956-3814.

University of Houston–Clear Lake, School of Education, Program in Foundations and Professional Studies, Houston, TX 77058-1098. Offers counseling (MS); instructional technology (MS); multicultural studies (MS). Part-time and evening/weekend programs available. *Faculty:* 15 full-time (11 women), 11 part-time/adjunct (6 women). *Students:* 35 full-time (29 women), 283 part-time (239 women); includes 111 minority (58 African Americans, 1 American Indian/Alaska Native, 10 Asian Americans or Pacific Islanders, 42 Hispanic Americans), 10 international. Average age 35. In 2006, 86 degrees awarded. *Degree requirements:* For master's, thesis optional. *Entrance requirements:* For master's, GRE or minimum GPA of 3.0 in last 60 hours. Additional exam requirements/recommendations for international students: Required—TOEFL (minimum score 550 paper-based; 213 computer-based). *Application deadline:* For fall admission, 7/1 for domestic students, 6/1 for international students; for spring admission, 10/1 for domestic and international students. Applications are processed on a rolling basis. Application fee: $35 ($75 for international students). Electronic applications accepted. *Financial support:* Career-related internships or fieldwork, Federal Work-Study, institutionally sponsored loans, and scholarships/grants available. Support available to part-time students. Financial award application deadline: 5/1; financial award applicants required to submit FAFSA. *Unit head:* Dr. Judy Marquez, Chair, 281-283-3580, E-mail: marquez@uhcl.edu. *Application contact:* Janis S. Bigelow, Assistant Director of Admissions, Recruitment and Communications, 281-283-2540, Fax: 281-283-2530, E-mail: bigelow@uhcl.edu.

University of Idaho, College of Graduate Studies, College of Education, Department of Counseling and School Psychology, Special Education, and Educational Leadership, Program in Counseling and Human Services, Moscow, ID 83844-2282. Offers M Ed, MS, Ed S. *Accreditation:* ACA (one or more programs are accredited); CORE. *Students:* 66 (49 women). Average age 38. In 2006, 51 degrees awarded. *Entrance requirements:* For master's, minimum GPA of 2.8. Application fee: $55 ($60 for international students). *Expenses:* Tuition, nonresident: full-time $9,600; part-time $140 per credit. Required fees: $4,740; $227 per credit. *Financial support:* Teaching assistantships available. *Unit head:* Dr. Russell A. Joki, Chair, Department of Counseling and School Psychology, Special Education, and Educational Leadership, 208-364-4099, E-mail: rjoki@uidaho.edu.

University of Idaho, College of Graduate Studies, College of Education, Doctoral Programs in Education, Moscow, ID 83844-2282. Offers adult and organizational learning (Ed D, PhD); counseliing and human services (PhD); counseling and human services (Ed D); curriculm and intstruction (Ed D); curriculum and instruction (PhD); educational leadership (Ed D, PhD); physical education (PhD); professional-technical and technology education (PhD); professional-technical and tecnology education (Ed D). *Students:* 208 (118 women). In 2006, 50 degrees awarded. *Expenses:* Tuition, nonresident: full-time $9,600; part-time $140 per credit. Required fees: $4,740; $227 per credit. *Application contact:* Shirley Green, Information Contact, 208-885-6773.

University of Illinois at Urbana–Champaign, Graduate College, College of Education, Department of Educational Psychology, Champaign, IL 61820. Offers Ed M, MA, MS, PhD, CAS. *Accreditation:* APA (one or more programs are accredited). Part-time programs available. *Faculty:* 24 full-time (16 women), 1 (woman) part-time/adjunct. *Students:* 92 full-time (66 women), 70 part-time (44 women); includes 25 minority (12 African Americans, 8 Asian Americans or Pacific Islanders, 5 Hispanic Americans), 53 international. 154 applicants, 32% accepted, 21 enrolled. In 2006, 30 master's, 12 doctorates awarded. *Degree requirements:* For doctorate, thesis/dissertation. *Entrance requirements:* For master's and doctorate, GRE General Test, minimum GPA of 3.5. *Application deadline:* Applications are processed on a rolling basis. Application fee: $50 ($60 for international students). Electronic applications accepted. *Financial support:* In 2006–07, 17 fellowships, 52 research assistantships, 51 teaching assistantships were awarded; tuition waivers (full and partial) also available. Financial award application deadline: 1/15. *Unit head:* Michelle Perry, Chair, 217-244-7766, Fax: 217-244-7620, E-mail: mperry@uiuc.edu. *Application contact:* Helen Katz, Secretary, 217-333-5242, Fax: 217-244-7620, E-mail: hnkatz@uiuc.edu.

The University of Iowa, Graduate College, College of Education, Department of Counseling, Rehabilitation, and Student Development, Iowa City, IA 52242-1316. Offers administration and research (PhD); counselor education and supervision (PhD); rehabilitation counseling (MA); rehabilitation counselor education (PhD); school counseling (MA); student development (MA, PhD). *Accreditation:* ACA (one or more programs are accredited); CORE (one or more programs are accredited). *Faculty:* 14 full-time, 3 part-time/adjunct. *Students:* 86 full-time (67 women), 31 part-time (21 women); includes 20 minority (15 African Americans, 2 Asian Americans or Pacific Islanders, 3 Hispanic Americans), 7 international. 63 applicants, 60% accepted, 25 enrolled. In 2006, 34 master's, 4 doctorates awarded. *Degree requirements:* For master's, exam, thesis optional; for doctorate, thesis/dissertation, comprehensive exam, registration. *Entrance requirements:* For master's and doctorate, GRE General Test, minimum GPA of 3.0. Additional exam requirements/recommendations for international students: Required—TOEFL (minimum score 550 paper-based; 213 computer-based; 81 iBT). Application fee: $60 ($85 for international students). Electronic applications accepted. *Financial support:* In 2006–07, 1 fellowship, 21 research assistantships with partial tuition reimbursements, 37 teaching assistantships with partial tuition reimbursements were awarded. Financial award applicants required to submit FAFSA. *Unit head:* Dr. Dennis R. Maki, Chair, 319-335-5275, Fax: 319-335-5291.

University of La Verne, College of Education and Organizational Leadership, Department of Education, Program in School Counseling, La Verne, CA 91750-4443. Offers pupil personnel services (Credential); school counseling (MS). Part-time programs available. *Faculty:* 18 full-time (13 women), 7 part-time/adjunct (all women). *Students:* 15 full-time (12 women), 59 part-time (53 women); includes 49 minority (6 African Americans, 2 American Indian/Alaska Native, 6 Asian Americans or Pacific Islanders, 35 Hispanic Americans). Average age 30. In 2006, 27 degrees awarded. *Degree requirements:* For master's, thesis optional. *Entrance requirements:* For master's, California Basic Educational Skills Test, minimum undergraduate GPA of 2.75, graduate 3.0; interview; 1 year's experience working with children; 3 letters of reference. Additional exam requirements/recommendations for international students: Required—TOEFL (minimum score 550 paper-based; 213 computer-based). *Application deadline:* Applications are processed on a rolling basis. Application fee: $50. *Expenses:* Contact institution. *Financial support:* Institutionally sponsored loans and unspecified assistantships available. Financial award application deadline: 3/2; financial award applicants required to submit FAFSA. *Unit head:* Dr. Robert Hansen, Chairperson, 909-593-3511 Ext. 4638, E-mail: hansenr@ulv.edu. *Application contact:* Jo Nell Baker, Director, Graduate Admissions and Academic Services, 909-593-3511 Ext. 4244, Fax: 909-392-2761, E-mail: gradadmt@ulv.edu.

University of La Verne, Regional Campus Administration, Master's Programs in Education, California Statewide Campus, La Verne, CA 91750-4443. Offers advanced teaching (M Ed); educational management (M Ed), including preliminary administrative services credential; reading (M Ed); school counseling (MS), including public personnel services credential. *Faculty:* 3 full-time (0 women), 60 part-time/adjunct (38 women). *Students:* 203 full-time (151 women), 268 part-time (210 women); includes 216 minority (42 African Americans, 5 American Indian/Alaska Native, 27 Asian Americans or Pacific Islanders, 142 Hispanic Americans). Average age 36. In 2006, 289 degrees awarded. *Entrance requirements:* For master's, California Basic Educational Skills Test, 3 letters of recommendation, teaching credential. *Application deadline:* Applications are processed on a rolling basis. Application fee: $50. *Expenses:* Contact institution. *Financial support:* Fellowships, institutionally sponsored loans available. Financial award application deadline: 3/2; financial award applicants required to submit FAFSA. *Unit head:* Juline Behrens, Director, 909-985-0944, Fax: 909-981-8695, E-mail: behrensj@ulv.edu.

University of Louisiana at Lafayette, Graduate School, Department of Counselor Education, Lafayette, LA 70504. Offers MS. *Faculty:* 6 full-time (2 women). *Students:* 37 full-time (31 women), 43 part-time (36 women); includes 5 minority (all African Americans) Average age 31. 48 applicants, 46% accepted, 15 enrolled. In 2006, 19 degrees awarded. *Degree requirements:* For master's, registration. *Entrance requirements:* For master's, GRE General Test, minimum GPA of 2.75. Additional exam requirements/recommendations for international students: Required—TOEFL (minimum score 550 paper-based; 213 computer-based). *Application deadline:* For fall admission, 5/15 for domestic and international students; for spring admission, 10/1 for domestic and international students. Applications are processed on a rolling basis. Application fee: $25 ($30 for international students). Electronic applications accepted. *Expenses:* Tuition, state resident: full-time $3,247; part-time $93 per credit hour. Tuition, nonresident: full-time $9,427; part-time $350 per credit hour. *Financial support:* In 2006–07, 3 research assistantships with full tuition reimbursements (averaging $5,500 per year) were awarded; Federal Work-Study and unspecified assistantships also available. Financial award application deadline: 5/1. *Unit head:* Dr. Irvin Esters, Director, 337-482-5261, Fax: 337-482-5262, E-mail: esters@louisiana.edu.

University of Louisiana at Monroe, Graduate Studies and Research, College of Education and Human Development, Department of Educational Leadership and Counseling, Program in Counseling, Monroe, LA 71209-0001. Offers M Ed. *Accreditation:* ACA; NCATE. Part-time and evening/weekend programs available. *Students:* 20 full-time (all women), 24 part-time (23 women); includes 22 minority (21 African Americans, 1 Hispanic American), 2 international. Average age 35. In 2006, 20 degrees awarded. *Degree requirements:* For master's, comprehensive exam. *Entrance requirements:* For master's, GRE General Test, minimum GPA of 2.8 in last 60 hours. *Application deadline:* For fall admission, 6/1 priority date for domestic students; for spring admission, 11/1 for domestic students. Applications are processed on a rolling basis. Application fee: $20 ($30 for international students). *Expenses:* Tuition, state resident: part-time $124 per credit hour. Tuition, nonresident: part-time $124 per credit hour.

Counselor Education

University of Louisiana at Monroe (continued)
Financial support: Research assistantships, teaching assistantships, career-related internships or fieldwork and unspecified assistantships available. Financial award application deadline: 7/1.

University of Louisville, Graduate School, College of Education and Human Development, Department of Educational and Counseling Psychology, Programs in Counseling and Personnel Services, Louisville, KY 40292-0001. Offers school counseling and guidance (M Ed, PhD). *Students:* 122 full-time (90 women), 124 part-time (99 women); includes 54 minority (48 African Americans, 1 American Indian/Alaska Native, 5 Asian Americans or Pacific Islanders), 6 international. Average age 35. In 2006, 78 master's, 9 doctorates awarded.

University of Maine, Graduate School, College of Education and Human Development, Program in Counselor Education, Orono, ME 04469. Offers M Ed, MA, MS, Ed D, CAS. *Accreditation:* NCATE. Part-time and evening/weekend programs available. *Students:* 70 full-time (58 women), 30 part-time (27 women); includes 3 minority (1 African American, 1 American Indian/Alaska Native, 1 Asian American or Pacific Islander), 1 international. Average age 34. 30 applicants, 83% accepted, 21 enrolled. In 2006, 28 master's, 2 doctorates, 1 other advanced degree awarded. *Degree requirements:* For master's, thesis or alternative. *Entrance requirements:* For master's, MAT; for doctorate, GRE General Test, MA, M Ed or MS; for CAS, MA, M Ed, or MS. Additional exam requirements/recommendations for international students: Required—TOEFL. *Application deadline:* For fall admission, 2/1 priority date for domestic students. Applications are processed on a rolling basis. Application fee: $50. Electronic applications accepted. *Financial support:* In 2006–07, teaching assistantships with tuition reimbursements (averaging $9,010 per year); research assistantships with tuition reimbursements, career-related internships or fieldwork, Federal Work-Study, institutionally sponsored loans, tuition waivers (full and partial), and unspecified assistantships also available. Financial award application deadline: 3/1. *Unit head:* Dr. Dorothy Breen, Coordinator, 207-581-2444, Fax: 207-581-2423. *Application contact:* Scott G. Delcourt, Associate Dean of the Graduate School, 207-581-3219, Fax: 207-581-3232, E-mail: graduate@maine.edu.

University of Manitoba, Faculty of Graduate Studies, Faculty of Education, Department of Educational Administration, Foundations and Psychology, Winnipeg, MB R3T 2N2, Canada. Offers adult education (M Ed); educational administration (M Ed); guidance and counseling (M Ed); inclusive special education (M Ed); special foundations education (M Ed). *Degree requirements:* For master's, thesis or alternative.

University of Mary Hardin-Baylor, College of Sciences and Humanities, Department of Psychology, Belton, TX 76513. Offers community counseling (MA); marriage and family Christian counseling (MA); psychology and counseling (MA); school counseling and psychology (MA). Part-time and evening/weekend programs available. *Faculty:* 5 full-time (3 women), 2 part-time/adjunct (1 woman). *Students:* 30 full-time (18 women), 29 part-time (21 women); includes 14 minority (6 African Americans, 2 Asian Americans or Pacific Islanders, 6 Hispanic Americans), 1 international. Average age 24. In 2006, 12 degrees awarded. *Degree requirements:* For master's, comprehensive exam. *Entrance requirements:* For master's, GRE General Test, minimum GPA of 3.0 in last 60 hours or 2.75 overall. *Application deadline:* For fall admission, 6/1 priority date for domestic students; for spring admission, 11/1 for domestic students. Applications are processed on a rolling basis. Application fee: $35 ($135 for international students). Electronic applications accepted. *Expenses:* Tuition: Full-time $8,910; part-time $495 per hour. Required fees: $906; $47 per hour. $30 per term. Tuition and fees vary according to course load. *Financial support:* Research assistantships with full tuition reimbursements, Federal Work-Study and scholarships (for some active duty military personnel only) available. Support available to part-time students. Financial award applicants required to submit FAFSA. *Unit head:* Dr. Raylene B. Statz, Director, Programs in Psychology and Counseling, 254-295-4548, E-mail: rstatz@umhb.edu.

University of Maryland, College Park, Graduate Studies, College of Education, Department of Counseling and Personnel Services, College Park, MD 20742. Offers college student personnel (M Ed, MA); college student personnel administration (PhD); community counseling (CAGS); community/career counseling (M Ed, MA); counseling and personnel services (M Ed, MA, PhD); counseling psychology (PhD); counselor education (PhD); rehabilitation counseling (M Ed, MA); school counseling (M Ed, MA); school psychology (M Ed, MA, PhD). *Accreditation:* ACA (one or more programs are accredited); APA (one or more programs are accredited); CORE (one or more programs are accredited); NCATE. Part-time and evening/weekend programs available. Postbaccalaureate distance learning degree programs offered (no on-campus study). *Faculty:* 41 full-time (26 women), 6 part-time/adjunct (5 women). *Students:* 169 full-time (124 women), 21 part-time (15 women); includes 76 minority (42 African Americans, 1 American Indian/Alaska Native, 14 Asian Americans or Pacific Islanders, 19 Hispanic Americans), 11 international. 382 applicants, 15% accepted, 31 enrolled. In 2006, 57 master's, 13 doctorates, 10 other advanced degrees awarded. *Degree requirements:* For master's, thesis (for some programs); for doctorate, thesis/dissertation. *Entrance requirements:* For master's, GRE General Test or MAT, minimum GPA of 3.0, 3 letters of recommendation; for doctorate, GRE General Test or MAT, minimum GPA of 3.5, 3 letters of recommendation. Additional exam requirements/recommendations for international students: Required—TOEFL. *Application deadline:* For fall admission, 3/1 for domestic students, 2/1 for international students; for spring admission, 9/1 for domestic students, 6/1 for international students. Applications are processed on a rolling basis. Application fee: $60. Electronic applications accepted. *Financial support:* In 2006–07, 11 fellowships with full tuition reimbursements (averaging $8,799 per year), 14 research assistantships (averaging $12,849 per year), 100 teaching assistantships with tuition reimbursements (averaging $14,265 per year) were awarded; career-related internships or fieldwork, Federal Work-Study, and scholarships/grants also available. Support available to part-time students. Financial award applicants required to submit FAFSA. *Faculty research:* Educational psychology, counseling, health. Total annual research expenditures: $2.1 million. *Unit head:* Dr. Ruth Fassingel, Dean, 301-405-2860, Fax: 301-405-9995, E-mail: rfassing@umd.edu. *Application contact:* Dean of Graduate School, 301-405-0358, Fax: 301-314-9305.

University of Maryland Eastern Shore, Graduate Programs, Department of Education, Program in Guidance and Counseling, Princess Anne, MD 21853-1299. Offers M Ed. Evening/weekend programs available. *Faculty:* 2 full-time (both women), 5 part-time/adjunct (3 women). *Students:* 15 full-time (11 women), 21 part-time (17 women); includes 21 minority (20 African Americans, 1 Hispanic American), 2 international. Average age 30. 14 applicants, 64% accepted, 9 enrolled. In 2006, 11 degrees awarded. *Degree requirements:* For master's, practicum, seminar paper. *Entrance requirements:* For master's, interview, minimum GPA of 3.0. Additional exam requirements/recommendations for international students: Required—TOEFL (minimum score 213 computer-based). *Application deadline:* For fall admission, 5/1 priority date for domestic and international students; for spring admission, 11/1 priority date for domestic and international students. Applications are processed on a rolling basis. Application fee: $30. Electronic applications accepted. *Financial support:* In 2006–07, 5 students received support, including 3 research assistantships with full and partial tuition reimbursements available (averaging $10,148 per year); career-related internships or fieldwork, scholarships/grants, and unspecified assistantships also available. Financial award application deadline: 3/1; financial award applicants required to submit FAFSA. *Unit head:* Dr. Cheryl Bowers, Coordinator, 410-651-6265, Fax: 410-651-7962, E-mail: cdbowers@mail.umes.edu.

University of Massachusetts Amherst, Graduate School, School of Education, Program in Education, Amherst, MA 01003. Offers cultural diversity and curriculum reform (M Ed, Ed D, CAGS); early childhood education and development (M Ed, Ed D, CAGS); educational administration (M Ed, Ed D, CAGS); elementary teacher education (M Ed, Ed D, CAGS); higher education (M Ed, Ed D, CAGS); international education (M Ed, Ed D, CAGS); mathematics, science, and instructional technology (M Ed, Ed D, CAGS); physical education teacher education (M Ed, Ed D, CAGS); reading and writing (M Ed, Ed D, CAGS); research and evaluation methods (M Ed, Ed D, CAGS); school psychology and school counseling (M Ed, Ed D, CAGS); secondary teacher education (M Ed, Ed D, CAGS); social justice education (M Ed, Ed D, CAGS); special education (M Ed, Ed D, CAGS). *Accreditation:* NCATE. *Students:* 418 full-time (286 women), 447 part-time (319 women); includes 147 minority (70 African Americans, 4 American Indian/Alaska Native, 28 Asian Americans or Pacific Islanders, 45 Hispanic Americans), 81 international. Average age 36. In 2006, 260 master's, 30 doctorates awarded. *Degree requirements:* For doctorate, thesis/dissertation. *Entrance requirements:* For master's and doctorate, GRE General Test. Additional exam requirements/recommendations for international students: Required—TOEFL (minimum score 530 paper-based; 197 computer-based). *Application deadline:* For fall admission, 1/15 for domestic and international students; for spring admission, 10/1 for domestic and international students. Applications are processed on a rolling basis. Application fee: $40 ($65 for international students). Electronic applications accepted. *Expenses:* Tuition, state resident: full-time $2,640; part-time $110 per credit. Tuition, nonresident: full-time $9,936; part-time $414 per credit. Required fees: $8,969; $3,129 per term. One-time fee: $257 full-time. Tuition and fees vary according to class time, course load, campus/location and reciprocity agreements. *Financial support:* Fellowships with full tuition reimbursements, research assistantships with full tuition reimbursements, teaching assistantships with full tuition reimbursements, career-related internships or fieldwork, Federal Work-Study, scholarships/grants, traineeships, and unspecified assistantships available. Support available to part-time students. Financial award application deadline: 1/15. *Unit head:* Linda L. Griffin, Professor, 413-545-6984.

University of Massachusetts Boston, Office of Graduate Studies, Graduate College of Education, Counseling and School Psychology Department, Program in School Guidance Counseling, Boston, MA 02125-3393. Offers M Ed, CAGS. *Expenses:* Tuition, state resident: full-time $2,590; part-time $301 per credit. Tuition, nonresident: full-time $9,758; part-time $427 per credit. One-time fee: $495 full-time. *Unit head:* Dr. Felicia Wilczenski, Director, 617-287-7592, E-mail: felicia.wilczenski@umb.edu.

University of Memphis, Graduate School, College of Education, Department of Counseling, Educational Psychology and Research, Memphis, TN 38152. Offers counseling and personnel services (MS, Ed D), including community agency counseling (MS), rehabilitation counseling (MS), school counseling (MS), student personnel services (MS); counseling psychology (PhD); educational psychology and research (MS, Ed D, PhD), including educational psychology (MS, Ed D), educational research (MS, Ed D). *Accreditation:* ACA (one or more programs are accredited); APA (one or more programs are accredited); CORE (one or more programs are accredited); NCATE. *Degree requirements:* For master's, thesis or alternative, comprehensive exam; for doctorate, thesis/dissertation, comprehensive exam. *Entrance requirements:* For master's, GRE General Test or MAT, minimum GPA of 2.5; for doctorate, GRE General Test. *Faculty research:* Anger management, aging and disability, supervision, multicultural counseling.

University of Miami, Graduate School, School of Education, Department of Educational and Psychological Studies, Program in Counseling, Coral Gables, FL 33124. Offers bilingual and bicultural counseling (Certificate); marriage and family therapy (MS Ed); mental health counseling (MS Ed). Part-time programs available. *Faculty:* 8 full-time (3 women), 10 part-time/adjunct (8 women). *Students:* 35 full-time (28 women), 19 part-time (17 women); includes 25 minority (4 African Americans, 1 Asian American or Pacific Islander, 20 Hispanic Americans), 2 international. Average age 25. 63 applicants, 81% accepted, 17 enrolled. In 2006, 33 degrees awarded. *Degree requirements:* For master's, comprehensive exam. *Entrance requirements:* For master's, GRE General Test; for Certificate, master's degree in a mental health field. Additional exam requirements/recommendations for international students: Required—TOEFL (minimum score 550 paper-based; 212 computer-based). *Application deadline:* For fall admission, 3/15 priority date for domestic and international students. Applications are processed on a rolling basis. Application fee: $50. Electronic applications accepted. *Financial support:* In 2006–07, 49 students received support; research assistantships, teaching assistantships, Federal Work-Study, institutionally sponsored loans, scholarships/grants, unspecified assistantships, and employee benefits available. Support available to part-time students. Financial award application deadline: 3/15; financial award applicants required to submit FAFSA. *Faculty research:* Cocaine recidivism, HIV, non-traditional families, health psychology, diversity. *Application contact:* Shelley Lue Foung, Senior Administrative Assistant, 305-284-3001, Fax: 305-284-3003, E-mail: sluefoung@miami.edu.

University of Minnesota, Twin Cities Campus, Graduate School, College of Education and Human Development, Department of Educational Psychology, Program in Counseling and Student Personnel Psychology, Minneapolis, MN 55455-0213. Offers MA, PhD, Ed S. *Students:* 109 full-time (88 women), 11 part-time (7 women); includes 16 minority (5 African Americans, 2 American Indian/Alaska Native, 7 Asian Americans or Pacific Islanders, 2 Hispanic Americans), 16 international. Average age 30. 127 applicants, 48% accepted, 39 enrolled. In 2006, 33 master's, 4 doctorates awarded. *Expenses:* Tuition, state resident: full-time $9,302; part-time $775 per credit. Tuition, nonresident: full-time $16,400; part-time $1,367 per credit. Full-time tuition and fees vary according to class time, course load, program, reciprocity agreements and student level. *Application contact:* Dr. Mary Bents, Associate Dean, 612-625-6501, Fax: 612-626-1580, E-mail: mbents@tc.umn.edu.

University of Mississippi, Graduate School, School of Education, Department of Educational Leadership and Counselor Education, Oxford, University, MS 38677. Offers counselor education (M Ed, PhD, Specialist); educational leadership (PhD); educational leadership and counselor education (M Ed, MA, Ed D, Ed S); higher education/student personnel (MA). *Accreditation:* ACA; NCATE. *Faculty:* 14 full-time (9 women), 4 part-time/adjunct (2 women). *Students:* 171 full-time (113 women), 158 part-time (110 women); includes 93 minority (88 African Americans, 2 Asian Americans or Pacific Islanders, 3 Hispanic Americans), 11 international. In 2006, 76 master's, 9 doctorates, 22 other advanced degrees awarded. *Degree requirements:* For doctorate, thesis/dissertation. *Entrance requirements:* For master's, GRE General Test, minimum GPA of 3.0; for doctorate, GRE General Test. Additional exam requirements/recommendations for international students: Required—TOEFL. *Application deadline:* For fall admission, 4/1 for domestic students; for spring admission, 10/1 for domestic students. Applications are processed on a rolling basis. Application fee: $25. Electronic applications accepted. *Expenses:* Tuition, state resident: full-time $4,602; part-time $256 per credit hour. Tuition, nonresident: full-time $10,566; part-time $587 per credit hour. *Financial support:* Scholarships/grants available. Financial award application deadline: 3/1; financial award applicants required to submit FAFSA. *Unit head:* Dr. Timothy Letzring, Acting Chair, 662-915-7069, E-mail: fdl@olemiss.edu.

University of Missouri–St. Louis, College of Education, Division of Counseling, St. Louis, MO 63121. Offers community counseling (M Ed); elementary school counseling (M Ed); secondary school counseling (M Ed). *Accreditation:* ACA; NCATE. *Faculty:* 7 full-time (3 women). *Students:* 58 full-time (49 women), 177 part-time (141 women); includes 50 minority (39 African Americans, 4 Asian Americans or Pacific Islanders, 7 Hispanic Americans), 5 international. Average age 32. In 2006, 47 master's awarded. *Entrance requirements:* For master's, 3 letters of recommendation, supplemental application. Additional exam requirements/recommendations for international students: Required—TOEFL (minimum score 550 paper-based; 213 computer-based). *Application deadline:* Applications are processed on a rolling basis. Application fee: $35 ($40 for international students). Electronic applications accepted. *Expenses:* Tuition, state resident: part-time $332 per credit hour. Tuition, nonresident: part-time $770 per credit hour. *Financial support:* In 2006–07, 2 research assistantships with full and partial tuition reimbursements (averaging $18,000 per year) were awarded. *Faculty research:* Vocational interests, self-concept, decision-making factors, developmental differences. *Unit head:* Dr. Mark Pope, Chair, 314-516-5782. *Application contact:* 314-516-5458, Fax: 314-516-6996, E-mail: gradadm@umsl.edu.

The University of Montana, Graduate School, School of Education, Department of Educational Leadership and Counseling, Program in Counselor Education, Missoula, MT 59812-0002. Offers counselor education (Ed S); counselor education and supervision (Ed D); mental health counseling (MA); school counseling (MA). *Accreditation:* ACA; NCATE. *Degree requirements:*

For doctorate, thesis/dissertation. *Entrance requirements:* For master's, doctorate, and Ed S, GRE General Test. Additional exam requirements/recommendations for international students: Required—TOEFL.

University of Montevallo, College of Education, Program in Guidance and Counseling, Montevallo, AL 35115. Offers M Ed. *Accreditation:* ACA; NCATE. Part-time and evening/weekend programs available. *Entrance requirements:* For master's, GRE General Test, MAT, minimum undergraduate GPA of 2.75 in last 60 hours or 2.5 overall, interview. Additional exam requirements/recommendations for international students: Required—TOEFL (minimum score 550 paper-based).

University of Nebraska at Kearney, College of Graduate Study, College of Education, Department of Counseling and School Psychology, Kearney, NE 68849-0001. Offers counseling (MS Ed, Ed S); school psychology (Ed S). *Accreditation:* ACA; NCATE. Part-time and evening/weekend programs available. *Faculty:* 6 full-time (3 women). *Students:* 44 full-time (35 women), 118 part-time (101 women); includes 2 minority (both Hispanic Americans), 4 international. 69 applicants, 52% accepted. In 2006, 47 master's, 7 other advanced degrees awarded. *Degree requirements:* For master's, thesis optional; for Ed S, thesis. *Entrance requirements:* For master's and Ed S, interview. Additional exam requirements/recommendations for international students: Required—TOEFL (minimum score 550 paper-based; 213 computer-based). *Application deadline:* For fall admission, 5/1 for domestic and international students; for spring admission, 8/15 for domestic students, 8/1 for international students. Applications are processed on a rolling basis. Application fee: $45. Electronic applications accepted. *Expenses:* Tuition, state resident: part-time $161 per hour. Tuition, nonresident: part-time $332 per hour. Required fees: $57 per hour. *Financial support:* In 2006–07, 7 research assistantships with full tuition reimbursements (averaging $8,200 per year), 1 teaching assistantship with full tuition reimbursement (averaging $8,200 per year) were awarded; career-related internships or fieldwork, scholarships/grants, and unspecified assistantships also available. Support available to part-time students. Financial award application deadline: 3/1; financial award applicants required to submit FAFSA. *Faculty research:* Multicultural counseling and diversity issues, team decision making, adult development, women's issues, brief therapy. *Unit head:* Dr. Max McFarland, Chair, 308-865-8508, E-mail: mcfarlandm@unk.edu.

University of Nebraska at Omaha, Graduate Studies and Research, College of Education, Department of Counseling, Omaha, NE 68182. Offers community counseling (MA, MS); counseling gerontology (MA, MS); school counseling-elementary (MA, MS); school counseling-secondary (MA, MS); student affairs practice in higher education (MA, MS). *Accreditation:* ACA (one or more programs are accredited); NCATE. Part-time and evening/weekend programs available. *Faculty:* 6 full-time (2 women). *Students:* 42 full-time (30 women), 114 part-time (98 women); includes 9 minority (6 African Americans, 2 Asian Americans or Pacific Islanders, 1 Hispanic American), 1 international. Average age 33. 55 applicants, 64% accepted, 23 enrolled. In 2006, 55 degrees awarded. *Degree requirements:* For master's, thesis (for some programs), comprehensive exam. *Entrance requirements:* For master's, GRE General Test, MAT, department test, interview, minimum GPA of 3.0. Additional exam requirements/recommendations for international students: Required—TOEFL (minimum score 550 paper-based; 213 computer-based; 80 iBT). *Application deadline:* For fall admission, 3/1 for domestic students; for spring admission, 10/1 for domestic students. Applications are processed on a rolling basis. Application fee: $45. Electronic applications accepted. *Financial support:* In 2006–07, 89 students received support, including 2 research assistantships with tuition reimbursements available; fellowships, Federal Work-Study, institutionally sponsored loans, scholarships/grants, tuition waivers (partial), and unspecified assistantships also available. Support available to part-time students. Financial award application deadline: 3/1; financial award applicants required to submit FAFSA. *Unit head:* Dr. Jeanette Seaberry, Chairperson, 402-554-2727.

University of Nevada, Las Vegas, Graduate College, College of Education, Department of Educational Psychology, Las Vegas, NV 89154-9900. Offers education psychology (MS); educational psychology (PhD); learning and technology (PhD); school counseling (M Ed); school counselor education (PhD); school psychology (PhD, Ed S). *Accreditation:* ACA (one or more programs are accredited); NCATE. Part-time and evening/weekend programs available. *Faculty:* 21 full-time (10 women), 1 (woman) part-time/adjunct. *Students:* 70 full-time (55 women), 95 part-time (68 women); includes 36 minority (18 African Americans, 12 Asian Americans or Pacific Islanders, 6 Hispanic Americans), 7 international. 104 applicants, 53% accepted, 47 enrolled. In 2006, 23 master's, 3 doctorates, 17 other advanced degrees awarded. *Degree requirements:* For master's, thesis (for some programs), comprehensive exam (for some programs); for doctorate, thesis/dissertation, oral exam, comprehensive exam. *Entrance requirements:* For master's, GRE General Test, minimum GPA of 3.0 during previous 2 years, 2.75 overall; for doctorate, GRE General Test, minimum GPA of 3.0. Additional exam requirements/recommendations for international students: Required—TOEFL (minimum score 550 paper-based; 213 computer-based; 80 iBT). *Application deadline:* For fall admission, 2/1 for domestic and international students. Application fee: $60 ($75 for international students). Electronic applications accepted. *Financial support:* In 2006–07, 17 research assistantships with partial tuition reimbursements (averaging $11,000 per year), 10 teaching assistantships with partial tuition reimbursements (averaging $12,000 per year) were awarded; career-related internships or fieldwork, Federal Work-Study, institutionally sponsored loans, scholarships/grants, health care benefits, and unspecified assistantships also available. Support available to part-time students. Financial award application deadline: 3/1. *Unit head:* Dr. Ralph E. Reynolds, Chair, 702-895-3787, E-mail: ralph.reynolds@unlv.edu. *Application contact:* Graduate College Admissions Evaluator, 702-895-3320, Fax: 702-895-4180, E-mail: gradcollege@unlv.edu.

University of Nevada, Reno, Graduate School, College of Education, Department of Counseling and Educational Psychology, Reno, NV 89557. Offers M Ed, MA, MS, Ed D, PhD, Ed S. *Accreditation:* ACA (one or more programs are accredited); NCATE. *Faculty:* 17. *Students:* 71 full-time (50 women), 64 part-time (52 women); includes 20 minority (4 African Americans, 5 American Indian/Alaska Native, 2 Asian Americans or Pacific Islanders, 9 Hispanic Americans), 5 international. Average age 36. 53 applicants, 85% accepted, 32 enrolled. In 2006, 24 master's, 10 doctorates, 4 other advanced degrees awarded. Terminal master's awarded for partial completion of doctoral program. *Degree requirements:* For master's, thesis optional; for doctorate, thesis/dissertation, qualifying exam, comprehensive exam. *Entrance requirements:* For master's, GRE, minimum GPA of 2.75; for doctorate, GRE, minimum GPA of 3.0. Additional exam requirements/recommendations for international students: Required—TOEFL. *Application deadline:* For fall admission, 2/15 priority date for domestic students; for spring admission, 9/15 for domestic students. Application fee: $60 ($95 for international students). *Financial support:* In 2006–07, 2 research assistantships with tuition reimbursements, 9 teaching assistantships with tuition reimbursements were awarded; Federal Work-Study, institutionally sponsored loans, and scholarships/grants also available. Financial award application deadline: 3/1. *Faculty research:* Marriage and family counseling, substance abuse attitudes of teachers, current supply of counseling educators, HIV-positive services for patients, family counseling for youth at risk. *Unit head:* Dr. Thomas Harrison, Chair, 775-784-6637.

University of New Hampshire, Graduate School, College of Liberal Arts, Department of Education, Program in Counseling, Durham, NH 03824. Offers M Ed, MA. Part-time programs available. *Faculty:* 32 full-time. *Students:* 34 full-time (27 women), 54 part-time (47 women). Average age 35. 34 applicants, 91% accepted, 19 enrolled. In 2006, 47 degrees awarded. *Degree requirements:* For master's, thesis (for some programs). *Entrance requirements:* For master's, GRE General Test. Additional exam requirements/recommendations for international students: Required—TOEFL (minimum score 550 paper-based; 213 computer-based). *Application deadline:* For fall admission, 3/1 priority date for domestic students, 4/1 for international students; for winter admission, 11/15 for domestic students; for spring admission, 3/1 for domestic students. Applications are processed on a rolling basis. Application fee: $60. Electronic applications accepted. *Expenses:* Tuition, state resident: full-time $8,540; part-time $474 per credit hour. Tuition, nonresident: full-time $20,990; part-time $862 per credit hour. Required fees: $1,343; $356 per term. Tuition and fees vary according to course load, program and reciprocity agreements. *Financial support:* In 2006–07, 4 fellowships, 4 teaching assistantships were awarded; research assistantships, career-related internships or fieldwork, Federal Work-Study, scholarships/grants, and tuition waivers (full and partial) also available. Support available to part-time students. Financial award application deadline: 2/15. *Faculty research:* Generic approach to counseling. *Unit head:* Dr. David Hebert, Coordinator, 603-862-3736, E-mail: education.department@unh.edu.

University of New Hampshire at Manchester, Center for Graduate and Professional Studies, Manchester, NH 03101-1113. Offers business administration (MBA); counseling (M Ed); education (M Ed, MAT); educational administration and supervision (M Ed, CAGS); industrial statistics (Certificate); public administration (MPA); public health (MPH, Certificate); social work (MSW).

University of New Mexico, Graduate School, College of Education, Department of Individual, Family and Community Education, Program in Counselor Education, Albuquerque, NM 87131-2039. Offers MA, PhD. *Accreditation:* ACA (one or more programs are accredited); NCATE. Part-time programs available. *Students:* 38 full-time (32 women), 51 part-time (40 women); includes 45 minority (5 African Americans, 8 American Indian/Alaska Native, 2 Asian Americans or Pacific Islanders, 30 Hispanic Americans), 1 international. Average age 37. 64 applicants, 19% accepted, 11 enrolled. In 2006, 30 master's, 2 doctorates awarded. *Degree requirements:* For master's, registration; for doctorate, thesis/dissertation, registration. *Entrance requirements:* For master's, 3 letters of recommendation, personal statement, departmental application; for doctorate, GRE General Test, 3 letters of recommendation, writing sample, personal statement, departmental application. Additional exam requirements/recommendations for international students: Required—TOEFL. *Application deadline:* For fall admission, 2/15 for domestic students; for spring admission, 9/15 for domestic students. Application fee: $50. Electronic applications accepted. *Financial support:* In 2006–07, 38 students received support, including 2 teaching assistantships with full and partial tuition reimbursements available (averaging $6,294 per year). Financial award application deadline: 3/1; financial award applicants required to submit FAFSA. *Faculty research:* Ethics, supervision, multiculturalism. *Unit head:* Program Coordinator, 505-277-1353. *Application contact:* Cynthia Salas, Department Administrator, 505-277-4535, Fax: 505-277-8361, E-mail: casalas@unm.edu.

University of New Orleans, Graduate School, College of Education and Human Development, Department of Educational Leadership, Counseling, and Foundations, Program in Counselor Education, New Orleans, LA 70148. Offers M Ed, PhD, GCE. *Accreditation:* ACA (one or more programs are accredited); NCATE. Evening/weekend programs available. *Students:* 88 (68 women). Average age 34. In 2006, 37 master's, 7 doctorates awarded. Terminal master's awarded for partial completion of doctoral program. *Degree requirements:* For master's, thesis (for some programs); for doctorate, variable foreign language requirement, thesis/dissertation. *Entrance requirements:* For master's and doctorate, GRE General Test. Additional exam requirements/recommendations for international students: Required—TOEFL (minimum score 550 paper-based; 213 computer-based). *Application deadline:* For fall admission, 7/1 priority date for domestic students, 6/1 for international students; for spring admission, 11/15 priority date for domestic students, 10/1 for international students. Applications are processed on a rolling basis. Application fee: $40. Electronic applications accepted. *Expenses:* Tuition, state resident: full-time $3,292. Tuition, nonresident: full-time $10,336. Required fees: $158. *Financial support:* Fellowships, research assistantships, teaching assistantships, career-related internships or fieldwork and tuition waivers (partial) available. Financial award application deadline: 3/15; financial award applicants required to submit FAFSA. *Unit head:* Dr. Diana Hulse-Killacky, Graduate Coordinator, 504-280-6662, Fax: 504-280-6065, E-mail: dhlseki@uno.edu.

University of North Alabama, College of Education, Department of Secondary Education, Program in Counseling, Florence, AL 35632-0001. Offers counseling (MA Ed); non-school-based counseling (MA); non-school-based teaching (MA). *Accreditation:* NCATE. Part-time and evening/weekend programs available. *Faculty:* 3 full-time (2 women), 4 part-time/adjunct (2 women). *Students:* 6 full-time (5 women), 25 part-time (18 women). Average age 34. In 2006, 8 degrees awarded. *Degree requirements:* For master's, comprehensive exam. *Entrance requirements:* For master's, GRE, MAT, or NTE, minimum GPA of 2.5, Alabama Class B Certificate or equivalent, teaching experience. *Application deadline:* For fall admission, 7/1 priority date for domestic students; for spring admission, 12/1 for domestic students. Applications are processed on a rolling basis. Application fee: $25. Electronic applications accepted. *Expenses:* Tuition, state resident: full-time $4,080. Tuition, nonresident: full-time $8,160. Required fees: $764. *Financial support:* Federal Work-Study available. Support available to part-time students. Financial award application deadline: 4/1. *Application contact:* Dr. Sue Wilson, Dean of Enrollment Management, 256-765-4316, Fax: 256-765-4349, E-mail: sjwilson@una.edu.

The University of North Carolina at Chapel Hill, Graduate School, School of Education, Program in School Counseling, Chapel Hill, NC 27599. Offers M Ed. *Accreditation:* ACA; NCATE. In 2006, 21 degrees awarded. *Degree requirements:* For master's, comprehensive exam. *Entrance requirements:* For master's, GRE General Test, minimum GPA of 3.0 during last 2 years of undergraduate course work. Additional exam requirements/recommendations for international students: Required—TOEFL (minimum score 550 paper-based; 213 computer-based). *Application deadline:* For fall admission, 1/1 priority date for domestic and international students. Applications are processed on a rolling basis. Application fee: $60. Electronic applications accepted. *Financial support:* Federal Work-Study available. Support available to part-time students. Financial award application deadline: 3/1; financial award applicants required to submit FAFSA. *Faculty research:* Career counseling, development and assessment, multicultural counseling, measurement. *Unit head:* Dr. John Galassi, Coordinator, 919-962-9196, E-mail: jgalassi@email.unc.edu. *Application contact:* Janet Carroll, Registrar, 919-962-8690, Fax: 919-962-1533, E-mail: jscarrol@email.unc.edu.

The University of North Carolina at Charlotte, Graduate School, College of Education, Department of Counseling, Charlotte, NC 28223-0001. Offers counseling (MA, PhD), including community and school counseling (MA), counseling (PhD). *Accreditation:* ACA. Part-time and evening/weekend programs available. Postbaccalaureate distance learning degree programs offered (no on-campus study). *Faculty:* 12 full-time (7 women), 2 part-time/adjunct (0 women). *Students:* 93 full-time (79 women), 74 part-time (66 women); includes 31 minority (27 African Americans, 3 Asian Americans or Pacific Islanders, 1 Hispanic American), 1 international. Average age 33. 146 applicants, 66% accepted, 69 enrolled. In 2006, 52 master's, 6 doctorates awarded. *Entrance requirements:* For master's, GRE or MAT. Additional exam requirements/recommendations for international students: Required—TOEFL (minimum score 557 paper-based; 220 computer-based). *Application deadline:* For fall admission, 7/1 for domestic students, 5/1 for international students; for spring admission, 11/1 for domestic students, 10/1 for international students. Applications are processed on a rolling basis. Application fee: $55. Electronic applications accepted. *Expenses:* Tuition, state resident: full-time $2,719; part-time $170 per credit. Tuition, nonresident: full-time $12,926; part-time $808 per credit. Required fees: $1,555. *Financial support:* In 2006–07, 13 teaching assistantships (averaging $8,231 per year) were awarded; fellowships, research assistantships, career-related internships or fieldwork, Federal Work-Study, institutionally sponsored loans, scholarships/grants, and unspecified assistantships also available. Support available to part-time students. Financial award application deadline: 4/1; financial award applicants required to submit FAFSA. *Unit head:* Dr. Susan R. Furr, Chair, 704-687-8960, Fax: 704-687-1013, E-mail: srfurr@email.uncc.edu. *Application contact:* Kathy B. Giddings, Director of Graduate Admissions, 704-687-3366, Fax: 704-687-3279, E-mail: gradadm@email.uncc.edu.

The University of North Carolina at Greensboro, Graduate School, School of Education, Department of Counseling and Educational Development, Greensboro, NC 27412-5001. Offers advanced school counseling (PMC); counseling and counselor education (PhD); counseling

Counselor Education

The University of North Carolina at Greensboro (continued)
and educational development (MS); couple and family counseling (PMC); school counseling (PMC); MS/Ed S. *Accreditation:* ACA (one or more programs are accredited); NCATE. *Faculty:* 10 full-time (5 women), 1 part-time/adjunct (0 women). *Students:* 106 full-time (92 women), 18 part-time (14 women); includes 21 minority (12 African Americans, 1 American Indian/Alaska Native, 4 Asian Americans or Pacific Islanders, 4 Hispanic Americans). 314 applicants, 22% accepted. *Degree requirements:* For master's, practicum, internship; for doctorate, thesis/dissertation, comprehensive exam. *Entrance requirements:* For master's, doctorate, and PMC, GRE General Test. Additional exam requirements/recommendations for international students: Required—TOEFL. *Application deadline:* For fall admission, 2/15 for domestic students. Application fee: $45. Electronic applications accepted. *Expenses:* Tuition, state resident: full-time $2,692. Tuition, nonresident: full-time $13,742. *Financial support:* In 2006–07, 57 students received support; fellowships with full tuition reimbursements available, research assistantships with full tuition reimbursements available, teaching assistantships with full tuition reimbursements available, career-related internships or fieldwork, Federal Work-Study, scholarships/grants, traineeships, and unspecified assistantships available. Support available to part-time students. *Faculty research:* Gerontology, invitational theory, career development, marriage and family therapy, drug and alcohol abuse prevention. *Unit head:* Dr. DiAnne Borders, Chair, 336-334-3425, Fax: 336-334-4120, E-mail: borders@uncg.edu. *Application contact:* Michelle Harkleroad, Director of Graduate Admissions, 336-334-4884, Fax: 336-334-4424, E-mail: mbharkle@uncg.edu.

The University of North Carolina at Pembroke, Graduate Studies, Department of Psychology and Counseling, Program in School Counseling, Pembroke, NC 28372-1510. Offers MA. *Accreditation:* NCATE. Part-time and evening/weekend programs available. *Faculty:* 4 full-time (3 women), 1 (woman) part-time/adjunct. *Students:* 6 full-time (all women), 54 part-time (47 women); includes 24 minority (7 African Americans, 16 American Indian/Alaska Native, 1 Asian American or Pacific Islander). Average age 37. 60 applicants, 100% accepted, 60 enrolled. In 2006, 7 degrees awarded. *Degree requirements:* For master's, thesis optional. *Entrance requirements:* For master's, GRE General Test or MAT, minimum GPA of 3.0 in major, 2.5 overall. Additional exam requirements/recommendations for international students: Required—TOEFL. *Application deadline:* For fall admission, 7/15 priority date for domestic and international students; for spring admission, 12/1 priority date for domestic and international students. Applications are processed on a rolling basis. Application fee: $40. *Expenses:* Tuition, state resident: full-time $3,516; part-time $1,091 per semester. Tuition, nonresident: full-time $12,924; part-time $4,619 per semester. Tuition and fees vary according to class time, course load, degree level and campus/location. *Financial support:* In 2006–07, 1 research assistantship with full tuition reimbursement (averaging $6,000 per year) was awarded; career-related internships or fieldwork and unspecified assistantships also available. Support available to part-time students. Financial award application deadline: 4/15; financial award applicants required to submit FAFSA. *Unit head:* Dr. David Pitner, 910-521-4037, Fax: 910-521-6165. *Application contact:* Dr. Kathleen C. Hilton, Dean of Graduate Studies, 910-521-6271, Fax: 910-521-6751, E-mail: grad@uncp.edu.

The University of North Carolina at Pembroke, Graduate Studies, Department of Psychology and Counseling, Program in Service Agency Counseling, Pembroke, NC 28372-1510. Offers MA. Part-time and evening/weekend programs available. *Faculty:* 4 full-time (3 women), 1 (woman) part-time/adjunct. *Students:* 3 full-time (all women), 13 part-time (10 women); includes 5 minority (2 African Americans, 3 American Indian/Alaska Native), 1 international. Average age 37. 16 applicants, 100% accepted, 16 enrolled. In 2006, 6 degrees awarded. *Degree requirements:* For master's, thesis optional. *Entrance requirements:* For master's, GRE General Test or MAT, minimum GPA of 3.0 in major, 2.5 overall. Additional exam requirements/recommendations for international students: Required—TOEFL. *Application deadline:* For fall admission, 7/15 priority date for domestic and international students; for spring admission, 12/1 priority date for domestic and international students. Applications are processed on a rolling basis. Application fee: $40. *Expenses:* Tuition, state resident: full-time $3,516; part-time $1,091 per semester. Tuition, nonresident: full-time $12,924; part-time $4,619 per semester. Tuition and fees vary according to class time, course load, degree level and campus/location. *Financial support:* In 2006–07, 1 research assistantship with full tuition reimbursement (averaging $6,000 per year) was awarded; career-related internships or fieldwork and unspecified assistantships also available. Support available to part-time students. Financial award application deadline: 4/15; financial award applicants required to submit FAFSA. *Unit head:* Dr. David Pitner, 910-521-4037, Fax: 910-521-6165. *Application contact:* Dr. Kathleen C. Hilton, Dean of Graduate Studies, 910-521-6271, Fax: 910-521-6751, E-mail: grad@uncp.edu.

University of Northern Colorado, Graduate School, College of Education and Behavioral Sciences, School of Applied Psychology and Counselor Education, Program in Counselor Education and Supervision, Greeley, CO 80639. Offers PhD. *Accreditation:* ACA. Part-time programs available. *Faculty:* 3 full-time (all women). *Students:* 29 full-time (20 women), 7 part-time (5 women); includes 3 minority (1 African American, 1 Asian American or Pacific Islander, 1 Hispanic American), 1 international. Average age 33. 30 applicants, 60% accepted, 12 enrolled. In 2006, 1 doctorate awarded. *Degree requirements:* For doctorate, thesis/dissertation, comprehensive exam. *Entrance requirements:* For doctorate, GRE General Test, 3 letters of recommendation. *Application deadline:* For fall admission, 1/1 for domestic and international students. Application fee: $50 ($60 for international students). *Expenses:* Tuition, state resident: full-time $5,118; part-time $213 per credit hour. Tuition, nonresident: full-time $14,832; part-time $618 per credit hour. Required fees: $674; $34 per credit hour. *Financial support:* In 2006–07, 29 students received support, including 7 fellowships (averaging $1,686 per year), 3 research assistantships (averaging $12,152 per year), 2 teaching assistantships (averaging $10,680 per year). Financial award application deadline: 3/1; financial award applicants required to submit FAFSA. *Unit head:* Dr. Michelle Athanasiou, Program Coordinator, 970-351-2731, Fax: 970-351-2625.

University of Northern Iowa, Graduate College, College of Education, Department of Educational Leadership, Counseling, and Postsecondary Education, Program in Counseling, Cedar Falls, IA 50614. Offers counseling (MA, Ed D); school counseling (MAE). *Accreditation:* ACA (one or more programs are accredited). Part-time and evening/weekend programs available. *Students:* 40 full-time (37 women), 30 part-time (25 women); includes 6 minority (3 African Americans, 1 Asian American or Pacific Islander, 2 Hispanic Americans). 54 applicants, 44% accepted, 16 enrolled. In 2006, 20 degrees awarded. *Degree requirements:* For master's, thesis or alternative, comprehensive exam; for doctorate, thesis/dissertation. *Entrance requirements:* For master's, minimum GPA of 3.5, 3 years of educational experience; for doctorate, minimum GPA of 3.2, 3 years of educational experience, master's degree. Additional exam requirements/recommendations for international students: Required—TOEFL (minimum score 500 paper-based; 180 computer-based; 61 iBT). *Application deadline:* For fall admission, 8/1 priority date for domestic students. Applications are processed on a rolling basis. Application fee: $30 ($50 for international students). Electronic applications accepted. *Expenses:* Tuition, state resident: full-time $5,936. Tuition, nonresident: full-time $14,074. *Financial support:* Career-related internships or fieldwork, Federal Work-Study, and tuition waivers (full and partial) available. Support available to part-time students. Financial award application deadline: 2/1. *Unit head:* Dr. Ann S. Vernon, Coordinator, 319-273-2226, Fax: 319-273-5175, E-mail: ann.vernon@uni.edu.

University of Northern Virginia, Graduate Programs, Manassas, VA 20109. Offers accountancy (MS); accounting (MBA); business administration (DBA); computer science (MS); counseling education (M Ed); early childhood education (M Ed); educational communication and instructional technology (M Ed); educational leadership (M Ed); finance (MBA); information systems technology (MS); management (MBA); marketing (MBA); project management (MBA); public administration (MPA); teaching English to speakers of other languages (M Ed). Part-time and evening/weekend programs available. Postbaccalaureate distance learning degree programs offered (no on-campus study). *Degree requirements:* For doctorate, thesis/dissertation, comprehensive exam, registration. *Entrance requirements:* Additional exam requirements/recommendations for international students: Required—TOEFL (minimum score 550 paper-based; 230 computer-based), IELTS (minimum score 6). Electronic applications accepted.

University of North Florida, College of Education and Human Services, Department of Counseling and Educational Leadership, Program in Counselor Education, Jacksonville, FL 32224-2645. Offers mental health counseling (M Ed); school counseling (M Ed). *Accreditation:* ACA; NCATE. Part-time and evening/weekend programs available. *Faculty:* 15 full-time (9 women). *Students:* 55 full-time (53 women), 21 part-time (20 women); includes 27 minority (20 African Americans, 2 Asian Americans or Pacific Islanders, 5 Hispanic Americans). Average age 33. 77 applicants, 39% accepted, 25 enrolled. In 2006, 34 degrees awarded. *Entrance requirements:* For master's, GRE General Test, minimum GPA of 3.0 in last 60 hours, 3 letters of recommendation, interview, writing sample. Additional exam requirements/recommendations for international students: Required—TOEFL (minimum score 500 paper-based; 173 computer-based). *Application deadline:* For fall admission, 5/1 for domestic students, 4/23 for international students; for spring admission, 9/26 for domestic students. Application fee: $30. Electronic applications accepted. *Expenses:* Tuition, state resident: full-time $4,948; part-time $206 per semester hour. Tuition, nonresident: full-time $19,140; part-time $408 per semester hour. *Financial support:* In 2006–07, 38 students received support, including 1 teaching assistantship (averaging $3,860 per year); career-related internships or fieldwork, Federal Work-Study, and tuition waivers (partial) also available. Support available to part-time students. Financial award application deadline: 4/1; financial award applicants required to submit FAFSA. *Faculty research:* Legal and ethical issues in working with minors in schools; gay, lesbian, bisexual, and transgender issues; collaboration between school counselors and classroom teachers; therapist distress and self care; school counselors as advocates for academic achievement. *Application contact:* Dr. David Whittinghill, Graduate Coordinator for Mental Health Counseling, 904-620-2838, E-mail: dwhittin@unf.edu.

University of North Texas, Robert B. Toulouse School of Graduate Studies, College of Education, Department of Counseling, Development and Higher Education, Program in Counseling, Denton, TX 76203. Offers counseling and student services (M Ed, MS, PhD); counselor education (MS). *Accreditation:* NCATE. Evening/weekend programs available. *Students:* 81 full-time (72 women), 245 part-time (201 women); includes 43 minority (21 African Americans, 1 American Indian/Alaska Native, 6 Asian Americans or Pacific Islanders, 15 Hispanic Americans), 17 international. Average age 30. 134 applicants, 38% accepted, 42 enrolled. In 2006, 101 master's, 8 doctorates awarded. *Degree requirements:* For master's, thesis optional; for doctorate, thesis/dissertation. *Entrance requirements:* For master's and doctorate, GRE General Test. Additional exam requirements/recommendations for international students: Recommended—TOEFL (minimum score 550 paper-based; 213 computer-based). *Application deadline:* For fall admission, 6/15 for domestic students; for spring admission, 11/15 for domestic students. Application fee: $50 ($75 for international students). *Expenses:* Tuition, state resident: full-time $3,573; part-time $198 per credit. Tuition, nonresident: full-time $8,577; part-time $476 per credit. Required fees: $1,258; $126 per credit. One-time fee: $150 full-time. Tuition and fees vary according to course load. *Financial support:* Teaching assistantships, career-related internships or fieldwork, Federal Work-Study, and institutionally sponsored loans available. Financial award application deadline: 4/1. *Application contact:* Jan Holden, Adviser, 940-565-2910, E-mail: holden@unt.edu.

University of Oklahoma, Graduate College, College of Education, Department of Educational Psychology, Program in School Counseling, Norman, OK 73019-0390. Offers M Ed. *Students:* 7 full-time (all women), 3 part-time (all women); includes 2 minority (1 African American, 1 American Indian/Alaska Native). 1 applicant, 0% accepted. In 2006, 5 degrees awarded. *Degree requirements:* For master's, comprehensive exam. *Entrance requirements:* For master's, GRE General Test, minimum GPA of 3.0. Additional exam requirements/recommendations for international students: Required—TOEFL (minimum score 550 paper-based; 213 computer-based). *Application deadline:* For fall admission, 1/31 for domestic students, 4/1 for international students. Applications are processed on a rolling basis. Application fee: $40 ($90 for international students). *Expenses:* Tuition, state resident: full-time $3,180; part-time $133 per credit hour. Tuition, nonresident: full-time $11,347; part-time $473 per credit hour. Required fees: $1,729; $62 per credit hour. $117 per semester. Tuition and fees vary according to course load and program. *Financial support:* In 2006–07, 8 students received support; research assistantships with partial tuition reimbursements available, teaching assistantships with partial tuition reimbursements available, Federal Work-Study, institutionally sponsored loans, scholarships/grants, and unspecified assistantships available. Financial award application deadline: 3/1; financial award applicants required to submit FAFSA. *Unit head:* Dr. Denise Beesley, Assistant Professor, 405-325-5974, Fax: 405-325-6655, E-mail: dbeesley@ou.edu. *Application contact:* Applications Officer, 405-325-4525, Fax: 405-325-6655, E-mail: gpoedpsych@ou.edu.

University of Phoenix–Southern Arizona Campus, The Artemis School, College of Education, Tucson, AZ 85712-2732. Offers curriculum instruction (MA Ed); educational counseling (MA Ed); elementary licensure (MA Ed); school counseling (MSC); secondary licensure (MA Ed); special education (Certificate). Evening/weekend programs available. *Faculty:* 101. *Students:* 75 full-time (55 women); includes 16 minority (2 African Americans, 1 American Indian/Alaska Native, 1 Asian American or Pacific Islander, 12 Hispanic Americans), 2 international. Average age 38. In 2006, 113 degrees awarded. *Degree requirements:* For master's, thesis (for some programs), registration. *Entrance requirements:* For master's, minimum undergraduate GPA of 2.5, 3 years of work experience. Additional exam requirements/recommendations for international students: Required—TOEFL (minimum score 550 paper-based; 213 computer-based; 79 iBT). *Application deadline:* Applications are processed on a rolling basis. Application fee: $45. Electronic applications accepted. *Expenses:* Tuition: Full-time $8,669. Required fees: $760. *Financial support:* Institutionally sponsored loans and scholarships/grants available. Financial award applicants required to submit FAFSA. *Unit head:* Dr. Marla LaRue, Dean/Executive Director, 480-557-1218, E-mail: marla.larue@phoenix.edu. *Application contact:* Campus College Chair, 520-881-6512, Fax: 520-795-6177.

University of Puerto Rico, Río Piedras, College of Education, Program in Guidance and Counseling, San Juan, PR 00931-3300. Offers M Ed, Ed D. Part-time programs available. *Students:* 44 full-time (37 women), 63 part-time (57 women); all minorities (all Hispanic Americans) Average age 25. In 2006, 8 master's, 2 doctorates awarded. *Degree requirements:* For master's, thesis; for doctorate, thesis/dissertation, internship. *Entrance requirements:* For master's, PAEG or GRE, interview, minimum GPA of 3.0, letter of recommendation; for doctorate, GRE or PAEG, master's degree, minimum GPA of 3.0, letter of recommendation (2), interview. *Application deadline:* For fall admission, 2/1 for domestic and international students. Application fee: $17. *Expenses:* Tuition, state resident: part-time $100 per credit. Tuition, nonresident: part-time $291 per credit. Required fees: $72 per semester. *Financial support:* Fellowships, research assistantships, teaching assistantships, career-related internships or fieldwork, Federal Work-Study, institutionally sponsored loans, and tuition waivers (partial) available. Financial award application deadline: 5/31. *Faculty research:* Graduation and retention rates-program evaluation. *Unit head:* Dr. Loyda Martinez, Coordinator, 787-764-0000 Ext. 4361, Fax: 787-763-4130.

University of Puget Sound, Graduate Studies, School of Education, Program in Education, Tacoma, WA 98416. Offers agency counseling (M Ed); counselor education (M Ed); pastoral counseling (M Ed). *Accreditation:* NCATE. Part-time programs available. *Faculty:* 2 full-time (both women), 1 (woman) part-time/adjunct. *Students:* 2 full-time (both women), 27 part-time (21 women); includes 7 minority (5 African Americans, 2 Asian Americans or Pacific Islanders), 1 international. Average age 31. 25 applicants, 48% accepted, 8 enrolled. In 2006, 19 degrees awarded. *Median time to degree:* Master's–1 year full-time, 2 years part-time. *Entrance requirements:* For master's, GRE General Test, minimum GPA of 3.0. Additional exam requirements/recommendations for international students: Required—TOEFL (minimum score 550 paper-based; 213 computer-based; 80 iBT). *Application deadline:* For fall admission, 3/1 priority date for domestic and international students. Applications are processed on a rolling basis. Application fee: $65. Electronic applications accepted. *Expenses:* *Contact institution.* Tuition and fees vary according to course load. *Financial support:* In 2006–07, 1 teaching assistantship with tuition reimbursement (averaging $12,250 per year) was awarded; career-related internships or fieldwork and tuition waivers (full) also available. Financial award application deadline: 3/31; financial award applicants required to submit FAFSA. *Faculty research:* Predictive use of test scores, cross-role professional preparation. *Application contact:* Dr. George H. Mills, Vice President for Enrollment, 253-879-3211, Fax: 253-879-3993, E-mail: admission@ups.edu.

University of Saint Francis, Graduate School, Department of Psychology and Counseling, Fort Wayne, IN 46808-3994. Offers general psychology (MS); mental health counseling (MS); pastoral counseling (MS); school counseling (MS Ed). Part-time and evening/weekend programs available. *Faculty:* 4 full-time (1 woman), 3 part-time/adjunct (0 women). *Students:* 28 full-time (24 women), 41 part-time (35 women); includes 7 minority (3 African Americans, 4 Hispanic Americans). Average age 35. 16 applicants, 88% accepted. In 2006, 8 degrees awarded. *Entrance requirements:* For master's, interview, minimum undergraduate GPA of 3.0. *Application deadline:* For fall admission, 7/1 for domestic students; for spring admission, 11/1 for domestic students. Applications are processed on a rolling basis. Application fee: $20. *Financial support:* In 2006–07, 4 students received support. Federal Work-Study, scholarships/grants, and unspecified assistantships available. *Unit head:* Dr. Rolf Daniel, Dean, 260-399-7700 Ext. 8403, Fax: 260-399-8170, E-mail: rdaniel@sf.edu. *Application contact:* Michelle Kuhlhorst, Admissions Counselor, 260-434-7748, Fax: 260-434-7590, E-mail: mkuhlhorst@st.edu.

University of San Diego, School of Leadership and Education Sciences, Program in Counseling, San Diego, CA 92110-2492. Offers MA. Part-time and evening/weekend programs available. *Faculty:* 5 full-time (2 women), 2 part-time/adjunct (both women). *Students:* 62 full-time (55 women), 24 part-time (20 women); includes 33 minority (1 American Indian/Alaska Native, 4 Asian Americans or Pacific Islanders, 28 Hispanic Americans). Average age 27. 97 applicants, 70% accepted, 34 enrolled. In 2006, 27 degrees awarded. *Degree requirements:* For master's, comprehensive exam. *Entrance requirements:* For master's, minimum GPA of 3.0, interview with faculty member. Additional exam requirements/recommendations for international students: Required—TOEFL (minimum score 580 paper-based; 237 computer-based), TWE. *Application deadline:* For fall admission, 3/1 priority date for domestic students. Applications are processed on a rolling basis. Application fee: $45. Electronic applications accepted. *Financial support:* Career-related internships or fieldwork, Federal Work-Study, institutionally sponsored loans, tuition waivers (partial), unspecified assistantships, and stipends available. Support available to part-time students. Financial award application deadline: 5/1; financial award applicants required to submit FAFSA. *Unit head:* Dr. Susan Zgliczynski, Graduate Program Director, 619-260-4287, Fax: 619-260-6835. *Application contact:* Stephen Pultz, Director of Admissions, 619-260-4524, Fax: 619-260-4158, E-mail: grads@sandiego.edu.

University of San Francisco, School of Education, Department of Counseling Psychology, San Francisco, CA 94117-1080. Offers counseling (MA), including educational counseling, life transitions counseling, marital and family therapy; counseling psychology (Ed D). *Faculty:* 7 full-time (3 women), 41 part-time/adjunct (27 women). *Students:* 225 full-time (185 women), 39 part-time (29 women); includes 89 minority (13 African Americans, 2 American Indian/Alaska Native, 31 Asian Americans or Pacific Islanders, 43 Hispanic Americans), 5 international. Average age 34. 281 applicants, 78% accepted, 108 enrolled. In 2006, 125 master's, 3 doctorates awarded. *Degree requirements:* For doctorate, thesis/dissertation. *Entrance requirements:* For doctorate, GRE General Test. Application fee: $55 ($65 for international students). *Expenses:* Tuition: Full-time $17,370; part-time $965 per unit. Tuition and fees vary according to degree level, campus/location and program. *Financial support:* In 2006–07, 194 students received support; fellowships, research assistantships, teaching assistantships available. Financial award application deadline: 3/2; financial award applicants required to submit FAFSA. *Unit head:* Dr. Brian Gerrard, Chair, 415-422-6868.

The University of Scranton, Graduate School, Department of Counseling and Human Services, Program in School Counseling, Scranton, PA 18510. Offers MS. *Accreditation:* ACA; NCATE. Part-time and evening/weekend programs available. *Students:* 51 full-time (44 women), 49 part-time (41 women); includes 3 minority (1 African American, 2 Hispanic Americans). Average age 27. 58 applicants, 91% accepted. In 2006, 30 degrees awarded. *Degree requirements:* For master's, capstone experience. *Entrance requirements:* For master's, minimum GPA of 2.75. Additional exam requirements/recommendations for international students: Required—TOEFL (minimum score 500 paper-based; 173 computer-based), IELTS (minimum score 6). *Application deadline:* For fall admission, 3/1 for domestic students. Application fee: $50. *Expenses:* Tuition: Part-time $684 per credit. Required fees: $25 per term. *Financial support:* Teaching assistantships, career-related internships or fieldwork and Federal Work-Study available. Support available to part-time students. Financial award application deadline: 3/1. *Unit head:* Dr. Lee Ann M. Eschbach, Director, 570-941-6299, Fax: 570-941-4201, E-mail: eschbach@scranton.edu.

University of South Alabama, Graduate School, College of Education, Department of Professional Studies, Mobile, AL 36688-0002. Offers community counseling (MS); educational media (M Ed, MS); instructional design and development (MS, PhD); rehabilitation counseling (MS); school counseling (M Ed); school psychometry (M Ed). *Accreditation:* NCATE. Part-time programs available. *Faculty:* 19 full-time (7 women). *Students:* 131 full-time (106 women), 192 part-time (155 women); includes 83 minority (74 African Americans, 5 American Indian/Alaska Native, 3 Asian Americans or Pacific Islanders, 1 Hispanic American), 10 international. 98 applicants, 69% accepted, 38 enrolled. In 2006, 59 master's, 2 doctorates awarded. *Degree requirements:* For master's, comprehensive exam. *Entrance requirements:* For master's, GRE General Test or MAT, minimum GPA of 3.0. *Application deadline:* For fall admission, 9/1 priority date for domestic students. Applications are processed on a rolling basis. Application fee: $25. *Financial support:* In 2006–07, 5 research assistantships were awarded; career-related internships or fieldwork also available. Support available to part-time students. Financial award application deadline: 4/1. *Faculty research:* Agency counseling, rehabilitation counseling, school psychometry. *Unit head:* Dr. Charles Guest, Chair, 251-380-2861.

University of South Carolina, The Graduate School, College of Education, Department of Educational Studies, Program in Counseling Education, Columbia, SC 29208. Offers PhD, Ed S. *Accreditation:* ACA (one or more programs are accredited); NCATE. *Degree requirements:* For doctorate, one foreign language, thesis/dissertation, comprehensive exam. *Entrance requirements:* For doctorate and Ed S, GRE General Test or MAT, interview. Electronic applications accepted. *Faculty research:* Multicultural counseling, children's fears, career development, family counseling.

The University of South Dakota, Graduate School, School of Education, Division of Counseling and Psychology in Education, Vermillion, SD 57069-2390. Offers MA, PhD, Ed S. *Accreditation:* ACA (one or more programs are accredited); NCATE. Part-time programs available. *Faculty:* 14 full-time (7 women), 2 part-time/adjunct (1 woman). *Students:* 135 (102 women). In 2006, 20 master's, 3 doctorates, 7 other advanced degrees awarded. *Degree requirements:* For master's and Ed S, thesis or alternative, comprehensive exam; for doctorate, thesis/dissertation, comprehensive exam. *Entrance requirements:* For master's and doctorate, GRE General Test, minimum GPA of 3.0. Additional exam requirements/recommendations for international students: Required—TOEFL (minimum score 550 paper-based; 213 computer-based; 79 iBT). *Application deadline:* Applications are processed on a rolling basis. Application fee: $35. Electronic applications accepted. *Expenses:* Tuition, state resident: part-time $120 per credit hour. Tuition, nonresident: part-time $355 per credit hour. Required fees: $90 per credit hour. *Financial support:* In 2006–07, research assistantships with partial tuition reimbursements (averaging $4,626 per year), teaching assistantships with partial tuition reimbursements (averaging $4,626 per year) were awarded; career-related internships or fieldwork, Federal Work-Study, and unspecified assistantships also available. Financial award applicants required to submit FAFSA. *Unit head:* Dr. Frank Main, Chair, 605-677-5250, Fax: 605-677-5438, E-mail: fmain@usd.edu.

University of Southern Maine, College of Education and Human Development, Program in Counselor Education, Portland, ME 04104-9300. Offers counseling (MS, CAS); mental health rehabilitation technician/community (Certificate). *Accreditation:* ACA (one or more programs are accredited); CORE; NCATE. Part-time and evening/weekend programs available. *Faculty:* 7 full-time (5 women), 2 part-time/adjunct (both women). *Students:* 42 full-time (36 women), 66 part-time (51 women); includes 1 minority (Asian American or Pacific Islander) 121 applicants, 49% accepted, 39 enrolled. In 2006, 31 master's, 3 other advanced degrees awarded. *Degree requirements:* For master's, thesis or alternative, comprehensive exam; for other advanced degree, thesis or alternative. *Entrance requirements:* For master's, GRE General Test or MAT, interview; for other advanced degree, master's degree. *Application deadline:* For fall admission, 2/1 for domestic students. Application fee: $50. Electronic applications accepted. *Expenses:* Tuition, state resident: full-time $4,860; part-time $270 per credit hour. Tuition, nonresident: full-time $13,572; part-time $754 per credit hour. Required fees: $222 per semester. Tuition and fees vary according to course load. *Financial support:* In 2006–07, 19 students received support, including 9 research assistantships with tuition reimbursements available (averaging $4,500 per year); career-related internships or fieldwork, Federal Work-Study, institutionally sponsored loans, scholarships/grants, and unspecified assistantships also available. Support available to part-time students. Financial award application deadline: 3/1; financial award applicants required to submit FAFSA. *Faculty research:* Counselor licensure. *Unit head:* Dr. E. Michael Brady, Chair, Human Resource Development Department, 207-780-5316, Fax: 207-780-5043, E-mail: mbrady@usm.maine.edu. *Application contact:* Robin Audesse, Associate Director of Graduate Admissions, 207-780-5306, Fax: 207-780-5193, E-mail: raudesse@usm.maine.edu.

University of South Florida, Graduate School, College of Education, Department of Psychological and Social Foundations of Education, Program in Counselor Education, Tampa, FL 33620-9951. Offers MA, PhD. *Accreditation:* ACA. *Students:* 57 full-time (51 women), 62 part-time (57 women); includes 25 minority (12 African Americans, 3 Asian Americans or Pacific Islanders, 10 Hispanic Americans), 2 international. 121 applicants, 48% accepted, 44 enrolled. In 2006, 37 degrees awarded. *Entrance requirements:* For master's, GRE General Test, minimum GPA of 3.0 in last 60 hours of coursework. *Application deadline:* For fall admission, 3/1 for domestic students. Application fee: $30. *Unit head:* Herbert A. Exum, Coordinator, 813-974-3515, Fax: 813-974-5814, E-mail: counseled@coedu.usf.edu. *Application contact:* Sandy Turner, Program Assistant, 813-974-3515, Fax: 813-974-5814.

The University of Tennessee, Graduate School, College of Education, Health and Human Sciences, Department of Educational Psychology and Counseling, Knoxville, TN 37996. Offers adult education (MS); applied educational psychology (MS); collaborative learning (Ed D); college student personnel (MS); mental health counseling (MS); rehabilitation counseling (MS); school counseling (MS). *Accreditation:* ACA (one or more programs are accredited); CORE (one or more programs are accredited); NCATE. Part-time and evening/weekend programs available. *Students:* 27 (20 women); includes 2 African Americans, 1 American Indian/Alaska Native 1 international. 69 applicants, 33% accepted. In 2006, 36 degrees awarded. *Degree requirements:* For master's, thesis optional. *Entrance requirements:* For master's, GRE General Test, minimum GPA of 2.7. Additional exam requirements/recommendations for international students: Required—TOEFL. *Application deadline:* For fall admission, 2/1 priority date for domestic students. Applications are processed on a rolling basis. Application fee: $35. Electronic applications accepted. *Expenses:* Tuition, state resident: full-time $5,574. Tuition, nonresident: full-time $16,840. Required fees: $792. *Financial support:* In 2006–07, 1 research assistantship, 2 teaching assistantships were awarded. Financial award application deadline: 2/1; financial award applicants required to submit FAFSA. *Unit head:* Dr. Olga Welch, Head, 865-974-5131, Fax: 865-974-8674, E-mail: owelch@utk.edu.

The University of Tennessee, Graduate School, College of Education, Health and Human Sciences, Program in Education, Knoxville, TN 37996. Offers art education (MS); counseling education (PhD); cultural studies in education (PhD); curriculum (MS, Ed S); curriculum, educational research and evaluation (Ed D, PhD); early childhood education (PhD); early childhood special education (MS); education of deaf and hard of hearing (MS); educational administration and policy studies (Ed D, PhD); educational administration and supervision (Ed S); educational psychology (Ed D, PhD); elementary education (MS, Ed S); elementary teaching (MS); English education (MS, Ed S); exercise science (PhD); foreign language/ESL education (MS, Ed S); instructional technology (MS, Ed D, PhD, Ed S); literacy, language and ESL education (PhD); literacy, language education, and ESL education (Ed D); mathematics education (MS, Ed S); modified and comprehensive special education (MS); reading education (MS, Ed S); school counseling (Ed S); school psychology (PhD, Ed S); science education (MS, Ed S); secondary teaching (MS); social foundations (MS); social science education (MS, Ed S); socio-cultural foundations of sports and education (PhD); special education (Ed S); teacher education (Ed D, PhD). *Accreditation:* NCATE. Part-time and evening/weekend programs available. *Students:* 529 (401 women); includes 39 minority (23 African Americans, 2 American Indian/Alaska Native, 9 Asian Americans or Pacific Islanders, 5 Hispanic Americans) 34 international. 420 applicants, 50% accepted. In 2006, 258 master's, 28 doctorates awarded. *Degree requirements:* For master's and Ed S, thesis optional; for doctorate, variable foreign language requirement, thesis/dissertation. *Entrance requirements:* For master's, minimum GPA of 2.7; for doctorate and Ed S, GRE General Test, minimum GPA of 2.7. Additional exam requirements/recommendations for international students: Required—TOEFL. *Application deadline:* For fall admission, 2/1 priority date for domestic students. Applications are processed on a rolling basis. Application fee: $35. Electronic applications accepted. *Expenses:* Tuition, state resident: full-time $5,574. Tuition, nonresident: full-time $16,840. Required fees: $792. *Financial support:* In 2006–07, 4 fellowships, 9 teaching assistantships were awarded; career-related internships or fieldwork, Federal Work-Study, institutionally sponsored loans, and unspecified assistantships also available. Financial award application deadline: 2/1; financial award applicants required to submit FAFSA. *Unit head:* Dr. Lester Knight, Head, 865-974-0907, Fax: 865-974-8718, E-mail: lknight@utk.edu.

The University of Tennessee at Chattanooga, Graduate School, College of Health, Education and Professional Studies, Graduate Studies Division of Education, Chattanooga, TN 37403-2598. Offers counseling (M Ed); educational leadership (Ed D); educational specialist (Ed S), including educational technology, school psychology; elementary education (M Ed); school leadership (M Ed); secondary education (M Ed); special education (M Ed). *Accreditation:* ACA; NCATE. Part-time and evening/weekend programs available. *Faculty:* 28 full-time (18 women), 7 part-time/adjunct (3 women). *Students:* 166 full-time (123 women), 309 part-time (238 women); includes 57 minority (46 African Americans, 2 American Indian/Alaska Native, 7 Asian Americans or Pacific Islanders, 2 Hispanic Americans). Average age 33. 138 applicants, 95% accepted, 66 enrolled. In 2006, 133 master's, 25 other advanced degrees awarded. *Degree requirements:* For master's, thesis optional; for doctorate, thesis/dissertation, comprehensive exam. *Entrance requirements:* For master's, GRE General Test or MAT, teaching certificate. *Application deadline:* For fall admission, 8/1 for domestic students; for spring admission, 12/1 for domestic students. Applications are processed on a rolling basis. Application fee: $30. *Expenses:* Tuition, state resident: full-time $5,434; part-time $339 per hour. Tuition, nonresident: full-time $14,830; part-time $861 per hour. Required fees: $940; $178 per hour. *Financial support:* Fellowships, research assistantships, Federal Work-Study and institutionally sponsored loans available. Support available to part-time students. Financial award application deadline: 4/1; financial award applicants required to submit FAFSA. *Faculty research:* School counseling, community counseling, elementary and secondary education, school leadership and administration. Total annual research expenditures: $258,901. *Unit head:* Dr. Anthony Lease, Head, 423-425-4211, Fax: 423-425-5380, E-mail: tony-lease@utc.edu. *Application contact:* Dr. Deborah E. Arfken, Dean of Graduate Studies, 423-425-4666, Fax: 423-425-5223, E-mail: deborah-arfken@utc.edu.

The University of Tennessee at Martin, Graduate Programs, College of Education and Behavioral Sciences, Programs in Counseling, Martin, TN 38238-1000. Offers mental health (MS Ed); school counseling (MS Ed). *Accreditation:* NCATE. Part-time programs available. *Students:* 56 (49 women); includes 15 African Americans. 29 applicants, 45% accepted, 9

Counselor Education

The University of Tennessee at Martin (continued)

enrolled. In 2006, 19 degrees awarded. *Degree requirements:* For master's, comprehensive exam. *Entrance requirements:* For master's, GRE General Test, minimum GPA of 2.5, resumé, letters of reference. Additional exam requirements/recommendations for international students: Required—TOEFL (minimum score 525 paper-based; 197 computer-based). *Application deadline:* For fall admission, 8/1 priority date for domestic students, 8/1 for international students; for spring admission, 1/1 priority date for domestic students, 1/1 for international students. Applications are processed on a rolling basis. Application fee: $30 ($50 for international students). Electronic applications accepted. *Expenses:* Tuition, state resident: part-time $303 per credit hour. Tuition, nonresident: part-time $829 per credit hour. *Financial support:* Career-related internships or fieldwork, scholarships/grants, tuition waivers (partial), and unspecified assistantships available. Support available to part-time students. Financial award application deadline: 3/1. *Unit head:* Dr. Suzanne Maniss, Coordinator, 731-881-7163, Fax: 731-881-7975, E-mail: smaniss@utm.edu.

The University of Texas at Austin, Graduate School, College of Education, Department of Educational Psychology, Austin, TX 78712-1111. Offers academic educational psychology (M Ed, MA); counseling education (M Ed); counseling psychology (PhD); human development and education (PhD); learning cognition and instruction (PhD); quantitative methods (PhD); school psychology (PhD). *Accreditation:* APA (one or more programs are accredited). *Degree requirements:* For master's, thesis optional; for doctorate, thesis/dissertation. *Entrance requirements:* For master's and doctorate, GRE General Test, 3 letters of recommendation. Additional exam requirements/recommendations for international students: Required—TOEFL.

The University of Texas at Brownsville, Graduate Studies, School of Education, Brownsville, TX 78520-4991. Offers bilingual education (M Ed); counseling and guidance (M Ed); curriculum and instruction (M Ed); early childhood education (M Ed); educational administration (M Ed); educational technology (M Ed); English as a second language (M Ed); reading specialist (M Ed); special education/educational diagnostician (M Ed). Part-time and evening/weekend programs available. Postbaccalaureate distance learning degree programs offered (minimal on-campus study). *Degree requirements:* For master's, thesis optional. *Entrance requirements:* For master's, GRE General Test. Additional exam requirements/recommendations for international students: Required—TOEFL.

The University of Texas at San Antonio, College of Education and Human Development, Department of Counseling, Educational Psychology, and Adult and Higher Education, San Antonio, TX 78249-0617. Offers counseling (MA); counselor education (PhD); education-adult and higher education (MA). Part-time programs available. *Faculty:* 17 full-time (9 women), 16 part-time/adjunct (4 women). *Students:* 154 full-time (125 women), 403 part-time (354 women); includes 299 minority (42 African Americans, 2 American Indian/Alaska Native, 7 Asian Americans or Pacific Islanders, 248 Hispanic Americans), 4 international. Average age 33. 210 applicants, 85% accepted, 172 enrolled. In 2006, 140 degrees awarded. *Degree requirements:* For master's, thesis optional. *Entrance requirements:* For master's, GRE General Test. Additional exam requirements/recommendations for international students: Required—TOEFL (minimum score 500 paper-based; 173 computer-based). *Application deadline:* For fall admission, 7/1 for domestic students, 4/1 for international students; for spring admission, 11/1 for domestic students, 9/1 for international students. Applications are processed on a rolling basis. Application fee: $45 ($80 for international students). Electronic applications accepted. *Expenses:* Tuition, state resident: full-time $1,730; part-time $192 per credit hour. Tuition, nonresident: full-time $6,680; part-time $742 per credit hour. Required fees: $733; $308,359 per credit hour. *Financial support:* In 2006–07, 1 research assistantship (averaging $18,720 per year) was awarded; career-related internships or fieldwork, Federal Work-Study, scholarships/grants, and unspecified assistantships also available. *Faculty research:* Early childhood, reading, special education, foundations, curriculum and instruction. *Unit head:* Dr. Marcheta P. Evans, Chair, 210-458-2600, Fax: 210-458-2605, E-mail: mevans@utsa.edu.

The University of Texas of the Permian Basin, Office of Graduate Studies, School of Education, Program in Counseling, Odessa, TX 79762-0001. Offers MA. *Degree requirements:* For master's, thesis (for some programs), comprehensive exam (for some programs), registration. *Entrance requirements:* For master's, GRE General Test. Additional exam requirements/recommendations for international students: Required—TOEFL (minimum score 550 paper-based; 213 computer-based).

The University of Texas–Pan American, College of Education, Department of Educational Psychology, Edinburg, TX 78541-2999. Offers counseling (M Ed); educational diagnostician (M Ed); gifted education (M Ed); school psychology (MA); special education (M Ed). Part-time and evening/weekend programs available. *Degree requirements:* For master's, thesis (for some programs), comprehensive exam (for some programs). *Entrance requirements:* For master's, GRE General Test, interview. *Expenses:* Tuition, state resident: full-time $2,577; part-time $143 per credit hour. Tuition, nonresident: full-time $7,527; part-time $418 per credit hour. Required fees: $561. *Faculty research:* Reading instruction, assessment practice, behavior interventions consultation, mental retardation.

University of the District of Columbia, College of Arts and Sciences, Department of Psychology and Counseling, Washington, DC 20008-1175. Offers clinical psychology (MS); counseling (MS). *Students:* 16 full-time (9 women), 20 part-time (13 women); includes 32 minority (26 African Americans, 2 Asian Americans or Pacific Islanders, 4 Hispanic Americans). Average age 31. *Degree requirements:* For master's, seminar paper, thesis optional. *Entrance requirements:* For master's, GRE General Test, writing proficiency exam. *Application deadline:* For fall admission, 6/15 priority date for domestic students; for spring admission, 11/1 for domestic students. Applications are processed on a rolling basis. Application fee: $20. *Unit head:* Dr. Eugene Johnson, Chairperson, 202-274-7406. *Application contact:* LaVerne Hill Flannigan, Director of Admission, 202-274-6069.

The University of Toledo, College of Graduate Studies, College of Health Science and Human Service, Division of Human Services, Toledo, OH 43606-3390. Offers counselor education and school psychology (MA, PhD, Ed S), including counselor education, guidance/counselor education (PhD), school psychology (MA, Ed S); criminal justice (MA, Certificate), including criminal justice (MA), juvenile justice (Certificate), severe behavioral spectrum (Certificate); health education (PhD); kinesiology (MSX, PhD), including exercise science; public health and rehabilitative services (MA, MPH), including public health (MPH), speech language pathology (MA); recreation and leisure (MA); social work (MS); speech-language pathology (MA). *Students:* 398 full-time (319 women), 270 part-time (194 women); includes 78 minority (60 African Americans, 8 Asian Americans or Pacific Islanders, 10 Hispanic Americans), 23 international. 641 applicants, 51% accepted, 246 enrolled.Application fee: $45. *Unit head:* Dr. Jerome M. Sulivan, Dean, College of Health Science and Human Service, 419-530-4180.

The University of Toledo, College of Graduate Studies, College of Health Science and Human Service, Division of Human Services, Department of Counselor Education and School Psychology, Program in Counselor Education, Toledo, OH 43606-3390. Offers community counseling (MA); counselor education (Ed S); counselor education and supervision (PhD). *Students:* 32 full-time (26 women), 59 part-time (51 women); includes 13 minority (12 African Americans, 1 Hispanic American), 2 international. Average age 33. 40 applicants, 40% accepted, 14 enrolled. In 2006, 29 master's, 8 doctorates awarded. *Financial support:* In 2006–07, 9 teaching assistantships with tuition reimbursements (averaging $12,000 per year) were awarded. *Unit head:* Dr. Jane A. Cox, Chair, Department of Counselor Education and School Psychology, 419-530-4311.

The University of Toledo, College of Graduate Studies, College of Health Science and Human Service, Division of Human Services, Department of Counselor Education and School Psychology, Program in School Psychology, Toledo, OH 43606-3390. Offers school counseling (MA); school psychology (Ed S). *Students:* 18 full-time (17 women), 10 part-time (8 women); includes 3 minority (all African Americans) Average age 28. 30 applicants, 53% accepted, 15 enrolled. In 2006, 10 master's, 8 Ed Ss awarded. *Entrance requirements:* For master's, GRE. *Application deadline:* For fall admission, 3/1 priority date for domestic students. Application fee: $45. *Unit head:* Dr. Paula Dupuy, Chair, 419-530-4064, E-mail: pdupuy@utnet.utoledo.edu. *Application contact:* Wendy Luellen, 419-530-2013, E-mail: wendy.luellen@utoledo.edu.

University of Utah, The Graduate School, College of Education, Department of Educational Psychology, Salt Lake City, UT 84112-1107. Offers counseling psychology (PhD); educational psychology (MA); professional counseling (MS); professional psychology (M Ed); school counseling (M Ed, MS); statistics (M Stat). *Accreditation:* APA (one or more programs are accredited). Evening/weekend programs available. *Faculty:* 16 full-time (7 women), 9 part-time/adjunct (3 women). *Students:* 83 full-time (55 women), 90 part-time (59 women); includes 24 minority (3 African Americans, 6 American Indian/Alaska Native, 3 Asian Americans or Pacific Islanders, 12 Hispanic Americans), 4 international. Average age 32. 166 applicants, 45% accepted, 32 enrolled. In 2006, 44 master's, 14 doctorates awarded. *Degree requirements:* For master's, variable foreign language requirement, thesis (for some programs), comprehensive exam; for doctorate, variable foreign language requirement, thesis/dissertation, oral exam. *Entrance requirements:* For master's and doctorate, GRE General Test, minimum GPA of 3.0. Additional exam requirements/recommendations for international students: Required—TOEFL (minimum score 500 paper-based; 173 computer-based). *Application deadline:* For fall admission, 4/1 for domestic and international students; for spring admission, 11/1 for domestic and international students. Applications are processed on a rolling basis. Application fee: $45 ($65 for international students). Electronic applications accepted. *Expenses:* Tuition, state resident: full-time $3,208. Tuition, nonresident: full-time $11,326. Required fees: $608. Tuition and fees vary according to class time and program. *Financial support:* Fellowships with full tuition reimbursements, research assistantships with full tuition reimbursements, teaching assistantships with partial tuition reimbursements, career-related internships or fieldwork, Federal Work-Study, institutionally sponsored loans, scholarships/grants, and unspecified assistantships available. Financial award application deadline: 2/1; financial award applicants required to submit FAFSA. *Faculty research:* Autism, computer technology and instruction, cognitive behavior, aging, group counseling. Total annual research expenditures: $37,452. *Unit head:* Dr. Robert D. Hill, Chair, 801-581-7148, Fax: 801-581-5566, E-mail: bob.hill@ed.utah.edu. *Application contact:* Sherrill Christensen, Academic Program Specialist, 801-581-7148, Fax: 801-581-5566, E-mail: sherrill.christensen@ed.utah.edu.

University of Vermont, Graduate College, College of Education and Social Services, Department of Integrated Professional Studies, Counseling Program, Burlington, VT 05405. Offers MS. *Accreditation:* ACA; NCATE. *Faculty:* 3 full-time (2 women), 6 part-time/adjunct (2 women). *Students:* 52 (38 women); includes 2 minority (1 American Indian/Alaska Native, 1 Hispanic American). 71 applicants, 62% accepted, 19 enrolled. In 2006, 14 degrees awarded. *Entrance requirements:* For master's, GRE General Test, resumé. Additional exam requirements/recommendations for international students: Required—TOEFL (minimum score 550 paper-based; 213 computer-based). *Application deadline:* For fall admission, 2/1 priority date for domestic students. Applications are processed on a rolling basis. Application fee: $40. Electronic applications accepted. *Expenses:* Tuition, state resident: part-time $434 per credit. Tuition, nonresident: part-time $1,096 per credit. *Financial support:* Fellowships, research assistantships, teaching assistantships available. Financial award application deadline: 2/1. *Faculty research:* Women and tenure, counseling children and adolescents. *Unit head:* Dr. Eric C. Nichols, Coordinator, 802-656-3888, Fax: 802-656-3173, E-mail: ecnichol@zoo.uvm.edu.

University of Victoria, Faculty of Graduate Studies, Faculty of Education, Department of Educational Psychology and Leadership Studies, Victoria, BC V8W 2Y2, Canada. Offers counseling (M Ed, MA); educational psychology (M Ed, MA, PhD), including counseling psychology (M Ed, MA), learning and development (PhD), learning development (MA), measurement and evaluation (PhD), measurement evaluation (M Ed, MA), special education (M Ed, MA); leadership studies (M Ed, MA). Part-time programs available. *Degree requirements:* For master's, thesis (for some programs), comprehensive exam (M Ed); for doctorate, thesis/dissertation, candidacy exam, comprehensive exam, registration. *Entrance requirements:* For master's, 2 years of work experience in a relevant field, minimum B average; for doctorate, GRE, 2 years of work experience in a relevant field, minimum B average. Additional exam requirements/recommendations for international students: Required—TOEFL (minimum score 575 paper-based; 233 computer-based), IELTS (minimum score 7). *Faculty research:* Learning and development (child, adolescent and adult), special education and exceptional children, evaluation and measurement.

University of Virginia, Curry School of Education, Department of Human Services, Program in Counselor Education, Charlottesville, VA 22903. Offers M Ed, Ed D, Ed S. *Accreditation:* ACA (one or more programs are accredited). *Students:* 48 full-time (44 women), 4 part-time (3 women); includes 7 minority (3 African Americans, 3 Asian Americans or Pacific Islanders, 1 Hispanic American), 1 international. Average age 26. 121 applicants, 54% accepted, 23 enrolled. In 2006, 26 degrees awarded. *Degree requirements:* For master's, comprehensive exam; for doctorate, thesis/dissertation, comprehensive exam. *Entrance requirements:* For master's, doctorate, and Ed S, GRE General Test. Additional exam requirements/recommendations for international students: Required—TOEFL (minimum score 600 paper-based; 250 computer-based). *Application deadline:* Applications are processed on a rolling basis. Application fee: $60. Electronic applications accepted. *Financial support:* Fellowships with tuition reimbursements available. Financial award applicants required to submit FAFSA. *Unit head:* Harriet Glossof, Associate Professor and Director, 434-243-8717. *Application contact:* Ila Crawford, Information Contact, 434-924-0772.

University of Washington, Graduate School, College of Education, Program in Educational Psychology, Seattle, WA 98195. Offers human development and cognition (M Ed, PhD); measurement and research (M Ed, PhD); school counseling (M Ed, PhD); school psychology (M Ed, PhD). *Accreditation:* APA. *Degree requirements:* For master's, thesis optional; for doctorate, thesis/dissertation. *Entrance requirements:* For master's and doctorate, GRE General Test, minimum GPA of 3.0. Additional exam requirements/recommendations for international students: Required—TOEFL.

The University of West Alabama, School of Graduate Studies, College of Education, Department of Teacher Education, Program in Guidance and Counseling, Livingston, AL 35470. Offers continuing education (MSCE); guidance and counseling (M Ed). *Accreditation:* NCATE. Part-time and evening/weekend programs available. *Faculty:* 3 full-time, 16 part-time/adjunct. *Students:* 477 full-time (411 women), 529 part-time (459 women); includes 460 minority (436 African Americans, 5 American Indian/Alaska Native, 10 Asian Americans or Pacific Islanders, 9 Hispanic Americans), 1 international. Average age 25. 10 applicants, 100% accepted. In 2006, 116 degrees awarded. *Entrance requirements:* For master's, GRE General Test, MAT, minimum GPA of 2.75. *Application deadline:* For fall admission, 9/10 priority date for domestic students; for spring admission, 3/21 for domestic students. Applications are processed on a rolling basis. Application fee: $20 ($50 for international students). *Financial support:* Career-related internships or fieldwork, Federal Work-Study, scholarships/grants, and unspecified assistantships available. Support available to part-time students.

The University of Western Ontario, Faculty of Graduate Studies, Social Sciences Division, Faculty of Education, Program in Counseling, London, ON N6A 5B8, Canada. Offers M Ed. Part-time programs available. *Entrance requirements:* For master's, minimum B average. *Application deadline:* For fall admission, 2/1 for domestic students. Application fee: $50. *Financial support:* Research assistantships, teaching assistantships, career-related internships or fieldwork available. Financial award application deadline: 4/1. *Faculty research:* Women's issues in counseling, causes for sexual harassment in the workplace, counselor memory and confidence in clinical judgements. *Unit head:* Allan Pitman, Graduate Chair, 519-661-2111 Ext. 88870, Fax: 519-661-3833, E-mail: pitman@uwo.ca. *Application contact:* L. Kulak, Graduate Supervisor, 519-661-2099, Fax: 519-661-3833, E-mail: kulak@edu.uwo.ca.

University of West Florida, College of Professional Studies, Division of Teacher Education, Master's Program in Curriculum and Instruction, Specialization in Guidance and Counseling,

Pensacola, FL 32514-5750. Offers M Ed. *Students:* 5 full-time (3 women), 8 part-time (7 women); includes 2 minority (1 African American, 1 American Indian/Alaska Native). Average age 26. 1 applicant, 100% accepted, 1 enrolled. In 2006, 6 degrees awarded. *Degree requirements:* For master's, thesis or alternative. *Entrance requirements:* Additional exam requirements/recommendations for international students: Required—TOEFL (minimum score 550 paper-based; 213 computer-based). *Application deadline:* For fall admission, 6/1 for domestic students, 5/15 for international students; for spring admission, 11/1 for domestic students, 10/1 for international students. Applications are processed on a rolling basis. Application fee: $30. *Expenses:* Tuition, state resident: full-time $5,871; part-time $245 per credit hour. Tuition, nonresident: full-time $21,241; part-time $885 per credit hour. *Financial support:* Fellowships, Federal Work-Study, scholarships/grants, and unspecified assistantships available.

University of West Georgia, Graduate School, College of Education, Department of Counseling and Educational Psychology, Carrollton, GA 30118. Offers counseling and guidance (M Ed, Ed S). *Accreditation:* ACA; NCATE. Part-time programs available. *Faculty:* 10 full-time (7 women), 2 part-time/adjunct (1 woman). *Students:* 52 full-time (47 women), 117 part-time (103 women); includes 51 minority (49 African Americans, 1 Asian American or Pacific Islander, 1 Hispanic American), 1 international. Average age 26. 49 applicants, 69% accepted, 34 enrolled. In 2006, 41 master's, 13 other advanced degrees awarded. *Degree requirements:* For master's, comprehensive exam; for Ed S, research project. *Entrance requirements:* For master's, GRE General Test, minimum GPA of 2.7, interview, letter of reference; for Ed S, GRE General Test, master's degree, minimum graduate GPA of 3.25, letter of reference. Additional exam requirements/recommendations for international students: Required—TOEFL. *Application deadline:* For fall admission, 6/1 for domestic and international students; for spring admission, 10/15 for domestic students, 10/5 for international students. Application fee: $20. *Expenses:* Tuition, state resident: full-time $2,286; part-time $127 per credit. Tuition, nonresident: full-time $9,144; part-time $508 per credit. Required fees: $494; $27 per credit. $121 per semester. *Financial support:* In 2006–07, 3 research assistantships with full tuition reimbursements (averaging $4,000 per year) were awarded; career-related internships or fieldwork, scholarships/grants, and unspecified assistantships also available. Support available to part-time students. Financial award applicants required to submit FAFSA. *Faculty research:* Academic and career development counseling, professional and ethical issues, transforming school counseling. *Unit head:* Dr. Brent M. Snow, Chair, 678-839-6554, Fax: 678-839-6099, E-mail: bsnow@westga.edu. *Application contact:* Dr. Charles W. Clark, Chair, 678-839-6508, E-mail: cclark@westga.edu.

University of Wisconsin–Madison, Graduate School, School of Education, Department of Counseling Psychology, Program in Counseling, Madison, WI 53706-1380. Offers MS. *Entrance requirements:* For master's, GRE General Test. *Application deadline:* For fall admission, 12/15 for domestic and international students. Application fee: $45. Electronic applications accepted. *Financial support:* Fellowships with full tuition reimbursements, research assistantships with full tuition reimbursements, teaching assistantships with full tuition reimbursements, project assistantships available. *Unit head:* Dr. Mary Lee Nelson, Chair, Department of Counseling Psychology, 608-263-3753.

University of Wisconsin–Oshkosh, The School of Graduate Studies, College of Education and Human Services, Department of Counselor Education, Oshkosh, WI 54901. Offers counseling (MSE). *Accreditation:* ACA; NCATE. Part-time and evening/weekend programs available. *Degree requirements:* For master's, practicum, thesis optional. *Entrance requirements:* For master's, interview, minimum GPA of 3.0, letters of recommendation. Additional exam requirements/recommendations for international students: Required—TOEFL (minimum score 550 paper-based; 213 computer-based). Electronic applications accepted. *Faculty research:* Gender issues, grief and loss, addictions, career development, close relationships.

University of Wisconsin–Platteville, School of Graduate Studies, College of Liberal Arts and Education, Counselor Education Program, Platteville, WI 53818-3099. Offers MSE. *Accreditation:* NCATE. Part-time programs available. *Faculty:* 5 full-time (2 women). *Students:* 45 full-time (39 women), 23 part-time (18 women); includes 1 minority (African American) 42 applicants, 40% accepted. In 2006, 27 degrees awarded. *Degree requirements:* For master's, thesis or alternative, comprehensive exam, registration. *Entrance requirements:* Additional exam requirements/recommendations for international students: Required—TOEFL (minimum score 500 paper-based). *Application deadline:* For fall admission, 7/1 priority date for domestic students; for spring admission, 11/1 for domestic students. Applications are processed on a rolling basis. Application fee: $45. Electronic applications accepted. *Expenses:* Tuition, state resident: part-time $365 per credit. Tuition, nonresident: part-time $955 per credit. *Financial support:* Research assistantships with partial tuition reimbursements, career-related internships or fieldwork, Federal Work-Study, institutionally sponsored loans, scholarships/grants, and unspecified assistantships available. Support available to part-time students. *Unit head:* Dr. Dominic Barraclough, Coordinator, 608-342-1252, Fax: 608-342-1986, E-mail: barracld@uwplatt.edu. *Application contact:* Kristal Prohaska, Admissions and Enrollment Management, 608-342-1125, Fax: 608-342-1122, E-mail: admit@uwplatt.edu.

University of Wisconsin–River Falls, Outreach and Graduate Studies, College of Education and Professional Studies, Department of Counseling and School Psychology, River Falls, WI 54022-5001. Offers counseling (MSE); school psychology (MSE, Ed S). *Accreditation:* NCATE. Part-time programs available. *Entrance requirements:* For master's, minimum GPA of 2.75, resumé, 3 letters of reference. Electronic applications accepted.

University of Wisconsin–Stevens Point, College of Professional Studies, School of Education, Program in Guidance and Counseling, Stevens Point, WI 54481-3897. Offers MSE. *Degree requirements:* For master's, thesis or alternative, comprehensive exam. *Application deadline:* Applications are processed on a rolling basis. Application fee: $45. *Expenses:* Tuition, state resident: full-time $5,910; part-time $328 per credit. Tuition, nonresident: full-time $16,520; part-time $918 per credit. Required fees: $756; $73 per credit. *Financial support:* Application deadline: 5/1. *Application contact:* Dr. Patricia Caro, Director, 715-346-4403, Fax: 715-346-4846, E-mail: pcaro@uwsp.edu.

University of Wisconsin–Superior, Graduate Division, Department of Counseling and Psychological Professions, Superior, WI 54880-4500. Offers community counseling (MSE); elementary school counseling (MSE); human relations (MSE); secondary school counseling (MSE). *Accreditation:* ACA. Part-time and evening/weekend programs available. *Degree requirements:* For master's, position paper, practicum. *Entrance requirements:* For master's, California Psychological Inventory, GRE and/or MAT, minimum GPA of 2.75. *Faculty research:* Women and power, intrafamily dynamics.

University of Wisconsin–Whitewater, School of Graduate Studies, College of Education, Department of Counselor Education, Whitewater, WI 53190-1790. Offers community counseling (MS Ed); higher education (MS Ed); school counseling (MS Ed). *Accreditation:* ACA; NCATE. Part-time and evening/weekend programs available. *Students:* 36 full-time (31 women), 91 part-time (76 women); includes 8 minority (2 African Americans, 1 Asian American or Pacific Islander, 5 Hispanic Americans). Average age 25. 52 applicants, 31% accepted, 13 enrolled. In 2006, 40 degrees awarded. *Degree requirements:* For master's, thesis or alternative. *Entrance requirements:* For master's, resumé, 2 letters of reference. Additional exam requirements/recommendations for international students: Required—TOEFL (minimum score 550 paper-based; 213 computer-based). *Application deadline:* For fall admission, 2/1 for domestic and international students. Application fee: $45. Electronic applications accepted. *Expenses:* Tuition, state resident: full-time $3,311. Tuition, nonresident: full-time $8,616. Required fees: $368 per credit. *Financial support:* In 2006–07, 1 research assistantship (averaging $9,875 per year) was awarded; Federal Work-Study, unspecified assistantships, and out of state fee waiver also available. Support available to part-time students. Financial award application deadline: 3/15; financial award applicants required to submit FAFSA. *Faculty research:* Alcohol and other drugs, counseling effectiveness, teacher mentoring. *Unit head:* Dr. Brenda O'Beirne, Coordinator, 262-472-1452, Fax: 262-472-2841, E-mail: obeirneb@uww.edu. *Application contact:* Sally A. Lange, School of Graduate Studies, 262-472-1006, Fax: 262-472-5027, E-mail: gradschl@uww.edu.

University of Wyoming, Graduate School, College of Education, Department of Counselor Education, Laramie, WY 82070. Offers MS, PhD. *Accreditation:* ACA (one or more programs are accredited). *Faculty:* 5 full-time (2 women), 1 (woman) part-time/adjunct. *Students:* 64 full-time (48 women), 26 part-time (20 women); includes 6 minority (2 African Americans, 2 American Indian/Alaska Native, 2 Hispanic Americans), 2 international. Average age 35. 52 applicants, 58% accepted. In 2006, 18 master's, 4 doctorates awarded. *Degree requirements:* For master's, thesis/dissertation, registration; for doctorate, thesis/dissertation, comprehensive exam, registration. *Entrance requirements:* For master's, GRE General Test, interview; for doctorate, video tape session, interview, writing sample. Additional exam requirements/recommendations for international students: Required—TOEFL. *Application deadline:* For fall admission, 3/15 for domestic students; for winter admission, 1/15 for domestic students; for spring admission, 11/15 for domestic students. Application fee: $50. *Financial support:* In 2006–07, 5 research assistantships with full tuition reimbursements (averaging $14,004 per year), 2 teaching assistantships with full tuition reimbursements (averaging $14,004 per year) were awarded. *Application contact:* Michael Day, Associate Dean, 307-766-3145, Fax: 307-766-6668, E-mail: mikeday@uwyo.edu.

Utah State University, School of Graduate Studies, College of Education and Human Services, Department of Psychology, Logan, UT 84322. Offers clinical/counseling/school psychology (PhD); research and evaluation methodology (PhD); school counseling (MS); school psychology (MS). *Accreditation:* APA (one or more programs are accredited). Part-time and evening/weekend programs available. Postbaccalaureate distance learning degree programs offered (no on-campus study). *Faculty:* 21 full-time (10 women), 35 part-time/adjunct (13 women). *Students:* 145 full-time (89 women), 24 part-time (16 women); includes 14 minority (3 African Americans, 3 American Indian/Alaska Native, 3 Asian Americans or Pacific Islanders, 5 Hispanic Americans), 14 international. Average age 34. 290 applicants, 66% accepted, 169 enrolled. In 2006, 44 master's, 5 doctorates awarded. Terminal master's awarded for partial completion of doctoral program. *Degree requirements:* For master's, thesis (for some programs); for doctorate, thesis/dissertation. *Entrance requirements:* For master's, GRE General Test (school psychology), MAT (school counseling), minimum GPA of 3.5; for doctorate, GRE General Test, minimum GPA of 3.5. Additional exam requirements/recommendations for international students: Required—TOEFL. *Application deadline:* For fall admission, 1/15 for domestic and international students; for spring admission, 10/15 for domestic and international students. Applications are processed on a rolling basis. Application fee: $50 ($60 for international students). *Financial support:* In 2006–07, 5 fellowships with full and partial tuition reimbursements (averaging $12,600 per year), 24 research assistantships with full and partial tuition reimbursements (averaging $11,500 per year), 12 teaching assistantships with full and partial tuition reimbursements (averaging $7,000 per year) were awarded; career-related internships or fieldwork, Federal Work-Study, institutionally sponsored loans, scholarships/grants, tuition waivers (partial), and unspecified assistantships also available. Financial award application deadline: 2/1. *Faculty research:* Hearing loss detection in infancy, ADHD, eating disorders, domestic violence, neuropsychology, bilingual/Spanish speaking students/parents. *Unit head:* David M. Stein, Head, 435-797-1460, Fax: 435-797-1448, E-mail: davids@coe.usu.edu. *Application contact:* Sheila Jessie, Staff Assistant IV, 435-797-1449, Fax: 435-797-1448, E-mail: sheilaj@coe.usu.edu.

Valdosta State University, Graduate School, College of Education, Department of Psychology and Counseling, Valdosta, GA 31698. Offers clinical/counseling psychology (MS); industrial/organizational psychology (MS); school counseling (M Ed, Ed S); school psychology (Ed S). Part-time and evening/weekend programs available. *Degree requirements:* For master's, thesis or alternative, comprehensive written and/or oral exams; for Ed S, thesis. *Entrance requirements:* For master's and Ed S, GRE General Test or MAT. Additional exam requirements/recommendations for international students: Required—TOEFL (minimum score 523 paper-based; 193 computer-based). Electronic applications accepted. *Faculty research:* Using Bender-Gestalt to predict graphomotor dimensions of the draw-a-person test, neurobehavioral hemispheric dominance.

Vanderbilt University, Peabody College, Department of Human and Organizational Development, Nashville, TN 37240-1001. Offers community development action (M Ed); human development counseling (M Ed). *Accreditation:* ACA; NCATE. Part-time programs available. *Faculty:* 17 full-time (8 women), 15 part-time/adjunct (10 women). *Students:* 52 full-time (47 women), 3 part-time (2 women); includes 12 minority (11 African Americans, 1 Hispanic American), 3 international. Average age 27. 91 applicants, 56% accepted, 24 enrolled. In 2006, 30 degrees awarded. *Degree requirements:* For master's, thesis optional. *Entrance requirements:* For master's, GRE General Test, MAT. Additional exam requirements/recommendations for international students: Required—TOEFL (minimum score 550 paper-based; 213 computer-based). *Application deadline:* For fall admission, 12/31 priority date for domestic and international students; for spring admission, 11/1 priority date for domestic and international students. Applications are processed on a rolling basis. Application fee: $0. Electronic applications accepted. *Expenses:* Tuition: Full-time $24,462. Required fees: $2,515. One-time fee: $30 full-time. Full-time tuition and fees vary according to course load, degree level and program. *Financial support:* In 2006–07, 41 students received support, including 11 fellowships with full and partial tuition reimbursements available, 10 research assistantships with full and partial tuition reimbursements available, 20 teaching assistantships with full and partial tuition reimbursements available; Federal Work-Study, institutionally sponsored loans, scholarships/grants, tuition waivers (partial), and unspecified assistantships also available. Support available to part-time students. Financial award application deadline: 2/1. *Faculty research:* Community psychology, international community development and urban policy, counseling and mental health services, organizational development and institutional change; youth physical and behavioral health in schools and neighborhoods. *Unit head:* Joseph Cunningham, Chair, 615-322-6881, Fax: 615-322-1141, E-mail: joe.cunningham@vanderbilt.edu. *Application contact:* Sherrie Lane, Office Assistant, 615-322-8484, Fax: 615-322-1141, E-mail: sherrie.a.lane@vanderbilt.edu.

Villanova University, Graduate School of Liberal Arts and Sciences, Department of Education and Human Services, Program in Community Counseling, Villanova, PA 19085-1699. Offers counseling and human relations (MS). *Students:* 18 full-time (16 women), 23 part-time (22 women); includes 2 minority (both African Americans) Average age 31. In 2006, 19 degrees awarded. *Degree requirements:* For master's, comprehensive exam. *Entrance requirements:* For master's, GRE or MAT, minimum GPA of 3.0. Additional exam requirements/recommendations for international students: Required—TOEFL. *Application deadline:* For fall admission, 8/1 priority date for domestic and international students; for spring admission, 12/1 for domestic and international students. Applications are processed on a rolling basis. Application fee: $50. Electronic applications accepted. *Expenses:* Tuition: Part-time $565 per credit. *Financial support:* Applicants required to submit FAFSA. *Unit head:* Dr. Kenneth M. Davis, Director, 610-519-4634.

See Close-Up on page 1617.

Villanova University, Graduate School of Liberal Arts and Sciences, Department of Education and Human Services, Program in Elementary School Counseling, Villanova, PA 19085-1699. Offers counseling and human relations (MS). Part-time and evening/weekend programs available. *Students:* 9 full-time (8 women), 12 part-time (10 women). Average age 27. In 2006, 14 degrees awarded. *Degree requirements:* For master's, comprehensive exam. *Entrance requirements:* For master's, GRE or MAT, minimum GPA of 3.0. *Application deadline:* For fall admission, 8/1 priority date for domestic students; for spring admission, 12/1 for domestic students. Applications are processed on a rolling basis. Application fee: $50. Electronic applications accepted. *Expenses:* Tuition: Part-time $565 per credit. *Financial support:* Career-related internships or fieldwork and Federal Work-Study available. Financial award applicants required to submit FAFSA. *Unit head:* Dr. Kenneth M. Davis, Director, 610-519-4634.

See Close-Up on page 1617.

Counselor Education

Villanova University, Graduate School of Liberal Arts and Sciences, Department of Education and Human Services, Program in Secondary School Counseling, Villanova, PA 19085-1699. Offers counseling and human relations (MS). *Students:* 24 full-time (20 women), 38 part-time (29 women); includes 4 minority (2 African Americans, 2 Asian Americans or Pacific Islanders). Average age 28. In 2006, 21 degrees awarded. *Degree requirements:* For master's, comprehensive exam. *Entrance requirements:* For master's, GRE or MAT, minimum GPA of 3.0. *Application deadline:* For fall admission, 8/1 priority date for domestic students; for spring admission, 12/1 for domestic students. Applications are processed on a rolling basis. Application fee: $50. Electronic applications accepted. *Expenses:* Tuition: Part-time $565 per credit. *Financial support:* Applicants required to submit FAFSA. *Unit head:* Dr. Kenneth M. Davis, Director, 610-519-4634.

See Close-Up on page 1617.

Virginia Commonwealth University, Graduate School, School of Education, Program in Counselor Education, Richmond, VA 23284-9005. Offers M Ed. *Accreditation:* NCATE. *Faculty:* 4 full-time (3 women). *Students:* 48 full-time (47 women), 40 part-time (36 women); includes 13 minority (12 African Americans, 1 Hispanic American). 65 applicants, 68% accepted, 27 enrolled. In 2006, 41 degrees awarded. *Entrance requirements:* For master's, GRE General Test or MAT. *Application deadline:* For fall admission, 5/15 for domestic students; for spring admission, 11/15 for domestic students. Application fee: $50. *Financial support:* Career-related internships or fieldwork and tuition waivers (full and partial) available. Support available to part-time students. Financial award application deadline: 3/1. *Unit head:* Dr. Susan Leone, Chair, 804-828-1332, E-mail: sdleone@vcu.edu. *Application contact:* Dr. Michael D. Davis, Director, Graduate Studies, 804-828-6530, Fax: 804-827-0676, E-mail: mddavis@vcu.edu.

See Close-Up on page 1621.

Virginia Polytechnic Institute and State University, Graduate School, College of Liberal Arts and Human Sciences, School of Education, Department of Educational Leadership and Policy Studies, Blacksburg, VA 24061. Offers administration and supervision of special education (Ed D, PhD, Ed S); adult and continuing education (MA Ed, Ed D, PhD); educational counseling (MA Ed, Ed D, PhD, Ed S); educational leadership (MA Ed, Ed D, PhD); educational research and evaluation (PhD). *Accreditation:* ACA; NCATE. *Students:* 139 full-time (107 women), 301 part-time (200 women); includes 119 minority (101 African Americans, 2 American Indian/Alaska Native, 4 Asian Americans or Pacific Islanders, 12 Hispanic Americans), 10 international. Average age 40. 175 applicants, 48% accepted, 82 enrolled. In 2006, 72 master's, 35 doctorates, 28 other advanced degrees awarded. *Degree requirements:* For doctorate, thesis/dissertation, comprehensive exam. *Entrance requirements:* Additional exam requirements/recommendations for international students: Required—TOEFL (minimum score 550 paper-based; 213 computer-based). *Application deadline:* For fall admission, 5/15 for international students; for spring admission, 10/15 for international students. Applications are processed on a rolling basis. Application fee: $45. Electronic applications accepted. *Expenses:* Tuition, state resident: full-time $7,017; part-time $390 per credit hour. Tuition, nonresident: full-time $12,414; part-time $690 per credit hour. International tuition: $11,296 full-time. Required fees: $1,523; $256 per term. *Financial support:* Career-related internships or fieldwork, Federal Work-Study, scholarships/grants, and unspecified assistantships available. Financial award application deadline: 4/1. *Unit head:* Dr. M. David Alexander, Head, 540-231-5642, Fax: 540-231-7845, E-mail: mdavid@vt.edu. *Application contact:* Kathy Tickle, Information Contact, 540-231-9721, Fax: 540-231-7845, E-mail: ktickle@vt.edu.

Virginia Polytechnic Institute and State University, Graduate School, College of Liberal Arts and Human Sciences, School of Education, Program in Counselor Education, Blacksburg, VA 24061. Offers MA Ed, Ed D, PhD, Ed S. *Accreditation:* ACA. *Expenses:* Tuition, state resident: full-time $7,017; part-time $390 per credit hour. Tuition, nonresident: full-time $12,414; part-time $690 per credit hour. International tuition: $11,296 full-time. Required fees: $1,523; $256 per term.

Virginia State University, School of Graduate Studies, Research, and Outreach, School of Liberal Arts and Education, Department of Educational Leadership and Administrative Systems Management, Program in Guidance, Petersburg, VA 23806-0001. Offers M Ed, MS. *Accreditation:* NCATE. *Degree requirements:* For master's, thesis optional.

Wake Forest University, Graduate School, Counseling Program, Winston-Salem, NC 27109. Offers MA. *Accreditation:* ACA. *Faculty:* 5 full-time (3 women). *Students:* 30 full-time (21 women), 2 part-time (both women); includes 4 minority (3 African Americans, 1 Hispanic American), 2 international. Average age 27. 148 applicants, 10% accepted, 15 enrolled. In 2006, 15 degrees awarded. *Degree requirements:* For master's, registration. *Entrance requirements:* For master's, GRE General Test. Additional exam requirements/recommendations for international students: Required—TOEFL (minimum score 213 computer-based). *Application deadline:* For fall admission, 1/15 for domestic and international students. Application fee: $45 ($55 for international students). Electronic applications accepted. *Financial support:* In 2006–07, 32 students received support, including 4 teaching assistantships with full tuition reimbursements available (averaging $6,000 per year); research assistantships with full tuition reimbursements available, scholarships/grants and tuition waivers (full) also available. Financial award application deadline: 1/15; financial award applicants required to submit FAFSA. *Unit head:* Dr. Sam Gladding, Director, 336-758-4882, Fax: 336-758-4591, E-mail: stg@wfu.edu.

Walsh University, Graduate Programs, Program in Counseling and Human Development, North Canton, OH 44720-3396. Offers mental health counseling (MA); school counseling (MA). *Accreditation:* ACA. Part-time and evening/weekend programs available. *Faculty:* 4 full-time (all women), 1 part-time/adjunct (0 women). *Students:* 32 full-time (27 women), 62 part-time (52 women); includes 4 minority (1 African American, 1 American Indian/Alaska Native, 2 Hispanic Americans), 1 international. Average age 30. 36 applicants, 56% accepted, 18 enrolled. In 2006, 16 degrees awarded. *Degree requirements:* For master's, internship, practicum. *Entrance requirements:* For master's, GRE General Test, MAT, interview, minimum GPA of 3.0, writing sample. Additional exam requirements/recommendations for international students: Required—TOEFL (minimum score 500 paper-based; 173 computer-based). *Application deadline:* For fall admission, 7/15 priority date for domestic students. Applications are processed on a rolling basis. Application fee: $25. Electronic applications accepted. *Expenses:* Tuition: Full-time $8,910; part-time $495 per credit. *Financial support:* In 2006–07, 18 students received support, including 6 research assistantships with tuition reimbursements available (averaging $3,862 per year); tuition waivers (partial) and tuition discounts also available. Financial award application deadline: 12/31. *Faculty research:* Introducing text for mental health counseling, treatment of violent or serious juvenile offenders, role of marketplace factors in practice of professional counseling, relationship between dispositional levels of forgiveness and wellness in counselors in training, wellness interventions for children diagnosed with Asperger's disorder. *Unit head:* Dr. Linda Barclay, Coordinator, 330-490-7264, Fax: 330-490-7165, E-mail: lbarclay@walsh.edu. *Application contact:* Brett D. Freshour, Vice President of Enrollment Management, 330-490-7286, Fax: 330-490-7165, E-mail: bfreshour@walsh.edu.

Washington State University Tri-Cities, Graduate Programs, Program in Education, Richland, WA 99352-1671. Offers counseling (Ed M); educational leadership (Ed M, Ed D); literacy (Ed M); secondary certification (Ed M); teaching (MIT). Part-time programs available. *Faculty:* 23. *Students:* 27 full-time (20 women), 82 part-time (68 women); includes 11 minority (all Hispanic Americans) Average age 36. 77 applicants, 71% accepted, 34 enrolled. *Degree requirements:* For master's, thesis or alternative, comprehensive exam, registration; for doctorate, thesis/dissertation, comprehensive exam. *Entrance requirements:* For master's, GRE, minimum GPA of 3.0, Working with Youth form, Character and Fitness form, 3 letters of recommendation. Additional exam requirements/recommendations for international students: Required—TOEFL. *Application deadline:* For fall admission, 2/1 priority date for domestic students, 3/1 for international students; for spring admission, 9/1 priority date for domestic students, 7/1 for international students. Applications are processed on a rolling basis. Application fee: $50. Electronic applications accepted. *Expenses:* Tuition, state resident: full-time $7,066. Tuition, nonresident: full-time $17,204. *Financial support:* In 2006–07, 59 students received support, including 1 fellowship (averaging $7,950 per year), teaching assistantships (averaging $13,056 per year); Federal Work-Study, scholarships/grants, and unspecified assistantships also available. *Faculty research:* Multicultural counseling, socio-cultural influences in schools, diverse learners, teacher education, K-12 educational leadership. *Unit head:* Dr. Nancy Kyle, Director, 509-372-7396.

Wayne State College, School of Education and Counseling, Department of Counseling and Special Education, Program in Guidance and Counseling, Wayne, NE 68787. Offers counseling (MSE); counselor education (MSE); school counseling (MSE). *Accreditation:* NCATE. Part-time and evening/weekend programs available. *Faculty:* 7 part-time/adjunct (3 women). *Students:* 10 full-time (8 women), 52 part-time (44 women); includes 3 minority (1 American Indian/Alaska Native, 2 Hispanic Americans). Average age 33. In 2006, 23 degrees awarded. *Degree requirements:* For master's, thesis optional. *Entrance requirements:* For master's, GRE General Test, minimum GPA of 3.0. Additional exam requirements/recommendations for international students: Required—TOEFL (minimum score 550 paper-based; 213 computer-based). *Application deadline:* Applications are processed on a rolling basis. Application fee: $30. Electronic applications accepted. *Expenses:* Tuition, state resident: full-time $3,114; part-time $130 per credit hour. Tuition, nonresident: full-time $6,228; part-time $260 per credit hour. Required fees: $894; $37 per credit hour. Tuition and fees vary according to course load. *Financial support:* Teaching assistantships available. Financial award applicants required to submit FAFSA.

Wayne State University, College of Education, Division of Theoretical and Behavioral Foundations, Detroit, MI 48202. Offers counseling (M Ed, MA, Ed D, PhD, Ed S); education evaluation and research (M Ed, Ed D, PhD); educational psychology (M Ed, Ed D, PhD, Ed S); educational sociology (M Ed, Ed D, PhD, Ed S); history and philosophy of education (M Ed, Ed D, PhD); rehabilitation counseling and community inclusion (MA, Ed S); school and community psychology (MA, Ed S); school clinical psychology (Ed S). *Accreditation:* ACA (one or more programs are accredited); CORE (one or more programs are accredited). Evening/weekend programs available. *Faculty:* 51 full-time (18 women), 11 part-time/adjunct (7 women). *Students:* 156 full-time (125 women), 232 part-time (191 women); includes 146 minority (140 African Americans, 1 American Indian/Alaska Native, 5 Hispanic Americans), 14 international. Average age 35. 146 applicants, 38% accepted, 39 enrolled. In 2006, 84 master's, 8 doctorates awarded. *Degree requirements:* For doctorate, thesis/dissertation. *Entrance requirements:* For master's, GRE (school and community psychology); for doctorate, GRE (educational psychology), interview, minimum GPA of 3.0. Additional exam requirements/recommendations for international students: Required—TOEFL (minimum score 550 paper-based; 213 computer-based), TWE (minimum score 6). *Application deadline:* For fall admission, 7/1 for domestic students, 6/1 for international students; for winter admission, 10/1 for international students; for spring admission, 2/1 for international students. Application fee: $20 ($30 for international students). Electronic applications accepted. *Financial support:* In 2006–07, 2 research assistantships (averaging $12,797 per year) were awarded; fellowships, career-related internships or fieldwork, Federal Work-Study, and institutionally sponsored loans also available. *Faculty research:* Adolescents at risk, supervision of counseling. *Unit head:* Dr. JoAnne Holbert, Assistant Dean, 313-577-1721, E-mail: jholbert@wayne.edu.

West Chester University of Pennsylvania, Graduate Studies, School of Education, Department of Counseling and Educational Psychology, West Chester, PA 19383. Offers elementary school counseling (M Ed); higher education counseling (MS); secondary school counseling (M Ed). *Accreditation:* NCATE. Part-time and evening/weekend programs available. *Students:* 93 full-time (84 women), 130 part-time (111 women); includes 26 African Americans, 1 Hispanic American, 1 international. Average age 28. 113 applicants, 89% accepted, 50 enrolled. In 2006, 71 degrees awarded. *Degree requirements:* For master's, comprehensive exam. *Entrance requirements:* For master's, GRE or MAT, interview. *Application deadline:* For fall admission, 4/15 priority date for domestic students; for spring admission, 10/15 for domestic students. Applications are processed on a rolling basis. Application fee: $35. *Financial support:* In 2006–07, 20 research assistantships with full tuition reimbursements (averaging $5,000 per year) were awarded; unspecified assistantships also available. Support available to part-time students. Financial award application deadline: 2/15; financial award applicants required to submit FAFSA. *Faculty research:* Teacher and student cognition, adolescent cognitive development. *Unit head:* Dr. Angelo Gadaleto, Chair, 610-436-2559, E-mail: agadaleto@wcupa.edu.

Western Carolina University, Graduate School, College of Education and Allied Professions, Department of Human Services, Cullowhee, NC 28723. Offers communication disorders (MS); comprehensive education-special education (MS); counseling (M Ed, MA Ed, MS), including community counseling (MS), school counseling (M Ed, MA Ed); general special education (MA Ed, MAT), including behavioral disorders (MA Ed), comprehensive education-special education (MA Ed), learning disabilities (MA Ed), mental retardation (MA Ed), special education-learning disabilities (MAT); human resource development (MS). *Accreditation:* ACA (one or more programs are accredited). Part-time and evening/weekend programs available. *Degree requirements:* For master's, comprehensive exam. *Entrance requirements:* For master's, GRE General Test. Additional exam requirements/recommendations for international students: Required—TOEFL (minimum score 550 paper-based; 213 computer-based).

Western Connecticut State University, Division of Graduate Studies, School of Professional Studies, Department of Education and Educational Psychology, Program in School Counseling, Danbury, CT 06810-6885. Offers MS. *Accreditation:* ACA. Part-time and evening/weekend programs available. *Faculty:* 12 full-time (7 women), 6 part-time/adjunct (3 women). *Students:* Average age 31. In 2006, 15 degrees awarded. *Entrance requirements:* For master's, minimum GPA of 2.8. *Application deadline:* For fall admission, 8/1 priority date for domestic students. Applications are processed on a rolling basis. Application fee: $40. *Financial support:* Fellowships, career-related internships or fieldwork available. Support available to part-time students. Financial award application deadline: 5/1; financial award applicants required to submit FAFSA. *Unit head:* Dr. Aram Aslanian, Unit Head, 203-837-8512. *Application contact:* Chris Shankle, Associate Director of Graduate Admissions, 203-837-8244, Fax: 203-837-8338, E-mail: shanklec@wcsu.edu.

Western Illinois University, School of Graduate Studies, College of Education and Human Services, Department of Counselor Education, Macomb, IL 61455-1390. Offers counseling (MS Ed). *Accreditation:* ACA. Part-time programs available. *Students:* 27 full-time (20 women), 75 part-time (64 women); includes 14 minority (6 African Americans, 1 American Indian/Alaska Native, 1 Asian American or Pacific Islander, 6 Hispanic Americans), 1 international. Average age 32. 34 applicants, 38% accepted. In 2006, 33 degrees awarded. *Degree requirements:* For master's, thesis or alternative. *Entrance requirements:* For master's, interview. Additional exam requirements/recommendations for international students: Required—TOEFL (minimum score 550 paper-based; 213 computer-based; 80 iBT). *Application deadline:* Applications are processed on a rolling basis. Application fee: $30. Electronic applications accepted. *Expenses:* Tuition, state resident: part-time $200 per credit hour. Tuition, nonresident: part-time $400 per credit hour. *Financial support:* In 2006–07, 10 students received support, including 10 research assistantships with full tuition reimbursements available (averaging $6,568 per year). Financial award applicants required to submit FAFSA. *Unit head:* Dr. Rori Carson, Interim Chairperson, 309-762-9481. *Application contact:* Dr. Barbara Baily, Director of Graduate Studies/Associate Provost, 309-298-1806, Fax: 309-298-2345, E-mail: grad-office@wiu.edu.

Western Kentucky University, Graduate Studies, College of Education and Behavioral Sciences, Department of Counseling and Student Affairs, Bowling Green, KY 42101. Offers business and marketing education (MA Ed); counseling (MA Ed); counselor education (Ed S); education and behavioral science (MA Ed); elementary education (MA Ed, Ed S); middle years education (MA Ed); secondary education (MA Ed, Ed S); student affairs (MA Ed). *Accreditation:* ACA; NCATE. Part-time and evening/weekend programs available. *Faculty:* 11 full-time (5 women), 9 part-time/adjunct (3 women). *Students:* 59 full-time (47 women), 157 part-time (126 women); includes 18 minority (13 African Americans, 1 American Indian/Alaska Native, 2 Asian Americans or Pacific Islanders, 2 Hispanic Americans), 1 international. Average age 31. 49 applicants, 67% accepted, 27 enrolled. In 2006, 89 master's, 4 other advanced degrees awarded. *Degree requirements:* For master's, thesis optional. *Entrance requirements:* For master's, GRE General Test. Additional exam requirements/recommendations for international students: Required—TOEFL (minimum score 555 paper-based; 213 computer-based; 79 iBT). *Application deadline:* For fall admission, 8/1 priority date for domestic students, 4/1 for international students; for spring admission, 12/1 for domestic students, 9/1 for international students. Applications are processed on a rolling basis. Application fee: $35. *Expenses:* Tuition, state resident: full-time $6,520; part-time $226 per hour. Tuition, nonresident: full-time $7,140; part-time $357 per hour. International tuition: $15,820 full-time. *Financial support:* In 2006–07, 1 research assistantship with partial tuition reimbursement (averaging $8,000 per year) was awarded; Federal Work-Study, institutionally sponsored loans, and service awards also available. Financial award application deadline: 4/1; financial award applicants required to submit FAFSA. *Faculty research:* Counselor education, research for residential workers. *Unit head:* Dr. Aaron W Hughey, Department Head, 270-745-4953, E-mail: aaron.hughey@wku.edu.

Western Michigan University, Graduate College, College of Education, Department of Counselor Education and Counseling Psychology, Kalamazoo, MI 49008-5202. Offers counseling psychology (PhD); counselor education (MA, Ed D, PhD); counselor education and counseling psychology (MA, PhD); counselor psychology (MA); marriage and family therapy (MA). *Accreditation:* ACA (one or more programs are accredited); APA (one or more programs are accredited); CORE; NCATE. *Degree requirements:* For doctorate, thesis/dissertation, oral exams. *Entrance requirements:* For doctorate, GRE General Test.

Western New Mexico University, Graduate Division, School of Education, Silver City, NM 88062-0680. Offers counselor education (MA); elementary education (MAT); reading education (MAT); school administration (MA); secondary education (MAT); special education (MAT). *Accreditation:* NCATE. *Degree requirements:* For master's, comprehensive exam. *Entrance requirements:* For master's, GRE General Test, GRE Subject Test, minimum GPA of 3.2 in last 64 hours of undergraduate study. Additional exam requirements/recommendations for international students: Required—TOEFL (minimum score 550 paper-based; 213 computer-based). Electronic applications accepted. *Expenses:* Tuition, state resident: full-time $1,329. Tuition, nonresident: full-time $4,779.

Western Washington University, Graduate School, College of Humanities and Social Sciences, Department of Psychology, Program in School Counseling, Bellingham, WA 98225-5996. Offers M Ed. *Accreditation:* ACA. *Faculty:* 24. *Students:* 12 full-time (10 women); includes 1 minority (African American) 33 applicants, 18% accepted, 6 enrolled. In 2006, 7 degrees awarded. *Degree requirements:* For master's, comprehensive exam. *Entrance requirements:* For master's, GRE General Test, minimum GPA of 3.0 in last 60 semester hours or last 90 quarter hours. Additional exam requirements/recommendations for international students: Required—TOEFL (minimum score 567 paper-based; 227 computer-based). *Application deadline:* For fall admission, 2/1 priority date for domestic students. Application fee: $50. *Expenses:* Tuition, state resident: full-time $6,609; part-time $199 per credit. Tuition, nonresident: full-time $16,845; part-time $540 per credit. *Financial support:* In 2006–07, 2 teaching assistantships with partial tuition reimbursements (averaging $9,339 per year) were awarded; career-related internships or fieldwork, Federal Work-Study, institutionally sponsored loans, scholarships/grants, tuition waivers (partial), and unspecified assistantships also available. Support available to part-time students. Financial award application deadline: 2/15; financial award applicants required to submit FAFSA. *Faculty research:* Peer helper program effectiveness, school counselor program accountability, psychosocial development for LGBT youth. *Unit head:* Dr. Arleen Lewis, Adviser, 360-650-3184. *Application contact:* Lynn Graham, Graduate Coordinator, 360-650-3184, E-mail: lynn.graham@wwu.edu.

Westfield State College, Division of Graduate and Continuing Education, Department of Psychology, Westfield, MA 01086. Offers mental health counseling (MA); school guidance (MA). Part-time and evening/weekend programs available. *Degree requirements:* For master's, comprehensive exam. *Entrance requirements:* For master's, GRE General Test, MAT, minimum undergraduate GPA of 2.7.

Westminster College, Programs in Education, Program in Guidance and Counseling, New Wilmington, PA 16172-0001. Offers M Ed, Certificate. Part-time and evening/weekend programs available. *Degree requirements:* For master's, comprehensive exam. *Entrance requirements:* For master's, minimum GPA of 3.0.

West Texas A&M University, College of Education and Social Sciences, Division of Education, Program in Counseling Education, Canyon, TX 79016-0001. Offers M Ed. Part-time and evening/weekend programs available. *Degree requirements:* For master's, thesis or alternative, comprehensive exam, registration. *Entrance requirements:* For master's, GRE General Test, interview. Additional exam requirements/recommendations for international students: Required—TOEFL (minimum score 550 paper-based). Electronic applications accepted. *Faculty research:* Reducing the somatoform patient's reliance on primary care through cognitive-relational group therapy, determining effects of premarital sex.

West Texas A&M University, College of Education and Social Sciences, Division of Education, Program in Professional Counseling, Canyon, TX 79016-0001. Offers MA. Part-time programs available. *Degree requirements:* For master's, comprehensive exam, registration. *Entrance requirements:* For master's, GRE General Test, interview, 12 semester hours in education and/or psychology, approval from the Counselor Admissions Committee. Additional exam requirements/recommendations for international students: Required—TOEFL (minimum score 550 paper-based). Electronic applications accepted.

West Virginia University, College of Human Resources and Education, Department of Counseling, Rehabilitation Counseling, and Counseling Psychology, Program in Counseling, Morgantown, WV 26506. Offers MA. *Accreditation:* ACA; APA. *Students:* 45 full-time (38 women), 11 part-time (7 women); includes 1 minority (Hispanic American), 1 international. Average age 28. 61 applicants, 49% accepted, 22 enrolled. In 2006, 46 degrees awarded. *Degree requirements:* For master's, content exams. *Entrance requirements:* For master's, GRE General Test, minimum GPA of 2.8, interview 2.8. Additional exam requirements/recommendations for international students: Required—TOEFL. *Application deadline:* For fall admission, 3/1 for domestic and international students; for winter admission, 10/15 for international students; for spring admission, 10/15 for domestic students. Application fee: $50. Electronic applications accepted. *Expenses:* Tuition, state resident: full-time $4,926; part-time $276 per credit hour. Tuition, nonresident: full-time $14,278; part-time $796 per credit hour. Tuition and fees vary according to program. *Financial support:* In 2006–07, 41 students received support, including 4 research assistantships with full tuition reimbursements available (averaging $8,264 per year), 7 teaching assistantships with full tuition reimbursements available (averaging $8,264 per year); career-related internships or fieldwork, Federal Work-Study, institutionally sponsored loans, tuition waivers (full and partial), and unspecified assistantships also available. Financial award application deadline: 2/1; financial award applicants required to submit FAFSA. *Faculty research:* Career development and placement, family therapy, conflict resolution, interviewing technique, multicultural counseling. *Unit head:* Dr. Ed Jacobs, Coordinator, 304-293-2177, Fax: 304-293-4082, E-mail: ed.jacobs@mail.wvu.edu.

Whitworth University, School of Education, Graduate Studies in Education, Program in Counseling, Spokane, WA 99251-0001. Offers school counselors (M Ed); social agency/church setting (M Ed). *Accreditation:* NCATE. Part-time and evening/weekend programs available. *Degree requirements:* For master's, internship, practicum, research project, or thesis. *Entrance requirements:* For master's, GRE General Test, MAT. *Application deadline:* For fall admission, 9/1 priority date for domestic students; for spring admission, 2/1 for domestic students. Applications are processed on a rolling basis. Application fee: $35. *Financial support:* Career-related internships or fieldwork available. Financial award application deadline: 2/1. *Faculty research:* Church counseling service support. *Unit head:* Dr. Diane Dempsey-Marr, Chair of Counseling Department, 509-777-4339, Fax: 509-777-4753, E-mail: dmarr@whitworth.edu. *Application contact:* Pat Bailey, Program Assistant, 509-777-3228, Fax: 509-777-4753, E-mail: gse@whitworth.edu.

Wichita State University, Graduate School, College of Education, Department of Administration, Counseling, Educational and School Psychology, Wichita, KS 67260. Offers counseling (M Ed); education administration (M Ed, Ed D); educational psychology (M Ed); school psychology (Ed S). *Accreditation:* NCATE. Part-time and evening/weekend programs available. *Degree requirements:* For master's, thesis optional; for doctorate, one foreign language, thesis/dissertation; for Ed S, internship, practicum. *Entrance requirements:* For master's, minimum GPA of 2.75; for doctorate, GRE General Test. Additional exam requirements/recommendations for international students: Required—TOEFL. Electronic applications accepted.

Widener University, School of Human Service Professions, Center for Education, Chester, PA 19013-5792. Offers adult education (M Ed); counseling in higher education (M Ed); counselor education (M Ed); early childhood education (M Ed); educational foundations (M Ed); educational leadership (M Ed); educational psychology (M Ed); elementary education (M Ed); English and language arts (M Ed); health education (M Ed); higher education leadership (Ed D); home and school visitor (M Ed); human sexuality (M Ed); mathematics education (M Ed); middle school education (M Ed); principalship (M Ed); reading and language arts (Ed D); reading education (M Ed); school administration (Ed D); science education (M Ed); social studies education (M Ed); special education (M Ed); technology education (M Ed). Part-time and evening/weekend programs available. Terminal master's awarded for partial completion of doctoral program. *Degree requirements:* For doctorate, thesis/dissertation. *Entrance requirements:* For master's, minimum GPA of 2.5; for doctorate, GRE or MAT, minimum GPA of 2.0 (undergraduate), 3.5 (graduate). Electronic applications accepted. Expenses: Contact institution. *Faculty research:* Reading and cognition, adult education, technology education, educational leadership, special education.

William Paterson University of New Jersey, College of Education, Department of Special Education and Counseling Services, Program in Counseling Services, Wayne, NJ 07470-8420. Offers counseling (M Ed). *Accreditation:* ACA; NCATE. *Students:* 17 full-time (13 women), 81 part-time (76 women); includes 10 minority (4 African Americans, 2 Asian Americans or Pacific Islanders, 4 Hispanic Americans). *Degree requirements:* For master's, thesis, research design, comprehensive exam. *Entrance requirements:* For master's, GRE General Test, MAT, minimum GPA of 2.75, teaching certificate. *Application deadline:* Applications are processed on a rolling basis. Application fee: $50. Electronic applications accepted. *Financial support:* Research assistantships with full tuition reimbursements, career-related internships or fieldwork and unspecified assistantships available. Support available to part-time students. Financial award application deadline: 4/1; financial award applicants required to submit FAFSA. *Unit head:* Dr. Paula Danzinger, Program Director, 973-720-3085. *Application contact:* Danielle Liautaud, Director, 973-720-3579, Fax: 973-720-2035, E-mail: liautaudd@wpunj.edu.

Wilmington College, Division of Education, New Castle, DE 19720-6491. Offers applied education technology (M Ed); career and technical education (M Ed); elementary and secondary school counseling (M Ed); elementary special education (M Ed); elementary studies (M Ed); instruction: gifted and talented (M Ed); instruction: teaching and learning (M Ed); literacy (M Ed); reading (M Ed); school leadership (M Ed); secondary teaching (MAT). Part-time and evening/weekend programs available. *Faculty:* 7 full-time (4 women). *Students:* 609 full-time (447 women), 1,350 part-time (1,013 women); includes 144 minority (131 African Americans, 3 American Indian/Alaska Native, 1 Asian American or Pacific Islander, 9 Hispanic Americans). Average age 34. 818 applicants, 100% accepted, 599 enrolled. In 2006, 737 degrees awarded. *Entrance requirements:* For master's, 2 letters of recommendation, interview. Additional exam requirements/recommendations for international students: Required—TOEFL (minimum score 500 paper-based; 173 computer-based). *Application deadline:* For fall admission, 4/30 for domestic students. Applications are processed on a rolling basis. Application fee: $25. *Financial support:* Applicants required to submit FAFSA. *Unit head:* Dr. Richard Gochnauer, Chair, 302-328-6795 Ext. 163, Fax: 302-328-7081. *Application contact:* Chris Ferguson, Director of Admissions and Financial Aid, 302-328-9407 Ext. 256, Fax: 302-328-5164, E-mail: inquire@wilmcoll.edu.

Winona State University, Graduate Studies, College of Education, Department of Counselor Education, Winona, MN 55987-5838. Offers community counseling (MS); professional development (MS); school counseling (MS). *Accreditation:* ACA; NCATE. Part-time and evening/weekend programs available. *Faculty:* 5 full-time (2 women). *Students:* 1 (woman) full-time, 104 part-time (88 women); includes 7 minority (1 American Indian/Alaska Native, 5 Asian Americans or Pacific Islanders, 1 Hispanic American). 52 applicants, 46% accepted, 19 enrolled. In 2006, 29 degrees awarded. *Degree requirements:* For master's, thesis or alternative. *Application deadline:* For fall admission, 8/8 priority date for domestic students; for spring admission, 2/17 for domestic students. Applications are processed on a rolling basis. Application fee: $20. *Financial support:* Career-related internships or fieldwork, Federal Work-Study, and unspecified assistantships available. Support available to part-time students. Financial award applicants required to submit FAFSA. *Unit head:* Dr. Tim Hatfield, Chairperson, 507-457-5337, E-mail: thatfield@winona.edu.

Winthrop University, College of Education, Program in Counseling and Development, Rock Hill, SC 29733. Offers agency counseling (M Ed); school counseling (M Ed). *Accreditation:* ACA; NCATE. Part-time programs available. *Students:* 29 full-time (all women), 10 part-time (7 women); includes 16 minority (all African Americans) Average age 26. In 2006, 22 degrees awarded. *Degree requirements:* For master's, comprehensive exam. *Entrance requirements:* For master's, GRE General Test or MAT, interview. Application fee: $35 ($50 for international students). Electronic applications accepted. *Expenses:* Tuition, state resident: full-time $9,148; part-time $383 per hour. Tuition, nonresident: full-time $16,864; part-time $704 per hour. *Financial support:* Career-related internships or fieldwork, Federal Work-Study, scholarships/grants, and unspecified assistantships available. Support available to part-time students. Financial award application deadline: 2/1; financial award applicants required to submit FAFSA. *Unit head:* Dr. Johnny Sanders, Unit Head, 803-323-4757, Fax: 803-323-4755, E-mail: sandersj@winthrop.edu. *Application contact:* 800-411-7041, Fax: 803-323-2292, E-mail: graduatestu@winthrop.edu.

Wright State University, School of Graduate Studies, College of Education and Human Services, Department of Human Services, Programs in Counseling, Dayton, OH 45435. Offers counseling (MA, MS), including business and industrial management, community counseling, exceptional children, marriage and family, mental health counseling; pupil personnel services (M Ed, MA), including school counseling. *Accreditation:* ACA (one or more programs are accredited); NCATE. *Students:* 52 full-time (43 women), 37 part-time (28 women); includes 12 minority (all African Americans) Average age 36. 38 applicants, 84% accepted. In 2006, 52 degrees awarded. *Degree requirements:* For master's, thesis (for some programs), comprehensive exam. *Entrance requirements:* For master's, GRE General Test, MAT, interview. Additional exam requirements/recommendations for international students: Required—TOEFL. Application fee: $25. *Financial support:* Tuition waivers (full and partial) and unspecified assistantships available. Support available to part-time students. Financial award applicants required to submit FAFSA. *Application contact:* John Kimble, Associate Director of Graduate Admissions and Records, 937-775-2957, Fax: 937-775-2453, E-mail: john.kimble@wright.edu.

Xavier University, College of Social Sciences, Health and Education, School of Education, Program in Community Counseling, Cincinnati, OH 45207. Offers MA. *Accreditation:* ACA. Part-time and evening/weekend programs available. *Faculty:* 5 full-time (2 women), 8 part-time/adjunct (4 women). *Students:* 54 full-time (50 women), 44 part-time (39 women); includes 15 minority (all African Americans), 1 international. Average age 33. 36 applicants, 56% accepted, 19 enrolled. In 2006, 19 degrees awarded. *Degree requirements:* For master's, internship. *Entrance requirements:* For master's, MAT or GRE, minimum GPA of 3.0, letters of reference,

Xavier University (continued)

interview, resumé. Additional exam requirements/recommendations for international students: Required—TOEFL (minimum score 550 paper-based; 213 computer-based). *Application deadline:* For fall admission, 5/1 priority date for domestic and international students; for spring admission, 10/1 priority date for domestic and international students. Application fee: $35. Electronic applications accepted. *Expenses:* Tuition: Part-time $462 per credit hour. Part-time tuition and fees vary according to degree level, campus/location and program. *Financial support:* Scholarships/grants and unspecified assistantships available. Support available to part-time students. Financial award applicants required to submit FAFSA. *Faculty research:* Reality therapy, career development, counselor supervision. *Unit head:* Dr. Lon Kriner, Director, 513-745-3822, Fax: 513-745-2920, E-mail: kriner@xavier.edu. *Application contact:* Roger Bosse, Interim Director of Graduate Studies, 513-745-3357, Fax: 513-745-1048, E-mail: bosse@xavier.edu.

Xavier University, College of Social Sciences, Health and Education, School of Education, Program in School Counseling, Cincinnati, OH 45207. Offers MA. *Accreditation:* ACA. Part-time and evening/weekend programs available. *Faculty:* 5 full-time (2 women), 8 part-time/adjunct (4 women). *Students:* 20 full-time (15 women), 62 part-time (51 women); includes 6 minority (5 African Americans, 1 Hispanic American), 1 international. Average age 32. 25 applicants, 40% accepted, 8 enrolled. In 2006, 32 degrees awarded. *Degree requirements:* For master's, internship. *Entrance requirements:* For master's, MAT or GRE, minimum GPA of 3.0, letters of reference, interview, resumé. Additional exam requirements/recommendations for international students: Required—TOEFL (minimum score 550 paper-based; 213 computer-based). *Application deadline:* For fall admission, 5/1 priority date for domestic students; for

spring admission, 10/1 priority date for domestic students. Applications are processed on a rolling basis. Application fee: $35. Electronic applications accepted. *Expenses:* Tuition: Part-time $462 per credit hour. Part-time tuition and fees vary according to degree level, campus/location and program. *Financial support:* Scholarships/grants and unspecified assistantships available. Support available to part-time students. Financial award applicants required to submit FAFSA. *Faculty research:* Counselor supervision, counseling challenging youth. *Unit head:* Dr. Lon Kriner, Director, 513-745-3822, Fax: 513-745-2920, E-mail: kriner@xavier.edu. *Application contact:* Roger Bosse, Interim Director of Graduate Studies, 513-745-3357, Fax: 513-745-1048, E-mail: bosse@xavier.edu.

Xavier University of Louisiana, Graduate School, Programs in Education, New Orleans, LA 70125-1098. Offers curriculum and instruction (MA); education administration and supervision (MA); guidance and counseling (MA). *Accreditation:* NCATE. Part-time and evening/weekend programs available. *Degree requirements:* For master's, thesis or alternative, comprehensive exam. *Entrance requirements:* For master's, GRE General Test, MAT, minimum GPA of 2.5. Additional exam requirements/recommendations for international students: Required—TOEFL.

Youngstown State University, Graduate School, College of Education, Department of Counseling, Youngstown, OH 44555-0001. Offers MS Ed. *Accreditation:* ACA; NCATE. Part-time and evening/weekend programs available. *Degree requirements:* For master's, comprehensive exam. *Entrance requirements:* For master's, MAT, interview, minimum GPA of 2.7. Additional exam requirements/recommendations for international students: Required—TOEFL. *Faculty research:* Suicide, euthanasia, ethical issues, marriage and family.

Developmental Education

Edinboro University of Pennsylvania, Graduate Studies and Research, School of Education, Department of Elementary Education, Program in Character Education, Edinboro, PA 16444. Offers Certificate. Part-time and evening/weekend programs available. *Students:* 3 full-time (1 woman), 20 part-time (17 women); includes 2 minority (both African Americans) Average age 35. In 2006, 9 degrees awarded. *Application deadline:* Applications are processed on a rolling basis. Application fee: $30. Electronic applications accepted. *Expenses:* Tuition, state resident: full-time $6,048; part-time $336 per credit. Tuition, nonresident: full-time $9,678; part-time $538 per credit. Required fees: $1,849; $42 per credit. *Financial support:* Application deadline: 2/15. *Unit head:* Dr. Patricia Flach, Coordinator, 814-732-1330, E-mail: pflach@edinboro.edu. *Application contact:* Dr. R. Scott Baldwin, Dean, 814-732-2752, Fax: 814-732-2268, E-mail: sbaldwin@edinboro.edu.

Ferris State University, College of Education and Human Services, School of Education, Big Rapids, MI 49307. Offers administration (MSCTE); curriculum and instruction (M Ed), including administration, elementary education, philanthropic education, reading, secondary education, special education, subject matter option; education technology (MSCTE); instructor (MSCTE); post-secondary administration (MSCTE); training and development (MSCTE). Part-time and evening/weekend programs available. Postbaccalaureate distance learning degree programs offered (no on-campus study). *Faculty:* 13 full-time (9 women), 26 part-time/adjunct (19 women). *Students:* 38 full-time (27 women), 254 part-time (164 women); includes 30 minority (22 African Americans, 1 American Indian/Alaska Native, 2 Asian Americans or Pacific Islanders, 5 Hispanic Americans), 1 international. Average age 37. 171 applicants, 99% accepted. In 2006, 92 degrees awarded. *Degree requirements:* For master's, thesis, research paper. *Entrance requirements:* For master's, 2 years of work experience, minimum GPA of 3.0. *Application deadline:* For fall admission, 6/1 priority date for domestic students; for winter admission, 12/10 priority date for domestic students. Applications are processed on a rolling basis. Application fee: $30. *Expenses:* Tuition, state resident: part-time $355 per credit hour. Tuition, nonresident: part-time $687 per credit hour. *Financial support:* Career-related internships or fieldwork and tuition waivers (full and partial) available. Support available to part-time students. Financial award applicants required to submit FAFSA. *Faculty research:* Suicide prevention, reading, women in education, special needs, administration. *Unit head:* Interim Director, 231-591-5362, Fax: 231-591-2041. *Application contact:* Sigrid Robertson, Secretary, 231-591-3511, Fax: 231-591-2041, E-mail: robertss@ferris.edu.

Grambling State University, School of Graduate Studies and Research, College of Education, Department of Educational Leadership, Grambling, LA 71245. Offers curriculum and instruction (Ed D); developmental education (Ed D); educational leadership (M Ed, Ed D); special education (M Ed). Part-time and evening/weekend programs available. Postbaccalaureate distance learning degree programs offered (minimal on-campus study). *Faculty:* 8 full-time (1 woman), 2 part-time/adjunct (0 women). *Students:* 19 full-time (17 women), 63 part-time (49 women); includes 59 minority (58 African Americans, 1 Asian American or Pacific Islander), 2 international. Average age 41. In 2006, 5 master's, 4 doctorates awarded. *Degree requirements:* For master's, thesis (for some programs), comprehensive exam; for doctorate, thesis/dissertation, comprehensive exam. *Entrance requirements:* For master's, GRE, TOEFL, minimum GPA of 2.5 on last degree; for doctorate, GRE, master's degree, minimum 1000 on GRE, minimum GPA of 3.0 on last degree, minimum 500 on GRE Verbal. *Application deadline:* For fall admission, 7/1 for domestic students; for spring admission, 12/1 for domestic students. Application fee: $20 ($30 for international students). *Expenses:* Tuition, state resident: full-time $2,232; part-time $124 per credit hour. Tuition, nonresident: full-time $7,582; part-time $124 per credit hour. Required fees: $1,127. *Financial support:* In 2006-07, 59 students received support, including 7 research assistantships (averaging $5,786 per year); institutionally sponsored loans and unspecified assistantships also available. Financial award application deadline: 5/31; financial award applicants required to submit FAFSA. *Unit head:* Dr. Olatunde Ogunyemi, Director, 318-274-6105, Fax: 318-274-2799, E-mail: ogunymio@gram.edu.

Instituto Tecnológico y de Estudios Superiores de Monterrey, Campus Ciudad Obregón, Programs in Education, Program in Cognitive Development, Ciudad Obregón, Mexico. Offers ME.

National-Louis University, College of Arts and Sciences, Division of Language and Academic Development, Program in Adult Literacy and Developmental Studies, Chicago, IL 60603. Offers M Ed, Certificate. Part-time and evening/weekend programs available. *Students:* Average age 40. 4 applicants, 100% accepted. In 2006, 7 master's, 2 Certificates awarded. *Entrance requirements:* For master's, GRE General Test, MAT, or Watson-Glaser Critical Thinking Appraisal, interview, minimum GPA of 3.0; for Certificate, GRE, MAT, or Watson-Glaser Critical Thinking Appraisal, interview, minimum GPA of 3.0. *Application deadline:* Applications are processed on a rolling basis. Application fee: $25. *Expenses:* Tuition: Full-time $17,685. One-time fee: $40 full-time. *Financial support:* Fellowships, career-related internships or fieldwork, Federal Work-Study, institutionally sponsored loans, scholarships/grants, and tuition waivers available. Support available to part-time students. Financial award application deadline: 4/15; financial award applicants required to submit FAFSA. *Faculty research:* Adult learning and development, learner-centered development, political and social foundations, reading development, curricular processes. *Application contact:* David McCulloch, Vice President for University Services, 800-443-5522 Ext. 5127, Fax: 847-465-0593, E-mail: dmcc@wheeling1.nl.edu.

North Carolina State University, Graduate School, College of Education, Department of Adult and Community College Education, Program in Training and Development, Raleigh, NC 27695. Offers M Ed, MS. *Degree requirements:* For master's, thesis optional. *Entrance*

requirements: For master's, GRE General Test or MAT, minimum GPA of 3.0 in major. Electronic applications accepted.

Rutgers, The State University of New Jersey, New Brunswick, Graduate School of Education, Department of Educational Psychology, Program in Learning, Cognition and Development, New Brunswick, NJ 08901-1281. Offers Ed M. Part-time and evening/weekend programs available. *Faculty:* 7 full-time (5 women). *Students:* 3 full-time (all women), 14 part-time (12 women). 13 applicants, 69% accepted, 8 enrolled. In 2006, 4 master's awarded. *Entrance requirements:* For master's, GRE General Test, 3 letters of recommendation. Additional exam requirements/recommendations for international students: Required—TOEFL (minimum score 550 paper-based; 233 computer-based; 83 iBT). *Application deadline:* For fall admission, 2/1 for domestic and international students; for spring admission, 11/1 for domestic and international students. Application fee: $60. Electronic applications accepted. *Financial support:* Application deadline: 3/15; *Faculty research:* Cognitive development, gender roles, cognition and instruction, peer learning, infancy and early childhood. *Unit head:* Dr. Susan Golbeck, Coordinator, 732-932-7496 Ext. 8323, Fax: 732-932-6829, E-mail: golbeck@rutgers.edu.

Texas State University-San Marcos, Graduate School, College of Education, Department of Educational Administration and Psychological Services, Program in Developmental and Adult Education, San Marcos, TX 78666. Offers MA, PhD. Part-time programs available. *Faculty:* 3 full-time (all women). *Students:* 1 (woman) full-time, 11 part-time (8 women); includes 8 minority (3 African Americans, 2 Asian Americans or Pacific Islanders, 3 Hispanic Americans), 1 international. Average age 40. 65 applicants, 45% accepted, 1 enrolled. In 2006, 4 master's, 4 doctorates awarded. *Degree requirements:* For master's, thesis, internship, comprehensive exam. *Entrance requirements:* For master's, GRE General Test, minimum GPA of 2.75 in last 60 hours of course work. Additional exam requirements/recommendations for international students: Required—TOEFL. *Application deadline:* For fall admission, 6/15 for domestic students, 6/1 for international students; for spring admission, 10/1 for domestic and international students. Applications are processed on a rolling basis. Application fee: $40 ($90 for international students). *Financial support:* In 2006-07, 12 students received support, including 7 research assistantships (averaging $6,948 per year), 5 teaching assistantships (averaging $9,468 per year); career-related internships or fieldwork, Federal Work-Study, and institutionally sponsored loans also available. Support available to part-time students. Financial award application deadline: 4/1; financial award applicants required to submit FAFSA. *Unit head:* Dr. Jovita Ross-Gordan, Graduate Advisor, 512-245-8084, Fax: 512-245-8872.

University of California, Berkeley, Graduate Division, School of Education, Division of Cognition and Development, Program in Developmental Teacher Education, Berkeley, CA 94720-1500. Offers MA/Credential. *Application deadline:* For fall admission, 12/1 for domestic students. Application fee: $60 ($80 for international students). Electronic applications accepted. *Financial support:* Unspecified assistantships available. *Unit head:* Paul Ammon, Director, 510-642-4201. *Application contact:* Admissions Office, 510-642-0841, Fax: 510-642-4808, E-mail: gse_info@uclink.berkeley.edu.

The University of Iowa, Graduate College, College of Education, Department of Teaching and Learning, Program in Early Childhood and Elementary Education, Iowa City, IA 52242-1316. Offers curriculum and supervision (MA, PhD); developmental reading (MA); early childhood education and care (MA); elementary education (MA, PhD); language, literature and culture (PhD). *Faculty:* 7 full-time, 4 part-time/adjunct. *Students:* 8 full-time (7 women), 23 part-time (all women); includes 2 minority (both African Americans), 5 international. 6 applicants, 67% accepted, 4 enrolled. In 2006, 11 master's, 1 doctorate awarded. *Degree requirements:* For master's, exam, thesis optional; for doctorate, thesis/dissertation, comprehensive exam, registration. *Entrance requirements:* For master's and doctorate, GRE General Test, minimum GPA of 3.0. Additional exam requirements/recommendations for international students: Required—TOEFL (minimum score 550 paper-based; 213 computer-based; 81 iBT). Application fee: $60 ($85 for international students). Electronic applications accepted. *Financial support:* In 2006-07, 1 fellowship, 2 research assistantships with partial tuition reimbursements, 8 teaching assistantships with partial tuition reimbursements were awarded. Financial award applicants required to submit FAFSA. *Unit head:* Gary Sasso, Chair, 319-335-5324, Fax: 319-335-5608.

The University of Iowa, Graduate College, College of Education, Department of Teaching and Learning, Program in Secondary Education, Iowa City, IA 52242-1316. Offers art education (MA, PhD); curriculum and supervision (PhD); curriculum supervision (MA); developmental reading (MA); English education (MA, MAT, PhD); foreign language education (MA, MAT); foreign language/ESL education (PhD); language, literature and culture (PhD); math education (PhD); mathematics education (MA); music education (MA, PhD); social studies (MA, PhD). *Faculty:* 11 full-time. *Students:* 53 full-time (33 women), 53 part-time (41 women); includes 5 minority (1 African American, 1 American Indian/Alaska Native, 2 Asian Americans or Pacific Islanders, 1 Hispanic American), 19 international. 66 applicants, 47% accepted, 17 enrolled. In 2006, 22 master's, 14 doctorates awarded. *Degree requirements:* For master's, exam, thesis optional; for doctorate, thesis/dissertation, comprehensive exam, registration. *Entrance requirements:* For master's and doctorate, GRE General Test, minimum GPA of 3.0. Additional exam requirements/recommendations for international students: Required—TOEFL (minimum score 550 paper-based; 213 computer-based; 81 iBT). Application fee: $60 ($85 for international students). Electronic applications accepted. *Financial support:* In 2006-07, 1 fellowship, 12 research assistantships with partial tuition reimbursements, 31 teaching assistantships with partial tuition reimbursements were awarded. Financial award applicants required to submit FAFSA. *Unit head:* Gary Sasso, Chair, 319-335-5324, Fax: 319-335-5608.

English Education

Agnes Scott College, Secondary English Program, Decatur, GA 30030-3797. Offers MAT. Evening/weekend programs available. *Faculty:* 5 full-time (3 women), 3 part-time/adjunct (2 women). *Students:* 12 full-time (11 women), 1 (woman) part-time; includes 3 minority (2 African Americans, 1 Asian American or Pacific Islander). Average age 32. 17 applicants, 88% accepted, 13 enrolled. In 2006, 25 degrees awarded. *Entrance requirements:* For master's, GRE, PRAXIS I, minimum GPA of 3.0, portfolio of writing samples, English major or significant study in English. *Application deadline:* For spring admission, 4/1 priority date for domestic and international students. Applications are processed on a rolling basis. Application fee: $35. *Expenses:* Tuition: Full-time $21,840; part-time $445 per hour. Required fees: $375. *Financial support:* Applicants required to submit FAFSA. *Faculty research:* Curriculum development, African-American literature, history of English, British and American modernism, instructional methods. *Unit head:* Dr. Willie Tolliver, Director, 404-471-5181, Fax: 404-471-5152, E-mail: wtolliver@agnesscott.edu. *Application contact:* Lisa M. Flowers, Education Faculty Coordinator, 404-471-5168, Fax: 404-471-5152, E-mail: lflowers@agnesscott.edu.

See Close-Up on page 1597.

Alabama State University, School of Graduate Studies, College of Education, Department of Curriculum and Instruction, Program in Secondary Education, Montgomery, AL 36101-0271. Offers biology education (M Ed, Ed S); English/language arts (M Ed); history education (M Ed, Ed S); mathematics education (M Ed); secondary education (Ed S); social studies (Ed S). Part-time programs available. *Students:* 31 full-time (23 women), 123 part-time (81 women); includes 114 minority (111 African Americans, 2 Asian Americans or Pacific Islanders, 1 Hispanic American), 1 international. In 2006, 27 degrees awarded. *Degree requirements:* For master's, comprehensive exam; for Ed S, thesis, comprehensive exam. *Entrance requirements:* For master's, GRE General Test, MAT, graduate writing competency test; for Ed S, graduate writing competency test, GRE, MAT. Additional exam requirements/recommendations for international students: Required—TOEFL (minimum score 500 paper-based; 173 computer-based). *Application deadline:* For fall admission, 7/15 for domestic students; for spring admission, 12/15 for domestic students. Applications are processed on a rolling basis. Application fee: $10. *Expenses:* Tuition, state resident: full-time $1,728; part-time $192 per hour. Tuition, nonresident: full-time $3,456; part-time $334 per hour. *Financial support:* In 2006–07, research assistantships (averaging $9,450 per year).

Albany State University, College of Education, Program in English Education, Albany, GA 31705-2717. Offers M Ed. *Accreditation:* NCATE. Part-time programs available. *Degree requirements:* For master's, thesis, comprehensive exam. *Entrance requirements:* For master's, GRE General Test, MAT or NTE. Electronic applications accepted. *Faculty research:* Creative writing for publication, Fulbright scholars.

Andrews University, School of Graduate Studies, College of Arts and Sciences, Department of English, Berrien Springs, MI 49104. Offers MA, MAT. Part-time programs available. *Degree requirements:* For master's, one foreign language, thesis optional. *Entrance requirements:* For master's, GRE Subject Test. *Faculty research:* Christianity and literature, Victorian literature, social linguistics, rhetoric, American literature.

Andrews University, School of Graduate Studies, School of Education, Department of Teaching, Learning, and Curriculum, Berrien Springs, MI 49104. Offers curriculum and instruction (MA, Ed D, PhD, Ed S); elementary education (MAT); reading (MA); secondary education (MAT), including biology, education, English, English as a second language, French, history, physics; special education/learning disabilities (MS); teacher education (MAT). *Entrance requirements:* For master's, GRE Subject Test.

Appalachian State University, Cratis D. Williams Graduate School, College of Arts and Sciences, Department of English, Boone, NC 28608. Offers English (MA); English education (MA). Part-time programs available. *Faculty:* 36 full-time (18 women). *Students:* 19 full-time (11 women), 37 part-time (19 women); includes 2 minority (both Asian Americans or Pacific Islanders) 40 applicants, 68% accepted, 22 enrolled. In 2006, 8 degrees awarded. *Degree requirements:* For master's, one foreign language, thesis (for some programs), comprehensive exam, registration. *Entrance requirements:* For master's, GRE General Test, minimum GPA of 3.2, 2 years teaching experience (English education). Additional exam requirements/recommendations for international students: Required—TOEFL (minimum score 570 paper-based; 230 computer-based). *Application deadline:* For fall admission, 7/1 priority date for domestic students, 1/1 for international students; for spring admission, 11/1 for domestic students, 6/1 for international students. Application fee: $50. *Expenses:* Tuition, state resident: full-time $2,600; part-time $127 per hour. Tuition, nonresident: full-time $13,200; part-time $597 per hour. Required fees: $2,000; $546 per term. *Financial support:* In 2006–07, 10 research assistantships (averaging $7,000 per year), 15 teaching assistantships (averaging $8,000 per year) were awarded; fellowships, career-related internships or fieldwork, Federal Work-Study, scholarships/grants, and unspecified assistantships also available. Support available to part-time students. Financial award application deadline: 7/1. *Faculty research:* Contemporary Irish literature, Romantic psychology, cultural practices of everyday life, Gullah linguistics, Renaissance women's writing. *Unit head:* Dr. Jeanne Dubino, Chair, 828-262-3098. *Application contact:* Dr. Bill Brewer, Graduate Adviser, 828-262-3098, E-mail: brewerwd@appstate.edu.

Arcadia University, Graduate Studies, Department of Education, Glenside, PA 19038-3295. Offers art education (M Ed, MA Ed); biology education (MA Ed); chemistry education (MA Ed); child development (CAS); computer education (M Ed, CAS); computer education 7–12 (MA Ed); early childhood education (M Ed, CAS), including individualized (M Ed), master teacher (M Ed), research in child development (M Ed); educational leadership (M Ed, CAS); educational psychology (CAS); elementary education (M Ed, CAS); English education (MA Ed); environmental education (MA Ed, CAS); history education (MA Ed); language arts (M Ed, CAS); mathematics education (M Ed, MA Ed, CAS); music education (MA Ed); psychology (MA Ed); pupil personnel services (CAS); reading (M Ed, CAS); school library science (M Ed); science education (M Ed, CAS); secondary education (M Ed, CAS); special education (M Ed, Ed D, CAS); theater arts (MA Ed); written communication (MA Ed). *Accreditation:* NASAD. Part-time and evening/weekend programs available. Postbaccalaureate distance learning degree programs offered (minimal on-campus study). *Faculty:* 12 full-time (8 women), 38 part-time/adjunct (26 women). *Students:* 60 full-time (56 women), 419 part-time (324 women); includes 70 minority (57 African Americans, 1 American Indian/Alaska Native, 6 Asian Americans or Pacific Islanders, 6 Hispanic Americans), 1 international. In 2006, 257 master's, 4 doctorates awarded. *Application deadline:* Applications are processed on a rolling basis. Application fee: $35. Electronic applications accepted. *Financial support:* Career-related internships or fieldwork, tuition waivers (partial), and unspecified assistantships available. *Unit head:* Dr. Steven P. Gulkus, Chair, 215-572-2120. *Application contact:* 215-572-2925, Fax: 215-572-2126, E-mail: grad@arcadia.edu.

Arkansas State University, Graduate School, College of Humanities and Social Sciences, Department of English and Philosophy, Jonesboro, State University, AR 72467. Offers English (MA); English education (MSE, SCCT). Part-time programs available. *Faculty:* 15 full-time (5 women), 1 part-time/adjunct (0 women). *Students:* 6 full-time (3 women), 20 part-time (17 women); includes 5 minority (all African Americans) Average age 31. 19 applicants, 89% accepted, 12 enrolled. In 2006, 9 degrees awarded. *Degree requirements:* For master's, one foreign language, thesis or alternative, comprehensive exam. *Entrance requirements:* For master's, GRE General Test or MAT, appropriate bachelor's degree, official transcript; for SCCT, GRE General Test or MAT, interview, master's degree, official transcript. Additional exam requirements/recommendations for international students: Required—TOEFL (minimum score 213 computer-based). *Application deadline:* Applications are processed on a rolling basis. Application fee: $30 ($40 for international students). Electronic applications accepted. *Expenses:* Tuition, state resident: full-time $3,393; part-time $189 per hour. Tuition, nonresident: full-time $8,577; part-time $477 per hour. Required fees: $752; $39 per hour. $25 per semester. *Financial support:* Teaching assistantships, scholarships/grants and unspecified assistantships available. Financial award application deadline: 7/1; financial award applicants required to submit FAFSA. *Unit head:* Dr. Charles Carr, Chair, 870-972-3043, Fax: 870-972-3045, E-mail: crcarr@astate.edu.

Arkansas Tech University, Graduate School, School of Education, Russellville, AR 72801. Offers college student personnel (MSE); educational leadership (M Ed, Ed S); English education (M Ed); gifted education (MSE); instructional improvement (M Ed); secondary education (M Ed); teaching, learning and leadership (M Ed). *Accreditation:* NCATE. Part-time programs available. *Students:* 44 full-time (33 women), 244 part-time (181 women); includes 20 minority (14 African Americans, 1 American Indian/Alaska Native, 3 Asian Americans or Pacific Islanders, 2 Hispanic Americans), 18 international. Average age 34. In 2006, 72 master's, 4 other advanced degrees awarded. *Degree requirements:* For master's, action research project, thesis optional. *Entrance requirements:* For master's, GRE General Test or MAT. Additional exam requirements/recommendations for international students: Required—TOEFL (minimum score 500 paper-based; 173 computer-based). *Application deadline:* For fall admission, 3/1 priority date for domestic students, 5/1 priority date for international students; for winter admission, 10/1 priority date for international students; for spring admission, 10/1 priority date for domestic and international students. Applications are processed on a rolling basis. Application fee: $0 ($30 for international students). Electronic applications accepted. *Expenses:* Tuition, state resident: full-time $3,060; part-time $170 per hour. Tuition, nonresident: full-time $6,120; part-time $340 per hour. Required fees: $312; $4 per hour. $84 per term. Part-time tuition and fees vary according to course load. *Financial support:* In 2006–07, teaching assistantships with full tuition reimbursements (averaging $4,000 per year); career-related internships or fieldwork, Federal Work-Study, scholarships/grants, health care benefits, and unspecified assistantships also available. Support available to part-time students. Financial award application deadline: 4/15; financial award applicants required to submit FAFSA. *Unit head:* Dr. C. Glenn Sheets, Dean, 479-968-0350, Fax: 479-968-0350, E-mail: glenn.sheets@atu.edu. *Application contact:* Dr. Eldon G. Clary, Dean of Graduate School, 479-968-0398, Fax: 479-964-0542, E-mail: graduate.school@atu.edu.

Arkansas Tech University, Graduate School, School of Liberal and Fine Arts, Russellville, AR 72801. Offers communication (MLA); English (M Ed, MA); fine arts (MLA); history (MA); multi-media journalism (MA); social science (MLA); social studies (M Ed); Spanish (MA, MLA); teaching English as a second language (MA, MLA). Part-time programs available. *Students:* 47 full-time (36 women), 102 part-time (82 women); includes 9 minority (2 African Americans, 1 American Indian/Alaska Native, 1 Asian American or Pacific Islander, 5 Hispanic Americans), 20 international. Average age 33. In 2006, 20 degrees awarded. *Degree requirements:* For master's, project. *Entrance requirements:* For master's, GRE General Test or MAT. Additional exam requirements/recommendations for international students: Required—TOEFL (minimum score 500 paper-based; 173 computer-based). *Application deadline:* For fall admission, 3/1 priority date for domestic students, 5/1 priority date for international students; for winter admission, 10/1 priority date for international students; for spring admission, 10/1 priority date for domestic and international students. Applications are processed on a rolling basis. Application fee: $0 ($30 for international students). Electronic applications accepted. *Expenses:* Tuition, state resident: full-time $3,060; part-time $170 per hour. Tuition, nonresident: full-time $6,120; part-time $340 per hour. Required fees: $312; $4 per hour. $84 per term. Part-time tuition and fees vary according to course load. *Financial support:* In 2006–07, teaching assistantships with full tuition reimbursements (averaging $4,000 per year); career-related internships or fieldwork, Federal Work-Study, scholarships/grants, health care benefits, and unspecified assistantships also available. Support available to part-time students. Financial award application deadline: 4/15; financial award applicants required to submit FAFSA. *Unit head:* Dr. Georgena Duncan, Dean, 479-968-0266, Fax: 479-968-0275, E-mail: georgena.duncan@atu.edu. *Application contact:* Dr. Eldon G. Clary, Dean of Graduate School, 479-968-0398, Fax: 479-964-0542, E-mail: graduate.school@atu.edu.

Armstrong Atlantic State University, School of Graduate Studies, Program in Education, Savannah, GA 31419-1997. Offers adult education (M Ed); early childhood education (M Ed); education (M Ed); elementary education (M Ed); middle grades education (M Ed); secondary education (M Ed), including business education, English education, mathematics education, science education, social science education; special education (M Ed), including behavioral disorders, curriculum and instruction, learning disabilities, speech-language pathology. *Accreditation:* NCATE. Part-time and evening/weekend programs available. Postbaccalaureate distance learning degree programs offered (minimal on-campus study). *Faculty:* 11 full-time (9 women), 13 part-time/adjunct (10 women). *Students:* 50 full-time (42 women), 219 part-time (175 women); includes 71 minority (67 African Americans, 3 Asian Americans or Pacific Islanders, 1 Hispanic American), 6 international. Average age 35. In 2006, 151 degrees awarded. *Degree requirements:* For master's, portfolio. *Entrance requirements:* For master's, GRE General Test or MAT, minimum GPA of 2.5, letters of recommendation. Additional exam requirements/recommendations for international students: Required—TOEFL (minimum score 523 paper-based; 193 computer-based). *Application deadline:* For fall admission, 7/1 priority date for domestic and international students; for spring admission, 11/15 priority date for domestic and international students. Applications are processed on a rolling basis. Application fee: $25. Electronic applications accepted. *Expenses:* Tuition, state resident: full-time $2,286; part-time $127 per credit. Tuition, nonresident: full-time $9,144; part-time $508 per credit. One-time fee: $257. *Financial support:* In 2006–07, research assistantships with partial tuition reimbursements (averaging $2,500 per year); career-related internships or fieldwork, Federal Work-Study, scholarships/grants, and unspecified assistantships also available. Support available to part-time students. Financial award applicants required to submit FAFSA. *Unit head:* Dr. Jane McHaney, College of Education Dean, 912-927-5398, Fax: 912-921-7425, E-mail: mchaneja@mail.armstrong.edu.

Auburn University, Graduate School, College of Education, Department of Curriculum and Teaching, Auburn University, AL 36849. Offers business education (M Ed, MS, PhD); early childhood education (M Ed, MS, PhD, Ed S); elementary education (M Ed, MS, PhD, Ed S); foreign languages (M Ed, MS); music education (M Ed, MS, PhD, Ed S); postsecondary education (PhD); reading education (PhD, Ed S); secondary education (M Ed, MS, PhD, Ed S), including English language arts, mathematics, science, social studies. *Accreditation:* NASM (one or more programs are accredited); NCATE. Part-time programs available. *Faculty:* 26 full-time (19 women). *Students:* 51 full-time (36 women), 116 part-time (86 women); includes 24 minority (23 African Americans, 1 Asian American or Pacific Islander). Average age 33. 181 applicants, 56% accepted, 68 enrolled. In 2006, 63 master's, 12 doctorates, 14 other advanced degrees awarded. *Degree requirements:* For master's, thesis (for some programs); for doctorate, thesis/dissertation; for Ed S, field project. *Entrance requirements:* For master's, doctorate, and Ed S, GRE General Test. *Application deadline:* For fall admission, 7/7 for domestic students; for spring admission, 11/24 for domestic students. Applications are processed on a rolling basis. Application fee: $25 ($50 for international students). Electronic applications accepted. *Expenses:* Tuition, state resident: full-time $5,000. Tuition, nonresident: full-time $15,000. Required fees: $416. Tuition and fees vary according to program. *Financial support:* Fellowships, teaching assistantships, career-related internships or fieldwork and Federal Work-Study available. Support available to part-time students. Financial award application deadline: 3/15. *Faculty research:* Emerging literacy, reading attitudes, music for at-risk youth, portfolio assessment. *Unit head:* Dr. Andrew M. Weaver, Head, 334-844-4434, E-mail: weaveam@mail.auburn.edu. *Application contact:* Dr. Joe Pittman, Interim Dean of the Graduate School, 334-844-4700.

Averett University, Graduate Studies in Education, Danville, VA 24541-3692. Offers art education (M Ed); biology (M Ed); chemistry (M Ed); curriculum and instruction (M Ed); elementary education (M Ed); English (M Ed); health and physical education (M Ed); history

English Education

Averett University (continued)
and social studies (M Ed); mathematics education (M Ed); physical science (M Ed); reading (M Ed); special education (learning disabilities specialization PK-12) (M Ed). Part-time and evening/weekend programs available. *Faculty:* 10 full-time (4 women), 7 part-time/adjunct (6 women). *Students:* 14 full-time (10 women), 85 part-time (67 women); includes 20 minority (18 African Americans, 2 Asian Americans or Pacific Islanders). Average age 33. 52 applicants, 100% accepted, 40 enrolled. In 2006, 48 degrees awarded. *Degree requirements:* For master's, thesis optional. *Entrance requirements:* For master's, PRAXIS, GRE General Test, MAT or NTE, writing proficiency exam, 3 letters of recommendation, current teacher's licensure or eligibility for licensure, minimum undergraduate GPA of 3.0 in previous 2 years. Additional exam requirements/recommendations for international students: Required—TOEFL (minimum score 600 paper-based; 200 computer-based). *Application deadline:* Applications are processed on a rolling basis. Application fee: $20. *Expenses: Contact institution. Financial support:* In 2006–07, 23 students received support. Federal Work-Study and scholarships/grants available. Financial award application deadline: 4/1; financial award applicants required to submit FAFSA. *Faculty research:* Literary assessment-PreK-6, handwriting instruction and assessment-PreK-6, written language instruction and assessment-PreK-6 and special needs students learning styles, curriculum and instruction processes. *Unit head:* Dr. Lynn H. Wolf, Chair, 434-793-3995, Fax: 434-791-4392, E-mail: lynn.wolf@averett.edu.

Belmont University, College of Arts and Sciences, School of Education, Nashville, TN 37212-3757. Offers education (MAT); elementary education (M Ed), including early childhood education, elementary education, gifted education, language arts education; English (M Ed); history (M Ed); mathematics (M Ed); middle grade education (M Ed); science (M Ed); secondary education (M Ed), including gifted education; sports administration (MSA); technology (M Ed). *Accreditation:* NCATE. Part-time and evening/weekend programs available. *Faculty:* 9 full-time (7 women), 20 part-time/adjunct (15 women). *Students:* 50 full-time (36 women), 116 part-time (76 women); includes 23 minority (20 African Americans, 1 Asian American or Pacific Islander, 2 Hispanic Americans), 1 international. Average age 30. 55 applicants, 60% accepted, 30 enrolled. In 2006, 82 degrees awarded. *Degree requirements:* For master's, thesis, comprehensive exam. *Entrance requirements:* For master's, MAT or GRE, minimum GPA of 2.75. Additional exam requirements/recommendations for international students: Required—TOEFL. *Application deadline:* For fall admission, 8/1 priority date for domestic students, 5/1 for international students; for spring admission, 12/1 priority date for domestic students, 9/1 for international students. Applications are processed on a rolling basis. Application fee: $50. *Expenses: Contact institution. Financial support:* In 2006–07, 25 students received support; fellowships with partial tuition reimbursements available, institutionally sponsored loans and tuition waivers (partial) available. Financial award application deadline: 4/15; financial award applicants required to submit FAFSA. *Faculty research:* Technology grant, professional development schools. Total annual research expenditures: $6,500. *Unit head:* Dr. Trevor F. Hutchins, Associate Dean, 615-460-6232, Fax: 615-460-6414, E-mail: hutchinst@mail.belmont.edu. *Application contact:* Julie Hullett, Admission/Licensure Officer, 615-460-6879, Fax: 615-460-5556, E-mail: hullettj@email.belmont.edu.

Bennington College, Graduate Programs, Program in Teaching, Bennington, VT 05201. Offers art education (MAT); early childhood (MAT); elementary education (MAT); English education (MAT); foreign language education (MAT); mathematics education (MAT); music education (MAT); science education (MAT); secondary education (MAT); social science education (MAT). *Faculty:* 4 part-time/adjunct (3 women). *Students:* 11 full-time (7 women), 1 (woman) part-time; includes 2 minority (both Hispanic Americans) Average age 31. 12 applicants, 75% accepted, 3 enrolled. In 2006, 13 degrees awarded. *Degree requirements:* For master's, 1 year teaching practicum, professional portfolio. *Entrance requirements:* For master's, interview. *Application deadline:* For fall admission, 3/1 for domestic students. Application fee: $60. *Expenses: Contact institution.* One-time fee: $75 full-time. Tuition and fees vary according to program. *Financial support:* In 2006–07, 10 students received support, including 4 fellowships (averaging $6,875 per year); scholarships/grants and unspecified assistantships also available. Financial award application deadline: 4/1; financial award applicants required to submit FAFSA. *Unit head:* George Kamberelis, Director of Center for Creative Teaching, 802-440-4863, E-mail: gkamberelis@bennington.edu. *Application contact:* Ken Himmelman, Dean of Admissions, 802-440-4312, Fax: 802-440-4320, E-mail: admissions@bennington.edu.

See Close-Up on page 861.

Bethel College, Program in Education, McKenzie, TN 38201. Offers administration and supervision (MA Ed); biology education K8-12 (MAT); elementary education (MAT); English education K8-12 (MAT); history education K8-12 (MAT); physical education K8-12 (MAT); special education K8-12 (MAT). Part-time and evening/weekend programs available. *Degree requirements:* For master's, thesis (for some programs). *Entrance requirements:* For master's, GRE General Test or MAT, minimum undergraduate GPA of 2.5.

Bob Jones University, Graduate Programs, Greenville, SC 29614. Offers accountancy (MS); Bible (MA); Bible translation (MA); Biblical studies (Certificate); broadcast management (MS); business administration (MBA); church history (MA, PhD); church ministries (MA); church music (MM); cinema and video production (MA); counseling (MS); curriculum and instruction (Ed D); divinity (M Div); dramatic production (MA); educational leadership (MS, Ed D, Ed S); elementary education (M Ed, MAT); English (M Ed, MA, MAT); fine arts (MA); graphic design (MA); history (M Ed, MA); illustration (MA); interpretative speech (MA); mathematics (M Ed, MAT); medical missions (Certificate); ministry (MM, D Min); multi-categorical special education (M Ed, MAT); music (M Ed); New Testament interpretation (PhD); Old Testament interpretation (PhD); orchestral instrument performance (MM); organ performance (MM); pastoral studies (MA); personnel services (MS, Ed S); piano pedagogy (MM); piano performance (MM); platform arts (MA); radio and television broadcasting (MS); rhetoric and public address (MA); secondary education (M Ed); studio art (MA); teaching Bible (MA); theology (MA, PhD); voice performance (MM); youth ministries (MA); M Div/MM.

Boston College, Lynch Graduate School of Education, Department of Teacher Education/Special Education and Curriculum and Instruction, Program in Secondary Education, Chestnut Hill, MA 02467-3800. Offers biology (MST); chemistry (MST); English (MAT); French (MAT); geology (MST); history (MAT); Latin and classical humanities (MAT); mathematics (MST); physics (MST); secondary teaching (M Ed), including biology, chemistry, English, French, geology, history, Latin and classical humanities, mathematics, physics, Spanish; Spanish (MAT). *Students:* 70 full-time (46 women), 28 part-time (15 women); includes 8 minority (4 African Americans, 1 American Indian/Alaska Native, 3 Asian Americans or Pacific Islanders), 2 international. 217 applicants, 72% accepted, 64 enrolled. In 2006, 48 degrees awarded. *Degree requirements:* For master's, comprehensive exam. *Entrance requirements:* For master's, GRE General Test or MAT. Additional exam requirements/recommendations for international students: Required—TOEFL. *Application deadline:* For fall admission, 1/1 priority date for domestic students. Application fee: $60. *Financial support:* Fellowships with full and partial tuition reimbursements, research assistantships with full and partial tuition reimbursements, teaching assistantships with full and partial tuition reimbursements, career-related internships or fieldwork, Federal Work-Study, scholarships/grants, traineeships, tuition waivers (full and partial), and unspecified assistantships available. Support available to part-time students. Financial award applicants required to submit FAFSA. *Faculty research:* Curriculum theory and practice, teacher preparation, learning styles, teacher research. *Application contact:* Timothy P. Blackman, Director, Graduate Admission and Financial Aid, 617-552-4214, Fax: 617-552-0398, E-mail: timothy.blackman.1@bc.edu.

Boston University, School of Education, Department of Curriculum and Teaching, Programs in English and Language Arts Education, Boston, MA 02215. Offers Ed M, CAGS. *Students:* 32 full-time (23 women), 1 (woman) part-time; includes 1 minority (Asian American or Pacific Islander), 1 international. Average age 25. 12 applicants, 92% accepted. *Degree requirements:* For master's, thesis optional. *Entrance requirements:* For master's and CAGS, GRE General Test or MAT. Additional exam requirements/recommendations for international students: Required—TOEFL. *Application deadline:* For fall admission, 2/15 priority date for domestic students; for winter admission, 10/1 priority date for domestic students. Applications are processed on a rolling basis. Application fee: $65. Electronic applications accepted. *Expenses:* Tuition: Full-time $33,330; part-time $1,042 per credit. Required fees: $462; $40. *Financial support:* Application deadline: 2/15. *Application contact:* 617-353-4237, Fax: 617-353-8937, E-mail: sedgrad@bu.edu.

Brooklyn College of the City University of New York, Division of Graduate Studies, School of Education, Program in Adolescence Education and Special Subjects, Brooklyn, NY 11210-2889. Offers art teacher (MA); biology teacher (MA); chemistry teacher (MA); English teacher (MA); French teacher (MA); health and nutrition sciences: health teacher (MS Ed); mathematics teacher (MA); music education (CAS); music teacher (MA); physical education teacher (MS Ed); physics teacher (MA); social studies teacher (MA); Spanish teacher (MA). Part-time and evening/weekend programs available. *Students:* 30 full-time (22 women), 450 part-time (257 women); includes 167 minority (101 African Americans, 21 Asian Americans or Pacific Islanders, 45 Hispanic Americans), 21 international. 277 applicants, 84% accepted, 113 enrolled. In 2006, 172 master's, 6 other advanced degrees awarded. *Degree requirements:* For master's, comprehensive exam (for some programs). *Entrance requirements:* For master's, LAST, previous course work in education, resumé, 2 letters of recommendation, essay. Additional exam requirements/recommendations for international students: Required—TOEFL. *Application deadline:* For fall admission, 3/1 priority date for domestic students, 2/1 priority date for international students; for spring admission, 11/1 priority date for domestic students, 10/1 priority date for international students. Applications are processed on a rolling basis. Application fee: $125. Electronic applications accepted. *Expenses:* Tuition, state resident: full-time $6,400; part-time $270 per credit. Tuition, nonresident: full-time $12,000; part-time $500 per credit. Required fees: $118 per semester. *Financial support:* Career-related internships or fieldwork, Federal Work-Study, institutionally sponsored loans, and scholarships/grants available. Support available to part-time students. Financial award application deadline: 5/1; financial award applicants required to submit FAFSA. *Faculty research:* Interdisciplinary education, semiotics, discourse analysis, autobiography, teacher identity. *Unit head:* Prof. Stephen Phillips, Program Facilitator, 718-951-5214, E-mail: phillips@brooklyn.cuny.edu. *Application contact:* Karen Alleyne-Pierre, Director of Admissions Services and Enrollment Communications, 718-951-5902, Fax: 718-951-4506, E-mail: grads@brooklyn.cuny.edu.

Brown University, Graduate School, Department of Education, Providence, RI 02912. Offers elementary education 1-6 (MAT); secondary biology (MAT); secondary English (MAT); secondary social studies/history (MAT). *Faculty:* 4 full-time (2 women), 7 part-time/adjunct (all women). *Students:* 28 full-time (23 women); includes 5 minority (2 African Americans, 1 Asian American or Pacific Islander, 2 Hispanic Americans). Average age 25. 89 applicants, 61% accepted, 28 enrolled. In 2006, 35 degrees awarded. *Degree requirements:* For master's, student teaching, portfolio. *Entrance requirements:* For master's, GRE General Test (secondary only), PRAXIS II (elementary), letters of recommendation, interview. *Application deadline:* For winter admission, 1/3 for domestic students. Application fee: $70. Electronic applications accepted. *Financial support:* In 2006–07, 23 students received support, including 2 fellowships (averaging $7,000 per year); Federal Work-Study, institutionally sponsored loans, scholarships/grants, tuition waivers (partial), and proctorships also available. Financial award application deadline: 2/1; financial award applicants required to submit FAFSA. *Faculty research:* Literacy, performance-based assessment, teaching English as a foreign language. *Unit head:* Lawrence Wakeford, Chairman, 401-863-3428, Fax: 401-863-1276, E-mail: lawrence_wakeford@brown.edu. *Application contact:* Carin Algava, Assistant Director, 401-863-3364, Fax: 401-863-1276, E-mail: carin_algava@brown.edu.

Buffalo State College, State University of New York, Graduate Studies and Research, Faculty of Arts and Humanities, Department of English, Buffalo, NY 14222-1095. Offers English (MA); secondary education (MS Ed), including English. Part-time and evening/weekend programs available. *Degree requirements:* For master's, thesis or project, 1 foreign language (MS Ed). *Entrance requirements:* For master's, minimum GPA of 2.75, 36 hours in English, New York teaching certificate (MS Ed). Additional exam requirements/recommendations for international students: Required—TOEFL (minimum score 550 paper-based; 213 computer-based).

California State University, San Bernardino, Graduate Studies, College of Education, San Bernardino, CA 92407-2397. Offers bilingual/cross-cultural education (MA); curriculum and instruction (MA); educational administration (MA); educational psychology and counseling (MA, MS), including counseling and guidance (MS), rehabilitation counseling (MA); elementary education (MA); English as a second language (MA); environmental education (MA); history and English for secondary teachers (MA); instructional technology (MA); reading (MA); secondary education (MA); special education and rehabilitation counseling (MA), including rehabilitation counseling, special education; teaching of science (MA); vocational and career education (MA). *Accreditation:* NCATE. Part-time and evening/weekend programs available. *Faculty:* 69 full-time, 145 part-time/adjunct. *Students:* 692 full-time (515 women), 345 part-time (245 women); includes 479 minority (145 African Americans, 12 American Indian/Alaska Native, 45 Asian Americans or Pacific Islanders, 277 Hispanic Americans), 17 international. Average age 33. 450 applicants, 82% accepted, 147 enrolled. In 2006, 349 degrees awarded. *Entrance requirements:* For master's, minimum GPA of 3.0 in education. *Application deadline:* For fall admission, 8/31 priority date for domestic students. Application fee: $55. *Financial support:* Career-related internships or fieldwork and Federal Work-Study available. Support available to part-time students. *Faculty research:* Multicultural education, brain-based learning, science education, social studies/global education. *Unit head:* Dr. Patricia Arlin, Dean, 909-537-5600, Fax: 909-537-7011, E-mail: parlin@csusb.edu.

Campbell University, Graduate and Professional Programs, School of Education, Buies Creek, NC 27506. Offers administration (MSA); community counseling (MA); elementary education (M Ed); English education (M Ed); interdisciplinary studies (M Ed); mathematics education (M Ed); middle grades education (M Ed); physical education (M Ed); school counseling (M Ed); secondary education (M Ed); social science education (M Ed). *Accreditation:* NCATE. Part-time and evening/weekend programs available. *Faculty:* 14 full-time (9 women), 12 part-time/adjunct (7 women). *Students:* 27 full-time (25 women), 183 part-time (146 women); includes 30 minority (24 African Americans, 3 American Indian/Alaska Native, 3 Hispanic Americans), 1 international. Average age 31. 112 applicants, 74% accepted, 74 enrolled. In 2006, 65 degrees awarded. *Degree requirements:* For master's, comprehensive exam. *Entrance requirements:* For master's, GRE General Test, minimum GPA of 2.7. *Application deadline:* For fall admission, 8/1 priority date for domestic students; for spring admission, 1/2 priority date for domestic students. Applications are processed on a rolling basis. Application fee: $65. *Expenses:* Tuition: Part-time $380 per semester hour. *Financial support:* In 2006–07, 67 students received support. Career-related internships or fieldwork and Federal Work-Study available. Financial award application deadline: 4/15; financial award applicants required to submit FAFSA. *Faculty research:* Spiritual values and wellness issues in counseling, stress and professional burnout among counselors, thinking strategies, leadership, adaptive technology. *Unit head:* Dr. Karen P. Nery, Dean, 910-893-1630, Fax: 910-893-1999, E-mail: nery@campbell.edu. *Application contact:* James S. Farthing, Director of Graduate Admissions for Business and Education, 910-893-1200 Ext. 1318, Fax: 910-814-4718, E-mail: farthing@campbell.edu.

Carthage College, Division of Teacher Education, Kenosha, WI 53140. Offers classroom guidance and counseling (M Ed); creative arts (M Ed); gifted and talented children (M Ed); language arts (M Ed); modern language (M Ed); natural sciences (M Ed); reading (M Ed, Certificate); social sciences (M Ed); teacher leadership (M Ed). Part-time and evening/weekend programs available. *Degree requirements:* For master's, thesis optional. *Entrance requirements:* For master's, MAT, minimum B average, letters of reference.

Chadron State College, School of Professional and Graduate Studies, Department of Education, Chadron, NE 69337. Offers business (MA Ed); community counseling (MA Ed); educational administration (MS Ed, Sp Ed); elementary education (MS Ed); history (MA Ed); language and literature (MA Ed); secondary administration (MS Ed); secondary education (MS Ed). *Accreditation:* NCATE. Part-time and evening/weekend programs available. Postbaccalaureate distance learning degree programs offered. *Degree requirements:* For master's, thesis optional. *Entrance requirements:* For master's, GRE General Test, GRE Writing Test, minimum GPA of 2.75 or 12 graduate hours at CSC with minimum GPA of 3.25. Additional exam requirements/recommendations for international students: Required—TOEFL. Electronic applications accepted. *Faculty research:* Rural education, technology, mental health.

Charleston Southern University, Programs in Education, Charleston, SC 29423-8087. Offers administration and supervision (M Ed), including elementary, secondary; elementary education (M Ed); English (MAT); science (MAT); secondary education (M Ed); social studies (MAT). *Accreditation:* NCATE. Part-time and evening/weekend programs available. *Degree requirements:* For master's, thesis optional. *Entrance requirements:* For master's, GRE or MAT. Expenses: Contact institution. *Faculty research:* Economic education, multicultural education, restructuring teacher education, participation in mathematics and science by minorities and women, at-risk children.

Chatham University, Program in Education, Pittsburgh, PA 15232-2826. Offers early childhood education (MAT); elementary education (MAT); English—secondary (MAT); environmental education (K-12) (MAT); secondary art (MAT); secondary biology education (MAT); secondary chemistry education (MAT); secondary English education (MAT); secondary math education (MAT); secondary physics education (MAT); secondary social studies education (MAT); special education (MAT). *Students:* 60 full-time (43 women), 23 part-time (22 women). Average age 29. 48 applicants, 77% accepted, 32 enrolled. In 2006, 59 degrees awarded. *Degree requirements:* For master's, thesis, teaching experience. *Entrance requirements:* For master's, PRAXIS I, minimum GPA of 3.0, sample of written work, recommendation letters. Additional exam requirements/recommendations for international students: Required—TOEFL (minimum score 600 paper-based; 250 computer-based; 100 iBT); Recommended—IELTS (minimum score 7), TWE (minimum score 5). *Application deadline:* For fall admission, 5/1 priority date for domestic and international students; for winter admission, 10/1 priority date for domestic and international students. Applications are processed on a rolling basis. Application fee: $45. Electronic applications accepted. *Financial support:* Career-related internships or fieldwork available. Financial award applicants required to submit FAFSA. *Faculty research:* Gifted education, environmental education, technology in education, writing as learning, class size and achievement. *Unit head:* Dr. Wendy Weiner, Director, 412-365-1146, Fax: 412-365-1505, E-mail: wweiner@chatham.edu. *Application contact:* 412-365-1825, Fax: 412-365-1609, E-mail: admissions@chatham.edu.

Christopher Newport University, Graduate Studies, Department of Teacher Preparation, Newport News, VA 23606-2998. Offers art (PK-12) (MAT); biology (6-12) (MAT); computer science (6-12) (MAT); elementary (PK-6) (MAT); English (6-12) (MAT); French (PK-12) (MAT); history (6-12) (MAT); history and social science (MAT); mathematics (6-12) (MAT); music (PK-12) (MAT), including choral, instrumental; physics (6-12) (MAT); Spanish (PK-12) (MAT); theater (PK-12) (MAT). Part-time and evening/weekend programs available. *Degree requirements:* For master's, thesis or alternative, comprehensive exam. *Entrance requirements:* For master's, PRAXIS I, minimum GPA of 3.0. Electronic applications accepted. *Faculty research:* Early literacy development, instructional innovations, professional teaching standards, multicultural issues, aesthetic education.

City College of the City University of New York, Graduate School, School of Education, Department of Secondary Education, New York, NY 10031-9198. Offers adolescent mathematics education (MA, AC); English education (MA); middle school mathematics education (MS); science education (MA); social studies education (AC). *Accreditation:* NCATE. *Students:* 286 applicants, 94% accepted, 219 enrolled. *Entrance requirements:* For master's, Liberal Arts and Sciences Test (LAST), Content Specialty Test (CST). Additional exam requirements/recommendations for international students: Required—TOEFL. *Application deadline:* For fall admission, 3/15 for domestic students; for spring admission, 10/15 for domestic students. Application fee: $125. *Unit head:* Susan Semel, Chair, 212-650-7262, E-mail: ssemel@ccny.cuny.edu. *Application contact:* Stacia Pusey, Graduate Admissions Adviser-Education, 212-650-5345, E-mail: spusey@ccny.cuny.edu.

Clarion University of Pennsylvania, Office of Research and Graduate Studies, College of Education and Human Services, Department of Education, Program in Education, Clarion, PA 16214. Offers curriculum and instruction (M Ed); early childhood (M Ed); English (M Ed); history (M Ed); literacy (M Ed); science (M Ed); technology (M Ed). *Accreditation:* NCATE. Part-time programs available. *Faculty:* 18 full-time (13 women). *Students:* 11 full-time (4 women), 54 part-time (37 women); includes 4 minority (3 African Americans, 1 Asian American or Pacific Islander). 50 applicants, 90% accepted. In 2006, 7 degrees awarded. *Degree requirements:* For master's, thesis or alternative, comprehensive exam. *Entrance requirements:* For master's, minimum QPA of 3.0, teacher certification. Additional exam requirements/recommendations for international students: Required—TOEFL (minimum score 550 paper-based; 213 computer-based; 80 iBT). *Application deadline:* For fall admission, 8/1 priority date for domestic students, 4/15 priority date for international students; for spring admission, 12/1 priority date for domestic students, 9/15 priority date for international students. Applications are processed on a rolling basis. Application fee: $30. Electronic applications accepted. *Expenses:* Tuition, state resident: part-time $336 per credit. Tuition, nonresident: part-time $538 per credit. *Financial support:* In 2006–07, 2 research assistantships with full tuition reimbursements (averaging $4,002 per year) were awarded. Support available to part-time students. Financial award application deadline: 3/1. *Application contact:* Dr. Brian Maguire, Coordinator, 814-393-2058, Fax: 814-393-2558, E-mail: bmaguire@clarion.edu.

Clemson University, Graduate School, College of Health, Education, and Human Development, School of Education, Program in Secondary Education, Clemson, SC 29634. Offers English (M Ed); mathematics (M Ed); natural sciences (M Ed). *Accreditation:* NCATE. *Students:* 5 full-time (2 women), 9 part-time (8 women); includes 1 minority (American Indian/Alaska Native). 11 applicants, 45% accepted, 2 enrolled. In 2006, 9 degrees awarded. *Entrance requirements:* For master's, teaching certificate. Additional exam requirements/recommendations for international students: Required—TOEFL. *Application deadline:* For fall admission, 6/1 for domestic students. Application fee: $50. *Expenses:* Tuition, state resident: full-time $8,812; part-time $450 per hour. Tuition, nonresident: full-time $18,036; part-time $760 per hour. Required fees: $474; $5 per term. *Financial support:* Application deadline: 6/1; *Unit head:* Dr. William Fisk, Graduate Coordinator, 864-656-5119, Fax: 864-656-1322, E-mail: bill252@clemson.edu.

See Close-Up on page 1273.

College of St. Joseph, Graduate Program, Division of Education, Program in Secondary Education, Rutland, VT 05701-3899. Offers English (M Ed); mathematics (M Ed); social studies (M Ed). Part-time and evening/weekend programs available. *Faculty:* 2 full-time (1 woman), 8 part-time/adjunct (5 women). *Students:* 4 full-time, 4 part-time. Average age 32. 7 applicants, 100% accepted, 6 enrolled. In 2006, 4 degrees awarded. *Entrance requirements:* For master's, PRAXIS I, 2 letters of recommendation, minimum GPA of 3.0, interview. *Application deadline:* Applications are processed on a rolling basis. Application fee: $35. *Expenses:* Tuition: Full-time $10,990; part-time $300 per credit. Part-time tuition and fees vary according to program. *Financial support:* Career-related internships or fieldwork, Federal Work-Study, and unspecified assistantships available. Support available to part-time students. Financial award application deadline: 3/1. *Unit head:* Dr. David Balfour, Director, 802-773-5900 Ext. 3230, Fax: 802-776-5258, E-mail: dbalfour@csj.edu. *Application contact:* Tracy Gallipo, Director of Admissions, 802-773-5900 Ext. 3262, Fax: 802-773-5900, E-mail: tracygallipo@csj.edu.

The College of William and Mary, School of Education, Program in Curriculum and Instruction, Williamsburg, VA 23187-8795. Offers elementary education (MA Ed); gifted education (MA Ed); reading education (MA Ed); secondary education (MA Ed), including English education, mathematics education, modern foreign languages education, science education, social studies education; special education (MA Ed), including emotionally disturbed, learning disabled, mental retardation, resource collaborating teaching. *Accreditation:* NCATE. Part-time programs available. *Faculty:* 15 full-time (6 women), 13 part-time/adjunct (10 women). *Students:* 51 full-time (39 women), 51 part-time (45 women); includes 6 minority (all African Americans) Average age 29. 161 applicants, 68% accepted, 61 enrolled. In 2006, 68 degrees awarded. *Degree requirements:* For master's, master's project. *Entrance requirements:* For master's, GRE or MAT, minimum GPA of 2.5. Additional exam requirements/recommendations for international students: Required—TOEFL. *Application deadline:* For fall admission, 2/1 for domestic and international students; for spring admission, 10/1 for domestic and international students. Application fee: $30. *Expenses:* Tuition, state resident: full-time $6,100; part-time $260 per credit. Tuition, nonresident: full-time $18,790; part-time $725 per credit. Required fees: $3,314. Tuition and fees vary according to program. *Financial support:* In 2006–07, 10 research assistantships with full and partial tuition reimbursements (averaging $5,000 per year) were awarded; career-related internships or fieldwork, Federal Work-Study, institutionally sponsored loans, scholarships/grants, and unspecified assistantships also available. Financial award application deadline: 2/1; financial award applicants required to submit FAFSA. *Faculty research:* National Council of Teachers of Mathematics Standards, counseling, self-concept and self-esteem, special education, curriculum development. *Unit head:* Dr. John Moore, Area Coordinator, 757-221-2333, E-mail: jnmoor@wm.edu. *Application contact:* Dorothy Osborne, Director of Admissions, 757-221-2317, E-mail: dsosbo@wm.edu.

The Colorado College, Department of Education, Program in Secondary Education, Colorado Springs, CO 80903-3294. Offers art teaching (MAT); English teaching (MAT); foreign language teaching (MAT); mathematics teaching (MAT); music teaching (MAT); science teaching (MAT); social studies teaching (MAT). *Faculty:* 2 full-time (1 woman), 10 part-time/adjunct (7 women). *Students:* 18 full-time (12 women); includes 2 minority (1 African American, 1 Asian American or Pacific Islander). Average age 27. 30 applicants, 90% accepted, 18 enrolled. In 2006, 16 degrees awarded. *Degree requirements:* For master's, thesis, internship. *Entrance requirements:* For master's, PRAXIS II or PLACE. *Application deadline:* For fall admission, 2/1 for domestic and international students. Application fee: $50. *Expenses:* Tuition: Full-time $23,567. One-time fee: $1,485 full-time. *Financial support:* In 2006–07, 15 teaching assistantships (averaging $16,000 per year) were awarded; career-related internships or fieldwork, institutionally sponsored loans, health care benefits, and tuition waivers (partial) also available. Financial award application deadline: 2/15; financial award applicants required to submit FAFSA. *Unit head:* Mike Taber, Director, 719-389-6026, Fax: 719-389-6473, E-mail: pveronesi@coloradocollege.edu. *Application contact:* Marsha E. Unruh, Director of Education Career Services, 719-389-6472, Fax: 719-389-6473, E-mail: munruh@coloradocollege.edu.

Columbia College Chicago, Graduate School, Department of Educational Studies, Chicago, IL 60605-1996. Offers elementary (MAT); English (MAT); interdisciplinary arts (MAT); multicultural education (MA); urban teaching (MA). Part-time and evening/weekend programs available. *Degree requirements:* For master's, thesis, student teaching experience, 100 pre-clinical hours. *Entrance requirements:* For master's, NTE, minimum GPA of 3.0, portfolio. Additional exam requirements/recommendations for international students: Required—TOEFL (minimum score 550 paper-based; 213 computer-based). Electronic applications accepted.

Columbus State University, Graduate Studies, College of Education, Department of Teacher Education, Columbus, GA 31907-5645. Offers early childhood education (M Ed, Ed S); instructional technology (MS); middle grades education (M Ed, Ed S); physical education (M Ed); secondary education (M Ed, Ed S), including English/language arts, general science (M Ed), mathematics, science (Ed S), social science; special education (Ed S), including behavior disorders, learning disabilities, mental retardation. *Accreditation:* NCATE. Part-time and evening/weekend programs available. Postbaccalaureate distance learning degree programs offered (minimal on-campus study). *Faculty:* 16 full-time (8 women), 2 part-time/adjunct (1 woman). *Students:* 61 full-time (45 women), 128 part-time (89 women); includes 44 minority (36 African Americans, 3 Asian Americans or Pacific Islanders, 5 Hispanic Americans), 1 international. Average age 36. 77 applicants, 49% accepted, 26 enrolled. In 2006, 66 master's, 13 other advanced degrees awarded. *Degree requirements:* For master's, thesis, exit exam; for Ed S, thesis or alternative. *Entrance requirements:* For master's, GRE General Test, minimum GPA of 2.75; for Ed S, GRE General Test. Additional exam requirements/recommendations for international students: Required—TOEFL (minimum score 550 paper-based; 213 computer-based). *Application deadline:* For fall admission, 5/1 priority date for domestic students, 5/1 for international students; for spring admission, 11/1 for domestic and international students. Applications are processed on a rolling basis. Application fee: $25. Electronic applications accepted. *Expenses:* Tuition, state resident: part-time $127 per semester hour. Tuition, nonresident: part-time $508 per semester hour. Required fees: $264 per semester. Tuition and fees vary according to course load. *Financial support:* In 2006–07, 118 students received support, including 21 research assistantships with partial tuition reimbursements available (averaging $3,000 per year); career-related internships or fieldwork, Federal Work-Study, institutionally sponsored loans, scholarships/grants, tuition waivers (partial), and unspecified assistantships also available. Support available to part-time students. Financial award application deadline: 5/1; financial award applicants required to submit FAFSA. *Unit head:* Dr. Deborah Gober, Acting Chair, 706-568-2255, Fax: 706-568-3134, E-mail: gober_deborah@colstate.edu. *Application contact:* Katie Thornton, Graduate Admissions Specialist, 706-568-2035, Fax: 706-568-2462, E-mail: thornton_katie@colstate.edu.

Connecticut College, Graduate School, Department of English, New London, CT 06320-4196. Offers MA, MAT. Part-time programs available. *Degree requirements:* For master's, one foreign language, thesis. *Entrance requirements:* For master's, GRE General Test, GRE Subject Test.

Converse College, School of Education and Graduate Studies, Program in Secondary Education, Spartanburg, SC 29302-0006. Offers biology (MAT); chemistry (MAT); English (M Ed, MAT); mathematics (M Ed, MAT); natural sciences (M Ed, MAT); social sciences (M Ed, MAT). Part-time programs available. *Students:* Average age 35. In 2006, 40 degrees awarded. *Degree requirements:* For master's, capstone paper. *Entrance requirements:* For master's, NTE or PRAXIS II (M Ed), minimum GPA of 2.75, 2 recommendations. *Application deadline:* For fall admission, 8/1 for domestic and international students; for winter admission, 11/15 for domestic and international students; for spring admission, 1/15 for domestic and international students. Applications are processed on a rolling basis. Application fee: $40. Electronic applications accepted. *Expenses:* Tuition: Part-time $305 per credit hour. Required fees: $20 per term. *Financial support:* Available to part-time students. Applicants required to submit FAFSA.

Delta State University, Graduate Programs, College of Arts and Sciences, Division of Languages and Literature, Cleveland, MS 38733-0001. Offers English education (M Ed). Part-time programs available. *Degree requirements:* For master's, thesis or alternative. *Application deadline:* For fall admission, 8/1 priority date for domestic students; for spring admission, 12/1 priority date for domestic students. Applications are processed on a rolling basis. Application fee: $0. *Financial support:* In 2006–07, research assistantships (averaging $4,000 per year); career-related internships or fieldwork, Federal Work-Study, and institutionally sponsored loans also available. Support available to part-time students. Financial award application deadline: 6/1. *Unit head:* Dr. Bill Hays, Chair, 662-846-4060, Fax: 662-846-4016.

DeSales University, Graduate Division, Program in Education, Center Valley, PA 18034-9568. Offers academic standards and information (Certificate); bilingual/ESL studies (Certificate); biology (M Ed); chemistry (M Ed); computers in education (K-12) (M Ed); computers in education (K-8) (M Ed); English (M Ed); instructional technology specialist (Certificate); mathematics (M Ed); special education (M Ed, Certificate); TESOL (M Ed). Part-time and evening/weekend programs available. Postbaccalaureate distance learning degree programs offered (minimal on-campus study). *Students:* 34 full-time, 190 part-time. In 2006, 30 degrees awarded. *Degree requirements:* For master's, thesis project. *Entrance requirements:* For master's, teaching certificate. *Application deadline:* Applications are processed on a rolling basis. Application fee: $35. Electronic applications accepted. *Expenses: Contact institution.*

English Education

DeSales University (continued)

Financial support: Unspecified assistantships available. Support available to part-time students. Financial award application deadline: 5/1. *Faculty research:* Effective teaching, computer interfacing in chemistry labs, computer applications to teaching, history of philosophy, aesthetics multidrug-resistant cancer. *Unit head:* Dr. Lujean Baab, Director of M.Ed. Program, 610-282-1100 Ext. 1739, Fax: 610-282-3734, E-mail: lujean.baab@desales.edu. *Application contact:* Donna L. Cressman, Program Secretary, 610-282-1100 Ext. 1461, Fax: 610-282-3734, E-mail: med@desales.edu.

Drake University, School of Education, Department of Teaching and Learning, Program in Secondary Education, Des Moines, IA 50311-4516. Offers art (MAT); biology (MAT); business (MAT); chemistry (MAT); English (MAT); general science (MAT); history-American (MAT); history-world (MAT); journalism (MAT); mathematics (MAT); physical science (MAT); physics (MAT); sociology (MAT); speech (MAT); speech communication (MAT); theatre (MAT). Part-time programs available. *Faculty:* 10 full-time (3 women), 28 part-time/adjunct (16 women). *Students:* 13 full-time (7 women), 33 part-time (20 women). 41 applicants, 56% accepted. In 2006, 12 degrees awarded. *Degree requirements:* For master's, thesis (for some programs), internships (s), comprehensive exam, registration. *Entrance requirements:* For master's, GRE General Test, MAT, or Drake Writing Assessment, resumé, 2 letters of recommendation. Additional exam requirements/recommendations for international students: Required—TOEFL (minimum score 550 paper-based; 213 computer-based). *Application deadline:* For fall admission, 7/1 priority date for domestic students, 6/1 priority date for international students; for spring admission, 11/1 priority date for domestic students, 10/1 priority date for international students. Applications are processed on a rolling basis. Application fee: $25. Electronic applications accepted. *Financial support:* Career-related internships or fieldwork and unspecified assistantships available. Support available to part-time students. *Faculty research:* Counseling and rehabilitation, behavioral supports, inquiry-based science methods, teacher quality enhancement. Total annual research expenditures: $1.5 million. *Unit head:* Dr. Linda Espey, Head, 515-271-1954, E-mail: linda.espey@drake.edu. *Application contact:* Ann J. Martin, Graduate Coordinator, 515-271-2034, Fax: 515-271-2831, E-mail: ann.martin@drake.edu.

East Carolina University, Graduate School, College of Education, Department of Curriculum and Instruction, Greenville, NC 27858-4353. Offers behavior/emotional disabilities (MA Ed); elementary education (MA Ed); English education (MA Ed); learning disabilities (MA Ed); low incidence disabilities (MA Ed); mental retardation (MA Ed); middle grade education (MA Ed); reading education (MA Ed); social studies education (MA Ed). Part-time programs available. Postbaccalaureate distance learning degree programs offered. *Students:* 92 full-time (85 women), 233 part-time (211 women); includes 42 minority (39 African Americans, 1 American Indian/Alaska Native, 1 Asian American or Pacific Islander, 1 Hispanic American). Average age 30. 25 applicants, 100% accepted, 25 enrolled. In 2006, 195 degrees awarded. *Degree requirements:* For master's, thesis optional. *Entrance requirements:* For master's, GRE General Test or MAT, interview, bachelor's degree in related field, minimum GPA of 2.5, teaching license. Additional exam requirements/recommendations for international students: Required—TOEFL. *Application deadline:* For fall admission, 6/1 priority date for domestic students. Applications are processed on a rolling basis. Application fee: $50. *Financial support:* Research assistantships, teaching assistantships, Federal Work-Study available. Support available to part-time students. Financial award application deadline: 6/1; financial award applicants required to submit FAFSA. *Unit head:* Dr. Sandra H. Warren, Interim Chair, 252-328-2699, E-mail: warrens@ecu.edu. *Application contact:* Dean of Graduate School, 252-328-6012, Fax: 252-328-6071, E-mail: gradschool@ecu.edu.

Eastern Kentucky University, The Graduate School, College of Education, Department of Curriculum and Instruction, Program in Secondary and Higher Education, Richmond, KY 40475-3102. Offers agricultural education (MA Ed); allied health sciences education (MA Ed); art education (MA Ed); biological sciences education (MA Ed); business education (MA Ed); chemistry education (MA Ed); earth science education (MA Ed); English education (MA Ed); general science education (MA Ed); geography education (MA Ed); history education (MA Ed); home economics education (MA Ed); industrial education (MA Ed); mathematical sciences education (MA Ed); physical education (MA Ed); physics education (MA Ed); political science education (MA Ed); psychology education (MA Ed); reading (MA Ed); school health education (MA Ed); sociology education (MA Ed). *Accreditation:* NCATE. Part-time programs available. *Students:* 16 full-time (8 women), 63 part-time (43 women); includes 5 minority (2 African Americans, 2 American Indian/Alaska Native, 1 Asian American or Pacific Islander). Average age 32. *Entrance requirements:* For master's, GRE General Test, minimum GPA of 2.5. Application fee: $30. *Expenses:* Tuition, state resident: full-time $5,610. Tuition, nonresident: full-time $15,910. *Financial support:* Research assistantships, teaching assistantships, Federal Work-Study available. Support available to part-time students. *Unit head:* Dr. Michael Martin, Chair, Department of Curriculum and Instruction, 859-622-2154, Fax: 859-622-2004.

Edinboro University of Pennsylvania, Graduate Studies and Research, School of Education, Department of Elementary Education, Program in Elementary Education, Edinboro, PA 16444. Offers character education (M Ed); early childhood education (M Ed); elementary education (M Ed), including language arts, mathematics, science, thesis focus. Part-time and evening/weekend programs available. *Students:* 31 full-time (26 women), 46 part-time (38 women). Average age 30. In 2006, 14 degrees awarded. *Degree requirements:* For master's, thesis or alternative, project, comprehensive exam. *Entrance requirements:* For master's, GRE or MAT, minimum QPA of 2.5, valid teaching certificate or current study to obtain certification. *Application deadline:* Applications are processed on a rolling basis. Application fee: $30. Electronic applications accepted. *Expenses:* Tuition, state resident: full-time $6,048; part-time $336 per credit. Tuition, nonresident: full-time $9,678; part-time $538 per credit. Required fees: $1,849; $42 per credit. *Financial support:* In 2006–07, 7 research assistantships with full and partial tuition reimbursements (averaging $3,850 per year) were awarded; career-related internships or fieldwork, Federal Work-Study, scholarships/grants, and unspecified assistantships also available. Support available to part-time students. Financial award application deadline: 2/15; financial award applicants required to submit FAFSA. *Unit head:* Dr. Kathleen Dailey, Coordinator, 814-732-2714, E-mail: dailey@edinboro.edu. *Application contact:* Dr. R. Scott Baldwin, Dean, 814-732-2752, Fax: 814-732-2268, E-mail: sbaldwin@edinboro.edu.

Elms College, Division of Education, Chicopee, MA 01013-2839. Offers early childhood education (MAT); education (M Ed, CAGS); elementary education (MAT); English as a second language (MAT); reading (MAT); secondary education (MAT), including biology education, English education, Spanish education; special education (MAT). Part-time and evening/weekend programs available. *Faculty:* 9 full-time (6 women), 4 part-time/adjunct (2 women). *Students:* 8 full-time (6 women), 97 part-time (89 women); includes 4 minority (2 Asian Americans or Pacific Islanders, 2 Hispanic Americans). Average age 36. 48 applicants, 90% accepted, 40 enrolled. In 2006, 37 master's, 8 other advanced degrees awarded. *Degree requirements:* For master's, thesis (for some programs). *Entrance requirements:* For master's, Massachusetts Educators Certification Test, minimum GPA of 3.0; for CAGS, master's degree in education. Additional exam requirements/recommendations for international students: Required—TOEFL. *Application deadline:* For fall admission, 7/1 priority date for domestic students; for spring admission, 11/1 priority date for domestic students. Applications are processed on a rolling basis. Application fee: $30. *Expenses:* Tuition: Full-time $9,180; part-time $510 per credit. Tuition and fees vary according to course load. *Financial support:* In 2006–07, 3 teaching assistantships with partial tuition reimbursements were awarded; tuition waivers (partial) also available. Support available to part-time students. Financial award application deadline: 4/15; financial award applicants required to submit FAFSA. *Unit head:* Dr. Mary Janeczek, Director, 413-594-2761, Fax: 413-592-4871, E-mail: janeczeke@elms.edu.

Emory & Henry College, Graduate Programs, Emory, VA 24327-0947. Offers American history (MA Ed); English and language arts (MA Ed); reading and language arts (MA Ed); reading specialist (MA Ed). Part-time and evening/weekend programs available. *Faculty:* 4 part-time/adjunct (2 women). *Students:* 1 full-time (0 women), 54 part-time (45 women). Average age 37. 53 applicants, 100% accepted, 53 enrolled. In 2006, 62 degrees awarded. *Median time to degree:* Master's–2.5 years part-time. *Entrance requirements:* For master's, GRE, recommendations. *Application deadline:* Applications are processed on a rolling basis. Application fee: $30. *Financial support:* Applicants required to submit FAFSA. *Unit head:* Dr. Jack Roper, Director of Graduate Studies, 276-944-6188, Fax: 276-944-5223, E-mail: jroper@ehc.edu.

Fitchburg State College, Division of Graduate and Continuing Education, Programs in English and Teaching English (Secondary Level), Fitchburg, MA 01420-2697. Offers MA, MAT. *Accreditation:* NCATE. Part-time and evening/weekend programs available. *Students:* 3 full-time (2 women), 38 part-time (30 women); includes 1 minority (African American) Average age 34. 16 applicants, 94% accepted, 9 enrolled. In 2006, 14 degrees awarded. *Entrance requirements:* For master's, GRE General Test or MAT, letters of recommendation, resumé. Additional exam requirements/recommendations for international students: Required—TOEFL (minimum score 550 paper-based; 213 computer-based; 79 iBT). *Application deadline:* Applications are processed on a rolling basis. Application fee: $25 ($50 for international students). *Expenses:* Tuition, state resident: part-time $150 per credit. Tuition, nonresident: part-time $150 per credit. Required fees: $90 per credit. *Financial support:* In 2006–07, research assistantships with partial tuition reimbursements (averaging $5,500 per year); Federal Work-Study, scholarships/grants, and unspecified assistantships also available. Support available to part-time students. Financial award application deadline: 3/1; financial award applicants required to submit FAFSA. *Unit head:* Dr. Chola Chisunka, Chair, 978-665-3445, Fax: 978-665-3658, E-mail: gce@fsc.edu. *Application contact:* Director of Admissions, 978-665-3144, Fax: 978-665-4540, E-mail: admissions@fsc.edu.

Florida Agricultural and Mechanical University, Division of Graduate Studies, Research, and Continuing Education, College of Education, Program in Secondary Education and Foundation, Tallahassee, FL 32307-3200. Offers biology (M Ed); chemistry (MS Ed); English (MS Ed); history (MS Ed); math (MS Ed); physics (MS Ed). *Accreditation:* NCATE. *Degree requirements:* For master's, thesis (for some programs). *Entrance requirements:* For master's, GRE General Test, minimum GPA of 3.0. Additional exam requirements/recommendations for international students: Required—TOEFL.

Florida Gulf Coast University, College of Education, Program in Secondary Education, Fort Myers, FL 33965-6565. Offers biology (MAT); English (MAT); mathematics (MAT); social sciences (MAT). Part-time and evening/weekend programs available. *Faculty:* 31 full-time (21 women), 30 part-time/adjunct (24 women). *Entrance requirements:* For master's, GRE General Test, MAT, minimum GPA of 3.0. Additional exam requirements/recommendations for international students: Required—TOEFL (minimum score 550 paper-based; 213 computer-based). *Application deadline:* For fall admission, 7/1 priority date for domestic students; for spring admission, 10/15 for domestic students. Applications are processed on a rolling basis. Application fee: $30. Electronic applications accepted. *Expenses:* Tuition, state resident: full-time $4,326. Tuition, nonresident: full-time $18,523. Required fees: $1,211. One-time fee: $5 full-time. *Faculty research:* Integration of technology in the classroom, year-round schools, school choice, virtual high schools. *Unit head:* Dr. Pat Wachholz, Associate Dean, 239-590-7808, Fax: 239-590-7801, E-mail: wachhol@fgcu.edu.

Florida International University, College of Education, Department of Curriculum and Instruction, Program in English Education, Miami, FL 33199. Offers MAT, MS, Ed D. *Accreditation:* NCATE. Part-time and evening/weekend programs available. *Faculty:* 2 full-time (both women). *Students:* 1 full-time (0 women), 4 part-time (3 women); includes 2 minority (both Hispanic Americans) Average age 28. 2 applicants, 50% accepted, 1 enrolled. *Entrance requirements:* For master's, GRE General Test, minimum GPA of 3.0; for doctorate, GRE General Test. Additional exam requirements/recommendations for international students: Required—TOEFL (minimum score 550 paper-based; 213 computer-based; 80 iBT), IELTS (minimum score 6). *Application deadline:* For fall admission, 6/1 priority date for domestic students, 4/1 for international students; for winter admission, 6/1 for domestic students, 9/1 for international students; for spring admission, 3/1 for domestic students, 2/1 for international students. Applications are processed on a rolling basis. Application fee: $30. *Expenses:* Tuition, state resident: part-time $249 per credit hour. Tuition, nonresident: part-time $753 per credit hour. Tuition and fees vary according to program. *Unit head:* Dr. Linda A. Spears-Bunto, Head, 305-348-2976.

Florida State University, Graduate Studies, College of Education, Department of Middle and Secondary Education, Program in English Education, Tallahassee, FL 32306. Offers MS, PhD, Ed S. Part-time programs available. *Faculty:* 3 full-time (all women), 1 (woman) part-time/adjunct. *Students:* 6 full-time (all women), 17 part-time (13 women); includes 8 minority (5 African Americans, 3 Hispanic Americans). 19 applicants, 58% accepted, 10 enrolled. In 2006, 12 degrees awarded. *Degree requirements:* For master's and Ed S, thesis optional; for doctorate, thesis/dissertation, comprehensive exam. *Entrance requirements:* For master's, doctorate, and Ed S, GRE General Test, minimum GPA of 3.0. *Application deadline:* For fall admission, 7/1 priority date for domestic students; for spring admission, 11/1 for domestic students. Applications are processed on a rolling basis. Application fee: $30. *Expenses:* Tuition, state resident: full-time $5,822; part-time $243 per credit hour. Tuition, nonresident: full-time $20,976; part-time $874 per credit hour. Tuition and fees vary according to program. *Financial support:* Fellowships, research assistantships, teaching assistantships available. Financial award applicants required to submit FAFSA. *Unit head:* Dr. Susan Wood, Head, 850-644-6553, Fax: 850-644-1880, E-mail: wood@coe.fsu.edu. *Application contact:* Christina Crotty, Office Manager, 850-644-7810, Fax: 850-644-1880, E-mail: crotty@mailer.fsu.edu.

Framingham State College, Division of Graduate and Continuing Education, Program in English, Framingham, MA 01701-9101. Offers M Ed. *Faculty:* 3 full-time, 1 part-time/adjunct. *Students:* 19. In 2006, 4 degrees awarded. *Unit head:* Dr. Julia Scandrett, Coordinator, 508-626-4815, Fax: 508-626-4030, E-mail: jscande@frc.mass.edu. *Application contact:* 508-626-4550, Fax: 508-626-4030, E-mail: dgce@frc.mass.edu.

Gardner-Webb University, Graduate School, Department of English, Boiling Springs, NC 28017. Offers English (MA); English education (MA). Part-time and evening/weekend programs available. *Faculty:* 4 full-time (2 women). *Students:* Average age 25. 2 applicants, 100% accepted, 2 enrolled. In 2006, 7 degrees awarded. *Degree requirements:* For master's, comprehensive exam. *Entrance requirements:* For master's, GRE General Test, MAT, or NTE; PRAXIS, minimum GPA of 2.5. *Application deadline:* For fall admission, 8/1 priority date for domestic students. Applications are processed on a rolling basis. Application fee: $25. Electronic applications accepted. *Expenses:* Tuition: Full-time $3,144; part-time $262 per hour. *Financial support:* Unspecified assistantships available. *Unit head:* Dr. Gayle B. Price, Chair, 704-406-4414, Fax: 704-406-3921, E-mail: gprice@gardner-webb.edu.

Georgia College & State University, Graduate School, School of Education, Department of Foundations and Secondary Education, Milledgeville, GA 31061. Offers English education (M Ed); instructional technology (M Ed); mathematics education (M Ed); natural science education (M Ed, Ed S); secondary education (MAT); social science education (M Ed, Ed S). *Accreditation:* NCATE. *Students:* 49 full-time (33 women), 66 part-time (47 women); includes 13 minority (11 African Americans, 2 Hispanic Americans), 2 international. Average age 32. 75 applicants, 27% accepted, 9 enrolled. In 2006, 83 master's awarded. *Degree requirements:* For master's and Ed S, comprehensive exam. *Entrance requirements:* For master's, GRE General Test or MAT, 2 letters of recommendation; for Ed S, GRE General Test or MAT, master's degree, 2 letters of recommendation, 2 years teaching experience. Additional exam requirements/recommendations for international students: Required—TOEFL. *Application deadline:* For fall admission, 7/1 priority date for domestic students. Applications are processed on a rolling basis. Application fee: $25. Electronic applications accepted. *Expenses:* Tuition, state resident: full-time $3,222; part-time $179 per credit hour. Tuition, nonresident: full-time $12,870; part-time $715 per credit hour. Required fees: $391 per semester. Tuition and fees vary according to course load. *Financial support:* In 2006–07, 10 research assistantships (averaging $3,800 per year) were awarded; career-related internships or fieldwork and Federal Work-Study also available. Support available to part-time students. Financial award application deadline: 3/15. *Unit head:* Dr. Cynthia Alby, Chair/MAT Cohort Leader, 478-445-2513, Fax: 478-445-7362, E-mail: cynthia.alby@gcsu.edu.

Georgia Southern University, Jack N. Averitt College of Graduate Studies, College of Education, Department of Teaching and Learning, Program in English Education, Statesboro, GA 30460. Offers M Ed, MAT. *Accreditation:* NCATE. Part-time and evening/weekend programs available. *Students:* 2 full-time (both women), 5 part-time (4 women); includes 1 minority (African American) Average age 32. 5 applicants, 100% accepted, 2 enrolled. In 2006, 4 degrees awarded. *Degree requirements:* For master's, exit assessment. *Entrance requirements:* For master's, GRE General Test or MAT, minimum GPA of 2.5. Additional exam requirements/recommendations for international students: Required—TOEFL (minimum score 550 paper-based; 213 computer-based; 80 iBT). *Application deadline:* For fall admission, 3/1 priority date for domestic students, 3/1 for international students; for spring admission, 10/1 priority date for domestic students, 10/1 for international students. Applications are processed on a rolling basis. Application fee: $30 ($50 for international students). Electronic applications accepted. *Financial support:* In 2006–07, 6 students received support, including research assistantships with partial tuition reimbursements available (averaging $5,500 per year), teaching assistantships with partial tuition reimbursements available (averaging $5,500 per year); Federal Work-Study, scholarships/grants, tuition waivers (partial), and unspecified assistantships also available. Support available to part-time students. Financial award application deadline: 4/15; financial award applicants required to submit FAFSA. *Faculty research:* Literacy for at-risk students. *Unit head:* Dr. Mary Bennett, Assistant Professor, 912-681-0356, Fax: 912-681-0026, E-mail: mbennett@georgiasouthern.edu. *Application contact:* 912-681-5384, Fax: 912-681-0740, E-mail: gradadmissions@georgiasouthern.edu.

Georgia State University, College of Education, Department of Middle-Secondary Education and Instructional Technology, Programs in Secondary Education, Atlanta, GA 30303-3083. Offers art education (Ed S); English education (M Ed, Ed S); mathematics education (M Ed, PhD, Ed S); music education (PhD); science education (M Ed, PhD, Ed S); social studies education (M Ed, PhD, Ed S). *Accreditation:* NASM (one or more programs are accredited); NCATE. Part-time and evening/weekend programs available. *Students:* 103 full-time (71 women), 140 part-time (92 women); includes 53 minority (48 African Americans, 2 Asian Americans or Pacific Islanders, 3 Hispanic Americans), 12 international. Average age 35. 36 applicants, 86% accepted. In 2006, 87 master's, 12 doctorates, 12 other advanced degrees awarded. *Degree requirements:* For master's, comprehensive exam; for doctorate, thesis/dissertation, comprehensive exam; for Ed S, project/exam. *Entrance requirements:* For master's, GRE General Test, minimum GPA of 2.5; for doctorate, GRE General Test or MAT, minimum GPA of 3.3; for Ed S, GRE General Test or MAT, minimum graduate GPA of 3.25. Application fee: $25. *Financial support:* Career-related internships or fieldwork, Federal Work-Study, and institutionally sponsored loans available. *Faculty research:* Women and science, problem solving in mathematics, dialects, economic education. *Unit head:* Dr. Ruth Hough, Acting Chair, Department of Middle-Secondary Education and Instructional Technology, 404-651-2510.

Grand Valley State University, College of Education, Program in Reading and Language Arts, Allendale, MI 49401-9403. Offers M Ed. *Accreditation:* NCATE. Part-time and evening/weekend programs available. *Faculty:* 5 full-time (4 women), 2 part-time/adjunct (both women). *Students:* 2 full-time (both women), 160 part-time (157 women); includes 10 minority (4 African Americans, 2 American Indian/Alaska Native, 2 Asian Americans or Pacific Islanders, 2 Hispanic Americans). Average age 31. 28 applicants, 93% accepted, 24 enrolled. In 2006, 32 degrees awarded. *Degree requirements:* For master's, thesis. *Entrance requirements:* For master's, GRE General Test or minimum GPA of 3.0. Additional exam requirements/recommendations for international students: Required—TOEFL. *Application deadline:* Applications are processed on a rolling basis. Application fee: $30. Electronic applications accepted. *Expenses:* Tuition, state resident: full-time $5,850; part-time $325 per credit. Tuition, nonresident: full-time $10,800; part-time $600 per credit. Tuition and fees vary according to course load. *Financial support:* In 2006–07, research assistantships with full and partial tuition reimbursements (averaging $8,000 per year); career-related internships or fieldwork, Federal Work-Study, scholarships/grants, and unspecified assistantships also available. *Faculty research:* Culture of literacy, literacy acquisition, assessment, content area literacy, writing pedagogy. *Unit head:* Dr. Nancy Patterson, Director, 616-331-6226, E-mail: patterson@gvsu.edu. *Application contact:* Dr. Douglas Busman, Director, Student Information and Services, 616-331-6831, Fax: 616-331-6217, E-mail: busmando@gvsu.edu.

Harding University, College of Education, Searcy, AR 72149-0001. Offers advanced studies in teaching and learning (M Ed); art (MSE); behavioral science (MSE); Bible and religion (MSE); counseling (MS, Ed S); early childhood education (M Ed); early childhood special education (M Ed, MSE); education (MSE); educational leadership (M Ed, Ed S); elementary education (M Ed); English (MSE); family and consumer science (MSE); French (MSE); history/social science (MSE); kinesiology (MSE); math (MSE); physical science (MSE); reading (M Ed); secondary education (M Ed); Spanish (MSE); special education licensure (M Ed); teaching (MAT). *Accreditation:* NCATE. Part-time programs available. *Faculty:* 8 full-time (2 women), 45 part-time/adjunct (30 women). *Students:* 153 full-time (123 women), 469 part-time (341 women); includes 72 minority (63 African Americans, 4 American Indian/Alaska Native, 1 Asian American or Pacific Islander, 4 Hispanic Americans), 9 international. Average age 35. 175 applicants, 90% accepted, 147 enrolled. In 2006, 241 degrees awarded. *Degree requirements:* For master's, portfolio(s), thesis optional; for Ed S, portfolio, specialist project. *Entrance requirements:* For master's, GRE, MAT, PRAXIS; for Ed S, MAT or GRE. Additional exam requirements/recommendations for international students: Required—TOEFL (minimum score 550 paper-based). *Application deadline:* For fall admission, 8/1 for domestic and international students; for spring admission, 1/1 for domestic and international students. Applications are processed on a rolling basis. Application fee: $35. *Expenses:* Tuition: Part-time $455 per semester hour. Required fees: $20 per semester hour. Tuition and fees vary according to course load. *Financial support:* Scholarships/grants and unspecified assistantships available. Support available to part-time students. *Faculty research:* Reading, comprehension, school violence, educational technology, behavior, college choice, differentiated instruction, brain based teaching. *Unit head:* Pat Bashaw, Chair, 501-279-4183, Fax: 501-279-4051, E-mail: pbashaw@harding.edu.

Henderson State University, Graduate Studies, School of Education, Department of Curriculum, Instruction and Leadership, Arkadelphia, AR 71999-0001. Offers early childhood (P-4) (MSE); English (MSE); English as a second language (MSE, CP); math (MSE); middle school (MSE); reading (MSE); social science (MSE). *Accreditation:* NCATE. Part-time programs available. *Faculty:* 19 full-time (6 women), 4 part-time/adjunct (2 women). *Students:* 38 full-time (36 women), 49 part-time (47 women); includes 6 minority (5 African Americans, 1 Hispanic American), 16 international. Average age 37. In 2006, 31 degrees awarded. *Entrance requirements:* For master's, GRE General Test or MAT, minimum GPA of 2.7, teacher certification. *Application deadline:* For fall admission, 5/1 priority date for domestic students, 5/1 for international students; for winter admission, 10/1 for international students; for spring admission, 12/1 priority date for domestic students, 4/1 for international students. Applications are processed on a rolling basis. Application fee: $0 ($30 for international students). *Expenses:* Tuition, state resident: full-time $3,294; part-time $183 per credit hour. Tuition, nonresident: full-time $6,588; part-time $366 per credit hour. Required fees: $176 per term. *Financial support:* In 2006–07, 1 teaching assistantship with full tuition reimbursement (averaging $4,000 per year) was awarded; research assistantships, Federal Work-Study and institutionally sponsored loans also available. Support available to part-time students. Financial award application deadline: 7/31. *Unit head:* Dr. Kenneth Harris, Chairperson, 870-230-5203, Fax: 870-230-5455, E-mail: harris@hsu.edu. *Application contact:* Dr. Marck L. Beggs, Graduate Dean, 870-230-5126, Fax: 870-230-5479, E-mail: beggsm@hsu.edu.

Hofstra University, School of Education and Allied Human Services, Department of Curriculum and Teaching, Program in English Education, Hempstead, NY 11549. Offers MA, MS Ed. *Students:* 24 full-time (14 women), 22 part-time (13 women); includes 3 minority (2 African Americans, 1 Hispanic American). Average age 28. 33 applicants, 97% accepted, 18 enrolled. In 2006, 24 degrees awarded. *Degree requirements:* For master's, fieldwork, electronic portfolio, and curriculum project (MA). *Entrance requirements:* For master's, 2 letters of recommendation, teacher certification (MA). Additional exam requirements/recommendations for international students: Required—TOEFL (minimum score 550 paper-based; 213 computer-based). *Application deadline:* Applications are processed on a rolling basis. Application fee: $60. Electronic applications accepted. *Expenses:* Tuition: Full-time $13,320; part-time $740 per credit. Required fees: $930; $155 per term. *Financial support:* In 2006–07, 25 students received support, including 3 research assistantships with full and partial tuition reimbursements available (averaging $6,725 per year); fellowships with tuition reimbursements available, Federal Work-Study, scholarships/grants, tuition waivers (full and partial), unspecified assistantships, and tuition vouchers for cooperating teachers also available. Support available to part-time students. *Faculty research:* Reading and writing across the curriculum, using technology to teach English language arts, immigrant literature, supervision of pre-service English language arts teachers, curriculum and instruction, the Reading/Writing Workshop. *Unit head:* Dr. Maureen O. Murphy, Director, 516-463-6775, E-mail: catmom@hofstra.edu. *Application contact:* Carol Drummer, Dean of Graduate Admissions, 516-463-4876, Fax: 516-463-4664, E-mail: gradstudent@hofstra.edu.

Hunter College of the City University of New York, Graduate School, School of Arts and Sciences, Department of English, New York, NY 10021-5085. Offers British and American literature (MA); creative writing (MFA); English education (MA). Part-time and evening/weekend programs available. *Faculty:* 39 full-time (26 women). *Students:* 4 full-time (3 women), 107 part-time (75 women); includes 10 minority (2 African Americans, 2 Asian Americans or Pacific Islanders, 6 Hispanic Americans). Average age 33. 336 applicants, 17% accepted, 40 enrolled. In 2006, 23 degrees awarded. *Entrance requirements:* Additional exam requirements/recommendations for international students: Required—TOEFL. *Application deadline:* For fall admission, 4/1 for domestic students, 2/1 for international students; for spring admission, 11/1 for domestic students, 9/1 for international students. Application fee: $125. *Expenses:* Tuition, state resident: part-time $270 per credit. Tuition, nonresident: part-time $500 per credit. Required fees: $45 per semester. *Financial support:* Fellowships, Federal Work-Study and tuition waivers (partial) available. Support available to part-time students. *Faculty research:* Medieval, early modern, late century, Asian American, post-colonial literatures. *Unit head:* Dr. Christina Leon-Alfar, Chair, 212-772-5187, Fax: 212-772-5411, E-mail: calfar@hunter.cuny.edu. *Application contact:* Sarah Chinn, Adviser, 212-772-5187, E-mail: gradenghish@hunter.cuny.edu.

Hunter College of the City University of New York, Graduate School, School of Education, Programs in Secondary Education, Concentration in English Education, New York, NY 10021-5085. Offers MA. *Accreditation:* NCATE. *Students:* 3 full-time (all women), 59 part-time (44 women); includes 8 minority (4 African Americans, 4 Hispanic Americans). Average age 31. 52 applicants, 35% accepted, 10 enrolled. In 2006, 6 degrees awarded. *Degree requirements:* For master's, thesis, professional teaching portfolio, N.Y. state teacher certification exam, research project. *Entrance requirements:* For master's, minimum GPA of 2.8, 2 letters of reference, minimum of 21 credits in English. Additional exam requirements/recommendations for international students: Required—TOEFL, TWE. *Application deadline:* For fall admission, 4/1 for domestic students, 2/1 for international students; for spring admission, 11/1 for domestic students, 9/1 for international students. Applications are processed on a rolling basis. Application fee: $125. *Expenses:* Tuition, state resident: part-time $270 per credit. Tuition, nonresident: part-time $500 per credit. Required fees: $45 per semester. *Financial support:* Federal Work-Study and tuition waivers (partial) available. Support available to part-time students. *Unit head:* Dr. Christina Leon-Alfar, Chair, 212-772-5187, Fax: 212-772-5411, E-mail: calfar@hunter.cuny.edu. *Application contact:* William Zlata, Director for Graduate Admissions, 212-772-4482, Fax: 212-650-3336, E-mail: admissions@hunter.cuny.edu.

Indiana University of Pennsylvania, School of Graduate Studies and Research, College of Humanities and Social Sciences, Department of English, Program in Composition and Teaching English to Speakers of Other Languages, Indiana, PA 15705-1087. Offers composition and teaching English to speakers of other languages (PhD); teaching English (MAT); teaching English to speakers of other languages (MA). *Faculty:* 39 full-time (20 women). *Students:* 169 full-time (95 women), 8 part-time (4 women); includes 12 minority (9 African Americans, 1 Asian American or Pacific Islander, 2 Hispanic Americans), 68 international. Average age 36. 208 applicants, 52% accepted. In 2006, 23 master's, 24 doctorates awarded. *Degree requirements:* For master's, thesis optional; for doctorate, one foreign language, thesis/dissertation, comprehensive exam. *Entrance requirements:* For master's and doctorate, 2 letters of recommendation. Additional exam requirements/recommendations for international students: Required—TOEFL. *Application deadline:* For fall admission, 7/1 priority date for domestic students; for spring admission, 11/1 for domestic students. Applications are processed on a rolling basis. Application fee: $30. *Expenses:* Tuition, state resident: full-time $6,048; part-time $336 per credit. Tuition, nonresident: full-time $9,678; part-time $538 per credit. Required fees: $1,069; $148 per year. *Financial support:* In 2006–07, 2 fellowships (averaging $5,000 per year), 18 research assistantships with full and partial tuition reimbursements (averaging $6,170 per year), 8 teaching assistantships with partial tuition reimbursements (averaging $17,001 per year) were awarded. Financial award application deadline: 3/15; financial award applicants required to submit FAFSA. *Unit head:* Dr. Ben Rafoth, Graduate Coordinator, 724-357-2272.

Indiana University–Purdue University Fort Wayne, College of Arts and Sciences, Department of English and Linguistics, Fort Wayne, IN 46805-1499. Offers English (MA, MAT); TENL (teaching English as a new language) (Certificate). Part-time programs available. *Faculty:* 28 full-time (17 women). *Students:* 7 full-time (4 women), 23 part-time (19 women); includes 2 minority (1 African American, 1 Hispanic American), 1 international. Average age 31. 12 applicants, 83% accepted, 10 enrolled. In 2006, 10 master's, 3 other advanced degrees awarded. *Degree requirements:* For master's, one foreign language, thesis (for some programs), teaching certificate (MAT). *Entrance requirements:* For master's, GRE General Test, minimum GPA of 3.0, major or minor in English, 3 letters of recommendation. Additional exam requirements/recommendations for international students: Required—TOEFL (minimum score 600 paper-based; 260 computer-based). *Application deadline:* For fall admission, 8/1 for domestic students; for spring admission, 10/15 for domestic students. Applications are processed on a rolling basis. Application fee: $30. *Expenses:* Tuition, state resident: full-time $4,039; part-time $224 per credit. Tuition, nonresident: full-time $9,220; part-time $512 per credit. Required fees: $429; $24 per credit. Tuition and fees vary according to course load. *Financial support:* In 2006–07, 9 teaching assistantships with partial tuition reimbursements (averaging $11,950 per year) were awarded; career-related internships or fieldwork, scholarships/grants, and unspecified assistantships also available. Support available to part-time students. Financial award application deadline: 3/1; financial award applicants required to submit FAFSA. *Faculty research:* Colloquial American English, parthenogenesis, Octoavio Paz and Theory of Static. Total annual research expenditures: $49,403. *Unit head:* Dr. Richard M. Ramsey, Chairperson, 260-481-6841, Fax: 260-481-6985, E-mail: ramseyr@ipfw.edu.

Indiana University–Purdue University Indianapolis, Department of English, Indianapolis, IN 46202-2896. Offers English (MA); teaching English (MA). *Faculty:* 20 full-time (8 women). *Students:* 6 full-time (3 women), 32 part-time (13 women); includes 2 minority (1 African American, 1 Hispanic American), 3 international. Average age 32. In 2006, 10 degrees awarded. *Entrance requirements:* For master's, GRE. Application fee: $50 ($60 for international students). *Expenses:* Tuition, state resident: full-time $5,437; part-time $227 per credit hour. Tuition, nonresident: full-time $15,694; part-time $654 per credit hour. Required fees: $620. Tuition and fees vary according to course load, campus/location and program. *Financial support:* Fellowships, research assistantships, career-related internships or fieldwork available. *Unit head:* Susanmarie Harrington, Chair, 317-2788-1153.

Iona College, School of Arts and Science, Program in Adolescence Education, New Rochelle, NY 10801-1890. Offers biology education (MS Ed, MST); English education (MS Ed, MST); mathematics education (MS Ed, MST); social studies education (MS Ed, MST); Spanish

English Education

Iona College (continued)
education (MS Ed, MST). *Accreditation:* NCATE. Part-time and evening/weekend programs available. *Faculty:* 11 full-time (6 women), 21 part-time/adjunct (13 women). *Students:* 15 full-time (9 women), 68 part-time (52 women); includes 6 minority (1 African American, 1 Asian American or Pacific Islander, 4 Hispanic Americans). Average age 28. 42 applicants, 57% accepted, 11 enrolled. In 2006, 29 degrees awarded. *Degree requirements:* For master's, thesis or alternative. *Entrance requirements:* For master's, minimum GPA of 2.5 (MST), New York teaching certificate (MS Ed). Additional exam requirements/recommendations for international students: Required—TOEFL (minimum score 550 paper-based; 213 computer-based). *Application deadline:* Applications are processed on a rolling basis. Application fee: $50. Electronic applications accepted. *Expenses:* Tuition: Part-time $665 per credit. Required fees: $150 per term. *Financial support:* Unspecified assistantships available. Support available to part-time students. *Faculty research:* Reading/writing, educational technology, administration, early literacy assessment, literacy development. *Unit head:* Dr. Patricia Antonacci, Chair, 914-633-2080, Fax: 914-633-2608, E-mail: pantonacci@iona.edu. *Application contact:* Veronica Jarek-Prinz, Graduate Admissions, 914-633-2289, Fax: 914-633-2012, E-mail: vjarekprinz@iona.edu.

Ithaca College, Graduate Studies, School of Humanities and Sciences, Program in Adolescent Education, Ithaca, NY 14850-7020. Offers biology 7-12 (MAT); chemistry 7-12 (MAT); English 7-12 (MAT); French 7-12 (MAT); math 7-12 (MAT); physics 7-12 (MAT); social studies 7-12 (MAT); Spanish (MAT). *Faculty:* 14 full-time (5 women), 1 (woman) part-time/adjunct. *Students:* 8 full-time (2 women), 2 part-time (both women); includes 1 minority (Hispanic American) Average age 28. 12 applicants, 92% accepted, 10 enrolled. *Entrance requirements:* For master's, minimum GPA of 3.0. *Application deadline:* For fall admission, 5/15 for domestic students; for spring admission, 12/1 for domestic students. Application fee: $40. *Expenses:* Contact institution. *Financial support:* In 2006–07, 10 students received support, including 8 teaching assistantships (averaging $5,820 per year). Financial award application deadline:3/1. *Unit head:* Linda Hanrahan, Chairperson, 607-274-3147, E-mail: lhanrahan@ithaca.edu.

Jackson State University, Graduate School, School of Liberal Arts, Department of English and Modern Foreign Languages, Jackson, MS 39217. Offers English (MA); teaching English (MAT). Part-time and evening/weekend programs available. *Faculty:* 11 full-time (10 women), 1 (woman) part-time/adjunct. *Students:* 6 full-time (3 women), 17 part-time (15 women); includes 20 minority (all African Americans), 1 international. In 2006, 6 degrees awarded. *Degree requirements:* For master's, thesis or alternative, comprehensive exam. *Entrance requirements:* For master's, GRE General Test. Additional exam requirements/recommendations for international students: Required—TOEFL. *Application deadline:* For fall admission, 3/1 priority date for domestic students; for spring admission, 10/1 for domestic students. Applications are processed on a rolling basis. Application fee: $20. *Financial support:* In 2006–07, 6 students received support. Career-related internships or fieldwork, Federal Work-Study, scholarships/grants, and unspecified assistantships available. Support available to part-time students. Financial award application deadline: 3/1; financial award applicants required to submit FAFSA. *Unit head:* Dr. Jean D. Chamberlain, Chair, 601-978-2111, Fax: 601-974-5942, E-mail: jean.d.chamberlain@jsums.edu. *Application contact:* Curtis Gore, Director of Graduate Admissions, 601-979-2455, Fax: 601-974-4325, E-mail: cgore@ccaix.jsums.edu.

Kent State University, College of Arts and Sciences, Department of English, Kent, OH 44242-0001. Offers comparative literature (MA); creative writing (MFA); English for teachers (MA); literature (PhD); literature and writing (MA); rhetoric and composition (PhD); teaching English as a second language (MA). Part-time programs available. Terminal master's awarded for partial completion of doctoral program. *Degree requirements:* For master's, one foreign language, thesis optional; for doctorate, one foreign language, thesis/dissertation, qualifying exams. *Entrance requirements:* For master's and doctorate, GRE General Test, writing sample, letters of recommendation. Additional exam requirements/recommendations for international students: Required—TOEFL (minimum score 600 paper-based). Electronic applications accepted. *Faculty research:* British and American literature, textual editing, rhetoric and composition, cultural studies, linguistic and critical theories.

Kutztown University of Pennsylvania, College of Graduate Studies and Extended Learning, College of Education, Program in Secondary Education, Kutztown, PA 19530-0730. Offers biology (M Ed); curriculum and instruction (M Ed); English (M Ed); mathematics (M Ed); secondary education (Certificate); social studies (M Ed). *Accreditation:* NCATE. Part-time and evening/weekend programs available. *Faculty:* 5 full-time (2 women). *Students:* 69 full-time (32 women), 80 part-time (44 women); includes 5 minority (1 African American, 1 American Indian/Alaska Native, 2 Asian Americans or Pacific Islanders, 1 Hispanic American), 3 international. Average age 32. 80 applicants, 88% accepted, 34 enrolled. In 2006, 26 degrees awarded. *Degree requirements:* For master's, thesis optional. *Entrance requirements:* For master's, GRE General Test. Additional exam requirements/recommendations for international students: Required—TOEFL. *Application deadline:* Applications are processed on a rolling basis. Application fee: $35. Electronic applications accepted. *Expenses:* Tuition, state resident: full-time $6,048; part-time $336 per credit. Tuition, nonresident: full-time $9,678; part-time $538 per credit. *Financial support:* In 2006–07, research assistantships with full tuition reimbursements (averaging $5,000 per year); career-related internships or fieldwork, Federal Work-Study, and unspecified assistantships also available. Financial award application deadline: 3/15; financial award applicants required to submit FAFSA. *Unit head:* Dr. Kathleen Dolgos, Chairperson, 610-683-4279, Fax: 610-683-1338, E-mail: dolgos@kutztown.edu.

Lehman College of the City University of New York, Division of Education, Department of Middle and High School Education, Program in English Education, Bronx, NY 10468-1589. Offers MS Ed. *Accreditation:* NCATE. *Entrance requirements:* For master's, minimum GPA of 3.0 in English, 2.8 overall; teaching certificate.

Long Island University, Brooklyn Campus, Richard L. Conolly College of Liberal Arts and Sciences, Department of English, Brooklyn, NY 11201-8423. Offers English literature (MA); professional and creative writing (MA); teaching of writing (MA). Part-time and evening/weekend programs available. *Degree requirements:* For master's, thesis or alternative. *Entrance requirements:* For master's, 2 letters of recommendation. Additional exam requirements/recommendations for international students: Required—TOEFL (minimum score 550 paper-based; 173 computer-based). Electronic applications accepted.

Long Island University, C.W. Post Campus, School of Education, Department of Curriculum and Instruction, Brookville, NY 11548-1300. Offers adolescence education (MS); adolescence education: biology (MS); adolescence education: earth science (MS); adolescence education: English (MS); adolescence education: mathematics (MS); adolescence education: social studies (MS); adolescence education: Spanish (MS); art education (MS); bilingual education (MS); childhood education (MS); early childhood education (MS); middle childhood education (MS); music education (MS); teaching English to speakers of other languages (MS). Part-time and evening/weekend programs available. *Degree requirements:* For master's, comprehensive exam or thesis, student teaching. *Entrance requirements:* For master's, minimum GPA of 2.75 in major, 2.5 overall. Electronic applications accepted. *Faculty research:* Ethics and education, teaching strategies.

Longwood University, Office of Graduate Studies, College of Education and Human Services, Farmville, VA 23909. Offers communication sciences and disorders (MS); community and college counseling (MS); curriculum and instruction specialist-elementary (MS), including mild disabilities, modern languages; curriculum and instruction specialist-secondary (MS), including English, mild disabilities, modern languages; educational leadership (MS); guidance and counseling (MS); literacy and culture (MS); school library media (MS). *Accreditation:* NCATE. Part-time and evening/weekend programs available. *Degree requirements:* For master's, thesis optional. *Entrance requirements:* For master's, GRE (communication sciences and disorders), minimum GPA of 2.75. Additional exam requirements/recommendations for international students: Required—TOEFL (minimum score 550 paper-based; 213 computer-based).

Longwood University, Office of Graduate Studies, Department of English and Modern Languages, Farmville, VA 23909. Offers 6-12 initial teaching/licensure (MA); creative writing (MA); English education and writing (MA); literature (MA). Part-time programs available. *Degree requirements:* For master's, thesis (for some programs), comprehensive exam (for some programs). *Entrance requirements:* For master's, minimum GPA of 2.75. Additional exam requirements/recommendations for international students: Required—TOEFL (minimum score 550 paper-based; 213 computer-based).

Louisiana Tech University, Graduate School, College of Education, Department of Curriculum, Instruction and Leadership, Ruston, LA 71272. Offers curriculum and instruction (MS, Ed D); educational leadership (Ed D); secondary education (M Ed), including business education, English education, foreign language education, health and physical education, mathematics education, science education, social studies education, speech education. *Accreditation:* NCATE. Part-time programs available. *Degree requirements:* For doctorate, thesis/dissertation. *Entrance requirements:* For master's and doctorate, GRE General Test.

Lynchburg College, Graduate Studies, School of Education and Human Development, Program in English Education, Lynchburg, VA 24501-3199. Offers M Ed. *Faculty:* 4 full-time (2 women). *Students:* 7 full-time (6 women), 3 part-time (all women); includes 1 American Indian/Alaska Native.. In 2006, 7 degrees awarded. *Median time to degree:* Master's–3 years full-time, 4 years part-time. *Expenses:* Tuition: Full-time $6,300; part-time $350 per credit. Required fees: $100. *Unit head:* Dr. James Koger, Program Coordinator, 434-544-8628.

Manhattanville College, Graduate Programs, School of Education, Program in Middle Childhood/Adolescence Education (Grades 5-12), Purchase, NY 10577-2132. Offers biology (MAT); biology and special education (MPS); chemistry (MAT); chemistry and special education (MPS); English (MAT); English and special education (MPS); literacy (MPS), including reading and writing, writing; literacy and special education (MPS); math (MAT); math and special education (MPS); second language (MAT), including French, Italian, Latin, Spanish; social studies (MAT); social studies and special education (MPS); special education (MPS). Part-time and evening/weekend programs available. *Students:* 76 full-time (53 women), 109 part-time (68 women); includes 8 African Americans, 1 Asian American or Pacific Islander, 10 Hispanic Americans, 1 international. In 2006, 165 degrees awarded. *Degree requirements:* For master's, comprehensive exam or research project, field experience. *Entrance requirements:* For master's, minimum undergraduate GPA of 3.0, 2 letters of recommendation. *Application deadline:* Applications are processed on a rolling basis. Application fee: $55. *Financial support:* Career-related internships or fieldwork and institutionally sponsored loans available. Support available to part-time students. *Application contact:* Alyce Ware Poli, Director of Admissions, 914-323-5142, Fax: 914-694-1732, E-mail: edschool@mville.edu.

Marymount University, School of Arts and Sciences, Program in Humanities, Arlington, VA 22207-4299. Offers humanities (MA); humanities: teaching licensure in secondary English (MA). Part-time and evening/weekend programs available. *Students:* 3 full-time (all women), 6 part-time (5 women); includes 3 minority (all African Americans), 1 international. Average age 28. 4 applicants, 100% accepted, 3 enrolled. In 2006, 3 degrees awarded. *Degree requirements:* For master's, thesis or alternative. *Entrance requirements:* For master's, GRE; GRE or MAT and Praxis I or SAT/ACT (for teaching licensure), interview, writing sample, 2 letters of recommendation. Additional exam requirements/recommendations for international students: Required—TOEFL (minimum score 600 paper-based; 250 computer-based). *Application deadline:* Applications are processed on a rolling basis. Application fee: $40. Electronic applications accepted. *Expenses:* Tuition: Full-time $11,160; part-time $620 per credit. Required fees: $113; $630 per credit. *Financial support:* Research assistantships with full tuition reimbursements, career-related internships or fieldwork, scholarships/grants, and unspecified assistantships available. Support available to part-time students. Financial award applicants required to submit FAFSA.

Maryville University of Saint Louis, School of Education, St. Louis, MO 63141-7299. Offers art education (MA Ed); early childhood education (MA Ed); education (Ed D); elementary education (MA Ed); elementary education/English (MA Ed); environmental education (MA Ed); gifted education (MA Ed); middle grades education (MA Ed); reading specialist (MA Ed); secondary education (MA Ed), including educational leadership, secondary teaching and inquiry. *Accreditation:* NASAD; NCATE. Part-time and evening/weekend programs available. *Students:* 17 full-time (14 women), 168 part-time (129 women); includes 20 African Americans, 2 Asian Americans or Pacific Islanders, 1 Hispanic American, 2 international. Average age 37. 39 applicants, 95% accepted, 24 enrolled. In 2006, 37 degrees awarded. *Degree requirements:* For master's, thesis, project. *Entrance requirements:* For master's and doctorate, minimum GPA of 3.0, 3 professional recommendations. Additional exam requirements/recommendations for international students: Required—TOEFL (minimum score 550 paper-based). *Application deadline:* Applications are processed on a rolling basis. Application fee: $35 ($50 for international students). Electronic applications accepted. *Expenses:* Tuition: Full-time $17,800; part-time $555 per credit. Required fees: $55 per semester. Tuition and fees vary according to degree level and program. *Financial support:* Career-related internships or fieldwork, Federal Work-Study, tuition waivers (partial), and professional educator discounts available. Financial award application deadline: 7/31; financial award applicants required to submit FAFSA. *Faculty research:* Collaboration with public schools, preservice program development, mathematics, diversity, literacy. *Unit head:* Dr. Sam Hausfather, Dean, 314-529-9466, Fax: 314-529-9921, E-mail: shausfather@maryville.edu. *Application contact:* Dr. Lillian Curtis, Graduate Admissions Coordinator, 314-529-9542, Fax: 314-529-9921, E-mail: teachered@maryville.edu.

Miami University, Graduate School, College of Arts and Sciences, Department of English, Oxford, OH 45056. Offers composition and rhetoric (MA, PhD); creative writing (MA); criticism (PhD); English and American literature and language (PhD); English education (MAT); library theory (PhD); literature (MA, MAT, PhD); technical and scientific communication (MTSC). Part-time programs available. *Degree requirements:* For master's, final exam; for doctorate, 2 foreign languages, thesis/dissertation, final exams, comprehensive exam. *Entrance requirements:* For master's, minimum undergraduate GPA of 3.0 during previous 2 years or 2.75 overall; for doctorate, GRE General Test, GRE Subject Test, minimum GPA of 2.75 (undergraduate), 3.0 (graduate). Additional exam requirements/recommendations for international students: Required—TOEFL (minimum score 550 paper-based; 213 computer-based), TWE (minimum score 4). Electronic applications accepted.

Millersville University of Pennsylvania, Graduate School, School of Humanities and Social Sciences, Department of English, Millersville, PA 17551-0302. Offers English (MA); English education (M Ed). Part-time and evening/weekend programs available. *Faculty:* 24 full-time (14 women), 12 part-time/adjunct (8 women). *Students:* 10 full-time (9 women), 23 part-time (17 women); includes 1 minority (Hispanic American) Average age 31. 14 applicants, 93% accepted, 7 enrolled. In 2006, 13 degrees awarded. *Degree requirements:* For master's, departmental exam, thesis optional. *Entrance requirements:* For master's, GRE or MAT. Additional exam requirements/recommendations for international students: Required—TOEFL (minimum score 500 paper-based; 183 computer-based). *Application deadline:* For fall admission, 3/1 priority date for domestic students; for spring admission, 10/1 priority date for domestic students. Applications are processed on a rolling basis. Application fee: $35. *Expenses:* Tuition, state resident: full-time $6,048; part-time $336 per credit. Tuition, nonresident: full-time $9,678; part-time $538 per credit. Required fees: $1,244. Tuition and fees vary according to course load. *Financial support:* In 2006–07, 9 students received support, including 9 research assistantships with full tuition reimbursements available (averaging $4,250 per year); Federal Work-Study, institutionally sponsored loans, and unspecified assistantships also available. Support available to part-time students. Financial award application deadline: 3/15; financial award applicants required to submit FAFSA. *Faculty research:* Literary criticism, rhetoric and composition studies, distance teaching, creative writing, journalism history. Total annual research expenditures: $7,500. *Unit head:* Dr. Beverly Schneller, Chair, 717-872-3994, Fax: 717-871-2446, E-mail: beverly.schneller@millersville.edu. *Application contact:* Dr. Victor S. DeSantis, Dean of Graduate Studies, 717-872-3099, Fax: 717-871-2022, E-mail: victor.desantis@millersville.edu.

Mills College, Graduate Studies, Education Department, Oakland, CA 94613-1000. Offers administration (Ed D); child life in health care settings (MA); early childhood education (MA); education (MA), including curriculum and instruction, elementary education, English education, mathematics education, science education, secondary education, social sciences education, teaching. Part-time and evening/weekend programs available. *Faculty:* 10 full-time (7 women), 15 part-time/adjunct (12 women). *Students:* 192 full-time (153 women), 41 part-time (36 women); includes 62 minority (28 African Americans, 13 Asian Americans or Pacific Islanders, 21 Hispanic Americans), 2 international. Average age 34. 160 applicants, 74% accepted, 73 enrolled. In 2006, 52 master's, 1 doctorate awarded. Terminal master's awarded for partial completion of doctoral program. *Degree requirements:* For master's, comprehensive exam. *Entrance requirements:* For doctorate, GRE General Test. Additional exam requirements/recommendations for international students: Required—TOEFL. *Application deadline:* For fall admission, 2/1 for domestic and international students; for spring admission, 11/1 for domestic and international students. Applications are processed on a rolling basis. Application fee: $50. Electronic applications accepted. *Financial support:* In 2006–07, 56 fellowships with tuition reimbursements (averaging $2,700 per year), 15 teaching assistantships (averaging $6,350 per year) were awarded; career-related internships or fieldwork, institutionally sponsored loans, scholarships/grants, and residence awards also available. Support available to part-time students. Financial award application deadline: 2/1; financial award applicants required to submit CSS PROFILE or FAFSA. *Faculty research:* Child development, gender and education, public policy, cross-cultural development, development of literacy. *Unit head:* Joseph Kahne, Chairperson, 510-430-3190, Fax: 510-430-3314, E-mail: grad-studies@mills.edu. *Application contact:* Randy McGlauthing, Director of Graduate Admissions, 510-430-2355, Fax: 510-430-2159, E-mail: rmglaut@mills.edu.

Minnesota State University Mankato, College of Graduate Studies, College of Arts and Humanities, Department of English, Mankato, MN 56001. Offers creative writing (MFA); English (MA, MS); English literature (MA); teaching English (MS, MT); teaching English as a second language (MA); technical communication (Certificate). Part-time programs available. *Students:* 53 full-time (32 women), 77 part-time (53 women). Average age 32. In 2006, 29 degrees awarded. *Degree requirements:* For master's, one foreign language, thesis or alternative, comprehensive exam. *Entrance requirements:* For master's, minimum GPA of 3.0 during previous 2 years, writing sample (MFA). *Application deadline:* Applications are processed on a rolling basis. Application fee: $40. Electronic applications accepted. *Financial support:* Research assistantships with full tuition reimbursements, teaching assistantships with full tuition reimbursements, career-related internships or fieldwork, Federal Work-Study, and unspecified assistantships available. Financial award application deadline: 3/15; financial award applicants required to submit FAFSA. *Faculty research:* Keats and Christianity. *Unit head:* Dr. John Banschbach, Chairperson, 507-389-2117. *Application contact:* 507-389-2321, E-mail: grad@mnsu.edu.

Mississippi College, Graduate School, School of Education, Department of Teacher Education and Leadership, Clinton, MS 39058. Offers art (M Ed); biological science (M Ed); business education (M Ed); computer science (M Ed); dyslexia therapy (M Ed); educational leadership (M Ed, Ed S); elementary education (M Ed, Ed S); English (M Ed); higher education administration (MS); mathematics (M Ed); secondary education (M Ed); social studies (history) (M Ed); teaching arts (M Ed). Part-time programs available. *Faculty:* 9 full-time (5 women), 14 part-time/adjunct (10 women). *Students:* 52 full-time (36 women), 286 part-time (247 women); includes 173 minority (171 African Americans, 1 American Indian/Alaska Native, 1 Hispanic American), 1 international. Average age 32. In 2006, 131 degrees awarded. *Degree requirements:* For master's, thesis optional. *Entrance requirements:* For master's, NTE. Additional exam requirements/recommendations for international students: Recommended—IELTS. *Application deadline:* Applications are processed on a rolling basis. Application fee: $25. Electronic applications accepted. *Expenses:* Tuition: Full-time $7,290; part-time $405 per hour. Required fees: $150 per term. Tuition and fees vary according to campus/location and program. *Financial support:* Teaching assistantships, career-related internships or fieldwork, Federal Work-Study, scholarships/grants, and unspecified assistantships available. Support available to part-time students. Financial award applicants required to submit FAFSA. *Unit head:* Dr. Tom Williams, Chair, 601-925-3844, E-mail: twilliams@mc.edu.

Montclair State University, The Graduate School, College of Education and Human Services, Department of Curriculum and Teaching, Montclair, NJ 07043-1624. Offers education (M Ed); educational technology (M Ed); school library media specialist (Certificate); teaching (MAT, Certificate), including art (MAT), biological science (MAT), early childhood education (P-3) (MAT), earth science (MAT), elementary education (K-8) (MAT), English (MAT), French (MAT), health and physical education (MAT), health education (MAT), home economics (MAT), mathematics (MAT), music (MAT), physical education (MAT), physical science (MAT), social studies (MAT), Spanish (MAT), teacher of ESL (MAT), teacher of students with disabilities (MAT). Part-time and evening/weekend programs available. *Faculty:* 16 full-time (12 women), 13 part-time/adjunct (8 women). *Students:* 147 full-time (113 women), 230 part-time (188 women); includes 58 minority (33 African Americans, 1 American Indian/Alaska Native, 12 Asian Americans or Pacific Islanders, 12 Hispanic Americans), 4 international. Average age 33. 118 applicants, 38% accepted, 37 enrolled. In 2006, 166 master's, 11 other advanced degrees awarded. *Degree requirements:* For master's, field experience. *Entrance requirements:* For master's, PRAXIS II, minimum GPA of 2.67, 2 letters of recommendation. Additional exam requirements/recommendations for international students: Required—TOEFL (minimum score 83 computer-based). *Application deadline:* For fall admission, 2/15 for domestic and international students; for spring admission, 9/15 for domestic and international students. Applications are processed on a rolling basis. Application fee: $60. Electronic applications accepted. *Expenses:* Tuition, state resident: part-time $450 per credit. Tuition, nonresident: part-time $682 per credit. Tuition and fees vary according to degree level and program. *Financial support:* In 2006–07, 7 research assistantships with full tuition reimbursements (averaging $7,000 per year) were awarded; Federal Work-Study, scholarships/grants, and unspecified assistantships also available. Support available to part-time students. Financial award application deadline: 3/1; financial award applicants required to submit FAFSA. *Unit head:* Dr. Deborah Eldridge, Chairperson, 973-655-5187.

National-Louis University, National College of Education, Programs in Reading and Language, Chicago, IL 60603. Offers language and literacy (M Ed, MS Ed, CAS); reading recovery (CAS); reading specialist (M Ed, MS Ed, CAS). Part-time and evening/weekend programs available. *Students:* 1 (woman) full-time, 237 part-time (231 women); includes 32 minority (11 African Americans, 2 American Indian/Alaska Native, 4 Asian Americans or Pacific Islanders, 15 Hispanic Americans). Average age 34. 15 applicants, 100% accepted. In 2006, 36 master's, 2 other advanced degrees awarded. *Degree requirements:* For master's, thesis (for some programs). *Entrance requirements:* For master's, MAT or GRE, minimum GPA of 3.0, teaching certificate; for CAS, master's degree, teaching certificate. *Application deadline:* Applications are processed on a rolling basis. Application fee: $25. *Expenses:* Tuition: Full-time $17,685. One-time fee: $40 full-time. *Financial support:* Fellowships, career-related internships or fieldwork, Federal Work-Study, institutionally sponsored loans, and scholarships/grants available. Support available to part-time students. Financial award applicants required to submit FAFSA. *Unit head:* Dr. Camille Blachowicz, Coordinator, 847-475-1100 Ext. 2558. *Application contact:* David McCulloch, Vice President for University Services, 800-443-5522 Ext. 5127, Fax: 847-465-0593, E-mail: dmcc@wheeling1.nl.edu.

New York University, Steinhardt School of Culture, Education and Human Development, Department of Music and Performing Arts Professions, Program in Educational Theatre, New York, NY 10012-1019. Offers educational theatre (Ed D, Advanced Certificate); educational theatre for colleges and communities (MA, PhD); educational theatre with English 7-12 (MA); teaching educational theatre, all grades (MA). Part-time and evening/weekend programs available. *Faculty:* 6 full-time (3 women). *Students:* 90 full-time (74 women), 49 part-time (37 women); includes 16 minority (8 African Americans, 3 Asian Americans or Pacific Islanders, 5 Hispanic Americans), 8 international. 100 applicants, 77% accepted, 53 enrolled. In 2006, 103 master's, 4 doctorates awarded. Terminal master's awarded for partial completion of doctoral program. *Degree requirements:* For master's, thesis (for some programs); for doctorate, thesis/dissertation. *Entrance requirements:* For master's, audition; for doctorate, GRE General Test, interview; for Advanced Certificate, master's degree. Additional exam requirements/recommendations for international students: Required—TOEFL. *Application deadline:* For fall admission, 12/15 priority date for domestic and international students; for spring admission, 11/1 for domestic and international students. Applications are processed on a rolling basis. Application fee: $50. *Expenses:* Tuition: Part-time $1,080 per unit. Required fees: $56 per unit. $329 per term. Tuition and fees vary according to program. *Financial support:* Teaching assistantships with partial tuition reimbursements, career-related internships or fieldwork, Federal Work-Study, and scholarships/grants available. Support available to part-time students. Financial award application deadline: 2/1; financial award applicants required to submit FAFSA. *Faculty research:* Theatre for young audiences, drama in education, applied theatre, arts education assessment, reflective praxis. *Unit head:* Dr. Philip Taylor, Director, 212-998-5424, Fax: 212-995-4043. *Application contact:* 212-998-5030, Fax: 212-995-4328, E-mail: steinhardt.gradadmissions@nyu.edu.

New York University, Steinhardt School of Culture, Education and Human Development, Department of Teaching and Learning, Program in English Education, New York, NY 10012-1019. Offers MA, PhD, Advanced Certificate. *Accreditation:* Teacher Education Accreditation Council. Part-time and evening/weekend programs available. *Faculty:* 5 full-time (2 women). *Students:* 62 full-time (48 women), 40 part-time (33 women); includes 19 minority (6 African Americans, 5 Asian Americans or Pacific Islanders, 8 Hispanic Americans), 5 international. 91 applicants, 85% accepted, 23 enrolled. In 2006, 50 master's, 3 doctorates awarded. Terminal master's awarded for partial completion of doctoral program. *Degree requirements:* For master's, thesis (for some programs); for doctorate, thesis/dissertation. *Entrance requirements:* For doctorate, GRE General Test, interview; for Advanced Certificate, master's degree. Additional exam requirements/recommendations for international students: Required—TOEFL. *Application deadline:* For fall admission, 12/15 priority date for domestic and international students; for spring admission, 11/1 for domestic and international students. Applications are processed on a rolling basis. Application fee: $50. *Expenses:* Tuition: Part-time $1,080 per unit. Required fees: $56 per unit. $329 per term. Tuition and fees vary according to program. *Financial support:* Fellowships with full and partial tuition reimbursements, teaching assistantships with full and partial tuition reimbursements, career-related internships or fieldwork, Federal Work-Study, institutionally sponsored loans, scholarships/grants, tuition waivers (partial), and unspecified assistantships available. Support available to part-time students. Financial award application deadline: 2/1; financial award applicants required to submit FAFSA. *Faculty research:* Educational linguistics and language development, making meaning of literature, teaching of literature, adolescent literacy, equity issues. *Unit head:* Dr. John Mayher, Director, 212-998-5460, Fax: 212-995-4049. *Application contact:* 212-998-5030, Fax: 212-995-4328, E-mail: steinhardt.gradadmissions@nyu.edu.

North Carolina Agricultural and Technical State University, Graduate School, School of Education, Department of Curriculum and Instruction, Program in Intermediate Education, Greensboro, NC 27411. Offers biology education (MS); chemistry education (MS); English education (MS); history education (MS); social science education (MS). *Accreditation:* NCATE. Part-time and evening/weekend programs available. *Degree requirements:* For master's, thesis (for some programs), qualifying exam, comprehensive exam. *Entrance requirements:* For master's, GRE General Test, minimum GPA of 3.0.

Northeastern Illinois University, Graduate College, College of Education, School of Teacher Education, Program in Instruction, Chicago, IL 60625-4699. Offers language arts (MSI). *Faculty:* 30 full-time (20 women), 39 part-time/adjunct (29 women). *Students:* 1 (woman) full-time, 23 part-time (19 women); includes 4 minority (1 African American, 1 American Indian/Alaska Native, 2 Hispanic Americans). Average age 31. In 2006, 4 degrees awarded. *Degree requirements:* For master's, 2 research papers, oral exam. *Entrance requirements:* For master's, minimum GPA of 2.75; previous course work in English, linguistics, or speech; teaching certificate. *Application deadline:* For fall admission, 4/1 priority date for domestic students; for spring admission, 8/15 for domestic students. Applications are processed on a rolling basis. Application fee: $25. *Financial support:* In 2006–07, 8 students received support, including research assistantships with full tuition reimbursements available (averaging $6,600 per year). *Faculty research:* Emergent literacy, literature-based literacy instruction, drama and literature in the classroom, curriculum integration, standards-based assessment, integrating technology.

Northeastern Illinois University, Graduate College, College of Education, School of Teacher Education, Program in Teaching, Chicago, IL 60625-4699. Offers language arts (MAT). *Accreditation:* NCATE. *Faculty:* 30 full-time (20 women), 39 part-time/adjunct (29 women). *Students:* 18 full-time (12 women), 42 part-time (32 women); includes 15 minority (4 African Americans, 3 Asian Americans or Pacific Islanders, 8 Hispanic Americans), 1 international. Average age 31. 13 applicants, 77% accepted. In 2006, 12 degrees awarded. *Degree requirements:* For master's, 2 research papers, oral exam. *Entrance requirements:* For master's, minimum GPA of 2.75; previous course work in English, speech, drama, or linguistics. *Application deadline:* For fall admission, 4/1 priority date for domestic students; for spring admission, 8/15 for domestic students. Applications are processed on a rolling basis. Application fee: $25. *Financial support:* In 2006–07, 13 students received support, including 5 research assistantships with full tuition reimbursements available (averaging $6,600 per year); career-related internships or fieldwork, Federal Work-Study, institutionally sponsored loans, and tuition waivers (full and partial) also available. Support available to part-time students. Financial award applicants required to submit CSS PROFILE. *Faculty research:* Emergent literacy, literature-based literacy, drama and literature in the classroom, curriculum integration, standards-based assessment.

Northern Arizona University, Graduate College, College of Arts and Letters, Department of English, Program in English, Flagstaff, AZ 86011. Offers creative writing (MA); English education (MA); general English (MA); literature (MA); rhetoric (MA). *Degree requirements:* For master's, departmental qualifying exam. *Entrance requirements:* For master's, GRE General Test, GRE Subject Test.

Northern State University, Division of Graduate Studies in Education, Program in Teaching and Learning, Aberdeen, SD 57401-7198. Offers educational studies (MS Ed); elementary classroom teaching (MS Ed); health, physical education, and coaching (MS Ed); language and literacy (MS Ed); secondary classroom teaching (MS Ed); special education (MS Ed). *Accreditation:* NCATE. Part-time and evening/weekend programs available. *Faculty:* 69 full-time (19 women). *Students:* 5 full-time (3 women), 70 part-time (51 women); includes 3 minority (1 African American, 1 American Indian/Alaska Native, 1 Asian American or Pacific Islander). Average age 32. In 2006, 23 degrees awarded. *Degree requirements:* For master's, thesis optional. *Entrance requirements:* For master's, minimum GPA of 2.75. Additional exam requirements/recommendations for international students: Required—TOEFL (minimum score 550 paper-based; 213 computer-based). *Application deadline:* For fall admission, 8/15 priority date for domestic students; for spring admission, 12/15 for domestic students. Applications are processed on a rolling basis. Application fee: $35. Electronic applications accepted. *Expenses:* Tuition, state resident: full-time $3,373; part-time $120 per credit. Tuition, nonresident: full-time $9,943; part-time $355 per credit. International tuition: $13,000 full-time. Required fees: $86 per credit. One-time fee: $35 full-time. Tuition and fees vary according to course load, degree level and reciprocity agreements. *Financial support:* In 2006–07, 17 teaching assistantships with partial tuition reimbursements (averaging $4,812 per year) were awarded; career-related internships or fieldwork, Federal Work-Study, institutionally sponsored loans, scholarships/grants, and unspecified assistantships also available. Support available to part-time students. Financial award application deadline: 3/1; financial award applicants required to

English Education

Northern State University (continued)
submit FAFSA. *Application contact:* Tammy K. Griffith, Senior Secretary, 605-626-2558, Fax: 605-626-2542, E-mail: griffith@northern.edu.

North Georgia College & State University, Graduate Studies, Program in Teacher Education, Dahlonega, GA 30597. Offers early childhood education (M Ed); educational leadership (Ed S); middle grades education (M Ed); secondary education (M Ed), including art education, biology education, chemistry education, English education, history education, mathematics education, physical education, science education; special education (M Ed), including interrelated special education, learning disabilities. *Accreditation:* NCATE. Part-time and evening/weekend programs available. Postbaccalaureate distance learning degree programs offered (minimal on-campus study). *Faculty:* 35 full-time (18 women), 9 part-time/adjunct (6 women). *Students:* 260. Average age 32. 120 applicants, 63% accepted. In 2006, 134 degrees awarded. *Degree requirements:* For master's, thesis optional. *Entrance requirements:* For master's, GRE General Test or MAT, minimum GPA of 2.75; for Ed S, GRE General Test or MAT, 3 years of teaching experience, master's degree, minimum graduate GPA of 3.25. *Application deadline:* For fall admission, 7/1 priority date for domestic students; for spring admission, 12/10 priority date for domestic students. Applications are processed on a rolling basis. Application fee: $25. Electronic applications accepted. *Expenses:* Tuition, state resident: full-time $3,044; part-time $127 per credit hour. Tuition, nonresident: full-time $12,172; part-time $508 per credit hour. Required fees: $892; $458 per semester. *Financial support:* Teaching assistantships, career-related internships or fieldwork and scholarships/grants available. Support available to part-time students. Financial award application deadline: 5/1. *Faculty research:* Computers and teachers' attitudes, rural versus urban teacher attitudes, teacher leadership roles, minority recruitment in teaching force. *Unit head:* Dr. Bob Michael, Dean, School of Education, 706-864-1998, Fax: 706-867-2850, E-mail: bmichael@ngcsu.edu. *Application contact:* Dr. Donna A. Gessell, Director of Graduate Studies and External Programs, 706-864-1528, Fax: 706-867-2795, E-mail: dgessell@ngcsu.edu.

Northwestern State University of Louisiana, Graduate Studies and Research, College of Education, Programs in Education, Natchitoches, LA 71497. Offers business and distributive education (M Ed); counseling (M Ed); early childhood education (M Ed); education (M Ed); education leadership (M Ed); educational technology (M Ed); elementary teaching (M Ed); English education (M Ed); home economics education (M Ed); mathematics education (M Ed); reading (M Ed); science education (M Ed); secondary teaching (M Ed); social sciences education (M Ed). *Students:* 49 full-time (41 women), 245 part-time (206 women); includes 78 minority (70 African Americans, 5 American Indian/Alaska Native, 2 Asian Americans or Pacific Islanders, 1 Hispanic American). Average age 35. In 2006, 158 degrees awarded. *Degree requirements:* For master's, thesis or alternative, comprehensive exam, registration. *Entrance requirements:* For master's, GRE General Test, minimum undergraduate GPA of 2.5. *Application contact:* Dr. Steven G. Horton, Associate Provost/Dean, Graduate Studies, Research, and Information Systems, 318-357-5851, Fax: 318-357-5019, E-mail: grad_school@nsula.edu.

Northwest Missouri State University, Graduate School, College of Arts and Sciences, Department of English, Maryville, MO 64468-6001. Offers English (MA); English with speech emphasis (MA); teaching English with speech emphasis (MS Ed). Part-time programs available. *Faculty:* 12 full-time (4 women). *Students:* 6 full-time (4 women), 8 part-time (3 women); includes 1 minority (Hispanic American) 10 applicants, 70% accepted, 4 enrolled. In 2006, 5 degrees awarded. *Degree requirements:* For master's, thesis optional. *Entrance requirements:* For master's, GRE General Test, minimum undergraduate GPA of 2.5, writing sample. Additional exam requirements/recommendations for international students: Required—TOEFL (minimum score 550 paper-based; 213 computer-based). *Application deadline:* For fall admission, 7/1 for domestic and international students; for spring admission, 11/15 for domestic and international students. Applications are processed on a rolling basis. Application fee: $0 ($50 for international students). *Financial support:* In 2006–07, 5 teaching assistantships with full tuition reimbursements (averaging $6,000 per year) were awarded. Financial award application deadline: 3/1; financial award applicants required to submit FAFSA. *Unit head:* Dr. Beth Richards, Chairperson, 660-562-1745. *Application contact:* Dr. Frances Shipley, Dean of Graduate School, 660-562-1145, Fax: 660-562-1096, E-mail: gradsch@nwmissouri.edu.

Nova Southeastern University, Fischler School of Education and Human Services, Graduate Teacher Education Program, Fort Lauderdale, FL 33314-7796. Offers athletic administration (MS); cognitive and behavioral disabilities (MS); computer science education (Ed S); computer science education (K-12) (MS); curriculum and teaching (Ed S); curriculum, instruction and technology (MS); curriculum, instruction, management and administration (Ed S); early childhood special education (MS); early literacy and reading (Ed S); early literacy education (MS); education technology (MS); educational leadership (administration K–12) (MS, Ed S); educational media (Ed S); educational media (K-12) (MS); elementary education (MS, Ed S), including ESOL endorsement (MS); English (MS, Ed S); exceptional student education (MS), including ESOL endorsement; gifted education (MS, Ed S); interdisciplinary arts education (MS); management and administration of educational programs (MS); mathematics (MS, Ed S); multicultural early intervention (MS); pre-kindergarten/primary (MS); preschool education (MS); reading (MS, Ed S); science (MS, Ed S); secondary education (MS, Ed S); social studies (MS, Ed S); Spanish language (MS); teaching and learning (MA, MS), including curriculum and instruction (MA), elementary mathematics (MA), elementary reading (MA), K-12 technology integration (MA); teaching English to speakers of other languages (MS, Ed S); technology management and administration (Ed S); urban studies education (MS); varying exceptionalities (Ed S). Part-time and evening/weekend programs available. Postbaccalaureate distance learning degree programs offered. *Faculty:* 131 full-time (78 women), 548 part-time/adjunct (342 women). *Students:* 1,418 full-time (1,139 women), 3,464 part-time (2,877 women); includes 2,462 minority (1,732 African Americans, 13 American Indian/Alaska Native, 44 Asian Americans or Pacific Islanders, 673 Hispanic Americans), 77 international. Average age 38. 1,771 applicants, 80% accepted, 1419 enrolled. In 2006, 2,078 master's, 425 other advanced degrees awarded. *Degree requirements:* For master's and Ed S, thesis, practicum, internship. *Entrance requirements:* For master's, MAT, GRE, CLAST, CBEST, PRAXIS I, GKT, minimum GPA of 2.5; for Ed S, MAT or GRE, master's degree, teaching certificate, minimum GPA of 3.0. Additional exam requirements/recommendations for international students: Recommended—TOEFL (minimum score 550 paper-based; 213 computer-based), IELTS (minimum score 6). *Application deadline:* For fall admission, 8/11 priority date for domestic and international students; for winter admission, 12/28 priority date for domestic and international students; for spring admission, 4/22 priority date for domestic and international students. Applications are processed on a rolling basis. Application fee: $50. Electronic applications accepted. *Financial support:* Federal Work-Study available. Support available to part-time students. Financial award application deadline: 1/7. *Faculty research:* School effectiveness, critical thinking, leadership skills acquisition, child education, multicultural education. *Unit head:* Dr. Meline Kevorkian, Associate Dean of Master's and Educational Programs, 954-262-8500, Fax: 954-262-3606, E-mail: melinek@nova.edu. *Application contact:* Jennifer Quiñones Nottingham, Dean of Student Affairs, 800-986-3223 Ext. 8624, Fax: 954-262-3911, E-mail: jlquinon@nova.edu.

Occidental College, Graduate Studies, Department of Education, Program in Secondary Education, Los Angeles, CA 90041-3314. Offers English and comparative literary studies (MAT); history (MAT); life science (MAT); mathematics (MAT); physical science (MAT); social science (MAT); Spanish (MAT). Part-time programs available. *Faculty:* 3 full-time (2 women), 2 part-time/adjunct (both women). *Students:* 4 full-time (all women), 3 part-time (1 woman); includes 5 minority (1 Asian American or Pacific Islander, 4 Hispanic Americans). Average age 25. 4 applicants, 100% accepted, 4 enrolled. In 2006, 4 degrees awarded. *Degree requirements:* For master's, final exam, graduate synthesis paper. *Entrance requirements:* For master's, GRE General Test, minimum GPA of 3.0. Additional exam requirements/recommendations for international students: Required—TOEFL (minimum score 625 paper-based). *Application deadline:* For fall admission, 3/1 for domestic and international students; for spring admission, 10/1 for domestic and international students. Applications are processed on a rolling basis. Application fee: $50. *Expenses:* Contact institution. *Financial support:* Fellowships, Federal Work-Study, institutionally sponsored loans, and scholarships/grants available. Support available to part-time students. Financial award application deadline: 3/1; financial award applicants required to submit FAFSA. *Unit head:* Chair, 323-259-2781, E-mail: edudept@oxy.edu. *Application contact:* Angela Allen, Credential Analyst/Department Services Coordinator, 323-259-2781, E-mail: edudept@oxy.edu.

Plymouth State University, College of Graduate Studies, Graduate Studies in Education, Program in English Education, Plymouth, NH 03264-1595. Offers M Ed. Part-time and evening/weekend programs available. *Students:* 1 (woman) full-time, 53 part-time (43 women); includes 1 minority (Asian American or Pacific Islander) Average age 34. 10 applicants, 100% accepted, 10 enrolled. In 2006, 15 degrees awarded. *Entrance requirements:* For master's, MAT. *Application deadline:* Applications are processed on a rolling basis. Application fee: $75. *Expenses:* Tuition, state resident: part-time $369 per credit. Tuition, nonresident: part-time $407 per credit. Tuition and fees vary according to course level. *Financial support:* Career-related internships or fieldwork, scholarships/grants, and unspecified assistantships available. Support available to part-time students. Financial award applicants required to submit FAFSA. *Unit head:* Dr. Meg Petersen, Program Coordinator, 603-535-2684, E-mail: mpetersen@plymouth.edu.

Purdue University, Graduate School, School of Education, Department of Curriculum and Instruction, West Lafayette, IN 47907. Offers agricultural and extension education (PhD, Ed S); agriculture and extension education (MS, MS Ed); art education (PhD); consumer and family sciences and extension education (MS Ed, PhD, Ed S); curriculum studies (MS Ed, PhD, Ed S); educational technology (MS Ed, PhD, Ed S); elementary education (MS Ed); foreign language education (MS Ed, PhD, Ed S); industrial technology (PhD, Ed S); language arts (MS Ed, PhD, Ed S); literacy (MS Ed, PhD, Ed S); mathematics/science education (MS, MS Ed, PhD, Ed S); social studies (MS Ed, PhD); social studies education (Ed S); vocational/industrial education (MS Ed, PhD, Ed S); vocational/technical education (MS Ed, PhD, Ed S). *Accreditation:* NCATE. Part-time and evening/weekend programs available. *Faculty:* 26 full-time (13 women), 3 part-time/adjunct (all women). *Students:* 59 full-time (37 women), 112 part-time (70 women); includes 24 minority (13 African Americans, 3 American Indian/Alaska Native, 4 Asian Americans or Pacific Islanders, 4 Hispanic Americans), 38 international. Average age 35. 92 applicants, 68% accepted, 38 enrolled. In 2006, 52 master's, 23 doctorates awarded. *Degree requirements:* For master's, thesis optional; for doctorate, thesis/dissertation, oral and written exams; for Ed S, oral presentation, project. *Entrance requirements:* For master's, GRE General Test, minimum B average; for doctorate, GRE General Test; for Ed S, GRE, minimum B average. Additional exam requirements/recommendations for international students: Required—TOEFL. *Application deadline:* For fall admission, 1/15 priority date for domestic students, 1/15 for international students; for spring admission, 9/15 for domestic and international students. Applications are processed on a rolling basis. Application fee: $55. Electronic applications accepted. *Financial support:* In 2006–07, 3 fellowships with full tuition reimbursements (averaging $10,500 per year), 11 research assistantships with full tuition reimbursements (averaging $11,500 per year), 43 teaching assistantships with full tuition reimbursements (averaging $10,800 per year) were awarded; career-related internships or fieldwork and tuition waivers (full) also available. Support available to part-time students. Financial award application deadline: 3/1; financial award applicants required to submit FAFSA. *Faculty research:* Literacy acquisition and development, teacher beliefs and knowledge, recruitment and retention of underrepresented students, economic education, literacy discourse. *Unit head:* Dr. James D Lehman, Head, 765-494-7935, Fax: 765-496-1622. *Application contact:* Patricia Mason, Coordinator of Graduate Studies, 765-494-2345, Fax: 765-494-5832, E-mail: gradoffice@soe.purdue.edu.

Queens College of the City University of New York, Division of Graduate Studies, Division of Education, Department of Secondary Education, Flushing, NY 11367-1597. Offers art (MS Ed); biology (MS Ed, AC); chemistry (MS Ed, AC); earth sciences (MS Ed, AC); English (MS Ed, AC); French (MS Ed, AC); Italian (MS Ed, AC); mathematics (MS Ed, AC); music (MS Ed, AC); physics (MS Ed, AC); social studies (MS Ed, AC); Spanish (MS Ed, AC). Part-time and evening/weekend programs available. *Faculty:* 22 full-time (14 women). *Students:* 50 full-time (28 women), 974 part-time (627 women). 633 applicants, 82% accepted, 407 enrolled. In 2006, 227 degrees awarded. *Degree requirements:* For master's, research project; for AC, thesis optional. *Entrance requirements:* For master's, minimum GPA of 3.0. Additional exam requirements/recommendations for international students: Required—TOEFL. *Application deadline:* For fall admission, 4/1 for domestic students; for spring admission, 11/1 for domestic students. Applications are processed on a rolling basis. Application fee: $125. *Financial support:* Career-related internships or fieldwork, Federal Work-Study, institutionally sponsored loans, and tuition waivers (partial) available. Support available to part-time students. Financial award application deadline: 4/1; financial award applicants required to submit FAFSA. *Unit head:* Dr. Eleanor Armour-Thomas, Chairperson, 718-997-5150, E-mail: armourthomas@yahoo.com. *Application contact:* Mario Caruso, Director of Graduate Admissions, 718-997-5200, Fax: 718-997-5193, E-mail: graduate_admissions@qc.edu.

Quinnipiac University, Division of Education, Program in Secondary Education, Hamden, CT 06518-1940. Offers biology (MAT); chemistry (MAT); English (MAT); French (MAT); history/social studies (MAT); mathematics (MAT); physics (MAT); Spanish (MAT). *Faculty:* 7 full-time (5 women), 23 part-time/adjunct (14 women). *Students:* 64 full-time (41 women); includes 5 minority (1 African American, 4 Hispanic Americans). Average age 26. 63 applicants, 87% accepted, 42 enrolled. In 2006, 37 degrees awarded. *Entrance requirements:* For master's, PRAXIS I, minimum GPA of 2.67, interview. Additional exam requirements/recommendations for international students: Required—TOEFL (minimum score 575 paper-based; 233 computer-based; 90 iBT), IELTS (minimum score 7). *Application deadline:* For fall admission, 3/15 priority date for domestic students. Applications are processed on a rolling basis. Application fee: $45. Electronic applications accepted. *Expenses:* Tuition: Part-time $675 per credit. Required fees: $30 per credit. *Financial support:* Career-related internships or fieldwork and tuition waivers (partial) available. Financial award application deadline: 4/15; financial award applicants required to submit FAFSA. *Faculty research:* Multicultural and urban education, role of technology in education, challenges of teaching divers learners, socio-cultural nature of learning. *Unit head:* Dr. Bernadine Krawczyk, Assistant Dean, Division of Education, 203-582-3510, Fax: 203-582-3473, E-mail: bernadine.krawczyk@quinnipiac.edu. *Application contact:* 800-462-1944, Fax: 203-582-3443, E-mail: graduate@quinnipiac.edu.

See Close-Up on page 911.

Rider University, Department of Graduate Education, Leadership and Counseling, Lawrenceville, NJ 08648-3001. Offers counseling services (MA, Ed S); curriculum, instruction and supervision (MA); director of school counseling services (Certificate); educational administration (MA); organizational leadership (MA); principal (Certificate); reading/language arts (MA, Certificate), including reading specialist (Certificate), reading/language arts (MA); school business administrator (Certificate); school counseling services (Certificate); school psychology (Ed S); special education (MA); supervisor (Certificate); teacher certification (Certificate), including business education, elementary education, English as a second language, English education, mathematics education, preschool to grade 3, science education, social studies education, world languages; teaching (MA). *Accreditation:* NCATE. Part-time and evening/weekend programs available. *Faculty:* 24 full-time (12 women), 30 part-time/adjunct (15 women). *Students:* 90 full-time (75 women), 457 part-time (369 women); includes 73 minority (50 African Americans, 2 American Indian/Alaska Native, 6 Asian Americans or Pacific Islanders, 15 Hispanic Americans), 1 international. Average age 32. 314 applicants, 61% accepted, 138 enrolled. In 2006, 116 master's, 19 other advanced degrees awarded. *Degree requirements:* For master's, thesis or alternative, internship, portfolios, comprehensive exam (for some programs); for other advanced degree, internship, professional portfolio. *Entrance requirements:* For master's, GRE (counseling, school psychology), MAT, interview, resumé, letters of recommendation; for other advanced degree, PRAXIS. Additional exam requirements/recommendations for international students: Required—TOEFL (minimum score 550 paper-based; 213 computer-based). *Application deadline:* For fall admission, 5/1 priority date for domestic students, 6/1 priority date for international students; for spring admission, 11/1 priority date for domestic and international students. Applications are processed on a rolling basis. Application fee: $50. Electronic applications accepted. *Expenses:* Tuition: Part-time $525 per credit. Required fees: $35 per course. $30 per semester. *Financial support:* In 2006–07, 271 students received support. Career-related internships or fieldwork, Federal Work-Study, institutionally sponsored loans, and unspecified assistantships available. Support available to part-time students. Financial award applicants required to submit FAFSA. *Faculty research:* Gifted students, self-esteem, hope and mental health, conflicts in group work, cultural diversity and counseling assessment of special needs in children. *Unit head:* Dr. Dennis C. Buss, Chair, 609-895-5353, Fax: 609-896-5362, E-mail: dbuss@rider.edu. *Application contact:* Jamie L Mitchell, Director of Graduate Admissions, 609-896-5036, Fax: 609-895-5680, E-mail: jmitchell@rider.edu.

See Close-Up on page 913.

Rockford College, Graduate Studies, Department of Education, Program in Secondary Education, Rockford, IL 61108-2393. Offers art education (MAT); English (MAT); history (MAT); political science (MAT); secondary education (MAT); social sciences (MAT). Part-time and evening/weekend programs available. *Degree requirements:* For master's, thesis optional. *Entrance requirements:* For master's, GRE General Test.

Rollins College, Hamilton Holt School, Program in Education, Winter Park, FL 32789-4499. Offers elementary education (M Ed, MAT); secondary education (MAT), including English, mathematics, music. Part-time and evening/weekend programs available. *Students:* 14 full-time (12 women), 36 part-time (32 women); includes 5 minority (2 African Americans, 1 Asian American or Pacific Islander, 2 Hispanic Americans), 1 international. Average age 35. In 2006, 14 degrees awarded. *Degree requirements:* For master's, comprehensive exam. *Entrance requirements:* For master's, GRE or MAT, interview. Additional exam requirements/recommendations for international students: Required—TOEFL. *Application deadline:* For fall admission, 7/16 for domestic students; for winter admission, 12/3 for domestic students; for spring admission, 4/22 for domestic students. Applications are processed on a rolling basis. Application fee: $50. Electronic applications accepted. *Expenses: Contact institution. Financial support:* Teaching assistantships, scholarships/grants available. Support available to part-time students. *Unit head:* Dr. J. Scott Hewit, Director, 407-646-2300, E-mail: jhewit@rollins.edu. *Application contact:* Rebecca Cordray, Coordinator of Records and Registration, 407-646-1568, Fax: 407-975-6430, E-mail: rcordray@rollins.edu.

Rutgers, The State University of New Jersey, New Brunswick, Graduate School of Education, Department of Learning and Teaching, Program in English Education, New Brunswick, NJ 08901-1281. Offers Ed M. Part-time programs available. *Students:* 31 full-time (26 women), 2 part-time (both women). 76 applicants, 55% accepted, 30 enrolled. In 2006, 22 degrees awarded. *Degree requirements:* For master's, comprehensive exam or paper. *Entrance requirements:* For master's, GRE General Test, minimum GPA of 3.0. Additional exam requirements/recommendations for international students: Required—TOEFL. *Application deadline:* For fall admission, 2/1 for domestic and international students. Application fee: $60. Electronic applications accepted. *Financial support:* Application deadline: 3/15; *Unit head:* Dr. Jennifer Rowsell, Coordinator, 732-932-7496 Ext. 8157, E-mail: jrowsell@rci.rutgers.edu.

Sage Graduate School, Graduate School, Division of Education, Program in Teaching, Troy, NY 12180-4115. Offers art education (MAT); biology (MAT); English (MAT); mathematics (MAT); social studies (MAT). Part-time and evening/weekend programs available. *Faculty:* 11 full-time (8 women), 20 part-time/adjunct (15 women). *Students:* 34 full-time (28 women), 41 part-time (29 women); includes 3 minority (1 African American, 1 Asian American or Pacific Islander, 1 Hispanic American). Average age 27. 72 applicants, 64% accepted, 33 enrolled. In 2006, 31 degrees awarded. *Entrance requirements:* For master's, minimum undergraduate GPA of 2.75 overall, minimum undergraduate GPA of 3.0 in content area. Additional exam requirements/recommendations for international students: Required—TOEFL (minimum score 550 paper-based; 213 computer-based). *Application deadline:* For fall admission, 8/1 for domestic students. Applications are processed on a rolling basis. Application fee: $40. *Expenses:* Tuition: Full-time $9,270; part-time $515 per credit hour. *Financial support:* Career-related internships or fieldwork, scholarships/grants, and unspecified assistantships available. Support available to part-time students. Financial award application deadline: 3/1; financial award applicants required to submit FAFSA. *Unit head:* Peter McDermott, Director, 518-244-2493, E-mail: mcderp@sage.edu. *Application contact:* Shannon K. Easton, Director of Graduate and Adult Admission, 518-244-2443, Fax: 518-244-6880, E-mail: sgsadm@sage.edu.

St. John Fisher College, Office of the Provost, Ralph C. Wilson Jr. School of Education, Adolescence Education Program, Rochester, NY 14618-3597. Offers adolescence English (MS Ed); adolescence French (MS Ed); adolescence social studies (MS Ed); adolescence Spanish (MS Ed). Part-time and evening/weekend programs available. *Faculty:* 4 full-time (2 women), 2 part-time/adjunct (1 woman). *Students:* Average age 31. 35 applicants, 91% accepted, 25 enrolled. In 2006, 13 degrees awarded. *Degree requirements:* For master's, student teaching, capstone project, field experiences; for degree. *Entrance requirements:* For master's, GRE (if GPA is below 3.0), minimum GPA of 3.0, 30 hours in certification area, 2 letters of reference, personal statement. Additional exam requirements/recommendations for international students: Required—TOEFL (minimum score 575 paper-based; 233 computer-based; 80 iBT). *Application deadline:* For fall admission, 4/1 for domestic students; for spring admission, 10/30 for domestic students. Applications are processed on a rolling basis. Application fee: $30. *Expenses:* Tuition: Part-time $615 per credit. Tuition and fees vary according to program. *Financial support:* In 2006–07, 1 student received support. Federal Work-Study and scholarships/grants available. Financial award application deadline: 2/15; financial award applicants required to submit FAFSA. *Faculty research:* Arts and humanities, urban schools, constructivist learning, at risk students, mentoring. *Unit head:* Dr. Russell Coward, Director, 585-385-8114, E-mail: rcoward@sjfc.edu. *Application contact:* Shannon Cleverley, Director of Graduate Admissions, 585-385-8161, Fax: 585-385-8344, E-mail: scleverley@sjfc.edu.

Salem State College, Graduate School, Program in English, Salem, MA 01970-5353. Offers English (MA, MAT, MA/MAT); English as a second language (MAT); MA/MAT. Part-time and evening/weekend programs available. *Faculty:* 3 part-time/adjunct (1 woman). *Students:* 13 full-time (8 women), 49 part-time (34 women); includes 1 minority (Asian American or Pacific Islander), 1 international. Average age 32. In 2006, 20 degrees awarded. *Degree requirements:* For master's, one foreign language. *Entrance requirements:* For master's, GRE General Test, MAT. *Application deadline:* Applications are processed on a rolling basis. Application fee: $35. *Unit head:* Nancy Schultz, Coordinator, 978-542-6105, E-mail: nschultz@salemstate.edu.

Salisbury University, Graduate Division, Department of Education, Salisbury, MD 21801-6837. Offers art (MAT); biology (MAT); business education (MAT); chemistry (MAT); early childhood education (M Ed); educational administration (M Ed); elementary education (M Ed); English (M Ed, MAT); French (MAT); geography (MAT); history (MAT); mathematics (MAT); media and technology (MAT); music (MAT); psychology (MAT); reading education (MAT); science (MAT); secondary education (MAT); social studies (MAT); Spanish (MAT). *Accreditation:* NCATE. Part-time and evening/weekend programs available. *Faculty:* 12 full-time (6 women), 10 part-time/adjunct (8 women). *Students:* 17 full-time (9 women), 84 part-time (72 women); includes 6 minority (5 African Americans, 1 Hispanic American). Average age 30. 15 applicants, 73% accepted, 11 enrolled. In 2006, 63 degrees awarded. *Degree requirements:* For master's, comprehensive exam (for some programs). *Entrance requirements:* For master's, PRAXIS, minimum GPA of 2.75. Additional exam requirements/recommendations for international students: Required—TOEFL (minimum score 550 paper-based; 213 computer-based). *Application deadline:* For fall admission, 8/1 priority date for domestic students; for spring admission, 1/1 for domestic students. Applications are processed on a rolling basis. Application fee: $45. *Expenses:* Tuition, state resident: part-time $260 per credit hour. Tuition, nonresident: part-time $546 per credit hour. Required fees: $52 per credit hour. *Financial support:* In 2006–07, 3 teaching assistantships with full tuition reimbursements were awarded; career-related internships or fieldwork and scholarships/grants also available. Support available to part-time students. Financial award applicants required to submit FAFSA. *Faculty research:* Middle-level education, student outcomes. *Unit head:* Dr. Edward C. Robeck, Program Coordinator, 410-543-6292, Fax: 410-548-2593, E-mail: ecrobeck@salisbury.edu. *Application contact:* Debra J. Clark, Administrative Assistant I, 410-543-6281, Fax: 410-548-2593, E-mail: djclark@salisbury.edu.

San Francisco State University, Division of Graduate Studies, College of Education, Department of Elementary Education, Program in Language and Literacy Education, San Francisco, CA 94132-1722. Offers MA. *Degree requirements:* For master's, thesis or alternative. *Entrance requirements:* For master's, minimum GPA of 2.5 in last 60 units. *Application deadline:* For fall admission, 11/30 priority date for domestic students. Applications are processed on a rolling basis. Application fee: $55. *Financial support:* Application deadline: 3/1. *Application contact:* Dr. Josie Arce, Graduate Coordinator, 415-338-2292, E-mail: jarce@sfsu.edu.

San Francisco State University, Division of Graduate Studies, College of Humanities, Department of English Language and Literature, San Francisco, CA 94132-1722. Offers composition (MA, Certificate); linguistics (MA); literature (MA); teaching composition (Certificate); teaching English to speakers of other languages (MA); teaching post-secondary reading (Certificate). Part-time programs available. *Faculty:* 58 full-time (22 women). *Students:* 180 (118 women). Average age 28. In 2006, 120 degrees awarded. *Entrance requirements:* For master's, minimum GPA of 2.5 in last 60 units. *Application deadline:* Applications are processed on a rolling basis. Application fee: $55. *Financial support:* Teaching assistantships available. Financial award application deadline: 3/1. *Faculty research:* Modern critical theory, composition theory and practice. *Unit head:* Dr. James Kohn, Chair, 415-338-2264.

San Jose State University, Graduate Studies and Research, College of Humanities and the Arts, Department of English and Comparative Literature, San Jose, CA 95192-0001. Offers creative writing (MFA); English (MA); secondary English education (Certificate). *Students:* 31 full-time (22 women), 59 part-time (45 women); includes 16 minority (3 African Americans, 1 American Indian/Alaska Native, 6 Asian Americans or Pacific Islanders, 6 Hispanic Americans), 2 international. Average age 34. 94 applicants, 73% accepted, 36 enrolled. In 2006, 37 degrees awarded. *Degree requirements:* For master's, one foreign language, thesis or alternative. *Entrance requirements:* For master's, GRE. Additional exam requirements/recommendations for international students: Required—TOEFL. *Application deadline:* For fall admission, 6/29 for domestic students; for spring admission, 11/30 for domestic students. Applications are processed on a rolling basis. Application fee: $59. Electronic applications accepted. *Financial support:* Applicants required to submit FAFSA. *Unit head:* John Engell, Chair, 408-924-4499, Fax: 408-924-4580, E-mail: jfengell@email.sjsu.edu. *Application contact:* Dr. Noelle Brada-Williams, Graduate Coordinator, 408-924-4435.

Smith College, Graduate Programs, Department of Education and Child Study, Program in Secondary Education, Northampton, MA 01063. Offers biological sciences education (MAT); chemistry education (MAT); English education (MAT); French education (MAT); geology education (MAT); government education (MAT); history education (MAT); mathematics education (MAT); physics education (MAT); Spanish education (MAT). Part-time programs available. *Faculty:* 6 full-time (4 women), 3 part-time/adjunct (2 women). *Students:* 4 full-time (2 women). Average age 36. 12 applicants, 67% accepted, 3 enrolled. In 2006, 5 master's awarded. *Entrance requirements:* For master's, GRE General Test. Additional exam requirements/recommendations for international students: Required—TOEFL. *Application deadline:* For fall admission, 4/1 for domestic students, 1/15 for international students; for spring admission, 12/1 for domestic students. Application fee: $60. *Expenses:* Tuition: Full-time $32,320; part-time $1,010 per credit. Tuition and fees vary according to course load. *Financial support:* In 2006–07, 3 students received support. Career-related internships or fieldwork, institutionally sponsored loans, and scholarships/grants available. Support available to part-time students. Financial award application deadline: 1/15; financial award applicants required to submit CSS PROFILE or FAFSA. *Unit head:* Rosetta Cohen, Graduate Student Advisor, 413-585-3266.

Smith College, Graduate Programs, Department of English Language and Literature, Northampton, MA 01063. Offers MAT. Part-time programs available. *Faculty:* 21 full-time (9 women). *Students:* 2 applicants, 100% accepted, 1 enrolled. In 2006, 2 degrees awarded. *Entrance requirements:* Additional exam requirements/recommendations for international students: Required—TOEFL. *Application deadline:* For fall admission, 1/15 for domestic and international students; for spring admission, 12/1 for domestic students. Application fee: $60. *Expenses:* Tuition: Full-time $32,320; part-time $1,010 per credit. Tuition and fees vary according to course load. *Unit head:* Michael Gorra, Department Chair, 413-585-3305, E-mail: mgorra@smith.edu.

South Carolina State University, School of Graduate Studies, Department of Education, Orangeburg, SC 29117-0001. Offers early childhood and special education (M Ed); early childhood education (MAT); elementary education (M Ed, MAT); engineering (MAT); general science (MAT); mathematics (MAT); secondary education (M Ed), including biology education, business education, counselor education, English education, home economics education, industrial education, mathematics education, science education, social studies education; special education (M Ed), including emotionally handicapped, learning disabilities, mentally handicapped. *Accreditation:* NCATE. Part-time and evening/weekend programs available. *Faculty:* 21 full-time (10 women), 4 part-time/adjunct (0 women). *Students:* 34 full-time (28 women), 33 part-time (25 women); includes 63 minority (61 African Americans, 1 American Indian/Alaska Native, 1 Asian American or Pacific Islander). Average age 35. 46 applicants, 67% accepted, 19 enrolled. In 2006, 28 degrees awarded. *Degree requirements:* For master's, departmental qualifying exam, thesis optional. *Entrance requirements:* For master's, GRE General Test, NTE, interview, teaching certificate. *Application deadline:* For fall admission, 6/15 priority date for domestic students, 6/15 for international students; for spring admission, 11/1 for domestic and international students. Applications are processed on a rolling basis. Application fee: $25. Electronic applications accepted. *Expenses:* Tuition, state resident: full-time $7,278. Tuition, nonresident: full-time $14,322. *Financial support:* Fellowships, research assistantships, career-related internships or fieldwork, Federal Work-Study, and institutionally sponsored loans available. Financial award application deadline: 6/1. *Faculty research:* Critical thinking, child abuse, stress, test-taking skills, conflict resolution, mainstreaming. *Unit head:* Dr. Gail Joyner-Fleming, Interim Chair, 803-533-3769, Fax: 803-536-8492, E-mail: zf-gfleming@scsu.edu. *Application contact:* Annette Hazzard-Jones, Program Coordinator II, 803-536-8809, Fax: 803-536-8812, E-mail: zs_ahazzard@scsu.edu.

Southern Illinois University Edwardsville, Graduate Studies and Research, College of Arts and Sciences, Department of English Language and Literature, Program in Teaching of Writing, Edwardsville, IL 62026-0001. Offers MA, Postbaccalaureate Certificate. Part-time and evening/weekend programs available. *Students:* 2 full-time (1 woman), 14 part-time (12 women). Average age 33. 7 applicants, 71% accepted. In 2006, 1 master's, 1 other advanced degree awarded. *Degree requirements:* For master's, thesis or alternative, final exam. *Entrance requirements:* Additional exam requirements/recommendations for international students: Required—TOEFL. *Application deadline:* For fall admission, 7/20 for domestic students, 6/1 for international students; for spring admission, 12/14 for domestic students, 10/1 for international students. Application fee: $30. Electronic applications accepted. *Financial support:* Fellowships with full tuition reimbursements, research assistantships with full tuition reimbursements, teaching assistantships with full tuition reimbursements, Federal Work-Study, institutionally sponsored loans, and unspecified assistantships available. Support available to part-time students. Financial award application deadline: 3/1. *Unit head:* Dr. Jack Voller, Director, 618-650-2460, E-mail: jvoller@siue.edu.

Southern Illinois University Edwardsville, Graduate Studies and Research, School of Education, Department of Curriculum and Instruction, Program in Secondary Education, Edwardsville, IL 62026-0001. Offers art (MS Ed); biology (MS Ed); chemistry (MS Ed); English (MS Ed); foreign languages (MS Ed); history (MS Ed); mathematics (MS Ed); physics (MS Ed); reading (MS Ed); science (MS Ed). *Accreditation:* NCATE. Part-time and evening/weekend programs available. *Students:* 2 full-time (both women), 23 part-time (14 women); includes 2 minority (both

English Education

Southern Illinois University Edwardsville (continued)
African Americans) Average age 33. 12 applicants, 42% accepted. In 2006, 10 degrees awarded. *Degree requirements:* For master's, thesis or alternative, final exam. *Entrance requirements:* For master's, MAT. Additional exam requirements/recommendations for international students: Required—TOEFL. *Application deadline:* For fall admission, 7/20 for domestic students, 6/1 for international students; for spring admission, 12/14 for domestic students, 10/1 for international students. Application fee: $30. Electronic applications accepted. *Financial support:* Fellowships, research assistantships, teaching assistantships, Federal Work-Study, institutionally sponsored loans, and unspecified assistantships available. Support available to part-time students. Financial award application deadline: 3/1; financial award applicants required to submit FAFSA. *Unit head:* Dr. David DeWeese, Director, 618-650-3432, E-mail: ddewees@siue.edu.

Southwestern Oklahoma State University, College of Arts and Sciences, Specialization in English, Weatherford, OK 73096-3098. Offers M Ed. M Ed distance learning degree program offered to Oklahoma residents only. *Accreditation:* NCATE. Part-time programs available. *Degree requirements:* For master's, exam. *Entrance requirements:* For master's, GRE General Test or minimum undergraduate GPA of 3.0. Additional exam requirements/recommendations for international students: Required—TOEFL.

Stanford University, School of Education, Program in Curriculum Studies and Teacher Education, Stanford, CA 94305-9991. Offers art education (MA, PhD); dance education (MA); English education (MA, PhD); general curriculum studies (MA, PhD); mathematics education (MA, PhD); science education (MA, PhD); social studies education (PhD); teacher education (MA, PhD). *Degree requirements:* For master's, thesis (for some programs); for doctorate, thesis/dissertation. *Entrance requirements:* For master's and doctorate, GRE General Test. Electronic applications accepted.

Stanford University, School of Education, Teacher Education Program, Stanford, CA 94305-9991. Offers English education (MA); languages education (MA); mathematics education (MA); science education (MA); social studies education (MA). *Degree requirements:* For master's, thesis. *Entrance requirements:* For master's, GRE General Test. Electronic applications accepted.

State University of New York at Binghamton, Graduate School, School of Education, Program in Secondary Education, Binghamton, NY 13902-6000. Offers biology education (MAT, MS Ed, MST); earth science education (MAT, MS Ed, MST); English education (MAT, MS Ed, MST); French education (MAT, MST); mathematical sciences education (MAT, MS Ed, MST); physics (MAT, MS Ed, MST); social studies (MAT, MS Ed, MST); Spanish education (MAT, MST). *Accreditation:* Teacher Education Accreditation Council. Part-time and evening/weekend programs available. *Students:* 89 full-time (50 women), 47 part-time (32 women); includes 6 minority (1 African American, 3 Asian Americans or Pacific Islanders, 2 Hispanic Americans). Average age 29. 72 applicants, 72% accepted, 23 enrolled. In 2006, 44 degrees awarded. *Entrance requirements:* For master's, GRE General Test. Additional exam requirements/recommendations for international students: Required—TOEFL. *Application deadline:* For fall admission, 4/15 priority date for domestic students, 1/15 priority date for international students; for spring admission, 11/1 for domestic students, 10/1 priority date for international students. Applications are processed on a rolling basis. Application fee: $60. Electronic applications accepted. *Financial support:* In 2006–07, 25 students received support, including 2 fellowships with partial tuition reimbursements available (averaging $2,350 per year), 4 research assistantships with full and partial tuition reimbursements available (averaging $6,638 per year), 13 teaching assistantships with full tuition reimbursements available (averaging $5,944 per year); career-related internships or fieldwork, Federal Work-Study, institutionally sponsored loans, tuition waivers (full and partial), and unspecified assistantships also available. Support available to part-time students. Financial award application deadline: 2/15. *Unit head:* Dr. Thomas O'Brien, Coordinator, 607-777-7329, E-mail: tobrien@binghamton.edu.

State University of New York at Plattsburgh, Division of Education, Health, and Human Services, Department of Adolescence Education/Health, Plattsburgh, NY 12901-2681. Offers adolescence education (MST); biology 7-12 (MST); chemistry 7-12 (MST); earth science 7-12 (MST); English 7-12 (MST); French 7-12 (MST); mathematics 7-12 (MST); physics 7-12 (MST); social studies 7-12 (MST); Spanish 7-12 (MST). *Faculty:* 4 full-time (3 women), 2 part-time/adjunct (0 women). *Students:* 58 full-time (38 women), 14 part-time (10 women); includes 5 minority (1 African American, 4 Hispanic Americans). Average age 30. 49 applicants, 78% accepted, 32 enrolled. In 2006, 30 degrees awarded. *Degree requirements:* For master's, comprehensive exam or research project. *Entrance requirements:* For master's, GRE General Test or MAT, minimum GPA of 2.5. *Application deadline:* For fall admission, 2/15 priority date for domestic students; for spring admission, 10/15 priority date for domestic students. Applications are processed on a rolling basis. Application fee: $50. *Expenses:* Tuition, state resident: full-time $6,900; part-time $288 per credit hour. Tuition, nonresident: full-time $10,920; part-time $455 per credit hour. *Financial support:* Application deadline: 4/15; *Unit head:* Dr. Lois Beach, Chair, 578-564-5750, E-mail: lois.beach@plattsburgh.edu. *Application contact:* Sharon Derr, Assistant Director, Graduate Admission, 518-564-4723, Fax: 518-564-4722, E-mail: derrsl@plattsburgh.edu.

State University of New York College at Brockport, School of Professions, Department of Education and Human Development, Program in Adolescence Education, Brockport, NY 14420-2997. Offers biology education (MS Ed); chemistry education (MS Ed); earth science education (MS Ed); English education (MS Ed); mathematics education (MS Ed); physics education (MS Ed); social studies education (MS Ed). *Accreditation:* NCATE. Part-time programs available. *Students:* 39 full-time (21 women), 117 part-time (66 women); includes 6 minority (3 African Americans, 1 Asian American or Pacific Islander, 2 Hispanic Americans). 57 applicants, 61% accepted, 32 enrolled. In 2006, 91 degrees awarded. *Degree requirements:* For master's, thesis or alternative. *Entrance requirements:* For master's, minimum GPA of 3.0, letters of recommendation. Additional exam requirements/recommendations for international students: Required—TOEFL (minimum score 550 paper-based; 213 computer-based; 80 iBT). *Application deadline:* For fall admission, 2/15 for domestic and international students; for spring admission, 9/15 for domestic and international students. Application fee: $50. *Expenses:* Tuition, state resident: full-time $6,900; part-time $288 per credit. Tuition, nonresident: full-time $10,920; part-time $455 per credit. *Financial support:* Career-related internships or fieldwork, Federal Work-Study, scholarships/grants, and unspecified assistantships available. Support available to part-time students. Financial award application deadline: 3/15; financial award applicants required to submit FAFSA. *Application contact:* Coordinator of Certification and Graduate Advisement, 585-395-2344.

State University of New York College at Cortland, Graduate Studies, School of Arts and Sciences, Programs in Adolescence Education, Cortland, NY 13045. Offers biology (MAT, MS Ed); chemistry (MAT, MS Ed); earth science (MAT, MS Ed); English (MS Ed); French (MS Ed); mathematics (MAT, MS Ed); physics (MAT, MS Ed); social studies (MS Ed); Spanish (MS Ed). *Accreditation:* NCATE. Part-time and evening/weekend programs available. *Degree requirements:* For master's, one foreign language, thesis (for some programs), comprehensive exam (for some programs). *Entrance requirements:* For master's, GRE General Test.

Stony Brook University, State University of New York, School of Professional Development, Stony Brook, NY 11794. Offers adolescence education: mathematics (Certificate); biology 7-12 (MAT); chemistry-grade 7-12 (MAT); coaching (Certificate); computer integrated engineering (Certificate); cultural studies (Certificate); earth science-grade 7-12 (MAT); educational computing (Advanced Certificate, Certificate); English-grade 7-12 (MAT); environmental and waste management (MS, Advanced Certificate); environmental systems management (Certificate); environmental/occupational health and safety (Certificate); French-grade 7-12 (MAT); German-grade 7-12 (MAT); human resource management (Certificate); industrial management (Certificate); information systems management (Certificate); Italian-grade 7-12 (MAT); liberal studies (MA); liberal studies online (MA); Long Island regional studies (Certificate); operation research (Certificate); physics-grade 7-12 (MAT); Russian-grade 7-12 (MAT); school administration and supervision (Certificate); school district administration (Certificate); social science and the professions (MPS), including human resources management, labor management, public affairs, waste management; social studies 7-12 (MAT); waste management (Certificate); women's studies (Certificate). Part-time and evening/weekend programs available. Postbaccalaureate distance learning degree programs offered. *Faculty:* 1 full-time (0 women), 118 part-time/adjunct (45 women). *Students:* 322 full-time (202 women), 1,188 part-time (728 women); includes 164 minority (69 African Americans, 2 American Indian/Alaska Native, 29 Asian Americans or Pacific Islanders, 64 Hispanic Americans), 11 international. Average age 28. In 2006, 738 master's, 405 other advanced degrees awarded. *Degree requirements:* For master's, one foreign language, thesis or alternative. *Application deadline:* Applications are processed on a rolling basis. Application fee: $62. *Expenses:* Tuition, state resident: full-time $6,900; part-time $288 per credit. Tuition, nonresident: full-time $10,920; part-time $455 per credit. *Financial support:* In 2006–07, 5 teaching assistantships were awarded; fellowships, research assistantships, career-related internships or fieldwork also available. Support available to part-time students. *Unit head:* Dr. Paul J. Edelson, Dean, 631-632-7052, Fax: 631-632-9046, E-mail: paul.edelson@sunysb.edu. *Application contact:* Sandra Romansky, Director of Admissions and Advisement, 631-632-7050, Fax: 631-632-9046, E-mail: sandra.romansky@sunysb.edu.

Syracuse University, Graduate School, School of Education, Department of Reading and Language Arts, Program in English Education, Syracuse, NY 13244. Offers PhD. Part-time programs available. *Students:* 3 full-time (all women), 1 (woman) part-time, 1 international. 4 applicants, 0% accepted. *Degree requirements:* For doctorate, thesis/dissertation; for degree. *Entrance requirements:* For doctorate, GRE. Additional exam requirements/recommendations for international students: Required—TOEFL. *Application deadline:* For fall admission, 2/1 priority date for domestic students. Applications are processed on a rolling basis. Application fee: $65. Electronic applications accepted. *Expenses:* Tuition: Full-time $16,920; part-time $940 per credit hour. Required fees: $930; $930 per year. *Financial support:* Fellowships with full tuition reimbursements, teaching assistantships with full tuition reimbursements available. *Unit head:* Dr. Kelly Chandler-Olcott, Director, 315-443-4757, E-mail: kpchandl@syr.edu. *Application contact:* Liza Rochelson, Graduate Admission Recruiter, 315-443-2505, Fax: 315-443-2258, E-mail: gradcrt@gwmail.syr.edu.

Syracuse University, Graduate School, School of Education, Department of Reading and Language Arts, Program in English Education: Preparation 7-12, Syracuse, NY 13244. Offers MS. Part-time programs available. *Students:* 12 full-time (10 women); includes 4 minority (2 African Americans, 2 Hispanic Americans). 11 applicants, 82% accepted, 6 enrolled. *Degree requirements:* For master's, thesis or alternative. *Entrance requirements:* For master's, GRE. Additional exam requirements/recommendations for international students: Required—TOEFL. *Application deadline:* For fall admission, 2/1 priority date for domestic students. Applications are processed on a rolling basis. Application fee: $65. Electronic applications accepted. *Expenses:* Tuition: Full-time $16,920; part-time $940 per credit hour. Required fees: $930; $930 per year. *Unit head:* Dr. Kelly Chandler-Olcott, Director, 315-443-4757, E-mail: kpchandl@syr.edu. *Application contact:* Liza Rochelson, Graduate Admission Recruiter, 315-443-2505, Fax: 315-443-2258, E-mail: gradcrt@gwmail.syr.edu.

Teachers College Columbia University, Graduate Faculty of Education, Department of Arts and Humanities, Program in Teaching of English and English Education, New York, NY 10027-6696. Offers Ed M, MA, Ed D, PhD. *Accreditation:* NCATE. Part-time and evening/weekend programs available. *Faculty:* 5 full-time (all women). *Students:* 60 full-time (48 women), 112 part-time (92 women); includes 32 minority (10 African Americans, 15 Asian Americans or Pacific Islanders, 7 Hispanic Americans), 13 international. Average age 31. 181 applicants, 78% accepted, 73 enrolled. In 2006, 110 master's, 7 doctorates awarded. Terminal master's awarded for partial completion of doctoral program. *Degree requirements:* For doctorate, 2 foreign languages, thesis/dissertation. *Application deadline:* For fall admission, 5/15 for domestic students; for spring admission, 12/1 for domestic students. Application fee: $65. *Expenses:* Tuition: Full-time $23,400; part-time $975 per credit. Required fees: $320 per term. *Financial support:* Fellowships, research assistantships, teaching assistantships, career-related internships or fieldwork, Federal Work-Study, institutionally sponsored loans, and tuition waivers (full and partial) available. Support available to part-time students. Financial award application deadline: 2/1. *Faculty research:* Teaching of writing and reading, language and curriculum, literacy and health, narrative and action research. *Application contact:* Mark E. Stearns, Associate Director of Admission, 212-678-3710, Fax: 212-678-4171.

Temple University, Graduate School, College of Education, Department of Curriculum, Instruction, and Technology in Education, Philadelphia, PA 19122-6096. Offers applied behavioral analysis (MS Ed); career and technical education (MS Ed); early childhood education and elementary education (MS Ed); English education (MS Ed); language arts education (Ed D); math/science education (Ed D); mathematics education (MS Ed); science education (MS Ed); second and foreign language education (MS Ed); special education (MS Ed); teaching English as a second language (MS Ed). Part-time and evening/weekend programs available. *Faculty:* 31 full-time (14 women). *Students:* 96 full-time (71 women), 482 part-time (336 women); includes 109 minority (67 African Americans, 3 American Indian/Alaska Native, 23 Asian Americans or Pacific Islanders, 16 Hispanic Americans), 28 international. 308 applicants, 64% accepted, 116 enrolled. In 2006, 225 master's, 21 doctorates awarded. Terminal master's awarded for partial completion of doctoral program. *Degree requirements:* For master's, thesis or alternative; for doctorate, thesis/dissertation. *Entrance requirements:* For master's and doctorate, GRE General Test or MAT, minimum GPA of 3.0. Additional exam requirements/recommendations for international students: Required—TOEFL (minimum score 550 paper-based; 213 computer-based; 79 iBT). *Application deadline:* For fall admission, 4/1 for domestic students, 12/15 for international students; for spring admission, 10/1 for domestic students, 8/1 for international students. Application fee: $50. Electronic applications accepted. *Expenses:* Tuition, state resident: full-time $12,264; part-time $511 per credit. Tuition, nonresident: full-time $17,904; part-time $746 per credit. Required fees: $84 per course. Tuition and fees vary according to program. *Financial support:* Fellowships, research assistantships with full tuition reimbursements, teaching assistantships with full tuition reimbursements available. Financial award application deadline: 1/15; financial award applicants required to submit FAFSA. *Faculty research:* School improvement, problem solving, literacy, language development. *Unit head:* Dr. Thomas Walker, Chair, 215-204-2117, Fax: 215-204-1414, E-mail: tjwalker@temple.edu.

Texas A&M University, College of Education and Human Development, Department of Teaching, Learning, and Culture, College Station, TX 77843. Offers curriculum and instruction (M Ed, MS, PhD); mathematics education (M Ed, MS, PhD); multicultural/urban/ESL/international education (M Ed, MS, PhD); reading/language arts (M Ed, MS, PhD); science education (M Ed, MS, PhD); social studies education (M Ed, MS, PhD). *Accreditation:* NCATE. Part-time programs available. *Faculty:* 25 full-time (9 women), 2 part-time/adjunct (both women). *Students:* 156 full-time (115 women), 226 part-time (191 women); includes 95 minority (43 African Americans, 1 American Indian/Alaska Native, 9 Asian Americans or Pacific Islanders, 42 Hispanic Americans), 36 international. Average age 36. 137 applicants, 83% accepted, 80 enrolled. In 2006, 69 master's, 15 doctorates awarded. *Median time to degree:* Of those who began their doctoral program in fall 1998, 77% received their degree in 8 years or less. *Degree requirements:* For master's, thesis (for some programs), comprehensive exam; for doctorate, thesis/dissertation, comprehensive exam. *Entrance requirements:* For master's, GRE General Test, minimum GPA of 3.0; for doctorate, GRE General Test, 3 years of teaching experience. Additional exam requirements/recommendations for international students: Required—TOEFL (minimum score 550 paper-based; 213 computer-based). *Application deadline:* For fall admission, 1/15 priority date for domestic and international students; for spring admission, 9/15 priority date for domestic and international students. Applications are processed on a rolling basis. Application fee: $50 ($75 for international students). Electronic applications accepted. *Expenses:* Tuition, state resident: full-time $4,697. Tuition, nonresident: full-time $11,297.

Required fees: $2,272. *Financial support:* In 2006–07, fellowships with partial tuition reimbursements (averaging $3,000 per year), teaching assistantships with partial tuition reimbursements (averaging $7,200 per year) were awarded; research assistantships with partial tuition reimbursements, career-related internships or fieldwork, Federal Work-Study, institutionally sponsored loans, scholarships/grants, tuition waivers (partial), and unspecified assistantships also available. Support available to part-time students. Financial award application deadline: 4/1; financial award applicants required to submit FAFSA. *Unit head:* Dr. Dennie Smith, Head, 979-845-8384, Fax: 979-845-9663. *Application contact:* Graduate Admissions Supervisor, 979-845-8382, Fax: 979-845-9663.

Texas A&M University–Commerce, Graduate School, College of Arts and Sciences, Department of Literature and Languages, Commerce, TX 75429-3011. Offers college teaching of English (PhD); English (MA, MS); Spanish (MA). Part-time programs available. Terminal master's awarded for partial completion of doctoral program. *Degree requirements:* For master's, thesis (for some programs), comprehensive exam; for doctorate, one foreign language, thesis/dissertation, departmental qualifying exam. *Entrance requirements:* For master's and doctorate, GRE General Test. Electronic applications accepted. *Faculty research:* Latino literature, American film studies, ethnographic research, Willa Carter.

Texas Tech University, Graduate School, College of Education, Division of Curriculum and Instruction, Lubbock, TX 79409. Offers bilingual education (M Ed); curriculum and instruction (M Ed, PhD); elementary education (M Ed); language and literacy education (M Ed); secondary education (M Ed). *Accreditation:* NCATE. Part-time programs available. *Students:* 68 full-time (48 women), 99 part-time (82 women); includes 35 minority (6 African Americans, 1 Asian American or Pacific Islander, 28 Hispanic Americans), 10 international. Average age 34. 165 applicants, 59% accepted, 10 enrolled. In 2006, 61 master's, 7 doctorates awarded. *Degree requirements:* For master's, thesis optional; for doctorate, thesis/dissertation. *Entrance requirements:* For master's and doctorate, GRE General Test. Additional exam requirements/recommendations for international students: Required—TOEFL (minimum score 550 paper-based; 213 computer-based). *Application deadline:* For fall admission, 3/1 priority date for international students; for spring admission, 11/1 priority date for international students. Applications are processed on a rolling basis. Application fee: $50 ($60 for international students). Electronic applications accepted. *Expenses:* Tuition, state resident: full-time $4,440. Tuition, nonresident: full-time $11,040. Required fees: $2,136. *Financial support:* In 2006–07, 100 students received support; research assistantships with partial tuition reimbursements available, teaching assistantships with partial tuition reimbursements available, career-related internships or fieldwork, Federal Work-Study, and institutionally sponsored loans available. Support available to part-time students. Financial award application deadline: 4/15; financial award applicants required to submit FAFSA. *Faculty research:* Multicultural foundations of education, teacher education, instruction and pedagogy in subject areas, curriculum theory, language and literary. *Unit head:* Dr. Peggy Johnson, Associate Dean, 806-742-1988 Ext. 437, Fax: 806-742-2179, E-mail: peggy.johnson@ttu.edu.

Trinity (Washington) University, School of Education, Washington, DC 20017-1094. Offers democracy, diversity, and social justice (M Ed); early childhood (MAT); educational administration (MSA); elementary education (MAT); English as a second language (M Ed, MAT); literacy and reading education (M Ed); school counseling (MA); secondary education (MAT), including English, math, science, social studies; special education (MAT). *Accreditation:* NCATE. Part-time and evening/weekend programs available. *Degree requirements:* For master's, thesis (for some programs), capstone project(s). *Entrance requirements:* For master's, PRAXIS I, minimum GPA of 2.8. Additional exam requirements/recommendations for international students: Required—TOEFL (minimum score 550 paper-based; 213 computer-based). *Faculty research:* Technology, literacy, special education, organizations, inclusion models.

Union Graduate College, School of Education, Schenectady, NY 12308-3107. Offers biology (MAT, MS); chemistry (MAT); earth science (MAT); English (MAT); French (MAT); general science (MAT); German (MAT); languages (MAT); Latin (MAT); mathematics (MAT); mathematics and technology (MS); physical science (MS); physics (MAT); social studies (MAT); Spanish (MAT). *Accreditation:* Teacher Education Accreditation Council. *Faculty:* 5 full-time (1 woman), 19 part-time/adjunct (10 women). *Students:* 57 full-time (36 women), 21 part-time (14 women); includes 2 African Americans, 2 Hispanic Americans, 2 international. Average age 31. 59 applicants, 83% accepted, 39 enrolled. In 2006, 56 degrees awarded. *Degree requirements:* For master's, thesis or project. *Entrance requirements:* For master's, minimum GPA of 3.0, letters of recommendation. Additional exam requirements/recommendations for international students: Required—TOEFL (minimum score 550 paper-based; 213 computer-based). Application fee: $60. *Expenses:* Contact institution. *Financial support:* In 2006–07, 12 research assistantships with tuition reimbursements (averaging $3,000 per year) were awarded; Federal Work-Study, scholarships/grants, health care benefits, and tuition waivers (partial) also available. Support available to part-time students. Financial award applicants required to submit FAFSA. *Unit head:* Dr. Patrick Allen, Dean, 518-388-6361, Fax: 518-388-6686, E-mail: mat@union.edu. *Application contact:* Rhonda Sheehan, Director of Graduate Admissions Registrar, 518-388-6238, Fax: 518-388-6686, E-mail: sheehanr@union.edu.

See Close-Up on page 923.

University at Buffalo, the State University of New York, Graduate School, Graduate School of Education, Department of Learning and Instruction, Buffalo, NY 14260. Offers adolescence education (Certificate); biology (Ed M); chemistry (Ed M); childhood education (Ed M); early childhood and childhood education with bilingual extension (Ed M); early childhood education (Ed M); earth science (Ed M); elementary education (Ed D, PhD); English (Ed M); English education (PhD); English for speakers of other languages (Ed M); foreign and second language education (PhD); French (Ed M); general education (Ed M); German (Ed M); Italian (Ed M); Japanese (Ed M); Latin (Ed M); literary specialist (Ed M); mathematics (Ed M); mathematics education (PhD); mentoring teachers (Certificate); music education (Ed M, Certificate); physics (Ed M); reading education (PhD); Russian (Ed M); school administrator and supervisor (Certificate); science education (PhD); social studies (Ed M); Spanish (Ed M); special education (PhD); teaching and leading for diversity (Certificate); teaching English to speakers of other languages (Ed M). Part-time and evening/weekend programs available. Postbaccalaureate distance learning degree programs offered (no on-campus study). *Faculty:* 30 full-time (20 women), 53 part-time/adjunct (38 women). *Students:* 368 full-time (269 women), 297 part-time (226 women); includes 50 minority (15 African Americans, 2 American Indian/Alaska Native, 14 Asian Americans or Pacific Islanders, 19 Hispanic Americans), 66 international. Average age 31. 638 applicants, 75% accepted, 298 enrolled. In 2006, 248 master's, 18 doctorates, 48 other advanced degrees awarded. Terminal master's awarded for partial completion of doctoral program. *Degree requirements:* For master's, comprehensive exam, registration; for doctorate, thesis/dissertation, research analysis exam, research experience component. *Entrance requirements:* For doctorate, GRE General Test or MAT, interview, writing sample, letters of recommendation. Additional exam requirements/recommendations for international students: Required—TOEFL (minimum score 600 paper-based; 250 computer-based). *Application deadline:* For fall admission, 2/1 priority date for domestic and international students; for spring admission, 11/15 priority date for domestic students, 10/1 for international students. Applications are processed on a rolling basis. Application fee: $50. Electronic applications accepted. *Financial support:* In 2006–07, 70 students received support, including 6 fellowships with full tuition reimbursements available (averaging $10,000 per year), 16 research assistantships with full tuition reimbursements available (averaging $9,000 per year), teaching assistantships with full tuition reimbursements available (averaging $9,000 per year); career-related internships or fieldwork, Federal Work-Study, institutionally sponsored loans, scholarships/grants, tuition waivers (partial), and unspecified assistantships also available. Financial award application deadline: 2/28; financial award applicants required to submit FAFSA. *Faculty research:* Science assessment, state-level testing, early learning, literacy, second language acquisition. Total annual research expenditures: $432,366. *Unit head:* Dr. Maria E. Runfola, Chair, 716-645-2455, Fax: 716-645-3161. *Application contact:* Barbara Belz, Admissions Secretary, 716-645-2110 Ext. 1159, Fax: 716-645-3161, E-mail: belz@buffalo.edu.

University of Alaska Fairbanks, School of Education, Fairbanks, AK 99775-7520. Offers cross cultural education (M Ed); curriculum instruction (M Ed); education (M Ed); guidance and counseling (M Ed); k-12 reading (M Ed); language and literacy (M Ed). *Accreditation:* NCATE. Part-time programs available. Postbaccalaureate distance learning degree programs offered. *Faculty:* 18 full-time (10 women), 3 part-time/adjunct (all women). *Students:* 56 full-time (40 women), 89 part-time (72 women); includes 31 minority (4 African Americans, 21 American Indian/Alaska Native, 2 Asian Americans or Pacific Islanders, 4 Hispanic Americans), 1 international. Average age 37. 69 applicants, 67% accepted, 42 enrolled. In 2006, 33 degrees awarded. *Degree requirements:* For master's, thesis or alternative, student teaching, comprehensive exam, registration. *Entrance requirements:* For master's, GRE General Test, PRAXIS I. Additional exam requirements/recommendations for international students: Required—TOEFL (minimum score 550 paper-based; 213 computer-based). *Application deadline:* For fall admission, 3/1 for domestic and international students; for spring admission, 10/1 for domestic students, 9/1 for international students. Application fee: $50. Electronic applications accepted. *Financial support:* In 2006–07, 2 research assistantships with tuition reimbursements (averaging $6,510 per year), 4 teaching assistantships with tuition reimbursements (averaging $10,441 per year) were awarded; fellowships with tuition reimbursements, career-related internships or fieldwork, Federal Work-Study, and scholarships/grants also available. Financial award applicants required to submit FAFSA. *Faculty research:* Native ways of knowing, classroom research in methods of literacy instruction, multiple intelligence theory, geometry concept development, mathematics and science curriculum development. *Unit head:* Dr. Eric C. Madsen, Dean, 907-474-7341, Fax: 907-474-5451, E-mail: fysoed@uaf.edu.

The University of Arizona, Graduate College, College of Humanities, Department of English, Rhetoric, Composition and the Teaching of English Program, Tucson, AZ 85721. Offers MA, PhD. *Degree requirements:* For master's, one foreign language, comprehensive exam, registration; for doctorate, one foreign language, thesis/dissertation, comprehensive exam, registration. *Entrance requirements:* For master's and doctorate, GRE, writing sample, 3 letters of reference. Additional exam requirements/recommendations for international students: Required—TOEFL (minimum score 550 paper-based; 213 computer-based).

University of Arkansas at Pine Bluff, Program in Education, Pine Bluff, AR 71601-2799. Offers elementary education (M Ed); secondary education (M Ed), including English, general science, mathematics, physical education, social studies. Part-time and evening/weekend programs available. *Degree requirements:* For master's, comprehensive exam. *Entrance requirements:* For master's, GRE, minimum GPA of 2.75, NTE or Standard Arkansas Teaching Certificate. *Faculty research:* Teacher certification, accreditation, assessment, standards, portfolio development, rehabilitation, technology.

University of Central Florida, College of Education, Department of Teaching and Learning Principles, Program in English Language Arts Education, Orlando, FL 32816. Offers M Ed, MA. *Accreditation:* NCATE. Part-time and evening/weekend programs available. *Students:* 13 full-time (5 women), 18 part-time (13 women); includes 4 minority (2 African Americans, 2 Hispanic Americans). In 2006, 9 master's awarded. *Degree requirements:* For master's, thesis or alternative, research project. *Entrance requirements:* For master's, GRE General Test. Additional exam requirements/recommendations for international students: Required—TOEFL. *Application deadline:* For fall admission, 7/15 for domestic students; for spring admission, 12/1 for domestic students. Application fee: $30. Electronic applications accepted. *Expenses:* Tuition, state resident: full-time $6,167; part-time $257 per credit hour. Tuition, nonresident: full-time $22,790; part-time $950 per credit hour. *Financial support:* In 2006–07, 3 research assistantships with partial tuition reimbursements (averaging $3,000 per year) were awarded; fellowships with partial tuition reimbursements, teaching assistantships with partial tuition reimbursements, career-related internships or fieldwork, Federal Work-Study, institutionally sponsored loans, tuition waivers (partial), and unspecified assistantships also available. Financial award application deadline: 3/1; financial award applicants required to submit FAFSA. *Unit head:* Dr. Jeffery Kaplan, Coordinator, 407-823-2041, Fax: 407-823-4880, E-mail: jkaplan@mail.ucf.edu.

University of Colorado at Denver and Health Sciences Center, College of Liberal Arts and Sciences, Department of English, Denver, CO 80217-3364. Offers applied linguistics (MA); English studies (MA); literature (MA); teaching English to speakers of other languages (Certificate); teaching of writing (MA). Part-time and evening/weekend programs available. *Faculty:* 31 full-time (20 women). *Students:* 3 full-time (1 woman), 60 part-time (40 women); includes 7 minority (4 Asian Americans or Pacific Islanders, 3 Hispanic Americans), 1 international. Average age 32. 33 applicants, 61% accepted, 14 enrolled. In 2006, 22 degrees awarded. *Degree requirements:* For master's, thesis optional. *Entrance requirements:* For master's, GRE General Test, minimum GPA of 3.0. Additional exam requirements/recommendations for international students: Required—TOEFL (minimum score 550 paper-based). *Application deadline:* For fall admission, 5/25 for domestic students; for spring admission, 10/25 for domestic students. Applications are processed on a rolling basis. Application fee: $50 ($75 for international students). Electronic applications accepted. *Financial support:* Research assistantships, teaching assistantships, Federal Work-Study available. Financial award application deadline: 4/1; financial award applicants required to submit FAFSA. *Unit head:* Prof. Nancy Ciccone, Chair, 303-556-8395, Fax: 303-556-2959, E-mail: nancy.ciccone@cudenver.edu. *Application contact:* Prof. Ian Ying, Program Advisor, 303-556-6728, Fax: 303-556-2959, E-mail: hongguang.ying@cudenver.edu.

University of Connecticut, Graduate School, Neag School of Education, Department of Curriculum and Instruction, Storrs, CT 06269. Offers curriculum and instruction (MA, PhD), including agriculture education, bilingual and bicultural education, elementary education, English education, history and social sciences education, mathematics education, reading education, science education, secondary education, world languages education. *Accreditation:* NCATE. *Faculty:* 28 full-time (12 women). *Students:* 158 full-time (120 women), 54 part-time (44 women); includes 24 minority (3 African Americans, 1 American Indian/Alaska Native, 3 Asian Americans or Pacific Islanders, 17 Hispanic Americans), 2 international. Average age 27. 268 applicants, 76% accepted, 203 enrolled. In 2006, 181 master's, 4 doctorates awarded. Terminal master's awarded for partial completion of doctoral program. *Degree requirements:* For master's, thesis or alternative, comprehensive exam; for doctorate, thesis/dissertation. *Entrance requirements:* For doctorate, GRE General Test. Additional exam requirements/recommendations for international students: Required—TOEFL (minimum score 550 paper-based; 213 computer-based). *Application deadline:* For fall admission, 2/1 priority date for domestic and international students; for spring admission, 11/1 for domestic students, 10/1 for international students. Applications are processed on a rolling basis. Application fee: $55. Electronic applications accepted. *Financial support:* In 2006–07, 14 research assistantships with full tuition reimbursements, 4 teaching assistantships with full tuition reimbursements were awarded; fellowships, Federal Work-Study, scholarships/grants, health care benefits, and unspecified assistantships also available. Financial award application deadline: 2/1; financial award applicants required to submit FAFSA. *Unit head:* Mary Anne Doyle, Head, 860-486-2433, Fax: 860-486-0280. *Application contact:* Lisa Rasicot, Graduate Coordinator, 860-486-3065, Fax: 860-486-0210, E-mail: soeadm02@uconnvm.uconn.edu.

University of Connecticut, Graduate School, Neag School of Education, Department of Curriculum and Instruction, Field of Curriculum and Instruction, Program in English Education, Storrs, CT 06269. Offers MA, PhD. *Accreditation:* NCATE. *Faculty:* 9 full-time (7 women). *Students:* 8 full-time (7 women), 2 part-time (both women); includes 1 minority (African American) Average age 26. 8 applicants, 100% accepted, 8 enrolled. In 2006, 7 degrees awarded. Terminal master's awarded for partial completion of doctoral program. *Degree requirements:* For master's, thesis or alternative, comprehensive exam; for doctorate, thesis/dissertation. *Entrance requirements:* For doctorate, GRE General Test. Additional exam requirements/recommendations for international students: Required—TOEFL (minimum score 550 paper-based; 213 computer-based). *Application deadline:* For fall admission, 2/1 priority date for domestic and international students; for spring admission, 11/1 for domestic students, 10/1 for international students. Applications are processed on a rolling basis. Application fee: $55. Electronic applications accepted. *Financial support:* Research assistantships with full tuition

English Education

University of Connecticut (continued)
reimbursements, teaching assistantships with full tuition reimbursements, Federal Work-Study, scholarships/grants, health care benefits, and unspecified assistantships available. Financial award application deadline: 2/1; financial award applicants required to submit FAFSA. *Application contact:* Lisa Rasicot, Graduate Coordinator, 860-486-3065, Fax: 860-486-0210, E-mail: soeadm02@uconnvm.uconn.edu.

University of Florida, Graduate School, College of Education, School of Teaching and Learning, Gainesville, FL 32611. Offers bilingual/ESOL education (M Ed, MAE, Ed D, PhD, Ed S); curriculum and instruction (M Ed, MAE, Ed D, PhD, Ed S); early childhood education (Ed D, PhD, Ed S); elementary education (M Ed, MAE); English education (M Ed, MAE); mathematics education (M Ed, MAE); reading education (M Ed, MAE); science education (M Ed, MAE); social foundations (M Ed, MAE, Ed D, PhD); social studies education (M Ed, MAE). *Accreditation:* NCATE. *Faculty:* 29 full-time (20 women). *Students:* 506 (406 women); includes 87 minority (20 African Americans, 3 American Indian/Alaska Native, 13 Asian Americans or Pacific Islanders, 51 Hispanic Americans) 34 international. In 2006, 278 master's, 8 doctorates awarded. *Degree requirements:* For master's, thesis optional; for doctorate, variable foreign language requirement, thesis/dissertation. *Entrance requirements:* For master's and doctorate, GRE General Test, minimum GPA of 3.0; for Ed S, GRE General Test. Additional exam requirements/recommendations for international students: Required—TOEFL (minimum score 550 paper-based; 213 computer-based). *Application deadline:* For fall admission, 6/1 for domestic students. Applications are processed on a rolling basis. Application fee: $30. Electronic applications accepted. *Expenses:* Tuition, state resident: full-time $6,827. Tuition, nonresident: full-time $21,951. Required fees: $999. *Financial support:* In 2006–07, 5 research assistantships (averaging $11,947 per year), 22 teaching assistantships (averaging $9,709 per year) were awarded; fellowships, career-related internships or fieldwork and unspecified assistantships also available. *Faculty research:* Teacher education, inclusive education, classroom processes, curriculum and technology. *Unit head:* Dr. Tom Dana, Director, 352-392-9191 Ext. 200, Fax: 352-392-9193, E-mail: tdana@coe.ufl.edu. *Application contact:* Dr. Linda C. Jones, Coordinator, 352-392-0761 Ext. 267, Fax: 352-392-9193, E-mail: lcjones@coe.ufl.edu.

University of Illinois at Chicago, Graduate College, College of Liberal Arts and Sciences, Department of English, Chicago, IL 60607-7128. Offers English (MA, PhD), including creative writing, language, literacy and rhetoric (PhD), literature, teaching of English (MA); language, literacy, and rhetoric (PhD); linguistics (MA), including applied linguistics (teaching English as a second language). Part-time and evening/weekend programs available. *Degree requirements:* For doctorate, variable foreign language requirement, thesis/dissertation, written and oral exams. *Entrance requirements:* For master's, GRE General Test, GRE Subject Test; for doctorate, GRE General Test, GRE Subject Test, minimum GPA of 2.0. Additional exam requirements/recommendations for international students: Required—TOEFL. Electronic applications accepted. *Faculty research:* Literary history and theory.

University of Indianapolis, Graduate Programs, School of Education, Indianapolis, IN 46227-3697. Offers art education (MAT); biology (MAT); chemistry (MAT); curriculum and instruction (MA); earth sciences (MAT); education (MA, MAT); educational leadership (MA); elementary education (MA); English (MAT); French (MAT); math (MAT); physical education (MAT); physics (MAT); secondary education (MA), including art education, education, English education, social studies education; social studies (MAT); Spanish (MAT). *Accreditation:* NCATE. Part-time and evening/weekend programs available. *Faculty:* 4 full-time (2 women), 6 part-time/adjunct (2 women). *Students:* 32 full-time (16 women), 70 part-time (42 women); includes 2 minority (1 African American, 1 Hispanic American). Average age 31. In 2006, 51 degrees awarded. *Entrance requirements:* For master's, GRE Subject Test, minimum GPA of 2.5, 3 letters of recommendation, interview, Praxis I, writing exercise, be within 9 hours of completing content requirements. Additional exam requirements/recommendations for international students: Required—TOEFL (minimum score 550 paper-based; 213 computer-based). *Application deadline:* Applications are processed on a rolling basis. Application fee: $50. *Financial support:* Federal Work-Study available. Financial award application deadline: 5/1; financial award applicants required to submit FAFSA. *Faculty research:* Assessment of teacher education, perceptions of prospective teachers by parents. *Unit head:* Dr. E. Lynne Weisenbach, Dean, 317-788-3446, Fax: 317-788-3300, E-mail: weisenbach@uindy.edu.

The University of Iowa, Graduate College, College of Education, Department of Teaching and Learning, Program in Early Childhood and Elementary Education, Iowa City, IA 52242-1316. Offers curriculum and supervision (MA, PhD); developmental reading (MA); early childhood education and care (MA); elementary education (MA, PhD); language, literature and culture (PhD). *Faculty:* 7 full-time, 4 part-time/adjunct. *Students:* 8 full-time (7 women), 23 part-time (all women); includes 2 minority (both African Americans), 5 international. 6 applicants, 67% accepted, 4 enrolled. In 2006, 11 master's, 1 doctorate awarded. *Degree requirements:* For master's, exam, thesis optional; for doctorate, thesis/dissertation, comprehensive exam, registration. *Entrance requirements:* For master's and doctorate, GRE General Test, minimum GPA of 3.0. Additional exam requirements/recommendations for international students: Required—TOEFL (minimum score 550 paper-based; 213 computer-based; 81 iBT). Application fee: $60 ($85 for international students). Electronic applications accepted. *Financial support:* In 2006–07, 1 fellowship, 2 research assistantships with partial tuition reimbursements, 8 teaching assistantships with partial tuition reimbursements were awarded. Financial award applicants required to submit FAFSA. *Unit head:* Gary Sasso, Chair, 319-335-5324, Fax: 319-335-5608.

The University of Iowa, Graduate College, College of Education, Department of Teaching and Learning, Program in Secondary Education, Iowa City, IA 52242-1316. Offers art education (MA, PhD); curriculum and supervision (PhD); curriculum supervision (MA); developmental reading (MA); English education (MA, MAT, PhD); foreign language education (MA, MAT); foreign language/ESL education (PhD); language, literature and culture (PhD); math education (PhD); mathematics education (MA); music education (MA, PhD); social studies (MA, PhD). *Faculty:* 11 full-time. *Students:* 53 full-time (33 women), 53 part-time (41 women); includes 5 minority (1 African American, 1 American Indian/Alaska Native, 2 Asian Americans or Pacific Islanders, 1 Hispanic American), 19 international. 66 applicants, 47% accepted, 17 enrolled. In 2006, 22 master's, 14 doctorates awarded. *Degree requirements:* For master's, exam, thesis optional; for doctorate, thesis/dissertation, comprehensive exam, registration. *Entrance requirements:* For master's and doctorate, GRE General Test, minimum GPA of 3.0. Additional exam requirements/recommendations for international students: Required—TOEFL (minimum score 550 paper-based; 213 computer-based; 81 iBT). Application fee: $60 ($85 for international students). Electronic applications accepted. *Financial support:* In 2006–07, 1 fellowship, 12 research assistantships with partial tuition reimbursements, 31 teaching assistantships with partial tuition reimbursements were awarded. Financial award applicants required to submit FAFSA. *Unit head:* Gary Sasso, Chair, 319-335-5324, Fax: 319-335-5608.

University of Manitoba, Faculty of Graduate Studies, Faculty of Education, Department of Curriculum, Teaching and Learning, Winnipeg, MB R3T 2N2, Canada. Offers general curriculum (M Ed); language and literacy (M Ed); post-secondary studies (M Ed); teaching English as a second language (M Ed). *Degree requirements:* For master's, thesis or alternative.

University of Michigan, Horace H. Rackham School of Graduate Studies, Joint Program in English and Education, Ann Arbor, MI 48109. Offers PhD. *Degree requirements:* For doctorate, one foreign language. *Entrance requirements:* For doctorate, GRE General Test, master's degree, teaching experience. Additional exam requirements/recommendations for international students: Required—TOEFL (minimum score 620 paper-based; 260 computer-based). Electronic applications accepted. *Faculty research:* Literacy, teacher education, discourse analysis, rhetoric and composition studies.

University of Michigan, Horace H. Rackham School of Graduate Studies, School of Education, Programs in Educational Studies, Ann Arbor, MI 48109. Offers curriculum development (MA); early childhood education (MA, PhD); educational administration and policy (MA, PhD); educational foundation, administration, policy, and research methods (MA); educational foundations and policy (MA, PhD); elementary education (MA-Certification); English education (MA); English language learning in school settings (MA); learning technologies (MA, PhD); literacy, language, and culture (MA, PhD); mathematics education (MA, PhD); research methods (MA); science education (MA, PhD); secondary education (MA-Certification); social studies education (MA); special education (PhD); teaching and teacher education (PhD); MA-Certification; MBA/MA; PhD/MA. Terminal master's awarded for partial completion of doctoral program. *Degree requirements:* For master's, thesis (for some programs); for doctorate, thesis/dissertation, comprehensive exam. *Entrance requirements:* For master's and doctorate, GRE General Test. Additional exam requirements/recommendations for international students: Required—TOEFL (minimum score 600 paper-based; 250 computer-based). *Application deadline:* For fall admission, 12/1 priority date for domestic students, 12/1 for international students. Application fee: $60 ($75 for international students). Electronic applications accepted. *Financial support:* Applicants required to submit FAFSA. *Unit head:* Dr. Addison Stone, Chairperson, 734-763-7500, Fax: 734-615-1290, E-mail: addison@umich.edu. *Application contact:* Roberta Perry, Office of Student Services, 734-764-7563, Fax: 734-763-1495, E-mail: ed.grad.admit@umich.edu.

University of Minnesota, Twin Cities Campus, Graduate School, College of Education and Human Development, Department of Curriculum and Instruction, Program in Teaching, Minneapolis, MN 55455-0213. Offers Chinese (M Ed); earth science (M Ed); elementary special education (M Ed); English (M Ed); English as a second language (M Ed); French (M Ed); German (M Ed); Hebrew (M Ed); Japanese (M Ed); life sciences (M Ed); mathematics (M Ed); middle school science (M Ed); science (M Ed); second languages and cultures (M Ed); social studies (M Ed); Spanish (M Ed). *Students:* 324 full-time (230 women), 132 part-time (86 women); includes 44 minority (5 African Americans, 2 American Indian/Alaska Native, 27 Asian Americans or Pacific Islanders, 10 Hispanic Americans), 4 international. Average age 27. 499 applicants, 74% accepted, 327 enrolled. In 2006, 545 degrees awarded. *Expenses:* Tuition, state resident: full-time $9,302; part-time $775 per credit. Tuition, nonresident: full-time $16,400; part-time $1,367 per credit. Full-time tuition and fees vary according to class time, course load, program, reciprocity agreements and student level. *Application contact:* Dr. Mary Bents, Associate Dean, 612-625-6501, Fax: 612-626-1580, E-mail: mbents@tc.umn.edu.

University of Missouri–Columbia, Graduate School, College of Education, Department of Curriculum and Instruction, Columbia, MO 65211. Offers agricultural education (M Ed, PhD, Ed S); art education (M Ed, PhD, Ed S); business and office education (M Ed, PhD, Ed S); early childhood education (M Ed, PhD, Ed S); elementary education (M Ed, PhD, Ed S); English education (M Ed, PhD, Ed S); foreign language education (M Ed, PhD, Ed S); health education and promotion (M Ed, PhD); learning and instruction (M Ed); marketing education (M Ed, PhD, Ed S); mathematics education (M Ed, PhD, Ed S); music education (M Ed, PhD, Ed S); reading education (M Ed, PhD, Ed S); science education (M Ed, PhD, Ed S); social studies education (M Ed, PhD, Ed S); vocational education (M Ed, PhD, Ed S). Part-time programs available. *Faculty:* 24 full-time (12 women). *Students:* 195 full-time (148 women), 260 part-time (214 women); includes 27 minority (8 African Americans, 1 American Indian/Alaska Native, 10 Asian Americans or Pacific Islanders, 8 Hispanic Americans), 19 international. In 2006, 186 master's, 12 doctorates awarded. Terminal master's awarded for partial completion of doctoral program. *Degree requirements:* For doctorate, thesis/dissertation. *Entrance requirements:* For master's and Ed S, GRE General Test or MAT, minimum GPA of 3.0; for doctorate, GRE General Test, minimum GPA of 3.0. *Application deadline:* Applications are processed on a rolling basis. Application fee: $45 ($60 for international students). *Financial support:* Fellowships, research assistantships, teaching assistantships, institutionally sponsored loans available. *Unit head:* Dr. Lloyd H. Barrow, Director of Graduate Studies, 573-882-8247, E-mail: robinsonr@missouri.edu.

The University of Montana, Graduate School, College of Arts and Sciences, Department of English, Program in Teaching, Missoula, MT 59812-0002. Offers MA. *Accreditation:* NCATE. *Entrance requirements:* For master's, GRE General Test, sample of written work.

University of Nevada, Las Vegas, Graduate College, College of Education, Department of Curriculum and Instruction, Las Vegas, NV 89154-9900. Offers curriculum and instruction (Ed D, PhD, Ed S); elementary education (M Ed, MS); English education (M Ed, MS); library science (M Ed, MS); literacy education (M Ed, MS); mathematics education (M Ed, MS); multicultural education (M Ed, MS); reading specialist (M Ed, MS); secondary education (M Ed, MS); teacher leadership (M Ed, MS); teaching English as a second language (M Ed, MS); technology integration and leadership (M Ed, MS). *Accreditation:* NCATE. Part-time and evening/weekend programs available. *Faculty:* 40 full-time (19 women), 21 part-time/adjunct (14 women). *Students:* 257 full-time (189 women), 387 part-time (296 women); includes 114 minority (28 African Americans, 5 American Indian/Alaska Native, 34 Asian Americans or Pacific Islanders, 47 Hispanic Americans), 7 international. 261 applicants, 70% accepted, 168 enrolled. In 2006, 231 master's, 5 doctorates awarded. *Degree requirements:* For master's, thesis (for some programs), comprehensive exam (for some programs); for doctorate, thesis/dissertation, oral exam. *Entrance requirements:* For master's, minimum GPA of 3.0; for doctorate, GRE General Test, minimum graduate GPA of 3.0. Additional exam requirements/recommendations for international students: Required—TOEFL (minimum score 550 paper-based; 213 computer-based; 80 iBT). *Application deadline:* For fall admission, 2/15 for domestic and international students; for spring admission, 9/30 for domestic and international students. Application fee: $60 ($75 for international students). Electronic applications accepted. *Financial support:* In 2006–07, 30 research assistantships with partial tuition reimbursements (averaging $10,000 per year), 7 teaching assistantships with partial tuition reimbursements (averaging $12,000 per year) were awarded; career-related internships or fieldwork, Federal Work-Study, institutionally sponsored loans, scholarships/grants, health care benefits, and unspecified assistantships also available. Support available to part-time students. Financial award application deadline: 3/1. *Unit head:* Dr. Greg Levitt, Chair, 702-895-3241. *Application contact:* Graduate College Admissions Evaluator, 702-895-3320, E-mail: gradcollege@unlv.edu.

University of New Hampshire, Graduate School, College of Liberal Arts, Department of English, Durham, NH 03824. Offers English (PhD); English education (MST); language and linguistics (MA); literature (MA); writing (MA). Part-time programs available. *Faculty:* 44 full-time. *Students:* 39 full-time (25 women), 63 part-time (42 women); includes 6 minority (1 American Indian/Alaska Native, 2 Asian Americans or Pacific Islanders, 3 Hispanic Americans), 2 international. Average age 34. 175 applicants, 51% accepted, 29 enrolled. In 2006, 44 master's, 3 doctorates awarded. *Degree requirements:* For master's, one foreign language; for doctorate, 2 foreign languages, thesis/dissertation. *Entrance requirements:* For master's, GRE General Test, sample of written work; for doctorate, GRE General Test, GRE Subject Test, sample of written work. Additional exam requirements/recommendations for international students: Required—TOEFL (minimum score 550 paper-based; 213 computer-based). *Application deadline:* For fall admission, 2/15 priority date for domestic students, 2/15 for international students. Applications are processed on a rolling basis. Application fee: $60. Electronic applications accepted. *Expenses:* Tuition, state resident: full-time $8,540; part-time $474 per credit hour. Tuition, nonresident: full-time $20,990; part-time $862 per credit hour. Required fees: $1,343; $356 per term. Tuition and fees vary according to course load, program and reciprocity agreements. *Financial support:* In 2006–07, 4 fellowships, 38 teaching assistantships were awarded; research assistantships, career-related internships or fieldwork, Federal Work-Study, scholarships/grants, and tuition waivers (full and partial) also available. Support available to part-time students. Financial award application deadline: 2/15. *Unit head:* Dr. Janet Aikins, Chairperson, 603-862-3977. *Application contact:* Sue Smith, Administrative Assistant, 603-862-3963, E-mail: engl.grad@unh.edu.

University of New Orleans, Graduate School, College of Liberal Arts, Department of English, New Orleans, LA 70148. Offers English (MA); English teaching (MAET). Part-time and evening/weekend programs available. *Students:* 62 (44 women). Average age 31. In 2006, 24 degrees awarded. *Entrance requirements:* For master's, GRE General Test. Additional exam requirements/recommendations for international students: Required—TOEFL (minimum score

550 paper-based; 213 computer-based). *Application deadline:* For fall admission, 7/1 priority date for domestic students, 6/1 for international students; for spring admission, 11/15 priority date for domestic students, 10/1 for international students. Applications are processed on a rolling basis. Application fee: $40. Electronic applications accepted. *Expenses:* Tuition, state resident: full-time $3,292. Tuition, nonresident: full-time $10,336. Required fees: $158. *Financial support:* Research assistantships, teaching assistantships, career-related internships or fieldwork and tuition waivers (partial) available. Financial award application deadline: 3/15; financial award applicants required to submit FAFSA. *Faculty research:* American, British, and world literature; linguistics. *Unit head:* Dr. Peter Schock, Chairperson, 504-280-6274, Fax: 504-280-7334, E-mail: pschock@uno.edu. *Application contact:* Dr. Barbara Fitzpatrick, Graduate Coordinator, 504-280-6975, Fax: 504-280-7334, E-mail: barbara.fitzpatrick@uno.edu.

The University of North Carolina at Chapel Hill, Graduate School, School of Education, Program in Secondary Education, Chapel Hill, NC 27599. Offers English (Grades 9-12) (MAT); French (Grades K-12) (MAT); German (Grades K-12) (MAT); Japanese (Grades K-12) (MAT); Latin (Grades 9-12) (MAT); mathematics (Grades 9-12) (MAT); music (Grades K-12) (MAT); science (Grades 9-12) (MAT); social studies/social science (Grades 9-12) (MAT); Spanish (Grades K-12) (MAT). *Accreditation:* NCATE. In 2006, 72 degrees awarded. *Degree requirements:* For master's, comprehensive exam. *Entrance requirements:* For master's, GRE General Test, minimum GPA of 3.0 during last 2 years of undergraduate course work. Additional exam requirements/recommendations for international students: Required—TOEFL (minimum score 550 paper-based; 213 computer-based), ACTFL oral proficiency interview. *Application deadline:* For fall admission, 1/1 priority date for domestic and international students. Applications are processed on a rolling basis. Application fee: $60. Electronic applications accepted. *Financial support:* Federal Work-Study available. Support available to part-time students. Financial award application deadline: 3/1; financial award applicants required to submit FAFSA. *Faculty research:* Curriculum and instruction, teacher education per subject. *Unit head:* Dr. James Trier, Coordinator, 919-843-4627. *Application contact:* Janet Carroll, Registrar, 919-962-8690, Fax: 919-962-1533, E-mail: jscarrol@email.unc.edu.

The University of North Carolina at Charlotte, Graduate School, College of Arts and Sciences, Department of English, Program in English Education, Charlotte, NC 28223-0001. Offers MA. Part-time and evening/weekend programs available. *Students:* 1 full-time (0 women), 7 part-time (6 women). Average age 28. 3 applicants, 67% accepted, 2 enrolled. In 2006, 2 degrees awarded. *Degree requirements:* For master's, thesis. *Entrance requirements:* For master's, GRE General Test or MAT, minimum GPA of 2.75. Additional exam requirements/recommendations for international students: Required—TOEFL (minimum score 557 paper-based; 220 computer-based). *Application deadline:* For fall admission, 7/15 for domestic students, 5/1 for international students; for spring admission, 11/15 for domestic students, 10/1 for international students. Application fee: $55. *Expenses:* Tuition, state resident: full-time $2,719; part-time $170 per credit. Tuition, nonresident: full-time $12,926; part-time $808 per credit. Required fees: $1,555. *Financial support:* Fellowships, research assistantships, teaching assistantships, career-related internships or fieldwork, Federal Work-Study, institutionally sponsored loans, scholarships/grants, and unspecified assistantships available. Support available to part-time students. Financial award application deadline: 4/1; financial award applicants required to submit FAFSA. *Unit head:* Dr. Lillian Brannon, Coordinator, 704-687-3220, Fax: 704-687-6988, E-mail: lbrannon@email.uncc.edu. *Application contact:* Kathy B. Giddings, Director of Graduate Admissions, 704-687-3366, Fax: 704-687-3279, E-mail: gradadm@email.uncc.edu.

The University of North Carolina at Greensboro, Graduate School, College of Arts and Sciences, Department of English, Program in English, Greensboro, NC 27412-5001. Offers American literature (PhD); English (M Ed, MA); English literature (PhD); rhetoric and composition (PhD). *Students:* 82 full-time (56 women), 35 part-time (24 women); includes 15 minority (13 African Americans, 1 American Indian/Alaska Native, 1 Asian American or Pacific Islander). *Degree requirements:* For master's, thesis or alternative, comprehensive exam; for doctorate, variable foreign language requirement, thesis/dissertation, preliminary exam. *Entrance requirements:* For master's, GRE General Test, GRE Subject Test, minimum GPA of 3.0; for doctorate, GRE General Test, GRE Subject Test, critical writing sample, minimum GPA of 3.0. Additional exam requirements/recommendations for international students: Required—TOEFL. *Application deadline:* For fall admission, 1/20 priority date for domestic students; for spring admission, 11/1 for domestic students. Application fee: $45. Electronic applications accepted. *Expenses:* Tuition, state resident: full-time $2,692. Tuition, nonresident: full-time $13,742. *Financial support:* Fellowships, research assistantships, teaching assistantships available. *Unit head:* Dr. Christian Moraru, Director of Graduate Studies, 336-334-3564, E-mail: c_moraru@uncg.edu. *Application contact:* Michelle Harkleroad, Director of Graduate Admissions, 336-334-4884, Fax: 336-334-4424, E-mail: mbharkle@uncg.edu.

The University of North Carolina at Pembroke, Graduate Studies, Department of English, Theater and Languages, Program in English Education, Pembroke, NC 28372-1510. Offers MA, MAT. *Accreditation:* NCATE. Part-time and evening/weekend programs available. *Faculty:* 4 full-time (2 women). *Students:* Average age 32. 13 applicants, 100% accepted, 13 enrolled. In 2006, 2 degrees awarded. *Degree requirements:* For master's, thesis optional. *Entrance requirements:* For master's, GRE, MAT, or NTE, minimum GPA of 3.0 in major or 2.5 overall. Additional exam requirements/recommendations for international students: Required—TOEFL. *Application deadline:* For fall admission, 7/15 priority date for domestic and international students; for spring admission, 12/1 priority date for domestic and international students. Applications are processed on a rolling basis. Application fee: $40. *Expenses:* Tuition, state resident: full-time $3,516; part-time $1,091 per semester. Tuition, nonresident: full-time $12,924; part-time $4,619 per semester. Tuition and fees vary according to class time, course load, degree level and campus/location. *Financial support:* In 2006–07, 1 research assistantship with full tuition reimbursement (averaging $6,000 per year) was awarded; unspecified assistantships also available. Support available to part-time students. Financial award application deadline: 4/15; financial award applicants required to submit FAFSA. *Unit head:* Dr. Roger A. Ladd, Director, 910-521-6624, Fax: 910-521-6646, E-mail: roger.ladd@uncp.edu. *Application contact:* Dr. Kathleen C. Hilton, Dean of Graduate Studies, 910-521-6271, Fax: 910-521-6751, E-mail: grad@uncp.edu.

University of Oklahoma, Graduate College, College of Education, Department of Instructional Leadership and Academic Curriculum, Norman, OK 73019-0390. Offers education (Certificate); instructional leadership and academic curriculum (M Ed, PhD), including bilingual education, early childhood education, elementary education, English education, math education, reading education, science education, secondary education, social studies education. *Accreditation:* NCATE. Part-time and evening/weekend programs available. *Faculty:* 20 full-time (11 women), 6 part-time/adjunct (all women). *Students:* 76 full-time (63 women), 115 part-time (89 women); includes 25 minority (8 African Americans, 12 American Indian/Alaska Native, 4 Asian Americans or Pacific Islanders, 1 Hispanic American), 12 international. 72 applicants, 96% accepted, 56 enrolled. In 2006, 11 master's, 10 doctorates awarded. *Degree requirements:* For doctorate, thesis/dissertation. *Entrance requirements:* For master's, 12 hours of course work in education; for doctorate, GRE General Test, master's degree, minimum graduate GPA of 3.0. Additional exam requirements/recommendations for international students: Required—TOEFL (minimum score 550 paper-based; 213 computer-based). *Application deadline:* For fall admission, 6/1 priority date for domestic students, 4/1 for international students; for spring admission, 11/1 for domestic students, 9/1 for international students. Applications are processed on a rolling basis. Application fee: $40 ($90 for international students). *Expenses:* Tuition, state resident: full-time $3,180; part-time $133 per credit hour. Tuition, nonresident: full-time $11,347; part-time $473 per credit hour. Required fees: $1,729; $62 per credit hour. $117 per semester. Tuition and fees vary according to course load and program. *Financial support:* In 2006–07, 76 students received support, including 5 research assistantships with partial tuition reimbursements available (averaging $9,773 per year), 7 teaching assistantships with partial tuition reimbursements available (averaging $10,403 per year); scholarships/grants and unspecified assistantships also available. Financial award applicants required to submit FAFSA. *Faculty research:* Early literacy, learning cycle, social justice, teacher education. Total annual research expenditures: $119,917. *Unit head:* Dr. Priscilla Griffith, Chair and Graduate Liaison, 405-325-1498, Fax: 405-325-4061, E-mail: pgriffith@ou.edu.

University of Phoenix–Omaha Campus, College of Education, Omaha, NE 68154-5240. Offers administration and supervision (MA Ed); curriculum and instruction (MA Ed); curriculum and instruction—English and language arts education (MA Ed); curriculum and instruction—adult education (MA Ed); curriculum and instruction—computer education (MA Ed); curriculum and instruction—English as a second language (MA Ed); curriculum and instruction—mathematics education (MA Ed); elementary teacher education (MA Ed); secondary teacher education (MA Ed); special education (MA Ed).

University of Phoenix Online Campus, The Artemis School, College of Education, Phoenix, AZ 85034-7209. Offers administration and supervision (MAEd); adult education and training (MAEd); curriculum and instruction-adult education (MAEd); curriculum and instruction-English and language arts education (MAEd); curriculum and instruction-mathematics education (MAEd); curriculum education (MAEd); curriculum instruction (MAEd); early childhood (MAEd); English as a second language (MAEd); teacher education elementary (MAEd); teacher education secondary (MAEd). Evening/weekend programs available. Postbaccalaureate distance learning degree programs offered (no on-campus study). *Faculty:* 12 full-time (5 women), 8,196 part-time/adjunct (6,937 women). *Students:* 11,937 full-time (9,375 women); includes 2,972 minority (2,210 African Americans, 74 American Indian/Alaska Native, 205 Asian Americans or Pacific Islanders, 483 Hispanic Americans), 906 international. Average age 36. *Degree requirements:* For master's, thesis (for some programs), registration. *Entrance requirements:* For master's, 3 years of work experience, minimum GPA of 2.5. Additional exam requirements/recommendations for international students: Required—TOEFL (minimum score 550 paper-based; 213 computer-based; 79 iBT). *Application deadline:* Applications are processed on a rolling basis. Application fee: $45. Electronic applications accepted. *Expenses:* Tuition: Full-time $12,664. Required fees: $760. *Financial support:* Institutionally sponsored loans and scholarships/grants available. Financial award applicants required to submit FAFSA. *Unit head:* Dr. Marla LaRue, Dean/Executive Director, 480-557-1218, E-mail: marla.larue@phoenix.edu. *Application contact:* Dr. Marla LaRue, Dean/Executive Director, 480-557-1218, E-mail: marla.larue@phoenix.edu.

University of Phoenix–Springfield Campus, College of Education, Springfield, MO 65804-7211. Offers administration and supervision (MA Ed); curriculum and instruction (MA Ed); curriculum and instruction/adult education (MA Ed); curriculum and instruction/computer education (MA Ed); curriculum and instruction/English as a second language (MA Ed); English and language arts education (MA Ed); mathematics education (MA Ed).

University of Pittsburgh, School of Education, Department of Instruction and Learning, Program in Secondary Education, Pittsburgh, PA 15260. Offers English/communications education (M Ed, MAT, Ed D, PhD); foreign languages education (M Ed, MAT, Ed D, PhD); mathematics education (M Ed, MAT, Ed D); reading education (PhD); science education (M Ed, MAT, MS, Ed D); social studies education (M Ed, MAT, Ed D, PhD). Part-time and evening/weekend programs available. *Students:* 157 full-time (111 women), 84 part-time (61 women); includes 18 minority (7 African Americans, 5 Asian Americans or Pacific Islanders, 6 Hispanic Americans), 13 international. 163 applicants, 74% accepted, 86 enrolled. In 2006, 114 master's, 7 doctorates awarded. *Degree requirements:* For master's and doctorate, thesis/dissertation. *Entrance requirements:* For master's, PRAXIS I; for doctorate, GRE General Test. Additional exam requirements/recommendations for international students: Required—TOEFL. *Application deadline:* For fall admission, 2/1 priority date for domestic students; for spring admission, 11/15 priority date for domestic students. Applications are processed on a rolling basis. Application fee: $50. Electronic applications accepted. *Financial support:* Fellowships, teaching assistantships, career-related internships or fieldwork, Federal Work-Study, tuition waivers (partial), and unspecified assistantships available. Support available to part-time students. Financial award application deadline: 3/15; financial award applicants required to submit FAFSA. *Application contact:* Joan M. Cutone, Director, School of Education Student Service Center, 412-648-2230, Fax: 412-648-1899, E-mail: soeinfo@pitt.edu.

University of Puerto Rico, Mayagüez Campus, Graduate Studies, College of Arts and Sciences, Department of English, Mayagüez, PR 00681-9000. Offers English education (MA). Part-time programs available. *Faculty:* 46 full-time (34 women). *Students:* 30 full-time (20 women), 36 part-time (29 women); includes 62 minority (all Hispanic Americans), 4 international. 21 applicants, 95% accepted, 15 enrolled. In 2006, 4 degrees awarded. *Degree requirements:* For master's, thesis optional. *Entrance requirements:* For master's, course work in linguistics or language, American literature, British literature, and structure/grammar or syntax. *Application deadline:* For fall admission, 2/15 for domestic and international students; for spring admission, 9/15 for domestic and international students. Applications are processed on a rolling basis. Application fee: $25. *Expenses:* Tuition, nonresident: full-time $4,655. Required fees: $210. One-time fee: $77 full-time. Part-time tuition and fees vary according to course load and reciprocity agreements. *Financial support:* In 2006–07, 20 students received support, including fellowships (averaging $12,000 per year), 1 research assistantship (averaging $15,000 per year), 19 teaching assistantships (averaging $8,500 per year); Federal Work-Study and institutionally sponsored loans also available. *Faculty research:* Teaching English as a second language, linguistics, American literature, British literature. *Unit head:* Dr. Betsy Morales, Director, 787-265-3847, Fax: 787-265-3847, E-mail: betsym@uprm.edu. *Application contact:* Prof. Gayle Griggs, Associate Director, 787-832-4040 Ext. 3064, Fax: 787-265-3847.

University of Puerto Rico, Río Piedras, College of Education, Program in Curriculum and Teaching, San Juan, PR 00931-3300. Offers biology education (M Ed); chemistry education (M Ed); curriculum and teaching (Ed D); English education (M Ed); history education (M Ed); mathematics education (M Ed); physics education (M Ed); secondary education (M Ed); Spanish education (M Ed). Part-time programs available. *Students:* 64 full-time (42 women), 123 part-time (91 women); all minorities (all Hispanic Americans) In 2006, 8 master's, 19 doctorates awarded. *Degree requirements:* For master's, thesis; for doctorate, thesis/dissertation, internship. *Entrance requirements:* For master's, PAEG or GRE, minimum GPA of 3.0, letter of recommendation; for doctorate, GRE or PAEG, master's degree, minimum GPA of 3.0, letter of recommendation (2), interview. *Application deadline:* For fall admission, 2/1 for domestic and international students. Application fee: $17. *Expenses:* Tuition, state resident: part-time $100 per credit. Tuition, nonresident: part-time $291 per credit. Required fees: $72 per semester. *Financial support:* Fellowships, research assistantships, teaching assistantships, career-related internships or fieldwork, Federal Work-Study, institutionally sponsored loans, and tuition waivers (partial) available. Financial award application deadline: 5/31. *Faculty research:* Science curriculum, administration management. *Unit head:* Dr. Loyda Martinez, Coordinator, 787-764-0000 Ext. 4361, Fax: 787-763-4130. *Application contact:* Information Contact, 787-764-0000 Ext. 4368, Fax: 787-763-4130.

University of St. Francis, College of Education, Joliet, IL 60435-6169. Offers curriculum and instruction (MS); educational leadership (MS), including reading, special education; elementary education certification (M Ed); secondary education certification (M Ed), including English education, math education, science education, social studies education; special education (M Ed); teaching and learning (MS). Part-time and evening/weekend programs available. *Faculty:* 11 full-time (10 women), 25 part-time/adjunct (12 women). *Students:* 52 full-time (38 women), 381 part-time (293 women); includes 38 minority (21 African Americans, 1 American Indian/Alaska Native, 4 Asian Americans or Pacific Islanders, 12 Hispanic Americans). Average age 33. 194 applicants, 80% accepted, 117 enrolled. In 2006, 165 degrees awarded. *Degree requirements:* For master's, comprehensive exam (for some programs), registration. *Entrance requirements:* For master's, minimum undergraduate GPA of 2.75, 2 letters of recommendation, computer competency. Additional exam requirements/recommendations for international students: Required—TOEFL (minimum score 550 paper-based; 213 computer-based). *Application deadline:* Applications are processed on a rolling basis. Application fee: $30. Electronic applications accepted. *Expenses:* Contact institution. Part-time tuition and fees vary according to campus/location and program. *Financial support:* In 2006–07, 272 students

English Education

University of St. Francis (continued)
received support. Scholarships/grants, tuition waivers (partial), and unspecified assistantships available. Support available to part-time students. Financial award applicants required to submit FAFSA. *Unit head:* Dr. John Gambro, Dean, 815-740-3456, Fax: 815-740-2264, E-mail: jgambro@stfrancis.edu. *Application contact:* Sandra Sloka, Director of Admissions for Graduate and Degree Completion Programs, 800-735-7500, Fax: 815-740-5032, E-mail: ssloka@stfrancis.edu.

University of South Carolina, The Graduate School, College of Arts and Sciences, Department of English, Columbia, SC 29208. Offers creative writing (MFA); English (MA, PhD); English education (MAT); MLIS/MA. MAT offered in cooperation with the College of Education. Part-time programs available. *Degree requirements:* For master's, one foreign language, thesis, comprehensive exam; for doctorate, 2 foreign languages, thesis/dissertation, comprehensive exam. *Entrance requirements:* For master's, GRE General Test (MFA), GRE Subject Test (MA, MAT), sample of written work; for doctorate, GRE General Test, GRE Subject Test, sample of written work. Additional exam requirements/recommendations for international students: Required—TOEFL. Electronic applications accepted. *Faculty research:* Nineteenth-and twentieth-century American and British literature, composition and rhetoric, linguistics, speech.

University of South Carolina, The Graduate School, College of Education, Department of Instruction and Teacher Education, Program in Secondary Education, Columbia, SC 29208. Offers art education (IMA, MAT); business education (IMA, MAT); English (MAT); foreign language (MAT); health education (MAT); mathematics (MAT); science (IMA, MAT); secondary education (M Ed, MA, MT, PhD); social studies (IMA, MAT); theatre and speech (IMA, MAT). IMA and MT offered jointly with the subject areas. *Accreditation:* NCATE. *Degree requirements:* For master's, thesis (for some programs), foreign language (MA), comprehensive exam; for doctorate, one foreign language, thesis/dissertation, comprehensive exam. *Entrance requirements:* For master's, GRE General Test or MAT, teaching certificate (IMA, M Ed), interview; for doctorate, GRE General Test or MAT, interview. *Faculty research:* Middle school programs, professional development, school collaboration.

University of South Florida, Graduate School, College of Education, Department of Secondary Education, Tampa, FL 33620-9951. Offers English education (M Ed, MA, PhD); foreign language education (M Ed, MA); instructional technology (M Ed); mathematics education (M Ed, MA, PhD, Ed S); middle school education (M Ed); science education (M Ed, MA, MAT, PhD); second language acquisition/instructional technology (PhD); secondary education (PhD); social science education (M Ed, MA). *Accreditation:* NCATE. Part-time and evening/weekend programs available. *Faculty:* 29 full-time (16 women), 15 part-time/adjunct (8 women). *Students:* 136 full-time (95 women), 279 part-time (188 women); includes 85 minority (35 African Americans, 1 American Indian/Alaska Native, 13 Asian Americans or Pacific Islanders, 36 Hispanic Americans), 19 international. 212 applicants, 71% accepted, 96 enrolled. In 2006, 87 master's, 12 doctorates awarded. *Entrance requirements:* For master's and doctorate, GRE General Test, minimum GPA of 3.5; for Ed S, GRE General Test. *Application deadline:* For fall admission, 6/1 for domestic students; for spring admission, 10/15 for domestic students. Application fee: $30. Electronic applications accepted. *Financial support:* Scholarships/grants and unspecified assistantships available. Total annual research expenditures: $477,202. *Unit head:* Dr. Jane H. Applegate, Interim Chairperson, 813-974-3533, Fax: 813-974-3837, E-mail: applegat@tempest.coedu.usf.edu.

The University of Tennessee, Graduate School, College of Education, Health and Human Sciences, Program in Education, Knoxville, TN 37996. Offers art education (MS); counseling education (PhD); cultural studies in education (PhD); curriculum (MS, Ed S); curriculum, educational research and evaluation (Ed D, PhD); early childhood education (PhD); early childhood special education (MS); education of deaf and hard of hearing (MS); educational administration and policy studies (Ed D, PhD); educational administration and supervision (Ed S); educational psychology (Ed D, PhD); elementary education (MS, Ed S); elementary teaching (MS); English education (MS, Ed S); exercise science (PhD); foreign language/ESL education (MS, Ed S); instructional technology (MS, Ed D, PhD, Ed S); literacy, language and ESL education (PhD); literacy, language education, and ESL education (Ed D); mathematics education (MS, Ed S); modified and comprehensive special education (MS); reading education (MS, Ed S); school counseling (Ed S); school psychology (PhD, Ed S); science education (MS, Ed S); secondary teaching (MS); social foundations (MS); social science education (MS, Ed S); socio-cultural foundations of sports and education (PhD); special education (Ed S); teacher education (Ed D, PhD). *Accreditation:* NCATE. Part-time and evening/weekend programs available. *Students:* 529 (401 women); includes 39 minority (23 African Americans, 2 American Indian/Alaska Native, 9 Asian Americans or Pacific Islanders, 5 Hispanic Americans) 34 international. 420 applicants, 50% accepted. In 2006, 258 master's, 28 doctorates awarded. *Degree requirements:* For master's and Ed S, thesis optional; for doctorate, variable foreign language requirement, thesis/dissertation. *Entrance requirements:* For master's, minimum GPA of 2.7; for doctorate and Ed S, GRE General Test, minimum GPA of 2.7. Additional exam requirements/recommendations for international students: Required—TOEFL. *Application deadline:* For fall admission, 2/1 priority date for domestic students. Applications are processed on a rolling basis. Application fee: $35. Electronic applications accepted. *Expenses:* Tuition, state resident: full-time $5,574. Tuition, nonresident: full-time $16,840. Required fees: $792. *Financial support:* In 2006–07, 4 fellowships, 9 teaching assistantships were awarded; career-related internships or fieldwork, Federal Work-Study, institutionally sponsored loans, and unspecified assistantships also available. Financial award application deadline: 2/1; financial award applicants required to submit FAFSA. *Unit head:* Dr. Lester Knight, Head, 865-974-0907, Fax: 865-974-8718, E-mail: lknight@utk.edu.

The University of Texas at El Paso, Graduate School, College of Liberal Arts, Department of English, El Paso, TX 79968-0001. Offers English and American literature (MA); professional writing and rhetoric (MA); teaching English (MAT). Part-time and evening/weekend programs available. *Degree requirements:* For master's, thesis optional. *Entrance requirements:* For master's, GRE General Test, minimum GPA of 3.0. Additional exam requirements/recommendations for international students: Required—TOEFL. Electronic applications accepted. *Faculty research:* Literature, creative writing, literary theory.

The University of Texas at Tyler, College of Education and Psychology, Department of Curriculum and Instruction, Tyler, TX 75799-0001. Offers curriculum and instruction (M Ed); secondary teaching (MAT), including art, biology, computer science, English, history, journalism, mathematics, music, political science, sociology, speech, theatre. Part-time programs available. *Faculty:* 10 full-time (6 women), 2 part-time/adjunct (1 woman). *Students:* 3 full-time (2 women), 7 part-time (6 women); includes 1 minority (African American) Average age 32. 1 applicant, 100% accepted, 1 enrolled. In 2006, 6 degrees awarded. *Degree requirements:* For master's, research project (M Ed). *Entrance requirements:* For master's, GRE or MAT. Application fee: $0 ($50 for international students). Electronic applications accepted. *Expenses:* Tuition, state resident: part-time $50 per credit hour. Tuition, nonresident: part-time $328 per credit hour. Required fees: $107 per credit hour. $426 per term. *Financial support:* Scholarships/grants available. *Unit head:* Dr. Robert Stevens, Chair/Professor of Education, 903-566-7315, E-mail: rstevens@uttyler.edu. *Application contact:* Bonnie Purser, Office of Graduate Studies, 903-566-7142, Fax: 903-566-7068, E-mail: bpurser@uttyler.edu.

The University of Toledo, College of Graduate Studies, College of Education, Department of Curriculum and Instruction, Program in Education and English, Toledo, OH 43606-3390. Offers MAE. *Students:* 1 full-time (0 women), 2 part-time (both women). Average age 29. 2 applicants, 50% accepted, 1 enrolled.

University of Victoria, Faculty of Graduate Studies, Faculty of Education, Department of Curriculum and Instruction, Victoria, BC V8W 2Y2, Canada. Offers art (M Ed, MA, PhD); curriculum studies (M Ed, MA, PhD); early childhood (M Ed, MA, PhD); language and literacy (M Ed, MA, PhD); mathematics (M Ed, MA, PhD); music (M Ed, MA); music education (PhD); science (M Ed, MA, PhD); social studies (M Ed, MA); social, cultural and foundational studies (PhD); technology and environmental education (PhD). Part-time programs available. *Degree requirements:* For master's, thesis, project (M Ed); for doctorate, thesis/dissertation, comprehensive exam, registration. *Entrance requirements:* For master's, minimum B average. Additional exam requirements/recommendations for international students: Required—TOEFL (minimum score 575 paper-based; 233 computer-based), IELTS (minimum score 7). Electronic applications accepted. *Faculty research:* Elementary and secondary English, language arts, curriculum theory and practice, educational media and technology, educational administration and leadership, history and philosophy of education.

University of Washington, Graduate School, College of Arts and Sciences, Department of English, Seattle, WA 98195. Offers English (MA, MAT, MFA, PhD); English as a second language (MAT). Part-time programs available. Terminal master's awarded for partial completion of doctoral program. *Degree requirements:* For master's, one foreign language, thesis (for some programs); for doctorate, one foreign language, thesis/dissertation. *Entrance requirements:* For master's, GRE General Test, GRE Subject Test (for English (MA, MAT) only), minimum GPA of 3.0; for doctorate, GRE General Test, GRE Subject Test. Additional exam requirements/recommendations for international students: Required—TOEFL. Electronic applications accepted. *Faculty research:* English and American literature, critical theory, creative writing, language theory.

University of Washington, Graduate School, College of Education, Seattle, WA 98195. Offers curriculum and instruction (M Ed, Ed D, PhD), including educational technology, general curriculum (Ed D, PhD), language, literacy, and culture, mathematics education, multicultural education, reading and language arts education (Ed D), science education, social studies education, teaching and curriculum (M Ed); educational leadership and policy studies (M Ed, Ed D, PhD), including administration, educational organization and policy, higher education, school district leadership (Ed D), social/cultural foundations; educational psychology (M Ed, PhD), including human development and cognition, measurement and research, school counseling (M Ed), school psychology; special education (M Ed, Ed D, PhD), including early childhood education, elementary special education, emotional and behavioral disabilities (M Ed), general special education, severe disabilities; teacher education (MIT). *Accreditation:* APA. Part-time and evening/weekend programs available. *Degree requirements:* For master's, thesis optional; for doctorate, thesis/dissertation. *Entrance requirements:* For master's and doctorate, GRE General Test, minimum GPA of 3.0. Additional exam requirements/recommendations for international students: Required—TOEFL. Electronic applications accepted. *Faculty research:* School restructuring/effective schools, special education interventions, literacy and writing, technology, school partnerships, teacher preparation.

The University of West Alabama, School of Graduate Studies, College of Liberal Arts, Department of English and Language Arts, Livingston, AL 35470. Offers language arts (MAT). *Accreditation:* NCATE. *Faculty:* 6 full-time (1 woman). *Students:* 20 full-time (18 women), 35 part-time (32 women); includes 26 minority (all African Americans) Application fee: $20 ($50 for international students). *Financial support:* Career-related internships or fieldwork, Federal Work-Study, scholarships/grants, and unspecified assistantships available. Support available to part-time students. *Unit head:* Dr. Pat Beatty, Chairperson, 800-621-8044 Ext. 3641.

University of West Georgia, Graduate School, College of Education, Department of Curriculum and Instruction, Program in Secondary Education—English, Carrollton, GA 30118. Offers M Ed, Ed S. *Accreditation:* NCATE. Part-time and evening/weekend programs available. *Students:* 1 (woman) full-time, 9 part-time (7 women); includes 1 minority (African American) Average age 34. In 2006, 2 master's, 4 other advanced degrees awarded. *Degree requirements:* For master's, comprehensive exam; for Ed S, research project. *Entrance requirements:* For master's, GRE General Test or MAT, minimum GPA of 2.7; for Ed S, GRE General Test or MAT, master's degree, minimum graduate GPA of 3.0. *Application deadline:* For fall admission, 8/1 for domestic students. Applications are processed on a rolling basis. Application fee: $20. *Expenses:* Tuition, state resident: full-time $2,286; part-time $127 per credit. Tuition, nonresident: full-time $9,144; part-time $508 per credit. Required fees: $494; $27 per credit. $121 per semester. *Financial support:* In 2006–07, research assistantships with full tuition reimbursements (averaging $3,000 per year); career-related internships or fieldwork, scholarships/grants, and unspecified assistantships also available. Support available to part-time students. Financial award applicants required to submit FAFSA. *Application contact:* Dr. Charles W. Clark, Chair, 678-839-6508, E-mail: cclark@westga.edu.

University of Wisconsin–Eau Claire, College of Education and Human Sciences, Program in Secondary Education, Eau Claire, WI 54702-4004. Offers biology (MAT, MST); education and professional development (MEPD); English (MAT, MST); history (MAT, MST); mathematics (MAT, MST). *Faculty:* 9 full-time (6 women). *Students:* 10 full-time (7 women), 23 part-time (20 women), 1 international. Average age 33. 21 applicants, 57% accepted, 4 enrolled. In 2006, 22 degrees awarded. *Degree requirements:* For master's, thesis optional. *Entrance requirements:* For master's, 2 years of teaching experience or the equivalent. *Application deadline:* For fall admission, 7/1 for domestic students; for spring admission, 12/1 for domestic students. Applications are processed on a rolling basis. Application fee: $45. *Expenses:* Tuition, state resident: full-time $6,533; part-time $363 per credit. Tuition, nonresident: full-time $17,143; part-time $952 per credit. Tuition and fees vary according to program and reciprocity agreements. *Financial support:* In 2006–07, 17 students received support, including 2 teaching assistantships (averaging $5,200 per year); Federal Work-Study also available. Financial award application deadline: 3/1; financial award applicants required to submit FAFSA. *Unit head:* Dr. Tamara Lindsey, Chair, 715-836-4737, Fax: 715-836-4868, E-mail: lindsetp@uwec.edu.

Vanderbilt University, Peabody College, Department of Teaching and Learning, Nashville, TN 37240-1001. Offers curriculum and instructional leadership (M Ed); early childhood education (M Ed); early childhood leadership (Ed D); elementary education (M Ed); English education (M Ed); English language learners (M Ed); mathematics education (M Ed); reading education (M Ed); science education (M Ed); secondary education (M Ed). *Accreditation:* NCATE. *Faculty:* 23 full-time (13 women), 28 part-time/adjunct (19 women). *Students:* 71 full-time (62 women), 21 part-time (15 women); includes 9 minority (8 African Americans, 1 Hispanic American), 2 international. Average age 27. 102 applicants, 60% accepted, 27 enrolled. In 2006, 53 master's, 3 doctorates awarded. *Degree requirements:* For master's, thesis optional. *Entrance requirements:* For master's, GRE General Test, MAT. Additional exam requirements/recommendations for international students: Required—TOEFL (minimum score 550 paper-based; 213 computer-based). *Application deadline:* For fall admission, 12/31 priority date for domestic and international students; for spring admission, 11/1 priority date for domestic and international students. Applications are processed on a rolling basis. Application fee: $0. Electronic applications accepted. *Expenses:* Tuition: Full-time $24,462. Required fees: $2,515. One-time fee: $30 full-time. Full-time tuition and fees vary according to course load, degree level and program. *Financial support:* In 2006–07, 62 students received support, including 36 fellowships with full and partial tuition reimbursements available, 13 research assistantships with full and partial tuition reimbursements available, 13 teaching assistantships with full and partial tuition reimbursements available; Federal Work-Study, institutionally sponsored loans, scholarships/grants, tuition waivers (partial), and unspecified assistantships also available. Support available to part-time students. Financial award application deadline: 2/1; financial award applicants required to submit FAFSA. *Faculty research:* Teaching and learning; development of subject matter knowledge; learning and policy; development students' mathematical and scientific knowledge, development of literacy. *Unit head:* Leona Schauble, Chair, 615-322-8100, Fax: 615-322-8999, E-mail: leona.schauble@vanderbilt.edu. *Application contact:* Angela Saylor, Educational Coordinator, 615-322-8092, Fax: 615-322-8999.

Washington State University, Graduate School, College of Liberal Arts, Department of English, Pullman, WA 99164. Offers composition (MA); English (MA, PhD); teaching of English (MA). *Faculty:* 34. *Students:* 56 full-time (33 women), 2 part-time (1 woman); includes 8 minority (1 African American, 2 American Indian/Alaska Native, 3 Asian Americans or Pacific Islanders, 2 Hispanic Americans), 6 international. Average age 32. 81 applicants, 25% accepted,

18 enrolled. In 2006, 9 master's, 10 doctorates awarded. *Degree requirements:* For master's, one foreign language, thesis (for some programs), oral exam, comprehensive exam (for some programs); for doctorate, 2 foreign languages, thesis/dissertation, oral exam, written exam, comprehensive exam. *Entrance requirements:* For master's and doctorate, GRE General Test, GRE Subject Test, minimum GPA of 3.0, 10 page writing sample, 3 letters of recommendation. Additional exam requirements/recommendations for international students: Required—TOEFL. *Application deadline:* For fall admission, 1/10 priority date for domestic students, 1/10 for international students. Applications are processed on a rolling basis. Application fee: $50. *Expenses:* Tuition, state resident: full-time $7,066. Tuition, nonresident: full-time $17,204. *Financial support:* In 2006–07, 48 students received support, including 1 fellowship (averaging $2,000 per year), 2 research assistantships with full and partial tuition reimbursements available (averaging $13,917 per year), 44 teaching assistantships with full and partial tuition reimbursements available (averaging $13,056 per year); career-related internships or fieldwork, Federal Work-Study, institutionally sponsored loans, scholarships/grants, health care benefits, and tuition waivers (partial) also available. Financial award application deadline: 4/1; financial award applicants required to submit FAFSA. *Faculty research:* Nationalism and gender in the American West, slavery and exploitation in 19th century Britain, photography and the color line, D.H. Lawrence and Mexico, social movement cultures and the arts. Total annual research expenditures: $81,455. *Unit head:* Dr. George E. Kennedy, Chair, 509-335-2581, Fax: 509-335-2582, E-mail: gkennedy@wsu.edu. *Application contact:* Graduate School Admissions, 800-GRADWSU, Fax: 509-335-1949, E-mail: gradsch@wsu.edu.

Wayne State College, School of Education and Counseling, Department of Educational Foundations and Leadership, Program in Curriculum and Instruction, Wayne, NE 68787. Offers alternative education (MSE); business education (MSE); communication arts education (MSE); curriculum and instruction (MSE); early childhood education (MSE); elementary education (MSE); English as a second language (MSE); English education (MSE); family consumer science of education (MSE); industrial technology education (MSE); learning communities (MSE); mathematics education (MSE); music education (MSE); science education (MSE); social science education (MSE). *Accreditation:* NCATE. Part-time and evening/weekend programs available. *Faculty:* 17 part-time/adjunct (11 women). *Students:* 17 full-time (10 women), 307 part-time (248 women); includes 6 minority (2 African Americans, 1 American Indian/Alaska Native, 2 Asian Americans or Pacific Islanders, 1 Hispanic American), 1 international. Average age 35. In 2006, 167 degrees awarded. *Degree requirements:* For master's, thesis optional. *Entrance requirements:* For master's, GRE General Test. Additional exam requirements/recommendations for international students: Required—TOEFL (minimum score 550 paper-based; 213 computer-based). *Application deadline:* Applications are processed on a rolling basis. Application fee: $30. *Expenses:* Tuition, state resident: full-time $3,114; part-time $130 per credit hour. Tuition, nonresident: full-time $6,228; part-time $260 per credit hour. Required fees: $894; $37 per credit hour. Tuition and fees vary according to course load. *Financial support:* Applicants required to submit FAFSA.

Wayne State University, College of Education, Division of Teacher Education, Detroit, MI 48202. Offers adult and continuing education (M Ed); art education (M Ed); bilingual/bicultural education (M Ed, MAT); business education (M Ed, MAT); career and technical education (M Ed, Ed D, PhD, Ed S); curriculum and instruction (Ed D, PhD, Ed S); distributive education (M Ed, MAT); early childhood education (M Ed); elementary education (M Ed, MAT, Ed D, PhD, Ed S); elementary education curriculum and instruction (M Ed); English education (M Ed); English education-secondary (M Ed, Ed S); foreign language education (M Ed); general education (Ed D, Ed S); health occupations education (M Ed); industrial education (M Ed); mathematics education (M Ed, Ed S); pre-school and parent education (M Ed); reading (M Ed, Ed D, Ed S); reading, languages and literature (Ed D); school music-vocal (M Ed); science education (M Ed, MAT, Ed S); secondary education (MAT); secondary school reading (M Ed); social studies education (M Ed, Ed S), including education-secondary (M Ed); special education (M Ed, Ed D, PhD, Ed S); teacher education (MAT, Ed D, PhD). *Faculty:* 41 full-time (22 women), 2 part-time/adjunct (both women). *Students:* 401 full-time (295 women), 1,021 part-time (784 women); includes 527 minority (452 African Americans, 6 American Indian/Alaska Native, 32 Asian Americans or Pacific Islanders, 37 Hispanic Americans), 18 international. Average age 36. 296 applicants, 81% accepted, 132 enrolled. In 2006, 386 master's, 1 doctorate awarded. *Degree requirements:* For doctorate, thesis/dissertation. *Entrance requirements:* For master's, minimum GPA of 2.6; for doctorate, minimum undergraduate GPA of 3.0, graduate 3.5; interview. Additional exam requirements/recommendations for international students: Required—TOEFL (minimum score 550 paper-based; 213 computer-based), TWE (minimum score 6). *Application deadline:* For fall admission, 7/1 for domestic students, 6/1 for international students; for winter admission, 10/1 for international students; for spring admission, 2/1 for international students. Application fee: $30 ($50 for international students). Electronic applications accepted. *Financial support:* In 2006–07, 1 fellowship (averaging $34,919 per year) was awarded; research assistantships. *Faculty research:* Reading and writing literacy and literature. Total annual research expenditures: $209,400. *Unit head:* Dr. Joann Snyder, Academic Director, 313-577-1644, E-mail: joanne.snyder@wayne.edu. *Application contact:* Sharon Elliott, Assistant Dean, 313-577-0902, E-mail: sharon.elliott@wayne.edu.

Western Carolina University, Graduate School, College of Education and Allied Professions, Department of Educational Leadership and Foundations, Programs in Secondary Education, Cullowhee, NC 28723. Offers art education (MAT); biology (MAT); chemistry (MAT); comprehensive education (MA Ed), including art, biology, English, mathematics, music, physical education, reading, social sciences; English (MAT); family and consumer sciences (MAT); mathematics (MAT); physical education (MAT); reading (MAT); social sciences (MAT). *Accreditation:* NCATE (one or more programs are accredited). Part-time and evening/weekend programs available. *Degree requirements:* For master's, comprehensive exam. *Entrance requirements:* For master's, GRE General Test, portfolio. Additional exam requirements/recommendations for international students: Required—TOEFL (minimum score 550 paper-based; 213 computer-based).

Western Connecticut State University, Division of Graduate Studies, School of Professional Studies, Department of Education and Educational Psychology, English Education Concentration, Danbury, CT 06810-6885. Offers MS. Part-time and evening/weekend programs available. *Students:* Average age 35. In 2006, 1 degree awarded. *Degree requirements:* For master's, thesis or comprehensive exam. *Entrance requirements:* For master's, minimum GPA of 2.8, teaching certificate. *Application deadline:* For fall admission, 8/1 priority date for domestic students. Applications are processed on a rolling basis. Application fee: $40. *Financial support:* Fellowships, career-related internships or fieldwork available. Support available to part-time students. Financial award applicants required to submit FAFSA. *Application contact:* Chris Shankle, Associate Director of Graduate Admissions, 203-837-8244, Fax: 203-837-8338, E-mail: shanklec@wcsu.edu.

Western Governors University, Teachers College, Salt Lake City, UT 84107. Offers English language learning (K-12) (MA); learning and technology (M Ed, MA); management and evaluation (M Ed); management and innovation (M Ed); mathematics education (5-12) (MA); mathematics education (5-9) (MA); mathematics education (K-6) (MA); science (5-12) (MA), including biology, geology; science education (509) (MA); technology (M Ed); technology for principals (Post-Graduate Certificate). *Accreditation:* NCATE. Part-time and evening/weekend programs available. Postbaccalaureate distance learning degree programs offered (no on-campus study). *Degree requirements:* For master's, comprehensive exam, registration. *Entrance requirements:* Additional exam requirements/recommendations for international students: Required—TOEFL (minimum score 450 paper-based). Electronic applications accepted. Expenses: Contact institution.

Western Kentucky University, Graduate Studies, Potter College of Arts and Letters, Department of English, Bowling Green, KY 42101. Offers education (MA); English (MA Ed); literature (MA), including American literature, British literature, literary theory, women writers, world literature; teaching English as a second language (MA); writing (MA). Part-time and evening/weekend programs available. *Faculty:* 16 full-time (11 women), 1 part-time/adjunct (0 women). *Students:* 16 full-time (9 women), 20 part-time (16 women); includes 4 minority (3 African Americans, 1 Hispanic American). Average age 29. 13 applicants, 62% accepted, 4 enrolled. In 2006, 17 master's awarded. *Degree requirements:* For master's, final exam, thesis optional. *Entrance requirements:* For master's, GRE General Test, minimum GPA of 2.75. Additional exam requirements/recommendations for international students: Required—TOEFL (minimum score 555 paper-based; 213 computer-based; 79 iBT). *Application deadline:* For fall admission, 7/1 priority date for domestic students, 4/1 for international students; for spring admission, 11/1 for domestic students, 9/1 for international students. Applications are processed on a rolling basis. Application fee: $35. *Expenses:* Tuition, state resident: full-time $6,520; part-time $226 per hour. Tuition, nonresident: full-time $7,140; part-time $357 per hour. International tuition: $15,820 full-time. *Financial support:* In 2006–07, 12 students received support, including 2 research assistantships with partial tuition reimbursements available (averaging $9,400 per year), 9 teaching assistantships with partial tuition reimbursements available (averaging $9,400 per year); Federal Work-Study, institutionally sponsored loans, tuition waivers (partial), and service awards also available. Support available to part-time students. Financial award application deadline: 4/1; financial award applicants required to submit FAFSA. *Faculty research:* Improving writing, linking teacher knowledge and performance, Victorian women writers, Kentucky women writers, Kentucky poets. Total annual research expenditures: $2,800. *Unit head:* Dr. Karen L Schneider, Head, 270-745-3046, Fax: 270-745-2533, E-mail: karen.scheider@wku.edu.

Western Michigan University, Graduate College, College of Arts and Sciences, Department of English, Kalamazoo, MI 49008-5202. Offers creative writing (MFA); English (MA, PhD); English education (MA, PhD); professional writing (MA). *Degree requirements:* For master's, oral exams; for doctorate, one foreign language, thesis/dissertation, oral exam, written exams. *Entrance requirements:* For master's and doctorate, GRE General Test, GRE Subject Test.

Western New England College, School of Arts and Sciences, Program in English for Teachers, Springfield, MA 01119. Offers MAET. Part-time and evening/weekend programs available.

Widener University, School of Human Service Professions, Center for Education, Chester, PA 19013-5792. Offers adult education (M Ed); counseling in higher education (M Ed); counselor education (M Ed); early childhood education (M Ed); educational foundations (M Ed); educational leadership (M Ed); educational psychology (M Ed); elementary education (M Ed); English and language arts (M Ed); health education (M Ed); higher education leadership (Ed D); home and school visitor (M Ed); human sexuality (M Ed); mathematics education (M Ed); middle school education (M Ed); principalship (M Ed); reading and language arts (Ed D); reading education (M Ed); school administration (Ed D); science education (M Ed); social studies education (M Ed); special education (M Ed); technology education (M Ed). Part-time and evening/weekend programs available. Terminal master's awarded for partial completion of doctoral program. *Degree requirements:* For doctorate, thesis/dissertation. *Entrance requirements:* For master's, minimum GPA of 2.5; for doctorate, GRE or MAT, minimum GPA of 2.0 (undergraduate), 3.5 (graduate). Electronic applications accepted. Expenses: Contact institution. *Faculty research:* Reading and cognition, adult education, technology education, educational leadership, special education.

Wilkes University, Graduate Studies and Continued Learning, College of Arts, Humanities and Social Sciences, Program in Teacher Education, Wilkes-Barre, PA 18766-0002. Offers classroom technology (MS Ed); educational computing (MS Ed); educational development and strategies (MS Ed); educational leadership (MS Ed); elementary education (MS Ed); instructional technology (MS Ed); school business leadership (MS Ed); secondary education (MS Ed), including biology, chemistry, English, history; special education (MS Ed). Part-time and evening/weekend programs available. Postbaccalaureate distance learning degree programs offered (minimal on-campus study). *Students:* 32 full-time (21 women), 1,588 part-time (1,106 women); includes 29 minority (6 African Americans, 2 American Indian/Alaska Native, 4 Asian Americans or Pacific Islanders, 17 Hispanic Americans). Average age 33. In 2006, 754 degrees awarded. *Entrance requirements:* Additional exam requirements/recommendations for international students: Required—TOEFL (minimum score 500 paper-based; 173 computer-based). *Application deadline:* Applications are processed on a rolling basis. Application fee: $40. *Expenses:* *Contact institution.* *Financial support:* Federal Work-Study and unspecified assistantships available. Financial award application deadline: 3/1; financial award applicants required to submit FAFSA. *Unit head:* Dr. Michael Speziale, Interim Dean, 570-408-4679, Fax: 570-408-4905, E-mail: michael.speziale@wilkes.edu. *Application contact:* Kathleen Houlihan, Director of Graduate Studies, 570-408-3235, Fax: 570-408-7846, E-mail: kathleen.houlihan@wilkes.edu.

William Carey University, Graduate Studies, School of Education, Hattiesburg, MS 39401-5499. Offers art education (M Ed); art of teaching (M Ed); elementary education (M Ed, Ed S); English education (M Ed); gifted education (M Ed); history and social science (M Ed); mild/moderate disabilities (M Ed); secondary education (M Ed). Part-time programs available. *Faculty:* 19 full-time (12 women), 25 part-time/adjunct (17 women). *Students:* 142 full-time (111 women), 412 part-time (343 women); includes 123 minority (121 African Americans, 1 Asian American or Pacific Islander, 1 Hispanic American). In 2006, 305 master's, 2 other advanced degrees awarded. *Degree requirements:* For master's, comprehensive exam. *Entrance requirements:* For master's, GRE, MAT, minimum GPA of 2.5, Class A teacher's license. Additional exam requirements/recommendations for international students: Required—TOEFL (minimum score 550 paper-based; 213 computer-based). *Application deadline:* For fall admission, 8/7 for domestic and international students; for winter admission, 10/30 for domestic and international students; for spring admission, 2/12 for domestic and international students. Application fee: $25. *Expenses:* Tuition: Full-time $5,040; part-time $240 per credit hour. Tuition and fees vary according to course load. *Financial support:* In 2006–07, 371 students received support. Federal Work-Study and scholarships/grants available. Support available to part-time students. *Unit head:* Dr. Patty Ward, Dean, 601-318-6139, Fax: 601-318-6185, E-mail: patty.ward@wmcarey.edu. *Application contact:* Jason Douglas, Clerical Assistant, Graduate Admissions, 601-318-6774, Fax: 601-318-6765, E-mail: jason.douglas@wmcarey.edu.

Worcester State College, Graduate Studies, Department of Education, Concentration in English, Worcester, MA 01602-2597. Offers M Ed. Part-time programs available. *Students:* 1 (woman) full-time, 4 part-time (2 women). Average age 32. 10 applicants, 80% accepted, 2 enrolled. In 2006, 2 degrees awarded. *Degree requirements:* For master's, thesis optional. *Entrance requirements:* For master's, GRE General Test or MAT, 18 undergraduate credits in English, excluding composition. Additional exam requirements/recommendations for international students: Required—TOEFL (minimum score 550 paper-based; 213 computer-based). *Application deadline:* Applications are processed on a rolling basis. Application fee: $30. *Expenses:* Tuition, state resident: full-time $4,518; part-time $251 per credit hour. Tuition, nonresident: full-time $4,518; part-time $251 per credit hour. *Financial support:* Career-related internships or fieldwork, Federal Work-Study, institutionally sponsored loans, scholarships/grants, and unspecified assistantships available. Support available to part-time students. Financial award application deadline: 3/1; financial award applicants required to submit FAFSA. *Unit head:* Dr. Ruth Haber, Coordinator, 508-929-8706. *Application contact:* Nicole Brown, Assistant Dean of Graduate and Continuing Education, 508-929-8787, Fax: 508-929-8100, E-mail: nbrown@worcester.edu.

Environmental Education

Alaska Pacific University, Graduate Programs, Environmental Science Department, Program in Outdoor and Environmental Education, Anchorage, AK 99508-4672. Offers MSOEE. Part-time programs available. *Faculty:* 1 full-time (0 women). *Students:* 9 full-time (all women), 1 part-time; includes 1 minority (Hispanic American) Average age 30. *Degree requirements:* For master's, thesis. *Entrance requirements:* For master's, MAT or GRE, minimum GPA of 3.0. Additional exam requirements/recommendations for international students: Required—TOEFL (minimum score 550 paper-based; 213 computer-based). *Application deadline:* For fall admission, 4/1 priority date for domestic students, 6/1 priority date for international students; for spring admission, 12/1 priority date for domestic students, 9/1 priority date for international students. Applications are processed on a rolling basis. Application fee: $25. *Expenses:* Tuition: Part-time $550 per credit hour. Required fees: $100 per semester. Tuition and fees vary according to program. *Financial support:* In 2006–07, 3 research assistantships (averaging $1,375 per year) were awarded; career-related internships or fieldwork, Federal Work-Study, scholarships/grants, and unspecified assistantships also available. Support available to part-time students. Financial award application deadline: 4/15; financial award applicants required to submit FAFSA. *Unit head:* Steven Rubinstein, Director, 907-746-2700. *Application contact:* Michael Warner, Director of Admissions, 907-564-8248, Fax: 907-564-8317, E-mail: mikew@alaskapacific.edu.

Antioch University New England, Graduate School, Department of Environmental Studies, Program in Environmental Studies, Keene, NH 03431-3552. Offers conservation biology (MS); environmental advocacy (MS); environmental education (MS); teacher certification in biology (7th-12th grade) (MS); teacher certification in general science (5th-9th grade) (MS). *Faculty:* 13 full-time (4 women), 10 part-time/adjunct (4 women). *Students:* 115 full-time (78 women), 37 part-time (25 women); includes 2 minority (1 American Indian/Alaska Native, 1 Hispanic American). Average age 31. 118 applicants, 86% accepted, 69 enrolled. In 2006, 35 degrees awarded. *Degree requirements:* For master's, practicum. *Entrance requirements:* For master's, previous undergraduate course work in biology, chemistry, mathematics (environmental biology). Additional exam requirements/recommendations for international students: Required—TOEFL (minimum score 550 paper-based; 213 computer-based). *Application deadline:* For fall admission, 8/1 for domestic and international students. Applications are processed on a rolling basis. Application fee: $50. Electronic applications accepted. *Expenses:* Contact institution. Tuition and fees vary according to program and student level. *Financial support:* In 2006–07, 114 students received support, including 2 fellowships (averaging $750 per year), 5 research assistantships (averaging $795 per year), 4 teaching assistantships (averaging $598 per year); Federal Work-Study and scholarships/grants also available. Financial award applicants required to submit FAFSA. *Faculty research:* Sustainability, natural resources inventory. *Unit head:* Dr. Jim Jordan, Associate Chair for Academic Affairs, 603-283-2339, Fax: 603-357-0718, E-mail: james_jordan@antiochne.edu. *Application contact:* Leatrice A. Oram, Co-Director of Admissions, 800-490-3310, Fax: 603-357-0718, E-mail: admissions@antiochne.edu.

Arcadia University, Graduate Studies, Department of Education, Glenside, PA 19038-3295. Offers art education (M Ed, MA Ed); biology education (MA Ed); chemistry education (MA Ed); child development (CAS); computer education (M Ed, CAS); computer education 7–12 (MA Ed); early childhood education (M Ed, CAS), including individualized (M Ed), master teacher (M Ed), research in child development (M Ed); educational leadership (M Ed, CAS); educational psychology (CAS); elementary education (M Ed, CAS); English education (MA Ed); environmental education (MA Ed, CAS); history education (MA Ed); language arts (M Ed, CAS); mathematics education (M Ed, MA Ed, CAS); music education (MA Ed); psychology (MA Ed); pupil personnel services (CAS); reading (M Ed, CAS); school library science (M Ed); science education (M Ed, CAS); secondary education (M Ed, CAS); special education (M Ed, Ed D, CAS); theater arts (MA Ed); written communication (MA Ed). *Accreditation:* NASAD. Part-time and evening/weekend programs available. Postbaccalaureate distance learning degree programs offered (minimal on-campus study). *Faculty:* 12 full-time (8 women), 38 part-time/adjunct (26 women). *Students:* 60 full-time (56 women), 419 part-time (324 women); includes 70 minority (57 African Americans, 1 American Indian/Alaska Native, 6 Asian Americans or Pacific Islanders, 6 Hispanic Americans), 1 international. In 2006, 257 master's, 4 doctorates awarded. *Application deadline:* Applications are processed on a rolling basis. Application fee: $35. Electronic applications accepted. *Financial support:* Career-related internships or fieldwork, tuition waivers (partial), and unspecified assistantships available. *Unit head:* Dr. Steven P. Gulkus, Chair, 215-572-2120. *Application contact:* 215-572-2925, Fax: 215-572-2126, E-mail: grad@arcadia.edu.

Brooklyn College of the City University of New York, Division of Graduate Studies, School of Education, Program in Childhood Education, Brooklyn, NY 11210-2889. Offers bilingual education (MS Ed); liberal arts (MS Ed); mathematics (MS Ed); science/environmental education (MS Ed). Part-time and evening/weekend programs available. *Students:* 10 full-time (9 women), 275 part-time (233 women); includes 130 minority (84 African Americans, 12 Asian Americans or Pacific Islanders, 34 Hispanic Americans), 11 international. 154 applicants, 81% accepted, 80 enrolled. In 2006, 214 degrees awarded. *Entrance requirements:* For master's, LAST, interview, previous course work in education, writing sample, resumé, 2 letters of recommendation. Additional exam requirements/recommendations for international students: Required—TOEFL. *Application deadline:* For fall admission, 3/1 priority date for domestic students, 2/1 priority date for international students; for spring admission, 11/1 priority date for domestic students, 10/1 priority date for international students. Applications are processed on a rolling basis. Application fee: $125. Electronic applications accepted. *Expenses:* Tuition, state resident: full-time $6,400; part-time $270 per credit. Tuition, nonresident: full-time $12,000; part-time $500 per credit. Required fees: $118 per semester. *Financial support:* Career-related internships or fieldwork, Federal Work-Study, institutionally sponsored loans, and scholarships/grants available. Support available to part-time students. Financial award application deadline: 5/1; financial award applicants required to submit FAFSA. *Faculty research:* Emotional intelligence, multiculturalism, arts immersion, the Holocaust. *Unit head:* Dr. Sharon O'Connor-Petruso, Program Head, 718-951-5214. *Application contact:* Karen Alleyne-Pierre, Director of Admissions Services and Enrollment Communications, 718-951-5902, Fax: 718-951-4506, E-mail: grads@brooklyn.cuny.edu.

California State University, Fullerton, Graduate Studies, College of Humanities and Social Sciences, Program in Environmental Studies, Fullerton, CA 92834-9480. Offers environmental education and communication (MS); environmental policy and planning (MS); environmental sciences (MS); technological studies (MS). Part-time programs available. *Students:* 25 full-time (13 women), 49 part-time (28 women); includes 21 minority (2 African Americans, 6 Asian Americans or Pacific Islanders, 13 Hispanic Americans), 9 international. Average age 32. 48 applicants, 71% accepted, 21 enrolled. In 2006, 22 degrees awarded. *Degree requirements:* For master's, thesis. *Entrance requirements:* For master's, minimum GPA of 2.5 in last 60 units of course work. Application fee: $55. *Expenses:* Tuition, nonresident: part-time $339 per unit. Required fees: $1,155 per semester. *Financial support:* Career-related internships or fieldwork, Federal Work-Study, institutionally sponsored loans, and scholarships/grants available. Support available to part-time students. Financial award application deadline: 3/1. *Unit head:* Dr. Robert Voeks, Coordinator, 714-278-4373.

California State University, San Bernardino, Graduate Studies, College of Education, Program in Environmental Education, San Bernardino, CA 92407-2397. Offers MA. *Accreditation:* NCATE. *Students:* 14 full-time (13 women), 15 part-time (14 women); includes 7 minority (1 American Indian/Alaska Native, 1 Asian American or Pacific Islander, 5 Hispanic Americans). Average age 33. 18 applicants, 94% accepted, 10 enrolled. In 2006, 14 degrees awarded. *Application deadline:* For fall admission, 8/31 priority date for domestic students. Application fee: $55. *Unit head:* Dr. Herbert Brunkhorst, Chair, 909-537-5290, Fax: 909-537-7522, E-mail: hkbrunkh@csusb.edu.

Chatham University, Program in Education, Pittsburgh, PA 15232-2826. Offers early childhood education (MAT); elementary education (MAT); English—secondary (MAT); environmental education (K-12) (MAT); secondary art (MAT); secondary biology education (MAT); secondary chemistry education (MAT); secondary English education (MAT); secondary math education (MAT); secondary physics education (MAT); secondary social studies education (MAT); special education (MAT). *Students:* 60 full-time (43 women), 23 part-time (22 women). Average age 29. 48 applicants, 77% accepted, 32 enrolled. In 2006, 59 degrees awarded. *Degree requirements:* For master's, thesis, teaching experience. *Entrance requirements:* For master's, PRAXIS I, minimum GPA of 3.0, sample of written work, recommendation letters. Additional exam requirements/recommendations for international students: Required—TOEFL (minimum score 600 paper-based; 250 computer-based; 100 iBT); Recommended—IELTS (minimum score 7), TWE (minimum score 5). *Application deadline:* For fall admission, 5/1 priority date for domestic and international students; for winter admission, 10/1 priority date for domestic and international students. Applications are processed on a rolling basis. Application fee: $45. Electronic applications accepted. *Financial support:* Career-related internships or fieldwork available. Financial award applicants required to submit FAFSA. *Faculty research:* Gifted education, environmental education, technology in education, writing as learning, class size and achievement. *Unit head:* Dr. Wendy Weiner, Director, 412-365-1146, Fax: 412-365-1505, E-mail: wweiner@chatham.edu. *Application contact:* 412-365-1825, Fax: 412-365-1609, E-mail: admissions@chatham.edu.

Concordia University Wisconsin, Graduate Programs, Department of Education, Mequon, WI 53097-2402. Offers art education (MS Ed); curriculum and instruction (MS Ed); early childhood (MS Ed); educational administration (MS Ed); environmental education (MS Ed); family studies (MS Ed); reading (MS Ed); school counseling (MS Ed); special education (MS Ed). Part-time and evening/weekend programs available. Postbaccalaureate distance learning degree programs offered (minimal on-campus study). *Faculty:* 30. *Students:* 396 (284 women). In 2006, 51 degrees awarded. *Degree requirements:* For master's, thesis or alternative, comprehensive exam. *Entrance requirements:* For master's, minimum GPA of 3.0, teaching license. Additional exam requirements/recommendations for international students: Required—TOEFL. Application fee: $35. *Financial support:* Career-related internships or fieldwork and tuition waivers (partial) available. Financial award application deadline: 8/1. *Faculty research:* Motivation, developmental learning, learning styles. *Unit head:* Dr. James Juergensen, Director, 262-243-4214, E-mail: james.juergensen@cuw.edu. *Application contact:* Graduate Admissions, 262-243-4248, Fax: 262-243-4428.

Florida Institute of Technology, Graduate Programs, College of Science, Department of Science and Mathematics Education, Melbourne, FL 32901-6975. Offers computer education (MS); elementary science education (M Ed); environmental education (MS); mathematics education (MS, Ed D, PhD, Ed S); science and mathematics education (MAT); science education (MS, Ed D, PhD, Ed S). Part-time and evening/weekend programs available. *Faculty:* 4 full-time (1 woman), 2 part-time/adjunct (1 woman). *Students:* 11 full-time (6 women), 21 part-time (14 women); includes 2 minority (1 African American, 1 American Indian/Alaska Native), 7 international. Average age 38. 40 applicants, 58% accepted, 5 enrolled. In 2006, 7 master's, 2 doctorates, 1 other advanced degree awarded. Terminal master's awarded for partial completion of doctoral program. *Degree requirements:* For master's, thesis (for some programs), comprehensive exam (for some programs), registration; for doctorate, thesis/dissertation, oral defense of dissertation, comprehensive exam, registration. *Entrance requirements:* For master's, minimum GPA of 3.0, resumé, 3 letters of recommendation (elementary science education); for doctorate, minimum GPA of 3.2, resumé, 3 letters of recommendation; for Ed S, minimum GPA of 3.0, resumé, 3 letters of recommendation. Additional exam requirements/recommendations for international students: Required—TOEFL (minimum score 550 paper-based; 213 computer-based). *Application deadline:* Applications are processed on a rolling basis. Application fee: $50. Electronic applications accepted. *Expenses:* Tuition: Part-time $900 per credit. *Financial support:* In 2006–07, 1 student received support, including 1 research assistantship with full and partial tuition reimbursement available (averaging $5,346 per year); career-related internships or fieldwork and tuition remissions also available. Support available to part-time students. Financial award application deadline: 3/1; financial award applicants required to submit FAFSA. *Faculty research:* Measurement and evaluation, computers in education, educational technology. Total annual research expenditures: $6,000. *Unit head:* Dr. David E. Cook, Department Head, 321-674-8126, Fax: 321-674-7598, E-mail: dcook@fit.edu. *Application contact:* Carolyn P. Farrior, Director of Graduate Admissions, 321-674-7118, Fax: 321-723-9468, E-mail: cfarrior@fit.edu.

Gannon University, School of Graduate Studies, College of Sciences, Engineering, and Health Sciences, School of Sciences, Program in Natural and Environmental Sciences, Erie, PA 16541-0001. Offers M Ed. Part-time and evening/weekend programs available. In 2006, 1 degree awarded. *Degree requirements:* For master's, thesis, comprehensive exam. *Entrance requirements:* For master's, GRE Subject Test. Additional exam requirements/recommendations for international students: Required—TOEFL (minimum score 500 paper-based; 173 computer-based). *Application deadline:* Applications are processed on a rolling basis. Application fee: $25. *Expenses:* Tuition: Full-time $12,240; part-time $680 per credit. Required fees: $496; $16 per credit. Tuition and fees vary according to course load, degree level, campus/location and program. *Financial support:* Career-related internships or fieldwork available. Support available to part-time students. Financial award application deadline: 7/1; financial award applicants required to submit FAFSA. *Unit head:* Dr. Harry Diz, Chair, 814-871-7633, E-mail: diz001@gannon.edu. *Application contact:* Debra Meszaros, Director of Graduate Recruitment, 814-871-5819, Fax: 814-871-5827, E-mail: cfal@gannon.edu.

Lesley University, Graduate School of Arts and Social Sciences, Cambridge, MA 02138-2790. Offers clinical mental health counseling (MA), including expressive therapies counseling, holistic counseling, school and community counseling; counseling psychology (MA, CAGS), including professional counseling (MA), school counseling (MA); creative arts in learning (CAGS); creative writing (MFA); ecological teaching and learning (MS); environmental education (MS); expressive therapies (MA, PhD, CAGS), including art (MA), dance (MA), expressive therapies, music (MA); independent studies (CAGS); independent study (MA); intercultural relations (MA, CAGS); interdisciplinary studies (MA), including individualized studies, integrative holistic health, women's studies; visual arts (MFA). Part-time and evening/weekend programs available. Postbaccalaureate distance learning degree programs offered (minimal on-campus study). *Faculty:* 49 full-time (41 women), 185 part-time/adjunct (137 women). *Students:* 721 full-time (648 women), 2,074 part-time (1,897 women); includes 182 minority (104 African Americans, 12 American Indian/Alaska Native, 14 Asian Americans or Pacific Islanders, 52 Hispanic Americans), 66 international. Average age 37. 1,005 applicants, 92% accepted, 717 enrolled. In 2006, 1,179 master's, 2 doctorates, 1 other advanced degree awarded. *Degree requirements:* For master's, internship, practicum, thesis (expressive therapies); for doctorate and CAGS, thesis/dissertation, arts apprenticeship, field placement; for CAGS, thesis, internship (counseling psychology, expressive therapies). *Entrance requirements:* For master's, MAT (counseling psychology), interview, writing samples, art portfolio; for doctorate, GRE or MAT; for CAGS, interview, master's degree. Additional exam requirements/recommendations for international students: Required—TOEFL (minimum score 550 paper-based; 213 computer-based; 80 iBT). *Application deadline:* Applications are processed on a rolling basis. Application fee: $50. Electronic applications accepted. *Financial support:* In 2006–07, 64 students received support, including research assistantships (averaging $3,400 per year), 1 teaching assistantship (averaging $7,298 per year); career-related internships or fieldwork, Federal Work-Study, scholarships/grants, and unspecified assistantships also available. Support available to part-time students. Financial award application deadline: 4/15; financial award applicants required to submit FAFSA. *Faculty research:* Psychotherapy and culture; psychotherapy and psychological trauma; women's issues in art, teaching and psychotherapy; community based art, psycho-spiritual inquiry. *Unit head:* Dr. Julia Halevy, Dean, 617-349-

8317, Fax: 617-349-8366, E-mail: jhalevy@lesley.edu. *Application contact:* Christina Murray, Senior Assistant Director, On-Campus Admissions, 617-349-8827, Fax: 617-349-8313, E-mail: cmurray3@lesley.edu.

Maryville University of Saint Louis, School of Education, St. Louis, MO 63141-7299. Offers art education (MA Ed); early childhood education (MA Ed); education (Ed D); elementary education (MA Ed); elementary education/English (MA Ed); environmental education (MA Ed); gifted education (MA Ed); middle grades education (MA Ed); reading specialist (MA Ed); secondary education (MA Ed), including educational leadership, secondary teaching and inquiry. *Accreditation:* NASAD; NCATE. Part-time and evening/weekend programs available. *Students:* 17 full-time (14 women), 168 part-time (129 women); includes 20 African Americans, 2 Asian Americans or Pacific Islanders, 1 Hispanic American, 2 international. Average age 37. 39 applicants, 95% accepted, 24 enrolled. In 2006, 37 degrees awarded. *Degree requirements:* For master's, thesis, project. *Entrance requirements:* For master's and doctorate, minimum GPA of 3.0, 3 professional recommendations. Additional exam requirements/recommendations for international students: Required—TOEFL (minimum score 550 paper-based). *Application deadline:* Applications are processed on a rolling basis. Application fee: $35 ($50 for international students). Electronic applications accepted. *Expenses:* Tuition: Full-time $17,800; part-time $555 per credit. Required fees: $55 per semester. Tuition and fees vary according to degree level and program. *Financial support:* Career-related internships or fieldwork, Federal Work-Study, tuition waivers (partial), and professional educator discounts available. Financial award application deadline: 7/31; financial award applicants required to submit FAFSA. *Faculty research:* Collaboration with public schools, preservice program development, mathematics, diversity, literacy. *Unit head:* Dr. Sam Hausfather, Dean, 314-529-9466, Fax: 314-529-9921, E-mail: shausfather@maryville.edu. *Application contact:* Dr. Lillian Curtis, Graduate Admissions Coordinator, 314-529-9542, Fax: 314-529-9921, E-mail: teachered@maryville.edu.

New York University, Steinhardt School of Culture, Education and Human Development, Department of Humanities and Social Sciences in the Professions, Program in Environmental Conservation Education, New York, NY 10012-1019. Offers MA. *Accreditation:* Teacher Education Accreditation Council. Part-time and evening/weekend programs available. *Faculty:* 1 full-time (0 women). *Students:* 11 full-time (8 women), 5 part-time (3 women); includes 1 minority (Hispanic American), 2 international. 14 applicants, 86% accepted, 7 enrolled. In 2006, 9 degrees awarded. *Degree requirements:* For master's, thesis (for some programs). *Entrance requirements:* Additional exam requirements/recommendations for international students: Required—TOEFL. *Application deadline:* For fall admission, 12/15 priority date for domestic and international students; for spring admission, 11/1 for domestic and international students. Applications are processed on a rolling basis. Application fee: $50. *Expenses:* Tuition: Part-time $1,080 per unit. Required fees: $56 per unit. $329 per term. Tuition and fees vary according to program. *Financial support:* Career-related internships or fieldwork, Federal Work-Study, institutionally sponsored loans, and tuition waivers (partial) available. Support available to part-time students. Financial award application deadline: 2/1; financial award applicants required to submit FAFSA. *Faculty research:* Environmental ethics, values and policy, philosophy and geography. *Unit head:* Dr. Mary Leou, Acting Director, 212-998-5474, Fax: 212-995-4832. *Application contact:* 212-998-5030, Fax: 212-995-4328, E-mail: steinhardt.gradadmissions@nyu.edu.

Prescott College, Graduate Programs, Program in Environmental Studies, Prescott, AZ 86301. Offers agroecology (MA); ecopsychology (MA); environmental education (MA); environmental studies (MA); sustainability (MA). MA in environmental education offered jointly with Teton Science School. Part-time programs available. Postbaccalaureate distance learning degree programs offered (minimal on-campus study). *Faculty:* 1 full-time (0 women), 32 part-time/adjunct (9 women). *Students:* 22 full-time (16 women), 20 part-time (6 women); includes 3 minority (1 African American, 1 American Indian/Alaska Native, 1 Hispanic American). Average age 35. In 2006, 16 degrees awarded. *Degree requirements:* For master's, thesis, fieldwork or internship, practicum. *Entrance requirements:* For master's, 2 letters of recommendation, resumé. *Application deadline:* For fall admission, 5/1 priority date for domestic students; for spring admission, 11/1 priority date for domestic students. Applications are processed on a rolling basis. Application fee: $40. Electronic applications accepted. *Expenses:* Tuition: Full-time $12,408; part-time $517 per credit. One-time fee: $130. *Financial support:* Career-related internships or fieldwork and Federal Work-Study available. Financial award applicants required to submit FAFSA. *Unit head:* Dr. Paul Sneed, Head, 928-350-3204. *Application contact:* Kerstin Alicki, Admissions Counselor, 877-350-2100 Ext. 2102, Fax: 928-776-5242, E-mail: admissions@prescott.edu.

Saint Vincent College, Program in Education, Latrobe, PA 15650-2690. Offers curriculum and instruction (MS); environmental education (MS); library media management (MS); school administration (MS); special education (MS). Part-time and evening/weekend programs available. *Degree requirements:* For master's, comprehensive exam. *Entrance requirements:* For master's, GRE (if undergraduate GPA is below 3.0). Additional exam requirements/recommendations for international students: Required—TOEFL (minimum score 550 paper-based; 213 computer-based). *Faculty research:* Assessment and instructional technology.

Slippery Rock University of Pennsylvania, Graduate Studies (Recruitment), College of Health, Environment, and Science, Department of Parks, Recreation, and Environmental Education, Slippery Rock, PA 16057-1383. Offers environmental education (M Ed); resource management (MS); sustainable systems (MS). Part-time and evening/weekend programs available. *Degree requirements:* For master's, thesis (for some programs), comprehensive exam (for some programs). *Entrance requirements:* For master's, GRE General Test, MAT, minimum GPA of 2.75. Additional exam requirements/recommendations for international students: Required—TOEFL (minimum score 550 paper-based; 213 computer-based). *Application deadline:* For fall admission, 7/1 priority date for domestic and international students; for spring admission, 11/1 priority date for domestic and international students. Applications are processed on a rolling basis. Application fee: $25. Electronic applications accepted. *Expenses:* Tuition, state resident: part-time $336 per credit. Tuition, nonresident: part-time $538 per credit. Required fees: $84 per credit. $37 per semester. *Financial support:* Career-related internships or fieldwork, Federal Work-Study, scholarships/grants, and unspecified assistantships available. Support available to part-time students. Financial award application deadline: 5/1; financial award applicants required to submit FAFSA. *Unit head:* Dr. Daniel Dziubek, Graduate Coordinator, 724-738-2068, Fax: 724-738-2938, E-mail: daniel.dziubek@sru.edu. *Application contact:* April Longwell, Interim Director of Graduate Studies, 724-738-2051 Ext. 2116, Fax: 724-738-2146, E-mail: graduate.studies@sru.edu.

Southern Connecticut State University, School of Graduate Studies, School of Arts and Sciences, Department of Environmental Education/Science Education, New Haven, CT 06515-1355. Offers environmental education (MS); science education (MS, Diploma). *Accreditation:* NCATE. Part-time and evening/weekend programs available. *Faculty:* 2 full-time, 1 part-time/adjunct. *Students:* 6 full-time (3 women), 19 part-time (12 women); includes 1 minority (African American) 31 applicants, 100% accepted, 23 enrolled. *Degree requirements:* For master's, thesis or alternative. *Entrance requirements:* For master's, interview; for Diploma, master's degree. *Application deadline:* For fall admission, 7/15 priority date for domestic students. Applications are processed on a rolling basis. Application fee: $50. Electronic applications accepted. *Financial support:* Application deadline: 4/15; *Unit head:* Dr. Susan Cusato, Coordinator, 203-392-6610, Fax: 203-392-6614, E-mail: hagemans1@southernct.edu.

Southern Oregon University, Graduate Studies, School of Sciences, Ashland, OR 97520. Offers environmental education (MA, MS); mathematics/computer science (MA, MS); science (MA, MS). Part-time programs available. *Degree requirements:* For master's, thesis (for some programs), comprehensive exam (MA). *Entrance requirements:* For master's, GRE General Test, minimum GPA of 3.0. *Faculty research:* Ferroelectric, ecology environmental science, biotechnology, material science.

Universidad Metropolitana, Graduate Programs in Education, Program in Environmental Education, San Juan, PR 00928-1150. Offers MA.

Universidad Metropolitana, School of Environmental Affairs, Program in Environmental Education, San Juan, PR 00928-1150. Offers MA. Part-time programs available. *Degree requirements:* For master's, thesis or alternative. *Entrance requirements:* For master's, EXADEP, interview. Electronic applications accepted.

Université du Québec à Montréal, Graduate Programs, Program in Education, Montréal, QC H3C 3P8, Canada. Offers education (M Ed, MA, PhD); education of the environmental sciences (Diploma). Part-time programs available. *Degree requirements:* For master's, thesis (for some programs); for doctorate, thesis/dissertation. *Entrance requirements:* For master's and Diploma, appropriate bachelor's degree or equivalent, proficiency in French; for doctorate, appropriate master's degree or equivalent, proficiency in French.

University of Minnesota, Twin Cities Campus, Graduate School, College of Education and Human Development, Department of Curriculum and Instruction, Minneapolis, MN 55455-0213. Offers art education (M Ed, MA, PhD); children's literature (M Ed, MA, PhD); curriculum and instruction (MA, PhD); early childhood education (M Ed, PhD); elementary education (M Ed, MA, PhD); English education (MA, PhD); environmental education (M Ed); family education (M Ed, MA, Ed D, PhD); instructional systems and technology (M Ed, MA, PhD); language arts (MA, PhD); language immersion education (Certificate); literacy education (MA); mathematics education (MA, PhD); reading education (MA, PhD); science education (MA, PhD); second languages and cultures education (MA, PhD); social studies education (MA, PhD); teaching (M Ed), including Chinese, earth science, elementary special education, English, English as a second language, French, German, Hebrew, Japanese, life sciences, mathematics, middle school science, science, second languages and cultures, social studies, Spanish; technology enhanced learning (Certificate); writing education (M Ed, MA, PhD). *Faculty:* 30 full-time (18 women). *Students:* 496 full-time (363 women), 338 part-time (235 women); includes 89 minority (26 African Americans, 4 American Indian/Alaska Native, 42 Asian Americans or Pacific Islanders, 17 Hispanic Americans), 33 international. Average age 29. 734 applicants, 66% accepted, 425 enrolled. In 2006, 644 master's, 18 doctorates, 11 other advanced degrees awarded. *Expenses:* Tuition, state resident: full-time $9,302; part-time $775 per credit. Tuition, nonresident: full-time $16,400; part-time $1,367 per credit. Full-time tuition and fees vary according to class time, course load, program, reciprocity agreements and student level. *Financial support:* In 2006–07, 7 fellowships (averaging $24,775 per year), 22 research assistantships with full tuition reimbursements (averaging $24,775 per year), 52 teaching assistantships with full tuition reimbursements (averaging $24,775 per year) were awarded. *Faculty research:* Educational practice for a democratic and just society; curriculum history and development/assessment; teacher preparation/induction/mentoring/development; cultural, linguistic, social, political, technological, and economic factors that influence teaching and learning. Total annual research expenditures: $1.2 million. *Unit head:* Dr. Ruth Thomas, Chair, 612-624-4772, Fax: 612-624-8277, E-mail: thoma006@umn.edu. *Application contact:* Dr. Mary Bents, Associate Dean, 612-625-6501, Fax: 612-626-1580, E-mail: mbents@tc.umn.edu.

University of New Hampshire, Graduate School, Interdisciplinary Programs, Program in Environmental Education, Durham, NH 03824. Offers MA. Program offered in summer only. Part-time programs available. *Faculty:* 32 full-time. *Students:* 6 full-time (4 women), 9 part-time (6 women). Average age 30. In 2006, 14 degrees awarded. *Entrance requirements:* Additional exam requirements/recommendations for international students: Required—TOEFL (minimum score 550 paper-based; 213 computer-based). *Application deadline:* Applications are processed on a rolling basis. Application fee: $60. Electronic applications accepted. *Expenses:* Tuition, state resident: full-time $8,540; part-time $474 per credit hour. Tuition, nonresident: full-time $20,990; part-time $862 per credit hour. Required fees: $1,343; $356 per term. Tuition and fees vary according to course load, program and reciprocity agreements. *Financial support:* Fellowships, research assistantships, teaching assistantships available. Financial award application deadline: 2/15. *Unit head:* Dr. Scott Fletcher, Chairperson, 603-862-3445, E-mail: education.department@unh.edu. *Application contact:* Lisa Canfield, Administrative Assistant, 603-862-2310, E-mail: education.department@unh.edu.

University of Victoria, Faculty of Graduate Studies, Faculty of Education, Department of Curriculum and Instruction, Victoria, BC V8W 2Y2, Canada. Offers art (M Ed, MA, PhD); curriculum studies (M Ed, MA, PhD); early childhood (M Ed, MA, PhD); language and literacy (M Ed, MA, PhD); mathematics (M Ed, MA, PhD); music (M Ed, MA); music education (PhD); science (M Ed, MA, PhD); social studies (M Ed, MA); social, cultural and foundational studies (PhD); technology and environmental education (PhD). Part-time programs available. *Degree requirements:* For master's, thesis, project (M Ed); for doctorate, thesis/dissertation, comprehensive exam, registration. *Entrance requirements:* For master's, minimum B average. Additional exam requirements/recommendations for international students: Required—TOEFL (minimum score 575 paper-based; 233 computer-based), IELTS (minimum score 7). Electronic applications accepted. *Faculty research:* Elementary and secondary English, language arts, curriculum theory and practice, educational media and technology, educational administration and leadership, history and philosophy of education.

Western Washington University, Graduate School, Huxley College of the Environment, Department of Environmental Studies, Program in Natural Science/Science Education, Bellingham, WA 98225-5996. Offers M Ed. Part-time programs available. *Faculty:* 26. *Students:* 17 full-time (11 women), 7 part-time (4 women); includes 2 minority (both Hispanic Americans) 6 applicants, 100% accepted, 5 enrolled. In 2006, 13 degrees awarded. *Degree requirements:* For master's, thesis optional. *Entrance requirements:* For master's, GRE or MAT, minimum GPA of 3.0 in last 60 semester hours. Additional exam requirements/recommendations for international students: Required—TOEFL (minimum score 567 paper-based; 227 computer-based). Application fee: $50. *Expenses:* Tuition, state resident: full-time $6,609; part-time $199 per credit. Tuition, nonresident: full-time $16,845; part-time $540 per credit. *Financial support:* Federal Work-Study, institutionally sponsored loans, scholarships/grants, tuition waivers (partial), and unspecified assistantships available. Support available to part-time students. Financial award application deadline: 2/15; financial award applicants required to submit FAFSA. *Faculty research:* Role of wilderness in national park history; history of the conservation movement and sense of place in environmental education; environmental care and responsibility; conservation psychology and environmental education. *Unit head:* Dr. John Miles, Graduate Program Adviser, 360-650-3896, E-mail: john.miles@wwu.edu.

West Virginia University, Davis College of Agriculture, Forestry and Consumer Sciences, Division of Resource Management and Sustainable Development, Program in Agricultural and Extension Education, Morgantown, WV 26506. Offers agricultural extension education (MS); teaching vocational-agriculture (MS). *Accreditation:* NCATE. Part-time programs available. *Students:* 5 full-time (4 women), 3 part-time (2 women). Average age 29. 6 applicants, 100% accepted, 3 enrolled. In 2006, 4 degrees awarded. *Degree requirements:* For master's, thesis, registration. *Entrance requirements:* For master's, GRE General Test, minimum GPA of 2.75. Additional exam requirements/recommendations for international students: Required—TOEFL. *Application deadline:* For fall admission, 7/1 priority date for domestic students. Applications are processed on a rolling basis. Application fee: $50. *Expenses:* Tuition, state resident: full-time $4,926; part-time $276 per credit hour. Tuition, nonresident: full-time $14,278; part-time $796 per credit hour. Tuition and fees vary according to program. *Financial support:* In 2006–07, 5 students received support, including 1 teaching assistantship with full tuition reimbursement available (averaging $8,100 per year); Federal Work-Study, institutionally sponsored loans, and tuition waivers (partial) also available. Financial award application deadline: 2/1; financial award applicants required to submit FAFSA. *Faculty research:* Program development in vocational agriculture, agricultural extension, supervised experience programs, leadership development. *Unit head:* Dr. Stacy A. Gartin, Chair, 304-293-3431 Ext. 4480, Fax: 304-293-3752, E-mail: stacy.gartin@mail.wvu.edu.

Foreign Languages Education

The American University in Cairo, Graduate Studies and Research, School of Humanities and Social Sciences, Arabic Language Institute, Cairo, Egypt. Offers teaching Arabic as a foreign language (MA). *Entrance requirements:* Additional exam requirements/recommendations for international students: Required—English entrance exam and/or TOEFL.

Andrews University, School of Graduate Studies, College of Arts and Sciences, Department of International Language Studies, Berrien Springs, MI 49104. Offers MAT.

Andrews University, School of Graduate Studies, School of Education, Department of Teaching, Learning, and Curriculum, Berrien Springs, MI 49104. Offers curriculum and instruction (MA, Ed D, PhD, Ed S); elementary education (MAT); reading (MA); secondary education (MAT), including biology, education, English, English as a second language, French, history, physics; special education/learning disabilities (MS); teacher education (MAT). *Entrance requirements:* For master's, GRE Subject Test.

Auburn University, Graduate School, College of Education, Department of Curriculum and Teaching, Auburn University, AL 36849. Offers business education (M Ed, MS, PhD); early childhood education (M Ed, MS, PhD, Ed S); elementary education (M Ed, MS, PhD, Ed S); foreign languages (M Ed, MS); music education (M Ed, MS, PhD, Ed S); postsecondary education (PhD); reading education (PhD, Ed S); secondary education (M Ed, MS, PhD, Ed S), including English language arts, mathematics, science, social studies. *Accreditation:* NASM (one or more programs are accredited); NCATE. Part-time programs available. *Faculty:* 26 full-time (19 women). *Students:* 51 full-time (36 women), 116 part-time (86 women); includes 24 minority (23 African Americans, 1 Asian American or Pacific Islander). Average age 33. 181 applicants, 56% accepted, 68 enrolled. In 2006, 63 master's, 12 doctorates, 14 other advanced degrees awarded. *Degree requirements:* For master's, thesis (for some programs); for doctorate, thesis/dissertation; for Ed S, field project. *Entrance requirements:* For master's, doctorate, and Ed S, GRE General Test. *Application deadline:* For fall admission, 7/7 for domestic students; for spring admission, 11/24 for domestic students. Applications are processed on a rolling basis. Application fee: $25 ($50 for international students). Electronic applications accepted. *Expenses:* Tuition, state resident: full-time $5,000. Tuition, nonresident: full-time $15,000. Required fees: $416. Tuition and fees vary according to program. *Financial support:* Fellowships, teaching assistantships, career-related internships or fieldwork and Federal Work-Study available. Support available to part-time students. Financial award application deadline: 3/15. *Faculty research:* Emerging literacy, reading attitudes, music for at-risk youth, portfolio assessment. *Unit head:* Dr. Andrew M. Weaver, Head, 334-844-4434, E-mail: weaveam@mail.auburn.edu. *Application contact:* Dr. Joe Pittman, Interim Dean of the Graduate School, 334-844-4700.

Bennington College, Graduate Programs, Program in Teaching, Bennington, VT 05201. Offers art education (MAT); early childhood (MAT); elementary education (MAT); English education (MAT); foreign language education (MAT); mathematics education (MAT); music education (MAT); science education (MAT); secondary education (MAT); social science education (MAT). *Faculty:* 4 part-time/adjunct (3 women). *Students:* 11 full-time (7 women), 1 (woman) part-time; includes 2 minority (both Hispanic Americans) Average age 31. 12 applicants, 75% accepted, 3 enrolled. In 2006, 13 degrees awarded. *Degree requirements:* For master's, 1 year teaching practicum, professional portfolio. *Entrance requirements:* For master's, interview. *Application deadline:* For fall admission, 3/1 for domestic students. Application fee: $60. *Expenses: Contact institution.* One-time fee: $75 full-time. Tuition and fees vary according to program. *Financial support:* In 2006–07, 10 students received support, including 4 fellowships (averaging $6,875 per year); scholarships/grants and unspecified assistantships also available. Financial award application deadline: 4/1; financial award applicants required to submit FAFSA. *Unit head:* George Kamberelis, Director of Center for Creative Teaching, 802-440-4863, E-mail: gkamberelis@bennington.edu. *Application contact:* Ken Himmelman, Dean of Admissions, 802-440-4312, Fax: 802-440-4320, E-mail: admissions@bennington.edu.

See Close-Up on page 861.

Bennington College, Graduate Programs, Program in Teaching a Second Language, Bennington, VT 05201. Offers education (MATSL); foreign language education (MATSL); French (MATSL); Spanish (MATSL). Part-time programs available. *Faculty:* 2 full-time (0 women), 5 part-time/adjunct (3 women). *Students:* Average age 40. 8 applicants, 75% accepted, 5 enrolled. In 2006, 5 degrees awarded. *Degree requirements:* For master's, one foreign language. *Entrance requirements:* For master's, oral proficiency interview (OPI). Additional exam requirements/recommendations for international students: Required—TOEFL (minimum score 577 paper-based; 233 computer-based). *Application deadline:* For spring admission, 4/1 priority date for domestic and international students. Applications are processed on a rolling basis. Application fee: $60. *Expenses: Contact institution.* One-time fee: $75 full-time. Tuition and fees vary according to program. *Financial support:* In 2006–07, 1 student received support. Scholarships/grants available. Financial award application deadline: 4/1; financial award applicants required to submit FAFSA. *Faculty research:* Acquisition, evaluation, assessment, conceptual teaching and learning content-driven communication, applied linguistics. *Unit head:* Carol Meyer, Director of Isabelle Kaplan Center for Languages and Cultures, 802-440-4710, Fax: 802-447-4269, E-mail: matsl@bennington.edu. *Application contact:* Nancy Pearlman, Assistant Director, 802-440-4710, Fax: 802-447-4269, E-mail: matsl@benington.edu.

Boston College, Lynch Graduate School of Education, Department of Teacher Education/Special Education and Curriculum and Instruction, Program in Secondary Education, Chestnut Hill, MA 02467-3800. Offers biology (MST); chemistry (MST); English (MAT); French (MAT); geology (MST); history (MAT); Latin and classical humanities (MAT); mathematics (MST); physics (MST); secondary teaching (M Ed), including biology, chemistry, English, French, geology, history, Latin and classical humanities, mathematics, physics, Spanish; Spanish (MAT). *Students:* 70 full-time (46 women), 28 part-time (15 women); includes 8 minority (4 African Americans, 1 American Indian/Alaska Native, 3 Asian Americans or Pacific Islanders), 2 international. 217 applicants, 72% accepted, 64 enrolled. In 2006, 48 degrees awarded. *Degree requirements:* For master's, comprehensive exam. *Entrance requirements:* For master's, GRE General Test or MAT. Additional exam requirements/recommendations for international students: Required—TOEFL. *Application deadline:* For fall admission, 1/1 priority date for domestic students. Application fee: $60. *Financial support:* Fellowships with full and partial tuition reimbursements, research assistantships with full and partial tuition reimbursements, teaching assistantships with full and partial tuition reimbursements, career-related internships or fieldwork, Federal Work-Study, scholarships/grants, traineeships, tuition waivers (full and partial), and unspecified assistantships available. Support available to part-time students. Financial award applicants required to submit FAFSA. *Faculty research:* Curriculum theory and practice, teacher preparation, learning styles, teacher research. *Application contact:* Timothy P. Blackman, Director, Graduate Admission and Financial Aid, 617-552-4214, Fax: 617-552-0398, E-mail: timothy.blackman.1@bc.edu.

Boston University, School of Education, Department of Literacy and Language, Counseling and Development, Program in Modern Foreign Language Education, Boston, MA 02215. Offers Ed M, MAT. *Students:* 5 full-time (4 women), 1 (woman) part-time. Average age 26. 18 applicants, 72% accepted. In 2006, 6 degrees awarded. *Degree requirements:* For master's, thesis or alternative. *Entrance requirements:* For master's, GRE General Test or MAT. Additional exam requirements/recommendations for international students: Required—TOEFL. *Application deadline:* For fall admission, 2/15 priority date for domestic students; for winter admission, 10/1 priority date for domestic students. Applications are processed on a rolling basis. Application fee: $70. Electronic applications accepted. *Expenses:* Tuition: Full-time $33,330; part-time $1,042 per credit. Required fees: $462; $40. *Financial support:* Application deadline: 2/15. *Unit head:* Dr. Julie Coppola, Head, 617-353-3260. *Application contact:* 617-353-4237, Fax: 617-353-8937, E-mail: sedgrad@bu.edu.

Bowling Green State University, Graduate College, College of Arts and Sciences, Department of German, Russian, and East Asian Languages, Bowling Green, OH 43403. Offers German (MA, MAT); MA/MA. Part-time programs available. *Faculty:* 8 full-time (3 women), 1 part-time/adjunct (0 women). *Students:* 16 full-time (11 women); includes 1 minority (African American), 1 international. Average age 25. 16 applicants, 81% accepted, 5 enrolled. In 2006, 11 degrees awarded. *Degree requirements:* For master's, one foreign language, thesis or alternative. *Entrance requirements:* For master's, GRE General Test. Additional exam requirements/recommendations for international students: Required—TOEFL. *Application deadline:* For fall admission, 3/1 priority date for domestic students. Application fee: $30. Electronic applications accepted. *Expenses:* Tuition, state resident: part-time $535 per hour. Tuition, nonresident: part-time $884 per hour. *Financial support:* In 2006–07, 12 teaching assistantships with full tuition reimbursements (averaging $7,145 per year) were awarded; research assistantships with full tuition reimbursements, Federal Work-Study, institutionally sponsored loans, tuition waivers (partial), and unspecified assistantships also available. Financial award applicants required to submit FAFSA. *Unit head:* Dr. Christina Guenther, Graduate Coordinator, 419-372-8028. *Application contact:* Dr. Geoffrey Howes, Graduate Coordinator, 419-372-7139.

Bowling Green State University, Graduate College, College of Arts and Sciences, Department of Romance Languages, Program in French, Bowling Green, OH 43403. Offers French (MA); French education (MAT). Part-time programs available. *Students:* 24 full-time (18 women), 2 part-time; includes 2 minority (1 African American, 1 Hispanic American), 1 international. Average age 27. 21 applicants, 76% accepted, 12 enrolled. In 2006, 6 degrees awarded. *Degree requirements:* For master's, one foreign language, thesis or alternative. *Entrance requirements:* For master's, GRE General Test. Additional exam requirements/recommendations for international students: Required—TOEFL. *Application deadline:* For fall admission, 2/28 priority date for domestic students. Application fee: $30. Electronic applications accepted. *Expenses:* Tuition, state resident: part-time $535 per hour. Tuition, nonresident: part-time $884 per hour. *Financial support:* In 2006–07, 3 research assistantships with full tuition reimbursements (averaging $6,171 per year), 8 teaching assistantships with full tuition reimbursements (averaging $6,171 per year) were awarded; Federal Work-Study and unspecified assistantships also available. Financial award applicants required to submit FAFSA. *Faculty research:* Francophone literature, French cinema, business French, nineteenth and twentieth century literature. *Application contact:* Dr. Deborah Shocket, Graduate Coordinator, 419-372-8632.

Bowling Green State University, Graduate College, College of Arts and Sciences, Department of Romance Languages, Program in Spanish, Bowling Green, OH 43403. Offers Spanish (MA); Spanish education (MAT). Part-time programs available. *Students:* 34 full-time (23 women), 4 part-time (all women); includes 7 minority (4 African Americans, 3 Hispanic Americans), 2 international. Average age 27. 30 applicants, 90% accepted, 21 enrolled. In 2006, 15 degrees awarded. *Degree requirements:* For master's, one foreign language, thesis or alternative. *Entrance requirements:* For master's, GRE General Test. Additional exam requirements/recommendations for international students: Required—TOEFL. *Application deadline:* For fall admission, 2/15 priority date for domestic students. Application fee: $30. Electronic applications accepted. *Expenses:* Tuition, state resident: part-time $535 per hour. Tuition, nonresident: part-time $884 per hour. *Financial support:* In 2006–07, 17 teaching assistantships with full tuition reimbursements (averaging $6,171 per year) were awarded; research assistantships with full tuition reimbursements, Federal Work-Study and unspecified assistantships also available. Financial award applicants required to submit FAFSA. *Faculty research:* U.S. Latino literature and culture, Latin American film and popular culture, applied linguistics, Spanish popular culture. *Application contact:* Dr. Ernesto Delgado, Graduate Coordinator, 419-372-7150.

Brigham Young University, Graduate Studies, College of Humanities, Center for Language Studies, Provo, UT 84602-1001. Offers language acquisition and teaching (MA). *Faculty:* 9 full-time (0 women). *Students:* 11 full-time (7 women), 11 part-time (10 women); includes 7 minority (6 Asian Americans or Pacific Islanders, 1 Hispanic American). Average age 31. 12 applicants, 67% accepted, 6 enrolled. In 2006, 6 degrees awarded. *Degree requirements:* For master's, 2 foreign languages, thesis. *Entrance requirements:* For master's, GRE General Test, interview, strong background in language of specialization, writing sample, minimum GPA of 3.5 (recommended). Additional exam requirements/recommendations for international students: Required—TOEFL (minimum score 575 paper-based; 213 computer-based). *Application deadline:* For fall admission, 2/1 for domestic and international students. Application fee: $50. Electronic applications accepted. *Financial support:* In 2006–07, 17 students received support, including 14 fellowships with partial tuition reimbursements available (averaging $4,000 per year); teaching assistantships with partial tuition reimbursements available, career-related internships or fieldwork, institutionally sponsored loans, scholarships/grants, traineeships, tuition waivers (partial), and unspecified assistantships also available. Support available to part-time students. Financial award application deadline: 2/1. *Faculty research:* Second language vocabulary, applied linguistics, computer-assisted learning and instructing, language comprehension, testing sociolinguists. Total annual research expenditures: $1 million. *Unit head:* Dr. Ray T. Clifford, Director, 801-422-3263, Fax: 801-422-9741, E-mail: rayc@byu.edu. *Application contact:* Agnes Y. Welch, Program Manager, 801-422-1201, Fax: 801-422-9741, E-mail: agnes_welch@byu.edu.

Brigham Young University, Graduate Studies, College of Humanities, Department of Spanish and Portuguese, Provo, UT 84602-1001. Offers Portuguese linguistics (MA); Portuguese literature (MA); Spanish linguistics (MA); Spanish teaching (MA); Spanish/Latin American Literature (MA); Spanish/Peninsular literature (MA). Part-time programs available. *Faculty:* 26 full-time (5 women). *Students:* 23 full-time (15 women), 23 part-time (15 women); includes 13 minority (all Hispanic Americans) Average age 26. 25 applicants, 64% accepted, 13 enrolled. In 2006, 18 degrees awarded. *Degree requirements:* For master's, one foreign language, thesis, 1 semester of teaching, comprehensive exam. *Entrance requirements:* For master's, minimum GPA of 3.5 in Spanish or Portuguese, 3.3 overall. Additional exam requirements/recommendations for international students: Required—TOEFL (minimum score 550 paper-based; 213 computer-based). *Application deadline:* For fall admission, 2/1 for domestic and international students. Application fee: $50. Electronic applications accepted. *Financial support:* In 2006–07, 44 students received support, including research assistantships with partial tuition reimbursements available (averaging $3,800 per year), teaching assistantships with partial tuition reimbursements available (averaging $6,200 per year); institutionally sponsored loans, tuition waivers (partial), and unspecified assistantships also available. Support available to part-time students. Financial award application deadline: 6/15. *Faculty research:* Mexican prose; Latin American theater, literature, phonetics, and phonology; pedagogy; classical Portuguese literature; Peninsular prose and theater. *Unit head:* Dr. Alvin F. Sherman, Chair, 801-422-3107, Fax: 801-422-0628, E-mail: alvin_sherman@byu.edu. *Application contact:* Arwen T. Wyatt, Graduate Secretary, 801-422-2196, Fax: 801-422-0628, E-mail: arwen_wyatt@byu.edu.

Brooklyn College of the City University of New York, Division of Graduate Studies, School of Education, Program in Adolescence Education and Special Subjects, Brooklyn, NY 11210-2889. Offers art teacher (MA); biology teacher (MA); chemistry teacher (MA); English teacher (MA); French teacher (MA); health and nutrition sciences: health teacher (MS Ed); mathematics teacher (MA); music education (CAS); music teacher (MA); physical education teacher (MS Ed); physics teacher (MA); social studies teacher (MA); Spanish teacher (MA). Part-time and evening/weekend programs available. *Students:* 30 full-time (22 women), 450 part-time (257 women); includes 167 minority (101 African Americans, 21 Asian Americans or Pacific Islanders, 45 Hispanic Americans), 21 international. 277 applicants, 84% accepted, 113 enrolled. In 2006, 172 master's, 6 other advanced degrees awarded. *Degree requirements:* For master's, comprehensive exam (for some programs). *Entrance requirements:* For master's, LAST, previous course work in education, resumé, 2 letters of recommendation, essay. Additional exam requirements/recommendations for international students: Required—TOEFL. *Application deadline:* For fall admission, 3/1 priority date for domestic students, 2/1 priority date for international students; for spring admission, 11/1 priority date for domestic students, 10/1 priority date for international students. Applications are processed on a rolling basis. Application fee: $125. Electronic applications accepted. *Expenses:* Tuition, state resident: full-time $6,400; part-time $270 per credit. Tuition, nonresident: full-time $12,000; part-time $500 per credit. Required fees: $118 per semester. *Financial support:* Career-related internships or fieldwork, Federal Work-Study, institutionally sponsored loans, and scholarships/grants available. Support available to part-time students. Financial award application deadline: 5/1; financial award applicants required to submit FAFSA. *Faculty research:* Interdisciplinary education, semiotics, discourse analysis, autobiography, teacher identity. *Unit head:* Prof. Stephen Phillips, Program Facilitator, 718-951-5214, E-mail: phillips@brooklyn.cuny.edu. *Application contact:* Karen Alleyne-Pierre, Director of Admissions Services and Enrollment Communications, 718-951-5902, Fax: 718-951-4506, E-mail: grads@brooklyn.cuny.edu.

California State University, Chico, Graduate School, Program in Teaching International Languages, Chico, CA 95929-0722. Offers MA. *Students:* 17 full-time (13 women), 13 part-time (6 women); includes 9 minority (2 American Indian/Alaska Native, 1 Asian American or Pacific Islander, 6 Hispanic Americans), 3 international. Average age 35. 16 applicants, 100% accepted, 7 enrolled. In 2006, 11 degrees awarded. *Entrance requirements:* Additional exam requirements/recommendations for international students: Required—TOEFL (minimum score 550 paper-based; 213 computer-based). *Application deadline:* For fall admission, 3/1 for domestic and international students; for spring admission, 9/15 for domestic and international students. Applications are processed on a rolling basis. Application fee: $55. Electronic applications accepted. *Unit head:* Hilda I. Hernandez, Graduate Coordinator, 530-898-6258.

California State University, Sacramento, Graduate Studies, College of Arts and Letters, Department of Foreign Languages, Sacramento, CA 95819-6048. Offers MA. Part-time programs available. *Students:* 11 full-time (8 women), 28 part-time (21 women); includes 28 minority (2 Asian Americans or Pacific Islanders, 26 Hispanic Americans). Average age 38. 30 applicants, 87% accepted, 13 enrolled. *Degree requirements:* For master's, one foreign language, thesis or alternative, writing proficiency exam. *Entrance requirements:* For master's, interview, minimum GPA of 2.5 during previous 2 years of course work. Additional exam requirements/recommendations for international students: Required—TOEFL. *Application deadline:* Applications are processed on a rolling basis. Application fee: $55. Electronic applications accepted. *Financial support:* Teaching assistantships, career-related internships or fieldwork and Federal Work-Study available. Support available to part-time students. Financial award application deadline: 3/1. *Unit head:* Dr. Wilfrido Corral, Chair, 916-278-6333, Fax: 916-278-5502.

Central Connecticut State University, School of Graduate Studies, School of Arts and Sciences, Department of Modern Languages, Program in Modern Language, New Britain, CT 06050-4010. Offers French (MA); Italian (Certificate); modern language (MA). Part-time and evening/weekend programs available. *Students:* 2 full-time (both women), 20 part-time (17 women); includes 5 minority (all Hispanic Americans) 14 applicants, 50% accepted, 5 enrolled. In 2006, 14 degrees awarded. *Degree requirements:* For master's, one foreign language, thesis or alternative, comprehensive exam. *Entrance requirements:* For master's, minimum GPA of 2.7, 24 credits of course work in French. Additional exam requirements/recommendations for international students: Required—TOEFL. *Application deadline:* For fall admission, 7/1 for domestic students; for spring admission, 12/1 for domestic students. Applications are processed on a rolling basis. Application fee: $50. Electronic applications accepted. *Expenses:* Tuition, area resident: Full-time $3,970; part-time $380 per credit. Tuition, state resident: full-time $5,955; part-time $380 per credit. Tuition, nonresident: full-time $11,061; part-time $380 per credit. Required fees: $3,189. One-time fee: $62 part-time. Tuition and fees vary according to degree level and program. *Faculty research:* Twentieth century French theater, seventeenth century French literature, French Middle Ages.

Christopher Newport University, Graduate Studies, Department of Teacher Preparation, Newport News, VA 23606-2998. Offers art (PK-12) (MAT); biology (6-12) (MAT); computer science (6-12) (MAT); elementary (PK-6) (MAT); English (6-12) (MAT); French (PK-12) (MAT); history (6-12) (MAT); history and social science (MAT); mathematics (6-12) (MAT); music (PK-12) (MAT), including choral, instrumental; physics (6-12) (MAT); Spanish (PK-12) (MAT); theater (PK-12) (MAT). Part-time and evening/weekend programs available. *Degree requirements:* For master's, thesis or alternative, comprehensive exam. *Entrance requirements:* For master's, PRAXIS I, minimum GPA of 3.0. Electronic applications accepted. *Faculty research:* Early literacy development, instructional innovations, professional teaching standards, multicultural issues, aesthetic education.

Cleveland State University, College of Graduate Studies, College of Education and Human Services, Department of Teacher Education, Cleveland, OH 44115. Offers art education (M Ed); early childhood education (M Ed); foreign language education (M Ed); mathematics and science education (M Ed); middle childhood education (M Ed); special education (M Ed), including mild/moderate disabilities, moderate/intensive disabilities; teaching English to speakers of other languages (M Ed). Part-time and evening/weekend programs available. *Faculty:* 14 full-time (8 women), 5 part-time/adjunct (4 women). *Students:* 120 full-time (96 women), 592 part-time (485 women); includes 145 minority (123 African Americans, 7 Asian Americans or Pacific Islanders, 15 Hispanic Americans), 7 international. Average age 34. 526 applicants, 41% accepted, 144 enrolled. In 2006, 324 degrees awarded. *Degree requirements:* For master's, thesis or alternative, comprehensive exam (for some programs). *Entrance requirements:* For master's, GRE General Test or MAT, minimum GPA of 2.75. Additional exam requirements/recommendations for international students: Required—TOEFL (minimum score 525 paper-based; 197 computer-based), IELTS (minimum score 6). *Application deadline:* For fall admission, 7/15 priority date for domestic students. Applications are processed on a rolling basis. Application fee: $30. *Financial support:* In 2006–07, 12 research assistantships with full tuition reimbursements (averaging $3,480 per year) were awarded; tuition waivers (partial) and unspecified assistantships also available. *Faculty research:* Early literacy, professional development in reading, reading recovery, dual language, induction programs. Total annual research expenditures: $6.2 million. *Unit head:* Dr. Clifford T. Bennett, Chairperson, 216-523-7105, Fax: 216-687-5379, E-mail: c.t.bennett@csuohio.edu.

College of Charleston, Graduate School, School of Education, Program in Languages, Charleston, SC 29424-0001. Offers M Ed. Electronic applications accepted.

The College of New Jersey, Graduate Division, School of Culture and Society, Department of Modern Language, Ewing, NJ 08628. Offers applied Spanish studies (MA). *Students:* 4 applicants, 100% accepted. In 2006, 2 degrees awarded. *Entrance requirements:* For master's, GRE, minimum GPA of 3.0 in field or 2.75 overall. Additional exam requirements/recommendations for international students: Required—TOEFL. *Application deadline:* For fall admission, 4/15 for domestic students; for spring admission, 10/15 for domestic students. Application fee: $60. Electronic applications accepted. *Financial support:* Application deadline: 5/1; *Unit head:* Deborah Compte, Coordinator, 609-771-2392, E-mail: dcompte@tcnj.edu. *Application contact:* Susan L. Hydro, Office of Graduate Studies, Assistant Dean, 609-771-2300, Fax: 609-637-5105, E-mail: graduate@tcnj.edu.

The College of William and Mary, School of Education, Program in Curriculum and Instruction, Williamsburg, VA 23187-8795. Offers elementary education (MA Ed); gifted education (MA Ed); reading education (MA Ed); secondary education (MA Ed), including English education, mathematics education, modern foreign languages education, science education, social studies education; special education (MA Ed), including emotionally disturbed, learning disabled, mental retardation, resource collaborating teaching. *Accreditation:* NCATE. Part-time programs available. *Faculty:* 15 full-time (6 women), 13 part-time/adjunct (10 women). *Students:* 51 full-time (39 women), 51 part-time (45 women); includes 6 minority (all African Americans) Average age 29. 161 applicants, 68% accepted, 61 enrolled. In 2006, 68 degrees awarded. *Degree requirements:* For master's, master's project. *Entrance requirements:* For master's, GRE or MAT, minimum GPA of 2.5. Additional exam requirements/recommendations for international students: Required—TOEFL. *Application deadline:* For fall admission, 2/1 for domestic and international students; for spring admission, 10/1 for domestic and international students. Application fee: $30. *Expenses:* Tuition, state resident: full-time $6,100; part-time $260 per credit. Tuition, nonresident: full-time $18,790; part-time $725 per credit. Required fees: $3,314. Tuition and fees vary according to program. *Financial support:* In 2006–07, 10 research assistantships with full and partial tuition reimbursements (averaging $5,000 per year) were awarded; career-related internships or fieldwork, Federal Work-Study, institutionally sponsored loans, scholarships/grants, and unspecified assistantships also available. Financial award application deadline: 2/1; financial award applicants required to submit FAFSA. *Faculty research:* National Council of Teachers of Mathematics Standards, counseling, self-concept and self-esteem, special education, curriculum development. *Unit head:* Dr. John Moore, Area Coordinator, 757-221-2333, E-mail: jnmoor@wm.edu. *Application contact:* Dorothy Osborne, Director of Admissions, 757-221-2317, E-mail: dsosbo@wm.edu.

The Colorado College, Department of Education, Program in Secondary Education, Colorado Springs, CO 80903-3294. Offers art teaching (MAT); English teaching (MAT); foreign language teaching (MAT); mathematics teaching (MAT); music teaching (MAT); science teaching (MAT); social studies teaching (MAT). *Faculty:* 2 full-time (1 woman), 10 part-time/adjunct (7 women). *Students:* 18 full-time (12 women); includes 2 minority (1 African American, 1 Asian American or Pacific Islander). Average age 27. 30 applicants, 90% accepted, 18 enrolled. In 2006, 16 degrees awarded. *Degree requirements:* For master's, thesis, internship. *Entrance requirements:* For master's, PRAXIS II or PLACE. *Application deadline:* For fall admission, 2/1 for domestic and international students. Application fee: $50. *Expenses:* Tuition: Full-time $23,567. One-time fee: $1,485 full-time. *Financial support:* In 2006–07, 15 teaching assistantships (averaging $16,000 per year) were awarded; career-related internships or fieldwork, institutionally sponsored loans, health care benefits, and tuition waivers (partial) also available. Financial award application deadline: 2/15; financial award applicants required to submit FAFSA. *Unit head:* Mike Taber, Director, 719-389-6026, Fax: 719-389-6473, E-mail: pveronesi@coloradocollege.edu. *Application contact:* Marsha E. Unruh, Director of Education Career Services, 719-389-6472, Fax: 719-389-6473, E-mail: munruh@coloradocollege.edu.

Colorado State University, Graduate School, College of Liberal Arts, Department of Foreign Languages and Literatures, Fort Collins, CO 80523-0015. Offers MA. TESL degrees are offered jointly with the Department of English. Part-time programs available. *Faculty:* 15 full-time (6 women), 1 (woman) part-time/adjunct. *Students:* 15 full-time (3 women), 9 part-time (4 women); includes 3 minority (all Hispanic Americans), 2 international. Average age 29. 21 applicants, 81% accepted, 9 enrolled. In 2006, 6 degrees awarded. *Degree requirements:* For master's, one foreign language, thesis (for some programs), thesis or paper, competitive exams, comprehensive exam, registration. *Entrance requirements:* For master's, minimum GPA of 3.0; undergraduate major/proficiency in foreign languages. Additional exam requirements/recommendations for international students: Required—TOEFL (minimum score 550 paper-based). *Application deadline:* For fall admission, 4/1 priority date for domestic students; for spring admission, 11/1 priority date for domestic students. Applications are processed on a rolling basis. Application fee: $50. Electronic applications accepted. *Expenses:* Tuition, state resident: full-time $4,248; part-time $236 per credit. Tuition, nonresident: full-time $15,642; part-time $869 per credit. Required fees: $66 per credit. Tuition and fees vary according to program. *Financial support:* In 2006–07, 15 students received support, including 12 teaching assistantships with full tuition reimbursements available; fellowships, career-related internships or fieldwork and scholarships/grants also available. Financial award application deadline: 2/1. *Faculty research:* French, German, and Hispanic literatures and cultures; video-assisted language learning; computer-assisted language learners; foreign language teaching methodologies; linguistics. Total annual research expenditures: $11,000. *Unit head:* Dr. Paola Malpezzi-Price, Chair, 970-491-6141, Fax: 970-491-2822, E-mail: paola.malpezzi_price@colostate.edu. *Application contact:* Dr. Maria del Mar Lopez-Cabrales, Graduate Coordinator, 970-491-5957, Fax: 970-491-2822, E-mail: maria.lopez-cabrales@colostate.edu.

Connecticut College, Graduate School, Department of French, New London, CT 06320-4196. Offers MA, MAT. Part-time programs available. *Degree requirements:* For master's, one foreign language, thesis or alternative.

Connecticut College, Graduate School, Department of German, New London, CT 06320-4196. Offers MAT. Part-time programs available. *Entrance requirements:* For master's, MAT.

Connecticut College, Graduate School, Department of Russian Studies, New London, CT 06320-4196. Offers MAT. Part-time programs available. *Entrance requirements:* For master's, MAT.

Cornell University, Graduate School, Graduate Fields of Arts and Sciences, Field of Linguistics, Ithaca, NY 14853-0001. Offers applied linguistics (MA, PhD); East Asian linguistics (MA, PhD); English linguistics (MA, PhD); general linguistics (MA, PhD); Germanic linguistics (MA, PhD); Indo-European linguistics (MA, PhD); phonetics (MA, PhD); phonological theory (MA, PhD); Romance linguistics (MA, PhD); second language acquisition (MA, PhD); semantics (MA, PhD); Slavic linguistics (MA, PhD); sociolinguistics (MA, PhD); South Asian linguistics (MA, PhD); Southeast Asian linguistics (MA, PhD); syntactic theory (MA, PhD). *Faculty:* 19 full-time (10 women). *Students:* 28 full-time (13 women); includes 2 minority (1 Asian American or Pacific Islander, 1 Hispanic American), 17 international. Average age 30. 87 applicants, 17% accepted, 6 enrolled. In 2006, 4 master's, 2 doctorates awarded. Terminal master's awarded for partial completion of doctoral program. *Degree requirements:* For master's, one foreign language, thesis/dissertation; for doctorate, one foreign language, thesis/dissertation, comprehensive exam. *Entrance requirements:* For master's and doctorate, GRE General Test, 2 letters of recommendation. Additional exam requirements/recommendations for international students: Required—TOEFL (minimum score 600 paper-based; 250 computer-based). *Application deadline:* For fall admission, 1/15 for domestic students. Application fee: $60. Electronic applications accepted. *Expenses:* Tuition: Full-time $32,800. Full-time tuition and fees vary according to program. *Financial support:* In 2006–07, 25 students received support, including 11 fellowships with full tuition reimbursements available, 14 teaching assistantships with full tuition reimbursements available; research assistantships with full tuition reimbursements available, institutionally sponsored loans, scholarships/grants, health care benefits, tuition waivers (full and partial), and unspecified assistantships also available. Financial award applicants required to submit FAFSA. *Faculty research:* Phonology and phonetics; syntax and semantics; historical linguistics; philosophy of language; language acquisition. *Unit head:* Director of Graduate Studies, 607-255-1105. *Application contact:* Graduate Field Assistant, 607-255-1105, E-mail: lingfield@cornell.edu.

Eastern Washington University, Graduate Studies, College of Arts and Letters, Department of Modern Languages and Literatures, Cheney, WA 99004-2431. Offers French education (M Ed). *Accreditation:* NCATE. *Degree requirements:* For master's, comprehensive exam. *Entrance requirements:* For master's, minimum GPA of 3.0.

Elms College, Division of Education, Chicopee, MA 01013-2839. Offers early childhood education (MAT); education (M Ed, CAGS); elementary education (MAT); English as a second language (MAT); reading (MAT); secondary education (MAT), including biology education, English education, Spanish education; special education (MAT). Part-time and evening/weekend programs available. *Faculty:* 9 full-time (6 women), 4 part-time/adjunct (2 women). *Students:* 8 full-time (6 women), 97 part-time (89 women); includes 4 minority (2 Asian Americans or Pacific Islanders, 2 Hispanic Americans). Average age 36. 48 applicants, 90% accepted, 40 enrolled. In 2006, 37 master's, 8 other advanced degrees awarded. *Degree requirements:* For master's, thesis (for some programs). *Entrance requirements:* For master's, Massachusetts Educators Certification Test, minimum GPA of 3.0; for CAGS, master's degree in education. Additional exam requirements/recommendations for international students: Required—TOEFL. *Application deadline:* For fall admission, 7/1 priority date for domestic students; for spring admission, 11/1 priority date for domestic students. Applications are processed on a rolling basis. Application fee: $30. *Expenses:* Tuition: Full-time $9,180; part-time $510 per credit. Tuition and fees vary according to course load. *Financial support:* In

Foreign Languages Education

Elms College (continued)
2006–07, 3 teaching assistantships with partial tuition reimbursements were awarded; tuition waivers (partial) also available. Support available to part-time students. Financial award application deadline: 4/15; financial award applicants required to submit FAFSA. *Unit head:* Dr. Mary Janeczek, Director, 413-594-2761, Fax: 413-592-4871, E-mail: janeczeke@elms.edu.

Fairfield University, Graduate School of Education and Allied Professions, Department of TESOL, Foreign Language and Bilingual/Multicultural Education, Fairfield, CT 06824-5195. Offers MA, CAS. Part-time and evening/weekend programs available. *Faculty:* 1 (woman) full-time, 2 part-time/adjunct (both women). *Students:* 9 full-time (7 women), 39 part-time (31 women). Average age 34. 14 applicants, 57% accepted, 7 enrolled. In 2006, 11 master's, 5 other advanced degrees awarded. *Degree requirements:* For master's, educational technology course, thesis optional. *Entrance requirements:* For master's, PRAXIS I (PPST), minimum QPA of 2.67, 2 recommendations, resumè. Additional exam requirements/recommendations for international students: Required—TOEFL (minimum score 550 paper-based; 213 computer-based; 79 iBT). *Application deadline:* Applications are processed on a rolling basis. Application fee: $55. Electronic applications accepted. *Financial support:* Scholarships/grants, tuition waivers (partial), and unspecified assistantships available. Financial award applicants required to submit FAFSA. *Faculty research:* Teacher education. *Unit head:* Sr. Julianna Poole, SSND, Chair, 203-254-4000 Ext. 2873, Fax: 203-254-4047, E-mail: jpoole@mail.fairfield.edu. *Application contact:* Marianne Gumpper, Director of Graduate and Continuing Studies Admissions, 203-254-4184, Fax: 203-254-4073, E-mail: gradadmis@mail.fairfield.edu.

Florida Atlantic University, Dorothy F. Schmidt College of Arts and Letters, Department of Languages and Linguistics, Boca Raton, FL 33431-0991. Offers comparative literature (MA); French (MA); German (MA); Spanish (MA); teaching French (MAT); teaching German (MAT); teaching Spanish (MAT). Part-time programs available. *Faculty:* 14 full-time (9 women). *Students:* 28 full-time (23 women), 12 part-time (9 women); includes 16 minority (2 African Americans, 2 Asian Americans or Pacific Islanders, 12 Hispanic Americans), 7 international. Average age 35. 26 applicants, 65% accepted, 13 enrolled. In 2006, 19 degrees awarded. *Degree requirements:* For master's, one foreign language, comprehensive exam, registration. *Entrance requirements:* For master's, GRE General Test, minimum GPA of 3.0. *Application deadline:* For fall admission, 6/1 priority date for domestic students; for spring admission, 11/1 for domestic students. Applications are processed on a rolling basis. Application fee: $30. *Expenses:* Tuition, area resident: Full-time $4,394. Tuition, nonresident: full-time $16,441. *Financial support:* In 2006–07, 15 teaching assistantships with partial tuition reimbursements (averaging $7,200 per year) were awarded; fellowships, research assistantships, Federal Work-Study and tuition waivers (partial) also available. Support available to part-time students. Financial award application deadline: 4/1. *Faculty research:* Modern European studies, modern Latin America, medieval Europe. *Unit head:* Dr. Myriam J. Ruthenberg, Chair, 561-297-3860, Fax: 561-297-2756.

Florida International University, College of Education, Department of Curriculum and Instruction, Program in Foreign Language Education—Teaching English to Speakers of Other Languages (TESOL), Miami, FL 33199. Offers foreign language education (Certificate); teaching English (MS). Part-time and evening/weekend programs available. *Faculty:* 3 full-time (all women). *Students:* 6 full-time (4 women), 15 part-time (13 women); includes 13 minority (3 African Americans, 2 Asian Americans or Pacific Islanders, 8 Hispanic Americans). Average age 35. 4 applicants, 75% accepted, 3 enrolled. In 2006, 12 degrees awarded. *Entrance requirements:* For master's, GRE General Test, minimum GPA of 3.0. Additional exam requirements/recommendations for international students: Required—TOEFL (minimum score 550 paper-based; 213 computer-based; 80 iBT), IELTS (minimum score 6). *Application deadline:* For fall admission, 6/1 priority date for domestic students, 4/1 for international students; for winter admission, 10/1 priority date for domestic students, 9/1 for international students; for spring admission, 3/1 priority date for domestic students, 2/1 for international students. Applications are processed on a rolling basis. Application fee: $30. Electronic applications accepted. *Expenses:* Tuition, state resident: part-time $249 per credit hour. Tuition, nonresident: part-time $753 per credit hour. Tuition and fees vary according to program. *Financial support:* Research assistantships, career-related internships or fieldwork and Federal Work-Study available. *Faculty research:* Methodology, applied languages. *Unit head:* Dr. Eric Dwyer, Program Director, 305-348-2078, E-mail: dwyere@fiu.edu. *Application contact:* Marisa Salazar, Student Recruiter, 305-348-3002, Fax: 305-348-3227, E-mail: marisa.salazar@fiu.edu.

Florida International University, College of Education, Department of Curriculum and Instruction, Program in French Education—Initial Teacher Preparation, Miami, FL 33199. Offers MAT. Part-time and evening/weekend programs available. *Faculty:* 1 full-time (0 women). *Students:* Average age 38. *Entrance requirements:* For master's, GRE General Test, minimum 1000, minimum GPA of 3.0. Additional exam requirements/recommendations for international students: Required—TOEFL (minimum score 550 paper-based; 213 computer-based; 80 iBT), IELTS (minimum score 6). *Application deadline:* For fall admission, 6/1 priority date for domestic students, 4/1 for international students; for winter admission, 10/1 priority date for domestic students, 9/1 for international students; for spring admission, 3/1 priority date for domestic students, 2/1 for international students. Applications are processed on a rolling basis. Application fee: $30. Electronic applications accepted. *Expenses:* Tuition, state resident: part-time $249 per credit hour. Tuition, nonresident: part-time $753 per credit hour. Tuition and fees vary according to program. *Financial support:* Fellowships, research assistantships with full and partial tuition reimbursements, teaching assistantships with full and partial tuition reimbursements, Federal Work-Study and tuition waivers (full and partial) available. Support available to part-time students. *Unit head:* Dr. Eric Dwyer, Program Director, 305-348-2078, E-mail: dwyere@fiu.edu. *Application contact:* Marisa Salazar, Student Recruiter, 305-348-3002, Fax: 305-348-3227, E-mail: marisa.salazar@fiu.edu.

Florida International University, College of Education, Department of Curriculum and Instruction, Program in Modern Language Education/Bilingual Education, Miami, FL 33199. Offers MS, Ed D. *Accreditation:* NCATE. Part-time and evening/weekend programs available. *Entrance requirements:* Additional exam requirements/recommendations for international students: Required—TOEFL. *Application deadline:* Applications are processed on a rolling basis. *Expenses:* Tuition, state resident: part-time $249 per credit hour. Tuition, nonresident: part-time $753 per credit hour. Tuition and fees vary according to program. *Faculty research:* Language and business, teaching English to speakers of other languages (TESOL). *Unit head:* Dr. Eric Dwyer, Program Director, 305-348-2078, E-mail: dwyere@fiu.edu.

Florida International University, College of Education, Department of Curriculum and Instruction, Program in Spanish Education—Initial Teacher Preparation, Miami, FL 33199. Offers MAT. Part-time and evening/weekend programs available. *Faculty:* 2 full-time (1 woman). *Entrance requirements:* For master's, GRE General Test, minimum 1000, minimum GPA of 3.0. Additional exam requirements/recommendations for international students: Required—TOEFL (minimum score 550 paper-based; 213 computer-based; 80 iBT), IELTS (minimum score 6). *Application deadline:* For fall admission, 6/1 priority date for domestic students, 4/1 for international students; for winter admission, 10/1 priority date for domestic students, 9/1 for international students; for spring admission, 3/1 priority date for domestic students, 2/1 for international students. Applications are processed on a rolling basis. Application fee: $30. Electronic applications accepted. *Expenses:* Tuition, state resident: part-time $249 per credit hour. Tuition, nonresident: part-time $753 per credit hour. Tuition and fees vary according to program. *Financial support:* Fellowships, research assistantships, teaching assistantships, Federal Work-Study and tuition waivers (full and partial) available. Support available to part-time students. *Unit head:* Dr. Eric Dwyer, Program Director, 305-348-2078, E-mail: dwyere@fiu.edu. *Application contact:* Marisa Salazar, Student Recruiter, 305-348-3002, Fax: 305-348-3227, E-mail: marisa.salazar@fiu.edu.

Framingham State College, Division of Graduate and Continuing Education, Program in Spanish, Framingham, MA 01701-9101. Offers M Ed. *Students:* 19. In 2006, 7 degrees awarded. *Unit head:* Dr. Michael Wong-Russell, Coordinator, 508-626-4680, Fax: 508-626-4030, E-mail: mwongru@frc.mass.edu. *Application contact:* 508-626-4550, Fax: 508-626-4030, E-mail: dgce@frc.mass.edu.

George Mason University, College of Humanities and Social Sciences, Department of Modern and Classical Languages, Fairfax, VA 22030. Offers foreign languages (MA). *Faculty:* 26 full-time (15 women), 47 part-time/adjunct (35 women). *Students:* 7 full-time (6 women), 32 part-time (29 women); includes 15 minority (3 African Americans, 3 Asian Americans or Pacific Islanders, 9 Hispanic Americans), 3 international. Average age 36. 24 applicants, 92% accepted, 11 enrolled. In 2006, 4 degrees awarded. *Degree requirements:* For master's, thesis optional. *Entrance requirements:* For master's, minimum GPA of 3.0 in last 60 hours. *Application deadline:* For fall admission, 5/1 for domestic students; for spring admission, 11/1 for domestic students. Application fee: $60 ($75 for international students). Electronic applications accepted. *Expenses:* Tuition, state resident: full-time $5,724; part-time $238 per credit. Tuition, nonresident: full-time $16,896; part-time $704 per credit. Required fees: $1,656; $69 per credit. *Financial support:* Available to part-time students. Application deadline: 3/1; *Unit head:* Jeffrey T. Chamberlain, Chairperson, 703-993-1230, Fax: 703-993-1245, E-mail: jchamber@gmu.edu. *Application contact:* Dr. Mark Goldin, Information Contact, 703-993-1231, E-mail: language@gmu.edu.

Georgia Southern University, Jack N. Averitt College of Graduate Studies, College of Education, Department of Teaching and Learning, Program in French Education, Statesboro, GA 30460. Offers M Ed. *Accreditation:* NCATE. Part-time and evening/weekend programs available. In 2006, 1 degree awarded. *Degree requirements:* For master's, one foreign language. *Entrance requirements:* For master's, GRE General Test or MAT, minimum GPA of 2.5. Additional exam requirements/recommendations for international students: Required—TOEFL (minimum score 550 paper-based; 213 computer-based; 80 iBT). *Application deadline:* For fall admission, 3/1 priority date for domestic students, 6/1 for international students; for spring admission, 10/1 priority date for domestic and international students. Applications are processed on a rolling basis. Application fee: $50. Electronic applications accepted. *Financial support:* In 2006–07, research assistantships with partial tuition reimbursements (averaging $5,500 per year), teaching assistantships with partial tuition reimbursements (averaging $5,500 per year) were awarded; Federal Work-Study, scholarships/grants, traineeships, and tuition waivers (partial) also available. Support available to part-time students. Financial award application deadline: 4/15; financial award applicants required to submit FAFSA. *Unit head:* Dr. David Alley, Professor, 912-681-0246, Fax: 912-681-0026, E-mail: dalley@georgiasouthern.edu. *Application contact:* 912-681-5384, Fax: 912-681-0740, E-mail: gradadmissions@georgiasouthern.edu.

Georgia Southern University, Jack N. Averitt College of Graduate Studies, College of Education, Department of Teaching and Learning, Program in Spanish Education, Statesboro, GA 30460. Offers MAT. *Accreditation:* NCATE. Part-time and evening/weekend programs available. *Students:* 1 (woman) full-time, 1 (woman) part-time. Average age 40. 1 applicant, 100% accepted, 0 enrolled. In 2006, 6 degrees awarded. *Degree requirements:* For master's, exit assessment. *Entrance requirements:* For master's, GRE General Test or MAT, minimum GPA of 2.5. Additional exam requirements/recommendations for international students: Required—TOEFL (minimum score 550 paper-based; 213 computer-based; 80 iBT). *Application deadline:* For fall admission, 3/1 for domestic and international students; for spring admission, 10/1 priority date for domestic students, 10/1 for international students. Applications are processed on a rolling basis. Application fee: $50. Electronic applications accepted. *Financial support:* In 2006–07, 1 student received support, including research assistantships with partial tuition reimbursements available (averaging $5,500 per year), teaching assistantships with partial tuition reimbursements available (averaging $5,500 per year); Federal Work-Study, scholarships/grants, tuition waivers (partial), and unspecified assistantships also available. Support available to part-time students. Financial award application deadline: 4/15; financial award applicants required to submit FAFSA. *Unit head:* Dr. David Alley, Professor, 912-681-0246, Fax: 912-681-0652, E-mail: dalley@georgiasouthern.edu. *Application contact:* 912-681-5384, Fax: 912-681-0740, E-mail: gradadmissions@georgiasouthern.edu.

Georgia Southern University, Jack N. Averitt College of Graduate Studies, College of Liberal Arts and Social Sciences, Department of Foreign Languages, Statesboro, GA 30460. Offers MA. Part-time and evening/weekend programs available. *Students:* 3 full-time (2 women), 6 part-time (all women); includes 4 minority (all Hispanic Americans) Average age 41. 3 applicants, 100% accepted, 3 enrolled. *Degree requirements:* For master's, one foreign language, thesis optional. *Entrance requirements:* For master's, GRE, minimum GPA of 3.0. Additional exam requirements/recommendations for international students: Required—TOEFL (minimum score 550 paper-based; 213 computer-based; 80 iBT). *Application deadline:* For fall admission, 3/1 priority date for domestic students, 3/1 for international students; for spring admission, 10/1 priority date for domestic students, 10/1 for international students. Applications are processed on a rolling basis. Application fee: $50. Electronic applications accepted. *Financial support:* In 2006–07, 5 students received support; research assistantships with partial tuition reimbursements available, teaching assistantships with partial tuition reimbursements available, career-related internships or fieldwork, Federal Work-Study, scholarships/grants, tuition waivers (partial), and unspecified assistantships available. Support available to part-time students. *Unit head:* Dr. Donnie Richards, Chair, 912-681-5281, Fax: 912-681-0652, E-mail: forlangs@georgiasouthern.edu. *Application contact:* 912-681-5384, Fax: 912-681-0740, E-mail: gradadmissions@georgiasouthern.edu.

Harding University, College of Education, Searcy, AR 72149-0001. Offers advanced studies in teaching and learning (M Ed); art (MSE); behavioral science (MSE); Bible and religion (MSE); counseling (MS, Ed S); early childhood education (M Ed); early childhood special education (M Ed, MSE); education (MSE); educational leadership (M Ed, Ed S); elementary education (M Ed); English (MSE); family and consumer science (MSE); French (MSE); history/social science (MSE); kinesiology (MSE); math (MSE); physical science (MSE); reading (M Ed); secondary education (M Ed); Spanish (MSE); special education licensure (M Ed); teaching (MAT). *Accreditation:* NCATE. Part-time programs available. *Faculty:* 8 full-time (2 women), 45 part-time/adjunct (30 women). *Students:* 153 full-time (123 women), 469 part-time (341 women); includes 72 minority (63 African Americans, 4 American Indian/Alaska Native, 1 Asian American or Pacific Islander, 4 Hispanic Americans), 9 international. Average age 35. 175 applicants, 90% accepted, 147 enrolled. In 2006, 241 degrees awarded. *Degree requirements:* For master's, portfolio(s), thesis optional; for Ed S, portfolio, specialist project. *Entrance requirements:* For master's, GRE, MAT, PRAXIS; for Ed S, MAT or GRE. Additional exam requirements/recommendations for international students: Required—TOEFL (minimum score 550 paper-based). *Application deadline:* For fall admission, 8/1 for domestic and international students; for spring admission, 1/1 for domestic and international students. Applications are processed on a rolling basis. Application fee: $35. *Expenses:* Tuition: Part-time $455 per semester hour. Required fees: $20 per semester hour. Tuition and fees vary according to course load. *Financial support:* Scholarships/grants and unspecified assistantships available. Support available to part-time students. *Faculty research:* Reading, comprehension, school violence, educational technology, behavior, college choice, differentiated instruction, brain based teaching. *Unit head:* Pat Bashaw, Chair, 501-279-4183, Fax: 501-279-4051, E-mail: pbashaw@harding.edu.

Hofstra University, College of Liberal Arts and Sciences, Department of Romance Languages and Literatures, Hempstead, NY 11549. Offers Spanish (MA). *Accreditation:* NCATE. Part-time and evening/weekend programs available. *Faculty:* 3 full-time (2 women), 2 part-time/adjunct (1 woman). *Students:* 3 full-time (all women), 4 part-time (all women); includes 5 minority (all Hispanic Americans) Average age 34. 7 applicants, 100% accepted, 4 enrolled. In 2006, 2 degrees awarded. *Degree requirements:* For master's, one foreign language, thesis, registration. *Entrance requirements:* For master's, interview, 2 letters of recommendation, essay. Additional exam requirements/recommendations for international students: Required—TOEFL (minimum score 550 paper-based; 213 computer-based). *Application deadline:* Applications are processed on a rolling basis. Application fee: $60. Electronic applications accepted.

Expenses: Tuition: Full-time $13,320; part-time $740 per credit. Required fees: $930; $155 per term. *Financial support:* In 2006–07, 5 students received support, including 1 fellowship with tuition reimbursement available (averaging $3,000 per year); research assistantships with full and partial tuition reimbursements available, scholarships/grants and tuition waivers (full and partial) also available. Financial award applicants required to submit FAFSA. *Faculty research:* Culture of food in Latin/American countries; Latin American poetry; contemporary Spanish cultural studies; Spanish and Cuban theater; medieval literature and politics of language; postcolonial, decolonization and imperial studies. *Unit head:* Dr. David A. Powell, Chairperson, 516-463-5485, Fax: 516-463-2310, E-mail: rlldap@mail1.hofstra.edu. *Application contact:* Carol Drummer, Dean of Graduate Admissions, 516-463-4876, Fax: 516-463-4664, E-mail: gradstudent@hofstra.edu.

Hofstra University, School of Education and Allied Human Services, Department of Curriculum and Teaching, Program in Foreign Language Education, Hempstead, NY 11549. Offers French (MA, MS Ed); German (MA, MS Ed); Russian (MA, MS Ed); Spanish (MA, MS Ed). Part-time programs available. *Students:* 7 full-time (all women), 3 part-time (all women); includes 2 minority (both Hispanic Americans) Average age 30. 4 applicants, 100% accepted, 1 enrolled. In 2006, 3 degrees awarded. *Degree requirements:* For master's, one foreign language. *Entrance requirements:* For master's, 2 letters of recommendation, teacher certification (MA), essay. Additional exam requirements/recommendations for international students: Required—TOEFL (minimum score 550 paper-based; 213 computer-based). *Application deadline:* Applications are processed on a rolling basis. Application fee: $60. Electronic applications accepted. *Expenses:* Tuition: Full-time $13,320; part-time $740 per credit. Required fees: $930; $155 per term. *Financial support:* In 2006–07, 1 student received support, including 1 fellowship with tuition reimbursement available (averaging $2,333 per year); research assistantships with full and partial tuition reimbursements available, tuition waivers (full and partial) also available. Financial award applicants required to submit FAFSA. *Unit head:* Dr. David A. Powell, Chairperson, 516-463-5485, Fax: 516-463-2310, E-mail: rlldap@mail1.hofstra.edu. *Application contact:* Carol Drummer, Dean of Graduate Admissions, 516-463-4876, Fax: 516-463-4664, E-mail: gradstudent@hofstra.edu.

Hood College, Graduate School, Program in Foreign Language Proficiency, Frederick, MD 21701-8575. Offers Certificate. Application fee: $35. *Expenses:* Tuition: Part-time $350 per credit. Required fees: $20 per semester. *Unit head:* Roser Caminals—Heath, Chair, 301-696-3474. *Application contact:* Dr. Kathleen C. Bands, Associate Dean of Graduate School, 301-696-3811, Fax: 301-696-3597, E-mail: gofurther@hood.edu.

Hunter College of the City University of New York, Graduate School, School of Arts and Sciences, Department of Romance Languages, Program in French, New York, NY 10021-5085. Offers French (MA); French education (MA). Part-time and evening/weekend programs available. *Faculty:* 6 full-time (4 women), 8 part-time/adjunct (3 women). *Students:* Average age 36. 3 applicants, 67% accepted, 1 enrolled. In 2006, 2 degrees awarded. *Degree requirements:* For master's, 2 foreign languages, comprehensive exam. *Entrance requirements:* For master's, GRE General Test, GRE Subject Test, ability to read, speak, and write French; interview. Additional exam requirements/recommendations for international students: Required—TOEFL. *Application deadline:* For fall admission, 4/1 for domestic students, 2/1 for international students; for spring admission, 11/1 for domestic students, 9/1 for international students. Application fee: $125. *Expenses:* Tuition, state resident: part-time $270 per credit. Tuition, nonresident: part-time $500 per credit. Required fees: $45 per semester. *Financial support:* Fellowships, Federal Work-Study, scholarships/grants, and tuition waivers (partial) available. Support available to part-time students. Financial award application deadline: 4/15. *Faculty research:* Contemporary French theater, Villiers-del Isle-Adam, Voltaire, medieval folklore, fin-de-siécle. *Application contact:* William Zlata, Director for Graduate Admissions, 212-772-4482, Fax: 212-650-3336, E-mail: admissions@hunter.cuny.edu.

Hunter College of the City University of New York, Graduate School, School of Arts and Sciences, Department of Romance Languages, Program in Italian, New York, NY 10021-5085. Offers Italian (MA); Italian education (MA). *Faculty:* 1 (woman) full-time, 10 part-time/adjunct (all women). *Students:* Average age 22. 6 applicants, 33% accepted, 1 enrolled. In 2006, 2 degrees awarded. *Degree requirements:* For master's, 2 foreign languages, comprehensive exam. *Entrance requirements:* For master's, GRE General Test, GRE Subject Test, ability to read, speak, and write Italian; interview. Additional exam requirements/recommendations for international students: Required—TOEFL. *Application deadline:* For fall admission, 4/1 for domestic students, 2/1 for international students; for spring admission, 11/1 for domestic students, 9/1 for international students. Application fee: $125. *Expenses:* Tuition, state resident: part-time $270 per credit. Tuition, nonresident: part-time $500 per credit. Required fees: $45 per semester. *Financial support:* Federal Work-Study, scholarships/grants, and tuition waivers (partial) available. Support available to part-time students. Financial award application deadline: 4/15. *Faculty research:* Dante, Middle Ages, Renaissance, contemporary Italian novel and poetry, late Renaissance and baroque. *Unit head:* Dr. Paolo Fasoli, Graduate Co-Adviser, 212-772-5129, Fax: 212-772-5094, E-mail: pfasoli@hunter.cuny.edu. *Application contact:* William Zlata, Director for Graduate Admissions, 212-772-4482, Fax: 212-650-3336, E-mail: admissions@hunter.cuny.edu.

Hunter College of the City University of New York, Graduate School, School of Arts and Sciences, Department of Romance Languages, Program in Spanish, New York, NY 10021-5085. Offers Spanish (MA); Spanish education (MA). Part-time and evening/weekend programs available. *Faculty:* 10 full-time (7 women), 17 part-time/adjunct (9 women). *Students:* Average age 36. 6 applicants, 33% accepted, 1 enrolled. In 2006, 11 degrees awarded. *Degree requirements:* For master's, 2 foreign languages, comprehensive exam. *Entrance requirements:* For master's, GRE General Test, GRE Subject Test, ability to read, speak, and write Spanish; interview. Additional exam requirements/recommendations for international students: Required—TOEFL. *Application deadline:* For fall admission, 4/1 for domestic students, 2/1 for international students; for spring admission, 11/1 for domestic students, 9/1 for international students. Application fee: $125. *Expenses:* Tuition, state resident: part-time $270 per credit. Tuition, nonresident: part-time $500 per credit. Required fees: $45 per semester. *Financial support:* Federal Work-Study and tuition waivers (partial) available. Support available to part-time students. Financial award application deadline: 4/15. *Faculty research:* Galician studies, contemporary Spanish poetry, Lope de Vega, comparative Hispanic literatures, contemporary Hispanic poetry. *Unit head:* Dr. Carlos Hortas, Graduate Adviser, 212-772-5009, E-mail: chortas@hunter.cuny.edu. *Application contact:* William Zlata, Director for Graduate Admissions, 212-772-4482, Fax: 212-650-3336, E-mail: admissions@hunter.cuny.edu.

Hunter College of the City University of New York, Graduate School, School of Education, Programs in Secondary Education, Concentration in French Education, New York, NY 10021-5085. Offers MA. *Accreditation:* NCATE. *Students:* 1 (woman) full-time, 6 part-time (5 women); includes 1 minority (African American) Average age 33. 6 applicants, 83% accepted, 3 enrolled. In 2006, 2 degrees awarded. *Degree requirements:* For master's, thesis, professional teaching portfolio, New York State Teacher Certification Exam. *Entrance requirements:* For master's, 24 credits in French, minimum GPA of 3.0 in French, minimum GPA of 2.8 overall, 2 letters of reference, interview. Additional exam requirements/recommendations for international students: Required—TOEFL, TWE. *Application deadline:* For fall admission, 4/1 for domestic students, 2/1 for international students; for spring admission, 11/1 for domestic students, 9/1 for international students. Applications are processed on a rolling basis. Application fee: $125. *Expenses:* Tuition, state resident: part-time $270 per credit. Tuition, nonresident: part-time $500 per credit. Required fees: $45 per semester. *Financial support:* Federal Work-Study and tuition waivers (partial) available. Support available to part-time students. *Unit head:* Dr. Julia Przybos, Graduate Advisor, 212-772-5097, E-mail: jprzybos@shiva.hunter.cuny.edu. *Application contact:* William Zlata, Director for Graduate Admissions, 212-772-4482, Fax: 212-650-3336, E-mail: admissions@hunter.cuny.edu.

Hunter College of the City University of New York, Graduate School, School of Education, Programs in Secondary Education, Concentration in Italian Education, New York, NY 10021-5085. Offers MA. *Accreditation:* NCATE. *Students:* Average age 44. 3 applicants, 0% accepted. *Degree requirements:* For master's, thesis, professional teaching portfolio, New York State Teacher Certification Exam, research project. *Entrance requirements:* For master's, minimum GPA of 3.0 in Italian, 2.8 overall; 24 credits of course work in Italian; 2 letters of reference; interview. Additional exam requirements/recommendations for international students: Required—TOEFL, TWE. *Application deadline:* For fall admission, 4/1 for domestic students, 2/1 for international students; for spring admission, 11/1 for domestic students, 9/1 for international students. Applications are processed on a rolling basis. Application fee: $125. *Expenses:* Tuition, state resident: part-time $270 per credit. Tuition, nonresident: part-time $500 per credit. Required fees: $45 per semester. *Financial support:* Federal Work-Study and tuition waivers (partial) available. Support available to part-time students. *Unit head:* Dr. Paolo Fasoli, Chair, 212-772-5129, Fax: 212-772-5094, E-mail: pfasoli@hunter.cuny.edu. *Application contact:* William Zlata, Director for Graduate Admissions, 212-772-4482, Fax: 212-650-3336, E-mail: admissions@hunter.cuny.edu.

Hunter College of the City University of New York, Graduate School, School of Education, Programs in Secondary Education, Concentration in Spanish Education, New York, NY 10021-5085. Offers MA. *Accreditation:* NCATE. *Students:* 1 (woman) full-time, 39 part-time (27 women); includes 31 minority (all Hispanic Americans) Average age 35. 9 applicants, 78% accepted, 4 enrolled. *Degree requirements:* For master's, thesis, professional teaching portfolio, New York State Teacher Certification Exam. *Entrance requirements:* For master's, minimum GPA of 3.0 in Spanish, 2.8 overall; 24 credits of course work in Spanish; 2 letters of reference; interview. Additional exam requirements/recommendations for international students: Required—TOEFL, TWE. *Application deadline:* For fall admission, 4/1 for domestic students, 2/1 for international students; for spring admission, 11/1 for domestic students, 9/1 for international students. Applications are processed on a rolling basis. Application fee: $125. *Expenses:* Tuition, state resident: part-time $270 per credit. Tuition, nonresident: part-time $500 per credit. Required fees: $45 per semester. *Financial support:* Federal Work-Study and tuition waivers (partial) available. Support available to part-time students. *Unit head:* Dr. Carlos Hortas, Graduate Adviser, 212-772-5009, E-mail: chortas@hunter.cuny.edu. *Application contact:* William Zlata, Director for Graduate Admissions, 212-772-4482, Fax: 212-650-3336, E-mail: admissions@hunter.cuny.edu.

Indiana University Bloomington, Graduate School, College of Arts and Sciences, Department of French and Italian, Bloomington, IN 47405-7000. Offers French (MA, PhD), including French instruction (MA), French linguistics, French literature; Italian (MA, PhD). PhD offered through the University Graduate School. Part-time programs available. *Faculty:* 17 full-time (5 women). *Students:* 37 full-time (22 women), 43 part-time (24 women); includes 6 minority (3 African Americans, 1 American Indian/Alaska Native, 2 Hispanic Americans), 30 international. Average age 30. In 2006, 9 degrees awarded. *Degree requirements:* For master's, one foreign language; for doctorate, 2 foreign languages, thesis/dissertation. *Entrance requirements:* For master's and doctorate, GRE General Test. Additional exam requirements/recommendations for international students: Required—TOEFL. *Application deadline:* For fall admission, 1/15 priority date for domestic students, 12/15 for international students; for spring admission, 9/1 priority date for domestic students, 9/1 for international students. Applications are processed on a rolling basis. Application fee: $50 ($60 for international students). Electronic applications accepted. *Expenses:* Tuition, state resident: full-time $5,791; part-time $241 per credit hour. Tuition, nonresident: full-time $16,866; part-time $703 per credit hour. *Financial support:* Fellowships with partial tuition reimbursements, teaching assistantships with partial tuition reimbursements, career-related internships or fieldwork, institutionally sponsored loans, and tuition waivers (full) available. Financial award application deadline: 2/15. *Faculty research:* French-Creole studies, history of rhetoric, medieval epic and romance, post seventeenth century novel and poetry, Renaissance narrative and poetry. *Unit head:* Dr. Andrea Ciccarelli, Chairman, 812-855-1952, Fax: 812-855-8877, E-mail: fritdept@indiana.edu. *Application contact:* Daniela Ortiz, Secretary, 812-855-1088, Fax: 812-855-8877, E-mail: fritdept@indiana.edu.

Indiana University Bloomington, Graduate School, College of Arts and Sciences, Department of Germanic Studies, Bloomington, IN 47405-7000. Offers German literature and studies (PhD); German studies (MA, PhD), including German and business studies (MA), German literature and culture (MA), German literature and linguistics (MA); medieval German studies (PhD); teaching German (MAT). PhD offered through the University Graduate School. *Faculty:* 12 full-time (3 women), 6 part-time/adjunct (2 women). *Students:* 35 full-time (18 women), 10 international. Average age 31. In 2006, 4 master's, 4 doctorates awarded. Terminal master's awarded for partial completion of doctoral program. *Degree requirements:* For master's, one foreign language, registration; for doctorate, one foreign language, thesis/dissertation, comprehensive exam, registration. *Entrance requirements:* For master's, GRE General Test, BA in German or equivalent; for doctorate, GRE General Test, MA in German or equivalent. Additional exam requirements/recommendations for international students: Required—TOEFL. *Application deadline:* For fall admission, 1/15 priority date for domestic students, 12/15 for international students; for spring admission, 9/1 priority date for domestic students, 9/1 for international students. Applications are processed on a rolling basis. Application fee: $50 ($60 for international students). *Expenses:* Tuition, state resident: full-time $5,791; part-time $241 per credit hour. Tuition, nonresident: full-time $16,866; part-time $703 per credit hour. *Financial support:* Fellowships with full and partial tuition reimbursements, teaching assistantships with full tuition reimbursements, Federal Work-Study, institutionally sponsored loans, scholarships/grants, and unspecified assistantships available. Support available to part-time students. Financial award application deadline: 1/15; financial award applicants required to submit FAFSA. *Faculty research:* German (and European) literature: medieval to modern/postmodern, German and culture studies, Germanic philology, literary theory, literature and the other arts. *Unit head:* Kari Ellen Gade, Professor and Acting Chair, 812-855-8138, Fax: 812-855-8292, E-mail: gade@indiana.edu. *Application contact:* Michelle Dunbar, Graduate Secretary, 812-855-7947, E-mail: germanic@indiana.edu.

Indiana University Bloomington, Graduate School, College of Arts and Sciences, Department of Spanish and Portuguese, Bloomington, IN 47405-7000. Offers Hispanic linguistics (MA, PhD); Hispanic literature (MA); Luso-Brazilian literature (MA); Luso-Brazilian studies (PhD); Spanish literatures (PhD); teaching Spanish (MAT). PhD offered through the University Graduate School. *Faculty:* 19 full-time (10 women). *Students:* 56 full-time (29 women), 14 part-time (8 women); includes 11 minority (1 African American, 10 Hispanic Americans), 17 international. Average age 30. *Degree requirements:* For master's, one foreign language; for doctorate, 3 foreign languages, thesis/dissertation. *Entrance requirements:* For master's, GRE General Test, GRE Subject Test, bachelor's degree in Portuguese or Spanish, minimum GPA of 3.25; for doctorate, GRE General Test, GRE Subject Test, master's degree in Portuguese or Spanish, minimum GPA of 3.25. Additional exam requirements/recommendations for international students: Required—TOEFL. *Application deadline:* For fall admission, 1/15 priority date for domestic students, 12/15 for international students; for spring admission, 9/1 for domestic and international students. Application fee: $50 ($60 for international students). *Expenses:* Tuition, state resident: full-time $5,791; part-time $241 per credit hour. Tuition, nonresident: full-time $16,866; part-time $703 per credit hour. *Financial support:* Fellowships with full tuition reimbursements, teaching assistantships with full tuition reimbursements, Federal Work-Study available. Financial award application deadline: 1/15. *Faculty research:* Spanish American literature, Spanish peninsular literature, Luso-Brazilian studies, Catalan studies. *Unit head:* Josep Miguel Sobrer, Chair, 812-855-8498. *Application contact:* Steven Wagschal, Student Contact, 812-855-9194.

Iona College, School of Arts and Science, Program in Adolescence Education, New Rochelle, NY 10801-1890. Offers biology education (MS Ed, MST); English education (MS Ed, MST); mathematics education (MS Ed, MST); social studies education (MS Ed, MST); Spanish education (MS Ed, MST). *Accreditation:* NCATE. Part-time and evening/weekend programs available. *Faculty:* 11 full-time (6 women), 21 part-time/adjunct (13 women). *Students:* 15 full-time (9 women), 68 part-time (52 women); includes 6 minority (1 African American, 1 Asian American or Pacific Islander, 4 Hispanic Americans). Average age 28. 42 applicants, 57% accepted, 11 enrolled. In 2006, 29 degrees awarded. *Degree requirements:* For master's,

Foreign Languages Education

Iona College (continued)

thesis or alternative. *Entrance requirements:* For master's, minimum GPA of 2.5 (MST), New York teaching certificate (MS Ed). Additional exam requirements/recommendations for international students: Required—TOEFL (minimum score 550 paper-based; 213 computer-based). *Application deadline:* Applications are processed on a rolling basis. Application fee: $50. Electronic applications accepted. *Expenses:* Tuition: Part-time $665 per credit. Required fees: $150 per term. *Financial support:* Unspecified assistantships available. Support available to part-time students. *Faculty research:* Reading/writing, educational technology, administration, early literacy assessment, literacy development. *Unit head:* Dr. Patricia Antonacci, Chair, 914-633-2080, Fax: 914-633-2608, E-mail: pantonacci@iona.edu. *Application contact:* Veronica Jarek-Prinz, Graduate Admissions, 914-633-2289, Fax: 914-633-2012, E-mail: vjarekprinz@iona.edu.

Ithaca College, Graduate Studies, School of Humanities and Sciences, Program in Adolescent Education, Ithaca, NY 14850-7020. Offers biology 7-12 (MAT); chemistry 7-12 (MAT); English 7-12 (MAT); French 7-12 (MAT); math 7-12 (MAT); physics 7-12 (MAT); social studies 7-12 (MAT); Spanish (MAT). *Faculty:* 14 full-time (5 women), 1 (woman) part-time/adjunct. *Students:* 8 full-time (2 women), 2 part-time (both women); includes 1 minority (Hispanic American). Average age 28. 12 applicants, 92% accepted, 10 enrolled. *Entrance requirements:* For master's, minimum GPA of 3.0. *Application deadline:* For fall admission, 5/15 for domestic students; for spring admission, 12/1 for domestic students. Application fee: $40. *Expenses:* Contact institution. *Financial support:* In 2006–07, 10 students received support, including 8 teaching assistantships (averaging $5,820 per year). Financial award application deadline:3/1. *Unit head:* Linda Hanrahan, Chairperson, 607-274-3147, E-mail: lhanrahan@ithaca.edu.

Long Island University, C.W. Post Campus, College of Liberal Arts and Sciences, Department of Foreign Languages, Brookville, NY 11548-1300. Offers Spanish (MA); Spanish education (MS). Part-time programs available. *Degree requirements:* For master's, 2 foreign languages, thesis or alternative, comprehensive exam, registration. *Entrance requirements:* For master's, 24 credits of undergraduate Spanish. Electronic applications accepted. *Faculty research:* Making of superhero, dialogue in the 19th century novel, nicknames, Menendez Pidal and Spanish School of Philology, women writers of Latin America.

Long Island University, C.W. Post Campus, School of Education, Department of Curriculum and Instruction, Brookville, NY 11548-1300. Offers adolescence education (MS); adolescence education: biology (MS); adolescence education: earth science (MS); adolescence education: English (MS); adolescence education: mathematics (MS); adolescence education: social studies (MS); adolescence education: Spanish (MS); art education (MS); bilingual education (MS); childhood education (MS); early childhood education (MS); middle childhood education (MS); music education (MS); teaching English to speakers of other languages (MS). Part-time and evening/weekend programs available. *Degree requirements:* For master's, comprehensive exam or thesis, student teaching. *Entrance requirements:* For master's, minimum GPA of 2.75 in major, 2.5 overall. Electronic applications accepted. *Faculty research:* Ethics and education, teaching strategies.

Louisiana Tech University, Graduate School, College of Education, Department of Curriculum, Instruction and Leadership, Ruston, LA 71272. Offers curriculum and instruction (MS, Ed D); educational leadership (Ed D); secondary education (M Ed), including business education, English education, foreign language education, health and physical education, mathematics education, science education, social studies education, speech education. *Accreditation:* NCATE. Part-time programs available. *Degree requirements:* For doctorate, thesis/dissertation. *Entrance requirements:* For master's and doctorate, GRE General Test.

Manhattanville College, Graduate Programs, School of Education, Program in Middle Childhood/Adolescence Education (Grades 5-12), Purchase, NY 10577-2132. Offers biology (MAT); biology and special education (MPS); chemistry (MAT); chemistry and special education (MPS); English (MAT); English and special education (MPS); literacy (MPS), including reading and writing, writing; literacy and special education (MPS); math (MAT); math and special education (MPS); second language (MAT), including French, Italian, Latin, Spanish; social studies (MAT); social studies and special education (MPS); special education (MPS). Part-time and evening/weekend programs available. *Students:* 76 full-time (53 women), 109 part-time (68 women); includes 8 African Americans, 1 Asian American or Pacific Islander, 10 Hispanic Americans, 1 international. In 2006, 165 degrees awarded. *Degree requirements:* For master's, comprehensive exam or research project, field experience. *Entrance requirements:* For master's, minimum undergraduate GPA of 3.0, 2 letters of recommendation. *Application deadline:* Applications are processed on a rolling basis. Application fee: $55. *Financial support:* Career-related internships or fieldwork and institutionally sponsored loans available. Support available to part-time students. *Application contact:* Alyce Ware Poli, Director of Admissions, 914-323-5142, Fax: 914-694-1732, E-mail: edschool@mville.edu.

Marquette University, Graduate School, College of Arts and Sciences, Department of Foreign Languages and Literatures, Milwaukee, WI 53201-1881. Offers Spanish (MA, MAT). Part-time programs available. *Faculty:* 45 full-time (33 women), 6 part-time/adjunct (5 women). *Students:* 8 full-time (6 women), 1 (woman) part-time; includes 5 minority (all Hispanic Americans), 1 international. Average age 27. 6 applicants, 100% accepted, 4 enrolled. In 2006, 3 degrees awarded. *Degree requirements:* For master's, one foreign language. *Entrance requirements:* Additional exam requirements/recommendations for international students: Required—TOEFL. Application fee: $40. *Financial support:* In 2006–07, 5 research assistantships were awarded; teaching assistantships, Federal Work-Study, institutionally sponsored loans, scholarships/grants, and tuition waivers (full and partial) also available. Support available to part-time students. Financial award application deadline: 2/15. *Faculty research:* Magic realism, African-Hispanic literature, women studies, Hispanic linguistics. *Unit head:* Dr. Belén Castaneda, Chair, 414-288-7063, Fax: 414-288-1578. *Application contact:* Dr. Armando Gonzáles-Percz, Director of Graduate Studies, 414-288-7268, Fax: 414-288-1578.

McGill University, Faculty of Graduate and Postdoctoral Studies, Faculty of Education, Department of Integrated Studies in Education, Montréal, QC H3A 2T5, Canada. Offers culture and values in education (MA, PhD); curriculum (MA); educational leadership (Certificate, Diploma); educational studies (PhD); integrated studies in education (M Ed); leadership (MA); second language education (MA, PhD). *Degree requirements:* For master's, thesis (for some programs), registration; for doctorate, thesis/dissertation, comprehensive exam, registration. *Entrance requirements:* For master's, 2 years of relevant experience, minimum GPA of 3.0; for doctorate, minimum GPA of 3.0, acquisition of prospective supervisor; for other advanced degree, minimum GPA of 3.0. Additional exam requirements/recommendations for international students: Required—TOEFL (minimum score 580 paper-based; 237 computer-based).

Michigan State University, The Graduate School, College of Arts and Letters, Program in Second Language Studies, East Lansing, MI 48824. Offers PhD. *Students:* 19 full-time (13 women), 1 (woman) part-time; includes 1 minority (African American), 13 international. Average age 31. 54 applicants, 26% accepted. *Entrance requirements:* Additional exam requirements/recommendations for international students: Required—TOEFL, Michigan State University ELT (85), Michigan ELAB (85). Electronic applications accepted. *Expenses:* Tuition: state resident: part-time $346 per credit hour. Tuition, nonresident: part-time $730 per credit hour. Tuition and fees vary according to program. *Financial support:* In 2006–07, 11 fellowships with tuition reimbursements, 14 research assistantships with tuition reimbursements (averaging $12,249 per year), 5 teaching assistantships with tuition reimbursements (averaging $12,335 per year) were awarded. *Unit head:* Dr. Susan Mary Gass, Director, 517-432-1812, Fax: 517-353-9637, E-mail: gass@msu.edu. *Application contact:* Anna Davis, Graduate Secretary, 517-432-1812, Fax: 517-353-9637, E-mail: sls@msu.edu.

Middle Tennessee State University, College of Graduate Studies, College of Liberal Arts, Department of Foreign Languages and Literatures, Murfreesboro, TN 37132. Offers MAT.

Part-time and evening/weekend programs available. Postbaccalaureate distance learning degree programs offered. *Faculty:* 14 full-time (8 women). *Students:* 4 full-time (3 women), 20 part-time (16 women); includes 8 minority (4 African Americans, 1 American Indian/Alaska Native, 3 Hispanic Americans). Average age 31. 7 applicants, 100% accepted. In 2006, 14 degrees awarded. *Degree requirements:* For master's, one foreign language, comprehensive exam. *Entrance requirements:* For master's, GRE. Additional exam requirements/recommendations for international students: Required—TOEFL (minimum score 525 paper-based; 195 computer-based). *Application deadline:* For fall admission, 8/1 priority date for domestic students. Applications are processed on a rolling basis. Application fee: $25. Electronic applications accepted. *Financial support:* In 2006–07, 10 students received support. Career-related internships or fieldwork and institutionally sponsored loans available. Support available to part-time students. Financial award application deadline: 5/1; financial award applicants required to submit FAFSA. *Faculty research:* Literature and linguistics, French literature, interactive material design, Holocaust literature, foreign language pedagogy. *Unit head:* Dr. Deborah Mistron, Chair, 615-898-2981, Fax: 615-898-5826.

Mississippi State University, College of Arts and Sciences, Department of Foreign Languages, Mississippi State, MS 39762. Offers French (MA); French/German (MA); German (MA); Spanish (MA); Spanish/French (MA); Spanish/German (MA). Part-time programs available. *Faculty:* 17 full-time (9 women), 4 part-time/adjunct (3 women). *Students:* 12 full-time (8 women), 1 (woman) part-time; includes 2 minority (1 African American, 1 Hispanic American), 2 international. Average age 26. 7 applicants, 86% accepted, 3 enrolled. In 2006, 12 degrees awarded. *Degree requirements:* For master's, one foreign language, comprehensive oral or written exam, thesis optional. *Entrance requirements:* For master's, minimum GPA of 2.75. Additional exam requirements/recommendations for international students: Required—TOEFL (minimum score 525 paper-based). *Application deadline:* For fall admission, 7/1 for domestic students; for spring admission, 11/1 for domestic students. Applications are processed on a rolling basis. Application fee: $30. *Expenses:* Tuition, state resident: full-time $4,550; part-time $253 per hour. Tuition, nonresident: full-time $10,552; part-time $584 per hour. International tuition: $10,882 full-time. Tuition and fees vary according to course load. *Financial support:* In 2006–07, 15 teaching assistantships with full tuition reimbursements (averaging $7,766 per year) were awarded; Federal Work-Study, institutionally sponsored loans, and unspecified assistantships also available. Financial award applicants required to submit FAFSA. *Faculty research:* French, German, Spanish literature from medieval to present; gender and cultural studies in French; Spanish American literature; foreign language methodology; linguistics. *Unit head:* Dr. Edmond A. Emplaincourt, Head, 662-325-3480, Fax: 662-325-8209, E-mail: eaempl@ra.msstate.edu. *Application contact:* Dr. Phil Bonfanti, Director of Admissions, 662-325-4104, Fax: 662-325-8872, E-mail: admit@msstate.edu.

Missouri State University, Graduate College, College of Arts and Letters, Department of Modern and Classical Languages, Springfield, MO 65804-0094. Offers secondary education (MS Ed), including French, German, Spanish. *Faculty:* 5 full-time (2 women). *Students:* 2 full-time (both women), 2 part-time (both women); includes 1 minority (Hispanic American). Average age 33. 2 applicants, 50% accepted, 1 enrolled. In 2006, 1 degree awarded. *Entrance requirements:* For master's, grades 9–12 teaching certification. Additional exam requirements/recommendations for international students: Required—TOEFL (minimum score 550 paper-based; 213 computer-based; 79 iBT), IELTS (minimum score 6). *Application deadline:* For fall admission, 7/20 priority date for domestic students; for spring admission, 12/20 priority date for domestic students. Application fee: $35. *Expenses:* Tuition, state resident: full-time $3,582; part-time $199 per credit hour. Tuition, nonresident: full-time $6,984; part-time $199 per credit hour. Required fees: $548. Full-time tuition and fees vary according to course level, course load, program and reciprocity agreements. *Financial support:* Teaching assistantships with full tuition reimbursements available. Financial award applicants required to submit FAFSA. *Unit head:* Dr. Madeleine Kernen, Head, 417-836-7626, E-mail: mcl@missouristate.edu.

Monterey Institute of International Studies, Graduate School of Language and Educational Linguistics, Program in Teaching Foreign Language, Monterey, CA 93940-2691. Offers MATFL. *Students:* 9 full-time (8 women), 54 part-time (34 women); includes 9 minority (1 African American, 8 Asian Americans or Pacific Islanders), 11 international. Average age 39. 31 applicants, 84% accepted, 17 enrolled. In 2006, 9 degrees awarded. *Degree requirements:* For master's, one foreign language. *Entrance requirements:* For master's, minimum GPA of 3.0, proficiency in foreign language. Additional exam requirements/recommendations for international students: Required—TOEFL. *Application deadline:* For fall admission, 3/15 priority date for domestic students; for spring admission, 10/1 priority date for domestic students. Applications are processed on a rolling basis. Application fee: $50. Electronic applications accepted. *Expenses:* Tuition: Full-time $26,500; part-time $1,200 per credit. Required fees: $200. *Financial support:* Application deadline: 3/15; *Unit head:* Dr. Jean Turner, Head, 831-647-3522, Fax: 831-647-6650, E-mail: gslel@miis.edu. *Application contact:* 831-647-4123, Fax: 831-647-6405, E-mail: admit@miis.edu.

See Close-Up on page 1369.

New College of California, School of Humanities, San Francisco, CA 94102-5206. Offers humanities and leadership (MA), including activism and social change, culture, ecology, and sustainable community; Irish studies (MA); media studies (MA); poetics (MA, MFA), including poetics (MA); poetics and writing (MFA); teaching (MAT); women's spirituality (MA); writing and consciousness (MA); MA/MFA. Part-time and evening/weekend programs available. *Degree requirements:* For master's, thesis.

New York University, Steinhardt School of Culture, Education and Human Development, Department of Teaching and Learning, Program in Multilingual/Multicultural Studies, New York, NY 10012-1019. Offers bilingual education (MA, PhD, Advanced Certificate); foreign language education (MA, Advanced Certificate); foreign language education/TESOL (MA); teaching English to speakers of other languages (MA, PhD, Advanced Certificate). *Accreditation:* Teacher Education Accreditation Council. Part-time and evening/weekend programs available. *Faculty:* 3 full-time (2 women). *Students:* 121 full-time (105 women), 103 part-time (89 women); includes 38 minority (3 African Americans, 19 Asian Americans or Pacific Islanders, 16 Hispanic Americans), 95 international. 272 applicants, 75% accepted, 87 enrolled. In 2006, 103 master's, 5 doctorates, 6 other advanced degrees awarded. Terminal master's awarded for partial completion of doctoral program. *Degree requirements:* For master's, thesis (for some programs); for doctorate, thesis/dissertation. *Entrance requirements:* For doctorate, GRE General Test, interview; for Advanced Certificate, master's degree. Additional exam requirements/recommendations for international students: Required—TOEFL. *Application deadline:* For fall admission, 12/15 priority date for domestic and international students; for spring admission, 11/1 for domestic and international students. Applications are processed on a rolling basis. Application fee: $50. *Expenses:* Tuition: Part-time $1,080 per unit. Required fees: $56 per unit. $329 per term. Tuition and fees vary according to program. *Financial support:* Fellowships with full and partial tuition reimbursements, career-related internships or fieldwork, Federal Work-Study, institutionally sponsored loans, scholarships/grants, and tuition waivers (partial) available. Support available to part-time students. Financial award application deadline: 2/1; financial award applicants required to submit FAFSA. *Faculty research:* Second language acquisition, cross-cultural communication, technology-enhanced language learning, language variation, action learning. *Unit head:* Dr. Miriam Eisenstein Ebsworth, Director, 212-998-5460, Fax: 212-995-4049. *Application contact:* 212-998-5030, Fax: 212-995-4328, E-mail: steinhardt.gradadmissions@nyu.edu.

Northern Arizona University, Graduate College, College of Arts and Letters, Department of Modern Languages, Flagstaff, AZ 86011. Offers MAT.

Occidental College, Graduate Studies, Department of Education, Program in Secondary Education, Los Angeles, CA 90041-3314. Offers English and comparative literary studies (MAT); history (MAT); life science (MAT); mathematics (MAT); physical science (MAT); social science (MAT); Spanish (MAT). Part-time programs available. *Faculty:* 3 full-time (2 women), 2 part-time/adjunct (both women). *Students:* 4 full-time (all women), 3 part-time (1 woman);

includes 5 minority (1 Asian American or Pacific Islander, 4 Hispanic Americans). Average age 25. 4 applicants, 100% accepted, 4 enrolled. In 2006, 4 degrees awarded. *Degree requirements:* For master's, final exam, graduate synthesis paper. *Entrance requirements:* For master's, GRE General Test, minimum GPA of 3.0. Additional exam requirements/recommendations for international students: Required—TOEFL (minimum score 625 paper-based). *Application deadline:* For fall admission, 3/1 for domestic and international students; for spring admission, 10/1 for domestic and international students. Applications are processed on a rolling basis. Application fee: $50. *Expenses: Contact institution. Financial support:* Fellowships, Federal Work-Study, institutionally sponsored loans, and scholarships/grants available. Support available to part-time students. Financial award application deadline: 3/1; financial award applicants required to submit FAFSA. *Unit head:* Chair, 323-259-2781, E-mail: edudept@oxy.edu. *Application contact:* Angela Allen, Credential Analyst/Department Services Coordinator, 323-259-2781, E-mail: edudept@oxy.edu.

Portland State University, Graduate Studies, College of Liberal Arts and Sciences, Department of Foreign Languages and Literatures, Portland, OR 97207-0751. Offers foreign literature and language (MA); French (MA); German (MA); Japanese (MA); Spanish (MA). Part-time programs available. *Faculty:* 36 full-time (20 women), 23 part-time/adjunct (17 women). *Students:* 37 full-time (22 women), 13 part-time (10 women); includes 6 minority (1 African American, 1 Asian American or Pacific Islander, 4 Hispanic Americans), 7 international. Average age 32. 28 applicants, 79% accepted, 16 enrolled. In 2006, 18 master's awarded. *Degree requirements:* For master's, one foreign language, thesis (for some programs). *Entrance requirements:* Additional exam requirements/recommendations for international students: Required—TOEFL (minimum score 550 paper-based; 213 computer-based). *Application deadline:* For fall admission, 4/1 for domestic students, 3/1 for international students; for winter admission, 8/1 for domestic students, 7/1 for international students; for spring admission, 11/1 for domestic and international students. Applications are processed on a rolling basis. Application fee: $50. *Expenses:* Tuition: state resident: full-time $6,426; part-time $238 per credit. Tuition, nonresident: full-time $11,016; part-time $408 per credit. Tuition and fees vary according to course load. *Financial support:* In 2006–07, 5 teaching assistantships with full tuition reimbursements (averaging $7,921 per year) were awarded; research assistantships with full tuition reimbursements, Federal Work-Study, scholarships/grants, and unspecified assistantships also available. Support available to part-time students. Financial award application deadline: 3/1; financial award applicants required to submit FAFSA. *Faculty research:* Foreign language pedagogy, applied and social linguistics, literary history and criticism. Total annual research expenditures: $11,193. *Unit head:* Dr. Sandra F. Freels, Chair, 503-725-3522, Fax: 503-725-5276. *Application contact:* Karen Popp, Office Coordinator, 503-725-3522, E-mail: poppk@pdx.edu.

Purdue University, Graduate School, College of Liberal Arts, Department of Foreign Languages and Literatures, West Lafayette, IN 47907. Offers French (MA, MAT, PhD), including French (MA, PhD), French education (MAT); German (MA, MAT, PhD), including German (MA, PhD), German education (MAT); Spanish (MA, MAT, PhD), including Spanish (MA, PhD), Spanish education (MAT). *Faculty:* 42 full-time (17 women). *Students:* 56 full-time (33 women), 24 part-time (20 women); includes 7 minority (1 Asian American or Pacific Islander, 6 Hispanic Americans), 47 international. Average age 32. 44 applicants, 77% accepted, 22 enrolled. In 2006, 13 master's, 6 doctorates awarded. Terminal master's awarded for partial completion of doctoral program. *Degree requirements:* For master's, one foreign language; for doctorate, 2 foreign languages, thesis/dissertation. *Entrance requirements:* For master's and doctorate, GRE, writing sample, sample recording of English and language of study. Additional exam requirements/recommendations for international students: Required—TOEFL. *Application deadline:* For fall admission, 5/1 for domestic and international students; for spring admission, 10/1 for domestic and international students. Applications are processed on a rolling basis. Application fee: $55. Electronic applications accepted. *Financial support:* In 2006–07, 1 fellowship was awarded; teaching assistantships. Support available to part-time students. Financial award applicants required to submit FAFSA. *Faculty research:* Linguistics, semiotics, literary criticism, pedagogy. *Unit head:* Dr. Paul B. Dixon, Head, 765-494-3867. *Application contact:* Betty Lewis, Graduate Content, 765-494-3841, E-mail: lewisbl@purdue.edu.

Purdue University, Graduate School, School of Education, Department of Curriculum and Instruction, West Lafayette, IN 47907. Offers agricultural and extension education (PhD, Ed S); agriculture and extension education (MS, MS Ed); art education (PhD); consumer and family sciences and extension education (MS Ed, PhD, Ed S); curriculum studies (MS Ed, PhD, Ed S); educational technology (MS Ed, PhD, Ed S); elementary education (MS Ed); foreign language education (MS Ed, PhD, Ed S); industrial technology (PhD, Ed S); language arts (MS Ed, PhD, Ed S); literacy (MS Ed, PhD, Ed S); mathematics/science education (MS, MS Ed, PhD, Ed S); social studies (MS Ed, PhD); social studies education (Ed S); vocational/industrial education (MS Ed, PhD, Ed S); vocational/technical education (MS Ed, PhD, Ed S). *Accreditation:* NCATE. Part-time and evening/weekend programs available. *Faculty:* 26 full-time (13 women), 3 part-time/adjunct (all women). *Students:* 59 full-time (37 women), 112 part-time (70 women); includes 24 minority (13 African Americans, 3 American Indian/Alaska Native, 4 Asian Americans or Pacific Islanders, 4 Hispanic Americans), 38 international. Average age 35. 92 applicants, 68% accepted, 38 enrolled. In 2006, 52 master's, 23 doctorates awarded. *Degree requirements:* For master's, thesis optional; for doctorate, thesis/dissertation, oral and written exams; for Ed S, oral presentation, project. *Entrance requirements:* For master's, GRE General Test, minimum B average; for doctorate, GRE General Test; for Ed S, GRE, minimum B average. Additional exam requirements/recommendations for international students: Required—TOEFL. *Application deadline:* For fall admission, 1/15 priority date for domestic students, 1/15 for international students; for spring admission, 9/15 for domestic and international students. Applications are processed on a rolling basis. Application fee: $55. Electronic applications accepted. *Financial support:* In 2006–07, 3 fellowships with full tuition reimbursements (averaging $10,500 per year), 11 research assistantships with full tuition reimbursements (averaging $11,500 per year), 43 teaching assistantships with full tuition reimbursements (averaging $10,800 per year) were awarded; career-related internships or fieldwork and tuition waivers (full) also available. Support available to part-time students. Financial award application deadline: 3/1; financial award applicants required to submit FAFSA. *Faculty research:* Literacy acquisition and development, teacher beliefs and knowledge, recruitment and retention of underrepresented students, economic education, literacy discourse. *Unit head:* Dr. James D Lehman, Head, 765-494-7935, Fax: 765-496-1622. *Application contact:* Patricia Mason, Coordinator of Graduate Studies, 765-494-2345, Fax: 765-494-5832, E-mail: gradoffice@soe.purdue.edu.

Queens College of the City University of New York, Division of Graduate Studies, Division of Education, Department of Secondary Education, Flushing, NY 11367-1597. Offers art (MS Ed); biology (MS Ed, AC); chemistry (MS Ed, AC); earth sciences (MS Ed, AC); English (MS Ed, AC); French (MS Ed, AC); Italian (MS Ed, AC); mathematics (MS Ed, AC); music (MS Ed, AC); physics (MS Ed, AC); social studies (MS Ed, AC); Spanish (MS Ed, AC). Part-time and evening/weekend programs available. *Faculty:* 22 full-time (14 women). *Students:* 50 full-time (28 women), 974 part-time (627 women). 633 applicants, 82% accepted, 407 enrolled. In 2006, 227 degrees awarded. *Degree requirements:* For master's, research project; for AC, thesis optional. *Entrance requirements:* For master's, minimum GPA of 3.0. Additional exam requirements/recommendations for international students: Required—TOEFL. *Application deadline:* For fall admission, 4/1 for domestic students; for spring admission, 11/1 for domestic students. Applications are processed on a rolling basis. Application fee: $125. *Financial support:* Career-related internships or fieldwork, Federal Work-Study, institutionally sponsored loans, and tuition waivers (partial) available. Support available to part-time students. Financial award application deadline: 4/1; financial award applicants required to submit FAFSA. *Unit head:* Dr. Eleanor Armour-Thomas, Chairperson, 718-997-5150, E-mail: armourthomas@yahoo.com. *Application contact:* Mario Caruso, Director of Graduate Admissions, 718-997-5200, Fax: 718-997-5193, E-mail: graduate_admissions@qc.edu.

Quinnipiac University, Division of Education, Program in Secondary Education, Hamden, CT 06518-1940. Offers biology (MAT); chemistry (MAT); English (MAT); French (MAT); history/social studies (MAT); mathematics (MAT); physics (MAT); Spanish (MAT). *Faculty:* 7 full-time

(5 women), 23 part-time/adjunct (14 women). *Students:* 64 full-time (41 women); includes 5 minority (1 African American, 4 Hispanic Americans). Average age 26. 63 applicants, 87% accepted, 42 enrolled. In 2006, 37 degrees awarded. *Entrance requirements:* For master's, PRAXIS I, minimum GPA of 2.67, interview. Additional exam requirements/recommendations for international students: Required—TOEFL (minimum score 575 paper-based; 233 computer-based; 90 iBT), IELTS (minimum score 7). *Application deadline:* For fall admission, 3/15 priority date for domestic students. Applications are processed on a rolling basis. Application fee: $45. Electronic applications accepted. *Expenses:* Tuition: Part-time $675 per credit. Required fees: $30 per credit. *Financial support:* Career-related internships or fieldwork and tuition waivers (partial) available. Financial award application deadline: 4/15; financial award applicants required to submit FAFSA. *Faculty research:* Multicultural and urban education, role of technology in education, challenges of teaching divers learners, socio-cultural nature of learning. *Unit head:* Dr. Bernadine Krawczyk, Assistant Dean, Division of Education, 203-582-3510, Fax: 203-582-3473, E-mail: bernadine.krawczyk@quinnipiac.edu. *Application contact:* 800-462-1944, Fax: 203-582-3443, E-mail: graduate@quinnipiac.edu.

See Close-Up on page 911.

Rider University, Department of Graduate Education, Leadership and Counseling, Lawrenceville, NJ 08648-3001. Offers counseling services (MA, Ed S); curriculum, instruction and supervision (MA); director of school counseling services (Certificate); educational administration (MA); organizational leadership (MA); principal (Certificate); reading/language arts (MA, Certificate), including reading specialist (Certificate), reading/language arts (MA); school business administrator (Certificate); school counseling services (Certificate); school psychology (Ed S); special education (MA); supervisor (Certificate); teacher certification (Certificate), including business education, elementary education, English as a second language, English education, mathematics education, preschool to grade 3, science education, social studies education, world languages; teaching (MA). *Accreditation:* NCATE. Part-time and evening/weekend programs available. *Faculty:* 24 full-time (12 women), 30 part-time/adjunct (15 women). *Students:* 90 full-time (75 women), 457 part-time (369 women); includes 73 minority (50 African Americans, 2 American Indian/Alaska Native, 6 Asian Americans or Pacific Islanders, 15 Hispanic Americans), 1 international. Average age 32. 314 applicants, 61% accepted, 138 enrolled. In 2006, 116 master's, 19 other advanced degrees awarded. *Degree requirements:* For master's, thesis or alternative, internship, portfolios, comprehensive exam (for some programs); for other advanced degree, internship, professional portfolio. *Entrance requirements:* For master's, GRE (counseling, school psychology), MAT, interview, resumé, letters of recommendation; for other advanced degree, PRAXIS. Additional exam requirements/recommendations for international students: Required—TOEFL (minimum score 550 paper-based; 213 computer-based). *Application deadline:* For fall admission, 5/1 priority date for domestic students, 6/1 priority date for international students; for spring admission, 11/1 priority date for domestic and international students. Applications are processed on a rolling basis. Application fee: $50. Electronic applications accepted. *Expenses:* Tuition: Part-time $525 per credit. Required fees: $35 per course. $30 per semester. *Financial support:* In 2006–07, 271 students received support. Career-related internships or fieldwork, Federal Work-Study, institutionally sponsored loans, and unspecified assistantships available. Support available to part-time students. Financial award applicants required to submit FAFSA. *Faculty research:* Gifted students, self-esteem, hope and mental health, conflicts in group work, cultural diversity and counseling assessment of special needs in children. *Unit head:* Dr. Dennis C. Buss, Chair, 609-895-5353, Fax: 609-896-5362, E-mail: dbuss@rider.edu. *Application contact:* Jamie L Mitchell, Director of Graduate Admissions, 609-896-5036, Fax: 609-895-5680, E-mail: jmitchell@rider.edu.

See Close-Up on page 913.

Rivier College, School of Graduate Studies, Department of Modern Languages, Nashua, NH 03060-5086. Offers Spanish (MAT). Part-time and evening/weekend programs available. *Faculty:* 1 full-time (0 women), 1 part-time/adjunct (0 women). *Students:* 1 (woman) full-time, 10 part-time (9 women); includes 1 Hispanic American. Average age 37. In 2006, 5 degrees awarded. *Degree requirements:* For master's, registration. *Application deadline:* Applications are processed on a rolling basis. Application fee: $25. *Financial support:* Available to part-time students. Application deadline: 2/1; *Unit head:* Dr. Barry Jackson, Chairperson, 603-888-1311 Ext. 8204. *Application contact:* Diane Monahan, Director of Graduate Admissions, 603-897-8129, Fax: 603-897-8810, E-mail: gradadm@rivier.edu.

Rutgers, The State University of New Jersey, New Brunswick, Graduate School of Education, Department of Learning and Teaching, Program in Language Education, New Brunswick, NJ 08901-1281. Offers English as a second language education (Ed M); language education (Ed M, Ed D). Part-time programs available. *Faculty:* 3 full-time (2 women). *Students:* 34 full-time (31 women), 25 part-time (19 women). 92 applicants, 53% accepted, 29 enrolled. In 2006, 22 master's awarded. Terminal master's awarded for partial completion of doctoral program. *Degree requirements:* For master's, comprehensive exam; for doctorate, thesis/dissertation, concept paper, qualifying exam. *Entrance requirements:* For master's, GRE General Test, minimum GPA of 3.0; for doctorate, GRE General Test, minimum GPA of 3.5. Additional exam requirements/recommendations for international students: Required—TOEFL. *Application deadline:* For fall admission, 2/1 for domestic and international students. Application fee: $60. Electronic applications accepted. *Financial support:* Application deadline: 3/15; *Faculty research:* Linguistics, sociolinguistics, cross-cultural/international communication. *Unit head:* Dr. Mary Curran, Coordinator, 732-932-7496 Ext. 8101, Fax: 732-932-7552, E-mail: mcurran@rci.rutgers.edu.

Rutgers, The State University of New Jersey, New Brunswick, Graduate School, Program in French, New Brunswick, NJ 08901-1281. Offers French (MA, PhD); French studies (MAT). Part-time and evening/weekend programs available. Terminal master's awarded for partial completion of doctoral program. *Degree requirements:* For master's, one foreign language, thesis optional; for doctorate, 3 foreign languages, thesis/dissertation. *Entrance requirements:* For master's and doctorate, GRE General Test. *Faculty research:* Literatures in French, literary history and theory, rhetoric and poetics.

Rutgers, The State University of New Jersey, New Brunswick, Graduate School, Program in Italian, New Brunswick, NJ 08901-1281. Offers Italian (MA); Italian literature and literary criticism (MA, PhD); language, literature and civilization (MAT). Part-time and evening/weekend programs available. Terminal master's awarded for partial completion of doctoral program. *Degree requirements:* For master's, one foreign language, thesis optional; for doctorate, 2 foreign languages, thesis/dissertation. *Entrance requirements:* For master's and doctorate, GRE General Test. Additional exam requirements/recommendations for international students: Required—TOEFL. *Faculty research:* Literature.

St. John Fisher College, Office of the Provost, Ralph C. Wilson Jr. School of Education, Adolescence Education Program, Rochester, NY 14618-3597. Offers adolescence English (MS Ed); adolescence French (MS Ed); adolescence social studies (MS Ed); adolescence Spanish (MS Ed). Part-time and evening/weekend programs available. *Faculty:* 4 full-time (2 women), 2 part-time/adjunct (1 woman). *Students:* Average age 31. 35 applicants, 91% accepted, 25 enrolled. In 2006, 13 degrees awarded. *Degree requirements:* For master's, student teaching, capstone project, field experiences; for degree. *Entrance requirements:* For master's, GRE (if GPA is below 3.0), minimum GPA of 3.0, 30 hours in certification area, 2 letters of reference, personal statement. Additional exam requirements/recommendations for international students: Required—TOEFL (minimum score 575 paper-based; 233 computer-based; 80 iBT). *Application deadline:* For fall admission, 4/1 for domestic students; for spring admission, 10/30 for domestic students. Applications are processed on a rolling basis. Application fee: $30. *Expenses:* Tuition: Part-time $615 per credit. Tuition and fees vary according to program. *Financial support:* In 2006–07, 1 student received support. Federal Work-Study and scholarships/grants available. Financial award application deadline: 2/15; financial award applicants required to submit FAFSA. *Faculty research:* Arts and humanities, urban schools, constructivist learning, at risk students, mentoring. *Unit head:* Dr. Russell Coward, Director,

Foreign Languages Education

St. John Fisher College (continued)
585-385-8114, E-mail: rcoward@sjfc.edu. *Application contact:* Shannon Cleverley, Director of Graduate Admissions, 585-385-8161, Fax: 585-385-8344, E-mail: scleverley@sjfc.edu.

Salisbury University, Graduate Division, Department of Education, Salisbury, MD 21801-6837. Offers art (MAT); biology (MAT); business education (MAT); chemistry (MAT); early childhood education (M Ed); educational administration (M Ed); elementary education (M Ed); English (M Ed, MAT); French (MAT); geography (MAT); history (MAT); mathematics (MAT); media and technology (MAT); music (MAT); psychology (MAT); reading education (MAT); science (MAT); secondary education (MAT); social studies (MAT); Spanish (MAT). *Accreditation:* NCATE. Part-time and evening/weekend programs available. *Faculty:* 12 full-time (6 women), 10 part-time/adjunct (8 women). *Students:* 17 full-time (9 women), 84 part-time (72 women); includes 6 minority (5 African Americans, 1 Hispanic American). Average age 30. 15 applicants, 73% accepted, 11 enrolled. In 2006, 63 degrees awarded. *Degree requirements:* For master's, comprehensive exam (for some programs). *Entrance requirements:* For master's, PRAXIS, minimum GPA of 2.75. Additional exam requirements/recommendations for international students: Required—TOEFL (minimum score 550 paper-based; 213 computer-based). *Application deadline:* For fall admission, 8/1 priority date for domestic students; for spring admission, 1/1 for domestic students. Applications are processed on a rolling basis. Application fee: $45. *Expenses:* Tuition, state resident: part-time $260 per credit hour. Tuition, nonresident: part-time $546 per credit hour. Required fees: $52 per credit hour. *Financial support:* In 2006–07, 3 teaching assistantships with full tuition reimbursements were awarded; career-related internships or fieldwork and scholarships/grants also available. Support available to part-time students. Financial award applicants required to submit FAFSA. *Faculty research:* Middle-level education, student outcomes. *Unit head:* Dr. Edward C. Robeck, Program Coordinator, 410-543-6292, Fax: 410-548-2593, E-mail: ecrobeck@salisbury.edu. *Application contact:* Debra J. Clark, Administrative Assistant I, 410-543-6281, Fax: 410-548-2593, E-mail: djclark@salisbury.edu.

School for International Training, Graduate Programs, Programs in Language Teacher Education, Brattleboro, VT 05302-0676. Offers English for speakers of other languages (MAT); French (MAT); Spanish (MAT). *Students:* 55 full-time (45 women), 85 part-time (61 women); includes 15 minority (6 African Americans, 2 American Indian/Alaska Native, 1 Asian American or Pacific Islander, 6 Hispanic Americans), 33 international. Average age 32. 186 applicants, 81% accepted, 85 enrolled. In 2006, 61 degrees awarded. *Degree requirements:* For master's, one foreign language, thesis, practice teaching. *Entrance requirements:* For master's, 4 letters of reference. Additional exam requirements/recommendations for international students: Required—TOEFL. *Application deadline:* Applications are processed on a rolling basis. Application fee: $50. *Expenses:* Tuition: Full-time $27,355; part-time $638 per credit hour. Required fees: $1,092. *Financial support:* Career-related internships or fieldwork, Federal Work-Study, institutionally sponsored loans, and scholarships/grants available. Financial award application deadline: 3/1; financial award applicants required to submit FAFSA. *Unit head:* Marla Solomon, Graduate Dean, 802-258-3325, Fax: 802-258-3241, E-mail: marla.solomon@sit.edu. *Application contact:* Information Contact, 800-336-1616, Fax: 802-258-3500, E-mail: admissions@sit.edu.

Smith College, Graduate Programs, Department of Education and Child Study, Program in Secondary Education, Northampton, MA 01063. Offers biological sciences education (MAT); chemistry education (MAT); English education (MAT); French education (MAT); geology education (MAT); government education (MAT); history education (MAT); mathematics education (MAT); physics education (MAT); Spanish education (MAT). Part-time programs available. *Faculty:* 6 full-time (4 women), 3 part-time/adjunct (2 women). *Students:* 4 full-time (2 women). Average age 36. 12 applicants, 67% accepted, 3 enrolled. In 2006, 5 master's awarded. *Entrance requirements:* For master's, GRE General Test. Additional exam requirements/recommendations for international students: Required—TOEFL. *Application deadline:* For fall admission, 4/1 for domestic students, 1/15 for international students; for spring admission, 12/1 for domestic students. Application fee: $60. *Expenses:* Tuition: Full-time $32,320; part-time $1,010 per credit. Tuition and fees vary according to course load. *Financial support:* In 2006–07, 3 students received support. Career-related internships or fieldwork, institutionally sponsored loans, and scholarships/grants available. Support available to part-time students. Financial award application deadline: 1/15; financial award applicants required to submit CSS PROFILE or FAFSA. *Unit head:* Rosetta Cohen, Graduate Student Advisor, 413-585-3266.

Southern Illinois University Edwardsville, Graduate Studies and Research, School of Education, Department of Curriculum and Instruction, Program in Secondary Education, Edwardsville, IL 62026-0001. Offers art (MS Ed); biology (MS Ed); chemistry (MS Ed); English (MS Ed); foreign languages (MS Ed); history (MS Ed); mathematics (MS Ed); physics (MS Ed); reading (MS Ed); science (MS Ed). *Accreditation:* NCATE. Part-time and evening/weekend programs available. *Students:* 2 full-time (both women), 23 part-time (14 women); includes 2 minority (both African Americans) Average age 33. 12 applicants, 42% accepted. In 2006, 10 degrees awarded. *Degree requirements:* For master's, thesis or alternative, final exam. *Entrance requirements:* For master's, MAT. Additional exam requirements/recommendations for international students: Required—TOEFL. *Application deadline:* For fall admission, 7/20 for domestic students, 6/1 for international students; for spring admission, 12/14 for domestic students, 10/1 for international students. Application fee: $30. Electronic applications accepted. *Financial support:* Fellowships, research assistantships, teaching assistantships, Federal Work-Study, institutionally sponsored loans, and unspecified assistantships available. Support available to part-time students. Financial award application deadline: 3/1; financial award applicants required to submit FAFSA. *Unit head:* Dr. David DeWeese, Director, 618-650-3432, E-mail: ddewees@siue.edu.

Stanford University, School of Education, Teacher Education Program, Stanford, CA 94305-9991. Offers English education (MA); languages education (MA); mathematics education (MA); science education (MA); social studies education (MA). *Degree requirements:* For master's, thesis. *Entrance requirements:* For master's, GRE General Test. Electronic applications accepted.

State University of New York at Binghamton, Graduate School, School of Education, Program in Secondary Education, Binghamton, NY 13902-6000. Offers biology education (MAT, MS Ed, MST); earth science education (MAT, MS Ed, MST); English education (MAT, MS Ed, MST); French education (MAT, MST); mathematical sciences education (MAT, MS Ed, MST); physics (MAT, MS Ed, MST); social studies (MAT, MS Ed, MST); Spanish education (MAT, MST). *Accreditation:* Teacher Education Accreditation Council. Part-time and evening/weekend programs available. *Students:* 89 full-time (50 women), 47 part-time (32 women); includes 6 minority (1 African American, 3 Asian Americans or Pacific Islanders, 2 Hispanic Americans). Average age 29. 72 applicants, 72% accepted, 23 enrolled. In 2006, 44 degrees awarded. *Entrance requirements:* For master's, GRE General Test. Additional exam requirements/recommendations for international students: Required—TOEFL. *Application deadline:* For fall admission, 4/15 priority date for domestic students, 1/15 priority date for international students; for spring admission, 11/1 for domestic students, 10/1 priority date for international students. Applications are processed on a rolling basis. Application fee: $60. Electronic applications accepted. *Financial support:* In 2006–07, 25 students received support, including 2 fellowships with partial tuition reimbursements available (averaging $2,350 per year), 4 research assistantships with full and partial tuition reimbursements available (averaging $6,638 per year), 13 teaching assistantships with full tuition reimbursements available (averaging $5,944 per year); career-related internships or fieldwork, Federal Work-Study, institutionally sponsored loans, tuition waivers (full and partial), and unspecified assistantships also available. Support available to part-time students. Financial award application deadline: 2/15. *Unit head:* Dr. Thomas O'Brien, Coordinator, 607-777-7329, E-mail: tobrien@binghamton.edu.

State University of New York at Plattsburgh, Division of Education, Health, and Human Services, Department of Adolescence Education/Health, Plattsburgh, NY 12901-2681. Offers adolescence education (MST); biology 7-12 (MST); chemistry 7-12 (MST); earth science 7-12 (MST); English 7-12 (MST); French 7-12 (MST); mathematics 7-12 (MST); physics 7-12 (MST); social studies 7-12 (MST); Spanish 7-12 (MST). *Faculty:* 4 full-time (3 women), 2 part-time/adjunct (0 women). *Students:* 58 full-time (38 women), 14 part-time (10 women); includes 5 minority (1 African American, 4 Hispanic Americans). Average age 30. 49 applicants, 78% accepted, 32 enrolled. In 2006, 30 degrees awarded. *Degree requirements:* For master's, comprehensive exam or research project. *Entrance requirements:* For master's, GRE General Test or MAT, minimum GPA of 2.5. *Application deadline:* For fall admission, 2/15 priority date for domestic students; for spring admission, 10/15 priority date for domestic students. Applications are processed on a rolling basis. Application fee: $50. *Expenses:* Tuition, state resident: full-time $6,900; part-time $288 per credit hour. Tuition, nonresident: full-time $10,920; part-time $455 per credit hour. *Financial support:* Application deadline: 4/15; *Unit head:* Dr. Lois Beach, Chair, 578-564-5750, E-mail: lois.beach@plattsburgh.edu. *Application contact:* Sharon Derr, Assistant Director, Graduate Admission, 518-564-4723, Fax: 518-564-4722, E-mail: derrsl@plattsburgh.edu.

State University of New York College at Cortland, Graduate Studies, School of Arts and Sciences, Programs in Adolescence Education, Cortland, NY 13045. Offers biology (MAT, MS Ed); chemistry (MAT, MS Ed); earth science (MAT, MS Ed); English (MS Ed); French (MS Ed); mathematics (MAT, MS Ed); physics (MAT, MS Ed); social studies (MS Ed); Spanish (MS Ed). *Accreditation:* NCATE. Part-time and evening/weekend programs available. *Degree requirements:* For master's, one foreign language, thesis (for some programs), comprehensive exam (for some programs). *Entrance requirements:* For master's, GRE General Test.

Stony Brook University, State University of New York, School of Professional Development, Stony Brook, NY 11794. Offers adolescence education: mathematics (Certificate); biology 7-12 (MAT); chemistry-grade 7-12 (MAT); coaching (Certificate); computer integrated engineering (Certificate); cultural studies (Certificate); earth science-grade 7-12 (MAT); educational computing (Advanced Certificate, Certificate); English-grade 7-12 (MAT); environmental and waste management (MS, Advanced Certificate); environmental systems management (Certificate); environmental/occupational health and safety (Certificate); French-grade 7-12 (MAT); German-grade 7-12 (MAT); human resource management (Certificate); industrial management (Certificate); information systems management (Certificate); Italian-grade 7-12 (MAT); liberal studies (MA); liberal studies online (MA); Long Island regional studies (Certificate); operation research (Certificate); physics-grade 7-12 (MAT); Russian-grade 7-12 (MAT); school administration and supervision (Certificate); school district administration (Certificate); social science and the professions (MPS), including human resources management, labor management, public affairs, waste management; social studies 7-12 (MAT); waste management (Certificate); women's studies (Certificate). Part-time and evening/weekend programs available. Postbaccalaureate distance learning degree programs offered. *Faculty:* 1 full-time (0 women), 118 part-time/adjunct (45 women). *Students:* 322 full-time (202 women), 1,188 part-time (728 women); includes 164 minority (69 African Americans, 2 American Indian/Alaska Native, 29 Asian Americans or Pacific Islanders, 64 Hispanic Americans), 11 international. Average age 28. In 2006, 738 master's, 405 other advanced degrees awarded. *Degree requirements:* For master's, one foreign language, thesis or alternative. *Application deadline:* Applications are processed on a rolling basis. Application fee: $62. *Expenses:* Tuition, state resident: full-time $6,900; part-time $288 per credit. Tuition, nonresident: full-time $10,920; part-time $455 per credit. *Financial support:* In 2006–07, 5 teaching assistantships were awarded; fellowships, research assistantships, career-related internships or fieldwork also available. Support available to part-time students. *Unit head:* Dr. Paul J. Edelson, Dean, 631-632-7052, Fax: 631-632-9046, E-mail: paul.edelson@sunysb.edu. *Application contact:* Sandra Romansky, Director of Admissions and Advisement, 631-632-7050, Fax: 631-632-9046, E-mail: sandra.romansky@sunysb.edu.

Teachers College Columbia University, Graduate Faculty of Education, Department of Arts and Humanities, Program in Teaching of Spanish, New York, NY 10027-6696. Offers Ed M, MA, Ed D, Ed DCT, PhD. *Accreditation:* NCATE. Part-time programs available. *Students:* Average age 58. In 2006, 1 degree awarded. Terminal master's awarded for partial completion of doctoral program. *Degree requirements:* For doctorate, thesis/dissertation. *Application deadline:* For fall admission, 5/15 for domestic students; for spring admission, 12/1 for domestic students. Application fee: $65. *Expenses:* Tuition: Full-time $23,400; part-time $975 per credit. Required fees: $320 per term. *Financial support:* Career-related internships or fieldwork, Federal Work-Study, institutionally sponsored loans, and tuition waivers (full and partial) available. Support available to part-time students. Financial award application deadline: 2/1. *Faculty research:* Content of teacher training, curriculum, applied linguistics in the teaching of Spanish, distance learning, poetry in Spanish. *Application contact:* Mark E. Stearns, Associate Director of Admission, 212-678-3710, Fax: 212-678-4171.

Temple University, Graduate School, College of Education, Department of Curriculum, Instruction, and Technology in Education, Philadelphia, PA 19122-6096. Offers applied behavioral analysis (MS Ed); career and technical education (MS Ed); early childhood education and elementary education (MS Ed); English education (MS Ed); language arts education (Ed D); math/science education (Ed D); mathematics education (MS Ed); science education (MS Ed); second and foreign language education (MS Ed); special education (MS Ed); teaching English as a second language (MS Ed). Part-time and evening/weekend programs available. *Faculty:* 31 full-time (14 women). *Students:* 96 full-time (71 women), 482 part-time (336 women); includes 109 minority (67 African Americans, 3 American Indian/Alaska Native, 23 Asian Americans or Pacific Islanders, 16 Hispanic Americans), 28 international. 308 applicants, 64% accepted, 116 enrolled. In 2006, 225 master's, 21 doctorates awarded. Terminal master's awarded for partial completion of doctoral program. *Degree requirements:* For master's, thesis or alternative; for doctorate, thesis/dissertation. *Entrance requirements:* For master's and doctorate, GRE General Test or MAT, minimum GPA of 3.0. Additional exam requirements/recommendations for international students: Required—TOEFL (minimum score 550 paper-based; 213 computer-based; 79 iBT). *Application deadline:* For fall admission, 4/1 for domestic students, 12/15 for international students; for spring admission, 10/1 for domestic students, 8/1 for international students. Application fee: $50. Electronic applications accepted. *Expenses:* Tuition, state resident: full-time $12,264; part-time $511 per credit. Tuition, nonresident: full-time $17,904; part-time $746 per credit. Required fees: $84 per course. Tuition and fees vary according to program. *Financial support:* Fellowships, research assistantships with full tuition reimbursements, teaching assistantships with full tuition reimbursements available. Financial award application deadline: 1/15; financial award applicants required to submit FAFSA. *Faculty research:* School improvement, problem solving, literacy, language development. *Unit head:* Dr. Thomas Walker, Chair, 215-204-2117, Fax: 215-204-1414, E-mail: tjwalker@temple.edu.

Texas A&M International University, Office of Graduate Studies and Research, College of Arts and Sciences, Department of Language and Literature, Laredo, TX 78041-1900. Offers English (MA); Hispanic studies (PhD); Spanish (MA). *Faculty:* 5 full-time (0 women). *Students:* 1 (woman) full-time, 12 part-time (10 women); all minorities (all Hispanic Americans) Average age 31. 6 applicants, 83% accepted, 1 enrolled. In 2006, 10 degrees awarded. *Entrance requirements:* For master's, GRE General Test. Additional exam requirements/recommendations for international students: Required—TOEFL (minimum score 550 paper-based; 213 computer-based). *Application deadline:* For fall admission, 7/15 priority date for domestic students; for spring admission, 11/12 for domestic students. Applications are processed on a rolling basis. Application fee: $25. *Expenses:* Tuition, state resident: full-time $1,580. Tuition, nonresident: full-time $5,432. Required fees: $3,808. *Financial support:* In 2006–07, 5 students received support. Application deadline: 11/1. *Unit head:* Dr. Sean Chadwell, Chair, 956-326-2471, E-mail: schadwell@tamiu.edu. *Application contact:* Rosie Espinoza-Dickinson, Director of Admissions, 956-326-2200, Fax: 956-326-2199, E-mail: enroll@tamiu.edu.

Texas A&M University–Kingsville, College of Graduate Studies, College of Arts and Sciences, Department of Language and Literature, Kingsville, TX 78363. Offers English (MA, MS); Spanish (MA). Part-time and evening/weekend programs available. *Degree requirements:*

For master's, thesis or alternative, comprehensive exam. *Entrance requirements:* For master's, GRE General Test, minimum GPA of 3.0. Additional exam requirements/recommendations for international students: Required—TOEFL. *Faculty research:* Linguistics, culture, Spanish American literature, Spanish peninsular literature, American literature.

Union Graduate College, School of Education, Schenectady, NY 12308-3107. Offers biology (MAT, MS); chemistry (MAT); earth science (MAT); English (MAT); French (MAT); general science (MAT); German (MAT); languages (MAT); Latin (MAT); mathematics (MAT); mathematics and technology (MS); physical science (MS); physics (MAT); social studies (MAT); Spanish (MAT). *Accreditation:* Teacher Education Accreditation Council. *Faculty:* 5 full-time (1 woman), 19 part-time/adjunct (10 women). *Students:* 57 full-time (36 women), 21 part-time (14 women); includes 2 African Americans, 2 Hispanic Americans, 2 international. Average age 31. 59 applicants, 83% accepted, 39 enrolled. In 2006, 56 degrees awarded. *Degree requirements:* For master's, thesis or project. *Entrance requirements:* For master's, minimum GPA of 3.0, letters of recommendation. Additional exam requirements/recommendations for international students: Required—TOEFL (minimum score 550 paper-based; 213 computer-based). Application fee: $60. *Expenses: Contact institution. Financial support:* In 2006–07, 12 research assistantships with tuition reimbursements (averaging $3,000 per year) were awarded; Federal Work-Study, scholarships/grants, health care benefits, and tuition waivers (partial) also available. Support available to part-time students. Financial award applicants required to submit FAFSA. *Unit head:* Dr. Patrick Allen, Dean, 518-388-6361, Fax: 518-388-6686, E-mail: mat@union.edu. *Application contact:* Rhonda Sheehan, Director of Graduate Admissions Registrar, 518-388-6238, Fax: 518-388-6686, E-mail: sheehanr@union.edu.

See Close-Up on page 923.

Universidad del Este, Graduate School, Carolina, PR 00983. Offers accounting (MBA); administration (M Ed); criminal justice and criminology (MA); education (M Ed); elementary education (M Ed); human resources (MBA); management (MBA); social work (MA); teaching English (M Ed); teaching Spanish (M Ed).

University at Buffalo, the State University of New York, Graduate School, Graduate School of Education, Department of Learning and Instruction, Buffalo, NY 14260. Offers adolescence education (Certificate); biology (Ed M); chemistry (Ed M); childhood education (Ed M); early childhood and childhood education with bilingual extension (Ed M); early childhood education (Ed M); earth science (Ed M); elementary education (Ed D, PhD); English (Ed M); English education (PhD); English for speakers of other languages (Ed M); foreign and second language education (PhD); French (Ed M); general education (Ed M); German (Ed M); Italian (Ed M); Japanese (Ed M); Latin (Ed M); literary specialist (Ed M); mathematics (Ed M); mathematics education (PhD); mentoring teachers (Certificate); music education (Ed M, Certificate); physics (Ed M); reading education (PhD); Russian (Ed M); school administrator and supervisor (Certificate); science education (PhD); social studies (Ed M); Spanish (Ed M); special education (PhD); teaching and leading for diversity (Certificate); teaching English to speakers of other languages (Ed M). Part-time and evening/weekend programs available. Postbaccalaureate distance learning degree programs offered (no on-campus study). *Faculty:* 30 full-time (20 women), 53 part-time/adjunct (38 women). *Students:* 368 full-time (269 women), 297 part-time (226 women); includes 50 minority (15 African Americans, 2 American Indian/Alaska Native, 14 Asian Americans or Pacific Islanders, 19 Hispanic Americans), 66 international. Average age 31. 638 applicants, 75% accepted, 298 enrolled. In 2006, 248 master's, 18 doctorates, 48 other advanced degrees awarded. Terminal master's awarded for partial completion of doctoral program. *Degree requirements:* For master's, comprehensive exam, registration; for doctorate, thesis/dissertation, research analysis exam, research experience component. *Entrance requirements:* For doctorate, GRE General Test or MAT, interview, writing sample, letters of recommendation. Additional exam requirements/recommendations for international students: Required—TOEFL (minimum score 600 paper-based; 250 computer-based). *Application deadline:* For fall admission, 2/1 priority date for domestic and international students; for spring admission, 11/15 priority date for domestic students, 10/1 for international students. Applications are processed on a rolling basis. Application fee: $50. Electronic applications accepted. *Financial support:* In 2006–07, 70 students received support, including 6 fellowships with full tuition reimbursements available (averaging $10,000 per year), 16 research assistantships with full tuition reimbursements available (averaging $9,000 per year), teaching assistantships with full tuition reimbursements available (averaging $9,000 per year); career-related internships or fieldwork, Federal Work-Study, institutionally sponsored loans, scholarships/grants, tuition waivers (partial), and unspecified assistantships also available. Financial award application deadline: 2/28; financial award applicants required to submit FAFSA. *Faculty research:* Science assessment, state-level testing, early learning, literacy, second language acquisition. Total annual research expenditures: $432,366. *Unit head:* Dr. Maria E. Runfola, Chair, 716-645-2455, Fax: 716-645-3161. *Application contact:* Barbara Belz, Admissions Secretary, 716-645-2110 Ext. 1159, Fax: 716-645-3161, E-mail: belz@buffalo.edu.

The University of Arizona, Graduate College, College of Humanities, Department of Russian and Slavic Studies, Tucson, AZ 85721. Offers Russian (M Ed, MA). Part-time programs available. *Faculty:* 8. *Students:* 10 full-time (5 women), 6 part-time (4 women); includes 1 minority (Hispanic American), 1 international. Average age 31. 8 applicants, 75% accepted, 5 enrolled. In 2006, 3 degrees awarded. *Degree requirements:* For master's, one foreign language, thesis (for some programs), comprehensive exam (for some programs). *Entrance requirements:* For master's, department language proficiency exam, minimum GPA of 3.0. Additional exam requirements/recommendations for international students: Required—TOEFL. *Application deadline:* For fall admission, 8/1 for domestic students. Applications are processed on a rolling basis. Application fee: $50. Electronic applications accepted. *Financial support:* In 2006–07, 16 students received support, including 7 teaching assistantships with full tuition reimbursements available (averaging $13,500 per year); fellowships, Federal Work-Study, scholarships/grants, and tuition waivers (full) also available. *Faculty research:* Russian literature, language/pedagogy, linguistics, Russian culture. *Unit head:* Dr. Teresa Polowy, Head, 520-621-7341, Fax: 520-626-4007, E-mail: tpolowy@email.arizona.edu. *Application contact:* Judi Greil, Coordinator, 520-621-3702, Fax: 520-626-4007, E-mail: greilj@u.arizona.edu.

The University of Arizona, Graduate College, College of Humanities, Department of Spanish and Portuguese, Tucson, AZ 85721. Offers Spanish (M Ed, MA, PhD). *Faculty:* 19 full-time (8 women), 5 part-time/adjunct (3 women). *Students:* 72 full-time (40 women), 8 part-time (5 women); includes 59 minority (all Hispanic Americans), 21 international. Average age 36. 42 applicants, 26% accepted, 11 enrolled. In 2006, 11 master's, 3 doctorates awarded. Terminal master's awarded for partial completion of doctoral program. *Median time to degree:* Of those who began their doctoral program in fall 1998, 50% received their degree in 8 years or less. *Degree requirements:* For master's, one foreign language, comprehensive exam; for doctorate, 3 foreign languages, thesis/dissertation, comprehensive exam. *Entrance requirements:* For master's and doctorate, GRE General Test, BA in Spanish, minimum GPA of 3.0. Additional exam requirements/recommendations for international students: Required—TOEFL (minimum score 550 paper-based; 213 computer-based). *Application deadline:* For fall admission, 2/15 for domestic and international students; for spring admission, 8/1 for domestic and international students. Applications are processed on a rolling basis. Application fee: $50. *Financial support:* In 2006–07, 7 fellowships with full tuition reimbursements (averaging $2,888 per year), 85 teaching assistantships with partial tuition reimbursements (averaging $12,597 per year) were awarded; institutionally sponsored loans, scholarships/grants, health care benefits, and tuition waivers (full) also available. Financial award application deadline: 2/15. *Faculty research:* Spanish and Latin American literature and linguistics, literary theory. *Unit head:* Dr. Malcolm A. Compitello, Head, 520-621-3123. *Application contact:* Isela Gonzales, Graduate Secretary, 520-621-3125, Fax: 520-621-6104, E-mail: iselag@email.arizona.edu.

University of Calgary, Faculty of Graduate Studies, Faculty of Education, Graduate Division of Educational Research, Calgary, AB T2N 1N4, Canada. Offers community rehabilitation and disability studies (M Ed, M Sc, Ed D, PhD, Graduate Certificate, Graduate Diploma); curriculum, teaching and learning (M Ed, M Sc, MA, Ed D, PhD, Graduate Certificate, Graduate Diploma); educational contexts (M Ed, MA, Ed D, PhD, Graduate Certificate, Graduate Diploma); educational leadership (M Ed, MA, Ed D, PhD, Graduate Certificate, Graduate Diploma); educational technology (M Ed, M Sc, MA, Ed D, PhD, Graduate Certificate, Graduate Diploma); gifted education (M Sc, MA, Ed D, PhD, Graduate Certificate, Graduate Diploma); higher education administration (Ed D); interpretive studies in education (M Ed, M Sc, MA, Ed D, PhD, Graduate Certificate, Graduate Diploma); second language teaching (M Ed, Ed D, PhD, Graduate Certificate, Graduate Diploma); teaching English as a second language (M Ed, M Sc, MA, Ed D, PhD, Graduate Certificate, Graduate Diploma); workplace and adult learning (M Ed, MA, Ed D, PhD, Graduate Certificate, Graduate Diploma). Ed D in both higher education administration and educational leadership offered via distance delivery. Part-time and evening/weekend programs available. Postbaccalaureate distance learning degree programs offered (minimal on-campus study). *Faculty:* 44 full-time, 52 part-time/adjunct. *Students:* 488 full-time, 550 part-time. 400 applicants, 50% accepted. In 2006, 102 master's, 18 doctorates awarded. *Degree requirements:* For master's, thesis (for some programs); for doctorate, thesis/dissertation, candidacy exam. *Entrance requirements:* For master's, minimum GPA of 3.0, 3 letters of reference; for doctorate, minimum GPA of 3.5, 3 letters of reference; for other advanced degree, minimum GPA of 3.0. Additional exam requirements/recommendations for international students: Required—TOEFL, IELTS. *Application deadline:* For fall admission, 2/15 for domestic students, 2/5 for international students; for winter admission, 6/15 for domestic and international students. Application fee: $100. Electronic applications accepted. *Financial support:* In 2006–07, research assistantships (averaging $3,920 per year); teaching assistantships, career-related internships or fieldwork, scholarships/grants, and unspecified assistantships also available. Financial award application deadline: 2/1. *Faculty research:* Curriculum, leadership, technology, contexts, gifted, second language teaching, work place and adult learning. *Unit head:* Dr. Charles F. Webber, Associate Dean, 403-220-5675, Fax: 403-282-3005, E-mail: cwebber@ucalgary.ca. *Application contact:* Patricia A. Brown, Program Officer, Graduate Division of Educational Research, 403-220-3178, Fax: 403-282-3005, E-mail: brownp@ucalgary.ca.

University of California, Irvine, Office of Graduate Studies, School of Humanities, Department of Spanish and Portuguese, Irvine, CA 92697. Offers Spanish (MA, MAT, PhD). *Students:* 40 full-time (27 women), 1 (woman) part-time; includes 25 minority (1 Asian American or Pacific Islander, 24 Hispanic Americans), 3 international. In 2006, 1 master's, 1 doctorate awarded. *Degree requirements:* For doctorate, thesis/dissertation. *Entrance requirements:* For master's and doctorate, GRE General Test, minimum GPA of 3.0. Additional exam requirements/recommendations for international students: Required—TOEFL (minimum score 550 paper-based; 213 computer-based). *Application deadline:* For fall admission, 1/15 priority date for domestic students; for winter admission, 10/15 priority date for domestic students. Applications are processed on a rolling basis. Application fee: $60. Electronic applications accepted. *Financial support:* Fellowships, teaching assistantships, institutionally sponsored loans, traineeships, health care benefits, and unspecified assistantships available. Financial award application deadline: 3/1; financial award applicants required to submit FAFSA. *Faculty research:* Latin American literature, Spanish literature, Spanish linguistics in Creole studies, Hispanic literature in the U.S., Luso-Brazilian literature. *Unit head:* Ana Paula Ferreira, Chair, 949-824-7265, Fax: 949-824-2803, E-mail: apferrei@uci.edu. *Application contact:* Linda T. Le, Graduate Coordinator, 949-824-8793, Fax: 949-824-2803, E-mail: ttle@uci.edu.

University of Central Arkansas, Graduate School, College of Liberal Arts, Department of Foreign Languages, Conway, AR 72035-0001. Offers MA. Part-time programs available. *Faculty:* 7 full-time (3 women). *Students:* 4 full-time (1 woman), 21 part-time (15 women); includes 2 minority (both African Americans) 18 applicants, 100% accepted, 18 enrolled. *Degree requirements:* For master's, one foreign language, comprehensive exam. *Entrance requirements:* For master's, GRE General Test, minimum GPA of 2.7. Additional exam requirements/recommendations for international students: Required—TOEFL (minimum score 550 paper-based; 213 computer-based). *Application deadline:* For fall admission, 3/1 priority date for domestic and international students; for spring admission, 10/1 priority date for domestic and international students. Application fee: $25 ($40 for international students). *Expenses:* Tuition, state resident: full-time $4,194; part-time $233 per semester. Tuition, nonresident: full-time $5,963; part-time $429 per semester. International tuition: $6,162 full-time. Required fees: $65; $23 per semester. One-time fee: $65 part-time. *Financial support:* In 2006–07, 2 teaching assistantships with partial tuition reimbursements (averaging $10,000 per year) were awarded. Financial award application deadline: 2/15; financial award applicants required to submit FAFSA. *Unit head:* Dr. Phillip Bailey, Chair, 501-450-5645, Fax: 501-450-5185, E-mail: phillipb@mail.uca.edu. *Application contact:* Brenda Herring, Admissions Assistant, 501-450-5065, Fax: 501-450-5678, E-mail: bherring@uca.edu.

University of Central Florida, College of Education, Department of Teaching and Learning Principles, Orlando, FL 32816. Offers art education (M Ed, MA); coaching (Certificate); educational media (M Ed); elementary education (M Ed, MA); English language arts education (M Ed, MA); foreign language education (Certificate); health and wellness (Certificate); K-8 mathematics and science education (M Ed, Certificate); mathematics education (M Ed, MA); music education (M Ed, MA); online educational media (Certificate); reading education (M Ed, MA, Certificate); science education (M Ed, MA); social science education (M Ed, MA); sports leadership (Certificate); vocational education (M Ed, MA); world studies education (Certificate); writing education (Certificate). Part-time and evening/weekend programs available. *Faculty:* 57 full-time (44 women), 62 part-time/adjunct (42 women). *Students:* 101 full-time (77 women), 323 part-time (269 women); includes 60 minority (24 African Americans, 13 Asian Americans or Pacific Islanders, 23 Hispanic Americans), 5 international. 221 applicants, 76% accepted, 115 enrolled. In 2006, 158 master's, 40 other advanced degrees awarded. *Degree requirements:* For Certificate, thesis or alternative. *Entrance requirements:* For degree, GRE General Test, minimum GPA of 3.0. Additional exam requirements/recommendations for international students: Required—TOEFL. *Application deadline:* For fall admission, 7/15 for domestic students; for spring admission, 12/15 for domestic students. Application fee: $30. Electronic applications accepted. *Expenses:* Tuition, state resident: full-time $6,167; part-time $257 per credit hour. Tuition, nonresident: full-time $22,790; part-time $950 per credit hour. *Financial support:* Fellowships with partial tuition reimbursements, research assistantships with partial tuition reimbursements, teaching assistantships with partial tuition reimbursements, career-related internships or fieldwork, Federal Work-Study, institutionally sponsored loans, tuition waivers (partial), and unspecified assistantships available. Financial award application deadline: 3/1; financial award applicants required to submit FAFSA. *Unit head:* Dr. Robert Williams, Chair, 407-823-1768, E-mail: rdwilliams@mail.ucf.edu. *Application contact:* Information Contact, 407-823-2053.

University of Connecticut, Graduate School, Neag School of Education, Department of Curriculum and Instruction, Storrs, CT 06269. Offers curriculum and instruction (MA, PhD), including agriculture education, bilingual and bicultural education, elementary education, English education, history and social sciences education, mathematics education, reading education, science education, secondary education, world languages education. *Accreditation:* NCATE. *Faculty:* 28 full-time (12 women). *Students:* 158 full-time (120 women), 54 part-time (44 women); includes 24 minority (3 African Americans, 1 American Indian/Alaska Native, 3 Asian Americans or Pacific Islanders, 17 Hispanic Americans), 2 international. Average age 27. 268 applicants, 76% accepted, 203 enrolled. In 2006, 181 master's, 4 doctorates awarded. Terminal master's awarded for partial completion of doctoral program. *Degree requirements:* For master's, thesis or alternative, comprehensive exam; for doctorate, thesis/dissertation. *Entrance requirements:* For doctorate, GRE General Test. Additional exam requirements/recommendations for international students: Required—TOEFL (minimum score 550 paper-based; 213 computer-based). *Application deadline:* For fall admission, 2/1 priority date for domestic and international students; for spring admission, 11/1 for domestic students, 10/1 for international students. Applications are processed on a rolling basis. Application fee: $55. Electronic applications accepted. *Financial support:* In 2006–07, 14 research assistantships with full tuition reimbursements, 4 teaching assistantships with full tuition reimbursements were awarded; fellowships, Federal Work-Study, scholarships/grants, health care benefits, and unspecified

Foreign Languages Education

University of Connecticut (continued)
assistantships also available. Financial award application deadline: 2/1; financial award applicants required to submit FAFSA. *Unit head:* Mary Anne Doyle, Head, 860-486-2433, Fax: 860-486-0280. *Application contact:* Lisa Rasicot, Graduate Coordinator, 860-486-3065, Fax: 860-486-0210, E-mail: soeadm02@uconnvm.uconn.edu.

University of Connecticut, Graduate School, Neag School of Education, Department of Curriculum and Instruction, Field of Curriculum and Instruction, Program in World Languages Education, Storrs, CT 06269. Offers MA, PhD. *Accreditation:* NCATE. *Faculty:* 9 full-time (7 women). Terminal master's awarded for partial completion of doctoral program. *Degree requirements:* For master's, thesis or alternative, comprehensive exam; for doctorate, thesis/dissertation. *Entrance requirements:* For doctorate, GRE General Test. Additional exam requirements/recommendations for international students: Required—TOEFL (minimum score 550 paper-based; 213 computer-based). *Application deadline:* For fall admission, 2/1 priority date for domestic and international students; for spring admission, 11/1 for domestic students, 10/1 for international students. Applications are processed on a rolling basis. Application fee: $55. Electronic applications accepted. *Financial support:* Teaching assistantships with full tuition reimbursements, Federal Work-Study, scholarships/grants, health care benefits, and unspecified assistantships available. Financial award application deadline: 2/1; financial award applicants required to submit FAFSA. *Application contact:* Lisa Rasicot, Graduate Coordinator, 860-486-3065, Fax: 860-486-0210, E-mail: soeadm02@uconnvm.uconn.edu.

University of Delaware, College of Arts and Sciences, Department of Foreign Languages and Literatures, Newark, DE 19716. Offers foreign languages and literatures (MA), including French, German, Spanish; foreign languages pedagogy (MA), including French, German, Spanish. *Degree requirements:* For master's, one foreign language, comprehensive exam. *Entrance requirements:* For master's, GRE General Test, letters of recommendation, writing sample. Additional exam requirements/recommendations for international students: Required—TOEFL. Electronic applications accepted. *Faculty research:* Computer-assisted instruction, literature by women, Spanish Golden Age, French realism, twentieth century German, French, Spanish literature.

University of Hawaii at Manoa, Graduate Division, Colleges of Arts and Sciences, College of Language, Linguistics and Literature, Department of Hawaiian and Indo-Pacific Languages and Literatures, Program in Hawaiian, Honolulu, HI 96822. Offers MA. *Faculty:* 12 full-time (6 women). *Students:* 8 full-time (4 women), 2 part-time (1 woman); includes 5 minority (all Asian Americans or Pacific Islanders) 8 applicants, 50% accepted, 2 enrolled. *Degree requirements:* For master's, thesis optional. *Entrance requirements:* Additional exam requirements/recommendations for international students: Required—TOEFL (minimum score 500 paper-based; 173 computer-based; 61 iBT). *Application deadline:* For fall admission, 3/1 for domestic and international students. Application fee: $50. *Financial support:* In 2006–07, 3 research assistantships (averaging $16,176 per year), 1 teaching assistantship (averaging $13,296 per year) were awarded. Total annual research expenditures: $797,832. *Application contact:* Emily Hawkins, Information Contact, 808-956-6419, Fax: 808-956-5978.

University of Hawaii at Manoa, Graduate Division, Colleges of Arts and Sciences, College of Language, Linguistics and Literature, Department of Second Language Studies, Honolulu, HI 96822. Offers English as a second language (MA, Graduate Certificate); second language acquisition (PhD). *Faculty:* 94 full-time (31 women), 1 part-time/adjunct (0 women). *Students:* 112 full-time (79 women), 26 part-time (11 women); includes 8 minority (6 Asian Americans or Pacific Islanders, 2 Hispanic Americans), 21 international. Average age 33. 96 applicants, 58% accepted, 37 enrolled. In 2006, 40 master's, 5 other advanced degrees awarded. *Degree requirements:* For master's, 2 foreign languages, thesis/dissertation; for doctorate, 2 foreign languages, thesis/dissertation, comprehensive exam. *Entrance requirements:* For master's, GRE General Test, minimum GPA of 3.0; for doctorate, GRE General Test, MA, scholarly publications. Additional exam requirements/recommendations for international students: Required—TOEFL (minimum score 600 paper-based; 250 computer-based; 100 iBT). *Application deadline:* For fall admission, 1/15 for domestic and international students; for spring admission, 9/1 for domestic and international students. Applications are processed on a rolling basis. Application fee: $50. *Financial support:* In 2006–07, 48 students received support, including 18 research assistantships (averaging $16,541 per year), 30 teaching assistantships (averaging $13,930 per year); fellowships, career-related internships or fieldwork, Federal Work-Study, institutionally sponsored loans, scholarships/grants, and tuition waivers (full and partial) also available. Financial award application deadline: 2/1; financial award applicants required to submit FAFSA. *Faculty research:* Second language use, second language analysis, second language pedagogy and testing, second language learning, qualitative and quantitative research methods for second languages. Total annual research expenditures: $339,700. *Application contact:* Thomas Hudson, Information Contact, 808-956-6131, Fax: 808-956-2802.

University of Illinois at Urbana–Champaign, Graduate College, College of Liberal Arts and Sciences, Department of Spanish, Italian and Portuguese, Champaign, IL 61820. Offers Italian (PhD); Spanish, Italian and Portuguese (MA). *Faculty:* 17 full-time (9 women), 1 (woman) part-time/adjunct. *Students:* 47 full-time (30 women), 19 part-time (15 women); includes 8 minority (1 African American, 7 Hispanic Americans), 35 international. 50 applicants, 66% accepted, 16 enrolled. In 2006, 7 master's, 6 doctorates awarded. *Degree requirements:* For doctorate, 2 foreign languages, thesis/dissertation. *Entrance requirements:* For master's, GRE General Test, GRE Subject Test, minimum GPA of 3.0. *Application deadline:* For fall admission, 3/1 for domestic students. Applications are processed on a rolling basis. Application fee: $50 ($60 for international students). Electronic applications accepted. *Financial support:* In 2006–07, 7 fellowships, 2 research assistantships, 59 teaching assistantships were awarded; tuition waivers (full and partial) also available. Financial award application deadline: 2/15. *Unit head:* Diane Musumeci, Head, 217-244-3250, Fax: 217-244-8430, E-mail: musumeci@uiuc.edu. *Application contact:* Lynn Stanke, Secretary, 217-333-6269, Fax: 214-244-8430, E-mail: stanke@uiuc.edu.

University of Illinois at Urbana–Champaign, Graduate College, College of Liberal Arts and Sciences, Second Language Acquisition and Teacher Education Program, Champaign, IL 61820. Offers CAS. *Unit head:* Dr. Sarah C. Mangelsdorf, Dean, College of Liberal Arts and Sciences, 217-333-1350, Fax: 217-333-9142, E-mail: smangels@uiuc.edu.

University of Indianapolis, Graduate Programs, School of Education, Indianapolis, IN 46227-3697. Offers art education (MAT); biology (MAT); chemistry (MAT); curriculum and instruction (MA); earth sciences (MAT); education (MA, MAT); educational leadership (MA); elementary education (MA); English (MAT); French (MAT); math (MAT); physical education (MAT); physics (MAT); secondary education (MA), including art education, education, English education, social studies education; social studies (MAT); Spanish (MAT). *Accreditation:* NCATE. Part-time and evening/weekend programs available. *Faculty:* 4 full-time (2 women), 6 part-time/adjunct (2 women). *Students:* 32 full-time (16 women), 70 part-time (42 women); includes 2 minority (1 African American, 1 Hispanic American). Average age 31. In 2006, 51 degrees awarded. *Entrance requirements:* For master's, GRE Subject Test, minimum GPA of 2.5, 3 letters of recommendation, interview, Praxis I, writing exercise, be within 9 hours of completing content requirements. Additional exam requirements/recommendations for international students: Required—TOEFL (minimum score 550 paper-based; 213 computer-based). *Application deadline:* Applications are processed on a rolling basis. Application fee: $50. *Financial support:* Federal Work-Study available. Financial award application deadline: 5/1; financial award applicants required to submit FAFSA. *Faculty research:* Assessment of teacher education, perceptions of prospective teachers by parents. *Unit head:* Dr. E. Lynne Weisenbach, Dean, 317-788-3446, Fax: 317-788-3300, E-mail: weisenbach@uindy.edu.

The University of Iowa, Graduate College, College of Education, Department of Teaching and Learning, Program in Secondary Education, Iowa City, IA 52242-1316. Offers art education (MA, PhD); curriculum and supervision (PhD); curriculum supervision (MA); developmental reading (MA); English education (MA, MAT, PhD); foreign language education (MA, MAT); foreign language/ESL education (PhD); language, literature and culture (PhD); math education (PhD); mathematics education (MA); music education (MA, PhD); social studies (MA, PhD). *Faculty:* 11 full-time. *Students:* 53 full-time (33 women), 53 part-time (41 women); includes 5 minority (1 African American, 1 American Indian/Alaska Native, 2 Asian Americans or Pacific Islanders, 1 Hispanic American), 19 international. 66 applicants, 47% accepted, 17 enrolled. In 2006, 22 master's, 14 doctorates awarded. *Degree requirements:* For master's, exam, thesis optional; for doctorate, thesis/dissertation, comprehensive exam, registration. *Entrance requirements:* For master's and doctorate, GRE General Test, minimum GPA of 3.0. Additional exam requirements/recommendations for international students: Required—TOEFL (minimum score 550 paper-based; 213 computer-based; 81 iBT). Application fee: $60 ($85 for international students). Electronic applications accepted. *Financial support:* In 2006–07, 1 fellowship, 12 research assistantships with partial tuition reimbursements, 31 teaching assistantships with partial tuition reimbursements were awarded. Financial award applicants required to submit FAFSA. *Unit head:* Gary Sasso, Chair, 319-335-5324, Fax: 319-335-5608.

The University of Iowa, Graduate College, Program in Second Language Acquisition, Iowa City, IA 52242-1316. Offers PhD. *Students:* 9 full-time (8 women), 10 part-time (7 women); includes 1 minority (Asian American or Pacific Islander), 13 international. 18 applicants, 22% accepted, 1 enrolled. In 2006, 5 degrees awarded. *Degree requirements:* For doctorate, thesis/dissertation, comprehensive exam, registration. *Entrance requirements:* For doctorate, GRE General Test, minimum GPA of 3.0. Additional exam requirements/recommendations for international students: Required—TOEFL (minimum score 550 paper-based; 213 computer-based; 81 iBT). *Application deadline:* For fall admission, 2/1 for domestic and international students. Application fee: $60 ($85 for international students). Electronic applications accepted. *Financial support:* In 2006–07, 2 fellowships, 4 research assistantships with partial tuition reimbursements, 11 teaching assistantships with partial tuition reimbursements were awarded. Financial award applicants required to submit FAFSA. *Unit head:* Dr. L. Kathy Heilenman, Co-Director, 319-335-0529.

University of Kentucky, Graduate School, College of Arts and Sciences and College of Education, Program in Teaching World Languages, Lexington, KY 40506-0032. Offers MA. *Faculty:* 28 full-time (10 women), 2 part-time/adjunct (1 woman). *Students:* 10 full-time (all women), 2 part-time (1 woman), 1 international. Average age 26. 3 applicants, 100% accepted, 3 enrolled. In 2006, 3 degrees awarded. *Entrance requirements:* For master's, GRE General Test, minimum undergraduate GPA of 2.75. Additional exam requirements/recommendations for international students: Required—TOEFL (minimum score 550 paper-based; 213 computer-based). *Application deadline:* For fall admission, 7/17 priority date for domestic students, 2/1 priority date for international students; for spring admission, 12/13 priority date for domestic students, 6/15 priority date for international students. Application fee: $40 ($55 for international students). Electronic applications accepted. *Expenses:* Tuition, state resident: full-time $7,670; part-time $401 per credit hour. Tuition, nonresident: full-time $16,158; part-time $873 per credit hour. *Financial support:* In 2006–07, 3 students received support, including 1 fellowship with full tuition reimbursement available, 2 teaching assistantships with full tuition reimbursements available (averaging $8,075 per year); research assistantships with full tuition reimbursements available, Federal Work-Study, scholarships/grants, traineeships, health care benefits, tuition waivers (partial), and unspecified assistantships also available. Support available to part-time students. Financial award application deadline: 3/15; financial award applicants required to submit FAFSA. *Unit head:* Dr. Stayc Dubravac, Head, 859-257-9562, Fax: 859-257-3743. *Application contact:* Brian Jackson, Senior Associate Dean, 859-257-4905, Fax: 859-323-1928, E-mail: brian.jackson@uky.edu.

University of Louisville, Graduate School, College of Education and Human Development, Department of Teaching and Learning, Louisville, KY 40292-0001. Offers art education (MAT); curriculum and instruction (Ed D); early elementary education (M Ed, MAT); foreign language education (MAT); instructional technology (M Ed); interdisciplinary early childhood education (M Ed); middle school education (M Ed, MAT); music education (MAT); reading education (M Ed); secondary education (M Ed, MAT); special education (M Ed, PhD). *Students:* 241 full-time (186 women), 462 part-time (345 women); includes 67 minority (51 African Americans, 2 American Indian/Alaska Native, 9 Asian Americans or Pacific Islanders, 5 Hispanic Americans), 19 international. Average age 33. In 2006, 243 master's, 62 doctorates awarded. *Entrance requirements:* For master's, GRE General Test. *Application deadline:* Applications are processed on a rolling basis. Application fee: $50. Electronic applications accepted. *Financial support:* Fellowships, research assistantships, teaching assistantships, Federal Work-Study and scholarships/grants available. *Unit head:* Dr. Karen S. Karp, Chair, 502-852-6431, Fax: 502-852-1497, E-mail: karen@louisville.edu.

University of Maine, Graduate School, College of Liberal Arts and Sciences, Department of Modern Languages and Classics, Orono, ME 04469. Offers French (MA, MAT). Part-time programs available. *Faculty:* 12 full-time (6 women). *Students:* 3 full-time (2 women), 6 part-time (all women). Average age 40. 4 applicants, 75% accepted, 3 enrolled. In 2006, 1 degree awarded. *Degree requirements:* For master's, one foreign language, thesis (for some programs). *Entrance requirements:* For master's, GRE General Test. Additional exam requirements/recommendations for international students: Required—TOEFL. *Application deadline:* For fall admission, 2/1 priority date for domestic students. Applications are processed on a rolling basis. Application fee: $50. Electronic applications accepted. *Financial support:* In 2006–07, fellowships with tuition reimbursements (averaging $14,000 per year), 3 teaching assistantships with tuition reimbursements (averaging $9,010 per year) were awarded; research assistantships with tuition reimbursements, Federal Work-Study, tuition waivers (full and partial), and instructorships also available. Financial award application deadline: 3/1. *Faculty research:* Narratology, poetics, Quebec literature, theater, women's studies. *Unit head:* Dr. Eugene DelVecchio, Chair, 207-581-2072, Fax: 207-581-1832. *Application contact:* Scott G. Delcourt, Associate Dean of the Graduate School, 207-581-3219, Fax: 207-581-3232, E-mail: graduate@maine.edu.

University of Maryland, College Park, Graduate Studies, College of Arts and Humanities, School of Languages, Literature, and Cultures, Program in Second Language Acquisition and Application, College Park, MD 20742. Offers French (MA); German (MA); Japanese (MA); Russian (MA); second language instruction (PhD); second language learning (PhD); second language measurement and assessment (PhD); second language use (PhD); Spanish (MA). *Students:* 21 full-time (15 women), 16 part-time (14 women); includes 5 minority (1 Asian American or Pacific Islander, 4 Hispanic Americans), 10 international. 40 applicants, 15% accepted, 4 enrolled. In 2006, 12 degrees awarded. *Entrance requirements:* For master's, BA or BS in related field, demonstrated language competency, 3 letters of reference. *Application deadline:* For fall admission, 1/15 for domestic students, 2/1 for international students; for spring admission, 9/15 for domestic students, 6/1 for international students. Applications are processed on a rolling basis. Application fee: $60. Electronic applications accepted. *Financial support:* In 2006–07, 4 fellowships (averaging $2,586 per year) were awarded. *Faculty research:* Second language acquisition, pedagogical perspectives, technological applications, language use in professional contexts. *Unit head:* Dr. Cynthia L. Martin, Acting Chair, 301-405-4244, E-mail: cmartin@umd.edu. *Application contact:* Dean of Graduate School, 301-405-0358, Fax: 301-314-9305.

University of Massachusetts Amherst, Graduate School, College of Humanities and Fine Arts, Department of French and Italian, Amherst, MA 01003. Offers French and Francophone studies (MA, MAT, PhD); Italian studies (MAT). Part-time programs available. *Faculty:* 12 full-time (7 women). *Students:* 9 full-time (8 women), 7 part-time (6 women), 3 international. Average age 29. 14 applicants, 86% accepted, 6 enrolled. In 2006, 7 degrees awarded. *Degree requirements:* For master's, thesis or alternative. *Entrance requirements:* For master's, GRE General Test. Additional exam requirements/recommendations for international students: Required—TOEFL (minimum score 530 paper-based; 197 computer-based). *Application deadline:* For fall admission, 2/1 priority date for domestic and international students; for spring admission, 10/1 for domestic and international students. Applications are processed on a rolling basis. Application fee: $40 ($65 for international students). Electronic applications accepted. *Expenses:* Tuition, state resident: full-time $2,640; part-time $110 per credit. Tuition, nonresident: full-time $9,936; part-time $414 per credit. Required fees: $8,969; $3,129 per term. One-time fee: $257 full-time. Tuition and fees vary according to class time, course load, campus/location and reciprocity agreements. *Financial support:* In 2006–07, 21 teaching assistantships with full tuition reimbursements (averaging $10,150 per year) were awarded; fellowships with full tuition reimbursements, research assistantships with full tuition reimbursements, career-related internships or fieldwork, Federal Work-Study, scholarships/ grants, traineeships, and unspecified assistantships also available. Support available to part-time students. Financial award application deadline: 2/1. *Unit head:* Dr. Michael Papio, Head, 412-545-6697, Fax: 412-545-2314, E-mail: papio@hfa.umass.edu.

University of Massachusetts Boston, Office of Graduate Studies, College of Liberal Arts, Program in Applied Linguistics, Boston, MA 02125-3393. Offers bilingual education (MA); English as a second language (MA); foreign language pedagogy (MA). Part-time and evening/ weekend programs available. *Students:* 21 full-time (16 women), 76 part-time (56 women); includes 23 minority (8 African Americans, 4 Asian Americans or Pacific Islanders, 11 Hispanic Americans), 12 international. Average age 36. 57 applicants, 79% accepted, 22 enrolled. In 2006, 44 degrees awarded. *Median time to degree:* Master's—4 years full-time. *Degree requirements:* For master's, one foreign language, comprehensive exam. *Entrance requirements:* For master's, minimum GPA of 2.75. *Application deadline:* For fall admission, 2/1 priority date for domestic students; for spring admission, 10/15 for domestic students. Application fee: $25 ($40 for international students). *Expenses:* Tuition, state resident: full-time $2,590; part-time $301 per credit. Tuition, nonresident: full-time $9,758; part-time $427 per credit. One-time fee: $495 full-time. *Financial support:* In 2006–07, 8 research assistantships with full tuition reimbursements (averaging $13,000 per year), 6 teaching assistantships with full tuition reimbursements (averaging $13,000 per year) were awarded; career-related internships or fieldwork, Federal Work-Study, and unspecified assistantships also available. Support available to part-time students. Financial award application deadline: 3/1; financial award applicants required to submit FAFSA. *Faculty research:* Multicultural theory and curriculum development, foreign language pedagogy, language and culture, applied psycholinguistics, bilingual education. *Unit head:* Dr. Donaldo Macedo, Director, 617-287-5760, E-mail: donalde.macedo@umb.edu. *Application contact:* Peggy Roldan, Graduate Admissions Coordinator, 617-287-6400, Fax: 617-287-6236, E-mail: bos.gadm@dpc.umassp.edu.

University of Michigan, Horace H. Rackham School of Graduate Studies, College of Literature, Science, and the Arts, Department of Classical Studies, Ann Arbor, MI 48109. Offers classical studies (PhD); Greek (AM); Latin (AM); teaching Latin (MAT). Terminal master's awarded for partial completion of doctoral program. *Degree requirements:* For master's, one foreign language, comprehensive exam; for doctorate, 4 foreign languages, thesis/dissertation, oral defense of dissertation, preliminary exam. *Entrance requirements:* For master's and doctorate, GRE General Test. Additional exam requirements/recommendations for international students: Required—TOEFL (minimum score 560 paper-based; 220 computer-based). Electronic applications accepted. *Faculty research:* Greek and Latin literature, ancient history, papyrology, archaeology.

University of Minnesota, Twin Cities Campus, Graduate School, College of Education and Human Development, Department of Curriculum and Instruction, Program in Teaching, Minneapolis, MN 55455-0213. Offers Chinese (M Ed); earth science (M Ed); elementary special education (M Ed); English (M Ed); English as a second language (M Ed); French (M Ed); German (M Ed); Hebrew (M Ed); Japanese (M Ed); life sciences (M Ed); mathematics (M Ed); middle school science (M Ed); science (M Ed); second languages and cultures (M Ed); social studies (M Ed); Spanish (M Ed). *Students:* 324 full-time (230 women), 132 part-time (86 women); includes 44 minority (5 African Americans, 2 American Indian/Alaska Native, 27 Asian Americans or Pacific Islanders, 10 Hispanic Americans), 4 international. Average age 27. 499 applicants, 74% accepted, 327 enrolled. In 2006, 545 degrees awarded. *Expenses:* Tuition, state resident: full-time $9,302; part-time $775 per credit. Tuition, nonresident: full-time $16,400; part-time $1,367 per credit. Full-time tuition and fees vary according to class time, course load, program, reciprocity agreements and student level. *Application contact:* Dr. Mary Bents, Associate Dean, 612-625-6501, Fax: 612-626-1580, E-mail: mbents@tc.umn.edu.

University of Missouri–Columbia, Graduate School, College of Arts and Sciences, Department of Romance Languages and Literature, Columbia, MO 65211. Offers French (MA, PhD); literature (MA); Spanish (MA, PhD); teaching (MA). *Faculty:* 22 full-time (10 women). *Students:* 24 full-time (19 women), 17 part-time (10 women); includes 7 minority (1 African American, 1 American Indian/Alaska Native, 1 Asian American or Pacific Islander, 4 Hispanic Americans), 8 international. In 2006, 11 degrees awarded. Terminal master's awarded for partial completion of doctoral program. *Degree requirements:* For master's, one foreign language; for doctorate, 4 foreign languages, thesis/dissertation. *Entrance requirements:* For master's and doctorate, GRE General Test, minimum GPA of 3.0. *Application deadline:* For fall admission, 1/15 priority date for domestic students. Applications are processed on a rolling basis. Application fee: $45 ($60 for international students). *Financial support:* Research assistantships, teaching assistantships, institutionally sponsored loans available. *Unit head:* Dr. Margaret M. Olsen, Director of Graduate Studies, 573-882-3767, E-mail: olsenm@missouri.edu.

University of Missouri–Columbia, Graduate School, College of Education, Department of Curriculum and Instruction, Columbia, MO 65211. Offers agricultural education (M Ed, PhD, Ed S); art education (M Ed, PhD, Ed S); business and office education (M Ed, PhD, Ed S); early childhood education (M Ed, PhD, Ed S); elementary education (M Ed, PhD, Ed S); English education (M Ed, PhD, Ed S); foreign language education (M Ed, PhD, Ed S); health education and promotion (M Ed, PhD); learning and instruction (M Ed); marketing education (M Ed, PhD, Ed S); mathematics education (M Ed, PhD, Ed S); music education (M Ed, PhD, Ed S); reading education (M Ed, PhD, Ed S); science education (M Ed, PhD, Ed S); social studies education (M Ed, PhD, Ed S); vocational education (M Ed, PhD, Ed S). Part-time programs available. *Faculty:* 24 full-time (12 women). *Students:* 195 full-time (148 women), 260 part-time (214 women); includes 27 minority (8 African Americans, 1 American Indian/ Alaska Native, 10 Asian Americans or Pacific Islanders, 8 Hispanic Americans), 19 international. In 2006, 186 master's, 12 doctorates awarded. Terminal master's awarded for partial completion of doctoral program. *Degree requirements:* For doctorate, thesis/dissertation. *Entrance requirements:* For master's and Ed S, GRE General Test or MAT, minimum GPA of 3.0; for doctorate, GRE General Test, minimum GPA of 3.0. *Application deadline:* Applications are processed on a rolling basis. Application fee: $45 ($60 for international students). *Financial support:* Fellowships, research assistantships, teaching assistantships, institutionally sponsored loans available. *Unit head:* Dr. Lloyd H. Barrow, Director of Graduate Studies, 573-882-8247, E-mail: robinsonr@missouri.edu.

University of Nebraska at Kearney, College of Graduate Study, College of Fine Arts and Humanities, Department of Modern Languages, Kearney, NE 68849-0001. Offers French (MA Ed); German (MA Ed); Spanish (MA Ed). *Accreditation:* NCATE. Part-time and evening/ weekend programs available. *Faculty:* 5 full-time (2 women). In 2006, 1 degree awarded. *Degree requirements:* For master's, thesis optional. *Entrance requirements:* For master's, GRE General Test. *Application deadline:* For fall admission, 5/1 for domestic and international students; for spring admission, 8/15 for domestic students, 8/1 for international students. Applications are processed on a rolling basis. Application fee: $45. Electronic applications accepted. *Expenses:* Tuition, state resident: part-time $161 per hour. Tuition, nonresident: part-time $332 per hour. Required fees: $57 per hour. *Financial support:* In 2006–07, 1 teaching assistantship with full tuition reimbursement (averaging $8,200 per year) was awarded; career-related internships or fieldwork also available. Support available to part-time students. Financial award application deadline: 3/1; financial award applicants required to submit FAFSA. *Faculty research:* Translation theory, Spanish linguistics; Heidegger, Rilke and Nietzsche; symotolistic poetry. *Unit head:* Dr. Sonja Kropp, Chair, 308-865-8536, Fax: 308-865-8806, E-mail: kropps@unk.edu.

University of Nebraska at Omaha, Graduate Studies and Research, College of Arts and Sciences, Program in Language Teaching, Omaha, NE 68182. Offers MA. Part-time and

evening/weekend programs available. *Faculty:* 8 full-time (7 women). *Students:* Average age 35. 13 applicants, 85% accepted, 8 enrolled. *Degree requirements:* For master's, thesis (for some programs), comprehensive exam. *Entrance requirements:* For master's, letters of recommendation, oral and written language sample. Additional exam requirements/recommendations for international students: Required—TOEFL (minimum score 600 paper-based; 250 computer-based; 100 iBT). *Application deadline:* For fall admission, 7/1 priority date for domestic students; for spring admission, 11/15 priority date for domestic students. Application fee: $45. *Financial support:* In 2006–07, 2 students received support. Tuition waivers (partial) available. Financial award application deadline: 3/1; financial award applicants required to submit FAFSA. *Unit head:* Dr. Carolyn Gascoigne, Chairperson, 402-554-4841.

University of Nevada, Reno, Graduate School, College of Liberal Arts, Department of Foreign Languages and Literatures, Reno, NV 89557. Offers French (MA); German (MA); Spanish (MA). *Faculty:* 18. *Students:* 6 full-time (4 women), 20 part-time (17 women); includes 6 minority (all Hispanic Americans), 1 international. Average age 31. 10 applicants, 80% accepted, 7 enrolled. In 2006, 10 degrees awarded. *Degree requirements:* For master's, one foreign language, thesis optional. *Entrance requirements:* For master's, GRE General Test, minimum GPA of 2.75. Additional exam requirements/recommendations for international students: Required—TOEFL. *Application deadline:* For fall admission, 3/1 priority date for domestic students; for spring admission, 11/1 for domestic students. Applications are processed on a rolling basis. Application fee: $60 ($95 for international students). *Financial support:* In 2006–07, 7 teaching assistantships were awarded; Federal Work-Study and institutionally sponsored loans also available. Financial award application deadline: 3/1. *Faculty research:* Thirteenth-century mysticism, contemporary Spanish and Latin American poetry and theater, French interrelation between narration and photography, exile literature and Holocaust. *Unit head:* Dr. Miriella Melara, Graduate Program Director, 775-682-8890.

The University of North Carolina at Chapel Hill, Graduate School, School of Education, Program in Secondary Education, Chapel Hill, NC 27599. Offers English (Grades 9–12) (MAT); French (Grades K–12) (MAT); German (Grades K–12) (MAT); Japanese (Grades K–12) (MAT); Latin (Grades 9–12) (MAT); mathematics (Grades 9–12) (MAT); music (Grades K–12) (MAT); science (Grades 9–12) (MAT); social studies/social science (Grades 9–12) (MAT); Spanish (Grades K–12) (MAT). *Accreditation:* NCATE. In 2006, 72 degrees awarded. *Degree requirements:* For master's, comprehensive exam. *Entrance requirements:* For master's, GRE General Test, minimum GPA of 3.0 during last 2 years of undergraduate course work. Additional exam requirements/recommendations for international students: Required—TOEFL (minimum score 550 paper-based; 213 computer-based), ACTFL oral proficiency interview. *Application deadline:* For fall admission, 1/1 priority date for domestic and international students. Applications are processed on a rolling basis. Application fee: $60. Electronic applications accepted. *Financial support:* Federal Work-Study available. Support available to part-time students. Financial award application deadline: 3/1; financial award applicants required to submit FAFSA. *Faculty research:* Curriculum and instruction, teacher education per subject. *Unit head:* Dr. James Trier, Coordinator, 919-843-4627. *Application contact:* Janet Carroll, Registrar, 919-962-8690, Fax: 919-962-1533, E-mail: jscarrol@email.unc.edu.

The University of North Carolina at Charlotte, Graduate School, College of Education, Program in Teacher Education, Charlotte, NC 28223-0001. Offers art education (K–12) (MAT); dance education (K–12) (MAT); elementary education (K–6) (MAT); English as a second language (K–12) (MAT); foreign language education (K–12) (MAT); general teacher education (MAT); middle grades education (6–9) (MAT); music education (K–12) (MAT); secondary education (9–12) (MAT); special education (K–12) (MAT); theatre education (K–12) (MAT). *Students:* 16 full-time (12 women), 200 part-time (170 women); includes 30 minority (22 African Americans, 2 American Indian/Alaska Native, 2 Asian Americans or Pacific Islanders, 4 Hispanic Americans), 2 international. Average age 33. 74 applicants, 85% accepted, 49 enrolled. In 2006, 43 degrees awarded. *Entrance requirements:* For master's, GRE or MAT. Additional exam requirements/recommendations for international students: Required—TOEFL (minimum score 557 paper-based; 220 computer-based). *Application deadline:* For fall admission, 7/1 for domestic students, 5/1 for international students; for spring admission, 11/1 for domestic students, 10/1 for international students. Applications are processed on a rolling basis. Application fee: $55. Electronic applications accepted. *Expenses:* Tuition, state resident: full-time $2,719; part-time $170 per credit. Tuition, nonresident: full-time $12,926; part-time $808 per credit. Required fees: $1,555. *Financial support:* Fellowships, research assistantships, teaching assistantships, career-related internships or fieldwork, Federal Work-Study, institutionally sponsored loans, scholarships/grants, and unspecified assistantships available. Support available to part-time students. Financial award application deadline: 4/1; financial award applicants required to submit FAFSA. *Unit head:* Dr. Kimberly J. Hartman, Coordinator, 704-687-8883, Fax: 704-687-6430, E-mail: khartman@email.uncc.edu. *Application contact:* Kathy B. Giddings, Director of Graduate Admissions, 704-687-3366, Fax: 704-687-3279, E-mail: gradadm@email.uncc.edu.

The University of North Carolina at Greensboro, Graduate School, School of Education, Department of Curriculum and Instruction, Greensboro, NC 27412-5001. Offers college teaching and adult learning (Certificate); curriculum and instruction (M Ed), including chemistry education, elementary education, English as a second language, French education, instructional technology, mathematics education, middle grades education, reading education, science education, social studies education, Spanish education; curriculum and teaching (PhD), including higher education, teacher education and development; English as a second language (Certificate); higher education (M Ed); supervision (M Ed). *Accreditation:* NCATE. Part-time programs available. *Faculty:* 27 full-time (18 women), 8 part-time/adjunct (3 women). *Students:* 137 full-time (114 women), 231 part-time (195 women); includes 63 minority (52 African Americans, 2 American Indian/Alaska Native, 5 Asian Americans or Pacific Islanders, 4 Hispanic Americans). 146 applicants, 32% accepted. *Degree requirements:* For doctorate, thesis/dissertation. *Entrance requirements:* For master's and doctorate, GRE General Test. Additional exam requirements/recommendations for international students: Required—TOEFL. Application fee: $45. Electronic applications accepted. *Expenses:* Tuition, state resident: full-time $2,692. Tuition, nonresident: full-time $13,742. *Financial support:* Fellowships, research assistantships with full tuition reimbursements, teaching assistantships with full tuition reimbursements, career-related internships or fieldwork, Federal Work-Study, scholarships/grants, traineeships, and unspecified assistantships available. Support available to part-time students. *Faculty research:* Community college literacy program, middle school mathematics/computer mathematics. *Unit head:* Dr. Sam Miller, Chair, 336-334-3445, Fax: 336-334-4120, E-mail: sdmille2@uncg.edu. *Application contact:* Michelle Harkleroad, Director of Graduate Admissions, 336-334-4884, Fax: 336-334-4424, E-mail: mbharkle@uncg.edu.

University of Northern Colorado, Graduate School, College of Humanities and Social Sciences, School of Modern Languages and Cultural Studies, Hispanic Studies Program, Greeley, CO 80639. Offers Spanish/teaching (MA). Part-time programs available. *Faculty:* 2 full-time (both women). *Students:* 1 (woman) full-time, 6 part-time (5 women); includes 4 minority (all Hispanic Americans) Average age 52. 1 applicant, 100% accepted, 0 enrolled. In 2006, 9 degrees awarded. *Degree requirements:* For master's, thesis or alternative, comprehensive exam. *Entrance requirements:* For master's, minimum undergraduate GPA of 3.0, BA in Spanish, 1 year of secondary teaching. *Application deadline:* Applications are processed on a rolling basis. Application fee: $50 ($60 for international students). Electronic applications accepted. *Expenses:* Tuition, state resident: full-time $5,118; part-time $213 per credit hour. Tuition, nonresident: full-time $14,832; part-time $618 per credit hour. Required fees: $674; $34 per credit hour. *Financial support:* In 2006–07, 3 students received support; fellowships, research assistantships, teaching assistantships, unspecified assistantships available. Financial award application deadline: 3/1; financial award applicants required to submit FAFSA. *Unit head:* Dr. Joy Landeira, Program Coordinator, 970-351-2221.

University of Pittsburgh, School of Education, Department of Instruction and Learning, Program in Secondary Education, Pittsburgh, PA 15260. Offers English/communications education (M Ed, MAT, Ed D, PhD); foreign languages education (M Ed, MAT, Ed D, PhD); mathemat-

Foreign Languages Education

University of Pittsburgh (continued)
ics education (M Ed, MAT, Ed D); reading education (PhD); science education (M Ed, MAT, MS, Ed D); social studies education (M Ed, MAT, Ed D, PhD). Part-time and evening/weekend programs available. *Students:* 157 full-time (111 women), 84 part-time (61 women); includes 18 minority (7 African Americans, 5 Asian Americans or Pacific Islanders, 6 Hispanic Americans), 13 international. 163 applicants, 74% accepted, 86 enrolled. In 2006, 114 master's, 7 doctorates awarded. *Degree requirements:* For master's and doctorate, thesis/dissertation. *Entrance requirements:* For master's, PRAXIS I; for doctorate, GRE General Test. Additional exam requirements/recommendations for international students: Required—TOEFL. *Application deadline:* For fall admission, 2/1 priority date for domestic students; for spring admission, 11/15 priority date for domestic students. Applications are processed on a rolling basis. Application fee: $50. Electronic applications accepted. *Financial support:* Fellowships, teaching assistantships, career-related internships or fieldwork, Federal Work-Study, tuition waivers (partial), and unspecified assistantships available. Support available to part-time students. Financial award application deadline: 3/15; financial award applicants required to submit FAFSA. *Application contact:* Joan M. Cutone, Director, School of Education Student Service Center, 412-648-2230, Fax: 412-648-1899, E-mail: soeinfo@pitt.edu.

University of Puerto Rico, Río Piedras, College of Education, Program in Curriculum and Teaching, San Juan, PR 00931-3300. Offers biology education (M Ed); chemistry education (M Ed); curriculum and teaching (Ed D); English education (M Ed); history education (M Ed); mathematics education (M Ed); physics education (M Ed); secondary education (M Ed); Spanish education (M Ed). Part-time programs available. *Students:* 64 full-time (42 women), 123 part-time (91 women); all minorities (all Hispanic Americans) In 2006, 8 master's, 19 doctorates awarded. *Degree requirements:* For master's, thesis; for doctorate, thesis/dissertation, internship. *Entrance requirements:* For master's, PAEG or GRE, minimum GPA of 3.0, letter of recommendation; for doctorate, GRE or PAEG, master's degree, minimum GPA of 3.0, letter of recommendation (2), interview. *Application deadline:* For fall admission, 2/1 for domestic and international students. Application fee: $17. *Expenses:* Tuition, state resident: part-time $100 per credit. Tuition, nonresident: part-time $291 per credit. Required fees: $72 per semester. *Financial support:* Fellowships, research assistantships, teaching assistantships, career-related internships or fieldwork, Federal Work-Study, institutionally sponsored loans, and tuition waivers (partial) available. Financial award application deadline: 5/31. *Faculty research:* Science curriculum, administration management. *Unit head:* Dr. Loyda Martinez, Coordinator, 787-764-0000 Ext. 4361, Fax: 787-763-4130. *Application contact:* Information Contact, 787-764-0000 Ext. 4368, Fax: 787-763-4130.

University of South Carolina, The Graduate School, College of Arts and Sciences, Department of Languages, Literatures, and Cultures, Columbia, SC 29208. Offers comparative literature (MA, PhD); foreign languages (MAT), including French, German, Spanish; French (MA); German (MA); Spanish (MA). MAT offered in cooperation with the College of Education. Part-time programs available. *Degree requirements:* For master's, one foreign language, comprehensive exam; for doctorate, 2 foreign languages, thesis/dissertation, comprehensive exam. *Entrance requirements:* For master's and doctorate, GRE General Test, writing sample. Additional exam requirements/recommendations for international students: Required—TOEFL. Electronic applications accepted. *Faculty research:* Modern literature, linguistics, literature and culture, medieval literature.

University of South Carolina, The Graduate School, College of Education, Department of Instruction and Teacher Education, Program in Secondary Education, Columbia, SC 29208. Offers art education (IMA, MAT); business education (IMA, MAT); English (MAT); foreign language (MAT); health education (MAT); mathematics (MAT); science (IMA, MAT); secondary education (M Ed, MA, MT, PhD); social studies (IMA, MAT); theatre and speech (IMA, MAT). IMA and MT offered jointly with the subject areas. *Accreditation:* NCATE. *Degree requirements:* For master's, thesis (for some programs), foreign language (MA), comprehensive exam; for doctorate, one foreign language, thesis/dissertation, comprehensive exam. *Entrance requirements:* For master's, GRE General Test or MAT, teaching certificate (IMA, M Ed), interview; for doctorate, GRE General Test or MAT, interview. *Faculty research:* Middle school programs, professional development, school collaboration.

University of Southern Mississippi, Graduate School, College of Arts and Letters, Department of Foreign Languages and Literatures, Hattiesburg, MS 39406-0001. Offers French (MATL); Spanish (MATL); teaching English to speakers of other languages (TESOL) (MATL). *Faculty:* 11 full-time (5 women). *Students:* 14 full-time (11 women), 23 part-time (20 women); includes 6 minority (2 African Americans, 1 Asian American or Pacific Islander, 3 Hispanic Americans), 4 international. Average age 35. 22 applicants, 55% accepted, 7 enrolled. In 2006, 24 degrees awarded. *Degree requirements:* For master's, comprehensive exam, registration. *Entrance requirements:* For master's, GRE General Test, minimum GPA of 3.0 in field of study, 2.75 in last 2 years. Additional exam requirements/recommendations for international students: Required—TOEFL. *Application deadline:* For fall admission, 3/1 for domestic and international students. Applications are processed on a rolling basis. Application fee: $25 ($30 for international students). *Financial support:* In 2006–07, 1 research assistantship (averaging $5,930 per year), 8 teaching assistantships with full tuition reimbursements (averaging $5,930 per year) were awarded; Federal Work-Study, scholarships/grants, and unspecified assistantships also available. Financial award application deadline: 3/15. *Unit head:* Dr. William J. Powell, Chair, 601-266-4964, Fax: 601-266-4853.

University of South Florida, Graduate School, College of Education, Department of Secondary Education, Tampa, FL 33620-9951. Offers English education (M Ed, MA, PhD); foreign language education (M Ed, MA); instructional technology (M Ed); mathematics education (M Ed, MA, PhD, Ed S); middle school education (M Ed); science education (M Ed, MA, MAT, PhD); second language acquisition/instructional technology (PhD); secondary education (PhD); social science education (M Ed, MA). *Accreditation:* NCATE. Part-time and evening/weekend programs available. *Faculty:* 29 full-time (16 women), 15 part-time/adjunct (8 women). *Students:* 136 full-time (95 women), 279 part-time (188 women); includes 85 minority (35 African Americans, 1 American Indian/Alaska Native, 13 Asian Americans or Pacific Islanders, 36 Hispanic Americans), 19 international. 212 applicants, 71% accepted, 96 enrolled. In 2006, 87 master's, 12 doctorates awarded. *Entrance requirements:* For master's and doctorate, GRE General Test, minimum GPA of 3.5; for Ed S, GRE General Test. *Application deadline:* For fall admission, 6/1 for domestic students; for spring admission, 10/15 for domestic students. Application fee: $30. Electronic applications accepted. *Financial support:* Scholarships/grants and unspecified assistantships available. Total annual research expenditures: $477,202. *Unit head:* Dr. Jane H. Applegate, Interim Chairperson, 813-974-3533, Fax: 813-974-3837, E-mail: applegat@tempest.coedu.usf.edu.

The University of Tennessee, Graduate School, College of Education, Health and Human Sciences, Program in Education, Knoxville, TN 37996. Offers art education (MS); counseling education (PhD); cultural studies in education (PhD); curriculum (MS, Ed S); curriculum, educational research and evaluation (Ed D, PhD); early childhood education (PhD); early childhood special education (MS); education of deaf and hard of hearing (MS); educational administration and policy studies (Ed D, PhD); educational administration and supervision (Ed S); educational psychology (Ed D, PhD); elementary education (MS, Ed S); elementary teaching (MS); English education (MS, Ed S); exercise science (PhD); foreign language/ESL education (MS, Ed S); instructional technology (MS, Ed D, PhD, Ed S); literacy, language and ESL education (PhD); literacy, language education, and ESL education (Ed D); mathematics education (MS, Ed S); modified and comprehensive special education (MS); reading education (MS, Ed S); school counseling (Ed S); school psychology (PhD, Ed S); science education (MS, Ed S); secondary teaching (MS); social foundations (MS); social science education (MS, Ed S); socio-cultural foundations of sports and education (PhD); special education (Ed S); teacher education (Ed D, PhD). *Accreditation:* NCATE. Part-time and evening/weekend programs available. *Students:* 529 (401 women); includes 39 minority (23 African Americans, 2 American Indian/Alaska Native, 9 Asian Americans or Pacific Islanders, 5 Hispanic Americans) 34 international. 420 applicants, 50% accepted. In 2006, 258 master's, 28 doctorates awarded. *Degree requirements:* For master's and Ed S, thesis optional; for doctorate, variable foreign language requirement, thesis/dissertation. *Entrance requirements:* For master's, minimum GPA of 2.7; for doctorate and Ed S, GRE General Test, minimum GPA of 2.7. Additional exam requirements/recommendations for international students: Required—TOEFL. *Application deadline:* For fall admission, 2/1 priority date for domestic students. Applications are processed on a rolling basis. Application fee: $35. Electronic applications accepted. *Expenses:* Tuition, state resident: full-time $5,574. Tuition, nonresident: full-time $16,840. Required fees: $792. *Financial support:* In 2006–07, 4 fellowships, 9 teaching assistantships were awarded; career-related internships or fieldwork, Federal Work-Study, institutionally sponsored loans, and unspecified assistantships also available. Financial award application deadline: 2/1; financial award applicants required to submit FAFSA. *Unit head:* Dr. Lester Knight, Head, 865-974-0907, Fax: 865-974-8718, E-mail: lknight@utk.edu.

The University of Texas at Austin, Graduate School, College of Education, Program in Foreign Language Education, Austin, TX 78712-1111. Offers MA, PhD. Part-time programs available. *Degree requirements:* For master's and doctorate, one foreign language, thesis/dissertation. *Entrance requirements:* For master's and doctorate, GRE General Test. Electronic applications accepted. *Faculty research:* Individual differences in language learning, culture, portfolio, assessment, biliteracy.

The University of Toledo, College of Graduate Studies, College of Education, Department of Curriculum and Instruction, Program in Education and French, Toledo, OH 43606-3390. Offers MAE.

The University of Toledo, College of Graduate Studies, College of Education, Department of Curriculum and Instruction, Program in Education and German, Toledo, OH 43606-3390. Offers MAE.

The University of Toledo, College of Graduate Studies, College of Education, Department of Curriculum and Instruction, Program in Education and Spanish, Toledo, OH 43606-3390. Offers MAE. *Students:* 1 (woman) full-time. 1 applicant, 100% accepted, 1 enrolled.

University of Utah, The Graduate School, College of Humanities, Department of Languages and Literature, Salt Lake City, UT 84112-1107. Offers comparative literature (MA, PhD); French (MA, MALP); German (MA, MALP, PhD); language pedagogy (MALP); Spanish (MA, MALP, PhD). *Faculty:* 35 full-time (18 women). *Students:* 27 full-time (18 women), 10 part-time (6 women); includes 4 minority (all Hispanic Americans), 5 international. Average age 35. 32 applicants, 47% accepted, 10 enrolled. In 2006, 14 master's, 4 doctorates awarded. Terminal master's awarded for partial completion of doctoral program. *Median time to degree:* Of those who began their doctoral program in fall 1998, 66% received their degree in 8 years or less. *Degree requirements:* For master's, 2 foreign languages, comprehensive exam, registration; for doctorate, 3 foreign languages, thesis/dissertation, comprehensive exam, registration. *Entrance requirements:* For doctorate, MA in target language. Additional exam requirements/recommendations for international students: Required—TOEFL (minimum score 500 paper-based; 173 computer-based). *Application deadline:* For fall admission, 2/1 priority date for domestic students, 1/15 priority date for international students; for spring admission, 10/15 priority date for domestic students. Applications are processed on a rolling basis. Application fee: $45 ($65 for international students). Electronic applications accepted. *Expenses:* Tuition, state resident: full-time $3,208. Tuition, nonresident: full-time $11,326. Required fees: $608. Tuition and fees vary according to class time and program. *Financial support:* In 2006–07, 35 students received support, including 35 teaching assistantships with full tuition reimbursements available (averaging $10,500 per year); fellowships with tuition reimbursements available, health care benefits also available. Financial award application deadline: 2/1; financial award applicants required to submit FAFSA. *Faculty research:* Literary theory, stylistics, Russian and Soviet literature, existentialism, theory of criticism. Total annual research expenditures: $42,903. *Unit head:* Dr. Christine A. Jones, Director of Graduate Studies, 801-585-3002, Fax: 801-581-7581, E-mail: cjones@hum.utah.edu. *Application contact:* Corky Reeser, Executive Graduate Secretary, 801-581-7570, Fax: 801-581-7581, E-mail: c.reeser@mail.hum.utah.edu.

University of Vermont, Graduate College, College of Arts and Sciences, Department of Classics, Burlington, VT 05405. Offers Greek (MA); Greek and Latin (MAT); Latin (MA). *Students:* 4 (1 woman). 10 applicants, 50% accepted, 3 enrolled. In 2006, 1 degree awarded. *Degree requirements:* For master's, one foreign language, thesis. *Entrance requirements:* For master's, GRE General Test. Additional exam requirements/recommendations for international students: Required—TOEFL (minimum score 550 paper-based; 213 computer-based). *Application deadline:* For fall admission, 4/1 priority date for domestic students. Applications are processed on a rolling basis. Application fee: $40. *Expenses:* Tuition, state resident: part-time $434 per credit. Tuition, nonresident: part-time $1,096 per credit. *Financial support:* Fellowships, teaching assistantships available. Financial award application deadline: 3/1. *Faculty research:* Early Greek literature. *Unit head:* Dr. Z. Philip Ambrose, Acting Chair, 802-656-3210.

University of Victoria, Faculty of Graduate Studies, Faculty of Humanities, Department of French, Victoria, BC V8W 2Y2, Canada. Offers literature (MA); teaching emphasis (MA). Part-time and evening/weekend programs available. *Degree requirements:* For master's, 2 foreign languages, thesis optional. *Entrance requirements:* For master's, BA in French. Additional exam requirements/recommendations for international students: Required—TOEFL (minimum score 575 paper-based; 233 computer-based), IELTS (minimum score 7). Electronic applications accepted. *Faculty research:* French-Canadian literature, stylistics, comparative literature, Francophone literature.

University of West Georgia, Graduate School, College of Education, Department of Curriculum and Instruction, Program in Education-French, Carrollton, GA 30118. Offers M Ed. *Entrance requirements:* For master's, GRE or MAT. *Expenses:* Tuition, state resident: full-time $2,286; part-time $127 per credit. Tuition, nonresident: full-time $9,144; part-time $508 per credit. Required fees: $494; $27 per credit. $121 per semester. *Application contact:* Dr. Charles W. Clark, Chair, 678-839-6508, E-mail: cclark@westga.edu.

University of West Georgia, Graduate School, College of Education, Department of Curriculum and Instruction, Program in Education-Spanish, Carrollton, GA 30118. Offers M Ed. *Students:* Average age 33. In 2006, 1 degree awarded. *Entrance requirements:* For master's, GRE or MAT. *Expenses:* Tuition, state resident: full-time $2,286; part-time $127 per credit. Tuition, nonresident: full-time $9,144; part-time $508 per credit. Required fees: $494; $27 per credit. $121 per semester. *Application contact:* Dr. Charles W. Clark, Chair, 678-839-6508, E-mail: cclark@westga.edu.

University of Wisconsin–Madison, Graduate School, School of Education, Department of Curriculum and Instruction, Madison, WI 53706-1380. Offers art education (MA); curriculum and instruction (MS, PhD); education and mathematics (MA); French education (MA); German education (MA); music education (MS); science education (MS); Spanish education (MA). *Accreditation:* NASM (one or more programs are accredited). *Degree requirements:* For doctorate, thesis/dissertation. Application fee: $45. *Financial support:* Project assistantships available. *Unit head:* Dr. Alan Lockwood, Chair, 608-262-4000.

Vanderbilt University, Graduate School, Department of French and Italian, Nashville, TN 37240-1001. Offers French (MA, MAT, PhD). *Faculty:* 14 full-time (10 women). *Students:* 10 full-time (8 women); includes 1 minority (African American), 1 international. 22 applicants, 23% accepted, 3 enrolled. In 2006, 1 degree awarded. *Degree requirements:* For master's, one foreign language, comprehensive exam; for doctorate, 2 foreign languages, thesis/dissertation, final and qualifying exams. *Entrance requirements:* For master's and doctorate, GRE General Test. *Application deadline:* For fall admission, 1/15 for domestic and international students. Application fee: $0. Electronic applications accepted. *Expenses:* Tuition: Full-time $24,462. Required fees: $2,515. One-time fee: $30 full-time. Full-time tuition and fees vary according to course load, degree level and program. *Financial support:* Fellowships with full tuition reimbursements, teaching assistantships with full tuition reimbursements, career-related internships or fieldwork, Federal Work-Study, and institutionally sponsored loans available. Financial award application deadline: 1/15. *Faculty research:* Baudelaire, Rabelais, voyage literature, postcolonial literature, medieval epic. *Unit head:* Virginia Scott, Chair, 615-322-6900, Fax: 615-343-6909, E-mail: virginia.m.scott@vanderbilt.edu. *Application contact:* Robert F. Barsky, Director of Graduate Studies, 615-322-6900, Fax: 615-343-6909, E-mail: robert.barsky@vanderbilt.edu.

Vanderbilt University, Graduate School, Department of Germanic and Slavic Languages, Nashville, TN 37240-1001. Offers German (MA, MAT, PhD). *Faculty:* 11 full-time (4 women). *Students:* 18 full-time (9 women); includes 1 minority (Asian American or Pacific Islander), 9 international. 14 applicants, 64% accepted, 6 enrolled. In 2006, 2 master's, 1 doctorate awarded. *Degree requirements:* For master's, one foreign language, thesis or alternative; for doctorate, 2 foreign languages, thesis/dissertation, qualifying and final exams, comprehensive exam. *Entrance requirements:* For master's and doctorate, GRE General Test, sample of written work. *Application deadline:* For fall admission, 1/15 for domestic and international students. Application fee: $0. Electronic applications accepted. *Expenses:* Tuition: Full-time $24,462. Required fees: $2,515. One-time fee: $30 full-time. Full-time tuition and fees vary according to course load, degree level and program. *Financial support:* Fellowships, teaching assistantships with full tuition reimbursements, career-related internships or fieldwork, Federal Work-Study, and institutionally sponsored loans available. Financial award application deadline: 1/15. *Faculty research:* 1750 to present, Middle Ages, baroque, language pedagogy, linguistics. Total annual research expenditures: $59,485. *Unit head:* Dieter H. O. Sevin, Chair, 615-322-2611, Fax: 615-343-7258. *Application contact:* Meike Werner, Director of Graduate Studies, 615-322-2611, Fax: 615-343-7258, E-mail: meike.werner@vanderbilt.edu.

Vanderbilt University, Graduate School, Department of Spanish and Portuguese, Nashville, TN 37240-1001. Offers Portuguese (MA); Spanish (MA, MAT, PhD); Spanish and Portuguese (PhD). *Faculty:* 20 full-time (11 women), 2 part-time/adjunct (1 woman). *Students:* 31 full-time (16 women); includes 2 minority (1 African American, 1 Hispanic American), 15 international. 47 applicants, 13% accepted, 4 enrolled. In 2006, 1 master's, 4 doctorates awarded. *Degree requirements:* For master's, one foreign language, thesis; for doctorate, 2 foreign languages, thesis/dissertation, final and qualifying exams. *Entrance requirements:* For master's and doctorate, GRE General Test. *Application deadline:* For fall admission, 1/15 for domestic and international students. Application fee: $0. Electronic applications accepted. *Expenses:* Tuition: Full-time $24,462. Required fees: $2,515. One-time fee: $30 full-time. Full-time tuition and fees vary according to course load, degree level and program. *Financial support:* Fellowships with full and partial tuition reimbursements, teaching assistantships with full tuition reimbursements, Federal Work-Study and institutionally sponsored loans available. Financial award application deadline: 1/15. *Faculty research:* Spanish, Portuguese, and Latin American literatures; foreign language pedagogy; Renaissance and baroque poetry; nineteenth century Spanish novel. *Unit head:* Cathy Jrade, Chair, 615-322-6930, Fax: 615-343-7260. *Application contact:* Benigno Trigo, Director of Graduate Studies, 615-322-6930, Fax: 615-343-7260, E-mail: benigno.trigo@vanderbilt.edu.

Wayne State University, College of Education, Division of Teacher Education, Detroit, MI 48202. Offers adult and continuing education (M Ed); art education (M Ed); bilingual/bicultural education (M Ed, MAT); business education (M Ed, MAT); career and technical education (M Ed, Ed D, PhD, Ed S); curriculum and instruction (Ed D, PhD, Ed S); distributive education (M Ed, MAT); early childhood education (M Ed); elementary education (M Ed, MAT, Ed D, PhD, Ed S); elementary education curriculum and instruction (M Ed); English education (M Ed); English education-secondary (M Ed, Ed S); foreign language education (M Ed); general education (Ed D, Ed S); health occupations education (M Ed); industrial education (M Ed); mathematics education (M Ed, Ed S); pre-school and parent education (M Ed); reading (M Ed, Ed D, Ed S); reading, languages and literature (Ed D); school music-vocal (M Ed); science education (M Ed, MAT, Ed S); secondary education (MAT); secondary school reading (M Ed); social studies education (M Ed, Ed S), including education-secondary (M Ed); special education (M Ed, Ed D, PhD, Ed S); teacher education (MAT, Ed D, PhD). *Faculty:* 41 full-time (22 women), 2 part-time/adjunct (both women). *Students:* 401 full-time (295 women), 1,021 part-time (784 women); includes 527 minority (452 African Americans, 6 American Indian/Alaska Native, 32 Asian Americans or Pacific Islanders, 37 Hispanic Americans), 18 international. Average age 36. 296 applicants, 81% accepted, 132 enrolled. In 2006, 386 master's, 1 doctorate awarded. *Degree requirements:* For doctorate, thesis/dissertation. *Entrance requirements:* For master's, minimum GPA of 2.6; for doctorate, minimum undergraduate GPA of 3.0, graduate 3.5; interview. Additional exam requirements/recommendations for international students: Required—TOEFL (minimum score 550 paper-based; 213 computer-based), TWE (minimum score 6). *Application deadline:* For fall admission, 7/1 for domestic students, 6/1 for international students; for winter admission, 10/1 for international students; for spring admission, 2/1 for international students. Application fee: $30 ($50 for international students). Electronic applications accepted. *Financial support:* In 2006–07, 1 fellowship (averaging $34,919 per year) was awarded; research assistantships. *Faculty research:* Reading and writing literacy and literature. Total annual research expenditures: $209,400. *Unit head:* Dr. Joann Snyder, Academic Director, 313-577-1644, E-mail: joanne.snyder@wayne.edu. *Application contact:* Sharon Elliott, Assistant Dean, 313-577-0902, E-mail: sharon.elliott@wayne.edu.

West Chester University of Pennsylvania, Graduate Studies, College of Arts and Sciences, Department of Foreign Languages, West Chester, PA 19383. Offers French (M Ed, MA); German (M Ed); Latin (M Ed); Spanish (M Ed, MA). Part-time and evening/weekend programs available. *Students:* 5 full-time (4 women), 9 part-time (8 women). Average age 35. 10 applicants, 100% accepted, 5 enrolled. In 2006, 6 degrees awarded. *Degree requirements:* For master's, one foreign language, comprehensive exam. *Entrance requirements:* For master's, GRE, placement test. *Application deadline:* For fall admission, 4/15 priority date for domestic students; for spring admission, 10/15 for domestic students. Applications are processed on a rolling basis. Application fee: $35. *Financial support:* In 2006–07, 2 research assistantships with full tuition reimbursements (averaging $5,000 per year) were awarded; unspecified assistantships also available. Support available to part-time students. Financial award application deadline: 2/15; financial award applicants required to submit FAFSA. *Faculty research:* Implementation of world languages curriculum framework. *Unit head:* Dr. Jerry Williams, Chair, 610-436-2700, Fax: 610-436-3048, E-mail: jwilliams2@wcupa.edu. *Application contact:* Dr. Rebecca Pauly, Graduate Coordinator, 610-436-2382, E-mail: rpauly@wcupa.edu.

Worcester State College, Graduate Studies, Department of Education, Concentration in Spanish, Worcester, MA 01602-2597. Offers M Ed. *Students:* Average age 32. 1 applicant, 100% accepted, 1 enrolled. *Expenses:* Tuition, state resident: full-time $4,518; part-time $251 per credit hour. Tuition, nonresident: full-time $4,518; part-time $251 per credit hour. *Financial support:* In 2006–07, 1 research assistantship with full tuition reimbursement (averaging $4,800 per year) was awarded. *Unit head:* Dr. Juan Orbe, 508-929-8704.

Health Education

Adams State College, The Graduate School, Department of Health and Physical Education, Alamosa, CO 81102. Offers MA. *Accreditation:* Teacher Education Accreditation Council. Part-time programs available. *Degree requirements:* For master's, comprehensive exam. *Entrance requirements:* For master's, GRE General Test or MAT, minimum undergraduate GPA of 2.75.

Adelphi University, School of Education, Program in Health Studies, Garden City, NY 11530-0701. Offers community health education (MA, Certificate); school health education (MA). Part-time and evening/weekend programs available. *Students:* 10 full-time (9 women), 95 part-time (51 women); includes 6 minority (3 African Americans, 3 Hispanic Americans), 1 international. Average age 29. In 2006, 30 degrees awarded. *Degree requirements:* For master's, internship. *Entrance requirements:* For master's, 3 letters of recommendation, resumé, minimum cumulative GPA of 2.75. Additional exam requirements/recommendations for international students: Required—TOEFL (minimum score 550 paper-based; 213 computer-based). *Application deadline:* Applications are processed on a rolling basis. Application fee: $50. Electronic applications accepted. *Financial support:* Fellowships, research assistantships with partial tuition reimbursements, teaching assistantships, career-related internships or fieldwork, Federal Work-Study, institutionally sponsored loans, and tuition waivers (full) available. Support available to part-time students. Financial award application deadline: 2/15; financial award applicants required to submit FAFSA. *Faculty research:* Alcohol abuse, tobacco cessation, drug abuse, healthy family lives, healthy personal living. *Unit head:* Dr. Stanley Snegroff, Director, 516-877-4283, E-mail: snegroff@adelphi.edu. *Application contact:* Christine Murphy, Director of Admissions, 516-877-3050, Fax: 516-877-3039, E-mail: graduateadmissions@adelphi.edu.

Alabama State University, School of Graduate Studies, College of Education, Department of Health, Physical Education, and Recreation, Montgomery, AL 36101-0271. Offers health education (M Ed); physical education (M Ed). Part-time programs available. *Faculty:* 4 full-time (all women), 1 part-time/adjunct (0 women). *Students:* 7 full-time (2 women), 15 part-time (8 women); includes 18 minority (all African Americans) In 2006, 8 degrees awarded. *Degree requirements:* For master's, comprehensive exam. *Entrance requirements:* For master's, GRE General Test, MAT, graduate writing competency test. Additional exam requirements/recommendations for international students: Required—TOEFL (minimum score 500 paper-based; 173 computer-based). *Application deadline:* For fall admission, 7/15 for domestic students; for spring admission, 12/15 for domestic students. Applications are processed on a rolling basis. Application fee: $10. *Expenses:* Tuition, state resident: full-time $1,728; part-time $192 per hour. Tuition, nonresident: full-time $3,456; part-time $334 per hour. *Financial support:* In 2006–07, research assistantships (averaging $9,450 per year). *Faculty research:* Risk factors for heart disease in the college-age population, cardiovascular reactivity for the Cold Pressor Test. *Unit head:* Dr. Doris Screws, Chair, 334-229-4504, Fax: 334-229-4928.

Albany State University, College of Education, Program in Health and Physical Education, Albany, GA 31705-2717. Offers M Ed. *Accreditation:* NCATE. Part-time programs available. *Degree requirements:* For master's, thesis optional. *Entrance requirements:* For master's, GRE General Test, MAT or NTE. Electronic applications accepted.

Alcorn State University, School of Graduate Studies, School of Psychology and Education, Alcorn State, MS 39096-7500. Offers agricultural education (MS Ed); elementary education (MS Ed, Ed S); guidance and counseling (MS Ed); industrial education (MS Ed); secondary education (MS Ed), including health and physical education; special education (MS Ed). *Accreditation:* NCATE. *Faculty:* 14 full-time (9 women), 21 part-time/adjunct (13 women). *Students:* 76 full-time (44 women), 271 part-time (226 women); includes 333 minority (all African Americans) In 2006, 119 degrees awarded. *Degree requirements:* For master's, thesis optional. *Application deadline:* For fall admission, 7/15 priority date for domestic students; for spring admission, 11/25 for domestic students. Applications are processed on a rolling basis. Application fee: $0 ($10 for international students). *Financial support:* Career-related internships or fieldwork available. Support available to part-time students. *Unit head:* Dr. Josephine M. Posey, Dean, 601-877-6141, Fax: 601-877-3867.

Allen College, Program in Nursing, Waterloo, IA 50703. Offers acute care nurse practitioner (MSN); family nurse practitioner (MSN); health education (MSN); leadership in health care delivery (MSN). *Accreditation:* AACN; NLN. Part-time and evening/weekend programs available. *Faculty:* 2 full-time (both women), 4 part-time/adjunct (all women). *Students:* 19 full-time (17 women), 42 part-time (39 women). Average age 37. 62 applicants, 94% accepted, 46 enrolled. In 2006, 3 degrees awarded. *Degree requirements:* For master's, thesis optional. *Entrance requirements:* For master's, minimum GPA of 3.0. Additional exam requirements/recommendations for international students: Required—TOEFL (minimum score 550 paper-based). *Application deadline:* For fall admission, 7/15 priority date for domestic students; for spring admission, 12/1 priority date for domestic students. Applications are processed on a rolling basis. Application fee: $50. Electronic applications accepted. *Expenses:* Tuition: Full-time $9,824; part-time $562 per credit hour. Required fees: $481. One-time fee: $220 part-time. Tuition and fees vary according to course load. *Financial support:* In 2006–07, 58 students received support, including 1 teaching assistantship (averaging $10,116 per year); institutionally sponsored loans, scholarships/grants, and traineeships also available. Support available to part-time students. Financial award application deadline: 8/15; financial award applicants required to submit FAFSA. *Faculty research:* Pain and aged, congestive heart failure. *Unit head:* Nancy Kramer, Chair, 319-226-2040, Fax: 319-226-2070, E-mail: kramerna@ihs.org.

Arcadia University, Graduate Studies, Department of Medical Science and Community Health, Program in Allied Health, Glenside, PA 19038-3295. Offers MSHE, MSPH. Part-time and evening/weekend programs available. *Faculty:* 1 (woman) full-time, 9 part-time/adjunct (5 women). *Students:* 11 full-time (7 women), 36 part-time (31 women); includes 9 minority (8 African Americans, 1 Hispanic American), 4 international. In 2006, 18 degrees awarded. *Entrance requirements:* For master's, GMAT or GRE (MHA). *Application deadline:* Applications are processed on a rolling basis. Application fee: $35. *Financial support:* Tuition waivers (partial) and unspecified assistantships available. *Unit head:* Dr. Andrea Crivelli-Kovach, Coordinator, 215-572-4014. *Application contact:* 215-572-2910, Fax: 215-572-4049, E-mail: admiss@arcadia.edu.

Arkansas State University, Graduate School, College of Nursing and Health Professions, Program in Health Sciences, Jonesboro, State University, AR 72467. Offers aging studies (Certificate); health sciences (MS); health sciences education (Certificate). Part-time programs available. *Faculty:* 3 full-time (2 women). *Students:* 4 full-time (all women), 10 part-time (7 women); includes 6 minority (all African Americans), 1 international. Average age 32. 10 applicants, 80% accepted, 8 enrolled. *Degree requirements:* For master's, comprehensive exam. *Entrance requirements:* For master's, GRE General Test, Allied Health Professions Admission Test, appropriate bachelor's degree, resumé, writing sample, letters of reference, official transcript. Additional exam requirements/recommendations for international students: Required—TOEFL (minimum score 213 computer-based). *Application deadline:* Applications are processed on a rolling basis. Application fee: $30 ($40 for international students). Electronic applications accepted. *Expenses:* Contact institution. *Financial support:* Scholarships/grants available. Financial award application deadline: 7/1; financial award applicants required to submit FAFSA. *Unit head:* Chris Hutchinson, Head, 870-972-3073, Fax: 870-972-2004, E-mail: hutch@astate.edu.

A.T. Still University of Health Sciences, School of Health Management, Kirksville, MO 63501. Offers geriatric healthcare (MGH); health administration (MHA); health education

Health Education

A.T. Still University of Health Sciences (continued)
(DH Ed, MH Ed); public health (MPH). Part-time and evening/weekend programs available. Postbaccalaureate distance learning degree programs offered (no on-campus study). *Faculty:* 1 full-time (0 women), 45 part-time/adjunct (17 women). *Students:* 18 full-time (14 women), 194 part-time (130 women); includes 39 minority (20 African Americans, 8 American Indian/Alaska Native, 9 Asian Americans or Pacific Islanders, 2 Hispanic Americans). Average age 34. In 2006, 75 degrees awarded. *Degree requirements:* For master's, thesis (for some programs), capstone project. *Entrance requirements:* For master's, minimum GPA of 2.5, bachelor's degree or equivalent from U.S. institution. Additional exam requirements/recommendations for international students: Required—TOEFL (minimum score 500 paper-based; 222 computer-based). *Application deadline:* For fall admission, 8/27 for domestic students, 8/4 for international students; for winter admission, 10/25 for domestic students, 11/26 for international students; for spring admission, 2/10 for domestic students, 3/17 for international students. Applications are processed on a rolling basis. Electronic applications accepted. *Expenses: Contact institution. Financial support:* Application deadline: 5/1; *Unit head:* Dr. Jon Persavich, Dean, 660-626-2820, Fax: 660-626-2826, E-mail: jpersavich@atsu.edu. *Application contact:* Donna Sparks, Associate Director for Admissions, 660-626-2237, Fax: 660-626-2969, E-mail: admissions@atsu.edu.

Auburn University, Graduate School, College of Education, Department of Health and Human Performance, Auburn University, AL 36849. Offers exercise science (M Ed, MS, PhD); health promotion (M Ed, MS); physical education/teacher education (M Ed, MS, Ed D, Ed S). *Accreditation:* NCATE. Part-time programs available. *Faculty:* 13 full-time (5 women). *Students:* 40 full-time (18 women), 27 part-time (6 women); includes 7 minority (5 African Americans, 2 Hispanic Americans), 6 international. Average age 28. 67 applicants, 79% accepted, 24 enrolled. In 2006, 17 master's, 2 doctorates awarded. *Degree requirements:* For master's, thesis (for some programs); for doctorate, thesis/dissertation; for Ed S, exam, field project. *Entrance requirements:* For master's, GRE General Test; for doctorate and Ed S, GRE General Test, interview, master's degree. *Application deadline:* For fall admission, 7/7 for domestic students; for spring admission, 11/24 for domestic students. Applications are processed on a rolling basis. Application fee: $25 ($50 for international students). Electronic applications accepted. *Expenses:* Tuition, state resident: full-time $5,000. Tuition, nonresident: full-time $15,000. Required fees: $416. Tuition and fees vary according to program. *Financial support:* Research assistantships, teaching assistantships, Federal Work-Study available. Support available to part-time students. Financial award application deadline: 3/15. *Faculty research:* Biomechanics, exercise physiology, motor skill learning, school health, curriculum development. *Unit head:* Dr. Mary E Rudisill, Acting Head, 334-844-4483. *Application contact:* Dr. Joe Pittman, Interim Dean of the Graduate School, 334-844-4700.

Augusta State University, Graduate Studies, College of Education, Program in Health and Physical Education, Augusta, GA 30904-2200. Offers M Ed. *Faculty:* 3 full-time (2 women). *Students:* 4 full-time (2 women), 4 part-time (all women); includes 1 minority (Asian American or Pacific Islander) Average age 31. 3 applicants, 100% accepted, 3 enrolled. In 2006, 3 degrees awarded. *Entrance requirements:* For master's, GRE, MAT, minimum GPA of 2.5. Application fee: $20. *Expenses:* Tuition, state resident: full-time $3,044; part-time $127 per credit hour. Tuition, nonresident: full-time $12,172; part-time $508 per credit hour. *Financial support:* Career-related internships or fieldwork, Federal Work-Study, institutionally sponsored loans, and unspecified assistantships available. Support available to part-time students. *Unit head:* Dr. Paula J Dohoney, Chair, 706-731-7922, Fax: 706-667-4140, E-mail: pdohoney@aug.edu. *Application contact:* Andrea M Scott, Secretary to the Dean, 706-737-1499, Fax: 706-667-4706, E-mail: ascott@aug.edu.

Austin Peay State University, College of Graduate Studies, College of Professional Programs and Social Sciences, Department of Health and Human Performance, Clarksville, TN 37044. Offers health and physical education (MS). Part-time and evening/weekend programs available. Postbaccalaureate distance learning degree programs offered. *Faculty:* 6 full-time (4 women), 1 (woman) part-time/adjunct. *Students:* 31 full-time (16 women), 35 part-time (25 women); includes 30 minority (26 African Americans, 4 Hispanic Americans). Average age 30. In 2006, 29 degrees awarded. *Degree requirements:* For master's, thesis optional. *Entrance requirements:* For master's, GRE General Test, minimum GPA of 2.5, 2 letters of recommendation. Additional exam requirements/recommendations for international students: Required—TOEFL (minimum score 500 paper-based; 173 computer-based). *Application deadline:* For fall admission, 7/31 priority date for domestic students; for spring admission, 12/17 priority date for domestic students. Applications are processed on a rolling basis. Application fee: $25. Electronic applications accepted. *Expenses:* Tuition, state resident: full-time $5,138; part-time $272 per credit hour. Tuition, nonresident: full-time $14,832; part-time $693 per credit hour. Required fees: $1,009. *Financial support:* In 2006–07, fellowships (averaging $9,000 per year), research assistantships (averaging $10,270 per year) were awarded; career-related internships or fieldwork, Federal Work-Study, institutionally sponsored loans, scholarships/grants, and unspecified assistantships also available. Support available to part-time students. Financial award application deadline: 3/1; financial award applicants required to submit FAFSA. *Faculty research:* Aging and physical activity. *Unit head:* Dr. Dixie Dennis, Professor and Chair, 931-221-6111, Fax: 931-221-7040, E-mail: dennisdi@apsu.edu.

Averett University, Graduate Studies in Education, Danville, VA 24541-3692. Offers art education (M Ed); biology (M Ed); chemistry (M Ed); curriculum and instruction (M Ed); elementary education (M Ed); English (M Ed); health and physical education (M Ed); history and social studies (M Ed); mathematics education (M Ed); physical science (M Ed); reading (M Ed); special education (learning disabilities specialization PK-12) (M Ed). Part-time and evening/weekend programs available. *Faculty:* 10 full-time (4 women), 7 part-time/adjunct (6 women). *Students:* 14 full-time (10 women), 85 part-time (67 women); includes 20 minority (18 African Americans, 2 Asian Americans or Pacific Islanders). Average age 33. 52 applicants, 100% accepted, 40 enrolled. In 2006, 43 degrees awarded. *Degree requirements:* For master's, thesis optional. *Entrance requirements:* For master's, PRAXIS, GRE General Test, MAT or NTE, writing proficiency exam, 3 letters of recommendation, current teacher's licensure or eligibility for licensure, minimum undergraduate GPA of 3.0 in previous 2 years. Additional exam requirements/recommendations for international students: Required—TOEFL (minimum score 600 paper-based; 200 computer-based). *Application deadline:* Applications are processed on a rolling basis. Application fee: $20. *Expenses: Contact institution. Financial support:* In 2006–07, 23 students received support. Federal Work-Study and scholarships/grants available. Financial award application deadline: 4/1; financial award applicants required to submit FAFSA. *Faculty research:* Literary assessment-PreK-6, handwriting instruction and assessment-PreK-6, written language instruction and assessment-PreK-6 and special needs students learning styles, curriculum and instruction processes. *Unit head:* Dr. Lynn H. Wolf, Chair, 434-793-3995, Fax: 434-791-4392, E-mail: lynn.wolf@averett.edu.

Ball State University, Graduate School, College of Sciences and Humanities, Department of Physiology and Health Science, Program in Health Education, Muncie, IN 47306-1099. Offers MA, MAE. *Accreditation:* NCATE. *Students:* 3 full-time (2 women), 4 part-time (3 women). Average age 26. 12 applicants, 75% accepted, 4 enrolled. In 2006, 5 degrees awarded. Application fee: $25 ($35 for international students). *Financial support:* Teaching assistantships with full tuition reimbursements available. Financial award application deadline: 3/1. *Unit head:* Dr. Martin Wood, Director, 765-285-8349, Fax: 765-285-3210.

Baylor University, Graduate School, School of Education, Department of Health, Human Performance and Recreation, Waco, TX 76798. Offers exercise, nutrition and preventive health (PhD); health, human performance and recreation (MS Ed). *Accreditation:* NCATE. Part-time programs available. *Faculty:* 13 full-time (5 women), 3 part-time/adjunct (1 woman). *Students:* 58 full-time (33 women), 31 part-time (16 women); includes 14 minority (7 African Americans, 4 American Indian/Alaska Native, 1 Asian American or Pacific Islander, 2 Hispanic Americans), 5 international. 30 applicants, 87% accepted. In 2006, 41 master's, 5 doctorates awarded. *Degree requirements:* For master's, thesis optional. *Entrance requirements:* For master's, GRE General Test. *Application deadline:* For fall admission, 4/1 priority date for domestic students; for spring admission, 10/1 for domestic students. Applications are processed on a rolling basis. Application fee: $25. Electronic applications accepted. *Financial support:* In 2006–07, 35 students received support, including 22 teaching assistantships; career-related internships or fieldwork, Federal Work-Study, institutionally sponsored loans, tuition waivers (partial), and recreation supplements also available. *Faculty research:* Behavior change theory, pedagogy, nutrition and enzyme therapy, exercise testing, health planning. *Unit head:* Dr. Mike Greenwood, Graduate Program Director, 254-710-3505, Fax: 254-710-3527, E-mail: mike_greenwood@baylor.edu. *Application contact:* Suzanne Keener, Administrative Assistant, 254-710-3588, Fax: 254-710-3870.

Boston University, School of Education, Department of Curriculum and Teaching, Program in Health Education, Boston, MA 02215. Offers Ed M, CAGS. *Students:* 1 (woman) full-time, 5 part-time (4 women); includes 1 minority (Asian American or Pacific Islander) Average age 29. 8 applicants, 88% accepted. In 2006, 4 degrees awarded. *Degree requirements:* For master's, thesis optional. *Entrance requirements:* For master's and CAGS, GRE General Test or MAT. Additional exam requirements/recommendations for international students: Required—TOEFL. *Application deadline:* For fall admission, 2/15 priority date for domestic students; for winter admission, 10/1 priority date for domestic students. Applications are processed on a rolling basis. Application fee: $70. Electronic applications accepted. *Expenses:* Tuition: Full-time $33,330; part-time $1,042 per credit. Required fees: $462; $40. *Financial support:* Application deadline: 2/15. *Faculty research:* Substance abuse, therapeutic recreation, motor development and performance, stress management. *Unit head:* Dr. Eileen C. Sullivan, Coordinator, 617-353-3300, E-mail: eileensu@bu.edu. *Application contact:* 617-353-4237, Fax: 617-353-8937, E-mail: sedgrad@bu.edu.

Brigham Young University, Graduate Studies, College of Health and Human Performance, Department of Health Science, Provo, UT 84602-1001. Offers MPH. *Faculty:* 14 full-time (3 women). *Students:* 25 full-time (19 women), 5 part-time (4 women); includes 4 minority (1 African American, 3 Asian Americans or Pacific Islanders). Average age 26. 49 applicants, 31% accepted, 12 enrolled. In 2006, 8 degrees awarded. *Degree requirements:* For master's, oral defense. *Entrance requirements:* For master's, GRE General Test, minimum GPA of 3.0 in last 60 hours. Additional exam requirements/recommendations for international students: Required—TOEFL (minimum score 580 paper-based; 237 computer-based; 85 iBT), IELTS (minimum score 7). *Application deadline:* For fall admission, 2/1 for domestic and international students. Application fee: $50. Electronic applications accepted. *Financial support:* In 2006–07, 23 students received support, including 19 research assistantships with partial tuition reimbursements available (averaging $2,419 per year); fellowships with partial tuition reimbursements available, teaching assistantships, career-related internships or fieldwork, scholarships/grants, and tuition waivers (partial) also available. Financial award application deadline: 3/1. *Faculty research:* Social marketing, health communication, cancer, epidemiology, tobacco prevention and control, maternal and child health. Total annual research expenditures:$578,773. *Unit head:* Dr. Brad Neiger, Chair, 801-422-3313, Fax: 801-422-0273, E-mail: brad_neiger@byu.edu. *Application contact:* Dr. Michael Barnes, Graduate Coordinator, 801-422-3327, Fax: 801-422-0273, E-mail: michael_barnes@byu.edu.

Brooklyn College of the City University of New York, Division of Graduate Studies, School of Education, Program in Adolescence Education and Special Subjects, Brooklyn, NY 11210-2889. Offers art teacher (MA); biology teacher (MA); chemistry teacher (MA); English teacher (MA); French teacher (MA); health and nutrition sciences: health teacher (MS Ed); mathematics teacher (MA); music education (CAS); music teacher (MA); physical education teacher (MS Ed); physics teacher (MA); social studies teacher (MA); Spanish teacher (MA). Part-time and evening/weekend programs available. *Students:* 30 full-time (22 women), 450 part-time (257 women); includes 167 minority (101 African Americans, 21 Asian Americans or Pacific Islanders, 45 Hispanic Americans), 21 international. 277 applicants, 84% accepted, 113 enrolled. In 2006, 172 master's, 6 other advanced degrees awarded. *Degree requirements:* For master's, comprehensive exam (for some programs). *Entrance requirements:* For master's, LAST, previous course work in education, resumé, 2 letters of recommendation, essay. Additional exam requirements/recommendations for international students: Required—TOEFL. *Application deadline:* For fall admission, 3/1 priority date for domestic students, 2/1 priority date for international students; for spring admission, 11/1 priority date for domestic students, 10/1 priority date for international students. Applications are processed on a rolling basis. Application fee: $125. Electronic applications accepted. *Expenses:* Tuition, state resident: full-time $6,400; part-time $270 per credit. Tuition, nonresident: full-time $12,000; part-time $500 per credit. Required fees: $118 per semester. *Financial support:* Career-related internships or fieldwork, Federal Work-Study, institutionally sponsored loans, and scholarships/grants available. Support available to part-time students. Financial award application deadline: 5/1; financial award applicants required to submit FAFSA. *Faculty research:* Interdisciplinary education, semiotics, discourse analysis, autobiography, teacher identity. *Unit head:* Prof. Stephen Phillips, Program Facilitator, 718-951-5214, E-mail: phillips@brooklyn.cuny.edu. *Application contact:* Karen Alleyne-Pierre, Director of Admissions Services and Enrollment Communications, 718-951-5902, Fax: 718-951-4506, E-mail: grads@brooklyn.cuny.edu.

California State University, Dominguez Hills, College of Health and Human Services, Division of Health Sciences, Carson, CA 90747-0001. Offers gerontology (MA); health sciences (MS). Part-time programs available. *Faculty:* 1 (woman) full-time, 3 part-time/adjunct (all women). *Students:* 7 full-time (5 women), 19 part-time (16 women); includes 16 minority (9 African Americans, 7 Hispanic Americans), 1 international. Average age 39. 14 applicants, 71% accepted, 5 enrolled. In 2006, 4 degrees awarded. *Degree requirements:* For master's, comprehensive exam. *Entrance requirements:* Additional exam requirements/recommendations for international students: Required—TOEFL, TWE. *Application deadline:* For fall admission, 8/15 priority date for domestic students. Applications are processed on a rolling basis. Electronic applications accepted. *Expenses:* Tuition, nonresident: part-time $339 per unit. Required fees: $1,148 per term. Tuition and fees vary according to program. *Faculty research:* International health, health promotion and disease prevention, public health. *Unit head:* Dr. Mitchell T. Maki, Dean, College of Health and Human Services, 301-243-2046, E-mail: mmaki@csudh.edu.

California State University, Long Beach, Graduate Studies, College of Health and Human Services, Department of Health Science, Long Beach, CA 90840. Offers MPH. *Accreditation:* CEPH; NCATE. Part-time programs available. *Faculty:* 12 full-time (6 women), 30 part-time/adjunct (22 women). *Students:* 28 full-time (23 women), 19 part-time (12 women); includes 32 minority (5 African Americans, 1 American Indian/Alaska Native, 11 Asian Americans or Pacific Islanders, 15 Hispanic Americans), 2 international. Average age 31. 63 applicants, 57% accepted, 17 enrolled. In 2006, 7 degrees awarded. *Degree requirements:* For master's, thesis optional. *Entrance requirements:* For master's, minimum GPA of 3.0. *Application deadline:* For fall admission, 7/1 for domestic students; for spring admission, 12/1 for domestic students. Applications are processed on a rolling basis. Application fee: $55. Electronic applications accepted. *Financial support:* Federal Work-Study, institutionally sponsored loans, and scholarships/grants available. Financial award application deadline: 3/2. *Unit head:* Dr. Robert Friis, Chair, 562-985-4057, Fax: 562-985-2384, E-mail: rfriis@csulb.edu. *Application contact:* Dr. Mohammed Forouzesh, Graduate Coordinator, 562-985-4014, Fax: 562-985-2384, E-mail: mforouze@csulb.edu.

California State University, Los Angeles, Graduate Studies, College of Health and Human Services, School of Nursing, Program in Health Science, Los Angeles, CA 90032-8530. Offers MA. *Degree requirements:* For master's, project or thesis. *Entrance requirements:* Additional exam requirements/recommendations for international students: Required—TOEFL. *Application deadline:* For fall admission, 6/30 for domestic students; for spring admission, 2/1 for domestic students. Applications are processed on a rolling basis. Application fee: $55. *Expenses:* Tuition, nonresident: part-time $226 per unit. *Financial support:* Career-related internships or fieldwork and Federal Work-Study available. Support available to part-time students. Financial award application deadline: 3/1. *Unit head:* Chair, 323-343-4748, Fax: 323-343-6454.

California State University, Northridge, Graduate Studies, College of Health and Human Development, Department of Health Sciences, Northridge, CA 91330. Offers health administration (MS); health education (MPH). *Accreditation:* CEPH. *Faculty:* 18 full-time (11 women), 32 part-time/adjunct (18 women). *Students:* 69 full-time (16 women), 64 part-time (22 women); includes 58 minority (18 African Americans, 20 Asian Americans or Pacific Islanders, 20 Hispanic Americans), 14 international. Average age 31. 127 applicants, 52% accepted, 39 enrolled. In 2006, 39 degrees awarded. *Entrance requirements:* For master's, GRE General Test or minimum GPA of 3.0. Additional exam requirements/recommendations for international students: Required—TOEFL. *Application deadline:* For fall admission, 11/30 for domestic students. Application fee: $55. *Expenses:* Tuition, nonresident: full-time $8,136; part-time $4,068 per year. Required fees: $3,624; $1,161 per term. *Financial support:* Teaching assistantships available. Financial award application deadline: 3/1. *Faculty research:* Labor market needs assessment, health education products, dental hygiene, independent practice prototype. *Unit head:* Dr. Brian Malec, Chair, 818-677-3101. *Application contact:* Dr. Janet T. Reagan, Graduate Coordinator, 818-677-3101.

California State University, San Bernardino, Graduate Studies, College of Natural Sciences, Program in Health Science, San Bernardino, CA 92407-2397. Offers MS. *Faculty:* 9 full-time, 14 part-time/adjunct. *Students:* 14 full-time (13 women), 4 part-time (all women); includes 9 minority (6 African Americans, 3 Hispanic Americans). Average age 34. 14 applicants, 64% accepted, 8 enrolled. *Unit head:* Dr. Cynthia Paxton, Chair, 909-537-5339, Fax: 909-537-7037, E-mail: cpaxton@csusb.edu.

Central Washington University, Graduate Studies, Research and Continuing Education, College of Education and Professional Studies, Department of Health, Human Performance and Nutrition, Ellensburg, WA 98926. Offers health, physical education and nutrition (MS). *Accreditation:* NCATE. Part-time programs available. *Faculty:* 19 full-time (5 women). *Students:* 6 full-time (3 women), 15 part-time (9 women); includes 3 minority (2 African Americans, 1 Asian American or Pacific Islander). 22 applicants, 77% accepted, 15 enrolled. In 2006, 11 degrees awarded. *Degree requirements:* For master's, thesis or alternative. *Entrance requirements:* For master's, minimum GPA of 3.0. Additional exam requirements/recommendations for international students: Required—TOEFL (minimum score 550 paper-based; 213 computer-based; 79 iBT). *Application deadline:* For fall admission, 4/1 priority date for domestic students; for winter admission, 10/1 for domestic students; for spring admission, 1/1 for domestic students. Applications are processed on a rolling basis. Application fee: $50. Electronic applications accepted. *Expenses:* Tuition, state resident: full-time $6,312. Tuition, nonresident: full-time $14,112. Tuition and fees vary according to course load and degree level. *Financial support:* In 2006–07, 18 teaching assistantships with partial tuition reimbursements (averaging $8,100 per year) were awarded; research assistantships, Federal Work-Study and health care benefits also available. Financial award application deadline: 3/1; financial award applicants required to submit FAFSA. *Unit head:* Dr. Robert McGowan, Chair, 509-963-1911. *Application contact:* Justine Eason, Admissions Program Coordinator, 509-963-3103, Fax: 509-963-1799, E-mail: masters@cwu.edu.

The Citadel, The Military College of South Carolina, College of Graduate and Professional Studies, Department of Health, Exercise, and Sport Science, Charleston, SC 29409. Offers health, exercise, and sports science (MS); physical education (MAT). *Accreditation:* NCATE. Part-time and evening/weekend programs available. *Students:* 3 full-time (all women), 29 part-time (13 women); includes 2 minority (both African Americans) Average age 26. In 2006, 13 degrees awarded. *Entrance requirements:* For master's, GRE General Test, MAT, or 12 hours of graduate course work with a minimum GPA of 3.0. Additional exam requirements/recommendations for international students: Required—TOEFL (minimum score 550 paper-based; 213 computer-based). *Application deadline:* Applications are processed on a rolling basis. Application fee: $30. *Expenses:* Tuition, state resident: part-time $259 per credit hour. Tuition, nonresident: part-time $482 per credit hour. *Financial support:* Application deadline: 7/1; *Unit head:* Dr. John Carter, Interim Head, 843-953-5060, Fax: 843-953-6798, E-mail: john.carter@citadel.edu. *Application contact:* Dr. Raymond S. Jones, Associate Dean, College of Graduate and Professional Studies, 843-953-5089, Fax: 843-953-7630, E-mail: ray.jones@citadel.edu.

Cleveland State University, College of Graduate Studies, College of Education and Human Services, Department of Health, Physical Education, Recreation and Dance, Cleveland, OH 44115. Offers community health education (M Ed); exercise science (M Ed); human performance (M Ed); physical education pedagogy (M Ed); school health education (M Ed); sport and exercise psychology (M Ed); sports management (M Ed). Part-time programs available. *Faculty:* 9 full-time (5 women), 3 part-time/adjunct (0 women). *Students:* 12 full-time (7 women), 62 part-time (32 women); includes 16 minority (15 African Americans, 1 Asian American or Pacific Islander), 4 international. Average age 30. 52 applicants, 52% accepted, 19 enrolled. In 2006, 36 degrees awarded. *Degree requirements:* For master's, thesis optional. *Entrance requirements:* For master's, GRE General Test or MAT (if undergraduate GPA is below 2.75), minimum undergraduate GPA of 2.75. Additional exam requirements/recommendations for international students: Required—TOEFL (minimum score 525 paper-based; 197 computer-based), IELTS (minimum score 6). *Application deadline:* For fall admission, 7/15 priority date for domestic students; for spring admission, 12/15 priority date for domestic students. Applications are processed on a rolling basis. Application fee: $30. Electronic applications accepted. *Financial support:* In 2006–07, 6 research assistantships with full and partial tuition reimbursements (averaging $3,480 per year), 1 teaching assistantship with full and partial tuition reimbursement (averaging $3,480 per year) were awarded; career-related internships or fieldwork, tuition waivers (full), and unspecified assistantships also available. Financial award application deadline: 3/15. *Faculty research:* Childhood obesity, bone density, marketing fitness centers, motor development of disabled, mental skills training. Total annual research expenditures: $102,615. *Unit head:* Dr. Sheila M. Patterson, Chairperson, 216-687-4870, Fax: 216-687-5410, E-mail: s.m.patterson@csuohio.edu.

The College of New Jersey, Graduate Division, School of Nursing, Health and Exercise Science, Department of Health and Exercise Science, Program in Health Education, Ewing, NJ 08628. Offers health (MAT); physical education (M Ed). *Accreditation:* NCATE. *Students:* 3 applicants, 100% accepted. *Degree requirements:* For master's, comprehensive exam. *Entrance requirements:* For master's, MAT or GRE, minimum GPA of 3.0 in field or 2.75 overall. Additional exam requirements/recommendations for international students: Required—TOEFL. *Application deadline:* For fall admission, 4/15 for domestic students; for spring admission, 10/15 for domestic students. Application fee: $60. Electronic applications accepted. *Financial support:* Unspecified assistantships available. Financial award application deadline: 5/1; financial award applicants required to submit FAFSA. *Unit head:* Dr. Aristomen Chilakos, Coordinator, 609-771-3160, Fax: 609-637-5153, E-mail: chilako@tcnj.edu. *Application contact:* Susan L. Hydro, Office of Graduate Studies, Assistant Dean, 609-771-2300, Fax: 609-637-5105, E-mail: graduate@tcnj.edu.

Dalhousie University, Faculty of Graduate Studies, Faculty of Health Professions, School of Health and Human Performance, Division of Health Education, Halifax, NS B3H 4R2, Canada. Offers MA. Part-time programs available. *Degree requirements:* For master's, thesis. *Entrance requirements:* Additional exam requirements/recommendations for international students: Required—TOEFL. *Faculty research:* AIDS research, health knowledge of adolescents, evaluating health promotion, program evaluation.

East Carolina University, Graduate School, College of Health and Human Performance, Department of Health Education and Promotion, Greenville, NC 27858-4353. Offers environmental health (MS); health education (MA, MA Ed). *Accreditation:* NCATE. *Students:* 36 full-time (23 women), 82 part-time (54 women); includes 32 minority (29 African Americans, 2 American Indian/Alaska Native, 1 Hispanic American), 1 international. Average age 29. 14 applicants, 29% accepted, 3 enrolled. In 2006, 29 degrees awarded. *Degree requirements:* For master's, thesis optional. *Entrance requirements:* For master's, GRE General Test or MAT. Additional exam requirements/recommendations for international students: Required—TOEFL. *Application deadline:* For fall admission, 6/1 priority date for domestic students. Applications are processed on a rolling basis. Application fee: $50. *Financial support:* In 2006–07, 4 fellowships (averaging $4,000 per year), 4 research assistantships (averaging $7,500 per year), 15 teaching assistantships (averaging $7,500 per year) were awarded; career-related internships or fieldwork also available. Support available to part-time students. Financial award application deadline: 6/1. *Faculty research:* Community health education, worksite health promotion, school health education, environmental health. Total annual research expenditures: $300,000. *Unit head:* Dr. David M. White, Chair, 252-328-6000, Fax: 252-328-1285, E-mail: whited@ecu.edu.

Eastern Kentucky University, The Graduate School, College of Education, Department of Curriculum and Instruction, Program in Secondary and Higher Education, Richmond, KY 40475-3102. Offers agricultural education (MA Ed); allied health sciences education (MA Ed); art education (MA Ed); biological sciences education (MA Ed); business education (MA Ed); chemistry education (MA Ed); earth science education (MA Ed); English education (MA Ed); general science education (MA Ed); geography education (MA Ed); history education (MA Ed); home economics education (MA Ed); industrial education (MA Ed); mathematical sciences education (MA Ed); physical education (MA Ed); physics education (MA Ed); political science education (MA Ed); psychology education (MA Ed); reading (MA Ed); school health education (MA Ed); sociology education (MA Ed). *Accreditation:* NCATE. Part-time programs available. *Students:* 16 full-time (8 women), 63 part-time (43 women); includes 5 minority (2 African Americans, 2 American Indian/Alaska Native, 1 Asian American or Pacific Islander). Average age 32. *Entrance requirements:* For master's, GRE General Test, minimum GPA of 2.5. Application fee: $30. *Expenses:* Tuition, state resident: full-time $5,610. Tuition, nonresident: full-time $15,910. *Financial support:* Research assistantships, teaching assistantships, Federal Work-Study available. Support available to part-time students. *Unit head:* Dr. Michael Martin, Chair, Department of Curriculum and Instruction, 859-622-2154, Fax: 859-622-2004.

Eastern Michigan University, Graduate School, College of Health and Human Services, School of Health Promotion and Human Performance, Programs in Health and Physical Education, Ypsilanti, MI 48197. Offers MS. Part-time and evening/weekend programs available. Postbaccalaureate distance learning degree programs offered (minimal on-campus study). *Students:* 2 full-time (0 women), 31 part-time (18 women); includes 3 minority (all African Americans), 4 international. Average age 32. In 2006, 10 degrees awarded. *Entrance requirements:* Additional exam requirements/recommendations for international students: Required—TOEFL. *Application deadline:* For fall admission, 5/15 priority date for domestic students, 5/1 priority date for international students; for winter admission, 10/15 priority date for domestic students, 10/1 priority date for international students; for spring admission, 3/15 priority date for domestic students, 3/1 priority date for international students. Applications are processed on a rolling basis. Application fee: $35. *Expenses:* Tuition, state resident: part-time $341 per credit hour. Tuition, nonresident: full-time $16,104; part-time $671 per credit hour. Required fees: $816; $34 per credit hour. $40 per term. One-time fee: $82 full-time. Tuition and fees vary according to course level, course load, degree level and reciprocity agreements. *Financial support:* Fellowships, research assistantships with full tuition reimbursements, teaching assistantships with full tuition reimbursements, career-related internships or fieldwork, Federal Work-Study, institutionally sponsored loans, scholarships/grants, tuition waivers (partial), and unspecified assistantships available. Support available to part-time students. Financial award applicants required to submit FAFSA.

Eastern University, Graduate Education Programs, Program in School Health Services, St. Davids, PA 19087-3696. Offers M Ed. *Entrance requirements:* For master's, minimum GPA of 2.5. Additional exam requirements/recommendations for international students: Required—TOEFL.

East Stroudsburg University of Pennsylvania, Graduate School, School of Health Sciences and Human Performance, Department of Exercise Science, East Stroudsburg, PA 18301-2999. Offers cardiac rehabilitation and exercise science (MS). Part-time and evening/weekend programs available. *Faculty:* 4 full-time (1 woman), 1 part-time/adjunct (0 women). *Students:* 25 full-time (16 women), 6 part-time (2 women); includes 1 minority (African American), 4 international. Average age 28. In 2006, 32 degrees awarded. *Degree requirements:* For master's, comprehensive exam. *Entrance requirements:* Additional exam requirements/recommendations for international students: Required—TOEFL (minimum score 560 paper-based; 220 computer-based; 83 iBT). *Application deadline:* For fall admission, 7/31 priority date for domestic students, 5/1 priority date for international students; for spring admission, 11/30 for domestic students, 10/1 for international students. Applications are processed on a rolling basis. Application fee: $50. *Expenses:* Tuition, state resident: full-time $6,048; part-time $336 per credit. Tuition, nonresident: full-time $9,678; part-time $538 per credit. Required fees: $1,353; $67 per credit. One-time fee: $37 part-time. *Financial support:* In 2006–07, 19 research assistantships with full and partial tuition reimbursements were awarded; Federal Work-Study and institutionally sponsored loans also available. Financial award application deadline: 3/1. *Unit head:* Dr. Shala Davis, Graduate Coordinator, 570-422-3302, Fax: 570-422-3616, E-mail: sdavis@po-box.esu.edu.

East Stroudsburg University of Pennsylvania, Graduate School, School of Health Sciences and Human Performance, Department of Health, East Stroudsburg, PA 18301-2999. Offers community health education (MPH); health education (MS). *Accreditation:* CEPH (one or more programs are accredited). Part-time and evening/weekend programs available. *Faculty:* 3 full-time (2 women). *Students:* 4 full-time (all women), 9 part-time (all women); includes 1 minority (Asian American or Pacific Islander) Average age 37. In 2006, 4 degrees awarded. *Degree requirements:* For master's, comprehensive exam. *Entrance requirements:* For master's, GRE General Test, minimum GPA of 3.0 in major, 2.8 overall. Additional exam requirements/recommendations for international students: Required—TOEFL (minimum score 560 paper-based; 220 computer-based; 83 iBT). *Application deadline:* For fall admission, 7/31 priority date for domestic students, 5/1 priority date for international students; for spring admission, 11/30 for domestic students, 10/1 for international students. Applications are processed on a rolling basis. Application fee: $50. *Expenses:* Tuition, state resident: full-time $6,048; part-time $336 per credit. Tuition, nonresident: full-time $9,678; part-time $538 per credit. Required fees: $1,353; $67 per credit. One-time fee: $37 part-time. *Financial support:* In 2006–07, 4 research assistantships with full and partial tuition reimbursements were awarded; Federal Work-Study and institutionally sponsored loans also available. Financial award application deadline: 3/1; financial award applicants required to submit FAFSA. *Faculty research:* HIV prevention, wellness, international health issues. *Unit head:* Dr. Kathleen Hillman, Graduate Coordinator, 570-422-3727, Fax: 570-422-3848, E-mail: khillman@po-box.esu.edu.

East Stroudsburg University of Pennsylvania, Graduate School, School of Health Sciences and Human Performance, Department of Physical Education, East Stroudsburg, PA 18301-2999. Offers health and physical education (M Ed). *Faculty:* 2 full-time (both women). *Students:* 17 full-time (9 women), 9 part-time (1 woman); includes 3 minority (2 African Americans, 1 Hispanic American). Average age 30. In 2006, 20 degrees awarded. *Entrance requirements:* Additional exam requirements/recommendations for international students: Required—TOEFL (minimum score 560 paper-based; 220 computer-based; 83 iBT). *Application deadline:* For fall admission, 7/31 for domestic students, 5/1 for international students; for spring admission, 11/30 for domestic students, 10/1 for international students. Applications are processed on a rolling basis. Application fee: $50. *Expenses:* Tuition, state resident: full-time $6,048; part-time $336 per credit. Tuition, nonresident: full-time $9,678; part-time $538 per credit. Required fees: $1,353; $67 per credit. One-time fee: $37 part-time. *Financial support:* In 2006–07, 5 research assistantships were awarded; Federal Work-Study and unspecified assistantships also available. Financial award application deadline: 3/1; financial award applicants required to submit FAFSA. *Unit head:* Dr. Suzanne Mueller, Graduate Coordinator, 570-422-3104, E-mail: smueller@po-box.esu.edu.

Felician College, Program in Advanced Practice Nursing, Lodi, NJ 07644-2117. Offers adult nurse practitioner (MSN, PMC); family nurse practitioner (MSN, PMC); school nurse/teacher of

Health Education

Felician College (continued)
health education (Certificate). *Accreditation:* AACN. Part-time and evening/weekend programs available. Postbaccalaureate distance learning degree programs offered (no on-campus study). *Students:* 29 applicants, 90% accepted, 24 enrolled. *Degree requirements:* For master's, scholarly project. *Entrance requirements:* For master's, BS in nursing or equivalent, minimum GPA of 3.0, 2 letters of recommendation, RN license; for other advanced degree, RN license, minimum GPA of 2.75. Additional exam requirements/recommendations for international students: Recommended—TOEFL (minimum score 550 paper-based; 213 computer-based). *Application deadline:* Applications are processed on a rolling basis. Application fee: $40. *Expenses:* Tuition: Part-time $675 per credit. Tuition and fees vary according to program. *Financial support:* In 2006–07, 10 students received support. Traineeships available. Financial award applicants required to submit FAFSA. *Faculty research:* Anxiety and fear, curriculum innovation, health promotion. *Unit head:* Dr. Muriel Shore, Dean, Division of Health Sciences, 201-559-6030, E-mail: shorem@inet.felician.edu. *Application contact:* Wendy Lin-Cook, Director of Adult and Graduate Admission, 201-559-6077, Fax: 201-559-6138, E-mail: adultandgraduate@felician.edu.

See Close-Up on page 1957.

Florida Agricultural and Mechanical University, Division of Graduate Studies, Research, and Continuing Education, College of Education, Department of Health, Physical Education, and Recreation, Tallahassee, FL 32307-3200. Offers M Ed, MS Ed. *Accreditation:* NCATE. Part-time and evening/weekend programs available. *Degree requirements:* For master's, thesis optional. *Entrance requirements:* For master's, GRE General Test, minimum GPA of 3.0. Additional exam requirements/recommendations for international students: Required—TOEFL. *Faculty research:* Administration/curriculum, work behavior, psychology.

Florida State University, Graduate Studies, College of Education, Department of Middle and Secondary Education, Program in Health Education, Tallahassee, FL 32306. Offers MS. Part-time programs available. *Faculty:* 1 (woman) full-time. *Students:* 4 full-time (0 women), 2 part-time (both women); includes 1 minority (Hispanic American) 5 applicants, 80% accepted, 4 enrolled. In 2006, 1 degree awarded. *Degree requirements:* For master's, thesis optional. *Entrance requirements:* For master's, GRE General Test, minimum GPA of 3.0. *Application deadline:* For fall admission, 7/1 priority date for domestic students; for spring admission, 11/1 for domestic students. Applications are processed on a rolling basis. Application fee: $30. *Expenses:* Tuition, state resident: full-time $5,822; part-time $243 per credit hour. Tuition, nonresident: full-time $20,976; part-time $874 per credit hour. Tuition and fees vary according to program. *Financial support:* Fellowships, career-related internships or fieldwork available. Financial award applicants required to submit FAFSA. *Unit head:* Dr. Mary Sutherland, Head, 850-644-6553, Fax: 850-644-1880, E-mail: msutherl@garnet.acns.fsu.edu. *Application contact:* Christina Crotty, Office Manager, 850-644-7810, Fax: 850-644-1880, E-mail: crotty@mailer.fsu.edu.

Florida State University, Graduate Studies, College of Human Sciences, Department of Nutrition, Food, and Exercise Sciences, Tallahassee, FL 32306. Offers exercise science (PhD), including exercise physiology, motor learning and control; nutrition and food science (PhD); nutrition and food sciences (MS), including clinical nutrition, food science, nutrition and sport, nutrition science, nutrition, education and health promotion. *Faculty:* 15 full-time (9 women). *Students:* 44 full-time (35 women), 28 part-time (16 women); includes 16 minority (9 African Americans, 2 Asian Americans or Pacific Islanders, 5 Hispanic Americans), 12 international. 76 applicants, 72% accepted, 28 enrolled. In 2006, 17 master's, 4 doctorates awarded. *Degree requirements:* For master's, thesis optional; for doctorate, thesis/dissertation, registration. *Entrance requirements:* For master's and doctorate, GRE General Test, minimum GPA of 3.0. Additional exam requirements/recommendations for international students: Required—TOEFL (minimum score 80 iBT). *Application deadline:* For fall admission, 7/1 for domestic students, 5/1 for international students; for spring admission, 11/1 for domestic students, 12/1 for international students. Application fee: $30. Electronic applications accepted. *Expenses:* Tuition, state resident: full-time $5,822; part-time $243 per credit hour. Tuition, nonresident: full-time $20,976; part-time $874 per credit hour. Tuition and fees vary according to program. *Financial support:* In 2006–07, 43 students received support, including 3 fellowships with partial tuition reimbursements available (averaging $10,000 per year), 9 research assistantships with partial tuition reimbursements available (averaging $8,000 per year), 22 teaching assistantships with partial tuition reimbursements available (averaging $8,000 per year); career-related internships or fieldwork, Federal Work-Study, institutionally sponsored loans, scholarships/grants, and unspecified assistantships also available. Financial award application deadline: 1/15; financial award applicants required to submit FAFSA. *Faculty research:* Nutrition and exercise, vitamin A deficiency, protein biochemistry, cardiovascular responses to exercises, physiological effects of cigarette smoking related to health and wellness. *Unit head:* Dr. Bahram Arjmandi, Chair, 850-644-1828, Fax: 850-645-5000. *Application contact:* Olga Garmash, Program Assistant, 850-644-4800, Fax: 850-645-5000, E-mail: ogarmash@fsu.edu.

Fort Hays State University, Graduate School, College of Health and Life Sciences, Department of Health and Human Performance, Hays, KS 67601-4099. Offers MS. Part-time programs available. *Faculty:* 7 full-time (1 woman). *Students:* 16 full-time (6 women), 22 part-time (7 women); includes 3 minority (2 African Americans, 1 Hispanic American). Average age 29. 21 applicants, 100% accepted. In 2006, 15 degrees awarded. *Degree requirements:* For master's, thesis optional. *Entrance requirements:* For master's, GRE General Test or MAT. Additional exam requirements/recommendations for international students: Required—TOEFL (minimum score 550 paper-based; 213 computer-based). *Application deadline:* For fall admission, 7/1 priority date for domestic students. Applications are processed on a rolling basis. Application fee: $35. Electronic applications accepted. *Financial support:* In 2006–07, 8 teaching assistantships (averaging $5,000 per year) were awarded; research assistantships. *Faculty research:* Isoproterenol hydrochloride and exercise, dehydrogenase and high-density lipoprotein levels in athletics, venous blood parameters to adipose fat. *Unit head:* Glen McNeil, Chair, 785-628-4352, E-mail: gmcneil@fhsu.edu.

Framingham State College, Division of Graduate and Continuing Education, Programs in Food and Nutrition, Program in Human Nutrition: Education and Media Technologies, Framingham, MA 01701-9101. Offers MS. *Accreditation:* ADtA. *Unit head:* Prof. Janet Schwartz, Coordinator, 508-626-4702, Fax: 508-626-4030, E-mail: jschwar@frc.mass.edu. *Application contact:* 508-626-4550, Fax: 508-626-4030, E-mail: dgce@frc.mass.edu.

Georgia College & State University, Graduate School, School of Health Sciences, Department of Kinesiology, Milledgeville, GA 31061. Offers health and physical education (M Ed, Ed S). *Accreditation:* NCATE (one or more programs are accredited). *Students:* 16 full-time (8 women), 5 part-time (4 women), 2 international. Average age 26. 19 applicants, 74% accepted, 10 enrolled. In 2006, 8 master's awarded. *Degree requirements:* For master's, comprehensive exam; for Ed S, research project. *Entrance requirements:* For master's, GRE General Test or MAT, minimum GPA of 2.75 in upper-level undergraduate courses; for Ed S, GRE General Test or MAT, master's degree, minimum graduate GPA of 3.25, 2 years teaching experience. Additional exam requirements/recommendations for international students: Required—TOEFL (minimum score 500 paper-based; 173 computer-based). *Application deadline:* For fall admission, 7/15 priority date for domestic students. Applications are processed on a rolling basis. Application fee: $25. Electronic applications accepted. *Expenses:* Tuition, state resident: full-time $3,222; part-time $179 per credit hour. Tuition, nonresident: full-time $12,870; part-time $715 per credit hour. Required fees: $391 per semester. Tuition and fees vary according to course load. *Financial support:* In 2006–07, 13 research assistantships were awarded; career-related internships or fieldwork, Federal Work-Study, and unspecified assistantships also available. Support available to part-time students. Financial award application deadline: 3/1; financial award applicants required to submit FAFSA. *Unit head:* Dr. James Lidstone, Chair, 478-445-4072, E-mail: jim.lidstone@gcsu.edu.

Georgia Southern University, Jack N. Averitt College of Graduate Studies, College of Education, Department of Teaching and Learning, Program in Health and Physical Education, Statesboro, GA 30460. Offers M Ed. *Accreditation:* NCATE. Part-time and evening/weekend programs available. *Students:* 2 full-time (1 woman). Average age 24. *Degree requirements:* For master's, comprehensive exam. *Entrance requirements:* For master's, GRE General Test or MAT, minimum GPA of 2.5. Additional exam requirements/recommendations for international students: Required—TOEFL (minimum score 550 paper-based; 213 computer-based; 80 iBT). *Application deadline:* For fall admission, 3/1 priority date for domestic students, 3/1 for international students; for spring admission, 10/1 priority date for domestic students, 10/1 for international students. Applications are processed on a rolling basis. Application fee: $50. Electronic applications accepted. *Financial support:* In 2006–07, 2 students received support, including research assistantships with partial tuition reimbursements available (averaging $5,500 per year), teaching assistantships with partial tuition reimbursements available (averaging $5,500 per year); career-related internships or fieldwork, Federal Work-Study, and tuition waivers (partial) also available. Support available to part-time students. Financial award application deadline: 4/15; financial award applicants required to submit FAFSA. *Unit head:* Dr. Tony Pritchard, Coordinator, 912-871-1323, Fax: 912-681-0026, E-mail: tpritchard@georgiasouthern.edu. *Application contact:* 912-681-5384, Fax: 912-681-0740, E-mail: gradadmissions@georgiasouthern.edu.

Georgia Southwestern State University, Graduate Studies, School of Education, Americus, GA 31709-4693. Offers early childhood education (M Ed, Ed S); health and physical education (M Ed); middle grades education (M Ed, Ed S); reading (M Ed); secondary education (M Ed); special education (M Ed). *Accreditation:* NCATE. *Degree requirements:* For master's, comprehensive exam. *Entrance requirements:* For master's, GRE General Test or MAT, minimum GPA of 2.5; for Ed S, GRE General Test or MAT, minimum graduate GPA of 3.25, M Ed from accredited college or university, 3 years teaching experience. Electronic applications accepted.

Georgia State University, College of Education, Department of Kinesiology and Health, Program in Health and Physical Education, Atlanta, GA 30303-3083. Offers M Ed. Part-time and evening/weekend programs available. *Students:* Average age 34. 1 applicant, 100% accepted. In 2006, 1 degree awarded. *Degree requirements:* For master's, comprehensive exam. *Entrance requirements:* For master's, GRE General Test, minimum GPA of 2.5. *Application deadline:* For fall admission, 5/1 for domestic students; for spring admission, 10/1 for domestic students. Application fee: $25. *Financial support:* Teaching assistantships, career-related internships or fieldwork available. *Faculty research:* Exercise science, teacher behavior. *Unit head:* Dr. J. Andrew Doyle, Chair, Department of Kinesiology and Health, 404-651-4258, E-mail: adoyle@gsu.edu.

Harding University, College of Education, Searcy, AR 72149-0001. Offers advanced studies in teaching and learning (M Ed); art (MSE); behavioral science (MSE); Bible and religion (MSE); counseling (MS, Ed S); early childhood education (M Ed); early childhood special education (M Ed, MSE); education (MSE); educational leadership (M Ed, Ed S); elementary education (M Ed); English (MSE); family and consumer science (MSE); French (MSE); history/social science (MSE); kinesiology (MSE); math (MSE); physical science (MSE); reading (M Ed); secondary education (M Ed); Spanish (MSE); special education licensure (M Ed); teaching (MAT). *Accreditation:* NCATE. Part-time programs available. *Faculty:* 8 full-time (2 women), 45 part-time/adjunct (30 women). *Students:* 153 full-time (123 women), 469 part-time (341 women); includes 72 minority (63 African Americans, 4 American Indian/Alaska Native, 1 Asian American or Pacific Islander, 4 Hispanic Americans), 9 international. Average age 35. 175 applicants, 90% accepted, 147 enrolled. In 2006, 241 degrees awarded. *Degree requirements:* For master's, portfolio(s), thesis optional; for Ed S, portfolio, specialist project. *Entrance requirements:* For master's, GRE, MAT, PRAXIS; for Ed S, MAT or GRE. Additional exam requirements/recommendations for international students: Required—TOEFL (minimum score 550 paper-based). *Application deadline:* For fall admission, 8/1 for domestic and international students; for spring admission, 1/1 for domestic and international students. Applications are processed on a rolling basis. Application fee: $35. *Expenses:* Tuition: Part-time $455 per semester hour. Required fees: $20 per semester hour. Tuition and fees vary according to course load. *Financial support:* Scholarships/grants and unspecified assistantships available. Support available to part-time students. *Faculty research:* Reading, comprehension, school violence, educational technology, behavior, college choice, differentiated instruction, brain based teaching. *Unit head:* Pat Bashaw, Chair, 501-279-4183, Fax: 501-279-4051, E-mail: pbashaw@harding.edu.

Hofstra University, School of Education and Allied Human Services, Department of Health Professions and Family Studies, Program in Health Education, Hempstead, NY 11549. Offers MS. *Accreditation:* NCATE. Part-time programs available. *Students:* 29 full-time (20 women), 59 part-time (29 women); includes 4 minority (1 African American, 3 Hispanic Americans), 1 international. Average age 27. 37 applicants, 100% accepted, 26 enrolled. In 2006, 27 degrees awarded. *Entrance requirements:* For master's, interview, 2 letters of recommendation, essay. Additional exam requirements/recommendations for international students: Required—TOEFL (minimum score 550 paper-based; 213 computer-based). *Application deadline:* Applications are processed on a rolling basis. Application fee: $60. Electronic applications accepted. *Expenses:* Tuition: Full-time $13,320; part-time $740 per credit. Required fees: $930; $155 per term. *Financial support:* In 2006–07, 18 students received support, including 4 fellowships with tuition reimbursements available (averaging $2,650 per year), 2 research assistantships with full and partial tuition reimbursements available (averaging $8,691 per year); institutionally sponsored loans, scholarships/grants, tuition waivers (full and partial), and unspecified assistantships also available. Support available to part-time students. Financial award applicants required to submit FAFSA. *Faculty research:* Decreasing adolescent unintended pregnancy, comprehensive school health/certified teachers; life skills education in the content area. *Unit head:* Prof. Andrew Herman, Director, 516-463-6673, Fax: 516-463-4810, E-mail: hprazh@hofstra.edu. *Application contact:* Carol Drummer, Dean of Graduate Admissions, 516-463-4876, Fax: 516-463-4664, E-mail: gradstudent@hofstra.edu.

Howard University, Graduate School, Department of Health, Human Performance and Leisure Studies, Washington, DC 20059-0002. Offers exercise physiology (MS); health education (MS); sport studies (MS), including sociology of sport, sport management; urban recreation (MS), including leisure studies. Part-time and evening/weekend programs available. *Degree requirements:* For master's, thesis, comprehensive exam, registration. *Entrance requirements:* For master's, BS in human performance or related field. Electronic applications accepted. *Faculty research:* Health promotion, cardiovascular hypertension, physical activity, sport and human rights issues.

Howard University, Graduate School, Department of Physical Education, Recreation, and Health Education, Washington, DC 20059-0002. Offers exercise physiology (MS); recreation and leisure studies (MS); school and community health education (MS). Part-time programs available. *Degree requirements:* For master's, thesis or alternative, comprehensive exam. *Entrance requirements:* For master's, GRE General Test, minimum GPA of 3.0. *Faculty research:* Women's health, work and health, AIDS, men's health, hypertension, sports nutrition, social science, urban recreation, therapeutic recreation, commercial recreation.

Idaho State University, Office of Graduate Studies, Kasiska College of Health Professions, Department of Health and Nutrition Sciences, Program in Health Education, Pocatello, ID 83209. Offers MHE. *Faculty:* 4 full-time (2 women). *Students:* 5 full-time (all women), 18 part-time (12 women); includes 1 minority (African American) Average age 36. In 2006, 6 degrees awarded. *Degree requirements:* For master's, thesis optional. *Entrance requirements:* For master's, GRE General Test, previous coursework in statistics, natural sciences, tests and measurements. Additional exam requirements/recommendations for international students: Required—TOEFL (minimum score 600 paper-based; 213 computer-based). *Application deadline:* For fall admission, 7/1 for domestic students, 6/1 for international students; for spring admission, 12/1 for domestic students, 11/1 for international students. Applications are processed on a rolling basis. Application fee: $55. *Financial support:* In 2006–07, teaching assistantships with full and partial tuition reimbursements (averaging $8,694 per year); career-related internships or fieldwork, Federal Work-Study, scholarships/grants, and unspecified assistantships also available. Financial award application deadline: 1/1. *Faculty research:* Health and wellness. *Application contact:* Ellen Combs, Graduate School Technical Records Specialist, 208-282-2150, Fax: 208-282-4847.

Illinois State University, Graduate School, College of Applied Science and Technology, School of Kinesiology and Recreation, Normal, IL 61790-2200. Offers health education (MS); physical education (MS). *Faculty:* 20 full-time (10 women). *Students:* 77 full-time (40 women), 17 part-time (10 women); includes 9 minority (3 African Americans, 1 Asian American or Pacific Islander, 5 Hispanic Americans), 7 international. 86 applicants, 80% accepted. In 2006, 44 degrees awarded. *Degree requirements:* For master's, thesis or alternative. *Entrance requirements:* For master's, GRE General Test, minimum GPA of 2.6 in last 60 hours of course work. *Application deadline:* Applications are processed on a rolling basis. Application fee: $40. *Expenses:* Tuition, state resident: full-time $3,330; part-time $185 per credit hour. Tuition, nonresident: full-time $6,948; part-time $438 per credit hour. Required fees: $1,259; $52 per credit hour. *Financial support:* In 2006–07, 38 teaching assistantships (averaging $6,694 per year) were awarded; career-related internships or fieldwork, Federal Work-Study, tuition waivers (full and partial), and unspecified assistantships also available. Financial award application deadline: 4/1. *Faculty research:* Physical education obesity prevention and lifestyle enhancement program, development of a physical activity and nutrition resource web page. *Unit head:* David Thomas, Acting Chairperson, 309-438-8661.

Indiana State University, School of Graduate Studies, College of Health and Human Performance, Department of Health, Safety, and Environmental Health Sciences, Terre Haute, IN 47809-1401. Offers community health promotion (MA, MS); occupational safety management (MA, MS); school health and safety (MA, MS). *Accreditation:* NCATE (one or more programs are accredited). *Faculty:* 9 full-time (1 woman), 2 part-time/adjunct (1 woman). *Students:* 3 full-time (2 women), 19 part-time (5 women); includes 4 minority (3 African Americans, 1 Hispanic American), 1 international. Average age 37. 8 applicants, 63% accepted, 2 enrolled. In 2006, 3 degrees awarded. *Degree requirements:* For master's, thesis or alternative. *Entrance requirements:* For master's, GRE General Test. *Application deadline:* For fall admission, 7/1 priority date for domestic students; for spring admission, 11/1 priority date for domestic students. Applications are processed on a rolling basis. Application fee: $35. Electronic applications accepted. *Expenses:* Tuition, state resident: part-time $278 per credit. Tuition, nonresident: part-time $552 per credit. *Financial support:* In 2006–07, 1 research assistantship (averaging $3,150 per year) was awarded; teaching assistantships, tuition waivers (full) and unspecified assistantships also available. Financial award application deadline: 3/1; financial award applicants required to submit FAFSA. *Unit head:* Dr. Ernest Sheldon, Interim Chairperson, 812-237-3071.

Indiana University Bloomington, School of Health, Physical Education and Recreation, Department of Applied Health Science, Bloomington, IN 47405-7000. Offers health behavior (PhD); health promotion (MS); human development/family studies (MS); nutrition science (MS); public health (MPH); safety management (MS); school and college health education (MS). PhD offered through the University Graduate School. *Accreditation:* CEPH (one or more programs are accredited). *Faculty:* 21 full-time (11 women), 1 (woman) part-time/adjunct. *Students:* 72 full-time (54 women), 44 part-time (30 women); includes 18 minority (15 African Americans, 2 Asian Americans or Pacific Islanders, 1 Hispanic American), 17 international. Average age 30. 94 applicants, 88% accepted, 54 enrolled. In 2006, 50 master's, 7 doctorates awarded. *Degree requirements:* For master's, thesis optional; for doctorate, thesis/dissertation, registration. *Entrance requirements:* For master's, GRE (MS in nutrition science), 3 recommendations; for doctorate, GRE, 3 recommendations. Additional exam requirements/recommendations for international students: Required—TOEFL (minimum score 550 paper-based; 213 computer-based; 79 iBT). *Application deadline:* For fall admission, 4/30 priority date for domestic students, 12/1 priority date for international students; for spring admission, 11/15 priority date for domestic students, 9/1 priority date for international students. Application fee: $50 ($60 for international students). *Expenses:* Tuition, state resident: full-time $5,791; part-time $241 per credit hour. Tuition, nonresident: full-time $16,866; part-time $703 per credit hour. *Financial support:* In 2006–07, teaching assistantships with full and partial tuition reimbursements (averaging $11,666 per year); fellowships, career-related internships or fieldwork, Federal Work-Study, institutionally sponsored loans, scholarships/grants, tuition waivers (partial), and fee remissions also available. Financial award application deadline: 3/1. *Faculty research:* Cancer education, HIV/AIDS and drug education, public health, parent-child interactions, safety education. *Unit head:* Dr. Mohammad R. Torabi, Chair, 812-855-4808, Fax: 812-855-3936, E-mail: torabi@indiana.edu.

Indiana University of Pennsylvania, School of Graduate Studies and Research, College of Health and Human Services, Department of Health and Physical Education, Indiana, PA 15705-1087. Offers aquatics administration and facilities management (MS); exercise science (MS); sport management (MS); sport science (MS). Part-time programs available. *Faculty:* 8 full-time (4 women). *Students:* 33 full-time (17 women), 39 part-time (21 women); includes 3 minority (2 African Americans, 1 Asian American or Pacific Islander), 12 international. Average age 27. 75 applicants, 75% accepted. In 2006, 18 degrees awarded. *Degree requirements:* For master's, thesis optional. *Entrance requirements:* For master's, 2 letters of recommendation. Additional exam requirements/recommendations for international students: Required—TOEFL. *Application deadline:* For fall admission, 7/1 priority date for domestic students; for spring admission, 11/1 for domestic students. Applications are processed on a rolling basis. Application fee: $30. *Expenses:* Tuition, state resident: full-time $6,048; part-time $336 per credit. Tuition, nonresident: full-time $9,678; part-time $538 per credit. Required fees: $1,069; $148 per year. *Financial support:* In 2006–07, 6 research assistantships with full and partial tuition reimbursements (averaging $4,990 per year) were awarded. Financial award application deadline: 3/15; financial award applicants required to submit FAFSA. *Unit head:* Dr. Elaine Blair, Chairperson, 724-357-2770, E-mail: eblair@iup.edu.

Indiana University–Purdue University Indianapolis, Indiana University School of Medicine, School of Health and Rehabilitation Sciences, Indianapolis, IN 46202-2896. Offers health sciences education (MS); nutrition and dietetics (MS); occupational therapy (MS); physical therapy (DPT). Part-time and evening/weekend programs available. *Faculty:* 8 full-time (5 women). *Students:* 180 full-time (149 women), 35 part-time (21 women); includes 17 minority (6 African Americans, 7 Asian Americans or Pacific Islanders, 4 Hispanic Americans), 3 international. Average age 27. In 2006, 9 master's, 32 doctorates awarded. *Degree requirements:* For master's, thesis (for some programs). *Entrance requirements:* For master's, GRE General Test, minimum GPA of 3.0. Additional exam requirements/recommendations for international students: Required—TOEFL. *Application deadline:* For fall admission, 1/15 priority date for domestic students; for spring admission, 10/15 for domestic students. Application fee: $50 ($60 for international students). *Expenses:* Tuition, state resident: full-time $5,437; part-time $227 per credit hour. Tuition, nonresident: full-time $15,694; part-time $654 per credit hour. Required fees: $620. Tuition and fees vary according to course load, campus/location and program. *Financial support:* Fellowships, research assistantships, teaching assistantships, Federal Work-Study, institutionally sponsored loans, and scholarships/grants available. Support available to part-time students. Financial award applicants required to submit FAFSA. *Unit head:* Dr. Mark S. Sothmann, Dean of the School of Allied Health Sciences, 317-274-4702, E-mail: msothman@iupui.edu.

Inter American University of Puerto Rico, Metropolitan Campus, Faculty of Education, Program in Health and Physical Education, San Juan, PR 00919-1293. Offers MA. *Degree requirements:* For master's, comprehensive exam. *Entrance requirements:* For master's, GRE or EXADEP, interview. Electronic applications accepted.

Iowa State University of Science and Technology, Graduate College, College of Human Sciences, Department of Health and Human Performance, Ames, IA 50011. Offers education (M Ed); exercise and sport science (MS); health and human performance (PhD). *Faculty:* 15 full-time. *Students:* 31 full-time (14 women), 5 part-time (4 women); includes 2 minority (both African Americans), 5 international. 40 applicants, 28% accepted, 8 enrolled. In 2006, 8 master's, 1 doctorate awarded. *Degree requirements:* For master's, thesis or alternative; for doctorate, thesis/dissertation. *Entrance requirements:* For master's and doctorate, GRE General Test. Additional exam requirements/recommendations for international students: Required—TOEFL (paper-based 560; computer-based 220; iBT 79) or IELTS (6.5). *Application deadline:* For fall admission, 2/1 priority date for domestic and international students; for spring admission, 11/1 priority date for domestic and international students. Application fee: $30 ($70 for international students). Electronic applications accepted. *Expenses:* Tuition, state resident: full-time $5,936; part-time $330 per credit. Tuition, nonresident: full-time $16,350; part-time $330 per credit. *Financial support:* In 2006–07, 17 research assistantships with full and partial tuition reimbursements (averaging $17,180 per year), 13 teaching assistantships with full and partial tuition reimbursements (averaging $16,096 per year) were awarded; fellowships, career-related internships or fieldwork, scholarships/grants, health care benefits, and unspecified assistantships also available. *Unit head:* Dr. Jerry Thomas, Chair, 515-294-8009, Fax: 515-294-8740, E-mail: hhpgrad@iastate.edu. *Application contact:* Dr. Warren Franke, Chair, 515-294-8257, Fax: 515-294-8740, E-mail: wfranke@iastate.edu.

Ithaca College, Graduate Studies, School of Health Sciences and Human Performance, Program in Health Education, Ithaca, NY 14850-7020. Offers MS. Part-time programs available. *Faculty:* 7 full-time (5 women). *Students:* 9 full-time (8 women), 1 (woman) part-time. Average age 22. 12 applicants, 92% accepted, 8 enrolled. *Degree requirements:* For master's, thesis optional. *Entrance requirements:* For master's, GRE General Test, minimum GPA of 3.0. Additional exam requirements/recommendations for international students: Required—TOEFL (minimum score 550 paper-based; 213 computer-based). *Application deadline:* For fall admission, 3/1 priority date for domestic students; for spring admission, 12/1 for domestic students. Application fee: $40. *Expenses:* Contact institution. *Financial support:* In 2006–07, 9 students received support, including 9 teaching assistantships (averaging $5,119 per year); career-related internships or fieldwork, Federal Work-Study, institutionally sponsored loans, scholarships/grants, and unspecified assistantships also available. Support available to part-time students. Financial award application deadline: 3/1; financial award applicants required to submit FAFSA. *Unit head:* Mary Bentley, Chairperson, 607-274-3105, Fax: 607-274-1263, E-mail: gradstudies@ithaca.edu.

Jackson State University, Graduate School, School of Education, Department of Health, Physical Education and Recreation, Jackson, MS 39217. Offers MS Ed. *Accreditation:* NCATE. Part-time and evening/weekend programs available. *Faculty:* 5 full-time (0 women). *Students:* 6 full-time (5 women), 8 part-time (1 woman); includes 13 minority (all African Americans) In 2006, 5 degrees awarded. *Degree requirements:* For master's, thesis or alternative, comprehensive exam. *Entrance requirements:* For master's, GRE General Test. Additional exam requirements/recommendations for international students: Required—TOEFL. *Application deadline:* For fall admission, 3/1 priority date for domestic students; for spring admission, 10/1 for domestic students. Applications are processed on a rolling basis. Application fee: $20. *Financial support:* In 2006–07, 8 students received support. Career-related internships or fieldwork, Federal Work-Study, scholarships/grants, and unspecified assistantships available. Support available to part-time students. Financial award application deadline: 3/1; financial award applicants required to submit FAFSA. *Unit head:* Dr. Hill Williams, Chair, 601-979-2373, Fax: 601-979-2374, E-mail: hill.williams@jsums.edu. *Application contact:* Curtis Gore, Director of Graduate Admissions, 601-979-2455, Fax: 601-974-4325, E-mail: cgore@ccaix.jsums.edu.

Jacksonville State University, College of Graduate Studies and Continuing Education, College of Education and Professional Studies, Program in Health and Physical Education, Jacksonville, AL 36265-1602. Offers MS Ed. *Accreditation:* NCATE. Part-time and evening/weekend programs available. *Faculty:* 4 full-time (0 women). *Students:* 7 full-time (2 women), 48 part-time (19 women); includes 7 minority (6 African Americans, 1 American Indian/Alaska Native). In 2006, 14 degrees awarded. *Entrance requirements:* For master's, GRE General Test or MAT. *Application deadline:* Applications are processed on a rolling basis. Application fee: $20. *Expenses:* Tuition, state resident: full-time $5,400; part-time $225 per credit hour. Tuition, nonresident: full-time $10,800; part-time $450 per credit hour. One-time fee: $20 full-time. *Financial support:* Available to part-time students. Application deadline: 4/1. *Unit head:* Dr. Jeff Chandler, Head, 256-782-5973. *Application contact:* 256-782-5329.

James Madison University, College of Graduate and Outreach Programs, College of Integrated Science and Technology, Department of Health Sciences, Program in Health Education, Harrisonburg, VA 22807. Offers MS, MS Ed. Part-time programs available. *Faculty:* 19 full-time (10 women), 2 part-time/adjunct (1 woman). *Students:* 30 full-time (28 women), 14 part-time (12 women); includes 3 minority (2 African Americans, 1 Asian American or Pacific Islander), 1 international. Average age 27. In 2006, 16 degrees awarded. *Entrance requirements:* For master's, GRE General Test. Additional exam requirements/recommendations for international students: Required—TOEFL. *Application deadline:* For fall admission, 5/1 priority date for domestic students; for spring admission, 9/1 priority date for domestic students. Application fee: $55. *Expenses:* Tuition, state resident: full-time $6,336; part-time $264 per credit hour. Tuition, nonresident: full-time $17,832; part-time $743 per credit hour. *Financial support:* In 2006–07, 14 students received support, including 1 teaching assistantship with full tuition reimbursement available (averaging $8,167 per year); unspecified assistantships also available. Financial award application deadline: 3/1. *Unit head:* Dr. Maria T. Wessel, Coordinator, 540-568-3955.

John F. Kennedy University, Graduate School of Holistic Studies, Department of Integral Studies, Program in Holistic Health Education, Pleasant Hill, CA 94523-4817. Offers MA. Part-time and evening/weekend programs available. *Degree requirements:* For master's, thesis or alternative. *Entrance requirements:* For master's, interview. Additional exam requirements/recommendations for international students: Required—TOEFL.

The Johns Hopkins University, Bloomberg School of Public Health, Department of Health, Behavior and Society, Baltimore, MD 21218-2699. Offers behavioral sciences and health education (MHS); genetic counseling (Sc M); social and behavioral sciences (PhD, Sc D). *Faculty:* 36 full-time (28 women), 27 part-time/adjunct (15 women). *Students:* 62 full-time (59 women), 3 part-time (all women); includes 16 minority (6 African Americans, 6 Asian Americans or Pacific Islanders, 4 Hispanic Americans), 6 international. Average age 27. 179 applicants, 31% accepted, 26 enrolled. In 2006, 10 master's, 6 doctorates awarded. *Degree requirements:* For master's, thesis (for some programs), comprehensive exam (for some programs), registration (for some programs); for doctorate, thesis/dissertation, comprehensive exam, registration. *Entrance requirements:* For master's and doctorate, GRE, transcripts, curriculum vitae, statement, 3 recommendation letters. *Application deadline:* For fall admission, 12/1 for domestic and international students. Electronic applications accepted. *Expenses:* Tuition: Full-time $32,976. Tuition and fees vary according to degree level and program. *Financial support:* In 2006–07, 2 fellowships with tuition reimbursements (averaging $24,000 per year), 7 teaching assistantships (averaging $4,770 per year) were awarded; career-related internships or fieldwork, Federal Work-Study, scholarships/grants, traineeships, health care benefits, and unspecified assistantships also available. Financial award application deadline: 3/15. *Faculty research:* Structural and community-level inventions to improve health communication and health education behavioral and social aspects of genetic counseling. Total annual research expenditures: $4.6 million. *Unit head:* Georgean Smith, Administrator, 410-502-3715, Fax: 410-502-4333, E-mail: gesmith@jhsph.edu. *Application contact:* Barbara W. Diehl, Senior Academic Program Coordinator, 410-502-4415, Fax: 410-502-4333, E-mail: bdiehl@jhsph.edu.

Kent State University, Graduate School of Education, Health, and Human Services, Department of Adult, Counseling, Health and Vocational Education, Program in Health Education and Promotion, Kent, OH 44242-0001. Offers M Ed, MA, PhD. *Accreditation:* NCATE. *Faculty:* 8 full-time (6 women), 8 part-time/adjunct (all women). *Students:* 22 full-time (20 women), 21 part-time (17 women); includes 9 minority (8 African Americans, 1 Hispanic American). 13

Health Education

Kent State University (continued)

applicants, 69% accepted. In 2006, 10 master's, 1 doctorate awarded. *Degree requirements:* For master's, registration; for doctorate, thesis/dissertation, comprehensive exam, registration. *Entrance requirements:* For doctorate, GRE General Test. Additional exam requirements/recommendations for international students: Required—TOEFL. *Application deadline:* Applications are processed on a rolling basis. Application fee: $30. Electronic applications accepted. *Financial support:* In 2006–07, fellowships with full tuition reimbursements (averaging $8,497 per year); research assistantships with full tuition reimbursements, teaching assistantships with full tuition reimbursements, career-related internships or fieldwork, Federal Work-Study, institutionally sponsored loans, scholarships/grants, health care benefits, and unspecified assistantships also available. Support available to part-time students. Financial award application deadline: 4/1; financial award applicants required to submit FAFSA. *Faculty research:* Substance use/abuse, sexuality, community health assessment, epidemiology, HIV/AIDS. *Unit head:* Dr. Dianne Kerr, Coordinator, 330-672-7977, E-mail: jbyrne@kent.edu. *Application contact:* Nancy Miller, Academic Program Coordinator, Office of Graduate Student Services, 330-672-2586, Fax: 330-672-9162, E-mail: ogs@kent.edu.

Lake Erie College of Osteopathic Medicine, Professional Programs, Erie, PA 16509-1025. Offers biomedical sciences (Postbaccalaureate Certificate); medical education (MS); osteopathic medicine (DO); pharmacy (Pharm D). *Accreditation:* ACPE; AOsA. *Faculty:* 85 full-time (20 women), 84 part-time/adjunct (19 women). *Students:* 1,355 full-time (700 women); includes 261 minority (57 African Americans, 3 American Indian/Alaska Native, 171 Asian Americans or Pacific Islanders, 30 Hispanic Americans). Average age 25. 4,526 applicants, 15% accepted, 366 enrolled. In 2006, 198 DOs, 88 other advanced degrees awarded. *Median time to degree:* First professional degree–4 years full-time; master's–2 years full-time; Postbaccalaureate Certificate–3 years full-time. *Degree requirements:* For first professional degree, National Osteopathic Medical Licensing Exam, Levels 1 and 2; for Postbaccalaureate Certificate, North American Pharmacist Licensure Examination (NAPLEX). *Entrance requirements:* For first professional degree, MCAT, minimum GPA of 3.2, letters of recommendation; for Postbaccalaureate Certificate, PCAT, letters of recommendation, minimum GPA of 3.5. *Application deadline:* For fall admission, 3/1 for domestic students. Applications are processed on a rolling basis. Application fee: $50. Electronic applications accepted. *Expenses:* Tuition: Full-time $25,000. Required fees: $1,095. *Financial support:* In 2006–07, 1,238 students received support. Institutionally sponsored loans and scholarships/grants available. Financial award application deadline: 6/30; financial award applicants required to submit FAFSA. *Faculty research:* Cardiac smooth and skeletal muscle mechanics, chemotherapeutics and vitamins, osteopathic manipulation. *Unit head:* Dr. Silvia M. Ferretti, Provost Dean Vice President of Academic Affairs, 814-866-6641, Fax: 814-866-8123. *Application contact:* Amy Rowe, Admissions Coordinator, 814-866-6641, Fax: 814-866-8123, E-mail: arowe@lecom.edu.

Lehman College of the City University of New York, Division of Natural and Social Sciences, Department of Health Sciences, Program in Health Education and Promotion, Bronx, NY 10468-1589. Offers MA. *Accreditation:* NCATE. Part-time and evening/weekend programs available. *Degree requirements:* For master's, thesis or alternative. *Entrance requirements:* For master's, minimum GPA of 2.7.

Lehman College of the City University of New York, Division of Natural and Social Sciences, Department of Health Sciences, Program in Health N–12 Teacher, Bronx, NY 10468-1589. Offers MS Ed. *Accreditation:* NCATE. *Degree requirements:* For master's, thesis or alternative.

Loma Linda University, School of Public Health, Programs in Health Promotion and Education, Loma Linda, CA 92350. Offers MPH, Dr PH. *Accreditation:* CEPH (one or more programs are accredited). *Degree requirements:* For doctorate, thesis/dissertation. *Entrance requirements:* For doctorate, GRE General Test. Additional exam requirements/recommendations for international students: Required—Michigan English Language Assessment Battery or TOEFL.

Long Island University, Brooklyn Campus, School of Health Professions, Division of Sports Sciences, Brooklyn, NY 11201-8423. Offers adapted physical education (MS); athletic training and sports sciences (MS); exercise physiology (MS); health sciences (MS). Part-time and evening/weekend programs available. *Entrance requirements:* For master's, 2 letters of recommendation. Additional exam requirements/recommendations for international students: Required—TOEFL (minimum score 500 paper-based; 173 computer-based). Electronic applications accepted.

Louisiana Tech University, Graduate School, College of Education, Department of Curriculum, Instruction and Leadership, Ruston, LA 71272. Offers curriculum and instruction (MS, Ed D); educational leadership (Ed D); secondary education (M Ed), including business education, English education, foreign language education, health and physical education, mathematics education, science education, social studies education, speech education. *Accreditation:* NCATE. Part-time programs available. *Degree requirements:* For doctorate, thesis/dissertation. *Entrance requirements:* For master's and doctorate, GRE General Test.

Louisiana Tech University, Graduate School, College of Education, Department of Health Exercise Science, Ruston, LA 71272. Offers MS. *Accreditation:* NCATE. Part-time programs available. *Degree requirements:* For master's, thesis or alternative. *Entrance requirements:* For master's, GRE General Test.

Marshall University, Academic Affairs Division, College of Information, Technology and Engineering, Division of Environmental Science and Safety Technology, Program in Safety, Huntington, WV 25755. Offers MS. *Accreditation:* NCATE. *Faculty:* 2 full-time (1 woman). *Students:* 6 full-time (2 women), 22 part-time (3 women); includes 1 minority (African American), 1 international. Average age 34. In 2006, 7 degrees awarded. *Degree requirements:* For master's, comprehensive assessment, thesis optional. Application fee: $40. *Application contact:* Information Contact, 304-746-1900, Fax: 304-746-1902, E-mail: services@marshall.edu.

Marywood University, Academic Affairs, College of Education and Human Development, Department of Human Development, Emphasis in Health Promotion, Scranton, PA 18509-1598. Offers PhD. *Students:* 2 full-time (both women), 20 part-time (15 women). Average age 44. *Expenses:* Tuition: Part-time $672 per credit. Tuition and fees vary according to degree level, campus/location and program. *Unit head:* Dr. Marie Loftus, Director, Department of Human Development, 570-348-6292, E-mail: loftus@es.marywood.edu.

Middle Tennessee State University, College of Graduate Studies, College of Education and Behavioral Science, Department of Health, Physical Education, Recreation and Safety, Murfreesboro, TN 37132. Offers exercise science and health promotion (MS); health, physical education, recreation and safety (MS); human performance (PhD); physical education (PhD). *Accreditation:* NCATE (one or more programs are accredited). Part-time and evening/weekend programs available. Postbaccalaureate distance learning degree programs offered. *Faculty:* 26 full-time (12 women). *Students:* 10 full-time (6 women), 130 part-time (64 women); includes 27 minority (21 African Americans, 1 American Indian/Alaska Native, 5 Asian Americans or Pacific Islanders). Average age 28. 64 applicants, 94% accepted. In 2006, 39 master's, 7 doctorates awarded. *Entrance requirements:* For master's and doctorate, GRE or MAT. Additional exam requirements/recommendations for international students: Required—TOEFL (minimum score 525 paper-based; 195 computer-based). *Application deadline:* For fall admission, 8/1 priority date for domestic students. Applications are processed on a rolling basis. Application fee: $25. Electronic applications accepted. *Financial support:* In 2006–07, 31 students received support. Application deadline: 5/1; *Faculty research:* Cardiovascular disease and psychosocial stress, pediatric health and fitness, obesity, fitness testing, anaerobic power and lactate kinetics. *Unit head:* Dr. Dianne Bartley, Chair, 615-898-2811, Fax: 615-898-5020, E-mail: dbartley@mtsu.edu.

Midwestern University, Glendale Campus, College of Health Sciences, Arizona Campus, Program in Health Professions Education, Glendale, AZ 85308. Offers MHPE. Part-time

programs available. *Faculty:* 3 full-time (1 woman), 2 part-time/adjunct (0 women). *Students:* Average age 45. 6 applicants, 83% accepted, 2 enrolled. In 2006, 4 degrees awarded. *Entrance requirements:* For master's, GRE. *Application deadline:* Applications are processed on a rolling basis. Application fee: $50. *Unit head:* Dr. Leonard B. Bell, Director, 623-572-3622. *Application contact:* James Walters, Director of Admissions, 888-247-9277, Fax: 623-572-3340, E-mail: admissaz@midwestern.edu.

Mills College, Graduate Studies, Education Department, Oakland, CA 94613-1000. Offers administration (Ed D); child life in health care settings (MA); early childhood education (MA); education (MA), including curriculum and instruction, elementary education, English education, mathematics education, science education, secondary education, social sciences education, teaching. Part-time and evening/weekend programs available. *Faculty:* 10 full-time (7 women), 15 part-time/adjunct (12 women). *Students:* 192 full-time (153 women), 41 part-time (36 women); includes 62 minority (28 African Americans, 13 Asian Americans or Pacific Islanders, 21 Hispanic Americans), 2 international. Average age 34. 160 applicants, 74% accepted, 73 enrolled. In 2006, 52 master's, 1 doctorate awarded. Terminal master's awarded for partial completion of doctoral program. *Degree requirements:* For master's, comprehensive exam. *Entrance requirements:* For doctorate, GRE General Test. Additional exam requirements/recommendations for international students: Required—TOEFL. *Application deadline:* For fall admission, 2/1 for domestic and international students; for spring admission, 11/1 for domestic and international students. Applications are processed on a rolling basis. Application fee: $50. Electronic applications accepted. *Financial support:* In 2006–07, 56 fellowships with tuition reimbursements (averaging $2,700 per year), 15 teaching assistantships (averaging $6,350 per year) were awarded; career-related internships or fieldwork, institutionally sponsored loans, scholarships/grants, and residence awards also available. Support available to part-time students. Financial award application deadline: 2/1; financial award applicants required to submit CSS PROFILE or FAFSA. *Faculty research:* Child development, gender and education, public policy, cross-cultural development, development of literacy. *Unit head:* Joseph Kahne, Chairperson, 510-430-3190, Fax: 510-430-3314, E-mail: grad-studies@mills.edu. *Application contact:* Randy McGlauthing, Director of Graduate Admissions, 510-430-2355, Fax: 510-430-2159, E-mail: rmglaut@mills.edu.

Minnesota State University Mankato, College of Graduate Studies, College of Allied Health and Nursing, Department of Health Science, Mankato, MN 56001. Offers chemical dependency studies (MS); community health (MS); health science (MS, MT); school health (MS). Part-time programs available. *Students:* 14 full-time (11 women), 35 part-time (28 women). Average age 32. In 2006, 10 degrees awarded. *Degree requirements:* For master's, thesis or alternative, comprehensive exam. *Entrance requirements:* For master's, minimum GPA of 3.0 during previous 2 years. *Application deadline:* For fall admission, 7/1 for domestic students, 5/1 for international students; for spring admission, 11/1 for domestic students, 10/1 for international students. Applications are processed on a rolling basis. Application fee: $40. Electronic applications accepted. *Financial support:* Research assistantships with full tuition reimbursements, teaching assistantships with full tuition reimbursements, career-related internships or fieldwork and Federal Work-Study available. Support available to part-time students. Financial award application deadline: 3/15; financial award applicants required to submit FAFSA. *Faculty research:* Teaching methods, stress prophylaxis and management, effects of alcohol. *Unit head:* Dr. Dawn Larsen, Graduate Coordinator, 507-389-2113. *Application contact:* 507-389-2321, E-mail: grad@mnsu.edu.

Mississippi State University, College of Education, Department of Kinesiology, Mississippi State, MS 39762. Offers exercise science (MS); health education/health promotion (MS); sports administration (MS); teaching/coaching (MS). Part-time programs available. Postbaccalaureate distance learning degree programs offered (minimal on-campus study). *Faculty:* 15 full-time (4 women), 6 part-time/adjunct (4 women). *Students:* 34 full-time (13 women), 13 part-time (6 women); includes 6 minority (all African Americans), 1 international. Average age 25. 49 applicants, 69% accepted, 26 enrolled. In 2006, 25 degrees awarded. *Degree requirements:* For master's, comprehensive oral or written exam, thesis optional. *Entrance requirements:* For master's, GRE General Test, minimum GPA of 3.0. Additional exam requirements/recommendations for international students: Required—TOEFL. *Application deadline:* For fall admission, 7/1 for domestic students; for spring admission, 11/1 for domestic students. Applications are processed on a rolling basis. Application fee: $30. Electronic applications accepted. *Expenses:* Tuition, state resident: full-time $4,550; part-time $253 per hour. Tuition, nonresident: full-time $10,552; part-time $584 per hour. International tuition: $10,882 full-time. Tuition and fees vary according to course load. *Financial support:* In 2006–07, 13 students received support, including 7 teaching assistantships with full tuition reimbursements available (averaging $7,772 per year); research assistantships with full tuition reimbursements available, career-related internships or fieldwork, Federal Work-Study, institutionally sponsored loans, and unspecified assistantships also available. Financial award applicants required to submit FAFSA. *Faculty research:* Static balance and stepping performance of older adults, organizational justice, public health, strength training and recovery drinks, high risk drinking perceptions and behaviors. *Unit head:* Dr. Joseph Chromiak, Interim Head, 662-325-2963, Fax: 662-325-4525, E-mail: jchrom@colled.msstate.edu. *Application contact:* Dr. Phil Bonfanti, Director of Admissions, 662-325-4104, Fax: 662-325-8872, E-mail: admit@msstate.edu.

Mississippi University for Women, Graduate School, Division of Health and Kinesiology, Columbus, MS 39701-9998. Offers health education (MS). *Degree requirements:* For master's, comprehensive exam.

Montana State University, College of Graduate Studies, College of Education, Health, and Human Development, Department of Health and Human Development, Bozeman, MT 59717. Offers MS. *Accreditation:* ACA. Part-time programs available. *Faculty:* 25 full-time (17 women), 9 part-time/adjunct (7 women). *Students:* 42 full-time (31 women), 36 part-time (29 women); includes 1 minority (Asian American or Pacific Islander), 2 international. Average age 28. 32 applicants, 53% accepted, 15 enrolled. In 2006, 27 degrees awarded. *Degree requirements:* For master's, comprehensive exam, registration. *Entrance requirements:* For master's, GRE General Test. Additional exam requirements/recommendations for international students: Required—TOEFL (minimum score 550 paper-based; 213 computer-based). *Application deadline:* For fall admission, 7/15 priority date for domestic students, 5/15 priority date for international students; for spring admission, 12/1 priority date for domestic students, 10/1 priority date for international students. Applications are processed on a rolling basis. Application fee: $30. Electronic applications accepted. *Expenses:* Tuition, state resident: full-time $5,113. Tuition, nonresident: full-time $12,501. *Financial support:* In 2006–07, 14 students received support, including research assistantships (averaging $8,000 per year), teaching assistantships (averaging $8,000 per year); tuition waivers (full and partial) also available. Financial award application deadline: 3/1; financial award applicants required to submit FAFSA. *Faculty research:* Gait analysis, cancer prevention, obesity prevention, energy expenditure, decision making. Total annual research expenditures: $3.1 million. *Unit head:* Dr. Craig Stewart, Head, 404-994-3242, Fax: 404-994-2013, E-mail: cstewart@montana.edu. *Application contact:* Dr. Craig Stewart, Head, 404-994-3242, Fax: 404-994-2013, E-mail: cstewart@montana.edu.

Montclair State University, The Graduate School, College of Education and Human Services, Department of Curriculum and Teaching, Montclair, NJ 07043-1624. Offers education (M Ed); educational technology (M Ed); school library media specialist (Certificate); teaching (MAT, Certificate), including art (MAT), biological science (MAT), early childhood education (P-3) (MAT), earth science (MAT), elementary education (K-8) (MAT), English (MAT), French (MAT), health and physical education (MAT), health education (MAT), home economics (MAT), mathematics (MAT), music (MAT), physical education (MAT), physical science (MAT), social studies (MAT), Spanish (MAT), teacher of ESL (MAT), teacher of students with disabilities (MAT). Part-time and evening/weekend programs available. *Faculty:* 16 full-time (12 women), 13 part-time/adjunct (8 women). *Students:* 147 full-time (113 women), 230 part-time (188 women); includes 58 minority (33 African Americans, 1 American Indian/Alaska Native, 12 Asian Americans or Pacific Islanders, 12 Hispanic Americans), 4 international. Average age 33. 118 applicants, 38% accepted, 37 enrolled. In 2006, 166 master's, 11 other advanced degrees awarded.

Degree requirements: For master's, field experience. *Entrance requirements:* For master's, PRAXIS II, minimum GPA of 2.67, 2 letters of recommendation. Additional exam requirements/recommendations for international students: Required—TOEFL (minimum score 83 computer-based). *Application deadline:* For fall admission, 2/15 for domestic and international students; for spring admission, 9/15 for domestic and international students. Applications are processed on a rolling basis. Application fee: $60. Electronic applications accepted. *Expenses:* Tuition, state resident: part-time $450 per credit. Tuition, nonresident: part-time $682 per credit. Tuition and fees vary according to degree level and program. *Financial support:* In 2006–07, 7 research assistantships with full tuition reimbursements (averaging $7,000 per year) were awarded; Federal Work-Study, scholarships/grants, and unspecified assistantships also available. Support available to part-time students. Financial award application deadline: 3/1; financial award applicants required to submit FAFSA. *Unit head:* Dr. Deborah Eldridge, Chairperson, 973-655-5187.

Montclair State University, The Graduate School, College of Education and Human Services, Department of Exercise Science and Physical Education, Montclair, NJ 07043-1624. Offers health and physical education (Certificate); nutrition and exercise science (Certificate); physical education (MA, Certificate), including coaching and sports administration (MA), exercise science (MA), physical education (MA), teaching and supervision of physical education (MA). Part-time and evening/weekend programs available. *Faculty:* 14 full-time (8 women), 12 part-time/adjunct (7 women). *Students:* 23 full-time (10 women), 54 part-time (33 women); includes 10 minority (5 African Americans, 1 Asian American or Pacific Islander, 4 Hispanic Americans). 36 applicants, 47% accepted, 12 enrolled. In 2006, 11 master's, 13 other advanced degrees awarded. *Degree requirements:* For master's, comprehensive exam. *Entrance requirements:* For master's, GRE General Test, 2 letters of recommendation; for Certificate, 2 letters of recommendation (nutrition and exercise science concentration). Additional exam requirements/recommendations for international students: Required—TOEFL (minimum score 83 computer-based). *Application deadline:* For fall admission, 6/1 for international students; for spring admission, 10/1 for international students. Applications are processed on a rolling basis. Application fee: $60. Electronic applications accepted. *Expenses:* Tuition, state resident: part-time $450 per credit. Tuition, nonresident: part-time $682 per credit. Tuition and fees vary according to degree level and program. *Financial support:* In 2006–07, 4 research assistantships with full tuition reimbursements (averaging $5,000 per year) were awarded; Federal Work-Study, scholarships/grants, and unspecified assistantships also available. Support available to part-time students. Financial award application deadline: 3/1; financial award applicants required to submit FAFSA. *Unit head:* Dr. Joseph Donnelly, Chairperson, 973-655-4154.

Montclair State University, The Graduate School, College of Education and Human Services, Department of Health and Nutrition Sciences, Montclair, NJ 07043-1624. Offers food safety instructor (Certificate); health education (MA); nutrition and exercise science (MS); nutrition and food science (MS). *Faculty:* 14 full-time (8 women), 12 part-time/adjunct (7 women). *Students:* 11 full-time (10 women), 25 part-time (22 women); includes 2 minority (1 African American, 1 Asian American or Pacific Islander), 1 international. Average age 33. 28 applicants, 64% accepted, 14 enrolled. In 2006, 9 master's, 4 other advanced degrees awarded. *Degree requirements:* For master's, thesis optional. *Entrance requirements:* For master's, GRE, 2 letters of recommendation. Additional exam requirements/recommendations for international students: Required—TOEFL (minimum score 83 computer-based). *Application deadline:* For fall admission, 6/1 for international students; for spring admission, 10/1 for international students. *Expenses:* Tuition, state resident: part-time $450 per credit. Tuition, nonresident: part-time $682 per credit. Tuition and fees vary according to degree level and program. *Financial support:* In 2006–07, 2 research assistantships (averaging $7,000 per year) were awarded. *Faculty research:* Adolescent physical activity. Total annual research expenditures: $182,000. *Unit head:* Dr. Shahla Wunderlich, Chairperson, 973-655-6854, E-mail: wunderlichs@mail.montclair.edu.

Morehead State University, Graduate Programs, College of Education, Department of Health, Physical Education and Sport Sciences, Morehead, KY 40351. Offers exercise physiology (MA); health and physical education (MA); sports management (MA). *Accreditation:* NCATE. Part-time and evening/weekend programs available. *Faculty:* 12 full-time (8 women), 5 part-time/adjunct (2 women). *Students:* 16 full-time (10 women), 12 part-time (7 women), 2 international. Average age 32. In 2006, 11 degrees awarded. *Degree requirements:* For master's, oral exam, written core exam, thesis optional. *Entrance requirements:* For master's, GRE General Test or MAT, minimum GPA of 2.5; undergraduate major/minor in health, physical education, or recreation. Additional exam requirements/recommendations for international students: Required—TOEFL (minimum score 500 paper-based; 173 computer-based). *Application deadline:* For fall admission, 8/1 priority date for domestic and international students; for spring admission, 12/1 priority date for domestic and international students. Applications are processed on a rolling basis. Application fee: $0 ($55 for international students). Electronic applications accepted. *Financial support:* In 2006–07, 4 teaching assistantships (averaging $6,000 per year) were awarded; career-related internships or fieldwork, Federal Work-Study, and unspecified assistantships also available. Financial award application deadline: 4/1; financial award applicants required to submit FAFSA. *Faculty research:* Child growth and performance, instructional strategies, outdoor leadership qualities, exercise science, athletic training. *Unit head:* Dr. Lynne Fitzgerald, Chair, 606-783-2180, Fax: 606-783-5058. *Application contact:* Michelle Barber, Graduate Admissions Counselor, 606-783-2039, Fax: 606-783-5061, E-mail: m.barber@moreheadstate.edu.

Mount Mary College, Graduate Programs, Program in Dietetics, Milwaukee, WI 53222-4597. Offers administrative dietetics (MS); clinical dietetics (MS); nutrition education (MS). Part-time and evening/weekend programs available. *Faculty:* 1 (woman) full-time, 3 part-time/adjunct (all women). *Students:* 10 full-time (all women), 20 part-time (all women), 1 international. Average age 25. 30 applicants, 47% accepted, 13 enrolled. In 2006, 1 degree awarded. *Degree requirements:* For master's, thesis. *Entrance requirements:* For master's, minimum GPA of 2.75, completion of ADA and DPD requirements. Additional exam requirements/recommendations for international students: Required—TOEFL (minimum score 500 paper-based; 173 computer-based). *Application deadline:* For fall admission, 2/15 priority date for domestic students. Application fee: $35 ($75 for international students). *Expenses:* Tuition: Part-time $490 per credit. Required fees: $48 per term. Tuition and fees vary according to course load and program. *Financial support:* Career-related internships or fieldwork and Federal Work-Study available. Support available to part-time students. Financial award application deadline: 5/1; financial award applicants required to submit FAFSA. *Unit head:* Lisa Stark, Director, 414-258-4810 Ext. 398, E-mail: starkl@mtmary.edu.

New Jersey City University, Graduate and Continuing Education, College of Professional Studies, Department of Health Sciences, Jersey City, NJ 07305-1597. Offers community health education (MS); health administration (MS); school health education (MS). Part-time and evening/weekend programs available. *Faculty:* 5. *Students:* Average age 42. In 2006, 25 degrees awarded. *Degree requirements:* For master's, thesis or alternative, internship. *Entrance requirements:* For master's, GRE General Test or MAT. Additional exam requirements/recommendations for international students: Required—TOEFL. *Application deadline:* For fall admission, 8/1 priority date for domestic students; for spring admission, 12/1 for domestic students. Applications are processed on a rolling basis. Application fee: $0. *Expenses:* Tuition, state resident: full-time $7,038; part-time $391 per credit. Tuition, nonresident: full-time $12,510; part-time $695 per credit. Required fees: $65 per credit. *Financial support:* Career-related internships or fieldwork and unspecified assistantships available. *Unit head:* Dr. Lilliam Rosado, Chairperson, 201-200-3461.

New Mexico Highlands University, Graduate Studies, School of Education, Department of Exercise and Sport Sciences, Las Vegas, NM 87701. Offers human performance and sport (MA); sports administration (MA); teacher education (MA). Part-time programs available. *Faculty:* 2 full-time (1 woman). *Students:* 16 full-time (5 women), 44 part-time (13 women); includes 29 minority (7 African Americans, 1 Asian American or Pacific Islander, 21 Hispanic Americans), 1 international. Average age 31. 23 applicants, 78% accepted, 8 enrolled. In 2006, 10 degrees awarded. *Degree requirements:* For master's, thesis or alternative, comprehensive exam, registration. *Entrance requirements:* For master's, minimum undergraduate GPA of 3.0. Additional exam requirements/recommendations for international students: Required—TOEFL (minimum score 540 paper-based; 190 computer-based). *Application deadline:* For fall admission, 8/1 priority date for domestic students. Applications are processed on a rolling basis. Application fee: $15. *Expenses:* Tuition, state resident: part-time $101 per credit hour. Tuition, nonresident: part-time $101 per credit hour. *Financial support:* In 2006–07, 22 students received support, including 8 teaching assistantships with full and partial tuition reimbursements available (averaging $6,500 per year); career-related internships or fieldwork, Federal Work-Study, institutionally sponsored loans, scholarships/grants, tuition waivers (partial), and unspecified assistantships also available. Support available to part-time students. Financial award application deadline: 3/1; financial award applicants required to submit FAFSA. *Unit head:* Dr. Kathy Jenkins, Chair, 505-454-3287, Fax: 505-454-3001, E-mail: kjenkins@nmhu.edu. *Application contact:* Diane Trujillo, Administrative Assistant Graduate Studies, 505-454-3266, Fax: 505-454-3558, E-mail: dtrujillo@nmhu.edu.

New York University, Steinhardt School of Culture, Education and Human Development, Department of Nutrition, Food Studies, and Public Health, Program in Community Public Health, New York, NY 10012-1019. Offers community health (MPH); international community health (MPH); public health (PhD); public health nutrition (MPH). *Accreditation:* CEPH. Part-time and evening/weekend programs available. *Faculty:* 5 full-time (4 women). *Students:* 64 full-time (54 women), 43 part-time (39 women); includes 38 minority (12 African Americans, 1 American Indian/Alaska Native, 20 Asian Americans or Pacific Islanders, 5 Hispanic Americans), 4 international. 188 applicants, 76% accepted, 42 enrolled. In 2006, 21 master's, 1 doctorate awarded. *Degree requirements:* For master's, thesis (for some programs). *Entrance requirements:* For master's, GRE General Test; for doctorate, GRE General Test, interview. Additional exam requirements/recommendations for international students: Required—TOEFL. *Application deadline:* For fall admission, 12/15 priority date for domestic and international students; for spring admission, 11/1 for domestic and international students. Applications are processed on a rolling basis. Application fee: $50. *Expenses:* Tuition: Part-time $1,080 per unit. Required fees: $56 per unit. $329 per term. Tuition and fees vary according to program. *Financial support:* Career-related internships or fieldwork, Federal Work-Study, scholarships/grants, and tuition waivers (partial) available. Support available to part-time students. Financial award application deadline: 2/1; financial award applicants required to submit FAFSA. *Faculty research:* Social epidemiology, primary health care, global health, immigrants and health, infectious disease prevention. *Unit head:* Sally Guttmacher, Director, 212-998-5580, Fax: 212-995-4192. *Application contact:* 212-998-5030, Fax: 212-995-4328, E-mail: steinhardt.gradadmissions@nyu.edu.

North Carolina Agricultural and Technical State University, Graduate School, School of Education, Department of Health and Physical Education, Greensboro, NC 27411. Offers MS. *Accreditation:* NCATE. Part-time and evening/weekend programs available. *Degree requirements:* For master's, thesis or alternative, qualifying exam, comprehensive exam. *Entrance requirements:* For master's, GRE General Test, minimum GPA of 3.0.

Northeastern State University, Graduate College, College of Education, Department of Health and Human Performance, Tahlequah, OK 74464-2399. Offers health and kinesiology (MS Ed). Part-time and evening/weekend programs available. *Students:* 9 full-time (3 women), 23 part-time (8 women); includes 15 minority (5 African Americans, 4 American Indian/Alaska Native, 6 Hispanic Americans), 1 international. In 2006, 6 degrees awarded. *Entrance requirements:* For master's, MAT or GRE, minimum GPA of 2.5. Additional exam requirements/recommendations for international students: Required—TOEFL (minimum score 213 computer-based). *Application deadline:* For fall admission, 6/1 for domestic students. Application fee: $0 ($25 for international students). *Unit head:* Dr. Mark Giese, Chair, 918-456-5511 Ext. 3950.

Northern Arizona University, Consortium of Professional Schools and Colleges, College of Health Professions, Program in Public Health, Flagstaff, AZ 86011. Offers health education and health promotion (MPH). *Degree requirements:* For master's, internship. *Entrance requirements:* For master's, GRE General Test or MCAT, minimum GPA of 3.0.

Northern State University, Division of Graduate Studies in Education, Program in Teaching and Learning, Aberdeen, SD 57401-7198. Offers educational studies (MS Ed); elementary classroom teaching (MS Ed); health, physical education, and coaching (MS Ed); language and literacy (MS Ed); secondary classroom teaching (MS Ed); special education (MS Ed). *Accreditation:* NCATE. Part-time and evening/weekend programs available. *Faculty:* 69 full-time (19 women). *Students:* 5 full-time (3 women), 70 part-time (51 women); includes 3 minority (1 African American, 1 American Indian/Alaska Native, 1 Asian American or Pacific Islander). Average age 32. In 2006, 23 degrees awarded. *Degree requirements:* For master's, thesis optional. *Entrance requirements:* For master's, minimum GPA of 2.75. Additional exam requirements/recommendations for international students: Required—TOEFL (minimum score 550 paper-based; 213 computer-based). *Application deadline:* For fall admission, 8/15 priority date for domestic students; for spring admission, 12/15 for domestic students. Applications are processed on a rolling basis. Application fee: $35. Electronic applications accepted. *Expenses:* Tuition, state resident: full-time $3,373; part-time $120 per credit. Tuition, nonresident: full-time $9,943; part-time $355 per credit. International tuition: $13,000 full-time. Required fees: $86 per credit. One-time fee: $35 full-time. Tuition and fees vary according to course load, degree level and reciprocity agreements. *Financial support:* In 2006–07, 17 teaching assistantships with partial tuition reimbursements (averaging $4,812 per year) were awarded; career-related internships or fieldwork, Federal Work-Study, institutionally sponsored loans, scholarships/grants, and unspecified assistantships also available. Support available to part-time students. Financial award application deadline: 3/1; financial award applicants required to submit FAFSA. *Application contact:* Tammy K. Griffith, Senior Secretary, 605-626-2558, Fax: 605-626-2542, E-mail: griffith@northern.edu.

Northwestern State University of Louisiana, Graduate Studies and Research, Department of Health and Human Performance, Natchitoches, LA 71497. Offers MS. *Faculty:* 5 full-time (3 women). *Students:* 40 full-time (24 women), 21 part-time (8 women); includes 23 minority (17 African Americans, 1 American Indian/Alaska Native, 2 Asian Americans or Pacific Islanders, 3 Hispanic Americans), 1 international. Average age 26. In 2006, 14 degrees awarded. *Degree requirements:* For master's, thesis or alternative, comprehensive exam, registration. *Entrance requirements:* For master's, GRE General Test, minimum undergraduate GPA of 2.5. *Application deadline:* For fall admission, 8/1 priority date for domestic students; for spring admission, 1/10 for domestic students. Applications are processed on a rolling basis. Application fee: $20 ($30 for international students). *Financial support:* Career-related internships or fieldwork available. Financial award application deadline: 7/15. *Unit head:* Dr. William Dickens, Acting Chairman, 318-357-5132, Fax: 318-357-5904. *Application contact:* Dr. Steven G. Horton, Associate Provost/Dean, Graduate Studies, Research, and Information Systems, 318-357-5851, Fax: 318-357-5019, E-mail: grad_school@nsula.edu.

Northwest Missouri State University, Graduate School, College of Education and Human Services, Department of Health, Physical Education, Recreation and Dance, Maryville, MO 64468-6001. Offers health and physical education (MS Ed); recreation (MS). *Accreditation:* NCATE. Part-time programs available. *Faculty:* 10 full-time (4 women). *Students:* 36 full-time (16 women), 6 part-time (1 woman); includes 2 minority (1 African American, 1 Asian American or Pacific Islander). 36 applicants, 69% accepted, 16 enrolled. In 2006, 12 degrees awarded. *Degree requirements:* For master's, comprehensive exam. *Entrance requirements:* For master's, GRE General Test, minimum undergraduate GPA of 2.75, teaching certificate, writing sample. Additional exam requirements/recommendations for international students: Required—TOEFL (minimum score 550 paper-based; 213 computer-based). *Application deadline:* For fall admission, 7/1 for domestic and international students; for spring admission, 11/15 for domestic and international students. Applications are processed on a rolling basis. Application fee: $0 ($50 for international students). *Financial support:* In 2006–07, 23 teaching assistantships with full

Health Education

Northwest Missouri State University (continued)
tuition reimbursements (averaging $6,000 per year) were awarded; research assistantships, unspecified assistantships also available. Financial award application deadline: 3/1; financial award applicants required to submit FAFSA. *Unit head:* Dr. Loren Butler, Program Director, 660-562-1066. *Application contact:* Dr. Frances Shipley, Dean of Graduate School, 660-562-1145, Fax: 660-562-1096, E-mail: gradsch@nwmissouri.edu.

Nova Southeastern University, Fischler School of Education and Human Services, Program in Education, Fort Lauderdale, FL 33314-7796. Offers educational leadership (Ed D); health care education (Ed D); higher education (Ed D); human serviced administration (Ed D); instructional leadership (Ed D); instructional technology distance education (Ed D); organizational leadership (Ed D); special education (Ed D); speech language pathology (Ed D). *Students:* 619 full-time (452 women), 615 part-time (473 women); includes 737 minority (616 African Americans, 2 American Indian/Alaska Native, 14 Asian Americans or Pacific Islanders, 105 Hispanic Americans), 8 international. Average age 38. 480 applicants, 83% accepted, 398 enrolled. *Degree requirements:* For doctorate, thesis/dissertation. *Entrance requirements:* For doctorate, MAT or GRE, master's degree, 2 letters of recommendation, work experience. Additional exam requirements/recommendations for international students: Required—TSE (recommended) with a minimum score of 50; Recommended—TOEFL (minimum score 550 paper-based; 213 computer-based), IELTS (minimum score 6). *Application deadline:* For fall admission, 8/11 priority date for domestic and international students; for winter admission, 12/28 priority date for domestic and international students; for spring admission, 4/22 priority date for domestic and international students. Applications are processed on a rolling basis. Application fee: $50. Electronic applications accepted. *Financial support:* In 2006–07, 2 fellowships (averaging $9,375 per year) were awarded; scholarships/grants and tuition waivers (full) also available. Support available to part-time students. Financial award application deadline: 1/7; financial award applicants required to submit FAFSA. *Unit head:* Dr. Karen D. Bowser, Associate Dean of Doctoral Programs, 954-262-8500, Fax: 954-262-3912, E-mail: bowserk@nova.edu. *Application contact:* Jennifer Quiñones Nottingham, Dean of Student Affairs, 800-986-3223 Ext. 8624, Fax: 954-262-3911, E-mail: jlquinon@nova.edu.

Nova Southeastern University, Fischler School of Education and Human Services, Programs for Higher Education, Fort Lauderdale, FL 33314-7796. Offers adult education (Ed D); computing and information technology (Ed D); health care education (Ed D); higher education (Ed D); vocational, occupational and technical education (Ed D). Part-time and evening/weekend programs available. *Students:* 35 full-time (22 women), 321 part-time (222 women); includes 134 minority (116 African Americans, 1 American Indian/Alaska Native, 17 Hispanic Americans), 1 international. 4 applicants, 75% accepted, 3 enrolled. In 2006, 40 degrees awarded. *Degree requirements:* For doctorate, thesis/dissertation, practicum. *Entrance requirements:* For doctorate, MAT or GRE, master's degree, work experience in field, minimum GPA of 3.0. Additional exam requirements/recommendations for international students: Recommended—TOEFL (minimum score 550 paper-based; 213 computer-based), IELTS (minimum score 6). *Application deadline:* For fall admission, 8/11 priority date for domestic and international students; for winter admission, 12/28 priority date for domestic and international students; for spring admission, 4/22 priority date for domestic and international students. Applications are processed on a rolling basis. Application fee: $50. Electronic applications accepted. *Expenses:* Contact institution. *Financial support:* In 2006–07, 2 fellowships were awarded; career-related internships or fieldwork and tuition waivers (full) also available. Financial award application deadline: 1/7. *Unit head:* Dr. Karen D. Bowser, Associate Dean of Doctoral Programs, 954-262-8500, Fax: 954-262-3912, E-mail: bowserk@nova.edu. *Application contact:* Jennifer Quiñones Nottingham, Dean of Student Affairs, 800-986-3223 Ext. 8624, Fax: 954-262-3911, E-mail: jlquinon@nova.edu.

Oklahoma State University, College of Education, School of Applied Health and Educational Psychology, Stillwater, OK 74078. Offers applied behavioral studies (MS, Ed D, PhD); counseling and student personnel (MS, PhD); educational psychology (PhD); health (MS, Ed D); leisure sciences (MS, Ed D); physical education (MS, Ed D); physical education and leisure sciences (Ed D); school psychology (Ed S). *Accreditation:* APA (one or more programs are accredited). Part-time programs available. *Faculty:* 37 full-time (17 women), 12 part-time/adjunct (8 women). *Students:* 189 full-time (137 women), 180 part-time (113 women); includes 75 minority (25 African Americans, 34 American Indian/Alaska Native, 5 Asian Americans or Pacific Islanders, 11 Hispanic Americans), 27 international. Average age 33. 275 applicants, 28% accepted, 64 enrolled. In 2006, 45 master's, 21 doctorates awarded. *Degree requirements:* For master's, thesis or alternative; for doctorate, thesis/dissertation. *Entrance requirements:* For master's, GRE or MAT; for doctorate, GRE (PhD). Additional exam requirements/recommendations for international students: Required—TOEFL. *Application deadline:* For fall admission, 7/1 priority date for domestic students, 3/1 priority date for international students; for spring admission, 8/1 priority date for international students. Applications are processed on a rolling basis. Application fee: $40 ($75 for international students). Electronic applications accepted. *Expenses:* Tuition, state resident: part-time $146 per credit hour. Tuition, nonresident: part-time $516 per credit hour. Required fees: $44 per credit hour. Tuition and fees vary according to program. *Financial support:* In 2006–07, 29 research assistantships (averaging $6,452 per year), 64 teaching assistantships (averaging $8,263 per year) were awarded; career-related internships or fieldwork, Federal Work-Study, scholarships/grants, health care benefits, tuition waivers (partial), and unspecified assistantships also available. Support available to part-time students. Financial award application deadline: 3/1. *Unit head:* Dr. John Romans, Head, 405-744-6040.

Penn State Harrisburg, Graduate School, School of Behavioral Sciences and Education, Middletown, PA 17057-4898. Offers adult education (D Ed); applied behavior analysis (MA); applied clinical psychology (MA); applied psychological research (MA); community psychology and social change (MA); health education (M Ed); teaching and curriculum (M Ed); training and development (M Ed). Part-time and evening/weekend programs available. *Expenses:* Tuition, state resident: full-time $13,224; part-time $551 per credit. Tuition, nonresident: full-time $18,652; part-time $777 per credit. Required fees: $84 per semester. *Financial support:* Career-related internships or fieldwork available. *Unit head:* Dr. William D. Milheim, Director, 717-948-6205, Fax: 717-948-6209, E-mail: wdm2@psu.edu.

Plymouth State University, College of Graduate Studies, Graduate Studies in Education, Program in Health Education, Plymouth, NH 03264-1595. Offers M Ed. Part-time and evening/weekend programs available. *Students:* 2 full-time (both women), 49 part-time (43 women). Average age 37. 12 applicants, 100% accepted, 12 enrolled. In 2006, 10 degrees awarded. *Degree requirements:* For master's, PRAXIS. *Entrance requirements:* For master's, MAT, minimum GPA of 3.0. *Application deadline:* Applications are processed on a rolling basis. Application fee: $75. *Expenses:* Tuition, state resident: part-time $369 per credit. Tuition, nonresident: part-time $407 per credit. Tuition and fees vary according to course level. *Financial support:* Career-related internships or fieldwork, scholarships/grants, and unspecified assistantships available. Support available to part-time students. Financial award applicants required to submit FAFSA. *Unit head:* Dr. Irene Cucina, Program Coordinator, 603-535-2517, E-mail: icucina@plymouth.edu.

Portland State University, Graduate Studies, College of Urban and Public Affairs, School of Community Health, Portland, OR 97207-0751. Offers gerontology (Certificate); health education (MA, MS); health education and health promotion (MPH); health studies (MPA, MPH), including health administration and policy. *Accreditation:* CEPH. Part-time programs available. *Faculty:* 13 full-time (9 women), 8 part-time/adjunct (6 women). *Students:* 36 full-time (30 women), 34 part-time (27 women); includes 9 minority (1 African American, 1 Asian American or Pacific Islander, 7 Hispanic Americans), 5 international. Average age 32. 73 applicants, 84% accepted, 34 enrolled. In 2006, 20 degrees awarded. *Degree requirements:* For master's, oral and written exams. *Entrance requirements:* For master's, GRE General Test, 3 letters of recommendation. Additional exam requirements/recommendations for international students: Required—TOEFL (minimum score 550 paper-based; 213 computer-based). *Application deadline:* For fall admission, 2/1 for domestic and international students. Application fee: $50. *Expenses:* Tuition, state resident: full-time $6,426; part-time $238 per credit. Tuition, nonresident: full-time $11,016; part-time $408 per credit. Tuition and fees vary according to course load. *Financial support:* In 2006–07, 4 research assistantships with full tuition reimbursements (averaging $7,286 per year) were awarded; fellowships, teaching assistantships, career-related internships or fieldwork, Federal Work-Study, scholarships/grants, and unspecified assistantships also available. Support available to part-time students. Financial award application deadline: 3/1; financial award applicants required to submit FAFSA. Total annual research expenditures: $766,046. *Unit head:* Carlos J. Crespo, Interim Director, 503-725-5102, Fax: 503-725-5100. *Application contact:* Elizabeth Bull, Assistant to the Director, 503-725-4592, Fax: 503-725-5100, E-mail: bulle@pdx.edu.

Prairie View A&M University, Graduate School, College of Education, Department of Health and Human Performance, Prairie View, TX 77446-0519. Offers health education (M Ed, MS); physical education (M Ed, MS). *Accreditation:* NCATE. Part-time and evening/weekend programs available. *Faculty:* 3 part-time/adjunct (2 women). *Students:* 6 full-time (2 women), 30 part-time (11 women); includes 35 minority (33 African Americans, 1 American Indian/Alaska Native, 1 Hispanic American). Average age 27. 36 applicants, 100% accepted, 36 enrolled. In 2006, 9 degrees awarded. *Entrance requirements:* For master's, GRE General Test. *Application deadline:* For fall admission, 10/2 priority date for domestic students; for spring admission, 2/19 for domestic students. Applications are processed on a rolling basis. Application fee: $50. *Financial support:* In 2006–07, 8 fellowships with tuition reimbursements (averaging $1,200 per year), 10 research assistantships with tuition reimbursements (averaging $15,000 per year) were awarded; teaching assistantships with tuition reimbursements, career-related internships or fieldwork, Federal Work-Study, and institutionally sponsored loans also available. Support available to part-time students. Financial award application deadline: 4/1. *Unit head:* Marsha Kay Washington, Head, 936-857-4210, Fax: 936-857-4422. *Application contact:* Dr. William H. Parker, Dean of Graduate School, 936-857-2312, Fax: 936-857-4127, E-mail: william_parker@pvamu.edu.

Rhode Island College, School of Graduate Studies, Feinstein School of Education and Human Development, Department of Health and Physical Education, Providence, RI 02908-1991. Offers health education (M Ed). *Accreditation:* NCATE. Part-time and evening/weekend programs available. *Faculty:* 4 full-time (2 women). *Students:* Average age 38. In 2006, 13 degrees awarded. *Entrance requirements:* For master's, GRE General Test or MAT, teaching certificate, 3 letters of recommendation, interview. *Application deadline:* For fall admission, 3/15 for domestic students; for spring admission, 11/1 for domestic students. Applications are processed on a rolling basis. Application fee: $50. *Expenses:* Tuition, state resident: part-time $244 per credit. Tuition, nonresident: part-time $512 per credit. Required fees: $12 per credit. $66 per term. Tuition and fees vary according to degree level, program and reciprocity agreements. *Financial support:* Teaching assistantships with full tuition reimbursements, Federal Work-Study, scholarships/grants, health care benefits, and unspecified assistantships available. Support available to part-time students. Financial award application deadline: 5/15; financial award applicants required to submit FAFSA. *Unit head:* Dr. Karen Castagno, Chair, 401-456-8046.

Rosalind Franklin University of Medicine and Science, College of Health Professions, Department of Nutrition, North Chicago, IL 60064-3095. Offers clinical education (MS); clinical nutrition (MS). Part-time and evening/weekend programs available. Postbaccalaureate distance learning degree programs offered (no on-campus study). *Degree requirements:* For master's, thesis optional. *Entrance requirements:* For master's, minimum GPA of 2.75, registered dietitian (RD), professional certificate or license. Expenses: Contact institution. *Faculty research:* Nutrition education, distance learning, computer-based graduate education, childhood obesity, nutrition medical education.

Sage Graduate School, Graduate School, Division of Education, Program in School Health Education, Troy, NY 12180-4115. Offers MS. *Accreditation:* NCATE. Part-time and evening/weekend programs available. *Faculty:* 11 full-time (8 women), 20 part-time/adjunct (15 women). *Students:* 9 full-time (4 women), 46 part-time (31 women); includes 3 minority (1 African American, 1 American Indian/Alaska Native, 1 Hispanic American). Average age 30. 31 applicants, 61% accepted, 14 enrolled. In 2006, 17 degrees awarded. *Degree requirements:* For master's, thesis optional. *Entrance requirements:* For master's, minimum GPA of 2.75. Additional exam requirements/recommendations for international students: Required—TOEFL (minimum score 550 paper-based; 213 computer-based). *Application deadline:* Applications are processed on a rolling basis. Application fee: $40. *Expenses:* Tuition: Full-time $9,270; part-time $515 per credit hour. *Financial support:* Career-related internships or fieldwork, scholarships/grants, and unspecified assistantships available. Support available to part-time students. Financial award application deadline: 3/1; financial award applicants required to submit FAFSA. *Faculty research:* Policy development in health education and health care. *Unit head:* Dr. John J. Pelizza, Director, 518-244-2326, Fax: 518-244-2334, E-mail: peliz@sage.edu. *Application contact:* Shannon K. Easton, Director of Graduate and Adult Admission, 518-244-2443, Fax: 518-244-6880, E-mail: sgsadm@sage.edu.

Sage Graduate School, Graduate School, Division of Management, Communications and Legal Studies, Program in Health Services Administration, Troy, NY 12180-4115. Offers gerontology (MS); health education (MS); management (MS). Part-time and evening/weekend programs available. *Faculty:* 3 full-time (1 woman), 4 part-time/adjunct (2 women). *Students:* 1 (woman) full-time, 13 part-time (11 women). Average age 32. 8 applicants, 100% accepted, 8 enrolled. In 2006, 5 degrees awarded. *Entrance requirements:* For master's, minimum GPA of 2.75. Additional exam requirements/recommendations for international students: Required—TOEFL (minimum score 550 paper-based; 213 computer-based). Application fee: $40. *Expenses:* Tuition: Full-time $9,270; part-time $515 per credit hour. *Financial support:* Career-related internships or fieldwork, scholarships/grants, and unspecified assistantships available. Support available to part-time students. Financial award application deadline: 3/1; financial award applicants required to submit FAFSA. *Application contact:* Shannon K. Easton, Director of Graduate and Adult Admission, 518-244-2443, Fax: 518-244-6880, E-mail: sgsadm@sage.edu.

Saint Francis University, Department of Physician Assistant Sciences, Health Science Program, Loretto, PA 15940-0600. Offers MHS. Part-time and evening/weekend programs available. Postbaccalaureate distance learning degree programs offered (no on-campus study). *Faculty:* 1 (woman) full-time, 4 part-time/adjunct (2 women). *Students:* 13 applicants, 100% accepted, 13 enrolled. *Entrance requirements:* For master's, 2 letters of reference, minimum QPA of 2.5. *Application deadline:* Applications are processed on a rolling basis. Application fee: $50. Electronic applications accepted. *Expenses:* Contact institution. *Financial support:* Available to part-time students. Applicants required to submit FAFSA. *Unit head:* Melissa M. Kagarise, Coordinator, 814-472-3919, Fax: 814-472-3137, E-mail: mkagarise@francis.edu. *Application contact:* Peggy Beiswenger, Office Assistant, 814-472-3136, E-mail: pbeiswenger@francis.edu.

Saint Joseph's University, College of Arts and Sciences, Department of Health Services, Philadelphia, PA 19131-1395. Offers health administration (MS); health education (MS); nurse anesthesia (MS). Evening/weekend programs available. *Faculty:* 5 full-time (2 women), 12 part-time/adjunct (6 women). *Students:* 45 full-time (27 women), 147 part-time (107 women); includes 51 minority (45 African Americans, 3 Asian Americans or Pacific Islanders, 3 Hispanic Americans), 9 international. Average age 34. In 2006, 62 degrees awarded. *Entrance requirements:* For master's, 2 letters of recommendation. Additional exam requirements/recommendations for international students: Required—TOEFL. *Application deadline:* For fall admission, 7/15 for domestic students. Application fee: $35. *Financial support:* Fellowships, career-related internships or fieldwork available. *Unit head:* Dr. John Newhouse, Chair, 610-660-1578.

Salem International University, School of Education, Salem, WV 26426-0500. Offers curriculum and instruction (M Ed), including curriculum and instruction, educational technology leadership, physical education/health, teaching English as a second language; educational administration (M Ed). Part-time and evening/weekend programs available. Postbaccalaureate distance learning degree programs offered. *Faculty:* 5 full-time (4 women), 17 part-time/adjunct (8 women). *Students:* 74 full-time (45 women), 154 part-time (75 women); includes 7 minority (2 African Americans, 5 Asian Americans or Pacific Islanders), 28 international. Average age 41. 200 applicants, 75% accepted, 130 enrolled. In 2006, 18 degrees awarded. *Degree requirements:* For master's, thesis (for some programs), comprehensive exam (for some programs), registration. *Entrance requirements:* For master's, GRE, MAT, NTE, 3 letters of recommendation. Additional exam requirements/recommendations for international students: Required—TOEFL (minimum score 550 paper-based; 213 computer-based). *Application deadline:* Applications are processed on a rolling basis. Application fee: $25. Electronic applications accepted. *Expenses: Contact institution.* One-time fee: $25 part-time. Tuition and fees vary according to program. *Financial support:* Application deadline: 4/15; *Faculty research:* Improved classroom effectiveness. *Unit head:* Dean, School of Education, 304-326-1253, Fax: 304-326-1246. *Application contact:* Thomas White, Director of Admissions, 304-326-1549, Fax: 304-326-1246, E-mail: admission@salemiu.edu.

San Francisco State University, Division of Graduate Studies, College of Behavioral and Social Sciences, Human Sexuality Studies Program, San Francisco, CA 94132-1722. Offers MA. *Entrance requirements:* For master's, GRE, 2 letters of recommendation. Additional exam requirements/recommendations for international students: Required—TOEFL (minimum score 550 paper-based; 213 computer-based). *Application deadline:* For fall admission, 2/15 for domestic students. *Unit head:* Dr. Gilbert Herdt, Program Director, 415-405-3570, E-mail: hmsxdept@sfsu.edu. *Application contact:* Prof. Rita Melendez, Graduate Student Advisor, 415-405-3571.

San Jose State University, Graduate Studies and Research, College of Applied Sciences and Arts, Department of Health Science, San Jose, CA 95192-0001. Offers applied social gerontology (Certificate); community health education (MPH). *Accreditation:* CEPH (one or more programs are accredited). *Students:* 26 full-time (22 women), 45 part-time (37 women); includes 30 minority (3 African Americans, 12 Asian Americans or Pacific Islanders, 15 Hispanic Americans), 4 international. Average age 35. 112 applicants, 33% accepted, 20 enrolled. In 2006, 30 degrees awarded. *Entrance requirements:* For master's, GRE General Test. *Application deadline:* For fall admission, 6/29 for domestic students; for spring admission, 11/30 for domestic students. Applications are processed on a rolling basis. Application fee: $59. Electronic applications accepted. *Financial support:* Career-related internships or fieldwork, Federal Work-Study, and institutionally sponsored loans available. Support available to part-time students. Financial award applicants required to submit FAFSA. *Faculty research:* Behavioral science in occupational and health care settings, epidemiology in health care settings. *Unit head:* Kathleen Roe, Chair, 408-924-2970, Fax: 408-924-2979.

Simmons College, Graduate School, College of Arts and Sciences Graduate Studies, Department of Education, Program in Special Education, Boston, MA 02115. Offers applied behavior analysis (PhD); assistive technology (MS Ed, Ed S); behavioral education (MS Ed, Ed S); health professions education (PhD); language and literacy (MS Ed, Ed S); moderate disabilities (Ed S); moderate special needs (MS Ed); severe disabilities (Ed S); severe special needs (MS Ed); special education administration (MS Ed, PhD, Ed S). Part-time and evening/weekend programs available. *Faculty:* 9 full-time (7 women), 34 part-time/adjunct (23 women). *Students:* 51 full-time (46 women), 405 part-time (339 women); includes 31 minority (13 African Americans, 2 American Indian/Alaska Native, 7 Asian Americans or Pacific Islanders, 9 Hispanic Americans), 2 international. Average age 28. 155 applicants, 91% accepted, 121 enrolled. In 2006, 122 master's, 27 other advanced degrees awarded. *Degree requirements:* For master's, practicum; for doctorate, thesis/dissertation. *Entrance requirements:* For doctorate, GRE, research proposal interview. Additional exam requirements/recommendations for international students: Required—TOEFL (minimum score 600 paper-based; 250 computer-based; 100 iBT). *Application deadline:* For fall admission, 8/1 priority date for domestic students; for spring admission, 12/1 priority date for domestic students. Applications are processed on a rolling basis. Application fee: $35. Electronic applications accepted. *Expenses: Contact institution. Financial support:* Career-related internships or fieldwork, Federal Work-Study, institutionally sponsored loans, scholarships/grants, and tuition waivers (partial) available. Support available to part-time students. Financial award application deadline: 3/1; financial award applicants required to submit FAFSA. *Faculty research:* Classroom-based research, inclusion strategies, beginning teacher development. *Unit head:* Dr. Cathryn Mercier, Associate Dean, 617-521-2091. *Application contact:* Kristen Haack, Director, Graduate Studies Admission, 617-521-2915, Fax: 617-521-3058, E-mail: gsa@simmons.edu.

Simmons College, School for Health Studies, Program in Primary Health Care Nursing, Boston, MA 02115. Offers health professions education (PhD); primary health care nursing (MS, CAGS). *Accreditation:* AACN. Part-time programs available. *Faculty:* 8 full-time (7 women), 2 part-time/adjunct (both women). *Students:* 74 full-time (65 women), 84 part-time (81 women); includes 16 minority (4 African Americans, 10 Asian Americans or Pacific Islanders, 2 Hispanic Americans). Average age 30. 194 applicants, 61% accepted, 61 enrolled. In 2006, 30 master's, 1 other advanced degree awarded. *Median time to degree:* 2 years part-time. *Degree requirements:* For master's, thesis/dissertation, registration; for doctorate, thesis/dissertation, comprehensive exam, registration. *Entrance requirements:* For master's, GRE, courses in statistics and health assessment; for CAGS, previous coursework in microbiology, statistics, developmental psychology, organic and inorganic chemistry. Additional exam requirements/recommendations for international students: Required—TOEFL (minimum score 550 paper-based; 230 computer-based). *Application deadline:* For fall admission, 6/1 for domestic and international students; for winter admission, 11/1 for domestic and international students; for spring admission, 11/1 for domestic and international students. Applications are processed on a rolling basis. Application fee: $50. Electronic applications accepted. *Expenses: Contact institution. Financial support:* In 2006–07, 10 fellowships with partial tuition reimbursements were awarded; research assistantships, teaching assistantships, institutionally sponsored loans, scholarships/grants, and traineeships also available. Financial award application deadline: 3/1; financial award applicants required to submit FAFSA. *Faculty research:* Nursing leadership and mentoring, gerontology/home care, nurse practitioner in occupational health, adolescent pregnancy, developmental disabilities. Total annual research expenditures: $392,500. *Unit head:* Dr. Judy A. Beal, Chairperson, 617-521-2139, Fax: 617-521-3045, E-mail: judy.beal@simmons.edu. *Application contact:* Vilma Torres, Administrative Assistant, 617-521-2654, Fax: 617-521-3137, E-mail: shs@simmons.edu.

South Dakota State University, Graduate School, College of Arts and Science, Department of Health, Physical Education and Recreation, Brookings, SD 57007. Offers MS. Part-time programs available. *Faculty:* 4 full-time (1 woman), 1 part-time/adjunct (0 women). *Students:* 13 full-time (5 women), 12 part-time (2 women); includes 1 minority (African American) In 2006, 12 degrees awarded. *Degree requirements:* For master's, thesis, oral and written exams. *Entrance requirements:* For master's, GRE. Additional exam requirements/recommendations for international students: Required—TOEFL (minimum score 550 paper-based; 213 computer-based). *Application deadline:* For fall admission, 10/15 priority date for domestic students, 4/15 for international students; for spring admission, 3/15 for domestic students, 8/15 for international students. Applications are processed on a rolling basis. Application fee: $35. *Financial support:* In 2006–07, 1 research assistantship with partial tuition reimbursement (averaging $15,750 per year), 9 teaching assistantships with partial tuition reimbursements (averaging $15,750 per year) were awarded; career-related internships or fieldwork, Federal Work-Study, scholarships/grants, and unspecified assistantships also available. *Faculty research:* Effective teaching behaviors in physical education, sports nutrition, muscle/bone interaction, hormonal response to exercise. *Unit head:* Fred Oien, Head, 605-688-4668, Fax: 605-688-6446, E-mail: fred.oien@sdstate.edu. *Application contact:* Dr. Matthew Vukovich, Graduate Coordinator, 605-688-4668, Fax: 605-688-6446, E-mail: matt.vukovich@sdstate.edu.

Southeastern Louisiana University, College of Nursing and Health Sciences, Department of Kinesiology and Health Studies, Hammond, LA 70402. Offers health and kinesiology (MA). *Accreditation:* NCATE. Part-time programs available. *Faculty:* 10 full-time (4 women). *Students:* 21 full-time (15 women), 22 part-time (19 women); includes 11 minority (all African Americans), 3 international. Average age 29. 20 applicants, 95% accepted, 13 enrolled. In 2006, 15 degrees awarded. *Degree requirements:* For master's, thesis optional. *Entrance requirements:* For master's, GRE General Test, 30 hours of physical education, minimum GPA of 2.5. Additional exam requirements/recommendations for international students: Required—TOEFL (minimum score 500 paper-based; 173 computer-based). *Application deadline:* For fall admission, 7/15 priority date for domestic students, 6/1 priority date for international students; for spring admission, 12/1 priority date for domestic students, 10/1 priority date for international students. Applications are processed on a rolling basis. Application fee: $20 ($30 for international students). Electronic applications accepted. *Expenses:* Tuition, state resident: full-time $2,216; part-time $123 per credit. Tuition, nonresident: full-time $6,212; part-time $345 per credit. Required fees: $986; $55 per credit. Part-time tuition and fees vary according to course load. *Financial support:* In 2006–07, 8 research assistantships with full tuition reimbursements (averaging $5,500 per year), 3 teaching assistantships with full tuition reimbursements (averaging $5,500 per year) were awarded; Federal Work-Study, institutionally sponsored loans, unspecified assistantships, and administrative assistantships also available. Support available to part-time students. Financial award application deadline: 5/1; financial award applicants required to submit FAFSA. *Faculty research:* Relationship of exercise on body hormones; sexuality knowledge, attitudes and behaviors; drug and tobacco use and abuse; relationship of health and spirituality; exercise adherence and motivation. *Unit head:* Dr. Edward Hebert, Department Head, 985-549-2130, Fax: 985-549-5119, E-mail: ehebert@selu.edu. *Application contact:* Sandra Meyers, Graduate Admissions Analyst, 985-549-2066, Fax: 985-549-5632, E-mail: admissions@selu.edu.

Southern Connecticut State University, School of Graduate Studies, School of Education, Program in School Health Education, New Haven, CT 06515-1355. Offers MS. *Accreditation:* NCATE. Part-time and evening/weekend programs available. *Students:* 9 full-time (7 women), 55 part-time (32 women); includes 2 minority (1 African American, 1 Hispanic American). 20 applicants, 85% accepted, 15 enrolled. In 2006, 33 degrees awarded. *Entrance requirements:* For master's, interview. *Application deadline:* For fall admission, 7/15 priority date for domestic students. Applications are processed on a rolling basis. Application fee: $50. Electronic applications accepted. *Financial support:* Application deadline: 4/15; *Unit head:* Dr. Sharon Misasi, Chairperson, 203-392-6910, Fax: 203-392-6911, E-mail: misasis1@southernct.edu. *Application contact:* Dr. Doris Marino, Graduate Coordinator, 203-392-6922, Fax: 203-392-6911, E-mail: marinod1@southernct.edu.

Southern Illinois University Carbondale, Graduate School, College of Education, Department of Health Education and Recreation, Program in Community Health Education, Carbondale, IL 62901-4701. Offers MPH. *Students:* 12 full-time (9 women), 12 part-time (10 women); includes 6 minority (5 African Americans, 1 American Indian/Alaska Native), 3 international. 21 applicants, 14% accepted, 2 enrolled. In 2006, 3 degrees awarded. *Application contact:* Carol Reynolds, Administrative Assistant, 618-453-2415, Fax: 618-453-1829, E-mail: creynolds@siu.edu.

Southern Illinois University Carbondale, Graduate School, College of Education, Department of Health Education and Recreation, Program in Health Education, Carbondale, IL 62901-4701. Offers MS Ed, PhD. *Accreditation:* NCATE. Part-time programs available. *Faculty:* 9 full-time (6 women). *Students:* 13 full-time (9 women), 60 part-time (50 women); includes 7 minority (6 African Americans, 1 Asian American or Pacific Islander), 9 international. Average age 30. 17 applicants, 29% accepted, 0 enrolled. In 2006, 1 master's, 5 doctorates awarded. *Degree requirements:* For master's and doctorate, thesis/dissertation. *Entrance requirements:* For master's, MAT, minimum GPA of 2.7; for doctorate, MAT, minimum GPA of 3.25. Additional exam requirements/recommendations for international students: Required—TOEFL. *Application deadline:* For fall admission, 2/15 for domestic students; for spring admission, 9/15 for domestic students. Application fee: $20. *Financial support:* In 2006–07, 33 students received support, including 1 fellowship with full tuition reimbursement available, 10 teaching assistantships with full tuition reimbursements available; research assistantships with full tuition reimbursements available, career-related internships or fieldwork, Federal Work-Study, institutionally sponsored loans, and tuition waivers (full) also available. Support available to part-time students. *Faculty research:* Sexuality education, research design, injury control, program evaluation. *Application contact:* Carol Reynolds, Administrative Assistant, 618-453-2415, Fax: 618-453-1829, E-mail: creynolds@siu.edu.

Announcement: Southern Illinois University Carbondale is proud to offer 2 master's degrees in health education. Students interested in school health education can earn an MS in health education; those interested in community health can earn a Master in Public Health (MPH) in Community Health Education. In addition, the University continues to offer a nationally acclaimed (and ranked) doctoral program in health education. All degree programs allow students to demonstrate excellence in and out of the classroom. Awards received by students include the Graduate Dean's Fellowship Award and the Illinois School Health Association's "Barbara Gray Student Recognition Award." The health education doctoral program continues to maintain its traditional level of excellence. Awards received by students include the Social Science Research Council Dissertation Fellowship ($10,000), American School Health Association's "Delbert Oberteuffer Award," and Eta Sigma Gamma "National Gamman of the Year."

See Close-Up on page 1609.

Southern Illinois University Edwardsville, Graduate Studies and Research, School of Education, Department of Kinesiology and Health Education, Edwardsville, IL 62026-0001. Offers exercise physiology (Postbaccalaureate Certificate); kinesiology (MS Ed); pedagogy administration (Postbaccalaureate Certificate); sport and exercise behavior (Postbaccalaureate Certificate). *Accreditation:* NCATE. Part-time and evening/weekend programs available. *Faculty:* 12 full-time (5 women). *Students:* 20 full-time (10 women), 55 part-time (26 women); includes 8 minority (7 African Americans, 1 Hispanic American), 4 international. Average age 33. 53 applicants, 70% accepted. In 2006, 23 degrees awarded. *Degree requirements:* For master's, thesis or alternative, final exam. *Entrance requirements:* Additional exam requirements/recommendations for international students: Required—TOEFL. *Application deadline:* For fall admission, 7/20 for domestic students, 6/1 for international students; for spring admission, 12/14 for domestic students, 10/1 for international students. Application fee: $30. Electronic applications accepted. *Financial support:* In 2006–07, 5 teaching assistantships with full tuition reimbursements were awarded; fellowships, research assistantships with full tuition reimbursements, Federal Work-Study, institutionally sponsored loans, and unspecified assistantships also available. Support available to part-time students. Financial award application deadline: 3/1; financial award applicants required to submit FAFSA. *Unit head:* Dr. E. William Vogler, Chair, 618-650-3252, E-mail: wvogler@siue.edu.

Springfield College, Graduate Programs, Programs in Physical Education, Springfield, MA 01109-3797. Offers adapted physical education (M Ed, MPE, MS); advanced level coaching (M Ed, MPE, MS); athletic administration (M Ed, MPE, MS); general physical education (DPE, CAS); health education licensure (MPE, MS); health education licensure program (M Ed); physical education licensure (MPE, MS); physical education licensure program (M Ed); sport performance (M Ed, MPE, MS); teaching and administration (MS). Part-time and evening/weekend programs available. *Faculty:* 25 full-time (13 women), 2 part-time/adjunct (0 women). *Students:* 97. Average age 27. 78 applicants, 86% accepted, 45 enrolled. In 2006, 22 master's, 4 doctorates awarded. Terminal master's awarded for partial completion of doctoral program. *Degree requirements:* For master's, research project; for doctorate, thesis/dissertation. *Entrance requirements:* For master's, GRE General Test; for doctorate, GRE General Test, interview. Additional exam requirements/recommendations for international students: Required—TOEFL (minimum score 550 paper-based; 213 computer-based). *Application deadline:* For fall admission, 1/15 priority date for domestic students; for winter admission, 11/1 for domestic students; for spring admission, 12/1 for domestic students. Applications are processed on a rolling basis. Application fee: $50. Electronic applications accepted. *Expenses:*

Health Education

Springfield College (continued)

Tuition: Full-time $12,222; part-time $679 per credit. Required fees: $25; $25 per year. One-time fee: $25 full-time. *Financial support:* Fellowships with partial tuition reimbursements, teaching assistantships with partial tuition reimbursements, career-related internships or fieldwork, Federal Work-Study, institutionally sponsored loans, and tuition waivers (full and partial) available. Financial award application deadline: 3/1. *Faculty research:* Pedagogy, motor learning, history of physical education. *Unit head:* Dr. Stephen C. Coulon, Director, 413-748-3029, Fax: 413-748-3537, E-mail: stephen_coulon@spfldcol.edu. *Application contact:* Donald James Shaw, Director of Graduate Admissions, 413-748-3060, Fax: 413-748-3069, E-mail: donald_shaw_jr@spfldcol.edu.

State University of New York College at Brockport, School of Professions, Department of Health Science, Brockport, NY 14420-2997. Offers MS Ed. Part-time programs available. *Students:* 3 full-time (2 women), 16 part-time (11 women); includes 2 minority (1 African American, 1 American Indian/Alaska Native). 21 applicants, 52% accepted, 9 enrolled. In 2006, 15 degrees awarded. *Degree requirements:* For master's, thesis or alternative. *Entrance requirements:* For master's, GRE General Test, minimum GPA of 3.0, letters of recommendation. Additional exam requirements/recommendations for international students: Required—TOEFL (minimum score 550 paper-based; 213 computer-based; 80 iBT). *Application deadline:* For fall admission, 4/1 for domestic and international students; for spring admission, 11/1 for domestic and international students. Application fee: $50. *Expenses:* Tuition, state resident: full-time $6,900; part-time $288 per credit. Tuition, nonresident: full-time $10,920; part-time $455 per credit. *Financial support:* In 2006–07, 1 teaching assistantship with tuition reimbursement (averaging $6,000 per year) was awarded; career-related internships or fieldwork, Federal Work-Study, scholarships/grants, and unspecified assistantships also available. Support available to part-time students. Financial award application deadline: 3/15; financial award applicants required to submit FAFSA. *Faculty research:* Nutrition, substance abuse, HIV/AIDS, bioethics, worksite health. *Unit head:* Dr. Douglas M. Scheidt, Chairperson, 585-395-2643, Fax: 585-395-5246, E-mail: dscheidt@brockport.edu. *Application contact:* Dr. Patti Follansbee, Admissions Coordinator, 585-395-5483, E-mail: pfollans@brockport.edu.

State University of New York College at Cortland, Graduate Studies, School of Professional Studies, Department of Health Education, Cortland, NY 13045. Offers MS Ed, MST. *Accreditation:* NCATE. Part-time and evening/weekend programs available. *Entrance requirements:* Additional exam requirements/recommendations for international students: Required—TOEFL.

Teachers College Columbia University, Graduate Faculty of Education, Department of Health and Behavioral Studies, Program in Health Education, New York, NY 10027-6696. Offers MA, MS, Ed D. *Accreditation:* NCATE. Part-time and evening/weekend programs available. *Faculty:* 6 full-time (3 women), 6 part-time/adjunct. *Students:* 37 full-time (28 women), 92 part-time (82 women); includes 51 minority (31 African Americans, 1 American Indian/Alaska Native, 11 Asian Americans or Pacific Islanders, 8 Hispanic Americans), 10 international. Average age 35. 46 applicants, 74% accepted, 20 enrolled. In 2006, 31 master's, 16 doctorates awarded. Terminal master's awarded for partial completion of doctoral program. *Degree requirements:* For master's, integrative project, thesis optional; for doctorate, thesis/dissertation. *Entrance requirements:* For doctorate, GRE or MAT. *Application deadline:* For fall admission, 5/15 for domestic students; for spring admission, 12/1 for domestic students. Application fee: $65. *Expenses:* Tuition: Full-time $23,400; part-time $975 per credit. Required fees: $320 per term. *Financial support:* Fellowships, research assistantships available. Financial award application deadline: 2/1. *Application contact:* Peter Shon, Assistant Director of Admission, 212-678-3305, Fax: 212-678-4171, E-mail: shon@exchange.tc.columbia.edu.

See Close-Up on page 1129.

Temple University, Health Sciences Center and Graduate School, College of Health Professions, Department of Public Health, Program in Community Health Education, Philadelphia, PA 19122-6096. Offers MPH. *Accreditation:* CEPH. Part-time programs available. *Entrance requirements:* For master's, GRE General Test. Additional exam requirements/recommendations for international students: Required—TOEFL (minimum score 550 paper-based; 213 computer-based; 79 iBT). *Application deadline:* For fall admission, 2/15 for domestic students, 12/15 for international students; for spring admission, 10/15 for domestic students, 8/1 for international students. Application fee: $50. Electronic applications accepted. *Expenses:* Tuition, state resident: full-time $12,264; part-time $511 per credit. Tuition, nonresident: full-time $17,904; part-time $746 per credit. Required fees: $84 per course. Tuition and fees vary according to program. *Financial support:* Application deadline: 1/15; *Unit head:* Dr. Brenda Seals, Director, 215-204-6780, Fax: 215-204-1854, E-mail: bseals4@temple.edu.

Temple University, Health Sciences Center and Graduate School, College of Health Professions, Department of Public Health, Program in School Health Education, Philadelphia, PA 19122-6096. Offers Ed M. Part-time and evening/weekend programs available. *Faculty:* 12 full-time (8 women). *Students:* 1 (woman) full-time, 3 part-time (all women). In 2006, 2 degrees awarded. *Entrance requirements:* For master's, GRE or MAT. Additional exam requirements/recommendations for international students: Required—TOEFL (minimum score 550 paper-based; 213 computer-based; 79 iBT). *Application deadline:* For fall admission, 2/15 for domestic students, 12/15 for international students; for spring admission, 10/15 for domestic students, 8/1 for international students. Applications are processed on a rolling basis. Application fee: $50. Electronic applications accepted. *Expenses:* Tuition, state resident: full-time $12,264; part-time $511 per credit. Tuition, nonresident: full-time $17,904; part-time $746 per credit. Required fees: $84 per course. Tuition and fees vary according to program. *Financial support:* Research assistantships with tuition reimbursements, teaching assistantships with tuition reimbursements available. Financial award application deadline: 1/15; financial award applicants required to submit FAFSA. *Unit head:* Dr. Nikki Franke, Director, 215-204-5111, Fax: 215-204-1854, E-mail: nfranke@temple.edu.

Tennessee Technological University, Graduate School, College of Education, Department of Exercise Science, Physical Education and Wellness, Cookeville, TN 38505. Offers MA. *Accreditation:* NCATE. Part-time programs available. *Faculty:* 7 full-time (0 women). *Students:* 12 full-time (7 women), 32 part-time (14 women); includes 5 minority (all African Americans) Average age 27. 24 applicants, 88% accepted, 17 enrolled. In 2006, 9 degrees awarded. *Entrance requirements:* For master's, MAT. Additional exam requirements/recommendations for international students: Required—TOEFL. *Application deadline:* For fall admission, 3/1 priority date for domestic students; for spring admission, 8/1 for domestic students. Application fee: $25 ($30 for international students). *Expenses:* Tuition, state resident: full-time $8,748; part-time $319 per hour. Tuition, nonresident: full-time $23,524; part-time $740 per hour. *Financial support:* In 2006–07, fellowships (averaging $8,000 per year), 3 research assistantships (averaging $4,000 per year), 4 teaching assistantships (averaging $4,000 per year) were awarded; career-related internships or fieldwork also available. Financial award application deadline: 4/1. *Unit head:* Dr. Patricia Jordan, Interim Chairperson, 931-372-3467, Fax: 931-372-6319. *Application contact:* Dr. Francis O. Otuonye, Associate Vice President for Research and Graduate Studies, 931-372-3233, Fax: 931-372-3497, E-mail: fotuonye@tntech.edu.

Texas A&M Health Science Center, Baylor College of Dentistry, Graduate Division, Program in Health Professions Education, College Station, TX 77840. Offers MS. Part-time programs available. *Degree requirements:* For master's, thesis. *Entrance requirements:* For master's, GRE General Test, DDS or DMD. Additional exam requirements/recommendations for international students: Required—TOEFL. *Faculty research:* Craniofacial biology, dermatoglyphics, alternative curricula, admissions criteria, competency-based program assessment.

Texas A&M University, College of Education and Human Development, Department of Health and Kinesiology, College Station, TX 77843. Offers health education (M Ed, MS, Ed D, PhD); kinesiology (M Ed, MS, Ed D, PhD), including kinesiology (MS, PhD), physical education (M Ed, Ed D). Part-time programs available. *Faculty:* 25 full-time (7 women). *Students:* 121 full-time (50 women), 19 part-time (7 women); includes 23 minority (10 African Americans, 2 Asian Americans or Pacific Islanders, 11 Hispanic Americans), 24 international. Average age

23. 110 applicants, 65% accepted, 48 enrolled. In 2006, 30 master's, 13 doctorates awarded. *Degree requirements:* For master's, thesis (for some programs), registration; for doctorate, thesis/dissertation, comprehensive exam, registration. *Entrance requirements:* For master's and doctorate, GRE General Test. Additional exam requirements/recommendations for international students: Required—TOEFL. *Application deadline:* Applications are processed on a rolling basis. Application fee: $50 ($75 for international students). Electronic applications accepted. *Expenses:* Tuition, state resident: full-time $4,697. Tuition, nonresident: full-time $11,297. Required fees: $2,272. *Financial support:* Fellowships with partial tuition reimbursements, research assistantships, teaching assistantships, career-related internships or fieldwork and institutionally sponsored loans available. Financial award application deadline: 2/15; financial award applicants required to submit FAFSA. *Unit head:* Dr. Steve Dorman, Head, 979-845-3109, Fax: 979-847-8987. *Application contact:* Eva Parkerson, Information Contact, 979-458-2673, Fax: 979-847-8987, E-mail: eva@hlkn.tamu.edu.

Texas A&M University–Commerce, Graduate School, College of Education and Human Services, Department of Health, Kinesiology and Sports Studies, Commerce, TX 75429-3011. Offers M Ed, MS, Ed D. Part-time programs available. *Degree requirements:* For master's, thesis (for some programs), comprehensive exam. *Entrance requirements:* For master's, GRE General Test. Electronic applications accepted. *Faculty research:* Teaching, physical fitness.

Texas A&M University–Kingsville, College of Graduate Studies, College of Education, Department of Health and Kinesiology, Kingsville, TX 78363. Offers MA, MS. Part-time programs available. *Degree requirements:* For master's, thesis or alternative, comprehensive exam. *Entrance requirements:* For master's, GRE General Test, minimum GPA of 3.0. *Faculty research:* Body composition, electromyography.

Texas Southern University, Graduate School, College of Education, Department of Health, Physical Education and Recreation, Houston, TX 77004-4584. Offers health education (MS); physical education (MS). Part-time and evening/weekend programs available. *Faculty:* 5 full-time (2 women). *Students:* 9 full-time (6 women), 10 part-time (5 women); includes 17 minority (16 African Americans, 1 Hispanic American), 1 international. Average age 32. 7 applicants, 57% accepted, 4 enrolled. In 2006, 10 degrees awarded. *Degree requirements:* For master's, thesis optional. *Entrance requirements:* For master's, GRE General Test, minimum GPA of 2.5. Additional exam requirements/recommendations for international students: Required—TOEFL. *Application deadline:* For fall admission, 7/15 priority date for domestic students. Applications are processed on a rolling basis. Application fee: $50 ($75 for international students). *Financial support:* In 2006–07, 1 fellowship (averaging $1,473 per year) was awarded. Financial award application deadline: 5/1. *Unit head:* Dr. T. Robinson, Head, 713-313-7087.

Texas State University–San Marcos, Graduate School, College of Education, Department of Health, Physical Education, and Recreation, Program in Health and Physical Education, San Marcos, TX 78666. Offers MA. Part-time and evening/weekend programs available. *Degree requirements:* For master's, thesis, comprehensive exam. *Entrance requirements:* For master's, GRE General Test, minimum GPA of 2.75 in last 60 hours of course work. Additional exam requirements/recommendations for international students: Required—TOEFL. *Application deadline:* For fall admission, 6/15 priority date for domestic students; for spring admission, 10/15 priority date for domestic students. Applications are processed on a rolling basis. Application fee: $40 ($90 for international students). *Financial support:* Teaching assistantships, career-related internships or fieldwork, Federal Work-Study, and institutionally sponsored loans available. Financial award application deadline: 4/1; financial award applicants required to submit FAFSA. *Faculty research:* HIV/AIDS, youth fitness, leisure behavior, leisure program services and management evaluation. *Unit head:* Dr. John Walker, Head, 512-245-8106, Fax: 512-245-8678, E-mail: jw18@txstate.edu.

Texas State University–San Marcos, Graduate School, College of Education, Department of Health, Physical Education, and Recreation, Program in Health Education, San Marcos, TX 78666. Offers M Ed. Part-time and evening/weekend programs available. *Faculty:* 1 full-time (0 women). *Students:* 4 full-time (3 women), 2 part-time (1 woman); includes 1 minority (Hispanic American) Average age 25. 6 applicants, 100% accepted, 2 enrolled. In 2006, 5 degrees awarded. *Degree requirements:* For master's, comprehensive exam. *Entrance requirements:* For master's, GRE General Test, minimum GPA of 2.75 in last 60 hours of course work. Additional exam requirements/recommendations for international students: Required—TOEFL. *Application deadline:* For fall admission, 6/15 priority date for domestic students; for spring admission, 10/15 priority date for domestic students. Applications are processed on a rolling basis. Application fee: $40 ($90 for international students). *Financial support:* In 2006–07, 6 students received support, including 2 teaching assistantships (averaging $5,751 per year); career-related internships or fieldwork, Federal Work-Study, and institutionally sponsored loans also available. Support available to part-time students. Financial award application deadline: 4/1; financial award applicants required to submit FAFSA. *Faculty research:* AIDS education, employee wellness, isometric strength evaluation. *Unit head:* Dr. Steve Furney, Graduate Adviser, 512-245-2939, Fax: 512-245-8678, E-mail: sf02@txstate.edu.

Texas Woman's University, Graduate School, College of Health Sciences, Department of Health Studies, Denton, TX 76201. Offers MS, Ed D, PhD. Part-time and evening/weekend programs available. *Students:* 21 full-time (18 women), 65 part-time (60 women); includes 25 minority (16 African Americans, 1 American Indian/Alaska Native, 6 Asian Americans or Pacific Islanders, 2 Hispanic Americans), 3 international. Average age 38. In 2006, 2 master's, 8 doctorates awarded. *Degree requirements:* For master's, thesis or alternative, comprehensive exam; for doctorate, thesis/dissertation, qualifying exam, comprehensive exam. *Entrance requirements:* For master's, GRE General Test, MAT, 2 letters of recommendation; for doctorate, GRE General Test, minimum GPA of 3.5, 2 letters of recommendation. Additional exam requirements/recommendations for international students: Required—TOEFL (minimum score 550 paper-based; 213 computer-based; 79 iBT). *Application deadline:* For fall admission, 4/1 for international students; for spring admission, 8/1 for international students. Applications are processed on a rolling basis. Application fee: $30 ($50 for international students). Electronic applications accepted. *Expenses:* Tuition, area resident: Part-time $168 per unit. Tuition, state resident: full-time $4,369. Tuition, nonresident: full-time $9,373; part-time $443 per unit. Required fees: $20 per unit. $177 per term. *Financial support:* In 2006–07, 5 research assistantships (averaging $11,592 per year), 3 teaching assistantships (averaging $11,592 per year) were awarded; career-related internships or fieldwork, Federal Work-Study, institutionally sponsored loans, scholarships/grants, traineeships, health care benefits, tuition waivers (partial), and unspecified assistantships also available. Support available to part-time students. Financial award application deadline: 3/1; financial award applicants required to submit FAFSA. *Faculty research:* Worksite health, adolescent health, minority health, women's health, HIV/AIDS prevention. *Unit head:* Dr. Gay James, Chair, 940-898-2860, Fax: 940-898-2859, E-mail: gjames@mail.twu.edu. *Application contact:* Samuel Wheeler, Coordinator of Graduate Admissions, 940-898-3188, Fax: 940-898-3081, E-mail: wheelersr@twu.edu.

Touro University International, College of Health Sciences, Program in Health Sciences, Cypress, CA 90630. Offers clinical research administration (MS, Certificate); emergency and disaster management (MS, Certificate); environmental health science (Certificate); health care administration (PhD); health care management (MS), including health informatics; health education (MS, Certificate); health informatics (Certificate); health sciences (PhD); international health (MS); international health: educator or researcher option (PhD); international health: practitioner option (PhD); law and expert witness studies (MS, Certificate); public health (MS); quality assurance (Certificate). Part-time and evening/weekend programs available. Postbaccalaureate distance learning degree programs offered (no on-campus study). In 2006, 322 master's, 21 doctorates awarded. *Degree requirements:* For doctorate, thesis/dissertation, defense of dissertation, comprehensive exam. *Entrance requirements:* For master's, minimum GPA of 3.0; for doctorate, minimum GPA of 3.4, curriculum vitae, course work in research methods or statistics. Additional exam requirements/recommendations for international students: Required—TOEFL (minimum score 550 paper-based). Application fee: $75. *Expenses:* Tuition: Part-time $300 per credit hour. Tuition and fees vary according to course level and program. *Unit head:* Dr. Edith Neumann, Vice President for Academic Affairs, College of Health Sciences, 714-816-0366 Ext. 2030, Fax: 714-226-9844, E-mail: eneumann@touro.edu.

Tulane University, School of Public Health and Tropical Medicine, Department of Community Health Sciences, Program in Health Education and Communication, New Orleans, LA 70118-5669. Offers MPH. *Accreditation:* CEPH. *Faculty:* 5 full-time (1 woman), 6 part-time/adjunct (4 women). *Students:* 44 full-time (32 women), 21 part-time (19 women). *Degree requirements:* For master's, comprehensive exam. *Entrance requirements:* For master's, GRE General Test. Additional exam requirements/recommendations for international students: Required—TOEFL. *Application deadline:* For fall admission, 4/15 priority date for domestic and international students; for spring admission, 10/15 for domestic students, 10/15 priority date for international students. Applications are processed on a rolling basis. Application fee: $40. *Financial support:* Application deadline: 4/15. *Unit head:* Dr. Ted Chen, Acting Section Chief, 504-588-5391, E-mail: tchen@tulane.edu.

Union College, Graduate Programs, Department of Education, Barbourville, KY 40906-1499. Offers elementary education (MA); health and physical education (MA); middle grades (MA); music education (MA); principalship (MA); reading specialist (MA); secondary education (MA); special education (MA). *Degree requirements:* For master's, thesis optional. *Entrance requirements:* For master's, GRE General Test, NTE.

Union College, Graduate Programs, Department of Health and Physical Education, Barbourville, KY 40906-1499. Offers health (MA Ed). *Degree requirements:* For master's, thesis optional. *Entrance requirements:* For master's, GRE General Test, NTE.

The University of Alabama, Graduate School, College of Human Environmental Sciences, Department of Health Science, Tuscaloosa, AL 35487. Offers health education and promotion (PhD); health studies (MA). Part-time and evening/weekend programs available. Post-baccalaureate distance learning degree programs offered (no on-campus study). *Faculty:* 3 full-time (1 woman), 3 part-time/adjunct (1 woman). *Students:* 39 full-time (25 women), 77 part-time (52 women); includes 27 minority (21 African Americans, 2 American Indian/Alaska Native, 3 Asian Americans or Pacific Islanders, 1 Hispanic American), 2 international. Average age 34. 52 applicants, 75% accepted, 33 enrolled. In 2006, 51 master's, 2 doctorates awarded. *Median time to degree:* Master's–1.3 years full-time, 2 years part-time. Of those who began their doctoral program in fall 1998, 100% received their degree in 8 years or less. *Degree requirements:* For doctorate, one foreign language, thesis/dissertation. *Entrance requirements:* For master's and doctorate, GRE General Test or MAT, minimum GPA of 3.0. Additional exam requirements/recommendations for international students: Required—TOEFL. *Application deadline:* For fall admission, 7/6 for domestic students. Applications are processed on a rolling basis. Application fee: $25. *Financial support:* In 2006–07, 8 research assistantships with full tuition reimbursements (averaging $8,100 per year), teaching assistantships with full tuition reimbursements (averaging $8,100 per year) were awarded; career-related internships or fieldwork, Federal Work-Study, and institutionally sponsored loans also available. Financial award application deadline: 7/14. *Faculty research:* Program planning, adolescent health, worksite health, data management, health behavior. Total annual research expenditures:$43,097. *Unit head:* Dr. Michael A. Perko, Department Head and Associate Professor, 205-348-2956, Fax: 205-348-7568.

The University of Alabama at Birmingham, School of Education, Department of Human Studies, Program in Health Education, Birmingham, AL 35294. Offers MA Ed. *Accreditation:* NCATE. *Students:* 9 full-time (7 women), 18 part-time (11 women); includes 10 minority (9 African Americans, 1 Hispanic American), 2 international. 11 applicants, 100% accepted. In 2006, 10 degrees awarded. *Degree requirements:* For master's, thesis optional. *Entrance requirements:* For master's, GRE General Test, MAT, or NTE, minimum GPA of 3.0. *Application deadline:* Applications are processed on a rolling basis. Application fee: $35 ($60 for international students). Electronic applications accepted. *Expenses:* Tuition, state resident: part-time $170 per credit hour. Tuition, nonresident: part-time $425 per credit hour. Required fees: $15 per credit hour. $122 per term. Tuition and fees vary according to program. *Unit head:* Dr. David M. Macrina, Chair, Department of Human Studies, 205-934-2446, Fax: 205-975-8040, E-mail: dmacrina@uab.edu.

The University of Alabama at Birmingham, School of Education, Department of Human Studies, Program in Health Education/Health Promotion, Birmingham, AL 35294. Offers PhD. *Accreditation:* NCATE. *Students:* 6 full-time (5 women), 26 part-time (20 women); includes 14 minority (13 African Americans, 1 Hispanic American). 11 applicants, 82% accepted. In 2006, 4 degrees awarded. *Degree requirements:* For doctorate, thesis/dissertation. *Entrance requirements:* For doctorate, GRE General Test, MAT, minimum GPA of 3.25. Application fee: $35 ($60 for international students). Electronic applications accepted. *Expenses:* Tuition, state resident: part-time $170 per credit hour. Tuition, nonresident: part-time $425 per credit hour. Required fees: $15 per credit hour. $122 per term. Tuition and fees vary according to program. *Unit head:* Dr. David M. Macrina, Chair, Department of Human Studies, 205-934-2446, Fax: 205-975-8040, E-mail: dmacrina@uab.edu.

The University of Alabama at Birmingham, School of Public Health, Department of Health Behavior, Program in Health Education Promotion, Birmingham, AL 35294. Offers PhD. *Students:* 9 full-time (8 women), 14 part-time (9 women); includes 10 minority (9 African Americans, 1 Asian American or Pacific Islander). 20 applicants, 55% accepted. In 2006, 3 degrees awarded. Application fee: $35 ($60 for international students). *Expenses:* Tuition, state resident: part-time $170 per credit hour. Tuition, nonresident: part-time $425 per credit hour. Required fees: $15 per credit hour. $122 per term. Tuition and fees vary according to program.

University of Arkansas, Graduate School, College of Education and Health Professions, Department of Health Science, Kinesiology, Recreation and Dance, Program in Health Science, Fayetteville, AR 72701-1201. Offers MS, PhD. *Accreditation:* NCATE. *Students:* 8 full-time (4 women), 14 part-time (11 women); includes 3 minority (2 African Americans, 1 Asian American or Pacific Islander), 2 international. 19 applicants, 37% accepted. In 2006, 9 master's, 4 doctorates awarded. *Degree requirements:* For doctorate, thesis/dissertation. *Entrance requirements:* For doctorate, GRE General Test. Application fee: $40 ($50 for international students). *Financial support:* In 2006–07, 3 fellowships with tuition reimbursements, 4 teaching assistantships were awarded; research assistantships, career-related internships or fieldwork and Federal Work-Study also available. Support available to part-time students. Financial award application deadline: 4/1; financial award applicants required to submit FAFSA. *Application contact:* Dr. Dean Gorman, Coordinator of Graduate Studies, 479-575-6625, E-mail: dgorman@comp.uark.edu.

University of Calgary, Faculty of Medicine and Faculty of Graduate Studies, Department of Medical Science, Calgary, AB T2N 1N4, Canada. Offers cancer biology (M Sc, PhD); immunology (M Sc, PhD); joint injury and arthritis research (M Sc, PhD); medical education (M Sc, PhD); medical science (M Sc, PhD); mountain medicine and high altitude physiology (M Sc). *Faculty:* 114 full-time (17 women), 5 part-time/adjunct (0 women). *Students:* 96 full-time (55 women), 14 part-time (7 women). 68 applicants, 29% accepted, 19 enrolled. In 2006, 20 master's, 11 doctorates awarded. *Median time to degree:* Of those who began their doctoral program in fall 1998, 100% received their degree in 8 years or less. *Degree requirements:* For master's, thesis; for doctorate, thesis/dissertation, candidacy exam. *Entrance requirements:* For master's, minimum undergraduate GPA of 3.2; for doctorate, minimum graduate GPA of 3.2. Additional exam requirements/recommendations for international students: Required—TOEFL (minimum score 600 paper-based; 250 computer-based). *Application deadline:* For fall admission, 6/15 priority date for domestic students, 5/15 for international students; for winter admission, 10/15 priority date for domestic students, 9/15 for international students; for spring admission, 3/15 priority date for domestic students, 1/15 for international students. Applications are processed on a rolling basis. Application fee: $100 ($130 for international students). Electronic applications accepted. *Financial support:* In 2006–07, 30 students received support, including 22 research assistantships, 2 teaching assistantships; scholarships/grants and tuition waivers (partial) also available. *Faculty research:* Cancer biology, immunology, joint injury and arthritis, medical education, population genomics. *Unit head:* Dr. Francine Smith, Graduate Coordinator, 403-220-6852, Fax: 403-210-8109, E-mail: fsmith@ucalgary.ca. *Application contact:* Christine Szefer, Graduate Program Administrator, 403-220-6852, Fax: 403-210-8109, E-mail: cszefer@ucalgary.ca.

University of California, Berkeley, Graduate Division, School of Public Health, Master's Internationalist Program, Berkeley, CA 94720-1500. Offers community health education (MPH); epidemiology (MPH); interdisciplinary (MPH); maternal and child health (MPH); public health nutrition (MPH). *Accreditation:* CEPH. *Entrance requirements:* For master's, GRE General Test, minimum GPA of 3.0. *Application deadline:* For fall admission, 12/1 for domestic students. Applications are processed on a rolling basis. Application fee: $60 ($80 for international students). *Financial support:* Fellowships, research assistantships, teaching assistantships, Federal Work-Study and unspecified assistantships available. *Application contact:* Information Contact, 510-643-0881, E-mail: sphinfo@berkeley.edu.

University of Central Arkansas, Graduate School, College of Health and Behavioral Sciences, Department of Health Sciences, Conway, AR 72035-0001. Offers health education (MS); health systems (MS). *Faculty:* 9 full-time (5 women), 1 part-time/adjunct (0 women). *Students:* 7 full-time (5 women), 15 part-time (10 women); includes 8 minority (5 African Americans, 1 American Indian/Alaska Native, 2 Asian Americans or Pacific Islanders), 1 international. 7 applicants, 100% accepted, 7 enrolled. In 2006, 7 degrees awarded. *Degree requirements:* For master's, thesis optional. *Entrance requirements:* For master's, GRE General Test, minimum GPA of 2.7. Additional exam requirements/recommendations for international students: Required—TOEFL (minimum score 550 paper-based; 213 computer-based). *Application deadline:* For fall admission, 3/1 priority date for domestic students; for spring admission, 10/1 for domestic students. Applications are processed on a rolling basis. Application fee: $25 ($40 for international students). *Expenses:* Tuition, state resident: full-time $4,194; part-time $233 per semester. Tuition, nonresident: full-time $5,963; part-time $429 per semester. International tuition: $6,162 full-time. Required fees: $65; $23 per semester. One-time fee: $65 part-time. *Financial support:* In 2006–07, 4 research assistantships (averaging $5,700 per year) were awarded; Federal Work-Study, scholarships/grants, tuition waivers (partial), and unspecified assistantships also available. Financial award application deadline: 2/15; financial award applicants required to submit FAFSA. *Unit head:* Emogene Fox, Chairperson, 501-450-5508, Fax: 501-450-5515, E-mail: emogenef@uca.edu. *Application contact:* Nanette Fitzhugh, Administrative Assistant, 501-450-5063, Fax: 501-450-5678, E-mail: fitzhugh@uca.edu.

University of Central Oklahoma, College of Graduate Studies and Research, College of Education, Department of Occupational and Technical Education, Program in Professional Health Occupations, Edmond, OK 73034-5209. Offers M Ed. *Accreditation:* NCATE. Part-time programs available. *Entrance requirements:* For master's, GRE General Test. Additional exam requirements/recommendations for international students: Required—TOEFL (minimum score 550 paper-based; 213 computer-based). Electronic applications accepted.

University of Cincinnati, Division of Research and Advanced Studies, College of Education, Criminal Justice, and Human Services, Division of Human Services, Program in Health Promotion/Education, Cincinnati, OH 45221. Offers community health (MS); health education (MS, PhD); health promotion and education (M Ed). *Accreditation:* NCATE. Part-time and evening/weekend programs available. *Students:* 35. *Degree requirements:* For master's, thesis or alternative. *Entrance requirements:* For master's and doctorate, GRE General Test. Additional exam requirements/recommendations for international students: Required—TOEFL (minimum score 580 paper-based; 237 computer-based), OEPT. *Application deadline:* For fall admission, 2/15 priority date for domestic students. Applications are processed on a rolling basis. Application fee: $40. Electronic applications accepted. *Financial support:* Teaching assistantships with full tuition reimbursements, tuition waivers (full) and unspecified assistantships available. Support available to part-time students. Total annual research expenditures: $2.1 million. *Unit head:* Randall Cottrell, Head, 513-556-3861, Fax: 513-556-3898, E-mail: randall.cottrell@uc.edu.

University of Colorado at Denver and Health Sciences Center, College of Liberal Arts and Sciences, Program in Health and Behavioral Sciences, Denver, CO 80217-3364. Offers PhD. Part-time and evening/weekend programs available. *Faculty:* 7 full-time (3 women). *Students:* 3 full-time (all women), 25 part-time (23 women); includes 2 minority (1 Asian American or Pacific Islander, 1 Hispanic American), 1 international. Average age 39. 29 applicants, 24% accepted, 4 enrolled. In 2006, 8 degrees awarded. *Degree requirements:* For doctorate, thesis/dissertation, comprehensive exam. *Entrance requirements:* For doctorate, GRE. Additional exam requirements/recommendations for international students: Required—TOEFL (minimum score 525 paper-based; 193 computer-based). *Application deadline:* For fall admission, 2/15 for domestic students. Applications are processed on a rolling basis. Application fee: $50 ($75 for international students). *Financial support:* Fellowships with tuition reimbursements, research assistantships with partial tuition reimbursements, career-related internships or fieldwork and Federal Work-Study available. Financial award application deadline: 4/1; financial award applicants required to submit FAFSA. *Faculty research:* HIV/AIDS prevention, tobacco control, globalization and primary health care, social inequality and health, maternal and child health. *Unit head:* Lorna Moore, Interim Director, 303-556-3535, Fax: 303-556-5801, E-mail: lorna.moore@cudenver.edu. *Application contact:* Abby Fitch, Program Assistant, 303-556-4300, Fax: 303-556-8501, E-mail: abby.fitch@cudenver.edu.

University of Florida, Graduate School, College of Health and Human Performance, Department of Health Education and Behavior, Gainesville, FL 32611. Offers health behavior (PhD); health communication (Graduate Certificate); health education and behavior (MS). *Accreditation:* NCATE (one or more programs are accredited). Part-time programs available. *Faculty:* 12 full-time (5 women). Terminal master's awarded for partial completion of doctoral program. *Degree requirements:* For master's, thesis (for some programs); for doctorate, thesis/dissertation. *Entrance requirements:* For master's and doctorate, GRE General Test, minimum GPA of 3.0. Additional exam requirements/recommendations for international students: Required—TOEFL (minimum score 550 paper-based; 213 computer-based). *Application deadline:* For fall admission, 6/1 priority date for domestic students. Applications are processed on a rolling basis. Application fee: $30. Electronic applications accepted. *Expenses:* Tuition, state resident: full-time $6,827. Tuition, nonresident: full-time $21,951. Required fees: $999. *Financial support:* In 2006–07, 4 research assistantships (averaging $8,082 per year), 13 teaching assistantships (averaging $9,162 per year) were awarded; fellowships, career-related internships or fieldwork and institutionally sponsored loans also available. *Faculty research:* Adolescent health, human sexuality and HIV/AIDS, substance use, nutrition. *Unit head:* Dr. Robert Weiler, Chair, 352-392-0583 Ext. 1282, Fax: 352-392-1909, E-mail: rweiler@hhp.ufl.edu. *Application contact:* Dr. Robert Morgan Pigg, Coordinator, 352-392-0583 Ext. 1281, Fax: 352-392-1909, E-mail: rmpigg@hhp.ufl.edu.

University of Georgia, College of Public Health, Department of Health Promotion and Behavior, Athens, GA 30602. Offers M Ed, MA, MPH, PhD, Ed S. *Accreditation:* NCATE (one or more programs are accredited). *Faculty:* 7 full-time (5 women). *Students:* 12 full-time (10 women), 4 part-time (all women); includes 6 minority (5 African Americans, 1 Hispanic American). 52 applicants, 77% accepted. In 2006, 4 master's, 4 doctorates awarded. *Degree requirements:* For master's, thesis (MA); for doctorate, thesis/dissertation. *Entrance requirements:* For master's, GRE General Test or MAT; for doctorate, GRE General Test. *Application deadline:* For fall admission, 7/1 priority date for domestic students; for spring admission, 11/15 for domestic students. Application fee: $50. Electronic applications accepted. *Financial support:* Fellowships, research assistantships, teaching assistantships, unspecified assistantships available. *Unit head:* Dr. Mark G. Wilson, Head, 706-542-4364, Fax: 706-542-4956, E-mail: mwilson@coe.uga.edu. *Application contact:* Pamela Orpinas, Graduate Coordinator, 706-542-4372, Fax: 706-542-4956, E-mail: porpinas@uga.edu.

University of Georgia, Graduate School, Biomedical and Health Sciences Institute, Athens, GA 30602. Offers neuroscience (PhD). *Students:* 6 full-time (5 women), 1 international. 6 applicants,

Health Education

University of Georgia (continued)

67% accepted, 3 enrolled. *Unit head:* Dr. Harry A. Dailey, Director, 706-542-5922, Fax: 706-542-4285, E-mail: hdailey@uga.edu.

University of Houston, College of Education, Department of Health and Human Performance, Houston, TX 77204. Offers allied health (M Ed, Ed D); exercise science (MS); health education (M Ed); kinesiology (PhD); physical education (M Ed, Ed D). *Accreditation:* NCATE (one or more programs are accredited). Part-time and evening/weekend programs available. *Faculty:* 11 full-time (5 women), 6 part-time/adjunct (3 women). *Students:* 35 full-time (19 women), 33 part-time (17 women); includes 22 minority (12 African Americans, 1 Asian American or Pacific Islander, 9 Hispanic Americans), 1 international. Average age 29. 35 applicants, 54% accepted, 11 enrolled. In 2006, 24 master's, 4 doctorates awarded. *Degree requirements:* For master's, comprehensive exam or thesis; for doctorate, thesis/dissertation, comprehensive exam. *Entrance requirements:* For master's, GRE General Test or MAT; for doctorate, GRE General Test, interview. *Application deadline:* For fall admission, 7/3 for domestic students. Application fee: $35 ($75 for international students). *Expenses:* Tuition, state resident: full-time $5,429; part-time $226 per credit. Tuition, nonresident: full-time $12,029; part-time $501 per credit. Required fees: $2,454. *Financial support:* In 2006–07, 5 fellowships with full tuition reimbursements (averaging $9,500 per year), 4 research assistantships with full tuition reimbursements (averaging $9,850 per year), 9 teaching assistantships with full tuition reimbursements (averaging $9,850 per year) were awarded; career-related internships or fieldwork, Federal Work-Study, institutionally sponsored loans, scholarships/grants, health care benefits, and unspecified assistantships also available. Support available to part-time students. Financial award application deadline: 3/10. *Faculty research:* Motor development, physical fitness, comprehensive school health, leadership, sports law. *Unit head:* Dr. Chuck Layne, Chairperson, 713-743-9868, Fax: 713-743-9860, E-mail: clayne2@uh.edu.

University of Illinois at Chicago, College of Medicine and Graduate College, Graduate Programs in Medicine, Department of Health Professions Education, Chicago, IL 60607-7128. Offers MHPE. Part-time programs available. *Degree requirements:* For master's, thesis. *Entrance requirements:* For master's, GRE General Test. Additional exam requirements/recommendations for international students: Required—TOEFL. Electronic applications accepted.

University of Louisville, Graduate School, College of Education and Human Development, Department of Health and Sports Sciences, Program in Health Education, Louisville, KY 40292-0001. Offers M Ed. *Students:* 5 full-time (4 women), 5 part-time (2 women); includes 4 minority (3 African Americans, 1 Asian American or Pacific Islander). Average age 31. *Unit head:* Dr. Carol Stinson, Program Head, 502-852-0547, Fax: 502-852-4534.

University of Maryland, Baltimore County, Graduate School, College of Arts, Humanities and Social Sciences, Department of Emergency Health Services, Baltimore, MD 21250. Offers administration, planning, and policy (MS); education (MS); emergency health services (MS); preventive medicine and epidemiology (MS). Part-time and evening/weekend programs available. Postbaccalaureate distance learning degree programs offered (no on-campus study). *Faculty:* 4 full-time (0 women), 7 part-time/adjunct (1 woman). *Students:* 3 full-time (2 women), 32 part-time (12 women); includes 3 African Americans, 1 American Indian/Alaska Native, 3 Hispanic Americans. Average age 33. 22 applicants, 59% accepted, 11 enrolled. In 2006, 9 degrees awarded. *Median time to degree:* Master's–2.3 years full-time, 5 years part-time. *Degree requirements:* For master's, thesis (for some programs), comprehensive exam. *Entrance requirements:* For master's, GRE General Test, minimum GPA of 3.0. Additional exam requirements/recommendations for international students: Required—TOEFL (minimum score 550 paper-based; 213 computer-based; 80 iBT). *Application deadline:* For fall admission, 7/1 for domestic students. Applications are processed on a rolling basis. Application fee: $45. *Expenses:* Tuition, state resident: part-time $412 per credit hour. Tuition, nonresident: part-time $681 per credit hour. Required fees: $91 per credit hour. One-time fee: $75 part-time. *Financial support:* In 2006–07, fellowships with tuition reimbursements (averaging $55,000 per year), research assistantships with tuition reimbursements (averaging $21,000 per year) were awarded; teaching assistantships, career-related internships or fieldwork, Federal Work-Study, health care benefits, and unspecified assistantships also available. Financial award application deadline: 5/30; financial award applicants required to submit FAFSA. *Faculty research:* EMS management, disaster health services, emergency management. Total annual research expenditures: $500,000. *Unit head:* Dr. Bruce Walz, Chairman, 410-455-3223. *Application contact:* Dr. Rick Bissell, Program Director, 410-455-3776, Fax: 410-455-3045, E-mail: bissell@umbc.edu.

University of Maryland, College Park, Graduate Studies, College of Health and Human Performance, Department of Public and Community Health, College Park, MD 20742. Offers community health education (MPH); public/community health (PhD). *Accreditation:* CEPH. Part-time and evening/weekend programs available. *Faculty:* 35 full-time (17 women), 6 part-time/adjunct (all women). *Students:* 48 full-time (44 women), 32 part-time (30 women); includes 29 minority (17 African Americans, 5 Asian Americans or Pacific Islanders, 7 Hispanic Americans), 7 international. 48 applicants, 27% accepted, 7 enrolled. In 2006, 19 master's, 3 doctorates awarded. *Median time to degree:* Of those who began their doctoral program in fall 1998, 33% received their degree in 8 years or less. *Degree requirements:* For master's, thesis optional; for doctorate, thesis/dissertation, comprehensive exam. *Entrance requirements:* For master's, GRE General Test, minimum GPA of 3.0, 3 letters of recommendation; for doctorate, GRE General Test, minimum GPA of 3.5, 3 letters of recommendation. Additional exam requirements/recommendations for international students: Required—TOEFL. *Application deadline:* For fall admission, 1/15 for domestic students, 2/1 for international students. Applications are processed on a rolling basis. Application fee: $60. Electronic applications accepted. *Financial support:* In 2006–07, 3 fellowships with full tuition reimbursements (averaging $15,139 per year), 6 research assistantships with tuition reimbursements (averaging $14,562 per year), 2 teaching assistantships with tuition reimbursements (averaging $14,467 per year) were awarded; career-related internships or fieldwork, Federal Work-Study, and scholarships/grants also available. Support available to part-time students. Financial award applicants required to submit FAFSA. *Faculty research:* Controlling stress and tension, women's health, aging and public policy, adolescent health, long term care. Total annual research expenditures: $2 million. *Unit head:* Dr. Elbert Glover, Chair, 301-405-2467, Fax: 301-314-9167, E-mail: eglover1@umd.edu. *Application contact:* Dean of Graduate School, 301-405-0358, Fax: 301-314-9305.

University of Medicine and Dentistry of New Jersey, School of Health Related Professions, Department of Interdisciplinary Studies, Program in Health Sciences, Newark, NJ 07107-1709. Offers cardiopulmonary sciences (PhD); clinical laboratory sciences (PhD); health sciences (MS); interdisciplinary studies (PhD); nutrition (PhD); physical therapy/movement science (PhD). *Degree requirements:* For doctorate, thesis/dissertation. *Entrance requirements:* For doctorate, interview, writing sample. Additional exam requirements/recommendations for international students: Required—TOEFL. *Application deadline:* For fall admission, 3/1 for domestic students. Applications are processed on a rolling basis. Application fee: $50. Electronic applications accepted. *Unit head:* Dr. Margaret Kildoff, Director, 973-972-4989, Fax: 973-972-7854, E-mail: ms-phd-hs@umdnj.edu.

University of Michigan–Flint, School of Health Professions and Studies, Program in Health Education, Flint, MI 48502-1950. Offers MS. Part-time programs available. *Faculty:* 4 full-time (all women), 1 (woman) part-time/adjunct. *Students:* 10 full-time (8 women), 13 part-time (12 women); includes 4 minority (3 African Americans, 1 Hispanic American). Average age 38. 14 applicants, 93% accepted, 7 enrolled. In 2006, 4 degrees awarded. *Degree requirements:* For master's, thesis, internship or current employment as health educator. *Entrance requirements:* For master's, GRE General Test, minimum GPA of 2.8; course work in anatomy, physiology, statistics, speech, and developmental psychology. Additional exam requirements/recommendations for international students: Required—TOEFL (minimum score 550 paper-based; 220 computer-based), IELTS (minimum score 7). *Application deadline:* For fall admission, 8/1 priority date for domestic students, 3/1 priority date for international students; for winter admission, 11/15 priority date for domestic students, 7/1 priority date for international students; for spring admission, 3/15 priority date for domestic students, 11/1 priority date for international students. Applications are processed on a rolling basis. Application fee: $55. *Expenses:* Contact institution. *Financial support:* Fellowships, career-related internships or fieldwork, Federal Work-Study, and scholarships/grants available. Support available to part-time students. Financial award applicants required to submit FAFSA. *Faculty research:* Minority health, health disparities, cultural competency, HIV/AIDS, women's health. *Unit head:* Dr. Suzanne M. Selig, Director, 810-762-3172, Fax: 810-762-3003, E-mail: sselig@umich.edu. *Application contact:* Bradley T. Maki, Director of Graduate Admissions, 810-762-3171, Fax: 810-766-6789, E-mail: bmaki@umflint.edu.

University of Missouri–Columbia, Graduate School, College of Education, Department of Curriculum and Instruction, Columbia, MO 65211. Offers agricultural education (M Ed, PhD, Ed S); art education (M Ed, PhD, Ed S); business and office education (M Ed, PhD, Ed S); early childhood education (M Ed, PhD, Ed S); elementary education (M Ed, PhD, Ed S); English education (M Ed, PhD, Ed S); foreign language education (M Ed, PhD, Ed S); health education and promotion (M Ed, PhD); learning and instruction (M Ed); marketing education (M Ed, PhD, Ed S); mathematics education (M Ed, PhD, Ed S); music education (M Ed, PhD, Ed S); reading education (M Ed, PhD, Ed S); science education (M Ed, PhD, Ed S); social studies education (M Ed, PhD, Ed S); vocational education (M Ed, PhD, Ed S). Part-time programs available. *Faculty:* 24 full-time (12 women). *Students:* 195 full-time (148 women), 260 part-time (214 women); includes 27 minority (8 African Americans, 1 American Indian/Alaska Native, 10 Asian Americans or Pacific Islanders, 8 Hispanic Americans), 19 international. In 2006, 186 master's, 12 doctorates awarded. Terminal master's awarded for partial completion of doctoral program. *Degree requirements:* For doctorate, thesis/dissertation. *Entrance requirements:* For master's and Ed S, GRE General Test or MAT, minimum GPA of 3.0; for doctorate, GRE General Test, minimum GPA of 3.0. *Application deadline:* Applications are processed on a rolling basis. Application fee: $45 ($60 for international students). *Financial support:* Fellowships, research assistantships, teaching assistantships, institutionally sponsored loans available. *Unit head:* Dr. Lloyd H. Barrow, Director of Graduate Studies, 573-882-8247, E-mail: robinsonr@missouri.edu.

The University of Montana, Graduate School, School of Education, Department of Health and Human Performance, Missoula, MT 59812-0002. Offers exercise science (MS); health and human performance (MS); health promotion (MS). *Accreditation:* NCATE. Part-time programs available. *Entrance requirements:* For master's, GRE General Test. Additional exam requirements/recommendations for international students: Required—TOEFL. *Faculty research:* Exercise physiology, performance psychology, nutrition, pre-employment physical screening, program evaluation.

University of Nebraska at Omaha, Graduate Studies and Research, College of Education, School of Health, Physical Education, and Recreation, Omaha, NE 68182. Offers MA, MS. Part-time and evening/weekend programs available. *Faculty:* 12 full-time (2 women). *Students:* 49 full-time (28 women), 52 part-time (37 women); includes 7 minority (3 Asian Americans or Pacific Islanders, 4 Hispanic Americans), 7 international. Average age 28. 66 applicants, 55% accepted, 21 enrolled. In 2006, 31 degrees awarded. *Degree requirements:* For master's, thesis (for some programs), comprehensive exam. *Entrance requirements:* For master's, minimum GPA of 3.0, vary by concentration. Additional exam requirements/recommendations for international students: Required—TOEFL (minimum score 550 paper-based; 213 computer-based; 80 iBT). *Application deadline:* For fall admission, 7/1 priority date for domestic students; for spring admission, 12/1 priority date for domestic students. Applications are processed on a rolling basis. Application fee: $45. Electronic applications accepted. *Financial support:* In 2006–07, 71 students received support, including 8 research assistantships with tuition reimbursements available; fellowships, Federal Work-Study, institutionally sponsored loans, scholarships/grants, tuition waivers (full), and unspecified assistantships also available. Support available to part-time students. Financial award application deadline: 3/1; financial award applicants required to submit FAFSA. *Unit head:* Dr. Dan Blanke, Director, 402-554-2670.

University of Nebraska–Lincoln, Graduate College, College of Education and Human Services, Department of Health and Human Performance, Lincoln, NE 68588. Offers health, physical education, and recreation (M Ed, MPE). *Accreditation:* NCATE. *Degree requirements:* For master's, thesis (for some programs). *Entrance requirements:* For master's, curriculum vitae. Additional exam requirements/recommendations for international students: Required—TOEFL (minimum score 500 paper-based; 173 computer-based). Electronic applications accepted. *Faculty research:* Exercise science, health behaviors, fitness, teacher effectiveness.

University of New Mexico, Graduate School, College of Education, Department of Physical Performance and Development, Program in Health Education, Albuquerque, NM 87131-2039. Offers MS. *Accreditation:* NCATE. Part-time programs available. *Students:* 4 full-time (all women), 25 part-time (23 women); includes 12 minority (3 American Indian/Alaska Native, 1 Asian American or Pacific Islander, 8 Hispanic Americans). Average age 35. 11 applicants, 73% accepted, 4 enrolled. In 2006, 17 degrees awarded. *Degree requirements:* For master's, thesis or alternative, comprehensive exam (for some programs). *Entrance requirements:* For master's, 3 letters of reference, resumé, minimum cumulative GPA of 3.0 in last 2 years of bachelor's degree. Additional exam requirements/recommendations for international students: Required—TOEFL (minimum score 550 paper-based; 213 computer-based). *Application deadline:* For fall admission, 3/15 priority date for domestic students; for spring admission, 11/1 priority date for domestic students. Application fee: $50. Electronic applications accepted. *Financial support:* In 2006–07, 13 students received support, including 3 teaching assistantships with full tuition reimbursements available (averaging $10,815 per year); career-related internships or fieldwork, institutionally sponsored loans, scholarships/grants, and health care benefits also available. Financial award application deadline: 3/1; financial award applicants required to submit FAFSA. *Faculty research:* Alcohol and families, health behaviors and sexuality, multicultural health behavior, health promotion policy, school-based prevention, health and aging. *Unit head:* Dr. Eli Duryea, Coordinator, 505-277-5151, Fax: 505-277-6227, E-mail: duryea@unm.edu. *Application contact:* Carol Catania, Graduate Coordinator, 505-277-5151, Fax: 505-277-6227, E-mail: catania@unm.edu.

The University of North Carolina at Chapel Hill, Graduate School, School of Public Health, Department of Health Behavior and Health Education, Chapel Hill, NC 27599. Offers MPH, PhD, MPH/MRP. *Accreditation:* CEPH (one or more programs are accredited). *Faculty:* 18 full-time (12 women), 36 part-time/adjunct. *Students:* 138 full-time (121 women); includes 36 minority (20 African Americans, 11 Asian Americans or Pacific Islanders, 5 Hispanic Americans), 12 international. Average age 26. 261 applicants, 44% accepted, 56 enrolled. In 2006, 37 master's, 3 doctorates awarded. *Median time to degree:* Of those who began their doctoral program in fall 1998, 100% received their degree in 8 years or less. *Degree requirements:* For master's, thesis, major paper, comprehensive exam, registration; for doctorate, thesis/dissertation, comprehensive exam, registration. *Entrance requirements:* For master's, GRE General Test, minimum GPA of 3.0; for doctorate, GRE General Test, minimum GPA of 3.0, master's degree. Additional exam requirements/recommendations for international students: Required—TOEFL. *Application deadline:* For fall admission, 1/1 priority date for domestic and international students. Applications are processed on a rolling basis. Application fee: $70. Electronic applications accepted. *Financial support:* In 2006–07, 20 fellowships with full and partial tuition reimbursements (averaging $8,379 per year), 58 research assistantships with full and partial tuition reimbursements (averaging $10,086 per year), 6 teaching assistantships with full and partial tuition reimbursements (averaging $12,415 per year) were awarded; career-related internships or fieldwork, Federal Work-Study, institutionally sponsored loans, scholarships/grants, traineeships, and unspecified assistantships also available. Financial award application deadline: 1/1; financial award applicants required to submit FAFSA. *Faculty research:* Cancer prevention and control, aging health promotion and disease prevention, adolescent health, nutrition intervention. Total annual research expenditures: $1.8 million. *Unit head:* Dr. Edwin B. Fisher, Chair, 919-966-3918, Fax: 919-966-2921, E-mail: fishere@email.unc.edu. *Application contact:* Linda W. Cook, Student Services Manager, 919-966-5771, Fax: 919-966-2921, E-mail: lwcook@email.unc.edu.

University of Northern Iowa, Graduate College, College of Education, School of Health, Physical Education, and Leisure Services, Program in Health Education, Cedar Falls, IA 50614. Offers MA, Ed D. Part-time and evening/weekend programs available. *Students:* 9 full-time (8 women), 10 part-time (7 women); includes 3 minority (2 African Americans, 1 Hispanic American), 3 international. 10 applicants, 70% accepted, 4 enrolled. In 2006, 8 degrees awarded. *Degree requirements:* For master's, thesis or alternative, comprehensive exam. *Entrance requirements:* For master's, minimum GPA of 3.5, 3 years of educational experience; for doctorate, GRE. Additional exam requirements/recommendations for international students: Required—TOEFL (minimum score 500 paper-based; 180 computer-based; 61 iBT). *Application deadline:* For fall admission, 8/1 priority date for domestic students. Applications are processed on a rolling basis. Application fee: $30 ($50 for international students). Electronic applications accepted. *Expenses:* Tuition, state resident: full-time $5,936. Tuition, nonresident: full-time $14,074. *Financial support:* Career-related internships or fieldwork, Federal Work-Study, and tuition waivers (full and partial) available. Support available to part-time students. Financial award application deadline: 2/1. *Unit head:* Dr. Thomas Davis, Chair, 319-273-6151, E-mail: thomas.davis@uni.edu.

University of Oklahoma Health Sciences Center, Graduate College, College of Allied Health, Department of Allied Health Sciences, Oklahoma City, OK 73190. Offers PhD. *Degree requirements:* For doctorate, one foreign language, comprehensive exam. *Entrance requirements:* For doctorate, GRE General Test, 3 letters of recommendation, master's degree. Additional exam requirements/recommendations for international students: Required—TOEFL (minimum score 550 paper-based).

University of Pennsylvania, Graduate School of Education, Division of Applied Psychology and Human Development, Program in Human Sexuality Education, Philadelphia, PA 19104. Offers MS Ed, Ed D, PhD. Part-time programs available. Terminal master's awarded for partial completion of doctoral program. *Degree requirements:* For master's, thesis, comprehensive exam; for doctorate, thesis/dissertation, oral exams, comprehensive exam. *Entrance requirements:* For master's and doctorate, GRE General Test. Electronic applications accepted. Expenses: Contact institution. *Faculty research:* Relationships, alternative life-styles, sexual orientation, AIDS education.

University of Pittsburgh, School of Medicine, Clinical Educator Training Program, Pittsburgh, PA 15260. Offers clinical research (MS, Certificate); medical education (MS); medical research (Certificate). Part-time programs available. Postbaccalaureate distance learning degree programs offered (minimal on-campus study). *Faculty:* 23 full-time (10 women). *Students:* Average age 32. 4 applicants, 100% accepted, 4 enrolled. In 2006, 3 master's, 3 other advanced degrees awarded. *Degree requirements:* For master's, thesis, registration. *Entrance requirements:* For master's and Certificate, GRE, LSAT, MCAT or GMAT (only required of students without previous doctoral level degree). *Application deadline:* For spring admission, 3/1 priority date for domestic and international students. Applications are processed on a rolling basis. Application fee: $0. Electronic applications accepted. *Financial support:* Scholarships/grants and tuition waivers (partial) available. *Faculty research:* Medical education. *Application contact:* Jennifer A. Kush, Coordinator of Student Services, 412-586-9673, Fax: 412-586-9672, E-mail: kushja@upmc.edu.

University of Pittsburgh, School of Medicine, Clinical Research Training Program, Pittsburgh, PA 15260. Offers clinical research (MS, Certificate); medical education (MS, Certificate). Part-time programs available. Postbaccalaureate distance learning degree programs offered (minimal on-campus study). *Faculty:* 46 full-time (16 women). *Students:* Average age 32. 34 applicants, 82% accepted, 28 enrolled. In 2006, 11 master's, 12 Certificates awarded. *Degree requirements:* For master's, thesis, registration. *Entrance requirements:* For master's, GRE, LSAT, MCAT, or GMAT (only required for students without previous doctoral level degree); for Certificate, GRE, LSAT, MCAT, or GMAT (only required of students without previous doctoral level degree). *Application deadline:* For spring admission, 3/1 priority date for domestic and international students. Applications are processed on a rolling basis. Application fee: $0. Electronic applications accepted. *Financial support:* Scholarships/grants and tuition waivers (partial) available. *Faculty research:* Quality of life, mood disorders in children, pediatric palliative care, female pelvic medicines, antibiotic use and racial variations medication use. *Application contact:* Tammy L. Dennis, Coordinator of Student Services, 412-692-2686, Fax: 412-586-9672, E-mail: dennistl@upmc.edu.

University of Puerto Rico, Medical Sciences Campus, Graduate School of Public Health, Department of Social Sciences, Program in Health Education, San Juan, PR 00936-5067. Offers MPHE. Part-time and evening/weekend programs available. *Students:* 46 (40 women). 35 applicants, 94% accepted. In 2006, 6 degrees awarded. *Degree requirements:* For master's, thesis. *Entrance requirements:* For master's, GRE, previous course work in education, social sciences, algebra, and natural sciences. *Application deadline:* For fall admission, 3/15 for domestic students. Application fee: $20. *Financial support:* Research assistantships, teaching assistantships, career-related internships or fieldwork, Federal Work-Study, and institutionally sponsored loans available. Financial award application deadline: 4/30. *Application contact:* Prof. Mayra E. Santiago-Vargas, Counselor, 787-756-5244, Fax: 787-759-6719, E-mail: msantiago@rcm.upr.edu.

University of Puerto Rico, Medical Sciences Campus, Graduate School of Public Health, Department of Social Sciences, Program in School Health Promotion, San Juan, PR 00936-5067. Offers Certificate. *Application contact:* Prof. Mayra E. Santiago-Vargas, Counselor, 787-756-5244, Fax: 787-759-6719, E-mail: msantiago@rcm.upr.edu.

University of Rhode Island, Graduate School, College of Human Science and Services, Department of Kinesiology, Kingston, RI 02881. Offers exercise science (MS); physical education (MS); physical therapy (DPT); psychosocial aspects of physical activity and sport (MS); teaching and administration (MS). *Accreditation:* NCATE (one or more programs are accredited). In 2006, 14 degrees awarded. *Entrance requirements:* For master's, MAT or GRE. *Application deadline:* For fall admission, 4/15 priority date for domestic students; for spring admission, 11/15 for domestic students. Applications are processed on a rolling basis. Application fee: $35. *Expenses:* Tuition, state resident: full-time $6,032; part-time $335 per credit. Tuition, nonresident: full-time $17,288; part-time $960 per credit. Required fees: $65 per credit. $30 per semester. One-time fee: $80 part-time. *Financial support:* Career-related internships or fieldwork available. *Unit head:* Dr. Deborah Riebe, Chair, 401-874-5444.

University of South Alabama, Graduate School, College of Education, Department of Health, Physical Education and Leisure Services, Mobile, AL 36688-0002. Offers exercise science (MS); health education (M Ed); physical education (M Ed); therapeutic recreation (MS). *Accreditation:* NCATE (one or more programs are accredited). Part-time programs available. *Faculty:* 9 full-time (1 woman). *Students:* 26 full-time (18 women), 11 part-time (8 women); includes 11 minority (9 African Americans, 1 Asian American or Pacific Islander, 1 Hispanic American), 2 international. 12 applicants, 83% accepted, 5 enrolled. In 2006, 17 degrees awarded. *Degree requirements:* For master's, comprehensive exam. *Entrance requirements:* For master's, GRE General Test or MAT. *Application deadline:* For fall admission, 9/1 priority date for domestic students. Applications are processed on a rolling basis. Application fee: $25. *Financial support:* In 2006–07, 10 teaching assistantships were awarded; career-related internships or fieldwork also available. Support available to part-time students. Financial award application deadline: 4/1. *Unit head:* Dr. Frederick M. Scaffidi, Chair, 251-460-7131.

University of South Carolina, The Graduate School, Arnold School of Public Health, Department of Health Promotion, Education and Behavior, Columbia, SC 29208. Offers alcohol and drug studies (Certificate); health education administration (Ed D); health promotion and education (MAT, MPH, MS, MSPH, Dr PH, PhD); school health education (Certificate). MAT and Ed D offered in cooperation with the College of Education. *Accreditation:* CEPH (one or more programs are accredited); NCATE (one or more programs are accredited). *Degree requirements:* For master's, thesis or alternative, practicum (MPH), project (MS), comprehensive exam; for doctorate, thesis/dissertation, comprehensive exam. *Entrance requirements:* For master's and doctorate, GRE General Test. Additional exam requirements/recommendations for international students: Required—TOEFL (minimum score 570 paper-based; 230 computer-based). Electronic applications accepted. *Faculty research:* Implementation and evaluation of health behavior change programs, nutrition behavior, work site health promotion, AIDS education.

University of South Carolina, The Graduate School, College of Education, Department of Instruction and Teacher Education and Department of Health Promotion, Education and Behavior, Program in Health Education Administration, Columbia, SC 29208. Offers Ed D. *Accreditation:* NCATE. *Degree requirements:* For doctorate, thesis/dissertation, comprehensive exam. *Entrance requirements:* For doctorate, GRE General Test, resumé. Additional exam requirements/recommendations for international students: Required—TOEFL. Electronic applications accepted. *Faculty research:* Behavioral and social science applied to public health problems.

University of South Carolina, The Graduate School, College of Education, Department of Instruction and Teacher Education, Program in Secondary Education, Columbia, SC 29208. Offers art education (IMA, MAT); business education (IMA, MAT); English (MAT); foreign language (MAT); health education (MAT); mathematics (MAT); science (IMA, MAT); secondary education (M Ed, MA, MT, PhD); social studies (IMA, MAT); theatre and speech (IMA, MAT). IMA and MT offered jointly with the subject areas. *Accreditation:* NCATE. *Degree requirements:* For master's, thesis (for some programs), foreign language (MA), comprehensive exam; for doctorate, one foreign language, thesis/dissertation, comprehensive exam. *Entrance requirements:* For master's, GRE General Test or MAT, teaching certificate (IMA, M Ed), interview; for doctorate, GRE General Test or MAT, interview. *Faculty research:* Middle school programs, professional development, school collaboration.

The University of South Dakota, Graduate School, School of Education, Division of Health, Physical Education and Recreation, Vermillion, SD 57069-2390. Offers MA. *Accreditation:* NCATE. Part-time programs available. *Faculty:* 5 full-time (2 women), 1 (woman) part-time/adjunct. *Students:* 26 (8 women). In 2006, 22 degrees awarded. *Degree requirements:* For master's, thesis or alternative, comprehensive exam. *Entrance requirements:* For master's, GRE General Test, MAT, minimum GPA of 2.7. Additional exam requirements/recommendations for international students: Required—TOEFL (minimum score 550 paper-based; 213 computer-based; 79 iBT). *Application deadline:* Applications are processed on a rolling basis. Application fee: $35. Electronic applications accepted. *Expenses:* Tuition, state resident: part-time $120 per credit hour. Tuition, nonresident: part-time $355 per credit hour. Required fees: $90 per credit hour. *Financial support:* In 2006–07, research assistantships with partial tuition reimbursements (averaging $4,626 per year), teaching assistantships with partial tuition reimbursements (averaging $4,626 per year) were awarded; Federal Work-Study and unspecified assistantships also available. Financial award applicants required to submit FAFSA. *Unit head:* Dr. Garreth Zalud, Acting Chair/Graduate Director, 605-677-5310, Fax: 605-677-5338, E-mail: rkoch@usd.edu.

University of Southern Mississippi, Graduate School, College of Health, Department of Community Health Sciences, Hattiesburg, MS 39406-0001. Offers epidemiology and biostatistics (MPH); health education (MPH); health policy/administration (MPH); occupational/environmental health (MPH); public health nutrition (MPH). *Accreditation:* CEPH. Part-time and evening/weekend programs available. *Faculty:* 10 full-time (3 women). *Students:* 53 full-time (32 women), 13 part-time (10 women); includes 25 minority (24 African Americans, 1 Asian American or Pacific Islander), 15 international. Average age 30. 114 applicants, 84% accepted, 35 enrolled. In 2006, 27 degrees awarded. *Degree requirements:* For master's, thesis (for some programs), comprehensive exam, registration. *Entrance requirements:* For master's, GRE General Test, minimum GPA of 2.75 in last 60 hours. Additional exam requirements/recommendations for international students: Required—TOEFL. *Application deadline:* For fall admission, 3/1 for domestic and international students. Applications are processed on a rolling basis. Application fee: $25 ($30 for international students). *Financial support:* In 2006–07, 9 research assistantships with full tuition reimbursements (averaging $5,906 per year) were awarded; teaching assistantships with full tuition reimbursements, career-related internships or fieldwork and Federal Work-Study also available. Financial award application deadline: 3/15. *Faculty research:* Rural health care delivery, school health, nutrition of pregnant teens, risk factor reduction, sexually transmitted diseases. *Unit head:* Dr. James McGuire, Chair, 601-266-5437, Fax: 601-266-5043.

The University of Tennessee, Graduate School, College of Education, Health and Human Sciences, Program in Health Promotion and Health Education, Knoxville, TN 37996. Offers MS. *Accreditation:* CEPH. Part-time programs available. *Students:* 4 full-time (3 women), 11 part-time (all women). 4 applicants, 50% accepted. In 2006, 1 degree awarded. *Degree requirements:* For master's, thesis optional. *Entrance requirements:* For master's, minimum GPA of 2.7. Additional exam requirements/recommendations for international students: Required—TOEFL. *Application deadline:* For fall admission, 2/1 priority date for domestic students. Applications are processed on a rolling basis. Application fee: $35. Electronic applications accepted. *Expenses:* Tuition, state resident: full-time $5,574. Tuition, nonresident: full-time $16,840. Required fees: $792. *Financial support:* Application deadline: 2/1; *Unit head:* Dr. Paula Zemel, Graduate Representative, 865-974-5041, E-mail: pzemel@utk.edu.

The University of Tennessee, Graduate School, College of Education, Health and Human Sciences, Program in Safety, Knoxville, TN 37996. Offers MS. *Accreditation:* NCATE. Part-time programs available. *Students:* 19 (5 women); includes 1 African American. In 2006, 12 degrees awarded. *Degree requirements:* For master's, thesis optional. *Entrance requirements:* For master's, minimum GPA of 2.7. Additional exam requirements/recommendations for international students: Required—TOEFL. *Application deadline:* For fall admission, 2/1 priority date for domestic students. Applications are processed on a rolling basis. Application fee: $35. Electronic applications accepted. *Expenses:* Tuition, state resident: full-time $5,574. Tuition, nonresident: full-time $16,840. Required fees: $792. *Financial support:* Application deadline: 2/1; *Unit head:* Dr. Susan Smith, Graduate Representative, 865-974-5041, E-mail: smsmith@utk.edu.

The University of Texas at Austin, Graduate School, College of Education, Department of Kinesiology and Health Education, Austin, TX 78712-1111. Offers health education (M Ed, MA, Ed D, PhD); kinesiology (M Ed, MA, Ed D, PhD). Part-time programs available. Terminal master's awarded for partial completion of doctoral program. *Degree requirements:* For master's, thesis (for some programs); for doctorate, thesis/dissertation. *Entrance requirements:* For master's and doctorate, GRE General Test. Additional exam requirements/recommendations for international students: Required—TOEFL. Electronic applications accepted. *Faculty research:* Health promotion, human performance and exercise biochemistry, motor behavior and biomechanics, sport management, aging and pediatric development.

The University of Texas at El Paso, Graduate School, College of Health Sciences, School of Allied Health, Department of Health and Physical Education, El Paso, TX 79968-0001. Offers MS. Part-time and evening/weekend programs available. *Degree requirements:* For master's, thesis optional. *Entrance requirements:* For master's, GRE General Test. Additional exam requirements/recommendations for international students: Required—TOEFL. Electronic applications accepted.

The University of Texas at Tyler, College of Nursing and Health Sciences, Department of Health and Kinesiology, Tyler, TX 75799-0001. Offers clinical exercise physiology (MS); health and kinesiology (M Ed); kinesiology (MS). Part-time programs available. Postbaccalaureate distance learning degree programs offered. *Faculty:* 8 full-time (2 women), 8 part-time/adjunct (5 women). *Students:* 16 full-time (10 women), 29 part-time (15 women); includes 7 minority (5 African Americans, 1 Asian American or Pacific Islander, 1 Hispanic American). Average age 27. 27 applicants, 21 enrolled. In 2006, 20 degrees awarded. *Degree requirements:* For master's, thesis (for some programs), comprehensive exam (for some programs). *Application deadline:* Applications are processed on a rolling basis. Application fee: $0 ($50 for international students). Electronic applications accepted. *Expenses:* Tuition, state resident:

Health Education

The University of Texas at Tyler (continued)
part-time $50 per credit hour. Tuition, nonresident: part-time $328 per credit hour. Required fees: $107 per credit hour. $426 per term. *Financial support:* In 2006–07, 2 teaching assistantships (averaging $6,000 per year) were awarded; research assistantships, Federal Work-Study and scholarships/grants also available. Financial award application deadline: 7/1. *Faculty research:* Osteoporosis, muscle soreness, economy of locomotion, adoption of rehabilitation programs, effect of inactivity and aging on muscle blood vessels, territoriality. *Unit head:* Dr. James Schwane, Chairperson, 903-566-7306, Fax: 903-566-7065, E-mail: jschwane@mail.uttyl.edu. *Application contact:* Bonnie Purser, Office of Graduate Studies, 903-566-7142, Fax: 903-566-7068, E-mail: bpurser@uttyler.edu.

The University of Toledo, College of Graduate Studies, College of Education, Department of Curriculum and Instruction, Program in Health Education, Toledo, OH 43606-3390. Offers ME. *Students:* 8 full-time (7 women). 2 applicants, 100% accepted, 1 enrolled. In 2006, 4 degrees awarded.

The University of Toledo, College of Graduate Studies, College of Health Science and Human Service, Division of Human Services, Department of Health Education, Toledo, OH 43606-3390. Offers PhD. *Students:* 22 full-time (17 women); includes 3 minority (all African Americans), 2 international. Average age 42. 7 applicants, 57% accepted, 3 enrolled. In 2006, 3 degrees awarded.

University of Utah, The Graduate School, College of Health, Department of Health Promotion and Education, Salt Lake City, UT 84112-1107. Offers M Phil, MS, Ed D, PhD. Part-time and evening/weekend programs available. *Faculty:* 7 full-time (3 women). *Students:* 26 full-time (20 women), 26 part-time (19 women); includes 1 minority (Hispanic American), 1 international. Average age 37. 24 applicants, 100% accepted, 19 enrolled. In 2006, 5 master's, 4 doctorates awarded. Terminal master's awarded for partial completion of doctoral program. *Median time to degree:* Of those who began their doctoral program in fall 1998, 100% received their degree in 8 years or less. *Degree requirements:* For master's and doctorate, thesis/dissertation or alternative, field experience, comprehensive exam. *Entrance requirements:* For master's, GRE General Test, minimum GPA of 3.0; for doctorate, GRE General Test, minimum GPA of 3.2. Additional exam requirements/recommendations for international students: Required—TOEFL (minimum score 500 paper-based; 173 computer-based). *Application deadline:* For winter admission, 2/15 for domestic students. Application fee: $45 ($65 for international students). *Expenses:* Tuition, state resident: full-time $3,208. Tuition, nonresident: full-time $11,326. Required fees: $608. Tuition and fees vary according to class time and program. *Financial support:* In 2006–07, 7 students received support, including 2 research assistantships with full tuition reimbursements available (averaging $10,650 per year), 3 teaching assistantships with full tuition reimbursements available (averaging $10,650 per year); career-related internships or fieldwork, Federal Work-Study, and institutionally sponsored loans also available. Financial award application deadline: 2/15; financial award applicants required to submit FAFSA. *Faculty research:* Health behavior and counseling, health service administration, evaluation of health programs. Total annual research expenditures: $151,482. *Unit head:* Les Chatelain, Interim Chair, 801-581-4512, Fax: 801-585-3646, E-mail: les.chatelain@health.utah.edu. *Application contact:* Tim Behrens, Graduate Director, 801-581-8114, E-mail: tim.behrens@hsc.utah.edu.

University of Virginia, Curry School of Education, Department of Human Services, Program in Health and Physical Education, Charlottesville, VA 22903. Offers kinesiology (M Ed, Ed D). *Students:* 37 full-time (19 women), 2 part-time; includes 2 minority (1 African American, 1 Asian American or Pacific Islander). Average age 25. 28 applicants, 68% accepted, 8 enrolled. In 2006, 33 degrees awarded. *Degree requirements:* For master's, thesis (for some programs), comprehensive exam (for some programs); for doctorate, thesis/dissertation, comprehensive exam. *Entrance requirements:* For master's and doctorate, GRE General Test. *Application deadline:* Applications are processed on a rolling basis. Application fee: $60. Electronic applications accepted. *Financial support:* Applicants required to submit FAFSA. *Unit head:* Glenn A. Gaesser, Chair, 434-924-3543. *Application contact:* Roberta Camb, Information Contact, 434-924-6207, E-mail: rcl8b@virginia.edu.

University of Waterloo, Graduate Studies, Faculty of Applied Health Sciences, Department of Health Studies and Gerontology, Waterloo, ON N2L 3G1, Canada. Offers M Sc, MPH, PhD. Part-time programs available. *Faculty:* 23 full-time (12 women), 22 part-time/adjunct (9 women). *Students:* 62 full-time (54 women), 31 part-time (23 women). 60 applicants, 52% accepted, 18 enrolled. In 2006, 13 master's, 2 doctorates awarded. *Degree requirements:* For master's, thesis/dissertation, registration; for doctorate, thesis/dissertation, comprehensive exam, registration. *Entrance requirements:* For master's, honors degree, minimum B average, resumé, writing sample; for doctorate, GRE (recommended), master's degree, minimum B average, resumé, writing sample. Additional exam requirements/recommendations for international students: Required—TOEFL, TWE. *Application deadline:* For fall admission, 2/1 for domestic and international students. Application fee: $75 Canadian dollars. Electronic applications accepted. *Financial support:* Research assistantships, teaching assistantships, career-related internships or fieldwork, Federal Work-Study, institutionally sponsored loans, and scholarships/grants available. *Faculty research:* Population health, health promotion and disease prevention, healthy aging, health policy, planning and evaluation, health information management and health informatics, aging, health and well-being, work and health. *Unit head:* Dr. Jose Arocha, Associate Chair, Graduate Studies, 519-888-4567 Ext. 32729, Fax: 519-746-2510, E-mail: jfarocha@uwaterloo.ca. *Application contact:* Tracy Taves, Graduate Studies Coordinator, 519-888-4567 Ext. 36149, Fax: 519-746-6776, E-mail: tltaves@uwaterloo.ca.

University of West Florida, College of Professional Studies, Division of Health, Leisure, and Exercise Science, Program in Health Education, Pensacola, FL 32514-5750. Offers MS. *Students:* 14 full-time (13 women), 7 part-time (6 women); includes 2 minority (1 African American, 1 American Indian/Alaska Native), 1 international. Average age 34. 9 applicants, 100% accepted, 6 enrolled. In 2006, 15 degrees awarded. *Degree requirements:* For master's, thesis or alternative. *Entrance requirements:* For master's, GRE General Test, minimum GPA of 3.0. Additional exam requirements/recommendations for international students: Required—TOEFL (minimum score 550 paper-based; 213 computer-based). *Application deadline:* For fall admission, 6/1 for domestic students, 5/15 for international students; for spring admission, 11/1 for domestic students, 10/1 for international students. Applications are processed on a rolling basis. Application fee: $30. *Expenses:* Tuition, state resident: full-time $5,871; part-time $245 per credit hour. Tuition, nonresident: full-time $21,241; part-time $885 per credit hour. *Financial support:* Fellowships, research assistantships with partial tuition reimbursements, teaching assistantships, Federal Work-Study, scholarships/grants, tuition waivers (full and partial), and unspecified assistantships available. *Unit head:* Dr. Stuart W. Ryan, Chairperson, Division of Health, Leisure, and Exercise Science, 850-474-2592.

University of West Florida, College of Professional Studies, Division of Health, Leisure, and Exercise Science, Program in Health, Leisure, and Exercise Science, Pensacola, FL 32514-5750. Offers exercise science (MS); physical education (MS). *Students:* 25 full-time (16 women), 21 part-time (16 women); includes 5 minority (4 African Americans, 1 Hispanic American), 1 international. Average age 31. 24 applicants, 83% accepted, 15 enrolled. In 2006, 6 degrees awarded. *Degree requirements:* For master's, thesis or alternative. *Entrance requirements:* For master's, GRE General Test, minimum GPA of 3.0. Additional exam requirements/recommendations for international students: Required—TOEFL (minimum score 550 paper-based; 213 computer-based). *Application deadline:* For fall admission, 6/1 for domestic students, 5/15 for international students; for spring admission, 11/1 for domestic students, 10/1 for international students. Applications are processed on a rolling basis. Application fee: $30. *Expenses:* Tuition, state resident: full-time $5,871; part-time $245 per credit hour. Tuition, nonresident: full-time $21,241; part-time $885 per credit hour. *Financial support:* Fellowships, research assistantships with partial tuition reimbursements, teaching assistantships, Federal Work-Study, scholarships/grants, tuition waivers (full and partial), and unspecified assistantships available. Financial award application deadline: 4/15; financial award applicants required to submit FAFSA. *Unit head:* Dr. Stuart W. Ryan, Chairperson, Division of Health, Leisure, and Exercise Science, 850-474-2592.

University of Wisconsin–La Crosse, Office of University Graduate Studies, College of Science and Health, Department of Health Education and Health Promotion, Program in Community Health Education, La Crosse, WI 54601-3742. Offers MPH, MS. *Accreditation:* CEPH. *Students:* 11 full-time (all women), 19 part-time (16 women); includes 2 minority (both African Americans), 3 international. Average age 33. 8 applicants, 75% accepted, 3 enrolled. In 2006, 6 degrees awarded. *Degree requirements:* For master's, thesis. *Entrance requirements:* For master's, GRE General Test, GRE Subject Test (MPH), 3 letters of recommendation. Additional exam requirements/recommendations for international students: Required—TOEFL (minimum score 550 paper-based; 213 computer-based). Application fee: $45. *Financial support:* In 2006–07, 3 students received support, including 3 research assistantships (averaging $6,479 per year). *Faculty research:* School-based and community-based wellness strategies, violence prevention, alcohol and drug abuse prevention, competencies update project for health education, exercise and healthful pregnancy. *Unit head:* Dr. Gary Gilmore, Director, 608-785-8163, E-mail: gilmore.gary@uwlax.edu. *Application contact:* Kathryn Kiefer, Associate Director of Admissions, 608-785-8939, E-mail: admissions@uwlax.edu.

University of Wisconsin–La Crosse, Office of University Graduate Studies, College of Science and Health, Department of Health Education and Health Promotion, Program in School Health Education, La Crosse, WI 54601-3742. Offers MS. *Students:* 3 full-time (all women), 2 part-time (1 woman). Average age 27. 1 applicant, 100% accepted, 0 enrolled. In 2006, 4 degrees awarded. *Entrance requirements:* For master's, GRE General Test, minimum GPA of 2.85. Additional exam requirements/recommendations for international students: Required—TOEFL (minimum score 550 paper-based; 213 computer-based). Application fee: $45. *Financial support:* In 2006–07, 1 research assistantship (averaging $6,323 per year) was awarded. *Unit head:* Tracy Caravella, Director, 608-785-6788, E-mail: caravell.trac@uwlax.edu. *Application contact:* Kathryn Kiefer, Associate Director of Admissions, 608-785-8939, E-mail: admissions@uwlax.edu.

University of Wyoming, Graduate School, College of Health Sciences, Division of Kinesiology and Health, Laramie, WY 82070. Offers MS. *Accreditation:* NCATE. Part-time programs available. Postbaccalaureate distance learning degree programs offered (no on-campus study). *Faculty:* 11 full-time (2 women). *Students:* 13 full-time (8 women), 24 part-time (13 women); includes 2 minority (both Hispanic Americans), 3 international. Average age 29. 25 applicants, 36% accepted. In 2006, 7 degrees awarded. *Degree requirements:* For master's, thesis (for some programs), comprehensive exam (for some programs), registration. *Entrance requirements:* For master's, GRE General Test, minimum GPA of 3.0. Additional exam requirements/recommendations for international students: Required—TOEFL. *Application deadline:* For fall admission, 6/1 priority date for domestic students; for spring admission, 11/1 for domestic students. Applications are processed on a rolling basis. Application fee: $50. Electronic applications accepted. *Financial support:* In 2006–07, 7 teaching assistantships with tuition reimbursements (averaging $10,062 per year) were awarded; career-related internships or fieldwork and unspecified assistantships also available. Financial award application deadline: 3/1. *Faculty research:* Teacher effectiveness, effects of exercising on heart function, physiological responses of overtraining, psychological benefits of physical activity, health behavior. Total annual research expenditures: $25,000. *Unit head:* Dr. Mark Byra, Director, 307-766-5285, Fax: 307-766-4098, E-mail: byra@uwyo.edu. *Application contact:* Dr. Mark Byra, Graduate Coordinator, 307-766-5227, Fax: 307-766-4098, E-mail: byra@uwyo.edu.

Utah State University, School of Graduate Studies, College of Education and Human Services, Department of Health, Physical Education and Recreation, Logan, UT 84322. Offers M Ed, MS. *Accreditation:* NCATE. Part-time and evening/weekend programs available. Postbaccalaureate distance learning degree programs offered (minimal on-campus study). *Faculty:* 6 full-time (1 woman). *Students:* 43 full-time (16 women), 9 part-time (6 women); includes 3 minority (2 African Americans, 1 Hispanic American), 5 international. Average age 34. 45 applicants, 80% accepted, 32 enrolled. In 2006, 15 degrees awarded. *Degree requirements:* For master's, thesis (for some programs). *Entrance requirements:* For master's, GRE General Test or MAT, minimum GPA of 3.0. Additional exam requirements/recommendations for international students: Required—TOEFL. *Application deadline:* For fall admission, 3/15 priority date for domestic students, 3/15 for international students; for spring admission, 6/15 priority date for domestic students, 6/15 for international students. Applications are processed on a rolling basis. Application fee: $50 ($60 for international students). *Financial support:* In 2006–07, 5 research assistantships with partial tuition reimbursements (averaging $6,488 per year), 15 teaching assistantships with partial tuition reimbursements (averaging $6,488 per year) were awarded; career-related internships or fieldwork, Federal Work-Study, institutionally sponsored loans, and tuition waivers (full) also available. Financial award application deadline: 2/10. *Faculty research:* Sport psychology intervention, motor learning biomechanics, pedagogy, physiology. Total annual research expenditures: $21,000. *Unit head:* Dr. Dennis A. Nelson, Interim Head, 435-797-1509, Fax: 435-797-3759, E-mail: dane@cc.usu.edu. *Application contact:* Dr. Richard D. Gordin, Graduate Chair, 435-797-1506, Fax: 435-797-3759, E-mail: gordin@cc.usu.edu.

Valdosta State University, Graduate School, College of Education, Department of Kinesiology and Physical Education, Valdosta, GA 31698. Offers health and physical education (M Ed). *Accreditation:* NCATE. Part-time and evening/weekend programs available. *Degree requirements:* For master's, comprehensive written and/or oral exams. *Entrance requirements:* For master's, GRE General Test or MAT. Additional exam requirements/recommendations for international students: Required—TOEFL (minimum score 523 paper-based; 193 computer-based). Electronic applications accepted.

Virginia Commonwealth University, Graduate School, School of Education, Department of Health and Human Performance, Richmond, VA 23284-9005. Offers athletic training (MS); exercise science (MS); rehabilitation and movement science (PhD); teacher education (MS). *Faculty:* 7 full-time (2 women). *Students:* 13 full-time (8 women), 28 part-time (17 women); includes 3 minority (2 African Americans, 1 American Indian/Alaska Native), 1 international. 8 applicants, 100% accepted, 8 enrolled. *Entrance requirements:* For master's, GRE General Test or MAT. *Application deadline:* For fall admission, 5/15 for domestic students; for spring admission, 11/15 for domestic students. Applications are processed on a rolling basis. Application fee: $50. *Financial support:* Career-related internships or fieldwork, Federal Work-Study, and institutionally sponsored loans available. Support available to part-time students. Financial award application deadline: 3/1. *Unit head:* Dr. Edmund Acevedo, Chair, 804-828-1948, Fax: 804-828-1946, E-mail: eoacevedo@vcu.edu. *Application contact:* Dr. Michael D. Davis, Director, Graduate Studies, 804-828-6530, Fax: 804-827-0676, E-mail: mddavis@vcu.edu.

See Close-Ups on pages 2333, 1751, and 2331.

Virginia Polytechnic Institute and State University, Graduate School, College of Liberal Arts and Human Sciences, School of Education, Department of Teaching and Learning, Blacksburg, VA 24061. Offers curriculum and instruction (MA Ed, Ed D, PhD, Ed S); health and physical education (MS Ed); instructional technology (ITMA). *Accreditation:* NCATE. Postbaccalaureate distance learning degree programs offered (no on-campus study). *Students:* 274 full-time (184 women), 400 part-time (271 women); includes 83 minority (55 African Americans, 2 American Indian/Alaska Native, 18 Asian Americans or Pacific Islanders, 8 Hispanic Americans), 36 international. Average age 34. 374 applicants, 71% accepted, 237 enrolled. In 2006, 245 master's, 21 doctorates, 4 other advanced degrees awarded. *Entrance requirements:* Additional exam requirements/recommendations for international students: Required—TOEFL (minimum score 550 paper-based; 213 computer-based). *Application deadline:* For fall admission, 5/15 for international students; for spring admission, 10/15 for international students. Applications are processed on a rolling basis. Application fee: $45. Electronic applications accepted. *Expenses:* Tuition, state resident: full-time $7,017; part-time $390 per credit hour. Tuition, nonresident: full-time $12,414; part-time $690 per credit hour. International tuition: $11,296 full-time. Required fees: $1,523; $256 per term. *Financial support:*

Career-related internships or fieldwork, Federal Work-Study, scholarships/grants, and unspecified assistantships available. Financial award application deadline: 4/1. *Faculty research:* Instructional technology, teacher evaluation, school change, literacy, teaching strategies. *Unit head:* Dr. Daisy L. Stewart, Head, 540-231-8327, Fax: 540-231-3717. *Application contact:* Nancy Nolen, Information Contact, 540-231-5348, Fax: 540-231-3717, E-mail: nanolen@vt.edu.

Wayne State University, College of Education, Division of Kinesiology, Health and Sports Studies, Detroit, MI 48202. Offers health education (M Ed); kinesiology (M Ed); physical education (M Ed); recreation and park services (MA); sports administration (MA). *Faculty:* 9 full-time (2 women). *Students:* 40 full-time (16 women), 73 part-time (24 women); includes 25 minority (22 African Americans, 1 Asian American or Pacific Islander, 2 Hispanic Americans), 6 international. Average age 31. 39 applicants, 95% accepted, 26 enrolled. In 2006, 39 degrees awarded. *Degree requirements:* For master's, thesis (for some programs). *Entrance requirements:* For master's, GRE General Test. Additional exam requirements/recommendations for international students: Required—TOEFL; Recommended—TWE (minimum score 6). *Application deadline:* For fall admission, 7/1 for domestic students, 6/1 for international students; for winter admission, 10/1 for international students; for spring admission, 2/1 for international students. Application fee: $30 ($50 for international students). Electronic applications accepted. *Financial support:* In 2006–07, 3 research assistantships with tuition reimbursements (averaging $13,222 per year), 2 teaching assistantships with tuition reimbursements (averaging $13,222 per year) were awarded; career-related internships or fieldwork also available. *Faculty research:* Fitness in urban children, motor development of crack babies, effects of caffeine on metabolism/exercise, body composition of elite youth sports participants, systematic observation of teaching. Total annual research expenditures: $437,871. *Unit head:* Dr. Sally Erbaugh, Assistant Dean, 313-577-6210, Fax: 313-577-5999, E-mail: serbaugh@coe.wayne.edu. *Application contact:* John Wirth, Assistant Professor, 313-993-7972, Fax: 313-577-5999, E-mail: johnwirth@wayne.edu.

Wayne State University, College of Education, Division of Teacher Education, Detroit, MI 48202. Offers adult and continuing education (M Ed); art education (M Ed); bilingual/bicultural education (M Ed, MAT); business education (M Ed, MAT); career and technical education (M Ed, Ed D, PhD, Ed S); curriculum and instruction (Ed D, PhD, Ed S); distributive education (M Ed, MAT); early childhood education (M Ed); elementary education (M Ed, MAT, Ed D, PhD, Ed S); elementary education curriculum and instruction (M Ed); English education (M Ed); English education-secondary (M Ed, Ed S); foreign language education (M Ed); general education (Ed D, Ed S); health occupations education (M Ed); industrial education (M Ed); mathematics education (M Ed, Ed S); pre-school and parent education (M Ed); reading (M Ed, Ed D, Ed S); reading, languages and literature (Ed D); school music-vocal (M Ed); science education (M Ed, MAT, Ed S); secondary education (MAT); secondary school reading (M Ed); social studies education (M Ed, Ed S), including education-secondary (M Ed); special education (M Ed, Ed D, PhD, Ed S); teacher education (MAT, Ed D, PhD). *Faculty:* 41 full-time (22 women), 2 part-time/adjunct (both women). *Students:* 401 full-time (295 women), 1,021 part-time (784 women); includes 527 minority (452 African Americans, 6 American Indian/Alaska Native, 32 Asian Americans or Pacific Islanders, 37 Hispanic Americans), 18 international. Average age 36. 296 applicants, 81% accepted, 132 enrolled. In 2006, 386 master's, 1 doctorate awarded. *Degree requirements:* For doctorate, thesis/dissertation. *Entrance requirements:* For master's, minimum GPA of 2.6; for doctorate, minimum undergraduate GPA of 3.0, graduate 3.5; interview. Additional exam requirements/recommendations for international students: Required—TOEFL (minimum score 550 paper-based; 213 computer-based), TWE (minimum score 6). *Application deadline:* For fall admission, 7/1 for domestic students, 6/1 for international students; for winter admission, 10/1 for international students; for spring admission, 2/1 for international students. Application fee: $30 ($50 for international students). Electronic applications accepted. *Financial support:* In 2006–07, 1 fellowship (averaging $34,919 per year) was awarded; research assistantships. *Faculty research:* Reading and writing literacy and literature. Total annual research expenditures: $209,400. *Unit head:* Dr. Joann Snyder, Academic Director, 313-577-1644, E-mail: joanne.snyder@wayne.edu. *Application contact:* Sharon Elliott, Assistant Dean, 313-577-0902, E-mail: sharon.elliott@wayne.edu.

Wayne State University, School of Medicine, Graduate Programs in Medicine, Medical Research Program, Detroit, MI 48202. Offers MS. *Faculty:* 1 full-time (0 women). *Students:* 1 full-time (0 women). Average age 46. 3 applicants, 0% accepted. In 2006, 3 degrees awarded. *Entrance requirements:* For master's, GRE or MCAT, minimum GPA of 3.0, MD. Additional exam requirements/recommendations for international students: Required—TOEFL (minimum score 550 paper-based; 213 computer-based); Recommended—TWE (minimum score 6). *Application deadline:* For fall admission, 6/1 for international students; for winter admission, 10/1 for international students; for spring admission, 2/1 for international students. Applications are processed on a rolling basis. Application fee: $30 ($50 for international students). Electronic applications accepted. Total annual research expenditures: $84,500. *Unit head:* Dr. Robert Pauley, Director, 313-577-6872, E-mail: rpauley@med.wayne.edu.

West Chester University of Pennsylvania, Graduate Studies, School of Health Sciences, Department of Health, West Chester, PA 19383. Offers emergency preparedness (Certificate); environmental health (MS); gerontology (MS); health care administration (Certificate); health services (MSA); integrative health (Certificate); public health (MPH, MS); school health (M Ed). Part-time and evening/weekend programs available. *Students:* 35 full-time (27 women), 65 part-time (50 women); includes 19 African Americans, 1 Asian American or Pacific Islander, 9 international. Average age 34. 58 applicants, 98% accepted, 30 enrolled. In 2006, 36 degrees awarded. *Degree requirements:* For master's, thesis (for some programs), comprehensive exam. *Entrance requirements:* For master's, GRE. *Application deadline:* For fall admission, 4/15 priority date for domestic students; for spring admission, 10/15 for domestic students. Applications are processed on a rolling basis. Application fee: $35. *Financial support:* In 2006–07, 9 research assistantships with full tuition reimbursements (averaging $5,000 per year) were awarded; unspecified assistantships also available. Support available to part-time students. Financial award application deadline: 2/15; financial award applicants required to submit FAFSA. *Faculty research:* HIV/AIDS education, teacher preparation, water quality. *Unit head:* Dr. Roger Mustalish, Chair, 610-436-2931, E-mail: rmustalish@wcupa.edu. *Application contact:* Dr. Bethann Cinelli, Graduate Coordinator, 610-436-2267, E-mail: bcinelli@wcupa.edu.

Western Illinois University, School of Graduate Studies, College of Education and Human Services, Department of Health Sciences, Macomb, IL 61455-1390. Offers health education (MS); health services administration (Certificate). *Accreditation:* NCATE. Part-time programs available. *Students:* 23 full-time (16 women), 34 part-time (30 women); includes 2 minority (1 African American, 1 Hispanic American), 4 international. Average age 32. 33 applicants, 88% accepted. In 2006, 15 degrees awarded. *Degree requirements:* For master's, thesis or alternative, comprehensive exam. *Entrance requirements:* For master's, minimum GPA of 2.75. Additional exam requirements/recommendations for international students: Required—TOEFL (minimum score 550 paper-based; 213 computer-based; 80 iBT). *Application deadline:* Applications are processed on a rolling basis. Application fee: $30. Electronic applications accepted. *Expenses:* Tuition, state resident: part-time $200 per credit hour. Tuition, nonresident: part-time $400 per credit hour. *Financial support:* In 2006–07, 10 students received support, including 10 research assistantships with full tuition reimbursements available (averaging $6,568 per year). Financial award applicants required to submit FAFSA. *Unit head:* Dr. Diane Hamilton-Hancock, Chairperson, 309-298-1076. *Application contact:* Dr. Barbara Baily, Director of Graduate Studies/Associate Provost, 309-298-1806, Fax: 309-298-2345, E-mail: grad-office@wiu.edu.

Western Oregon University, Graduate Programs, College of Education, Division of Teacher Education, Program in Secondary Education, Monmouth, OR 97361-1394. Offers bilingual education (MS Ed); health (MS Ed); humanities (MAT, MS Ed); initial licensure (MAT); mathematics (MAT, MS Ed); science (MAT, MS Ed); social science (MAT, MS Ed). *Accreditation:* NCATE. Part-time and evening/weekend programs available. *Faculty:* 7 full-time (4 women), 15 part-time/adjunct (7 women). *Students:* 12 full-time (4 women), 21 part-time (10 women). Average age 32. In 2006, 31 degrees awarded. *Degree requirements:* For master's, written exam, thesis optional. *Entrance requirements:* For master's, minimum GPA of 3.0, teaching license. *Application deadline:* Applications are processed on a rolling basis. Application fee: $50. *Expenses:* Tuition, state resident: full-time $8,250; part-time $250 per credit. Tuition, nonresident: full-time $14,025; part-time $250 per credit. Required fees: $1,173. *Financial support:* In 2006–07, 16 teaching assistantships with full tuition reimbursements (averaging $706 per year) were awarded; research assistantships with full tuition reimbursements, career-related internships or fieldwork, Federal Work-Study, and tuition waivers (full and partial) also available. Support available to part-time students. Financial award application deadline: 3/1; financial award applicants required to submit FAFSA. *Faculty research:* Literacy, science in primary grades, geography education, retention, teacher burnout. *Unit head:* Dr. Mary Bucy, Unit Head, 503-838-8794, Fax: 503-838-8228. *Application contact:* Dr. David McDonald, Dean of Admissions, Retention and Enrollment Management, 503-838-8919, Fax: 503-838-8067, E-mail: mcdonald@wou.edu.

Western University of Health Sciences, College of Allied Health Professions, Program in Health Sciences, Pomona, CA 91766-1854. Offers MS. Part-time and evening/weekend programs available. *Faculty:* 2 full-time (1 woman). *Students:* 20 full-time (12 women), 8 part-time (6 women); includes 11 minority (1 African American, 8 Asian Americans or Pacific Islanders, 2 Hispanic Americans), 1 international. Average age 32. 10 applicants, 60% accepted, 6 enrolled. In 2006, 7 degrees awarded. *Entrance requirements:* For master's, minimum undergraduate GPA of 2.5, graduate 3.0; letters of recommendation; interview. *Application deadline:* For fall admission, 11/15 priority date for domestic students; for spring admission, 7/15 priority date for domestic students. Applications are processed on a rolling basis. Application fee: $35. *Expenses:* Contact institution. *Financial support:* Institutionally sponsored loans, scholarships/grants, and Veterans Educational Benefits available. Financial award application deadline: 3/2; financial award applicants required to submit FAFSA. *Unit head:* Tina Meyer, Chair, 909-469-5586, Fax: 909-469-5407. *Application contact:* Audrey Navarro, Information Contact, 909-469-5335, Fax: 909-469-5570, E-mail: admissions@westernu.edu.

West Virginia University, School of Physical Education, Morgantown, WV 26506. Offers athletic coaching (MS); athletic training (MS); exercise physiology (Ed D); physical education/teacher education (MS, Ed D), including administration of physical education (Ed D), curriculum and instruction (Ed D), motor development (Ed D), special physical education (Ed D); sport management (MS); sport psychology (MS, Ed D). *Degree requirements:* For doctorate, thesis/dissertation, oral exam, comprehensive exam. *Entrance requirements:* For master's, GRE or MAT, minimum GPA of 3.0; for doctorate, GRE General Test or MAT, minimum GPA of 3.5. Additional exam requirements/recommendations for international students: Required—TOEFL (minimum score 550 paper-based; 213 computer-based). Electronic applications accepted. *Expenses:* Tuition, state resident: full-time $4,926; part-time $276 per credit hour. Tuition, nonresident: full-time $14,278; part-time $796 per credit hour. Tuition and fees vary according to program. *Faculty research:* Sport psychosociology, teacher education, exercise psychology, counseling.

Widener University, School of Human Service Professions, Center for Education, Chester, PA 19013-5792. Offers adult education (M Ed); counseling in higher education (M Ed); counselor education (M Ed); early childhood education (M Ed); educational foundations (M Ed); educational leadership (M Ed); educational psychology (M Ed); elementary education (M Ed); English and language arts (M Ed); health education (M Ed); higher education leadership (Ed D); home and school visitor (M Ed); human sexuality (M Ed); mathematics education (M Ed); middle school education (M Ed); principalship (M Ed); reading and language arts (Ed D); reading education (M Ed); school administration (Ed D); science education (M Ed); social studies education (M Ed); special education (M Ed); technology education (M Ed). Part-time and evening/weekend programs available. Terminal master's awarded for partial completion of doctoral program. *Degree requirements:* For doctorate, thesis/dissertation. *Entrance requirements:* For master's, minimum GPA of 2.5; for doctorate, GRE or MAT, minimum GPA of 2.0 (undergraduate), 3.5 (graduate). Electronic applications accepted. Expenses: Contact institution. *Faculty research:* Reading and cognition, adult education, technology education, educational leadership, special education.

Worcester State College, Graduate Studies, Department of Education, Concentration in Health Education, Worcester, MA 01602-2597. Offers M Ed. Part-time programs available. *Students:* Average age 45. 8 applicants, 63% accepted, 2 enrolled. In 2006, 10 degrees awarded. *Degree requirements:* For master's, thesis optional. *Entrance requirements:* For master's, GRE General Test or MAT. Additional exam requirements/recommendations for international students: Required—TOEFL (minimum score 550 paper-based; 213 computer-based). *Application deadline:* Applications are processed on a rolling basis. Application fee: $30. *Expenses:* Tuition, state resident: full-time $4,518; part-time $251 per credit hour. Tuition, nonresident: full-time $4,518; part-time $251 per credit hour. *Financial support:* In 2006–07, 1 research assistantship with full tuition reimbursement (averaging $4,000 per year) was awarded; career-related internships or fieldwork, Federal Work-Study, institutionally sponsored loans, scholarships/grants, and unspecified assistantships also available. Support available to part-time students. Financial award application deadline: 3/1; financial award applicants required to submit FAFSA. *Unit head:* Dr. Nancy Brewer, Coordinator, 508-929-8838, Fax: 508-929-8164, E-mail: nbrewer@worcester.edu. *Application contact:* Nicole Brown, Assistant Dean of Graduate and Continuing Education, 508-929-8787, Fax: 508-929-8100, E-mail: nbrown@worcester.edu.

Wright State University, School of Graduate Studies, College of Education and Human Services, Department of Health, Physical Education, and Recreation, Dayton, OH 45435. Offers M Ed, MA. *Accreditation:* NCATE. *Students:* 1 (woman) full-time, 2 part-time (1 woman). Average age 30. 3 applicants, 67% accepted. In 2006, 3 degrees awarded. *Degree requirements:* For master's, thesis (for some programs), comprehensive exam. *Entrance requirements:* For master's, GRE General Test, MAT. Additional exam requirements/recommendations for international students: Required—TOEFL. Application fee: $25. *Financial support:* Available to part-time students. Applicants required to submit FAFSA. *Faculty research:* Motor learning, motor development, exercise physiology, adapted physical education. *Unit head:* Dr. D. Drew Pringle, Chair, 937-775-3223, Fax: 937-775-4252, E-mail: d.pringle@wright.edu. *Application contact:* John Kimble, Associate Director of Graduate Admissions and Records, 937-775-2957, Fax: 937-775-2453, E-mail: john.kimble@wright.edu.

Wright State University, School of Medicine, Program in Public Health, Dayton, OH 45435. Offers health promotion and education (MPH); public health management (MPH); public health nursing (MPH). *Accreditation:* CEPH. *Unit head:* Dr. Richard J. Schuster, Director, 937-258-5555, Fax: 937-258-5544, E-mail: richard.schuster@wright.edu.

Home Economics Education

Appalachian State University, Cratis D. Williams Graduate School, College of Fine and Applied Arts, Department of Family and Consumer Sciences, Boone, NC 28608. Offers child development (MA); family and consumer science (MA); family and consumer science education (MA). Part-time programs available. *Faculty:* 9 full-time (8 women). *Students:* 11 full-time (10 women), 7 part-time (all women); includes 1 minority (Asian American or Pacific Islander) 14 applicants, 71% accepted, 8 enrolled. In 2006, 9 degrees awarded. *Degree requirements:* For master's, thesis or alternative, comprehensive exam. *Entrance requirements:* For master's, GRE General Test. Additional exam requirements/recommendations for international students: Required—TOEFL (minimum score 550 paper-based; 230 computer-based). *Application deadline:* For fall admission, 7/1 priority date for domestic students, 1/1 for international students; for spring admission, 11/1 for domestic students, 6/1 for international students. Application fee: $50. *Expenses:* Tuition, state resident: full-time $2,600; part-time $127 per hour. Tuition, nonresident: full-time $13,200; part-time $597 per hour. Required fees: $2,000; $546 per term. *Financial support:* In 2006–07, 4 teaching assistantships (averaging $7,000 per year) were awarded; fellowships, research assistantships, career-related internships or fieldwork, scholarships/grants, and unspecified assistantships also available. Support available to part-time students. Financial award application deadline: 7/1; financial award applicants required to submit FAFSA. *Faculty research:* Food antioxidants, preschool curriculum, children with special needs, family child care, FCS curriculum content. Total annual research expenditures:$138,358. *Unit head:* Dr. Sarah Jordan, Chairperson, 828-262-2661. *Application contact:* Dr. Sammie Garner, Graduate Director, 828-262-2698, E-mail: garnersg@appstate.edu.

Central Washington University, Graduate Studies, Research and Continuing Education, College of Education and Professional Studies, Department of Family and Consumer Sciences, Ellensburg, WA 98926. Offers family and consumer sciences education (MS); family studies (MS); nutrition (MS). Part-time programs available. *Faculty:* 9 full-time (7 women). *Students:* 10 full-time (8 women), 6 part-time (5 women). 9 applicants, 22% accepted, 2 enrolled. In 2006, 6 degrees awarded. *Degree requirements:* For master's, thesis or alternative. *Entrance requirements:* For master's, GRE General Test (nutrition), minimum GPA of 3.0. Additional exam requirements/recommendations for international students: Required—TOEFL (minimum score 550 paper-based; 213 computer-based; 79 iBT). *Application deadline:* For fall admission, 4/1 priority date for domestic students; for winter admission, 10/1 for domestic students; for spring admission, 1/1 for domestic students. Applications are processed on a rolling basis. Application fee: $50. Electronic applications accepted. *Expenses:* Tuition, state resident: full-time $6,312. Tuition, nonresident: full-time $14,112. Tuition and fees vary according to course load and degree level. *Financial support:* In 2006–07, 1 teaching assistantship with partial tuition reimbursement (averaging $8,100 per year) was awarded; research assistantships, Federal Work-Study, health care benefits, and unspecified assistantships also available. Financial award application deadline: 3/1; financial award applicants required to submit FAFSA. *Unit head:* Dr. Jan Bowers, Chair, 509-963-2766. *Application contact:* Justine Eason, Admissions Program Coordinator, 509-963-3103, Fax: 509-963-1799, E-mail: masters@cwu.edu.

Eastern Kentucky University, The Graduate School, College of Education, Department of Curriculum and Instruction, Program in Secondary and Higher Education, Richmond, KY 40475-3102. Offers agricultural education (MA Ed); allied health sciences education (MA Ed); art education (MA Ed); biological sciences education (MA Ed); business education (MA Ed); chemistry education (MA Ed); earth science education (MA Ed); English education (MA Ed); general science education (MA Ed); geography education (MA Ed); history education (MA Ed); home economics education (MA Ed); industrial education (MA Ed); mathematical sciences education (MA Ed); physical education (MA Ed); physics education (MA Ed); political science education (MA Ed); psychology education (MA Ed); reading (MA Ed); school health education (MA Ed); sociology education (MA Ed). *Accreditation:* NCATE. Part-time programs available. *Students:* 16 full-time (8 women), 63 part-time (43 women); includes 5 minority (2 African Americans, 2 American Indian/Alaska Native, 1 Asian American or Pacific Islander). Average age 32. *Entrance requirements:* For master's, GRE General Test, minimum GPA of 2.5. Application fee: $30. *Expenses:* Tuition, state resident: full-time $5,610. Tuition, nonresident: full-time $15,910. *Financial support:* Research assistantships, teaching assistantships, Federal Work-Study available. Support available to part-time students. *Unit head:* Dr. Michael Martin, Chair, Department of Curriculum and Instruction, 859-622-2154, Fax: 859-622-2004.

Harding University, College of Education, Searcy, AR 72149-0001. Offers advanced studies in teaching and learning (M Ed); art (MSE); behavioral science (MSE); Bible and religion (MSE); counseling (MS, Ed S); early childhood education (M Ed); early childhood special education (M Ed, MSE); education (MSE); educational leadership (M Ed, Ed S); elementary education (M Ed); English (MSE); family and consumer science (MSE); French (MSE); history/social science (MSE); kinesiology (MSE); math (MSE); physical science (MSE); reading (M Ed); secondary education (M Ed); Spanish (MSE); special education licensure (M Ed); teaching (MAT). *Accreditation:* NCATE. Part-time programs available. *Faculty:* 8 full-time (2 women), 45 part-time/adjunct (30 women). *Students:* 153 full-time (123 women), 469 part-time (341 women); includes 72 minority (63 African Americans, 4 American Indian/Alaska Native, 1 Asian American or Pacific Islander, 4 Hispanic Americans), 9 international. Average age 35. 175 applicants, 90% accepted, 147 enrolled. In 2006, 241 degrees awarded. *Degree requirements:* For master's, portfolio(s), thesis optional; for Ed S, portfolio, specialist project. *Entrance requirements:* For master's, GRE, MAT, PRAXIS; for Ed S, MAT or GRE. Additional exam requirements/recommendations for international students: Required—TOEFL (minimum score 550 paper-based). *Application deadline:* For fall admission, 8/1 for domestic and international students; for spring admission, 1/1 for domestic and international students. Applications are processed on a rolling basis. Application fee: $35. *Expenses:* Tuition: Part-time $455 per semester hour. Required fees: $20 per semester hour. Tuition and fees vary according to course load. *Financial support:* Scholarships/grants and unspecified assistantships available. Support available to part-time students. *Faculty research:* Reading, comprehension, school violence, educational technology, behavior, college choice, differentiated instruction, brain based teaching. *Unit head:* Pat Bashaw, Chair, 501-279-4183, Fax: 501-279-4051, E-mail: pbashaw@harding.edu.

Indiana State University, School of Graduate Studies, College of Arts and Sciences, Department of Family and Consumer Sciences, Terre Haute, IN 47809-1401. Offers child development and family life (MS); clothing and textiles (MS); dietetics (MS); family and consumer sciences education (MS); nutrition and foods (MS). *Accreditation:* ADtA. Part-time programs available. *Faculty:* 6 full-time (4 women). *Students:* 10 full-time (all women), 12 part-time (10 women); includes 5 minority (3 African Americans, 2 Asian Americans or Pacific Islanders), 2 international. Average age 31. 14 applicants, 100% accepted, 7 enrolled. In 2006, 8 degrees awarded. *Degree requirements:* For master's, thesis optional. *Application deadline:* For fall admission, 7/1 priority date for domestic students; for spring admission, 11/1 priority date for domestic students. Applications are processed on a rolling basis. Application fee: $35. Electronic applications accepted. *Expenses:* Tuition, state resident: part-time $278 per credit. Tuition, nonresident: part-time $552 per credit. *Financial support:* In 2006–07, 2 research assistantships with partial tuition reimbursements (averaging $6,300 per year) were awarded; teaching assistantships, tuition waivers (partial) also available. Financial award application deadline: 3/1; financial award applicants required to submit FAFSA. *Unit head:* Dr. Frederica Kramer, Chairperson, 812-237-3297.

Iowa State University of Science and Technology, Graduate College, College of Human Sciences, Department of Apparel, Education Studies, and Hospitality Management, Program in Family and Consumer Sciences Education and Studies, Ames, IA 50011. Offers M Ed, MS, PhD. *Students:* 11 full-time (10 women), 30 part-time (29 women); includes 7 minority (all African Americans), 3 international. 16 applicants, 75% accepted, 11 enrolled. In 2006, 4 degrees awarded. *Degree requirements:* For master's, thesis (for some programs); for doctorate, thesis/dissertation. *Entrance requirements:* For master's and doctorate, GRE General Test. Additional exam requirements/recommendations for international students: Required—

TOEFL (paper-based 550; computer-based 213; iBT 80) or IELTS (6.5). *Application deadline:* For fall admission, 1/15 priority date for domestic and international students. Applications are processed on a rolling basis. Application fee: $30 ($70 for international students). Electronic applications accepted. *Expenses:* Tuition, state resident: full-time $5,936; part-time $330 per credit. Tuition, nonresident: full-time $16,350; part-time $330 per credit. *Financial support:* In 2006–07, 2 research assistantships with full and partial tuition reimbursements (averaging $17,508 per year), 1 teaching assistantship with full and partial tuition reimbursement (averaging $17,508 per year) were awarded; scholarships/grants also available. *Unit head:* Dr. Cheryl O. Hausafus, Director of Graduate Education, 515-294-5307, E-mail: haus@iastate.edu.

Louisiana State University and Agricultural and Mechanical College, Graduate School, College of Agriculture, School of Human Resource Education and Workforce Development, Baton Rouge, LA 70803. Offers comprehensive vocational education (MS, PhD); extension and international education (MS, PhD); industrial education (MS); vocational agriculture education (MS, PhD); vocational business education (MS); vocational home economics education (MS). *Accreditation:* NCATE. Part-time programs available. *Faculty:* 13 full-time (6 women). *Students:* 39 full-time (24 women), 68 part-time (42 women); includes 12 African Americans, 3 Hispanic Americans, 9 international. Average age 38. 20 applicants, 60% accepted, 3 enrolled. In 2006, 18 master's, 33 doctorates awarded. Terminal master's awarded for partial completion of doctoral program. *Degree requirements:* For master's, thesis (for some programs); for doctorate, thesis/dissertation. *Entrance requirements:* For master's and doctorate, GRE General Test, minimum GPA of 3.0. Additional exam requirements/recommendations for international students: Required—TOEFL (minimum score 550 paper-based; 213 computer-based; 79 iBT). *Application deadline:* For fall admission, 1/25 priority date for domestic students, 5/15 for international students; for spring admission, 10/15 for international students. Applications are processed on a rolling basis. Application fee: $25. Electronic applications accepted. *Financial support:* In 2006–07, 23 students received support, including 1 fellowship with full and partial tuition reimbursement available (averaging $23,678 per year), 10 research assistantships with full and partial tuition reimbursements available (averaging $11,750 per year), 5 teaching assistantships with partial tuition reimbursements available (averaging $10,210 per year); career-related internships or fieldwork, institutionally sponsored loans, tuition waivers (full and partial), and unspecified assistantships also available. Financial award application deadline: 3/1; financial award applicants required to submit FAFSA. *Faculty research:* Adult education, history and philosophy of vocational education, curriculum and instruction, career decision making. *Unit head:* Dr. Michael F. Burnett, Director, 225-578-5748, Fax: 225-578-2526, E-mail: vocbur@lsu.edu.

Montclair State University, The Graduate School, College of Education and Human Services, Department of Curriculum and Teaching, Montclair, NJ 07043-1624. Offers education (M Ed); educational technology (M Ed); school library media specialist (Certificate); teaching (MAT, Certificate), including art (MAT), biological science (MAT), early childhood education (P-3) (MAT), earth science (MAT), elementary education (K-8) (MAT), English (MAT), French (MAT), health and physical education (MAT), health education (MAT), home economics (MAT), mathematics (MAT), music (MAT), physical education (MAT), physical science (MAT), social studies (MAT), Spanish (MAT), teacher of ESL (MAT), teacher of students with disabilities (MAT). Part-time and evening/weekend programs available. *Faculty:* 16 full-time (12 women), 13 part-time/adjunct (8 women). *Students:* 147 full-time (113 women), 230 part-time (188 women); includes 58 minority (33 African Americans, 1 American Indian/Alaska Native, 12 Asian Americans or Pacific Islanders, 12 Hispanic Americans), 4 international. Average age 33. 118 applicants, 38% accepted, 37 enrolled. In 2006, 166 master's, 11 other advanced degrees awarded. *Degree requirements:* For master's, field experience. *Entrance requirements:* For master's, PRAXIS II, minimum GPA of 2.67, 2 letters of recommendation. Additional exam requirements/recommendations for international students: Required—TOEFL (minimum score 83 computer-based). *Application deadline:* For fall admission, 2/15 for domestic and international students; for spring admission, 9/15 for domestic and international students. Applications are processed on a rolling basis. Application fee: $60. Electronic applications accepted. *Expenses:* Tuition, state resident: part-time $450 per credit. Tuition, nonresident: part-time $682 per credit. Tuition and fees vary according to degree level and program. *Financial support:* In 2006–07, 7 research assistantships with full tuition reimbursements (averaging $7,000 per year) were awarded; Federal Work-Study, scholarships/grants, and unspecified assistantships also available. Support available to part-time students. Financial award application deadline: 3/1; financial award applicants required to submit FAFSA. *Unit head:* Dr. Deborah Eldridge, Chairperson, 973-655-5187.

Northwestern State University of Louisiana, Graduate Studies and Research, College of Education, Programs in Education, Natchitoches, LA 71497. Offers business and distributive education (M Ed); counseling (M Ed); early childhood education (M Ed); education (M Ed); education leadership (M Ed); educational technology (M Ed); elementary teaching (M Ed); English education (M Ed); home economics education (M Ed); mathematics education (M Ed); reading (M Ed); science education (M Ed); secondary teaching (M Ed); social sciences education (M Ed). *Students:* 49 full-time (41 women), 245 part-time (206 women); includes 78 minority (70 African Americans, 5 American Indian/Alaska Native, 2 Asian Americans or Pacific Islanders, 1 Hispanic American). Average age 35. In 2006, 158 degrees awarded. *Degree requirements:* For master's, thesis or alternative, comprehensive exam, registration. *Entrance requirements:* For master's, GRE General Test, minimum undergraduate GPA of 2.5. *Application contact:* Dr. Steven G. Horton, Associate Provost/Dean, Graduate Studies, Research, and Information Systems, 318-357-5851, Fax: 318-357-5019, E-mail: grad_school@nsula.edu.

The Ohio State University, Graduate School, College of Education and Human Ecology, Program in Family and Consumer Sciences Education, Columbus, OH 43210. Offers M Ed, MS. *Accreditation:* ADtA. *Faculty:* 8. *Students:* Average age 47. *Degree requirements:* For master's, thesis optional. *Entrance requirements:* For master's, GRE General Test. Additional exam requirements/recommendations for international students: Required—TOEFL (minimum score 577 paper-based; 233 computer-based). *Application deadline:* For fall admission, 8/15 priority date for domestic students, 7/1 priority date for international students; for winter admission, 12/1 priority date for domestic students, 11/1 priority date for international students; for spring admission, 3/1 priority date for domestic students, 2/1 priority date for international students. Applications are processed on a rolling basis. Application fee: $40 ($50 for international students). Electronic applications accepted. *Expenses:* Tuition, state resident: full-time $9,438. Tuition, nonresident: full-time $22,791. Tuition and fees vary according to course load, campus/location and program. *Financial support:* Fellowships, research assistantships, teaching assistantships, Federal Work-Study and institutionally sponsored loans available. Support available to part-time students. *Unit head:* Albert Davis, Graduate Studies Committee Chair, 614-292-7705, Fax: 614-292-2581, E-mail: davis.7@osu.edu. *Application contact:* 614-292-9444, Fax: 614-292-3895, E-mail: domestic.grad@osu.edu.

Purdue University, Graduate School, School of Education, Department of Curriculum and Instruction, West Lafayette, IN 47907. Offers agricultural and extension education (PhD, Ed S); agriculture and extension education (MS, MS Ed); art education (PhD); consumer and family sciences and extension education (MS Ed, PhD, Ed S); curriculum studies (MS Ed, PhD, Ed S); educational technology (MS Ed, PhD, Ed S); elementary education (MS Ed); foreign language education (MS Ed, PhD, Ed S); industrial technology (PhD, Ed S); language arts (MS Ed, PhD, Ed S); literacy (MS Ed, PhD, Ed S); mathematics/science education (MS, MS Ed, PhD, Ed S); social studies (MS Ed, PhD); social studies education (Ed S); vocational/industrial education (MS Ed, PhD, Ed S); vocational/technical education (MS Ed, PhD, Ed S). *Accreditation:* NCATE. Part-time and evening/weekend programs available. *Faculty:* 26 full-time (13 women), 3 part-time/adjunct (all women). *Students:* 59 full-time (37 women), 112 part-time (70 women); includes 24 minority (13 African Americans, 3 American Indian/Alaska Native, 4 Asian Americans or Pacific Islanders, 4 Hispanic Americans), 38 international. Average age 35. 92 applicants, 68% accepted, 38 enrolled. In 2006, 52 master's, 23 doctorates awarded. *Degree requirements:* For master's, thesis optional; for doctorate, thesis/dissertation, oral and written exams; for Ed S, oral presentation, project. *Entrance requirements:* For master's, GRE General Test, minimum B average; for doctorate, GRE General Test; for Ed S, GRE, minimum B average. Additional exam requirements/recommendations for international students: Required—TOEFL. *Application deadline:* For fall admission, 1/15 priority date for domestic students, 1/15 for international students; for spring admission, 9/15 for domestic and international students. Applications are processed on a rolling basis. Application fee: $55. Electronic applications accepted. *Financial support:* In 2006–07, 3 fellowships with full tuition reimbursements (averaging $10,500 per year), 11 research assistantships with full tuition reimbursements (averaging $11,500 per year), 43 teaching assistantships with full tuition reimbursements (averaging $10,800 per year) were awarded; career-related internships or fieldwork and tuition waivers (full) also available. Support available to part-time students. Financial award application deadline: 3/1; financial award applicants required to submit FAFSA. *Faculty research:* Literacy acquisition and development, teacher beliefs and knowledge, recruitment and retention of underrepresented students, economic education, literacy discourse. *Unit head:* Dr. James D Lehman, Head, 765-494-7935, Fax: 765-496-1622. *Application contact:* Patricia Mason, Coordinator of Graduate Studies, 765-494-2345, Fax: 765-494-5832, E-mail: gradoffice@soe.purdue.edu.

Queens College of the City University of New York, Division of Graduate Studies, Mathematics and Natural Sciences Division, Department of Family, Nutrition and Exercise Sciences, Flushing, NY 11367-1597. Offers home economics (MS Ed); physical education and exercise sciences (MS Ed). Part-time and evening/weekend programs available. *Faculty:* 12 full-time (7 women). *Students:* 2 full-time (0 women), 57 part-time (46 women). 53 applicants, 100% accepted, 32 enrolled. In 2006, 2 degrees awarded. *Degree requirements:* For master's, research project. *Entrance requirements:* For master's, minimum GPA of 3.0. Additional exam requirements/recommendations for international students: Required—TOEFL. *Application deadline:* For fall admission, 4/1 for domestic students; for spring admission, 11/1 for domestic students. Applications are processed on a rolling basis. Application fee: $125. *Financial support:* Career-related internships or fieldwork, Federal Work-Study, institutionally sponsored loans, tuition waivers (partial), and adjunct lectureships available. Support available to part-time students. Financial award application deadline: 4/1; financial award applicants required to submit FAFSA. *Faculty research:* Exercise and environmental physiology, interdisciplinary approaches to school curricula using outdoor education, program development in cardiac rehabilitation and adult fitness, nutrition education. *Unit head:* Dr. Elizabeth Lowe, Chairperson, 718-997-4168. *Application contact:* Mario Caruso, Director of Graduate Admissions, 718-997-5200, Fax: 718-997-5193, E-mail: graduate_admissions@qc.edu.

South Carolina State University, School of Graduate Studies, Department of Education, Orangeburg, SC 29117-0001. Offers early childhood and special education (M Ed); early childhood education (MAT); elementary education (M Ed, MAT); engineering (MAT); general science (MAT); mathematics (MAT); secondary education (M Ed), including biology education, business education, counselor education, English education, home economics education, industrial education, mathematics education, science education, social studies education; special education (M Ed), including emotionally handicapped, learning disabilities, mentally handicapped. *Accreditation:* NCATE. Part-time and evening/weekend programs available. *Faculty:* 21 full-time (10 women), 4 part-time/adjunct (0 women). *Students:* 34 full-time (28 women), 33 part-time (25 women); includes 63 minority (61 African Americans, 1 American Indian/Alaska Native, 1 Asian American or Pacific Islander). Average age 35. 46 applicants, 67% accepted, 19 enrolled. In 2006, 28 degrees awarded. *Degree requirements:* For master's, departmental qualifying exam, thesis optional. *Entrance requirements:* For master's, GRE General Test, NTE, interview, teaching certificate. *Application deadline:* For fall admission, 6/15 priority date for domestic students, 6/15 for international students; for spring admission, 11/1 for domestic and international students. Applications are processed on a rolling basis. Application fee: $25. Electronic applications accepted. *Expenses:* Tuition, state resident: full-time $7,278. Tuition, nonresident: full-time $14,322. *Financial support:* Fellowships, research assistantships, career-related internships or fieldwork, Federal Work-Study, and institutionally sponsored loans available. Financial award application deadline: 6/1. *Faculty research:* Critical thinking, child abuse, stress, test-taking skills, conflict resolution, mainstreaming. *Unit head:* Dr. Gail Joyner-Fleming, Interim Chair, 803-533-3769, Fax: 803-536-8492, E-mail: zf-gfleming@scsu.edu. *Application contact:* Annette Hazzard-Jones, Program Coordinator II, 803-536-8809, Fax: 803-536-8812, E-mail: zs_ahazzard@scsu.edu.

State University of New York College at Oneonta, Graduate Studies, Division of Education, Department of Adolescence Education, Oneonta, NY 13820-4015. Offers adolescence education (MS Ed); family and consumer science education (MS Ed). *Accreditation:* NCATE. Part-time and evening/weekend programs available. *Entrance requirements:* For master's, GRE General Test.

Texas Tech University, Graduate School, College of Human Sciences, Department of Applied and Professional Studies, Program in Family and Consumer Sciences Education, Lubbock, TX 79409. Offers MS, PhD, Certificate. Part-time and evening/weekend programs available. *Students:* 6 full-time (5 women), 19 part-time (13 women); includes 2 minority (1 American Indian/Alaska Native, 1 Hispanic American), 3 international. Average age 36. 16 applicants, 63% accepted, 5 enrolled. In 2006, 4 master's, 3 doctorates awarded. Terminal master's awarded for partial completion of doctoral program. *Degree requirements:* For master's, thesis optional; for doctorate, thesis/dissertation. *Entrance requirements:* For master's and doctorate, GRE General Test. Additional exam requirements/recommendations for international students: Required—TOEFL (minimum score 500 paper-based; 213 computer-based). *Application deadline:* For fall admission, 3/1 priority date for international students; for spring admission, 11/1 priority date for international students. Applications are processed on a rolling basis. Application fee: $50 ($60 for international students). Electronic applications accepted. *Expenses:* Tuition, state resident: full-time $4,440. Tuition, nonresident: full-time $11,040. Required fees: $2,136. *Financial support:* Research assistantships with partial tuition reimbursements, teaching assistantships with partial tuition reimbursements, career-related internships or fieldwork, Federal Work-Study, institutionally sponsored loans, and scholarships/grants available. Support available to part-time students. Financial award application deadline: 4/15; financial award applicants required to submit FAFSA. *Faculty research:* Work and family interaction, intergenerational initiatives, gender equity, curriculum, supervision. *Unit head:* Sue Couch, Director, 806-742-5050.

The University of British Columbia, Faculty of Graduate Studies, Faculty of Education, Department of Curriculum Studies, Vancouver, BC V6T 1Z1, Canada. Offers art education (M Ed, MA); curriculum studies (M Ed, MA, PhD); home economics education (M Ed, MA); math education (M Ed, MA); music education (M Ed, MA); physical education (M Ed, MA); science education (M Ed, MA); social studies education (M Ed, MA); technical studies education (M Ed, MA). Part-time programs available. *Faculty:* 31 full-time (17 women), 1 (woman) part-time/adjunct. *Students:* 153 full-time (102 women), 101 part-time (67 women), 25 international. Average age 40. 118 applicants, 64% accepted, 62 enrolled. In 2006, 46 master's, 4 doctorates awarded. *Degree requirements:* For master's, thesis (MA); for doctorate, thesis/dissertation, comprehensive exam, registration. *Entrance requirements:* Additional exam requirements/recommendations for international students: Required—TOEFL (minimum score 580 paper-based; 237 computer-based). *Application deadline:* For fall admission, 2/1 for domestic students, 1/1 for international students; for spring admission, 10/1 for domestic students, 9/1 for international students. Application fee: $90 ($150 for international students). Electronic applications accepted. *Expenses:* Contact institution. *Financial support:* In 2006–07, 10 fellowships with partial tuition reimbursements (averaging $16,000 per year), 11 research assistantships with partial tuition reimbursements (averaging $14,000 per year), 27 teaching assistantships with partial tuition reimbursements (averaging $14,000 per year) were awarded; tuition waivers (partial) also available. *Faculty research:* School subjects, teaching and learning. *Unit head:* Dr. Linda Peterat, Interim Head, 604-822-5422, Fax: 604-822-4714. *Application contact:* Basia Zurek, Graduate Secretary, 604-822-5367, Fax: 604-822-4714, E-mail: cust.grad@ubc.ca.

University of Central Oklahoma, College of Graduate Studies and Research, College of Education, Department of Human Environmental Sciences, Edmond, OK 73034-5209. Offers family and child studies (MS); family and consumer science education (MS); interior design (MS); nutrition-food management (MS). Part-time programs available. *Entrance requirements:* Additional exam requirements/recommendations for international students: Required—TOEFL (minimum score 550 paper-based; 213 computer-based). Electronic applications accepted. *Faculty research:* Dietetics and food science.

University of Indianapolis, Graduate Programs, School of Business, Graduate Business Programs, Indianapolis, IN 46227-3697. Offers business (EMBA); business administration (MBA); finance (Graduate Certificate); global supply chains management (Graduate Certificate); marketing (Graduate Certificate); organizational leadership (Graduate Certificate); technology management (Graduate Certificate). *Accreditation:* ACBSP. Part-time and evening/weekend programs available. *Faculty:* 6 full-time (2 women), 6 part-time/adjunct (1 woman). *Students:* 50 full-time (16 women), 92 part-time (32 women); includes 12 minority (4 African Americans, 7 Asian Americans or Pacific Islanders, 1 Hispanic American), 10 international. Average age 32. In 2006, 57 degrees awarded. *Entrance requirements:* For master's, GMAT, interview, minimum GPA of 2.8, 2 letters of recommendation, resumé. Additional exam requirements/recommendations for international students: Required—TOEFL (minimum score 550 paper-based; 213 computer-based). *Application deadline:* Applications are processed on a rolling basis. Application fee: $50. *Expenses:* Contact institution. *Financial support:* Federal Work-Study and unspecified assistantships available. Financial award application deadline: 5/1; financial award applicants required to submit FAFSA. *Faculty research:* Integration of microcomputers into decision making, communication skills, application of synthesized theories. *Unit head:* Dr. Matthew Will, Associate Dean, 317-788-3370, E-mail: mwill@uindy.edu.

Utah State University, School of Graduate Studies, College of Agriculture, Department of Agricultural Systems Technology and Education, Logan, UT 84322. Offers agricultural systems technology (MS), including agricultural extension education, agricultural mechanization, international agricultural extension, secondary and postsecondary agricultural education; family and consumer sciences education (MS). Part-time programs available. Postbaccalaureate distance learning degree programs offered (minimal on-campus study). *Faculty:* 11 full-time (4 women), 2 part-time/adjunct (1 woman). *Students:* 14 full-time (7 women), 6 part-time (4 women); includes 1 minority (Hispanic American) Average age 30. 20 applicants, 100% accepted, 15 enrolled. In 2006, 14 degrees awarded. *Degree requirements:* For master's, thesis (for some programs), comprehensive exam (for some programs), registration. *Entrance requirements:* For master's, GRE General Test, MAT, BS in agricultural education, agricultural extension, or related agricultural or science discipline; minimum GPA of 3.0. Additional exam requirements/recommendations for international students: Required—TOEFL. *Application deadline:* For fall admission, 7/1 priority date for domestic and international students; for spring admission, 11/1 priority date for domestic and international students. Applications are processed on a rolling basis. Application fee: $50 ($60 for international students). *Financial support:* In 2006–07, 3 research assistantships (averaging $10,000 per year) were awarded; career-related internships or fieldwork, Federal Work-Study, institutionally sponsored loans, and tuition waivers (partial) also available. Support available to part-time students. Financial award application deadline: 2/1. *Faculty research:* Extension and adult education; structures and environment; low-input agriculture; farm safety, systems, and mechanizations. Total annual research expenditures: $310,000. *Unit head:* Dr. Bruce E. Miller, Head, 435-797-2232, Fax: 435-797-4002, E-mail: bruce.miller@usu.edu. *Application contact:* Lazell W. Allen, Staff Assistant II, 435-797-2230, Fax: 435-797-4002, E-mail: lazella@cc.usu.edu.

Wayne State College, School of Education and Counseling, Department of Educational Foundations and Leadership, Program in Curriculum and Instruction, Wayne, NE 68787. Offers alternative education (MSE); business education (MSE); communication arts education (MSE); curriculum and instruction (MSE); early childhood education (MSE); elementary education (MSE); English as a second language (MSE); English education (MSE); family consumer science of education (MSE); industrial technology education (MSE); learning communities (MSE); mathematics education (MSE); music education (MSE); science education (MSE); social science education (MSE). *Accreditation:* NCATE. Part-time and evening/weekend programs available. *Faculty:* 17 part-time/adjunct (11 women). *Students:* 17 full-time (10 women), 307 part-time (248 women); includes 6 minority (2 African Americans, 1 American Indian/Alaska Native, 2 Asian Americans or Pacific Islanders, 1 Hispanic American), 1 international. Average age 35. In 2006, 167 degrees awarded. *Degree requirements:* For master's, thesis optional. *Entrance requirements:* For master's, GRE General Test. Additional exam requirements/recommendations for international students: Required—TOEFL (minimum score 550 paper-based; 213 computer-based). *Application deadline:* Applications are processed on a rolling basis. Application fee: $30. *Expenses:* Tuition, state resident: full-time $3,114; part-time $130 per credit hour. Tuition, nonresident: full-time $6,228; part-time $260 per credit hour. Required fees: $894; $37 per credit hour. Tuition and fees vary according to course load. *Financial support:* Applicants required to submit FAFSA.

Wayne State College, School of Natural and Social Sciences, Department of Health, Human Performance and Sport, Wayne, NE 68787. Offers exercise science (MSE); organization management (MSE), including sport and recreation management. Part-time and evening/weekend programs available. *Faculty:* 6 part-time/adjunct (2 women). *Students:* 15 full-time (3 women), 6 part-time (1 woman); includes 3 minority (all African Americans), 2 international. Average age 27. In 2006, 11 degrees awarded. *Degree requirements:* For master's, thesis optional. *Entrance requirements:* For master's, GRE General Test, minimum GPA of 3.0. Additional exam requirements/recommendations for international students: Required—TOEFL (minimum score 550 paper-based; 213 computer-based). *Application deadline:* Applications are processed on a rolling basis. Application fee: $30. Electronic applications accepted. *Expenses:* Tuition, state resident: full-time $3,114; part-time $130 per credit hour. Tuition, nonresident: full-time $6,228; part-time $260 per credit hour. Required fees: $894; $37 per credit hour. Tuition and fees vary according to course load. *Financial support:* In 2006–07, 3 teaching assistantships with full tuition reimbursements (averaging $4,000 per year) were awarded; career-related internships or fieldwork also available. Financial award applicants required to submit FAFSA. *Unit head:* Dr. Kevin Hill, Dean, 402-375-7030.

Western Carolina University, Graduate School, College of Education and Allied Professions, Department of Educational Leadership and Foundations, Programs in Secondary Education, Cullowhee, NC 28723. Offers art education (MAT); biology (MAT); chemistry (MAT); comprehensive education (MA Ed), including art, biology, English, mathematics, music, physical education, reading, social sciences; English (MAT); family and consumer sciences (MAT); mathematics (MAT); physical education (MAT); reading (MAT); social sciences (MAT). *Accreditation:* NCATE (one or more programs are accredited). Part-time and evening/weekend programs available. *Degree requirements:* For master's, comprehensive exam. *Entrance requirements:* For master's, GRE General Test, portfolio. Additional exam requirements/recommendations for international students: Required—TOEFL (minimum score 550 paper-based; 213 computer-based).

Mathematics Education

Acadia University, Faculty of Professional Studies, School of Education, Program in Curriculum Studies, Wolfville, NS B4P 2R6, Canada. Offers cultural and media studies (M Ed); inclusive education (M Ed); learning and technology (M Ed); science, math and technology (M Ed). Evening/weekend programs available. *Faculty:* 12 full-time (5 women). *Students:* 2 full-time (both women), 27 part-time (19 women). In 2006, 25 degrees awarded. *Degree requirements:* For master's, thesis optional. *Entrance requirements:* For master's, B Ed or the equivalent, minimum B average in undergraduate course work, 2 years of teaching experience. Additional exam requirements/recommendations for international students: Required—TOEFL (minimum score 580 paper-based; 237 computer-based). *Application deadline:* For fall admission, 3/15 priority date for domestic and international students. Application fee: $50. Electronic applications accepted. *Financial support:* Teaching assistantships available. Financial award application deadline: 2/1. *Faculty research:* Literacy development, postmodern philosophy and curriculum theory, historiography, philosophy of education, learning and technology. *Application contact:* Sheila Langille, Secretary, 902-585-1229, Fax: 902-585-1071, E-mail: sheila.langille@acadiau.ca.

Agnes Scott College, Secondary Mathematics and Science Program, Decatur, GA 30030-3797. Offers secondary biology (MAT); secondary chemistry (MAT); secondary math (MAT); secondary physics (MAT). *Faculty:* 5 full-time (3 women), 3 part-time/adjunct (2 women). *Students:* 3 full-time (all women). Average age 38. 3 applicants, 100% accepted, 3 enrolled. *Entrance requirements:* For master's, GRE, PRAXIS I, minimum GPA of 3.0, undergraduate major in the discipline. *Application deadline:* For spring admission, 4/1 priority date for domestic and international students. Application fee: $35. *Expenses:* Tuition: Full-time $21,840; part-time $445 per hour. Required fees: $375. *Faculty research:* Science education in urban high schools, inquiry-based science curricula, pedagogy and gender equity in teaching mathematics. *Unit head:* Dr. Myrtle H. Lewin, Professor and Chair, 404-471-6201, Fax: 404-471-5152, E-mail: mlewin@agnesscott.edu. *Application contact:* Lisa M. Flowers, Education Faculty Coordinator, 404-471-5168, Fax: 404-471-5152, E-mail: lflowers@agnesscott.edu.

See Close-Up on page 1599.

Alabama State University, School of Graduate Studies, College of Arts and Sciences, Department of Mathematics and Computer Science, Montgomery, AL 36101-0271. Offers mathematics (M Ed, MS, Ed S). Part-time programs available. *Faculty:* 5 full-time (0 women). *Students:* 5 full-time (1 woman), 2 part-time (1 woman). In 2006, 3 degrees awarded. *Degree requirements:* For Ed S, thesis. *Entrance requirements:* For master's, GRE, GRE Subject Test, graduate writing competence test; for Ed S, graduate writing competency test, GRE, MAT. Additional exam requirements/recommendations for international students: Required—TOEFL (minimum score 500 paper-based; 173 computer-based). *Application deadline:* For fall admission, 7/15 for domestic students; for spring admission, 12/15 for domestic students. Applications are processed on a rolling basis. Application fee: $10. *Expenses:* Tuition, area resident: Part-time $192 per hour. Tuition, state resident: full-time $1,728; part-time $334 per hour. Tuition, nonresident: full-time $3,456. *Financial support:* In 2006–07, 1 research assistantship (averaging $9,450 per year) was awarded. *Faculty research:* Discrete mathematics, symbolic dynamics, mathematical social sciences. Total annual research expenditures: $25,000. *Unit head:* Dr. Wallace Maryland, Chair, 334-229-4464, Fax: 334-229-4902, E-mail: wmaryl@asunet.alasu.edu.

Alabama State University, School of Graduate Studies, College of Education, Department of Curriculum and Instruction, Program in Secondary Education, Montgomery, AL 36101-0271. Offers biology education (M Ed, Ed S); English/language arts (M Ed); history education (M Ed, Ed S); mathematics education (M Ed); secondary education (Ed S); social studies (Ed S). Part-time programs available. *Students:* 31 full-time (23 women), 123 part-time (81 women); includes 114 minority (111 African Americans, 2 Asian Americans or Pacific Islanders, 1 Hispanic American), 1 international. In 2006, 27 degrees awarded. *Degree requirements:* For master's, comprehensive exam; for Ed S, thesis, comprehensive exam. *Entrance requirements:* For master's, GRE General Test, MAT, graduate writing competency test; for Ed S, graduate writing competency test, GRE, MAT. Additional exam requirements/recommendations for international students: Required—TOEFL (minimum score 500 paper-based; 173 computer-based). *Application deadline:* For fall admission, 7/15 for domestic students; for spring admission, 12/15 for domestic students. Applications are processed on a rolling basis. Application fee: $10. *Expenses:* Tuition, state resident: full-time $1,728; part-time $192 per hour. Tuition, nonresident: full-time $3,456; part-time $334 per hour. *Financial support:* In 2006–07, research assistantships (averaging $9,450 per year).

Albany State University, College of Education, Program in Mathematics Education, Albany, GA 31705-2717. Offers M Ed. *Accreditation:* NCATE. Part-time programs available. *Degree requirements:* For master's, comprehensive exam. *Entrance requirements:* For master's, GRE General Test, MAT or NTE. Electronic applications accepted. *Faculty research:* Instructional technology.

Appalachian State University, Cratis D. Williams Graduate School, College of Arts and Sciences, Department of Mathematics, Boone, NC 28608. Offers mathematics (MA); mathematics education (MA). Part-time programs available. *Faculty:* 19 full-time (9 women). *Students:* 16 full-time (6 women), 13 part-time (9 women); includes 2 minority (both African Americans) Average age 24. 13 applicants, 100% accepted, 12 enrolled. In 2006, 11 degrees awarded. *Degree requirements:* For master's, one foreign language, comprehensive exam, registration. *Entrance requirements:* For master's, GRE General Test. Additional exam requirements/recommendations for international students: Required—TOEFL (minimum score 570 paper-based; 230 computer-based). *Application deadline:* For fall admission, 7/1 for domestic students, 1/1 for international students; for spring admission, 11/1 for domestic students, 6/1 for international students. Application fee: $50. *Expenses:* Tuition, state resident: full-time $2,600; part-time $127 per hour. Tuition, nonresident: full-time $13,200; part-time $597 per hour. Required fees: $2,000; $546 per term. *Financial support:* In 2006–07, 16 teaching assistantships were awarded; fellowships, research assistantships, career-related internships or fieldwork, Federal Work-Study, scholarships/grants, and unspecified assistantships also available. Support available to part-time students. Financial award application deadline: 7/1. *Faculty research:* Graph theory, differential equations, logic, geometry, complex analysis. *Unit head:* Dr. Mark Ginn, Chair, 828-262-3050, Fax: 828-265-8617, E-mail: ginnmc@appstate.edu. *Application contact:* Dr. Richard Klima, Graduate Director, 828-262-3050, E-mail: klimare@math.appstate.edu.

Arcadia University, Graduate Studies, Department of Education, Glenside, PA 19038-3295. Offers art education (M Ed, MA Ed); biology education (MA Ed); chemistry education (MA Ed); child development (CAS); computer education (M Ed, CAS); computer education 7–12 (MA Ed); early childhood education (M Ed, CAS), including individualized (M Ed), master teacher (M Ed), research in child development (M Ed); educational leadership (M Ed, CAS); educational psychology (CAS); elementary education (M Ed, CAS); English education (MA Ed); environmental education (MA Ed, CAS); history education (MA Ed); language arts (M Ed, CAS); mathematics education (M Ed, MA Ed, CAS); music education (MA Ed); psychology (MA Ed); pupil personnel services (CAS); reading (M Ed, CAS); school library science (M Ed); science education (M Ed, CAS); secondary education (M Ed, CAS); special education (M Ed, Ed D, CAS); theater arts (MA Ed); written communication (MA Ed). *Accreditation:* NASAD. Part-time and evening/weekend programs available. Postbaccalaureate distance learning degree programs offered (minimal on-campus study). *Faculty:* 12 full-time (8 women), 38 part-time/adjunct (26 women). *Students:* 60 full-time (56 women), 419 part-time (324 women); includes 70 minority (57 African Americans, 1 American Indian/Alaska Native, 6 Asian Americans or Pacific Islanders, 6 Hispanic Americans), 1 international. In 2006, 257 master's, 4 doctorates awarded. *Application deadline:* Applications are processed on a rolling basis. Application fee: $35. Electronic applications accepted. *Financial support:* Career-related internships or fieldwork, tuition waivers (partial), and unspecified assistantships available. *Unit head:* Dr. Steven P. Gulkus, Chair, 215-572-2120. *Application contact:* 215-572-2925, Fax: 215-572-2126, E-mail: grad@arcadia.edu.

Arkansas Tech University, Graduate School, School of System Science, Russellville, AR 72801. Offers information technology (MS); mathematics (M Ed). Part-time programs available. *Students:* 45 full-time (8 women), 30 part-time (8 women); includes 2 minority (1 American Indian/Alaska Native, 1 Asian American or Pacific Islander), 40 international. Average age 29. In 2006, 29 degrees awarded. *Degree requirements:* For master's, internship. *Entrance requirements:* For master's, GRE General Test. Additional exam requirements/recommendations for international students: Required—TOEFL (minimum score 500 paper-based; 173 computer-based). *Application deadline:* For fall admission, 3/1 priority date for domestic students, 5/1 priority date for international students; for winter admission, 10/1 priority date for international students; for spring admission, 10/1 priority date for domestic and international students. Applications are processed on a rolling basis. Application fee: $0 ($30 for international students). Electronic applications accepted. *Expenses:* Tuition, state resident: full-time $3,060; part-time $170 per hour. Tuition, nonresident: full-time $6,120; part-time $340 per hour. Required fees: $312; $4 per hour. $84 per term. Part-time tuition and fees vary according to course load. *Financial support:* In 2006–07, teaching assistantships with full tuition reimbursements (averaging $4,000 per year); career-related internships or fieldwork, Federal Work-Study, scholarships/grants, health care benefits, and unspecified assistantships also available. Support available to part-time students. Financial award application deadline: 4/15; financial award applicants required to submit FAFSA. *Unit head:* Dr. John Watson, Dean, 479-968-0353 Ext. 501, E-mail: john.watson@atu.edu. *Application contact:* Dr. Eldon G. Clary, Dean of Graduate School, 479-968-0398, Fax: 479-964-0542, E-mail: graduate.school@atu.edu.

Armstrong Atlantic State University, School of Graduate Studies, Program in Education, Savannah, GA 31419-1997. Offers adult education (M Ed); early childhood education (M Ed); education (M Ed); elementary education (M Ed); middle grades education (M Ed); secondary education (M Ed), including business education, English education, mathematics education, science education, social science education; special education (M Ed), including behavioral disorders, curriculum and instruction, learning disabilities, speech-language pathology. *Accreditation:* NCATE. Part-time and evening/weekend programs available. Postbaccalaureate distance learning degree programs offered (minimal on-campus study). *Faculty:* 11 full-time (9 women), 13 part-time/adjunct (10 women). *Students:* 50 full-time (42 women), 219 part-time (175 women); includes 71 minority (67 African Americans, 3 Asian Americans or Pacific Islanders, 1 Hispanic American), 6 international. Average age 35. In 2006, 151 degrees awarded. *Degree requirements:* For master's, portfolio. *Entrance requirements:* For master's, GRE General Test or MAT, minimum GPA of 2.5, letters of recommendation. Additional exam requirements/recommendations for international students: Required—TOEFL (minimum score 523 paper-based; 193 computer-based). *Application deadline:* For fall admission, 7/1 priority date for domestic and international students; for spring admission, 11/15 priority date for domestic and international students. Applications are processed on a rolling basis. Application fee: $25. Electronic applications accepted. *Expenses:* Tuition, state resident: full-time $2,286; part-time $127 per credit. Tuition, nonresident: full-time $9,144; part-time $508 per credit. One-time fee: $257. *Financial support:* In 2006–07, research assistantships with partial tuition reimbursements (averaging $2,500 per year); career-related internships or fieldwork, Federal Work-Study, scholarships/grants, and unspecified assistantships also available. Support available to part-time students. Financial award applicants required to submit FAFSA. *Unit head:* Dr. Jane McHaney, College of Education Dean, 912-927-5398, Fax: 912-921-7425, E-mail: mchaneia@mail.armstrong.edu.

Asbury College, Graduate Programs, Wilmore, KY 40390-1198. Offers biology: alternative certificate (MA Ed); chemistry: alternative certificate (MA Ed); English (Certificate); English as a second language (MA Ed); ESL (Certificate); French (Certificate); mathematics: alternative certificate (MA Ed); reading / writing (MA Ed); social studies (Certificate); Spanish (Certificate); special education (MA Ed); special education: alternative certificate (MA Ed). *Accreditation:* NCATE. Part-time programs available. *Faculty:* 8 full-time (7 women), 9 part-time/adjunct (4 women). *Students:* Average age 36. 14 applicants, 100% accepted, 10 enrolled. In 2006, 17 degrees awarded. *Median time to degree:* Master's–2.5 years part-time. *Degree requirements:* For master's, action research project, portfolio. *Entrance requirements:* For master's, PRAXIS/NTE or GRE, minimum GPA of 2.75, letters of recommendation. Additional exam requirements/recommendations for international students: Recommended—TOEFL (minimum score 550 paper-based). *Application deadline:* Applications are processed on a rolling basis. Application fee: $25. *Expenses:* Tuition: Part-time $335 per credit hour. *Financial support:* Scholarships/grants and traineeships available. Financial award applicants required to submit FAFSA. *Unit head:* Dr. Bonnie J. Banker, Director, 859-858-3511 Ext. 2221, Fax: 859-858-3921, E-mail: bonnie.banker@asbury.edu. *Application contact:* Melanie S. Kinnell, Graduate Program Assistant and Certification Specialist, 859-858-3511 Ext. 2304, Fax: 859-858-3921, E-mail: graded@asbury.edu.

Auburn University, Graduate School, College of Education, Department of Curriculum and Teaching, Auburn University, AL 36849. Offers business education (M Ed, MS, PhD); early childhood education (M Ed, MS, PhD, Ed S); elementary education (M Ed, MS, PhD, Ed S); foreign languages (M Ed, MS); music education (M Ed, MS, PhD, Ed S); postsecondary education (PhD); reading education (PhD, Ed S); secondary education (M Ed, MS, PhD, Ed S), including English language arts, mathematics, science, social studies. *Accreditation:* NASM (one or more programs are accredited); NCATE. Part-time programs available. *Faculty:* 26 full-time (19 women). *Students:* 51 full-time (36 women), 116 part-time (86 women); includes 24 minority (23 African Americans, 1 Asian American or Pacific Islander). Average age 33. 181 applicants, 56% accepted, 68 enrolled. In 2006, 63 master's, 12 doctorates, 14 other advanced degrees awarded. *Degree requirements:* For master's, thesis (for some programs); for doctorate, thesis/dissertation; for Ed S, field project. *Entrance requirements:* For master's, doctorate, and Ed S, GRE General Test. *Application deadline:* For fall admission, 7/7 for domestic students; for spring admission, 11/24 for domestic students. Applications are processed on a rolling basis. Application fee: $25 ($50 for international students). Electronic applications accepted. *Expenses:* Tuition, state resident: full-time $5,000. Tuition, nonresident: full-time $15,000. Required fees: $416. Tuition and fees vary according to program. *Financial support:* Fellowships, teaching assistantships, career-related internships or fieldwork and Federal Work-Study available. Support available to part-time students. Financial award application deadline: 3/15. *Faculty research:* Emerging literacy, reading attitudes, music for at-risk youth, portfolio assessment. *Unit head:* Dr. Andrew M. Weaver, Head, 334-844-4434, E-mail: weaveam@mail.auburn.edu. *Application contact:* Dr. Joe Pittman, Interim Dean of the Graduate School, 334-844-4700.

Averett University, Graduate Studies in Education, Danville, VA 24541-3692. Offers art education (M Ed); biology (M Ed); chemistry (M Ed); curriculum and instruction (M Ed); elementary education (M Ed); English (M Ed); health and physical education (M Ed); history and social studies (M Ed); mathematics education (M Ed); physical science (M Ed); reading (M Ed); special education (learning disabilities specialization PK-12) (M Ed). Part-time and evening/weekend programs available. *Faculty:* 10 full-time (4 women), 7 part-time/adjunct (6 women). *Students:* 14 full-time (10 women), 85 part-time (67 women); includes 20 minority (18 African Americans, 2 Asian Americans or Pacific Islanders). Average age 33. 52 applicants, 100% accepted, 40 enrolled. In 2006, 48 degrees awarded. *Degree requirements:* For master's, thesis optional. *Entrance requirements:* For master's, PRAXIS, GRE General Test, MAT or NTE, writing proficiency exam, 3 letters of recommendation, current teacher's licensure or eligibility for licensure, minimum undergraduate GPA of 3.0 in previous 2 years. Additional exam requirements/recommendations for international students: Required—TOEFL (minimum score 600 paper-based; 200 computer-based). *Application deadline:* Applications are processed on a rolling basis. Application fee: $20. *Expenses:* Contact institution. *Financial support:* In

2006–07, 23 students received support. Federal Work-Study and scholarships/grants available. Financial award application deadline: 4/1; financial award applicants required to submit FAFSA. *Faculty research:* Literary assessment-PreK-6, handwriting instruction and assessment-PreK-6, written language instruction and assessment-PreK-6 and special needs students learning styles, curriculum and instruction processes. *Unit head:* Dr. Lynn H. Wolf, Chair, 434-793-3995, Fax: 434-791-4392, E-mail: lynn.wolf@averett.edu.

Ball State University, Graduate School, College of Sciences and Humanities, Department of Mathematical Sciences, Program in Mathematics, Muncie, IN 47306-1099. Offers mathematics (MA, MS); mathematics education (MAE). *Students:* 6 full-time (2 women), 9 part-time (7 women); includes 1 minority (Asian American or Pacific Islander), 2 international. Average age 39. 16 applicants, 69% accepted, 6 enrolled. In 2006, 1 degree awarded. Application fee: $25 ($35 for international students). *Financial support:* Research assistantships with full tuition reimbursements, teaching assistantships with tuition reimbursements available. Financial award application deadline: 3/1. *Unit head:* Dr. Richard Stankewitz, Director, 765-285-8662, Fax: 765-285-1721.

Bank Street College of Education, Graduate School, Department of Educational Leadership, New York, NY 10025. Offers early childhood leadership (MS Ed); educational leadership (MS Ed); leadership for educational change (Ed M, MS Ed); leadership in mathematics education (MS Ed); leadership in museum education (MS Ed); leadership in the arts (MS Ed). *Students:* 59 full-time (35 women), 137 part-time (100 women); includes 75 minority (31 African Americans, 1 American Indian/Alaska Native, 10 Asian Americans or Pacific Islanders, 33 Hispanic Americans), 5 international. Average age 36. 107 applicants, 89% accepted, 89 enrolled. In 2006, 88 degrees awarded. *Degree requirements:* For master's, thesis, registration. *Entrance requirements:* For master's, interview, minimum of 2 years experience in the classroom. Additional exam requirements/recommendations for international students: Required—TOEFL (minimum score 600 paper-based; 250 computer-based). *Application deadline:* For fall admission, 3/1 priority date for domestic students; for spring admission, 11/1 priority date for domestic students. Applications are processed on a rolling basis. Application fee: $50. *Expenses:* Tuition: Part-time $940 per credit. Required fees: $100 per term. *Financial support:* Career-related internships or fieldwork, Federal Work-Study, scholarships/grants, and unspecified assistantships available. Support available to part-time students. Financial award application deadline: 4/15; financial award applicants required to submit FAFSA. *Faculty research:* Leadership in small schools, mathematics education in elementary schools, professional development in early childhood, leadership in arts education, leadership in special education. *Unit head:* Dr. Rima Shore, Chairperson, 212-875-4478, Fax: 212-875-8753, E-mail: rshore@bankstreet.edu. *Application contact:* Ann Morgan, Director of Graduate Admissions, 212-875-4403, Fax: 212-875-4678, E-mail: amorgan@bankstreet.edu.

Belmont University, College of Arts and Sciences, School of Education, Nashville, TN 37212-3757. Offers education (MAT); elementary education (M Ed), including early childhood education, elementary education, gifted education, language arts education; English (M Ed); history (M Ed); mathematics (M Ed); middle grade education (M Ed); science (M Ed); secondary education (M Ed), including gifted education; sports administration (MSA); technology (M Ed). *Accreditation:* NCATE. Part-time and evening/weekend programs available. *Faculty:* 9 full-time (7 women), 20 part-time/adjunct (15 women). *Students:* 50 full-time (36 women), 116 part-time (76 women); includes 23 minority (20 African Americans, 1 Asian American or Pacific Islander, 2 Hispanic Americans), 1 international. Average age 30. 55 applicants, 60% accepted, 30 enrolled. In 2006, 82 degrees awarded. *Degree requirements:* For master's, thesis, comprehensive exam. *Entrance requirements:* For master's, MAT or GRE, minimum GPA of 2.75. Additional exam requirements/recommendations for international students: Required—TOEFL. *Application deadline:* For fall admission, 8/1 priority date for domestic students, 5/1 for international students; for spring admission, 12/1 priority date for domestic students, 9/1 for international students. Applications are processed on a rolling basis. Application fee: $50. *Expenses: Contact institution. Financial support:* In 2006–07, 25 students received support; fellowships with partial tuition reimbursements available, institutionally sponsored loans and tuition waivers (partial) available. Financial award application deadline: 4/15; financial award applicants required to submit FAFSA. *Faculty research:* Technology grant, professional development schools. Total annual research expenditures: $6,500. *Unit head:* Dr. Trevor F. Hutchins, Associate Dean, 615-460-6232, Fax: 615-460-6414, E-mail: hutchinst@mail.belmont.edu. *Application contact:* Julie Hullett, Admission/Licensure Officer, 615-460-6879, Fax: 615-460-5556, E-mail: hullettj@email.belmont.edu.

Bemidji State University, School of Graduate Studies, College of Social and Natural Sciences, Field of Mathematics, Bemidji, MN 56601-2699. Offers MS. Part-time programs available. *Faculty:* 12 full-time (3 women). *Students:* 1 full-time (0 women), 5 part-time (2 women). Average age 24. 3 applicants, 100% accepted. In 2006, 2 degrees awarded. *Entrance requirements:* Additional exam requirements/recommendations for international students: Required—TOEFL. *Application deadline:* For fall admission, 5/1 for domestic students. Applications are processed on a rolling basis. Application fee: $20. Electronic applications accepted. *Expenses:* Tuition, nonresident: part-time $284 per credit. Required fees: $86 per credit. *Financial support:* In 2006–07, 2 teaching assistantships with partial tuition reimbursements (averaging $8,250 per year) were awarded; career-related internships or fieldwork, Federal Work-Study, scholarships/grants, health care benefits, and unspecified assistantships also available. Support available to part-time students. Financial award application deadline: 5/1. *Unit head:* Dr. Randy Westhoff, Chair, 218-755-2831, Fax: 218-755-2822, E-mail: rwesthoff@bemidjistate.edu.

Bennington College, Graduate Programs, Program in Teaching, Bennington, VT 05201. Offers art education (MAT); early childhood (MAT); elementary education (MAT); English education (MAT); foreign language education (MAT); mathematics education (MAT); music education (MAT); science education (MAT); secondary education (MAT); social science education (MAT). *Faculty:* 4 part-time/adjunct (3 women). *Students:* 11 full-time (7 women), 1 (woman) part-time; includes 2 minority (both Hispanic Americans) Average age 31. 12 applicants, 75% accepted, 3 enrolled. In 2006, 13 degrees awarded. *Degree requirements:* For master's, 1 year teaching practicum, professional portfolio. *Entrance requirements:* For master's, interview. *Application deadline:* For fall admission, 3/1 for domestic students. Application fee: $60. *Expenses: Contact institution.* One-time fee: $75 full-time. Tuition and fees vary according to program. *Financial support:* In 2006–07, 10 students received support, including 4 fellowships (averaging $6,875 per year); scholarships/grants and unspecified assistantships also available. Financial award application deadline: 4/1; financial award applicants required to submit FAFSA. *Unit head:* George Kamberelis, Director of Center for Creative Teaching, 802-440-4863, E-mail: gkamberelis@bennington.edu. *Application contact:* Ken Himmelman, Dean of Admissions, 802-440-4312, Fax: 802-440-4320, E-mail: admissions@bennington.edu.

See Close-Up on page 861.

Bob Jones University, Graduate Programs, Greenville, SC 29614. Offers accountancy (MS); Bible (MA); Bible translation (MA); Biblical studies (Certificate); broadcast management (MS); business administration (MBA); church history (MA, PhD); church ministries (MA); church music (MM); cinema and video production (MA); counseling (MS); curriculum and instruction (Ed D); divinity (M Div); dramatic production (MA); educational leadership (MS, Ed D, Ed S); elementary education (M Ed, MAT); English (M Ed, MA, MAT); fine arts (MA); graphic design (MA); history (M Ed, MA); illustration (MA); interpretative speech (MA); mathematics (M Ed, MAT); medical missions (Certificate); ministry (MM, D Min); multi-categorical special education (M Ed, MAT); music (M Ed); New Testament interpretation (PhD); Old Testament interpretation (PhD); orchestral instrument performance (MM); organ performance (MM); pastoral studies (MA); personnel services (MS, Ed S); piano pedagogy (MM); piano performance (MM); platform arts (MA); radio and television broadcasting (MS); rhetoric and public address (MA); secondary education (M Ed); studio art (MA); teaching Bible (MA); theology (MA, PhD); voice performance (MM); youth ministries (MA); M Div/MM.

Boston College, Lynch Graduate School of Education, Department of Teacher Education/Special Education and Curriculum and Instruction, Program in Secondary Education, Chestnut Hill, MA 02467-3800. Offers biology (MST); chemistry (MST); English (MAT); French (MAT); geology (MST); history (MAT); Latin and classical humanities (MAT); mathematics (MST); physics (MST); secondary teaching (M Ed), including biology, chemistry, English, French, geology, history, Latin and classical humanities, mathematics, physics, Spanish; Spanish (MAT). *Students:* 70 full-time (46 women), 28 part-time (15 women); includes 8 minority (4 African Americans, 1 American Indian/Alaska Native, 3 Asian Americans or Pacific Islanders), 2 international. 217 applicants, 72% accepted, 64 enrolled. In 2006, 48 degrees awarded. *Degree requirements:* For master's, comprehensive exam. *Entrance requirements:* For master's, GRE General Test or MAT. Additional exam requirements/recommendations for international students: Required—TOEFL. *Application deadline:* For fall admission, 1/1 priority date for domestic students. Application fee: $60. *Financial support:* Fellowships with full and partial tuition reimbursements, research assistantships with full and partial tuition reimbursements, teaching assistantships with full and partial tuition reimbursements, career-related internships or fieldwork, Federal Work-Study, scholarships/grants, traineeships, tuition waivers (full and partial), and unspecified assistantships available. Support available to part-time students. Financial award applicants required to submit FAFSA. *Faculty research:* Curriculum theory and practice, teacher preparation, learning styles, teacher research. *Application contact:* Timothy P. Blackman, Director, Graduate Admission and Financial Aid, 617-552-4214, Fax: 617-552-0398, E-mail: timothy.blackman.1@bc.edu.

Boston University, School of Education, Department of Curriculum and Teaching, Program in Mathematics Education, Boston, MA 02215. Offers Ed M, MAT, Ed D, CAGS. *Students:* 7 full-time (4 women), 11 part-time (9 women); includes 3 minority (1 African American, 2 Asian Americans or Pacific Islanders), 1 international. Average age 27. 36 applicants, 78% accepted. In 2006, 9 degrees awarded. *Degree requirements:* For master's, thesis optional; for doctorate, thesis/dissertation, comprehensive exam. *Entrance requirements:* For master's, doctorate, and CAGS, GRE General Test or MAT. Additional exam requirements/recommendations for international students: Required—TOEFL. *Application deadline:* For fall admission, 2/15 priority date for domestic students; for winter admission, 10/1 priority date for domestic students. Applications are processed on a rolling basis. Application fee: $70. Electronic applications accepted. *Expenses:* Tuition: Full-time $33,330; part-time $1,042 per credit. Required fees: $462; $40. *Financial support:* Application deadline: 2/15. *Faculty research:* Learning theory, impact of computers, problem solving. *Unit head:* Dr. Carol Findell, Coordinator, 617-353-4226, E-mail: cfindell@bu.edu. *Application contact:* 617-353-4237, Fax: 617-353-8937, E-mail: sedgrad@bu.edu.

Bowling Green State University, Graduate College, College of Arts and Sciences, Department of Mathematics and Statistics, Bowling Green, OH 43403. Offers applied statistics (MS); mathematics (MA, MAT, PhD); probability and statistics (PhD). Part-time programs available. *Faculty:* 26 full-time (4 women), 2 part-time/adjunct (both women). *Students:* 59 full-time (23 women), 10 part-time (8 women); includes 1 minority (Asian American or Pacific Islander), 32 international. Average age 28. 144 applicants, 73% accepted, 12 enrolled. In 2006, 14 master's, 10 doctorates awarded. *Degree requirements:* For master's, thesis or alternative; for doctorate, thesis/dissertation, comprehensive exam; for degree. *Entrance requirements:* For master's and doctorate, GRE General Test. Additional exam requirements/recommendations for international students: Required—TOEFL. *Application deadline:* For fall admission, 1/31 priority date for domestic students. Application fee: $30. Electronic applications accepted. *Expenses:* Tuition, state resident: part-time $535 per hour. Tuition, nonresident: part-time $884 per hour. *Financial support:* In 2006–07, 3 research assistantships with full tuition reimbursements (averaging $8,271 per year), 46 teaching assistantships with full tuition reimbursements (averaging $12,280 per year) were awarded; Federal Work-Study, institutionally sponsored loans, and unspecified assistantships also available. Financial award applicants required to submit FAFSA. *Faculty research:* Statistics and probability, algebra, analysis. *Unit head:* Dr. Neal Carothers, Chair, 419-372-7453. *Application contact:* Dr. Hanfeng Chen, Graduate Coordinator, 419-372-7463, Fax: 419-372-6092.

Bridgewater State College, School of Graduate Studies, School of Arts and Sciences, Department of Mathematics and Computer Science, Bridgewater, MA 02325-0001. Offers computer science (MS); mathematics (MAT). Part-time and evening/weekend programs available. *Entrance requirements:* For master's, GRE General Test. *Application deadline:* For fall admission, 3/1 priority date for domestic students; for spring admission, 10/1 priority date for domestic students. Application fee: $50. *Financial support:* Career-related internships or fieldwork, health care benefits, and unspecified assistantships available. Support available to part-time students.

Brigham Young University, Graduate Studies, College of Physical and Mathematical Sciences, Department of Mathematics Education, Provo, UT 84602-1001. Offers MA. Part-time programs available. *Faculty:* 12 full-time (2 women). *Students:* 14 full-time (11 women), 3 part-time (all women); includes 2 minority (1 Asian American or Pacific Islander, 1 Hispanic American), 1 international. 10 applicants, 50% accepted, 5 enrolled. In 2006, 5 degrees awarded. *Degree requirements:* For master's, project or thesis, written exam. *Entrance requirements:* For master's, GRE General Test, teaching certificate, bachelor's degree in math education. Additional exam requirements/recommendations for international students: Required—TOEFL. *Application deadline:* For fall admission, 3/1 priority date for domestic and international students; for winter admission, 3/1 priority date for domestic and international students; for spring admission, 2/15 priority date for domestic and international students. Applications are processed on a rolling basis. Application fee: $50. Electronic applications accepted. *Financial support:* In 2006–07, 12 students received support, including 12 teaching assistantships with full tuition reimbursements available (averaging $14,000 per year); research assistantships with full tuition reimbursements available, institutionally sponsored loans and tuition waivers (partial) also available. Support available to part-time students. Financial award application deadline: 3/15. *Faculty research:* Pre-service math teacher education, teaching and learning with technology, cognition, algebraic geometry, communication in math classrooms. *Unit head:* Gerald M. Armstrong, Chair, 801-422-7407, Fax: 801-422-0511, E-mail: gma@byu.edu. *Application contact:* Jill Fielding, Administrative Assistant, 801-422-1840, Fax: 801-422-0511, E-mail: fielding@mathed.byu.edu.

Brooklyn College of the City University of New York, Division of Graduate Studies, Department of Mathematics, Brooklyn, NY 11210-2889. Offers mathematics (MA, PhD); secondary mathematics education (MA). The department offers courses at Brooklyn College that are creditable toward the CUNY doctoral degree (with permission of the executive officer of the doctoral program). Part-time and evening/weekend programs available. *Degree requirements:* For master's, comprehensive exam (mathematics). *Entrance requirements:* For master's, minimum GPA of 3.0, 2 letters of recommendation. Additional exam requirements/recommendations for international students: Required—TOEFL. *Application deadline:* For fall admission, 3/1 priority date for domestic students, 2/1 priority date for international students; for spring admission, 11/1 priority date for domestic students, 10/1 priority date for international students. Applications are processed on a rolling basis. Application fee: $125. Electronic applications accepted. *Expenses:* Tuition, state resident: full-time $6,400; part-time $270 per credit. Tuition, nonresident: full-time $12,000; part-time $500 per credit. Required fees: $118 per semester. *Financial support:* Federal Work-Study, institutionally sponsored loans, and scholarships/grants available. Support available to part-time students. Financial award application deadline: 5/1; financial award applicants required to submit FAFSA. *Faculty research:* Differential geometry, gauge theory, complex analysis, orthogonal functions. *Unit head:* Dr. George Shapiro, Chairperson, 718-951-5246, E-mail: gshapiro@brooklyn.cuny.edu. *Application contact:* Karen Alleyne-Pierre, Director of Admissions Services and Enrollment Communications, 718-951-5902, Fax: 718-951-4506, E-mail: grads@brooklyn.cuny.edu.

Brooklyn College of the City University of New York, Division of Graduate Studies, School of Education, Program in Adolescence Education and Special Subjects, Brooklyn, NY 11210-2889. Offers art teacher (MA); biology teacher (MA); chemistry teacher (MA); English teacher

Mathematics Education

Brooklyn College of the City University of New York (continued)
(MA); French teacher (MA); health and nutrition sciences: health teacher (MS Ed); mathematics teacher (MA); music education (CAS); music teacher (MA); physical education teacher (MS Ed); physics teacher (MA); social studies teacher (MA); Spanish teacher (MA). Part-time and evening/weekend programs available. *Students:* 30 full-time (22 women), 450 part-time (257 women); includes 167 minority (101 African Americans, 21 Asian Americans or Pacific Islanders, 45 Hispanic Americans), 21 international. 277 applicants, 84% accepted, 113 enrolled. In 2006, 172 master's, 6 other advanced degrees awarded. *Degree requirements:* For master's, comprehensive exam (for some programs). *Entrance requirements:* For master's, LAST, previous course work in education, resumé, 2 letters of recommendation, essay. Additional exam requirements/recommendations for international students: Required—TOEFL. *Application deadline:* For fall admission, 3/1 priority date for domestic students, 2/1 priority date for international students; for spring admission, 11/1 priority date for domestic students, 10/1 priority date for international students. Applications are processed on a rolling basis. Application fee: $125. Electronic applications accepted. *Expenses:* Tuition, state resident: full-time $6,400; part-time $270 per credit. Tuition, nonresident: full-time $12,000; part-time $500 per credit. Required fees: $118 per semester. *Financial support:* Career-related internships or fieldwork, Federal Work-Study, institutionally sponsored loans, and scholarships/grants available. Support available to part-time students. Financial award application deadline: 5/1; financial award applicants required to submit FAFSA. *Faculty research:* Interdisciplinary education, semiotics, discourse analysis, autobiography, teacher identity. *Unit head:* Prof. Stephen Phillips, Program Facilitator, 718-951-5214, E-mail: phillips@brooklyn.cuny.edu. *Application contact:* Karen Alleyne-Pierre, Director of Admissions Services and Enrollment Communications, 718-951-5902, Fax: 718-951-4506, E-mail: grads@brooklyn.cuny.edu.

Brooklyn College of the City University of New York, Division of Graduate Studies, School of Education, Program in Childhood Education, Brooklyn, NY 11210-2889. Offers bilingual education (MS Ed); liberal arts (MS Ed); mathematics (MS Ed); science/environmental education (MS Ed). Part-time and evening/weekend programs available. *Students:* 10 full-time (9 women), 275 part-time (233 women); includes 130 minority (84 African Americans, 12 Asian Americans or Pacific Islanders, 34 Hispanic Americans), 11 international. 154 applicants, 81% accepted, 80 enrolled. In 2006, 214 degrees awarded. *Entrance requirements:* For master's, LAST, interview, previous course work in education, writing sample, resumé, 2 letters of recommendation. Additional exam requirements/recommendations for international students: Required—TOEFL. *Application deadline:* For fall admission, 3/1 priority date for domestic students, 2/1 priority date for international students; for spring admission, 11/1 priority date for domestic students, 10/1 priority date for international students. Applications are processed on a rolling basis. Application fee: $125. Electronic applications accepted. *Expenses:* Tuition, state resident: full-time $6,400; part-time $270 per credit. Tuition, nonresident: full-time $12,000; part-time $500 per credit. Required fees: $118 per semester. *Financial support:* Career-related internships or fieldwork, Federal Work-Study, institutionally sponsored loans, and scholarships/grants available. Support available to part-time students. Financial award application deadline: 5/1; financial award applicants required to submit FAFSA. *Faculty research:* Emotional intelligence, multiculturalism, arts immersion, the Holocaust. *Unit head:* Dr. Sharon O'Connor-Petruso, Program Head, 718-951-5214. *Application contact:* Karen Alleyne-Pierre, Director of Admissions Services and Enrollment Communications, 718-951-5902, Fax: 718-951-4506, E-mail: grads@brooklyn.cuny.edu.

Brooklyn College of the City University of New York, Division of Graduate Studies, School of Education, Program in Middle Childhood Education (Math), Brooklyn, NY 11210-2889. Offers MS Ed. *Students:* 7 full-time (3 women), 194 part-time (102 women); includes 95 minority (60 African Americans, 25 Asian Americans or Pacific Islanders, 10 Hispanic Americans), 10 international. 84 applicants, 87% accepted, 59 enrolled. In 2006, 52 degrees awarded. *Entrance requirements:* For master's, LAST, 2 letters of recommendation, essay, resumé. Additional exam requirements/recommendations for international students: Required—TOEFL. *Application deadline:* For fall admission, 3/1 priority date for domestic students, 2/1 priority date for international students; for spring admission, 11/1 priority date for domestic students, 10/1 priority date for international students. Applications are processed on a rolling basis. Electronic applications accepted. *Expenses:* Tuition, state resident: full-time $6,400; part-time $270 per credit. Tuition, nonresident: full-time $12,000; part-time $500 per credit. Required fees: $118 per semester. *Financial support:* Federal Work-Study, institutionally sponsored loans, and scholarships/grants available. Support available to part-time students. Financial award application deadline: 5/1; financial award applicants required to submit FAFSA. *Unit head:* Prof. Mary Chiusano, Program Head, 718-951-5214, E-mail: mchiusano@brooklyn.cuny.edu. *Application contact:* Karen Alleyne-Pierre, Director of Admissions Services and Enrollment Communications, 718-951-5902, Fax: 718-951-4506, E-mail: grads@brooklyn.cuny.edu.

Buffalo State College, State University of New York, Graduate Studies and Research, Faculty of Natural and Social Sciences, Department of Mathematics, Buffalo, NY 14222-1095. Offers mathematics education (MS Ed). *Accreditation:* NCATE. Part-time and evening/weekend programs available. *Degree requirements:* For master's, thesis or alternative. *Entrance requirements:* For master's, 18 undergraduate hours in upper-level mathematics, minimum GPA of 2.5 in undergraduate math courses. Additional exam requirements/recommendations for international students: Required—TOEFL (minimum score 550 paper-based; 213 computer-based).

California State University, Bakersfield, Division of Graduate Studies and Research, School of Natural Sciences and Mathematics, Program in Secondary School Mathematics Teaching, Bakersfield, CA 93311-1022. Offers MA.

California State University, Chico, Graduate School, College of Natural Sciences, Program in Math Education, Chico, CA 95929-0722. Offers MS. *Application contact:* Dr. Rapti deSilva, Graduate Coordinator, 530-898-5767.

California State University, Dominguez Hills, College of Natural and Behavioral Science, Program in Teaching of Mathematics, Carson, CA 90747-0001. Offers MA. Part-time and evening/weekend programs available. *Faculty:* 5 full-time (2 women). *Students:* 1 full-time (0 women), 18 part-time (6 women); includes 9 minority (2 African Americans, 2 Asian Americans or Pacific Islanders, 5 Hispanic Americans). Average age 39. 8 applicants, 88% accepted, 2 enrolled. In 2006, 3 degrees awarded. *Degree requirements:* For master's, thesis, comprehensive exam, registration. *Entrance requirements:* For master's, 2 years of teaching experience, math competency. Additional exam requirements/recommendations for international students: Required—TOEFL. *Application deadline:* For fall admission, 6/1 priority date for domestic students; for spring admission, 11/1 priority date for domestic students. Applications are processed on a rolling basis. Application fee: $55. Electronic applications accepted. *Expenses:* Tuition, nonresident: part-time $339 per unit. Required fees: $1,148 per term. Tuition and fees vary according to program. *Unit head:* Dr. Serban Raianu, Chair, 310-243-3139, E-mail: sraianu@csudh.edu. *Application contact:* John Wilkins, Associate Professor, 310-243-2203, Fax: 310-516-3627, E-mail: jwilkins@csudh.edu.

California State University, Fresno, Division of Graduate Studies, College of Science and Mathematics, Department of Mathematics, Fresno, CA 93740-8027. Offers mathematics (MA); teaching (MA). Part-time programs available. *Degree requirements:* For master's, thesis or alternative. *Entrance requirements:* For master's, GRE General Test. Additional exam requirements/recommendations for international students: Required—TOEFL. Electronic applications accepted. *Faculty research:* Diagnostic testing project.

California State University, Fullerton, Graduate Studies, College of Education, Department of Secondary Education, Fullerton, CA 92834-9480. Offers middle school mathematics (MS); secondary education (MS); teacher induction (MS). *Students:* 2 full-time (both women), 30 part-time (20 women); includes 12 minority (7 Asian Americans or Pacific Islanders, 5 Hispanic Americans). Average age 31. 43 applicants, 70% accepted, 25 enrolled. In 2006, 28 degrees awarded. *Expenses:* Tuition, nonresident: part-time $339 per unit. Required fees: $1,155 per semester. *Unit head:* Dr. Victoria Costa, Head, 714-278-7037.

California State University, Fullerton, Graduate Studies, College of Natural Science and Mathematics, Department of Mathematics, Fullerton, CA 92834-9480. Offers applied mathematics (MA); mathematics (MA); mathematics for secondary school teachers (MA). Part-time programs available. *Students:* 8 full-time (6 women), 66 part-time (43 women); includes 40 minority (1 African American, 1 American Indian/Alaska Native, 22 Asian Americans or Pacific Islanders, 16 Hispanic Americans), 5 international. Average age 32. 67 applicants, 73% accepted, 22 enrolled. In 2006, 33 degrees awarded. *Degree requirements:* For master's, comprehensive exam or project. *Entrance requirements:* For master's, minimum GPA of 2.5 in last 60 units of course work, major in mathematics or related field. Application fee: $55. *Expenses:* Tuition, nonresident: part-time $339 per unit. Required fees: $1,155 per semester. *Financial support:* Research assistantships, teaching assistantships, career-related internships or fieldwork, Federal Work-Study, institutionally sponsored loans, and scholarships/grants available. Support available to part-time students. Financial award application deadline: 3/1. *Unit head:* Dr. Paul Deland, Chair, 714-278-3631.

California State University, Long Beach, Graduate Studies, College of Natural Sciences and Mathematics, Department of Mathematics and Statistics, Long Beach, CA 90840. Offers mathematics (MS); mathematics and science education (MS). Part-time programs available. *Faculty:* 43 full-time (9 women), 49 part-time/adjunct (21 women). *Students:* 47 full-time (23 women), 73 part-time (35 women); includes 56 minority (1 African American, 35 Asian Americans or Pacific Islanders, 20 Hispanic Americans), 13 international. Average age 33. 95 applicants, 62% accepted, 44 enrolled. In 2006, 15 degrees awarded. *Degree requirements:* For master's, comprehensive exam or thesis. *Application deadline:* For fall admission, 7/1 for domestic students; for spring admission, 12/1 for domestic students. Applications are processed on a rolling basis. Application fee: $55. Electronic applications accepted. *Financial support:* Teaching assistantships, Federal Work-Study, institutionally sponsored loans, scholarships/grants, and traineeships available. Financial award application deadline: 3/2. *Faculty research:* Algebra, functional analysis, partial differential equations, operator theory, numerical analysis. *Unit head:* Dr. Robert A Mena, Chair, 562-985-4721, Fax: 562-985-8227, E-mail: rmena@csulb.edu. *Application contact:* Dr. Ngo Viet, Graduate Coordinator, 562-985-5610, Fax: 562-985-8227, E-mail: viet@csulb.edu.

California State University, Northridge, Graduate Studies, College of Science and Mathematics, Department of Mathematics, Northridge, CA 91330. Offers applied mathematics (MS); mathematics (MS); mathematics for educational careers (MS). Part-time and evening/weekend programs available. *Faculty:* 38 full-time (11 women), 39 part-time/adjunct (19 women). *Students:* 25 full-time (9 women), 57 part-time (30 women); includes 23 minority (3 African Americans, 7 Asian Americans or Pacific Islanders, 13 Hispanic Americans), 3 international. Average age 34. 43 applicants, 72% accepted, 22 enrolled. In 2006, 13 degrees awarded. *Degree requirements:* For master's, thesis (for some programs). *Entrance requirements:* Additional exam requirements/recommendations for international students: Required—TOEFL. *Application deadline:* For fall admission, 11/30 for domestic students. Application fee: $55. *Expenses:* Tuition, nonresident: full-time $8,136; part-time $4,068 per year. Required fees: $3,624; $1,161 per term. *Financial support:* Teaching assistantships, Federal Work-Study and institutionally sponsored loans available. Support available to part-time students. Financial award application deadline: 3/1. *Unit head:* Dr. Helena Noronha, Chair, 818-677-2721. *Application contact:* Dr. Werner Horn, Graduate Coordinator, 818-677-7794.

Campbell University, Graduate and Professional Programs, School of Education, Buies Creek, NC 27506. Offers administration (MSA); community counseling (MA); elementary education (M Ed); English education (M Ed); interdisciplinary studies (M Ed); mathematics education (M Ed); middle grades education (M Ed); physical education (M Ed); school counseling (M Ed); secondary education (M Ed); social science education (M Ed). *Accreditation:* NCATE. Part-time and evening/weekend programs available. *Faculty:* 14 full-time (9 women), 12 part-time/adjunct (7 women). *Students:* 27 full-time (25 women), 183 part-time (146 women); includes 30 minority (24 African Americans, 3 American Indian/Alaska Native, 3 Hispanic Americans), 1 international. Average age 31. 112 applicants, 74% accepted, 74 enrolled. In 2006, 65 degrees awarded. *Degree requirements:* For master's, comprehensive exam. *Entrance requirements:* For master's, GRE General Test, minimum GPA of 2.7. *Application deadline:* For fall admission, 8/1 priority date for domestic students; for spring admission, 1/2 priority date for domestic students. Applications are processed on a rolling basis. Application fee: $65. *Expenses:* Tuition: Part-time $380 per semester hour. *Financial support:* In 2006–07, 67 students received support. Career-related internships or fieldwork and Federal Work-Study available. Financial award application deadline: 4/15; financial award applicants required to submit FAFSA. *Faculty research:* Spiritual values and wellness issues in counseling, stress and professional burnout among counselors, thinking strategies, leadership, adaptive technology. *Unit head:* Dr. Karen P. Nery, Dean, 910-893-1630, Fax: 910-893-1999, E-mail: nery@campbell.edu. *Application contact:* James S. Farthing, Director of Graduate Admissions for Business and Education, 910-893-1200 Ext. 1318, Fax: 910-814-4718, E-mail: farthing@campbell.edu.

Chatham University, Program in Education, Pittsburgh, PA 15232-2826. Offers early childhood education (MAT); elementary education (MAT); English—secondary (MAT); environmental education (K-12) (MAT); secondary art (MAT); secondary biology education (MAT); secondary chemistry education (MAT); secondary English education (MAT); secondary math education (MAT); secondary physics education (MAT); secondary social studies education (MAT); special education (MAT). *Students:* 60 full-time (43 women), 23 part-time (22 women). Average age 29. 48 applicants, 77% accepted, 32 enrolled. In 2006, 59 degrees awarded. *Degree requirements:* For master's, thesis, teaching experience. *Entrance requirements:* For master's, PRAXIS I, minimum GPA of 3.0, sample of written work, recommendation letters. Additional exam requirements/recommendations for international students: Required—TOEFL (minimum score 600 paper-based; 250 computer-based; 100 iBT); Recommended—IELTS (minimum score 7), TWE (minimum score 5). *Application deadline:* For fall admission, 5/1 priority date for domestic and international students; for winter admission, 10/1 priority date for domestic and international students. Applications are processed on a rolling basis. Application fee: $45. Electronic applications accepted. *Financial support:* Career-related internships or fieldwork available. Financial award applicants required to submit FAFSA. *Faculty research:* Gifted education, environmental education, technology in education, writing as learning, class size and achievement. *Unit head:* Dr. Wendy Weiner, Director, 412-365-1146, Fax: 412-365-1505, E-mail: wweiner@chatham.edu. *Application contact:* 412-365-1825, Fax: 412-365-1609, E-mail: admissions@chatham.edu.

Cheyney University of Pennsylvania, School of Education, Program in Mathematics Education, Cheyney, PA 19319-0200. Offers Certificate.

Christopher Newport University, Graduate Studies, Department of Teacher Preparation, Newport News, VA 23606-2998. Offers art (PK-12) (MAT); biology (6-12) (MAT); computer science (6-12) (MAT); elementary (PK-6) (MAT); English (6-12) (MAT); French (PK-12) (MAT); history (6-12) (MAT); history and social science (MAT); mathematics (6-12) (MAT); music (PK-12) (MAT), including choral, instrumental; physics (6-12) (MAT); Spanish (PK-12) (MAT); theater (PK-12) (MAT). Part-time and evening/weekend programs available. *Degree requirements:* For master's, thesis or alternative, comprehensive exam. *Entrance requirements:* For master's, PRAXIS I, minimum GPA of 3.0. Electronic applications accepted. *Faculty research:* Early literacy development, instructional innovations, professional teaching standards, multicultural issues, aesthetic education.

City College of the City University of New York, Graduate School, School of Education, Department of Secondary Education, New York, NY 10031-9198. Offers adolescent mathematics education (MA, AC); English education (MA); middle school mathematics education (MS); science education (MA); social studies education (AC). *Accreditation:* NCATE. *Students:* 286 applicants, 94% accepted, 219 enrolled. *Entrance requirements:* For master's, Liberal Arts and Sciences Test (LAST), Content Specialty Test (CST). Additional exam requirements/

recommendations for international students: Required—TOEFL. *Application deadline:* For fall admission, 3/15 for domestic students; for spring admission, 10/15 for domestic students. Application fee: $125. *Unit head:* Susan Semel, Chair, 212-650-7262, E-mail: ssemel@ccny.cuny.edu. *Application contact:* Stacia Pusey, Graduate Admissions Adviser-Education, 212-650-5345, E-mail: spusey@ccny.cuny.edu.

Clemson University, Graduate School, College of Health, Education, and Human Development, School of Education, Program in Secondary Education, Clemson, SC 29634. Offers English (M Ed); mathematics (M Ed); natural sciences (M Ed). *Accreditation:* NCATE. *Students:* 5 full-time (2 women), 9 part-time (8 women); includes 1 minority (American Indian/Alaska Native). 11 applicants, 45% accepted, 2 enrolled. In 2006, 9 degrees awarded. *Entrance requirements:* For master's, teaching certificate. Additional exam requirements/recommendations for international students: Required—TOEFL. *Application deadline:* For fall admission, 6/1 for domestic students. Application fee: $50. *Expenses:* Tuition, state resident: full-time $8,812; part-time $450 per hour. Tuition, nonresident: full-time $18,036; part-time $760 per hour. Required fees: $474; $5 per term. *Financial support:* Application deadline: 6/1; *Unit head:* Dr. William Fisk, Graduate Coordinator, 864-656-5119, Fax: 864-656-1322, E-mail: bill252@clemson.edu.

See Close-Up on page 1273.

Cleveland State University, College of Graduate Studies, College of Education and Human Services, Department of Teacher Education, Cleveland, OH 44115. Offers art education (M Ed); early childhood education (M Ed); foreign language education (M Ed); mathematics and science education (M Ed); middle childhood education (M Ed); special education (M Ed), including mild/moderate disabilities, moderate/intensive disabilities; teaching English to speakers of other languages (M Ed). Part-time and evening/weekend programs available. *Faculty:* 14 full-time (8 women), 5 part-time/adjunct (4 women). *Students:* 120 full-time (96 women), 592 part-time (485 women); includes 145 minority (123 African Americans, 7 Asian Americans or Pacific Islanders, 15 Hispanic Americans), 7 international. Average age 34. 526 applicants, 41% accepted, 144 enrolled. In 2006, 324 degrees awarded. *Degree requirements:* For master's, thesis or alternative, comprehensive exam (for some programs). *Entrance requirements:* For master's, GRE General Test or MAT, minimum GPA of 2.75. Additional exam requirements/recommendations for international students: Required—TOEFL (minimum score 525 paper-based; 197 computer-based), IELTS (minimum score 6). *Application deadline:* For fall admission, 7/15 priority date for domestic students. Applications are processed on a rolling basis. Application fee: $30. *Financial support:* In 2006–07, 12 research assistantships with full tuition reimbursements (averaging $3,480 per year) were awarded; tuition waivers (partial) and unspecified assistantships also available. *Faculty research:* Early literacy, professional development in reading, reading recovery, dual language, induction programs. Total annual research expenditures: $6.2 million. *Unit head:* Dr. Clifford T. Bennett, Chairperson, 216-523-7105, Fax: 216-687-5379, E-mail: c.t.bennett@csuohio.edu.

College of Charleston, Graduate School, School of Education, Program in Science and Mathematics for Teachers, Charleston, SC 29424-0001. Offers M Ed. *Accreditation:* NCATE. Electronic applications accepted.

College of St. Joseph, Graduate Program, Division of Education, Program in Secondary Education, Rutland, VT 05701-3899. Offers English (M Ed); mathematics (M Ed); social studies (M Ed). Part-time and evening/weekend programs available. *Faculty:* 2 full-time (1 woman), 8 part-time/adjunct (5 women). *Students:* 4 full-time, 4 part-time. Average age 32. 7 applicants, 100% accepted, 6 enrolled. In 2006, 4 degrees awarded. *Entrance requirements:* For master's, PRAXIS I, 2 letters of recommendation, minimum GPA of 3.0, interview. *Application deadline:* Applications are processed on a rolling basis. Application fee: $35. *Expenses:* Tuition: Full-time $10,990; part-time $300 per credit. Part-time tuition and fees vary according to program. *Financial support:* Career-related internships or fieldwork, Federal Work-Study, and unspecified assistantships available. Support available to part-time students. Financial award application deadline: 3/1. *Unit head:* Dr. David Balfour, Director, 802-773-5900 Ext. 3230, Fax: 802-776-5258, E-mail: dbalfour@csj.edu. *Application contact:* Tracy Gallipo, Director of Admissions, 802-773-5900 Ext. 3262, Fax: 802-773-5900, E-mail: tracygallipo@csj.edu.

The College of William and Mary, School of Education, Program in Curriculum and Instruction, Williamsburg, VA 23187-8795. Offers elementary education (MA Ed); gifted education (MA Ed); reading education (MA Ed); secondary education (MA Ed), including English education, mathematics education, modern foreign languages education, science education, social studies education; special education (MA Ed), including emotionally disturbed, learning disabled, mental retardation, resource collaborating teaching. *Accreditation:* NCATE. Part-time programs available. *Faculty:* 15 full-time (6 women), 13 part-time/adjunct (10 women). *Students:* 51 full-time (39 women), 51 part-time (45 women); includes 6 minority (all African Americans) Average age 29. 161 applicants, 68% accepted, 61 enrolled. In 2006, 68 degrees awarded. *Degree requirements:* For master's, master's project. *Entrance requirements:* For master's, GRE or MAT, minimum GPA of 2.5. Additional exam requirements/recommendations for international students: Required—TOEFL. *Application deadline:* For fall admission, 2/1 for domestic and international students; for spring admission, 10/1 for domestic and international students. Application fee: $30. *Expenses:* Tuition, state resident: full-time $6,100; part-time $260 per credit. Tuition, nonresident: full-time $18,790; part-time $725 per credit. Required fees: $3,314. Tuition and fees vary according to program. *Financial support:* In 2006–07, 10 research assistantships with full and partial tuition reimbursements (averaging $5,000 per year) were awarded; career-related internships or fieldwork, Federal Work-Study, institutionally sponsored loans, scholarships/grants, and unspecified assistantships also available. Financial award application deadline: 2/1; financial award applicants required to submit FAFSA. *Faculty research:* National Council of Teachers of Mathematics Standards, counseling, self-concept and self-esteem, special education, curriculum development. *Unit head:* Dr. John Moore, Area Coordinator, 757-221-2333, E-mail: jnmoor@wm.edu. *Application contact:* Dorothy Osborne, Director of Admissions, 757-221-2317, E-mail: dsosbo@wm.edu.

The Colorado College, Department of Education, Program in Secondary Education, Colorado Springs, CO 80903-3294. Offers art teaching (MAT); English teaching (MAT); foreign language teaching (MAT); mathematics teaching (MAT); music teaching (MAT); science teaching (MAT); social studies teaching (MAT). *Faculty:* 2 full-time (1 woman), 10 part-time/adjunct (7 women). *Students:* 18 full-time (12 women); includes 2 minority (1 African American, 1 Asian American or Pacific Islander). Average age 27. 30 applicants, 90% accepted, 18 enrolled. In 2006, 16 degrees awarded. *Degree requirements:* For master's, thesis, internship. *Entrance requirements:* For master's, PRAXIS II or PLACE. *Application deadline:* For fall admission, 2/1 for domestic and international students. Application fee: $50. *Expenses:* Tuition: Full-time $23,567. One-time fee: $1,485 full-time. *Financial support:* In 2006–07, 15 teaching assistantships (averaging $16,000 per year) were awarded; career-related internships or fieldwork, institutionally sponsored loans, health care benefits, and tuition waivers (partial) also available. Financial award application deadline: 2/15; financial award applicants required to submit FAFSA. *Unit head:* Mike Taber, Director, 719-389-6026, Fax: 719-389-6473, E-mail: pveronesi@coloradocollege.edu. *Application contact:* Marsha E. Unruh, Director of Education Career Services, 719-389-6472, Fax: 719-389-6473, E-mail: munruh@coloradocollege.edu.

Columbus State University, Graduate Studies, College of Education, Department of Teacher Education, Columbus, GA 31907-5645. Offers early childhood education (M Ed, Ed S); instructional technology (MS); middle grades education (M Ed, Ed S); physical education (M Ed); secondary education (M Ed, Ed S), including English/language arts, general science (M Ed), mathematics, science (Ed S), social science; special education (Ed S), including behavior disorders, learning disabilities, mental retardation. *Accreditation:* NCATE. Part-time and evening/weekend programs available. Postbaccalaureate distance learning degree programs offered (minimal on-campus study). *Faculty:* 16 full-time (8 women), 2 part-time/adjunct (1 woman). *Students:* 61 full-time (45 women), 128 part-time (89 women); includes 44 minority (36 African Americans, 3 Asian Americans or Pacific Islanders, 5 Hispanic Americans), 1 international. Average age 36. 77 applicants, 49% accepted, 26 enrolled. In 2006, 66 master's, 13 other advanced degrees awarded. *Degree requirements:* For master's, thesis, exit exam; for Ed S, thesis or alternative. *Entrance requirements:* For master's, GRE General Test, minimum GPA of 2.75; for Ed S, GRE General Test. Additional exam requirements/recommendations for international students: Required—TOEFL (minimum score 550 paper-based; 213 computer-based). *Application deadline:* For fall admission, 5/1 priority date for domestic students, 5/1 for international students; for spring admission, 11/1 for domestic and international students. Applications are processed on a rolling basis. Application fee: $25. Electronic applications accepted. *Expenses:* Tuition, state resident: part-time $127 per semester hour. Tuition, nonresident: part-time $508 per semester hour. Required fees: $264 per semester. Tuition and fees vary according to course load. *Financial support:* In 2006–07, 118 students received support, including 21 research assistantships with partial tuition reimbursements available (averaging $3,000 per year); career-related internships or fieldwork, Federal Work-Study, institutionally sponsored loans, scholarships/grants, tuition waivers (partial), and unspecified assistantships also available. Support available to part-time students. Financial award application deadline: 5/1; financial award applicants required to submit FAFSA. *Unit head:* Dr. Deborah Gober, Acting Chair, 706-568-2255, Fax: 706-568-3134, E-mail: gober_deborah@colstate.edu. *Application contact:* Katie Thornton, Graduate Admissions Specialist, 706-568-2035, Fax: 706-568-2462, E-mail: thornton_katie@colstate.edu.

Concordia University, School of Graduate Studies, Faculty of Arts and Science, Department of Mathematics and Statistics, Montréal, QC H3G 1M8, Canada. Offers mathematics (M Sc, MA, PhD); teaching of mathematics (MTM). *Students:* 59 full-time (32 women), 27 part-time (13 women). 144 applicants, 33% accepted, 24 enrolled. In 2006, 13 master's, 1 doctorate awarded. *Degree requirements:* For master's, thesis optional; for doctorate, thesis/dissertation, comprehensive exam. *Entrance requirements:* For master's, honors degree in mathematics or equivalent. *Application deadline:* For fall admission, 5/1 for domestic students; for winter admission, 3/31 for domestic students; for spring admission, 10/31 for domestic students. Application fee: $50. *Financial support:* Fellowships, research assistantships, teaching assistantships available. Financial award application deadline: 2/1. *Faculty research:* Number theory, computational algebra, mathematical physics, differential geometry, dynamical systems and statistics. *Unit head:* Dr. Yogendra Chaubey, Chair, 514-848-2424 Ext. 3234, Fax: 514-848-2831. *Application contact:* Dr. Galia Dafni, Director, 514-848-3257 Ext. 3216, Fax: 514-848-2831.

Connecticut College, Graduate School, Department of Mathematics, New London, CT 06320-4196. Offers MAT. Part-time programs available. *Entrance requirements:* For master's, MAT.

Converse College, School of Education and Graduate Studies, Program in Secondary Education, Spartanburg, SC 29302-0006. Offers biology (MAT); chemistry (MAT); English (M Ed, MAT); mathematics (M Ed, MAT); natural sciences (M Ed); social sciences (M Ed, MAT). Part-time programs available. *Students:* Average age 35. In 2006, 40 degrees awarded. *Degree requirements:* For master's, capstone paper. *Entrance requirements:* For master's, NTE or PRAXIS II (M Ed), minimum GPA of 2.75, 2 recommendations. *Application deadline:* For fall admission, 8/1 for domestic and international students; for winter admission, 11/15 for domestic and international students; for spring admission, 1/15 for domestic and international students. Applications are processed on a rolling basis. Application fee: $40. Electronic applications accepted. *Expenses:* Tuition: Part-time $305 per credit hour. Required fees: $20 per term. *Financial support:* Available to part-time students. Applicants required to submit FAFSA.

Cornell University, Graduate School, Graduate Fields of Agriculture and Life Sciences, Field of Education, Ithaca, NY 14853-0001. Offers agricultural education (MAT); biology (7-12) (MAT); chemistry (7-12) (MAT); curriculum and instruction (MPS, MS, PhD); earth science (7-12) (MAT); extension, and adult education (MPS, MS, PhD); mathematics (7-12) (MAT); physics (7-12) (MAT). *Faculty:* 26 full-time (9 women). *Students:* 56 full-time (33 women); includes 10 minority (1 African American, 5 Asian Americans or Pacific Islanders, 4 Hispanic Americans), 4 international. Average age 31. 96 applicants, 40% accepted, 18 enrolled. In 2006, 22 master's, 8 doctorates awarded. Terminal master's awarded for partial completion of doctoral program. *Degree requirements:* For master's, thesis (MS); for doctorate, thesis/dissertation, comprehensive exam. *Entrance requirements:* For master's and doctorate, GRE General Test, sample of written work (recommended), 2 letters of recommendation. Additional exam requirements/recommendations for international students: Required—TOEFL (minimum score 550 paper-based; 213 computer-based). *Application deadline:* For fall admission, 2/15 for domestic students. Application fee: $60. Electronic applications accepted. *Expenses:* Tuition: Full-time $32,800. Full-time tuition and fees vary according to program. *Financial support:* In 2006–07, 31 students received support, including 4 fellowships with full tuition reimbursements available, 7 research assistantships with full tuition reimbursements available, 20 teaching assistantships with full tuition reimbursements available; institutionally sponsored loans, scholarships/grants, health care benefits, tuition waivers (full and partial), and unspecified assistantships also available. Financial award applicants required to submit FAFSA. *Faculty research:* Moral development and professional ethics; public issues education and community development; socio/political issues in public education; teacher education and curriculum in agricultural science, and mathematics; extension research. *Unit head:* Director of Graduate Studies, 607-255-4278, Fax: 607-255-7905. *Application contact:* Graduate Field Assistant, 607-255-4278, Fax: 607-255-7905, E-mail: rh22@cornell.edu.

Delta State University, Graduate Programs, College of Arts and Sciences, Department of Mathematics, Cleveland, MS 38733-0001. Offers mathematics education (M Ed). Part-time programs available. *Degree requirements:* For master's, thesis or alternative. *Application deadline:* For fall admission, 8/1 priority date for domestic students; for spring admission, 12/1 priority date for domestic students. Applications are processed on a rolling basis. Application fee: $0. *Financial support:* In 2006–07, research assistantships (averaging $3,500 per year); career-related internships or fieldwork and institutionally sponsored loans also available. Support available to part-time students. Financial award application deadline: 6/1. *Unit head:* Dr. Rose Strahan, Chair, 662-846-4475, Fax: 662-846-4498, E-mail: rstrahan@deltastate.edu.

DePaul University, College of Liberal Arts and Sciences, Department of Mathematical Sciences, Chicago, IL 60604-2287. Offers applied mathematics (MS); applied statistics (MS, Certificate); mathematics education (MA). Part-time and evening/weekend programs available. *Faculty:* 23 full-time (6 women), 18 part-time/adjunct (5 women). *Students:* 78 full-time (42 women), 60 part-time (33 women); includes 31 minority (12 African Americans, 11 Asian Americans or Pacific Islanders, 8 Hispanic Americans), 6 international. Average age 30. 40 applicants, 100% accepted. In 2006, 30 degrees awarded. *Application deadline:* Applications are processed on a rolling basis. Application fee: $25. *Financial support:* In 2006–07, 8 students received support, including research assistantships with partial tuition reimbursements available (averaging $3,700 per year); teaching assistantships, tuition waivers (full and partial) also available. *Faculty research:* Verbally prime algebras, enveloping algebras of Lie, superalgebras and related rings, harmonic analysis, estimation theory. *Unit head:* Dr. Ahmed I Zayed, Chairperson, 773-325-7806, E-mail: azayed@depaul.edu.

DeSales University, Graduate Division, Program in Education, Center Valley, PA 18034-9568. Offers academic standards and information (Certificate); bilingual/ESL studies (Certificate); biology (M Ed); chemistry (M Ed); computers in education (K-12) (M Ed); computers in education (K-8) (M Ed); English (M Ed); instructional technology specialist (Certificate); mathematics (M Ed); special education (M Ed, Certificate); TESOL (M Ed). Part-time and evening/weekend programs available. Postbaccalaureate distance learning degree programs offered (minimal on-campus study). *Students:* 34 full-time, 190 part-time. In 2006, 30 degrees awarded. *Degree requirements:* For master's, thesis project. *Entrance requirements:* For master's, teaching certificate. *Application deadline:* Applications are processed on a rolling basis. Application fee: $35. Electronic applications accepted. *Expenses:* Contact institution. *Financial support:* Unspecified assistantships available. Support available to part-time students. Financial award application deadline: 5/1. *Faculty research:* Effective teaching, computer interfacing in chemistry labs, computer applications to teaching, history of philosophy, aesthetics multidrug-resistant cancer. *Unit head:* Dr. Lujean Baab, Director of M.Ed. Program, 610-

Mathematics Education

DeSales University (continued)
282-1100 Ext. 1739, Fax: 610-282-3734, E-mail: lujean.baab@desales.edu. *Application contact:* Donna L. Cressman, Program Secretary, 610-282-1100 Ext. 1461, Fax: 610-282-3734, E-mail: med@desales.edu.

Drake University, School of Education, Department of Teaching and Learning, Program in Secondary Education, Des Moines, IA 50311-4516. Offers art (MAT); biology (MAT); business (MAT); chemistry (MAT); English (MAT); general science (MAT); history-American (MAT); history-world (MAT); journalism (MAT); mathematics (MAT); physical science (MAT); physics (MAT); sociology (MAT); speech (MAT); speech communication (MAT); theatre (MAT). Part-time programs available. *Faculty:* 10 full-time (3 women), 28 part-time/adjunct (16 women). *Students:* 13 full-time (7 women), 33 part-time (20 women). 41 applicants, 56% accepted. In 2006, 12 degrees awarded. *Degree requirements:* For master's, thesis (for some programs), internships (s), comprehensive exam, registration. *Entrance requirements:* For master's, GRE General Test, MAT, or Drake Writing Assessment, resumé, 2 letters of recommendation. Additional exam requirements/recommendations for international students: Required—TOEFL (minimum score 550 paper-based; 213 computer-based). *Application deadline:* For fall admission, 7/1 priority date for domestic students, 6/1 priority date for international students; for spring admission, 11/1 priority date for domestic students, 10/1 priority date for international students. Applications are processed on a rolling basis. Application fee: $25. Electronic applications accepted. *Financial support:* Career-related internships or fieldwork and unspecified assistantships available. Support available to part-time students. *Faculty research:* Counseling and rehabilitation, behavioral supports, inquiry-based science methods, teacher quality enhancement. Total annual research expenditures: $1.5 million. *Unit head:* Dr. Linda Espey, Head, 515-271-1954, E-mail: linda.espey@drake.edu. *Application contact:* Ann J. Martin, Graduate Coordinator, 515-271-2034, Fax: 515-271-2831, E-mail: ann.martin@drake.edu.

East Carolina University, Graduate School, College of Education, Department of Mathematics and Science Education, Greenville, NC 27858-4353. Offers mathematics (MA Ed); science education (MA, MA Ed). Part-time and evening/weekend programs available. *Students:* 8 full-time (5 women), 74 part-time (68 women); includes 7 minority (6 African Americans, 1 Asian American or Pacific Islander). Average age 35. 16 applicants, 75% accepted, 8 enrolled. In 2006, 36 degrees awarded. *Degree requirements:* For master's, thesis optional. *Entrance requirements:* For master's, GRE General Test or MAT, interview, minimum GPA of 2.5, bachelor's degree in related field, teaching license (MA Ed). Additional exam requirements/recommendations for international students: Required—TOEFL. *Application deadline:* For fall admission, 6/1 priority date for domestic students. Applications are processed on a rolling basis. Application fee: $50. *Financial support:* Research assistantships, teaching assistantships, Federal Work-Study available. Support available to part-time students. Financial award application deadline: 6/1. *Unit head:* Dr. Ronald Preston, Chairperson, 252-328-9353, E-mail: prestonr@ecu.edu. *Application contact:* Dean of Graduate School, 252-328-6012, Fax: 252-328-6071, E-mail: gradschool@ecu.edu.

Eastern Illinois University, Graduate School, College of Sciences, Department of Mathematics and Computer Science, Charleston, IL 61920-3099. Offers mathematics (MA); mathematics education (MA). *Faculty:* 30 full-time (6 women). In 2006, 9 degrees awarded. *Entrance requirements:* For master's, GRE General Test. *Application deadline:* For fall admission, 7/31 priority date for domestic students. Applications are processed on a rolling basis. Application fee: $30. *Expenses:* Tuition, state resident: part-time $169 per semester hour. Tuition, nonresident: part-time $508 per semester hour. Required fees: $60 per semester hour. *Financial support:* In 2006–07, research assistantships with tuition reimbursements (averaging $7,200 per year), 8 teaching assistantships with tuition reimbursements (averaging $7,200 per year) were awarded. *Unit head:* Dr. Peter Andrews, Chair, 217-581-6275, Fax: 217-581-6284, E-mail: pgandrews@eiu.edu. *Application contact:* Dr. Kenneth Wolcott, Coordinator, 217-581-6279, Fax: 217-581-6284, E-mail: kwolcott@eiu.edu.

Eastern Kentucky University, The Graduate School, College of Education, Department of Curriculum and Instruction, Program in Secondary and Higher Education, Richmond, KY 40475-3102. Offers agricultural education (MA Ed); allied health sciences education (MA Ed); art education (MA Ed); biological sciences education (MA Ed); business education (MA Ed); chemistry education (MA Ed); earth science education (MA Ed); English education (MA Ed); general science education (MA Ed); geography education (MA Ed); history education (MA Ed); home economics education (MA Ed); industrial education (MA Ed); mathematical sciences education (MA Ed); physical education (MA Ed); physics education (MA Ed); political science education (MA Ed); psychology education (MA Ed); reading (MA Ed); school health education (MA Ed); sociology education (MA Ed). *Accreditation:* NCATE. Part-time programs available. *Students:* 16 full-time (8 women), 63 part-time (43 women); includes 5 minority (2 African Americans, 2 American Indian/Alaska Native, 1 Asian American or Pacific Islander). Average age 32. *Entrance requirements:* For master's, GRE General Test, minimum GPA of 2.5. Application fee: $30. *Expenses:* Tuition, state resident: full-time $5,610. Tuition, nonresident: full-time $15,910. *Financial support:* Research assistantships, teaching assistantships, Federal Work-Study available. Support available to part-time students. *Unit head:* Dr. Michael Martin, Chair, Department of Curriculum and Instruction, 859-622-2154, Fax: 859-622-2004.

Eastern Michigan University, Graduate School, College of Arts and Sciences, Department of Mathematics, Ypsilanti, MI 48197. Offers computer science (MA); mathematics (MA); mathematics education (MA); statistics (MA). Part-time and evening/weekend programs available. Postbaccalaureate distance learning degree programs offered (minimal on-campus study). *Faculty:* 25 full-time (10 women). *Students:* 5 full-time (4 women), 39 part-time (23 women); includes 7 minority (2 African Americans, 3 Asian Americans or Pacific Islanders, 2 Hispanic Americans), 8 international. Average age 33. In 2006, 6 degrees awarded. *Degree requirements:* For master's, thesis optional. *Entrance requirements:* Additional exam requirements/recommendations for international students: Required—TOEFL. *Application deadline:* For fall admission, 5/15 priority date for domestic students, 5/1 priority date for international students; for winter admission, 10/15 priority date for domestic students, 10/1 priority date for international students; for spring admission, 3/15 priority date for domestic students, 3/1 priority date for international students. Applications are processed on a rolling basis. Application fee: $35. *Expenses:* Tuition, state resident: part-time $341 per credit hour. Tuition, nonresident: full-time $16,104; part-time $671 per credit hour. Required fees: $816; $34 per credit hour. $40 per term. One-time fee: $82 full-time. Tuition and fees vary according to course level, course load, degree level and reciprocity agreements. *Financial support:* Fellowships, research assistantships with full tuition reimbursements, teaching assistantships with full tuition reimbursements, career-related internships or fieldwork, Federal Work-Study, institutionally sponsored loans, scholarships/grants, tuition waivers (partial), and unspecified assistantships available. Support available to part-time students. Financial award applicants required to submit FAFSA. *Unit head:* Dr. Bette Warren, Head, 734-487-1444, Fax: 734-487-2489, E-mail: bette.warren@emich.edu. *Application contact:* Dr. Walter Parry, Graduate Advisor, 734-487-5044, E-mail: walter.parry@emich.edu.

Eastern Washington University, Graduate Studies, College of Science, Mathematics and Technology, Department of Mathematics, Cheney, WA 99004-2431. Offers MS. *Accreditation:* NCATE. Part-time programs available. *Degree requirements:* For master's, thesis (for some programs), comprehensive exam. *Entrance requirements:* For master's, GRE General Test, departmental qualifying exam, minimum GPA of 3.0.

Edinboro University of Pennsylvania, Graduate Studies and Research, School of Education, Department of Elementary Education, Program in Elementary Education, Edinboro, PA 16444. Offers character education (M Ed); early childhood education (M Ed); elementary education (M Ed), including language arts, mathematics, science, thesis focus. Part-time and evening/weekend programs available. *Students:* 31 full-time (26 women), 46 part-time (38 women). Average age 30. In 2006, 14 degrees awarded. *Degree requirements:* For master's, thesis or alternative, project, comprehensive exam. *Entrance requirements:* For master's, GRE or MAT, minimum QPA of 2.5, valid teaching certificate or current study to obtain certification.

Application deadline: Applications are processed on a rolling basis. Application fee: $30. Electronic applications accepted. *Expenses:* Tuition, state resident: full-time $6,048; part-time $336 per credit. Tuition, nonresident: full-time $9,678; part-time $538 per credit. Required fees: $1,849; $42 per credit. *Financial support:* In 2006–07, 7 research assistantships with full and partial tuition reimbursements (averaging $3,850 per year) were awarded; career-related internships or fieldwork, Federal Work-Study, scholarships/grants, and unspecified assistantships also available. Support available to part-time students. Financial award application deadline: 2/15; financial award applicants required to submit FAFSA. *Unit head:* Dr. Kathleen Dailey, Coordinator, 814-732-2714, E-mail: dailey@edinboro.edu. *Application contact:* Dr. R. Scott Baldwin, Dean, 814-732-2752, Fax: 814-732-2268, E-mail: sbaldwin@edinboro.edu.

Florida Agricultural and Mechanical University, Division of Graduate Studies, Research, and Continuing Education, College of Education, Program in Secondary Education and Foundation, Tallahassee, FL 32307-3200. Offers biology (M Ed); chemistry (MS Ed); English (MS Ed); history (MS Ed); math (MS Ed); physics (MS Ed). *Accreditation:* NCATE. *Degree requirements:* For master's, thesis (for some programs). *Entrance requirements:* For master's, GRE General Test, minimum GPA of 3.0. Additional exam requirements/recommendations for international students: Required—TOEFL.

Florida Gulf Coast University, College of Education, Program in Secondary Education, Fort Myers, FL 33965-6565. Offers biology (MAT); English (MAT); mathematics (MAT); social sciences (MAT). Part-time and evening/weekend programs available. *Faculty:* 31 full-time (21 women), 30 part-time/adjunct (24 women). *Entrance requirements:* For master's, GRE General Test, MAT, minimum GPA of 3.0. Additional exam requirements/recommendations for international students: Required—TOEFL (minimum score 550 paper-based; 213 computer-based). *Application deadline:* For fall admission, 7/1 priority date for domestic students; for spring admission, 10/15 for domestic students. Applications are processed on a rolling basis. Application fee: $30. Electronic applications accepted. *Expenses:* Tuition, state resident: full-time $4,326. Tuition, nonresident: full-time $18,523. Required fees: $1,211. One-time fee: $5 full-time. *Faculty research:* Integration of technology in the classroom, year-round schools, school choice, virtual high schools. *Unit head:* Dr. Pat Wachholz, Associate Dean, 239-590-7808, Fax: 239-590-7801, E-mail: wachhol@fgcu.edu.

Florida Institute of Technology, Graduate Programs, College of Science, Department of Science and Mathematics Education, Melbourne, FL 32901-6975. Offers computer education (MS); elementary science education (M Ed); environmental education (MS); mathematics education (MS, Ed D, PhD, Ed S); science and mathematics education (MAT); science education (MS, Ed D, PhD, Ed S). Part-time and evening/weekend programs available. *Faculty:* 4 full-time (1 woman), 2 part-time/adjunct (1 woman). *Students:* 11 full-time (6 women), 21 part-time (14 women); includes 2 minority (1 African American, 1 American Indian/Alaska Native), 7 international. Average age 38. 40 applicants, 58% accepted, 5 enrolled. In 2006, 7 master's, 2 doctorates, 1 other advanced degree awarded. Terminal master's awarded for partial completion of doctoral program. *Degree requirements:* For master's, thesis (for some programs), comprehensive exam (for some programs), registration; for doctorate, thesis/dissertation, oral defense of dissertation, comprehensive exam, registration. *Entrance requirements:* For master's, minimum GPA of 3.0, resumé, 3 letters of recommendation (elementary science education); for doctorate, minimum GPA of 3.2, resumé, 3 letters of recommendation; for Ed S, minimum GPA of 3.0, resumé, 3 letters of recommendation. Additional exam requirements/recommendations for international students: Required—TOEFL (minimum score 550 paper-based; 213 computer-based). *Application deadline:* Applications are processed on a rolling basis. Application fee: $50. Electronic applications accepted. *Expenses:* Tuition: Part-time $900 per credit. *Financial support:* In 2006–07, 1 student received support, including 1 research assistantship with full and partial tuition reimbursement available (averaging $5,346 per year); career-related internships or fieldwork and tuition remissions also available. Support available to part-time students. Financial award application deadline: 3/1; financial award applicants required to submit FAFSA. *Faculty research:* Measurement and evaluation, computers in education, educational technology. Total annual research expenditures: $6,000. *Unit head:* Dr. David E. Cook, Department Head, 321-674-8126, Fax: 321-674-7598, E-mail: dcook@fit.edu. *Application contact:* Carolyn P. Farrior, Director of Graduate Admissions, 321-674-7118, Fax: 321-723-9468, E-mail: cfarrior@fit.edu.

Florida International University, College of Education, Department of Curriculum and Instruction, Program in Mathematics Education, Miami, FL 33199. Offers MAT, MS, Ed D, PhD. *Accreditation:* NCATE. Part-time and evening/weekend programs available. *Entrance requirements:* Additional exam requirements/recommendations for international students: Required—TOEFL. *Application deadline:* Applications are processed on a rolling basis. Application fee: $25. *Expenses:* Tuition, state resident: part-time $249 per credit hour. Tuition, nonresident: part-time $753 per credit hour. Tuition and fees vary according to program. *Faculty research:* Problem solving, heuristics, microcomputers. *Unit head:* Dr. Cengiz Alacaci, Head, 305-348-1067.

Florida State University, Graduate Studies, College of Education, Department of Middle and Secondary Education, Program in Mathematics Education, Tallahassee, FL 32306. Offers MS, PhD, Ed S. Part-time programs available. Postbaccalaureate distance learning degree programs offered. *Faculty:* 4 full-time (3 women). *Students:* 17 full-time (9 women), 66 part-time (47 women); includes 21 minority (10 African Americans, 1 American Indian/Alaska Native, 9 Asian Americans or Pacific Islanders, 1 Hispanic American). 59 applicants, 51% accepted, 20 enrolled. In 2006, 20 master's, 5 doctorates, 1 other advanced degree awarded. *Degree requirements:* For master's and Ed S, thesis optional; for doctorate, thesis/dissertation, comprehensive exam. *Entrance requirements:* For master's, doctorate, and Ed S, GRE General Test, minimum GPA of 3.0. *Application deadline:* For fall admission, 7/1 priority date for domestic students; for spring admission, 11/1 for domestic students. Applications are processed on a rolling basis. Application fee: $30. *Expenses:* Tuition, state resident: full-time $5,822; part-time $243 per credit hour. Tuition, nonresident: full-time $20,976; part-time $874 per credit hour. Tuition and fees vary according to program. *Financial support:* Fellowships, research assistantships, teaching assistantships, career-related internships or fieldwork available. Financial award applicants required to submit FAFSA. *Unit head:* Dr. Elizabeth Jakubowski, Head, 850-644-6553, Fax: 850-644-1880, E-mail: ejakubowski@coe.fsu.edu. *Application contact:* Christina Crotty, Office Manager, 850-644-7810, Fax: 850-644-1880, E-mail: crotty@mailer.fsu.edu.

Framingham State College, Division of Graduate and Continuing Education, Program in Mathematics, Framingham, MA 01701-9101. Offers M Ed. *Faculty:* 3 full-time. *Students:* 16. In 2006, 2 degrees awarded. *Entrance requirements:* For master's, GRE General Test, minimum GPA of 3.0. *Unit head:* Dr. Walter Czarnec, Coordinator, 508-626-4729, Fax: 508-626-4030, E-mail: czarnec@frc.mass.edu. *Application contact:* 508-626-4550, Fax: 508-626-4030, E-mail: dgce@frc.mass.edu.

Fresno Pacific University, Graduate Programs, Programs in Education, Fresno, CA 93702-4709. Offers administration (MA Ed), including administrative services; foundations, curriculum and teaching (MA Ed), including curriculum and teaching, school library and information technology; language, literacy, and culture (MA Ed), including bilingual/cross-cultural education, language development, multilingual contexts, reading; mathematics/science/computer education (MA Ed), including educational technology, integrated mathematics/science education, mathematics education; pupil personnel services (MA Ed), including school counseling, school psychology; special education (MA Ed), including mild/moderate, moderate/severe, physical and health impairments. Part-time and evening/weekend programs available. *Faculty:* 12 full-time (5 women), 19 part-time/adjunct (9 women). *Students:* 73 full-time (59 women), 399 part-time (295 women); includes 136 minority (9 African Americans, 5 American Indian/Alaska Native, 12 Asian Americans or Pacific Islanders, 110 Hispanic Americans), 2 international. Average age 39. 124 applicants, 73% accepted, 10 enrolled. In 2006, 128 degrees awarded. *Degree requirements:* For master's, thesis (for some programs), registration. *Entrance requirements:* For master's, interview; GMAT, GRE, MAT, or 6 units of course work with a faculty recommendation. Additional exam requirements/recommendations for international students: Required—TOEFL (minimum score 550 paper-based; 213 computer-based). *Application deadline:* For fall admission, 7/15 for domestic and international students; for spring admission, 11/15 for domestic and international students. Applications are processed on a rolling basis. Application fee: $90. Electronic applications accepted. *Expenses:* Tuition: Full-time $7,470; part-time $415 per credit. *Financial support:* In 2006–07, 260 students received support. Career-related internships or fieldwork, scholarships/grants, and tuition waivers (full and partial) available. Support available to part-time students. Financial award applicants required to submit FAFSA.

Fresno Pacific University, Graduate Programs, Programs in Education, Division of Mathematics/Science/Computer Education, Program in Integrated Mathematics/Science Education, Fresno, CA 93702-4709. Offers MA Ed. Part-time and evening/weekend programs available. *Students:* Average age 39. 6 applicants, 50% accepted, 1 enrolled. In 2006, 40 degrees awarded. *Degree requirements:* For master's, thesis or alternative, registration. *Entrance requirements:* Additional exam requirements/recommendations for international students: Required—TOEFL (minimum score 550 paper-based; 213 computer-based). *Application deadline:* For fall admission, 7/15 for domestic and international students; for spring admission, 11/15 for domestic and international students. Applications are processed on a rolling basis. Application fee: $90. *Expenses:* Tuition: Full-time $7,470; part-time $415 per credit. *Financial support:* In 2006–07, 24 students received support. Scholarships/grants and tuition waivers (full and partial) available. Support available to part-time students. Financial award applicants required to submit FAFSA.

Fresno Pacific University, Graduate Programs, Programs in Education, Division of Mathematics/Science/Computer Education, Program in Mathematics Education, Fresno, CA 93702-4709. Offers middle school mathematics (MA Ed); secondary school mathematics (MA Ed). Part-time and evening/weekend programs available. *Students:* Average age 38. 5 applicants, 40% accepted, 0 enrolled. In 2006, 11 degrees awarded. *Degree requirements:* For master's, thesis or alternative, registration. *Entrance requirements:* Additional exam requirements/recommendations for international students: Required—TOEFL (minimum score 550 paper-based; 213 computer-based). *Application deadline:* For fall admission, 7/15 for domestic and international students; for spring admission, 11/15 for domestic and international students. Applications are processed on a rolling basis. Application fee: $90. *Expenses:* Tuition: Full-time $7,470; part-time $415 per credit. *Financial support:* In 2006–07, 44 students received support. Scholarships/grants and tuition waivers (full and partial) available. Support available to part-time students. Financial award applicants required to submit FAFSA. *Unit head:* Ron D. Koop, Director, 559-453-2028, Fax: 559-453-2001, E-mail: rdkoop@fresno.edu.

Georgia College & State University, Graduate School, School of Education, Department of Foundations and Secondary Education, Milledgeville, GA 31061. Offers English education (M Ed); instructional technology (M Ed); mathematics education (M Ed); natural science education (M Ed, Ed S); secondary education (MAT); social science education (M Ed, Ed S). *Accreditation:* NCATE. *Students:* 49 full-time (33 women), 66 part-time (47 women); includes 13 minority (11 African Americans, 2 Hispanic Americans), 2 international. Average age 32. 75 applicants, 27% accepted, 9 enrolled. In 2006, 83 master's awarded. *Degree requirements:* For master's and Ed S, comprehensive exam. *Entrance requirements:* For master's, GRE General Test or MAT, 2 letters of recommendation; for Ed S, GRE General Test or MAT, master's degree, 2 letters of recommendation, 2 years teaching experience. Additional exam requirements/recommendations for international students: Required—TOEFL. *Application deadline:* For fall admission, 7/1 priority date for domestic students. Applications are processed on a rolling basis. Application fee: $25. Electronic applications accepted. *Expenses:* Tuition, state resident: full-time $3,222; part-time $179 per credit hour. Tuition, nonresident: full-time $12,870; part-time $715 per credit hour. Required fees: $391 per semester. Tuition and fees vary according to course load. *Financial support:* In 2006–07, 10 research assistantships (averaging $3,800 per year) were awarded; career-related internships or fieldwork and Federal Work-Study also available. Support available to part-time students. Financial award application deadline: 3/15. *Unit head:* Dr. Cynthia Alby, Chair/MAT Cohort Leader, 478-445-2513, Fax: 478-445-7362, E-mail: cynthia.alby@gcsu.edu.

Georgia Southern University, Jack N. Averitt College of Graduate Studies, College of Education, Department of Teaching and Learning, Program in Mathematics Education, Statesboro, GA 30460. Offers M Ed, MAT. *Accreditation:* NCATE. Part-time and evening/weekend programs available. *Students:* 1 (woman) full-time, 6 part-time (5 women); includes 1 minority (African American) Average age 31. 1 applicant, 0% accepted. In 2006, 5 degrees awarded. *Degree requirements:* For master's, exit assessment. *Entrance requirements:* For master's, GRE General Test or MAT, minimum GPA of 2.5. Additional exam requirements/recommendations for international students: Required—TOEFL (minimum score 550 paper-based; 213 computer-based; 80 iBT). *Application deadline:* For fall admission, 3/1 priority date for domestic students, 3/1 for international students; for spring admission, 10/1 priority date for domestic students, 10/1 for international students. Applications are processed on a rolling basis. Application fee: $50. Electronic applications accepted. *Financial support:* In 2006–07, 4 students received support, including research assistantships with partial tuition reimbursements available (averaging $5,500 per year), teaching assistantships with partial tuition reimbursements available (averaging $5,500 per year); Federal Work-Study, scholarships/grants, tuition waivers (partial), and unspecified assistantships also available. Support available to part-time students. Financial award application deadline: 4/15; financial award applicants required to submit FAFSA. *Faculty research:* Technology applications. *Unit head:* Dr. Mary Bennett, Assistant Professor, 912-681-0356, Fax: 912-681-0026, E-mail: mbennett@georgiasouthern.edu. *Application contact:* 912-681-5384, Fax: 912-681-0740, E-mail: gradadmissions@georgiasouthern.edu.

Georgia State University, College of Education, Department of Middle-Secondary Education and Instructional Technology, Programs in Secondary Education, Atlanta, GA 30303-3083. Offers art education (Ed S); English education (M Ed, Ed S); mathematics education (M Ed, PhD, Ed S); music education (PhD); science education (M Ed, PhD, Ed S); social studies education (M Ed, PhD, Ed S). *Accreditation:* NASM (one or more programs are accredited); NCATE. Part-time and evening/weekend programs available. *Students:* 103 full-time (71 women), 140 part-time (92 women); includes 53 minority (48 African Americans, 2 Asian Americans or Pacific Islanders, 3 Hispanic Americans), 12 international. Average age 35. 36 applicants, 86% accepted. In 2006, 87 master's, 12 doctorates, 12 other advanced degrees awarded. *Degree requirements:* For master's, comprehensive exam; for doctorate, thesis/dissertation, comprehensive exam; for Ed S, project/exam. *Entrance requirements:* For master's, GRE General Test, minimum GPA of 2.5; for doctorate, GRE General Test or MAT, minimum GPA of 3.3; for Ed S, GRE General Test or MAT, minimum graduate GPA of 3.25. Application fee: $25. *Financial support:* Career-related internships or fieldwork, Federal Work-Study, and institutionally sponsored loans available. *Faculty research:* Women and science, problem solving in mathematics, dialects, economic education. *Unit head:* Dr. Ruth Hough, Acting Chair, Department of Middle-Secondary Education and Instructional Technology, 404-651-2510.

Harding University, College of Education, Searcy, AR 72149-0001. Offers advanced studies in teaching and learning (M Ed); art (MSE); behavioral science (MSE); Bible and religion (MSE); counseling (MS, Ed S); early childhood education (M Ed); early childhood special education (M Ed, MSE); education (MSE); educational leadership (M Ed, Ed S); elementary education (M Ed); English (MSE); family and consumer science (MSE); French (MSE); history/social science (MSE); kinesiology (MSE); math (MSE); physical science (MSE); reading (M Ed); secondary education (M Ed); Spanish (MSE); special education licensure (M Ed); teaching (MAT). *Accreditation:* NCATE. Part-time programs available. *Faculty:* 8 full-time (2 women), 45 part-time/adjunct (30 women). *Students:* 153 full-time (123 women), 469 part-time (341 women); includes 72 minority (63 African Americans, 4 American Indian/Alaska Native, 1 Asian American or Pacific Islander, 4 Hispanic Americans), 9 international. Average age 35. 175 applicants, 90% accepted, 147 enrolled. In 2006, 241 degrees awarded. *Degree requirements:* For master's, portfolio(s), thesis optional; for Ed S, portfolio, specialist project. *Entrance requirements:* For master's, GRE, MAT, PRAXIS; for Ed S, MAT or GRE. Additional exam requirements/recommendations for international students: Required—TOEFL (minimum score 550 paper-based). *Application deadline:* For fall admission, 8/1 for domestic and international students; for spring admission, 1/1 for domestic and international students. Applications are processed on a rolling basis. Application fee: $35. *Expenses:* Tuition: Part-time $455 per semester hour. Required fees: $20 per semester hour. Tuition and fees vary according to course load. *Financial support:* Scholarships/grants and unspecified assistantships available. Support available to part-time students. *Faculty research:* Reading, comprehension, school violence, educational technology, behavior, college choice, differentiated instruction, brain based teaching. *Unit head:* Pat Bashaw, Chair, 501-279-4183, Fax: 501-279-4051, E-mail: pbashaw@harding.edu.

Harvard University, Extension School, Cambridge, MA 02138-3722. Offers applied sciences (CAS); biotechnology (ALM); educational technologies (ALM); educational technology (CET); English for graduate and professional studies (DGP); environmental management (ALM, CEM); information technology (ALM); journalism (ALM); liberal arts (ALM); management (ALM, CM); mathematics for teaching (ALM); museum studies (ALM); premedical studies (Diploma); publication and communication (CPC). Part-time and evening/weekend programs available. *Faculty:* 236 part-time/adjunct. *Students:* 101 full-time (56 women), 564 part-time (278 women); includes 167 minority (35 African Americans, 1 American Indian/Alaska Native, 84 Asian Americans or Pacific Islanders, 47 Hispanic Americans). Average age 36. In 2006, 112 master's, 184 Diplomas awarded. *Degree requirements:* For master's, thesis. *Entrance requirements:* For master's, 3 completed graduate courses with grade of B or higher. Additional exam requirements/recommendations for international students: Required—TOEFL (minimum score 600 paper-based; 250 computer-based), TWE (minimum score 5). *Application deadline:* Applications are processed on a rolling basis. Application fee: $75. *Expenses: Contact institution.* Full-time tuition and fees vary according to program and student level. *Financial support:* In 2006–07, 268 students received support. Scholarships/grants available. Support available to part-time students. Financial award application deadline: 8/6; financial award applicants required to submit FAFSA. *Unit head:* Michael Shinagel, Dean. *Application contact:* Program Director, 617-495-4024, Fax: 617-495-9176.

Harvard University, Graduate School of Education, Master's Programs in Education, Cambridge, MA 02138. Offers arts in education (Ed M); education policy and management (Ed M); higher education (Ed M); human development and psychology (Ed M); international education policy (Ed M); language and literacy (Ed M); learning and teaching (Ed M); mid-career mathematics and science (teaching certificate) (Ed M); mind brain and education (Ed M); risk and prevention (Ed M); school leadership (Ed M); special studies (Ed M); teaching and curriculum (teaching certificate) (Ed M); technology innovation and education (Ed M). Part-time programs available. *Faculty:* 58 full-time (25 women), 40 part-time/adjunct (22 women). *Students:* 540 full-time (412 women), 90 part-time (70 women); includes 137 minority (49 African Americans, 2 American Indian/Alaska Native, 61 Asian Americans or Pacific Islanders, 25 Hispanic Americans), 70 international. Average age 29. 1,211 applicants, 61% accepted, 585 enrolled. In 2006, 591 degrees awarded. *Entrance requirements:* For master's, GRE General Test, 3 letters of recommendation, official transcripts, statement of purpose. Additional exam requirements/recommendations for international students: Required—TOEFL (minimum score 600 paper-based; 250 computer-based; 100 iBT), TWE (minimum score 5). *Application deadline:* For fall admission, 1/2 for domestic and international students. Application fee: $85. Electronic applications accepted. *Expenses: Contact institution. Financial support:* In 2006–07, 392 students received support, including 23 fellowships (averaging $15,870 per year); career-related internships or fieldwork, Federal Work-Study, institutionally sponsored loans, scholarships/grants, health care benefits, tuition waivers (full and partial), and unspecified assistantships also available. Support available to part-time students. Financial award application deadline: 2/2; financial award applicants required to submit FAFSA. *Faculty research:* Learning and development; educational leadership and organizations; educational policy analysis. Total annual research expenditures: $14.8 million. *Unit head:* Dr. James Stiles, Associate Dean for Degree Programs. *Application contact:* Information Contact, 617-495-3414, Fax: 617-496-3577, E-mail: gseadmissions@harvard.edu.

Henderson State University, Graduate Studies, School of Education, Department of Curriculum, Instruction and Leadership, Arkadelphia, AR 71999-0001. Offers early childhood (P-4) (MSE); English (MSE); English as a second language (MSE, CP); math (MSE); middle school (MSE); reading (MSE); social science (MSE). *Accreditation:* NCATE. Part-time programs available. *Faculty:* 19 full-time (6 women), 4 part-time/adjunct (2 women). *Students:* 38 full-time (36 women), 49 part-time (47 women); includes 6 minority (5 African Americans, 1 Hispanic American), 16 international. Average age 37. In 2006, 31 degrees awarded. *Entrance requirements:* For master's, GRE General Test or MAT, minimum GPA of 2.7, teacher certification. *Application deadline:* For fall admission, 5/1 priority date for domestic students, 5/1 for international students; for winter admission, 10/1 for international students; for spring admission, 12/1 priority date for domestic students, 4/1 for international students. Applications are processed on a rolling basis. Application fee: $0 ($30 for international students). *Expenses:* Tuition, state resident: full-time $3,294; part-time $183 per credit hour. Tuition, nonresident: full-time $6,588; part-time $366 per credit hour. Required fees: $176 per term. *Financial support:* In 2006–07, 1 teaching assistantship with full tuition reimbursement (averaging $4,000 per year) was awarded; research assistantships, Federal Work-Study and institutionally sponsored loans also available. Support available to part-time students. Financial award application deadline: 7/31. *Unit head:* Dr. Kenneth Harris, Chairperson, 870-230-5203, Fax: 870-230-5455, E-mail: harris@hsu.edu. *Application contact:* Dr. Marck L. Beggs, Graduate Dean, 870-230-5126, Fax: 870-230-5479, E-mail: beggsm@hsu.edu.

Hofstra University, School of Education and Allied Human Services, Department of Curriculum and Teaching, Program in Elementary Education-Math/Science/Technology, Hempstead, NY 11549. Offers MA. *Accreditation:* NCATE. Part-time and evening/weekend programs available. *Students:* 8 full-time (7 women), 30 part-time (27 women); includes 5 minority (2 African Americans, 3 Hispanic Americans). Average age 25. 8 applicants, 88% accepted, 4 enrolled. In 2006, 26 degrees awarded. *Degree requirements:* For master's, thesis, BA or BS in elementary education. *Entrance requirements:* For master's, 2 letters of recommendation, interview, teaching certificate (MA), essay. Additional exam requirements/recommendations for international students: Required—TOEFL (minimum score 550 paper-based; 213 computer-based). *Application deadline:* Applications are processed on a rolling basis. Application fee: $60. Electronic applications accepted. *Expenses:* Tuition: Full-time $13,320; part-time $740 per credit. Required fees: $930; $155 per term. *Financial support:* In 2006–07, 5 students received support, including 4 fellowships with tuition reimbursements available (averaging $300 per year); research assistantships with tuition reimbursements available, scholarships/grants, tuition waivers (full and partial), and unspecified assistantships also available. Support available to part-time students. Financial award applicants required to submit FAFSA. *Faculty research:* Constructivism, mathematical reasoning, concept formation, science of learning, interdisciplinary curriculum. *Unit head:* Dr. Jacqueline Grennon Brooks, Program Director, 516-463-5371, Fax: 516-463-6196, E-mail: catjzk@hofstra.edu. *Application contact:* Carol Drummer, Dean of Graduate Admissions, 516-463-4876, Fax: 516-463-4664, E-mail: gradstudent@hofstra.edu.

Hofstra University, School of Education and Allied Human Services, Department of Curriculum and Teaching, Program in Mathematics Education, Hempstead, NY 11549. Offers MA, MS Ed. Part-time programs available. *Students:* 21 full-time (13 women), 25 part-time (17 women); includes 5 minority (2 African Americans, 2 Asian Americans or Pacific Islanders, 1 Hispanic American). Average age 27. 32 applicants, 97% accepted, 16 enrolled. In 2006, 33 degrees awarded. *Degree requirements:* For master's, one foreign language, thesis (for some programs), 100 hours of field placement, student teaching. *Entrance requirements:* For master's, 2 letters of recommendation, teacher certification (MA), essay. Additional exam requirements/recommendations for international students: Required—TOEFL (minimum score 550 paper-based; 213 computer-based). *Application deadline:* Applications are processed on a rolling basis. Application fee: $60. Electronic applications accepted. *Expenses:* Tuition: Full-time $13,320; part-time $740 per credit. Required fees: $930; $155 per term. *Financial support:* In

Mathematics Education

Hofstra University (continued)

2006–07, 12 students received support, including 4 fellowships with tuition reimbursements available (averaging $2,513 per year), 2 research assistantships with full and partial tuition reimbursements available (averaging $6,804 per year); Federal Work-Study, scholarships/grants, tuition waivers (full and partial), and unspecified assistantships also available. Financial award applicants required to submit FAFSA. *Faculty research:* Teaching modalities that appeal to low-achieving math students; equity in mathematics instruction; multicultural issues in math education; teaching enhanced mathematics; teaching modalities for fostering algebraic thinking in the elementary student. Total annual research expenditures: $2 million. *Unit head:* Dr. Sharon Whitton, Director, 516-463-6456, Fax: 516-463-6196, E-mail: catszw@hofstra.edu. *Application contact:* Carol Drummer, Dean of Graduate Admissions, 516-463-4876, Fax: 516-463-4664, E-mail: gradstudent@hofstra.edu.

Hood College, Graduate School, Department of Education, Frederick, MD 21701-8575. Offers curriculum and instruction (MS), including early childhood education, elementary education, elementary school science and mathematics, secondary education, special education; educational leadership (MS); reading specialization (MS); teaching the struggling reader (Certificate). Part-time and evening/weekend programs available. *Faculty:* 4 full-time (3 women), 32 part-time/adjunct (16 women). *Students:* 5 full-time (3 women), 371 part-time (313 women); includes 30 minority (23 African Americans, 4 Asian Americans or Pacific Islanders, 3 Hispanic Americans). Average age 32. 71 applicants, 99% accepted, 59 enrolled. In 2006, 67 degrees awarded. *Degree requirements:* For master's, action research project, portfolio (reading). *Entrance requirements:* For master's, minimum GPA of 2.5, teaching certification. *Application deadline:* Applications are processed on a rolling basis. Application fee: $35. *Expenses:* Tuition: Part-time $350 per credit. Required fees: $20 per semester. *Financial support:* Applicants required to submit FAFSA. *Faculty research:* Leadership, action research, brain research, learning styles. *Unit head:* Dr. John George, Chairperson, 301-696-3471, Fax: 301-696-3597, E-mail: george@hood.edu. *Application contact:* Dr. Kathleen C. Bands, Associate Dean of Graduate School, 301-696-3811, Fax: 301-696-3597, E-mail: gofurther@hood.edu.

Hood College, Graduate School, Program in Secondary Mathematics Education, Frederick, MD 21701-8575. Offers Certificate. *Students:* 2 applicants, 100% accepted, 1 enrolled. Application fee: $35. *Expenses:* Tuition: Part-time $350 per credit. Required fees: $20 per semester. *Unit head:* Dr. Betty Mayfield, Chairperson, 301-696-3763, E-mail: mayfield@hood.edu. *Application contact:* Dr. Kathleen C. Bands, Associate Dean of Graduate School, 301-696-3811, Fax: 301-696-3597, E-mail: gofurther@hood.edu.

Hunter College of the City University of New York, Graduate School, School of Arts and Sciences, Department of Mathematics and Statistics, New York, NY 10021-5085. Offers applied mathematics (MA); mathematics for secondary education (MA); pure mathematics (MA). Part-time and evening/weekend programs available. *Faculty:* 1 full-time (0 women), 19 part-time/adjunct (9 women). *Students:* 5 full-time (3 women), 24 part-time (10 women); includes 12 minority (1 African American, 8 Asian Americans or Pacific Islanders, 3 Hispanic Americans). Average age 34. 46 applicants, 50% accepted, 16 enrolled. In 2006, 17 degrees awarded. *Degree requirements:* For master's, one foreign language, thesis (for some programs), comprehensive exam. *Entrance requirements:* For master's, GRE General Test, 24 credits in mathematics. Additional exam requirements/recommendations for international students: Required—TOEFL. *Application deadline:* For fall admission, 4/1 for domestic students, 2/1 for international students; for spring admission, 11/1 for domestic students, 9/1 for international students. Application fee: $125. *Expenses:* Tuition, state resident: full-time $3,200; part-time $270 per credit. Tuition, nonresident: part-time $500 per credit. Required fees: $45 per semester. *Financial support:* Federal Work-Study, institutionally sponsored loans, scholarships/grants, and tuition waivers (partial) available. Support available to part-time students. *Faculty research:* Data analysis, dynamical systems, computer graphics, topology, statistical decision theory. *Unit head:* Ada Peluso, Chairperson, 212-772-5300, Fax: 212-772-4858, E-mail: peluso@math.hunter.cuny.edu. *Application contact:* William Zlata, Director for Graduate Admissions, 212-772-4482, Fax: 212-650-3336, E-mail: admissions@hunter.cuny.edu.

Hunter College of the City University of New York, Graduate School, School of Education, Programs in Secondary Education, Concentration in Mathematics Education, New York, NY 10021-5085. Offers MA. *Accreditation:* NCATE. *Faculty:* 1 full-time (0 women). *Students:* 1 full-time (0 women), 45 part-time (32 women); includes 11 minority (2 African Americans, 5 Asian Americans or Pacific Islanders, 4 Hispanic Americans). Average age 35. 31 applicants, 42% accepted, 10 enrolled. In 2006, 13 degrees awarded. *Degree requirements:* For master's, thesis, professional teaching portfolio, New York State Teacher Certification Exam, research project. *Entrance requirements:* For master's, minimum GPA of 2.8 overall, 2.7 in mathematics courses; 24 credits of course work in mathematics. Additional exam requirements/recommendations for international students: Required—TOEFL, TWE. *Application deadline:* For fall admission, 4/1 for domestic students, 2/1 for international students; for spring admission, 11/1 for domestic students, 9/1 for international students. Applications are processed on a rolling basis. Application fee: $125. *Expenses:* Tuition, state resident: part-time $270 per credit. Tuition, nonresident: part-time $500 per credit. Required fees: $45 per semester. *Financial support:* Federal Work-Study and tuition waivers (partial) available. Support available to part-time students. *Unit head:* Dr. Edward Binkowski, Graduate Adviser, 212-772-4715, E-mail: binkowski@math.hunter.cuny.edu. *Application contact:* William Zlata, Director for Graduate Admissions, 212-772-4482, Fax: 212-650-3336, E-mail: admissions@hunter.cuny.edu.

Idaho State University, Office of Graduate Studies, College of Arts and Sciences, Department of Mathematics, Pocatello, ID 83209. Offers mathematics (MS, DA); mathematics for secondary teachers (MA). *Faculty:* 14 full-time (3 women). *Students:* 12 full-time (3 women), 4 part-time (all women); includes 2 minority (1 Asian American or Pacific Islander, 1 Hispanic American), 3 international. Average age 33. In 2006, 2 master's, 1 doctorate awarded. *Degree requirements:* For master's, thesis (for some programs), comprehensive exam, registration; for doctorate, thesis/dissertation, teaching internships, comprehensive exam, registration. *Entrance requirements:* For master's, GRE General Test, GRE Subject Test, course work in modern algebra, differential equations, advanced calculus, introductory analysis; for doctorate, GRE General Test, GRE Subject Test, minimum GPA of 3.5 (graduate), MS in mathematics, teaching experience, 3 letters of recommendation. Additional exam requirements/recommendations for international students: Required—TOEFL (minimum score 550 paper-based; 213 computer-based; 80 iBT). *Application deadline:* For fall admission, 7/1 for domestic students, 6/1 for international students; for spring admission, 12/1 for domestic students, 11/1 for international students. Applications are processed on a rolling basis. Application fee: $55. *Expenses:* Tuition, state resident: part-time $251 per credit. Tuition, nonresident: part-time $366 per credit. Tuition and fees vary according to degree level, program and reciprocity agreements. *Financial support:* In 2006–07, 6 fellowships with full and partial tuition reimbursements (averaging $12,164 per year), 12 teaching assistantships with full and partial tuition reimbursements (averaging $8,694 per year) were awarded; career-related internships or fieldwork, Federal Work-Study, scholarships/grants, tuition waivers (full and partial), and unspecified assistantships also available. Financial award application deadline: 1/1. *Faculty research:* Algebra, analysis geometry, statistics, applied mathematics. Total annual research expenditures: $20,000. *Unit head:* Dr. Robert Fisher, Chairman, 208-282-3604, E-mail: fishrobe@isu.edu. *Application contact:* Ellen Combs, Graduate School Technical Records Specialist, 208-282-2150, Fax: 208-282-4847.

Illinois Institute of Technology, Graduate College, College of Science and Letters, Department of Mathematics and Science Education, Chicago, IL 60616-3793. Offers mathematics education (MME, MS, PhD); science education (MS, MSE, PhD). *Faculty:* 8 full-time (3 women), 1 (woman) part-time/adjunct. *Students:* 38 full-time (25 women), 37 part-time (23 women); includes 25 minority (14 African Americans, 5 Asian Americans or Pacific Islanders, 6 Hispanic Americans), 6 international. Average age 38. 36 applicants, 64% accepted, 7 enrolled. In 2006, 25 master's, 2 doctorates awarded. *Degree requirements:* For master's, thesis or alternative, comprehensive exam (for some programs); for doctorate, thesis/dissertation, comprehensive exam. *Entrance requirements:* For master's, GRE General Test, minimum undergraduate GPA of 3.0; for doctorate, GRE General Test, minimum GPA of 3.0, 3 years of teaching experience. Additional exam requirements/recommendations for international students: Required—TOEFL (minimum score 550 paper-based; 213 computer-based). *Application deadline:* For fall admission, 5/1 for domestic and international students; for spring admission, 10/15 for domestic and international students. Applications are processed on a rolling basis. Application fee: $40. Electronic applications accepted. *Expenses:* Tuition: Full-time $13,086; part-time $727 per credit. Required fees: $7 per credit. $235 per term. Tuition and fees vary according to class time, course level, course load, program and student level. *Financial support:* In 2006–07, 12 research assistantships with full tuition reimbursements (averaging $18,000 per year) were awarded; fellowships, career-related internships or fieldwork, Federal Work-Study, institutionally sponsored loans, scholarships/grants, health care benefits, tuition waivers (partial), and unspecified assistantships also available. Support available to part-time students. *Faculty research:* Nature of science, scientific inquiry, pedagogical content knowledge, classroom discourse, model eliciting activities. Total annual research expenditures: $348,657. *Unit head:* Dr. Norman G. Lederman, Chair, Professor, 312-567-3658, Fax: 312-567-3659, E-mail: ledermann@iit.edu.

Illinois State University, Graduate School, College of Arts and Sciences, Department of Mathematics, Program in Mathematics Education, Normal, IL 61790-2200. Offers PhD. *Students:* 8 full-time (5 women), 14 part-time (11 women); includes 2 minority (both African Americans), 6 international. 7 applicants, 57% accepted. In 2006, 2 degrees awarded. *Degree requirements:* For doctorate, variable foreign language requirement, thesis/dissertation, 2 terms of residency, comprehensive exam. *Entrance requirements:* For doctorate, GRE General Test. *Application deadline:* Applications are processed on a rolling basis. Application fee: $40. *Expenses:* Tuition, state resident: full-time $3,330; part-time $185 per credit hour. Tuition, nonresident: full-time $6,948; part-time $438 per credit hour. Required fees: $1,259; $52 per credit hour. *Financial support:* In 2006–07, 3 teaching assistantships (averaging $11,745 per year) were awarded. Financial award application deadline: 4/1. *Unit head:* Dr. George Seelinger, Chairperson, Department of Mathematics, 309-438-8781.

Indiana University Bloomington, Graduate School, College of Arts and Sciences, Department of Mathematics, Bloomington, IN 47405-7000. Offers applied mathematics–numerical analysis (MA, PhD); mathematics education (MAT); probability-statistics (MA, PhD). PhD offered through the University Graduate School. *Faculty:* 36 full-time (1 woman). *Students:* 94 full-time (25 women), 31 part-time (6 women); includes 6 minority (all Asian Americans or Pacific Islanders), 56 international. Average age 28. In 2006, 32 master's, 11 doctorates awarded. Terminal master's awarded for partial completion of doctoral program. *Degree requirements:* For doctorate, one foreign language, thesis/dissertation. *Entrance requirements:* For master's and doctorate, GRE General Test, GRE Subject Test. Additional exam requirements/recommendations for international students: Required—TOEFL. *Application deadline:* For fall admission, 1/15 priority date for domestic students, 12/15 for international students; for spring admission, 9/1 priority date for domestic students, 9/1 for international students. Applications are processed on a rolling basis. Application fee: $50 ($60 for international students). Electronic applications accepted. *Expenses:* Tuition, state resident: full-time $5,791; part-time $241 per credit hour. Tuition, nonresident: full-time $16,866; part-time $703 per credit hour. *Financial support:* Fellowships with full tuition reimbursements, research assistantships, teaching assistantships with full tuition reimbursements, Federal Work-Study available. Support available to part-time students. Financial award application deadline: 2/1. *Faculty research:* Topology, geometry, algebra. *Unit head:* James F. Davis, Chair, 812-855-2200. *Application contact:* Misty Cummings, Graduate Secretary, 812-855-2645, Fax: 812-855-0046, E-mail: gradmath@indiana.edu.

Indiana University Bloomington, School of Education, Department of Curriculum and Instruction, Bloomington, IN 47405-7000. Offers art education (MS, Ed D, PhD); curriculum studies (Ed D, PhD); elementary education (MS, Ed D, PhD, Ed S); mathematics education (MS, Ed D, PhD); science education (MS, Ed D, PhD); secondary education (MS, Ed D, PhD); social studies education (MS, PhD); special education (MS, Ed D, PhD, Ed S). PhD offered through the University Graduate School. *Accreditation:* NCATE. Part-time and evening/weekend programs available. *Students:* 39 full-time (28 women), 82 part-time (54 women); includes 15 minority (5 African Americans, 1 American Indian/Alaska Native, 6 Asian Americans or Pacific Islanders, 3 Hispanic Americans), 33 international. Average age 37. In 2006, 1 degree awarded. Terminal master's awarded for partial completion of doctoral program. *Degree requirements:* For doctorate, thesis/dissertation; for Ed S, comprehensive exam or project. *Entrance requirements:* For master's, doctorate, and Ed S, GRE General Test. *Application deadline:* For fall admission, 6/1 priority date for domestic students, 3/1 for international students; for winter admission, 11/1 priority date for domestic students; for spring admission, 9/1 for international students. Applications are processed on a rolling basis. Application fee: $50 ($60 for international students). Electronic applications accepted. *Expenses:* Tuition, state resident: full-time $5,791; part-time $241 per credit hour. Tuition, nonresident: full-time $16,866; part-time $703 per credit hour. *Financial support:* Fellowships with full and partial tuition reimbursements, research assistantships with full and partial tuition reimbursements, teaching assistantships with full and partial tuition reimbursements, career-related internships or fieldwork, Federal Work-Study, institutionally sponsored loans, and tuition waivers (partial) available. Support available to part-time students. *Unit head:* Cary Buzzelli, Chairperson, 812-856-8100. *Application contact:* Bobbie Partenheimer, Admissions Services Coordinator, 812-856-8127, Fax: 812-856-8333, E-mail: partenhe@indiana.edu.

Indiana University of Pennsylvania, School of Graduate Studies and Research, College of Natural Sciences and Mathematics, Department of Mathematics, Program in Elementary and Middle School Mathematics Education, Indiana, PA 15705-1087. Offers M Ed. *Accreditation:* NCATE. *Students:* 1 (woman) full-time, 12 part-time (8 women), 1 international. Average age 33. 2 applicants, 50% accepted. In 2006, 11 degrees awarded. *Degree requirements:* For master's, thesis optional. *Entrance requirements:* For master's, 2 letters of recommendation. Additional exam requirements/recommendations for international students: Required—TOEFL. *Application deadline:* For fall admission, 7/1 priority date for domestic students; for spring admission, 11/1 for domestic students. Applications are processed on a rolling basis. Application fee: $30. *Expenses:* Tuition, state resident: full-time $6,048; part-time $336 per credit. Tuition, nonresident: full-time $9,678; part-time $538 per credit. Required fees: $1,069; $148 per year. *Financial support:* In 2006–07, 2 research assistantships with full and partial tuition reimbursements (averaging $2,495 per year) were awarded; Federal Work-Study also available. Support available to part-time students. Financial award application deadline: 3/15; financial award applicants required to submit FAFSA. *Unit head:* Dr. James Myers, Graduate Coordinator, 724-357-4764, E-mail: jrmyers@iup.edu.

Indiana University of Pennsylvania, School of Graduate Studies and Research, College of Natural Sciences and Mathematics, Department of Mathematics, Program in Mathematics Education, Indiana, PA 15705-1087. Offers M Ed. *Accreditation:* NCATE. Part-time programs available. *Students:* Average age 25. 6 applicants, 33% accepted. *Degree requirements:* For master's, thesis optional. *Entrance requirements:* For master's, 2 letters of recommendation. Additional exam requirements/recommendations for international students: Required—TOEFL. *Application deadline:* For fall admission, 7/1 priority date for domestic students; for spring admission, 11/1 for domestic students. Applications are processed on a rolling basis. Application fee: $30. *Expenses:* Tuition, state resident: full-time $6,048; part-time $336 per credit. Tuition, nonresident: full-time $9,678; part-time $538 per credit. Required fees: $1,069; $148 per year. *Financial support:* In 2006–07, research assistantships (averaging $4,740 per year); career-related internships or fieldwork and Federal Work-Study also available. Support available to part-time students. Financial award application deadline: 3/15; financial award applicants required to submit FAFSA. *Unit head:* Dr. Michael Bosse, Graduate Coordinator, 724-357-3791, E-mail: mbosse@iup.edu.

Indiana University–Purdue University Indianapolis, School of Science, Department of Mathematical Sciences, Program in Math Education, Indianapolis, IN 46202-2896. Offers MS.

Expenses: Tuition, state resident: full-time $5,437; part-time $227 per credit hour. Tuition, nonresident: full-time $15,694; part-time $654 per credit hour. Required fees: $620. Tuition and fees vary according to course load, campus/location and program.

Instituto Tecnológico y de Estudios Superiores de Monterrey, Campus Ciudad Obregón, Programs in Education, Program in Mathematics, Ciudad Obregón, Mexico. Offers ME.

Inter American University of Puerto Rico, Ponce Campus, Graduate School, Mercedita, PR 00715-1602. Offers accounting (MBA); biology (M Ed); chemistry (M Ed); criminal justice (MA); elementary education (M Ed); English as a Second Language (M Ed); finance (MBA); history (M Ed); human resources (MBA); mathematics (M Ed); Spanish (M Ed); trade (MBA). *Entrance requirements:* For master's, minimum GPA of 2.5.

Iona College, School of Arts and Science, Program in Adolescence Education, New Rochelle, NY 10801-1890. Offers biology education (MS Ed, MST); English education (MS Ed, MST); mathematics education (MS Ed, MST); social studies education (MS Ed, MST); Spanish education (MS Ed, MST). *Accreditation:* NCATE. Part-time and evening/weekend programs available. *Faculty:* 11 full-time (6 women), 21 part-time/adjunct (13 women). *Students:* 15 full-time (9 women), 68 part-time (52 women); includes 6 minority (1 African American, 1 Asian American or Pacific Islander, 4 Hispanic Americans). Average age 28. 42 applicants, 57% accepted, 11 enrolled. In 2006, 29 degrees awarded. *Degree requirements:* For master's, thesis or alternative. *Entrance requirements:* For master's, minimum GPA of 2.5 (MST), New York teaching certificate (MS Ed). Additional exam requirements/recommendations for international students: Required—TOEFL (minimum score 550 paper-based; 213 computer-based). *Application deadline:* Applications are processed on a rolling basis. Application fee: $50. Electronic applications accepted. *Expenses:* Tuition: Part-time $665 per credit. Required fees: $150 per term. *Financial support:* Unspecified assistantships available. Support available to part-time students. *Faculty research:* Reading/writing, educational technology, administration, early literacy assessment, literacy development. *Unit head:* Dr. Patricia Antonacci, Chair, 914-633-2080, Fax: 914-633-2608, E-mail: pantonacci@iona.edu. *Application contact:* Veronica Jarek-Prinz, Graduate Admissions, 914-633-2289, Fax: 914-633-2012, E-mail: vjarekprinz@iona.edu.

Iowa State University of Science and Technology, Graduate College, College of Liberal Arts and Sciences, Department of Mathematics, Ames, IA 50011. Offers applied mathematics (MS, PhD); mathematics (MS, PhD); school mathematics (MSM). *Faculty:* 46 full-time, 1 part-time/adjunct. *Students:* 59 full-time (17 women), 13 part-time (3 women); includes 1 minority (Asian American or Pacific Islander), 33 international. 114 applicants, 28% accepted, 21 enrolled. In 2006, 11 master's, 6 doctorates awarded. *Degree requirements:* For master's, thesis or alternative; for doctorate, thesis/dissertation. *Entrance requirements:* For master's and doctorate, GRE General Test. Additional exam requirements/recommendations for international students: Required—TOEFL (paper-based 550; computer-based 213; iBT 79) or IELTS (6.5). *Application deadline:* For fall admission, 2/1 priority date for domestic and international students; for spring admission, 10/1 priority date for domestic and international students. Application fee: $30 ($70 for international students). Electronic applications accepted. *Expenses:* Tuition, state resident: full-time $5,936; part-time $330 per credit. Tuition, nonresident: full-time $16,350; part-time $330 per credit. *Financial support:* In 2006–07, 2 research assistantships with full and partial tuition reimbursements (averaging $17,838 per year), 53 teaching assistantships with full and partial tuition reimbursements (averaging $19,680 per year) were awarded; fellowships, scholarships/grants, health care benefits, and unspecified assistantships also available. *Unit head:* Dr. Justin R. Peters, Chair, 515-294-1752, Fax: 515-294-5454, E-mail: gradmath@iastate.edu. *Application contact:* Dr. Paul Sacks, Director of Graduate Education, 515-294-0393, E-mail: gradmath@iastate.edu.

Ithaca College, Graduate Studies, School of Humanities and Sciences, Program in Adolescent Education, Ithaca, NY 14850-7020. Offers biology 7-12 (MAT); chemistry 7-12 (MAT); English 7-12 (MAT); French 7-12 (MAT); math 7-12 (MAT); physics 7-12 (MAT); social studies 7-12 (MAT); Spanish (MAT). *Faculty:* 14 full-time (5 women), 1 (woman) part-time/adjunct. *Students:* 8 full-time (2 women), 2 part-time (both women); includes 1 minority (Hispanic American) Average age 28. 12 applicants, 92% accepted, 10 enrolled. *Entrance requirements:* For master's, minimum GPA of 3.0. *Application deadline:* For fall admission, 5/15 for domestic students; for spring admission, 12/1 for domestic students. Application fee: $40. *Expenses:* Contact institution. *Financial support:* In 2006–07, 10 students received support, including 8 teaching assistantships (averaging $5,820 per year). Financial award application deadline:3/1. *Unit head:* Linda Hanrahan, Chairperson, 607-274-3147, E-mail: lhanrahan@ithaca.edu.

Jackson State University, Graduate School, School of Science and Technology, Department of Mathematics, Jackson, MS 39217. Offers mathematics (MS); mathematics education (MST). Part-time and evening/weekend programs available. *Faculty:* 20 full-time (4 women). *Students:* 6 full-time (4 women), 1 (woman) part-time; includes 6 minority (all African Americans), 1 international. In 2006, 2 degrees awarded. *Degree requirements:* For master's, thesis (for some programs), comprehensive exam. *Entrance requirements:* For master's, GRE General Test. Additional exam requirements/recommendations for international students: Required—TOEFL. *Application deadline:* For fall admission, 3/1 priority date for domestic students; for spring admission, 10/1 for domestic students. Applications are processed on a rolling basis. Application fee: $20. *Financial support:* In 2006–07, 6 students received support. Career-related internships or fieldwork, Federal Work-Study, scholarships/grants, and unspecified assistantships available. Support available to part-time students. Financial award application deadline: 3/1; financial award applicants required to submit FAFSA. *Unit head:* Dr. Tor A. Kwembe, Chair, 601-979-2161, E-mail: tor.a.kwembe@jsums.edu. *Application contact:* Mae Robinson, Admissions Coordinator, 601-968-2455, Fax: 601-968-8246, E-mail: mrobinson@ccaix.jsums.edu.

Jacksonville University, College of Arts and Sciences, School of Education, Program in Mathematics Education, Jacksonville, FL 32211-3394. Offers MAT. Part-time and evening/weekend programs available. *Degree requirements:* For master's, comprehensive exam. *Entrance requirements:* For master's, GRE General Test. Additional exam requirements/recommendations for international students: Required—TOEFL.

Kean University, College of Education, Program in Classroom Instruction and Curriculum, Union, NJ 07083. Offers bilingual/bicultural education (MA); classroom instruction (MA); earth science (MA); educational technology (MA); elementary education (MA); mathematics/science/computer education (MA); teaching (MA); teaching English as a second language (MA). *Accreditation:* NCATE. Part-time and evening/weekend programs available. *Faculty:* 19 full-time (10 women). *Students:* 34 full-time (29 women), 174 part-time (139 women); includes 73 minority (9 African Americans, 7 Asian Americans or Pacific Islanders, 57 Hispanic Americans), 4 international. Average age 34. 103 applicants, 93% accepted, 67 enrolled. In 2006, 82 degrees awarded. *Degree requirements:* For master's, 2 foreign languages, thesis, comprehensive exam. *Entrance requirements:* For master's, GRE General Test or MAT, PRAXIS, minimum GPA of 2.75, 2 letters of recommendation, interview. *Application deadline:* For fall admission, 5/1 for domestic students; for spring admission, 11/1 for domestic students. Application fee: $60 ($150 for international students). Electronic applications accepted. *Expenses:* Tuition, state resident: full-time $8,856; part-time $369 per credit. Tuition, nonresident: full-time $11,256; part-time $469 per credit. *Financial support:* In 2006–07, 2 research assistantships with full tuition reimbursements (averaging $3,217 per year) were awarded; unspecified assistantships also available. *Unit head:* Dr. Frank H. Osborn, Program Coordinator, 908-737-4289, E-mail: fosborne@kean.edu. *Application contact:* Joanne Morris, Director of Graduate Admissions, 908-737-3355, Fax: 908-737-3354, E-mail: grad-adm@kean.edu.

Kean University, College of Natural, Applied and Health Sciences, Program in Mathematics Education, Union, NJ 07083. Offers computer applications (MA); supervision of math education (MA); teaching of math (MA). Part-time and evening/weekend programs available. *Faculty:* 24 full-time (6 women). *Students:* 2 full-time (1 woman), 11 part-time (2 women); includes 6 minority (2 African Americans, 2 Asian Americans or Pacific Islanders, 2 Hispanic Americans), 1 international. Average age 40. 4 applicants, 100% accepted, 1 enrolled. In 2006, 8 degrees awarded. *Degree requirements:* For master's, thesis, comprehensive exam. *Entrance requirements:* For master's, GRE General Test, undergraduate major or strong minor in math, 2 letters of recommendation, interview. *Application deadline:* For fall admission, 5/1 for domestic students; for spring admission, 11/1 for domestic students. Application fee: $60 ($150 for international students). *Expenses:* Tuition, state resident: full-time $8,856; part-time $369 per credit. Tuition, nonresident: full-time $11,256; part-time $469 per credit. *Financial support:* In 2006–07, 1 research assistantship with full tuition reimbursement (averaging $3,217 per year) was awarded. *Unit head:* Dr. Francine Abeles, Program Coordinator, 908-737-3714, E-mail: fabeles@kean.edu. *Application contact:* Joanne Morris, Director of Graduate Admissions, 908-737-3355, Fax: 908-737-3354, E-mail: grad-adm@kean.edu.

Kutztown University of Pennsylvania, College of Graduate Studies and Extended Learning, College of Education, Program in Secondary Education, Kutztown, PA 19530-0730. Offers biology (M Ed); curriculum and instruction (M Ed); English (M Ed); mathematics (M Ed); secondary education (Certificate); social studies (M Ed). *Accreditation:* NCATE. Part-time and evening/weekend programs available. *Faculty:* 5 full-time (2 women). *Students:* 69 full-time (32 women), 80 part-time (44 women); includes 5 minority (1 African American, 1 American Indian/Alaska Native, 2 Asian Americans or Pacific Islanders, 1 Hispanic American), 3 international. Average age 32. 80 applicants, 88% accepted, 34 enrolled. In 2006, 26 degrees awarded. *Degree requirements:* For master's, thesis optional. *Entrance requirements:* For master's, GRE General Test. Additional exam requirements/recommendations for international students: Required—TOEFL. *Application deadline:* Applications are processed on a rolling basis. Application fee: $35. Electronic applications accepted. *Expenses:* Tuition, state resident: full-time $6,048; part-time $336 per credit. Tuition, nonresident: full-time $9,678; part-time $538 per credit. *Financial support:* In 2006–07, research assistantships with full tuition reimbursements (averaging $5,000 per year); career-related internships or fieldwork, Federal Work-Study, and unspecified assistantships also available. Financial award application deadline: 3/15; financial award applicants required to submit FAFSA. *Unit head:* Dr. Kathleen Dolgos, Chairperson, 610-683-4279, Fax: 610-683-1338, E-mail: dolgos@kutztown.edu.

Lehman College of the City University of New York, Division of Education, Department of Middle and High School Education, Program in Mathematics 7–12, Bronx, NY 10468-1589. Offers MS Ed. *Accreditation:* NCATE. Part-time and evening/weekend programs available. *Degree requirements:* For master's, comprehensive exam or thesis. *Entrance requirements:* For master's, 18 credits in mathematics, 12 credits in education. *Faculty research:* Mathematical problem solving, Piagetian cognitive theory.

Long Island University, Brooklyn Campus, School of Education, Department of Teaching and Learning, Program in Secondary Education, Brooklyn, NY 11201-8423. Offers mathematics education (MS Ed). Part-time and evening/weekend programs available. *Degree requirements:* For master's, thesis optional. *Entrance requirements:* For master's, 2 letters of recommendation. Additional exam requirements/recommendations for international students: Required—TOEFL (minimum score 500 paper-based; 173 computer-based). Electronic applications accepted.

Long Island University, C.W. Post Campus, College of Liberal Arts and Sciences, Department of Mathematics, Brookville, NY 11548-1300. Offers applied mathematics (MS); mathematics education (MS); mathematics for secondary school teachers (MS). Part-time and evening/weekend programs available. *Degree requirements:* For master's, thesis or alternative, oral presentation. *Entrance requirements:* Additional exam requirements/recommendations for international students: Required—TOEFL. Electronic applications accepted. *Faculty research:* Differential geometry, topological groups, general topology, number theory, analysis and statistics, numerical analysis.

Long Island University, C.W. Post Campus, School of Education, Department of Curriculum and Instruction, Brookville, NY 11548-1300. Offers adolescence education (MS); adolescence education: biology (MS); adolescence education: earth science (MS); adolescence education: English (MS); adolescence education: mathematics (MS); adolescence education: social studies (MS); adolescence education: Spanish (MS); art education (MS); bilingual education (MS); childhood education (MS); early childhood education (MS); middle childhood education (MS); music education (MS); teaching English to speakers of other languages (MS). Part-time and evening/weekend programs available. *Degree requirements:* For master's, comprehensive exam or thesis, student teaching. *Entrance requirements:* For master's, minimum GPA of 2.75 in major, 2.5 overall. Electronic applications accepted. *Faculty research:* Ethics and education, teaching strategies.

Louisiana Tech University, Graduate School, College of Education, Department of Curriculum, Instruction and Leadership, Ruston, LA 71272. Offers curriculum and instruction (MS, Ed D); educational leadership (Ed D); secondary education (M Ed), including business education, English education, foreign language education, health and physical education, mathematics education, science education, social studies education, speech education. *Accreditation:* NCATE. Part-time programs available. *Degree requirements:* For doctorate, thesis/dissertation. *Entrance requirements:* For master's and doctorate, GRE General Test.

Loyola Marymount University, Graduate Division, College of Science and Engineering, Program in Mathematics, Los Angeles, CA 90045-2659. Offers MAT. *Faculty:* 19 full-time (7 women), 13 part-time/adjunct (6 women). *Students:* 1 full-time (0 women), 4 part-time (2 women); includes 4 minority (1 African American, 2 Asian Americans or Pacific Islanders, 1 Hispanic American). Average age 30. 2 applicants, 50% accepted, 1 enrolled.Application fee: $50. *Financial support:* In 2006–07, 2 students received support, including research assistantships (averaging $12,370 per year). Financial award application deadline: 6/1. *Unit head:* Dr. Michael Grady, Director, E-mail: mgrady@lmu.edu.

Manhattanville College, Graduate Programs, School of Education, Program in Middle Childhood/Adolescence Education (Grades 5-12), Purchase, NY 10577-2132. Offers biology (MAT); biology and special education (MPS); chemistry (MAT); chemistry and special education (MPS); English (MAT); English and special education (MPS); literacy (MPS), including reading and writing, writing; literacy and special education (MPS); math (MAT); math and special education (MPS); second language (MAT), including French, Italian, Latin, Spanish; social studies (MAT); social studies and special education (MPS); special education (MPS). Part-time and evening/weekend programs available. *Students:* 76 full-time (53 women), 109 part-time (68 women); includes 8 African Americans, 1 Asian American or Pacific Islander, 10 Hispanic Americans, 1 international. In 2006, 165 degrees awarded. *Degree requirements:* For master's, comprehensive exam or research project, field experience. *Entrance requirements:* For master's, minimum undergraduate GPA of 3.0, 2 letters of recommendation. *Application deadline:* Applications are processed on a rolling basis. Application fee: $55. *Financial support:* Career-related internships or fieldwork and institutionally sponsored loans available. Support available to part-time students. *Application contact:* Alyce Ware Poli, Director of Admissions, 914-323-5142, Fax: 914-694-1732, E-mail: edschool@mville.edu.

Marquette University, Graduate School, College of Arts and Sciences, Department of Mathematics, Statistics, and Computer Science, Milwaukee, WI 53201-1881. Offers algebra (PhD); bio-mathematical modeling (PhD); computers (MS); mathematics (MS); mathematics education (MS); statistics (MS). Part-time programs available. *Faculty:* 28 full-time (10 women), 9 part-time/adjunct (4 women). *Students:* 16 full-time (4 women), 9 part-time (4 women); includes 1 minority (Hispanic American), 13 international. Average age 31. 56 applicants, 82% accepted, 19 enrolled. In 2006, 3 master's, 1 doctorate awarded. Terminal master's awarded for partial completion of doctoral program. *Degree requirements:* For master's, thesis or alternative, comprehensive exam; for doctorate, 2 foreign languages, thesis/dissertation, comprehensive exam. *Entrance requirements:* For doctorate, sample of scholarly writing. Additional exam requirements/recommendations for international students: Required—TOEFL. Application fee: $40. *Financial support:* In 2006–07, 2 research assistantships, 20 teaching

Mathematics Education

Marquette University (continued)
assistantships were awarded; Federal Work-Study, institutionally sponsored loans, scholarships/grants, and tuition waivers (full and partial) also available. Support available to part-time students. Financial award application deadline: 2/15. *Faculty research:* Models of physiological systems, mathematical immunology, computational group theory, mathematical logic. Total annual research expenditures: $77,233. *Unit head:* Dr. Peter Jones, Chair, 414-288-3263, Fax: 414-288-1578. *Application contact:* Dr. Gary Krenz, Director of Graduate Studies, 414-288-6345.

Miami University, Graduate School, College of Arts and Sciences, Department of Mathematics and Statistics, Program in Mathematics, Oxford, OH 45056. Offers mathematics (MA, MAT, MS); mathematics/operations research (MS). Part-time programs available. *Degree requirements:* For master's, final exam. *Entrance requirements:* For master's, minimum undergraduate GPA of 3.0 during previous 2 years or 2.75 overall. Additional exam requirements/recommendations for international students: Required—TOEFL, TWE. Electronic applications accepted.

Miami University, Graduate School, School of Education and Allied Professions, Department of Teacher Education, Program in Secondary Education, Oxford, OH 45056. Offers adolescent education (MAT), including integrated English, integrated mathematics, integrated social studies, language arts; elementary mathematics education (M Ed); secondary education (M Ed, MAT). *Accreditation:* NCATE. Part-time programs available. *Degree requirements:* For master's, thesis (for some programs), final exam. *Entrance requirements:* For master's, MAT, minimum undergraduate GPA of 3.0 during previous 2 years or 2.75 overall. *Faculty research:* Teacher effectiveness, collaboration models.

Michigan State University, The Graduate School, College of Natural Science, Department of Mathematics, East Lansing, MI 48824. Offers applied mathematics (MS, PhD); industrial mathematics (MS); mathematics (MAT, MS, PhD); mathematics education (PhD). *Faculty:* 57 full-time (10 women). *Students:* 127 full-time (32 women), 5 part-time (2 women); includes 9 minority (1 African American, 1 American Indian/Alaska Native, 3 Asian Americans or Pacific Islanders, 4 Hispanic Americans), 66 international. Average age 27. 179 applicants, 23% accepted. In 2006, 18 master's, 15 doctorates awarded. *Entrance requirements:* Additional exam requirements/recommendations for international students: Required—TOEFL. Electronic applications accepted. *Expenses:* Tuition, state resident: part-time $346 per credit hour. Tuition, nonresident: part-time $730 per credit hour. Tuition and fees vary according to program. *Financial support:* In 2006–07, 14 fellowships with tuition reimbursements (averaging $4,370 per year), 15 research assistantships with tuition reimbursements (averaging $15,579 per year), 102 teaching assistantships with tuition reimbursements (averaging $14,026 per year) were awarded. Total annual research expenditures: $2.9 million. *Unit head:* Dr. Peter W. Bates, Chairperson, 517-355-9681, Fax: 517-432-1562, E-mail: bates@math.msu.edu. *Application contact:* Barbara S. Miller, Graduate Secretary, 517-353-6338, Fax: 517-432-1562, E-mail: bmiller@math.msu.edu.

Michigan State University, The Graduate School, College of Natural Science and College of Education, Division of Science and Mathematics Education, Program in Mathematics Education, East Lansing, MI 48824. Offers MS, PhD. *Students:* 10 full-time (5 women); includes 2 minority (1 African American, 1 American Indian/Alaska Native), 3 international. Average age 31. 14 applicants, 21% accepted. *Expenses:* Tuition, state resident: part-time $346 per credit hour. Tuition, nonresident: part-time $730 per credit hour. Tuition and fees vary according to program. *Financial support:* In 2006–07, 4 fellowships with tuition reimbursements, 9 research assistantships with tuition reimbursements (averaging $13,705 per year), 5 teaching assistantships with tuition reimbursements (averaging $13,914 per year) were awarded. *Application contact:* Program Information, 517-355-1708, Fax: 517-432-6868, E-mail: mathed@msu.edu.

Middle Tennessee State University, College of Graduate Studies, College of Basic and Applied Sciences, Department of Mathematical Sciences, Murfreesboro, TN 37132. Offers mathematics (MS); mathematics education (MST). Part-time and evening/weekend programs available. Postbaccalaureate distance learning degree programs offered. *Faculty:* 21 full-time (9 women). *Students:* 1 full-time (0 women), 29 part-time (13 women); includes 3 minority (2 African Americans, 1 Asian American or Pacific Islander). Average age 31. 7 applicants, 100% accepted. In 2006, 3 degrees awarded. *Degree requirements:* For master's, comprehensive exam. *Entrance requirements:* For master's, GRE General Test or MAT. Additional exam requirements/recommendations for international students: Required—TOEFL (minimum score 525 paper-based; 195 computer-based). *Application deadline:* For fall admission, 8/1 priority date for domestic students. Applications are processed on a rolling basis. Application fee: $25. Electronic applications accepted. *Financial support:* In 2006–07, 9 students received support. Institutionally sponsored loans available. Support available to part-time students. Financial award application deadline: 5/1; financial award applicants required to submit FAFSA. *Unit head:* Dr. Michaele Chappell, Interim Chair, 615-898-2669, Fax: 615-898-5422, E-mail: chappell@mtsu.edu.

Millersville University of Pennsylvania, Graduate School, School of Science and Mathematics, Department of Mathematics, Millersville, PA 17551-0302. Offers M Ed. *Accreditation:* NCATE. Part-time and evening/weekend programs available. *Faculty:* 20 full-time (4 women), 6 part-time/adjunct (all women). *Students:* 3 full-time (2 women), 8 part-time (6 women). Average age 29. 6 applicants, 100% accepted, 6 enrolled. In 2006, 6 degrees awarded. *Degree requirements:* For master's, thesis optional. *Entrance requirements:* For master's, GRE or MAT, minimum undergraduate GPA of 2.75, bachelor's degree in mathematics, mathematical proficiency. *Application deadline:* For fall admission, 3/1 priority date for domestic students; for spring admission, 10/1 priority date for domestic students. Applications are processed on a rolling basis. Application fee: $35. *Expenses:* Tuition, state resident: full-time $6,048; part-time $336 per credit. Tuition, nonresident: full-time $9,678; part-time $538 per credit. Required fees: $1,244. Tuition and fees vary according to course load. *Financial support:* Research assistantships with full tuition reimbursements, Federal Work-Study, institutionally sponsored loans, and unspecified assistantships available. Support available to part-time students. Financial award application deadline: 3/15; financial award applicants required to submit FAFSA. *Faculty research:* Math education statistics, applied mathematics, pure mathematics. *Unit head:* Dr. Robert T. Smith, Chair, 717-872-3780, Fax: 717-871-2320. *Application contact:* Dr. Victor S. DeSantis, Dean of Graduate Studies, 717-872-3099, Fax: 717-871-2022, E-mail: victor.desantis@millersville.edu.

Mills College, Graduate Studies, Education Department, Oakland, CA 94613-1000. Offers administration (Ed D); child life in health care settings (MA); early childhood education (MA); education (MA), including curriculum and instruction, elementary education, English education, mathematics education, science education, secondary education, social sciences education, teaching. Part-time and evening/weekend programs available. *Faculty:* 10 full-time (7 women), 15 part-time/adjunct (12 women). *Students:* 192 full-time (153 women), 41 part-time (36 women); includes 62 minority (28 African Americans, 13 Asian Americans or Pacific Islanders, 21 Hispanic Americans), 2 international. Average age 34. 160 applicants, 74% accepted, 73 enrolled. In 2006, 52 master's, 1 doctorate awarded. Terminal master's awarded for partial completion of doctoral program. *Degree requirements:* For master's, comprehensive exam. *Entrance requirements:* For doctorate, GRE General Test. Additional exam requirements/recommendations for international students: Required—TOEFL. *Application deadline:* For fall admission, 2/1 for domestic and international students; for spring admission, 11/1 for domestic and international students. Applications are processed on a rolling basis. Application fee: $50. Electronic applications accepted. *Financial support:* In 2006–07, 56 fellowships with tuition reimbursements (averaging $2,700 per year), 15 teaching assistantships (averaging $6,350 per year) were awarded; career-related internships or fieldwork, institutionally sponsored loans, scholarships/grants, and residence awards also available. Support available to part-time students. Financial award application deadline: 2/1; financial award applicants required to submit CSS PROFILE or FAFSA. *Faculty research:* Child development, gender and education, public policy, cross-cultural development, development of literacy. *Unit head:* Joseph Kahne, Chairperson, 510-430-3190, Fax: 510-430-3314, E-mail: grad-studies@mills.edu. *Application contact:* Randy McGlauthing, Director of Graduate Admissions, 510-430-2355, Fax: 510-430-2159, E-mail: rmglaut@mills.edu.

Minnesota State University Mankato, College of Graduate Studies, College of Science, Engineering and Technology, Department of Mathematics and Statistics, Mankato, MN 56001. Offers mathematics (MA, MS); mathematics education (MAT, MS); statistics (MS). *Students:* 5 full-time (2 women), 12 part-time (6 women). Average age 32. In 2006, 5 degrees awarded. *Degree requirements:* For master's, one foreign language, thesis or alternative, comprehensive exam. *Entrance requirements:* For master's, GRE General Test (if GPA is below 2.75), minimum GPA of 2.75 during previous 2 years of course work. Additional exam requirements/recommendations for international students: Required—TOEFL. *Application deadline:* For fall admission, 7/1 priority date for domestic students; for spring admission, 11/1 for domestic students. Applications are processed on a rolling basis. Application fee: $40. Electronic applications accepted. *Financial support:* Fellowships with partial tuition reimbursements, research assistantships with full tuition reimbursements, teaching assistantships with full tuition reimbursements, Federal Work-Study, institutionally sponsored loans, and unspecified assistantships available. Support available to part-time students. Financial award application deadline: 3/15; financial award applicants required to submit FAFSA. *Unit head:* Dr. Larry Pearson, Chairperson, 507-389-1453. *Application contact:* 507-389-2321, E-mail: grad@mnsu.edu.

Minot State University, Graduate School, Program in Mathematics and Computer Science, Minot, ND 58707-0002. Offers mathematics (MAT). *Faculty:* 4 full-time (0 women). *Students:* 31. 2 applicants, 100% accepted. In 2006, 10 degrees awarded. *Degree requirements:* For master's, thesis or alternative. *Entrance requirements:* For master's, minimum GPA of 2.75, undergraduate major in mathematics, teaching certificate. Additional exam requirements/recommendations for international students: Required—TOEFL. *Application deadline:* Applications are processed on a rolling basis. Application fee: $35. *Financial support:* In 2006–07, 2 students received support, including 1 research assistantship with partial tuition reimbursement available (averaging $500 per year), 1 teaching assistantship with partial tuition reimbursement available (averaging $500 per year); career-related internships or fieldwork, institutionally sponsored loans, and tuition waivers (partial) also available. Support available to part-time students. Financial award application deadline: 4/1. *Faculty research:* Mathematics education. *Unit head:* Dr. Selmer Moen, Chairperson, 701-858-3077. *Application contact:* Brenda Anderson, Administrative Assistant, 701-858-3250, Fax: 701-858-4286, E-mail: brenda.anderson@minotstateu.edu.

Mississippi College, Graduate School, School of Education, Department of Teacher Education and Leadership, Clinton, MS 39058. Offers art (M Ed); biological science (M Ed); business education (M Ed); computer science (M Ed); dyslexia therapy (M Ed); educational leadership (M Ed, Ed S); elementary education (M Ed, Ed S); English (M Ed); higher education administration (MS); mathematics (M Ed); secondary education (M Ed); social studies (history) (M Ed); teaching arts (M Ed). Part-time programs available. *Faculty:* 9 full-time (5 women), 14 part-time/adjunct (10 women). *Students:* 52 full-time (36 women), 286 part-time (247 women); includes 173 minority (171 African Americans, 1 American Indian/Alaska Native, 1 Hispanic American), 1 international. Average age 32. In 2006, 131 degrees awarded. *Degree requirements:* For master's, thesis optional. *Entrance requirements:* For master's, NTE. Additional exam requirements/recommendations for international students: Recommended—IELTS. *Application deadline:* Applications are processed on a rolling basis. Application fee: $25. Electronic applications accepted. *Expenses:* Tuition: Full-time $7,290; part-time $405 per hour. Required fees: $150 per term. Tuition and fees vary according to campus/location and program. *Financial support:* Teaching assistantships, career-related internships or fieldwork, Federal Work-Study, scholarships/grants, and unspecified assistantships available. Support available to part-time students. Financial award applicants required to submit FAFSA. *Unit head:* Dr. Tom Williams, Chair, 601-925-3844, E-mail: twilliams@mc.edu.

Montclair State University, The Graduate School, College of Education and Human Services, Center of Pedagogy, Montclair, NJ 07043-1624. Offers mathematics education (Ed D); philosophy for children (Ed D). Part-time programs available. *Faculty:* 18. *Degree requirements:* For doctorate, thesis/dissertation. *Entrance requirements:* For doctorate, GRE, 3 letters of recommendation. Additional exam requirements/recommendations for international students: Required—TOEFL (minimum score 117 computer-based). *Application deadline:* For fall admission, 2/1 for domestic students, 11/15 for international students. Application fee: $60. Electronic applications accepted. *Expenses:* Tuition, state resident: part-time $450 per credit. Tuition, nonresident: part-time $682 per credit. Tuition and fees vary according to degree level and program. *Financial support:* Research assistantships with full tuition reimbursements, institutionally sponsored loans and scholarships/grants available. Financial award application deadline: 3/1; financial award applicants required to submit FAFSA. *Unit head:* Jennifer Robinson, Director, 973-655-4262.

See Close-Up on page 1115.

Montclair State University, The Graduate School, College of Education and Human Services, Department of Curriculum and Teaching, Montclair, NJ 07043-1624. Offers education (M Ed); educational technology (M Ed); school library media specialist (Certificate); teaching (MAT, Certificate), including art (MAT), biological science (MAT), early childhood education (P-3) (MAT), earth science (MAT), elementary education (K-8) (MAT), English (MAT), French (MAT), health and physical education (MAT), health education (MAT), home economics (MAT), mathematics (MAT), music (MAT), physical education (MAT), physical science (MAT), social studies (MAT), Spanish (MAT), teacher of ESL (MAT), teacher of students with disabilities (MAT). Part-time and evening/weekend programs available. *Faculty:* 16 full-time (12 women), 13 part-time/adjunct (8 women). *Students:* 147 full-time (113 women), 230 part-time (188 women); includes 58 minority (33 African Americans, 1 American Indian/Alaska Native, 12 Asian Americans or Pacific Islanders, 12 Hispanic Americans), 4 international. Average age 33. 118 applicants, 38% accepted, 37 enrolled. In 2006, 166 master's, 11 other advanced degrees awarded. *Degree requirements:* For master's, field experience. *Entrance requirements:* For master's, PRAXIS II, minimum GPA of 2.67, 2 letters of recommendation. Additional exam requirements/recommendations for international students: Required—TOEFL (minimum score 83 computer-based). *Application deadline:* For fall admission, 2/15 for domestic and international students; for spring admission, 9/15 for domestic and international students. Applications are processed on a rolling basis. Application fee: $60. Electronic applications accepted. *Expenses:* Tuition, state resident: part-time $450 per credit. Tuition, nonresident: part-time $682 per credit. Tuition and fees vary according to degree level and program. *Financial support:* In 2006–07, 7 research assistantships with full tuition reimbursements (averaging $7,000 per year) were awarded; Federal Work-Study, scholarships/grants, and unspecified assistantships also available. Support available to part-time students. Financial award application deadline: 3/1; financial award applicants required to submit FAFSA. *Unit head:* Dr. Deborah Eldridge, Chairperson, 973-655-5187.

Montclair State University, The Graduate School, College of Education and Human Services, Department of Educational Foundations, Montclair, NJ 07043-1624. Offers critical thinking (M Ed); mathematics education (Ed D); philosophy for children (M Ed, Ed D, Certificate). Part-time and evening/weekend programs available. *Faculty:* 9 full-time (3 women), 7 part-time/adjunct (3 women). *Students:* 12 full-time (6 women), 42 part-time (29 women); includes 10 minority (7 African Americans, 1 Asian American or Pacific Islander, 2 Hispanic Americans), 8 international. Average age 33. 11 applicants, 27% accepted, 2 enrolled. In 2006, 18 master's, 4 doctorates, 1 other advanced degree awarded. *Degree requirements:* For master's, field experience; for doctorate, thesis/dissertation, comprehensive exam. *Entrance requirements:* For master's, GRE or MAT, minimum GPA of 2.67, 2 letters of recommendation, teaching certificate; for doctorate, GRE General Test, 3 years of classroom teaching experience, interview, writing sample. Additional exam requirements/recommendations for international students: Required—TOEFL (minimum score 117 computer-based). *Application deadline:* For fall admission, 2/1 for domestic students, 2/15 for international students; for spring admission,

10/15 for domestic and international students. Applications are processed on a rolling basis. Application fee: $60. Electronic applications accepted. *Expenses:* Tuition, state resident: part-time $450 per credit. Tuition, nonresident: part-time $682 per credit. Tuition and fees vary according to degree level and program. *Financial support:* In 2006–07, 1 research assistantship with full tuition reimbursement (averaging $7,000 per year) was awarded; Federal Work-Study and scholarships/grants also available. Support available to part-time students. Financial award application deadline: 3/1; financial award applicants required to submit FAFSA. *Unit head:* Dr. Mark Weinstein, Chairperson, 973-655-5170.

Montclair State University, The Graduate School, College of Science and Mathematics, Department of Mathematics, Montclair, NJ 07043-1624. Offers mathematics (MS), including mathematics education, pure and applied mathematics, statistics; teaching middle grades math (Certificate). Part-time and evening/weekend programs available. *Faculty:* 29 full-time (10 women), 26 part-time/adjunct (11 women). *Students:* 20 full-time (15 women), 146 part-time (104 women); includes 26 minority (11 African Americans, 9 Asian Americans or Pacific Islanders, 6 Hispanic Americans), 6 international. 60 applicants, 55% accepted, 24 enrolled. In 2006, 21 master's, 15 other advanced degrees awarded. *Degree requirements:* For master's, comprehensive exam. *Entrance requirements:* For master's, GRE General Test, minimum GPA of 2.67, 2 letters of recommendation. Additional exam requirements/recommendations for international students: Required—TOEFL (minimum score 83 computer-based). *Application deadline:* For fall admission, 6/1 for international students; for spring admission, 10/1 for international students. Applications are processed on a rolling basis. Application fee: $60. *Expenses:* Tuition, state resident: part-time $450 per credit. Tuition, nonresident: part-time $682 per credit. Tuition and fees vary according to degree level and program. *Financial support:* In 2006–07, 8 research assistantships with full tuition reimbursements (averaging $7,000 per year) were awarded; Federal Work-Study, scholarships/grants, and unspecified assistantships also available. Support available to part-time students. Financial award application deadline: 3/1; financial award applicants required to submit FAFSA. *Faculty research:* Infectious disease. Total annual research expenditures: $130,000. *Unit head:* Dr. Helen Roberts, Chairperson, 973-655-5132. *Application contact:* Dr. Ted Williamson, Advisor, 973-655-5146, E-mail: williamsont@mail.montclair.edu.

Morgan State University, School of Graduate Studies, School of Education and Urban Studies, Program in Mathematics Education, Baltimore, MD 21251. Offers MS, Ed D. *Students:* 19; includes 1 Asian American or Pacific Islander. *Degree requirements:* For doctorate, thesis/dissertation, comprehensive exam. *Entrance requirements:* For doctorate, GRE General Test or MAT. Additional exam requirements/recommendations for international students: Required—TOEFL (minimum score 550 paper-based; 213 computer-based). *Application deadline:* For fall admission, 2/1 priority date for domestic students; for spring admission, 10/1 priority date for domestic students. Application fee: $0. *Expenses:* Tuition, state resident: part-time $272 per credit. Tuition, nonresident: part-time $478 per credit. Required fees: $38 per credit. *Financial support:* Application deadline: 2/1. *Unit head:* Dr. Glenda Prime, Coordinator, 443-885-3780, E-mail: glprime@moac.morgan.edu. *Application contact:* Dr. Maurice C. Taylor, Dean, 443-885-3185, Fax: 443-885-8226, E-mail: mctaylor@moac.morgan.edu.

National-Louis University, National College of Education, Program in Mathematics Education, Chicago, IL 60603. Offers M Ed, MS Ed, CAS. Part-time and evening/weekend programs available. *Students:* Average age 45. 1 applicant, 100% accepted. *Degree requirements:* For master's, thesis (for some programs). *Entrance requirements:* For master's, MAT or GRE, minimum GPA of 3.0, teaching certificate; for CAS, master's degree, teaching certificate. *Application deadline:* Applications are processed on a rolling basis. Application fee: $25. *Expenses:* Tuition: Full-time $17,685. One-time fee: $40 full-time. *Financial support:* Fellowships, career-related internships or fieldwork, Federal Work-Study, institutionally sponsored loans, and scholarships/grants available. Support available to part-time students. Financial award applicants required to submit FAFSA. *Unit head:* Dr. Arthur Hyde, Coordinator, 847-475-1100 Ext. 4520. *Application contact:* David McCulloch, Vice President for University Services, 800-443-5522 Ext. 5127, Fax: 847-465-0593, E-mail: dmcc@wheeling1.nl.edu.

New Jersey City University, Graduate and Continuing Education, College of Arts and Sciences, Department of Mathematics, Jersey City, NJ 07305-1597. Offers mathematics education (MA). Evening/weekend programs available. *Faculty:* 10. In 2006, 19 degrees awarded. *Degree requirements:* For master's, thesis optional. *Entrance requirements:* For master's, GRE General Test or MAT. Additional exam requirements/recommendations for international students: Required—TOEFL. *Application deadline:* For fall admission, 8/1 priority date for domestic students; for spring admission, 12/1 for domestic students. Applications are processed on a rolling basis. Application fee: $0. *Expenses:* Tuition, state resident: full-time $7,038; part-time $391 per credit. Tuition, nonresident: full-time $12,510; part-time $695 per credit. Required fees: $65 per credit. *Financial support:* Unspecified assistantships available. *Unit head:* Dr. Richard Riggs, Chairperson, 201-200-3202, E-mail: rriggs@njcu.edu.

New York University, Steinhardt School of Culture, Education and Human Development, Department of Teaching and Learning, Program in Mathematics Education, New York, NY 10012-1019. Offers MA. *Accreditation:* Teacher Education Accreditation Council. Part-time and evening/weekend programs available. *Faculty:* 7 full-time (4 women). *Students:* 31 full-time (19 women), 16 part-time (12 women); includes 9 minority (8 Asian Americans or Pacific Islanders, 1 Hispanic American). 25 applicants, 76% accepted, 9 enrolled. In 2006, 29 degrees awarded. *Degree requirements:* For master's, thesis (for some programs). *Entrance requirements:* Additional exam requirements/recommendations for international students: Required—TOEFL. *Application deadline:* For fall admission, 12/15 priority date for domestic and international students; for spring admission, 11/1 for domestic and international students. Applications are processed on a rolling basis. Application fee: $50. *Expenses:* Tuition: Part-time $1,080 per unit. Required fees: $56 per unit. $329 per term. Tuition and fees vary according to program. *Financial support:* Fellowships with full and partial tuition reimbursements, teaching assistantships with partial tuition reimbursements, career-related internships or fieldwork, Federal Work-Study, institutionally sponsored loans, scholarships/grants, and tuition waivers (partial) available. Support available to part-time students. Financial award application deadline: 2/1; financial award applicants required to submit FAFSA. *Faculty research:* Mathematics anxiety, women and mathematics learning disabilities, technology in teaching of mathematics, mathematical modeling. *Unit head:* Dr. Kenneth Goldberg, Director, 212-998-5460, Fax: 212-995-4049. *Application contact:* 212-998-5030, Fax: 212-995-4328, E-mail: steinhardt.gradadmissions@nyu.edu.

Nicholls State University, Graduate Studies, College of Arts and Sciences, Department of Mathematics and Computer Science, Thibodaux, LA 70310. Offers community/technical college mathematics (MS). Part-time and evening/weekend programs available. *Faculty:* 5 full-time (1 woman). *Students:* 6 full-time (3 women), 3 part-time (1 woman); includes 1 minority (Hispanic American), 1 international. Average age 31. 7 applicants, 100% accepted, 7 enrolled. *Degree requirements:* For master's, comprehensive exam. *Entrance requirements:* For master's, GRE General Test. *Application deadline:* For fall admission, 6/17 priority date for domestic students; for spring admission, 11/15 priority date for domestic students. Applications are processed on a rolling basis. Application fee: $20 ($30 for international students). Electronic applications accepted. *Expenses:* Tuition, state resident: part-time $450 per hour. Tuition, nonresident: part-time $450 per hour. *Financial support:* In 2006–07, teaching assistantships with full tuition reimbursements (averaging $10,000 per year); Federal Work-Study, scholarships/grants, and unspecified assistantships also available. Support available to part-time students. Financial award application deadline: 6/17. *Faculty research:* Operations research, statistics, numerical analysis, algebra, topology. *Unit head:* Dr. Scott J. Beslin, Head, 985-448-4384, Fax: 985-448-4927, E-mail: scott.beslin@nicholls.edu.

North Carolina Agricultural and Technical State University, Graduate School, College of Arts and Sciences, Department of Mathematics, Greensboro, NC 27411. Offers mathematics education (MS), including applied mathematics, mathematics, secondary education. *Accreditation:* NCATE. Part-time and evening/weekend programs available. *Degree requirements:*

For master's, thesis or alternative, qualifying exam, comprehensive exam. *Entrance requirements:* For master's, GRE General Test, minimum GPA of 3.0.

North Carolina State University, Graduate School, College of Education, Department of Mathematics, Science, and Technology Education, Program in Mathematics Education, Raleigh, NC 27695. Offers M Ed, MS, PhD. *Accreditation:* NCATE. Part-time programs available. *Degree requirements:* For master's, thesis (for some programs), oral exam; for doctorate, one foreign language, thesis/dissertation, oral and written exams. *Entrance requirements:* For master's, GRE General Test or MAT, minimum GPA of 3.0; for doctorate, GRE General Test, minimum GPA of 3.0, interview. Electronic applications accepted. *Faculty research:* Teacher education using technology, curriculum development, scientific visualization, problem solving.

North Dakota State University, The Graduate School, College of Human Development and Education, School of Education, Fargo, ND 58105. Offers agricultural education (M Ed, MS), including agricultural education, agricultural extension education (MS); counseling (M Ed, MS, PhD); curriculum and instruction (M Ed, MS), including pedagogy, physical education and athletic administration; education (PhD); educational leadership (M Ed, MS, Ed S); family and consumer sciences education (M Ed, MS); history education (M Ed, MS); mathematics education (M Ed, MS); music education (M Ed, MS); science education (M Ed, MS). *Accreditation:* NCATE. Part-time and evening/weekend programs available. Postbaccalaureate distance learning degree programs offered (minimal on-campus study). *Faculty:* 25 full-time (9 women), 3 part-time/adjunct (1 woman). *Students:* 29 full-time (25 women), 207 part-time (132 women); includes 15 minority (4 African Americans, 6 American Indian/Alaska Native, 3 Asian Americans or Pacific Islanders, 2 Hispanic Americans), 4 international. 88 applicants, 67% accepted, 56 enrolled. In 2006, 44 master's, 5 doctorates awarded. *Degree requirements:* For master's, comprehensive exam; for doctorate and Ed S, thesis/dissertation. *Entrance requirements:* For degree, GRE General Test, master's degree, minimum GPA of 3.25. Additional exam requirements/recommendations for international students: Required—TOEFL. *Application deadline:* Applications are processed on a rolling basis. Application fee: $45 ($60 for international students). *Financial support:* Research assistantships, teaching assistantships, career-related internships or fieldwork, Federal Work-Study, institutionally sponsored loans, and tuition waivers (full) available. Financial award application deadline: 4/15. *Unit head:* Dr. William O. Martin, Chair, 701-231-7104, Fax: 701-231-7416, E-mail: william.martin@ndsu.edu.

Northeastern Illinois University, Graduate College, College of Arts and Sciences, Department of Mathematics, Programs in Mathematics, Chicago, IL 60625-4699. Offers mathematics (MS); mathematics for elementary school teachers (MA). Part-time and evening/weekend programs available. *Faculty:* 16 full-time (5 women), 13 part-time/adjunct (5 women). *Students:* 5 full-time (4 women), 56 part-time (33 women); includes 8 minority (1 African American, 4 Asian Americans or Pacific Islanders, 3 Hispanic Americans). Average age 35. *Degree requirements:* For master's, project, thesis optional. *Entrance requirements:* For master's, minimum GPA of 2.75, 6 undergraduate courses in mathematics. *Financial support:* In 2006–07, 1 research assistantship with full tuition reimbursement (averaging $6,600 per year) was awarded; career-related internships or fieldwork, Federal Work-Study, institutionally sponsored loans, and tuition waivers (full and partial) also available. Support available to part-time students. Financial award applicants required to submit FAFSA. *Faculty research:* Numerical analysis, mathematical biology, operations research, statistics, geometry and mathematics of finance.

Northeastern State University, Graduate College, College of Education, Program in Mathematics Education, Tahlequah, OK 74464-2399. Offers M Ed. *Students:* 1 full-time (0 women), 10 part-time (9 women); includes 1 minority (American Indian/Alaska Native). In 2006, 4 degrees awarded. *Entrance requirements:* For master's, GRE or MAT, minimum GPA of 2.5. Additional exam requirements/recommendations for international students: Required—TOEFL (minimum score 213 computer-based). *Application deadline:* For fall admission, 6/1 priority date for domestic students. Applications are processed on a rolling basis. Application fee: $0 ($25 for international students). Electronic applications accepted. *Unit head:* Dr. Darryl Linde, Department Chair—Mathematics, 918-456-5511 Ext. 3809, E-mail: linded@nsuok.edu.

Northern Arizona University, Graduate College, College of Engineering and Natural Science, Department of Mathematics and Statistics, Flagstaff, AZ 86011. Offers mathematics (MAT, MS); statistics (MS). Part-time programs available. *Degree requirements:* For master's, thesis optional. *Faculty research:* Topology, statistics, groups, ring theory, number theory.

North Georgia College & State University, Graduate Studies, Program in Teacher Education, Dahlonega, GA 30597. Offers early childhood education (M Ed); educational leadership (Ed S); middle grades education (M Ed); secondary education (M Ed), including art education, biology education, chemistry education, English education, history education, mathematics education, physical education, science education; special education (M Ed), including inter-related special education, learning disabilities. *Accreditation:* NCATE. Part-time and evening/weekend programs available. Postbaccalaureate distance learning degree programs offered (minimal on-campus study). *Faculty:* 35 full-time (18 women), 9 part-time/adjunct (6 women). *Students:* 260. Average age 32. 120 applicants, 63% accepted. In 2006, 134 degrees awarded. *Degree requirements:* For master's, thesis optional. *Entrance requirements:* For master's, GRE General Test or MAT, minimum GPA of 2.75; for Ed S, GRE General Test or MAT, 3 years of teaching experience, master's degree, minimum graduate GPA of 3.25. *Application deadline:* For fall admission, 7/1 priority date for domestic students; for spring admission, 12/10 priority date for domestic students. Applications are processed on a rolling basis. Application fee: $25. Electronic applications accepted. *Expenses:* Tuition, state resident: full-time $3,044; part-time $127 per credit hour. Tuition, nonresident: full-time $12,172; part-time $508 per credit hour. Required fees: $892; $458 per semester. *Financial support:* Teaching assistantships, career-related internships or fieldwork and scholarships/grants available. Support available to part-time students. Financial award application deadline: 5/1. *Faculty research:* Computers and teachers' attitudes, rural versus urban teacher attitudes, teacher leadership roles, minority recruitment in teaching force. *Unit head:* Dr. Bob Michael, Dean, School of Education, 706-864-1998, Fax: 706-867-2850, E-mail: bmichael@ngcsu.edu. *Application contact:* Dr. Donna A. Gessell, Director of Graduate Studies and External Programs, 706-864-1528, Fax: 706-867-2795, E-mail: dgessell@ngcsu.edu.

Northwestern State University of Louisiana, Graduate Studies and Research, College of Education, Programs in Education, Natchitoches, LA 71497. Offers business and distributive education (M Ed); counseling (M Ed); early childhood education (M Ed); education (M Ed); education leadership (M Ed); educational technology (M Ed); elementary teaching (M Ed); English education (M Ed); home economics education (M Ed); mathematics education (M Ed); reading (M Ed); science education (M Ed); secondary teaching (M Ed); social sciences education (M Ed). *Students:* 49 full-time (41 women), 245 part-time (206 women); includes 78 minority (70 African Americans, 5 American Indian/Alaska Native, 2 Asian Americans or Pacific Islanders, 1 Hispanic American). Average age 35. In 2006, 158 degrees awarded. *Degree requirements:* For master's, thesis or alternative, comprehensive exam, registration. *Entrance requirements:* For master's, GRE General Test, minimum undergraduate GPA of 2.5. *Application contact:* Dr. Steven G. Horton, Associate Provost/Dean, Graduate Studies, Research, and Information Systems, 318-357-5851, Fax: 318-357-5019, E-mail: grad_school@nsula.edu.

Northwest Missouri State University, Graduate School, College of Arts and Sciences, Department of Mathematics and Statistics, Maryville, MO 64468-6001. Offers teaching mathematics (MS Ed). Part-time programs available. *Faculty:* 8 full-time (2 women). *Students:* 1 (woman) full-time, 4 part-time (2 women). 1 applicant, 100% accepted, 1 enrolled. In 2006, 3 degrees awarded. *Degree requirements:* For master's, comprehensive exam. *Entrance requirements:* For master's, GRE General Test, minimum undergraduate GPA of 2.5, writing sample. Additional exam requirements/recommendations for international students: Required—TOEFL (minimum score 550 paper-based; 213 computer-based). *Application deadline:* For fall admission, 7/1 for domestic and international students; for spring admission, 11/15 for domestic and international students. Applications are processed on a rolling basis. Application fee: $0 ($50 for international students). *Financial support:* In 2006–07, 3 teaching assistantships with

Mathematics Education

Northwest Missouri State University (continued)
full tuition reimbursements (averaging $6,000 per year) were awarded. Financial award application deadline: 3/1; financial award applicants required to submit FAFSA. *Unit head:* Dr. Dennis Malm, Chairperson, 660-562-1807. *Application contact:* Dr. Frances Shipley, Dean of Graduate School, 660-562-1145, Fax: 660-562-1096, E-mail: gradsch@nwmissouri.edu.

Nova Southeastern University, Fischler School of Education and Human Services, Graduate Teacher Education Program, Fort Lauderdale, FL 33314-7796. Offers athletic administration (MS); cognitive and behavioral disabilities (MS); computer science education (Ed S); computer science education (K-12) (MS); curriculum and teaching (Ed S); curriculum, instruction and technology (MS); curriculum, instruction, management and administration (Ed S); early childhood special education (MS); early literacy and reading (Ed S); early literacy education (MS); education technology (MS); educational leadership (administration K–12) (MS, Ed S); educational media (Ed S); educational media (K-12) (MS); elementary education (MS, Ed S), including ESOL endorsement (MS); English (MS, Ed S); exceptional student education (MS), including ESOL endorsement; gifted education (MS, Ed S); interdisciplinary arts education (MS); management and administration of educational programs (MS); mathematics (MS, Ed S); multicultural early intervention (MS); pre-kindergarten/primary (MS); preschool education (MS); reading (MS, Ed S); science (MS, Ed S); secondary education (MS); social studies (MS, Ed S); Spanish language (MS); teaching and learning (MA, MS), including curriculum and instruction (MA), elementary mathematics (MA), elementary reading (MA), K-12 technology integration (MA); teaching English to speakers of other languages (MS, Ed S); technology management and administration (Ed S); urban studies education (MS); varying exceptionalities (Ed S). Part-time and evening/weekend programs available. Postbaccalaureate distance learning degree programs offered. *Faculty:* 131 full-time (78 women), 548 part-time/adjunct (342 women). *Students:* 1,418 full-time (1,139 women), 3,464 part-time (2,877 women); includes 2,462 minority (1,732 African Americans, 13 American Indian/Alaska Native, 44 Asian Americans or Pacific Islanders, 673 Hispanic Americans), 77 international. Average age 38. 1,771 applicants, 80% accepted, 1419 enrolled. In 2006, 2,078 master's, 425 other advanced degrees awarded. *Degree requirements:* For master's and Ed S, thesis, practicum, internship. *Entrance requirements:* For master's, MAT, GRE, CLAST, CBEST, PRAXIS I, GKT, minimum GPA of 2.5; for Ed S, MAT or GRE, master's degree, teaching certificate, minimum GPA of 3.0. Additional exam requirements/recommendations for international students: Recommended—TOEFL (minimum score 550 paper-based; 213 computer-based), IELTS (minimum score 6). *Application deadline:* For fall admission, 8/11 priority date for domestic and international students; for winter admission, 12/28 priority date for domestic and international students; for spring admission, 4/22 priority date for domestic and international students. Applications are processed on a rolling basis. Application fee: $50. Electronic applications accepted. *Financial support:* Federal Work-Study available. Support available to part-time students. Financial award application deadline: 1/7. *Faculty research:* School effectiveness, critical thinking, leadership skills acquisition, child education, multicultural education. *Unit head:* Dr. Meline Kevorkian, Associate Dean of Master's and Educational Programs, 954-262-8500, Fax: 954-262-3606, E-mail: melinek@nova.edu. *Application contact:* Jennifer Quiñones Nottingham, Dean of Student Affairs, 800-986-3223 Ext. 8624, Fax: 954-262-3911, E-mail: jlquinon@nova.edu.

Oakland University, Graduate Study and Lifelong Learning, School of Education and Human Services, Department of Human Development and Child Studies, Program in Early Childhood Education, Rochester, MI 48309-4401. Offers early childhood education (M Ed, PhD, Certificate); early mathematics education (Certificate). *Students:* 25 full-time (23 women), 149 part-time (142 women); includes 27 minority (23 African Americans, 1 American Indian/Alaska Native, 1 Asian American or Pacific Islander, 2 Hispanic Americans), 1 international. Average age 36. 43 applicants, 93% accepted, 28 enrolled. In 2006, 45 master's, 2 doctorates awarded. *Degree requirements:* For doctorate, thesis/dissertation. *Entrance requirements:* For master's, minimum GPA of 3.0 for unconditional admission; for doctorate, GRE General Test, minimum GPA of 3.0 for unconditional admission. Additional exam requirements/recommendations for international students: Required—TOEFL (minimum score 550 paper-based; 213 computer-based). *Application deadline:* For fall admission, 5/1 for domestic students, 5/1 priority date for international students; for winter admission, 2/1 for domestic students, 9/1 priority date for international students. Application fee: $35. *Expenses:* Tuition, state resident: full-time $9,936; part-time $414 per credit. Tuition, nonresident: full-time $17,202; part-time $716 per credit. *Financial support:* Career-related internships or fieldwork, Federal Work-Study, institutionally sponsored loans, and tuition waivers (full) available. Financial award application deadline: 3/1; financial award applicants required to submit FAFSA. *Unit head:* Dr. Sherri Oden, Coordinator, 248-370-3027, E-mail: oden@oakland.edu.

Occidental College, Graduate Studies, Department of Education, Program in Secondary Education, Los Angeles, CA 90041-3314. Offers English and comparative literary studies (MAT); history (MAT); life science (MAT); mathematics (MAT); physical science (MAT); social science (MAT); Spanish (MAT). Part-time programs available. *Faculty:* 3 full-time (2 women), 2 part-time/adjunct (both women). *Students:* 4 full-time (all women), 3 part-time (1 woman); includes 5 minority (1 Asian American or Pacific Islander, 4 Hispanic Americans). Average age 25. 4 applicants, 100% accepted, 4 enrolled. In 2006, 4 degrees awarded. *Degree requirements:* For master's, final exam, graduate synthesis paper. *Entrance requirements:* For master's, GRE General Test, minimum GPA of 3.0. Additional exam requirements/recommendations for international students: Required—TOEFL (minimum score 625 paper-based). *Application deadline:* For fall admission, 3/1 for domestic and international students; for spring admission, 10/1 for domestic and international students. Applications are processed on a rolling basis. Application fee: $50. *Expenses:* Contact institution. *Financial support:* Fellowships, Federal Work-Study, institutionally sponsored loans, and scholarships/grants available. Support available to part-time students. Financial award application deadline: 3/1; financial award applicants required to submit FAFSA. *Unit head:* Chair, 323-259-2781, E-mail: edudept@oxy.edu. *Application contact:* Angela Allen, Credential Analyst/Department Services Coordinator, 323-259-2781, E-mail: edudept@oxy.edu.

Ohio University, Graduate Studies, College of Education, Department of Teacher Education, Athens, OH 45701-2979. Offers adolescent to young adult education (M Ed); curriculum and instruction (M Ed, PhD); mathematics education (PhD); middle child education (M Ed); reading and language arts (PhD); reading education (M Ed); social studies education (PhD); special education (M Ed, PhD). Part-time and evening/weekend programs available. *Faculty:* 21 full-time (13 women), 7 part-time/adjunct (all women). *Students:* 57 full-time (44 women), 61 part-time (46 women); includes 4 minority (2 African Americans, 1 Asian American or Pacific Islander, 1 Hispanic American), 36 international. 93 applicants, 61% accepted, 37 enrolled. *Median time to degree:* Of those who began their doctoral program in fall 1998, 92% received their degree in 8 years or less. *Degree requirements:* For master's, thesis or alternative, registration; for doctorate, thesis/dissertation, comprehensive exam, registration. *Entrance requirements:* For master's, GRE General Test or MAT if GPA is less than 2.9; for doctorate, GRE General Test, minimum GPA of 3.4, work experience. Additional exam requirements/recommendations for international students: Required—TOEFL (minimum score 550 paper-based; 213 computer-based). *Application deadline:* For fall admission, 4/1 priority date for domestic and international students. Applications are processed on a rolling basis. Application fee: $45. Electronic applications accepted. *Financial support:* In 2006–07, 52 students received support, including 31 research assistantships with full tuition reimbursements available (averaging $6,500 per year), teaching assistantships with full tuition reimbursements available (averaging $7,200 per year); Federal Work-Study, institutionally sponsored loans, tuition waivers (full), and unspecified assistantships also available. Financial award application deadline: 3/15. *Faculty research:* Cognition literacy, character education, teacher's education reform, disabilities. Total annual research expenditures: $605,070. *Unit head:* Dr. William Earl Smith, Chair, 740-593-4483, Fax: 740-593-0477, E-mail: smithw@ohio.edu. *Application contact:* Floyd J. Doney, Director of Student Affairs, 740-593-4400, Fax: 740-593-9310, E-mail: doney@ohio.edu.

Oklahoma State University, College of Arts and Sciences, Department of Mathematics, Stillwater, OK 74078. Offers applied mathematics (MS); mathematics (pure and applied) (PhD); mathematics (pure) (MS); mathematics education (MS, PhD). *Faculty:* 37 full-time (5 women), 7 part-time/adjunct (4 women). *Students:* 14 full-time (3 women), 22 part-time (11 women); includes 2 minority (both Asian Americans or Pacific Islanders), 20 international. Average age 31. 58 applicants, 26% accepted, 10 enrolled. In 2006, 12 master's, 1 doctorate awarded. *Degree requirements:* For master's, report or thesis; for doctorate, one foreign language, thesis/dissertation, comprehensive exam. *Entrance requirements:* For master's and doctorate, GRE. Additional exam requirements/recommendations for international students: Required—TOEFL. *Application deadline:* For fall admission, 6/1 priority date for domestic students, 3/1 priority date for international students; for spring admission, 8/1 priority date for international students. Applications are processed on a rolling basis. Application fee: $40 ($75 for international students). Electronic applications accepted. *Expenses:* Tuition, state resident: part-time $146 per credit hour. Tuition, nonresident: part-time $516 per credit hour. Required fees: $44 per credit hour. Tuition and fees vary according to program. *Financial support:* In 2006–07, 31 teaching assistantships (averaging $17,673 per year) were awarded; research assistantships, career-related internships or fieldwork, Federal Work-Study, scholarships/grants, health care benefits, tuition waivers (partial), and unspecified assistantships also available. Support available to part-time students. Financial award application deadline: 3/1. *Unit head:* Dr. Dale Alspach, Head, 405-744-5688, Fax: 405-744-8275.

Oregon State University, Graduate School, College of Science, Department of Science and Mathematics Education, Program in Advanced Mathematics Education, Corvallis, OR 97331. Offers MAT. *Accreditation:* NCATE. In 2006, 11 master's awarded. *Entrance requirements:* For master's, minimum GPA of 3.0 in last 90 hours. Additional exam requirements/recommendations for international students: Required—TOEFL. Application fee: $50. *Financial support:* Application deadline: 2/1. *Unit head:* M. Janice Rosenberg, Program Coordinator, 541-737-4031, Fax: 541-737-1817.

Oregon State University, Graduate School, College of Science, Department of Science and Mathematics Education, Program in Mathematics Education, Corvallis, OR 97331. Offers MA, MAT, MS, PhD. *Accreditation:* NCATE. *Students:* 17 full-time (10 women), 4 part-time (1 woman), 3 international. Average age 34. In 2006, 11 master's, 4 doctorates awarded. *Entrance requirements:* For master's, minimum GPA of 3.0 in last 90 hours of course work; for doctorate, GRE or MAT, minimum GPA of 3.0 in last 90 hours of course work. Additional exam requirements/recommendations for international students: Required—TOEFL. *Application deadline:* For fall admission, 3/1 for domestic students. Applications are processed on a rolling basis. Application fee: $50. *Financial support:* Teaching assistantships, Federal Work-Study and institutionally sponsored loans available. Support available to part-time students. Financial award application deadline: 2/1. *Faculty research:* Teacher action when focused on standards, teacher belief, integration of technology. *Unit head:* M. Janice Rosenberg, Program Coordinator, 541-737-4031, Fax: 541-737-1817.

Plymouth State University, College of Graduate Studies, Graduate Studies in Education, Program in Mathematics Education, Plymouth, NH 03264-1595. Offers M Ed. Part-time and evening/weekend programs available. *Students:* 1 (woman) full-time, 47 part-time (36 women). Average age 39. 10 applicants, 100% accepted, 10 enrolled. In 2006, 18 degrees awarded. *Degree requirements:* For master's, thesis optional. *Entrance requirements:* For master's, MAT, minimum GPA of 3.0. *Application deadline:* Applications are processed on a rolling basis. Application fee: $75. *Expenses:* Tuition, state resident: part-time $369 per credit. Tuition, nonresident: part-time $407 per credit. Tuition and fees vary according to course level. *Financial support:* Career-related internships or fieldwork, scholarships/grants, and unspecified assistantships available. Support available to part-time students. Financial award applicants required to submit FAFSA. *Unit head:* Dr. Richard Evans, Program Coordinator, 603-535-2487, E-mail: evans@plymouth.edu.

Portland State University, Graduate Studies, College of Liberal Arts and Sciences, Department of Mathematics and Statistics, Portland, OR 97207-0751. Offers mathematical sciences (PhD); mathematics education (PhD); statistics (MS); MA/MS. *Faculty:* 31 full-time (8 women), 14 part-time/adjunct (6 women). *Students:* 49 full-time (16 women), 62 part-time (21 women); includes 21 minority (4 African Americans, 2 American Indian/Alaska Native, 10 Asian Americans or Pacific Islanders, 5 Hispanic Americans), 10 international. Average age 33. 70 applicants, 93% accepted, 33 enrolled. In 2006, 21 master's, 1 doctorate awarded. *Degree requirements:* For master's, thesis or alternative, exams; for doctorate, 2 foreign languages, thesis/dissertation, exams. *Entrance requirements:* For master's, minimum GPA of 3.0 in upper-division course work or 2.75 overall; for doctorate, GRE General Test. Additional exam requirements/recommendations for international students: Required—TOEFL (minimum score 550 paper-based; 213 computer-based). *Application deadline:* For fall admission, 4/1 for domestic students, 3/1 for international students; for winter admission, 9/1 for domestic students, 8/1 for international students; for spring admission, 11/1 for domestic and international students. Applications are processed on a rolling basis. Application fee: $50. *Expenses:* Tuition, state resident: full-time $6,426; part-time $238 per credit. Tuition, nonresident: full-time $11,016; part-time $408 per credit. Required fees: $1,226; $23 per credit. $59 per term. Tuition and fees vary according to course load. *Financial support:* In 2006–07, 3 research assistantships (averaging $9,441 per year), 20 teaching assistantships with full tuition reimbursements (averaging $9,828 per year) were awarded; Federal Work-Study, scholarships/grants, tuition waivers (partial), and unspecified assistantships also available. Support available to part-time students. Financial award application deadline: 3/1; financial award applicants required to submit FAFSA. *Faculty research:* Algebra, topology, statistical distribution theory, control theory, statistical robustness. Total annual research expenditures: $287,717. *Unit head:* Marek Elzanowski, Chair, 503-725-3621, Fax: 503-725-3661, E-mail: elzanowskim@pdx.edu. *Application contact:* John Erdman, Coordinator, 503-725-3621, Fax: 503-725-3661, E-mail: erdman@pdx.edu.

Providence College, Graduate Studies, Department of Mathematics, Providence, RI 02918. Offers MAT. Part-time and evening/weekend programs available. *Faculty:* 4 full-time (1 woman). *Students:* 1 (woman) full-time, 21 part-time (12 women). Average age 40. 17 applicants, 71% accepted. In 2006, 8 degrees awarded. *Entrance requirements:* Additional exam requirements/recommendations for international students: Required—TOEFL (minimum score 550 paper-based; 213 computer-based). *Application deadline:* For fall admission, 8/1 for domestic students; for spring admission, 12/1 for domestic students. Applications are processed on a rolling basis. Application fee: $55. *Expenses:* Tuition: Full-time $6,573; part-time $939 per unit. *Financial support:* In 2006–07, research assistantships with full tuition reimbursements (averaging $8,400 per year); institutionally sponsored loans and unspecified assistantships also available. Support available to part-time students. Financial award application deadline: 8/1; financial award applicants required to submit FAFSA. *Faculty research:* Mathematics education, history of mathematics, differential equations. *Unit head:* Dr. Clement DeMayo, Director, 401-865-2633, Fax: 401-865-2057, E-mail: cdemayo@providence.edu.

Purdue University, Graduate School, School of Education, Department of Curriculum and Instruction, West Lafayette, IN 47907. Offers agricultural and extension education (PhD, Ed S); agriculture and extension education (MS, MS Ed); art education (PhD); consumer and family sciences and extension education (MS Ed, PhD, Ed S); curriculum studies (MS Ed, PhD, Ed S); educational technology (MS Ed, PhD, Ed S); elementary education (MS Ed); foreign language education (MS Ed, PhD, Ed S); industrial technology (PhD, Ed S); language arts (MS Ed, PhD, Ed S); literacy (MS Ed, PhD, Ed S); mathematics/science education (MS, MS Ed, PhD, Ed S); social studies (MS Ed, PhD); social studies education (Ed S); vocational/industrial education (MS Ed, PhD, Ed S); vocational/technical education (MS Ed, PhD, Ed S). *Accreditation:* NCATE. Part-time and evening/weekend programs available. *Faculty:* 26 full-time (13 women), 3 part-time/adjunct (all women). *Students:* 59 full-time (37 women), 112 part-time (70 women); includes 24 minority (13 African Americans, 3 American Indian/Alaska Native, 4 Asian Americans or Pacific Islanders, 4 Hispanic Americans), 38 international. Average age 35. 92 applicants, 68% accepted, 38 enrolled. In 2006, 52 master's, 23 doctorates awarded. *Degree requirements:* For master's, thesis optional; for doctorate, thesis/dissertation, oral and written exams; for Ed S, oral presentation, project. *Entrance requirements:*

For master's, GRE General Test, minimum B average; for doctorate, GRE General Test; for Ed S, GRE, minimum B average. Additional exam requirements/recommendations for international students: Required—TOEFL. *Application deadline:* For fall admission, 1/15 priority date for domestic students, 1/15 for international students; for spring admission, 9/15 for domestic and international students. Applications are processed on a rolling basis. Application fee: $55. Electronic applications accepted. *Financial support:* In 2006–07, 3 fellowships with full tuition reimbursements (averaging $10,500 per year), 11 research assistantships with full tuition reimbursements (averaging $11,500 per year), 43 teaching assistantships with full tuition reimbursements (averaging $10,800 per year) were awarded; career-related internships or fieldwork and tuition waivers (full) also available. Support available to part-time students. Financial award application deadline: 3/1; financial award applicants required to submit FAFSA. *Faculty research:* Literacy acquisition and development, teacher beliefs and knowledge, recruitment and retention of underrepresented students, economic education, literacy discourse. *Unit head:* Dr. James D Lehman, Head, 765-494-7935, Fax: 765-496-1622. *Application contact:* Patricia Mason, Coordinator of Graduate Studies, 765-494-2345, Fax: 765-494-5832, E-mail: gradoffice@soe.purdue.edu.

Purdue University Calumet, Graduate School, School of Engineering, Mathematics, and Science, Department of Mathematics, Computer Science, and Statistics, Hammond, IN 46323-2094. Offers mathematics (MAT, MS). Part-time programs available. *Entrance requirements:* Additional exam requirements/recommendations for international students: Required—TOEFL. *Faculty research:* Topology, analysis, algebra, mathematics education.

Queens College of the City University of New York, Division of Graduate Studies, Division of Education, Department of Secondary Education, Flushing, NY 11367-1597. Offers art (MS Ed); biology (MS Ed, AC); chemistry (MS Ed, AC); earth sciences (MS Ed, AC); English (MS Ed, AC); French (MS Ed, AC); Italian (MS Ed, AC); mathematics (MS Ed, AC); music (MS Ed, AC); physics (MS Ed, AC); social studies (MS Ed, AC); Spanish (MS Ed, AC). Part-time and evening/weekend programs available. *Faculty:* 22 full-time (14 women). *Students:* 50 full-time (28 women), 974 part-time (627 women). 633 applicants, 82% accepted, 407 enrolled. In 2006, 227 degrees awarded. *Degree requirements:* For master's, research project; for AC, thesis optional. *Entrance requirements:* For master's, minimum GPA of 3.0. Additional exam requirements/recommendations for international students: Required—TOEFL. *Application deadline:* For fall admission, 4/1 for domestic students; for spring admission, 11/1 for domestic students. Applications are processed on a rolling basis. Application fee: $125. *Financial support:* Career-related internships or fieldwork, Federal Work-Study, institutionally sponsored loans, and tuition waivers (partial) available. Support available to part-time students. Financial award application deadline: 4/1; financial award applicants required to submit FAFSA. *Unit head:* Dr. Eleanor Armour-Thomas, Chairperson, 718-997-5150, E-mail: armourthomas@yahoo.com. *Application contact:* Mario Caruso, Director of Graduate Admissions, 718-997-5200, Fax: 718-997-5193, E-mail: graduate_admissions@qc.edu.

Quinnipiac University, Division of Education, Program in Secondary Education, Hamden, CT 06518-1940. Offers biology (MAT); chemistry (MAT); English (MAT); French (MAT); history/social studies (MAT); mathematics (MAT); physics (MAT); Spanish (MAT). *Faculty:* 7 full-time (5 women), 23 part-time/adjunct (14 women). *Students:* 64 full-time (41 women); includes 5 minority (1 African American, 4 Hispanic Americans). Average age 26. 63 applicants, 87% accepted, 42 enrolled. In 2006, 37 degrees awarded. *Entrance requirements:* For master's, PRAXIS I, minimum GPA of 2.67, interview. Additional exam requirements/recommendations for international students: Required—TOEFL (minimum score 575 paper-based; 233 computer-based; 90 iBT), IELTS (minimum score 7). *Application deadline:* For fall admission, 3/15 priority date for domestic students. Applications are processed on a rolling basis. Application fee: $45. Electronic applications accepted. *Expenses:* Tuition: Part-time $675 per credit. Required fees: $30 per credit. *Financial support:* Career-related internships or fieldwork and tuition waivers (partial) available. Financial award application deadline: 4/15; financial award applicants required to submit FAFSA. *Faculty research:* Multicultural and urban education, role of technology in education, challenges of teaching divers learners, socio-cultural nature of learning. *Unit head:* Dr. Bernadine Krawczyk, Assistant Dean, Division of Education, 203-582-3510, Fax: 203-582-3473, E-mail: bernadine.krawczyk@quinnipiac.edu. *Application contact:* 800-462-1944, Fax: 203-582-3443, E-mail: graduate@quinnipiac.edu.

See Close-Up on page 911.

Rider University, Department of Graduate Education, Leadership and Counseling, Lawrenceville, NJ 08648-3001. Offers counseling services (MA, Ed S); curriculum, instruction and supervision (MA); director of school counseling services (Certificate); educational administration (MA); organizational leadership (MA); principal (Certificate); reading/language arts (MA, Certificate), including reading specialist (Certificate), reading/language arts (MA); school business administrator (Certificate); school counseling services (Certificate); school psychology (Ed S); special education (MA); supervisor (Certificate); teacher certification (Certificate), including business education, elementary education, English as a second language, English education, mathematics education, preschool to grade 3, science education, social studies education, world languages; teaching (MA). *Accreditation:* NCATE. Part-time and evening/weekend programs available. *Faculty:* 24 full-time (12 women), 30 part-time/adjunct (15 women). *Students:* 90 full-time (75 women), 457 part-time (369 women); includes 73 minority (50 African Americans, 2 American Indian/Alaska Native, 6 Asian Americans or Pacific Islanders, 15 Hispanic Americans), 1 international. Average age 32. 314 applicants, 61% accepted, 138 enrolled. In 2006, 116 master's, 19 other advanced degrees awarded. *Degree requirements:* For master's, thesis or alternative, internship, portfolios, comprehensive exam (for some programs); for other advanced degree, internship, professional portfolio. *Entrance requirements:* For master's, GRE (counseling, school psychology), MAT, interview, resumé, letters of recommendation; for other advanced degree, PRAXIS. Additional exam requirements/recommendations for international students: Required—TOEFL (minimum score 550 paper-based; 213 computer-based). *Application deadline:* For fall admission, 5/1 priority date for domestic students, 6/1 priority date for international students; for spring admission, 11/1 priority date for domestic and international students. Applications are processed on a rolling basis. Application fee: $50. Electronic applications accepted. *Expenses:* Tuition: Part-time $525 per credit. Required fees: $35 per course. $30 per semester. *Financial support:* In 2006–07, 271 students received support. Career-related internships or fieldwork, Federal Work-Study, institutionally sponsored loans, and unspecified assistantships available. Support available to part-time students. Financial award applicants required to submit FAFSA. *Faculty research:* Gifted students, self-esteem, hope and mental health, conflicts in group work, cultural diversity and counseling assessment of special needs in children. *Unit head:* Dr. Dennis C. Buss, Chair, 609-895-5353, Fax: 609-896-5362, E-mail: dbuss@rider.edu. *Application contact:* Jamie L Mitchell, Director of Graduate Admissions, 609-896-5036, Fax: 609-895-5680, E-mail: jmitchell@rider.edu.

See Close-Up on page 913.

Rollins College, Hamilton Holt School, Program in Education, Winter Park, FL 32789-4499. Offers elementary education (M Ed, MAT); secondary education (MAT), including English, mathematics, music. Part-time and evening/weekend programs available. *Students:* 14 full-time (12 women), 36 part-time (32 women); includes 5 minority (2 African Americans, 1 Asian American or Pacific Islander, 2 Hispanic Americans), 1 international. Average age 35. In 2006, 14 degrees awarded. *Degree requirements:* For master's, comprehensive exam. *Entrance requirements:* For master's, GRE or MAT, interview. Additional exam requirements/recommendations for international students: Required—TOEFL. *Application deadline:* For fall admission, 7/16 for domestic students; for winter admission, 12/3 for domestic students; for spring admission, 4/22 for domestic students. Applications are processed on a rolling basis. Application fee: $50. Electronic applications accepted. *Expenses:* Contact institution. *Financial support:* Teaching assistantships, scholarships/grants available. Support available to part-time students. *Unit head:* Dr. J. Scott Hewit, Director, 407-646-2300, E-mail: jhewit@rollins.edu. *Application contact:* Rebecca Cordray, Coordinator of Records and Registration, 407-646-1568, Fax: 407-975-6430, E-mail: rcordray@rollins.edu.

Rutgers, The State University of New Jersey, New Brunswick, Graduate School of Education, Department of Learning and Teaching, Program in Mathematics Education, New Brunswick, NJ 08901-1281. Offers Ed M, Ed D. Part-time programs available. *Faculty:* 5 full-time (3 women). *Students:* 36 full-time (24 women), 41 part-time (29 women). 62 applicants, 76% accepted, 34 enrolled. In 2006, 22 master's, 1 doctorate awarded. Terminal master's awarded for partial completion of doctoral program. *Degree requirements:* For master's, comprehensive exam (for some programs); for doctorate, thesis/dissertation, qualifying exam. *Entrance requirements:* For master's, GRE General Test, minimum GPA of 3.0; for doctorate, GRE General Test, minimum GPA of 3.5. Additional exam requirements/recommendations for international students: Required—TOEFL. *Application deadline:* For fall admission, 2/1 for domestic and international students. Application fee: $60. Electronic applications accepted. *Financial support:* Application deadline: 3/15; *Unit head:* Dr. Eva Thanheiser, Coordinator, 732-932-7496 Ext. 8153, Fax: 732-932-7552, E-mail: evat@rci.rutgers.edu.

Rutgers, The State University of New Jersey, New Brunswick, Graduate School of Education, Doctoral Program in Education, New Brunswick, NJ 08901-1281. Offers educational policy (PhD); educational psychology (PhD); literacy education (PhD); mathematics education (PhD). Part-time programs available. *Faculty:* 63 full-time (30 women). *Students:* 29 full-time (21 women), 45 part-time (34 women); includes 7 minority (4 African Americans, 3 Asian Americans or Pacific Islanders), 15 international. 85 applicants, 33% accepted, 13 enrolled. In 2006, 8 degrees awarded. *Degree requirements:* For doctorate, thesis/dissertation, qualifying exam. *Entrance requirements:* For doctorate, GRE General Test, GRE Subject Test (for mathematics education). Additional exam requirements/recommendations for international students: Required—TOEFL (minimum score 575 paper-based; 233 computer-based). *Application deadline:* For fall admission, 2/1 for domestic and international students. Application fee: $60. Electronic applications accepted. *Financial support:* In 2006–07, research assistantships with full tuition reimbursements (averaging $15,730 per year). Financial award application deadline: 3/15. *Faculty research:* Literacy education, math education, educational psychology, educational policy. *Unit head:* Prof. Clark Chinn, Director, 732-932-7496 Ext. 8319, Fax: 732-932-6829, E-mail: cchinn@rci.rutgers.edu. *Application contact:* Kristine Spaventa, Administrative Assistant, 732-932-7496 Ext. 8104, Fax: 732-932-8206, E-mail: sparenta@rci.rutgers.edu.

Sage Graduate School, Graduate School, Division of Education, Program in Teaching, Troy, NY 12180-4115. Offers art education (MAT); biology (MAT); English (MAT); mathematics (MAT); social studies (MAT). Part-time and evening/weekend programs available. *Faculty:* 11 full-time (8 women), 20 part-time/adjunct (15 women). *Students:* 34 full-time (28 women), 41 part-time (29 women); includes 3 minority (1 African American, 1 Asian American or Pacific Islander, 1 Hispanic American). Average age 27. 72 applicants, 64% accepted, 33 enrolled. In 2006, 31 degrees awarded. *Entrance requirements:* For master's, minimum undergraduate GPA of 2.75 overall, minimum undergraduate GPA of 3.0 in content area. Additional exam requirements/recommendations for international students: Required—TOEFL (minimum score 550 paper-based; 213 computer-based). *Application deadline:* For fall admission, 8/1 for domestic students. Applications are processed on a rolling basis. Application fee: $40. *Expenses:* Tuition: Full-time $9,270; part-time $515 per credit hour. *Financial support:* Career-related internships or fieldwork, scholarships/grants, and unspecified assistantships available. Support available to part-time students. Financial award application deadline: 3/1; financial award applicants required to submit FAFSA. *Unit head:* Peter McDermott, Director, 518-244-2493, E-mail: mcderp@sage.edu. *Application contact:* Shannon K. Easton, Director of Graduate and Adult Admission, 518-244-2443, Fax: 518-244-6880, E-mail: sgsadm@sage.edu.

St. John Fisher College, Office of the Provost, School of Arts and Sciences, Mathematics/Science/Technology Education Program, Rochester, NY 14618-3597. Offers MS. Part-time and evening/weekend programs available. *Faculty:* 3 full-time (1 woman), 1 part-time/adjunct (0 women). *Students:* 6 full-time (4 women), 83 part-time (59 women); includes 2 African Americans, 1 Asian American or Pacific Islander, 1 Hispanic American. Average age 32. 29 applicants, 66% accepted, 12 enrolled. In 2006, 24 degrees awarded. *Degree requirements:* For master's, thesis. *Entrance requirements:* For master's, minimum GPA of 3.0, interview, essay, recommendations. Additional exam requirements/recommendations for international students: Required—TOEFL (minimum score 575 paper-based; 233 computer-based; 80 iBT). *Application deadline:* For fall admission, 7/1 for domestic students; for spring admission, 10/30 for domestic students. Applications are processed on a rolling basis. Application fee: $30. *Expenses:* Tuition: Part-time $615 per credit. Tuition and fees vary according to program. *Financial support:* Federal Work-Study and scholarships/grants available. Financial award application deadline: 2/15; financial award applicants required to submit FAFSA. *Faculty research:* Mathematics education, science and technology education. *Unit head:* Dr. Diane Barrett, Graduate Director, 585-385-8366, E-mail: dbarrett@sjfc.edu. *Application contact:* Shannon Cleverley, Director of Graduate Admissions, 585-385-8161, Fax: 585-385-8344, E-mail: scleverley@sjfc.edu.

Salisbury University, Graduate Division, Department of Education, Salisbury, MD 21801-6837. Offers art (MAT); biology (MAT); business education (MAT); chemistry (MAT); early childhood education (M Ed); educational administration (M Ed); elementary education (M Ed); English (M Ed, MAT); French (MAT); geography (MAT); history (MAT); mathematics (MAT); media and technology (MAT); music (MAT); psychology (MAT); reading education (MAT); science (MAT); secondary education (MAT); social studies (MAT); Spanish (MAT). *Accreditation:* NCATE. Part-time and evening/weekend programs available. *Faculty:* 12 full-time (6 women), 10 part-time/adjunct (8 women). *Students:* 17 full-time (9 women), 84 part-time (72 women); includes 6 minority (5 African Americans, 1 Hispanic American). Average age 30. 15 applicants, 73% accepted, 11 enrolled. In 2006, 63 degrees awarded. *Degree requirements:* For master's, comprehensive exam (for some programs). *Entrance requirements:* For master's, PRAXIS, minimum GPA of 2.75. Additional exam requirements/recommendations for international students: Required—TOEFL (minimum score 550 paper-based; 213 computer-based). *Application deadline:* For fall admission, 8/1 priority date for domestic students; for spring admission, 1/1 for domestic students. Applications are processed on a rolling basis. Application fee: $45. *Expenses:* Tuition, state resident: part-time $260 per credit hour. Tuition, nonresident: part-time $546 per credit hour. Required fees: $52 per credit hour. *Financial support:* In 2006–07, 3 teaching assistantships with full tuition reimbursements were awarded; career-related internships or fieldwork and scholarships/grants also available. Support available to part-time students. Financial award applicants required to submit FAFSA. *Faculty research:* Middle-level education, student outcomes. *Unit head:* Dr. Edward C. Robeck, Program Coordinator, 410-543-6292, Fax: 410-548-2593, E-mail: ecrobeck@salisbury.edu. *Application contact:* Debra J. Clark, Administrative Assistant I, 410-543-6281, Fax: 410-548-2593, E-mail: djclark@salisbury.edu.

Salisbury University, Graduate Division, Program in Mathematics Education, Salisbury, MD 21801-6837. Offers MS. Part-time and evening/weekend programs available. *Faculty:* 5 full-time (2 women). *Students:* 1 (woman) full-time, 11 part-time (9 women). Average age 31. 3 applicants, 100% accepted, 3 enrolled. In 2006, 7 degrees awarded. *Entrance requirements:* Additional exam requirements/recommendations for international students: Required—TOEFL (minimum score 550 paper-based; 213 computer-based). *Application deadline:* Applications are processed on a rolling basis. Application fee: $45. Electronic applications accepted. *Expenses:* Tuition, state resident: part-time $260 per credit hour. Tuition, nonresident: part-time $546 per credit hour. Required fees: $52 per credit hour. *Financial support:* Applicants required to submit FAFSA. *Unit head:* Dr. Donald C. Cathcart, Coordinator, 410-543-5381, Fax: 410-548-5559, E-mail: dccathcart@salisbury.edu.

San Diego State University, Graduate and Research Affairs, College of Sciences, Department of Mathematical Sciences, San Diego, CA 92182. Offers applied mathematics (MS); mathematics (MA); mathematics and science education (PhD); statistics (MS). Part-time programs available. *Students:* 18 full-time (7 women), 26 part-time (17 women). 81 applicants, 74% accepted, 14 enrolled. In 2006, 28 master's, 3 doctorates awarded. *Degree requirements:* For doctorate, thesis/dissertation. *Entrance requirements:* For master's, GRE General Test; for

Mathematics Education

San Diego State University (continued)
doctorate, GRE, minimum GPA of 3.25 in last 30 undergraduate semester units, minimum graduate GPA of 3.5, MSE recommendation form, 3 letters of recommendation. Additional exam requirements/recommendations for international students: Required—TOEFL. *Application deadline:* For fall admission, 5/1 for domestic and international students; for spring admission, 11/1 for domestic students, 10/1 for international students. Applications are processed on a rolling basis. Application fee: $55. Electronic applications accepted. *Financial support:* Teaching assistantships, unspecified assistantships available. Financial award applicants required to submit FAFSA. *Faculty research:* Teacher education in mathematics. Total annual research expenditures: $1.3 million. *Unit head:* David Lesley, Chair, 619-594-6191, Fax: 619-594-6746, E-mail: lesley@math.sdsu.edu. *Application contact:* Larry Sowder, Graduate Coordinator, 619-594-7246, Fax: 619-594-6746, E-mail: lsowder@sciences.sdsu.edu.

San Francisco State University, Division of Graduate Studies, College of Education, Department of Elementary Education, Program in Mathematics Education, San Francisco, CA 94132-1722. Offers MA. *Accreditation:* NCATE. Part-time programs available. *Degree requirements:* For master's, thesis or alternative. *Entrance requirements:* For master's, minimum GPA of 2.5 in last 60 units. *Application deadline:* For fall admission, 11/30 priority date for domestic students. Applications are processed on a rolling basis. Application fee: $55. *Financial support:* Application deadline: 3/1. *Application contact:* Carol Langbort, Graduate Coordinator, 415-338-1584, E-mail: clangbo@sfsu.edu.

San Jose State University, Graduate Studies and Research, College of Science, Department of Mathematics, San Jose, CA 95192-0001. Offers mathematics (MA, MS); mathematics education (MA). Part-time and evening/weekend programs available. *Students:* 13 full-time (4 women), 31 part-time (19 women); includes 17 minority (2 African Americans, 11 Asian Americans or Pacific Islanders, 4 Hispanic Americans), 5 international. Average age 36. 37 applicants, 51% accepted, 11 enrolled. In 2006, 11 degrees awarded. *Degree requirements:* For master's, thesis (for some programs), comprehensive exam. *Entrance requirements:* For master's, GRE Subject Test. *Application deadline:* For fall admission, 6/29 for domestic students; for spring admission, 11/30 for domestic students. Applications are processed on a rolling basis. Application fee: $59. Electronic applications accepted. *Financial support:* In 2006–07, 20 teaching assistantships were awarded; career-related internships or fieldwork and Federal Work-Study also available. Support available to part-time students. Financial award applicants required to submit FAFSA. *Faculty research:* Artificial intelligence, algorithms, numerical analysis, software database, number theory. *Unit head:* Brad Jackson, Chair, 408-924-5100, Fax: 408-924-5080. *Application contact:* Richard Kubelka, Graduate Coordinator, 408-924-5132, E-mail: kubelka@math.sjsu.edu.

Slippery Rock University of Pennsylvania, Graduate Studies (Recruitment), College of Education, Department of Elementary Education and Early Childhood, Slippery Rock, PA 16057-1383. Offers early childhood education (M Ed); math/science (M Ed); reading (M Ed). *Accreditation:* NCATE. Part-time and evening/weekend programs available. *Degree requirements:* For master's, thesis (for some programs), reflective presentation, comprehensive exam (for some programs). *Entrance requirements:* For master's, GRE General Test, MAT, minimum GPA of 2.75 (minimum GPA of 3.0 for initial certification programs). Additional exam requirements/recommendations for international students: Required—TOEFL (minimum score 550 paper-based; 213 computer-based). *Application deadline:* For fall admission, 7/1 priority date for domestic and international students; for spring admission, 11/1 priority date for domestic and international students. Applications are processed on a rolling basis. Application fee: $25. Electronic applications accepted. *Expenses:* Tuition, state resident: part-time $336 per credit. Tuition, nonresident: part-time $538 per credit. Required fees: $84 per credit. $37 per semester. *Financial support:* Career-related internships or fieldwork, Federal Work-Study, scholarships/grants, and unspecified assistantships available. Support available to part-time students. Financial award application deadline: 5/1; financial award applicants required to submit FAFSA. *Unit head:* Dr. Suzanne Rose, Graduate Coordinator, 724-738-2863, Fax: 724-738-2880, E-mail: suzanne.rose@sn.edu. *Application contact:* April Longwell, Interim Director of Graduate Studies, 724-738-2051 Ext. 2116, Fax: 724-738-2146, E-mail: graduate.studies@sru.edu.

Slippery Rock University of Pennsylvania, Graduate Studies (Recruitment), College of Education, Department of Secondary Education/Foundations of Education, Slippery Rock, PA 16057-1383. Offers secondary education in math/science (M Ed). *Accreditation:* NCATE. *Degree requirements:* For master's, thesis (for some programs), comprehensive exam (for some programs). *Entrance requirements:* For master's, GRE General Test, MAT, minimum GPA of 2.75 (minimum GPA of 3.0 for initial certification programs). Additional exam requirements/recommendations for international students: Required—TOEFL (minimum score 550 paper-based; 213 computer-based). *Application deadline:* For fall admission, 7/1 priority date for domestic and international students; for spring admission, 11/1 priority date for domestic and international students. Applications are processed on a rolling basis. Application fee: $25. Electronic applications accepted. *Expenses:* Tuition, state resident: part-time $336 per credit. Tuition, nonresident: part-time $538 per credit. Required fees: $84 per credit. $37 per semester. *Financial support:* Career-related internships or fieldwork, Federal Work-Study, scholarships/grants, and unspecified assistantships available. Support available to part-time students. Financial award application deadline: 5/1; financial award applicants required to submit FAFSA. *Unit head:* Graduate Coordinator, 724-738-2041, Fax: 724-738-2880. *Application contact:* April Longwell, Interim Director of Graduate Studies, 724-738-2051 Ext. 2116, Fax: 724-738-2146, E-mail: graduate.studies@sru.edu.

Smith College, Graduate Programs, Department of Education and Child Study, Program in Secondary Education, Northampton, MA 01063. Offers biological sciences education (MAT); chemistry education (MAT); English education (MAT); French education (MAT); geology education (MAT); government education (MAT); history education (MAT); mathematics education (MAT); physics education (MAT); Spanish education (MAT). Part-time programs available. *Faculty:* 6 full-time (4 women), 3 part-time/adjunct (2 women). *Students:* 4 full-time (2 women). Average age 36. 12 applicants, 67% accepted, 3 enrolled. In 2006, 5 master's awarded. *Entrance requirements:* For master's, GRE General Test. Additional exam requirements/recommendations for international students: Required—TOEFL. *Application deadline:* For fall admission, 4/1 for domestic students, 1/15 for international students; for spring admission, 12/1 for domestic students. Application fee: $60. *Expenses:* Tuition: Full-time $32,320; part-time $1,010 per credit. Tuition and fees vary according to course load. *Financial support:* In 2006–07, 3 students received support. Career-related internships or fieldwork, institutionally sponsored loans, and scholarships/grants available. Support available to part-time students. Financial award application deadline: 1/15; financial award applicants required to submit CSS PROFILE or FAFSA. *Unit head:* Rosetta Cohen, Graduate Student Advisor, 413-585-3266.

South Carolina State University, School of Graduate Studies, Department of Education, Orangeburg, SC 29117-0001. Offers early childhood and special education (M Ed); early childhood education (MAT); elementary education (M Ed, MAT); engineering (MAT); general science (MAT); mathematics (MAT); secondary education (M Ed), including biology education, business education, counselor education, English education, home economics education, industrial education, mathematics education, science education, social studies education; special education (M Ed), including emotionally handicapped, learning disabilities, mentally handicapped. *Accreditation:* NCATE. Part-time and evening/weekend programs available. *Faculty:* 21 full-time (10 women), 4 part-time/adjunct (0 women). *Students:* 34 full-time (28 women), 33 part-time (25 women); includes 63 minority (61 African Americans, 1 American Indian/Alaska Native, 1 Asian American or Pacific Islander). Average age 35. 46 applicants, 67% accepted, 19 enrolled. In 2006, 28 degrees awarded. *Degree requirements:* For master's, departmental qualifying exam, thesis optional. *Entrance requirements:* For master's, GRE General Test, NTE, interview, teaching certificate. *Application deadline:* For fall admission, 6/15 priority date for domestic students, 6/15 for international students; for spring admission, 11/1 for domestic and international students. Applications are processed on a rolling basis. Application fee: $25. Electronic applications accepted. *Expenses:* Tuition, state resident: full-time $7,278. Tuition, nonresident: full-time $14,322. *Financial support:* Fellowships, research assistantships, career-related internships or fieldwork, Federal Work-Study, and institutionally sponsored loans available. Financial award application deadline: 6/1. *Faculty research:* Critical thinking, child abuse, stress, test-taking skills, conflict resolution, mainstreaming. *Unit head:* Dr. Gail Joyner-Fleming, Interim Chair, 803-533-3769, Fax: 803-536-8492, E-mail: zf-gfleming@scsu.edu. *Application contact:* Annette Hazzard-Jones, Program Coordinator II, 803-536-8809, Fax: 803-536-8812, E-mail: zs_ahazzard@scsu.edu.

Southern Illinois University Edwardsville, Graduate Studies and Research, School of Education, Department of Curriculum and Instruction, Program in Secondary Education, Edwardsville, IL 62026-0001. Offers art (MS Ed); biology (MS Ed); chemistry (MS Ed); English (MS Ed); foreign languages (MS Ed); history (MS Ed); mathematics (MS Ed); physics (MS Ed); reading (MS Ed); science (MS Ed). *Accreditation:* NCATE. Part-time and evening/weekend programs available. *Students:* 2 full-time (both women), 23 part-time (14 women); includes 2 minority (both African Americans) Average age 33. 12 applicants, 42% accepted. In 2006, 10 degrees awarded. *Degree requirements:* For master's, thesis or alternative, final exam. *Entrance requirements:* For master's, MAT. Additional exam requirements/recommendations for international students: Required—TOEFL. *Application deadline:* For fall admission, 7/20 for domestic students, 6/1 for international students; for spring admission, 12/14 for domestic students, 10/1 for international students. Application fee: $30. Electronic applications accepted. *Financial support:* Fellowships, research assistantships, teaching assistantships, Federal Work-Study, institutionally sponsored loans, and unspecified assistantships available. Support available to part-time students. Financial award application deadline: 3/1; financial award applicants required to submit FAFSA. *Unit head:* Dr. David DeWeese, Director, 618-650-3432, E-mail: ddewees@siue.edu.

Southern University and Agricultural and Mechanical College, Graduate School, Department of Science/Mathematics Education, Baton Rouge, LA 70813. Offers PhD. *Accreditation:* NCATE. *Degree requirements:* For doctorate, thesis/dissertation. *Entrance requirements:* For doctorate, GRE General Test. Additional exam requirements/recommendations for international students: Required—TOEFL (minimum score 525 paper-based; 193 computer-based). *Faculty research:* Performance assessment in science/mathematics education, equity in science/mathematics education, technology and distance learning, science/mathematics concept formation, cognitive themes, problem solving in science/mathematics education.

Southwestern Oklahoma State University, College of Arts and Sciences, Department of Mathematics, Weatherford, OK 73096-3098. Offers M Ed. Part-time programs available. *Degree requirements:* For master's, exam. *Entrance requirements:* For master's, GRE General Test or minimum undergraduate GPA of 3.0. Additional exam requirements/recommendations for international students: Required—TOEFL.

Stanford University, School of Education, Program in Curriculum Studies and Teacher Education, Stanford, CA 94305-9991. Offers art education (MA, PhD); dance education (MA); English education (MA, PhD); general curriculum studies (MA, PhD); mathematics education (MA, PhD); science education (MA, PhD); social studies education (PhD); teacher education (MA, PhD). *Degree requirements:* For master's, thesis (for some programs); for doctorate, thesis/dissertation. *Entrance requirements:* For master's and doctorate, GRE General Test. Electronic applications accepted.

Stanford University, School of Education, Teacher Education Program, Stanford, CA 94305-9991. Offers English education (MA); languages education (MA); mathematics education (MA); science education (MA); social studies education (MA). *Degree requirements:* For master's, thesis. *Entrance requirements:* For master's, GRE General Test. Electronic applications accepted.

State University of New York at Binghamton, Graduate School, School of Education, Program in Secondary Education, Binghamton, NY 13902-6000. Offers biology education (MAT, MS Ed, MST); earth science education (MAT, MS Ed, MST); English education (MAT, MS Ed, MST); French education (MAT, MST); mathematical sciences education (MAT, MS Ed, MST); physics (MAT, MS Ed, MST); social studies (MAT, MS Ed, MST); Spanish education (MAT, MST). *Accreditation:* Teacher Education Accreditation Council. Part-time and evening/weekend programs available. *Students:* 89 full-time (50 women), 47 part-time (32 women); includes 6 minority (1 African American, 3 Asian Americans or Pacific Islanders, 2 Hispanic Americans). Average age 29. 72 applicants, 72% accepted, 23 enrolled. In 2006, 44 degrees awarded. *Entrance requirements:* For master's, GRE General Test. Additional exam requirements/recommendations for international students: Required—TOEFL. *Application deadline:* For fall admission, 4/15 priority date for domestic students, 1/15 priority date for international students; for spring admission, 11/1 for domestic students, 10/1 priority date for international students. Applications are processed on a rolling basis. Application fee: $60. Electronic applications accepted. *Financial support:* In 2006–07, 25 students received support, including 2 fellowships with partial tuition reimbursements available (averaging $2,350 per year), 4 research assistantships with full and partial tuition reimbursements available (averaging $6,638 per year), 13 teaching assistantships with full tuition reimbursements available (averaging $5,944 per year); career-related internships or fieldwork, Federal Work-Study, institutionally sponsored loans, tuition waivers (full and partial), and unspecified assistantships also available. Support available to part-time students. Financial award application deadline: 2/15. *Unit head:* Dr. Thomas O'Brien, Coordinator, 607-777-7329, E-mail: tobrien@binghamton.edu.

State University of New York at Plattsburgh, Division of Education, Health, and Human Services, Department of Adolescence Education/Health, Plattsburgh, NY 12901-2681. Offers adolescence education (MST); biology 7-12 (MST); chemistry 7-12 (MST); earth science 7-12 (MST); English 7-12 (MST); French 7-12 (MST); mathematics 7-12 (MST); physics 7-12 (MST); social studies 7-12 (MST); Spanish 7-12 (MST). *Faculty:* 4 full-time (3 women), 2 part-time/adjunct (0 women). *Students:* 58 full-time (38 women), 14 part-time (10 women); includes 5 minority (1 African American, 4 Hispanic Americans). Average age 30. 49 applicants, 78% accepted, 32 enrolled. In 2006, 30 degrees awarded. *Degree requirements:* For master's, comprehensive exam or research project. *Entrance requirements:* For master's, GRE General Test or MAT, minimum GPA of 2.5. *Application deadline:* For fall admission, 2/15 priority date for domestic students; for spring admission, 10/15 priority date for domestic students. Applications are processed on a rolling basis. Application fee: $50. *Expenses:* Tuition, state resident: full-time $6,900; part-time $288 per credit hour. Tuition, nonresident: full-time $10,920; part-time $455 per credit hour. *Financial support:* Application deadline: 4/15; *Unit head:* Dr. Lois Beach, Chair, 578-564-5750, E-mail: lois.beach@plattsburgh.edu. *Application contact:* Sharon Derr, Assistant Director, Graduate Admission, 518-564-4723, Fax: 518-564-4722, E-mail: derrsl@plattsburgh.edu.

State University of New York College at Brockport, School of Professions, Department of Education and Human Development, Program in Adolescence Education, Brockport, NY 14420-2997. Offers biology education (MS Ed); chemistry education (MS Ed); earth science education (MS Ed); English education (MS Ed); mathematics education (MS Ed); physics education (MS Ed); social studies education (MS Ed). *Accreditation:* NCATE. Part-time programs available. *Students:* 39 full-time (21 women), 117 part-time (66 women); includes 6 minority (3 African Americans, 1 Asian American or Pacific Islander, 2 Hispanic Americans). 57 applicants, 61% accepted, 32 enrolled. In 2006, 91 degrees awarded. *Degree requirements:* For master's, thesis or alternative. *Entrance requirements:* For master's, minimum GPA of 3.0, letters of recommendation. Additional exam requirements/recommendations for international students: Required—TOEFL (minimum score 550 paper-based; 213 computer-based; 80 iBT). *Application deadline:* For fall admission, 2/15 for domestic and international students; for spring admission, 9/15 for domestic and international students. Application fee: $50. *Expenses:* Tuition, state resident: full-time $6,900; part-time $288 per credit. Tuition, nonresident: full-time $10,920; part-time $455 per credit. *Financial support:* Career-related internships or fieldwork, Federal Work-Study, scholarships/grants, and unspecified assistantships available. Support available to part-time students. Financial award application deadline: 3/15; financial award applicants required to submit FAFSA. *Application contact:* Coordinator of Certification and Graduate Advisement, 585-395-2344.

State University of New York College at Cortland, Graduate Studies, School of Arts and Sciences, Programs in Adolescence Education, Cortland, NY 13045. Offers biology (MAT, MS Ed); chemistry (MAT, MS Ed); earth science (MAT, MS Ed); English (MS Ed); French (MS Ed); mathematics (MAT, MS Ed); physics (MAT, MS Ed); social studies (MS Ed); Spanish (MS Ed). *Accreditation:* NCATE. Part-time and evening/weekend programs available. *Degree requirements:* For master's, one foreign language, thesis (for some programs), comprehensive exam (for some programs). *Entrance requirements:* For master's, GRE General Test.

Stephen F. Austin State University, Graduate School, College of Sciences and Mathematics, Department of Mathematics and Statistics, Nacogdoches, TX 75962. Offers mathematics (MS); mathematics education (MS); statistics (MS). *Degree requirements:* For master's, thesis optional. *Entrance requirements:* For master's, GRE General Test, minimum GPA of 2.8 in last 60 hours, 2.5 overall. Additional exam requirements/recommendations for international students: Required—TOEFL. *Faculty research:* Kernel type estimators, fractal mappings, spline curve fitting, robust regression continua theory.

Stony Brook University, State University of New York, School of Professional Development, Stony Brook, NY 11794. Offers adolescence education: mathematics (Certificate); biology 7-12 (MAT); chemistry-grade 7-12 (MAT); coaching (Certificate); computer integrated engineering (Certificate); cultural studies (Certificate); earth science-grade 7-12 (MAT); educational computing (Advanced Certificate, Certificate); English-grade 7-12 (MAT); environmental and waste management (MS, Advanced Certificate); environmental systems management (Certificate); environmental/occupational health and safety (Certificate); French-grade 7-12 (MAT); German-grade 7-12 (MAT); human resource management (Certificate); industrial management (Certificate); information systems management (Certificate); Italian-grade 7-12 (MAT); liberal studies (MA); liberal studies online (MA); Long Island regional studies (Certificate); operation research (Certificate); physics-grade 7-12 (MAT); Russian-grade 7-12 (MAT); school administration and supervision (Certificate); school district administration (Certificate); social science and the professions (MPS), including human resources management, labor management, public affairs, waste management; social studies 7-12 (MAT); waste management (Certificate); women's studies (Certificate). Part-time and evening/weekend programs available. Postbaccalaureate distance learning degree programs offered. *Faculty:* 1 full-time (0 women), 118 part-time/adjunct (45 women). *Students:* 322 full-time (202 women), 1,188 part-time (728 women); includes 164 minority (69 African Americans, 2 American Indian/Alaska Native, 29 Asian Americans or Pacific Islanders, 64 Hispanic Americans), 11 international. Average age 28. In 2006, 738 master's, 405 other advanced degrees awarded. *Degree requirements:* For master's, one foreign language, thesis or alternative. *Application deadline:* Applications are processed on a rolling basis. Application fee: $62. *Expenses:* Tuition, state resident: full-time $6,900; part-time $288 per credit. Tuition, nonresident: full-time $10,920; part-time $455 per credit. *Financial support:* In 2006–07, 5 teaching assistantships were awarded; fellowships, research assistantships, career-related internships or fieldwork also available. Support available to part-time students. *Unit head:* Dr. Paul J. Edelson, Dean, 631-632-7052, Fax: 631-632-9046, E-mail: paul.edelson@sunysb.edu. *Application contact:* Sandra Romansky, Director of Admissions and Advisement, 631-632-7050, Fax: 631-632-9046, E-mail: sandra.romansky@sunysb.edu.

Syracuse University, Graduate School, School of Education, Department of Teaching and Leadership, Program in Mathematics Education, Syracuse, NY 13244. Offers mathematics education (PhD); mathematics education: preparation 7-12 (MS). Part-time and evening/weekend programs available. *Students:* 11 full-time (3 women), 2 part-time (both women); includes 1 minority (African American), 3 international. 13 applicants, 46% accepted, 4 enrolled. *Degree requirements:* For master's, thesis or alternative; for doctorate, thesis/dissertation. *Entrance requirements:* For master's and doctorate, GRE. Additional exam requirements/recommendations for international students: Required—TOEFL. *Application deadline:* For fall admission, 2/1 priority date for domestic students. Applications are processed on a rolling basis. Application fee: $65. Electronic applications accepted. *Expenses:* Tuition: Full-time $16,920; part-time $940 per credit hour. Required fees: $930; $930 per year. *Financial support:* Fellowships with full tuition reimbursements, teaching assistantships with full tuition reimbursements available. *Unit head:* Dr. Joanna Masingila, Chair, 315-443-1483, E-mail: jomasing@syr.edu. *Application contact:* Liza Rochelson, Graduate Admission Recruiter, 315-443-2505, Fax: 315-443-2258, E-mail: gradcrt@gwmail.syr.edu.

Teachers College Columbia University, Graduate Faculty of Education, Department of Math, Science and Technology, Program in Mathematics Education, New York, NY 10027-6696. Offers Ed M, MA, MS, Ed D, Ed DCT, PhD. *Accreditation:* NCATE. *Faculty:* 3 full-time (1 woman). *Students:* 53 full-time (31 women), 93 part-time (46 women); includes 46 minority (18 African Americans, 22 Asian Americans or Pacific Islanders, 6 Hispanic Americans), 8 international. Average age 35. 122 applicants, 80% accepted, 44 enrolled. In 2006, 79 master's, 8 doctorates awarded. *Degree requirements:* For doctorate, thesis/dissertation. *Entrance requirements:* For master's, undergraduate major or minor in mathematics; for doctorate, MA in mathematics or mathematics education. *Application deadline:* For fall admission, 5/15 for domestic students; for spring admission, 12/1 for domestic students. Application fee: $65. *Expenses:* Tuition: Full-time $23,400; part-time $975 per credit. Required fees: $320 per term. *Financial support:* Career-related internships or fieldwork, Federal Work-Study, institutionally sponsored loans, and tuition waivers (full and partial) available. Support available to part-time students. Financial award application deadline: 2/1. *Faculty research:* Problem solving, curriculum development, international education, history of mathematics. *Application contact:* Deanna Ghozati, Assistant Director of Admission, 212-678-4018, Fax: 212-678-4171, E-mail: ghozati@tc.edu.

See Close-Up on page 1615.

Temple University, Graduate School, College of Education, Department of Curriculum, Instruction, and Technology in Education, Philadelphia, PA 19122-6096. Offers applied behavioral analysis (MS Ed); career and technical education (MS Ed); early childhood education and elementary education (MS Ed); English education (MS Ed); language arts education (Ed D); math/science education (Ed D); mathematics education (MS Ed); science education (MS Ed); second and foreign language education (MS Ed); special education (MS Ed); teaching English as a second language (MS Ed). Part-time and evening/weekend programs available. *Faculty:* 31 full-time (14 women). *Students:* 96 full-time (71 women), 482 part-time (336 women); includes 109 minority (67 African Americans, 3 American Indian/Alaska Native, 23 Asian Americans or Pacific Islanders, 16 Hispanic Americans), 28 international. 308 applicants, 64% accepted, 116 enrolled. In 2006, 225 master's, 21 doctorates awarded. Terminal master's awarded for partial completion of doctoral program. *Degree requirements:* For master's, thesis or alternative; for doctorate, thesis/dissertation. *Entrance requirements:* For master's and doctorate, GRE General Test or MAT, minimum GPA of 3.0. Additional exam requirements/recommendations for international students: Required—TOEFL (minimum score 550 paper-based; 213 computer-based; 79 iBT). *Application deadline:* For fall admission, 4/1 for domestic students, 12/15 for international students; for spring admission, 10/1 for domestic students, 8/1 for international students. Application fee: $50. Electronic applications accepted. *Expenses:* Tuition, state resident: full-time $12,264; part-time $511 per credit. Tuition, nonresident: full-time $17,904; part-time $746 per credit. Required fees: $84 per course. Tuition and fees vary according to program. *Financial support:* Fellowships, research assistantships with full tuition reimbursements, teaching assistantships with full tuition reimbursements available. Financial award application deadline: 1/15; financial award applicants required to submit FAFSA. *Faculty research:* School improvement, problem solving, literacy, language development. *Unit head:* Dr. Thomas Walker, Chair, 215-204-2117, Fax: 215-204-1414, E-mail: tjwalker@temple.edu.

Texas A&M University, College of Education and Human Development, Department of Teaching, Learning, and Culture, College Station, TX 77843. Offers curriculum and instruction (M Ed, MS, PhD); mathematics education (M Ed, MS, PhD); multicultural/urban/ESL/international education (M Ed, MS, PhD); reading/language arts (M Ed, MS, PhD); science education (M Ed, MS, PhD); social studies education (M Ed, MS, PhD). *Accreditation:* NCATE. Part-time programs available. *Faculty:* 25 full-time (9 women), 2 part-time/adjunct (both women). *Students:* 156 full-time (115 women), 226 part-time (191 women); includes 95 minority (43 African Americans, 1 American Indian/Alaska Native, 9 Asian Americans or Pacific Islanders, 42 Hispanic Americans), 36 international. Average age 36. 137 applicants, 83% accepted, 80 enrolled. In 2006, 69 master's, 15 doctorates awarded. *Median time to degree:* Of those who began their doctoral program in fall 1998, 77% received their degree in 8 years or less. *Degree requirements:* For master's, thesis (for some programs), comprehensive exam; for doctorate, thesis/dissertation, comprehensive exam. *Entrance requirements:* For master's, GRE General Test, minimum GPA of 3.0; for doctorate, GRE General Test, 3 years of teaching experience. Additional exam requirements/recommendations for international students: Required—TOEFL (minimum score 550 paper-based; 213 computer-based). *Application deadline:* For fall admission, 1/15 priority date for domestic and international students; for spring admission, 9/15 priority date for domestic and international students. Applications are processed on a rolling basis. Application fee: $50 ($75 for international students). Electronic applications accepted. *Expenses:* Tuition, state resident: full-time $4,697. Tuition, nonresident: full-time $11,297. Required fees: $2,272. *Financial support:* In 2006–07, fellowships with partial tuition reimbursements (averaging $3,000 per year), teaching assistantships with partial tuition reimbursements (averaging $7,200 per year) were awarded; research assistantships with partial tuition reimbursements, career-related internships or fieldwork, Federal Work-Study, institutionally sponsored loans, scholarships/grants, tuition waivers (partial), and unspecified assistantships also available. Support available to part-time students. Financial award application deadline: 4/1; financial award applicants required to submit FAFSA. *Unit head:* Dr. Dennie Smith, Head, 979-845-8384, Fax: 979-845-9663. *Application contact:* Graduate Admissions Supervisor, 979-845-8382, Fax: 979-845-9663.

Texas A&M University–Corpus Christi, Graduate Studies and Research, College of Science and Technology, Program in Mathematics, Corpus Christi, TX 78412-5503. Offers applied and computational mathematics (MS); curriculum content (MS). Part-time programs available. *Degree requirements:* For master's, thesis (for some programs). *Entrance requirements:* For master's, 2 letters of recommendation.

Texas State University-San Marcos, Graduate School, College of Science, Department of Mathematics, Program in Middle School Mathematics Teaching, San Marcos, TX 78666. Offers M Ed. *Students:* 1 (woman) full-time, 15 part-time (12 women); includes 2 minority (both Hispanic Americans) Average age 37. 16 applicants, 100% accepted, 13 enrolled. In 2006, 14 degrees awarded. *Entrance requirements:* For master's, GRE, minimum GPA of 2.75 in last 60 hours of undergraduate course work. *Application deadline:* For fall admission, 6/15 priority date for domestic students, 6/1 priority date for international students; for spring admission, 10/15 priority date for domestic students, 10/1 priority date for international students. Applications are processed on a rolling basis. Application fee: $40 ($90 for international students). *Financial support:* In 2006–07, 12 students received support, including 6 teaching assistantships (averaging $8,100 per year). Financial award application deadline: 4/1; financial award applicants required to submit FAFSA. *Unit head:* Dr. Maria Acosta, Graduate Adviser, 512-245-2497, E-mail: ma05@txstate.edu.

Texas State University-San Marcos, Graduate School, Interdisciplinary Studies Program in Elementary Mathematics, Science, and Technology, San Marcos, TX 78666. Offers MSIS. *Students:* 3 applicants, 0% accepted. In 2006, 2 degrees awarded. *Degree requirements:* For master's, comprehensive exam. *Application deadline:* For fall admission, 6/15 priority date for domestic students; for spring admission, 10/15 priority date for domestic students. Applications are processed on a rolling basis. Application fee: $40 ($90 for international students). *Financial support:* Application deadline: 4/1; *Unit head:* Dr. Sandra Mody, Acting Dean, 512-245-3381, Fax: 512-245-8095, E-mail: sw04@txstate.edu.

Texas Woman's University, Graduate School, College of Arts and Sciences, Department of Mathematics and Computer Science, Denton, TX 76201. Offers mathematics (MA, MS); mathematics teaching (MS). Part-time and evening/weekend programs available. *Students:* 13 full-time (10 women), 13 part-time (12 women); includes 6 minority (3 African Americans, 1 American Indian/Alaska Native, 2 Asian Americans or Pacific Islanders), 2 international. Average age 33. In 2006, 9 degrees awarded. *Degree requirements:* For master's, thesis (for some programs), comprehensive exam. *Entrance requirements:* For master's, 2 letters of reference. Additional exam requirements/recommendations for international students: Required—TOEFL (minimum score 550 paper-based; 213 computer-based; 79 iBT). *Application deadline:* For fall admission, 4/1 for international students; for spring admission, 8/1 for international students. Applications are processed on a rolling basis. Application fee: $30 ($50 for international students). Electronic applications accepted. *Expenses:* Tuition, area resident: Part-time $168 per unit. Tuition, state resident: full-time $4,369. Tuition, nonresident: full-time $9,373; part-time $443 per unit. Required fees: $20 per unit. $177 per term. *Financial support:* In 2006–07, 3 research assistantships (averaging $10,188 per year), 6 teaching assistantships (averaging $10,188 per year) were awarded; career-related internships or fieldwork, Federal Work-Study, institutionally sponsored loans, scholarships/grants, traineeships, health care benefits, and unspecified assistantships also available. Support available to part-time students. Financial award application deadline: 3/1; financial award applicants required to submit FAFSA. *Faculty research:* Biopharmaceutical statistics, dynamical systems and control theory, Bayesian inference, math and computer science curriculum innovation, computer modeling of physical phenomenon. *Unit head:* Dr. Don E. Edwards, Chair, 940-898-2166, Fax: 940-898-2179, E-mail: dedwards@mail.twu.edu. *Application contact:* Samuel Wheeler, Coordinator of Graduate Admissions, 940-898-3188, Fax: 940-898-3081, E-mail: wheelersr@twu.edu.

Towson University, Graduate School, Program in Mathematics Education, Towson, MD 21252-0001. Offers MS. *Accreditation:* NCATE. *Students:* 2 full-time (both women), 65 part-time (51 women); includes 10 minority (7 African Americans, 1 American Indian/Alaska Native, 2 Asian Americans or Pacific Islanders), 3 international. 19 applicants, 79% accepted, 8 enrolled. In 2006, 12 degrees awarded. *Entrance requirements:* For master's, current certification for teaching secondary school mathematics, minimum GPA of 3.0. *Application deadline:* Applications are processed on a rolling basis. Application fee: $50. Electronic applications accepted. *Expenses:* Tuition, state resident: part-time $275 per unit. Tuition, nonresident: part-time $577 per unit. Required fees: $72 per unit. *Financial support:* Application deadline: 4/1; *Unit head:* Dr. Wei Sun, Graduate Program Director, 410-704-4921, Fax: 410-704-4143, E-mail: wsun@towson.edu. *Application contact:* 410-704-2501, Fax: 410-704-4675, E-mail: grads@towson.edu.

Trinity (Washington) University, School of Education, Washington, DC 20017-1094. Offers democracy, diversity, and social justice (M Ed); early childhood (MAT); educational administration (MSA); elementary education (MAT); English as a second language (M Ed, MAT); literacy and reading education (M Ed); school counseling (MA); secondary education (MAT), including English, math, science, social studies; special education (MAT). *Accreditation:* NCATE. Part-time and evening/weekend programs available. *Degree requirements:* For master's, thesis (for some programs), capstone project(s). *Entrance requirements:* For master's, PRAXIS I, minimum GPA of 2.8. Additional exam requirements/recommendations for international students: Required—TOEFL (minimum score 550 paper-based; 213 computer-based). *Faculty research:* Technology, literacy, special education, organizations, inclusion models.

Union Graduate College, School of Education, Schenectady, NY 12308-3107. Offers biology (MAT, MS); chemistry (MAT); earth science (MAT); English (MAT); French (MAT); general science (MAT); German (MAT); languages (MAT); Latin (MAT); mathematics (MAT); mathematics and technology (MS); physical science (MS); physics (MAT); social studies (MAT); Spanish (MAT). *Accreditation:* Teacher Education Accreditation Council. *Faculty:* 5 full-time (1 woman), 19 part-time/adjunct (10 women). *Students:* 57 full-time (36 women), 21 part-time (14 women); includes 2 African Americans, 2 Hispanic Americans, 2 international. Average age 31.

Mathematics Education

Union Graduate College (continued)

59 applicants, 83% accepted, 39 enrolled. In 2006, 56 degrees awarded. *Degree requirements:* For master's, thesis or project. *Entrance requirements:* For master's, minimum GPA of 3.0, letters of recommendation. Additional exam requirements/recommendations for international students: Required—TOEFL (minimum score 550 paper-based; 213 computer-based). Application fee: $60. *Expenses:* Contact institution. *Financial support:* In 2006–07, 12 research assistantships with tuition reimbursements (averaging $3,000 per year) were awarded; Federal Work-Study, scholarships/grants, health care benefits, and tuition waivers (partial) also available. Support available to part-time students. Financial award applicants required to submit FAFSA. *Unit head:* Dr. Patrick Allen, Dean, 518-388-6361, Fax: 518-388-6686, E-mail: mat@union.edu. *Application contact:* Rhonda Sheehan, Director of Graduate Admissions Registrar, 518-388-6238, Fax: 518-388-6686, E-mail: sheehanr@union.edu.

See Close-Up on page 923.

University at Albany, State University of New York, College of Arts and Sciences, Department of Mathematics and Statistics, Albany, NY 12222-0001. Offers mathematics (PhD); secondary teaching (MA); statistics (MA). Evening/weekend programs available. *Students:* 36 full-time (15 women), 15 part-time (4 women). Average age 31. In 2006, 10 master's, 1 doctorate awarded. *Degree requirements:* For doctorate, one foreign language, thesis/dissertation. *Entrance requirements:* For doctorate, GRE General Test. Additional exam requirements/recommendations for international students: Required—TOEFL (minimum score 550 paper-based; 213 computer-based). *Application deadline:* For fall admission, 3/15 for domestic students, 5/1 for international students; for spring admission, 11/1 for international students. Applications are processed on a rolling basis. Application fee: $75. Electronic applications accepted. *Expenses:* Tuition, state resident: full-time $6,900; part-time $288 per credit. Tuition, nonresident: full-time $10,920; part-time $455 per credit. Required fees: $1,139. *Financial support:* Fellowships, research assistantships, teaching assistantships, minority assistantships available. Financial award application deadline: 3/15. *Unit head:* Edward C. Turner, Chair, 518-442-4602.

University at Buffalo, the State University of New York, Graduate School, Graduate School of Education, Department of Learning and Instruction, Buffalo, NY 14260. Offers adolescence education (Certificate); biology (Ed M); chemistry (Ed M); childhood education (Ed M); early childhood and childhood education with bilingual extension (Ed M); early childhood education (Ed M); earth science (Ed M); elementary education (Ed D, PhD); English (Ed M); English education (PhD); English for speakers of other languages (Ed M); foreign and second language education (PhD); French (Ed M); general education (Ed M); German (Ed M); Italian (Ed M); Japanese (Ed M); Latin (Ed M); literary specialist (Ed M); mathematics (Ed M); mathematics education (PhD); mentoring teachers (Certificate); music education (Ed M, Certificate); physics (Ed M); reading education (PhD); Russian (Ed M); school administrator and supervisor (Certificate); science education (PhD); social studies (Ed M); Spanish (Ed M); special education (PhD); teaching and leading for diversity (Certificate); teaching English to speakers of other languages (Ed M). Part-time and evening/weekend programs available. Postbaccalaureate distance learning degree programs offered (no on-campus study). *Faculty:* 30 full-time (20 women), 53 part-time/adjunct (38 women). *Students:* 368 full-time (269 women), 297 part-time (226 women); includes 50 minority (15 African Americans, 2 American Indian/Alaska Native, 14 Asian Americans or Pacific Islanders, 19 Hispanic Americans), 66 international. Average age 31. 638 applicants, 75% accepted, 298 enrolled. In 2006, 248 master's, 18 doctorates, 48 other advanced degrees awarded. Terminal master's awarded for partial completion of doctoral program. *Degree requirements:* For master's, comprehensive exam, registration; for doctorate, thesis/dissertation, research analysis exam, research experience component. *Entrance requirements:* For doctorate, GRE General Test or MAT, interview, writing sample, letters of recommendation. Additional exam requirements/recommendations for international students: Required—TOEFL (minimum score 600 paper-based; 250 computer-based). *Application deadline:* For fall admission, 2/1 priority date for domestic and international students; for spring admission, 11/15 priority date for domestic students, 10/1 for international students. Applications are processed on a rolling basis. Application fee: $50. Electronic applications accepted. *Financial support:* In 2006–07, 70 students received support, including 6 fellowships with full tuition reimbursements available (averaging $10,000 per year), 16 research assistantships with full tuition reimbursements available (averaging $9,000 per year), teaching assistantships with full tuition reimbursements available (averaging $9,000 per year); career-related internships or fieldwork, Federal Work-Study, institutionally sponsored loans, scholarships/grants, tuition waivers (partial), and unspecified assistantships also available. Financial award application deadline: 2/28; financial award applicants required to submit FAFSA. *Faculty research:* Science assessment, state-level testing, early learning, literacy, second language acquisition. Total annual research expenditures: $432,366. *Unit head:* Dr. Maria E. Runfola, Chair, 716-645-2455, Fax: 716-645-3161. *Application contact:* Barbara Belz, Admissions Secretary, 716-645-2110 Ext. 1159, Fax: 716-645-3161, E-mail: belz@buffalo.edu.

University of Arkansas, Graduate School, J. William Fulbright College of Arts and Sciences, Department of Mathematical Sciences, Program in Secondary Mathematics, Fayetteville, AR 72701-1201. Offers MA. *Accreditation:* NCATE. *Degree requirements:* For master's, written exam. Application fee: $40 ($50 for international students). *Financial support:* Fellowships, research assistantships, teaching assistantships, career-related internships or fieldwork and Federal Work-Study available. Support available to part-time students. Financial award application deadline: 4/1; financial award applicants required to submit FAFSA. *Unit head:* Dr. Mark Arnold, Graduate Coordinator, 479-575-3351, Fax: 479-575-8630, E-mail: arnold@uark.edu.

University of Arkansas at Pine Bluff, Program in Education, Pine Bluff, AR 71601-2799. Offers elementary education (M Ed); secondary education (M Ed), including English, general science, mathematics, physical education, social studies. Part-time and evening/weekend programs available. *Degree requirements:* For master's, comprehensive exam. *Entrance requirements:* For master's, GRE, minimum GPA of 2.75, NTE or Standard Arkansas Teaching Certificate. *Faculty research:* Teacher certification, accreditation, assessment, standards, portfolio development, rehabilitation, technology.

The University of British Columbia, Faculty of Graduate Studies, Faculty of Education, Department of Curriculum Studies, Vancouver, BC V6T 1Z1, Canada. Offers art education (M Ed, MA); curriculum studies (M Ed, MA, PhD); home economics education (M Ed, MA); math education (M Ed, MA); music education (M Ed, MA); physical education (M Ed, MA); science education (M Ed, MA); social studies education (M Ed, MA); technical studies education (M Ed, MA). Part-time programs available. *Faculty:* 31 full-time (17 women), 1 (woman) part-time/adjunct. *Students:* 153 full-time (102 women), 101 part-time (67 women), 25 international. Average age 40. 118 applicants, 64% accepted, 62 enrolled. In 2006, 46 master's, 4 doctorates awarded. *Degree requirements:* For master's, thesis (MA); for doctorate, thesis/dissertation, comprehensive exam, registration. *Entrance requirements:* Additional exam requirements/recommendations for international students: Required—TOEFL (minimum score 580 paper-based; 237 computer-based). *Application deadline:* For fall admission, 2/1 for domestic students, 1/1 for international students; for spring admission, 10/1 for domestic students, 9/1 for international students. Application fee: $90 ($150 for international students). Electronic applications accepted. *Expenses:* Contact institution. *Financial support:* In 2006–07, 10 fellowships with partial tuition reimbursements (averaging $16,000 per year), 11 research assistantships with partial tuition reimbursements (averaging $14,000 per year), 27 teaching assistantships with partial tuition reimbursements (averaging $14,000 per year) were awarded; tuition waivers (partial) also available. *Faculty research:* School subjects, teaching and learning. *Unit head:* Dr. Linda Peterat, Interim Head, 604-822-5422, Fax: 604-822-4714. *Application contact:* Basia Zurek, Graduate Secretary, 604-822-5367, Fax: 604-822-4714, E-mail: cust.grad@ubc.ca.

University of California, Berkeley, Graduate Division, School of Education, Division of Cognition and Development, Program in Development in Mathematics and Science, Berkeley, CA 94720-1500. Offers MA, PhD/MA. *Application deadline:* For fall admission, 12/1 for domestic students. Application fee: $60 ($80 for international students). *Application contact:* Admissions Office, 510-642-0841, Fax: 510-642-4808, E-mail: gse_info@uclink.berkeley.edu.

University of California, Berkeley, Graduate Division, School of Education, Division of Cognition and Development, Program in Education in Mathematics, Science, and Technology, Berkeley, CA 94720-1500. Offers MA, PhD, PhD/MA. *Entrance requirements:* For master's and doctorate, GRE General Test, minimum GPA of 3.0 during last 2 years of undergraduate course work. *Application deadline:* For fall admission, 12/1 for domestic students. Application fee: $60. Electronic applications accepted. *Financial support:* Unspecified assistantships available. Financial award application deadline: 12/15. *Application contact:* Admissions Office, 510-642-0841, Fax: 510-642-4808, E-mail: gse_info@uclink.berkeley.edu.

University of California, Berkeley, Graduate Division, School of Education, Division of Cognition and Development, Program in Science and Mathematics Education, Berkeley, CA 94720-1500. Offers MA/Credential. *Application deadline:* For fall admission, 12/1 for domestic students. Application fee: $60 ($80 for international students). Electronic applications accepted. *Financial support:* Unspecified assistantships available. *Unit head:* Daniel Zimmerlin, Academic Coordinator, 510-642-4206. *Application contact:* Admissions Office, 510-642-0841, Fax: 510-642-4808, E-mail: gse_info@uclink.berkeley.edu.

University of California, San Diego, Office of Graduate Studies, Program in Mathematics and Science Education, La Jolla, CA 92093. Offers PhD. *Entrance requirements:* For doctorate, GRE General Test. Electronic applications accepted.

University of Central Florida, College of Education, Department of Teaching and Learning Principles, Program in K-8 Mathematics and Science Education, Orlando, FL 32816. Offers M Ed, Certificate. *Accreditation:* NCATE. *Students:* 1 (woman) full-time, 23 part-time (17 women); includes 3 minority (all African Americans) Average age 36. In 2006, 8 master's awarded. Application fee: $30. *Expenses:* Tuition, state resident: full-time $6,167; part-time $257 per credit hour. Tuition, nonresident: full-time $22,790; part-time $950 per credit hour. *Financial support:* Fellowships available. *Unit head:* Dr. Michael C. Hynes, Coordinator, 407-823-6076, E-mail: hynes@mail.ucf.edu.

University of Central Florida, College of Education, Department of Teaching and Learning Principles, Program in Mathematics Education, Orlando, FL 32816. Offers M Ed, MA. *Accreditation:* NCATE. Part-time and evening/weekend programs available. *Students:* 17 full-time (13 women), 24 part-time (14 women); includes 11 minority (2 African Americans, 3 Asian Americans or Pacific Islanders, 6 Hispanic Americans), 1 international. In 2006, 20 master's awarded. *Entrance requirements:* For master's, GRE General Test. Additional exam requirements/recommendations for international students: Required—TOEFL. *Application deadline:* For fall admission, 7/15 for domestic students; for spring admission, 12/1 for domestic students. Application fee: $30. Electronic applications accepted. *Expenses:* Tuition, state resident: full-time $6,167; part-time $257 per credit hour. Tuition, nonresident: full-time $22,790; part-time $950 per credit hour. *Financial support:* In 2006–07, 2 fellowships with partial tuition reimbursements (averaging $5,000 per year), 2 research assistantships with partial tuition reimbursements (averaging $6,200 per year) were awarded; teaching assistantships with partial tuition reimbursements, career-related internships or fieldwork, Federal Work-Study, institutionally sponsored loans, tuition waivers (partial), and unspecified assistantships also available. Financial award application deadline: 3/1; financial award applicants required to submit FAFSA. *Unit head:* Dr. Michael C. Hynes, Coordinator, 407-823-6076, E-mail: hynes@mail.ucf.edu.

University of Central Florida, College of Education, Doctoral Program in Education, Orlando, FL 32816. Offers communication sciences and disorders (PhD); counselor education (PhD); curriculum and instruction (PhD); elementary education (PhD); exceptional education (PhD); hospitality education (PhD); instructional technology (PhD); mathematics education (PhD). *Students:* 86 full-time (63 women), 9 part-time (4 women); includes 21 minority (15 African Americans, 2 Asian Americans or Pacific Islanders, 4 Hispanic Americans), 19 international. Average age 39. In 2006, 16 degrees awarded. Application fee: $30. Electronic applications accepted. *Expenses:* Tuition, state resident: full-time $6,167; part-time $257 per credit hour. Tuition, nonresident: full-time $22,790; part-time $950 per credit hour. *Financial support:* In 2006–07, 44 fellowships with partial tuition reimbursements (averaging $3,700 per year), 54 research assistantships with partial tuition reimbursements (averaging $7,000 per year), 9 teaching assistantships with partial tuition reimbursements (averaging $7,000 per year) were awarded.

University of Central Oklahoma, College of Graduate Studies and Research, College of Mathematics and Science, Department of Mathematics and Statistics, Edmond, OK 73034-5209. Offers applied mathematical sciences (MS), including computer science, mathematics, mathematics/computer science teaching, statistics. Part-time programs available. *Degree requirements:* For master's, thesis. *Entrance requirements:* Additional exam requirements/recommendations for international students: Required—TOEFL (minimum score 550 paper-based; 213 computer-based). Electronic applications accepted. *Faculty research:* Curvature, FAA, math education.

University of Cincinnati, Division of Research and Advanced Studies, McMicken College of Arts and Sciences, Department of Mathematical Sciences, Cincinnati, OH 45221. Offers applied mathematics (MS, PhD); mathematics education (MAT); pure mathematics (MS, PhD); statistics (MS, PhD). Part-time programs available. *Faculty:* 39 full-time (4 women), 12 part-time/adjunct (4 women). *Students:* 64 full-time (31 women), 6 part-time (1 woman); includes 2 minority (1 African American, 1 Asian American or Pacific Islander), 40 international. Average age 25. 91 applicants, 35% accepted, 27 enrolled. In 2006, 33 master's, 2 doctorates awarded. Terminal master's awarded for partial completion of doctoral program. *Median time to degree:* Of those who began their doctoral program in fall 1998, 6% received their degree in 8 years or less. *Degree requirements:* For master's, thesis or alternative, comprehensive exam; for doctorate, one foreign language, thesis/dissertation, comprehensive exam. *Entrance requirements:* For master's, GRE, teacher certification (MAT); for doctorate, GRE. Additional exam requirements/recommendations for international students: Required—TOEFL. *Application deadline:* For fall admission, 2/1 priority date for domestic and international students. Applications are processed on a rolling basis. Application fee: $40. Electronic applications accepted. *Financial support:* In 2006–07, 38 students received support, including 2 fellowships with full tuition reimbursements available (averaging $13,500 per year), 2 research assistantships with full tuition reimbursements available (averaging $15,000 per year), 33 teaching assistantships with full tuition reimbursements available (averaging $13,850 per year); career-related internships or fieldwork, scholarships/grants, tuition waivers (partial), and unspecified assistantships also available. Financial award application deadline: 2/1. *Faculty research:* Algebra, analysis, differential equations, numerical analysis, statistics. Total annual research expenditures:$127,952. *Unit head:* Dr. Timothy Hodges, Head, 513-556-4052, Fax: 513-556-3417, E-mail: timothy.hodges@uc.edu. *Application contact:* Dr. Bingyu Zhang, Graduate Program Director, 513-556-4060, Fax: 513-556-3417, E-mail: grad.director@math.uc.edu.

University of Connecticut, Graduate School, Neag School of Education, Department of Curriculum and Instruction, Storrs, CT 06269. Offers curriculum and instruction (MA, PhD), including agriculture education, bilingual and bicultural education, elementary education, English education, history and social sciences education, mathematics education, reading education, science education, secondary education, world languages education. *Accreditation:* NCATE. *Faculty:* 28 full-time (12 women). *Students:* 158 full-time (120 women), 54 part-time (44 women); includes 24 minority (3 African Americans, 1 American Indian/Alaska Native, 3 Asian Americans or Pacific Islanders, 17 Hispanic Americans), 2 international. Average age 27. 268 applicants, 76% accepted, 203 enrolled. In 2006, 181 master's, 4 doctorates awarded. Terminal master's awarded for partial completion of doctoral program. *Degree requirements:* For master's, thesis or alternative, comprehensive exam; for doctorate, thesis/dissertation. *Entrance requirements:* For doctorate, GRE General Test. Additional exam requirements/recommendations for international students: Required—TOEFL (minimum score 550 paper-based; 213 computer-based). *Application deadline:* For fall admission, 2/1 priority date for domestic and international students; for spring admission, 11/1 for domestic students, 10/1 for international students. Applications are processed on a rolling basis. Application fee: $55. Electronic applications accepted. *Financial support:* In 2006–07, 14 research assistantships with full tuition reimbursements, 4 teaching assistantships with full tuition reimbursements were awarded; fellowships, Federal Work-Study, scholarships/grants, health care benefits, and unspecified assistantships also available. Financial award application deadline: 2/1; financial award applicants required to submit FAFSA. *Unit head:* Mary Anne Doyle, Head, 860-486-2433, Fax: 860-486-0280. *Application contact:* Lisa Rasicot, Graduate Coordinator, 860-486-3065, Fax: 860-486-0210, E-mail: soeadm02@uconnvm.uconn.edu.

University of Connecticut, Graduate School, Neag School of Education, Department of Curriculum and Instruction, Field of Curriculum and Instruction, Program in Mathematics Education, Storrs, CT 06269. Offers MA, PhD. *Accreditation:* NCATE. *Faculty:* 9 full-time (7 women). *Students:* 5 full-time (4 women), 7 part-time (6 women). Average age 32. 12 applicants, 42% accepted, 5 enrolled. In 2006, 4 degrees awarded. Terminal master's awarded for partial completion of doctoral program. *Degree requirements:* For master's, comprehensive exam; for doctorate, thesis/dissertation. *Entrance requirements:* For doctorate, GRE General Test. Additional exam requirements/recommendations for international students: Required—TOEFL (minimum score 550 paper-based; 213 computer-based). *Application deadline:* For fall admission, 2/1 priority date for domestic and international students; for spring admission, 11/1 for domestic students, 10/1 for international students. Applications are processed on a rolling basis. Application fee: $55. Electronic applications accepted. *Financial support:* In 2006–07, 1 teaching assistantship with full tuition reimbursement was awarded; fellowships, research assistantships with full tuition reimbursements, Federal Work-Study, scholarships/grants, health care benefits, and unspecified assistantships also available. Financial award application deadline: 2/1; financial award applicants required to submit FAFSA. *Application contact:* Lisa Rasicot, Graduate Coordinator, 860-486-3065, Fax: 860-486-0210, E-mail: soeadm02@uconnvm.uconn.edu.

University of Dayton, Graduate School, College of Arts and Sciences, Department of Mathematics, Dayton, OH 45469-1300. Offers applied mathematics (MS); financial mathematics (MS); mathematics education (MS). Part-time and evening/weekend programs available. *Faculty:* 15 full-time (5 women). *Students:* 13 full-time (6 women), 4 part-time (1 woman); includes 3 minority (all African Americans), 5 international. Average age 25. 41 applicants, 37% accepted, 5 enrolled. *Entrance requirements:* For master's, minimum undergraduate GPA of 2.8. Additional exam requirements/recommendations for international students: Required—TOEFL (minimum score 550 paper-based; 213 computer-based). *Application deadline:* For fall admission, 3/1 priority date for domestic and international students. Electronic applications accepted. *Expenses:* Tuition: Part-time $601 per semester hour. Tuition and fees vary according to degree level and program. *Financial support:* In 2006–07, 7 teaching assistantships with full tuition reimbursements (averaging $11,572 per year) were awarded; institutionally sponsored loans, health care benefits, and unspecified assistantships also available. Financial award applicants required to submit FAFSA. *Faculty research:* Differential equations, integral equations, general topology, measure theory, graph theory, financial math, math education, and numerical analysis. *Unit head:* Dr. Paul W. Eloe, Chair, 937-229-2511, Fax: 937-229-2566, E-mail: paul.eloe@notes.udayton.edu. *Application contact:* Erika Eavers, Graduate Admission Processor, 937-229-3065, Fax: 937-229-4729, E-mail: erika.eavers@notes.udayton.edu.

University of Detroit Mercy, College of Engineering and Science, Department of Mathematics and Computer Science, Program in Teaching of Mathematics, Detroit, MI 48221. Offers MATM. *Expenses:* Tuition: Full-time $15,750; part-time $875 per credit hour. Required fees: $570.

University of Florida, Graduate School, College of Education, School of Teaching and Learning, Gainesville, FL 32611. Offers bilingual/ESOL education (M Ed, MAE, Ed D, PhD, Ed S); curriculum and instruction (M Ed, MAE, Ed D, PhD, Ed S); early childhood education (Ed D, PhD, Ed S); elementary education (M Ed, MAE); English education (M Ed, MAE); mathematics education (M Ed, MAE); reading education (M Ed, MAE); science education (M Ed, MAE); social foundations (M Ed, MAE, Ed D, PhD); social studies education (M Ed, MAE). *Accreditation:* NCATE. *Faculty:* 29 full-time (20 women). *Students:* 506 (406 women); includes 87 minority (20 African Americans, 3 American Indian/Alaska Native, 13 Asian Americans or Pacific Islanders, 51 Hispanic Americans) 34 international. In 2006, 278 master's, 8 doctorates awarded. *Degree requirements:* For master's, thesis optional; for doctorate, variable foreign language requirement, thesis/dissertation. *Entrance requirements:* For master's and doctorate, GRE General Test, minimum GPA of 3.0; for Ed S, GRE General Test. Additional exam requirements/recommendations for international students: Required—TOEFL (minimum score 550 paper-based; 213 computer-based). *Application deadline:* For fall admission, 6/1 for domestic students. Applications are processed on a rolling basis. Application fee: $30. Electronic applications accepted. *Expenses:* Tuition, state resident: full-time $6,827. Tuition, nonresident: full-time $21,951. Required fees: $999. *Financial support:* In 2006–07, 5 research assistantships (averaging $11,947 per year), 22 teaching assistantships (averaging $9,709 per year) were awarded; fellowships, career-related internships or fieldwork and unspecified assistantships also available. *Faculty research:* Teacher education, inclusive education, classroom processes, curriculum and technology. *Unit head:* Dr. Tom Dana, Director, 352-392-9191 Ext. 200, Fax: 352-392-9193, E-mail: tdana@coe.ufl.edu. *Application contact:* Dr. Linda C. Jones, Coordinator, 352-392-0761 Ext. 267, Fax: 352-392-9193, E-mail: lcjones@coe.ufl.edu.

University of Georgia, Graduate School, College of Education, Department of Mathematics and Science Education, Athens, GA 30602. Offers M Ed, MA, Ed D, PhD, Ed S. *Faculty:* 17 full-time (7 women). *Students:* 107 full-time (67 women), 113 part-time (89 women); includes 28 minority (19 African Americans, 5 Asian Americans or Pacific Islanders, 4 Hispanic Americans), 23 international. 35 applicants, 31% accepted. In 2006, 35 master's, 11 doctorates, 12 other advanced degrees awarded. *Application deadline:* For fall admission, 7/1 priority date for domestic students; for spring admission, 11/15 for domestic students. Application fee: $50. *Unit head:* Dr. Denise S. Mewborn, Head, 706-542-4548, Fax: 706-542-4551, E-mail: dmewborn@uga.edu.

University of Houston, College of Education, Department of Curriculum and Instruction, Houston, TX 77204. Offers art education (M Ed); bilingual education (M Ed); curriculum and instruction (Ed D); early childhood education (M Ed); education of the gifted (M Ed); elementary education (M Ed); mathematics education (M Ed); reading and language arts education (M Ed); science education (M Ed); second language education (M Ed); secondary education (M Ed); social studies education (M Ed); teaching (M Ed). *Accreditation:* NCATE. Part-time and evening/weekend programs available. *Faculty:* 24 full-time (11 women), 16 part-time/adjunct (14 women). *Students:* 134 full-time (102 women), 327 part-time (256 women); includes 142 minority (49 African Americans, 1 American Indian/Alaska Native, 29 Asian Americans or Pacific Islanders, 63 Hispanic Americans), 19 international. Average age 37. 113 applicants, 72% accepted, 61 enrolled. In 2006, 106 master's, 32 doctorates awarded. *Degree requirements:* For master's, comprehensive exam or thesis; for doctorate, thesis/dissertation, comprehensive exam. *Entrance requirements:* For master's, GRE General Test or MAT; for doctorate, GRE General Test, interview. *Application deadline:* For fall admission, 7/3 priority date for domestic students. Applications are processed on a rolling basis. Application fee: $35 ($75 for international students). *Expenses:* Tuition, state resident: full-time $5,429; part-time $226 per credit. Tuition, nonresident: full-time $12,029; part-time $501 per credit. Required fees: $2,454. *Financial support:* In 2006–07, 2 fellowships with full tuition reimbursements (averaging $9,500 per year), 6 research assistantships with full tuition reimbursements (averaging $8,800 per year), 25 teaching assistantships with full tuition reimbursements (averaging $8,800 per year) were awarded; career-related internships or fieldwork, Federal Work-Study, institutionally sponsored loans, scholarships/grants, health care benefits, and unspecified assistantships also available. Support available to part-time students. Financial award application deadline: 3/10. *Faculty research:* Teaching-learning process, instructional technology in schools, teacher education, classroom management, at-risk students. *Unit head:* Dr. Juanita Copley, Chairperson, 713-743-4950, Fax: 713-743-4990, E-mail: ncopley@aol.com.

University of Illinois at Chicago, Graduate College, College of Liberal Arts and Sciences, Department of Mathematics, Statistics, and Computer Science, Program in Teaching of Mathematics, Chicago, IL 60607-7128. Offers MST. Part-time programs available. *Degree requirements:* For master's, comprehensive exam. *Entrance requirements:* For master's, GRE General Test, minimum GPA of 2.75. Additional exam requirements/recommendations for international students: Required—TOEFL. Electronic applications accepted.

University of Illinois at Urbana–Champaign, Graduate College, College of Liberal Arts and Sciences, Department of Mathematics, Champaign, IL 61820. Offers applied mathematics (MS); mathematics (MA, MS, PhD); teaching of mathematics (MS). *Faculty:* 70 full-time (5 women), 7 part-time/adjunct (3 women). *Students:* 171 full-time (37 women), 40 part-time (15 women); includes 16 minority (1 African American, 1 American Indian/Alaska Native, 12 Asian Americans or Pacific Islanders, 2 Hispanic Americans), 111 international. 339 applicants, 36% accepted, 27 enrolled. In 2006, 54 master's, 13 doctorates awarded. *Degree requirements:* For doctorate, 2 foreign languages, thesis/dissertation. *Entrance requirements:* For master's, GRE, minimum GPA of 3.0. *Application deadline:* For fall admission, 2/6 for domestic students. Applications are processed on a rolling basis. Application fee: $50 ($60 for international students). Electronic applications accepted. *Financial support:* In 2006–07, 23 fellowships, 47 research assistantships, 151 teaching assistantships were awarded; tuition waivers (full and partial) also available. Financial award application deadline: 2/15. *Unit head:* Sheldon Katz, Chair, 217-333-6209, Fax: 217-333-9576. *Application contact:* Lori Dick, Administrative Assistant, 217-333-3350, Fax: 217-333-9576, E-mail: ldick@math.uiuc.edu.

University of Indianapolis, Graduate Programs, School of Education, Indianapolis, IN 46227-3697. Offers art education (MAT); biology (MAT); chemistry (MAT); curriculum and instruction (MA); earth sciences (MAT); education (MA, MAT); educational leadership (MA); elementary education (MA); English (MAT); French (MAT); math (MAT); physical education (MAT); physics (MAT); secondary education (MA), including art education, education, English education, social studies education; social studies (MAT); Spanish (MAT). *Accreditation:* NCATE. Part-time and evening/weekend programs available. *Faculty:* 4 full-time (2 women), 6 part-time/adjunct (2 women). *Students:* 32 full-time (16 women), 70 part-time (42 women); includes 2 minority (1 African American, 1 Hispanic American). Average age 31. In 2006, 51 degrees awarded. *Entrance requirements:* For master's, GRE Subject Test, minimum GPA of 2.5, 3 letters of recommendation, interview, Praxis I, writing exercise, be within 9 hours of completing content requirements. Additional exam requirements/recommendations for international students: Required—TOEFL (minimum score 550 paper-based; 213 computer-based). *Application deadline:* Applications are processed on a rolling basis. Application fee: $50. *Financial support:* Federal Work-Study available. Financial award application deadline: 5/1; financial award applicants required to submit FAFSA. *Faculty research:* Assessment of teacher education, perceptions of prospective teachers by parents. *Unit head:* Dr. E. Lynne Weisenbach, Dean, 317-788-3446, Fax: 317-788-3300, E-mail: weisenbach@uindy.edu.

The University of Iowa, Graduate College, College of Education, Department of Teaching and Learning, Program in Secondary Education, Iowa City, IA 52242-1316. Offers art education (MA, PhD); curriculum and supervision (PhD); curriculum supervision (MA); developmental reading (MA); English education (MA, MAT, PhD); foreign language education (MA, MAT); foreign language/ESL education (PhD); language, literature and culture (PhD); math education (PhD); mathematics education (MA); music education (MA, PhD); social studies (MA, PhD). *Faculty:* 11 full-time. *Students:* 53 full-time (33 women), 53 part-time (41 women); includes 5 minority (1 African American, 1 American Indian/Alaska Native, 2 Asian Americans or Pacific Islanders, 1 Hispanic American), 19 international. 66 applicants, 47% accepted, 17 enrolled. In 2006, 22 master's, 14 doctorates awarded. *Degree requirements:* For master's, exam, thesis optional; for doctorate, thesis/dissertation, comprehensive exam, registration. *Entrance requirements:* For master's and doctorate, GRE General Test, minimum GPA of 3.0. Additional exam requirements/recommendations for international students: Required—TOEFL (minimum score 550 paper-based; 213 computer-based; 81 iBT). Application fee: $60 ($85 for international students). Electronic applications accepted. *Financial support:* In 2006–07, 1 fellowship, 12 research assistantships with partial tuition reimbursements, 31 teaching assistantships with partial tuition reimbursements were awarded. Financial award applicants required to submit FAFSA. *Unit head:* Gary Sasso, Chair, 319-335-5324, Fax: 319-335-5608.

University of Massachusetts Lowell, Graduate School, Graduate School of Education, Lowell, MA 01854-2881. Offers administration, planning, and policy (CAGS); curriculum and instruction (M Ed, CAGS); educational administration (M Ed); language arts and literacy (Ed D); leadership in schooling (Ed D); math and science education (Ed D); reading and language (M Ed, CAGS). *Accreditation:* NCATE. Part-time and evening/weekend programs available. Postbaccalaureate distance learning degree programs offered (no on-campus study). Terminal master's awarded for partial completion of doctoral program. *Degree requirements:* For doctorate, thesis/dissertation. *Entrance requirements:* For master's and doctorate, GRE General Test. Additional exam requirements/recommendations for international students: Required—TOEFL. Electronic applications accepted.

University of Miami, Graduate School, School of Education, Department of Teaching and Learning, Program in Mathematics and Science Resource Teaching, Coral Gables, FL 33124. Offers MS Ed, Ed S. Part-time and evening/weekend programs available. *Students:* 1 full-time (0 women), 15 part-time (all women); includes 10 minority (5 African Americans, 5 Hispanic Americans). 12 applicants, 50% accepted, 6 enrolled. In 2006, 13 degrees awarded. *Degree requirements:* For master's, comprehensive exam (for some programs). *Application deadline:* Applications are processed on a rolling basis. Electronic applications accepted. *Financial support:* In 2006–07, 15 students received support. Application deadline: 3/1; *Faculty research:* Mathematics education.

University of Miami, Graduate School, School of Education, Department of Teaching and Learning, Program in Teaching and Learning, Coral Gables, FL 33124. Offers exceptional student education (PhD); mathematics and science education (PhD); reading (PhD); teaching English to speakers of other languages (PhD). Part-time and evening/weekend programs available. *Students:* 25 full-time (20 women), 6 part-time (5 women); includes 11 minority (2 African Americans, 9 Hispanic Americans), 5 international. Average age 38. 23 applicants, 61% accepted, 4 enrolled. In 2006, 3 doctorates awarded. *Median time to degree:* Of those who began their doctoral program in fall 1998, 100% received their degree in 8 years or less. *Degree requirements:* For doctorate, thesis/dissertation. *Entrance requirements:* For doctorate, GRE General Test, GRE Subject Test. Additional exam requirements/recommendations for international students: Required—TOEFL (minimum score 550 paper-based; 212 computer-based). Application fee: $50. Electronic applications accepted. *Financial support:* In 2006–07, 16 research assistantships with full tuition reimbursements (averaging $13,000 per year), 3 teaching assistantships with full tuition reimbursements (averaging $13,000 per year) were awarded; fellowships, tuition waivers (partial) also available. Financial award application deadline: 3/1; financial award applicants required to submit FAFSA. *Faculty research:* Teacher education, multicultural education, technology, second language acquisition.

University of Michigan, Horace H. Rackham School of Graduate Studies, School of Education, Programs in Educational Studies, Ann Arbor, MI 48109. Offers curriculum development (MA); early childhood education (MA, PhD); educational administration and policy (MA, PhD); educational foundation, administration, policy, and research methods (MA); educational foundations and policy (MA, PhD); elementary education (MA-Certification); English education (MA); English language learning in school settings (MA); learning technologies (MA, PhD); literacy, language, and culture (MA, PhD); mathematics education (MA, PhD); research methods (MA); science education (MA, PhD); secondary education (MA-Certification); social studies education (MA); special education (PhD); teaching and teacher education (PhD); MA-Certification; MBA/MA; PhD/MA. Terminal master's awarded for partial completion of doctoral program. *Degree requirements:* For master's, thesis (for some programs); for doctorate, thesis/

Mathematics Education

University of Michigan (continued)
dissertation, comprehensive exam. *Entrance requirements:* For master's and doctorate, GRE General Test. Additional exam requirements/recommendations for international students: Required—TOEFL (minimum score 600 paper-based; 250 computer-based). *Application deadline:* For fall admission, 12/1 priority date for domestic students, 12/1 for international students. Application fee: $60 ($75 for international students). Electronic applications accepted. *Financial support:* Applicants required to submit FAFSA. *Unit head:* Dr. Addison Stone, Chairperson, 734-763-7500, Fax: 734-615-1290, E-mail: addison@umich.edu. *Application contact:* Roberta Perry, Office of Student Services, 734-764-7563, Fax: 734-763-1495, E-mail: ed.grad.admit@umich.edu.

University of Minnesota, Twin Cities Campus, Graduate School, College of Education and Human Development, Department of Curriculum and Instruction, Program in Teaching, Minneapolis, MN 55455-0213. Offers Chinese (M Ed); earth science (M Ed); elementary special education (M Ed); English (M Ed); English as a second language (M Ed); French (M Ed); German (M Ed); Hebrew (M Ed); Japanese (M Ed); life sciences (M Ed); mathematics (M Ed); middle school science (M Ed); science (M Ed); second languages and cultures (M Ed); social studies (M Ed); Spanish (M Ed). *Students:* 324 full-time (230 women), 132 part-time (86 women); includes 44 minority (5 African Americans, 2 American Indian/Alaska Native, 27 Asian Americans or Pacific Islanders, 10 Hispanic Americans), 4 international. Average age 27. 499 applicants, 74% accepted, 327 enrolled. In 2006, 545 degrees awarded. *Expenses:* Tuition, state resident: full-time $9,302; part-time $775 per credit. Tuition, nonresident: full-time $16,400; part-time $1,367 per credit. Full-time tuition and fees vary according to class time, course load, program, reciprocity agreements and student level. *Application contact:* Dr. Mary Bents, Associate Dean, 612-625-6501, Fax: 612-626-1580, E-mail: mbents@tc.umn.edu.

University of Missouri–Columbia, Graduate School, College of Arts and Sciences, Department of Mathematics, Columbia, MO 65211. Offers applied mathematics (MS); mathematics (MA, MST, PhD). *Faculty:* 44 full-time (7 women). *Students:* 64 full-time (21 women), 4 part-time (1 woman); includes 1 minority (African American), 29 international. In 2006, 18 master's, 11 doctorates awarded. *Degree requirements:* For doctorate, 2 foreign languages, thesis/dissertation. *Entrance requirements:* For master's and doctorate, GRE General Test, minimum GPA of 3.0. *Application deadline:* Applications are processed on a rolling basis. Application fee: $45 ($60 for international students). *Financial support:* Fellowships, research assistantships, teaching assistantships, institutionally sponsored loans available. *Unit head:* Dr. Jan Segert, Director of Graduate Studies, 573-882-6953, E-mail: segertj@missouri.edu.

University of Missouri–Columbia, Graduate School, College of Education, Department of Curriculum and Instruction, Columbia, MO 65211. Offers agricultural education (M Ed, PhD, Ed S); art education (M Ed, PhD, Ed S); business and office education (M Ed, PhD, Ed S); early childhood education (M Ed, PhD, Ed S); elementary education (M Ed, PhD, Ed S); English education (M Ed, PhD, Ed S); foreign language education (M Ed, PhD, Ed S); health education and promotion (M Ed, PhD); learning and instruction (M Ed); marketing education (M Ed, PhD, Ed S); mathematics education (M Ed, PhD, Ed S); music education (M Ed, PhD, Ed S); reading education (M Ed, PhD, Ed S); science education (M Ed, PhD, Ed S); social studies education (M Ed, PhD, Ed S); vocational education (M Ed, PhD, Ed S). Part-time programs available. *Faculty:* 24 full-time (12 women). *Students:* 195 full-time (148 women), 260 part-time (214 women); includes 27 minority (8 African Americans, 1 American Indian/Alaska Native, 10 Asian Americans or Pacific Islanders, 8 Hispanic Americans), 19 international. In 2006, 186 master's, 12 doctorates awarded. Terminal master's awarded for partial completion of doctoral program. *Degree requirements:* For doctorate, thesis/dissertation. *Entrance requirements:* For master's and Ed S, GRE General Test or MAT, minimum GPA of 3.0; for doctorate, GRE General Test, minimum GPA of 3.0. *Application deadline:* Applications are processed on a rolling basis. Application fee: $45 ($60 for international students). *Financial support:* Fellowships, research assistantships, teaching assistantships, institutionally sponsored loans available. *Unit head:* Dr. Lloyd H. Barrow, Director of Graduate Studies, 573-882-8247, E-mail: robinsonr@missouri.edu.

University of Missouri–Rolla, Graduate School, College of Arts and Sciences, Department of Mathematics and Statistics, Program in Mathematics, Rolla, MO 65409-0910. Offers mathematics (PhD); mathematics education (MST). *Degree requirements:* For master's, thesis or alternative; for doctorate, one foreign language, thesis/dissertation. *Entrance requirements:* For master's and doctorate, GRE General Test. Electronic applications accepted. *Faculty research:* Analysis, differential equations, topology, statistics.

The University of Montana, Graduate School, College of Arts and Sciences, Department of Mathematical Sciences, Missoula, MT 59812-0002. Offers mathematics (MA, PhD), including college teaching (PhD); traditional mathematics research (PhD); mathematics education (MA). Part-time programs available. Terminal master's awarded for partial completion of doctoral program. *Degree requirements:* For doctorate, thesis/dissertation. *Entrance requirements:* For master's and doctorate, GRE General Test. Additional exam requirements/recommendations for international students: Required—TOEFL (minimum score 525 paper-based; 195 computer-based).

University of Nevada, Las Vegas, Graduate College, College of Education, Department of Curriculum and Instruction, Las Vegas, NV 89154-9900. Offers curriculum and instruction (Ed D, PhD, Ed S); elementary education (M Ed, MS); English education (M Ed, MS); library science (M Ed, MS); literacy education (M Ed, MS); mathematics education (M Ed, MS); multicultural education (M Ed, MS); reading specialist (M Ed, MS); secondary education (M Ed, MS); teacher leadership (M Ed, MS); teaching English as a second language (M Ed, MS); technology integration and leadership (M Ed, MS). *Accreditation:* NCATE. Part-time and evening/weekend programs available. *Faculty:* 40 full-time (19 women), 21 part-time/adjunct (14 women). *Students:* 257 full-time (189 women), 387 part-time (296 women); includes 114 minority (28 African Americans, 5 American Indian/Alaska Native, 34 Asian Americans or Pacific Islanders, 47 Hispanic Americans), 7 international. 261 applicants, 70% accepted, 168 enrolled. In 2006, 231 master's, 5 doctorates awarded. *Degree requirements:* For master's, thesis (for some programs), comprehensive exam (for some programs); for doctorate, thesis/dissertation, oral exam. *Entrance requirements:* For master's, minimum GPA of 3.0; for doctorate, GRE General Test, minimum graduate GPA of 3.0. Additional exam requirements/recommendations for international students: Required—TOEFL (minimum score 550 paper-based; 213 computer-based; 80 iBT). *Application deadline:* For fall admission, 2/15 for domestic and international students; for spring admission, 9/30 for domestic and international students. Application fee: $60 ($75 for international students). Electronic applications accepted. *Financial support:* In 2006–07, 30 research assistantships with partial tuition reimbursements (averaging $10,000 per year), 7 teaching assistantships with partial tuition reimbursements (averaging $12,000 per year) were awarded; career-related internships or fieldwork, Federal Work-Study, institutionally sponsored loans, scholarships/grants, health care benefits, and unspecified assistantships also available. Support available to part-time students. Financial award application deadline: 3/1. *Unit head:* Dr. Greg Levitt, Chair, 702-895-3241. *Application contact:* Graduate College Admissions Evaluator, 702-895-3320, E-mail: gradcollege@unlv.edu.

University of Nevada, Las Vegas, Graduate College, College of Science, Department of Mathematical Sciences, Las Vegas, NV 89154-9900. Offers applied mathematics (MS, PhD); applied statistics (MS); computational mathematics (PhD); pure mathematics (MS, PhD); statistics (PhD); teaching mathematics (MS). Part-time programs available. *Faculty:* 26 full-time (3 women), 1 part-time/adjunct (0 women). *Students:* 29 full-time (11 women), 22 part-time (7 women); includes 9 minority (1 African American, 4 Asian Americans or Pacific Islanders, 4 Hispanic Americans), 15 international. 42 applicants, 31% accepted, 10 enrolled. In 2006, 12 degrees awarded. *Degree requirements:* For master's, thesis (for some programs), oral exam, comprehensive exam (for some programs). *Entrance requirements:* For master's, minimum GPA of 3.0 during previous 2 years, 2.75 overall. Additional exam requirements/recommendations for international students: Required—TOEFL (minimum score 550 paper-based; 213 computer-based; 80 iBT). *Application deadline:* For fall admission, 2/1 for domestic

and international students; for spring admission, 10/1 for domestic and international students. Application fee: $60 ($75 for international students). Electronic applications accepted. *Financial support:* In 2006–07, 40 teaching assistantships with partial tuition reimbursements (averaging $10,500 per year) were awarded; career-related internships or fieldwork, Federal Work-Study, institutionally sponsored loans, scholarships/grants, health care benefits, and unspecified assistantships also available. Support available to part-time students. Financial award application deadline: 3/1. *Unit head:* Dr. Chih-Hsiang Ho, Chair, 702-895-0396. *Application contact:* Graduate College Admissions Evaluator, 702-895-3320, Fax: 702-895-4180, E-mail: gradcollege@unlv.edu.

University of Nevada, Reno, Graduate School, College of Science, Department of Mathematics and Statistics, Reno, NV 89557. Offers mathematics (MS); teaching mathematics (MATM). *Faculty:* 17. *Students:* 20 full-time (8 women), 11 part-time (4 women); includes 4 minority (all Asian Americans or Pacific Islanders), 6 international. Average age 30. 21 applicants, 86% accepted, 13 enrolled. In 2006, 6 degrees awarded. *Degree requirements:* For master's, thesis optional. *Entrance requirements:* For master's, GRE General Test, minimum GPA of 2.75. Additional exam requirements/recommendations for international students: Required—TOEFL. *Application deadline:* For fall admission, 3/1 priority date for domestic students; for spring admission, 11/1 for domestic students. Applications are processed on a rolling basis. Application fee: $60 ($95 for international students). *Financial support:* In 2006–07, 2 research assistantships, 6 teaching assistantships were awarded; institutionally sponsored loans also available. Financial award application deadline: 3/1. *Faculty research:* Operator algebra, nonlinear systems, differential equations. *Unit head:* Dr. Aleksey Telyakovskiy, Graduate Program Director, 775-784-1364.

University of New Hampshire, Graduate School, College of Engineering and Physical Sciences, Department of Mathematics and Statistics, Durham, NH 03824. Offers applied mathematics (MS); mathematics (MS, MST, PhD); mathematics education (PhD); statistics (MS). *Faculty:* 26 full-time. *Students:* 16 full-time (8 women), 35 part-time (15 women); includes 2 minority (both Asian Americans or Pacific Islanders), 20 international. Average age 28. 54 applicants, 46% accepted, 16 enrolled. In 2006, 12 master's, 4 doctorates awarded. Terminal master's awarded for partial completion of doctoral program. *Degree requirements:* For doctorate, 2 foreign languages, thesis/dissertation. *Entrance requirements:* Additional exam requirements/recommendations for international students: Required—TOEFL (minimum score 550 paper-based; 213 computer-based). *Application deadline:* For fall admission, 4/1 priority date for domestic students, 4/1 for international students; for winter admission, 12/1 priority date for domestic students. Applications are processed on a rolling basis. Application fee: $60. Electronic applications accepted. *Expenses:* Tuition, state resident: full-time $8,540; part-time $474 per credit hour. Tuition, nonresident: full-time $20,990; part-time $862 per credit hour. Required fees: $1,343; $356 per term. Tuition and fees vary according to course load, program and reciprocity agreements. *Financial support:* In 2006–07, 2 fellowships, 1 research assistantship, 26 teaching assistantships were awarded; Federal Work-Study, scholarships/grants, and tuition waivers (full and partial) also available. Support available to part-time students. Financial award application deadline: 2/15. *Faculty research:* Operator theory, complex analysis, algebra, nonlinear dynamics, statistics. *Unit head:* Dr. Eric Grinberg, Chairperson, 603-862-5772. *Application contact:* Jan Jankowski, Administrative Assistant, 603-862-2320, E-mail: jan.jankowski@unh.edu.

The University of North Carolina at Chapel Hill, Graduate School, School of Education, Program in Secondary Education, Chapel Hill, NC 27599. Offers English (Grades 9-12) (MAT); French (Grades K-12) (MAT); German (Grades K-12) (MAT); Japanese (Grades K-12) (MAT); Latin (Grades 9-12) (MAT); mathematics (Grades 9-12) (MAT); music (Grades K-12) (MAT); science (Grades 9-12) (MAT); social studies/social science (Grades 9-12) (MAT); Spanish (Grades K-12) (MAT). *Accreditation:* NCATE. In 2006, 72 degrees awarded. *Degree requirements:* For master's, comprehensive exam. *Entrance requirements:* For master's, GRE General Test, minimum GPA of 3.0 during last 2 years of undergraduate course work. Additional exam requirements/recommendations for international students: Required—TOEFL (minimum score 550 paper-based; 213 computer-based), ACTFL oral proficiency interview. *Application deadline:* For fall admission, 1/1 priority date for domestic and international students. Applications are processed on a rolling basis. Application fee: $60. Electronic applications accepted. *Financial support:* Federal Work-Study available. Support available to part-time students. Financial award application deadline: 3/1; financial award applicants required to submit FAFSA. *Faculty research:* Curriculum and instruction, teacher education per subject. *Unit head:* Dr. James Trier, Coordinator, 919-843-4627. *Application contact:* Janet Carroll, Registrar, 919-962-8690, Fax: 919-962-1533, E-mail: jscarrol@email.unc.edu.

The University of North Carolina at Charlotte, Graduate School, College of Arts and Sciences, Department of Mathematics and Statistics, Program in Mathematics Education, Charlotte, NC 28223-0001. Offers MA. *Students:* Average age 27. 6 applicants, 100% accepted, 4 enrolled. In 2006, 3 degrees awarded. *Degree requirements:* For master's, comprehensive exam. *Entrance requirements:* For master's, GRE General Test, minimum GPA of 2.75 overall. Additional exam requirements/recommendations for international students: Required—TOEFL (minimum score 557 paper-based; 220 computer-based). *Application deadline:* For fall admission, 7/15 for domestic students, 5/1 for international students; for spring admission, 11/15 for domestic students, 10/1 for international students. Application fee: $55. *Expenses:* Tuition, state resident: full-time $2,719; part-time $170 per credit. Tuition, nonresident: full-time $12,926; part-time $808 per credit. Required fees: $1,555. *Financial support:* Career-related internships or fieldwork, Federal Work-Study, institutionally sponsored loans, scholarships/grants, and unspecified assistantships available. Support available to part-time students. Financial award application deadline: 4/1; financial award applicants required to submit FAFSA. *Unit head:* Dr. Victor V. Cifarelli, Coordinator, 704-687-4579, Fax: 704-687-0415, E-mail: cifare@email.uncc.edu. *Application contact:* Kathy B. Giddings, Director of Graduate Admissions, 704-687-3366, Fax: 704-687-3279, E-mail: gradadm@email.uncc.edu.

The University of North Carolina at Greensboro, Graduate School, School of Education, Department of Curriculum and Instruction, Greensboro, NC 27412-5001. Offers college teaching and adult learning (Certificate); curriculum and instruction (M Ed), including chemistry education, elementary education, English as a second language, French education, instructional technology, mathematics education, middle grades education, reading education, science education, social studies education, Spanish education; curriculum and teaching (PhD), including higher education, teacher education and development; English as a second language (Certificate); higher education (M Ed); supervision (M Ed). *Accreditation:* NCATE. Part-time programs available. *Faculty:* 27 full-time (18 women), 8 part-time/adjunct (3 women). *Students:* 137 full-time (114 women), 231 part-time (195 women); includes 63 minority (52 African Americans, 2 American Indian/Alaska Native, 5 Asian Americans or Pacific Islanders, 4 Hispanic Americans). 146 applicants, 32% accepted. *Degree requirements:* For doctorate, thesis/dissertation. *Entrance requirements:* For master's and doctorate, GRE General Test. Additional exam requirements/recommendations for international students: Required—TOEFL. Application fee: $45. Electronic applications accepted. *Expenses:* Tuition, state resident: full-time $2,692. Tuition, nonresident: full-time $13,742. *Financial support:* Fellowships, research assistantships with full tuition reimbursements, teaching assistantships with full tuition reimbursements, career-related internships or fieldwork, Federal Work-Study, scholarships/grants, traineeships, and unspecified assistantships available. Support available to part-time students. *Faculty research:* Community college literacy program, middle school mathematics/computer mathematics. *Unit head:* Dr. Sam Miller, Chair, 336-334-3445, Fax: 336-334-4120, E-mail: sdmille2@uncg.edu. *Application contact:* Michelle Harkleroad, Director of Graduate Admissions, 336-334-4884, Fax: 336-334-4424, E-mail: mbharkle@uncg.edu.

The University of North Carolina at Pembroke, Graduate Studies, Department of Mathematics and Computer Science, Program in Mathematics Education, Pembroke, NC 28372-1510. Offers MA, MAT. *Accreditation:* NCATE. Part-time and evening/weekend programs available. *Faculty:* 2 full-time (0 women). *Students:* Average age 29. 6 applicants, 100% accepted, 6 enrolled. In 2006, 2 degrees awarded. *Degree requirements:* For master's, thesis optional.

Entrance requirements: For master's, GRE General Test or MAT, bachelor's degree in mathematics or mathematics education; minimum GPA of 3.0 in major, 2.5 overall. Additional exam requirements/recommendations for international students: Required—TOEFL. *Application deadline:* For fall admission, 7/15 priority date for domestic students; for spring admission, 12/1 priority date for domestic students. Applications are processed on a rolling basis. Application fee: $40. *Expenses:* Tuition, state resident: full-time $3,516; part-time $1,091 per semester. Tuition, nonresident: full-time $12,924; part-time $4,619 per semester. Tuition and fees vary according to class time, course load, degree level and campus/location. *Financial support:* Unspecified assistantships available. Support available to part-time students. Financial award application deadline: 4/15; financial award applicants required to submit FAFSA.

University of Northern Colorado, Graduate School, College of Natural and Health Sciences, Graduate Interdisciplinary Degree Program: Middle Level Mathematics, Greeley, CO 80639. Offers MA. *Students:* 1 full-time (0 women), 7 part-time (4 women); includes 1 minority (Hispanic American) Average age 47. 3 applicants, 100% accepted, 2 enrolled. *Degree requirements:* For master's, comprehensive exam. *Application deadline:* Applications are processed on a rolling basis. Application fee: $50 ($60 for international students). Electronic applications accepted. *Expenses:* Tuition, state resident: full-time $5,118; part-time $213 per credit hour. Tuition, nonresident: full-time $14,832; part-time $618 per credit hour. Required fees: $674; $34 per credit hour. *Financial support:* In 2006–07, 2 students received support; fellowships, research assistantships, teaching assistantships available. Financial award application deadline: 3/1. *Unit head:* Dr. Dean Allison, Program Coordinator, 970-351-2820.

University of Northern Colorado, Graduate School, College of Natural and Health Sciences, School of Mathematical Sciences, Greeley, CO 80639. Offers mathematical teaching (MA); mathematics education (PhD); mathematics: liberal arts (MA). Part-time programs available. *Faculty:* 12 full-time (4 women). *Students:* 17 full-time (11 women), 30 part-time (19 women); includes 4 minority (1 African American, 1 Asian American or Pacific Islander, 2 Hispanic Americans). Average age 32. 14 applicants, 93% accepted, 7 enrolled. In 2006, 9 master's, 2 doctorates awarded. *Degree requirements:* For master's, thesis or alternative, comprehensive exam; for doctorate, thesis/dissertation, comprehensive exam. *Entrance requirements:* For master's, GRE General Test (liberal arts), 3 letters of recommendation; for doctorate, GRE General Test, 3 letters of recommendation. *Application deadline:* Applications are processed on a rolling basis. Application fee: $50 ($60 for international students). Electronic applications accepted. *Expenses:* Tuition, state resident: full-time $5,118; part-time $213 per credit hour. Tuition, nonresident: full-time $14,832; part-time $618 per credit hour. Required fees: $674; $34 per credit hour. *Financial support:* In 2006–07, 18 students received support, including 2 fellowships (averaging $1,675 per year), 2 research assistantships (averaging $14,350 per year), 8 teaching assistantships (averaging $13,723 per year); unspecified assistantships also available. Financial award application deadline: 3/1; financial award applicants required to submit FAFSA. *Unit head:* Dr. Jeff Farmer, Director, 970-351-2820, Fax: 970-351-2155.

University of Northern Iowa, Graduate College, College of Natural Sciences, Department of Mathematics, Cedar Falls, IA 50614. Offers mathematics (MA); mathematics for middle grades (MA). Part-time programs available. *Students:* 7 full-time (3 women), 18 part-time (14 women); includes 4 minority (all African Americans), 1 international. 10 applicants, 70% accepted, 6 enrolled. In 2006, 6 degrees awarded. *Degree requirements:* For master's, thesis or alternative, comprehensive exam (for some programs). *Entrance requirements:* Additional exam requirements/recommendations for international students: Required—TOEFL (minimum score 600 paper-based; 250 computer-based; 100 iBT). *Application deadline:* For fall admission, 8/1 priority date for domestic students. Applications are processed on a rolling basis. Application fee: $30 ($50 for international students). Electronic applications accepted. *Expenses:* Tuition, state resident: full-time $5,936. Tuition, nonresident: full-time $14,074. Required fees: $1,026. *Financial support:* Career-related internships or fieldwork, Federal Work-Study, scholarships/grants, and tuition waivers (full and partial) available. Support available to part-time students. Financial award application deadline: 2/1. *Unit head:* Dr. Jerry Ridenhour, Head, 319-273-2631, Fax: 319-273-2546, E-mail: jerry.ridenhour@uni.edu.

University of Oklahoma, Graduate College, College of Education, Department of Instructional Leadership and Academic Curriculum, Norman, OK 73019-0390. Offers education (Certificate); instructional leadership and academic curriculum (M Ed, PhD), including bilingual education, early childhood education, elementary education, English education, math education, reading education, science education, secondary education, social studies education. *Accreditation:* NCATE. Part-time and evening/weekend programs available. *Faculty:* 20 full-time (11 women), 6 part-time/adjunct (all women). *Students:* 76 full-time (63 women), 115 part-time (89 women); includes 25 minority (8 African Americans, 12 American Indian/Alaska Native, 4 Asian Americans or Pacific Islanders, 1 Hispanic American), 12 international. 72 applicants, 96% accepted, 56 enrolled. In 2006, 11 master's, 10 doctorates awarded. *Degree requirements:* For doctorate, thesis/dissertation. *Entrance requirements:* For master's, 12 hours of course work in education; for doctorate, GRE General Test, master's degree, minimum graduate GPA of 3.0. Additional exam requirements/recommendations for international students: Required—TOEFL (minimum score 550 paper-based; 213 computer-based). *Application deadline:* For fall admission, 6/1 priority date for domestic students, 4/1 for international students; for spring admission, 11/1 for domestic students, 9/1 for international students. Applications are processed on a rolling basis. Application fee: $40 ($90 for international students). *Expenses:* Tuition, state resident: full-time $3,180; part-time $133 per credit hour. Tuition, nonresident: full-time $11,347; part-time $473 per credit hour. Required fees: $1,729; $62 per credit hour. $117 per semester. Tuition and fees vary according to course load and program. *Financial support:* In 2006–07, 76 students received support, including 5 research assistantships with partial tuition reimbursements available (averaging $9,773 per year), 7 teaching assistantships with partial tuition reimbursements available (averaging $10,403 per year); scholarships/grants and unspecified assistantships also available. Financial award applicants required to submit FAFSA. *Faculty research:* Early literacy, learning cycle, social justice, teacher education. Total annual research expenditures: $119,917. *Unit head:* Dr. Priscilla Griffith, Chair and Graduate Liaison, 405-325-1498, Fax: 405-325-4061, E-mail: pgriffith@ou.edu.

University of Phoenix–Omaha Campus, College of Education, Omaha, NE 68154-5240. Offers administration and supervision (MA Ed); curriculum and instruction (MA Ed); curriculum and instruction—English and language arts education (MA Ed); curriculum and instruction—adult education (MA Ed); curriculum and instruction—computer education (MA Ed); curriculum and instruction—English as a second language (MA Ed); curriculum and instruction—mathematics education (MA Ed); elementary teacher education (MA Ed); secondary teacher education (MA Ed); special education (MA Ed).

University of Phoenix Online Campus, The Artemis School, College of Education, Phoenix, AZ 85034-7209. Offers administration and supervision (MAEd); adult education and training (MAEd); curriculum and instruction-adult education (MAEd); curriculum and instruction-English and language arts education (MAEd); curriculum and instruction-mathematics education (MAEd); curriculum education (MAEd); curriculum instruction (MAEd); early childhood (MAEd); English as a second language (MAEd); teacher education elementary (MAEd); teacher education secondary (MAEd). Evening/weekend programs available. Postbaccalaureate distance learning degree programs offered (no on-campus study). *Faculty:* 12 full-time (5 women), 8,196 part-time/adjunct (6,937 women). *Students:* 11,937 full-time (9,375 women); includes 2,972 minority (2,210 African Americans, 74 American Indian/Alaska Native, 205 Asian Americans or Pacific Islanders, 483 Hispanic Americans), 906 international. Average age 36. *Degree requirements:* For master's, thesis (for some programs), registration. *Entrance requirements:* For master's, 3 years of work experience, minimum GPA of 2.5. Additional exam requirements/recommendations for international students: Required—TOEFL (minimum score 550 paper-based; 213 computer-based; 79 iBT). *Application deadline:* Applications are processed on a rolling basis. Application fee: $45. Electronic applications accepted. *Expenses:* Tuition: Full-time $12,664. Required fees: $760. *Financial support:* Institutionally sponsored loans and scholarships/grants available. Financial award applicants required to submit FAFSA. *Unit head:* Dr. Marla LaRue, Dean/Executive Director, 480-557-1218, E-mail: marla.larue@phoenix.edu. *Application contact:* Dr. Marla LaRue, Dean/Executive Director, 480-557-1218, E-mail: marla.larue@phoenix.edu.

University of Phoenix–Springfield Campus, College of Education, Springfield, MO 65804-7211. Offers administration and supervision (MA Ed); curriculum and instruction (MA Ed); curriculum and instruction/adult education (MA Ed); curriculum and instruction/computer education (MA Ed); curriculum and instruction/English as a second language (MA Ed); English and language arts education (MA Ed); mathematics education (MA Ed).

University of Pittsburgh, School of Education, Department of Instruction and Learning, Program in Secondary Education, Pittsburgh, PA 15260. Offers English/communications education (M Ed, MAT, Ed D, PhD); foreign languages education (M Ed, MAT, Ed D, PhD); mathematics education (M Ed, MAT, Ed D); reading education (PhD); science education (M Ed, MAT, MS, Ed D); social studies education (M Ed, MAT, Ed D, PhD). Part-time and evening/weekend programs available. *Students:* 157 full-time (111 women), 84 part-time (61 women); includes 18 minority (7 African Americans, 5 Asian Americans or Pacific Islanders, 6 Hispanic Americans), 13 international. 163 applicants, 74% accepted, 86 enrolled. In 2006, 114 master's, 7 doctorates awarded. *Degree requirements:* For master's and doctorate, thesis/dissertation. *Entrance requirements:* For master's, PRAXIS I; for doctorate, GRE General Test. Additional exam requirements/recommendations for international students: Required—TOEFL. *Application deadline:* For fall admission, 2/1 priority date for domestic students; for spring admission, 11/15 priority date for domestic students. Applications are processed on a rolling basis. Application fee: $50. Electronic applications accepted. *Financial support:* Fellowships, teaching assistantships, career-related internships or fieldwork, Federal Work-Study, tuition waivers (partial), and unspecified assistantships available. Support available to part-time students. Financial award application deadline: 3/15; financial award applicants required to submit FAFSA. *Application contact:* Joan M. Cutone, Director, School of Education Student Service Center, 412-648-2230, Fax: 412-648-1899, E-mail: soeinfo@pitt.edu.

University of Puerto Rico, Río Piedras, College of Education, Program in Curriculum and Teaching, San Juan, PR 00931-3300. Offers biology education (M Ed); chemistry education (M Ed); curriculum and teaching (Ed D); English education (M Ed); history education (M Ed); mathematics education (M Ed); physics education (M Ed); secondary education (M Ed); Spanish education (M Ed). Part-time programs available. *Students:* 64 full-time (42 women), 123 part-time (91 women); all minorities (all Hispanic Americans) In 2006, 8 master's, 19 doctorates awarded. *Degree requirements:* For master's, thesis; for doctorate, thesis/dissertation, internship. *Entrance requirements:* For master's, PAEG or GRE, minimum GPA of 3.0, letter of recommendation; for doctorate, GRE or PAEG, master's degree, minimum GPA of 3.0, letter of recommendation (2), interview. *Application deadline:* For fall admission, 2/1 for domestic and international students. Application fee: $17. *Expenses:* Tuition, state resident: part-time $100 per credit. Tuition, nonresident: part-time $291 per credit. Required fees: $72 per semester. *Financial support:* Fellowships, research assistantships, teaching assistantships, career-related internships or fieldwork, Federal Work-Study, institutionally sponsored loans, and tuition waivers (partial) available. Financial award application deadline: 5/31. *Faculty research:* Science curriculum, administration management. *Unit head:* Dr. Loyda Martinez, Coordinator, 787-764-0000 Ext. 4361, Fax: 787-763-4130. *Application contact:* Information Contact, 787-764-0000 Ext. 4368, Fax: 787-763-4130.

University of Rio Grande, Graduate School, Rio Grande, OH 45674. Offers classroom teaching (M Ed), including fine arts, learning disabilities, mathematics, reading education. Part-time and evening/weekend programs available. *Degree requirements:* For master's, final research project, portfolio. *Entrance requirements:* For master's, minimum GPA of 2.7 in major, 2.5 overall. *Faculty research:* Interagency collaboration, reading and mathematics, learning styles, college access, literacy.

University of St. Francis, College of Education, Joliet, IL 60435-6169. Offers curriculum and instruction (MS); educational leadership (MS), including reading, special education; elementary education certification (M Ed); secondary education certification (M Ed), including English education, math education, science education, social studies education; special education (M Ed); teaching and learning (MS). Part-time and evening/weekend programs available. *Faculty:* 11 full-time (10 women), 25 part-time/adjunct (12 women). *Students:* 52 full-time (38 women), 381 part-time (293 women); includes 38 minority (21 African Americans, 1 American Indian/Alaska Native, 4 Asian Americans or Pacific Islanders, 12 Hispanic Americans). Average age 33. 194 applicants, 80% accepted, 117 enrolled. In 2006, 165 degrees awarded. *Degree requirements:* For master's, comprehensive exam (for some programs), registration. *Entrance requirements:* For master's, minimum undergraduate GPA of 2.75, 2 letters of recommendation, computer competency. Additional exam requirements/recommendations for international students: Required—TOEFL (minimum score 550 paper-based; 213 computer-based). *Application deadline:* Applications are processed on a rolling basis. Application fee: $30. Electronic applications accepted. *Expenses: Contact institution.* Part-time tuition and fees vary according to campus/location and program. *Financial support:* In 2006–07, 272 students received support. Scholarships/grants, tuition waivers (partial), and unspecified assistantships available. Support available to part-time students. Financial award applicants required to submit FAFSA. *Unit head:* Dr. John Gambro, Dean, 815-740-3456, Fax: 815-740-2264, E-mail: jgambro@stfrancis.edu. *Application contact:* Sandra Sloka, Director of Admissions for Graduate and Degree Completion Programs, 800-735-7500, Fax: 815-740-5032, E-mail: ssloka@stfrancis.edu.

University of South Carolina, The Graduate School, College of Education, Department of Instruction and Teacher Education, Program in Secondary Education, Columbia, SC 29208. Offers art education (IMA, MAT); business education (IMA, MAT); English (MAT); foreign language (MAT); health education (MAT); mathematics (MAT); science (IMA, MAT); secondary education (M Ed, MA, MT, PhD); social studies (IMA, MAT); theatre and speech (IMA, MAT). IMA and MT offered jointly with the subject areas. *Accreditation:* NCATE. *Degree requirements:* For master's, thesis (for some programs), foreign language (MA), comprehensive exam; for doctorate, one foreign language, thesis/dissertation, comprehensive exam. *Entrance requirements:* For master's, GRE General Test or MAT, teaching certificate (IMA, M Ed), interview; for doctorate, GRE General Test or MAT, interview. *Faculty research:* Middle school programs, professional development, school collaboration.

University of South Carolina, The Graduate School, College of Science and Mathematics, Department of Mathematics, Columbia, SC 29208. Offers mathematics (MA, MS, PhD); mathematics education (M Math, MAT). MAT offered in cooperation with the College of Education. Part-time programs available. Terminal master's awarded for partial completion of doctoral program. *Degree requirements:* For master's, thesis; for doctorate, one foreign language, thesis/dissertation. *Entrance requirements:* For master's and doctorate, GRE General Test. Electronic applications accepted. *Faculty research:* Applied mathematics, analysis, discrete mathematics, algebra, topology.

University of Southern Mississippi, Graduate School, College of Science and Technology, Center for Science and Mathematics Education, Hattiesburg, MS 39406-0001. Offers MS, PhD. *Faculty:* 1 (woman) full-time. *Students:* 15 full-time (10 women), 25 part-time (18 women); includes 1 African American, 3 international. Average age 36. 13 applicants, 62% accepted, 7 enrolled. In 2006, 2 master's, 2 doctorates awarded. *Degree requirements:* For master's, thesis or alternative, comprehensive exam, registration; for doctorate, thesis/dissertation, comprehensive exam, registration. *Entrance requirements:* For master's, GRE General Test, minimum GPA of 2.75 in last 60 hours; for doctorate, GRE General Test, minimum GPA of 3.5. Additional exam requirements/recommendations for international students: Required—TOEFL. *Application deadline:* For fall admission, 3/15 priority date for domestic students, 3/15 for international students. Applications are processed on a rolling basis. Application fee: $25 ($30 for international students). *Financial support:* In 2006–07, 7 research assistantships (averaging $7,490 per year), 4 teaching assistantships with full tuition reimbursements (averaging $7,490 per year) were awarded; fellowships with full tuition reimbursements, Federal Work-

Mathematics Education

University of Southern Mississippi (continued)
Study also available. Financial award application deadline: 3/15. *Unit head:* Dr. Sherry Herron, Director, 601-266-4739, Fax: 601-266-4741.

University of South Florida, Graduate School, College of Education, Department of Secondary Education, Tampa, FL 33620-9951. Offers English education (M Ed, MA, PhD); foreign language education (M Ed, MA); instructional technology (M Ed); mathematics education (M Ed, MA, PhD, Ed S); middle school education (M Ed); science education (M Ed, MA, MAT, PhD); second language acquisition/instructional technology (PhD); secondary education (PhD); social science education (M Ed, MA). *Accreditation:* NCATE. Part-time and evening/weekend programs available. *Faculty:* 29 full-time (16 women), 15 part-time/adjunct (8 women). *Students:* 136 full-time (95 women), 279 part-time (188 women); includes 85 minority (35 African Americans, 1 American Indian/Alaska Native, 13 Asian Americans or Pacific Islanders, 36 Hispanic Americans), 19 international. 212 applicants, 71% accepted, 96 enrolled. In 2006, 87 master's, 12 doctorates awarded. *Entrance requirements:* For master's and doctorate, GRE General Test, minimum GPA of 3.5; for Ed S, GRE General Test. *Application deadline:* For fall admission, 6/1 for domestic students; for spring admission, 10/15 for domestic students. Application fee: $30. Electronic applications accepted. *Financial support:* Scholarships/grants and unspecified assistantships available. Total annual research expenditures: $477,202. *Unit head:* Dr. Jane H. Applegate, Interim Chairperson, 813-974-3533, Fax: 813-974-3837, E-mail: applegat@tempest.coedu.usf.edu.

The University of Tampa, Program in Teaching, Tampa, FL 33606-1490. Offers education (MAT); math education (MAT); reading (M Ed); science education (MAT). *Students:* 66 applicants, 71% accepted, 40 enrolled.Application fee: $40. *Expenses:* Tuition: Part-time $426 per credit hour. Required fees: $35 per year. *Unit head:* Dr. Martine Harrison, Associate Professor of Education, 813-253-3333 Ext. 3373, E-mail: mharrison@ut.edu.

The University of Tennessee, Graduate School, College of Education, Health and Human Sciences, Program in Education, Knoxville, TN 37996. Offers art education (MS); counseling education (PhD); cultural studies in education (PhD); curriculum (MS, Ed S); curriculum, educational research and evaluation (Ed D, PhD); early childhood education (PhD); early childhood special education (MS); education of deaf and hard of hearing (MS); educational administration and policy studies (Ed D, PhD); educational administration and supervision (Ed S); educational psychology (Ed D, PhD); elementary education (MS, Ed S); elementary teaching (MS); English education (MS, Ed S); exercise science (PhD); foreign language/ESL education (MS, Ed S); instructional technology (MS, Ed D, PhD, Ed S); literacy, language and ESL education (PhD); literacy, language education, and ESL education (Ed D); mathematics education (MS, Ed S); modified and comprehensive special education (MS); reading education (MS, Ed S); school counseling (Ed S); school psychology (PhD, Ed S); science education (MS, Ed S); secondary teaching (MS); social foundations (MS); social science education (MS, Ed S); socio-cultural foundations of sports and education (PhD); special education (Ed S); teacher education (Ed D, PhD). *Accreditation:* NCATE. Part-time and evening/weekend programs available. *Students:* 529 (401 women); includes 39 minority (23 African Americans, 2 American Indian/Alaska Native, 9 Asian Americans or Pacific Islanders, 5 Hispanic Americans) 34 international. 420 applicants, 50% accepted. In 2006, 258 master's, 28 doctorates awarded. *Degree requirements:* For master's and Ed S, thesis optional; for doctorate, variable foreign language requirement, thesis/dissertation. *Entrance requirements:* For master's, minimum GPA of 2.7; for doctorate and Ed S, GRE General Test, minimum GPA of 2.7. Additional exam requirements/recommendations for international students: Required—TOEFL. *Application deadline:* For fall admission, 2/1 priority date for domestic students. Applications are processed on a rolling basis. Application fee: $35. Electronic applications accepted. *Expenses:* Tuition, state resident: full-time $5,574. Tuition, nonresident: full-time $16,840. Required fees: $792. *Financial support:* In 2006–07, 4 fellowships, 9 teaching assistantships were awarded; career-related internships or fieldwork, Federal Work-Study, institutionally sponsored loans, and unspecified assistantships also available. Financial award application deadline: 2/1; financial award applicants required to submit FAFSA. *Unit head:* Dr. Lester Knight, Head, 865-974-0907, Fax: 865-974-8718, E-mail: lknight@utk.edu.

The University of Texas at Austin, Graduate School, College of Education, Programs in Science/Mathematics Education, Program in Mathematics Education, Austin, TX 78712-1111. Offers M Ed, MA, PhD. *Entrance requirements:* For master's and doctorate, GRE General Test. Electronic applications accepted.

The University of Texas at Dallas, School of Natural Sciences and Mathematics, Program in Mathematics and Science Education, Richardson, TX 75083-0688. Offers mathematics education (MAT); science education (MAT). Part-time and evening/weekend programs available. *Faculty:* 3 full-time (all women), 1 part-time/adjunct (0 women). *Students:* 6 full-time (5 women), 54 part-time (41 women); includes 18 minority (8 African Americans, 4 Asian Americans or Pacific Islanders, 6 Hispanic Americans), 5 international. Average age 37. 43 applicants, 79% accepted, 23 enrolled. In 2006, 27 degrees awarded. *Entrance requirements:* For master's, GRE General Test, minimum GPA of 3.0 in upper-level coursework in field. Additional exam requirements/recommendations for international students: Required—TOEFL (minimum score 550 paper-based; 213 computer-based). *Application deadline:* For fall admission, 7/15 for domestic students; for spring admission, 11/15 for domestic students. Applications are processed on a rolling basis. Application fee: $50 ($100 for international students). Electronic applications accepted. *Financial support:* In 2006–07, 2 students received support, including 1 teaching assistantship (averaging $9,550 per year); fellowships, research assistantships, career-related internships or fieldwork, Federal Work-Study, institutionally sponsored loans, and scholarships/grants also available. Support available to part-time students. Financial award application deadline: 4/30; financial award applicants required to submit FAFSA. *Faculty research:* Techniques for training teachers, philosophic definitions of science held by working scientists, science teachers, science students. Total annual research expenditures: $18,210. *Unit head:* Dr. Cynthia Ledbetter, Head, 972-883-2496, Fax: 972-883-6371, E-mail: ledbetter@utdallas.edu.

The University of Texas at San Antonio, College of Sciences, Department of Mathematics, San Antonio, TX 78249-0617. Offers mathematics education (MS). Part-time and evening/weekend programs available. *Faculty:* 10 full-time (3 women). *Students:* 18 full-time (6 women), 46 part-time (25 women); includes 5 African Americans, 7 Asian Americans or Pacific Islanders, 1 international. Average age 35. 30 applicants, 83% accepted, 25 enrolled. In 2006, 19 degrees awarded. *Degree requirements:* For master's, thesis optional. *Entrance requirements:* For master's, GRE General Test, minimum GPA of 3.0 in last 60 hours. Additional exam requirements/recommendations for international students: Required—TOEFL (minimum score 500 paper-based; 173 computer-based). *Application deadline:* For fall admission, 7/1 for domestic students, 4/1 for international students; for spring admission, 11/1 for domestic students, 9/1 for international students. Applications are processed on a rolling basis. Application fee: $45 ($80 for international students). Electronic applications accepted. *Expenses:* Tuition, state resident: full-time $1,730; part-time $192 per credit hour. Tuition, nonresident: full-time $6,680; part-time $742 per credit hour. Required fees: $733; $308,359 per credit hour. *Financial support:* In 2006–07, 1 research assistantship (averaging $31,200 per year), 15 teaching assistantships (averaging $21,760 per year) were awarded. *Unit head:* Dr. Francis A. Norman, Interim Chair, 210-458-4494, Fax: 210-458-4439, E-mail: sandy.norman@utsa.edu.

The University of Texas at Tyler, College of Education and Psychology, Department of Curriculum and Instruction, Tyler, TX 75799-0001. Offers curriculum and instruction (M Ed); secondary teaching (MAT), including art, biology, computer science, English, history, journalism, mathematics, music, political science, sociology, speech, theatre. Part-time programs available. *Faculty:* 10 full-time (6 women), 2 part-time/adjunct (1 woman). *Students:* 3 full-time (2 women), 7 part-time (6 women); includes 1 minority (African American) Average age 32. 1 applicant, 100% accepted, 1 enrolled. In 2006, 6 degrees awarded. *Degree requirements:* For master's, research project (M Ed). *Entrance requirements:* For master's, GRE or MAT. Application fee: $0 ($50 for international students). Electronic applications accepted. *Expenses:* Tuition, state resident: part-time $50 per credit hour. Tuition, nonresident: part-time $328 per credit hour. Required fees: $107 per credit hour. $426 per term. *Financial support:* Scholarships/grants available. *Unit head:* Dr. Robert Stevens, Chair/Professor of Education, 903-566-7315, E-mail: rstevens@uttyler.edu. *Application contact:* Bonnie Purser, Office of Graduate Studies, 903-566-7142, Fax: 903-566-7068, E-mail: bpurser@uttyler.edu.

University of the District of Columbia, College of Arts and Sciences, Department of Mathematics, Washington, DC 20008-1175. Offers MST. Part-time and evening/weekend programs available. *Students:* 2 full-time (1 woman), 1 (woman) part-time; includes 2 minority (both African Americans) Average age 29. 33 applicants, 30% accepted, 3 enrolled. In 2006, 1 degree awarded. *Degree requirements:* For master's, comprehensive exam. *Entrance requirements:* For master's, GRE General Test, writing proficiency exam. *Application deadline:* For fall admission, 6/15 priority date for domestic students; for spring admission, 11/1 for domestic students. Applications are processed on a rolling basis. Application fee: $20. *Unit head:* Dr. Vernise Steadman, Chair, 202-274-5153. *Application contact:* LaVerne Hill Flannigan, Director of Admission, 202-274-6069.

University of the Incarnate Word, School of Graduate Studies and Research, Dreeben School of Education, Programs in Education, San Antonio, TX 78209-6397. Offers adult education (M Ed, MA); diversity education (M Ed, MA); early childhood education (M Ed, MA); instructional technology (M Ed, MA); international education and entrepreneurship (PhD); kinesiology (M Ed, MA); mathematics education (PhD); organizational leadership (PhD); organizational learning (M Ed, MA); reading (M Ed, MA); special education (M Ed, MA). *Students:* 15 full-time (8 women), 179 part-time (117 women); includes 70 minority (20 African Americans, 1 American Indian/Alaska Native, 1 Asian American or Pacific Islander, 48 Hispanic Americans), 54 international. Average age 39. In 2006, 15 degrees awarded. Application fee: $20. *Expenses:* Tuition: Part-time $570 per credit hour. Required fees: $54 per credit hour. One-time fee: $195 part-time. Tuition and fees vary according to degree level. *Financial support:* Federal Work-Study and scholarships/grants available. *Unit head:* Dr. Richard Gray, Director, 210-829-3138, Fax: 210-829-3134, E-mail: gray@uiwtx.edu. *Application contact:* Andrea Cyterski-Acosta, Dean of Enrollment, 210-829-6005, Fax: 210-829-3921, E-mail: cyterski@uiwtx.edu.

University of the Virgin Islands, Graduate Programs, Division of Science and Mathematics, Program in Mathematics, Saint Thomas, VI 00802-9990. Offers mathematics for secondary teachers (MA). *Faculty:* 2 full-time (1 woman). *Students:* 7 applicants, 57% accepted, 3 enrolled. *Degree requirements:* For master's, courses, action research paper. *Entrance requirements:* For master's, GRE or similar, minimum GPA 2.5 BA or BS specific experience and courses. *Application deadline:* For fall admission, 4/30 for domestic and international students; for spring admission, 10/30 for domestic and international students. Application fee: $25. *Expenses:* Tuition, area resident: Full-time $4,950; part-time $275 per credit. Tuition, nonresident: full-time $9,900; part-time $550 per credit. Required fees: $130 per term. Tuition and fees vary according to course load and degree level. *Financial support:* Fellowships, research assistantships, teaching assistantships, tuition waivers (full) and paid by Department of Education, Virgin Islands available. Financial award application deadline: 4/15. *Unit head:* Dr. Adam Parr, Chairperson, 340-693-1333, Fax: 340-693-1245, E-mail: aparr@uvi.edu. *Application contact:* Carolyn Cook-Roberts, Director of Admissions, 340-693-1224, Fax: 340-693-1155, E-mail: ccook@uvi.edu.

The University of Toledo, College of Graduate Studies, College of Education, Department of Curriculum and Instruction, Program in Education and Mathematics, Toledo, OH 43606-3390. Offers MAE, MES. *Students:* Average age 44.

University of Tulsa, Graduate School, College of Arts and Sciences, School of Education, Program in Mathematics and Science Education, Tulsa, OK 74104-3189. Offers MSMSE. Part-time programs available. *Students:* 2 full-time (both women), 1 (woman) part-time, 1 international. Average age 23. 4 applicants, 25% accepted, 1 enrolled. *Entrance requirements:* For master's, GRE General Test. Additional exam requirements/recommendations for international students: Required—TOEFL (minimum score 575 paper-based; 231 computer-based), IELTS (minimum score 7). *Application deadline:* Applications are processed on a rolling basis. Application fee: $40. Electronic applications accepted. *Expenses:* Tuition: Full-time $13,338; part-time $741 per credit hour. *Financial support:* In 2006–07, 2 students received support, including 1 research assistantship (averaging $10,300 per year), 1 teaching assistantship with full and partial tuition reimbursement available (averaging $10,300 per year); fellowships with full and partial tuition reimbursements available, Federal Work-Study, scholarships/grants, tuition waivers (full and partial), and unspecified assistantships also available. Support available to part-time students. Financial award application deadline: 2/1; financial award applicants required to submit FAFSA. *Unit head:* Dr. Alexander W. Wiseman, Head, 918-631-2371, Fax: 918-631-2133, E-mail: alexander-wiseman@utulsa.edu.

University of Vermont, Graduate College, College of Engineering and Mathematics, Department of Mathematics and Statistics, Program in Mathematics, Burlington, VT 05405. Offers mathematics (MS, PhD); mathematics education (MST). *Students:* 24 (10 women) 3 international. 41 applicants, 73% accepted, 9 enrolled. In 2006, 2 master's, 1 doctorate awarded. *Degree requirements:* For doctorate, thesis/dissertation. *Entrance requirements:* For master's and doctorate, GRE General Test. Additional exam requirements/recommendations for international students: Required—TOEFL (minimum score 550 paper-based; 213 computer-based). *Application deadline:* For fall admission, 4/1 priority date for domestic students. Applications are processed on a rolling basis. Application fee: $40. Electronic applications accepted. *Expenses:* Tuition, state resident: part-time $434 per credit. Tuition, nonresident: part-time $1,096 per credit. *Financial support:* Fellowships, research assistantships, teaching assistantships available. Financial award application deadline: 3/1. *Unit head:* Dr. J. Yang, Coordinator, 802-656-2940.

University of Victoria, Faculty of Graduate Studies, Faculty of Education, Department of Curriculum and Instruction, Victoria, BC V8W 2Y2, Canada. Offers art (M Ed, MA, PhD); curriculum studies (M Ed, MA, PhD); early childhood (M Ed, MA, PhD); language and literacy (M Ed, MA, PhD); mathematics (M Ed, MA, PhD); music (M Ed, MA); music education (PhD); science (M Ed, MA, PhD); social studies (M Ed, MA); social, cultural and foundational studies (PhD); technology and environmental education (PhD). Part-time programs available. *Degree requirements:* For master's, thesis, project (M Ed); for doctorate, thesis/dissertation, comprehensive exam, registration. *Entrance requirements:* For master's, minimum B average. Additional exam requirements/recommendations for international students: Required—TOEFL (minimum score 575 paper-based; 233 computer-based), IELTS (minimum score 7). Electronic applications accepted. *Faculty research:* Elementary and secondary English, language arts, curriculum theory and practice, educational media and technology, educational administration and leadership, history and philosophy of education.

University of Washington, Graduate School, College of Education, Seattle, WA 98195. Offers curriculum and instruction (M Ed, Ed D, PhD), including educational technology, general curriculum (Ed D, PhD), language, literacy, and culture, mathematics education, multicultural education, reading and language arts education (Ed D), science education, social studies education, teaching and curriculum (M Ed); educational leadership and policy studies (M Ed, Ed D, PhD), including administration, educational organization and policy, higher education, school district leadership (Ed D), social/cultural foundations; educational psychology (M Ed, PhD), including human development and cognition, measurement and research, school counseling (M Ed), school psychology; special education (M Ed, Ed D, PhD), including early childhood education, elementary special education, emotional and behavioral disabilities (M Ed), general special education, severe disabilities; teacher education (MIT). *Accreditation:* APA. Part-time and evening/weekend programs available. *Degree requirements:* For master's, thesis optional; for doctorate, thesis/dissertation. *Entrance requirements:* For master's and doctorate, GRE General Test, minimum GPA of 3.0. Additional exam requirements/recommendations for international students: Required—TOEFL. Electronic applications accepted. *Faculty research:* School restructuring/effective schools, special education interventions, literacy and writing, technology, school partnerships, teacher preparation.

The University of West Alabama, School of Graduate Studies, College of Natural Sciences and Mathematics, Department of Mathematics, Livingston, AL 35470. Offers MAT. *Accreditation:* NCATE. *Faculty:* 1 full-time (0 women). *Students:* 2 full-time (both women), 16 part-time (12 women); includes 12 minority (all African Americans) Application fee: $20 ($50 for international students). *Financial support:* Career-related internships or fieldwork, Federal Work-Study, scholarships/grants, and unspecified assistantships available. Support available to part-time students. *Unit head:* Dr. Thomas Ratkovich, Interim Chair, 800-621-3442, E-mail: tratkovich@uwa.edu.

University of West Georgia, Graduate School, College of Education, Department of Curriculum and Instruction, Program in Secondary Education—Mathematics, Carrollton, GA 30118. Offers M Ed, Ed S. Part-time and evening/weekend programs available. *Students:* 4 full-time (2 women), 12 part-time (9 women). Average age 26. In 2006, 5 master's, 1 other advanced degree awarded. *Degree requirements:* For master's, comprehensive exam; for Ed S, research project. *Entrance requirements:* For master's and Ed S, GRE or MAT. *Application deadline:* For fall admission, 8/1 for domestic students. Applications are processed on a rolling basis. Application fee: $20. *Expenses:* Tuition, state resident: full-time $2,286; part-time $127 per credit. Tuition, nonresident: full-time $9,144; part-time $508 per credit. Required fees: $494; $27 per credit. $121 per semester. *Financial support:* In 2006–07, research assistantships with full tuition reimbursements (averaging $3,000 per year). Financial award applicants required to submit FAFSA. *Application contact:* Dr. Charles W. Clark, Chair, 678-839-6508, E-mail: cclark@westga.edu.

University of Wisconsin–Eau Claire, College of Education and Human Sciences, Program in Secondary Education, Eau Claire, WI 54702-4004. Offers biology (MAT, MST); education and professional development (MEPD); English (MAT, MST); history (MAT, MST); mathematics (MAT, MST). *Faculty:* 9 full-time (6 women). *Students:* 10 full-time (7 women), 23 part-time (20 women), 1 international. Average age 33. 21 applicants, 57% accepted, 4 enrolled. In 2006, 22 degrees awarded. *Degree requirements:* For master's, thesis optional. *Entrance requirements:* For master's, 2 years of teaching experience or the equivalent. *Application deadline:* For fall admission, 7/1 for domestic students; for spring admission, 12/1 for domestic students. Applications are processed on a rolling basis. Application fee: $45. *Expenses:* Tuition, state resident: full-time $6,533; part-time $363 per credit. Tuition, nonresident: full-time $17,143; part-time $952 per credit. Tuition and fees vary according to program and reciprocity agreements. *Financial support:* In 2006–07, 17 students received support, including 2 teaching assistantships (averaging $5,200 per year); Federal Work-Study also available. Financial award application deadline: 3/1; financial award applicants required to submit FAFSA. *Unit head:* Dr. Tamara Lindsey, Chair, 715-836-4737, Fax: 715-836-4868, E-mail: lindsetp@uwec.edu.

University of Wisconsin–Madison, Graduate School, School of Education, Department of Curriculum and Instruction, Madison, WI 53706-1380. Offers art education (MA); curriculum and instruction (MS, PhD); education and mathematics (MA); French education (MA); German education (MA); music education (MS); science education (MS); Spanish education (MA). *Accreditation:* NASM (one or more programs are accredited). *Degree requirements:* For doctorate, thesis/dissertation. Application fee: $45. *Financial support:* Project assistantships available. *Unit head:* Dr. Alan Lockwood, Chair, 608-262-4000.

University of Wisconsin–Oshkosh, The School of Graduate Studies, College of Letters and Science, Department of Mathematics, Oshkosh, WI 54901. Offers mathematics education (MS). Part-time programs available. *Degree requirements:* For master's, thesis optional. *Entrance requirements:* For master's, 30 undergraduate credits in mathematics. Additional exam requirements/recommendations for international students: Required—TOEFL (minimum score 550 paper-based; 213 computer-based). Electronic applications accepted. *Faculty research:* Problem solving, number theory, discrete mathematics, statistics.

University of Wisconsin–River Falls, Outreach and Graduate Studies, College of Arts and Science, Program in Mathematics, River Falls, WI 54022-5001. Offers mathematics education (MSE). *Accreditation:* NCATE. Part-time programs available. *Degree requirements:* For master's, thesis (for some programs). *Entrance requirements:* For master's, minimum GPA of 2.75. Electronic applications accepted.

University of Wyoming, Graduate School, College of Arts and Sciences, Department of Mathematics, Laramie, WY 82070. Offers mathematics (MA, MAT, MS, MST, PhD); mathematics/computer science (PhD). Part-time programs available. *Faculty:* 27 full-time (7 women). *Students:* 24 full-time (5 women), 7 part-time (3 women); includes 1 minority (American Indian/Alaska Native), 10 international. Average age 31. 49 applicants, 24% accepted. In 2006, 3 master's, 2 doctorates awarded. Terminal master's awarded for partial completion of doctoral program. *Degree requirements:* For master's, thesis or alternative, qualifying exam; for doctorate, one foreign language, thesis/dissertation, preliminary exam. *Entrance requirements:* For master's and doctorate, GRE General Test, minimum GPA of 3.0. Additional exam requirements/recommendations for international students: Required—TOEFL. *Application deadline:* For fall admission, 3/1 priority date for domestic students. Applications are processed on a rolling basis. Application fee: $50. *Financial support:* In 2006–07, 1 research assistantship with full tuition reimbursement (averaging $12,032 per year), 19 teaching assistantships with full tuition reimbursements (averaging $12,032 per year) were awarded; institutionally sponsored loans also available. Financial award application deadline: 3/1. *Faculty research:* Numerical analysis, classical analysis, mathematical modeling, algebraic combinations. *Unit head:* Dr. Sivaguru Sritharon, Head, 307-766-4221. *Application contact:* Dr. Sivaguru Sritharon, Head, 307-766-4221.

Vanderbilt University, Peabody College, Department of Teaching and Learning, Nashville, TN 37240-1001. Offers curriculum and instructional leadership (M Ed); early childhood education (M Ed); early childhood leadership (Ed D); elementary education (M Ed); English education (M Ed); English language learners (M Ed); mathematics education (M Ed); reading education (M Ed); science education (M Ed); secondary education (M Ed). *Accreditation:* NCATE. *Faculty:* 23 full-time (13 women), 28 part-time/adjunct (19 women). *Students:* 71 full-time (62 women), 21 part-time (15 women); includes 9 minority (8 African Americans, 1 Hispanic American), 2 international. Average age 27. 102 applicants, 60% accepted, 27 enrolled. In 2006, 53 master's, 3 doctorates awarded. *Degree requirements:* For master's, thesis optional. *Entrance requirements:* For master's, GRE General Test, MAT. Additional exam requirements/recommendations for international students: Required—TOEFL (minimum score 550 paper-based; 213 computer-based). *Application deadline:* For fall admission, 12/31 priority date for domestic and international students; for spring admission, 11/1 priority date for domestic and international students. Applications are processed on a rolling basis. Application fee: $0. Electronic applications accepted. *Expenses:* Tuition: Full-time $24,462. Required fees: $2,515. One-time fee: $30 full-time. Full-time tuition and fees vary according to course load, degree level and program. *Financial support:* In 2006–07, 62 students received support, including 36 fellowships with full and partial tuition reimbursements available, 13 research assistantships with full and partial tuition reimbursements available, 13 teaching assistantships with full and partial tuition reimbursements available; Federal Work-Study, institutionally sponsored loans, scholarships/grants, tuition waivers (partial), and unspecified assistantships also available. Support available to part-time students. Financial award application deadline: 2/1; financial award applicants required to submit FAFSA. *Faculty research:* Teaching and learning; development of subject matter knowledge; learning and policy; development students' mathematical and scientific knowledge, development of literacy. *Unit head:* Leona Schauble, Chair, 615-322-8100, Fax: 615-322-8999, E-mail: leona.schauble@vanderbilt.edu. *Application contact:* Angela Saylor, Educational Coordinator, 615-322-8092, Fax: 615-322-8999.

Virginia State University, School of Graduate Studies, Research, and Outreach, School of Engineering, Science and Technology, Department of Mathematics, Petersburg, VA 23806-0001. Offers mathematics (MS); mathematics education (M Ed). *Degree requirements:* For master's, thesis (for some programs).

Washington State University, Graduate School, College of Education, Department of Teaching and Learning, Pullman, WA 99164. Offers curriculum and instruction (Ed D, PhD); diverse languages (M Ed, MA); elementary education (M Ed, MA, MIT); exercise science (MS); literacy education (M Ed, MA, PhD); math education (PhD); secondary education (M Ed, MA). *Accreditation:* NCATE. *Faculty:* 27. *Students:* 54 full-time (43 women), 20 part-time (14 women); includes 13 minority (4 African Americans, 2 American Indian/Alaska Native, 2 Asian Americans or Pacific Islanders, 5 Hispanic Americans), 5 international. Average age 34. 244 applicants, 16% accepted, 11 enrolled. In 2006, 20 master's, 3 doctorates awarded. *Degree requirements:* For master's, thesis (for some programs), oral or written exam, comprehensive exam (for some programs); for doctorate, thesis/dissertation, oral, written exam, comprehensive exam. *Entrance requirements:* For master's and doctorate, GRE General Test, minimum GPA of 3.0, 3 letters of recommendation. Additional exam requirements/recommendations for international students: Required—TOEFL. *Application deadline:* For fall admission, 2/1 for domestic students, 3/1 for international students; for spring admission, 9/1 for domestic students, 7/1 for international students. Applications are processed on a rolling basis. Application fee: $50. *Expenses:* Tuition, state resident: full-time $7,066. Tuition, nonresident: full-time $17,204. *Financial support:* In 2006–07, 13 research assistantships with partial tuition reimbursements (averaging $13,917 per year), 22 teaching assistantships with partial tuition reimbursements (averaging $13,056 per year) were awarded; career-related internships or fieldwork, Federal Work-Study, institutionally sponsored loans, tuition waivers (partial), unspecified assistantships, and staff assistantships, teaching associateships also available. Financial award application deadline: 4/1. *Faculty research:* Evolution of middle school education issues in special education, computer-assisted language learning. Total annual research expenditures: $1.1 million. *Unit head:* Dr. Corinne Mantle-Bromley, Chair, 509-335-5027. *Application contact:* Graduate School Admissions, 800-GRADWSU, Fax: 509-335-1949, E-mail: gradsch@wsu.edu.

Washington State University, Graduate School, College of Sciences, Department of Mathematics, Pullman, WA 99164. Offers applied mathematics (MS, PhD); mathematics teaching (MS, PhD). *Faculty:* 27. *Students:* 41 full-time (17 women), 2 part-time (both women); includes 3 minority (all Asian Americans or Pacific Islanders), 12 international. Average age 29. 158 applicants, 19% accepted, 13 enrolled. In 2006, 6 master's, 3 doctorates awarded. *Degree requirements:* For master's, thesis (for some programs), oral exam, project, comprehensive exam (for some programs); for doctorate, 2 foreign languages, thesis/dissertation, oral exam, written exam, comprehensive exam. *Entrance requirements:* For master's and doctorate, minimum GPA of 3.0, 3 letters of recommendation. Additional exam requirements/recommendations for international students: Required—TOEFL (minimum score 600 paper-based; 250 computer-based). *Application deadline:* For fall admission, 2/1 for domestic and international students; for spring admission, 9/1 for domestic students, 7/1 for international students. Applications are processed on a rolling basis. Application fee: $50. Electronic applications accepted. *Expenses:* Tuition, state resident: full-time $7,066. Tuition, nonresident: full-time $17,204. Required fees: $510. *Financial support:* In 2006–07, 33 students received support, including 2 fellowships with tuition reimbursements available (averaging $2,500 per year), 3 research assistantships with full and partial tuition reimbursements available (averaging $13,917 per year), 27 teaching assistantships with full and partial tuition reimbursements available (averaging $13,056 per year); career-related internships or fieldwork, Federal Work-Study, institutionally sponsored loans, and tuition waivers (partial) also available. Financial award application deadline: 2/1; financial award applicants required to submit FAFSA. *Faculty research:* Computational mathematics, operations research, modeling in the natural sciences, applied statistics. Total annual research expenditures: $425,725. *Unit head:* Dr. V.S. Manoranjan, Chair, 509-335-4918, Fax: 509-335-1188, E-mail: chair@math.wsu.edu. *Application contact:* Graduate School Admissions, 800-GRADWSU, Fax: 509-335-1949, E-mail: gradsch@wsu.edu.

Washington University in St. Louis, Graduate School of Arts and Sciences, Department of Mathematics, St. Louis, MO 63130-4899. Offers mathematics (MA, PhD); mathematics education (MAT); statistics (MA, PhD). Terminal master's awarded for partial completion of doctoral program. *Degree requirements:* For master's, thesis or alternative; for doctorate, thesis/dissertation. *Entrance requirements:* For master's and doctorate, GRE General Test. Electronic applications accepted.

Wayne State College, School of Education and Counseling, Department of Educational Foundations and Leadership, Program in Curriculum and Instruction, Wayne, NE 68787. Offers alternative education (MSE); business education (MSE); communication arts education (MSE); curriculum and instruction (MSE); early childhood education (MSE); elementary education (MSE); English as a second language (MSE); English education (MSE); family consumer science of education (MSE); industrial technology education (MSE); learning communities (MSE); mathematics education (MSE); music education (MSE); science education (MSE); social science education (MSE). *Accreditation:* NCATE. Part-time and evening/weekend programs available. *Faculty:* 17 part-time/adjunct (11 women). *Students:* 17 full-time (10 women), 307 part-time (248 women); includes 6 minority (2 African Americans, 1 American Indian/Alaska Native, 2 Asian Americans or Pacific Islanders, 1 Hispanic American), 1 international. Average age 35. In 2006, 167 degrees awarded. *Degree requirements:* For master's, thesis optional. *Entrance requirements:* For master's, GRE General Test. Additional exam requirements/recommendations for international students: Required—TOEFL (minimum score 550 paper-based; 213 computer-based). *Application deadline:* Applications are processed on a rolling basis. Application fee: $30. *Expenses:* Tuition, state resident: full-time $3,114; part-time $130 per credit hour. Tuition, nonresident: full-time $6,228; part-time $260 per credit hour. Required fees: $894; $37 per credit hour. Tuition and fees vary according to course load. *Financial support:* Applicants required to submit FAFSA.

Wayne State University, College of Education, Division of Teacher Education, Detroit, MI 48202. Offers adult and continuing education (M Ed); art education (M Ed); bilingual/bicultural education (M Ed, MAT); business education (M Ed, MAT); career and technical education (M Ed, Ed D, PhD, Ed S); curriculum and instruction (Ed D, PhD, Ed S); distributive education (M Ed, MAT); early childhood education (M Ed); elementary education (M Ed, MAT, Ed D, PhD, Ed S); elementary education curriculum and instruction (M Ed); English education (M Ed); English education-secondary (M Ed, Ed S); foreign language education (M Ed); general education (Ed D, Ed S); health occupations education (M Ed); industrial education (M Ed); mathematics education (M Ed, Ed S); pre-school and parent education (M Ed); reading (M Ed, Ed D, Ed S); reading, languages and literature (Ed D); school music-vocal (M Ed); science education (M Ed, MAT, Ed S); secondary education (MAT); secondary school reading (M Ed); social studies education (M Ed, Ed S), including education-secondary (M Ed); special education (M Ed, Ed D, PhD, Ed S); teacher education (MAT, Ed D, PhD). *Faculty:* 41 full-time (22 women), 2 part-time/adjunct (both women). *Students:* 401 full-time (295 women), 1,021 part-time (784 women); includes 527 minority (452 African Americans, 6 American Indian/Alaska Native, 32 Asian Americans or Pacific Islanders, 37 Hispanic Americans), 18 international. Average age 36. 296 applicants, 81% accepted, 132 enrolled. In 2006, 386 master's, 1 doctorate awarded. *Degree requirements:* For doctorate, thesis/dissertation. *Entrance requirements:* For master's, minimum GPA of 2.6; for doctorate, minimum undergraduate GPA of 3.0, graduate 3.5; interview. Additional exam requirements/recommendations for international students: Required—TOEFL (minimum score 550 paper-based; 213 computer-based), TWE (minimum score 6). *Application deadline:* For fall admission, 7/1 for domestic students, 6/1 for international students; for winter admission, 10/1 for international students; for spring admission, 2/1 for international students. Application fee: $30 ($50 for international students). Electronic applications accepted. *Financial support:* In 2006–07, 1 fellowship (averaging $34,919 per year) was awarded; research assistantships. *Faculty research:* Reading and writing literacy and literature. Total annual research expenditures: $209,400. *Unit head:* Dr. Joann Snyder, Academic Director, 313-577-1644, E-mail: joanne.snyder@wayne.edu. *Application contact:* Sharon Elliott, Assistant Dean, 313-577-0902, E-mail: sharon.elliott@wayne.edu.

Webster University, School of Education, Department of Multidisciplinary Studies, St. Louis, MO 63119-3194. Offers administrative leadership (Ed S); education leadership (Ed S);

Mathematics Education

Webster University (continued)
educational technology (MAT); mathematics (MAT); multidisciplinary studies (MAT); school systems, superintendency and leadership (Ed S); social science (MAT); special education (MAT). Part-time programs available. *Students:* 97 full-time (83 women), 687 part-time (573 women); includes 173 minority (142 African Americans, 2 American Indian/Alaska Native, 13 Asian Americans or Pacific Islanders, 16 Hispanic Americans), 6 international. Average age 34. In 2006, 14 degrees awarded. *Entrance requirements:* For master's, minimum GPA of 2.5. *Application deadline:* Applications are processed on a rolling basis. Application fee: $25 ($50 for international students). *Expenses:* Tuition: Full-time $8,820; part-time $490 per credit. Tuition and fees vary according to degree level, campus/location and program. *Financial support:* Federal Work-Study available. Support available to part-time students. Financial award application deadline: 4/1; financial award applicants required to submit FAFSA. *Unit head:* Dr. Donna Campbell, Chair, 314-961-2660 Ext. 7042, Fax: 314-968-7118. *Application contact:* Director of Graduate and Evening Student Admissions, Fax: 314-968-7116, E-mail: gadmit@webster.edu.

Wesleyan College, Department of Education, Program in Middle-Level Mathematics and Middle-Level Science Education, Macon, GA 31210-4462. Offers MA. Offered during summer only. Part-time programs available. *Faculty:* 4 full-time (3 women), 2 part-time/adjunct (both women). *Students:* 4 full-time (3 women), 8 part-time (all women); includes 6 minority (all African Americans) Average age 32. 6 applicants, 67% accepted, 4 enrolled. In 2006, 2 degrees awarded. *Degree requirements:* For master's, thesis or alternative, practicum, professional portfolio. *Entrance requirements:* For master's, GRE or MAT. Additional exam requirements/recommendations for international students: Required—TOEFL. *Application deadline:* For fall admission, 7/1 priority date for domestic students; for spring admission, 12/1 priority date for domestic students. Applications are processed on a rolling basis. Application fee: $25. *Expenses:* Tuition: Full-time $14,500. Tuition and fees vary according to program. *Financial support:* Federal Work-Study available. Financial award application deadline: 4/1; financial award applicants required to submit FAFSA. *Faculty research:* Instructional technology, cognitive development, verbal classroom interactions.

Western Carolina University, Graduate School, College of Education and Allied Professions, Department of Educational Leadership and Foundations, Programs in Secondary Education, Cullowhee, NC 28723. Offers art education (MAT); biology (MAT); chemistry (MAT); comprehensive education (MA Ed), including art, biology, English, mathematics, music, physical education, reading, social sciences; English (MAT); family and consumer sciences (MAT); mathematics (MAT); physical education (MAT); reading (MAT); social sciences (MAT). *Accreditation:* NCATE (one or more programs are accredited). Part-time and evening/weekend programs available. *Degree requirements:* For master's, comprehensive exam. *Entrance requirements:* For master's, GRE General Test, portfolio. Additional exam requirements/recommendations for international students: Required—TOEFL (minimum score 550 paper-based; 213 computer-based).

Western Connecticut State University, Division of Graduate Studies, School of Professional Studies, Department of Education and Educational Psychology, Mathematics Education Concentration, Danbury, CT 06810-6885. Offers MS. Part-time and evening/weekend programs available. *Students:* Average age 30. In 2006, 2 degrees awarded. *Degree requirements:* For master's, thesis optional. *Entrance requirements:* For master's, minimum GPA of 2.8, teaching certificate. *Application deadline:* For fall admission, 8/1 priority date for domestic students. Applications are processed on a rolling basis. Application fee: $40. *Financial support:* Fellowships, career-related internships or fieldwork available. Support available to part-time students. Financial award application deadline: 5/1; financial award applicants required to submit FAFSA. *Application contact:* Chris Shankle, Associate Director of Graduate Admissions, 203-837-8244, Fax: 203-837-8338, E-mail: shanklec@wcsu.edu.

Western Governors University, Teachers College, Salt Lake City, UT 84107. Offers English language learning (K-12) (MA); learning and technology (M Ed, MA); management and evaluation (M Ed); management and innovation (M Ed); mathematics education (5-12) (MA); mathematics education (5-9) (MA); mathematics education (K-6) (MA); science (5-12) (MA), including biology, geology; science education (509) (MA); technology (M Ed); technology for principals (Post-Graduate Certificate). *Accreditation:* NCATE. Part-time and evening/weekend programs available. Postbaccalaureate distance learning degree programs offered (no on-campus study). *Degree requirements:* For master's, comprehensive exam, registration. *Entrance requirements:* Additional exam requirements/recommendations for international students: Required—TOEFL (minimum score 450 paper-based). Electronic applications accepted. Expenses: Contact institution.

Western Michigan University, Graduate College, College of Arts and Sciences, Department of Mathematics, Programs in Mathematics, Kalamazoo, MI 49008-5202. Offers mathematics (MA); mathematics education (MA, PhD). *Degree requirements:* For master's, oral exams; for doctorate, one foreign language, thesis/dissertation, oral exams, 3 comprehensive exams, internship. *Entrance requirements:* For doctorate, GRE General Test.

Western New England College, School of Arts and Sciences, Program in Mathematics for Teachers, Springfield, MA 01119. Offers MAMT. Part-time and evening/weekend programs available.

Western Oregon University, Graduate Programs, College of Education, Division of Teacher Education, Program in Secondary Education, Monmouth, OR 97361-1394. Offers bilingual education (MS Ed); health (MS Ed); humanities (MAT, MS Ed); initial licensure (MAT); mathematics (MAT, MS Ed); science (MAT, MS Ed); social science (MAT, MS Ed). *Accreditation:* NCATE. Part-time and evening/weekend programs available. *Faculty:* 7 full-time (4 women), 15 part-time/adjunct (7 women). *Students:* 12 full-time (4 women), 21 part-time (10 women). Average age 32. In 2006, 31 degrees awarded. *Degree requirements:* For master's, written exam, thesis optional. *Entrance requirements:* For master's, minimum GPA of 3.0, teaching license. *Application deadline:* Applications are processed on a rolling basis. Application fee: $50. *Expenses:* Tuition, state resident: full-time $8,250; part-time $250 per credit. Tuition, nonresident: full-time $14,025; part-time $250 per credit. Required fees: $1,173. *Financial support:* In 2006–07, 16 teaching assistantships with full tuition reimbursements (averaging $706 per year) were awarded; research assistantships with full tuition reimbursements, career-related internships or fieldwork, Federal Work-Study, and tuition waivers (full and partial) also available. Support available to part-time students. Financial award application deadline: 3/1; financial award applicants required to submit FAFSA. *Faculty research:* Literacy, science in primary grades, geography education, retention, teacher burnout. *Unit head:* Dr. Mary Bucy, Unit Head, 503-838-8794, Fax: 503-838-8228. *Application contact:* Dr. David McDonald, Dean of Admissions, Retention and Enrollment Management, 503-838-8919, Fax: 503-838-8067, E-mail: mcdonald@wou.edu.

West Virginia University, Eberly College of Arts and Sciences, Department of Mathematics, Morgantown, WV 26506. Offers applied mathematics (MS, PhD); discrete mathematics (PhD); interdisciplinary mathematics (MS); mathematics for secondary education (MS); pure mathematics (MS). Part-time programs available. *Faculty:* 26 full-time (3 women), 19 part-time/adjunct (11 women). *Students:* 40 full-time (17 women), 3 part-time (1 woman), 23 international. Average age 29. 44 applicants, 91% accepted, 17 enrolled. In 2006, 10 master's, 4 doctorates awarded. Terminal master's awarded for partial completion of doctoral program. *Degree requirements:* For master's, thesis optional; for doctorate, one foreign language, thesis/dissertation, comprehensive exam. *Entrance requirements:* For master's, minimum GPA of 2.5; for doctorate, master's degree in mathematics. Additional exam requirements/recommendations for international students: Required—TOEFL (paper-based 550; computer-based 213) or IELTS (paper-based 6). *Application deadline:* For fall admission, 2/15 priority date for domestic and international students. Applications are processed on a rolling basis. Application fee: $50. *Expenses:* Tuition, state resident: full-time $4,926; part-time $276 per credit hour. Tuition, nonresident: full-time $14,278; part-time $796 per credit hour. Tuition and fees vary according to program. *Financial support:* In 2006–07, 41 students received support, including 6 research assistantships with full tuition reimbursements available (averaging $12,000 per year), 18 teaching assistantships with full tuition reimbursements available (averaging $10,000 per year); Federal Work-Study, institutionally sponsored loans, and tuition waivers (full and partial) also available. Financial award application deadline: 2/15; financial award applicants required to submit FAFSA. *Faculty research:* Combinatorics and graph theory, topology, differential equations, applied and computational mathematics. Total annual research expenditures: $578,444. *Unit head:* Dr. Sherman D. Riemenschneider, Chair, 304-293-2011 Ext. 2322, Fax: 304-293-3982, E-mail: sherm.riemenschneider@mail.wvu.edu. *Application contact:* Dr. Harvey R. Diamond, Director of Graduate Studies, 304-293-2011 Ext. 2347, Fax: 304-293-3982, E-mail: harvey.diamond@mail.wvu.edu.

Widener University, School of Human Service Professions, Center for Education, Chester, PA 19013-5792. Offers adult education (M Ed); counseling in higher education (M Ed); counselor education (M Ed); early childhood education (M Ed); educational foundations (M Ed); educational leadership (M Ed); educational psychology (M Ed); elementary education (M Ed); English and language arts (M Ed); health education (M Ed); higher education leadership (Ed D); home and school visitor (M Ed); human sexuality (M Ed); mathematics education (M Ed); middle school education (M Ed); principalship (M Ed); reading and language arts (Ed D); reading education (M Ed); school administration (Ed D); science education (M Ed); social studies education (M Ed); special education (M Ed); technology education (M Ed). Part-time and evening/weekend programs available. Terminal master's awarded for partial completion of doctoral program. *Degree requirements:* For doctorate, thesis/dissertation. *Entrance requirements:* For master's, minimum GPA of 2.5; for doctorate, GRE or MAT, minimum GPA of 2.0 (undergraduate), 3.5 (graduate). Electronic applications accepted. Expenses: Contact institution. *Faculty research:* Reading and cognition, adult education, technology education, educational leadership, special education.

Wilkes University, Graduate Studies and Continued Learning, College of Science and Engineering, Department of Mathematics and Computer Science, Wilkes-Barre, PA 18766-0002. Offers mathematics (MS, MS Ed). Part-time programs available. *Students:* 1 (woman) full-time, 4 part-time (2 women). Average age 34. *Degree requirements:* For master's, thesis or alternative. *Entrance requirements:* For master's, GRE General Test. Additional exam requirements/recommendations for international students: Required—TOEFL (minimum score 500 paper-based; 173 computer-based). *Application deadline:* Applications are processed on a rolling basis. Application fee: $40. *Financial support:* Federal Work-Study and unspecified assistantships available. Financial award application deadline: 3/1; financial award applicants required to submit FAFSA. *Unit head:* Dr. Ming Lew, Chair, 570-408-4844, Fax: 570-408-7860, E-mail: ming.lew@wilkes.edu. *Application contact:* Kathleen Houlihan, Director of Graduate Studies, 570-408-3235, Fax: 570-408-7846, E-mail: kathleen.houlihan@wilkes.edu.

Wright State University, School of Graduate Studies, College of Science and Mathematics, Interdisciplinary Program in Science and Mathematics, Dayton, OH 45435. Offers MST. *Students:* 4 full-time (all women), 2 part-time (1 woman); includes 1 minority (African American) *Unit head:* Dr. Beth Basista, Director, 937-775-2954, Fax: 937-775-2571, E-mail: beth.basista@wright.edu.

Museum Education

Bank Street College of Education, Graduate School, Department of Curriculum and Instruction, Program in Museum Education, New York, NY 10025. Offers museum education (MS Ed); museum education: elementary education certification (MS Ed); museum education: middle school certification (MS Ed); museum studies (MS Ed). *Students:* 30 full-time (28 women), 27 part-time (all women); includes 8 minority (3 African Americans, 5 Asian Americans or Pacific Islanders). Average age 27. 37 applicants, 84% accepted, 23 enrolled. In 2006, 20 degrees awarded. *Degree requirements:* For master's, thesis, registration. *Entrance requirements:* For master's, interview. Additional exam requirements/recommendations for international students: Required—TOEFL (minimum score 600 paper-based; 250 computer-based). *Application deadline:* For fall admission, 3/1 priority date for domestic and international students; for spring admission, 11/1 priority date for domestic and international students. Applications are processed on a rolling basis. Application fee: $50. *Expenses:* Tuition: Part-time $940 per credit. Required fees: $100 per term. *Financial support:* Federal Work-Study and scholarships/grants available. Support available to part-time students. Financial award application deadline: 4/15; financial award applicants required to submit FAFSA. *Faculty research:* Equitable access and openness to diversity in museum settings, exhibition display and development, museum/school partnerships. *Unit head:* Nina Jensen, Director, 212-875-4491, Fax: 212-875-4753, E-mail: ninajensen@bankstreet.edu. *Application contact:* Ann Morgan, Director of Graduate Admissions, 212-875-4403, Fax: 212-875-4678, E-mail: amorgan@bankstreet.edu.

Bank Street College of Education, Graduate School, Department of Educational Leadership, New York, NY 10025. Offers early childhood leadership (MS Ed); educational leadership (MS Ed); leadership for educational change (Ed M, MS Ed); leadership in mathematics education (MS Ed); leadership in museum education (MS Ed); leadership in the arts (MS Ed). *Students:* 59 full-time (35 women), 137 part-time (100 women); includes 75 minority (31 African Americans, 1 American Indian/Alaska Native, 10 Asian Americans or Pacific Islanders, 33 Hispanic Americans), 5 international. Average age 36. 107 applicants, 89% accepted, 89 enrolled. In 2006, 88 degrees awarded. *Degree requirements:* For master's, thesis, registration. *Entrance requirements:* For master's, interview, minimum of 2 years experience in the classroom. Additional exam requirements/recommendations for international students: Required—TOEFL (minimum score 600 paper-based; 250 computer-based). *Application deadline:* For fall admission, 3/1 priority date for domestic students; for spring admission, 11/1 priority date for domestic students. Applications are processed on a rolling basis. Application fee: $50. *Expenses:* Tuition: Part-time $940 per credit. Required fees: $100 per term. *Financial support:* Career-related internships or fieldwork, Federal Work-Study, scholarships/grants, and unspecified assistantships available. Support available to part-time students. Financial award application deadline: 4/15; financial award applicants required to submit FAFSA. *Faculty research:* Leadership in small schools, mathematics education in elementary schools, professional development in early childhood, leadership in arts education, leadership in special education. *Unit head:* Dr. Rima Shore, Chairperson, 212-875-4478, Fax: 212-875-8753, E-mail: rshore@bankstreet.edu. *Application contact:* Ann Morgan, Director of Graduate Admissions, 212-875-4403, Fax: 212-875-4678, E-mail: amorgan@bankstreet.edu.

The College of New Rochelle, Graduate School, Division of Art and Communication Studies, Program in Art Museum Education, New Rochelle, NY 10805-2308. Offers Certificate. *Degree requirements:* For Certificate, internship. *Application deadline:* For fall admission, 8/1 priority date for domestic students. Applications are processed on a rolling basis. Application fee: $35. *Expenses:* Tuition: Part-time $575 per credit. Required fees: $90 per term. *Financial support:* Scholarships/grants available. *Unit head:* Dr. John Patton, Head, Division of Art and Communication Studies, 914-654-5208, Fax: 914-654-5593.

The George Washington University, Graduate School of Education and Human Development, Department of Educational Leadership, Program in Museum Education, Washington, DC 20052. Offers MAT. *Degree requirements:* For master's, comprehensive exam. *Entrance requirements:* For master's, GRE General Test or MAT, minimum GPA of 2.75.

The University of the Arts, College of Art and Design, Department of Museum Studies, Philadelphia, PA 19102-4944. Offers museum communication (MA); museum education (MA); museum exhibition planning and design (MFA). *Accreditation:* NASAD. Part-time programs available. *Degree requirements:* For master's, thesis, internship. *Entrance requirements:* For master's, portfolio. Additional exam requirements/recommendations for international students: Required—TOEFL (minimum score 550 paper-based; 213 computer-based).

Music Education

Alabama Agricultural and Mechanical University, School of Graduate Studies, School of Education, Department of Curriculum and Instruction, Area in Music Education, Huntsville, AL 35811. Offers music (MS); music education (M Ed). *Accreditation:* NCATE. Part-time and evening/weekend programs available. *Faculty:* 1 (woman) full-time, 1 part-time/adjunct (0 women). *Degree requirements:* For master's, comprehensive exam. *Entrance requirements:* For master's, GRE General Test. *Application deadline:* For fall admission, 5/1 for domestic students. Applications are processed on a rolling basis. Application fee: $25. Electronic applications accepted. *Financial support:* Career-related internships or fieldwork and traineeships available. Financial award application deadline: 4/1. *Faculty research:* Jazz and black music, Alabama folk music. *Unit head:* Dr. Horace Carney, Chairperson, 256-372-5512.

Albany State University, College of Education, Program in Music Education, Albany, GA 31705-2717. Offers M Ed. *Accreditation:* NCATE. Part-time programs available. *Degree requirements:* For master's, teaching demonstration. *Entrance requirements:* For master's, GRE General Test, MAT or NTE, minimum GPA of 2.5, previous course work in music history and theory. Electronic applications accepted.

Appalachian State University, Cratis D. Williams Graduate School, School of Music, Program in Music Therapy, Boone, NC 28608. Offers MMT. *Accreditation:* NASM; NCATE. *Students:* 3 full-time (all women), 1 (woman) part-time. 2 applicants, 100% accepted, 2 enrolled. *Degree requirements:* For master's, thesis or alternative, comprehensive exam. *Entrance requirements:* For master's, GRE General Test. Additional exam requirements/recommendations for international students: Required—TOEFL (minimum score 550 paper-based; 230 computer-based). *Application deadline:* For fall admission, 7/1 for domestic students, 1/1 for international students; for spring admission, 11/1 for domestic students, 6/1 for international students. Application fee: $50. *Expenses:* Tuition: state resident: full-time $2,600; part-time $127 per hour. Tuition, nonresident: full-time $13,200; part-time $597 per hour. Required fees: $2,000; $546 per term. *Financial support:* Fellowships, research assistantships, teaching assistantships, career-related internships or fieldwork, tuition waivers (partial), and unspecified assistantships available. Financial award application deadline: 7/1. *Unit head:* Dr. Nancy Schneeloch-Bingham, Graduate Program Director, 828-262-6463, E-mail: schneelochna@appstate.edu.

Arcadia University, Graduate Studies, Department of Education, Glenside, PA 19038-3295. Offers art education (M Ed, MA Ed); biology education (MA Ed); chemistry education (MA Ed); child development (CAS); computer education (M Ed, CAS); computer education 7–12 (MA Ed); early childhood education (M Ed, CAS), including individualized (M Ed), master teacher (M Ed), research in child development (M Ed); educational leadership (M Ed, CAS); educational psychology (CAS); elementary education (M Ed, CAS); English education (MA Ed); environmental education (MA Ed, CAS); history education (MA Ed); language arts (M Ed, CAS); mathematics education (M Ed, MA Ed, CAS); music education (MA Ed); psychology (MA Ed); pupil personnel services (CAS); reading (M Ed, CAS); school library science (M Ed); science education (M Ed, CAS); secondary education (M Ed, CAS); special education (M Ed, Ed D, CAS); theater arts (MA Ed); written communication (MA Ed). *Accreditation:* NASAD. Part-time and evening/weekend programs available. Postbaccalaureate distance learning degree programs offered (minimal on-campus study). *Faculty:* 12 full-time (8 women), 38 part-time/adjunct (26 women). *Students:* 60 full-time (56 women), 419 part-time (324 women); includes 70 minority (57 African Americans, 1 American Indian/Alaska Native, 6 Asian Americans or Pacific Islanders, 6 Hispanic Americans), 1 international. In 2006, 257 master's, 4 doctorates awarded. *Application deadline:* Applications are processed on a rolling basis. Application fee: $35. Electronic applications accepted. *Financial support:* Career-related internships or fieldwork, tuition waivers (partial), and unspecified assistantships available. *Unit head:* Dr. Steven P. Gulkus, Chair, 215-572-2120. *Application contact:* 215-572-2925, Fax: 215-572-2126, E-mail: grad@arcadia.edu.

Arkansas State University, Graduate School, College of Fine Arts, Department of Music, Jonesboro, State University, AR 72467. Offers music education (MME, SCCT); performance (MM). *Accreditation:* NASM (one or more programs are accredited). Part-time programs available. *Faculty:* 12 full-time (2 women), 2 part-time/adjunct (0 women). *Students:* 7 full-time (4 women), 14 part-time (6 women); includes 1 minority (African American), 1 international. Average age 29. 13 applicants, 77% accepted, 7 enrolled. In 2006, 2 master's, 1 other advanced degree awarded. *Degree requirements:* For master's, 2 foreign languages, thesis or alternative, comprehensive exam. *Entrance requirements:* For master's, GRE General Test or MAT (MME), university entrance exam, appropriate bachelor's degree, audition, official transcript; for SCCT, GRE General Test or MAT, interview, master's degree, official transcript. Additional exam requirements/recommendations for international students: Required—TOEFL (minimum score 213 computer-based). *Application deadline:* Applications are processed on a rolling basis. Application fee: $30 ($40 for international students). Electronic applications accepted. *Expenses:* Tuition: state resident: full-time $3,393; part-time $189 per hour. Tuition, nonresident: full-time $8,577; part-time $477 per hour. Required fees: $752; $39 per hour. $25 per semester. *Financial support:* Teaching assistantships, scholarships/grants and unspecified assistantships available. Financial award application deadline: 7/1; financial award applicants required to submit FAFSA. *Unit head:* Dr. Tom O'Connor, Chair, 870-972-2094, Fax: 870-972-3932, E-mail: toconnor@astate.edu.

Auburn University, Graduate School, College of Education, Department of Curriculum and Teaching, Auburn University, AL 36849. Offers business education (M Ed, MS, PhD); early childhood education (M Ed, MS, PhD, Ed S); elementary education (M Ed, MS, PhD, Ed S); foreign languages (M Ed, MS); music education (M Ed, MS, PhD, Ed S); postsecondary education (PhD); reading education (PhD, Ed S); secondary education (M Ed, MS, PhD, Ed S), including English language arts, mathematics, science, social studies. *Accreditation:* NASM (one or more programs are accredited); NCATE. Part-time programs available. *Faculty:* 26 full-time (19 women). *Students:* 51 full-time (36 women), 116 part-time (86 women); includes 24 minority (23 African Americans, 1 Asian American or Pacific Islander). Average age 33. 181 applicants, 56% accepted, 68 enrolled. In 2006, 63 master's, 12 doctorates, 14 other advanced degrees awarded. *Degree requirements:* For master's, thesis (for some programs); for doctorate, thesis/dissertation; for Ed S, field project. *Entrance requirements:* For master's, doctorate, and Ed S, GRE General Test. *Application deadline:* For fall admission, 7/7 for domestic students; for spring admission, 11/24 for domestic students. Applications are processed on a rolling basis. Application fee: $25 ($50 for international students). Electronic applications accepted. *Expenses:* Tuition: state resident: full-time $5,000. Tuition, nonresident: full-time $15,000. Required fees: $416. Tuition and fees vary according to program. *Financial support:* Fellowships, teaching assistantships, career-related internships or fieldwork and Federal Work-Study available. Support available to part-time students. Financial award application deadline: 3/15. *Faculty research:* Emerging literacy, reading attitudes, music for at-risk youth, portfolio assessment. *Unit head:* Dr. Andrew M. Weaver, Head, 334-844-4434, E-mail: weaveam@mail.auburn.edu. *Application contact:* Dr. Joe Pittman, Interim Dean of the Graduate School, 334-844-4700.

Austin College, Program in Education, Sherman, TX 75090-4400. Offers art education (MA); elementary education (MA); middle school education (MA); music education (MA); physical education and coaching (MA); secondary education (MA). Applicants must meet Austin College's undergraduate curriculum requirements. Part-time programs available. *Faculty:* 5 full-time (3 women), 1 (woman) part-time/adjunct. *Students:* 33 full-time (26 women); includes 3 minority (2 Asian Americans or Pacific Islanders, 1 Hispanic American). Average age 25. In 2006, 24 degrees awarded. *Degree requirements:* For master's, one foreign language, thesis or alternative. *Entrance requirements:* For master's, Texas Academic Skills Program Test. *Application deadline:* For fall admission, 5/1 priority date for domestic students; for spring admission, 1/15 priority date for domestic students. Applications are processed on a rolling basis. Application fee: $35. Electronic applications accepted. *Expenses:* Tuition: Full-time $27,385. Required fees: $160. *Financial support:* In 2006–07, 27 students received support. Career-related internships or fieldwork, Federal Work-Study, scholarships/grants, and unspecified assistantships available. Support available to part-time students. Financial award application deadline: 4/1; financial award applicants required to submit FAFSA. *Unit head:* Dr. Barbara Sylvester, Director of Teaching Program, 903-813-2498, Fax: 903-813-2326, E-mail: bsylvester@austincollege.edu.

Austin Peay State University, College of Graduate Studies, College of Arts and Letters, Department of Music, Clarksville, TN 37044. Offers music education (M Mu); performance (M Mu). *Accreditation:* NASM. Part-time programs available. *Faculty:* 16 full-time (7 women), 5 part-time/adjunct (2 women). *Students:* 16 full-time (9 women), 4 part-time (1 woman); includes 1 minority (African American) Average age 26. In 2006, 7 degrees awarded. *Degree requirements:* For master's, thesis optional. *Entrance requirements:* For master's, GRE General Test, diagnostic exams, audition. Additional exam requirements/recommendations for international students: Required—TOEFL (minimum score 500 paper-based; 173 computer-based). *Application deadline:* For fall admission, 7/31 priority date for domestic students; for spring admission, 12/17 priority date for domestic students. Applications are processed on a rolling basis. Application fee: $25. Electronic applications accepted. *Expenses:* Tuition: state resident: full-time $5,138; part-time $272 per credit hour. Tuition, nonresident: full-time $14,832; part-time $693 per credit hour. Required fees: $1,009. *Financial support:* In 2006–07, research assistantships (averaging $10,270 per year); fellowships, career-related internships or fieldwork, Federal Work-Study, institutionally sponsored loans, scholarships/grants, and unspecified assistantships also available. Support available to part-time students. Financial award application deadline: 3/1; financial award applicants required to submit FAFSA. *Faculty research:* American sacred music, Cecilian music, hypermedia instructional systems, Chinese music, baroque guitar. *Unit head:* Dr. Gail M. Robinson-Oturu, Chair, 931-221-7818, Fax: 931-221-7529, E-mail: oturug@apsu.edu.

Azusa Pacific University, School of Music, Azusa, CA 91702-7000. Offers education (M Mus); performance (M Mus). Part-time and evening/weekend programs available. *Students:* 16 full-time (12 women), 29 part-time (15 women); includes 12 minority (1 African American, 5 Asian Americans or Pacific Islanders, 6 Hispanic Americans), 11 international. 35 applicants, 94% accepted, 33 enrolled. In 2006, 11 degrees awarded. *Degree requirements:* For master's, recital. *Entrance requirements:* For master's, interview, audition. Additional exam requirements/recommendations for international students: Required—TOEFL (minimum score 550 paper-based). Application fee: $45 ($65 for international students). *Expenses:* Tuition: Part-time $475 per credit. *Financial support:* In 2006–07, 7 students received support, including 1 teaching assistantship with partial tuition reimbursement available (averaging $4,000 per year); career-related internships or fieldwork also available. Support available to part-time students. Financial award applicants required to submit FAFSA. *Faculty research:* Tribal music of northeast India, rare Motown recordings in England. *Unit head:* Dr. Duane Funderburk, Dean, 626-812-3020, E-mail: dfunderburk@apu.edu. *Application contact:* Graduate Admissions, 626-815-5470, Fax: 626-815-3867, E-mail: dfunderburk@apu.edu.

Ball State University, Graduate School, College of Fine Arts, School of Music, Muncie, IN 47306-1099. Offers music education (MA, MM, DA). *Accreditation:* NASM; NCATE (one or more programs are accredited). *Faculty:* 48. *Students:* 34 full-time (19 women), 39 part-time (18 women); includes 6 minority (3 African Americans, 1 American Indian/Alaska Native, 1 Asian American or Pacific Islander, 1 Hispanic American), 19 international. Average age 25. 46 applicants, 76% accepted, 24 enrolled. In 2006, 20 master's, 5 doctorates awarded. *Degree requirements:* For doctorate, thesis/dissertation. *Entrance requirements:* For master's, audition; for doctorate, GRE General Test, audition, minimum graduate GPA of 3.2, writing sample. Application fee: $25 ($35 for international students). *Financial support:* In 2006–07, 42 teaching assistantships with full tuition reimbursements (averaging $6,505 per year) were awarded; research assistantships with full tuition reimbursements. Financial award application deadline: 3/1. *Unit head:* Dr. Meryl Montione, Unit Head, 765-285-5400, Fax: 765-285-5401. *Application contact:* Kirby Koriath, Coordinator, 765-285-5502, Fax: 765-285-5401, E-mail: kkoriat2@bsu.edu.

Baylor University, Graduate School, School of Music, Waco, TX 76798. Offers church music (MM); composition (MM); conducting (MM); music education (MM); music history and literature (MM); music theory (MM); performance (MM); piano accompanying (MM); piano pedagogy and performance (MM); M Div/MM. *Accreditation:* NASM. *Students:* 14 full-time (9 women), 40 part-time (19 women); includes 6 minority (1 African American, 1 American Indian/Alaska Native, 4 Hispanic Americans), 11 international. In 2006, 32 degrees awarded. *Degree requirements:* For master's, variable foreign language requirement, thesis (for some programs). *Entrance requirements:* For master's, GRE General Test. *Application deadline:* For fall admission, 8/1 for domestic students; for spring admission, 12/1 for domestic students. Applications are processed on a rolling basis. Application fee: $25. *Financial support:* Federal Work-Study and institutionally sponsored loans available. *Unit head:* Dr. Harry Elzinga, Graduate Program Director, 254-710-1161, Fax: 254-710-1191, E-mail: harry_elzinga@baylor.edu. *Application contact:* Suzanne Keener, Administrative Assistant, 254-710-3588, Fax: 254-710-3870.

Belmont University, College of Visual and Performing Arts, School of Music, Nashville, TN 37212-3757. Offers church music (MM); composition (MM); music education (MM); pedagogy (MM); performance (MM). *Accreditation:* NASM. Part-time programs available. *Faculty:* 24

Music Education

Belmont University (continued)
full-time (7 women), 16 part-time/adjunct (8 women). *Students:* 12 full-time (7 women), 34 part-time (17 women); includes 3 minority (1 Asian American or Pacific Islander, 2 Hispanic Americans), 2 international. Average age 27. 19 applicants, 89% accepted, 13 enrolled. In 2006, 11 degrees awarded. *Degree requirements:* For master's, thesis (for some programs), comprehensive exam, registration. *Entrance requirements:* For master's, placement exam, GRE or MAT, audition, interview, minimum GPA of 2.75. Additional exam requirements/recommendations for international students: Required—TOEFL (minimum score 500 paper-based; 173 computer-based). *Application deadline:* For fall admission, 5/1 priority date for domestic students, 5/1 for international students; for spring admission, 11/1 priority date for domestic students, 11/1 for international students. Applications are processed on a rolling basis. Application fee: $50. Electronic applications accepted. *Financial support:* In 2006–07, 33 fellowships (averaging $1,000 per year), 5 teaching assistantships (averaging $2,000 per year) were awarded; career-related internships or fieldwork, scholarships/grants, and unspecified assistantships also available. Financial award application deadline: 3/1; financial award applicants required to submit FAFSA. *Unit head:* Dr. Robert Gregg, Director, 615-460-8106, Fax: 615-386-0239, E-mail: greggr@mail.belmont.edu. *Application contact:* Tish Mosley, Graduate Secretary, 615-460-8117, Fax: 615-386-0239, E-mail: mosleyt@mail.belmont.edu.

Bennington College, Graduate Programs, Program in Teaching, Bennington, VT 05201. Offers art education (MAT); early childhood (MAT); elementary education (MAT); English education (MAT); foreign language education (MAT); mathematics education (MAT); music education (MAT); science education (MAT); secondary education (MAT); social science education (MAT). *Faculty:* 4 part-time/adjunct (3 women). *Students:* 11 full-time (7 women), 1 (woman) part-time; includes 2 minority (both Hispanic Americans) Average age 31. 12 applicants, 75% accepted, 3 enrolled. In 2006, 13 degrees awarded. *Degree requirements:* For master's, 1 year teaching practicum, professional portfolio. *Entrance requirements:* For master's, interview. *Application deadline:* For fall admission, 3/1 for domestic students. Application fee: $60. *Expenses: Contact institution.* One-time fee: $75 full-time. Tuition and fees vary according to program. *Financial support:* In 2006–07, 10 students received support, including 4 fellowships (averaging $6,875 per year); scholarships/grants and unspecified assistantships also available. Financial award application deadline: 4/1; financial award applicants required to submit FAFSA. *Unit head:* George Kamberelis, Director of Center for Creative Teaching, 802-440-4863, E-mail: gkamberelis@bennington.edu. *Application contact:* Ken Himmelman, Dean of Admissions, 802-440-4312, Fax: 802-440-4320, E-mail: admissions@bennington.edu.

See Close-Up on page 861.

Bob Jones University, Graduate Programs, Greenville, SC 29614. Offers accountancy (MS); Bible (MA); Bible translation (MA); Biblical studies (Certificate); broadcast management (MS); business administration (MBA); church history (MA, PhD); church ministries (MA); church music (MM); cinema and video production (MA); counseling (MS); curriculum and instruction (Ed D); divinity (M Div); dramatic production (MA); educational leadership (MS, Ed D, Ed S); elementary education (M Ed, MAT); English (M Ed, MA, MAT); fine arts (MA); graphic design (MA); history (M Ed, MA); illustration (MA); interpretative speech (MA); mathematics (M Ed, MAT); medical missions (Certificate); ministry (MM, D Min); multi-categorical special education (M Ed, MAT); music (M Ed); New Testament interpretation (PhD); Old Testament interpretation (PhD); orchestral instrument performance (MM); organ performance (MM); pastoral studies (MA); personnel services (MS, Ed S); piano pedagogy (MM); piano performance (MM); platform arts (MA); radio and television broadcasting (MS); rhetoric and public address (MA); secondary education (M Ed); studio art (MA); teaching Bible (MA); theology (MA, PhD); voice performance (MM); youth ministries (MA); M Div/MM.

Boise State University, Graduate College, College of Arts and Sciences, Department of Music, Program in Music Education, Boise, ID 83725-0399. Offers MM. *Accreditation:* NASM; NCATE. Part-time programs available. *Students:* Average age 35. 3 applicants, 100% accepted, 0 enrolled. *Degree requirements:* For master's, thesis optional. *Entrance requirements:* For master's, minimum GPA of 3.0, performance demonstration. *Application deadline:* For fall admission, 7/17 priority date for domestic students; for spring admission, 12/5 priority date for domestic students. Applications are processed on a rolling basis. Application fee: $0. Electronic applications accepted. *Financial support:* Career-related internships or fieldwork, Federal Work-Study, institutionally sponsored loans, and unspecified assistantships available. Support available to part-time students. Financial award application deadline: 3/1. *Unit head:* Dr. Jeanne Belfy, Coordinator, 208-426-1216.

Boise State University, Graduate College, College of Arts and Sciences, Department of Music, Program in Pedagogy, Boise, ID 83725-0399. Offers MM. *Accreditation:* NCATE. Part-time programs available. *Students:* 1 (woman) full-time, 3 part-time (all women). Average age 41. In 2006, 1 degree awarded. *Degree requirements:* For master's, thesis optional. *Entrance requirements:* For master's, minimum GPA of 3.0, performance demonstration. *Application deadline:* For fall admission, 7/17 priority date for domestic students; for spring admission, 12/5 priority date for domestic students. Applications are processed on a rolling basis. Application fee: $0. Electronic applications accepted. *Financial support:* Career-related internships or fieldwork, Federal Work-Study, and institutionally sponsored loans available. Support available to part-time students. Financial award application deadline: 3/1. *Unit head:* Dr. Jeanne Belfy, Coordinator, 208-426-1216.

The Boston Conservatory, Graduate Division, Boston, MA 02215. Offers choral conducting (MM); composition (MM); music (MM, ADP, Certificate), including music, music education (MM); music performance (MM, ADP, Certificate); opera (MM, ADP, Certificate); theater (MM). *Accreditation:* NASM (one or more programs are accredited). Part-time programs available. *Degree requirements:* For master's, recital or performance; for other advanced degree, recital. *Entrance requirements:* For master's and other advanced degree, audition. Additional exam requirements/recommendations for international students: Required—TOEFL (minimum score 580 paper-based; 237 computer-based). Electronic applications accepted.

The Boston Conservatory, Graduate Division, Music Division, Department of Music Education, Boston, MA 02215. Offers MM. *Accreditation:* NASM. Part-time programs available. *Degree requirements:* For master's, comprehensive oral exam, thesis or recital. *Entrance requirements:* For master's, audition, interview. Additional exam requirements/recommendations for international students: Required—TOEFL (minimum score 580 paper-based; 237 computer-based). Electronic applications accepted.

Boston University, College of Fine Arts, School of Music, Program in Music Education, Boston, MA 02215. Offers MM, DMA. *Accreditation:* NASM. *Students:* 353 full-time (172 women), 156 part-time (79 women); includes 72 minority (44 African Americans, 6 American Indian/Alaska Native, 6 Asian Americans or Pacific Islanders, 16 Hispanic Americans), 24 international. Average age 36. 31 applicants, 74% accepted, 15 enrolled. In 2006, 8 degrees awarded. *Degree requirements:* For master's, thesis; for doctorate, 2 foreign languages, thesis/dissertation. *Entrance requirements:* Additional exam requirements/recommendations for international students: Required—TOEFL. *Application deadline:* For fall admission, 1/15 priority date for domestic and international students. Applications are processed on a rolling basis. Application fee: $60. *Expenses:* Tuition: Full-time $33,330; part-time $1,042 per credit. Required fees: $462; $40. *Financial support:* Fellowships, teaching assistantships available. Financial award application deadline: 1/15. *Unit head:* William McManus, Chairman. *Application contact:* Mark Krone, Manager, Graduate Admissions, 617-353-3350, E-mail: arts@bu.edu.

Boston University, Graduate School of Arts and Sciences, Department of Music, Boston, MA 02215. Offers composition (MA); music education (MA); music history/theory (PhD); musicology (MA, PhD). *Accreditation:* NASM. *Students:* 3 full-time (1 woman). Average age 26. 13 applicants, 38% accepted, 0 enrolled. In 2006, 6 degrees awarded. *Degree requirements:* For master's and doctorate, 2 foreign languages, thesis/dissertation, comprehensive exam, registration. *Entrance requirements:* For master's and doctorate, GRE General Test, musical composition or research paper, 3 letters of recommendation. Additional exam requirements/recommendations for international students: Required—TOEFL (minimum score 550 paper-based; 213 computer-based). *Application deadline:* For fall admission, 3/15 for domestic and international students; for spring admission, 10/15 for domestic and international students. Application fee: $70. *Expenses:* Tuition: Full-time $33,330; part-time $1,042 per credit. Required fees: $462; $40. *Financial support:* Federal Work-Study, scholarships/grants, and unspecified assistantships available. Support available to part-time students. Financial award application deadline: 1/15; financial award applicants required to submit FAFSA. *Unit head:* Victor Coelho, Director, 617-358-4412, Fax: 617-353-7455, E-mail: blues@bu.edu. *Application contact:* Student Contact, 617-353-8789, Fax: 617-353-7455.

Bowling Green State University, Graduate College, College of Musical Arts, Bowling Green, OH 43403. Offers composition (MM); contemporary music (DMA), including composition, performance; ethnomusicology (MM); music education (MM), including choral, comprehensive, instrumental; music history (MM); music theory (MM); performance (MM). *Accreditation:* NASM. Part-time programs available. *Faculty:* 55 full-time (20 women), 14 part-time/adjunct (6 women). *Students:* 109 full-time (56 women), 19 part-time (11 women); includes 7 minority (5 African Americans, 2 Hispanic Americans), 31 international. Average age 26. 176 applicants, 55% accepted, 49 enrolled. In 2006, 45 degrees awarded. *Degree requirements:* For master's, thesis or alternative, recitals; for doctorate, thesis/dissertation, comprehensive exam. *Entrance requirements:* For master's, GRE General Test, diagnostic placement exams in music history and theory, audition, interview. Additional exam requirements/recommendations for international students: Required—TOEFL. *Application deadline:* For fall admission, 3/1 priority date for domestic students. Application fee: $30. Electronic applications accepted. *Expenses:* Tuition, state resident: part-time $535 per hour. Tuition, nonresident: part-time $884 per hour. *Financial support:* In 2006–07, 14 research assistantships with full tuition reimbursements (averaging $4,923 per year), 74 teaching assistantships with full tuition reimbursements (averaging $5,479 per year) were awarded; career-related internships or fieldwork, Federal Work-Study, and unspecified assistantships also available. Financial award applicants required to submit FAFSA. *Faculty research:* Ethnomusicology. *Unit head:* Dr. Richard Kennell, Dean, 419-372-2188. *Application contact:* Dr. Robert Satterlee, Graduate Coordinator, 419-372-2360.

Brandon University, School of Music, Brandon, MB R7A 6A9, Canada. Offers music education (M Mus); performance and literature (M Mus), including piano, strings. Part-time programs available. *Degree requirements:* For master's, thesis (for some programs), comprehensive exam (for some programs). *Entrance requirements:* For master's, B Mus. Additional exam requirements/recommendations for international students: Required—TOEFL (580 paper-based; 237 computer-based) or IELTS. Electronic applications accepted. *Faculty research:* Philosophy of music.

Brigham Young University, Graduate Studies, College of Fine Arts and Communications, School of Music, Provo, UT 84602-1001. Offers composition (MM); conducting (MM); music education (MA, MM); musicology (MA); performance (MM). *Accreditation:* NASM. *Faculty:* 46 full-time (9 women), 3 part-time/adjunct (1 woman). *Students:* 54 full-time (32 women), 13 part-time (4 women); includes 5 minority (all Asian Americans or Pacific Islanders) Average age 26. 64 applicants, 53% accepted, 30 enrolled. In 2006, 20 degrees awarded. *Degree requirements:* For master's, thesis (for some programs), recital, project or composition (for some programs), comprehensive exam (for some programs), registration. *Entrance requirements:* For master's, graduate placement exam, minimum GPA of 3.0 in last 60 hours, bachelor of music degree. Additional exam requirements/recommendations for international students: Required—TOEFL (minimum score 580 paper-based; 237 computer-based), IELTS. *Application deadline:* For fall admission, 2/1 priority date for domestic students, 1/1 priority date for international students. Application fee: $50. Electronic applications accepted. *Financial support:* In 2006–07, 43 teaching assistantships (averaging $5,000 per year) were awarded; research assistantships, career-related internships or fieldwork, institutionally sponsored loans, scholarships/grants, tuition waivers (partial), and unspecified assistantships also available. Support available to part-time students. Financial award application deadline: 2/1; financial award applicants required to submit FAFSA. *Faculty research:* Pergolesi, Louis Armstrong, NY Art School, rock and roll, beauty and the voice. *Unit head:* Dr. Dale E. Monson, Director, 801-422-6304, Fax: 801-422-0533, E-mail: dale_monson@byu.edu. *Application contact:* Dr. Thomas L. Durham, Graduate Coordinator, 801-422-3226, Fax: 801-422-0533, E-mail: thomas_durham@byu.edu.

Brooklyn College of the City University of New York, Division of Graduate Studies, Conservatory of Music, Brooklyn, NY 11210-2889. Offers composition (MM); music (DMA, PhD); music education (MA); musicology (MA); performance practice (MM). The department offers courses at Brooklyn College that are creditable toward the CUNY doctoral degree (with permission of the executive officer of the doctoral program). Part-time programs available. *Students:* 2 full-time (1 woman), 52 part-time (32 women); includes 10 minority (3 African Americans, 1 Asian American or Pacific Islander, 6 Hispanic Americans), 25 international. 46 applicants, 74% accepted, 20 enrolled. In 2006, 24 degrees awarded. *Degree requirements:* For master's, one foreign language, thesis. *Entrance requirements:* For master's, 36 credits in music, audition, completed composition, writing sample. Additional exam requirements/recommendations for international students: Required—TOEFL. *Application deadline:* For fall admission, 3/1 priority date for domestic students, 2/1 priority date for international students; for spring admission, 11/1 priority date for domestic students, 10/1 priority date for international students. Applications are processed on a rolling basis. Application fee: $125. Electronic applications accepted. *Expenses:* Tuition, state resident: full-time $6,400; part-time $270 per credit. Tuition, nonresident: full-time $12,000; part-time $500 per credit. Required fees: $118 per semester. *Financial support:* Career-related internships or fieldwork, Federal Work-Study, institutionally sponsored loans, and scholarships/grants available. Support available to part-time students. Financial award application deadline: 5/1; financial award applicants required to submit FAFSA. *Faculty research:* American music, computer music. *Unit head:* Dr. Bruce MacIntyre, Chairperson, 718-951-5286, E-mail: brucem@brooklyn.cuny.edu. *Application contact:* Karen Alleyne-Pierre, Director of Admissions Services and Enrollment Communications, 718-951-5902, Fax: 718-951-4506, E-mail: grads@brooklyn.cuny.edu.

Brooklyn College of the City University of New York, Division of Graduate Studies, School of Education, Program in Adolescence Education and Special Subjects, Brooklyn, NY 11210-2889. Offers art teacher (MA); biology teacher (MA); chemistry teacher (MA); English teacher (MA); French teacher (MA); health and nutrition sciences: health teacher (MS Ed); mathematics teacher (MA); music education (CAS); music teacher (MA); physical education teacher (MS Ed); physics teacher (MA); social studies teacher (MA); Spanish teacher (MA). Part-time and evening/weekend programs available. *Students:* 30 full-time (22 women), 450 part-time (257 women); includes 167 minority (101 African Americans, 21 Asian Americans or Pacific Islanders, 45 Hispanic Americans), 21 international. 277 applicants, 84% accepted, 113 enrolled. In 2006, 172 master's, 6 other advanced degrees awarded. *Degree requirements:* For master's, comprehensive exam (for some programs). *Entrance requirements:* For master's, LAST, previous course work in education, resumé, 2 letters of recommendation, essay. Additional exam requirements/recommendations for international students: Required—TOEFL. *Application deadline:* For fall admission, 3/1 priority date for domestic students, 2/1 priority date for international students; for spring admission, 11/1 priority date for domestic students, 10/1 priority date for international students. Applications are processed on a rolling basis. Application fee: $125. Electronic applications accepted. *Expenses:* Tuition, state resident: full-time $6,400; part-time $270 per credit. Tuition, nonresident: full-time $12,000; part-time $500 per credit. Required fees: $118 per semester. *Financial support:* Career-related internships or fieldwork, Federal Work-Study, institutionally sponsored loans, and scholarships/grants available. Support available to part-time students. Financial award application deadline: 5/1; financial award applicants required to submit FAFSA. *Faculty research:* Interdisciplinary education, semiotics, discourse analysis, autobiography, teacher identity. *Unit head:* Prof. Stephen Phillips, Program Facilitator, 718-951-5214, E-mail: phillips@brooklyn.cuny.edu. *Application contact:* Karen Alleyne-Pierre, Director of Admissions Services and Enrollment Communications, 718-951-5902, Fax: 718-951-4506, E-mail: grads@brooklyn.cuny.edu.

Butler University, Jordan College of Fine Arts, Department of Music, Indianapolis, IN 46208-3485. Offers composition (MM); conducting (MM); music (MM); music education (MM); music history (MM); organ (MM); performance (MM). *Accreditation:* NASM. Part-time and evening/weekend programs available. *Faculty:* 19 full-time (4 women), 11 part-time/adjunct (3 women). *Students:* 16 full-time (6 women), 26 part-time (17 women); includes 3 minority (2 Asian Americans or Pacific Islanders, 1 Hispanic American), 3 international. Average age 28. 37 applicants, 62% accepted, 15 enrolled. In 2006, 17 degrees awarded. *Degree requirements:* For master's, thesis (for some programs). *Entrance requirements:* For master's, GRE General Test, GRE Subject Test, audition, interview. *Application deadline:* For fall admission, 8/15 priority date for domestic students. Applications are processed on a rolling basis. Application fee: $35. Electronic applications accepted. *Expenses:* Tuition: Full-time $6,030; part-time $335 per credit. Tuition and fees vary according to program. *Financial support:* In 2006–07, 15 teaching assistantships with full tuition reimbursements (averaging $2,500 per year) were awarded; fellowships, career-related internships or fieldwork, institutionally sponsored loans, and scholarships/grants also available. Support available to part-time students. Financial award application deadline: 7/15; financial award applicants required to submit FAFSA. *Unit head:* Dr. Andrea Gullickson, Head, 317-940-9988, Fax: 317-940-9658, E-mail: agullick@butler.edu. *Application contact:* Kathy Lang, Admission Representative, 317-940-9646, Fax: 317-940-9658, E-mail: klang@butler.edu.

California State University, Fresno, Division of Graduate Studies, College of Arts and Humanities, Department of Music, Fresno, CA 93740-8027. Offers music (MA); music education (MA); performance (MA). *Accreditation:* NASM. Part-time programs available. *Degree requirements:* For master's, thesis or alternative. *Entrance requirements:* For master's, GRE General Test, BA in music, minimum GPA of 3.0. Additional exam requirements/recommendations for international students: Required—TOEFL. Electronic applications accepted. *Faculty research:* Technology transfer, folk art.

California State University, Fullerton, Graduate Studies, College of the Arts, Department of Music, Fullerton, CA 92834-9480. Offers music education (MA); music history and literature (MA); performance (MM); theory-composition (MM). *Accreditation:* NASM. Part-time programs available. *Students:* 8 full-time (5 women), 50 part-time (30 women); includes 18 minority (2 African Americans, 11 Asian Americans or Pacific Islanders, 5 Hispanic Americans), 12 international. Average age 31. 55 applicants, 56% accepted, 14 enrolled. In 2006, 19 degrees awarded. *Degree requirements:* For master's, project or thesis. *Entrance requirements:* For master's, audition, major in music or related field, minimum GPA of 2.5 in last 60 units of course work. Application fee: $55. *Expenses:* Tuition, nonresident: part-time $339 per unit. Required fees: $1,155 per semester. *Financial support:* Teaching assistantships, Federal Work-Study, institutionally sponsored loans, and scholarships/grants available. Support available to part-time students. Financial award application deadline: 3/1. *Unit head:* Dr. Marc Dickey, Chair, 714-278-3511. *Application contact:* Dr. Mitch Fennell, Adviser, 714-278-3511.

California State University, Los Angeles, Graduate Studies, College of Arts and Letters, Department of Music, Los Angeles, CA 90032-8530. Offers music composition (MM); music education (MA); musicology (MA); performance (MM). *Accreditation:* NASM. Part-time and evening/weekend programs available. *Faculty:* 16 full-time (5 women), 40 part-time/adjunct (14 women). *Students:* 33 full-time (20 women), 71 part-time (29 women); includes 43 minority (8 African Americans, 15 Asian Americans or Pacific Islanders, 20 Hispanic Americans), 10 international. In 2006, 20 degrees awarded. *Degree requirements:* For master's, project or thesis. *Entrance requirements:* For master's, audition. Additional exam requirements/recommendations for international students: Required—TOEFL. *Application deadline:* For fall admission, 6/30 for domestic students; for spring admission, 2/1 for domestic students. Applications are processed on a rolling basis. Application fee: $55. *Expenses:* Tuition, nonresident: part-time $226 per unit. *Financial support:* Career-related internships or fieldwork and Federal Work-Study available. Support available to part-time students. Financial award application deadline: 3/1. *Faculty research:* Gregorian semiology, baroque opera. *Unit head:* 1st Lt. David Connors, Chair, 323-343-4060, Fax: 323-343-4063.

California State University, Northridge, Graduate Studies, College of Arts, Media, and Communication, Department of Music, Northridge, CA 91330. Offers composition (MM); conducting (MM); music education (MA); performance (MM). *Accreditation:* NASM. *Faculty:* 21 full-time (6 women), 46 part-time/adjunct (15 women). *Students:* 16 full-time (7 women), 36 part-time (16 women); includes 13 minority (10 Asian Americans or Pacific Islanders, 3 Hispanic Americans), 8 international. Average age 31. 67 applicants, 42% accepted, 24 enrolled. In 2006, 6 degrees awarded. *Degree requirements:* For master's, thesis. *Entrance requirements:* For master's, audition, GRE General Test or minimum GPA of 3.0. Additional exam requirements/recommendations for international students: Required—TOEFL. *Application deadline:* For fall admission, 11/30 for domestic students. Application fee: $55. *Expenses:* Tuition, nonresident: full-time $8,136; part-time $4,068 per year. Required fees: $3,624; $1,161 per term. *Financial support:* Application deadline: 3/1. *Faculty research:* Touring program. *Unit head:* Dr. Katherine Ramos Baker, Chair, 818-677-4752. *Application contact:* Graduate Coordinator, 818-677-3181.

Campbellsville University, School of Music, Campbellsville, KY 42718-2799. Offers church music (MM); music (MA); music education (MM). *Accreditation:* NASM. Part-time programs available. *Faculty:* 8 full-time (2 women), 3 part-time/adjunct (1 woman). *Students:* 50 full-time (32 women), 29 part-time (16 women); includes 30 minority (all Asian Americans or Pacific Islanders), 36 international. Average age 31. 29 applicants, 97% accepted, 27 enrolled. In 2006, 12 degrees awarded. *Degree requirements:* For master's, thesis (for some programs), paper or recital. *Entrance requirements:* For master's, GRE General Test or PRAXIS, minimum GPA of 2.75. Additional exam requirements/recommendations for international students: Required—TOEFL (minimum score 550 paper-based). *Application deadline:* For fall admission, 6/1 priority date for domestic students, 5/1 priority date for international students; for spring admission, 11/1 priority date for domestic students, 10/1 priority date for international students. Applications are processed on a rolling basis. Application fee: $25. Electronic applications accepted. *Expenses:* Tuition: Full-time $6,570; part-time $365 per hour. Tuition and fees vary according to program. *Financial support:* In 2006–07, 24 students received support, including 1 fellowship (averaging $4,300 per year); institutionally sponsored loans and scholarships/grants also available. Support available to part-time students. Financial award application deadline: 6/1; financial award applicants required to submit FAFSA. *Unit head:* Dr. J. Robert Gaddis, Dean, 270-789-5269, Fax: 270-789-5524, E-mail: jrgaddis@campbellsville.edu. *Application contact:* Karla Deaton, Assistant Director of Admissions, 270-789-5078, Fax: 270-789-5071, E-mail: krdeaton@campbellsville.edu.

Capital University, Conservatory of Music, Columbus, OH 43209-2394. Offers music education (MM), including instrumental emphasis, Kodály emphasis. Program offered only in summer. *Accreditation:* NASM. Part-time programs available. *Faculty:* 6 full-time (1 woman), 14 part-time/adjunct (8 women). *Students:* 73 full-time (63 women), 2 part-time (both women); includes 3 minority (1 African American, 1 American Indian/Alaska Native, 1 Asian American or Pacific Islander), 4 international. Average age 30. In 2006, 17 degrees awarded. *Degree requirements:* For master's, thesis or alternative, chamber performance exam, comprehensive exam, registration. *Entrance requirements:* For master's, music theory exam, minimum undergraduate GPA of 3.0. Additional exam requirements/recommendations for international students: Required—TOEFL (minimum score 550 paper-based; 213 computer-based; 80 iBT). *Application deadline:* 3/15 priority date for domestic and international students. Applications are processed on a rolling basis. Application fee: $25. Electronic applications accepted. *Expenses:* Contact institution. Part-time tuition and fees vary according to program. *Financial support:* Scholarships/grants and tuition waivers (partial) available. *Faculty research:* Folk song research, Kodály method, performance, composition. *Unit head:* Dr. William B. Dederer, Dean, 614-236-6474, Fax: 614-236-6935. *Application contact:* Dr. Sandra Mathias, Director, Kod[00e1]ly Institute/Graduate Coordinator, 614-236-6267, Fax: 614-236-6935, E-mail: smathias@capital.edu.

Carnegie Mellon University, College of Fine Arts, School of Music, Pittsburgh, PA 15213-3891. Offers composition (MM); conducting (MM); music education (MM); performance (MM). *Accreditation:* NASM. Part-time programs available. *Degree requirements:* For master's, recital. *Entrance requirements:* For master's, audition. *Faculty research:* Computer music, music history.

Case Western Reserve University, School of Graduate Studies, Department of Music, Program in Music Education, Cleveland, OH 44106. Offers MA, PhD. *Accreditation:* NASM. *Faculty:* 4 full-time (1 woman). *Students:* 11 full-time (6 women), 7 part-time (3 women); includes 2 minority (1 African American, 1 Asian American or Pacific Islander). Average age 28. 14 applicants, 50% accepted, 7 enrolled. In 2006, 3 master's, 1 doctorate awarded. *Degree requirements:* For master's, thesis (for some programs); for doctorate, thesis/dissertation. *Entrance requirements:* For master's and doctorate, audition. Additional exam requirements/recommendations for international students: Required—TOEFL. Application fee: $50. *Financial support:* In 2006–07, 14 teaching assistantships were awarded; fellowships, career-related internships or fieldwork and tuition waivers (full) also available. *Faculty research:* Psychology of music, creative thinking, computer applications, educational psychology. *Application contact:* Susanne Petrick, Admissions, 216-368-2400, Fax: 216-368-6557, E-mail: stp8@case.edu.

The Catholic University of America, The Benjamin T. Rome School of Music, Program in Music Education, Washington, DC 20064. Offers MM, DMA. *Students:* 4 full-time (3 women), 17 part-time (14 women); includes 1 minority (Asian American or Pacific Islander), 3 international. Average age 38. 12 applicants, 67% accepted, 3 enrolled. *Degree requirements:* For master's, thesis/dissertation, recital; for doctorate, thesis/dissertation, recital, comprehensive exam. *Entrance requirements:* For master's, theory placement test, audition or recital, 2 letters of recommendation; for doctorate, school qualifying exam, recital, 2 letters of recommendation. Additional exam requirements/recommendations for international students: Required—TOEFL (minimum score 580 paper-based; 237 computer-based). *Application deadline:* For fall admission, 2/1 priority date for domestic students; for spring admission, 11/15 priority date for domestic students. Applications are processed on a rolling basis. Electronic applications accepted. *Expenses:* Tuition: Full-time $27,700; part-time $1,045 per credit hour. Required fees: $1,290. Part-time tuition and fees vary according to campus/location and program. *Financial support:* Career-related internships or fieldwork, Federal Work-Study, scholarships/grants, tuition waivers (full and partial), and unspecified assistantships available. Support available to part-time students. Financial award application deadline: 2/1; financial award applicants required to submit FAFSA. *Application contact:* Christine Mica, Director, University Admissions, 202-319-5305, Fax: 202-319-6533, E-mail: cua-admissions@cua.edu.

The Catholic University of America, The Benjamin T. Rome School of Music, Program in Piano, Washington, DC 20064. Offers accompanying and chamber music (MM); chamber music (DMA); performance (MM, DMA); piano pedagogy (MM, DMA); vocal accompanying (DMA). *Accreditation:* NASM. Part-time programs available. *Students:* 6 full-time (5 women), 16 part-time (15 women); includes 5 minority (1 African American, 4 Asian Americans or Pacific Islanders), 10 international. Average age 34. 15 applicants, 47% accepted, 1 enrolled. In 2006, 1 master's, 1 doctorate awarded. *Entrance requirements:* For master's, theory placement test, audition or recital, 2 letters of recommendation, experience record; for doctorate, school qualifying exams, recital, 2 letters of recommendation, experience record. Additional exam requirements/recommendations for international students: Required—TOEFL (minimum score 580 paper-based; 237 computer-based). *Application deadline:* For fall admission, 2/1 priority date for domestic students; for spring admission, 11/15 priority date for domestic students. Applications are processed on a rolling basis. Application fee: $55. Electronic applications accepted. *Expenses:* Tuition: Full-time $27,700; part-time $1,045 per credit hour. Required fees: $1,290. Part-time tuition and fees vary according to campus/location and program. *Financial support:* Career-related internships or fieldwork, Federal Work-Study, scholarships/grants, tuition waivers (full and partial), and unspecified assistantships available. Support available to part-time students. Financial award application deadline: 2/1; financial award applicants required to submit FAFSA. *Application contact:* Christine Mica, Director, University Admissions, 202-319-5305, Fax: 202-319-6533, E-mail: cua-admissions@cua.edu.

The Catholic University of America, The Benjamin T. Rome School of Music, Program in Voice, Washington, DC 20064. Offers vocal pedagogy (MM); vocal performance (MM); voice pedagogy and performance (DMA). *Accreditation:* NASM. Part-time programs available. *Students:* 14 full-time (all women), 13 part-time (9 women); includes 7 minority (5 African Americans, 1 Asian American or Pacific Islander, 1 Hispanic American), 4 international. Average age 31. 29 applicants, 76% accepted, 10 enrolled. In 2006, 4 master's, 2 doctorates awarded. *Degree requirements:* For master's, 3 foreign languages, thesis (for some programs), recital; for doctorate, 3 foreign languages, thesis/dissertation, recitals, comprehensive exam. *Entrance requirements:* For master's, theory placement test, audition or recital; 2 letters of recommendation; proficiency in French, German and Italian; for doctorate, school qualifying exams, recital; 2 letters of recommendation; proficiency in French, German and Italian. Additional exam requirements/recommendations for international students: Required—TOEFL (minimum score 580 paper-based; 237 computer-based). *Application deadline:* For fall admission, 2/1 priority date for domestic students; for spring admission, 11/15 priority date for domestic students. Applications are processed on a rolling basis. Application fee: $55. Electronic applications accepted. *Expenses:* Tuition: Full-time $27,700; part-time $1,045 per credit hour. Required fees: $1,290. Part-time tuition and fees vary according to campus/location and program. *Financial support:* Career-related internships or fieldwork, Federal Work-Study, scholarships/grants, tuition waivers (full and partial), and unspecified assistantships available. Support available to part-time students. Financial award application deadline: 2/1; financial award applicants required to submit FAFSA. *Application contact:* Christine Mica, Director, University Admissions, 202-319-5305, Fax: 202-319-6533, E-mail: cua-admissions@cua.edu.

Central Connecticut State University, School of Graduate Studies, School of Arts and Sciences, Department of Music, New Britain, CT 06050-4010. Offers music education (MS, Certificate). *Accreditation:* NASM. Part-time and evening/weekend programs available. *Faculty:* 10 full-time (5 women), 30 part-time/adjunct (14 women). *Students:* 3 full-time (all women), 18 part-time (7 women). Average age 21. 17 applicants, 65% accepted, 5 enrolled. In 2006, 10 master's, 2 other advanced degrees awarded. *Degree requirements:* For master's, thesis or alternative, comprehensive exam or special project. *Entrance requirements:* For master's, audition, minimum GPA of 2.7. Additional exam requirements/recommendations for international students: Required—TOEFL. *Application deadline:* For fall admission, 7/10 for domestic students; for spring admission, 12/10 for domestic students. Applications are processed on a rolling basis. Application fee: $50. Electronic applications accepted. *Expenses:* Tuition, area resident: Full-time $3,970; part-time $380 per credit. Tuition, state resident: full-time $5,955; part-time $380 per credit. Tuition, nonresident: full-time $11,061; part-time $380 per credit. Required fees: $3,189. One-time fee: $62 part-time. Tuition and fees vary according to degree level and program. *Financial support:* In 2006–07, 1 student received support, including 1 research assistantship; career-related internships or fieldwork, Federal Work-Study, scholarships/grants, and unspecified assistantships also available. Support available to part-time students. Financial award application deadline: 3/1; financial award applicants required to submit FAFSA. *Faculty research:* Applied music. *Unit head:* Dr. Daniel D'Addio, Chair, 860-832-2912.

Central Michigan University, College of Graduate Studies, College of Communication and Fine Arts, School of Music, Concentration in Music Education and Supervision, Mount Pleasant, MI 48859. Offers MM. *Accreditation:* NASM; NCATE. *Degree requirements:* For master's, thesis or alternative, registration. *Entrance requirements:* For master's, GRE Revised Music Test, audition, interview, minimum undergraduate GPA of 3.0 in music minimum GPA of 2.7 overall.

Christopher Newport University, Graduate Studies, Department of Teacher Preparation, Newport News, VA 23606-2998. Offers art (PK-12) (MAT); biology (6-12) (MAT); computer

Music Education

Christopher Newport University (continued)
science (6-12) (MAT); elementary (PK-6) (MAT); English (6-12) (MAT); French (PK-12) (MAT); history (6-12) (MAT); history and social science (MAT); mathematics (6-12) (MAT); music (PK-12) (MAT), including choral, instrumental; physics (6-12) (MAT); Spanish (PK-12) (MAT); theater (PK-12) (MAT). Part-time and evening/weekend programs available. *Degree requirements:* For master's, thesis or alternative, comprehensive exam. *Entrance requirements:* For master's, PRAXIS I, minimum GPA of 3.0. Electronic applications accepted. *Faculty research:* Early literacy development, instructional innovations, professional teaching standards, multicultural issues, aesthetic education.

Cleveland State University, College of Graduate Studies, College of Liberal Arts and Social Sciences, Department of Music, Cleveland, OH 44115. Offers composition (MM); music education (MM); performance (MM). *Accreditation:* NASM. Part-time and evening/weekend programs available. *Faculty:* 12 full-time (5 women). *Students:* 15 full-time (10 women), 44 part-time (27 women); includes 7 minority (5 African Americans, 2 Asian Americans or Pacific Islanders), 3 international. Average age 30. 41 applicants, 73% accepted, 19 enrolled. In 2006, 12 degrees awarded. *Degree requirements:* For master's, thesis or recital. *Entrance requirements:* For master's, departmental assessment in music history, minimum undergraduate GPA of 2.75. Additional exam requirements/recommendations for international students: Required—TOEFL (minimum score 525 paper-based; 197 computer-based). *Application deadline:* For fall admission, 7/15 priority date for domestic students. Applications are processed on a rolling basis. Application fee: $30. *Financial support:* In 2006–07, 15 students received support, including 9 research assistantships with full tuition reimbursements available (averaging $3,480 per year); tuition waivers (partial) and unspecified assistantships also available. Financial award application deadline: 3/1. *Faculty research:* Ethnomusicology, classical-romantic music, new performance practices, electronic music, interdisciplinary studies. Total annual research expenditures: $121,000. *Unit head:* Dr. Eric E. Ziolek, Chairperson, 216-687-2301, Fax: 216-687-9279, E-mail: e.ziolek@csuohio.edu. *Application contact:* Dr. Birch Browning, Coordinator of Graduate Studies and Admission, 216-687-3768, Fax: 216-687-9279, E-mail: b.browning@csuohio.edu.

College of Mount St. Joseph, Graduate Education Program, Cincinnati, OH 45233-1670. Offers adolescent young adult education (MA); art (MA); inclusive early childhood education (MA); instructional leadership (MA); middle childhood education (MA); multicultural special education (MA); music (MA); reading (MA). *Accreditation:* Teacher Education Accreditation Council. Part-time and evening/weekend programs available. Postbaccalaureate distance learning degree programs offered (minimal on-campus study). *Faculty:* 22 full-time (14 women), 11 part-time/adjunct (6 women). *Students:* 68 full-time (54 women), 115 part-time (96 women); includes 21 minority (16 African Americans, 2 American Indian/Alaska Native, 1 Asian American or Pacific Islander, 2 Hispanic Americans). Average age 34. 91 applicants, 98% accepted, 62 enrolled. In 2006, 61 degrees awarded. *Degree requirements:* For master's, research project. *Entrance requirements:* For master's, GRE, PRAXIS II in teaching content area (math or science), 2 letters of recommendation, interview, resumé, prerequisite courses in communications, behavioral sciences and mathematics. Additional exam requirements/recommendations for international students: Required—TOEFL (minimum score 560 paper-based; 220 computer-based). *Application deadline:* Applications are processed on a rolling basis. Application fee: $50. Electronic applications accepted. *Expenses: Contact institution. Financial support:* In 2006–07, 3 students received support. Career-related internships or fieldwork and scholarships/grants available. Support available to part-time students. Financial award application deadline: 6/1; financial award applicants required to submit FAFSA. *Faculty research:* Foreign and second language learning problems/reading disabilities/hyperlexia, multicultural/bilingual special education, alternative educator licensure, science education, pedagogical content knowledge. *Unit head:* Dr. Mifrando Obach, Chair, 513-244-3263, Fax: 513-244-4867, E-mail: mifrando_obach@mail.msj.edu. *Application contact:* Marilyn Hoskins, Assistant Director of Admissions for Graduate Recruitment, 513-244-4723, Fax: 513-244-4629, E-mail: marilyn_hoskins@mail.msg.edu.

The College of Saint Rose, Graduate Studies, School of Arts and Humanities, Music Department, Program in Music Education, Albany, NY 12203-1419. Offers MS Ed, Certificate. *Accreditation:* NASM; NCATE. *Degree requirements:* For master's, final project, thesis optional. *Entrance requirements:* For master's, audition, minimum undergraduate GPA of 3.0; for Certificate, placement test if undergraduate degree is not in music, audition. Additional exam requirements/recommendations for international students: Required—TOEFL (minimum score 550 paper-based; 213 computer-based). Electronic applications accepted.

Announcement: Since the founding of The College of Saint Rose more than 80 years ago, music and art have played a pivotal role in enriching the lives of students. Soon these outstanding programs will be showcased in the new $14-million Massry Center for the Arts, a striking, modern facility that will demonstrate the College's commitment to the visual and performing arts and their importance in the life of New York's capital city. The Center will be a hub of musical and visual arts activity; a gathering space for students, performers, composers, scholars, and teachers; and a place for the community to celebrate these Saint Rose programs, which are increasing both in popularity and prominence.

The Colorado College, Department of Education, Program in Secondary Education, Colorado Springs, CO 80903-3294. Offers art teaching (MAT); English teaching (MAT); foreign language teaching (MAT); mathematics teaching (MAT); music teaching (MAT); science teaching (MAT); social studies teaching (MAT). *Faculty:* 2 full-time (1 woman), 10 part-time/adjunct (7 women). *Students:* 18 full-time (12 women); includes 2 minority (1 African American, 1 Asian American or Pacific Islander). Average age 27. 30 applicants, 90% accepted, 18 enrolled. In 2006, 16 degrees awarded. *Degree requirements:* For master's, thesis, internship. *Entrance requirements:* For master's, PRAXIS II or PLACE. *Application deadline:* For fall admission, 2/1 for domestic and international students. Application fee: $50. *Expenses:* Tuition: Full-time $23,567. One-time fee: $1,485 full-time. *Financial support:* In 2006–07, 15 teaching assistantships (averaging $16,000 per year) were awarded; career-related internships or fieldwork, institutionally sponsored loans, health care benefits, and tuition waivers (partial) also available. Financial award application deadline: 2/15; financial award applicants required to submit FAFSA. *Unit head:* Mike Taber, Director, 719-389-6026, Fax: 719-389-6473, E-mail: pveronesi@coloradocollege.edu. *Application contact:* Marsha E. Unruh, Director of Education Career Services, 719-389-6472, Fax: 719-389-6473, E-mail: munruh@coloradocollege.edu.

Columbus State University, Graduate Studies, College of Arts and Letters, Schwob School of Music, Columbus, GA 31907-5645. Offers music education (MM). *Accreditation:* NASM; NCATE. Part-time and evening/weekend programs available. *Faculty:* 4 full-time (1 woman). *Students:* 8 full-time (4 women), 1 part-time; includes 1 minority (African American), 1 international. Average age 36. 11 applicants, 45% accepted, 4 enrolled. In 2006, 3 degrees awarded. *Degree requirements:* For master's, exit exam. *Entrance requirements:* For master's, GRE General Test, MAT. Additional exam requirements/recommendations for international students: Required—TOEFL (minimum score 550 paper-based; 213 computer-based). *Application deadline:* For fall admission, 5/1 priority date for domestic students, 5/1 for international students; for spring admission, 11/1 for domestic and international students. Applications are processed on a rolling basis. Application fee: $25. Electronic applications accepted. *Expenses:* Tuition, state resident: part-time $127 per semester hour. Tuition, nonresident: part-time $508 per semester hour. Required fees: $264 per semester. Tuition and fees vary according to course load. *Financial support:* In 2006–07, 6 students received support, including 6 research assistantships with partial tuition reimbursements available (averaging $3,000 per year); career-related internships or fieldwork, Federal Work-Study, institutionally sponsored loans, scholarships/grants, tuition waivers (full), and unspecified assistantships also available. Support available to part-time students. Financial award application deadline: 5/1; financial award applicants required to submit FAFSA. *Unit head:* Prof. Earl Coleman, Acting Director, 706-649-7375, E-mail: coleman_earl@colstate.edu. *Application contact:* Katie Thornton, Graduate Admissions Specialist, 706-568-2035, Fax: 706-568-2462, E-mail: thornton_katie@colstate.edu.

Connecticut College, Graduate School, Department of Music, New London, CT 06320-4196. Offers MA, MAT. Part-time programs available. *Degree requirements:* For master's, one foreign language, thesis. *Entrance requirements:* For master's, MAT, audition. *Faculty research:* Applied music, composition, history, theory.

Conservatorio de Musica, Program in Music Education, San Juan, PR 00918-2199. Offers MM Ed. *Faculty:* 2 full-time (0 women), 1 part-time/adjunct (0 women). *Students:* 19 full-time (4 women), 13 part-time (3 women); all minorities (all Hispanic Americans) 8 applicants, 100% accepted, 7 enrolled. *Entrance requirements:* For master's, EXADEP, 3 letters of recommendation, audition, bachelor's degree in music education, •interview, minimum GPA of 2.5, performance video, teaching video. Additional exam requirements/recommendations for international students: Required—TOEFL. *Application deadline:* For fall admission, 3/24 for domestic and international students; for winter admission, 10/27 for domestic and international students. Application fee: $100. *Financial support:* Fellowships, research assistantships, teaching assistantships, scholarships/grants available. Financial award application deadline: 7/31; financial award applicants required to submit FAFSA. *Application contact:* Eutimia Santiago, Director of Admissions, 787-751-0160 Ext. 275, Fax: 787-754-6284, E-mail: admisiones@cmpr.edu.

Converse College, Carroll McDaniel Petrie School of Music, Spartanburg, SC 29302-0006. Offers instrumental performance (M Mus); music education (M Mus); piano pedagogy (M Mus); vocal performance (M Mus). *Accreditation:* NASM. Part-time and evening/weekend programs available. *Faculty:* 21 full-time (11 women), 13 part-time/adjunct (6 women). *Students:* 13 full-time (10 women), 7 part-time (3 women); includes 5 minority (all African Americans), 3 international. Average age 30. 14 applicants, 86% accepted, 7 enrolled. In 2006, 9 degrees awarded. *Degree requirements:* For master's, variable foreign language requirement, thesis (for some programs), recitals, comprehensive exam. *Entrance requirements:* For master's, NTE (music education), audition, 3 letters of recommendation. Additional exam requirements/recommendations for international students: Required—TOEFL. *Application deadline:* For spring admission, 3/1 priority date for domestic and international students. Applications are processed on a rolling basis. Application fee: $35. Electronic applications accepted. *Expenses:* Tuition: Part-time $305 per credit hour. Required fees: $20 per term. *Financial support:* In 2006–07, 8 students received support, including 8 teaching assistantships with full and partial tuition reimbursements available (averaging $3,125 per year); fellowships, career-related internships or fieldwork, Federal Work-Study, institutionally sponsored loans, and unspecified assistantships also available. Support available to part-time students. Financial award application deadline: 4/15. *Faculty research:* Chamber music, opera, performance, composition, recording. Total annual research expenditures: $16,000. *Unit head:* Dr. Scott M. Robbins, Sr., Interim Dean, 864-596-9021, Fax: 864-596-9167, E-mail: scott.robbins@converse.edu. *Application contact:* Dr. Patricia S. Foy, Interim Assistant Dean/Director of Graduate Studies in Music, 864-596-9021, Fax: 864-596-9167, E-mail: pattifoy@converse.edu.

DePaul University, School of Music, Chicago, IL 60604-2287. Offers applied music (performance) (MM, Certificate); jazz studies (MM), including composition, performance; music composition (MM); music education (MM). *Accreditation:* NASM (one or more programs are accredited). Part-time and evening/weekend programs available. *Faculty:* 11 full-time (2 women), 50 part-time/adjunct (14 women). *Students:* 9 full-time (1 woman), 18 part-time (3 women); includes 1 minority (African American), 1 international. Average age 27. 175 applicants, 46% accepted. In 2006, 40 master's, 5 Certificates awarded. *Degree requirements:* For master's, terminal project. *Entrance requirements:* For master's, bachelor's degree in music or related field, audition, minimum GPA of 3.0; for Certificate, master's degree in performance or related field. Additional exam requirements/recommendations for international students: Required—TOEFL (minimum score 550 paper-based; 213 computer-based; 80 iBT). *Application deadline:* For fall admission, 1/15 priority date for domestic and international students. Applications are processed on a rolling basis. Electronic applications accepted. *Expenses: Contact institution. Financial support:* In 2006–07, 4 fellowships with partial tuition reimbursements were awarded; teaching assistantships, career-related internships or fieldwork, Federal Work-Study, scholarships/grants, and tuition waivers also available. Support available to part-time students. Financial award application deadline: 1/15. *Unit head:* Dr. Donald E. Casey, Dean, 773-325-7256. *Application contact:* Ross Beacraft, Director of Admissions, 773-325-7444, Fax: 773-325-7429, E-mail: rbeacraft@depaul.edu.

Duquesne University, Mary Pappert School of Music, Pittsburgh, PA 15282-0001. Offers music composition (MM); music education (MM); music performance (MM, AD); music technology (MM); music theory (MM); sacred music (MM). *Accreditation:* NASM. Part-time programs available. Postbaccalaureate distance learning degree programs offered (minimal on-campus study). *Faculty:* 26 full-time (9 women), 74 part-time/adjunct (13 women). *Students:* 64 full-time (20 women), 10 part-time, 19 international. Average age 23. 76 applicants, 92% accepted, 37 enrolled. In 2006, 43 master's, 5 ADs awarded. *Degree requirements:* For master's, thesis (for some programs), recital (music performance), comprehensive exam; for AD, recital. *Entrance requirements:* For master's, audition, minimum undergraduate QPA of 3.0 in music, portfolio of original compositions, theoretical papers, or music education experience; for AD, audition. Additional exam requirements/recommendations for international students: Required—TOEFL (minimum score 550 paper-based; 213 computer-based; 79 iBT). *Application deadline:* For fall admission, 8/1 priority date for domestic students; for spring admission, 12/1 for domestic students. Applications are processed on a rolling basis. Application fee: $50. *Expenses: Contact institution.* Tuition and fees vary according to degree level and program. *Financial support:* In 2006–07, 50 fellowships with full and partial tuition reimbursements were awarded; career-related internships or fieldwork, Federal Work-Study, institutionally sponsored loans, and tuition waivers (full and partial) also available. Support available to part-time students. Financial award application deadline: 4/1. *Faculty research:* Performance; computer-assisted instruction in music at elementary and secondary levels; electronic music; contemporary music, theory, and analysis; development of on-line graduate music courses. Total annual research expenditures: $7,500. *Unit head:* Dr. Edward W. Kocher, Dean, 412-396-6082, Fax: 412-396-1524, E-mail: kocher@duq.edu. *Application contact:* Peggy Eiseman, Administrative Assistant of Admissions, 412-396-5064, Fax: 412-396-5479, E-mail: eiseman@duq.edu.

East Carolina University, Graduate School, College of Fine Arts and Communication, School of Music, Greenville, NC 27858-4353. Offers music education (MM); music therapy (MM); performance (MM); theory and composition (MM). *Accreditation:* NASM. Part-time programs available. *Faculty:* 37 full-time (10 women). *Students:* 37 full-time (20 women), 20 part-time (12 women); includes 6 minority (4 African Americans, 1 Asian American or Pacific Islander, 1 Hispanic American), 4 international. Average age 28. 24 applicants, 13% accepted, 3 enrolled. In 2006, 22 degrees awarded. *Degree requirements:* For master's, thesis optional. *Entrance requirements:* For master's, GRE General Test or MAT. Additional exam requirements/recommendations for international students: Required—TOEFL. *Application deadline:* For fall admission, 6/1 priority date for domestic students. Applications are processed on a rolling basis. Application fee: $50. *Financial support:* Fellowships, research assistantships, teaching assistantships, Federal Work-Study available. Support available to part-time students. Financial award application deadline: 6/1. *Unit head:* Dr. J. Christopher Buddo, Director. *Application contact:* Dean of Graduate School, 252-328-6012, Fax: 252-328-6071, E-mail: gradschool@ecu.edu.

Eastern Kentucky University, The Graduate School, College of Education, Department of Curriculum and Instruction, Richmond, KY 40475-3102. Offers elementary education general (MA Ed), including early elementary education, elementary education general, reading; music education (MA Ed); secondary and higher education (MA Ed), including agricultural education, allied health sciences education, art education, biological sciences education, business education, chemistry education, earth science education, English education, general science education, geography education, history education, home economics education, industrial education, mathematical sciences education, physical education, physics education, political science education, psychology education, reading, school health education, sociology education. *Accreditation:* NCATE. Part-time programs available. *Faculty:* 22 full-time (13 women), 18 part-time/adjunct (14 women). *Students:* 62 full-time (51 women), 300 part-time (257 women);

includes 9 minority (5 African Americans, 2 American Indian/Alaska Native, 1 Asian American or Pacific Islander, 1 Hispanic American), 1 international. Average age 32. 437 applicants, 22% accepted. In 2006, 166 degrees awarded. *Entrance requirements:* For master's, GRE General Test, minimum GPA of 2.5. Application fee: $35. *Expenses:* Tuition, state resident: full-time $5,610. Tuition, nonresident: full-time $15,910. *Financial support:* In 2006–07, research assistantships (averaging $6,500 per year), teaching assistantships (averaging $6,500 per year) were awarded; career-related internships or fieldwork and Federal Work-Study also available. Support available to part-time students. *Faculty research:* Technology in education, reading instruction, e-portfolios, induction to teacher education, dispositions of teachers. *Unit head:* Dr. Michael Martin, Chair, 859-622-2154, Fax: 859-622-2004.

Eastern Michigan University, Graduate School, College of Arts and Sciences, Department of Music and Dance, Ypsilanti, MI 48197. Offers music (MA); music education (MA); music performance (MA); music theory-literature (MA); piano pedagogy (MA). *Accreditation:* NASM. Part-time and evening/weekend programs available. Postbaccalaureate distance learning degree programs offered (minimal on-campus study). *Faculty:* 31 full-time (13 women). *Students:* 6 full-time (3 women), 38 part-time (22 women); includes 3 minority (2 African Americans, 1 Asian American or Pacific Islander), 8 international. Average age 31. In 2006, 7 degrees awarded. *Entrance requirements:* Additional exam requirements/recommendations for international students: Required—TOEFL. *Application deadline:* For fall admission, 5/15 priority date for domestic students, 5/1 priority date for international students; for winter admission, 10/15 priority date for domestic students, 10/1 priority date for international students; for spring admission, 3/15 priority date for domestic students, 3/1 priority date for international students. Applications are processed on a rolling basis. Application fee: $35. *Expenses:* Tuition, state resident: part-time $341 per credit hour. Tuition, nonresident: full-time $16,104; part-time $671 per credit hour. Required fees: $816; $34 per credit hour. $40 per term. One-time fee: $82 full-time. Tuition and fees vary according to course level, course load, degree level and reciprocity agreements. *Financial support:* Fellowships, research assistantships with full tuition reimbursements, teaching assistantships with full tuition reimbursements, career-related internships or fieldwork, Federal Work-Study, institutionally sponsored loans, scholarships/grants, tuition waivers (partial), and unspecified assistantships available. Support available to part-time students. Financial award applicants required to submit FAFSA. *Unit head:* Dr. David Woike, Head, 734-487-4380, Fax: 734-487-6939, E-mail: dave.woike@emich.edu. *Application contact:* Dr. David Pierce, Head, 734-487-4114, E-mail: dvid.pierce@emich.edu.

Eastern Washington University, Graduate Studies, College of Arts and Letters, Department of Music, Cheney, WA 99004-2431. Offers composition (MA); instrumental/vocal performance (MA); music education (MA); music history and literature (MA). *Accreditation:* NASM. Part-time programs available. *Degree requirements:* For master's, thesis or alternative, comprehensive exam. *Entrance requirements:* For master's, GRE General Test, minimum GPA of 3.0.

Emporia State University, School of Graduate Studies, College of Liberal Arts and Sciences, Department of Music, Emporia, KS 66801-5087. Offers music education (MM), including instrumental, vocal; performance (MM). *Accreditation:* NASM. Part-time programs available. *Faculty:* 14 full-time (4 women), 5 part-time/adjunct (4 women). *Students:* 4 full-time (1 woman), 12 part-time (7 women), 1 international. 4 applicants, 100% accepted, 2 enrolled. In 2006, 3 degrees awarded. *Degree requirements:* For master's, comprehensive exam or thesis. *Entrance requirements:* For master's, music qualifying exam, appropriate undergraduate degree. Additional exam requirements/recommendations for international students: Required—TOEFL (minimum score 450 paper-based; 133 computer-based). *Application deadline:* For fall admission, 8/15 priority date for domestic students. Applications are processed on a rolling basis. Application fee: $30 ($75 for international students). Electronic applications accepted. *Expenses:* Tuition, state resident: full-time $3,438; part-time $143 per credit hour. Tuition, nonresident: full-time $10,398; part-time $433 per credit hour. Required fees: $724; $44 per credit hour. *Financial support:* In 2006–07, 1 research assistantship with full tuition reimbursement (averaging $6,752 per year), 5 teaching assistantships with full tuition reimbursements (averaging $6,752 per year) were awarded; Federal Work-Study, institutionally sponsored loans, health care benefits, and unspecified assistantships also available. Financial award application deadline: 3/15; financial award applicants required to submit FAFSA. *Unit head:* Dr. Marie C. Miller, Chair, 620-341-5431, E-mail: mmiller@emporia.edu. *Application contact:* Dr. Andrew Houchins, Graduate Coordinator, 620-341-6089, E-mail: ahouchin@emporia.edu.

Five Towns College, Department of Music, Dix Hills, NY 11746-6055. Offers jazz/commercial music (MM); music (DMA); music education (MM). Part-time programs available. *Faculty:* 13 full-time (all women), 12 part-time/adjunct (2 women). *Students:* 25 full-time (19 women), 48 part-time (30 women); includes 10 minority (4 African Americans, 4 Asian Americans or Pacific Islanders, 2 Hispanic Americans). Average age 35. 82 applicants, 100% accepted. In 2006, 20 degrees awarded. *Degree requirements:* For master's, exams, major composition or capstone project, recital; for doctorate, thesis/dissertation, final oral exam, comprehensive exam, registration. *Entrance requirements:* For master's, audition, bachelor's degree in music or music education, minimum GPA of 2.75, 36 hours of course work in performance; for doctorate, master's degree in music, minimum GPA of 3.0, 3 letters of recommendation. Additional exam requirements/recommendations for international students: Required—TOEFL (minimum score 550 paper-based; 213 computer-based; 80 iBT). *Application deadline:* Applications are processed on a rolling basis. Application fee: $50. *Financial support:* Fellowships with tuition reimbursements, tuition waivers (partial) available. Financial award applicants required to submit FAFSA. *Faculty research:* Teaching methods, teaching strategies and techniques, analysis of modern music, jazz. *Unit head:* Dr. Jill Miller-Thorn, Dean of Graduate Studies, 631-656-2100, Fax: 631-656-2172, E-mail: jmillerthorn@ftc.edu. *Application contact:* Jerry Cohen, Dean of Enrollment, 631-656-2121, Fax: 631-656-2172, E-mail: admissions@ftc.edu.

Florida International University, College of Architecture and the Arts, Miami, FL 33199. Offers architecture (MS); art and art history (MFA), including visual arts; landscape architecture (MS); music (MM, MS), including music (MM), music education (MS). *Accreditation:* ASLA. Part-time and evening/weekend programs available. *Faculty:* 67 full-time (23 women). *Students:* 166 full-time (84 women), 37 part-time (22 women); includes 121 minority (17 African Americans, 6 Asian Americans or Pacific Islanders, 98 Hispanic Americans), 23 international. Average age 31. 126 applicants, 55% accepted, 53 enrolled. In 2006, 62 degrees awarded. *Degree requirements:* For master's, thesis. *Entrance requirements:* For master's, GRE General Test. Additional exam requirements/recommendations for international students: Required—TOEFL. *Application deadline:* For fall admission, 4/1 priority date for domestic students; for spring admission, 10/1 for domestic students. Applications are processed on a rolling basis. Application fee: $25. *Expenses:* Tuition, state resident: part-time $249 per credit hour. Tuition, nonresident: part-time $753 per credit hour. Tuition and fees vary according to program. *Unit head:* Juan A. Bueno, Dean, 305-348-3176, Fax: 305-348-6716, E-mail: buenoj@fiu.edu.

Florida International University, College of Arts and Sciences, School of Music, Program in Music Education, Miami, FL 33199. Offers MS. *Accreditation:* NASM. Part-time and evening/weekend programs available. *Students:* Average age 41. In 2006, 2 degrees awarded. *Entrance requirements:* For master's, GRE General Test or minimum GPA of 3.0. Additional exam requirements/recommendations for international students: Required—TOEFL. *Application deadline:* For fall admission, 4/1 priority date for domestic students; for spring admission, 10/1 for domestic students. Applications are processed on a rolling basis. Application fee: $25. *Expenses:* Tuition, state resident: part-time $249 per credit hour. Tuition, nonresident: part-time $753 per credit hour. Tuition and fees vary according to program. *Faculty research:* Psychology of music teaching, classroom methodology, biofeedback. *Unit head:* Dr. Joseph Rohm, Director, School of Music, 305-348-3354, Fax: 305-348-4073, E-mail: joseph.rohm@fiu.edu.

Florida State University, Graduate Studies, College of Music, Program in Music Education, Tallahassee, FL 32306. Offers MM Ed, Ed D, PhD. *Accreditation:* NASM. *Faculty:* 25 full-time. *Students:* 61 full-time (22 women); includes 14 minority (10 African Americans, 1 Asian American or Pacific Islander, 3 Hispanic Americans). Average age 23. 60 applicants, 90% accepted, 37 enrolled. In 2006, 23 master's, 11 doctorates awarded. *Degree requirements:* For master's, departmental qualifying exam, thesis optional; for doctorate, thesis/dissertation, departmental qualifying exam. *Entrance requirements:* For master's and doctorate, minimum GPA of 3.0 or GRE General Test. Additional exam requirements/recommendations for international students: Required—TOEFL (minimum score 650 paper-based; 213 computer-based). *Application deadline:* For fall admission, 7/1 for domestic students, 5/2 for international students; for spring admission, 11/3 for domestic students, 9/1 for international students. Applications are processed on a rolling basis. Application fee: $30. *Expenses:* Tuition, state resident: full-time $5,822; part-time $243 per credit hour. Tuition, nonresident: full-time $20,976; part-time $874 per credit hour. Tuition and fees vary according to program. *Financial support:* In 2006–07, 9 students received support, including 9 teaching assistantships with full tuition reimbursements available (averaging $3,000 per year); career-related internships or fieldwork, Federal Work-Study, and tuition waivers (partial) also available. Support available to part-time students. Financial award application deadline: 2/28; financial award applicants required to submit FAFSA. *Application contact:* Dr. Seth Beckman, Assistant Dean for Academic Affairs/Director of Graduate Studies, 850-644-5848, Fax: 850-644-2033, E-mail: sbeckman@mailer.fsu.edu.

George Mason University, College of Visual and Performing Arts, Department of Music, Fairfax, VA 22030. Offers music (MA); music education (MA). *Accreditation:* NASM. *Faculty:* 14 full-time (6 women), 26 part-time/adjunct (14 women). *Students:* 15 full-time (8 women), 38 part-time (24 women); includes 8 minority (6 African Americans, 1 Asian American or Pacific Islander, 1 Hispanic American), 2 international. Average age 30. 42 applicants, 60% accepted, 18 enrolled. In 2006, 10 degrees awarded. *Degree requirements:* For master's, thesis (for some programs). *Entrance requirements:* For master's, music teaching certificate. *Application deadline:* For fall admission, 5/1 for domestic students; for spring admission, 11/1 for domestic students. Application fee: $60 ($75 for international students). Electronic applications accepted. *Expenses:* Tuition, state resident: full-time $5,724; part-time $238 per credit. Tuition, nonresident: full-time $16,896; part-time $704 per credit. Required fees: $1,656; $69 per credit. *Financial support:* Available to part-time students. Application deadline: 3/1. *Unit head:* James Gardner, Chairman, 703-993-1380, Fax: 703-993-1394, E-mail: jgardne2@gmu.edu. *Application contact:* Dr. Tom Owens, Information Contact, 703-993-1236, E-mail: music@gmu.edu.

Georgia State University, College of Education, Department of Middle-Secondary Education and Instructional Technology, Programs in Secondary Education, Atlanta, GA 30303-3083. Offers art education (Ed S); English education (M Ed, Ed S); mathematics education (M Ed, PhD, Ed S); music education (PhD); science education (M Ed, PhD, Ed S); social studies education (M Ed, PhD, Ed S). *Accreditation:* NASM (one or more programs are accredited); NCATE. Part-time and evening/weekend programs available. *Students:* 103 full-time (71 women), 140 part-time (92 women); includes 53 minority (48 African Americans, 2 Asian Americans or Pacific Islanders, 3 Hispanic Americans), 12 international. Average age 35. 36 applicants, 86% accepted. In 2006, 87 master's, 12 doctorates, 12 other advanced degrees awarded. *Degree requirements:* For master's, comprehensive exam; for doctorate, thesis/dissertation, comprehensive exam; for Ed S, project/exam. *Entrance requirements:* For master's, GRE General Test, minimum GPA of 2.5; for doctorate, GRE General Test or MAT, minimum GPA of 3.3; for Ed S, GRE General Test or MAT, minimum graduate GPA of 3.25. Application fee: $25. *Financial support:* Career-related internships or fieldwork, Federal Work-Study, and institutionally sponsored loans available. *Faculty research:* Women and science, problem solving in mathematics, dialects, economic education. *Unit head:* Dr. Ruth Hough, Acting Chair, Department of Middle-Secondary Education and Instructional Technology, 404-651-2510.

Gordon College, Graduate Education, Wenham, MA 01984-1899. Offers education (M Ed, MAT); music education (MME). *Accreditation:* NASM. Part-time and evening/weekend programs available. *Faculty:* 5 full-time (4 women), 9 part-time/adjunct (5 women). *Students:* 2 full-time (both women), 131 part-time (107 women); includes 2 minority (both Asian Americans or Pacific Islanders) Average age 28. 133 applicants, 100% accepted, 133 enrolled. In 2006, 12 degrees awarded. *Entrance requirements:* For master's, GRE or MAT, references. Additional exam requirements/recommendations for international students: Required—TOEFL (minimum score 550 paper-based; 213 computer-based). *Application deadline:* Applications are processed on a rolling basis. Application fee: $50. *Faculty research:* Reading, early childhood development, ELL (English Language Learners). *Unit head:* Dr. Malcolm L. Patterson, Dean of Graduate Studies, 978-867-4355, Fax: 978-867-4663, E-mail: malcolm.patterson@gordon.edu. *Application contact:* E. Jean Bilsbury, Program Coordinator, 978-867-4322, Fax: 978-867-4663, E-mail: jean.bilsbury@gordon.edu.

Hardin-Simmons University, Graduate School, School of Music, Abilene, TX 79698-0001. Offers church music (MM); music education (MM); music performance (MM); theory-composition (MM). *Accreditation:* NASM. Part-time programs available. *Faculty:* 12 full-time (6 women). *Students:* 6 full-time (1 woman), 2 part-time. Average age 27. 3 applicants, 100% accepted, 1 enrolled. In 2006, 2 degrees awarded. *Degree requirements:* For master's, one foreign language, thesis (for some programs), comprehensive exam. *Entrance requirements:* For master's, minimum undergraduate GPA of 3.0 in major, 2.7 overall; performance; writing sample; demonstrated knowledge in chosen area. Additional exam requirements/recommendations for international students: Required—TOEFL (minimum score 550 paper-based; 213 computer-based). *Application deadline:* For fall admission, 8/15 priority date for domestic students; for spring admission, 1/5 priority date for domestic students. Applications are processed on a rolling basis. Application fee: $50 ($100 for international students). *Expenses:* Tuition: Full-time $9,090; part-time $505 per hour. Required fees: $490; $66 per semester. One-time fee: $50. Tuition and fees vary according to course load and degree level. *Financial support:* In 2006–07, 5 fellowships (averaging $1,200 per year) were awarded; career-related internships or fieldwork and scholarships/grants also available. Support available to part-time students. Financial award application deadline: 6/30; financial award applicants required to submit FAFSA. *Unit head:* Dr. Leigh Anne Hunsaker, Director, 325-670-1391, Fax: 325-670-5873, E-mail: hunsaker@hsutx.edu. *Application contact:* Dr. Gary Stanlake, Dean of Graduate Studies, 325-670-1298, Fax: 325-670-1564, E-mail: gradoff@hsutx.edu.

Hebrew College, Program in Jewish Studies, Newton Centre, MA 02459. Offers Jewish liturgical music (Certificate); Jewish music education (Certificate); Jewish studies (MA). Part-time and evening/weekend programs available. Postbaccalaureate distance learning degree programs offered (minimal on-campus study). *Faculty:* 6 full-time (1 woman), 19 part-time/adjunct (7 women). *Students:* 39 (24 women). Average age 30. 26 applicants, 69% accepted, 14 enrolled. *Degree requirements:* For master's, one foreign language. *Entrance requirements:* For master's, GRE, interview. Additional exam requirements/recommendations for international students: Required—TOEFL. *Application deadline:* For fall admission, 12/15 priority date for domestic and international students; for winter admission, 2/15 priority date for domestic and international students; for spring admission, 5/30 priority date for domestic and international students. Applications are processed on a rolling basis. Application fee: $50. *Financial support:* In 2006–07, fellowships (averaging $5,000 per year); tuition waivers (partial) also available. Support available to part-time students. Financial award application deadline: 4/15; financial award applicants required to submit FAFSA. *Unit head:* Dr. Barry Mesch, Provost, 617-559-8600, Fax: 617-559-8601, E-mail: bmesch@hebrewcollege.edu. *Application contact:* Kate Nachman, Director of Admissions, 617-559-8610, Fax: 617-559-8601, E-mail: admissions@hebrewcollege.edu.

Hofstra University, School of Education and Allied Human Services, Department of Curriculum and Teaching, Program in Music Education, Hempstead, NY 11549. Offers music education (MA, MS Ed); wind conducting (MA). Part-time programs available. *Students:* 16 full-time (6 women), 37 part-time (22 women); includes 4 minority (1 African American, 1 Asian American or Pacific Islander, 2 Hispanic Americans). Average age 26. 40 applicants, 100% accepted, 21 enrolled. In 2006, 20 degrees awarded. *Degree requirements:* For master's, one foreign language, thesis (for some programs). *Entrance requirements:* For master's, 2 letters of recommendation, teacher certification (MA), essay. Additional exam requirements/recommendations for international students: Required—TOEFL (minimum score 550 paper-

Music Education

Hofstra University (continued)

based; 213 computer-based). *Application deadline:* Applications are processed on a rolling basis. Application fee: $60. Electronic applications accepted. *Expenses:* Tuition: Full-time $13,320; part-time $740 per credit. Required fees: $930; $155 per term. *Financial support:* In 2006–07, 6 students received support, including 3 fellowships with tuition reimbursements available (averaging $3,667 per year); research assistantships with full and partial tuition reimbursements available, scholarships/grants, tuition waivers (full and partial), and unspecified assistantships also available. Support available to part-time students. Financial award applicants required to submit FAFSA. *Faculty research:* Creative thinking, musical thinking, curriculum design, teacher preparation. *Unit head:* Dr. Nathalie G. Robinson, Program Director, 516-463-4514, Fax: 516-463-6393, E-mail: musngr@hofstra.edu. *Application contact:* Carol Drummer, Dean of Graduate Admissions, 516-463-4876, Fax: 516-463-4664, E-mail: gradstudent@hofstra.edu.

Holy Names University, Graduate Division, Department of Music, Oakland, CA 94619-1699. Offers Kodály music education (Certificate); music education with a Kodály emphasis (MM); performance (MM); piano pedagogy (MM); piano pedagogy with Suzuki emphasis (Certificate). *Faculty:* 2 full-time (1 woman), 9 part-time/adjunct (5 women). *Students:* 8 full-time (7 women), 14 part-time (13 women); includes 5 minority (1 African American, 3 Asian Americans or Pacific Islanders, 1 Hispanic American), 2 international. Average age 37. 15 applicants, 80% accepted, 11 enrolled. In 2006, 7 degrees awarded. *Degree requirements:* For master's, recital. *Entrance requirements:* For master's, audition, minimum undergraduate GPA of 2.6 overall, 3.0 in major. Additional exam requirements/recommendations for international students: Required—TOEFL. *Application deadline:* For fall admission, 8/1 priority date for domestic students; for spring admission, 12/1 priority date for domestic students. Applications are processed on a rolling basis. Application fee: $50. *Expenses:* Tuition: Full-time $10,800; part-time $600 per unit. Required fees: $240; $120 per term. *Financial support:* In 2006–07, 10 students received support. Scholarships/grants available. Support available to part-time students. Financial award application deadline: 3/2; financial award applicants required to submit FAFSA. *Faculty research:* Performance practice with special interest in baroque, Romantic, and twentieth-century instrumental and vocal music; choral pedagogy; Hungarian music education. *Unit head:* Anne Laskey, Director, 510-436-1234. *Application contact:* 800-430-1351, Fax: 510-436-1325, E-mail: admissions@hnu.edu.

Howard University, Graduate School, Division of Fine Arts, Department of Music, Washington, DC 20059-0002. Offers applied music (MM); jazz studies (MM); music education (MM Ed). *Accreditation:* NASM. Part-time programs available. *Degree requirements:* For master's, thesis or alternative, departmental qualifying exam, recital, comprehensive exam. *Entrance requirements:* For master's, minimum GPA of 3.0, bachelor's degree in music or music education. Additional exam requirements/recommendations for international students: Required—TOEFL.

Hunter College of the City University of New York, Graduate School, School of Arts and Sciences, Department of Music, New York, NY 10021-5085. Offers music (MA); music education (MA). Part-time and evening/weekend programs available. *Faculty:* 10 full-time (3 women), 3 part-time/adjunct (1 woman). *Students:* 2 full-time (1 woman), 47 part-time (19 women); includes 7 minority (3 African Americans, 2 Asian Americans or Pacific Islanders, 2 Hispanic Americans). Average age 33. 25 applicants, 96% accepted, 17 enrolled. In 2006, 18 degrees awarded. *Degree requirements:* For master's, one foreign language, thesis, composition, essay, or recital; proficiency exam. *Entrance requirements:* For master's, undergraduate major in music (minimum 24 credits) or equivalent, sample of work, research paper. Additional exam requirements/recommendations for international students: Required—TOEFL. *Application deadline:* For fall admission, 4/1 for domestic students, 2/1 for international students; for spring admission, 11/1 for domestic students, 9/1 for international students. Applications are processed on a rolling basis. Application fee: $125. *Expenses:* Tuition, state resident: part-time $270 per credit. Tuition, nonresident: part-time $500 per credit. Required fees: $45 per semester. *Financial support:* In 2006–07, 4 fellowships (averaging $1,000 per year) were awarded; Federal Work-Study, tuition waivers (partial), and lesson stipends also available. Support available to part-time students. Financial award application deadline: 4/15. *Faculty research:* African and African-American music, Bach, Renaissance music, early romantic music, theory of tonal music. *Unit head:* Dr. Paul F. Mueller, Chair, 212-772-5020, Fax: 212-772-5022, E-mail: music@hunter.cuny.edu. *Application contact:* Dr. L. Poundie Burstein, Graduate Adviser, 212-650-5152, E-mail: huntermus@aol.com.

Hunter College of the City University of New York, Graduate School, School of Education, Program in Music Education, New York, NY 10021-5085. Offers MA. *Accreditation:* NCATE. *Faculty:* 1 (woman) full-time, 4 part-time/adjunct (0 women). *Students:* 3 full-time (2 women), 22 part-time (10 women); includes 1 minority (African American) Average age 35. 15 applicants, 60% accepted, 7 enrolled. In 2006, 3 degrees awarded. *Degree requirements:* For master's, one foreign language, thesis, professional teaching portfolio, New York State Teacher Certification Exams, comprehensive exam. *Entrance requirements:* For master's, minimum GPA of 2.8, 2 letters of reference. Additional exam requirements/recommendations for international students: Required—TOEFL, TWE. *Application deadline:* For fall admission, 4/1 for domestic students, 2/1 for international students; for spring admission, 11/1 for domestic students, 9/1 for international students. Applications are processed on a rolling basis. Application fee: $125. *Expenses:* Tuition, state resident: part-time $270 per credit. Tuition, nonresident: part-time $500 per credit. Required fees: $45 per semester. *Financial support:* Federal Work-Study and tuition waivers (partial) available. Support available to part-time students. *Unit head:* Dr. Victor Bobetsky, Graduate Adviser, Director, 212-650-3574. E-mail: vbobetsky@aol.com. *Application contact:* William Zlata, Director for Graduate Admissions, 212-772-4482, Fax: 212-650-3336, E-mail: admissions@hunter.cuny.edu.

Indiana University of Pennsylvania, School of Graduate Studies and Research, College of Fine Arts, Department of Music and Music Education, Program in Music, Indiana, PA 15705-1087. Offers music education (MA); music history and literature (MA); music theory and composition (MA); performance (MA). *Accreditation:* NASM. Part-time programs available. *Faculty:* 15 full-time (2 women), 1 part-time/adjunct (0 women). *Students:* 9 full-time (6 women), 9 part-time (5 women), 3 international. Average age 26. 26 applicants, 38% accepted. In 2006, 6 degrees awarded. *Degree requirements:* For master's, thesis optional. *Entrance requirements:* For master's, 2 letters of recommendation, audition. Additional exam requirements/recommendations for international students: Required—TOEFL. *Application deadline:* For fall admission, 7/1 priority date for domestic students; for spring admission, 11/1 for domestic students. Applications are processed on a rolling basis. Application fee: $30. *Expenses:* Tuition, state resident: full-time $6,048; part-time $336 per credit. Tuition, nonresident: full-time $9,678; part-time $538 per credit. Required fees: $1,069; $148 per year. *Financial support:* In 2006–07, 1 fellowship (averaging $500 per year), 6 research assistantships with full and partial tuition reimbursements (averaging $2,495 per year) were awarded; Federal Work-Study also available. Support available to part-time students. Financial award application deadline: 3/15; financial award applicants required to submit FAFSA. *Unit head:* Dr. Keith Young, Head, 724-357-4408.

Inter American University of Puerto Rico, San Germán Campus, Graduate Studies Center, Graduate Program in Music Education, San Germán, PR 00683-5008. Offers MA. Part-time and evening/weekend programs available. *Faculty:* 8 full-time, 7 part-time/adjunct. *Students:* 42. In 2006, 26 degrees awarded. Application fee: $31. *Expenses:* Tuition: Part-time $175 per credit. Required fees: $238 per semester. Tuition and fees vary according to degree level. *Financial support:* Federal Work-Study available. *Application contact:* Dr. Raquel Montalvo, Graduate Coordinator, 787-264-1912, Fax: 787-892-7510, E-mail: ramontalvo@sg.inter.edu.

Ithaca College, Graduate Studies, School of Music, Program in Music and Music Education, Ithaca, NY 14850-7020. Offers composition (MM); conducting (MM); music education (MM, MS); performance (MM); Suzuki pedagogy (MM). *Accreditation:* NASM. Part-time programs available. *Faculty:* 59 full-time (21 women), 1 part-time/adjunct (0 women). *Students:* 39 full-time (19 women), 7 part-time (5 women); includes 1 minority (Hispanic American), 2 international. Average age 25. 112 applicants, 29% accepted, 27 enrolled. In 2006, 37 degrees awarded. *Degree requirements:* For master's, thesis (for some programs), comprehensive exam, registration. *Entrance requirements:* For master's, audition, minimum GPA of 3.0. Additional exam requirements/recommendations for international students: Required—TOEFL (minimum score 550 paper-based; 213 computer-based). *Application deadline:* For fall admission, 3/1 for domestic students; for spring admission, 12/1 for domestic students. Applications are processed on a rolling basis. Application fee: $40. *Financial support:* In 2006–07, 39 students received support, including 29 teaching assistantships (averaging $8,767 per year); career-related internships or fieldwork, Federal Work-Study, institutionally sponsored loans, scholarships/grants, and unspecified assistantships also available. Support available to part-time students. Financial award application deadline: 3/1; financial award applicants required to submit FAFSA. *Faculty research:* Musical performance and performance studies; musical composition, music theory and analysis; music history and musicology; musical direction and conducting. *Unit head:* Dr. Verna Brummett, Chairperson, 607-274-3386, Fax: 607-274-1727.

Jackson State University, Graduate School, School of Liberal Arts, Department of Music, Jackson, MS 39217. Offers music education (MM Ed). *Accreditation:* NASM. Part-time and evening/weekend programs available. *Faculty:* 9 full-time (4 women). *Students:* 4 full-time (1 woman), 2 part-time (1 woman); includes 5 minority (all African Americans) In 2006, 3 degrees awarded. *Degree requirements:* For master's, thesis or alternative, comprehensive exam. *Entrance requirements:* For master's, GRE General Test. Additional exam requirements/recommendations for international students: Required—TOEFL. *Application deadline:* For fall admission, 3/1 priority date for domestic students; for spring admission, 10/1 for domestic students. Applications are processed on a rolling basis. Application fee: $20. *Financial support:* In 2006–07, 5 students received support. Career-related internships or fieldwork, Federal Work-Study, scholarships/grants, and unspecified assistantships available. Support available to part-time students. Financial award application deadline: 3/1; financial award applicants required to submit FAFSA. *Unit head:* Dr. Jimmie James, Chair, 601-979-2141, Fax: 601-979-2568. *Application contact:* Curtis Gore, Director of Graduate Admissions, 601-979-2455, Fax: 601-974-4325, E-mail: cgore@ccaix.jsums.edu.

Jacksonville University, College of Arts and Sciences, School of Education, Program in Music Education, Jacksonville, FL 32211-3394. Offers MAT. *Accreditation:* NASM. Part-time and evening/weekend programs available. *Degree requirements:* For master's, comprehensive exam. *Entrance requirements:* For master's, GRE General Test, minimum GPA of 3.0. Additional exam requirements/recommendations for international students: Required—TOEFL.

James Madison University, College of Graduate and Outreach Programs, College of Visual and Performing Arts, School of Music, Harrisonburg, VA 22807. Offers conducting (MM); music education (MM); performance (MM); theory-composition (MM). *Accreditation:* NASM. Part-time programs available. *Faculty:* 20 full-time (6 women), 5 part-time/adjunct (1 woman). *Students:* 13 full-time (8 women), 3 part-time (1 woman). Average age 27. In 2006, 2 degrees awarded. *Degree requirements:* For master's, comprehensive exam. *Entrance requirements:* For master's, GRE General Test, audition. Additional exam requirements/recommendations for international students: Required—TOEFL. *Application deadline:* For fall admission, 5/1 priority date for domestic students; for spring admission, 9/1 priority date for domestic students. Applications are processed on a rolling basis. Application fee: $55. Electronic applications accepted. *Expenses:* Tuition, state resident: full-time $6,336; part-time $264 per credit hour. Tuition, nonresident: full-time $17,832; part-time $743 per credit hour. *Financial support:* In 2006–07, 12 students received support, including 3 teaching assistantships with full tuition reimbursements available (averaging $8,167 per year); Federal Work-Study and unspecified assistantships also available. Financial award application deadline: 3/1; financial award applicants required to submit FAFSA. *Unit head:* Dr. Jeffrey A. Showell, Academic Unit Head, 540-568-6197.

Kansas State University, Graduate School, College of Arts and Sciences, Department of Music, Manhattan, KS 66506. Offers music education (MM); music education/band conducting (MM); music history and literature (MM); performance (MM); performance with pedagogy emphasis (MM); theory and composition (MM). *Accreditation:* NASM. Part-time programs available. *Faculty:* 19 full-time (5 women). *Students:* 20 full-time (9 women), 1 international. Average age 25. 6 applicants, 100% accepted, 6 enrolled. In 2006, 6 degrees awarded. *Degree requirements:* For master's, thesis optional. *Entrance requirements:* For master's, GRE, audition (in person or recording), interview (music education). Additional exam requirements/recommendations for international students: Required—TOEFL (minimum score 600 paper-based). *Application deadline:* For fall admission, 2/1 priority date for domestic and international students; for spring admission, 10/1 priority date for domestic students, 8/1 priority date for international students. Applications are processed on a rolling basis. Application fee: $30 ($55 for international students). Electronic applications accepted. *Expenses:* Tuition, state resident: full-time $6,352; part-time $240 per credit hour. Tuition, nonresident: full-time $14,296; part-time $571 per credit hour. Required fees: $585. *Financial support:* In 2006–07, 11 teaching assistantships with full tuition reimbursements (averaging $7,091 per year) were awarded; institutionally sponsored loans, scholarships/grants, and tuition waivers (full and partial) also available. Support available to part-time students. Financial award application deadline: 3/1; financial award applicants required to submit FAFSA. *Faculty research:* Music since 1945, music by women composers, American music, opera, current performance practices. Total annual research expenditures: $28,070. *Unit head:* Dr. Gary Mortenson, Head, 785-532-3828, Fax: 785-532-7732, E-mail: garym@ksu.edu. *Application contact:* Fred Burrack, Director of Graduate Programs, 785-532-5764, Fax: 785-532-7732, E-mail: fburrack@ksu.edu.

Kent State University, College of Fine and Professional Arts, Hugh A. Glauser School of Music, Kent, OH 44242-0001. Offers composition (MA); conducting (MM); ethnomusicology (MA); music education (MM, PhD); musicology (MA); musicology-ethnomusicology (PhD); performance (MM); theory (MA); theory and composition (PhD). *Accreditation:* NASM. *Degree requirements:* For master's, variable foreign language requirement, comprehensive exam, 2 recitals, essay and recital, or thesis; for doctorate, variable foreign language requirement, thesis/dissertation, comprehensive exam. *Entrance requirements:* For master's, diagnostic exams in music history and theory, audition, minimum GPA of 2.75; for doctorate, diagnostic exams in music history and theory, master's thesis or scholarly paper, minimum GPA of 3.0. Additional exam requirements/recommendations for international students: Required—TOEFL. Electronic applications accepted. *Faculty research:* Music composition, performance, teaching and history.

Kutztown University of Pennsylvania, College of Graduate Studies and Extended Learning, College of Visual and Performing Arts, Program in Music Education, Kutztown, PA 19530-0730. Offers Certificate. *Students:* 4 full-time (2 women), 5 part-time (3 women), 1 international. 8 applicants, 100% accepted, 3 enrolled. *Expenses:* Tuition, state resident: full-time $6,048; part-time $336 per credit. Tuition, nonresident: full-time $9,678; part-time $538 per credit. *Unit head:* Dr. William Mowder, Dean, College of Visual and Performing Arts, 610-683-4500, Fax: 610-683-4547, E-mail: mowder@kutztown.edu.

LaGrange College, Graduate Programs, Department of Education, LaGrange, GA 30240-2999. Offers art education (MAT); curriculum and instruction (M Ed); music education (MAT); secondary education (MAT). Part-time and evening/weekend programs available. *Degree requirements:* For master's, comprehensive exam. *Entrance requirements:* For master's, GRE, MAT, or NTE, minimum GPA of 2.5. Additional exam requirements/recommendations for international students: Required—TOEFL (minimum score 550 paper-based).

Lamar University, College of Graduate Studies, College of Fine Arts and Communication, Department of Music, Theatre, and Dance, Beaumont, TX 77710. Offers music education (MM Ed); music performance (MM); theatre (MS). *Accreditation:* NASM (one or more programs are accredited). *Faculty:* 11 full-time (4 women), 3 part-time/adjunct (1 woman). *Students:* 8

full-time (7 women), 6 part-time (3 women); includes 4 minority (3 African Americans, 1 Hispanic American). Average age 30. 13 applicants, 31% accepted, 1 enrolled. In 2006, 5 degrees awarded. *Degree requirements:* For master's, thesis optional. *Entrance requirements:* For master's, GRE General Test, theory placement exams, audition. Additional exam requirements/recommendations for international students: Required—TOEFL. *Application deadline:* For fall admission, 8/1 for domestic students; for spring admission, 12/1 for domestic students. Applications are processed on a rolling basis. Application fee: $25 ($50 for international students). *Expenses:* Tuition, nonresident: part-time $33 per hour. Required fees: $43 per hour. $110 per semester. *Financial support:* In 2006–07, 4 fellowships with tuition reimbursements (averaging $2,000 per year), 2 teaching assistantships were awarded; institutionally sponsored loans and tuition waivers (partial) also available. Support available to part-time students. Financial award application deadline: 4/1. *Faculty research:* Performance: ensembles and personal. *Unit head:* Dr. L. Randolph Babin, Chair, 409-880-8144, Fax: 409-880-8143, E-mail: babinlr@hal.lamar.edu. *Application contact:* Dr. Robert M. Culbertson, Adviser, 409-880-8073, Fax: 409-880-8143, E-mail: culbertsrm@hal.lamar.edu.

Lebanon Valley College, Graduate Studies and Continuing Education, Program in Music Education, Annville, PA 17003-1400. Offers MME. *Accreditation:* NASM. Part-time programs available. *Faculty:* 4 full-time (1 woman), 2 part-time/adjunct (1 woman). *Students:* Average age 42. *Degree requirements:* For master's, thesis, registration. *Entrance requirements:* For master's, minimum GPA of 3.0, teaching certificate. *Application deadline:* Applications are processed on a rolling basis. Application fee: $30. Electronic applications accepted. *Expenses:* Tuition: Full-time $28,280; part-time $390 per credit. Required fees: $575. *Financial support:* Application deadline: 5/1; *Unit head:* Dr. Mark L Mecham, Head, 717-867-6276.

Lee University, Program in Music, Cleveland, TN 37320-3450. Offers church music (MCM); music education (MME); performance (MMMP). *Accreditation:* NASM. Part-time programs available. *Faculty:* 21 full-time (4 women), 1 part-time/adjunct (0 women). *Students:* 26 full-time (12 women), 3 part-time (all women); includes 12 minority (1 African American, 10 American Indian/Alaska Native, 1 Hispanic American), 4 international. 24 applicants, 71% accepted, 9 enrolled. In 2006, 2 degrees awarded. *Degree requirements:* For master's, variable foreign language requirement, thesis, internship, comprehensive exam. *Entrance requirements:* For master's, audition, resumé, interview, minimum GPA of 2.75. Additional exam requirements/recommendations for international students: Required—TOEFL. *Application deadline:* For fall admission, 4/1 for domestic students; for spring admission, 10/1 for domestic students. Applications are processed on a rolling basis. Application fee: $25. *Expenses:* Tuition: Part-time $412 per credit. Required fees: $10 per semester. Tuition and fees vary according to course load. *Financial support:* In 2006–07, 13 teaching assistantships (averaging $2,275 per year) were awarded; career-related internships or fieldwork, Federal Work-Study, institutionally sponsored loans, and scholarships/grants also available. Financial award application deadline: 4/15; financial award applicants required to submit FAFSA. *Unit head:* Dr. Jim W. Burns, Director, 423-614-8240, Fax: 423-614-8242, E-mail: gradmusic@leeuniversity.edu. *Application contact:* Vicki Glasscock, Graduate Admissions Director, 423-614-8059, E-mail: vglasscock@leeuniversity.edu.

Lehman College of the City University of New York, Division of Arts and Humanities, Department of Music, Bronx, NY 10468-1589. Offers MAT. *Accreditation:* NCATE. Part-time and evening/weekend programs available. *Entrance requirements:* For master's, audition. *Faculty research:* Music and music education.

Lehman College of the City University of New York, Division of Education, Department of Middle and High School Education, Program in Music Education, Bronx, NY 10468-1589. Offers MS Ed. Part-time and evening/weekend programs available.

Long Island University, C.W. Post Campus, School of Education, Department of Curriculum and Instruction, Brookville, NY 11548-1300. Offers adolescence education (MS); adolescence education: biology (MS); adolescence education: earth science (MS); adolescence education: English (MS); adolescence education: mathematics (MS); adolescence education: social studies (MS); adolescence education: Spanish (MS); art education (MS); bilingual education (MS); childhood education (MS); early childhood education (MS); middle childhood education (MS); music education (MS); teaching English to speakers of other languages (MS). Part-time and evening/weekend programs available. *Degree requirements:* For master's, comprehensive exam or thesis, student teaching. *Entrance requirements:* For master's, minimum GPA of 2.75 in major, 2.5 overall. Electronic applications accepted. *Faculty research:* Ethics and education, teaching strategies.

Long Island University, C.W. Post Campus, School of Visual and Performing Arts, Department of Music, Brookville, NY 11548-1300. Offers music (MA); music education (MS). Part-time programs available. *Degree requirements:* For master's, thesis. *Entrance requirements:* For master's, GRE General Test (MA), GRE Subject Test in music, minimum undergraduate GPA of 3.0, 2 professional and/or academic letters of recommendation, current resumé. Electronic applications accepted. *Faculty research:* Performance, composing, musicology, conducting, computer-based music technology.

Louisiana State University and Agricultural and Mechanical College, Graduate School, College of Music and Dramatic Arts, School of Music, Baton Rouge, LA 70803. Offers music (MM, DMA, PhD); music education (PhD). *Accreditation:* NASM. Part-time programs available. *Faculty:* 48 full-time (15 women), 3 part-time/adjunct (2 women). *Students:* 125 full-time (73 women), 35 part-time (21 women); includes 17 minority (7 African Americans, 6 Asian Americans or Pacific Islanders, 4 Hispanic Americans), 29 international. Average age 30. 125 applicants, 58% accepted, 40 enrolled. In 2006, 51 master's, 18 doctorates awarded. Terminal master's awarded for partial completion of doctoral program. *Degree requirements:* For doctorate, thesis/dissertation (for some programs). *Entrance requirements:* For master's, minimum GPA of 3.0, audition/interview; for doctorate, GRE General Test, minimum GPA of 3.0, audition/interview. Additional exam requirements/recommendations for international students: Required—TOEFL (minimum score 550 paper-based; 213 computer-based; 79 iBT). *Application deadline:* For fall admission, 3/15 priority date for domestic students, 5/15 for international students; for spring admission, 10/15 for international students. Applications are processed on a rolling basis. Application fee: $25. Electronic applications accepted. *Financial support:* In 2006–07, 3 fellowships (averaging $30,670 per year), 84 teaching assistantships with full and partial tuition reimbursements (averaging $9,735 per year) were awarded; research assistantships with full and partial tuition reimbursements, Federal Work-Study, institutionally sponsored loans, scholarships/grants, tuition waivers (full and partial), and unspecified assistantships also available. Support available to part-time students. Financial award applicants required to submit FAFSA. *Faculty research:* Music education, music literature, formal and harmonic analysis, pedagogy, performance. Total annual research expenditures: $359,795. *Application contact:* Dr. Sara Lyn Baird, Interim Dean, 225-578-3261, Fax: 225-578-2562.

Manhattanville College, Graduate Programs, School of Education, Program in Music Education, Purchase, NY 10577-2132. Offers MAT. Part-time and evening/weekend programs available. *Students:* 4 full-time (3 women), 5 part-time (4 women). In 2006, 1 degree awarded. *Degree requirements:* For master's, comprehensive exam or research project, field experience. *Entrance requirements:* For master's, audition, minimum undergraduate GPA of 3.0, 2 letters of recommendation. *Application deadline:* Applications are processed on a rolling basis. Application fee: $55. *Financial support:* Career-related internships or fieldwork and institutionally sponsored loans available. Support available to part-time students. *Application contact:* Alyce Ware Poli, Director of Admissions, 914-323-5142, Fax: 914-694-1732, E-mail: edschool@mville.edu.

Marywood University, Academic Affairs, Insalaco College of Creative Arts and Management, Music Department, Program in Music Education, Scranton, PA 18509-1598. Offers MA. *Accreditation:* NASM; NCATE. Part-time and evening/weekend programs available. *Students:* Average age 31. In 2006, 1 degree awarded. *Degree requirements:* For master's, thesis or alternative, comprehensive exam. *Entrance requirements:* For master's, GRE Subject Test, audition. Additional exam requirements/recommendations for international students: Required—TOEFL (minimum score 550 paper-based; 213 computer-based). *Application deadline:* For fall admission, 4/15 priority date for domestic and international students; for spring admission, 11/15 priority date for domestic and international students. Applications are processed on a rolling basis. Application fee: $30. Electronic applications accepted. *Expenses:* Tuition: Part-time $672 per credit. Tuition and fees vary according to degree level, campus/location and program. *Financial support:* Research assistantships with tuition reimbursements, career-related internships or fieldwork, scholarships/grants, tuition waivers (partial), and unspecified assistantships available. Support available to part-time students. Financial award application deadline: 2/15; financial award applicants required to submit FAFSA. *Application contact:* Dr. Deborah M. Flynn, Coordinator of Graduate Advising (Enrollment Management), 570-348-6211, E-mail: flynn@ac.marywood.edu.

McGill University, Faculty of Graduate and Postdoctoral Studies, Schulich School of Music, Montréal, QC H3A 2T5, Canada. Offers composition (M Mus, D Mus, PhD); music education (MA, PhD); music technology (MA, PhD); musicology (MA, PhD); performance (M Mus); performance studies (D Mus); sound recording (M Mus, PhD); theory (MA, PhD). *Degree requirements:* For master's, thesis (for some programs), registration; for doctorate, thesis/dissertation, comprehensive exam, registration. *Entrance requirements:* For master's, minimum GPA of 3.0, audition (for performance programs); for doctorate, minimum GPA of 3.0; audition (for performance programs); M Mus in composition, scores and/or tape (D Mus in composition). Additional exam requirements/recommendations for international students: Required—TOEFL (minimum score 550 paper-based; 213 computer-based), IELTS (minimum score 7). Electronic applications accepted. *Faculty research:* Music in social context, nineteenth-century analysis and theory, digital audio production.

McNeese State University, Graduate School, College of Liberal Arts, Department of Performing Arts, Program in Music Education, Lake Charles, LA 70609. Offers MM Ed. *Accreditation:* NASM; NCATE. Evening/weekend programs available. *Faculty:* 5 full-time (1 woman), 1 (woman) part-time/adjunct. *Students:* 2 full-time (1 woman), 4 part-time (2 women); includes 2 minority (both African Americans) *Entrance requirements:* For master's, GRE General Test. *Application deadline:* For fall admission, 7/15 priority date for domestic students. Applications are processed on a rolling basis. Application fee: $20 ($30 for international students). *Expenses:* Tuition, area resident: Full-time $2,226; part-time $193 per hour. Required fees: $919; $106 per hour. *Financial support:* Teaching assistantships available. Financial award application deadline: 5/1. *Unit head:* Michele Martin, Head, Department of Performing Arts, 337-475-5028, Fax: 337-475-5063, E-mail: mmartin@mcneese.edu.

Miami University, Graduate School, School of Fine Arts, Department of Music, Program in Music Education, Oxford, OH 45056. Offers MM. *Accreditation:* NASM. *Degree requirements:* For master's, final and oral exams, recital. *Entrance requirements:* For master's, audition, minimum undergraduate GPA of 3.0 during previous 2 years or 3.0 overall. Additional exam requirements/recommendations for international students: Required—TOEFL, TWE.

Michigan State University, The Graduate School, College of Music, East Lansing, MI 48824. Offers music (PhD); music composition (M Mus, DMA); music conducting (M Mus, DMA); music education (M Mus); music performance (M Mus, DMA); music theory (M Mus); music therapy (M Mus); musicology (MA); piano pedagogy (M Mus). *Accreditation:* NASM. *Faculty:* 56 full-time (15 women), 3 part-time/adjunct (1 woman). *Students:* 234 full-time (126 women), 51 part-time (31 women); includes 27 minority (5 African Americans, 1 American Indian/Alaska Native, 17 Asian Americans or Pacific Islanders, 4 Hispanic Americans), 107 international. Average age 29. 316 applicants, 44% accepted. In 2006, 34 master's, 23 doctorates awarded. *Entrance requirements:* Additional exam requirements/recommendations for international students: Required—TOEFL. Electronic applications accepted. *Expenses:* Tuition, state resident: part-time $346 per credit hour. Tuition, nonresident: part-time $730 per credit hour. Tuition and fees vary according to program. *Financial support:* In 2006–07, 24 fellowships with tuition reimbursements, 21 research assistantships with tuition reimbursements (averaging $12,247 per year), 84 teaching assistantships with tuition reimbursements (averaging $12,181 per year) were awarded. *Unit head:* Prof. James B. Forger, Dean, 517-355-4583, Fax: 517-432-2880, E-mail: forger@msu.edu. *Application contact:* Anne Simon, Assistant to the Associate Director for Graduate Studies, 517-353-9122, Fax: 517-432-2880, E-mail: gradprograms@music.msu.edu.

Minot State University, Graduate School, Program in Music, Minot, ND 58707-0002. Offers music education (MME). Program offered during summer only. *Accreditation:* NASM. *Faculty:* 6 full-time (1 woman). *Students:* 7 applicants, 100% accepted. *Degree requirements:* For master's, thesis or alternative. *Entrance requirements:* For master's, music exam, minimum GPA of 2.75. Additional exam requirements/recommendations for international students: Required—TOEFL. *Application deadline:* Applications are processed on a rolling basis. Application fee: $35. *Financial support:* Research assistantships with partial tuition reimbursements, teaching assistantships with partial tuition reimbursements, career-related internships or fieldwork, institutionally sponsored loans, scholarships/grants, traineeships, tuition waivers (partial), and unspecified assistantships available. Support available to part-time students. Financial award application deadline: 4/1. *Unit head:* Sandra Starr, Chairperson, 701-858-3185, Fax: 701-839-6933. *Application contact:* Brenda Anderson, Administrative Assistant, 701-858-3250, Fax: 701-858-4286, E-mail: brenda.anderson@minotstateu.edu.

Mississippi College, Graduate School, College of Arts and Sciences, School of Christian Studies and the Arts, Department of Music, Clinton, MS 39058. Offers applied music performance (MM); conducting (MM); music education (MM); music performance: organ (MM); vocal pedagogy (MM). *Accreditation:* NASM. Part-time and evening/weekend programs available. *Faculty:* 8 full-time (4 women), 5 part-time/adjunct (4 women). *Students:* 2 full-time (both women), 12 part-time (7 women); includes 3 minority (2 African Americans, 1 Hispanic American), 4 international. Average age 27. In 2006, 2 degrees awarded. *Degree requirements:* For master's, recital. *Entrance requirements:* For master's, GRE, minimum GPA of 2.5. Additional exam requirements/recommendations for international students: Recommended—IELTS. *Application deadline:* For fall admission, 8/15 priority date for domestic students. Applications are processed on a rolling basis. Application fee: $25. Electronic applications accepted. *Expenses:* Tuition: Full-time $7,290; part-time $405 per hour. Required fees: $150 per term. Tuition and fees vary according to campus/location and program. *Financial support:* Teaching assistantships, Federal Work-Study, scholarships/grants, and unspecified assistantships available. Support available to part-time students. Financial award application deadline: 4/1; financial award applicants required to submit FAFSA. *Unit head:* Dr. James Meaders, Chair, 601-925-3441, Fax: 601-925-3945, E-mail: meaders@mc.edu.

Montclair State University, The Graduate School, College of Education and Human Services, Department of Curriculum and Teaching, Montclair, NJ 07043-1624. Offers education (M Ed); educational technology (M Ed); school library media specialist (Certificate); teaching (MAT, Certificate), including art (MAT), biological science (MAT), early childhood education (P-3) (MAT), earth science (MAT), elementary education (K-8) (MAT), English (MAT), French (MAT), health and physical education (MAT), health education (MAT), home economics (MAT), mathematics (MAT), music (MAT), physical education (MAT), physical science (MAT), social studies (MAT), Spanish (MAT), teacher of ESL (MAT), teacher of students with disabilities (MAT). Part-time and evening/weekend programs available. *Faculty:* 16 full-time (12 women), 13 part-time/adjunct (8 women). *Students:* 147 full-time (113 women), 230 part-time (188 women); includes 58 minority (33 African Americans, 1 American Indian/Alaska Native, 12 Asian Americans or Pacific Islanders, 12 Hispanic Americans), 4 international. Average age 33. 118 applicants, 38% accepted, 37 enrolled. In 2006, 166 master's, 11 other advanced degrees awarded. *Degree requirements:* For master's, field experience. *Entrance requirements:* For master's, PRAXIS II, minimum GPA of 2.67, 2 letters of recommendation. Additional exam requirements/recommendations for international students: Required—TOEFL (minimum score 83 computer-based). *Application deadline:* For fall admission, 2/15 for domestic and international students; for spring admission, 9/15 for domestic and international students. Applications are processed

Music Education

Montclair State University (continued)
on a rolling basis. Application fee: $60. Electronic applications accepted. *Expenses:* Tuition, state resident: part-time $450 per credit. Tuition, nonresident: part-time $682 per credit. Tuition and fees vary according to degree level and program. *Financial support:* In 2006–07, 7 research assistantships with full tuition reimbursements (averaging $7,000 per year) were awarded; Federal Work-Study, scholarships/grants, and unspecified assistantships also available. Support available to part-time students. Financial award application deadline: 3/1; financial award applicants required to submit FAFSA. *Unit head:* Dr. Deborah Eldridge, Chairperson, 973-655-5187.

Montclair State University, The Graduate School, School of the Arts, Department of Music, Montclair, NJ 07043-1624. Offers music (AD); music education (MA); music therapy (MA); performance (MA, Certificate); theory/composition (MA). *Accreditation:* NASM. Part-time and evening/weekend programs available. *Faculty:* 18 full-time (6 women), 64 part-time/adjunct (31 women). *Students:* 17 full-time (11 women), 30 part-time (19 women); includes 3 minority (1 African American, 1 Asian American or Pacific Islander, 1 Hispanic American), 5 international. 40 applicants, 40% accepted, 11 enrolled. In 2006, 11 master's, 1 other advanced degree awarded. *Degree requirements:* For master's, compositions, recitals, or thesis. *Entrance requirements:* For master's, GRE General Test, audition; undergraduate degree in music or at least 40 semester hours of work in theory, music history, performance; 2 letters of recommendation; teaching certificate (MA in music education). Additional exam requirements/recommendations for international students: Required—TOEFL (minimum score 83 computer-based). *Application deadline:* For fall admission, 6/1 for international students; for spring admission, 10/1 for international students. Applications are processed on a rolling basis. Application fee: $60. Electronic applications accepted. *Expenses:* Tuition, state resident: part-time $450 per credit. Tuition, nonresident: part-time $682 per credit. Tuition and fees vary according to degree level and program. *Financial support:* In 2006–07, 2 research assistantships with full tuition reimbursements (averaging $7,000 per year) were awarded; Federal Work-Study, scholarships/grants, and unspecified assistantships also available. Support available to part-time students. Financial award application deadline: 3/1; financial award applicants required to submit FAFSA. *Unit head:* Prof. Robert Aldridge, Chairperson, 973-655-7212.

Morehead State University, Graduate Programs, Caudill College of Humanities, Department of Music, Morehead, KY 40351. Offers music education (MM); music performance (MM). *Accreditation:* NASM. Part-time and evening/weekend programs available. *Faculty:* 23 full-time (18 women), 3 part-time/adjunct (1 woman). *Students:* 8 full-time (4 women), 14 part-time (7 women); includes 2 minority (1 African American, 1 Asian American or Pacific Islander), 3 international. Average age 32. In 2006, 8 degrees awarded. *Degree requirements:* For master's, oral and written exams. *Entrance requirements:* For master's, minimum GPA of 3.0 in music, 2.5 overall; audition. Additional exam requirements/recommendations for international students: Required—TOEFL (minimum score 550 paper-based; 173 computer-based). *Application deadline:* For fall admission, 8/1 priority date for domestic and international students; for spring admission, 12/1 priority date for domestic and international students. Applications are processed on a rolling basis. Application fee: $0 ($55 for international students). Electronic applications accepted. *Financial support:* In 2006–07, 8 teaching assistantships (averaging $6,000 per year) were awarded; career-related internships or fieldwork, Federal Work-Study, and unspecified assistantships also available. Financial award application deadline: 4/1; financial award applicants required to submit FAFSA. *Faculty research:* Musical instrument digital interface (MIDI) applications, tonal concepts of euphonium and baritone horn, digital synthesis, computer-assisted instruction in music, musical composition. *Unit head:* Dr. Scott McBride, Chair, 606-783-2473, Fax: 606-783-5004, E-mail: s.mcbride@moreheadstate.edu. *Application contact:* Michelle Barber, Graduate Admissions Counselor, 606-783-2039, Fax: 606-783-5061, E-mail: m.barber@moreheadstate.edu.

Murray State University, College of Humanities and Fine Arts, Program in Music, Murray, KY 42071. Offers music education (MME). *Accreditation:* NASM. Part-time programs available. *Faculty:* 10 full-time (3 women). *Students:* 6. 1 applicant, 100% accepted. In 2006, 6 degrees awarded. *Entrance requirements:* For master's, GRE General Test or MAT. Additional exam requirements/recommendations for international students: Required—TOEFL. *Application deadline:* Applications are processed on a rolling basis. Application fee: $25. *Financial support:* In 2006–07, 1 research assistantship (averaging $4,500 per year), 2 teaching assistantships (averaging $4,500 per year) were awarded; Federal Work-Study also available. Financial award application deadline: 4/1. *Unit head:* Dr. Pamela Wurgler, Graduate Coordinator, 270-809-6337, Fax: 270-809-3965, E-mail: pamela.wurgler@murraystate.edu.

Nazareth College of Rochester, Graduate Studies, Department of Music, Program in Music Education, Rochester, NY 14618-3790. Offers MS Ed. *Accreditation:* NASM; Teacher Education Accreditation Council. Part-time and evening/weekend programs available. *Faculty:* 1 (woman) full-time, 4 part-time/adjunct (2 women). *Students:* 9 applicants, 89% accepted, 5 enrolled. In 2006, 5 degrees awarded. *Entrance requirements:* For master's, audition, minimum GPA of 3.0. *Application deadline:* For fall admission, 4/1 for domestic students; for spring admission, 10/1 for domestic students. Application fee: $40. *Financial support:* Research assistantships with partial tuition reimbursements available. Financial award application deadline: 3/1; financial award applicants required to submit FAFSA. *Unit head:* Dr. Mary Carlson, Director, 585-389-2697, Fax: 585-389-2698, E-mail: mccarlso@naz.edu. *Application contact:* Judith G. Baker, Director, Graduate Admissions, 585-389-2050, Fax: 585-389-2817, E-mail: gradstudies@naz.edu.

New Jersey City University, Graduate and Continuing Education, College of Arts and Sciences, Department of Music, Dance and Theatre, Jersey City, NJ 07305-1597. Offers music education (MA); performance (MM). *Accreditation:* NASM. Evening/weekend programs available. *Faculty:* 9. *Students:* 1 (woman) full-time, 13 part-time (6 women); includes 4 minority (1 African American, 2 Asian Americans or Pacific Islanders, 1 Hispanic American), 1 international. Average age 33. In 2006, 9 degrees awarded. *Degree requirements:* For master's, recital, thesis optional. *Entrance requirements:* For master's, GRE General Test or MAT. Additional exam requirements/recommendations for international students: Required—TOEFL. *Application deadline:* For fall admission, 8/1 priority date for domestic students; for spring admission, 12/1 for domestic students. Applications are processed on a rolling basis. Application fee: $0. *Expenses:* Tuition, state resident: full-time $7,038; part-time $391 per credit. Tuition, nonresident: full-time $12,510; part-time $695 per credit. Required fees: $65 per credit. *Financial support:* Unspecified assistantships available. *Unit head:* Dr. Edward Raditz, Chairperson, 201-200-3157, E-mail: eraditz@njcu.edu.

New York University, Steinhardt School of Culture, Education and Human Development, Department of Music and Performing Arts Professions, Program in Music Education, New York, NY 10012-1019. Offers MA, Ed D, PhD, Advanced Certificate. *Accreditation:* Teacher Education Accreditation Council. Part-time and evening/weekend programs available. *Faculty:* 5 full-time (1 woman). *Students:* 23 full-time (20 women), 22 part-time (14 women); includes 10 minority (2 African Americans, 7 Asian Americans or Pacific Islanders, 1 Hispanic American), 15 international. 40 applicants, 85% accepted, 18 enrolled. In 2006, 15 master's, 2 other advanced degrees awarded. Terminal master's awarded for partial completion of doctoral program. *Degree requirements:* For master's, thesis (for some programs); for doctorate, thesis/dissertation. *Entrance requirements:* For master's, audition; for doctorate, GRE General Test, interview; for Advanced Certificate, master's degree. Additional exam requirements/recommendations for international students: Required—TOEFL. *Application deadline:* For fall admission, 12/15 priority date for domestic and international students; for spring admission, 11/1 for domestic and international students. Applications are processed on a rolling basis. Application fee: $50. *Expenses:* Tuition: Part-time $1,080 per unit. Required fees: $56 per unit. $329 per term. Tuition and fees vary according to program. *Financial support:* Fellowships with full and partial tuition reimbursements, career-related internships or fieldwork, Federal Work-Study, scholarships/grants, and tuition waivers (partial) available. Support available to part-time students. Financial award application deadline: 2/1; financial award applicants required to submit FAFSA. *Faculty research:* Music education philosophy, community music education, integrated curriculum, multiple intelligences, technology in arts education. *Unit head:* Dr. John Gilbert, Director, 212-998-5424, E-mail: john.gilbert@nyu.edu. *Application contact:* 212-998-5030, Fax: 212-995-4328, E-mail: steinhardt.gradadmissions@nyu.edu.

Norfolk State University, School of Graduate Studies, School of Liberal Arts, Department of Music, Norfolk, VA 23504. Offers music (MM); music education (MM); performance (MM); theory and composition (MM). *Accreditation:* NASM. Part-time programs available. *Degree requirements:* For master's, thesis or alternative. *Entrance requirements:* For master's, minimum GPA of 2.7, letters of recommendation. Additional exam requirements/recommendations for international students: Required—TOEFL.

North Dakota State University, The Graduate School, College of Human Development and Education, School of Education, Fargo, ND 58105. Offers agricultural education (M Ed, MS), including agricultural education, agricultural extension education (MS); counseling (M Ed, MS, PhD); curriculum and instruction (M Ed, MS), including pedagogy, physical education and athletic administration; education (PhD); educational leadership (M Ed, MS, Ed S); family and consumer sciences education (M Ed, MS); history education (M Ed, MS); mathematics education (M Ed, MS); music education (M Ed, MS); science education (M Ed, MS). *Accreditation:* NCATE. Part-time and evening/weekend programs available. Postbaccalaureate distance learning degree programs offered (minimal on-campus study). *Faculty:* 25 full-time (9 women), 3 part-time/adjunct (1 woman). *Students:* 29 full-time (25 women), 207 part-time (132 women); includes 15 minority (4 African Americans, 6 American Indian/Alaska Native, 3 Asian Americans or Pacific Islanders, 2 Hispanic Americans), 4 international. 88 applicants, 67% accepted, 56 enrolled. In 2006, 44 master's, 5 doctorates awarded. *Degree requirements:* For master's, comprehensive exam; for doctorate and Ed S, thesis/dissertation. *Entrance requirements:* For degree, GRE General Test, master's degree, minimum GPA of 3.25. Additional exam requirements/recommendations for international students: Required—TOEFL. *Application deadline:* Applications are processed on a rolling basis. Application fee: $45 ($60 for international students). *Financial support:* Research assistantships, teaching assistantships, career-related internships or fieldwork, Federal Work-Study, institutionally sponsored loans, and tuition waivers (full) available. Financial award application deadline: 4/15. *Unit head:* Dr. William O. Martin, Chair, 701-231-7104, Fax: 701-231-7416, E-mail: william.martin@ndsu.edu.

Northern Arizona University, Graduate College, College of Arts and Letters, School of Music, Flagstaff, AZ 86011. Offers choral conducting (MM); instrumental conducting (MM); instrumental performance (MM); music education (MM); music history (MM); theory and composition (MM); vocal performance (MM). *Accreditation:* NASM.

Northwestern University, School of Music, Department of Music Academic Studies and Composition, Evanston, IL 60208. Offers music cognition (PhD); music composition (MM, DM); music education (MM, PhD); music technology (MM, PhD); music theory (MM, PhD); musicology (MM, PhD). PhD admissions and degree offered through The Graduate School. *Accreditation:* NASM. *Degree requirements:* For doctorate, thesis/dissertation, comprehensive exam. *Entrance requirements:* For master's, portfolio or research papers; for doctorate, GRE General Test, portfolio, research papers. Additional exam requirements/recommendations for international students: Required—TOEFL (paper-based 560; computer-based 220) or IELTS (paper-based 6). *Faculty research:* Music cognition, cognitive learning, aesthetic education, computer music, technology in education.

Northwest Missouri State University, Graduate School, College of Arts and Sciences, Department of Music, Maryville, MO 64468-6001. Offers teaching music (MS Ed). *Accreditation:* NASM. Part-time programs available. *Faculty:* 4 full-time (0 women). *Students:* 5 full-time (2 women), 3 part-time (all women). 2 applicants, 100% accepted, 2 enrolled. In 2006, 2 degrees awarded. *Degree requirements:* For master's, comprehensive exam. *Entrance requirements:* For master's, GRE General Test, minimum undergraduate GPA of 2.5, writing sample. Additional exam requirements/recommendations for international students: Required—TOEFL (minimum score 550 paper-based; 213 computer-based). *Application deadline:* For fall admission, 7/1 for domestic and international students; for spring admission, 11/15 for domestic and international students. Applications are processed on a rolling basis. Application fee: $0 ($50 for international students). *Financial support:* In 2006–07, 3 research assistantships with full tuition reimbursements (averaging $6,000 per year) were awarded. Financial award application deadline: 3/1; financial award applicants required to submit FAFSA. *Unit head:* Dr. Ernest Woodruff, Chairperson, 660-562-1317. *Application contact:* Dr. Frances Shipley, Dean of Graduate School, 660-562-1145, Fax: 660-562-1096, E-mail: gradsch@nwmissouri.edu.

Notre Dame de Namur University, Division of Academic Affairs, School of Arts and Humanities, Department of Music, Belmont, CA 94002-1908. Offers music (MM); pedagogy (MM); performance (MM). *Accreditation:* NASM. Part-time and evening/weekend programs available. *Faculty:* 3 full-time (2 women), 8 part-time/adjunct (4 women). *Students:* 2 full-time (1 woman), 12 part-time (11 women); includes 5 Asian Americans or Pacific Islanders, 1 international. Average age 32. 3 applicants, 100% accepted, 3 enrolled. In 2006, 1 degree awarded. *Degree requirements:* For master's, exams. *Entrance requirements:* For master's, audition, appropriate bachelor's degree, minimum GPA of 2.5. Additional exam requirements/recommendations for international students: Required—TOEFL. *Application deadline:* For fall admission, 8/1 priority date for domestic students; for spring admission, 12/1 priority date for domestic students. Applications are processed on a rolling basis. Application fee: $50. Electronic applications accepted. *Expenses:* Tuition: Part-time $655 per credit. *Financial support:* Available to part-time students. Applicants required to submit FAFSA. *Unit head:* Debra Lambert, Chair, 650-580-3694. *Application contact:* Helen Valine, Director of Graduate Admissions, 650-508-3534, Fax: 650-508-3426, E-mail: grad.admit@ndnu.edu.

Oakland University, Graduate Study and Lifelong Learning, College of Arts and Sciences, Department of Music, Rochester, MI 48309-4401. Offers music (MM); music education (PhD). *Accreditation:* NASM. *Faculty:* 12 full-time (2 women), 6 part-time/adjunct (4 women). *Students:* 10 full-time (6 women), 56 part-time (39 women); includes 7 minority (5 African Americans, 1 Asian American or Pacific Islander, 1 Hispanic American), 3 international. Average age 32. 21 applicants, 90% accepted, 13 enrolled. In 2006, 8 master's, 2 doctorates awarded. *Entrance requirements:* For master's, minimum GPA of 3.0 for unconditional admission. Additional exam requirements/recommendations for international students: Required—TOEFL (minimum score 550 paper-based; 213 computer-based). *Application deadline:* For fall admission, 7/15 priority date for domestic students, 5/1 priority date for international students; for winter admission, 12/1 priority date for domestic students, 9/1 priority date for international students; for spring admission, 3/15 priority date for domestic students. Applications are processed on a rolling basis. Application fee: $35. Electronic applications accepted. *Expenses:* Contact institution. *Financial support:* Federal Work-Study, institutionally sponsored loans, and tuition waivers (full) available. Financial award application deadline: 3/1; financial award applicants required to submit FAFSA. *Unit head:* Dr. Jacqueline H. Wiggins, Acting Chair, 248-370-2030, Fax: 248-370-2041, E-mail: jwiggins@oakland.edu.

Ohio University, Graduate Studies, College of Fine Arts, School of Music, Athens, OH 45701-2979. Offers accompanying (MM); composition (MM); conducting (MM); history/literature (MM); music education (MM); music therapy (MM); performance (MM, Certificate); performance/pedagogy (MM); theory (MM). *Accreditation:* NASM. Postbaccalaureate distance learning degree programs offered (minimal on-campus study). *Faculty:* 35 full-time (10 women), 1 part-time/adjunct (0 women). *Students:* 31 full-time (15 women), 13 part-time (7 women); includes 2 minority (both African Americans), 12 international. 49 applicants, 55% accepted, 16 enrolled. In 2006, 22 degrees awarded. *Degree requirements:* For master's, thesis (for some programs), oral exam. *Entrance requirements:* For master's, audition, interview, and/or portfolio. Additional exam requirements/recommendations for international students: Required—TOEFL. *Application deadline:* For fall admission, 8/15 priority date for domestic students. Application fee: $45. *Financial support:* In 2006–07, 35 students received support, including 35 teaching assistantships with full and partial tuition reimbursements available (averaging $4,500 per year); career-related internships or fieldwork, Federal Work-Study, institutionally sponsored loans, and tuition waivers (full and partial) also available. Financial award application deadline: 3/15. *Unit head:* Dr. Richard D. Wetzel, Director, 740-593-4244, Fax: 740-593-1429, E-mail: wetzel@ohio.edu.

Oklahoma State University, College of Arts and Sciences, Department of Music, Stillwater, OK 74078. Offers pedagogy and performance (MM). *Accreditation:* NASM. *Faculty:* 27 full-time (11 women), 4 part-time/adjunct (1 woman). *Students:* 8 full-time (1 woman), 6 part-time (3 women); includes 1 minority (American Indian/Alaska Native), 1 international. Average age 29. 13 applicants, 54% accepted, 7 enrolled. In 2006, 2 degrees awarded. *Degree requirements:* For master's, final project and oral exam. *Entrance requirements:* For master's, audition, minimum GPA of 3.0. Additional exam requirements/recommendations for international students: Required—TOEFL. *Application deadline:* For fall admission, 3/1 priority date for international students; for spring admission, 8/1 priority date for international students. Applications are processed on a rolling basis. Application fee: $40 ($75 for international students). Electronic applications accepted. *Expenses:* Tuition, state resident: part-time $146 per credit hour. Tuition, nonresident: part-time $516 per credit hour. Required fees: $44 per credit hour. Tuition and fees vary according to program. *Financial support:* In 2006–07, 9 teaching assistantships (averaging $8,715 per year) were awarded; scholarships/grants, health care benefits, and unspecified assistantships also available. Financial award application deadline: 3/1. *Faculty research:* Discovery and presentation of music literature of other countries, transportation of ancient music literature to modern notation. *Unit head:* Dr. Julia Combs, Head, 405-744-8997, Fax: 405-744-9324, E-mail: julie.combs@okstate.edu.

Old Dominion University, College of Arts and Letters, Program in Music Education, Norfolk, VA 23529. Offers MME. *Students:* 1 full-time (0 women), 4 part-time (3 women). Average age 34. In 2006, 11 degrees awarded. *Degree requirements:* For master's, thesis (for some programs), recital, comprehensive exam, registration. *Entrance requirements:* For master's, music theory exam, diagnostic examination, baccalaureate degree in music theory, history education, or applied music; audition. *Expenses:* Tuition, area resident: Part-time $285 per credit hour. Tuition, nonresident: part-time $715 per credit hour. Required fees: $94 per semester. *Financial support:* Scholarships/grants and unspecified assistantships available. *Unit head:* Dr. Alfred S. Townsend, Graduate Program Director, 757-683-6562, E-mail: atownsen@odu.edu.

Oregon State University, Graduate School, College of Education, Program in Music Education, Corvallis, OR 97331. Offers MAT. In 2006, 10 degrees awarded. *Degree requirements:* For master's, thesis optional. *Entrance requirements:* For master's, minimum GPA of 3.0 in last 90 hours of course work. Additional exam requirements/recommendations for international students: Required—TOEFL. *Application deadline:* For fall admission, 3/1 for domestic students. Applications are processed on a rolling basis. Application fee: $50. *Financial support:* Teaching assistantships, career-related internships or fieldwork, Federal Work-Study, and institutionally sponsored loans available. Support available to part-time students. Financial award application deadline: 2/1. *Faculty research:* Teaching skills and methods, verbal and nonverbal classroom teaching techniques. *Unit head:* Dr. Kenneth J. Winograd, Chair, 541-737-4661.

Oregon State University, Graduate School, College of Liberal Arts, Department of Music, Corvallis, OR 97331. Offers music education (MAT). *Accreditation:* NCATE. *Degree requirements:* For master's, thesis. *Entrance requirements:* For master's, GRE General Test, NTE, California Basic Educational Skills Test, minimum GPA of 3.0 in last 90 hours of course work. Additional exam requirements/recommendations for international students: Required—TOEFL. *Application deadline:* For fall admission, 3/1 for domestic students. Applications are processed on a rolling basis. Application fee: $50. *Financial support:* Career-related internships or fieldwork, Federal Work-Study, and institutionally sponsored loans available. Support available to part-time students. Financial award application deadline: 2/1. *Unit head:* Dr. Marlan G. Carlson, Chair, 541-737-4061, Fax: 541-737-4268, E-mail: mcarlson@orst.edu. *Application contact:* Dr. Tina Scott, Coordinator, 541-737-5603, Fax: 541-737-2434, E-mail: tscott@orst.edu.

Penn State University Park, Graduate School, College of Arts and Architecture, School of Music, State College, University Park, PA 16802-1503. Offers composition/theory (M Mus); conducting (M Mus); music education (MME, PhD); music theory (MA); music theory and history (MA); musicology (MA); performance (M Mus); piano, pedagogy and performance (M Mus); voice performance and pedagogy (M Mus). *Accreditation:* NASM. *Unit head:* Sue E. Haug, Director, 814-863-0431, Fax: 814-865-6785, E-mail: seh22@psu.edu. *Application contact:* Sue E. Haug, Director, 814-863-0431, Fax: 814-865-6785, E-mail: seh22@psu.edu.

Pittsburg State University, Graduate School, College of Arts and Sciences, Department of Music, Pittsburg, KS 66762. Offers instrumental music education (MM); music history/music literature (MM); performance (MM), including orchestral performance, organ, piano, voice; theory and composition (MM); vocal music education (MM). *Accreditation:* NASM. *Students:* 11. *Degree requirements:* For master's, thesis or alternative. Application fee: $35 ($60 for international students). *Expenses:* Tuition, state resident: full-time $2,144; part-time $181 per credit hour. Tuition, nonresident: full-time $5,273; part-time $442 per credit hour. Tuition and fees vary according to course load and campus/location. *Financial support:* In 2006–07, teaching assistantships (averaging $5,000 per year); career-related internships or fieldwork, Federal Work-Study, and unspecified assistantships also available. *Unit head:* Dr. Craig Fuchs, Chairperson, 620-235-4466. *Application contact:* Jamie Vanderbeck, Assistant Director, 620-235-4223, Fax: 620-235-4219, E-mail: jvanderb@pittstate.edu.

Portland State University, Graduate Studies, School of Fine and Performing Arts, Department of Music, Portland, OR 97207-0751. Offers conducting (MMC); music education (MAT, MST); performance (MMP). *Accreditation:* NASM. Part-time programs available. *Faculty:* 23 full-time (6 women), 19 part-time/adjunct (6 women). *Students:* 24 full-time (12 women), 10 part-time (5 women); includes 2 minority (both Asian Americans or Pacific Islanders), 2 international. Average age 30. 18 applicants, 94% accepted, 14 enrolled. In 2006, 14 degrees awarded. *Entrance requirements:* For master's, departmental exam, GRE General Test, minimum GPA of 3.0 in upper-division course work or 2.75 overall. Additional exam requirements/recommendations for international students: Required—TOEFL (minimum score 550 paper-based; 213 computer-based). *Application deadline:* For fall admission, 8/1 priority date for domestic students, 8/1 for international students; for winter admission, 10/1 for domestic and international students; for spring admission, 2/1 for domestic and international students. Applications are processed on a rolling basis. Application fee: $50. *Expenses:* Tuition, state resident: full-time $6,426; part-time $238 per credit. Tuition, nonresident: full-time $11,016; part-time $408 per credit. Tuition and fees vary according to course load. *Financial support:* Research assistantships with full tuition reimbursements, teaching assistantships with full tuition reimbursements, Federal Work-Study, scholarships/grants, and unspecified assistantships available. Support available to part-time students. Financial award application deadline: 3/1; financial award applicants required to submit FAFSA. *Faculty research:* Composition, music analysis, music history, jazz. Total annual research expenditures: $11,406. *Unit head:* Bryan Johanson, Chair, 503-725-3003, Fax: 503-725-8215.

Queens College of the City University of New York, Division of Graduate Studies, Division of Education, Department of Secondary Education, Flushing, NY 11367-1597. Offers art (MS Ed); biology (MS Ed, AC); chemistry (MS Ed, AC); earth sciences (MS Ed, AC); English (MS Ed, AC); French (MS Ed, AC); Italian (MS Ed, AC); mathematics (MS Ed, AC); music (MS Ed, AC); physics (MS Ed, AC); social studies (MS Ed, AC); Spanish (MS Ed, AC). Part-time and evening/weekend programs available. *Faculty:* 22 full-time (14 women). *Students:* 50 full-time (28 women), 974 part-time (627 women). 633 applicants, 82% accepted, 407 enrolled. In 2006, 227 degrees awarded. *Degree requirements:* For master's, research project; for AC, thesis optional. *Entrance requirements:* For master's, minimum GPA of 3.0. Additional exam requirements/recommendations for international students: Required—TOEFL. *Application deadline:* For fall admission, 4/1 for domestic students; for spring admission, 11/1 for domestic students. Applications are processed on a rolling basis. Application fee: $125. *Financial support:* Career-related internships or fieldwork, Federal Work-Study, institutionally sponsored loans, and tuition waivers (partial) available. Support available to part-time students. Financial award application deadline: 4/1; financial award applicants required to submit FAFSA. *Unit head:* Dr. Eleanor Armour-Thomas, Chairperson, 718-997-5150, E-mail: armourthomas@yahoo.com. *Application contact:* Mario Caruso, Director of Graduate Admissions, 718-997-5200, Fax: 718-997-5193, E-mail: graduate_admissions@qc.edu.

Rhode Island College, School of Graduate Studies, Faculty of Arts and Sciences, Department of Music, Theatre, and Dance, Providence, RI 02908-1991. Offers music education (MAT, MM Ed); theatre (MFA). Part-time and evening/weekend programs available. *Faculty:* 3 full-time (0 women), 5 part-time/adjunct (3 women). *Students:* 18 full-time (12 women), 8 part-time (5 women); includes 1 minority (African American) Average age 31. In 2006, 9 degrees awarded. *Degree requirements:* For master's, thesis, final MFA project, comprehensive exam, registration. *Entrance requirements:* For master's, GRE General Test or MAT, exams in music education, theory, history and literature, audition, 3 letters of recommendation, evidence of musicianship, interview. *Application deadline:* For fall admission, 4/1 for domestic students; for spring admission, 11/1 for domestic students. Applications are processed on a rolling basis. Application fee: $50. *Expenses:* Tuition, state resident: part-time $244 per credit. Tuition, nonresident: part-time $512 per credit. Required fees: $12 per credit. $66 per term. Tuition and fees vary according to degree level, program and reciprocity agreements. *Financial support:* Teaching assistantships with full tuition reimbursements, Federal Work-Study, scholarships/grants, health care benefits, and unspecified assistantships available. Support available to part-time students. Financial award application deadline: 5/15; financial award applicants required to submit FAFSA. *Unit head:* Prof. William Wilson, Chair, 401-456-9516.

Rollins College, Hamilton Holt School, Program in Education, Winter Park, FL 32789-4499. Offers elementary education (M Ed, MAT); secondary education (MAT), including English, mathematics, music. Part-time and evening/weekend programs available. *Students:* 14 full-time (12 women), 36 part-time (32 women); includes 5 minority (2 African Americans, 1 Asian American or Pacific Islander, 2 Hispanic Americans), 1 international. Average age 35. In 2006, 14 degrees awarded. *Degree requirements:* For master's, comprehensive exam. *Entrance requirements:* For master's, GRE or MAT, interview. Additional exam requirements/recommendations for international students: Required—TOEFL. *Application deadline:* For fall admission, 7/16 for domestic students; for winter admission, 12/3 for domestic students; for spring admission, 4/22 for domestic students. Applications are processed on a rolling basis. Application fee: $50. Electronic applications accepted. *Expenses: Contact institution. Financial support:* Teaching assistantships, scholarships/grants available. Support available to part-time students. *Unit head:* Dr. J. Scott Hewit, Director, 407-646-2300, E-mail: jhewit@rollins.edu. *Application contact:* Rebecca Cordray, Coordinator of Records and Registration, 407-646-1568, Fax: 407-975-6430, E-mail: rcordray@rollins.edu.

Roosevelt University, Graduate Division, Chicago College of Performing Arts, The Music Conservatory, Chicago, IL 60605-1394. Offers music (MM); piano pedagogy (Diploma). Part-time and evening/weekend programs available. *Students:* 128 full-time (70 women), 13 part-time (7 women); includes 13 minority (3 African Americans, 4 Asian Americans or Pacific Islanders, 6 Hispanic Americans), 45 international. Average age 27. 256 applicants, 53% accepted, 61 enrolled. In 2006, 44 degrees awarded. *Application deadline:* For fall admission, 6/1 priority date for domestic students. Applications are processed on a rolling basis. Application fee: $25 ($35 for international students). *Financial support:* Federal Work-Study available. Support available to part-time students. Financial award application deadline: 2/15. *Unit head:* Linda Berna, Director, 312-341-3785. *Application contact:* Joanne Canyon-Heller, Coordinator of Graduate Admission, 877-APPLY RU, Fax: 312-281-3356, E-mail: applyru@roosevelt.edu.

Rowan University, Graduate School, College of Education, Department of Special Educational Services/Instruction, Glassboro, NJ 08028-1701. Offers counseling in educational settings (MA); learning disabilities (MA); music education (MA); school psychology (MA, Ed S); special education (MA). *Accreditation:* NCATE. Part-time and evening/weekend programs available. *Students:* 55 full-time (49 women), 167 part-time (151 women); includes 21 minority (10 African Americans, 2 American Indian/Alaska Native, 4 Asian Americans or Pacific Islanders, 5 Hispanic Americans). Average age 31. In 2006, 110 degrees awarded. *Degree requirements:* For master's, thesis, comprehensive exam; for Ed S, thesis or alternative. *Entrance requirements:* For master's and Ed S, GRE General Test. *Application deadline:* Applications are processed on a rolling basis. Application fee: $50. Electronic applications accepted. *Expenses:* Tuition, state resident: full-time $9,882; part-time $549 per credit. Tuition, nonresident: full-time $9,882; part-time $549 per credit. Tuition and fees vary according to degree level. *Financial support:* Career-related internships or fieldwork, Federal Work-Study, and unspecified assistantships available. Support available to part-time students. *Unit head:* Dr. Donna Cook, Chair, 856-256-4767.

Rutgers, The State University of New Jersey, New Brunswick, Mason Gross School of the Arts, Program in Music, New Brunswick, NJ 08901-1281. Offers collaborative piano (MM, DMA); conducting: choral (MM, DMA); conducting: instrumental (MM, DMA); conducting: orchestral (MM, DMA); jazz studies (MM); music (DMA, AD); music education (MM, DMA); music performance (MM). *Accreditation:* NASM. *Faculty:* 36 full-time (10 women), 24 part-time/adjunct (7 women). *Students:* 116 full-time (66 women), 99 part-time (60 women); includes 90 minority (13 African Americans, 71 Asian Americans or Pacific Islanders, 6 Hispanic Americans). Average age 30. 307 applicants, 27% accepted, 51 enrolled. In 2006, 28 master's, 20 doctorates awarded. *Degree requirements:* For doctorate, one foreign language. *Entrance requirements:* For doctorate, audition. Additional exam requirements/recommendations for international students: Required—TOEFL (minimum score 550 paper-based; 213 computer-based). *Application deadline:* For fall admission, 2/1 for domestic students, 11/1 for international students; for spring admission, 11/1 for domestic students, 2/1 for international students. Applications are processed on a rolling basis. Application fee: $50. Electronic applications accepted. *Financial support:* In 2006–07, 98 students received support, including 16 fellowships with full tuition reimbursements available (averaging $6,000 per year), 13 teaching assistantships with partial tuition reimbursements available (averaging $8,860 per year); Federal Work-Study, institutionally sponsored loans, scholarships/grants, and tuition waivers also available. Support available to part-time students. Financial award application deadline: 2/1; financial award applicants required to submit FAFSA. *Faculty research:* Performance, twentieth century music, jazz. *Unit head:* Dr. Richard Chrisman, Graduate Director, 732-932-9272, Fax: 732-932-1517, E-mail: chrisman@rci.rutgers.edu. *Application contact:* Lois Fromer, Senior Administrative Assistant, 732-932-9190, Fax: 732-932-1517, E-mail: fromer@rci.rutgers.edu.

St. Cloud State University, School of Graduate Studies, College of Fine Arts and Humanities, Department of Music, St. Cloud, MN 56301-4498. Offers conducting and literature (MM); music education (MM); piano pedagogy (MM). *Accreditation:* NASM. *Faculty:* 16 full-time (7 women), 1 part-time/adjunct (0 women). *Students:* 8 full-time (4 women), 14 part-time (7 women), 1 international. 6 applicants, 100% accepted. In 2006, 2 degrees awarded. *Degree requirements:* For master's, thesis or alternative, comprehensive exam (for some programs). *Entrance requirements:* For master's, GRE General Test, minimum GPA of 2.75. Additional exam requirements/recommendations for international students: Required—MELAB; Recommended—TOEFL (minimum score 550 paper-based; 213 computer-based), IELTS (minimum score 7). *Application deadline:* For fall admission, 6/1 priority date for domestic students, 4/1 for international students; for spring admission, 10/1 priority date for domestic students, 8/1 for international students. Applications are processed on a rolling basis. Application fee: $35. Electronic applications accepted. *Financial support:* Federal Work-Study, scholarships/grants, and unspecified assistantships available. Financial award application deadline: 3/1. *Unit head:* Dr. Mark Springer, Chairperson, 320-308-3223, Fax: 320-308-2902. *Application contact:* Linda Lou Krueger, School of Graduate Studies, 320-308-2113, Fax: 320-308-5371, E-mail: lekrueger@stcloudstate.edu.

Salisbury University, Graduate Division, Department of Education, Salisbury, MD 21801-6837. Offers art (MAT); biology (MAT); business education (MAT); chemistry (MAT); early childhood education (M Ed); educational administration (M Ed); elementary education (M Ed); English (M Ed, MAT); French (MAT); geography (MAT); history (MAT); mathematics (MAT);

Music Education

Salisbury University (continued)

media and technology (MAT); music (MAT); psychology (MAT); reading education (MAT); science (MAT); secondary education (MAT); social studies (MAT); Spanish (MAT). *Accreditation:* NCATE. Part-time and evening/weekend programs available. *Faculty:* 12 full-time (6 women), 10 part-time/adjunct (8 women). *Students:* 17 full-time (9 women), 84 part-time (72 women); includes 6 minority (5 African Americans, 1 Hispanic American). Average age 30. 15 applicants, 73% accepted, 11 enrolled. In 2006, 63 degrees awarded. *Degree requirements:* For master's, comprehensive exam (for some programs). *Entrance requirements:* For master's, PRAXIS, minimum GPA of 2.75. Additional exam requirements/recommendations for international students: Required—TOEFL (minimum score 550 paper-based; 213 computer-based). *Application deadline:* For fall admission, 8/1 priority date for domestic students; for spring admission, 1/1 for domestic students. Applications are processed on a rolling basis. Application fee: $45. *Expenses:* Tuition, state resident: part-time $260 per credit hour. Tuition, nonresident: part-time $546 per credit hour. Required fees: $52 per credit hour. *Financial support:* In 2006–07, 3 teaching assistantships with full tuition reimbursements were awarded; career-related internships or fieldwork and scholarships/grants also available. Support available to part-time students. Financial award applicants required to submit FAFSA. *Faculty research:* Middle-level education, student outcomes. *Unit head:* Dr. Edward C. Robeck, Program Coordinator, 410-543-6292, Fax: 410-548-2593, E-mail: ecrobeck@salisbury.edu. *Application contact:* Debra J. Clark, Administrative Assistant I, 410-543-6281, Fax: 410-548-2593, E-mail: djclark@salisbury.edu.

Samford University, School of Performing Arts, Birmingham, AL 35229-0002. Offers church music (MM); music education (MME). *Accreditation:* NASM. Part-time programs available. *Faculty:* 11 full-time (3 women), 2 part-time/adjunct (0 women). *Students:* 6 full-time (2 women), 3 part-time (2 women). Average age 24. 1 applicant, 100% accepted, 1 enrolled. In 2006, 3 degrees awarded. *Entrance requirements:* For master's, GRE General Test or MAT. Additional exam requirements/recommendations for international students: Required—TOEFL (minimum score 550 paper-based; 213 computer-based). *Application deadline:* For fall admission, 9/1 for domestic students; for spring admission, 1/20 for domestic students. Application fee: $25. *Expenses:* Tuition: Part-time $500 per credit. One-time fee: $25 part-time. Full-time tuition and fees vary according to program and student level. *Financial support:* In 2006–07, 7 students received support. Federal Work-Study, scholarships/grants, and tuition waivers (partial) available. Financial award application deadline: 9/1. *Faculty research:* Hymnology, choral techniques, assessment of music learning at elementary and secondary levels, piano pedagogy. *Unit head:* Dr. Joseph H. Hopkins, Dean, 205-726-2165, E-mail: jhhopkin@samford.edu. *Application contact:* Dr. Paul Richardson, Assistant Dean for Graduate Studies, 205-726-2496, Fax: 205-726-2165.

Sam Houston State University, College of Arts and Sciences, School of Music, Huntsville, TX 77341. Offers conducting (MM); music (MM); music education (M Ed, MM). *Accreditation:* NASM. Part-time programs available. *Faculty:* 8 full-time (3 women). *Students:* 7 full-time (2 women), 1 (woman) part-time; includes 1 minority (Hispanic American), 2 international. Average age 26. In 2006, 9 degrees awarded. *Degree requirements:* For master's, thesis (for some programs), departmental qualifying exam. *Entrance requirements:* For master's, GRE General Test. Additional exam requirements/recommendations for international students: Required—TOEFL (minimum score 550 paper-based; 213 computer-based). *Application deadline:* For fall admission, 8/1 for domestic students; for spring admission, 12/1 for domestic students. Applications are processed on a rolling basis. Application fee: $20. *Expenses:* Tuition, state resident: full-time $5,904; part-time $164 per semester hour. Tuition, nonresident: full-time $15,804; part-time $439 per semester hour. Required fees: $1,374; $462 per semester. *Financial support:* Teaching assistantships, Federal Work-Study and scholarships/grants available. Financial award application deadline: 5/31; financial award applicants required to submit FAFSA. *Unit head:* Dr. James Bankhead, Chair, 936-294-3808, Fax: 936-294-3765, E-mail: bankhead@shsu.edu. *Application contact:* Scott Plugge, Advisor, 936-294-1393, E-mail: plugge@shsu.edu.

San Diego State University, Graduate and Research Affairs, College of Professional Studies and Fine Arts, School of Music and Dance, San Diego, CA 92182. Offers composition (acoustic and electronic) (MM); conducting (MM); ethnomusicology (MA); jazz studies (MM); musicology (MA); performance (MM); piano pedagogy (MA); theory (MA). *Students:* 31 full-time (16 women), 26 part-time (13 women); includes 10 minority (2 African Americans, 3 Asian Americans or Pacific Islanders, 5 Hispanic Americans), 4 international. Average age 29. 41 applicants, 56% accepted, 9 enrolled. In 2006, 13 degrees awarded. *Degree requirements:* For master's, thesis (for some programs), comprehensive exam (for some programs). *Entrance requirements:* For master's, GRE General Test, bachelor's degree in related field, 2 letters of reference. Additional exam requirements/recommendations for international students: Required—TOEFL. *Application deadline:* For fall admission, 5/1 for domestic and international students; for spring admission, 11/1 for domestic students, 10/1 for international students. Applications are processed on a rolling basis. Application fee: $55. Electronic applications accepted. *Financial support:* Fellowships, teaching assistantships, career-related internships or fieldwork and unspecified assistantships available. Financial award applicants required to submit FAFSA. Total annual research expenditures: $14,000. *Unit head:* Martin Chambers, Director, 619-594-1691, Fax: 619-594-1692, E-mail: mchambers@mail.sdsu.edu. *Application contact:* Martin Chambers, Director, 619-594-1691, Fax: 619-594-1692, E-mail: mchambers@mail.sdsu.edu.

San Francisco State University, Division of Graduate Studies, College of Creative Arts, School of Music and Dance, San Francisco, CA 94132-1722. Offers chamber music (MM); classical performance (MM); composition (MA); conducting (MM); music education (MA); music history (MA). *Accreditation:* NASM. Part-time programs available. *Faculty:* 13 full-time (4 women), 14 part-time/adjunct (3 women). *Students:* 25 (15 women). Average age 29. In 2006, 14 degrees awarded. *Degree requirements:* For master's, thesis (for some programs), culminating project (composition or recital). *Entrance requirements:* For master's, classification exams in music history and theory, minimum GPA of 2.5 in last 60 units. *Application deadline:* For fall admission, 11/30 priority date for domestic students. Applications are processed on a rolling basis. Application fee: $55. *Financial support:* Fellowships, teaching assistantships, Federal Work-Study available. Financial award application deadline: 3/1. *Faculty research:* Music composition, minimal music, conducting, chamber music, performance. *Unit head:* Dr. George DeGaffenreid, Director, 415-338-1432, Fax: 415-338-6159. *Application contact:* Dr. Victoria Neve, Graduate Coordinator, 415-338-1430, E-mail: docvic@sfsu.edu.

Shenandoah University, Shenandoah Conservatory, Winchester, VA 22601-5195. Offers arts administration (MS); church music (MM, Certificate); composition (MM); conducting (MM); dance (MA, MFA, MS); dance accompanying (MM); music (MS); music education (MME, DMA); music therapy (MMT); pedagogy (MM); performance (MM, DMA, Artist Diploma); piano accompanying (MM). *Accreditation:* NASM. Part-time and evening/weekend programs available. *Faculty:* 46 full-time (20 women), 20 part-time/adjunct (7 women). *Students:* 45 full-time (28 women), 113 part-time (67 women), 20 international. Average age 36. 88 applicants, 48% accepted, 33 enrolled. In 2006, 37 master's, 10 doctorates, 4 other advanced degrees awarded. *Degree requirements:* For master's, thesis (for some programs), internship (MS), recital (MM), research teaching project or thesis (MME), project (MA), comprehensive exam (for some programs); for doctorate, thesis/dissertation (for some programs), dissertation or teaching project, comprehensive exam. *Entrance requirements:* Additional exam requirements/recommendations for international students: Required—TOEFL (minimum score 527 paper-based; 197 computer-based; 71 iBT). *Application deadline:* Applications are processed on a rolling basis. Application fee: $30. Electronic applications accepted. *Expenses:* Tuition: Full-time $12,200; part-time $610 per credit. Required fees: $150. Full-time tuition and fees vary according to course load and program. *Financial support:* In 2006–07, 158 students received support, including fellowships with partial tuition reimbursements available (averaging $2,020 per year), teaching assistantships with partial tuition reimbursements available (averaging $5,727 per year); career-related internships or fieldwork, institutionally sponsored loans, scholarships/grants, and unspecified assistantships also available. Support available to part-time students. Financial award application deadline: 3/15; financial award applicants required to submit FAFSA. *Faculty research:* Creative activity, performance practice, music therapy aging, composition, choreography. Total annual research expenditures: $4,272. *Unit head:* Dr. Laurence A. Kaptain, Dean, 540-665-4600, Fax: 540-665-5402, E-mail: lkaptain@su.edu. *Application contact:* David Anthony, Dean of Admissions, 540-665-4581, Fax: 540-665-4627, E-mail: admit@su.edu.

Silver Lake College, Division of Graduate Studies, Program in Music Education, Manitowoc, WI 54220-9319. Offers music education-Kodaly emphasis (MM). *Accreditation:* NASM; NCATE. Part-time programs available. *Faculty:* 1 (woman) full-time, 1 (woman) part-time/adjunct. *Students:* Average age 32. 3 applicants, 67% accepted, 0 enrolled. In 2006, 1 degree awarded. *Degree requirements:* For master's, thesis, comprehensive exam, registration. *Entrance requirements:* For master's, music performance exam, exam in music history and theory and conducting, interview, minimum undergraduate GPA of 3.0, writing sample, three letters of recommendation, audition. Additional exam requirements/recommendations for international students: Required—TOEFL. *Application deadline:* Applications are processed on a rolling basis. Application fee: $35. Electronic applications accepted. *Expenses:* Tuition: Full-time $6,120; part-time $340 per credit. *Financial support:* Career-related internships or fieldwork, Federal Work-Study, and scholarships/grants available. Support available to part-time students. Financial award applicants required to submit FAFSA. *Faculty research:* Effects of prenatal music on bonding and stimulation, music and the brain, early childhood music. *Unit head:* Sr. Lorna Zemke, OSF, DMA, Director, 920-686-6161, Fax: 920-684-7082, E-mail: lzemke@silver.sl.edu. *Application contact:* Jamie Grant, Associate Director- Admissions, 800-236-4752 Ext. 186, Fax: 920-684-7082, E-mail: jgrant@silver.sl.edu.

Southeast Missouri State University, School of Graduate Studies, Department of Music, Cape Girardeau, MO 63701-4799. Offers music education (MME). *Accreditation:* NASM; NCATE. Part-time programs available. *Faculty:* 8 full-time (3 women). *Students:* 1 full-time (0 women), 2 part-time (1 woman). Average age 26. 1 applicant, 100% accepted. In 2006, 2 degrees awarded. *Degree requirements:* For master's, thesis or alternative, project, comprehensive exam (for some programs). *Entrance requirements:* For master's, departmental exam in music theory, audition, minimum GPA of 2.5. *Application deadline:* For fall admission, 8/1 for domestic students, 4/1 for international students; for spring admission, 11/21 for domestic students, 10/1 for international students. Applications are processed on a rolling basis. Application fee: $20 ($100 for international students). Electronic applications accepted. *Financial support:* In 2006–07, 1 student received support. Applicants required to submit FAFSA. *Unit head:* Dr. Christopher Goeke, Chairperson, 573-651-2544, E-mail: cgoeke@semo.edu. *Application contact:* Marsha L. Arant, Senior Administrative Assistant, Office of Graduate Studies, 573-651-2192, Fax: 573-651-2001, E-mail: marant@semo.edu.

Southern Illinois University Carbondale, Graduate School, College of Liberal Arts, School of Music, Carbondale, IL 62901-4701. Offers composition and theory (MM); history and literature (MM); music education (MM); opera/music theater (MM); performance (MM); piano pedagogy (MM). *Accreditation:* NASM. Part-time programs available. *Faculty:* 22 full-time (6 women). *Students:* 11 full-time (4 women), 20 part-time (12 women); includes 4 minority (2 African Americans, 1 Asian American or Pacific Islander, 1 Hispanic American), 4 international. Average age 24. 38 applicants, 50% accepted, 7 enrolled. In 2006, 8 degrees awarded. *Degree requirements:* For master's, one foreign language, thesis or alternative. *Entrance requirements:* For master's, audition, minimum GPA of 2.7. Additional exam requirements/recommendations for international students: Required—TOEFL. *Application deadline:* Applications are processed on a rolling basis. Application fee: $0. *Financial support:* In 2006–07, 16 students received support, including 2 fellowships with full tuition reimbursements available, 12 teaching assistantships with full tuition reimbursements available; research assistantships with full tuition reimbursements available, Federal Work-Study, institutionally sponsored loans, and tuition waivers (full) also available. Support available to part-time students. Financial award application deadline: 4/1. *Faculty research:* Performance practices, historical research, operatic development. *Unit head:* Dr. Robert Weiss, Director, 618-453-2541, E-mail: rweiss@siu.edu. *Application contact:* Dr. Frank Stemper, Graduate Coordinator, 618-536-7505, E-mail: gradmus@siu.edu.

Southern Illinois University Edwardsville, Graduate Studies and Research, College of Arts and Sciences, Department of Music, Edwardsville, IL 62026-0001. Offers music education (MM); music performance (MM). *Accreditation:* NASM. Part-time programs available. *Faculty:* 16 full-time (5 women). *Students:* 10 full-time (5 women), 18 part-time (13 women); includes 2 minority (both African Americans) Average age 33. 14 applicants, 57% accepted. In 2006, 10 degrees awarded. *Degree requirements:* For master's, one foreign language, thesis or alternative, departmental qualifying exam, final exam, recital. *Entrance requirements:* For master's, audition (music performance). Additional exam requirements/recommendations for international students: Required—TOEFL. *Application deadline:* For fall admission, 7/20 for domestic students, 6/1 for international students; for spring admission, 12/14 for domestic students, 10/1 for international students. Application fee: $30. Electronic applications accepted. *Financial support:* In 2006–07, 1 teaching assistantship with full tuition reimbursement was awarded; fellowships with full tuition reimbursements, research assistantships with full tuition reimbursements, Federal Work-Study, institutionally sponsored loans, and unspecified assistantships also available. Support available to part-time students. Financial award application deadline: 3/1. *Unit head:* Dr. Prince Wells, Chair, 618-650-3900, E-mail: pwells@siue.edu. *Application contact:* Dr. Darryl Coan, Director, 618-650-2012, E-mail: dcoan@siue.edu.

Southern Methodist University, Meadows School of the Arts, Division of Music, Dallas, TX 75275. Offers conducting (MM); music composition (MM); music education (MM); music history (MM); music theory (MM); performance (MM, Certificate); piano performance and pedagogy (MM); sacred music (MSM). *Accreditation:* NASM. Part-time programs available. *Faculty:* 34 full-time (10 women), 29 part-time/adjunct (10 women). *Students:* 115 full-time (65 women), 19 part-time (12 women); includes 13 minority (6 African Americans, 1 Asian American or Pacific Islander, 6 Hispanic Americans), 45 international. Average age 25. 125 applicants, 70% accepted, 56 enrolled. In 2006, 39 master's, 12 Certificates awarded. *Entrance requirements:* For master's, placement exams in music history and theory, audition, bachelor's degree in music or equivalent, minimum GPA of 3.0 (research paper in history; theory; education). Additional exam requirements/recommendations for international students: Required—TOEFL (minimum score 550 paper-based; 213 computer-based; 80 iBT). *Application deadline:* For fall admission, 3/1 priority date for domestic and international students; for spring admission, 11/1 for domestic and international students. Applications are processed on a rolling basis. Application fee: $75. *Financial support:* In 2006–07, 77 students received support, including 70 teaching assistantships with full and partial tuition reimbursements available (averaging $4,000 per year); career-related internships or fieldwork, Federal Work-Study, scholarships/grants, tuition waivers (full and partial), and unspecified assistantships also available. Financial award application deadline: 3/1; financial award applicants required to submit FAFSA. *Faculty research:* Music perception and cognition, computer-based instruction, music medicine and therapy, theoretical and historical analysis–medieval to contemporary. *Unit head:* Nancy Cochran, Director, 214-768-1951, Fax: 214-768-4669, E-mail: ncochran@smu.edu. *Application contact:* Jean Cherry, Director of Graduate Admissions and Records, 214-768-3765, Fax: 214-768-3272, E-mail: jcherry@smu.edu.

Southwestern Oklahoma State University, College of Arts and Sciences, Department of Music, Weatherford, OK 73096-3098. Offers music education (MM); performance (MM). *Accreditation:* NASM. Part-time programs available. *Degree requirements:* For master's, recital (music performance). *Entrance requirements:* For master's, minimum GPA of 2.5. Additional exam requirements/recommendations for international students: Required—TOEFL.

State University of New York at Fredonia, Graduate Studies, School of Music, Program in Music Education, Fredonia, NY 14063-1136. Offers MM. *Accreditation:* NASM. Part-time and evening/weekend programs available. *Faculty:* 6 full-time (2 women), 2 part-time/adjunct (1 woman). *Students:* 9 full-time (7 women), 13 part-time (11 women). Average age 27. In 2006,

14 degrees awarded. *Degree requirements:* For master's, thesis optional. *Application deadline:* For fall admission, 8/5 for domestic students; for spring admission, 12/1 for domestic students. Application fee: $50. *Expenses:* Tuition, state resident: full-time $6,900; part-time $288 per credit hour. Tuition, nonresident: full-time $10,920; part-time $455 per credit hour. Required fees: $1,132; $47 per credit hour. *Financial support:* In 2006–07, 3 teaching assistantships with partial tuition reimbursements (averaging $6,620 per year) were awarded; research assistantships, tuition waivers (full and partial) also available. Support available to part-time students. Financial award application deadline: 3/15. *Unit head:* Dr. Karl Boelter, Director, School of Music, 716-673-3151, E-mail: karl.boelter@fredonia.edu.

State University of New York College at Potsdam, Crane School of Music, Potsdam, NY 13676. Offers composition (MM); history and literature (MM); music education (MM); music theory (MM); performance (MM). Part-time programs available. *Faculty:* 12 full-time (4 women), 1 part-time/adjunct (0 women). *Students:* 16 full-time (10 women), 4 part-time (3 women), 1 international. In 2006, 20 degrees awarded. *Degree requirements:* For master's, variable foreign language requirement, thesis. *Entrance requirements:* For master's, audition, minimum GPA of 3.0. Additional exam requirements/recommendations for international students: Required—TOEFL (minimum score 550 paper-based; 213 computer-based). *Application deadline:* For fall admission, 3/1 for domestic students. Applications are processed on a rolling basis. Application fee: $50. *Financial support:* Teaching assistantships with full tuition reimbursements, career-related internships or fieldwork, Federal Work-Study, and scholarships/grants available. Support available to part-time students. Financial award applicants required to submit FAFSA. *Unit head:* Dr. Alan Solomon, Dean, 315-267-2415, Fax: 315-267-2413, E-mail: solomon@postsdam.edu. *Application contact:* Peter Cutler, Graduate Admissions Counselor, 315-267-3154, Fax: 315-267-4802, E-mail: cutlerpj@potsdam.edu.

Syracuse University, Graduate School, School of Education, Department of Teaching and Leadership, Program in Music Education, Syracuse, NY 13244. Offers music education/professional certification (M Mus, MS); music education: teacher preparation (MS). *Accreditation:* NASM. Part-time and evening/weekend programs available. *Students:* 19 full-time (16 women), 9 part-time (6 women); includes 3 minority (1 African American, 1 Asian American or Pacific Islander, 1 Hispanic American). 11 applicants, 82% accepted, 5 enrolled. *Degree requirements:* For master's, thesis or alternative. *Entrance requirements:* For master's, GRE. Additional exam requirements/recommendations for international students: Required—TOEFL. *Application deadline:* For fall admission, 2/1 priority date for domestic students. Applications are processed on a rolling basis. Application fee: $65. Electronic applications accepted. *Expenses:* Tuition: Full-time $16,920; part-time $940 per credit hour. Required fees: $930; $930 per year. *Unit head:* Dr. John Coggiola, Chair, 315-443-5896, E-mail: jecoggio@syr.edu. *Application contact:* Liza Rochelson, Graduate Admission Recruiter, 315-443-2505, Fax: 315-443-2258, E-mail: gradcrt@gwmail.syr.edu.

Teachers College Columbia University, Graduate Faculty of Education, Department of Arts and Humanities, Program in Music and Music Education, New York, NY 10027-6696. Offers Ed M, MA, Ed D, Ed DCT. *Accreditation:* NCATE. Part-time programs available. *Faculty:* 4 full-time (2 women), 12 part-time/adjunct. *Students:* 36 full-time (27 women), 154 part-time (106 women); includes 48 minority (12 African Americans, 29 Asian Americans or Pacific Islanders, 7 Hispanic Americans), 21 international. Average age 32. 127 applicants, 72% accepted, 63 enrolled. In 2006, 75 master's, 15 doctorates awarded. Terminal master's awarded for partial completion of doctoral program. *Degree requirements:* For master's, thesis, project; for doctorate, variable foreign language requirement, thesis/dissertation. *Entrance requirements:* For master's and doctorate, diagnostic exam. *Application deadline:* For fall admission, 5/15 for domestic students. Application fee: $65. *Expenses:* Tuition: Full-time $23,400; part-time $975 per credit. Required fees: $320 per term. *Financial support:* Fellowships, research assistantships, teaching assistantships, career-related internships or fieldwork, Federal Work-Study, institutionally sponsored loans, and tuition waivers (full and partial) available. Support available to part-time students. Financial award application deadline: 2/1. *Faculty research:* Artistry, creativity, and proficiency in production and performance; educational theory and practice; piano pedagogy; research strategies in music pedagogy. *Application contact:* Mark E. Stearns, Associate Director of Admission, 212-678-3710, Fax: 212-678-4171.

Temple University, Graduate School, Esther Boyer College of Music and Dance, Department of Keyboard Instruction, Philadelphia, PA 19122-6096. Offers MM, DMA. Part-time programs available. *Entrance requirements:* Additional exam requirements/recommendations for international students: Required—TOEFL. *Application deadline:* For fall admission, 12/15 for international students; for spring admission, 8/1 for international students. Applications are processed on a rolling basis. Application fee: $50. Electronic applications accepted. *Expenses:* Tuition, state resident: full-time $12,264; part-time $511 per credit. Tuition, nonresident: full-time $17,904; part-time $746 per credit. Required fees: $84 per course. Tuition and fees vary according to program. *Financial support:* Application deadline: 1/15; *Unit head:* Harvey Wedeen, Chair, 215-204-7388, E-mail: hwedeen@temple.edu.

Temple University, Graduate School, Esther Boyer College of Music and Dance, Department of Music Education and Therapy, Philadelphia, PA 19122-6096. Offers music education (MM, PhD); music therapy (MMT, PhD). *Accreditation:* NASM. Part-time and evening/weekend programs available. *Faculty:* 43 full-time (9 women), 75 part-time/adjunct (30 women). *Students:* 16 full-time (13 women), 60 part-time (45 women); includes 4 minority (2 African Americans, 1 Asian American or Pacific Islander, 1 Hispanic American), 9 international. 60 applicants, 50% accepted, 19 enrolled. In 2006, 13 master's, 4 doctorates awarded. *Degree requirements:* For master's and doctorate, thesis/dissertation. *Entrance requirements:* Additional exam requirements/recommendations for international students: Required—TOEFL. *Application deadline:* For fall admission, 12/15 for international students. Applications are processed on a rolling basis. Application fee: $50. Electronic applications accepted. *Expenses:* Tuition, state resident: full-time $12,264; part-time $511 per credit. Tuition, nonresident: full-time $17,904; part-time $746 per credit. Required fees: $84 per course. Tuition and fees vary according to program. *Financial support:* Fellowships, teaching assistantships, career-related internships or fieldwork and Federal Work-Study available. Financial award application deadline: 1/15; financial award applicants required to submit FAFSA. *Faculty research:* Music learning theory, guided imagery in music, computer learning theory. *Unit head:* Dr. Beth Bolton, Chair, 215-204-8310, Fax: 215-204-4957, E-mail: bbolton@temple.edu.

Tennessee State University, The School of Graduate Studies and Research, College of Arts and Sciences, Department of Music, Nashville, TN 37209-1561. Offers music education (MS). *Accreditation:* NASM. *Faculty:* 6 full-time (1 woman). *Students:* 6 full-time (3 women), 4 part-time (2 women); includes 6 minority (5 African Americans, 1 Asian American or Pacific Islander). Average age 30. 5 applicants, 100% accepted, 3 enrolled. In 2006, 2 degrees awarded. *Degree requirements:* For master's, thesis optional. *Entrance requirements:* For master's, MAT. *Application deadline:* Applications are processed on a rolling basis. Application fee: $25. *Faculty research:* Applications of technology in music education; K-12 Jocal, instrumental and general music pedagogy: historical research in American Music education; classical guitar performance practice. *Unit head:* Dr. Robert Elliott, Head, 615-963-5341, E-mail: relliott@tnstate.edu.

Texas A&M University–Commerce, Graduate School, College of Arts and Sciences, Department of Music, Commerce, TX 75429-3011. Offers music (MA, MS); music composition (MA, MM); music education (MA, MM, MS); music literature (MA); music performance (MA, MM); music theory (MA, MM). *Accreditation:* NASM. Part-time programs available. *Degree requirements:* For master's, thesis (for some programs), comprehensive exam. *Entrance requirements:* For master's, GRE General Test. Electronic applications accepted.

Texas A&M University–Kingsville, College of Graduate Studies, College of Arts and Sciences, Department of Music, Kingsville, TX 78363. Offers music education (MM). *Accreditation:* NASM. *Degree requirements:* For master's, thesis or alternative, comprehensive exam. *Entrance requirements:* For master's, GRE General Test, minimum GPA of 3.0. Additional exam requirements/recommendations for international students: Required—TOEFL.

Texas Christian University, College of Fine Arts, School of Music, Fort Worth, TX 76129-0002. Offers conducting (M Mus); music education (MM Ed); musicology (M Mus); organ performance (M Mus); piano (Artist Diploma); piano pedagogy (M Mus); piano performance (M Mus); string performance (M Mus); theory/composition (M Mus); vocal performance (M Mus); voice pedagogy (M Mus); wind and percussion performance (M Mus). *Accreditation:* NASM. Part-time and evening/weekend programs available. *Degree requirements:* For master's, one foreign language, thesis (for some programs). *Entrance requirements:* For master's, GRE General Test, audition or composition/theory, letters of recommendation. Additional exam requirements/recommendations for international students: Required—TOEFL. *Application deadline:* For fall admission, 3/1 for domestic students; for spring admission, 12/1 for domestic students. Applications are processed on a rolling basis. Application fee: $0. *Expenses:* Tuition: Part-time $800 per credit hour. *Financial support:* Unspecified assistantships available. Financial award application deadline: 3/1. *Unit head:* Dr. Richard Gipson, Director, 817-257-7602. *Application contact:* Dr. Joseph Butler, Associate Dean, College of Fine Arts, E-mail: j.butler@tcu.edu.

Texas State University-San Marcos, Graduate School, College of Fine Arts and Communication, School of Music, Program in Music Education, San Marcos, TX 78666. Offers MM. *Accreditation:* NASM. Part-time programs available. *Faculty:* 14 full-time (3 women). *Students:* 2 full-time (1 woman), 6 part-time (3 women); includes 1 minority (Hispanic American) Average age 29. 2 applicants, 100% accepted, 2 enrolled. In 2006, 9 degrees awarded. *Degree requirements:* For master's, comprehensive exam. *Entrance requirements:* For master's, GRE General Test, minimum GPA of 2.75 in last 60 hours of course work. Additional exam requirements/recommendations for international students: Required—TOEFL. *Application deadline:* For fall admission, 6/15 priority date for domestic students; for spring admission, 10/15 priority date for domestic students. Applications are processed on a rolling basis. Application fee: $40 ($90 for international students). *Financial support:* In 2006–07, 4 students received support; teaching assistantships, career-related internships or fieldwork, Federal Work-Study, institutionally sponsored loans, and scholarships/grants available. Support available to part-time students. Financial award application deadline: 4/1; financial award applicants required to submit FAFSA. *Unit head:* Dr. Nico Schuler, Graduate Advisor, 512-245-3396, Fax: 512-245-8181, E-mail: ns13@txstate.edu.

Texas Tech University, Graduate School, College of Visual and Performing Arts, School of Music, Lubbock, TX 79409. Offers composition (MM, DMA); conducting (DMA); music performance (MM); music theory (MM); musicology (MM); pedagogy (MM); performance (DMA); piano pedagogy (DMA). *Accreditation:* NASM. Part-time programs available. *Faculty:* 39 full-time (12 women). *Students:* 85 full-time (32 women), 28 part-time (15 women); includes 9 minority (2 African Americans, 1 American Indian/Alaska Native, 2 Asian Americans or Pacific Islanders, 4 Hispanic Americans), 24 international. Average age 40. 84 applicants, 63% accepted, 28 enrolled. In 2006, 21 master's, 10 doctorates awarded. *Degree requirements:* For master's, thesis (for some programs); for doctorate, thesis/dissertation. *Entrance requirements:* For master's and doctorate, GRE General Test. Additional exam requirements/recommendations for international students: Required—TOEFL (minimum score 550 paper-based; 213 computer-based). *Application deadline:* For fall admission, 3/1 priority date for international students; for spring admission, 11/1 priority date for international students. Applications are processed on a rolling basis. Application fee: $50 ($60 for international students). Electronic applications accepted. *Expenses:* Tuition, state resident: full-time $4,440. Tuition, nonresident: full-time $11,040. Required fees: $2,136. *Financial support:* In 2006–07, 72 students received support, including 1 research assistantship with partial tuition reimbursement available (averaging $7,350 per year), 67 teaching assistantships with partial tuition reimbursements available (averaging $7,525 per year); Federal Work-Study and institutionally sponsored loans also available. Support available to part-time students. Financial award application deadline: 4/15; financial award applicants required to submit FAFSA. *Faculty research:* Strategies for music pedagogy in grades K-12, performance practice of traditional music, role of the woman piano virtuoso, vernacular music center; voice health and culture. *Unit head:* Prof. William Ballenger, School of Music Director, 806-742-2270, Fax: 806-742-2294, E-mail: william.ballenger@ttu.edu. *Application contact:* Janeen Gilliam, Admissions and Scholarship Coordinator, 806-742-2270 Ext. 225, Fax: 806-742-2294, E-mail: janeen.gilliam@ttu.edu.

Towson University, Graduate School, Program in Music Education, Towson, MD 21252-0001. Offers Dalcroze (Certificate); Kodaly (Certificate); music education (MS); Orff (Certificate). *Accreditation:* NASM; NCATE. Part-time and evening/weekend programs available. *Faculty:* 12 full-time (2 women). *Students:* 8 full-time (5 women), 42 part-time (29 women); includes 2 African Americans, 2 Hispanic Americans, 1 international. Average age 24. 12 applicants, 100% accepted, 9 enrolled. In 2006, 9 degrees awarded. *Degree requirements:* For master's, exam, thesis optional. *Entrance requirements:* For master's, bachelor's degree in music education or certification as public school music teacher, minimum GPA of 3.0; for Certificate, bachelor's degree in music or certification as public school music teacher. *Application deadline:* Applications are processed on a rolling basis. Application fee: $50. Electronic applications accepted. *Expenses:* Tuition, state resident: part-time $275 per unit. Tuition, nonresident: part-time $577 per unit. Required fees: $72 per unit. *Financial support:* Federal Work-Study and unspecified assistantships available. Financial award application deadline: 4/1; financial award applicants required to submit FAFSA. *Unit head:* Dr. Michael Jothen, Graduate Program Director, 410-704-2257, Fax: 410-704-3434, E-mail: mjothen@towson.edu. *Application contact:* 410-704-2501, Fax: 410-704-4675, E-mail: grads@towson.edu.

Union College, Graduate Programs, Department of Education, Program in Music Education, Barbourville, KY 40906-1499. Offers MA. *Degree requirements:* For master's, thesis optional. *Entrance requirements:* For master's, GRE General Test, NTE.

Université Laval, Faculty of Music, Programs in Music, Québec, QC G1K 7P4, Canada. Offers composition (M Mus); instrumental didactics (M Mus); interpretation (M Mus); music (PhD); music education (M Mus); musicology (M Mus). Terminal master's awarded for partial completion of doctoral program. *Degree requirements:* For master's, thesis (for some programs); for doctorate, thesis/dissertation, comprehensive exam. *Entrance requirements:* For master's, English exam, audition, knowledge of French; for doctorate, English exam, knowledge of French, third language. Electronic applications accepted.

University at Buffalo, the State University of New York, Graduate School, Graduate School of Education, Department of Learning and Instruction, Buffalo, NY 14260. Offers adolescence education (Certificate); biology (Ed M); chemistry (Ed M); childhood education (Ed M); early childhood and childhood education with bilingual extension (Ed M); early childhood education (Ed M); earth science (Ed M); elementary education (Ed D, PhD); English (Ed M); English education (PhD); English for speakers of other languages (Ed M); foreign and second language education (PhD); French (Ed M); general education (Ed M); German (Ed M); Italian (Ed M); Japanese (Ed M); Latin (Ed M); literary specialist (Ed M); mathematics (Ed M); mathematics education (PhD); mentoring teachers (Certificate); music education (Ed M, Certificate); physics (Ed M); reading education (PhD); Russian (Ed M); school administrator and supervisor (Certificate); science education (PhD); social studies (Ed M); Spanish (Ed M); special education (PhD); teaching and leading for diversity (Certificate); teaching English to speakers of other languages (Ed M). Part-time and evening/weekend programs available. Postbaccalaureate distance learning degree programs offered (no on-campus study). *Faculty:* 30 full-time (20 women), 53 part-time/adjunct (38 women). *Students:* 368 full-time (269 women), 297 part-time (226 women); includes 50 minority (15 African Americans, 2 American Indian/Alaska Native, 14 Asian Americans or Pacific Islanders, 19 Hispanic Americans), 66 international. Average age 31. 638 applicants, 75% accepted, 298 enrolled. In 2006, 248 master's, 18 doctorates, 48 other advanced degrees awarded. Terminal master's awarded for partial completion of doctoral program. *Degree requirements:* For master's, comprehensive exam, registration; for doctorate, thesis/dissertation, research analysis exam, research experience component. *Entrance requirements:* For doctorate, GRE General Test or MAT, interview, writing sample, letters of recommendation. Additional exam requirements/recommendations for international

Music Education

University at Buffalo, the State University of New York (continued)
students: Required—TOEFL (minimum score 600 paper-based; 250 computer-based). *Application deadline:* For fall admission, 2/1 priority date for domestic and international students; for spring admission, 11/15 priority date for domestic students, 10/1 for international students. Applications are processed on a rolling basis. Application fee: $50. Electronic applications accepted. *Financial support:* In 2006–07, 70 students received support, including 6 fellowships with full tuition reimbursements available (averaging $10,000 per year), 16 research assistantships with full tuition reimbursements available (averaging $9,000 per year), teaching assistantships with full tuition reimbursements available (averaging $9,000 per year); career-related internships or fieldwork, Federal Work-Study, institutionally sponsored loans, scholarships/grants, tuition waivers (partial), and unspecified assistantships also available. Financial award application deadline: 2/28; financial award applicants required to submit FAFSA. *Faculty research:* Science assessment, state-level testing, early learning, literacy, second language acquisition. Total annual research expenditures: $432,366. *Unit head:* Dr. Maria E. Runfola, Chair, 716-645-2455, Fax: 716-645-3161. *Application contact:* Barbara Belz, Admissions Secretary, 716-645-2110 Ext. 1159, Fax: 716-645-3161, E-mail: belz@buffalo.edu.

The University of Akron, Graduate School, College of Fine and Applied Arts, School of Music, Program in Music Education, Akron, OH 44325. Offers MM. *Accreditation:* NCATE. *Students:* 7 full-time (6 women), 22 part-time (12 women); includes 2 minority (both African Americans), 1 international. Average age 30. 5 applicants, 60% accepted, 1 enrolled. In 2006, 11 degrees awarded. *Degree requirements:* For master's, thesis optional. *Entrance requirements:* For master's, minimum GPA of 2.75, interview, audition. Additional exam requirements/recommendations for international students: Required—TOEFL (minimum score 550 paper-based; 213 computer-based; 79 iBT). *Application deadline:* For fall admission, 3/31 for domestic students. Applications are processed on a rolling basis. Application fee: $30 ($40 for international students). Electronic applications accepted. *Expenses:* Tuition, state resident: full-time $6,164; part-time $342 per credit. Tuition, nonresident: full-time $10,575; part-time $588 per credit. Required fees: $806; $43 per credit. $12 per term. Tuition and fees vary according to course load, degree level and program. *Unit head:* Laurie Lafferty, Head, 330-972-5761, E-mail: laffert@uakron.edu. *Application contact:* Laurie Lafferty, Head, 330-972-5761, E-mail: laffert@uakron.edu.

The University of Alabama, Graduate School, College of Education, Department of Music Education, Tuscaloosa, AL 35487. Offers choral music education (MA); instrumental music education (MA); music education (Ed D, PhD, Ed S). *Accreditation:* NASM. Part-time programs available. *Students:* Average age 28. 2 applicants. In 2006, 4 master's, 1 doctorate awarded. *Median time to degree:* Of those who began their doctoral program in fall 1998, 100% received their degree in 8 years or less. *Degree requirements:* For master's, thesis optional; for doctorate, thesis/dissertation, oral exam (PhD), comprehensive exam, registration. *Entrance requirements:* For master's and Ed S, GRE or MAT; for doctorate, GRE or MAT, interview, writing sample. Additional exam requirements/recommendations for international students: Required—TOEFL (minimum score 550 paper-based; 213 computer-based). *Application deadline:* For fall admission, 7/1 priority date for domestic students; for spring admission, 11/1 priority date for domestic students. Application fee: $25. *Financial support:* Research assistantships with full and partial tuition reimbursements, teaching assistantships with full and partial tuition reimbursements available. Financial award application deadline: 3/1. *Faculty research:* Elementary music, music for students with special needs, choral music. *Unit head:* Dr. Carol A. Prickett, Department Head and Professor, 205-348-1432, Fax: 205-348-1675, E-mail: cpricket@bama.ua.edu. *Application contact:* Cathie A. Daniels, Office Associate Senior, 205-348-6054, Fax: 205-348-1675, E-mail: cdaniels@bama.ua.edu.

University of Alaska Fairbanks, College of Liberal Arts, Department of Music, Fairbanks, AK 99775-7520. Offers Alaskan ethnomusicology (MA); music education (MA); music history (MA); music theory (MA); performance (MA). *Accreditation:* NASM. Part-time programs available. *Faculty:* 11 full-time (4 women). *Students:* 5 full-time (1 woman), 5 part-time (3 women); includes 1 minority (American Indian/Alaska Native). Average age 35. 6 applicants, 33% accepted, 1 enrolled. In 2006, 1 degree awarded. *Degree requirements:* For master's, thesis or alternative, oral exam, comprehensive exam, registration. *Entrance requirements:* For master's, GRE General Test, BA in music. Additional exam requirements/recommendations for international students: Required—TOEFL (minimum score 550 paper-based; 213 computer-based). *Application deadline:* For fall admission, 6/1 for domestic students, 3/1 for international students; for spring admission, 10/15 for domestic students, 9/1 for international students. Applications are processed on a rolling basis. Application fee: $50. Electronic applications accepted. *Financial support:* In 2006–07, 5 teaching assistantships with tuition reimbursements (averaging $11,093 per year) were awarded; fellowships with tuition reimbursements, Federal Work-Study and scholarships/grants also available. Financial award application deadline: 6/1; financial award applicants required to submit FAFSA. *Faculty research:* Symphony, opera, jazz, chamber and solo performance. *Unit head:* Dr. John R. Hopkins, Chair, 907-474-7555, Fax: 907-474-6420, E-mail: fymusic@uaf.edu.

The University of Arizona, Graduate College, College of Fine Arts, School of Music and Dance, Tucson, AZ 85721. Offers composition (MM, A Mus D); conducting (MM, A Mus D); music education (MM, PhD); music theory (MM, PhD); musicology (MM); performance (MM, A Mus D). *Accreditation:* NASD (one or more programs are accredited); NASM (one or more programs are accredited). Part-time programs available. *Faculty:* 47 full-time (11 women), 10 part-time/adjunct (4 women). *Students:* 125 full-time (64 women), 56 part-time (24 women); includes 21 minority (4 African Americans, 2 American Indian/Alaska Native, 7 Asian Americans or Pacific Islanders, 8 Hispanic Americans), 34 international. Average age 32. 152 applicants, 55% accepted, 54 enrolled. In 2006, 24 master's, 12 doctorates awarded. *Degree requirements:* For master's, thesis or alternative, orals; for doctorate, thesis/dissertation or alternative, comprehensive exam, registration. *Entrance requirements:* For master's and doctorate, minimum GPA of 3.0, audition. Additional exam requirements/recommendations for international students: Required—TOEFL. *Application deadline:* For fall admission, 2/1 for domestic students; for winter admission, 8/1 for domestic students; for spring admission, 8/1 for domestic students. Applications are processed on a rolling basis. Application fee: $50. *Financial support:* In 2006–07, 151 students received support, including 2 fellowships with partial tuition reimbursements available (averaging $10,000 per year), 82 teaching assistantships with partial tuition reimbursements available (averaging $5,225 per year); career-related internships or fieldwork, institutionally sponsored loans, scholarships/grants, health care benefits, and tuition waivers (full) also available. Support available to part-time students. Financial award application deadline: 2/1. *Faculty research:* Music in general education, psychology of music learning, innovation in string music education, Zarzuela, Franz Liszt's work. Total annual research expenditures: $52,880. *Unit head:* Peter McAllister, Director, 520-621-7023, Fax: 520-621-1351, E-mail: pmcallis@email.arizona.edu. *Application contact:* Rex A. Woods, Director of Academic Student Services and Graduate Studies, 520-621-1454, Fax: 520-621-8118, E-mail: rawoods@u.arizona.edu.

The University of British Columbia, Faculty of Graduate Studies, Faculty of Education, Department of Curriculum Studies, Vancouver, BC V6T 1Z1, Canada. Offers art education (M Ed, MA); curriculum studies (M Ed, MA, PhD); home economics education (M Ed, MA); math education (M Ed, MA); music education (M Ed, MA); physical education (M Ed, MA); science education (M Ed, MA); social studies education (M Ed, MA); technical studies education (M Ed, MA). Part-time programs available. *Faculty:* 31 full-time (17 women), 1 (woman) part-time/adjunct. *Students:* 153 full-time (102 women), 101 part-time (67 women), 25 international. Average age 40. 118 applicants, 64% accepted, 62 enrolled. In 2006, 46 master's, 4 doctorates awarded. *Degree requirements:* For master's, thesis (MA); for doctorate, thesis/dissertation, comprehensive exam, registration. *Entrance requirements:* Additional exam requirements/recommendations for international students: Required—TOEFL (minimum score 580 paper-based; 237 computer-based). *Application deadline:* For fall admission, 2/1 for domestic students, 1/1 for international students; for spring admission, 10/1 for domestic students, 9/1 for international students. Application fee: $90 ($150 for international students). Electronic applications accepted. *Expenses: Contact institution. Financial support:* In 2006–07, 10 fellowships with partial tuition reimbursements (averaging $16,000 per year), 11 research assistantships with partial tuition reimbursements (averaging $14,000 per year), 27 teaching assistantships with partial tuition reimbursements (averaging $14,000 per year) were awarded; tuition waivers (partial) also available. *Faculty research:* School subjects, teaching and learning. *Unit head:* Dr. Linda Peterat, Interim Head, 604-822-5422, Fax: 604-822-4714. *Application contact:* Basia Zurek, Graduate Secretary, 604-822-5367, Fax: 604-822-4714, E-mail: cust.grad@ubc.ca.

University of Central Arkansas, Graduate School, College of Fine Arts and Communication, Department of Music, Conway, AR 72035-0001. Offers choral conducting (MM); instrumental conducting (MM); music education (MM); music theory (MM); performance (MM). *Accreditation:* NASM. Part-time programs available. *Faculty:* 17 full-time (4 women), 1 part-time/adjunct (0 women). *Students:* 15 full-time (7 women), 3 part-time; includes 1 minority (African American), 1 international. 10 applicants, 100% accepted, 10 enrolled. In 2006, 5 degrees awarded. *Degree requirements:* For master's, thesis optional. *Entrance requirements:* For master's, GRE General Test, minimum GPA of 2.7. Additional exam requirements/recommendations for international students: Required—TOEFL (minimum score 550 paper-based; 213 computer-based). *Application deadline:* For fall admission, 3/1 priority date for domestic students; for spring admission, 10/1 priority date for domestic students. Applications are processed on a rolling basis. Application fee: $25 ($40 for international students). *Expenses:* Tuition, state resident: full-time $4,194; part-time $233 per semester. Tuition, nonresident: full-time $5,963; part-time $429 per semester. International tuition: $6,162 full-time. Required fees: $65; $23 per semester. One-time fee: $65 part-time. *Financial support:* Federal Work-Study, scholarships/grants, tuition waivers (partial), and unspecified assistantships available. Financial award application deadline: 2/15; financial award applicants required to submit FAFSA. *Unit head:* Jeffrey Jarvis, Unit Head, 501-450-3163. *Application contact:* Brenda Herring, Admissions Assistant, 501-450-5065, Fax: 501-450-5678, E-mail: bherring@uca.edu.

University of Central Florida, College of Education, Department of Teaching and Learning Principles, Program in Music Education, Orlando, FL 32816. Offers M Ed, MA. *Accreditation:* NASM; NCATE. Part-time and evening/weekend programs available. *Students:* 2 full-time (1 woman), 22 part-time (15 women); includes 4 minority (3 African Americans, 1 Hispanic American). In 2006, 8 degrees awarded. *Entrance requirements:* For master's, GRE General Test. Additional exam requirements/recommendations for international students: Required—TOEFL. *Application deadline:* For fall admission, 7/15 for domestic students; for spring admission, 12/1 for domestic students. Application fee: $30. Electronic applications accepted. *Expenses:* Tuition, state resident: full-time $6,167; part-time $257 per credit hour. Tuition, nonresident: full-time $22,790; part-time $950 per credit hour. *Financial support:* Fellowships with partial tuition reimbursements, research assistantships with partial tuition reimbursements, teaching assistantships with partial tuition reimbursements, career-related internships or fieldwork, Federal Work-Study, institutionally sponsored loans, tuition waivers (partial), and unspecified assistantships available. Financial award application deadline: 3/1; financial award applicants required to submit FAFSA. *Unit head:* Dr. Mary Palmer, Coordinator, 407-823-3397, E-mail: mpalmer@pagasus.cc.ucf.edu.

University of Central Oklahoma, College of Graduate Studies and Research, College of Arts, Media, and Design, Department of Music, Edmond, OK 73034-5209. Offers music education (MM); performance (MM). *Accreditation:* NASM. Part-time programs available. *Entrance requirements:* Additional exam requirements/recommendations for international students: Required—TOEFL (minimum score 550 paper-based; 213 computer-based). Electronic applications accepted. *Faculty research:* Opera/orchestral composition, western/world music, ethnomusicology, literature for librettos.

University of Cincinnati, Division of Research and Advanced Studies, College-Conservatory of Music, Division of Music Education, Cincinnati, OH 45221. Offers MM. *Accreditation:* NASM; NCATE. *Degree requirements:* For master's, paper or thesis. *Entrance requirements:* For master's, GRE General Test, interview. Additional exam requirements/recommendations for international students: Required—TOEFL (minimum score 520 paper-based; 190 computer-based). Electronic applications accepted. *Faculty research:* Choral, orchestral, and wind conducting; Kodaly; Orff-Schulwerk; jazz studies; string education.

University of Colorado at Boulder, Graduate School, College of Music, Boulder, CO 80309. Offers church music (M Mus); composition (M Mus, D Mus A); conducting (M Mus, D Mus A); music education (M Mus Ed, PhD); music literature (M Mus); musicology (PhD); pedagogy (M Mus, D Mus A); performance (M Mus, D Mus A). *Accreditation:* NASM. *Faculty:* 48 full-time (18 women). *Students:* 192 full-time (98 women), 52 part-time (23 women); includes 22 minority (2 African Americans, 2 American Indian/Alaska Native, 10 Asian Americans or Pacific Islanders, 8 Hispanic Americans), 32 international. Average age 31. 186 applicants, 82% accepted. In 2006, 46 master's, 14 doctorates awarded. Terminal master's awarded for partial completion of doctoral program. *Degree requirements:* For master's, variable foreign language requirement, thesis or alternative, recital, comprehensive exam; for doctorate, variable foreign language requirement, thesis/dissertation. *Entrance requirements:* For master's, GRE General Test, GRE Subject Test (music literature), minimum undergraduate GPA of 2.75; for doctorate, GRE General Test, GRE Subject Test, audition, sample of research. *Application deadline:* For fall admission, 3/1 priority date for domestic students, 12/1 for international students. Applications are processed on a rolling basis. Application fee: $50 ($60 for international students). *Financial support:* In 2006–07, 150 fellowships (averaging $3,030 per year), 11 teaching assistantships (averaging $8,294 per year) were awarded; tuition waivers (full) also available. Financial award application deadline: 3/1. Total annual research expenditures: $14,833. *Unit head:* Daniel P. Sher, Dean, 303-492-7505, Fax: 303-492-5619, E-mail: daniel.sher@colorado.edu. *Application contact:* Associate Dean for Graduate Studies, 303-492-2207, Fax: 303-492-5619, E-mail: gradmusc@colorado.edu.

University of Connecticut, Graduate School, School of Fine Arts, Department of Music, Field of Music, Storrs, CT 06269. Offers conducting (M Mus, DMA); historical musicology (MA); music (Performer's Certificate); music education (M Mus, PhD); music theory (MA); music theory and history (PhD); performance (M Mus, DMA). *Accreditation:* NASM. *Faculty:* 17 full-time (3 women). *Students:* 35 full-time (17 women), 29 part-time (17 women); includes 4 minority (2 Asian Americans or Pacific Islanders, 2 Hispanic Americans), 11 international. Average age 31. 73 applicants, 48% accepted, 31 enrolled. In 2006, 14 master's, 1 doctorate, 1 other advanced degree awarded. Terminal master's awarded for partial completion of doctoral program. *Degree requirements:* For master's, comprehensive exam; for doctorate, thesis/dissertation. *Entrance requirements:* For master's, GRE General Test, GRE Subject Test, audition; for doctorate, GRE Subject Test, MAT, audition. Additional exam requirements/recommendations for international students: Required—TOEFL (minimum score 550 paper-based; 213 computer-based). *Application deadline:* For fall admission, 2/1 priority date for domestic and international students; for spring admission, 11/1 for domestic students, 10/1 for international students. Applications are processed on a rolling basis. Application fee: $55. Electronic applications accepted. *Financial support:* In 2006–07, 6 research assistantships, 23 teaching assistantships with full tuition reimbursements were awarded; fellowships, Federal Work-Study, health care benefits, and unspecified assistantships also available. Financial award application deadline: 2/1; financial award applicants required to submit FAFSA. *Unit head:* Richard Bass, Director, 860-486-4197, E-mail: richard.bass@uconn.edu. *Application contact:* Debbie Trahan, Administrative Assistant, 860-486-3731, E-mail: dtrahan@finearts.sfa.uconn.edu.

University of Dayton, Graduate School, School of Education and Allied Professions, Department of Teacher Education, Dayton, OH 45469-1300. Offers adolescent/young adult (MS Ed); art education (MS Ed); early childhood education (MS Ed); inclusive early childhood (MS Ed); interdisciplinary education (MS Ed); intervention specialist education, mild/moderate (MS Ed); literacy (MS Ed); middle childhood (MS Ed); multi-age education (MS Ed); music education (MS Ed); teacher as leader (MS Ed); technology in education (MS Ed). Part-time and evening/

weekend programs available. *Faculty:* 13 full-time (9 women), 33 part-time/adjunct (25 women). *Students:* 149 full-time (120 women), 284 part-time (241 women); includes 37 minority (31 African Americans, 3 Asian Americans or Pacific Islanders, 3 Hispanic Americans), 3 international. Average age 33. 201 applicants, 58% accepted, 31 enrolled. In 2006, 150 degrees awarded. *Degree requirements:* For master's, thesis, capstone research project. *Entrance requirements:* For master's, GRE General Test, minimum GPA of 2.75. Additional exam requirements/recommendations for international students: Required—TOEFL (minimum score 550 paper-based; 213 computer-based). *Application deadline:* For fall admission, 3/15 priority date for domestic students, 3/1 priority date for international students. Applications are processed on a rolling basis. Application fee: $0. Electronic applications accepted. *Expenses: Contact institution. Financial support:* In 2006–07, 8 teaching assistantships with partial tuition reimbursements (averaging $7,600 per year) were awarded; career-related internships or fieldwork, institutionally sponsored loans, health care benefits, and unspecified assistantships also available. Financial award applicants required to submit FAFSA. *Faculty research:* Diversity, literacy, art representation by young children, preservice teacher preparation. Total annual research expenditures: $330,000. *Unit head:* Dr. Katie A. Kinnucan-Welsch, Chair, 937-229-3346. *Application contact:* Erika Eavers, Graduate Admission Processor, 937-229-3065, Fax: 937-229-4729, E-mail: erika.eavers@notes.udayton.edu.

University of Delaware, College of Arts and Sciences, Department of Music, Newark, DE 19716. Offers composition (MM); music education (MM); performance (MM). *Accreditation:* NASM. Part-time programs available. *Entrance requirements:* For master's, audition. Additional exam requirements/recommendations for international students: Required—TOEFL. Electronic applications accepted. *Faculty research:* Teaching of music.

University of Denver, Faculty of Arts and Humanities/Social Sciences, Lamont School of Music, Denver, CO 80208. Offers composition (MA); conducting (MA); jazz and commercial music (Certificate); music (MM); music education (MA); music history and literature (MA); Orff-Schulwerk (MA); performance (MA); piano pedagogy (MA); Suzuki pedagogy (MA); Suzuki teaching (Certificate); theory (MA). *Accreditation:* NASM. Part-time programs available. *Faculty:* 24 full-time (6 women). *Students:* 18 full-time (8 women), 40 part-time (15 women); includes 3 minority (all Hispanic Americans), 8 international. Average age 30. 61 applicants, 67% accepted. In 2006, 13 degrees awarded. *Degree requirements:* For master's, thesis (for some programs), recital or project, 2 years language (performance, music history and literature). *Entrance requirements:* For master's, GRE General Test, music history and theory qualifying exams. Additional exam requirements/recommendations for international students: Required—TOEFL. *Application deadline:* Applications are processed on a rolling basis. Application fee: $50. Electronic applications accepted. *Expenses:* Tuition: Full-time $29,628; part-time $823 per credit. *Financial support:* In 2006–07, 36 teaching assistantships with full and partial tuition reimbursements (averaging $4,300 per year) were awarded; career-related internships or fieldwork, Federal Work-Study, institutionally sponsored loans, and scholarships/grants also available. Support available to part-time students. Financial award application deadline: 4/15; financial award applicants required to submit FAFSA. *Unit head:* Joseph Docksey, Director, 303-871-6973. *Application contact:* Graduate Adviser, 303-871-6973, E-mail: marhuels@du.edu.

University of Florida, Graduate School, College of Fine Arts, School of Music, Gainesville, FL 32611. Offers choral conducting (MM, PhD); composition/theory (MM, PhD); ethnomusicology (PhD); instrumental conducting (MM, PhD); music (MM, PhD); music education (MM, PhD); music history and literature (MM); musicology (PhD); performance (MM); sacred music (MM). *Accreditation:* NASM. *Faculty:* 37 full-time (9 women). *Students:* 118 (61 women); includes 18 minority (6 African Americans, 1 American Indian/Alaska Native, 2 Asian Americans or Pacific Islanders, 9 Hispanic Americans) 21 international. In 2006, 29 master's, 9 doctorates awarded. *Degree requirements:* For master's, variable foreign language requirement, thesis; for doctorate, thesis/dissertation. *Entrance requirements:* For master's and doctorate, audition, GRE General Test or minimum GPA of 3.0. Additional exam requirements/recommendations for international students: Required—TOEFL (minimum score 550 paper-based; 213 computer-based). *Application deadline:* For fall admission, 6/1 priority date for domestic students. Applications are processed on a rolling basis. Application fee: $30. Electronic applications accepted. *Expenses:* Tuition, state resident: full-time $6,827. Tuition, nonresident: full-time $21,951. Required fees: $999. *Financial support:* In 2006–07, 1 research assistantship with tuition reimbursement (averaging $8,000 per year), 27 teaching assistantships with tuition reimbursements (averaging $9,632 per year) were awarded; fellowships with full tuition reimbursements, unspecified assistantships also available. *Unit head:* Will Kesling, Program Director, 352-392-0223 Ext. 207. *Application contact:* Dr. Leslie Odom, Coordinator, 352-392-0223 Ext. 231, Fax: 352-352-0461, E-mail: lodom@ufl.edu.

University of Georgia, Graduate School, College of Education, Program in Music Education, Athens, GA 30602. Offers MM Ed, Ed D, Ed S. *Accreditation:* NASM; NCATE. *Students:* 15 full-time (8 women), 43 part-time (25 women); includes 5 minority (4 African Americans, 1 Hispanic American). 36 applicants, 67% accepted, 11 enrolled. In 2006, 16 master's, 7 other advanced degrees awarded. *Degree requirements:* For doctorate, thesis/dissertation. *Entrance requirements:* For master's, GRE General Test, MAT; for doctorate, GRE General Test; for Ed S, GRE General Test or MAT. *Application deadline:* For fall admission, 7/1 priority date for domestic students; for spring admission, 11/15 for domestic students. Application fee: $50. Electronic applications accepted. *Financial support:* Fellowships, research assistantships, teaching assistantships, unspecified assistantships available. *Unit head:* Dr. Donald R. Lowe, Director, 706-542-3737, Fax: 706-542-2773, E-mail: dlowe@uga.edu. *Application contact:* Dr. Kenneth M. Fischer, Graduate Coordinator, 206-542-2743, Fax: 206-542-2773, E-mail: kfischer@uga.edu.

University of Hartford, The Hartt School, West Hartford, CT 06117-1599. Offers choral conducting (MM Ed); composition (MM, DMA, Artist Diploma, Diploma); conducting (MM, DMA, Artist Diploma, Diploma), including choral (MM, Diploma), instrumental (MM, Diploma); early childhood education (MM Ed); instrumental conducting (MM Ed); Kodály (MM Ed); music (CAGS); music education (DMA, PhD); music history (MM); music theory (MM); pedagogy (MM Ed); performance (MM, MM Ed, DMA, Artist Diploma, Diploma); research (MM Ed); technology (MM Ed). *Accreditation:* NASM. Part-time programs available. *Faculty:* 37 full-time (5 women), 33 part-time/adjunct (16 women). *Students:* 108 full-time (53 women), 31 part-time (19 women); includes 11 minority (6 African Americans, 4 Asian Americans or Pacific Islanders, 1 Hispanic American), 31 international. Average age 29. 163 applicants, 55% accepted, 55 enrolled. In 2006, 49 master's, 9 doctorates, 10 other advanced degrees awarded. *Degree requirements:* For master's and doctorate, variable foreign language requirement, thesis/dissertation (for some programs), recital; for other advanced degree, recital. *Entrance requirements:* For master's, audition, letters of recommendation; for doctorate, proficiency exam, audition, interview, research paper; for other advanced degree, audition. Additional exam requirements/recommendations for international students: Required—TOEFL. *Application deadline:* For fall admission, 4/1 priority date for domestic students. Applications are processed on a rolling basis. Application fee: $40 ($55 for international students). Electronic applications accepted. *Expenses: Contact institution. Financial support:* Fellowships, teaching assistantships, Federal Work-Study available. Support available to part-time students. Financial award application deadline: 6/1; financial award applicants required to submit FAFSA. *Unit head:* Dr. Malcolm Morrison, Dean, 860-768-4468, E-mail: morrison@mail.hartford.edu. *Application contact:* Lynne Johnson, Director of Admissions, 860-768-4115, Fax: 860-768-4441, E-mail: johnson@hartford.edu.

University of Houston, College of Liberal Arts and Social Sciences, Moores School of Music, Houston, TX 77204. Offers accompanying (MM); applied music (MM); composition (MM, DMA); conducting (DMA); music education (MM, DMA); music literature (MM); music performance and pedagogy (MM); music theory (MM); performance (DMA). *Accreditation:* NASM. Part-time programs available. *Faculty:* 27 full-time (7 women), 19 part-time/adjunct (8 women). *Students:* 88 full-time (40 women), 34 part-time (18 women); includes 18 minority (7 African Americans, 4 Asian Americans or Pacific Islanders, 7 Hispanic Americans), 22 international. Average age 30. 81 applicants, 60% accepted, 34 enrolled. In 2006, 35 master's, 7 doctorates awarded. *Degree requirements:* For master's, variable foreign language requirement, thesis (for some programs), departmental comprehensive exam, recital; for doctorate, one foreign language, thesis/dissertation, departmental qualifying exam, recitals. *Entrance requirements:* For master's, GRE General Test, audition; for doctorate, GRE General Test, GRE Subject Test, audition. *Application deadline:* For fall admission, 7/1 priority date for domestic students. Applications are processed on a rolling basis. Application fee: $0 ($75 for international students). *Expenses:* Tuition, state resident: full-time $5,429; part-time $226 per credit. Tuition, nonresident: full-time $12,029; part-time $501 per credit. Required fees: $2,454. *Financial support:* In 2006–07, 48 teaching assistantships with full tuition reimbursements (averaging $9,800 per year) were awarded; fellowships with full tuition reimbursements, research assistantships with full tuition reimbursements, career-related internships or fieldwork, Federal Work-Study, institutionally sponsored loans, scholarships/grants, health care benefits, and unspecified assistantships also available. Support available to part-time students. Financial award application deadline: 3/10. *Faculty research:* Twentieth century music, baroque music, history of music theory, music analysis. *Unit head:* David Ashley White, Chairperson, 713-743-3009, Fax: 713-743-3166, E-mail: daw@orpheus.music.uh.edu. *Application contact:* Howard Pollack, Director of Graduate Studies, 713-743-3314, Fax: 713-743-3166.

The University of Iowa, Graduate College, College of Education, Department of Teaching and Learning, Program in Secondary Education, Iowa City, IA 52242-1316. Offers art education (MA, PhD); curriculum and supervision (PhD); curriculum supervision (MA); developmental reading (MA); English education (MA, MAT, PhD); foreign language education (MA, MAT); foreign language/ESL education (PhD); language, literature and culture (PhD); math education (PhD); mathematics education (MA); music education (MA, PhD); social studies (MA, PhD). *Faculty:* 11 full-time. *Students:* 53 full-time (33 women), 53 part-time (41 women); includes 5 minority (1 African American, 1 American Indian/Alaska Native, 2 Asian Americans or Pacific Islanders, 1 Hispanic American), 19 international. 66 applicants, 47% accepted, 17 enrolled. In 2006, 22 master's, 14 doctorates awarded. *Degree requirements:* For master's, exam, thesis optional; for doctorate, thesis/dissertation, comprehensive exam, registration. *Entrance requirements:* For master's and doctorate, GRE General Test, minimum GPA of 3.0. Additional exam requirements/recommendations for international students: Required—TOEFL (minimum score 550 paper-based; 213 computer-based; 81 iBT). Application fee: $60 ($85 for international students). Electronic applications accepted. *Financial support:* In 2006–07, 1 fellowship, 12 research assistantships with partial tuition reimbursements, 31 teaching assistantships with partial tuition reimbursements were awarded. Financial award applicants required to submit FAFSA. *Unit head:* Gary Sasso, Chair, 319-335-5324, Fax: 319-335-5608.

University of Kansas, Graduate Studies, School of Fine Arts, Department of Music and Dance, Program in Music Education, Lawrence, KS 66045. Offers MME, PhD. *Faculty:* 7 full-time (4 women), 1 part-time/adjunct (0 women). *Students:* 6 full-time (all women), 19 part-time (15 women); includes 1 minority (Asian American or Pacific Islander), 1 international. Average age 35. 12 applicants, 42% accepted. In 2006, 2 master's, 2 doctorates awarded. *Degree requirements:* For master's, thesis optional; for doctorate, thesis/dissertation, comprehensive exam, registration. *Entrance requirements:* For master's, GRE, minimum GPA of 3.0; for doctorate, GRE, MEMT diagnostic exam, minimum graduate GPA of 3.5. Additional exam requirements/recommendations for international students: Required—TOEFL. *Application deadline:* For fall admission, 3/15 for domestic and international students; for spring admission, 8/15 for domestic and international students. Applications are processed on a rolling basis. Application fee: $55 ($60 for international students). Electronic applications accepted. *Expenses:* Tuition, area resident: Part-time $227 per credit. Tuition, state resident: part-time $543 per credit. Tuition and fees vary according to course load, campus/location, program and reciprocity agreements. *Financial support:* Fellowships, research assistantships with partial tuition reimbursements, teaching assistantships with full and partial tuition reimbursements, institutionally sponsored loans, scholarships/grants, and unspecified assistantships available. Financial award application deadline: 12/15; financial award applicants required to submit FAFSA. *Faculty research:* Music theory. *Application contact:* George Duerksen, Director of Graduate Studies, 785-864-9632, Fax: 785-864-5866, E-mail: gduerksen@ku.edu.

University of Kentucky, Graduate School, College of Fine Arts, Program in Music, Lexington, KY 40506-0032. Offers music (PhD); music composition (MM); music education (MM); music performance (MM); music theory (MA); musical arts (DMA); musicology (MA). *Accreditation:* NASM. Part-time and evening/weekend programs available. *Faculty:* 31 full-time (8 women). *Students:* 122 full-time (62 women), 30 part-time (15 women); includes 18 minority (11 African Americans, 2 American Indian/Alaska Native, 2 Asian Americans or Pacific Islanders, 3 Hispanic Americans), 14 international. Average age 34. 103 applicants, 50% accepted, 30 enrolled. In 2006, 20 master's, 7 doctorates awarded. *Median time to degree:* Of those who began their doctoral program in fall 1998, 67% received their degree in 8 years or less. *Degree requirements:* For master's, variable foreign language requirement, thesis (for some programs), comprehensive exam; for doctorate, variable foreign language requirement, thesis/dissertation, comprehensive exam. *Entrance requirements:* For master's, GRE General Test, minimum undergraduate GPA of 2.75; for doctorate, GRE General Test, minimum undergraduate GPA of 2.75, graduate work GPA of 3.0. Additional exam requirements/recommendations for international students: Required—TOEFL (minimum score 550 paper-based; 213 computer-based). *Application deadline:* For fall admission, 7/17 priority date for domestic students, 2/1 priority date for international students; for spring admission, 12/13 priority date for domestic students, 6/15 priority date for international students. Application fee: $40 ($55 for international students). Electronic applications accepted. *Expenses:* Tuition, state resident: full-time $7,670; part-time $401 per credit hour. Tuition, nonresident: full-time $16,158; part-time $873 per credit hour. *Financial support:* In 2006–07, 10 fellowships with full tuition reimbursements (averaging $3,845 per year), 14 research assistantships with full tuition reimbursements (averaging $7,603 per year), 45 teaching assistantships with full tuition reimbursements (averaging $10,438 per year) were awarded; Federal Work-Study, institutionally sponsored loans, scholarships/grants, traineeships, health care benefits, tuition waivers (partial), and unspecified assistantships also available. Support available to part-time students. Financial award application deadline: 3/15; financial award applicants required to submit FAFSA. *Faculty research:* Musicology, music theory, jazz, music education, performance and conducting. Total annual research expenditures: $23,000. *Unit head:* Dr. Cecilia Wang, Director of Graduate Studies, 859-230-2306, Fax: 859-257-9576. *Application contact:* Dr. Brian Jackson, Senior Associate Dean, 859-257-4667, Fax: 859-257-4676, E-mail: brian.jackson@uky.edu.

University of Louisiana at Lafayette, Graduate School, College of the Arts, School of Music, Lafayette, LA 70504. Offers conducting (MM); pedagogy (MM); vocal and instrumental performance (MM). *Accreditation:* NASM. *Faculty:* 14 full-time (5 women). *Students:* 13 full-time (6 women), 4 part-time (1 woman), 1 international. Average age 25. 8 applicants, 63% accepted, 5 enrolled. In 2006, 7 degrees awarded. *Degree requirements:* For master's, thesis or alternative, registration. *Entrance requirements:* For master's, GRE General Test, minimum GPA of 2.75. Additional exam requirements/recommendations for international students: Required—TOEFL (minimum score 550 paper-based; 213 computer-based). *Application deadline:* For fall admission, 5/15 for domestic and international students; for spring admission, 10/1 for domestic and international students. Applications are processed on a rolling basis. Application fee: $25 ($30 for international students). Electronic applications accepted. *Expenses:* Tuition, state resident: full-time $3,247; part-time $93 per credit hour. Tuition, nonresident: full-time $9,427; part-time $350 per credit hour. *Financial support:* In 2006–07, 12 research assistantships with full tuition reimbursements (averaging $5,500 per year) were awarded; fellowships, teaching assistantships, Federal Work-Study and unspecified assistantships also available. Financial award application deadline: 5/1. *Faculty research:* Nineteenth century American music, trumpet pedagogy, fifteenth century Renaissance polyphony, Charles Ives. *Unit head:* Dr. A. C. Himes, Head, 337-482-6016, Fax: 337-482-5017, E-mail: ach5291@louisiana.edu. *Application contact:* Dr. Andrea Loewy, Graduate Coordinator, 337-482-5214, Fax: 337-482-5017, E-mail: akl9749@louisiana.edu.

University of Louisville, Graduate School, College of Education and Human Development, Department of Teaching and Learning, Program in Music Education, Louisville, KY 40292-

Music Education

University of Louisville (continued)
0001. Offers MAT. *Accreditation:* NCATE. *Students:* 4 full-time (all women). Average age 24. In 2006, 4 degrees awarded. *Entrance requirements:* For master's, GRE General Test. *Application deadline:* Applications are processed on a rolling basis. Application fee: $50. Electronic applications accepted. *Financial support:* Fellowships, research assistantships, teaching assistantships, Federal Work-Study and scholarships/grants available. *Unit head:* Dr. Robert Amchin, Head, 502-852-0536, Fax: 502-852-0520, E-mail: robert.amchin@louisville.edu.

University of Louisville, Graduate School, School of Music, Program in Music Education, Louisville, KY 40292-0001. Offers MAT, MME. *Accreditation:* NASM. Part-time programs available. *Students:* 1 full-time (0 women), 4 part-time (2 women); includes 1 minority (African American) Average age 30. In 2006, 1 degree awarded. *Degree requirements:* For master's, thesis. *Entrance requirements:* For master's, GRE General Test, music history and theory exam, audition. *Application deadline:* For fall admission, 3/15 priority date for domestic students; for winter admission, 10/1 priority date for domestic students. Applications are processed on a rolling basis. Application fee: $50. *Financial support:* Teaching assistantships with full and partial tuition reimbursements available. *Unit head:* Dr. Robert A. Amchin, Division Head, 502-852-0536, Fax: 502-852-0520, E-mail: raamch01@louisville.edu.

University of Maryland, College Park, Graduate Studies, College of Arts and Humanities, School of Music, Program in Music, College Park, MD 20742. Offers M Ed, MA, MM, DMA, Ed D, PhD. *Students:* 208 full-time (125 women), 73 part-time (38 women); includes 36 minority (9 African Americans, 21 Asian Americans or Pacific Islanders, 6 Hispanic Americans), 78 international. 534 applicants, 19% accepted, 58 enrolled. In 2006, 45 master's, 49 doctorates awarded. *Median time to degree:* Of those who began their doctoral program in fall 1998, 53% received their degree in 8 years or less. *Entrance requirements:* Additional exam requirements/recommendations for international students: Required—TOEFL. *Application deadline:* For fall admission, 12/1 for domestic students, 2/1 for international students; for spring admission, 11/1 for domestic students, 6/1 for international students. Application fee: $60. *Financial support:* In 2006–07, 2 fellowships (averaging $13,476 per year) were awarded. *Application contact:* Dean of Graduate School, 301-405-0358, Fax: 301-314-9305.

University of Massachusetts Lowell, Graduate School, College of Arts and Sciences, Department of Music, Department of Music Education, Lowell, MA 01854-2881. Offers MM. *Accreditation:* NASM; NCATE. Part-time programs available. *Degree requirements:* For master's, one foreign language, thesis. *Entrance requirements:* For master's, MAT, audition.

University of Memphis, Graduate School, College of Communication and Fine Arts, Rudi E. Scheidt School of Music, Memphis, TN 38152. Offers applied music (M Mu); composition (M Mu, DMA); music education (M Mu, DMA); music history (M Mu); musicology (PhD); Orff-Schulwerk (M Mu); performance (DMA); piano pedagogy (M Mu); sacred music (M Mu, DMA); Suzuki pedagogy-piano/strings (M Mu). *Accreditation:* NASM. Part-time programs available. Terminal master's awarded for partial completion of doctoral program. *Degree requirements:* For master's, thesis or alternative, comprehensive exam; for doctorate, one foreign language, thesis/dissertation, exam, comprehensive exam, registration. *Entrance requirements:* For master's, GRE General Test or MAT, proficiency exam, audition; for doctorate, GRE General Test or MAT, proficiency exam, audition, master's degree. Additional exam requirements/recommendations for international students: Required—TOEFL. *Faculty research:* Spanish Renaissance, twentieth century music, Project OPTIMUS, composition, musical performance, regional music, performance, performance practice, composition.

University of Miami, Graduate School, Frost School of Music, Department of Music Education and Music Therapy, Coral Gables, FL 33124. Offers music education (MM, PhD, Spec M); music therapy (MM). *Accreditation:* NASM; NCATE. *Students:* 19 full-time (12 women), 4 part-time (3 women); includes 2 minority (both Hispanic Americans), 6 international. Average age 30. 25 applicants, 56% accepted, 8 enrolled. In 2006, 6 master's, 6 doctorates awarded. *Degree requirements:* For master's, thesis; for doctorate and Spec M, thesis/dissertation, 2 research tools; for Spec M, thesis, research project. *Entrance requirements:* For master's and doctorate, GRE General Test. Additional exam requirements/recommendations for international students: Required—TOEFL. *Application deadline:* For fall admission, 2/1 priority date for domestic and international students; for spring admission, 11/1 priority date for domestic and international students. Applications are processed on a rolling basis. Application fee: $65. Electronic applications accepted. *Financial support:* In 2006–07, fellowships with full tuition reimbursements (averaging $8,000 per year), 4 teaching assistantships with full tuition reimbursements (averaging $7,850 per year) were awarded; tuition waivers (partial) also available. Financial award application deadline: 2/1. *Unit head:* Dr. Joyce Jordan, Chair and Director, 305-284-6252. *Application contact:* Dr. Edward Paul Asmus, Associate Dean for Graduate Studies, 305-284-2241, Fax: 305-284-6475, E-mail: ed.asmus@miami.edu.

University of Michigan, Horace H. Rackham School of Graduate Studies, The School of Music, Theatre, and Dance, Program in Music Education, Ann Arbor, MI 48109. Offers MM, PhD, Spec M. *Accreditation:* NASM. *Degree requirements:* For doctorate, 2 foreign languages, thesis/dissertation, oral and preliminary exams. *Entrance requirements:* For doctorate, MAT, writing sample, portfolio. Additional exam requirements/recommendations for international students: Required—TOEFL (minimum score 600 paper-based; 250 computer-based). Electronic applications accepted.

University of Minnesota, Duluth, Graduate School, School of Fine Arts, Department of Music, Duluth, MN 55812-2496. Offers music education (MM); performance (MM). *Accreditation:* NASM. Part-time programs available. *Faculty:* 14 full-time (4 women), 2 part-time/adjunct (1 woman). *Students:* 5 full-time (3 women), 4 part-time (3 women). Average age 31. 1 applicant, 100% accepted, 1 enrolled. In 2006, 3 degrees awarded. *Degree requirements:* For master's, thesis (for some programs), recital (MM in performance), comprehensive exam. *Entrance requirements:* For master's, audition, minimum GPA of 3.0, sample of written work, interview, bachelor's degree in music, video of teaching. Additional exam requirements/recommendations for international students: Required—TOEFL (minimum score 550 paper-based; 213 computer-based). *Application deadline:* For fall admission, 7/15 for domestic students; for spring admission, 11/15 for domestic students. Applications are processed on a rolling basis. Application fee: $55 ($75 for international students). *Financial support:* In 2006–07, 9 students received support, including 8 fellowships (averaging $1,200 per year), 1 teaching assistantship with tuition reimbursement available (averaging $6,000 per year); Federal Work-Study, institutionally sponsored loans, scholarships/grants, and unspecified assistantships also available. *Faculty research:* Band composition, music aesthetics, learning theory, value theory, music advocacy. *Unit head:* Dr. Judith Kritzmire, Director of Graduate Studies, 218-726-8260, Fax: 218-726-8210, E-mail: jkritzmire@d.umn.edu.

University of Missouri–Columbia, Graduate School, College of Education, Department of Curriculum and Instruction, Columbia, MO 65211. Offers agricultural education (M Ed, PhD, Ed S); art education (M Ed, PhD, Ed S); business and office education (M Ed, PhD, Ed S); early childhood education (M Ed, PhD, Ed S); elementary education (M Ed, PhD, Ed S); English education (M Ed, PhD, Ed S); foreign language education (M Ed, PhD, Ed S); health education and promotion (M Ed, PhD); learning and instruction (M Ed); marketing education (M Ed, PhD, Ed S); mathematics education (M Ed, PhD, Ed S); music education (M Ed, PhD, Ed S); reading education (M Ed, PhD, Ed S); science education (M Ed, PhD, Ed S); social studies education (M Ed, PhD, Ed S); vocational education (M Ed, PhD, Ed S). Part-time programs available. *Faculty:* 24 full-time (12 women). *Students:* 195 full-time (148 women), 260 part-time (214 women); includes 27 minority (8 African Americans, 1 American Indian/Alaska Native, 10 Asian Americans or Pacific Islanders, 8 Hispanic Americans), 19 international. In 2006, 186 master's, 12 doctorates awarded. Terminal master's awarded for partial completion of doctoral program. *Degree requirements:* For doctorate, thesis/dissertation. *Entrance requirements:* For master's and Ed S, GRE General Test or MAT, minimum GPA of 3.0; for doctorate, GRE General Test, minimum GPA of 3.0. *Application deadline:* Applications are processed on a rolling basis. Application fee: $45 ($60 for international students). *Financial support:* Fellowships, research assistantships, teaching assistantships, institutionally sponsored loans available. *Unit head:* Dr. Lloyd H. Barrow, Director of Graduate Studies, 573-882-8247, E-mail: robinsonr@missouri.edu.

University of Missouri–Kansas City, Conservatory of Music, Kansas City, MO 64110-2499. Offers composition (MM, DMA); conducting (MM, DMA); music (MA); music education (MME, PhD); music history and literature (MM); music theory (MM); performance (MM, DMA). *Accreditation:* NASM. Part-time programs available. *Faculty:* 52 full-time (21 women), 35 part-time/adjunct (17 women). *Students:* 138 full-time (78 women), 100 part-time (50 women); includes 14 minority (3 African Americans, 3 American Indian/Alaska Native, 6 Asian Americans or Pacific Islanders, 2 Hispanic Americans), 54 international. Average age 29. 228 applicants, 56% accepted, 74 enrolled. In 2006, 36 master's, 9 doctorates awarded. *Degree requirements:* For master's, variable foreign language requirement, thesis (for some programs), comprehensive exam; for doctorate, variable foreign language requirement, thesis/dissertation or alternative, comprehensive exam. *Entrance requirements:* For master's, minimum GPA of 3.0 in major, auditions (performance); for doctorate, minimum graduate GPA of 3.5, auditions (performance degrees), portfolio of compositions. Additional exam requirements/recommendations for international students: Required—TOEFL (minimum score 550 paper-based; 213 computer-based). *Application deadline:* For fall admission, 3/1 priority date for domestic students, 2/1 for international students; for winter admission, 1/5 priority date for domestic students, 11/1 for international students; for spring admission, 4/15 for domestic students. Application fee: $35 ($50 for international students). *Expenses:* Tuition, state resident: full-time $4,975; part-time $276 per credit. Tuition, nonresident: full-time $12,847; part-time $713 per credit. Required fees: $595; $595 per year. *Financial support:* In 2006–07, 135 students received support, including 95 teaching assistantships with partial tuition reimbursements available (averaging $8,526 per year); fellowships with partial tuition reimbursements available, career-related internships or fieldwork, Federal Work-Study, institutionally sponsored loans, scholarships/grants, tuition waivers (partial), and unspecified assistantships also available. Support available to part-time students. *Faculty research:* Electro-acoustic composition, affective music responses, American music theatre, Russian choral music, music therapy and Alzheimer's. *Unit head:* Dr. Randall G. Pembrook, Dean, 816-235-2731, Fax: 816-235-5265, E-mail: pembrookr@umkc.edu. *Application contact:* James Elswick, Associate Director, 816-235-2932, Fax: 816-235-5264, E-mail: cadmissions@umkc.edu.

University of Missouri–St. Louis, College of Fine Arts and Communication, Program in Music Education, St. Louis, MO 63121. Offers MME. *Accreditation:* NASM. Part-time and evening/weekend programs available. *Faculty:* 16 full-time (7 women). *Students:* 2 full-time (1 woman), 28 part-time (16 women); includes 2 minority (1 African American, 1 Hispanic American). Average age 32. In 2006, 5 degrees awarded. *Entrance requirements:* For master's, departmental test, 3 letters of recommendation. Additional exam requirements/recommendations for international students: Required—TOEFL (minimum score 550 paper-based; 213 computer-based). *Application deadline:* For fall admission, 7/15 priority date for domestic students; for spring admission, 12/15 for domestic students. Applications are processed on a rolling basis. Application fee: $35 ($40 for international students). Electronic applications accepted. *Expenses:* Tuition, state resident: part-time $332 per credit hour. Tuition, nonresident: part-time $770 per credit hour. *Faculty research:* Music technology, musicology, music education methods, history of music education, psychology of music. *Unit head:* Dr. Fred Willman, Director of Graduate Studies, 314-516-5980, Fax: 314-516-6593, E-mail: fred_willman@umsl.edu. *Application contact:* 314-516-5458, Fax: 314-516-6996, E-mail: gradadm@umsl.edu.

The University of Montana, Graduate School, School of Fine Arts, Department of Music, Missoula, MT 59812-0002. Offers music (MM), including composition/technology, music education, musical theater, performance. *Accreditation:* NASM. *Entrance requirements:* For master's, GRE General Test, GRE Subject Test, portfolio.

University of Nebraska at Kearney, College of Graduate Study, College of Fine Arts and Humanities, Department of Music, Kearney, NE 68849-0001. Offers music education (MA Ed). *Accreditation:* NASM; NCATE. Part-time and evening/weekend programs available. *Faculty:* 11 full-time (4 women). *Students:* 1 applicant, 0% accepted. *Degree requirements:* For master's, thesis optional. *Entrance requirements:* For master's, interview/audition, portfolio, letters of recommendation. *Application deadline:* For fall admission, 5/1 for domestic and international students; for spring admission, 8/15 for domestic and international students. Application fee: $45. *Expenses:* Tuition, state resident: part-time $161 per hour. Tuition, nonresident: part-time $332 per hour. Required fees: $57 per hour. *Financial support:* Career-related internships or fieldwork and scholarships/grants available. Support available to part-time students. Financial award application deadline: 3/1; financial award applicants required to submit FAFSA. *Faculty research:* Contemporary American music, musical theatre, opera, woodwind performance and pedagogy. *Unit head:* Dr. Valerie Cisler, Chair, 308-865-8618, E-mail: cislerv@unk.edu.

University of Nevada, Las Vegas, Graduate College, College of Fine Arts, Department of Music, Las Vegas, NV 89154-9900. Offers applied music (performance) (MM); composition/theory (MM); music education (MM); performance studies (DMA). *Accreditation:* NASM. Part-time programs available. *Faculty:* 30 full-time (6 women), 12 part-time/adjunct (1 woman). *Students:* 55 full-time (21 women), 35 part-time (16 women); includes 10 minority (4 African Americans, 1 American Indian/Alaska Native, 4 Asian Americans or Pacific Islanders, 1 Hispanic American), 9 international. 67 applicants, 64% accepted, 31 enrolled. In 2006, 25 degrees awarded. *Degree requirements:* For master's, oral and/or written comprehensive exam, thesis optional; for doctorate, lecture-recital and document. *Entrance requirements:* For master's, minimum GPA of 3.0. Additional exam requirements/recommendations for international students: Required—TOEFL (minimum score 550 paper-based; 213 computer-based; 80 iBT). *Application deadline:* For fall admission, 6/15 for domestic students, 5/1 for international students; for spring admission, 11/15 for domestic students, 10/1 for international students. Application fee: $60 ($75 for international students). Electronic applications accepted. *Financial support:* In 2006–07, 20 teaching assistantships with partial tuition reimbursements (averaging $11,000 per year) were awarded; career-related internships or fieldwork, Federal Work-Study, institutionally sponsored loans, scholarships/grants, health care benefits, and unspecified assistantships also available. Support available to part-time students. Financial award application deadline: 3/1. *Unit head:* Dr. Bill Bernatis, Interim Chair, 702-895-3332. *Application contact:* Graduate College Admissions Evaluator, 702-895-3320, Fax: 702-895-4180, E-mail: gradcollege@unlv.edu.

University of New Hampshire, Graduate School, College of Liberal Arts, Department of Music, Durham, NH 03824. Offers music education (MA); music history (MA). *Accreditation:* NASM. *Faculty:* 15 full-time. *Students:* 2 full-time (both women), 10 part-time (3 women). Average age 35. 4 applicants, 100% accepted, 1 enrolled. In 2006, 7 degrees awarded. *Degree requirements:* For master's, one foreign language. *Entrance requirements:* For master's, audition. Additional exam requirements/recommendations for international students: Required—TOEFL (minimum score 550 paper-based; 213 computer-based). *Application deadline:* For fall admission, 4/1 priority date for domestic students; for winter admission, 12/1 for domestic students. Applications are processed on a rolling basis. Application fee: $60. Electronic applications accepted. *Expenses:* Tuition, state resident: full-time $8,540; part-time $474 per credit hour. Tuition, nonresident: full-time $20,990; part-time $862 per credit hour. Required fees: $1,343; $356 per term. Tuition and fees vary according to course load, program and reciprocity agreements. *Financial support:* In 2006–07, 4 teaching assistantships were awarded; fellowships, research assistantships, career-related internships or fieldwork, Federal Work-Study, scholarships/grants, and tuition waivers (full and partial) also available. Support available to part-time students. Financial award application deadline: 2/15. *Unit head:* Dr. Mark DeTurk, Chairperson, 603-862-3244. *Application contact:* Dr. Isabel Gray, Administrative Assistant, 603-862-2418, E-mail: grad.music@unh.edu.

The University of North Carolina at Chapel Hill, Graduate School, School of Education, Program in Secondary Education, Chapel Hill, NC 27599. Offers English (Grades 9-12) (MAT); French (Grades K-12) (MAT); German (Grades K-12) (MAT); Japanese (Grades K-12) (MAT);

Latin (Grades 9-12) (MAT); mathematics (Grades 9-12) (MAT); music (Grades K-12) (MAT); science (Grades 9-12) (MAT); social studies/social science (Grades 9-12) (MAT); Spanish (Grades K-12) (MAT). *Accreditation:* NCATE. In 2006, 72 degrees awarded. *Degree requirements:* For master's, comprehensive exam. *Entrance requirements:* For master's, GRE General Test, minimum GPA of 3.0 during last 2 years of undergraduate course work. Additional exam requirements/recommendations for international students: Required—TOEFL (minimum score 550 paper-based; 213 computer-based), ACTFL oral proficiency interview. *Application deadline:* For fall admission, 1/1 priority date for domestic and international students. Applications are processed on a rolling basis. Application fee: $60. Electronic applications accepted. *Financial support:* Federal Work-Study available. Support available to part-time students. Financial award application deadline: 3/1; financial award applicants required to submit FAFSA. *Faculty research:* Curriculum and instruction, teacher education per subject. *Unit head:* Dr. James Trier, Coordinator, 919-843-4627. *Application contact:* Janet Carroll, Registrar, 919-962-8690, Fax: 919-962-1533, E-mail: jscarrol@email.unc.edu.

The University of North Carolina at Charlotte, Graduate School, College of Education, Program in Teacher Education, Charlotte, NC 28223-0001. Offers art education (K-12) (MAT); dance education (K-12) (MAT); elementary education (K-6) (MAT); English as a second language (K-12) (MAT); foreign language education (K-12) (MAT); general teacher education (MAT); middle grades education (6-9) (MAT); music education (K-12) (MAT); secondary education (9-12) (MAT); special education (K-12) (MAT); theatre education (K-12) (MAT). *Students:* 16 full-time (12 women), 200 part-time (170 women); includes 30 minority (22 African Americans, 2 American Indian/Alaska Native, 2 Asian Americans or Pacific Islanders, 4 Hispanic Americans), 2 international. Average age 33. 74 applicants, 85% accepted, 49 enrolled. In 2006, 43 degrees awarded. *Entrance requirements:* For master's, GRE or MAT. Additional exam requirements/recommendations for international students: Required—TOEFL (minimum score 557 paper-based; 220 computer-based). *Application deadline:* For fall admission, 7/1 for domestic students, 5/1 for international students; for spring admission, 11/1 for domestic students, 10/1 for international students. Applications are processed on a rolling basis. Application fee: $55. Electronic applications accepted. *Expenses:* Tuition, state resident: full-time $2,719; part-time $170 per credit. Tuition, nonresident: full-time $12,926; part-time $808 per credit. Required fees: $1,555. *Financial support:* Fellowships, research assistantships, teaching assistantships, career-related internships or fieldwork, Federal Work-Study, institutionally sponsored loans, scholarships/grants, and unspecified assistantships available. Support available to part-time students. Financial award application deadline: 4/1; financial award applicants required to submit FAFSA. *Unit head:* Dr. Kimberly J. Hartman, Coordinator, 704-687-8883, Fax: 704-687-6430, E-mail: khartman@email.uncc.edu. *Application contact:* Kathy B. Giddings, Director of Graduate Admissions, 704-687-3366, Fax: 704-687-3279, E-mail: gradadm@email.uncc.edu.

The University of North Carolina at Greensboro, Graduate School, School of Music, Greensboro, NC 27412-5001. Offers composition (MM); education (MM); music education (PhD); performance (MM, DMA). *Faculty:* 56 full-time (14 women), 11 part-time/adjunct (5 women). *Students:* 138 full-time (79 women), 56 part-time (34 women); includes 26 minority (13 African Americans, 1 American Indian/Alaska Native, 10 Asian Americans or Pacific Islanders, 2 Hispanic Americans). 213 applicants, 41% accepted. *Degree requirements:* For master's, variable foreign language requirement, thesis (for some programs), recital; for doctorate, thesis/dissertation, diagnostic exam, recital, comprehensive exam. *Entrance requirements:* For master's, GRE General Test, NTE, audition; for doctorate, GRE General Test, GRE Subject Test (music), audition. Additional exam requirements/recommendations for international students: Required—TOEFL. *Application deadline:* For fall admission, 3/1 for domestic students. Application fee: $45. Electronic applications accepted. *Expenses:* Tuition, state resident: full-time $2,692. Tuition, nonresident: full-time $13,742. *Financial support:* Fellowships with full tuition reimbursements, research assistantships with full tuition reimbursements, teaching assistantships with full tuition reimbursements, unspecified assistantships available. *Unit head:* Dr. John J. Deal, Dean, 336-334-5789, Fax: 336-334-5497, E-mail: jjdeal@uncg.edu. *Application contact:* Michelle Harkleroad, Director of Graduate Admissions, 336-334-4884, Fax: 336-334-4424, E-mail: mbharkle@uncg.edu.

The University of North Carolina at Pembroke, Graduate Studies, Program in Music Education, Pembroke, NC 28372-1510. Offers MA, MAT. *Accreditation:* NASM. *Faculty:* 2 full-time (1 woman). *Students:* 7 applicants, 100% accepted, 7 enrolled. In 2006, 5 degrees awarded. *Entrance requirements:* For master's, GRE or MAT, minimum GPA of 3.0 in major, 2.5 overall; audition, philosophy of music statement. Additional exam requirements/recommendations for international students: Required—TOEFL. *Application deadline:* For fall admission, 7/15 priority date for domestic and international students; for spring admission, 12/1 priority date for domestic and international students. Application fee: $40. *Expenses:* Tuition, state resident: full-time $3,516; part-time $1,091 per semester. Tuition, nonresident: full-time $12,924; part-time $4,619 per semester. Tuition and fees vary according to class time, course load, degree level and campus/location. *Financial support:* In 2006–07, research assistantships with full tuition reimbursements (averaging $6,000 per year); unspecified assistantships also available. Support available to part-time students. *Unit head:* Dr. Janita K. Byars, Director, 910-521-5704, Fax: 910-521-6390, E-mail: janita.byars@uncp.edu. *Application contact:* Dr. Kathleen C. Hilton, Dean of Graduate Studies, 910-521-6271, Fax: 910-521-6751, E-mail: grad@uncp.edu.

University of North Dakota, Graduate School, College of Arts and Sciences, Department of Music, Grand Forks, ND 58202. Offers music (M Mus); music education (M Mus, DMEd). *Accreditation:* NASM. Part-time programs available. *Faculty:* 15 full-time (6 women). *Students:* 6 full-time (4 women), 7 part-time (3 women); includes 1 Asian American or Pacific Islander, 2 international. 6 applicants, 17% accepted, 1 enrolled. In 2006, 4 degrees awarded. *Degree requirements:* For master's, thesis or alternative, comprehensive exam. *Entrance requirements:* For master's, minimum GPA of 3.0. Additional exam requirements/recommendations for international students: Required—TOEFL (minimum score 550 paper-based; 213 computer-based; 79 iBT), IELTS (minimum score 6). *Application deadline:* For fall admission, 2/15 priority date for domestic and international students; for spring admission, 10/15 priority date for domestic and international students. Applications are processed on a rolling basis. Application fee: $35. Electronic applications accepted. *Expenses:* Tuition, state resident: full-time $5,650; part-time $214 per credit. Tuition, nonresident: full-time $14,248; part-time $572 per credit. Required fees: $1,008; $42 per credit. Tuition and fees vary according to reciprocity agreements. *Financial support:* In 2006–07, 2 teaching assistantships with full tuition reimbursements (averaging $5,950 per year) were awarded; fellowships, research assistantships, Federal Work-Study, institutionally sponsored loans, scholarships/grants, and tuition waivers (full and partial) also available. Support available to part-time students. Financial award application deadline: 3/15; financial award applicants required to submit FAFSA. *Unit head:* Dr. Royce Blackburn, Graduate Director, 701-777-2644, Fax: 701-777-3320, E-mail: royce_blackburn@und.nodak.edu. *Application contact:* Brenda Halle, Admissions Specialist, 701-777-2947, Fax: 701-777-3619, E-mail: brendahalle@mail.und.edu.

University of Northern Colorado, Graduate School, College of Performing and Visual Arts, School of Music, Greeley, CO 80639. Offers collaborative keyboard (MM); conducting (MM); instrumental performance (MM); jazz studies (MM); music conducting (DA); music education (MM, DA); music history and literature (MM, DA); music performance (DA); music theory and composition (MM, DA); vocal performance (MM). *Accreditation:* NASM; NCATE (one or more programs are accredited). Part-time programs available. *Faculty:* 29 full-time (10 women). *Students:* 78 full-time (37 women), 16 part-time (5 women); includes 2 minority (1 African American, 1 Asian American or Pacific Islander), 8 international. Average age 31. 63 applicants, 94% accepted, 32 enrolled. In 2006, 23 master's, 8 doctorates awarded. *Degree requirements:* For master's, thesis or alternative, comprehensive exam; for doctorate, thesis/dissertation, comprehensive exam. *Entrance requirements:* For master's, audition; for doctorate, GRE General Test, audition, 3 letters of recommendation. *Application deadline:* Applications are processed on a rolling basis. Application fee: $50 ($60 for international students). Electronic applications accepted. *Expenses:* Tuition, state resident: full-time $5,118; part-time $213 per credit hour. Tuition, nonresident: full-time $14,832; part-time $618 per credit hour. Required fees: $674; $34 per credit hour. *Financial support:* In 2006–07, 66 students received support, including 6 fellowships (averaging $2,513 per year), 24 research assistantships (averaging $6,104 per year), 16 teaching assistantships (averaging $5,430 per year); unspecified assistantships also available. Financial award application deadline: 3/1; financial award applicants required to submit FAFSA. *Unit head:* H. David Caffey, Director, 970-351-2679.

University of Northern Iowa, Graduate College, College of Humanities and Fine Arts, School of Music, Program in Music Education, Cedar Falls, IA 50614. Offers jazz pedagogy (MM); music (MA); music education (MM); piano performance and pedagogy (MM). *Accreditation:* NASM. Part-time and evening/weekend programs available. *Students:* 7 full-time (2 women), 9 part-time (6 women); includes 1 minority (African American), 2 international. 5 applicants, 60% accepted, 0 enrolled. *Degree requirements:* For master's, thesis or alternative, comprehensive exam. *Entrance requirements:* Additional exam requirements/recommendations for international students: Required—TOEFL (minimum score 500 paper-based; 180 computer-based; 61 iBT). *Application deadline:* For fall admission, 8/1 priority date for domestic students. Applications are processed on a rolling basis. Application fee: $30 ($50 for international students). Electronic applications accepted. *Expenses:* Tuition, state resident: full-time $5,936. Tuition, nonresident: full-time $14,074. *Financial support:* Career-related internships or fieldwork, Federal Work-Study, and tuition waivers (full and partial) available. Support available to part-time students. Financial award application deadline: 2/1. *Unit head:* Dr. Rebecca Burkhardt, Coordinator, 319-273-6272, Fax: 319-273-7320, E-mail: rebecca.burkhardt@uni.edu.

University of North Texas, Robert B. Toulouse School of Graduate Studies, College of Music, Denton, TX 76203. Offers composition (MM, DMA, PhD); jazz studies (MM); music (MA); music education (MM, MME, PhD); music theory (MM, PhD); musicology (MM, PhD); performance (MM, DMA), including conducting. *Accreditation:* NASM. *Faculty:* 103 full-time (26 women). *Students:* 351 full-time (156 women), 185 part-time (67 women); includes 72 minority (10 African Americans, 3 American Indian/Alaska Native, 24 Asian Americans or Pacific Islanders, 35 Hispanic Americans), 147 international. Average age 29. 416 applicants, 66% accepted, 141 enrolled. In 2006, 83 master's, 30 doctorates awarded. Terminal master's awarded for partial completion of doctoral program. *Degree requirements:* For master's, variable foreign language requirement, thesis (for some programs), qualifying exam, recital; for doctorate, variable foreign language requirement, thesis/dissertation, qualifying exam, recitals. *Entrance requirements:* For master's, GRE General Test, GRE Subject Test, College of Music graduate admission exam, audition (MM in performance); for doctorate, GRE General Test, GRE Subject Test, College of Music graduate admission exam, audition (DMA in performance). *Application deadline:* For fall admission, 7/15 for domestic students. Application fee: $50 ($75 for international students). *Expenses:* Tuition, state resident: full-time $3,573; part-time $198 per credit. Tuition, nonresident: full-time $8,577; part-time $476 per credit. Required fees: $1,258; $126 per credit. One-time fee: $150 full-time. Tuition and fees vary according to course load. *Financial support:* Fellowships, research assistantships, teaching assistantships, career-related internships or fieldwork, Federal Work-Study, institutionally sponsored loans, and scholarships/grants available. Financial award application deadline: 4/1. *Faculty research:* Organology; Latin American music; computer-aided training in music theory, electro-acoustical music, and intermedia. *Unit head:* Dr. James C. Scott, Dean, 940-565-3704, Fax: 940-565-2002. *Application contact:* Dr. Graham Phipps, Graduate Adviser, 940-565-4566, Fax: 940-565-2002, E-mail: phipps@music.unt.edu.

University of Oklahoma, Graduate College, College of Fine Arts, School of Music, Norman, OK 73019-0390. Offers choral conducting (M Mus); conducting (M Mus Ed, DMA); general (M Mus Ed); instrumental (M Mus Ed); instrumental conducting (M Mus); music composition (M Mus, DMA); music education (M Mus Ed, PhD); music theory (M Mus); musicology (M Mus); organ (M Mus, DMA); piano (M Mus, DMA); voice (M Mus, DMA); wind/percussion/string (M Mus, DMA). *Accreditation:* NASM. *Faculty:* 61 full-time (22 women), 1 part-time/adjunct (0 women). *Students:* 98 full-time (55 women), 62 part-time (33 women); includes 8 minority (1 African American, 4 American Indian/Alaska Native, 2 Asian Americans or Pacific Islanders, 1 Hispanic American), 20 international. 68 applicants, 76% accepted, 34 enrolled. In 2006, 28 master's, 15 doctorates awarded. *Degree requirements:* For master's, variable foreign language requirement, thesis (for some programs), departmental qualifying exam, oral and preliminary exams; for doctorate, variable foreign language requirement, thesis/dissertation, departmental qualifying exam, general and oral exams. *Entrance requirements:* For master's, audition, BA in music, minimum GPA of 3.0; for doctorate, audition, minimum GPA of 3.0. Additional exam requirements/recommendations for international students: Required—TOEFL (minimum score 550 paper-based; 213 computer-based). *Application deadline:* For fall admission, 6/1 priority date for domestic students, 4/1 for international students; for spring admission, 11/1 for domestic students, 9/1 for international students. Applications are processed on a rolling basis. Application fee: $40 ($90 for international students). *Expenses:* Tuition, state resident: full-time $3,180; part-time $133 per credit hour. Tuition, nonresident: full-time $11,347; part-time $473 per credit hour. Required fees: $1,729; $62 per credit hour. $117 per semester. Tuition and fees vary according to course load and program. *Financial support:* In 2006–07, 6 fellowships with full tuition reimbursements (averaging $5,000 per year), 14 research assistantships with partial tuition reimbursements (averaging $9,548 per year), 75 teaching assistantships with partial tuition reimbursements (averaging $9,673 per year) were awarded; scholarships/grants, health care benefits, and unspecified assistantships also available. Financial award application deadline: 4/7; financial award applicants required to submit FAFSA. Total annual research expenditures: $2,449. *Unit head:* Dr. Steven Curtis, Director, 405-325-2081, Fax: 405-325-7574, E-mail: scurtis@ou.edu. *Application contact:* Jan Russell, Graduate Admission and Recruiting, 405-325-5393, Fax: 405-325-7574, E-mail: jrussell@ou.edu.

University of Oregon, Graduate School, School of Music, Program in Music Education, Eugene, OR 97403. Offers M Mus, DMA, PhD. *Accreditation:* NASM. Part-time programs available. *Faculty:* 30 full-time (9 women), 4 part-time/adjunct (1 woman). *Students:* 3 applicants, 100% accepted. In 2006, 7 master's, 1 doctorate awarded. Terminal master's awarded for partial completion of doctoral program. *Degree requirements:* For master's, variable foreign language requirement, thesis (for some programs); for doctorate, one foreign language, thesis/dissertation, comprehensive exam. *Entrance requirements:* For master's, minimum GPA of 3.0, videotape or interview; for doctorate, GRE General Test, minimum GPA of 3.0, videotape or interview. Additional exam requirements/recommendations for international students: Required—TOEFL. *Application deadline:* For fall admission, 7/1 for domestic students. Application fee: $50. *Financial support:* In 2006–07, 5 teaching assistantships were awarded; career-related internships or fieldwork and Federal Work-Study also available. Financial award application deadline: 3/1. *Faculty research:* Psalms of DeLasso, stress and muscular tension in stringed instrument performance, piano music of Stravinsky, learning aptitudes in elementary music. *Unit head:* Ann Tedards, Associate Dean, 541-346-5664. *Application contact:* Anne Merydith, Admissions Contact, 541-346-5664, E-mail: gradmus@uoregon.edu.

University of Ottawa, Faculty of Graduate and Postdoctoral Studies, Faculty of Arts, Department of Music, Ottawa, ON K1N 6N5, Canada. Offers music (M Mus, MA); orchestral studies (Certificate); piano pedagogy research (Certificate). *Degree requirements:* For master's, thesis optional. *Entrance requirements:* For master's, honors degree or equivalent, minimum B+ average. Electronic applications accepted. *Faculty research:* Performance, theory, musicology.

University of Rhode Island, Graduate School, College of Human Science and Services, School of Education, Kingston, RI 02881. Offers adult education (MA); elementary education (MA); music education (MM); reading education (MA); secondary education (MA); MS/PhD. *Accreditation:* NCATE. Evening/weekend programs available. In 2006, 40 degrees awarded. *Entrance requirements:* For master's, GRE or MAT. Additional exam requirements/recommendations for international students: Required—TOEFL. *Application deadline:* For fall admission, 4/15 priority date for domestic students; for spring admission, 11/15 for domestic students. Applications are processed on a rolling basis. Application fee: $35. *Expenses:* Tuition, state resident: full-time $6,032; part-time $335 per credit. Tuition, nonresident: full-time $17,288; part-time $960 per credit. Required fees: $65 per credit. $30 per semester. One-time

Music Education

University of Rhode Island (continued)
fee: $80 part-time. *Financial support:* Career-related internships or fieldwork available. *Unit head:* Dr. David Byrd, Director, 401-874-5484.

University of Rochester, Eastman School of Music, Rochester, NY 14627-0250. Offers composition (MA, MM, DMA, PhD); conducting (MM, DMA); education (MA, PhD); jazz studies/contemporary media (MM); music education (MM, DMA); musicology (MA, PhD); pedagogy of music theory (MA); performance and literature (MM, DMA); piano accompanying and chamber music (MM, DMA); theory (MA, PhD). *Accreditation:* NASM. Part-time programs available. *Degree requirements:* For master's, thesis/dissertation (for some programs); for doctorate, thesis/dissertation (for some programs), comprehensive exam (for some programs). *Entrance requirements:* For master's and doctorate, GRE. Expenses: Contact institution.

University of St. Thomas, Graduate Studies, College of Arts and Sciences, Program in Music Education, St. Paul, MN 55105-1096. Offers MA. *Accreditation:* NASM; NCATE. Part-time programs available. *Faculty:* 2 full-time (0 women), 37 part-time/adjunct (19 women). *Students:* Average age 33. 6 applicants, 100% accepted, 6 enrolled. In 2006, 6 degrees awarded. *Median time to degree:* Master's–4 years part-time. *Degree requirements:* For master's, thesis, 2 teaching videotape assessments, comprehensive exam, registration. *Entrance requirements:* For master's, teaching videotape, performance assessment hearing, interview, interview essay. Additional exam requirements/recommendations for international students: Required—TOEFL (minimum score 550 paper-based). *Application deadline:* For fall admission, 7/1 for domestic students; for winter admission, 12/1 for domestic students; for spring admission, 4/1 for domestic students. Applications are processed on a rolling basis. Application fee: $50. *Financial support:* In 2006–07, 9 students received support, including 8 fellowships (averaging $1,300 per year); research assistantships, teaching assistantships, career-related internships or fieldwork, institutionally sponsored loans, scholarships/grants, and tuition waivers (partial) also available. Financial award application deadline: 4/1. *Faculty research:* Kodaly, choral conducting, piano pedagogy. *Unit head:* Jill L. Trinka, Director, 800-328-6819 Ext. 25871, Fax: 651-962-5886, E-mail: jltrinka@stthomas.edu. *Application contact:* Beverly H. Johnson, Program Coordinator, 800-328-6819, Fax: 651-962-5886, E-mail: bhjohnson@stthomas.edu.

University of South Carolina, The Graduate School, School of Music, Columbia, SC 29208. Offers composition (MM, DMA); conducting (MM, DMA); jazz studies (MM); music education (MM Ed, PhD); music history (MM); music performance (Certificate); music theory (MM); opera theater (MM); performance (MM, DMA); piano pedagogy (MM, DMA). *Accreditation:* NASM (one or more programs are accredited). Part-time programs available. *Degree requirements:* For master's, thesis (for some programs), comprehensive exam; for doctorate, one foreign language, thesis/dissertation, comprehensive exam; for Certificate, recitals. *Entrance requirements:* For master's and doctorate, GRE General Test or MAT, music diagnostic exam. Additional exam requirements/recommendations for international students: Required—TOEFL (minimum score 600 paper-based; 250 computer-based). Electronic applications accepted. Expenses: Contact institution. *Faculty research:* Music skills in pre-school children, evaluation of school performing ensembles.

University of Southern California, Graduate School, Thornton School of Music, Program in Music Education, Los Angeles, CA 90089. Offers MM, MM Ed, DMA. *Accreditation:* NASM. Part-time programs available. *Students:* 20 full-time (13 women), 8 part-time (3 women); includes 10 minority (3 Asian Americans or Pacific Islanders, 7 Hispanic Americans), 4 international. In 2006, 3 master's, 1 doctorate awarded. Terminal master's awarded for partial completion of doctoral program. *Degree requirements:* For master's, thesis (for some programs); for doctorate, one foreign language, thesis/dissertation. *Application deadline:* For fall admission, 12/1 priority date for domestic students. Application fee: $85. *Expenses:* Tuition: Full-time $33,314; part-time $1,121 per credit. Required fees: $522. Full-time tuition and fees vary according to program. *Financial support:* In 2006–07, research assistantships (averaging $18,500 per year), teaching assistantships with full tuition reimbursements (averaging $18,500 per year) were awarded; fellowships, Federal Work-Study, institutionally sponsored loans, and scholarships/grants also available. Financial award application deadline: 2/15; financial award applicants required to submit FAFSA. *Faculty research:* Vocal jazz, jazz improvisation, creative thinking, Broadway musical, music appreciation, technology. *Unit head:* Gwendolyn McGraw, Chair, 213-740-3211.

University of Southern Mississippi, Graduate School, College of Arts and Letters, School of Music, Hattiesburg, MS 39406-0001. Offers conducting (MM); history and literature (MM); music education (MME, PhD); performance (MM); performance and pedagogy (DMA); theory and composition (MM); woodwind performance (MM). *Accreditation:* NASM. *Faculty:* 36 full-time (9 women). *Students:* 66 full-time (30 women), 19 part-time (8 women); includes 12 minority (7 African Americans, 1 American Indian/Alaska Native, 4 Hispanic Americans), 13 international. Average age 29. 46 applicants, 70% accepted, 24 enrolled. In 2006, 31 master's, 8 doctorates awarded. Terminal master's awarded for partial completion of doctoral program. *Degree requirements:* For master's, thesis (for some programs), comprehensive exam, registration; for doctorate, thesis/dissertation, comprehensive exam, registration. *Entrance requirements:* For master's, GRE General Test, minimum GPA of 2.75 in last 60 hours; for doctorate, GRE General Test, minimum GPA of 3.5. Additional exam requirements/recommendations for international students: Required—TOEFL. *Application deadline:* For fall admission, 3/1 priority date for domestic students; for spring admission, 12/13 for domestic students. Applications are processed on a rolling basis. Application fee: $25 ($30 for international students). *Financial support:* In 2006–07, 60 teaching assistantships with full tuition reimbursements (averaging $5,554 per year) were awarded; research assistantships, Federal Work-Study, scholarships/grants, tuition waivers (partial), and unspecified assistantships also available. Financial award application deadline: 3/15. *Faculty research:* Music theory, composition. *Unit head:* Dr. Charles Elliott, Director, 601-266-5543, Fax: 601-266-6427, E-mail: celliott@usm.edu. *Application contact:* Graduate Coordinator, 601-266-5369, Fax: 601-266-6427.

University of South Florida, Graduate School, College of Visual and Performing Arts, School of Music, Tampa, FL 33620-9951. Offers chamber music (MM); composition (MM); conducting (MM); electro-acoustic music (MM); jazz studies (MM), including composition, performance; performance (MM), including percussion, piano, string, voice, wind; piano pedagogy (MM); theory (MM). *Accreditation:* NASM. Part-time and evening/weekend programs available. *Degree requirements:* For master's, thesis (for some programs), comprehensive exam. *Entrance requirements:* For master's, GRE General Test, diagnostic exam in theory and history, audition, portfolio. Additional exam requirements/recommendations for international students: Required—TOEFL (minimum score 550 paper-based; 213 computer-based). *Application deadline:* For fall admission, 8/1 priority date for domestic students, 6/1 for international students; for spring admission, 12/1 for domestic students, 10/1 for international students. Application fee: $30. *Financial support:* Fellowships with full tuition reimbursements, research assistantships with full tuition reimbursements, teaching assistantships with full tuition reimbursements, scholarships/grants, health care benefits, and unspecified assistantships available. Financial award application deadline: 2/1. *Faculty research:* Medieval and Renaissance musicology, nonverbal conducting. *Unit head:* Dr. Wade P. Weast, Director, 813-974-2311, Fax: 813-974-8721, E-mail: wweast@arts.usf.edu. *Application contact:* Dr. William P. Hayden, Associate Director for Student Affairs, 813-974-1753, Fax: 813-974-4165, E-mail: wphayden@arts.usf.edu.

The University of Tennessee, Graduate School, College of Arts and Sciences, School of Music, Knoxville, TN 37996. Offers accompanying (MM); choral conducting (MM); composition (MM); instrumental conducting (MM); jazz (MM); music education (MM); music theory (MM); musicology (MM); performance (MM); piano pedagogy and literature (MM). Part-time programs available. *Students:* 70 (38 women); includes 7 African Americans, 1 Asian American or Pacific Islander 4 international. In 2006, 30 degrees awarded. *Degree requirements:* For master's, thesis (for some programs). *Entrance requirements:* For master's, audition, minimum GPA of 2.7. Additional exam requirements/recommendations for international students: Required—TOEFL. *Application deadline:* For fall admission, 2/1 priority date for domestic students. Applications are processed on a rolling basis. Application fee: $35. Electronic applications accepted. *Expenses:* Tuition, state resident: full-time $5,574. Tuition, nonresident: full-time $16,840. Required fees: $792. *Financial support:* In 2006–07, 1 fellowship, 14 teaching assistantships were awarded; research assistantships, Federal Work-Study, institutionally sponsored loans, and unspecified assistantships also available. Financial award application deadline: 2/1; financial award applicants required to submit FAFSA. *Unit head:* Dr. Roger Stephens, Head, 865-974-3241, Fax: 865-974-1941. *Application contact:* Dr. Cathy Leach, Graduate Representative, 865-974-6558, E-mail: cathyfl726@aol.com.

The University of Texas at El Paso, Graduate School, College of Liberal Arts, Department of Music, El Paso, TX 79968-0001. Offers music education (MM); music performance (MM). *Accreditation:* NASM. Part-time and evening/weekend programs available. *Degree requirements:* For master's, thesis. *Entrance requirements:* For master's, departmental exam. Additional exam requirements/recommendations for international students: Required—TOEFL. Electronic applications accepted.

The University of Texas at Tyler, College of Education and Psychology, Department of Curriculum and Instruction, Tyler, TX 75799-0001. Offers curriculum and instruction (M Ed); secondary teaching (MAT), including art, biology, computer science, English, history, journalism, mathematics, music, political science, sociology, speech, theatre. Part-time programs available. *Faculty:* 10 full-time (6 women), 2 part-time/adjunct (1 woman). *Students:* 3 full-time (2 women), 7 part-time (6 women); includes 1 minority (African American) Average age 32. 1 applicant, 100% accepted, 1 enrolled. In 2006, 6 degrees awarded. *Degree requirements:* For master's, research project (M Ed). *Entrance requirements:* For master's, GRE or MAT. Application fee: $0 ($50 for international students). Electronic applications accepted. *Expenses:* Tuition, state resident: part-time $50 per credit hour. Tuition, nonresident: part-time $328 per credit hour. Required fees: $107 per credit hour. $426 per term. *Financial support:* Scholarships/grants available. *Unit head:* Dr. Robert Stevens, Chair/Professor of Education, 903-566-7315, E-mail: rstevens@uttyler.edu. *Application contact:* Bonnie Purser, Office of Graduate Studies, 903-566-7142, Fax: 903-566-7068, E-mail: bpurser@uttyler.edu.

The University of Texas–Pan American, College of Arts and Humanities, Department of Music, Edinburg, TX 78541-2999. Offers ethnomusicology (M Mus); interdisciplinary studies (MAIS); music education (M Mus); performance (M Mus). Part-time programs available. *Degree requirements:* For master's, recital (performance), thesis optional. *Entrance requirements:* For master's, audition for performance area, bachelor's degree in music. *Expenses:* Tuition, state resident: full-time $2,577; part-time $143 per credit hour. Tuition, nonresident: full-time $7,527; part-time $418 per credit hour. Required fees: $561. *Faculty research:* Music history, instrumental pedagogy, vocal pedagogy, music education, ethnomusicology.

The University of the Arts, College of Performing Arts, School of Music, Division of Music Education, Philadelphia, PA 19102-4944. Offers MAT. *Accreditation:* NASM. Part-time programs available. *Degree requirements:* For master's, student teaching experience. *Entrance requirements:* For master's, audition. Additional exam requirements/recommendations for international students: Required—TOEFL (minimum score 550 paper-based; 213 computer-based).

University of the Pacific, Conservatory of Music, Program in Music Education, Stockton, CA 95211-0197. Offers MM. *Faculty:* 1 (woman) full-time, 4 part-time/adjunct (2 women). *Students:* 1 (woman) full-time, 2 part-time; includes 2 minority (1 Asian American or Pacific Islander, 1 Hispanic American). Average age 25. 3 applicants, 100% accepted, 3 enrolled. In 2006, 1 degree awarded. *Entrance requirements:* For master's, 3 letters of recommendation. Additional exam requirements/recommendations for international students: Required—TOEFL (minimum score 475 paper-based; 150 computer-based). *Application deadline:* For fall admission, 3/1 priority date for domestic students; for spring admission, 10/1 priority date for domestic students. Applications are processed on a rolling basis. Application fee: $75. *Expenses:* Tuition: Full-time $26,920. Required fees: $430. Tuition and fees vary according to course load. *Financial support:* Application deadline: 3/1; *Unit head:* Dr. Ruth Brittin, Associate Professor, 209-946-2408, E-mail: rbrittin@pacific.edu.

The University of Toledo, College of Graduate Studies, College of Education, Department of Curriculum and Instruction, Program in Music Education, Toledo, OH 43606-3390. Offers MME. *Students:* 2 full-time (both women), 3 part-time (2 women). Average age 42. 3 applicants, 100% accepted, 2 enrolled.

University of Toronto, School of Graduate Studies, Humanities Division, Department of Music, Toronto, ON M5S 1A1, Canada. Offers composition (Mus M, Mus Doc); music education (Mus M, PhD); musicology/theory (MA, PhD). Part-time programs available. *Degree requirements:* For master's, oral examination (Mus M in composition), 1 language (MA); for doctorate, thesis/dissertation (for some programs), recital of original works (Mus Doc), thesis (PhD). *Entrance requirements:* For master's, Bachelor of Music in area of specialization with minimum B average in final 2 years, original compositions (Mus M in composition); for doctorate, master's degree in area of specialization, minimum B+ average, at least 2 extended compositions (Mus Doc).

University of Victoria, Faculty of Graduate Studies, Faculty of Education, Department of Curriculum and Instruction, Victoria, BC V8W 2Y2, Canada. Offers art (M Ed, MA, PhD); curriculum studies (M Ed, MA, PhD); early childhood (M Ed, MA, PhD); language and literacy (M Ed, MA, PhD); mathematics (M Ed, MA, PhD); music (M Ed, MA); music education (PhD); science (M Ed, MA, PhD); social studies (M Ed, MA); social, cultural and foundational studies (PhD); technology and environmental education (PhD). Part-time programs available. *Degree requirements:* For master's, thesis, project (M Ed); for doctorate, thesis/dissertation, comprehensive exam, registration. *Entrance requirements:* For master's, minimum B average. Additional exam requirements/recommendations for international students: Required—TOEFL (minimum score 575 paper-based; 233 computer-based), IELTS (minimum score 7). Electronic applications accepted. *Faculty research:* Elementary and secondary English, language arts, curriculum theory and practice, educational media and technology, educational administration and leadership, history and philosophy of education.

University of Washington, Graduate School, College of Arts and Sciences, School of Music, Concentration in Music Education, Seattle, WA 98195. Offers MA, PhD. *Accreditation:* NASM. *Degree requirements:* For doctorate, thesis/dissertation. *Entrance requirements:* For master's, GRE General Test, GRE Subject Test, minimum GPA of 3.0; for doctorate, GRE General Test, GRE Subject Test, minimum GPA of 3.0, sample of scholarly writing, videotape of teaching, 1 year of teaching experience. Additional exam requirements/recommendations for international students: Required—TOEFL. Electronic applications accepted. *Faculty research:* Multiethnic issues in music instruction, affective responses to music.

University of West Georgia, Graduate School, College of Arts and Sciences, Department of Music, Program in Music Education, Carrollton, GA 30118. Offers M Mus. *Accreditation:* NASM; NCATE. Part-time programs available. *Students:* 4 applicants, 100% accepted, 4 enrolled. In 2006, 3 degrees awarded. *Degree requirements:* For master's, thesis optional. *Entrance requirements:* For master's, GRE General Test or MAT, qualifying exam, minimum GPA of 2.5, bachelor's degree in music education or teacher certification, performance evaluation. *Application deadline:* For fall admission, 8/1 priority date for domestic students; for spring admission, 1/2 for domestic students. Application fee: $20. Electronic applications accepted. *Expenses:* Tuition, state resident: full-time $2,286; part-time $127 per credit. Tuition, nonresident: full-time $9,144; part-time $508 per credit. Required fees: $494; $27 per credit. $121 per semester. *Financial support:* In 2006–07, 2 students received support, including 2 research assistantships with full tuition reimbursements available (averaging $6,000 per year); career-related internships or fieldwork and unspecified assistantships also available. Support available to part-time students. Financial award applicants required to submit FAFSA.

Faculty research: Musicology, band music, music education. *Application contact:* Dr. Charles W. Clark, Chair, 678-839-6508, E-mail: cclark@westga.edu.

University of Wisconsin–Madison, Graduate School, College of Letters and Science, School of Music, Program in Music Education, Madison, WI 53706-1380. Offers curriculum and instruction (PhD); music education (MM). *Accreditation:* NASM. *Degree requirements:* For doctorate, 2 foreign languages, thesis/dissertation. *Entrance requirements:* For doctorate, GRE General Test.

University of Wisconsin–Madison, Graduate School, School of Education, Department of Curriculum and Instruction, Madison, WI 53706-1380. Offers art education (MA); curriculum and instruction (MS, PhD); education and mathematics (MA); French education (MA); German education (MA); music education (MS); science education (MS); Spanish education (MA). *Accreditation:* NASM (one or more programs are accredited). *Degree requirements:* For doctorate, thesis/dissertation. Application fee: $45. *Financial support:* Project assistantships available. *Unit head:* Dr. Alan Lockwood, Chair, 608-262-4000.

University of Wisconsin–Stevens Point, College of Fine Arts and Communication, Department of Music, Stevens Point, WI 54481-3897. Offers MM Ed. *Accreditation:* NASM. Part-time programs available. *Faculty:* 20 full-time (7 women), 3 part-time/adjunct (0 women). *Students:* 1 (woman) full-time, 4 part-time (3 women). In 2006, 2 degrees awarded. *Degree requirements:* For master's, thesis or alternative. *Entrance requirements:* For master's, teaching certificate. *Application deadline:* For fall admission, 5/1 priority date for domestic students. Applications are processed on a rolling basis. Application fee: $45. *Expenses:* Tuition, state resident: full-time $5,910; part-time $328 per credit. Tuition, nonresident: full-time $16,520; part-time $918 per credit. Required fees: $756; $73 per credit. *Financial support:* Career-related internships or fieldwork, Federal Work-Study, institutionally sponsored loans, and unspecified assistantships available. Support available to part-time students. Financial award application deadline: 5/1; financial award applicants required to submit FAFSA. *Faculty research:* Music education, music composition, music performance. *Unit head:* Robert Kase, Chair, 715-346-3107, Fax: 715-346-2718, E-mail: rkase@uwfp.edu. *Application contact:* Patricia Holland, Information Contact, 715-346-3107, Fax: 715-346-3163, E-mail: pholland@uwsp.edu.

University of Wyoming, Graduate School, College of Arts and Sciences, Department of Music, Laramie, WY 82070. Offers music education (MA); performance (MM). *Accreditation:* NASM. *Faculty:* 12. *Students:* 13 full-time (5 women), 6 part-time (3 women); includes 2 minority (1 African American, 1 Asian American or Pacific Islander), 6 international. Average age 27. 16 applicants, 81% accepted. In 2006, 12 degrees awarded. *Degree requirements:* For master's, thesis, performance, comprehensive exam, registration. *Entrance requirements:* For master's, minimum GPA of 3.0. Additional exam requirements/recommendations for international students: Required—TOEFL (minimum score 540 paper-based; 207 computer-based). *Application deadline:* For fall admission, 3/1 priority date for domestic and international students. Application fee: $50. Electronic applications accepted. *Financial support:* In 2006–07, 8 students received support, including 8 teaching assistantships with full tuition reimbursements available (averaging $10,384 per year); unspecified assistantships also available. Financial award application deadline: 3/1. *Unit head:* Dr. David Brinkman, Head, 307-766-5242, Fax: 307-766-5326, E-mail: brinkman@uwyo.edu.

Valdosta State University, Graduate School, College of the Fine Arts, Department of Music, Valdosta, GA 31698. Offers music education (MME); performance (MMP). *Accreditation:* NASM. Part-time programs available. *Degree requirements:* For master's, comprehensive written and/or oral exams. *Entrance requirements:* For master's, GRE General Test or MAT. Additional exam requirements/recommendations for international students: Required—TOEFL (minimum score 523 paper-based; 193 computer-based).

VanderCook College of Music, Program in Music Education, Chicago, IL 60616-3731. Offers MM Ed. Offered during summer only. *Accreditation:* NASM. Part-time programs available. *Degree requirements:* For master's, thesis optional. *Entrance requirements:* For master's, minimum GPA of 3.0. *Faculty research:* Pedagogy in elementary music.

Virginia Commonwealth University, Graduate School, School of the Arts, Department of Music, Richmond, VA 23284-9005. Offers education (MM). *Accreditation:* NASM. *Faculty:* 11 full-time (4 women). *Students:* 1 applicant, 100% accepted, 0 enrolled. In 2006, 12 degrees awarded. *Degree requirements:* For master's, departmental qualifying exam, recital. *Entrance requirements:* For master's, department examination, audition or tapes, portfolio. *Application deadline:* For fall admission, 7/1 for domestic students; for spring admission, 12/1 for domestic students. Application fee: $50. *Financial support:* Fellowships, teaching assistantships, career-related internships or fieldwork, Federal Work-Study, and institutionally sponsored loans available. Support available to part-time students. Financial award application deadline: 3/15. *Faculty research:* Composition, conducting, education, performance. *Unit head:* Dr. John Guthmiller, Acting Chair, 804-828-1166, Fax: 804-828-6469, E-mail: jguthmil@vcu.edu.

See Close-Up on page 1623.

Washington State University, Graduate School, College of Liberal Arts, School of Music and Theatre Arts, Pullman, WA 99164. Offers composition (MA); jazz (MA); music (MA); music education (MA); performance (MA). *Accreditation:* NASM. *Faculty:* 16. *Students:* 18 full-time (6 women), 2 part-time (1 woman); includes 1 minority (Hispanic American) Average age 30. 16 applicants, 44% accepted, 7 enrolled. In 2006, 11 degrees awarded. *Degree requirements:* For master's, thesis (for some programs), oral exam, comprehensive exam (for some programs). *Entrance requirements:* For master's, audition, minimum GPA of 3.0, 3 letters of recommendation, composition portfolio and recording (composition), writing sample and written philosophy (music education), writing sample (music history), in-depth audition (performance). Additional exam requirements/recommendations for international students: Required—TOEFL. *Application deadline:* For fall admission, 3/1 priority date for domestic students, 3/1 for international students; for spring admission, 9/1 for domestic students, 7/1 for international students. Applications are processed on a rolling basis. Application fee: $50. Electronic applications accepted. *Expenses:* Tuition, state resident: full-time $7,066. Tuition, nonresident: full-time $17,204. *Financial support:* In 2006–07, 20 students received support, including 1 fellowship (averaging $3,500 per year), research assistantships (averaging $13,917 per year), 11 teaching assistantships with full and partial tuition reimbursements available (averaging $13,056 per year); career-related internships or fieldwork, Federal Work-Study, institutionally sponsored loans, and tuition waivers (partial) also available. Financial award application deadline: 4/1; financial award applicants required to submit FAFSA. Total annual research expenditures: $4,950. *Unit head:* Dr. Gerald Berthiaume, Director, 509-335-3898, Fax: 509-335-4245, E-mail: berthia@wsu.edu. *Application contact:* Graduate School Admissions, 800-GRADWSU, Fax: 509-335-1949, E-mail: gradsch@wsu.edu.

Wayne State College, School of Education and Counseling, Department of Educational Foundations and Leadership, Program in Curriculum and Instruction, Wayne, NE 68787. Offers alternative education (MSE); business education (MSE); communication arts education (MSE); curriculum and instruction (MSE); early childhood education (MSE); elementary education (MSE); English as a second language (MSE); English education (MSE); family consumer science of education (MSE); industrial technology education (MSE); learning communities (MSE); mathematics education (MSE); music education (MSE); science education (MSE); social science education (MSE). *Accreditation:* NCATE. Part-time and evening/weekend programs available. *Faculty:* 17 part-time/adjunct (11 women). *Students:* 17 full-time (10 women), 307 part-time (248 women); includes 6 minority (2 African Americans, 1 American Indian/Alaska Native, 2 Asian Americans or Pacific Islanders, 1 Hispanic American), 1 international. Average age 35. In 2006, 167 degrees awarded. *Degree requirements:* For master's, thesis optional. *Entrance requirements:* For master's, GRE General Test. Additional exam requirements/recommendations for international students: Required—TOEFL (minimum score 550 paper-based; 213 computer-based). *Application deadline:* Applications are processed on a rolling basis. Application fee: $30. *Expenses:* Tuition, state resident: full-time $3,114; part-time $130 per credit hour. Tuition, nonresident: full-time $6,228; part-time $260 per credit hour. Required fees: $894; $37 per credit hour. Tuition and fees vary according to course load. *Financial support:* Applicants required to submit FAFSA.

Wayne State University, College of Fine, Performing and Communication Arts, Department of Music, Detroit, MI 48202. Offers choral conducting (MM); composition (MM); music (MA, MM); music education (MM); orchestral studies (Certificate); performance (MM); theory (MM). *Accreditation:* NASM. *Faculty:* 53 full-time (15 women). *Students:* 9 full-time (4 women), 17 part-time (7 women); includes 4 minority (2 African Americans, 2 Asian Americans or Pacific Islanders), 4 international. Average age 31. 16 applicants, 81% accepted, 8 enrolled. In 2006, 10 degrees awarded. *Entrance requirements:* For master's, audition, interview. Additional exam requirements/recommendations for international students: Required—TOEFL (minimum score 550 paper-based; 213 computer-based); Recommended—TWE (minimum score 6). *Application deadline:* For fall admission, 4/1 for domestic students, 6/1 for international students; for winter admission, 10/1 for international students; for spring admission, 2/1 for international students. Applications are processed on a rolling basis. Application fee: $30 ($50 for international students). Electronic applications accepted. *Financial support:* In 2006–07, 12 students received support; research assistantships, career-related internships or fieldwork, Federal Work-Study, institutionally sponsored loans, and scholarships/grants available. Support available to part-time students. *Faculty research:* Teacher training, pedagogy, musicology, composition/theory, conducting/performance practice. *Unit head:* Dr. John Van Der Weg, Chair, 313-577-1800, Fax: 313-577-5420, E-mail: music.chair@wayne.edu. *Application contact:* Mary Wischusen, Graduate Director, 313-577-2612, E-mail: mary.wischusen@wayne.edu.

Webster University, Leigh Gerdine College of Fine Arts, Department of Music, St. Louis, MO 63119-3194. Offers church music (MM); composition (MM); conducting (MM); jazz studies (MM); music (MA); music education (MM); performance (MM); piano (MM). *Accreditation:* NASM. *Students:* 7 full-time (4 women), 19 part-time (7 women), 2 international. Average age 31. In 2006, 6 degrees awarded. *Application deadline:* Applications are processed on a rolling basis. Application fee: $25 ($50 for international students). *Expenses:* Tuition: Full-time $8,820; part-time $490 per credit. Tuition and fees vary according to degree level, campus/location and program. *Financial support:* Teaching assistantships, Federal Work-Study available. Support available to part-time students. Financial award application deadline: 4/1; financial award applicants required to submit FAFSA. *Unit head:* Michael Parkinson, Chair, 314-968-7033, Fax: 314-963-6048, E-mail: parkinmi@webster.edu. *Application contact:* Denise Harrell, Associate Director of Graduate and Evening Student Admissions, 314-968-6983, Fax: 314-968-7116, E-mail: gadmit@webster.edu.

West Chester University of Pennsylvania, Graduate Studies, College of Visual and Performing Arts, Department of Music Education, West Chester, PA 19383. Offers MM. *Accreditation:* NASM; NCATE. Part-time and evening/weekend programs available. *Students:* 2 full-time (1 woman), 31 part-time (21 women). Average age 28. 30 applicants, 90% accepted, 9 enrolled. In 2006, 6 degrees awarded. *Degree requirements:* For master's, recital, thesis optional. *Entrance requirements:* For master's, GRE General Test, audition. *Application deadline:* For fall admission, 4/15 priority date for domestic students; for spring admission, 10/15 for domestic students. Applications are processed on a rolling basis. Application fee: $35. *Financial support:* Research assistantships with full tuition reimbursements, unspecified assistantships available. Support available to part-time students. Financial award application deadline: 2/15; financial award applicants required to submit FAFSA. *Faculty research:* Developing music listening skills. *Unit head:* Prof. Kristen Albert, Chair, 610-436-0495, E-mail: kalbert@wcupa.edu. *Application contact:* Dr. J. Bryan Burton, Graduate Coordinator, 610-436-2222, E-mail: jburton@wcupa.edu.

Western Carolina University, Graduate School, College of Education and Allied Professions, Department of Educational Leadership and Foundations, Programs in Secondary Education, Cullowhee, NC 28723. Offers art education (MAT); biology (MAT); chemistry (MAT); comprehensive education (MA Ed), including art, biology, English, mathematics, music, physical education, reading, social sciences; English (MAT); family and consumer sciences (MAT); mathematics (MAT); physical education (MAT); reading (MAT); social sciences (MAT). *Accreditation:* NCATE (one or more programs are accredited). Part-time and evening/weekend programs available. *Degree requirements:* For master's, comprehensive exam. *Entrance requirements:* For master's, GRE General Test, portfolio. Additional exam requirements/recommendations for international students: Required—TOEFL (minimum score 550 paper-based; 213 computer-based).

Western Connecticut State University, Division of Graduate Studies, School of Visual and Performing Arts, Music Department, Danbury, CT 06810-6885. Offers music education (MS). *Accreditation:* NASM. Part-time and evening/weekend programs available. *Faculty:* 5 full-time (1 woman). *Students:* Average age 29. In 2006, 20 degrees awarded. *Degree requirements:* For master's, thesis or comprehensive exam. *Entrance requirements:* For master's, minimum GPA of 2.8, teaching certificate. *Application deadline:* For fall admission, 8/1 priority date for domestic students. Applications are processed on a rolling basis. Application fee: $40. *Financial support:* Fellowships, career-related internships or fieldwork available. Support available to part-time students. Financial award application deadline: 5/1; financial award applicants required to submit FAFSA. *Unit head:* Dr. Kevin Isaacs, Professor, 203-837-8354. *Application contact:* Chris Shankle, Associate Director of Graduate Admissions, 203-837-8244, Fax: 203-837-8338, E-mail: shanklec@wcsu.edu.

Western Kentucky University, Graduate Studies, Potter College of Arts and Letters, Department of Music, Bowling Green, KY 42101. Offers MA Ed. *Accreditation:* NASM; NCATE. Part-time and evening/weekend programs available. *Faculty:* 6 full-time (1 woman). *Students:* 5 full-time (1 woman), 4 part-time (all women). Average age 30. 6 applicants, 83% accepted, 3 enrolled. In 2006, 3 degrees awarded. *Degree requirements:* For master's, written exam. *Entrance requirements:* For master's, GRE General Test, minimum GPA of 3.0. Additional exam requirements/recommendations for international students: Required—TOEFL (minimum score 555 paper-based; 213 computer-based; 79 iBT). *Application deadline:* For fall admission, 7/1 priority date for domestic students, 4/1 for international students; for spring admission, 11/1 for domestic students, 9/1 for international students. Applications are processed on a rolling basis. Application fee: $35. *Expenses:* Tuition, state resident: full-time $6,520; part-time $226 per hour. Tuition, nonresident: full-time $7,140; part-time $357 per hour. International tuition: $15,820 full-time. *Financial support:* Federal Work-Study, institutionally sponsored loans, tuition waivers (partial), unspecified assistantships, and service awards available. Support available to part-time students. Financial award application deadline: 4/1; financial award applicants required to submit FAFSA. *Faculty research:* Music education, music technology, performance. *Unit head:* Dr. Mary Groom, Head, 270-745-3751, Fax: 270-745-6855, E-mail: mitzi.groom@wku.edu.

Westminster Choir College of Rider University, Graduate Programs in Music, Program in Music Education, Princeton, NJ 08540-3899. Offers MM, MME. *Accreditation:* NASM. *Entrance requirements:* For master's, audition, interview, repertoire list, 2 letters of reference, resumé. Additional exam requirements/recommendations for international students: Required—TOEFL (minimum score 525 paper-based; 195 computer-based). *Application deadline:* Applications are processed on a rolling basis. Application fee: $45. Electronic applications accepted. *Financial support:* Research assistantships, career-related internships or fieldwork, Federal Work-Study, and unspecified assistantships available. Support available to part-time students. Financial award application deadline: 3/1; financial award applicants required to submit FAFSA. *Unit head:* Robert L. Annis, Dean, 609-921-7100 Ext. 8206, Fax: 609-683-8856, E-mail: annis@rider.edu. *Application contact:* Kate Shields, Director of Admissions, 609-921-7100 Ext. 8103, Fax: 609-921-2538, E-mail: wccadmission@rider.edu.

See Close-Up on page 1629.

West Virginia University, College of Creative Arts, Division of Music, Morgantown, WV 26506. Offers music composition (MM, DMA); music education (MM, PhD); music history

Music Education

West Virginia University (continued)
(MM); music performance (MM, DMA); music theory (MM). *Accreditation:* NASM. *Faculty:* 37 full-time (15 women), 10 part-time/adjunct (3 women). *Students:* 54 full-time (29 women), 33 part-time (14 women); includes 4 minority (2 African Americans, 2 Asian Americans or Pacific Islanders), 23 international. Average age 28. 65 applicants, 68% accepted, 22 enrolled. In 2006, 21 master's, 5 doctorates awarded. *Degree requirements:* For master's, thesis (for some programs), recitals, comprehensive exam; for doctorate, variable foreign language requirement, thesis/dissertation, recitals (DMA), comprehensive exam. *Entrance requirements:* For master's, GRE General Test (music history), minimum GPA of 3.0, audition; for doctorate, GRE General Test (music education), minimum GPA of 3.0, audition. Additional exam requirements/recommendations for international students: Required—TOEFL. *Application deadline:* For fall admission, 3/15 priority date for domestic students, 2/15 priority date for international students; for spring admission, 10/15 for domestic students, 9/15 for international students. Applications are processed on a rolling basis. Application fee: $45. *Expenses:* Tuition, state resident: full-time $4,926; part-time $276 per credit hour. Tuition, nonresident: full-time $14,278; part-time $796 per credit hour. Tuition and fees vary according to program. *Financial support:* In 2006–07, 57 students received support, including 3 research assistantships with full and partial tuition reimbursements available (averaging $8,400 per year), 10 teaching assistantships with full and partial tuition reimbursements available (averaging $8,400 per year); Federal Work-Study, institutionally sponsored loans, and tuition waivers (partial) also available. Financial award application deadline: 2/1; financial award applicants required to submit FAFSA. *Faculty research:* Jazz history, seventeenth century French court music, nineteenth century composition theory. *Unit head:* Dr. David M. Bess, Chair, 304-293-4617 Ext. 3174, Fax: 304-293-7491, E-mail: david.bess@mail.wvu.edu. *Application contact:* Dr. Howard Keith Jackson, Director of Graduate Studies, 304-293-4841 Ext. 3224, Fax: 304-293-7941, E-mail: keith.jackson@mail.wvu.edu.

Wichita State University, Graduate School, College of Fine Arts, School of Music, Wichita, KS 67260. Offers music (MM); music education (MME). *Accreditation:* NASM. Part-time programs available. *Degree requirements:* For master's, one foreign language, thesis, recital, research project. *Entrance requirements:* For master's, GRE, audition, BM or BME. Additional exam requirements/recommendations for international students: Required—TOEFL. Electronic applications accepted.

Winthrop University, College of Visual and Performing Arts, Department of Music, Rock Hill, SC 29733. Offers conducting (MM); music education (MME); performance (MM). *Accreditation:* NASM. Part-time programs available. *Faculty:* 13 full-time (5 women), 13 part-time/adjunct (4 women). *Students:* 11 full-time (6 women), 10 part-time (4 women); includes 1 minority (African American), 2 international. Average age 27. In 2006, 10 degrees awarded. *Degree requirements:* For master's, oral and written exams, recital (MM). *Entrance requirements:* For master's, GRE General Test, audition, minimum GPA of 3.0, 2 recitals. *Application deadline:* For fall admission, 7/15 priority date for domestic students; for spring admission, 12/1 for domestic students. Applications are processed on a rolling basis. Application fee: $35 ($50 for international students). Electronic applications accepted. *Expenses:* Tuition, state resident: full-time $9,148; part-time $383 per hour. Tuition, nonresident: full-time $16,864; part-time $704 per hour. *Financial support:* Federal Work-Study, scholarships/grants, and unspecified assistantships available. Support available to part-time students. Financial award application deadline: 2/1; financial award applicants required to submit FAFSA. *Unit head:* Dr. Donald Rogers, Chair, 803-323-2255, Fax: 803-323-2343, E-mail: rogersd@winthrop.edu. *Application contact:* Sharon B. Johnson, Director of Graduate Studies, 800-411-7041, Fax: 803-323-2292, E-mail: johnsons@winthrop.edu.

Wright State University, School of Graduate Studies, College of Liberal Arts, Department of Music, Dayton, OH 45435. Offers music education (M Mus); performance (M Mus). *Accreditation:* NASM. Part-time programs available. *Students:* 5 full-time (3 women), 11 part-time (8 women). Average age 29. 12 applicants, 100% accepted. In 2006, 4 degrees awarded. *Degree requirements:* For master's, thesis or alternative, oral exam. *Entrance requirements:* For master's, theory placement test, BA in music. Additional exam requirements/recommendations for international students: Required—TOEFL. Application fee: $25. *Financial support:* Fellowships, research assistantships, teaching assistantships, unspecified assistantships available. Support available to part-time students. Financial award applicants required to submit FAFSA. *Faculty research:* General music, current needs, role of teacher, expectations in music education. *Unit head:* Dr. Herbert E. Dregalla, Chair, 937-775-2346, Fax: 937-775-3786, E-mail: herbert.dregalla@wright.edu.

Youngstown State University, Graduate School, College of Fine and Performing Arts, School of Music, Youngstown, OH 44555-0001. Offers music education (MM); music history and literature (MM); music theory and composition (MM); performance (MM). *Accreditation:* NASM. Part-time and evening/weekend programs available. *Degree requirements:* For master's, one foreign language, final qualifying exam, thesis optional. *Entrance requirements:* For master's, audition; GRE General Test or minimum GPA of 2.7. Additional exam requirements/recommendations for international students: Required—TOEFL. *Faculty research:* Teaching education, use of computers, conducting.

Reading Education

Abilene Christian University, Graduate School, College of Education and Human Services, Graduate Studies in Education, Reading Specialist Program, Abilene, TX 79699-9100. Offers M Ed. Part-time programs available. *Faculty:* 6 part-time/adjunct (2 women). *Students:* 1 (woman) full-time. 2 applicants, 50% accepted, 1 enrolled. *Degree requirements:* For master's, comprehensive exam. *Entrance requirements:* For master's, GRE General Test or MAT. *Application deadline:* For fall admission, 4/1 priority date for domestic students; for spring admission, 11/1 for domestic students. Applications are processed on a rolling basis. Application fee: $40 ($45 for international students). Electronic applications accepted. *Expenses:* Tuition: Full-time $12,504; part-time $521 per hour. Required fees: $700; $34 per hour. *Financial support:* Federal Work-Study available. Support available to part-time students. Financial award application deadline: 4/1. *Application contact:* William Horn, Graduate Admissions Counselor, 325-674-2656, Fax: 325-674-6717, E-mail: gradinfo@acu.edu.

Adelphi University, School of Education, Program in Literacy, Garden City, NY 11530-0701. Offers birth-grade 12 (MS); birth-grade 6 (MS); grades 5-12 (MS). Part-time and evening/weekend programs available. *Students:* Average age 28. In 2006, 73 degrees awarded. *Entrance requirements:* For master's, 2 letters of recommendation, resumé, valid New York state teaching certification. Additional exam requirements/recommendations for international students: Required—TOEFL (minimum score 550 paper-based; 213 computer-based). *Application deadline:* For fall admission, 4/1 priority date for domestic students; for spring admission, 11/1 priority date for domestic students. Applications are processed on a rolling basis. Application fee: $50. Electronic applications accepted. *Financial support:* Fellowships, research assistantships with partial tuition reimbursements, teaching assistantships, career-related internships or fieldwork, Federal Work-Study, institutionally sponsored loans, and tuition waivers (full) available. Support available to part-time students. Financial award application deadline: 2/15; financial award applicants required to submit FAFSA. *Faculty research:* Assessment and intervention, literacy education and development, higher and teacher education, human and adult development, achieving styles and human motivation. *Unit head:* Anne Mungai, Director, 516-877-4096, E-mail: mungai@adelphi.edu. *Application contact:* Christine Murphy, Director of Admissions, 516-877-3050, Fax: 516-877-3039, E-mail: graduateadmissions@adelphi.edu.

Albany State University, College of Education, Program in Reading Education, Albany, GA 31705-2717. Offers M Ed. *Degree requirements:* For master's, comprehensive exam. Electronic applications accepted. *Faculty research:* Development of language arts, general mathematics textbook evaluation, implications for reading professionals.

Alfred University, Graduate School, Division of Education, Alfred, NY 14802-1205. Offers counseling (MS Ed, CAS); literacy teacher (MS Ed). Part-time programs available. *Students:* 12 full-time (all women), 26 part-time (18 women). Average age 24. 62 applicants, 61% accepted, 30 enrolled. In 2006, 48 master's, 19 other advanced degrees awarded. *Entrance requirements:* For master's, LAST, Assessment of Teaching Skills (written), Content Specialty Test. Additional exam requirements/recommendations for international students: Required—TOEFL (minimum score 590 paper-based; 243 computer-based; 90 iBT), IELTS (minimum score 7). *Application deadline:* Applications are processed on a rolling basis. Application fee: $50. Electronic applications accepted. *Expenses:* Tuition: Full-time $29,600; part-time $630 per credit hour. Required fees: $850; $70 per semester. Tuition and fees vary according to program. *Financial support:* In 2006–07, 12 students received support, including research assistantships (averaging $14,225 per year); tuition waivers (partial) and unspecified assistantships also available. Financial award applicants required to submit FAFSA. *Faculty research:* Whole language, ethics in counseling and psychotherapy. *Unit head:* Dr. James Curl, Chair, 607-871-2219, E-mail: fcurl@alfred.edu. *Application contact:* Valerie Stephens, Coordinator of Graduate Admissions, 607-871-2141, Fax: 607-871-2198, E-mail: gradinquiry@alfred.edu.

Alverno College, School of Education, Milwaukee, WI 53234-3922. Offers adaptive education (MA); administrative leadership (MA); adult education and organizational development (MA); adult educational and instructional design (MA); adult educational and instructional technology (MA); instructional leadership (MA); instructional technology for K-12 settings (MA); professional development (MA); reading education (MA); reading education with adaptive education (MA); science education (MA); teaching in alternative schools (MA). *Accreditation:* NCATE. Part-time and evening/weekend programs available. *Faculty:* 12 full-time (11 women), 12 part-time/adjunct (10 women). *Students:* 83 full-time (68 women), 74 part-time (60 women); includes 37 minority (32 African Americans, 2 American Indian/Alaska Native, 3 Hispanic Americans). Average age 35. 61 applicants, 82% accepted, 41 enrolled. In 2006, 46 degrees awarded. *Degree requirements:* For master's, presentation/defense of proposal, conference presentation of inquiry projects. *Entrance requirements:* For master's, bachelor's degree in related field, communication samples from work setting, 3 letters of recommendation. Additional exam requirements/recommendations for international students: Required—TOEFL. *Application deadline:* For fall admission, 8/1 priority date for domestic and international students; for spring admission, 12/15 priority date for domestic and international students. Applications are processed on a rolling basis. Application fee: $20. Electronic applications accepted. *Expenses:* Tuition: Full-time $9,288; part-time $516 per credit. Required fees: $250; $125 per semester. Tuition and fees vary according to program. *Financial support:* In 2006–07, 92 students received support. Federal Work-Study available. Support available to part-time students. Financial award application deadline: 4/15; financial award applicants required to submit FAFSA. *Faculty research:* Student self-assessment, self-reflection, integration of curriculum, identifying needs of students in strategic situations and designing appropriate classroom strategies, implementing guided. *Unit head:* Dr. Mary Diez, Graduate Dean, 414-382-6214, Fax: 414-382-6332, E-mail: mary.diez@alverno.edu. *Application contact:* Sarajane Kennedy, Associate Director, Admissions Graduate Programs, 414-382-6104, Fax: 414-382-6332, E-mail: sarajane.kennedy@alverno.edu.

American International College, School of Psychology and Education, Department of Education, Springfield, MA 01109-3189. Offers administration (M Ed, CAGS); child development (MA, Ed D), including educational psychology; elementary education (M Ed, CAGS); reading (M Ed, CAGS); secondary education (M Ed, CAGS); special education (M Ed, CAGS); teaching (MAT). Part-time and evening/weekend programs available. *Faculty:* 5 full-time (3 women), 15 part-time/adjunct (9 women). *Students:* 31 full-time (27 women), 268 part-time (217 women); includes 25 minority (13 African Americans, 4 Asian Americans or Pacific Islanders, 8 Hispanic Americans), 2 international. Average age 39. In 2006, 38 master's, 2 doctorates, 5 other advanced degrees awarded. Terminal master's awarded for partial completion of doctoral program. *Degree requirements:* For master's, thesis (for some programs), practicum, comprehensive exam (for some programs), registration; for doctorate, thesis/dissertation, comprehensive exam (for some programs), registration; for CAGS, practicum. *Entrance requirements:* For master's, minimum B- average in undergraduate course work; for doctorate, GRE General Test, interview. Additional exam requirements/recommendations for international students: Required—TOEFL. *Application deadline:* For fall admission, 7/1 priority date for domestic and international students; for spring admission, 12/1 priority date for domestic and international students. Applications are processed on a rolling basis. Application fee: $50. *Expenses:* Tuition: Part-time $585 per semester hour. Required fees: $100 per year. Full-time tuition and fees vary according to program. *Financial support:* Career-related internships or fieldwork and institutionally sponsored loans available. Financial award applicants required to submit FAFSA. *Unit head:* Dr. Barbara Dautrich, Chair, 413-205-3407, Fax: 413-205-3943, E-mail: barbara.dautrich@aic.edu. *Application contact:* Keshawn Dodds, Associate Director of Graduate Admissions, 413-205-3549, Fax: 413-205-3911, E-mail: keshawn.dodds@aic.edu.

Andrews University, School of Graduate Studies, School of Education, Department of Teaching, Learning, and Curriculum, Program in Reading, Berrien Springs, MI 49104. Offers MA. *Degree requirements:* For master's, thesis optional. *Entrance requirements:* For master's, GRE Subject Test.

Angelo State University, College of Graduate Studies, College of Education, Department of Teacher Education, Program in Reading Specialist, San Angelo, TX 76909. Offers M Ed. Part-time and evening/weekend programs available. *Faculty:* 17 full-time (12 women). *Students:* Average age 26. 2 applicants, 100% accepted, 1 enrolled. In 2006, 5 degrees awarded. *Degree requirements:* For master's, comprehensive exam. *Entrance requirements:* For master's, GRE General Test. Additional exam requirements/recommendations for international students: Required—TOEFL or IELTS. *Application deadline:* For fall admission, 7/15 priority date for domestic students, 6/15 for international students; for spring admission, 12/8 for domestic students, 11/1 for international students. Applications are processed on a rolling basis. Application fee: $40 ($50 for international students). Electronic applications accepted. *Expenses:* Tuition, state resident: full-time $2,340; part-time $130 per hour. Tuition, nonresident: full-time $7,290; part-time $405 per hour. Required fees: $906; $56 per hour. *Financial support:* In 2006–07, 3 students received support. Career-related internships or fieldwork, Federal Work-Study, scholarships/grants, tuition waivers (partial), and unspecified assistantships available. Support available to part-time students. Financial award application deadline: 3/1; financial award applicants required to submit FAFSA. *Application contact:* Dr. Cheryl Hines, Graduate Advisor, 325-942-2052 Ext. 283, E-mail: cheryl.hines@angelo.edu.

Anna Maria College, Graduate Division, Program in Education, Paxton, MA 01612. Offers early childhood development (M Ed); education (CAGS); elementary education (M Ed); reading (M Ed). Part-time and evening/weekend programs available. *Faculty:* 6 full-time (5 women), 16 part-time/adjunct (15 women). *Students:* 13 full-time (all women), 84 part-time (82 women); includes 1 minority (Hispanic American) Average age 34. In 2006, 30 master's, 2 other advanced degrees awarded. *Degree requirements:* For master's, action research project. *Entrance requirements:* For master's, bachelor's degree in liberal arts or sciences, minimum GPA of 3.0. *Application deadline:* For fall admission, 3/1 priority date for domestic and international students; for spring admission, 11/1 priority date for domestic and international students. Applications are processed on a rolling basis. Application fee: $40. Electronic applications accepted. *Financial support:* Applicants required to submit FAFSA. *Unit head:* Christine Holmes, Director, 508-849-3418, Fax: 508-849-3343, E-mail: cholmes@annamaria.edu. *Application contact:* Janet LaPointe, Admissions Coordinator, Graduate and Continuing Education, 508-849-3234, Fax: 508-819-3362, E-mail: jlapointe@annamaria.edu.

Appalachian State University, Cratis D. Williams Graduate School, College of Education, Department of Language, Reading, and Exceptionalities, Program in Reading Education, Boone, NC 28608. Offers MA. Part-time programs available. Postbaccalaureate distance learning degree programs offered (minimal on-campus study). *Students:* 5 full-time (all women), 94 part-time (92 women); includes 10 minority (all African Americans) 33 applicants, 97% accepted, 28 enrolled. In 2006, 40 degrees awarded. *Degree requirements:* For master's, thesis optional. *Entrance requirements:* For master's, GRE General Test or MAT, minimum GPA of 2.7 in last 60 hours of course work. Additional exam requirements/recommendations for international students: Required—TOEFL (minimum score 570 paper-based; 230 computer-based). *Application deadline:* For fall admission, 7/1 for domestic students, 1/1 for international students; for spring admission, 11/1 for domestic students, 6/1 for international students. Applications are processed on a rolling basis. Application fee: $50. *Expenses:* Tuition, state resident: full-time $2,600; part-time $127 per hour. Tuition, nonresident: full-time $13,200; part-time $597 per hour. Required fees: $2,000; $546 per term. *Financial support:* Research assistantships, teaching assistantships available. Financial award application deadline: 7/1. *Faculty research:* Technology and literacy, beginning reading process, developmental acquisition of English orthography, severe reading disability, comprehension strategy instruction. *Unit head:* Dr. Woodrow Trathen, Director, 828-262-6056.

Arcadia University, Graduate Studies, Department of Education, Glenside, PA 19038-3295. Offers art education (M Ed, MA Ed); biology education (MA Ed); chemistry education (MA Ed); child development (CAS); computer education (M Ed, CAS); computer education 7–12 (MA Ed); early childhood education (M Ed, CAS), including individualized (M Ed), master teacher (M Ed), research in child development (M Ed); educational leadership (M Ed, CAS); educational psychology (CAS); elementary education (M Ed, CAS); English education (MA Ed); environmental education (MA Ed, CAS); history education (MA Ed); language arts (M Ed, CAS); mathematics education (M Ed, MA Ed, CAS); music education (MA Ed); psychology (MA Ed); pupil personnel services (CAS); reading (M Ed, CAS); school library science (M Ed); science education (M Ed, CAS); secondary education (M Ed, CAS); special education (M Ed, Ed D, CAS); theater arts (MA Ed); written communication (MA Ed). *Accreditation:* NASAD. Part-time and evening/weekend programs available. Postbaccalaureate distance learning degree programs offered (minimal on-campus study). *Faculty:* 12 full-time (8 women), 38 part-time/adjunct (26 women). *Students:* 60 full-time (56 women), 419 part-time (324 women); includes 70 minority (57 African Americans, 1 American Indian/Alaska Native, 6 Asian Americans or Pacific Islanders, 6 Hispanic Americans), 1 international. In 2006, 257 master's, 4 doctorates awarded. *Application deadline:* Applications are processed on a rolling basis. Application fee: $35. Electronic applications accepted. *Financial support:* Career-related internships or fieldwork, tuition waivers (partial), and unspecified assistantships available. *Unit head:* Dr. Steven P. Gulkus, Chair, 215-572-2120. *Application contact:* 215-572-2925, Fax: 215-572-2126, E-mail: grad@arcadia.edu.

Arkansas State University, Graduate School, College of Education, Department of Teacher Education, Jonesboro, State University, AR 72467. Offers early childhood education (MSE); early childhood services (MS); elementary education (MSE); reading (MSE, SCCT). *Accreditation:* NCATE. Part-time programs available. *Faculty:* 6 full-time (3 women). *Students:* 2 full-time (both women), 30 part-time (29 women); includes 3 minority (2 African Americans, 1 Asian American or Pacific Islander). Average age 32. 22 applicants, 82% accepted, 12 enrolled. In 2006, 35 degrees awarded. *Degree requirements:* For master's, thesis or alternative, comprehensive exam. *Entrance requirements:* For master's, GRE General Test or MAT, appropriate bachelor's degree, official transcript; for SCCT, GRE General Test or MAT, interview, master's degree, official transcript. Additional exam requirements/recommendations for international students: Required—TOEFL (minimum score 213 computer-based). *Application deadline:* Applications are processed on a rolling basis. Application fee: $30 ($40 for international students). Electronic applications accepted. *Expenses:* Tuition, state resident: full-time $3,393; part-time $189 per hour. Tuition, nonresident: full-time $8,577; part-time $477 per hour. Required fees: $752; $39 per hour. $25 per semester. *Financial support:* Teaching assistantships, career-related internships or fieldwork, scholarships/grants, and unspecified assistantships available. Financial award application deadline: 7/1; financial award applicants required to submit FAFSA. *Unit head:* Dr. Dianne Lawler-Prince, Interim Chair, 870-972-3059, Fax: 870-972-3344, E-mail: dprince@astate.edu.

Asbury College, Graduate Programs, Wilmore, KY 40390-1198. Offers biology: alternative certificate (MA Ed); chemistry: alternative certificate (MA Ed); English (Certificate); English as a second language (MA Ed); ESL (Certificate); French (Certificate); mathematics: alternative certificate (MA Ed); reading / writing (MA Ed); social studies (Certificate); Spanish (Certificate); special education (MA Ed); special education: alternative certificate (MA Ed). *Accreditation:* NCATE. Part-time programs available. *Faculty:* 8 full-time (7 women), 9 part-time/adjunct (4 women). *Students:* Average age 36. 14 applicants, 100% accepted, 10 enrolled. In 2006, 17 degrees awarded. *Median time to degree:* Master's–2.5 years part-time. *Degree requirements:* For master's, action research project, portfolio. *Entrance requirements:* For master's, PRAXIS/NTE or GRE, minimum GPA of 2.75, letters of recommendation. Additional exam requirements/recommendations for international students: Recommended—TOEFL (minimum score 550 paper-based). *Application deadline:* Applications are processed on a rolling basis. Application fee: $25. *Expenses:* Tuition: Part-time $335 per credit hour. *Financial support:* Scholarships/grants and traineeships available. Financial award applicants required to submit FAFSA. *Unit head:* Dr. Bonnie J. Banker, Director, 859-858-3511 Ext. 2221, Fax: 859-858-3921, E-mail: bonnie.banker@asbury.edu. *Application contact:* Melanie S. Kinnell, Graduate Program Assistant and Certification Specialist, 859-858-3511 Ext. 2304, Fax: 859-858-3921, E-mail: graded@asbury.edu.

Auburn University, Graduate School, College of Education, Department of Curriculum and Teaching, Auburn University, AL 36849. Offers business education (M Ed, MS, PhD); early childhood education (M Ed, MS, PhD, Ed S); elementary education (M Ed, MS, PhD, Ed S); foreign languages (M Ed, MS); music education (M Ed, MS, PhD, Ed S); postsecondary education (PhD); reading education (PhD, Ed S); secondary education (M Ed, MS, PhD, Ed S), including English language arts, mathematics, science, social studies. *Accreditation:* NASM (one or more programs are accredited); NCATE. Part-time programs available. *Faculty:* 26 full-time (19 women). *Students:* 51 full-time (36 women), 116 part-time (86 women); includes 24 minority (23 African Americans, 1 Asian American or Pacific Islander). Average age 33. 181 applicants, 56% accepted, 68 enrolled. In 2006, 63 master's, 12 doctorates, 14 other advanced degrees awarded. *Degree requirements:* For master's, thesis (for some programs); for doctorate, thesis/dissertation; for Ed S, field project. *Entrance requirements:* For master's, doctorate, and Ed S, GRE General Test. *Application deadline:* For fall admission, 7/7 for domestic students; for spring admission, 11/24 for domestic students. Applications are processed on a rolling basis. Application fee: $25 ($50 for international students). Electronic applications accepted. *Expenses:* Tuition, state resident: full-time $5,000. Tuition, nonresident: full-time $15,000. Required fees: $416. Tuition and fees vary according to program. *Financial support:* Fellowships, teaching assistantships, career-related internships or fieldwork and Federal Work-Study available. Support available to part-time students. Financial award application deadline: 3/15. *Faculty research:* Emerging literacy, reading attitudes, music for at-risk youth, portfolio assessment. *Unit head:* Dr. Andrew M. Weaver, Head, 334-844-4434, E-mail: weaveam@mail.auburn.edu. *Application contact:* Dr. Joe Pittman, Interim Dean of the Graduate School, 334-844-4700.

Auburn University Montgomery, School of Education, Department of Early Childhood, Elementary, and Reading Education, Montgomery, AL 36124-4023. Offers early childhood education (M Ed, Ed S); elementary education (M Ed, Ed S); reading education (M Ed, Ed S). *Accreditation:* NCATE. Part-time and evening/weekend programs available. *Faculty:* 6 full-time (all women). *Students:* 38 full-time (32 women), 88 part-time (83 women); includes 47 minority (43 African Americans, 1 American Indian/Alaska Native, 2 Asian Americans or Pacific Islanders, 1 Hispanic American), 1 international. Average age 32. In 2006, 33 master's, 5 other advanced degrees awarded. *Degree requirements:* For master's and Ed S, comprehensive exam. *Entrance requirements:* For master's, GRE General Test or MAT, certification, BS in teaching; for Ed S, GRE General Test or MAT, certification. *Application deadline:* Applications are processed on a rolling basis. Application fee: $25. Electronic applications accepted. *Financial support:* In 2006–07, 1 teaching assistantship was awarded; career-related internships or fieldwork and scholarships/grants also available. Support available to part-time students. Financial award application deadline: 3/1; financial award applicants required to submit FAFSA. *Unit head:* Dr. Lynne Mills, Head, 334-244-3283, Fax: 334-244-3835, E-mail: lmills@mail.aum.edu.

Aurora University, College of Education, Aurora, IL 60506-4892. Offers curriculum and instruction (Ed D); education (MAT); education and administration (Ed D); educational leadership (MEL); reading instruction (MA). Part-time and evening/weekend programs available. *Faculty:* 20 full-time (10 women), 99 part-time/adjunct (55 women). *Students:* 144 full-time (102 women), 1,156 part-time (832 women); includes 169 minority (32 African Americans, 2 American Indian/Alaska Native, 10 Asian Americans or Pacific Islanders, 125 Hispanic Americans). Average age 36. 451 applicants, 99% accepted, 421 enrolled. In 2006, 439 master's, 9 doctorates awarded. *Degree requirements:* For doctorate, thesis/dissertation. *Entrance requirements:* For master's, 2 years of teaching experience, valid teaching certificate. Additional exam requirements/recommendations for international students: Required—TOEFL (minimum score 550 paper-based; 213 computer-based). *Application deadline:* For fall admission, 8/23 priority date for domestic students. Applications are processed on a rolling basis. Application fee: $25. Electronic applications accepted. *Expenses:* Contact institution. Tuition and fees vary according to campus/location and program. *Financial support:* In 2006–07, 355 students received support; fellowships, research assistantships, teaching assistantships, Federal Work-Study and scholarships/grants available. Support available to part-time students. Financial award application deadline: 4/15; financial award applicants required to submit FAFSA. *Unit head:* Dr. Donald C. Wold, Dean, 630-844-1542, Fax: 630-844-5530, E-mail: dwold@aurora.edu. *Application contact:* Donna DeSpain, Dean of Adult and Graduate Studies, 800-742-5281, Fax: 630-844-5535, E-mail: auadmission@aurora.edu.

Austin Peay State University, College of Graduate Studies, College of Professional Programs and Social Sciences, School of Education, Clarksville, TN 37044. Offers curriculum and instruction (MA Ed); education (M Ed, Ed S); educational leadership studies (MA Ed); reading (MA Ed). *Accreditation:* NCATE. Part-time and evening/weekend programs available. Postbaccalaureate distance learning degree programs offered. *Faculty:* 24 full-time (14 women), 8 part-time/adjunct (4 women). *Students:* 81 full-time (65 women), 225 part-time (180 women); includes 48 minority (37 African Americans, 2 American Indian/Alaska Native, 1 Asian American or Pacific Islander, 8 Hispanic Americans). Average age 35. In 2006, 81 master's, 16 other advanced degrees awarded. *Degree requirements:* For master's, teaching license, thesis optional. *Entrance requirements:* For master's, GRE General Test, 3 letters of recommendation; for Ed S, GRE General Test, master's degree, minimum graduate GPA of 3.0, 3 letters of recommendation. Additional exam requirements/recommendations for international students: Required—TOEFL (minimum score 500 paper-based; 173 computer-based). *Application deadline:* For fall admission, 7/31 priority date for domestic students; for spring admission, 12/17 priority date for domestic students. Applications are processed on a rolling basis. Application fee: $25. Electronic applications accepted. *Expenses:* Tuition, state resident: full-time $5,138; part-time $272 per credit hour. Tuition, nonresident: full-time $14,832; part-time $693 per credit hour. Required fees: $1,009. *Financial support:* In 2006–07, research assistantships (averaging $10,270 per year); career-related internships or fieldwork, Federal Work-Study, institutionally sponsored loans, scholarships/grants, and unspecified assistantships also available. Support available to part-time students. Financial award application deadline: 3/1; financial award applicants required to submit FAFSA. *Unit head:* Dr. Carlette Hardin, Director, 931-221-7696, Fax: 931-221-1292, E-mail: forbusl@apsu.edu.

Averett University, Graduate Studies in Education, Danville, VA 24541-3692. Offers art education (M Ed); biology (M Ed); chemistry (M Ed); curriculum and instruction (M Ed); elementary education (M Ed); English (M Ed); health and physical education (M Ed); history and social studies (M Ed); mathematics education (M Ed); physical science (M Ed); reading (M Ed); special education (learning disabilities specialization PK-12) (M Ed). Part-time and evening/weekend programs available. *Faculty:* 10 full-time (4 women), 7 part-time/adjunct (6 women). *Students:* 14 full-time (10 women), 85 part-time (67 women); includes 20 minority (18 African Americans, 2 Asian Americans or Pacific Islanders). Average age 33. 52 applicants, 100% accepted, 40 enrolled. In 2006, 48 degrees awarded. *Degree requirements:* For master's, thesis optional. *Entrance requirements:* For master's, PRAXIS, GRE General Test, MAT or NTE, writing proficiency exam, 3 letters of recommendation, current teacher's licensure or eligibility for licensure, minimum undergraduate GPA of 3.0 in previous 2 years. Additional exam requirements/recommendations for international students: Required—TOEFL (minimum score 600 paper-based; 200 computer-based). *Application deadline:* Applications are processed on a rolling basis. Application fee: $20. *Expenses:* Contact institution. *Financial support:* In 2006–07, 23 students received support. Federal Work-Study and scholarships/grants available. Financial award application deadline: 4/1; financial award applicants required to submit FAFSA. *Faculty research:* Literary assessment-PreK-6, handwriting instruction and assessment-PreK-6, written language instruction and assessment-PreK-6 and special needs students learning styles, curriculum and instruction processes. *Unit head:* Dr. Lynn H. Wolf, Chair, 434-793-3995, Fax: 434-791-4392, E-mail: lynn.wolf@averett.edu.

Avila University, School of Education, Kansas City, MO 64145-1698. Offers education (MA); English for speakers of other languages (Advanced Certificate); special reading (Advanced Certificate). Part-time and evening/weekend programs available. *Faculty:* 7 full-time (5 women), 17 part-time/adjunct (13 women). *Students:* 144 full-time (112 women), 42 part-time (24 women); includes 17 minority (15 African Americans, 2 Hispanic Americans). Average age 37. 72 applicants, 42% accepted, 14 enrolled. In 2006, 34 degrees awarded. *Entrance requirements:* For master's, minimum GPA of 3.0. *Application deadline:* Applications are processed on a rolling basis. Application fee: $0. Electronic applications accepted. *Expenses:* Tuition: Full-time $7,470; part-time $415 per credit. *Financial support:* In 2006–07, 1 research assistantship was awarded; career-related internships or fieldwork also available. Support available to part-time students. Financial award applicants required to submit FAFSA. *Unit head:* Dr. Laura Sloan, Dean, 816-501-3663, Fax: 816-501-2455, E-mail: laura.sloan@avila.edu. *Application contact:* Deana Angotti, Director of Graduate Education, 816-501-2446, Fax: 816-501-2915, E-mail: deana.augotti@avila.edu.

Baldwin-Wallace College, Graduate Programs, Division of Education, Specialization in Reading, Berea, OH 44017-2088. Offers MA Ed. *Accreditation:* NCATE. Part-time and evening/weekend programs available. *Students:* 27 full-time (22 women), 37 part-time (36 women); includes 8 minority (5 African Americans, 1 Asian American or Pacific Islander, 2 Hispanic Americans). Average age 31. 34 applicants, 88% accepted, 19 enrolled. In 2006, 63 degrees awarded. *Degree requirements:* For master's, comprehensive exam. *Entrance requirements:* For master's, bachelor's degree in field, MAT or minimum GPA of 2.75. *Application deadline:* For fall admission, 8/15 priority date for domestic students; for spring admission, 12/15 priority date for domestic students. Applications are processed on a rolling basis. Application fee: $25. Electronic applications accepted. *Expenses:* Tuition: Part-time $760 per

Reading Education

Baldwin-Wallace College (continued)
credit hour. Tuition and fees vary according to program. *Financial support:* Career-related internships or fieldwork available. Financial award applicants required to submit FAFSA. *Application contact:* Winifred W. Gerhardt, Director of Admission for the Evening and Weekend College, 440-826-2222, Fax: 440-826-3830, E-mail: admission@bw.edu.

Bank Street College of Education, Graduate School, Department of Curriculum and Instruction, Program in Reading and Literacy, New York, NY 10025. Offers advanced literacy specialization (Ed M); reading and literacy (MS Ed); teaching literacy (MS Ed); teaching literacy and elementary education (MS Ed). *Accreditation:* NCATE. *Students:* 35 full-time (33 women), 71 part-time (70 women); includes 25 minority (9 African Americans, 6 Asian Americans or Pacific Islanders, 10 Hispanic Americans). Average age 30. 71 applicants, 75% accepted, 40 enrolled. In 2006, 30 degrees awarded. *Degree requirements:* For master's, thesis, registration. *Entrance requirements:* For master's, interview. Additional exam requirements/recommendations for international students: Required—TOEFL (minimum score 600 paper-based; 250 computer-based). *Application deadline:* For fall admission, 3/1 priority date for domestic students; for spring admission, 11/1 priority date for domestic students. Applications are processed on a rolling basis. Application fee: $50. *Expenses:* Tuition: Part-time $940 per credit. Required fees: $100 per term. *Financial support:* Career-related internships or fieldwork, Federal Work-Study, scholarships/grants, and unspecified assistantships available. Support available to part-time students. Financial award application deadline: 4/15; financial award applicants required to submit FAFSA. *Faculty research:* Language development, reading and the writing process, reading difficulties in multi-cultural classrooms. *Unit head:* Dr. Margaret McNamara, Director, 212-875-4586, Fax: 212-875-4753, E-mail: mam@bankstreet.edu. *Application contact:* Ann Morgan, Director of Graduate Admissions, 212-875-4403, Fax: 212-875-4678, E-mail: amorgan@bankstreet.edu.

Barry University, School of Education, Program in Curriculum and Instruction, Miami Shores, FL 33161-6695. Offers accomplished teacher (Ed S); culture, language and literacy (TESOL) (PhD); curriculum evaluation and research (PhD); early childhood (Ed S); early childhood education (PhD); elementary (Ed S); elementary education (PhD); ESOL (Ed S); gifted (Ed S); Montessori (Ed S); PKP/elementary (Ed S); reading (Ed S); reading, language and cognition (PhD). *Students:* 2 full-time (both women), 36 part-time (27 women); includes 21 minority (12 African Americans, 9 Hispanic Americans), 6 international. 45 applicants, 33% accepted, 4 enrolled. In 2006, 4 degrees awarded. *Entrance requirements:* For doctorate, GRE, minimum GPA of 3.25. Application fee: $30. *Unit head:* Dr. Jill Farrell, Director, 305-899-3198, Fax: 305-899-4708, E-mail: jfarrell@mail.barry.edu. *Application contact:* Dave Fletcher, Director of Graduate Admissions, 305-899-3113, Fax: 305-899-2971, E-mail: dfletcher@mail.barry.edu.

Barry University, School of Education, Program in Reading, Miami Shores, FL 33161-6695. Offers MS, Ed S. Part-time and evening/weekend programs available. *Students:* 43 full-time (42 women), 86 part-time (82 women); includes 74 minority (31 African Americans, 2 Asian Americans or Pacific Islanders, 41 Hispanic Americans), 1 international. 79 applicants, 76% accepted, 41 enrolled. In 2006, 61 master's, 4 other advanced degrees awarded. *Degree requirements:* For master's, practicum; for Ed S, practicum. *Entrance requirements:* For master's, GRE General Test or MAT, minimum GPA of 3.0, course work in children's literature; for Ed S, GRE General Test, minimum GPA of 3.0. *Application deadline:* For fall admission, 5/1 priority date for domestic students. Applications are processed on a rolling basis. Application fee: $30. Electronic applications accepted. *Unit head:* Dr. Joyce Warner, Director, 305-899-3713, Fax: 305-899-4708, E-mail: jwarner@mail.barry.edu. *Application contact:* Dave Fletcher, Director of Graduate Admissions, 305-899-3113, Fax: 305-899-2971, E-mail: dfletcher@mail.barry.edu.

Bellarmine University, Annsley Frazier Thornton School of Education, Louisville, KY 40205-0671. Offers early elementary education (MA, MAT); instructional leadership and school administration/school principal (MA); learning and behavior disorders (MA); middle school education (MA, MAT); reading and writing endorsement (MA); secondary school education (MAT); Waldorf inspired curriculum (MA);). *Accreditation:* NCATE. Part-time and evening/weekend programs available. *Faculty:* 10 full-time (8 women), 5 part-time/adjunct (all women). *Students:* 92 full-time (68 women), 140 part-time (104 women); includes 16 minority (11 African Americans, 1 Asian American or Pacific Islander, 4 Hispanic Americans). Average age 32. In 2006, 98 degrees awarded. *Degree requirements:* For master's, thesis (for some programs), comprehensive exam. *Entrance requirements:* For master's, minimum overall GPA of 2.75, 3.0 in major; letters of recommendation; valid Kentucky provisional or professional certificate. Additional exam requirements/recommendations for international students: Required—TOEFL (minimum score 550 paper-based; 213 computer-based; 80 iBT), GRE. *Application deadline:* Applications are processed on a rolling basis. Application fee: $25. Electronic applications accepted. *Expenses:* Contact institution. Tuition and fees vary according to program. *Faculty research:* Social justice, service learning dispositions, educational technology, special education. *Unit head:* Dr. Milton Brown, Dean (Interim), 502-452-8486, Fax: 502-452-8189, E-mail: mbrown@bellarmine.edu. *Application contact:* Theresa Klapheke, Director of Graduate Programs, 502-452-8033, Fax: 502-452-8189, E-mail: tklapheke@bellarmine.edu.

Benedictine University, Graduate Programs, Program in Education, Lisle, IL 60532-0900. Offers curriculum and instruction and collaborative teaching (M Ed); elementary education (MA Ed); leadership and administration (M Ed); reading and literacy (M Ed); secondary education (MA Ed); special education (MA Ed). Part-time and evening/weekend programs available. *Faculty:* 4 full-time (2 women), 52 part-time/adjunct (30 women). *Students:* 257 (196 women); includes 22 minority (4 African Americans, 1 American Indian/Alaska Native, 3 Asian Americans or Pacific Islanders, 14 Hispanic Americans) 2 international. Average age 33. 130 applicants, 93% accepted, 13 enrolled. In 2006, 181 degrees awarded. *Degree requirements:* For master's, thesis (for some programs), comprehensive exam. *Entrance requirements:* For master's, GRE or MAT. Additional exam requirements/recommendations for international students: Required—TOEFL (minimum score 550 paper-based; 213 computer-based). *Application deadline:* For fall admission, 9/1 for domestic students; for winter admission, 12/1 for domestic students; for spring admission, 2/15 for domestic students. Applications are processed on a rolling basis. Application fee: $40. Electronic applications accepted. *Expenses:* Contact institution. *Financial support:* Career-related internships or fieldwork and health care benefits available. Support available to part-time students. *Unit head:* Dr. Richard Campbell, Director, 630-829-6242, Fax: 630-960-1126, E-mail: rcampbell@ben.edu. *Application contact:* Kari Gibbons, Director, Admissions, 630-829-6200, Fax: 630-829-6584, E-mail: kgibbons@ben.edu.

Berry College, Graduate Programs, Graduate Programs in Education, Program in Middle-Grades Education and Reading, Mount Berry, GA 30149-0159. Offers M Ed. *Accreditation:* NCATE. Part-time programs available. *Faculty:* 9 part-time/adjunct (5 women). *Students:* 1 full-time (0 women), 30 part-time (23 women); includes 1 Hispanic American. Average age 34. In 2006, 11 degrees awarded. *Degree requirements:* For master's, oral exams, thesis optional. *Entrance requirements:* For master's, GRE General Test, MAT, or NTE, minimum GPA of 2.5. Additional exam requirements/recommendations for international students: Required—TOEFL (minimum score 550 paper-based; 213 computer-based). *Application deadline:* For fall admission, 5/1 for domestic students; for spring admission, 10/1 for domestic students. Applications are processed on a rolling basis. Application fee: $25 ($30 for international students). *Expenses:* Contact institution. *Financial support:* In 2006–07, 27 students received support, including 2 research assistantships with full tuition reimbursements available (averaging $3,500 per year); scholarships/grants, tuition waivers (partial), and unspecified assistantships also available. Support available to part-time students. Financial award application deadline: 4/1; financial award applicants required to submit FAFSA. *Faculty research:* Curriculum development, teacher training, pedagogy. *Application contact:* Richard D. Paul, Dean of Admissions and Financial Aid, 706-236-2215, Fax: 706-290-2178, E-mail: dpaul@berry.edu.

Bethel University, Graduate School, Department of Education, St. Paul, MN 55112-6999. Offers education K-12 (MA); educational administration (Ed D); literacy (Certificate); literacy education (MA); secondary education (MA); special education (M Ed). Evening/weekend programs available. *Faculty:* 20 full-time (10 women), 34 part-time/adjunct (18 women). *Students:* 192 full-time (119 women), 110 part-time (71 women); includes 16 minority (6 African Americans, 5 Asian Americans or Pacific Islanders, 5 Hispanic Americans). Average age 35. In 2006, 58 master's, 9 other advanced degrees awarded. *Degree requirements:* For master's, thesis, practicum; for doctorate, thesis/dissertation, registration. *Entrance requirements:* For master's, interview, current teaching license, minimum GPA of 3.0, teaching experience (if applicable), letters of reference; for doctorate, MAT or GRE, minimum GPA of 3.5, letters of reference, master's degree. Additional exam requirements/recommendations for international students: Required—TOEFL (minimum score 550 paper-based; 213 computer-based). *Application deadline:* For fall admission, 8/1 priority date for domestic students; for winter admission, 12/10 priority date for domestic students; for spring admission, 5/1 priority date for domestic students. Applications are processed on a rolling basis. Application fee: $25. Electronic applications accepted. *Expenses:* Contact institution. Tuition and fees vary according to program. *Financial support:* Institutionally sponsored loans and scholarships/grants available. Financial award applicants required to submit FAFSA. *Unit head:* Dr. Jay B. Rasmussen, Director, 651-638-6237, Fax: 651-638-8004, E-mail: jay-rasmussen@bethel.edu. *Application contact:* Michael Price, Director of Admissions, 651-635-8000 Ext. 8017, Fax: 651-635-8004, E-mail: m_price@bethel.edu.

Bloomsburg University of Pennsylvania, School of Graduate Studies, College of Professional Studies, School of Education, Department of Exceptionality Programs, Program in Reading, Bloomsburg, PA 17815-1301. Offers M Ed. *Accreditation:* NCATE. *Faculty:* 2 full-time (both women). *Students:* 3 full-time (all women), 65 part-time (62 women); includes 1 minority (Asian American or Pacific Islander) Average age 30. 22 applicants, 100% accepted, 15 enrolled. In 2006, 35 degrees awarded. *Entrance requirements:* For master's, teaching certificate, minimum QPA of 3.0. Additional exam requirements/recommendations for international students: Required—TOEFL (minimum score 550 paper-based; 213 computer-based; 79 iBT). *Application deadline:* Applications are processed on a rolling basis. Application fee: $30. Electronic applications accepted. *Expenses:* Tuition, state resident: full-time $6,048; part-time $336 per credit. Tuition, nonresident: full-time $9,678; part-time $538 per credit. Required fees: $1,415. *Financial support:* Unspecified assistantships available. *Faculty research:* Diagnosis, remediation, parental involvement, language arts, child literacy. *Unit head:* Dr. Elaine Pongratz, Coordinator, 570-389-5119, Fax: 570-389-3980, E-mail: epongrat@bloomu.edu.

Boise State University, Graduate College, College of Education, Programs in Teacher Education, Program in Reading, Boise, ID 83725-0399. Offers MA. *Accreditation:* NCATE. Part-time programs available. *Faculty:* 5 full-time (3 women). *Students:* 5 full-time (all women), 43 part-time (41 women); includes 5 minority (2 American Indian/Alaska Native, 1 Asian American or Pacific Islander, 2 Hispanic Americans). Average age 41. 16 applicants, 100% accepted, 5 enrolled. In 2006, 10 degrees awarded. *Degree requirements:* For master's, thesis optional. *Entrance requirements:* For master's, minimum GPA of 3.0. *Application deadline:* For fall admission, 7/1 priority date for domestic students; for spring admission, 11/15 priority date for domestic students. Applications are processed on a rolling basis. Application fee: $0. Electronic applications accepted. *Financial support:* Career-related internships or fieldwork, Federal Work-Study, institutionally sponsored loans, and unspecified assistantships available. Support available to part-time students. Financial award application deadline: 3/1. *Unit head:* Dr. Lee Dubert, Head, 208-426-3271, Fax: 208-426-4365, E-mail: ldubert@boisestate.edu.

Boston College, Lynch Graduate School of Education, Department of Teacher Education/Special Education and Curriculum and Instruction, Reading Specialist Program, Chestnut Hill, MA 02467-3800. Offers M Ed, CAES. *Students:* 6 full-time (all women), 6 part-time (5 women); includes 2 minority (both Hispanic Americans) 25 applicants, 64% accepted, 5 enrolled. In 2006, 7 degrees awarded. *Degree requirements:* For master's and CAES, comprehensive exam. *Entrance requirements:* For master's and CAES, GRE General Test or MAT. Additional exam requirements/recommendations for international students: Required—TOEFL. *Application deadline:* For fall admission, 1/1 priority date for domestic students. Application fee: $60. *Financial support:* Fellowships with full and partial tuition reimbursements, research assistantships with full and partial tuition reimbursements, teaching assistantships with full and partial tuition reimbursements, career-related internships or fieldwork, Federal Work-Study, scholarships/grants, traineeships, tuition waivers (full and partial), and unspecified assistantships available. Support available to part-time students. Financial award applicants required to submit FAFSA. *Faculty research:* Reading instruction, educational publishing, children's literature, teaching writing, literacy. *Application contact:* Timothy P. Blackman, Director, Graduate Admission and Financial Aid, 617-552-4214, Fax: 617-552-0398, E-mail: timothy.blackman.1@bc.edu.

Boston University, School of Education, Department of Literacy and Language, Counseling and Development, Program in Reading Education, Boston, MA 02215. Offers literacy and language (Ed D); reading education (Ed M, CAGS). *Students:* 6 full-time (all women), 9 part-time (8 women). Average age 32. 23 applicants, 87% accepted. In 2006, 6 degrees awarded. *Degree requirements:* For doctorate, thesis/dissertation, comprehensive exam. *Entrance requirements:* For master's, doctorate, and CAGS, GRE General Test or MAT. Additional exam requirements/recommendations for international students: Required—TOEFL. *Application deadline:* For fall admission, 2/15 priority date for domestic students; for winter admission, 10/1 priority date for domestic students. Applications are processed on a rolling basis. Application fee: $65. Electronic applications accepted. *Expenses:* Tuition: Full-time $33,330; part-time $1,042 per credit. Required fees: $462; $40. *Financial support:* Application deadline: 2/15. *Faculty research:* Reading diagnosis (disabilities), professional preparation. *Unit head:* Dr. Jeanne Paratore, Head, 617-353-3285, E-mail: jparator@bu.edu. *Application contact:* 617-353-4237, Fax: 617-353-8937, E-mail: sedgrad@bu.edu.

Bowie State University, Graduate Programs, Program in Reading Education, Bowie, MD 20715-9465. Offers M Ed. *Accreditation:* NCATE. Part-time and evening/weekend programs available. *Faculty:* 1 (woman) full-time. *Students:* 42 full-time (39 women), 69 part-time (60 women); includes 72 minority (67 African Americans, 2 Asian Americans or Pacific Islanders, 3 Hispanic Americans). Average age 36. In 2006, 17 degrees awarded. *Degree requirements:* For master's, research paper, thesis optional. *Entrance requirements:* For master's, minimum GPA of 2.5, teaching certificate, teaching experience. *Application deadline:* For fall admission, 4/1 priority date for domestic students, 4/1 for international students; for spring admission, 11/1 for domestic and international students. Applications are processed on a rolling basis. Application fee: $40. *Expenses:* Tuition, state resident: full-time $7,344; part-time $306 per credit. Tuition, nonresident: full-time $14,304; part-time $396 per credit. Required fees: $1,078; $77 per credit. $539 per term. One-time fee: $40. *Financial support:* Application deadline: 4/1. *Faculty research:* Literacy education, multicultural education. *Unit head:* Dr. Lucille Strain, Coordinator, 301-860-3129, E-mail: lstrain@bowiestate.edu. *Application contact:* Angela Issac, Information Contact.

Bowling Green State University, Graduate College, College of Education and Human Development, School of Education and Intervention Services, Teacher and Learning Division, Program in Reading, Bowling Green, OH 43403. Offers M Ed, Ed S. *Accreditation:* NCATE. Part-time programs available. *Students:* 10 full-time (all women), 10 part-time (all women); includes 1 minority (Hispanic American) Average age 29. 6 applicants, 83% accepted, 0 enrolled. In 2006, 20 degrees awarded. *Degree requirements:* For master's, thesis or alternative; for Ed S, practicum or field experience. *Entrance requirements:* For master's and Ed S, GRE General Test. Additional exam requirements/recommendations for international students: Required—TOEFL. *Application deadline:* For fall admission, 2/15 priority date for domestic students. Applications are processed on a rolling basis. Application fee: $30. Electronic applications accepted. *Expenses:* Tuition, state resident: part-time $535 per hour. Tuition, nonresident: part-time $884 per hour. *Financial support:* In 2006–07, 10 research assistantships with tuition reimbursements (averaging $7,774 per year) were awarded; teaching assistantships with tuition reimbursements, career-related internships or fieldwork, Federal Work-Study, institutionally sponsored loans, and unspecified assistantships also available. Financial award applicants required to submit FAFSA. *Faculty research:* Children's literature, attention deficit disorder

(ADD)/reading correlation, content area reading, reading instruction, reading/writing connection. *Unit head:* Dr. Cindy Hendricks, Director, 419-372-7341.

Bridgewater State College, School of Graduate Studies, School of Education and Allied Science, Department of Elementary and Early Childhood Education, Program in Reading, Bridgewater, MA 02325-0001. Offers M Ed, CAGS. *Accreditation:* NCATE. Part-time and evening/weekend programs available. *Entrance requirements:* For master's, GRE General Test, 1 year of teaching experience. *Application deadline:* For fall admission, 3/1 priority date for domestic students; for spring admission, 10/1 priority date for domestic students. Application fee: $50. *Financial support:* Career-related internships or fieldwork, health care benefits, and unspecified assistantships available. Support available to part-time students.

Brigham Young University, Graduate Studies, David O. McKay School of Education, Department of Teacher Education, Provo, UT 84602-1001. Offers literacy education (M Ed, MA); teacher education (M Ed, MA). *Accreditation:* NCATE. *Faculty:* 19 full-time (9 women). *Students:* Average age 33. 18 applicants, 78% accepted, 12 enrolled. In 2006, 10 master's awarded. *Median time to degree:* Master's–2 years part-time. *Degree requirements:* For master's, thesis (for some programs), thesis or project (MA). *Entrance requirements:* For master's, GRE General Test, minimum 1 year of teaching experience, minimum GPA of 3.25 in last 60 hours of course work, valid teaching credential. Additional exam requirements/recommendations for international students: Required—TOEFL (minimum score 500 paper-based). *Application deadline:* For fall admission, 2/1 priority date for domestic and international students. Application fee: $50. Electronic applications accepted. *Financial support:* In 2006–07, 19 students received support; research assistantships, teaching assistantships with full tuition reimbursements available, scholarships/grants and tuition waivers (partial) available. *Faculty research:* Elementary mathematics education, elementary school curriculum, teaching of reading, balanced literacy, teaching and learning. Total annual research expenditures: $378,450. *Unit head:* Dr. M. Winston Egan, Chair, 801-422-4542, Fax: 801-422-0652, E-mail: winn_egan@byu.edu. *Application contact:* Kristine Abbott, Department Secretary, 801-422-4078, Fax: 801-422-0652, E-mail: kristine_abbott@byu.edu.

Bucknell University, Graduate Studies, College of Arts and Sciences, Department of Education, Specialization in Reading, Lewisburg, PA 17837. Offers MA, MS Ed. *Degree requirements:* For master's, thesis or alternative. *Entrance requirements:* For master's, GRE General Test, minimum GPA of 2.8. Additional exam requirements/recommendations for international students: Required—TOEFL.

Buffalo State College, State University of New York, Graduate Studies and Research, Faculty of Applied Science and Education, Department of Elementary Education and Reading, Programs in Literacy Specialist, Buffalo, NY 14222-1095. Offers literacy specialist (birth-grade 6) (MS Ed); literacy specialist (grades 5-12) (MPS). *Accreditation:* NCATE. Part-time and evening/weekend programs available. *Degree requirements:* For master's, project. *Entrance requirements:* For master's, minimum GPA of 3.0 in last 60 hours. Additional exam requirements/recommendations for international students: Required—TOEFL (minimum score 550 paper-based; 213 computer-based).

Butler University, College of Education, Indianapolis, IN 46208-3485. Offers administration (MS); elementary education (MS); reading (MS); school counseling (MS); secondary education (MS); special education (MS). *Accreditation:* ACA; NCATE. Part-time and evening/weekend programs available. *Faculty:* 12 full-time (6 women), 11 part-time/adjunct (8 women). *Students:* 18 full-time (10 women), 156 part-time (125 women); includes 21 minority (16 African Americans, 2 Asian Americans or Pacific Islanders, 3 Hispanic Americans), 7 international. Average age 31. 56 applicants, 57% accepted, 29 enrolled. In 2006, 72 degrees awarded. *Entrance requirements:* For master's, GRE General Test, MAT, interview. *Application deadline:* For fall admission, 8/15 priority date for domestic students. Applications are processed on a rolling basis. Application fee: $35. Electronic applications accepted. *Expenses:* Tuition: Full-time $6,030; part-time $335 per credit. Tuition and fees vary according to program. *Financial support:* Institutionally sponsored loans available. Support available to part-time students. Financial award application deadline: 7/15; financial award applicants required to submit FAFSA. *Faculty research:* Ethics in cybercounseling, history of sports for disabled effect of fetal alcohol syndrome on perceptual learning, Reading Recovery's theoretical framework in teacher education. *Unit head:* Dr. Ena Shelley, Dean, 317-940-9752, Fax: 317-940-6481. *Application contact:* Karen Farrell, Department Secretary, 317-940-9220, E-mail: kfarrell@butler.edu.

California Baptist University, Program in Education, Riverside, CA 92504-3206. Offers cross-cultural language and academic development (MA Ed); educational leadership (MS Ed); educational technology (MS Ed); instructional computer applications (MS Ed); reading (MS Ed); special education (MS Ed); teaching (MS Ed). Part-time programs available. *Faculty:* 16 full-time (10 women), 16 part-time/adjunct (13 women). *Students:* 77 full-time (64 women), 408 part-time (342 women); includes 157 minority (41 African Americans, 12 American Indian/Alaska Native, 18 Asian Americans or Pacific Islanders, 86 Hispanic Americans), 2 international. 282 applicants, 70% accepted, 171 enrolled. In 2006, 63 degrees awarded. *Degree requirements:* For master's, thesis optional. *Entrance requirements:* For master's, minimum undergraduate GPA of 2.75, 12 semester hours of course work in education. Additional exam requirements/recommendations for international students: Required—TOEFL (minimum score 575 paper-based; 230 computer-based), IELTS (minimum score 7). *Application deadline:* For fall admission, 9/1 for domestic students, 7/15 priority date for international students; for spring admission, 1/3 for domestic students, 11/1 priority date for international students. Applications are processed on a rolling basis. Application fee: $45. Electronic applications accepted. *Expenses:* Tuition: Full-time $7,812; part-time $434 per unit. Required fees: $120 per semester. Tuition and fees vary according to program. *Financial support:* In 2006–07, 19 students received support. Career-related internships or fieldwork, Federal Work-Study, and scholarships/grants available. Support available to part-time students. Financial award applicants required to submit FAFSA. *Unit head:* Dr. Mary Crist, Dean, School of Education, 951-343-4313, Fax: 951-343-4516, E-mail: mcrist@calbaptist.edu. *Application contact:* Gail Ronveaux, Dean of Graduate Enrollment, 951-343-5045, Fax: 951-343-5095, E-mail: graduateadmissions@calbaptist.edu.

California Lutheran University, Graduate Studies, School of Education, Emphasis in Curriculum and Instruction, Thousand Oaks, CA 91360-2787. Offers reading education (MA). *Accreditation:* NCATE. Part-time and evening/weekend programs available. *Degree requirements:* For master's, thesis or comprehensive exam. *Entrance requirements:* For master's, GRE General Test, interview, minimum GPA of 3.0.

California State University, Chico, Graduate School, College of Communication and Education, Department of Education, Chico, CA 95929-0222. Offers education (MA), including curriculum and instruction, educational administration, linguistically and culturally diverse learners, reading/language arts, special education. *Students:* 29 full-time (20 women), 66 part-time (53 women); includes 11 minority (2 African Americans, 1 American Indian/Alaska Native, 1 Asian American or Pacific Islander, 7 Hispanic Americans), 1 international. Average age 36. 47 applicants, 100% accepted, 39 enrolled. In 2006, 37 degrees awarded. *Entrance requirements:* Additional exam requirements/recommendations for international students: Required—TOEFL (minimum score 550 paper-based; 213 computer-based). *Application deadline:* For fall admission, 3/1 for domestic and international students; for spring admission, 9/15 for domestic and international students. Applications are processed on a rolling basis. Application fee: $55. Electronic applications accepted. *Financial support:* Fellowships, teaching assistantships, career-related internships or fieldwork and stipends available. *Unit head:* Dr. Deborah Summers, Chair, 530-898-6421.

California State University, Chico, Graduate School, College of Communication and Education, Department of Education, Program in Education, Option in Reading/Language Arts, Chico, CA 95929-0722. Offers MA. *Students:* 6 full-time (all women), 8 part-time (all women); includes 1 minority (Hispanic American) Average age 34. 8 applicants, 100% accepted, 7 enrolled. *Unit head:* Dr. James Richmond, Graduate Coordinator, 530-898-6610.

California State University, Fresno, Division of Graduate Studies, School of Education and Human Development, Department of Literacy and Early Education, Fresno, CA 93740-8027. Offers education (MA), including early childhood education, reading/language arts. *Accreditation:* NCATE. Part-time and evening/weekend programs available. *Degree requirements:* For master's, thesis or alternative. *Entrance requirements:* For master's, GRE General Test, MAT, minimum GPA of 2.75. Additional exam requirements/recommendations for international students: Required—TOEFL. Electronic applications accepted. *Faculty research:* Reading recovery, monitoring/tutoring programs, character and academics, professional ethics, low-performing partnership schools.

California State University, Fullerton, Graduate Studies, College of Education, Department of Reading, Fullerton, CA 92834-9480. Offers MS. *Students:* 12 full-time (all women), 161 part-time (149 women); includes 49 minority (1 African American, 14 Asian Americans or Pacific Islanders, 34 Hispanic Americans). Average age 37. 72 applicants, 83% accepted, 47 enrolled. In 2006, 95 degrees awarded. Application fee: $55. *Expenses:* Tuition, nonresident: part-time $339 per unit. Required fees: $1,155 per semester. *Unit head:* Dr. Jo Ann Carter-Wells, Chair, 714-278-3357.

California State University, Los Angeles, Graduate Studies, Charter College of Education, Division of Curriculum and Instruction, Los Angeles, CA 90032-8530. Offers elementary teaching (MA); reading (MA); secondary teaching (MA). Part-time and evening/weekend programs available. *Faculty:* 13 full-time (8 women), 8 part-time/adjunct (all women). *Students:* 269 full-time (184 women), 572 part-time (406 women); includes 528 minority (48 African Americans, 1 American Indian/Alaska Native, 142 Asian Americans or Pacific Islanders, 337 Hispanic Americans), 20 international. In 2006, 134 degrees awarded. *Entrance requirements:* For master's, minimum GPA of 2.75 in last 90 units of course work, teaching certificate. Additional exam requirements/recommendations for international students: Required—TOEFL. *Application deadline:* For fall admission, 6/30 for domestic students; for spring admission, 2/1 for domestic students. Applications are processed on a rolling basis. Application fee: $55. *Expenses:* Tuition, nonresident: part-time $226 per unit. *Financial support:* Federal Work-Study available. Support available to part-time students. Financial award application deadline: 3/1. *Faculty research:* Media, language arts, mathematics, computers, drug-free schools. *Unit head:* Dr. Andrea Maxie, Chair, 323-343-4350, Fax: 323-343-5458.

California State University, Sacramento, Graduate Studies, College of Education, Department of Teacher Education, Program in Reading Education, Sacramento, CA 95819-6048. Offers MA. Part-time programs available. *Degree requirements:* For master's, thesis or alternative, writing proficiency exam. *Entrance requirements:* For master's, minimum GPA of 3.0, teaching credentials. Additional exam requirements/recommendations for international students: Required—TOEFL. *Application deadline:* Applications are processed on a rolling basis. Application fee: $55. Electronic applications accepted. *Financial support:* Career-related internships or fieldwork and Federal Work-Study available. Support available to part-time students. Financial award application deadline: 3/1.

California State University, San Bernardino, Graduate Studies, College of Education, Program in Reading, San Bernardino, CA 92407-2397. Offers MA. *Accreditation:* NCATE. Part-time and evening/weekend programs available. *Students:* 55 full-time (49 women), 41 part-time (34 women); includes 37 minority (11 African Americans, 3 Asian Americans or Pacific Islanders, 23 Hispanic Americans). Average age 38. 29 applicants, 90% accepted, 12 enrolled. In 2006, 34 degrees awarded. *Degree requirements:* For master's, thesis or alternative. *Entrance requirements:* For master's, minimum GPA of 3.0 in education. *Application deadline:* For fall admission, 8/31 priority date for domestic students. Application fee: $55. *Financial support:* Career-related internships or fieldwork and Federal Work-Study available. Support available to part-time students. *Unit head:* Dr. Mary Jo Skillings, Chair, 909-537-5639, Fax: 909-537-5992, E-mail: maryjosk@csusb.edu.

California State University, Stanislaus, Graduate School, College of Education, Department of Teacher Education, Turlock, CA 95382. Offers curriculum and instruction (MA Ed), including elementary education, multilingual education, reading education, secondary education. Part-time and evening/weekend programs available. *Degree requirements:* For master's, thesis. *Entrance requirements:* For master's, MAT or GRE, minimum GPA of 3.0. Additional exam requirements/recommendations for international students: Required—TOEFL (minimum score 550 paper-based; 213 computer-based).

California University of Pennsylvania, School of Graduate Studies and Research, School of Education, Department of Elementary Education, Program in Reading Specialist, California, PA 15419-1394. Offers M Ed. *Accreditation:* NCATE. Part-time and evening/weekend programs available. *Faculty:* 6 full-time (3 women). *Students:* 7 full-time (all women), 68 part-time (65 women). Average age 36. 34 applicants, 97% accepted, 33 enrolled. In 2006, 33 degrees awarded. *Median time to degree:* Master's–1.5 years full-time, 3 years part-time. *Degree requirements:* For master's, practicum, thesis optional. *Entrance requirements:* For master's, MAT, PRAXIS, minimum GPA of 3.0, teaching certificate. Additional exam requirements/recommendations for international students: Required—TOEFL (minimum score 550 paper-based; 213 computer-based; 80 iBT). *Application deadline:* For fall admission, 8/1 priority date for domestic and international students; for winter admission, 12/1 priority date for domestic and international students; for spring admission, 5/1 priority date for domestic and international students. Applications are processed on a rolling basis. Application fee: $25. Electronic applications accepted. *Expenses:* Tuition, state resident: full-time $6,048; part-time $336 per credit. Tuition, nonresident: full-time $9,678; part-time $538 per credit. Required fees: $1,854; $263 per credit. Full-time tuition and fees vary according to course load, campus/location and program. *Financial support:* Career-related internships or fieldwork, scholarships/grants, traineeships, and unspecified assistantships available. Financial award applicants required to submit FAFSA. *Faculty research:* Online education in reading supervision, phonetics education, remedial reading, injury and reading remediation in brain patients. *Unit head:* Prof. Jane Bonari, Graduate Coordinator, 724-938-4569, Fax: 724-938-5873, E-mail: bonari@cup.edu.

Calvin College, Graduate Programs in Education, Grand Rapids, MI 49546-4388. Offers curriculum and instruction (M Ed); educational leadership (M Ed); learning disabilities (M Ed); literacy (M Ed). *Accreditation:* NCATE. Part-time programs available. *Faculty:* 2 full-time (both women), 6 part-time/adjunct (2 women). *Students:* 6 full-time (5 women), 87 part-time (66 women); includes 9 minority (3 African Americans, 1 American Indian/Alaska Native, 4 Asian Americans or Pacific Islanders, 1 Hispanic American). Average age 29. 26 applicants, 100% accepted. In 2006, 14 degrees awarded. *Degree requirements:* For master's, thesis or seminar; for degree. *Entrance requirements:* For master's, teaching certificate. Additional exam requirements/recommendations for international students: Required—TOEFL (minimum score 550 paper-based; 213 computer-based). *Application deadline:* For fall admission, 8/1 priority date for domestic students, 5/1 priority date for international students; for spring admission, 1/1 priority date for domestic students, 11/1 priority date for international students. Applications are processed on a rolling basis. Application fee: $0. Electronic applications accepted. *Expenses:* Tuition: Part-time $420 per credit hour. *Financial support:* In 2006–07, 19 students received support. Federal Work-Study, scholarships/grants, and tuition waivers (full and partial) available. Support available to part-time students. Financial award application deadline: 4/3. *Faculty research:* Literacy, racialized gender and gendered identity, teacher learning, learning disabilities identification. *Unit head:* Dr. Susan S. Hasseler, Associate Dean for Teacher Education, 616-526-6597, Fax: 616-526-6505, E-mail: shassele@calvin.edu. *Application contact:* Deb Abbott, Administrative Assistant, 616-526-6105, Fax: 616-526-6505, E-mail: dka2@calvin.edu.

Canisius College, Graduate Division, School of Education and Human Services, Department of Graduate Education, Buffalo, NY 14208-1098. Offers business education (MS); childhood education (MS); college student personnel (MS); differentiated instruction (MS Ed); early childhood education (MS); education administration (MS); education of the deaf and hard of hearing (MS); general education (MS Ed); literacy education (MS Ed); reading education (MS Ed); secondary education (MS); special education (MS). *Accreditation:* NCATE. Part-time

Reading Education

Canisius College (continued)

and evening/weekend programs available. *Faculty:* 13 full-time (12 women), 74 part-time/adjunct (44 women). *Students:* 377 full-time (267 women), 303 part-time (219 women); includes 43 minority (27 African Americans, 2 American Indian/Alaska Native, 6 Asian Americans or Pacific Islanders, 8 Hispanic Americans), 187 international. Average age 30. In 2006, 296 degrees awarded. Application fee: $25. *Expenses:* Tuition: Part-time $645 per credit hour. Required fees: $19 per credit hour. Tuition and fees vary according to program. *Financial support:* Research assistantships with full tuition reimbursements, career-related internships or fieldwork, institutionally sponsored loans, scholarships/grants, health care benefits, tuition waivers (full and partial), and unspecified assistantships available. *Faculty research:* Autism, Asperger's disease, private higher education, reading strategies. *Unit head:* Rev. Paul Nochelski, Chair of Graduate Education and Leadership, 716-888-3297, Fax: 716-888-3299. *Application contact:* James D. Bagwell, Director of Graduate Recruitment and Admissions, 716-888-2544, Fax: 716-888-3290, E-mail: bagwellj@canisius.edu.

Capella University, School of Education, Minneapolis, MN 55402. Offers college teaching (Certificate); curriculum and instruction (MS, PhD); education (MS); enrollment management (MS); instructional design for online learning (MS, PhD); k-12 studies in education (MS, PhD); leadership for higher education (MS, PhD); leadership in education administration (Certificate); leadership in educational administration (MS, PhD); postsecondary and adult education (MS, PhD); professional studies in education (MS, PhD); reading and literacy (MS); training and performance improvement (MS, PhD). Part-time and evening/weekend programs available. Postbaccalaureate distance learning degree programs offered (minimal on-campus study). Terminal master's awarded for partial completion of doctoral program. *Degree requirements:* For master's, integrative project, thesis optional; for doctorate, thesis/dissertation, comprehensive exam, registration. *Entrance requirements:* Additional exam requirements/recommendations for international students: Required—TOEFL (minimum score 550 paper-based; 213 computer-based), TWE (minimum score 4). Electronic applications accepted. *Faculty research:* Higher education administration, distance learning, adult education, training and curriculum design.

Cardinal Stritch University, College of Education, Department of Reading/Language Arts, Reading/Learning Disability, Milwaukee, WI 53217-3985. Offers reading/language arts (MA); reading/learning disability (MA). *Accreditation:* NCATE. Part-time and evening/weekend programs available. *Degree requirements:* For master's, thesis, faculty recommendation, research project, comprehensive exam. *Entrance requirements:* For master's, letters of recommendation (2), minimum GPA of 2.75.

Carthage College, Division of Teacher Education, Kenosha, WI 53140. Offers classroom guidance and counseling (M Ed); creative arts (M Ed); gifted and talented children (M Ed); language arts (M Ed); modern language (M Ed); natural sciences (M Ed); reading (M Ed, Certificate); social sciences (M Ed); teacher leadership (M Ed). Part-time and evening/weekend programs available. *Degree requirements:* For master's, thesis optional. *Entrance requirements:* For master's, MAT, minimum B average, letters of reference.

Castleton State College, Division of Graduate Studies, Department of Education, Program in Language Arts and Reading, Castleton, VT 05735. Offers MA Ed, CAGS. Part-time and evening/weekend programs available. *Degree requirements:* For master's, thesis or alternative; for CAGS, publishable paper, written exams. *Entrance requirements:* For master's, GRE General Test, MAT, interview, minimum undergraduate GPA of 3.0; for CAGS, educational research, master's degree, minimum undergraduate GPA of 3.0.

Central Connecticut State University, School of Graduate Studies, School of Education and Professional Studies, Department of Reading, New Britain, CT 06050-4010. Offers MS, Sixth Year Certificate. Part-time and evening/weekend programs available. *Faculty:* 8 full-time (6 women), 6 part-time/adjunct (3 women). *Students:* 1 (woman) full-time, 159 part-time (150 women); includes 5 minority (2 African Americans, 1 Asian American or Pacific Islander, 2 Hispanic Americans). Average age 34. 63 applicants, 71% accepted, 33 enrolled. In 2006, 108 master's, 18 other advanced degrees awarded. *Degree requirements:* For master's, thesis or alternative, comprehensive exam; for Sixth Year Certificate, qualifying exam. *Entrance requirements:* For master's, minimum GPA of 2.7. Additional exam requirements/recommendations for international students: Required—TOEFL. *Application deadline:* For fall admission, 7/1 for domestic students; for spring admission, 12/1 for domestic students. Applications are processed on a rolling basis. Application fee: $50. Electronic applications accepted. *Expenses:* Tuition, area resident: Full-time $3,970; part-time $380 per credit. Tuition, state resident: full-time $5,955; part-time $380 per credit. Tuition, nonresident: full-time $11,061; part-time $380 per credit. Required fees: $3,189. One-time fee: $62 part-time. Tuition and fees vary according to degree level and program. *Financial support:* In 2006–07, 5 students received support; research assistantships, career-related internships or fieldwork, Federal Work-Study, scholarships/grants, and unspecified assistantships available. Support available to part-time students. Financial award application deadline: 3/1; financial award applicants required to submit FAFSA. *Faculty research:* Developmental, clinical, and administrative aspects of reading and language arts instruction. *Unit head:* Dr. Helen Abadiano, Chair, 860-832-2175.

Central Michigan University, Central Michigan University Off-Campus Programs, Program in Education, Mount Pleasant, MI 48859. Offers education (MA); educational technology (MA); reading and literacy (MA). Part-time and evening/weekend programs available. *Entrance requirements:* For master's, minimum GPA of 2.7 in major. Additional exam requirements/recommendations for international students: Required—TOEFL. *Application deadline:* Applications are processed on a rolling basis. Application fee: $50. Electronic applications accepted. *Financial support:* Scholarships/grants available. Support available to part-time students. *Unit head:* Jennifer Cochran, Director, 989-774-2584, E-mail: jennifer.cochran@cmich.edu. *Application contact:* 877-268-4636, E-mail: cmuoffcampus@cmich.edu.

Central Michigan University, College of Graduate Studies, College of Education and Human Services, Department of Teacher Education and Professional Development, Mount Pleasant, MI 48859. Offers educational technology· (MA); elementary education (MA), including classroom teaching, early childhood education, reading in the elementary school; library, media, and technology (MA), including library media, media and technology; middle level education (MA); reading improvement (MA); secondary education (MA); teaching senior high (MA). *Accreditation:* NCATE. *Degree requirements:* For master's, thesis or alternative, registration. *Faculty research:* Reading instruction and reading disabilities, teaching and learning styles, school and business partnerships, school restructuring and improvement, mathematics learning and instruction.

Central State University, Program in Education, Wilberforce, OH 45384. Offers educational technology (M Ed); leadership (M Ed); literacy (M Ed). Part-time and evening/weekend programs available. *Degree requirements:* For master's, thesis or alternative. *Entrance requirements:* For master's, GRE.

Central Washington University, Graduate Studies, Research and Continuing Education, College of Education and Professional Studies, Department of Education, Program in Reading Education, Ellensburg, WA 98926. Offers M Ed. Part-time programs available. *Faculty:* 21 full-time (10 women). *Students:* 6 applicants, 67% accepted, 4 enrolled. In 2006, 11 degrees awarded. *Degree requirements:* For master's, thesis or alternative. *Entrance requirements:* For master's, minimum GPA of 3.0. Additional exam requirements/recommendations for international students: Required—TOEFL (minimum score 550 paper-based; 213 computer-based; 79 iBT). *Application deadline:* For fall admission, 4/1 priority date for domestic students; for winter admission, 10/1 for domestic students; for spring admission, 1/1 for domestic students. Applications are processed on a rolling basis. Application fee: $50. *Expenses:* Tuition, state resident: full-time $6,312. Tuition, nonresident: full-time $14,112. Tuition and fees vary according to course load and degree level. *Financial support:* Research assistantships with partial tuition reimbursements, teaching assistantships with partial tuition reimbursements, Federal Work-Study, health care benefits, and unspecified assistantships

available. Financial award application deadline: 3/1; financial award applicants required to submit FAFSA. *Application contact:* Justine Eason, Admissions Program Coordinator, 509-963-3103, Fax: 509-963-1799, E-mail: masters@cwu.edu.

Chapman University, Graduate Studies, School of Education, Concentration in Reading Education, Orange, CA 92866. Offers MA. Part-time and evening/weekend programs available. *Faculty:* 16 full-time (11 women), 25 part-time/adjunct (14 women). *Students:* Average age 30. *Degree requirements:* For master's, thesis optional. *Entrance requirements:* For master's, GRE General Test, MAT, or California Subject Examinations for Teachers, minimum undergraduate GPA of 2.5. Additional exam requirements/recommendations for international students: Required—TOEFL (minimum score 550 paper-based). *Application deadline:* Applications are processed on a rolling basis. Application fee: $55. Electronic applications accepted. *Expenses:* Contact institution. *Financial support:* In 2006–07, 3 students received support; fellowships, Federal Work-Study available. Financial award application deadline: 6/30; financial award applicants required to submit FAFSA. *Unit head:* Dr. Sally Thomas, Coordinator, 714-997-6781, E-mail: sthomas@chapman.edu. *Application contact:* Rika Judd, Information Contact, 714-997-6786, Fax: 714-997-6713, E-mail: rjudd@chapman.edu.

Chicago State University, School of Graduate and Professional Studies, College of Education, Department of Reading, Elementary Education, Library Information and Media Studies, Program in Reading, Chicago, IL 60628. Offers teaching of reading (MS Ed). *Accreditation:* NCATE. *Entrance requirements:* For master's, minimum GPA of 2.75.

The Citadel, The Military College of South Carolina, College of Graduate and Professional Studies, School of Education, Program in Reading, Charleston, SC 29409. Offers M Ed. *Accreditation:* NCATE. Part-time and evening/weekend programs available. *Students:* 5 full-time (all women), 34 part-time (all women); includes 6 minority (all African Americans) Average age 28. In 2006, 14 degrees awarded. *Entrance requirements:* For master's, GRE General Test, MAT, or 12 hours of graduate course work with a minimum GPA of 3.5. Additional exam requirements/recommendations for international students: Required—TOEFL (minimum score 550 paper-based; 213 computer-based). *Application deadline:* Applications are processed on a rolling basis. Application fee: $30. *Expenses:* Tuition, state resident: part-time $259 per credit hour. Tuition, nonresident: part-time $482 per credit hour. *Financial support:* Application deadline: 7/1; *Unit head:* Dr. Jennifer L. Altieri, Head, 843-953-3162, Fax: 843-953-7258, E-mail: jennifer.altieri@citadel.edu. *Application contact:* Dr. Raymond S. Jones, Associate Dean, College of Graduate and Professional Studies, 843-953-5089, Fax: 843-953-7630, E-mail: ray.jones@citadel.edu.

City College of the City University of New York, Graduate School, College of Liberal Arts and Science, Division of the Humanities and Arts, Department of English, Program in Language and Literacy, New York, NY 10031-9198. Offers MA. *Accreditation:* NCATE. *Students:* 26. *Entrance requirements:* For master's, GRE, 2 writing samples. Additional exam requirements/recommendations for international students: Required—TOEFL (minimum score 600 paper-based; 250 computer-based). *Application deadline:* For fall admission, 5/1 for domestic students; for spring admission, 11/1 for domestic students. Application fee: $125. *Unit head:* Barbara Gleason, Head, 212-650-6694.

City University, Graduate Division, Gordon Albright School of Education, Bellevue, WA 98005. Offers curriculum and instruction (M Ed); educational leadership (M Ed); educational leadership: principal certification (M Ed, Certificate); educational leadership: principal/program administrator certification (Certificate); educational leadership: program administrator certification (M Ed, Certificate); guidance and counseling (M Ed, Certificate); integrated arts and performance learning (M Ed); professional certification-teachers (Certificate); reading (Certificate); reading and literacy (M Ed); reading, literacy, and ESL/ELL (M Ed); teacher certification (MIT); technology, curriculum and instruction (M Ed). Part-time and evening/weekend programs available. Postbaccalaureate distance learning degree programs offered (no on-campus study). *Entrance requirements:* Additional exam requirements/recommendations for international students: Required—TOEFL (minimum score 540 paper-based; 207 computer-based); Recommended—IELTS. Electronic applications accepted.

Clarion University of Pennsylvania, Office of Research and Graduate Studies, College of Education and Human Services, Department of Education, Program in Education, Clarion, PA 16214. Offers curriculum and instruction (M Ed); early childhood (M Ed); English (M Ed); history (M Ed); literacy (M Ed); science (M Ed); technology (M Ed). *Accreditation:* NCATE.Part-time programs available. *Faculty:* 18 full-time (13 women). *Students:* 11 full-time (4 women), 54 part-time (37 women); includes 4 minority (3 African Americans, 1 Asian American or Pacific Islander). 50 applicants, 90% accepted. In 2006, 7 degrees awarded. *Degree requirements:* For master's, thesis or alternative, comprehensive exam. *Entrance requirements:* For master's, minimum QPA of 3.0, teacher certification. Additional exam requirements/recommendations for international students: Required—TOEFL (minimum score 550 paper-based; 213 computer-based; 80 iBT). *Application deadline:* For fall admission, 8/1 priority date for domestic students, 4/15 priority date for international students; for spring admission, 12/1 priority date for domestic students, 9/15 priority date for international students. Applications are processed on a rolling basis. Application fee: $30. Electronic applications accepted. *Expenses:* Tuition, state resident: part-time $336 per credit. Tuition, nonresident: part-time $538 per credit. *Financial support:* In 2006–07, 2 research assistantships with full tuition reimbursements (averaging $4,002 per year) were awarded. Support available to part-time students. Financial award application deadline: 3/1. *Application contact:* Dr. Brian Maguire, Coordinator, 814-393-2058, Fax: 814-393-2558, E-mail: bmaguire@clarion.edu.

Clarion University of Pennsylvania, Office of Research and Graduate Studies, College of Education and Human Services, Department of Education, Program in Reading, Clarion, PA 16214. Offers M Ed. *Accreditation:* NCATE. Part-time programs available. *Faculty:* 18 full-time (13 women). *Students:* 2 full-time (both women), 21 part-time (all women). 4 applicants, 75% accepted. In 2006, 11 degrees awarded. *Degree requirements:* For master's, thesis or alternative, National Teacher Exam, Reading Specialist, comprehensive exam. *Entrance requirements:* For master's, minimum QPA of 3.0, teacher certification. Additional exam requirements/recommendations for international students: Required—TOEFL (minimum score 550 paper-based; 213 computer-based; 80 iBT). *Application deadline:* For fall admission, 8/1 priority date for domestic students, 4/15 priority date for international students; for spring admission, 12/1 priority date for domestic students, 9/15 priority date for international students. Applications are processed on a rolling basis. Application fee: $30. Electronic applications accepted. *Expenses:* Tuition, state resident: part-time $336 per credit. Tuition, nonresident: part-time $538 per credit. *Financial support:* In 2006–07, 2 research assistantships with full tuition reimbursements (averaging $4,002 per year) were awarded. Support available to part-time students. Financial award application deadline: 3/1. *Application contact:* Dr. Brian Maguire, Coordinator, 814-393-2058, Fax: 814-393-2558, E-mail: bmaguire@clarion.edu.

Clarke College, Program in Education, Dubuque, IA 52001-3198. Offers early childhood/special education (MA); educational administration: elementary and secondary (MA); educational media: elementary and secondary (MA); multi-categorical resource K–12 (MA); multidisciplinary studies (MA); reading: elementary (MA); technology in education (MA). Part-time and evening/weekend programs available. Postbaccalaureate distance learning degree programs offered (minimal on-campus study). *Degree requirements:* For master's, thesis optional. *Entrance requirements:* For master's, GRE General Test or MAT, minimum GPA of 2.75. Electronic applications accepted.

Clemson University, Graduate School, College of Health, Education, and Human Development, School of Education, Program in Reading, Clemson, SC 29634. Offers M Ed. *Accreditation:* NCATE. *Students:* 1 (woman) full-time, 30 part-time (29 women); includes 1 minority (African American) 3 applicants, 33% accepted, 0 enrolled. In 2006, 27 degrees awarded. *Entrance requirements:* For master's, teaching certificate. Additional exam requirements/recommendations for international students: Required—TOEFL. *Application deadline:* For fall admission, 6/1 for domestic students. Applications are processed on a rolling basis. Application fee: $50. Electronic applications accepted. *Expenses:* Tuition, state resident: full-time $8,812; part-time $450 per hour. Tuition, nonresident: full-time $18,036; part-time $760 per hour. Required fees: $474; $5 per term. *Financial support:* Application deadline: 6/1; *Faculty research:* Literature, writing, reading recovery across the curriculum. *Unit head:* Dr. Kathy Headley, Graduate Coordinator, 864-656-5119.

See Close-Up on page 1605.

College of Mount St. Joseph, Graduate Education Program, Cincinnati, OH 45233-1670. Offers adolescent young adult education (MA); art (MA); inclusive early childhood education (MA); instructional leadership (MA); middle childhood education (MA); multicultural special education (MA); music (MA); reading (MA). *Accreditation:* Teacher Education Accreditation Council. Part-time and evening/weekend programs available. Postbaccalaureate distance learning degree programs offered (minimal on-campus study). *Faculty:* 22 full-time (14 women), 11 part-time/adjunct (6 women). *Students:* 68 full-time (54 women), 115 part-time (96 women); includes 21 minority (16 African Americans, 2 American Indian/Alaska Native, 1 Asian American or Pacific Islander, 2 Hispanic Americans). Average age 34. 91 applicants, 98% accepted, 62 enrolled. In 2006, 61 degrees awarded. *Degree requirements:* For master's, research project. *Entrance requirements:* For master's, GRE, PRAXIS II in teaching content area (math or science), 2 letters of recommendation, interview, resumé, prerequisite courses in communications, behavioral sciences and mathematics. Additional exam requirements/recommendations for international students: Required—TOEFL (minimum score 560 paper-based; 220 computer-based). *Application deadline:* Applications are processed on a rolling basis. Application fee: $50. Electronic applications accepted. *Expenses: Contact institution. Financial support:* In 2006–07, 3 students received support. Career-related internships or fieldwork and scholarships/grants available. Support available to part-time students. Financial award application deadline: 6/1; financial award applicants required to submit FAFSA. *Faculty research:* Foreign and second language learning problems/reading disabilities/hyperlexia, multicultural/bilingual special education, alternative educator licensure, science education, pedagogical content knowledge. *Unit head:* Dr. Mifrando Obach, Chair, 513-244-3263, Fax: 513-244-4867, E-mail: mifrando_obach@mail.msj.edu. *Application contact:* Marilyn Hoskins, Assistant Director of Admissions for Graduate Recruitment, 513-244-4723, Fax: 513-244-4629, E-mail: marilyn_hoskins@mail.msg.edu.

The College of New Jersey, Graduate Division, School of Education, Department of Special Education, Language and Literacy, Program in Developmental Reading, Ewing, NJ 08628. Offers M Ed. *Accreditation:* NCATE. *Students:* 3 applicants, 100% accepted. In 2006, 10 degrees awarded. *Degree requirements:* For master's, comprehensive exam. *Entrance requirements:* For master's, GRE General Test, minimum GPA of 3.0 in field or 2.75 overall. Additional exam requirements/recommendations for international students: Required—TOEFL. *Application deadline:* For fall admission, 4/15 for domestic students; for spring admission, 10/15 for domestic students. Application fee: $60. Electronic applications accepted. *Financial support:* Application deadline: 5/1. *Unit head:* Dr. Susan Blair-Larsen, Graduate Coordinator, 609-771-2321. *Application contact:* Susan L. Hydro, Office of Graduate Studies, Assistant Dean, 609-771-2300, Fax: 609-637-5105, E-mail: graduate@tcnj.edu.

The College of New Jersey, Graduate Division, School of Education, Department of Special Education, Language and Literacy, Program in Reading Certification, Ewing, NJ 08628. Offers Certificate. *Students:* 3 applicants, 100% accepted. *Entrance requirements:* Additional exam requirements/recommendations for international students: Required—TOEFL. *Application deadline:* For fall admission, 4/15 for domestic students; for spring admission, 10/15 for domestic students. Application fee: $60. Electronic applications accepted. *Unit head:* Dr. Susan Blair-Larsen, Graduate Coordinator, 609-771-2321. *Application contact:* Susan L. Hydro, Office of Graduate Studies, Assistant Dean, 609-771-2300, Fax: 609-637-5105, E-mail: graduate@tcnj.edu.

The College of New Rochelle, Graduate School, Division of Education, Program in Literacy Education, New Rochelle, NY 10805-2308. Offers MS Ed. Part-time and evening/weekend programs available. *Faculty:* 3 full-time (all women), 6 part-time/adjunct (5 women). *Students:* 7 full-time (all women), 132 part-time (130 women); includes 10 minority (3 African Americans, 1 American Indian/Alaska Native, 6 Hispanic Americans). Average age 29. In 2006, 62 degrees awarded. *Degree requirements:* For master's, practicum. *Entrance requirements:* For master's, interview, minimum GPA of 3.0 in field, 2.7 overall, early elementary teacher certification. *Application deadline:* For fall admission, 8/1 priority date for domestic students; for spring admission, 4/6 for domestic students. Applications are processed on a rolling basis. Application fee: $35. *Expenses:* Tuition: Part-time $575 per credit. Required fees: $90 per term. *Financial support:* In 2006–07, 1 research assistantship was awarded; scholarships/grants also available. *Unit head:* Dr. Marie Ribarich, Acting Division Head, Division of Education, 914-654-5333, Fax: 914-654-5593, E-mail: mribarich@cnr.edu.

College of St. Joseph, Graduate Program, Division of Education, Program in Reading, Rutland, VT 05701-3899. Offers M Ed. Part-time and evening/weekend programs available. *Faculty:* 3 full-time (2 women), 8 part-time/adjunct (5 women). *Students:* 3 full-time, 14 part-time. Average age 32. 11 applicants, 100% accepted, 11 enrolled. In 2006, 6 degrees awarded. *Degree requirements:* For master's, comprehensive exam, registration. *Entrance requirements:* For master's, interview, current licensure in another area, 2 letters of reference. *Application deadline:* Applications are processed on a rolling basis. Application fee: $35. *Expenses:* Tuition: Full-time $10,990; part-time $300 per credit. Part-time tuition and fees vary according to program. *Financial support:* Career-related internships or fieldwork, Federal Work-Study, and unspecified assistantships available. Support available to part-time students. Financial award application deadline: 3/1. *Application contact:* Tracy Gallipo, Director of Admissions, 802-773-5900 Ext. 3262, Fax: 802-773-5900, E-mail: tracygallipo@csj.edu.

The College of Saint Rose, Graduate Studies, School of Education, Reading/Special Education Department, Albany, NY 12203-1419. Offers literacy: birth-grade 6 (MS Ed); literacy: grades 5-12 (MS Ed); reading (Certificate), including literacy: birth—grade 6, literacy: grades 5-12; special education (MS Ed), including adolescent education, childhood education, special education advanced study. Part-time and evening/weekend programs available. *Entrance requirements:* For master's, minimum undergraduate GPA of 3.0. Additional exam requirements/recommendations for international students: Required—TOEFL (minimum score 550 paper-based; 213 computer-based). Electronic applications accepted.

The College of William and Mary, School of Education, Program in Curriculum and Instruction, Williamsburg, VA 23187-8795. Offers elementary education (MA Ed); gifted education (MA Ed); reading education (MA Ed); secondary education (MA Ed), including English education, mathematics education, modern foreign languages education, science education, social studies education; special education (MA Ed), including emotionally disturbed, learning disabled, mental retardation, resource collaborating teaching. *Accreditation:* NCATE. Part-time programs available. *Faculty:* 15 full-time (6 women), 13 part-time/adjunct (10 women). *Students:* 51 full-time (39 women), 51 part-time (45 women); includes 6 minority (all African Americans) Average age 29. 161 applicants, 68% accepted, 61 enrolled. In 2006, 68 degrees awarded. *Degree requirements:* For master's, master's project. *Entrance requirements:* For master's, GRE or MAT, minimum GPA of 2.5. Additional exam requirements/recommendations for international students: Required—TOEFL. *Application deadline:* For fall admission, 2/1 for domestic and international students; for spring admission, 10/1 for domestic and international students. Application fee: $30. *Expenses:* Tuition, state resident: full-time $6,100; part-time $260 per credit. Tuition, nonresident: full-time $18,790; part-time $725 per credit. Required fees: $3,314. Tuition and fees vary according to program. *Financial support:* In 2006–07, 10 research assistantships with full and partial tuition reimbursements (averaging $5,000 per year) were awarded; career-related internships or fieldwork, Federal Work-Study, institutionally sponsored loans, scholarships/grants, and unspecified assistantships also available. Financial award application deadline: 2/1; financial award applicants required to submit FAFSA. *Faculty research:* National Council of Teachers of Mathematics Standards, counseling, self-concept and self-esteem, special education, curriculum development. *Unit head:* Dr. John Moore, Area Coordinator, 757-221-2333, E-mail: jnmoor@wm.edu. *Application contact:* Dorothy Osborne, Director of Admissions, 757-221-2317, E-mail: dsosbo@wm.edu.

Concordia University, College of Education, Program in Reading Education, River Forest, IL 60305-1499. Offers MA. Part-time and evening/weekend programs available. *Degree requirements:* For master's, thesis optional. *Entrance requirements:* For master's, minimum GPA of 2.9. Additional exam requirements/recommendations for international students: Required—TOEFL (minimum score 550 paper-based; 195 computer-based). Electronic applications accepted. *Faculty research:* Early literacy, classroom management and organization in reading, minority students and reading.

Concordia University, Graduate Programs in Education, Program in Literacy Education, Seward, NE 68434-1599. Offers M Ed. *Accreditation:* NCATE. Part-time programs available. *Degree requirements:* For master's, thesis or alternative. *Entrance requirements:* For master's, GRE, MAT, or NTE, minimum GPA of 3.0, BS in education or equivalent.

Concordia University Wisconsin, Graduate Programs, Department of Education, Program in Reading, Mequon, WI 53097-2402. Offers MS Ed. Part-time and evening/weekend programs available. Postbaccalaureate distance learning degree programs offered (minimal on-campus study). *Students:* 58 (55 women). In 2006, 4 degrees awarded. *Degree requirements:* For master's, thesis or alternative, comprehensive exam. *Entrance requirements:* For master's, minimum GPA of 3.0. Additional exam requirements/recommendations for international students: Required—TOEFL. Application fee: $35. *Financial support:* Application deadline: 8/1. *Unit head:* Dr. Marsha K. Konz, Dean of Graduate Studies, 262-243-4253, Fax: 262-243-4428, E-mail: marsha.konz@cuw.edu. *Application contact:* Graduate Admissions, 262-243-4248, Fax: 262-243-4428.

Coppin State University, Division of Graduate Studies, Division of Education, Baltimore, MD 21216-3698. Offers adult and general education (MS); curriculum and instruction (M Ed, MA, MS), including curriculum and instruction (M Ed), reading education (MS), teaching (MA); special education (M Ed). *Accreditation:* NCATE. Part-time and evening/weekend programs available. Postbaccalaureate distance learning degree programs offered. *Faculty:* 18 full-time (13 women), 8 part-time/adjunct (4 women). *Students:* 34 full-time (25 women), 126 part-time (91 women); includes 131 minority (all African Americans), 4 international. Average age 37. 97 applicants, 76% accepted, 66 enrolled. In 2006, 21 degrees awarded. *Degree requirements:* For master's, thesis (for some programs), comprehensive exam (for some programs), registration. *Application deadline:* For fall admission, 8/15 priority date for domestic students; for spring admission, 12/15 priority date for domestic students. Applications are processed on a rolling basis. Application fee: $45. *Financial support:* Career-related internships or fieldwork, Federal Work-Study, institutionally sponsored loans, and scholarships/grants available. Support available to part-time students. Financial award application deadline: 6/30; financial award applicants required to submit FAFSA. *Unit head:* Dr. Julius Chapman, Chair, 410-951-3082, Fax: 410-951-3089, E-mail: jchapman@coppin.edu.

Coppin State University, Division of Graduate Studies, Division of Education, Department of Curriculum and Instruction, Program in Reading Education, Baltimore, MD 21216-3698. Offers MS. Part-time programs available. *Faculty:* 2 full-time (both women), 1 (woman) part-time/adjunct. *Students:* Average age 33. 17 applicants, 76% accepted, 12 enrolled. In 2006, 3 degrees awarded. *Degree requirements:* For master's, 3 hours of capstone experience in urban literacy. *Entrance requirements:* For master's, MAT or GRE, resumé, references, teacher certification, 3 years of teaching experience. *Application deadline:* For fall admission, 8/15 priority date for domestic students; for spring admission, 12/15 priority date for domestic students. Applications are processed on a rolling basis. Application fee: $45. *Financial support:* Application deadline: 6/30; *Unit head:* Dr. Delores S. Harvey, Coordinator, 410-951-3068.

Curry College, Division of Continuing Education and Graduate Studies, Program in Education, Milton, MA 02186-9984. Offers adult education (Certificate); educational administration (M Ed); educational therapy (Certificate); elementary education (M Ed); foundations (non-license) (M Ed); learning disabilities across the lifespan (Certificate); reading (M Ed, Certificate); special education (M Ed). Part-time and evening/weekend programs available. *Faculty:* 6 full-time (4 women), 11 part-time/adjunct (7 women). *Degree requirements:* For master's, research project. *Entrance requirements:* For master's, MAT, interview, recommendations, resumé. Additional exam requirements/recommendations for international students: Required—TOEFL (minimum score 550 paper-based). *Application deadline:* For fall admission, 8/1 priority date for domestic students; for spring admission, 1/1 for domestic students. Applications are processed on a rolling basis. Application fee: $50. *Expenses: Contact institution. Financial support:* Career-related internships or fieldwork and tuition waivers (partial) available. *Faculty research:* Classroom trauma, therapeutic writing, inclusionary practices. *Unit head:* Dr. Donald Gratz, Director and Associate Professor, 617-333-2243, E-mail: dgratz0703@curry.edu. *Application contact:* John Bresnahan, Director of Graduate Enrollment and Student Services, 617-333-2243, Fax: 617-333-2045, E-mail: jbresnah0104@curry.edu.

Dallas Baptist University, Dorothy M. Bush College of Education, Education Program, Dallas, TX 75211-9299. Offers early childhood education (M Ed); educational leadership (M Ed); elementary reading education (M Ed); general elementary education (M Ed); reading specialist (M Ed). Part-time and evening/weekend programs available. *Faculty:* 49 full-time (21 women), 112 part-time/adjunct (46 women). *Students:* 47 full-time, 149 part-time. 65 applicants, 58% accepted, 36 enrolled. In 2006, 67 degrees awarded. *Entrance requirements:* For master's, GRE General Test, minimum GPA of 3.0. Additional exam requirements/recommendations for international students: Required—TOEFL. *Application deadline:* Applications are processed on a rolling basis. Application fee: $25. Electronic applications accepted. *Expenses:* Tuition: Full-time $8,370; part-time $465 per credit hour. Required fees: $465 per credit hour. *Financial support:* Federal Work-Study, institutionally sponsored loans, scholarships/grants, and tuition waivers (full and partial) available. Support available to part-time students. *Faculty research:* Emerging literacy, self-directed schools. *Unit head:* Dr. Elaine Wilmore, Interim Director, 214-333-5413, Fax: 214-333-5551, E-mail: graduate@dbu.edu. *Application contact:* Kit P. Montgomery, Director of Graduate Programs, 214-333-5242, Fax: 214-333-5579, E-mail: graduate@dbu.edu.

Dallas Baptist University, Dorothy M. Bush College of Education, Program in Education in Reading and ESL, Dallas, TX 75211-9299. Offers M Ed. *Faculty:* 49 full-time (21 women), 112 part-time/adjunct (46 women). Application fee: $25. *Expenses:* Tuition: Full-time $8,370; part-time $465 per credit hour. Required fees: $465 per credit hour. *Unit head:* Amie Sarker, Director, 214-333-5413, E-mail: graduate@dbu.edu. *Application contact:* Kit P. Montgomery, Director of Graduate Programs, 214-333-5242, Fax: 214-333-5579, E-mail: graduate@dbu.edu.

DePaul University, School of Education, Chicago, IL 60604-2287. Offers bilingual and bicultural education (M Ed, MA); curriculum studies (M Ed, MA); education (Ed D), including curriculum studies, educational leadership; educational leadership (M Ed, MA), including administration and supervision, Catholic school leadership, physical education; human development and learning (MA); human services and counseling (M Ed, MA), including agencies, family concerns, and higher education, elementary schools, human services management, secondary schools; reading and learning disabilities (M Ed, MA); social culture studies in education and development (M Ed, MA), including curriculum studies/development; teaching and learning (early childhood, elementary and secondary) (M Ed), including elementary education (M Ed, MA), secondary education (M Ed, MA); teaching and learning (early childhood, elementary, and secondary) (MA), including elementary education (M Ed, MA), secondary education (M Ed, MA). *Accreditation:* NCATE. Part-time and evening/weekend programs available. *Faculty:* 61 full-time (40 women), 76 part-time/adjunct (46 women). *Students:* 1,371 full-time (1,103 women), 474 part-time (362 women); includes 435 minority (144 African Americans, 7 American Indian/Alaska Native, 89 Asian Americans or Pacific Islanders, 195 Hispanic Americans), 11 international. Average age 30. 993 applicants, 80% accepted, 617 enrolled. In 2006, 324 master's, 7 doctorates awarded. *Degree requirements:* For doctorate, thesis/dissertation.

Reading Education

DePaul University (continued)
Entrance requirements: For master's, interview, minimum GPA of 2.75, 2 letters of recommendation; for doctorate, interview, master's degree, 2 years of work experience (recommended), writing sample, 3 letters of recommendation. Application fee: $25. Electronic applications accepted. *Financial support:* In 2006–07, 16 research assistantships with tuition reimbursements (averaging $4,370 per year), 1 teaching assistantship (averaging $6,000 per year) were awarded; career-related internships or fieldwork also available. *Faculty research:* Reflective teaching, children at risk, loss, ethnicity, urban education. Total annual research expenditures: $556,194. *Unit head:* Dr. Clara Jennings, Dean, 773-325-7581, Fax: 773-325-7728, E-mail: cjennings@depaul.edu. *Application contact:* Dr. John Bollwark, Data Project Manager, 773-325-7582, Fax: 773-325-7713, E-mail: jbollwar@depaul.edu.

Dominican University, School of Education, River Forest, IL 60305-1099. Offers curriculum and instruction (MA Ed); early childhood education (MS); education (MAT); educational administration (MA); literacy (MS); special education (MS). Part-time and evening/weekend programs available. *Faculty:* 17 full-time (14 women), 37 part-time/adjunct (24 women). *Students:* 65 full-time (46 women), 514 part-time (425 women); includes 78 minority (23 African Americans, 16 Asian Americans or Pacific Islanders, 39 Hispanic Americans), 2 international. Average age 34. 130 applicants, 89% accepted, 100 enrolled. In 2006, 203 degrees awarded. *Entrance requirements:* For master's, Illinois certification test of basic skills. Additional exam requirements/recommendations for international students: Required—TOEFL (minimum score 550 paper-based; 213 computer-based). *Application deadline:* Applications are processed on a rolling basis. Application fee: $25. *Expenses: Contact institution.* Tuition and fees vary according to campus/location and program. *Financial support:* In 2006–07, 63 students received support. Career-related internships or fieldwork, scholarships/grants, and tuition waivers (partial) available. Support available to part-time students. Financial award application deadline: 8/15; financial award applicants required to submit FAFSA. *Faculty research:* Governance of private education institutions, reading and language arts, inclusion, organizational planning, leadership and vision. *Unit head:* Sr. Colleen McNicholas, Dean, 708-524-6830, Fax: 708-524-6665, E-mail: educate@dom.edu. *Application contact:* Keven Hansen, Coordinator of Admissions and Recruitment, 708-524-6921, Fax: 708-524-6665, E-mail: educate@dom.edu.

Dowling College, Graduate Programs in Education, Oakdale, NY 11769-1999. Offers educational administration (Ed D, PD), including computers in education (PD), educational administration (Ed D), school administration and supervision (PD), school district administration (PD); human development and learning (MS Ed); literacy (MS Ed); literacy/special education (MS Ed); secondary education (MS Ed); special education (MS Ed). *Accreditation:* NCATE. Part-time and evening/weekend programs available. Postbaccalaureate distance learning degree programs offered. *Faculty:* 29 full-time (13 women), 91 part-time/adjunct (60 women). *Students:* 496 full-time (364 women), 1,083 part-time (827 women); includes 119 minority (37 African Americans, 20 Asian Americans or Pacific Islanders, 62 Hispanic Americans), 2 international. Average age 38. 618 applicants, 86% accepted, 300 enrolled. In 2006, 641 master's, 25 doctorates awarded. *Degree requirements:* For master's and PD, comprehensive exam; for doctorate, thesis/dissertation. *Entrance requirements:* For master's, minimum GPA of 3.0; for doctorate, GRE, master's degree; for PD, teaching certificate. Additional exam requirements/recommendations for international students: Required—TOEFL (minimum score 550 paper-based). *Application deadline:* For fall admission, 9/1 priority date for domestic students; for winter admission, 1/1 priority date for domestic students; for spring admission, 2/1 priority date for domestic students. Applications are processed on a rolling basis. Application fee: $25. Electronic applications accepted. *Expenses:* Tuition: Full-time $16,008; part-time $667 per credit. Tuition and fees vary according to course load. *Financial support:* In 2006–07, 358 students received support, including 20 research assistantships with tuition reimbursements available (averaging $3,150 per year); career-related internships or fieldwork, Federal Work-Study, scholarships/grants, tuition waivers (partial), and unspecified assistantships also available. Support available to part-time students. Financial award application deadline: 6/30; financial award applicants required to submit FAFSA. *Faculty research:* Natural readers, Korean styles and learning strategies, mothers of children with disabilities, computers in instruction, cultural background and organizational roadblocks to problem solving. *Unit head:* Dr. Clyde Payne, Associate Provost, 631-244-3404, Fax: 631-589-6644, E-mail: paynec@dowling.edu. *Application contact:* Franks S. Pizzardi, Director of Admissions Operations, 631-244-3227, Fax: 631-244-1059, E-mail: pizzardf@dowling.edu.

Duquesne University, School of Education, Department of Instruction and Leadership, Program in Reading and Language Arts, Pittsburgh, PA 15282-0001. Offers MS Ed. Part-time and evening/weekend programs available. *Faculty:* 1 (woman) full-time, 4 part-time/adjunct (2 women). *Students:* 47. 16 applicants, 94% accepted, 14 enrolled. In 2006, 19 degrees awarded. *Degree requirements:* For master's, thesis optional. *Entrance requirements:* For master's, MAT, minimum GPA of 3.0. Additional exam requirements/recommendations for international students: Required—TOEFL. *Application deadline:* For fall admission, 8/1 for domestic students; for spring admission, 12/1 for domestic students. Applications are processed on a rolling basis. Application fee: $50. *Expenses:* Tuition: Part-time $723 per credit. Required fees: $71 per credit. Tuition and fees vary according to degree level and program. *Financial support:* In 2006–07, 1 research assistantship with full and partial tuition reimbursement (averaging $5,200 per year) was awarded; Federal Work-Study also available. Support available to part-time students. *Unit head:* Dr. Rosemary T. Mautino, Coordinator, 412-396-6089, Fax: 412-396-5388, E-mail: mautino@duq.edu.

East Carolina University, Graduate School, College of Education, Department of Curriculum and Instruction, Greenville, NC 27858-4353. Offers behavior/emotional disabilities (MA Ed); elementary education (MA Ed); English education (MA Ed); learning disabilities (MA Ed); low incidence disabilities (MA Ed); mental retardation (MA Ed); middle grade education (MA Ed); reading education (MA Ed); social studies education (MA Ed). Part-time programs available. Postbaccalaureate distance learning degree programs offered. *Students:* 92 full-time (85 women), 233 part-time (211 women); includes 42 minority (39 African Americans, 1 American Indian/Alaska Native, 1 Asian American or Pacific Islander, 1 Hispanic American). Average age 30. 25 applicants, 100% accepted, 25 enrolled. In 2006, 195 degrees awarded. *Degree requirements:* For master's, thesis optional. *Entrance requirements:* For master's, GRE General Test or MAT, interview, bachelor's degree in related field, minimum GPA of 2.5, teaching license. Additional exam requirements/recommendations for international students: Required—TOEFL. *Application deadline:* For fall admission, 6/1 priority date for domestic students. Applications are processed on a rolling basis. Application fee: $50. *Financial support:* Research assistantships, teaching assistantships, Federal Work-Study available. Support available to part-time students. Financial award application deadline: 6/1; financial award applicants required to submit FAFSA. *Unit head:* Dr. Sandra H. Warren, Interim Chair, 252-328-2699, E-mail: warrens@ecu.edu. *Application contact:* Dean of Graduate School, 252-328-6012, Fax: 252-328-6071, E-mail: gradschool@ecu.edu.

Eastern Connecticut State University, School of Education and Professional Studies/Graduate Division, Program in Reading and Language Arts, Willimantic, CT 06226-2295. Offers MS. *Accreditation:* NCATE. Part-time and evening/weekend programs available. *Faculty:* 2 full-time (both women), 2 part-time/adjunct (both women). *Students:* 2 full-time (both women), 45 part-time (44 women); includes 1 minority (African American) Average age 35. 4 applicants, 100% accepted, 3 enrolled. In 2006, 16 degrees awarded. *Degree requirements:* For master's, comprehensive exam or thesis. *Entrance requirements:* For master's, minimum GPA of 2.7, teaching certificate. Additional exam requirements/recommendations for international students: Required—TOEFL (minimum score 550 paper-based; 213 computer-based). *Application deadline:* For fall admission, 7/6 priority date for domestic and international students; for spring admission, 11/3 priority date for domestic and international students. Applications are processed on a rolling basis. Application fee: $50. *Expenses:* Tuition, state resident: full-time $3,970. Tuition, nonresident: full-time $11,061; part-time $336 per credit. Required fees: $35 per credit. *Financial support:* Teaching assistantships, career-related internships or fieldwork, scholarships/grants, and unspecified assistantships available. Support available to part-time students. Financial award application deadline: 3/15. *Unit head:* Dr. Susannah Richards, Advisor, 860-465-4533, Fax: 860-465-5099, E-mail: richardss@easternct.edu. *Application contact:* Dr. Tuesday L. Cooper, Associate Dean, 860-465-4543, Fax: 860-465-4538, E-mail: coopert@easternct.edu.

Eastern Kentucky University, The Graduate School, College of Education, Department of Curriculum and Instruction, Program in Secondary and Higher Education, Richmond, KY 40475-3102. Offers agricultural education (MA Ed); allied health sciences education (MA Ed); art education (MA Ed); biological sciences education (MA Ed); business education (MA Ed); chemistry education (MA Ed); earth science education (MA Ed); English education (MA Ed); general science education (MA Ed); geography education (MA Ed); history education (MA Ed); home economics education (MA Ed); industrial education (MA Ed); mathematical sciences education (MA Ed); physical education (MA Ed); physics education (MA Ed); political science education (MA Ed); psychology education (MA Ed); reading (MA Ed); school health education (MA Ed); sociology education (MA Ed). *Accreditation:* NCATE. Part-time programs available. *Students:* 16 full-time (8 women), 63 part-time (43 women); includes 5 minority (2 African Americans, 2 American Indian/Alaska Native, 1 Asian American or Pacific Islander). Average age 32. *Entrance requirements:* For master's, GRE General Test, minimum GPA of 2.5. Application fee: $30. *Expenses:* Tuition, state resident: full-time $5,610. Tuition, nonresident: full-time $15,910. *Financial support:* Research assistantships, teaching assistantships, Federal Work-Study available. Support available to part-time students. *Unit head:* Dr. Michael Martin, Chair, Department of Curriculum and Instruction, 859-622-2154, Fax: 859-622-2004.

Eastern Michigan University, Graduate School, College of Education, Department of Teacher Education, Program in Reading, Ypsilanti, MI 48197. Offers MA. *Accreditation:* NCATE. Part-time and evening/weekend programs available. Postbaccalaureate distance learning degree programs offered (minimal on-campus study). *Students:* Average age 32. In 2006, 38 degrees awarded. *Entrance requirements:* For master's, GRE. Additional exam requirements/recommendations for international students: Required—TOEFL. *Application deadline:* For fall admission, 5/15 priority date for domestic students, 5/1 priority date for international students; for winter admission, 10/15 priority date for domestic students, 10/1 priority date for international students; for spring admission, 3/15 priority date for domestic students, 3/1 priority date for international students. Applications are processed on a rolling basis. Application fee: $35. *Expenses:* Tuition, state resident: part-time $341 per credit hour. Tuition, nonresident: full-time $16,104; part-time $671 per credit hour. Required fees: $816; $34 per credit hour. $40 per term. One-time fee: $82 full-time. Tuition and fees vary according to course level, course load, degree level and reciprocity agreements. *Financial support:* Fellowships, research assistantships with full tuition reimbursements, teaching assistantships with full tuition reimbursements, career-related internships or fieldwork, Federal Work-Study, institutionally sponsored loans, scholarships/grants, tuition waivers (partial), and unspecified assistantships available. Support available to part-time students. Financial award applicants required to submit FAFSA.

Eastern Nazarene College, Adult and Graduate Studies, Division of Education, Quincy, MA 02170-2999. Offers early childhood education (M Ed, Certificate); elementary education (M Ed, Certificate); English as a second language (M Ed, Certificate); instructional enrichment and development (M Ed, Certificate); middle school education (M Ed, Certificate); moderate special needs education (M Ed, Certificate); principal (Certificate); program development and supervision (M Ed, Certificate); secondary education (M Ed, Certificate); special education administrator (Certificate); supervisor (Certificate); teacher of reading (M Ed, Certificate). M Ed and Certificate also available through weekend program for administration, special needs, and reading only. Part-time and evening/weekend programs available. *Faculty:* 9 full-time (5 women), 11 part-time/adjunct (5 women). *Students:* 135. Average age 35. 20 applicants, 100% accepted. In 2006, 2 degrees awarded. *Entrance requirements:* Additional exam requirements/recommendations for international students: Required—TOEFL (minimum score 550 paper-based). *Application deadline:* Applications are processed on a rolling basis. Application fee: $35. *Financial support:* Career-related internships or fieldwork available. Support available to part-time students. Financial award applicants required to submit FAFSA. *Unit head:* Dr. Lorne Ranstrom, Chair, 617-745-3528, E-mail: randstrol@enc.edu. *Application contact:* Christine Galbraith, Graduate Studies Recruiter, 617-774-6703, Fax: 617-984-4901, E-mail: christine.galbraith@enc.edu.

Eastern Washington University, Graduate Studies, College of Education and Human Development, Department of Education, Program in Literacy Specialist, Cheney, WA 99004-2431. Offers M Ed. *Accreditation:* NCATE. *Degree requirements:* For master's, comprehensive exam. *Entrance requirements:* For master's, minimum GPA of 3.0.

East Stroudsburg University of Pennsylvania, Graduate School, School of Professional Studies, Department of Reading, East Stroudsburg, PA 18301-2999. Offers M Ed. Part-time and evening/weekend programs available. *Faculty:* 4 full-time (all women), 6 part-time/adjunct (all women). *Students:* 14 full-time (all women), 135 part-time (128 women); includes 9 minority (2 African Americans, 1 Asian American or Pacific Islander, 6 Hispanic Americans). Average age 32. In 2006, 61 degrees awarded. *Degree requirements:* For master's, comprehensive exam. *Entrance requirements:* For master's, PRAXIS/teacher certification, letter of recommendation, Pennsylvania Department of Education requirements. Additional exam requirements/recommendations for international students: Required—TOEFL (minimum score 560 paper-based; 220 computer-based; 83 iBT). *Application deadline:* For fall admission, 7/31 priority date for domestic students, 5/1 priority date for international students; for spring admission, 11/30 for domestic students, 10/1 for international students. Applications are processed on a rolling basis. Application fee: $50. *Expenses:* Tuition, state resident: full-time $6,048; part-time $336 per credit. Tuition, nonresident: full-time $9,678; part-time $538 per credit. Required fees: $1,353; $67 per credit. One-time fee: $37 part-time. *Financial support:* In 2006–07, 3 research assistantships with full and partial tuition reimbursements were awarded; Federal Work-Study and institutionally sponsored loans also available. Financial award application deadline: 3/1; financial award applicants required to submit FAFSA. *Faculty research:* Portfolio assessment, reading assessment. *Unit head:* Dr. Mary Beth Allen, Interim Graduate Coordinator, 570-422-3411, Fax: 570-422-3924, E-mail: mballen@po-box.esu.edu.

East Tennessee State University, School of Graduate Studies, College of Education, Department of Curriculum and Instruction, Johnson City, TN 37614. Offers 7-12 (MAT); classroom technology (M Ed); educational communication (M Ed); educational media/educational technology (M Ed); elementary education (M Ed, MAT); K-12 (MAT); reading and storytelling (M Ed, MA); reading education (M Ed, MA); school library media (M Ed); secondary education (M Ed, MAT). *Accreditation:* NCATE. Part-time and evening/weekend programs available. *Degree requirements:* For master's, thesis (for some programs). *Entrance requirements:* For master's, GRE, minimum GPA of 3.0. Additional exam requirements/recommendations for international students: Required—TOEFL (minimum score 550 paper-based; 213 computer-based). *Faculty research:* Critical thinking, curriculum development, cultural diversity, cognitive processes, effective teaching strategies.

Edinboro University of Pennsylvania, Graduate Studies and Research, School of Education, Department of Elementary Education, Program in Reading, Edinboro, PA 16444. Offers reading (M Ed); reading specialist (Certificate). Part-time and evening/weekend programs available. *Students:* 11 full-time (all women), 112 part-time (104 women); includes 1 minority (African American) Average age 31. In 2006, 48 degrees awarded. *Degree requirements:* For master's, thesis or alternative, project, comprehensive exam; for Certificate, thesis or alternative, competency exam. *Entrance requirements:* For master's, GRE or MAT, minimum QPA of 2.5, valid elementary teaching certificate or current study to obtain certification; for Certificate, GRE or MAT, reading section of National Teacher's Exam, minimum QPA of 2.5. *Application deadline:* Applications are processed on a rolling basis. Application fee: $30. Electronic applications accepted. *Expenses:* Tuition, state resident: full-time $6,048; part-time $336 per credit. Tuition, nonresident: full-time $9,678; part-time $538 per credit. Required fees: $1,849; $42 per credit. *Financial support:* In 2006–07, 5 research assistantships with full and partial tuition reimbursements (averaging $3,850 per year) were awarded; Federal Work-

Study, scholarships/grants, and unspecified assistantships also available. Support available to part-time students. Financial award application deadline: 2/15; financial award applicants required to submit FAFSA. *Unit head:* Dr. Marian Beckman, Coordinator, 814-732-2355, E-mail: mbeckman@edinboro.edu. *Application contact:* Dr. R. Scott Baldwin, Dean, 814-732-2752, Fax: 814-732-2268, E-mail: sbaldwin@edinboro.edu.

Elms College, Division of Education, Chicopee, MA 01013-2839. Offers early childhood education (MAT); education (M Ed, CAGS); elementary education (MAT); English as a second language (MAT); reading (MAT); secondary education (MAT), including biology education, English education, Spanish education; special education (MAT). Part-time and evening/weekend programs available. *Faculty:* 9 full-time (6 women), 4 part-time/adjunct (2 women). *Students:* 8 full-time (6 women), 97 part-time (89 women); includes 4 minority (2 Asian Americans or Pacific Islanders, 2 Hispanic Americans). Average age 36. 48 applicants, 90% accepted, 40 enrolled. In 2006, 37 master's, 8 other advanced degrees awarded. *Degree requirements:* For master's, thesis (for some programs). *Entrance requirements:* For master's, Massachusetts Educators Certification Test, minimum GPA of 3.0; for CAGS, master's degree in education. Additional exam requirements/recommendations for international students: Required—TOEFL. *Application deadline:* For fall admission, 7/1 priority date for domestic students; for spring admission, 11/1 priority date for domestic students. Applications are processed on a rolling basis. Application fee: $30. *Expenses:* Tuition: Full-time $9,180; part-time $510 per credit. Tuition and fees vary according to course load. *Financial support:* In 2006–07, 3 teaching assistantships with partial tuition reimbursements were awarded; tuition waivers (partial) also available. Support available to part-time students. Financial award application deadline: 4/15; financial award applicants required to submit FAFSA. *Unit head:* Dr. Mary Janeczek, Director, 413-594-2761, Fax: 413-592-4871, E-mail: janeczeke@elms.edu.

Emory & Henry College, Graduate Programs, Emory, VA 24327-0947. Offers American history (MA Ed); English and language arts (MA Ed); reading and language arts (MA Ed); reading specialist (MA Ed). Part-time and evening/weekend programs available. *Faculty:* 4 part-time/adjunct (2 women). *Students:* 1 full-time (0 women), 54 part-time (45 women). Average age 37. 53 applicants, 100% accepted, 53 enrolled. In 2006, 62 degrees awarded. *Median time to degree:* Master's–2.5 years part-time. *Entrance requirements:* For master's, GRE, recommendations. *Application deadline:* Applications are processed on a rolling basis. Application fee: $30. *Financial support:* Applicants required to submit FAFSA. *Unit head:* Dr. Jack Roper, Director of Graduate Studies, 276-944-6188, Fax: 276-944-5223, E-mail: jroper@ehc.edu.

Emporia State University, School of Graduate Studies, The Teachers College, Department of Early Childhood/Elementary Teacher Education, Program in Master Teacher, Emporia, KS 66801-5087. Offers master teacher (MS), including elementary subject matter, English as a second language, reading, secondary subject matter. *Accreditation:* NCATE. Part-time programs available. *Students:* 1 (woman) full-time, 83 part-time (82 women); includes 2 minority (1 American Indian/Alaska Native, 1 Hispanic American). 14 applicants, 93% accepted, 13 enrolled. In 2006, 23 degrees awarded. *Degree requirements:* For master's, comprehensive exam or thesis, practicum. *Entrance requirements:* For master's, GRE General Test or MAT, graduate essay exam, appropriate bachelor's degree, letters of recommendation. Additional exam requirements/recommendations for international students: Required—TOEFL. *Application deadline:* For fall admission, 8/15 priority date for domestic students. Applications are processed on a rolling basis. Application fee: $30 ($75 for international students). Electronic applications accepted. *Expenses:* Tuition, state resident: full-time $3,438; part-time $143 per credit hour. Tuition, nonresident: full-time $10,398; part-time $433 per credit hour. Required fees: $724; $44 per credit hour. *Financial support:* Federal Work-Study, institutionally sponsored loans, health care benefits, and unspecified assistantships available. Financial award application deadline: 3/15; financial award applicants required to submit FAFSA. *Unit head:* Dr. Jean Morrow, Chair, Department of Early Childhood/Elementary Teacher Education, 620-341-5766, E-mail: jmorrow@emporia.edu.

Endicott College, Van Loan School of Graduate and Professional Studies, Program in Reading and Literacy, Beverly, MA 01915-2096. Offers initial and professional licensure (M Ed). Part-time and evening/weekend programs available. *Faculty:* 25 part-time/adjunct (14 women). *Students:* Average age 35. *Degree requirements:* For master's, comprehensive exam, registration. *Entrance requirements:* For master's, MAT or GRE, Massachusetts teaching certificate, letters of recommendation. *Application deadline:* Applications are processed on a rolling basis. Application fee: $50. *Expenses:* Tuition: Part-time $279 per credit. Tuition and fees vary according to program. *Financial support:* Career-related internships or fieldwork, Federal Work-Study, and institutionally sponsored loans available. *Unit head:* Dr. John D. MacLean, Director of Licensure Programs, 978-232-2408, E-mail: jmaclean@endicott.edu.

Evangel University, Department of Education, Springfield, MO 65802-2191. Offers educational leadership (M Ed); reading education (M Ed); secondary teaching (M Ed); teaching (MA). Part-time and evening/weekend programs available. *Faculty:* 4 full-time (2 women), 6 part-time/adjunct (5 women). *Students:* 2 full-time (both women), 17 part-time (14 women); includes 2 minority (1 Asian American or Pacific Islander, 1 Hispanic American). Average age 26. 10 applicants, 100% accepted, 10 enrolled. In 2006, 13 degrees awarded. *Degree requirements:* For master's, thesis optional. *Entrance requirements:* For master's, PRAXIS II (preferred), GRE (accepted). Additional exam requirements/recommendations for international students: Required—TOEFL (minimum score 550 paper-based; 213 computer-based). *Application deadline:* For fall admission, 7/15 priority date for domestic students; for spring admission, 11/15 priority date for domestic students. Applications are processed on a rolling basis. Application fee: $25. *Financial support:* In 2006–07, 6 students received support. Career-related internships or fieldwork, institutionally sponsored loans, and scholarships/grants available. Support available to part-time students. Financial award application deadline: 3/1; financial award applicants required to submit FAFSA. *Unit head:* Dr. Jeff Hittenberger, Chair, 417-865-2815 Ext. 8559, E-mail: hittenbergerj@evangel.edu. *Application contact:* Charity H. Fahlstrom, Director of Graduate and Professional Studies Admissions, 417-865-2811 Ext. 1227, Fax: 417-575-5484.

Fairleigh Dickinson University, College at Florham, University College: Arts, Sciences, and Professional Studies, Peter Sammartino School of Education, Madison, NJ 07940-1099. Offers education for certified teachers (MA, Certificate); educational leadership (MA); instructional technology (Certificate); literacy/reading (Certificate); teaching (MAT). *Students:* 62 full-time (52 women), 58 part-time (41 women). Average age 29. 77 applicants, 83% accepted, 58 enrolled. In 2006, 86 degrees awarded. *Application deadline:* Applications are processed on a rolling basis. Application fee: $40.

Fairleigh Dickinson University, Metropolitan Campus, University College: Arts, Sciences, and Professional Studies, Peter Sammartino School of Education, Teaneck, NJ 07666-1914. Offers dyslexia specialist (Certificate); education for certified teachers (MA); educational leadership (MA); instructional technology (Certificate); learning disabilities (MA); literacy/reading (Certificate); multilingual education (MA); teacher of the handicapped (Certificate); teaching (MAT). Part-time programs available. *Students:* 70 full-time (54 women), 515 part-time (424 women), 14 international. Average age 36. 290 applicants, 92% accepted, 130 enrolled. In 2006, 106 degrees awarded. *Degree requirements:* For master's, research project (MAT). *Application deadline:* Applications are processed on a rolling basis. Application fee: $40. *Unit head:* Dr. Vicki Cohen, Director, 201-692-2525, Fax: 201-692-2603, E-mail: vicki_cohen@fdu.edu.

See Close-Up on page 877.

Fayetteville State University, Graduate School, Program in Middle Grades, Secondary and Special Education, Fayetteville, NC 28301-4298. Offers biology (MA Ed); history (MA Ed); mathematics (MA Ed); middle grades (MA Ed); political science (MA Ed); reading (MA Ed); sociology (MA Ed); special education (MA Ed), including behavioral-emotional handicaps, mentally handicapped, specific training disability. *Accreditation:* NCATE. Part-time and evening/weekend programs available. *Faculty:* 19 full-time (12 women), 3 part-time/adjunct (2 women). *Students:* 14 full-time (10 women), 48 part-time (40 women); includes 44 minority (40 African Americans, 2 American Indian/Alaska Native, 1 Asian American or Pacific Islander, 1 Hispanic American). Average age 39. 16 applicants, 100% accepted, 16 enrolled. In 2006, 33 degrees awarded. *Degree requirements:* For master's, internship. *Application deadline:* For fall admission, 7/1 for domestic students; for spring admission, 12/1 for domestic students. Applications are processed on a rolling basis. Application fee: $25. Electronic applications accepted. *Expenses:* Tuition, state resident: full-time $2,118. Tuition, nonresident: full-time $11,708. Required fees: $1,099. Tuition and fees vary according to course load. *Unit head:* Dr. Charletta Barringer-Brown, Interim Chair, 910-672-1182, E-mail: cbarringerbrown@uncfsu.edu.

Ferris State University, College of Education and Human Services, School of Education, Big Rapids, MI 49307. Offers administration (MSCTE); curriculum and instruction (M Ed), including administration, elementary education, philanthropic education, reading, secondary education, special education, subject matter option; education technology (MSCTE); instructor (MSCTE); post-secondary administration (MSCTE); training and development (MSCTE). Part-time and evening/weekend programs available. Postbaccalaureate distance learning degree programs offered (no on-campus study). *Faculty:* 13 full-time (9 women), 26 part-time/adjunct (19 women). *Students:* 38 full-time (27 women), 254 part-time (164 women); includes 30 minority (22 African Americans, 1 American Indian/Alaska Native, 2 Asian Americans or Pacific Islanders, 5 Hispanic Americans), 1 international. Average age 37. 171 applicants, 99% accepted. In 2006, 92 degrees awarded. *Degree requirements:* For master's, thesis, research paper. *Entrance requirements:* For master's, 2 years of work experience, minimum GPA of 3.0. *Application deadline:* For fall admission, 6/1 priority date for domestic students; for winter admission, 12/10 priority date for domestic students. Applications are processed on a rolling basis. Application fee: $30. *Expenses:* Tuition, state resident: part-time $355 per credit hour. Tuition, nonresident: part-time $687 per credit hour. *Financial support:* Career-related internships or fieldwork and tuition waivers (full and partial) available. Support available to part-time students. Financial award applicants required to submit FAFSA. *Faculty research:* Suicide prevention, reading, women in education, special needs, administration. *Unit head:* Interim Director, 231-591-5362, Fax: 231-591-2041. *Application contact:* Sigrid Robertson, Secretary, 231-591-3511, Fax: 231-591-2041, E-mail: robertss@ferris.edu.

Florida Atlantic University, College of Education, Department of Teacher Education, Boca Raton, FL 33431-0991. Offers art teacher education (M Ed); curriculum and instruction (M Ed, Ed D, Ed S); educational psychology (MSF); elementary education (M Ed); foundations of education (M Ed); multicultural education (MSF); reading teacher education (M Ed). *Accreditation:* NCATE. Part-time and evening/weekend programs available. *Faculty:* 29 full-time (23 women), 75 part-time/adjunct (50 women). *Students:* 78 full-time (65 women), 176 part-time (159 women); includes 50 minority (20 African Americans, 1 American Indian/Alaska Native, 6 Asian Americans or Pacific Islanders, 23 Hispanic Americans), 1 international. Average age 35. 132 applicants, 64% accepted, 62 enrolled. In 2006, 95 master's, 2 doctorates awarded. *Degree requirements:* For master's, registration; for doctorate, thesis/dissertation, departmental qualifying exam, comprehensive exam, registration; for Ed S, departmental qualifying exam. *Entrance requirements:* For master's, GRE General Test, minimum GPA of 3.0 in last 2 years of undergraduate course work; for doctorate, GRE General Test, GRE Subject Test, minimum graduate GPA of 3.2, 3.0 in last 2 years of undergraduate course work; for Ed S, GRE General Test. Additional exam requirements/recommendations for international students: Required—TOEFL. *Application deadline:* Applications are processed on a rolling basis. Application fee: $30. *Expenses:* Tuition, area resident: Full-time $4,394. Tuition, nonresident: full-time $16,441. *Financial support:* In 2006–07, 4 research assistantships with partial tuition reimbursements (averaging $8,000 per year), 3 teaching assistantships with partial tuition reimbursements (averaging $8,000 per year) were awarded; fellowships with partial tuition reimbursements, career-related internships or fieldwork, scholarships/grants, and unspecified assistantships also available. *Faculty research:* Technology, teaching English to speakers of other languages, math teaching, electronic portfolio assessment, global perspectives through social studies. *Unit head:* Dr. Penelope Fritzer, Chairperson, 561-297-3584.

Florida Atlantic University, Jupiter Campus, College of Education, Jupiter, FL 33458. Offers exceptional student education (M Ed); reading (M Ed).

Florida Gulf Coast University, College of Education, Program in Reading Education, Fort Myers, FL 33965-6565. Offers M Ed. Part-time and evening/weekend programs available. *Faculty:* 31 full-time (21 women), 30 part-time/adjunct (24 women). *Students:* 39 full-time (37 women), 15 part-time (13 women); includes 6 minority (1 American Indian/Alaska Native, 5 Hispanic Americans). Average age 36. 24 applicants, 88% accepted, 21 enrolled. In 2006, 29 degrees awarded. *Entrance requirements:* For master's, GRE General Test, MAT, minimum GPA of 3.0. Additional exam requirements/recommendations for international students: Required—TOEFL (minimum score 550 paper-based; 213 computer-based). *Application deadline:* For fall admission, 7/1 priority date for domestic students; for spring admission, 10/15 for domestic students. Applications are processed on a rolling basis. Application fee: $30. Electronic applications accepted. *Expenses:* Tuition, state resident: full-time $4,326. Tuition, nonresident: full-time $18,523. Required fees: $1,211. One-time fee: $5 full-time. *Faculty research:* Struggling readers, reading and writing connection, involving families in reading. *Unit head:* Dr. Patricia Wachholz, Head, 239-590-7808, Fax: 239-590-7801, E-mail: pwachhol@fgcu.edu.

Florida International University, College of Education, Department of Curriculum and Instruction, Program in Reading Education, Miami, FL 33199. Offers MS, Ed D. *Accreditation:* NCATE. Part-time and evening/weekend programs available. *Faculty:* 3 full-time (all women). *Students:* 11 full-time (all women), 103 part-time (101 women); includes 87 minority (17 African Americans, 3 Asian Americans or Pacific Islanders, 67 Hispanic Americans). Average age 32. 53 applicants, 96% accepted, 36 enrolled. In 2006, 88 degrees awarded. *Degree requirements:* For master's, thesis optional. *Entrance requirements:* For master's, minimum GPA of 3.0, professional certification. Additional exam requirements/recommendations for international students: Required—TOEFL (minimum score 550 paper-based; 213 computer-based; 80 iBT), IELTS (minimum score 6). *Application deadline:* For fall admission, 6/1 priority date for domestic students, 4/1 for international students; for winter admission, 10/1 priority date for domestic students, 9/1 for international students; for spring admission, 3/1 priority date for domestic students, 2/1 for international students. Applications are processed on a rolling basis. Application fee: $30. Electronic applications accepted. *Expenses:* Tuition, state resident: part-time $249 per credit hour. Tuition, nonresident: part-time $753 per credit hour. Tuition and fees vary according to program. *Faculty research:* Understanding reading comprehension, improving reading instruction, racial issues in reading and learning. *Unit head:* Dr. Joyce Fine, Program Director, 305-348-6152, E-mail: finej@fiu.edu. *Application contact:* Marisa Salazar, Student Recruiter, 305-348-3002, Fax: 305-348-3227, E-mail: marisa.salazar@fiu.edu.

Florida State University, Graduate Studies, College of Education, Department of Childhood Education, Reading, and Disability Services, Tallahassee, FL 32306. Offers early childhood education (MS, Ed D, PhD, Ed S); elementary education (MS, Ed D, PhD, Ed S); reading education/language arts (MS, Ed D, PhD, Ed S); special education (MS, PhD, Ed S), including emotional disturbance/learning disabilities (MS), mental retardation (MS), rehabilitation counseling, special education (PhD, Ed S), visual disabilities (MS). Part-time programs available. *Faculty:* 24 full-time (19 women), 3 part-time/adjunct (all women). *Students:* 85 full-time (73 women), 205 part-time (189 women); includes 60 minority (36 African Americans, 2 American Indian/Alaska Native, 13 Asian Americans or Pacific Islanders, 9 Hispanic Americans). 189 applicants, 61% accepted, 71 enrolled. In 2006, 76 master's, 7 doctorates, 5 other advanced degrees awarded. *Degree requirements:* For master's and Ed S, thesis optional; for doctorate, thesis/dissertation, comprehensive exam. *Entrance requirements:* For master's, doctorate, and Ed S, GRE General Test, minimum GPA of 3.0. *Application deadline:* For fall admission, 7/1 priority date for domestic students; for spring admission, 11/1 for domestic students. Applications are processed on a rolling basis. Application fee: $30. *Expenses:* Tuition, state resident: full-time $5,822; part-time $243 per credit hour. Tuition, nonresident: full-time $20,976;

Reading Education

Florida State University (continued)
part-time $874 per credit hour. Tuition and fees vary according to program. *Financial support:* In 2006–07, 2 fellowships, 4 research assistantships, 12 teaching assistantships were awarded; career-related internships or fieldwork also available. Financial award applicants required to submit FAFSA. *Unit head:* Dr. Mary Frances Hanline, Chair, 850-644-5458, Fax: 850-644-7736, E-mail: mhanline@coe.fsu.edu. *Application contact:* Timolin Lynette Bodison-Baker, Program Assistant, 850-644-5458, Fax: 850-644-7736, E-mail: bodison@coe.fsu.edu.

Fordham University, Graduate School of Education, Division of Curriculum and Teaching, New York, NY 10023. Offers adult education (MS, MSE); bilingual teacher education (MSE); curriculum and teaching (MSE); early childhood education (MSE); elementary education (MST); language, literacy, and learning (PhD); reading education (MSE, Adv C); secondary education (MAT, MSE); special education (MSE, Adv C); teaching English as a second language (MSE). *Accreditation:* NCATE. *Faculty:* 22 full-time (18 women), 38 part-time/adjunct (28 women). *Students:* 68 full-time (51 women), 663 part-time (612 women); includes 200 minority (74 African Americans, 1 American Indian/Alaska Native, 37 Asian Americans or Pacific Islanders, 88 Hispanic Americans), 3 international. Average age 32. 636 applicants, 86% accepted, 322 enrolled. In 2006, 351 master's, 8 doctorates awarded. *Degree requirements:* For doctorate and Adv C, thesis/dissertation. *Entrance requirements:* For doctorate, MAT, GRE General Test. Application fee: $65. *Financial support:* Applicants required to submit FAFSA. *Unit head:* Dr. Terry Osborn, Chairperson, 212-636-6450.

Framingham State College, Division of Graduate and Continuing Education, Program in Literacy and Language, Framingham, MA 01701-9101. Offers M Ed. Part-time and evening/weekend programs available. *Faculty:* 3 part-time/adjunct. *Students:* 67. In 2006, 30 degrees awarded. *Entrance requirements:* For master's, MAT. *Unit head:* Dr. Diane Lowe, Coordinator, 508-626-4887, Fax: 508-626-4030, E-mail: dlowe@frc.mass.edu. *Application contact:* 508-626-4550, Fax: 508-626-4030, E-mail: dgce@frc.mass.edu.

Fresno Pacific University, Graduate Programs, Programs in Education, Fresno, CA 93702-4709. Offers administration (MA Ed), including administrative services; foundations, curriculum and teaching (MA Ed), including curriculum and teaching, school library and information technology; language, literacy, and culture (MA Ed), including bilingual/cross-cultural education, language development, multilingual contexts, reading; mathematics/science/computer education (MA Ed), including educational technology, integrated mathematics/science education, mathematics education; pupil personnel services (MA Ed), including school counseling, school psychology; special education (MA Ed), including mild/moderate, moderate/severe, physical and health impairments. Part-time and evening/weekend programs available. *Faculty:* 12 full-time (5 women), 19 part-time/adjunct (9 women). *Students:* 73 full-time (59 women), 399 part-time (295 women); includes 136 minority (9 African Americans, 5 American Indian/Alaska Native, 12 Asian Americans or Pacific Islanders, 110 Hispanic Americans), 2 international. Average age 39. 124 applicants, 73% accepted, 10 enrolled. In 2006, 128 degrees awarded. *Degree requirements:* For master's, thesis (for some programs), registration. *Entrance requirements:* For master's, interview; GMAT, GRE, MAT, or 6 units of course work with a faculty recommendation. Additional exam requirements/recommendations for international students: Required—TOEFL (minimum score 550 paper-based; 213 computer-based). *Application deadline:* For fall admission, 7/15 for domestic and international students; for spring admission, 11/15 for domestic and international students. Applications are processed on a rolling basis. Application fee: $90. Electronic applications accepted. *Expenses:* Tuition: Full-time $7,470; part-time $415 per credit. *Financial support:* In 2006–07, 260 students received support. Career-related internships or fieldwork, scholarships/grants, and tuition waivers (full and partial) available. Support available to part-time students. Financial award applicants required to submit FAFSA.

Fresno Pacific University, Graduate Programs, Programs in Education, Division of Language, Literacy, and Culture, Program in Language Development, Fresno, CA 93702-4709. Offers MA Ed. Part-time and evening/weekend programs available. *Students:* Average age 46. *Degree requirements:* For master's, thesis or alternative, registration. *Entrance requirements:* Additional exam requirements/recommendations for international students: Required—TOEFL (minimum score 550 paper-based; 213 computer-based). *Application deadline:* For fall admission, 7/15 for domestic and international students; for spring admission, 11/15 for domestic and international students. Applications are processed on a rolling basis. Application fee: $90. Electronic applications accepted. *Expenses:* Tuition: Full-time $7,470; part-time $415 per credit. *Financial support:* In 2006–07, 1 student received support. Scholarships/grants and tuition waivers (full and partial) available. Support available to part-time students. Financial award applicants required to submit FAFSA.

Fresno Pacific University, Graduate Programs, Programs in Education, Division of Language, Literacy, and Culture, Program in Reading, Fresno, CA 93702-4709. Offers reading/English as a second language (MA Ed); reading/language arts (MA Ed). Part-time and evening/weekend programs available. *Students:* 1 (woman) full-time, 27 part-time (26 women); includes 12 minority (2 Asian Americans or Pacific Islanders, 10 Hispanic Americans). Average age 41. 3 applicants, 100% accepted, 1 enrolled. In 2006, 3 degrees awarded. *Degree requirements:* For master's, thesis or alternative, registration. *Entrance requirements:* Additional exam requirements/recommendations for international students: Required—TOEFL (minimum score 550 paper-based; 213 computer-based). *Application deadline:* For fall admission, 7/15 for domestic and international students; for spring admission, 11/15 for domestic and international students. Applications are processed on a rolling basis. Application fee: $90. Electronic applications accepted. *Expenses:* Tuition: Full-time $7,470; part-time $415 per credit. *Financial support:* In 2006–07, 9 students received support. Scholarships/grants and tuition waivers (full and partial) available. Support available to part-time students. Financial award applicants required to submit FAFSA.

Frostburg State University, Graduate School, College of Education, Department of Educational Professions, Program in Reading, Frostburg, MD 21532-1099. Offers M Ed. *Accreditation:* NCATE. *Degree requirements:* For master's, thesis or alternative, in-service. *Entrance requirements:* For master's, teaching certificate. Electronic applications accepted.

Furman University, Graduate Division, Department of Education, Greenville, SC 29613. Offers early childhood education (MA); elementary education (MA); English as a second language (MA); middle school education (MA); reading (MA); school administration (MA); special education (MA). *Accreditation:* NCATE. Part-time and evening/weekend programs available. *Faculty:* 17 full-time (12 women), 19 part-time/adjunct (15 women). *Students:* 114 full-time (89 women), 72 part-time (59 women); includes 27 minority (23 African Americans, 4 Hispanic Americans). Average age 32. 36 applicants, 100% accepted, 36 enrolled. In 2006, 111 degrees awarded. *Degree requirements:* For master's, thesis (for some programs), comprehensive exam. *Entrance requirements:* For master's, GRE General Test or PRAXIS. *Application deadline:* For fall admission, 8/1 priority date for domestic and international students; for winter admission, 12/1 priority date for domestic and international students; for spring admission, 2/1 priority date for domestic and international students. Applications are processed on a rolling basis. Application fee: $50. *Expenses:* Tuition: Part-time $347 per credit. *Financial support:* In 2006–07, 97 students received support; fellowships, scholarships/grants and unspecified assistantships available. Financial award application deadline: 1/15; financial award applicants required to submit FAFSA. *Unit head:* Dr. Nelly Hecker, Head, 864-294-3385.

Gannon University, School of Graduate Studies, College of Humanities, Business, and Education, School of Education, Program in Reading, Erie, PA 16541-0001. Offers M Ed, Certificate. Part-time and evening/weekend programs available. *Students:* 1 (woman) full-time, 13 part-time (all women). Average age 28. 8 applicants, 75% accepted, 5 enrolled. In 2006, 3 master's, 1 other advanced degree awarded. *Degree requirements:* For master's, thesis, comprehensive exam. *Entrance requirements:* For master's, GRE General Test or MAT, NTE, interview, teaching certificate. Additional exam requirements/recommendations for international students: Required—TOEFL (minimum score 500 paper-based; 173 computer-based). *Application deadline:* Applications are processed on a rolling basis. Application fee: $25. *Expenses:* Tuition: Full-time $12,240; part-time $680 per credit. Required fees: $496; $16 per credit. Tuition and fees vary according to course load, degree level, campus/location and program. *Financial support:* Application deadline: 7/1; *Application contact:* Debra Meszaros, Director of Graduate Recruitment, 814-871-5819, Fax: 814-871-5827, E-mail: cfal@gannon.edu.

George Mason University, Graduate School of Education, Programs in Curriculum and Instruction, Fairfax, VA 22030. Offers bilingual/multicultural/English as a second language education (M Ed); early childhood education (M Ed); instructional technology (M Ed); middle education (M Ed); reading (M Ed); secondary education (M Ed); special education (M Ed). Part-time and evening/weekend programs available. *Faculty:* 108 full-time (70 women), 193 part-time/adjunct (140 women). *Students:* 185 full-time (144 women), 816 part-time (683 women); includes 148 minority (46 African Americans, 2 American Indian/Alaska Native, 44 Asian Americans or Pacific Islanders, 56 Hispanic Americans), 28 international. Average age 34. 822 applicants, 72% accepted, 473 enrolled. In 2006, 606 master's awarded. *Entrance requirements:* For master's, minimum GPA of 3.0 in last 60 hours. *Application deadline:* For fall admission, 5/1 for domestic students; for spring admission, 11/1 for domestic students. Application fee: $60 ($75 for international students). Electronic applications accepted. *Expenses:* Tuition, state resident: full-time $5,724; part-time $238 per credit. Tuition, nonresident: full-time $16,896; part-time $704 per credit. Required fees: $1,656; $69 per credit. *Financial support:* Career-related internships or fieldwork available. Support available to part-time students. Financial award application deadline: 3/1; financial award applicants required to submit FAFSA. *Unit head:* Martin E. Ford, Senior Associate Dean, 703-993-2008.

Georgia Southern University, Jack N. Averitt College of Graduate Studies, College of Education, Department of Curriculum, Foundations, and Reading, Program in Reading Education, Statesboro, GA 30460. Offers M Ed. *Accreditation:* NCATE. Part-time programs available. *Students:* 8 full-time (all women), 34 part-time (29 women); includes 2 minority (both African Americans) Average age 32. 9 applicants, 78% accepted, 5 enrolled. In 2006, 17 degrees awarded. *Degree requirements:* For master's, comprehensive exam. *Entrance requirements:* For master's, GRE General Test or MAT, minimum GPA of 2.5. Additional exam requirements/recommendations for international students: Required—TOEFL (minimum score 550 paper-based; 213 computer-based; 80 iBT). *Application deadline:* For fall admission, 3/1 priority date for domestic and international students; for spring admission, 10/1 priority date for domestic students, 10/1 for international students. Applications are processed on a rolling basis. Application fee: $50. Electronic applications accepted. *Financial support:* In 2006–07, 17 students received support, including research assistantships with partial tuition reimbursements available (averaging $5,500 per year), teaching assistantships with partial tuition reimbursements available (averaging $5,500 per year); career-related internships or fieldwork, Federal Work-Study, scholarships/grants, tuition waivers (partial), and unspecified assistantships also available. Support available to part-time students. Financial award application deadline: 4/15; financial award applicants required to submit FAFSA. *Faculty research:* Emerging literacy, content literacy, literature groups, phonics/whole language, qualitative research methods. *Unit head:* Dr. Michael Moore, Coordinator, 912-681-0211, Fax: 912-681-5382, E-mail: mmoore@georgiasouthern.edu. *Application contact:* Office of Graduate Admissions, 912-681-5384, Fax: 912-681-0740, E-mail: gradadmissions@georgiasouthern.edu.

Georgia Southwestern State University, Graduate Studies, School of Education, Americus, GA 31709-4693. Offers early childhood education (M Ed, Ed S); health and physical education (M Ed); middle grades education (M Ed, Ed S); reading (M Ed); secondary education (M Ed); special education (M Ed). *Accreditation:* NCATE. *Degree requirements:* For master's, comprehensive exam. *Entrance requirements:* For master's, GRE General Test or MAT, minimum GPA of 2.5; for Ed S, GRE General Test or MAT, minimum graduate GPA of 3.25, M Ed from accredited college or university, 3 years teaching experience. Electronic applications accepted.

Georgia State University, College of Education, Department of Middle-Secondary Education and Instructional Technology, Program in Reading Instruction, Atlanta, GA 30303-3083. Offers reading, language and literacy (M Ed); reading, language, and literacy (PhD, Ed S); teaching English as a second language (M Ed). *Accreditation:* NCATE. Part-time and evening/weekend programs available. *Students:* 6 full-time (all women), 24 part-time (20 women); includes 4 minority (3 African Americans, 1 Asian American or Pacific Islander), 1 international. Average age 29. 14 applicants, 71% accepted. In 2006, 11 degrees awarded. *Degree requirements:* For master's, comprehensive exam; for Ed S, project/exam. *Entrance requirements:* For master's, GRE General Test, minimum GPA of 2.5; for Ed S, GRE General Test or MAT, minimum graduate GPA of 3.25. *Application deadline:* For fall admission, 7/15 for domestic students; for spring admission, 1/15 for domestic students. Application fee: $25. *Financial support:* Career-related internships or fieldwork, Federal Work-Study, and institutionally sponsored loans available. *Faculty research:* Language development, attribution theory, linguistics. *Unit head:* Dr. Ruth Hough, Acting Chair, Department of Middle-Secondary Education and Instructional Technology, 404-651-2510.

Governors State University, College of Education, Program in Reading, University Park, IL 60466-0975. Offers MA. *Accreditation:* NCATE. *Students:* Average age 32.Application fee: $25. *Expenses:* Tuition, state resident: full-time $4,104; part-time $171 per hour. Tuition, nonresident: part-time $513 per hour.

Grand Canyon University, College of Education, Phoenix, AZ 85017-1097. Offers elementary education (M Ed, MA); reading education (MA); secondary education (M Ed); teaching (MAT); teaching English as a second language (MA). Part-time and evening/weekend programs available. Postbaccalaureate distance learning degree programs offered (no on-campus study). *Degree requirements:* For master's, publishable research paper (M Ed). *Entrance requirements:* For master's, MAT, GRE or minimum GPA of 3.0.

See Close-Up on page 885.

Grand Valley State University, College of Education, Program in Reading and Language Arts, Allendale, MI 49401-9403. Offers M Ed. *Accreditation:* NCATE. Part-time and evening/weekend programs available. *Faculty:* 5 full-time (4 women), 2 part-time/adjunct (both women). *Students:* 2 full-time (both women), 160 part-time (157 women); includes 10 minority (4 African Americans, 2 American Indian/Alaska Native, 2 Asian Americans or Pacific Islanders, 2 Hispanic Americans). Average age 31. 28 applicants, 93% accepted, 24 enrolled. In 2006, 32 degrees awarded. *Degree requirements:* For master's, thesis. *Entrance requirements:* For master's, GRE General Test or minimum GPA of 3.0. Additional exam requirements/recommendations for international students: Required—TOEFL. *Application deadline:* Applications are processed on a rolling basis. Application fee: $30. Electronic applications accepted. *Expenses:* Tuition, state resident: full-time $5,850; part-time $325 per credit. Tuition, nonresident: full-time $10,800; part-time $600 per credit. Tuition and fees vary according to course load. *Financial support:* In 2006–07, research assistantships with full and partial tuition reimbursements (averaging $8,000 per year); career-related internships or fieldwork, Federal Work-Study, scholarships/grants, and unspecified assistantships also available. *Faculty research:* Culture of literacy, literacy acquisition, assessment, content area literacy, writing pedagogy. *Unit head:* Dr. Nancy Patterson, Director, 616-331-6226, E-mail: patterson@gvsu.edu. *Application contact:* Dr. Douglas Busman, Director, Student Information and Services, 616-331-6831, Fax: 616-331-6217, E-mail: busmando@gvsu.edu.

Gwynedd-Mercy College, School of Education, Gwynedd Valley, PA 19437-0901. Offers educational administration (MS); master teacher (MS); reading (MS); school counseling (MS); special education (MS). Part-time and evening/weekend programs available. *Faculty:* 9 full-time (5 women), 37 part-time/adjunct (17 women). *Students:* 92 full-time (66 women), 464 part-time (374 women); includes 52 minority (49 African Americans, 3 Hispanic Americans), 1 international. Average age 34. In 2006, 160 degrees awarded. *Degree requirements:* For master's, thesis, internship, practicum. *Entrance requirements:* For master's, GRE or MAT; PPST Praxis Test, minimum GPA of 3.0. *Application deadline:* Applications are processed on a rolling basis. Application fee: $25. *Expenses:* Tuition: Part-time $525 per credit hour. *Financial support:* In 2006–07, 2 research assistantships were awarded; career-related internships or fieldwork, Federal Work-Study, tuition waivers (full and partial), and unspecified assistantships also available. Financial award applicants required to submit FAFSA. *Faculty research:* Learning and the brain, reading literacy, ethics and moral judgment, leadership, teaching and multicultural education. *Unit head:* Dr. Lorraine Cavaliere, EdD, Dean, 215-641-5549, Fax: 215-542-4695, E-mail: cavaliere.l@gmc.edu. *Application contact:* Marian Watkins, Graduate Program Coordinator, 215-641-5561, Fax: 215-542-4695, E-mail: watkins.m@gmc.edu.

Harding University, College of Education, Searcy, AR 72149-0001. Offers advanced studies in teaching and learning (M Ed); art (MSE); behavioral science (MSE); Bible and religion (MSE); counseling (MS, Ed S); early childhood education (M Ed); early childhood special education (M Ed, MSE); education (MSE); educational leadership (M Ed, Ed S); elementary education (M Ed); English (MSE); family and consumer science (MSE); French (MSE); history/social science (MSE); kinesiology (MSE); math (MSE); physical science (MSE); reading (M Ed); secondary education (M Ed); Spanish (MSE); special education licensure (M Ed); teaching (MAT). *Accreditation:* NCATE. Part-time programs available. *Faculty:* 8 full-time (2 women), 45 part-time/adjunct (30 women). *Students:* 153 full-time (123 women), 469 part-time (341 women); includes 72 minority (63 African Americans, 4 American Indian/Alaska Native, 1 Asian American or Pacific Islander, 4 Hispanic Americans), 9 international. Average age 35. 175 applicants, 90% accepted, 147 enrolled. In 2006, 241 degrees awarded. *Degree requirements:* For master's, portfolio(s), thesis optional; for Ed S, portfolio, specialist project. *Entrance requirements:* For master's, GRE, MAT, PRAXIS; for Ed S, MAT or GRE. Additional exam requirements/recommendations for international students: Required—TOEFL (minimum score 550 paper-based). *Application deadline:* For fall admission, 8/1 for domestic and international students; for spring admission, 1/1 for domestic and international students. Applications are processed on a rolling basis. Application fee: $35. *Expenses:* Tuition: Part-time $455 per semester hour. Required fees: $20 per semester hour. Tuition and fees vary according to course load. *Financial support:* Scholarships/grants and unspecified assistantships available. Support available to part-time students. *Faculty research:* Reading, comprehension, school violence, educational technology, behavior, college choice, differentiated instruction, brain based teaching. *Unit head:* Pat Bashaw, Chair, 501-279-4183, Fax: 501-279-4051, E-mail: pbashaw@harding.edu.

Hardin-Simmons University, Graduate School, Irvin School of Education, Department of Education, Reading Specialist Program, Abilene, TX 79698-0001. Offers M Ed. Part-time programs available. *Faculty:* 2 full-time (both women), 1 (woman) part-time/adjunct. *Students:* Average age 32. 3 applicants, 100% accepted, 2 enrolled. In 2006, 3 degrees awarded. *Degree requirements:* For master's, comprehensive exam. *Entrance requirements:* For master's, minimum undergraduate GPA of 3.0 in major, 2.7 overall. Additional exam requirements/recommendations for international students: Required—TOEFL (minimum score 550 paper-based; 213 computer-based). *Application deadline:* For fall admission, 8/15 priority date for domestic students; for spring admission, 1/5 priority date for domestic students. Applications are processed on a rolling basis. Application fee: $50 ($100 for international students). *Expenses:* Tuition: Full-time $9,090; part-time $505 per hour. Required fees: $490; $66 per semester. One-time fee: $50. Tuition and fees vary according to course load and degree level. *Financial support:* In 2006–07, 3 students received support, including 2 fellowships (averaging $1,200 per year); scholarships/grants also available. Support available to part-time students. Financial award application deadline: 6/30; financial award applicants required to submit FAFSA. *Faculty research:* Social networking as a gatekeeper, reflective process of teachers, growth of reflective practice in pre-service teachers, multicultural children's literature. *Unit head:* Dr. Lori Copeland, Director, 325-670-1348, E-mail: lcope@hsutx.edu. *Application contact:* Dr. Gary Stanlake, Dean of Graduate Studies, 325-670-1298, Fax: 325-670-1564, E-mail: gradoff@hsutx.edu.

Harvard University, Graduate School of Education, Master's Programs in Education, Cambridge, MA 02138. Offers arts in education (Ed M); education policy and management (Ed M); higher education (Ed M); human development and psychology (Ed M); international education policy (Ed M); language and literacy (Ed M); learning and teaching (Ed M); mid-career mathematics and science (teaching certificate) (Ed M); mind brain and education (Ed M); risk and prevention (Ed M); school leadership (Ed M); special studies (Ed M); teaching and curriculum (teaching certificate) (Ed M); technology innovation and education (Ed M). Part-time programs available. *Faculty:* 58 full-time (25 women), 40 part-time/adjunct (22 women). *Students:* 540 full-time (412 women), 90 part-time (70 women); includes 137 minority (49 African Americans, 2 American Indian/Alaska Native, 61 Asian Americans or Pacific Islanders, 25 Hispanic Americans), 70 international. Average age 29. 1,211 applicants, 61% accepted, 585 enrolled. In 2006, 591 degrees awarded. *Entrance requirements:* For master's, GRE General Test, 3 letters of recommendation, official transcripts, statement of purpose. Additional exam requirements/recommendations for international students: Required—TOEFL (minimum score 600 paper-based; 250 computer-based; 100 iBT), TWE (minimum score 5). *Application deadline:* For fall admission, 1/2 for domestic and international students. Application fee: $85. Electronic applications accepted. *Expenses:* Contact institution. *Financial support:* In 2006–07, 392 students received support, including 23 fellowships (averaging $15,870 per year); career-related internships or fieldwork, Federal Work-Study, institutionally sponsored loans, scholarships/grants, health care benefits, tuition waivers (full and partial), and unspecified assistantships also available. Support available to part-time students. Financial award application deadline: 2/2; financial award applicants required to submit FAFSA. *Faculty research:* Learning and development; educational leadership and organizations; educational policy analysis. Total annual research expenditures: $14.8 million. *Unit head:* Dr. James Stiles, Associate Dean for Degree Programs. *Application contact:* Information Contact, 617-495-3414, Fax: 617-496-3577, E-mail: gseadmissions@harvard.edu.

Henderson State University, Graduate Studies, School of Education, Department of Curriculum, Instruction and Leadership, Arkadelphia, AR 71999-0001. Offers early childhood (P-4) (MSE); English (MSE); English as a second language (MSE, CP); math (MSE); middle school (MSE); reading (MSE); social science (MSE). *Accreditation:* NCATE. Part-time programs available. *Faculty:* 19 full-time (6 women), 4 part-time/adjunct (2 women). *Students:* 38 full-time (36 women), 49 part-time (47 women); includes 6 minority (5 African Americans, 1 Hispanic American), 16 international. Average age 37. In 2006, 31 degrees awarded. *Entrance requirements:* For master's, GRE General Test or MAT, minimum GPA of 2.7, teacher certification. *Application deadline:* For fall admission, 5/1 priority date for domestic students, 5/1 for international students; for winter admission, 10/1 for international students; for spring admission, 12/1 priority date for domestic students, 4/1 for international students. Applications are processed on a rolling basis. Application fee: $0 ($30 for international students). *Expenses:* Tuition, state resident: full-time $3,294; part-time $183 per credit hour. Tuition, nonresident: full-time $6,588; part-time $366 per credit hour. Required fees: $176 per term. *Financial support:* In 2006–07, 1 teaching assistantship with full tuition reimbursement (averaging $4,000 per year) was awarded; research assistantships, Federal Work-Study and institutionally sponsored loans also available. Support available to part-time students. Financial award application deadline: 7/31. *Unit head:* Dr. Kenneth Harris, Chairperson, 870-230-5203, Fax: 870-230-5455, E-mail: harris@hsu.edu. *Application contact:* Dr. Marck L. Beggs, Graduate Dean, 870-230-5126, Fax: 870-230-5479, E-mail: beggsm@hsu.edu.

Heritage University, Graduate Programs in Education, Program in Professional Studies, Toppenish, WA 98948-9599. Offers bilingual education/ESL (M Ed); biology (M Ed); English and literature (M Ed); reading/literacy (M Ed); special education (M Ed). Part-time and evening/weekend programs available. *Students:* 174 (125 women); includes 52 minority (1 African American, 4 American Indian/Alaska Native, 6 Asian Americans or Pacific Islanders, 41 Hispanic Americans). Average age 37. In 2006, 84 degrees awarded. *Degree requirements:* For master's, thesis (for some programs), comprehensive exam (for some programs), registration. *Application deadline:* Applications are processed on a rolling basis. Application fee: $50 ($100 for international students). *Financial support:* Career-related internships or fieldwork, Federal Work-Study, institutionally sponsored loans, and tuition waivers (partial) available. Support available to part-time students. *Unit head:* Dr. Jack McPherson, Head, 509-865-8626, E-mail: mcpherson_j@heritage.edu. *Application contact:* Kathy Otto, Coordinator of Administrative Services, 509-865-8635, Fax: 509-865-8629, E-mail: otto_k@heritage.edu.

Hofstra University, School of Education and Allied Human Services, Department of Counseling, Research, Special Education and Rehabilitation, Program in Special Education, Hempstead, NY 11549. Offers early childhood special education (MS Ed, Advanced Certificate); gifted education (Advanced Certificate); inclusive early childhood special education (MS Ed); inclusive elementary special education (MS Ed); inclusive secondary special education (MS Ed); literacy studies and special education (MS Ed); special education (MA, MS Ed, PD); special education assessment and diagnosis (Advanced Certificate); teaching students with severe/multiple disabilities (Advanced Certificate). *Accreditation:* NCATE. Part-time and evening/weekend programs available. Postbaccalaureate distance learning degree programs offered. *Students:* 87 full-time (82 women), 116 part-time (110 women); includes 21 minority (8 African Americans, 4 Asian Americans or Pacific Islanders, 9 Hispanic Americans). Average age 28. 110 applicants, 79% accepted, 61 enrolled. In 2006, 74 master's, 7 other advanced degrees awarded. *Degree requirements:* For master's, thesis (for some programs), seminars, student teaching, comprehensive exam (for some programs), registration; for other advanced degree, fieldwork. *Entrance requirements:* For master's, interview, 3 letters of reference, resumé, minimum GPA of 3.0; for other advanced degree, interview, 3 letters of recommendation, resumé. Additional exam requirements/recommendations for international students: Required—TOEFL (minimum score 550 paper-based; 213 computer-based). *Application deadline:* Applications are processed on a rolling basis. Application fee: $60. Electronic applications accepted. *Expenses:* Tuition: Full-time $13,320; part-time $740 per credit. Required fees: $930; $155 per term. *Financial support:* In 2006–07, 64 students received support, including 6 fellowships with tuition reimbursements available (averaging $2,552 per year), 4 research assistantships with full and partial tuition reimbursements available (averaging $4,378 per year); Federal Work-Study, scholarships/grants, tuition waivers (full and partial), and unspecified assistantships also available. Support available to part-time students. Financial award applicants required to submit FAFSA. *Faculty research:* Inclusive schooling, autism spectrum disorders related services, parent participation in the special education process, co-teaching student teaching. *Unit head:* Dr. George Guiliani, Director, 516-463-5778, Fax: 516-463-6184, E-mail: cprdcs@hofstra.edu. *Application contact:* Carol Drummer, Dean of Graduate Admissions, 516-463-4876, Fax: 516-463-4664, E-mail: gradstudent@hofstra.edu.

Hofstra University, School of Education and Allied Human Services, Department of Literacy Studies, Hempstead, NY 11549. Offers literacy studies (MA, MS Ed, Ed D, PhD, CAS, PD), including advanced literacy studies (birth-6) (PD), advanced literacy studies (grades 5–12) (PD), literacy studies (Ed D, PhD), literacy studies (birth–grade 6) (MS Ed, CAS), literacy studies (birth-grade 6) and special education (birth-grade 2) (MS Ed), literacy studies (birth-grade 6) and special education (grades 1-6) (MS Ed), literacy studies (grades 5–12) (MS Ed, CAS), teaching of writing (birth–grade 6) (MA), teaching of writing (grades 5–12) (MA). *Accreditation:* NCATE. Part-time and evening/weekend programs available. *Faculty:* 8 full-time (7 women), 8 part-time/adjunct (all women). *Students:* 28 full-time (all women), 166 part-time (159 women); includes 12 minority (4 African Americans, 3 Asian Americans or Pacific Islanders, 5 Hispanic Americans), 2 international. Average age 29. 101 applicants, 70% accepted, 58 enrolled. In 2006, 76 master's, 2 doctorates, 5 other advanced degrees awarded. *Degree requirements:* For master's, portfolio; for doctorate, one foreign language, thesis/dissertation, comprehensive exam, registration. *Entrance requirements:* For master's, interview, teaching certificate, 2 letters of recommendation, essay; for doctorate, GRE, 2 letters of recommendation, interview, resumé, teaching certificate, essay; for other advanced degree, 2 letters of recommendation, interview, teaching certificate, essay. Additional exam requirements/recommendations for international students: Required—TOEFL (minimum score 550 paper-based; 213 computer-based). *Application deadline:* Applications are processed on a rolling basis. Application fee: $60. Electronic applications accepted. *Expenses:* Tuition: Full-time $13,320; part-time $740 per credit. Required fees: $930; $155 per term. *Financial support:* In 2006–07, 75 students received support, including 21 fellowships with tuition reimbursements available (averaging $3,873 per year), 2 research assistantships with full and partial tuition reimbursements available (averaging $5,908 per year); career-related internships or fieldwork, Federal Work-Study, scholarships/grants, health care benefits, tuition waivers (full and partial), and unspecified assistantships also available. Support available to part-time students. Financial award applicants required to submit FAFSA. *Faculty research:* Miscue analysis, literacy and technology, teacher research in literacy, issues in bilingual and biliteracy education, literacy in the lives of children in trauma. *Unit head:* Dr. Debra Goodman, Chairperson, 516-463-5563, Fax: 516-463-5949, E-mail: readzg@hofstra.edu. *Application contact:* Carol Drummer, Dean of Graduate Admissions, 516-463-4876, Fax: 516-463-4664, E-mail: gradstudent@hofstra.edu.

Holy Family University, Graduate School, School of Education, Philadelphia, PA 19114-2094. Offers education (M Ed); elementary education (M Ed); reading specialist (M Ed); secondary education (M Ed). Part-time and evening/weekend programs available. *Degree requirements:* For master's, thesis optional. *Entrance requirements:* For master's, GRE or MAT, interview. *Faculty research:* Cognition, developmental issues, sociological issues in education.

Hood College, Graduate School, Department of Education, Frederick, MD 21701-8575. Offers curriculum and instruction (MS), including early childhood education, elementary education, elementary school science and mathematics, secondary education, special education; educational leadership (MS); reading specialization (MS); teaching the struggling reader (Certificate). Part-time and evening/weekend programs available. *Faculty:* 4 full-time (3 women), 32 part-time/adjunct (16 women). *Students:* 5 full-time (3 women), 371 part-time (313 women); includes 30 minority (23 African Americans, 4 Asian Americans or Pacific Islanders, 3 Hispanic Americans). Average age 32. 71 applicants, 99% accepted, 59 enrolled. In 2006, 67 degrees awarded. *Degree requirements:* For master's, action research project, portfolio (reading). *Entrance requirements:* For master's, minimum GPA of 2.5, teaching certification. *Application deadline:* Applications are processed on a rolling basis. Application fee: $35. *Expenses:* Tuition: Part-time $350 per credit. Required fees: $20 per semester. *Financial support:* Applicants required to submit FAFSA. *Faculty research:* Leadership, action research, brain research, learning styles. *Unit head:* Dr. John George, Chairperson, 301-696-3471, Fax: 301-696-3597, E-mail: george@hood.edu. *Application contact:* Dr. Kathleen C. Bands, Associate Dean of Graduate School, 301-696-3811, Fax: 301-696-3597, E-mail: gofurther@hood.edu.

Houston Baptist University, College of Education and Behavioral Sciences, Programs in Education, Houston, TX 77074-3298. Offers bilingual education (M Ed); counselor education (M Ed); curriculum and instruction (M Ed); educational administration (M Ed); educational diagnostician (M Ed); reading education (M Ed). Part-time programs available. *Degree requirements:* For master's, registration. *Entrance requirements:* For master's, GRE General Test or MAT. Additional exam requirements/recommendations for international students: Required—TOEFL (minimum score 550 paper-based; 213 computer-based).

Howard University, School of Education, Department of Curriculum and Instruction, Program in Reading, Washington, DC 20059-0002. Offers M Ed, MA, MAT, CAGS. MA offered through the Graduate School of Arts and Sciences. *Accreditation:* NCATE. Part-time programs available. *Faculty:* 1 (woman) part-time/adjunct. *Students:* 1 (woman) full-time; minority (African American) Average age 25. *Degree requirements:* For master's, thesis (for some programs), expository writing exam, internships, practicum, comprehensive exam; for CAGS, thesis or alternative. *Entrance requirements:* For master's, GRE General Test (MA), minimum GPA of 2.7. *Application deadline:* For fall admission, 4/1 priority date for domestic students; for spring admission, 11/1 for domestic students. Applications are processed on a rolling basis. Application fee: $45. *Financial support:* Fellowships, research assistantships, teaching assistantships, career-related internships or fieldwork, Federal Work-Study, institutionally sponsored loans, scholarships/grants, and unspecified assistantships available. Financial award application

Reading Education

Howard University (continued)
deadline: 4/1. *Faculty research:* Recruiting teachers, multicultural literature, early reading, teacher-made materials.

Hunter College of the City University of New York, Graduate School, School of Education, Department of Curriculum and Teaching, New York, NY 10021-5085. Offers bilingual education (MS); corrective reading (K–12) (MS Ed); early childhood education (MS); educational supervision and administration (AC); elementary education (MS); literacy education (MS); teaching English as a second language (MA). *Faculty:* 84 full-time (68 women), 112 part-time/adjunct (79 women). *Students:* 272 full-time (238 women), 1,353 part-time (1,237 women); includes 393 minority (127 African Americans, 103 Asian Americans or Pacific Islanders, 163 Hispanic Americans). Average age 36. 778 applicants, 48% accepted, 256 enrolled. In 2006, 291 degrees awarded. *Degree requirements:* For master's, thesis; for AC, portfolio review. *Entrance requirements:* For degree, minimum B average in graduate course work, teaching certificate, minimum 3 years of full-time teaching experience, interview, 2 letters of support. Additional exam requirements/recommendations for international students: Required—TOEFL, TWE. *Application deadline:* For fall admission, 4/1 for domestic students; for spring admission, 11/1 for domestic students. Applications are processed on a rolling basis. Application fee: $125. *Expenses:* Tuition, state resident: part-time $270 per credit. Tuition, nonresident: part-time $500 per credit. Required fees: $45 per semester. *Financial support:* Federal Work-Study, scholarships/grants, and tuition waivers (partial) available. Support available to part-time students. *Faculty research:* Teacher opportunity corps-mentor program for first-year teachers, adult literacy, student literacy corporation. *Unit head:* Dr. Anne M. Ediger, Head, 212-777-4763, E-mail: anne.ediger@hunter.cuny.edu. *Application contact:* William Zlata, Director for Graduate Admissions, 212-772-4482, Fax: 212-650-3336, E-mail: admissions@hunter.cuny.edu.

Idaho State University, Office of Graduate Studies, College of Education, Department of Educational Foundations, Pocatello, ID 83209. Offers child and family studies (M Ed); curriculum leadership (M Ed); education (M Ed); educational administration (M Ed); educational foundations (5th Year Certificate); elementary education (M Ed), including K-12 education, literacy, secondary education. Part-time and evening/weekend programs available. Postbaccalaureate distance learning degree programs offered (no on-campus study). *Faculty:* 12 full-time (8 women). *Students:* 16 full-time (11 women), 161 part-time (102 women); includes 2 minority (1 Asian American or Pacific Islander, 1 Hispanic American), 2 international. Average age 40. In 2006, 15 degrees awarded. *Degree requirements:* For master's, oral exam, written exam, thesis optional; for 5th Year Certificate, thesis (for some programs), oral exam, written exam, comprehensive exam, registration (for some programs). *Entrance requirements:* For master's, GRE General Test or MAT, minimum undergraduate GPA of 3.0; for 5th Year Certificate, GRE General Test, minimum undergraduate GPA of 3.0, master's degree. Additional exam requirements/recommendations for international students: Required—TOEFL (minimum score 550 paper-based; 213 computer-based; 80 iBT). *Application deadline:* For fall admission, 7/1 for domestic students, 6/1 for international students; for spring admission, 12/1 for domestic students, 11/1 for international students. Applications are processed on a rolling basis. Application fee: $55. *Expenses:* Tuition, state resident: part-time $251 per credit. Tuition, nonresident: part-time $366 per credit. Tuition and fees vary according to degree level, program and reciprocity agreements. *Financial support:* Career-related internships or fieldwork, Federal Work-Study, institutionally sponsored loans, scholarships/grants, tuition waivers, and unspecified assistantships available. Support available to part-time students. Financial award application deadline: 1/1. *Faculty research:* Child and families studies; business education; special education; math, science, and technology education. *Unit head:* Dr. Jack Newsome, Chair, 208-282-4838, E-mail: newsjack@isu.edu. *Application contact:* Dr. Peter Denner, Assistant Dean, 208-282-3807, Fax: 208-282-4697, E-mail: dennpete@isu.edu.

Illinois State University, Graduate School, College of Education, Department of Curriculum and Instruction, Program in Reading, Normal, IL 61790-2200. Offers MS Ed. *Accreditation:* NCATE. *Students:* 3 full-time (all women), 91 part-time (89 women); includes 5 minority (3 African Americans, 1 Asian American or Pacific Islander, 1 Hispanic American). 14 applicants, 100% accepted. In 2006, 53 degrees awarded. *Degree requirements:* For master's, practicum. *Entrance requirements:* For master's, GRE General Test, minimum GPA of 3.0 in last 60 hours of course work, course work in reading. *Application deadline:* Applications are processed on a rolling basis. Application fee: $40. *Expenses:* Tuition, state resident: full-time $3,330; part-time $185 per credit hour. Tuition, nonresident: full-time $6,948; part-time $438 per credit hour. Required fees: $1,259; $52 per credit hour. *Financial support:* In 2006–07, 2 research assistantships (averaging $7,313 per year) were awarded; tuition waivers (full) also available. Financial award application deadline: 4/1. *Unit head:* Dr. Barbara Nourie, Acting Chairperson, Department of Curriculum and Instruction, 309-438-5425.

Indiana State University, School of Graduate Studies, College of Education, Department of Elementary and Special Education, Terre Haute, IN 47809-1401. Offers early childhood education (M Ed); elementary education (M Ed); literacy (M Ed). *Accreditation:* NCATE. *Faculty:* 9 full-time (7 women), 5 part-time/adjunct (4 women). *Students:* 6 full-time (all women), 46 part-time (43 women); includes 3 minority (2 African Americans, 1 Asian American or Pacific Islander), 2 international. Average age 35. 26 applicants, 96% accepted, 12 enrolled. In 2006, 26 degrees awarded. *Application deadline:* For fall admission, 7/1 priority date for domestic students; for spring admission, 11/1 priority date for domestic students. Applications are processed on a rolling basis. Application fee: $35. Electronic applications accepted. *Expenses:* Tuition, state resident: part-time $278 per credit. Tuition, nonresident: part-time $552 per credit. *Financial support:* In 2006–07, research assistantships with partial tuition reimbursements (averaging $6,500 per year); teaching assistantships with partial tuition reimbursements, tuition waivers (partial) also available. Financial award application deadline: 3/1; financial award applicants required to submit FAFSA. *Unit head:* Dr. Diana Quatroche, Interim Chairperson, 812-237-2852.

Indiana University Bloomington, School of Education, Department of Language Education, Bloomington, IN 47405-7000. Offers MS, Ed D, PhD, Ed S. PhD offered through the University Graduate School. *Accreditation:* NCATE. Part-time and evening/weekend programs available. Postbaccalaureate distance learning degree programs offered. *Students:* 54 full-time (39 women), 91 part-time (70 women); includes 5 minority (1 African American, 2 Asian Americans or Pacific Islanders, 2 Hispanic Americans), 61 international. Average age 34. In 2006, 48 master's, 1 doctorate awarded. Terminal master's awarded for partial completion of doctoral program. *Degree requirements:* For doctorate, thesis/dissertation, internship; for Ed S, comprehensive exam or project. *Entrance requirements:* For master's, GRE General Test, minimum GPA of 3.3; for doctorate, GRE General Test, minimum graduate GPA of 3.5; for Ed S, GRE General Test. *Application deadline:* For fall admission, 6/1 for domestic students, 3/1 for international students; for spring admission, 9/1 for international students. Application fee: $50 ($60 for international students). *Expenses:* Tuition, state resident: full-time $5,791; part-time $241 per credit hour. Tuition, nonresident: full-time $16,866; part-time $703 per credit hour. *Financial support:* Fellowships with tuition reimbursements, research assistantships with partial tuition reimbursements, teaching assistantships with partial tuition reimbursements, career-related internships or fieldwork, Federal Work-Study, institutionally sponsored loans, and tuition waivers (full and partial) available. Support available to part-time students. *Faculty research:* Relationship of reading, writing, and speaking; job related literacy; assessment; sociolinguistics. *Unit head:* MaryBeth Hines, Chair, 812-856-8270, Fax: 812-856-8287. *Application contact:* Office Manager, 812-856-8270.

Indiana University of Pennsylvania, School of Graduate Studies and Research, College of Education and Educational Technology, Department of Professional Studies in Education, Program in Literacy, Indiana, PA 15705-1087. Offers literacy (M Ed); reading (M Ed). *Accreditation:* NCATE. Part-time programs available. *Faculty:* 3 full-time (all women). *Students:* 4 full-time (all women), 62 part-time (56 women); includes 1 minority (African American) Average age 29. 39 applicants, 87% accepted. In 2006, 28 degrees awarded. *Degree requirements:* For master's, thesis optional. *Entrance requirements:* For master's, 2 letters of recommendation. Additional exam requirements/recommendations for international students: Required—TOEFL. *Application deadline:* For fall admission, 7/1 priority date for domestic students; for spring admission, 11/1 for domestic students. Applications are processed on a rolling basis. Application fee: $30. *Expenses:* Tuition, state resident: full-time $6,048; part-time $336 per credit. Tuition, nonresident: full-time $9,678; part-time $538 per credit. Required fees: $1,069; $148 per year. *Financial support:* In 2006–07, 2 research assistantships with full and partial tuition reimbursements (averaging $2,495 per year) were awarded; career-related internships or fieldwork and Federal Work-Study also available. Support available to part-time students. Financial award application deadline: 3/15; financial award applicants required to submit FAFSA. *Unit head:* Dr. Anne Creany, Graduate Coordinator, 724-357-2409.

Jacksonville State University, College of Graduate Studies and Continuing Education, College of Education and Professional Studies, Program in Reading Specialist, Jacksonville, AL 36265-1602. Offers MS Ed. *Faculty:* 3 full-time (all women). In 2006, 6 degrees awarded. *Application deadline:* Applications are processed on a rolling basis. Application fee: $20. *Expenses:* Tuition, state resident: full-time $5,400; part-time $225 per credit hour. Tuition, nonresident: full-time $10,800; part-time $450 per credit hour. One-time fee: $20 full-time. *Financial support:* Available to part-time students. Application deadline: 4/1. *Unit head:* Dr. Carol Uline, Head, 256-782-5853. *Application contact:* 256-782-5329.

Jacksonville University, College of Arts and Sciences, School of Education, Program in Reading Education, Jacksonville, FL 32211-3394. Offers MAT. Part-time and evening/weekend programs available. *Degree requirements:* For master's, comprehensive exam. *Entrance requirements:* For master's, GRE General Test, minimum GPA of 3.0. Additional exam requirements/recommendations for international students: Required—TOEFL.

James Madison University, College of Graduate and Outreach Programs, College of Education, Early, Elementary, and Reading Education Department, Program in Reading Education, Harrisonburg, VA 22807. Offers M Ed. *Accreditation:* NCATE. Part-time programs available. *Students:* Average age 27. *Entrance requirements:* For master's, GRE General Test. Additional exam requirements/recommendations for international students: Required—TOEFL. *Application deadline:* For fall admission, 5/1 priority date for domestic students; for spring admission, 9/1 priority date for domestic students. Applications are processed on a rolling basis. Application fee: $55. Electronic applications accepted. *Expenses:* Tuition, state resident: full-time $6,336; part-time $264 per credit hour. Tuition, nonresident: full-time $17,832; part-time $743 per credit hour. *Financial support:* Federal Work-Study and unspecified assistantships available. Financial award application deadline: 3/1; financial award applicants required to submit FAFSA. *Unit head:* Dr. Martha Ross, Academic Unit Head, 540-568-6255.

The Johns Hopkins University, School of Professional Studies in Business and Education, School of Education, Department of Teacher Development and Leadership, Baltimore, MD 21218-2699. Offers adult learning (Certificate); business leadership for independent schools (Certificate); earth/space science (Certificate); educational leadership for independent schools (Certificate); educational studies (MS); effective teaching of reading (Certificate); ESL instruction (Certificate); gifted education (Certificate); leadership for school, family and community collaboration (Certificate); reading (MS); school administration and supervision (MS, Certificate); teacher development and leadership (Ed D); teacher leadership (Certificate); technology for educators (MS); urban education (Certificate). Part-time and evening/weekend programs available. Postbaccalaureate distance learning degree programs offered (minimal on-campus study). *Students:* 19 full-time (18 women), 535 part-time (413 women); includes 98 minority (76 African Americans, 1 American Indian/Alaska Native, 18 Asian Americans or Pacific Islanders, 3 Hispanic Americans), 2 international. Average age 31. 544 applicants, 79% accepted, 374 enrolled. In 2006, 151 master's, 180 other advanced degrees awarded. *Degree requirements:* For master's and Certificate, portfolio; for doctorate, thesis/dissertation, comprehensive exam, registration. *Entrance requirements:* For master's and Certificate, minimum GPA of 3.0; for doctorate, GRE, interview, master's degree, minimum GPA of 3.0, resumé, letters of recommendation. Additional exam requirements/recommendations for international students: Required—TOEFL (minimum score 600 paper-based; 250 computer-based; 100 iBT). *Application deadline:* For fall admission, 5/1 for international students; for spring admission, 10/15 for international students. Applications are processed on a rolling basis. Application fee: $60. *Expenses:* Tuition: Full-time $32,976. Tuition and fees vary according to degree level and program. *Financial support:* Scholarships/grants available. Support available to part-time students. Financial award application deadline: 6/1; financial award applicants required to submit FAFSA. *Unit head:* Dr. Edward Pajak, Chair, 410-309-1265, Fax: 410-290-0467. *Application contact:* Carol Herrman, Admissions Coordinator, 410-872-1234, Fax: 410-872-1251, E-mail: onestop.admissions@jhu.edu.

Johnson State College, Graduate Program in Education, Program in Reading Education, Johnson, VT 05656-9405. Offers MA Ed. *Faculty:* 1 (woman) full-time. *Students:* 1 (woman) full-time, 8 part-time (all women). *Degree requirements:* For master's, thesis or alternative, comprehensive exam. *Entrance requirements:* For master's, interview. Additional exam requirements/recommendations for international students: Required—TOEFL. *Application deadline:* For fall admission, 7/15 priority date for domestic students, 4/15 priority date for international students; for spring admission, 11/1 priority date for domestic students, 8/15 priority date for international students. Applications are processed on a rolling basis. Application fee: $35. *Financial support:* Career-related internships or fieldwork, Federal Work-Study, and institutionally sponsored loans available. Support available to part-time students. Financial award application deadline: 3/1; financial award applicants required to submit FAFSA. *Application contact:* Catherine H. Higley, Administrative Assistant for Graduate Programs, 800-635-2356 Ext. 1244, Fax: 802-635-1248, E-mail: higleyc@jsc.vsc.edu.

Kean University, College of Education, Program in Reading Specialization, Union, NJ 07083. Offers adult literacy (MA); basic skills (MA); reading specialization (MA). *Faculty:* 10 full-time (8 women). *Students:* 3 full-time (all women), 90 part-time (89 women); includes 10 minority (7 African Americans, 1 Asian American or Pacific Islander, 2 Hispanic Americans). Average age 33. 33 applicants, 97% accepted, 20 enrolled. In 2006, 20 degrees awarded. *Degree requirements:* For master's, thesis, practicum, clinic, research seminar. *Entrance requirements:* For master's, GRE General Test or MAT, 2 letters of recommendation, interview, teaching certification, minimum GPA of 2.75. *Application deadline:* For fall admission, 5/1 for domestic students; for spring admission, 11/1 for domestic students. Application fee: $60 ($150 for international students). Electronic applications accepted. *Expenses:* Tuition, state resident: full-time $8,856; part-time $369 per credit. Tuition, nonresident: full-time $11,256; part-time $469 per credit. *Financial support:* In 2006–07, 1 research assistantship with full tuition reimbursement (averaging $3,217 per year) was awarded. *Unit head:* Dr. Joan M. Kastner, Program Coordinator, 908-737-3942, E-mail: jkastner@kean.edu. *Application contact:* Joanne Morris, Director of Graduate Admissions, 908-737-3355, Fax: 908-737-3354, E-mail: gradadm@kean.edu.

Kent State University, Graduate School of Education, Health, and Human Services, Department of Teaching, Leadership, and Curriculum Studies, Program in Reading, Kent, OH 44242-0001. Offers M Ed, MA. *Accreditation:* NCATE. Part-time programs available. *Faculty:* 9 full-time (7 women). *Students:* 5 full-time (all women), 113 part-time (all women); includes 5 minority (3 African Americans, 2 Hispanic Americans). 29 applicants, 97% accepted. In 2006, 37 degrees awarded. *Degree requirements:* For master's, thesis (for some programs), registration. *Entrance requirements:* Additional exam requirements/recommendations for international students: Required—TOEFL. *Application deadline:* Applications are processed on a rolling basis. Application fee: $30. Electronic applications accepted. *Financial support:* In 2006–07, fellowships with full tuition reimbursements (averaging $7,210 per year); research assistantships with full tuition reimbursements, teaching assistantships with full tuition reimbursements, career-related internships or fieldwork, Federal Work-Study, institutionally sponsored loans, scholarships/grants, health care benefits, and unspecified assistantships also available. Support available to part-time students. Financial award application deadline: 4/1; financial award applicants required to submit FAFSA. *Faculty research:* Adolescent literacy, adult and family literacy, school change in literacy education, struggling readers. *Unit head:* Dr. Nancy Padak, Coordinator, 330-672-2836, E-mail: npadak@kent.edu. *Application contact:* Nancy Miller, Academic Program Coordinator, Office of Graduate Student Services, 330-672-2576, Fax: 330-672-9162, E-mail: ogs@kent.edu.

King's College, Program in Reading, Wilkes-Barre, PA 18711-0801. Offers M Ed. Part-time and evening/weekend programs available. *Faculty:* 3 full-time (2 women), 9 part-time/adjunct (6 women). *Students:* Average age 27. In 2006, 16 degrees awarded. *Degree requirements:* For master's, thesis. *Entrance requirements:* For master's, GRE. Additional exam requirements/recommendations for international students: Required—TOEFL (minimum score 600 paper-based; 250 computer-based). *Application deadline:* Applications are processed on a rolling basis. Application fee: $35. *Expenses:* Tuition: Full-time $26,598; part-time $625 per credit. Required fees: $900. *Unit head:* Dr. Elizabeth S. Lott, Director of Graduate Programs, 570-208-5991, Fax: 570-825-9049, E-mail: eslott@kings.edu.

Kutztown University of Pennsylvania, College of Graduate Studies and Extended Learning, College of Education, Program in Reading, Kutztown, PA 19530-0730. Offers M Ed. *Accreditation:* NCATE. Part-time and evening/weekend programs available. *Students:* 3 full-time (2 women), 87 part-time (85 women); includes 2 minority (both Hispanic Americans) Average age 30. 37 applicants, 89% accepted, 16 enrolled. In 2006, 15 degrees awarded. *Degree requirements:* For master's, comprehensive project. *Entrance requirements:* For master's, GRE General Test. Additional exam requirements/recommendations for international students: Required—TOEFL. *Application deadline:* Applications are processed on a rolling basis. Application fee: $35. Electronic applications accepted. *Expenses:* Tuition, state resident: full-time $6,048; part-time $336 per credit. Tuition, nonresident: full-time $9,678; part-time $538 per credit. *Financial support:* In 2006–07, research assistantships with full tuition reimbursements (averaging $5,000 per year); career-related internships or fieldwork, Federal Work-Study, and unspecified assistantships also available. Financial award application deadline: 3/15; financial award applicants required to submit FAFSA. *Unit head:* Dr. Beth Herbine, Coordinator, 610-683-4271.

Lake Erie College, Division of Education, Painesville, OH 44077-3389. Offers curriculum and instruction (MS Ed); education (MS Ed); educational leadership (MS Ed); reading (MS Ed). Part-time and evening/weekend programs available. *Faculty:* 4 full-time (1 woman), 4 part-time/adjunct (1 woman). *Students:* Average age 37. 9 applicants, 89% accepted, 5 enrolled. In 2006, 20 degrees awarded. *Degree requirements:* For master's, thesis, applied research project, comprehensive exam. *Entrance requirements:* For master's, GRE General Test or minimum GPA of 3.0. Additional exam requirements/recommendations for international students: Required—TOEFL (minimum score 590 paper-based). *Application deadline:* For fall admission, 8/1 priority date for domestic students, 6/1 for international students; for spring admission, 12/15 for domestic students, 10/1 for international students. Applications are processed on a rolling basis. Application fee: $25 ($50 for international students). Electronic applications accepted. *Expenses: Contact institution. Financial support:* Applicants required to submit FAFSA. *Faculty research:* Cooperative learning, portfolio assessment, education systems in England, video case-based instruction. *Unit head:* Dr. Richard Bonde, Associate Dean, 440-375-7156, Fax: 440-375-7005, E-mail: rbonde@lec.edu. *Application contact:* 440-375-7050, Fax: 440-375-7005, E-mail: admissions@lec.edu.

Lehman College of the City University of New York, Division of Education, Department of Specialized Services in Education, Program in Reading Teacher, Bronx, NY 10468-1589. Offers MS Ed. *Accreditation:* NCATE. Evening/weekend programs available. *Entrance requirements:* For master's, interview, minimum GPA of 2.7. *Faculty research:* Emergent literacy, language-based classrooms, primary and secondary social contexts of language and literacy, innovative in-service education models, adult literacy.

Lenoir-Rhyne College, Graduate Programs, School of Education, Program in Literacy Education (K-12), Hickory, NC 28603. Offers MA. Part-time and evening/weekend programs available. *Degree requirements:* For master's, thesis optional. *Entrance requirements:* For master's, GRE General Test or MAT, minimum undergraduate GPA of 2.7, graduate 3.0. Additional exam requirements/recommendations for international students: Required—TOEFL (minimum score 600 paper-based). Electronic applications accepted.

Lesley University, School of Education, Cambridge, MA 02138-2790. Offers curriculum and instruction (M Ed, CAGS); early childhood education (M Ed); educational studies (PhD); elementary education (M Ed); individually designed (M Ed); middle school education (M Ed); moderate special needs (M Ed); reading (M Ed, CAGS); science in education (M Ed); severe special needs (M Ed); special needs (CAGS); technology in education (M Ed, CAGS). Part-time and evening/weekend programs available. Postbaccalaureate distance learning degree programs offered (no on-campus study). *Faculty:* 47 full-time (39 women), 208 part-time/adjunct (135 women). *Students:* 242 full-time (222 women), 2,903 part-time (2,495 women); includes 279 minority (179 African Americans, 7 American Indian/Alaska Native, 25 Asian Americans or Pacific Islanders, 68 Hispanic Americans), 10 international. Average age 36. 1,186 applicants, 96% accepted, 792 enrolled. In 2006, 1,724 master's, 6 doctorates, 17 other advanced degrees awarded. *Degree requirements:* For master's, practicum; for doctorate, thesis/dissertation. *Entrance requirements:* For doctorate, GRE General Test or MAT, interview, master's degree, resumé; for CAGS, interview, master's degree. Additional exam requirements/recommendations for international students: Required—TOEFL (minimum score 550 paper-based; 213 computer-based; 80 iBT). *Application deadline:* Applications are processed on a rolling basis. Application fee: $50. Electronic applications accepted. *Financial support:* In 2006–07, 26 students received support, including research assistantships (averaging $3,400 per year), teaching assistantships (averaging $3,400 per year); career-related internships or fieldwork, Federal Work-Study, scholarships/grants, and unspecified assistantships also available. Support available to part-time students. Financial award application deadline: 4/15; financial award applicants required to submit FAFSA. *Faculty research:* Assessment in literacy, mathematics and science; autism spectrum disorders; instructional technology and online learning; multicultural education and ELL. *Unit head:* Dr. Mario Borunda, Dean, 617-349-8375, Fax: 617-349-8607, E-mail: mborunda@lesley.edu. *Application contact:* Kristen Card, Associate Director of On-Campus Admissions, 617-349-8734, Fax: 617-349-8313, E-mail: kmcard@lesley.edu.

See Close-Up on page 893.

Liberty University, School of Education, Lynchburg, VA 24502. Offers administration and supervision (M Ed); curriculum and instruction (M Ed); early childhood education (M Ed); education specialist (Ed S); educational leadership (Ed D); elementary education (M Ed); gifted education (M Ed); reading specialist (M Ed); school counseling (M Ed); secondary education (M Ed); special education (M Ed). *Accreditation:* NCATE. Part-time programs available. Postbaccalaureate distance learning degree programs offered (minimal on-campus study). *Faculty:* 8 full-time (3 women), 7 part-time/adjunct (3 women). *Students:* 33 full-time (22 women), 308 part-time (180 women); includes 22 minority (12 African Americans, 2 American Indian/Alaska Native, 2 Asian Americans or Pacific Islanders, 6 Hispanic Americans), 5 international. Average age 39. 434 applicants, 77% accepted, 111 enrolled. In 2006, 39 master's, 12 doctorates, 16 other advanced degrees awarded. *Degree requirements:* For doctorate, thesis/dissertation, comprehensive exam. *Entrance requirements:* For master's, GRE General Test or MAT (if taken on or before 1999), 2 letters of recommendation, minimum undergraduate GPA of 3.0, curriculum vitae, graduate status record; for doctorate, GRE General Test or MAT (if taken before 1999), minimum master's GPA of 3.0, 3 years of teacher experience; for Ed S, GRE General Test or MAT (if taken before 1999), minimum master's GPA of 3.0, 3 years of teaching experience. Additional exam requirements/recommendations for international students: Required—TOEFL (minimum score 600 paper-based; 250 computer-based). *Application deadline:* For fall admission, 6/1 priority date for domestic students; for spring admission, 11/1 for domestic students. Applications are processed on a rolling basis. Application fee: $35. Electronic applications accepted. *Expenses: Contact institution. Financial support:* In 2006–07, 226 students received support. Federal Work-Study and tuition waivers (partial) available. *Faculty research:* Self-determination, character education, bibliotherapy, learning styles, distance education. *Unit head:* Dr. Karen L. Parker, Dean, 434-582-2195, Fax: 434-582-2468, E-mail: kparker@liberty.edu. *Application contact:* Kyle A Falce, Director of Graduate Admissions, 800-424-9596, Fax: 800-628-7977, E-mail: gradadmissions@liberty.edu.

Long Island University, Brentwood Campus, School of Education, Brentwood, NY 11717. Offers elementary education (MS); reading (MS); school counseling (MS); school district administration and supervision (MS); special education (MS). Part-time and evening/weekend programs available.

Long Island University, Brooklyn Campus, School of Education, Department of Teaching and Learning, Program in Reading, Brooklyn, NY 11201-8423. Offers MS Ed. Part-time and evening/weekend programs available. *Degree requirements:* For master's, thesis optional. *Entrance requirements:* For master's, 2 letters of recommendation. Additional exam requirements/recommendations for international students: Required—TOEFL (minimum score 500 paper-based; 173 computer-based). Electronic applications accepted.

Long Island University, C.W. Post Campus, School of Education, Department of Special Education and Literacy, Brookville, NY 11548-1300. Offers childhood education/literacy (MS); childhood education/special education (MS); literacy (MS Ed); special education (MS Ed). Part-time and evening/weekend programs available. *Degree requirements:* For master's, research project, comprehensive exam or thesis. *Entrance requirements:* For master's, interview; minimum GPA of 2.75 in major, 2.5 overall. Electronic applications accepted. *Faculty research:* Autism, mainstreaming, robotics and microcomputers in special education, transition from school to work.

Long Island University, Rockland Graduate Campus, Graduate School, Programs in Special Education and Literacy, Orangeburg, NY 10962. Offers childhood literacy (MS); childhood special education (MS); literacy (MS Ed); special education (MS Ed).

Long Island University, Southampton Graduate Campus, Education Division, Program in Literacy Education, Southampton, NY 11968-4198. Offers MS Ed. Part-time programs available. *Faculty:* 4 full-time, 6 part-time/adjunct. *Students:* 12 full-time (9 women), 18 part-time (12 women). Average age 31. 35 applicants, 100% accepted, 30 enrolled. In 2006, 14 degrees awarded. *Degree requirements:* For master's, comprehensive exam. *Entrance requirements:* For master's, minimum undergraduate GPA of 2.75, NYSTC-New York State Provisional or Initial Teacher Certification. Additional exam requirements/recommendations for international students: Required—TOEFL (minimum score 550 paper-based; 250 computer-based). *Application deadline:* For fall admission, 4/15 priority date for domestic and international students; for spring admission, 11/30 priority date for domestic and international students. Applications are processed on a rolling basis. Application fee: $30. Electronic applications accepted. *Expenses:* Tuition: Part-time $790 per credit. Required fees: $220 per semester. *Financial support:* In 2006–07, 8 students received support, including 1 research assistantship with full tuition reimbursement available; scholarships/grants and unspecified assistantships also available. Support available to part-time students. Financial award applicants required to submit FAFSA. *Unit head:* Dr. David Schultz, Unit Head, 631-287-8010. *Application contact:* Joyce Tuttle, Director of Graduate Admissions and Program Administration, 631-287-8010, Fax: 631-287-8253, E-mail: joyce.tuttle@liu.edu.

Long Island University, Westchester Graduate Campus, Programs in Education-Teaching, Program in Literacy Education, Purchase, NY 10577. Offers MS Ed. Part-time and evening/weekend programs available. *Faculty:* 1 (woman) full-time, 9 part-time/adjunct (6 women). *Students:* 10 applicants, 100% accepted, 8 enrolled. In 2006, 5 degrees awarded. *Application deadline:* Applications are processed on a rolling basis. Application fee: $30. *Expenses:* Tuition: Part-time $790 per credit. *Financial support:* In 2006–07, 4 students received support. Scholarships/grants, tuition waivers (partial), and unspecified assistantships available. *Unit head:* Dr. Rebecca Rich, Director, 914-831-2714, Fax: 914-251-5955, E-mail: rebecca.rich@liu.edu. *Application contact:* Ellen Brief, Coordinator of Admissions, Marketing, Student Services and Public Relations, 914-831-2701, Fax: 914-251-5959, E-mail: ellen.brief@liu.edu.

Longwood University, Office of Graduate Studies, College of Education and Human Services, Farmville, VA 23909. Offers communication sciences and disorders (MS); community and college counseling (MS); curriculum and instruction specialist-elementary (MS), including mild disabilities, modern languages; curriculum and instruction specialist-secondary (MS), including English, mild disabilities, modern languages; educational leadership (MS); guidance and counseling (MS); literacy and culture (MS); school library media (MS). *Accreditation:* NCATE. Part-time and evening/weekend programs available. *Degree requirements:* For master's, thesis optional. *Entrance requirements:* For master's, GRE (communication sciences and disorders), minimum GPA of 2.75. Additional exam requirements/recommendations for international students: Required—TOEFL (minimum score 550 paper-based; 213 computer-based).

Loyola College in Maryland, Graduate Programs, College of Arts and Sciences, Department of Education, Program in Reading, Baltimore, MD 21210-2699. Offers M Ed, CAS. *Accreditation:* NCATE. Part-time and evening/weekend programs available. *Students:* Average age 31. In 2006, 47 master's, 1 other advanced degree awarded. *Entrance requirements:* For master's and CAS, GRE General Test, GRE Subject Test (recommended). Additional exam requirements/recommendations for international students: Required—TOEFL (minimum score 550 paper-based; 213 computer-based). *Application deadline:* For fall admission, 7/1 priority date for domestic students; for spring admission, 10/1 priority date for domestic students. Applications are processed on a rolling basis. Application fee: $50. *Financial support:* Career-related internships or fieldwork available. Financial award applicants required to submit FAFSA. *Unit head:* Debby Deal, Director, 410-617-2000 Ext. 2134, E-mail: ddeal@loyola.edu.

Loyola Marymount University, Graduate Division, School of Education, Program in Child/Adolescent Literacy, Los Angeles, CA 90045-2659. Offers MA. *Students:* 61 full-time (54 women), 12 part-time (11 women); includes 29 minority (3 African Americans, 1 American Indian/Alaska Native, 1 Asian American or Pacific Islander, 24 Hispanic Americans). Average age 31. In 2006, 30 degrees awarded. *Degree requirements:* For master's, comprehensive exam. *Application deadline:* For fall admission, 7/15 for domestic students; for spring admission, 11/15 for domestic students. Application fee: $50. Electronic applications accepted. *Financial support:* In 2006–07, 20 students received support. Application deadline: 6/1; *Unit head:* Dr. Candace Poindexter, Coordinator, 310-338-7310, E-mail: cpoindex@lmu.edu.

Loyola Marymount University, Graduate Division, School of Education, Program in Literacy/Language Arts, Los Angeles, CA 90045-2659. Offers M Ed. Part-time and evening/weekend programs available. *Students:* 27 full-time (25 women), 3 part-time (all women); includes 15 minority (3 African Americans, 1 Asian American or Pacific Islander, 11 Hispanic Americans). Average age 30. In 2006, 2 degrees awarded. *Degree requirements:* For master's, comprehensive exam. *Entrance requirements:* For master's, GRE General Test, interview. Additional exam requirements/recommendations for international students: Required—TOEFL (minimum score 600 paper-based; 250 computer-based). *Application deadline:* For fall admission, 7/15 for domestic students; for spring admission, 11/15 for domestic students. Application fee: $50. Electronic applications accepted. *Financial support:* In 2006–07, 11 students received support. Federal Work-Study and scholarships/grants available. Support available to part-time students. Financial award application deadline: 6/1; financial award applicants required to submit FAFSA. *Unit head:* Dr. Candace Poindexter, Coordinator, 310-338-7310, E-mail: cpoindex@lmu.edu.

Loyola University Chicago, School of Education, Program in Initial Teacher Preparation, Chicago, IL 60611-2196. Offers elementary education (M Ed); reading specialist (M Ed); school technology (M Ed); science education (M Ed); secondary education (M Ed); special education (M Ed). *Accreditation:* NCATE. *Faculty:* 11 full-time (9 women), 6 part-time/adjunct (4 women). *Students:* 138. Average age 28. 95 applicants, 65% accepted, 39 enrolled.

Reading Education

Loyola University Chicago (continued)

In 2006, 84 degrees awarded. *Degree requirements:* For master's, comprehensive exam. *Entrance requirements:* For master's, Illinois Basic Skills Test, 3 letters of recommendation, minimum GPA of 3.0, resumé. Additional exam requirements/recommendations for international students: Required—TOEFL (minimum score 550 paper-based; 213 computer-based; 79 iBT). *Application deadline:* For fall admission, 7/1 priority date for domestic and international students; for spring admission, 11/1 priority date for domestic and international students. Applications are processed on a rolling basis. Application fee: $50. Electronic applications accepted. *Financial support:* In 2006–07, 2 research assistantships with full tuition reimbursements (averaging $8,500 per year), 1 teaching assistantship were awarded. Financial award application deadline: 2/15. *Faculty research:* Positive behavior support, school reform, school improvement. *Unit head:* Dr. Dorothy Giroux, Director, 312-915-7027, E-mail: dgiroux@luc.edu. *Application contact:* Marie Rosin-Dittmar, Information Contact, 312-915-6800, E-mail: schleduc@luc.edu.

Loyola University New Orleans, College of Arts and Sciences, Department of Education and Counseling, New Orleans, LA 70118-6195. Offers counseling (MS); elementary education (MS); reading education (MS); secondary education (MS). Part-time and evening/weekend programs available. *Degree requirements:* For master's, comprehensive exam. *Entrance requirements:* For master's, GRE or MAT (preferred), interview, letters of recommendation, writing sample. Additional exam requirements/recommendations for international students: Required—TOEFL (minimum score 550 paper-based; 213 computer-based). Electronic applications accepted. *Faculty research:* Counseling theory, spirituality issues, group counseling, multicultural application.

Lyndon State College, Graduate Programs in Education, Department of Education, Lyndonville, VT 05851-0919. Offers curriculum and instruction (M Ed); reading specialist (M Ed); special education (M Ed); teaching and counseling (M Ed). Part-time and evening/weekend programs available. *Degree requirements:* For master's, exam or major field project. *Entrance requirements:* Additional exam requirements/recommendations for international students: Recommended—TOEFL (minimum score 500 paper-based; 173 computer-based).

Madonna University, Programs in Education, Livonia, MI 48150-1173. Offers Catholic school leadership (MSA); educational leadership (MSA); learning disabilities (MAT); literacy education (MAT); teaching and learning (MAT). *Accreditation:* NCATE. Part-time and evening/weekend programs available. *Faculty:* 11 full-time (7 women), 8 part-time/adjunct (2 women). *Students:* 2 full-time (both women), 154 part-time (134 women); includes 10 minority (6 African Americans, 1 Asian American or Pacific Islander, 3 Hispanic Americans), 2 international. Average age 36. 20 applicants, 85% accepted. In 2006, 133 degrees awarded. *Degree requirements:* For master's, thesis or alternative. *Application deadline:* For fall admission, 8/1 priority date for domestic students; for winter admission, 12/1 priority date for domestic students; for spring admission, 4/1 priority date for domestic students. Applications are processed on a rolling basis. Application fee: $25 ($200 for international students). Electronic applications accepted. *Financial support:* Career-related internships or fieldwork, Federal Work-Study, institutionally sponsored loans, and scholarships/grants available. Support available to part-time students. *Unit head:* Dr. Robert Kimball, Dean, 734-432-5652, E-mail: rkimball@madonna.edu. *Application contact:* Sandra Kellums, Coordinator of Graduate Admissions and Records, 734-432-5667, Fax: 734-432-5862, E-mail: skellum@madonna.edu.

Malone College, School of Education, Graduate Program in Education, Canton, OH 44709-3897. Offers curriculum and instruction (MA); curriculum, instruction, and professional development (MA); instructional technology (MA); intervention specialist (MA); reading (MA). Part-time and evening/weekend programs available. *Faculty:* 11 full-time (4 women), 12 part-time/adjunct (9 women). *Students:* 4 full-time (2 women), 96 part-time (78 women); includes 5 minority (1 African American, 2 Asian Americans or Pacific Islanders, 2 Hispanic Americans). Average age 33. In 2006, 26 degrees awarded. *Degree requirements:* For master's, research project. *Entrance requirements:* For master's, minimum GPA of 3.0, teaching license. *Application deadline:* Applications are processed on a rolling basis. Application fee: $25. *Expenses:* Tuition: Part-time $399 per credit hour. *Financial support:* Tuition waivers (partial) available. Support available to part-time students. Financial award application deadline: 6/30. *Faculty research:* The Bible as children's literature, special needs students and literacy development, middle level education, school/university partnerships and professional development, child/adolescent literature and popular culture. *Unit head:* Dr. Donald Williams, Director, 330-471-8509, Fax: 330-471-8563, E-mail: dwilliams@malone.edu. *Application contact:* Dr. David Kleffman, Recruiter, 330-471-8447, Fax: 330-471-8343, E-mail: dkleffman@malone.edu.

Manhattanville College, Graduate Programs, School of Education, Program in Early Childhood Education, Purchase, NY 10577-2132. Offers childhood and early childhood education (MAT); early childhood education (birth-grade 2) (MAT); literacy (birth-grade 6) (MPS), including reading, writing; literacy (birth-grade 6) and special education (grades 1-6) (MPS); special education (birth-grade 2) (MPS); special education (birth-grade 6) (MPS). Part-time and evening/weekend programs available. *Students:* 43 full-time (42 women), 62 part-time (59 women); includes 1 African American, 1 Asian American or Pacific Islander, 7 Hispanic Americans. In 2006, 5 degrees awarded. *Degree requirements:* For master's, comprehensive exam or research project, field experience. *Entrance requirements:* For master's, minimum undergraduate GPA of 3.0, 2 letters of recommendation. *Application deadline:* Applications are processed on a rolling basis. Application fee: $55. *Financial support:* Career-related internships or fieldwork and institutionally sponsored loans available. Support available to part-time students. *Application contact:* Alyce Ware Poli, Director of Admissions, 914-323-5142, Fax: 914-694-1732, E-mail: edschool@mville.edu.

Manhattanville College, Graduate Programs, School of Education, Program in Middle Childhood/Adolescence Education (Grades 5-12), Purchase, NY 10577-2132. Offers biology (MAT); biology and special education (MPS); chemistry (MAT); chemistry and special education (MPS); English (MAT); English and special education (MPS); literacy (MPS), including reading and writing, writing; literacy and special education (MPS); math (MAT); math and special education (MPS); second language (MAT), including French, Italian, Latin, Spanish; social studies (MAT); social studies and special education (MPS); special education (MPS). Part-time and evening/weekend programs available. *Students:* 76 full-time (53 women), 109 part-time (68 women); includes 8 African Americans, 1 Asian American or Pacific Islander, 10 Hispanic Americans, 1 international. In 2006, 165 degrees awarded. *Degree requirements:* For master's, comprehensive exam or research project, field experience. *Entrance requirements:* For master's, minimum undergraduate GPA of 3.0, 2 letters of recommendation. *Application deadline:* Applications are processed on a rolling basis. Application fee: $55. *Financial support:* Career-related internships or fieldwork and institutionally sponsored loans available. Support available to part-time students. *Application contact:* Alyce Ware Poli, Director of Admissions, 914-323-5142, Fax: 914-694-1732, E-mail: edschool@mville.edu.

Marshall University, Academic Affairs Division, College of Education and Human Services, Graduate School of Education and Professional Development, Program in Reading Education, Huntington, WV 25755. Offers MA, Ed S. *Accreditation:* NCATE. Part-time and evening/weekend programs available. *Faculty:* 2 full-time (1 woman), 22 part-time/adjunct (18 women). *Students:* 34 full-time (33 women), 206 part-time (203 women); includes 2 minority (both African Americans) Average age 36. In 2006, 93 degrees awarded. *Degree requirements:* For master's, comprehensive or oral assessment, final project, thesis optional; for Ed S, research project, thesis optional. *Entrance requirements:* For master's, GRE General Test or MAT; for Ed S, master's degree in reading, minimum GPA of 3.0. Application fee: $40. *Financial support:* Federal Work-Study, tuition waivers (full and partial), and unspecified assistantships available. Support available to part-time students. Financial award applicants required to submit FAFSA. *Unit head:* Dr. Noel E. Bowling, Director, 304-746-2024, E-mail: nbowling@marshall.edu. *Application contact:* Information Contact, 304-746-1900, Fax: 304-746-1902, E-mail: services@marshall.edu.

Marygrove College, Graduate Division, Education Unit, Program in Reading Education, Detroit, MI 48221-2599. Offers M Ed. Part-time and evening/weekend programs available. *Degree requirements:* For master's, practicum, research project. *Entrance requirements:* For master's, MAT, interview, minimum undergraduate GPA of 3.0, teaching certificate.

Maryville University of Saint Louis, School of Education, St. Louis, MO 63141-7299. Offers art education (MA Ed); early childhood education (MA Ed); education (Ed D); elementary education (MA Ed); elementary education/English (MA Ed); environmental education (MA Ed); gifted education (MA Ed); middle grades education (MA Ed); reading specialist (MA Ed); secondary education (MA Ed), including educational leadership, secondary teaching and inquiry. *Accreditation:* NASAD; NCATE. Part-time and evening/weekend programs available. *Students:* 17 full-time (14 women), 168 part-time (129 women); includes 20 African Americans, 2 Asian Americans or Pacific Islanders, 1 Hispanic American, 2 international. Average age 37. 39 applicants, 95% accepted, 24 enrolled. In 2006, 37 degrees awarded. *Degree requirements:* For master's, thesis, project. *Entrance requirements:* For master's and doctorate, minimum GPA of 3.0, 3 professional recommendations. Additional exam requirements/recommendations for international students: Required—TOEFL (minimum score 550 paper-based). *Application deadline:* Applications are processed on a rolling basis. Application fee: $35 ($50 for international students). Electronic applications accepted. *Expenses:* Tuition: Full-time $17,800; part-time $555 per credit. Required fees: $55 per semester. Tuition and fees vary according to degree level and program. *Financial support:* Career-related internships or fieldwork, Federal Work-Study, tuition waivers (partial), and professional educator discounts available. Financial award application deadline: 7/31; financial award applicants required to submit FAFSA. *Faculty research:* Collaboration with public schools, preservice program development, mathematics, diversity, literacy. *Unit head:* Dr. Sam Hausfather, Dean, 314-529-9466, Fax: 314-529-9921, E-mail: shausfather@maryville.edu. *Application contact:* Dr. Lillian Curtis, Graduate Admissions Coordinator, 314-529-9542, Fax: 314-529-9921, E-mail: teachered@maryville.edu.

Marywood University, Academic Affairs, College of Education and Human Development, Department of Education, Program in Reading Education, Scranton, PA 18509-1598. Offers MS. *Accreditation:* NCATE. Part-time and evening/weekend programs available. *Students:* 1 (woman) full-time, 25 part-time (24 women). Average age 31. 4 applicants, 100% accepted. In 2006, 8 degrees awarded. *Degree requirements:* For master's, thesis or alternative, internship/practicum. *Entrance requirements:* For master's, GRE or MAT. Additional exam requirements/recommendations for international students: Required—TOEFL (minimum score 550 paper-based; 213 computer-based). *Application deadline:* For fall admission, 4/15 priority date for domestic and international students; for spring admission, 11/15 priority date for domestic and international students. Applications are processed on a rolling basis. Application fee: $30. Electronic applications accepted. *Expenses:* Tuition: Part-time $672 per credit. Tuition and fees vary according to degree level, campus/location and program. *Financial support:* Research assistantships with tuition reimbursements, career-related internships or fieldwork, scholarships/grants, tuition waivers (partial), and unspecified assistantships available. Support available to part-time students. Financial award application deadline: 2/15; financial award applicants required to submit FAFSA. *Faculty research:* Design of school reading programs, whole language. *Application contact:* Dr. Deborah M. Flynn, Coordinator of Graduate Advising (Enrollment Management), 570-348-6211, E-mail: flynn@ac.marywood.edu.

Massachusetts College of Liberal Arts, Program in Education, North Adams, MA 01247-4100. Offers curriculum and instruction (M Ed); educational administration (M Ed); reading (M Ed); special education (M Ed). Part-time and evening/weekend programs available. *Degree requirements:* For master's, thesis. *Entrance requirements:* For master's, writing sample. *Faculty research:* Anxiety, methodology, mainstreaming.

McDaniel College, Graduate and Professional Studies, Program in Reading Education, Westminster, MD 21157-4390. Offers MS. *Accreditation:* NCATE. Part-time and evening/weekend programs available. *Degree requirements:* For master's, thesis optional. *Entrance requirements:* For master's, GRE General Test, MAT, or NTE/PRAXIS I, letters of reference (3). Additional exam requirements/recommendations for international students: Required—TOEFL (minimum score 213 computer-based).

Medaille College, Program in Education, Buffalo, NY 14214-2695. Offers curriculum and instruction (MS Ed); education preparation (MS Ed); literacy (MS Ed); special education (MS). Part-time and evening/weekend programs available. *Faculty:* 30 full-time (20 women), 28 part-time/adjunct (18 women). *Students:* 516 full-time (417 women), 334 part-time (276 women); includes 16 minority (13 African Americans, 2 Asian Americans or Pacific Islanders, 1 Hispanic American), 654 international. Average age 27. 725 applicants, 97% accepted, 655 enrolled. In 2006, 229 degrees awarded. *Degree requirements:* For master's, thesis or alternative. *Entrance requirements:* For master's, minimum undergraduate GPA of 2.7. Additional exam requirements/recommendations for international students: Required—TOEFL (minimum score 550 paper-based; 213 computer-based). *Application deadline:* For fall admission, 8/15 priority date for domestic students; for spring admission, 1/15 priority date for domestic students. Applications are processed on a rolling basis. Application fee: $35. Electronic applications accepted. *Expenses:* Tuition: Part-time $580 per credit hour. Full-time tuition and fees vary according to program. *Financial support:* In 2006–07, 390 students received support. Federal Work-Study available. Financial award applicants required to submit FAFSA. *Faculty research:* Curriculum planning, truancy, tracking minority students, curriculum design, mentoring students. *Unit head:* Dr. Robert DiSibio, Director of Graduate Programs, 716-635-5033 Ext. 2017, Fax: 716-634-2232, E-mail: rdisibio@medaille.edu. *Application contact:* Susan Greenwald, Executive Director of Admissions, 716-635-5033 Ext. 2011, Fax: 716-631-1380, E-mail: sgreenwald@medaille.edu.

Mercer University, Graduate Studies, Cecil B. Day Campus, Tift College of Education, Macon, GA 31207-0003. Offers early childhood education (M Ed, MAT); educational leadership (M Ed, PhD); middle grades education (M Ed, MAT); reading education (M Ed); secondary education (M Ed, MAT); teacher leadership (Ed S). Part-time and evening/weekend programs available. *Faculty:* 13 full-time (6 women), 7 part-time/adjunct (3 women). *Students:* 31 full-time (23 women), 211 part-time (174 women); includes 111 minority (101 African Americans, 2 American Indian/Alaska Native, 6 Asian Americans or Pacific Islanders, 2 Hispanic Americans), 2 international. Average age 33. In 2006, 57 master's, 4 other advanced degrees awarded. *Degree requirements:* For master's and Ed S, research project; for doctorate, thesis/dissertation. *Entrance requirements:* For master's, GRE or MAT, minimum undergraduate GPA of 2.75; for doctorate, GRE; for Ed S, GRE or MAT, minimum GPA of 3.25, 3 years of teaching experience. *Application deadline:* For fall admission, 8/1 for domestic and international students; for spring admission, 12/1 for domestic and international students. Applications are processed on a rolling basis. Application fee: $25. *Expenses:* Contact institution. *Financial support:* Federal Work-Study available. Support available to part-time students. Financial award application deadline: 5/1. *Faculty research:* Educational computing, content area reading, concept learning, importance of play for young children, multicultural literature. *Unit head:* Dr. Carl R. Martray, Dean, 478-301-5397, Fax: 478-301-2280, E-mail: martray_cr@mercer.edu. *Application contact:* Dr. Allison Gilmore, Associate Dean for Graduate Teacher Education, 678-547-6330, Fax: 678-547-6055, E-mail: gilmore_a@mercer.edu.

Mercy College, Division of Education, Dobbs Ferry, NY 10522-1189. Offers adolescence education: grades 7-12 (MS); applied behavior analysis (MS); bilingual education (MS); childhood education: grades 1-6 (MS); early childhood education: birth—grade 2 (MS); education (MS); elementary education (MS); learning technology (MS); middle childhood education: grades 5-9 (MS); reading (MS); school administration and supervision (MS); school building leadership (MS); school business administration (MS); secondary education (MS); special education (MS); students with disabilities: grades 5-9 (MS); students with disabilities: grades 7-12 (MS); teaching English to speakers of other languages (MS); teaching literacy: birth—grade 6 (MS); teaching literacy: grades 5-12 (MS); urban education (MS). *Students:* 572 full-time (467 women), 1,719 part-time (1,287 women); includes 943 minority (470 African Americans, 7 American Indian/Alaska Native, 48 Asian Americans or Pacific Islanders, 418

Hispanic Americans), 6 international. Average age 33. In 2006, 1090 degrees awarded. *Entrance requirements:* For master's, teaching certificate. *Application deadline:* For fall admission, 2/1 for domestic students. Applications are processed on a rolling basis. Application fee: $37. *Expenses:* *Contact institution.* Tuition and fees vary according to program. *Financial support:* Institutionally sponsored loans, scholarships/grants, and unspecified assistantships available. Support available to part-time students. *Faculty research:* Distance learning, literacy, assessment, community schools, impact of staff development. *Unit head:* Dr. William Prattella, Chairperson, 914-674-7555, Fax: 914-674-7352, E-mail: wprattella@mercy.edu. *Application contact:* Kathleen Jackson, Director of Admissions, 800-Mercy-NY, Fax: 914-674-7382, E-mail: admissions@mercy.edu.

MGH Institute of Health Professions, Graduate Programs, Program in Communication Sciences and Disorders, Boston, MA 02129. Offers reading (Certificate); speech-language pathology (MS). *Accreditation:* ASHA (one or more programs are accredited). Part-time programs available. *Faculty:* 11 full-time (7 women), 8 part-time/adjunct (6 women). *Students:* 74 full-time (72 women), 26 part-time (24 women); includes 5 minority (1 African American, 3 Asian Americans or Pacific Islanders, 1 Hispanic American). Average age 28. 173 applicants, 57% accepted, 47 enrolled. In 2006, 37 master's, 13 other advanced degrees awarded. *Degree requirements:* For master's, thesis or alternative, research proposal. *Entrance requirements:* For master's, GRE General Test. Additional exam requirements/recommendations for international students: Required—TOEFL (minimum score 550 paper-based; 213 computer-based). *Application deadline:* For fall admission, 1/28 for domestic and international students. Application fee: $50. Electronic applications accepted. *Financial support:* In 2006–07, 68 students received support; research assistantships, teaching assistantships, career-related internships or fieldwork, scholarships/grants, tuition waivers (full and partial), and unspecified assistantships available. Support available to part-time students. Financial award application deadline: 3/3; financial award applicants required to submit FAFSA. *Faculty research:* Children's language disorders, reading, speech disorders, voice disorders, augmentative communication, autism. *Unit head:* Kevin P. Kearns, Director, 617-724-6361, Fax: 617-726-8022, E-mail: kkearns@partners.org. *Application contact:* Maureen Rika Judd, Manager of Admissions, 617-726-6069, Fax: 617-726-8010, E-mail: admissions@mghihp.edu.

See Close-Up on page 1963.

Miami University, Graduate School, School of Education and Allied Professions, Department of Teacher Education, Program in Reading Education, Oxford, OH 45056. Offers M Ed. *Accreditation:* NCATE. Part-time programs available. *Degree requirements:* For master's, final exam. *Entrance requirements:* For master's, MAT, minimum undergraduate GPA of 3.0 during previous 2 years or 2.75 overall. Additional exam requirements/recommendations for international students: Required—TOEFL (minimum score 550 paper-based; 213 computer-based), TWE (minimum score 4). *Faculty research:* Teacher effectiveness.

Michigan State University, The Graduate School, College of Education, Program in Literacy Instruction, East Lansing, MI 48824. Offers MA. Part-time programs available. *Students:* 2 full-time (both women), 45 part-time (44 women); includes 3 minority (2 African Americans, 1 Hispanic American). Average age 30. 17 applicants, 76% accepted. In 2006, 27 degrees awarded. *Degree requirements:* For master's, final exam or portfolio. *Entrance requirements:* Additional exam requirements/recommendations for international students: Required—TOEFL, Michigan State University ELT (85), Michigan ELAB (83). Electronic applications accepted. *Expenses:* Tuition, state resident: part-time $346 per credit hour. Tuition, nonresident: part-time $730 per credit hour. Tuition and fees vary according to program. *Unit head:* Dr. Susan Florio-Ruane, Coordinator, 517-432-4867, E-mail: susanfr@msu.edu. *Application contact:* Rosario Garcia, Program Secretary, 517-355-1872, E-mail: malit@msu.edu.

Middle Tennessee State University, College of Graduate Studies, College of Education and Behavioral Science, Department of Elementary and Special Education, Major in Reading, Murfreesboro, TN 37132. Offers M Ed. *Accreditation:* NCATE. Part-time and evening/weekend programs available. Postbaccalaureate distance learning degree programs offered. *Students:* 1 (woman) full-time, 15 part-time (all women); includes 1 minority (African American) 4 applicants, 100% accepted. In 2006, 10 degrees awarded. *Entrance requirements:* For master's, GRE or MAT. Additional exam requirements/recommendations for international students: Required—TOEFL (minimum score 525 paper-based; 195 computer-based). *Application deadline:* For fall admission, 8/1 priority date for domestic students. Applications are processed on a rolling basis. Application fee: $25. Electronic applications accepted. *Financial support:* Application deadline: 5/1. *Unit head:* Dr. Connie Jones, Chair, Department of Elementary and Special Education, 615-898-2680, Fax: 615-898-5309, E-mail: cojones@mtsu.edu.

Midwestern State University, Graduate Studies, College of Education, Program in Reading Education, Wichita Falls, TX 76308. Offers M Ed. Part-time and evening/weekend programs available. *Faculty:* 9 full-time (6 women), 3 part-time/adjunct (all women). *Students:* Average age 28. 2 applicants, 50% accepted, 0 enrolled. In 2006, 5 degrees awarded. *Degree requirements:* For master's, comprehensive exam. *Entrance requirements:* For master's, GRE General Test, MAT or GMAT. Additional exam requirements/recommendations for international students: Required—TOEFL (minimum score 550 paper-based; 213 computer-based). *Application deadline:* For fall admission, 7/1 for domestic students, 4/1 for international students; for spring admission, 11/1 for domestic students, 8/1 for international students. Applications are processed on a rolling basis. Application fee: $35 ($50 for international students). Electronic applications accepted. *Financial support:* In 2006–07, 3 students received support. Career-related internships or fieldwork, Federal Work-Study, institutionally sponsored loans, scholarships/grants, tuition waivers (partial), and unspecified assistantships available. Support available to part-time students. Financial award application deadline: 5/1; financial award applicants required to submit FAFSA. *Unit head:* Dr. Ann Estrada, Chair, 940-397-4136, Fax: 940-397-4672, E-mail: ann.estrada@mwsu.edu. *Application contact:* 800-842-1922, Fax: 940-397-4672, E-mail: admissions@mwsu.edu.

Millersville University of Pennsylvania, Graduate School, School of Education, Department of Elementary and Early Childhood Education, Program in Reading/Language Arts Education, Millersville, PA 17551-0302. Offers M Ed. *Accreditation:* NCATE. Part-time and evening/weekend programs available. *Faculty:* 20 full-time (15 women), 11 part-time/adjunct (6 women). *Students:* 1 (woman) full-time, 67 part-time (61 women). Average age 29. 7 applicants, 100% accepted, 7 enrolled. In 2006, 32 degrees awarded. *Degree requirements:* For master's, thesis optional. *Entrance requirements:* For master's, GRE or MAT, minimum undergraduate GPA of 2.75, Pennsylvania Instructional Certificate. *Application deadline:* For fall admission, 3/1 priority date for domestic students; for spring admission, 10/1 priority date for domestic students. Applications are processed on a rolling basis. Application fee: $35. *Expenses:* Tuition, state resident: full-time $6,048; part-time $336 per credit. Tuition, nonresident: full-time $9,678; part-time $538 per credit. Required fees: $1,244. Tuition and fees vary according to course load. *Financial support:* In 2006–07, 1 student received support, including 1 research assistantship with full tuition reimbursement available (averaging $4,250 per year); career-related internships or fieldwork, Federal Work-Study, institutionally sponsored loans, and unspecified assistantships also available. Support available to part-time students. Financial award application deadline: 3/15; financial award applicants required to submit FAFSA. *Faculty research:* Teaching grammar, content area literacy, multicultural children's literature, writing motivation. *Unit head:* Dr. Mary Ann Gray-Schlegel, Coordinator for Language and Literacy, 717-872-3397, Fax: 717-871-5462, E-mail: mary.gray-schlegel@millersville.edu. *Application contact:* Dr. Victor S. DeSantis, Dean of Graduate Studies, 717-872-3099, Fax: 717-871-2022, E-mail: victor.desantis@millersville.edu.

Minnesota State University Moorhead, Graduate Studies, College of Education and Human Services, Program in Reading, Moorhead, MN 56563-0002. Offers MS. *Accreditation:* NCATE. Part-time and evening/weekend programs available. *Faculty:* 7 part-time/adjunct (6 women). *Students:* 3 applicants, 100% accepted. In 2006, 3 degrees awarded. *Degree requirements:* For master's, final oral exam, project or thesis. *Entrance requirements:* For master's, MAT, minimum GPA of 2.75, 2 years of teaching experience. Additional exam requirements/recommendations for international students: Required—TOEFL (minimum score 550 paper-based; 213 computer-based). *Application deadline:* For fall admission, 4/15 priority date for domestic students, 3/15 for international students; for spring admission, 11/1 priority date for domestic students. Applications are processed on a rolling basis. Application fee: $20. Electronic applications accepted. *Financial support:* In 2006–07, 1 research assistantship (averaging $1,000 per year) was awarded; career-related internships or fieldwork, Federal Work-Study, and unspecified assistantships also available. Financial award application deadline: 7/15; financial award applicants required to submit FAFSA. *Unit head:* Dr. Peggy Rittenhouse, Coordinator, 218-477-2696, E-mail: rittenps@mnstate.edu.

Missouri State University, Graduate College, College of Education, School of Teacher Education, Program in Reading Education, Springfield, MO 65804-0094. Offers MS Ed. Part-time and evening/weekend programs available. *Students:* 5 full-time (all women), 44 part-time (42 women); includes 3 minority (1 African American, 1 American Indian/Alaska Native, 1 Hispanic American). Average age 35. 6 applicants, 100% accepted, 6 enrolled. In 2006, 21 degrees awarded. *Degree requirements:* For master's, thesis or alternative, comprehensive exam. *Entrance requirements:* For master's, GRE or minimum GPA of 3.0, teaching certificate. Additional exam requirements/recommendations for international students: Required—TOEFL (minimum score 550 paper-based; 213 computer-based; 79 iBT). *Application deadline:* For fall admission, 7/20 priority date for domestic students; for spring admission, 12/20 for domestic students. Applications are processed on a rolling basis. Application fee: $35. *Expenses:* Tuition, state resident: full-time $3,582; part-time $199 per credit hour. Tuition, nonresident: full-time $6,984; part-time $199 per credit hour. Required fees: $548. Full-time tuition and fees vary according to course level, course load, program and reciprocity agreements. *Financial support:* Teaching assistantships with full tuition reimbursements, Federal Work-Study and scholarships/grants available. Financial award application deadline: 3/31; financial award applicants required to submit FAFSA. *Unit head:* Dr. Deanne Camp, Graduate Program Director, 417-836-6983, E-mail: deannecamp@missouristate.edu.

Monmouth University, Graduate School, School of Education, West Long Branch, NJ 07764-1898. Offers educational counseling (MS Ed); elementary education (MAT), including certified teachers, non-certified teachers; learning disabilities-teacher consultant (Certificate); principal studies (MS Ed); reading specialist (MS Ed, Certificate); special education (MS Ed); supervisor (Certificate); teacher of the handicapped (Certificate). Part-time and evening/weekend programs available. *Faculty:* 24 full-time (15 women), 25 part-time/adjunct (17 women). *Students:* 169 full-time (133 women), 426 part-time (374 women); includes 45 minority (21 African Americans, 2 American Indian/Alaska Native, 2 Asian Americans or Pacific Islanders, 20 Hispanic Americans). Average age 31. 355 applicants, 96% accepted, 138 enrolled. In 2006, 209 degrees awarded. *Entrance requirements:* For master's, minimum GPA of 3.0 in major, 2.75 overall. Additional exam requirements/recommendations for international students: Required—TOEFL (minimum score 550 paper-based; 213 computer-based; 79 iBT), IELTS (minimum score 5), MELAB 77, Cambridge A, B, C. *Application deadline:* For fall admission, 7/15 priority date for domestic students; for spring admission, 11/15 priority date for domestic students. Applications are processed on a rolling basis. Application fee: $50. Electronic applications accepted. *Expenses:* Tuition: Full-time $12,780; part-time $710 per credit. Required fees: $628; $314 per term. *Financial support:* In 2006–07, 221 fellowships (averaging $2,053 per year), 17 research assistantships (averaging $6,527 per year) were awarded; career-related internships or fieldwork, scholarships/grants, tuition waivers (partial), and unspecified assistantships also available. Support available to part-time students. Financial award application deadline: 3/1; financial award applicants required to submit FAFSA. *Faculty research:* Multicultural literacy, science and mathematics teaching strategies, teacher as reflective practitioner, children with disabilities, varied contexts of learning. *Unit head:* Dr. Lynn Romeo, Program Director, 732-571-4484, Fax: 732-263-5277, E-mail: lromeo@monmouth.edu. *Application contact:* Kevin Roane, Director, Office of Graduate Admission, 732-571-3452, Fax: 732-263-5123, E-mail: gradadm@monmouth.edu.

Montana State University–Billings, College of Education and Human Services, Department of Special Education, Counseling, Reading and Early Childhood, Option in Reading, Billings, MT 59101-0298. Offers M Ed. *Accreditation:* NCATE. Part-time programs available. *Students:* 20. 7 applicants, 100% accepted, 7 enrolled. In 2006, 10 degrees awarded. *Degree requirements:* For master's, thesis or professional paper and/or field experience, thesis optional. *Entrance requirements:* For master's, GRE General Test or MAT, minimum GPA of 3.0 (undergraduate), 3.25 (graduate). *Application deadline:* Applications are processed on a rolling basis. Application fee: $40. *Expenses:* Tuition, state resident: full-time $4,599. Tuition, nonresident: full-time $10,786. *Financial support:* Teaching assistantships, career-related internships or fieldwork, Federal Work-Study, institutionally sponsored loans, scholarships/grants, tuition waivers (partial), and unspecified assistantships available. Support available to part-time students. Financial award application deadline: 5/1; financial award applicants required to submit FAFSA. *Application contact:* David M. Sullivan, Graduate Studies Counselor, 406-657-2053, Fax: 406-657-2299, E-mail: dsullivan@msubillings.edu.

Montclair State University, The Graduate School, College of Education and Human Services, Department of Early Childhood, Elementary and Literacy Education, Montclair, NJ 07043-1624. Offers early childhood /elementary education (M Ed); early childhood education and teaching students in disabilities (MAT); early childhood special education (M Ed, Certificate); elementary education with disabilities (MAT); elementary school teacher (Certificate); learning disabilities (Certificate); reading (MA, Certificate); reading specialist (Certificate). Part-time and evening/weekend programs available. *Faculty:* 15 full-time (13 women), 65 part-time/adjunct (52 women). *Students:* 27 full-time (24 women), 189 part-time (179 women); includes 24 minority (12 African Americans, 3 Asian Americans or Pacific Islanders, 9 Hispanic Americans), 1 international. 116 applicants, 47% accepted, 35 enrolled. In 2006, 40 master's, 53 other advanced degrees awarded. *Degree requirements:* For master's, clinical experience, portfolio. *Entrance requirements:* For master's, GRE, PRAXIS II, 2 letters of recommendation. Additional exam requirements/recommendations for international students: Required—TOEFL (minimum score 83 computer-based). *Application deadline:* For fall admission, 6/1 for international students; for spring admission, 10/1 for international students. Applications are processed on a rolling basis. Application fee: $60. Electronic applications accepted. *Expenses:* Tuition, state resident: part-time $450 per credit. Tuition, nonresident: part-time $682 per credit. Tuition and fees vary according to degree level and program. *Financial support:* In 2006–07, 15 research assistantships with full tuition reimbursements (averaging $7,000 per year) were awarded; Federal Work-Study, scholarships/grants, and unspecified assistantships also available. Support available to part-time students. Financial award application deadline: 3/1; financial award applicants required to submit FAFSA. *Unit head:* Dr. Nancy Lauter, Chairperson, 973-655-5407, E-mail: lautern@mail.montclair.edu. *Application contact:* Dr. Linda Luise, Adviser, 973-655-4247, E-mail: wisel@mail.montclair.edu.

Morehead State University, Graduate Programs, College of Education, Department of Curriculum and Instruction, Program in Elementary Education, Morehead, KY 40351. Offers elementary education (MA Ed); international education (MA Ed); middle school education (MA Ed, MAT); reading (MA Ed). *Accreditation:* NCATE. Part-time and evening/weekend programs available. *Students:* 2 full-time (both women), 84 part-time (80 women); includes 1 minority (American Indian/Alaska Native). Average age 32. In 2006, 52 degrees awarded. *Degree requirements:* For master's, thesis optional. *Entrance requirements:* For master's, GRE General Test, minimum GPA of 2.75, teaching certificate. Additional exam requirements/recommendations for international students: Required—TOEFL (minimum score 500 paper-based; 173 computer-based). *Application deadline:* For fall admission, 8/1 priority date for domestic and international students; for spring admission, 12/1 priority date for domestic and international students. Applications are processed on a rolling basis. Application fee: $0 ($55 for international students). Electronic applications accepted. *Financial support:* In 2006–07, teaching assistantships (averaging $6,000 per year); career-related internships or fieldwork, Federal Work-Study, and unspecified assistantships also available. Financial award application deadline: 4/1; financial award applicants required to submit FAFSA. *Faculty research:* Teaching through journal writing, gifted children, reading instruction in elementary schools,

Reading Education

Morehead State University *(continued)*

teaching social studies in elementary schools, ungraded elementary schools. *Application contact:* Michelle Barber, Graduate Admissions Counselor, 606-783-2039, Fax: 606-783-5061, E-mail: m.barber@moreheadstate.edu.

Morningside College, Graduate Division, Department of Education, Program in Reading Specialist, Sioux City, IA 51106. Offers MAT. Part-time and evening/weekend programs available. *Entrance requirements:* For master's, MAT, writing sample.

Mount Saint Mary College, Division of Education, Newburgh, NY 12550-3494. Offers adolescence and special education (MS Ed); adolescence education (MS Ed); childhood and special education (MS Ed); childhood education (MS Ed); literacy and special education (MS Ed); literacy/childhood (MS Ed); middle school (5-6) (MS Ed); middle school (7-9) (MS Ed); special education (1-6) (MS Ed); special education (7-12) (MS Ed). *Accreditation:* NCATE. Part-time and evening/weekend programs available. *Faculty:* 11 full-time (8 women), 21 part-time/adjunct (18 women). *Students:* 87 full-time (74 women), 368 part-time (303 women); includes 38 minority (12 African Americans, 2 American Indian/Alaska Native, 5 Asian Americans or Pacific Islanders, 19 Hispanic Americans). Average age 31. 164 applicants, 45% accepted, 58 enrolled. In 2006, 131 degrees awarded. *Application deadline:* Applications are processed on a rolling basis. Application fee: $35. *Expenses:* Tuition: Full-time $11,880; part-time $660 per credit. *Financial support:* In 2006–07, 30 students received support. Unspecified assistantships available. Financial award application deadline: 3/15. *Faculty research:* Learning and teaching styles, computers in special education, language development. *Unit head:* Theresa Lewis, Coordinator, 845-569-3149, Fax: 845-569-3535, E-mail: tlewis@msmc.edu.

Mount Saint Vincent University, Graduate Programs, Faculty of Education, Program in Literacy Education, Halifax, NS B3M 2J6, Canada. Offers M Ed, MA Ed, MA-R. Part-time and evening/weekend programs available. Postbaccalaureate distance learning degree programs offered (no on-campus study). *Degree requirements:* For master's, thesis (for some programs). *Entrance requirements:* For master's, minimum B average, 1 year of teaching experience, bachelor's degree in related field. Electronic applications accepted. *Faculty research:* Writing processes and instruction, assessment and evaluation of literacy education, critical literacy, early literacy development, gender and literacy.

Murray State University, College of Education, Department of Early Childhood and Elementary Education, Program in Elementary Education and Reading and Writing, Murray, KY 42071. Offers MA Ed, Ed S. *Accreditation:* NCATE. Part-time programs available. *Faculty:* 6 part-time/adjunct (5 women). *Students:* 108; includes 4 minority (all African Americans), 2 international. 18 applicants, 100% accepted, 18 enrolled. In 2006, 34 master's awarded. *Median time to degree:* Of those who began their doctoral program in fall 1998, 100% received their degree in 8 years or less. *Degree requirements:* For master's, thesis optional. *Entrance requirements:* For master's, minimum GPA of 2.5 for conditional admittance, 3.0 for unconditional; for Ed S, GRE General Test or MAT. Additional exam requirements/recommendations for international students: Required—TOEFL. *Application deadline:* Applications are processed on a rolling basis. Application fee: $25. *Financial support:* Research assistantships, teaching assistantships, Federal Work-Study available. Financial award application deadline: 4/1.

Murray State University, College of Education, Department of Early Childhood and Elementary Education, Program in Reading and Writing, Murray, KY 42071. Offers MA Ed. *Accreditation:* NCATE. *Degree requirements:* For master's, portfolio, thesis optional. *Entrance requirements:* Additional exam requirements/recommendations for international students: Required—TOEFL.

National-Louis University, National College of Education, Doctoral Programs in Education, Program in Reading and Language, Chicago, IL 60603. Offers Ed D. Part-time and evening/weekend programs available. *Students:* 1 (woman) full-time, 18 part-time (all women); includes 3 minority (1 African American, 1 Asian American or Pacific Islander, 1 Hispanic American). Average age 44. 2 applicants, 100% accepted. In 2006, 4 degrees awarded. *Degree requirements:* For doctorate, thesis/dissertation, internship, comprehensive exam. *Entrance requirements:* For doctorate, GRE General Test, minimum GPA of 3.25, interview, resumé, writing sample. *Application deadline:* For fall admission, 5/1 for domestic students; for spring admission, 1/15 for domestic students. Application fee: $25. *Expenses:* Tuition: Full-time $17,685. One-time fee: $40 full-time. *Financial support:* Fellowships, research assistantships, teaching assistantships, career-related internships or fieldwork, Federal Work-Study, institutionally sponsored loans, and scholarships/grants available. Support available to part-time students. Financial award application deadline: 4/15; financial award applicants required to submit FAFSA. *Application contact:* David McCulloch, Vice President for University Services, 800-443-5522 Ext. 5127, Fax: 847-465-0593, E-mail: dmcc@wheeling1.nl.edu.

National-Louis University, National College of Education, Programs in Reading and Language, Chicago, IL 60603. Offers language and literacy (M Ed, MS Ed, CAS); reading recovery (CAS); reading specialist (M Ed, MS Ed, CAS). Part-time and evening/weekend programs available. *Students:* 1 (woman) full-time, 237 part-time (231 women); includes 32 minority (11 African Americans, 2 American Indian/Alaska Native, 4 Asian Americans or Pacific Islanders, 15 Hispanic Americans). Average age 34. 15 applicants, 100% accepted. In 2006, 36 master's, 2 other advanced degrees awarded. *Degree requirements:* For master's, thesis (for some programs). *Entrance requirements:* For master's, MAT or GRE, minimum GPA of 3.0, teaching certificate; for CAS, master's degree, teaching certificate. *Application deadline:* Applications are processed on a rolling basis. Application fee: $25. *Expenses:* Tuition: Full-time $17,685. One-time fee: $40 full-time. *Financial support:* Fellowships, career-related internships or fieldwork, Federal Work-Study, institutionally sponsored loans, and scholarships/grants available. Support available to part-time students. Financial award applicants required to submit FAFSA. *Unit head:* Dr. Camille Blachowicz, Coordinator, 847-475-1100 Ext. 2558. *Application contact:* David McCulloch, Vice President for University Services, 800-443-5522 Ext. 5127, Fax: 847-465-0593, E-mail: dmcc@wheeling1.nl.edu.

Nazareth College of Rochester, Graduate Studies, Department of Education, Program in Literacy Education, Rochester, NY 14618-3790. Offers MS Ed. *Accreditation:* Teacher Education Accreditation Council. Part-time and evening/weekend programs available. *Faculty:* 3 full-time (all women), 11 part-time/adjunct (8 women). *Students:* 27 full-time (26 women), 98 part-time (94 women); includes 6 minority (3 African Americans, 3 Hispanic Americans). Average age 33. 69 applicants, 99% accepted, 39 enrolled. In 2006, 73 degrees awarded. *Degree requirements:* For master's, comprehensive exam. *Entrance requirements:* For master's, minimum GPA of 3.0. *Application deadline:* For fall admission, 4/1 for domestic students; for spring admission, 10/1 for domestic students. Application fee: $40. *Financial support:* Research assistantships with partial tuition reimbursements available. Financial award application deadline: 3/1; financial award applicants required to submit FAFSA. *Unit head:* Dr. Naomi Erdmann, Director, 585-389-2614, Fax: 585-389-2452, E-mail: nerdman0@naz.edu. *Application contact:* Judith G. Baker, Director, Graduate Admissions, 585-389-2050, Fax: 585-389-2817, E-mail: gradstudies@naz.edu.

New Jersey City University, Graduate and Continuing Education, College of Education, Department of Literacy Education, Jersey City, NJ 07305-1597. Offers elementary school reading (MA); reading specialist (MA); secondary school reading (MA). Evening/weekend programs available. *Faculty:* 10. *Students:* Average age 32. In 2006, 16 degrees awarded. *Degree requirements:* For master's, comprehensive exam. *Entrance requirements:* For master's, GRE General Test or MAT. Additional exam requirements/recommendations for international students: Required—TOEFL. *Application deadline:* For fall admission, 8/1 priority date for domestic students; for spring admission, 12/1 for domestic students. Applications are processed on a rolling basis. Application fee: $0. *Expenses:* Tuition, state resident: full-time $7,038; part-time $391 per credit. Tuition, nonresident: full-time $12,510; part-time $695 per credit. Required fees: $65 per credit. *Financial support:* Research assistantships, unspecified assistantships available. *Faculty research:* Reading clinic. *Unit head:* Peter Incardone, Chairperson, 201-200-3521, E-mail: pincardone@njcu.edu.

New Mexico State University, Graduate School, College of Education, Department of Curriculum and Instruction, Las Cruces, NM 88003-8001. Offers curriculum and instruction (MAT, Ed D, PhD, Ed S); general education (MA); reading (Ed S). *Accreditation:* NCATE. Part-time programs available. Postbaccalaureate distance learning degree programs offered (minimal on-campus study). *Faculty:* 22 full-time (10 women), 11 part-time/adjunct (3 women). *Students:* 200 full-time (155 women), 399 part-time (312 women); includes 267 minority (16 African Americans, 12 American Indian/Alaska Native, 7 Asian Americans or Pacific Islanders, 232 Hispanic Americans), 33 international. Average age 37. 233 applicants, 82% accepted. In 2006, 213 master's, 17 doctorates awarded. *Degree requirements:* For master's, thesis optional; for doctorate, thesis/dissertation, comprehensive exam. *Entrance requirements:* For master's, minimum GPA of 2.5 in last 12 hours of course work; for doctorate, portfolio. *Application deadline:* For fall admission, 7/1 priority date for domestic students; for spring admission, 11/1 for domestic students. Applications are processed on a rolling basis. Application fee: $30 ($50 for international students). *Financial support:* In 2006–07, 1 fellowship, 20 teaching assistantships were awarded; research assistantships, career-related internships or fieldwork, Federal Work-Study, scholarships/grants, health care benefits, and unspecified assistantships also available. Support available to part-time students. Financial award application deadline: 3/1. *Faculty research:* Multicultural education, literacy/biliteracy education, bilingual and English as a second language education, critical pedagogy, education for democratic society. *Unit head:* Dr. James O'Donnell, Head, 505-646-2990, Fax: 505-646-5436, E-mail: jodonnel@nmsu.edu.

New York University, Steinhardt School of Culture, Education and Human Development, Department of Teaching and Learning, Program in Literacy Education, New York, NY 10012-1019. Offers literacy education (MA), including literacy education: birth-grade 6, literacy education: grades 5-12. *Accreditation:* Teacher Education Accreditation Council. Part-time and evening/weekend programs available. *Faculty:* 1 (woman) full-time. *Students:* 8 full-time (all women), 19 part-time (17 women); includes 4 minority (2 African Americans, 1 Asian American or Pacific Islander, 1 Hispanic American). 46 applicants, 98% accepted, 14 enrolled. In 2006, 28 degrees awarded. *Degree requirements:* For master's, thesis (for some programs). *Entrance requirements:* For master's, teacher certification. Additional exam requirements/recommendations for international students: Required—TOEFL. *Application deadline:* For fall admission, 12/15 priority date for domestic and international students; for spring admission, 11/1 for domestic and international students. Applications are processed on a rolling basis. Application fee: $50. *Expenses:* Tuition: Part-time $1,080 per unit. Required fees: $56 per unit. $329 per term. Tuition and fees vary according to program. *Financial support:* Career-related internships or fieldwork, Federal Work-Study, institutionally sponsored loans, scholarships/grants, and tuition waivers (partial) available. Support available to part-time students. Financial award application deadline: 2/1; financial award applicants required to submit FAFSA. *Faculty research:* Early literacy intervention and development, psycho and sociolinguistics, multicultural education, literacy assessment and instruction. *Unit head:* Cynthia McCallister, Director, 212-998-5416, Fax: 212-995-4049. *Application contact:* Office of Graduate Admissions, 212-998-5030, Fax: 212-995-4328, E-mail: steinhardt.gradadmissions@nyu.edu.

Niagara University, Graduate Division of Education, Concentration in Literacy Instruction, Niagara Falls, Niagara University, NY 14109. Offers MS Ed. *Students:* 38 full-time (36 women), 51 part-time (47 women); includes 3 minority (1 African American, 2 Hispanic Americans), 1 international. In 2006, 34 degrees awarded. *Unit head:* Dr. Chandra Foote, Chair, 716-286-8549.

North Carolina Agricultural and Technical State University, Graduate School, School of Education, Department of Curriculum and Instruction, Program in Reading, Greensboro, NC 27411. Offers MS. *Accreditation:* NCATE. Part-time and evening/weekend programs available. *Degree requirements:* For master's, thesis or alternative, qualifying exam, comprehensive exam. *Entrance requirements:* For master's, GRE General Test, minimum GPA of 3.0.

Northeastern Illinois University, Graduate College, College of Education, School of Teacher Education, Program in Reading, Chicago, IL 60625-4699. Offers MA. Part-time and evening/weekend programs available. *Faculty:* 30 full-time (20 women), 39 part-time/adjunct (29 women). *Students:* 1 (woman) full-time, 166 part-time (150 women); includes 31 minority (5 African Americans, 1 Asian American or Pacific Islander, 25 Hispanic Americans). Average age 33. 70 applicants, 94% accepted. In 2006, 34 degrees awarded. *Degree requirements:* For master's, thesis optional. *Entrance requirements:* For master's, previous course work in psychology or tests and measurements, minimum GPA of 2.75. *Application deadline:* For fall admission, 4/1 priority date for domestic students; for spring admission, 8/15 for domestic students. Applications are processed on a rolling basis. Application fee: $25. *Financial support:* In 2006–07, 40 students received support, including 2 research assistantships with full tuition reimbursements available (averaging $6,600 per year); career-related internships or fieldwork, Federal Work-Study, institutionally sponsored loans, and tuition waivers (full and partial) also available. Support available to part-time students. Financial award applicants required to submit FAFSA. *Faculty research:* Early literacy, reading disabilities, cognitive processes, multicultural and linguistic diversity, use of literature in the classroom.

Northeastern State University, Graduate College, College of Education, Department of Curriculum and Instruction, Program in Reading, Tahlequah, OK 74464-2399. Offers M Ed. Part-time and evening/weekend programs available. *Students:* 16 full-time (all women), 61 part-time (59 women); includes 12 minority (2 African Americans, 8 American Indian/Alaska Native, 1 Asian American or Pacific Islander, 1 Hispanic American). In 2006, 28 degrees awarded. *Degree requirements:* For master's, thesis. *Entrance requirements:* For master's, MAT or GRE, minimum GPA of 2.5. Additional exam requirements/recommendations for international students: Required—TOEFL (minimum score 213 computer-based). *Application deadline:* For fall admission, 6/1 priority date for domestic students. Applications are processed on a rolling basis. Application fee: $0 ($25 for international students). Electronic applications accepted. *Financial support:* Teaching assistantships, Federal Work-Study available. Financial award application deadline: 3/1. *Unit head:* Dr. Steve Sargents, Coordinator, 918-449-6000 Ext. 6587, Fax: 918-458-2351, E-mail: sargents@nsuok.edu.

Northern Illinois University, Graduate School, College of Education, Department of Literacy Education, De Kalb, IL 60115-2854. Offers curriculum and instruction (Ed D), including reading; literacy education (MS Ed). Part-time and evening/weekend programs available. *Faculty:* 12 full-time (10 women), 1 part-time/adjunct (0 women). *Students:* 3 full-time (2 women), 220 part-time (202 women); includes 40 minority (4 African Americans, 3 Asian Americans or Pacific Islanders, 33 Hispanic Americans). Average age 38. 45 applicants, 36% accepted, 12 enrolled. In 2006, 52 degrees awarded. *Degree requirements:* For master's, thesis optional; for doctorate, thesis/dissertation, candidacy exam, dissertation defense. *Entrance requirements:* For master's, GRE General Test or MAT, minimum undergraduate GPA of 2.75; for doctorate, GRE General Test, minimum GPA of 2.75 (undergraduate), 3.2 (graduate). Additional exam requirements/recommendations for international students: Required—TOEFL (minimum score 550 paper-based; 213 computer-based). *Application deadline:* For fall admission, 3/1 priority date for domestic students, 5/1 for international students; for spring admission, 11/1 for domestic students, 10/1 for international students. Applications are processed on a rolling basis. Application fee: $30. Electronic applications accepted. *Financial support:* In 2006–07, 1 research assistantship with full tuition reimbursement, 21 teaching assistantships with full tuition reimbursements were awarded; fellowships with full tuition reimbursements, career-related internships or fieldwork, Federal Work-Study, scholarships/grants, tuition waivers (full), and unspecified assistantships also available. Support available to part-time students. Financial award applicants required to submit FAFSA. *Faculty research:* Early reading development, literacy for bilingual students, family literacy, expository writing, fluency. *Unit head:* Dr. Norm Stahl, Chair, 815-753-9032, E-mail: stahl@niu.edu.

Northern State University, Division of Graduate Studies in Education, Program in Teaching and Learning, Aberdeen, SD 57401-7198. Offers educational studies (MS Ed); elementary classroom teaching (MS Ed); health, physical education, and coaching (MS Ed); language and literacy (MS Ed); secondary classroom teaching (MS Ed); special education (MS Ed).

Accreditation: NCATE. Part-time and evening/weekend programs available. *Faculty:* 69 full-time (19 women). *Students:* 5 full-time (3 women), 70 part-time (51 women); includes 3 minority (1 African American, 1 American Indian/Alaska Native, 1 Asian American or Pacific Islander). Average age 32. In 2006, 23 degrees awarded. *Degree requirements:* For master's, thesis optional. *Entrance requirements:* For master's, minimum GPA of 2.75. Additional exam requirements/recommendations for international students: Required—TOEFL (minimum score 550 paper-based; 213 computer-based). *Application deadline:* For fall admission, 8/15 priority date for domestic students; for spring admission, 12/15 for domestic students. Applications are processed on a rolling basis. Application fee: $35. Electronic applications accepted. *Expenses:* Tuition, state resident: full-time $3,373; part-time $120 per credit. Tuition, nonresident: full-time $9,943; part-time $355 per credit. International tuition: $13,000 full-time. Required fees: $86 per credit. One-time fee: $35 full-time. Tuition and fees vary according to course load, degree level and reciprocity agreements. *Financial support:* In 2006–07, 17 teaching assistantships with partial tuition reimbursements (averaging $4,812 per year) were awarded; career-related internships or fieldwork, Federal Work-Study, institutionally sponsored loans, scholarships/grants, and unspecified assistantships also available. Support available to part-time students. Financial award application deadline: 3/1; financial award applicants required to submit FAFSA. *Application contact:* Tammy K. Griffith, Senior Secretary, 605-626-2558, Fax: 605-626-2542, E-mail: griffith@northern.edu.

Northwestern Oklahoma State University, School of Professional Studies, Reading Specialist Program, Alva, OK 73717-2799. Offers M Ed. *Accreditation:* NCATE. Part-time programs available. *Faculty:* 4 full-time (3 women). In 2006, 8 degrees awarded. *Degree requirements:* For master's, portfolio, thesis optional. *Entrance requirements:* For master's, GRE General Test or MAT, minimum GPA of 2.75. *Application deadline:* Applications are processed on a rolling basis. Application fee: $15. *Expenses:* Tuition, state resident: part-time $700 per year. Tuition, nonresident: part-time $1,715 per year. *Financial support:* Application deadline: 5/1. *Unit head:* Dr. Martie Young, Coordinator, 580-327-8449.

Northwestern State University of Louisiana, Graduate Studies and Research, College of Education, Programs in Education, Natchitoches, LA 71497. Offers business and distributive education (M Ed); counseling (M Ed); early childhood education (M Ed); education (M Ed); education leadership (M Ed); educational technology (M Ed); elementary teaching (M Ed); English education (M Ed); home economics education (M Ed); mathematics education (M Ed); reading (M Ed); science education (M Ed); secondary teaching (M Ed); social sciences education (M Ed). *Students:* 49 full-time (41 women), 245 part-time (206 women); includes 78 minority (70 African Americans, 5 American Indian/Alaska Native, 2 Asian Americans or Pacific Islanders, 1 Hispanic American). Average age 35. In 2006, 158 degrees awarded. *Degree requirements:* For master's, thesis or alternative, comprehensive exam, registration. *Entrance requirements:* For master's, GRE General Test, minimum undergraduate GPA of 2.5. *Application contact:* Dr. Steven G. Horton, Associate Provost/Dean, Graduate Studies, Research, and Information Systems, 318-357-5851, Fax: 318-357-5019, E-mail: grad_school@nsula.edu.

Northwestern State University of Louisiana, Graduate Studies and Research, College of Education, Programs in Educational Leadership and Instruction, Natchitoches, LA 71497. Offers counseling (Ed S); educational leadership (Ed S); educational technology (Ed S); elementary teaching (Ed S); reading (Ed S); secondary teaching (Ed S); special education (Ed S). *Students:* 17 full-time (15 women), 114 part-time (87 women); includes 55 minority (51 African Americans, 1 Asian American or Pacific Islander, 3 Hispanic Americans). Average age 39. In 2006, 11 degrees awarded. *Entrance requirements:* For degree, GRE General Test. *Application contact:* Dr. Steven G. Horton, Associate Provost/Dean, Graduate Studies, Research, and Information Systems, 318-357-5851, Fax: 318-357-5019, E-mail: grad_school@nsula.edu.

Northwest Missouri State University, Graduate School, College of Education and Human Services, Department of Curriculum and Instruction, Program in Reading, Maryville, MO 64468-6001. Offers MS Ed. *Accreditation:* NCATE. Part-time programs available. *Faculty:* 10 full-time (all women). *Students:* 2 full-time (both women), 41 part-time (all women); includes 1 minority (Hispanic American) 6 applicants, 83% accepted, 4 enrolled. In 2006, 6 degrees awarded. *Degree requirements:* For master's, comprehensive exam. *Entrance requirements:* For master's, GRE General Test, minimum undergraduate GPA of 2.75, teaching certificate, writing sample. Additional exam requirements/recommendations for international students: Required—TOEFL (minimum score 550 paper-based; 213 computer-based). *Application deadline:* For fall admission, 7/1 for domestic and international students; for spring admission, 11/15 for domestic and international students. Applications are processed on a rolling basis. Application fee: $0 ($50 for international students). *Financial support:* Application deadline: 3/1; *Unit head:* Dr. Margaret Drew, Director, 660-562-1668, E-mail: mdrew@mail.nwmissouri.edu. *Application contact:* Dr. Frances Shipley, Dean of Graduate School, 660-562-1145, Fax: 660-562-1096, E-mail: gradsch@nwmissouri.edu.

Northwest Nazarene University, Graduate Studies, Program in Teacher Education, Nampa, ID 83686-5897. Offers curriculum and instruction (M Ed); educational leadership (M Ed); exceptional child (M Ed); reading education (M Ed); school counseling (M Ed). *Accreditation:* ACA; NCATE. Part-time programs available. *Faculty:* 11 full-time (4 women), 10 part-time/adjunct (6 women). *Students:* 113 full-time (79 women), 20 part-time (18 women); includes 4 minority (2 Asian Americans or Pacific Islanders, 2 Hispanic Americans). Average age 34. In 2006, 35 degrees awarded. *Degree requirements:* For master's, action research project. *Entrance requirements:* For master's, minimum undergraduate GPA of 2.8 overall or 3.0 during final 30 semester credits. *Application deadline:* For fall admission, 9/1 for domestic students. Applications are processed on a rolling basis. Application fee: $25. *Faculty research:* Action research, cooperative learning, accountability, institutional accreditation. *Unit head:* Dr. Karen Blacklock, Chair, 208-467-8399, Fax: 208-467-8562.

Notre Dame College, Graduate Studies, South Euclid, OH 44121-4293. Offers accounting (Certificate); creative critical thinking (M Ed); financial services management (Certificate); information systems (Certificate); learning disabilities (M Ed); management (Certificate); paralegal (Certificate); pastoral ministry (Certificate); reading (M Ed); teacher education (Certificate). Part-time and evening/weekend programs available. *Degree requirements:* For master's, thesis. *Entrance requirements:* For master's, GRE General Test, MAT, minimum GPA of 2.75, valid teaching certificate. *Faculty research:* Cognitive psychology, teaching critical thinking in the classroom.

Notre Dame de Namur University, Division of Academic Affairs, School of Education and Leadership, Program in Reading, Belmont, CA 94002-1908. Offers MA, Certificate. *Expenses:* Tuition: Part-time $655 per credit. *Unit head:* Dr. Anabel Jensen, Head, 650-508-3696. *Application contact:* Helen Valine, Director of Graduate Admissions, 650-508-3534, Fax: 650-508-3426, E-mail: grad.admit@ndnu.edu.

Nova Southeastern University, Fischler School of Education and Human Services, Graduate Teacher Education Program, Fort Lauderdale, FL 33314-7796. Offers athletic administration (MS); cognitive and behavioral disabilities (MS); computer science education (Ed S); computer science education (K-12) (MS); curriculum and teaching (Ed S); curriculum, instruction and technology (MS); curriculum, instruction, management and administration (Ed S); early childhood special education (MS); early literacy and reading (Ed S); early literacy education (MS); education technology (MS); educational leadership (administration K–12) (MS, Ed S); educational media (Ed S); educational media (K-12) (MS); elementary education (MS, Ed S), including ESOL endorsement (MS); English (MS, Ed S); exceptional student education (MS), including ESOL endorsement; gifted education (MS, Ed S); interdisciplinary arts education (MS); management and administration of educational programs (MS); mathematics (MS, Ed S); multicultural early intervention (MS); pre-kindergarten/primary (MS); preschool education (MS); reading (MS, Ed S); science (MS, Ed S); secondary education (MS); social studies (MS, Ed S); Spanish language (MS); teaching and learning (MA, MS), including curriculum and instruction (MA), elementary mathematics (MA), elementary reading (MA), K-12 technology integration (MA); teaching English to speakers of other languages (MS, Ed S); technology management and administration (Ed S); urban studies education (MS); varying exceptionalities (Ed S). Part-time and evening/weekend programs available. Postbaccalaureate distance learning degree programs offered. *Faculty:* 131 full-time (78 women), 548 part-time/adjunct (342 women). *Students:* 1,418 full-time (1,139 women), 3,464 part-time (2,877 women); includes 2,462 minority (1,732 African Americans, 13 American Indian/Alaska Native, 44 Asian Americans or Pacific Islanders, 673 Hispanic Americans), 77 international. Average age 38. 1,771 applicants, 80% accepted, 1419 enrolled. In 2006, 2,078 master's, 425 other advanced degrees awarded. *Degree requirements:* For master's and Ed S, thesis, practicum, internship. *Entrance requirements:* For master's, MAT, GRE, CLAST, CBEST, PRAXIS I, GKT, minimum GPA of 2.5; for Ed S, MAT or GRE, master's degree, teaching certificate, minimum GPA of 3.0. Additional exam requirements/recommendations for international students: Recommended—TOEFL (minimum score 550 paper-based; 213 computer-based), IELTS (minimum score 6). *Application deadline:* For fall admission, 8/11 priority date for domestic and international students; for winter admission, 12/28 priority date for domestic and international students; for spring admission, 4/22 priority date for domestic and international students. Applications are processed on a rolling basis. Application fee: $50. Electronic applications accepted. *Financial support:* Federal Work-Study available. Support available to part-time students. Financial award application deadline: 1/7. *Faculty research:* School effectiveness, critical thinking, leadership skills acquisition, child education, multicultural education. *Unit head:* Dr. Meline Kevorkian, Associate Dean of Master's and Educational Programs, 954-262-8500, Fax: 954-262-3606, E-mail: melinek@nova.edu. *Application contact:* Jennifer Quiñones Nottingham, Dean of Student Affairs, 800-986-3223 Ext. 8624, Fax: 954-262-3911, E-mail: jlquinon@nova.edu.

Oakland University, Graduate Study and Lifelong Learning, School of Education and Human Services, Program in Reading and Language Arts, Rochester, MI 48309-4401. Offers reading (Certificate); reading and language arts (MAT); reading education (PhD); reading, language arts and literature (Certificate). *Faculty:* 8 full-time (4 women), 9 part-time/adjunct (all women). *Students:* 49 full-time (46 women), 263 part-time (241 women); includes 16 minority (9 African Americans, 2 American Indian/Alaska Native, 1 Asian American or Pacific Islander, 4 Hispanic Americans). Average age 32. 64 applicants, 98% accepted, 57 enrolled. In 2006, 127 master's, 9 doctorates awarded. *Degree requirements:* For doctorate, thesis/dissertation. *Entrance requirements:* For master's, minimum GPA of 3.0 for unconditional admission; for doctorate, MAT, minimum GPA of 3.0 for unconditional admission. *Application deadline:* For fall admission, 3/1 for domestic and international students. Application fee: $35. Electronic applications accepted. *Expenses:* Tuition, state resident: full-time $9,936; part-time $414 per credit. Tuition, nonresident: full-time $17,202; part-time $716 per credit. *Financial support:* Career-related internships or fieldwork, Federal Work-Study, institutionally sponsored loans, and tuition waivers (full) available. Financial award application deadline: 3/1; financial award applicants required to submit FAFSA. *Unit head:* Dr. Jane Cipielewski, Chair, 248-370-3065, Fax: 248-370-4367. *Application contact:* Dr. Toni Walters, Coordinator, 248-370-4205, Fax: 248-370-4367, E-mail: twalters@oakland.edu.

Ohio University, Graduate Studies, College of Education, Department of Teacher Education, Athens, OH 45701-2979. Offers adolescent to young adult education (M Ed); curriculum and instruction (M Ed, PhD); mathematics education (PhD); middle child education (M Ed); reading and language arts (PhD); reading education (M Ed); social studies education (PhD); special education (M Ed, PhD). Part-time and evening/weekend programs available. *Faculty:* 21 full-time (13 women), 7 part-time/adjunct (all women). *Students:* 57 full-time (44 women), 61 part-time (46 women); includes 4 minority (2 African Americans, 1 Asian American or Pacific Islander, 1 Hispanic American), 36 international. 93 applicants, 61% accepted, 37 enrolled. *Median time to degree:* Of those who began their doctoral program in fall 1998, 92% received their degree in 8 years or less. *Degree requirements:* For master's, thesis or alternative, registration; for doctorate, thesis/dissertation, comprehensive exam, registration. *Entrance requirements:* For master's, GRE General Test or MAT if GPA is less than 2.9; for doctorate, GRE General Test, minimum GPA of 3.4, work experience. Additional exam requirements/recommendations for international students: Required—TOEFL (minimum score 550 paper-based; 213 computer-based). *Application deadline:* For fall admission, 4/1 priority date for domestic and international students. Applications are processed on a rolling basis. Application fee: $45. Electronic applications accepted. *Financial support:* In 2006–07, 52 students received support, including 31 research assistantships with full tuition reimbursements available (averaging $6,500 per year), teaching assistantships with full tuition reimbursements available (averaging $7,200 per year); Federal Work-Study, institutionally sponsored loans, tuition waivers (full), and unspecified assistantships also available. Financial award application deadline: 3/15. *Faculty research:* Cognition literacy, character education, teacher's education reform, disabilities. Total annual research expenditures: $605,070. *Unit head:* Dr. William Earl Smith, Chair, 740-593-4483, Fax: 740-593-0477, E-mail: smithw@ohio.edu. *Application contact:* Floyd J. Doney, Director of Student Affairs, 740-593-4400, Fax: 740-593-9310, E-mail: doney@ohio.edu.

Old Dominion University, Darden College of Education, Doctoral Program in Literacy Leadership, Norfolk, VA 23529. Offers PhD. Part-time and evening/weekend programs available. *Faculty:* 7 full-time (6 women). *Students:* 1 (woman) full-time, 2 part-time (both women). Average age 55. *Degree requirements:* For doctorate, thesis/dissertation, comprehensive exam, registration. *Entrance requirements:* For doctorate, GRE, minimum GPA of 3.0, MS in reading or related degree. *Application deadline:* Applications are processed on a rolling basis. Application fee: $40. Electronic applications accepted. *Expenses:* Tuition, area resident: Part-time $285 per credit hour. Tuition, nonresident: part-time $715 per credit hour. Required fees: $94 per semester. *Financial support:* In 2006–07, 1 fellowship with full tuition reimbursement was awarded; career-related internships or fieldwork, scholarships/grants, and unspecified assistantships also available. *Faculty research:* Literacy with special needs, children reading first instruction, reading in the content area diverse and literacy. Total annual research expenditures: $600,000. *Unit head:* Dr. Jane Hager, Graduate Program Director, 757-683-4734.

Old Dominion University, Darden College of Education, Program in Reading Education, Norfolk, VA 23529. Offers MS Ed. *Accreditation:* NCATE. Part-time and evening/weekend programs available. Postbaccalaureate distance learning degree programs offered (no on-campus study). *Faculty:* 7 full-time (6 women), 14 part-time/adjunct (12 women). *Students:* 2 full-time (both women), 63 part-time (55 women); includes 11 minority (10 African Americans, 1 American Indian/Alaska Native). Average age 35. 23 applicants, 91% accepted, 21 enrolled. In 2006, 32 degrees awarded. *Degree requirements:* For master's, thesis optional. *Entrance requirements:* For master's, GRE General Test or MAT, minimum GPA of 3.0 in major, 2.8 overall; teaching certificate. *Application deadline:* For fall admission, 7/1 for domestic students. Applications are processed on a rolling basis. Application fee: $40. Electronic applications accepted. *Expenses:* Tuition, area resident: Part-time $285 per credit hour. Tuition, nonresident: part-time $715 per credit hour. Required fees: $94 per semester. *Financial support:* In 2006–07, 7 students received support, including 1 research assistantship with partial tuition reimbursement available (averaging $9,000 per year); career-related internships or fieldwork, Federal Work-Study, institutionally sponsored loans, scholarships/grants, and unspecified assistantships also available. Support available to part-time students. Financial award application deadline: 2/15; financial award applicants required to submit FAFSA. *Faculty research:* Metacognition and reading, strategies for improving comprehension in reading science, reading in content areas, vocabulary instruction for adolescents, literacy with special needs children, Reading First instruction, reading in the content area, vocabulary, diversity and literacy. Total annual research expenditures: $150,000. *Unit head:* Dr. Charlene Fleener, Graduate Program Director, 757-683-5103, Fax: 757-683-5862, E-mail: cfleener@odu.edu.

Oregon State University, Graduate School, College of Education, Program in Language Arts Education, Corvallis, OR 97331. Offers MAT. *Accreditation:* NCATE. Part-time programs available. In 2006, 7 degrees awarded. *Degree requirements:* For master's, thesis (for some programs). *Entrance requirements:* For master's, California Basic Educational Skills Test, NTE, minimum GPA of 3.0 in last 90 hours of course work. Additional exam requirements/recommendations for international students: Required—TOEFL. *Application deadline:* For fall admission, 3/1 for

Reading Education

Oregon State University (continued)
domestic students. Applications are processed on a rolling basis. Application fee: $50. *Financial support:* Research assistantships, teaching assistantships, career-related internships or fieldwork, Federal Work-Study, and institutionally sponsored loans available. Support available to part-time students. Financial award application deadline: 2/1. *Unit head:* Dr. Kenneth J. Winograd, Chair, 541-737-4661.

Penn State University Park, Graduate School, College of Education, Department of Curriculum and Instruction, State College, University Park, PA 16802-1503. Offers bilingual education (M Ed, MS, PhD); early childhood education (M Ed, MS, PhD); elementary education (M Ed, MS, PhD); instructional systems (M Ed, MS, PhD); language arts and reading (M Ed, MS, PhD); science education (M Ed, MS, PhD); social studies education (MS, PhD); supervisor and curriculum development (M Ed, MS, PhD). *Accreditation:* NCATE. *Unit head:* Dr. Murry R. Nelson, Head, 814-865-6321, Fax: 814-863-7602, E-mail: mrn2@psu.edu. *Application contact:* Judy Nastase, Graduate Staff Assistant, 814-865-2168, E-mail: jcn3@psu.edu.

Pittsburg State University, Graduate School, College of Education, Department of Curriculum and Instruction, Pittsburg, KS 66762. Offers classroom reading teacher (MS); early childhood education (MS); elementary education (MS); reading (MS); reading specialist (MS); secondary education (MS); teaching (MAT). *Accreditation:* NCATE. *Students:* 141. *Degree requirements:* For master's, thesis or alternative. *Entrance requirements:* For master's, GRE or MAT. Application fee: $35 ($60 for international students). *Expenses:* Tuition, state resident: full-time $2,144; part-time $181 per credit hour. Tuition, nonresident: full-time $5,273; part-time $442 per credit hour. Tuition and fees vary according to course load and campus/location. *Financial support:* In 2006–07, teaching assistantships (averaging $5,000 per year); career-related internships or fieldwork, Federal Work-Study, and unspecified assistantships also available. *Unit head:* Dr. V. June Taylor, Chairperson, 620-235-4508. *Application contact:* Jamie Vanderbeck, Assistant Director, 620-235-4223, Fax: 620-235-4219, E-mail: jvanderb@pittstate.edu.

Plymouth State University, College of Graduate Studies, Graduate Studies in Education, Program in Reading and Writing Specialist, Plymouth, NH 03264-1595. Offers M Ed. Part-time and evening/weekend programs available. *Students:* 1 (woman) full-time, 74 part-time (73 women). 14 applicants, 100% accepted, 14 enrolled. In 2006, 10 degrees awarded. *Degree requirements:* For master's, PRAXIS. *Entrance requirements:* For master's, GRE General Test or MAT, minimum GPA of 3.0. *Application deadline:* Applications are processed on a rolling basis. Application fee: $75. *Expenses:* Tuition, state resident: part-time $369 per credit. Tuition, nonresident: part-time $407 per credit. Tuition and fees vary according to course level. *Financial support:* Career-related internships or fieldwork, scholarships/grants, and unspecified assistantships available. Support available to part-time students. Financial award applicants required to submit FAFSA. *Unit head:* Dr. Dennise M. Maslakowski, Associate Vice President, 603-535-2286, Fax: 603-535-2572, E-mail: dmmaslakowski@plymouth.edu.

Portland State University, Graduate Studies, School of Education, Department of Curriculum and Instruction, Portland, OR 97207-0751. Offers early childhood education (MA, MS); education (M Ed, MA, MS); educational leadership: curriculum and instruction (Ed D); educational media/school librarianship (MA, MS); elementary education (M Ed, MAT, MST); reading (MA, MS); secondary education (M Ed, MAT, MST). *Accreditation:* NCATE. Part-time programs available. *Faculty:* 20 full-time (14 women), 18 part-time/adjunct (9 women). *Students:* 185 full-time (135 women), 209 part-time (160 women); includes 53 minority (7 African Americans, 4 American Indian/Alaska Native, 13 Asian Americans or Pacific Islanders, 29 Hispanic Americans), 13 international. Average age 32. 372 applicants, 87% accepted, 171 enrolled. In 2006, 352 master's, 4 doctorates awarded. *Degree requirements:* For master's, special project or thesis, written exam; for doctorate, thesis/dissertation. *Entrance requirements:* For master's, California Basic Educational Skills Test, minimum GPA of 3.0 in upper-division course work or 2.75 overall. Additional exam requirements/recommendations for international students: Required—TOEFL (minimum score 550 paper-based; 213 computer-based). *Application deadline:* For fall admission, 4/1 for domestic and international students; for winter admission, 9/1 for domestic and international students; for spring admission, 11/1 for domestic and international students. Applications are processed on a rolling basis. Application fee: $50. *Expenses:* Tuition, state resident: full-time $6,426; part-time $238 per credit. Tuition, nonresident: full-time $11,016; part-time $408 per credit. Tuition and fees vary according to course load. *Financial support:* In 2006–07, 5 research assistantships with full tuition reimbursements (averaging $5,508 per year) were awarded; teaching assistantships with full tuition reimbursements, career-related internships or fieldwork, Federal Work-Study, and institutionally sponsored loans also available. Support available to part-time students. Financial award application deadline: 3/1; financial award applicants required to submit FAFSA. *Faculty research:* Early literacy, characteristics of successful teachers of at-risk students, participation of women/minorities in technology courses, selection of cooperating teachers. Total annual research expenditures: $308,420. *Unit head:* Steven Lee, Head, 503-725-4689, Fax: 503-725-8475. *Application contact:* Majken Elek, Department Secretary, 503-725-4756, Fax: 503-725-8475, E-mail: majkene@pdx.edu.

Providence College, Graduate Studies, Department of Education, Program in Education Literacy, Providence, RI 02918. Offers M Ed. Part-time and evening/weekend programs available. *Faculty:* 6 full-time (5 women), 45 part-time/adjunct (25 women). *Students:* 24 full-time (18 women), 58 part-time (52 women); includes 1 minority (Hispanic American) Average age 31. 22 applicants, 55% accepted. In 2006, 36 degrees awarded. *Degree requirements:* For master's, comprehensive exam. *Entrance requirements:* For master's, GRE General Test. Additional exam requirements/recommendations for international students: Required—TOEFL (minimum score 550 paper-based; 213 computer-based). *Application deadline:* For fall admission, 8/1 for domestic students; for spring admission, 12/1 for domestic students. Applications are processed on a rolling basis. Application fee: $55. *Expenses:* Tuition: Full-time $6,573; part-time $939 per unit. *Financial support:* In 2006–07, 1 research assistantship with full tuition reimbursement (averaging $8,400 per year) was awarded; career-related internships or fieldwork, institutionally sponsored loans, and unspecified assistantships also available. Support available to part-time students. Financial award application deadline: 8/1; financial award applicants required to submit FAFSA. *Unit head:* E. Sharon Capobianco, Director, 401-865-1987, Fax: 401-865-1147, E-mail: escapobi@providence.edu.

Purdue University, Graduate School, School of Education, Department of Curriculum and Instruction, West Lafayette, IN 47907. Offers agricultural and extension education (PhD, Ed S); agriculture and extension education (MS, MS Ed); art education (PhD); consumer and family sciences and extension education (MS Ed, PhD, Ed S); curriculum studies (MS Ed, PhD, Ed S); educational technology (MS Ed, PhD, Ed S); elementary education (MS Ed); foreign language education (MS Ed, PhD, Ed S); industrial technology (PhD, Ed S); language arts (MS Ed, PhD, Ed S); literacy (MS Ed, PhD, Ed S); mathematics/science education (MS, MS Ed, PhD, Ed S); social studies (MS Ed, PhD); social studies education (Ed S); vocational/industrial education (MS Ed, PhD, Ed S); vocational/technical education (MS Ed, PhD, Ed S). *Accreditation:* NCATE. Part-time and evening/weekend programs available. *Faculty:* 26 full-time (13 women), 3 part-time/adjunct (all women). *Students:* 59 full-time (37 women), 112 part-time (70 women); includes 24 minority (13 African Americans, 3 American Indian/Alaska Native, 4 Asian Americans or Pacific Islanders, 4 Hispanic Americans), 38 international. Average age 35. 92 applicants, 68% accepted, 38 enrolled. In 2006, 52 master's, 23 doctorates awarded. *Degree requirements:* For master's, thesis optional; for doctorate, thesis/dissertation, oral and written exams; for Ed S, oral presentation, project. *Entrance requirements:* For master's, GRE General Test, minimum B average; for doctorate, GRE General Test; for Ed S, GRE, minimum B average. Additional exam requirements/recommendations for international students: Required—TOEFL. *Application deadline:* For fall admission, 1/15 priority date for domestic students, 1/15 for international students; for spring admission, 9/15 for domestic and international students. Applications are processed on a rolling basis. Application fee: $55. Electronic applications accepted. *Financial support:* In 2006–07, 3 fellowships with full tuition reimbursements (averaging $10,500 per year), 11 research assistantships with full tuition reimbursements (averaging $11,500 per year), 43 teaching assistantships with full tuition reimbursements (averaging $10,800 per year) were awarded; career-related internships or fieldwork and tuition waivers (full) also available. Support available to part-time students. Financial award application deadline: 3/1; financial award applicants required to submit FAFSA. *Faculty research:* Literacy acquisition and development, teacher beliefs and knowledge, recruitment and retention of underrepresented students, economic education, literacy discourse. *Unit head:* Dr. James D Lehman, Head, 765-494-7935, Fax: 765-496-1622. *Application contact:* Patricia Mason, Coordinator of Graduate Studies, 765-494-2345, Fax: 765-494-5832, E-mail: gradoffice@soe.purdue.edu.

Queens College of the City University of New York, Division of Graduate Studies, Division of Education, Department of Elementary and Early Childhood Education, Program in Literacy, Flushing, NY 11367-1597. Offers MS Ed. Part-time programs available. *Faculty:* 8 full-time (6 women). *Students:* 11 applicants, 100% accepted, 11 enrolled. In 2006, 44 degrees awarded. *Degree requirements:* For master's, research project. *Entrance requirements:* For master's, minimum GPA of 3.0. Additional exam requirements/recommendations for international students: Required—TOEFL. *Application deadline:* For fall admission, 4/1 for domestic students; for spring admission, 11/1 for domestic students. Applications are processed on a rolling basis. Application fee: $125. *Financial support:* Career-related internships or fieldwork, Federal Work-Study, institutionally sponsored loans, and tuition waivers (partial) available. Support available to part-time students. Financial award application deadline: 4/1; financial award applicants required to submit FAFSA. *Unit head:* Dr. Evelyn O'Connor, Coordinator, 718-997-5387. *Application contact:* Mario Caruso, Director of Graduate Admissions, 718-997-5200, Fax: 718-997-5193, E-mail: graduate_admissions@qc.edu.

Radford University, Graduate College, College of Education and Human Development, School of Teacher and Educational Leadership, Program in Reading, Radford, VA 24142. Offers MS. *Accreditation:* NCATE. Part-time and evening/weekend programs available. Postbaccalaureate distance learning degree programs offered (minimal on-campus study). *Faculty:* 3 full-time (2 women), 1 (woman) part-time/adjunct. *Students:* 3 full-time (all women), 46 part-time (all women). Average age 33. 1 applicant, 100% accepted, 1 enrolled. In 2006, 4 degrees awarded. *Degree requirements:* For master's, comprehensive exam. *Entrance requirements:* Additional exam requirements/recommendations for international students: Required—TOEFL. *Application deadline:* For fall admission, 3/1 priority date for domestic students, 4/1 for international students; for spring admission, 10/1 for domestic students, 8/1 for international students. Applications are processed on a rolling basis. Application fee: $40. Electronic applications accepted. *Expenses:* Tuition, state resident: full-time $4,680; part-time $260 per credit hour. Tuition, nonresident: full-time $8,604; part-time $478 per credit hour. *Financial support:* In 2006–07, research assistantships with partial tuition reimbursements (averaging $8,000 per year), teaching assistantships with partial tuition reimbursements (averaging $8,700 per year) were awarded; career-related internships or fieldwork, Federal Work-Study, institutionally sponsored loans, scholarships/grants, and unspecified assistantships also available. Financial award application deadline: 3/1; financial award applicants required to submit FAFSA. *Unit head:* Dr. Donald B. Langrehr, Coordinator, 540-831-6580, Fax: 540-831-5059, E-mail: dlangreh@radford.edu.

Regis University, School for Professional Studies, Program in Teacher Education, Denver, CO 80221-1099. Offers adult learning, training, and development (M Ed); curriculum, instruction, and assessment (M Ed); early childhood (M Ed); educational technology (Certificate); elementary (M Ed); ESL (M Ed); fine arts (M Ed), including arts, music; instructional technology (M Ed); professional leadership (M Ed); reading (M Ed); secondary (M Ed); self-designed (M Ed); space studies (M Ed); special education (M Ed); teacher licensure (M Ed). Program also offered in Henderson and Las Vegas (Summerlin), NV. Postbaccalaureate distance learning degree programs offered. *Unit head:* Dr. Suzie Perry, Dean, 303-458-4302. *Application contact:* Partick Lowenthal, Assistant Director, 303-458-4300 Ext. 4314, E-mail: masters@regis.edu.

Rhode Island College, School of Graduate Studies, Feinstein School of Education and Human Development, Department of Elementary Education, Providence, RI 02908-1991. Offers early childhood education (M Ed); elementary education (M Ed, MAT); reading (M Ed). *Accreditation:* NCATE. Part-time and evening/weekend programs available. *Faculty:* 17 full-time (10 women), 5 part-time/adjunct (all women). *Students:* 33 full-time (28 women), 75 part-time (69 women); includes 4 minority (all Hispanic Americans) Average age 33. In 2006, 56 degrees awarded. *Entrance requirements:* For master's, GRE General Test or MAT, Praxis II (elementary content knowledge), 3 letters of recommendation, interview. *Application deadline:* For fall admission, 3/15 for domestic students; for spring admission, 11/1 for domestic students. Applications are processed on a rolling basis. Application fee: $50. *Expenses:* Tuition, state resident: part-time $244 per credit. Tuition, nonresident: part-time $512 per credit. Required fees: $12 per credit. $66 per term. Tuition and fees vary according to degree level, program and reciprocity agreements. *Financial support:* Teaching assistantships with full tuition reimbursements, Federal Work-Study, scholarships/grants, and health care benefits available. Support available to part-time students. Financial award application deadline: 5/15; financial award applicants required to submit FAFSA. *Unit head:* Dr. Lisa Owen, Chair, 401-456-8016, E-mail: lowen@ric.edu.

Rider University, Department of Graduate Education, Leadership and Counseling, Lawrenceville, NJ 08648-3001. Offers counseling services (MA, Ed S); curriculum, instruction and supervision (MA); director of school counseling services (Certificate); educational administration (MA); organizational leadership (MA); principal (Certificate); reading/language arts (MA, Certificate), including reading specialist (Certificate), reading/language arts (MA); school business administrator (Certificate); school counseling services (Certificate); school psychology (Ed S); special education (MA); supervisor (Certificate); teacher certification (Certificate), including business education, elementary education, English as a second language, English education, mathematics education, preschool to grade 3, science education, social studies education, world languages; teaching (MA). *Accreditation:* NCATE. Part-time and evening/weekend programs available. *Faculty:* 24 full-time (12 women), 30 part-time/adjunct (15 women). *Students:* 90 full-time (75 women), 457 part-time (369 women); includes 73 minority (50 African Americans, 2 American Indian/Alaska Native, 6 Asian Americans or Pacific Islanders, 15 Hispanic Americans), 1 international. Average age 32. 314 applicants, 61% accepted, 138 enrolled. In 2006, 116 master's, 19 other advanced degrees awarded. *Degree requirements:* For master's, thesis or alternative, internship, portfolios, comprehensive exam (for some programs); for other advanced degree, internship, professional portfolio. *Entrance requirements:* For master's, GRE (counseling, school psychology), MAT, interview, resumé, letters of recommendation; for other advanced degree, PRAXIS. Additional exam requirements/recommendations for international students: Required—TOEFL (minimum score 550 paper-based; 213 computer-based). *Application deadline:* For fall admission, 5/1 priority date for domestic students, 6/1 priority date for international students; for spring admission, 11/1 priority date for domestic and international students. Applications are processed on a rolling basis. Application fee: $50. Electronic applications accepted. *Expenses:* Tuition: Part-time $525 per credit. Required fees: $35 per course. $30 per semester. *Financial support:* In 2006–07, 271 students received support. Career-related internships or fieldwork, Federal Work-Study, institutionally sponsored loans, and unspecified assistantships available. Support available to part-time students. Financial award applicants required to submit FAFSA. *Faculty research:* Gifted students, self-esteem, hope and mental health, conflicts in group work, cultural diversity and counseling assessment of special needs in children. *Unit head:* Dr. Dennis C. Buss, Chair, 609-895-5353, Fax: 609-896-5362, E-mail: dbuss@rider.edu. *Application contact:* Jamie L Mitchell, Director of Graduate Admissions, 609-896-5036, Fax: 609-895-5680, E-mail: jmitchell@rider.edu.

See Close-Up on page 913.

Rivier College, School of Graduate Studies, Department of Education, Nashua, NH 03060-5086. Offers curriculum and instruction (M Ed); early childhood education (M Ed); educational administration (M Ed); educational studies (M Ed); elementary education (M Ed); elementary education and general special education (M Ed); emotional and behavioral disorders (M Ed); general social education (M Ed); leadership and learning (CAGS); learning disabilities (M Ed); learning disabilities and reading (M Ed); mental health counseling (MA); reading (M Ed); school counseling (M Ed). Part-time and evening/weekend programs available. *Faculty:* 11 full-time (7 women), 40 part-time/adjunct (29 women). *Students:* 41 full-time (33 women), 221 part-time (192 women); includes 4 minority (2 African Americans, 2 Hispanic Americans). Average age 37. In 2006, 134 degrees awarded. *Degree requirements:* For master's, internships. *Entrance requirements:* For master's, GRE General Test or MAT. *Application deadline:* Applications are processed on a rolling basis. Application fee: $25. *Financial support:* Available to part-time students. Application deadline: 2/1; *Unit head:* Dr. Charles L. Mitsakos, Chairman, 603-888-1311 Ext. 8582. *Application contact:* Diane Monahan, Director of Graduate Admissions, 603-897-8129, Fax: 603-897-8810, E-mail: gradadm@rivier.edu.

Roberts Wesleyan College, Division of Teacher Education, Rochester, NY 14624-1997. Offers adolescence education (M Ed); childhood and special education (M Ed); literacy education (M Ed); urban education (M Ed). Part-time and evening/weekend programs available. *Faculty:* 17 part-time/adjunct (7 women). *Students:* 1 (woman) full-time, 66 part-time (47 women). Average age 33. 52 applicants, 63% accepted. In 2006, 20 degrees awarded. *Degree requirements:* For master's, thesis. *Application deadline:* For fall admission, 8/1 priority date for domestic students; for spring admission, 12/1 for domestic students. Applications are processed on a rolling basis. Application fee: $35. *Financial support:* In 2006–07, 7 students received support. Career-related internships or fieldwork available. Financial award application deadline: 9/1; financial award applicants required to submit FAFSA. *Unit head:* Dr. Richard Mace, Chair, 585-594-6934. *Application contact:* Paula Finch, Graduate Admissions Coordinator, 585-594-6683, E-mail: finch_paula@roberts.edu.

Rockford College, Graduate Studies, Department of Education, Program in Reading, Rockford, IL 61108-2393. Offers MAT. Part-time and evening/weekend programs available. *Degree requirements:* For master's, thesis optional. *Entrance requirements:* For master's, GRE General Test.

Roger Williams University, School of Education, Program in Literacy Education, Bristol, RI 02809. Offers literacy (MA). Part-time programs available. *Faculty:* 3 full-time (all women), 1 (woman) part-time/adjunct. *Students:* Average age 30. 10 applicants, 100% accepted, 9 enrolled. In 2006, 7 degrees awarded. *Degree requirements:* For master's, state-mandated exams. *Entrance requirements:* For master's, GRE or MAT. *Application deadline:* Applications are processed on a rolling basis. Application fee: $50. Electronic applications accepted. *Expenses:* Tuition: Part-time $362 per credit. Tuition and fees vary according to program. *Financial support:* Career-related internships or fieldwork and health care benefits available. Financial award applicants required to submit FAFSA. *Faculty research:* Assessment of reading difficulties, action research in reading, comprehension and writing, student mediation techniques. *Application contact:* Suzanne Faubl, Director of Graduate Admissions, 401-254-3809, Fax: 401-254-3557, E-mail: sfaubl@rwu.edu.

Roosevelt University, Graduate Division, College of Education, Program in Language and Literacy, Chicago, IL 60605-1394. Offers reading teacher education (MA). *Students:* 1 (woman) full-time, 53 part-time (52 women); includes 11 minority (8 African Americans, 1 American Indian/Alaska Native, 1 Asian American or Pacific Islander, 1 Hispanic American). Average age 32. 14 applicants, 64% accepted, 8 enrolled. In 2006, 40 degrees awarded. *Unit head:* Dr. Sharon Grant, Chair, 847-619-8831.

Rowan University, Graduate School, College of Education, Department of Reading Education, Glassboro, NJ 08028-1701. Offers MA. *Accreditation:* NCATE. Part-time and evening/weekend programs available. *Students:* 1 (woman) full-time, 50 part-time (all women). Average age 34. 7 applicants, 57% accepted, 4 enrolled. In 2006, 18 degrees awarded. *Degree requirements:* For master's, thesis, comprehensive exam. *Entrance requirements:* For master's, GRE General Test, GRE Subject Test, interview, minimum GPA of 2.8. Additional exam requirements/recommendations for international students: Required—TOEFL. *Application deadline:* Applications are processed on a rolling basis. Application fee: $50. Electronic applications accepted. *Expenses:* Tuition, state resident: full-time $9,882; part-time $549 per credit. Tuition, nonresident: full-time $9,882; part-time $549 per credit. Tuition and fees vary according to degree level. *Financial support:* Career-related internships or fieldwork, Federal Work-Study, and unspecified assistantships available. Support available to part-time students. *Unit head:* Dr. Stacey Leftwich, Adviser, 856-256-3821.

Rutgers, The State University of New Jersey, New Brunswick, Graduate School of Education, Department of Learning and Teaching, Program in Literacy Education, New Brunswick, NJ 08901-1281. Offers Ed M, Ed D. Part-time programs available. *Faculty:* 2 full-time (both women). *Students:* 24 applicants, 54% accepted, 11 enrolled. In 2006, 6 master's, 1 doctorate awarded. Terminal master's awarded for partial completion of doctoral program. *Degree requirements:* For master's, comprehensive exam; for doctorate, thesis/dissertation, qualifying exam. *Entrance requirements:* For master's, GRE General Test, minimum undergraduate GPA of 3.0; for doctorate, GRE General Test, 2 years of teaching experience, certification, minimum graduate GPA of 3.5. Additional exam requirements/recommendations for international students: Required—TOEFL. *Application deadline:* For fall admission, 2/1 for domestic and international students; for spring admission, 10/1 for domestic and international students. Application fee: $60. Electronic applications accepted. *Financial support:* Teaching assistantships available. Financial award application deadline: 3/15; financial award applicants required to submit FAFSA. *Faculty research:* Early childhood literacy development, discourse analysis-adult literacy. *Unit head:* Dr. Lesley Morrow, Coordinator, 732-932-7496 Ext. 8119, E-mail: lmorro@rci.rutgers.edu.

Rutgers, The State University of New Jersey, New Brunswick, Graduate School of Education, Department of Learning and Teaching, Program in Reading Education, New Brunswick, NJ 08901-1281. Offers Ed M. Part-time programs available. *Faculty:* 4 full-time (all women). *Students:* 1 (woman) full-time, 23 part-time (22 women). 19 applicants, 79% accepted, 12 enrolled. In 2006, 12 degrees awarded. *Degree requirements:* For master's, comprehensive exam or paper. *Entrance requirements:* For master's, GRE General Test. *Application deadline:* For fall admission, 2/1 for domestic and international students. Application fee: $60. Electronic applications accepted. *Financial support:* Application deadline: 3/15; *Unit head:* Dr. Dorothy Strickland, Coordinator, 732-932-7496 Ext. 8353, E-mail: strickla@rci.rutgers.edu.

Rutgers, The State University of New Jersey, New Brunswick, Graduate School of Education, Doctoral Program in Education, New Brunswick, NJ 08901-1281. Offers educational policy (PhD); educational psychology (PhD); literacy education (PhD); mathematics education (PhD). Part-time programs available. *Faculty:* 63 full-time (30 women). *Students:* 29 full-time (21 women), 45 part-time (34 women); includes 7 minority (4 African Americans, 3 Asian Americans or Pacific Islanders), 15 international. 85 applicants, 33% accepted, 13 enrolled. In 2006, 8 degrees awarded. *Degree requirements:* For doctorate, thesis/dissertation, qualifying exam. *Entrance requirements:* For doctorate, GRE General Test, GRE Subject Test (for mathematics education). Additional exam requirements/recommendations for international students: Required—TOEFL (minimum score 575 paper-based; 233 computer-based). *Application deadline:* For fall admission, 2/1 for domestic and international students. Application fee: $60. Electronic applications accepted. *Financial support:* In 2006–07, research assistantships with full tuition reimbursements (averaging $15,730 per year). Financial award application deadline: 3/15. *Faculty research:* Literacy education, math education, educational psychology, educational policy. *Unit head:* Prof. Clark Chinn, Director, 732-932-7496 Ext. 8319, Fax: 732-932-6829, E-mail: cchinn@rci.rutgers.edu. *Application contact:* Kristine Spaventa, Administrative Assistant, 732-932-7496 Ext. 8104, Fax: 732-932-8206, E-mail: sparenta@rci.rutgers.edu.

Sacred Heart University, Graduate Studies, College of Education and Health Professions, Department of Education, Fairfield, CT 06825-1000. Offers administration (CAS); educational

technology (MAT); elementary education (MAT); reading (CAS); secondary education (MAT); teaching (CAS). Part-time and evening/weekend programs available. Postbaccalaureate distance learning degree programs offered (minimal on-campus study). *Faculty:* 23 full-time (10 women). *Students:* 360 full-time (285 women), 710 part-time (520 women); includes 39 minority (15 African Americans, 4 American Indian/Alaska Native, 5 Asian Americans or Pacific Islanders, 15 Hispanic Americans), 4 international. Average age 34. 335 applicants, 87% accepted, 270 enrolled. In 2006, 312 master's, 59 other advanced degrees awarded. *Degree requirements:* For master's, thesis or alternative. *Entrance requirements:* For master's, PRAXIS (teacher certification/MAT); for CAS, PRAXIS I. Additional exam requirements/recommendations for international students: Required—TOEFL (minimum score 550 paper-based; 213 computer-based). *Application deadline:* Applications are processed on a rolling basis. Application fee: $50 ($100 for international students). Electronic applications accepted. *Expenses:* Contact institution. Full-time tuition and fees vary according to degree level and program. *Financial support:* Teaching assistantships with partial tuition reimbursements, career-related internships or fieldwork, institutionally sponsored loans, traineeships, tuition waivers (partial), and unspecified assistantships available. Support available to part-time students. Financial award applicants required to submit FAFSA. *Faculty research:* Reading education, learning theory, teacher preparation, education of underachievers. *Unit head:* Dr. Edward Malin, Director, 203-371-7800, Fax: 203-365-7513. *Application contact:* Alexis Haakonsen, Dean of Graduate Admissions, 203-365-7619, Fax: 203-365-4732, E-mail: haakonsena@sacredheart.edu.

Sage Graduate School, Graduate School, Division of Education, Program in Childhood Education/Literacy, Troy, NY 12180-4115. Offers MS. Part-time and evening/weekend programs available. *Faculty:* 11 full-time (8 women), 20 part-time/adjunct (15 women). *Students:* 7 full-time (all women), 12 part-time (all women). Average age 27. 15 applicants, 73% accepted, 6 enrolled. In 2006, 3 degrees awarded. *Degree requirements:* For master's, thesis optional. *Entrance requirements:* Additional exam requirements/recommendations for international students: Required—TOEFL (minimum score 550 paper-based; 213 computer-based). *Application deadline:* Applications are processed on a rolling basis. Application fee: $40. *Expenses:* Tuition; Full-time $9,270; part-time $515 per credit hour. *Financial support:* Career-related internships or fieldwork, scholarships/grants, and unspecified assistantships available. Support available to part-time students. Financial award application deadline: 3/1. *Application contact:* Shannon K. Easton, Director of Graduate and Adult Admission, 518-244-2443, Fax: 518-244-6880, E-mail: sgsadm@sage.edu.

Sage Graduate School, Graduate School, Division of Education, Program in Literacy, Troy, NY 12180-4115. Offers MS Ed. *Accreditation:* NCATE. Part-time and evening/weekend programs available. *Faculty:* 11 full-time (8 women), 20 part-time/adjunct (15 women). *Students:* 14 full-time (all women), 39 part-time (38 women); includes 1 minority (Hispanic American) Average age 27. 26 applicants, 85% accepted, 15 enrolled. In 2006, 33 degrees awarded. *Entrance requirements:* For master's, minimum GPA of 2.75. Additional exam requirements/recommendations for international students: Required—TOEFL (minimum score 550 paper-based; 213 computer-based). *Application deadline:* Applications are processed on a rolling basis. Application fee: $40. *Expenses:* Tuition: Full-time $9,270; part-time $515 per credit hour. *Financial support:* Career-related internships or fieldwork, scholarships/grants, and unspecified assistantships available. Support available to part-time students. Financial award application deadline: 3/1; financial award applicants required to submit FAFSA. *Faculty research:* Literacy development in at-risk children. *Unit head:* Ellen Adams, Director, 518-244-2054, Fax: 518-244-2334, E-mail: adamse@sage.edu. *Application contact:* Shannon K. Easton, Director of Graduate and Adult Admission, 518-244-2443, Fax: 518-244-6880, E-mail: sgsadm@sage.edu.

Sage Graduate School, Graduate School, Division of Education, Program in Literacy/Childhood Special Education, Troy, NY 12180-4115. Offers MS Ed. *Accreditation:* NCATE.Part-time and evening/weekend programs available. *Faculty:* 11 full-time (8 women), 20 part-time/adjunct (15 women). *Students:* 8 full-time (all women), 12 part-time (all women); includes 2 minority (both African Americans) Average age 27. 8 applicants, 63% accepted, 3 enrolled. In 2006, 6 degrees awarded. *Entrance requirements:* For master's, minimum GPA of 2.75. Additional exam requirements/recommendations for international students: Required—TOEFL (minimum score 550 paper-based; 213 computer-based). *Application deadline:* Applications are processed on a rolling basis. Application fee: $40. *Expenses:* Tuition: Full-time $9,270; part-time $515 per credit hour. *Financial support:* Career-related internships or fieldwork, scholarships/grants, and unspecified assistantships available. Support available to part-time students. Financial award application deadline: 3/1; financial award applicants required to submit FAFSA. *Faculty research:* Commonalities in the roles of reading specialists and resource/consultant teachers. *Application contact:* Shannon K. Easton, Director of Graduate and Adult Admission, 518-244-2443, Fax: 518-244-6880, E-mail: sgsadm@sage.edu.

Saginaw Valley State University, College of Education, Program in Reading Education, University Center, MI 48710. Offers MAT. *Accreditation:* NCATE. Part-time and evening/weekend programs available. *Students:* 2 full-time (both women), 117 part-time (112 women); includes 4 minority (3 African Americans, 1 Hispanic American). Average age 33. 27 applicants, 100% accepted, 23 enrolled. In 2006, 28 degrees awarded. *Degree requirements:* For master's, capstone course, practicum. *Entrance requirements:* For master's, minimum GPA of 3.0, teaching certificate. *Application deadline:* Applications are processed on a rolling basis. Application fee: $25. Electronic applications accepted. *Expenses:* Tuition, state resident: full-time $7,225; part-time $301 per credit hour. Tuition, nonresident: full-time $13,888; part-time $579 per credit hour. Required fees: $330; $14 per credit hour. Tuition and fees vary according to course load. *Financial support:* Applicants required to submit FAFSA. *Faculty research:* Preservice, middle school, secondary teacher, literacy education. *Application contact:* Jeanne Chipman, Certification Officer, 989-964-4083, Fax: 989-964-4385, E-mail: jdc@svsu.edu.

St. Bonaventure University, School of Graduate Studies, School of Education, Program in Literacy, St. Bonaventure, NY 14778-2284. Offers MS Ed. *Accreditation:* NCATE. Part-time and evening/weekend programs available. *Degree requirements:* For master's, thesis optional. *Entrance requirements:* Additional exam requirements/recommendations for international students: Required—TOEFL. Electronic applications accepted. *Faculty research:* Children's literary tastes, reading diagnosis.

Saint Francis University, Department of Education and Educational Leadership. Loretto, PA 15940-0600. Offers education (M Ed); educational leadership (MEDL); reading (M Ed). Part-time and evening/weekend programs available. *Faculty:* 24 part-time/adjunct (8 women). *Students:* Average age 30. 19 applicants, 100% accepted, 19 enrolled. In 2006, 35 degrees awarded. *Degree requirements:* For master's, thesis optional. *Entrance requirements:* For master's, GRE or MAT if undergraduate GPA is less than 2.8, minimum undergraduate QPA of 2.5. *Application deadline:* Applications are processed on a rolling basis. Application fee: $30. *Expenses:* Contact institution. Tuition and fees vary according to program. *Financial support:* Research assistantships with full and partial tuition reimbursements, teaching assistantships with full and partial tuition reimbursements, career-related internships or fieldwork and unspecified assistantships available. *Unit head:* Dr. Janette D. Kelly, Director, Graduate Education, 814-472-3058, Fax: 814-472-3864, E-mail: jkelly@francis.edu.

St. John Fisher College, Office of the Provost, Ralph C. Wilson Jr. School of Education, Literacy Education Program, Rochester, NY 14618-3597. Offers literacy birth to grade 6 (MS); literacy grades 5 to 12 (MS). Part-time and evening/weekend programs available. *Faculty:* 7 full-time (4 women), 8 part-time/adjunct (all women). *Students:* 24 full-time (21 women), 111 part-time (101 women); includes 3 African Americans, 1 American Indian/Alaska Native. Average age 28. 46 applicants, 91% accepted, 28 enrolled. In 2006, 63 degrees awarded. *Degree requirements:* For master's, research project. *Entrance requirements:* For master's, minimum GPA of 3.0, teacher certification, letters of reference. Additional exam requirements/recommendations for international students: Required—TOEFL (minimum score 575 paper-based; 233 computer-based; 80 iBT). *Application deadline:* For fall admission, 4/1 for domestic students; for spring admission, 10/30 for domestic students. Applications are processed on a

Reading Education

St. John Fisher College (continued)
rolling basis. Application fee: $30. *Expenses:* Tuition: Part-time $615 per credit. Tuition and fees vary according to program. *Financial support:* Federal Work-Study and scholarships/grants available. Financial award application deadline: 2/15; financial award applicants required to submit FAFSA. *Faculty research:* Adolescent use of new literacies (instant messaging), referral practices, at risk early literacy, new literacies (Internet, technology), equity in education. *Unit head:* Dr. Kathleen Broikou, Director, 585-385-8112, E-mail: broikou@sjfc.edu. *Application contact:* Shannon Cleverley, Director of Graduate Admissions, 585-385-8161, Fax: 585-385-8344, E-mail: scleverley@sjfc.edu.

St. John's University, The School of Education, Division of Human Services and Counseling, Literacy Program, Queens, NY 11439. Offers MS Ed, PD. Part-time and evening/weekend programs available. *Students:* 7 full-time (all women), 95 part-time (89 women); includes 14 minority (5 African Americans, 1 Asian American or Pacific Islander, 8 Hispanic Americans). Average age 25. 60 applicants, 95% accepted, 41 enrolled. In 2006, 63 master's, 1 PD awarded. *Entrance requirements:* For master's, minimum GPA of 3.0, New York teaching certificate; for PD, minimum GPA of 3.0, MS Ed, New York teaching certificate. Additional exam requirements/recommendations for international students: Required—TOEFL (minimum score 500 paper-based). *Application deadline:* For fall admission, 4/1 for domestic students, 5/1 priority date for international students; for spring admission, 11/1 for domestic students, 11/1 priority date for international students. Applications are processed on a rolling basis. Application fee: $40. Electronic applications accepted. *Expenses:* Tuition: Full-time $18,480; part-time $770 per credit. Required fees: $125 per semester. Tuition and fees vary according to program. *Financial support:* Research assistantships, career-related internships or fieldwork and scholarships/grants available. Support available to part-time students. Financial award application deadline: 3/1; financial award applicants required to submit FAFSA. *Faculty research:* Visual fluency and reading proficiency, semantic mapping and literacy proficiency, beginning literacy, literature approaches to literacy. *Application contact:* Kelly Ronayne, Assistant Dean, 718-990-2303, Fax: 718-990-6069, E-mail: graded@stjohns.edu.

St. Joseph's College, New York, Graduate Programs, Program in Education, Field of Literacy and Cognition, Brooklyn, NY 11205-3688. Offers MA.

See Close-Up on page 915.

St. Joseph's College, Suffolk Campus, Program in Literacy and Cognition, Patchogue, NY 11772-2399. Offers MA.

Saint Joseph's University, College of Arts and Sciences, Department of Education, Philadelphia, PA 19131-1395. Offers educational leadership (Ed D); elementary education (MS); instructional technology (MS); professional education (MS); reading (MS); secondary education (MS); special education (MS); training and organizational development (MS, Certificate). Part-time and evening/weekend programs available. *Faculty:* 18 full-time (9 women), 67 part-time/adjunct (34 women). *Students:* 77 full-time (63 women), 551 part-time (417 women); includes 115 minority (94 African Americans, 2 American Indian/Alaska Native, 8 Asian Americans or Pacific Islanders, 11 Hispanic Americans), 12 international. In 2006, 286 master's, 5 doctorates awarded. *Entrance requirements:* For master's, 2 letters of recommendation, minimum GPA of 3.0; for doctorate, GRE/MAT, 2 letters of recommendation, resumé. Additional exam requirements/recommendations for international students: Required—TOEFL. *Application deadline:* For fall admission, 7/15 for domestic students. Application fee: $35. *Expenses:* Contact institution. *Financial support:* Fellowships, research assistantships, career-related internships or fieldwork and Federal Work-Study available. Support available to part-time students. *Unit head:* Dr. Encarnacion Rodriguez, Director of Graduate Education, 610-660-3348.

Saint Leo University, Graduate Studies in Education, Saint Leo, FL 33574-6665. Offers education (MAT); educational leadership (M Ed); exceptional student education (M Ed); instructional leadership (M Ed); reading (M Ed). Part-time and evening/weekend programs available. Postbaccalaureate distance learning degree programs offered (minimal on-campus study). *Faculty:* 8 full-time (5 women), 10 part-time/adjunct (all women). *Students:* 96 full-time (77 women), 169 part-time (143 women); includes 22 minority (16 African Americans, 6 Hispanic Americans), 2 international. Average age 35. 365 applicants, 54% accepted, 116 enrolled. In 2006, 39 degrees awarded. *Degree requirements:* For master's, comprehensive exam or passing FELE scores. *Entrance requirements:* For master's, GRE General Test or MAT, 2 letters of recommendation, minimum undergraduate GPA of 3.0 or GRE or MAT, professional teaching certificate, resumé. Additional exam requirements/recommendations for international students: Required—TOEFL (minimum score 550 paper-based; 213 computer-based). *Application deadline:* For fall admission, 7/1 priority date for domestic students; for spring admission, 11/12 priority date for domestic students. Applications are processed on a rolling basis. Application fee: $45. Electronic applications accepted. *Financial support:* In 2006–07, 242 students received support. Career-related internships or fieldwork, Federal Work-Study, and scholarships/grants available. Support available to part-time students. Financial award application deadline: 3/1; financial award applicants required to submit FAFSA. *Faculty research:* The role of the school leader in (1) data analysis of student achievement (2) teacher recruitment (3) teacher effectiveness. *Unit head:* Dr. John Smith, Director, 352-588-8309, Fax: 352-588-8861, E-mail: med@saintleo.edu. *Application contact:* Scott Cathcart, Vice President of Enrollment, 800-707-8846, Fax: 352-588-7873, E-mail: grad.admission@saintleo.edu.

Saint Martin's University, Graduate Programs, Department of Education, Lacey, WA 98503-1297. Offers administration (M Ed); English as a second language (M Ed); guidance and counseling (M Ed); reading (M Ed); special education (M Ed); teaching (MIT); technology in education (M Ed). Part-time and evening/weekend programs available. *Degree requirements:* For master's, thesis or alternative, project or comprehensives, comprehensive exam (for some programs). *Entrance requirements:* For master's, GRE General Test or MAT, resumé. Additional exam requirements/recommendations for international students: Required—TOEFL (minimum score 560 paper-based). *Faculty research:* Reader's theatre and reader/writer workshops, curriculum and assessment integration, gender and equity, classroom evaluations, organizational leadership.

Saint Mary's College of California, School of Education, Program in Reading Leadership, Moraga, CA 94575. Offers MA. Part-time and evening/weekend programs available. *Faculty:* 2 full-time (both women), 1 (woman) part-time/adjunct. *Students:* Average age 38. 11 applicants, 64% accepted, 7 enrolled. In 2006, 2 degrees awarded. *Median time to degree:* Master's–2 years full-time. *Degree requirements:* For master's, thesis or alternative. *Entrance requirements:* For master's, interview, minimum GPA of 3.0. *Application deadline:* Applications are processed on a rolling basis. Application fee: $50. *Financial support:* Career-related internships or fieldwork available. Support available to part-time students. Financial award application deadline: 2/15. *Unit head:* Dr. Mary Kay Moskal, Director, 925-631-4726, Fax: 925-376-8379, E-mail: mmoskal@stmarys-ca.edu.

Saint Mary's University of Minnesota, School of Graduate and Professional Programs, Program in Literacy Education, Winona, MN 55987-1399. Offers K-12 reading teacher (Certificate); literacy education (MA). *Unit head:* Dr. Jane Anderson, Director, 507-457-6621, E-mail: janders1@smumn.edu.

St. Mary's University of San Antonio, Graduate School, Department of Teacher Education, Program in Reading, San Antonio, TX 78228-8507. Offers MA. Part-time programs available. Postbaccalaureate distance learning degree programs offered (no on-campus study). *Faculty:* 1 (woman) full-time. *Students:* 6 full-time (5 women), 26 part-time (22 women); includes 10 minority (all Hispanic Americans) Average age 34. In 2006, 11 degrees awarded. *Degree requirements:* For master's, comprehensive exam, registration. *Entrance requirements:* For master's, GRE. *Application deadline:* Applications are processed on a rolling basis. Application fee: $30. Electronic applications accepted. *Expenses:* Tuition: Full-time $10,890; part-time $605 per hour. Required fees: $500. Tuition and fees vary according to degree level. *Financial support:* Career-related internships or fieldwork, Federal Work-Study, institutionally sponsored loans, scholarships/grants, health care benefits, and unspecified assistantships available. Financial award application deadline: 3/31; financial award applicants required to submit FAFSA. *Unit head:* Dr. Neva A. Davenport, Director, 210-436-3121, Fax: 210-431-2246, E-mail: edneva@stmarytx.edu.

Saint Michael's College, Graduate Programs, Program in Education, Colchester, VT 05439. Offers administration (M Ed, CAGS); arts in education (CAGS); curriculum and instruction (M Ed, CAGS); information technology (CAGS); reading (M Ed); special education (M Ed, CAGS); technology (M Ed). Part-time and evening/weekend programs available. *Faculty:* 5 full-time (3 women), 35 part-time/adjunct (29 women). *Students:* 26 full-time (18 women), 114 part-time (86 women), 2 international. Average age 34. 48 applicants, 81% accepted, 36 enrolled. In 2006, 46 degrees awarded. *Degree requirements:* For master's, thesis. *Entrance requirements:* For master's, minimum GPA of 3.0. *Application deadline:* Applications are processed on a rolling basis. Application fee: $35. Electronic applications accepted. *Financial support:* Fellowships, scholarships/grants available. Support available to part-time students. Financial award applicants required to submit FAFSA. *Faculty research:* Integrative curriculum, moral and spiritual dimensions of education, learning styles, multiple intelligences, integrating technology into the curriculum. *Unit head:* Dr. Anne P. Judson, Director, 802-654-2649, Fax: 802-654-2664, E-mail: ajudson@smcvt.edu.

Saint Peter's College, Graduate Programs in Education, Reading Specialist Program, Jersey City, NJ 07306-5997. Offers MA. Part-time and evening/weekend programs available. *Degree requirements:* For master's, departmental qualifying exam. *Entrance requirements:* For master's, GRE or MAT.

St. Thomas Aquinas College, Division of Teacher Education, Sparkill, NY 10976. Offers adolescence education (MST); childhood and special education (MST); childhood education (MST); reading (MS Ed, PMC); special education (MS Ed, PMC); teaching (MS Ed), including elementary education, middle school education, secondary education. *Accreditation:* NCATE. Part-time and evening/weekend programs available. *Degree requirements:* For master's, comprehensive professional portfolio; for PMC, action research project. *Entrance requirements:* For master's, New York State Qualifying Exam, GRE General Test or minimum GPA of 3.0, teaching certificate; for PMC, GRE General Test or minimum GPA of 3.0. Electronic applications accepted. *Faculty research:* Computer applications in education, adolescent special education students, literacy development, inclusive practices for special education students.

See Close-Up on page 917.

St. Thomas University, School of Graduate Studies, Department of Education, Miami Gardens, FL 33054-6459. Offers educational administration (MS, Certificate); educational leadership (Ed D); elementary education (MS); reading (MS); special education (MS). Part-time and evening/weekend programs available. *Degree requirements:* For master's, comprehensive exam; for doctorate, thesis/dissertation, comprehensive exam. *Entrance requirements:* For master's, interview, minimum GPA of 3.0 or GRE; for doctorate, GRE or MAT. Additional exam requirements/recommendations for international students: Required—TOEFL. Electronic applications accepted.

Saint Xavier University, Graduate Studies, School of Education, Chicago, IL 60655-3105. Offers counseling (MA); counselor education (MA); curriculum and instruction (MA); early childhood education (MA); education (CAS); educational administration (MA); elementary education (MA); field-based education (MA); general educational studies (MA); individualized program (MA); learning disabilities (MA); reading (MA); secondary education (MA). *Accreditation:* NCATE. Part-time and evening/weekend programs available. *Faculty:* 92. *Students:* 45 full-time (35 women), 1,529 part-time (1,309 women). In 2006, 474 degrees awarded. *Degree requirements:* For master's, thesis or project. *Entrance requirements:* For master's, minimum GPA of 3.0. *Application deadline:* For fall admission, 8/15 priority date for domestic students. Applications are processed on a rolling basis. Application fee: $35. *Expenses:* Contact institution. *Financial support:* Career-related internships or fieldwork available. Support available to part-time students. Financial award applicants required to submit FAFSA. *Unit head:* Dr. Beverly Gulley, Dean, 773-298-3221, Fax: 773-779-9061, E-mail: gulley@sxu.edu. *Application contact:* Beth Gierach, Managing Director of Admission, 773-298-3053, Fax: 773-298-3076, E-mail: gierach@sxu.edu.

Salem College, Department of Education, Winston-Salem, NC 27108-0548. Offers early education and leadership (MAT); elementary education (MAT); English as a second language (MAT); language and literacy (M Ed); middle school education (MAT); secondary education (MAT); special education (MAT). *Accreditation:* NCATE. Part-time and evening/weekend programs available. *Faculty:* 8 full-time (6 women), 5 part-time/adjunct (all women). *Students:* 8 full-time (all women), 250 part-time (238 women); includes 19 minority (16 African Americans, 1 Asian American or Pacific Islander, 2 Hispanic Americans). Average age 33. 110 applicants, 65% accepted, 68 enrolled. In 2006, 34 degrees awarded. *Degree requirements:* For master's, practicum (MAT), project (M Ed), oral and written comprehensive exams. *Entrance requirements:* For master's, GRE, minimum GPA of 2.5. *Application deadline:* Applications are processed on a rolling basis. Application fee: $30. *Financial support:* In 2006–07, 152 students received support. Federal Work-Study and scholarships/grants available. Support available to part-time students. Financial award applicants required to submit FAFSA. *Faculty research:* Content area reading strategies, literacy development, brain compatible instruction. *Unit head:* Dr. Paula Grubbs, Director of Teacher Education, 336-721-2610, Fax: 336-721-2683, E-mail: grubbs@salem.edu.

Salem State College, Graduate School, Program in Reading, Salem, MA 01970-5353. Offers M Ed, CAGS. *Accreditation:* NCATE. Part-time and evening/weekend programs available. *Faculty:* 4 part-time/adjunct (all women). *Students:* 9 full-time (all women), 90 part-time (88 women); includes 3 minority (1 Asian American or Pacific Islander, 2 Hispanic Americans). Average age 36. In 2006, 23 degrees awarded. *Entrance requirements:* For master's, GRE General Test, MAT. *Application deadline:* Applications are processed on a rolling basis. Application fee: $35. *Unit head:* Francesca Pomerantz, Coordinator, 978-542-7042, Fax: 978-542-7023, E-mail: fpomerantz@salemstate.edu.

Salisbury University, Graduate Division, Department of Education, Salisbury, MD 21801-6837. Offers art (MAT); biology (MAT); business education (MAT); chemistry (MAT); early childhood education (M Ed); educational administration (M Ed); elementary education (M Ed); English (M Ed, MAT); French (MAT); geography (MAT); history (MAT); mathematics (MAT); media and technology (MAT); music (MAT); psychology (MAT); reading education (MAT); science (MAT); secondary education (MAT); social studies (MAT); Spanish (MAT). *Accreditation:* NCATE. Part-time and evening/weekend programs available. *Faculty:* 12 full-time (6 women), 10 part-time/adjunct (8 women). *Students:* 17 full-time (9 women), 84 part-time (72 women); includes 6 minority (5 African Americans, 1 Hispanic American). Average age 30. 15 applicants, 73% accepted, 11 enrolled. In 2006, 63 degrees awarded. *Degree requirements:* For master's, comprehensive exam (for some programs). *Entrance requirements:* For master's, PRAXIS, minimum GPA of 2.75. Additional exam requirements/recommendations for international students: Required—TOEFL (minimum score 550 paper-based; 213 computer-based). *Application deadline:* For fall admission, 8/1 priority date for domestic students; for spring admission, 1/1 for domestic students. Applications are processed on a rolling basis. Application fee: $45. *Expenses:* Tuition, state resident: part-time $260 per credit hour. Tuition, nonresident: part-time $546 per credit hour. Required fees: $52 per credit hour. *Financial support:* In 2006–07, 3 teaching assistantships with full tuition reimbursements were awarded; career-related internships or fieldwork and scholarships/grants also available. Support available to part-time students. Financial award applicants required to submit FAFSA. *Faculty research:* Middle-level education, student outcomes. *Unit head:* Dr. Edward C. Robeck, Program Coordinator, 410-543-6292, Fax: 410-548-2593, E-mail: ecrobeck@salisbury.edu. *Application contact:* Debra J. Clark, Administrative Assistant I, 410-543-6281, Fax: 410-548-2593, E-mail: djclark@salisbury.edu.

Salisbury University, Graduate Division, Program in Reading, Salisbury, MD 21801-6837. Offers M Ed. *Faculty:* 3 full-time (2 women). *Students:* Average age 31. 4 applicants, 25% accepted, 1 enrolled. In 2006, 3 degrees awarded. *Entrance requirements:* Additional exam requirements/recommendations for international students: Required—TOEFL (minimum score 550 paper-based; 213 computer-based). *Application deadline:* Applications are processed on a rolling basis. Application fee: $45. Electronic applications accepted. *Expenses:* Tuition, state resident: part-time $260 per credit hour. Tuition, nonresident: part-time $546 per credit hour. Required fees: $52 per credit hour. *Financial support:* Applicants required to submit FAFSA. *Unit head:* Dr. Edward C. Robeck, Coordinator, 410-543-6292, E-mail: ecrobeck@salisbury.edu. *Application contact:* Debra J. Clark, Administrative Assistant, 410-543-6281, E-mail: djclark@salisbury.edu.

Sam Houston State University, College of Education and Applied Science, Department of Language, Literacy, and Special Populations, Huntsville, TX 77341. Offers early childhood education (M Ed); reading (M Ed, MA); special education (M Ed, MA). Part-time and evening/weekend programs available. *Faculty:* 6 full-time (4 women). *Students:* 2 full-time (both women), 104 part-time (100 women); includes 18 minority (6 African Americans, 1 American Indian/Alaska Native, 11 Hispanic Americans), 2 international. Average age 37. In 2006, 26 degrees awarded. *Entrance requirements:* For master's, GRE General Test, minimum GPA of 2.5. *Application deadline:* For fall admission, 8/1 for domestic students; for spring admission, 12/1 for domestic students. Application fee: $20. *Expenses:* Tuition, state resident: full-time $5,904; part-time $164 per semester hour. Tuition, nonresident: full-time $15,804; part-time $439 per semester hour. Required fees: $1,374; $462 per semester. *Financial support:* Teaching assistantships available. Financial award application deadline: 5/31; financial award applicants required to submit FAFSA. *Unit head:* Dr. Mary Robbins, Chair, 936-294-3890, Fax: 936-294-1131, E-mail: edu_mer@shsu.edu. *Application contact:* Molly Doughtie, Advisor, 936-294-1105, E-mail: edu_mxd@shsu.edu.

San Diego State University, Graduate and Research Affairs, College of Education, School of Teacher Education, Program in Reading Education, San Diego, CA 92182. Offers MA. *Accreditation:* NCATE. Part-time programs available. *Students:* 4 full-time (all women), 47 part-time (44 women); includes 8 minority (1 American Indian/Alaska Native, 4 Asian Americans or Pacific Islanders, 3 Hispanic Americans), 1 international. Average age 29. 25 applicants, 84% accepted, 6 enrolled. In 2006, 17 degrees awarded. *Entrance requirements:* For master's, GRE General Test, letters of reference. Additional exam requirements/recommendations for international students: Required—TOEFL. *Application deadline:* For fall admission, 5/1 for domestic and international students; for spring admission, 11/1 for domestic students, 10/1 for international students. Applications are processed on a rolling basis. Application fee: $55. Electronic applications accepted. *Financial support:* Applicants required to submit FAFSA. *Faculty research:* Literacy, writing, reading/writing connection, class size reduction in reading, book clubs, evaluation instruments in reading/language arts. *Unit head:* Pamela Ross, Graduate Advisor, 619-594-7033, Fax: 619-594-7828, E-mail: pross@mail.sdsu.edu.

San Francisco State University, Division of Graduate Studies, College of Education, Department of Elementary Education, Program in Language and Literacy Education, San Francisco, CA 94132-1722. Offers MA. *Degree requirements:* For master's, thesis or alternative. *Entrance requirements:* For master's, minimum GPA of 2.5 in last 60 units. *Application deadline:* For fall admission, 11/30 priority date for domestic students. Applications are processed on a rolling basis. Application fee: $55. *Financial support:* Application deadline: 3/1. *Application contact:* Dr. Josie Arce, Graduate Coordinator, 415-338-2292, E-mail: jarce@sfsu.edu.

San Francisco State University, Division of Graduate Studies, College of Humanities, Department of English Language and Literature, San Francisco, CA 94132-1722. Offers composition (MA, Certificate); linguistics (MA); literature (MA); teaching composition (Certificate); teaching English to speakers of other languages (MA); teaching post-secondary reading (Certificate). Part-time programs available. *Faculty:* 58 full-time (22 women). *Students:* 180 (118 women). Average age 28. In 2006, 120 degrees awarded. *Entrance requirements:* For master's, minimum GPA of 2.5 in last 60 units. *Application deadline:* Applications are processed on a rolling basis. Application fee: $55. *Financial support:* Teaching assistantships available. Financial award application deadline: 3/1. *Faculty research:* Modern critical theory, composition theory and practice. *Unit head:* Dr. James Kohn, Chair, 415-338-2264.

Seattle Pacific University, Graduate School, School of Education, Program in Curriculum and Instruction, Seattle, WA 98119-1997. Offers reading/language arts education (M Ed). *Accreditation:* NCATE. Part-time and evening/weekend programs available. *Students:* 9 full-time (8 women), 36 part-time (31 women); includes 1 African American, 1 Asian American or Pacific Islander. 24 applicants, 75% accepted, 14 enrolled. In 2006, 19 degrees awarded. *Entrance requirements:* For master's, GRE General Test or MAT, minimum GPA of 3.0. *Application deadline:* For fall admission, 7/1 priority date for domestic students; for spring admission, 3/1 priority date for domestic students. Applications are processed on a rolling basis. Application fee: $50. *Expenses: Contact institution. Financial support:* Applicants required to submit FAFSA. *Faculty research:* Educational technology, classroom environments, character education. *Unit head:* Dr. Greg Fritzberg, Chair, 206-281-2623, E-mail: gregf@spu.edu. *Application contact:* Allan Blomquist, Graduate Programs Manager, 206-281-2378, Fax: 206-281-2756, E-mail: blomqa@spu.edu.

Seattle University, College of Education, Program in Literacy, Seattle, WA 98122-1090. Offers M Ed, Post-Master's Certificate. *Students:* 1 (woman) full-time, 8 part-time (7 women). Average age 34. *Entrance requirements:* For master's, GRE, MAT or minimum GPA of 3.0, 1 year of K-12 work experience; for Post-Master's Certificate, GRE, MAT or minimum GPA of 3.0, master's degree, WA state teaching certification. Additional exam requirements/recommendations for international students: Required—TOEFL. *Application deadline:* For fall admission, 8/20 priority date for domestic students; for winter admission, 11/20 priority date for domestic students; for spring admission, 2/20 priority date for domestic students. Application fee: $55. *Unit head:* Dr. Katherine Schlick Noe, Director, 206-296-5768, E-mail: kschlnoe@seattleu.edu. *Application contact:* Janet Shandley, Associate Dean of Graduate Admissions, 206-296-5900, Fax: 206-298-5656, E-mail: grad_admissions@seattleu.edu.

Shippensburg University of Pennsylvania, School of Graduate Studies, College of Education and Human Services, Department of Teacher Education, Shippensburg, PA 17257-2299. Offers curriculum and instruction (M Ed); reading (M Ed); special education (M Ed). *Accreditation:* NCATE. Part-time and evening/weekend programs available. *Faculty:* 16 full-time (11 women), 3 part-time/adjunct (all women). *Students:* 14 full-time (9 women), 201 part-time (181 women); includes 4 minority (3 African Americans, 1 Hispanic American). Average age 30. 66 applicants, 52% accepted, 28 enrolled. In 2006, 75 degrees awarded. *Degree requirements:* For master's, practicum or internship required for some programs. *Entrance requirements:* For master's, MAT (if GPA is below 2.75), interview, letters of recommendation, writing sample, resumé. Additional exam requirements/recommendations for international students: Required—TOEFL (minimum score 560 paper-based; 220 computer-based). *Application deadline:* For fall admission, 6/1 priority date for domestic students, 3/1 for international students; for spring admission, 9/1 priority date for domestic students, 7/1 for international students. Applications are processed on a rolling basis. Application fee: $30. Electronic applications accepted. *Expenses:* Tuition, state resident: part-time $336 per credit. Tuition, nonresident: part-time $538 per credit. *Financial support:* In 2006–07, 10 research assistantships with full tuition reimbursements (averaging $3,125 per year) were awarded; career-related internships or fieldwork, scholarships/grants, and unspecified assistantships also available. Support available to part-time students. Financial award application deadline: 3/1; financial award applicants required to submit FAFSA. *Unit head:* Dr. Elizabeth Vaughan, Chairperson, 717-477-1688, Fax: 717-477-4046, E-mail: ejvaug@ship.edu. *Application contact:* Renee Payne, Associate Dean of Graduate Admissions, 717-477-1231, Fax: 717-477-4016, E-mail: rmpayn@ship.edu.

Siena Heights University, Graduate College, Program in Teacher Education, Concentration in Elementary Education, Adrian, MI 49221-1796. Offers elementary education/reading (MA). Part-time programs available. *Degree requirements:* For master's, thesis, presentation. *Entrance requirements:* For master's, interview, minimum GPA of 3.0.

Siena Heights University, Graduate College, Program in Teacher Education, Concentration in Secondary Education, Adrian, MI 49221-1796. Offers secondary education/reading (MA). Part-time programs available. *Degree requirements:* For master's, thesis, presentation. *Entrance requirements:* For master's, minimum GPA of 3.0, interview.

Slippery Rock University of Pennsylvania, Graduate Studies (Recruitment), College of Education, Department of Elementary Education and Early Childhood, Slippery Rock, PA 16057-1383. Offers early childhood education (M Ed); math/science (M Ed); reading (M Ed). *Accreditation:* NCATE. Part-time and evening/weekend programs available. *Degree requirements:* For master's, thesis (for some programs), reflective presentation, comprehensive exam (for some programs). *Entrance requirements:* For master's, GRE General Test, MAT, minimum GPA of 2.75 (minimum GPA of 3.0 for initial certification programs). Additional exam requirements/recommendations for international students: Required—TOEFL (minimum score 550 paper-based; 213 computer-based). *Application deadline:* For fall admission, 7/1 priority date for domestic and international students; for spring admission, 11/1 priority date for domestic and international students. Applications are processed on a rolling basis. Application fee: $25. Electronic applications accepted. *Expenses:* Tuition, state resident: part-time $336 per credit. Tuition, nonresident: part-time $538 per credit. Required fees: $84 per credit. $37 per semester. *Financial support:* Career-related internships or fieldwork, Federal Work-Study, scholarships/grants, and unspecified assistantships available. Support available to part-time students. Financial award application deadline: 5/1; financial award applicants required to submit FAFSA. *Unit head:* Dr. Suzanne Rose, Graduate Coordinator, 724-738-2863, Fax: 724-738-2880, E-mail: suzanne.rose@sn.edu. *Application contact:* April Longwell, Interim Director of Graduate Studies, 724-738-2051 Ext. 2116, Fax: 724-738-2146, E-mail: graduate.studies@sru.edu.

Sojourner-Douglass College, Graduate Program, Baltimore, MD 21205-1814. Offers human services (MASS); public administration (MASS); urban education (reading) (MASS).

Southern Adventist University, School of Education and Psychology, Collegedale, TN 37315-0370. Offers curriculum and instruction (MS Ed); educational administration and supervision (MS Ed); inclusive education (MS Ed); literacy education (MS Ed); outdoor teacher education (MS Ed); professional counseling (MS); school counseling (MS). *Accreditation:* NCATE. Part-time and evening/weekend programs available. *Faculty:* 11 full-time (5 women), 1 (woman) part-time/adjunct. *Students:* 36 full-time (29 women), 7 part-time (6 women); includes 8 minority (6 African Americans, 2 Hispanic Americans). Average age 30. 15 applicants, 100% accepted, 15 enrolled. In 2006, 25 degrees awarded. *Degree requirements:* For master's, position paper (MS), portfolio (MS Ed in outdoor teacher education), thesis optional. *Entrance requirements:* For master's, GRE General Test, interview (MS); 9 semester hours of upper division course work in psychology or related field, including 1 course in psychology research or statistics; 9 semester hours of education (MS Ed). Additional exam requirements/recommendations for international students: Required—TOEFL (minimum score 600 paper-based; 250 computer-based; 100 iBT). *Application deadline:* For fall admission, 5/15 priority date for domestic and international students; for winter admission, 10/15 priority date for domestic and international students; for spring admission, 3/31 priority date for domestic and international students. Applications are processed on a rolling basis. Application fee: $25. Electronic applications accepted. *Financial support:* In 2006–07, 7 students received support, including 4 research assistantships with full tuition reimbursements available (averaging $10,000 per year); career-related internships or fieldwork, scholarships/grants, tuition waivers (partial), and unspecified assistantships also available. Support available to part-time students. Financial award application deadline: 4/1; financial award applicants required to submit FAFSA. *Unit head:* Dr. Denise Dunzweiler, Dean, 423-236-2776, Fax: 423-236-1765, E-mail: denise@southern.edu. *Application contact:* Mikhaile Spence, Information Contact, 423-236-2496, Fax: 423-236-1765, E-mail: maspence@southern.edu.

Southern Connecticut State University, School of Graduate Studies, School of Education, Program in Reading, New Haven, CT 06515-1355. Offers MS, Diploma. Part-time and evening/weekend programs available. *Students:* 5 full-time (all women), 193 part-time (189 women); includes 2 minority (1 Asian American or Pacific Islander, 1 Hispanic American). 50 applicants, 94% accepted, 27 enrolled. In 2006, 37 master's, 16 Diplomas awarded. *Degree requirements:* For master's, thesis or alternative. *Entrance requirements:* For master's, interview, teaching certificate; for Diploma, master's degree. *Application deadline:* For fall admission, 7/15 priority date for domestic students. Applications are processed on a rolling basis. Application fee: $50. Electronic applications accepted. *Financial support:* Application deadline: 4/15; *Unit head:* Dr. Pamela Brucker, Interim Chairperson, 203-392-5950, Fax: 203-392-5927, E-mail: bruckerp1@southernct.edu. *Application contact:* Dr. Nancy Boyles, Graduate Coordinator, 203-392-5946, E-mail: boylesn1@southernct.edu.

Southern Illinois University Edwardsville, Graduate Studies and Research, School of Education, Department of Curriculum and Instruction, Program in Literacy Education, Edwardsville, IL 62026-0001. Offers MS Ed. *Students:* 1 (woman) full-time, 50 part-time (47 women). 9 applicants, 44% accepted. In 2006, 9 degrees awarded. *Degree requirements:* For master's, comprehensive exam. *Application deadline:* For fall admission, 7/20 for domestic students, 6/1 for international students; for spring admission, 12/14 for domestic students, 10/1 for international students. Application fee: $30. Electronic applications accepted. *Unit head:* Dr. Stephanie McAndrews, Director, 618-650-3426, E-mail: smcandr@siue.edu.

Southern Illinois University Edwardsville, Graduate Studies and Research, School of Education, Department of Curriculum and Instruction, Program in Secondary Education, Edwardsville, IL 62026-0001. Offers art (MS Ed); biology (MS Ed); chemistry (MS Ed); English (MS Ed); foreign languages (MS Ed); history (MS Ed); mathematics (MS Ed); physics (MS Ed); reading (MS Ed); science (MS Ed). *Accreditation:* NCATE. Part-time and evening/weekend programs available. *Students:* 2 full-time (both women), 23 part-time (14 women); includes 2 minority (both African Americans) Average age 33. 12 applicants, 42% accepted. In 2006, 10 degrees awarded. *Degree requirements:* For master's, thesis or alternative, final exam. *Entrance requirements:* For master's, MAT. Additional exam requirements/recommendations for international students: Required—TOEFL. *Application deadline:* For fall admission, 7/20 for domestic students, 6/1 for international students; for spring admission, 12/14 for domestic students, 10/1 for international students. Application fee: $30. Electronic applications accepted. *Financial support:* Fellowships, research assistantships, teaching assistantships, Federal Work-Study, institutionally sponsored loans, and unspecified assistantships available. Support available to part-time students. Financial award application deadline: 3/1; financial award applicants required to submit FAFSA. *Unit head:* Dr. David DeWeese, Director, 618-650-3432, E-mail: ddewees@siue.edu.

Southern Oregon University, Graduate Studies, School of Social Sciences, Department of Education, Ashland, OR 97520. Offers elementary education (MA Ed, MS Ed), including classroom teacher, early childhood, handicapped learner, reading, supervision; secondary education (MA Ed, MS Ed), including classroom teacher, handicapped learner, reading, supervision; teaching (MAT). *Degree requirements:* For master's, thesis optional. *Entrance requirements:* For master's, GRE General Test, minimum GPA of 3.0. Electronic applications accepted.

State University of New York at Binghamton, Graduate School, School of Education, Program in Reading Education, Binghamton, NY 13902-6000. Offers MS Ed. *Accreditation:* Teacher Education Accreditation Council. Part-time and evening/weekend programs available. *Students:* 2 full-time (both women), 35 part-time (34 women); includes 1 minority (Hispanic American) Average age 29. 2 applicants, 0% accepted. In 2006, 14 degrees awarded. *Entrance requirements:* For master's, GRE General Test. Additional exam requirements/recommendations for international students: Required—TOEFL. *Application deadline:* For fall admission, 4/15 priority date for domestic students, 1/15 priority date for international students; for spring admission, 11/1 for domestic students, 10/1 priority date for international students. Applications are processed on a rolling basis. Application fee: $60. Electronic applications accepted.

Reading Education

State University of New York at Binghamton (continued)
Financial support: In 2006–07, 1 student received support, including 1 fellowship with full tuition reimbursement available (averaging $4,050 per year); research assistantships, career-related internships or fieldwork, Federal Work-Study, institutionally sponsored loans, and unspecified assistantships also available. Support available to part-time students. Financial award application deadline: 2/15. *Unit head:* Dr. Karen M. Bromley, Coordinator, 607-777-2301, E-mail: kbromley@binghamton.edu.

State University of New York at Fredonia, Graduate Studies, College of Education, Program in Literacy, Fredonia, NY 14063-1136. Offers MS Ed. *Accreditation:* NCATE. Part-time and evening/weekend programs available. *Faculty:* 1 (woman) part-time/adjunct. *Students:* 22 full-time (20 women), 48 part-time (44 women); includes 1 minority (American Indian/Alaska Native). Average age 26. In 2006, 35 degrees awarded. *Degree requirements:* For master's, thesis optional. *Application deadline:* For fall admission, 8/5 for domestic students; for spring admission, 12/1 for domestic students. Application fee: $50. *Expenses:* Tuition, state resident: full-time $6,900; part-time $288 per credit hour. Tuition, nonresident: full-time $10,920; part-time $455 per credit hour. Required fees: $1,132; $47 per credit hour. *Financial support:* In 2006–07, 2 teaching assistantships with partial tuition reimbursements (averaging $4,965 per year) were awarded; research assistantships, career-related internships or fieldwork and tuition waivers (full and partial) also available. Support available to part-time students. Financial award application deadline: 3/15. *Unit head:* Dr. Christine Givner, Dean, College of Education, 716-673-3311, E-mail: christine.givner@fredonia.edu.

State University of New York at New Paltz, Graduate School, Faculty of Education, Department of Elementary Education, New Paltz, NY 12561. Offers childhood education (MS Ed); childhood education (1-6) (MST); early childhood education (B-2) (MST); literacy education (5-12) (MS Ed); literacy education (B-6) (MS Ed). *Accreditation:* NCATE. Part-time and evening/weekend programs available. *Faculty:* 10 full-time (6 women), 42 part-time/adjunct (33 women). *Students:* 53 full-time (47 women), 135 part-time (124 women); includes 11 minority (4 African Americans, 1 Asian American or Pacific Islander, 6 Hispanic Americans). Average age 30. 142 applicants. In 2006, 91 degrees awarded. *Degree requirements:* For master's, portfolio. *Entrance requirements:* For master's, GRE/MAT (MST), minimum GPA of 3.0, teaching certificate (MS Ed). Additional exam requirements/recommendations for international students: Required—TOEFL (minimum score 550 paper-based; 213 computer-based; 80 iBT). *Application deadline:* For fall admission, 4/1 for domestic and international students; for spring admission, 11/1 for domestic and international students. Application fee: $50. Electronic applications accepted. *Expenses:* Tuition, state resident: full-time $6,900; part-time $288 per credit hour. Tuition, nonresident: full-time $10,920; part-time $455 per credit hour. *Financial support:* Federal Work-Study and institutionally sponsored loans available. *Unit head:* Dr. Winifred Montgomery, Chair, 845-257-2860, E-mail: montgomw@newpaltz.edu.

State University of New York at Oswego, Graduate Studies, School of Education, Department of Curriculum and Instruction, Oswego, NY 13126. Offers art education (MAT); elementary education (MS Ed); literacy education (MS Ed); secondary education (MS Ed); special education (MS Ed). Part-time and evening/weekend programs available. *Faculty:* 23 full-time, 45 part-time/adjunct. *Students:* 184 full-time (139 women), 220 part-time (185 women); includes 12 minority (5 African Americans, 1 American Indian/Alaska Native, 1 Asian American or Pacific Islander, 5 Hispanic Americans), 1 international. Average age 33. 266 applicants, 89% accepted. In 2006, 255 degrees awarded. *Degree requirements:* For master's, thesis optional. *Entrance requirements:* For master's, GRE General Test, minimum GPA of 2.7, provisional teaching certificate. Additional exam requirements/recommendations for international students: Required—TOEFL (minimum score 560 paper-based; 220 computer-based). *Application deadline:* For fall admission, 3/1 for domestic students; for spring admission, 10/1 for domestic students. Application fee: $50. *Expenses:* Tuition, state resident: part-time $288 per credit. Tuition, nonresident: part-time $455 per credit. Tuition and fees vary according to program. *Financial support:* In 2006–07, 9 students received support, including 3 fellowships, 6 teaching assistantships with full tuition reimbursements available; career-related internships or fieldwork, Federal Work-Study, institutionally sponsored loans, scholarships/grants, and unspecified assistantships also available. Support available to part-time students. Financial award application deadline: 4/1; financial award applicants required to submit FAFSA. *Faculty research:* Classroom applications for microcomputers; classroom questioning, wait-time, and achievement; values clarification and academic achievement. *Unit head:* Dr. Pamela Michel, Chair, 315-312-4052. *Application contact:* Dr. Joyce Smith, Coordinator, Graduate Education, 315-312-4052.

State University of New York at Plattsburgh, Division of Education, Health, and Human Services, Program in Literacy Education, Plattsburgh, NY 12901-2681. Offers birth-grade 6 (MS Ed); grades 5-12 (MS Ed). *Faculty:* 5 full-time (4 women), 8 part-time/adjunct (7 women). *Students:* 15 full-time (all women), 19 part-time (16 women); includes 1 minority (Asian American or Pacific Islander) Average age 31. 20 applicants, 75% accepted, 15 enrolled. In 2006, 27 degrees awarded. *Degree requirements:* For master's, comprehensive exam or research project, thesis optional. *Entrance requirements:* For master's, GRE General Test or MAT, minimum GPA of 2.5. *Application deadline:* Applications are processed on a rolling basis. Application fee: $50. *Expenses:* Tuition, state resident: full-time $6,900; part-time $288 per credit hour. Tuition, nonresident: full-time $10,920; part-time $455 per credit hour. *Financial support:* In 2006–07, 9 students received support. Federal Work-Study available. Support available to part-time students. Financial award application deadline: 4/15; financial award applicants required to submit FAFSA. *Faculty research:* Reading pedagogy, early childhood literacy, children's literature, integrated language arts. *Unit head:* Dr. Robert Ackland, Coordinator, 518-564-5147. *Application contact:* Sharon Derr, Assistant Director, Graduate Admission, 518-564-4723, Fax: 518-564-4722, E-mail: derrsl@plattsburgh.edu.

State University of New York College at Brockport, School of Professions, Department of Education and Human Development, Program in Childhood Literacy, Brockport, NY 14420-2997. Offers MS Ed. *Accreditation:* NCATE. *Students:* 19 full-time (18 women). 33 applicants, 73% accepted. In 2006, 14 degrees awarded. *Degree requirements:* For master's, thesis or alternative. *Entrance requirements:* For master's, minimum GPA of 3.0, letters of recommendation, interview. Additional exam requirements/recommendations for international students: Required—TOEFL (minimum score 550 paper-based; 213 computer-based; 80 iBT). *Application deadline:* For fall admission, 2/15 for domestic and international students. Application fee: $50. *Expenses:* Tuition, state resident: full-time $6,900; part-time $288 per credit. Tuition, nonresident: full-time $10,920; part-time $455 per credit. *Financial support:* Career-related internships or fieldwork, Federal Work-Study, and scholarships/grants available. Financial award application deadline: 3/15; financial award applicants required to submit FAFSA. *Application contact:* Coordinator of Certification and Graduate Advisement, 585-395-2344.

State University of New York College at Cortland, Graduate Studies, School of Education, Program in Literacy, Cortland, NY 13045. Offers MS Ed. *Accreditation:* NCATE. Part-time and evening/weekend programs available. *Degree requirements:* For master's, one foreign language, thesis (for some programs), comprehensive exam. *Entrance requirements:* Additional exam requirements/recommendations for international students: Required—TOEFL.

State University of New York College at Geneseo, Graduate Studies, School of Education, Program in Reading, Geneseo, NY 14454-1401. Offers MS Ed. Part-time and evening/weekend programs available. *Faculty:* 5 full-time (3 women). *Students:* 18 full-time (16 women), 42 part-time (37 women); includes 1 minority (Asian American or Pacific Islander), 1 international. Average age 24. 30 applicants. In 2006, 28 degrees awarded. *Degree requirements:* For master's, thesis optional. *Entrance requirements:* For master's, GRE General Test. *Application deadline:* For fall admission, 6/1 priority date for domestic students; for spring admission, 10/1 for domestic students. Application fee: $50. *Financial support:* In 2006–07, 4 students received support; teaching assistantships with tuition reimbursements available, career-related internships or fieldwork, Federal Work-Study, and institutionally sponsored loans available. Financial

award application deadline: 4/1; financial award applicants required to submit FAFSA. *Unit head:* Dr. Osman Alawiye, Chairperson, School of Education, 585-245-5560, Fax: 585-245-5220.

State University of New York College at Oneonta, Graduate Studies, Division of Education, Department of Elementary and Reading Education, Oneonta, NY 13820-4015. Offers childhood education (MS Ed); literacy education (MS Ed). *Accreditation:* NCATE. Part-time and evening/weekend programs available. *Entrance requirements:* For master's, GRE General Test.

State University of New York College at Potsdam, School of Education, Program in Literacy Education, Potsdam, NY 13676. Offers MS Ed. *Accreditation:* NCATE. Part-time and evening/weekend programs available. Postbaccalaureate distance learning degree programs offered (minimal on-campus study). *Faculty:* 5 full-time (3 women), 1 (woman) part-time/adjunct. *Students:* 56 full-time (50 women), 54 part-time (48 women). In 2006, 190 degrees awarded. *Degree requirements:* For master's, culminating experience, thesis optional. *Entrance requirements:* For master's, minimum GPA of 2.75 in last 60 hours of course work. Additional exam requirements/recommendations for international students: Required—TOEFL (minimum score 550 paper-based; 213 computer-based). *Application deadline:* Applications are processed on a rolling basis. Application fee: $50. *Financial support:* Fellowships, teaching assistantships with full tuition reimbursements, career-related internships or fieldwork, Federal Work-Study, and scholarships/grants available. Support available to part-time students. Financial award application deadline: 3/1. *Unit head:* Dr. Richard J. Bates, Chairperson, Literacy Department, 315-267-2535, Fax: 315-267-4802, E-mail: batesrj@potsdam.edu. *Application contact:* Peter Cutler, Graduate Admissions Counselor, 315-267-3154, Fax: 315-267-4802, E-mail: cutlerpj@potsdam.edu.

Stetson University, College of Arts and Sciences, Division of Education, Department of Teacher Education, Program in Reading Education, DeLand, FL 32723. Offers M Ed. *Students:* 1 (woman) full-time, 19 part-time (all women), 1 international. Average age 33. In 2006, 17 degrees awarded. *Application contact:* Midge McDaniel, Office of Graduate Studies, 386-822-7075, Fax: 386-822-7388, E-mail: mmcdanie@stetson.edu.

Sul Ross State University, Rio Grande College of Sul Ross State University, Alpine, TX 79832. Offers business administration (MBA); teacher education (M Ed), including bilingual education, counseling, educational diagnostics, elementary education, general education, reading, school administration, secondary education. Part-time and evening/weekend programs available. *Degree requirements:* For master's, thesis optional. *Entrance requirements:* For master's, GMAT or GRE General Test, minimum GPA of 2.5 in last 60 hours of undergraduate work. *Faculty research:* Drug and substance abuse counseling, U.S.-Mexico border economic development.

Sul Ross State University, School of Professional Studies, Department of Teacher Education, Program in Reading Specialist, Alpine, TX 79832. Offers M Ed. Part-time and evening/weekend programs available. *Degree requirements:* For master's, thesis optional. *Entrance requirements:* For master's, GMAT or GRE General Test, minimum GPA of 2.5 in last 60 hours of undergraduate work.

Syracuse University, Graduate School, School of Education, Department of Reading and Language Arts, Program in Literacy Education, Syracuse, NY 13244. Offers literacy education: birth-grade 6 (MS); literacy education: grades 5-12 (MS). Part-time programs available. *Students:* 13 full-time (12 women), 21 part-time (20 women); includes 2 minority (1 African American, 1 Asian American or Pacific Islander), 1 international. 20 applicants, 95% accepted, 8 enrolled. *Degree requirements:* For master's, thesis or alternative. *Entrance requirements:* For master's, GRE. Additional exam requirements/recommendations for international students: Required—TOEFL. *Application deadline:* For fall admission, 2/1 priority date for domestic students. Applications are processed on a rolling basis. Application fee: $65. Electronic applications accepted. *Expenses:* Tuition: Full-time $16,920; part-time $940 per credit hour. Required fees: $930; $930 per year. *Financial support:* Fellowships with tuition reimbursements, research assistantships with tuition reimbursements, teaching assistantships with tuition reimbursements available. *Faculty research:* Literacy, knowledge modeling, assessment, teaching of literature, writing. *Unit head:* Dr. Rachel Brown, Chair, 315-443-5180. *Application contact:* Liza Rochelson, Graduate Admission Recruiter, 315-443-2505, Fax: 315-443-2258, E-mail: gradcrt@gwmail.syr.edu.

Syracuse University, Graduate School, School of Education, Department of Reading and Language Arts, Program in Reading Education, Syracuse, NY 13244. Offers PhD. Part-time programs available. *Students:* 5 full-time (all women), 11 part-time (10 women). 2 applicants, 100% accepted, 1 enrolled. *Degree requirements:* For doctorate, thesis/dissertation; for degree. *Entrance requirements:* For doctorate, GRE. Additional exam requirements/recommendations for international students: Required—TOEFL. *Application deadline:* For fall admission, 2/1 priority date for domestic students. Applications are processed on a rolling basis. Application fee: $65. Electronic applications accepted. *Expenses:* Tuition: Full-time $16,920; part-time $940 per credit hour. Required fees: $930; $930 per year. *Unit head:* Dr. Kathleen Hinchman, Graduate Chair, 315-443-4757. *Application contact:* Liza Rochelson, Graduate Admission Recruiter, 315-443-2505, Fax: 315-443-2258, E-mail: gradcrt@gwmail.syr.edu.

Teachers College Columbia University, Graduate Faculty of Education, Department of Curriculum and Teaching, Program in Literacy Specialist, New York, NY 10027-6696. Offers MA. *Students:* 13 full-time (all women), 13 part-time (12 women); includes 2 minority (1 African American, 1 Asian American or Pacific Islander), 2 international. 44 applicants, 61% accepted, 17 enrolled. Application fee: $65. *Expenses:* Tuition: Full-time $23,400; part-time $975 per credit. Required fees: $320 per term. *Application contact:* Peter Shon, Assistant Director of Admission, 212-678-3305, Fax: 212-678-4171, E-mail: shon@exchange.tc.columbia.edu.

Teachers College Columbia University, Graduate Faculty of Education, Department of Health and Behavioral Studies, Program in Reading Specialist, New York, NY 10027-6696. Offers MA. *Faculty:* 2 full-time (both women), 6 part-time/adjunct. *Students:* 12 full-time (all women), 69 part-time (68 women); includes 6 minority (2 African Americans, 4 Asian Americans or Pacific Islanders), 4 international. Average age 28. 42 applicants, 57% accepted, 17 enrolled. In 2006, 30 degrees awarded. *Application deadline:* For fall admission, 5/15 for domestic students. Application fee: $65. *Expenses:* Tuition: Full-time $23,400; part-time $975 per credit. Required fees: $320 per term. *Financial support:* Application deadline: 2/1. *Application contact:* Peter Shon, Assistant Director of Admission, 212-678-3305, Fax: 212-678-4171, E-mail: shon@exchange.tc.columbia.edu.

See Close-Up on page 1129.

Teachers College Columbia University, Graduate Faculty of Education, Program in Reading/Learning Disability, New York, NY 10027-6696. Offers Ed M. *Application deadline:* For fall admission, 5/15 for domestic students. Application fee: $50. *Expenses:* Tuition: Full-time $23,400; part-time $975 per credit. Required fees: $320 per term. *Financial support:* Career-related internships or fieldwork, Federal Work-Study, institutionally sponsored loans, and tuition waivers (partial) available. Support available to part-time students. Financial award application deadline: 2/1. *Faculty research:* Reading and spelling disorders, workplace literacy, reading and writing among children and adults. *Application contact:* Director of Admissions, 212-678-3083, Fax: 212-678-4171.

Temple University, Graduate School, College of Education, Department of Curriculum, Instruction, and Technology in Education, Philadelphia, PA 19122-6096. Offers applied behavioral analysis (MS Ed); career and technical education (MS Ed); early childhood education and elementary education (MS Ed); English education (MS Ed); language arts education (Ed D); math/science education (Ed D); mathematics education (MS Ed); science education (MS Ed); second and foreign language education (MS Ed); special education (MS Ed); teaching English as a second language (MS Ed). Part-time and evening/weekend programs available. *Faculty:* 31 full-time (14 women). *Students:* 96 full-time (71 women), 482 part-time (336 women);

includes 109 minority (67 African Americans, 3 American Indian/Alaska Native, 23 Asian Americans or Pacific Islanders, 16 Hispanic Americans), 28 international. 308 applicants, 64% accepted, 116 enrolled. In 2006, 225 master's, 21 doctorates awarded. Terminal master's awarded for partial completion of doctoral program. *Degree requirements:* For master's, thesis or alternative; for doctorate, thesis/dissertation. *Entrance requirements:* For master's and doctorate, GRE General Test or MAT, minimum GPA of 3.0. Additional exam requirements/recommendations for international students: Required—TOEFL (minimum score 550 paper-based; 213 computer-based; 79 iBT). *Application deadline:* For fall admission, 4/1 for domestic students, 12/15 for international students; for spring admission, 10/1 for domestic students, 8/1 for international students. Application fee: $50. Electronic applications accepted. *Expenses:* Tuition, state resident: full-time $12,264; part-time $511 per credit. Tuition, nonresident: full-time $17,904; part-time $746 per credit. Required fees: $84 per course. Tuition and fees vary according to program. *Financial support:* Fellowships, research assistantships with full tuition reimbursements, teaching assistantships with full tuition reimbursements available. Financial award application deadline: 1/15; financial award applicants required to submit FAFSA. *Faculty research:* School improvement, problem solving, literacy, language development. *Unit head:* Dr. Thomas Walker, Chair, 215-204-2117, Fax: 215-204-1414, E-mail: tjwalker@temple.edu.

Tennessee Technological University, Graduate School, College of Education, Department of Curriculum and Instruction, Program in Reading, Cookeville, TN 38505. Offers MA, Ed S. *Accreditation:* NCATE. Part-time and evening/weekend programs available. *Faculty:* 2 full-time (both women). *Students:* 4 full-time (all women), 18 part-time (16 women). Average age 27. 15 applicants, 73% accepted, 5 enrolled. In 2006, 9 master's, 1 other advanced degree awarded. *Degree requirements:* For Ed S, thesis or alternative. *Entrance requirements:* For master's, MAT; for Ed S, MAT, NTE. Additional exam requirements/recommendations for international students: Required—TOEFL. *Application deadline:* For fall admission, 3/1 priority date for domestic students; for spring admission, 8/1 for domestic students. Application fee: $25 ($30 for international students). *Expenses:* Tuition, state resident: full-time $8,748; part-time $319 per hour. Tuition, nonresident: full-time $23,524; part-time $740 per hour. *Financial support:* In 2006–07, fellowships (averaging $8,000 per year), 4 teaching assistantships (averaging $4,000 per year) were awarded; research assistantships, career-related internships or fieldwork also available. Financial award application deadline: 4/1. *Application contact:* Dr. Francis O. Otuonye, Associate Vice President for Research and Graduate Studies, 931-372-3233, Fax: 931-372-3497, E-mail: fotuonye@tntech.edu.

Texas A&M International University, Office of Graduate Studies and Research, College of Education, Department of Curriculum and Instruction, Laredo, TX 78041-1900. Offers bilingual education (PhD); curriculum and instruction (MS, PhD); early childhood education (PhD); reading (MS). *Expenses:* Tuition, state resident: full-time $1,580. Tuition, nonresident: full-time $5,432. Required fees: $3,808. *Unit head:* Dr. Barbara Greybeck, Interim Chair, 956-326-2678, E-mail: bgreybeck@tamiu.edu. *Application contact:* Rosie Dickinson, Director of Admissions, 956-326-2200.

Texas A&M University, College of Education and Human Development, Department of Teaching, Learning, and Culture, College Station, TX 77843. Offers curriculum and instruction (M Ed, MS, PhD); mathematics education (M Ed, MS, PhD); multicultural/urban/ESL/international education (M Ed, MS, PhD); reading/language arts (M Ed, MS, PhD); science education (M Ed, MS, PhD); social studies education (M Ed, MS, PhD). *Accreditation:* NCATE. Part-time programs available. *Faculty:* 25 full-time (9 women), 2 part-time/adjunct (both women). *Students:* 156 full-time (115 women), 226 part-time (191 women); includes 95 minority (43 African Americans, 1 American Indian/Alaska Native, 9 Asian Americans or Pacific Islanders, 42 Hispanic Americans), 36 international. Average age 36. 137 applicants, 83% accepted, 80 enrolled. In 2006, 69 master's, 15 doctorates awarded. *Median time to degree:* Of those who began their doctoral program in fall 1998, 77% received their degree in 8 years or less. *Degree requirements:* For master's, thesis (for some programs), comprehensive exam; for doctorate, thesis/dissertation, comprehensive exam. *Entrance requirements:* For master's, GRE General Test, minimum GPA of 3.0; for doctorate, GRE General Test, 3 years of teaching experience. Additional exam requirements/recommendations for international students: Required—TOEFL (minimum score 550 paper-based; 213 computer-based). *Application deadline:* For fall admission, 1/15 priority date for domestic and international students; for spring admission, 9/15 priority date for domestic and international students. Applications are processed on a rolling basis. Application fee: $50 ($75 for international students). Electronic applications accepted. *Expenses:* Tuition, state resident: full-time $4,697. Tuition, nonresident: full-time $11,297. Required fees: $2,272. *Financial support:* In 2006–07, fellowships with partial tuition reimbursements (averaging $3,000 per year), teaching assistantships with partial tuition reimbursements (averaging $7,200 per year) were awarded; research assistantships with partial tuition reimbursements, career-related internships or fieldwork, Federal Work-Study, institutionally sponsored loans, scholarships/grants, tuition waivers (partial), and unspecified assistantships also available. Support available to part-time students. Financial award application deadline: 4/1; financial award applicants required to submit FAFSA. *Unit head:* Dr. Dennie Smith, Head, 979-845-8384, Fax: 979-845-9663. *Application contact:* Graduate Admissions Supervisor, 979-845-8382, Fax: 979-845-9663.

Texas A&M University–Commerce, Graduate School, College of Education and Human Services, Department of Elementary Education, Commerce, TX 75429-3011. Offers early childhood education (M Ed, MA, MS); elementary education (M Ed, MS); reading (M Ed, MA, MS); supervision of curriculum and instruction: elementary education (Ed D). Part-time programs available. Terminal master's awarded for partial completion of doctoral program. *Degree requirements:* For master's, thesis (for some programs), comprehensive exam; for doctorate, 2 foreign languages, thesis/dissertation, departmental qualifying exam. *Entrance requirements:* For master's and doctorate, GRE General Test. Electronic applications accepted. *Faculty research:* Literacy and learning, early childhood, preservice teacher education, technology.

Texas A&M University–Corpus Christi, Graduate Studies and Research, College of Education, Corpus Christi, TX 78412-5503. Offers counseling (MS, PhD), including counseling (MS), counselor education (PhD); curriculum and instruction (MS, Ed D); early childhood education (MS); educational administration (MS); educational leadership (Ed D); educational technology (MS); elementary education (MS); kinesiology (MS); occupational training and development (MS); reading (MS); secondary education (MS); special education (MS). Part-time and evening/weekend programs available. *Degree requirements:* For master's, thesis (for some programs), comprehensive exam, registration; for doctorate, thesis/dissertation, comprehensive exam, registration. *Entrance requirements:* For master's, GRE General Test. Additional exam requirements/recommendations for international students: Required—TOEFL. Electronic applications accepted.

Texas A&M University–Kingsville, College of Graduate Studies, College of Education, Department of Education, Program in Reading Specialization, Kingsville, TX 78363. Offers MS. Part-time and evening/weekend programs available. *Degree requirements:* For master's, minithesis. *Entrance requirements:* For master's, GRE General Test, MAT, minimum GPA of 3.0. *Faculty research:* Reading programs for preparing the handicapped, reading methods in elementary education, literature-based reading instruction.

Texas Southern University, Graduate School, College of Education, Area of Curriculum and Instruction, Houston, TX 77004-4584. Offers bilingual education (M Ed); curriculum, instruction, and urban education (Ed D); early childhood education (M Ed); elementary education (M Ed); reading education (M Ed); secondary education (M Ed); special education (M Ed). Part-time and evening/weekend programs available. *Faculty:* 8 full-time (6 women), 1 part-time/adjunct (0 women). *Students:* 41 full-time (36 women), 43 part-time (38 women); includes 82 minority (77 African Americans, 2 Asian Americans or Pacific Islanders, 3 Hispanic Americans). Average age 36. 34 applicants, 82% accepted, 24 enrolled. In 2006, 6 master's, 13 doctorates awarded. *Degree requirements:* For master's, comprehensive exam; for doctorate, thesis/dissertation, comprehensive exam. *Entrance requirements:* For master's, GRE General Test, minimum GPA of 2.5; for doctorate, GRE General Test or MAT, master's degree, minimum B+ average. Additional exam requirements/recommendations for international students: Required—TOEFL. *Application deadline:* For fall admission, 7/15 priority date for domestic students. Applications are processed on a rolling basis. Application fee: $50 ($75 for international students). *Financial support:* Federal Work-Study and institutionally sponsored loans available. Financial award application deadline: 5/1. *Unit head:* Dr. Cherry Gooden, Chair, 713-313-7496, Fax: 713-313-7496, E-mail: gooden_cr@tsu.edu.

Texas State University-San Marcos, Graduate School, College of Education, Department of Curriculum and Instruction, Program in Reading Education, San Marcos, TX 78666. Offers M Ed. Part-time and evening/weekend programs available. *Faculty:* 4 full-time (3 women), 2 part-time/adjunct (both women). *Students:* 1 (woman) full-time, 12 part-time (all women); includes 3 minority (all Hispanic Americans) Average age 33. 5 applicants, 100% accepted, 4 enrolled. In 2006, 3 degrees awarded. *Degree requirements:* For master's, thesis optional. *Entrance requirements:* For master's, GRE General Test, minimum GPA of 2.75 in last 60 hours of course work, teaching experience. Additional exam requirements/recommendations for international students: Required—TOEFL. *Application deadline:* For fall admission, 6/15 priority date for domestic students; for spring admission, 10/15 priority date for domestic students. Applications are processed on a rolling basis. Application fee: $40 ($90 for international students). *Financial support:* In 2006–07, 8 students received support, including 1 research assistantship (averaging $6,570 per year); career-related internships or fieldwork, Federal Work-Study, and institutionally sponsored loans also available. Support available to part-time students. Financial award application deadline: 4/1; financial award applicants required to submit FAFSA. *Faculty research:* Reading comprehension, computer-assisted instruction. *Unit head:* Dr. Gwynne Ash, Graduate Advisor, 512-245-2581, Fax: 512-245-8365, E-mail: ga13@txstate.edu. *Application contact:* Dr. J. Michael Willoughby, Dean of Graduate School, 512-245-2581, Fax: 512-245-8365, E-mail: gradcollege@txstate.edu.

Texas Tech University, Graduate School, College of Education, Division of Curriculum and Instruction, Lubbock, TX 79409. Offers bilingual education (M Ed); curriculum and instruction (M Ed, PhD); elementary education (M Ed); language and literacy education (M Ed); secondary education (M Ed). *Accreditation:* NCATE. Part-time programs available. *Students:* 68 full-time (48 women), 99 part-time (82 women); includes 35 minority (6 African Americans, 1 Asian American or Pacific Islander, 28 Hispanic Americans), 10 international. Average age 34. 165 applicants, 59% accepted, 10 enrolled. In 2006, 61 master's, 7 doctorates awarded. *Degree requirements:* For master's, thesis optional; for doctorate, thesis/dissertation. *Entrance requirements:* For master's and doctorate, GRE General Test. Additional exam requirements/recommendations for international students: Required—TOEFL (minimum score 550 paper-based; 213 computer-based). *Application deadline:* For fall admission, 3/1 priority date for international students; for spring admission, 11/1 priority date for international students. Applications are processed on a rolling basis. Application fee: $50 ($60 for international students). Electronic applications accepted. *Expenses:* Tuition, state resident: full-time $4,440. Tuition, nonresident: full-time $11,040. Required fees: $2,136. *Financial support:* In 2006–07, 100 students received support; research assistantships with partial tuition reimbursements available, teaching assistantships with partial tuition reimbursements available, career-related internships or fieldwork, Federal Work-Study, and institutionally sponsored loans available. Support available to part-time students. Financial award application deadline: 4/15; financial award applicants required to submit FAFSA. *Faculty research:* Multicultural foundations of education, teacher education, instruction and pedagogy in subject areas, curriculum theory, language and literary. *Unit head:* Dr. Peggy Johnson, Associate Dean, 806-742-1988 Ext. 437, Fax: 806-742-2179, E-mail: peggy.johnson@ttu.edu.

Texas Woman's University, Graduate School, College of Professional Education, Department of Reading, Denton, TX 76201. Offers reading education (M Ed, MA, MS, Ed D, PhD). Part-time and evening/weekend programs available. *Students:* 2 full-time (both women), 76 part-time (75 women); includes 16 minority (5 African Americans, 3 Asian Americans or Pacific Islanders, 8 Hispanic Americans), 1 international. Average age 40. 19 applicants, 26% accepted. In 2006, 9 master's, 4 doctorates awarded. Terminal master's awarded for partial completion of doctoral program. *Degree requirements:* For master's, thesis/dissertation; for doctorate, thesis/dissertation, comprehensive exam. *Entrance requirements:* For master's, GRE General Test; for doctorate, GRE General Test, minimum graduate GPA of 3.5, on-site writing sample, teaching experience, interview, MS degree, 3 letters of reference, resumé. Additional exam requirements/recommendations for international students: Required—TOEFL (minimum score 550 paper-based; 213 computer-based; 79 iBT). *Application deadline:* For fall admission, 4/1 for international students; for spring admission, 8/1 for international students. Applications are processed on a rolling basis. Application fee: $30 ($50 for international students). Electronic applications accepted. *Expenses:* Tuition, area resident: Part-time $168 per unit. Tuition, state resident: full-time $4,369. Tuition, nonresident: full-time $9,373; part-time $443 per unit. Required fees: $20 per unit. $177 per term. *Financial support:* In 2006–07, 1 research assistantship (averaging $10,206 per year), teaching assistantships (averaging $10,206 per year) were awarded; fellowships, career-related internships or fieldwork, Federal Work-Study, institutionally sponsored loans, scholarships/grants, traineeships, health care benefits, and unspecified assistantships also available. Support available to part-time students. Financial award application deadline: 3/1; financial award applicants required to submit FAFSA. *Faculty research:* Teacher change, home/school partnerships, literacy-middle grades, literacy, language acquisition. *Unit head:* Dr. Margaret Compton, Chair, 940-898-2227, Fax: 940-898-2224, E-mail: mcomptonhall@twu.edu. *Application contact:* Samuel Wheeler, Coordinator of Graduate Admissions, 940-898-3188, Fax: 940-898-3081, E-mail: wheelersr@twu.edu.

Touro University International, College of Education, Program in Education, Cypress, CA 90630. Offers adult education (MA Ed); aviation education (MA Ed); children's literacy development (MA Ed); e-learning (MA Ed); early childhood education (MA Ed); enrollment management (MA Ed); higher education (MA Ed); teaching and instruction (MA Ed); training and development (MA Ed). Part-time and evening/weekend programs available. Postbaccalaureate distance learning degree programs offered (no on-campus study). In 2006, 193 degrees awarded. *Degree requirements:* For master's, capstone project with integrative paper. *Entrance requirements:* For master's, minimum GPA of 3.0. Additional exam requirements/recommendations for international students: Required—TOEFL (minimum score 550 paper-based). Application fee: $75. *Expenses:* Tuition: Part-time $300 per credit hour. Tuition and fees vary according to course level and program. *Unit head:* Dr. Edith Neumann, Vice President for Academic Affairs, College of Education, 714-816-0366 Ext. 2030, Fax: 714-226-9844, E-mail: eneumann@tourou.edu.

Towson University, Graduate School, Program in Reading, Towson, MD 21252-0001. Offers reading (M Ed); reading education (CAS). *Accreditation:* NCATE. Part-time and evening/weekend programs available. Postbaccalaureate distance learning degree programs offered (minimal on-campus study). *Faculty:* 6 full-time (5 women), 8 part-time/adjunct (all women). *Students:* 14 full-time (11 women), 245 part-time (226 women); includes 37 minority (32 African Americans, 2 Asian Americans or Pacific Islanders, 3 Hispanic Americans). Average age 28. 54 applicants, 80% accepted, 23 enrolled. In 2006, 77 degrees awarded. *Degree requirements:* For master's, exam. *Entrance requirements:* For master's, minimum GPA of 3.0; for CAS, letters of reference, portfolio, master's degree in reading or related field. *Application deadline:* Applications are processed on a rolling basis. Application fee: $50. Electronic applications accepted. *Expenses:* Tuition, state resident: part-time $275 per unit. Tuition, nonresident: part-time $577 per unit. Required fees: $72 per unit. *Financial support:* In 2006–07, 4 students received support. Federal Work-Study, scholarships/grants, and unspecified assistantships available. Financial award application deadline: 4/1; financial award applicants required to submit FAFSA. *Faculty research:* Teacher training, early literacy, adolescent literacy, reading clinics, family literacy. *Unit head:* Dr. Barbara Laster, Graduate Program Director, 410-704-2556, Fax: 410-704-3434, E-mail: blaster@towson.edu. *Application contact:* 410-704-2501, Fax: 410-704-4675, E-mail: grads@towson.edu.

Trevecca Nazarene University, Graduate Division, School of Education, Major in Reading PreK-12, Nashville, TN 37210-2877. Offers M Ed. Part-time and evening/weekend programs avail-

Reading Education

Trevecca Nazarene University *(continued)*
able. *Students:* 18 full-time (all women); includes 4 minority (3 African Americans, 1 American Indian/Alaska Native). *Degree requirements:* For master's, exit assessment. *Entrance requirements:* For master's, GRE General Test, MAT, minimum GPA of 2.7, 2 reference forms. Additional exam requirements/recommendations for international students: Required—TOEFL (minimum score 500 paper-based; 173 computer-based). *Application deadline:* Applications are processed on a rolling basis. Application fee: $25. *Expenses:* Contact institution. Tuition and fees vary according to degree level and program. *Financial support:* Applicants required to submit FAFSA. *Application contact:* Admissions Office, 615-248-1201, Fax: 615-248-1597, E-mail: admissions_ged@trevecca.edu.

Trinity (Washington) University, School of Education, Washington, DC 20017-1094. Offers democracy, diversity, and social justice (M Ed); early childhood (MAT); educational administration (MSA); elementary education (MAT); English as a second language (M Ed, MAT); literacy and reading education (M Ed); school counseling (MA); secondary education (MAT), including English, math, science, social studies; special education (MAT). *Accreditation:* NCATE. Part-time and evening/weekend programs available. *Degree requirements:* For master's, thesis (for some programs), capstone project(s). *Entrance requirements:* For master's, PRAXIS I, minimum GPA of 2.8. Additional exam requirements/recommendations for international students: Required—TOEFL (minimum score 550 paper-based; 213 computer-based). *Faculty research:* Technology, literacy, special education, organizations, inclusion models.

Union College, Graduate Programs, Department of Education, Reading Specialist Program, Barbourville, KY 40906-1499. Offers MA. *Degree requirements:* For master's, thesis optional. *Entrance requirements:* For master's, GRE General Test, NTE.

University at Albany, State University of New York, School of Education, Department of Reading, Albany, NY 12222-0001. Offers MS, Ed D, CAS. Evening/weekend programs available. *Students:* 50 full-time (45 women), 224 part-time (206 women). Average age 38. 83 applicants, 71% accepted, 51 enrolled. In 2006, 145 master's, 2 doctorates, 1 other advanced degree awarded. *Degree requirements:* For doctorate, one foreign language, thesis/dissertation. *Entrance requirements:* For doctorate, GRE General Test. Additional exam requirements/recommendations for international students: Required—TOEFL (minimum score 550 paper-based; 213 computer-based). *Application deadline:* For fall admission, 3/1 for domestic students. Applications are processed on a rolling basis. Application fee: $75. Electronic applications accepted. *Expenses:* Tuition, state resident: full-time $6,900; part-time $288 per credit. Tuition, nonresident: full-time $10,920; part-time $455 per credit. Required fees: $1,139. *Financial support:* Fellowships available. Financial award application deadline: 4/15. *Unit head:* Sean Walmsley, Chair, 518-442-5100.

University at Buffalo, the State University of New York, Graduate School, Graduate School of Education, Department of Learning and Instruction, Buffalo, NY 14260. Offers adolescence education (Certificate); biology (Ed M); chemistry (Ed M); childhood education (Ed M); early childhood and childhood education with bilingual extension (Ed M); early childhood education (Ed M); earth science (Ed M); elementary education (Ed D, PhD); English (Ed M); English education (PhD); English for speakers of other languages (Ed M); foreign and second language education (PhD); French (Ed M); general education (Ed M); German (Ed M); Italian (Ed M); Japanese (Ed M); Latin (Ed M); literary specialist (Ed M); mathematics (Ed M); mathematics education (PhD); mentoring teachers (Certificate); music education (Ed M, Certificate); physics (Ed M); reading education (PhD); Russian (Ed M); school administrator and supervisor (Certificate); science education (PhD); social studies (Ed M); Spanish (Ed M); special education (PhD); teaching and leading for diversity (Certificate); teaching English to speakers of other languages (Ed M). Part-time and evening/weekend programs available. Postbaccalaureate distance learning degree programs offered (no on-campus study). *Faculty:* 30 full-time (20 women), 53 part-time/adjunct (38 women). *Students:* 368 full-time (269 women), 297 part-time (226 women); includes 50 minority (15 African Americans, 2 American Indian/Alaska Native, 14 Asian Americans or Pacific Islanders, 19 Hispanic Americans), 66 international. Average age 31. 638 applicants, 75% accepted, 298 enrolled. In 2006, 248 master's, 18 doctorates, 48 other advanced degrees awarded. Terminal master's awarded for partial completion of doctoral program. *Degree requirements:* For master's, comprehensive exam, registration; for doctorate, thesis/dissertation, research analysis exam, research experience component. *Entrance requirements:* For doctorate, GRE General Test or MAT, interview, writing sample, letters of recommendation. Additional exam requirements/recommendations for international students: Required—TOEFL (minimum score 600 paper-based; 250 computer-based). *Application deadline:* For fall admission, 2/1 priority date for domestic and international students; for spring admission, 11/15 priority date for domestic students, 10/1 for international students. Applications are processed on a rolling basis. Application fee: $50. Electronic applications accepted. *Financial support:* In 2006–07, 70 students received support, including 6 fellowships with full tuition reimbursements available (averaging $10,000 per year), 16 research assistantships with full tuition reimbursements available (averaging $9,000 per year), teaching assistantships with full tuition reimbursements available (averaging $9,000 per year); career-related internships or fieldwork, Federal Work-Study, institutionally sponsored loans, scholarships/grants, tuition waivers (partial), and unspecified assistantships also available. Financial award application deadline: 2/28; financial award applicants required to submit FAFSA. *Faculty research:* Science assessment, state-level testing, early learning, literacy, second language acquisition. Total annual research expenditures: $432,366. *Unit head:* Dr. Maria E. Runfola, Chair, 716-645-2455, Fax: 716-645-3161. *Application contact:* Barbara Belz, Admissions Secretary, 716-645-2110 Ext. 1159, Fax: 716-645-3161, E-mail: belz@buffalo.edu.

University of Alaska Fairbanks, School of Education, Fairbanks, AK 99775-7520. Offers cross cultural education (M Ed); curriculum instruction (M Ed); education (M Ed); guidance and counseling (M Ed); k-12 reading (M Ed); language and literacy (M Ed). *Accreditation:* NCATE. Part-time programs available. Postbaccalaureate distance learning degree programs offered. *Faculty:* 18 full-time (10 women), 3 part-time/adjunct (all women). *Students:* 56 full-time (40 women), 89 part-time (72 women); includes 31 minority (4 African Americans, 21 American Indian/Alaska Native, 2 Asian Americans or Pacific Islanders, 4 Hispanic Americans), 1 international. Average age 37. 69 applicants, 67% accepted, 42 enrolled. In 2006, 33 degrees awarded. *Degree requirements:* For master's, thesis or alternative, student teaching, comprehensive exam, registration. *Entrance requirements:* For master's, GRE General Test, PRAXIS I. Additional exam requirements/recommendations for international students: Required—TOEFL (minimum score 550 paper-based; 213 computer-based). *Application deadline:* For fall admission, 3/1 for domestic and international students; for spring admission, 10/1 for domestic students, 9/1 for international students. Application fee: $50. Electronic applications accepted. *Financial support:* In 2006–07, 2 research assistantships with tuition reimbursements (averaging $6,510 per year), 4 teaching assistantships with tuition reimbursements (averaging $10,441 per year) were awarded; fellowships with tuition reimbursements, career-related internships or fieldwork, Federal Work-Study, and scholarships/grants also available. Financial award applicants required to submit FAFSA. *Faculty research:* Native ways of knowing, classroom research in methods of literacy instruction, multiple intelligence theory, geometry concept development, mathematics and science curriculum development. *Unit head:* Dr. Eric C. Madsen, Dean, 907-474-7341, Fax: 907-474-5451, E-mail: fysoed@uaf.edu.

The University of Arizona, Graduate College, College of Education, Department of Language, Reading, and Culture, Tucson, AZ 85721. Offers bilingual education (M Ed); bilingual/multicultural education (MA); language, reading and culture (MA, Ed D, PhD, Ed S). Part-time programs available. *Faculty:* 9 full-time (6 women), 12 part-time/adjunct (9 women). *Students:* 81 full-time (62 women), 89 part-time (71 women); includes 54 minority (4 African Americans, 13 American Indian/Alaska Native, 5 Asian Americans or Pacific Islanders, 32 Hispanic Americans), 20 international. Average age 40. 56 applicants, 75% accepted, 37 enrolled. In 2006, 28 master's, 13 doctorates awarded. Terminal master's awarded for partial completion of doctoral program. *Degree requirements:* For master's, thesis (MA), thesis optional; for doctorate, thesis/dissertation, comprehensive exam, registration; for Ed S, thesis optional. *Entrance*

requirements: For doctorate and Ed S, GRE, MAT. Additional exam requirements/recommendations for international students: Required—TOEFL. *Application deadline:* For fall admission, 2/1 for domestic students; for spring admission, 10/1 for domestic students. Application fee: $50. *Financial support:* In 2006–07, 12 fellowships with full and partial tuition reimbursements (averaging $1,333 per year), 6 research assistantships with full and partial tuition reimbursements (averaging $5,200 per year), 5 teaching assistantships with full and partial tuition reimbursements (averaging $5,500 per year) were awarded; career-related internships or fieldwork, scholarships/grants, health care benefits, tuition waivers (full and partial), and unspecified assistantships also available. Financial award application deadline: 3/7; financial award applicants required to submit FAFSA. *Faculty research:* Reading, Native American education, language policy, children's literature, bilingual/bicultural literacy. Total annual research expenditures: $500,000. *Unit head:* Dr. Patricia L. Anders, Head, 520-621-1311, Fax: 520-621-1853. *Application contact:* Maria Fierro, Graduate Coordinator, 520-621-1311, Fax: 520-621-1853.

University of Arkansas at Little Rock, Graduate School, College of Education, Department of Teacher Education, Program in Middle Childhood Education, Little Rock, AR 72204-1099. Offers middle childhood education (M Ed); reading (M Ed).

University of Bridgeport, School of Education and Human Resources, Division of Education, Program in Secondary Education, Bridgeport, CT 06604. Offers computer specialist (Diploma); international education (Diploma); reading specialist (MS, Diploma); secondary education (MS, Diploma). Part-time and evening/weekend programs available. *Faculty:* 12 full-time (5 women), 72 part-time/adjunct (44 women). *Students:* 1 full-time (0 women), 5 part-time (all women). Average age 37. 8 applicants, 63% accepted, 1 enrolled. In 2006, 4 degrees awarded. *Degree requirements:* For master's, final exam, final project, or thesis; for Diploma, thesis or alternative, final project. *Entrance requirements:* For master's, GRE General Test, MAT, minimum undergraduate QPA of 2.5; for Diploma, GRE General Test or MAT, minimum graduate QPA of 3.0. *Application deadline:* For fall admission, 8/1 priority date for domestic students; for spring admission, 12/1 priority date for domestic students. Applications are processed on a rolling basis. Application fee: $25 ($35 for international students). Electronic applications accepted. *Financial support:* Career-related internships or fieldwork, Federal Work-Study, and institutionally sponsored loans available. Support available to part-time students. Financial award application deadline: 6/1; financial award applicants required to submit FAFSA. *Faculty research:* Self-concept, internship assessment, stress and situational development, follow-up of graduation, trend analysis. *Unit head:* Dr. Allen P. Cook, Associate Dean, Division of Education, 203-576-4206, Fax: 203-576-4200, E-mail: acook@bridgeport.edu.

The University of British Columbia, Faculty of Graduate Studies, Faculty of Education, Program in Language and Literacy Education, Vancouver, BC V6T 1Z1, Canada. Offers library education (M Ed, MA, PhD); literacy education (M Ed, MA, PhD); modern language education (M Ed, MA, PhD); teaching English as a second language (M Ed, MA, PhD). Part-time and evening/weekend programs available. *Faculty:* 27 full-time (14 women). *Students:* 127 (102 women). 80 applicants, 73% accepted, 42 enrolled. In 2006, 28 master's, 2 doctorates awarded. *Degree requirements:* For master's, thesis (MA); for doctorate, thesis/dissertation. *Entrance requirements:* For master's and doctorate, minimum B+ average in last 2 years with minimum 2 courses at A standing. Additional exam requirements/recommendations for international students: Required—TOEFL (minimum score 550 paper-based; 213 computer-based), TWE (minimum score 4.5). *Application deadline:* For fall admission, 2/1 priority date for domestic students, 12/15 for international students; for spring admission, 8/1 for domestic students. Applications are processed on a rolling basis. Application fee: $90 Canadian dollars ($150 Canadian dollars for international students). Electronic applications accepted. *Financial support:* In 2006–07, fellowships with partial tuition reimbursements (averaging $16,000 per year), research assistantships (averaging $4,000 per year), teaching assistantships (averaging $5,344 per year) were awarded; institutionally sponsored loans, scholarships/grants, tuition waivers (full and partial), and unspecified assistantships also available. *Faculty research:* Language and literacy development, second language acquisition, Asia Pacific language curriculum, children's literature, whole language instruction. Total annual research expenditures: $500,000. *Unit head:* Dr. Geoff Williams, Head, 604-827-5785, Fax: 604-822-3154, E-mail: lled.educ@ubc.ca. *Application contact:* Graduate Secretary, 604-822-8259, Fax: 604-822-3154, E-mail: lled.educ@ubc.ca.

University of California, Berkeley, Graduate Division, School of Education, Division of Language and Literacy, Society and Culture, Berkeley, CA 94720-1500. Offers education and single subject credential: English (MA); language, literacy, and culture (MA, Ed D, PhD), including athletes and academic achievement (MA), language, literacy, and culture (MA); social and cultural studies in education (MA, PhD); PhD/MA. *Degree requirements:* For master's, exam or thesis; for doctorate, thesis/dissertation, oral qualifying exam (PhD). *Entrance requirements:* For master's and doctorate, GRE General Test, minimum GPA of 3.0 during last 2 years of undergraduate course work. *Application deadline:* For fall admission, 12/1 for domestic students. Application fee: $60 ($80 for international students). Electronic applications accepted. *Financial support:* Fellowships, research assistantships, teaching assistantships, unspecified assistantships available. *Faculty research:* Literature, English education, reading education, second language teaching and learning, teacher education. *Application contact:* Admissions Office, 510-642-0841, Fax: 510-642-4808, E-mail: gse_info@uclink.berkeley.edu.

University of Central Arkansas, Graduate School, College of Education, Department of Early Childhood and Special Education, Program in Reading Education, Conway, AR 72035-0001. Offers MSE. *Accreditation:* NCATE. Part-time programs available. *Students:* 1 (woman) full-time, 77 part-time (all women); includes 5 minority (3 African Americans, 2 Hispanic Americans), 1 international. 36 applicants, 100% accepted, 36 enrolled. In 2006, 9 degrees awarded. *Degree requirements:* For master's, thesis optional. *Entrance requirements:* For master's, GRE General Test, minimum GPA of 2.7. Additional exam requirements/recommendations for international students: Required—TOEFL (minimum score 550 paper-based; 213 computer-based). *Application deadline:* For fall admission, 3/1 priority date for domestic and international students; for spring admission, 10/1 priority date for domestic and international students. Applications are processed on a rolling basis. Application fee: $25 ($40 for international students). *Expenses:* Tuition, state resident: full-time $4,194; part-time $233 per semester. Tuition, nonresident: full-time $5,963; part-time $429 per semester. International tuition: $6,162 full-time. Required fees: $65; $23 per semester. One-time fee: $65 part-time. *Financial support:* Federal Work-Study, scholarships/grants, tuition waivers (partial), and unspecified assistantships available. Support available to part-time students. Financial award application deadline: 2/15; financial award applicants required to submit FAFSA. *Unit head:* Mary Mosley, Coordinator, 501-450-5461, Fax: 501-450-5358, E-mail: marym@uca.edu. *Application contact:* Brenda Herring, Admissions Assistant, 501-450-5065, Fax: 501-450-5678, E-mail: bherring@uca.edu.

University of Central Florida, College of Education, Department of Teaching and Learning Principles, Program in Reading Education, Orlando, FL 32816. Offers M Ed, MA, Certificate. *Accreditation:* NCATE. Part-time and evening/weekend programs available. *Students:* 9 full-time (all women), 82 part-time (80 women); includes 7 minority (3 African Americans, 4 Hispanic Americans). In 2006, 34 master's, 18 other advanced degrees awarded. *Degree requirements:* For master's, thesis or alternative. *Entrance requirements:* For master's, GRE General Test. Additional exam requirements/recommendations for international students: Required—TOEFL. *Application deadline:* For fall admission, 7/15 for domestic students; for spring admission, 12/1 for domestic students. Application fee: $30. Electronic applications accepted. *Expenses:* Tuition, state resident: full-time $6,167; part-time $257 per credit hour. Tuition, nonresident: full-time $22,790; part-time $950 per credit hour. *Financial support:* In 2006–07, 1 research assistantship with partial tuition reimbursement (averaging $8,800 per year) was awarded; fellowships with partial tuition reimbursements, teaching assistantships with partial tuition reimbursements, career-related internships or fieldwork, Federal Work-Study, institutionally sponsored loans, tuition waivers (full), and unspecified assistantships also available. Financial award application deadline: 3/1; financial award applicants required to submit FAFSA. *Unit head:* Dr. Karri Williams, Coordinator, 321-632-1111, E-mail: kjwilliams@mail.ucf.edu.

University of Central Missouri, The Graduate School, College of Education, Department of Curriculum and Instruction, Warrensburg, MO 64093. Offers curriculum and instruction (Ed S); elementary education (MSE); K–12 education (MSE); literacy education (MSE); secondary education (MSE). *Accreditation:* NCATE. Part-time programs available. *Faculty:* 22 full-time (14 women). *Students:* 43 full-time (33 women), 309 part-time (237 women); includes 27 minority (23 African Americans, 1 Asian American or Pacific Islander, 3 Hispanic Americans), 3 international. Average age 33. 81 applicants, 81% accepted, 65 enrolled. In 2006, 70 master's, 1 other advanced degree awarded. *Degree requirements:* For master's, comprehensive exam or thesis; for Ed S, thesis, comprehensive exam. *Entrance requirements:* For master's, GRE General Test, minimum GPA of 2.75, teaching certificate; for Ed S, GRE General Test, minimum GPA of 3.25, teaching certificate. Additional exam requirements/recommendations for international students: Required—TOEFL (minimum score 500 paper-based; 173 computer-based). *Application deadline:* For fall admission, 6/1 priority date for domestic students, 5/1 priority date for international students; for spring admission, 10/1 priority date for domestic students, 10/1 for international students. Applications are processed on a rolling basis. Application fee: $30 ($50 for international students). *Expenses:* Tuition, state resident: full-time $5,448; part-time $227 per credit hour. Tuition, nonresident: full-time $10,896; part-time $454 per credit hour. Required fees: $336; $14 per credit hour. *Financial support:* In 2006–07, 4 students received support. Federal Work-Study, scholarships/grants, unspecified assistantships, and administrative and laboratory assistantships available. Support available to part-time students. Financial award application deadline: 3/1; financial award applicants required to submit FAFSA. *Faculty research:* Reading maturity, student and faculty evaluation, online teaching and learning, video documentation, teacher candidates' assessment of student thinking and learning. *Unit head:* Dr. Sharon Lamson, Chair, 660-543-4235, Fax: 660-543-4167, E-mail: lamson@ucmo.edu.

University of Central Oklahoma, College of Graduate Studies and Research, College of Education, Department of Curriculum and Instruction, Program in Reading, Edmond, OK 73034-5209. Offers M Ed. *Accreditation:* NCATE. Part-time programs available. *Entrance requirements:* For master's, GRE General Test. Additional exam requirements/recommendations for international students: Required—TOEFL (minimum score 550 paper-based; 213 computer-based). Electronic applications accepted.

University of Cincinnati, Division of Research and Advanced Studies, College of Education, Criminal Justice, and Human Services, Division of Teacher Education, Program in Reading/Literacy, Cincinnati, OH 45221. Offers M Ed, Ed D. *Accreditation:* NCATE. Part-time programs available. *Students:* 22. *Degree requirements:* For master's, thesis or alternative; for doctorate, thesis/dissertation. *Entrance requirements:* For master's, GRE General Test. Additional exam requirements/recommendations for international students: Required—TOEFL (minimum score 550 paper-based; 213 computer-based), TWE (minimum score 4.5), OEPT. *Application deadline:* For fall admission, 2/1 for domestic students. Application fee: $40. Electronic applications accepted. *Financial support:* Fellowships, tuition waivers (partial) and unspecified assistantships available. *Application contact:* Cheri Williams, Chair, 513-556-3571, Fax: 513-556-1001, E-mail: cheri.williams@uc.edu.

University of Connecticut, Graduate School, Neag School of Education, Department of Curriculum and Instruction, Storrs, CT 06269. Offers curriculum and instruction (MA, PhD), including agriculture education, bilingual and bicultural education, elementary education, English education, history and social sciences education, mathematics education, reading education, science education, secondary education, world languages education. *Accreditation:* NCATE. *Faculty:* 28 full-time (12 women). *Students:* 158 full-time (120 women), 54 part-time (44 women); includes 24 minority (3 African Americans, 1 American Indian/Alaska Native, 3 Asian Americans or Pacific Islanders, 17 Hispanic Americans), 2 international. Average age 27. 268 applicants, 76% accepted, 203 enrolled. In 2006, 181 master's, 4 doctorates awarded. Terminal master's awarded for partial completion of doctoral program. *Degree requirements:* For master's, thesis or alternative, comprehensive exam; for doctorate, thesis/dissertation. *Entrance requirements:* For doctorate, GRE General Test. Additional exam requirements/recommendations for international students: Required—TOEFL (minimum score 550 paper-based; 213 computer-based). *Application deadline:* For fall admission, 2/1 priority date for domestic and international students; for spring admission, 11/1 for domestic students, 10/1 for international students. Applications are processed on a rolling basis. Application fee: $55. Electronic applications accepted. *Financial support:* In 2006–07, 14 research assistantships with full tuition reimbursements, 4 teaching assistantships with full tuition reimbursements were awarded; fellowships, Federal Work-Study, scholarships/grants, health care benefits, and unspecified assistantships also available. Financial award application deadline: 2/1; financial award applicants required to submit FAFSA. *Unit head:* Mary Anne Doyle, Head, 860-486-2433, Fax: 860-486-0280. *Application contact:* Lisa Rasicot, Graduate Coordinator, 860-486-3065, Fax: 860-486-0210, E-mail: soeadm02@uconnvm.uconn.edu.

University of Connecticut, Graduate School, Neag School of Education, Department of Curriculum and Instruction, Field of Curriculum and Instruction, Program in Reading Education, Storrs, CT 06269. Offers MA, PhD. *Accreditation:* NCATE. *Faculty:* 9 full-time (7 women). *Students:* 8 full-time (all women), 12 part-time (all women). Average age 35. 21 applicants, 67% accepted, 12 enrolled. In 2006, 9 degrees awarded. Terminal master's awarded for partial completion of doctoral program. *Degree requirements:* For master's, thesis or alternative, comprehensive exam; for doctorate, thesis/dissertation. *Entrance requirements:* For doctorate, GRE General Test. Additional exam requirements/recommendations for international students: Required—TOEFL (minimum score 550 paper-based; 213 computer-based). *Application deadline:* For fall admission, 2/1 priority date for domestic and international students; for spring admission, 11/1 for domestic students, 10/1 for international students. Applications are processed on a rolling basis. Application fee: $55. Electronic applications accepted. *Financial support:* In 2006–07, 1 research assistantship with full tuition reimbursement was awarded; fellowships, teaching assistantships with full tuition reimbursements, Federal Work-Study, scholarships/grants, health care benefits, and unspecified assistantships also available. Financial award application deadline: 2/1; financial award applicants required to submit FAFSA. *Application contact:* Lisa Rasicot, Graduate Coordinator, 860-486-3065, Fax: 860-486-0210, E-mail: soeadm02@uconnvm.uconn.edu.

University of Dayton, Graduate School, School of Education and Allied Professions, Department of Teacher Education, Dayton, OH 45469-1300. Offers adolescent/young adult (MS Ed); art education (MS Ed); early childhood education (MS Ed); inclusive early childhood (MS Ed); interdisciplinary education (MS Ed); intervention specialist education, mild/moderate (MS Ed); literacy (MS Ed); middle childhood (MS Ed); multi-age education (MS Ed); music education (MS Ed); teacher as leader (MS Ed); technology in education (MS Ed). Part-time and evening/weekend programs available. *Faculty:* 13 full-time (9 women), 33 part-time/adjunct (25 women). *Students:* 149 full-time (120 women), 284 part-time (241 women); includes 37 minority (31 African Americans, 3 Asian Americans or Pacific Islanders, 3 Hispanic Americans), 3 international. Average age 33. 201 applicants, 58% accepted, 31 enrolled. In 2006, 150 degrees awarded. *Degree requirements:* For master's, thesis, capstone research project. *Entrance requirements:* For master's, GRE General Test, minimum GPA of 2.75. Additional exam requirements/recommendations for international students: Required—TOEFL (minimum score 550 paper-based; 213 computer-based). *Application deadline:* For fall admission, 3/15 priority date for domestic students, 3/1 priority date for international students. Applications are processed on a rolling basis. Application fee: $0. Electronic applications accepted. *Expenses: Contact institution. Financial support:* In 2006–07, 8 teaching assistantships with partial tuition reimbursements (averaging $7,600 per year) were awarded; career-related internships or fieldwork, institutionally sponsored loans, health care benefits, and unspecified assistantships also available. Financial award applicants required to submit FAFSA. *Faculty research:* Diversity, literacy, art representation by young children, preservice teacher preparation. Total annual research expenditures: $330,000. *Unit head:* Dr. Katie A. Kinnucan-Welsch, Chair, 937-229-3346. *Application contact:* Erika Eavers, Graduate Admission Processor, 937-229-3065, Fax: 937-229-4729, E-mail: erika.eavers@notes.udayton.edu.

University of Florida, Graduate School, College of Education, School of Teaching and Learning, Gainesville, FL 32611. Offers bilingual/ESOL education (M Ed, MAE, Ed D, PhD, Ed S); curriculum and instruction (M Ed, MAE, Ed D, PhD, Ed S); early childhood education (Ed D, PhD, Ed S); elementary education (M Ed, MAE); English education (M Ed, MAE); mathematics education (M Ed, MAE); reading education (M Ed, MAE); science education (M Ed, MAE); social foundations (M Ed, MAE, Ed D, PhD); social studies education (M Ed, MAE). *Accreditation:* NCATE. *Faculty:* 29 full-time (20 women). *Students:* 506 (406 women); includes 87 minority (20 African Americans, 3 American Indian/Alaska Native, 13 Asian Americans or Pacific Islanders, 51 Hispanic Americans) 34 international. In 2006, 278 master's, 8 doctorates awarded. *Degree requirements:* For master's, thesis optional; for doctorate, variable foreign language requirement, thesis/dissertation. *Entrance requirements:* For master's and doctorate, GRE General Test, minimum GPA of 3.0; for Ed S, GRE General Test. Additional exam requirements/recommendations for international students: Required—TOEFL (minimum score 550 paper-based; 213 computer-based). *Application deadline:* For fall admission, 6/1 for domestic students. Applications are processed on a rolling basis. Application fee: $30. Electronic applications accepted. *Expenses:* Tuition, state resident: full-time $6,827. Tuition, nonresident: full-time $21,951. Required fees: $999. *Financial support:* In 2006–07, 5 research assistantships (averaging $11,947 per year), 22 teaching assistantships (averaging $9,709 per year) were awarded; fellowships, career-related internships or fieldwork and unspecified assistantships also available. *Faculty research:* Teacher education, inclusive education, classroom processes, curriculum and technology. *Unit head:* Dr. Tom Dana, Director, 352-392-9191 Ext. 200, Fax: 352-392-9193, E-mail: tdana@coe.ufl.edu. *Application contact:* Dr. Linda C. Jones, Coordinator, 352-392-0761 Ext. 267, Fax: 352-392-9193, E-mail: lcjones@coe.ufl.edu.

University of Georgia, Graduate School, College of Education, Department of Language and Literacy Education, Athens, GA 30602. Offers M Ed, MA, Ed D, PhD, Ed S. *Accreditation:* NCATE. *Faculty:* 17 full-time (10 women). *Students:* 82 full-time (68 women), 111 part-time (96 women); includes 23 minority (12 African Americans, 1 Asian American or Pacific Islander, 10 Hispanic Americans), 14 international. 110 applicants, 39% accepted, 17 enrolled. In 2006, 54 master's, 8 doctorates, 12 other advanced degrees awarded. *Entrance requirements:* For master's and Ed S, GRE General Test or MAT; for doctorate, GRE General Test. Additional exam requirements/recommendations for international students: Required—TOEFL (minimum score 550 paper-based; 213 computer-based). *Application deadline:* For fall admission, 7/1 priority date for domestic students; for spring admission, 11/15 for domestic students. Application fee: $50. Electronic applications accepted. *Faculty research:* Comprehension, critical literacy, literacy and technology, vocabulary instruction, content area reading. *Unit head:* Dr. Joel A. Taxel, Head, 706-542-4511, Fax: 706-542-3817, E-mail: jtaxel@uga.edu. *Application contact:* Dr. Mark A. Faust, Graduate Coordinator, 706-542-4516, Fax: 706-542-4509, E-mail: mfaust@uga.edu.

University of Guam, Graduate School and Research, College of Education, Program in Language and Literacy, Mangilao, GU 96923. Offers M Ed. Part-time programs available. *Degree requirements:* For master's, comprehensive oral and written exams, special project or thesis. *Entrance requirements:* For master's, GRE General Test. Additional exam requirements/recommendations for international students: Required—TOEFL.

University of Houston, College of Education, Department of Curriculum and Instruction, Houston, TX 77204. Offers art education (M Ed); bilingual education (M Ed); curriculum and instruction (Ed D); early childhood education (M Ed); education of the gifted (M Ed); elementary education (M Ed); mathematics education (M Ed); reading and language arts education (M Ed); science education (M Ed); second language education (M Ed); secondary education (M Ed); social studies education (M Ed); teaching (M Ed). *Accreditation:* NCATE. Part-time and evening/weekend programs available. *Faculty:* 24 full-time (11 women), 16 part-time/adjunct (14 women). *Students:* 134 full-time (102 women), 327 part-time (256 women); includes 142 minority (49 African Americans, 1 American Indian/Alaska Native, 29 Asian Americans or Pacific Islanders, 63 Hispanic Americans), 19 international. Average age 37. 113 applicants, 72% accepted, 61 enrolled. In 2006, 106 master's, 32 doctorates awarded. *Degree requirements:* For master's, comprehensive exam or thesis; for doctorate, thesis/dissertation, comprehensive exam. *Entrance requirements:* For master's, GRE General Test or MAT; for doctorate, GRE General Test, interview. *Application deadline:* For fall admission, 7/3 priority date for domestic students. Applications are processed on a rolling basis. Application fee: $35 ($75 for international students). *Expenses:* Tuition, state resident: full-time $5,429; part-time $226 per credit. Tuition, nonresident: full-time $12,029; part-time $501 per credit. Required fees: $2,454. *Financial support:* In 2006–07, 2 fellowships with full tuition reimbursements (averaging $9,500 per year), 6 research assistantships with full tuition reimbursements (averaging $8,800 per year), 25 teaching assistantships with full tuition reimbursements (averaging $8,800 per year) were awarded; career-related internships or fieldwork, Federal Work-Study, institutionally sponsored loans, scholarships/grants, health care benefits, and unspecified assistantships also available. Support available to part-time students. Financial award application deadline: 3/10. *Faculty research:* Teaching-learning process, instructional technology in schools, teacher education, classroom management, at-risk students. *Unit head:* Dr. Juanita Copley, Chairperson, 713-743-4950, Fax: 713-743-4990, E-mail: ncopley@aol.com.

University of Houston–Clear Lake, School of Education, Program in Curriculum and Instruction, Houston, TX 77058-1098. Offers curriculum and instruction (MS); early childhood education (MS); reading (MS); school library and information science (MS). Part-time and evening/weekend programs available. *Faculty:* 17 full-time (15 women), 9 part-time/adjunct (7 women). *Students:* 40 full-time (39 women), 185 part-time (176 women); includes 66 minority (32 African Americans, 7 Asian Americans or Pacific Islanders, 27 Hispanic Americans), 6 international. Average age 34. In 2006, 80 degrees awarded. *Degree requirements:* For master's, thesis (for some programs). *Entrance requirements:* For master's, GRE or minimum GPA of 3.0 in last 60 hours. Additional exam requirements/recommendations for international students: Required—TOEFL (minimum score 550 paper-based; 213 computer-based). *Application deadline:* For fall admission, 7/1 for domestic students, 6/1 for international students; for spring admission, 10/1 for domestic and international students. Applications are processed on a rolling basis. Application fee: $35 ($75 for international students). Electronic applications accepted. *Financial support:* Career-related internships or fieldwork, Federal Work-Study, institutionally sponsored loans, and scholarships/grants available. Support available to part-time students. Financial award application deadline: 5/1; financial award applicants required to submit FAFSA. *Unit head:* Dr. Suzanne Brown, Chair, 281-283-3540, E-mail: brownsue@uhcl.edu. *Application contact:* Janis S. Bigelow, Assistant Director of Admissions, Recruitment and Communications, 281-283-2540, Fax: 281-283-2530, E-mail: bigelow@uhcl.edu.

University of Illinois at Chicago, Graduate College, College of Education, Department of Curriculum and Instruction, Chicago, IL 60607-7128. Offers curriculum and instruction (PhD); educational psychology (PhD); instructional leadership (M Ed), including elementary education, reading, secondary education; leadership and administration (M Ed); policy and administration (PhD); policy studies in urban education (PhD). Part-time and evening/weekend programs available. *Degree requirements:* For doctorate, thesis/dissertation. *Entrance requirements:* For master's, minimum GPA of 2.75; for doctorate, GRE General Test, minimum GPA of 2.75. Additional exam requirements/recommendations for international students: Required—TOEFL. Electronic applications accepted. *Faculty research:* Curriculum theory, curriculum development, research on teaching, curriculum and context, reading/literacy.

University of La Verne, College of Education and Organizational Leadership, Department of Education, Program in Reading, La Verne, CA 91750-4443. Offers reading (M Ed, Certificate); reading and language arts specialist (Credential). *Faculty:* 15 full-time (10 women), 6 part-time/adjunct (all women). *Students:* 1 (woman) full-time, 45 part-time (41 women); includes 21 minority (1 African American, 2 Asian Americans or Pacific Islanders, 18 Hispanic Americans).

Reading Education

University of La Verne (continued)

Average age 35. In 2006, 13 degrees awarded. *Degree requirements:* For master's, thesis optional. *Entrance requirements:* For master's, MAT, California Basic Educational Skills Test, minimum GPA of 3.0, basic teaching credential, interview, 3 letters of reference. *Application deadline:* Applications are processed on a rolling basis. Application fee: $50. *Expenses:* Contact institution. *Financial support:* Institutionally sponsored loans, scholarships/grants, and unspecified assistantships available. Financial award application deadline: 3/2; financial award applicants required to submit FAFSA. *Unit head:* Dr. Janice Pilgreen, Chairperson, 909-593-3511 Ext. 4624, E-mail: pilgreen@ulv.edu. *Application contact:* Jo Nell Baker, Director, Graduate Admissions and Academic Services, 909-593-3511 Ext. 4244, Fax: 909-392-2761, E-mail: gradadmt@ulv.edu.

University of La Verne, Regional Campus Administration, Master's Programs in Education, California Statewide Campus, La Verne, CA 91750-4443. Offers advanced teaching (M Ed); educational management (M Ed), including preliminary administrative services credential; reading (M Ed); school counseling (MS), including public personnel services credential. *Faculty:* 3 full-time (0 women), 60 part-time/adjunct (38 women). *Students:* 203 full-time (151 women), 268 part-time (210 women); includes 216 minority (42 African Americans, 5 American Indian/Alaska Native, 27 Asian Americans or Pacific Islanders, 142 Hispanic Americans). Average age 36. In 2006, 289 degrees awarded. *Entrance requirements:* For master's, California Basic Educational Skills Test, 3 letters of recommendation, teaching credential. *Application deadline:* Applications are processed on a rolling basis. Application fee: $50. *Expenses:* Contact institution. *Financial support:* Fellowships, institutionally sponsored loans available. Financial award application deadline: 3/2; financial award applicants required to submit FAFSA. *Unit head:* Juline Behrens, Director, 909-985-0944, Fax: 909-981-8695, E-mail: behrensj@ulv.edu.

University of Louisiana at Monroe, Graduate Studies and Research, College of Education and Human Development, Department of Curriculum and Instruction, Program in Reading, Monroe, LA 71209-0001. Offers M Ed. *Accreditation:* NCATE. *Students:* 1 (woman) full-time. Average age 29. *Entrance requirements:* For master's, GRE General Test, minimum GPA of 2.5. *Application deadline:* For fall admission, 6/1 priority date for domestic students; for spring admission, 11/1 for domestic students. Applications are processed on a rolling basis. Application fee: $20 ($30 for international students). *Expenses:* Tuition, state resident: part-time $124 per credit hour. Tuition, nonresident: part-time $124 per credit hour. *Financial support:* Research assistantships, teaching assistantships available. Financial award application deadline: 7/1. *Unit head:* Dr. Gary Stringer, Head, Department of Curriculum and Instruction, 318-342-1266, Fax: 318-342-1240, E-mail: stringer@ulm.edu.

University of Louisville, Graduate School, College of Education and Human Development, Department of Teaching and Learning, Program in Reading Education, Louisville, KY 40292-0001. Offers M Ed. *Accreditation:* NCATE. *Students:* 9 full-time (8 women), 13 part-time (all women), 2 international. Average age 39. In 2006, 10 degrees awarded. *Entrance requirements:* For master's, GRE General Test. *Application deadline:* Applications are processed on a rolling basis. Application fee: $50. Electronic applications accepted. *Financial support:* Fellowships, research assistantships, teaching assistantships available. *Unit head:* Dr. Brenda Overturf, Head, 502-852-6431, Fax: 502-852-1497, E-mail: b0over01@louisville.edu.

University of Maine, Graduate School, College of Education and Human Development, Program in Literacy Education, Orono, ME 04469. Offers M Ed, MA, MS, Ed D, CAS. *Accreditation:* NCATE. Part-time and evening/weekend programs available. *Students:* 19 full-time (18 women), 27 part-time (26 women), 1 international. Average age 42. 11 applicants, 82% accepted, 9 enrolled. In 2006, 20 master's, 6 other advanced degrees awarded. *Degree requirements:* For master's, thesis or alternative; for doctorate, thesis/dissertation. *Entrance requirements:* For master's, MAT; for doctorate, GRE General Test, MA, M Ed, or MS; for CAS, MAT, MA, M Ed, or MS. Additional exam requirements/recommendations for international students: Required—TOEFL. *Application deadline:* For fall admission, 2/1 priority date for domestic students. Applications are processed on a rolling basis. Application fee: $50. Electronic applications accepted. *Financial support:* In 2006–07, teaching assistantships with tuition reimbursements (averaging $9,010 per year); career-related internships or fieldwork, Federal Work-Study, institutionally sponsored loans, tuition waivers (full and partial), and unspecified assistantships also available. Support available to part-time students. Financial award application deadline: 3/1. *Unit head:* Dr. Dorothy Breen, Coordinator, 207-581-2444, Fax: 207-581-2423. *Application contact:* Scott G. Delcourt, Associate Dean of the Graduate School, 207-581-3219, Fax: 207-581-3232, E-mail: graduate@maine.edu.

University of Mary, Program in Education, Bismarck, ND 58504-9652. Offers college teaching (MS Ed); curriculum and instruction (MS Ed); early childhood education (MS Ed); early childhood special education (MS Ed); elementary education administration (MS Ed); reading (MS Ed); secondary education administration (MS Ed); special education (MS Ed). Part-time programs available. *Faculty:* 8 full-time (4 women), 12 part-time/adjunct (7 women). *Students:* 2 full-time (1 woman), 34 part-time (25 women), 2 international. Average age 35. In 2006, 17 degrees awarded. *Degree requirements:* For master's, portfolio or thesis. *Entrance requirements:* For master's, interview, letters of reference. *Application deadline:* Applications are processed on a rolling basis. Application fee: $40. *Financial support:* In 2006–07, 1 teaching assistantship with full tuition reimbursement was awarded; career-related internships or fieldwork also available. Support available to part-time students. Financial award application deadline: 8/1; financial award applicants required to submit FAFSA. *Faculty research:* Innovative pedagogy in higher education, technology in education, content standards, children of poverty, children with diverse learning needs. *Unit head:* Dr. Rebecca Yunker Salveson, Director, 701-355-8186, E-mail: rysalves@umary.edu. *Application contact:* Leona Friedig, Administrative Secretary, 701-355-8058, E-mail: lfriedig@umary.edu.

University of Mary Hardin-Baylor, College of Education, Belton, TX 76513. Offers educational administration (M Ed, Ed D); educational psychology (M Ed); exercise and sport science (M Ed); general studies (M Ed); reading education (M Ed). Part-time and evening/weekend programs available. *Faculty:* 10 full-time (5 women), 1 part-time/adjunct (0 women). *Students:* 8 full-time (3 women), 36 part-time (26 women); includes 8 minority (3 African Americans, 5 Hispanic Americans). Average age 24. In 2006, 18 degrees awarded. *Degree requirements:* For master's, comprehensive exam, registration. *Entrance requirements:* For master's, GRE General Test, minimum GPA of 2.75, Texas teaching certificate. *Application deadline:* For fall admission, 6/1 priority date for domestic students; for spring admission, 11/1 for domestic students. Applications are processed on a rolling basis. Application fee: $35 ($135 for international students). Electronic applications accepted. *Expenses:* Tuition: Full-time $8,910; part-time $495 per hour. Required fees: $906; $47 per hour. $30 per term. Tuition and fees vary according to course load. *Financial support:* Federal Work-Study, scholarships/grants, and scholarships (for some active duty military personnel only) available. Support available to part-time students. Financial award application deadline: 6/1; financial award applicants required to submit FAFSA. *Unit head:* Dr. Marlene Zipperlen, Dean, 254-295-4572, Fax: 254-295-4480, E-mail: mzipperlen@umhb.edu. *Application contact:* Dr. Shirley Dahl, Director, Graduate Programs in Education, 254-295-4185, Fax: 254-295-4480, E-mail: sdahl@umhb.edu.

University of Maryland, College Park, Graduate Studies, College of Education, Department of Curriculum and Instruction, College Park, MD 20742. Offers reading (M Ed, MA, PhD, CAGS); secondary education (M Ed, MA, Ed D, PhD, CAGS); teaching English to speakers of other languages (M Ed). *Accreditation:* NCATE. Part-time and evening/weekend programs available. Postbaccalaureate distance learning degree programs offered (no on-campus study). *Faculty:* 52 full-time (32 women), 33 part-time/adjunct (30 women). *Students:* 200 full-time (159 women), 189 part-time (155 women); includes 101 minority (48 African Americans, 30 Asian Americans or Pacific Islanders, 23 Hispanic Americans), 33 international. 258 applicants, 62% accepted, 101 enrolled. In 2006, 118 master's, 14 doctorates awarded. *Median time to degree:* Of those who began their doctoral program in fall 1998, 38% received their degree in 8 years or less. *Degree requirements:* For master's, seminar paper; for doctorate, thesis/dissertation, published paper, oral exam, comprehensive exam. *Entrance requirements:* For master's, GRE General Test or MAT, minimum GPA of 3.0, 3 letters of recommendation; for doctorate, GRE General Test or MAT, minimum undergraduate GPA of 3.0, graduate 3.5; 3 letters of recommendation. *Application deadline:* For fall admission, 1/15 for domestic students, 2/1 for international students; for spring admission, 9/1 for domestic students, 6/1 for international students. Applications are processed on a rolling basis. Application fee: $60. Electronic applications accepted. *Financial support:* In 2006–07, 3 fellowships with full tuition reimbursements (averaging $5,677 per year), 25 research assistantships with tuition reimbursements (averaging $16,943 per year), 53 teaching assistantships with tuition reimbursements (averaging $14,810 per year) were awarded; Federal Work-Study and scholarships/grants also available. Support available to part-time students. Financial award applicants required to submit FAFSA. *Faculty research:* Teacher preparation, curriculum study, in-service education. Total annual research expenditures: $3.3 million. *Unit head:* Dr. Stephen M. Koziol, Chairman, 301-405-3117, Fax: 301-314-9055, E-mail: skoziol@umd.edu. *Application contact:* Dean of Graduate School, 301-405-0358, Fax: 301-314-9305.

University of Massachusetts Amherst, Graduate School, School of Education, Program in Education, Amherst, MA 01003. Offers cultural diversity and curriculum reform (M Ed, Ed D, CAGS); early childhood education and development (M Ed, Ed D, CAGS); educational administration (M Ed, Ed D, CAGS); elementary teacher education (M Ed, Ed D, CAGS); higher education (M Ed, Ed D, CAGS); international education (M Ed, Ed D, CAGS); mathematics, science, and instructional technology (M Ed, Ed D, CAGS); physical education teacher education (M Ed, Ed D, CAGS); reading and writing (M Ed, Ed D, CAGS); research and evaluation methods (M Ed, Ed D, CAGS); school psychology and school counseling (M Ed, Ed D, CAGS); secondary teacher education (M Ed, Ed D, CAGS); social justice education (M Ed, Ed D, CAGS); special education (M Ed, Ed D, CAGS). *Accreditation:* NCATE. *Students:* 418 full-time (286 women), 447 part-time (319 women); includes 147 minority (70 African Americans, 4 American Indian/Alaska Native, 28 Asian Americans or Pacific Islanders, 45 Hispanic Americans), 81 international. Average age 36. In 2006, 260 master's, 30 doctorates awarded. *Degree requirements:* For doctorate, thesis/dissertation. *Entrance requirements:* For master's and doctorate, GRE General Test. Additional exam requirements/recommendations for international students: Required—TOEFL (minimum score 530 paper-based; 197 computer-based). *Application deadline:* For fall admission, 1/15 for domestic and international students; for spring admission, 10/1 for domestic and international students. Applications are processed on a rolling basis. Application fee: $40 ($65 for international students). Electronic applications accepted. *Expenses:* Tuition, state resident: full-time $2,640; part-time $110 per credit. Tuition, nonresident: full-time $9,936; part-time $414 per credit. Required fees: $8,969; $3,129 per term. One-time fee: $257 full-time. Tuition and fees vary according to class time, course load, campus/location and reciprocity agreements. *Financial support:* Fellowships with full tuition reimbursements, research assistantships with full tuition reimbursements, teaching assistantships with full tuition reimbursements, career-related internships or fieldwork, Federal Work-Study, scholarships/grants, traineeships, and unspecified assistantships available. Support available to part-time students. Financial award application deadline: 1/15. *Unit head:* Linda L. Griffin, Professor, 413-545-6984.

University of Massachusetts Lowell, Graduate School, Graduate School of Education, Lowell, MA 01854-2881. Offers administration, planning, and policy (CAGS); curriculum and instruction (M Ed, CAGS); educational administration (M Ed); language arts and literacy (Ed D); leadership in schooling (Ed D); math and science education (Ed D); reading and language (M Ed, CAGS). *Accreditation:* NCATE. Part-time and evening/weekend programs available. Postbaccalaureate distance learning degree programs offered (no on-campus study). Terminal master's awarded for partial completion of doctoral program. *Degree requirements:* For doctorate, thesis/dissertation. *Entrance requirements:* For master's and doctorate, GRE General Test. Additional exam requirements/recommendations for international students: Required—TOEFL. Electronic applications accepted.

University of Memphis, Graduate School, College of Education, Department of Instruction and Curriculum Leadership, Memphis, TN 38152. Offers early childhood education (MAT, MS, Ed D); elementary education (MAT); instruction and curriculum (MS, Ed D); instruction design and technology (MS, Ed D); reading (MS, Ed D); secondary education (MAT); special education (MAT, MS, Ed D). *Accreditation:* NCATE (one or more programs are accredited). Part-time programs available. Terminal master's awarded for partial completion of doctoral program. *Degree requirements:* For master's, thesis or alternative, comprehensive exam; for doctorate, thesis/dissertation, comprehensive exam. *Entrance requirements:* For master's, GRE General Test, minimum GPA of 2.5; for doctorate, GRE General Test, GRE Subject Test, 2 years of teaching experience. Electronic applications accepted. *Faculty research:* Effective urban teachers, preparation and retention of urban teachers, technology utilization in schools, field-based preparation teacher preparation programs, effective use of online instruction.

University of Miami, Graduate School, School of Education, Department of Teaching and Learning, Program in Exceptional Student Education, Reading and ESOL, Coral Gables, FL 33124. Offers MS Ed, Ed S. Part-time and evening/weekend programs available. *Students:* 11 full-time (all women), 37 part-time (31 women); includes 32 minority (11 African Americans, 21 Hispanic Americans), 1 international. 24 applicants, 75% accepted, 15 enrolled. In 2006, 72 degrees awarded. *Degree requirements:* For master's, electronic portfolio review; for Ed S, thesis optional. *Entrance requirements:* For master's and Ed S, GRE General Test. Additional exam requirements/recommendations for international students: Required—TOEFL (minimum score 550 paper-based; 212 computer-based). *Application deadline:* Applications are processed on a rolling basis. Electronic applications accepted. *Financial support:* Tuition waivers (full and partial) available. Financial award application deadline: 3/1; financial award applicants required to submit FAFSA. *Faculty research:* Inclusion, behavior disorders, emotional disorders, learning disabilities, math problem solving and special education. *Unit head:* Dr. Marjorie Montague, Coordinator, 305-284-2902, Fax: 305-284-3003, E-mail: mmontague@miami.edu.

University of Miami, Graduate School, School of Education, Department of Teaching and Learning, Program in Reading, Coral Gables, FL 33124. Offers MS Ed, Ed S. *Accreditation:* NCATE. Part-time and evening/weekend programs available. *Students:* Average age 31. 41 applicants, 76% accepted, 28 enrolled. In 2006, 20 degrees awarded. *Degree requirements:* For master's, electronic portfolio review; for Ed S, thesis optional. *Entrance requirements:* For master's and Ed S, GRE General Test. Additional exam requirements/recommendations for international students: Required—TOEFL (minimum score 550 paper-based; 212 computer-based). *Application deadline:* Applications are processed on a rolling basis. Application fee: $50. Electronic applications accepted. *Financial support:* In 2006–07, 41 students received support; teaching assistantships with tuition reimbursements available, Federal Work-Study, tuition waivers (full and partial), and unspecified assistantships available. Financial award application deadline: 3/1; financial award applicants required to submit FAFSA. *Faculty research:* Inclusion, behavior disorders, learning disabilities, literacy, emotional and behavior disorders. *Unit head:* Dr. William Blanton, Advisor, 305-284-5053, Fax: 305-284-3003, E-mail: blantonw@miami.edu.

University of Miami, Graduate School, School of Education, Department of Teaching and Learning, Program in Teaching and Learning, Coral Gables, FL 33124. Offers exceptional student education (PhD); mathematics and science education (PhD); reading (PhD); teaching English to speakers of other languages (PhD). Part-time and evening/weekend programs available. *Students:* 25 full-time (20 women), 6 part-time (5 women); includes 11 minority (2 African Americans, 9 Hispanic Americans), 5 international. Average age 38. 23 applicants, 61% accepted, 4 enrolled. In 2006, 3 doctorates awarded. *Median time to degree:* Of those who began their doctoral program in fall 1998, 100% received their degree in 8 years or less. *Degree requirements:* For doctorate, thesis/dissertation. *Entrance requirements:* For doctorate, GRE General Test, GRE Subject Test. Additional exam requirements/recommendations for international students: Required—TOEFL (minimum score 550 paper-based; 212 computer-based). Application fee: $50. Electronic applications accepted. *Financial support:* In 2006–07, 16 research assistantships with full tuition reimbursements (averaging $13,000 per year), 3 teaching assistantships with full tuition reimbursements (averaging $13,000 per year) were awarded; fellowships, tuition waivers (partial) also available. Financial award application deadline: 3/1; financial award applicants required to submit FAFSA. *Faculty research:* Teacher education, multicultural education, technology, second language acquisition.

University of Michigan, Horace H. Rackham School of Graduate Studies, School of Education, Programs in Educational Studies, Ann Arbor, MI 48109. Offers curriculum development (MA); early childhood education (MA, PhD); educational administration and policy (MA, PhD); educational foundation, administration, policy, and research methods (MA); educational foundations and policy (MA, PhD); elementary education (MA-Certification); English education (MA); English language learning in school settings (MA); learning technologies (MA, PhD); literacy, language, and culture (MA, PhD); mathematics education (MA, PhD); research methods (MA); science education (MA, PhD); secondary education (MA-Certification); social studies education (MA); special education (PhD); teaching and teacher education (PhD); MA-Certification; MBA/MA; PhD/MA. Terminal master's awarded for partial completion of doctoral program. *Degree requirements:* For master's, thesis (for some programs); for doctorate, thesis/dissertation, comprehensive exam. *Entrance requirements:* For master's and doctorate, GRE General Test. Additional exam requirements/recommendations for international students: Required—TOEFL (minimum score 600 paper-based; 250 computer-based). *Application deadline:* For fall admission, 12/1 priority date for domestic students, 12/1 for international students. Application fee: $60 ($75 for international students). Electronic applications accepted. *Financial support:* Applicants required to submit FAFSA. *Unit head:* Dr. Addison Stone, Chairperson, 734-763-7500, Fax: 734-615-1290, E-mail: addison@umich.edu. *Application contact:* Roberta Perry, Office of Student Services, 734-764-7563, Fax: 734-763-1495, E-mail: ed.grad.admit@umich.edu.

University of Michigan–Flint, School of Education and Human Services, Department of Education, Flint, MI 48502-1950. Offers early childhood education (MA Ed); education (MA Ed); elementary education with teaching certificate (MA Ed); literacy (K-12) (MA Ed); special education (MA Ed); urban and multicultural education (MA Ed). Part-time programs available. *Faculty:* 19 full-time (15 women), 9 part-time/adjunct (6 women). *Students:* 20 full-time (18 women), 193 part-time (167 women); includes 15 minority (12 African Americans, 1 American Indian/Alaska Native, 2 Hispanic Americans), 2 international. 109 applicants, 80% accepted, 65 enrolled. In 2006, 54 degrees awarded. *Entrance requirements:* Additional exam requirements/recommendations for international students: Required—TOEFL (minimum score 550 paper-based; 220 computer-based), IELTS (minimum score 7). *Application deadline:* For fall admission, 8/1 priority date for domestic students, 3/1 priority date for international students; for winter admission, 11/15 priority date for domestic students, 7/15 priority date for international students; for spring admission, 3/15 priority date for domestic students, 11/15 priority date for international students. Application fee: $55. *Expenses:* Contact institution. *Unit head:* Dr. Beverly Schumer, Director, 810-424-5215, E-mail: bschumer@umflint.edu. *Application contact:* Beulah Alexander, Executive Secretary, 810-766-6879, Fax: 810-766-6891, E-mail: beulaha@umflint.edu.

University of Minnesota, Twin Cities Campus, Graduate School, College of Education and Human Development, Department of Curriculum and Instruction, Minneapolis, MN 55455-0213. Offers art education (M Ed, MA, PhD); children's literature (M Ed, MA, PhD); curriculum and instruction (MA, PhD); early childhood education (M Ed, PhD); elementary education (M Ed, MA, PhD); English education (MA, PhD); environmental education (M Ed); family education (M Ed, MA, Ed D, PhD); instructional systems and technology (M Ed, MA, PhD); language arts (MA, PhD); language immersion education (Certificate); literacy education (MA); mathematics education (MA, PhD); reading education (MA, PhD); science education (MA, PhD); second languages and cultures education (MA, PhD); social studies education (MA, PhD); teaching (M Ed), including Chinese, earth science, elementary special education, English, English as a second language, French, German, Hebrew, Japanese, life sciences, mathematics, middle school science, science, second languages and cultures, social studies, Spanish; technology enhanced learning (Certificate); writing education (M Ed, MA, PhD). *Faculty:* 30 full-time (18 women). *Students:* 496 full-time (363 women), 338 part-time (235 women); includes 89 minority (26 African Americans, 4 American Indian/Alaska Native, 42 Asian Americans or Pacific Islanders, 17 Hispanic Americans), 33 international. Average age 29. 734 applicants, 66% accepted, 425 enrolled. In 2006, 644 master's, 18 doctorates, 11 other advanced degrees awarded. *Expenses:* Tuition, state resident: full-time $9,302; part-time $775 per credit. Tuition, nonresident: full-time $16,400; part-time $1,367 per credit. Full-time tuition and fees vary according to class time, course load, program, reciprocity agreements and student level. *Financial support:* In 2006–07, 7 fellowships (averaging $24,775 per year), 22 research assistantships with full tuition reimbursements (averaging $24,775 per year), 52 teaching assistantships with full tuition reimbursements (averaging $24,775 per year) were awarded. *Faculty research:* Educational practice for a democratic and just society; curriculum history and development/assessment; teacher preparation/induction/mentoring/development; cultural, linguistic, social, political, technological, and economic factors that influence teaching and learning. Total annual research expenditures: $1.2 million. *Unit head:* Dr. Ruth Thomas, Chair, 612-624-4772, Fax: 612-624-8277, E-mail: thoma006@umn.edu. *Application contact:* Dr. Mary Bents, Associate Dean, 612-625-6501, Fax: 612-626-1580, E-mail: mbents@tc.umn.edu.

University of Missouri–Columbia, Graduate School, College of Education, Department of Curriculum and Instruction, Columbia, MO 65211. Offers agricultural education (M Ed, PhD, Ed S); art education (M Ed, PhD, Ed S); business and office education (M Ed, PhD, Ed S); early childhood education (M Ed, PhD, Ed S); elementary education (M Ed, PhD, Ed S); English education (M Ed, PhD, Ed S); foreign language education (M Ed, PhD, Ed S); health education and promotion (M Ed, PhD); learning and instruction (M Ed); marketing education (M Ed, PhD, Ed S); mathematics education (M Ed, PhD, Ed S); music education (M Ed, PhD, Ed S); reading education (M Ed, PhD, Ed S); science education (M Ed, PhD, Ed S); social studies education (M Ed, PhD, Ed S); vocational education (M Ed, PhD, Ed S). Part-time programs available. *Faculty:* 24 full-time (12 women). *Students:* 195 full-time (148 women), 260 part-time (214 women); includes 27 minority (8 African Americans, 1 American Indian/Alaska Native, 10 Asian Americans or Pacific Islanders, 8 Hispanic Americans), 19 international. In 2006, 186 master's, 12 doctorates awarded. Terminal master's awarded for partial completion of doctoral program. *Degree requirements:* For doctorate, thesis/dissertation. *Entrance requirements:* For master's and Ed S, GRE General Test or MAT, minimum GPA of 3.0; for doctorate, GRE General Test, minimum GPA of 3.0. *Application deadline:* Applications are processed on a rolling basis. Application fee: $45 ($60 for international students). *Financial support:* Fellowships, research assistantships, teaching assistantships, institutionally sponsored loans available. *Unit head:* Dr. Lloyd H. Barrow, Director of Graduate Studies, 573-882-8247, E-mail: robinsonr@missouri.edu.

University of Missouri–Kansas City, School of Education, Kansas City, MO 64110-2499. Offers administration (Ed D); counseling and guidance (MA, Ed S); counseling psychology (PhD); curriculum and instruction (MA, Ed S); education (PhD); educational administration (Ed S); reading education (MA, Ed S); special education (MA). *Accreditation:* NCATE. Part-time and evening/weekend programs available. *Faculty:* 59 full-time (46 women), 39 part-time/adjunct (29 women). *Students:* 182 full-time (151 women), 470 part-time (344 women); includes 148 minority (117 African Americans, 5 American Indian/Alaska Native, 8 Asian Americans or Pacific Islanders, 18 Hispanic Americans), 9 international. Average age 34. 560 applicants, 79% accepted, 253 enrolled. In 2006, 196 master's, 4 doctorates, 41 other advanced degrees awarded. *Degree requirements:* For doctorate, thesis/dissertation, internship, practicum. *Entrance requirements:* For master's, GRE, minimum GPA of 2.75, 2 letters of references, a written statement of purpose; for doctorate, GRE, minimum GPA of 3.0; for Ed S, minimum GPA of 3.0. Additional exam requirements/recommendations for international students: Required—TOEFL (minimum score 550 paper-based; 213 computer-based). *Application deadline:* For fall admission, 4/1 priority date for domestic students, 4/1 for international students; for winter admission, 10/1 priority date for domestic students, 10/1 for international students; for spring admission, 10/1 priority date for domestic students, 10/1 for international students. Applications are processed on a rolling basis. Application fee: $35 ($50 for international students). *Expenses:* Tuition, state resident: full-time $4,975; part-time $276 per credit. Tuition, nonresident: full-time $12,847; part-time $713 per credit. Required fees: $595; $595 per year. *Financial support:* In 2006–07, 361 students received support, including 13 research assistantships with partial tuition reimbursements available (averaging $10,560 per year); fellowships with full tuition reimbursements available, teaching assistantships, career-related internships or fieldwork, Federal Work-Study, institutionally sponsored loans, and tuition waivers (full and partial) also available. Support available to part-time students. Financial award application deadline: 3/1. *Faculty research:* Urban education, inquiry-based field study, theories of counseling and psychotherapy, school literacy, educational technology. Total annual research expenditures: $94,515. *Unit head:* Dr. Linda Edwards, Dean, 816-235-2236, Fax: 816-235-5270, E-mail: edwardsli@umkc.edu. *Application contact:* Dr. Lori Reesor, Assistant Dean, 816-235-1473, Fax: 816-235-5270, E-mail: reesorl@umkc.edu.

University of Missouri–St. Louis, College of Education, Division of Teaching and Learning, St. Louis, MO 63121. Offers elementary education (M Ed), including reading; secondary education (M Ed), including curriculum and instruction, middle school, reading; special education (M Ed), including behavioral disorders, early childhood special education, learning disabilities, mentally retardation; teaching-learning processes (Ed D, PhD). *Faculty:* 20 full-time (13 women), 5 part-time/adjunct (4 women). *Students:* 118 full-time (84 women), 353 part-time (311 women); includes 90 minority (75 African Americans, 1 American Indian/Alaska Native, 3 Asian Americans or Pacific Islanders, 11 Hispanic Americans), 4 international. Average age 36. In 2006, 136 master's, 3 doctorates awarded. *Entrance requirements:* For doctorate, GRE General Test, 3 letters of recommendation. *Application deadline:* For fall admission, 7/15 for domestic students; for spring admission, 12/15 for domestic students. *Expenses:* Tuition, state resident: part-time $332 per credit hour. Tuition, nonresident: part-time $770 per credit hour. *Financial support:* In 2006–07, 9 teaching assistantships (averaging $14,250 per year) were awarded; research assistantships. *Unit head:* Dr. Gayle Wilkinson, Chair, 314-516-5791. *Application contact:* 314-516-5458, Fax: 314-516-6996, E-mail: gadadm@umsl.edu.

University of Nebraska at Kearney, College of Graduate Study, College of Education, Department of Teacher Education, Kearney, NE 68849-0001. Offers curriculum and instruction (MS Ed); instructional technology (MS Ed); reading education (MA Ed); special education (MA Ed). Part-time and evening/weekend programs available. *Faculty:* 9 full-time (5 women). *Students:* 15 full-time (10 women), 226 part-time (173 women); includes 5 minority (1 African American, 1 Asian American or Pacific Islander, 3 Hispanic Americans), 4 international. 46 applicants, 78% accepted. In 2006, 66 degrees awarded. *Degree requirements:* For master's, thesis optional. *Entrance requirements:* For master's, portfolio or GRE. Additional exam requirements/recommendations for international students: Required—TOEFL (minimum score 550 paper-based; 213 computer-based). *Application deadline:* For fall admission, 5/1 for domestic and international students; for spring admission, 8/15 for domestic students, 8/1 for international students. Applications are processed on a rolling basis. Application fee: $45. Electronic applications accepted. *Expenses:* Tuition, state resident: part-time $161 per hour. Tuition, nonresident: part-time $332 per hour. Required fees: $57 per hour. *Financial support:* In 2006–07, 8 research assistantships with full tuition reimbursements (averaging $8,200 per year) were awarded; career-related internships or fieldwork, scholarships/grants, and unspecified assistantships also available. Support available to part-time students. *Unit head:* Dr. Dennis Pottnoff, Chair, 308-865-8513, E-mail: pottnoffd@unk.edu.

University of Nebraska at Omaha, Graduate Studies and Research, College of Education, Department of Teacher Education, Program in Reading Education, Omaha, NE 68182. Offers MS. *Accreditation:* NCATE. Part-time and evening/weekend programs available. *Faculty:* 4 full-time (3 women). *Students:* 3 full-time (all women), 59 part-time (all women). Average age 34. 17 applicants, 88% accepted, 12 enrolled. In 2006, 17 degrees awarded. *Degree requirements:* For master's, thesis (for some programs), comprehensive exam. *Entrance requirements:* For master's, minimum GPA of 3.0. Additional exam requirements/recommendations for international students: Required—TOEFL (minimum score 550 paper-based; 213 computer-based; 80 iBT). *Application deadline:* For fall admission, 7/1 priority date for domestic students; for spring admission, 12/1 priority date for domestic students. Applications are processed on a rolling basis. Application fee: $45. Electronic applications accepted. *Financial support:* In 2006–07, 10 students received support; fellowships, teaching assistantships with tuition reimbursements available, Federal Work-Study, institutionally sponsored loans, scholarships/grants, tuition waivers (full), and unspecified assistantships available. Support available to part-time students. Financial award application deadline: 3/1.

University of Nevada, Las Vegas, Graduate College, College of Education, Department of Curriculum and Instruction, Las Vegas, NV 89154-9900. Offers curriculum and instruction (Ed D, PhD, Ed S); elementary education (M Ed, MS); English education (M Ed, MS); library science (M Ed, MS); literacy education (M Ed, MS); mathematics education (M Ed, MS); multicultural education (M Ed, MS); reading specialist (M Ed, MS); secondary education (M Ed, MS); teacher leadership (M Ed, MS); teaching English as a second language (M Ed, MS); technology integration and leadership (M Ed, MS). *Accreditation:* NCATE. Part-time and evening/weekend programs available. *Faculty:* 40 full-time (19 women), 21 part-time/adjunct (14 women). *Students:* 257 full-time (189 women), 387 part-time (296 women); includes 114 minority (28 African Americans, 5 American Indian/Alaska Native, 34 Asian Americans or Pacific Islanders, 47 Hispanic Americans), 7 international. 261 applicants, 70% accepted, 168 enrolled. In 2006, 231 master's, 5 doctorates awarded. *Degree requirements:* For master's, thesis (for some programs), comprehensive exam (for some programs); for doctorate, thesis/dissertation, oral exam. *Entrance requirements:* For master's, minimum GPA of 3.0; for doctorate, GRE General Test, minimum graduate GPA of 3.0. Additional exam requirements/recommendations for international students: Required—TOEFL (minimum score 550 paper-based; 213 computer-based; 80 iBT). *Application deadline:* For fall admission, 2/15 for domestic and international students; for spring admission, 9/30 for domestic and international students. Application fee: $60 ($75 for international students). Electronic applications accepted. *Financial support:* In 2006–07, 30 research assistantships with partial tuition reimbursements (averaging $10,000 per year), 7 teaching assistantships with partial tuition reimbursements (averaging $12,000 per year) were awarded; career-related internships or fieldwork, Federal Work-Study, institutionally sponsored loans, scholarships/grants, health care benefits, and unspecified assistantships also available. Support available to part-time students. Financial award application deadline: 3/1. *Unit head:* Dr. Greg Levitt, Chair, 702-895-3241. *Application contact:* Graduate College Admissions Evaluator, 702-895-3320, E-mail: gradcollege@unlv.edu.

University of Nevada, Reno, Graduate School, College of Education, Department of Educational Specialties, Reno, NV 89557. Offers educational specialties (MA, MS, PhD, Ed S); literacy studies (M Ed, MA, Ed D, PhD); special education (M Ed); teaching English as a second language (MA). *Students:* 75 full-time (58 women), 188 part-time (161 women); includes 29 minority (2 African Americans, 1 American Indian/Alaska Native, 10 Asian Americans or Pacific Islanders, 16 Hispanic Americans), 20 international. Average age 38. 123 applicants, 82% accepted, 50 enrolled. In 2006, 50 master's, 1 doctorate awarded. *Degree requirements:* For master's, thesis optional; for doctorate, thesis/dissertation, comprehensive exam. *Entrance requirements:* For master's, minimum GPA of 2.75; for doctorate, GRE. Additional exam requirements/recommendations for international students: Required—TOEFL (minimum score 500 paper-based; 173 computer-based). *Application deadline:* For fall admission, 3/1 priority date for domestic students; for spring admission, 10/1 for domestic students. Applications are processed on a rolling basis. Application fee: $60 ($95 for international students). Electronic applications accepted. *Unit head:* Dr. Chris Cheney, Head, 775-784-7853.

University of New England, College of Arts and Sciences, Program in Education, Biddeford, ME 04005-9526. Offers general studies (MS Ed); literacy (MS Ed); teaching methodologies (MS Ed). Part-time programs available. Postbaccalaureate distance learning degree programs offered (minimal on-campus study). *Faculty:* 4 full-time (2 women), 22 part-time/adjunct (13 women). *Students:* 12 full-time (9 women), 435 part-time (322 women); includes 11 minority (3 African Americans, 1 American Indian/Alaska Native, 3 Asian Americans or Pacific Islanders, 4 Hispanic Americans), 1 international. Average age 36. 148 applicants, 100%

Reading Education

University of New England (continued)
accepted, 116 enrolled. In 2006, 241 degrees awarded. *Degree requirements:* For master's, collaborative action research project, integrative seminar portfolio. *Entrance requirements:* For master's, teaching certificate, 2 years of teaching experience. Additional exam requirements/recommendations for international students: Required—TOEFL. *Application deadline:* For fall admission, 9/15 for domestic students; for spring admission, 1/15 for domestic students. Applications are processed on a rolling basis. Application fee: $40. Electronic applications accepted. *Expenses:* Contact institution. *Financial support:* Application deadline: 5/1; *Faculty research:* Distance learning, effective teaching, transition planning, adult learning. *Unit head:* Dr. Susan Hillman, Chair of Education Department, 207-283-0171 Ext. 2888, E-mail: shillman@une.edu. *Application contact:* Robert Pecchia, Associate Dean of Admissions, 207-283-0171 Ext. 2297, Fax: 207-602-5900, E-mail: admissions@une.edu.

University of New Hampshire, Graduate School, College of Liberal Arts, Department of Education, Program in Reading, Durham, NH 03824. Offers M Ed. Part-time programs available. *Faculty:* 32 full-time. *Students:* 5 full-time (4 women), 24 part-time (all women). Average age 41. 12 applicants, 100% accepted, 10 enrolled. In 2006, 9 degrees awarded. *Degree requirements:* For master's, thesis or alternative. *Entrance requirements:* For master's, GRE General Test. Additional exam requirements/recommendations for international students: Required—TOEFL (minimum score 550 paper-based; 213 computer-based). *Application deadline:* For fall admission, 4/1 for domestic and international students. Applications are processed on a rolling basis. Application fee: $50. Electronic applications accepted. *Expenses:* Tuition, state resident: full-time $8,540; part-time $474 per credit hour. Tuition, nonresident: full-time $20,990; part-time $862 per credit hour. Required fees: $1,343; $356 per term. Tuition and fees vary according to course load, program and reciprocity agreements. *Financial support:* In 2006–07, 2 fellowships, 3 teaching assistantships were awarded; research assistantships, career-related internships or fieldwork, Federal Work-Study, scholarships/grants, and tuition waivers (full and partial) also available. Support available to part-time students. Financial award application deadline: 2/15. *Faculty research:* Reading foundations; clinical components; consultant, supervisory, and research skills. *Unit head:* Dr. John Carney, Coordinator, 603-862-2373, E-mail: education.department@unh.edu.

The University of North Carolina at Chapel Hill, Graduate School, School of Education, Program in Education, Chapel Hill, NC 27599. Offers culture, curriculum and change (PhD); culture, curriculum, and change (MA); early childhood, families, and literacy studies (MA, PhD); educational psychology measurements, and evaluation (PhD); educational psychology, measurement, and evaluation (MA). *Accreditation:* NCATE. In 2006, 11 master's, 10 doctorates awarded. *Degree requirements:* For master's, thesis/dissertation; for doctorate, thesis/dissertation, comprehensive exam, registration. *Entrance requirements:* For master's, GRE General Test, minimum GPA of 3.0 during last 2 years of undergraduates course work; for doctorate, GRE General Test, minimum GPA of 3.0 during last 2 years of undergraduate course work. Additional exam requirements/recommendations for international students: Required—TOEFL (minimum score 550 paper-based; 213 computer-based). *Application deadline:* For fall admission, 1/1 priority date for domestic and international students. Applications are processed on a rolling basis. Application fee: $60. Electronic applications accepted. *Financial support:* Federal Work-Study available. Support available to part-time students. Financial award application deadline: 3/1; financial award applicants required to submit FAFSA. *Application contact:* Janet Carroll, Registrar, 919-962-8690, Fax: 919-962-1533, E-mail: jscarrol@email.unc.edu.

The University of North Carolina at Charlotte, Graduate School, College of Education, Department of Reading and Elementary Education, Charlotte, NC 28223-0001. Offers elementary education (M Ed); reading education (M Ed). Part-time and evening/weekend programs available. Postbaccalaureate distance learning degree programs offered (no on-campus study). *Faculty:* 17 full-time (8 women), 2 part-time/adjunct (0 women). *Students:* 4 full-time (all women), 80 part-time (78 women); includes 4 minority (3 African Americans, 1 American Indian/Alaska Native). Average age 30. 28 applicants, 89% accepted, 20 enrolled. In 2006, 28 degrees awarded. *Entrance requirements:* For master's, GRE or MAT. Additional exam requirements/recommendations for international students: Required—TOEFL (minimum score 557 paper-based; 220 computer-based). *Application deadline:* For fall admission, 7/1 for domestic students, 5/1 for international students; for spring admission, 11/1 for domestic students, 10/1 for international students. Applications are processed on a rolling basis. Application fee: $55. Electronic applications accepted. *Expenses:* Tuition, state resident: full-time $2,719; part-time $170 per credit. Tuition, nonresident: full-time $12,926; part-time $808 per credit. Required fees: $1,555. *Financial support:* In 2006–07, 4 teaching assistantships (averaging $8,500 per year) were awarded; fellowships, research assistantships, career-related internships or fieldwork, Federal Work-Study, institutionally sponsored loans, scholarships/grants, and unspecified assistantships also available. Support available to part-time students. Financial award application deadline: 4/1; financial award applicants required to submit FAFSA. *Unit head:* Dr. Robert J. Rickelman, Chair, 704-687-8889, Fax: 704-687-3749, E-mail: rjrickel@email.uncc.edu. *Application contact:* Kathy B. Giddings, Director of Graduate Admissions, 704-687-3366, Fax: 704-687-3279, E-mail: gradadm@email.uncc.edu.

The University of North Carolina at Greensboro, Graduate School, School of Education, Department of Curriculum and Instruction, Greensboro, NC 27412-5001. Offers college teaching and adult learning (Certificate); curriculum and instruction (M Ed), including chemistry education, elementary education, English as a second language, French education, instructional technology, mathematics education, middle grades education, reading education, science education, social studies education, Spanish education; curriculum and teaching (PhD), including higher education, teacher education and development; English as a second language (Certificate); higher education (M Ed); supervision (M Ed). *Accreditation:* NCATE. Part-time programs available. *Faculty:* 27 full-time (18 women), 8 part-time/adjunct (3 women). *Students:* 137 full-time (114 women), 231 part-time (195 women); includes 63 minority (52 African Americans, 2 American Indian/Alaska Native, 5 Asian Americans or Pacific Islanders, 4 Hispanic Americans). 146 applicants, 32% accepted. *Degree requirements:* For doctorate, thesis/dissertation. *Entrance requirements:* For master's and doctorate, GRE General Test. Additional exam requirements/recommendations for international students: Required—TOEFL. Application fee: $45. Electronic applications accepted. *Expenses:* Tuition, state resident: full-time $2,692. Tuition, nonresident: full-time $13,742. *Financial support:* Fellowships, research assistantships with full tuition reimbursements, teaching assistantships with full tuition reimbursements, career-related internships or fieldwork, Federal Work-Study, scholarships/grants, traineeships, and unspecified assistantships available. Support available to part-time students. *Faculty research:* Community college literacy program, middle school mathematics/computer mathematics. *Unit head:* Dr. Sam Miller, Chair, 336-334-3445, Fax: 336-334-4120, E-mail: sdmille2@uncg.edu. *Application contact:* Michelle Harkleroad, Director of Graduate Admissions, 336-334-4884, Fax: 336-334-4424, E-mail: mbharkle@uncg.edu.

The University of North Carolina at Pembroke, Graduate Studies, School of Education, Program in Reading Education, Pembroke, NC 28372-1510. Offers MA Ed. *Accreditation:* NCATE. Part-time and evening/weekend programs available. *Faculty:* 2 full-time (0 women). *Students:* 3 full-time (all women), 49 part-time (47 women); includes 4 minority (2 African Americans, 2 American Indian/Alaska Native). Average age 35. 52 applicants, 100% accepted, 52 enrolled. In 2006, 10 degrees awarded. *Degree requirements:* For master's, thesis optional. *Entrance requirements:* For master's, GRE General Test or MAT, minimum GPA of 3.0 in major, 2.5 overall; teaching license. Additional exam requirements/recommendations for international students: Required—TOEFL. *Application deadline:* For fall admission, 7/15 priority date for domestic students; for winter admission, 7/15 for international students; for spring admission, 12/1 priority date for domestic and international students. Applications are processed on a rolling basis. Application fee: $40. *Expenses:* Tuition, state resident: full-time $3,516; part-time $1,091 per semester. Tuition, nonresident: full-time $12,924; part-time $4,619 per semester. Tuition and fees vary according to class time, course load, degree level and campus/location. *Financial support:* In 2006–07, research assistantships with full tuition reimbursements (averaging $6,000 per year); career-related internships or fieldwork and unspecified assistantships also available. Support available to part-time students. Financial award application deadline: 4/15; financial award applicants required to submit FAFSA. *Unit head:* Dr. Betty W. Brown, Director, 910-521-6856, Fax: 910-521-6165, E-mail: betty.brown@uncp.edu. *Application contact:* Dr. Kathleen C. Hilton, Dean of Graduate Studies, 910-521-6271, Fax: 910-521-6751, E-mail: grad@uncp.edu.

The University of North Carolina Wilmington, School of Education, Department of Elementary, Middle Level and Literacy Education, Program in Language and Literacy Education, Wilmington, NC 28403-3297. Offers M Ed. *Accreditation:* NCATE. Part-time and evening/weekend programs available. *Students:* 9 full-time (all women), 27 part-time (25 women). Average age 38. 20 applicants, 70% accepted, 12 enrolled. In 2006, 22 degrees awarded. *Degree requirements:* For master's, comprehensive exam. *Entrance requirements:* For master's, GRE General Test, MAT, minimum B average in upper-division undergraduate course work. *Application deadline:* For fall admission, 6/1 for domestic students. Applications are processed on a rolling basis. Application fee: $45. *Financial support:* Unspecified assistantships available. Financial award application deadline: 3/15. *Unit head:* Dr. Barbara Honchell, Coordinator, 910-962-3382. *Application contact:* Dr. Robert D. Roer, Dean, Graduate School, 910-962-4117, Fax: 910-962-3787, E-mail: roer@uncw.edu.

University of North Dakota, Graduate School, College of Education and Human Development, Program in Reading Education, Grand Forks, ND 58202. Offers M Ed, MS. *Accreditation:* NCATE. Part-time programs available. Postbaccalaureate distance learning degree programs offered (minimal on-campus study). *Faculty:* 1 (woman) full-time. *Students:* 4 applicants, 75% accepted, 3 enrolled. In 2006, 3 degrees awarded. *Degree requirements:* For master's, thesis or alternative, comprehensive exam. *Entrance requirements:* For master's, minimum GPA of 3.0. Additional exam requirements/recommendations for international students: Required—TOEFL (minimum score 550 paper-based; 213 computer-based; 79 iBT), IELTS (minimum score 6). *Application deadline:* For fall admission, 2/15 priority date for domestic and international students; for spring admission, 10/15 priority date for domestic and international students. Applications are processed on a rolling basis. Application fee: $35. Electronic applications accepted. *Expenses:* Tuition, state resident: full-time $5,650; part-time $214 per credit. Tuition, nonresident: full-time $14,248; part-time $572 per credit. Required fees: $1,008; $42 per credit. Tuition and fees vary according to reciprocity agreements. *Financial support:* In 2006–07, 3 students received support; fellowships, research assistantships, teaching assistantships, career-related internships or fieldwork, Federal Work-Study, institutionally sponsored loans, scholarships/grants, and tuition waivers (full and partial) available. Support available to part-time students. Financial award application deadline: 3/15; financial award applicants required to submit FAFSA. *Faculty research:* Whole language, multicultural education, child-focused learning, experiential science, cooperative learning. *Unit head:* Dr. Anne Walker, Director, 701-777-3162, Fax: 701-777-4393, E-mail: anne_walker@und.nodak.edu. *Application contact:* Linda M. Baeza, Admissions Officer, 701-777-2945, Fax: 701-777-3619, E-mail: gradschool@mail.und.nodak.edu.

University of Northern Colorado, Graduate School, College of Education and Behavioral Sciences, School of Teacher Education, Reading Program, Greeley, CO 80639. Offers MA. *Accreditation:* NCATE. Part-time and evening/weekend programs available. Postbaccalaureate distance learning degree programs offered (no on-campus study). *Faculty:* 3 full-time (1 woman). *Students:* 8 full-time (all women), 16 part-time (15 women); includes 1 minority (Hispanic American) Average age 35. 7 applicants, 71% accepted, 2 enrolled. In 2006, 26 degrees awarded. *Degree requirements:* For master's, thesis or alternative, comprehensive exam. *Entrance requirements:* For master's, GRE General Test (if undergraduate GPA is below 3.0), resumé, letters of reference. *Application deadline:* Applications are processed on a rolling basis. Application fee: $50 ($60 for international students). Electronic applications accepted. *Expenses:* Tuition, state resident: full-time $5,118; part-time $213 per credit hour. Tuition, nonresident: full-time $14,832; part-time $618 per credit hour. Required fees: $674; $34 per credit hour. *Financial support:* In 2006–07, 14 students received support; fellowships, research assistantships, teaching assistantships, unspecified assistantships available. Financial award application deadline: 3/1; financial award applicants required to submit FAFSA. *Unit head:* Dr. Roger Eldridge, Program Coordinator, 970-351-1605.

University of Northern Iowa, Graduate College, College of Education, Department of Curriculum and Instruction, Program in Reading, Cedar Falls, IA 50614. Offers elementary reading and language arts (MAE); reading education (MAE); secondary reading (MAE). Part-time and evening/weekend programs available. *Students:* 3 full-time (all women), 47 part-time (45 women); includes 3 minority (1 African American, 2 Hispanic Americans). 17 applicants, 82% accepted, 14 enrolled. In 2006, 2 degrees awarded. *Degree requirements:* For master's, thesis or alternative, comprehensive exam. *Entrance requirements:* For master's, minimum GPA of 3.5, 3 years of educational experience. Additional exam requirements/recommendations for international students: Required—TOEFL (minimum score 500 paper-based; 180 computer-based; 61 iBT). *Application deadline:* For fall admission, 8/1 priority date for domestic students. Applications are processed on a rolling basis. Application fee: $30 ($50 for international students). Electronic applications accepted. *Expenses:* Tuition, state resident: full-time $5,936. Tuition, nonresident: full-time $14,074. *Financial support:* Career-related internships or fieldwork, Federal Work-Study, and tuition waivers (full and partial) available. Support available to part-time students. Financial award application deadline: 2/1. *Unit head:* Dr. Deborah Tidwell, Coordinator, 319-273-2070, Fax: 319-273-5886, E-mail: deborah.tidwell@uni.edu.

University of North Texas, Robert B. Toulouse School of Graduate Studies, College of Education, Department of Teacher Education and Administration, Program in Reading, Denton, TX 76203. Offers M Ed, MS, Ed D, PhD. *Accreditation:* NCATE. *Students:* 2 full-time (both women), 19 part-time (17 women); includes 2 minority (1 African American, 1 Hispanic American), 1 international. Average age 36. 19 applicants, 68% accepted, 7 enrolled. In 2006, 2 master's, 3 doctorates awarded. *Degree requirements:* For doctorate, thesis/dissertation. *Entrance requirements:* For master's and doctorate, GRE General Test. *Application deadline:* For fall admission, 7/15 for domestic students. Application fee: $50 ($75 for international students). *Expenses:* Tuition, state resident: full-time $3,573; part-time $198 per credit. Tuition, nonresident: full-time $8,577; part-time $476 per credit. Required fees: $1,258; $126 per credit. One-time fee: $150 full-time. Tuition and fees vary according to course load. *Financial support:* Fellowships, research assistantships, teaching assistantships, career-related internships or fieldwork, Federal Work-Study, and institutionally sponsored loans available. Financial award application deadline: 4/1. *Unit head:* Dr. Janelle Mathis, Coordinator, 940-565-2754, E-mail: mathis@coe.unt.edu.

University of Oklahoma, Graduate College, College of Education, Department of Instructional Leadership and Academic Curriculum, Norman, OK 73019-0390. Offers education (Certificate); instructional leadership and academic curriculum (M Ed, PhD), including bilingual education, early childhood education, elementary education, English education, math education, reading education, science education, secondary education, social studies education. *Accreditation:* NCATE. Part-time and evening/weekend programs available. *Faculty:* 20 full-time (11 women), 6 part-time/adjunct (all women). *Students:* 76 full-time (63 women), 115 part-time (89 women); includes 25 minority (8 African Americans, 12 American Indian/Alaska Native, 4 Asian Americans or Pacific Islanders, 1 Hispanic American), 12 international. 72 applicants, 96% accepted, 56 enrolled. In 2006, 11 master's, 10 doctorates awarded. *Degree requirements:* For doctorate, thesis/dissertation. *Entrance requirements:* For master's, 12 hours of course work in education; for doctorate, GRE General Test, master's degree, minimum graduate GPA of 3.0. Additional exam requirements/recommendations for international students: Required—TOEFL (minimum score 550 paper-based; 213 computer-based). *Application deadline:* For fall admission, 6/1 priority date for domestic students, 4/1 for international students; for spring admission, 11/1 for domestic students, 9/1 for international students. Applications are processed on a rolling basis. Application fee: $40 ($90 for international students). *Expenses:* Tuition, state resident: full-time $3,180; part-time $133 per credit hour. Tuition, nonresident: full-time $11,347; part-time $473 per credit hour. Required fees: $1,729; $62 per credit hour. $117 per semester.

Tuition and fees vary according to course load and program. *Financial support:* In 2006–07, 76 students received support, including 5 research assistantships with partial tuition reimbursements available (averaging $9,773 per year), 7 teaching assistantships with partial tuition reimbursements available (averaging $10,403 per year); scholarships/grants and unspecified assistantships also available. Financial award applicants required to submit FAFSA. *Faculty research:* Early literacy, learning cycle, social justice, teacher education. Total annual research expenditures: $119,917. *Unit head:* Dr. Priscilla Griffith, Chair and Graduate Liaison, 405-325-1498, Fax: 405-325-4061, E-mail: pgriffith@ou.edu.

University of Pennsylvania, Graduate School of Education, Division of Language in Education, Program in Reading, Writing, and Literacy, Philadelphia, PA 19104. Offers MS Ed, Ed D, PhD. Part-time programs available. *Degree requirements:* For master's, comprehensive exam; for doctorate, one foreign language, thesis/dissertation, preliminary exam. *Entrance requirements:* For master's and doctorate, GRE General Test or MAT. Additional exam requirements/recommendations for international students: Required—TOEFL. Electronic applications accepted. Expenses: Contact institution. *Faculty research:* Reading and writing relationships, classroom teachers as researchers, comprehension processes.

University of Pittsburgh, School of Education, Department of Instruction and Learning, Program in Reading Education, Pittsburgh, PA 15260. Offers M Ed, Ed D, PhD. *Students:* 11 full-time (all women), 82 part-time (76 women); includes 7 minority (6 African Americans, 1 Hispanic American). 51 applicants, 88% accepted, 18 enrolled. In 2006, 17 master's, 3 doctorates awarded. *Degree requirements:* For master's and doctorate, thesis/dissertation. *Entrance requirements:* For master's, PRAXIS I; for doctorate, GRE General Test. Additional exam requirements/recommendations for international students: Required—TOEFL. *Application deadline:* For fall admission, 2/1 for domestic students. Application fee: $50. *Financial support:* Application deadline: 3/15; *Application contact:* Joan M. Cutone, Director, School of Education Student Service Center, 412-648-2230, Fax: 412-648-1899, E-mail: soeinfo@pitt.edu.

University of Pittsburgh, School of Education, Department of Instruction and Learning, Program in Secondary Education, Pittsburgh, PA 15260. Offers English/communications education (M Ed, MAT, Ed D, PhD); foreign languages education (M Ed, MAT, Ed D, PhD); mathematics education (M Ed, MAT, Ed D); reading education (PhD); science education (M Ed, MAT, MS, Ed D); social studies education (M Ed, MAT, Ed D, PhD). Part-time and evening/weekend programs available. *Students:* 157 full-time (111 women), 84 part-time (61 women); includes 18 minority (7 African Americans, 5 Asian Americans or Pacific Islanders, 6 Hispanic Americans), 13 international. 163 applicants, 74% accepted, 86 enrolled. In 2006, 114 master's, 7 doctorates awarded. *Degree requirements:* For master's and doctorate, thesis/dissertation. *Entrance requirements:* For master's, PRAXIS I; for doctorate, GRE General Test. Additional exam requirements/recommendations for international students: Required—TOEFL. *Application deadline:* For fall admission, 2/1 priority date for domestic students; for spring admission, 11/15 priority date for domestic students. Applications are processed on a rolling basis. Application fee: $50. Electronic applications accepted. *Financial support:* Fellowships, teaching assistantships, career-related internships or fieldwork, Federal Work-Study, tuition waivers (partial), and unspecified assistantships available. Support available to part-time students. Financial award application deadline: 3/15; financial award applicants required to submit FAFSA. *Application contact:* Joan M. Cutone, Director, School of Education Student Service Center, 412-648-2230, Fax: 412-648-1899, E-mail: soeinfo@pitt.edu.

University of Rhode Island, Graduate School, College of Human Science and Services, School of Education, Program in Reading Education, Kingston, RI 02881. Offers MA. *Accreditation:* NCATE. *Entrance requirements:* For master's, GRE or MAT. Additional exam requirements/recommendations for international students: Required—TOEFL. *Application deadline:* For fall admission, 4/15 priority date for domestic students; for spring admission, 11/15 for domestic students. Applications are processed on a rolling basis. Application fee: $35. *Expenses:* Tuition, state resident: full-time $6,032; part-time $335 per credit. Tuition, nonresident: full-time $17,288; part-time $960 per credit. Required fees: $65 per credit. $30 per semester. One-time fee: $80 part-time. *Financial support:* Career-related internships or fieldwork available. *Unit head:* Dr. Theresa Deeney, Advisor, 401-874-2682.

University of Rio Grande, Graduate School, Rio Grande, OH 45674. Offers classroom teaching (M Ed), including fine arts, learning disabilities, mathematics, reading education. Part-time and evening/weekend programs available. *Degree requirements:* For master's, final research project, portfolio. *Entrance requirements:* For master's, minimum GPA of 2.7 in major, 2.5 overall. *Faculty research:* Interagency collaboration, reading and mathematics, learning styles, college access, literacy.

University of St. Francis, College of Education, Joliet, IL 60435-6169. Offers curriculum and instruction (MS); educational leadership (MS), including reading, special education; elementary education certification (M Ed); secondary education certification (M Ed), including English education, math education, science education, social studies education; special education (M Ed); teaching and learning (MS). Part-time and evening/weekend programs available. *Faculty:* 11 full-time (10 women), 25 part-time/adjunct (12 women). *Students:* 52 full-time (38 women), 381 part-time (293 women); includes 38 minority (21 African Americans, 1 American Indian/Alaska Native, 4 Asian Americans or Pacific Islanders, 12 Hispanic Americans). Average age 33. 194 applicants, 80% accepted, 117 enrolled. In 2006, 165 degrees awarded. *Degree requirements:* For master's, comprehensive exam (for some programs), registration. *Entrance requirements:* For master's, minimum undergraduate GPA of 2.75, 2 letters of recommendation, computer competency. Additional exam requirements/recommendations for international students: Required—TOEFL (minimum score 550 paper-based; 213 computer-based). *Application deadline:* Applications are processed on a rolling basis. Application fee: $30. Electronic applications accepted. *Expenses: Contact institution.* Part-time tuition and fees vary according to campus/location and program. *Financial support:* In 2006–07, 272 students received support. Scholarships/grants, tuition waivers (partial), and unspecified assistantships available. Support available to part-time students. Financial award applicants required to submit FAFSA. *Unit head:* Dr. John Gambro, Dean, 815-740-3456, Fax: 815-740-2264, E-mail: jgambro@stfrancis.edu. *Application contact:* Sandra Sloka, Director of Admissions for Graduate and Degree Completion Programs, 800-735-7500, Fax: 815-740-5032, E-mail: ssloka@stfrancis.edu.

University of St. Thomas, Graduate Studies, School of Education, Department of Curriculum and Instruction, St. Paul, MN 55105-1096. Offers critical pedagogy (Ed D); curriculum and instruction (MA, Ed S), including elementary (MA), K-12 (MA), secondary (MA); gifted, creative, and talented education (MA, Certificate); learning technology (MA, Certificate); reading (MA). Part-time and evening/weekend programs available. Postbaccalaureate distance learning degree programs offered (minimal on-campus study). *Students:* 5 full-time (all women), 109 part-time (91 women); includes 12 minority (7 African Americans, 1 American Indian/Alaska Native, 2 Asian Americans or Pacific Islanders, 2 Hispanic Americans), 2 international. Average age 35. 103 applicants, 91% accepted, 89 enrolled. In 2006, 13 master's, 7 doctorates, 11 other advanced degrees awarded. *Degree requirements:* For master's, thesis (for some programs), registration; for doctorate and other advanced degree, thesis/dissertation, registration. *Entrance requirements:* For master's, minimum GPA of 2.75 or MAT; for doctorate, minimum 3 years of experience as an educator; master's degree; minimum graduate GPA of 2.75, interview, writing sample; for other advanced degree, MAT, minimum graduate GPA of 2.75. Additional exam requirements/recommendations for international students: Required—TOEFL (minimum score 550 paper-based; 213 computer-based). *Application deadline:* For fall admission, 6/1 priority date for domestic students; for spring admission, 11/1 priority date for domestic students. Applications are processed on a rolling basis. Application fee: $50. *Financial support:* In 2006–07, 59 students received support; fellowships, research assistantships, institutionally sponsored loans and scholarships/grants available. Support available to part-time students. *Faculty research:* Multicultural education for gifted children, education plans for gifted children, globalization and adult learning, best gifted practices in Minnesota, exploring cultural tools. *Unit head:* Dr. Karen L. Westberg, Department Chair, 651-962-4985, Fax: 651-962-4169, E-mail: klwestberg@stthomas.edu. *Application contact:* Daniel Vevang, Department Assistant, 651-962-4460, Fax: 651-962-4169, E-mail: dvevang@stthomas.edu.

The University of Scranton, Graduate School, Department of Education, Program in Reading Education, Scranton, PA 18510. Offers MS. *Accreditation:* NCATE. Part-time and evening/weekend programs available. *Students:* 3 full-time (all women), 6 part-time (3 women). Average age 27. 11 applicants, 100% accepted. In 2006, 8 degrees awarded. *Degree requirements:* For master's, thesis (for some programs), capstone experience, comprehensive exam, registration. *Entrance requirements:* For master's, minimum GPA of 2.75. Additional exam requirements/recommendations for international students: Required—TOEFL (minimum score 500 paper-based; 173 computer-based), IELTS (minimum score 6). *Application deadline:* Applications are processed on a rolling basis. Application fee: $50. *Expenses:* Tuition: Part-time $684 per credit. Required fees: $25 per term. *Financial support:* Fellowships, teaching assistantships, career-related internships or fieldwork, Federal Work-Study, and unspecified assistantships available. Support available to part-time students. Financial award application deadline: 3/1. *Unit head:* Dr. Derry Stufft, Director, 570-941-7421, Fax: 570-941-7401, E-mail: stufftda@scranton.edu.

University of Sioux Falls, Program in Education, Sioux Falls, SD 57105-1699. Offers leadership (M Ed); reading (M Ed); superintendent (Ed S); teaching (M Ed); technology (M Ed). Summer admission only. *Accreditation:* NCATE. Part-time and evening/weekend programs available. Postbaccalaureate distance learning degree programs offered (minimal on-campus study). *Faculty:* 12 full-time (8 women), 13 part-time/adjunct (7 women). *Students:* 9 applicants, 100% accepted, 7 enrolled. In 2006, 46 master's, 26 other advanced degrees awarded. *Median time to degree:* Master's–2.5 years part-time; Ed S–2 years part-time. *Degree requirements:* For master's, research application project; for Ed S, portfolio. *Entrance requirements:* For master's, minimum GPA of 3.0, 1 year of teaching experience; for Ed S, administrative exam, minimum 3 years of teaching experience, minimum cumulative GPA of 3.5. Additional exam requirements/recommendations for international students: Required—TOEFL. *Application deadline:* Applications are processed on a rolling basis. Application fee: $25. *Expenses:* Tuition: Part-time $300 per semester hour. Required fees: $15 per term. Part-time tuition and fees vary according to program. *Financial support:* In 2006–07, 58 students received support. Scholarships/grants available. Support available to part-time students. *Unit head:* Dawn Olson, Director of Graduate Education, 605-575-2063, Fax: 605-575-2079, E-mail: dawn.olson@usiouxfalls.edu.

University of South Alabama, Graduate School, College of Education, Department of Leadership and Teacher Education, Mobile, AL 36688-0002. Offers early childhood education (M Ed); educational administration (Ed S); educational leadership (M Ed); elementary education (M Ed); reading education (M Ed); science education (M Ed); secondary education (M Ed); special education (M Ed, Ed S). *Accreditation:* NCATE. Part-time programs available. *Faculty:* 22 full-time (13 women). *Students:* 287 full-time (251 women), 229 part-time (194 women); includes 137 minority (125 African Americans, 8 American Indian/Alaska Native, 3 Asian Americans or Pacific Islanders, 1 Hispanic American), 4 international. 43 applicants, 84% accepted, 20 enrolled. In 2006, 169 master's, 12 other advanced degrees awarded. *Degree requirements:* For master's, comprehensive exam. *Entrance requirements:* For master's, GRE General Test or MAT, minimum GPA of 3.0. *Application deadline:* For fall admission, 9/1 priority date for domestic students. Applications are processed on a rolling basis. Application fee: $25. *Financial support:* In 2006–07, 6 research assistantships were awarded; career-related internships or fieldwork also available. Support available to part-time students. Financial award application deadline: 4/1. *Unit head:* Dr. David L. Gray, Chair, 251-380-2894.

University of South Carolina, The Graduate School, College of Education, Department of Instruction and Teacher Education, Program in Language and Literacy, Columbia, SC 29208. Offers M Ed, PhD. *Accreditation:* NCATE. *Degree requirements:* For master's, comprehensive exam; for doctorate, one foreign language, thesis/dissertation, comprehensive exam. *Entrance requirements:* For master's, GRE General Test, MAT, teaching certificate, resumé; for doctorate, GRE General Test, resumé. *Faculty research:* Remedial and compensatory education, metacognition and learning, literacy, learning, teacher change.

University of Southern Maine, College of Education and Human Development, Program in Literacy Education, Portland, ME 04104-9300. Offers applied literacy (MS Ed); English as a second language (MS Ed, CAS); literacy education (MS Ed, CAS, Certificate). *Accreditation:* NCATE. Part-time and evening/weekend programs available. *Faculty:* 4 full-time (3 women), 3 part-time/adjunct (0 women). *Students:* 2 full-time (both women), 51 part-time (47 women); includes 1 minority (Asian American or Pacific Islander) 18 applicants, 89% accepted, 13 enrolled. In 2006, 28 degrees awarded. *Degree requirements:* For master's, thesis or alternative, comprehensive exam; for other advanced degree, thesis or alternative. *Entrance requirements:* For master's, GRE General Test or MAT; for other advanced degree, master's degree. *Application deadline:* For fall admission, 2/1 for domestic students; for spring admission, 9/15 for domestic students. Application fee: $50. Electronic applications accepted. *Expenses:* Tuition, state resident: full-time $4,860; part-time $270 per credit hour. Tuition, nonresident: full-time $13,572; part-time $754 per credit hour. Required fees: $222 per semester. Tuition and fees vary according to course load. *Financial support:* In 2006–07, 4 students received support, including 1 research assistantship with tuition reimbursement available (averaging $4,500 per year); career-related internships or fieldwork, Federal Work-Study, institutionally sponsored loans, scholarships/grants, and unspecified assistantships also available. Support available to part-time students. Financial award application deadline: 3/1; financial award applicants required to submit FAFSA. *Unit head:* Dr. James Curry, Chair, Professional Education Department, 207-780-5400, Fax: 207-780-8277, E-mail: jcurry@usm.maine.edu. *Application contact:* Robin Audesse, Associate Director of Graduate Admissions, 207-780-5306, Fax: 207-780-5193, E-mail: raudesse@usm.maine.edu.

University of Southern Mississippi, Graduate School, College of Education and Psychology, Department of Curriculum, Instruction, and Special Education, Hattiesburg, MS 39406-0001. Offers alternative secondary teacher education (MAT); early childhood education (M Ed, Ed S); education of the gifted (M Ed, Ed D, PhD, Ed S); elementary education (M Ed, Ed D, PhD, Ed S); reading (M Ed, MS, Ed S); secondary education (M Ed, MS, Ed D, PhD, Ed S); special education (M Ed, Ed D, PhD, Ed S). *Faculty:* 16 full-time (11 women). *Students:* 31 full-time (28 women), 54 part-time (51 women); includes 5 minority (4 African Americans, 1 Hispanic American), 1 international. Average age 35. 59 applicants, 27% accepted, 11 enrolled. In 2006, 43 master's, 3 doctorates, 4 other advanced degrees awarded. *Degree requirements:* For master's, thesis (for some programs), comprehensive exam, registration; for doctorate and Ed S, thesis/dissertation, comprehensive exam, registration. *Entrance requirements:* For master's, GRE General Test, MAT, minimum GPA of 3.0; for doctorate, GRE General Test, minimum GPA of 3.5; for Ed S, GRE General Test, MAT, minimum GPA of 3.25. Additional exam requirements/recommendations for international students: Required—TOEFL. *Application deadline:* For fall admission, 3/1 priority date for domestic students, 3/1 for international students. Applications are processed on a rolling basis. Application fee: $25 ($30 for international students). *Financial support:* In 2006–07, 10 research assistantships with full tuition reimbursements (averaging $22,333 per year), 2 teaching assistantships with full tuition reimbursements (averaging $22,333 per year) were awarded; Federal Work-Study, institutionally sponsored loans, and tuition waivers (partial) also available. Financial award application deadline: 3/15. *Faculty research:* Mathematical problem solving, integrative curriculum, writing process, teacher education models. Total annual research expenditures: $100,000. *Unit head:* Dr. Dana Thames, Chair, 601-266-4547, Fax: 601-266-4175. *Application contact:* B.J. Davis, Administrative Assistant, 601-266-6987, Fax: 601-266-4548.

University of South Florida, Graduate School, College of Education, Department of Childhood Education, Program in Reading Education, Tampa, FL 33620-9951. Offers MA. *Students:* 92 applicants, 84% accepted, 54 enrolled. In 2006, 59 degrees awarded. *Entrance requirements:* For master's, GRE, minimum GPA of 2.5. *Application deadline:* For fall admission, 6/1 for domestic students; for spring admission, 10/15 for domestic students. Application fee: $30.

Reading Education

University of South Florida *(continued)*
Unit head: Nancy Williams, Program Coordinator, 813-974-3460, Fax: 813-974-0938, E-mail: nwilliam@tempest.coedu.usf.edu. *Application contact:* Christine Miranda, Admissions/Registrar's Officer, 813-974-3463, Fax: 813-974-0936, E-mail: miranda@tempest.coedu.usf.edu.

The University of Tampa, Program in Teaching, Tampa, FL 33606-1490. Offers education (MAT); math education (MAT); reading (M Ed); science education (MAT). *Students:* 66 applicants, 71% accepted, 40 enrolled. Application fee: $40. *Expenses:* Tuition: Part-time $426 per credit hour. Required fees: $35 per year. *Unit head:* Dr. Martine Harrison, Associate Professor of Education, 813-253-3333 Ext. 3373, E-mail: mharrison@ut.edu.

The University of Tennessee, Graduate School, College of Education, Health and Human Sciences, Program in Education, Knoxville, TN 37996. Offers art education (MS); counseling education (PhD); cultural studies in education (PhD); curriculum (MS, Ed S); curriculum, educational research and evaluation (Ed D, PhD); early childhood education (PhD); early childhood special education (MS); education of deaf and hard of hearing (MS); educational administration and policy studies (Ed D, PhD); educational administration and supervision (Ed S); educational psychology (Ed D, PhD); elementary education (MS, Ed S); elementary teaching (MS); English education (MS, Ed S); exercise science (PhD); foreign language/ESL education (MS, Ed S); instructional technology (MS, Ed D, PhD, Ed S); literacy, language and ESL education (PhD); literacy, language education, and ESL education (Ed D); mathematics education (MS, Ed S); modified and comprehensive special education (MS); reading education (MS, Ed S); school counseling (Ed S); school psychology (PhD, Ed S); science education (MS, Ed S); secondary teaching (MS); social foundations (MS); social science education (MS, Ed S); socio-cultural foundations of sports and education (PhD); special education (Ed S); teacher education (Ed D, PhD). *Accreditation:* NCATE. Part-time and evening/weekend programs available. *Students:* 529 (401 women); includes 39 minority (23 African Americans, 2 American Indian/Alaska Native, 9 Asian Americans or Pacific Islanders, 5 Hispanic Americans) 34 international. 420 applicants, 50% accepted. In 2006, 258 master's, 28 doctorates awarded. *Degree requirements:* For master's and Ed S, thesis optional; for doctorate, variable foreign language requirement, thesis/dissertation. *Entrance requirements:* For master's, minimum GPA of 2.7; for doctorate and Ed S, GRE General Test, minimum GPA of 2.7. Additional exam requirements/recommendations for international students: Required—TOEFL. *Application deadline:* For fall admission, 2/1 priority date for domestic students. Applications are processed on a rolling basis. Application fee: $35. Electronic applications accepted. *Expenses:* Tuition, state resident: full-time $5,574. Tuition, nonresident: full-time $16,840. Required fees: $792. *Financial support:* In 2006–07, 4 fellowships, 9 teaching assistantships were awarded; career-related internships or fieldwork, Federal Work-Study, institutionally sponsored loans, and unspecified assistantships also available. Financial award application deadline: 2/1; financial award applicants required to submit FAFSA. *Unit head:* Dr. Lester Knight, Head, 865-974-0907, Fax: 865-974-8718, E-mail: lknight@utk.edu.

The University of Texas at Brownsville, Graduate Studies, School of Education, Brownsville, TX 78520-4991. Offers bilingual education (M Ed); counseling and guidance (M Ed); curriculum and instruction (M Ed); early childhood education (M Ed); educational administration (M Ed); educational technology (M Ed); English as a second language (M Ed); reading specialist (M Ed); special education/educational diagnostician (M Ed). Part-time and evening/weekend programs available. Postbaccalaureate distance learning degree programs offered (minimal on-campus study). *Degree requirements:* For master's, thesis optional. *Entrance requirements:* For master's, GRE General Test. Additional exam requirements/recommendations for international students: Required—TOEFL.

The University of Texas at San Antonio, College of Education and Human Development, Department of Interdisciplinary Learning and Teaching, San Antonio, TX 78249-0617. Offers curriculum and instruction (MA); early childhood and elementary education (MA); educational psychology/special education (MA); instructional technology (MA); reading and literacy (MA). Part-time and evening/weekend programs available. *Faculty:* 26 full-time (all women), 1 part-time/adjunct (0 women). *Students:* 40 full-time (32 women), 240 part-time (207 women); includes 155 minority (20 African Americans, 1 American Indian/Alaska Native, 6 Asian Americans or Pacific Islanders, 128 Hispanic Americans), 3 international. Average age 35. 94 applicants, 100% accepted, 94 enrolled. In 2006, 61 degrees awarded. *Degree requirements:* For master's, thesis optional. *Entrance requirements:* For master's, GRE General Test. Additional exam requirements/recommendations for international students: Required—TOEFL (minimum score 500 paper-based; 173 computer-based). *Application deadline:* For fall admission, 7/1 for domestic students, 4/1 for international students; for spring admission, 11/1 for domestic students, 9/1 for international students. Applications are processed on a rolling basis. Application fee: $45 ($80 for international students). Electronic applications accepted. *Expenses:* Tuition, state resident: full-time $1,730; part-time $192 per credit hour. Tuition, nonresident: full-time $6,680; part-time $742 per credit hour. Required fees: $733; $308,359 per credit hour. *Financial support:* In 2006–07, 3 research assistantships (averaging $28,891 per year) were awarded; career-related internships or fieldwork, Federal Work-Study, scholarships/grants, and unspecified assistantships also available. *Faculty research:* Early childhood, reading, special education, foundations, curriculum and instruction. Total annual research expenditures: $570,791. *Unit head:* Dr. Belinda B. Flores, Chair, 210-458-5969, Fax: 210-458-7281, E-mail: belinda.flores@utsa.edu.

The University of Texas at Tyler, College of Education and Psychology, Department of Early Childhood Education, Reading and Special Education, Tyler, TX 75799-0001. Offers early childhood education (M Ed, MA); reading (M Ed, MA); special education (M Ed, MA). Part-time and evening/weekend programs available. *Faculty:* 13 full-time (11 women), 3 part-time/adjunct (2 women). *Students:* 9 full-time (8 women), 46 part-time (42 women); includes 8 minority (6 African Americans, 2 Hispanic Americans), 2 international. Average age 36. 5 applicants, 4 enrolled. In 2006, 16 degrees awarded. *Degree requirements:* For master's, thesis (for some programs), research project, comprehensive exam. *Entrance requirements:* For master's, GRE General Test. *Application deadline:* For fall admission, 11/1 for domestic students. Applications are processed on a rolling basis. Application fee: $0 ($50 for international students). Electronic applications accepted. *Expenses:* Tuition, state resident: part-time $50 per credit hour. Tuition, nonresident: part-time $328 per credit hour. Required fees: $107 per credit hour. $426 per term. *Financial support:* In 2006–07, 2 research assistantships (averaging $12,000 per year) were awarded; scholarships/grants also available. Financial award application deadline: 7/1. *Faculty research:* Improving quality in childcare settings, play and creativity, teacher interactions, effects of modeling on early childhood teachers, biofeedback, literacy instruction. *Unit head:* Dr. Brenda Gilliam, Head, 903-566-7087, Fax: 903-565-5527, E-mail: bgilliam@mail.uttyl.edu. *Application contact:* Bonnie Purser, Office of Graduate Studies, 903-566-7142, Fax: 903-566-7068, E-mail: bpurser@uttyler.edu.

The University of Texas of the Permian Basin, Office of Graduate Studies, School of Education, Program in Reading, Odessa, TX 79762-0001. Offers MA. *Degree requirements:* For master's, thesis (for some programs), comprehensive exam (for some programs), registration. *Entrance requirements:* For master's, GRE General Test. Additional exam requirements/recommendations for international students: Required—TOEFL (minimum score 550 paper-based; 213 computer-based).

The University of Texas–Pan American, College of Education, Department of Curriculum and Instruction: Elementary and Secondary, Edinburg, TX 78541-2999. Offers bilingual education (M Ed); early childhood education (M Ed); elementary education (M Ed); reading (M Ed); secondary education (M Ed). Part-time programs available. *Degree requirements:* For master's, thesis optional. *Entrance requirements:* For master's, GRE. Additional exam requirements/recommendations for international students: Required—TOEFL, IELTS. *Expenses:* Tuition, state resident: full-time $2,577; part-time $143 per credit hour. Tuition, nonresident: full-time $7,527; part-time $418 per credit hour. Required fees: $561. *Faculty research:* Dual language instruction, literacy and technology, teacher education in diverse populations, mathematics and science education.

University of the Cumberlands, Graduate Programs in Education, Reading and Writing Specialist Program, Williamsburg, KY 40769-1372. Offers MA Ed. Evening/weekend programs available. *Degree requirements:* For master's, comprehensive exam. *Entrance requirements:* For master's, GRE or NTE, Kentucky teaching certificate.

University of the Incarnate Word, School of Graduate Studies and Research, Dreeben School of Education, Programs in Education, San Antonio, TX 78209-6397. Offers adult education (M Ed, MA); diversity education (M Ed, MA); early childhood education (M Ed, MA); instructional technology (M Ed, MA); international education and entrepreneurship (PhD); kinesiology (M Ed, MA); mathematics education (PhD); organizational leadership (PhD); organizational learning (M Ed, MA); reading (M Ed, MA); special education (M Ed, MA). *Students:* 15 full-time (8 women), 179 part-time (117 women); includes 70 minority (20 African Americans, 1 American Indian/Alaska Native, 1 Asian American or Pacific Islander, 48 Hispanic Americans), 54 international. Average age 39. In 2006, 15 degrees awarded. Application fee: $20. *Expenses:* Tuition: Part-time $570 per credit hour. Required fees: $54 per credit hour. One-time fee: $195 part-time. Tuition and fees vary according to degree level. *Financial support:* Federal Work-Study and scholarships/grants available. *Unit head:* Dr. Richard Gray, Director, 210-829-3138, Fax: 210-829-3134, E-mail: gray@uiwtx.edu. *Application contact:* Andrea Cyterski-Acosta, Dean of Enrollment, 210-829-6005, Fax: 210-829-3921, E-mail: cyterski@uiwtx.edu.

University of Vermont, Graduate College, College of Education and Social Services, Department of Education, Program in Reading and Language Arts, Burlington, VT 05405. Offers M Ed. *Accreditation:* NCATE. *Students:* 15 (14 women). 11 applicants, 82% accepted, 9 enrolled. In 2006, 4 degrees awarded. *Degree requirements:* For master's, thesis or alternative. *Entrance requirements:* Additional exam requirements/recommendations for international students: Required—TOEFL (minimum score 550 paper-based; 213 computer-based). *Application deadline:* For fall admission, 8/1 priority date for domestic students. Applications are processed on a rolling basis. Application fee: $40. *Expenses:* Tuition, state resident: part-time $434 per credit. Tuition, nonresident: part-time $1,096 per credit. *Financial support:* Teaching assistantships, career-related internships or fieldwork available. Financial award application deadline: 3/1. *Unit head:* Dr. Russell M. Agne, Chairperson, 802-656-3356.

University of Victoria, Faculty of Graduate Studies, Faculty of Education, Department of Curriculum and Instruction, Victoria, BC V8W 2Y2, Canada. Offers art (M Ed, MA, PhD); curriculum studies (M Ed, MA, PhD); early childhood (M Ed, MA, PhD); language and literacy (M Ed, MA, PhD); mathematics (M Ed, MA, PhD); music (M Ed, MA); music education (PhD); science (M Ed, MA, PhD); social studies (M Ed, MA); social, cultural and foundational studies (PhD); technology and environmental education (PhD). Part-time programs available. *Degree requirements:* For master's, thesis, project (M Ed); for doctorate, thesis/dissertation, comprehensive exam, registration. *Entrance requirements:* For master's, minimum B average. Additional exam requirements/recommendations for international students: Required—TOEFL (minimum score 575 paper-based; 233 computer-based), IELTS (minimum score 7). Electronic applications accepted. *Faculty research:* Elementary and secondary English, language arts, curriculum theory and practice, educational media and technology, educational administration and leadership, history and philosophy of education.

University of Washington, Graduate School, College of Education, Seattle, WA 98195. Offers curriculum and instruction (M Ed, Ed D, PhD), including educational technology, general curriculum (Ed D, PhD), language, literacy, and culture, mathematics education, multicultural education, reading and language arts education (Ed D), science education, social studies education, teaching and curriculum (M Ed); educational leadership and policy studies (M Ed, Ed D, PhD), including administration, educational organization and policy, higher education, school district leadership (Ed D), social/cultural foundations; educational psychology (M Ed, PhD), including human development and cognition, measurement and research, school counseling (M Ed), school psychology; special education (M Ed, Ed D, PhD), including early childhood education, elementary special education, emotional and behavioral disabilities (M Ed), general special education, severe disabilities; teacher education (MIT). *Accreditation:* APA. Part-time and evening/weekend programs available. *Degree requirements:* For master's, thesis optional; for doctorate, thesis/dissertation. *Entrance requirements:* For master's and doctorate, GRE General Test, minimum GPA of 3.0. Additional exam requirements/recommendations for international students: Required—TOEFL. Electronic applications accepted. *Faculty research:* School restructuring/effective schools, special education interventions, literacy and writing, technology, school partnerships, teacher preparation.

University of West Florida, College of Professional Studies, Division of Teacher Education, Program in Reading Education, Pensacola, FL 32514-5750. Offers M Ed. Part-time and evening/weekend programs available. *Students:* 5 full-time (all women), 42 part-time (40 women); includes 6 minority (4 African Americans, 1 American Indian/Alaska Native, 1 Hispanic American). Average age 36. 12 applicants, 100% accepted, 8 enrolled. In 2006, 32 degrees awarded. *Entrance requirements:* For master's, GRE General Test or minimum GPA of 3.0. Additional exam requirements/recommendations for international students: Required—TOEFL (minimum score 550 paper-based; 213 computer-based). *Application deadline:* For fall admission, 6/1 for domestic students, 5/15 for international students; for spring admission, 11/1 for domestic students, 10/1 for international students. Applications are processed on a rolling basis. Application fee: $30. *Expenses:* Tuition, state resident: full-time $5,871; part-time $245 per credit hour. Tuition, nonresident: full-time $21,241; part-time $885 per credit hour. *Financial support:* Fellowships, teaching assistantships, career-related internships or fieldwork, Federal Work-Study, scholarships/grants, and unspecified assistantships available. Financial award application deadline: 4/15; financial award applicants required to submit FAFSA. *Unit head:* Dr. Joseph M. Peters, Chairperson and Associate Dean, Division of Teacher Education, 850-474-2768.

University of West Georgia, Graduate School, College of Education, Department of Curriculum and Instruction, Program in Reading Education, Carrollton, GA 30118. Offers M Ed. Part-time and evening/weekend programs available. *Students:* 2 full-time (both women), 26 part-time (23 women); includes 4 minority (all African Americans) Average age 23. In 2006, 12 degrees awarded. *Degree requirements:* For master's, comprehensive exam. *Entrance requirements:* For master's, GRE or MAT. *Application deadline:* For fall admission, 8/1 for domestic students. Applications are processed on a rolling basis. Application fee: $20. *Expenses:* Tuition, state resident: full-time $2,286; part-time $127 per credit. Tuition, nonresident: full-time $9,144; part-time $508 per credit. Required fees: $494; $27 per credit. $121 per semester. *Financial support:* In 2006–07, research assistantships with full tuition reimbursements (averaging $3,000 per year). Financial award applicants required to submit FAFSA. *Application contact:* Dr. Charles W. Clark, Chair, 678-839-6508, E-mail: cclark@westga.edu.

University of Wisconsin–Eau Claire, College of Education and Human Sciences, Program in Reading, Eau Claire, WI 54702-4004. Offers MST. *Faculty:* 9 full-time (6 women). *Students:* Average age 30. 10 applicants, 80% accepted, 2 enrolled. In 2006, 1 degree awarded. *Degree requirements:* For master's, thesis optional. *Application deadline:* For fall admission, 7/1 for domestic students; for spring admission, 12/1 for domestic students. Applications are processed on a rolling basis. Application fee: $45. *Expenses:* Tuition, state resident: full-time $6,533; part-time $363 per credit. Tuition, nonresident: full-time $17,143; part-time $952 per credit. Tuition and fees vary according to program and reciprocity agreements. *Financial support:* Federal Work-Study available. Financial award application deadline: 3/1; financial award applicants required to submit FAFSA. *Unit head:* Dr. Tamara Lindsey, Chair, 715-836-4737, Fax: 715-836-4868, E-mail: lindsetp@uwec.edu.

University of Wisconsin–La Crosse, Office of University Graduate Studies, College of Liberal Studies, Department of Educational Studies, Program in Reading, La Crosse, WI 54601-3742. Offers MS Ed. Part-time programs available. *Students:* Average age 40. 2 applicants, 100% accepted, 2 enrolled. In 2006, 7 degrees awarded. *Degree requirements:* For master's, thesis or alternative. *Entrance requirements:* For master's, certification prior to completion of student teaching or equivalent at elementary or secondary level, portfolio. Additional exam requirements/recommendations for international students: Required—TOEFL (minimum score

550 paper-based; 213 computer-based). *Application deadline:* Applications are processed on a rolling basis. Application fee: $45. Electronic applications accepted. *Financial support:* Research assistantships with partial tuition reimbursements, Federal Work-Study, health care benefits, and unspecified assistantships available. Financial award application deadline: 3/15; financial award applicants required to submit FAFSA. *Faculty research:* Pre-service teacher education; literacy development; emergent literacy; instructional strategies in literacy; vocabulary development. *Unit head:* Dr. Delores Heiden, Director, 608-785-8149, E-mail: heiden.delo@uwlax.edu. *Application contact:* Kathryn Kiefer, Associate Director of Admissions, 608-785-8939, E-mail: admissions@uwlax.edu.

University of Wisconsin–Milwaukee, Graduate School, School of Education, Department of Curriculum and Instruction, Milwaukee, WI 53201-0413. Offers curriculum planning and instruction improvement (MS); early childhood education (MS); elementary education (MS); junior high/middle school education (MS); reading education (MS); secondary education (MS); teaching in an urban setting (MS). Part-time programs available. *Faculty:* 27 full-time (17 women). *Students:* 21 full-time (17 women), 67 part-time (54 women); includes 15 minority (8 African Americans, 3 Asian Americans or Pacific Islanders, 4 Hispanic Americans), 3 international. 44 applicants, 43% accepted, 19 enrolled. In 2006, 38 degrees awarded. *Degree requirements:* For master's, thesis or alternative. *Application deadline:* For fall admission, 1/1 priority date for domestic students; for spring admission, 9/1 for domestic students. Applications are processed on a rolling basis. Application fee: $45 ($75 for international students). *Expenses:* Tuition, state resident: part-time $510 per credit. Tuition, nonresident: part-time $1,408 per credit. Tuition and fees vary according to program. *Financial support:* Fellowships, research assistantships, teaching assistantships, career-related internships or fieldwork and unspecified assistantships available. Support available to part-time students. Financial award application deadline: 4/15. *Unit head:* Linda Post, Chair, 414-229-4884, Fax: 414-229-5571, E-mail: lpost@uwm.edu.

University of Wisconsin–Oshkosh, The School of Graduate Studies, College of Education and Human Services, Department of Reading Education, Oshkosh, WI 54901. Offers MSE. *Accreditation:* NCATE. Part-time programs available. *Degree requirements:* For master's, thesis or alternative, reflective journey course. *Entrance requirements:* For master's, interview, teaching certificate, undergraduate degree in teacher education, letters of recommendation. Additional exam requirements/recommendations for international students: Required—TOEFL (minimum score 550 paper-based; 213 computer-based). Electronic applications accepted. *Faculty research:* Writing and reading, assessment, learner-centered instruction, multicultural literature, family literacy.

University of Wisconsin–River Falls, Outreach and Graduate Studies, College of Education and Professional Studies, Department of Teacher Education, River Falls, WI 54022-5001. Offers elementary education (MSE); reading (MSE). *Accreditation:* NCATE. Part-time programs available. *Degree requirements:* For master's, thesis or alternative, comprehensive exam, registration. *Entrance requirements:* For master's, minimum GPA of 2.75. Electronic applications accepted.

University of Wisconsin–Stevens Point, College of Professional Studies, School of Education, Program in Education—General/Reading, Stevens Point, WI 54481-3897. Offers MSE. Part-time programs available. *Faculty:* 13 full-time (11 women). *Students:* 5 full-time (1 woman), 58 part-time (47 women); includes 3 minority (2 Asian Americans or Pacific Islanders, 1 Hispanic American). Average age 26. In 2006, 68 degrees awarded. *Degree requirements:* For master's, thesis or alternative, comprehensive exam. *Entrance requirements:* For master's, minimum undergraduate GPA of 3.0, teacher certification, 2 years teaching experience, letters of recommendation. Additional exam requirements/recommendations for international students: Required—TOEFL (minimum score 523 paper-based; 193 computer-based). *Application deadline:* For fall admission, 5/1 priority date for domestic students. Applications are processed on a rolling basis. Application fee: $45. *Expenses:* Tuition, state resident: full-time $5,910; part-time $328 per credit. Tuition, nonresident: full-time $16,520; part-time $918 per credit. Required fees: $756; $73 per credit. *Financial support:* In 2006–07, 4 research assistantships with partial tuition reimbursements (averaging $9,807 per year) were awarded; Federal Work-Study and unspecified assistantships also available. Support available to part-time students. Financial award application deadline: 5/1; financial award applicants required to submit FAFSA. *Faculty research:* Reading strategies in the content areas, gifted education, curriculum and instruction, standards-based education. *Application contact:* Dr. Patricia Caro, Director, 715-346-4403, Fax: 715-346-4846, E-mail: pcaro@uwsp.edu.

University of Wisconsin–Superior, Graduate Division, Department of Teacher Education, Program in Teaching Reading, Superior, WI 54880-4500. Offers MSE. Part-time and evening/weekend programs available. *Degree requirements:* For master's, thesis or alternative, research project, comprehensive exam. *Entrance requirements:* For master's, minimum GPA of 2.75, teaching certificate.

University of Wisconsin–Whitewater, School of Graduate Studies, College of Education, Program in Reading, Whitewater, WI 53190-1790. Offers MS Ed. Part-time and evening/weekend programs available. Postbaccalaureate distance learning degree programs offered (no on-campus study). *Students:* 2 full-time (both women), 22 part-time (21 women); includes 1 minority (African American) Average age 32. 3 applicants, 100% accepted, 3 enrolled. In 2006, 10 degrees awarded. *Entrance requirements:* Additional exam requirements/recommendations for international students: Required—TOEFL (minimum score 550 paper-based; 213 computer-based). *Application deadline:* For fall admission, 7/15 priority date for domestic students; for spring admission, 12/1 priority date for domestic students. Application fee: $45. *Expenses:* Tuition, state resident: full-time $3,311. Tuition, nonresident: full-time $8,616. Required fees: $368 per credit. *Financial support:* Research assistantships, Federal Work-Study, scholarships/grants, and unspecified assistantships available. Support available to part-time students. Financial award application deadline: 3/15; financial award applicants required to submit FAFSA. *Unit head:* Anne Stinson, Coordinator, 262-472-1973, Fax: 262-472-1988. *Application contact:* Sally A. Lange, School of Graduate Studies, 262-472-1006, Fax: 262-472-5027, E-mail: gradschl@uww.edu.

Valdosta State University, Graduate School, College of Education, Department of Early Childhood and Reading Education, Valdosta, GA 31698. Offers early childhood education (M Ed, Ed S); reading education (M Ed). *Accreditation:* NCATE. Part-time and evening/weekend programs available. *Degree requirements:* For master's, comprehensive written and/or oral exams; for Ed S, thesis. *Entrance requirements:* For master's and Ed S, GRE General Test or MAT. Additional exam requirements/recommendations for international students: Required—TOEFL (minimum score 523 paper-based; 193 computer-based). Electronic applications accepted.

Vanderbilt University, Peabody College, Department of Teaching and Learning, Nashville, TN 37240-1001. Offers curriculum and instructional leadership (M Ed); early childhood education (M Ed); early childhood leadership (Ed D); elementary education (M Ed); English education (M Ed); English language learners (M Ed); mathematics education (M Ed); reading education (M Ed); science education (M Ed); secondary education (M Ed). *Accreditation:* NCATE. *Faculty:* 23 full-time (13 women), 28 part-time/adjunct (19 women). *Students:* 71 full-time (62 women), 21 part-time (15 women); includes 9 minority (8 African Americans, 1 Hispanic American), 2 international. Average age 27. 102 applicants, 60% accepted, 27 enrolled. In 2006, 53 master's, 3 doctorates awarded. *Degree requirements:* For master's, thesis optional. *Entrance requirements:* For master's, GRE General Test, MAT. Additional exam requirements/recommendations for international students: Required—TOEFL (minimum score 550 paper-based; 213 computer-based). *Application deadline:* For fall admission, 12/31 priority date for domestic and international students; for spring admission, 11/1 priority date for domestic and international students. Applications are processed on a rolling basis. Application fee: $0. Electronic applications accepted. *Expenses:* Tuition: Full-time $24,462. Required fees: $2,515. One-time fee: $30 full-time. Full-time tuition and fees vary according to course load, degree level and program. *Financial support:* In 2006–07, 62 students received support, including 36 fellowships with full and partial tuition reimbursements available, 13 research assistantships with full and partial tuition reimbursements available, 13 teaching assistantships with full and partial tuition reimbursements available; Federal Work-Study, institutionally sponsored loans, scholarships/grants, tuition waivers (partial), and unspecified assistantships also available. Support available to part-time students. Financial award application deadline: 2/1; financial award applicants required to submit FAFSA. *Faculty research:* Teaching and learning; development of subject matter knowledge; learning and policy; development students' mathematical and scientific knowledge, development of literacy. *Unit head:* Leona Schauble, Chair, 615-322-8100, Fax: 615-322-8999, E-mail: leona.schauble@vanderbilt.edu. *Application contact:* Angela Saylor, Educational Coordinator, 615-322-8092, Fax: 615-322-8999.

Virginia Commonwealth University, Graduate School, School of Education, Program in Adult and Organizational Learning, Richmond, VA 23284-9005. Offers adult literacy (M Ed); adults with disabilities (M Ed); human resource development (M Ed). *Accreditation:* NCATE. Part-time programs available. *Students:* 1 applicant, 0% accepted. In 2006, 14 degrees awarded. *Entrance requirements:* For master's, GRE General Test or MAT. *Application deadline:* For fall admission, 5/15 for domestic students; for spring admission, 11/15 for domestic students. Applications are processed on a rolling basis. Application fee: $50. *Financial support:* Career-related internships or fieldwork and Federal Work-Study available. Financial award application deadline: 3/1. *Faculty research:* Adult development and learning, program planning and evaluation. *Unit head:* James McMillan, Division Head, 804-828-1305. *Application contact:* Dr. Michael D. Davis, Director, Graduate Studies, 804-828-6530, Fax: 804-827-0676, E-mail: mddavis@vcu.edu.

See Close-Up on page 1279.

Virginia Commonwealth University, Graduate School, School of Education, Program in Reading, Richmond, VA 23284-9005. Offers M Ed. *Accreditation:* NCATE. In 2006, 1 degree awarded. *Degree requirements:* For master's, comprehensive exam. *Entrance requirements:* For master's, GRE General Test or MAT. *Application deadline:* For fall admission, 5/15 for domestic students; for spring admission, 11/15 for domestic students. Applications are processed on a rolling basis. Application fee: $50. *Financial support:* Federal Work-Study, institutionally sponsored loans, and tuition waivers (partial) available. Financial award application deadline: 3/1. *Unit head:* James McMillan, Division Head, 804-828-1305. *Application contact:* Dr. Michael D. Davis, Director, Graduate Studies, 804-828-6530, Fax: 804-827-0676, E-mail: mddavis@vcu.edu.

See Close-Up on page 1625.

Wagner College, Division of Graduate Studies, Department of Education, Program in Literacy (B-6), Staten Island, NY 10301-4495. Offers MS Ed. Part-time programs available. *Students:* 10 full-time (9 women), 3 part-time (2 women). 8 applicants, 88% accepted, 6 enrolled. In 2006, 9 degrees awarded. *Degree requirements:* For master's, thesis. *Entrance requirements:* For master's, minimum GPA of 2.75. Additional exam requirements/recommendations for international students: Required—TOEFL (minimum score 550 paper-based; 217 computer-based). *Application deadline:* For fall admission, 8/1 priority date for domestic students, 6/30 priority date for international students; for spring admission, 12/10 for domestic students, 11/15 for international students. Applications are processed on a rolling basis. Application fee: $50 ($85 for international students). *Expenses:* Tuition: Full-time $15,120; part-time $840 per credit. *Financial support:* Fellowships, unspecified assistantships available. Financial award applicants required to submit FAFSA. *Application contact:* Susan Rosenberg, Office of Graduate Studies, 718-390-3106, Fax: 718-390-3456, E-mail: graduate@wagner.edu.

Walla Walla College, Graduate School, School of Education and Psychology, Specialization in Literacy Instruction, College Place, WA 99324-1198. Offers M Ed, MA, MAT. *Faculty:* 8 full-time (3 women), 3 part-time/adjunct (1 woman). *Degree requirements:* For master's, thesis (for some programs). *Entrance requirements:* For master's, GRE General Test, minimum GPA of 2.75. *Application deadline:* For fall admission, 4/1 priority date for domestic students. Applications are processed on a rolling basis. Application fee: $50. Electronic applications accepted. *Expenses:* Tuition: Full-time $20,124; part-time $516 per quarter hour. *Financial support:* Teaching assistantships with partial tuition reimbursements available. Financial award application deadline: 4/1; financial award applicants required to submit FAFSA. *Application contact:* Dr. Joe G. Galusha, Dean of Graduate Studies, 509-527-2421, Fax: 509-527-2237, E-mail: galujo@wwc.edu.

Washburn University, College of Arts and Sciences, Department of Education, Program in Reading, Topeka, KS 66621. Offers M Ed. *Accreditation:* NCATE. Part-time programs available. *Degree requirements:* For master's, portfolio. *Entrance requirements:* For master's, GRE General Test, MAT, minimum GPA of 3.0 during previous 2 years. *Expenses:* Tuition, state resident: full-time $4,338; part-time $241 per credit hour. Tuition, nonresident: full-time $8,820; part-time $490 per credit hour. Required fees: $62; $31 per semester. *Application contact:* Tara Porter, Licensure Officer, 785-670-1434, Fax: 785-670-1046, E-mail: tara.porter@washburn.edu.

Washington State University, Graduate School, College of Education, Department of Teaching and Learning, Pullman, WA 99164. Offers curriculum and instruction (Ed D, PhD); diverse languages (M Ed, MA); elementary education (M Ed, MA, MIT); exercise science (MS); literacy education (M Ed, MA, PhD); math education (PhD); secondary education (M Ed, MA). *Accreditation:* NCATE. *Faculty:* 27. *Students:* 54 full-time (43 women), 20 part-time (14 women); includes 13 minority (4 African Americans, 2 American Indian/Alaska Native, 2 Asian Americans or Pacific Islanders, 5 Hispanic Americans), 5 international. Average age 34. 244 applicants, 16% accepted, 11 enrolled. In 2006, 20 master's, 3 doctorates awarded. *Degree requirements:* For master's, thesis (for some programs), oral or written exam, comprehensive exam (for some programs); for doctorate, thesis/dissertation, oral, written exam, comprehensive exam. *Entrance requirements:* For master's and doctorate, GRE General Test, minimum GPA of 3.0, 3 letters of recommendation. Additional exam requirements/recommendations for international students: Required—TOEFL. *Application deadline:* For fall admission, 2/1 for domestic students, 3/1 for international students; for spring admission, 9/1 for domestic students, 7/1 for international students. Applications are processed on a rolling basis. Application fee: $50. *Expenses:* Tuition, state resident: full-time $7,066. Tuition, nonresident: full-time $17,204. *Financial support:* In 2006–07, 13 research assistantships with partial tuition reimbursements (averaging $13,917 per year), 22 teaching assistantships with partial tuition reimbursements (averaging $13,056 per year) were awarded; career-related internships or fieldwork, Federal Work-Study, institutionally sponsored loans, tuition waivers (partial), unspecified assistantships, and staff assistantships, teaching associateships also available. Financial award application deadline: 4/1. *Faculty research:* Evolution of middle school education issues in special education, computer-assisted language learning. Total annual research expenditures: $1.1 million. *Unit head:* Dr. Corinne Mantle-Bromley, Chair, 509-335-5027. *Application contact:* Graduate School Admissions, 800-GRADWSU, Fax: 509-335-1949, E-mail: gradsch@wsu.edu.

Washington State University Tri-Cities, Graduate Programs, Program in Education, Richland, WA 99352-1671. Offers counseling (Ed M); educational leadership (Ed M, Ed D); literacy (Ed M); secondary certification (Ed M); teaching (MIT). Part-time programs available. *Faculty:* 23. *Students:* 27 full-time (20 women), 82 part-time (68 women); includes 11 minority (all Hispanic Americans) Average age 36. 77 applicants, 71% accepted, 34 enrolled. *Degree requirements:* For master's, thesis or alternative, comprehensive exam, registration; for doctorate, thesis/dissertation, comprehensive exam. *Entrance requirements:* For master's, GRE, minimum GPA of 3.0, Working with Youth form, Character and Fitness form, 3 letters of recommendation. Additional exam requirements/recommendations for international students: Required—TOEFL. *Application deadline:* For fall admission, 2/1 priority date for domestic students, 3/1 for international students; for spring admission, 9/1 priority date for domestic students, 7/1 for international students. Applications are processed on a rolling basis. Application fee: $50. Electronic applications accepted. *Expenses:* Tuition, state resident: full-time $7,066. Tuition, nonresident: full-time $17,204. *Financial support:* In 2006–07, 59 students

Reading Education

Washington State University Tri-Cities (continued)

received support, including 1 fellowship (averaging $7,950 per year), teaching assistantships (averaging $13,056 per year); Federal Work-Study, scholarships/grants, and unspecified assistantships also available. *Faculty research:* Multicultural counseling, socio-cultural influences in schools, diverse learners, teacher education, K-12 educational leadership. *Unit head:* Dr. Nancy Kyle, Director, 509-372-7396.

Wayne State University, College of Education, Division of Teacher Education, Detroit, MI 48202. Offers adult and continuing education (M Ed); art education (M Ed); bilingual/bicultural education (M Ed, MAT); business education (M Ed, MAT); career and technical education (M Ed, Ed D, PhD, Ed S); curriculum and instruction (Ed D, PhD, Ed S); distributive education (M Ed, MAT); early childhood education (M Ed); elementary education (M Ed, MAT, Ed D, PhD, Ed S); elementary education curriculum and instruction (M Ed); English education (M Ed); English education-secondary (M Ed, Ed S); foreign language education (M Ed); general education (Ed D, Ed S); health occupations education (M Ed); industrial education (M Ed); mathematics education (M Ed, Ed S); pre-school and parent education (M Ed); reading (M Ed, Ed D, Ed S); reading, languages and literature (Ed D); school music-vocal (M Ed); science education (M Ed, MAT, Ed S); secondary education (MAT); secondary school reading (M Ed); social studies education (M Ed, Ed S), including education-secondary (M Ed); special education (M Ed, Ed D, PhD, Ed S); teacher education (MAT, Ed D, PhD). *Faculty:* 41 full-time (22 women), 2 part-time/adjunct (both women). *Students:* 401 full-time (295 women), 1,021 part-time (784 women); includes 527 minority (452 African Americans, 6 American Indian/Alaska Native, 32 Asian Americans or Pacific Islanders, 37 Hispanic Americans), 18 international. Average age 36. 296 applicants, 81% accepted, 132 enrolled. In 2006, 386 master's, 1 doctorate awarded. *Degree requirements:* For doctorate, thesis/dissertation. *Entrance requirements:* For master's, minimum GPA of 2.6; for doctorate, minimum undergraduate GPA of 3.0, graduate 3.5; interview. Additional exam requirements/recommendations for international students: Required—TOEFL (minimum score 550 paper-based; 213 computer-based), TWE (minimum score 6). *Application deadline:* For fall admission, 7/1 for domestic students, 6/1 for international students; for winter admission, 10/1 for international students; for spring admission, 2/1 for international students. Application fee: $30 ($50 for international students). Electronic applications accepted. *Financial support:* In 2006-07, 1 fellowship (averaging $34,919 per year) was awarded; research assistantships. *Faculty research:* Reading and writing literacy and literature. Total annual research expenditures: $209,400. *Unit head:* Dr. Joann Snyder, Academic Director, 313-577-1644, E-mail: joanne.snyder@wayne.edu. *Application contact:* Sharon Elliott, Assistant Dean, 313-577-0902, E-mail: sharon.elliott@wayne.edu.

West Chester University of Pennsylvania, Graduate Studies, School of Education, Department of Literacy, West Chester, PA 19383. Offers reading (M Ed). Part-time and evening/weekend programs available. *Students:* 2 full-time (both women), 141 part-time (134 women); includes 1 African American, 2 Hispanic Americans. Average age 29. 40 applicants, 100% accepted, 26 enrolled. In 2006, 40 degrees awarded. *Degree requirements:* For master's, comprehensive exam. *Entrance requirements:* For master's, GRE or MAT, minimum GPA of 3.0, teaching certificate. *Application deadline:* For fall admission, 4/15 priority date for domestic students; for spring admission, 10/15 priority date for domestic students. Applications are processed on a rolling basis. Application fee: $35. *Financial support:* In 2006-07, 3 research assistantships with full tuition reimbursements (averaging $5,000 per year) were awarded; unspecified assistantships also available. Support available to part-time students. Financial award application deadline: 2/15; financial award applicants required to submit FAFSA. *Faculty research:* Teaching and mentoring pre-service teachers to teach reading in urban settings. *Unit head:* Dr. Susan Klerzien, Chair, 610-436-3225, E-mail: sklerzien@wcupa.edu. *Application contact:* Dr. Dena Beeghly, Graduate Coordinator, 610-436-3070, E-mail: dbeeghly@wcupa.edu.

Western Carolina University, Graduate School, College of Education and Allied Professions, Department of Birth-Kindergarten, Elementary and Middle Grades Education, Program in Reading Education, Cullowhee, NC 28723. Offers comprehensive education-reading (MA Ed); reading education (MAT). *Accreditation:* NCATE. Part-time and evening/weekend programs available. *Degree requirements:* For master's, comprehensive exam. *Entrance requirements:* For master's, GRE General Test. Additional exam requirements/recommendations for international students: Required—TOEFL (minimum score 550 paper-based; 213 computer-based).

Western Carolina University, Graduate School, College of Education and Allied Professions, Department of Educational Leadership and Foundations, Programs in Secondary Education, Cullowhee, NC 28723. Offers art education (MAT); biology (MAT); chemistry (MAT); comprehensive education (MA Ed), including art, biology, English, mathematics, music, physical education, reading, social sciences; English (MAT); family and consumer sciences (MAT); mathematics (MAT); physical education (MAT); reading (MAT); social sciences (MAT). *Accreditation:* NCATE (one or more programs are accredited). Part-time and evening/weekend programs available. *Degree requirements:* For master's, comprehensive exam. *Entrance requirements:* For master's, GRE General Test, portfolio. Additional exam requirements/recommendations for international students: Required—TOEFL (minimum score 550 paper-based; 213 computer-based).

Western Connecticut State University, Division of Graduate Studies, School of Professional Studies, Department of Education and Educational Psychology, Reading Option, Danbury, CT 06810-6885. Offers MS. Part-time and evening/weekend programs available. *Students:* 1 (woman) full-time, 58 part-time (54 women); includes 1 minority (Hispanic American), 1 international. Average age 31. 8 applicants, 100% accepted. In 2006, 27 degrees awarded. *Degree requirements:* For master's, thesis or research project. *Entrance requirements:* For master's, minimum GPA of 2.8, teaching certificate in elementary education. *Application deadline:* For fall admission, 8/1 priority date for domestic students. Applications are processed on a rolling basis. Application fee: $40. *Financial support:* Career-related internships or fieldwork available. Support available to part-time students. Financial award application deadline: 5/1; financial award applicants required to submit FAFSA. *Application contact:* Chris Shankle, Associate Director of Graduate Admissions, 203-837-8244, Fax: 203-837-8338, E-mail: shanklec@wcsu.edu.

Western Illinois University, School of Graduate Studies, College of Education and Human Services, Department of Curriculum and Instruction, Program in Reading, Macomb, IL 61455-1390. Offers MS Ed. *Accreditation:* NCATE. Part-time programs available. *Students:* 5 full-time (all women), 195 part-time (190 women); includes 6 minority (3 African Americans, 3 Hispanic Americans). Average age 34. 53 applicants, 98% accepted. In 2006, 42 degrees awarded. *Degree requirements:* For master's, thesis or alternative. *Entrance requirements:* For master's, minimum GPA of 2.75, teacher certification. Additional exam requirements/recommendations for international students: Required—TOEFL (minimum score 550 paper-based; 213 computer-based; 80 iBT). *Application deadline:* Applications are processed on a rolling basis. Application fee: $30. Electronic applications accepted. *Expenses:* Tuition, state resident: part-time $200 per credit hour. Tuition, nonresident: part-time $400 per credit hour. *Financial support:* In 2006-07, research assistantships with full tuition reimbursements (averaging $6,568 per year). Financial award applicants required to submit FAFSA. *Application contact:* Dr. Barbara Baily, Director of Graduate Studies/Associate Provost, 309-298-1806, Fax: 309-298-2345, E-mail: grad-office@wiu.edu.

Western Kentucky University, Graduate Studies, College of Education and Behavioral Sciences, Department of Special Instructional Programs, Bowling Green, KY 42101. Offers exceptional child education (MAE); interdisciplinary early child education (MAE); library media education (MS); literacy (MAE). Part-time and evening/weekend programs available. Postbaccalaureate distance learning degree programs offered (minimal on-campus study). *Faculty:* 15 full-time (12 women), 1 (woman) part-time/adjunct. *Students:* 38 full-time (35 women), 347 part-time (296 women); includes 18 minority (8 African Americans, 2 American Indian/Alaska Native, 1 Asian American or Pacific Islander, 7 Hispanic Americans), 2 international. Average

age 33. 131 applicants, 66% accepted, 57 enrolled. In 2006, 146 degrees awarded. *Degree requirements:* For master's, comprehensive exam. *Entrance requirements:* For master's, GRE General Test. Additional exam requirements/recommendations for international students: Required—TOEFL (minimum score 555 paper-based; 213 computer-based; 79 iBT). *Application deadline:* For fall admission, 7/1 for domestic students, 4/1 for international students; for spring admission, 11/1 for domestic students, 9/1 for international students. Application fee: $35. *Expenses:* Tuition, state resident: full-time $6,520; part-time $226 per hour. Tuition, nonresident: full-time $7,140; part-time $357 per hour. International tuition: $15,820 full-time. *Financial support:* In 2006-07, 2 research assistantships with partial tuition reimbursements (averaging $8,000 per year) were awarded; tuition waivers (partial) and unspecified assistantships also available. *Faculty research:* Teacher preparation in moderate/severe disabilities. Total annual research expenditures: $125,538. *Unit head:* Dr. Sherry Powers, Department Head, 270-745-4607, Fax: 270-745-3441, E-mail: sherry.powers@wku.edu.

Western Michigan University, Graduate College, College of Education, Department of Teaching, Learning, and Leadership, Program in Reading, Kalamazoo, MI 49008-5202. Offers MA. *Accreditation:* NCATE.

Western New Mexico University, Graduate Division, School of Education, Silver City, NM 88062-0680. Offers counselor education (MA); elementary education (MAT); reading education (MAT); school administration (MA); secondary education (MAT); special education (MAT). *Accreditation:* NCATE. *Degree requirements:* For master's, comprehensive exam. *Entrance requirements:* For master's, GRE General Test, GRE Subject Test, minimum GPA of 3.2 in last 64 hours of undergraduate study. Additional exam requirements/recommendations for international students: Required—TOEFL (minimum score 550 paper-based; 213 computer-based). Electronic applications accepted. *Expenses:* Tuition, state resident: full-time $1,329. Tuition, nonresident: full-time $4,779.

Westfield State College, Division of Graduate and Continuing Education, Department of Education, Program in Reading, Westfield, MA 01086. Offers M Ed. *Accreditation:* NCATE. Part-time and evening/weekend programs available. *Degree requirements:* For master's, practicum. *Entrance requirements:* For master's, GRE General Test or MAT, minimum undergraduate GPA of 2.7.

Westminster College, Programs in Education, Program in Reading, New Wilmington, PA 16172-0001. Offers M Ed, Certificate. Part-time and evening/weekend programs available. *Degree requirements:* For master's, portfolio. *Entrance requirements:* For master's, minimum GPA of 3.0.

West Texas A&M University, College of Education and Social Sciences, Division of Education, Program in Reading, Canyon, TX 79016-0001. Offers M Ed. Part-time and evening/weekend programs available. *Degree requirements:* For master's, comprehensive exam, registration. *Entrance requirements:* For master's, GRE General Test, interview with master's committee chairperson, state certification as a reading specialist with 3 years of teaching experience. Electronic applications accepted. *Faculty research:* Multicultural child and adolescent literature, bilingual, dual language, monolingual classrooms.

West Virginia University, College of Human Resources and Education, Department of Curriculum and Instruction-Literacy, Program in Reading, Morgantown, WV 26506. Offers MA. *Accreditation:* NCATE. Part-time programs available. *Students:* 18 full-time (17 women), 69 part-time (64 women); includes 2 minority (both African Americans) Average age 31. In 2006, 80 degrees awarded. *Degree requirements:* For master's, content exams, thesis optional. *Entrance requirements:* For master's, minimum GPA of 2.75. Additional exam requirements/recommendations for international students: Required—TOEFL. *Application deadline:* Applications are processed on a rolling basis. Application fee: $50. Electronic applications accepted. *Expenses:* Tuition, state resident: full-time $4,926; part-time $276 per credit hour. Tuition, nonresident: full-time $14,278; part-time $796 per credit hour. Tuition and fees vary according to program. *Financial support:* In 2006-07, 38 students received support, including 1 teaching assistantship with full tuition reimbursement available (averaging $8,264 per year); Federal Work-Study, institutionally sponsored loans, tuition waivers (full and partial), and graduate administrative assistantships also available. Financial award application deadline: 2/1; financial award applicants required to submit FAFSA. *Faculty research:* Teacher education, current practices, protocol research, metacognitive studies. *Unit head:* Dr. Steven D. Rinehart, Program Coordinator, 304-293-3441, Fax: 304-293-3802, E-mail: steve.rinehart@mail.wvu.edu.

Wheelock College, Graduate Programs, Division of Education, Boston, MA 02215-4176. Offers early childhood education (MS); education leadership (MS); elementary education (MS); language, literacy, and reading (MS); teaching students with moderate disabilities (MS). *Accreditation:* NCATE. Postbaccalaureate distance learning degree programs offered (minimal on-campus study). *Degree requirements:* For master's, comprehensive exam. *Entrance requirements:* Additional exam requirements/recommendations for international students: Required—TOEFL. Electronic applications accepted. *Faculty research:* Symbolic learning, emergent literacy, diversity inclusion, beginning reading language and culture, math education.

Widener University, School of Human Service Professions, Center for Education, Chester, PA 19013-5792. Offers adult education (M Ed); counseling in higher education (M Ed); counselor education (M Ed); early childhood education (M Ed); educational foundations (M Ed); educational leadership (M Ed); educational psychology (M Ed); elementary education (M Ed); English and language arts (M Ed); health education (M Ed); higher education leadership (Ed D); home and school visitor (M Ed); human sexuality (M Ed); mathematics education (M Ed); middle school education (M Ed); principalship (M Ed); reading and language arts (Ed D); reading education (M Ed); school administration (Ed D); science education (M Ed); social studies education (M Ed); special education (M Ed); technology education (M Ed). Part-time and evening/weekend programs available. Terminal master's awarded for partial completion of doctoral program. *Degree requirements:* For doctorate, thesis/dissertation. *Entrance requirements:* For master's, minimum GPA of 2.5; for doctorate, GRE or MAT, minimum GPA of 2.0 (undergraduate), 3.5 (graduate). Electronic applications accepted. Expenses: Contact institution. *Faculty research:* Reading and cognition, adult education, technology education, educational leadership, special education.

William Paterson University of New Jersey, College of Education, Program in Reading, Wayne, NJ 07470-8420. Offers M Ed. *Accreditation:* NCATE. *Students:* 24 applicants, 38% accepted, 8 enrolled. *Degree requirements:* For master's, research design. *Entrance requirements:* For master's, GRE General Test, MAT, minimum GPA of 2.75, teaching certificate. *Application deadline:* Applications are processed on a rolling basis. Application fee: $50. Electronic applications accepted. *Financial support:* In 2006-07, 1 student received support; research assistantships with full tuition reimbursements available, career-related internships or fieldwork and unspecified assistantships available. Support available to part-time students. Financial award application deadline: 4/1; financial award applicants required to submit FAFSA. *Faculty research:* Reading improvement, urban education. *Unit head:* Dr. Geraldine Mongillo, Graduate Coordinator, 973-720-3139. *Application contact:* Danielle Liautaud, Director, 973-720-3579, Fax: 973-720-2035, E-mail: liautaudd@wpunj.edu.

Wilmington College, Department of Education, Wilmington, OH 45177. Offers reading (M Ed); special education (M Ed). Part-time programs available. *Degree requirements:* For master's, comprehensive exam. *Entrance requirements:* For master's, GRE or MAT, minimum GPA of 3.0, 2 letters of recommendation. Additional exam requirements/recommendations for international students: Required—TOEFL. *Faculty research:* Reading instruction, special education practices, conflict resolution in the schools, models of higher education for teachers.

Wilmington College, Division of Education, New Castle, DE 19720-6491. Offers applied education technology (M Ed); career and technical education (M Ed); elementary and secondary school counseling (M Ed); elementary special education (M Ed); elementary studies (M Ed); instruction: gifted and talented (M Ed); instruction: teaching and learning (M Ed);

literacy (M Ed); reading (M Ed); school leadership (M Ed); secondary teaching (MAT). Part-time and evening/weekend programs available. *Faculty:* 7 full-time (4 women). *Students:* 609 full-time (447 women), 1,350 part-time (1,013 women); includes 144 minority (131 African Americans, 3 American Indian/Alaska Native, 1 Asian American or Pacific Islander, 9 Hispanic Americans). Average age 34. 818 applicants, 100% accepted, 599 enrolled. In 2006, 737 degrees awarded. *Entrance requirements:* For master's, 2 letters of recommendation, interview. Additional exam requirements/recommendations for international students: Required—TOEFL (minimum score 500 paper-based; 173 computer-based). *Application deadline:* For fall admission, 4/30 for domestic students. Applications are processed on a rolling basis. Application fee: $25. *Financial support:* Applicants required to submit FAFSA. *Unit head:* Dr. Richard Gochnauer, Chair, 302-328-6795 Ext. 163, Fax: 302-328-7081. *Application contact:* Chris Ferguson, Director of Admissions and Financial Aid, 302-328-9407 Ext. 256, Fax: 302-328-5164, E-mail: inquire@wilmcoll.edu.

Winthrop University, College of Education, Program in Reading Education, Rock Hill, SC 29733. Offers M Ed. *Accreditation:* NCATE. Part-time programs available. *Students:* 3 full-time (all women), 15 part-time (13 women). Average age 26. In 2006, 23 degrees awarded. *Entrance requirements:* For master's, PRAXIS, South Carolina Class III Teaching Certificate, 1 year of teaching experience. *Application deadline:* For fall admission, 7/15 priority date for domestic students; for spring admission, 12/1 for domestic students. Applications are processed on a rolling basis. Application fee: $35. Electronic applications accepted. *Expenses:* Tuition, state resident: full-time $9,148; part-time $383 per hour. Tuition, nonresident: full-time $16,864; part-time $704 per hour. *Financial support:* Career-related internships or fieldwork, Federal Work-Study, scholarships/grants, and unspecified assistantships available. Support available to part-time students. Financial award application deadline: 2/1; financial award applicants required to submit FAFSA. *Unit head:* Dr. Richard Ingram, Acting Chair, 803-323-2158, E-mail: ingramr@winthrop.edu. *Application contact:* 800-411-7041, Fax: 803-323-2292, E-mail: graduatestu@winthrop.edu.

Worcester State College, Graduate Studies, Department of Education, Concentration in Reading, Worcester, MA 01602-2597. Offers M Ed. Part-time and evening/weekend programs available. *Students:* Average age 37. 14 applicants, 64% accepted, 3 enrolled. In 2006, 2 degrees awarded. *Degree requirements:* For master's, thesis optional. *Entrance requirements:* For master's, GRE General Test or MAT, teaching certificate. Additional exam requirements/recommendations for international students: Required—TOEFL (minimum score 550 paper-based; 213 computer-based). *Application deadline:* Applications are processed on a rolling basis. Application fee: $30. *Expenses:* Tuition, state resident: full-time $4,518; part-time $251 per credit hour. Tuition, nonresident: full-time $4,518; part-time $251 per credit hour. *Financial support:* Career-related internships or fieldwork, Federal Work-Study, institutionally sponsored loans, scholarships/grants, and unspecified assistantships available. Support available to part-time students. Financial award application deadline: 3/1; financial award applicants required to submit FAFSA. *Unit head:* Dr. Margaret Pray-Bouchard, Coordinator, 508-929-8840, Fax: 508-929-8164, E-mail: mbouchard@worcester.edu. *Application contact:* Nicole Brown, Assistant Dean of Graduate and Continuing Education, 508-929-8787, Fax: 508-929-8100, E-mail: nbrown@worcester.edu.

Xavier University, College of Social Sciences, Health and Education, School of Education, Program in Reading Specialist, Cincinnati, OH 45207. Offers M Ed. Part-time and evening/weekend programs available. *Faculty:* 3 full-time (2 women), 10 part-time/adjunct (7 women). *Students:* 3 full-time (all women), 50 part-time (49 women); includes 3 minority (2 African Americans, 1 American Indian/Alaska Native). Average age 31. 14 applicants, 50% accepted, 5 enrolled. In 2006, 39 degrees awarded. *Degree requirements:* For master's, research project. *Entrance requirements:* For master's, GRE or MAT, minimum GPA of 2.8. Additional exam requirements/recommendations for international students: Required—TOEFL (minimum score 550 paper-based; 213 computer-based). *Application deadline:* For fall admission, 8/15 priority date for domestic students. Applications are processed on a rolling basis. Application fee: $35. *Expenses:* Tuition: Part-time $462 per credit hour. Part-time tuition and fees vary according to degree level, campus/location and program. *Financial support:* Scholarships/grants and unspecified assistantships available. Support available to part-time students. Financial award applicants required to submit FAFSA. *Faculty research:* Emergent reading, Mische analysis, analysis of reader response to children's literature in the U.S. and Canada. *Unit head:* Dr. Leslie Prosak-Beres, Director, 513-745-3652, Fax: 513-745-1052, E-mail: prosak@xavier.edu. *Application contact:* Roger Bosse, Interim Director of Graduate Studies, 513-745-3357, Fax: 513-745-1048, E-mail: bosse@xavier.edu.

Youngstown State University, Graduate School, College of Education, Department of Teacher Education, Program in Early and Middle Childhood Education, Youngstown, OH 44555-0001. Offers teaching—elementary education (MS Ed); teaching—secondary reading (MS Ed). *Accreditation:* NCATE. Part-time and evening/weekend programs available. *Degree requirements:* For master's, comprehensive exam. *Entrance requirements:* For master's, GRE, MAT, or teaching certificate; minimum GPA of 2.7. Additional exam requirements/recommendations for international students: Required—TOEFL.

Religious Education

Alliance University College, Canadian Theological Seminary, Calgary, AB T2P 3T5, Canada. Offers biblical/theological studies (MA); Chinese ministries (Certificate); Christian studies (Diploma); church education (M Div); intercultural ministries (M Div, MA, Diploma); leadership and ministry (MA); pastoral ministries (M Div). *Accreditation:* ATS (one or more programs are accredited). Part-time programs available. Postbaccalaureate distance learning degree programs offered (minimal on-campus study). *Degree requirements:* For M Div, one foreign language; for master's, internship. *Entrance requirements:* Additional exam requirements/recommendations for international students: Required—TOEFL (minimum score 220 computer-based). Electronic applications accepted. *Faculty research:* Evangelicalism and sociology, missiological trends, chaplaincy, intertestamental studies.

Andover Newton Theological School, Graduate and Professional Programs, Newton Centre, MA 02459-2243. Offers divinity (M Div); general (MA); psychology and religion (MA); religious education (MA); research (MA); sacred theology (STM); theology (D Min); theology and the arts (MA). *Accreditation:* ACIPE; ATS. Part-time programs available. *Degree requirements:* For M Div, registration; for master's, thesis (for some programs), comprehensive exam (for some programs), registration; for doctorate, thesis/dissertation, comprehensive exam, registration. *Entrance requirements:* For doctorate, M Div or equivalent. Additional exam requirements/recommendations for international students: Required—TOEFL (minimum score 550 paper-based; 213 computer-based). Electronic applications accepted.

Andrews University, School of Graduate Studies, Seventh-day Adventist Theological Seminary, Program in Religious Education, Berrien Springs, MI 49104. Offers MA, Ed D, PhD, Ed S. Part-time programs available. Terminal master's awarded for partial completion of doctoral program. *Degree requirements:* For doctorate, thesis/dissertation. *Entrance requirements:* For master's, GRE Subject Test. *Faculty research:* Marriage and family, spiritual gifts and temperament.

Asbury Theological Seminary, Graduate and Professional Programs, School of Practical Theology, Wilmore, KY 40390-1199. Offers Christian education (MACE); Christian leadership (MA); Christian studies (Certificate); counseling (MAC); pastoral counseling (MAPC); youth ministry (MA). *Accreditation:* ACIPE; ATS. *Unit head:* Dr. Catherine Stonehouse, Dean. *Application contact:* Janelle Vernon, Admissions Director, 859-858-2211, Fax: 859-858-2287, E-mail: admissions_office@asburyseminary.edu.

Azusa Pacific University, Haggard School of Theology, Program in Christian Education in Youth Ministry, Azusa, CA 91702-7000. Offers Christian education (MA). *Accreditation:* NCATE. *Students:* 1 (woman) full-time, 23 part-time (7 women); includes 6 minority (1 African American, 1 American Indian/Alaska Native, 1 Asian American or Pacific Islander, 3 Hispanic Americans), 2 international. In 2006, 5 degrees awarded. Application fee: $45 ($65 for international students). *Expenses:* Tuition: Part-time $475 per credit.

Baptist Bible College of Pennsylvania, Graduate School, Clarks Summit, PA 18411-1297. Offers Christian school education (MS); counseling (MS). Part-time and evening/weekend programs available. *Entrance requirements:* Additional exam requirements/recommendations for international students: Required—TOEFL.

Baptist Theological Seminary at Richmond, Graduate and Professional Program, Richmond, VA 23227. Offers children and family ministry (M Div); Christian education (M Div); church music (M Div); theology (D Min); youth and student ministry (M Div); M Div/MS; M Div/MSW. *Accreditation:* ATS. Part-time programs available. Postbaccalaureate distance learning degree programs offered (minimal on-campus study). *Faculty:* 14 full-time (6 women), 8 part-time/adjunct (1 woman). *Students:* 146 full-time (70 women), 27 part-time (18 women); includes 15 minority (13 African Americans, 1 American Indian/Alaska Native, 1 Hispanic American), 4 international. Average age 39. 66 applicants, 88% accepted, 45 enrolled. In 2006, 26 first professional degrees, 7 doctorates awarded. *Median time to degree:* Of those who began their doctoral program in fall 1998, 92% received their degree in 8 years or less. *Degree requirements:* For M Div, one foreign language, comprehensive exam (for some programs), registration, mission immersion experience, internship, thesis optional; for doctorate, one foreign language, thesis/dissertation, field study, independent study, comprehensive exam, registration. *Entrance requirements:* For doctorate, MAT, M Div, 3 years of full-time ministry experience. Additional exam requirements/recommendations for international students: Required—TOEFL (minimum score 481 paper-based; 213 computer-based). *Application deadline:* For fall admission, 8/1 priority date for domestic students, 5/1 priority date for international students; for winter admission, 12/1 priority date for domestic students, 9/1 priority date for international students; for spring admission, 1/1 priority date for domestic students, 10/1 priority date for international students. Applications are processed on a rolling basis. Application fee: $35. *Expenses:* Tuition: Full-time $6,500; part-time $650 per credit. Required fees: $45 per term. Full-time tuition and fees vary according to degree level. *Financial support:* In 2006–07, 135 students received support, including 16 teaching assistantships (averaging $1,300 per year); scholarships/grants and tuition waivers (partial) also available. Financial award application deadline: 2/1. *Faculty research:* New Testament studies, Old Testament studies, pastoral care, church history, theology. *Unit head:* Dr. Ronald W. Crawford, President, 804-355-8135, Fax: 804-355-8182. *Application contact:* Director of Admissions, 804-355-8135, Fax: 804-355-8182.

Bethel Seminary, Graduate and Professional Programs, St. Paul, MN 55112-6998. Offers biblical studies (MATS, Certificate); children's and family ministry (MACFM); Christian education (MACE); Christian thought (M Div, MACT); church leadership (D Min); congregation and family care (D Min); global and contextual studies (MA); global missions (Certificate); lay ministry (Certificate); marriage and family studies (M Div); marriage and family therapy (MAMFT); missions (MATS); pastoral ministries (M Div); theological studies (MATS, Certificate); transformational leadership (MATL); youth ministries (MACE). *Accreditation:* ACIPE; ATS (one or more programs are accredited). Part-time and evening/weekend programs available. Postbaccalaureate distance learning degree programs offered (minimal on-campus study). *Faculty:* 26 full-time (3 women), 72 part-time/adjunct. *Students:* 494 full-time (148 women), 582 part-time (242 women); includes 164 minority (77 African Americans, 1 American Indian/Alaska Native, 60 Asian Americans or Pacific Islanders, 26 Hispanic Americans), 6 international. Average age 36. 314 applicants, 86% accepted. In 2006, 62 first professional degrees, 102 master's, 14 doctorates awarded. *Degree requirements:* For M Div, one foreign language; for master's, variable foreign language requirement, thesis (for some programs); for doctorate, thesis/dissertation. *Entrance requirements:* For M Div and master's, letters of reference; for doctorate, M Div, letters of reference. Additional exam requirements/recommendations for international students: Required—TOEFL (minimum score 550 paper-based; 213 computer-based). *Application deadline:* For fall admission, 8/1 priority date for domestic students; for winter admission, 12/1 priority date for domestic students; for spring admission, 1/1 priority date for domestic students. Applications are processed on a rolling basis. Application fee: $20. Electronic applications accepted. *Expenses:* Tuition: Full-time $10,080; part-time $280 per credit. *Financial support:* In 2006–07, 375 students received support, including 20 teaching assistantships; career-related internships or fieldwork, Federal Work-Study, institutionally sponsored loans, and scholarships/grants also available. Financial award application deadline: 7/15; financial award applicants required to submit FAFSA. *Faculty research:* Nature of theology, ethics, biblical commentaries, nature of God, science and theology. *Unit head:* Dr. Leland Eliason, Executive Vice President and Provost, 651-638-6182. *Application contact:* Joseph V. Dworak, Director of Admissions, 651-638-6288, Fax: 651-638-6002, E-mail: j-dworak@bethel.edu.

Biola University, Talbot School of Theology, La Mirada, CA 90639-0001. Offers Bible exposition (MA); biblical and theological studies (MA); Christian education (MACE); Christian ministry and leadership (MA); divinity (M Div); education (PhD); ministry (MA Min); New Testament (MA); Old Testament (MA); philosophy of religion and ethics (MA); spiritual formation (MA); spiritual formation and soul care (MA); theology (MA, Th M, D Min). *Accreditation:* ATS. Part-time and evening/weekend programs available. *Degree requirements:* For M Div, thesis or alternative; for master's, variable foreign language requirement, thesis or alternative; for doctorate, variable foreign language requirement, thesis/dissertation. *Entrance requirements:* For M Div, minimum GPA of 2.6; for master's, minimum undergraduate GPA of 3.0; for doctorate, minimum GPA of 3.25. Additional exam requirements/recommendations for international students: Required—TOEFL (minimum score 550 paper-based; 213 computer-based). *Faculty research:* Moral development; biological, medical, and social ethics; ancient Near Eastern historical philosophy.

Boston College, Graduate School of Arts and Sciences, Institute of Religious Education and Pastoral Ministry, Chestnut Hill, MA 02467-3800. Offers church leadership (MA); pastoral ministry (MA), including Hispanic ministry, liturgy and worship, pastoral care and counseling, spirituality; religious education (MA, PhD); social justice/social ministry (MA); youth ministry (MA); MA/MA; MS/MA; MSW/MA. Part-time programs available. *Students:* 103 applicants, 54% accepted, 46 enrolled. In 2006, 37 master's, 4 doctorates awarded. *Degree requirements:* For doctorate, one foreign language, thesis/dissertation. *Entrance requirements:* For doctorate, GRE. Additional exam requirements/recommendations for international students: Required—TOEFL (minimum score 550 paper-based; 213 computer-based). *Application deadline:* For fall admission, 3/1 priority date for domestic students. Application fee: $70. Electronic applications accepted. *Financial support:* Fellowships with tuition reimbursements, career-related internships or fieldwork, Federal Work-Study, and tuition waivers (full and partial) available. Support available to part-time students. Financial award application deadline: 3/1; financial award applicants required to submit FAFSA. *Faculty research:* Philosophy and practice of

Religious Education

Boston College (continued)

religious education, pastoral psychology, liturgical and spiritual theology, spiritual formation for the practice of ministry. *Unit head:* Dr. Thomas Groome, Chairperson, 617-552-8449, Fax: 617-552-0811. *Application contact:* Dr. Jennifer Bader, Assistant Director, Academic Affairs, 617-552-4478, Fax: 617-552-0811, E-mail: jennifer.bader@bc.edu.

Boston College, Lynch Graduate School of Education, Department of Teacher Education/ Special Education and Curriculum and Instruction, Religious Education Specialization, Chestnut Hill, MA 02467-3800. Offers M Ed, CAES. *Students:* 12 full-time (5 women), 11 part-time (9 women); includes 1 minority (Hispanic American), 4 international. In 2006, 8 degrees awarded. *Degree requirements:* For master's and CAES, comprehensive exam. *Entrance requirements:* For master's, GRE General Test or MAT. Additional exam requirements/recommendations for international students: Required—TOEFL. Application fee: $60. *Financial support:* Fellowships with full and partial tuition reimbursements, research assistantships with full and partial tuition reimbursements, teaching assistantships with full and partial tuition reimbursements, career-related internships or fieldwork, Federal Work-Study, scholarships/grants, traineeships, tuition waivers (full and partial), and unspecified assistantships available. Support available to part-time students. Financial award applicants required to submit FAFSA. *Faculty research:* Curriculum development, inter-religious dialogue, ethical and value issues and pedagogy. *Application contact:* Timothy P. Blackman, Director, Graduate Admission and Financial Aid, 617-552-4214, Fax: 617-552-0398, E-mail: timothy.blackman.1@bc.edu.

Brandeis University, Graduate School of Arts and Sciences, Program in Elementary Education, Waltham, MA 02454-9110. Offers Jewish day school (MAT); public education elementary (MAT); secondary education (English, history, biology, Bible) (MAT). *Faculty:* 6 full-time (2 women), 9 part-time/adjunct (all women). *Students:* 7 full-time (5 women); includes 1 African American. Average age 27. In 2006, 9 degrees awarded. *Degree requirements:* For master's, research program MTEL. *Application deadline:* For fall admission, 1/15 priority date for domestic students, 1/15 for international students. Applications are processed on a rolling basis. Application fee: $55. Electronic applications accepted. *Financial support:* In 2006–07, 7 students received support, including 7 fellowships with tuition reimbursements available; scholarships/grants also available. Financial award applicants required to submit CSS PROFILE. *Faculty research:* Teacher education, induction, philosophy, education, democracy education. *Unit head:* Dr. Dirck Roosevelt, Director, MAT Program, 781-736-2020, Fax: 781-736-5020, E-mail: drooseve@brandeis.edu. *Application contact:* Marlene Mihalsky, Department Coordinator, 781-736-2022, Fax: 781-736-5020.

Brigham Young University, Graduate Studies, College of Religious Education, Provo, UT 84602-1001. Offers MRE. *Faculty:* 63 full-time (5 women). *Students:* 8 full-time (1 woman), 6 part-time. In 2006, 3 degrees awarded. *Degree requirements:* For master's, thesis, registration. *Entrance requirements:* For master's, GRE, minimum GPA of 3.0 in last 60 hours, letter of recommendation. *Application deadline:* For fall admission, 12/1 for international students; for winter admission, 12/1 for domestic students. Application fee: $50. *Financial support:* In 2006–07, 14 students received support. Scholarships/grants available. *Unit head:* Dr. Terry B. Ball, Dean, 801-422-2736, Fax: 801-422-0616, E-mail: terry_ball@byu.edu. *Application contact:* Dr. Clyde J. Williams, Professor of Ancient Scripture, 801-422-2124, Fax: 801-422-0616.

Calvin Theological Seminary, Graduate and Professional Programs, Grand Rapids, MI 49546-4387. Offers divinity (M Div); educational ministry (MA); historical theology (PhD); missions: church growth (MA); philosophical and moral theology (PhD); systematic theology (PhD); theological studies (MTS); theology (Th M). *Accreditation:* ACIPE; ATS. Part-time programs available. *Faculty:* 22 full-time (1 woman), 8 part-time/adjunct (2 women). *Students:* 236 full-time (35 women), 64 part-time (15 women); includes 27 minority (7 African Americans, 15 Asian Americans or Pacific Islanders, 5 Hispanic Americans), 93 international. Average age 31. 174 applicants, 77% accepted, 99 enrolled. In 2006, 23 first professional degrees, 42 master's, 2 doctorates awarded. *Median time to degree:* Of those who began their doctoral program in fall 1998, 80% received their degree in 8 years or less. *Degree requirements:* For M Div, 2 foreign languages; for master's, thesis (for some programs); for doctorate, 4 foreign languages, thesis/dissertation, comprehensive exam. *Entrance requirements:* For doctorate, GRE General Test, Hebrew, Greek, and a modern foreign language. Additional exam requirements/ recommendations for international students: Required—TOEFL (minimum score 550 paper-based; 213 computer-based), TWE (minimum score 4). *Application deadline:* For fall admission, 3/1 priority date for domestic and international students. Applications are processed on a rolling basis. Application fee: $25. *Expenses:* Tuition: Full-time $9,766; part-time $217 per hour. *Financial support:* In 2006–07, 187 students received support, including 4 fellowships with full tuition reimbursements available (averaging $8,405 per year), 4 teaching assistantships with full tuition reimbursements available (averaging $5,760 per year); career-related internships or fieldwork, institutionally sponsored loans, scholarships/grants, and tuition waivers (full) also available. Support available to part-time students. Financial award application deadline: 3/1; financial award applicants required to submit FAFSA. *Faculty research:* Recent Trinity theory, Christian anthropology, Proverbs, reformed confessions, Paul's view of law. *Unit head:* Dr. Cornelius Plantinga, Head, 616-957-6024, Fax: 616-957-6536, E-mail: sempres@calvinseminary.edu. *Application contact:* Rev. Gregory Janke, Director of Admissions, 616-957-7035, Fax: 616-957-8621, E-mail: gjanke@calvinseminary.edu.

Campbell University, Graduate and Professional Programs, Divinity School, Buies Creek, NC 27506. Offers Christian education (MA); divinity (M Div); ministry (D Min); M Div/MA; M Div/MBA. *Accreditation:* ATS. *Faculty:* 9 full-time (1 woman), 10 part-time/adjunct (3 women). *Students:* 148 full-time (55 women), 82 part-time (41 women); includes 40 minority (35 African Americans, 1 American Indian/Alaska Native, 4 Hispanic Americans), 2 international. Average age 38. 74 applicants, 81% accepted, 48 enrolled. In 2006, 27 degrees awarded. *Degree requirements:* For doctorate, final project. *Entrance requirements:* For master's, minimum GPA of 2.5; for doctorate, MAT, M Div, minimum graduate GPA of 3.0. Additional exam requirements/ recommendations for international students: Required—TOEFL (minimum score 580 paper-based; 237 computer-based). *Application deadline:* For fall admission, 7/1 for domestic students; for spring admission, 11/15 for domestic students. Applications are processed on a rolling basis. Application fee: $20. *Expenses: Contact institution. Financial support:* In 2006–07, 193 students received support, including 143 fellowships (averaging $800 per year); scholarships/ grants and unspecified assistantships also available. Support available to part-time students. Financial award application deadline: 5/1. *Faculty research:* New Testament, theology, spiritual formation, Old Testament, Christian leadership. Total annual research expenditures: $15,000. *Unit head:* Dr. Michael Glenn Cogdill, Dean, 910-893-1830, Fax: 910-893-1835, E-mail: cogdill@campbell.edu. *Application contact:* Kelly M. Jones, Director of Admissions, 910-893-1830, Fax: 910-893-1835, E-mail: kjones@campbell.edu.

Chicago Theological Seminary, Graduate and Professional Programs, Chicago, IL 60637-1507. Offers clinical pastoral education (D Min); Jewish-Christian studies (PhD); pastoral counseling (D Min); preaching (D Min); religious studies (MA); spiritual leadership (D Min); theology (M Div); theology and the human sciences (PhD), including theology and society, theology and the personality sciences; M Div/MSW. *Accreditation:* ACIPE; ATS. Part-time programs available. *Faculty:* 12 full-time (4 women). *Students:* 78 full-time (34 women), 153 part-time (76 women); includes 76 minority (65 African Americans, 8 Asian Americans or Pacific Islanders, 3 Hispanic Americans), 30 international. 94 applicants, 84% accepted, 53 enrolled. In 2006, 20 first professional degrees, 4 master's, 13 doctorates awarded. *Degree requirements:* For M Div and master's, thesis; for doctorate, 2 foreign languages, thesis/ dissertation, comprehensive exam. *Entrance requirements:* For doctorate, GRE General Test. Additional exam requirements/recommendations for international students: Required—TOEFL (minimum score 217 computer-based). *Application deadline:* For fall admission, 3/1 priority date for domestic and international students; for spring admission, 11/1 for domestic and international students. Applications are processed on a rolling basis. Application fee: $50. *Expenses:* Tuition: Full-time $9,920; part-time $1,240 per course. Tuition and fees vary according to program. *Financial support:* In 2006–07, 94 students received support, including 15 fellowships (averaging $15,000 per year); institutionally sponsored loans and scholarships/ grants also available. Support available to part-time students. Financial award application deadline: 3/1; financial award applicants required to submit FAFSA. *Faculty research:* Bible, culture and hermeneutics/theology, gender & sexuality/black faith and life/spirituality and psychology/practical theology. Total annual research expenditures: $150,000. *Unit head:* Dr. Dow Edgerton, Dean, 773-752-5757, Fax: 773-752-5925, E-mail: dedgerton@ctschicago.edu. *Application contact:* Rev. Alison Buttrick Patton, Director of Admissions, Recruitment and Financial Aid, 773-322-0229, Fax: 773-752-1903, E-mail: apatton@ctschicago.edu.

Claremont School of Theology, Graduate and Professional Programs, Program in Religion, Claremont, CA 91711-3199. Offers practical theology (PhD); religion and theology (MA); religious education (MARE). *Accreditation:* ACIPE; ATS. *Faculty:* 18 full-time (7 women), 27 part-time/adjunct (12 women). *Students:* 39 full-time (21 women), 77 part-time (40 women); includes 36 minority (14 African Americans, 19 Asian Americans or Pacific Islanders, 3 Hispanic Americans), 16 international. Average age 37. 75 applicants, 64% accepted, 21 enrolled. In 2006, 24 master's, 6 doctorates awarded. Terminal master's awarded for partial completion of doctoral program. *Median time to degree:* Of those who began their doctoral program in fall 1998, 66% received their degree in 8 years or less. *Degree requirements:* For master's, thesis; for doctorate, 2 foreign languages, thesis/dissertation. *Entrance requirements:* For doctorate, GRE General Test. Additional exam requirements/recommendations for international students: Required—TOEFL (minimum score 250 computer-based). *Application deadline:* For fall admission, 1/15 for domestic and international students. Application fee: $50. Electronic applications accepted. *Expenses:* Tuition: Part-time $520 per unit. Required fees: $190 per semester. Tuition and fees vary according to degree level. *Financial support:* In 2006–07, 87 students received support, including 9 research assistantships (averaging $1,200 per year), 7 teaching assistantships (averaging $2,000 per year); career-related internships or fieldwork, Federal Work-Study, institutionally sponsored loans, scholarships/grants, and tuition waivers (full and partial) also available. Support available to part-time students. Financial award application deadline: 4/1; financial award applicants required to submit FAFSA. *Application contact:* Director of Admissions, 866-274-6500, Fax: 909-447-6389, E-mail: admission@cst.edu.

Columbia International University, Columbia Biblical Seminary and School of Missions, Columbia, SC 29230-3122. Offers academic ministries (M Div); bible exposition (M Div, MABE); biblical studies (Certificate); counseling ministries (Certificate); divinity (M Div); educational ministries (M Div, MAEM, Certificate); intercultural studies (M Div, MAIS, Certificate); leadership (D Min); leadership for evangelism/mobilization (MALM); member care (D Min); ministry (Certificate); missions (D Min); pastoral counseling and spiritual formation (M Div, MAPS); preaching (D Min); theology (MA). *Accreditation:* ATS (one or more programs are accredited). Part-time and evening/weekend programs available. *Faculty:* 14 full-time (1 woman), 9 part-time/adjunct (1 woman). *Students:* 180 full-time (59 women), 218 part-time (61 women); includes 81 minority (58 African Americans, 1 American Indian/Alaska Native, 18 Asian Americans or Pacific Islanders, 4 Hispanic Americans), 22 international. Average age 36. 277 applicants, 81% accepted, 117 enrolled. In 2006, 20 first professional degrees, 54 master's, 3 doctorates, 15 other advanced degrees awarded. *Degree requirements:* For M Div, internship; for master's, integrative seminar; for doctorate, thesis/dissertation, comprehensive exam. *Entrance requirements:* For master's, minimum GPA of 2.7; for doctorate, 3 years of ministerial experience, M Div. Additional exam requirements/recommendations for international students: Required—TOEFL. *Application deadline:* For fall admission, 8/1 priority date for domestic and international students; for winter admission, 12/15 priority date for domestic and international students; for spring admission, 1/15 priority date for domestic and international students. Applications are processed on a rolling basis. Application fee: $45. Electronic applications accepted. *Expenses:* Tuition: Part-time $400 per semester hour. Tuition and fees vary according to course load and program. *Financial support:* In 2006–07, 120 students received support. Career-related internships or fieldwork, Federal Work-Study, institutionally sponsored loans, and scholarships/grants available. Financial award application deadline: 3/15; financial award applicants required to submit FAFSA. *Unit head:* Dr. Junias Venugopal, Dean, 803-754-4100 Ext. 5330, Fax: 803-786-4209, E-mail: jvenugopal@ciu.edu. *Application contact:* Michelle MacGregor, Director of Admissions, 800-777-2227 Ext. 5335, Fax: 803-786-4209, E-mail: yescbs@ciu.edu.

Columbia International University, Columbia Graduate School, Columbia, SC 29230-3122. Offers Bible teaching (MABT); Christian higher education leadership (Ed D); Christian school educational leadership (Ed D); counseling (MACN); curriculum and instruction (M Ed), including Christian school guidance, English as a second language, learning disabilities, school technology; early childhood and elementary education (MAT); educational administration (M Ed); teaching English as a foreign language (Certificate); teaching English as a foreign language and intercultural studies (MATF). Part-time and evening/weekend programs available. *Faculty:* 11 full-time (4 women), 7 part-time/adjunct (5 women). *Students:* 52 full-time (44 women), 93 part-time (59 women); includes 17 minority (11 African Americans, 2 Asian Americans or Pacific Islanders, 4 Hispanic Americans), 10 international. Average age 35. 107 applicants, 56% accepted, 41 enrolled. In 2006, 62 degrees awarded. *Degree requirements:* For master's, internships, professional project. *Entrance requirements:* For master's, Minnesota Multiphasic Personality Inventory, MAT, minimum GPA of 2.7. Additional exam requirements/ recommendations for international students: Required—TOEFL. *Application deadline:* For fall admission, 8/1 priority date for domestic and international students; for winter admission, 12/15 priority date for domestic and international students; for spring admission, 1/15 priority date for domestic and international students. Applications are processed on a rolling basis. Application fee: $45. Electronic applications accepted. *Expenses:* Tuition: Part-time $400 per semester hour. Tuition and fees vary according to course load and program. *Financial support:* In 2006–07, 35 students received support. Career-related internships or fieldwork, Federal Work-Study, institutionally sponsored loans, and scholarships/grants available. Financial award application deadline: 3/17; financial award applicants required to submit FAFSA. *Unit head:* Dr. Milton Uecker, Dean, 803-807-5319, Fax: 803-786-4209, E-mail: muecker@ciu.edu. *Application contact:* Michelle MacGregor, Director of Admissions, 800-777-2227 Ext. 5335, Fax: 803-786-4209, E-mail: yescbs@ciu.edu.

Concordia University, College of Education, Program in Christian Education, River Forest, IL 60305-1499. Offers MA. *Entrance requirements:* Additional exam requirements/ recommendations for international students: Required—TOEFL (minimum score 550 paper-based; 195 computer-based). Electronic applications accepted.

Concordia University, Graduate Programs in Education, Program in Parish Education, Seward, NE 68434-1599. Offers MPE. *Accreditation:* NCATE. Part-time and evening/weekend programs available. *Degree requirements:* For master's, thesis or alternative. *Entrance requirements:* For master's, GRE, MAT, or NTE, minimum GPA of 3.0, BS in education or equivalent.

Concordia University, St. Paul, College of Vocation and Ministry, St. Paul, MN 55104-5494. Offers Christian education (Certificate); Christian outreach (MA). Part-time and evening/ weekend programs available. Postbaccalaureate distance learning degree programs offered (minimal on-campus study). *Faculty:* 4 full-time (0 women), 7 part-time/adjunct (3 women). *Students:* Average age 35. In 2006, 8 master's, 2 other advanced degrees awarded. *Entrance requirements:* Additional exam requirements/recommendations for international students: Required—TOEFL. *Application deadline:* Applications are processed on a rolling basis. Application fee: $50. Electronic applications accepted. *Financial support:* Federal Work-Study and scholarships/grants available. Financial award applicants required to submit FAFSA. *Unit head:* Dr. Steven Arnold, Dean, 651-641-8213, E-mail: sarnold@csp.edu. *Application contact:* Kimberly Craig, Director of Graduate and Cohort Admission, 651-603-6223, Fax: 651-603-6320, E-mail: craig@csp.edu.

Cornerstone University, Graduate Programs, Grand Rapids, MI 49525-5897. Offers chaplaincy ministries (M Div); counseling ministries (M Div, MA); educational ministries (M Div, MA); historical theology (MA, Th M); intercultural ministries (MA); intercultural studies (M Div);

interdisciplinary studies (MA); ministry leadership (MA); New Testament (MA, Th M); Old Testament (MA, Th M); pastoral ministries (M Div); systematic theology (MA, Th M). Part-time programs available. Postbaccalaureate distance learning degree programs offered. *Degree requirements:* For M Div, 2 foreign languages, registration; for master's, thesis (for some programs), comprehensive exam (for some programs), registration. *Entrance requirements:* For M Div and master's, minimum GPA of 2.5, 2 letters of reference. Additional exam requirements/recommendations for international students: Required—TOEFL (minimum score 575 paper-based; 235 computer-based). Electronic applications accepted.

Dallas Baptist University, School of Leadership and Christian Education, Program in Christian Education, Dallas, TX 75211-9299. Offers adult ministry (MA); Baptist student ministry (MA); business ministry (MA); children's ministry (MA); collegiate ministry (MA); counseling ministry (MA); education ministry (MA); general ministry (MA); ministry with students (MA); missions ministry (MA); worship ministry (MA); youth ministry (MA). Part-time and evening/weekend programs available. *Faculty:* 49 full-time (21 women), 112 part-time/adjunct (46 women). *Students:* 40 full-time, 45 part-time. 50 applicants, 32% accepted, 15 enrolled. In 2006, 19 degrees awarded. *Entrance requirements:* For master's, GRE, ACT or SAT, minimum GPA of 2.8. Additional exam requirements/recommendations for international students: Required—TOEFL. *Application deadline:* Applications are processed on a rolling basis. Application fee: $25. Electronic applications accepted. *Expenses:* Tuition: Full-time $8,370; part-time $465 per credit hour. Required fees: $465 per credit hour. *Financial support:* Federal Work-Study, institutionally sponsored loans, scholarships/grants, and tuition waivers (full and partial) available. Support available to part-time students. *Unit head:* Dr. Judy Morris, Director, 214-333-5246, Fax: 214-333-5115, E-mail: graduate@dbu.edu. *Application contact:* Kit P. Montgomery, Director of Graduate Programs, 214-333-5242, Fax: 214-333-5579, E-mail: graduate@dbu.edu.

Dallas Baptist University, School of Leadership and Christian Education, Program in Christian Education: Childhood Ministry, Dallas, TX 75211-9299. Offers MA. *Faculty:* 49 full-time (21 women), 112 part-time/adjunct (46 women). *Students:* 3 applicants, 67% accepted, 1 enrolled. Application fee: $25. *Expenses:* Tuition: Full-time $8,370; part-time $465 per credit hour. Required fees: $465 per credit hour. *Unit head:* Tommy Sanders, Director, 214-333-6851, Fax: 214-333-6955, E-mail: graduate@dbu.edu. *Application contact:* Kit P. Montgomery, Director of Graduate Programs, 214-333-5242, Fax: 214-333-5579, E-mail: graduate@dbu.edu.

Dallas Baptist University, School of Leadership and Christian Education, Program in Christian Education: Student Ministry, Dallas, TX 75211-9299. Offers MA. *Faculty:* 49 full-time (21 women), 112 part-time/adjunct (46 women). *Students:* 2 full-time, 5 part-time. Application fee: $25. *Expenses:* Tuition: Full-time $8,370; part-time $465 per credit hour. Required fees: $465 per credit hour. *Unit head:* Dr. Dwayne Ulmer, Director, 214-333-5387, Fax: 214-333-6955, E-mail: graduate@dbu.edu. *Application contact:* Kit P. Montgomery, Director of Graduate Programs, 214-333-5242, Fax: 214-333-5579, E-mail: graduate@dbu.edu.

Dallas Theological Seminary, Graduate Programs, Dallas, TX 75204-6499. Offers academic ministries (Th M); Bible translation (Th M); biblical and theological studies (CGS); biblical counseling (MA); biblical exegesis and linguistics (MA); biblical studies (MA, PhD); Christian education (MA, D Min); cross-cultural ministries (MA, Th M); educational leadership (Th M); evangelism and discipleship (Th M); interdisciplinary studies (Th M); media arts in ministry (Th M); ministry (D Min); parachurch ministries (Th M); pastoral ministries (Th M); sacred theology (STM); theological studies (PhD); women's ministry (Th M). MA (biblical exegesis and linguistics) offered jointly with the Summer Institute of Linguistics; extension branches located in Chattanooga (TN), Houston (TX), Philadelphia (PA), San Antonio (TX), and the Tampa Bay area (FL). *Accreditation:* ATS (one or more programs are accredited). Part-time and evening/weekend programs available. *Degree requirements:* For master's, variable foreign language requirement, thesis (for some programs); for doctorate, 2 foreign languages, thesis/dissertation. *Entrance requirements:* Additional exam requirements/recommendations for international students: Required—TOEFL, TWE. Electronic applications accepted.

Felician College, Program in Religious Education, Lodi, NJ 07644-2117. Offers MA, Certificate, PMC. Part-time and evening/weekend programs available. Postbaccalaureate distance learning degree programs offered (no on-campus study). *Students:* 24 applicants, 79% accepted, 18 enrolled. *Degree requirements:* For master's, thesis. *Entrance requirements:* For master's, minimum GPA of 3.0, 1 letter of recommendation. Additional exam requirements/recommendations for international students: Recommended—TOEFL (minimum score 550 paper-based; 213 computer-based). *Application deadline:* Applications are processed on a rolling basis. Application fee: $40. *Expenses:* Tuition: Part-time $675 per credit. Tuition and fees vary according to program. *Financial support:* Scholarships/grants and tuition waivers (partial) available. *Faculty research:* Spirituality, race and ethnicity in religious settings. *Unit head:* Dr. Dolores M. Henchy, Director, 201-559-6053, Fax: 973-472-8936, E-mail: henchyd@inet.felician.edu. *Application contact:* Wendy Lin-Cook, Director of Adult and Graduate Admission, 201-559-6077, Fax: 201-559-6138, E-mail: adultandgraduate@felician.edu.

Fordham University, Graduate School of Religion and Religious Education, New York, NY 10458. Offers pastoral counseling and spiritual care (MA); pastoral ministry/spirituality/pastoral counseling (D Min); religion and religious education (MA); religious education (MS, PhD, PD); spiritual direction (Certificate). Part-time programs available. *Faculty:* 9 full-time (3 women), 10 part-time/adjunct (3 women). *Students:* 70 full-time (28 women), 121 part-time (50 women); includes 29 minority (5 African Americans, 7 Asian Americans or Pacific Islanders, 17 Hispanic Americans), 75 international. Average age 37. 78 applicants, 96% accepted, 53 enrolled. In 2006, 38 master's, 8 doctorates, 3 other advanced degrees awarded. Terminal master's awarded for partial completion of doctoral program. *Degree requirements:* For master's, research paper; for doctorate, thesis/dissertation, comprehensive exam. *Entrance requirements:* For doctorate, MAT. *Application deadline:* For fall admission, 7/1 priority date for domestic students, 5/1 priority date for international students; for spring admission, 12/1 priority date for domestic students, 10/1 priority date for international students. Applications are processed on a rolling basis. Application fee: $65. Electronic applications accepted. *Expenses:* Contact institution. *Financial support:* In 2006–07, 140 students received support, including 3 research assistantships with full tuition reimbursements available (averaging $4,400 per year); scholarships/grants, unspecified assistantships, and university work-study also available. Support available to part-time students. Financial award application deadline: 2/1. *Faculty research:* Spirituality and spiritual direction, pastoral care and counseling, adult family and community, growth and young adult. *Unit head:* Rev. Anthony J. Ciorra, Dean, 718-817-4804, Fax: 718-817-3352, E-mail: ciorra@fordham.edu. *Application contact:* Dr. Robert Binder, Associate Dean, 718-817-4808, Fax: 718-817-3352, E-mail: binder@fordham.edu.

Gardner-Webb University, M. Christopher White School of Divinity, Boiling Springs, NC 28017. Offers business administration (MA); Christian education (M Div); English (MA); ministry (D Min); missiology (M Div); pastoral care and counseling (M Div); pastoral ministry (M Div). *Accreditation:* ACIPE; ATS. Part-time programs available. *Faculty:* 9 full-time (2 women), 7 part-time/adjunct (1 woman). *Students:* 106 full-time (29 women), 58 part-time (12 women); includes 29 minority (27 African Americans, 2 Hispanic Americans). Average age 34. 69 applicants, 97% accepted, 59 enrolled. In 2006, 33 master's, 5 doctorates awarded. *Degree requirements:* For first-professional, 2 foreign languages. *Entrance requirements:* For M Div, minimum GPA of 2.0; for master's, minimum GPA of 2.5; for doctorate, minimum GPA of 2.75. *Application deadline:* For fall admission, 8/1 priority date for domestic students; for spring admission, 12/15 priority date for domestic students. Applications are processed on a rolling basis. Application fee: $25. *Expenses:* Contact institution. *Financial support:* Fellowships, institutionally sponsored loans and unspecified assistantships available. Support available to part-time students. Financial award application deadline: 5/15. *Faculty research:* Jewish Christian dialogue, Islam. *Unit head:* Dr. Robert W. Canoy, Dean, 704-406-4400, Fax: 704-406-3935, E-mail: rcanoy@gardner-webb.edu. *Application contact:* Dr. Toby Ziglar, Director of Admissions, 704-406-3205, Fax: 704-406-3935, E-mail: tziglar@gardner-webb.edu.

Garrett-Evangelical Theological Seminary, Graduate and Professional Programs, Evanston, IL 60201-3298. Offers Bible and culture (PhD); Christian education (MA); Christian education and congregational studies (PhD); contemporary theology and culture (PhD); divinity (M Div); ethics, church, and society (MA); liturgical studies (PhD); ministry (D Min); music ministry (MA); pastoral care and counseling (MA); pastoral theology, personality, and culture (PhD); spiritual formation and evangelism (MA); theological studies (MTS); M Div/MSW. *Accreditation:* ACIPE; ATS (one or more programs are accredited). Part-time programs available. *Degree requirements:* For master's, thesis (for some programs); for doctorate, thesis/dissertation. *Entrance requirements:* For doctorate, GRE (PhD). Additional exam requirements/recommendations for international students: Required—TOEFL (minimum score 560 paper-based; 230 computer-based). Electronic applications accepted.

Global University of the Assemblies of God, School of Graduate Studies, Springfield, MO 65804. Offers biblical studies (MA); divinity (M Div); ministerial studies (MA), including education, leadership, missions, New Testament, Old Testament. Part-time and evening/weekend programs available. Postbaccalaureate distance learning degree programs offered (no on-campus study). *Degree requirements:* For master's, thesis (for some programs). *Entrance requirements:* For M Div, minimum undergraduate GPA of 3.0; for master's, minimum undergraduate GPA of 3.0, 15 undergraduate credit hours of course work in Bible or theology. Electronic applications accepted. *Faculty research:* Higher education, cross-cultural missions.

Gordon-Conwell Theological Seminary, Graduate and Professional Programs, South Hamilton, MA 01982. Offers Christian education (MACE); church history (MACH); counseling (MACO); ministry (D Min); missions/evangelism (MAME); New Testament (MANT); Old Testament (MAOT); religion (MAR); theology (M Div, MATH, Th M). *Accreditation:* ACIPE; ATS (one or more programs are accredited). Part-time and evening/weekend programs available. *Degree requirements:* For M Div, 2 foreign languages; for master's, one foreign language, thesis optional; for doctorate, 2 foreign languages, thesis/dissertation. *Entrance requirements:* For M Div and master's, minimum GPA of 2.5; for doctorate, minimum GPA of 3.0.

Grand Rapids Theological Seminary of Cornerstone University, Graduate Programs, Grand Rapids, MI 49525-5897. Offers biblical counseling (MA); chaplaincy (M Div); Christian education (M Div, MA); intercultural studies (MA); missions (M Div); New Testament (MA, Th M); Old Testament (MA, Th M); pastoral studies (M Div); systematic theology (MA); theology (Th M). *Accreditation:* ATS. Part-time programs available. Postbaccalaureate distance learning degree programs offered (minimal on-campus study). *Degree requirements:* For master's, 2 foreign languages, thesis (for some programs), oral exam. Electronic applications accepted.

Gratz College, Graduate Programs, Program in Jewish Education, Melrose Park, PA 19027. Offers MA, Certificate, MA/Certificate, MA/MA. Part-time and evening/weekend programs available. *Degree requirements:* For master's, one foreign language. *Entrance requirements:* For master's, interview.

Harding University, College of Education, Searcy, AR 72149-0001. Offers advanced studies in teaching and learning (M Ed); art (MSE); behavioral science (MSE); Bible and religion (MSE); counseling (MS, Ed S); early childhood education (M Ed); early childhood special education (M Ed, MSE); education (MSE); educational leadership (M Ed, Ed S); elementary education (M Ed); English (MSE); family and consumer science (MSE); French (MSE); history/social science (MSE); kinesiology (MSE); math (MSE); physical science (MSE); reading (M Ed); secondary education (M Ed); Spanish (MSE); special education licensure (M Ed); teaching (MAT). *Accreditation:* NCATE. Part-time programs available. *Faculty:* 8 full-time (2 women), 45 part-time/adjunct (30 women). *Students:* 153 full-time (123 women), 469 part-time (341 women); includes 72 minority (63 African Americans, 4 American Indian/Alaska Native, 1 Asian American or Pacific Islander, 4 Hispanic Americans), 9 international. Average age 35. 175 applicants, 90% accepted, 147 enrolled. In 2006, 241 degrees awarded. *Degree requirements:* For master's, portfolio(s), thesis optional; for Ed S, portfolio, specialist project. *Entrance requirements:* For master's, GRE, MAT, PRAXIS; for Ed S, MAT or GRE. Additional exam requirements/recommendations for international students: Required—TOEFL (minimum score 550 paper-based). *Application deadline:* For fall admission, 8/1 for domestic and international students; for spring admission, 1/1 for domestic and international students. Applications are processed on a rolling basis. Application fee: $35. *Expenses:* Tuition: Part-time $455 per semester hour. Required fees: $20 per semester hour. Tuition and fees vary according to course load. *Financial support:* Scholarships/grants and unspecified assistantships available. Support available to part-time students. *Faculty research:* Reading, comprehension, school violence, educational technology, behavior, college choice, differentiated instruction, brain based teaching. *Unit head:* Pat Bashaw, Chair, 501-279-4183, Fax: 501-279-4051, E-mail: pbashaw@harding.edu.

Hebrew College, Shoolman Graduate School of Education, Newton Centre, MA 02459. Offers early childhood Jewish education (Certificate); Jewish day school education (Certificate); Jewish education (MJ Ed); Jewish family education (Certificate); Jewish special education (Certificate); Jewish youth education, informal education and camping (Certificate). Part-time and evening/weekend programs available. Postbaccalaureate distance learning degree programs offered. *Faculty:* 6 full-time (1 woman), 19 part-time/adjunct (7 women). *Students:* 51 (42 women). Average age 37. 33 applicants, 79% accepted, 19 enrolled. In 2006, 5 degrees awarded. *Degree requirements:* For master's, one foreign language. *Entrance requirements:* For master's, GRE, interview. Additional exam requirements/recommendations for international students: Required—TOEFL. *Application deadline:* For fall admission, 12/15 priority date for domestic and international students; for winter admission, 2/15 priority date for domestic and international students; for spring admission, 5/30 priority date for domestic and international students. Application fee: $50. *Financial support:* Fellowships, career-related internships or fieldwork and tuition waivers (partial) available. Support available to part-time students. Financial award application deadline: 4/15; financial award applicants required to submit FAFSA. *Unit head:* Dr. Barry Mesch, Provost, 617-559-8600, Fax: 617-559-8601, E-mail: bmesch@hebrewcollege.edu. *Application contact:* Kate Nachman, Director of Admissions, 617-559-8610, Fax: 617-559-8601, E-mail: admissions@hebrewcollege.edu.

Hebrew Union College–Jewish Institute of Religion, Rhea Hirsch School of Education, Los Angeles, CA 90007-3796. Offers day school teaching (Certificate); Jewish education (MAJE, PhD); MAJCS/MAJE. *Faculty:* 3 full-time (2 women), 7 part-time/adjunct (5 women). *Students:* 21 full-time (15 women), 1 international. Average age 29. 11 applicants, 100% accepted, 11 enrolled. In 2006, 6 master's, 5 other advanced degrees awarded. Terminal master's awarded for partial completion of doctoral program. *Median time to degree:* Master's–3 years full-time. *Degree requirements:* For master's, one foreign language, thesis or alternative, Hebrew; for doctorate, one foreign language, thesis/dissertation, Hebrew. *Entrance requirements:* For master's, GRE General Test, Hebrew, interview, minimum undergraduate GPA of 3.0; for doctorate, GRE General Test, interview, knowledge of Hebrew, minimum GPA of 3.0. Additional exam requirements/recommendations for international students: Required—TOEFL (minimum score 550 paper-based). *Application deadline:* For fall admission, 2/1 for domestic and international students. Application fee: $50. *Expenses:* Tuition: Full-time $16,000; part-time $680 per unit. One-time fee: $100 full-time. *Financial support:* Career-related internships or fieldwork and scholarships/grants available. Support available to part-time students. Financial award application deadline: 3/2; financial award applicants required to submit FAFSA. *Unit head:* Dr. Michael Zeldin, Director, 213-749-3424 Ext. 4216, Fax: 213-747-6128, E-mail: mzeldin@huc.edu. *Application contact:* Director of Admissions and Recruitment, 213-749-3424 Ext. 4221, Fax: 213-7476128.

Hebrew Union College–Jewish Institute of Religion, School of Education, New York, NY 10012-1186. Offers MARE. Part-time programs available. *Faculty:* 21 full-time (9 women), 10 part-time/adjunct (4 women). *Students:* 8 full-time (6 women), 16 part-time (10 women), 3 international. Average age 32. In 2006, 5 degrees awarded. *Degree requirements:* For master's, one foreign language, thesis. *Entrance requirements:* For master's, GRE, minimum 2 years of college-level Hebrew. *Application deadline:* Applications are processed on a rolling basis. Application fee: $35. *Expenses:* Tuition: Full-time $16,000; part-time $680 per credit. Required fees: $35. One-time fee: $75 full-time. *Financial support:* Career-related internships

Religious Education

Hebrew Union College–Jewish Institute of Religion (continued) or fieldwork and scholarships/grants available. Financial award application deadline: 6/1; financial award applicants required to submit FAFSA. *Unit head:* Jo Kay, Director, 212-674-5300 Ext. 2213, Fax: 212-388-1720, E-mail: jkay@huc.edu. *Application contact:* Merline Denis, Administrative Assistant, 212-824-2252, Fax: 212-388-1720, E-mail: mdenis@huc.edu.

Indiana Wesleyan University, College of Graduate Studies, Program in Ministry, Marion, IN 46953-4974. Offers ministerial education (MA); ministry (MA). Part-time programs available. Postbaccalaureate distance learning degree programs offered. *Faculty:* 5 part-time/adjunct (0 women). *Students:* 114 full-time (19 women), 11 part-time (2 women); includes 21 minority (18 African Americans, 2 American Indian/Alaska Native, 1 Hispanic American), 2 international. Average age 36. In 2006, 18 degrees awarded. *Degree requirements:* For master's, practicum or project. *Application deadline:* Applications are processed on a rolling basis. Application fee: $0. Electronic applications accepted. *Expenses: Contact institution.* Tuition and fees vary according to degree level, campus/location and program. *Financial support:* Career-related internships or fieldwork available. *Faculty research:* History of worship innovation, history of New Testament afterlife traditions, second century Mantanism, cross-cultural ministry. *Unit head:* Dr. Russ Gunsalus, Chair, 765-677 Ext. 2259, E-mail: russ.gunsalus@indwes.edu. *Application contact:* David McMillan, Assistant Director of Enrollment Management, 765-677-2688, E-mail: david.mcmillan@indwes.edu.

The Jewish Theological Seminary, William Davidson Graduate School of Jewish Education, New York, NY 10027-4649. Offers MA, Ed D. Offered in conjunction with Rabbinical School; H. L. Miller Cantorial School and College of Jewish Music; Teacher's College, Columbia University; and Union Theological Seminary. Part-time programs available. Postbaccalaureate distance learning degree programs offered (minimal on-campus study). *Faculty:* 62 full-time (19 women), 59 part-time/adjunct (28 women). *Students:* 83 full-time (56 women), 42 part-time (23 women); includes 2 minority (both Hispanic Americans) Average age 33. 56 applicants, 80% accepted, 32 enrolled. In 2006, 6 master's, 1 doctorate awarded. *Degree requirements:* For master's, one foreign language, thesis optional; for doctorate, one foreign language, thesis/dissertation, comprehensive exam. *Entrance requirements:* For master's, GRE or MAT, 3 letters of recommendation; for doctorate, GRE or MAT, writing sample, 3 letters of recommendation. *Application deadline:* For fall admission, 2/1 priority date for domestic students. Applications are processed on a rolling basis. Application fee: $50. *Expenses:* Tuition: Full-time $18,880; part-time $900 per credit. Required fees: $250; $125 per semester. Tuition and fees vary according to program. *Financial support:* Fellowships, career-related internships or fieldwork available. Financial award application deadline: 3/1. *Unit head:* Dr. Steven Brown, Dean, 212-678-8030, Fax: 212-749-9085, E-mail: stbrown@jtsa.edu. *Application contact:* Jamie Beth Schindler, Director of Admissions, 212-678-8866, Fax: 212-749-9085, E-mail: jaschindler@jtsa.edu.

See Close-Up on page 1607.

Jewish University of America, Graduate School, Program in Jewish Education, Skokie, IL 60077-3248. Offers MJ Ed, DJ Ed. *Degree requirements:* For master's, thesis optional; for doctorate, one foreign language, thesis/dissertation. *Entrance requirements:* For master's and doctorate, interview.

La Sierra University, School of Religion, Riverside, CA 92515. Offers religion (MA); religious education (MA); religious studies (MA). *Accreditation:* ATS. Part-time programs available. *Degree requirements:* For master's, one foreign language, thesis or alternative. *Entrance requirements:* For master's, GRE General Test, minimum GPA of 3.0.

Laura and Alvin Siegal College of Judaic Studies, Graduate Programs, Program in Religious Education, Beachwood, OH 44122-7116. Offers Jewish education (MAJS); Judaic studies (MAJS). Part-time and evening/weekend programs available. Postbaccalaureate distance learning degree programs offered (minimal on-campus study). *Degree requirements:* For master's, one foreign language, thesis. *Entrance requirements:* For master's, interview.

Loyola Marymount University, Graduate Division, School of Education, Program in Catholic Inclusive Education, Los Angeles, CA 90045-2659. Offers MA. *Students:* 4 full-time (2 women), 25 part-time (22 women); includes 17 minority (3 African Americans, 2 Asian Americans or Pacific Islanders, 12 Hispanic Americans), 2 international. Average age 40. *Application fee:* $50. *Financial support:* Application deadline: 6/1; *Unit head:* Dr. Victoria L. Graf, Head, 310-338-7305, E-mail: vgraf@lmu.edu.

Loyola University Chicago, Institute of Pastoral Studies, Chicago, IL 60611-2196. Offers divinity (M Div); pastoral counseling (MA, Certificate), including pastoral counseling (MA), pastoral studies (MA); pastoral studies (MA); religious education (Certificate); social justice (MA); spiritual direction (Certificate); spirituality (MA); M Div/MA; M Div/MSN; M Div/MSW. *Accreditation:* ACIPE. Part-time and evening/weekend programs available. *Faculty:* 6 full-time (1 woman), 33 part-time/adjunct (16 women). *Students:* 106 full-time (57 women), 118 part-time (82 women); includes 20 minority (13 African Americans, 1 Asian American or Pacific Islander, 6 Hispanic Americans), 15 international. Average age 42. 93 applicants, 91% accepted, 72 enrolled. In 2006, 29 degrees awarded. *Degree requirements:* For M Div, project; for master's, project, thesis optional. *Entrance requirements:* For master's, interview. Additional exam requirements/recommendations for international students: Required—TOEFL. *Application deadline:* Applications are processed on a rolling basis. Application fee: $50. Electronic applications accepted. *Expenses: Contact institution.* *Financial support:* In 2006–07, 84 students received support. Career-related internships or fieldwork, Federal Work-Study, institutionally sponsored loans, scholarships/grants, and tuition waivers (partial) available. Support available to part-time students. Financial award application deadline: 3/1; financial award applicants required to submit FAFSA. *Faculty research:* Catholic theology, skills of religious ministry, family ministries, spirituality and divorced men. *Unit head:* Dr. Robert A. Ludwig, Director, 312-915-7467, Fax: 312-915-7410, E-mail: rludwig@luc.edu. *Application contact:* Randy Gibbons, Administrative Assistant, 312-915-7450, Fax: 312-915-7410, E-mail: rgibbon@luc.edu.

Luther Rice University, Graduate Programs, Lithonia, GA 30038-2454. Offers Bible/theology (M Div); Christian education (M Div); Christian studies (MA); church ministry (D Min); counseling (M Div); discipleship counseling (MA); ministry (M Div, MA); missions/evangelism (M Div). Part-time programs available. Postbaccalaureate distance learning degree programs offered (no on-campus study). *Degree requirements:* For doctorate, thesis/dissertation. *Entrance requirements:* Additional exam requirements/recommendations for international students: Required—TOEFL (minimum score 500 paper-based; 173 computer-based).

Michigan Theological Seminary, Graduate Programs, Plymouth, MI 48170. Offers Christian education (MA); counseling psychology (MA); divinity (M Div); expository communication (D Min); theological studies (MA). Part-time and evening/weekend programs available. *Degree requirements:* For M Div, 2 foreign languages; for master's, one foreign language, thesis; for doctorate, 2 foreign languages, thesis/dissertation. *Faculty research:* Judaism, cults, world religions.

Midwestern Baptist Theological Seminary, Graduate and Professional Programs, Kansas City, MO 64118-4697. Offers Biblical studies (MA); Christian education (MACE); divinity/ministry (M Div); ministry (D Min); sacred music (MCM). *Accreditation:* ATS. Part-time programs available. Postbaccalaureate distance learning degree programs offered (minimal on-campus study). *Degree requirements:* For M Div, 2 foreign languages; for doctorate, thesis/dissertation. *Entrance requirements:* For doctorate, MAT. Electronic applications accepted. *Faculty research:* Ministerial studies, Biblical and theological studies, missions, counseling.

Midwest University, Graduate Programs, Wentzville, MO 63385. Offers church music (MA, D Min); theology (M Div, MA, D Min), including Christian mission (M Div, D Min), counseling (M Div, D Min), education (M Div, D Min), leadership (M Div, D Min). Part-time programs available. Postbaccalaureate distance learning degree programs offered (minimal on-campus study).

Entrance requirements: Additional exam requirements/recommendations for international students: Recommended—TOEFL (minimum score 550 paper-based).

Nazarene Theological Seminary, Graduate and Professional Programs, Kansas City, MO 64131-1263. Offers Christian education (MA); intercultural studies (MA); theological studies (MA); theology (M Div, D Min). *Accreditation:* ACIPE; ATS. Part-time programs available. *Faculty:* 20 full-time (3 women), 12 part-time/adjunct (2 women). *Students:* 166 full-time (46 women), 141 part-time (34 women); includes 23 minority (9 African Americans, 2 American Indian/Alaska Native, 4 Asian Americans or Pacific Islanders, 8 Hispanic Americans), 4 international. Average age 31. 115 applicants, 83% accepted, 78 enrolled. In 2006, 37 first professional degrees, 24 master's, 9 doctorates awarded. *Degree requirements:* For master's, thesis (for some programs), comprehensive exam; for doctorate, thesis/dissertation. *Entrance requirements:* Additional exam requirements/recommendations for international students: Required—TOEFL. *Application deadline:* For fall admission, 8/1 priority date for domestic students; for spring admission, 12/1 for domestic students. Applications are processed on a rolling basis. Application fee: $25 ($200 for international students). Electronic applications accepted. *Expenses:* Tuition: Full-time $8,136; part-time $339 per credit. Required fees: $75 per semester. *Financial support:* In 2006–07, 235 students received support, including 15 teaching assistantships (averaging $1,400 per year); institutionally sponsored loans and scholarships/grants also available. Support available to part-time students. Financial award application deadline: 3/1; financial award applicants required to submit FAFSA. *Unit head:* Dr. Roger L. Hahn, Dean of the Faculty, 816-333-6254 Ext. 220, Fax: 816-333-6271, E-mail: rlhahn@nts.edu. *Application contact:* Jay A. Sandbloom, Director of Admissions, 816-333-6254 Ext. 211, Fax: 816-333-6271, E-mail: jasandbloom@nts.edu.

Newman Theological College, Religious Education Program, Edmonton, AB T6V 1H3, Canada. Offers Catholic school administration (CCSA); religious education (MRE, GDRE). Part-time programs available. Postbaccalaureate distance learning degree programs offered (no on-campus study). *Faculty:* 1 full-time (0 women), 5 part-time/adjunct (3 women). *Students:* Average age 44. 50 applicants, 80% accepted, 32 enrolled. In 2006, 4 master's, 8 other advanced degrees awarded. *Degree requirements:* For master's, thesis or alternative. *Entrance requirements:* For master's, 2 years of successful teaching experience; graduate diploma in religious education; for other advanced degree, bachelor's degree in education, teaching certificate. Additional exam requirements/recommendations for international students: Required—TOEFL (minimum score 560 paper-based; 220 computer-based). *Application deadline:* For fall admission, 8/30 priority date for domestic students; for winter admission, 12/21 for domestic students; for spring admission, 4/30 for domestic students. Application fee: $25. *Expenses:* Tuition: Full-time $9,000; part-time $900 per term. Required fees: $50; $20 per term. One-time fee: $40 full-time. *Financial support:* Tuition bursaries available. Support available to part-time students. Financial award application deadline: 5/30. *Unit head:* Dr. Dan Kingdon, Director, 780-447-2993 Ext. 224, Fax: 780-447-2685, E-mail: dan.kingdon@newman.edu. *Application contact:* Carol Anne Seed, Registrar, 780-447-2993 Ext. 227, Fax: 780-447-2685.

New Orleans Baptist Theological Seminary, Graduate and Professional Programs, Division of Christian Education Ministries, New Orleans, LA 70126-4858. Offers Christian education (M Div, MACE, D Min, DEM, PhD). Evening/weekend programs available. *Degree requirements:* For M Div, project report; for doctorate, thesis/dissertation. *Entrance requirements:* For doctorate, GRE General Test.

North Park Theological Seminary, Graduate and Professional Programs, Program in Religious Education, Chicago, IL 60625-4895. Offers MACE. Part-time programs available. *Entrance requirements:* For master's, minimum GPA of 2.5. Additional exam requirements/recommendations for international students: Required—TOEFL.

Nova Southeastern University, Fischler School of Education and Human Services, Graduate Teacher Education Program, Fort Lauderdale, FL 33314-7796. Offers athletic administration (MS); cognitive and behavioral disabilities (MS); computer science education (Ed S); computer science education (K-12) (MS); curriculum and teaching (Ed S); curriculum, instruction and technology (MS); curriculum, instruction, management and administration (Ed S); early childhood special education (MS); early literacy and reading (Ed S); early literacy education (MS); education technology (MS); educational leadership (administration K–12) (MS, Ed S); educational media (Ed S); educational media (K-12) (MS); elementary education (MS, Ed S), including ESOL endorsement (MS); English (MS, Ed S); exceptional student education (MS), including ESOL endorsement; gifted education (MS, Ed S); interdisciplinary arts education (MS); management and administration of educational programs (MS); mathematics (MS, Ed S); multicultural early intervention (MS); pre-kindergarten/primary (MS); preschool education (MS); reading (MS, Ed S); science (MS, Ed S); secondary education (MS); social studies (MS, Ed S); Spanish language (MS); teaching and learning (MA, MS), including curriculum and instruction (MA), elementary mathematics (MA), elementary reading (MA), K-12 technology integration (MA); teaching English to speakers of other languages (MS, Ed S); technology management and administration (Ed S); urban studies education (MS); varying exceptionalities (Ed S). Part-time and evening/weekend programs available. Postbaccalaureate distance learning degree programs offered. *Faculty:* 131 full-time (78 women), 548 part-time/adjunct (342 women). *Students:* 1,418 full-time (1,139 women), 3,464 part-time (2,877 women); includes 2,462 minority (1,732 African Americans, 13 American Indian/Alaska Native, 44 Asian Americans or Pacific Islanders, 673 Hispanic Americans), 77 international. Average age 38. 1,771 applicants, 80% accepted, 1419 enrolled. In 2006, 2,078 master's, 425 other advanced degrees awarded. *Degree requirements:* For master's and Ed S, thesis, practicum, internship. *Entrance requirements:* For master's, MAT, GRE, CLAST, CBEST, PRAXIS I, GKT, minimum GPA of 2.5; for Ed S, MAT or GRE, master's degree, teaching certificate, minimum GPA of 3.0. Additional exam requirements/recommendations for international students: Recommended—TOEFL (minimum score 550 paper-based; 213 computer-based), IELTS (minimum score 6). *Application deadline:* For fall admission, 8/11 priority date for domestic and international students; for winter admission, 12/28 priority date for domestic and international students; for spring admission, 4/22 priority date for domestic and international students. Applications are processed on a rolling basis. Application fee: $50. Electronic applications accepted. *Financial support:* Federal Work-Study available. Support available to part-time students. Financial award application deadline: 1/7. *Faculty research:* School effectiveness, critical thinking, leadership skills acquisition, child education, multicultural education. *Unit head:* Dr. Meline Kevorkian, Associate Dean of Master's and Educational Programs, 954-262-8500, Fax: 954-262-3606, E-mail: melinek@nova.edu. *Application contact:* Jennifer Quiñones Nottingham, Dean of Student Affairs, 800-986-3223 Ext. 8624, Fax: 954-262-3911, E-mail: jlquinon@nova.edu.

Oral Roberts University, School of Education, Tulsa, OK 74171-0001. Offers Christian school administration (MA Ed, Ed D); Christian school administration (K-12) (MA Ed, Ed D); Christian school curriculum development (MA Ed); college and higher education administration (MA Ed, Ed D); public school administration (K-12) (MA Ed, Ed D); public school teaching (MA Ed); teaching English as a second language (MA Ed). *Accreditation:* NCATE. Part-time programs available. Postbaccalaureate distance learning degree programs offered (minimal on-campus study). *Faculty:* 9 full-time (2 women), 9 part-time/adjunct (4 women). *Students:* 331 full-time (217 women); includes 118 minority (96 African Americans, 7 American Indian/Alaska Native, 10 Asian Americans or Pacific Islanders, 5 Hispanic Americans). 125 applicants, 96% accepted, 116 enrolled. In 2006, 25 master's, 10 doctorates awarded. *Degree requirements:* For master's, thesis (for some programs), comprehensive exam; for doctorate, thesis/dissertation, comprehensive exam. *Entrance requirements:* For master's, GRE General Test or MAT, minimum GPA of 3.0; for doctorate, minimum GPA of 3.0. Additional exam requirements/recommendations for international students: Required—TOEFL (minimum score 500 paper-based; 173 computer-based). *Application deadline:* For fall admission, 7/1 priority date for domestic students, 5/1 priority date for international students; for spring admission, 12/1 priority date for domestic students, 10/1 priority date for international students. Applications are processed on a rolling basis. Application fee: $35. *Expenses: Contact institution.* *Financial support:* In 2006–07, 4 research assistantships (averaging $5,000 per year) were awarded; scholarships/grants and unspecified assistantships also available. Financial award application deadline: 6/1; financial award applicants required to submit FAFSA. *Faculty research:* Teacher effectiveness, college success in high achieving, African-Americans, professional development practices. *Unit head:* Dr. David Hand, Dean, 918-495-7084, Fax: 918-495-6050, E-mail: dhand@oru.edu. *Application contact:* Kim Schmeisser, Graduate Admissions, 918-495-6058, Fax: 918-495-6222, E-mail: gradeducation@oru.edu.

Oral Roberts University, School of Theology and Missions, Tulsa, OK 74171-0001. Offers biblical literature (MA); Christian counseling (MA); Christian education (MA); divinity (M Div); missions (MA); practical theology (MA); theological/historical studies (MA); theology (D Min). *Accreditation:* ATS; NASM. Part-time programs available. Postbaccalaureate distance learning degree programs offered (minimal on-campus study). *Faculty:* 17 full-time (2 women). *Students:* 346 full-time (142 women), 133 part-time (61 women); includes 188 minority (129 African Americans, 32 Asian Americans or Pacific Islanders, 27 Hispanic Americans), 52 international. Average age 36. 170 applicants, 95% accepted, 124 enrolled. In 2006, 41 first professional degrees, 51 master's, 21 doctorates awarded. *Degree requirements:* For M Div, one foreign language; for master's, thesis (for some programs), practicum/internship; for doctorate, thesis/dissertation, applied research project. *Entrance requirements:* For M Div and master's, GRE General Test or MAT, minimum GPA of 2.5; for doctorate, M Div, minimum GPA of 3.0, 3 years of full-time ministry experience. Additional exam requirements/recommendations for international students: Required—TOEFL (minimum score 500 paper-based; 173 computer-based). *Application deadline:* For fall admission, 7/1 priority date for domestic students, 5/1 priority date for international students; for spring admission, 12/1 priority date for domestic students, 10/1 priority date for international students. Applications are processed on a rolling basis. Application fee: $35. *Financial support:* In 2006–07, teaching assistantships (averaging $3,600 per year); scholarships/grants and employment assistantships also available. Financial award application deadline: 6/1; financial award applicants required to submit FAFSA. *Unit head:* Dr. Thomson K. Mathew, Dean, 918-495-7016, Fax: 918-495-6259, E-mail: tmathew@oru.edu. *Application contact:* 918-495-6989, Fax: 918-495-7965, E-mail: alsc@oru.edu.

Pfeiffer University, School of Religion and Christian Education, Misenheimer, NC 28109-0960. Offers MACE. Part-time and evening/weekend programs available. *Faculty:* 4 full-time (2 women). *Students:* 1 (woman) full-time, 51 part-time (40 women); includes 12 minority (all African Americans), 1 international. Average age 40. In 2006, 12 degrees awarded. *Entrance requirements:* For master's, minimum GPA of 2.75. *Application deadline:* For fall admission, 8/21 priority date for domestic students. Applications are processed on a rolling basis. Application fee: $75. *Expenses:* Tuition: Part-time $380 per semester hour. Tuition and fees vary according to campus/location. *Financial support:* Scholarships/grants available. Support available to part-time students. Financial award applicants required to submit FAFSA. *Unit head:* Kathleen Kilbourne, Coordinator, 704-521-9116 Ext. 236, E-mail: kbourne@pfeiffer.edu.

Phillips Theological Seminary, Programs in Theology, Tulsa, OK 74116. Offers administration of church agencies (M Div); campus ministry (M Div); church-related social work (M Div); college and seminary teaching (M Div); global mission work (M Div); institutional chaplaincy (M Div); ministerial vocations in Christian education (M Div); ministry (D Min), including parish ministry, pastoral counseling, practices of ministry; ministry and culture (MAMC), including Christian education, congregational leadership, history and practice of Christian spirituality, theology, ethics, and culture; ministry of music (M Div); pastoral care and counseling (M Div); pastoral ministry (M Div); theological studies (MTS). *Accreditation:* ATS. Part-time programs available. Postbaccalaureate distance learning degree programs offered (minimal on-campus study). *Degree requirements:* For master's, thesis (for some programs); for doctorate, thesis/dissertation. *Entrance requirements:* For master's, minimum GPA of 2.5; for doctorate, M Div, minimum GPA of 3.0. *Faculty research:* Biblical studies, historical studies, theology and culture, practical theology, theology and film.

Pontifical Catholic University of Puerto Rico, College of Education, Ponce, PR 00717-0777. Offers commercial education (MRE); curriculum instruction (M Ed); education (PhD); education-general (MRE); English as a second language (MRE); religious education (MA Ed); scholar psychology (MRE). Part-time and evening/weekend programs available. *Degree requirements:* For master's, thesis (for some programs), comprehensive exam. *Entrance requirements:* For master's, GRE, 2 letters of recommendation, interview, minimum GPA of 2.75; for doctorate, EXADEP, GRE or MAT, 3 letters of recommendation. *Faculty research:* Teaching English as a second language, learning styles, leadership styles.

Providence College and Theological Seminary, Theological Seminary, Otterburne, MB R0A 1G0, Canada. Offers children's ministry (Certificate); Christian studies (MA, Certificate); counseling (MA); cross-cultural discipleship (Certificate); divinity (M Div); educational studies (MA), including counseling psychology, educational ministries, student development, teaching English to speakers of other languages, training teachers of English to speakers of other languages; global studies (MA); lay counseling (Diploma); ministry (D Min); teaching English to speakers of other languages (Certificate); theological studies (MA); training teacher of English to speakers of other languages (Certificate); youth ministry (Certificate). *Accreditation:* ATS. Part-time programs available. *Degree requirements:* For M Div, 2 foreign languages, thesis (for some programs), comprehensive exam; for master's, variable foreign language requirement, thesis (for some programs); for doctorate, thesis/dissertation. *Entrance requirements:* Additional exam requirements/recommendations for international students: Recommended—TOEFL (minimum score 550 paper-based; 213 computer-based). *Faculty research:* Studies in Isaiah, theology of sin.

Reformed Theological Seminary–Charlotte Campus, Graduate and Professional Programs, Charlotte, NC 28226-6318. Offers biblical studies (MA); Christian education/youth ministry (M Div); ministry (D Min); theological studies (MA). Part-time programs available. Postbaccalaureate distance learning degree programs offered (minimal on-campus study). *Faculty:* 9 full-time. *Students:* 362. *Degree requirements:* For M Div, 2 foreign languages; for doctorate, thesis/dissertation. *Entrance requirements:* For master's, minimum GPA of 2.6; for doctorate, minimum GPA of 3.0. *Application deadline:* For fall admission, 5/1 priority date for domestic students; for winter admission, 10/1 priority date for domestic students; for spring admission, 11/1 priority date for domestic students. Applications are processed on a rolling basis. Application fee: $25. *Expenses:* Tuition: Part-time $325 per semester hour. *Financial support:* In 2006–07, teaching assistantships (averaging $1,600 per year). Financial award application deadline: 5/1. *Application contact:* Stephane Jeanrenaud, Director of Admissions, 800-755-2429, E-mail: admissions.charlotte@rts.edu.

Reformed Theological Seminary–Jackson Campus, Graduate and Professional Programs, Jackson, MS 39209-3099. Offers Bible, theology, and missions (Certificate); biblical studies (MA); Christian education (M Div, MA); counseling (M Div); divinity (M Div, Diploma); marriage and family therapy (MA); ministry (D Min); missions (M Div, MA, D Min); New Testament (Th M); Old Testament (Th M); theological studies (MA); theology (Th M); M Div/MA. *Accreditation:* AAMFT/COAMFTE (one or more programs are accredited); ATS (one or more programs are accredited). *Degree requirements:* For M Div, 2 foreign languages, thesis (for some programs); for master's, thesis (for some programs), fieldwork; for doctorate, 2 foreign languages, thesis/dissertation. *Entrance requirements:* For M Div and master's, minimum GPA of 2.6; for doctorate, minimum GPA of 3.0. Additional exam requirements/recommendations for international students: Required—TOEFL.

Regent University, Graduate School, School of Education, Virginia Beach, VA 23464-9800. Offers Christian school program (M Ed); cross-categorical special education (M Ed); education (M Ed, Ed D); educational leadership (M Ed); elementary education (M Ed); individual degree plan (M Ed); master teacher (M Ed); special education leadership (Ed S); TESOL (M Ed). Part-time and evening/weekend programs available. Postbaccalaureate distance learning degree programs offered (minimal on-campus study). *Faculty:* 25 full-time (11 women), 132 part-time/adjunct (90 women). *Students:* 220 full-time (176 women), 501 part-time (374 women); includes 264 minority (229 African Americans, 9 Asian Americans or Pacific Islanders, 26 Hispanic Americans), 13 international. Average age 38. 472 applicants, 79% accepted, 256 enrolled. In 2006, 185 master's, 5 doctorates awarded. *Degree requirements:* For master's, thesis or alternative; for doctorate, thesis/dissertation, comprehensive exam. *Entrance requirements:* For master's, MAT, minimum undergraduate GPA of 2.75, writing sample, resumé; for doctorate, GRE, writing sample, 3 years of relevant professional experience, master's-level paper, copies of published work. Additional exam requirements/recommendations for international students: Required—TOEFL (minimum score 577 paper-based; 233 computer-based). *Application deadline:* For fall admission, 4/1 priority date for domestic students; for spring admission, 10/15 priority date for domestic students. Applications are processed on a rolling basis. Application fee: $50. Electronic applications accepted. *Expenses:* Contact institution. *Financial support:* In 2006–07, 721 students received support; fellowships, career-related internships or fieldwork, scholarships/grants, tuition waivers (full and partial), and unspecified assistantships available. Support available to part-time students. Financial award application deadline: 4/1; financial award applicants required to submit FAFSA. *Faculty research:* Character development and discipline for children, education leadership development, diversity in schools, classroom management, technology in education settings. *Unit head:* Dr. Alan A. Arroyo, Dean, 757-226-4261, Fax: 757-226-4318, E-mail: alanarr@regent.edu. *Application contact:* Althea Bishard, Registrar and Executive Director of Enrollment and Academic Services, 800-373-5504, Fax: 757-226-4381, E-mail: admissions@regent.edu.

St. Augustine's Seminary of Toronto, Graduate and Professional Programs, Scarborough, ON M1M 1M3, Canada. Offers divinity (M Div); lay ministry (Diploma); religious education (MRE); theological studies (MTS, Diploma). *Accreditation:* ATS. Part-time and evening/weekend programs available. Postbaccalaureate distance learning degree programs offered (minimal on-campus study). *Faculty:* 11 full-time (4 women), 20 part-time/adjunct (4 women). *Students:* 53 full-time (2 women), 141 part-time (62 women), 16 international. Average age 42. 45 applicants, 91% accepted, 37 enrolled. In 2006, 7 first professional degrees, 12 master's awarded. *Degree requirements:* For first-professional, field education, thesis optional. *Entrance requirements:* Course work in philosophy. Additional exam requirements/recommendations for international students: Required—TOEFL (minimum score 580 paper-based; 237 computer-based), TWE (minimum score 5). *Application deadline:* For fall admission, 7/15 priority date for domestic and international students; for winter admission, 11/15 priority date for domestic and international students; for spring admission, 4/15 priority date for domestic and international students. Application fee: $25 Canadian dollars. *Expenses:* Tuition: Full-time $4,352; part-time $435 per course. Required fees: $54 per term. Tuition and fees vary according to course load. *Unit head:* Rev. Michael Mcgourty, Dean of Studies, 416-261-7207, Fax: 416-261-2529. *Application contact:* Theresa Mary Vicioso, Registrar/Administrative Assistant to the Dean of Studies, 416-261-7207 Ext. 230, Fax: 416-261-2529, E-mail: t.vicioso@utoronto.ca.

Saints Cyril and Methodius Seminary, Graduate and Professional Programs, Orchard Lake, MI 48324. Offers pastoral ministry (MAPM); religious education (MARE); theology (M Div, MA). *Accreditation:* ATS. Part-time programs available.

St. Vladimir's Orthodox Theological Seminary, Graduate School of Theology, Crestwood, NY 10707-1699. Offers general theological studies (MA); liturgical music (MA); religious education (MA); theology (M Div, M Th, D Min); M Div/MA. MA in general theological studies, M Div offered jointly with St. Nersess Seminary. *Accreditation:* ATS. Part-time programs available. *Degree requirements:* For M Div and master's, one foreign language, thesis, fieldwork; for doctorate, thesis/dissertation, fieldwork. *Entrance requirements:* For doctorate, M Div, minimum GPA of 3.0. Additional exam requirements/recommendations for international students: Required—TOEFL (minimum score 250 computer-based).

Shasta Bible College, Program in Biblical Counseling, Redding, CA 96002. Offers biblical counseling and Christian family life education (MA). Part-time programs available. *Degree requirements:* For master's, thesis or alternative, comprehensive exam (for some programs), registration. *Entrance requirements:* For master's, minimum GPA of 2.5. Additional exam requirements/recommendations for international students: Required—TOEFL.

Southeastern Baptist Theological Seminary, Graduate and Professional Programs, Wake Forest, NC 27588-1889. Offers advanced biblical studies (M Div); Christian education (M Div, MACE); Christian ethics (PhD); Christian ministry (M Div); Christian planting (M Div); church music (MACM); counseling (MACO); evangelism (PhD); language (M Div); ministry (D Min); New Testament (PhD); Old Testament (PhD); philosophy (PhD); theology (Th M, PhD); women's studies (M Div). *Accreditation:* ACIPE; ATS (one or more programs are accredited). *Degree requirements:* For M Div, supervised ministry; for master's, thesis (for some programs), oral exam; for doctorate, thesis/dissertation, fieldwork. *Entrance requirements:* For master's, Cooperative English Test, minimum GPA of 2.0, M Div or equivalent (Th M); for doctorate, GRE General Test or MAT, Cooperative English Test, M Div or equivalent, 3 years of professional experience.

Southern Adventist University, School of Religion, Collegedale, TN 37315-0370. Offers church leadership and management (MA); evangelism (MA); homiletics (MA); religious education (MA); religious studies (MA). Summer program only. Part-time programs available. *Faculty:* 10 full-time (0 women), 5 part-time/adjunct (0 women). *Students:* 3 full-time (0 women), 6 part-time (1 woman); includes 3 minority (1 African American, 2 Asian Americans or Pacific Islanders). Average age 36. 9 applicants, 100% accepted, 9 enrolled. In 2006, 6 degrees awarded. *Degree requirements:* For master's, thesis (for some programs), comprehensive exam. *Entrance requirements:* Additional exam requirements/recommendations for international students: Required—TOEFL (minimum score 550 paper-based). *Application deadline:* For spring admission, 4/30 priority date for domestic students, 12/30 for international students. Applications are processed on a rolling basis. Application fee: $25. *Financial support:* In 2006–07, 4 students received support. Tuition waivers (full) available. Support available to part-time students. Financial award application deadline: 4/1; financial award applicants required to submit FAFSA. *Faculty research:* Biblical archaeology. *Unit head:* Dr. Greg A. King, Dean, 423-236-2975, Fax: 423-236-1976, E-mail: gking@southern.edu. *Application contact:* Susan L. Brown, Administrative Assistant, 423-236-2977, Fax: 423-236-1977, E-mail: sbrown@southern.edu.

Southern Baptist Theological Seminary, School of Leadership and Church Ministry, Louisville, KY 40280-0004. Offers M Div, MACE, Ed D, PhD. Part-time programs available. Postbaccalaureate distance learning degree programs offered (minimal on-campus study). *Degree requirements:* For M Div, 2 foreign languages; for doctorate, thesis/dissertation. *Entrance requirements:* For doctorate, GRE General Test, field essay, interview, M Div or MACE. Additional exam requirements/recommendations for international students: Required—TWE. *Faculty research:* Gerontology, creative teaching methods, faith development in children, faith development in youth, transformational learning.

Southern Evangelical Seminary, Graduate School of Ministry and Missions, Matthews, NC 28105. Offers Christian education (MA); church ministry (MA, Certificate); divinity (Certificate), including apologetics (M Div, Certificate); Islamic studies (Certificate); theology (M Div), including apologetics (M Div, Certificate), Biblical studies. Part-time and evening/weekend programs available. Postbaccalaureate distance learning degree programs offered. *Students:* 31 applicants, 100% accepted, 20 enrolled. In 2006, 1 first professional degree, 5 master's awarded. *Degree requirements:* For M Div, 2 foreign languages, registration; for master's, thesis (for some programs), registration. *Entrance requirements:* Additional exam requirements/recommendations for international students: Required—TOEFL (minimum score 600 paper-based; 250 computer-based). *Application deadline:* For fall admission, 8/15 priority date for domestic students, 8/5 priority date for international students; for winter admission, 12/15 priority date for domestic and international students; for spring admission, 1/15 priority date for domestic and international students. Applications are processed on a rolling basis. Application fee: $25. *Financial support:* Scholarships/grants available. *Unit head:* Dr. Barry R. Leventhal, Dean, 704-847-5600 Ext. 204, Fax: 704-845-1747, E-mail: dean@ses.edu.

Southwestern Assemblies of God University, Thomas F. Harrison School of Graduate Studies, Program in Education, Waxahachie, TX 75165-5735. Offers Christian school administra-

Religious Education

Southwestern Assemblies of God University (continued)
tion (MS); curriculum development (MS); MS/MA. *Degree requirements:* For master's, comprehensive written and oral exams. *Entrance requirements:* For master's, GRE General Test, minimum GPA of 2.5. Electronic applications accepted.

Southwestern Baptist Theological Seminary, School of Educational Ministries, Fort Worth, TX 76122-0000. Offers MA Comm, MACC, MACCM, MACE, MACSE, MAMFC, DEM, PhD, SPEM. Part-time and evening/weekend programs available. Terminal master's awarded for partial completion of doctoral program. *Degree requirements:* For master's, thesis, registration; for doctorate, thesis/dissertation, statistics comprehensive exam, comprehensive exam, registration. *Entrance requirements:* For doctorate, GRE or MAT, MACE or equivalent, minimum GPA of 3.0; for SPEM, 3 years of ministry experience after master's degree, MACE or equivalent. Additional exam requirements/recommendations for international students: Required—TOEFL (minimum score 550 paper-based; 213 computer-based), TWE. Electronic applications accepted. *Faculty research:* Youth ministry.

Spertus Institute of Jewish Studies, Graduate Programs, Program in Jewish Education, Chicago, IL 60605-1901. Offers MAJ Ed. Part-time and evening/weekend programs available. *Faculty:* 9 part-time/adjunct (1 woman). *Degree requirements:* For master's, one foreign language, thesis. *Entrance requirements:* For master's, bachelor of arts in Jewish studies. *Application deadline:* Applications are processed on a rolling basis. Application fee: $50. *Financial support:* Scholarships/grants available. Financial award applicants required to submit FAFSA. *Unit head:* Dr. Dean Phillip Bell, Dean, 312-322-1791, Fax: 312-994-5360, E-mail: dbell@spertus.edu. *Application contact:* Nadia Whiteside, Recruitment Manager, 312-322-1707, Fax: 312-922-6406, E-mail: mwhiteside@spertus.edu.

Teachers College Columbia University, Graduate Faculty of Education, Department of Arts and Humanities, Program in Religion and Education, New York, NY 10027-6696. Offers Ed M, MA, Ed D. *Accreditation:* NCATE. *Students:* Average age 59. *Degree requirements:* For doctorate, thesis/dissertation. *Application deadline:* For fall admission, 5/15 for domestic students; for spring admission, 12/1 for domestic students. Application fee: $65. *Expenses:* Tuition: Full-time $23,400; part-time $975 per credit. Required fees: $320 per term. *Financial support:* Career-related internships or fieldwork, Federal Work-Study, institutionally sponsored loans, and tuition waivers (full and partial) available. Support available to part-time students. Financial award application deadline: 2/1. *Faculty research:* Epistemology; science and education; Waldorf education; epistemological, cultural, and spiritual foundations of education. *Application contact:* Mark E. Stearns, Associate Director of Admission, 212-678-3710, Fax: 212-678-4171.

Trinity Baptist College, Graduate Programs, Jacksonville, FL 32221. Offers Bible (M Ed); Christian school administration (M Ed); classroom practices (M Ed); ministry (M Min); special education (M Ed). Postbaccalaureate distance learning degree programs offered. *Faculty:* 10. *Entrance requirements:* For master's, GRE (M Ed), 2 letters of recommendation; minimum GPA of 2.5 (M Min) or 3.0 (M Ed); computer proficiency.

Trinity International University, Trinity Evangelical Divinity School, Deerfield, IL 60015-1284. Offers Biblical and Near Eastern archaeology and languages (MA); Christian studies (MA, Certificate); Christian thought (MA); church history (MA, Th M); congregational ministry: pastor-teacher (M Div); congregational ministry: team ministry (M Div); counseling ministries (MA); counseling psychology (MA); cross-cultural ministry (M Div); educational studies (PhD); evangelism (MA); general studies (MAR); history of Christianity in America (MA); intercultural studies (MA, PhD); leadership and ministry management (D Min); military chaplaincy (D Min); ministry (MA); mission and evangelism (Th M); missions and evangelism (D Min); New Testament (MA, Th M); Old Testament (Th M); Old Testament and Semitic languages (MA); pastoral care (M Div); pastoral care and counseling (D Min); pastoral counseling and psychology (Th M); pastoral theology (Th M); philosophy of religion (MA); preaching (D Min); research ministry (M Div); systematic theology (Th M); theological studies (PhD); urban ministry (MA, MAR). *Accreditation:* ATS (one or more programs are accredited). Part-time programs available. Postbaccalaureate distance learning degree programs offered (minimal on-campus study). *Faculty:* 39 full-time (3 women), 68 part-time/adjunct (10 women). *Students:* 515 full-time (105 women), 716 part-time (180 women); includes 163 minority (32 African Americans, 1 American Indian/Alaska Native, 119 Asian Americans or Pacific Islanders, 11 Hispanic Americans), 135 international. 489 applicants, 88% accepted, 212 enrolled. In 2006, 76 first professional degrees, 136 master's, 47 doctorates, 31 other advanced degrees awarded. *Degree requirements:* For M Div, 2 foreign languages; for master's, thesis, fieldwork, comprehensive exam; for doctorate, thesis/dissertation, comprehensive exam (for some programs); for Certificate, integrative papers. *Entrance requirements:* For M Div, GRE, MAT; for master's, GRE, MAT, minimum cumulative undergraduate GPA of 3.0; for doctorate, GRE, minimum cumulative graduate GPA of 3.2; for Certificate, GRE, MAT, minimum undergraduate GPA of 2.5. Additional exam requirements/recommendations for international students: Required—TOEFL (minimum score 580 paper-based; 237 computer-based), TWE (minimum score 4). *Application deadline:* For fall admission, 7/15 priority date for domestic and international students. Applications are processed on a rolling basis. Application fee: $25. Electronic applications accepted. *Expenses: Contact institution. Financial support:* In 2006–07, 929 students received support, including 6 fellowships with partial tuition reimbursements available, 12 teaching assistantships with partial tuition reimbursements available; career-related internships or fieldwork, Federal Work-Study, scholarships/grants, and tuition waivers (partial) also available. Financial award application deadline: 4/1; financial award applicants required to submit FAFSA. *Unit head:* Dr. Tite Tiénou, Academic Dean, 847-317-8086, Fax: 847-317-8014, E-mail: ttienou@teds.edu. *Application contact:* Ron Campbell, Director of Admissions, 800-345-8337, Fax: 847-317-8097, E-mail: rcampbel@tiu.edu.

Union Theological Seminary and Presbyterian School of Christian Education, School of Christian Education, Richmond, VA 23227-4597. Offers MA, MATS, M Div/MA, M Div/MSW, MSW/MA. Part-time and evening/weekend programs available. Postbaccalaureate distance learning degree programs offered (minimal on-campus study). *Degree requirements:* For master's, oral and written exams. *Entrance requirements:* Additional exam requirements/recommendations for international students: Required—TOEFL (minimum score 550 paper-based; 213 computer-based), TWE (minimum score 4).

University of St. Michael's College, Faculty of Theology, Toronto, ON M5S 1J4, Canada. Offers Catholic leadership (MA); eastern Christian studies (Certificate, Diploma); religious education (Diploma); theological studies (Diploma); theology (M Div, MA, MRE, MTS, D Min, PhD, Th D); theology and ecology (Certificate); theology and Jewish studies (MA). *Accreditation:* ATS (one or more programs are accredited). Part-time programs available. *Faculty:* 10 full-time (3 women), 17 part-time/adjunct (6 women). *Students:* 106 full-time (41 women), 129 part-time (75 women); includes 10 African Americans, 18 Asian Americans or Pacific Islanders, 23 international. Average age 40. 89 applicants, 76% accepted, 66 enrolled. In 2006, 4 first professional degrees, 12 master's, 8 doctorates, 13 other advanced degrees awarded. *Degree requirements:* For M Div and other advanced degree, thesis optional; for master's, thesis (for some programs), 1 foreign language (MA), 2 foreign languages (Th M); for doctorate, 3 foreign languages, thesis/dissertation, comprehensive exam, registration. *Entrance requirements:* For M Div and other advanced degree, minimum GPA of 2.7; for master's, M Div or BA, course work in an ancient or modern language, minimum GPA of 3.3; for doctorate, MA in theology, Th M, or M Div with thesis, minimum GPA of 3.7. Additional exam requirements/recommendations for international students: Required—TOEFL (minimum score 600 paper-based; 250 computer-based). *Application deadline:* For fall admission, 1/15 for domestic and international students. Applications are processed on a rolling basis. Application fee: $25 Canadian dollars. Electronic applications accepted. *Expenses:* Tuition: Full-time $5,495. Tuition and fees vary according to course load and program. *Financial support:* In 2006–07, 45 students received support, including fellowships with partial tuition reimbursements available (averaging $2,500 per year), research assistantships with partial tuition reimbursements available (averaging $2,500 per year), 11 teaching assistantships with partial tuition reimbursements available (averaging $2,400 per year); scholarships/grants, tuition waivers (partial), and bursaries also available. Financial award application deadline: 2/1. *Faculty research:* Patristics, eastern Christianity, ecology and theology, ecumenism, Jewish Christian studies. *Unit head:* Dr. Anne Anderson, CSJ, Dean, 416-926-7265, Fax: 416-926-7294, E-mail: anne.anderson@utoronto.ca. *Application contact:* Student Services Officer, 416-926-7140, Fax: 416-926-7294, E-mail: usmtheology.registrar@utoronto.ca.

University of St. Thomas, Graduate Studies, Saint Paul Seminary School of Divinity, Program in Theology/Pastoral Studies, St. Paul, MN 55105-1096. Offers religious education (MARE); theology (MA). *Accreditation:* ACIPE; ATS. Part-time and evening/weekend programs available. *Faculty:* 13 full-time (5 women), 5 part-time/adjunct (2 women). *Students:* 8 full-time (2 women), 15 part-time (5 women), 2 international. Average age 37. 4 applicants, 100% accepted, 4 enrolled. In 2006, 23 degrees awarded. *Degree requirements:* For master's, one foreign language, thesis or alternative, comprehensive exam, registration. *Entrance requirements:* For master's, GRE, interview, 3 letters of recommendation. Additional exam requirements/recommendations for international students: Required—TOEFL (minimum score 550 paper-based; 213 computer-based). *Application deadline:* Applications are processed on a rolling basis. Application fee: $40. Electronic applications accepted. *Expenses: Contact institution. Financial support:* Fellowships, research assistantships, institutionally sponsored loans and scholarships/grants available. Support available to part-time students. Financial award application deadline: 4/1; financial award applicants required to submit FAFSA. *Faculty research:* Theological education. *Unit head:* Dr. Christopher J. Thompson, Academic Dean, 651-962-5771, Fax: 651-962-5790, E-mail: cjthompson@stthomas.edu. *Application contact:* Rev. Peter A. Laird, Vice Rector and Admissions Chair, 651-962-5070, Fax: 651-962-5790, E-mail: palaird@stthomas.edu.

University of San Francisco, School of Education, Department of Catholic Educational Leadership, San Francisco, CA 94117-1080. Offers Catholic school leadership (MA, Ed D); Catholic school teaching (MA); private school administration (Ed D). *Faculty:* 1 (woman) full-time, 3 part-time/adjunct (2 women). *Students:* 9 full-time (5 women), 32 part-time (18 women); includes 10 minority (6 Asian Americans or Pacific Islanders, 4 Hispanic Americans), 3 international. Average age 37. 33 applicants, 97% accepted, 13 enrolled. In 2006, 4 master's, 6 doctorates awarded. *Degree requirements:* For doctorate, thesis/dissertation. Application fee: $55 ($65 for international students). *Expenses:* Tuition: Full-time $17,370; part-time $965 per unit. Tuition and fees vary according to degree level, campus/location and program. *Financial support:* In 2006–07, 14 students received support; fellowships, research assistantships, teaching assistantships available. Financial award application deadline: 3/2; financial award applicants required to submit FAFSA. *Unit head:* Br. Ray Vercruysse, Chair, 415-422-6226.

Western Seminary, Graduate Programs, Program in Church Education, Portland, OR 97215-3367. Offers MA, D Min. *Degree requirements:* For master's, thesis or alternative, practicum.

Wheaton College, Graduate School, Department of Christian Formation and Ministry, Wheaton, IL 60187-5593. Offers MA. Part-time programs available. *Students:* 36. 22 applicants, 91% accepted, 12 enrolled. In 2006, 27 degrees awarded. *Degree requirements:* For master's, thesis or alternative. *Entrance requirements:* For master's, GRE General Test or MAT. *Application deadline:* For fall admission, 3/1 priority date for domestic students; for spring admission, 11/1 for domestic students. Applications are processed on a rolling basis. Application fee: $30. *Financial support:* Career-related internships or fieldwork, scholarships/grants, and unspecified assistantships available. Financial award application deadline: 3/1. *Unit head:* Dr. Barrett McRay, Coordinator, 630-752-5198. *Application contact:* Julie A. Huebner, Director of Graduate Admissions, 630-752-5195, Fax: 630-752-5935, E-mail: gradadm@wheaton.edu.

Yeshiva University, Azrieli Graduate School of Jewish Education and Administration, New York, NY 10033-4391. Offers MS, Ed D, Specialist. Part-time and evening/weekend programs available. Terminal master's awarded for partial completion of doctoral program. *Degree requirements:* For master's, one foreign language; for doctorate, one foreign language, thesis/dissertation, certifying exams, internship, comprehensive exam; for Specialist, one foreign language, comprehensive exam, certifying exams, internship. *Entrance requirements:* For master's, GRE General Test, BA in Jewish studies or equivalent; for doctorate and Specialist, GRE General Test, master's degree in Jewish education, 2 years of teaching experience. Expenses: Contact institution. *Faculty research:* Social patterns of American and Israeli Jewish population, special education, adult education, technology in education, return to religious values.

Science Education

Acadia University, Faculty of Professional Studies, School of Education, Program in Curriculum Studies, Wolfville, NS B4P 2R6, Canada. Offers cultural and media studies (M Ed); inclusive education (M Ed); learning and technology (M Ed); science, math and technology (M Ed). Evening/weekend programs available. *Faculty:* 12 full-time (5 women). *Students:* 2 full-time (both women), 27 part-time (19 women). In 2006, 25 degrees awarded. *Degree requirements:* For master's, thesis optional. *Entrance requirements:* For master's, B Ed or the equivalent, minimum B average in undergraduate course work, 2 years of teaching experience. Additional exam requirements/recommendations for international students: Required—TOEFL (minimum score 580 paper-based; 237 computer-based). *Application deadline:* For fall admission, 3/15 priority date for domestic and international students. Application fee: $50. Electronic applications accepted. *Financial support:* Teaching assistantships available. Financial award application deadline: 2/1. *Faculty research:* Literacy development, postmodern philosophy and curriculum theory, historiography, philosophy of education, learning and technology. *Application contact:* Sheila Langille, Secretary, 902-585-1229, Fax: 902-585-1071, E-mail: sheila.langille@acadiau.ca.

Agnes Scott College, Secondary Mathematics and Science Program, Decatur, GA 30030-3797. Offers secondary biology (MAT); secondary chemistry (MAT); secondary math (MAT); secondary physics (MAT). *Faculty:* 5 full-time (3 women), 3 part-time/adjunct (2 women). *Students:* 3 full-time (all women). Average age 38. 3 applicants, 100% accepted, 3 enrolled. *Entrance requirements:* For master's, GRE, PRAXIS I, minimum GPA of 3.0, undergraduate major in the discipline. *Application deadline:* For spring admission, 4/1 priority date for domestic and international students. Application fee: $35. *Expenses:* Tuition: Full-time $21,840; part-time $445 per hour. Required fees: $375. *Faculty research:* Science education in urban high schools, inquiry-based science curricula, pedagogy and gender equity in teaching mathematics.

Unit head: Dr. Myrtle H. Lewin, Professor and Chair, 404-471-6201, Fax: 404-471-5152, E-mail: mlewin@agnesscott.edu. *Application contact:* Lisa M. Flowers, Education Faculty Coordinator, 404-471-5168, Fax: 404-471-5152, E-mail: lflowers@agnesscott.edu.

See Close-Up on page 1599.

Alabama State University, School of Graduate Studies, College of Education, Department of Curriculum and Instruction, Program in Secondary Education, Montgomery, AL 36101-0271. Offers biology education (M Ed, Ed S); English/language arts (M Ed); history education (M Ed, Ed S); mathematics education (M Ed); secondary education (Ed S); social studies (Ed S). Part-time programs available. *Students:* 31 full-time (23 women), 123 part-time (81 women); includes 114 minority (111 African Americans, 2 Asian Americans or Pacific Islanders, 1 Hispanic American), 1 international. In 2006, 27 degrees awarded. *Degree requirements:* For master's, comprehensive exam; for Ed S, thesis, comprehensive exam. *Entrance requirements:* For master's, GRE General Test, MAT, graduate writing competency test; for Ed S, graduate writing competency test, GRE, MAT. Additional exam requirements/recommendations for international students: Required—TOEFL (minimum score 500 paper-based; 173 computer-based). *Application deadline:* For fall admission, 7/15 for domestic students; for spring admission, 12/15 for domestic students. Applications are processed on a rolling basis. Application fee: $10. *Expenses:* Tuition, state resident: full-time $1,728; part-time $192 per hour. Tuition, nonresident: full-time $3,456; part-time $334 per hour. *Financial support:* In 2006–07, research assistantships (averaging $9,450 per year).

Albany State University, College of Education, Program in Science Education, Albany, GA 31705-2717. Offers biology (M Ed); chemistry (M Ed). *Accreditation:* NCATE. Part-time programs available. *Degree requirements:* For master's, comprehensive exam. *Entrance requirements:* For master's, GRE General Test, MAT or NTE. Electronic applications accepted.

Alverno College, School of Education, Milwaukee, WI 53234-3922. Offers adaptive education (MA); administrative leadership (MA); adult education and organizational development (MA); adult educational and instructional design (MA); adult educational and instructional technology (MA); instructional leadership (MA); instructional technology for K-12 settings (MA); professional development (MA); reading education (MA); reading education with adaptive education (MA); science education (MA); teaching in alternative schools (MA). *Accreditation:* NCATE. Part-time and evening/weekend programs available. *Faculty:* 12 full-time (11 women), 12 part-time/adjunct (10 women). *Students:* 83 full-time (68 women), 74 part-time (60 women); includes 37 minority (32 African Americans, 2 American Indian/Alaska Native, 3 Hispanic Americans). Average age 35. 61 applicants, 82% accepted, 41 enrolled. In 2006, 46 degrees awarded. *Degree requirements:* For master's, presentation/defense of proposal, conference presentation of inquiry projects. *Entrance requirements:* For master's, bachelor's degree in related field, communication samples from work setting, 3 letters of recommendation. Additional exam requirements/recommendations for international students: Required—TOEFL. *Application deadline:* For fall admission, 8/1 priority date for domestic and international students; for spring admission, 12/15 priority date for domestic and international students. Applications are processed on a rolling basis. Application fee: $20. Electronic applications accepted. *Expenses:* Tuition: Full-time $9,288; part-time $516 per credit. Required fees: $250; $125 per semester. Tuition and fees vary according to program. *Financial support:* In 2006–07, 92 students received support. Federal Work-Study available. Support available to part-time students. Financial award application deadline: 4/15; financial award applicants required to submit FAFSA. *Faculty research:* Student self-assessment, self-reflection, integration of curriculum, identifying needs of students in strategic situations and designing appropriate classroom strategies, implementing guided. *Unit head:* Dr. Mary Diez, Graduate Dean, 414-382-6214, Fax: 414-382-6332, E-mail: mary.diez@alverno.edu. *Application contact:* Sarajane Kennedy, Associate Director, Admissions Graduate Programs, 414-382-6104, Fax: 414-382-6332, E-mail: sarajane.kennedy@alverno.edu.

American University of Puerto Rico, Program in Education, Bayamón, PR 00960-2037. Offers art history (M Ed); elementary education (4-6) (M Ed); elementary education (k-3) (M Ed); general science education (M Ed); physical education (k-12) (M Ed); special education at secondary level (transition) (M Ed). *Entrance requirements:* For master's, EXADEP or GRE or MAT, 2 letters of recommendation, minimum GPA of 2.5.

Andrews University, School of Graduate Studies, College of Arts and Sciences, Department of Biology, Berrien Springs, MI 49104. Offers MAT, MS. *Degree requirements:* For master's, thesis, comprehensive exam. *Entrance requirements:* For master's, GRE Subject Test.

Andrews University, School of Graduate Studies, School of Education, Department of Teaching, Learning, and Curriculum, Berrien Springs, MI 49104. Offers curriculum and instruction (MA, Ed D, PhD, Ed S); elementary education (MAT); reading (MA); secondary education (MAT), including biology, education, English, English as a second language, French, history, physics; special education/learning disabilities (MS); teacher education (MAT). *Entrance requirements:* For master's, GRE Subject Test.

Antioch University New England, Graduate School, Department of Environmental Studies, Program in Environmental Studies, Keene, NH 03431-3552. Offers conservation biology (MS); environmental advocacy (MS); environmental education (MS); teacher certification in biology (7th-12th grade) (MS); teacher certification in general science (5th-9th grade) (MS). *Faculty:* 13 full-time (4 women), 10 part-time/adjunct (4 women). *Students:* 115 full-time (78 women), 37 part-time (25 women); includes 2 minority (1 American Indian/Alaska Native, 1 Hispanic American). Average age 31. 118 applicants, 86% accepted, 69 enrolled. In 2006, 35 degrees awarded. *Degree requirements:* For master's, practicum. *Entrance requirements:* For master's, previous undergraduate course work in biology, chemistry, mathematics (environmental biology). Additional exam requirements/recommendations for international students: Required—TOEFL (minimum score 550 paper-based; 213 computer-based). *Application deadline:* For fall admission, 8/1 for domestic and international students. Applications are processed on a rolling basis. Application fee: $50. Electronic applications accepted. *Expenses: Contact institution.* Tuition and fees vary according to program and student level. *Financial support:* In 2006–07, 114 students received support, including 2 fellowships (averaging $750 per year), 5 research assistantships (averaging $795 per year), 4 teaching assistantships (averaging $598 per year); Federal Work-Study and scholarships/grants also available. Financial award applicants required to submit FAFSA. *Faculty research:* Sustainability, natural resources inventory. *Unit head:* Dr. Jim Jordan, Associate Chair for Academic Affairs, 603-283-2339, Fax: 603-357-0718, E-mail: james_jordan@antiochne.edu. *Application contact:* Leatrice A. Oram, Co-Director of Admissions, 800-490-3310, Fax: 603-357-0718, E-mail: admissions@antiochne.edu.

Arcadia University, Graduate Studies, Department of Education, Glenside, PA 19038-3295. Offers art education (M Ed, MA Ed); biology education (MA Ed); chemistry education (MA Ed); child development (CAS); computer education (M Ed, CAS); computer education 7–12 (MA Ed); early childhood education (M Ed, CAS), including individualized (M Ed), master teacher (M Ed), research in child development (M Ed); educational leadership (M Ed, CAS); educational psychology (CAS); elementary education (M Ed, CAS); English education (MA Ed); environmental education (MA Ed, CAS); history education (MA Ed); language arts (M Ed, CAS); mathematics education (M Ed, MA Ed, CAS); music education (MA Ed); psychology (MA Ed); pupil personnel services (CAS); reading (M Ed, CAS); school library science (M Ed); science education (M Ed, CAS); secondary education (M Ed, CAS); special education (M Ed, Ed D, CAS); theater arts (MA Ed); written communication (MA Ed). *Accreditation:* NASAD. Part-time and evening/weekend programs available. Postbaccalaureate distance learning degree programs offered (minimal on-campus study). *Faculty:* 12 full-time (8 women), 38 part-time/adjunct (26 women). *Students:* 60 full-time (56 women), 419 part-time (324 women); includes 70 minority (57 African Americans, 1 American Indian/Alaska Native, 6 Asian Americans or Pacific Islanders, 6 Hispanic Americans), 1 international. In 2006, 257 master's, 4 doctorates awarded. *Application deadline:* Applications are processed on a rolling basis. Application fee: $35. Electronic applications accepted. *Financial support:* Career-related internships or fieldwork, tuition waivers (partial), and unspecified assistantships available. *Unit head:* Dr. Steven P. Gulkus, Chair, 215-572-2120. *Application contact:* 215-572-2925, Fax: 215-572-2126, E-mail: grad@arcadia.edu.

Arizona State University, Division of Graduate Studies, College of Liberal Arts and Sciences, Department of Biology, Program in Biology Education, Tempe, AZ 85287. Offers MS, PhD. Terminal master's awarded for partial completion of doctoral program. *Degree requirements:* For master's, thesis; for doctorate, thesis/dissertation, oral exam. *Entrance requirements:* For master's and doctorate, GRE General Test, GRE Subject Test. Additional exam requirements/recommendations for international students: Required—TOEFL (minimum score 600 paper-based; 250 computer-based).

Arkansas State University, Graduate School, College of Sciences and Mathematics, Department of Biological Sciences, Jonesboro, State University, AR 72467. Offers biological sciences (MA); biology (MS); biology education (MSE, SCCT); environmental sciences (MS, PhD); molecular biosciences (PhD). Part-time programs available. *Faculty:* 22 full-time (7 women), 3 part-time/adjunct (2 women). *Students:* 37 full-time (17 women), 26 part-time (13 women); includes 4 minority (2 African Americans, 2 American Indian/Alaska Native), 9 international. Average age 27. 68 applicants, 50% accepted, 27 enrolled. In 2006, 14 master's, 4 doctorates awarded. *Degree requirements:* For master's, thesis (for some programs), comprehensive exam; for doctorate, thesis/dissertation, comprehensive exam. *Entrance requirements:* For master's, GRE General Test, appropriate bachelor's degree, letters of reference, official transcript; for doctorate, master's degree, interview, letters of reference, personal statement, official transcript; for SCCT, GRE General Test or MAT, interview, master's degree, letters of reference, official transcript. Additional exam requirements/recommendations for international students: Required—TOEFL (minimum score 213 computer-based). *Application deadline:* Applications are processed on a rolling basis. Application fee: $30 ($40 for international students). Electronic applications accepted. *Expenses:* Tuition, state resident: full-time $3,393; part-time $189 per hour. Tuition, nonresident: full-time $8,577; part-time $477 per hour. Required fees: $752; $39 per hour. $25 per semester. *Financial support:* Fellowships, research assistantships, teaching assistantships, career-related internships or fieldwork, scholarships/grants, and unspecified assistantships available. Financial award application deadline: 7/1; financial award applicants required to submit FAFSA. *Unit head:* Dr. Aldemaro Romero, Chair, 870-972-3082, Fax: 870-972-2638, E-mail: aromero@astate.edu.

Arkansas State University, Graduate School, College of Sciences and Mathematics, Department of Chemistry and Physics, Jonesboro, State University, AR 72467. Offers chemistry (MS); chemistry education (MSE, SCCT). Part-time programs available. *Faculty:* 8 full-time (1 woman). *Students:* 3 full-time (all women), 7 part-time (3 women); includes 4 minority (2 African Americans, 2 Hispanic Americans), 1 international. Average age 26. 3 applicants, 100% accepted, 3 enrolled. *Degree requirements:* For master's, thesis or alternative, comprehensive exam. *Entrance requirements:* For master's, GRE General Test or MAT, appropriate bachelor's degree, official transcript; for SCCT, GRE General Test or MAT, interview, master's degree, official transcript. Additional exam requirements/recommendations for international students: Required—TOEFL (minimum score 213 computer-based). *Application deadline:* Applications are processed on a rolling basis. Application fee: $30 ($40 for international students). Electronic applications accepted. *Expenses:* Tuition, state resident: full-time $3,393; part-time $189 per hour. Tuition, nonresident: full-time $8,577; part-time $477 per hour. Required fees: $752; $39 per hour. $25 per semester. *Financial support:* Teaching assistantships, career-related internships or fieldwork, scholarships/grants, and unspecified assistantships available. Financial award application deadline: 7/1; financial award applicants required to submit FAFSA. *Unit head:* Dr. John Pratte, Chair, 870-972-3086, Fax: 890-972-3089, E-mail: jpratte@astate.edu.

Armstrong Atlantic State University, School of Graduate Studies, Program in Education, Savannah, GA 31419-1997. Offers adult education (M Ed); early childhood education (M Ed); education (M Ed); elementary education (M Ed); middle grades education (M Ed); secondary education (M Ed), including business education, English education, mathematics education, science education, social science education; special education (M Ed), including behavioral disorders, curriculum and instruction, learning disabilities, speech-language pathology. *Accreditation:* NCATE. Part-time and evening/weekend programs available. Postbaccalaureate distance learning degree programs offered (minimal on-campus study). *Faculty:* 11 full-time (9 women), 13 part-time/adjunct (10 women). *Students:* 50 full-time (42 women), 219 part-time (175 women); includes 71 minority (67 African Americans, 3 Asian Americans or Pacific Islanders, 1 Hispanic American), 6 international. Average age 35. In 2006, 151 degrees awarded. *Degree requirements:* For master's, portfolio. *Entrance requirements:* For master's, GRE General Test or MAT, minimum GPA of 2.5, letters of recommendation. Additional exam requirements/recommendations for international students: Required—TOEFL (minimum score 523 paper-based; 193 computer-based). *Application deadline:* For fall admission, 7/1 priority date for domestic and international students; for spring admission, 11/15 priority date for domestic and international students. Applications are processed on a rolling basis. Application fee: $25. Electronic applications accepted. *Expenses:* Tuition, state resident: full-time $2,286; part-time $127 per credit. Tuition, nonresident: full-time $9,144; part-time $508 per credit. One-time fee: $257. *Financial support:* In 2006–07, research assistantships with partial tuition reimbursements (averaging $2,500 per year); career-related internships or fieldwork, Federal Work-Study, scholarships/grants, and unspecified assistantships also available. Support available to part-time students. Financial award applicants required to submit FAFSA. *Unit head:* Dr. Jane McHaney, College of Education Dean, 912-927-5398, Fax: 912-921-7425, E-mail: mchaneja@mail.armstrong.edu.

Asbury College, Graduate Programs, Wilmore, KY 40390-1198. Offers biology: alternative certificate (MA Ed); chemistry: alternative certificate (MA Ed); English (Certificate); English as a second language (MA Ed); ESL (Certificate); French (Certificate); mathematics: alternative certificate (MA Ed); reading / writing (MA Ed); social studies (Certificate); Spanish (Certificate); special education (MA Ed); special education: alternative certificate (MA Ed). *Accreditation:* NCATE. Part-time programs available. *Faculty:* 8 full-time (7 women), 9 part-time/adjunct (4 women). *Students:* Average age 36. 14 applicants, 100% accepted, 10 enrolled. In 2006, 17 degrees awarded. *Median time to degree:* Master's–2.5 years part-time. *Degree requirements:* For master's, action research project, portfolio. *Entrance requirements:* For master's, PRAXIS/NTE or GRE, minimum GPA of 2.75, letters of recommendation. Additional exam requirements/recommendations for international students: Recommended—TOEFL (minimum score 550 paper-based). *Application deadline:* Applications are processed on a rolling basis. Application fee: $25. *Expenses:* Tuition: Part-time $335 per credit hour. *Financial support:* Scholarships/grants and traineeships available. Financial award applicants required to submit FAFSA. *Unit head:* Dr. Bonnie J. Banker, Director, 859-858-3511 Ext. 2221, Fax: 859-858-3921, E-mail: bonnie.banker@asbury.edu. *Application contact:* Melanie S. Kinnell, Graduate Program Assistant and Certification Specialist, 859-858-3511 Ext. 2304, Fax: 859-858-3921, E-mail: graded@asbury.edu.

Auburn University, Graduate School, College of Education, Department of Curriculum and Teaching, Auburn University, AL 36849. Offers business education (M Ed, MS, PhD); early childhood education (M Ed, MS, PhD, Ed S); elementary education (M Ed, MS, PhD, Ed S); foreign languages (M Ed, MS); music education (M Ed, MS, PhD, Ed S); postsecondary education (PhD); reading education (PhD, Ed S); secondary education (M Ed, MS, PhD, Ed S), including English language arts, mathematics, science, social studies. *Accreditation:* NASM (one or more programs are accredited); NCATE. Part-time programs available. *Faculty:* 26 full-time (19 women). *Students:* 51 full-time (36 women), 116 part-time (86 women); includes 24 minority (23 African Americans, 1 Asian American or Pacific Islander). Average age 33. 181 applicants, 56% accepted, 68 enrolled. In 2006, 63 master's, 12 doctorates, 14 other advanced degrees awarded. *Degree requirements:* For master's, thesis (for some programs); for doctorate, thesis/dissertation; for Ed S, field project. *Entrance requirements:* For master's, doctorate, and Ed S, GRE General Test. *Application deadline:* For fall admission, 7/7 for domestic students; for spring admission, 11/24 for domestic students. Applications are

Science Education

Auburn University (continued)

processed on a rolling basis. Application fee: $25 ($50 for international students). Electronic applications accepted. *Expenses:* Tuition, state resident: full-time $5,000. Tuition, nonresident: full-time $15,000. Required fees: $416. Tuition and fees vary according to program. *Financial support:* Fellowships, teaching assistantships, career-related internships or fieldwork and Federal Work-Study available. Support available to part-time students. Financial award application deadline: 3/15. *Faculty research:* Emerging literacy, reading attitudes, music for at-risk youth, portfolio assessment. *Unit head:* Dr. Andrew M. Weaver, Head, 334-844-4434, E-mail: weaveam@mail.auburn.edu. *Application contact:* Dr. Joe Pittman, Interim Dean of the Graduate School, 334-844-4700.

Averett University, Graduate Studies in Education, Danville, VA 24541-3692. Offers art education (M Ed); biology (M Ed); chemistry (M Ed); curriculum and instruction (M Ed); elementary education (M Ed); English (M Ed); health and physical education (M Ed); history and social studies (M Ed); mathematics education (M Ed); physical science (M Ed); reading (M Ed); special education (learning disabilities specialization PK-12) (M Ed). Part-time and evening/weekend programs available. *Faculty:* 10 full-time (4 women), 7 part-time/adjunct (6 women). *Students:* 14 full-time (10 women), 85 part-time (67 women); includes 20 minority (18 African Americans, 2 Asian Americans or Pacific Islanders). Average age 33. 52 applicants, 100% accepted, 40 enrolled. In 2006, 48 degrees awarded. *Degree requirements:* For master's, thesis optional. *Entrance requirements:* For master's, PRAXIS, GRE General Test, MAT or NTE, writing proficiency exam, 3 letters of recommendation, current teacher's licensure or eligibility for licensure, minimum undergraduate GPA of 3.0 in previous 2 years. Additional exam requirements/recommendations for international students: Required—TOEFL (minimum score 600 paper-based; 200 computer-based). *Application deadline:* Applications are processed on a rolling basis. Application fee: $20. *Expenses: Contact institution. Financial support:* In 2006–07, 23 students received support. Federal Work-Study and scholarships/grants available. Financial award application deadline: 4/1; financial award applicants required to submit FAFSA. *Faculty research:* Literary assessment-PreK-6, handwriting instruction and assessment-PreK-6, written language instruction and assessment-PreK-6 and special needs students learning styles, curriculum and instruction processes. *Unit head:* Dr. Lynn H. Wolf, Chair, 434-793-3995, Fax: 434-791-4392, E-mail: lynn.wolf@averett.edu.

Ball State University, Graduate School, College of Sciences and Humanities, Department of Biology, Muncie, IN 47306-1099. Offers biology (MA, MAE, MS); biology education (Ed D). *Faculty:* 22. *Students:* 20 full-time (10 women), 27 part-time (17 women); includes 4 minority (2 Asian Americans or Pacific Islanders, 2 Hispanic Americans), 8 international. Average age 24. 41 applicants, 78% accepted, 15 enrolled. In 2006, 16 master's, 3 doctorates awarded. *Degree requirements:* For doctorate, thesis/dissertation. *Entrance requirements:* For master's, GRE General Test; for doctorate, GRE General Test, minimum graduate GPA of 3.2. Application fee: $25 ($35 for international students). *Financial support:* In 2006–07, 1 research assistantship with full tuition reimbursement (averaging $12,565 per year), 34 teaching assistantships with full tuition reimbursements (averaging $8,750 per year) were awarded; career-related internships or fieldwork also available. Financial award application deadline: 3/1. *Faculty research:* Aquatics and fisheries, tumors, water and air pollution, developmental biology and genetics. *Unit head:* Dr. Kemuel Badger, Chairman, 765-285-8820, Fax: 765-285-8804.

Belmont University, College of Arts and Sciences, School of Education, Nashville, TN 37212-3757. Offers education (MAT); elementary education (M Ed), including early childhood education, elementary education, gifted education, language arts education; English (M Ed); history (M Ed); mathematics (M Ed); middle grade education (M Ed); science (M Ed); secondary education (M Ed), including gifted education; sports administration (MSA); technology (M Ed). *Accreditation:* NCATE. Part-time and evening/weekend programs available. *Faculty:* 9 full-time (7 women), 20 part-time/adjunct (15 women). *Students:* 50 full-time (36 women), 116 part-time (76 women); includes 23 minority (20 African Americans, 1 Asian American or Pacific Islander, 2 Hispanic Americans), 1 international. Average age 30. 55 applicants, 60% accepted, 30 enrolled. In 2006, 82 degrees awarded. *Degree requirements:* For master's, thesis, comprehensive exam. *Entrance requirements:* For master's, MAT or GRE, minimum GPA of 2.75. Additional exam requirements/recommendations for international students: Required—TOEFL. *Application deadline:* For fall admission, 8/1 priority date for domestic students, 5/1 for international students; for spring admission, 12/1 priority date for domestic students, 9/1 for international students. Applications are processed on a rolling basis. Application fee: $50. *Expenses: Contact institution. Financial support:* In 2006–07, 25 students received support; fellowships with partial tuition reimbursements available, institutionally sponsored loans and tuition waivers (partial) available. Financial award application deadline: 4/15; financial award applicants required to submit FAFSA. *Faculty research:* Technology grant, professional development schools. Total annual research expenditures: $6,500. *Unit head:* Dr. Trevor F. Hutchins, Associate Dean, 615-460-6232, Fax: 615-460-6414, E-mail: hutchinst@mail.belmont.edu. *Application contact:* Julie Hullett, Admission/Licensure Officer, 615-460-6879, Fax: 615-460-5556, E-mail: hullettj@email.belmont.edu.

Bemidji State University, School of Graduate Studies, College of Social and Natural Sciences, Field of Science, Bemidji, MN 56601-2699. Offers MS. Part-time programs available. *Faculty:* 3 full-time (0 women), 1 part-time/adjunct (0 women). *Students:* Average age 29. In 2006, 7 degrees awarded. *Entrance requirements:* Additional exam requirements/recommendations for international students: Required—TOEFL. *Application deadline:* For fall admission, 5/1 for domestic students. Applications are processed on a rolling basis. Application fee: $20. Electronic applications accepted. *Expenses:* Tuition, nonresident: part-time $284 per credit. Required fees: $86 per credit. *Financial support:* Career-related internships or fieldwork, Federal Work-Study, scholarships/grants, health care benefits, and unspecified assistantships available. Support available to part-time students. Financial award application deadline: 5/1. *Unit head:* Dr. John Truedson, Coordinator, 218-755-2796, Fax: 218-755-4107, E-mail: jtruedson@bemidjistate.edu.

Benedictine University, Graduate Programs, Program in Science Content and Process, Lisle, IL 60532-0900. Offers MS. *Expenses:* Tuition: Full-time $12,150; part-time $450 per credit hour. *Unit head:* Dr. John Mickus, Director, 630-829-6539.

Bennington College, Graduate Programs, Program in Teaching, Bennington, VT 05201. Offers art education (MAT); early childhood (MAT); elementary education (MAT); English education (MAT); foreign language education (MAT); mathematics education (MAT); music education (MAT); science education (MAT); secondary education (MAT); social science education (MAT). *Faculty:* 4 part-time/adjunct (3 women). *Students:* 11 full-time (7 women), 1 (woman) part-time; includes 2 minority (both Hispanic Americans) Average age 31. 12 applicants, 75% accepted, 3 enrolled. In 2006, 13 degrees awarded. *Degree requirements:* For master's, 1 year teaching practicum, professional portfolio. *Entrance requirements:* For master's, interview. *Application deadline:* For fall admission, 3/1 for domestic students. Application fee: $60. *Expenses: Contact institution.* One-time fee: $75 full-time. Tuition and fees vary according to program. *Financial support:* In 2006–07, 10 students received support, including 4 fellowships (averaging $6,875 per year); scholarships/grants and unspecified assistantships also available. Financial award application deadline: 4/1; financial award applicants required to submit FAFSA. *Unit head:* George Kamberelis, Director of Center for Creative Teaching, 802-440-4863, E-mail: gkamberelis@bennington.edu. *Application contact:* Ken Himmelman, Dean of Admissions, 802-440-4312, Fax: 802-440-4320, E-mail: admissions@bennington.edu.

See Close-Up on page 861.

Bethel College, Program in Education, McKenzie, TN 38201. Offers administration and supervision (MA Ed); biology education K8-12 (MAT); elementary education (MAT); English education K8-12 (MAT); history education K8-12 (MAT); physical education K8-12 (MAT); special education K8-12 (MAT). Part-time and evening/weekend programs available. *Degree requirements:* For master's, thesis (for some programs). *Entrance requirements:* For master's, GRE General Test or MAT, minimum undergraduate GPA of 2.5.

Bloomsburg University of Pennsylvania, School of Graduate Studies, College of Science and Technology, Department of Biological and Allied Health Sciences, Program in Biology Education, Bloomsburg, PA 17815-1301. Offers M Ed. *Accreditation:* NCATE. *Faculty:* 19 full-time (5 women). *Degree requirements:* For master's, thesis or alternative. *Entrance requirements:* For master's, teaching certificate, minimum QPA of 3.0. Additional exam requirements/recommendations for international students: Required—TOEFL (minimum score 550 paper-based; 213 computer-based; 79 iBT). *Application deadline:* Applications are processed on a rolling basis. Application fee: $30. Electronic applications accepted. *Expenses:* Tuition, state resident: full-time $6,048; part-time $336 per credit. Tuition, nonresident: full-time $9,678; part-time $538 per credit. Required fees: $1,415. *Unit head:* Dr. Kristen Brubaker, Coordinator, 570-389-4137, Fax: 570-389-3028, E-mail: kbrubake@bloomu.edu.

Boise State University, Graduate College, College of Arts and Sciences, Department of Geosciences, Boise, ID 83725-0399. Offers earth science (MS); geology (MS, PhD); geophysics (MS, PhD). Part-time programs available. *Faculty:* 14 full-time (0 women), 24 part-time/adjunct (3 women). *Students:* 13 full-time (7 women), 22 part-time (7 women), 4 international. Average age 34. 18 applicants, 83% accepted, 6 enrolled. In 2006, 5 degrees awarded. *Degree requirements:* For master's, thesis. *Entrance requirements:* For master's, GRE General Test, BS in related field, minimum GPA of 3.0; for doctorate, GRE General Test. *Application deadline:* For fall admission, 3/1 priority date for domestic students; for spring admission, 10/1 priority date for domestic students. Applications are processed on a rolling basis. Application fee: $0. Electronic applications accepted. *Financial support:* In 2006–07, 11 fellowships with full and partial tuition reimbursements (averaging $11,333 per year), 6 research assistantships with full tuition reimbursements (averaging $11,153 per year), 10 teaching assistantships (averaging $10,834 per year) were awarded; career-related internships or fieldwork, Federal Work-Study, institutionally sponsored loans, scholarships/grants, tuition waivers (partial), and unspecified assistantships also available. Support available to part-time students. Financial award application deadline: 3/1. *Faculty research:* Seismology, geothermal aquifers, sedimentation, tectonics, seismo-acoustic propagation. *Unit head:* Dr. Clyde J. Northrup, Chairman, 208-426-1631, Fax: 208-426-4061.

Boston College, Graduate School of Arts and Sciences, Department of Chemistry, Chestnut Hill, MA 02467-3800. Offers biochemistry (PhD); inorganic chemistry (PhD); organic chemistry (PhD); physical chemistry (PhD); science education (MST). MST is offered through the School of Education for secondary school science teaching. Part-time programs available. *Students:* 119 full-time (51 women), 2 part-time (1 woman); includes 13 minority (2 African Americans, 8 Asian Americans or Pacific Islanders, 3 Hispanic Americans), 39 international. 208 applicants, 41359% accepted, 17 enrolled. In 2006, 4 master's, 5 doctorates awarded. *Degree requirements:* For doctorate, thesis/dissertation, qualifying exam. *Entrance requirements:* For doctorate, GRE General Test, GRE Subject Test. Additional exam requirements/recommendations for international students: Required—TOEFL (minimum score 550 paper-based; 213 computer-based). *Application deadline:* For fall admission, 1/2 for domestic students. Application fee: $70. Electronic applications accepted. *Financial support:* Fellowships with full tuition reimbursements, research assistantships with full tuition reimbursements, teaching assistantships with full tuition reimbursements, Federal Work-Study available. Support available to part-time students. Financial award application deadline: 3/1; financial award applicants required to submit FAFSA. *Unit head:* Dr. Amir Hoveyda, Chairperson, 617-552-1735, E-mail: amir.hoveyda@bc.edu. *Application contact:* Dr. Marc Snapper, Graduate Program Director, 617-552-8096, Fax: 617-552-0833, E-mail: marc.snapper@bc.edu.

Boston College, Lynch Graduate School of Education, Department of Teacher Education/Special Education and Curriculum and Instruction, Program in Secondary Education, Chestnut Hill, MA 02467-3800. Offers biology (MST); chemistry (MST); English (MAT); French (MAT); geology (MST); history (MAT); Latin and classical humanities (MAT); mathematics (MST); physics (MST); secondary teaching (M Ed), including biology, chemistry, English, French, geology, history, Latin and classical humanities, mathematics, physics, Spanish; Spanish (MAT). *Students:* 70 full-time (46 women), 28 part-time (15 women); includes 8 minority (4 African Americans, 1 American Indian/Alaska Native, 3 Asian Americans or Pacific Islanders), 2 international. 217 applicants, 72% accepted, 64 enrolled. In 2006, 48 degrees awarded. *Degree requirements:* For master's, comprehensive exam. *Entrance requirements:* For master's, GRE General Test or MAT. Additional exam requirements/recommendations for international students: Required—TOEFL. *Application deadline:* For fall admission, 1/1 priority date for domestic students. Application fee: $60. *Financial support:* Fellowships with full and partial tuition reimbursements, research assistantships with full and partial tuition reimbursements, teaching assistantships with full and partial tuition reimbursements, career-related internships or fieldwork, Federal Work-Study, scholarships/grants, traineeships, tuition waivers (full and partial), and unspecified assistantships available. Support available to part-time students. Financial award applicants required to submit FAFSA. *Faculty research:* Curriculum theory and practice, teacher preparation, learning styles, teacher research. *Application contact:* Timothy P. Blackman, Director, Graduate Admission and Financial Aid, 617-552-4214, Fax: 617-552-0398, E-mail: timothy.blackman.1@bc.edu.

Boston University, School of Education, Department of Curriculum and Teaching, Program in Science Education, Boston, MA 02215. Offers Ed M, MAT, Ed D, CAGS. *Students:* 10 full-time (all women), 3 part-time (all women); includes 1 minority (Asian American or Pacific Islander), 1 international. Average age 26. 34 applicants, 97% accepted. In 2006, 13 degrees awarded. *Degree requirements:* For master's, thesis optional; for doctorate, thesis/dissertation, comprehensive exam. *Entrance requirements:* For master's, doctorate, and CAGS, GRE General Test or MAT. Additional exam requirements/recommendations for international students: Required—TOEFL. *Application deadline:* For fall admission, 2/15 priority date for domestic students; for winter admission, 10/1 priority date for domestic students. Applications are processed on a rolling basis. Application fee: $70. Electronic applications accepted. *Expenses:* Tuition: Full-time $33,330; part-time $1,042 per credit. Required fees: $462; $40. *Financial support:* Application deadline: 2/15. *Faculty research:* Teacher training, leadership. *Unit head:* Dr. Douglas Zook, Head, 617-353-2030, E-mail: dzook@bu.edu. *Application contact:* 617-353-4237, Fax: 617-353-8937, E-mail: sedgrad@bu.edu.

Bowling Green State University, Graduate College, College of Arts and Sciences, Department of Physics and Astronomy, Bowling Green, OH 43403. Offers geophysics (MS); physics (MAT, MS). *Faculty:* 8 full-time (0 women). *Students:* 11 full-time (1 woman), 12 part-time (7 women); includes 1 minority (Asian American or Pacific Islander), 6 international. Average age 33. 21 applicants, 57% accepted, 5 enrolled. In 2006, 7 degrees awarded. *Degree requirements:* For master's, thesis or alternative. *Entrance requirements:* For master's, GRE General Test. Additional exam requirements/recommendations for international students: Required—TOEFL. *Application deadline:* For fall admission, 2/15 priority date for domestic students. Application fee: $30. Electronic applications accepted. *Expenses:* Tuition, state resident: part-time $535 per hour. Tuition, nonresident: part-time $884 per hour. *Financial support:* In 2006–07, 10 teaching assistantships with full tuition reimbursements (averaging $10,380 per year) were awarded; research assistantships with full tuition reimbursements, career-related internships or fieldwork, institutionally sponsored loans, and unspecified assistantships also available. Financial award applicants required to submit FAFSA. *Faculty research:* Computational physics, solid-state physics, materials science, theoretical physics. *Unit head:* Dr. John Laird, Chair, 419-372-7244. *Application contact:* Dr. Lewis Fulcher, Graduate Coordinator, 419-372-2635.

Bridgewater State College, School of Graduate Studies, School of Arts and Sciences, Department of Biological Sciences, Bridgewater, MA 02325-0001. Offers MAT. Part-time and evening/weekend programs available. *Entrance requirements:* For master's, GRE General Test. *Application deadline:* For fall admission, 3/1 priority date for domestic students; for spring admission, 10/1 priority date for domestic students. Application fee: $50. *Financial support:*

Career-related internships or fieldwork, health care benefits, and unspecified assistantships available. Support available to part-time students.

Bridgewater State College, School of Graduate Studies, School of Arts and Sciences, Department of Physics, Bridgewater, MA 02325-0001. Offers MAT. *Accreditation:* NCATE. Part-time and evening/weekend programs available. *Entrance requirements:* For master's, GRE General Test. *Application deadline:* For fall admission, 3/1 priority date for domestic students; for spring admission, 10/1 priority date for domestic students. Application fee: $50. *Financial support:* Career-related internships or fieldwork, health care benefits, and unspecified assistantships available. Support available to part-time students.

Bridgewater State College, School of Graduate Studies, School of Arts and Sciences, Program in Physical Sciences, Bridgewater, MA 02325-0001. Offers MAT. *Accreditation:* NCATE. Part-time and evening/weekend programs available. *Entrance requirements:* For master's, GRE General Test. *Application deadline:* For fall admission, 3/1 priority date for domestic students; for spring admission, 10/1 priority date for domestic students. Application fee: $50. *Financial support:* Career-related internships or fieldwork, health care benefits, and unspecified assistantships available. Support available to part-time students.

Brigham Young University, Graduate Studies, College of Life Sciences, Department of Integrative Biology, Provo, UT 84602-1001. Offers biological science education (MS); integrative biology (MS, PhD). *Faculty:* 23 full-time (3 women). *Students:* 33 full-time (16 women); includes 2 minority (1 Asian American or Pacific Islander, 1 Hispanic American). Average age 27. 24 applicants, 58% accepted, 14 enrolled. In 2006, 1 master's, 1 doctorate awarded. *Median time to degree:* Of those who began their doctoral program in fall 1998, 100% received their degree in 8 years or less. *Degree requirements:* For master's and doctorate, thesis/dissertation, comprehensive exam, registration. *Entrance requirements:* For master's and doctorate, GRE General Test, minimum GPA of 3.0 for last 60 credit hours of course work. Additional exam requirements/recommendations for international students: Required—TOEFL (minimum score 550 paper-based; 213 computer-based; 85 iBT). *Application deadline:* For fall admission, 1/31 for domestic and international students. Application fee: $50. Electronic applications accepted. *Financial support:* In 2006–07, 33 students received support, including 1 fellowship with full and partial tuition reimbursement available (averaging $5,500 per year), 22 research assistantships with full and partial tuition reimbursements available (averaging $12,000 per year), 33 teaching assistantships with full and partial tuition reimbursements available (averaging $12,000 per year); career-related internships or fieldwork, institutionally sponsored loans, scholarships/grants, tuition waivers (full and partial), and unspecified assistantships also available. Financial award application deadline: 3/1. *Faculty research:* Systematics, bioinformatics, conservation. Total annual research expenditures: $1.9 million. *Unit head:* Dr. Keith A. Crandall, Chair, 801-422-3495, Fax: 801-422-0090, E-mail: keith_crandall@byu.edu. *Application contact:* Carolyn W. Hansen, Graduate Secretary, 801-422-2010, Fax: 801-422-0090, E-mail: carolyn_hansen@byu.edu.

Brooklyn College of the City University of New York, Division of Graduate Studies, School of Education, Program in Adolescence Education and Special Subjects, Brooklyn, NY 11210-2889. Offers art teacher (MA); biology teacher (MA); chemistry teacher (MA); English teacher (MA); French teacher (MA); health and nutrition sciences: health teacher (MS Ed); mathematics teacher (MA); music education (CAS); music teacher (MA); physical education teacher (MS Ed); physics teacher (MA); social studies teacher (MA); Spanish teacher (MA). Part-time and evening/weekend programs available. *Students:* 30 full-time (22 women), 450 part-time (257 women); includes 167 minority (101 African Americans, 21 Asian Americans or Pacific Islanders, 45 Hispanic Americans), 21 international. 277 applicants, 84% accepted, 113 enrolled. In 2006, 172 master's, 6 other advanced degrees awarded. *Degree requirements:* For master's, comprehensive exam (for some programs). *Entrance requirements:* For master's, LAST, previous course work in education, resumé, 2 letters of recommendation, essay. Additional exam requirements/recommendations for international students: Required—TOEFL. *Application deadline:* For fall admission, 3/1 priority date for domestic students, 2/1 priority date for international students; for spring admission, 11/1 priority date for domestic students, 10/1 priority date for international students. Applications are processed on a rolling basis. Application fee: $125. Electronic applications accepted. *Expenses:* Tuition, state resident: full-time $6,400; part-time $270 per credit. Tuition, nonresident: full-time $12,000; part-time $500 per credit. Required fees: $118 per semester. *Financial support:* Career-related internships or fieldwork, Federal Work-Study, institutionally sponsored loans, and scholarships/grants available. Support available to part-time students. Financial award application deadline: 5/1; financial award applicants required to submit FAFSA. *Faculty research:* Interdisciplinary education, semiotics, discourse analysis, autobiography, teacher identity. *Unit head:* Prof. Stephen Phillips, Program Facilitator, 718-951-5214, E-mail: phillips@brooklyn.cuny.edu. *Application contact:* Karen Alleyne-Pierre, Director of Admissions Services and Enrollment Communications, 718-951-5902, Fax: 718-951-4506, E-mail: grads@brooklyn.cuny.edu.

Brooklyn College of the City University of New York, Division of Graduate Studies, School of Education, Program in Childhood Education, Brooklyn, NY 11210-2889. Offers bilingual education (MS Ed); liberal arts (MS Ed); mathematics (MS Ed); science/environmental education (MS Ed). Part-time and evening/weekend programs available. *Students:* 10 full-time (9 women), 275 part-time (233 women); includes 130 minority (84 African Americans, 12 Asian Americans or Pacific Islanders, 34 Hispanic Americans), 11 international. 154 applicants, 81% accepted, 80 enrolled. In 2006, 214 degrees awarded. *Entrance requirements:* For master's, LAST, interview, previous course work in education, writing sample, resumé, 2 letters of recommendation. Additional exam requirements/recommendations for international students: Required—TOEFL. *Application deadline:* For fall admission, 3/1 priority date for domestic students, 2/1 priority date for international students; for spring admission, 11/1 priority date for domestic students, 10/1 priority date for international students. Applications are processed on a rolling basis. Application fee: $125. Electronic applications accepted. *Expenses:* Tuition, state resident: full-time $6,400; part-time $270 per credit. Tuition, nonresident: full-time $12,000; part-time $500 per credit. Required fees: $118 per semester. *Financial support:* Career-related internships or fieldwork, Federal Work-Study, institutionally sponsored loans, and scholarships/grants available. Support available to part-time students. Financial award application deadline: 5/1; financial award applicants required to submit FAFSA. *Faculty research:* Emotional intelligence, multiculturalism, arts immersion, the Holocaust. *Unit head:* Dr. Sharon O'Connor-Petruso, Program Head, 718-951-5214. *Application contact:* Karen Alleyne-Pierre, Director of Admissions Services and Enrollment Communications, 718-951-5902, Fax: 718-951-4506, E-mail: grads@brooklyn.cuny.edu.

Brooklyn College of the City University of New York, Division of Graduate Studies, School of Education, Program in Middle Childhood Education (Science), Brooklyn, NY 11210-2889. Offers MS Ed. Part-time and evening/weekend programs available. *Students:* 19 applicants, 100% accepted, 11 enrolled. In 2006, 10 degrees awarded. *Entrance requirements:* For master's, LAST, interview, previous course work in education and mathematics, resumé, 2 letters of recommendation, essay. Additional exam requirements/recommendations for international students: Required—TOEFL. *Application deadline:* For fall admission, 3/1 priority date for domestic students, 2/1 priority date for international students; for spring admission, 11/1 priority date for domestic students, 10/1 priority date for international students. Applications are processed on a rolling basis. Application fee: $125. Electronic applications accepted. *Expenses:* Tuition, state resident: full-time $6,400; part-time $270 per credit. Tuition, nonresident: full-time $12,000; part-time $500 per credit. Required fees: $118 per semester. *Financial support:* Federal Work-Study, institutionally sponsored loans, and scholarships/grants available. Support available to part-time students. Financial award application deadline: 5/1; financial award applicants required to submit FAFSA. *Faculty research:* Geometric thinking, mastery of basic facts, problem-solving strategies, history of mathematics. *Unit head:* Dr. Eleanor Miele, Program Head, 718-951-5214, E-mail: emiele@brooklyn.cuny.edu. *Application contact:* Karen Alleyne-Pierre, Director of Admissions Services and Enrollment Communications, 718-951-5902, Fax: 718-951-4506, E-mail: grads@brooklyn.cuny.edu.

Brown University, Graduate School, Department of Education, Providence, RI 02912. Offers elementary education 1-6 (MAT); secondary biology (MAT); secondary English (MAT); secondary social studies/history (MAT). *Faculty:* 4 full-time (2 women), 7 part-time/adjunct (all women). *Students:* 28 full-time (23 women); includes 5 minority (2 African Americans, 1 Asian American or Pacific Islander, 2 Hispanic Americans). Average age 25. 89 applicants, 61% accepted, 28 enrolled. In 2006, 35 degrees awarded. *Degree requirements:* For master's, student teaching, portfolio. *Entrance requirements:* For master's, GRE General Test (secondary only), PRAXIS II (elementary), letters of recommendation, interview. *Application deadline:* For winter admission, 1/3 for domestic students. Application fee: $70. Electronic applications accepted. *Financial support:* In 2006–07, 23 students received support, including 2 fellowships (averaging $7,000 per year); Federal Work-Study, institutionally sponsored loans, scholarships/grants, tuition waivers (partial), and proctorships also available. Financial award application deadline: 2/1; financial award applicants required to submit FAFSA. *Faculty research:* Literacy, performance-based assessment, teaching English as a foreign language. *Unit head:* Lawrence Wakeford, Chairman, 401-863-3428, Fax: 401-863-1276, E-mail: lawrence_wakeford@brown.edu. *Application contact:* Carin Algava, Assistant Director, 401-863-3364, Fax: 401-863-1276, E-mail: carin_algava@brown.edu.

Buffalo State College, State University of New York, Graduate Studies and Research, Faculty of Natural and Social Sciences, Department of Biology, Buffalo, NY 14222-1095. Offers biology (MA); secondary education (MS Ed), including biology. Evening/weekend programs available. *Degree requirements:* For master's, thesis (for some programs), project. *Entrance requirements:* For master's, minimum GPA of 2.75. Additional exam requirements/recommendations for international students: Required—TOEFL (minimum score 550 paper-based; 213 computer-based).

Buffalo State College, State University of New York, Graduate Studies and Research, Faculty of Natural and Social Sciences, Department of Chemistry, Buffalo, NY 14222-1095. Offers chemistry (MA); secondary education (MS Ed), including chemistry. Part-time and evening/weekend programs available. *Degree requirements:* For master's, thesis (for some programs), project. *Entrance requirements:* For master's, minimum GPA of 2.6, New York teaching certificate (MS Ed). Additional exam requirements/recommendations for international students: Required—TOEFL (minimum score 550 paper-based; 213 computer-based).

Buffalo State College, State University of New York, Graduate Studies and Research, Faculty of Natural and Social Sciences, Department of Earth Science and Science Education, Buffalo, NY 14222-1095. Offers secondary education (MS Ed), including geoscience, science. *Accreditation:* NCATE. Part-time and evening/weekend programs available. *Degree requirements:* For master's, thesis or alternative, project. *Entrance requirements:* For master's, 36 undergraduate hours in mathematics and science. Additional exam requirements/recommendations for international students: Required—TOEFL (minimum score 550 paper-based; 213 computer-based).

Buffalo State College, State University of New York, Graduate Studies and Research, Faculty of Natural and Social Sciences, Department of Physics, Buffalo, NY 14222-1095. Offers secondary education physics (MS Ed). *Degree requirements:* For master's, project. *Entrance requirements:* For master's, minimum GPA of 2.5, New York State teaching certification. Additional exam requirements/recommendations for international students: Required—TOEFL (minimum score 550 paper-based; 213 computer-based).

California State University, Chico, Graduate School, Interdisciplinary Programs, Chico, CA 95929-0234. Offers interdisciplinary studies (MA, MS); science teaching (MS); simulation science (MS). Part-time programs available. *Students:* 17 full-time (13 women), 13 part-time (6 women); includes 9 minority (2 American Indian/Alaska Native, 1 Asian American or Pacific Islander, 6 Hispanic Americans), 3 international. Average age 35. 16 applicants, 100% accepted, 7 enrolled. In 2006, 23 degrees awarded. *Degree requirements:* For master's, thesis or alternative, oral exam. *Entrance requirements:* For master's, GRE General Test or MAT, 3 letters of recommendation, purposed program plan. Additional exam requirements/recommendations for international students: Required—TOEFL (minimum score 550 paper-based; 213 computer-based). *Application deadline:* For fall admission, 3/1 for domestic and international students; for spring admission, 9/15 for domestic and international students. Applications are processed on a rolling basis. Application fee: $55. *Financial support:* Fellowships, Federal Work-Study available. Support available to part-time students. *Unit head:* Dr. Jane Rysberg, Graduate Coordinator, 530-895-5178.

California State University, Fullerton, Graduate Studies, College of Natural Science and Mathematics, Program in Science Education, Fullerton, CA 92834-9480. Offers teaching science (MAT). Part-time programs available. *Students:* Average age 30. 1 applicant, 100% accepted, 1 enrolled. In 2006, 3 degrees awarded. *Degree requirements:* For master's, project or thesis. *Entrance requirements:* For master's, diagnostic exam, minimum GPA of 2.5 in last 60 units of course work, teaching credential, bachelor's degree in science. Application fee: $55. *Expenses:* Tuition, nonresident: part-time $339 per unit. Required fees: $1,155 per semester. *Financial support:* Federal Work-Study, institutionally sponsored loans, and scholarships/grants available. Support available to part-time students. Financial award application deadline: 3/1. *Faculty research:* Earth and space science education. *Unit head:* Dr. Richard Lodyga, Director, 714-278-3942.

California State University, Long Beach, Graduate Studies, College of Natural Sciences and Mathematics, Department of Mathematics and Statistics, Long Beach, CA 90840. Offers mathematics (MS); mathematics and science education (MS). Part-time programs available. *Faculty:* 43 full-time (9 women), 49 part-time/adjunct (21 women). *Students:* 47 full-time (23 women), 73 part-time (35 women); includes 56 minority (1 African American, 35 Asian Americans or Pacific Islanders, 20 Hispanic Americans), 13 international. Average age 33. 95 applicants, 62% accepted, 44 enrolled. In 2006, 15 degrees awarded. *Degree requirements:* For master's, comprehensive exam or thesis. *Application deadline:* For fall admission, 7/1 for domestic students; for spring admission, 12/1 for domestic students. Applications are processed on a rolling basis. Application fee: $55. Electronic applications accepted. *Financial support:* Teaching assistantships, Federal Work-Study, institutionally sponsored loans, scholarships/grants, and traineeships available. Financial award application deadline: 3/2. *Faculty research:* Algebra, functional analysis, partial differential equations, operator theory, numerical analysis. *Unit head:* Dr. Robert A Mena, Chair, 562-985-4721, Fax: 562-985-8227, E-mail: rmena@csulb.edu. *Application contact:* Dr. Ngo Viet, Graduate Coordinator, 562-985-5610, Fax: 562-985-8227, E-mail: viet@csulb.edu.

California State University, San Bernardino, Graduate Studies, College of Education, Program in Teaching of Science, San Bernardino, CA 92407-2397. Offers MA. *Accreditation:* NCATE. *Students:* 9 full-time (3 women), 3 part-time (2 women); includes 5 minority (1 African American, 1 American Indian/Alaska Native, 3 Hispanic Americans). Average age 29. 8 applicants, 75% accepted, 2 enrolled. In 2006, 3 degrees awarded. Application fee: $55. *Unit head:* Dr. Robert Stein, Coordinator, 909-537-5377, Fax: 909-537-7119, E-mail: bstein@csusb.edu.

Carthage College, Division of Teacher Education, Kenosha, WI 53140. Offers classroom guidance and counseling (M Ed); creative arts (M Ed); gifted and talented children (M Ed); language arts (M Ed); modern language (M Ed); natural sciences (M Ed); reading (M Ed, Certificate); social sciences (M Ed); teacher leadership (M Ed). Part-time and evening/weekend programs available. *Degree requirements:* For master's, thesis optional. *Entrance requirements:* For master's, MAT, minimum B average, letters of reference.

Central Michigan University, College of Graduate Studies, College of Science and Technology, Department of Chemistry, Mount Pleasant, MI 48859. Offers chemistry (MS); teaching chemistry (MA). *Degree requirements:* For master's, thesis or alternative. *Faculty research:* Biochemistry, analytical and organic-inorganic chemistry, polymer chemistry.

Charleston Southern University, Programs in Education, Charleston, SC 29423-8087. Offers administration and supervision (M Ed), including elementary, secondary; elementary education

Science Education

Charleston Southern University (continued)
(M Ed); English (MAT); science (MAT); secondary education (M Ed); social studies (MAT). *Accreditation:* NCATE. Part-time and evening/weekend programs available. *Degree requirements:* For master's, thesis optional. *Entrance requirements:* For master's, GRE or MAT. Expenses: Contact institution. *Faculty research:* Economic education, multicultural education, restructuring teacher education, participation in mathematics and science by minorities and women, at-risk children.

Chatham University, Program in Education, Pittsburgh, PA 15232-2826. Offers early childhood education (MAT); elementary education (MAT); English—secondary (MAT); environmental education (K-12) (MAT); secondary art (MAT); secondary biology education (MAT); secondary chemistry education (MAT); secondary English education (MAT); secondary math education (MAT); secondary physics education (MAT); secondary social studies education (MAT); special education (MAT). *Students:* 60 full-time (43 women), 23 part-time (22 women). Average age 29. 48 applicants, 77% accepted, 32 enrolled. In 2006, 59 degrees awarded. *Degree requirements:* For master's, thesis, teaching experience. *Entrance requirements:* For master's, PRAXIS I, minimum GPA of 3.0, sample of written work, recommendation letters. Additional exam requirements/recommendations for international students: Required—TOEFL (minimum score 600 paper-based; 250 computer-based; 100 iBT); Recommended—IELTS (minimum score 7), TWE (minimum score 5). *Application deadline:* For fall admission, 5/1 priority date for domestic and international students; for winter admission, 10/1 priority date for domestic and international students. Applications are processed on a rolling basis. Application fee: $45. Electronic applications accepted. *Financial support:* Career-related internships or fieldwork available. Financial award applicants required to submit FAFSA. *Faculty research:* Gifted education, environmental education, technology in education, writing as learning, class size and achievement. *Unit head:* Dr. Wendy Weiner, Director, 412-365-1146, Fax: 412-365-1505, E-mail: wweiner@chatham.edu. *Application contact:* 412-365-1825, Fax: 412-365-1609, E-mail: admissions@chatham.edu.

Christopher Newport University, Graduate Studies, Department of Teacher Preparation, Newport News, VA 23606-2998. Offers art (PK-12) (MAT); biology (6-12) (MAT); computer science (6-12) (MAT); elementary (PK-6) (MAT); English (6-12) (MAT); French (PK-12) (MAT); history (6-12) (MAT); history and social science (MAT); mathematics (6-12) (MAT); music (PK-12) (MAT), including choral, instrumental; physics (6-12) (MAT); Spanish (PK-12) (MAT); theater (PK-12) (MAT). Part-time and evening/weekend programs available. *Degree requirements:* For master's, thesis or alternative, comprehensive exam. *Entrance requirements:* For master's, PRAXIS I, minimum GPA of 3.0. Electronic applications accepted. *Faculty research:* Early literacy development, instructional innovations, professional teaching standards, multicultural issues, aesthetic education.

City College of the City University of New York, Graduate School, School of Education, Department of Secondary Education, Program in Science Education, New York, NY 10031-9198. Offers MA. *Accreditation:* NCATE. *Students:* 287. 89 applicants, 100% accepted, 71 enrolled. *Entrance requirements:* For master's, Liberal Arts and Sciences Test (LAST), Content Specialty Test (CST). Additional exam requirements/recommendations for international students: Required—TOEFL. *Application deadline:* For fall admission, 3/15 for domestic students; for spring admission, 10/15 for domestic students. Application fee: $125. *Unit head:* Prof. R. Steinberg, Head, 212-650-5617, E-mail: steinberg@ccny.cuny.edu. *Application contact:* Stacia Pusey, Graduate Admissions Adviser-Education, 212-650-5345, E-mail: spusey@ccny.cuny.edu.

Clarion University of Pennsylvania, Office of Research and Graduate Studies, College of Education and Human Services, Department of Education, Program in Education, Clarion, PA 16214. Offers curriculum and instruction (M Ed); early childhood (M Ed); English (M Ed); history (M Ed); literacy (M Ed); science (M Ed); technology (M Ed). *Accreditation:* NCATE. Part-time programs available. *Faculty:* 18 full-time (13 women). *Students:* 11 full-time (4 women), 54 part-time (37 women); includes 4 minority (3 African Americans, 1 Asian American or Pacific Islander). 50 applicants, 90% accepted. In 2006, 7 degrees awarded. *Degree requirements:* For master's, thesis or alternative, comprehensive exam. *Entrance requirements:* For master's, minimum QPA of 3.0, teacher certification. Additional exam requirements/recommendations for international students: Required—TOEFL (minimum score 550 paper-based; 213 computer-based; 80 iBT). *Application deadline:* For fall admission, 8/1 priority date for domestic students, 4/15 priority date for international students; for spring admission, 12/1 priority date for domestic students, 9/15 priority date for international students. Applications are processed on a rolling basis. Application fee: $30. Electronic applications accepted. *Expenses:* Tuition, state resident: part-time $336 per credit. Tuition, nonresident: part-time $538 per credit. *Financial support:* In 2006–07, 2 research assistantships with full tuition reimbursements (averaging $4,002 per year) were awarded. Support available to part-time students. Financial award application deadline: 3/1. *Application contact:* Dr. Brian Maguire, Coordinator, 814-393-2058, Fax: 814-393-2558, E-mail: bmaguire@clarion.edu.

Clarion University of Pennsylvania, Office of Research and Graduate Studies, College of Education and Human Services, Department of Education, Program in Science Education, Clarion, PA 16214. Offers M Ed. *Faculty:* 4 full-time (3 women). *Students:* 7 full-time (2 women), 14 part-time (7 women). 5 applicants, 100% accepted. In 2006, 16 degrees awarded. *Degree requirements:* For master's, thesis or alternative, comprehensive exam. *Entrance requirements:* For master's, minimum QPA of 3.0. Additional exam requirements/recommendations for international students: Required—TOEFL (minimum score 550 paper-based; 213 computer-based; 80 iBT). *Application deadline:* For fall admission, 8/1 priority date for domestic students, 4/15 priority date for international students; for spring admission, 12/1 priority date for domestic students, 9/15 priority date for international students. Applications are processed on a rolling basis. Application fee: $30. Electronic applications accepted. *Expenses:* Tuition, state resident: part-time $336 per credit. Tuition, nonresident: part-time $538 per credit. *Financial support:* In 2006–07, 3 research assistantships with full tuition reimbursements (averaging $4,002 per year) were awarded. Financial award application deadline: 3/1. *Application contact:* Dr. Bruce Smith, Graduate Coordinator, 814-393-2646, Fax: 814-393-2731, E-mail: bsmith@clarion.edu.

Clark Atlanta University, School of Arts and Sciences, Department of Chemistry, Atlanta, GA 30314. Offers inorganic chemistry (MS, PhD); organic chemistry (MS, PhD); physical chemistry (MS, PhD); science education (DA). Part-time programs available. *Degree requirements:* For master's, one foreign language, thesis, comprehensive exam; for doctorate, 2 foreign languages, thesis/dissertation, cumulative exam. *Entrance requirements:* For master's, GRE General Test, minimum GPA of 2.5; for doctorate, GRE General Test, GRE Subject Test, minimum graduate GPA of 3.0.

Clemson University, Graduate School, College of Health, Education, and Human Development, School of Education, Program in Secondary Education, Clemson, SC 29634. Offers English (M Ed); mathematics (M Ed); natural sciences (M Ed). *Accreditation:* NCATE. *Students:* 5 full-time (2 women), 9 part-time (8 women); includes 1 minority (American Indian/Alaska Native). 11 applicants, 45% accepted, 2 enrolled. In 2006, 9 degrees awarded. *Entrance requirements:* For master's, teaching certificate. Additional exam requirements/recommendations for international students: Required—TOEFL. *Application deadline:* For fall admission, 6/1 for domestic students. Application fee: $50. *Expenses:* Tuition, state resident: full-time $8,812; part-time $450 per hour. Tuition, nonresident: full-time $18,036; part-time $760 per hour. Required fees: $474; $5 per term. *Financial support:* Application deadline: 6/1; *Unit head:* Dr. William Fisk, Graduate Coordinator, 864-656-5119, Fax: 864-656-1322, E-mail: bill252@clemson.edu.

See Close-Up on page 1273.

Cleveland State University, College of Graduate Studies, College of Education and Human Services, Department of Teacher Education, Cleveland, OH 44115. Offers art education (M Ed); early childhood education (M Ed); foreign language education (M Ed); mathematics and science education (M Ed); middle childhood education (M Ed); special education (M Ed), including mild/moderate disabilities, moderate/intensive disabilities; teaching English to speakers of other languages (M Ed). Part-time and evening/weekend programs available. *Faculty:* 14 full-time (8 women), 5 part-time/adjunct (4 women). *Students:* 120 full-time (96 women), 592 part-time (485 women); includes 145 minority (123 African Americans, 7 Asian Americans or Pacific Islanders, 15 Hispanic Americans), 7 international. Average age 34. 526 applicants, 41% accepted, 144 enrolled. In 2006, 324 degrees awarded. *Degree requirements:* For master's, thesis or alternative, comprehensive exam (for some programs). *Entrance requirements:* For master's, GRE General Test or MAT, minimum GPA of 2.75. Additional exam requirements/recommendations for international students: Required—TOEFL (minimum score 525 paper-based; 197 computer-based), IELTS (minimum score 6). *Application deadline:* For fall admission, 7/15 priority date for domestic students. Applications are processed on a rolling basis. Application fee: $30. *Financial support:* In 2006–07, 12 research assistantships with full tuition reimbursements (averaging $3,480 per year) were awarded; tuition waivers (partial) and unspecified assistantships also available. *Faculty research:* Early literacy, professional development in reading, reading recovery, dual language, induction programs. Total annual research expenditures: $6.2 million. *Unit head:* Dr. Clifford T. Bennett, Chairperson, 216-523-7105, Fax: 216-687-5379, E-mail: c.t.bennett@csuohio.edu.

College of Charleston, Graduate School, School of Education, Program in Science and Mathematics for Teachers, Charleston, SC 29424-0001. Offers M Ed. *Accreditation:* NCATE. Electronic applications accepted.

College of the Humanities and Sciences, Harrison Middleton University, Graduate Program, Tempe, AZ 85282. Offers education (MA, Ed D); humanities (MA); imaginative literature (MA); jurisprudence (MA); natural science (MA); philosophy and religion (MA); social science (MA). Part-time and evening/weekend programs available. Postbaccalaureate distance learning degree programs offered (no on-campus study). *Faculty:* 17 full-time (7 women), 5 part-time/adjunct (2 women). *Students:* 38 full-time (9 women). In 2006, 10 degrees awarded. Application fee: $50. *Expenses:* Tuition: Part-time $275 per credit hour. *Application contact:* Kathleen Mirabile, Vice-President, Provost, 877-248-6724, Fax: 800-762-1622, E-mail: kmirabile@chumsci.edu.

The College of William and Mary, School of Education, Program in Curriculum and Instruction, Williamsburg, VA 23187-8795. Offers elementary education (MA Ed); gifted education (MA Ed); reading education (MA Ed); secondary education (MA Ed), including English education, mathematics education, modern foreign languages education, science education, social studies education; special education (MA Ed), including emotionally disturbed, learning disabled, mental retardation, resource collaborating teaching. *Accreditation:* NCATE. Part-time programs available. *Faculty:* 15 full-time (6 women), 13 part-time/adjunct (10 women). *Students:* 51 full-time (39 women), 51 part-time (45 women); includes 6 minority (all African Americans) Average age 29. 161 applicants, 68% accepted, 61 enrolled. In 2006, 68 degrees awarded. *Degree requirements:* For master's, master's project. *Entrance requirements:* For master's, GRE or MAT, minimum GPA of 2.5. Additional exam requirements/recommendations for international students: Required—TOEFL. *Application deadline:* For fall admission, 2/1 for domestic and international students; for spring admission, 10/1 for domestic and international students. Application fee: $30. *Expenses:* Tuition, state resident: full-time $6,100; part-time $260 per credit. Tuition, nonresident: full-time $18,790; part-time $725 per credit. Required fees: $3,314. Tuition and fees vary according to program. *Financial support:* In 2006–07, 10 research assistantships with full and partial tuition reimbursements (averaging $5,000 per year) were awarded; career-related internships or fieldwork, Federal Work-Study, institutionally sponsored loans, scholarships/grants, and unspecified assistantships also available. Financial award application deadline: 2/1; financial award applicants required to submit FAFSA. *Faculty research:* National Council of Teachers of Mathematics Standards, counseling, self-concept and self-esteem, special education, curriculum development. *Unit head:* Dr. John Moore, Area Coordinator, 757-221-2333, E-mail: jnmoor@wm.edu. *Application contact:* Dorothy Osborne, Director of Admissions, 757-221-2317, E-mail: dsosbo@wm.edu.

The Colorado College, Department of Education, Program in Secondary Education, Colorado Springs, CO 80903-3294. Offers art teaching (MAT); English teaching (MAT); foreign language teaching (MAT); mathematics teaching (MAT); music teaching (MAT); science teaching (MAT); social studies teaching (MAT). *Faculty:* 2 full-time (1 woman), 10 part-time/adjunct (7 women). *Students:* 18 full-time (12 women); includes 2 minority (1 African American, 1 Asian American or Pacific Islander). Average age 27. 30 applicants, 90% accepted, 18 enrolled. In 2006, 16 degrees awarded. *Degree requirements:* For master's, thesis, internship. *Entrance requirements:* For master's, PRAXIS II or PLACE. *Application deadline:* For fall admission, 2/1 for domestic and international students. Application fee: $50. *Expenses:* Tuition: Full-time $23,567. One-time fee: $1,485 full-time. *Financial support:* In 2006–07, 15 teaching assistantships (averaging $16,000 per year) were awarded; career-related internships or fieldwork, institutionally sponsored loans, health care benefits, and tuition waivers (partial) also available. Financial award application deadline: 2/15; financial award applicants required to submit FAFSA. *Unit head:* Mike Taber, Director, 719-389-6026, Fax: 719-389-6473, E-mail: pveronesi@coloradocollege.edu. *Application contact:* Marsha E. Unruh, Director of Education Career Services, 719-389-6472, Fax: 719-389-6473, E-mail: munruh@coloradocollege.edu.

The Colorado College, Programs for Experienced Teachers, Colorado Springs, CO 80903-3294. Offers American Southwest studies for all teachers (MAT); arts and humanities for secondary school teachers and administrators (MAT); integrated natural science for all teachers (MAT); liberal arts for elementary school teachers and administrators (MAT). Programs offered during summer only. Part-time programs available. *Faculty:* 18 part-time/adjunct (8 women). *Students:* 78; includes 2 minority (both Hispanic Americans) Average age 31. In 2006, 28 degrees awarded. *Degree requirements:* For master's, thesis, oral exam, 50 page paper. *Application deadline:* Applications are processed on a rolling basis. Application fee: $50. *Expenses:* Contact institution. One-time fee: $1,485 full-time. *Financial support:* Institutionally sponsored loans and half-tuition waivers to teachers with a contract available. *Unit head:* Dr. Libby Rittenberg, Dean of Summer Programs, 719-389-6657, Fax: 719-389-6955. *Application contact:* Ann H. Van Horn, Assistant Dean of Summer Session, 719-389-6656, Fax: 719-389-6955, E-mail: avanhorn@coloradocollege.edu.

Columbus State University, Graduate Studies, College of Education, Department of Teacher Education, Columbus, GA 31907-5645. Offers early childhood education (M Ed, Ed S); instructional technology (MS); middle grades education (M Ed, Ed S); physical education (M Ed); secondary education (M Ed, Ed S), including English/language arts, general science (M Ed), mathematics, science (Ed S), social science; special education (Ed S), including behavior disorders, learning disabilities, mental retardation. *Accreditation:* NCATE. Part-time and evening/weekend programs available. Postbaccalaureate distance learning degree programs offered (minimal on-campus study). *Faculty:* 16 full-time (8 women), 2 part-time/adjunct (1 woman). *Students:* 61 full-time (45 women), 128 part-time (89 women); includes 44 minority (36 African Americans, 3 Asian Americans or Pacific Islanders, 5 Hispanic Americans), 1 international. Average age 36. 77 applicants, 49% accepted, 26 enrolled. In 2006, 66 master's, 13 other advanced degrees awarded. *Degree requirements:* For master's, thesis, exit exam; for Ed S, thesis or alternative. *Entrance requirements:* For master's, GRE General Test, minimum GPA of 2.75; for Ed S, GRE General Test. Additional exam requirements/recommendations for international students: Required—TOEFL (minimum score 550 paper-based; 213 computer-based). *Application deadline:* For fall admission, 5/1 priority date for domestic students, 5/1 for international students; for spring admission, 11/1 for domestic and international students. Applications are processed on a rolling basis. Application fee: $25. Electronic applications accepted. *Expenses:* Tuition, state resident: part-time $127 per semester hour. Tuition, nonresident: part-time $508 per semester hour. Required fees: $264 per semester. Tuition and fees vary according to course load. *Financial support:* In 2006–07, 118 students received support, including 21 research assistantships with partial tuition reimbursements available (averaging $3,000 per year); career-related internships or fieldwork, Federal Work-Study, institutionally sponsored loans, scholarships/grants, tuition waivers (partial), and unspecified assistantships also available. Support available to part-time students. Financial award application deadline: 5/1; financial award applicants required to submit FAFSA. *Unit head:* Dr. Deborah Gober, Acting Chair, 706-568-2255, Fax: 706-568-3134, E-mail: gober_deborah@colstate.edu. *Application contact:* Katie Thornton, Graduate Admissions Specialist, 706-568-2035, Fax: 706-568-2462, E-mail: thornton_katie@colstate.edu.

Connecticut College, Graduate School, Department of Botany, New London, CT 06320-4196. Offers MA, MAT. Part-time programs available. *Degree requirements:* For master's, thesis. *Entrance requirements:* For master's, GRE or MAT. *Faculty research:* Tidal marsh ecology, upland vegetation dynamics, plant development, halophyte physiology.

Connecticut College, Graduate School, Department of Chemistry, New London, CT 06320-4196. Offers MAT. Part-time programs available. *Entrance requirements:* For master's, MAT.

Connecticut College, Graduate School, Department of Physics, New London, CT 06320-4196. Offers MAT. Part-time programs available. *Entrance requirements:* For master's, MAT.

Converse College, School of Education and Graduate Studies, Program in Secondary Education, Spartanburg, SC 29302-0006. Offers biology (MAT); chemistry (MAT); English (M Ed, MAT); mathematics (M Ed, MAT); natural sciences (M Ed); social sciences (M Ed, MAT). Part-time programs available. *Students:* Average age 35. In 2006, 40 degrees awarded. *Degree requirements:* For master's, capstone paper. *Entrance requirements:* For master's, NTE or PRAXIS II (M Ed), minimum GPA of 2.75, 2 recommendations. *Application deadline:* For fall admission, 8/1 for domestic and international students; for winter admission, 11/15 for domestic and international students; for spring admission, 1/15 for domestic and international students. Applications are processed on a rolling basis. Application fee: $40. Electronic applications accepted. *Expenses:* Tuition: Part-time $305 per credit hour. Required fees: $20 per term. *Financial support:* Available to part-time students. Applicants required to submit FAFSA.

Cornell University, Graduate School, Graduate Fields of Agriculture and Life Sciences, Field of Education, Ithaca, NY 14853-0001. Offers agricultural education (MAT); biology (7-12) (MAT); chemistry (7-12) (MAT); curriculum and instruction (MPS, MS, PhD); earth science (7-12) (MAT); extension, and adult education (MPS, MS, PhD); mathematics (7-12) (MAT); physics (7-12) (MAT). *Faculty:* 26 full-time (9 women). *Students:* 56 full-time (33 women); includes 10 minority (1 African American, 5 Asian Americans or Pacific Islanders, 4 Hispanic Americans), 4 international. Average age 31. 96 applicants, 40% accepted, 18 enrolled. In 2006, 22 master's, 8 doctorates awarded. Terminal master's awarded for partial completion of doctoral program. *Degree requirements:* For master's, thesis (MS); for doctorate, thesis/dissertation, comprehensive exam. *Entrance requirements:* For master's and doctorate, GRE General Test, sample of written work (recommended), 2 letters of recommendation. Additional exam requirements/recommendations for international students: Required—TOEFL (minimum score 550 paper-based; 213 computer-based). *Application deadline:* For fall admission, 2/15 for domestic students. Application fee: $60. Electronic applications accepted. *Expenses:* Tuition: Full-time $32,800. Full-time tuition and fees vary according to program. *Financial support:* In 2006–07, 31 students received support, including 4 fellowships with full tuition reimbursements available, 7 research assistantships with full tuition reimbursements available, 20 teaching assistantships with full tuition reimbursements available; institutionally sponsored loans, scholarships/grants, health care benefits, tuition waivers (full and partial), and unspecified assistantships also available. Financial award applicants required to submit FAFSA. *Faculty research:* Moral development and professional ethics; public issues education and community development; socio/political issues in public education; teacher education and curriculum in agricultural science, and mathematics; extension research. *Unit head:* Director of Graduate Studies, 607-255-4278, Fax: 607-255-7905. *Application contact:* Graduate Field Assistant, 607-255-4278, Fax: 607-255-7905, E-mail: rh22@cornell.edu.

Delaware State University, Graduate Programs, Department of Biology, Dover, DE 19901-2277. Offers biology (MS); biology education (MS). Part-time and evening/weekend programs available. *Degree requirements:* For master's, thesis (for some programs). *Entrance requirements:* For master's, GRE, minimum GPA of 3.0 in major, 2.75 overall. Electronic applications accepted. *Faculty research:* Cell biology, immunology, microbiology, genetics, ecology.

Delaware State University, Graduate Programs, Department of Education, Program in Science Education, Dover, DE 19901-2277. Offers MA. Part-time and evening/weekend programs available. *Degree requirements:* For master's, thesis optional. *Entrance requirements:* For master's, GRE General Test, minimum GPA of 3.0 in major, 2.75 overall. Electronic applications accepted. *Faculty research:* Science reform in schools, inquiry science.

Delaware State University, Graduate Programs, Department of Physics, Dover, DE 19901-2277. Offers physics (MS); physics teaching (MS). Part-time and evening/weekend programs available. *Entrance requirements:* For master's, minimum GPA of 3.0 in major, 2.75 overall. Electronic applications accepted. *Faculty research:* Thermal properties of solids, nuclear physics, radiation damage in solids.

DeSales University, Graduate Division, Program in Education, Center Valley, PA 18034-9568. Offers academic standards and information (Certificate); bilingual/ESL studies (Certificate); biology (M Ed); chemistry (M Ed); computers in education (K-12) (M Ed); computers in education (K-8) (M Ed); English (M Ed); instructional technology specialist (Certificate); mathematics (M Ed); special education (M Ed, Certificate); TESOL (M Ed). Part-time and evening/weekend programs available. Postbaccalaureate distance learning degree programs offered (minimal on-campus study). *Students:* 34 full-time, 190 part-time. In 2006, 30 degrees awarded. *Degree requirements:* For master's, thesis project. *Entrance requirements:* For master's, teaching certificate. *Application deadline:* Applications are processed on a rolling basis. Application fee: $35. Electronic applications accepted. *Expenses: Contact institution. Financial support:* Unspecified assistantships available. Support available to part-time students. Financial award application deadline: 5/1. *Faculty research:* Effective teaching, computer interfacing in chemistry labs, computer applications to teaching, history of philosophy, aesthetics multidrug-resistant cancer. *Unit head:* Dr. Lujean Baab, Director of M.Ed. Program, 610-282-1100 Ext. 1739, Fax: 610-282-3734, E-mail: lujean.baab@desales.edu. *Application contact:* Donna L. Cressman, Program Secretary, 610-282-1100 Ext. 1461, Fax: 610-282-3734, E-mail: med@desales.edu.

Drake University, School of Education, Department of Teaching and Learning, Program in Secondary Education, Des Moines, IA 50311-4516. Offers art (MAT); biology (MAT); business (MAT); chemistry (MAT); English (MAT); general science (MAT); history-American (MAT); history-world (MAT); journalism (MAT); mathematics (MAT); physical science (MAT); physics (MAT); sociology (MAT); speech (MAT); speech communication (MAT); theatre (MAT). Part-time programs available. *Faculty:* 10 full-time (3 women), 28 part-time/adjunct (16 women). *Students:* 13 full-time (7 women), 33 part-time (20 women). 41 applicants, 56% accepted. In 2006, 12 degrees awarded. *Degree requirements:* For master's, thesis (for some programs), internships (s), comprehensive exam, registration. *Entrance requirements:* For master's, GRE General Test, MAT, or Drake Writing Assessment, resumé, 2 letters of recommendation. Additional exam requirements/recommendations for international students: Required—TOEFL (minimum score 550 paper-based; 213 computer-based). *Application deadline:* For fall admission, 7/1 priority date for domestic students, 6/1 priority date for international students; for spring admission, 11/1 priority date for domestic students, 10/1 priority date for international students. Applications are processed on a rolling basis. Application fee: $25. Electronic applications accepted. *Financial support:* Career-related internships or fieldwork and unspecified assistantships available. Support available to part-time students. *Faculty research:* Counseling and rehabilitation, behavioral supports, inquiry-based science methods, teacher quality enhancement. Total annual research expenditures: $1.5 million. *Unit head:* Dr. Linda Espey, Head, 515-271-1954, E-mail: linda.espey@drake.edu. *Application contact:* Ann J. Martin, Graduate Coordinator, 515-271-2034, Fax: 515-271-2831, E-mail: ann.martin@drake.edu.

East Carolina University, Graduate School, College of Education, Department of Mathematics and Science Education, Greenville, NC 27858-4353. Offers mathematics (MA Ed); science education (MA, MA Ed). Part-time and evening/weekend programs available. *Students:* 8 full-time (5 women), 74 part-time (68 women); includes 7 minority (6 African Americans, 1 Asian American or Pacific Islander). Average age 35. 16 applicants, 75% accepted, 8 enrolled. In 2006, 36 degrees awarded. *Degree requirements:* For master's, thesis optional. *Entrance requirements:* For master's, GRE General Test or MAT, interview, minimum GPA of 2.5, bachelor's degree in related field, teaching license (MA Ed). Additional exam requirements/recommendations for international students: Required—TOEFL. *Application deadline:* For fall admission, 6/1 priority date for domestic students. Applications are processed on a rolling basis. Application fee: $50. *Financial support:* Research assistantships, teaching assistantships, Federal Work-Study available. Support available to part-time students. Financial award application deadline: 6/1. *Unit head:* Dr. Ronald Preston, Chairperson, 252-328-9353, E-mail: prestonr@ecu.edu. *Application contact:* Dean of Graduate School, 252-328-6012, Fax: 252-328-6071, E-mail: gradschool@ecu.edu.

Eastern Connecticut State University, School of Education and Professional Studies/Graduate Division, Program in Science Education, Willimantic, CT 06226-2295. Offers MS. *Accreditation:* NCATE. Part-time and evening/weekend programs available. *Faculty:* 1 (woman) full-time. *Students:* Average age 41. 1 applicant, 100% accepted, 0 enrolled. In 2006, 1 degree awarded. *Degree requirements:* For master's, comprehensive exam or thesis. *Entrance requirements:* For master's, minimum GPA of 2.7, teaching certificate. Additional exam requirements/recommendations for international students: Required—TOEFL (minimum score 550 paper-based; 213 computer-based). *Application deadline:* For fall admission, 7/6 priority date for domestic and international students; for spring admission, 11/3 priority date for domestic and international students. Applications are processed on a rolling basis. Application fee: $50. *Expenses:* Tuition, state resident: full-time $3,970. Tuition, nonresident: full-time $11,061; part-time $336 per credit. Required fees: $35 per credit. *Financial support:* Teaching assistantships, career-related internships or fieldwork, scholarships/grants, and unspecified assistantships available. Support available to part-time students. Financial award application deadline: 3/15. *Unit head:* Dr. Jeanelle Bland, Advisor, 860-465-4532, Fax: 860-465-5099, E-mail: blandj@easternct.edu. *Application contact:* Dr. Tuesday L. Cooper, Associate Dean, 860-465-4543, Fax: 860-465-4538, E-mail: coopert@easternct.edu.

Eastern Kentucky University, The Graduate School, College of Education, Department of Curriculum and Instruction, Program in Secondary and Higher Education, Richmond, KY 40475-3102. Offers agricultural education (MA Ed); allied health sciences education (MA Ed); art education (MA Ed); biological sciences education (MA Ed); business education (MA Ed); chemistry education (MA Ed); earth science education (MA Ed); English education (MA Ed); general science education (MA Ed); geography education (MA Ed); history education (MA Ed); home economics education (MA Ed); industrial education (MA Ed); mathematical sciences education (MA Ed); physical education (MA Ed); physics education (MA Ed); political science education (MA Ed); psychology education (MA Ed); reading (MA Ed); school health education (MA Ed); sociology education (MA Ed). *Accreditation:* NCATE. Part-time programs available. *Students:* 16 full-time (8 women), 63 part-time (43 women); includes 5 minority (2 African Americans, 2 American Indian/Alaska Native, 1 Asian American or Pacific Islander). Average age 32. *Entrance requirements:* For master's, GRE General Test, minimum GPA of 2.5. Application fee: $30. *Expenses:* Tuition, state resident: full-time $5,610. Tuition, nonresident: full-time $15,910. *Financial support:* Research assistantships, teaching assistantships, Federal Work-Study available. Support available to part-time students. *Unit head:* Dr. Michael Martin, Chair, Department of Curriculum and Instruction, 859-622-2154, Fax: 859-622-2004.

Eastern Michigan University, Graduate School, College of Arts and Sciences, Department of Physics and Astronomy, Ypsilanti, MI 48197. Offers general science (MS); physics (MS); physics education (MS). Part-time and evening/weekend programs available. Postbaccalaureate distance learning degree programs offered (minimal on-campus study). *Faculty:* 11 full-time (2 women). *Students:* 2 full-time (0 women), 11 part-time (3 women), 1 international. Average age 33. In 2006, 8 degrees awarded. *Entrance requirements:* Additional exam requirements/recommendations for international students: Required—TOEFL. *Application deadline:* For fall admission, 5/15 priority date for domestic students, 5/1 priority date for international students; for winter admission, 10/15 priority date for domestic students, 10/1 priority date for international students; for spring admission, 3/15 priority date for domestic students, 3/1 priority date for international students. Applications are processed on a rolling basis. Application fee: $35. *Expenses:* Tuition, state resident: part-time $341 per credit hour. Tuition, nonresident: full-time $16,104; part-time $671 per credit hour. Required fees: $816; $34 per credit hour. $40 per term. One-time fee: $82 full-time. Tuition and fees vary according to course level, course load, degree level and reciprocity agreements. *Financial support:* Fellowships, research assistantships with full tuition reimbursements, teaching assistantships with full tuition reimbursements, career-related internships or fieldwork, Federal Work-Study, institutionally sponsored loans, scholarships/grants, tuition waivers, and unspecified assistantships available. Support available to part-time students. Financial award applicants required to submit FAFSA. *Unit head:* Dr. Alexandria Oakes, Head, 734-487-4144, Fax: 734-487-0989, E-mail: aoakes@emich.edu.

Eastern Washington University, Graduate Studies, College of Education and Human Development, Department of Education, Cheney, WA 99004-2431. Offers adult education (M Ed); college instruction (MA, MS); curriculum and instruction (M Ed); early childhood education (M Ed); educational leadership (M Ed); elementary teaching (M Ed); foundations of education (M Ed); instructional media and technology (M Ed); literacy specialist (M Ed); school library media administration (M Ed); science education (M Ed); social science education (M Ed); supervising (clinic) teaching (M Ed). *Accreditation:* NCATE. Part-time programs available. *Degree requirements:* For master's, comprehensive exam. *Entrance requirements:* For master's, minimum GPA of 3.0.

East Stroudsburg University of Pennsylvania, Graduate School, School of Arts and Sciences, Department of Biology, East Stroudsburg, PA 18301-2999. Offers biology (M Ed, MS). Part-time and evening/weekend programs available. *Faculty:* 12 full-time (4 women). *Students:* 19 full-time (9 women), 36 part-time (18 women); includes 2 minority (1 African American, 1 Hispanic American), 2 international. Average age 30. In 2006, 18 degrees awarded. *Degree requirements:* For master's, thesis or alternative, comprehensive exam. *Entrance requirements:* For master's, GRE, undergraduate major in life sciences, 2 semesters in chemistry, 3 letters of recommendation, letter of intent from student. Additional exam requirements/recommendations for international students: Required—TOEFL (minimum score 560 paper-based; 220 computer-based; 83 iBT). *Application deadline:* For fall admission, 7/31 for domestic students, 5/1 priority date for international students; for spring admission, 11/30 for domestic students, 10/1 for international students. Applications are processed on a rolling basis. Application fee: $50. *Expenses:* Tuition, state resident: full-time $6,048; part-time $336 per credit. Tuition, nonresident: full-time $9,678; part-time $538 per credit. Required fees: $1,353; $67 per credit. One-time fee: $37 part-time. *Financial support:* In 2006–07, 12 research assistantships with full and partial tuition reimbursements were awarded; Federal Work-Study and institutionally sponsored loans also available. Financial award application deadline: 3/1; financial award applicants required to submit FAFSA. *Unit head:* Dr. Jane Huffman, Graduate Coordinator, 570-422-3725, Fax: 570-422-3724, E-mail: jhuffman@po-box.esu.edu.

Edinboro University of Pennsylvania, Graduate Studies and Research, School of Education, Department of Elementary Education, Program in Elementary Education, Edinboro, PA 16444. Offers character education (M Ed); early childhood education (M Ed); elementary education (M Ed), including language arts, mathematics, science, thesis focus. Part-time and evening/weekend programs available. *Students:* 31 full-time (26 women), 46 part-time (38 women). Average age 30. In 2006, 14 degrees awarded. *Degree requirements:* For master's, thesis or alternative, project, comprehensive exam. *Entrance requirements:* For master's, GRE or MAT, minimum QPA of 2.5, valid teaching certificate or current study to obtain certification. *Application deadline:* Applications are processed on a rolling basis. Application fee: $30. Electronic applications accepted. *Expenses:* Tuition, state resident: full-time $6,048; part-time $336 per credit. Tuition, nonresident: full-time $9,678; part-time $538 per credit. Required fees: $1,849; $42 per credit. *Financial support:* In 2006–07, 7 research assistantships with full and

Science Education

Edinboro University of Pennsylvania (continued)

partial tuition reimbursements (averaging $3,850 per year) were awarded; career-related internships or fieldwork, Federal Work-Study, scholarships/grants, and unspecified assistantships also available. Support available to part-time students. Financial award application deadline: 2/15; financial award applicants required to submit FAFSA. *Unit head:* Dr. Kathleen Dailey, Coordinator, 814-732-2714, E-mail: dailey@edinboro.edu. *Application contact:* Dr. R. Scott Baldwin, Dean, 814-732-2752, Fax: 814-732-2268, E-mail: sbaldwin@edinboro.edu.

Elms College, Division of Education, Chicopee, MA 01013-2839. Offers early childhood education (MAT); education (M Ed, CAGS); elementary education (MAT); English as a second language (MAT); reading (MAT); secondary education (MAT), including biology education, English education, Spanish education; special education (MAT). Part-time and evening/weekend programs available. *Faculty:* 9 full-time (6 women), 4 part-time/adjunct (2 women). *Students:* 8 full-time (6 women), 97 part-time (89 women); includes 4 minority (2 Asian Americans or Pacific Islanders, 2 Hispanic Americans). Average age 36. 48 applicants, 90% accepted, 40 enrolled. In 2006, 37 master's, 8 other advanced degrees awarded. *Degree requirements:* For master's, thesis (for some programs). *Entrance requirements:* For master's, Massachusetts Educators Certification Test, minimum GPA of 3.0; for CAGS, master's degree in education. Additional exam requirements/recommendations for international students: Required—TOEFL. *Application deadline:* For fall admission, 7/1 priority date for domestic students; for spring admission, 11/1 priority date for domestic students. Applications are processed on a rolling basis. Application fee: $30. *Expenses:* Tuition: Full-time $9,180; part-time $510 per credit. Tuition and fees vary according to course load. *Financial support:* In 2006–07, 3 teaching assistantships with partial tuition reimbursements were awarded; tuition waivers (partial) also available. Support available to part-time students. Financial award application deadline: 4/15; financial award applicants required to submit FAFSA. *Unit head:* Dr. Mary Janeczek, Director, 413-594-2761, Fax: 413-592-4871, E-mail: janeczeke@elms.edu.

Fairleigh Dickinson University, Metropolitan Campus, University College: Arts, Sciences, and Professional Studies, School of Natural Sciences, Program in Science, Teaneck, NJ 07666-1914. Offers MA. *Students:* 10 full-time (8 women), 28 part-time (19 women), 4 international. Average age 30. 23 applicants, 61% accepted, 7 enrolled. In 2006, 23 degrees awarded. *Application deadline:* Applications are processed on a rolling basis. Application fee: $40. *Unit head:* Dr. Irwin Isquith, Director, School of Natural Sciences, 201-692-2000.

Fitchburg State College, Division of Graduate and Continuing Education, Program in Science Education, Fitchburg, MA 01420-2697. Offers M Ed. *Accreditation:* NCATE. Part-time and evening/weekend programs available. *Students:* 1 full-time (0 women), 4 part-time (3 women). Average age 41. In 2006, 2 degrees awarded. *Entrance requirements:* For master's, GRE General Test, teaching certificate, appropriate bachelor's degree, letters of recommendation, resumé. Additional exam requirements/recommendations for international students: Required—TOEFL (minimum score 550 paper-based; 213 computer-based; 79 iBT). *Application deadline:* Applications are processed on a rolling basis. Application fee: $25 ($50 for international students). *Expenses:* Tuition, state resident: part-time $150 per credit. Tuition, nonresident: part-time $150 per credit. Required fees: $90 per credit. *Financial support:* In 2006–07, research assistantships with partial tuition reimbursements (averaging $5,500 per year); Federal Work-Study, scholarships/grants, and unspecified assistantships also available. Support available to part-time students. Financial award application deadline: 3/1; financial award applicants required to submit FAFSA. *Unit head:* Dr. Christopher Cratsley, Chair, 978-665-3617, Fax: 978-665-3658, E-mail: gce@fsc.edu. *Application contact:* Director of Admissions, 978-665-3144, Fax: 978-665-4540, E-mail: admissions@fsc.edu.

Fitchburg State College, Division of Graduate and Continuing Education, Programs in Biology and Teaching Biology (Secondary Level), Fitchburg, MA 01420-2697. Offers MA, MAT. *Accreditation:* NCATE. Part-time and evening/weekend programs available. *Students:* 2 full-time (both women), 9 part-time (7 women). Average age 35. 4 applicants, 100% accepted, 4 enrolled. In 2006, 4 degrees awarded. *Entrance requirements:* For master's, GRE General Test, letters of recommendation, resumé. Additional exam requirements/recommendations for international students: Required—TOEFL (minimum score 550 paper-based; 213 computer-based; 79 iBT). *Application deadline:* Applications are processed on a rolling basis. Application fee: $25 ($50 for international students). *Expenses:* Tuition, state resident: part-time $150 per credit. Tuition, nonresident: part-time $150 per credit. Required fees: $90 per credit. *Financial support:* In 2006–07, research assistantships with partial tuition reimbursements (averaging $5,500 per year); Federal Work-Study, scholarships/grants, and unspecified assistantships also available. Support available to part-time students. Financial award application deadline: 3/1; financial award applicants required to submit FAFSA. *Unit head:* Dr. Christopher Cratsley, Chair, 978-665-3617, Fax: 978-665-3658, E-mail: gce@fsc.edu. *Application contact:* Director of Admissions, 978-665-3144, Fax: 978-665-4540, E-mail: admissions@fsc.edu.

Florida Agricultural and Mechanical University, Division of Graduate Studies, Research, and Continuing Education, College of Education, Program in Secondary Education and Foundation, Tallahassee, FL 32307-3200. Offers biology (M Ed); chemistry (MS Ed); English (MS Ed); history (MS Ed); math (MS Ed); physics (MS Ed). *Accreditation:* NCATE. *Degree requirements:* For master's, thesis (for some programs). *Entrance requirements:* For master's, GRE General Test, minimum GPA of 3.0. Additional exam requirements/recommendations for international students: Required—TOEFL.

Florida Gulf Coast University, College of Education, Program in Secondary Education, Fort Myers, FL 33965-6565. Offers biology (MAT); English (MAT); mathematics (MAT); social sciences (MAT). Part-time and evening/weekend programs available. *Faculty:* 31 full-time (21 women), 30 part-time/adjunct (24 women). *Entrance requirements:* For master's, GRE General Test, MAT, minimum GPA of 3.0. Additional exam requirements/recommendations for international students: Required—TOEFL (minimum score 550 paper-based; 213 computer-based). *Application deadline:* For fall admission, 7/1 priority date for domestic students; for spring admission, 10/15 for domestic students. Applications are processed on a rolling basis. Application fee: $30. Electronic applications accepted. *Expenses:* Tuition, state resident: full-time $4,326. Tuition, nonresident: full-time $18,523. Required fees: $1,211. One-time fee: $5 full-time. *Faculty research:* Integration of technology in the classroom, year-round schools, school choice, virtual high schools. *Unit head:* Dr. Pat Wachholz, Associate Dean, 239-590-7808, Fax: 239-590-7801, E-mail: wachhol@fgcu.edu.

Florida Institute of Technology, Graduate Programs, College of Science, Department of Science and Mathematics Education, Melbourne, FL 32901-6975. Offers computer education (MS); elementary science education (M Ed); environmental education (MS); mathematics education (MS, Ed D, PhD, Ed S); science and mathematics education (MAT); science education (MS, Ed D, PhD, Ed S). Part-time and evening/weekend programs available. *Faculty:* 4 full-time (1 woman), 2 part-time/adjunct (1 woman). *Students:* 11 full-time (6 women), 21 part-time (14 women); includes 2 minority (1 African American, 1 American Indian/Alaska Native), 7 international. Average age 38. 40 applicants, 58% accepted, 5 enrolled. In 2006, 7 master's, 2 doctorates, 1 other advanced degree awarded. Terminal master's awarded for partial completion of doctoral program. *Degree requirements:* For master's, thesis (for some programs), comprehensive exam (for some programs); registration; for doctorate, thesis/dissertation, oral defense of dissertation, comprehensive exam, registration. *Entrance requirements:* For master's, minimum GPA of 3.0, resumé, 3 letters of recommendation (elementary science education); for doctorate, minimum GPA of 3.2, resumé, 3 letters of recommendation; for Ed S, minimum GPA of 3.0, resumé, 3 letters of recommendation. Additional exam requirements/recommendations for international students: Required—TOEFL (minimum score 550 paper-based; 213 computer-based). *Application deadline:* Applications are processed on a rolling basis. Application fee: $50. Electronic applications accepted. *Expenses:* Tuition: Part-time $900 per credit. *Financial support:* In 2006–07, 1 student received support, including 1 research assistantship with full and partial tuition reimbursement available (averaging $5,346 per year); career-related internships or fieldwork and tuition remissions also available. Support available to part-time students. Financial award application deadline: 3/1;

financial award applicants required to submit FAFSA. *Faculty research:* Measurement and evaluation, computers in education, educational technology. Total annual research expenditures: $6,000. *Unit head:* Dr. David E. Cook, Department Head, 321-674-8126, Fax: 321-674-7598, E-mail: dcook@fit.edu. *Application contact:* Carolyn P. Farrior, Director of Graduate Admissions, 321-674-7118, Fax: 321-723-9468, E-mail: cfarrior@fit.edu.

Florida International University, College of Education, Department of Curriculum and Instruction, Program in Science Education, Miami, FL 33199. Offers MAT, MS, Ed D, PhD. *Accreditation:* NCATE. Part-time and evening/weekend programs available. *Entrance requirements:* Additional exam requirements/recommendations for international students: Required—TOEFL. *Application deadline:* Applications are processed on a rolling basis. *Expenses:* Tuition, state resident: part-time $249 per credit hour. Tuition, nonresident: part-time $753 per credit hour. Tuition and fees vary according to program. *Faculty research:* Science processes, attitudes, bilingual science education, computers in science education. *Unit head:* Dr. George O'Brien, Head, 305-348-2599.

Florida State University, Graduate Studies, College of Education, Department of Middle and Secondary Education, Program in Science Education, Tallahassee, FL 32306. Offers MS, PhD, Ed S. Part-time programs available. Postbaccalaureate distance learning degree programs offered. *Faculty:* 3 full-time (2 women), 1 part-time/adjunct (0 women). *Students:* 6 full-time (4 women), 35 part-time (22 women); includes 11 minority (5 African Americans, 2 Asian Americans or Pacific Islanders, 4 Hispanic Americans). 24 applicants, 46% accepted, 7 enrolled. In 2006, 4 master's, 2 doctorates awarded. *Degree requirements:* For master's and Ed S, thesis optional; for doctorate, thesis/dissertation, comprehensive exam. *Entrance requirements:* For master's, doctorate, and Ed S, GRE General Test, minimum GPA of 3.0. *Application deadline:* For fall admission, 7/1 priority date for domestic students; for spring admission, 11/1 for domestic students. Applications are processed on a rolling basis. Application fee: $30. *Expenses:* Tuition, state resident: full-time $5,822; part-time $243 per credit hour. Tuition, nonresident: full-time $20,976; part-time $874 per credit hour. Tuition and fees vary according to program. *Financial support:* Fellowships, research assistantships, teaching assistantships, career-related internships or fieldwork available. Financial award applicants required to submit FAFSA. *Unit head:* Dr. Sherry Southerland, Head, 850-644-6553, Fax: 850-644-1880, E-mail: southerl@coe.fsu.edu. *Application contact:* Christina Crotty, Office Manager, 850-644-7810, Fax: 850-644-1880, E-mail: crotty@mailer.fsu.edu.

Framingham State College, Division of Graduate and Continuing Education, Program in Biology, Framingham, MA 01701-9101. Offers M Ed. *Students:* 15. In 2006, 1 degree awarded. *Unit head:* Dr. Eugene Muller, Coordinator, 508-626-4798, Fax: 508-626-4030, E-mail: gmuller@frc.mass.edu. *Application contact:* Graduate Office, 508-626-4550, Fax: 508-626-4030, E-mail: dgce@frc.mass.edu.

Fresno Pacific University, Graduate Programs, Programs in Education, Fresno, CA 93702-4709. Offers administration (MA Ed), including administrative services; foundations, curriculum and teaching (MA Ed), including curriculum and teaching, school library and information technology; language, literacy, and culture (MA Ed), including bilingual/cross-cultural education, language development, multilingual contexts, reading; mathematics/science/computer education (MA Ed), including educational technology, integrated mathematics/science education, mathematics education; pupil personnel services (MA Ed), including school counseling, school psychology; special education (MA Ed), including mild/moderate, moderate/severe, physical and health impairments. Part-time and evening/weekend programs available. *Faculty:* 12 full-time (5 women), 19 part-time/adjunct (9 women). *Students:* 73 full-time (59 women), 399 part-time (295 women); includes 136 minority (9 African Americans, 5 American Indian/Alaska Native, 12 Asian Americans or Pacific Islanders, 110 Hispanic Americans), 2 international. Average age 39. 124 applicants, 73% accepted, 10 enrolled. In 2006, 128 degrees awarded. *Degree requirements:* For master's, thesis (for some programs), registration. *Entrance requirements:* For master's, interview, GMAT, GRE, MAT, or 6 units of course work with a faculty recommendation. Additional exam requirements/recommendations for international students: Required—TOEFL (minimum score 550 paper-based; 213 computer-based). *Application deadline:* For fall admission, 7/15 for domestic and international students; for spring admission, 11/15 for domestic and international students. Applications are processed on a rolling basis. Application fee: $90. Electronic applications accepted. *Expenses:* Tuition: Full-time $7,470; part-time $415 per credit. *Financial support:* In 2006–07, 260 students received support. Career-related internships or fieldwork, scholarships/grants, and tuition waivers (full and partial) available. Support available to part-time students. Financial award applicants required to submit FAFSA.

Fresno Pacific University, Graduate Programs, Programs in Education, Division of Mathematics/Science/Computer Education, Program in Integrated Mathematics/Science Education, Fresno, CA 93702-4709. Offers MA Ed. Part-time and evening/weekend programs available. *Students:* Average age 39. 6 applicants, 50% accepted, 1 enrolled. In 2006, 40 degrees awarded. *Degree requirements:* For master's, thesis or alternative, registration. *Entrance requirements:* Additional exam requirements/recommendations for international students: Required—TOEFL (minimum score 550 paper-based; 213 computer-based). *Application deadline:* For fall admission, 7/15 for domestic and international students; for spring admission, 11/15 for domestic and international students. Applications are processed on a rolling basis. Application fee: $90. *Expenses:* Tuition: Full-time $7,470; part-time $415 per credit. *Financial support:* In 2006–07, 24 students received support. Scholarships/grants and tuition waivers (full and partial) available. Support available to part-time students. Financial award applicants required to submit FAFSA.

Gannon University, School of Graduate Studies, College of Sciences, Engineering, and Health Sciences, School of Sciences, Program in Natural and Environmental Sciences, Erie, PA 16541-0001. Offers M Ed. Part-time and evening/weekend programs available. In 2006, 1 degree awarded. *Degree requirements:* For master's, thesis, comprehensive exam. *Entrance requirements:* For master's, GRE Subject Test. Additional exam requirements/recommendations for international students: Required—TOEFL (minimum score 500 paper-based; 173 computer-based). *Application deadline:* Applications are processed on a rolling basis. Application fee: $25. *Expenses:* Tuition: Full-time $12,240; part-time $680 per credit. Required fees: $496; $16 per credit. Tuition and fees vary according to course load, degree level, campus/location and program. *Financial support:* Career-related internships or fieldwork available. Support available to part-time students. Financial award application deadline: 7/1; financial award applicants required to submit FAFSA. *Unit head:* Dr. Harry Diz, Chair, 814-871-7633, E-mail: diz001@gannon.edu. *Application contact:* Debra Meszaros, Director of Graduate Recruitment, 814-871-5819, Fax: 814-871-5827, E-mail: cfal@gannon.edu.

Georgia College & State University, Graduate School, School of Education, Department of Foundations and Secondary Education, Milledgeville, GA 31061. Offers English education (M Ed); instructional technology (M Ed); mathematics education (M Ed); natural science education (M Ed, Ed S); secondary education (MAT); social science education (M Ed, Ed S). *Accreditation:* NCATE. *Students:* 49 full-time (33 women), 66 part-time (47 women); includes 13 minority (11 African Americans, 2 Hispanic Americans), 2 international. Average age 32. 75 applicants, 27% accepted, 9 enrolled. In 2006, 83 master's awarded. *Degree requirements:* For master's and Ed S, comprehensive exam. *Entrance requirements:* For master's, GRE General Test or MAT, 2 letters of recommendation; for Ed S, GRE General Test or MAT, master's degree, 2 letters of recommendation, 2 years teaching experience. Additional exam requirements/recommendations for international students: Required—TOEFL. *Application deadline:* For fall admission, 7/1 priority date for domestic students. Applications are processed on a rolling basis. Application fee: $25. Electronic applications accepted. *Expenses:* Tuition, state resident: full-time $3,222; part-time $179 per credit hour. Tuition, nonresident: full-time $12,870; part-time $715 per credit hour. Required fees: $391 per semester. Tuition and fees vary according to course load. *Financial support:* In 2006–07, 10 research assistantships (averaging $3,800 per year) were awarded; career-related internships or fieldwork and Federal Work-Study also available. Support available to part-time students. Financial award application deadline: 3/15. *Unit head:* Dr. Cynthia Alby, Chair/MAT Cohort Leader, 478-445-2513, Fax: 478-445-7362, E-mail: cynthia.alby@gcsu.edu.

Georgia Southern University, Jack N. Averitt College of Graduate Studies, College of Education, Department of Teaching and Learning, Program in Science Education, Statesboro, GA 30460. Offers M Ed, MAT. *Accreditation:* NCATE. Part-time and evening/weekend programs available. *Students:* 3 full-time (2 women), 3 part-time (2 women). Average age 28. 1 applicant, 100% accepted, 1 enrolled. In 2006, 3 degrees awarded. *Degree requirements:* For master's, exit assessment. *Entrance requirements:* For master's, GRE General Test or MAT, minimum GPA of 2.5. Additional exam requirements/recommendations for international students: Required—TOEFL (minimum score 550 paper-based; 213 computer-based; 80 iBT). *Application deadline:* For fall admission, 3/1 priority date for domestic students, 3/1 for international students; for spring admission, 10/1 priority date for domestic students, 10/1 for international students. Applications are processed on a rolling basis. Application fee: $50. Electronic applications accepted. *Financial support:* In 2006–07, 5 students received support, including research assistantships with partial tuition reimbursements available (averaging $5,500 per year), teaching assistantships with partial tuition reimbursements available (averaging $5,500 per year); Federal Work-Study, scholarships/grants, tuition waivers (partial), and unspecified assistantships also available. Support available to part-time students. Financial award application deadline: 4/15; financial award applicants required to submit FAFSA. *Faculty research:* Gender. *Unit head:* Dr. Mary Bennett, Assistant Professor, 912-681-0356, Fax: 912-681-0026, E-mail: mbennett@georgiasouthern.edu. *Application contact:* 912-681-5384, Fax: 912-681-0740, E-mail: gradadmissions@georgiasouthern.edu.

Georgia State University, College of Education, Department of Middle-Secondary Education and Instructional Technology, Programs in Secondary Education, Atlanta, GA 30303-3083. Offers art education (Ed S); English education (M Ed, Ed S); mathematics education (M Ed, PhD, Ed S); music education (PhD); science education (M Ed, PhD, Ed S); social studies education (M Ed, PhD, Ed S). *Accreditation:* NASM (one or more programs are accredited); NCATE. Part-time and evening/weekend programs available. *Students:* 103 full-time (71 women), 140 part-time (92 women); includes 53 minority (48 African Americans, 2 Asian Americans or Pacific Islanders, 3 Hispanic Americans), 12 international. Average age 35. 36 applicants, 86% accepted. In 2006, 87 master's, 12 doctorates, 12 other advanced degrees awarded. *Degree requirements:* For master's, comprehensive exam; for doctorate, thesis/dissertation, comprehensive exam; for Ed S, project/exam. *Entrance requirements:* For master's, GRE General Test, minimum GPA of 2.5; for doctorate, GRE General Test or MAT, minimum GPA of 3.3; for Ed S, GRE General Test or MAT, minimum graduate GPA of 3.25. Application fee: $25. *Financial support:* Career-related internships or fieldwork, Federal Work-Study, and institutionally sponsored loans available. *Faculty research:* Women and science, problem solving in mathematics, dialects, economic education. *Unit head:* Dr. Ruth Hough, Acting Chair, Department of Middle-Secondary Education and Instructional Technology, 404-651-2510.

Grambling State University, School of Graduate Studies and Research, College of Professional Studies, Grambling, LA 71245. Offers MA, MS, MSN, MSW, PMC. Part-time programs available. *Faculty:* 16 full-time (8 women), 7 part-time/adjunct (2 women). *Students:* 152 full-time (127 women), 42 part-time (32 women); includes 148 minority (147 African Americans, 1 Asian American or Pacific Islander), 3 international. Average age 32. In 2006, 75 degrees awarded. *Entrance requirements:* For master's, GRE General Test. *Application deadline:* For fall admission, 7/1 for domestic students; for spring admission, 12/1 for domestic students. Applications are processed on a rolling basis. Application fee: $20 ($30 for international students). *Expenses:* Tuition, state resident: full-time $2,232; part-time $124 per credit hour. Tuition, nonresident: full-time $7,582; part-time $124 per credit hour. Required fees: $1,127. *Financial support:* In 2006–07, 137 students received support, including 19 research assistantships (averaging $3,342 per year); teaching assistantships, institutionally sponsored loans and unspecified assistantships also available. Financial award application deadline: 5/31; financial award applicants required to submit FAFSA. *Unit head:* Dr. Marianne Fisher-Giorlando, Acting Dean, 318-274-3234, Fax: 318-273-6041, E-mail: giorlando@gram.edu.

Harding University, College of Education, Searcy, AR 72149-0001. Offers advanced studies in teaching and learning (M Ed); art (MSE); behavioral science (MSE); Bible and religion (MSE); counseling (MS, Ed S); early childhood education (M Ed); early childhood special education (M Ed, MSE); education (MSE); educational leadership (M Ed, Ed S); elementary education (M Ed); English (MSE); family and consumer science (MSE); French (MSE); history/social science (MSE); kinesiology (MSE); math (MSE); physical science (MSE); reading (M Ed); secondary education (M Ed); Spanish (MSE); special education licensure (M Ed); teaching (MAT). *Accreditation:* NCATE. Part-time programs available. *Faculty:* 8 full-time (2 women), 45 part-time/adjunct (30 women). *Students:* 153 full-time (123 women), 469 part-time (341 women); includes 72 minority (63 African Americans, 4 American Indian/Alaska Native, 1 Asian American or Pacific Islander, 4 Hispanic Americans), 9 international. Average age 35. 175 applicants, 90% accepted, 147 enrolled. In 2006, 241 degrees awarded. *Degree requirements:* For master's, portfolio(s), thesis optional; for Ed S, portfolio, specialist project. *Entrance requirements:* For master's, GRE, MAT, PRAXIS; for Ed S, MAT or GRE. Additional exam requirements/recommendations for international students: Required—TOEFL (minimum score 550 paper-based). *Application deadline:* For fall admission, 8/1 for domestic and international students; for spring admission, 1/1 for domestic and international students. Applications are processed on a rolling basis. Application fee: $35. *Expenses:* Tuition: Part-time $455 per semester hour. Required fees: $20 per semester hour. Tuition and fees vary according to course load. *Financial support:* Scholarships/grants and unspecified assistantships available. Support available to part-time students. *Faculty research:* Reading, comprehension, school violence, educational technology, behavior, college choice, differentiated instruction, brain based teaching. *Unit head:* Pat Bashaw, Chair, 501-279-4183, Fax: 501-279-4051, E-mail: pbashaw@harding.edu.

Hardin-Simmons University, Graduate School, Holland School of Sciences and Mathematics, Abilene, TX 79698-0001. Offers MS, DPT. Part-time programs available. *Faculty:* 4 full-time (1 woman). *Students:* 5 full-time (4 women), 5 part-time (2 women), 1 international. Average age 38. 2 applicants, 100% accepted, 2 enrolled. In 2006, 4 degrees awarded. *Degree requirements:* For master's, thesis or alternative, Internship, comprehensive exam. *Entrance requirements:* For master's, minimum undergraduate GPA of 3.0 in major 2.7 overall; 2 semesters of course work in each biology, chemistry and geology; interview, writing sample, occupational experience. Additional exam requirements/recommendations for international students: Required—TOEFL (minimum score 550 paper-based; 213 computer-based). *Application deadline:* For fall admission, 8/15 priority date for domestic students; for spring admission, 1/5 priority date for domestic students. Applications are processed on a rolling basis. Application fee: $50 ($100 for international students). *Expenses:* Tuition: Full-time $9,090; part-time $505 per hour. Required fees: $490; $66 per semester. One-time fee: $50. Tuition and fees vary according to course load and degree level. *Financial support:* In 2006–07, 10 students received support, including 1 fellowship (averaging $1,200 per year); career-related internships or fieldwork and scholarships/grants also available. Support available to part-time students. Financial award application deadline: 6/30; financial award applicants required to submit FAFSA. *Unit head:* Dr. Christopher McNair, Dean, 325-670-1401, Fax: 325-670-1385, E-mail: cmcnair@hsutx.edu. *Application contact:* Dr. Gary Stanlake, Dean of Graduate Studies, 325-670-1298, Fax: 325-670-1564, E-mail: gradoff@hsutx.edu.

Harvard University, Graduate School of Education, Master's Programs in Education, Cambridge, MA 02138. Offers arts in education (Ed M); education policy and management (Ed M); higher education (Ed M); human development and psychology (Ed M); international education policy (Ed M); language and literacy (Ed M); learning and teaching (Ed M); mid-career mathematics and science (teaching certificate) (Ed M); mind brain and education (Ed M); risk and prevention (Ed M); school leadership (Ed M); special studies (Ed M); teaching and curriculum (teaching certificate) (Ed M); technology innovation and education (Ed M). Part-time programs available. *Faculty:* 58 full-time (25 women), 40 part-time/adjunct (22 women). *Students:* 540 full-time (412 women), 90 part-time (70 women); includes 137 minority (49 African Americans, 2 American Indian/Alaska Native, 61 Asian Americans or Pacific Islanders, 25 Hispanic Americans), 70 international. Average age 29. 1,211 applicants, 61% accepted, 585 enrolled. In 2006, 591 degrees awarded. *Entrance requirements:* For master's, GRE General Test, 3 letters of recommendation, official transcripts, statement of purpose. Additional exam requirements/recommendations for international students: Required—TOEFL (minimum score 600 paper-based; 250 computer-based; 100 iBT), TWE (minimum score 5). *Application deadline:* For fall admission, 1/2 for domestic and international students. Application fee: $85. Electronic applications accepted. *Expenses:* Contact institution. *Financial support:* In 2006–07, 392 students received support, including 23 fellowships (averaging $15,870 per year); career-related internships or fieldwork, Federal Work-Study, institutionally sponsored loans, scholarships/grants, health care benefits, tuition waivers (full and partial), and unspecified assistantships also available. Support available to part-time students. Financial award application deadline: 2/2; financial award applicants required to submit FAFSA. *Faculty research:* Learning and development; educational leadership and organizations; educational policy analysis. Total annual research expenditures: $14.8 million. *Unit head:* Dr. James Stiles, Associate Dean for Degree Programs. *Application contact:* Information Contact, 617-495-3414, Fax: 617-496-3577, E-mail: gseadmissions@harvard.edu.

Heritage University, Graduate Programs in Education, Toppenish, WA 98948-9599. Offers counseling (M Ed); educational administration (M Ed); professional studies (M Ed), including bilingual education/ESL, biology, English and literature, reading/literacy, special education; teaching (MIT). Part-time and evening/weekend programs available. *Faculty:* 21 full-time (13 women), 67 part-time/adjunct (35 women). *Students:* 328 full-time (232 women), 146 part-time (96 women); includes 135 minority (11 African Americans, 11 American Indian/Alaska Native, 12 Asian Americans or Pacific Islanders, 101 Hispanic Americans). Average age 38. 245 applicants, 76% accepted, 134 enrolled. In 2006, 254 degrees awarded. *Degree requirements:* For master's, thesis (for some programs), comprehensive exam, registration. *Entrance requirements:* For master's, interview, letters of recommendation, teaching certificate. Additional exam requirements/recommendations for international students: Recommended—TOEFL (minimum score 550 paper-based; 213 computer-based). *Application deadline:* For fall admission, 3/15 priority date for domestic and international students; for spring admission, 2/1 priority date for domestic and international students. Applications are processed on a rolling basis. Application fee: $50 ($100 for international students). *Financial support:* Career-related internships or fieldwork, Federal Work-Study, institutionally sponsored loans, and tuition waivers (partial) available. Support available to part-time students. Financial award application deadline: 2/10; financial award applicants required to submit FAFSA. *Unit head:* Jim Borst, Dean of the College of Education and Psychology, 509-865-8652, Fax: 509-865-8629, E-mail: borst_j@heritage.edu. *Application contact:* Kathy Otto, Coordinator of Administrative Services, 509-865-8635, Fax: 509-865-8629, E-mail: otto_k@heritage.edu.

Hofstra University, School of Education and Allied Human Services, Department of Curriculum and Teaching, Program in Elementary Education-Math/Science/Technology, Hempstead, NY 11549. Offers MA. *Accreditation:* NCATE. Part-time and evening/weekend programs available. *Students:* 8 full-time (7 women), 30 part-time (27 women); includes 5 minority (2 African Americans, 3 Hispanic Americans). Average age 25. 8 applicants, 88% accepted, 4 enrolled. In 2006, 26 degrees awarded. *Degree requirements:* For master's, thesis, BA or BS in elementary education. *Entrance requirements:* For master's, 2 letters of recommendation, interview, teaching certificate (MA), essay. Additional exam requirements/recommendations for international students: Required—TOEFL (minimum score 550 paper-based; 213 computer-based). *Application deadline:* Applications are processed on a rolling basis. Application fee: $60. Electronic applications accepted. *Expenses:* Tuition: Full-time $13,320; part-time $740 per credit. Required fees: $930; $155 per term. *Financial support:* In 2006–07, 5 students received support, including 4 fellowships with tuition reimbursements available (averaging $300 per year); research assistantships with tuition reimbursements available, scholarships/grants, tuition waivers (full and partial), and unspecified assistantships also available. Support available to part-time students. Financial award applicants required to submit FAFSA. *Faculty research:* Constructivism, mathematical reasoning, concept formation, science of learning, interdisciplinary curriculum. *Unit head:* Dr. Jacqueline Grennon Brooks, Program Director, 516-463-5371, Fax: 516-463-6196, E-mail: catjzk@hofstra.edu. *Application contact:* Carol Drummer, Dean of Graduate Admissions, 516-463-4876, Fax: 516-463-4664, E-mail: gradstudent@hofstra.edu.

Hofstra University, School of Education and Allied Human Services, Department of Curriculum and Teaching, Program in Science Education, Hempstead, NY 11549. Offers science education (biology, chemistry, geology, physics, earth science) (MA); science education (biology, chemistry, physics, earth science, geology) (MS Ed); secondary education (intensive program) (CAS). *Students:* 15 full-time (13 women), 14 part-time (7 women); includes 2 minority (both Asian Americans or Pacific Islanders) Average age 26. 27 applicants, 89% accepted, 15 enrolled. In 2006, 17 degrees awarded. *Degree requirements:* For master's, one foreign language, comprehensive exam (for some programs), registration, electronic portfolio, thesis optional; for CAS, one foreign language. *Entrance requirements:* For master's, 2 letters of recommendation, teacher certification (MA), essay. Additional exam requirements/recommendations for international students: Required—TOEFL (minimum score 550 paper-based; 213 computer-based). *Application deadline:* Applications are processed on a rolling basis. Application fee: $60. Electronic applications accepted. *Expenses:* Tuition: Full-time $13,320; part-time $740 per credit. Required fees: $930; $155 per term. *Financial support:* In 2006–07, 7 students received support, including 4 fellowships with tuition reimbursements available (averaging $3,338 per year), 1 research assistantship (averaging $5,685 per year); Federal Work-Study, traineeships, tuition waivers (full and partial), and unspecified assistantships also available. Financial award applicants required to submit FAFSA. *Faculty research:* Multicultural science education, hard to staff school research, concept-based curriculum, use of technology in science teaching and learning. *Unit head:* Dr. S. Maxwell Hines, Director, 516-463-5774, Fax: 516-463-6196, E-mail: catsmh@hofstra.edu. *Application contact:* Carol Drummer, Dean of Graduate Admissions, 516-463-4876, Fax: 516-463-4664, E-mail: gradstudent@hofstra.edu.

Hood College, Graduate School, Department of Education, Frederick, MD 21701-8575. Offers curriculum and instruction (MS), including early childhood education, elementary education, elementary school science and mathematics, secondary education, special education; educational leadership (MS); reading specialization (MS); teaching the struggling reader (Certificate). Part-time and evening/weekend programs available. *Faculty:* 4 full-time (3 women), 32 part-time/adjunct (16 women). *Students:* 5 full-time (3 women), 371 part-time (313 women); includes 30 minority (23 African Americans, 4 Asian Americans or Pacific Islanders, 3 Hispanic Americans). Average age 32. 71 applicants, 99% accepted, 59 enrolled. In 2006, 67 degrees awarded. *Degree requirements:* For master's, action research project, portfolio (reading). *Entrance requirements:* For master's, minimum GPA of 2.5, teaching certification. *Application deadline:* Applications are processed on a rolling basis. Application fee: $35. *Expenses:* Tuition: Part-time $350 per credit. Required fees: $20 per semester. *Financial support:* Applicants required to submit FAFSA. *Faculty research:* Leadership, action research, brain research, learning styles. *Unit head:* Dr. John George, Chairperson, 301-696-3471, Fax: 301-696-3597, E-mail: george@hood.edu. *Application contact:* Dr. Kathleen C. Bands, Associate Dean of Graduate School, 301-696-3811, Fax: 301-696-3597, E-mail: gofurther@hood.edu.

Hunter College of the City University of New York, Graduate School, School of Arts and Sciences, Department of Geography, New York, NY 10021-5085. Offers analytical geography (MA); earth system science (MA); environmental and social issues (MA); geographic information science (Certificate); geographic information systems (MA); teaching earth science (MA). Part-time and evening/weekend programs available. *Faculty:* 3 full-time (1 woman), 10 part-time/adjunct (0 women). *Students:* 2 full-time (0 women), 34 part-time (19 women); includes 2 minority (1 African American, 1 Hispanic American). Average age 33. 18 applicants, 94% accepted, 13 enrolled. In 2006, 14 degrees awarded. *Degree requirements:* For master's, comprehensive exam or thesis. *Entrance requirements:* For master's, GRE General Test, minimum B average in major, minimum B- average overall, 18 credits of course work in geography, 2 letters of recommendation; for Certificate, minimum of B average in major, B-

Science Education

Hunter College of the City University of New York (continued)

overall. Additional exam requirements/recommendations for international students: Required—TOEFL. *Application deadline:* For fall admission, 4/1 for domestic students; for spring admission, 11/1 for domestic students. Applications are processed on a rolling basis. Application fee: $125. *Expenses:* Tuition, state resident: full-time $3,200; part-time $270 per credit. Tuition, nonresident: part-time $500 per credit. Required fees: $45 per semester. *Financial support:* In 2006–07, 1 fellowship (averaging $3,000 per year), 2 research assistantships (averaging $10,000 per year), 10 teaching assistantships (averaging $6,000 per year) were awarded; career-related internships or fieldwork, Federal Work-Study, institutionally sponsored loans, and unspecified assistantships also available. Financial award application deadline: 3/1. *Faculty research:* Urban geography, economic geography, geographic information science, demographic methods, climate change. *Unit head:* Prof. William Solecki, Chair, 212-772-4536, Fax: 212-772-5268, E-mail: wsolecki@hunter.cuny.edu. *Application contact:* Prof. Marianna Pavlovskaya, Graduate Adviser, 212-772-5320, Fax: 212-772-5268, E-mail: mpavlov@geo.hunter.cuny.edu.

Hunter College of the City University of New York, Graduate School, School of Education, Programs in Secondary Education, Concentration in Biology Education, New York, NY 10021-5085. Offers MA. *Accreditation:* NCATE. *Students:* Average age 35. 16 applicants, 19% accepted, 2 enrolled. In 2006, 5 degrees awarded. *Degree requirements:* For master's, thesis, professional teaching portfolio, New York State Teacher Certification Exams, research project. *Entrance requirements:* For master's, minimum GPA of 2.8, 2 letters of reference, 21 credits of course work in biology. Additional exam requirements/recommendations for international students: Required—TOEFL, TWE. *Application deadline:* For fall admission, 4/1 for domestic students, 2/1 for international students; for spring admission, 11/1 for domestic students, 9/1 for international students. Application fee: $125. *Expenses:* Tuition, state resident: part-time $270 per credit. Tuition, nonresident: part-time $500 per credit. Required fees: $45 per semester. *Financial support:* Federal Work-Study and tuition waivers (partial) available. Support available to part-time students. *Unit head:* Dr. Steve Demeo, Program Advisor, 212-772-4776, E-mail: sdemeo@hunter.cuny.edu. *Application contact:* William Zlata, Director for Graduate Admissions, 212-772-4482, Fax: 212-650-3336, E-mail: admissions@hunter.cuny.edu.

Hunter College of the City University of New York, Graduate School, School of Education, Programs in Secondary Education, Concentration in Chemistry Education, New York, NY 10021-5085. Offers MA. *Accreditation:* NCATE. *Students:* Average age 32. 1 applicant, 0% accepted. In 2006, 2 degrees awarded. *Degree requirements:* For master's, thesis, professional teaching portfolio, New York State Teacher Certification Exam. *Entrance requirements:* For master's, minimum GPA of 2.8, 2 letters of reference, minimum of 29 credits in science and mathematics. *Application deadline:* For fall admission, 4/1 for domestic students, 2/1 for international students; for spring admission, 11/1 for domestic students, 9/1 for international students. Application fee: $125. *Expenses:* Tuition, state resident: part-time $270 per credit. Tuition, nonresident: part-time $500 per credit. Required fees: $45 per semester. *Financial support:* Federal Work-Study and tuition waivers (partial) available. Support available to part-time students. *Unit head:* Dr. Klaus Grohmann, Program Advisor, 212-772-5333, E-mail: gklaus@patsy.hunter.cuny.edu. *Application contact:* William Zlata, Director for Graduate Admissions, 212-772-4482, Fax: 212-650-3336, E-mail: admissions@hunter.cuny.edu.

Hunter College of the City University of New York, Graduate School, School of Education, Programs in Secondary Education, Concentration in Physics Education, New York, NY 10021-5085. Offers MA. *Accreditation:* NCATE. *Students:* Average age 31. 1 applicant, 0% accepted. In 2006, 1 degree awarded. *Degree requirements:* For master's, thesis, professional teaching portfolio, N.Y. State Teacher Certification Exam, research project. *Entrance requirements:* For master's, minimum GPA of 2.8, undergraduate major in physics, 2 letters of reference. Additional exam requirements/recommendations for international students: Required—TOEFL, TWE. *Application deadline:* For fall admission, 4/1 for domestic students, 2/1 for international students; for spring admission, 11/1 for domestic students, 9/1 for international students. Application fee: $125. *Expenses:* Tuition, state resident: part-time $270 per credit. Tuition, nonresident: part-time $500 per credit. Required fees: $45 per semester. *Financial support:* Federal Work-Study and tuition waivers (partial) available. Support available to part-time students. *Unit head:* Dr. Rodney Varley, Program Adviser, 212-772-5252, E-mail: rvarley@shiva.hunter.cuny.edu. *Application contact:* William Zlata, Director for Graduate Admissions, 212-772-4482, Fax: 212-650-3336, E-mail: admissions@hunter.cuny.edu.

ICR Graduate School, Graduate Programs, Santee, CA 92071. Offers astro/geophysics (MS); biology (MS); geology (MS); science education (MS). Part-time programs available. *Faculty:* 5 full-time (1 woman), 1 part-time/adjunct (0 women). *Students:* 6 full-time (2 women), 6 part-time (3 women). Average age 45. In 2006, 4 degrees awarded. *Degree requirements:* For master's, thesis (for some programs), comprehensive exam (for some programs). *Entrance requirements:* For master's, minimum undergraduate GPA of 3.0, bachelor's degree in science or science education. *Application deadline:* Applications are processed on a rolling basis. Application fee: $30. *Expenses:* Tuition: Part-time $200 per semester. *Faculty research:* Age of the earth, limits of variation, catastrophe, optimum methods for teaching. Total annual research expenditures: $200,000. *Unit head:* Dr. Kenneth B. Cumming, Dean, 619-448-0900, Fax: 619-448-3469. *Application contact:* Dr. Jack Kriege, Registrar, 619-448-0900 Ext. 6016, Fax: 619-448-3469, E-mail: jkriege@icr.org.

Illinois Institute of Technology, Graduate College, College of Science and Letters, Department of Computer Science, Chicago, IL 60616-3793. Offers computer science (MCS, MS, PhD); teaching (MST); telecommunications and software engineering (MTSE); MS/M Ch E. Part-time and evening/weekend programs available. Postbaccalaureate distance learning degree programs offered (no on-campus study). *Faculty:* 28 full-time (6 women), 6 part-time/adjunct (0 women). *Students:* 314 full-time (74 women), 139 part-time (33 women); includes 30 minority (6 African Americans, 22 Asian Americans or Pacific Islanders, 2 Hispanic Americans), 375 international. Average age 26. 1,189 applicants, 58% accepted, 151 enrolled. In 2006, 135 master's, 15 doctorates awarded. Terminal master's awarded for partial completion of doctoral program. *Degree requirements:* For master's, thesis (for some programs); for doctorate, thesis/dissertation, comprehensive exam. *Entrance requirements:* For master's and doctorate, GRE General Test, minimum undergraduate GPA of 3.0. Additional exam requirements/recommendations for international students: Required—TOEFL (minimum score 550 paper-based; 213 computer-based). *Application deadline:* For fall admission, 5/1 for domestic and international students; for spring admission, 10/15 for domestic and international students. Applications are processed on a rolling basis. Application fee: $40. Electronic applications accepted. *Expenses:* Tuition: Full-time $13,086; part-time $727 per credit. Required fees: $7 per credit. $235 per term. Tuition and fees vary according to class time, course level, course load, program and student level. *Financial support:* In 2006–07, 28 research assistantships with full tuition reimbursements (averaging $12,000 per year), 31 teaching assistantships with full tuition reimbursements (averaging $12,000 per year) were awarded; fellowships, career-related internships or fieldwork, Federal Work-Study, institutionally sponsored loans, scholarships/grants, traineeships, health care benefits, tuition waivers (partial), and unspecified assistantships also available. Support available to part-time students. Financial award applicants required to submit FAFSA. *Faculty research:* Information retrieval, parallel and distributed computing, networking, algorithms, natural language processing. Total annual research expenditures: $1.9 million. *Unit head:* Cynthia S. Hood, Associate Chair, 312-567-3309, Fax: 312-567-5067. *Application contact:* Morgan Frederick, Assistant Director of Graduate Communications, 866-472-3448, Fax: 312-567-3138, E-mail: inquiry.grad@iit.edu.

Illinois Institute of Technology, Graduate College, College of Science and Letters, Department of Mathematics and Science Education, Chicago, IL 60616-3793. Offers mathematics education (MME, MS, PhD); science education (MS, MSE, PhD). *Faculty:* 8 full-time (3 women), 1 (woman) part-time/adjunct. *Students:* 38 full-time (25 women), 37 part-time (23 women); includes 25 minority (14 African Americans, 5 Asian Americans or Pacific Islanders, 6 Hispanic Americans), 6 international. Average age 38. 36 applicants, 64% accepted, 7 enrolled. In 2006, 25 master's, 2 doctorates awarded. *Degree requirements:* For master's, thesis or alternative, comprehensive exam (for some programs); for doctorate, thesis/dissertation, comprehensive exam. *Entrance requirements:* For master's, GRE General Test, minimum undergraduate GPA of 3.0; for doctorate, GRE General Test, minimum GPA of 3.0, 3 years of teaching experience. Additional exam requirements/recommendations for international students: Required—TOEFL (minimum score 550 paper-based; 213 computer-based). *Application deadline:* For fall admission, 5/1 for domestic and international students; for spring admission, 10/15 for domestic and international students. Applications are processed on a rolling basis. Application fee: $40. Electronic applications accepted. *Expenses:* Tuition: Full-time $13,086; part-time $727 per credit. Required fees: $7 per credit. $235 per term. Tuition and fees vary according to class time, course level, course load, program and student level. *Financial support:* In 2006–07, 12 research assistantships with full tuition reimbursements (averaging $18,000 per year) were awarded; fellowships, career-related internships or fieldwork, Federal Work-Study, institutionally sponsored loans, scholarships/grants, health care benefits, tuition waivers (partial), and unspecified assistantships also available. Support available to part-time students. *Faculty research:* Nature of science, scientific inquiry, pedagogical content knowledge, classroom discourse, model eliciting activities. Total annual research expenditures: $348,657. *Unit head:* Dr. Norman G. Lederman, Chair, Professor, 312-567-3658, Fax: 312-567-3659, E-mail: ledermann@iit.edu.

Indiana State University, School of Graduate Studies, College of Arts and Sciences, Department of Life Sciences, Terre Haute, IN 47809-1401. Offers ecology (PhD); life sciences (MS); microbiology (PhD); physiology (PhD); science education (MS); sports medicine (PhD). *Faculty:* 22 full-time (6 women), 4 part-time/adjunct (1 woman). *Students:* 49 full-time (21 women), 15 part-time (7 women); includes 2 minority (both Asian Americans or Pacific Islanders), 14 international. Average age 28. 42 applicants, 64% accepted, 21 enrolled. In 2006, 14 master's, 2 doctorates awarded. *Degree requirements:* For master's, thesis (for some programs); for doctorate, thesis/dissertation, comprehensive exam. *Entrance requirements:* For master's and doctorate, GRE General Test. *Application deadline:* For fall admission, 7/1 priority date for domestic students; for spring admission, 11/1 priority date for domestic students. Applications are processed on a rolling basis. Application fee: $35. Electronic applications accepted. *Expenses:* Tuition, state resident: part-time $278 per credit. Tuition, nonresident: part-time $552 per credit. *Financial support:* In 2006–07, 23 teaching assistantships with partial tuition reimbursements (averaging $8,478 per year) were awarded; research assistantships with partial tuition reimbursements, Federal Work-Study, institutionally sponsored loans, and tuition waivers (partial) also available. Financial award application deadline: 3/1; financial award applicants required to submit FAFSA. *Unit head:* Dr. Swapan Ghosh, Interim Chairperson, 812-237-2400.

Indiana State University, School of Graduate Studies, College of Arts and Sciences, Department of Science Education, Terre Haute, IN 47809-1401. Offers MS. *Accreditation:* NCATE. *Faculty:* 1 part-time/adjunct (0 women). *Students:* 1 (woman) full-time, 5 part-time (4 women). Average age 30. 1 applicant, 100% accepted, 0 enrolled. In 2006, 1 degree awarded. *Degree requirements:* For master's, thesis optional. *Application deadline:* For fall admission, 7/1 priority date for domestic students; for spring admission, 11/1 priority date for domestic students. Applications are processed on a rolling basis. Application fee: $35. Electronic applications accepted. *Expenses:* Tuition, state resident: part-time $278 per credit. Tuition, nonresident: part-time $552 per credit. *Financial support:* Teaching assistantships, tuition waivers (partial) available. Financial award application deadline: 3/1; financial award applicants required to submit FAFSA. *Unit head:* Dr. Susan Berta, Interim Coordinator, 812-237-3297.

Indiana Tech, Program in Science, Fort Wayne, IN 46803-1297. Offers MSE. Part-time and evening/weekend programs available. *Entrance requirements:* Additional exam requirements/recommendations for international students: Required—TOEFL (minimum score 550 paper-based). Electronic applications accepted.

Indiana University Bloomington, Graduate School, College of Arts and Sciences, Department of Biology, Bloomington, IN 47405-7000. Offers biology teaching (MAT); evolution, ecology, and behavior (MA, PhD); genetics (PhD); microbiology (MA, PhD); molecular, cellular, and developmental biology (PhD); plant sciences (MA, PhD); zoology (MA, PhD). PhD offered through the University Graduate School. Part-time programs available. *Faculty:* 42 full-time (8 women), 21 part-time/adjunct (6 women). *Students:* 85 full-time (53 women), 78 part-time (49 women); includes 21 minority (6 African Americans, 1 American Indian/Alaska Native, 5 Asian Americans or Pacific Islanders, 9 Hispanic Americans), 33 international. Average age 27. In 2006, 3 master's, 22 doctorates awarded. Terminal master's awarded for partial completion of doctoral program. *Degree requirements:* For master's and doctorate, thesis/dissertation, oral defense. *Entrance requirements:* For master's and doctorate, GRE General Test. Additional exam requirements/recommendations for international students: Required—TOEFL. *Application deadline:* For fall admission, 1/5 priority date for domestic students; for spring admission, 9/1 priority date for domestic students. Applications are processed on a rolling basis. Application fee: $45. Electronic applications accepted. *Expenses:* Tuition, state resident: full-time $5,791; part-time $241 per credit hour. Tuition, nonresident: full-time $16,866; part-time $703 per credit hour. *Financial support:* In 2006–07, fellowships with tuition reimbursements (averaging $19,500 per year), research assistantships with tuition reimbursements (averaging $19,500 per year), teaching assistantships with tuition reimbursements (averaging $18,000 per year) were awarded; scholarships/grants and tuition waivers (full) also available. *Unit head:* Dr. Elizabeth C. Raff, Chair, 812-855-5522. *Application contact:* Gretchen Clearwater, Adviser for Graduate Affairs, 812-855-1861, Fax: 812-855-6705, E-mail: biograd@bio.indiana.edu.

Indiana University Bloomington, Graduate School, College of Arts and Sciences, Department of Chemistry, Bloomington, IN 47405-7000. Offers analytical chemistry (PhD); biological chemistry (PhD); chemistry (MAT); inorganic chemistry (PhD); physical chemistry (PhD). PhD offered through the University Graduate School. *Faculty:* 29 full-time (2 women). *Students:* 95 full-time (25 women), 60 part-time (20 women); includes 10 minority (3 African Americans, 5 Asian Americans or Pacific Islanders, 2 Hispanic Americans), 57 international. Average age 27. In 2006, 6 master's, 12 doctorates awarded. Terminal master's awarded for partial completion of doctoral program. *Degree requirements:* For master's and doctorate, thesis/dissertation. *Entrance requirements:* For master's and doctorate, GRE General Test, GRE Subject Test. Additional exam requirements/recommendations for international students: Required—TOEFL. *Application deadline:* For fall admission, 1/15 priority date for domestic students, 12/15 for international students; for spring admission, 9/1 priority date for domestic students, 9/1 for international students. Applications are processed on a rolling basis. Application fee: $50 ($60 for international students). *Expenses:* Tuition, state resident: full-time $5,791; part-time $241 per credit hour. Tuition, nonresident: full-time $16,866; part-time $703 per credit hour. *Financial support:* In 2006–07, 23 fellowships with full tuition reimbursements, 57 research assistantships with full tuition reimbursements, 78 teaching assistantships with full tuition reimbursements were awarded; Federal Work-Study and institutionally sponsored loans also available. *Faculty research:* Synthesis of complex natural products, organic reaction mechanisms, organic electrochemistry, transitive-metal chemistry, solid-state and surface chemistry. Total annual research expenditures: $7.7 million. *Unit head:* Richard DiMarchi, Chairperson, 812-855-2268. *Application contact:* Mary Vayne, Admissions, 812-855-2069.

Indiana University Bloomington, School of Education, Department of Curriculum and Instruction, Bloomington, IN 47405-7000. Offers art education (MS, Ed D, PhD); curriculum studies (Ed D, PhD); elementary education (MS, Ed D, PhD, Ed S); mathematics education (MS, Ed D, PhD); science education (MS, Ed D, PhD); secondary education (MS, Ed D, PhD); social studies education (MS, PhD); special education (MS, Ed D, PhD, Ed S). PhD offered through the University Graduate School. *Accreditation:* NCATE. Part-time and evening/weekend programs available. *Students:* 39 full-time (28 women), 82 part-time (54 women); includes 15 minority (5 African Americans, 1 American Indian/Alaska Native, 6 Asian Americans or Pacific Islanders, 3 Hispanic Americans), 33 international. Average age 37. In 2006, 1 degree awarded. Terminal master's awarded for partial completion of doctoral program. *Degree requirements:* For doctorate, thesis/dissertation; for Ed S, comprehensive exam or project. *Entrance requirements:* For master's, doctorate, and Ed S, GRE General Test. *Application* *deadline:* For fall admission, 6/1 priority date for domestic students, 3/1 for international students; for winter admission, 11/1 priority date for domestic students; for spring admission, 9/1 for international students. Applications are processed on a rolling basis. Application fee: $50 ($60 for international students). Electronic applications accepted. *Expenses:* Tuition, state resident: full-time $5,791; part-time $241 per credit hour. Tuition, nonresident: full-time $16,866; part-time $703 per credit hour. *Financial support:* Fellowships with full and partial tuition reimbursements, research assistantships with full and partial tuition reimbursements, teaching assistantships with full and partial tuition reimbursements, career-related internships or fieldwork, Federal Work-Study, institutionally sponsored loans, and tuition waivers (partial) available. Support available to part-time students. *Unit head:* Cary Buzzelli, Chairperson, 812-856-8100. *Application contact:* Bobbie Partenheimer, Admissions Services Coordinator, 812-856-8127, Fax: 812-856-8333, E-mail: partenhe@indiana.edu.

Instituto Tecnológico y de Estudios Superiores de Monterrey, Campus Monterrey, Graduate and Research Division, Program in Natural and Social Sciences, Monterrey, Mexico. Offers biotechnology (MS); chemistry (MS, PhD); communications (MS); education (MA). Part-time programs available. *Degree requirements:* For master's and doctorate, one foreign language, thesis/dissertation. *Entrance requirements:* For master's, EXADEP; for doctorate, EXADEP, master's degree in related field. Additional exam requirements/recommendations for international students: Required—TOEFL. *Faculty research:* Cultural industries, mineral substances, bioremediation, food processing, CQ in industrial chemical processing.

Inter American University of Puerto Rico, Metropolitan Campus, Faculty of Education, Program in Teaching of Science, San Juan, PR 00919-1293. Offers MA Ed. *Degree requirements:* For master's, comprehensive exam. *Entrance requirements:* For master's, GRE or EXADEP, interview. Electronic applications accepted.

Inter American University of Puerto Rico, Ponce Campus, Graduate School, Mercedita, PR 00715-1602. Offers accounting (MBA); biology (M Ed); chemistry (M Ed); criminal justice (MA); elementary education (M Ed); English as a Second Language (M Ed); finance (MBA); history (M Ed); human resources (MBA); mathematics (M Ed); Spanish (M Ed); trade (MBA). *Entrance requirements:* For master's, minimum GPA of 2.5.

Inter American University of Puerto Rico, San Germán Campus, Graduate Studies Center, Graduate Program in Science Education, San Germán, PR 00683-5008. Offers MA. Part-time and evening/weekend programs available. *Faculty:* 8 full-time, 11 part-time/adjunct. *Students:* 28. In 2006, 9 degrees awarded. *Degree requirements:* For master's, comprehensive exam. *Entrance requirements:* For master's, GRE General Test or EXADEP, minimum GPA of 3.0. *Application deadline:* For fall admission, 4/30 priority date for domestic students; for spring admission, 11/15 for domestic students. Applications are processed on a rolling basis. Application fee: $31. *Expenses:* Tuition: Part-time $175 per credit. Required fees: $238 per semester. Tuition and fees vary according to degree level. *Financial support:* Teaching assistantships, unspecified assistantships available. *Application contact:* Dr. Aurora Graniela, Graduate Coordinator, 787-264-1912 Ext. 7355, Fax: 787-892-7510, E-mail: aurora@sg.inter.edu.

Iona College, School of Arts and Science, Program in Adolescence Education, New Rochelle, NY 10801-1890. Offers biology education (MS Ed, MST); English education (MS Ed, MST); mathematics education (MS Ed, MST); social studies education (MS Ed, MST); Spanish education (MS Ed, MST). *Accreditation:* NCATE. Part-time and evening/weekend programs available. *Faculty:* 11 full-time (6 women), 21 part-time/adjunct (13 women). *Students:* 15 full-time (9 women), 68 part-time (52 women); includes 6 minority (1 African American, 1 Asian American or Pacific Islander, 4 Hispanic Americans). Average age 28. 42 applicants, 57% accepted, 11 enrolled. In 2006, 29 degrees awarded. *Degree requirements:* For master's, thesis or alternative. *Entrance requirements:* For master's, minimum GPA of 2.5 (MST), New York teaching certificate (MS Ed). Additional exam requirements/recommendations for international students: Required—TOEFL (minimum score 550 paper-based; 213 computer-based). *Application deadline:* Applications are processed on a rolling basis. Application fee: $50. Electronic applications accepted. *Expenses:* Tuition: Part-time $665 per credit. Required fees: $150 per term. *Financial support:* Unspecified assistantships available. Support available to part-time students. *Faculty research:* Reading/writing, educational technology, administration, early literacy assessment, literacy development. *Unit head:* Dr. Patricia Antonacci, Chair, 914-633-2080, Fax: 914-633-2608, E-mail: pantonacci@iona.edu. *Application contact:* Veronica Jarek-Prinz, Graduate Admissions, 914-633-2289, Fax: 914-633-2012, E-mail: vjarekprinz@iona.edu.

Ithaca College, Graduate Studies, School of Humanities and Sciences, Program in Adolescent Education, Ithaca, NY 14850-7020. Offers biology 7-12 (MAT); chemistry 7-12 (MAT); English 7-12 (MAT); French 7-12 (MAT); math 7-12 (MAT); physics 7-12 (MAT); social studies 7-12 (MAT); Spanish (MAT). *Faculty:* 14 full-time (5 women), 1 (woman) part-time/adjunct. *Students:* 8 full-time (2 women), 2 part-time (both women); includes 1 minority (Hispanic American) Average age 28. 12 applicants, 92% accepted, 10 enrolled. *Entrance requirements:* For master's, minimum GPA of 3.0. *Application deadline:* For fall admission, 5/15 for domestic students; for spring admission, 12/1 for domestic students. Application fee: $40. *Expenses:* Contact institution. *Financial support:* In 2006–07, 10 students received support, including 8 teaching assistantships (averaging $5,820 per year). Financial award application deadline:3/1. *Unit head:* Linda Hanrahan, Chairperson, 607-274-3147, E-mail: lhanrahan@ithaca.edu.

Jackson State University, Graduate School, School of Science and Technology, Department of Biology, Jackson, MS 39217. Offers biology education (MST); environmental science (MS, PhD). Part-time and evening/weekend programs available. *Faculty:* 9 full-time (1 woman), 2 part-time/adjunct (1 woman). *Students:* 47 full-time (30 women), 37 part-time (18 women); includes 71 minority (67 African Americans, 1 American Indian/Alaska Native, 2 Asian Americans or Pacific Islanders, 1 Hispanic American), 8 international. In 2006, 10 master's, 7 doctorates awarded. *Degree requirements:* For master's, thesis (alternative accepted for MST); for doctorate, thesis/dissertation, comprehensive exam. *Entrance requirements:* For master's, GRE General Test; for doctorate, MAT. Additional exam requirements/recommendations for international students: Required—TOEFL. *Application deadline:* For fall admission, 3/1 priority date for domestic students; for spring admission, 10/1 for domestic students. Applications are processed on a rolling basis. Application fee: $20. *Financial support:* In 2006–07, 13 students received support. Career-related internships or fieldwork, Federal Work-Study, scholarships/grants, and unspecified assistantships available. Support available to part-time students. Financial award application deadline: 3/1; financial award applicants required to submit FAFSA. *Faculty research:* Comparative studies on the carbohydrate composition of marine macroalgae, host-parasite relationship between the spruce budworm and entomepathogen fungus. *Unit head:* Dr. Gregorie Begonia, Acting Chair, 601-979-2586, Fax: 601-979-5853, E-mail: gregorie.begonia@jsums.edu. *Application contact:* Curtis Gore, Director of Graduate Admissions, 601-979-2455, Fax: 601-974-4325, E-mail: cgore@ccaix.jsums.edu.

Jackson State University, Graduate School, School of Science and Technology, Department of Physics, Atmospheric Sciences, and General Science, Jackson, MS 39217. Offers science education (MST). Part-time and evening/weekend programs available. *Faculty:* 2 full-time (0 women). *Students:* 1 (woman) full-time, 3 part-time (2 women); includes 3 minority (all African Americans) In 2006, 3 degrees awarded. *Degree requirements:* For master's, comprehensive exam. *Entrance requirements:* For master's, GRE General Test. Additional exam requirements/recommendations for international students: Required—TOEFL. *Application deadline:* For fall admission, 3/1 priority date for domestic students; for spring admission, 10/1 for domestic students. Applications are processed on a rolling basis. Application fee: $20. *Financial support:* Application deadline: 3/1. *Unit head:* Dr. Quinton L. Williams, Chair, 601-979-7012, Fax: 601-979-6196, E-mail: quinton.l.williams@jsums.edu. *Application contact:* Curtis Gore, Director of Graduate Admissions, 601-979-2455, Fax: 601-974-4325, E-mail: cgore@ccaix.jsums.edu.

John Carroll University, Graduate School, Program in Integrated Science, University Heights, OH 44118-4581. Offers MA. Part-time programs available. *Students:* 18 applicants, 94% accepted, 16 enrolled. In 2006, 15 degrees awarded. *Median time to degree:* Master's–2 years part-time. *Degree requirements:* For master's, thesis optional. *Entrance requirements:* For master's, minimum GPA of 2.5. Application fee: $25 ($35 for international students). *Expenses:* Tuition: Full-time $9,675; part-time $645 per credit hour. Tuition and fees vary according to program. *Financial support:* Tuition waivers (partial) available. Support available to part-time students. *Unit head:* Michael Kimmel, Director, Integrated Science Program, 216-397-1507, Fax: 216-397-1835, E-mail: mkimmel@jcu.edu.

The Johns Hopkins University, School of Professional Studies in Business and Education, School of Education, Department of Teacher Development and Leadership, Baltimore, MD 21218-2699. Offers adult learning (Certificate); business leadership for independent schools (Certificate); earth/space science (Certificate); educational leadership for independent schools (Certificate); educational studies (MS); effective teaching of reading (Certificate); ESL instruction (Certificate); gifted education (Certificate); leadership for school, family and community collaboration (Certificate); reading (MS); school administration and supervision (MS, Certificate); teacher development and leadership (Ed D); teacher leadership (Certificate); technology for educators (MS); urban education (Certificate). Part-time and evening/weekend programs available. Postbaccalaureate distance learning degree programs offered (minimal on-campus study). *Students:* 19 full-time (18 women), 535 part-time (413 women); includes 98 minority (76 African Americans, 1 American Indian/Alaska Native, 18 Asian Americans or Pacific Islanders, 3 Hispanic Americans), 2 international. Average age 31. 544 applicants, 79% accepted, 374 enrolled. In 2006, 151 master's, 180 other advanced degrees awarded. *Degree requirements:* For master's and Certificate, portfolio; for doctorate, thesis/dissertation, comprehensive exam, registration. *Entrance requirements:* For master's and Certificate, minimum GPA of 3.0; for doctorate, GRE, interview, master's degree, minimum GPA of 3.0, resumé, letters of recommendation. Additional exam requirements/recommendations for international students: Required—TOEFL (minimum score 600 paper-based; 250 computer-based; 100 iBT). *Application deadline:* For fall admission, 5/1 for international students; for spring admission, 10/15 for international students. Applications are processed on a rolling basis. Application fee: $60. *Expenses:* Tuition: Full-time $32,976. Tuition and fees vary according to degree level and program. *Financial support:* Scholarships/grants available. Support available to part-time students. Financial award application deadline: 6/1; financial award applicants required to submit FAFSA. *Unit head:* Dr. Edward Pajak, Chair, 410-309-1265, Fax: 410-290-0467. *Application contact:* Carol Herrman, Admissions Coordinator, 410-872-1234, Fax: 410-872-1251, E-mail: onestop.admissions@jhu.edu.

Johnson State College, Graduate Program in Education, Program in Science Education, Johnson, VT 05656-9405. Offers MA Ed. *Faculty:* 3 full-time (2 women), 3 part-time/adjunct (2 women). *Financial support:* Federal Work-Study and unspecified assistantships available. Support available to part-time students. Financial award application deadline: 3/1; financial award applicants required to submit FAFSA. *Application contact:* Catherine H. Higley, Administrative Assistant for Graduate Programs, 800-635-2356 Ext. 1244, Fax: 802-635-1248, E-mail: higleyc@jsc.vsc.edu.

Kean University, College of Education, Program in Classroom Instruction and Curriculum, Union, NJ 07083. Offers bilingual/bicultural education (MA); classroom instruction (MA); earth science (MA); educational technology (MA); elementary education (MA); mathematics/science/computer education (MA); teaching (MA); teaching English as a second language (MA). *Accreditation:* NCATE. Part-time and evening/weekend programs available. *Faculty:* 19 full-time (10 women). *Students:* 34 full-time (29 women), 174 part-time (139 women); includes 73 minority (9 African Americans, 7 Asian Americans or Pacific Islanders, 57 Hispanic Americans), 4 international. Average age 34. 103 applicants, 93% accepted, 67 enrolled. In 2006, 82 degrees awarded. *Degree requirements:* For master's, 2 foreign languages, thesis, comprehensive exam. *Entrance requirements:* For master's, GRE General Test or MAT, PRAXIS, minimum GPA of 2.75, 2 letters of recommendation, interview. *Application deadline:* For fall admission, 5/1 for domestic students; for spring admission, 11/1 for domestic students. Application fee: $60 ($150 for international students). Electronic applications accepted. *Expenses:* Tuition, state resident: full-time $8,856; part-time $369 per credit. Tuition, nonresident: full-time $11,256; part-time $469 per credit. *Financial support:* In 2006–07, 2 research assistantships with full tuition reimbursements (averaging $3,217 per year) were awarded; unspecified assistantships also available. *Unit head:* Dr. Frank H. Osborn, Program Coordinator, 908-737-4289, E-mail: fosborne@kean.edu. *Application contact:* Joanne Morris, Director of Graduate Admissions, 908-737-3355, Fax: 908-737-3354, E-mail: grad-adm@kean.edu.

Kutztown University of Pennsylvania, College of Graduate Studies and Extended Learning, College of Education, Program in Secondary Education, Kutztown, PA 19530-0730. Offers biology (M Ed); curriculum and instruction (M Ed); English (M Ed); mathematics (M Ed); secondary education (Certificate); social studies (M Ed). *Accreditation:* NCATE. Part-time and evening/weekend programs available. *Faculty:* 5 full-time (2 women). *Students:* 69 full-time (32 women), 80 part-time (44 women); includes 5 minority (1 African American, 1 American Indian/Alaska Native, 2 Asian Americans or Pacific Islanders, 1 Hispanic American), 3 international. Average age 32. 80 applicants, 88% accepted, 34 enrolled. In 2006, 26 degrees awarded. *Degree requirements:* For master's, thesis optional. *Entrance requirements:* For master's, GRE General Test. Additional exam requirements/recommendations for international students: Required—TOEFL. *Application deadline:* Applications are processed on a rolling basis. Application fee: $35. Electronic applications accepted. *Expenses:* Tuition, state resident: full-time $6,048; part-time $336 per credit. Tuition, nonresident: full-time $9,678; part-time $538 per credit. *Financial support:* In 2006–07, research assistantships with full tuition reimbursements (averaging $5,000 per year); career-related internships or fieldwork, Federal Work-Study, and unspecified assistantships also available. Financial award application deadline: 3/15; financial award applicants required to submit FAFSA. *Unit head:* Dr. Kathleen Dolgos, Chairperson, 610-683-4279, Fax: 610-683-1338, E-mail: dolgos@kutztown.edu.

Lawrence Technological University, College of Arts and Sciences, Southfield, MI 48075-1058. Offers computer science (MS); educational technology (MET); science education (MSE); technical communication (MS). Part-time and evening/weekend programs available. *Faculty:* 9 full-time (3 women), 8 part-time/adjunct (0 women). *Students:* 5 full-time (0 women), 100 part-time (59 women); includes 21 minority (8 African Americans, 13 Asian Americans or Pacific Islanders), 2 international. Average age 33. 87 applicants, 87% accepted, 39 enrolled. In 2006, 42 degrees awarded. *Entrance requirements:* For master's, GRE. Additional exam requirements/recommendations for international students: Required—TOEFL (minimum score 550 paper-based; 213 computer-based). *Application deadline:* For fall admission, 8/1 priority date for domestic students; for winter admission, 12/1 priority date for domestic students; for spring admission, 5/1 for domestic students. Applications are processed on a rolling basis. Application fee: $50. Electronic applications accepted. *Financial support:* Application deadline: 3/1; *Unit head:* Dr. Hsiao-Ping Moore, Interim Dean, 248-204-3500, Fax: 248-204-3518, E-mail: scidean@ltu.edu. *Application contact:* Jane Rohrback, Director of Admissions, 248-204-3160, Fax: 248-204-3188, E-mail: admissions@ltu.edu.

Lebanon Valley College, Graduate Studies and Continuing Education, Program in Science Education, Annville, PA 17003-1400. Offers MSE. Part-time programs available. *Faculty:* 4 part-time/adjunct (2 women). *Students:* Average age 33. In 2006, 14 degrees awarded. *Degree requirements:* For master's, thesis, registration. *Entrance requirements:* For master's, minimum GPA of 3.0, teacher certification. *Application deadline:* Applications are processed on a rolling basis. Application fee: $30. *Expenses:* Tuition: Full-time $28,280; part-time $390 per credit. Required fees: $575. *Financial support:* In 2006–07, 2 students received support. Application deadline: 5/1; *Unit head:* Patricia Woods, Coordinator, 717-867-6190, Fax: 717-867-6018.

Lehman College of the City University of New York, Division of Education, Department of Middle and High School Education, Program in Science Education, Bronx, NY 10468-1589. Offers MS Ed. *Accreditation:* NCATE.

Science Education

Lesley University, School of Education, Cambridge, MA 02138-2790. Offers curriculum and instruction (M Ed, CAGS); early childhood education (M Ed); educational studies (PhD); elementary education (M Ed); individually designed (M Ed); middle school education (M Ed); moderate special needs (M Ed); reading (M Ed, CAGS); science in education (M Ed); severe special needs (M Ed); special needs (CAGS); technology in education (M Ed, CAGS). Part-time and evening/weekend programs available. Postbaccalaureate distance learning degree programs offered (no on-campus study). *Faculty:* 47 full-time (39 women), 208 part-time/adjunct (135 women). *Students:* 242 full-time (222 women), 2,903 part-time (2,495 women); includes 279 minority (179 African Americans, 7 American Indian/Alaska Native, 25 Asian Americans or Pacific Islanders, 68 Hispanic Americans), 10 international. Average age 36. 1,186 applicants, 96% accepted, 792 enrolled. In 2006, 1,724 master's, 6 doctorates, 17 other advanced degrees awarded. *Degree requirements:* For master's, practicum; for doctorate, thesis/dissertation. *Entrance requirements:* For doctorate, GRE General Test or MAT, interview, master's degree, resumé; for CAGS, interview, master's degree. Additional exam requirements/recommendations for international students: Required—TOEFL (minimum score 550 paper-based; 213 computer-based; 80 iBT). *Application deadline:* Applications are processed on a rolling basis. Application fee: $50. Electronic applications accepted. *Financial support:* In 2006–07, 26 students received support, including research assistantships (averaging $3,400 per year), teaching assistantships (averaging $3,400 per year); career-related internships or fieldwork, Federal Work-Study, scholarships/grants, and unspecified assistantships also available. Support available to part-time students. Financial award application deadline: 4/15; financial award applicants required to submit FAFSA. *Faculty research:* Assessment in literacy, mathematics and science; autism spectrum disorders; instructional technology and online learning; multicultural education and ELL. *Unit head:* Dr. Mario Borunda, Dean, 617-349-8375, Fax: 617-349-8607, E-mail: mborunda@lesley.edu. *Application contact:* Kristen Card, Associate Director of On-Campus Admissions, 617-349-8734, Fax: 617-349-8313, E-mail: kmcard@lesley.edu.

See Close-Up on page 893.

Long Island University, C.W. Post Campus, College of Liberal Arts and Sciences, Department of Biology, Brookville, NY 11548-1300. Offers biology (MS); biology education (MS). Part-time and evening/weekend programs available. *Degree requirements:* For master's, thesis optional. *Entrance requirements:* For master's, GRE General Test, minimum GPA of 2.75 in major. Electronic applications accepted. *Faculty research:* Immunology, molecular biology, systematics, behavioral ecology, microbiology.

Long Island University, C.W. Post Campus, School of Education, Department of Curriculum and Instruction, Brookville, NY 11548-1300. Offers adolescence education (MS); adolescence education: biology (MS); adolescence education: earth science (MS); adolescence education: English (MS); adolescence education: mathematics (MS); adolescence education: social studies (MS); adolescence education: Spanish (MS); art education (MS); bilingual education (MS); childhood education (MS); early childhood education (MS); middle childhood education (MS); music education (MS); teaching English to speakers of other languages (MS). Part-time and evening/weekend programs available. *Degree requirements:* For master's, comprehensive exam or thesis, student teaching. *Entrance requirements:* For master's, minimum GPA of 2.75 in major, 2.5 overall. Electronic applications accepted. *Faculty research:* Ethics and education, teaching strategies.

Louisiana Tech University, Graduate School, College of Education, Department of Curriculum, Instruction and Leadership, Ruston, LA 71272. Offers curriculum and instruction (MS, Ed D); educational leadership (Ed D); secondary education (M Ed), including business education, English education, foreign language education, health and physical education, mathematics education, science education, social studies education, speech education. *Accreditation:* NCATE. Part-time programs available. *Degree requirements:* For doctorate, thesis/dissertation. *Entrance requirements:* For master's and doctorate, GRE General Test.

Loyola University Chicago, School of Education, Program in Initial Teacher Preparation, Chicago, IL 60611-2196. Offers elementary education (M Ed); reading specialist (M Ed); school technology (M Ed); science education (M Ed); secondary education (M Ed); special education (M Ed). *Accreditation:* NCATE. *Faculty:* 11 full-time (9 women), 6 part-time/adjunct (4 women). *Students:* 138. Average age 28. 95 applicants, 65% accepted, 39 enrolled. In 2006, 84 degrees awarded. *Degree requirements:* For master's, comprehensive exam. *Entrance requirements:* For master's, Illinois Basic Skills Test, 3 letters of recommendation, minimum GPA of 3.0, resumé. Additional exam requirements/recommendations for international students: Required—TOEFL (minimum score 550 paper-based; 213 computer-based; 79 iBT). *Application deadline:* For fall admission, 7/1 priority date for domestic and international students; for spring admission, 11/1 priority date for domestic and international students. Applications are processed on a rolling basis. Application fee: $50. Electronic applications accepted. *Financial support:* In 2006–07, 2 research assistantships with full tuition reimbursements (averaging $8,500 per year), 1 teaching assistantship were awarded. Financial award application deadline: 2/15. *Faculty research:* Positive behavior support, school reform, school improvement. *Unit head:* Dr. Dorothy Giroux, Director, 312-915-7027, E-mail: dgiroux@luc.edu. *Application contact:* Marie Rosin-Dittmar, Information Contact, 312-915-6800, E-mail: schleduc@luc.edu.

Lynchburg College, Graduate Studies, School of Education and Human Development, Program in Science Education, Lynchburg, VA 24501-3199. Offers M Ed. *Faculty:* 3 full-time (1 woman). *Students:* 1 (woman) full-time, 5 part-time (2 women). In 2006, 1 degree awarded. *Median time to degree:* Master's–2 years full-time. *Expenses:* Tuition: Full-time $6,300; part-time $350 per credit. Required fees: $100. *Financial support:* Fellowships, teaching assistantships, career-related internships or fieldwork, scholarships/grants, and unspecified assistantships available. *Unit head:* Dr. Woody McKenzie, Program Coordinator, 434-544-8480, E-mail: mckenzie_w@lynchburg.edu.

Lyndon State College, Graduate Programs in Education, Department of Natural Sciences, Lyndonville, VT 05851-0919. Offers science education (MST). Part-time programs available. *Degree requirements:* For master's, exam or major field project. *Entrance requirements:* Additional exam requirements/recommendations for international students: Recommended—TOEFL (minimum score 500 paper-based; 173 computer-based). *Faculty research:* Fern genetics, comparative butterfly research.

Manhattanville College, Graduate Programs, School of Education, Program in Middle Childhood/Adolescence Education (Grades 5-12), Purchase, NY 10577-2132. Offers biology (MAT); biology and special education (MPS); chemistry (MAT); chemistry and special education (MPS); English (MAT); English and special education (MPS); literacy (MPS), including reading and writing, writing; literacy and special education (MPS); math (MAT); math and special education (MPS); second language (MAT), including French, Italian, Latin, Spanish; social studies (MAT); social studies and special education (MPS); special education (MPS). Part-time and evening/weekend programs available. *Students:* 76 full-time (53 women), 109 part-time (68 women); includes 8 African Americans, 1 Asian American or Pacific Islander, 10 Hispanic Americans, 1 international. In 2006, 165 degrees awarded. *Degree requirements:* For master's, comprehensive exam or research project, field experience. *Entrance requirements:* For master's, minimum undergraduate GPA of 3.0, 2 letters of recommendation. *Application deadline:* Applications are processed on a rolling basis. Application fee: $55. *Financial support:* Career-related internships or fieldwork and institutionally sponsored loans available. Support available to part-time students. *Application contact:* Alyce Ware Poli, Director of Admissions, 914-323-5142, Fax: 914-694-1732, E-mail: edschool@mville.edu.

McNeese State University, Graduate School, College of Science, Department of Biological and Environmental Sciences, Program in Environmental and Chemical Sciences, Lake Charles, LA 70609. Offers chemistry environmental science education (MS); environmental sciences (MS). Evening/weekend programs available. *Faculty:* 3 full-time (0 women). *Students:* 7 full-time (4 women), 2 part-time; includes 4 minority (1 African American, 1 Asian American or Pacific Islander, 2 Hispanic Americans), 3 international. In 2006, 3 degrees awarded. *Degree requirements:* For master's, thesis or alternative, comprehensive exam. *Entrance requirements:* For master's, GRE. *Application deadline:* For fall admission, 5/15 priority date for domestic students. Applications are processed on a rolling basis. Application fee: $20 ($30 for international students). *Expenses:* Tuition, area resident: Full-time $2,226; part-time $193 per hour. Required fees: $919; $106 per hour. *Financial support:* Application deadline: 5/1. *Unit head:* Dr. Harold Stevenson, Coordinator, 337-475-5663, Fax: 337-475-5677, E-mail: hstevens@mcneese.edu.

McNeese State University, Graduate School, College of Science, Department of Chemistry, Program in Environmental and Chemical Sciences, Lake Charles, LA 70609. Offers chemistry (MS); chemistry environmental science education (MS). Evening/weekend programs available. *Faculty:* 4 full-time. *Students:* 18 full-time (10 women), 1 part-time; includes 5 African Americans, 7 international. In 2006, 5 degrees awarded. *Degree requirements:* For master's, thesis or alternative, comprehensive exam. *Entrance requirements:* For master's, GRE. *Application deadline:* For fall admission, 5/15 priority date for domestic students. Applications are processed on a rolling basis. Application fee: $20 ($30 for international students). *Expenses:* Tuition, area resident: Full-time $2,226; part-time $193 per hour. Required fees: $919; $106 per hour. *Financial support:* Application deadline: 5/1. *Unit head:* Dr. Harold Stevenson, Coordinator, 337-475-5663, Fax: 337-475-5677, E-mail: hstevens@mcneese.edu.

Michigan State University, The Graduate School, College of Natural Science and College of Education, Division of Science and Mathematics Education, Program in Biological, Physical and General Science for Teachers, East Lansing, MI 48824. Offers biological science (MS); general science (MAT); physical science (MS). *Students:* 4 applicants, 0% accepted. *Expenses:* Tuition, state resident: part-time $346 per credit hour. Tuition, nonresident: part-time $730 per credit hour. Tuition and fees vary according to program. *Application contact:* Margaret Iding.

Michigan Technological University, Graduate School, College of Sciences and Arts, Department of Education, Program in Applied Science Education, Houghton, MI 49931-1295. Offers MS. Part-time programs available. *Degree requirements:* For master's, internship, project, final paper, defense. *Entrance requirements:* For master's, teaching certification (science or math preferred), 1 year of teaching experience. Additional exam requirements/recommendations for international students: Required—TOEFL. Electronic applications accepted.

Middle Tennessee State University, College of Graduate Studies, College of Basic and Applied Sciences, Department of Aerospace, Murfreesboro, TN 37132. Offers aerospace education (M Ed); aviation administration (MS). Part-time and evening/weekend programs available. Postbaccalaureate distance learning degree programs offered. *Faculty:* 4 full-time (1 woman). *Students:* 9 full-time (3 women), 15 part-time (3 women); includes 3 minority (all African Americans) Average age 28. 7 applicants, 100% accepted. In 2006, 6 degrees awarded. *Degree requirements:* For master's, one foreign language, comprehensive exam. *Entrance requirements:* For master's, GRE General Test or MAT. Additional exam requirements/recommendations for international students: Required—TOEFL (minimum score 525 paper-based; 195 computer-based). *Application deadline:* For fall admission, 8/1 priority date for domestic students. Applications are processed on a rolling basis. Application fee: $25. Electronic applications accepted. *Financial support:* In 2006–07, 3 students received support. Application deadline: 5/1. *Unit head:* Dr. Paul Craig, Coordinator, 615-898-2788, E-mail: pcraig@mtsu.edu.

Mills College, Graduate Studies, Education Department, Oakland, CA 94613-1000. Offers administration (Ed D); child life in health care settings (MA); early childhood education (MA); education (MA), including curriculum and instruction, elementary education, English education, mathematics education, science education, secondary education, social sciences education, teaching. Part-time and evening/weekend programs available. *Faculty:* 10 full-time (7 women), 15 part-time/adjunct (12 women). *Students:* 192 full-time (153 women), 41 part-time (36 women); includes 62 minority (28 African Americans, 13 Asian Americans or Pacific Islanders, 21 Hispanic Americans), 2 international. Average age 34. 160 applicants, 74% accepted, 73 enrolled. In 2006, 52 master's, 1 doctorate awarded. Terminal master's awarded for partial completion of doctoral program. *Degree requirements:* For master's, comprehensive exam. *Entrance requirements:* For doctorate, GRE General Test. Additional exam requirements/recommendations for international students: Required—TOEFL. *Application deadline:* For fall admission, 2/1 for domestic and international students; for spring admission, 11/1 for domestic and international students. Applications are processed on a rolling basis. Application fee: $50. Electronic applications accepted. *Financial support:* In 2006–07, 56 fellowships with tuition reimbursements (averaging $2,700 per year), 15 teaching assistantships (averaging $6,350 per year) were awarded; career-related internships or fieldwork, institutionally sponsored loans, scholarships/grants, and residence awards also available. Support available to part-time students. Financial award application deadline: 2/1; financial award applicants required to submit CSS PROFILE or FAFSA. *Faculty research:* Child development, gender and education, public policy, cross-cultural development, development of literacy. *Unit head:* Joseph Kahne, Chairperson, 510-430-3190, Fax: 510-430-3314, E-mail: grad-studies@mills.edu. *Application contact:* Randy McGlauthing, Director of Graduate Admissions, 510-430-2355, Fax: 510-430-2159, E-mail: rmglaut@mills.edu.

Minnesota State University Mankato, College of Graduate Studies, College of Science, Engineering and Technology, Department of Biological Sciences, Mankato, MN 56001. Offers biology (MS); biology education (MS); environmental science (MS), including ecology, economic and political systems, human ecosystems, physical science, technology. Part-time programs available. *Students:* 8 full-time (4 women), 26 part-time (13 women). Average age 31. In 2006, 7 degrees awarded. *Degree requirements:* For master's, one foreign language, thesis or alternative, comprehensive exam. *Entrance requirements:* For master's, minimum GPA of 3.0 during previous 2 years of course work. Additional exam requirements/recommendations for international students: Required—TOEFL. *Application deadline:* For fall admission, 7/1 priority date for domestic students; for spring admission, 11/1 for domestic students. Applications are processed on a rolling basis. Application fee: $40. Electronic applications accepted. *Financial support:* Fellowships, research assistantships with full tuition reimbursements, teaching assistantships with full tuition reimbursements, career-related internships or fieldwork, Federal Work-Study, institutionally sponsored loans, and unspecified assistantships available. Support available to part-time students. Financial award application deadline: 3/15; financial award applicants required to submit FAFSA. *Faculty research:* Limnology, enzyme analysis, membrane engineering, converters. *Unit head:* Dr. Gregg Marg, Chairperson, 507-389-2786. *Application contact:* 507-389-2321, E-mail: grad@mnsu.edu.

Minot State University, Graduate School, Program in Biological and Agricultural Sciences, Minot, ND 58707-0002. Offers science (MAT). *Faculty:* 9 full-time (2 women). *Students:* 3. *Degree requirements:* For master's, thesis. *Entrance requirements:* For master's, minimum GPA of 3.0 or GRE General Test, secondary teaching certificate. Additional exam requirements/recommendations for international students: Required—TOEFL. *Application deadline:* Applications are processed on a rolling basis. Application fee: $35. *Financial support:* In 2006–07, 1 research assistantship with partial tuition reimbursement (averaging $500 per year), 1 teaching assistantship with partial tuition reimbursement (averaging $500 per year) were awarded; career-related internships or fieldwork, institutionally sponsored loans, scholarships/grants, traineeships, tuition waivers (partial), and unspecified assistantships also available. Support available to part-time students. Financial award application deadline: 4/1. *Unit head:* Dr. John Webster, Chairperson, 701-858-3066, Fax: 701-858-3163, E-mail: webster@minotstateu.edu. *Application contact:* Brenda Anderson, Administrative Assistant, 701-858-3250 Ext. 3150, Fax: 701-858-4286, E-mail: brenda.anderson@minotstateu.edu.

Mississippi College, Graduate School, School of Education, Department of Teacher Education and Leadership, Clinton, MS 39058. Offers art (M Ed); biological science (M Ed); business education (M Ed); computer science (M Ed); dyslexia therapy (M Ed); educational leadership (M Ed, Ed S); elementary education (M Ed, Ed S); English (M Ed); higher education administration (MS); mathematics (M Ed); secondary education (M Ed); social studies (history) (M Ed);

teaching arts (M Ed). Part-time programs available. *Faculty:* 9 full-time (5 women), 14 part-time/adjunct (10 women). *Students:* 52 full-time (36 women), 286 part-time (247 women); includes 173 minority (171 African Americans, 1 American Indian/Alaska Native, 1 Hispanic American), 1 international. Average age 32. In 2006, 131 degrees awarded. *Degree requirements:* For master's, thesis optional. *Entrance requirements:* For master's, NTE. Additional exam requirements/recommendations for international students: Recommended—IELTS. *Application deadline:* Applications are processed on a rolling basis. Application fee: $25. Electronic applications accepted. *Expenses:* Tuition: Full-time $7,290; part-time $405 per hour. Required fees: $150 per term. Tuition and fees vary according to campus/location and program. *Financial support:* Teaching assistantships, career-related internships or fieldwork, Federal Work-Study, scholarships/grants, and unspecified assistantships available. Support available to part-time students. Financial award applicants required to submit FAFSA. *Unit head:* Dr. Tom Williams, Chair, 601-925-3844, E-mail: twilliams@mc.edu.

Missouri State University, Graduate College, College of Natural and Applied Sciences, Department of Physics, Astronomy, and Materials Science, Springfield, MO 65804-0094. Offers materials science (MS); physics, astronomy, and materials science (MNAS); secondary education (MS Ed), including physics. Part-time programs available. *Faculty:* 11 full-time (0 women). *Students:* 11 full-time (2 women), 3 part-time; includes 1 minority (Hispanic American), 7 international. Average age 26. 12 applicants, 42% accepted, 1 enrolled. In 2006, 5 degrees awarded. *Degree requirements:* For master's, thesis, comprehensive exam. *Entrance requirements:* For master's, GRE (MS, MNAS), minimum undergraduate GPA of 3.0 (MS and MNAS), 9-12 teaching certification (MS Ed). Additional exam requirements/recommendations for international students: Required—TOEFL (minimum score 550 paper-based; 213 computer-based; 79 iBT). *Application deadline:* For fall admission, 7/20 priority date for domestic students; for spring admission, 12/20 priority date for domestic students. Applications are processed on a rolling basis. Application fee: $35. Electronic applications accepted. *Expenses:* Tuition, state resident: full-time $3,582; part-time $199 per credit hour. Tuition, nonresident: full-time $6,984; part-time $199 per credit hour. Required fees: $548. Full-time tuition and fees vary according to course level, course load, program and reciprocity agreements. *Financial support:* In 2006–07, 8 research assistantships with full tuition reimbursements (averaging $9,000 per year), 1 teaching assistantship with full tuition reimbursement (averaging $9,000 per year) were awarded; Federal Work-Study, scholarships/grants, and unspecified assistantships also available. Financial award application deadline: 3/31; financial award applicants required to submit FAFSA. *Faculty research:* Nanocomposites, ferroelectricity, infrared focal plane array sensors, biosensors. *Unit head:* Dr. Pawan Kahol, Head, 417-836-5131, Fax: 417-836-6226, E-mail: materialsscience@missouristate.edu.

Montclair State University, The Graduate School, College of Education and Human Services, Department of Curriculum and Teaching, Montclair, NJ 07043-1624. Offers education (M Ed); educational technology (M Ed); school library media specialist (Certificate); teaching (MAT, Certificate), including art (MAT), biological science (MAT), early childhood education (P-3) (MAT), earth science (MAT), elementary education (K-8) (MAT), English (MAT), French (MAT), health and physical education (MAT), health education (MAT), home economics (MAT), mathematics (MAT), music (MAT), physical education (MAT), physical science (MAT), social studies (MAT), Spanish (MAT), teacher of ESL (MAT), teacher of students with disabilities (MAT). Part-time and evening/weekend programs available. *Faculty:* 16 full-time (12 women), 13 part-time/adjunct (8 women). *Students:* 147 full-time (113 women), 230 part-time (188 women); includes 58 minority (33 African Americans, 1 American Indian/Alaska Native, 12 Asian Americans or Pacific Islanders, 12 Hispanic Americans), 4 international. Average age 33. 118 applicants, 38% accepted, 37 enrolled. In 2006, 166 master's, 11 other advanced degrees awarded. *Degree requirements:* For master's, field experience. *Entrance requirements:* For master's, PRAXIS II, minimum GPA of 2.67, 2 letters of recommendation. Additional exam requirements/recommendations for international students: Required—TOEFL (minimum score 83 computer-based). *Application deadline:* For fall admission, 2/15 for domestic and international students; for spring admission, 9/15 for domestic and international students. Applications are processed on a rolling basis. Application fee: $60. Electronic applications accepted. *Expenses:* Tuition, state resident: part-time $450 per credit. Tuition, nonresident: part-time $682 per credit. Tuition and fees vary according to degree level and program. *Financial support:* In 2006–07, 7 research assistantships with full tuition reimbursements (averaging $7,000 per year) were awarded; Federal Work-Study, scholarships/grants, and unspecified assistantships also available. Support available to part-time students. Financial award application deadline: 3/1; financial award applicants required to submit FAFSA. *Unit head:* Dr. Deborah Eldridge, Chairperson, 973-655-5187.

Montclair State University, The Graduate School, College of Science and Mathematics, Department of Biology and Molecular Biology, Montclair, NJ 07043-1624. Offers biology (MS), including biology science education, molecular biology; molecular biology (Certificate). Part-time and evening/weekend programs available. *Faculty:* 19 full-time (8 women), 20 part-time/adjunct (9 women). *Students:* 19 full-time (10 women), 52 part-time (38 women); includes 19 minority (5 African Americans, 4 Asian Americans or Pacific Islanders, 10 Hispanic Americans), 1 international. 50 applicants, 48% accepted, 19 enrolled. In 2006, 18 master's, 7 other advanced degrees awarded. *Degree requirements:* For master's, thesis or alternative, comprehensive exam. *Entrance requirements:* For master's, GRE General Test, 24 credits of course work in undergraduate biology, 2 letters of recommendation, teaching certificate (biology sciences education concentration). Additional exam requirements/recommendations for international students: Required—TOEFL (minimum score 83 computer-based). *Application deadline:* For fall admission, 6/1 for international students; for spring admission, 10/1 for international students. Applications are processed on a rolling basis. Application fee: $60. Electronic applications accepted. *Expenses:* Tuition, state resident: part-time $450 per credit. Tuition, nonresident: part-time $682 per credit. Tuition and fees vary according to degree level and program. *Financial support:* In 2006–07, 7 research assistantships with full tuition reimbursements (averaging $7,000 per year) were awarded; Federal Work-Study, scholarships/grants, and unspecified assistantships also available. Support available to part-time students. Financial award application deadline: 3/1; financial award applicants required to submit FAFSA. *Faculty research:* Cells, algea blooms, scallops, NJ bays, Barnegat Bay. Total annual research expenditures: $48,000. *Unit head:* Dr. Scott Kight, Chairperson, 973-655-7047. *Application contact:* Dr. Reginald Halaby, Adviser, 973-655-4397, E-mail: halabyr@mail.montclair.edu.

Montclair State University, The Graduate School, College of Science and Mathematics, Department of Earth and Environmental Studies, Montclair, NJ 07043-1624. Offers environmental management (MA, D Env M); environmental studies (MS), including environmental education, environmental health, environmental management, environmental science; geoscience (MS, Certificate), including geoscience (MS), water resource management (Certificate). Part-time and evening/weekend programs available. *Faculty:* 17 full-time (3 women), 9 part-time/adjunct (3 women). *Students:* 24 full-time (11 women), 45 part-time (20 women); includes 6 minority (3 African Americans, 1 Asian American or Pacific Islander, 2 Hispanic Americans), 8 international. 33 applicants, 39% accepted, 7 enrolled. In 2006, 18 master's, 3 other advanced degrees awarded. *Degree requirements:* For master's, thesis or alternative, comprehensive exam; for doctorate, thesis/dissertation. *Entrance requirements:* For master's, GRE General Test, 2 letters of recommendation. Additional exam requirements/recommendations for international students: Required—TOEFL (minimum score 83 computer-based). *Application deadline:* For fall admission, 6/1 for international students; for spring admission, 10/1 for international students. Applications are processed on a rolling basis. Application fee: $60. Electronic applications accepted. *Expenses:* Tuition, state resident: part-time $450 per credit. Tuition, nonresident: part-time $682 per credit. Tuition and fees vary according to degree level and program. *Financial support:* In 2006–07, 14 research assistantships with full tuition reimbursements were awarded; Federal Work-Study, scholarships/grants, and unspecified assistantships also available. Support available to part-time students. Financial award application deadline: 3/1; financial award applicants required to submit FAFSA. *Faculty research:* Antarctica, carbon pools, contaminated sediments, wetlands. Total annual research expenditures: $127,880. *Unit head:* Dr. Gregory Pope, Chairperson, 973-655-7385. *Application contact:* Dr. Harbans Singh, Adviser, 973-655-7383.

Morgan State University, School of Graduate Studies, School of Education and Urban Studies, Program in Science Education, Baltimore, MD 21251. Offers MS, Ed D. *Students:* 24 (18 women); includes 16 minority (15 African Americans, 1 Asian American or Pacific Islander) 6 international. Average age 30. *Entrance requirements:* Additional exam requirements/recommendations for international students: Required—TOEFL (minimum score 550 paper-based; 213 computer-based). *Application deadline:* For fall admission, 2/1 priority date for domestic students; for spring admission, 10/1 priority date for domestic students. *Expenses:* Tuition, state resident: part-time $272 per credit. Tuition, nonresident: part-time $478 per credit. Required fees: $38 per credit. *Unit head:* Dr. Glenda Prime, Coordinator, 443-885-3780, E-mail: glprime@moac.morgan.edu. *Application contact:* Dr. Maurice C. Taylor, Dean, 443-885-3185, Fax: 443-885-8226, E-mail: mctaylor@moac.morgan.edu.

National-Louis University, National College of Education, Program in Science Education, Chicago, IL 60603. Offers M Ed, MS Ed, CAS. Part-time and evening/weekend programs available. *Students:* Average age 41. In 2006, 12 degrees awarded. *Degree requirements:* For master's, thesis (for some programs). *Entrance requirements:* For master's, MAT or GRE, minimum GPA of 3.0, teaching certificate; for CAS, master's degree, teaching certificate. *Application deadline:* Applications are processed on a rolling basis. Application fee: $25. *Expenses:* Tuition: Full-time $17,685. One-time fee: $40 full-time. *Financial support:* Fellowships, career-related internships or fieldwork, Federal Work-Study, institutionally sponsored loans, and scholarships/grants available. Support available to part-time students. Financial award applicants required to submit FAFSA. *Unit head:* Dr. Vito Dipinto, Coordinator, 847-475-1100 Ext. 2559. *Application contact:* David McCulloch, Vice President for University Services, 800-443-5522 Ext. 5127, Fax: 847-465-0593, E-mail: dmcc@wheeling1.nl.edu.

New Mexico Institute of Mining and Technology, Graduate Studies, Program in Science Teaching, Socorro, NM 87801. Offers MST. *Faculty:* 1 (woman) full-time, 7 part-time/adjunct (1 woman). *Students:* 1 (woman) full-time, 49 part-time (36 women); includes 7 minority (1 Asian American or Pacific Islander, 6 Hispanic Americans), 1 international. Average age 41. 4 applicants, 75% accepted, 3 enrolled. In 2006, 16 degrees awarded. *Degree requirements:* For master's, thesis optional. *Entrance requirements:* For master's, GRE General Test. Additional exam requirements/recommendations for international students: Required—TOEFL (minimum score 540 paper-based; 207 computer-based). *Application deadline:* For fall admission, 3/1 priority date for domestic students; for spring admission, 6/1 for domestic students. Applications are processed on a rolling basis. Application fee: $16. Electronic applications accepted. *Expenses:* Tuition, state resident: full-time $3,593; part-time $200 per credit. Tuition, nonresident: full-time $11,554; part-time $642 per credit. Required fees: $419; $16 per credit. $34 per term. Tuition and fees vary according to course load. *Financial support:* In 2006–07, 1 research assistantship (averaging $17,598 per year) was awarded; fellowships, teaching assistantships, Federal Work-Study and institutionally sponsored loans also available. Financial award application deadline: 3/1; financial award applicants required to submit CSS PROFILE or FAFSA. *Faculty research:* Teaching secondary school science and/or mathematics. *Unit head:* Dr. Peter Gerity, Vice President for Academic Affairs, 505-835-5227, Fax: 505-835-5678, E-mail: science@nmt.edu. *Application contact:* Dr. David B. Johnson, Dean of Graduate Studies, 505-835-5513, Fax: 505-835-5476, E-mail: graduate@nmt.edu.

New York University, Steinhardt School of Culture, Education and Human Development, Department of Teaching and Learning, Program in Science Education, New York, NY 10012-1019. Offers biology grades 7-12 (MA); chemistry grades 7-12 (MA); physics grades 7-12 (MA). Part-time and evening/weekend programs available. *Faculty:* 4 full-time (3 women). *Students:* 11 full-time (9 women), 10 part-time (6 women); includes 12 minority (5 African Americans, 4 Asian Americans or Pacific Islanders, 3 Hispanic Americans), 1 international. 10 applicants, 100% accepted, 6 enrolled. In 2006, 13 degrees awarded. *Degree requirements:* For master's, thesis (for some programs). *Entrance requirements:* Additional exam requirements/recommendations for international students: Required—TOEFL. *Application deadline:* For fall admission, 12/15 priority date for domestic and international students; for spring admission, 11/1 for domestic and international students. Applications are processed on a rolling basis. Application fee: $50. *Expenses:* Tuition: Part-time $1,080 per unit. Required fees: $56 per unit. $329 per term. Tuition and fees vary according to program. *Financial support:* Career-related internships or fieldwork, Federal Work-Study, institutionally sponsored loans, scholarships/grants, and tuition waivers (partial) available. Support available to part-time students. Financial award application deadline: 2/1; financial award applicants required to submit FAFSA. *Faculty research:* Science curriculum development, gender and ethnicity, technology use, history and philosophy of school science, science in urban schools. *Unit head:* Dr. Pamela Fraser-Abder, Director, 212-998-5460, Fax: 212-995-4049. *Application contact:* 212-998-5030, Fax: 212-995-4328, E-mail: steinhardt.gradadmissions@nyu.edu.

North Carolina Agricultural and Technical State University, Graduate School, School of Education, Department of Curriculum and Instruction, Program in Intermediate Education, Greensboro, NC 27411. Offers biology education (MS); chemistry education (MS); English education (MS); history education (MS); social science education (MS). *Accreditation:* NCATE. Part-time and evening/weekend programs available. *Degree requirements:* For master's, thesis (for some programs), qualifying exam, comprehensive exam. *Entrance requirements:* For master's, GRE General Test, minimum GPA of 3.0.

North Carolina State University, Graduate School, College of Education, Department of Mathematics, Science, and Technology Education, Program in Science Education, Raleigh, NC 27695. Offers M Ed, MS, PhD. *Accreditation:* NCATE. Part-time programs available. *Degree requirements:* For master's, thesis (for some programs), oral exam; for doctorate, one foreign language, thesis/dissertation, oral and written exams. *Entrance requirements:* For master's, GRE General Test or MAT, minimum GPA of 3.0; for doctorate, GRE General Test, minimum GPA of 3.0, interview. Electronic applications accepted. *Faculty research:* Teacher development, sociocultural issues in learning, student science misconceptions, technical applications to science teaching.

North Dakota State University, The Graduate School, College of Human Development and Education, School of Education, Fargo, ND 58105. Offers agricultural education (M Ed, MS), including agricultural education, agricultural extension education (MS); counseling (M Ed, MS, PhD); curriculum and instruction (M Ed, MS), including pedagogy, physical education and athletic administration; education (PhD); educational leadership (M Ed, MS, Ed S); family and consumer sciences education (M Ed, MS); history education (M Ed, MS); mathematics education (M Ed, MS); music education (M Ed, MS); science education (M Ed, MS). *Accreditation:* NCATE. Part-time and evening/weekend programs available. Postbaccalaureate distance learning degree programs offered (minimal on-campus study). *Faculty:* 25 full-time (9 women), 3 part-time/adjunct (1 woman). *Students:* 29 full-time (25 women), 207 part-time (132 women); includes 15 minority (4 African Americans, 6 American Indian/Alaska Native, 3 Asian Americans or Pacific Islanders, 2 Hispanic Americans), 4 international. 88 applicants, 67% accepted, 56 enrolled. In 2006, 44 master's, 5 doctorates awarded. *Degree requirements:* For master's, comprehensive exam; for doctorate and Ed S, thesis/dissertation. *Entrance requirements:* For degree, GRE General Test, master's degree, minimum GPA of 3.25. Additional exam requirements/recommendations for international students: Required—TOEFL. *Application deadline:* Applications are processed on a rolling basis. Application fee: $45 ($60 for international students). *Financial support:* Research assistantships, teaching assistantships, career-related internships or fieldwork, Federal Work-Study, institutionally sponsored loans, and tuition waivers (full) available. Financial award application deadline: 4/15. *Unit head:* Dr. William O. Martin, Chair, 701-231-7104, Fax: 701-231-7416, E-mail: william.martin@ndsu.edu.

Northeastern State University, Graduate College, College of Science and Health Professions, Program in Science Education, Tahlequah, OK 74464-2399. Offers M Ed. Part-time and evening/weekend programs available. In 2006, 4 degrees awarded. *Entrance requirements:* For master's, MAT or GRE, minimum GPA of 2.5. *Application deadline:* For fall admission, 6/1 for domestic students. Application fee: $0 ($25 for international students). *Unit head:* Dr. April Adams, Chair, 918-456-5511 Ext. 3819.

Science Education

Northern Arizona University, Graduate College, College of Engineering and Natural Science, Department of Biological Sciences, Flagstaff, AZ 86011. Offers biology (MS, PhD); biology education (MAT). *Degree requirements:* For master's, final exam (MAT), thesis (MS), oral exam; for doctorate, thesis/dissertation. *Entrance requirements:* For master's, GRE General Test, GRE Subject Test; for doctorate, GRE General Test. Electronic applications accepted. *Faculty research:* Genetic levels of trophic levels, plant hybrid zones, insect biodiversity, natural history and cognition of wild jays.

Northern Arizona University, Graduate College, College of Engineering and Natural Science, Department of Physics and Astronomy, Flagstaff, AZ 86011. Offers applied physics (MS); physical science (MAT). Part-time programs available. *Degree requirements:* For master's, thesis optional. *Entrance requirements:* For master's, GRE.

North Georgia College & State University, Graduate Studies, Program in Teacher Education, Dahlonega, GA 30597. Offers early childhood education (M Ed); educational leadership (Ed S); middle grades education (M Ed); secondary education (M Ed), including art education, biology education, chemistry education, English education, history education, mathematics education, physical education, science education; special education (M Ed), including interrelated special education, learning disabilities. *Accreditation:* NCATE. Part-time and evening/weekend programs available. Postbaccalaureate distance learning degree programs offered (minimal on-campus study). *Faculty:* 35 full-time (18 women), 9 part-time/adjunct (6 women). *Students:* 260. Average age 32. 120 applicants, 63% accepted. In 2006, 134 degrees awarded. *Degree requirements:* For master's, thesis optional. *Entrance requirements:* For master's, GRE General Test or MAT, minimum GPA of 2.75; for Ed S, GRE General Test or MAT, 3 years of teaching experience, master's degree, minimum graduate GPA of 3.25. *Application deadline:* For fall admission, 7/1 priority date for domestic students; for spring admission, 12/10 priority date for domestic students. Applications are processed on a rolling basis. Application fee: $25. Electronic applications accepted. *Expenses:* Tuition, state resident: full-time $3,044; part-time $127 per credit hour. Tuition, nonresident: full-time $12,172; part-time $508 per credit hour. Required fees: $892; $458 per semester. *Financial support:* Teaching assistantships, career-related internships or fieldwork and scholarships/grants available. Support available to part-time students. Financial award application deadline: 5/1. *Faculty research:* Computers and teachers' attitudes, rural versus urban teacher attitudes, teacher leadership roles, minority recruitment in teaching force. *Unit head:* Dr. Bob Michael, Dean, School of Education, 706-864-1998, Fax: 706-867-2850, E-mail: bmichael@ngcsu.edu. *Application contact:* Dr. Donna A. Gessell, Director of Graduate Studies and External Programs, 706-864-1528, Fax: 706-867-2795, E-mail: dgessell@ngcsu.edu.

Northwestern State University of Louisiana, Graduate Studies and Research, College of Education, Programs in Education, Natchitoches, LA 71497. Offers business and distributive education (M Ed); counseling (M Ed); early childhood education (M Ed); education (M Ed); education leadership (M Ed); educational technology (M Ed); elementary teaching (M Ed); English education (M Ed); home economics education (M Ed); mathematics education (M Ed); reading (M Ed); science education (M Ed); secondary teaching (M Ed); social sciences education (M Ed). *Students:* 49 full-time (41 women), 245 part-time (206 women); includes 78 minority (70 African Americans, 5 American Indian/Alaska Native, 2 Asian Americans or Pacific Islanders, 1 Hispanic American). Average age 35. In 2006, 158 degrees awarded. *Degree requirements:* For master's, thesis or alternative, comprehensive exam, registration. *Entrance requirements:* For master's, GRE General Test, minimum undergraduate GPA of 2.5. *Application contact:* Dr. Steven G. Horton, Associate Provost/Dean, Graduate Studies, Research, and Information Systems, 318-357-5851, Fax: 318-357-5019, E-mail: grad_school@nsula.edu.

Northwest Missouri State University, Graduate School, College of Education and Human Services, Program in Teaching: Science, Maryville, MO 64468-6001. Offers MS Ed. *Accreditation:* NCATE. Part-time programs available. *Faculty:* 3 full-time (all women). *Students:* 6 full-time (all women), 40 part-time (25 women). 1 applicant, 100% accepted, 1 enrolled. In 2006, 1 degree awarded. *Degree requirements:* For master's, thesis optional. *Entrance requirements:* For master's, GRE General Test, minimum GPA of 2.75 in major, 2.5 overall; teaching certificate; writing sample. Additional exam requirements/recommendations for international students: Required—TOEFL (minimum score 550 paper-based; 213 computer-based). *Application deadline:* For fall admission, 7/1 for domestic and international students; for spring admission, 11/15 for domestic and international students. Applications are processed on a rolling basis. Application fee: $0 ($50 for international students). *Financial support:* In 2006–07, 3 research assistantships with full tuition reimbursements (averaging $6,000 per year) were awarded; teaching assistantships. Financial award application deadline: 3/1; financial award applicants required to submit FAFSA. *Unit head:* Dr. Pat Lucido, Chairperson, 660-562-1605. *Application contact:* Dr. Frances Shipley, Dean of Graduate School, 660-562-1145, Fax: 660-562-1096, E-mail: gradsch@nwmissouri.edu.

Nova Southeastern University, Fischler School of Education and Human Services, Graduate Teacher Education Program, Fort Lauderdale, FL 33314-7796. Offers athletic administration (MS); cognitive and behavioral disabilities (MS); computer science education (Ed S); computer science education (K-12) (MS); curriculum and teaching (Ed S); curriculum, instruction and technology (MS); curriculum, instruction, management and administration (Ed S); early childhood special education (MS); early literacy and reading (Ed S); early literacy education (MS); education technology (MS); educational leadership (administration K–12) (MS, Ed S); educational media (Ed S); educational media (K-12) (MS); elementary education (MS, Ed S), including ESOL endorsement (MS); English (MS, Ed S); exceptional student education (MS), including ESOL endorsement; gifted education (MS, Ed S); interdisciplinary arts education (MS); management and administration of educational programs (MS); mathematics (MS, Ed S); multicultural early intervention (MS); pre-kindergarten/primary (MS); preschool education (MS); reading (MS, Ed S); science (MS, Ed S); secondary education (MS); social studies (MS, Ed S); Spanish language (MS); teaching and learning (MA, MS), including curriculum and instruction (MA), elementary mathematics (MA), elementary reading (MA), K-12 technology integration (MA); teaching English to speakers of other languages (MS, Ed S); technology management and administration (Ed S); urban studies education (MS); varying exceptionalities (Ed S). Part-time and evening/weekend programs available. Postbaccalaureate distance learning degree programs offered. *Faculty:* 131 full-time (78 women), 548 part-time/adjunct (342 women). *Students:* 1,418 full-time (1,139 women), 3,464 part-time (2,877 women); includes 2,462 minority (1,732 African Americans, 13 American Indian/Alaska Native, 44 Asian Americans or Pacific Islanders, 673 Hispanic Americans), 77 international. Average age 38. 1,771 applicants, 80% accepted, 1419 enrolled. In 2006, 2,078 master's, 425 other advanced degrees awarded. *Degree requirements:* For master's and Ed S, thesis, practicum, internship. *Entrance requirements:* For master's, MAT, GRE, CLAST, CBEST, PRAXIS I, GKT, minimum GPA of 2.5; for Ed S, MAT or GRE, master's degree, teaching certificate, minimum GPA of 3.0. Additional exam requirements/recommendations for international students: Recommended—TOEFL (minimum score 550 paper-based; 213 computer-based), IELTS (minimum score 6). *Application deadline:* For fall admission, 8/11 priority date for domestic and international students; for winter admission, 12/28 priority date for domestic and international students; for spring admission, 4/22 priority date for domestic and international students. Applications are processed on a rolling basis. Application fee: $50. Electronic applications accepted. *Financial support:* Federal Work-Study available. Support available to part-time students. Financial award application deadline: 1/7. *Faculty research:* School effectiveness, critical thinking, leadership skills acquisition, child education, multicultural education. *Unit head:* Dr. Meline Kevorkian, Associate Dean of Master's and Educational Programs, 954-262-8500, Fax: 954-262-3606, E-mail: melinek@nova.edu. *Application contact:* Jennifer Quiñones Nottingham, Dean of Student Affairs, 800-986-3223 Ext. 8624, Fax: 954-262-3911, E-mail: jlquinon@nova.edu.

Occidental College, Graduate Studies, Department of Education, Program in Secondary Education, Los Angeles, CA 90041-3314. Offers English and comparative literary studies (MAT); history (MAT); life science (MAT); mathematics (MAT); physical science (MAT); social science (MAT); Spanish (MAT). Part-time programs available. *Faculty:* 3 full-time (2 women), 2 part-time/adjunct (both women). *Students:* 4 full-time (all women), 3 part-time (1 woman); includes 5 minority (1 Asian American or Pacific Islander, 4 Hispanic Americans). Average age 25. 4 applicants, 100% accepted, 4 enrolled. In 2006, 4 degrees awarded. *Degree requirements:* For master's, final exam, graduate synthesis paper. *Entrance requirements:* For master's, GRE General Test, minimum GPA of 3.0. Additional exam requirements/recommendations for international students: Required—TOEFL (minimum score 625 paper-based). *Application deadline:* For fall admission, 3/1 for domestic and international students; for spring admission, 10/1 for domestic and international students. Applications are processed on a rolling basis. Application fee: $50. *Expenses:* Contact institution. *Financial support:* Fellowships, Federal Work-Study, institutionally sponsored loans, and scholarships/grants available. Support available to part-time students. Financial award application deadline: 3/1; financial award applicants required to submit FAFSA. *Unit head:* Chair, 323-259-2781, E-mail: edudept@oxy.edu. *Application contact:* Angela Allen, Credential Analyst/Department Services Coordinator, 323-259-2781, E-mail: edudept@oxy.edu.

Ohio University, Graduate Studies, College of Arts and Sciences, Department of Geological Sciences, Athens, OH 45701-2979. Offers environmental geochemistry (MS); environmental geology (MS); environmental/hydrology (MS); geology (MS); geology education (MS); geomorphology/surficial processes (MS); geophysics (MS); hydrogeology (MS); sedimentology (MS); structure/tectonics (MS). Part-time programs available. *Faculty:* 10 full-time (4 women), 4 part-time/adjunct (1 woman). *Students:* 22 full-time (6 women), 3 part-time (2 women); includes 1 minority (Hispanic American), 4 international. Average age 23. 15 applicants, 67% accepted, 8 enrolled. In 2006, 7 degrees awarded. *Degree requirements:* For master's, thesis, thesis proposal defense and thesis defense. *Entrance requirements:* Additional exam requirements/recommendations for international students: Required—TOEFL (minimum score 550 paper-based; 217 computer-based). *Application deadline:* For fall admission, 2/1 priority date for domestic students, 1/1 priority date for international students. Application fee: $45. Electronic applications accepted. *Financial support:* In 2006–07, 18 students received support, including 3 research assistantships with full tuition reimbursements available (averaging $11,900 per year), 13 teaching assistantships with full tuition reimbursements available (averaging $11,900 per year); institutionally sponsored loans, scholarships/grants, tuition waivers (full), and unspecified assistantships also available. Financial award application deadline: 2/1. *Faculty research:* Geoscience education, tectonics, flurial geomorphology, invertebrate paleontology, mine/hydrology. Total annual research expenditures: $649,020. *Unit head:* Dr. David Kidder, Chair, 740-593-1101, Fax: 740-593-0486, E-mail: kidder@ohio.edu. *Application contact:* Dr. David Schneider, Graduate Chair, 740-593-1101, Fax: 740-593-0486, E-mail: schneidd@ohio.edu.

Old Dominion University, Darden College of Education, Programs in Secondary Education, Norfolk, VA 23529. Offers biology (MS Ed); chemistry (MS Ed); English (MS Ed); instructional technology (MS Ed); library science (MS Ed); secondary education (MS Ed). *Accreditation:* NCATE. Part-time and evening/weekend programs available. Postbaccalaureate distance learning degree programs offered (minimal on-campus study). *Faculty:* 28 full-time (11 women). *Students:* 61 full-time (45 women), 119 part-time (72 women); includes 21 minority (13 African Americans, 4 Asian Americans or Pacific Islanders, 4 Hispanic Americans), 1 international. Average age 35. 47 applicants, 87% accepted. In 2006, 119 degrees awarded. *Degree requirements:* For master's, thesis optional. *Entrance requirements:* For master's, GRE General Test, or MAT, PRAXIS I for master's with licensure, minimum GPA of 2.8, teaching certificate. Additional exam requirements/recommendations for international students: Required—TOEFL. *Application deadline:* Applications are processed on a rolling basis. Application fee: $40. Electronic applications accepted. *Expenses:* Tuition, area resident: Part-time $285 per credit hour. Tuition, nonresident: part-time $715 per credit hour. Required fees: $94 per semester. *Financial support:* In 2006–07, 58 students received support, including 2 research assistantships with tuition reimbursements available (averaging $6,777 per year), 3 teaching assistantships with tuition reimbursements available (averaging $5,333 per year); fellowships, career-related internships or fieldwork, Federal Work-Study, institutionally sponsored loans, scholarships/grants, and tuition waivers (partial) also available. Support available to part-time students. Financial award application deadline: 2/15; financial award applicants required to submit FAFSA. *Faculty research:* Mathematics retraining, writing project for teachers, geography teaching, reading. *Unit head:* Dr. Robert Lucking, Graduate Program Director, 757-683-5545, Fax: 757-683-5862, E-mail: rlucking@odu.edu.

Oregon State University, Graduate School, College of Science, Department of Science and Mathematics Education, Program in Biology Education, Corvallis, OR 97331. Offers MAT. *Accreditation:* NCATE. *Entrance requirements:* For master's, minimum GPA of 3.0 in last 90 hours. Additional exam requirements/recommendations for international students: Required—TOEFL. *Application deadline:* For fall admission, 1/15 for domestic students. Application fee: $50. *Unit head:* M. Janice Rosenberg, Program Coordinator, 541-737-4031, Fax: 541-737-1817.

Oregon State University, Graduate School, College of Science, Department of Science and Mathematics Education, Program in Chemistry Education, Corvallis, OR 97331. Offers MAT. *Accreditation:* NCATE. *Entrance requirements:* For master's, minimum GPA of 3.0 in last 90 hours of course work. Additional exam requirements/recommendations for international students: Required—TOEFL. *Application deadline:* For fall admission, 1/15 for domestic students. Application fee: $50. *Unit head:* M. Janice Rosenberg, Program Coordinator, 541-737-4031, Fax: 541-737-1817.

Oregon State University, Graduate School, College of Science, Department of Science and Mathematics Education, Program in Integrated Science Education, Corvallis, OR 97331. Offers MAT. *Accreditation:* NCATE. In 2006, 30 master's awarded. *Entrance requirements:* For master's, minimum GPA of 3.0 in last 90 hours. Additional exam requirements/recommendations for international students: Required—TOEFL. *Application deadline:* For fall admission, 3/1 for domestic students. Application fee: $50. *Financial support:* Application deadline: 2/1. *Unit head:* M. Janice Rosenberg, Program Coordinator, 541-737-4031, Fax: 541-737-1817.

Oregon State University, Graduate School, College of Science, Department of Science and Mathematics Education, Program in Physics Education, Corvallis, OR 97331. Offers MAT. *Accreditation:* NCATE. Part-time programs available. *Degree requirements:* For master's, thesis (for some programs). *Entrance requirements:* For master's, minimum GPA of 3.0 in last 90 hours of course work. Additional exam requirements/recommendations for international students: Required—TOEFL. *Application deadline:* For fall admission, 1/15 for domestic students. Application fee: $50. *Financial support:* Application deadline: 2/1. *Unit head:* M. Janice Rosenberg, Program Coordinator, 541-737-4031, Fax: 541-737-1817.

Oregon State University, Graduate School, College of Science, Department of Science and Mathematics Education, Program in Science Education, Corvallis, OR 97331. Offers MA, MAT, MS, PhD. *Accreditation:* NCATE. *Students:* 34 full-time (20 women), 7 part-time (4 women); includes 2 minority (1 African American, 1 Hispanic American), 3 international. Average age 32. In 2006, 30 master's, 3 doctorates awarded. *Degree requirements:* For doctorate, thesis/dissertation. *Entrance requirements:* For master's, minimum GPA of 3.0 in last 90 hours; for doctorate, GRE or MAT, minimum GPA of 3.0 in last 90 hours. Additional exam requirements/recommendations for international students: Required—TOEFL. *Application deadline:* For fall admission, 3/1 for domestic students. Application fee: $50. *Financial support:* Teaching assistantships, Federal Work-Study and institutionally sponsored loans available. Support available to part-time students. Financial award application deadline: 2/1. *Faculty research:* Teacher thought processes, pedagogical content knowledge and teacher preparation. *Unit head:* Dr. Lawrence B. Flick, Chair, 541-737-4031, Fax: 541-737-1817.

Penn State University Park, Graduate School, College of Education, Department of Curriculum and Instruction, State College, University Park, PA 16802-1503. Offers bilingual education (M Ed, MS, PhD); early childhood education (M Ed, MS, PhD); elementary education (M Ed, MS, PhD); instructional systems (M Ed, MS, PhD); language arts and reading (M Ed, MS, PhD); science education (M Ed, MS, PhD); social studies education (MS, PhD); supervisor and curriculum development (M Ed, MS, PhD). *Accreditation:* NCATE. *Unit head:* Dr. Murry

R. Nelson, Head, 814-865-6321, Fax: 814-863-7602, E-mail: mrn2@psu.edu. *Application contact:* Judy Nastase, Graduate Staff Assistant, 814-865-2168, E-mail: jcn3@psu.edu.

Plymouth State University, College of Graduate Studies, Graduate Studies in Education, Program in Science, Plymouth, NH 03264-1595. Offers applied meteorology (MS); environmental science and policy (MS); science education (MS). *Students:* 1 (woman) full-time, 36 part-time (17 women). Average age 30. 21 applicants, 100% accepted, 21 enrolled. *Expenses:* Tuition, state resident: part-time $369 per credit. Tuition, nonresident: part-time $407 per credit. Tuition and fees vary according to course level. *Unit head:* Dr. Steve Kahl, Director of the Center for the Environment, E-mail: jskahl@plymouth.edu.

Portland State University, Graduate Studies, College of Liberal Arts and Sciences, Department of Geology, Portland, OR 97207-0751. Offers environmental sciences and resources (PhD); geology (MA, MS); science/geology (MAT, MST). Part-time programs available. *Faculty:* 12 full-time (2 women), 1 (woman) part-time/adjunct. *Students:* 12 full-time (5 women), 15 part-time (7 women). Average age 30. 13 applicants, 54% accepted, 5 enrolled. In 2006, 5 degrees awarded. *Degree requirements:* For master's, thesis, field comprehensive; for doctorate, thesis/dissertation, 2 years of residency. *Entrance requirements:* For master's, GRE General Test, GRE Subject Test, BA/BS in geology, minimum GPA of 3.0 in upper-division course work or 2.75 overall. Additional exam requirements/recommendations for international students: Required—TOEFL (minimum score 550 paper-based; 213 computer-based). *Application deadline:* 1/31 priority date for domestic and international students. Applications are processed on a rolling basis. Application fee: $50. *Expenses:* Tuition, state resident: full-time $6,426; part-time $238 per credit. Tuition, nonresident: full-time $11,016; part-time $408 per credit. Required fees: $1,226; $23 per credit. $59 per term. Tuition and fees vary according to course load. *Financial support:* In 2006–07, 9 teaching assistantships with full tuition reimbursements (averaging $10,100 per year) were awarded; research assistantships with full tuition reimbursements, career-related internships or fieldwork, Federal Work-Study, scholarships/grants, and unspecified assistantships also available. Support available to part-time students. Financial award application deadline: 3/1; financial award applicants required to submit FAFSA. *Faculty research:* Sediment transport, volcanic environmental geology, coastal and fluvial processes. Total annual research expenditures: $1.6 million. *Unit head:* Dr. Michael L. Cummings, Head, 503-725-3022, Fax: 503-725-3025. *Application contact:* Nancy Eriksson, Office Coordinator, 503-725-3022, Fax: 503-725-3025, E-mail: erikssonn@pdx.edu.

Portland State University, Graduate Studies, College of Liberal Arts and Sciences, Interdisciplinary Program in Environmental Sciences and Resources, Portland, OR 97207-0751. Offers environmental management (MEM); environmental sciences/biology (PhD); environmental sciences/chemistry (PhD); environmental sciences/civil engineering (PhD); environmental sciences/geography (PhD); environmental sciences/geology (PhD); environmental sciences/physics (PhD); environmental studies (MS); science/environmental science (MST). Part-time programs available. *Faculty:* 9 full-time (1 woman), 1 part-time/adjunct (0 women). *Students:* 82 full-time (34 women), 39 part-time (19 women); includes 10 minority (1 African American, 1 American Indian/Alaska Native, 6 Asian Americans or Pacific Islanders, 2 Hispanic Americans), 33 international. Average age 32. 66 applicants, 73% accepted, 29 enrolled. In 2006, 16 master's, 7 doctorates awarded. *Degree requirements:* For doctorate, variable foreign language requirement, thesis/dissertation, oral and qualifying exams. *Entrance requirements:* For doctorate, minimum GPA of 3.0 in upper-division course work or 2.75 overall. Additional exam requirements/recommendations for international students: Required—TOEFL (minimum score 550 paper-based; 213 computer-based). *Application deadline:* For fall admission, 4/1 priority date for domestic students, 3/1 priority date for international students. Applications are processed on a rolling basis. Application fee: $50. *Expenses:* Tuition, state resident: full-time $6,426; part-time $238 per credit. Tuition, nonresident: full-time $11,016; part-time $408 per credit. Required fees: $1,226; $23 per credit. $59 per term. Tuition and fees vary according to course load. *Financial support:* In 2006–07, 2 research assistantships with full tuition reimbursements (averaging $10,577 per year), 3 teaching assistantships with full tuition reimbursements (averaging $9,909 per year) were awarded; Federal Work-Study, scholarships/grants, tuition waivers (partial), and unspecified assistantships also available. Support available to part-time students. Financial award application deadline: 3/1; financial award applicants required to submit FAFSA. *Faculty research:* Environmental aspects of biology, chemistry, civil engineering, geology, physics. Total annual research expenditures: $1.8 million. *Unit head:* John Rueter, Director, 503-725-4980, Fax: 503-725-3888.

Portland State University, Graduate Studies, College of Liberal Arts and Sciences, Interdisciplinary Programs in General Science, General Social Science, and General Arts and Letters, Portland, OR 97207-0751. Offers general arts and letters education (MAT, MST); general science education (MAT, MST); general social science education (MAT, MST). Part-time and evening/weekend programs available. *Students:* 23 full-time (18 women), 15 part-time (13 women); includes 2 minority (1 American Indian/Alaska Native, 1 Asian American or Pacific Islander), 5 international. Average age 37. 15 applicants, 80% accepted, 11 enrolled. In 2006, 6 degrees awarded. *Entrance requirements:* For master's, minimum GPA of 3.0 in upper-division course work or 2.75 overall. Additional exam requirements/recommendations for international students: Required—TOEFL (minimum score 550 paper-based; 213 computer-based). *Application deadline:* For fall admission, 4/1 priority date for domestic students, 3/1 priority date for international students. Application fee: $50. *Expenses:* Tuition, state resident: full-time $6,426; part-time $238 per credit. Tuition, nonresident: full-time $11,016; part-time $408 per credit. Tuition and fees vary according to course load. *Financial support:* In 2006–07, 2 research assistantships with full tuition reimbursements (averaging $9,930 per year) were awarded; fellowships with full tuition reimbursements, teaching assistantships with full tuition reimbursements, Federal Work-Study and unspecified assistantships also available. Support available to part-time students. Financial award application deadline: 3/1; financial award applicants required to submit FAFSA. *Unit head:* Robert Mercer, Senior Academic Adviser, 503-725-5059.

Purdue University, Graduate School, College of Science, Department of Chemistry, West Lafayette, IN 47907. Offers analytical chemistry (MS, PhD); biochemistry (MS, PhD); chemical education (MS, PhD); inorganic chemistry (MS, PhD); organic chemistry (MS, PhD); physical chemistry (MS, PhD). *Faculty:* 45 full-time (10 women), 8 part-time/adjunct (2 women). *Students:* 295 full-time (111 women), 48 part-time (28 women); includes 49 minority (22 African Americans, 9 Asian Americans or Pacific Islanders, 18 Hispanic Americans), 141 international. Average age 28. 499 applicants, 25% accepted, 52 enrolled. In 2006, 15 master's, 47 doctorates awarded. Terminal master's awarded for partial completion of doctoral program. *Degree requirements:* For master's and doctorate, thesis/dissertation. *Entrance requirements:* Additional exam requirements/recommendations for international students: Required—TOEFL. *Application deadline:* For fall admission, 4/1 priority date for domestic students, 3/1 for international students; for spring admission, 10/1 priority date for domestic students, 9/1 for international students. Applications are processed on a rolling basis. Application fee: $55. Electronic applications accepted. *Financial support:* In 2006–07, 2 fellowships with partial tuition reimbursements (averaging $18,000 per year), 55 teaching assistantships with partial tuition reimbursements (averaging $18,000 per year) were awarded; research assistantships with partial tuition reimbursements, tuition waivers (partial) also available. Support available to part-time students. Financial award applicants required to submit FAFSA. *Unit head:* Dr. Timothy S. Zwier, Head, 765-494-5203. *Application contact:* R. E. Wild, Director of Graduate Admissions, 765-494-5200, E-mail: wild@purdue.edu.

Purdue University, Graduate School, School of Education, Department of Curriculum and Instruction, West Lafayette, IN 47907. Offers agricultural and extension education (PhD, Ed S); agriculture and extension education (MS, MS Ed); art education (PhD); consumer and family sciences and extension education (MS Ed, PhD, Ed S); curriculum studies (MS Ed, PhD, Ed S); educational technology (MS Ed, PhD, Ed S); elementary education (MS Ed); foreign language education (MS Ed, PhD, Ed S); industrial technology (PhD, Ed S); language arts (MS Ed, PhD, Ed S); literacy (MS Ed, PhD, Ed S); mathematics/science education (MS, MS Ed, PhD, Ed S); social studies (MS Ed, PhD); social studies education (Ed S); vocational/industrial education (MS Ed, PhD, Ed S); vocational/technical education (MS Ed, PhD, Ed S). *Accreditation:* NCATE. Part-time and evening/weekend programs available. *Faculty:* 26 full-time (13 women), 3 part-time/adjunct (all women). *Students:* 59 full-time (37 women), 112 part-time (70 women); includes 24 minority (13 African Americans, 3 American Indian/Alaska Native, 4 Asian Americans or Pacific Islanders, 4 Hispanic Americans), 38 international. Average age 35. 92 applicants, 68% accepted, 38 enrolled. In 2006, 52 master's, 23 doctorates awarded. *Degree requirements:* For master's, thesis optional; for doctorate, thesis/dissertation, oral and written exams; for Ed S, oral presentation, project. *Entrance requirements:* For master's, GRE General Test, minimum B average; for doctorate, GRE General Test; for Ed S, GRE, minimum B average. Additional exam requirements/recommendations for international students: Required—TOEFL. *Application deadline:* For fall admission, 1/15 priority date for domestic students, 1/15 for international students; for spring admission, 9/15 for domestic and international students. Applications are processed on a rolling basis. Application fee: $55. Electronic applications accepted. *Financial support:* In 2006–07, 3 fellowships with full tuition reimbursements (averaging $10,500 per year), 11 research assistantships with full tuition reimbursements (averaging $11,500 per year), 43 teaching assistantships with full tuition reimbursements (averaging $10,800 per year) were awarded; career-related internships or fieldwork and tuition waivers (full) also available. Support available to part-time students. Financial award application deadline: 3/1; financial award applicants required to submit FAFSA. *Faculty research:* Literacy acquisition and development, teacher beliefs and knowledge, recruitment and retention of underrepresented students, economic education, literacy discourse. *Unit head:* Dr. James D Lehman, Head, 765-494-7935, Fax: 765-496-1622. *Application contact:* Patricia Mason, Coordinator of Graduate Studies, 765-494-2345, Fax: 765-494-5832, E-mail: gradoffice@soe.purdue.edu.

Purdue University Calumet, Graduate School, School of Engineering, Mathematics, and Science, Department of Biological Sciences, Hammond, IN 46323-2094. Offers biology (MS); biology teaching (MS); biotechnology (MS). *Entrance requirements:* For master's, GRE. Additional exam requirements/recommendations for international students: Required—TOEFL. Electronic applications accepted. *Faculty research:* Cell biology, molecular biology, genetics, microbiology, neurophysiology.

Queens College of the City University of New York, Division of Graduate Studies, Division of Education, Department of Secondary Education, Flushing, NY 11367-1597. Offers art (MS Ed); biology (MS Ed, AC); chemistry (MS Ed, AC); earth sciences (MS Ed, AC); English (MS Ed, AC); French (MS Ed, AC); Italian (MS Ed, AC); mathematics (MS Ed, AC); music (MS Ed, AC); physics (MS Ed, AC); social studies (MS Ed, AC); Spanish (MS Ed, AC). Part-time and evening/weekend programs available. *Faculty:* 22 full-time (14 women). *Students:* 50 full-time (28 women), 974 part-time (627 women). 633 applicants, 82% accepted, 407 enrolled. In 2006, 227 degrees awarded. *Degree requirements:* For master's, research project; for AC, thesis optional. *Entrance requirements:* For master's, minimum GPA of 3.0. Additional exam requirements/recommendations for international students: Required—TOEFL. *Application deadline:* For fall admission, 4/1 for domestic students; for spring admission, 11/1 for domestic students. Applications are processed on a rolling basis. Application fee: $125. *Financial support:* Career-related internships or fieldwork, Federal Work-Study, institutionally sponsored loans, and tuition waivers (partial) available. Support available to part-time students. Financial award application deadline: 4/1; financial award applicants required to submit FAFSA. *Unit head:* Dr. Eleanor Armour-Thomas, Chairperson, 718-997-5150, E-mail: armourthomas@yahoo.com. *Application contact:* Mario Caruso, Director of Graduate Admissions, 718-997-5200, Fax: 718-997-5193, E-mail: graduate_admissions@qc.edu.

Quinnipiac University, Division of Education, Program in Secondary Education, Hamden, CT 06518-1940. Offers biology (MAT); chemistry (MAT); English (MAT); French (MAT); history/social studies (MAT); mathematics (MAT); physics (MAT); Spanish (MAT). *Faculty:* 7 full-time (5 women), 23 part-time/adjunct (14 women). *Students:* 64 full-time (41 women); includes 5 minority (1 African American, 4 Hispanic Americans). Average age 26. 63 applicants, 87% accepted, 42 enrolled. In 2006, 37 degrees awarded. *Entrance requirements:* For master's, PRAXIS I, minimum GPA of 2.67, interview. Additional exam requirements/recommendations for international students: Required—TOEFL (minimum score 575 paper-based; 233 computer-based; 90 iBT), IELTS (minimum score 7). *Application deadline:* For fall admission, 3/15 priority date for domestic students. Applications are processed on a rolling basis. Application fee: $45. Electronic applications accepted. *Expenses:* Tuition: Part-time $675 per credit. Required fees: $30 per credit. *Financial support:* Career-related internships or fieldwork and tuition waivers (partial) available. Financial award application deadline: 4/15; financial award applicants required to submit FAFSA. *Faculty research:* Multicultural and urban education, role of technology in education, challenges of teaching divers learners, socio-cultural nature of learning. *Unit head:* Dr. Bernadine Krawczyk, Assistant Dean, Division of Education, 203-582-3510, Fax: 203-582-3473, E-mail: bernadine.krawczyk@quinnipiac.edu. *Application contact:* 800-462-1944, Fax: 203-582-3443, E-mail: graduate@quinnipiac.edu.

See Close-Up on page 911.

Regis University, School for Professional Studies, Program in Teacher Education, Denver, CO 80221-1099. Offers adult learning, training, and development (M Ed); curriculum, instruction, and assessment (M Ed); early childhood (M Ed); educational technology (Certificate); elementary (M Ed); ESL (M Ed); fine arts (M Ed), including arts, music; instructional technology (M Ed); professional leadership (M Ed); reading (M Ed); secondary (M Ed); self-designed (M Ed); space studies (M Ed); special education (M Ed); teacher licensure (M Ed). Program also offered in Henderson and Las Vegas (Summerlin), NV. Postbaccalaureate distance learning degree programs offered. *Unit head:* Dr. Suzie Perry, Dean, 303-458-4302. *Application contact:* Partick Lowenthal, Assistant Director, 303-458-4300 Ext. 4314, E-mail: masters@regis.edu.

Rider University, Department of Graduate Education, Leadership and Counseling, Lawrenceville, NJ 08648-3001. Offers counseling services (MA, Ed S); curriculum, instruction and supervision (MA); director of school counseling services (Certificate); educational administration (MA); organizational leadership (MA); principal (Certificate); reading/language arts (MA, Certificate), including reading specialist (Certificate), reading/language arts (MA); school business administrator (Certificate); school counseling services (Certificate); school psychology (Ed S); special education (MA); supervisor (Certificate); teacher certification (Certificate), including business education, elementary education, English as a second language, English education, mathematics education, preschool to grade 3, science education, social studies education, world languages; teaching (MA). *Accreditation:* NCATE. Part-time and evening/weekend programs available. *Faculty:* 24 full-time (12 women), 30 part-time/adjunct (15 women). *Students:* 90 full-time (75 women), 457 part-time (369 women); includes 73 minority (50 African Americans, 2 American Indian/Alaska Native, 6 Asian Americans or Pacific Islanders, 15 Hispanic Americans), 1 international. Average age 32. 314 applicants, 61% accepted, 138 enrolled. In 2006, 116 master's, 19 other advanced degrees awarded. *Degree requirements:* For master's, thesis or alternative, internship, portfolios, comprehensive exam (for some programs); for other advanced degree, internship, professional portfolio. *Entrance requirements:* For master's, GRE (counseling, school psychology), MAT, interview, resumé, letters of recommendation; for other advanced degree, PRAXIS. Additional exam requirements/recommendations for international students: Required—TOEFL (minimum score 550 paper-based; 213 computer-based). *Application deadline:* For fall admission, 5/1 priority date for domestic students, 6/1 priority date for international students; for spring admission, 11/1 priority date for domestic and international students. Applications are processed on a rolling basis. Application fee: $50. Electronic applications accepted. *Expenses:* Tuition: Part-time $525 per credit. Required fees: $35 per course. $30 per semester. *Financial support:* In 2006–07, 271 students received support. Career-related internships or fieldwork, Federal Work-Study, institutionally sponsored loans, and unspecified assistantships available. Support available to part-time students. Financial award applicants required to submit FAFSA. *Faculty research:* Gifted students, self-esteem, hope and mental health, conflicts in group work, cultural diversity and counseling assessment of special needs in children. *Unit head:* Dr.

Science Education

Rider University (continued)

Dennis C. Buss, Chair, 609-895-5353, Fax: 609-896-5362, E-mail: dbuss@rider.edu. *Application contact:* Jamie L Mitchell, Director of Graduate Admissions, 609-896-5036, Fax: 609-895-5680, E-mail: jmitchell@rider.edu.

See Close-Up on page 913.

Rutgers, The State University of New Jersey, New Brunswick, Graduate School of Education, Department of Learning and Teaching, Program in Science Education, New Brunswick, NJ 08901-1281. Offers Ed M, Ed D. Part-time programs available. *Faculty:* 3 full-time (2 women). *Students:* 24 full-time (17 women), 19 part-time (13 women). 47 applicants, 62% accepted, 20 enrolled. In 2006, 20 master's, 2 doctorates awarded. Terminal master's awarded for partial completion of doctoral program. *Degree requirements:* For master's, comprehensive exam (for some programs); for doctorate, thesis/dissertation, qualifying exam. *Entrance requirements:* For master's, GRE General Test, minimum GPA of 3.0; for doctorate, GRE General Test, minimum GPA of 3.5. Additional exam requirements/recommendations for international students: Required—TOEFL. *Application deadline:* For fall admission, 2/1 for domestic and international students. Application fee: $60. Electronic applications accepted. *Financial support:* Application deadline: 3/15; *Unit head:* Dr. Eugenia Etkina, Coordinator, 732-932-7496 Ext. 8339, E-mail: etkina@rci.rutgers.edu.

Rutgers, The State University of New Jersey, New Brunswick, Graduate School, Program in Chemistry and Chemical Biology, New Brunswick, NJ 08901-1281. Offers analytical chemistry (MS, PhD); biological chemistry (PhD); chemistry education (MST); inorganic chemistry (MS, PhD); organic chemistry (MS, PhD); physical chemistry (MS, PhD). Part-time and evening/weekend programs available. Terminal master's awarded for partial completion of doctoral program. *Degree requirements:* For master's, thesis or alternative, exam, comprehensive exam, registration; for doctorate, thesis/dissertation, cumulative exams, 1 year residency, comprehensive exam, registration. *Entrance requirements:* For master's and doctorate, GRE General Test, GRE Subject Test. Additional exam requirements/recommendations for international students: Required—TOEFL. Electronic applications accepted. *Faculty research:* Biophysical organic/bioorganic, inorganic/bioinorganic, theoretical, and solid-state/surface chemistry.

Sage Graduate School, Graduate School, Division of Education, Program in Teaching, Troy, NY 12180-4115. Offers art education (MAT); biology (MAT); English (MAT); mathematics (MAT); social studies (MAT). Part-time and evening/weekend programs available. *Faculty:* 11 full-time (8 women), 20 part-time/adjunct (15 women). *Students:* 34 full-time (28 women), 41 part-time (29 women); includes 3 minority (1 African American, 1 Asian American or Pacific Islander, 1 Hispanic American). Average age 27. 72 applicants, 64% accepted, 33 enrolled. In 2006, 31 degrees awarded. *Entrance requirements:* For master's, minimum undergraduate GPA of 2.75 overall, minimum undergraduate GPA of 3.0 in content area. Additional exam requirements/recommendations for international students: Required—TOEFL (minimum score 550 paper-based; 213 computer-based). *Application deadline:* For fall admission, 8/1 for domestic students. Applications are processed on a rolling basis. Application fee: $40. *Expenses:* Tuition: Full-time $9,270; part-time $515 per credit hour. *Financial support:* Career-related internships or fieldwork, scholarships/grants, and unspecified assistantships available. Support available to part-time students. Financial award application deadline: 3/1; financial award applicants required to submit FAFSA. *Unit head:* Peter McDermott, Director, 518-244-2493, E-mail: mcderp@sage.edu. *Application contact:* Shannon K. Easton, Director of Graduate and Adult Admission, 518-244-2443, Fax: 518-244-6880, E-mail: sgsadm@sage.edu.

Saginaw Valley State University, College of Education, Program in Natural Science Teaching, University Center, MI 48710. Offers elementary (MAT); middle school (MAT); secondary school (MAT). *Accreditation:* NCATE. Part-time and evening/weekend programs available. *Students:* 1 (woman) full-time, 22 part-time (16 women). Average age 36. 3 applicants, 100% accepted, 3 enrolled. In 2006, 15 degrees awarded. *Degree requirements:* For master's, capstone course. *Entrance requirements:* For master's, minimum GPA of 3.0, teaching certificate. *Application deadline:* Applications are processed on a rolling basis. Application fee: $25. Electronic applications accepted. *Expenses:* Tuition, state resident: full-time $7,225; part-time $301 per credit hour. Tuition, nonresident: full-time $13,888; part-time $579 per credit hour. Required fees: $330; $14 per credit hour. Tuition and fees vary according to course load. *Financial support:* Applicants required to submit FAFSA. *Application contact:* Jeanne Chipman, Certification Officer, 989-964-4083, Fax: 989-964-4385, E-mail: jdc@svsu.edu.

St. John Fisher College, Office of the Provost, School of Arts and Sciences, Mathematics/Science/Technology Education Program, Rochester, NY 14618-3597. Offers MS. Part-time and evening/weekend programs available. *Faculty:* 3 full-time (1 woman), 1 part-time/adjunct (0 women). *Students:* 6 full-time (4 women), 83 part-time (59 women); includes 2 African Americans, 1 Asian American or Pacific Islander, 1 Hispanic American. Average age 32. 29 applicants, 66% accepted, 12 enrolled. In 2006, 24 degrees awarded. *Degree requirements:* For master's, thesis. *Entrance requirements:* For master's, minimum GPA of 3.0, interview, essay, recommendations. Additional exam requirements/recommendations for international students: Required—TOEFL (minimum score 575 paper-based; 233 computer-based; 80 iBT). *Application deadline:* For fall admission, 7/1 for domestic students; for spring admission, 10/30 for domestic students. Applications are processed on a rolling basis. Application fee: $30. *Expenses:* Tuition: Part-time $615 per credit. Tuition and fees vary according to program. *Financial support:* Federal Work-Study and scholarships/grants available. Financial award application deadline: 2/15; financial award applicants required to submit FAFSA. *Faculty research:* Mathematics education, science and technology education. *Unit head:* Dr. Diane Barrett, Graduate Director, 585-385-8366, E-mail: dbarrett@sjfc.edu. *Application contact:* Shannon Cleverley, Director of Graduate Admissions, 585-385-8161, Fax: 585-385-8344, E-mail: scleverley@sjfc.edu.

Salem State College, Graduate School, Program in Biology, Salem, MA 01970-5353. Offers MAT. Part-time and evening/weekend programs available. *Students:* Average age 28. *Application deadline:* Applications are processed on a rolling basis. Application fee: $35. *Unit head:* Mark Fregeau, Professor, 978-542-6310, E-mail: mfregeau@salemstate.edu.

Salem State College, Graduate School, Program in Chemistry, Salem, MA 01970-5353. Offers MAT. Part-time and evening/weekend programs available. *Students:* Average age 27. *Application deadline:* Applications are processed on a rolling basis. Application fee: $35. *Unit head:* William Adams, Professor, 978-542-6310, E-mail: wadams@salemstate.edu.

Salisbury University, Graduate Division, Department of Education, Salisbury, MD 21801-6837. Offers art (MAT); biology (MAT); business education (MAT); chemistry (MAT); early childhood education (M Ed); educational administration (M Ed); elementary education (M Ed); English (M Ed, MAT); French (MAT); geography (MAT); history (MAT); mathematics (MAT); media and technology (MAT); music (MAT); psychology (MAT); reading education (MAT); science (MAT); secondary education (MAT); social studies (MAT); Spanish (MAT). *Accreditation:* NCATE. Part-time and evening/weekend programs available. *Faculty:* 12 full-time (6 women), 10 part-time/adjunct (8 women). *Students:* 17 full-time (9 women), 84 part-time (72 women); includes 6 minority (5 African Americans, 1 Hispanic American). Average age 30. 15 applicants, 73% accepted, 11 enrolled. In 2006, 63 degrees awarded. *Degree requirements:* For master's, comprehensive exam (for some programs). *Entrance requirements:* For master's, PRAXIS, minimum GPA of 2.75. Additional exam requirements/recommendations for international students: Required—TOEFL (minimum score 550 paper-based; 213 computer-based). *Application deadline:* For fall admission, 8/1 priority date for domestic students; for spring admission, 1/1 for domestic students. Applications are processed on a rolling basis. Application fee: $45. *Expenses:* Tuition, state resident: part-time $260 per credit hour. Tuition, nonresident: part-time $546 per credit hour. Required fees: $52 per credit hour. *Financial support:* In 2006–07, 3 teaching assistantships with full tuition reimbursements were awarded; career-related internships or fieldwork and scholarships/grants also available. Support available to part-time students. Financial award applicants required to submit FAFSA. *Faculty research:* Middle-level education, student outcomes. *Unit head:* Dr. Edward C. Robeck, Program Coordinator, 410-543-6292, Fax: 410-548-2593, E-mail: ecrobeck@salisbury.edu. *Application contact:* Debra J. Clark, Administrative Assistant I, 410-543-6281, Fax: 410-548-2593, E-mail: djclark@salisbury.edu.

San Diego State University, Graduate and Research Affairs, College of Sciences, Department of Mathematical Sciences, San Diego, CA 92182. Offers applied mathematics (MS); mathematics (MA); mathematics and science education (PhD); statistics (MS). Part-time programs available. *Students:* 18 full-time (7 women), 26 part-time (17 women). 81 applicants, 74% accepted, 14 enrolled. In 2006, 28 master's, 3 doctorates awarded. *Degree requirements:* For doctorate, thesis/dissertation. *Entrance requirements:* For master's, GRE General Test; for doctorate, GRE, minimum GPA of 3.25 in last 30 undergraduate semester units, minimum graduate GPA of 3.5, MSE recommendation form, 3 letters of recommendation. Additional exam requirements/recommendations for international students: Required—TOEFL. *Application deadline:* For fall admission, 5/1 for domestic and international students; for spring admission, 11/1 for domestic students, 10/1 for international students. Applications are processed on a rolling basis. Application fee: $55. Electronic applications accepted. *Financial support:* Teaching assistantships, unspecified assistantships available. Financial award applicants required to submit FAFSA. *Faculty research:* Teacher education in mathematics. Total annual research expenditures: $1.3 million. *Unit head:* David Lesley, Chair, 619-594-6191, Fax: 619-594-6746, E-mail: lesley@math.sdsu.edu. *Application contact:* Larry Sowder, Graduate Coordinator, 619-594-7246, Fax: 619-594-6746, E-mail: lsowder@sciences.sdsu.edu.

Slippery Rock University of Pennsylvania, Graduate Studies (Recruitment), College of Education, Department of Elementary Education and Early Childhood, Slippery Rock, PA 16057-1383. Offers early childhood education (M Ed); math/science (M Ed); reading (M Ed). *Accreditation:* NCATE. Part-time and evening/weekend programs available. *Degree requirements:* For master's, thesis (for some programs), reflective presentation, comprehensive exam (for some programs). *Entrance requirements:* For master's, GRE General Test, MAT, minimum GPA of 2.75 (minimum GPA of 3.0 for initial certification programs). Additional exam requirements/recommendations for international students: Required—TOEFL (minimum score 550 paper-based; 213 computer-based). *Application deadline:* For fall admission, 7/1 priority date for domestic and international students; for spring admission, 11/1 priority date for domestic and international students. Applications are processed on a rolling basis. Application fee: $25. Electronic applications accepted. *Expenses:* Tuition, state resident: part-time $336 per credit. Tuition, nonresident: part-time $538 per credit. Required fees: $84 per credit. $37 per semester. *Financial support:* Career-related internships or fieldwork, Federal Work-Study, scholarships/grants, and unspecified assistantships available. Support available to part-time students. Financial award application deadline: 5/1; financial award applicants required to submit FAFSA. *Unit head:* Dr. Suzanne Rose, Graduate Coordinator, 724-738-2863, Fax: 724-738-2880, E-mail: suzanne.rose@sn.edu. *Application contact:* April Longwell, Interim Director of Graduate Studies, 724-738-2051 Ext. 2116, Fax: 724-738-2146, E-mail: graduate.studies@sru.edu.

Slippery Rock University of Pennsylvania, Graduate Studies (Recruitment), College of Education, Department of Secondary Education/Foundations of Education, Slippery Rock, PA 16057-1383. Offers secondary education in math/science (M Ed). *Accreditation:* NCATE. *Degree requirements:* For master's, thesis (for some programs), comprehensive exam (for some programs). *Entrance requirements:* For master's, GRE General Test, MAT, minimum GPA of 2.75 (minimum GPA of 3.0 for initial certification programs). Additional exam requirements/recommendations for international students: Required—TOEFL (minimum score 550 paper-based; 213 computer-based). *Application deadline:* For fall admission, 7/1 priority date for domestic and international students; for spring admission, 11/1 priority date for domestic and international students. Applications are processed on a rolling basis. Application fee: $25. Electronic applications accepted. *Expenses:* Tuition, state resident: part-time $336 per credit. Tuition, nonresident: part-time $538 per credit. Required fees: $84 per credit. $37 per semester. *Financial support:* Career-related internships or fieldwork, Federal Work-Study, scholarships/grants, and unspecified assistantships available. Support available to part-time students. Financial award application deadline: 5/1; financial award applicants required to submit FAFSA. *Unit head:* Graduate Coordinator, 724-738-2041, Fax: 724-738-2880. *Application contact:* April Longwell, Interim Director of Graduate Studies, 724-738-2051 Ext. 2116, Fax: 724-738-2146, E-mail: graduate.studies@sru.edu.

Smith College, Graduate Programs, Department of Education and Child Study, Program in Secondary Education, Northampton, MA 01063. Offers biological sciences education (MAT); chemistry education (MAT); English education (MAT); French education (MAT); geology education (MAT); government education (MAT); history education (MAT); mathematics education (MAT); physics education (MAT); Spanish education (MAT). Part-time programs available. *Faculty:* 6 full-time (4 women), 3 part-time/adjunct (2 women). *Students:* 4 full-time (2 women). Average age 36. 12 applicants, 67% accepted, 3 enrolled. In 2006, 5 master's awarded. *Entrance requirements:* For master's, GRE General Test. Additional exam requirements/recommendations for international students: Required—TOEFL. *Application deadline:* For fall admission, 4/1 for domestic students, 1/15 for international students; for spring admission, 12/1 for domestic students. Application fee: $60. *Expenses:* Tuition: Full-time $32,320; part-time $1,010 per credit. Tuition and fees vary according to course load. *Financial support:* In 2006–07, 3 students received support. Career-related internships or fieldwork, institutionally sponsored loans, and scholarships/grants available. Support available to part-time students. Financial award application deadline: 1/15; financial award applicants required to submit CSS PROFILE or FAFSA. *Unit head:* Rosetta Cohen, Graduate Student Advisor, 413-585-3266.

South Carolina State University, School of Graduate Studies, Department of Education, Orangeburg, SC 29117-0001. Offers early childhood and special education (M Ed); early childhood education (MAT); elementary education (M Ed, MAT); engineering (MAT); general science (MAT); mathematics (MAT); secondary education (M Ed), including biology education, business education, counselor education, English education, home economics education, industrial education, mathematics education, science education, social studies education; special education (M Ed), including emotionally handicapped, learning disabilities, mentally handicapped. *Accreditation:* NCATE. Part-time and evening/weekend programs available. *Faculty:* 21 full-time (10 women), 4 part-time/adjunct (0 women). *Students:* 34 full-time (28 women), 33 part-time (25 women); includes 63 minority (61 African Americans, 1 American Indian/Alaska Native, 1 Asian American or Pacific Islander). Average age 35. 46 applicants, 67% accepted, 19 enrolled. In 2006, 28 degrees awarded. *Degree requirements:* For master's, departmental qualifying exam, thesis optional. *Entrance requirements:* For master's, GRE General Test, NTE, interview, teaching certificate. *Application deadline:* For fall admission, 6/15 priority date for domestic students, 6/15 for international students; for spring admission, 11/1 for domestic and international students. Applications are processed on a rolling basis. Application fee: $25. Electronic applications accepted. *Expenses:* Tuition, state resident: full-time $7,278. Tuition, nonresident: full-time $14,322. *Financial support:* Fellowships, research assistantships, career-related internships or fieldwork, Federal Work-Study, and institutionally sponsored loans available. Financial award application deadline: 6/1. *Faculty research:* Critical thinking, child abuse, stress, test-taking skills, conflict resolution, mainstreaming. *Unit head:* Dr. Gail Joyner-Fleming, Interim Chair, 803-533-3769, Fax: 803-536-8492, E-mail: zf-gfleming@scsu.edu. *Application contact:* Annette Hazzard-Jones, Program Coordinator II, 803-536-8809, Fax: 803-536-8812, E-mail: zs_ahazzard@scsu.edu.

Southeast Missouri State University, School of Graduate Studies, Godwin Center for Science and Mathematics Education, Cape Girardeau, MO 63701-4799. Offers science education (MNS). Part-time programs available. *Students:* 1 (woman) full-time, 7 part-time (5 women). Average age 32. 2 applicants, 100% accepted. In 2006, 3 degrees awarded. *Degree requirements:* For master's, thesis or alternative, comprehensive exam (for some programs). *Entrance requirements:* For master's, minimum GPA of 2.75, valid teaching certificate. Additional exam requirements/recommendations for international students: Required—TOEFL (minimum score 550 paper-based; 213 computer-based). *Application deadline:* For fall admission, 8/1 for domestic students, 4/1 for international students; for spring admission, 11/21 for domestic students, 10/1 for international students. Applications are processed on a rolling basis. Application fee: $20 ($100 for international students). Electronic applications accepted. *Financial support:* In 2006–07, 1 student received support. Applicants required to submit FAFSA. *Unit head:* Dr. Sharon Coleman, Director, 573-651-2372, Fax: 573-986-6792, E-mail: godwin@semo.edu. *Application contact:* Marsha L. Arant, Senior Administrative Assistant, Office of Graduate Studies, 573-651-2192, Fax: 573-651-2001, E-mail: marant@semo.edu.

Southern Connecticut State University, School of Graduate Studies, School of Arts and Sciences, Department of Environmental Education/Science Education, New Haven, CT 06515-1355. Offers environmental education (MS); science education (MS, Diploma). *Accreditation:* NCATE. Part-time and evening/weekend programs available. *Faculty:* 2 full-time, 1 part-time/adjunct. *Students:* 6 full-time (3 women), 19 part-time (12 women); includes 1 minority (African American) 31 applicants, 100% accepted, 23 enrolled. *Degree requirements:* For master's, thesis or alternative. *Entrance requirements:* For master's, interview; for Diploma, master's degree. *Application deadline:* For fall admission, 7/15 priority date for domestic students. Applications are processed on a rolling basis. Application fee: $50. Electronic applications accepted. *Financial support:* Application deadline: 4/15; *Unit head:* Dr. Susan Cusato, Coordinator, 203-392-6610, Fax: 203-392-6614, E-mail: hagemans1@southernct.edu.

Southern Illinois University Edwardsville, Graduate Studies and Research, School of Education, Department of Curriculum and Instruction, Program in Secondary Education, Edwardsville, IL 62026-0001. Offers art (MS Ed); biology (MS Ed); chemistry (MS Ed); English (MS Ed); foreign languages (MS Ed); history (MS Ed); mathematics (MS Ed); physics (MS Ed); reading (MS Ed); science (MS Ed). *Accreditation:* NCATE. Part-time and evening/weekend programs available. *Students:* 2 full-time (both women), 23 part-time (14 women); includes 2 minority (both African Americans) Average age 33. 12 applicants, 42% accepted. In 2006, 10 degrees awarded. *Degree requirements:* For master's, thesis or alternative, final exam. *Entrance requirements:* For master's, MAT. Additional exam requirements/recommendations for international students: Required—TOEFL. *Application deadline:* For fall admission, 7/20 for domestic students, 6/1 for international students; for spring admission, 12/14 for domestic students, 10/1 for international students. Application fee: $30. Electronic applications accepted. *Financial support:* Fellowships, research assistantships, teaching assistantships, Federal Work-Study, institutionally sponsored loans, and unspecified assistantships available. Support available to part-time students. Financial award application deadline: 3/1; financial award applicants required to submit FAFSA. *Unit head:* Dr. David DeWeese, Director, 618-650-3432, E-mail: ddewees@siue.edu.

Southern University and Agricultural and Mechanical College, Graduate School, Department of Science/Mathematics Education, Baton Rouge, LA 70813. Offers PhD. *Accreditation:* NCATE. *Degree requirements:* For doctorate, thesis/dissertation. *Entrance requirements:* For doctorate, GRE General Test. Additional exam requirements/recommendations for international students: Required—TOEFL (minimum score 525 paper-based; 193 computer-based). *Faculty research:* Performance assessment in science/mathematics education, equity in science/mathematics education, technology and distance learning, science/mathematics concept formation, cognitive themes, problem solving in science/mathematics education.

Southwestern Oklahoma State University, College of Arts and Sciences, Specialization in Natural Sciences, Weatherford, OK 73096-3098. Offers M Ed. Part-time programs available. *Degree requirements:* For master's, exam. *Entrance requirements:* For master's, GRE General Test or minimum undergraduate GPA of 3.0. Additional exam requirements/recommendations for international students: Required—TOEFL.

Stanford University, School of Education, Program in Curriculum Studies and Teacher Education, Stanford, CA 94305-9991. Offers art education (MA, PhD); dance education (MA); English education (MA, PhD); general curriculum studies (MA, PhD); mathematics education (MA, PhD); science education (MA, PhD); social studies education (PhD); teacher education (MA, PhD). *Degree requirements:* For master's, thesis (for some programs); for doctorate, thesis/dissertation. *Entrance requirements:* For master's and doctorate, GRE General Test. Electronic applications accepted.

Stanford University, School of Education, Teacher Education Program, Stanford, CA 94305-9991. Offers English education (MA); languages education (MA); mathematics education (MA); science education (MA); social studies education (MA). *Degree requirements:* For master's, thesis. *Entrance requirements:* For master's, GRE General Test. Electronic applications accepted.

State University of New York at Binghamton, Graduate School, School of Education, Program in Secondary Education, Binghamton, NY 13902-6000. Offers biology education (MAT, MS Ed, MST); earth science education (MAT, MS Ed, MST); English education (MAT, MS Ed, MST); French education (MAT, MST); mathematical sciences education (MAT, MS Ed, MST); physics (MAT, MS Ed, MST); social studies (MAT, MS Ed, MST); Spanish education (MAT, MST). *Accreditation:* Teacher Education Accreditation Council. Part-time and evening/weekend programs available. *Students:* 89 full-time (50 women), 47 part-time (32 women); includes 6 minority (1 African American, 3 Asian Americans or Pacific Islanders, 2 Hispanic Americans). Average age 29. 72 applicants, 72% accepted, 23 enrolled. In 2006, 44 degrees awarded. *Entrance requirements:* For master's, GRE General Test. Additional exam requirements/recommendations for international students: Required—TOEFL. *Application deadline:* For fall admission, 4/15 priority date for domestic students, 1/15 priority date for international students; for spring admission, 11/1 for domestic students, 10/1 priority date for international students. Applications are processed on a rolling basis. Application fee: $60. Electronic applications accepted. *Financial support:* In 2006–07, 25 students received support, including 2 fellowships with partial tuition reimbursements available (averaging $2,350 per year), 4 research assistantships with full and partial tuition reimbursements available (averaging $6,638 per year), 13 teaching assistantships with full tuition reimbursements available (averaging $5,944 per year); career-related internships or fieldwork, Federal Work-Study, institutionally sponsored loans, tuition waivers (full and partial), and unspecified assistantships also available. Support available to part-time students. Financial award application deadline: 2/15. *Unit head:* Dr. Thomas O'Brien, Coordinator, 607-777-7329, E-mail: tobrien@binghamton.edu.

State University of New York at Fredonia, Graduate Studies, Department of Chemistry and Biochemistry, Fredonia, NY 14063-1136. Offers chemistry (MS); curriculum and instruction science education (MS Ed). Part-time and evening/weekend programs available. *Faculty:* 1 full-time (0 women). *Students:* 1 (woman) full-time, 1 (woman) part-time; includes 1 minority (Asian American or Pacific Islander) Average age 24. In 2006, 1 degree awarded. *Degree requirements:* For master's, thesis optional. *Application deadline:* For fall admission, 8/5 for domestic students; for spring admission, 12/1 for domestic students. Application fee: $50. *Expenses:* Tuition, state resident: full-time $6,900; part-time $288 per credit hour. Tuition, nonresident: full-time $10,920; part-time $455 per credit hour. Required fees: $1,132; $47 per credit hour. *Financial support:* Research assistantships, teaching assistantships with partial tuition reimbursements, tuition waivers (full and partial) available. Support available to part-time students. Financial award application deadline: 3/15. *Unit head:* Dr. Thomas Janik, Chairman, 716-673-3281, E-mail: thomas.janik@fredonia.edu.

State University of New York at Plattsburgh, Division of Education, Health, and Human Services, Department of Adolescence Education/Health, Plattsburgh, NY 12901-2681. Offers adolescence education (MST); biology 7-12 (MST); chemistry 7-12 (MST); earth science 7-12 (MST); English 7-12 (MST); French 7-12 (MST); mathematics 7-12 (MST); social studies 7-12 (MST); Spanish 7-12 (MST). *Faculty:* 4 full-time (3 women), 2 part-time/adjunct (0 women). *Students:* 58 full-time (38 women), 14 part-time (10 women); includes 5 minority (1 African American, 4 Hispanic Americans). Average age 30. 49 applicants, 78% accepted, 32 enrolled. In 2006, 30 degrees awarded. *Degree requirements:* For master's, comprehensive exam or research project. *Entrance requirements:* For master's, GRE General Test or MAT, minimum GPA of 2.5. *Application deadline:* For fall admission, 2/15 priority date for domestic students; for spring admission, 10/15 priority date for domestic students. Applications are processed on a rolling basis. Application fee: $50. *Expenses:* Tuition, state resident: full-time $6,900; part-time $288 per credit hour. Tuition, nonresident: full-time $10,920; part-time $455 per credit hour. *Financial support:* Application deadline: 4/15; *Unit head:* Dr. Lois Beach, Chair, 578-564-5750, E-mail: lois.beach@plattsburgh.edu. *Application contact:* Sharon Derr, Assistant Director, Graduate Admission, 518-564-4723, Fax: 518-564-4722, E-mail: derrsl@plattsburgh.edu.

State University of New York College at Brockport, School of Professions, Department of Education and Human Development, Program in Adolescence Education, Brockport, NY 14420-2997. Offers biology education (MS Ed); chemistry education (MS Ed); earth science education (MS Ed); English education (MS Ed); mathematics education (MS Ed); physics education (MS Ed); social studies education (MS Ed). *Accreditation:* NCATE. Part-time programs available. *Students:* 39 full-time (21 women), 117 part-time (66 women); includes 6 minority (3 African Americans, 1 Asian American or Pacific Islander, 2 Hispanic Americans). 57 applicants, 61% accepted, 32 enrolled. In 2006, 91 degrees awarded. *Degree requirements:* For master's, thesis or alternative. *Entrance requirements:* For master's, minimum GPA of 3.0, letters of recommendation. Additional exam requirements/recommendations for international students: Required—TOEFL (minimum score 550 paper-based; 213 computer-based; 80 iBT). *Application deadline:* For fall admission, 2/15 for domestic and international students; for spring admission, 9/15 for domestic and international students. Application fee: $50. *Expenses:* Tuition, state resident: full-time $6,900; part-time $288 per credit. Tuition, nonresident: full-time $10,920; part-time $455 per credit. *Financial support:* Career-related internships or fieldwork, Federal Work-Study, scholarships/grants, and unspecified assistantships available. Support available to part-time students. Financial award application deadline: 3/15; financial award applicants required to submit FAFSA. *Application contact:* Coordinator of Certification and Graduate Advisement, 585-395-2344.

State University of New York College at Cortland, Graduate Studies, School of Arts and Sciences, Programs in Adolescence Education, Cortland, NY 13045. Offers biology (MAT, MS Ed); chemistry (MAT, MS Ed); earth science (MAT, MS Ed); English (MS Ed); French (MS Ed); mathematics (MAT, MS Ed); physics (MAT, MS Ed); social studies (MS Ed); Spanish (MS Ed). *Accreditation:* NCATE. Part-time and evening/weekend programs available. *Degree requirements:* For master's, one foreign language, thesis (for some programs), comprehensive exam (for some programs). *Entrance requirements:* For master's, GRE General Test.

Stony Brook University, State University of New York, School of Professional Development, Stony Brook, NY 11794. Offers adolescence education: mathematics (Certificate); biology 7-12 (MAT); chemistry-grade 7-12 (MAT); coaching (Certificate); computer integrated engineering (Certificate); cultural studies (Certificate); earth science-grade 7-12 (MAT); educational computing (Advanced Certificate, Certificate); English-grade 7-12 (MAT); environmental and waste management (MS, Advanced Certificate); environmental systems management (Certificate); environmental/occupational health and safety (Certificate); French-grade 7-12 (MAT); German-grade 7-12 (MAT); human resource management (Certificate); industrial management (Certificate); information systems management (Certificate); Italian-grade 7-12 (MAT); liberal studies (MA); liberal studies online (MA); Long Island regional studies (Certificate); operation research (Certificate); physics-grade 7-12 (MAT); Russian-grade 7-12 (MAT); school administration and supervision (Certificate); school district administration (Certificate); social science and the professions (MPS), including human resources management, labor management, public affairs, waste management; social studies 7-12 (MAT); waste management (Certificate); women's studies (Certificate). Part-time and evening/weekend programs available. Postbaccalaureate distance learning degree programs offered. *Faculty:* 1 full-time (0 women), 118 part-time/adjunct (45 women). *Students:* 322 full-time (202 women), 1,188 part-time (728 women); includes 164 minority (69 African Americans, 2 American Indian/Alaska Native, 29 Asian Americans or Pacific Islanders, 64 Hispanic Americans), 11 international. Average age 28. In 2006, 738 master's, 405 other advanced degrees awarded. *Degree requirements:* For master's, one foreign language, thesis or alternative. *Application deadline:* Applications are processed on a rolling basis. Application fee: $62. *Expenses:* Tuition, state resident: full-time $6,900; part-time $288 per credit. Tuition, nonresident: full-time $10,920; part-time $455 per credit. *Financial support:* In 2006–07, 5 teaching assistantships were awarded; fellowships, research assistantships, career-related internships or fieldwork also available. Support available to part-time students. *Unit head:* Dr. Paul J. Edelson, Dean, 631-632-7052, Fax: 631-632-9046, E-mail: paul.edelson@sunysb.edu. *Application contact:* Sandra Romansky, Director of Admissions and Advisement, 631-632-7050, Fax: 631-632-9046, E-mail: sandra.romansky@sunysb.edu.

Syracuse University, Graduate School, College of Arts and Sciences, Program in College Science Teaching, Syracuse, NY 13244. Offers PhD. Part-time programs available. Postbaccalaureate distance learning degree programs offered. *Students:* 3 full-time (2 women), 6 part-time (4 women); includes 1 minority (Asian American or Pacific Islander) *Entrance requirements:* For doctorate, GRE General Test, GRE Subject Test. *Application deadline:* For fall admission, 1/10 priority date for domestic students. Applications are processed on a rolling basis. Application fee: $65. Electronic applications accepted. *Expenses:* Tuition: Full-time $16,920; part-time $940 per credit hour. Required fees: $930; $930 per year. *Financial support:* Fellowships with full tuition reimbursements, teaching assistantships with full and partial tuition reimbursements available. *Unit head:* Dr. Marvin Druger, Chair, 315-443-3820, Fax: 315-443-1140, E-mail: mdruger@syr.edu. *Application contact:* Cynthia Daley, 315-443-2586.

Syracuse University, Graduate School, School of Education, Department of Teaching and Leadership, Program in Science Education, Syracuse, NY 13244. Offers science education (PhD); science/biology education: preparation 7-12 (MS); science/chemistry education: preparation 7-12 (MS); science/earth science education: preparation 7-12 (MS); science/physics education: preparation 7-12 (MS). Part-time and evening/weekend programs available. *Students:* 25 full-time (17 women), 13 part-time (8 women); includes 2 minority (both Asian Americans or Pacific Islanders), 1 international. 18 applicants, 89% accepted, 10 enrolled. *Degree requirements:* For master's, thesis or alternative; for doctorate, thesis/dissertation. *Entrance requirements:* For master's and doctorate, GRE. Additional exam requirements/recommendations for international students: Required—TOEFL. *Application deadline:* For fall admission, 2/1 priority date for domestic students. Applications are processed on a rolling basis. Application fee: $65. Electronic applications accepted. *Expenses:* Tuition: Full-time $16,920; part-time $940 per credit hour. Required fees: $930; $930 per year. *Financial support:* Fellowships with tuition reimbursements, research assistantships with tuition reimbursements, teaching assistantships with tuition reimbursements available. *Unit head:* Dr. John Tillotson, Program Director, 315-443-2586. *Application contact:* Liza Rochelson, Graduate Admission Recruiter, 315-443-2505, Fax: 315-443-2258, E-mail: gradcrt@gwmail.syr.edu.

Teachers College Columbia University, Graduate Faculty of Education, Department of Math, Science and Technology, Programs in Science Education, New York, NY 10027-6696. Offers Ed M, MA, MS, Ed D, Ed DCT, PhD. *Accreditation:* NCATE. Part-time and evening/weekend programs available. *Faculty:* 4 full-time (2 women), 5 part-time/adjunct. *Students:* 18 full-time (12 women), 70 part-time (42 women); includes 24 minority (14 African Americans, 6 Asian Americans or Pacific Islanders, 4 Hispanic Americans), 5 international. Average age 30. 95 applicants, 59% accepted, 18 enrolled. In 2006, 42 master's, 7 doctorates awarded. Terminal master's awarded for partial completion of doctoral program. *Degree requirements:* For master's, culminating paper; for doctorate, thesis/dissertation. *Entrance requirements:* For master's and doctorate, 24 credits in science. *Application deadline:* For fall admission, 5/15 for domestic students; for spring admission, 12/1 for domestic students. Application fee: $65. *Expenses:* Tuition: Full-time $23,400; part-time $975 per credit. Required fees: $320 per term. *Financial support:* Fellowships, career-related internships or fieldwork, Federal Work-Study, institutionally sponsored loans, and tuition waivers (full and partial) available. Support available to part-time students. Financial award application deadline: 2/1. *Faculty research:* Cell biology and physiological ecology of protozoa, teaching and learning of pre-college and

Science Education

Teachers College Columbia University (continued)
college sciences, homelessness. Total annual research expenditures: $100,000. *Application contact:* Deanna Ghozati, Assistant Director of Admission, 212-678-4018, Fax: 212-678-4171, E-mail: ghozati@tc.edu.

See Close-Up on page 1615.

Temple University, Graduate School, College of Education, Department of Curriculum, Instruction, and Technology in Education, Philadelphia, PA 19122-6096. Offers applied behavioral analysis (MS Ed); career and technical education (MS Ed); early childhood education and elementary education (MS Ed); English education (MS Ed); language arts education (Ed D); math/science education (Ed D); mathematics education (MS Ed); science education (MS Ed); second and foreign language education (MS Ed); special education (MS Ed); teaching English as a second language (MS Ed). Part-time and evening/weekend programs available. *Faculty:* 31 full-time (14 women). *Students:* 96 full-time (71 women), 482 part-time (336 women); includes 109 minority (67 African Americans, 3 American Indian/Alaska Native, 23 Asian Americans or Pacific Islanders, 16 Hispanic Americans), 28 international. 308 applicants, 64% accepted, 116 enrolled. In 2006, 225 master's, 21 doctorates awarded. Terminal master's awarded for partial completion of doctoral program. *Degree requirements:* For master's, thesis or alternative; for doctorate, thesis/dissertation. *Entrance requirements:* For master's and doctorate, GRE General Test or MAT, minimum GPA of 3.0. Additional exam requirements/recommendations for international students: Required—TOEFL (minimum score 550 paper-based; 213 computer-based; 79 iBT). *Application deadline:* For fall admission, 4/1 for domestic students, 12/15 for international students; for spring admission, 10/1 for domestic students, 8/1 for international students. Application fee: $50. Electronic applications accepted. *Expenses:* Tuition, state resident: full-time $12,264; part-time $511 per credit. Tuition, nonresident: full-time $17,904; part-time $746 per credit. Required fees: $84 per course. Tuition and fees vary according to program. *Financial support:* Fellowships, research assistantships with full tuition reimbursements, teaching assistantships with full tuition reimbursements available. Financial award application deadline: 1/15; financial award applicants required to submit FAFSA. *Faculty research:* School improvement, problem solving, literacy, language development. *Unit head:* Dr. Thomas Walker, Chair, 215-204-2117, Fax: 215-204-1414, E-mail: tjwalker@temple.edu.

Texas A&M University, College of Education and Human Development, Department of Teaching, Learning, and Culture, College Station, TX 77843. Offers curriculum and instruction (M Ed, MS, PhD); mathematics education (M Ed, MS, PhD); multicultural/urban/ESL/international education (M Ed, MS, PhD); reading/language arts (M Ed, MS, PhD); science education (M Ed, MS, PhD); social studies education (M Ed, MS, PhD). *Accreditation:* NCATE. Part-time programs available. *Faculty:* 25 full-time (9 women), 2 part-time/adjunct (both women). *Students:* 156 full-time (115 women), 226 part-time (191 women); includes 95 minority (43 African Americans, 1 American Indian/Alaska Native, 9 Asian Americans or Pacific Islanders, 42 Hispanic Americans), 36 international. Average age 36. 137 applicants, 83% accepted, 80 enrolled. In 2006, 69 master's, 15 doctorates awarded. *Median time to degree:* Of those who began their doctoral program in fall 1998, 77% received their degree in 8 years or less. *Degree requirements:* For master's, thesis (for some programs), comprehensive exam; for doctorate, thesis/dissertation, comprehensive exam. *Entrance requirements:* For master's, GRE General Test, minimum GPA of 3.0; for doctorate, GRE General Test, 3 years of teaching experience. Additional exam requirements/recommendations for international students: Required—TOEFL (minimum score 550 paper-based; 213 computer-based). *Application deadline:* For fall admission, 1/15 priority date for domestic and international students; for spring admission, 9/15 priority date for domestic and international students. Applications are processed on a rolling basis. Application fee: $50 ($75 for international students). Electronic applications accepted. *Expenses:* Tuition, state resident: full-time $4,697. Tuition, nonresident: full-time $11,297. Required fees: $2,272. *Financial support:* In 2006–07, fellowships with partial tuition reimbursements (averaging $3,000 per year), teaching assistantships with partial tuition reimbursements (averaging $7,200 per year) were awarded; research assistantships with partial tuition reimbursements, career-related internships or fieldwork, Federal Work-Study, institutionally sponsored loans, scholarships/grants, tuition waivers (partial), and unspecified assistantships also available. Support available to part-time students. Financial award application deadline: 4/1; financial award applicants required to submit FAFSA. *Unit head:* Dr. Dennie Smith, Head, 979-845-8384, Fax: 979-845-9663. *Application contact:* Graduate Admissions Supervisor, 979-845-8382, Fax: 979-845-9663.

Texas Christian University, School of Education, Program in Educational Studies: Science Education, Fort Worth, TX 76129-0002. Offers PhD. *Expenses:* Tuition: Part-time $800 per credit hour. *Application contact:* Director of Graduate Studies, 817-257-7664.

Texas Christian University, School of Education, Program in Science Education, Fort Worth, TX 76129-0002. Offers M Ed. Part-time and evening/weekend programs available. *Degree requirements:* For master's, thesis optional. *Entrance requirements:* Additional exam requirements/recommendations for international students: Required—TOEFL. *Application deadline:* For fall admission, 3/1 for domestic students; for spring admission, 12/1 for domestic students. Applications are processed on a rolling basis. Application fee: $0. *Expenses:* Tuition: Part-time $800 per credit hour. *Financial support:* Career-related internships or fieldwork and unspecified assistantships available. Financial award application deadline: 3/1. *Application contact:* Director of Graduate Studies, 817-257-7664.

Texas State University-San Marcos, Graduate School, Interdisciplinary Studies Program in Elementary Mathematics, Science, and Technology, San Marcos, TX 78666. Offers MSIS. *Students:* 3 applicants, 0% accepted. In 2006, 2 degrees awarded. *Degree requirements:* For master's, comprehensive exam. *Application deadline:* For fall admission, 6/15 priority date for domestic students; for spring admission, 10/15 priority date for domestic students. Applications are processed on a rolling basis. Application fee: $40 ($90 for international students). *Financial support:* Application deadline: 4/1; *Unit head:* Dr. Sandra Mody, Acting Dean, 512-245-3381, Fax: 512-245-8095, E-mail: sw04@txstate.edu.

Texas Woman's University, Graduate School, College of Arts and Sciences, Department of Biology, Denton, TX 76201. Offers biology (MS); biology teaching (MS); molecular biology (PhD). Part-time programs available. *Students:* 28 full-time (17 women), 8 part-time (6 women); includes 8 minority (6 African Americans, 2 Hispanic Americans), 21 international. Average age 29. In 2006, 1 degree awarded. Terminal master's awarded for partial completion of doctoral program. *Degree requirements:* For master's, thesis (for some programs), comprehensive exam; for doctorate, thesis/dissertation, residency, comprehensive exam. *Entrance requirements:* For master's and doctorate, GRE General Test, 3 letters of reference. Additional exam requirements/recommendations for international students: Required—TOEFL (minimum score 550 paper-based; 213 computer-based; 79 iBT). *Application deadline:* For fall admission, 4/1 for international students; for spring admission, 8/1 for international students. Applications are processed on a rolling basis. Application fee: $30 ($50 for international students). Electronic applications accepted. *Expenses:* Tuition, area resident: Part-time $168 per unit. Tuition, state resident: full-time $4,369. Tuition, nonresident: full-time $9,373; part-time $443 per unit. Required fees: $20 per unit. $177 per term. *Financial support:* In 2006–07, 42 research assistantships (averaging $11,592 per year), teaching assistantships (averaging $11,592 per year) were awarded; career-related internships or fieldwork, Federal Work-Study, institutionally sponsored loans, scholarships/grants, traineeships, health care benefits, and unspecified assistantships also available. Support available to part-time students. Financial award application deadline: 3/1; financial award applicants required to submit FAFSA. *Faculty research:* Plants and plant viruses, plasmia DNA in bacteria, transcriptional regulation of RNA, hormone actions, serotonin modulation of female reproductive behavior. *Unit head:* Dr. Sarah McIntire, Chair, 940-898-2351, Fax: 940-898-2382, E-mail: smcintire@mail.twu.edu. *Application contact:* Samuel Wheeler, Coordinator of Graduate Admissions, 940-898-3188, Fax: 940-898-3081, E-mail: wheelersr@twu.edu.

Texas Woman's University, Graduate School, College of Arts and Sciences, Department of Chemistry and Physics, Denton, TX 76201. Offers chemistry (MS); chemistry teaching (MS); science teaching (MS). Part-time programs available. *Students:* 4 full-time (3 women), 1 (woman) part-time; includes 2 minority (both African Americans), 1 international. Average age 28. *Degree requirements:* For master's, thesis, comprehensive exam. *Entrance requirements:* For master's, GRE General Test, bachelor's degree in chemistry or equivalent, 2 reference contacts. Additional exam requirements/recommendations for international students: Required—TOEFL (minimum score 550 paper-based; 213 computer-based; 79 iBT). *Application deadline:* For fall admission, 4/1 for international students; for spring admission, 8/1 for international students. Applications are processed on a rolling basis. Application fee: $30 ($50 for international students). Electronic applications accepted. *Expenses:* Tuition, area resident: Part-time $168 per unit. Tuition, state resident: full-time $4,369. Tuition, nonresident: full-time $9,373; part-time $443 per unit. Required fees: $20 per unit. $177 per term. *Financial support:* In 2006–07, 2 research assistantships (averaging $10,188 per year), teaching assistantships (averaging $10,188 per year) were awarded; career-related internships or fieldwork, Federal Work-Study, institutionally sponsored loans, scholarships/grants, traineeships, health care benefits, and unspecified assistantships also available. Support available to part-time students. Financial award application deadline: 3/1; financial award applicants required to submit FAFSA. *Faculty research:* Mechanisms and kinetics of organic reactions, mechanisms of enzyme catalysis, chelation chemistry of macrocyclic ligands. *Unit head:* Dr. Richard Sheardy, Chair, 940-898-2550, Fax: 940-898-2548, E-mail: rsheardy@mail.twu.edu. *Application contact:* Samuel Wheeler, Coordinator of Graduate Admissions, 940-898-3188, Fax: 940-898-3081, E-mail: wheelersr@twu.edu.

Towson University, Graduate School, Program in Science Education, Towson, MD 21252-0001. Offers MS. *Entrance requirements:* For master's, secondary school teacher certification, 24 credits in related course work, minimum GPA of 3.0. Application fee: $50. *Expenses:* Tuition, state resident: part-time $275 per unit. Tuition, nonresident: part-time $577 per unit. Required fees: $72 per unit. *Unit head:* Sarah Haines, Graduate Program Director, 410-704-2926. *Application contact:* 410-704-2501, Fax: 410-704-4675, E-mail: grads@towson.edu.

Trinity (Washington) University, School of Education, Washington, DC 20017-1094. Offers democracy, diversity, and social justice (M Ed); early childhood (MAT); educational administration (MSA); elementary education (MAT); English as a second language (M Ed, MAT); literacy and reading education (M Ed); school counseling (MA); secondary education (MAT), including English, math, science, social studies; special education (MAT). *Accreditation:* NCATE. Part-time and evening/weekend programs available. *Degree requirements:* For master's, thesis (for some programs), capstone project(s). *Entrance requirements:* For master's, PRAXIS I, minimum GPA of 2.8. Additional exam requirements/recommendations for international students: Required—TOEFL (minimum score 550 paper-based; 213 computer-based). *Faculty research:* Technology, literacy, special education, organizations, inclusion models.

Union Graduate College, School of Education, Schenectady, NY 12308-3107. Offers biology (MAT, MS); chemistry (MAT); earth science (MAT); English (MAT); French (MAT); general science (MAT); German (MAT); languages (MAT); Latin (MAT); mathematics (MAT); mathematics and technology (MS); physical science (MS); physics (MAT); social studies (MAT); Spanish (MAT). *Accreditation:* Teacher Education Accreditation Council. *Faculty:* 5 full-time (1 woman), 19 part-time/adjunct (10 women). *Students:* 57 full-time (36 women), 21 part-time (14 women); includes 2 African Americans, 2 Hispanic Americans, 2 international. Average age 31. 59 applicants, 83% accepted, 39 enrolled. In 2006, 56 degrees awarded. *Degree requirements:* For master's, thesis or project. *Entrance requirements:* For master's, minimum GPA of 3.0, letters of recommendation. Additional exam requirements/recommendations for international students: Required—TOEFL (minimum score 550 paper-based; 213 computer-based). Application fee: $60. *Expenses:* Contact institution. *Financial support:* In 2006–07, 12 research assistantships with tuition reimbursements (averaging $3,000 per year) were awarded; Federal Work-Study, scholarships/grants, health care benefits, and tuition waivers (partial) also available. Support available to part-time students. Financial award applicants required to submit FAFSA. *Unit head:* Dr. Patrick Allen, Dean, 518-388-6361, Fax: 518-388-6686, E-mail: mat@union.edu. *Application contact:* Rhonda Sheehan, Director of Graduate Admissions Registrar, 518-388-6238, Fax: 518-388-6686, E-mail: sheehanr@union.edu.

See Close-Up on page 923.

University at Albany, State University of New York, College of Arts and Sciences, Department of Mathematics and Statistics, Albany, NY 12222-0001. Offers mathematics (PhD); secondary teaching (MA); statistics (MA). Evening/weekend programs available. *Students:* 36 full-time (15 women), 15 part-time (4 women). Average age 31. In 2006, 10 master's, 1 doctorate awarded. *Degree requirements:* For doctorate, one foreign language, thesis/dissertation. *Entrance requirements:* For doctorate, GRE General Test. Additional exam requirements/recommendations for international students: Required—TOEFL (minimum score 550 paper-based; 213 computer-based). *Application deadline:* For fall admission, 3/15 for domestic students, 5/1 for international students; for spring admission, 11/1 for international students. Applications are processed on a rolling basis. Application fee: $75. Electronic applications accepted. *Expenses:* Tuition, state resident: full-time $6,900; part-time $288 per credit. Tuition, nonresident: full-time $10,920; part-time $455 per credit. Required fees: $1,139. *Financial support:* Fellowships, research assistantships, teaching assistantships, minority assistantships available. Financial award application deadline: 3/15. *Unit head:* Edward C. Turner, Chair, 518-442-4602.

University at Buffalo, the State University of New York, Graduate School, Graduate School of Education, Department of Learning and Instruction, Buffalo, NY 14260. Offers adolescence education (Certificate); biology (Ed M); chemistry (Ed M); childhood education (Ed M); early childhood and childhood education with bilingual extension (Ed M); early childhood education (Ed M); earth science (Ed M); elementary education (Ed D, PhD); English (Ed M); English education (PhD); English for speakers of other languages (Ed M); foreign and second language education (PhD); French (Ed M); general education (Ed M); German (Ed M); Italian (Ed M); Japanese (Ed M); Latin (Ed M); literary specialist (Ed M); mathematics (Ed M); mathematics education (PhD); mentoring teachers (Certificate); music education (Ed M, Certificate); physics (Ed M); reading education (PhD); Russian (Ed M); school administrator and supervisor (Certificate); science education (PhD); social studies (Ed M); Spanish (Ed M); special education (PhD); teaching and leading for diversity (Certificate); teaching English to speakers of other languages (Ed M). Part-time and evening/weekend programs available. Postbaccalaureate distance learning degree programs offered (no on-campus study). *Faculty:* 30 full-time (20 women), 53 part-time/adjunct (38 women). *Students:* 368 full-time (269 women), 297 part-time (226 women); includes 50 minority (15 African Americans, 2 American Indian/Alaska Native, 14 Asian Americans or Pacific Islanders, 19 Hispanic Americans), 66 international. Average age 31. 638 applicants, 75% accepted, 298 enrolled. In 2006, 248 master's, 18 doctorates, 48 other advanced degrees awarded. Terminal master's awarded for partial completion of doctoral program. *Degree requirements:* For master's, comprehensive exam, registration; for doctorate, thesis/dissertation, research analysis exam, research experience component. *Entrance requirements:* For doctorate, GRE General Test or MAT, interview, writing sample, letters of recommendation. Additional exam requirements/recommendations for international students: Required—TOEFL (minimum score 600 paper-based; 250 computer-based). *Application deadline:* For fall admission, 2/1 priority date for domestic and international students; for spring admission, 11/15 priority date for domestic students, 10/1 for international students. Applications are processed on a rolling basis. Application fee: $50. Electronic applications accepted. *Financial support:* In 2006–07, 70 students received support, including 6 fellowships with full tuition reimbursements available (averaging $10,000 per year), 16 research assistantships with full tuition reimbursements available (averaging $9,000 per year), teaching assistantships with full tuition reimbursements available (averaging $9,000 per year); career-related internships or fieldwork, Federal Work-Study, institutionally sponsored loans, scholarships/grants, tuition waivers (partial), and unspecified assistantships also available. Financial award application deadline: 2/28; financial award applicants required to submit FAFSA. *Faculty research:* Science assessment, state-level testing, early learning, literacy, second language acquisition. Total annual research expenditures: $432,366. *Unit head:* Dr. Maria E. Runfola,

Chair, 716-645-2455, Fax: 716-645-3161. *Application contact:* Barbara Belz, Admissions Secretary, 716-645-2110 Ext. 1159, Fax: 716-645-3161, E-mail: belz@buffalo.edu.

University of Arkansas at Pine Bluff, Program in Education, Pine Bluff, AR 71601-2799. Offers elementary education (M Ed); secondary education (M Ed), including English, general science, mathematics, physical education, social studies. Part-time and evening/weekend programs available. *Degree requirements:* For master's, comprehensive exam. *Entrance requirements:* For master's, GRE, minimum GPA of 2.75, NTE or Standard Arkansas Teaching Certificate. *Faculty research:* Teacher certification, accreditation, assessment, standards, portfolio development, rehabilitation, technology.

The University of British Columbia, Faculty of Graduate Studies, Faculty of Education, Department of Curriculum Studies, Vancouver, BC V6T 1Z1, Canada. Offers art education (M Ed, MA); curriculum studies (M Ed, MA, PhD); home economics education (M Ed, MA); math education (M Ed, MA); music education (M Ed, MA); physical education (M Ed, MA); science education (M Ed, MA); social studies education (M Ed, MA); technical studies education (M Ed, MA). Part-time programs available. *Faculty:* 31 full-time (17 women), 1 (woman) part-time/adjunct. *Students:* 153 full-time (102 women), 101 part-time (67 women), 25 international. Average age 40. 118 applicants, 64% accepted, 62 enrolled. In 2006, 46 master's, 4 doctorates awarded. *Degree requirements:* For master's, thesis (MA); for doctorate, thesis/dissertation, comprehensive exam, registration. *Entrance requirements:* Additional exam requirements/recommendations for international students: Required—TOEFL (minimum score 580 paper-based; 237 computer-based). *Application deadline:* For fall admission, 2/1 for domestic students, 1/1 for international students; for spring admission, 10/1 for domestic students, 9/1 for international students. Application fee: $90 ($150 for international students). Electronic applications accepted. *Expenses:* Contact institution. *Financial support:* In 2006–07, 10 fellowships with partial tuition reimbursements (averaging $16,000 per year), 11 research assistantships with partial tuition reimbursements (averaging $14,000 per year), 27 teaching assistantships with partial tuition reimbursements (averaging $14,000 per year) were awarded; tuition waivers (partial) also available. *Faculty research:* School subjects, teaching and learning. *Unit head:* Dr. Linda Peterat, Interim Head, 604-822-5422, Fax: 604-822-4714. *Application contact:* Basia Zurek, Graduate Secretary, 604-822-5367, Fax: 604-822-4714, E-mail: cust.grad@ubc.ca.

University of California, Berkeley, Graduate Division, School of Education, Division of Cognition and Development, Program in Development in Mathematics and Science, Berkeley, CA 94720-1500. Offers MA, PhD/MA. *Application deadline:* For fall admission, 12/1 for domestic students. Application fee: $60 ($80 for international students). *Application contact:* Admissions Office, 510-642-0841, Fax: 510-642-4808, E-mail: gse_info@uclink.berkeley.edu.

University of California, Berkeley, Graduate Division, School of Education, Division of Cognition and Development, Program in Education in Mathematics, Science, and Technology, Berkeley, CA 94720-1500. Offers MA, PhD, PhD/MA. *Entrance requirements:* For master's and doctorate, GRE General Test, minimum GPA of 3.0 during last 2 years of undergraduate course work. *Application deadline:* For fall admission, 12/1 for domestic students. Application fee: $60. Electronic applications accepted. *Financial support:* Unspecified assistantships available. Financial award application deadline: 12/15. *Application contact:* Admissions Office, 510-642-0841, Fax: 510-642-4808, E-mail: gse_info@uclink.berkeley.edu.

University of California, Berkeley, Graduate Division, School of Education, Division of Cognition and Development, Program in Science and Mathematics Education, Berkeley, CA 94720-1500. Offers MA/Credential. *Application deadline:* For fall admission, 12/1 for domestic students. Application fee: $60 ($80 for international students). Electronic applications accepted. *Financial support:* Unspecified assistantships available. *Unit head:* Daniel Zimmerlin, Academic Coordinator, 510-642-4206. *Application contact:* Admissions Office, 510-642-0841, Fax: 510-642-4808, E-mail: gse_info@uclink.berkeley.edu.

University of California, Los Angeles, Graduate Division, College of Letters and Science, Department of Physics and Astronomy, Program in Physics, Los Angeles, CA 90095. Offers physics (MS, PhD); physics education (MAT). MAT admits only applicants whose objective is PhD. *Degree requirements:* For master's, comprehensive exam or thesis; for doctorate, thesis/dissertation, oral and written qualifying exams. *Entrance requirements:* For master's, GRE General Test, GRE Subject Test (physics), minimum GPA of 3.0; for doctorate, GRE General Test, GRE Subject Test (physics), minimum undergraduate GPA of 3.0. Electronic applications accepted.

University of California, San Diego, Office of Graduate Studies, Program in Mathematics and Science Education, La Jolla, CA 92093. Offers PhD. *Entrance requirements:* For doctorate, GRE General Test. Electronic applications accepted.

University of Central Florida, College of Education, Department of Teaching and Learning Principles, Program in K-8 Mathematics and Science Education, Orlando, FL 32816. Offers M Ed, Certificate. *Accreditation:* NCATE. *Students:* 1 (woman) full-time, 23 part-time (17 women); includes 3 minority (all African Americans) Average age 36. In 2006, 8 master's awarded. Application fee: $30. *Expenses:* Tuition, state resident: full-time $6,167; part-time $257 per credit hour. Tuition, nonresident: full-time $22,790; part-time $950 per credit hour. *Financial support:* Fellowships available. *Unit head:* Dr. Michael C. Hynes, Coordinator, 407-823-6076, E-mail: hynes@mail.ucf.edu.

University of Central Florida, College of Education, Department of Teaching and Learning Principles, Program in Science Education, Orlando, FL 32816. Offers M Ed, MA. *Accreditation:* NCATE. Part-time and evening/weekend programs available. *Students:* 9 full-time (6 women), 21 part-time (15 women); includes 6 minority (3 African Americans, 2 Asian Americans or Pacific Islanders, 1 Hispanic American). In 2006, 13 degrees awarded. *Entrance requirements:* For master's, GRE General Test. Additional exam requirements/recommendations for international students: Required—TOEFL. *Application deadline:* For fall admission, 7/15 for domestic students; for spring admission, 12/1 for domestic students. Application fee: $30. Electronic applications accepted. *Expenses:* Tuition, state resident: full-time $6,167; part-time $257 per credit hour. Tuition, nonresident: full-time $22,790; part-time $950 per credit hour. *Financial support:* In 2006–07, 1 research assistantship with partial tuition reimbursement (averaging $6,000 per year) was awarded; fellowships with partial tuition reimbursements, teaching assistantships with partial tuition reimbursements, career-related internships or fieldwork, Federal Work-Study, institutionally sponsored loans, tuition waivers (partial), and unspecified assistantships also available. Financial award application deadline: 3/1; financial award applicants required to submit FAFSA. *Unit head:* Dr. Aldrin Sweeney, Coordinator, 407-823-2561, E-mail: asweeney@pegasus.cc.ucf.edu.

University of Chicago, Division of Social Sciences, Committee on Conceptual and Historical Studies of Science, Chicago, IL 60637-1513. Offers PhD. *Students:* 3. *Degree requirements:* For doctorate, thesis/dissertation, registration. *Entrance requirements:* For doctorate, GRE General Test, GRE Subject Test. Additional exam requirements/recommendations for international students: Required—TOEFL, IELTS (minimum score 7). *Application deadline:* For fall admission, 12/28 for domestic and international students. Application fee: $55. Electronic applications accepted. *Expenses:* Tuition: Full-time $34,920. Required fees: $612. One-time fee: $35 full-time. Full-time tuition and fees vary according to course load, degree level and program. *Financial support:* Fellowships, teaching assistantships, Federal Work-Study, institutionally sponsored loans, scholarships/grants, traineeships, health care benefits, and unspecified assistantships available. Financial award application deadline: 12/28; financial award applicants required to submit FAFSA. *Unit head:* Prof. Adrian Johns, Chair, 773-702-8261. *Application contact:* Office of the Dean of Students, 773-702-8415.

University of Cincinnati, Division of Research and Advanced Studies, College of Education, Criminal Justice, and Human Services, Division of Teacher Education, Cincinnati, OH 45221. Offers curriculum and instruction (M Ed, Ed D); deaf studies (Certificate); early childhood education (M Ed); middle childhood education (M Ed); postsecondary literacy instruction (Certificate); reading/literacy (M Ed, Ed D); secondary education (M Ed); special education (M Ed, Ed D); teaching English as a second language (M Ed, Ed D, Certificate); teaching science (MS). Part-time programs available. *Degree requirements:* For doctorate, thesis/dissertation. *Entrance requirements:* For master's, GRE General Test. *Application deadline:* For fall admission, 2/1 for domestic students. Application fee: $30. Electronic applications accepted. *Financial support:* Fellowships, career-related internships or fieldwork, tuition waivers (partial), and unspecified assistantships available. *Unit head:* David Naylor, Student Contact, 513-556-3563, Fax: 513-556-2483, E-mail: david.naylor@uc.edu. *Application contact:* Dr. Richard Kretschmer, Graduate Program Director, 513-556-4547, Fax: 513-556-1001, E-mail: richard.kretschmer@uc.edu.

University of Connecticut, Graduate School, Neag School of Education, Department of Curriculum and Instruction, Storrs, CT 06269. Offers curriculum and instruction (MA, PhD), including agriculture education, bilingual and bicultural education, elementary education, English education, history and social sciences education, mathematics education, reading education, science education, secondary education, world languages education. *Accreditation:* NCATE. *Faculty:* 28 full-time (12 women). *Students:* 158 full-time (120 women), 54 part-time (44 women); includes 24 minority (3 African Americans, 1 American Indian/Alaska Native, 3 Asian Americans or Pacific Islanders, 17 Hispanic Americans), 2 international. Average age 27. 268 applicants, 76% accepted, 203 enrolled. In 2006, 181 master's, 4 doctorates awarded. Terminal master's awarded for partial completion of doctoral program. *Degree requirements:* For master's, thesis or alternative, comprehensive exam; for doctorate, thesis/dissertation. *Entrance requirements:* For doctorate, GRE General Test. Additional exam requirements/recommendations for international students: Required—TOEFL (minimum score 550 paper-based; 213 computer-based). *Application deadline:* For fall admission, 2/1 priority date for domestic and international students; for spring admission, 11/1 for domestic students, 10/1 for international students. Applications are processed on a rolling basis. Application fee: $55. Electronic applications accepted. *Financial support:* In 2006–07, 14 research assistantships with full tuition reimbursements, 4 teaching assistantships with full tuition reimbursements were awarded; fellowships, Federal Work-Study, scholarships/grants, health care benefits, and unspecified assistantships also available. Financial award application deadline: 2/1; financial award applicants required to submit FAFSA. *Unit head:* Mary Anne Doyle, Head, 860-486-2433, Fax: 860-486-0280. *Application contact:* Lisa Rasicot, Graduate Coordinator, 860-486-3065, Fax: 860-486-0210, E-mail: soeadm02@uconnvm.uconn.edu.

University of Connecticut, Graduate School, Neag School of Education, Department of Curriculum and Instruction, Field of Curriculum and Instruction, Program in Science Education, Storrs, CT 06269. Offers MA, PhD. *Accreditation:* NCATE. *Faculty:* 9 full-time (7 women). *Students:* 8 full-time (4 women), 1 (woman) part-time; includes 1 minority (African American) Average age 26. 11 applicants, 73% accepted, 8 enrolled. In 2006, 1 degree awarded. Terminal master's awarded for partial completion of doctoral program. *Degree requirements:* For master's, thesis or alternative, comprehensive exam; for doctorate, thesis/dissertation. *Entrance requirements:* For doctorate, GRE General Test. Additional exam requirements/recommendations for international students: Required—TOEFL (minimum score 550 paper-based; 213 computer-based). *Application deadline:* For fall admission, 2/1 priority date for domestic and international students; for spring admission, 11/1 for domestic students, 10/1 for international students. Applications are processed on a rolling basis. Application fee: $55. Electronic applications accepted. *Financial support:* In 2006–07, 2 research assistantships with full tuition reimbursements were awarded; fellowships, teaching assistantships with full tuition reimbursements, Federal Work-Study, scholarships/grants, health care benefits, and unspecified assistantships also available. Financial award application deadline: 2/1; financial award applicants required to submit FAFSA. *Application contact:* Lisa Rasicot, Graduate Coordinator, 860-486-3065, Fax: 860-486-0210, E-mail: soeadm02@uconnvm.uconn.edu.

University of Florida, Graduate School, College of Education, School of Teaching and Learning, Gainesville, FL 32611. Offers bilingual/ESOL education (M Ed, MAE, Ed D, PhD, Ed S); curriculum and instruction (M Ed, MAE, Ed D, PhD, Ed S); early childhood education (Ed D, PhD, Ed S); elementary education (M Ed, MAE); English education (M Ed, MAE); mathematics education (M Ed, MAE); reading education (M Ed, MAE); science education (M Ed, MAE); social foundations (M Ed, MAE, Ed D, PhD); social studies education (M Ed, MAE). *Accreditation:* NCATE. *Faculty:* 29 full-time (20 women). *Students:* 506 (406 women); includes 87 minority (20 African Americans, 3 American Indian/Alaska Native, 13 Asian Americans or Pacific Islanders, 51 Hispanic Americans) 34 international. In 2006, 278 master's, 8 doctorates awarded. *Degree requirements:* For master's, thesis optional; for doctorate, variable foreign language requirement, thesis/dissertation. *Entrance requirements:* For master's and doctorate, GRE General Test, minimum GPA of 3.0; for Ed S, GRE General Test. Additional exam requirements/recommendations for international students: Required—TOEFL (minimum score 550 paper-based; 213 computer-based). *Application deadline:* For fall admission, 6/1 for domestic students. Applications are processed on a rolling basis. Application fee: $30. Electronic applications accepted. *Expenses:* Tuition, state resident: full-time $6,827. Tuition, nonresident: full-time $21,951. Required fees: $999. *Financial support:* In 2006–07, 5 research assistantships (averaging $11,947 per year), 22 teaching assistantships (averaging $9,709 per year) were awarded; fellowships, career-related internships or fieldwork and unspecified assistantships also available. *Faculty research:* Teacher education, inclusive education, classroom processes, curriculum and technology. *Unit head:* Dr. Tom Dana, Director, 352-392-9191 Ext. 200, Fax: 352-392-9193, E-mail: tdana@coe.ufl.edu. *Application contact:* Dr. Linda C. Jones, Coordinator, 352-392-0761 Ext. 267, Fax: 352-392-9193, E-mail: lcjones@coe.ufl.edu.

University of Florida, Graduate School, College of Liberal Arts and Sciences, Department of Geological Sciences, Gainesville, FL 32611. Offers geology (MS, MST, PhD). *Faculty:* 18 full-time (2 women). *Students:* 39 (18 women); includes 1 minority (Hispanic American) 12 international. In 2006, 5 master's, 2 doctorates awarded. Terminal master's awarded for partial completion of doctoral program. *Degree requirements:* For master's, thesis (for some programs); for doctorate, one foreign language, thesis/dissertation. *Entrance requirements:* For master's and doctorate, GRE General Test, GRE Subject Test, minimum GPA of 3.0. Additional exam requirements/recommendations for international students: Required—TOEFL (minimum score 550 paper-based; 213 computer-based). *Application deadline:* For fall admission, 6/1 priority date for domestic students; for spring admission, 10/1 priority date for domestic students. Applications are processed on a rolling basis. Application fee: $30. Electronic applications accepted. *Expenses:* Tuition, state resident: full-time $6,827. Tuition, nonresident: full-time $21,951. Required fees: $999. *Financial support:* In 2006–07, 5 research assistantships with full tuition reimbursements (averaging $12,528 per year), 24 teaching assistantships with full tuition reimbursements (averaging $12,382 per year) were awarded; fellowships with full tuition reimbursements, career-related internships or fieldwork, Federal Work-Study, institutionally sponsored loans, and scholarships/grants also available. Support available to part-time students. Financial award application deadline: 3/1. *Faculty research:* Paleoclimatology, tectonophysics, petrochemistry, marine geology, geochemistry, hydrology. *Unit head:* Dr. Paul Mueller, Chair, 352-392-2231, Fax: 352-392-9294, E-mail: mueller@geology.ufl.edu. *Application contact:* Dr. Michael R. Perfit, Graduate Coordinator, 352-392-2128, Fax: 352-392-9294, E-mail: perfit@geology.ufl.edu.

University of Georgia, Graduate School, College of Education, Department of Mathematics and Science Education, Athens, GA 30602. Offers M Ed, MA, Ed D, PhD, Ed S. *Faculty:* 17 full-time (7 women). *Students:* 107 full-time (67 women), 113 part-time (89 women); includes 28 minority (19 African Americans, 5 Asian Americans or Pacific Islanders, 4 Hispanic Americans), 23 international. 35 applicants, 31% accepted. In 2006, 35 master's, 11 doctorates, 12 other advanced degrees awarded. *Application deadline:* For fall admission, 7/1 priority date for domestic students; for spring admission, 11/15 for domestic students. Application fee: $50. *Unit head:* Dr. Denise S. Mewborn, Head, 706-542-4548, Fax: 706-542-4551, E-mail: dmewborn@uga.edu.

University of Houston, College of Education, Department of Curriculum and Instruction, Houston, TX 77204. Offers art education (M Ed); bilingual education (M Ed); curriculum and

Science Education

University of Houston (continued)
instruction (Ed D); early childhood education (M Ed); education of the gifted (M Ed); elementary education (M Ed); mathematics education (M Ed); reading and language arts education (M Ed); science education (M Ed); second language education (M Ed); secondary education (M Ed); social studies education (M Ed); teaching (M Ed). *Accreditation:* NCATE. Part-time and evening/weekend programs available. *Faculty:* 24 full-time (11 women), 16 part-time/adjunct (14 women). *Students:* 134 full-time (102 women), 327 part-time (256 women); includes 142 minority (49 African Americans, 1 American Indian/Alaska Native, 29 Asian Americans or Pacific Islanders, 63 Hispanic Americans), 19 international. Average age 37. 113 applicants, 72% accepted, 61 enrolled. In 2006, 106 master's, 32 doctorates awarded. *Degree requirements:* For master's, comprehensive exam or thesis; for doctorate, thesis/dissertation, comprehensive exam. *Entrance requirements:* For master's, GRE General Test or MAT; for doctorate, GRE General Test, interview. *Application deadline:* For fall admission, 7/3 priority date for domestic students. Applications are processed on a rolling basis. Application fee: $35 ($75 for international students). *Expenses:* Tuition, state resident: full-time $5,429; part-time $226 per credit. Tuition, nonresident: full-time $12,029; part-time $501 per credit. Required fees: $2,454. *Financial support:* In 2006–07, 2 fellowships with full tuition reimbursements (averaging $9,500 per year), 6 research assistantships with full tuition reimbursements (averaging $8,800 per year), 25 teaching assistantships with full tuition reimbursements (averaging $8,800 per year) were awarded; career-related internships or fieldwork, Federal Work-Study, institutionally sponsored loans, scholarships/grants, health care benefits, and unspecified assistantships also available. Support available to part-time students. Financial award application deadline: 3/10. *Faculty research:* Teaching-learning process, instructional technology in schools, teacher education, classroom management, at-risk students. *Unit head:* Dr. Juanita Copley, Chairperson, 713-743-4950, Fax: 713-743-4990, E-mail: ncopley@aol.com.

University of Idaho, College of Graduate Studies, College of Science, Department of Geological Sciences, Moscow, ID 83844-2282. Offers earth science (MAT); geology (MS, PhD); hydrology (MS). *Students:* 37 (15 women). Average age 29. In 2006, 13 master's, 1 doctorate awarded. *Degree requirements:* For doctorate, one foreign language, thesis/dissertation. *Entrance requirements:* For master's, minimum GPA of 2.8; for doctorate, minimum undergraduate GPA of 2.8, 3.0 graduate. *Application deadline:* For fall admission, 8/1 for domestic students; for spring admission, 12/15 for domestic students. Application fee: $55 ($60 for international students). *Expenses:* Tuition, nonresident: full-time $9,600; part-time $140 per credit. Required fees: $4,740; $227 per credit. *Financial support:* Fellowships, research assistantships, teaching assistantships available. Financial award application deadline: 2/15. *Unit head:* Dr. Dennis Geist, Head, 208-885-6491.

University of Idaho, College of Graduate Studies, College of Science, Department of Physics, Moscow, ID 83844-2282. Offers physics (MS, PhD); physics education (MAT). *Students:* 20 (4 women). Average age 28. In 2006, 3 master's, 4 doctorates awarded. *Degree requirements:* For master's and doctorate, thesis/dissertation. *Entrance requirements:* For master's, GRE, minimum GPA of 2.8; for doctorate, GRE, minimum undergraduate GPA of 2.8, 3.0 graduate. *Application deadline:* For fall admission, 8/1 for domestic students; for spring admission, 12/15 for domestic students. Application fee: $55 ($60 for international students). *Expenses:* Tuition, nonresident: full-time $9,600; part-time $140 per credit. Required fees: $4,740; $227 per credit. *Financial support:* Research assistantships, teaching assistantships available. Financial award application deadline: 2/15. *Unit head:* Dr. Wei Jiang Yeh, Interim Chair, 208-885-5768.

University of Indianapolis, Graduate Programs, School of Education, Indianapolis, IN 46227-3697. Offers art education (MAT); biology (MAT); chemistry (MAT); curriculum and instruction (MA); earth sciences (MAT); education (MA, MAT); educational leadership (MA); elementary education (MA); English (MAT); French (MAT); math (MAT); physical education (MAT); physics (MAT); secondary education (MA), including art education, education, English education, social studies education; social studies (MAT); Spanish (MAT). *Accreditation:* NCATE. Part-time and evening/weekend programs available. *Faculty:* 4 full-time (2 women), 6 part-time/adjunct (2 women). *Students:* 32 full-time (16 women), 70 part-time (42 women); includes 2 minority (1 African American, 1 Hispanic American). Average age 31. In 2006, 51 degrees awarded. *Entrance requirements:* For master's, GRE Subject Test, minimum GPA of 2.5, 3 letters of recommendation, interview, Praxis I, writing exercise, be within 9 hours of completing content requirements. Additional exam requirements/recommendations for international students: Required—TOEFL (minimum score 550 paper-based; 213 computer-based). *Application deadline:* Applications are processed on a rolling basis. Application fee: $50. *Financial support:* Federal Work-Study available. Financial award application deadline: 5/1; financial award applicants required to submit FAFSA. *Faculty research:* Assessment of teacher education, perceptions of prospective teachers by parents. *Unit head:* Dr. E. Lynne Weisenbach, Dean, 317-788-3446, Fax: 317-788-3300, E-mail: weisenbach@uindy.edu.

The University of Iowa, Graduate College, College of Liberal Arts and Sciences, Program in Science Education, Iowa City, IA 52242-1316. Offers MS, PhD. *Faculty:* 5 full-time. *Students:* 18 full-time (10 women), 13 part-time (6 women); includes 1 minority (Hispanic American), 10 international. 14 applicants, 71% accepted, 6 enrolled. In 2006, 7 master's, 8 doctorates awarded. *Degree requirements:* For master's, exam, thesis optional; for doctorate, thesis/dissertation, comprehensive exam, registration. *Entrance requirements:* For master's and doctorate, GRE General Test, minimum GPA of 3.0. Additional exam requirements/recommendations for international students: Required—TOEFL (minimum score 550 paper-based; 213 computer-based; 81 iBT). Application fee: $60 ($85 for international students). Electronic applications accepted. *Financial support:* In 2006–07, 10 research assistantships with partial tuition reimbursements, 8 teaching assistantships with partial tuition reimbursements were awarded; fellowships also available. Financial award applicants required to submit FAFSA. *Unit head:* Gary Sasso, Chair, 319-335-5324, Fax: 319-335-5608.

University of Maine, Graduate School, College of Education and Human Development, Program in Science Education, Orono, ME 04469. Offers M Ed, MS, CAS. *Accreditation:* NCATE. Part-time and evening/weekend programs available. *Students:* 5 full-time (4 women), 6 part-time (4 women); includes 1 minority (American Indian/Alaska Native). Average age 33. 8 applicants, 88% accepted, 4 enrolled. In 2006, 7 master's, 1 other advanced degree awarded. *Degree requirements:* For master's, thesis or alternative. *Entrance requirements:* For master's, MAT; for CAS, MA, M Ed, or MS. Additional exam requirements/recommendations for international students: Required—TOEFL. *Application deadline:* For fall admission, 2/1 priority date for domestic students. Applications are processed on a rolling basis. Application fee: $50. Electronic applications accepted. *Financial support:* In 2006–07, research assistantships with tuition reimbursements (averaging $9,450 per year), teaching assistantships with tuition reimbursements (averaging $9,010 per year) were awarded; Federal Work-Study, institutionally sponsored loans, and tuition waivers (full and partial) also available. Financial award application deadline: 3/1. *Unit head:* Dr. Dorothy Breen, Coordinator, 207-581-2444, Fax: 207-581-2423. *Application contact:* Scott G. Delcourt, Associate Dean of the Graduate School, 207-581-3219, Fax: 207-581-3232, E-mail: graduate@maine.edu.

University of Massachusetts Lowell, Graduate School, Graduate School of Education, Lowell, MA 01854-2881. Offers administration, planning, and policy (CAGS); curriculum and instruction (M Ed, CAGS); educational administration (M Ed); language arts and literacy (Ed D); leadership in schooling (Ed D); math and science education (Ed D); reading and language (M Ed, CAGS). *Accreditation:* NCATE. Part-time and evening/weekend programs available. Postbaccalaureate distance learning degree programs offered (no on-campus study). Terminal master's awarded for partial completion of doctoral program. *Degree requirements:* For doctorate, thesis/dissertation. *Entrance requirements:* For master's and doctorate, GRE General Test. Additional exam requirements/recommendations for international students: Required—TOEFL. Electronic applications accepted.

University of Miami, Graduate School, School of Education, Department of Teaching and Learning, Program in Mathematics and Science Resource Teaching, Coral Gables, FL 33124. Offers MS Ed, Ed S. Part-time and evening/weekend programs available. *Students:* 1 full-time (0 women), 15 part-time (all women); includes 10 minority (5 African Americans, 5 Hispanic Americans). 12 applicants, 50% accepted, 6 enrolled. In 2006, 13 degrees awarded. *Degree requirements:* For master's, comprehensive exam (for some programs). *Application deadline:* Applications are processed on a rolling basis. Electronic applications accepted. *Financial support:* In 2006–07, 15 students received support. Application deadline: 3/1; *Faculty research:* Mathematics education.

University of Miami, Graduate School, School of Education, Department of Teaching and Learning, Program in Teaching and Learning, Coral Gables, FL 33124. Offers exceptional student education (PhD); mathematics and science education (PhD); reading (PhD); teaching English to speakers of other languages (PhD). Part-time and evening/weekend programs available. *Students:* 25 full-time (20 women), 6 part-time (5 women); includes 11 minority (2 African Americans, 9 Hispanic Americans), 5 international. Average age 38. 23 applicants, 61% accepted, 4 enrolled. In 2006, 3 doctorates awarded. *Median time to degree:* Of those who began their doctoral program in fall 1998, 100% received their degree in 8 years or less. *Degree requirements:* For doctorate, thesis/dissertation. *Entrance requirements:* For doctorate, GRE General Test, GRE Subject Test. Additional exam requirements/recommendations for international students: Required—TOEFL (minimum score 550 paper-based; 212 computer-based). Application fee: $50. Electronic applications accepted. *Financial support:* In 2006–07, 16 research assistantships with full tuition reimbursements (averaging $13,000 per year), 3 teaching assistantships with full tuition reimbursements (averaging $13,000 per year) were awarded; fellowships, tuition waivers (partial) also available. Financial award application deadline: 3/1; financial award applicants required to submit FAFSA. *Faculty research:* Teacher education, multicultural education, technology, second language acquisition.

University of Michigan, Horace H. Rackham School of Graduate Studies, School of Education, Programs in Educational Studies, Ann Arbor, MI 48109. Offers curriculum development (MA); early childhood education (MA, PhD); educational administration and policy (MA, PhD); educational foundation, administration, policy, and research methods (MA); educational foundations and policy (MA, PhD); elementary education (MA-Certification); English education (MA); English language learning in school settings (MA); learning technologies (MA, PhD); literacy, language, and culture (MA, PhD); mathematics education (MA, PhD); research methods (MA); science education (MA, PhD); secondary education (MA-Certification); social studies education (MA); special education (PhD); teaching and teacher education (PhD); MA-Certification; MBA/MA; PhD/MA. Terminal master's awarded for partial completion of doctoral program. *Degree requirements:* For master's, thesis (for some programs); for doctorate, thesis/dissertation, comprehensive exam. *Entrance requirements:* For master's and doctorate, GRE General Test. Additional exam requirements/recommendations for international students: Required—TOEFL (minimum score 600 paper-based; 250 computer-based). *Application deadline:* For fall admission, 12/1 priority date for domestic students, 12/1 for international students. Application fee: $60 ($75 for international students). Electronic applications accepted. *Financial support:* Applicants required to submit FAFSA. *Unit head:* Dr. Addison Stone, Chairperson, 734-763-7500, Fax: 734-615-1290, E-mail: addison@umich.edu. *Application contact:* Roberta Perry, Office of Student Services, 734-764-7563, Fax: 734-763-1495, E-mail: ed.grad.admit@umich.edu.

University of Minnesota, Twin Cities Campus, Graduate School, College of Education and Human Development, Department of Curriculum and Instruction, Program in Teaching, Minneapolis, MN 55455-0213. Offers Chinese (M Ed); earth science (M Ed); elementary special education (M Ed); English (M Ed); English as a second language (M Ed); French (M Ed); German (M Ed); Hebrew (M Ed); Japanese (M Ed); life sciences (M Ed); mathematics (M Ed); middle school science (M Ed); science (M Ed); second languages and cultures (M Ed); social studies (M Ed); Spanish (M Ed). *Students:* 324 full-time (230 women), 132 part-time (86 women); includes 44 minority (5 African Americans, 2 American Indian/Alaska Native, 27 Asian Americans or Pacific Islanders, 10 Hispanic Americans), 4 international. Average age 27. 499 applicants, 74% accepted, 327 enrolled. In 2006, 545 degrees awarded. *Expenses:* Tuition, state resident: full-time $9,302; part-time $775 per credit. Tuition, nonresident: full-time $16,400; part-time $1,367 per credit. Full-time tuition and fees vary according to class time, course load, program, reciprocity agreements and student level. *Application contact:* Dr. Mary Bents, Associate Dean, 612-625-6501, Fax: 612-626-1580, E-mail: mbents@tc.umn.edu.

University of Missouri–Columbia, Graduate School, College of Education, Department of Curriculum and Instruction, Columbia, MO 65211. Offers agricultural education (M Ed, PhD, Ed S); art education (M Ed, PhD, Ed S); business and office education (M Ed, PhD, Ed S); early childhood education (M Ed, PhD, Ed S); elementary education (M Ed, PhD, Ed S); English education (M Ed, PhD, Ed S); foreign language education (M Ed, PhD, Ed S); health education and promotion (M Ed, PhD); learning and instruction (M Ed); marketing education (M Ed, PhD, Ed S); mathematics education (M Ed, PhD, Ed S); music education (M Ed, PhD, Ed S); reading education (M Ed, PhD, Ed S); science education (M Ed, PhD, Ed S); social studies education (M Ed, PhD, Ed S); vocational education (M Ed, PhD, Ed S). Part-time programs available. *Faculty:* 24 full-time (12 women). *Students:* 195 full-time (148 women), 260 part-time (214 women); includes 27 minority (8 African Americans, 1 American Indian/Alaska Native, 10 Asian Americans or Pacific Islanders, 8 Hispanic Americans), 19 international. In 2006, 186 master's, 12 doctorates awarded. Terminal master's awarded for partial completion of doctoral program. *Degree requirements:* For doctorate, thesis/dissertation. *Entrance requirements:* For master's and Ed S, GRE General Test or MAT, minimum GPA of 3.0; for doctorate, GRE General Test, minimum GPA of 3.0. *Application deadline:* Applications are processed on a rolling basis. Application fee: $45 ($60 for international students). *Financial support:* Fellowships, research assistantships, teaching assistantships, institutionally sponsored loans available. *Unit head:* Dr. Lloyd H. Barrow, Director of Graduate Studies, 573-882-8247, E-mail: robinsonr@missouri.edu.

University of Missouri–Rolla, Graduate School, College of Arts and Sciences, Department of Chemistry, Rolla, MO 65409-0910. Offers chemistry (MS, PhD); chemistry education (MST). Terminal master's awarded for partial completion of doctoral program. *Degree requirements:* For doctorate, one foreign language, thesis/dissertation. *Entrance requirements:* For master's and doctorate, minimum GPA of 3.0. Electronic applications accepted. *Faculty research:* Structure and properties of materials; bioanalytical, environmental, and polymer chemistry.

University of Nebraska at Kearney, College of Graduate Study, College of Natural and Social Sciences, Department of Biology, Kearney, NE 68849-0001. Offers biology (MS); science education (MS Ed). Part-time and evening/weekend programs available. *Faculty:* 14 full-time (6 women). *Students:* 20 full-time (12 women), 145 part-time (91 women); includes 13 minority (6 African Americans, 1 American Indian/Alaska Native, 5 Asian Americans or Pacific Islanders, 1 Hispanic American), 4 international. 57 applicants, 77% accepted. In 2006, 23 degrees awarded. *Degree requirements:* For master's, thesis optional. *Entrance requirements:* For master's, GRE General Test. Additional exam requirements/recommendations for international students: Required—TOEFL (minimum score 550 paper-based; 213 computer-based). *Application deadline:* For fall admission, 5/1 for domestic and international students; for spring admission, 8/15 for domestic students, 8/1 for international students. Applications are processed on a rolling basis. Application fee: $45. Electronic applications accepted. *Expenses:* Tuition, state resident: part-time $161 per hour. Tuition, nonresident: part-time $332 per hour. Required fees: $57 per hour. *Financial support:* In 2006–07, 4 research assistantships with full tuition reimbursements (averaging $8,200 per year), 4 teaching assistantships with full tuition reimbursements (averaging $8,200 per year) were awarded; career-related internships or fieldwork, scholarships/grants, and unspecified assistantships also available. Support available to part-time students. Financial award application deadline: 3/1; financial award applicants required to submit FAFSA. *Faculty research:* Pollution injury, molecular biology-viral gene expression, prairie range condition modeling, evolution of symbiotic nitrogen fixation. *Unit head:* Dr. John Hertner, Chair, 308-865-8548, Fax: 308-865-8045, E-mail: hertnerj@unk.edu.

University of New Hampshire, Graduate School, College of Engineering and Physical Sciences, Department of Chemistry, Durham, NH 03824. Offers chemistry (MS, MST, PhD);

chemistry education (PhD). *Faculty:* 14 full-time. *Students:* 28 full-time (9 women), 22 part-time (9 women); includes 4 minority (2 African Americans, 1 Asian American or Pacific Islander, 1 Hispanic American), 14 international. Average age 26. 24 applicants, 96% accepted, 11 enrolled. In 2006, 4 master's, 2 doctorates awarded. Terminal master's awarded for partial completion of doctoral program. *Degree requirements:* For master's, thesis; for doctorate, one foreign language, thesis/dissertation. *Entrance requirements:* Additional exam requirements/recommendations for international students: Required—TOEFL (minimum score 550 paper-based; 213 computer-based). *Application deadline:* For fall admission, 4/1 priority date for domestic students, 4/1 for international students; for winter admission, 12/1 priority date for domestic students. Applications are processed on a rolling basis. Application fee: $60. *Expenses:* Tuition, state resident: full-time $8,540; part-time $474 per credit hour. Tuition, nonresident: full-time $20,990; part-time $862 per credit hour. Required fees: $1,343; $356 per term. Tuition and fees vary according to course load, program and reciprocity agreements. *Financial support:* In 2006–07, 11 research assistantships, 33 teaching assistantships were awarded; fellowships, Federal Work-Study, scholarships/grants, and tuition waivers (full and partial) also available. Support available to part-time students. Financial award application deadline: 2/15. *Faculty research:* Analytical, physical, organic, and inorganic chemistry. *Unit head:* Dr. Chris Bauer, Chairperson, 603-862-1550. *Application contact:* Cindi Rohwer, Coordinator, 603-862-1550, E-mail: chem.dept@unh.edu.

University of New Orleans, Graduate School, College of Sciences, Program in Science Teaching, New Orleans, LA 70148. Offers MAST. *Accreditation:* NCATE. *Students:* 3 (2 women). Average age 39. In 2006, 2 degrees awarded. *Entrance requirements:* Additional exam requirements/recommendations for international students: Required—TOEFL (minimum score 550 paper-based; 213 computer-based). *Application deadline:* For fall admission, 7/1 priority date for domestic students, 6/1 for international students; for spring admission, 11/15 priority date for domestic students, 10/1 for international students. Applications are processed on a rolling basis. Application fee: $40. Electronic applications accepted. *Expenses:* Tuition, state resident: full-time $3,292. Tuition, nonresident: full-time $10,336. Required fees: $158. *Financial support:* Application deadline: 3/15; *Unit head:* Dr. Steve Stevenson, Associate Dean, 504-280-6783, Fax: 504-280-7483, E-mail: mmsteven@uno.edu.

The University of North Carolina at Chapel Hill, Graduate School, School of Education, Program in Secondary Education, Chapel Hill, NC 27599. Offers English (Grades 9-12) (MAT); French (Grades K-12) (MAT); German (Grades K-12) (MAT); Japanese (Grades K-12) (MAT); Latin (Grades 9-12) (MAT); mathematics (Grades 9-12) (MAT); music (Grades K-12) (MAT); science (Grades 9-12) (MAT); social studies/social science (Grades 9-12) (MAT); Spanish (Grades K-12) (MAT). *Accreditation:* NCATE. In 2006, 72 degrees awarded. *Degree requirements:* For master's, comprehensive exam. *Entrance requirements:* For master's, GRE General Test, minimum GPA of 3.0 during last 2 years of undergraduate course work. Additional exam requirements/recommendations for international students: Required—TOEFL (minimum score 550 paper-based; 213 computer-based), ACTFL oral proficiency interview. *Application deadline:* For fall admission, 1/1 priority date for domestic and international students. Applications are processed on a rolling basis. Application fee: $60. Electronic applications accepted. *Financial support:* Federal Work-Study available. Support available to part-time students. Financial award application deadline: 3/1; financial award applicants required to submit FAFSA. *Faculty research:* Curriculum and instruction, teacher education per subject. *Unit head:* Dr. James Trier, Coordinator, 919-843-4627. *Application contact:* Janet Carroll, Registrar, 919-962-8690, Fax: 919-962-1533, E-mail: jscarrol@email.unc.edu.

The University of North Carolina at Greensboro, Graduate School, School of Education, Department of Curriculum and Instruction, Greensboro, NC 27412-5001. Offers college teaching and adult learning (Certificate); curriculum and instruction (M Ed), including chemistry education, elementary education, English as a second language, French education, instructional technology, mathematics education, middle grades education, reading education, science education, social studies education, Spanish education; curriculum and teaching (PhD), including higher education, teacher education and development; English as a second language (Certificate); higher education (M Ed); supervision (M Ed). *Accreditation:* NCATE. Part-time programs available. *Faculty:* 27 full-time (18 women), 8 part-time/adjunct (3 women). *Students:* 137 full-time (114 women), 231 part-time (195 women); includes 63 minority (52 African Americans, 2 American Indian/Alaska Native, 5 Asian Americans or Pacific Islanders, 4 Hispanic Americans). 146 applicants, 32% accepted. *Degree requirements:* For doctorate, thesis/dissertation. *Entrance requirements:* For master's and doctorate, GRE General Test. Additional exam requirements/recommendations for international students: Required—TOEFL. Application fee: $45. Electronic applications accepted. *Expenses:* Tuition, state resident: full-time $2,692. Tuition, nonresident: full-time $13,742. *Financial support:* Fellowships, research assistantships with full tuition reimbursements, teaching assistantships with full tuition reimbursements, career-related internships or fieldwork, Federal Work-Study, scholarships/grants, traineeships, and unspecified assistantships available. Support available to part-time students. *Faculty research:* Community college literacy program, middle school mathematics/computer mathematics. *Unit head:* Dr. Sam Miller, Chair, 336-334-3445, Fax: 336-334-4120, E-mail: sdmille2@uncg.edu. *Application contact:* Michelle Harkleroad, Director of Graduate Admissions, 336-334-4884, Fax: 336-334-4424, E-mail: mbharkle@uncg.edu.

The University of North Carolina at Pembroke, Graduate Studies, Department of Biology, Pembroke, NC 28372-1510. Offers science education (MA). Part-time and evening/weekend programs available. *Faculty:* 3 full-time (1 woman), 1 part-time/adjunct (0 women). *Students:* 1 (woman) full-time, 6 part-time (4 women). Average age 34. 7 applicants, 100% accepted, 7 enrolled. In 2006, 3 degrees awarded. *Degree requirements:* For master's, thesis. *Entrance requirements:* For master's, GRE or MAT, minimum GPA of 3.0 in major or 2.5 overall. *Application deadline:* For fall admission, 7/15 priority date for domestic and international students; for spring admission, 12/1 priority date for domestic and international students. Applications are processed on a rolling basis. Application fee: $40. *Expenses:* Tuition, state resident: full-time $3,516; part-time $1,091 per semester. Tuition, nonresident: full-time $12,924; part-time $4,619 per semester. Tuition and fees vary according to class time, course load, degree level and campus/location. *Financial support:* In 2006–07, 1 research assistantship with full tuition reimbursement (averaging $6,000 per year) was awarded; unspecified assistantships also available. Support available to part-time students. Financial award application deadline: 4/15; financial award applicants required to submit FAFSA. *Unit head:* Dr. Peter A. Wish, Director, 910-521-6427, Fax: 910-521-6638, E-mail: pete.wish@uncp.edu. *Application contact:* Dr. Kathleen C. Hilton, Dean of Graduate Studies, 910-521-6271, Fax: 910-521-6751, E-mail: grad@uncp.edu.

University of Northern Colorado, Graduate School, College of Natural and Health Sciences, School of Biological Sciences, Greeley, CO 80639. Offers biological education (PhD); biological sciences (MS). Part-time programs available. *Faculty:* 16 full-time (8 women). *Students:* 20 full-time (9 women), 5 part-time (3 women); includes 1 minority (Asian American or Pacific Islander) Average age 31. 4 applicants, 100% accepted, 2 enrolled. In 2006, 5 master's, 3 doctorates awarded. *Degree requirements:* For master's, comprehensive exam; for doctorate, thesis/dissertation, comprehensive exam. *Entrance requirements:* For master's and doctorate, GRE General Test, 3 letters of recommendation. *Application deadline:* Applications are processed on a rolling basis. Application fee: $50 ($60 for international students). Electronic applications accepted. *Expenses:* Tuition, state resident: full-time $5,118; part-time $213 per credit hour. Tuition, nonresident: full-time $14,832; part-time $618 per credit hour. Required fees: $674; $34 per credit hour. *Financial support:* In 2006–07, 24 students received support, including 8 fellowships (averaging $959 per year), research assistantships (averaging $17,950 per year), 12 teaching assistantships (averaging $14,360 per year); unspecified assistantships also available. Financial award application deadline: 3/1; financial award applicants required to submit FAFSA. *Unit head:* Dr. Catherine Gardiner, Director, 970-351-2921, Fax: 970-351-2335.

University of Northern Colorado, Graduate School, College of Natural and Health Sciences, School of Chemistry, Earth Sciences and Physics, Program in Chemistry, Greeley, CO 80639. Offers chemistry education (PhD); chemistry: education (MS); chemistry: research (MS). Part-time programs available. *Faculty:* 5 full-time (1 woman). *Students:* 15 full-time (12 women), 5 part-time (2 women); includes 2 minority (both Hispanic Americans), 1 international. Average age 30. 11 applicants, 82% accepted, 5 enrolled. In 2006, 2 master's, 3 doctorates awarded. *Degree requirements:* For master's, thesis or alternative, comprehensive exam; for doctorate, thesis/dissertation, comprehensive exam. *Entrance requirements:* For master's, 3 letters of reference; for doctorate, GRE General Test, 3 letters of reference. *Application deadline:* Applications are processed on a rolling basis. Application fee: $50 ($60 for international students). Electronic applications accepted. *Expenses:* Tuition, state resident: full-time $5,118; part-time $213 per credit hour. Tuition, nonresident: full-time $14,832; part-time $618 per credit hour. Required fees: $674; $34 per credit hour. *Financial support:* In 2006–07, 14 students received support, including 2 fellowships (averaging $6,735 per year), 6 research assistantships (averaging $12,859 per year), teaching assistantships (averaging $12,555 per year); unspecified assistantships also available. Financial award application deadline: 3/1; financial award applicants required to submit FAFSA. *Unit head:* Dr. Richard Schwenz, Program Coordinator, 970-351-2559.

University of Northern Iowa, Graduate College, College of Natural Sciences, Program in Science Education, Cedar Falls, IA 50614. Offers MA, SP. *Faculty:* 8 full-time (4 women). *Students:* 3 full-time (1 woman), 24 part-time (17 women); includes 1 minority (African American) 7 applicants, 71% accepted, 4 enrolled. In 2006, 8 degrees awarded. *Degree requirements:* For master's, thesis or alternative, comprehensive exam (for some programs). *Entrance requirements:* Additional exam requirements/recommendations for international students: Required—TOEFL (minimum score 500 paper-based; 180 computer-based; 61 iBT). *Application deadline:* For fall admission, 8/1 priority date for domestic students. Applications are processed on a rolling basis. Application fee: $30 ($50 for international students). Electronic applications accepted. *Expenses:* Tuition, state resident: full-time $5,936. Tuition, nonresident: full-time $14,074. *Financial support:* Application deadline: 2/1. *Unit head:* Dr. Cherin A. Lee, Director, 319-273-2499, Fax: 319-273-7124, E-mail: cherin.lee@uni.edu.

University of North Texas Health Science Center at Fort Worth, Graduate School of Biomedical Sciences, Fort Worth, TX 76107-2699. Offers anatomy and cell biology (MS, PhD); biochemistry and molecular biology (MS, PhD); biomedical sciences (MS, PhD); biotechnology (MS); forensic genetics (MS); integrative physiology (MS, PhD); medical science (MS); microbiology and immunology (MS, PhD); pharmacology (MS, PhD); science education (MS); DO/MS; DO/PhD. Terminal master's awarded for partial completion of doctoral program. *Degree requirements:* For master's and doctorate, thesis/dissertation. *Entrance requirements:* For master's and doctorate, GRE General Test. Additional exam requirements/recommendations for international students: Required—TOEFL. Expenses: Contact institution. *Faculty research:* Alzheimer's disease, aging, eye diseases, cancer, cardiovascular disease.

University of Oklahoma, Graduate College, College of Education, Department of Instructional Leadership and Academic Curriculum, Norman, OK 73019-0390. Offers education (Certificate); instructional leadership and academic curriculum (M Ed, PhD), including bilingual education, early childhood education, elementary education, English education, math education, reading education, science education, secondary education, social studies education. *Accreditation:* NCATE. Part-time and evening/weekend programs available. *Faculty:* 20 full-time (11 women), 6 part-time/adjunct (all women). *Students:* 76 full-time (63 women), 115 part-time (89 women); includes 25 minority (8 African Americans, 12 American Indian/Alaska Native, 4 Asian Americans or Pacific Islanders, 1 Hispanic American), 12 international. 72 applicants, 96% accepted, 56 enrolled. In 2006, 11 master's, 10 doctorates awarded. *Degree requirements:* For doctorate, thesis/dissertation. *Entrance requirements:* For master's, 12 hours of course work in education; for doctorate, GRE General Test, master's degree, minimum graduate GPA of 3.0. Additional exam requirements/recommendations for international students: Required—TOEFL (minimum score 550 paper-based; 213 computer-based). *Application deadline:* For fall admission, 6/1 priority date for domestic students, 4/1 for international students; for spring admission, 11/1 for domestic students, 9/1 for international students. Applications are processed on a rolling basis. Application fee: $40 ($90 for international students). *Expenses:* Tuition, state resident: full-time $3,180; part-time $133 per credit hour. Tuition, nonresident: full-time $11,347; part-time $473 per credit hour. Required fees: $1,729; $62 per credit hour. $117 per semester. Tuition and fees vary according to course load and program. *Financial support:* In 2006–07, 76 students received support, including 5 research assistantships with partial tuition reimbursements available (averaging $9,773 per year), 7 teaching assistantships with partial tuition reimbursements available (averaging $10,403 per year); scholarships/grants and unspecified assistantships also available. Financial award applicants required to submit FAFSA. *Faculty research:* Early literacy, learning cycle, social justice, teacher education. Total annual research expenditures: $119,917. *Unit head:* Dr. Priscilla Griffith, Chair and Graduate Liaison, 405-325-1498, Fax: 405-325-4061, E-mail: pgriffith@ou.edu.

University of Pittsburgh, School of Education, Department of Instruction and Learning, Program in Secondary Education, Pittsburgh, PA 15260. Offers English/communications education (M Ed, MAT, Ed D, PhD); foreign languages education (M Ed, MAT, Ed D, PhD); mathematics education (M Ed, MAT, Ed D); reading education (PhD); science education (M Ed, MAT, MS, Ed D); social studies education (M Ed, MAT, Ed D, PhD). Part-time and evening/weekend programs available. *Students:* 157 full-time (111 women), 84 part-time (61 women); includes 18 minority (7 African Americans, 5 Asian Americans or Pacific Islanders, 6 Hispanic Americans), 13 international. 163 applicants, 74% accepted, 86 enrolled. In 2006, 114 master's, 7 doctorates awarded. *Degree requirements:* For master's and doctorate, thesis/dissertation. *Entrance requirements:* For master's, PRAXIS I; for doctorate, GRE General Test. Additional exam requirements/recommendations for international students: Required—TOEFL. *Application deadline:* For fall admission, 2/1 priority date for domestic students; for spring admission, 11/15 priority date for domestic students. Applications are processed on a rolling basis. Application fee: $50. Electronic applications accepted. *Financial support:* Fellowships, teaching assistantships, career-related internships or fieldwork, Federal Work-Study, tuition waivers (partial), and unspecified assistantships available. Support available to part-time students. Financial award application deadline: 3/15; financial award applicants required to submit FAFSA. *Application contact:* Joan M. Cutone, Director, School of Education Student Service Center, 412-648-2230, Fax: 412-648-1899, E-mail: soeinfo@pitt.edu.

University of Puerto Rico, Río Piedras, College of Education, Program in Curriculum and Teaching, San Juan, PR 00931-3300. Offers biology education (M Ed); chemistry education (M Ed); curriculum and teaching (Ed D); English education (M Ed); history education (M Ed); mathematics education (M Ed); physics education (M Ed); secondary education (M Ed); Spanish education (M Ed). Part-time programs available. *Students:* 64 full-time (42 women), 123 part-time (91 women); all minorities (all Hispanic Americans) In 2006, 8 master's, 19 doctorates awarded. *Degree requirements:* For master's, thesis; for doctorate, thesis/dissertation, internship. *Entrance requirements:* For master's, PAEG or GRE, minimum GPA of 3.0, letter of recommendation; for doctorate, GRE or PAEG, master's degree, minimum GPA of 3.0, letter of recommendation (2), interview. *Application deadline:* For fall admission, 2/1 for domestic and international students. Application fee: $17. *Expenses:* Tuition, state resident: part-time $100 per credit. Tuition, nonresident: part-time $291 per credit. Required fees: $72 per semester. *Financial support:* Fellowships, research assistantships, teaching assistantships, career-related internships or fieldwork, Federal Work-Study, institutionally sponsored loans, and tuition waivers (partial) available. Financial award application deadline: 5/31. *Faculty research:* Science curriculum, administration management. *Unit head:* Dr. Loyda Martinez, Coordinator, 787-764-0000 Ext. 4361, Fax: 787-763-4130. *Application contact:* Information Contact, 787-764-0000 Ext. 4368, Fax: 787-763-4130.

University of St. Francis, College of Education, Joliet, IL 60435-6169. Offers curriculum and instruction (MS); educational leadership (MS), including reading, special education; elementary education certification (M Ed); secondary education certification (M Ed), including English education, math education, science education, social studies education; special education (M Ed); teaching and learning (MS). Part-time and evening/weekend programs available.

Science Education

University of St. Francis (continued)
Faculty: 11 full-time (10 women), 25 part-time/adjunct (12 women). *Students:* 52 full-time (38 women), 381 part-time (293 women); includes 38 minority (21 African Americans, 1 American Indian/Alaska Native, 4 Asian Americans or Pacific Islanders, 12 Hispanic Americans). Average age 33. 194 applicants, 80% accepted, 117 enrolled. In 2006, 165 degrees awarded. *Degree requirements:* For master's, comprehensive exam (for some programs), registration. *Entrance requirements:* For master's, minimum undergraduate GPA of 2.75, 2 letters of recommendation, computer competency. Additional exam requirements/recommendations for international students: Required—TOEFL (minimum score 550 paper-based; 213 computer-based). *Application deadline:* Applications are processed on a rolling basis. Application fee: $30. Electronic applications accepted. *Expenses: Contact institution.* Part-time tuition and fees vary according to campus/location and program. *Financial support:* In 2006–07, 272 students received support. Scholarships/grants, tuition waivers (partial), and unspecified assistantships available. Support available to part-time students. Financial award applicants required to submit FAFSA. *Unit head:* Dr. John Gambro, Dean, 815-740-3456, Fax: 815-740-2264, E-mail: jgambro@stfrancis.edu. *Application contact:* Sandra Sloka, Director of Admissions for Graduate and Degree Completion Programs, 800-735-7500, Fax: 815-740-5032, E-mail: ssloka@stfrancis.edu.

University of South Alabama, Graduate School, College of Education, Department of Leadership and Teacher Education, Mobile, AL 36688-0002. Offers early childhood education (M Ed); educational administration (Ed S); educational leadership (M Ed); elementary education (M Ed); reading education (M Ed); science education (M Ed); secondary education (M Ed); special education (M Ed, Ed S). *Accreditation:* NCATE. Part-time programs available. *Faculty:* 22 full-time (13 women). *Students:* 287 full-time (251 women), 229 part-time (194 women); includes 137 minority (125 African Americans, 8 American Indian/Alaska Native, 3 Asian Americans or Pacific Islanders, 1 Hispanic American), 4 international. 43 applicants, 84% accepted, 20 enrolled. In 2006, 169 master's, 12 other advanced degrees awarded. *Degree requirements:* For master's, comprehensive exam. *Entrance requirements:* For master's, GRE General Test or MAT, minimum GPA of 3.0. *Application deadline:* For fall admission, 9/1 priority date for domestic students. Applications are processed on a rolling basis. Application fee: $25. *Financial support:* In 2006–07, 6 research assistantships were awarded; career-related internships or fieldwork also available. Support available to part-time students. Financial award application deadline: 4/1. *Unit head:* Dr. David L. Gray, Chair, 251-380-2894.

University of South Carolina, The Graduate School, College of Arts and Sciences, Department of Geography, Columbia, SC 29208. Offers geography (MA, MS, PhD); geography education (IMA). IMA and MAT offered in cooperation with the College of Education. Part-time programs available. *Degree requirements:* For master's, thesis (for some programs), comprehensive exam, registration; for doctorate, thesis/dissertation, comprehensive exam, registration. *Entrance requirements:* For master's, GRE General Test; for doctorate, GRE General Test, master's degree. Electronic applications accepted. *Faculty research:* Geographic information processing; economic, cultural, physical, and environmental geography.

University of South Carolina, The Graduate School, College of Education, Department of Instruction and Teacher Education, Program in Secondary Education, Columbia, SC 29208. Offers art education (IMA, MAT); business education (IMA, MAT); English (MAT); foreign language (MAT); health education (MAT); mathematics (MAT); science (IMA, MAT); secondary education (M Ed, MA, MT, PhD); social studies (IMA, MAT); theatre and speech (IMA, MAT). IMA and MT offered jointly with the subject areas. *Accreditation:* NCATE. *Degree requirements:* For master's, thesis (for some programs), foreign language (MA), comprehensive exam; for doctorate, one foreign language, thesis/dissertation, comprehensive exam. *Entrance requirements:* For master's, GRE General Test or MAT, teaching certificate (IMA, M Ed), interview; for doctorate, GRE General Test or MAT, interview. *Faculty research:* Middle school programs, professional development, school collaboration.

University of South Carolina, The Graduate School, College of Science and Mathematics, Department of Biological Sciences, Columbia, SC 29208. Offers biology (MS, PhD); biology education (IMA, MAT); ecology, evolution and organismal biology (MS, PhD); molecular, cellular, and developmental biology (MS, PhD). IMA and MAT offered in cooperation with the College of Education. Terminal master's awarded for partial completion of doctoral program. *Degree requirements:* For master's, one foreign language, thesis (for some programs); for doctorate, one foreign language, thesis/dissertation. *Entrance requirements:* For master's and doctorate, GRE General Test, minimum GPA of 3.0 in science. Electronic applications accepted. *Faculty research:* Marine ecology, population and evolutionary biology, molecular biology and genetics, development.

University of Southern Mississippi, Graduate School, College of Science and Technology, Center for Science and Mathematics Education, Hattiesburg, MS 39406-0001. Offers MS, PhD. *Faculty:* 1 (woman) full-time. *Students:* 15 full-time (10 women), 25 part-time (18 women); includes 1 African American, 3 international. Average age 36. 13 applicants, 62% accepted, 7 enrolled. In 2006, 2 master's, 2 doctorates awarded. *Degree requirements:* For master's, thesis or alternative, comprehensive exam, registration; for doctorate, thesis/dissertation, comprehensive exam, registration. *Entrance requirements:* For master's, GRE General Test, minimum GPA of 2.75 in last 60 hours; for doctorate, GRE General Test, minimum GPA of 3.5. Additional exam requirements/recommendations for international students: Required—TOEFL. *Application deadline:* For fall admission, 3/15 priority date for domestic students, 3/15 for international students. Applications are processed on a rolling basis. Application fee: $25 ($30 for international students). *Financial support:* In 2006–07, 7 research assistantships (averaging $7,490 per year), 4 teaching assistantships with full tuition reimbursements (averaging $7,490 per year) were awarded; fellowships with full tuition reimbursements, Federal Work-Study also available. Financial award application deadline: 3/15. *Unit head:* Dr. Sherry Herron, Director, 601-266-4739, Fax: 601-266-4741.

University of South Florida, Graduate School, College of Education, Department of Secondary Education, Program in Science Education, Tampa, FL 33620-9951. Offers MAT, PhD. *Students:* 6 full-time (5 women), 10 part-time (7 women); includes 1 minority (African American), 1 international. 6 applicants, 67% accepted, 3 enrolled. In 2006, 1 degree awarded. *Entrance requirements:* For master's, GRE General Test, minimum GPA of 3.0 in last 60 hours of coursework. Additional exam requirements/recommendations for international students: Required—TOEFL. *Application deadline:* For fall admission, 6/1 for domestic students; for spring admission, 10/15 for domestic students. Application fee: $30. *Unit head:* Elaine Howes, Program Director, 813-974-2816, Fax: 813-974-3837, E-mail: eshowes@coedu.usf.edu. *Application contact:* Dana L. Zeidler, Information Contact, 813-974-2816, Fax: 813-974-3837.

The University of Tampa, Program in Teaching, Tampa, FL 33606-1490. Offers education (MAT); math education (MAT); reading (M Ed); science education (MAT). *Students:* 66 applicants, 71% accepted, 40 enrolled.Application fee: $40. *Expenses:* Tuition: Part-time $426 per credit hour. Required fees: $35 per year. *Unit head:* Dr. Martine Harrison, Associate Professor of Education, 813-253-3333 Ext. 3373, E-mail: mharrison@ut.edu.

The University of Tennessee, Graduate School, College of Education, Health and Human Sciences, Program in Education, Knoxville, TN 37996. Offers art education (MS); counseling education (PhD); cultural studies in education (PhD); curriculum (MS, Ed S); curriculum, educational research and evaluation (Ed D, PhD); early childhood education (PhD); early childhood special education (MS); education of deaf and hard of hearing (MS); educational administration and policy studies (Ed D, PhD); educational administration and supervision (Ed S); educational psychology (Ed D, PhD); elementary education (MS, Ed S); elementary teaching (MS); English education (MS, Ed S); exercise science (PhD); foreign language/ESL education (MS, Ed S); instructional technology (MS, Ed D, PhD, Ed S); literacy, language and ESL education (PhD); literacy, language education, and ESL education (Ed D); mathematics education (MS, Ed S); modified and comprehensive special education (MS); reading education (MS, Ed S); school counseling (Ed S); school psychology (PhD, Ed S); science education (MS, Ed S); secondary teaching (MS); social foundations (MS); social science education (MS, Ed S); socio-cultural foundations of sports and education (PhD); special education (Ed S); teacher education (Ed D, PhD). *Accreditation:* NCATE. Part-time and evening/weekend programs available. *Students:* 529 (401 women); includes 39 minority (23 African Americans, 2 American Indian/Alaska Native, 9 Asian Americans or Pacific Islanders, 5 Hispanic Americans) 34 international. 420 applicants, 50% accepted. In 2006, 258 master's, 28 doctorates awarded. *Degree requirements:* For master's and Ed S, thesis optional; for doctorate, variable foreign language requirement, thesis/dissertation. *Entrance requirements:* For master's, minimum GPA of 2.7; for doctorate and Ed S, GRE General Test, minimum GPA of 2.7. Additional exam requirements/recommendations for international students: Required—TOEFL. *Application deadline:* For fall admission, 2/1 priority date for domestic students. Applications are processed on a rolling basis. Application fee: $35. Electronic applications accepted. *Expenses:* Tuition, state resident: full-time $5,574. Tuition, nonresident: full-time $16,840. Required fees: $792. *Financial support:* In 2006–07, 4 fellowships, 9 teaching assistantships were awarded; career-related internships or fieldwork, Federal Work-Study, institutionally sponsored loans, and unspecified assistantships also available. Financial award application deadline: 2/1; financial award applicants required to submit FAFSA. *Unit head:* Dr. Lester Knight, Head, 865-974-0907, Fax: 865-974-8718, E-mail: lknight@utk.edu.

The University of Texas at Austin, Graduate School, College of Education, Programs in Science/Mathematics Education, Program in Science Education, Austin, TX 78712-1111. Offers M Ed, MA, PhD. *Entrance requirements:* For master's and doctorate, GRE General Test.

The University of Texas at Dallas, School of Natural Sciences and Mathematics, Program in Mathematics and Science Education, Richardson, TX 75083-0688. Offers mathematics education (MAT); science education (MAT). Part-time and evening/weekend programs available. *Faculty:* 3 full-time (all women), 1 part-time/adjunct (0 women). *Students:* 6 full-time (5 women), 54 part-time (41 women); includes 18 minority (8 African Americans, 4 Asian Americans or Pacific Islanders, 6 Hispanic Americans), 5 international. Average age 37. 43 applicants, 79% accepted, 23 enrolled. In 2006, 27 degrees awarded. *Entrance requirements:* For master's, GRE General Test, minimum GPA of 3.0 in upper-level coursework in field. Additional exam requirements/recommendations for international students: Required—TOEFL (minimum score 550 paper-based; 213 computer-based). *Application deadline:* For fall admission, 7/15 for domestic students; for spring admission, 11/15 for domestic students. Applications are processed on a rolling basis. Application fee: $50 ($100 for international students). Electronic applications accepted. *Financial support:* In 2006–07, 2 students received support, including 1 teaching assistantship (averaging $9,550 per year); fellowships, research assistantships, career-related internships or fieldwork, Federal Work-Study, institutionally sponsored loans, and scholarships/grants also available. Support available to part-time students. Financial award application deadline: 4/30; financial award applicants required to submit FAFSA. *Faculty research:* Techniques for training teachers, philosophic definitions of science held by working scientists, science teachers, science students. Total annual research expenditures: $18,210. *Unit head:* Dr. Cynthia Ledbetter, Head, 972-883-2496, Fax: 972-883-6371, E-mail: ledbetter@utdallas.edu.

The University of Texas at Tyler, College of Education and Psychology, Department of Curriculum and Instruction, Tyler, TX 75799-0001. Offers curriculum and instruction (M Ed); secondary teaching (MAT), including art, biology, computer science, English, history, journalism, mathematics, music, political science, sociology, speech, theatre. Part-time programs available. *Faculty:* 10 full-time (6 women), 2 part-time/adjunct (1 woman). *Students:* 3 full-time (2 women), 7 part-time (6 women); includes 1 minority (African American) Average age 32. 1 applicant, 100% accepted, 1 enrolled. In 2006, 6 degrees awarded. *Degree requirements:* For master's, research project (M Ed). *Entrance requirements:* For master's, GRE or MAT. Application fee: $0 ($50 for international students). Electronic applications accepted. *Expenses:* Tuition, state resident: part-time $50 per credit hour. Tuition, nonresident: part-time $328 per credit hour. Required fees: $107 per credit hour. $426 per term. *Financial support:* Scholarships/grants available. *Unit head:* Dr. Robert Stevens, Chair/Professor of Education, 903-566-7315, E-mail: rstevens@uttyler.edu. *Application contact:* Bonnie Purser, Office of Graduate Studies, 903-566-7142, Fax: 903-566-7068, E-mail: bpurser@uttyler.edu.

University of the Incarnate Word, School of Graduate Studies and Research, School of Mathematics, Sciences, and Engineering, Program in Mathematics, San Antonio, TX 78209-6397. Offers mathematics (MS); teaching (MA). Part-time and evening/weekend programs available. *Students:* 1 (woman) full-time, 11 part-time (10 women); includes 5 minority (2 African Americans, 3 Hispanic Americans). Average age 39. In 2006, 8 degrees awarded. *Entrance requirements:* For master's, GRE General Test. Additional exam requirements/recommendations for international students: Required—TOEFL. *Application deadline:* For fall admission, 8/15 priority date for domestic students; for spring admission, 12/31 for domestic students. Applications are processed on a rolling basis. Application fee: $20. *Expenses:* Tuition: Part-time $570 per credit hour. Required fees: $54 per credit hour. One-time fee: $195 part-time. Tuition and fees vary according to degree level. *Financial support:* Federal Work-Study and scholarships/grants available. *Faculty research:* Topology, set theory, mathematics education. *Unit head:* Dr. Elizabeth Kreston, Chair, 210-805-1225, Fax: 210-829-3153, E-mail: kreston@universe.uiwtx.edu. *Application contact:* Andrea Cyterski-Acosta, Dean of Enrollment, 210-829-6005, Fax: 210-829-3921, E-mail: cyterski@uiwtx.edu.

The University of Toledo, College of Graduate Studies, College of Education, Department of Curriculum and Instruction, Program in Education and Biology, Toledo, OH 43606-3390. Offers MES. *Students:* 1 (woman) full-time, 1 (woman) part-time. 1 applicant, 100% accepted, 1 enrolled. In 2006, 1 degree awarded.

The University of Toledo, College of Graduate Studies, College of Education, Department of Curriculum and Instruction, Program in Education and Chemistry, Toledo, OH 43606-3390. Offers MES. *Students:* 2 applicants, 50% accepted, 1 enrolled. In 2006, 1 degree awarded.

The University of Toledo, College of Graduate Studies, College of Education, Department of Curriculum and Instruction, Program in Education and Geology, Toledo, OH 43606-3390. Offers MES.

The University of Toledo, College of Graduate Studies, College of Education, Department of Curriculum and Instruction, Program in Education and Physics, Toledo, OH 43606-3390. Offers MES.

University of Tulsa, Graduate School, College of Arts and Sciences, School of Education, Program in Mathematics and Science Education, Tulsa, OK 74104-3189. Offers MSMSE. Part-time programs available. *Students:* 2 full-time (both women), 1 (woman) part-time, 1 international. Average age 23. 4 applicants, 25% accepted, 1 enrolled. *Entrance requirements:* For master's, GRE General Test. Additional exam requirements/recommendations for international students: Required—TOEFL (minimum score 575 paper-based; 231 computer-based), IELTS (minimum score 7). *Application deadline:* Applications are processed on a rolling basis. Application fee: $40. Electronic applications accepted. *Expenses:* Tuition: Full-time $13,338; part-time $741 per credit hour. *Financial support:* In 2006–07, 2 students received support, including 1 research assistantship (averaging $10,300 per year), 1 teaching assistantship with full and partial tuition reimbursement available (averaging $10,300 per year); fellowships with full and partial tuition reimbursements available, Federal Work-Study, scholarships/grants, tuition waivers (full and partial), and unspecified assistantships also available. Support available to part-time students. Financial award application deadline: 2/1; financial award applicants required to submit FAFSA. *Unit head:* Dr. Alexander W. Wiseman, Head, 918-631-2371, Fax: 918-631-2133, E-mail: alexander-wiseman@utulsa.edu.

University of Utah, The Graduate School, College of Science, Department of Chemistry, Salt Lake City, UT 84112-1107. Offers chemical physics (PhD); chemistry (M Phil, MA, MS, PhD); science teacher education (MS). Part-time programs available. Postbaccalaureate distance learning degree programs offered. *Faculty:* 27 full-time (4 women), 2 part-time/adjunct (0 women). *Students:* 146 full-time (61 women), 31 part-time (12 women); includes 8 minority (5 Asian Americans or Pacific Islanders, 3 Hispanic Americans), 84 international. Average age 28. 328 applicants, 29% accepted, 32 enrolled. In 2006, 12 master's, 14 doctorates awarded. Terminal master's awarded for partial completion of doctoral program. *Median time to degree:* Of those who began their doctoral program in fall 1998, 100% received their degree in 8 years or less. *Degree requirements:* For master's, 20 hours course work, 10 hours research, thesis optional; for doctorate, thesis/dissertation, 18 hours course work, 14 hours research. *Entrance requirements:* For master's and doctorate, GRE General Test, minimum GPA of 3.0. Additional exam requirements/recommendations for international students: Required—TOEFL (minimum score 620 paper-based; 260 computer-based; 105 iBT). *Application deadline:* For fall admission, 4/1 for domestic and international students; for winter admission, 3/15 for domestic and international students; for spring admission, 11/1 for domestic and international students. Applications are processed on a rolling basis. Application fee: $45 ($65 for international students). Electronic applications accepted. *Expenses:* Tuition, state resident: full-time $3,208. Tuition, nonresident: full-time $11,326. Required fees: $608. Tuition and fees vary according to class time and program. *Financial support:* In 2006–07, research assistantships with tuition reimbursements (averaging $21,500 per year), teaching assistantships with tuition reimbursements (averaging $20,500 per year) were awarded; fellowships with tuition reimbursements, scholarships/grants and tuition waivers (full) also available. Financial award application deadline: 4/1; financial award applicants required to submit FAFSA. *Faculty research:* Biological, theoretical, inorganic, organic, and physical-analytical chemistry. Total annual research expenditures: $11.1 million. *Unit head:* Peter B. Armentrout, Chair, 801-581-6681, Fax: 801-581-8433, E-mail: armentrout@chemistry.utah.edu. *Application contact:* Jo Hoovey, Graduate Coordinator, 801-581-4393, Fax: 801-581-5408, E-mail: jhoovey@chem.utah.edu.

University of Vermont, Graduate College, College of Arts and Sciences, Department of Biology, Burlington, VT 05405. Offers biology (MS, PhD); biology education (MST). *Faculty:* 17. *Students:* 34 (20 women) 16 international. 51 applicants, 31% accepted, 7 enrolled. In 2006, 1 master's, 2 doctorates awarded. *Degree requirements:* For master's and doctorate, thesis/dissertation. *Entrance requirements:* For master's and doctorate, GRE General Test. Additional exam requirements/recommendations for international students: Required—TOEFL (minimum score 550 paper-based; 213 computer-based). *Application deadline:* For fall admission, 2/1 priority date for domestic students. Applications are processed on a rolling basis. Application fee: $40. Electronic applications accepted. *Expenses:* Tuition, state resident: part-time $434 per credit. Tuition, nonresident: part-time $1,096 per credit. *Financial support:* Fellowships, research assistantships, teaching assistantships available. *Unit head:* Dr. Judith Van Houten, Chairperson, 802-656-2922. *Application contact:* N. Gotelli, Coordinator, 802-656-2922.

University of Victoria, Faculty of Graduate Studies, Faculty of Education, Department of Curriculum and Instruction, Victoria, BC V8W 2Y2, Canada. Offers art (M Ed, MA, PhD); curriculum studies (M Ed, MA, PhD); early childhood (M Ed, MA, PhD); language and literacy (M Ed, MA, PhD); mathematics (M Ed, MA, PhD); music (M Ed, MA); music education (PhD); science (M Ed, MA, PhD); social studies (M Ed, MA); social, cultural and foundational studies (PhD); technology and environmental education (PhD). Part-time programs available. *Degree requirements:* For master's, thesis, project (M Ed); for doctorate, thesis/dissertation, comprehensive exam, registration. *Entrance requirements:* For master's, minimum B average. Additional exam requirements/recommendations for international students: Required—TOEFL (minimum score 575 paper-based; 233 computer-based), IELTS (minimum score 7). Electronic applications accepted. *Faculty research:* Elementary and secondary English, language arts, curriculum theory and practice, educational media and technology, educational administration and leadership, history and philosophy of education.

University of Virginia, College and Graduate School of Arts and Sciences, Department of Physics, Charlottesville, VA 22903. Offers physics (MA, MS, PhD); physics education (MA). *Faculty:* 32 full-time (3 women). *Students:* 89 full-time (17 women); includes 3 minority (2 Asian Americans or Pacific Islanders, 1 Hispanic American), 40 international. Average age 27. 175 applicants, 30% accepted, 12 enrolled. In 2006, 13 master's, 11 doctorates awarded. *Degree requirements:* For master's and doctorate, thesis/dissertation. *Entrance requirements:* For master's and doctorate, GRE General Test, GRE Subject Test. *Application deadline:* Applications are processed on a rolling basis. Application fee: $60. Electronic applications accepted. *Financial support:* Applicants required to submit FAFSA. *Unit head:* Dinko Pocanic, Chair, 434-924-3781, Fax: 434-924-4576, E-mail: phys-chair@physics.virginia.edu. *Application contact:* Peter C. Brunjes, Associate Dean for Graduate Programs and Research, 434-924-7184, Fax: 434-924-6737, E-mail: grad-a-s@virginia.edu.

University of Washington, Graduate School, College of Education, Seattle, WA 98195. Offers curriculum and instruction (M Ed, Ed D, PhD), including educational technology, general curriculum (Ed D, PhD), language, literacy, and culture, mathematics education, multicultural education, reading and language arts education (Ed D), science education, social studies education, teaching and curriculum (M Ed); educational leadership and policy studies (M Ed, Ed D, PhD), including administration, educational organization and policy, higher education, school district leadership (Ed D), social/cultural foundations; educational psychology (M Ed, PhD), including human development and cognition, measurement and research, school counseling (M Ed), school psychology; special education (M Ed, Ed D, PhD), including early childhood education, elementary special education, emotional and behavioral disabilities (M Ed), general special education, severe disabilities; teacher education (MIT). *Accreditation:* APA. Part-time and evening/weekend programs available. *Degree requirements:* For master's, thesis optional; for doctorate, thesis/dissertation. *Entrance requirements:* For master's and doctorate, GRE General Test, minimum GPA of 3.0. Additional exam requirements/recommendations for international students: Required—TOEFL. Electronic applications accepted. *Faculty research:* School restructuring/effective schools, special education interventions, literacy and writing, technology, school partnerships, teacher preparation.

University of Washington, Graduate School, Interdisciplinary Graduate Program in Biology for Teachers, Seattle, WA 98195. Offers MS. Part-time programs available. *Degree requirements:* For master's, research project and oral exam. *Entrance requirements:* For master's, GRE General Test, minimum GPA of 3.0, teaching certificate or professional teaching experience. Electronic applications accepted.

The University of West Alabama, School of Graduate Studies, College of Natural Sciences and Mathematics, Department of Biological Sciences, Livingston, AL 35470. Offers MAT. *Accreditation:* NCATE. *Faculty:* 4 full-time (0 women). *Students:* 7 full-time (5 women), 19 part-time (11 women); includes 16 minority (all African Americans) Application fee: $20 ($50 for international students). *Financial support:* Career-related internships or fieldwork, Federal Work-Study, scholarships/grants, and unspecified assistantships available. Support available to part-time students. *Unit head:* Dr. John McCall, Chairperson, 800-621-8044 Ext. 3724.

University of West Florida, College of Arts and Sciences: Sciences, Division of Life and Health Sciences, Department of Biology, Pensacola, FL 32514-5750. Offers biological chemistry (MS); biology (MS); biology education (MST); coastal zone studies (MS); environmental biology (MS). *Faculty:* 16 full-time (5 women), 2 part-time/adjunct (0 women). *Students:* 7 full-time (6 women), 34 part-time (23 women); includes 3 minority (2 Asian Americans or Pacific Islanders, 1 Hispanic American), 2 international. Average age 28. 12 applicants, 58% accepted, 6 enrolled. In 2006, 11 degrees awarded. *Degree requirements:* For master's, thesis. *Entrance requirements:* For master's, GRE General Test. Additional exam requirements/recommendations for international students: Required—TOEFL (minimum score 550 paper-based; 213 computer-based). *Application deadline:* For fall admission, 6/1 for domestic students, 5/15 for international students; for spring admission, 11/1 for domestic students, 10/1 for international students. Applications are processed on a rolling basis. Application fee: $30. *Expenses:* Tuition, state resident: full-time $5,871; part-time $245 per credit hour. Tuition, nonresident: full-time $21,241; part-time $885 per credit hour. *Financial support:* In 2006–07, 20 students received support, including 5 research assistantships with partial tuition reimbursements available (averaging $5,000 per year), 11 teaching assistantships with partial tuition reimbursements available (averaging $8,000 per year). Financial award application deadline: 4/15; financial award applicants required to submit FAFSA.

University of West Georgia, Graduate School, College of Education, Department of Curriculum and Instruction, Program in Secondary Education—Science, Carrollton, GA 30118. Offers M Ed, Ed S. Part-time and evening/weekend programs available. *Students:* 2 full-time (both women), 7 part-time (6 women); includes 1 minority (African American) Average age 33. In 2006, 3 master's, 2 other advanced degrees awarded. *Degree requirements:* For master's, comprehensive exam; for Ed S, research project. *Entrance requirements:* For master's and Ed S, GRE or MAT. *Application deadline:* For fall admission, 8/1 for domestic students. Applications are processed on a rolling basis. Application fee: $20. *Expenses:* Tuition, state resident: full-time $2,286; part-time $127 per credit. Tuition, nonresident: full-time $9,144; part-time $508 per credit. Required fees: $494; $27 per credit. $121 per semester. *Financial support:* In 2006–07, research assistantships with full tuition reimbursements (averaging $3,000 per year). Financial award applicants required to submit FAFSA. *Application contact:* Dr. Charles W. Clark, Chair, 678-839-6508, E-mail: cclark@westga.edu.

University of Wisconsin–Eau Claire, College of Education and Human Sciences, Program in Secondary Education, Eau Claire, WI 54702-4004. Offers biology (MAT, MST); education and professional development (MEPD); English (MAT, MST); history (MAT, MST); mathematics (MAT, MST). *Faculty:* 9 full-time (6 women). *Students:* 10 full-time (7 women), 23 part-time (20 women), 1 international. Average age 33. 21 applicants, 57% accepted, 4 enrolled. In 2006, 22 degrees awarded. *Degree requirements:* For master's, thesis optional. *Entrance requirements:* For master's, 2 years of teaching experience or the equivalent. *Application deadline:* For fall admission, 7/1 for domestic students; for spring admission, 12/1 for domestic students. Applications are processed on a rolling basis. Application fee: $45. *Expenses:* Tuition, state resident: full-time $6,533; part-time $363 per credit. Tuition, nonresident: full-time $17,143; part-time $952 per credit. Tuition and fees vary according to program and reciprocity agreements. *Financial support:* In 2006–07, 17 students received support, including 2 teaching assistantships (averaging $5,200 per year); Federal Work-Study also available. Financial award application deadline: 3/1; financial award applicants required to submit FAFSA. *Unit head:* Dr. Tamara Lindsey, Chair, 715-836-4737, Fax: 715-836-4868, E-mail: lindsetp@uwec.edu.

University of Wisconsin–Madison, Graduate School, School of Education, Department of Curriculum and Instruction, Madison, WI 53706-1380. Offers art education (MA); curriculum and instruction (MS, PhD); education and mathematics (MA); French education (MA); German education (MA); music education (MS); science education (MS); Spanish education (MA). *Accreditation:* NASM (one or more programs are accredited). *Degree requirements:* For doctorate, thesis/dissertation. Application fee: $45. *Financial support:* Project assistantships available. *Unit head:* Dr. Alan Lockwood, Chair, 608-262-4000.

University of Wisconsin–River Falls, Outreach and Graduate Studies, College of Arts and Science, Program in Science, River Falls, WI 54022-5001. Offers science education (MSE). Part-time programs available. *Degree requirements:* For master's, thesis or alternative, comprehensive exam, registration. *Entrance requirements:* For master's, minimum GPA of 2.75. Electronic applications accepted.

University of Wisconsin–Stevens Point, College of Letters and Science, Department of Biology, Stevens Point, WI 54481-3897. Offers MST. *Faculty:* 22 full-time (6 women), 1 part-time/adjunct (0 women). *Degree requirements:* For master's, thesis or alternative. *Entrance requirements:* For master's, minimum overall undergraduate GPA of 2.75, bachelor's degree in biology with minimum 3.0 GPA, teacher's license. *Application deadline:* For fall admission, 5/1 priority date for domestic students. Applications are processed on a rolling basis. Application fee: $45. *Expenses:* Tuition, state resident: full-time $5,910; part-time $328 per credit. Tuition, nonresident: full-time $16,520; part-time $918 per credit. Required fees: $756; $73 per credit. *Financial support:* Federal Work-Study available. Financial award application deadline: 5/1; financial award applicants required to submit FAFSA. *Unit head:* Dr. Robert Bell, Chair, 715-346-2159, E-mail: rbell@uwsp.edu. *Application contact:* Dr. Eric Wild, Coordinator, 715-346-2159, Fax: 715-346-3624, E-mail: ewild@uwsp.edu.

University of Wyoming, Graduate School, College of Education, Science and Mathematics Teaching Center, Laramie, WY 82070. Offers MS, MST. *Faculty:* 6 full-time (3 women), 39 part-time/adjunct (9 women). *Students:* 3 full-time (1 woman), 18 part-time (15 women). Average age 39. 1 applicant, 0% accepted. In 2006, 6 degrees awarded. *Degree requirements:* For master's, thesis. *Entrance requirements:* For master's, GRE General Test, minimum GPA of 3.0, writing sample, 3 letters of recommendation. *Application deadline:* For fall admission, 6/1 priority date for domestic students. Applications are processed on a rolling basis. Application fee: $50. Electronic applications accepted. *Financial support:* In 2006–07, 1 teaching assistantship with full tuition reimbursement (averaging $10,384 per year) was awarded; unspecified assistantships also available. Financial award applicants required to submit FAFSA. *Unit head:* Dr. Robert L. Mayes, Director, 307-766-3776, Fax: 307-766-3792, E-mail: smtc@uwyo.edu. *Application contact:* Jami Salo, Office Associate, 307-766-6381, Fax: 307-766-3792, E-mail: smtc@uwyo.edu.

Vanderbilt University, Graduate School, Department of Physics and Astronomy, Nashville, TN 37240-1001. Offers astronomy (MS); physics (MA, MAT, MS, PhD). *Faculty:* 65 full-time (3 women). *Students:* 74 full-time (18 women); includes 4 minority (3 African Americans, 1 Hispanic American), 36 international. 180 applicants, 13% accepted, 13 enrolled. In 2006, 8 master's, 5 doctorates awarded. *Degree requirements:* For master's, thesis; for doctorate, thesis/dissertation, final and qualifying exams. *Entrance requirements:* For master's, GRE General Test; for doctorate, GRE General Test, GRE Subject Test. *Application deadline:* For fall admission, 1/15 for domestic and international students. Application fee: $0. Electronic applications accepted. *Expenses:* Tuition: Full-time $24,462. Required fees: $2,515. One-time fee: $30 full-time. Full-time tuition and fees vary according to course load, degree level and program. *Financial support:* Fellowships with full and partial tuition reimbursements, research assistantships with full tuition reimbursements, teaching assistantships with full tuition reimbursements, career-related internships or fieldwork, Federal Work-Study, and institutionally sponsored loans available. Financial award application deadline: 1/15. *Faculty research:* Experimental and theoretical physics, free electron laser, living-state physics, heavy-ion physics, nuclear structure. *Unit head:* Robert J. Scherrer, Chair, 615-322-2828, Fax: 615-343-7263. *Application contact:* Vicky Greene, Director of Graduate Studies, 615-322-2828, Fax: 615-343-7263, E-mail: senta.greene@vanderbilt.edu.

Vanderbilt University, Peabody College, Department of Teaching and Learning, Nashville, TN 37240-1001. Offers curriculum and instructional leadership (M Ed); early childhood education (M Ed); early childhood leadership (Ed D); elementary education (M Ed); English education (M Ed); English language learners (M Ed); mathematics education (M Ed); reading education (M Ed); science education (M Ed); secondary education (M Ed). *Accreditation:* NCATE. *Faculty:* 23 full-time (13 women), 28 part-time/adjunct (19 women). *Students:* 71 full-time (62 women), 21 part-time (15 women); includes 9 minority (8 African Americans, 1 Hispanic American), 2 international. Average age 27. 102 applicants, 60% accepted, 27 enrolled. In 2006, 53 master's, 3 doctorates awarded. *Degree requirements:* For master's, thesis optional. *Entrance requirements:* For master's, GRE General Test, MAT. Additional exam requirements/recommendations for international students: Required—TOEFL (minimum score 550 paper-based; 213 computer-based). *Application deadline:* For fall admission, 12/31 priority date for domestic and international students; for spring admission, 11/1 priority date for domestic and international students. Applications are processed on a rolling basis. Application fee: $0. Electronic applications accepted. *Expenses:* Tuition: Full-time $24,462. Required fees: $2,515. One-time fee: $30 full-time. Full-time tuition and fees vary according to course load, degree level and program. *Financial support:* In 2006–07, 62 students received support, including 36 fellowships with full and partial tuition reimbursements available, 13 research assistantships with full and partial tuition reimbursements available, 13 teaching assistantships

Science Education

Vanderbilt University (continued)
with full and partial tuition reimbursements available; Federal Work-Study, institutionally sponsored loans, scholarships/grants, tuition waivers (partial), and unspecified assistantships also available. Support available to part-time students. Financial award application deadline: 2/1; financial award applicants required to submit FAFSA. *Faculty research:* Teaching and learning; development of subject matter knowledge; learning and policy; development students' mathematical and scientific knowledge, development of literacy. *Unit head:* Leona Schauble, Chair, 615-322-8100, Fax: 615-322-8999, E-mail: leona.schauble@vanderbilt.edu. *Application contact:* Angela Saylor, Educational Coordinator, 615-322-8092, Fax: 615-322-8999.

Wayne State College, School of Education and Counseling, Department of Educational Foundations and Leadership, Program in Curriculum and Instruction, Wayne, NE 68787. Offers alternative education (MSE); business education (MSE); communication arts education (MSE); curriculum and instruction (MSE); early childhood education (MSE); elementary education (MSE); English as a second language (MSE); English education (MSE); family consumer science of education (MSE); industrial technology education (MSE); learning communities (MSE); mathematics education (MSE); music education (MSE); science education (MSE); social science education (MSE). *Accreditation:* NCATE. Part-time and evening/weekend programs available. *Faculty:* 17 part-time/adjunct (11 women). *Students:* 17 full-time (10 women), 307 part-time (248 women); includes 6 minority (2 African Americans, 1 American Indian/Alaska Native, 2 Asian Americans or Pacific Islanders, 1 Hispanic American), 1 international. Average age 35. In 2006, 167 degrees awarded. *Degree requirements:* For master's, thesis optional. *Entrance requirements:* For master's, GRE General Test. Additional exam requirements/recommendations for international students: Required—TOEFL (minimum score 550 paper-based; 213 computer-based). *Application deadline:* Applications are processed on a rolling basis. Application fee: $30. *Expenses:* Tuition, state resident: full-time $3,114; part-time $130 per credit hour. Tuition, nonresident: full-time $6,228; part-time $260 per credit hour. Required fees: $894; $37 per credit hour. Tuition and fees vary according to course load. *Financial support:* Applicants required to submit FAFSA.

Wayne State University, College of Education, Division of Teacher Education, Detroit, MI 48202. Offers adult and continuing education (M Ed); art education (M Ed); bilingual/bicultural education (M Ed, MAT); business education (M Ed, MAT); career and technical education (M Ed, Ed D, PhD, Ed S); curriculum and instruction (Ed D, PhD, Ed S); distributive education (M Ed, MAT); early childhood education (M Ed); elementary education (M Ed, MAT, Ed D, PhD, Ed S); elementary education curriculum and instruction (M Ed); English education (M Ed); English education-secondary (M Ed, Ed S); foreign language education (M Ed); general education (Ed D, Ed S); health occupations education (M Ed); industrial education (M Ed); mathematics education (M Ed, Ed S); pre-school and parent education (M Ed); reading (M Ed, Ed D, Ed S); reading, languages and literature (Ed D); school music-vocal (M Ed); science education (M Ed, MAT, Ed S); secondary education (MAT); secondary school reading (M Ed); social studies education (M Ed, Ed S), including education-secondary (M Ed); special education (M Ed, Ed D, PhD, Ed S); teacher education (MAT, Ed D, PhD). *Faculty:* 41 full-time (22 women), 2 part-time/adjunct (both women). *Students:* 401 full-time (295 women), 1,021 part-time (784 women); includes 527 minority (452 African Americans, 6 American Indian/Alaska Native, 32 Asian Americans or Pacific Islanders, 37 Hispanic Americans), 18 international. Average age 36. 296 applicants, 81% accepted, 132 enrolled. In 2006, 386 master's, 1 doctorate awarded. *Degree requirements:* For doctorate, thesis/dissertation. *Entrance requirements:* For master's, minimum GPA of 2.6; for doctorate, minimum undergraduate GPA of 3.0, graduate 3.5; interview. Additional exam requirements/recommendations for international students: Required—TOEFL (minimum score 550 paper-based; 213 computer-based), TWE (minimum score 6). *Application deadline:* For fall admission, 7/1 for domestic students, 6/1 for international students; for winter admission, 10/1 for international students; for spring admission, 2/1 for international students. Application fee: $30 ($50 for international students). Electronic applications accepted. *Financial support:* In 2006–07, 1 fellowship (averaging $34,919 per year) was awarded; research assistantships. *Faculty research:* Reading and writing literacy and literature. Total annual research expenditures: $209,400. *Unit head:* Dr. Joann Snyder, Academic Director, 313-577-1644, E-mail: joanne.snyder@wayne.edu. *Application contact:* Sharon Elliott, Assistant Dean, 313-577-0902, E-mail: sharon.elliott@wayne.edu.

Wesleyan College, Department of Education, Program in Middle-Level Mathematics and Middle-Level Science Education, Macon, GA 31210-4462. Offers MA. Offered during summer only. Part-time programs available. *Faculty:* 4 full-time (3 women), 2 part-time/adjunct (both women). *Students:* 4 full-time (3 women), 8 part-time (all women); includes 6 minority (all African Americans) Average age 32. 6 applicants, 67% accepted, 4 enrolled. In 2006, 2 degrees awarded. *Degree requirements:* For master's, thesis or alternative, practicum, professional portfolio. *Entrance requirements:* For master's, GRE or MAT. Additional exam requirements/recommendations for international students: Required—TOEFL. *Application deadline:* For fall admission, 7/1 priority date for domestic students; for spring admission, 12/1 priority date for domestic students. Applications are processed on a rolling basis. Application fee: $25. *Expenses:* Tuition: Full-time $14,500. Tuition and fees vary according to program. *Financial support:* Federal Work-Study available. Financial award application deadline: 4/1; financial award applicants required to submit FAFSA. *Faculty research:* Instructional technology, cognitive development, verbal classroom interactions.

West Chester University of Pennsylvania, Graduate Studies, College of Arts and Sciences, Department of Chemistry, West Chester, PA 19383. Offers chemistry (M Ed, MS); clinical chemistry (MS); physical science (MA). Part-time and evening/weekend programs available. *Students:* Average age 47. In 2006, 1 degree awarded. *Degree requirements:* For master's, one foreign language, comprehensive exam. *Entrance requirements:* For master's, GRE General Test (recommended). *Application deadline:* For fall admission, 4/15 priority date for domestic students; for spring admission, 10/15 for domestic students. Applications are processed on a rolling basis. Application fee: $35. *Financial support:* In 2006–07, research assistantships with full tuition reimbursements (averaging $5,000 per year). Support available to part-time students. Financial award application deadline: 2/15; financial award applicants required to submit FAFSA. *Faculty research:* Solid phase rates into monodisperse polymers and palladium-mediated rates into novel materials. *Unit head:* Dr. Blaise Frost, Chair, 610-436-2631, Fax: 610-436-2840, E-mail: bfrost@wcupa.edu. *Application contact:* Dr. Naseer Ahmad, Graduate Coordinator, 610-436-2476, E-mail: anaseer@wcupa.edu.

Western Carolina University, Graduate School, College of Education and Allied Professions, Department of Educational Leadership and Foundations, Programs in Secondary Education, Cullowhee, NC 28723. Offers art education (MAT); biology (MAT); chemistry (MAT); comprehensive education (MA Ed), including art, biology, English, mathematics, music, physical education, reading, social sciences; English (MAT); family and consumer sciences (MAT); mathematics (MAT); physical education (MAT); reading (MAT); social sciences (MAT). *Accreditation:* NCATE (one or more programs are accredited). Part-time and evening/weekend programs available. *Degree requirements:* For master's, comprehensive exam. *Entrance requirements:* For master's, GRE General Test, portfolio. Additional exam requirements/recommendations for international students: Required—TOEFL (minimum score 550 paper-based; 213 computer-based).

Western Governors University, Teachers College, Salt Lake City, UT 84107. Offers English language learning (K-12) (MA); learning and technology (M Ed, MA); management and evaluation (M Ed); management and innovation (M Ed); mathematics education (5-12) (MA); mathematics education (5-9) (MA); mathematics education (K-6) (MA); science (5-12) (MA), including biology, geology; science education (509) (MA); technology (M Ed); technology for principals (Post-Graduate Certificate). *Accreditation:* NCATE. Part-time and evening/weekend programs available. Postbaccalaureate distance learning degree programs offered (no on-campus study). *Degree requirements:* For master's, comprehensive exam, registration. *Entrance requirements:* Additional exam requirements/recommendations for international students: Required—TOEFL (minimum score 450 paper-based). Electronic applications accepted. Expenses: Contact institution.

Western Kentucky University, Graduate Studies, Ogden College of Science and Engineering, Department of Biology, Bowling Green, KY 42101. Offers biology (MA Ed, MS). *Faculty:* 11 full-time (3 women). *Students:* 19 full-time (11 women), 13 part-time (11 women); includes 1 minority (Asian American or Pacific Islander), 11 international. Average age 28. 28 applicants, 64% accepted, 12 enrolled. In 2006, 5 degrees awarded. *Degree requirements:* For master's, research tool, thesis optional. *Entrance requirements:* For master's, GRE General Test, minimum GPA of 2.75. Additional exam requirements/recommendations for international students: Required—TOEFL (minimum score 555 paper-based; 213 computer-based; 79 iBT). *Application deadline:* For fall admission, 7/1 priority date for domestic students, 4/1 for international students; for spring admission, 11/1 for domestic students, 9/1 for international students. Applications are processed on a rolling basis. Application fee: $35. *Expenses:* Tuition, state resident: full-time $6,520; part-time $226 per hour. Tuition, nonresident: full-time $7,140; part-time $357 per hour. International tuition: $15,820 full-time. *Financial support:* In 2006–07, 7 research assistantships with partial tuition reimbursements (averaging $10,000 per year), 10 teaching assistantships with partial tuition reimbursements (averaging $10,000 per year) were awarded; Federal Work-Study, institutionally sponsored loans, tuition waivers (partial), unspecified assistantships, and service awards also available. Support available to part-time students. Financial award application deadline: 4/1; financial award applicants required to submit FAFSA. *Faculty research:* Phytoremediation, culturing of salt water organisms, PCR-based standards, biological monitoring (water) bioremediation, genetic diversity. Total annual research expenditures: $81,235. *Unit head:* Dr. Richard G. Bowker, Interim Dean, Graduate Studies, 270-745-3696, Fax: 270-745-6856, E-mail: richard.bowker@wku.edu.

Western Kentucky University, Graduate Studies, Ogden College of Science and Engineering, Department of Chemistry, Bowling Green, KY 42101. Offers chemistry (MA Ed, MS). *Faculty:* 9 full-time (3 women). *Students:* 9 full-time (6 women), 6 part-time (4 women), 5 international. Average age 26. 9 applicants, 56% accepted, 5 enrolled. In 2006, 4 degrees awarded. *Degree requirements:* For master's, thesis, comprehensive exam. *Entrance requirements:* For master's, GRE General Test, minimum GPA of 2.75. Additional exam requirements/recommendations for international students: Required—TOEFL (minimum score 555 paper-based; 213 computer-based). *Application deadline:* For fall admission, 7/1 priority date for domestic students, 4/1 for international students; for spring admission, 11/1 for domestic students, 9/1 for international students. Applications are processed on a rolling basis. Application fee: $35. *Expenses:* Tuition, state resident: full-time $6,520; part-time $226 per hour. Tuition, nonresident: full-time $7,140; part-time $357 per hour. International tuition: $15,820 full-time. *Financial support:* In 2006–07, 3 research assistantships with partial tuition reimbursements (averaging $8,000 per year), 8 teaching assistantships with partial tuition reimbursements (averaging $8,000 per year) were awarded; Federal Work-Study, institutionally sponsored loans, tuition waivers (partial), and service awards also available. Support available to part-time students. Financial award application deadline: 4/1; financial award applicants required to submit FAFSA. *Faculty research:* Catatonic surfactants, directed orthometalation reactions, thermal stability and degradation mechanisms, co-firing refused derived fuels, laser fluorescence. Total annual research expenditures: $202,172. *Unit head:* Dr. Cathleen J Webb, Head, 270-745-3457, Fax: 270-745-5361, E-mail: cathleen.webb@wku.edu.

Western Michigan University, Graduate College, College of Arts and Sciences, Mallinson Institute for Science Education, Kalamazoo, MI 49008-5202. Offers PhD. *Degree requirements:* For doctorate, thesis/dissertation, oral and written exams, comprehensive exam. *Entrance requirements:* For doctorate, GRE General Test. Electronic applications accepted. *Faculty research:* History and philosophy of science, curriculum and instruction, science content learning, college science teaching and learning, social and cultural factors in science education.

See Close-Up on page 1627.

Western Oregon University, Graduate Programs, College of Education, Division of Teacher Education, Program in Secondary Education, Monmouth, OR 97361-1394. Offers bilingual education (MS Ed); health (MS Ed); humanities (MAT, MS Ed); initial licensure (MAT); mathematics (MAT, MS Ed); science (MAT, MS Ed); social science (MAT, MS Ed). *Accreditation:* NCATE. Part-time and evening/weekend programs available. *Faculty:* 7 full-time (4 women), 15 part-time/adjunct (7 women). *Students:* 12 full-time (4 women), 21 part-time (10 women). Average age 32. In 2006, 31 degrees awarded. *Degree requirements:* For master's, written exam, thesis optional. *Entrance requirements:* For master's, minimum GPA of 3.0, teaching license. *Application deadline:* Applications are processed on a rolling basis. Application fee: $50. *Expenses:* Tuition, state resident: full-time $8,250; part-time $250 per credit. Tuition, nonresident: full-time $14,025; part-time $250 per credit. Required fees: $1,173. *Financial support:* In 2006–07, 16 teaching assistantships with full tuition reimbursements (averaging $706 per year) were awarded; research assistantships with full tuition reimbursements, career-related internships or fieldwork, Federal Work-Study, and tuition waivers (full and partial) also available. Support available to part-time students. Financial award application deadline: 3/1; financial award applicants required to submit FAFSA. *Faculty research:* Literacy, science in primary grades, geography education, retention, teacher burnout. *Unit head:* Dr. Mary Bucy, Unit Head, 503-838-8794, Fax: 503-838-8228. *Application contact:* Dr. David McDonald, Dean of Admissions, Retention and Enrollment Management, 503-838-8919, Fax: 503-838-8067, E-mail: mcdonald@wou.edu.

Western Washington University, Graduate School, Huxley College of the Environment, Department of Environmental Studies, Bellingham, WA 98225-5996. Offers geography (MS); natural science/science education (M Ed). Part-time programs available. *Faculty:* 26. *Degree requirements:* For master's, thesis. *Entrance requirements:* For master's, GRE General Test, minimum GPA of 3.0 in last 60 semester hours or last 90 quarter hours. Additional exam requirements/recommendations for international students: Required—TOEFL (minimum score 567 paper-based; 227 computer-based). *Application deadline:* For fall admission, 2/1 priority date for domestic students. Applications are processed on a rolling basis. Application fee: $50. *Expenses:* Tuition, state resident: full-time $6,609; part-time $199 per credit. Tuition, nonresident: full-time $16,845; part-time $540 per credit. *Financial support:* In 2006–07, 9 teaching assistantships with partial tuition reimbursements (averaging $9,339 per year) were awarded; Federal Work-Study, institutionally sponsored loans, scholarships/grants, tuition waivers (partial), and unspecified assistantships also available. Support available to part-time students. Financial award application deadline: 2/15; financial award applicants required to submit FAFSA. *Faculty research:* Geomorphology; pedogenesis; quaternary studies and climate change in the western U.S. landscape ecology, biogeography, pyrogeography, and spatial analysis. *Unit head:* Dr. Gigi Berardi, Chair, 360-650-3277, E-mail: gigi.berardi@wwu.edu.

Widener University, School of Human Service Professions, Center for Education, Chester, PA 19013-5792. Offers adult education (M Ed); counseling in higher education (M Ed); counselor education (M Ed); early childhood education (M Ed); educational foundations (M Ed); educational leadership (M Ed); educational psychology (M Ed); elementary education (M Ed); English and language arts (M Ed); health education (M Ed); higher education leadership (Ed D); home and school visitor (M Ed); human sexuality (M Ed); mathematics education (M Ed); middle school education (M Ed); principalship (M Ed); reading and language arts (Ed D); reading education (M Ed); school administration (Ed D); science education (M Ed); social studies education (M Ed); special education (M Ed); technology education (M Ed). Part-time and evening/weekend programs available. Terminal master's awarded for partial completion of doctoral program. *Degree requirements:* For doctorate, thesis/dissertation. *Entrance requirements:* For master's, minimum GPA of 2.5; for doctorate, GRE or MAT, minimum GPA of 2.0 (undergraduate), 3.5 (graduate). Electronic applications accepted. Expenses: Contact institution. *Faculty research:* Reading and cognition, adult education, technology education, educational leadership, special education.

Wilkes University, Graduate Studies and Continued Learning, College of Arts, Humanities and Social Sciences, Program in Teacher Education, Wilkes-Barre, PA 18766-0002. Offers classroom technology (MS Ed); educational computing (MS Ed); educational development and strategies (MS Ed); educational leadership (MS Ed); elementary education (MS Ed); instructional technology (MS Ed); school business leadership (MS Ed); secondary education (MS Ed), including biology, chemistry, English, history; special education (MS Ed). Part-time and evening/weekend programs available. Postbaccalaureate distance learning degree programs offered (minimal on-campus study). *Students:* 32 full-time (21 women), 1,588 part-time (1,106 women); includes 29 minority (6 African Americans, 2 American Indian/Alaska Native, 4 Asian Americans or Pacific Islanders, 17 Hispanic Americans). Average age 33. In 2006, 754 degrees awarded. *Entrance requirements:* Additional exam requirements/recommendations for international students: Required—TOEFL (minimum score 500 paper-based; 173 computer-based). *Application deadline:* Applications are processed on a rolling basis. Application fee: $40. *Expenses:* Contact institution. *Financial support:* Federal Work-Study and unspecified assistantships available. Financial award application deadline: 3/1; financial award applicants required to submit FAFSA. *Unit head:* Dr. Michael Speziale, Interim Dean, 570-408-4679, Fax: 570-408-4905, E-mail: michael.speziale@wilkes.edu. *Application contact:* Kathleen Houlihan, Director of Graduate Studies, 570-408-3235, Fax: 570-408-7846, E-mail: kathleen.houlihan@wilkes.edu.

Wright State University, School of Graduate Studies, College of Science and Mathematics, Department of Earth and Environmental Sciences, Program in Earth Science Education, Dayton, OH 45435. Offers MST. *Students:* 36 full-time (27 women), 8 part-time (5 women); includes 2 minority (1 African American, 1 Asian American or Pacific Islander). 10 applicants, 100% accepted. In 2006, 24 degrees awarded. *Entrance requirements:* For master's, GRE General Test. Additional exam requirements/recommendations for international students: Required—TOEFL. Application fee: $25. *Financial support:* Fellowships, research assistantships, teaching assistantships available. Support available to part-time students. Financial award application deadline: 3/1; financial award applicants required to submit FAFSA. *Faculty research:* Pedagogy. *Unit head:* Dr. William Slattery, Program Director, 937-775-3441, Fax: 937-775-3462, E-mail: william.slattery@wright.edu. *Application contact:* Deborah L. Cowles, Assistant to Chair, 937-775-3455, Fax: 937-775-3462, E-mail: deborah.cowles@wright.edu.

Wright State University, School of Graduate Studies, College of Science and Mathematics, Department of Physics, Program in Physics Education, Dayton, OH 45435. Offers MST. Part-time and evening/weekend programs available. *Students:* Average age 35. 4 applicants, 75% accepted. In 2006, 3 degrees awarded. *Entrance requirements:* Additional exam requirements/recommendations for international students: Required—TOEFL. *Application deadline:* For fall admission, 3/1 priority date for domestic students. Applications are processed on a rolling basis. Application fee: $25. *Financial support:* Fellowships, research assistantships, teaching assistantships, Federal Work-Study, institutionally sponsored loans, and tuition waivers (full and partial) available. Support available to part-time students. Financial award application deadline: 3/1; financial award applicants required to submit FAFSA. *Faculty research:* Pedagogy. *Unit head:* Dr. Lok Lew Yan Voon, Chair, Department of Physics, 937-775-2954, Fax: 937-775-2222, E-mail: lok.lewyanvoon@wright.edu.

Wright State University, School of Graduate Studies, College of Science and Mathematics, Interdisciplinary Program in Science and Mathematics, Dayton, OH 45435. Offers MST. *Students:* 4 full-time (all women), 2 part-time (1 woman); includes 1 minority (African American) *Unit head:* Dr. Beth Basista, Director, 937-775-2954, Fax: 937-775-2571, E-mail: beth.basista@wright.edu.

Social Sciences Education

Acadia University, Faculty of Professional Studies, School of Education, Program in Curriculum Studies, Wolfville, NS B4P 2R6, Canada. Offers cultural and media studies (M Ed); inclusive education (M Ed); learning and technology (M Ed); science, math and technology (M Ed). Evening/weekend programs available. *Faculty:* 12 full-time (5 women). *Students:* 2 full-time (both women), 27 part-time (19 women). In 2006, 25 degrees awarded. *Degree requirements:* For master's, thesis optional. *Entrance requirements:* For master's, B Ed or the equivalent, minimum B average in undergraduate course work, 2 years of teaching experience. Additional exam requirements/recommendations for international students: Required—TOEFL (minimum score 580 paper-based; 237 computer-based). *Application deadline:* For fall admission, 3/15 priority date for domestic and international students. Application fee: $50. Electronic applications accepted. *Financial support:* Teaching assistantships available. Financial award application deadline: 2/1. *Faculty research:* Literacy development, postmodern philosophy and curriculum theory, historiography, philosophy of education, learning and technology. *Application contact:* Sheila Langille, Secretary, 902-585-1229, Fax: 902-585-1071, E-mail: sheila.langille@acadiau.ca.

Alabama State University, School of Graduate Studies, College of Education, Department of Curriculum and Instruction, Program in Secondary Education, Montgomery, AL 36101-0271. Offers biology education (M Ed, Ed S); English/language arts (M Ed); history education (M Ed, Ed S); mathematics education (M Ed); secondary education (Ed S); social studies (Ed S). Part-time programs available. *Students:* 31 full-time (23 women), 123 part-time (81 women); includes 114 minority (111 African Americans, 2 Asian Americans or Pacific Islanders, 1 Hispanic American), 1 international. In 2006, 27 degrees awarded. *Degree requirements:* For master's, comprehensive exam; for Ed S, thesis, comprehensive exam. *Entrance requirements:* For master's, GRE General Test, MAT, graduate writing competency test; for Ed S, graduate writing competency test, GRE, MAT. Additional exam requirements/recommendations for international students: Required—TOEFL (minimum score 500 paper-based; 173 computer-based). *Application deadline:* For fall admission, 7/15 for domestic students; for spring admission, 12/15 for domestic students. Applications are processed on a rolling basis. Application fee: $10. *Expenses:* Tuition, state resident: full-time $1,728; part-time $192 per hour. Tuition, nonresident: full-time $3,456; part-time $334 per hour. *Financial support:* In 2006–07, research assistantships (averaging $9,450 per year).

Albany State University, College of Education, Program in Social Science Education, Albany, GA 31705-2717. Offers M Ed. *Degree requirements:* For master's, comprehensive exam. Electronic applications accepted.

Andrews University, School of Graduate Studies, College of Arts and Sciences, Department of History, Berrien Springs, MI 49104. Offers MA, MAT. Part-time programs available. *Degree requirements:* For master's, variable foreign language requirement, thesis optional. *Entrance requirements:* For master's, GRE Subject Test. *Faculty research:* American intellectual history, Civil War, American church history, modern German history.

Andrews University, School of Graduate Studies, School of Education, Department of Teaching, Learning, and Curriculum, Berrien Springs, MI 49104. Offers curriculum and instruction (MA, Ed D, PhD, Ed S); elementary education (MAT); reading (MA); secondary education (MAT), including biology, education, English, English as a second language, French, history, physics; special education/learning disabilities (MS); teacher education (MAT). *Entrance requirements:* For master's, GRE Subject Test.

Appalachian State University, Cratis D. Williams Graduate School, College of Arts and Sciences, Department of History, Boone, NC 28608. Offers history (MA); history education (MA); public history (MA). Part-time programs available. *Faculty:* 28 full-time (8 women). *Students:* 21 full-time (9 women), 18 part-time (7 women); includes 2 minority (1 Asian American or Pacific Islander, 1 Hispanic American), 1 international. 32 applicants, 97% accepted, 27 enrolled. In 2006, 16 degrees awarded. *Degree requirements:* For master's, one foreign language, thesis (for some programs), comprehensive exam. *Entrance requirements:* For master's, GRE General Test, minimum GPA of 3.0. Additional exam requirements/recommendations for international students: Required—TOEFL (minimum score 570 paper-based; 230 computer-based). *Application deadline:* For fall admission, 7/1 for domestic students, 1/1 for international students; for spring admission, 11/1 for domestic students, 6/1 for international students. Applications are processed on a rolling basis. Application fee: $50. *Expenses:* Tuition, state resident: full-time $2,600; part-time $127 per hour. Tuition, nonresident: full-time $13,200; part-time $597 per hour. Required fees: $2,000; $546 per term. *Financial support:* In 2006–07, 12 teaching assistantships (averaging $7,000 per year) were awarded; fellowships, research assistantships, career-related internships or fieldwork, Federal Work-Study, scholarships/grants, and unspecified assistantships also available. Support available to part-time students. Financial award application deadline: 7/1; financial award applicants required to submit FAFSA. *Faculty research:* Women's history, social/cultural history, US history, Latin America, medieval studies. *Unit head:* Dr. Michael Krenn, Chairperson, 828-262-2282. *Application contact:* Dr. James Goff, Director, 828-262-6019, E-mail: goffjr@appstate.edu.

Arcadia University, Graduate Studies, Department of Education, Glenside, PA 19038-3295. Offers art education (M Ed, MA Ed); biology education (MA Ed); chemistry education (MA Ed); child development (CAS); computer education (M Ed, CAS); computer education 7–12 (MA Ed); early childhood education (M Ed, CAS), including individualized (M Ed), master teacher (M Ed), research in child development (M Ed); educational leadership (M Ed, CAS); educational psychology (CAS); elementary education (M Ed, CAS); English education (MA Ed); environmental education (MA Ed, CAS); history education (MA Ed); language arts (M Ed, CAS); mathematics education (M Ed, MA Ed, CAS); music education (MA Ed); psychology (MA Ed); pupil personnel services (CAS); reading (M Ed, CAS); school library science (M Ed); science education (M Ed, CAS); secondary education (M Ed, CAS); special education (M Ed, Ed D, CAS); theater arts (MA Ed); written communication (MA Ed). *Accreditation:* NASAD. Part-time and evening/weekend programs available. Postbaccalaureate distance learning degree programs offered (minimal on-campus study). *Faculty:* 12 full-time (8 women), 38 part-time/adjunct (26 women). *Students:* 60 full-time (56 women), 419 part-time (324 women); includes 70 minority (57 African Americans, 1 American Indian/Alaska Native, 6 Asian Americans or Pacific Islanders, 6 Hispanic Americans), 1 international. In 2006, 257 master's, 4 doctorates awarded. *Application deadline:* Applications are processed on a rolling basis. Application fee: $35. Electronic applications accepted. *Financial support:* Career-related internships or fieldwork, tuition waivers (partial), and unspecified assistantships available. *Unit head:* Dr. Steven P. Gulkus, Chair, 215-572-2120. *Application contact:* 215-572-2925, Fax: 215-572-2126, E-mail: grad@arcadia.edu.

Arkansas State University, Graduate School, College of Humanities and Social Sciences, Department of History, Jonesboro, State University, AR 72467. Offers heritage studies (PhD); history (MA, SCCT); social science (MSE). Part-time programs available. *Faculty:* 14 full-time (7 women), 2 part-time/adjunct (1 woman). *Students:* 22 full-time (13 women), 45 part-time (29 women); includes 6 minority (all African Americans), 2 international. Average age 38. 75 applicants, 84% accepted, 49 enrolled. In 2006, 17 master's, 2 doctorates awarded. *Degree requirements:* For master's, thesis or alternative, comprehensive exam; for doctorate, thesis/dissertation, comprehensive exam. *Entrance requirements:* For master's, GRE General Test or MAT, GMAT, appropriate bachelor's degree, letters of reference, official transcript; for doctorate, appropriate master's degree, interview, letters of reference, official transcript; for SCCT, GRE General Test or MAT, interview, master's degree, letters of reference, official transcript. Additional exam requirements/recommendations for international students: Required—TOEFL (minimum score 213 computer-based). *Application deadline:* Applications are processed on a rolling basis. Application fee: $30 ($40 for international students). Electronic applications accepted. *Expenses:* Tuition, state resident: full-time $3,393; part-time $189 per hour. Tuition, nonresident: full-time $8,577; part-time $477 per hour. Required fees: $752; $39 per hour. $25 per semester. *Financial support:* Fellowships, teaching assistantships, scholarships/grants, tuition waivers, and unspecified assistantships available. Financial award application deadline: 7/1; financial award applicants required to submit FAFSA. *Unit head:* Dr. Pamela Hronek, Chair, 870-972-3046, Fax: 870-972-2880, E-mail: phronek@astate.edu.

Arkansas Tech University, Graduate School, School of Liberal and Fine Arts, Russellville, AR 72801. Offers communication (MLA); English (M Ed, MA); fine arts (MLA); history (MA); multi-media journalism (MA); social science (MLA); social studies (M Ed); Spanish (MA, MLA); teaching English as a second language (MA, MLA). Part-time programs available. *Students:* 47 full-time (36 women), 102 part-time (82 women); includes 9 minority (2 African Americans, 1 American Indian/Alaska Native, 1 Asian American or Pacific Islander, 5 Hispanic Americans), 20 international. Average age 33. In 2006, 20 degrees awarded. *Degree requirements:* For master's, project. *Entrance requirements:* For master's, GRE General Test or MAT. Additional exam requirements/recommendations for international students: Required—TOEFL (minimum score 500 paper-based; 173 computer-based). *Application deadline:* For fall admission, 3/1 priority date for domestic students, 5/1 priority date for international students; for winter admission, 10/1 priority date for international students; for spring admission, 10/1 priority date for domestic and international students. Applications are processed on a rolling basis. Application fee: $0 ($30 for international students). Electronic applications accepted. *Expenses:* Tuition, state resident: full-time $3,060; part-time $170 per hour. Tuition, nonresident: full-time $6,120; part-time $340 per hour. Required fees: $312; $4 per hour. $84 per term. Part-time tuition and fees vary according to course load. *Financial support:* In 2006–07, teaching assistantships with full tuition reimbursements (averaging $4,000 per year); career-related internships or fieldwork, Federal Work-Study, scholarships/grants, health care benefits, and unspecified assistantships also available. Support available to part-time students. Financial award application deadline: 4/15; financial award applicants required to submit FAFSA. *Unit head:* Dr. Georgena Duncan, Dean, 479-968-0266, Fax: 479-968-0275, E-mail: georgena.duncan@atu.edu. *Application contact:* Dr. Eldon G. Clary, Dean of Graduate School, 479-968-0398, Fax: 479-964-0542, E-mail: graduate.school@atu.edu.

Armstrong Atlantic State University, School of Graduate Studies, Program in Education, Savannah, GA 31419-1997. Offers adult education (M Ed); early childhood education (M Ed); education (M Ed); elementary education (M Ed); middle grades education (M Ed); secondary education (M Ed), including business education, English education, mathematics education, science education, social science education; special education (M Ed), including behavioral disorders, curriculum and instruction, learning disabilities, speech-language pathology. *Accreditation:* NCATE. Part-time and evening/weekend programs available. Postbaccalaureate distance learning degree programs offered (minimal on-campus study). *Faculty:* 11 full-time (9 women), 13 part-time/adjunct (10 women). *Students:* 50 full-time (42 women), 219 part-time (175 women); includes 71 minority (67 African Americans, 3 Asian Americans or Pacific Islanders, 1 Hispanic American), 6 international. Average age 35. In 2006, 151 degrees awarded. *Degree requirements:* For master's, portfolio. *Entrance requirements:* For master's, GRE General Test or MAT, minimum GPA of 2.5, letters of recommendation. Additional exam

Social Sciences Education

Armstrong Atlantic State University (continued)
requirements/recommendations for international students: Required—TOEFL (minimum score 523 paper-based; 193 computer-based). *Application deadline:* For fall admission, 7/1 priority date for domestic and international students; for spring admission, 11/15 priority date for domestic and international students. Applications are processed on a rolling basis. Application fee: $25. Electronic applications accepted. *Expenses:* Tuition, state resident: full-time $2,286; part-time $127 per credit. Tuition, nonresident: full-time $9,144; part-time $508 per credit. One-time fee: $257. *Financial support:* In 2006–07, research assistantships with partial tuition reimbursements (averaging $2,500 per year); career-related internships or fieldwork, Federal Work-Study, scholarships/grants, and unspecified assistantships also available. Support available to part-time students. Financial award applicants required to submit FAFSA. *Unit head:* Dr. Jane McHaney, College of Education Dean, 912-927-5398, Fax: 912-921-7425, E-mail: mchaneia@mail.armstrong.edu.

Asbury College, Graduate Programs, Wilmore, KY 40390-1198. Offers biology: alternative certificate (MA Ed); chemistry: alternative certificate (MA Ed); English (Certificate); English as a second language (MA Ed); ESL (Certificate); French (Certificate); mathematics: alternative certificate (MA Ed); reading / writing (MA Ed); social studies (Certificate); Spanish (Certificate); special education (MA Ed); special education: alternative certificate (MA Ed). *Accreditation:* NCATE. Part-time programs available. *Faculty:* 8 full-time (7 women), 9 part-time/adjunct (4 women). *Students:* Average age 36. 14 applicants, 100% accepted, 10 enrolled. In 2006, 17 degrees awarded. *Median time to degree:* Master's–2.5 years part-time. *Degree requirements:* For master's, action research project, portfolio. *Entrance requirements:* For master's, PRAXIS/NTE or GRE, minimum GPA of 2.75, letters of recommendation. Additional exam requirements/recommendations for international students: Recommended—TOEFL (minimum score 550 paper-based). *Application deadline:* Applications are processed on a rolling basis. Application fee: $25. *Expenses:* Tuition: Part-time $335 per credit hour. *Financial support:* Scholarships/grants and traineeships available. Financial award applicants required to submit FAFSA. *Unit head:* Dr. Bonnie J. Banker, Director, 859-858-3511 Ext. 2221, Fax: 859-858-3921, E-mail: bonnie.banker@asbury.edu. *Application contact:* Melanie S. Kinnell, Graduate Program Assistant and Certification Specialist, 859-858-3511 Ext. 2304, Fax: 859-858-3921, E-mail: graded@asbury.edu.

Auburn University, Graduate School, College of Education, Department of Curriculum and Teaching, Auburn University, AL 36849. Offers business education (M Ed, MS, PhD); early childhood education (M Ed, MS, PhD, Ed S); elementary education (M Ed, MS, PhD, Ed S); foreign languages (M Ed, MS); music education (M Ed, MS, PhD, Ed S); postsecondary education (PhD); reading education (PhD, Ed S); secondary education (M Ed, MS, PhD, Ed S), including English language arts, mathematics, science, social studies. *Accreditation:* NASM (one or more programs are accredited); NCATE. Part-time programs available. *Faculty:* 26 full-time (19 women). *Students:* 51 full-time (36 women), 116 part-time (86 women); includes 24 minority (23 African Americans, 1 Asian American or Pacific Islander). Average age 33. 181 applicants, 56% accepted, 68 enrolled. In 2006, 63 master's, 12 doctorates, 14 other advanced degrees awarded. *Degree requirements:* For master's, thesis (for some programs); for doctorate, thesis/dissertation; for Ed S, field project. *Entrance requirements:* For master's, doctorate, and Ed S, GRE General Test. *Application deadline:* For fall admission, 7/7 for domestic students; for spring admission, 11/24 for domestic students. Applications are processed on a rolling basis. Application fee: $25 ($50 for international students). Electronic applications accepted. *Expenses:* Tuition, state resident: full-time $5,000. Tuition, nonresident: full-time $15,000. Required fees: $416. Tuition and fees vary according to program. *Financial support:* Fellowships, teaching assistantships, career-related internships or fieldwork and Federal Work-Study available. Support available to part-time students. Financial award application deadline: 3/15. *Faculty research:* Emerging literacy, reading attitudes, music for at-risk youth, portfolio assessment. *Unit head:* Dr. Andrew M. Weaver, Head, 334-844-4434, E-mail: weaveam@mail.auburn.edu. *Application contact:* Dr. Joe Pittman, Interim Dean of the Graduate School, 334-844-4700.

Averett University, Graduate Studies in Education, Danville, VA 24541-3692. Offers art education (M Ed); biology (M Ed); chemistry (M Ed); curriculum and instruction (M Ed); elementary education (M Ed); English (M Ed); health and physical education (M Ed); history and social studies (M Ed); mathematics education (M Ed); physical science (M Ed); reading (M Ed); special education (learning disabilities specialization PK-12) (M Ed). Part-time and evening/weekend programs available. *Faculty:* 10 full-time (4 women), 7 part-time/adjunct (6 women). *Students:* 14 full-time (10 women), 85 part-time (67 women); includes 20 minority (18 African Americans, 2 Asian Americans or Pacific Islanders). Average age 33. 52 applicants, 100% accepted, 40 enrolled. In 2006, 48 degrees awarded. *Degree requirements:* For master's, thesis optional. *Entrance requirements:* For master's, PRAXIS, GRE General Test, MAT or NTE, writing proficiency exam, 3 letters of recommendation, current teacher's licensure or eligibility for licensure, minimum undergraduate GPA of 3.0 in previous 2 years. Additional exam requirements/recommendations for international students: Required—TOEFL (minimum score 600 paper-based; 200 computer-based). *Application deadline:* Applications are processed on a rolling basis. Application fee: $20. *Expenses:* Contact institution. *Financial support:* In 2006–07, 23 students received support. Federal Work-Study and scholarships/grants available. Financial award application deadline: 4/1; financial award applicants required to submit FAFSA. *Faculty research:* Literary assessment-PreK-6, handwriting instruction and assessment-PreK-6, written language instruction and assessment-PreK-6 and special needs students learning styles, curriculum and instruction processes. *Unit head:* Dr. Lynn H. Wolf, Chair, 434-793-3995, Fax: 434-791-4392, E-mail: lynn.wolf@averett.edu.

Belmont University, College of Arts and Sciences, School of Education, Nashville, TN 37212-3757. Offers education (MAT); elementary education (M Ed), including early childhood education, elementary education, gifted education, language arts education; English (M Ed); history (M Ed); mathematics (M Ed); middle grade education (M Ed); science (M Ed); secondary education (M Ed), including gifted education; sports administration (MSA); technology (M Ed). *Accreditation:* NCATE. Part-time and evening/weekend programs available. *Faculty:* 9 full-time (7 women), 20 part-time/adjunct (15 women). *Students:* 50 full-time (36 women), 116 part-time (76 women); includes 23 minority (20 African Americans, 1 Asian American or Pacific Islander, 2 Hispanic Americans), 1 international. Average age 30. 55 applicants, 60% accepted, 30 enrolled. In 2006, 82 degrees awarded. *Degree requirements:* For master's, thesis, comprehensive exam. *Entrance requirements:* For master's, MAT or GRE, minimum GPA of 2.75. Additional exam requirements/recommendations for international students: Required—TOEFL. *Application deadline:* For fall admission, 8/1 priority date for domestic students, 5/1 for international students; for spring admission, 12/1 priority date for domestic students, 9/1 for international students. Applications are processed on a rolling basis. Application fee: $50. *Expenses:* Contact institution. *Financial support:* In 2006–07, 25 students received support; fellowships with partial tuition reimbursements available, institutionally sponsored loans and tuition waivers (partial) available. Financial award application deadline: 4/15; financial award applicants required to submit FAFSA. *Faculty research:* Technology grant, professional development schools. Total annual research expenditures: $6,500. *Unit head:* Dr. Trevor F. Hutchins, Associate Dean, 615-460-6232, Fax: 615-460-6414, E-mail: hutchinst@mail.belmont.edu. *Application contact:* Julie Hullett, Admission/Licensure Officer, 615-460-6879, Fax: 615-460-5556, E-mail: hullettj@email.belmont.edu.

Bennington College, Graduate Programs, Program in Teaching, Bennington, VT 05201. Offers art education (MAT); early childhood (MAT); elementary education (MAT); English education (MAT); foreign language education (MAT); mathematics education (MAT); music education (MAT); science education (MAT); secondary education (MAT); social science education (MAT). *Faculty:* 4 part-time/adjunct (3 women). *Students:* 11 full-time (7 women), 1 (woman) part-time; includes 2 minority (both Hispanic Americans) Average age 31. 12 applicants, 75% accepted, 3 enrolled. In 2006, 13 degrees awarded. *Degree requirements:* For master's, 1 year teaching practicum, professional portfolio. *Entrance requirements:* For master's, interview. *Application deadline:* For fall admission, 3/1 for domestic students. Application fee: $60. *Expenses:* Contact institution. One-time fee: $75 full-time. Tuition and fees vary according to program. *Financial support:* In 2006–07, 10 students received support, including 4 fellowships (averaging $6,875 per year); scholarships/grants and unspecified assistantships also available. Financial award application deadline: 4/1; financial award applicants required to submit FAFSA. *Unit head:* George Kamberelis, Director of Center for Creative Teaching, 802-440-4863, E-mail: gkamberelis@bennington.edu. *Application contact:* Ken Himmelman, Dean of Admissions, 802-440-4312, Fax: 802-440-4320, E-mail: admissions@bennington.edu.

See Close-Up on page 861.

Bethel College, Program in Education, McKenzie, TN 38201. Offers administration and supervision (MA Ed); biology education K8-12 (MAT); elementary education (MAT); English education K8-12 (MAT); history education K8-12 (MAT); physical education K8-12 (MAT); special education K8-12 (MAT). Part-time and evening/weekend programs available. *Degree requirements:* For master's, thesis (for some programs). *Entrance requirements:* For master's, GRE General Test or MAT, minimum undergraduate GPA of 2.5.

Bob Jones University, Graduate Programs, Greenville, SC 29614. Offers accountancy (MS); Bible (MA); Bible translation (MA); Biblical studies (Certificate); broadcast management (MS); business administration (MBA); church history (MA, PhD); church ministries (MA); church music (MM); cinema and video production (MA); counseling (MS); curriculum and instruction (Ed D); divinity (M Div); dramatic production (MA); educational leadership (MS, Ed D, Ed S); elementary education (M Ed, MAT); English (M Ed, MA, MAT); fine arts (MA); graphic design (MA); history (M Ed, MA); illustration (MA); interpretative speech (MA); mathematics (M Ed, MAT); medical missions (Certificate); ministry (MM, D Min); multi-categorical special education (M Ed, MAT); music (M Ed); New Testament interpretation (PhD); Old Testament interpretation (PhD); orchestral instrument performance (MM); organ performance (MM); pastoral studies (MA); personnel services (MS, Ed S); piano pedagogy (MM); piano performance (MM); platform arts (MA); radio and television broadcasting (MS); rhetoric and public address (MA); secondary education (M Ed); studio art (MA); teaching Bible (MA); theology (MA, PhD); voice performance (MM); youth ministries (MA); M Div/MM.

Boston College, Lynch Graduate School of Education, Department of Teacher Education/Special Education and Curriculum and Instruction, Program in Secondary Education, Chestnut Hill, MA 02467-3800. Offers biology (MST); chemistry (MST); English (MAT); French (MAT); geology (MST); history (MAT); Latin and classical humanities (MAT); mathematics (MST); physics (MST); secondary teaching (M Ed), including biology, chemistry, English, French, geology, history, Latin and classical humanities, mathematics, physics, Spanish; Spanish (MAT). *Students:* 70 full-time (46 women), 28 part-time (15 women); includes 8 minority (4 African Americans, 1 American Indian/Alaska Native, 3 Asian Americans or Pacific Islanders), 2 international. 217 applicants, 72% accepted, 64 enrolled. In 2006, 48 degrees awarded. *Degree requirements:* For master's, comprehensive exam. *Entrance requirements:* For master's, GRE General Test or MAT. Additional exam requirements/recommendations for international students: Required—TOEFL. *Application deadline:* For fall admission, 1/1 priority date for domestic students. Application fee: $60. *Financial support:* Fellowships with full and partial tuition reimbursements, research assistantships with full and partial tuition reimbursements, teaching assistantships with full and partial tuition reimbursements, career-related internships or fieldwork, Federal Work-Study, scholarships/grants, traineeships, tuition waivers (full and partial), and unspecified assistantships available. Support available to part-time students. Financial award applicants required to submit FAFSA. *Faculty research:* Curriculum theory and practice, teacher preparation, learning styles, teacher research. *Application contact:* Timothy P. Blackman, Director, Graduate Admission and Financial Aid, 617-552-4214, Fax: 617-552-0398, E-mail: timothy.blackman.1@bc.edu.

Boston University, School of Education, Department of Curriculum and Teaching, Program in Social Studies Education, Boston, MA 02215. Offers Ed M, MAT, Ed D, CAGS. *Students:* 12 full-time (6 women), 3 part-time (1 woman); includes 1 minority (Hispanic American) Average age 26. 58 applicants, 74% accepted. In 2006, 11 degrees awarded. *Degree requirements:* For master's, thesis optional; for doctorate, thesis/dissertation, comprehensive exam. *Entrance requirements:* For master's, doctorate, and CAGS, GRE General Test or MAT. Additional exam requirements/recommendations for international students: Required—TOEFL. *Application deadline:* For fall admission, 2/15 priority date for domestic students; for winter admission, 11/1 priority date for domestic students. Applications are processed on a rolling basis. Application fee: $70. Electronic applications accepted. *Expenses:* Tuition: Full-time $33,330; part-time $1,042 per credit. Required fees: $462; $40. *Financial support:* Application deadline: 2/15. *Faculty research:* Law-focused and intercultural education. *Unit head:* Dr. Dan Davis, Head, 617-353-3314, E-mail: dfdavis@bu.edu. *Application contact:* 617-353-4237, Fax: 617-353-8937, E-mail: sedgrad@bu.edu.

Bridgewater State College, School of Graduate Studies, School of Arts and Sciences, Department of History, Bridgewater, MA 02325-0001. Offers MAT. Part-time and evening/weekend programs available. *Entrance requirements:* For master's, GRE General Test. *Application deadline:* For fall admission, 3/1 priority date for domestic students; for spring admission, 10/1 priority date for domestic students. Application fee: $50. *Financial support:* Career-related internships or fieldwork, health care benefits, and unspecified assistantships available. Support available to part-time students.

Brooklyn College of the City University of New York, Division of Graduate Studies, School of Education, Program in Adolescence Education and Special Subjects, Brooklyn, NY 11210-2889. Offers art teacher (MA); biology teacher (MA); chemistry teacher (MA); English teacher (MA); French teacher (MA); health and nutrition sciences: health teacher (MS Ed); mathematics teacher (MA); music education (CAS); music teacher (MA); physical education teacher (MS Ed); physics teacher (MA); social studies teacher (MA); Spanish teacher (MA). Part-time and evening/weekend programs available. *Students:* 30 full-time (22 women), 450 part-time (257 women); includes 167 minority (101 African Americans, 21 Asian Americans or Pacific Islanders, 45 Hispanic Americans), 21 international. 277 applicants, 84% accepted, 113 enrolled. In 2006, 172 master's, 6 other advanced degrees awarded. *Degree requirements:* For master's, comprehensive exam (for some programs). *Entrance requirements:* For master's, LAST, previous course work in education, resumé, 2 letters of recommendation, essay. Additional exam requirements/recommendations for international students: Required—TOEFL. *Application deadline:* For fall admission, 3/1 priority date for domestic students, 2/1 priority date for international students; for spring admission, 11/1 priority date for domestic students, 10/1 priority date for international students. Applications are processed on a rolling basis. Application fee: $125. Electronic applications accepted. *Expenses:* Tuition, state resident: full-time $6,400; part-time $270 per credit. Tuition, nonresident: full-time $12,000; part-time $500 per credit. Required fees: $118 per semester. *Financial support:* Career-related internships or fieldwork, Federal Work-Study, institutionally sponsored loans, and scholarships/grants available. Support available to part-time students. Financial award application deadline: 5/1; financial award applicants required to submit FAFSA. *Faculty research:* Interdisciplinary education, semiotics, discourse analysis, autobiography, teacher identity. *Unit head:* Prof. Stephen Phillips, Program Facilitator, 718-951-5214, E-mail: phillips@brooklyn.cuny.edu. *Application contact:* Karen Alleyne-Pierre, Director of Admissions Services and Enrollment Communications, 718-951-5902, Fax: 718-951-4506, E-mail: grads@brooklyn.cuny.edu.

Brown University, Graduate School, Department of Education, Providence, RI 02912. Offers elementary education 1-6 (MAT); secondary biology (MAT); secondary English (MAT); secondary social studies/history (MAT). *Faculty:* 4 full-time (2 women), 7 part-time/adjunct (all women). *Students:* 28 full-time (23 women); includes 5 minority (2 African Americans, 1 Asian American or Pacific Islander, 2 Hispanic Americans). Average age 25. 89 applicants, 61% accepted, 28 enrolled. In 2006, 35 degrees awarded. *Degree requirements:* For master's, student teaching, portfolio. *Entrance requirements:* For master's, GRE General Test (secondary only), PRAXIS II (elementary), letters of recommendation, interview. *Application deadline:* For winter admission, 1/3 for domestic students. Application fee: $70. Electronic applications accepted. *Financial support:* In 2006–07, 23 students received support, including 2 fellowships (averaging $7,000 per year); Federal Work-Study, institutionally sponsored loans, scholarships/grants, tuition waivers (partial), and proctorships also available. Financial award application deadline: 2/1; financial award applicants required to submit FAFSA. *Faculty research:* Literacy, performance-based assessment, teaching English as a foreign language. *Unit head:* Lawrence Wakeford, Chairman, 401-863-3428, Fax: 401-863-1276, E-mail: lawrence_wakeford@brown.edu. *Application contact:* Carin Algava, Assistant Director, 401-863-3364, Fax: 401-863-1276, E-mail: carin_algava@brown.edu.

Buffalo State College, State University of New York, Graduate Studies and Research, Faculty of Natural and Social Sciences, Department of History and Social Studies, Buffalo, NY 14222-1095. Offers history (MA); secondary education (MS Ed), including social studies. Part-time and evening/weekend programs available. *Degree requirements:* For master's, one foreign language, thesis (for some programs), project (MS Ed). *Entrance requirements:* For master's, minimum GPA of 2.75, 30 hours in history (MA), 36 hours in history or social sciences (MS Ed). Additional exam requirements/recommendations for international students: Required—TOEFL (minimum score 550 paper-based; 213 computer-based).

California State University, Chico, Graduate School, College of Behavioral and Social Sciences, Social Science Program, Chico, CA 95929-0445. Offers social science (MA); social science education (MA). *Students:* 7 full-time (3 women), 4 part-time (2 women); includes 2 minority (1 African American, 1 Hispanic American). Average age 35. 5 applicants, 100% accepted, 5 enrolled. In 2006, 5 degrees awarded. *Degree requirements:* For master's, thesis or alternative, oral exam. *Entrance requirements:* For master's, GRE General Test or MAT. Additional exam requirements/recommendations for international students: Required—TOEFL (minimum score 550 paper-based; 213 computer-based). *Application deadline:* For fall admission, 3/1 for domestic and international students; for spring admission, 9/15 for domestic and international students. Applications are processed on a rolling basis. Application fee: $55. Electronic applications accepted. *Financial support:* Fellowships, teaching assistantships available. *Unit head:* Dr. Gwen Sheldon, Graduate Coordinator, 530-895-5204.

California State University, San Bernardino, Graduate Studies, College of Education, San Bernardino, CA 92407-2397. Offers bilingual/cross-cultural education (MA); curriculum and instruction (MA); educational administration (MA); educational psychology and counseling (MA, MS), including counseling and guidance (MS), rehabilitation counseling (MA); elementary education (MA); English as a second language (MA); environmental education (MA); history and English for secondary teachers (MA); instructional technology (MA); reading (MA); secondary education (MA); special education and rehabilitation counseling (MA), including rehabilitation counseling, special education; teaching of science (MA); vocational and career education (MA). *Accreditation:* NCATE. Part-time and evening/weekend programs available. *Faculty:* 69 full-time, 145 part-time/adjunct. *Students:* 692 full-time (515 women), 345 part-time (245 women); includes 479 minority (145 African Americans, 12 American Indian/Alaska Native, 45 Asian Americans or Pacific Islanders, 277 Hispanic Americans), 17 international. Average age 33. 450 applicants, 82% accepted, 147 enrolled. In 2006, 349 degrees awarded. *Entrance requirements:* For master's, minimum GPA of 3.0 in education. *Application deadline:* For fall admission, 8/31 priority date for domestic students. Application fee: $55. *Financial support:* Career-related internships or fieldwork and Federal Work-Study available. Support available to part-time students. *Faculty research:* Multicultural education, brain-based learning, science education, social studies/global education. *Unit head:* Dr. Patricia Arlin, Dean, 909-537-5600, Fax: 909-537-7011, E-mail: parlin@csusb.edu.

Campbell University, Graduate and Professional Programs, School of Education, Buies Creek, NC 27506. Offers administration (MSA); community counseling (MA); elementary education (M Ed); English education (M Ed); interdisciplinary studies (M Ed); mathematics education (M Ed); middle grades education (M Ed); physical education (M Ed); school counseling (M Ed); secondary education (M Ed); social science education (M Ed). *Accreditation:* NCATE. Part-time and evening/weekend programs available. *Faculty:* 14 full-time (9 women), 12 part-time/adjunct (7 women). *Students:* 27 full-time (25 women), 183 part-time (146 women); includes 30 minority (24 African Americans, 3 American Indian/Alaska Native, 3 Hispanic Americans), 1 international. Average age 31. 112 applicants, 74% accepted, 74 enrolled. In 2006, 65 degrees awarded. *Degree requirements:* For master's, comprehensive exam. *Entrance requirements:* For master's, GRE General Test, minimum GPA of 2.7. *Application deadline:* For fall admission, 8/1 priority date for domestic students; for spring admission, 1/2 priority date for domestic students. Applications are processed on a rolling basis. Application fee: $65. *Expenses:* Tuition: Part-time $380 per semester hour. *Financial support:* In 2006–07, 67 students received support. Career-related internships or fieldwork and Federal Work-Study available. Financial award application deadline: 4/15; financial award applicants required to submit FAFSA. *Faculty research:* Spiritual values and wellness issues in counseling, stress and professional burnout among counselors, thinking strategies, leadership, adaptive technology. *Unit head:* Dr. Karen P. Nery, Dean, 910-893-1630, Fax: 910-893-1999, E-mail: nery@campbell.edu. *Application contact:* James S. Farthing, Director of Graduate Admissions for Business and Education, 910-893-1200 Ext. 1318, Fax: 910-814-4718, E-mail: farthing@campbell.edu.

Carthage College, Division of Teacher Education, Kenosha, WI 53140. Offers classroom guidance and counseling (M Ed); creative arts (M Ed); gifted and talented children (M Ed); language arts (M Ed); modern language (M Ed); natural sciences (M Ed); reading (M Ed, Certificate); social sciences (M Ed); teacher leadership (M Ed). Part-time and evening/weekend programs available. *Degree requirements:* For master's, thesis optional. *Entrance requirements:* For master's, MAT, minimum B average, letters of reference.

Chadron State College, School of Professional and Graduate Studies, Department of Education, Chadron, NE 69337. Offers business (MA Ed); community counseling (MA Ed); educational administration (MS Ed, Sp Ed); elementary education (MS Ed); history (MA Ed); language and literature (MA Ed); secondary administration (MS Ed); secondary education (MS Ed). *Accreditation:* NCATE. Part-time and evening/weekend programs available. Postbaccalaureate distance learning degree programs offered. *Degree requirements:* For master's, thesis optional. *Entrance requirements:* For master's, GRE General Test, GRE Writing Test, minimum GPA of 2.75 or 12 graduate hours at CSC with minimum GPA of 3.25. Additional exam requirements/recommendations for international students: Required—TOEFL. Electronic applications accepted. *Faculty research:* Rural education, technology, mental health.

Chaminade University of Honolulu, Graduate Services, Program in Education, Honolulu, HI 96816-1578. Offers social science via peace education (M Ed). Part-time and evening/weekend programs available. Postbaccalaureate distance learning degree programs offered (minimal on-campus study). *Faculty:* 7 full-time (6 women), 19 part-time/adjunct (17 women). *Students:* 197 full-time (148 women), 127 part-time (97 women); includes 225 minority (19 African Americans, 1 American Indian/Alaska Native, 191 Asian Americans or Pacific Islanders, 14 Hispanic Americans), 2 international. Average age 35. 236 applicants, 81% accepted. In 2006, 102 degrees awarded. *Degree requirements:* For master's, thesis or alternative. *Entrance requirements:* For master's, minimum GPA of 2.75. Additional exam requirements/recommendations for international students: Required—TOEFL (minimum score 550 paper-based). *Application deadline:* For fall admission, 9/15 priority date for domestic students; for winter admission, 12/15 priority date for domestic students; for spring admission, 3/1 priority date for domestic students. Applications are processed on a rolling basis. Application fee: $50. *Expenses:* Tuition: Part-time $465 per credit. *Financial support:* In 2006–07, 172 students received support. Career-related internships or fieldwork, Federal Work-Study, institutionally sponsored loans, scholarships/grants, and tuition waivers (partial) available. Support available to part-time students. Financial award application deadline: 3/1; financial award applicants required to submit FAFSA. *Faculty research:* Peace and curriculum education. *Unit head:* Dr. David Jelinek, Dean, 808-440-4251, Fax: 808-739-4607. *Application contact:* Steve Wheeler, Graduate Services Representative, 808-739-4664, Fax: 808-739-8329, E-mail: swheeler@chaminade.edu.

Charleston Southern University, Programs in Education, Charleston, SC 29423-8087. Offers administration and supervision (M Ed), including elementary, secondary; elementary education (M Ed); English (MAT); science (MAT); secondary education (M Ed); social studies (MAT). *Accreditation:* NCATE. Part-time and evening/weekend programs available. *Degree requirements:* For master's, thesis optional. *Entrance requirements:* For master's, GRE or MAT. Expenses: Contact institution. *Faculty research:* Economic education, multicultural education, restructuring teacher education, participation in mathematics and science by minorities and women, at-risk children.

Chatham University, Program in Education, Pittsburgh, PA 15232-2826. Offers early childhood education (MAT); elementary education (MAT); English—secondary (MAT); environmental education (K-12) (MAT); secondary art (MAT); secondary biology education (MAT); secondary chemistry education (MAT); secondary English education (MAT); secondary math education (MAT); secondary physics education (MAT); secondary social studies education (MAT); special education (MAT). *Students:* 60 full-time (43 women), 23 part-time (22 women). Average age 29. 48 applicants, 77% accepted, 32 enrolled. In 2006, 59 degrees awarded. *Degree requirements:* For master's, thesis, teaching experience. *Entrance requirements:* For master's, PRAXIS I, minimum GPA of 3.0, sample of written work, recommendation letters. Additional exam requirements/recommendations for international students: Required—TOEFL (minimum score 600 paper-based; 250 computer-based; 100 iBT); Recommended—IELTS (minimum score 7), TWE (minimum score 5). *Application deadline:* For fall admission, 5/1 priority date for domestic and international students; for winter admission, 10/1 priority date for domestic and international students. Applications are processed on a rolling basis. Application fee: $45. Electronic applications accepted. *Financial support:* Career-related internships or fieldwork available. Financial award applicants required to submit FAFSA. *Faculty research:* Gifted education, environmental education, technology in education, writing as learning, class size and achievement. *Unit head:* Dr. Wendy Weiner, Director, 412-365-1146, Fax: 412-365-1505, E-mail: wweiner@chatham.edu. *Application contact:* 412-365-1825, Fax: 412-365-1609, E-mail: admissions@chatham.edu.

Christopher Newport University, Graduate Studies, Department of Teacher Preparation, Newport News, VA 23606-2998. Offers art (PK-12) (MAT); biology (6-12) (MAT); computer science (6-12) (MAT); elementary (PK-6) (MAT); English (6-12) (MAT); French (PK-12) (MAT); history (6-12) (MAT); history and social science (MAT); mathematics (6-12) (MAT); music (PK-12) (MAT), including choral, instrumental; physics (6-12) (MAT); Spanish (PK-12) (MAT); theater (PK-12) (MAT). Part-time and evening/weekend programs available. *Degree requirements:* For master's, thesis or alternative, comprehensive exam. *Entrance requirements:* For master's, PRAXIS I, minimum GPA of 3.0. Electronic applications accepted. *Faculty research:* Early literacy development, instructional innovations, professional teaching standards, multicultural issues, aesthetic education.

City College of the City University of New York, Graduate School, School of Education, Department of Secondary Education, New York, NY 10031-9198. Offers adolescent mathematics education (MA, AC); English education (MA); middle school mathematics education (MS); science education (MA); social studies education (AC). *Accreditation:* NCATE. *Students:* 286 applicants, 94% accepted, 219 enrolled. *Entrance requirements:* For master's, Liberal Arts and Sciences Test (LAST), Content Specialty Test (CST). Additional exam requirements/recommendations for international students: Required—TOEFL. *Application deadline:* For fall admission, 3/15 for domestic students; for spring admission, 10/15 for domestic students. Application fee: $125. *Unit head:* Susan Semel, Chair, 212-650-7262, E-mail: ssemel@ccny.cuny.edu. *Application contact:* Stacia Pusey, Graduate Admissions Adviser-Education, 212-650-5345, E-mail: spusey@ccny.cuny.edu.

Clarion University of Pennsylvania, Office of Research and Graduate Studies, College of Education and Human Services, Department of Education, Program in Education, Clarion, PA 16214. Offers curriculum and instruction (M Ed); early childhood (M Ed); English (M Ed); history (M Ed); literacy (M Ed); science (M Ed); technology (M Ed). *Accreditation:* NCATE. Part-time programs available. *Faculty:* 18 full-time (13 women). *Students:* 11 full-time (4 women), 54 part-time (37 women); includes 4 minority (3 African Americans, 1 Asian American or Pacific Islander). 50 applicants, 90% accepted. In 2006, 7 degrees awarded. *Degree requirements:* For master's, thesis or alternative, comprehensive exam. *Entrance requirements:* For master's, minimum QPA of 3.0, teacher certification. Additional exam requirements/recommendations for international students: Required—TOEFL (minimum score 550 paper-based; 213 computer-based; 80 iBT). *Application deadline:* For fall admission, 8/1 priority date for domestic students, 4/15 priority date for international students; for spring admission, 12/1 priority date for domestic students, 9/15 priority date for international students. Applications are processed on a rolling basis. Application fee: $30. Electronic applications accepted. *Expenses:* Tuition, state resident: part-time $336 per credit. Tuition, nonresident: part-time $538 per credit. *Financial support:* In 2006–07, 2 research assistantships with full tuition reimbursements (averaging $4,002 per year) were awarded. Support available to part-time students. Financial award application deadline: 3/1. *Application contact:* Dr. Brian Maguire, Coordinator, 814-393-2058, Fax: 814-393-2558, E-mail: bmaguire@clarion.edu.

College of St. Joseph, Graduate Program, Division of Education, Program in Secondary Education, Rutland, VT 05701-3899. Offers English (M Ed); mathematics (M Ed); social studies (M Ed). Part-time and evening/weekend programs available. *Faculty:* 2 full-time (1 woman), 8 part-time/adjunct (5 women). *Students:* 4 full-time, 4 part-time. Average age 32. 7 applicants, 100% accepted, 6 enrolled. In 2006, 4 degrees awarded. *Entrance requirements:* For master's, PRAXIS I, 2 letters of recommendation, minimum GPA of 3.0, interview. *Application deadline:* Applications are processed on a rolling basis. Application fee: $35. *Expenses:* Tuition: Full-time $10,990; part-time $300 per credit. Part-time tuition and fees vary according to program. *Financial support:* Career-related internships or fieldwork, Federal Work-Study, and unspecified assistantships available. Support available to part-time students. Financial award application deadline: 3/1. *Unit head:* Dr. David Balfour, Director, 802-773-5900 Ext. 3230, Fax: 802-776-5258, E-mail: dbalfour@csj.edu. *Application contact:* Tracy Gallipo, Director of Admissions, 802-773-5900 Ext. 3262, Fax: 802-773-5900, E-mail: tracygallipo@csj.edu.

The College of William and Mary, School of Education, Program in Curriculum and Instruction, Williamsburg, VA 23187-8795. Offers elementary education (MA Ed); gifted education (MA Ed); reading education (MA Ed); secondary education (MA Ed), including English education, mathematics education, modern foreign languages education, science education, social studies education; special education (MA Ed), including emotionally disturbed, learning disabled, mental retardation, resource collaborating teaching. *Accreditation:* NCATE. Part-time programs available. *Faculty:* 15 full-time (6 women), 13 part-time/adjunct (10 women). *Students:* 51 full-time (39 women), 51 part-time (45 women); includes 6 minority (all African Americans) Average age 29. 161 applicants, 68% accepted, 61 enrolled. In 2006, 68 degrees awarded. *Degree requirements:* For master's, master's project. *Entrance requirements:* For master's, GRE or MAT, minimum GPA of 2.5. Additional exam requirements/recommendations for international students: Required—TOEFL. *Application deadline:* For fall admission, 2/1 for domestic and international students; for spring admission, 10/1 for domestic and international students. Application fee: $30. *Expenses:* Tuition, state resident: full-time $6,100; part-time $260 per credit. Tuition, nonresident: full-time $18,790; part-time $725 per credit. Required fees: $3,314. Tuition and fees vary according to program. *Financial support:* In 2006–07, 10 research assistantships with full and partial tuition reimbursements (averaging $5,000 per year) were awarded; career-related internships or fieldwork, Federal Work-Study, institutionally sponsored loans, scholarships/grants, and unspecified assistantships also available. Financial award application deadline: 2/1; financial award applicants required to submit FAFSA. *Faculty research:* National Council of Teachers of Mathematics Standards, counseling, self-concept and self-esteem, special education, curriculum development. *Unit head:* Dr. John Moore, Area Coordinator, 757-221-2333, E-mail: jnmoor@wm.edu. *Application contact:* Dorothy Osborne, Director of Admissions, 757-221-2317, E-mail: dsosbo@wm.edu.

The Colorado College, Department of Education, Program in Secondary Education, Colorado Springs, CO 80903-3294. Offers art teaching (MAT); English teaching (MAT); foreign language teaching (MAT); mathematics teaching (MAT); music teaching (MAT); science teaching (MAT);

Social Sciences Education

The Colorado College (continued)

social studies teaching (MAT). *Faculty:* 2 full-time (1 woman), 10 part-time/adjunct (7 women). *Students:* 18 full-time (12 women); includes 2 minority (1 African American, 1 Asian American or Pacific Islander). Average age 27. 30 applicants, 90% accepted, 18 enrolled. In 2006, 16 degrees awarded. *Degree requirements:* For master's, thesis, internship. *Entrance requirements:* For master's, PRAXIS II or PLACE. *Application deadline:* For fall admission, 2/1 for domestic and international students. Application fee: $50. *Expenses:* Tuition: Full-time $23,567. One-time fee: $1,485 full-time. *Financial support:* In 2006–07, 15 teaching assistantships (averaging $16,000 per year) were awarded; career-related internships or fieldwork, institutionally sponsored loans, health care benefits, and tuition waivers (partial) also available. Financial award application deadline: 2/15; financial award applicants required to submit FAFSA. *Unit head:* Mike Taber, Director, 719-389-6026, Fax: 719-389-6473, E-mail: pveronesi@coloradocollege.edu. *Application contact:* Marsha E. Unruh, Director of Education Career Services, 719-389-6472, Fax: 719-389-6473, E-mail: munruh@coloradocollege.edu.

Columbus State University, Graduate Studies, College of Education, Department of Teacher Education, Columbus, GA 31907-5645. Offers early childhood education (M Ed, Ed S); instructional technology (MS); middle grades education (M Ed, Ed S); physical education (M Ed); secondary education (M Ed, Ed S), including English/language arts, general science (M Ed), mathematics, science (Ed S), social science; special education (Ed S), including behavior disorders, learning disabilities, mental retardation. *Accreditation:* NCATE. Part-time and evening/weekend programs available. Postbaccalaureate distance learning degree programs offered (minimal on-campus study). *Faculty:* 16 full-time (8 women), 2 part-time/adjunct (1 woman). *Students:* 61 full-time (45 women), 128 part-time (89 women); includes 44 minority (36 African Americans, 3 Asian Americans or Pacific Islanders, 5 Hispanic Americans), 1 international. Average age 36. 77 applicants, 49% accepted, 26 enrolled. In 2006, 66 master's, 13 other advanced degrees awarded. *Degree requirements:* For master's, thesis, exit exam; for Ed S, thesis or alternative. *Entrance requirements:* For master's, GRE General Test, minimum GPA of 2.75; for Ed S, GRE General Test. Additional exam requirements/recommendations for international students: Required—TOEFL (minimum score 550 paper-based; 213 computer-based). *Application deadline:* For fall admission, 5/1 priority date for domestic students, 5/1 for international students; for spring admission, 11/1 for domestic and international students. Applications are processed on a rolling basis. Application fee: $25. Electronic applications accepted. *Expenses:* Tuition, state resident: part-time $127 per semester hour. Tuition, nonresident: part-time $508 per semester hour. Required fees: $264 per semester. Tuition and fees vary according to course load. *Financial support:* In 2006–07, 118 students received support, including 21 research assistantships with partial tuition reimbursements available (averaging $3,000 per year); career-related internships or fieldwork, Federal Work-Study, institutionally sponsored loans, scholarships/grants, tuition waivers (partial), and unspecified assistantships also available. Support available to part-time students. Financial award application deadline: 5/1; financial award applicants required to submit FAFSA. *Unit head:* Dr. Deborah Gober, Acting Chair, 706-568-2255, Fax: 706-568-3134, E-mail: gober_deborah@colstate.edu. *Application contact:* Katie Thornton, Graduate Admissions Specialist, 706-568-2035, Fax: 706-568-2462, E-mail: thornton_katie@colstate.edu.

Converse College, School of Education and Graduate Studies, Program in Secondary Education, Spartanburg, SC 29302-0006. Offers biology (MAT); chemistry (MAT); English (M Ed, MAT); mathematics (M Ed, MAT); natural sciences (M Ed); social sciences (M Ed, MAT). Part-time programs available. *Students:* Average age 35. In 2006, 40 degrees awarded. *Degree requirements:* For master's, capstone paper. *Entrance requirements:* For master's, NTE or PRAXIS II (M Ed), minimum GPA of 2.75, 2 recommendations. *Application deadline:* For fall admission, 8/1 for domestic and international students; for winter admission, 11/15 for domestic and international students; for spring admission, 1/15 for domestic and international students. Applications are processed on a rolling basis. Application fee: $40. Electronic applications accepted. *Expenses:* Tuition: Part-time $305 per credit hour. Required fees: $20 per term. *Financial support:* Available to part-time students. Applicants required to submit FAFSA.

Delta State University, Graduate Programs, College of Arts and Sciences, Department of History, Cleveland, MS 38733-0001. Offers history education (M Ed). Part-time programs available. *Degree requirements:* For master's, thesis or alternative. *Entrance requirements:* For master's, GRE General Test or MAT. *Application deadline:* For fall admission, 8/1 priority date for domestic students; for spring admission, 12/1 priority date for domestic students. Applications are processed on a rolling basis. Application fee: $0. *Financial support:* In 2006–07, research assistantships (averaging $3,500 per year); career-related internships or fieldwork, Federal Work-Study, and institutionally sponsored loans also available. Support available to part-time students. Financial award application deadline: 6/1. *Unit head:* Dr. Chester Morgan, Chair, 662-846-4170, Fax: 662-846-4136, E-mail: bmorgan@deltastate.edu.

Delta State University, Graduate Programs, College of Arts and Sciences, Division of Social Sciences, Program in Social Science Secondary Education, Cleveland, MS 38733-0001. Offers M Ed. Part-time programs available. *Degree requirements:* For master's, thesis or alternative. *Application deadline:* For fall admission, 8/1 priority date for domestic students; for spring admission, 12/1 priority date for domestic students. Applications are processed on a rolling basis. Application fee: $0. *Financial support:* Research assistantships, career-related internships or fieldwork, Federal Work-Study, and institutionally sponsored loans available. Support available to part-time students. Financial award application deadline: 6/1.

Drake University, School of Education, Department of Teaching and Learning, Program in Secondary Education, Des Moines, IA 50311-4516. Offers art (MAT); biology (MAT); business (MAT); chemistry (MAT); English (MAT); general science (MAT); history-American (MAT); history-world (MAT); journalism (MAT); mathematics (MAT); physical science (MAT); physics (MAT); sociology (MAT); speech (MAT); speech communication (MAT); theatre (MAT). Part-time programs available. *Faculty:* 10 full-time (3 women), 28 part-time/adjunct (16 women). *Students:* 13 full-time (7 women), 33 part-time (20 women). 41 applicants, 56% accepted. In 2006, 12 degrees awarded. *Degree requirements:* For master's, thesis (for some programs), internships (s), comprehensive exam, registration. *Entrance requirements:* For master's, GRE General Test, MAT, or Drake Writing Assessment, resumé, 2 letters of recommendation. Additional exam requirements/recommendations for international students: Required—TOEFL (minimum score 550 paper-based; 213 computer-based). *Application deadline:* For fall admission, 7/1 priority date for domestic students, 6/1 priority date for international students; for spring admission, 11/1 priority date for domestic students, 10/1 priority date for international students. Applications are processed on a rolling basis. Application fee: $25. Electronic applications accepted. *Financial support:* Career-related internships or fieldwork and unspecified assistantships available. Support available to part-time students. *Faculty research:* Counseling and rehabilitation, behavioral supports, inquiry-based science methods, teacher quality enhancement. Total annual research expenditures: $1.5 million. *Unit head:* Dr. Linda Espey, Head, 515-271-1954, E-mail: linda.espey@drake.edu. *Application contact:* Ann J. Martin, Graduate Coordinator, 515-271-2034, Fax: 515-271-2831, E-mail: ann.martin@drake.edu.

East Carolina University, Graduate School, College of Education, Department of Curriculum and Instruction, Greenville, NC 27858-4353. Offers behavior/emotional disabilities (MA Ed); elementary education (MA Ed); English education (MA Ed); learning disabilities (MA Ed); low incidence disabilities (MA Ed); mental retardation (MA Ed); middle grade education (MA Ed); reading education (MA Ed); social studies education (MA Ed). Part-time programs available. Postbaccalaureate distance learning degree programs offered. *Students:* 92 full-time (85 women), 233 part-time (211 women); includes 42 minority (39 African Americans, 1 American Indian/Alaska Native, 1 Asian American or Pacific Islander, 1 Hispanic American). Average age 30. 25 applicants, 100% accepted, 25 enrolled. In 2006, 195 degrees awarded. *Degree requirements:* For master's, thesis optional. *Entrance requirements:* For master's, GRE General Test or MAT, interview, bachelor's degree in related field, minimum GPA of 2.5, teaching license. Additional exam requirements/recommendations for international students: Required—TOEFL. *Application deadline:* For fall admission, 6/1 priority date for domestic students. Applications are processed on a rolling basis. Application fee: $50. *Financial support:* Research assistantships, teaching assistantships, Federal Work-Study available. Support available to part-time students. Financial award application deadline: 6/1; financial award applicants required to submit FAFSA. *Unit head:* Dr. Sandra H. Warren, Interim Chair, 252-328-2699, E-mail: warrens@ecu.edu. *Application contact:* Dean of Graduate School, 252-328-6012, Fax: 252-328-6071, E-mail: gradschool@ecu.edu.

Eastern Kentucky University, The Graduate School, College of Education, Department of Curriculum and Instruction, Program in Secondary and Higher Education, Richmond, KY 40475-3102. Offers agricultural education (MA Ed); allied health sciences education (MA Ed); art education (MA Ed); biological sciences education (MA Ed); business education (MA Ed); chemistry education (MA Ed); earth science education (MA Ed); English education (MA Ed); general science education (MA Ed); geography education (MA Ed); history education (MA Ed); home economics education (MA Ed); industrial education (MA Ed); mathematical sciences education (MA Ed); physical education (MA Ed); physics education (MA Ed); political science education (MA Ed); psychology education (MA Ed); reading (MA Ed); school health education (MA Ed); sociology education (MA Ed). *Accreditation:* NCATE. Part-time programs available. *Students:* 16 full-time (8 women), 63 part-time (43 women); includes 5 minority (2 African Americans, 2 American Indian/Alaska Native, 1 Asian American or Pacific Islander). Average age 32. *Entrance requirements:* For master's, GRE General Test, minimum GPA of 2.5. Application fee: $30. *Expenses:* Tuition, state resident: full-time $5,610. Tuition, nonresident: full-time $15,910. *Financial support:* Research assistantships, teaching assistantships, Federal Work-Study available. Support available to part-time students. *Unit head:* Dr. Michael Martin, Chair, Department of Curriculum and Instruction, 859-622-2154, Fax: 859-622-2004.

Eastern Washington University, Graduate Studies, College of Education and Human Development, Department of Education, Cheney, WA 99004-2431. Offers adult education (M Ed); college instruction (MA, MS); curriculum and instruction (M Ed); early childhood education (M Ed); educational leadership (M Ed); elementary teaching (M Ed); foundations of education (M Ed); instructional media and technology (M Ed); literacy specialist (M Ed); school library media administration (M Ed); science education (M Ed); social science education (M Ed); supervising (clinic) teaching (M Ed). *Accreditation:* NCATE. Part-time programs available. *Degree requirements:* For master's, comprehensive exam. *Entrance requirements:* For master's, minimum GPA of 3.0.

East Stroudsburg University of Pennsylvania, Graduate School, School of Arts and Sciences, Department of History, East Stroudsburg, PA 18301-2999. Offers history (M Ed, MA). Part-time and evening/weekend programs available. *Faculty:* 5 full-time (0 women). *Students:* 11 full-time (2 women), 20 part-time (10 women); includes 2 minority (both African Americans) Average age 33. In 2006, 7 degrees awarded. *Degree requirements:* For master's, variable foreign language requirement, thesis (for some programs), comprehensive exam. *Entrance requirements:* Additional exam requirements/recommendations for international students: Required—TOEFL (minimum score 560 paper-based; 220 computer-based; 83 iBT). *Application deadline:* For fall admission, 7/31 priority date for domestic students, 5/1 priority date for international students; for spring admission, 11/30 for domestic students, 10/1 for international students. Applications are processed on a rolling basis. Application fee: $50. *Expenses:* Tuition, state resident: full-time $6,048; part-time $336 per credit. Tuition, nonresident: full-time $9,678; part-time $538 per credit. Required fees: $1,353; $67 per credit. One-time fee: $37 part-time. *Financial support:* In 2006–07, 6 research assistantships with full and partial tuition reimbursements were awarded; Federal Work-Study and institutionally sponsored loans also available. Financial award application deadline: 3/1; financial award applicants required to submit FAFSA. *Unit head:* Dr. Lawrence Squeri, Graduate Coordinator, 570-422-3284, Fax: 570-422-3506, E-mail: lsqueri@po-box.edu.

East Stroudsburg University of Pennsylvania, Graduate School, School of Arts and Sciences, Department of Political Science, East Stroudsburg, PA 18301-2999. Offers political science (M Ed, MA). Part-time and evening/weekend programs available. *Faculty:* 8 full-time (2 women). *Students:* 27 full-time (12 women), 19 part-time (11 women); includes 9 minority (5 African Americans, 4 Hispanic Americans), 3 international. Average age 31. In 2006, 10 degrees awarded. *Degree requirements:* For master's, variable foreign language requirement, thesis or alternative, comprehensive exam. *Entrance requirements:* Additional exam requirements/recommendations for international students: Required—TOEFL (minimum score 560 paper-based; 220 computer-based; 83 iBT). *Application deadline:* For fall admission, 7/31 priority date for domestic students, 5/1 priority date for international students; for spring admission, 11/30 for domestic students, 10/1 for international students. Applications are processed on a rolling basis. Application fee: $50. *Expenses:* Tuition, state resident: full-time $6,048; part-time $336 per credit. Tuition, nonresident: full-time $9,678; part-time $538 per credit. Required fees: $1,353; $67 per credit. One-time fee: $37 part-time. *Financial support:* In 2006–07, 16 research assistantships with full and partial tuition reimbursements were awarded; Federal Work-Study and institutionally sponsored loans also available. Financial award application deadline: 3/1; financial award applicants required to submit FAFSA. *Unit head:* Dr. Patricia Crotty, Graduate Coordinator, 570-422-3271, Fax: 570-422-3506, E-mail: pcrotty@po-box.esu.edu.

Emporia State University, School of Graduate Studies, College of Liberal Arts and Sciences, Department of Social Sciences, Program in Social Sciences, Emporia, KS 66801-5087. Offers American history (MAT); anthropology (MAT); economics (MAT); geography (MAT); political science (MAT); social studies education (MAT); sociology (MAT); world history (MAT). *Accreditation:* NCATE. Part-time programs available. *Students:* 2 applicants, 100% accepted, 2 enrolled. In 2006, 7 degrees awarded. *Degree requirements:* For master's, comprehensive exam or thesis. *Entrance requirements:* For master's, appropriate bachelor's degree, teacher certification. Additional exam requirements/recommendations for international students: Required—TOEFL. *Application deadline:* For fall admission, 8/15 priority date for domestic students. Applications are processed on a rolling basis. Application fee: $30 ($75 for international students). Electronic applications accepted. *Expenses:* Tuition, state resident: full-time $3,438; part-time $143 per credit hour. Tuition, nonresident: full-time $10,398; part-time $433 per credit hour. Required fees: $724; $44 per credit hour. *Financial support:* Federal Work-Study, institutionally sponsored loans, health care benefits, and unspecified assistantships available. Financial award application deadline: 3/15; financial award applicants required to submit FAFSA. *Application contact:* Dr. Christopher Lovett, Associate Professor, 620-341-5577, E-mail: clovett@emporia.edu.

Fayetteville State University, Graduate School, Program in Middle Grades, Secondary and Special Education, Fayetteville, NC 28301-4298. Offers biology (MA Ed); history (MA Ed); mathematics (MA Ed); middle grades (MA Ed); political science (MA Ed); reading (MA Ed); sociology (MA Ed); special education (MA Ed), including behavioral-emotional handicaps, mentally handicapped, specific training disability. *Accreditation:* NCATE. Part-time and evening/weekend programs available. *Faculty:* 19 full-time (12 women), 3 part-time/adjunct (2 women). *Students:* 14 full-time (10 women), 48 part-time (40 women); includes 44 minority (40 African Americans, 2 American Indian/Alaska Native, 1 Asian American or Pacific Islander, 1 Hispanic American). Average age 39. 16 applicants, 100% accepted, 16 enrolled. In 2006, 33 degrees awarded. *Degree requirements:* For master's, internship. *Application deadline:* For fall admission, 7/1 for domestic students; for spring admission, 12/1 for domestic students. Applications are processed on a rolling basis. Application fee: $25. Electronic applications accepted. *Expenses:* Tuition, state resident: full-time $2,118. Tuition, nonresident: full-time $11,708. Required fees: $1,099. Tuition and fees vary according to course load. *Unit head:* Dr. Charletta Barringer-Brown, Interim Chair, 910-672-1182, E-mail: cbarringerbrown@uncfsu.edu.

Fitchburg State College, Division of Graduate and Continuing Education, Programs in History and Teaching History (Secondary Level), Fitchburg, MA 01420-2697. Offers MA, MAT. *Accreditation:* NCATE. Part-time and evening/weekend programs available. *Students:* Average age 36. 9 applicants, 89% accepted, 5 enrolled. In 2006, 3 degrees awarded. *Entrance requirements:* For master's, GRE General Test or MAT, appropriate bachelor's degree, letters of recommendation, resumé. Additional exam requirements/recommendations for international students: Required—TOEFL (minimum score 550 paper-based; 213 computer-based; 79 iBT). *Application deadline:* Applications are processed on a rolling basis. Application fee: $25 ($50 for international students). *Expenses:* Tuition, state resident: part-time $150 per credit. Tuition, nonresident: part-time $150 per credit. Required fees: $90 per credit. *Financial support:* In 2006–07, research assistantships with partial tuition reimbursements (averaging $5,500 per year); Federal Work-Study, scholarships/grants, and unspecified assistantships also available. Support available to part-time students. Financial award application deadline: 3/1; financial award applicants required to submit FAFSA. *Unit head:* Dr. Laura Baker, Chair, 978-665-3379, Fax: 978-665-3658, E-mail: gce@fsc.edu. *Application contact:* Director of Admissions, 978-665-3144, Fax: 978-665-4540, E-mail: admissions@fsc.edu.

Florida Agricultural and Mechanical University, Division of Graduate Studies, Research, and Continuing Education, College of Education, Program in Secondary Education and Foundation, Tallahassee, FL 32307-3200. Offers biology (M Ed); chemistry (MS Ed); English (MS Ed); history (MS Ed); math (MS Ed); physics (MS Ed). *Accreditation:* NCATE. *Degree requirements:* For master's, thesis (for some programs). *Entrance requirements:* For master's, GRE General Test, minimum GPA of 3.0. Additional exam requirements/recommendations for international students: Required—TOEFL.

Florida Gulf Coast University, College of Education, Program in Secondary Education, Fort Myers, FL 33965-6565. Offers biology (MAT); English (MAT); mathematics (MAT); social sciences (MAT). Part-time and evening/weekend programs available. *Faculty:* 31 full-time (21 women), 30 part-time/adjunct (24 women). *Entrance requirements:* For master's, GRE General Test, MAT, minimum GPA of 3.0. Additional exam requirements/recommendations for international students: Required—TOEFL (minimum score 550 paper-based; 213 computer-based). *Application deadline:* For fall admission, 7/1 priority date for domestic students; for spring admission, 10/15 for domestic students. Applications are processed on a rolling basis. Application fee: $30. Electronic applications accepted. *Expenses:* Tuition, state resident: full-time $4,326. Tuition, nonresident: full-time $18,523. Required fees: $1,211. One-time fee: $5 full-time. *Faculty research:* Integration of technology in the classroom, year-round schools, school choice, virtual high schools. *Unit head:* Dr. Pat Wachholz, Associate Dean, 239-590-7808, Fax: 239-590-7801, E-mail: wachhol@fgcu.edu.

Florida International University, College of Education, Department of Curriculum and Instruction, Program in Social Studies Education, Miami, FL 33199. Offers MAT, MS, Ed D. *Accreditation:* NCATE. Part-time and evening/weekend programs available. *Entrance requirements:* Additional exam requirements/recommendations for international students: Required—TOEFL. *Application deadline:* Applications are processed on a rolling basis. *Expenses:* Tuition, state resident: part-time $249 per credit hour. Tuition, nonresident: part-time $753 per credit hour. Tuition and fees vary according to program. *Faculty research:* Pedagogical knowledge base for teaching social studies, global education. *Unit head:* Dr. Hilary Landorf, Assistant Professor, 305-348-2410, E-mail: landorf@fiu.edu. *Application contact:* Marisa Salazar, Student Recruiter, 305-348-3002, Fax: 305-348-3227, E-mail: marisa.salazar@fiu.edu.

Florida State University, Graduate Studies, College of Education, Department of Middle and Secondary Education, Program in Social Science Education, Tallahassee, FL 32306. Offers MS, Ed D, PhD, Ed S. Part-time programs available. *Faculty:* 3 full-time (2 women), 1 part-time/adjunct (0 women). *Students:* 9 full-time (4 women), 14 part-time (3 women); includes 2 minority (both African Americans) 7 applicants, 43% accepted, 1 enrolled. In 2006, 3 master's, 2 doctorates awarded. *Degree requirements:* For master's and Ed S, thesis optional; for doctorate, thesis/dissertation, comprehensive exam. *Entrance requirements:* For master's, doctorate, and Ed S, GRE General Test, minimum GPA of 3.0. *Application deadline:* For fall admission, 7/1 priority date for domestic students; for spring admission, 11/1 for domestic students. Applications are processed on a rolling basis. Application fee: $30. *Expenses:* Tuition, state resident: full-time $5,822; part-time $243 per credit hour. Tuition, nonresident: full-time $20,976; part-time $874 per credit hour. Tuition and fees vary according to program. *Financial support:* Fellowships, research assistantships, teaching assistantships, career-related internships or fieldwork available. Financial award applicants required to submit FAFSA. *Unit head:* Dr. Robert Gutierrez, Head, 850-644-6553, Fax: 850-644-1880, E-mail: gutierre@coe.fsu.edu. *Application contact:* Christina Crotty, Office Manager, 850-644-7810, Fax: 850-644-1880, E-mail: crotty@mailer.fsu.edu.

Framingham State College, Division of Graduate and Continuing Education, Program in History, Framingham, MA 01701-9101. Offers M Ed. *Faculty:* 2 full-time, 2 part-time/adjunct. *Students:* 25. In 2006, 4 degrees awarded. *Unit head:* Dr. Brad Nutting, Coordinator, 508-626-4822, Fax: 508-626-4030, E-mail: bnuttin@frc.mass.edu. *Application contact:* 508-626-4550, Fax: 508-626-4030, E-mail: dgce@frc.mass.edu.

Georgia College & State University, Graduate School, School of Education, Department of Foundations and Secondary Education, Milledgeville, GA 31061. Offers English education (M Ed); instructional technology (M Ed); mathematics education (M Ed); natural science education (M Ed, Ed S); secondary education (MAT); social science education (M Ed, Ed S). *Accreditation:* NCATE. *Students:* 49 full-time (33 women), 66 part-time (47 women); includes 13 minority (11 African Americans, 2 Hispanic Americans), 2 international. Average age 32. 75 applicants, 27% accepted, 9 enrolled. In 2006, 83 master's awarded. *Degree requirements:* For master's and Ed S, comprehensive exam. *Entrance requirements:* For master's, GRE General Test or MAT, 2 letters of recommendation; for Ed S, GRE General Test or MAT, master's degree, 2 letters of recommendation, 2 years teaching experience. Additional exam requirements/recommendations for international students: Required—TOEFL. *Application deadline:* For fall admission, 7/1 priority date for domestic students. Applications are processed on a rolling basis. Application fee: $25. Electronic applications accepted. *Expenses:* Tuition, state resident: full-time $3,222; part-time $179 per credit hour. Tuition, nonresident: full-time $12,870; part-time $715 per credit hour. Required fees: $391 per semester. Tuition and fees vary according to course load. *Financial support:* In 2006–07, 10 research assistantships (averaging $3,800 per year) were awarded; career-related internships or fieldwork and Federal Work-Study also available. Support available to part-time students. Financial award application deadline: 3/15. *Unit head:* Dr. Cynthia Alby, Chair/MAT Cohort Leader, 478-445-2513, Fax: 478-445-7362, E-mail: cynthia.alby@gcsu.edu.

Georgia Southern University, Jack N. Averitt College of Graduate Studies, College of Education, Department of Teaching and Learning, Program in Social Science Education, Statesboro, GA 30460. Offers M Ed. *Accreditation:* NCATE. Part-time and evening/weekend programs available. *Students:* 4 full-time (3 women), 6 part-time (2 women); includes 2 minority (both African Americans) Average age 25. 2 applicants, 100% accepted, 1 enrolled. *Degree requirements:* For master's, exit assessment. *Entrance requirements:* For master's, GRE General Test or MAT, minimum GPA of 2.5. Additional exam requirements/recommendations for international students: Required—TOEFL (minimum score 550 paper-based; 213 computer-based; 80 iBT). *Application deadline:* For fall admission, 3/1 priority date for domestic students, 3/1 for international students; for spring admission, 10/1 priority date for domestic students, 10/1 for international students. Applications are processed on a rolling basis. Application fee: $50. Electronic applications accepted. *Financial support:* In 2006–07, 7 students received support, including 1 research assistantship with partial tuition reimbursement available (averaging $5,500 per year), teaching assistantships with partial tuition reimbursements available (averaging $5,500 per year); Federal Work-Study, scholarships/grants, tuition waivers (partial), and unspecified assistantships also available. Support available to part-time students. Financial award application deadline: 4/15; financial award applicants required to submit FAFSA. *Faculty research:* Environmental issues. *Unit head:* Dr. Mary Bennett, Assistant Professor, 912-681-0356, Fax: 912-681-0026, E-mail: mbennett@georgiasouthern.edu. *Application contact:* 912-681-5384, Fax: 912-681-0740, E-mail: gradadmissions@georgiasouthern.edu.

Georgia State University, College of Education, Department of Middle-Secondary Education and Instructional Technology, Programs in Secondary Education, Atlanta, GA 30303-3083. Offers art education (Ed S); English education (M Ed, Ed S); mathematics education (M Ed, PhD, Ed S); music education (PhD); science education (M Ed, PhD, Ed S); social studies education (M Ed, PhD, Ed S). *Accreditation:* NASM (one or more programs are accredited); NCATE. Part-time and evening/weekend programs available. *Students:* 103 full-time (71 women), 140 part-time (92 women); includes 53 minority (48 African Americans, 2 Asian Americans or Pacific Islanders, 3 Hispanic Americans), 12 international. Average age 35. 36 applicants, 86% accepted. In 2006, 87 master's, 12 doctorates, 12 other advanced degrees awarded. *Degree requirements:* For master's, comprehensive exam; for doctorate, thesis/dissertation, comprehensive exam; for Ed S, project/exam. *Entrance requirements:* For master's, GRE General Test, minimum GPA of 2.5; for doctorate, GRE General Test or MAT, minimum GPA of 3.3; for Ed S, GRE General Test or MAT, minimum graduate GPA of 3.25. Application fee: $25. *Financial support:* Career-related internships or fieldwork, Federal Work-Study, and institutionally sponsored loans available. *Faculty research:* Women and science, problem solving in mathematics, dialects, economic education. *Unit head:* Dr. Ruth Hough, Acting Chair, Department of Middle-Secondary Education and Instructional Technology, 404-651-2510.

Grambling State University, School of Graduate Studies and Research, College of Arts and Sciences, Program in Teaching Social Sciences, Grambling, LA 71245. Offers social studies (MAT). Part-time programs available. *Faculty:* 3 full-time (2 women), 1 (woman) part-time/adjunct. *Students:* 25 full-time (16 women), 9 part-time (7 women); all minorities (all African Americans) Average age 32. In 2006, 10 degrees awarded. *Degree requirements:* For master's, thesis optional. *Entrance requirements:* For master's, GRE, minimum GPA of 3.0 on last degree. Additional exam requirements/recommendations for international students: Required—TOEFL. *Application deadline:* For fall admission, 7/1 for domestic students; for spring admission, 12/1 for domestic students. Applications are processed on a rolling basis. Application fee: $20 ($30 for international students). *Expenses:* Tuition, state resident: full-time $2,232; part-time $124 per credit hour. Tuition, nonresident: full-time $7,582; part-time $124 per credit hour. Required fees: $1,127. *Financial support:* In 2006–07, 29 students received support, including 8 teaching assistantships (averaging $3,500 per year); institutionally sponsored loans and unspecified assistantships also available. Financial award application deadline: 5/31; financial award applicants required to submit FAFSA. *Unit head:* Dr. Ronnie L. Davis, Director, 318-274-2235, E-mail: davisr@gram.edu.

Harding University, College of Education, Searcy, AR 72149-0001. Offers advanced studies in teaching and learning (M Ed); art (MSE); behavioral science (MSE); Bible and religion (MSE); counseling (MS, Ed S); early childhood education (M Ed); early childhood special education (M Ed, MSE); education (MSE); educational leadership (M Ed, Ed S); elementary education (M Ed); English (MSE); family and consumer science (MSE); French (MSE); history/social science (MSE); kinesiology (MSE); math (MSE); physical science (MSE); reading (M Ed); secondary education (M Ed); Spanish (MSE); special education licensure (M Ed); teaching (MAT). *Accreditation:* NCATE. Part-time programs available. *Faculty:* 8 full-time (2 women), 45 part-time/adjunct (30 women). *Students:* 153 full-time (123 women), 469 part-time (341 women); includes 72 minority (63 African Americans, 4 American Indian/Alaska Native, 1 Asian American or Pacific Islander, 4 Hispanic Americans), 9 international. Average age 35. 175 applicants, 90% accepted, 147 enrolled. In 2006, 241 degrees awarded. *Degree requirements:* For master's, portfolio(s), thesis optional; for Ed S, portfolio, specialist project. *Entrance requirements:* For master's, GRE, MAT, PRAXIS; for Ed S, MAT or GRE. Additional exam requirements/recommendations for international students: Required—TOEFL (minimum score 550 paper-based). *Application deadline:* For fall admission, 8/1 for domestic and international students; for spring admission, 1/1 for domestic and international students. Applications are processed on a rolling basis. Application fee: $35. *Expenses:* Tuition: Part-time $455 per semester hour. Required fees: $20 per semester hour. Tuition and fees vary according to course load. *Financial support:* Scholarships/grants and unspecified assistantships available. Support available to part-time students. *Faculty research:* Reading, comprehension, school violence, educational technology, behavior, college choice, differentiated instruction, brain based teaching. *Unit head:* Pat Bashaw, Chair, 501-279-4183, Fax: 501-279-4051, E-mail: pbashaw@harding.edu.

Henderson State University, Graduate Studies, School of Education, Department of Curriculum, Instruction and Leadership, Arkadelphia, AR 71999-0001. Offers early childhood (P-4) (MSE); English (MSE); English as a second language (MSE, CP); math (MSE); middle school (MSE); reading (MSE); social science (MSE). *Accreditation:* NCATE. Part-time programs available. *Faculty:* 19 full-time (6 women), 4 part-time/adjunct (2 women). *Students:* 38 full-time (36 women), 49 part-time (47 women); includes 6 minority (5 African Americans, 1 Hispanic American), 16 international. Average age 37. In 2006, 31 degrees awarded. *Entrance requirements:* For master's, GRE General Test or MAT, minimum GPA of 2.7, teacher certification. *Application deadline:* For fall admission, 5/1 priority date for domestic students, 5/1 for international students; for winter admission, 10/1 for international students; for spring admission, 12/1 priority date for domestic students, 4/1 for international students. Applications are processed on a rolling basis. Application fee: $0 ($30 for international students). *Expenses:* Tuition, state resident: full-time $3,294; part-time $183 per credit hour. Tuition, nonresident: full-time $6,588; part-time $366 per credit hour. Required fees: $176 per term. *Financial support:* In 2006–07, 1 teaching assistantship with full tuition reimbursement (averaging $4,000 per year) was awarded; research assistantships, Federal Work-Study and institutionally sponsored loans also available. Support available to part-time students. Financial award application deadline: 7/31. *Unit head:* Dr. Kenneth Harris, Chairperson, 870-230-5203, Fax: 870-230-5455, E-mail: harris@hsu.edu. *Application contact:* Dr. Marck L. Beggs, Graduate Dean, 870-230-5126, Fax: 870-230-5479, E-mail: beggsm@hsu.edu.

Hofstra University, School of Education and Allied Human Services, Department of Curriculum and Teaching, Program in Social Studies Education, Hempstead, NY 11549. Offers MA, MS Ed. Part-time programs available. *Students:* 40 full-time (19 women), 24 part-time (13 women); includes 9 minority (2 African Americans, 2 Asian Americans or Pacific Islanders, 5 Hispanic Americans). Average age 27. 60 applicants, 90% accepted, 33 enrolled. In 2006, 44 degrees awarded. *Degree requirements:* For master's, one foreign language, comprehensive exam, state exam. *Entrance requirements:* For master's, 2 letters of recommendation, teacher certification (MA), essay. Additional exam requirements/recommendations for international students: Required—TOEFL (minimum score 550 paper-based; 213 computer-based). *Application deadline:* Applications are processed on a rolling basis. Application fee: $60. Electronic applications accepted. *Expenses:* Tuition: Full-time $13,320; part-time $740 per credit. Required fees: $930; $155 per term. *Financial support:* In 2006–07, 49 students received support, including 1 fellowship with tuition reimbursement available (averaging $3,000 per year), 1 research assistantship with full and partial tuition reimbursement available (averaging $4,700 per year); scholarships/grants and tuition waivers (full and partial) also available. Financial award applicants required to submit FAFSA. *Faculty research:* New York and slavery, religion and history. Total annual research expenditures: $1,000. *Unit head:* Dr. Alan J. Singer, Director, 516-463-5853, Fax: 516-463-6196, E-mail: catajs@hofstra.edu. *Application contact:* Carol Drummer, Dean of Graduate Admissions, 516-463-4876, Fax: 516-463-4664, E-mail: gradstudent@hofstra.edu.

Hunter College of the City University of New York, Graduate School, School of Education, Programs in Secondary Education, Concentration in Social Studies Education, New York, NY 10021-5085. Offers MA. *Accreditation:* NCATE. *Students:* 2 full-time (both women), 49 part-time (23 women); includes 7 minority (2 African Americans, 2 Asian Americans or Pacific Islanders, 3 Hispanic Americans). Average age 31. 45 applicants, 47% accepted, 12 enrolled. In 2006, 5 degrees awarded. *Degree requirements:* For master's, thesis, professional teaching portfolio, New York State Teacher Certification Exam, research project. *Entrance requirements:* For master's, minimum GPA of 3.0 in history, 2.8 overall; 2 letters of reference; minimum of 30 credits in social studies areas. Additional exam requirements/recommendations for international students: Required—TOEFL, TWE. *Application deadline:* For fall admission, 4/1 for domestic students, 2/1 for international students; for spring admission, 11/1 for domestic students, 9/1 for international students. Applications are processed on a rolling basis. Application fee: $125. *Expenses:* Tuition, state resident: part-time $270 per credit. Tuition, nonresident: part-time $500 per credit. Required fees: $45 per semester. *Financial support:* Federal Work-

Social Sciences Education

Hunter College of the City University of New York (continued)
Study and tuition waivers (partial) available. Support available to part-time students. *Unit head:* Dr. Barbara Welter, Graduate Advisor, 212-772-5480, E-mail: bwelter@shiva.hunter.cuny.edu. *Application contact:* William Zlata, Director for Graduate Admissions, 212-772-4482, Fax: 212-650-3336, E-mail: admissions@hunter.cuny.edu.

Indiana University Bloomington, School of Education, Department of Curriculum and Instruction, Bloomington, IN 47405-7000. Offers art education (MS, Ed D, PhD); curriculum studies (Ed D, PhD); elementary education (MS, Ed D, PhD, Ed S); mathematics education (MS, Ed D, PhD); science education (MS, Ed D, PhD); secondary education (MS, Ed D, PhD); social studies education (MS, PhD); special education (MS, Ed D, PhD, Ed S). PhD offered through the University Graduate School. *Accreditation:* NCATE. Part-time and evening/weekend programs available. *Students:* 39 full-time (28 women), 82 part-time (54 women); includes 15 minority (5 African Americans, 1 American Indian/Alaska Native, 6 Asian Americans or Pacific Islanders, 3 Hispanic Americans), 33 international. Average age 37. In 2006, 1 degree awarded. Terminal master's awarded for partial completion of doctoral program. *Degree requirements:* For doctorate, thesis/dissertation; for Ed S, comprehensive exam or project. *Entrance requirements:* For master's, doctorate, and Ed S, GRE General Test. *Application deadline:* For fall admission, 6/1 priority date for domestic students, 3/1 for international students; for winter admission, 11/1 priority date for domestic students; for spring admission, 9/1 for international students. Applications are processed on a rolling basis. Application fee: $50 ($60 for international students). Electronic applications accepted. *Expenses:* Tuition, state resident: full-time $5,791; part-time $241 per credit hour. Tuition, nonresident: full-time $16,866; part-time $703 per credit hour. *Financial support:* Fellowships with full and partial tuition reimbursements, research assistantships with full and partial tuition reimbursements, teaching assistantships with full and partial tuition reimbursements, career-related internships or fieldwork, Federal Work-Study, institutionally sponsored loans, and tuition waivers (partial) available. Support available to part-time students. *Unit head:* Cary Buzzelli, Chairperson, 812-856-8100. *Application contact:* Bobbie Partenheimer, Admissions Services Coordinator, 812-856-8127, Fax: 812-856-8333, E-mail: partenhe@indiana.edu.

Instituto Tecnologico de Santo Domingo, Graduate School, Santo Domingo, Dominican Republic. Offers corporate finance (M Mgmt); education (M Ed); engineering (M Eng), including data telecommunications, industrial engineering, sanitary and environmental engineering, structural engineering; environmental science (M En S); human resources administration (M Mgmt); management (M Mgmt); psychology (MA); social science (M Ed). *Entrance requirements:* For master's, birth certificate, minimum GPA of 2.0.

Inter American University of Puerto Rico, Ponce Campus, Graduate School, Mercedita, PR 00715-1602. Offers accounting (MBA); biology (M Ed); chemistry (M Ed); criminal justice (MA); elementary education (M Ed); English as a Second Language (M Ed); finance (MBA); history (M Ed); human resources (MBA); mathematics (M Ed); Spanish (M Ed); trade (MBA). *Entrance requirements:* For master's, minimum GPA of 2.5.

Iona College, School of Arts and Science, Program in Adolescence Education, New Rochelle, NY 10801-1890. Offers biology education (MS Ed, MST); English education (MS Ed, MST); mathematics education (MS Ed, MST); social studies education (MS Ed, MST); Spanish education (MS Ed, MST). *Accreditation:* NCATE. Part-time and evening/weekend programs available. *Faculty:* 11 full-time (6 women), 21 part-time/adjunct (13 women). *Students:* 15 full-time (9 women), 68 part-time (52 women); includes 6 minority (1 African American, 1 Asian American or Pacific Islander, 4 Hispanic Americans). Average age 28. 42 applicants, 57% accepted, 11 enrolled. In 2006, 29 degrees awarded. *Degree requirements:* For master's, thesis or alternative. *Entrance requirements:* For master's, minimum GPA of 2.5 (MST), New York teaching certificate (MS Ed). Additional exam requirements/recommendations for international students: Required—TOEFL (minimum score 550 paper-based; 213 computer-based). *Application deadline:* Applications are processed on a rolling basis. Application fee: $50. Electronic applications accepted. *Expenses:* Tuition: Part-time $665 per credit. Required fees: $150 per term. *Financial support:* Unspecified assistantships available. Support available to part-time students. *Faculty research:* Reading/writing, educational technology, administration, early literacy assessment, literacy development. *Unit head:* Dr. Patricia Antonacci, Chair, 914-633-2080, Fax: 914-633-2608, E-mail: pantonacci@iona.edu. *Application contact:* Veronica Jarek-Prinz, Graduate Admissions, 914-633-2289, Fax: 914-633-2012, E-mail: vjarekprinz@iona.edu.

Ithaca College, Graduate Studies, School of Humanities and Sciences, Program in Adolescent Education, Ithaca, NY 14850-7020. Offers biology 7-12 (MAT); chemistry 7-12 (MAT); English 7-12 (MAT); French 7-12 (MAT); math 7-12 (MAT); physics 7-12 (MAT); social studies 7-12 (MAT); Spanish (MAT). *Faculty:* 14 full-time (5 women), 1 (woman) part-time/adjunct. *Students:* 8 full-time (2 women), 2 part-time (both women); includes 1 minority (Hispanic American) Average age 28. 12 applicants, 92% accepted, 10 enrolled. *Entrance requirements:* For master's, minimum GPA of 3.0. *Application deadline:* For fall admission, 5/15 for domestic students; for spring admission, 12/1 for domestic students. Application fee: $40. *Expenses:* Contact institution. *Financial support:* In 2006–07, 10 students received support, including 8 teaching assistantships (averaging $5,820 per year). Financial award application deadline: 3/1. *Unit head:* Linda Hanrahan, Chairperson, 607-274-3147, E-mail: lhanrahan@ithaca.edu.

Kutztown University of Pennsylvania, College of Graduate Studies and Extended Learning, College of Education, Program in Secondary Education, Kutztown, PA 19530-0730. Offers biology (M Ed); curriculum and instruction (M Ed); English (M Ed); mathematics (M Ed); secondary education (Certificate); social studies (M Ed). *Accreditation:* NCATE. Part-time and evening/weekend programs available. *Faculty:* 5 full-time (2 women). *Students:* 69 full-time (32 women), 80 part-time (44 women); includes 5 minority (1 African American, 1 American Indian/Alaska Native, 2 Asian Americans or Pacific Islanders, 1 Hispanic American), 3 international. Average age 32. 80 applicants, 88% accepted, 34 enrolled. In 2006, 26 degrees awarded. *Degree requirements:* For master's, thesis optional. *Entrance requirements:* For master's, GRE General Test. Additional exam requirements/recommendations for international students: Required—TOEFL. *Application deadline:* Applications are processed on a rolling basis. Application fee: $35. Electronic applications accepted. *Expenses:* Tuition, state resident: full-time $6,048; part-time $336 per credit. Tuition, nonresident: full-time $9,678; part-time $538 per credit. *Financial support:* In 2006–07, research assistantships with full tuition reimbursements (averaging $5,000 per year); career-related internships or fieldwork, Federal Work-Study, and unspecified assistantships also available. Financial award application deadline: 3/15; financial award applicants required to submit FAFSA. *Unit head:* Dr. Kathleen Dolgos, Chairperson, 610-683-4279, Fax: 610-683-1338, E-mail: dolgos@kutztown.edu.

Lehman College of the City University of New York, Division of Education, Department of Middle and High School Education, Program in Social Studies 7–12, Bronx, NY 10468-1589. Offers MA. *Accreditation:* NCATE. *Entrance requirements:* For master's, minimum GPA of 3.0 in social sciences, 2.7 overall.

Louisiana Tech University, Graduate School, College of Education, Department of Curriculum, Instruction and Leadership, Ruston, LA 71272. Offers curriculum and instruction (MS, Ed D); educational leadership (Ed D); secondary education (M Ed), including business education, English education, foreign language education, health and physical education, mathematics education, science education, social studies education, speech education. *Accreditation:* NCATE. Part-time programs available. *Degree requirements:* For doctorate, thesis/dissertation. *Entrance requirements:* For master's and doctorate, GRE General Test.

Manhattanville College, Graduate Programs, School of Education, Program in Middle Childhood/Adolescence Education (Grades 5-12), Purchase, NY 10577-2132. Offers biology (MAT); biology and special education (MPS); chemistry (MAT); chemistry and special education (MPS); English (MAT); English and special education (MPS); literacy (MPS), including reading and writing, writing; literacy and special education (MPS); math (MAT); math and special education (MPS); second language (MAT), including French, Italian, Latin, Spanish; social studies (MAT); social studies and special education (MPS); special education (MPS). Part-time and evening/weekend programs available. *Students:* 76 full-time (53 women), 109 part-time (68 women); includes 8 African Americans, 1 Asian American or Pacific Islander, 10 Hispanic Americans, 1 international. In 2006, 165 degrees awarded. *Degree requirements:* For master's, comprehensive exam or research project, field experience. *Entrance requirements:* For master's, minimum undergraduate GPA of 3.0, 2 letters of recommendation. *Application deadline:* Applications are processed on a rolling basis. Application fee: $55. *Financial support:* Career-related internships or fieldwork and institutionally sponsored loans available. Support available to part-time students. *Application contact:* Alyce Ware Poli, Director of Admissions, 914-323-5142, Fax: 914-694-1732, E-mail: edschool@mville.edu.

McNeese State University, Graduate School, College of Education, Department of Teacher Education, Program in Teaching, Lake Charles, LA 70609. Offers elementary education (MAT); secondary education (MAT); special education (mild/moderate) (MAT). Evening/weekend programs available. *Faculty:* 12 full-time (8 women), 2 part-time/adjunct (1 woman). *Students:* 37 full-time (30 women), 168 part-time (146 women); includes 53 minority (47 African Americans, 2 Asian Americans or Pacific Islanders, 4 Hispanic Americans), 2 international. In 2006, 26 degrees awarded. *Entrance requirements:* For master's, GRE, PRAXIS. *Application deadline:* For fall admission, 5/15 priority date for domestic students. Applications are processed on a rolling basis. Application fee: $20 ($30 for international students). *Expenses:* Tuition, area resident: Full-time $2,226; part-time $193 per hour. Required fees: $919; $106 per hour. *Financial support:* Application deadline: 5/1. *Unit head:* Dr. Wayne R Fetter, Dean, College of Education, 337-475-5432, Fax: 337-475-5467, E-mail: wfetter@mcneese.edu.

Miami University, Graduate School, School of Education and Allied Professions, Department of Teacher Education, Program in Secondary Education, Oxford, OH 45056. Offers adolescent education (MAT), including integrated English, integrated mathematics, integrated social studies, language arts; elementary mathematics education (M Ed); secondary education (M Ed, MAT). *Accreditation:* NCATE. Part-time programs available. *Degree requirements:* For master's, thesis (for some programs), final exam. *Entrance requirements:* For master's, MAT, minimum undergraduate GPA of 3.0 during previous 2 years or 2.75 overall. *Faculty research:* Teacher effectiveness, collaboration models.

Michigan State University, The Graduate School, College of Arts and Letters, Department of History, East Lansing, MI 48824. Offers history (MA, PhD); history-secondary school teaching (MA). *Faculty:* 45 full-time (21 women). *Students:* 58 full-time (31 women), 8 part-time (1 woman); includes 17 minority (11 African Americans, 1 Asian American or Pacific Islander, 5 Hispanic Americans), 9 international. Average age 32. 47 applicants, 45% accepted. In 2006, 1 master's, 8 doctorates awarded. *Entrance requirements:* Additional exam requirements/recommendations for international students: Required—TOEFL. Electronic applications accepted. *Expenses:* Tuition, state resident: part-time $346 per credit hour. Tuition, nonresident: part-time $730 per credit hour. Tuition and fees vary according to program. *Financial support:* In 2006–07, 25 fellowships with tuition reimbursements, 8 research assistantships with tuition reimbursements (averaging $12,820 per year), 33 teaching assistantships with tuition reimbursements (averaging $12,627 per year) were awarded. Total annual research expenditures:$30,302. *Unit head:* Dr. Mark L. Kornbluh, Chairperson, 517-355-7502, Fax: 517-353-5599, E-mail: kornbluh@msu.edu. *Application contact:* Janell Kebler, Graduate Secretary, 517-355-7501, Fax: 517-353-5599, E-mail: history@msu.edu.

Mills College, Graduate Studies, Education Department, Oakland, CA 94613-1000. Offers administration (Ed D); child life in health care settings (MA); early childhood education (MA); education (MA), including curriculum and instruction, elementary education, English education, mathematics education, science education, secondary education, social sciences education, teaching. Part-time and evening/weekend programs available. *Faculty:* 10 full-time (7 women), 15 part-time/adjunct (12 women). *Students:* 192 full-time (153 women), 41 part-time (36 women); includes 62 minority (28 African Americans, 13 Asian Americans or Pacific Islanders, 21 Hispanic Americans), 2 international. Average age 34. 160 applicants, 74% accepted, 73 enrolled. In 2006, 52 master's, 1 doctorate awarded. Terminal master's awarded for partial completion of doctoral program. *Degree requirements:* For master's, comprehensive exam. *Entrance requirements:* For doctorate, GRE General Test. Additional exam requirements/recommendations for international students: Required—TOEFL. *Application deadline:* For fall admission, 2/1 for domestic and international students; for spring admission, 11/1 for domestic and international students. Applications are processed on a rolling basis. Application fee: $50. Electronic applications accepted. *Financial support:* In 2006–07, 56 fellowships with tuition reimbursements (averaging $2,700 per year), 15 teaching assistantships (averaging $6,350 per year) were awarded; career-related internships or fieldwork, institutionally sponsored loans, scholarships/grants, and residence awards also available. Support available to part-time students. Financial award application deadline: 2/1; financial award applicants required to submit CSS PROFILE or FAFSA. *Faculty research:* Child development, gender and education, public policy, cross-cultural development, development of literacy. *Unit head:* Joseph Kahne, Chairperson, 510-430-3190, Fax: 510-430-3314, E-mail: grad-studies@mills.edu. *Application contact:* Randy McGlauthing, Director of Graduate Admissions, 510-430-2355, Fax: 510-430-2159, E-mail: rmglaut@mills.edu.

Minnesota State University Mankato, College of Graduate Studies, College of Social and Behavioral Sciences, Department of Geography, Mankato, MN 56001. Offers geography (MS); geography education (MT). Part-time programs available. *Students:* 8 full-time (5 women), 22 part-time (3 women). Average age 30. In 2006, 7 degrees awarded. *Degree requirements:* For master's, one foreign language, comprehensive exam. *Entrance requirements:* For master's, GRE General Test (if GPA is below 2.8 for the last 2 years), minimum GPA of 3.0 during previous 2 years. *Application deadline:* For fall admission, 7/1 priority date for domestic students; for spring admission, 11/1 for domestic students. Applications are processed on a rolling basis. Application fee: $40. Electronic applications accepted. *Financial support:* Research assistantships, teaching assistantships with full tuition reimbursements, career-related internships or fieldwork, Federal Work-Study, institutionally sponsored loans, and unspecified assistantships available. Support available to part-time students. Financial award application deadline: 3/15; financial award applicants required to submit FAFSA. *Unit head:* Dr. Donald Friend, Chairperson, 507-389-1610. *Application contact:* 507-389-2321, E-mail: grad@mnsu.edu.

Minnesota State University Mankato, College of Graduate Studies, College of Social and Behavioral Sciences, Department of History, Mankato, MN 56001. Offers history (MA, MS); social studies (MS); teaching history (MS, MT). *Students:* 9 full-time (5 women), 17 part-time (4 women). Average age 35. In 2006, 7 degrees awarded. *Degree requirements:* For master's, one foreign language, thesis or alternative, comprehensive exam. *Entrance requirements:* For master's, minimum GPA of 3.0 during previous 2 years. Additional exam requirements/recommendations for international students: Required—TOEFL. *Application deadline:* For fall admission, 7/1 priority date for domestic students; for spring admission, 11/1 for domestic students. Applications are processed on a rolling basis. Application fee: $40. Electronic applications accepted. *Financial support:* Research assistantships, teaching assistantships with full tuition reimbursements, career-related internships or fieldwork, Federal Work-Study, institutionally sponsored loans, and unspecified assistantships available. Support available to part-time students. Financial award application deadline: 3/15. *Faculty research:* Charivaris, Lindbergh in the U.S., Dutch trade to South America in the seventeenth and eighteenth centuries. *Unit head:* Dr. Charles Piehl, Graduate Coordinator, 507-389-5316. *Application contact:* 507-389-2321, E-mail: grad@mnsu.edu.

Mississippi College, Graduate School, School of Education, Department of Teacher Education and Leadership, Clinton, MS 39058. Offers art (M Ed); biological science (M Ed); business education (M Ed); computer science (M Ed); dyslexia therapy (M Ed); educational leadership (M Ed, Ed S); elementary education (M Ed, Ed S); English (M Ed); higher education administration (MS); mathematics (M Ed); secondary education (M Ed); social studies (history) (M Ed);

teaching arts (M Ed). Part-time programs available. *Faculty:* 9 full-time (5 women), 14 part-time/adjunct (10 women). *Students:* 52 full-time (36 women), 286 part-time (247 women); includes 173 minority (171 African Americans, 1 American Indian/Alaska Native, 1 Hispanic American), 1 international. Average age 32. In 2006, 131 degrees awarded. *Degree requirements:* For master's, thesis optional. *Entrance requirements:* For master's, NTE. Additional exam requirements/recommendations for international students: Recommended—IELTS. *Application deadline:* Applications are processed on a rolling basis. Application fee: $25. Electronic applications accepted. *Expenses:* Tuition: Full-time $7,290; part-time $405 per hour. Required fees: $150 per term. Tuition and fees vary according to campus/location and program. *Financial support:* Teaching assistantships, career-related internships or fieldwork, Federal Work-Study, scholarships/grants, and unspecified assistantships available. Support available to part-time students. Financial award applicants required to submit FAFSA. *Unit head:* Dr. Tom Williams, Chair, 601-925-3844, E-mail: twilliams@mc.edu.

Missouri State University, Graduate College, College of Humanities and Public Affairs, Department of History, Springfield, MO 65804-0094. Offers history (MA); secondary education (MS Ed), including history, social science. Part-time programs available. *Faculty:* 16 full-time (1 woman). *Students:* 12 full-time (5 women), 58 part-time (24 women); includes 2 minority (1 American Indian/Alaska Native, 1 Hispanic American). Average age 34. 23 applicants, 83% accepted, 12 enrolled. In 2006, 9 degrees awarded. *Degree requirements:* For master's, thesis or alternative, comprehensive exam. *Entrance requirements:* For master's, minimum GPA of 2.75, 24 hours of undergraduate course work in history (MA), 9-12 teaching certification (MS Ed). Additional exam requirements/recommendations for international students: Required—TOEFL (minimum score 550 paper-based; 213 computer-based; 79 iBT), IELTS (minimum score 6). *Application deadline:* For fall admission, 7/20 priority date for domestic students; for spring admission, 12/20 priority date for domestic students. Applications are processed on a rolling basis. Application fee: $35. Electronic applications accepted. *Expenses:* Tuition, state resident: full-time $3,582; part-time $199 per credit hour. Tuition, nonresident: full-time $6,984; part-time $199 per credit hour. Required fees: $548. Full-time tuition and fees vary according to course level, course load, program and reciprocity agreements. *Financial support:* In 2006–07, 2 research assistantships with full tuition reimbursements (averaging $9,000 per year), 2 teaching assistantships with full tuition reimbursements (averaging $9,000 per year) were awarded; Federal Work-Study, scholarships/grants, and unspecified assistantships also available. Support available to part-time students. Financial award application deadline: 3/31; financial award applicants required to submit FAFSA. *Faculty research:* Recent U.S. history, Native American history, legal history, women's history, ancient Near East. *Unit head:* Michael Sheng, Head, 417-836-5511, Fax: 417-836-5523, E-mail: history@missouristate.edu.

Montclair State University, The Graduate School, College of Humanities and Social Sciences, Department of History, Montclair, NJ 07043-1624. Offers social sciences (MA), including history. Part-time and evening/weekend programs available. *Faculty:* 16 full-time (6 women), 15 part-time/adjunct (5 women). *Students:* 11 applicants, 73% accepted, 5 enrolled. In 2006, 16 degrees awarded. *Degree requirements:* For master's, comprehensive exam. *Entrance requirements:* For master's, GRE General Test, 2 letters of recommendation. Additional exam requirements/recommendations for international students: Required—TOEFL (minimum score 550 paper-based; 213 computer-based). *Application deadline:* For fall admission, 6/1 for international students; for spring admission, 11/1 for international students. Applications are processed on a rolling basis. Application fee: $60. Electronic applications accepted. *Expenses:* Tuition, state resident: part-time $450 per credit. Tuition, nonresident: part-time $682 per credit. Tuition and fees vary according to degree level and program. *Financial support:* Research assistantships with full tuition reimbursements, Federal Work-Study, scholarships/grants, and unspecified assistantships available. Support available to part-time students. Financial award application deadline: 3/1. *Unit head:* Dr. Leslie Wilson, Adviser, 973-655-5261.

New York University, Steinhardt School of Culture, Education and Human Development, Department of Humanities and Social Sciences in the Professions, Program in Studies in Arts and Humanities Education, New York, NY 10012-1019. Offers MA, PhD. Part-time and evening/weekend programs available. *Faculty:* 6 full-time (4 women). *Students:* 17 full-time (15 women), 17 part-time (10 women); includes 7 minority (2 African Americans, 2 Asian Americans or Pacific Islanders, 3 Hispanic Americans), 2 international. 24 applicants, 83% accepted, 10 enrolled. In 2006, 9 master's, 1 doctorate awarded. Terminal master's awarded for partial completion of doctoral program. *Degree requirements:* For master's, thesis (for some programs); for doctorate, thesis/dissertation. *Entrance requirements:* For doctorate, GRE General Test, interview. Additional exam requirements/recommendations for international students: Required—TOEFL. *Application deadline:* For fall admission, 12/15 priority date for domestic and international students; for spring admission, 11/1 for domestic and international students. Applications are processed on a rolling basis. Application fee: $50. *Expenses:* Tuition: Part-time $1,080 per unit. Required fees: $56 per unit. $329 per term. Tuition and fees vary according to program. *Financial support:* Fellowships with full and partial tuition reimbursements, Federal Work-Study, institutionally sponsored loans, scholarships/grants, and tuition waivers (partial) available. Support available to part-time students. Financial award application deadline: 2/1; financial award applicants required to submit FAFSA. *Faculty research:* Interrelationships between film and literature; literary rhetoric, stylistics, and the creative process; relationships among culture, aesthetic response, and learning. *Unit head:* Dr. Joy G. Boyum, Director, 212-992-9475, Fax: 212-995-4832, E-mail: jgb2@nyu.edu. *Application contact:* 212-998-5030, Fax: 212-995-4328, E-mail: steinhardt.gradadmissions@nyu.edu.

New York University, Steinhardt School of Culture, Education and Human Development, Department of Teaching and Learning, Program in Social Studies Education, New York, NY 10012-1019. Offers MA. *Accreditation:* Teacher Education Accreditation Council. Part-time and evening/weekend programs available. *Faculty:* 2 full-time (1 woman). *Students:* 19 full-time (13 women), 18 part-time (9 women); includes 12 minority (4 African Americans, 5 Asian Americans or Pacific Islanders, 3 Hispanic Americans). 36 applicants, 86% accepted, 7 enrolled. In 2006, 21 degrees awarded. *Degree requirements:* For master's, thesis (for some programs). *Entrance requirements:* Additional exam requirements/recommendations for international students: Required—TOEFL. *Application deadline:* For fall admission, 12/15 priority date for domestic and international students; for spring admission, 11/1 for domestic and international students. Applications are processed on a rolling basis. Application fee: $50. *Expenses:* Tuition: Part-time $1,080 per unit. Required fees: $56 per unit. $329 per term. Tuition and fees vary according to program. *Financial support:* Career-related internships or fieldwork, Federal Work-Study, institutionally sponsored loans, scholarships/grants, and tuition waivers (partial) available. Support available to part-time students. Financial award application deadline: 2/1; financial award applicants required to submit FAFSA. *Faculty research:* Social studies education reform, ethnography and oral history, civic education, labor history and social studies curriculum, material culture. *Application contact:* 212-998-5030, Fax: 212-995-4328, E-mail: steinhardt.gradadmissions@nyu.edu.

North Carolina Agricultural and Technical State University, Graduate School, College of Arts and Sciences, Department of History and Social Science Education, Greensboro, NC 27411. Offers history education (MS); social science education (MS). *Accreditation:* NCATE. *Degree requirements:* For master's, qualifying exam. *Entrance requirements:* For master's, GRE General Test.

North Carolina Agricultural and Technical State University, Graduate School, School of Education, Department of Curriculum and Instruction, Program in Intermediate Education, Greensboro, NC 27411. Offers biology education (MS); chemistry education (MS); English education (MS); history education (MS); social science education (MS). *Accreditation:* NCATE. Part-time and evening/weekend programs available. *Degree requirements:* For master's, thesis (for some programs), qualifying exam, comprehensive exam. *Entrance requirements:* For master's, GRE General Test, minimum GPA of 3.0.

North Dakota State University, The Graduate School, College of Human Development and Education, School of Education, Fargo, ND 58105. Offers agricultural education (M Ed, MS), including agricultural education, agricultural extension education (MS); counseling (M Ed, MS, PhD); curriculum and instruction (M Ed, MS), including pedagogy, physical education and athletic administration; education (PhD); educational leadership (M Ed, MS, Ed S); family and consumer sciences education (M Ed, MS); history education (M Ed, MS); mathematics education (M Ed, MS); music education (M Ed, MS); science education (M Ed, MS). *Accreditation:* NCATE. Part-time and evening/weekend programs available. Postbaccalaureate distance learning degree programs offered (minimal on-campus study). *Faculty:* 25 full-time (9 women), 3 part-time/adjunct (1 woman). *Students:* 29 full-time (25 women), 207 part-time (132 women); includes 15 minority (4 African Americans, 6 American Indian/Alaska Native, 3 Asian Americans or Pacific Islanders, 2 Hispanic Americans), 4 international. 88 applicants, 67% accepted, 56 enrolled. In 2006, 44 master's, 5 doctorates awarded. *Degree requirements:* For master's, comprehensive exam; for doctorate and Ed S, thesis/dissertation. *Entrance requirements:* For degree, GRE General Test, master's degree, minimum GPA of 3.25. Additional exam requirements/recommendations for international students: Required—TOEFL. *Application deadline:* Applications are processed on a rolling basis. Application fee: $45 ($60 for international students). *Financial support:* Research assistantships, teaching assistantships, career-related internships or fieldwork, Federal Work-Study, institutionally sponsored loans, and tuition waivers (full) available. Financial award application deadline: 4/15. *Unit head:* Dr. William O. Martin, Chair, 701-231-7104, Fax: 701-231-7416, E-mail: william.martin@ndsu.edu.

North Georgia College & State University, Graduate Studies, Program in Teacher Education, Dahlonega, GA 30597. Offers early childhood education (M Ed); educational leadership (Ed S); middle grades education (M Ed); secondary education (M Ed), including art education, biology education, chemistry education, English education, history education, mathematics education, physical education, science education; special education (M Ed), including interrelated special education, learning disabilities. *Accreditation:* NCATE. Part-time and evening/weekend programs available. Postbaccalaureate distance learning degree programs offered (minimal on-campus study). *Faculty:* 35 full-time (18 women), 9 part-time/adjunct (6 women). *Students:* 260. Average age 32. 120 applicants, 63% accepted. In 2006, 134 degrees awarded. *Degree requirements:* For master's, thesis optional. *Entrance requirements:* For master's, GRE General Test or MAT, minimum GPA of 2.75; for Ed S, GRE General Test or MAT, 3 years of teaching experience, master's degree, minimum graduate GPA of 3.25. *Application deadline:* For fall admission, 7/1 priority date for domestic students; for spring admission, 12/10 priority date for domestic students. Applications are processed on a rolling basis. Application fee: $25. Electronic applications accepted. *Expenses:* Tuition, state resident: full-time $3,044; part-time $127 per credit hour. Tuition, nonresident: full-time $12,172; part-time $508 per credit hour. Required fees: $892; $458 per semester. *Financial support:* Teaching assistantships, career-related internships or fieldwork and scholarships/grants available. Support available to part-time students. Financial award application deadline: 5/1. *Faculty research:* Computers and teachers' attitudes, rural versus urban teacher attitudes, teacher leadership roles, minority recruitment in teaching force. *Unit head:* Dr. Bob Michael, Dean, School of Education, 706-864-1998, Fax: 706-867-2850, E-mail: bmichael@ngcsu.edu. *Application contact:* Dr. Donna A. Gessell, Director of Graduate Studies and External Programs, 706-864-1528, Fax: 706-867-2795, E-mail: dgessell@ngcsu.edu.

Northwestern State University of Louisiana, Graduate Studies and Research, College of Education, Programs in Education, Natchitoches, LA 71497. Offers business and distributive education (M Ed); counseling (M Ed); early childhood education (M Ed); education (M Ed); education leadership (M Ed); educational technology (M Ed); elementary teaching (M Ed); English education (M Ed); home economics education (M Ed); mathematics education (M Ed); reading (M Ed); science education (M Ed); secondary teaching (M Ed); social sciences education (M Ed). *Students:* 49 full-time (41 women), 245 part-time (206 women); includes 78 minority (70 African Americans, 5 American Indian/Alaska Native, 2 Asian Americans or Pacific Islanders, 1 Hispanic American). Average age 35. In 2006, 158 degrees awarded. *Degree requirements:* For master's, thesis or alternative, comprehensive exam, registration. *Entrance requirements:* For master's, GRE General Test, minimum undergraduate GPA of 2.5. *Application contact:* Dr. Steven G. Horton, Associate Provost/Dean, Graduate Studies, Research, and Information Systems, 318-357-5851, Fax: 318-357-5019, E-mail: grad_school@nsula.edu.

Northwest Missouri State University, Graduate School, College of Arts and Sciences, Department of History, Humanities, and Political Science, Maryville, MO 64468-6001. Offers history (MA); teaching history (MS Ed). Part-time programs available. *Faculty:* 5 full-time (1 woman). *Students:* 8 full-time (2 women), 2 part-time (1 woman); includes 1 minority (Asian American or Pacific Islander) 10 applicants, 100% accepted, 9 enrolled. In 2006, 1 degree awarded. *Degree requirements:* For master's, thesis, comprehensive exam. *Entrance requirements:* For master's, GRE General Test, undergraduate major/minor in social studies/humanities, minimum undergraduate GPA of 2.5, writing sample. Additional exam requirements/recommendations for international students: Required—TOEFL (minimum score 550 paper-based; 213 computer-based). *Application deadline:* For fall admission, 7/1 for domestic and international students; for spring admission, 11/15 for domestic and international students. Applications are processed on a rolling basis. Application fee: $0 ($50 for international students). *Financial support:* In 2006–07, 2 research assistantships with full tuition reimbursements (averaging $6,000 per year) were awarded. Financial award application deadline: 3/1; financial award applicants required to submit FAFSA. *Unit head:* Dr. Richard Frucht, Chairperson, 660-562-1614. *Application contact:* Dr. Frances Shipley, Dean of Graduate School, 660-562-1145, Fax: 660-562-1096, E-mail: gradsch@nwmissouri.edu.

Nova Southeastern University, Fischler School of Education and Human Services, Graduate Teacher Education Program, Fort Lauderdale, FL 33314-7796. Offers athletic administration (MS); cognitive and behavioral disabilities (MS); computer science education (Ed S); computer science education (K-12) (MS); curriculum and teaching (Ed S); curriculum, instruction and technology (MS); curriculum, instruction, management and administration (Ed S); early childhood special education (MS); early literacy and reading (Ed S); early literacy education (MS); education technology (MS); educational leadership (administration K–12) (MS, Ed S); educational media (Ed S); educational media (K-12) (MS); elementary education (MS, Ed S), including ESOL endorsement (MS); English (MS, Ed S); exceptional student education (MS), including ESOL endorsement; gifted education (MS, Ed S); interdisciplinary arts education (MS); management and administration of educational programs (MS); mathematics (MS, Ed S); multicultural early intervention (MS); pre-kindergarten/primary (MS); preschool education (MS); reading (MS, Ed S); science (MS, Ed S); secondary education (MS); social studies (MS, Ed S); Spanish language (MS); teaching and learning (MA, MS), including curriculum and instruction (MA), elementary mathematics (MA), elementary reading (MA), K-12 technology integration (MA); teaching English to speakers of other languages (MS, Ed S); technology management and administration (Ed S); urban studies education (MS); varying exceptionalities (Ed S). Part-time and evening/weekend programs available. Postbaccalaureate distance learning degree programs offered. *Faculty:* 131 full-time (78 women), 548 part-time/adjunct (342 women). *Students:* 1,418 full-time (1,139 women), 3,464 part-time (2,877 women); includes 2,462 minority (1,732 African Americans, 13 American Indian/Alaska Native, 44 Asian Americans or Pacific Islanders, 673 Hispanic Americans), 77 international. Average age 38. 1,771 applicants, 80% accepted, 1419 enrolled. In 2006, 2,078 master's, 425 other advanced degrees awarded. *Degree requirements:* For master's and Ed S, thesis, practicum, internship. *Entrance requirements:* For master's, MAT, GRE, CLAST, CBEST, PRAXIS I, GKT, minimum GPA of 2.5; for Ed S, MAT or GRE, master's degree, teaching certificate, minimum GPA of 3.0. Additional exam requirements/recommendations for international students: Recommended—TOEFL (minimum score 550 paper-based; 213 computer-based), IELTS (minimum score 6). *Application deadline:* For fall admission, 8/11 priority date for domestic and international students; for winter admission, 12/28 priority date for domestic and international students; for spring admission, 4/22 priority date for domestic and international students. Applications are processed on a rolling basis. Application fee: $50. Electronic applications accepted. *Financial support:* Federal Work-Study available. Support available to part-time students. Financial award application deadline: 1/7. *Faculty research:* School effectiveness, critical thinking, leadership skills acquisition, child education, multicultural education. *Unit head:* Dr. Meline Kevorkian, Associ-

Social Sciences Education

Nova Southeastern University (continued)
ate Dean of Master's and Educational Programs, 954-262-8500, Fax: 954-262-3606, E-mail: melinek@nova.edu. *Application contact:* Jennifer Quiñones Nottingham, Dean of Student Affairs, 800-986-3223 Ext. 8624, Fax: 954-262-3911, E-mail: jlquinon@nova.edu.

Occidental College, Graduate Studies, Department of Education, Program in Secondary Education, Los Angeles, CA 90041-3314. Offers English and comparative literary studies (MAT); history (MAT); life science (MAT); mathematics (MAT); physical science (MAT); social science (MAT); Spanish (MAT). Part-time programs available. *Faculty:* 3 full-time (2 women), 2 part-time/adjunct (both women). *Students:* 4 full-time (all women), 3 part-time (1 woman); includes 5 minority (1 Asian American or Pacific Islander, 4 Hispanic Americans). Average age 25. 4 applicants, 100% accepted, 4 enrolled. In 2006, 4 degrees awarded. *Degree requirements:* For master's, final exam, graduate synthesis paper. *Entrance requirements:* For master's, GRE General Test, minimum GPA of 3.0. Additional exam requirements/recommendations for international students: Required—TOEFL (minimum score 625 paper-based). *Application deadline:* For fall admission, 3/1 for domestic and international students; for spring admission, 10/1 for domestic and international students. Applications are processed on a rolling basis. Application fee: $50. *Expenses: Contact institution. Financial support:* Fellowships, Federal Work-Study, institutionally sponsored loans, and scholarships/grants available. Support available to part-time students. Financial award application deadline: 3/1; financial award applicants required to submit FAFSA. *Unit head:* Chair, 323-259-2781, E-mail: edudept@oxy.edu. *Application contact:* Angela Allen, Credential Analyst/Department Services Coordinator, 323-259-2781, E-mail: edudept@oxy.edu.

Ohio University, Graduate Studies, College of Education, Department of Teacher Education, Athens, OH 45701-2979. Offers adolescent to young adult education (M Ed); curriculum and instruction (M Ed, PhD); mathematics education (PhD); middle child education (M Ed); reading and language arts (PhD); reading education (M Ed); social studies education (PhD); special education (M Ed, PhD). Part-time and evening/weekend programs available. *Faculty:* 21 full-time (13 women), 7 part-time/adjunct (all women). *Students:* 57 full-time (44 women), 61 part-time (46 women); includes 4 minority (2 African Americans, 1 Asian American or Pacific Islander, 1 Hispanic American), 36 international. 93 applicants, 61% accepted, 37 enrolled. *Median time to degree:* Of those who began their doctoral program in fall 1998, 92% received their degree in 8 years or less. *Degree requirements:* For master's, thesis or alternative, registration; for doctorate, thesis/dissertation, comprehensive exam, registration. *Entrance requirements:* For master's, GRE General Test or MAT if GPA is less than 2.9; for doctorate, GRE General Test, minimum GPA of 3.4, work experience. Additional exam requirements/recommendations for international students: Required—TOEFL (minimum score 550 paper-based; 213 computer-based). *Application deadline:* For fall admission, 4/1 priority date for domestic and international students. Applications are processed on a rolling basis. Application fee: $45. Electronic applications accepted. *Financial support:* In 2006–07, 52 students received support, including 31 research assistantships with full tuition reimbursements available (averaging $6,500 per year), teaching assistantships with full tuition reimbursements available (averaging $7,200 per year); Federal Work-Study, institutionally sponsored loans, tuition waivers (full), and unspecified assistantships also available. Financial award application deadline: 3/15. *Faculty research:* Cognition literacy, character education, teacher's education reform, disabilities. Total annual research expenditures: $605,070. *Unit head:* Dr. William Earl Smith, Chair, 740-593-4483, Fax: 740-593-0477, E-mail: smithw@ohio.edu. *Application contact:* Floyd J. Doney, Director of Student Affairs, 740-593-4400, Fax: 740-593-9310, E-mail: doney@ohio.edu.

Penn State University Park, Graduate School, College of Education, Department of Curriculum and Instruction, State College, University Park, PA 16802-1503. Offers bilingual education (M Ed, MS, PhD); early childhood education (M Ed, MS, PhD); elementary education (M Ed, MS, PhD); instructional systems (M Ed, MS, PhD); language arts and reading (M Ed, MS, PhD); science education (M Ed, MS, PhD); social studies education (MS, PhD); supervisor and curriculum development (M Ed, MS, PhD). *Accreditation:* NCATE. *Unit head:* Dr. Murry R. Nelson, Head, 814-865-6321, Fax: 814-863-7602, E-mail: mrn2@psu.edu. *Application contact:* Judy Nastase, Graduate Staff Assistant, 814-865-2168, E-mail: jcn3@psu.edu.

Portland State University, Graduate Studies, College of Liberal Arts and Sciences, Interdisciplinary Programs in General Science, General Social Science, and General Arts and Letters, Portland, OR 97207-0751. Offers general arts and letters education (MAT, MST); general science education (MAT, MST); general social science education (MAT, MST). Part-time and evening/weekend programs available. *Students:* 23 full-time (18 women), 15 part-time (13 women); includes 2 minority (1 American Indian/Alaska Native, 1 Asian American or Pacific Islander), 5 international. Average age 37. 15 applicants, 80% accepted, 11 enrolled. In 2006, 6 degrees awarded. *Entrance requirements:* For master's, minimum GPA of 3.0 in upper-division course work or 2.75 overall. Additional exam requirements/recommendations for international students: Required—TOEFL (minimum score 550 paper-based; 213 computer-based). *Application deadline:* For fall admission, 4/1 priority date for domestic students, 3/1 priority date for international students. Application fee: $50. *Expenses:* Tuition, state resident: full-time $6,426; part-time $238 per credit. Tuition, nonresident: full-time $11,016; part-time $408 per credit. Tuition and fees vary according to course load. *Financial support:* In 2006–07, 2 research assistantships with full tuition reimbursements (averaging $9,930 per year) were awarded; fellowships with full tuition reimbursements, teaching assistantships with full tuition reimbursements, Federal Work-Study and unspecified assistantships also available. Support available to part-time students. Financial award application deadline: 3/1; financial award applicants required to submit FAFSA. *Unit head:* Robert Mercer, Senior Academic Adviser, 503-725-5059.

Princeton University, Graduate School, Department of History, Princeton, NJ 08544-1019. Offers community college history teaching (PhD); history (PhD); history of science (PhD). *Degree requirements:* For doctorate, variable foreign language requirement, thesis/dissertation, comprehensive exam. *Entrance requirements:* For doctorate, GRE General Test, sample of written work. Additional exam requirements/recommendations for international students: Required—TOEFL (minimum score 600 paper-based; 250 computer-based). Electronic applications accepted. *Faculty research:* World comparative, Europe-early modern, modern, late antique, medieval.

Purdue University, Graduate School, School of Education, Department of Curriculum and Instruction, West Lafayette, IN 47907. Offers agricultural and extension education (PhD, Ed S); agriculture and extension education (MS, MS Ed); art education (PhD); consumer and family sciences and extension education (MS Ed, PhD, Ed S); curriculum studies (MS Ed, PhD, Ed S); educational technology (MS Ed, PhD, Ed S); elementary education (MS Ed); foreign language education (MS Ed, PhD, Ed S); industrial technology (PhD, Ed S); language arts (MS Ed, PhD, Ed S); literacy (MS Ed, PhD, Ed S); mathematics/science education (MS, MS Ed, PhD, Ed S); social studies (MS Ed, PhD); social studies education (Ed S); vocational/industrial education (MS Ed, PhD, Ed S); vocational/technical education (MS Ed, PhD, Ed S). *Accreditation:* NCATE. Part-time and evening/weekend programs available. *Faculty:* 26 full-time (13 women), 3 part-time/adjunct (all women). *Students:* 59 full-time (37 women), 112 part-time (70 women); includes 24 minority (13 African Americans, 3 American Indian/Alaska Native, 4 Asian Americans or Pacific Islanders, 4 Hispanic Americans), 38 international. Average age 35. 92 applicants, 68% accepted, 38 enrolled. In 2006, 52 master's, 23 doctorates awarded. *Degree requirements:* For master's, thesis optional; for doctorate, thesis/dissertation, oral and written exams; for Ed S, oral presentation, project. *Entrance requirements:* For master's, GRE General Test, minimum B average; for doctorate, GRE General Test; for Ed S, GRE, minimum B average. Additional exam requirements/recommendations for international students: Required—TOEFL. *Application deadline:* For fall admission, 1/15 priority date for domestic students, 1/15 for international students; for spring admission, 9/15 for domestic and international students. Applications are processed on a rolling basis. Application fee: $55. Electronic applications accepted. *Financial support:* In 2006–07, 3 fellowships with full tuition reimbursements (averaging $10,500 per year), 11 research assistantships with full tuition reimbursements (averaging $11,500 per year), 43 teaching assistantships with full tuition reimbursements (averaging $10,800 per year) were awarded; career-related internships or fieldwork and tuition waivers (full) also available. Support available to part-time students. Financial award application deadline: 3/1; financial award applicants required to submit FAFSA. *Faculty research:* Literacy acquisition and development, teacher beliefs and knowledge, recruitment and retention of underrepresented students, economic education, literacy discourse. *Unit head:* Dr. James D Lehman, Head, 765-494-7935, Fax: 765-496-1622. *Application contact:* Patricia Mason, Coordinator of Graduate Studies, 765-494-2345, Fax: 765-494-5832, E-mail: gradoffice@soe.purdue.edu.

Queens College of the City University of New York, Division of Graduate Studies, Division of Education, Department of Secondary Education, Flushing, NY 11367-1597. Offers art (MS Ed); biology (MS Ed, AC); chemistry (MS Ed, AC); earth sciences (MS Ed, AC); English (MS Ed, AC); French (MS Ed, AC); Italian (MS Ed, AC); mathematics (MS Ed, AC); music (MS Ed, AC); physics (MS Ed, AC); social studies (MS Ed, AC); Spanish (MS Ed, AC). Part-time and evening/weekend programs available. *Faculty:* 22 full-time (14 women). *Students:* 50 full-time (28 women), 974 part-time (627 women). 633 applicants, 82% accepted, 407 enrolled. In 2006, 227 degrees awarded. *Degree requirements:* For master's, research project; for AC, thesis optional. *Entrance requirements:* For master's, minimum GPA of 3.0. Additional exam requirements/recommendations for international students: Required—TOEFL. *Application deadline:* For fall admission, 4/1 for domestic students; for spring admission, 11/1 for domestic students. Applications are processed on a rolling basis. Application fee: $125. *Financial support:* Career-related internships or fieldwork, Federal Work-Study, institutionally sponsored loans, and tuition waivers (partial) available. Support available to part-time students. Financial award application deadline: 4/1; financial award applicants required to submit FAFSA. *Unit head:* Dr. Eleanor Armour-Thomas, Chairperson, 718-997-5150, E-mail: armourthomas@yahoo.com. *Application contact:* Mario Caruso, Director of Graduate Admissions, 718-997-5200, Fax: 718-997-5193, E-mail: graduate_admissions@qc.edu.

Quinnipiac University, Division of Education, Program in Secondary Education, Hamden, CT 06518-1940. Offers biology (MAT); chemistry (MAT); English (MAT); French (MAT); history/social studies (MAT); mathematics (MAT); physics (MAT); Spanish (MAT). *Faculty:* 7 full-time (5 women), 23 part-time/adjunct (14 women). *Students:* 64 full-time (41 women); includes 5 minority (1 African American, 4 Hispanic Americans). Average age 26. 63 applicants, 87% accepted, 42 enrolled. In 2006, 37 degrees awarded. *Entrance requirements:* For master's, PRAXIS I, minimum GPA of 2.67, interview. Additional exam requirements/recommendations for international students: Required—TOEFL (minimum score 575 paper-based; 233 computer-based; 90 iBT), IELTS (minimum score 7). *Application deadline:* For fall admission, 3/15 priority date for domestic students. Applications are processed on a rolling basis. Application fee: $45. Electronic applications accepted. *Expenses:* Tuition: Part-time $675 per credit. Required fees: $30 per credit. *Financial support:* Career-related internships or fieldwork and tuition waivers (partial) available. Financial award application deadline: 4/15; financial award applicants required to submit FAFSA. *Faculty research:* Multicultural and urban education, role of technology in education, challenges of teaching divers learners, socio-cultural nature of learning. *Unit head:* Dr. Bernadine Krawczyk, Assistant Dean, Division of Education, 203-582-3510, Fax: 203-582-3473, E-mail: bernadine.krawczyk@quinnipiac.edu. *Application contact:* 800-462-1944, Fax: 203-582-3443, E-mail: graduate@quinnipiac.edu.

See Close-Up on page 911.

Rider University, Department of Graduate Education, Leadership and Counseling, Lawrenceville, NJ 08648-3001. Offers counseling services (MA, Ed S); curriculum, instruction and supervision (MA); director of school counseling services (Certificate); educational administration (MA); organizational leadership (MA); principal (Certificate); reading/language arts (MA, Certificate), including reading specialist (Certificate), reading/language arts (MA); school business administrator (Certificate); school counseling services (Certificate); school psychology (Ed S); special education (MA); supervisor (Certificate); teacher certification (Certificate), including business education, elementary education, English as a second language, English education, mathematics education, preschool to grade 3, science education, social studies education, world languages; teaching (MA). *Accreditation:* NCATE. Part-time and evening/weekend programs available. *Faculty:* 24 full-time (12 women), 30 part-time/adjunct (15 women). *Students:* 90 full-time (75 women), 457 part-time (369 women); includes 73 minority (50 African Americans, 2 American Indian/Alaska Native, 6 Asian Americans or Pacific Islanders, 15 Hispanic Americans), 1 international. Average age 32. 314 applicants, 61% accepted, 138 enrolled. In 2006, 116 master's, 19 other advanced degrees awarded. *Degree requirements:* For master's, thesis or alternative, internship, portfolios, comprehensive exam (for some programs); for other advanced degree, internship, professional portfolio. *Entrance requirements:* For master's, GRE (counseling, school psychology), MAT, interview, resumé, letters of recommendation; for other advanced degree, PRAXIS. Additional exam requirements/recommendations for international students: Required—TOEFL (minimum score 550 paper-based; 213 computer-based). *Application deadline:* For fall admission, 5/1 priority date for domestic students, 6/1 priority date for international students; for spring admission, 11/1 priority date for domestic and international students. Applications are processed on a rolling basis. Application fee: $50. Electronic applications accepted. *Expenses:* Tuition: Part-time $525 per credit. Required fees: $35 per course. $30 per semester. *Financial support:* In 2006–07, 271 students received support. Career-related internships or fieldwork, Federal Work-Study, institutionally sponsored loans, and unspecified assistantships available. Support available to part-time students. Financial award applicants required to submit FAFSA. *Faculty research:* Gifted students, self-esteem, hope and mental health, conflicts in group work, cultural diversity and counseling assessment of special needs in children. *Unit head:* Dr. Dennis C. Buss, Chair, 609-895-5353, Fax: 609-896-5362, E-mail: dbuss@rider.edu. *Application contact:* Jamie L Mitchell, Director of Graduate Admissions, 609-896-5036, Fax: 609-895-5680, E-mail: jmitchell@rider.edu.

See Close-Up on page 913.

Rivier College, School of Graduate Studies, Department of History, Law and Government, Nashua, NH 03060-5086. Offers social studies education (MAT). *Faculty:* 2 full-time (0 women). *Students:* Average age 37. In 2006, 6 degrees awarded. *Degree requirements:* For master's, registration. Application fee: $25. *Unit head:* Dr. George Kaloudis, Chairperson, 603-897-8574. *Application contact:* Diane Monahan, Director of Graduate Admissions, 603-897-8129, Fax: 603-897-8810, E-mail: gradadm@rivier.edu.

Rockford College, Graduate Studies, Department of Education, Program in Secondary Education, Rockford, IL 61108-2393. Offers art education (MAT); English (MAT); history (MAT); political science (MAT); secondary education (MAT); social sciences (MAT). Part-time and evening/weekend programs available. *Degree requirements:* For master's, thesis optional. *Entrance requirements:* For master's, GRE General Test.

Rutgers, The State University of New Jersey, New Brunswick, Graduate School of Education, Department of Educational Theory, Policy and Administration, Program in Social Studies Education, New Brunswick, NJ 08901-1281. Offers Ed M, Ed D. Part-time and evening/weekend programs available. *Faculty:* 3 full-time (2 women). *Students:* 22 full-time (9 women), 7 part-time (3 women). Average age 28. 73 applicants, 48% accepted, 26 enrolled. In 2006, 25 degrees awarded. Terminal master's awarded for partial completion of doctoral program. *Degree requirements:* For master's, comprehensive exam; for doctorate, thesis/dissertation, qualifying exam. *Entrance requirements:* For master's and doctorate, GRE General Test. Additional exam requirements/recommendations for international students: Required—TOEFL. *Application deadline:* For fall admission, 2/1 for domestic and international students. Application fee: $60. Electronic applications accepted. *Financial support:* Application deadline: 3/15; *Faculty research:* Academic freedom, equal educational opportunity, social studies curricula. *Unit head:* Dr. Benjamin Justice, Coordinator, 732-932-7496 Ext. 8110, Fax: 732-932-6803,

E-mail: bjust@rci.rutgers.edu. *Application contact:* Sandy Chubrick, Administrative Assistant, 732-932-7496 Ext. 8239, Fax: 732-932-6803, E-mail: chubrick@rci.rutgers.edu.

Sage Graduate School, Graduate School, Division of Education, Program in Teaching, Troy, NY 12180-4115. Offers art education (MAT); biology (MAT); English (MAT); mathematics (MAT); social studies (MAT). Part-time and evening/weekend programs available. *Faculty:* 11 full-time (8 women), 20 part-time/adjunct (15 women). *Students:* 34 full-time (28 women), 41 part-time (29 women); includes 3 minority (1 African American, 1 Asian American or Pacific Islander, 1 Hispanic American). Average age 27. 72 applicants, 64% accepted, 33 enrolled. In 2006, 31 degrees awarded. *Entrance requirements:* For master's, minimum undergraduate GPA of 2.75 overall, minimum undergraduate GPA of 3.0 in content area. Additional exam requirements/recommendations for international students: Required—TOEFL (minimum score 550 paper-based; 213 computer-based). *Application deadline:* For fall admission, 8/1 for domestic students. Applications are processed on a rolling basis. Application fee: $40. *Expenses:* Tuition: Full-time $9,270; part-time $515 per credit hour. *Financial support:* Career-related internships or fieldwork, scholarships/grants, and unspecified assistantships available. Support available to part-time students. Financial award application deadline: 3/1; financial award applicants required to submit FAFSA. *Unit head:* Peter McDermott, Director, 518-244-2493, E-mail: mcderp@sage.edu. *Application contact:* Shannon K. Easton, Director of Graduate and Adult Admission, 518-244-2443, Fax: 518-244-6880, E-mail: sgsadm@sage.edu.

St. John Fisher College, Office of the Provost, Ralph C. Wilson Jr. School of Education, Adolescence Education Program, Rochester, NY 14618-3597. Offers adolescence English (MS Ed); adolescence French (MS Ed); adolescence social studies (MS Ed); adolescence Spanish (MS Ed). Part-time and evening/weekend programs available. *Faculty:* 4 full-time (2 women), 2 part-time/adjunct (1 woman). *Students:* Average age 31. 35 applicants, 91% accepted, 25 enrolled. In 2006, 13 degrees awarded. *Degree requirements:* For master's, student teaching, capstone project, field experiences; for degree. *Entrance requirements:* For master's, GRE (if GPA is below 3.0), minimum GPA of 3.0, 30 hours in certification area, 2 letters of reference, personal statement. Additional exam requirements/recommendations for international students: Required—TOEFL (minimum score 575 paper-based; 233 computer-based; 80 iBT). *Application deadline:* For fall admission, 4/1 for domestic students; for spring admission, 10/30 for domestic students. Applications are processed on a rolling basis. Application fee: $30. *Expenses:* Tuition: Part-time $615 per credit. Tuition and fees vary according to program. *Financial support:* In 2006–07, 1 student received support. Federal Work-Study and scholarships/grants available. Financial award application deadline: 2/15; financial award applicants required to submit FAFSA. *Faculty research:* Arts and humanities, urban schools, constructivist learning, at risk students, mentoring. *Unit head:* Dr. Russell Coward, Director, 585-385-8114, E-mail: rcoward@sjfc.edu. *Application contact:* Shannon Cleverley, Director of Graduate Admissions, 585-385-8161, Fax: 585-385-8344, E-mail: scleverley@sjfc.edu.

Salisbury University, Graduate Division, Department of Education, Salisbury, MD 21801-6837. Offers art (MAT); biology (MAT); business education (MAT); chemistry (MAT); early childhood education (M Ed); educational administration (M Ed); elementary education (M Ed); English (M Ed, MAT); French (MAT); geography (MAT); history (MAT); mathematics (MAT); media and technology (MAT); music (MAT); psychology (MAT); reading education (MAT); science (MAT); secondary education (MAT); social studies (MAT); Spanish (MAT). *Accreditation:* NCATE. Part-time and evening/weekend programs available. *Faculty:* 12 full-time (6 women), 10 part-time/adjunct (8 women). *Students:* 17 full-time (9 women), 84 part-time (72 women); includes 6 minority (5 African Americans, 1 Hispanic American). Average age 30. 15 applicants, 73% accepted, 11 enrolled. In 2006, 63 degrees awarded. *Degree requirements:* For master's, comprehensive exam (for some programs). *Entrance requirements:* For master's, PRAXIS, minimum GPA of 2.75. Additional exam requirements/recommendations for international students: Required—TOEFL (minimum score 550 paper-based; 213 computer-based). *Application deadline:* For fall admission, 8/1 priority date for domestic students; for spring admission, 1/1 for domestic students. Applications are processed on a rolling basis. Application fee: $45. *Expenses:* Tuition, state resident: part-time $260 per credit hour. Tuition, nonresident: part-time $546 per credit hour. Required fees: $52 per credit hour. *Financial support:* In 2006–07, 3 teaching assistantships with full tuition reimbursements were awarded; career-related internships or fieldwork and scholarships/grants also available. Support available to part-time students. Financial award applicants required to submit FAFSA. *Faculty research:* Middle-level education, student outcomes. *Unit head:* Dr. Edward C. Robeck, Program Coordinator, 410-543-6292, Fax: 410-548-2593, E-mail: ecrobeck@salisbury.edu. *Application contact:* Debra J. Clark, Administrative Assistant I, 410-543-6281, Fax: 410-548-2593, E-mail: djclark@salisbury.edu.

Smith College, Graduate Programs, Department of Education and Child Study, Program in Secondary Education, Northampton, MA 01063. Offers biological sciences education (MAT); chemistry education (MAT); English education (MAT); French education (MAT); geology education (MAT); government education (MAT); history education (MAT); mathematics education (MAT); physics education (MAT); Spanish education (MAT). Part-time programs available. *Faculty:* 6 full-time (4 women), 3 part-time/adjunct (2 women). *Students:* 4 full-time (2 women). Average age 36. 12 applicants, 67% accepted, 3 enrolled. In 2006, 5 master's awarded. *Entrance requirements:* For master's, GRE General Test. Additional exam requirements/recommendations for international students: Required—TOEFL. *Application deadline:* For fall admission, 4/1 for domestic students, 1/15 for international students; for spring admission, 12/1 for domestic students. Application fee: $60. *Expenses:* Tuition: Full-time $32,320; part-time $1,010 per credit. Tuition and fees vary according to course load. *Financial support:* In 2006–07, 3 students received support. Career-related internships or fieldwork, institutionally sponsored loans, and scholarships/grants available. Support available to part-time students. Financial award application deadline: 1/15; financial award applicants required to submit CSS PROFILE or FAFSA. *Unit head:* Rosetta Cohen, Graduate Student Advisor, 413-585-3266.

South Carolina State University, School of Graduate Studies, Department of Education, Orangeburg, SC 29117-0001. Offers early childhood and special education (M Ed); early childhood education (MAT); elementary education (M Ed, MAT); engineering (MAT); general science (MAT); mathematics (MAT); secondary education (M Ed), including biology education, business education, counselor education, English education, home economics education, industrial education, mathematics education, science education, social studies education; special education (M Ed), including emotionally handicapped, learning disabilities, mentally handicapped. *Accreditation:* NCATE. Part-time and evening/weekend programs available. *Faculty:* 21 full-time (10 women), 4 part-time/adjunct (0 women). *Students:* 34 full-time (28 women), 33 part-time (25 women); includes 63 minority (61 African Americans, 1 American Indian/Alaska Native, 1 Asian American or Pacific Islander). Average age 35. 46 applicants, 67% accepted, 19 enrolled. In 2006, 28 degrees awarded. *Degree requirements:* For master's, departmental qualifying exam, thesis optional. *Entrance requirements:* For master's, GRE General Test, NTE, interview, teaching certificate. *Application deadline:* For fall admission, 6/15 priority date for domestic students, 6/15 for international students; for spring admission, 11/1 for domestic and international students. Applications are processed on a rolling basis. Application fee: $25. Electronic applications accepted. *Expenses:* Tuition, state resident: full-time $7,278. Tuition, nonresident: full-time $14,322. *Financial support:* Fellowships, research assistantships, career-related internships or fieldwork, Federal Work-Study, and institutionally sponsored loans available. Financial award application deadline: 6/1. *Faculty research:* Critical thinking, child abuse, stress, test-taking skills, conflict resolution, mainstreaming. *Unit head:* Dr. Gail Joyner-Fleming, Interim Chair, 803-533-3769, Fax: 803-536-8492, E-mail: zf-gfleming@scsu.edu. *Application contact:* Annette Hazzard-Jones, Program Coordinator II, 803-536-8809, Fax: 803-536-8812, E-mail: zs_ahazzard@scsu.edu.

Southern Illinois University Edwardsville, Graduate Studies and Research, School of Education, Department of Curriculum and Instruction, Program in Secondary Education, Edwardsville, IL 62026-0001. Offers art (MS Ed); biology (MS Ed); chemistry (MS Ed); English (MS Ed); foreign languages (MS Ed); history (MS Ed); mathematics (MS Ed); physics (MS Ed); reading (MS Ed); science (MS Ed). *Accreditation:* NCATE. Part-time and evening/weekend programs available. *Students:* 2 full-time (both women), 23 part-time (14 women); includes 2 minority (both African Americans) Average age 33. 12 applicants, 42% accepted. In 2006, 10 degrees awarded. *Degree requirements:* For master's, thesis or alternative, final exam. *Entrance requirements:* For master's, MAT. Additional exam requirements/recommendations for international students: Required—TOEFL. *Application deadline:* For fall admission, 7/20 for domestic students, 6/1 for international students; for spring admission, 12/14 for domestic students, 10/1 for international students. Application fee: $30. Electronic applications accepted. *Financial support:* Fellowships, research assistantships, teaching assistantships, Federal Work-Study, institutionally sponsored loans, and unspecified assistantships available. Support available to part-time students. Financial award application deadline: 3/1; financial award applicants required to submit FAFSA. *Unit head:* Dr. David DeWeese, Director, 618-650-3432, E-mail: ddewees@siue.edu.

Southwestern Oklahoma State University, College of Arts and Sciences, Department of Social Sciences, Weatherford, OK 73096-3098. Offers M Ed. *Degree requirements:* For master's, exam. *Entrance requirements:* For master's, GRE General Test or minimum undergraduate GPA of 3.0. Additional exam requirements/recommendations for international students: Required—TOEFL.

Stanford University, School of Education, Program in Curriculum Studies and Teacher Education, Stanford, CA 94305-9991. Offers art education (MA, PhD); dance education (MA); English education (MA, PhD); general curriculum studies (MA, PhD); mathematics education (MA, PhD); science education (MA, PhD); social studies education (PhD); teacher education (MA, PhD). *Degree requirements:* For master's, thesis (for some programs); for doctorate, thesis/dissertation. *Entrance requirements:* For master's and doctorate, GRE General Test. Electronic applications accepted.

Stanford University, School of Education, Teacher Education Program, Stanford, CA 94305-9991. Offers English education (MA); languages education (MA); mathematics education (MA); science education (MA); social studies education (MA). *Degree requirements:* For master's, thesis. *Entrance requirements:* For master's, GRE General Test. Electronic applications accepted.

State University of New York at Binghamton, Graduate School, School of Education, Program in Secondary Education, Binghamton, NY 13902-6000. Offers biology education (MAT, MS Ed, MST); earth science education (MAT, MS Ed, MST); English education (MAT, MS Ed, MST); French education (MAT, MST); mathematical sciences education (MAT, MS Ed, MST); physics (MAT, MS Ed, MST); social studies (MAT, MS Ed, MST); Spanish education (MAT, MST). *Accreditation:* Teacher Education Accreditation Council. Part-time and evening/weekend programs available. *Students:* 89 full-time (50 women), 47 part-time (32 women); includes 6 minority (1 African American, 3 Asian Americans or Pacific Islanders, 2 Hispanic Americans). Average age 29. 72 applicants, 72% accepted, 23 enrolled. In 2006, 44 degrees awarded. *Entrance requirements:* For master's, GRE General Test. Additional exam requirements/recommendations for international students: Required—TOEFL. *Application deadline:* For fall admission, 4/15 priority date for domestic students, 1/15 priority date for international students; for spring admission, 11/1 for domestic students, 10/1 priority date for international students. Applications are processed on a rolling basis. Application fee: $60. Electronic applications accepted. *Financial support:* In 2006–07, 25 students received support, including 2 fellowships with partial tuition reimbursements available (averaging $2,350 per year), 4 research assistantships with full and partial tuition reimbursements available (averaging $6,638 per year), 13 teaching assistantships with full tuition reimbursements available (averaging $5,944 per year); career-related internships or fieldwork, Federal Work-Study, institutionally sponsored loans, tuition waivers (full and partial), and unspecified assistantships also available. Support available to part-time students. Financial award application deadline: 2/15. *Unit head:* Dr. Thomas O'Brien, Coordinator, 607-777-7329, E-mail: tobrien@binghamton.edu.

State University of New York at Plattsburgh, Division of Education, Health, and Human Services, Department of Adolescence Education/Health, Plattsburgh, NY 12901-2681. Offers adolescence education (MST); biology 7-12 (MST); chemistry 7-12 (MST); earth science 7-12 (MST); English 7-12 (MST); French 7-12 (MST); mathematics 7-12 (MST); physics 7-12 (MST); social studies 7-12 (MST); Spanish 7-12 (MST). *Faculty:* 4 full-time (3 women), 2 part-time/adjunct (0 women). *Students:* 58 full-time (38 women), 14 part-time (10 women); includes 5 minority (1 African American, 4 Hispanic Americans). Average age 30. 49 applicants, 78% accepted, 32 enrolled. In 2006, 30 degrees awarded. *Degree requirements:* For master's, comprehensive exam or research project. *Entrance requirements:* For master's, GRE General Test or MAT, minimum GPA of 2.5. *Application deadline:* For fall admission, 2/15 priority date for domestic students; for spring admission, 10/15 priority date for domestic students. Applications are processed on a rolling basis. Application fee: $50. *Expenses:* Tuition, state resident: full-time $6,900; part-time $288 per credit hour. Tuition, nonresident: full-time $10,920; part-time $455 per credit hour. *Financial support:* Application deadline: 4/15; *Unit head:* Dr. Lois Beach, Chair, 578-564-5750, E-mail: lois.beach@plattsburgh.edu. *Application contact:* Sharon Derr, Assistant Director, Graduate Admission, 518-564-4723, Fax: 518-564-4722, E-mail: derrsl@plattsburgh.edu.

State University of New York College at Brockport, School of Professions, Department of Education and Human Development, Program in Adolescence Education, Brockport, NY 14420-2997. Offers biology education (MS Ed); chemistry education (MS Ed); earth science education (MS Ed); English education (MS Ed); mathematics education (MS Ed); physics education (MS Ed); social studies education (MS Ed). *Accreditation:* NCATE. Part-time programs available. *Students:* 39 full-time (21 women), 117 part-time (66 women); includes 6 minority (3 African Americans, 1 Asian American or Pacific Islander, 2 Hispanic Americans). 57 applicants, 61% accepted, 32 enrolled. In 2006, 91 degrees awarded. *Degree requirements:* For master's, thesis or alternative. *Entrance requirements:* For master's, minimum GPA of 3.0, letters of recommendation. Additional exam requirements/recommendations for international students: Required—TOEFL (minimum score 550 paper-based; 213 computer-based; 80 iBT). *Application deadline:* For fall admission, 2/15 for domestic and international students; for spring admission, 9/15 for domestic and international students. Application fee: $50. *Expenses:* Tuition, state resident: full-time $6,900; part-time $288 per credit. Tuition, nonresident: full-time $10,920; part-time $455 per credit. *Financial support:* Career-related internships or fieldwork, Federal Work-Study, scholarships/grants, and unspecified assistantships available. Support available to part-time students. Financial award application deadline: 3/15; financial award applicants required to submit FAFSA. *Application contact:* Coordinator of Certification and Graduate Advisement, 585-395-2344.

State University of New York College at Cortland, Graduate Studies, School of Arts and Sciences, Programs in Adolescence Education, Cortland, NY 13045. Offers biology (MAT, MS Ed); chemistry (MAT, MS Ed); earth science (MAT, MS Ed); English (MS Ed); French (MS Ed); mathematics (MAT, MS Ed); physics (MAT, MS Ed); social studies (MS Ed); Spanish (MS Ed). *Accreditation:* NCATE. Part-time and evening/weekend programs available. *Degree requirements:* For master's, one foreign language, thesis (for some programs), comprehensive exam (for some programs). *Entrance requirements:* For master's, GRE General Test.

Stony Brook University, State University of New York, School of Professional Development, Stony Brook, NY 11794. Offers adolescence education: mathematics (Certificate); biology 7-12 (MAT); chemistry-grade 7-12 (MAT); coaching (Certificate); computer integrated engineering (Certificate); cultural studies (Certificate); earth science-grade 7-12 (MAT); educational computing (Advanced Certificate, Certificate); English-grade 7-12 (MAT); environmental and waste management (MS, Advanced Certificate); environmental systems management (Certificate); environmental/occupational health and safety (Certificate); French-grade 7-12 (MAT); German-grade 7-12 (MAT); human resource management (Certificate); industrial management (Certificate); information systems management (Certificate); Italian-grade 7-12 (MAT); liberal studies (MA); liberal studies online (MA); Long Island regional studies (Certificate);

Social Sciences Education

Stony Brook University, State University of New York (continued)
operation research (Certificate); physics-grade 7-12 (MAT); Russian-grade 7-12 (MAT); school administration and supervision (Certificate); school district administration (Certificate); social science and the professions (MPS), including human resources management, labor management, public affairs, waste management; social studies 7-12 (MAT); waste management (Certificate); women's studies (Certificate). Part-time and evening/weekend programs available. Postbaccalaureate distance learning degree programs offered. *Faculty:* 1 full-time (0 women), 118 part-time/adjunct (45 women). *Students:* 322 full-time (202 women), 1,188 part-time (728 women); includes 164 minority (69 African Americans, 2 American Indian/Alaska Native, 29 Asian Americans or Pacific Islanders, 64 Hispanic Americans), 11 international. Average age 28. In 2006, 738 master's, 405 other advanced degrees awarded. *Degree requirements:* For master's, one foreign language, thesis or alternative. *Application deadline:* Applications are processed on a rolling basis. Application fee: $62. *Expenses:* Tuition, state resident: full-time $6,900; part-time $288 per credit. Tuition, nonresident: full-time $10,920; part-time $455 per credit. *Financial support:* In 2006–07, 5 teaching assistantships were awarded; fellowships, research assistantships, career-related internships or fieldwork also available. Support available to part-time students. *Unit head:* Dr. Paul J. Edelson, Dean, 631-632-7052, Fax: 631-632-9046, E-mail: paul.edelson@sunysb.edu. *Application contact:* Sandra Romansky, Director of Admissions and Advisement, 631-632-7050, Fax: 631-632-9046, E-mail: sandra.romansky@sunysb.edu.

Syracuse University, Graduate School, School of Education, Department of Teaching and Leadership, Program in Social Studies Education, Syracuse, NY 13244. Offers social studies education (CAS); social studies education: preparation 7-12 (MS). Part-time and evening/weekend programs available. *Students:* 10 full-time (4 women), 1 (woman) part-time; includes 1 minority (African American) 7 applicants, 100% accepted, 5 enrolled. *Degree requirements:* For master's, thesis or alternative; for CAS, thesis. *Entrance requirements:* Additional exam requirements/recommendations for international students: Required—TOEFL. *Application deadline:* For fall admission, 2/1 priority date for domestic students. Applications are processed on a rolling basis. Application fee: $65. Electronic applications accepted. *Expenses:* Tuition: Full-time $16,920; part-time $940 per credit hour. Required fees: $930; $930 per year. *Application contact:* Liza Rochelson, Graduate Admission Recruiter, 315-443-2505, Fax: 315-443-2258, E-mail: gradcrt@gwmail.syr.edu.

Teachers College Columbia University, Graduate Faculty of Education, Department of Arts and Humanities, Program in Social Studies Education, New York, NY 10027-6696. Offers Ed M, MA, Ed D, PhD. *Accreditation:* NCATE. Part-time and evening/weekend programs available. *Faculty:* 4 full-time (3 women). *Students:* 37 full-time (26 women), 40 part-time (20 women); includes 15 minority (3 African Americans, 5 Asian Americans or Pacific Islanders, 7 Hispanic Americans), 5 international. Average age 29. 149 applicants, 74% accepted, 43 enrolled. In 2006, 67 master's, 2 doctorates awarded. Terminal master's awarded for partial completion of doctoral program. *Degree requirements:* For doctorate, thesis/dissertation. *Application deadline:* For fall admission, 5/15 for domestic students. Application fee: $65. *Expenses:* Tuition: Full-time $23,400; part-time $975 per credit. Required fees: $320 per term. *Financial support:* Fellowships, research assistantships, teaching assistantships, career-related internships or fieldwork, Federal Work-Study, institutionally sponsored loans, and tuition waivers (full and partial) available. Support available to part-time students. Financial award application deadline: 2/1. *Faculty research:* History of social studies education, social studies curriculum and teaching, women's history, gender and diversity issues in the classroom. *Application contact:* Mark E. Stearns, Associate Director of Admission, 212-678-3710, Fax: 212-678-4171.

Texas A&M University–Commerce, Graduate School, College of Arts and Sciences, Department of History, Commerce, TX 75429-3011. Offers history (MA, MS); social sciences (M Ed, MS). Part-time programs available. *Degree requirements:* For master's, thesis (for some programs), comprehensive exam. *Entrance requirements:* For master's, GRE General Test. Electronic applications accepted. *Faculty research:* American foreign policy, colonial America, Texas politics, Medieval England.

Texas State University-San Marcos, Graduate School, College of Liberal Arts, Department of Geography, Program in Environmental Geography, Geography Education, and Geography Information Science, San Marcos, TX 78666. Offers environmental geography (PhD); geography education (PhD); information science (PhD). Part-time programs available. *Students:* 34 full-time (18 women), 23 part-time (8 women); includes 15 minority (2 African Americans, 8 Asian Americans or Pacific Islanders, 5 Hispanic Americans), 4 international. Average age 39. 24 applicants, 67% accepted, 13 enrolled. In 2006, 8 degrees awarded. *Degree requirements:* For doctorate, thesis/dissertation. *Entrance requirements:* For doctorate, GRE General Test, minimum GPA of 3.5, master's degree in geography, demonstrated scholarly research. Additional exam requirements/recommendations for international students: Required—TOEFL. *Application deadline:* For fall admission, 6/15 priority date for domestic students, 6/1 for international students; for spring admission, 10/15 priority date for domestic students, 10/1 for international students. Applications are processed on a rolling basis. Application fee: $40 ($90 for international students). *Financial support:* In 2006–07, 46 students received support, including 17 research assistantships (averaging $7,807 per year), 19 teaching assistantships (averaging $8,735 per year); career-related internships or fieldwork, Federal Work-Study, and institutionally sponsored loans also available. Support available to part-time students. Financial award application deadline: 4/1; financial award applicants required to submit FAFSA. *Unit head:* Dr. David Butler, Graduate Adviser, 512-245-7977, Fax: 512-245-8353, E-mail: db25@txstate.edu.

Trinity (Washington) University, School of Education, Washington, DC 20017-1094. Offers democracy, diversity, and social justice (M Ed); early childhood (MAT); educational administration (MSA); elementary education (MAT); English as a second language (M Ed, MAT); literacy and reading education (M Ed); school counseling (MA); secondary education (MAT), including English, math, science, social studies; special education (MAT). *Accreditation:* NCATE. Part-time and evening/weekend programs available. *Degree requirements:* For master's, thesis (for some programs), capstone project(s). *Entrance requirements:* For master's, PRAXIS I, minimum GPA of 2.8. Additional exam requirements/recommendations for international students: Required—TOEFL (minimum score 550 paper-based; 213 computer-based). *Faculty research:* Technology, literacy, special education, organizations, inclusion models.

Union Graduate College, School of Education, Schenectady, NY 12308-3107. Offers biology (MAT, MS); chemistry (MAT); earth science (MAT); English (MAT); French (MAT); general science (MAT); German (MAT); languages (MAT); Latin (MAT); mathematics (MAT); mathematics and technology (MS); physical science (MS); physics (MAT); social studies (MAT); Spanish (MAT). *Accreditation:* Teacher Education Accreditation Council. *Faculty:* 5 full-time (1 woman), 19 part-time/adjunct (10 women). *Students:* 57 full-time (36 women), 21 part-time (14 women); includes 2 African Americans, 2 Hispanic Americans, 2 international. Average age 31. 59 applicants, 83% accepted, 39 enrolled. In 2006, 56 degrees awarded. *Degree requirements:* For master's, thesis or project. *Entrance requirements:* For master's, minimum GPA of 3.0, letters of recommendation. Additional exam requirements/recommendations for international students: Required—TOEFL (minimum score 550 paper-based; 213 computer-based). Application fee: $60. *Expenses: Contact institution. Financial support:* In 2006–07, 12 research assistantships with tuition reimbursements (averaging $3,000 per year) were awarded; Federal Work-Study, scholarships/grants, health care benefits, and tuition waivers (partial) also available. Support available to part-time students. Financial award applicants required to submit FAFSA. *Unit head:* Dr. Patrick Allen, Dean, 518-388-6361, Fax: 518-388-6686, E-mail: mat@union.edu. *Application contact:* Rhonda Sheehan, Director of Graduate Admissions Registrar, 518-388-6238, Fax: 518-388-6686, E-mail: sheehanr@union.edu.

See Close-Up on page 923.

University at Buffalo, the State University of New York, Graduate School, Graduate School of Education, Department of Learning and Instruction, Buffalo, NY 14260. Offers adolescence education (Certificate); biology (Ed M); chemistry (Ed M); childhood education (Ed M); early childhood and childhood education with bilingual extension (Ed M); early childhood education (Ed M); earth science (Ed M); elementary education (Ed D, PhD); English (Ed M); English education (PhD); English for speakers of other languages (Ed M); foreign and second language education (PhD); French (Ed M); general education (Ed M); German (Ed M); Italian (Ed M); Japanese (Ed M); Latin (Ed M); literary specialist (Ed M); mathematics (Ed M); mathematics education (PhD); mentoring teachers (Certificate); music education (Ed M, Certificate); physics (Ed M); reading education (PhD); Russian (Ed M); school administrator and supervisor (Certificate); science education (PhD); social studies (Ed M); Spanish (Ed M); special education (PhD); teaching and leading for diversity (Certificate); teaching English to speakers of other languages (Ed M). Part-time and evening/weekend programs available. Postbaccalaureate distance learning degree programs offered (no on-campus study). *Faculty:* 30 full-time (20 women), 53 part-time/adjunct (38 women). *Students:* 368 full-time (269 women), 297 part-time (226 women); includes 50 minority (15 African Americans, 2 American Indian/Alaska Native, 14 Asian Americans or Pacific Islanders, 19 Hispanic Americans), 66 international. Average age 31. 638 applicants, 75% accepted, 298 enrolled. In 2006, 248 master's, 18 doctorates, 48 other advanced degrees awarded. Terminal master's awarded for partial completion of doctoral program. *Degree requirements:* For master's, comprehensive exam, registration; for doctorate, thesis/dissertation, research analysis exam, research experience component. *Entrance requirements:* For doctorate, GRE General Test or MAT, interview, writing sample, letters of recommendation. Additional exam requirements/recommendations for international students: Required—TOEFL (minimum score 600 paper-based; 250 computer-based). *Application deadline:* For fall admission, 2/1 priority date for domestic and international students; for spring admission, 11/15 priority date for domestic students, 10/1 for international students. Applications are processed on a rolling basis. Application fee: $50. Electronic applications accepted. *Financial support:* In 2006–07, 70 students received support, including 6 fellowships with full tuition reimbursements available (averaging $10,000 per year), 16 research assistantships with full tuition reimbursements available (averaging $9,000 per year), teaching assistantships with full tuition reimbursements available (averaging $9,000 per year); career-related internships or fieldwork, Federal Work-Study, institutionally sponsored loans, scholarships/grants, tuition waivers (partial), and unspecified assistantships also available. Financial award application deadline: 2/28; financial award applicants required to submit FAFSA. *Faculty research:* Science assessment, state-level testing, early learning, literacy, second language acquisition. Total annual research expenditures: $432,366. *Unit head:* Dr. Maria E. Runfola, Chair, 716-645-2455, Fax: 716-645-3161. *Application contact:* Barbara Belz, Admissions Secretary, 716-645-2110 Ext. 1159, Fax: 716-645-3161, E-mail: belz@buffalo.edu.

University of Arkansas at Pine Bluff, Program in Education, Pine Bluff, AR 71601-2799. Offers elementary education (M Ed); secondary education (M Ed), including English, general science, mathematics, physical education, social studies. Part-time and evening/weekend programs available. *Degree requirements:* For master's, comprehensive exam. *Entrance requirements:* For master's, GRE, minimum GPA of 2.75, NTE or Standard Arkansas Teaching Certificate. *Faculty research:* Teacher certification, accreditation, assessment, standards, portfolio development, rehabilitation, technology.

The University of British Columbia, Faculty of Graduate Studies, Faculty of Education, Department of Curriculum Studies, Vancouver, BC V6T 1Z1, Canada. Offers art education (M Ed, MA); curriculum studies (M Ed, MA, PhD); home economics education (M Ed, MA); math education (M Ed, MA); music education (M Ed, MA); physical education (M Ed, MA); science education (M Ed, MA); social studies education (M Ed, MA); technical studies education (M Ed, MA). Part-time programs available. *Faculty:* 31 full-time (17 women), 1 (woman) part-time/adjunct. *Students:* 153 full-time (102 women), 101 part-time (67 women), 25 international. Average age 40. 118 applicants, 64% accepted, 62 enrolled. In 2006, 46 master's, 4 doctorates awarded. *Degree requirements:* For master's, thesis (MA); for doctorate, thesis/dissertation, comprehensive exam, registration. *Entrance requirements:* Additional exam requirements/recommendations for international students: Required—TOEFL (minimum score 580 paper-based; 237 computer-based). *Application deadline:* For fall admission, 2/1 for domestic students, 1/1 for international students; for spring admission, 10/1 for domestic students, 9/1 for international students. Application fee: $90 ($150 for international students). Electronic applications accepted. *Expenses: Contact institution. Financial support:* In 2006–07, 10 fellowships with partial tuition reimbursements (averaging $16,000 per year), 11 research assistantships with partial tuition reimbursements (averaging $14,000 per year), 27 teaching assistantships with partial tuition reimbursements (averaging $14,000 per year) were awarded; tuition waivers (partial) also available. *Faculty research:* School subjects, teaching and learning. *Unit head:* Dr. Linda Peterat, Interim Head, 604-822-5422, Fax: 604-822-4714. *Application contact:* Basia Zurek, Graduate Secretary, 604-822-5367, Fax: 604-822-4714, E-mail: cust.grad@ubc.ca.

University of California, Santa Cruz, Division of Graduate Studies, Division of Social Sciences, Program in Social Documentation, Santa Cruz, CA 95064. Offers MA.

University of Central Florida, College of Education, Department of Teaching and Learning Principles, Program in Social Science Education, Orlando, FL 32816. Offers M Ed, MA. *Accreditation:* NCATE. Part-time and evening/weekend programs available. *Students:* 15 full-time (9 women), 20 part-time (12 women); includes 6 minority (1 African American, 1 Asian American or Pacific Islander, 4 Hispanic Americans). In 2006, 11 master's awarded. *Entrance requirements:* For master's, GRE General Test. Additional exam requirements/recommendations for international students: Required—TOEFL. *Application deadline:* For fall admission, 7/15 for domestic students; for spring admission, 12/1 for domestic students. Application fee: $30. Electronic applications accepted. *Expenses:* Tuition, state resident: full-time $6,167; part-time $257 per credit hour. Tuition, nonresident: full-time $22,790; part-time $950 per credit hour. *Financial support:* Fellowships with partial tuition reimbursements, research assistantships with partial tuition reimbursements, teaching assistantships with partial tuition reimbursements, career-related internships or fieldwork, Federal Work-Study, institutionally sponsored loans, tuition waivers (partial), and unspecified assistantships available. Financial award application deadline: 3/1; financial award applicants required to submit FAFSA. *Unit head:* Dr. Scott Waring, Coordinator, 407-823-1766, E-mail: swaring@mail.ucf.edu.

University of Cincinnati, Division of Research and Advanced Studies, College of Education, Criminal Justice, and Human Services, Division of Teacher Education, Cincinnati, OH 45221. Offers curriculum and instruction (M Ed, Ed D); deaf studies (Certificate); early childhood education (M Ed); middle childhood education (M Ed); postsecondary literacy instruction (Certificate); reading/literacy (M Ed, Ed D); secondary education (M Ed); special education (M Ed, Ed D); teaching English as a second language (M Ed, Ed D, Certificate); teaching science (MS). Part-time programs available. *Degree requirements:* For doctorate, thesis/dissertation. *Entrance requirements:* For master's, GRE General Test. *Application deadline:* For fall admission, 2/1 for domestic students. Application fee: $30. Electronic applications accepted. *Financial support:* Fellowships, career-related internships or fieldwork, tuition waivers (partial), and unspecified assistantships available. *Unit head:* David Naylor, Student Contact, 513-556-3563, Fax: 513-556-2483, E-mail: david.naylor@uc.edu. *Application contact:* Dr. Richard Kretschmer, Graduate Program Director, 513-556-4547, Fax: 513-556-1001, E-mail: richard.kretschmer@uc.edu.

University of Colorado at Denver and Health Sciences Center, School of Education and Human Development, Program in Initial Professional Teacher Education, Denver, CO 80217-3364. Offers special education (MA). *Accreditation:* NCATE. Part-time and evening/weekend programs available. *Faculty:* 26 full-time (20 women). *Students:* 177 full-time (142 women), 389 part-time (345 women); includes 58 minority (10 African Americans, 3 American Indian/Alaska Native, 14 Asian Americans or Pacific Islanders, 31 Hispanic Americans), 3 international. Average age 32. 170 applicants, 86% accepted, 91 enrolled. In 2006, 270 degrees awarded. *Degree requirements:* For master's, thesis or alternative. *Entrance requirements:* For master's, GRE, MAT, minimum GPA of 2.75, 3 letters of recommendation. Additional exam requirements/recommendations for international students: Required—TOEFL (minimum score 525 paper-based; 197 computer-based). *Application deadline:* For fall admission, 3/1 for domestic students; for spring admission, 9/15 for domestic students. Applications are processed on a rolling basis. Application fee: $50 ($75 for international students). Electronic applications accepted. *Financial support:* Research assistantships, teaching assistantships, Federal Work-Study available. Financial award application deadline: 4/1; financial award applicants required to submit FAFSA. *Unit head:* Carole Basile, Coordinator, 303-556-3336, Fax: 303-556-4479, E-mail: carole.basile@cudenver.edu. *Application contact:* Orlando Green, Academic Advisor, 303-556-5274, Fax: 303-556-4479, E-mail: orlando.green@cudenver.edu.

University of Connecticut, Graduate School, Neag School of Education, Department of Curriculum and Instruction, Storrs, CT 06269. Offers curriculum and instruction (MA, PhD), including agriculture education, bilingual and bicultural education, elementary education, English education, history and social sciences education, mathematics education, reading education, science education, secondary education, world languages education. *Accreditation:* NCATE. *Faculty:* 28 full-time (12 women). *Students:* 158 full-time (120 women), 54 part-time (44 women); includes 24 minority (3 African Americans, 1 American Indian/Alaska Native, 3 Asian Americans or Pacific Islanders, 17 Hispanic Americans), 2 international. Average age 27. 268 applicants, 76% accepted, 203 enrolled. In 2006, 181 master's, 4 doctorates awarded. Terminal master's awarded for partial completion of doctoral program. *Degree requirements:* For master's, thesis or alternative, comprehensive exam; for doctorate, thesis/dissertation. *Entrance requirements:* For doctorate, GRE General Test. Additional exam requirements/recommendations for international students: Required—TOEFL (minimum score 550 paper-based; 213 computer-based). *Application deadline:* For fall admission, 2/1 priority date for domestic and international students; for spring admission, 11/1 for domestic students, 10/1 for international students. Applications are processed on a rolling basis. Application fee: $55. Electronic applications accepted. *Financial support:* In 2006–07, 14 research assistantships with full tuition reimbursements, 4 teaching assistantships with full tuition reimbursements were awarded; fellowships, Federal Work-Study, scholarships/grants, health care benefits, and unspecified assistantships also available. Financial award application deadline: 2/1; financial award applicants required to submit FAFSA. *Unit head:* Mary Anne Doyle, Head, 860-486-2433, Fax: 860-486-0280. *Application contact:* Lisa Rasicot, Graduate Coordinator, 860-486-3065, Fax: 860-486-0210, E-mail: soeadm02@uconnvm.uconn.edu.

University of Connecticut, Graduate School, Neag School of Education, Department of Curriculum and Instruction, Field of Curriculum and Instruction, Program in History and Social Sciences Education, Storrs, CT 06269. Offers MA, PhD. *Accreditation:* NCATE. *Faculty:* 9 full-time (7 women). *Students:* 7 full-time (3 women), 1 (woman) part-time. Average age 23. 9 applicants, 67% accepted, 6 enrolled. In 2006, 3 degrees awarded. Terminal master's awarded for partial completion of doctoral program. *Degree requirements:* For master's, thesis or alternative, comprehensive exam; for doctorate, thesis/dissertation. *Entrance requirements:* For doctorate, GRE General Test. Additional exam requirements/recommendations for international students: Required—TOEFL (minimum score 550 paper-based; 213 computer-based). *Application deadline:* For fall admission, 2/1 priority date for domestic and international students; for spring admission, 11/1 for domestic students, 10/1 for international students. Applications are processed on a rolling basis. Application fee: $55. Electronic applications accepted. *Financial support:* In 2006–07, 1 teaching assistantship with full tuition reimbursement was awarded; fellowships, research assistantships with full tuition reimbursements, Federal Work-Study, scholarships/grants, health care benefits, and unspecified assistantships also available. Financial award application deadline: 2/1; financial award applicants required to submit FAFSA. *Application contact:* Lisa Rasicot, Graduate Coordinator, 860-486-3065, Fax: 860-486-0210, E-mail: soeadm02@uconnvm.uconn.edu.

University of Florida, Graduate School, College of Education, School of Teaching and Learning, Gainesville, FL 32611. Offers bilingual/ESOL education (M Ed, MAE, Ed D, PhD, Ed S); curriculum and instruction (M Ed, MAE, Ed D, PhD, Ed S); early childhood education (Ed D, PhD, Ed S); elementary education (M Ed, MAE); English education (M Ed, MAE); mathematics education (M Ed, MAE); reading education (M Ed, MAE); science education (M Ed, MAE); social foundations (M Ed, MAE, Ed D, PhD); social studies education (M Ed, MAE). *Accreditation:* NCATE. *Faculty:* 29 full-time (20 women). *Students:* 506 (406 women); includes 87 minority (20 African Americans, 3 American Indian/Alaska Native, 13 Asian Americans or Pacific Islanders, 51 Hispanic Americans) 34 international. In 2006, 278 master's, 8 doctorates awarded. *Degree requirements:* For master's, thesis optional; for doctorate, variable foreign language requirement, thesis/dissertation. *Entrance requirements:* For master's and doctorate, GRE General Test, minimum GPA of 3.0; for Ed S, GRE General Test. Additional exam requirements/recommendations for international students: Required—TOEFL (minimum score 550 paper-based; 213 computer-based). *Application deadline:* For fall admission, 6/1 for domestic students. Applications are processed on a rolling basis. Application fee: $30. Electronic applications accepted. *Expenses:* Tuition, state resident: full-time $6,827. Tuition, nonresident: full-time $21,951. Required fees: $999. *Financial support:* In 2006–07, 5 research assistantships (averaging $11,947 per year), 22 teaching assistantships (averaging $9,709 per year) were awarded; fellowships, career-related internships or fieldwork and unspecified assistantships also available. *Faculty research:* Teacher education, inclusive education, classroom processes, curriculum and technology. *Unit head:* Dr. Tom Dana, Director, 352-392-9191 Ext. 200, Fax: 352-392-9193, E-mail: tdana@coe.ufl.edu. *Application contact:* Dr. Linda C. Jones, Coordinator, 352-392-0761 Ext. 267, Fax: 352-392-9193, E-mail: lcjones@coe.ufl.edu.

University of Florida, Graduate School, College of Liberal Arts and Sciences, Department of Political Science, Gainesville, FL 32611. Offers international development policy and administration (MA, Certificate); international relations (MA, MAT); political campaigning (MA, Certificate); political science (MA, MAT, PhD); public affairs (MA, Certificate); JD/MA. Part-time programs available. *Faculty:* 33 full-time (8 women), 1 (woman) part-time/adjunct. *Students:* 120 (46 women); includes 9 minority (5 African Americans, 1 Asian American or Pacific Islander, 3 Hispanic Americans) 13 international. In 2006, 20 master's, 9 doctorates awarded. Terminal master's awarded for partial completion of doctoral program. *Degree requirements:* For master's, variable foreign language requirement, thesis or alternative; for doctorate, variable foreign language requirement, thesis/dissertation. *Entrance requirements:* For master's and doctorate, GRE General Test, minimum GPA of 3.0. Additional exam requirements/recommendations for international students: Required—TOEFL (minimum score 550 paper-based; 213 computer-based). *Application deadline:* For fall admission, 3/16 priority date for domestic students. Applications are processed on a rolling basis. Application fee: $30. Electronic applications accepted. *Expenses:* Tuition, state resident: full-time $6,827. Tuition, nonresident: full-time $21,951. Required fees: $999. *Financial support:* In 2006–07, 3 research assistantships (averaging $17,922 per year), 40 teaching assistantships (averaging $17,340 per year) were awarded; fellowships, career-related internships or fieldwork, Federal Work-Study, institutionally sponsored loans, and unspecified assistantships also available. Financial award application deadline: 1/15. *Faculty research:* U.S. political development, religion and politics, environmental politics and policy, developing societies, international relations. *Unit head:* Philip J. Williams, Chair, 352-392-0262 Ext. 247, Fax: 352-392-8127, E-mail: pjw@polisci.ufl.edu. *Application contact:* Dr. J. Samuel Barkin, Coordinator, 352-392-0262 Ext. 222, Fax: 352-392-8127, E-mail: barkin@polisci.ufl.edu.

University of Georgia, Graduate School, College of Education, Department of Elementary and Social Studies Education, Athens, GA 30602. Offers early childhood education (M Ed, PhD, Ed S); elementary and middle school education (M Ed, PhD, Ed S), including elementary education (PhD), middle school education; social foundations of education (PhD). *Faculty:* 15 full-time (8 women). *Students:* 113 full-time (88 women), 122 part-time (95 women); includes 25 minority (19 African Americans, 4 Asian Americans or Pacific Islanders, 2 Hispanic Americans), 14 international. 170 applicants, 69% accepted, 88 enrolled. In 2006, 77 master's, 6 doctorates, 6 other advanced degrees awarded. *Entrance requirements:* For master's and Ed S, GRE General Test or MAT; for doctorate, GRE General Test. *Application deadline:* For fall admission, 7/1 priority date for domestic students; for spring admission, 11/15 for domestic students. Application fee: $50. Electronic applications accepted. *Financial support:* Fellowships, research assistantships, teaching assistantships, unspecified assistantships available. *Unit head:* Dr. Ronald J. Vansickle, Head, 706-542-7265, Fax: 706-542-6506, E-mail: rvansick@uga.edu. *Application contact:* Dr. John D. Hoge, Graduate Coordinator, 706-542-4416, Fax: 706-542-4277, E-mail: jdhoge@uga.edu.

University of Houston, College of Education, Department of Curriculum and Instruction, Houston, TX 77204. Offers art education (M Ed); bilingual education (M Ed); curriculum and instruction (Ed D); early childhood education (M Ed); education of the gifted (M Ed); elementary education (M Ed); mathematics education (M Ed); reading and language arts education (M Ed); science education (M Ed); second language education (M Ed); secondary education (M Ed); social studies education (M Ed); teaching (M Ed). *Accreditation:* NCATE. Part-time and evening/weekend programs available. *Faculty:* 24 full-time (11 women), 16 part-time/adjunct (14 women). *Students:* 134 full-time (102 women), 327 part-time (256 women); includes 142 minority (49 African Americans, 1 American Indian/Alaska Native, 29 Asian Americans or Pacific Islanders, 63 Hispanic Americans), 19 international. Average age 37. 113 applicants, 72% accepted, 61 enrolled. In 2006, 106 master's, 32 doctorates awarded. *Degree requirements:* For master's, comprehensive exam or thesis; for doctorate, thesis/dissertation, comprehensive exam. *Entrance requirements:* For master's, GRE General Test or MAT; for doctorate, GRE General Test, interview. *Application deadline:* For fall admission, 7/3 priority date for domestic students. Applications are processed on a rolling basis. Application fee: $35 ($75 for international students). *Expenses:* Tuition, state resident: full-time $5,429; part-time $226 per credit. Tuition, nonresident: full-time $12,029; part-time $501 per credit. Required fees: $2,454. *Financial support:* In 2006–07, 2 fellowships with full tuition reimbursements (averaging $9,500 per year), 6 research assistantships with full tuition reimbursements (averaging $8,800 per year), 25 teaching assistantships with full tuition reimbursements (averaging $8,800 per year) were awarded; career-related internships or fieldwork, Federal Work-Study, institutionally sponsored loans, scholarships/grants, health care benefits, and unspecified assistantships also available. Support available to part-time students. Financial award application deadline: 3/10. *Faculty research:* Teaching-learning process, instructional technology in schools, teacher education, classroom management, at-risk students. *Unit head:* Dr. Juanita Copley, Chairperson, 713-743-4950, Fax: 713-743-4990, E-mail: ncopley@aol.com.

University of Indianapolis, Graduate Programs, School of Education, Indianapolis, IN 46227-3697. Offers art education (MAT); biology (MAT); chemistry (MAT); curriculum and instruction (MA); earth sciences (MAT); education (MA, MAT); educational leadership (MA); elementary education (MA); English (MAT); French (MAT); math (MAT); physical education (MAT); physics (MAT); secondary education (MA), including art education, education, English education, social studies education; social studies (MAT); Spanish (MAT). *Accreditation:* NCATE. Part-time and evening/weekend programs available. *Faculty:* 4 full-time (2 women), 6 part-time/adjunct (2 women). *Students:* 32 full-time (16 women), 70 part-time (42 women); includes 2 minority (1 African American, 1 Hispanic American). Average age 31. In 2006, 51 degrees awarded. *Entrance requirements:* For master's, GRE Subject Test, minimum GPA of 2.5, 3 letters of recommendation, interview, Praxis I, writing exercise, be within 9 hours of completing content requirements. Additional exam requirements/recommendations for international students: Required—TOEFL (minimum score 550 paper-based; 213 computer-based). *Application deadline:* Applications are processed on a rolling basis. Application fee: $50. *Financial support:* Federal Work-Study available. Financial award application deadline: 5/1; financial award applicants required to submit FAFSA. *Faculty research:* Assessment of teacher education, perceptions of prospective teachers by parents. *Unit head:* Dr. E. Lynne Weisenbach, Dean, 317-788-3446, Fax: 317-788-3300, E-mail: weisenbach@uindy.edu.

The University of Iowa, Graduate College, College of Education, Department of Teaching and Learning, Program in Secondary Education, Iowa City, IA 52242-1316. Offers art education (MA, PhD); curriculum and supervision (PhD); curriculum supervision (MA); developmental reading (MA); English education (MA, MAT, PhD); foreign language education (MA, MAT); foreign language/ESL education (PhD); language, literature and culture (PhD); math education (PhD); mathematics education (MA); music education (MA, PhD); social studies (MA, PhD). *Faculty:* 11 full-time. *Students:* 53 full-time (33 women), 53 part-time (41 women); includes 5 minority (1 African American, 1 American Indian/Alaska Native, 2 Asian Americans or Pacific Islanders, 1 Hispanic American), 19 international. 66 applicants, 47% accepted, 17 enrolled. In 2006, 22 master's, 14 doctorates awarded. *Degree requirements:* For master's, exam, thesis optional; for doctorate, thesis/dissertation, comprehensive exam, registration. *Entrance requirements:* For master's and doctorate, GRE General Test, minimum GPA of 3.0. Additional exam requirements/recommendations for international students: Required—TOEFL (minimum score 550 paper-based; 213 computer-based; 81 iBT). Application fee: $60 ($85 for international students). Electronic applications accepted. *Financial support:* In 2006–07, 1 fellowship, 12 research assistantships with partial tuition reimbursements, 31 teaching assistantships with partial tuition reimbursements were awarded. Financial award applicants required to submit FAFSA. *Unit head:* Gary Sasso, Chair, 319-335-5324, Fax: 319-335-5608.

University of Maine, Graduate School, College of Education and Human Development, Program in Social Studies Education, Orono, ME 04469. Offers M Ed, MA, MS, CAS. *Accreditation:* NCATE. Part-time and evening/weekend programs available. *Students:* 1 (woman) full-time, 1 (woman) part-time. Average age 43. 1 applicant, 0% accepted. In 2006, 2 degrees awarded. *Degree requirements:* For master's, thesis or alternative. *Entrance requirements:* For master's, MAT; for CAS, MA, M Ed, or MS. Additional exam requirements/recommendations for international students: Required—TOEFL. *Application deadline:* For fall admission, 2/1 priority date for domestic students. Applications are processed on a rolling basis. Application fee: $50. Electronic applications accepted. *Financial support:* In 2006–07, teaching assistantships with tuition reimbursements (averaging $9,010 per year); tuition waivers (full and partial) also available. Financial award application deadline: 3/1. *Unit head:* Dr. Dorothy Breen, Coordinator, 207-581-2444, Fax: 207-581-2423. *Application contact:* Scott G. Delcourt, Associate Dean of the Graduate School, 207-581-3219, Fax: 207-581-3232, E-mail: graduate@maine.edu.

University of Michigan, Horace H. Rackham School of Graduate Studies, School of Education, Programs in Educational Studies, Ann Arbor, MI 48109. Offers curriculum development (MA); early childhood education (MA, PhD); educational administration and policy (MA, PhD); educational foundation, administration, policy, and research methods (MA); educational foundations and policy (MA, PhD); elementary education (MA-Certification); English education (MA); English language learning in school settings (MA); learning technologies (MA, PhD); literacy, language, and culture (MA, PhD); mathematics education (MA, PhD); research methods (MA); science education (MA, PhD); secondary education (MA-Certification); social studies education (MA); special education (PhD); teaching and teacher education (PhD); MA-Certification; MBA/MA; PhD/MA. Terminal master's awarded for partial completion of doctoral program. *Degree requirements:* For master's, thesis (for some programs); for doctorate, thesis/dissertation, comprehensive exam. *Entrance requirements:* For master's and doctorate, GRE General Test. Additional exam requirements/recommendations for international students: Required—TOEFL (minimum score 600 paper-based; 250 computer-based). *Application deadline:* For fall admission, 12/1 priority date for domestic students, 12/1 for international students. Application fee: $60 ($75 for international students). Electronic applications accepted. *Financial support:* Applicants required to submit FAFSA. *Unit head:* Dr. Addison Stone, Chairperson, 734-763-7500, Fax: 734-615-1290, E-mail: addison@umich.edu. *Application contact:* Roberta Perry, Office of Student Services, 734-764-7563, Fax: 734-763-1495, E-mail: ed.grad.admit@umich.edu.

University of Minnesota, Twin Cities Campus, Graduate School, College of Education and Human Development, Department of Curriculum and Instruction, Program in Teaching, Minneapolis, MN 55455-0213. Offers Chinese (M Ed); earth science (M Ed); elementary special education (M Ed); English (M Ed); English as a second language (M Ed); French (M Ed); German (M Ed); Hebrew (M Ed); Japanese (M Ed); life sciences (M Ed); mathematics (M Ed); middle school science (M Ed); science (M Ed); second languages and cultures (M Ed); social studies (M Ed); Spanish (M Ed). *Students:* 324 full-time (230 women), 132 part-time (86 women); includes 44 minority (5 African Americans, 2 American Indian/Alaska Native, 27 Asian

Social Sciences Education

University of Minnesota, Twin Cities Campus (continued)
Americans or Pacific Islanders, 10 Hispanic Americans), 4 international. Average age 27. 499 applicants, 74% accepted, 327 enrolled. In 2006, 545 degrees awarded. *Expenses:* Tuition, state resident: full-time $9,302; part-time $775 per credit. Tuition, nonresident: full-time $16,400; part-time $1,367 per credit. Full-time tuition and fees vary according to class time, course load, program, reciprocity agreements and student level. *Application contact:* Dr. Mary Bents, Associate Dean, 612-625-6501, Fax: 612-626-1580, E-mail: mbents@tc.umn.edu.

University of Missouri–Columbia, Graduate School, College of Education, Department of Curriculum and Instruction, Columbia, MO 65211. Offers agricultural education (M Ed, PhD, Ed S); art education (M Ed, PhD, Ed S); business and office education (M Ed, PhD, Ed S); early childhood education (M Ed, PhD, Ed S); elementary education (M Ed, PhD, Ed S); English education (M Ed, PhD, Ed S); foreign language education (M Ed, PhD, Ed S); health education and promotion (M Ed, PhD); learning and instruction (M Ed); marketing education (M Ed, PhD, Ed S); mathematics education (M Ed, PhD, Ed S); music education (M Ed, PhD, Ed S); reading education (M Ed, PhD, Ed S); science education (M Ed, PhD, Ed S); social studies education (M Ed, PhD, Ed S); vocational education (M Ed, PhD, Ed S). Part-time programs available. *Faculty:* 24 full-time (12 women). *Students:* 195 full-time (148 women), 260 part-time (214 women); includes 27 minority (8 African Americans, 1 American Indian/Alaska Native, 10 Asian Americans or Pacific Islanders, 8 Hispanic Americans), 19 international. In 2006, 186 master's, 12 doctorates awarded. Terminal master's awarded for partial completion of doctoral program. *Degree requirements:* For doctorate, thesis/dissertation. *Entrance requirements:* For master's and Ed S, GRE General Test or MAT, minimum GPA of 3.0; for doctorate, GRE General Test, minimum GPA of 3.0. *Application deadline:* Applications are processed on a rolling basis. Application fee: $45 ($60 for international students). *Financial support:* Fellowships, research assistantships, teaching assistantships, institutionally sponsored loans available. *Unit head:* Dr. Lloyd H. Barrow, Director of Graduate Studies, 573-882-8247, E-mail: robinsonr@missouri.edu.

University of New Orleans, Graduate School, College of Liberal Arts, Department of History, New Orleans, LA 70148. Offers history (MA); history teaching (MAHT). *Students:* 36 (18 women). Average age 34. In 2006, 6 degrees awarded. *Degree requirements:* For master's, one foreign language, thesis (for some programs). *Entrance requirements:* For master's, GRE General Test. Additional exam requirements/recommendations for international students: Required—TOEFL (minimum score 550 paper-based; 213 computer-based). *Application deadline:* For fall admission, 7/1 priority date for domestic students, 6/1 for international students; for spring admission, 11/15 priority date for domestic students, 10/1 for international students. Applications are processed on a rolling basis. Application fee: $40. Electronic applications accepted. *Expenses:* Tuition, state resident: full-time $3,292. Tuition, nonresident: full-time $10,336. Required fees: $158. *Financial support:* Research assistantships available. Financial award application deadline: 3/15; financial award applicants required to submit FAFSA. *Faculty research:* Recent U.S. political, military, urban, regional, and legal history. *Unit head:* Dr. Gunter Bischot, Chairperson, 504-280-6611, Fax: 504-280-6883, E-mail: gjbischo@uno.edu. *Application contact:* Dr. Molly Mitchell, Graduate Coordinator, Fax: 504-280-6883, E-mail: mnmitche@uno.edu.

The University of North Carolina at Chapel Hill, Graduate School, School of Education, Program in Secondary Education, Chapel Hill, NC 27599. Offers English (Grades 9-12) (MAT); French (Grades K-12) (MAT); German (Grades K-12) (MAT); Japanese (Grades K-12) (MAT); Latin (Grades 9-12) (MAT); mathematics (Grades 9-12) (MAT); music (Grades K-12) (MAT); science (Grades 9-12) (MAT); social studies/social science (Grades 9-12) (MAT); Spanish (Grades K-12) (MAT). *Accreditation:* NCATE. In 2006, 72 degrees awarded. *Degree requirements:* For master's, comprehensive exam. *Entrance requirements:* For master's, GRE General Test, minimum GPA of 3.0 during last 2 years of undergraduate course work. Additional exam requirements/recommendations for international students: Required—TOEFL (minimum score 550 paper-based; 213 computer-based), ACTFL oral proficiency interview. *Application deadline:* For fall admission, 1/1 priority date for domestic and international students. Applications are processed on a rolling basis. Application fee: $60. Electronic applications accepted. *Financial support:* Federal Work-Study available. Support available to part-time students. Financial award application deadline: 3/1; financial award applicants required to submit FAFSA. *Faculty research:* Curriculum and instruction, teacher education per subject. *Unit head:* Dr. James Trier, Coordinator, 919-843-4627. *Application contact:* Janet Carroll, Registrar, 919-962-8690, Fax: 919-962-1533, E-mail: jscarrol@email.unc.edu.

The University of North Carolina at Greensboro, Graduate School, School of Education, Department of Curriculum and Instruction, Greensboro, NC 27412-5001. Offers college teaching and adult learning (Certificate); curriculum and instruction (M Ed), including chemistry education, elementary education, English as a second language, French education, instructional technology, mathematics education, middle grades education, reading education, science education, social studies education, Spanish education; curriculum and teaching (PhD), including higher education, teacher education and development; English as a second language (Certificate); higher education (M Ed); supervision (M Ed). *Accreditation:* NCATE. Part-time programs available. *Faculty:* 27 full-time (18 women), 8 part-time/adjunct (3 women). *Students:* 137 full-time (114 women), 231 part-time (195 women); includes 63 minority (52 African Americans, 2 American Indian/Alaska Native, 5 Asian Americans or Pacific Islanders, 4 Hispanic Americans). 146 applicants, 32% accepted. *Degree requirements:* For doctorate, thesis/dissertation. *Entrance requirements:* For master's and doctorate, GRE General Test. Additional exam requirements/recommendations for international students: Required—TOEFL. Application fee: $45. Electronic applications accepted. *Expenses:* Tuition, state resident: full-time $2,692. Tuition, nonresident: full-time $13,742. *Financial support:* Fellowships, research assistantships with full tuition reimbursements, teaching assistantships with full tuition reimbursements, career-related internships or fieldwork, Federal Work-Study, scholarships/grants, traineeships, and unspecified assistantships available. Support available to part-time students. *Faculty research:* Community college literacy program, middle school mathematics/computer mathematics. *Unit head:* Dr. Sam Miller, Chair, 336-334-3445, Fax: 336-334-4120, E-mail: sdmille2@uncg.edu. *Application contact:* Michelle Harkleroad, Director of Graduate Admissions, 336-334-4884, Fax: 336-334-4424, E-mail: mbharkle@uncg.edu.

The University of North Carolina at Pembroke, Graduate Studies, Department of History, Program in Social Studies Education, Pembroke, NC 28372-1510. Offers MA, MAT. Part-time and evening/weekend programs available. *Faculty:* 3 full-time (1 woman). *Students:* 1 (woman) full-time, 11 part-time (3 women); includes 2 minority (both American Indian/Alaska Native). Average age 34. 12 applicants, 100% accepted, 12 enrolled. *Degree requirements:* For master's, thesis optional. *Entrance requirements:* For master's, GRE or MAT, minimum GPA of 3.0 in major, 2.5 overall. Additional exam requirements/recommendations for international students: Required—TOEFL. *Application deadline:* For fall admission, 7/15 priority date for domestic and international students; for spring admission, 12/1 priority date for domestic and international students. Applications are processed on a rolling basis. Application fee: $40. *Expenses:* Tuition, state resident: full-time $3,516; part-time $1,091 per semester. Tuition, nonresident: full-time $12,924; part-time $4,619 per semester. Tuition and fees vary according to class time, course load, degree level and campus/location. *Financial support:* In 2006–07, research assistantships with full tuition reimbursements (averaging $6,000 per year); unspecified assistantships also available. Support available to part-time students. Financial award application deadline: 4/15; financial award applicants required to submit FAFSA. *Unit head:* Dr. Scott C. Billingsley, Director, 910-521-6807, Fax: 910-775-4026, E-mail: scott.billingsley@uncp.edu.

University of Oklahoma, Graduate College, College of Education, Department of Instructional Leadership and Academic Curriculum, Norman, OK 73019-0390. Offers education (Certificate); instructional leadership and academic curriculum (M Ed, PhD), including bilingual education, early childhood education, elementary education, English education, math education, reading education, science education, secondary education, social studies education. *Accreditation:* NCATE. Part-time and evening/weekend programs available. *Faculty:* 20 full-time (11 women), 6 part-time/adjunct (all women). *Students:* 76 full-time (63 women), 115 part-time (89 women); includes 25 minority (8 African Americans, 12 American Indian/Alaska Native, 4 Asian Americans or Pacific Islanders, 1 Hispanic American), 12 international. 72 applicants, 96% accepted, 56 enrolled. In 2006, 11 master's, 10 doctorates awarded. *Degree requirements:* For doctorate, thesis/dissertation. *Entrance requirements:* For master's, 12 hours of course work in education; for doctorate, GRE General Test, master's degree, minimum graduate GPA of 3.0. Additional exam requirements/recommendations for international students: Required—TOEFL (minimum score 550 paper-based; 213 computer-based). *Application deadline:* For fall admission, 6/1 priority date for domestic students, 4/1 for international students; for spring admission, 11/1 for domestic students, 9/1 for international students. Applications are processed on a rolling basis. Application fee: $40 ($90 for international students). *Expenses:* Tuition, state resident: full-time $3,180; part-time $133 per credit hour. Tuition, nonresident: full-time $11,347; part-time $473 per credit hour. Required fees: $1,729; $62 per credit hour. $117 per semester. Tuition and fees vary according to course load and program. *Financial support:* In 2006–07, 76 students received support, including 5 research assistantships with partial tuition reimbursements available (averaging $9,773 per year), 7 teaching assistantships with partial tuition reimbursements available (averaging $10,403 per year); scholarships/grants and unspecified assistantships also available. Financial award applicants required to submit FAFSA. *Faculty research:* Early literacy, learning cycle, social justice, teacher education. Total annual research expenditures: $119,917. *Unit head:* Dr. Priscilla Griffith, Chair and Graduate Liaison, 405-325-1498, Fax: 405-325-4061, E-mail: pgriffith@ou.edu.

University of Pittsburgh, School of Education, Department of Instruction and Learning, Program in Secondary Education, Pittsburgh, PA 15260. Offers English/communications education (M Ed, MAT, Ed D, PhD); foreign languages education (M Ed, MAT, Ed D, PhD); mathematics education (M Ed, MAT, Ed D); reading education (PhD); science education (M Ed, MAT, MS, Ed D); social studies education (M Ed, MAT, Ed D, PhD). Part-time and evening/weekend programs available. *Students:* 157 full-time (111 women), 84 part-time (61 women); includes 18 minority (7 African Americans, 5 Asian Americans or Pacific Islanders, 6 Hispanic Americans), 13 international. 163 applicants, 74% accepted, 86 enrolled. In 2006, 114 master's, 7 doctorates awarded. *Degree requirements:* For master's and doctorate, thesis/dissertation. *Entrance requirements:* For master's, PRAXIS I; for doctorate, GRE General Test. Additional exam requirements/recommendations for international students: Required—TOEFL. *Application deadline:* For fall admission, 2/1 priority date for domestic students; for spring admission, 11/15 priority date for domestic students. Applications are processed on a rolling basis. Application fee: $50. Electronic applications accepted. *Financial support:* Fellowships, teaching assistantships, career-related internships or fieldwork, Federal Work-Study, tuition waivers (partial), and unspecified assistantships available. Support available to part-time students. Financial award application deadline: 3/15; financial award applicants required to submit FAFSA. *Application contact:* Joan M. Cutone, Director, School of Education Student Service Center, 412-648-2230, Fax: 412-648-1899, E-mail: soeinfo@pitt.edu.

University of Puerto Rico, Río Piedras, College of Education, Program in Curriculum and Teaching, San Juan, PR 00931-3300. Offers biology education (M Ed); chemistry education (M Ed); curriculum and teaching (Ed D); English education (M Ed); history education (M Ed); mathematics education (M Ed); physics education (M Ed); secondary education (M Ed); Spanish education (M Ed). Part-time programs available. *Students:* 64 full-time (42 women), 123 part-time (91 women); all minorities (all Hispanic Americans) In 2006, 8 master's, 19 doctorates awarded. *Degree requirements:* For master's, thesis; for doctorate, thesis/dissertation, internship. *Entrance requirements:* For master's, PAEG or GRE, minimum GPA of 3.0, letter of recommendation; for doctorate, GRE or PAEG, master's degree, minimum GPA of 3.0, letter of recommendation (2), interview. *Application deadline:* For fall admission, 2/1 for domestic and international students. Application fee: $17. *Expenses:* Tuition, state resident: part-time $100 per credit. Tuition, nonresident: part-time $291 per credit. Required fees: $72 per semester. *Financial support:* Fellowships, research assistantships, teaching assistantships, career-related internships or fieldwork, Federal Work-Study, institutionally sponsored loans, and tuition waivers (partial) available. Financial award application deadline: 5/31. *Faculty research:* Science curriculum, administration management. *Unit head:* Dr. Loyda Martinez, Coordinator, 787-764-0000 Ext. 4361, Fax: 787-763-4130. *Application contact:* Information Contact, 787-764-0000 Ext. 4368, Fax: 787-763-4130.

University of St. Francis, College of Education, Joliet, IL 60435-6169. Offers curriculum and instruction (MS); educational leadership (MS), including reading, special education; elementary education certification (M Ed); secondary education certification (M Ed), including English education, math education, science education, social studies education; special education (M Ed); teaching and learning (MS). Part-time and evening/weekend programs available. *Faculty:* 11 full-time (10 women), 25 part-time/adjunct (12 women). *Students:* 52 full-time (38 women), 381 part-time (293 women); includes 38 minority (21 African Americans, 1 American Indian/Alaska Native, 4 Asian Americans or Pacific Islanders, 12 Hispanic Americans). Average age 33. 194 applicants, 80% accepted, 117 enrolled. In 2006, 165 degrees awarded. *Degree requirements:* For master's, comprehensive exam (for some programs), registration. *Entrance requirements:* For master's, minimum undergraduate GPA of 2.75, 2 letters of recommendation, computer competency. Additional exam requirements/recommendations for international students: Required—TOEFL (minimum score 550 paper-based; 213 computer-based). *Application deadline:* Applications are processed on a rolling basis. Application fee: $30. Electronic applications accepted. *Expenses: Contact institution.* Part-time tuition and fees vary according to campus/location and program. *Financial support:* In 2006–07, 272 students received support. Scholarships/grants, tuition waivers (partial), and unspecified assistantships available. Support available to part-time students. Financial award applicants required to submit FAFSA. *Unit head:* Dr. John Gambro, Dean, 815-740-3456, Fax: 815-740-2264, E-mail: jgambro@stfrancis.edu. *Application contact:* Sandra Sloka, Director of Admissions for Graduate and Degree Completion Programs, 800-735-7500, Fax: 815-740-5032, E-mail: ssloka@stfrancis.edu.

University of South Carolina, The Graduate School, College of Arts and Sciences, Department of History, Columbia, SC 29208. Offers history (MA, PhD); history education (IMA, MAT); public history (MA, Certificate), including archives (MA), historic preservation (MA), museum (MA), museum management (Certificate); MLIS/MA. IMA and MAT offered in cooperation with the College of Education. Part-time programs available. Terminal master's awarded for partial completion of doctoral program. *Degree requirements:* For master's and doctorate, one foreign language, thesis/dissertation. *Entrance requirements:* For master's and doctorate, GRE General Test. Additional exam requirements/recommendations for international students: Required—TOEFL. Electronic applications accepted. *Faculty research:* American history, especially Southern and South Carolina; modern European history, especially Germany, France, Russian, and Great Britain; medieval, Renaissance, and late ancient history; Latin American history, especially Brazil and Mexico.

University of South Carolina, The Graduate School, College of Education, Department of Instruction and Teacher Education, Program in Secondary Education, Columbia, SC 29208. Offers art education (IMA, MAT); business education (IMA, MAT); English (MAT); foreign language (MAT); health education (MAT); mathematics (MAT); science (IMA, MAT); secondary education (M Ed, MA, MT, PhD); social studies (IMA, MAT); theatre and speech (IMA, MAT). IMA and MT offered jointly with the subject areas. *Accreditation:* NCATE. *Degree requirements:* For master's, thesis (for some programs), foreign language (MA), comprehensive exam; for doctorate, one foreign language, thesis/dissertation, comprehensive exam. *Entrance requirements:* For master's, GRE General Test or MAT, teaching certificate (IMA, M Ed), interview; for doctorate, GRE General Test or MAT, interview. *Faculty research:* Middle school programs, professional development, school collaboration.

University of Southern Mississippi, Graduate School, College of Education and Psychology, Department of Curriculum, Instruction, and Special Education, Hattiesburg, MS 39406-0001. Offers alternative secondary teacher education (MAT); early childhood education (M Ed,

Ed S); education of the gifted (M Ed, Ed D, PhD, Ed S); elementary education (M Ed, Ed D, PhD, Ed S); reading (M Ed, MS, Ed S); secondary education (M Ed, MS, Ed D, PhD, Ed S); special education (M Ed, Ed D, PhD, Ed S). *Faculty:* 16 full-time (11 women). *Students:* 31 full-time (28 women), 54 part-time (51 women); includes 5 minority (4 African Americans, 1 Hispanic American), 1 international. Average age 35. 59 applicants, 27% accepted, 11 enrolled. In 2006, 43 master's, 3 doctorates, 4 other advanced degrees awarded. *Degree requirements:* For master's, thesis (for some programs), comprehensive exam, registration; for doctorate and Ed S, thesis/dissertation, comprehensive exam, registration. *Entrance requirements:* For master's, GRE General Test, MAT, minimum GPA of 3.0; for doctorate, GRE General Test, minimum GPA of 3.5; for Ed S, GRE General Test, MAT, minimum GPA of 3.25. Additional exam requirements/recommendations for international students: Required—TOEFL. *Application deadline:* For fall admission, 3/1 priority date for domestic students, 3/1 for international students. Applications are processed on a rolling basis. Application fee: $25 ($30 for international students). *Financial support:* In 2006–07, 10 research assistantships with tuition reimbursements (averaging $22,333 per year), 2 teaching assistantships with full tuition reimbursements (averaging $22,333 per year) were awarded; Federal Work-Study, institutionally sponsored loans, and tuition waivers (partial) also available. Financial award application deadline: 3/15. *Faculty research:* Mathematical problem solving, integrative curriculum, writing process, teacher education models. Total annual research expenditures: $100,000. *Unit head:* Dr. Dana Thames, Chair, 601-266-4547, Fax: 601-266-4175. *Application contact:* B.J. Davis, Administrative Assistant, 601-266-6987, Fax: 601-266-4548.

University of South Florida, Graduate School, College of Education, Department of Secondary Education, Tampa, FL 33620-9951. Offers English education (M Ed, MA, PhD); foreign language education (M Ed, MA); instructional technology (M Ed); mathematics education (M Ed, MA, PhD, Ed S); middle school education (M Ed); science education (M Ed, MA, MAT, PhD); second language acquisition/instructional technology (PhD); secondary education (PhD); social science education (M Ed, MA). *Accreditation:* NCATE. Part-time and evening/weekend programs available. *Faculty:* 29 full-time (16 women), 15 part-time/adjunct (8 women). *Students:* 136 full-time (95 women), 279 part-time (188 women); includes 85 minority (35 African Americans, 1 American Indian/Alaska Native, 13 Asian Americans or Pacific Islanders, 36 Hispanic Americans), 19 international. 212 applicants, 71% accepted, 96 enrolled. In 2006, 87 master's, 12 doctorates awarded. *Entrance requirements:* For master's and doctorate, GRE General Test, minimum GPA of 3.5; for Ed S, GRE General Test. *Application deadline:* For fall admission, 6/1 for domestic students; for spring admission, 10/15 for domestic students. Application fee: $30. Electronic applications accepted. *Financial support:* Scholarships/grants and unspecified assistantships available. Total annual research expenditures: $477,202. *Unit head:* Dr. Jane H. Applegate, Interim Chairperson, 813-974-3533, Fax: 813-974-3837, E-mail: applegat@tempest.coedu.usf.edu.

The University of Tennessee, Graduate School, College of Education, Health and Human Sciences, Program in Education, Knoxville, TN 37996. Offers art education (MS); counseling education (PhD); cultural studies in education (PhD); curriculum (MS, Ed S); curriculum, educational research and evaluation (Ed D, PhD); early childhood education (PhD); early childhood special education (MS); education of deaf and hard of hearing (MS); educational administration and policy studies (Ed D, PhD); educational administration and supervision (Ed S); educational psychology (Ed D, PhD); elementary education (MS, Ed S); elementary teaching (MS); English education (MS, Ed S); exercise science (PhD); foreign language/ESL education (MS, Ed S); instructional technology (MS, Ed D, PhD, Ed S); literacy, language and ESL education (PhD); literacy, language education, and ESL education (Ed D); mathematics education (MS, Ed S); modified and comprehensive special education (MS); reading education (MS, Ed S); school counseling (Ed S); school psychology (PhD, Ed S); science education (MS, Ed S); secondary teaching (MS); social foundations (MS); social science education (MS, Ed S); socio-cultural foundations of sports and education (PhD); special education (Ed S); teacher education (Ed D, PhD). *Accreditation:* NCATE. Part-time and evening/weekend programs available. *Students:* 529 (401 women); includes 39 minority (23 African Americans, 2 American Indian/Alaska Native, 9 Asian Americans or Pacific Islanders, 5 Hispanic Americans) 34 international. 420 applicants, 50% accepted. In 2006, 258 master's, 28 doctorates awarded. *Degree requirements:* For master's and Ed S, thesis optional; for doctorate, variable foreign language requirement, thesis/dissertation. *Entrance requirements:* For master's, minimum GPA of 2.7; for doctorate and Ed S, GRE General Test, minimum GPA of 2.7. Additional exam requirements/recommendations for international students: Required—TOEFL. *Application deadline:* For fall admission, 2/1 priority date for domestic students. Applications are processed on a rolling basis. Application fee: $35. Electronic applications accepted. *Expenses:* Tuition, state resident: full-time $5,574. Tuition, nonresident: full-time $16,840. Required fees: $792. *Financial support:* In 2006–07, 4 fellowships, 9 teaching assistantships were awarded; career-related internships or fieldwork, Federal Work-Study, institutionally sponsored loans, and unspecified assistantships also available. Financial award application deadline: 2/1; financial award applicants required to submit FAFSA. *Unit head:* Dr. Lester Knight, Head, 865-974-0907, Fax: 865-974-8718, E-mail: lknight@utk.edu.

The University of Texas at Tyler, College of Arts and Sciences, Department of History, Tyler, TX 75799-0001. Offers history (MA, MAT). Part-time and evening/weekend programs available. *Faculty:* 5 full-time (1 woman). *Students:* 1 (woman) full-time, 17 part-time (10 women); includes 4 minority (2 African Americans, 1 American Indian/Alaska Native, 1 Hispanic American). Average age 38. 7 applicants, 5 enrolled. In 2006, 6 degrees awarded. *Degree requirements:* For master's, one foreign language, comprehensive exam. *Entrance requirements:* For master's, GRE General Test, minimum GPA of 3.0. *Application deadline:* Applications are processed on a rolling basis. Application fee: $0. Electronic applications accepted. *Expenses:* Tuition, state resident: part-time $50 per credit hour. Tuition, nonresident: part-time $328 per credit hour. Required fees: $107 per credit hour. $426 per term. *Financial support:* Federal Work-Study and unspecified assistantships available. Support available to part-time students. Financial award application deadline: 7/1; financial award applicants required to submit FAFSA. *Faculty research:* Early and modern U.S. history, early modern European history. *Unit head:* Dr. Vincent J. Falzone, Chair, 903-566-7395, Fax: 903-565-5700, E-mail: vfalzone@mail.uttyl.edu. *Application contact:* Bonnie Purser, Office of Graduate Studies, 903-566-7142, Fax: 903-566-7068, E-mail: bpurser@uttyler.edu.

The University of Texas at Tyler, College of Education and Psychology, Department of Curriculum and Instruction, Tyler, TX 75799-0001. Offers curriculum and instruction (M Ed); secondary teaching (MAT), including art, biology, computer science, English, history, journalism, mathematics, music, political science, sociology, speech, theatre. Part-time programs available. *Faculty:* 10 full-time (6 women), 2 part-time/adjunct (1 woman). *Students:* 3 full-time (2 women), 7 part-time (6 women); includes 1 minority (African American) Average age 32. 1 applicant, 100% accepted, 1 enrolled. In 2006, 6 degrees awarded. *Degree requirements:* For master's, research project (M Ed). *Entrance requirements:* For master's, GRE or MAT. Application fee: $0 ($50 for international students). Electronic applications accepted. *Expenses:* Tuition, state resident: part-time $50 per credit hour. Tuition, nonresident: part-time $328 per credit hour. Required fees: $107 per credit hour. $426 per term. *Financial support:* Scholarships/grants available. *Unit head:* Dr. Robert Stevens, Chair/Professor of Education, 903-566-7315, E-mail: rstevens@uttyler.edu. *Application contact:* Bonnie Purser, Office of Graduate Studies, 903-566-7142, Fax: 903-566-7068, E-mail: bpurser@uttyler.edu.

The University of Toledo, College of Graduate Studies, College of Education, Department of Curriculum and Instruction, Program in Education and History, Toledo, OH 43606-3390. Offers MAE. *Students:* 1 applicant, 0% accepted. In 2006, 1 degree awarded.

The University of Toledo, College of Graduate Studies, College of Education, Department of Curriculum and Instruction, Program in Education and Political Science, Toledo, OH 43606-3390. Offers MAE.

The University of Toledo, College of Graduate Studies, College of Education, Department of Curriculum and Instruction, Program in Education and Sociology, Toledo, OH 43606-3390. Offers MAE.

The University of Toledo, College of Graduate Studies, College of Education, Department of Foundations of Education, Toledo, OH 43606-3390. Offers education and sociology (MAE); educational psychology (ME, DE, PhD); educational research and measurement (ME, PhD); educational sociology (DE, PhD); educational theory and social foundations (ME); foundations of education (DE, PhD); history of education (DE, PhD); philosophy of education (DE, PhD). *Accreditation:* NCATE. *Faculty:* 13 full-time (7 women), 4 part-time/adjunct (3 women). *Students:* 18 full-time (12 women), 18 part-time (15 women); includes 7 minority (5 African Americans, 2 Hispanic Americans), 8 international. Average age 37. 14 applicants, 43% accepted, 4 enrolled. In 2006, 4 master's, 4 doctorates awarded. *Degree requirements:* For master's, thesis or alternative, comprehensive exam. *Entrance requirements:* For master's, minimum GPA of 2.7. *Application deadline:* For fall admission, 8/1 priority date for domestic students. Applications are processed on a rolling basis. Application fee: $45. Electronic applications accepted. *Financial support:* In 2006–07, 5 research assistantships with full tuition reimbursements (averaging $6,500 per year), 5 teaching assistantships with full tuition reimbursements (averaging $9,429 per year) were awarded; career-related internships or fieldwork, Federal Work-Study, and institutionally sponsored loans also available. Support available to part-time students. Financial award application deadline: 4/1; financial award applicants required to submit FAFSA. *Unit head:* Dr. Dale Snauwaert, Chair, 419-530-2478, Fax: 419-530-8337.

University of Victoria, Faculty of Graduate Studies, Faculty of Education, Department of Curriculum and Instruction, Victoria, BC V8W 2Y2, Canada. Offers art (M Ed, MA, PhD); curriculum studies (M Ed, MA, PhD); early childhood (M Ed, MA, PhD); language and literacy (M Ed, MA, PhD); mathematics (M Ed, MA, PhD); music (M Ed, MA); music education (PhD); science (M Ed, MA, PhD); social studies (M Ed, MA); social, cultural and foundational studies (PhD); technology and environmental education (PhD). Part-time programs available. *Degree requirements:* For master's, thesis, project (M Ed); for doctorate, thesis/dissertation, comprehensive exam, registration. *Entrance requirements:* For master's, minimum B average. Additional exam requirements/recommendations for international students: Required—TOEFL (minimum score 575 paper-based; 233 computer-based), IELTS (minimum score 7). Electronic applications accepted. *Faculty research:* Elementary and secondary English, language arts, curriculum theory and practice, educational media and technology, educational administration and leadership, history and philosophy of education.

University of Washington, Graduate School, College of Education, Seattle, WA 98195. Offers curriculum and instruction (M Ed, Ed D, PhD), including educational technology, general curriculum (Ed D, PhD), language, literacy, and culture, mathematics education, multicultural education, reading and language arts education (Ed D), science education, social studies education, teaching and curriculum (M Ed); educational leadership and policy studies (M Ed, Ed D, PhD), including administration, educational organization and policy, higher education, school district leadership (Ed D), social/cultural foundations; educational psychology (M Ed, PhD), including human development and cognition, measurement and research, school counseling (M Ed), school psychology; special education (M Ed, Ed D, PhD), including early childhood education, elementary special education, emotional and behavioral disabilities (M Ed), general special education, severe disabilities; teacher education (MIT). *Accreditation:* APA. Part-time and evening/weekend programs available. *Degree requirements:* For master's, thesis optional; for doctorate, thesis/dissertation. *Entrance requirements:* For master's and doctorate, GRE General Test, minimum GPA of 3.0. Additional exam requirements/recommendations for international students: Required—TOEFL. Electronic applications accepted. *Faculty research:* School restructuring/effective schools, special education interventions, literacy and writing, technology, school partnerships, teacher preparation.

The University of West Alabama, School of Graduate Studies, College of Liberal Arts, Department of History and Social Sciences, Livingston, AL 35470. Offers history (MAT); social science (MAT). *Accreditation:* NCATE. *Faculty:* 5 full-time (0 women). *Students:* 20 full-time (10 women), 44 part-time (28 women); includes 29 minority (all African Americans) Application fee: $20 ($50 for international students). *Financial support:* Career-related internships or fieldwork, Federal Work-Study, scholarships/grants, and unspecified assistantships available. Support available to part-time students. *Unit head:* Dr. David Bowen, Chairperson, 800-621-8044 Ext. 3467.

University of West Georgia, Graduate School, College of Education, Department of Curriculum and Instruction, Program in Secondary Education—Social Studies, Carrollton, GA 30118. Offers M Ed, Ed S. Part-time and evening/weekend programs available. *Students:* 1 full-time (0 women), 5 part-time (2 women); includes 1 minority (African American) Average age 20. In 2006, 3 master's, 1 other advanced degree awarded. *Degree requirements:* For master's, comprehensive exam; for Ed S, research project. *Entrance requirements:* For master's and Ed S, GRE or MAT. *Application deadline:* For fall admission, 8/1 for domestic students. Applications are processed on a rolling basis. Application fee: $20. *Expenses:* Tuition, state resident: full-time $2,286; part-time $127 per credit. Tuition, nonresident: full-time $9,144; part-time $508 per credit. Required fees: $494; $27 per credit. $121 per semester. *Financial support:* In 2006–07, research assistantships with full tuition reimbursements (averaging $3,000 per year). Financial award applicants required to submit FAFSA. *Application contact:* Dr. Charles W. Clark, Chair, 678-839-6508, E-mail: cclark@westga.edu.

University of Wisconsin–Eau Claire, College of Education and Human Sciences, Program in Secondary Education, Eau Claire, WI 54702-4004. Offers biology (MAT, MST); education and professional development (MEPD); English (MAT, MST); history (MAT, MST); mathematics (MAT, MST). *Faculty:* 9 full-time (6 women). *Students:* 10 full-time (7 women), 23 part-time (20 women), 1 international. Average age 33. 21 applicants, 57% accepted, 4 enrolled. In 2006, 22 degrees awarded. *Degree requirements:* For master's, thesis optional. *Entrance requirements:* For master's, 2 years of teaching experience or the equivalent. *Application deadline:* For fall admission, 7/1 for domestic students; for spring admission, 12/1 for domestic students. Applications are processed on a rolling basis. Application fee: $45. *Expenses:* Tuition, state resident: full-time $6,533; part-time $363 per credit. Tuition, nonresident: full-time $17,143; part-time $952 per credit. Tuition and fees vary according to program and reciprocity agreements. *Financial support:* In 2006–07, 17 students received support, including 2 teaching assistantships (averaging $5,200 per year); Federal Work-Study also available. Financial award application deadline: 3/1; financial award applicants required to submit FAFSA. *Unit head:* Dr. Tamara Lindsey, Chair, 715-836-4737, Fax: 715-836-4868, E-mail: lindsetp@uwec.edu.

University of Wisconsin–River Falls, Outreach and Graduate Studies, College of Arts and Science, Department of History and Philosophy, River Falls, WI 54022-5001. Offers social science education (MSE). Part-time programs available. *Degree requirements:* For master's, thesis (for some programs). *Entrance requirements:* For master's, minimum GPA of 2.75. Electronic applications accepted. *Faculty research:* WW II, Hitler, modern China, women's history, immigration history.

Virginia Commonwealth University, Graduate School, School of Education, Program in Teaching and Learning, Richmond, VA 23284-9005. Offers early education (MT); middle education (MT); secondary education (MT, Certificate); special education (MT). *Accreditation:* NCATE. Part-time programs available. *Faculty:* 22 full-time (12 women). *Students:* 152 full-time (130 women), 126 part-time (111 women); includes 42 minority (35 African Americans, 2 American Indian/Alaska Native, 4 Asian Americans or Pacific Islanders, 1 Hispanic American), 4 international. 551 applicants, 74% accepted. In 2006, 77 degrees awarded. *Entrance requirements:* For master's, GRE General Test or MAT. *Application deadline:* For fall admission, 5/15 for domestic students; for spring admission, 11/15 for domestic students. Applications are processed on a rolling basis. Application fee: $50. *Financial support:* Application deadline: 3/1. *Unit head:* Dr. Michael D. Davis, Director, Graduate Studies, 804-828-6530, Fax: 804-827-0676, E-mail: mddavis@vcu.edu. *Application contact:* Dr. Michael D. Davis, Director, Graduate Studies, 804-828-6530, Fax: 804-827-0676, E-mail: mddavis@vcu.edu.

See Close-Up on page 1137.

Social Sciences Education

Wayne State College, School of Education and Counseling, Department of Educational Foundations and Leadership, Program in Curriculum and Instruction, Wayne, NE 68787. Offers alternative education (MSE); business education (MSE); communication arts education (MSE); curriculum and instruction (MSE); early childhood education (MSE); elementary education (MSE); English as a second language (MSE); English education (MSE); family consumer science of education (MSE); industrial technology education (MSE); learning communities (MSE); mathematics education (MSE); music education (MSE); science education (MSE); social science education (MSE). *Accreditation:* NCATE. Part-time and evening/weekend programs available. *Faculty:* 17 part-time/adjunct (11 women). *Students:* 17 full-time (10 women), 307 part-time (248 women); includes 6 minority (2 African Americans, 1 American Indian/Alaska Native, 2 Asian Americans or Pacific Islanders, 1 Hispanic American), 1 international. Average age 35. In 2006, 167 degrees awarded. *Degree requirements:* For master's, thesis optional. *Entrance requirements:* For master's, GRE General Test. Additional exam requirements/recommendations for international students: Required—TOEFL (minimum score 550 paper-based; 213 computer-based). *Application deadline:* Applications are processed on a rolling basis. Application fee: $30. *Expenses:* Tuition, state resident: full-time $3,114; part-time $130 per credit hour. Tuition, nonresident: full-time $6,228; part-time $260 per credit hour. Required fees: $894; $37 per credit hour. Tuition and fees vary according to course load. *Financial support:* Applicants required to submit FAFSA.

Wayne State University, College of Education, Division of Teacher Education, Detroit, MI 48202. Offers adult and continuing education (M Ed); art education (M Ed); bilingual/bicultural education (M Ed, MAT); business education (M Ed, MAT); career and technical education (M Ed, Ed D, PhD, Ed S); curriculum and instruction (Ed D, PhD, Ed S); distributive education (M Ed, MAT); early childhood education (M Ed); elementary education (M Ed, MAT, Ed D, PhD, Ed S); elementary education curriculum and instruction (M Ed); English education (M Ed); English education-secondary (M Ed, Ed S); foreign language education (M Ed); general education (Ed D, Ed S); health occupations education (M Ed); industrial education (M Ed); mathematics education (M Ed, Ed S); pre-school and parent education (M Ed); reading (M Ed, Ed D, Ed S); reading, languages and literature (Ed D); school music-vocal (M Ed); science education (M Ed, MAT, Ed S); secondary education (MAT); secondary school reading (M Ed); social studies education (M Ed, Ed S), including education-secondary (M Ed); special education (M Ed, Ed D, PhD, Ed S); teacher education (MAT, Ed D, PhD). *Faculty:* 41 full-time (22 women), 2 part-time/adjunct (both women). *Students:* 401 full-time (295 women), 1,021 part-time (784 women); includes 527 minority (452 African Americans, 6 American Indian/Alaska Native, 32 Asian Americans or Pacific Islanders, 37 Hispanic Americans), 18 international. Average age 36. 296 applicants, 81% accepted, 132 enrolled. In 2006, 386 master's, 1 doctorate awarded. *Degree requirements:* For doctorate, thesis/dissertation. *Entrance requirements:* For master's, minimum GPA of 2.6; for doctorate, minimum undergraduate GPA of 3.0, graduate 3.5; interview. Additional exam requirements/recommendations for international students: Required—TOEFL (minimum score 550 paper-based; 213 computer-based), TWE (minimum score 6). *Application deadline:* For fall admission, 7/1 for domestic students, 6/1 for international students; for winter admission, 10/1 for international students; for spring admission, 2/1 for international students. Application fee: $30 ($50 for international students). Electronic applications accepted. *Financial support:* In 2006–07, 1 fellowship (averaging $34,919 per year) was awarded; research assistantships. *Faculty research:* Reading and writing literacy and literature. Total annual research expenditures: $209,400. *Unit head:* Dr. Joann Snyder, Academic Director, 313-577-1644, E-mail: joanne.snyder@wayne.edu. *Application contact:* Sharon Elliott, Assistant Dean, 313-577-0902, E-mail: sharon.elliott@wayne.edu.

Wayne State University, College of Education, Division of Theoretical and Behavioral Foundations, Detroit, MI 48202. Offers counseling (M Ed, MA, Ed D, PhD, Ed S); education evaluation and research (M Ed, Ed D, PhD); educational psychology (M Ed, Ed D, PhD, Ed S); educational sociology (M Ed, Ed D, PhD, Ed S); history and philosophy of education (M Ed, Ed D, PhD); rehabilitation counseling and community inclusion (MA, Ed S); school and community psychology (MA, Ed S); school clinical psychology (Ed S). *Accreditation:* ACA (one or more programs are accredited); CORE (one or more programs are accredited). Evening/weekend programs available. *Faculty:* 51 full-time (18 women), 11 part-time/adjunct (7 women). *Students:* 156 full-time (125 women), 232 part-time (191 women); includes 146 minority (140 African Americans, 1 American Indian/Alaska Native, 5 Hispanic Americans), 14 international. Average age 35. 146 applicants, 38% accepted, 39 enrolled. In 2006, 84 master's, 8 doctorates awarded. *Degree requirements:* For doctorate, thesis/dissertation. *Entrance requirements:* For master's, GRE (school and community psychology); for doctorate, GRE (educational psychology), interview, minimum GPA of 3.0. Additional exam requirements/recommendations for international students: Required—TOEFL (minimum score 550 paper-based; 213 computer-based), TWE (minimum score 6). *Application deadline:* For fall admission, 7/1 for domestic students, 6/1 for international students; for winter admission, 10/1 for international students; for spring admission, 2/1 for international students. Application fee: $20 ($30 for international students). Electronic applications accepted. *Financial support:* In 2006–07, 2 research assistantships (averaging $12,797 per year) were awarded; fellowships, career-related internships or fieldwork, Federal Work-Study, and institutionally sponsored loans also available. *Faculty research:* Adolescents at risk, supervision of counseling. *Unit head:* Dr. JoAnne Holbert, Assistant Dean, 313-577-1721, E-mail: jholbert@wayne.edu.

Webster University, School of Education, Department of Multidisciplinary Studies, St. Louis, MO 63119-3194. Offers administrative leadership (Ed S); education leadership (Ed S); educational technology (MAT); mathematics (MAT); multidisciplinary studies (MAT); school systems, superintendency and leadership (Ed S); social science (MAT); special education (MAT). Part-time programs available. *Students:* 97 full-time (83 women), 687 part-time (573 women); includes 173 minority (142 African Americans, 2 American Indian/Alaska Native, 13 Asian Americans or Pacific Islanders, 16 Hispanic Americans), 6 international. Average age 34. In 2006, 14 degrees awarded. *Entrance requirements:* For master's, minimum GPA of 2.5. *Application deadline:* Applications are processed on a rolling basis. Application fee: $25 ($50 for international students). *Expenses:* Tuition: Full-time $8,820; part-time $490 per credit. Tuition and fees vary according to degree level, campus/location and program. *Financial support:* Federal Work-Study available. Support available to part-time students. Financial award application deadline: 4/1; financial award applicants required to submit FAFSA. *Unit head:* Dr. Donna Campbell, Chair, 314-961-2660 Ext. 7042, Fax: 314-968-7118. *Application contact:* Director of Graduate and Evening Student Admissions, Fax: 314-968-7116, E-mail: gadmit@webster.edu.

Western Carolina University, Graduate School, College of Arts and Sciences, Department of History, Cullowhee, NC 28723. Offers American history (MA); comprehensive education (MA Ed), including social sciences; history (MA); social sciences (MAT). Part-time and evening/weekend programs available. *Degree requirements:* For master's, one foreign language, thesis (for some programs), comprehensive exam. *Entrance requirements:* For master's, GRE General Test. Additional exam requirements/recommendations for international students: Required—TOEFL (minimum score 550 paper-based; 213 computer-based).

Western Carolina University, Graduate School, College of Education and Allied Professions, Department of Educational Leadership and Foundations, Programs in Secondary Education, Cullowhee, NC 28723. Offers art education (MAT); biology (MAT); chemistry (MAT); comprehensive education (MA Ed), including art, biology, English, mathematics, music, physical education, reading, social sciences; English (MAT); family and consumer sciences (MAT); mathematics (MAT); physical education (MAT); reading (MAT); social sciences (MAT). *Accreditation:* NCATE (one or more programs are accredited). Part-time and evening/weekend programs available. *Degree requirements:* For master's, comprehensive exam. *Entrance requirements:* For master's, GRE General Test, portfolio. Additional exam requirements/recommendations for international students: Required—TOEFL (minimum score 550 paper-based; 213 computer-based).

Western Oregon University, Graduate Programs, College of Education, Division of Teacher Education, Program in Secondary Education, Monmouth, OR 97361-1394. Offers bilingual education (MS Ed); health (MS Ed); humanities (MAT, MS Ed); initial licensure (MAT); mathematics (MAT, MS Ed); science (MAT, MS Ed); social science (MAT, MS Ed). *Accreditation:* NCATE. Part-time and evening/weekend programs available. *Faculty:* 7 full-time (4 women), 15 part-time/adjunct (7 women). *Students:* 12 full-time (4 women), 21 part-time (10 women). Average age 32. In 2006, 31 degrees awarded. *Degree requirements:* For master's, written exam, thesis optional. *Entrance requirements:* For master's, minimum GPA of 3.0, teaching license. *Application deadline:* Applications are processed on a rolling basis. Application fee: $50. *Expenses:* Tuition, state resident: full-time $8,250; part-time $250 per credit. Tuition, nonresident: full-time $14,025; part-time $250 per credit. Required fees: $1,173. *Financial support:* In 2006–07, 16 teaching assistantships with full tuition reimbursements (averaging $706 per year) were awarded; research assistantships with full tuition reimbursements, career-related internships or fieldwork, Federal Work-Study, and tuition waivers (full and partial) also available. Support available to part-time students. Financial award application deadline: 3/1; financial award applicants required to submit FAFSA. *Faculty research:* Literacy, science in primary grades, geography education, retention, teacher burnout. *Unit head:* Dr. Mary Bucy, Unit Head, 503-838-8794, Fax: 503-838-8228. *Application contact:* Dr. David McDonald, Dean of Admissions, Retention and Enrollment Management, 503-838-8919, Fax: 503-838-8067, E-mail: mcdonald@wou.edu.

Widener University, School of Human Service Professions, Center for Education, Chester, PA 19013-5792. Offers adult education (M Ed); counseling in higher education (M Ed); counselor education (M Ed); early childhood education (M Ed); educational foundations (M Ed); educational leadership (M Ed); educational psychology (M Ed); elementary education (M Ed); English and language arts (M Ed); health education (M Ed); higher education leadership (Ed D); home and school visitor (M Ed); human sexuality (M Ed); mathematics education (M Ed); middle school education (M Ed); principalship (M Ed); reading and language arts (Ed D); reading education (M Ed); school administration (Ed D); science education (M Ed); social studies education (M Ed); special education (M Ed); technology education (M Ed). Part-time and evening/weekend programs available. Terminal master's awarded for partial completion of doctoral program. *Degree requirements:* For doctorate, thesis/dissertation. *Entrance requirements:* For master's, minimum GPA of 2.5; for doctorate, GRE or MAT, minimum GPA of 2.0 (undergraduate), 3.5 (graduate). Electronic applications accepted. Expenses: Contact institution. *Faculty research:* Reading and cognition, adult education, technology education, educational leadership, special education.

Wilkes University, Graduate Studies and Continued Learning, College of Arts, Humanities and Social Sciences, Program in Teacher Education, Wilkes-Barre, PA 18766-0002. Offers classroom technology (MS Ed); educational computing (MS Ed); educational development and strategies (MS Ed); educational leadership (MS Ed); elementary education (MS Ed); instructional technology (MS Ed); school business leadership (MS Ed); secondary education (MS Ed), including biology, chemistry, English, history; special education (MS Ed). Part-time and evening/weekend programs available. Postbaccalaureate distance learning degree programs offered (minimal on-campus study). *Students:* 32 full-time (21 women), 1,588 part-time (1,106 women); includes 29 minority (6 African Americans, 2 American Indian/Alaska Native, 4 Asian Americans or Pacific Islanders, 17 Hispanic Americans). Average age 33. In 2006, 754 degrees awarded. *Entrance requirements:* Additional exam requirements/recommendations for international students: Required—TOEFL (minimum score 500 paper-based; 173 computer-based). *Application deadline:* Applications are processed on a rolling basis. Application fee: $40. *Expenses:* Contact institution. *Financial support:* Federal Work-Study and unspecified assistantships available. Financial award application deadline: 3/1; financial award applicants required to submit FAFSA. *Unit head:* Dr. Michael Speziale, Interim Dean, 570-408-4679, Fax: 570-408-4905, E-mail: michael.speziale@wilkes.edu. *Application contact:* Kathleen Houlihan, Director of Graduate Studies, 570-408-3235, Fax: 570-408-7846, E-mail: kathleen.houlihan@wilkes.edu.

William Carey University, Graduate Studies, School of Education, Hattiesburg, MS 39401-5499. Offers art education (M Ed); art of teaching (M Ed); elementary education (M Ed, Ed S); English education (M Ed); gifted education (M Ed); history and social science (M Ed); mild/moderate disabilities (M Ed); secondary education (M Ed). Part-time programs available. *Faculty:* 19 full-time (12 women), 25 part-time/adjunct (17 women). *Students:* 142 full-time (111 women), 412 part-time (343 women); includes 123 minority (121 African Americans, 1 Asian American or Pacific Islander, 1 Hispanic American). In 2006, 305 master's, 2 other advanced degrees awarded. *Degree requirements:* For master's, comprehensive exam. *Entrance requirements:* For master's, GRE, MAT, minimum GPA of 2.5, Class A teacher's license. Additional exam requirements/recommendations for international students: Required—TOEFL (minimum score 550 paper-based; 213 computer-based). *Application deadline:* For fall admission, 8/7 for domestic and international students; for winter admission, 10/30 for domestic and international students; for spring admission, 2/12 for domestic and international students. Application fee: $25. *Expenses:* Tuition: Full-time $5,040; part-time $240 per credit hour. Tuition and fees vary according to course load. *Financial support:* In 2006–07, 371 students received support. Federal Work-Study and scholarships/grants available. Support available to part-time students. *Unit head:* Dr. Patty Ward, Dean, 601-318-6139, Fax: 601-318-6185, E-mail: patty.ward@wmcarey.edu. *Application contact:* Jason Douglas, Clerical Assistant, Graduate Admissions, 601-318-6774, Fax: 601-318-6765, E-mail: jason.douglas@wmcarey.edu.

Worcester State College, Graduate Studies, Department of Education, Concentration in History, Worcester, MA 01602-2597. Offers M Ed. Part-time programs available. *Students:* 1 (woman) full-time, 11 part-time (4 women); includes 1 minority (Hispanic American) Average age 31. 19 applicants, 74% accepted, 3 enrolled. In 2006, 7 degrees awarded. *Degree requirements:* For master's, thesis optional. *Entrance requirements:* For master's, GRE General Test or MAT, 18 undergraduate credits in history, including US history and Western civilizations. Additional exam requirements/recommendations for international students: Required—TOEFL (minimum score 550 paper-based; 213 computer-based). *Application deadline:* Applications are processed on a rolling basis. Application fee: $30. *Expenses:* Tuition, state resident: full-time $4,518; part-time $251 per credit hour. Tuition, nonresident: full-time $4,518; part-time $251 per credit hour. *Financial support:* In 2006–07, 1 research assistantship with full tuition reimbursement (averaging $4,800 per year) was awarded; career-related internships or fieldwork, Federal Work-Study, institutionally sponsored loans, scholarships/grants, and unspecified assistantships also available. Support available to part-time students. Financial award application deadline: 3/1; financial award applicants required to submit FAFSA. *Faculty research:* Labor history, Middle East politics, American-Russian relations, American–East Asian relations. *Unit head:* Dr. Charlotte Haller, Coordinator, 508-929-8046, E-mail: challer1@worcester.edu. *Application contact:* Nicole Brown, Assistant Dean of Graduate and Continuing Education, 508-929-8787, Fax: 508-929-8100, E-mail: nbrown@worcester.edu.

Vocational and Technical Education

Alabama Agricultural and Mechanical University, School of Graduate Studies, School of Engineering and Technology, Department of Industrial Technology, Huntsville, AL 35811. Offers M Ed, MS. *Accreditation:* NCATE. Part-time and evening/weekend programs available. *Faculty:* 4 full-time (1 woman). *Students:* 11 full-time (5 women), 14 part-time (11 women); includes 19 minority (all African Americans), 4 international. *Degree requirements:* For master's, thesis optional. *Entrance requirements:* For master's, GRE General Test. *Application deadline:* For fall admission, 5/1 for domestic students. Applications are processed on a rolling basis. Application fee: $25. Electronic applications accepted. *Financial support:* Research assistantships with tuition reimbursements, career-related internships or fieldwork available. Financial award application deadline: 4/1. *Faculty research:* Ionized gases, hypersonic flow, phenomenology, robotic systems development. *Unit head:* Dr. Theodore Dixie, Chairperson, 256-372-5400.

Alcorn State University, School of Graduate Studies, Department of Advanced Technologies, Alcorn State, MS 39096-7500. Offers workforce education leadership (MS). *Faculty:* 4 full-time (0 women). *Students:* 2 full-time (both women), 9 part-time (8 women); all minorities (all African Americans) *Unit head:* Dr. Kwabena Aypegong, Chairperson, 601-877-6482, Fax: 601-877-3941.

Alcorn State University, School of Graduate Studies, School of Psychology and Education, Alcorn State, MS 39096-7500. Offers agricultural education (MS Ed); elementary education (MS Ed, Ed S); guidance and counseling (MS Ed); industrial education (MS Ed); secondary education (MS Ed), including health and physical education; special education (MS Ed). *Accreditation:* NCATE. *Faculty:* 14 full-time (9 women), 21 part-time/adjunct (13 women). *Students:* 76 full-time (44 women), 271 part-time (226 women); includes 333 minority (all African Americans) In 2006, 119 degrees awarded. *Degree requirements:* For master's, thesis optional. *Application deadline:* For fall admission, 7/15 priority date for domestic students; for spring admission, 11/25 for domestic students. Applications are processed on a rolling basis. Application fee: $0 ($10 for international students). *Financial support:* Career-related internships or fieldwork available. Support available to part-time students. *Unit head:* Dr. Josephine M. Posey, Dean, 601-877-6141, Fax: 601-877-3867.

Appalachian State University, Cratis D. Williams Graduate School, College of Fine and Applied Arts, Department of Technology, Boone, NC 28608. Offers industrial technology (MA); technology education (MA). *Faculty:* 15 full-time (5 women). *Students:* 18 full-time (5 women), 7 part-time (2 women). Average age 23. 10 applicants, 100% accepted, 9 enrolled. In 2006, 16 degrees awarded. *Degree requirements:* For master's, comprehensive exam. *Entrance requirements:* For master's, GRE General Test. Additional exam requirements/recommendations for international students: Required—TOEFL (minimum score 550 paper-based; 230 computer-based). *Application deadline:* For fall admission, 7/1 priority date for domestic students, 1/1 for international students; for spring admission, 11/1 for domestic students, 6/1 for international students. Applications are processed on a rolling basis. Application fee: $50. *Expenses:* Tuition, state resident: full-time $2,600; part-time $127 per hour. Tuition, nonresident: full-time $13,200; part-time $597 per hour. Required fees: $2,000; $546 per term. *Financial support:* In 2006–07, 7 research assistantships (averaging $7,000 per year) were awarded; fellowships, teaching assistantships, career-related internships or fieldwork, Federal Work-Study, institutionally sponsored loans, scholarships/grants, and unspecified assistantships also available. Support available to part-time students. Financial award application deadline: 7/1; financial award applicants required to submit FAFSA. *Unit head:* Dr. Sidney Connor, Chair, 828-262-6351. *Application contact:* Dr. Marie Hoepfl, Coordinator, 828-262-3110.

Ball State University, Graduate School, College of Applied Science and Technology, Department of Industry and Technology, Muncie, IN 47306-1099. Offers MA, MAE. *Accreditation:* NCATE (one or more programs are accredited). *Faculty:* 5. *Students:* Average age 38. 14 applicants, 71% accepted, 4 enrolled. In 2006, 27 degrees awarded. Application fee: $25 ($35 for international students). *Financial support:* In 2006–07, 5 teaching assistantships with full tuition reimbursements (averaging $9,195 per year) were awarded. Financial award application deadline: 3/1. *Unit head:* Dr. Jack Wescott, Chairperson, 765-285-5641, Fax: 765-285-2162, E-mail: jwescott@bsu.edu.

Bemidji State University, School of Graduate Studies, College of Professional Studies, Field of Industrial Technology, Bemidji, MN 56601-2699. Offers technical education (MS). Part-time programs available. *Faculty:* 10 full-time (2 women). *Students:* Average age 38. 3 applicants, 100% accepted. In 2006, 1 degree awarded. *Degree requirements:* For master's, thesis. *Entrance requirements:* Additional exam requirements/recommendations for international students: Required—TOEFL. *Application deadline:* For fall admission, 5/1 for domestic students. Applications are processed on a rolling basis. Application fee: $20. Electronic applications accepted. *Expenses:* Tuition, nonresident: part-time $284 per credit. Required fees: $86 per credit. *Financial support:* In 2006–07, 3 teaching assistantships with partial tuition reimbursements (averaging $8,250 per year) were awarded; career-related internships or fieldwork, Federal Work-Study, scholarships/grants, health care benefits, and unspecified assistantships also available. Support available to part-time students. Financial award application deadline: 5/1. *Unit head:* Dr. Darren Olson, Chair, 218-755-2948, Fax: 218-755-4011, E-mail: dolson@bemidjistate.edu.

Bemidji State University, School of Graduate Studies, College of Professional Studies, Field of Technology/Career Technical Education, Bemidji, MN 56601-2699. Offers MS. Part-time programs available. *Faculty:* 10 full-time (2 women). *Students:* 1 (woman) full-time, 9 part-time (5 women). Average age 38. 4 applicants, 100% accepted. In 2006, 2 degrees awarded. *Application deadline:* For fall admission, 5/1 for domestic students. Applications are processed on a rolling basis. Application fee: $20. Electronic applications accepted. *Expenses:* Tuition, nonresident: part-time $284 per credit. Required fees: $86 per credit. *Unit head:* Dr. Darren Olson, Chair, 218-755-2948, Fax: 218-755-4011, E-mail: dolson@bemidjistate.edu.

Bowling Green State University, Graduate College, College of Technology, Program in Visual Communication and Technology Education, Bowling Green, OH 43403. Offers career and technology education (M Ed), including technology. Part-time programs available. *Faculty:* 12 full-time (3 women), 9 part-time/adjunct (4 women). *Students:* 21 full-time (8 women), 13 part-time (7 women); includes 9 minority (6 African Americans, 1 Asian American or Pacific Islander, 2 Hispanic Americans), 3 international. Average age 31. 21 applicants, 86% accepted, 8 enrolled. In 2006, 20 degrees awarded. *Degree requirements:* For master's, thesis or alternative. *Entrance requirements:* For master's, GRE General Test. Additional exam requirements/recommendations for international students: Required—TOEFL. *Application deadline:* For fall admission, 3/1 for domestic students. Application fee: $30. Electronic applications accepted. *Expenses:* Tuition, state resident: part-time $535 per hour. Tuition, nonresident: part-time $884 per hour. *Financial support:* In 2006–07, 8 research assistantships with full tuition reimbursements (averaging $7,024 per year), 7 teaching assistantships with full tuition reimbursements (averaging $7,981 per year) were awarded; career-related internships or fieldwork, Federal Work-Study, tuition waivers (full and partial), and unspecified assistantships also available. Financial award applicants required to submit FAFSA. *Faculty research:* Curriculum in technology education. *Unit head:* Dr. Larry Hatch, Chair, 419-372-2437. *Application contact:* Dr. Donna Trautman, Graduate Coordinator, 419-372-7575.

Buffalo State College, State University of New York, Graduate Studies and Research, Faculty of Applied Science and Education, Department of Educational Foundations, Program in Career and Technical Education, Buffalo, NY 14222-1095. Offers MS Ed. *Accreditation:* NCATE. Part-time and evening/weekend programs available. *Degree requirements:* For master's, thesis, thesis or project. *Entrance requirements:* For master's, minimum GPA of 2.5 in last 60 hours, New York teaching certificate. Additional exam requirements/recommendations for international students: Required—TOEFL (minimum score 550 paper-based; 213 computer-based).

Buffalo State College, State University of New York, Graduate Studies and Research, Faculty of Applied Science and Education, Department of Technology, Program in Technology Education, Buffalo, NY 14222-1095. Offers MS Ed. *Accreditation:* NCATE. *Degree requirements:* For master's, thesis or project. *Entrance requirements:* For master's, minimum GPA of 2.5 in last 60 hours, New York teaching certificate. Additional exam requirements/recommendations for international students: Required—TOEFL (minimum score 550 paper-based; 213 computer-based).

California Baptist University, Program in Education, Riverside, CA 92504-3206. Offers cross-cultural language and academic development (MA Ed); educational leadership (MS Ed); educational technology (MS Ed); instructional computer applications (MS Ed); reading (MS Ed); special education (MS Ed); teaching (MS Ed). Part-time programs available. *Faculty:* 16 full-time (10 women), 16 part-time/adjunct (13 women). *Students:* 77 full-time (64 women), 408 part-time (342 women); includes 157 minority (41 African Americans, 12 American Indian/Alaska Native, 18 Asian Americans or Pacific Islanders, 86 Hispanic Americans), 2 international. 282 applicants, 70% accepted, 171 enrolled. In 2006, 63 degrees awarded. *Degree requirements:* For master's, thesis optional. *Entrance requirements:* For master's, minimum undergraduate GPA of 2.75, 12 semester hours of course work in education. Additional exam requirements/recommendations for international students: Required—TOEFL (minimum score 575 paper-based; 230 computer-based), IELTS (minimum score 7). *Application deadline:* For fall admission, 9/1 for domestic students, 7/15 priority date for international students; for spring admission, 1/3 for domestic students, 11/1 priority date for international students. Applications are processed on a rolling basis. Application fee: $45. Electronic applications accepted. *Expenses:* Tuition: Full-time $7,812; part-time $434 per unit. Required fees: $120 per semester. Tuition and fees vary according to program. *Financial support:* In 2006–07, 19 students received support. Career-related internships or fieldwork, Federal Work-Study, and scholarships/grants available. Support available to part-time students. Financial award applicants required to submit FAFSA. *Unit head:* Dr. Mary Crist, Dean, School of Education, 951-343-4313, Fax: 951-343-4516, E-mail: mcrist@calbaptist.edu. *Application contact:* Gail Ronveaux, Dean of Graduate Enrollment, 951-343-5045, Fax: 951-343-5095, E-mail: graduateadmissions@calbaptist.edu.

California State University, Long Beach, Graduate Studies, College of Health and Human Services, Department of Professional Studies, Long Beach, CA 90840. Offers emergency services administration (MS); occupational studies (MA). *Accreditation:* NCATE. Part-time and evening/weekend programs available. Postbaccalaureate distance learning degree programs offered (no on-campus study). *Faculty:* 13 full-time (4 women), 11 part-time/adjunct (5 women). *Students:* 30 full-time (12 women), 188 part-time (50 women). Average age 44. 94 applicants, 89% accepted, 41 enrolled. In 2006, 19 degrees awarded. *Degree requirements:* For master's, comprehensive exam or thesis. *Application deadline:* For fall admission, 7/1 for domestic students; for spring admission, 12/1 for domestic students. Applications are processed on a rolling basis. Application fee: $55. Electronic applications accepted. *Financial support:* Federal Work-Study, institutionally sponsored loans, and scholarships/grants available. Financial award application deadline: 3/2. *Faculty research:* Special needs, leadership, training and development. *Unit head:* Dr. Paul Bott, Chair, 562-985-5633, Fax: 562-985-8815, E-mail: pbott@csulb.edu. *Application contact:* Dr. Peter Kreysa, Graduate Coordinator, 562-985-8111, Fax: 562-985-8815, E-mail: pkreysa@csulb.edu.

California State University, Sacramento, Graduate Studies, College of Education, Department of Special Education, Rehabilitation, and School Psychology, Sacramento, CA 95819-6048. Offers school psychology (MS); special education (MA); vocational rehabilitation (MS). *Accreditation:* CORE. Part-time programs available. *Students:* 130 full-time (112 women), 71 part-time (57 women); includes 48 minority (16 African Americans, 1 American Indian/Alaska Native, 10 Asian Americans or Pacific Islanders, 21 Hispanic Americans), 3 international. Average age 33. 103 applicants, 69% accepted, 45 enrolled. *Degree requirements:* For master's, thesis or alternative, writing proficiency exam. *Entrance requirements:* For master's, minimum GPA of 2.5. Additional exam requirements/recommendations for international students: Required—TOEFL. *Application deadline:* Applications are processed on a rolling basis. Application fee: $55. Electronic applications accepted. *Financial support:* Career-related internships or fieldwork and Federal Work-Study available. Support available to part-time students. Financial award application deadline: 3/1. *Unit head:* Bernice Bassde Martinez, Chair, 916-278-6622, Fax: 916-278-3498.

California State University, San Bernardino, Graduate Studies, College of Education, Program in Vocational and Career Education, San Bernardino, CA 92407-2397. Offers MA. *Accreditation:* NCATE. Part-time and evening/weekend programs available. *Students:* 23 full-time (19 women), 9 part-time (3 women); includes 18 minority (9 African Americans, 1 American Indian/Alaska Native, 2 Asian Americans or Pacific Islanders, 6 Hispanic Americans). Average age 42. 11 applicants, 55% accepted, 4 enrolled. *Degree requirements:* For master's, thesis. *Entrance requirements:* For master's, minimum GPA of 3.0 in education, vocational teaching credential. *Application deadline:* For fall admission, 8/31 priority date for domestic students. Application fee: $55. *Financial support:* Career-related internships or fieldwork and Federal Work-Study available. Support available to part-time students. *Unit head:* Dr. Herbert Brunkhorst, Coordinator, Designated Subjects, 909-537-5637, Fax: 909-537-7522, E-mail: hkbrunkh@csusb.edu.

California University of Pennsylvania, School of Graduate Studies and Research, School of Education, Department of Technology Education, California, PA 15419-1394. Offers M Ed. *Accreditation:* NCATE. Part-time and evening/weekend programs available. *Faculty:* 4 full-time (0 women). *Students:* 1 full-time (0 women), 20 part-time (4 women). Average age 29. 6 applicants, 67% accepted. In 2006, 6 degrees awarded. *Median time to degree:* Master's–1.5 years full-time, 3 years part-time. *Degree requirements:* For master's, thesis optional. *Entrance requirements:* For master's, MAT, minimum GPA of 3.0, teaching experience in industrial arts. Additional exam requirements/recommendations for international students: Required—TOEFL (minimum score 550 paper-based; 213 computer-based; 80 iBT). *Application deadline:* For fall admission, 8/1 priority date for domestic and international students; for winter admission, 12/1 priority date for domestic and international students; for spring admission, 5/1 priority date for domestic and international students. Applications are processed on a rolling basis. Application fee: $25. Electronic applications accepted. *Expenses:* Tuition, state resident: full-time $6,048; part-time $336 per credit. Tuition, nonresident: full-time $9,678; part-time $538 per credit. Required fees: $1,854; $263 per credit. Full-time tuition and fees vary according to course load, campus/location and program. *Financial support:* Career-related internships or fieldwork, scholarships/grants, traineeships, and unspecified assistantships available. Financial award applicants required to submit FAFSA. *Faculty research:* Curriculum, trends in technology, standards-based assessment. Total annual research expenditures: $110,000. *Unit head:* Dr. Glenn Hider, Coordinator, 724-938-5861, Fax: 724-938-4572.

Central Connecticut State University, School of Graduate Studies, School of Technology, Department of Technology Education, New Britain, CT 06050-4010. Offers MS, Certificate. Part-time and evening/weekend programs available. *Faculty:* 5 full-time (1 woman), 2 part-time/adjunct (0 women). *Students:* 5 full-time (1 woman), 26 part-time (4 women); includes 2 minority (both Hispanic Americans), 2 international. Average age 40. 16 applicants, 88% accepted, 5 enrolled. In 2006, 12 degrees awarded. *Degree requirements:* For master's, thesis or alternative, comprehensive exam or special project. *Entrance requirements:* For master's, minimum GPA of 2.7. Additional exam requirements/recommendations for international students: Required—TOEFL. *Application deadline:* For fall admission, 7/1 for domestic students; for spring admission, 12/1 for domestic students. Applications are processed on a rolling basis. Application fee: $50. Electronic applications accepted. *Expenses:* Tuition, area resident: Full-time $3,970; part-time $380 per credit. Tuition, state resident: full-time $5,955; part-time $380 per credit. Tuition, nonresident: full-time $11,061; part-time $380 per credit. Required fees: $3,189. One-time fee: $62 part-time. Tuition and fees vary according to degree level

Vocational and Technical Education

Central Connecticut State University (continued)
and program. *Financial support:* Research assistantships, career-related internships or fieldwork, Federal Work-Study, scholarships/grants, and unspecified assistantships available. Support available to part-time students. Financial award application deadline: 3/1; financial award applicants required to submit FAFSA. *Faculty research:* Instruction, curriculum development, administration, occupational training. *Unit head:* Dr. James DeLaura, Chair, 860-832-1850.

Central Michigan University, College of Graduate Studies, College of Science and Technology, Department of Engineering Technology, Mount Pleasant, MI 48859. Offers industrial education (MA); industrial management and technology (MA). *Degree requirements:* For master's, thesis or alternative, registration. *Entrance requirements:* For master's, 2 years of teaching experience, undergraduate major/minor in industrial engineering or related field (industrial education). *Faculty research:* Computer applications, manufacturing process control, automation, industrial activities.

Chicago State University, School of Graduate and Professional Studies, College of Education, Department of Technology and Education, Chicago, IL 60628. Offers secondary education (MAT); technology and education (MS Ed). Postbaccalaureate distance learning degree programs offered. *Degree requirements:* For master's, thesis optional. *Entrance requirements:* For master's, minimum GPA of 2.75.

Clarion University of Pennsylvania, Office of Research and Graduate Studies, College of Education and Human Services, Department of Education, Program in Education, Clarion, PA 16214. Offers curriculum and instruction (M Ed); early childhood (M Ed); English (M Ed); history (M Ed); literacy (M Ed); science (M Ed); technology (M Ed). *Accreditation:* NCATE. Part-time programs available. *Faculty:* 18 full-time (13 women). *Students:* 11 full-time (4 women), 54 part-time (37 women); includes 4 minority (3 African Americans, 1 Asian American or Pacific Islander). 50 applicants, 90% accepted. In 2006, 7 degrees awarded. *Degree requirements:* For master's, thesis or alternative, comprehensive exam. *Entrance requirements:* For master's, minimum QPA of 3.0, teacher certification. Additional exam requirements/recommendations for international students: Required—TOEFL (minimum score 550 paper-based; 213 computer-based; 80 iBT). *Application deadline:* For fall admission, 8/1 priority date for domestic students, 4/15 priority date for international students; for spring admission, 12/1 priority date for domestic students, 9/15 priority date for international students. Applications are processed on a rolling basis. Application fee: $30. Electronic applications accepted. *Expenses:* Tuition, state resident: part-time $336 per credit. Tuition, nonresident: part-time $538 per credit. *Financial support:* In 2006–07, 2 research assistantships with full tuition reimbursements (averaging $4,002 per year) were awarded. Support available to part-time students. Financial award application deadline: 3/1. *Application contact:* Dr. Brian Maguire, Coordinator, 814-393-2058, Fax: 814-393-2558, E-mail: bmaguire@clarion.edu.

Colorado State University, Graduate School, College of Applied Human Sciences, School of Education, Fort Collins, CO 80523-0015. Offers education and human resource studies (M Ed, PhD); student affairs in higher education (MS). PhD is offered in conjunction with the Department of Occupational Therapy. *Accreditation:* ACA; NCATE. Part-time programs available. Postbaccalaureate distance learning degree programs offered. *Faculty:* 19 full-time (8 women). *Students:* 137 full-time (96 women), 487 part-time (301 women); includes 91 minority (28 African Americans, 7 American Indian/Alaska Native, 15 Asian Americans or Pacific Islanders, 41 Hispanic Americans), 16 international. Average age 38. 349 applicants, 53% accepted, 143 enrolled. In 2006, 134 master's, 38 doctorates awarded. *Degree requirements:* For master's, thesis optional; for doctorate, thesis/dissertation, comprehensive exam, registration. *Entrance requirements:* For master's, GRE, minimum undergraduate GPA of 3.0, 3 letters of recommendation, curriculum vitae/resumé, additional School of Education application; for doctorate, minimum GPA of 3.0, 3 letters of recommendation, curriculum vitae. Additional exam requirements/recommendations for international students: Required—TOEFL (minimum score 550 paper-based; 213 computer-based). *Application deadline:* For fall admission, 3/15 for domestic and international students. Applications are processed on a rolling basis. Application fee: $50. Electronic applications accepted. *Expenses:* Tuition, state resident: full-time $4,248; part-time $236 per credit. Tuition, nonresident: full-time $15,642; part-time $869 per credit. Required fees: $66 per credit. Tuition and fees vary according to program. *Financial support:* In 2006–07, 6 fellowships (averaging $3,833 per year), 4 research assistantships with full tuition reimbursements (averaging $10,225 per year), 13 teaching assistantships with full tuition reimbursements (averaging $9,000 per year) were awarded; career-related internships or fieldwork, Federal Work-Study, institutionally sponsored loans, and traineeships also available. *Faculty research:* Innovative instruction, diverse learners, transition, scientifically-based evaluation methods, leadership and organizational development. Total annual research expenditures: $926,884. *Unit head:* Dr. Jean P. Lehmann, Interim Director, 970-491-6317, Fax: 970-491-1317, E-mail: jean.lehmann@colostate.edu. *Application contact:* Randi Fuller, Administrative Assistant, 970-491-0545, Fax: 970-491-1317, E-mail: fuller@cahs.colostate.edu.

East Carolina University, Graduate School, College of Education, Department of Business, Career, and Technical Education, Greenville, NC 27858-4353. Offers information technologies (MS); vocation education (MA Ed). *Accreditation:* NCATE. Part-time and evening/weekend programs available. Postbaccalaureate distance learning degree programs offered (no on-campus study). *Students:* 5 full-time (3 women), 40 part-time (25 women); includes 13 minority (11 African Americans, 1 American Indian/Alaska Native, 1 Hispanic American). Average age 35. 11 applicants, 9% accepted, 1 enrolled. In 2006, 14 degrees awarded. *Degree requirements:* For master's, thesis optional. *Entrance requirements:* For master's, GRE or MAT, minimum GPA of 2.5, bachelor's degree in related field, teaching license (MA Ed). Additional exam requirements/recommendations for international students: Required—TOEFL. *Application deadline:* For fall admission, 6/1 priority date for domestic students. Applications are processed on a rolling basis. Application fee: $50. *Financial support:* Federal Work-Study available. Support available to part-time students. Financial award application deadline: 6/1. *Unit head:* Dr. Ivan Wallace, Chair, 252-328-6983, Fax: 252-328-6835, E-mail: wallacei@ecu.edu. *Application contact:* Dean of Graduate School, 252-328-6012, Fax: 252-328-6071, E-mail: gradschool@ecu.edu.

Eastern Kentucky University, The Graduate School, College of Business and Technology, Department of Technology, Program in Industrial Education, Richmond, KY 40475-3102. Offers occupational training and development (MS); technical administration (MS); technology education (MS). *Accreditation:* NCATE. Part-time programs available. *Students:* 1 full-time (0 women), 8 part-time (3 women); includes 3 minority (1 African American, 1 Asian American or Pacific Islander, 1 Hispanic American), 2 international. Average age 37. 16 applicants, 69% accepted, 6 enrolled. *Entrance requirements:* For master's, GRE General Test, minimum GPA of 2.5. Application fee: $35. *Expenses:* Tuition, state resident: full-time $5,610. Tuition, nonresident: full-time $15,910. *Financial support:* Research assistantships, teaching assistantships, Federal Work-Study available. Support available to part-time students.

Eastern Kentucky University, The Graduate School, College of Education, Department of Curriculum and Instruction, Program in Secondary and Higher Education, Richmond, KY 40475-3102. Offers agricultural education (MA Ed); allied health sciences education (MA Ed); art education (MA Ed); biological sciences education (MA Ed); business education (MA Ed); chemistry education (MA Ed); earth science education (MA Ed); English education (MA Ed); general science education (MA Ed); geography education (MA Ed); history education (MA Ed); home economics education (MA Ed); industrial education (MA Ed); mathematical sciences education (MA Ed); physical education (MA Ed); physics education (MA Ed); political science education (MA Ed); psychology education (MA Ed); reading (MA Ed); school health education (MA Ed); sociology education (MA Ed). *Accreditation:* NCATE. Part-time programs available. *Students:* 16 full-time (8 women), 63 part-time (43 women); includes 5 minority (2 African Americans, 2 American Indian/Alaska Native, 1 Asian American or Pacific Islander). Average age 32. *Entrance requirements:* For master's, GRE General Test, minimum GPA of 2.5. Application fee: $30. *Expenses:* Tuition, state resident: full-time $5,610. Tuition, nonresident: full-time $15,910. *Financial support:* Research assistantships, teaching assistantships, Federal Work-Study available. Support available to part-time students. *Unit head:* Dr. Michael Martin, Chair, Department of Curriculum and Instruction, 859-622-2154, Fax: 859-622-2004.

Eastern Michigan University, Graduate School, College of Technology, School of Technology Studies, Program in Career, Technical and Workforce Education, Ypsilanti, MI 48197. Offers MS. Part-time and evening/weekend programs available. Postbaccalaureate distance learning degree programs offered (minimal on-campus study). *Students:* 1 (woman) full-time, 10 part-time (2 women); includes 3 minority (2 African Americans, 1 American Indian/Alaska Native). Average age 39. In 2006, 4 degrees awarded. *Entrance requirements:* Additional exam requirements/recommendations for international students: Required—TOEFL. *Application deadline:* For fall admission, 5/15 priority date for domestic students, 5/1 priority date for international students; for winter admission, 10/15 priority date for domestic students, 10/1 priority date for international students; for spring admission, 3/15 priority date for domestic students, 3/1 priority date for international students. Applications are processed on a rolling basis. Application fee: $35. *Expenses:* Tuition, state resident: part-time $341 per credit hour. Tuition, nonresident: full-time $16,104; part-time $671 per credit hour. Required fees: $816; $34 per credit hour. $40 per term. One-time fee: $82 full-time. Tuition and fees vary according to course level, course load, degree level and reciprocity agreements. *Financial support:* Fellowships, research assistantships with full tuition reimbursements, teaching assistantships with full tuition reimbursements, career-related internships or fieldwork, Federal Work-Study, institutionally sponsored loans, scholarships/grants, tuition waivers (partial), and unspecified assistantships available. Support available to part-time students. Financial award applicants required to submit FAFSA. *Unit head:* Dr. John Boyless, Director, School of Technology Studies, 734-487-1161, Fax: 734-487-7690, E-mail: john.boyless@emich.edu.

East Tennessee State University, School of Graduate Studies, College of Business and Technology, Department of Technology and Geomatics, Johnson City, TN 37614. Offers digital media (MS); engineering technology (MS); industrial arts/technology education (MS). Part-time programs available. *Degree requirements:* For master's, thesis or alternative, final oral exam. *Entrance requirements:* For master's, bachelor's degree in technical or related area, minimum GPA of 3.0. Additional exam requirements/recommendations for international students: Required—TOEFL (minimum score 550 paper-based; 213 computer-based). *Faculty research:* Computer-integrated manufacturing, technology education, CAD/CAM, organizational change.

Fitchburg State College, Division of Graduate and Continuing Education, Program in Occupational Education, Fitchburg, MA 01420-2697. Offers M Ed. *Accreditation:* NCATE. Part-time and evening/weekend programs available. *Students:* Average age 38. 4 applicants, 100% accepted, 2 enrolled. In 2006, 11 degrees awarded. *Entrance requirements:* For master's, GRE General Test or MAT, teaching certificate, letters of recommendation, resumé. Additional exam requirements/recommendations for international students: Required—TOEFL (minimum score 550 paper-based; 213 computer-based; 79 iBT). *Application deadline:* Applications are processed on a rolling basis. Application fee: $25 ($50 for international students). *Expenses:* Tuition, state resident: part-time $150 per credit. Tuition, nonresident: part-time $150 per credit. Required fees: $90 per credit. *Financial support:* In 2006–07, research assistantships with partial tuition reimbursements (averaging $5,500 per year); Federal Work-Study, scholarships/grants, and unspecified assistantships also available. Support available to part-time students. Financial award application deadline: 3/1; financial award applicants required to submit FAFSA. *Unit head:* Dr. James Alicata, Chair, 978-665-3047, Fax: 978-665-3658, E-mail: gce@fsc.edu. *Application contact:* Director of Admissions, 978-665-3144, Fax: 978-665-4540, E-mail: admissions@fsc.edu.

Fitchburg State College, Division of Graduate and Continuing Education, Program in Technology Education, Fitchburg, MA 01420-2697. Offers M Ed. *Accreditation:* NCATE. Part-time and evening/weekend programs available. *Students:* Average age 37. 4 applicants, 100% accepted, 2 enrolled. In 2006, 6 degrees awarded. *Entrance requirements:* For master's, GRE General Test or MAT, teaching certificate, letters of recommendation, resumé. Additional exam requirements/recommendations for international students: Required—TOEFL (minimum score 550 paper-based; 213 computer-based; 79 iBT). *Application deadline:* Applications are processed on a rolling basis. Application fee: $25 ($50 for international students). *Expenses:* Tuition, state resident: part-time $150 per credit. Tuition, nonresident: part-time $150 per credit. Required fees: $90 per credit. *Financial support:* In 2006–07, research assistantships with partial tuition reimbursements (averaging $5,500 per year); Federal Work-Study, scholarships/grants, and unspecified assistantships also available. Support available to part-time students. Financial award application deadline: 3/1; financial award applicants required to submit FAFSA. *Unit head:* Steven Therrien, Chair, 978-665-3384, Fax: 978-665-3658, E-mail: gce@fsc.edu. *Application contact:* Director of Admissions, 978-665-3144, Fax: 978-665-4540, E-mail: admissions@fsc.edu.

Florida Agricultural and Mechanical University, Division of Graduate Studies, Research, and Continuing Education, College of Education, Department of Vocational Education, Tallahassee, FL 32307-3200. Offers business education (MBE); industrial education (M Ed, MS Ed). *Accreditation:* NCATE. *Degree requirements:* For master's, thesis (for some programs). *Entrance requirements:* For master's, GRE General Test, minimum GPA of 3.0. Additional exam requirements/recommendations for international students: Required—TOEFL.

Georgia Southern University, Jack N. Averitt College of Graduate Studies, College of Education, Department of Teaching and Learning, Program in Technology Education, Statesboro, GA 30460. Offers M Ed. Part-time and evening/weekend programs available. *Students:* Average age 28. 2 applicants, 100% accepted, 1 enrolled. In 2006, 4 degrees awarded. *Degree requirements:* For master's, exit assessment. *Entrance requirements:* For master's, GRE General Test or MAT, minimum GPA of 2.5. Additional exam requirements/recommendations for international students: Required—TOEFL (minimum score 550 paper-based; 213 computer-based; 80 iBT). *Application deadline:* For fall admission, 3/1 priority date for domestic students, 3/1 for international students; for spring admission, 10/1 priority date for domestic students, 10/1 for international students. Applications are processed on a rolling basis. Application fee: $50. Electronic applications accepted. *Financial support:* In 2006–07, research assistantships with partial tuition reimbursements (averaging $5,500 per year), teaching assistantships with partial tuition reimbursements (averaging $5,500 per year) were awarded; Federal Work-Study, scholarships/grants, tuition waivers (partial), and unspecified assistantships also available. Support available to part-time students. Financial award application deadline: 4/15; financial award applicants required to submit FAFSA. *Unit head:* Dr. N. Creighton Alexander, Associate Professor, 912-871-1549, Fax: 912-871-1549, E-mail: calexand@georgiasouthern.edu. *Application contact:* 912-681-5384, Fax: 912-681-0740, E-mail: gradadmissions@georgiasouthern.edu.

Idaho State University, Office of Graduate Studies, College of Technology, Department of Human Resource Training and Development, Pocatello, ID 83209. Offers training and development (MTD). Part-time and evening/weekend programs available. Postbaccalaureate distance learning degree programs offered (minimal on-campus study). *Faculty:* 3 full-time (1 woman). *Students:* 23 full-time (13 women), 53 part-time (23 women); includes 5 minority (2 American Indian/Alaska Native, 1 Asian American or Pacific Islander, 2 Hispanic Americans), 1 international. Average age 42. In 2006, 7 degrees awarded. *Degree requirements:* For master's, thesis optional. *Entrance requirements:* For master's, GRE or MAT, minimum GPA of 3.0 upper division courses. Additional exam requirements/recommendations for international students: Required—TOEFL (minimum score 550 paper-based; 213 computer-based; 80 iBT). *Application deadline:* For fall admission, 7/1 for domestic students, 6/1 for international students; for spring admission, 12/1 for domestic students, 11/1 for international students. Applications are processed on a rolling basis. Application fee: $55. *Expenses:* Tuition, state resident: part-time $251 per credit. Tuition, nonresident: part-time $366 per credit. Tuition and fees vary according to degree level, program and reciprocity agreements. *Financial support:* In 2006–07, 2 teaching assistantships with full and partial tuition reimbursements (averaging $8,694 per year) were awarded; career-related internships or fieldwork, Federal Work-Study, scholarships/

grants, tuition waivers (full and partial), and unspecified assistantships also available. Support available to part-time students. Financial award application deadline: 1/1. *Faculty research:* Learning styles, instructional methodology, leadership administration. *Unit head:* Dr. Robert Croker, Chair, 208-282-2884, Fax: 208-282-4496, E-mail: crocobe@isu.edu. *Application contact:* Debra K. Ronneburg, Director of Admissions/Student Services, 208-282-2622, Fax: 208-282-5195, E-mail: ctech@isu.edu.

Indiana State University, School of Graduate Studies, College of Technology, Department of Industrial Technology Education, Terre Haute, IN 47809-1401. Offers career and technical education (MS); human resource development (MS); technology education (MS). *Accreditation:* NCATE. *Faculty:* 5 full-time (0 women), 1 part-time/adjunct (0 women). *Students:* 33 full-time (18 women), 120 part-time (70 women); includes 39 minority (29 African Americans, 6 Asian Americans or Pacific Islanders, 4 Hispanic Americans), 15 international. Average age 34. 70 applicants, 96% accepted, 35 enrolled. In 2006, 65 degrees awarded. *Entrance requirements:* For master's, bachelor's degree in industrial technology or related field. Additional exam requirements/recommendations for international students: Required—TOEFL. *Application deadline:* For fall admission, 7/1 priority date for domestic students; for spring admission, 11/1 priority date for domestic students. Applications are processed on a rolling basis. Application fee: $35. Electronic applications accepted. *Expenses:* Tuition, state resident: part-time $278 per credit. Tuition, nonresident: part-time $552 per credit. *Financial support:* In 2006–07, 6 research assistantships with partial tuition reimbursements (averaging $7,000 per year) were awarded; fellowships with partial tuition reimbursements, teaching assistantships with partial tuition reimbursements, institutionally sponsored loans and tuition waivers (partial) also available. Financial award application deadline: 3/1; financial award applicants required to submit FAFSA. *Unit head:* Dr. James Smallwood, Interim Chairperson, 812-237-2642.

Inter American University of Puerto Rico, Metropolitan Campus, Faculty of Education, Program in Occupational Education, San Juan, PR 00919-1293. Offers MA. *Degree requirements:* For master's, comprehensive exam. *Entrance requirements:* For master's, GRE or EXADEP, interview. Electronic applications accepted.

Inter American University of Puerto Rico, Metropolitan Campus, Faculty of Education, Program in Vocational Evaluation, San Juan, PR 00919-1293. Offers MA. *Degree requirements:* For master's, comprehensive exam. *Entrance requirements:* For master's, GRE or EXADEP, interview. Electronic applications accepted.

Iowa State University of Science and Technology, Graduate College, College of Agriculture, Program in Industrial Education and Technology, Ames, IA 50011. Offers MS, PhD. *Faculty:* 1 full-time. *Students:* 12 full-time (3 women), 10 part-time (2 women); includes 4 minority (all African Americans), 8 international. 6 applicants, 33% accepted, 1 enrolled. In 2006, 2 master's, 6 doctorates awarded. *Degree requirements:* For master's, thesis or alternative; for doctorate, thesis/dissertation. *Entrance requirements:* For master's and doctorate, GRE General Test. Additional exam requirements/recommendations for international students: Required—TOEFL (paper-based 550; computer-based 213; iBT 79) or IELTS (6.5). *Application deadline:* For fall admission, 2/1 priority date for domestic students, 6/1 priority date for international students; for spring admission, 7/1 for domestic students, 11/1 for international students. Application fee: $30 ($70 for international students). Electronic applications accepted. *Expenses:* Tuition, state resident: full-time $5,936; part-time $330 per credit. Tuition, nonresident: full-time $16,350; part-time $330 per credit. *Financial support:* In 2006–07, 11 research assistantships with full and partial tuition reimbursements (averaging $17,551 per year), 1 teaching assistantship with full and partial tuition reimbursement (averaging $17,551 per year) were awarded; fellowships, scholarships/grants, health care benefits, and unspecified assistantships also available. *Faculty research:* Industrial technology, technology education, training and development, technical education. *Unit head:* Dr. Ramesh Kanwar, Chair, 515-294-1434. *Application contact:* Dr. Steven Freeman, Director of Graduate Education, 515-294-9541, E-mail: sfreeman@iastate.edu.

Jackson State University, Graduate School, School of Science and Technology, Department of Technology and Industrial Arts, Jackson, MS 39217. Offers hazardous materials management (MS); industrial arts education (MS Ed). Part-time and evening/weekend programs available. *Faculty:* 3 full-time (0 women). *Students:* 9 full-time (3 women), 12 part-time (4 women); includes 19 minority (all African Americans), 1 international. In 2006, 10 degrees awarded. *Degree requirements:* For master's, thesis or alternative, comprehensive exam. *Entrance requirements:* For master's, GRE General Test. Additional exam requirements/recommendations for international students: Required—TOEFL. *Application deadline:* For fall admission, 3/1 priority date for domestic students; for spring admission, 10/1 for domestic students. Applications are processed on a rolling basis. Application fee: $20. *Financial support:* In 2006–07, 6 students received support. Career-related internships or fieldwork, Federal Work-Study, scholarships/grants, and unspecified assistantships available. Support available to part-time students. Financial award application deadline: 3/1; financial award applicants required to submit FAFSA. *Unit head:* Dr. James Ejiwale, Interim Chair, 601-968-2466, E-mail: james.ejiwale@jsums.edu. *Application contact:* Curtis Gore, Director of Graduate Admissions, 601-979-2455, Fax: 601-974-4325, E-mail: cgore@ccaix.jsums.edu.

James Madison University, College of Graduate and Outreach Programs, College of Education, Learning, Technology, and Leadership Department, Program in Adult Education/Human Resource Development, Harrisonburg, VA 22807. Offers MS Ed. *Accreditation:* NCATE. Part-time and evening/weekend programs available. *Students:* 10 full-time (8 women), 7 part-time (all women); includes 3 minority (all African Americans) Average age 27. In 2006, 9 degrees awarded. *Entrance requirements:* For master's, GRE General Test. Additional exam requirements/recommendations for international students: Required—TOEFL. *Application deadline:* For fall admission, 5/1 priority date for domestic students; for spring admission, 9/1 priority date for domestic students. Applications are processed on a rolling basis. Application fee: $55. Electronic applications accepted. *Expenses:* Tuition, state resident: full-time $6,336; part-time $264 per credit hour. Tuition, nonresident: full-time $17,832; part-time $743 per credit hour. *Financial support:* In 2006–07, 9 students received support. Unspecified assistantships available. Financial award application deadline: 3/1; financial award applicants required to submit FAFSA. *Unit head:* Dr. Diane Foucar-Szocki, Academic Unit Head, 540-568-6794.

Kent State University, Graduate School of Education, Health, and Human Services, Department of Adult, Counseling, Health and Vocational Education, Program in Career Technical Teacher Education, Kent, OH 44242-0001. Offers M Ed, MA, Ed S. *Faculty:* 1 full-time (0 women), 6 part-time/adjunct (3 women). *Students:* 1 (woman) full-time, 46 part-time (23 women); includes 7 minority (all African Americans) In 2006, 13 degrees awarded. *Degree requirements:* For master's, thesis (for some programs), registration. *Entrance requirements:* For degree, GRE General Test. Additional exam requirements/recommendations for international students: Required—TOEFL. *Application deadline:* Applications are processed on a rolling basis. Application fee: $30. Electronic applications accepted. *Financial support:* In 2006–07, fellowships with full tuition reimbursements (averaging $7,210 per year); research assistantships with full tuition reimbursements, teaching assistantships with full tuition reimbursements, career-related internships or fieldwork, Federal Work-Study, institutionally sponsored loans, scholarships/grants, health care benefits, and unspecified assistantships also available. Support available to part-time students. Financial award application deadline: 4/1; financial award applicants required to submit FAFSA. *Faculty research:* Workforce education/development, adult education, training and organizational change. *Unit head:* Dr. Patrick O'Connor, Coordinator, 330-672-2656, E-mail: poconnor@kent.edu. *Application contact:* Nancy Miller, Academic Program Coordinator, Office of Graduate Student Services, 330-672-2576, Fax: 330-672-9162, E-mail: ogs@kent.edu.

Louisiana State University and Agricultural and Mechanical College, Graduate School, College of Agriculture, School of Human Resource Education and Workforce Development, Baton Rouge, LA 70803. Offers comprehensive vocational education (MS, PhD); extension and international education (MS, PhD); industrial education (MS); vocational agriculture education (MS, PhD); vocational business education (MS); vocational home economics education (MS). *Accreditation:* NCATE. Part-time programs available. *Faculty:* 13 full-time (6 women). *Students:* 39 full-time (24 women), 68 part-time (42 women); includes 12 African Americans, 3 Hispanic Americans, 9 international. Average age 38. 20 applicants, 60% accepted, 3 enrolled. In 2006, 18 master's, 33 doctorates awarded. Terminal master's awarded for partial completion of doctoral program. *Degree requirements:* For master's, thesis (for some programs); for doctorate, thesis/dissertation. *Entrance requirements:* For master's and doctorate, GRE General Test, minimum GPA of 3.0. Additional exam requirements/recommendations for international students: Required—TOEFL (minimum score 550 paper-based; 213 computer-based; 79 iBT). *Application deadline:* For fall admission, 1/25 priority date for domestic students, 5/15 for international students; for spring admission, 10/15 for international students. Applications are processed on a rolling basis. Application fee: $25. Electronic applications accepted. *Financial support:* In 2006–07, 23 students received support, including 1 fellowship with full and partial tuition reimbursement available (averaging $23,678 per year), 10 research assistantships with full and partial tuition reimbursements available (averaging $11,750 per year), 5 teaching assistantships with partial tuition reimbursements available (averaging $10,210 per year); career-related internships or fieldwork, institutionally sponsored loans, tuition waivers (full and partial), and unspecified assistantships also available. Financial award application deadline: 3/1; financial award applicants required to submit FAFSA. *Faculty research:* Adult education, history and philosophy of vocational education, curriculum and instruction, career decision making. *Unit head:* Dr. Michael F. Burnett, Director, 225-578-5748, Fax: 225-578-2526, E-mail: vocbur@lsu.edu.

Marshall University, Academic Affairs Division, College of Education and Human Services, Division of Human Development and Allied Technology, Program in Adult and Technical Education, Huntington, WV 25755. Offers MS. *Accreditation:* NCATE. Evening/weekend programs available. *Faculty:* 2 full-time (both women). *Students:* 146 full-time (87 women), 104 part-time (68 women); includes 38 minority (34 African Americans, 2 Asian Americans or Pacific Islanders, 2 Hispanic Americans), 53 international. Average age 34. In 2006, 59 degrees awarded. *Degree requirements:* For master's, comprehensive assessment, thesis optional. Application fee: $40. *Application contact:* Information Contact, 304-746-1900, Fax: 304-746-1902, E-mail: services@marshall.edu.

Middle Tennessee State University, College of Graduate Studies, College of Basic and Applied Sciences, Department of Engineering Technology and Industrial Studies, Murfreesboro, TN 37132. Offers MS, MVTE. Part-time and evening/weekend programs available. Postbaccalaureate distance learning degree programs offered. *Faculty:* 11 full-time (3 women). *Students:* 2 full-time (1 woman), 27 part-time (5 women); all minorities (17 African Americans, 1 American Indian/Alaska Native, 10 Asian Americans or Pacific Islanders, 1 Hispanic American). Average age 34. 8 applicants, 100% accepted. In 2006, 11 degrees awarded. *Degree requirements:* For master's, one foreign language, comprehensive exam. *Entrance requirements:* For master's, GRE or MAT(MVTE), GRE (MS). Additional exam requirements/recommendations for international students: Required—TOEFL (minimum score 525 paper-based; 195 computer-based). *Application deadline:* For fall admission, 8/1 priority date for domestic students. Applications are processed on a rolling basis. Application fee: $25. Electronic applications accepted. *Financial support:* In 2006–07, 8 students received support. Institutionally sponsored loans available. Support available to part-time students. Financial award application deadline: 5/1; financial award applicants required to submit FAFSA. *Faculty research:* Concrete pavement technology and management, high temperature gas properties, metal forming, modeling and simulation, robotics work cell design. *Unit head:* Dr. Walter W. Boles, Chair, 615-898-2776, Fax: 615-898-5697.

Millersville University of Pennsylvania, Graduate School, School of Education, Department of Industry and Technology, Millersville, PA 17551-0302. Offers technology education (M Ed). *Accreditation:* NCATE. Part-time and evening/weekend programs available. *Faculty:* 18 full-time (1 woman), 7 part-time/adjunct (0 women). *Students:* 5 full-time (0 women), 8 part-time. Average age 31. 2 applicants, 50% accepted, 1 enrolled. In 2006, 2 degrees awarded. *Degree requirements:* For master's, departmental exam, thesis optional. *Entrance requirements:* For master's, GRE General Test or MAT, minimum undergraduate GPA of 2.75, teaching certificate. *Application deadline:* For fall admission, 3/1 priority date for domestic students; for spring admission, 10/1 priority date for domestic students. Applications are processed on a rolling basis. Application fee: $35. *Expenses:* Tuition, state resident: full-time $6,048; part-time $336 per credit. Tuition, nonresident: full-time $9,678; part-time $538 per credit. Required fees: $1,244. Tuition and fees vary according to course load. *Financial support:* In 2006–07, 2 students received support, including 2 research assistantships with full tuition reimbursements available (averaging $4,250 per year); career-related internships or fieldwork, Federal Work-Study, institutionally sponsored loans, and unspecified assistantships also available. Support available to part-time students. Financial award application deadline: 3/15; financial award applicants required to submit FAFSA. *Faculty research:* 2+2+2 articulated advanced manufacturing, resources to teach design to pre-service technology education teachers, advanced robotics center development, battery thermal management systems, design for production. *Unit head:* Dr. Perry Gemmill, Chair, 717-872-3316, Fax: 717-872-3318, E-mail: perry.gemmill@millersville.edu. *Application contact:* Dr. Victor S. DeSantis, Dean of Graduate Studies, 717-872-3099, Fax: 717-871-2022, E-mail: victor.desantis@millersville.edu.

Mississippi State University, College of Education, Department of Instructional Systems, Leadership, and Workforce Development, Mississippi State, MS 39762. Offers instructional technology (MSIT); technology (MS, Ed D, PhD, Ed S); workforce education leadership (MS). *Faculty:* 20 full-time (7 women), 1 (woman) part-time/adjunct. *Students:* 48 full-time (30 women), 62 part-time (48 women); includes 54 minority (53 African Americans, 1 Hispanic American). Average age 34. 28 applicants, 75% accepted, 17 enrolled. In 2006, 65 master's, 8 doctorates awarded. *Degree requirements:* For master's, comprehensive oral or written exam, thesis optional; for doctorate, thesis/dissertation, comprehensive oral and written exam. *Entrance requirements:* For master's, GRE, minimum GPA of 2.75 in junior and senior courses; for doctorate, GRE. Additional exam requirements/recommendations for international students: Required—TOEFL. *Application deadline:* For fall admission, 7/1 for domestic students; for spring admission, 11/1 for domestic students. Applications are processed on a rolling basis. Application fee: $30. *Expenses:* Tuition, state resident: full-time $4,550; part-time $253 per hour. Tuition, nonresident: full-time $10,552; part-time $584 per hour. International tuition: $10,882 full-time. Tuition and fees vary according to course load. *Financial support:* In 2006–07, 6 teaching assistantships with full tuition reimbursements (averaging $8,923 per year) were awarded; Federal Work-Study, institutionally sponsored loans, and unspecified assistantships also available. Financial award applicants required to submit FAFSA. *Faculty research:* Computer technology, nontraditional students, interactive video, instructional technology, educational leadership. *Unit head:* Dr. Linda Cornelius, Interim Head, 662-325-2281, Fax: 662-325-7599, E-mail: lcornelius@colled.msstate.edu. *Application contact:* Dr. Phil Bonfanti, Director of Admissions, 662-325-4104, Fax: 662-325-8872, E-mail: admit@msstate.edu.

Morehead State University, Graduate Programs, College of Science and Technology, Program in Career and Technical Education, Morehead, KY 40351. Offers MS. *Accreditation:* NCATE. Part-time and evening/weekend programs available. *Students:* 3 full-time (1 woman), 20 part-time (11 women). Average age 32. In 2006, 13 degrees awarded. *Degree requirements:* For master's, oral and/or written final exam, thesis optional. *Entrance requirements:* For master's, GRE General Test, minimum GPA of 3.0 in major, 2.5 overall. Additional exam requirements/recommendations for international students: Required—TOEFL (minimum score 500 paper-based; 173 computer-based). *Application deadline:* For fall admission, 8/1 priority date for domestic and international students; for spring admission, 12/1 priority date for domestic and international students. Applications are processed on a rolling basis. Application fee: $0. Electronic applications accepted. *Financial support:* In 2006–07, teaching assistantships (averaging $6,000 per year); career-related internships or fieldwork and Federal Work-Study also available. Financial award application deadline: 4/1; financial award applicants required to submit FAFSA. *Faculty research:* Robotics, herbicide safeness and forage grass species, computer-animated learning modules. *Unit head:* Dr. Lane Cowsert, Chair, 606-783-

Vocational and Technical Education

Morehead State University (continued)
2662, E-mail: l.cowser@moreheadstate.edu. *Application contact:* Michelle Barber, Graduate Admissions Counselor, 606-783-2039, Fax: 606-783-5061, E-mail: m.barber@moreheadstate.edu.

Murray State University, College of Education, Department of Adolescent, Career and Special Education, Program in Industrial and Technical Education, Murray, KY 42071. Offers MS. *Accreditation:* NCATE. Part-time programs available. *Students:* 11. 3 applicants, 100% accepted. *Degree requirements:* For master's, thesis (for some programs), portfolio. *Entrance requirements:* For master's, GRE General Test. Additional exam requirements/recommendations for international students: Required—TOEFL. *Application deadline:* Applications are processed on a rolling basis. Application fee: $25. *Financial support:* Research assistantships, teaching assistantships, Federal Work-Study available. Financial award application deadline: 4/1. *Unit head:* Paul McNeary, Graduate Coordinator, 270-809-6908, Fax: 270-809-2540, E-mail: paul.mcneary@coe.murraystate.edu.

North Carolina Agricultural and Technical State University, Graduate School, School of Technology, Department of Graphic Communication Systems and Technological Studies, Greensboro, NC 27411. Offers industrial arts education (MS); technology education (MS); vocational-industrial education (MS). *Accreditation:* NCATE. Part-time and evening/weekend programs available. *Degree requirements:* For master's, thesis or alternative, qualifying exam, comprehensive exam. *Entrance requirements:* For master's, GRE General Test, minimum GPA of 3.0.

Northern Arizona University, Graduate College, College of Education, Program in Career and Technical Education, Flagstaff, AZ 86011. Offers administration (M Ed); educational technology (M Ed); teaching (M Ed). *Degree requirements:* For master's, final oral exam, project, thesis optional.

Nova Southeastern University, Fischler School of Education and Human Services, Programs for Higher Education, Fort Lauderdale, FL 33314-7796. Offers adult education (Ed D); computing and information technology (Ed D); health care education (Ed D); higher education (Ed D); vocational, occupational and technical education (Ed D). Part-time and evening/weekend programs available. *Students:* 35 full-time (22 women), 321 part-time (222 women); includes 134 minority (116 African Americans, 1 American Indian/Alaska Native, 17 Hispanic Americans), 1 international. 4 applicants, 75% accepted, 3 enrolled. In 2006, 40 degrees awarded. *Degree requirements:* For doctorate, thesis/dissertation, practicum. *Entrance requirements:* For doctorate, MAT or GRE, master's degree, work experience in field, minimum GPA of 3.0. Additional exam requirements/recommendations for international students: Recommended—TOEFL (minimum score 550 paper-based; 213 computer-based), IELTS (minimum score 6). *Application deadline:* For fall admission, 8/11 priority date for domestic and international students; for winter admission, 12/28 priority date for domestic and international students; for spring admission, 4/22 priority date for domestic and international students. Applications are processed on a rolling basis. Application fee: $50. Electronic applications accepted. *Expenses:* Contact institution. *Financial support:* In 2006–07, 2 fellowships were awarded; career-related internships or fieldwork and tuition waivers (full) also available. Financial award application deadline: 1/7. *Unit head:* Dr. Karen D. Bowser, Associate Dean of Doctoral Programs, 954-262-8500, Fax: 954-262-3912, E-mail: bowserk@nova.edu. *Application contact:* Jennifer Quiñones Nottingham, Dean of Student Affairs, 800-986-3223 Ext. 8624, Fax: 954-262-3911, E-mail: jlquinon@nova.edu.

The Ohio State University, Graduate School, College of Food, Agricultural, and Environmental Sciences, Comprehensive Program in Vocational Education, Columbus, OH 43210. Offers PhD. *Faculty:* 10. *Students:* Average age 56. In 2006, 1 degree awarded. *Degree requirements:* For doctorate, thesis/dissertation. *Entrance requirements:* For doctorate, interview, minimum graduate GPA of 3.5. Additional exam requirements/recommendations for international students: Required—TOEFL (paper-based 550; computer-based 213) or IELTS (7) or Michigan English Language Assessment Battery (83). *Application deadline:* For fall admission, 8/15 priority date for domestic students, 7/1 priority date for international students; for winter admission, 12/1 priority date for domestic students, 11/1 priority date for international students; for spring admission, 3/1 priority date for domestic students, 2/1 priority date for international students. Applications are processed on a rolling basis. Application fee: $40 ($50 for international students). Electronic applications accepted. *Expenses:* Tuition, state resident: full-time $9,438. Tuition, nonresident: full-time $22,791. Tuition and fees vary according to course load, campus/location and program. *Financial support:* Fellowships, Federal Work-Study and institutionally sponsored loans available. Support available to part-time students. *Unit head:* Dr. Joseph A. Gliem, Graduate Studies Committee Chair, 614-292-6321, Fax: 614-292-7007, E-mail: gliem.2@osu.edu. *Application contact:* Graduate Admissions, 614-292-9444, Fax: 614-292-3895, E-mail: domestic.grad@osu.edu.

Oklahoma State University, College of Education, School of Educational Studies, Stillwater, OK 74078. Offers educational administration (MS); higher education (MS, Ed D); technical education (MS, Ed D); trade and industrial education (MS, Ed D). *Faculty:* 28 full-time (10 women), 25 part-time/adjunct (6 women). *Students:* 40 full-time (28 women), 160 part-time (93 women); includes 34 minority (14 African Americans, 11 American Indian/Alaska Native, 5 Asian Americans or Pacific Islanders, 4 Hispanic Americans), 8 international. Average age 40. 124 applicants, 43% accepted, 37 enrolled. In 2006, 34 master's, 29 doctorates awarded. *Degree requirements:* For master's, thesis or alternative; for doctorate, thesis/dissertation. *Entrance requirements:* For master's and doctorate, GRE or MAT. Additional exam requirements/recommendations for international students: Required—TOEFL. *Application deadline:* For fall admission, 7/1 priority date for domestic students, 3/1 priority date for international students; for spring admission, 8/1 priority date for international students. Applications are processed on a rolling basis. Application fee: $40 ($75 for international students). Electronic applications accepted. *Expenses:* Tuition, state resident: part-time $146 per credit hour. Tuition, nonresident: part-time $516 per credit hour. Required fees: $44 per credit hour. Tuition and fees vary according to program. *Financial support:* In 2006–07, 13 research assistantships (averaging $8,838 per year), 7 teaching assistantships (averaging $7,586 per year) were awarded; career-related internships or fieldwork, Federal Work-Study, and tuition waivers (partial) also available. Support available to part-time students. Financial award application deadline: 3/1. *Unit head:* Dr. Bert Jacobson, Head, 405-744-6275.

Old Dominion University, Darden College of Education, Programs in Occupational and Technical Studies, Norfolk, VA 23529. Offers business and industry training (MS); career and technical education (PhD); community college teaching (MS); human resources training (PhD); middle and secondary teaching (MS); technology education (PhD). *Accreditation:* NCATE (one or more programs are accredited). Part-time and evening/weekend programs available. Postbaccalaureate distance learning degree programs offered (minimal on-campus study). *Faculty:* 7 full-time (1 woman), 5 part-time/adjunct (2 women). *Students:* 15 full-time (11 women), 68 part-time (39 women); includes 13 minority (9 African Americans, 2 American Indian/Alaska Native, 2 Asian Americans or Pacific Islanders), 1 international. Average age 39. 44 applicants, 95% accepted, 37 enrolled. In 2006, 29 degrees awarded. *Degree requirements:* For master's, writing exam, candidacy exam, thesis optional; for doctorate, thesis/dissertation, writing exam, candidacy exam, comprehensive exam, registration. *Entrance requirements:* For master's, GRE General Test or MAT, minimum GPA of 2.8; for doctorate, GRE, minimum GPA of 3.0, 3 letters of reference. Additional exam requirements/recommendations for international students: Required—TOEFL. *Application deadline:* For fall admission, 6/1 priority date for domestic students, 6/1 for international students; for winter admission, 11/1 priority date for domestic students, 11/1 for international students; for spring admission, 3/1 priority date for domestic students, 3/1 for international students. Applications are processed on a rolling basis. Application fee: $40. Electronic applications accepted. *Expenses:* Tuition, area resident: Part-time $285 per credit hour. Tuition, nonresident: part-time $715 per credit hour. Required fees: $94 per semester. *Financial support:* In 2006–07, 19 students received support, including 1 fellowship with full tuition reimbursement available (averaging $15,000 per year), 2 research assistantships with partial tuition reimbursements available (averaging $9,000 per year), 5 teaching assistantships with partial tuition reimbursements available (averaging $12,600 per year); career-related internships or fieldwork, scholarships/grants, tuition waivers (partial), and unspecified assistantships also available. Support available to part-time students. Financial award application deadline: 2/15; financial award applicants required to submit FAFSA. *Faculty research:* Training and development, marketing, technology, special populations, support of academic subjects. Total annual research expenditures: $799,773. *Unit head:* Dr. John M. Ritz, Graduate Program Director, 757-683-4305, Fax: 757-683-5227, E-mail: otsgpd@odu.edu.

Penn State University Park, Graduate School, College of Education, Department of Learning and Performance Systems, State College, University Park, PA 16802-1503. Offers adult education (M Ed, D Ed, PhD); instructional systems (M Ed, MS, D Ed, PhD); workforce education and development (M Ed, MS, D Ed, PhD). *Unit head:* Dr. Edgar I. Farmer, Head, 814-863-3858, Fax: 814-865-2632, E-mail: eif1@psu.edu.

Pittsburg State University, Graduate School, College of Technology, Department of Graphics and Imaging Technologies and Technology Management, Pittsburg, KS 66762. Offers human resource development (MS); industrial education (Ed S); technology (MS), including printing management. *Faculty:* 3 full-time (0 women). *Students:* 59. *Degree requirements:* For master's, thesis or alternative. Application fee: $35 ($60 for international students). *Expenses:* Tuition, state resident: full-time $2,144; part-time $181 per credit hour. Tuition, nonresident: full-time $5,273; part-time $442 per credit hour. Tuition and fees vary according to course load and campus/location. *Financial support:* In 2006–07, teaching assistantships (averaging $5,000 per year); career-related internships or fieldwork also available. *Unit head:* Dr. Jesus Rodriguez, Chairperson, 620-235-4420. *Application contact:* Jamie Vanderbeck, Assistant Director, 620-235-4223, Fax: 620-235-4219, E-mail: jvanderb@pittstate.edu.

Pittsburg State University, Graduate School, College of Technology, Department of Technology Studies, Pittsburg, KS 66762. Offers human resource development (MS, Ed S); technical teacher education (MS); technology education (MS). *Students:* 17 full-time (4 women), 7 part-time (1 woman). *Degree requirements:* For master's, thesis or alternative. Application fee: $35 ($60 for international students). *Expenses:* Tuition, state resident: full-time $2,144; part-time $181 per credit hour. Tuition, nonresident: full-time $5,273; part-time $442 per credit hour. Tuition and fees vary according to course load and campus/location. *Financial support:* In 2006–07, teaching assistantships (averaging $5,000 per year); career-related internships or fieldwork and Federal Work-Study also available. *Unit head:* Dr. John Iley, Chairperson, 620-235-4371. *Application contact:* Marvene Darraugh, Administrative Officer, 620-235-4220, Fax: 620-235-4219, E-mail: mdarraug@pittstate.edu.

Purdue University, Graduate School, College of Technology, Graduate Program in Industrial Technology, West Lafayette, IN 47907. Offers MS. Part-time programs available. Postbaccalaureate distance learning degree programs offered (minimal on-campus study). *Faculty:* 143 full-time (21 women). *Students:* 79 full-time (24 women), 119 part-time (25 women); includes 14 minority (7 African Americans, 1 American Indian/Alaska Native, 4 Asian Americans or Pacific Islanders, 2 Hispanic Americans), 38 international. Average age 29. 143 applicants, 64% accepted, 66 enrolled. In 2006, 67 master's awarded. *Degree requirements:* For master's, oral exam. *Entrance requirements:* For master's, GRE General Test, minimum GPA of 3.0. Additional exam requirements/recommendations for international students: Required—TOEFL. *Application deadline:* For fall admission, 4/1 priority date for domestic students; for spring admission, 10/1 priority date for domestic students. Applications are processed on a rolling basis. Application fee: $55. Electronic applications accepted. *Financial support:* In 2006–07, 37 teaching assistantships were awarded; fellowships also available. Support available to part-time students. Financial award applicants required to submit FAFSA. *Unit head:* Dr. Matthew Stephans, Interim Head, 765-494-2554, Fax: 765-494-0486. *Application contact:* Debbie L. Hulsey, Graduate Contact, 765-494-6875, E-mail: dhulsey@purdue.edu.

Purdue University, Graduate School, School of Education, Department of Curriculum and Instruction, West Lafayette, IN 47907. Offers agricultural and extension education (PhD, Ed S); agriculture and extension education (MS, MS Ed); art education (PhD); consumer and family sciences and extension education (MS Ed, PhD, Ed S); curriculum studies (MS Ed, PhD, Ed S); educational technology (MS Ed, PhD, Ed S); elementary education (MS Ed); foreign language education (MS Ed, PhD, Ed S); industrial technology (PhD, Ed S); language arts (MS Ed, PhD, Ed S); literacy (MS Ed, PhD, Ed S); mathematics/science education (MS, MS Ed, PhD, Ed S); social studies (MS Ed, PhD); social studies education (Ed S); vocational/industrial education (MS Ed, PhD, Ed S); vocational/technical education (MS Ed, PhD, Ed S). *Accreditation:* NCATE. Part-time and evening/weekend programs available. *Faculty:* 26 full-time (13 women), 3 part-time/adjunct (all women). *Students:* 59 full-time (37 women), 112 part-time (70 women); includes 24 minority (13 African Americans, 3 American Indian/Alaska Native, 4 Asian Americans or Pacific Islanders, 4 Hispanic Americans), 38 international. Average age 35. 92 applicants, 68% accepted, 38 enrolled. In 2006, 52 master's, 23 doctorates awarded. *Degree requirements:* For master's, thesis optional; for doctorate, thesis/dissertation, oral and written exams; for Ed S, oral presentation, project. *Entrance requirements:* For master's, GRE General Test, minimum B average; for doctorate, GRE General Test; for Ed S, GRE, minimum B average. Additional exam requirements/recommendations for international students: Required—TOEFL. *Application deadline:* For fall admission, 1/15 priority date for domestic students, 1/15 for international students; for spring admission, 9/15 for domestic and international students. Applications are processed on a rolling basis. Application fee: $55. Electronic applications accepted. *Financial support:* In 2006–07, 3 fellowships with full tuition reimbursements (averaging $10,500 per year), 11 research assistantships with full tuition reimbursements (averaging $11,500 per year), 43 teaching assistantships with full tuition reimbursements (averaging $10,800 per year) were awarded; career-related internships or fieldwork and tuition waivers (full) also available. Support available to part-time students. Financial award application deadline: 3/1; financial award applicants required to submit FAFSA. *Faculty research:* Literacy acquisition and development, teacher beliefs and knowledge, recruitment and retention of underrepresented students, economic education, literacy discourse. *Unit head:* Dr. James D Lehman, Head, 765-494-7935, Fax: 765-496-1622. *Application contact:* Patricia Mason, Coordinator of Graduate Studies, 765-494-2345, Fax: 765-494-5832, E-mail: gradoffice@soe.purdue.edu.

Saint Martin's University, Graduate Programs, Department of Education, Lacey, WA 98503-1297. Offers administration (M Ed); English as a second language (M Ed); guidance and counseling (M Ed); reading (M Ed); special education (M Ed); teaching (MIT); technology in education (M Ed). Part-time and evening/weekend programs available. *Degree requirements:* For master's, thesis or alternative, project or comprehensives, comprehensive exam (for some programs). *Entrance requirements:* For master's, GRE General Test or MAT, resumé. Additional exam requirements/recommendations for international students: Required—TOEFL (minimum score 560 paper-based). *Faculty research:* Reader's theatre and reader/writer workshops, curriculum and assessment integration, gender and equity, classroom evaluations, organizational leadership.

Sam Houston State University, College of Arts and Sciences, Department of Agricultural Sciences, Huntsville, TX 77341. Offers agriculture (MS); industrial education (M Ed, MA); industrial technology (MA); vocational education (M Ed). Part-time and evening/weekend programs available. *Faculty:* 5 full-time (0 women). *Students:* 18 full-time (7 women), 17 part-time (11 women); includes 3 minority (1 Asian American or Pacific Islander, 2 Hispanic Americans), 2 international. Average age 28. In 2006, 13 degrees awarded. *Degree requirements:* For master's, thesis optional. *Entrance requirements:* For master's, GRE General Test, minimum GPA of 2.5. *Application deadline:* For fall admission, 8/1 for domestic students; for spring admission, 12/1 for domestic students. Application fee: $20. *Expenses:* Tuition, state resident: full-time $5,904; part-time $164 per semester hour. Tuition, nonresident: full-time $15,804; part-time $439 per semester hour. Required fees: $1,374; $462 per semester. *Financial support:* Teaching assistantships, career-related internships or fieldwork available. Financial award application deadline: 5/31; financial award applicants required to submit FAFSA.

Unit head: Dr. Doug R. Ullrich, Chair Interim, 936-294-1188, Fax: 936-294-1232, E-mail: agr_dru@shsu.edu.

South Carolina State University, School of Graduate Studies, Department of Education, Orangeburg, SC 29117-0001. Offers early childhood and special education (M Ed); early childhood education (MAT); elementary education (M Ed, MAT); engineering (MAT); general science (MAT); mathematics (MAT); secondary education (M Ed), including biology education, business education, counselor education, English education, home economics education, industrial education, mathematics education, science education, social studies education; special education (M Ed), including emotionally handicapped, learning disabilities, mentally handicapped. *Accreditation:* NCATE. Part-time and evening/weekend programs available. *Faculty:* 21 full-time (10 women), 4 part-time/adjunct (0 women). *Students:* 34 full-time (28 women), 33 part-time (25 women); includes 63 minority (61 African Americans, 1 American Indian/Alaska Native, 1 Asian American or Pacific Islander). Average age 35. 46 applicants, 67% accepted, 19 enrolled. In 2006, 28 degrees awarded. *Degree requirements:* For master's, departmental qualifying exam, thesis optional. *Entrance requirements:* For master's, GRE General Test, NTE, interview, teaching certificate. *Application deadline:* For fall admission, 6/15 priority date for domestic students, 6/15 for international students; for spring admission, 11/1 for domestic and international students. Applications are processed on a rolling basis. *Application fee:* $25. Electronic applications accepted. *Expenses:* Tuition, state resident: full-time $7,278. Tuition, nonresident: full-time $14,322. *Financial support:* Fellowships, research assistantships, career-related internships or fieldwork, Federal Work-Study, and institutionally sponsored loans available. Financial award application deadline: 6/1. *Faculty research:* Critical thinking, child abuse, stress, test-taking skills, conflict resolution, mainstreaming. *Unit head:* Dr. Gail Joyner-Fleming, Interim Chair, 803-533-3769, Fax: 803-536-8492, E-mail: zf-gfleming@scsu.edu. *Application contact:* Annette Hazzard-Jones, Program Coordinator II, 803-536-8809, Fax: 803-536-8812, E-mail: zs_ahazzard@scsu.edu.

Southern Illinois University Carbondale, Graduate School, College of Education, Department of Workforce Education and Development, Carbondale, IL 62901-4701. Offers MS Ed, PhD. *Accreditation:* NCATE. Part-time programs available. *Faculty:* 15 full-time (6 women), 1 part-time/adjunct (0 women). *Students:* 72 full-time (39 women), 196 part-time (108 women); includes 71 minority (58 African Americans, 5 Asian Americans or Pacific Islanders, 8 Hispanic Americans), 30 international. Average age 32. 83 applicants, 69% accepted, 9 enrolled. In 2006, 68 master's, 10 doctorates awarded. *Degree requirements:* For master's and doctorate, thesis/dissertation. *Entrance requirements:* For master's, minimum GPA of 2.7; for doctorate, GRE General Test, minimum GPA of 3.25. Additional exam requirements/recommendations for international students: Required—TOEFL. *Application deadline:* Applications are processed on a rolling basis. *Application fee:* $20. *Financial support:* In 2006–07, 38 students received support, including 4 research assistantships with full tuition reimbursements available, 10 teaching assistantships with full tuition reimbursements available; fellowships with full tuition reimbursements available, career-related internships or fieldwork, Federal Work-Study, institutionally sponsored loans, tuition waivers (full), and unspecified assistantships also available. Support available to part-time students. *Faculty research:* Career education, technical training, curriculum development, competency-based instruction, impact of technology on workplace and workforce. *Unit head:* Dr. Keith Waugh, Chair, 618-453-3321, Fax: 618-453-1909, E-mail: ckwaugh@siu.edu. *Application contact:* Dr. Marcia Anderson, Coordinator, 618-453-3321, Fax: 618-453-1909, E-mail: mandersn@siu.edu.

Announcement: To enhance graduate research opportunities in the doctoral program in workforce education and development, the Center for Workforce Development was created to serve as a broker in the exchange and sharing of information and resources. Program enhancements in e-learning and student and professional affiliations are ongoing.

See Close-Up on page 1611.

Southern New Hampshire University, School of Education, Manchester, NH 03106-1045. Offers business education (MS); child development (M Ed); computer technology education (Certificate); curriculum and instruction (M Ed); education (M Ed, CAS); elementary education (M Ed); general special education (Certificate); school business administrator (Certificate); school counseling (M Ed); school psychology (M Ed); secondary education (M Ed); training and development (Certificate). Part-time and evening/weekend programs available. Postbaccalaureate distance learning degree programs offered. *Faculty:* 6 full-time (3 women), 9 part-time/adjunct (7 women). *Students:* Average age 35. In 2006, 52 degrees awarded. *Degree requirements:* For master's, thesis or alternative, comprehensive exam (for some programs). *Entrance requirements:* For master's, GRE General Test or MAT, minimum GPA of 3.0. Additional exam requirements/recommendations for international students: Required—TOEFL (minimum score 550 paper-based; 213 computer-based). *Application deadline:* Applications are processed on a rolling basis. *Application fee:* $25. Electronic applications accepted. *Expenses:* Contact institution. *Financial support:* Institutionally sponsored loans available. Financial award applicants required to submit FAFSA. *Unit head:* Dr. Patrick J. Hartwick, Dean, 603-668-2211 Ext. 4698, Fax: 603-629-4673, E-mail: p.hartwick@snhu.edu. *Application contact:* Scott Durand, Director of Graduate Enrollment Services, 603-644-3102 Ext. 3338, Fax: 603-644-3144, E-mail: s.durand@snhu.edu.

State University of New York at Oswego, Graduate Studies, School of Education, Department of Technology, Oswego, NY 13126. Offers MS Ed. *Accreditation:* NCATE. Part-time programs available. *Faculty:* 2 full-time, 2 part-time/adjunct. *Students:* 4 full-time (0 women), 24 part-time (1 woman). Average age 25. 17 applicants, 100% accepted. In 2006, 26 degrees awarded. *Degree requirements:* For master's, departmental exam, thesis optional. *Entrance requirements:* For master's, provisional teaching certificate in technology education. Additional exam requirements/recommendations for international students: Required—TOEFL (minimum score 560 paper-based; 220 computer-based). *Application deadline:* For fall admission, 4/1 for domestic students; for spring admission, 10/1 for domestic students. Applications are processed on a rolling basis. *Application fee:* $50. *Expenses:* Tuition, state resident: part-time $288 per credit. Tuition, nonresident: part-time $455 per credit. Tuition and fees vary according to program. *Financial support:* In 2006–07, 1 student received support, including 1 teaching assistantship with full tuition reimbursement available; Federal Work-Study, institutionally sponsored loans, scholarships/grants, health care benefits, and unspecified assistantships also available. Support available to part-time students. Financial award application deadline: 4/1; financial award applicants required to submit FAFSA. *Faculty research:* Curriculum development, microcomputer applications. *Unit head:* Dr. Phillip Gaines, Chair, 315-312-3011.

State University of New York at Oswego, Graduate Studies, School of Education, Department of Vocational Teacher Preparation, Oswego, NY 13126. Offers agriculture (MS Ed); business and marketing (MS Ed); family and consumer sciences (MS Ed); health careers (MS Ed); technical education (MS Ed); trade education (MS Ed). *Accreditation:* NCATE. Part-time and evening/weekend programs available. *Faculty:* 3 full-time, 8 part-time/adjunct. *Students:* 24 full-time (10 women), 52 part-time (23 women); includes 4 minority (3 African Americans, 1 Hispanic American). Average age 40. 50 applicants, 100% accepted. In 2006, 31 degrees awarded. *Degree requirements:* For master's, thesis or alternative. *Entrance requirements:* Additional exam requirements/recommendations for international students: Required—TOEFL (minimum score 560 paper-based; 220 computer-based). *Application deadline:* For fall admission, 4/1 for domestic students; for spring admission, 10/1 for domestic students. Applications are processed on a rolling basis. *Application fee:* $50. *Expenses:* Tuition, state resident: part-time $288 per credit. Tuition, nonresident: part-time $455 per credit. Tuition and fees vary according to program. *Financial support:* In 2006–07, 3 students received support, including 2 fellowships, 1 teaching assistantship; career-related internships or fieldwork, Federal Work-Study, institutionally sponsored loans, health care benefits, and unspecified assistantships also available. Support available to part-time students. Financial award application deadline: 4/1; financial award applicants required to submit FAFSA. *Unit head:* Dr. Margaret Martin, Chair, 315-312-2480.

Sul Ross State University, School of Professional Studies, Department of Industrial Technology, Alpine, TX 79832. Offers industrial arts (M Ed). Part-time programs available. *Entrance requirements:* For master's, GMAT or GRE General Test, minimum GPA of 2.5 in last 60 hours of undergraduate work.

Temple University, Graduate School, College of Education, Department of Curriculum, Instruction, and Technology in Education, Philadelphia, PA 19122-6096. Offers applied behavioral analysis (MS Ed); career and technical education (MS Ed); early childhood education and elementary education (MS Ed); English education (MS Ed); language arts education (Ed D); math/science education (Ed D); mathematics education (MS Ed); science education (MS Ed); second and foreign language education (MS Ed); special education (MS Ed); teaching English as a second language (MS Ed). Part-time and evening/weekend programs available. *Faculty:* 31 full-time (14 women). *Students:* 96 full-time (71 women), 482 part-time (336 women); includes 109 minority (67 African Americans, 3 American Indian/Alaska Native, 23 Asian Americans or Pacific Islanders, 16 Hispanic Americans), 28 international. 308 applicants, 64% accepted, 116 enrolled. In 2006, 225 master's, 21 doctorates awarded. Terminal master's awarded for partial completion of doctoral program. *Degree requirements:* For master's, thesis or alternative; for doctorate, thesis/dissertation. *Entrance requirements:* For master's and doctorate, GRE General Test or MAT, minimum GPA of 3.0. Additional exam requirements/recommendations for international students: Required—TOEFL (minimum score 550 paper-based; 213 computer-based; 79 iBT). *Application deadline:* For fall admission, 4/1 for domestic students, 12/15 for international students; for spring admission, 10/1 for domestic students, 8/1 for international students. *Application fee:* $50. Electronic applications accepted. *Expenses:* Tuition, state resident: full-time $12,264; part-time $511 per credit. Tuition, nonresident: full-time $17,904; part-time $746 per credit. Required fees: $84 per course. Tuition and fees vary according to program. *Financial support:* Fellowships, research assistantships with full tuition reimbursements, teaching assistantships with full tuition reimbursements available. Financial award application deadline: 1/15; financial award applicants required to submit FAFSA. *Faculty research:* School improvement, problem solving, literacy, language development. *Unit head:* Dr. Thomas Walker, Chair, 215-204-2117, Fax: 215-204-1414, E-mail: tjwalker@temple.edu.

Texas A&M University–Corpus Christi, Graduate Studies and Research, College of Education, Program in Occupational Training and Development, Corpus Christi, TX 78412-5503. Offers MS. Part-time and evening/weekend programs available. *Degree requirements:* For master's, thesis (for some programs), comprehensive exam, registration. *Entrance requirements:* For master's, GRE General Test. Additional exam requirements/recommendations for international students: Required—TOEFL. Electronic applications accepted.

Texas State University–San Marcos, Graduate School, College of Applied Arts, Program in Management of Technical Education, San Marcos, TX 78666. Offers M Ed. Part-time and evening/weekend programs available. *Faculty:* 2 full-time (1 woman), 1 part-time/adjunct (0 women). *Students:* 5 full-time (3 women), 31 part-time (15 women); includes 18 minority (6 African Americans, 1 Asian American or Pacific Islander, 11 Hispanic Americans), 1 international. Average age 40. 23 applicants, 100% accepted, 12 enrolled. In 2006, 9 degrees awarded. *Degree requirements:* For master's, comprehensive exam. *Entrance requirements:* For master's, GRE General Test, minimum GPA of 2.75 in last 60 hours of course work. Additional exam requirements/recommendations for international students: Required—TOEFL. *Application deadline:* For fall admission, 6/15 for domestic students; for spring admission, 10/15 for domestic students. Applications are processed on a rolling basis. *Application fee:* $40 ($90 for international students). *Financial support:* In 2006–07, 34 students received support; research assistantships, career-related internships or fieldwork, Federal Work-Study, and institutionally sponsored loans available. Support available to part-time students. Financial award application deadline: 4/1; financial award applicants required to submit FAFSA. *Faculty research:* Vocational teaching, counseling, coordinating, and supervising. *Unit head:* Dr. Stephen Springer, Director, 512-245-2115, E-mail: ss01@txstate.edu.

Texas State University–San Marcos, Graduate School, Interdisciplinary Studies Program in Occupational Education, San Marcos, TX 78666. Offers MAIS, MSIS. *Faculty:* 4 full-time (1 woman). *Students:* 3 full-time (2 women), 25 part-time (10 women); includes 4 African Americans, 9 Hispanic Americans, 1 international. Average age 39. 22 applicants, 100% accepted, 11 enrolled. In 2006, 12 degrees awarded. *Degree requirements:* For master's, comprehensive exam. *Application deadline:* For fall admission, 6/15 priority date for domestic students; for spring admission, 10/15 priority date for domestic students. Applications are processed on a rolling basis. *Application fee:* $40 ($90 for international students). *Financial support:* In 2006–07, 21 students received support. Application deadline: 4/1; *Unit head:* Dr. Stephen Springer, Director, 512-245-2115, E-mail: ss01@txstate.edu.

Trevecca Nazarene University, Graduate Division, School of Education, Major in Instructional Technology, Nashville, TN 37210-2877. Offers M Ed. Part-time and evening/weekend programs available. *Students:* 6 full-time (4 women), 2 part-time (both women); includes 3 minority (all African Americans) In 2006, 10 degrees awarded. *Degree requirements:* For master's, exit assessment. *Entrance requirements:* For master's, GRE General Test, MAT, minimum GPA of 2.7, 2 reference forms. Additional exam requirements/recommendations for international students: Required—TOEFL (minimum score 500 paper-based; 173 computer-based). *Application deadline:* Applications are processed on a rolling basis. *Application fee:* $25. *Expenses:* Contact institution. Tuition and fees vary according to degree level and program. *Financial support:* Applicants required to submit FAFSA. *Application contact:* Admissions Office, 615-248-1201, Fax: 615-248-1597, E-mail: admissions_ged@trevecca.edu.

The University of Akron, Graduate School, College of Education, Department of Educational Foundations and Leadership, Program in Technical Education, Akron, OH 44325. Offers technical education guidance (MS); technical education instructional technology (MS); technical education teaching (MS); technical education training (MS). *Accreditation:* NCATE. *Students:* 3 full-time (2 women), 15 part-time (13 women); includes 4 minority (all African Americans), 1 international. Average age 40. 4 applicants, 100% accepted, 3 enrolled. In 2006, 7 degrees awarded. *Degree requirements:* For master's, cumulative portfolio. *Entrance requirements:* For master's, minimum GPA of 2.75. Additional exam requirements/recommendations for international students: Required—TOEFL (minimum score 550 paper-based; 213 computer-based; 79 iBT). *Application deadline:* For fall admission, 8/15 for domestic students. Applications are processed on a rolling basis. *Application fee:* $30 ($40 for international students). Electronic applications accepted. *Expenses:* Tuition, state resident: full-time $6,164; part-time $342 per credit. Tuition, nonresident: full-time $10,575; part-time $588 per credit. Required fees: $806; $43 per credit. $12 per term. Tuition and fees vary according to course load, degree level and program. *Financial support:* Fellowships with full tuition reimbursements, research assistantships with full tuition reimbursements, teaching assistantships with full tuition reimbursements, Federal Work-Study and unspecified assistantships available. *Unit head:* Dr. Qetler Jensrud, Head, 330-972-6403.

University of Arkansas, Graduate School, College of Education and Health Professions, Department of Rehabilitation, Human Resources and Communication Disorders, Program in Workforce Development Education, Fayetteville, AR 72701-1201. Offers M Ed. Part-time and evening/weekend programs available. Postbaccalaureate distance learning degree programs offered. *Students:* 16 full-time (8 women), 116 part-time (88 women); includes 33 minority (31 African Americans, 1 American Indian/Alaska Native, 1 Hispanic American). 53 applicants, 70% accepted. In 2006, 27 degrees awarded. *Financial support:* In 2006–07, 5 fellowships were awarded; research assistantships, teaching assistantships, career-related internships or fieldwork and Federal Work-Study also available. Support available to part-time students. Financial award application deadline: 4/1; financial award applicants required to submit FAFSA. *Application contact:* Dr. Frederick Nafukho, Graduate Coordinator, 479-575-4899, E-mail: nafukho@uark.edu.

University of Arkansas, Graduate School, College of Education and Health Professions, Department of Vocational and Adult Education, Program in Vocational Education, Fayetteville, AR 72701-1201. Offers M Ed, MAT, Ed D, Ed S. *Accreditation:* NCATE. Part-time and evening/

Vocational and Technical Education

University of Arkansas (continued)
weekend programs available. Postbaccalaureate distance learning degree programs offered. *Students:* 6 full-time (all women), 3 part-time (2 women); includes 1 minority (African American), 1 international. 10 applicants, 20% accepted. In 2006, 13 degrees awarded. *Degree requirements:* For master's, thesis optional; for doctorate, thesis/dissertation. Application fee: $40 ($50 for international students). *Financial support:* Fellowships with tuition reimbursements, research assistantships, teaching assistantships, career-related internships or fieldwork and Federal Work-Study available. Support available to part-time students. Financial award application deadline: 4/1; financial award applicants required to submit FAFSA. *Application contact:* Dr. Frederick Nafukho, Graduate Coordinator, 479-575-4899, E-mail: nafukho@uark.edu.

The University of British Columbia, Faculty of Graduate Studies, Faculty of Education, Department of Curriculum Studies, Vancouver, BC V6T 1Z1, Canada. Offers art education (M Ed, MA); curriculum studies (M Ed, MA, PhD); home economics education (M Ed, MA); math education (M Ed, MA); music education (M Ed, MA); physical education (M Ed, MA); science education (M Ed, MA); social studies education (M Ed, MA); technical studies education (M Ed, MA). Part-time programs available. *Faculty:* 31 full-time (17 women), 1 (woman) part-time/adjunct. *Students:* 153 full-time (102 women), 101 part-time (67 women), 25 international. Average age 40. 118 applicants, 64% accepted, 62 enrolled. In 2006, 46 master's, 4 doctorates awarded. *Degree requirements:* For master's, thesis (MA); for doctorate, thesis/dissertation, comprehensive exam, registration. *Entrance requirements:* Additional exam requirements/recommendations for international students: Required—TOEFL (minimum score 580 paper-based; 237 computer-based). *Application deadline:* For fall admission, 2/1 for domestic students, 1/1 for international students; for spring admission, 10/1 for domestic students, 9/1 for international students. Application fee: $90 ($150 for international students). Electronic applications accepted. *Expenses:* Contact institution. *Financial support:* In 2006–07, 10 fellowships with partial tuition reimbursements (averaging $16,000 per year), 11 research assistantships with partial tuition reimbursements (averaging $14,000 per year), 27 teaching assistantships with partial tuition reimbursements (averaging $14,000 per year) were awarded; tuition waivers (partial) also available. *Faculty research:* School subjects, teaching and learning. *Unit head:* Dr. Linda Peterat, Interim Head, 604-822-5422, Fax: 604-822-4714. *Application contact:* Basia Zurek, Graduate Secretary, 604-822-5367, Fax: 604-822-4714, E-mail: cust.grad@ubc.ca.

University of Calgary, Faculty of Graduate Studies, Faculty of Education, Graduate Division of Educational Research, Calgary, AB T2N 1N4, Canada. Offers community rehabilitation and disability studies (M Ed, M Sc, Ed D, PhD, Graduate Certificate, Graduate Diploma); curriculum, teaching and learning (M Ed, M Sc, MA, Ed D, PhD, Graduate Certificate, Graduate Diploma); educational contexts (M Ed, MA, Ed D, PhD, Graduate Certificate, Graduate Diploma); educational leadership (M Ed, MA, Ed D, PhD, Graduate Certificate, Graduate Diploma); educational technology (M Ed, M Sc, MA, Ed D, PhD, Graduate Certificate, Graduate Diploma); gifted education (M Sc, MA, Ed D, PhD, Graduate Certificate, Graduate Diploma); higher education administration (Ed D); interpretive studies in education (M Ed, M Sc, MA, Ed D, PhD, Graduate Certificate, Graduate Diploma); second language teaching (M Ed, Ed D, PhD, Graduate Certificate, Graduate Diploma); teaching English as a second language (M Ed, M Sc, MA, Ed D, PhD, Graduate Certificate, Graduate Diploma); workplace and adult learning (M Ed, MA, Ed D, PhD, Graduate Certificate, Graduate Diploma). Ed D in both higher education administration and educational leadership offered via distance delivery. Part-time and evening/weekend programs available. Postbaccalaureate distance learning degree programs offered (minimal on-campus study). *Faculty:* 44 full-time, 52 part-time/adjunct. *Students:* 488 full-time, 550 part-time. 400 applicants, 50% accepted. In 2006, 102 master's, 18 doctorates awarded. *Degree requirements:* For master's, thesis (for some programs); for doctorate, thesis/dissertation, candidacy exam. *Entrance requirements:* For master's, minimum GPA of 3.0, 3 letters of reference; for doctorate, minimum GPA of 3.5, 3 letters of reference; for other advanced degree, minimum GPA of 3.0. Additional exam requirements/recommendations for international students: Required—TOEFL, IELTS. *Application deadline:* For fall admission, 2/15 for domestic students, 2/5 for international students; for winter admission, 6/15 for domestic and international students. Application fee: $100. Electronic applications accepted. *Financial support:* In 2006–07, research assistantships (averaging $3,920 per year); teaching assistantships, career-related internships or fieldwork, scholarships/grants, and unspecified assistantships also available. Financial award application deadline: 2/1. *Faculty research:* Curriculum, leadership, technology, contexts, gifted, second language teaching, work place and adult learning. *Unit head:* Dr. Charles F. Webber, Associate Dean, 403-220-5675, Fax: 403-282-3005, E-mail: cwebber@ucalgary.ca. *Application contact:* Patricia A. Brown, Program Officer, Graduate Division of Educational Research, 403-220-3178, Fax: 403-282-3005, E-mail: brownp@ucalgary.ca.

University of Central Florida, College of Education, Department of Teaching and Learning Principles, Program in Vocational Education, Orlando, FL 32816. Offers M Ed, MA. *Accreditation:* NCATE. Part-time and evening/weekend programs available. *Students:* 3 full-time (2 women), 11 part-time (7 women); includes 3 minority (1 African American, 2 Asian Americans or Pacific Islanders). Average age 40. In 2006, 2 degrees awarded. *Entrance requirements:* For master's, GRE General Test. Additional exam requirements/recommendations for international students: Required—TOEFL. *Application deadline:* For fall admission, 7/15 for domestic students; for spring admission, 12/1 for domestic students. Electronic applications accepted. *Expenses:* Tuition, state resident: full-time $6,167; part-time $257 per credit hour. Tuition, nonresident: full-time $22,790; part-time $950 per credit hour. *Financial support:* Fellowships with partial tuition reimbursements, research assistantships with partial tuition reimbursements, teaching assistantships with partial tuition reimbursements, career-related internships or fieldwork, Federal Work-Study, institutionally sponsored loans, tuition waivers (partial), and unspecified assistantships available. Financial award application deadline: 3/1; financial award applicants required to submit FAFSA. *Unit head:* Dr. JoAnn Whiteman, Coordinator, 386-506-4041, E-mail: jwhitema@mail.ucf.edu. *Application contact:* Dr. JoAnn Whiteman, Coordinator, 386-506-4041, E-mail: jwhitema@mail.ucf.edu.

University of Central Missouri, The Graduate School, College of Education, Department of Career and Technology Education, Warrensburg, MO 64093. Offers human services/ technology and occupational education (Ed S); secondary education/business and office education (MSE); technology and occupational education (MS). *Accreditation:* NCATE (one or more programs are accredited). Part-time programs available. *Faculty:* 19 full-time (11 women). *Students:* 5 full-time (3 women), 34 part-time (17 women); includes 5 minority (2 African Americans, 1 Asian American or Pacific Islander, 2 Hispanic Americans), 2 international. Average age 39. 10 applicants. In 2006, 16 master's, 5 other advanced degrees awarded. *Degree requirements:* For master's, comprehensive exam (MS), comprehensive exam or thesis (MSE); for Ed S, thesis, comprehensive exam. *Entrance requirements:* For master's, GRE General Test (MSE), minimum GPA of 2.5 (MS); minimum GPA of 2.75, teaching certificate (MSE); for Ed S, GRE General Test, minimum graduate GPA of 3.25, teaching certificate. Additional exam requirements/recommendations for international students: Required—TOEFL (minimum score 500 paper-based; 173 computer-based). *Application deadline:* For fall admission, 6/1 priority date for domestic students, 5/1 priority date for international students; for spring admission, 10/1 priority date for domestic students, 10/1 for international students. Applications are processed on a rolling basis. Application fee: $30 ($50 for international students). *Expenses:* Tuition, state resident: full-time $5,448; part-time $227 per credit hour. Tuition, nonresident: full-time $10,896; part-time $454 per credit hour. Required fees: $336; $14 per credit hour. *Financial support:* In 2006–07, 2 students received support; teaching assistantships with full and partial tuition reimbursements available, Federal Work-Study, scholarships/grants, unspecified assistantships, and administrative and laboratory assistantships available. Support available to part-time students. Financial award application deadline: 3/1; financial award applicants required to submit FAFSA. *Unit head:* Richard Kahoe, Chair, 660-543-4452, Fax: 660-543-8753, E-mail: kahoe@ucmo.edu.

University of Georgia, Graduate School, College of Education, Department of Workforce Education, Leadership and Social Foundations, Athens, GA 30602. Offers M Ed, MA, MAT, Ed D, PhD, Ed S. *Accreditation:* NCATE. *Faculty:* 19 full-time (10 women). *Students:* 45 full-time (27 women), 181 part-time (109 women); includes 37 minority (34 African Americans, 1 American Indian/Alaska Native, 1 Asian American or Pacific Islander, 1 Hispanic American), 5 international. 139 applicants, 72% accepted, 62 enrolled. In 2006, 52 master's, 18 doctorates, 7 other advanced degrees awarded. *Entrance requirements:* For master's, GRE General Test, MAT; for doctorate, GRE General Test; for Ed S, GRE General Test or MAT. *Application deadline:* For fall admission, 7/1 priority date for domestic students; for spring admission, 11/15 for domestic students. Application fee: $50. Electronic applications accepted. *Financial support:* Fellowships, research assistantships, teaching assistantships, unspecified assistantships available. *Unit head:* Dr. Roger B. Hill, Head, 706-542-4100, Fax: 706-542-4054, E-mail: rbhill@uga.edu. *Application contact:* Dr. Mura N. Womble, Graduate Coordinator, 706-542-4503, Fax: 706-542-4054, E-mail: mwomble@uga.edu.

University of Idaho, College of Graduate Studies, College of Education, Department of Adult, Career, and Technology Education, Program in Professional-Technical and Technology Education, Moscow, ID 83844-2282. Offers M Ed, MS, Ed Sp PTE. *Accreditation:* NCATE. *Students:* 22. Average age 37. In 2006, 14 master's, 2 other advanced degrees awarded. *Entrance requirements:* For master's, minimum GPA of 2.8. *Application deadline:* For fall admission, 8/1 for domestic students; for spring admission, 12/15 for domestic students. Application fee: $55 ($60 for international students). *Expenses:* Tuition, nonresident: full-time $9,600; part-time $140 per credit. Required fees: $4,740; $227 per credit. *Financial support:* Application deadline: 2/15. *Unit head:* Dr. James A. Gregson, Head, Department of Adult, Career, and Technology Education, 208-885-2768.

University of Idaho, College of Graduate Studies, College of Education, Doctoral Programs in Education, Moscow, ID 83844-2282. Offers adult and organizational learning (Ed D, PhD); counseliing and human services (PhD); counseling and human services (Ed D); curriculum and intstruction (Ed D); curriculum and instruction (PhD); educational leadership (Ed D, PhD); physical education (PhD); professional-technical and technology education (PhD); professional-technical and tecnology education (Ed D). *Students:* 208 (118 women). In 2006, 50 degrees awarded. *Expenses:* Tuition, nonresident: full-time $9,600; part-time $140 per credit. Required fees: $4,740; S227 per credit. *Application contact:* Shirley Green, Information Contact, 208-885-6773.

University of Illinois at Urbana–Champaign, Graduate College, College of Education, Department of Human Resource Education, Champaign, IL 61820. Offers Ed M, MA, MS, Ed D, PhD, CAS, MBA/M Ed. Part-time programs available. *Faculty:* 6 full-time (2 women), 3 part-time/ adjunct (0 women). *Students:* 51 full-time (34 women), 138 part-time (96 women); includes 37 minority (24 African Americans, 11 Asian Americans or Pacific Islanders, 2 Hispanic Americans), 28 international. 82 applicants, 71% accepted, 57 enrolled. In 2006, 58 master's, 7 doctorates, 2 other advanced degrees awarded. *Degree requirements:* For master's, thesis (for some programs); for doctorate, thesis/dissertation. *Application deadline:* For fall admission, 5/15 for domestic students; for spring admission, 10/16 for domestic students. Applications are processed on a rolling basis. Application fee: $50 ($60 for international students). Electronic applications accepted. *Financial support:* In 2006–07, 2 fellowships, 10 research assistantships, 20 teaching assistantships were awarded; career-related internships or fieldwork and tuition waivers (full and partial) also available. Financial award application deadline: 2/15. *Unit head:* Scott D. Johnson, Interim Head, 217-333-0807, Fax: 217-244-5632, E-mail: sjohnson@uiuc.edu. *Application contact:* Laura Irle, Secretary, 217-333-0807, Fax: 217-244-5632, E-mail: lirle@uiuc.edu.

University of Kentucky, Graduate School, College of Agriculture, Program in Career, Technology and Leadership Education, Lexington, KY 40506-0032. Offers MS. *Accreditation:* NCATE. *Students:* 24 full-time (16 women), 50 part-time (28 women); includes 2 minority (both African Americans) Average age 31. In 2006, 26 degrees awarded. Terminal master's awarded for partial completion of doctoral program. *Degree requirements:* For master's, thesis optional. *Entrance requirements:* For master's, GRE General Test, minimum undergraduate GPA of 2.75. Additional exam requirements/recommendations for international students: Required—TOEFL (minimum score 550 paper-based; 213 computer-based). *Application deadline:* For fall admission, 7/17 priority date for domestic students, 2/1 priority date for international students; for spring admission, 12/13 priority date for domestic students, 6/15 priority date for international students. Application fee: $40 ($55 for international students). Electronic applications accepted. *Expenses:* Tuition, state resident: full-time $7,670; part-time $401 per credit hour. Tuition, nonresident: full-time $16,158; part-time $873 per credit hour. *Financial support:* In 2006–07, 4 fellowships with full tuition reimbursements, 16 research assistantships with full tuition reimbursements (averaging $14,000 per year), 16 teaching assistantships with full tuition reimbursements (averaging $10,500 per year) were awarded; career-related internships or fieldwork, Federal Work-Study, institutionally sponsored loans, scholarships/grants, traineeships, health care benefits, tuition waivers (partial), and unspecified assistantships also available. Support available to part-time students. Financial award application deadline: 3/15; financial award applicants required to submit FAFSA. *Unit head:* Dr. Randy Weckman, Director of Graduate Studies, 859-257-3937, Fax: 859-257-4354. *Application contact:* Dr. Brian Jackson, Senior Associate Dean, 859-257-4667, Fax: 859-257-4676, E-mail: brian.jackson@uky.edu.

University of Louisville, Graduate School, College of Education and Human Development, Department of Leadership, Foundations and Human Resource Education, Program in Occupational Training and Development, Louisville, KY 40292-0001. Offers M Ed. In 2006, 1 degree awarded. Application fee: $50. *Unit head:* Dr. Joe Petrosko, Chair, Department of Leadership, Foundations and Human Resource Education, 502-852-6667, Fax: 502-852-4563, E-mail: joseph.petrosko@louisville.edu.

University of Maryland Eastern Shore, Graduate Programs, Department of Technology, Princess Anne, MD 21853-1299. Offers career and technology education (M Ed). Part-time and evening/weekend programs available. *Faculty:* 1 full-time (0 women), 6 part-time/ adjunct (0 women). *Students:* 1 full-time (0 women), 17 part-time (5 women); includes 6 minority (4 African Americans, 1 American Indian/Alaska Native, 1 Asian American or Pacific Islander). Average age 38. In 2006, 19 degrees awarded. *Degree requirements:* For master's, seminar paper. *Entrance requirements:* For master's, PRAXIS, writing sample. Additional exam requirements/recommendations for international students: Required—TOEFL (minimum score 213 computer-based). *Application deadline:* For fall admission, 5/1 priority date for domestic and international students; for spring admission, 11/1 priority date for domestic and international students. Applications are processed on a rolling basis. Application fee: $30. Electronic applications accepted. *Financial support:* In 2006–07, 8 students received support. Scholarships/grants available. Financial award application deadline: 3/1; financial award applicants required to submit FAFSA. *Faculty research:* Doppler Radar study. Total annual research expenditures: $23,640. *Unit head:* Dr. Leon Copeland, Chair, 410-651-6465, Fax: 410-651-7959. *Application contact:* Dr. Gerald Day, Coordinator, 410-659-5332, Fax: 410-685-0032, E-mail: gfday@umes.edu.

University of Minnesota, Twin Cities Campus, Graduate School, College of Education and Human Development, Department of Work and Human Resource Education, Minneapolis, MN 55455-0213. Offers adult education (M Ed, MA, Ed D, PhD, Certificate); agricultural, food and environmental education (M Ed, MA, Ed D, PhD); business and industry education (M Ed, MA, Ed D, PhD); business education (M Ed); human resource development (M Ed, MA, Ed D, PhD, Certificate); marketing education (M Ed); postsecondary administration (Ed D); school-to-work (Certificate); technical education (Certificate); technology education (M Ed, MA); work and human resource education (M Ed, MA, Ed D, PhD); youth development leadership (M Ed). *Faculty:* 10 full-time (3 women). *Students:* 160 full-time (98 women), 215 part-time (143 women); includes 42 minority (24 African Americans, 2 American Indian/Alaska Native, 10 Asian Americans or Pacific Islanders, 6 Hispanic Americans), 56 international. Average age 38. 168 applicants, 80% accepted, 104 enrolled. In 2006, 79 master's, 23 doctorates, 50 other advanced degrees awarded. *Expenses:* Tuition, state resident: full-time $9,302; part-time $775 per credit. Tuition, nonresident: full-time $16,400; part-time $1,367 per credit. Full-time tuition and fees vary according to class time, course load, program, reciprocity agreements and student level. *Financial support:* In 2006–07, 9 research assistantships with full tuition reimbursements (averaging $24,775 per year), 16 teaching assistantships with full tuition reimbursements (averaging $24,775 per year) were awarded; fellowships also available. *Faculty research:* Assessment of career and technical education; adult education literacy; international human resource development; technology education; education and leadership related to agriculture, food, and the environment. Total annual research expenditures: $2.1 million. *Unit head:* Ken Bartlett, Chair, 612-624-4935, Fax: 612-624-2231. *Application contact:* Dr. Mary Bents, Associate Dean, 612-625-6501, Fax: 612-626-1580, E-mail: mbents@tc.umn.edu.

University of Missouri–Columbia, Graduate School, College of Education, Department of Curriculum and Instruction, Columbia, MO 65211. Offers agricultural education (M Ed, PhD, Ed S); art education (M Ed, PhD, Ed S); business and office education (M Ed, PhD, Ed S); early childhood education (M Ed, PhD, Ed S); elementary education (M Ed, PhD, Ed S); English education (M Ed, PhD, Ed S); foreign language education (M Ed, PhD, Ed S); health education and promotion (M Ed, PhD); learning and instruction (M Ed); marketing education (M Ed, PhD, Ed S); mathematics education (M Ed, PhD, Ed S); music education (M Ed, PhD, Ed S); reading education (M Ed, PhD, Ed S); science education (M Ed, PhD, Ed S); social studies education (M Ed, PhD, Ed S); vocational education (M Ed, PhD, Ed S). Part-time programs available. *Faculty:* 24 full-time (12 women). *Students:* 195 full-time (148 women), 260 part-time (214 women); includes 27 minority (8 African Americans, 1 American Indian/Alaska Native, 10 Asian Americans or Pacific Islanders, 8 Hispanic Americans), 19 international. In 2006, 186 master's, 12 doctorates awarded. Terminal master's awarded for partial completion of doctoral program. *Degree requirements:* For doctorate, thesis/dissertation. *Entrance requirements:* For master's and Ed S, GRE General Test or MAT, minimum GPA of 3.0; for doctorate, GRE General Test, minimum GPA of 3.0. *Application deadline:* Applications are processed on a rolling basis. Application fee: $45 ($60 for international students). *Financial support:* Fellowships, research assistantships, teaching assistantships, institutionally sponsored loans available. *Unit head:* Dr. Lloyd H. Barrow, Director of Graduate Studies, 573-882-8247, E-mail: robinsonr@missouri.edu.

University of North Dakota, Graduate School, College of Business and Public Administration, Department of Career and Technical Education, Grand Forks, ND 58202. Offers MS. *Faculty:* 4 full-time (2 women). In 2006, 2 degrees awarded. *Entrance requirements:* For master's, minimum GPA of 3.0. Additional exam requirements/recommendations for international students: Required—TOEFL (minimum score 550 paper-based; 213 computer-based; 79 iBT), IELTS (minimum score 6). *Application deadline:* For fall admission, 2/15 priority date for domestic and international students; for spring admission, 10/15 priority date for domestic and international students. Applications are processed on a rolling basis. Application fee: $35. Electronic applications accepted. *Expenses:* Tuition, state resident: full-time $5,650; part-time $214 per credit. Tuition, nonresident: full-time $14,248; part-time $572 per credit. Required fees: $1,008; $42 per credit. Tuition and fees vary according to reciprocity agreements. *Unit head:* Dr. Sandra Braathen, Chair, 701-777-3507, E-mail: sandy.braathen@mail.business.und.edu. *Application contact:* Linda M. Baeza, Admissions Officer, 701-777-2945, Fax: 701-777-3619, E-mail: gradschool@mail.und.nodak.edu.

University of Northern Iowa, Graduate College, College of Natural Sciences, Department of Industrial Technology, Cedar Falls, IA 50614. Offers MA, PSM, DIT. *Students:* 9 full-time (1 woman), 13 part-time (2 women), 8 international. 9 applicants, 78% accepted, 7 enrolled. In 2006, 5 master's, 3 doctorates awarded. *Degree requirements:* For master's, thesis or alternative, comprehensive exam; for doctorate, thesis/dissertation. *Entrance requirements:* For master's and doctorate, GRE. Additional exam requirements/recommendations for international students: Required—TOEFL (minimum score 600 paper-based; 250 computer-based; 100 iBT). *Application deadline:* For fall admission, 8/1 priority date for domestic students. Applications are processed on a rolling basis. Application fee: $30 ($50 for international students). Electronic applications accepted. *Expenses:* Tuition, state resident: full-time $5,936. Tuition, nonresident: full-time $14,074. *Financial support:* Teaching assistantships, career-related internships or fieldwork, Federal Work-Study, scholarships/grants, and tuition waivers (full and partial) available. Support available to part-time students. Financial award application deadline: 2/1. *Unit head:* Dr. Mohammed Fahmy, Head, 319-273-2561, Fax: 319-273-5818, E-mail: mohammed.fahmy@uni.edu.

University of North Texas, Robert B. Toulouse School of Graduate Studies, College of Education, Department of Technology and Cognition, Program in Applied Technology, Training and Development, Denton, TX 76203. Offers M Ed, MS, Ed D, PhD. *Accreditation:* NCATE. *Students:* 15 full-time (10 women), 52 part-time (30 women); includes 19 minority (12 African Americans, 4 Asian Americans or Pacific Islanders, 3 Hispanic Americans), 1 international. Average age 41. 22 applicants, 45% accepted, 7 enrolled. In 2006, 2 master's, 2 doctorates awarded. *Degree requirements:* For doctorate, one foreign language, thesis/dissertation, internship. *Entrance requirements:* For master's, GRE General Test; for doctorate, GRE General Test, admissions exam. Additional exam requirements/recommendations for international students: Recommended—TOEFL (minimum score 550 paper-based; 213 computer-based). *Application deadline:* For fall admission, 7/15 for domestic students. Application fee: $50 ($75 for international students). *Expenses:* Tuition, state resident: full-time $3,573; part-time $198 per credit. Tuition, nonresident: full-time $8,577; part-time $476 per credit. Required fees: $1,258; $126 per credit. One-time fee: $150 full-time. Tuition and fees vary according to course load. *Financial support:* Fellowships, research assistantships, teaching assistantships, career-related internships or fieldwork, Federal Work-Study, and institutionally sponsored loans available. Financial award application deadline: 4/1. *Unit head:* Dr. Jeff Allen, Head, 940-565-2093, Fax: 940-565-2185, E-mail: jallen@unt.edu.

University of South Carolina, The Graduate School, College of Education, Department of Educational Leadership and Policies, Columbia, SC 29208. Offers community and adult education (M Ed); curriculum and instruction (Ed D); educational administration (M Ed, MA, PhD, Ed S); higher education and student affairs (M Ed); higher education leadership (Certificate). *Accreditation:* NCATE. Part-time and evening/weekend programs available. Terminal master's awarded for partial completion of doctoral program. *Degree requirements:* For master's, foreign language (MA); for doctorate, one foreign language, thesis/dissertation, comprehensive exam. *Entrance requirements:* For master's and other advanced degree, GRE General Test or MAT; for doctorate, GRE General Test or MAT, interview. Electronic applications accepted.

University of Southern Maine, College of Education and Human Development, Program in Industrial/Technology Education, Portland, ME 04104-9300. Offers MS Ed. *Accreditation:* NCATE. Part-time and evening/weekend programs available. Postbaccalaureate distance learning degree programs offered. *Faculty:* 1 full-time (0 women). *Degree requirements:* For master's, thesis or alternative, practicum. *Application deadline:* For fall admission, 2/1 for domestic students. Application fee: $50. Electronic applications accepted. *Expenses:* Tuition, state resident: full-time $4,860; part-time $270 per credit hour. Tuition, nonresident: full-time $13,572; part-time $754 per credit hour. Required fees: $222 per semester. Tuition and fees vary according to course load. *Financial support:* Career-related internships or fieldwork, Federal Work-Study, institutionally sponsored loans, and unspecified assistantships available. Financial award application deadline: 3/1; financial award applicants required to submit FAFSA. *Unit head:* Dr. Robert Nannay, Coordinator, Technology Education, 207-780-5450. *Application contact:* Robin Audesse, Associate Director of Graduate Admissions, 207-780-5306, Fax: 207-780-5193, E-mail: raudesse@usm.maine.edu.

University of Southern Mississippi, Graduate School, College of Education and Psychology, Department of Technology Education, Hattiesburg, MS 39406-0001. Offers business technology education (MS); instructional technology (MS); technical occupational education (MS).

Part-time programs available. *Faculty:* 8 full-time (5 women). *Students:* 1 (woman) full-time, 26 part-time (18 women); includes 6 minority (5 African Americans, 1 Hispanic American), 1 international. Average age 38. 15 applicants, 13% accepted, 2 enrolled. In 2006, 21 degrees awarded. *Degree requirements:* For master's, thesis (for some programs), comprehensive exam, registration. *Entrance requirements:* For master's, GRE General Test, MAT, minimum GPA of 2.75 in last 60 hours. Additional exam requirements/recommendations for international students: Required—TOEFL. *Application deadline:* For fall admission, 3/1 priority date for domestic students, 3/1 for international students. Applications are processed on a rolling basis. Application fee: $25 ($30 for international students). *Financial support:* In 2006–07, 2 teaching assistantships with tuition reimbursements (averaging $6,500 per year) were awarded; research assistantships, Federal Work-Study also available. Financial award application deadline: 3/15. *Faculty research:* Occupational competency, professional development for vocational-technical. Total annual research expenditures: $166,068. *Unit head:* Dr. Edward C. Mann, Chair, 601-266-4446, Fax: 601-266-5957, E-mail: edward.mann@usm.edu.

University of South Florida, Graduate School, College of Education, Department of Adult, Career and Higher Education, Tampa, FL 33620-9951. Offers adult education (MA, Ed D, PhD, Ed S); career and technical education (MA); higher education/community college teaching (MA, PhD, Ed S); industrial-technical education (MA); vocational education (Ed D, PhD, Ed S). *Faculty:* 11 full-time (5 women), 2 part-time/adjunct (0 women). *Students:* 30 full-time (23 women), 176 part-time (121 women); includes 52 minority (32 African Americans, 1 American Indian/Alaska Native, 1 Asian American or Pacific Islander, 18 Hispanic Americans), 4 international. 104 applicants, 71% accepted, 55 enrolled. In 2006, 56 master's, 5 doctorates awarded. *Entrance requirements:* For master's, GRE General Test, minimum GPA of 3.0 in last 60 hours. *Application deadline:* For fall admission, 6/1 for domestic students; for spring admission, 10/15 for domestic students. Application fee: $30. *Financial support:* Career-related internships or fieldwork, scholarships/grants, and unspecified assistantships available. Total annual research expenditures: $191,880. *Unit head:* Robert Sullins, Interim Dean, E-mail: rsullins@ugs.usf.edu.

The University of Texas at Tyler, Graduate Studies, College of Business and Technology, Department of Human Resource Development and Technology, Tyler, TX 75799-0001. Offers human resource development (MS); industrial distribution (MS); industrial safety (MS); industrial technology (MS); instructional technology (MS); technology systems (MS). Part-time and evening/weekend programs available. Postbaccalaureate distance learning degree programs offered (no on-campus study). *Degree requirements:* For master's, comprehensive exam. *Entrance requirements:* For master's, GRE General Test or MAT. Additional exam requirements/recommendations for international students: Required—TOEFL. Electronic applications accepted. *Expenses:* Tuition, state resident: part-time $50 per credit hour. Tuition, nonresident: part-time $328 per credit hour. Required fees: $107 per credit hour. $426 per term. *Faculty research:* Human resource development.

The University of Toledo, College of Graduate Studies, College of Education, Department of Curriculum and Instruction, Program in Career and Technical Education, Toledo, OH 43606-3390. Offers Ed S. *Students:* 6 full-time (3 women), 17 part-time (12 women); includes 4 minority (2 African Americans, 1 American Indian/Alaska Native, 1 Hispanic American). Average age 36.

The University of Toledo, College of Graduate Studies, College of Education, Department of Educational Leadership, Program in Career and Technical Training, Toledo, OH 43606-3390. Offers ME. *Students:* 6 full-time (3 women), 17 part-time (12 women); includes 4 minority (2 African Americans, 1 American Indian/Alaska Native, 1 Hispanic American). 5 applicants, 80% accepted, 4 enrolled. In 2006, 6 degrees awarded. *Application contact:* Doctoral Program Director, 419-530-2461, Fax: 419-530-4912, E-mail: edleadr@utnet.utoledo.edu.

University of Victoria, Faculty of Graduate Studies, Faculty of Education, Department of Curriculum and Instruction, Victoria, BC V8W 2Y2, Canada. Offers art (M Ed, MA, PhD); curriculum studies (M Ed, MA, PhD); early childhood (M Ed, MA, PhD); language and literacy (M Ed, MA, PhD); mathematics (M Ed, MA, PhD); music (M Ed, MA); music education (PhD); science (M Ed, MA, PhD); social studies (M Ed, MA); social, cultural and foundational studies (PhD); technology and environmental education (PhD). Part-time programs available. *Degree requirements:* For master's, thesis, project (M Ed); for doctorate, thesis/dissertation, comprehensive exam, registration. *Entrance requirements:* For master's, minimum B average. Additional exam requirements/recommendations for international students: Required—TOEFL (minimum score 575 paper-based; 233 computer-based), IELTS (minimum score 7). Electronic applications accepted. *Faculty research:* Elementary and secondary English, language arts, curriculum theory and practice, educational media and technology, educational administration and leadership, history and philosophy of education.

University of West Florida, College of Professional Studies, Division of Teacher Education, Master's Program in Curriculum and Instruction, Specialization in Career and Technical Studies, Pensacola, FL 32514-5750. Offers M Ed. *Accreditation:* NCATE. Part-time and evening/weekend programs available. *Students:* Average age 47. 2 applicants, 100% accepted, 2 enrolled. In 2006, 1 degree awarded. *Entrance requirements:* For master's, GRE General Test or minimum GPA of 3.0. Additional exam requirements/recommendations for international students: Required—TOEFL (minimum score 550 paper-based; 213 computer-based). *Application deadline:* For fall admission, 6/1 for domestic students, 5/15 for international students; for spring admission, 11/1 for domestic students, 10/1 for international students. Applications are processed on a rolling basis. Application fee: $30. *Expenses:* Tuition, state resident: full-time $5,871; part-time $245 per credit hour. Tuition, nonresident: full-time $21,241; part-time $885 per credit hour. *Financial support:* Fellowships, career-related internships or fieldwork available. *Faculty research:* Dropout prevention, technology/educational enhancement.

University of Wisconsin–Platteville, School of Graduate Studies, College of Liberal Arts and Education, School of Education, Platteville, WI 53818-3099. Offers adult education (MSE); elementary education (MSE); middle school education (MSE); secondary education (MSE); vocational and technical education (MSE). *Accreditation:* NCATE. Part-time programs available. *Faculty:* 8 part-time/adjunct (3 women). *Students:* 48 full-time (37 women), 103 part-time (72 women); includes 33 minority (27 African Americans, 1 Asian American or Pacific Islander, 5 Hispanic Americans), 39 international. 39 applicants, 72% accepted. In 2006, 55 degrees awarded. *Degree requirements:* For master's, thesis or alternative, comprehensive exam, registration. *Entrance requirements:* Additional exam requirements/recommendations for international students: Required—TOEFL (minimum score 500 paper-based; 173 computer-based). *Application deadline:* For fall admission, 7/1 priority date for domestic students; for spring admission, 11/1 for domestic students. Applications are processed on a rolling basis. Application fee: $45. Electronic applications accepted. *Expenses:* Tuition, state resident: part-time $365 per credit. Tuition, nonresident: part-time $955 per credit. *Financial support:* Research assistantships with partial tuition reimbursements, career-related internships or fieldwork, Federal Work-Study, institutionally sponsored loans, scholarships/grants, and unspecified assistantships available. Support available to part-time students. *Unit head:* Dr. Michael Anderson, Director, 608-342-1131, Fax: 608-342-1133, E-mail: andersonmi@uwplatt.edu. *Application contact:* Kristal Prohaska, Admissions and Enrollment Management, 608-342-1125, Fax: 608-342-1122, E-mail: admit@uwplatt.edu.

University of Wisconsin–Stout, Graduate School, School of Education, Program in Career and Technical Education, Menomonie, WI 54751. Offers MS, Ed S. Part-time programs available. *Faculty:* 28 full-time (13 women). *Students:* 5 full-time (2 women), 50 part-time (31 women); includes 4 minority (all African Americans), 1 international. Average age 40. 33 applicants, 91% accepted, 8 enrolled. In 2006, 19 master's, 4 Ed Ss awarded. *Degree requirements:* For master's and Ed S, thesis. *Entrance requirements:* For master's, minimum GPA of 2.75; for Ed S, minimum GPA of 3.25. Additional exam requirements/recommendations for international students: Required—TOEFL (minimum score 500 paper-based; 173 computer-based; 61 iBT). *Application deadline:* Applications are processed on a rolling basis. Application fee: $45. Electronic applications accepted. *Expenses:* Tuition, state resident: part-time

Vocational and Technical Education

University of Wisconsin–Stout (continued)
$317 per credit. Tuition, nonresident: part-time $543 per credit. Tuition and fees vary according to reciprocity agreements. *Financial support:* In 2006–07, 1 research assistantship with partial tuition reimbursement (averaging $6,518 per year) was awarded; Federal Work-Study, scholarships/grants, health care benefits, tuition waivers (full and partial), and unspecified assistantships also available. Support available to part-time students. Financial award application deadline: 4/1; financial award applicants required to submit FAFSA. *Faculty research:* Needs assessment, task analysis, instructional development, learning technologies. *Unit head:* Dr. Howard Lee, Director, 715-232-1251, E-mail: leeh@uwstout.edu. *Application contact:* Anne E. Johnson, Graduate Student Evaluator, 715-232-1322, Fax: 715-232-2413, E-mail: johnsona@uwstout.edu.

University of Wisconsin–Stout, Graduate School, School of Education, Program in Industrial/Technology Education, Menomonie, WI 54751. Offers MS. Part-time programs available. *Faculty:* 12 full-time (2 women). *Students:* Average age 28. 3 applicants, 67% accepted, 0 enrolled. In 2006, 4 degrees awarded. *Degree requirements:* For master's, thesis. *Entrance requirements:* For master's, minimum GPA of 2.75. Additional exam requirements/recommendations for international students: Required—TOEFL (minimum score 500 paper-based; 173 computer-based; 61 iBT). *Application deadline:* Applications are processed on a rolling basis. Application fee: $45. Electronic applications accepted. *Expenses:* Tuition, state resident: part-time $317 per credit. Tuition, nonresident: part-time $543 per credit. Tuition and fees vary according to reciprocity agreements. *Financial support:* In 2006–07, 1 research assistantship with partial tuition reimbursement (averaging $2,459 per year) was awarded; Federal Work-Study, scholarships/grants, health care benefits, tuition waivers (full and partial), and unspecified assistantships also available. Support available to part-time students. Financial award application deadline: 4/1; financial award applicants required to submit FAFSA. *Faculty research:* Gender equity, instructional design, cognitive processes, socio-cultural impacts. *Unit head:* Dr. Brian McAlister, Director, 715-232-5609, E-mail: mcalisterb@uwstout.edu. *Application contact:* Anne E. Johnson, Graduate Student Evaluator, 715-232-1322, Fax: 715-232-2413, E-mail: johnsona@uwstout.edu.

Utah State University, School of Graduate Studies, College of Engineering, Department of Engineering and Technology Education, Logan, UT 84322. Offers industrial technology (MS). Part-time and evening/weekend programs available. *Faculty:* 6 full-time (0 women), 2 part-time/adjunct (0 women). *Students:* 5 full-time (1 woman), 4 part-time; includes 1 minority (Hispanic American) Average age 31. 14 applicants, 79% accepted, 9 enrolled. In 2006, 4 degrees awarded. *Degree requirements:* For master's, thesis optional. *Entrance requirements:* For master's, GRE General Test, MAT, minimum GPA of 3.0 in last 30 hours of course work. Additional exam requirements/recommendations for international students: Required—TOEFL. *Application deadline:* For fall admission, 6/15 priority date for domestic students; for spring admission, 10/15 for domestic students. Applications are processed on a rolling basis. Application fee: $50 ($60 for international students). *Financial support:* In 2006–07, 1 teaching assistantship with partial tuition reimbursement was awarded; fellowships, research assistantships with partial tuition reimbursements, career-related internships or fieldwork, institutionally sponsored loans, and tuition waivers (partial) also available. *Faculty research:* Computer-aided design drafting, technology and the public school, materials, electronics, aviation. Total annual research expenditures: $500,000. *Unit head:* Kurt H. Becker, Head, 435-797-1795, Fax: 435-797-2567, E-mail: kbecker@cc.usu.edu. *Application contact:* Dr. Edward M. Reeve, Information Contact, 435-797-3642, Fax: 435-797-2567, E-mail: fast@cc.usu.edu.

Valdosta State University, Graduate School, College of Education, Department of Adult and Career Education, Valdosta, GA 31698. Offers adult and career education (M Ed, Ed D); business education (M Ed). *Accreditation:* NCATE. Evening/weekend programs available. *Degree requirements:* For master's, portfolio; for doctorate, thesis/dissertation, comprehensive written and/or oral exams. *Entrance requirements:* For master's, GRE General Test or MAT, minimum GPA of 2.5; for doctorate, GRE General Test, minimum GPA of 3.5, 3 years of experience. Additional exam requirements/recommendations for international students: Required—TOEFL (minimum score 523 paper-based; 193 computer-based). Electronic applications accepted.

Virginia Polytechnic Institute and State University, Graduate School, College of Liberal Arts and Human Sciences, School of Education, Program in Career and Technical Education, Blacksburg, VA 24061. Offers MS Ed, Ed D, PhD, Ed S. *Expenses:* Tuition, state resident: full-time $7,017; part-time $390 per credit hour. Tuition, nonresident: full-time $12,414; part-time $690 per credit hour. International tuition: $11,296 full-time. Required fees: $1,523; $256 per term.

Virginia State University, School of Graduate Studies, Research, and Outreach, School of Liberal Arts and Education, Department of Educational Leadership and Administrative Systems Management, Program in Vocational Technical Education, Petersburg, VA 23806-0001. Offers M Ed, MS, CAGS. *Degree requirements:* For master's, thesis (for some programs).

Wayne State College, School of Education and Counseling, Department of Educational Foundations and Leadership, Program in Curriculum and Instruction, Wayne, NE 68787. Offers alternative education (MSE); business education (MSE); communication arts education (MSE); curriculum and instruction (MSE); early childhood education (MSE); elementary education (MSE); English as a second language (MSE); English education (MSE); family consumer science of education (MSE); industrial technology education (MSE); learning communities (MSE); mathematics education (MSE); music education (MSE); science education (MSE); social science education (MSE). *Accreditation:* NCATE. Part-time and evening/weekend programs available. *Faculty:* 17 part-time/adjunct (11 women). *Students:* 17 full-time (10 women), 307 part-time (248 women); includes 6 minority (2 African Americans, 1 American Indian/Alaska Native, 2 Asian Americans or Pacific Islanders, 1 Hispanic American), 1 international. Average age 35. In 2006, 167 degrees awarded. *Degree requirements:* For master's, thesis optional. *Entrance requirements:* For master's, GRE General Test. Additional exam requirements/recommendations for international students: Required—TOEFL (minimum score 550 paper-based; 213 computer-based). *Application deadline:* Applications are processed on a rolling basis. Application fee: $30. *Expenses:* Tuition, state resident: full-time $3,114; part-time $130 per credit hour. Tuition, nonresident: full-time $6,228; part-time $260 per credit hour. Required fees: $894; $37 per credit hour. Tuition and fees vary according to course load. *Financial support:* Applicants required to submit FAFSA.

Wayne State University, College of Education, Division of Teacher Education, Detroit, MI 48202. Offers adult and continuing education (M Ed); art education (M Ed); bilingual/bicultural education (M Ed, MAT); business education (M Ed, MAT); career and technical education (M Ed, Ed D, PhD, Ed S); curriculum and instruction (Ed D, PhD, Ed S); distributive education (M Ed, MAT); early childhood education (M Ed); elementary education (M Ed, MAT, Ed D, PhD, Ed S); elementary education curriculum and instruction (M Ed); English education (M Ed); English education-secondary (M Ed, Ed S); foreign language education (M Ed); general education (Ed D, Ed S); health occupations education (M Ed); industrial education (M Ed); mathematics education (M Ed, Ed S); pre-school and parent education (M Ed); reading (M Ed, Ed D, Ed S); reading, languages and literature (Ed D); school music-vocal (M Ed); science education (M Ed, MAT, Ed S); secondary education (MAT); secondary school reading (M Ed); social studies education (M Ed, Ed S), including education-secondary (M Ed); special education (M Ed, Ed D, PhD, Ed S); teacher education (MAT, Ed D, PhD). *Faculty:* 41 full-time (22 women), 2 part-time/adjunct (both women). *Students:* 401 full-time (295 women), 1,021 part-time (784 women); includes 527 minority (452 African Americans, 6 American Indian/Alaska Native, 32 Asian Americans or Pacific Islanders, 37 Hispanic Americans), 18 international. Average age 36. 296 applicants, 81% accepted, 132 enrolled. In 2006, 386 master's, 1 doctorate awarded. *Degree requirements:* For doctorate, thesis/dissertation. *Entrance requirements:* For master's, minimum GPA of 2.6; for doctorate, minimum undergraduate GPA of 3.0, graduate 3.5; interview. Additional exam requirements/recommendations for international students: Required—TOEFL (minimum score 550 paper-based; 213 computer-based), TWE (minimum score 6). *Application deadline:* For fall admission, 7/1 for domestic students, 6/1 for international students; for winter admission, 10/1 for international students; for spring admission, 2/1 for international students. Application fee: $30 ($50 for international students). Electronic applications accepted. *Financial support:* In 2006–07, 1 fellowship (averaging $34,919 per year) was awarded; research assistantships. *Faculty research:* Reading and writing literacy and literature. Total annual research expenditures: $209,400. *Unit head:* Dr. Joann Snyder, Academic Director, 313-577-1644, E-mail: joanne.snyder@wayne.edu. *Application contact:* Sharon Elliott, Assistant Dean, 313-577-0902, E-mail: sharon.elliott@wayne.edu.

Western Michigan University, Graduate College, College of Education, Department of Family and Consumer Sciences, Program in Career and Technical Education, Kalamazoo, MI 49008-5202. Offers MA. *Accreditation:* NCATE.

Westfield State College, Division of Graduate and Continuing Education, Department of Education, Program in Occupational Education, Westfield, MA 01086. Offers M Ed, CAGS. *Accreditation:* NCATE. Part-time and evening/weekend programs available. *Degree requirements:* For master's, comprehensive exam. *Entrance requirements:* For master's, GRE General Test or MAT, minimum undergraduate GPA of 2.7.

West Virginia University, College of Human Resources and Education, Department of Technology, Learning and Culture, Program in Technology Education, Morgantown, WV 26506. Offers information and communication systems (MA); instructional design and technology (MA); professional development (MA); technology and society (MA). *Accreditation:* NCATE. *Students:* 23 full-time (15 women), 27 part-time (16 women); includes 6 minority (3 African Americans, 3 Asian Americans or Pacific Islanders), 16 international. Average age 40. 22 applicants, 68% accepted, 9 enrolled. In 2006, 6 master's awarded. *Degree requirements:* For master's, thesis. *Entrance requirements:* For master's, GRE General Test, minimum GPA of 2.5. Additional exam requirements/recommendations for international students: Required—TOEFL. *Application deadline:* Applications are processed on a rolling basis. Application fee: $50. *Expenses:* Tuition, state resident: full-time $4,926; part-time $276 per credit hour. Tuition, nonresident: full-time $14,278; part-time $796 per credit hour. Tuition and fees vary according to program. *Financial support:* In 2006–07, 35 students received support, including 2 research assistantships with full tuition reimbursements available (averaging $14,400 per year); teaching assistantships, career-related internships or fieldwork, Federal Work-Study, institutionally sponsored loans, and tuition waivers (full and partial) also available. Financial award application deadline: 2/1; financial award applicants required to submit FAFSA. *Faculty research:* Appropriate technology, alternative energy, computer applications for education and training, telecommunication, professional development. Total annual research expenditures: $73,822. *Unit head:* Dr. Daniel Hursh, Chairperson, Department of Technology, Learning and Culture, 304-293-2076, Fax: 304-293-9424, E-mail: dan.hursh@mail.wvu.edu.

Wilmington College, Division of Education, New Castle, DE 19720-6491. Offers applied education technology (M Ed); career and technical education (M Ed); elementary and secondary school counseling (M Ed); elementary special education (M Ed); elementary studies (M Ed); instruction: gifted and talented (M Ed); instruction: teaching and learning (M Ed); literacy (M Ed); reading (M Ed); school leadership (M Ed); secondary teaching (MAT). Part-time and evening/weekend programs available. *Faculty:* 7 full-time (4 women). *Students:* 609 full-time (447 women), 1,350 part-time (1,013 women); includes 144 minority (131 African Americans, 3 American Indian/Alaska Native, 1 Asian American or Pacific Islander, 9 Hispanic Americans). Average age 34. 818 applicants, 100% accepted, 599 enrolled. In 2006, 737 degrees awarded. *Entrance requirements:* For master's, 2 letters of recommendation, interview. Additional exam requirements/recommendations for international students: Required—TOEFL (minimum score 500 paper-based; 173 computer-based). *Application deadline:* For fall admission, 4/30 for domestic students. Applications are processed on a rolling basis. Application fee: $25. *Financial support:* Applicants required to submit FAFSA. *Unit head:* Dr. Richard Gochnauer, Chair, 302-328-6795 Ext. 163, Fax: 302-328-7081. *Application contact:* Chris Ferguson, Director of Admissions and Financial Aid, 302-328-9407 Ext. 256, Fax: 302-328-5164, E-mail: inquire@wilmcoll.edu.

Wright State University, School of Graduate Studies, College of Education and Human Services, Department of Educational Leadership, Programs in Educational Leadership, Dayton, OH 45435. Offers curriculum and instruction: teacher leader (MA); educational administrative specialist: teacher leader (M Ed); educational administrative specialist: vocational education administration (M Ed, MA); student affairs in higher education-administration (M Ed, MA). *Accreditation:* NCATE. *Students:* 26 full-time (22 women), 430 part-time (344 women); includes 10 minority (8 African Americans, 1 American Indian/Alaska Native, 1 Hispanic American), 1 international. Average age 33. 179 applicants, 97% accepted. In 2006, 211 degrees awarded. *Degree requirements:* For master's, thesis (for some programs). *Entrance requirements:* For master's, GRE General Test, MAT. Additional exam requirements/recommendations for international students: Required—TOEFL. Application fee: $25. *Financial support:* Available to part-time students. Applicants required to submit FAFSA. *Unit head:* Dr. Charles W. Ryan, Director and Director of Graduate Programs in Education, 937-775-3286, Fax: 937-775-2405, E-mail: charles.ryan@wright.edu. *Application contact:* John Kimble, Associate Director of Graduate Admissions and Records, 937-775-2957, Fax: 937-775-2453, E-mail: john.kimble@wright.edu.

Wright State University, School of Graduate Studies, College of Education and Human Services, Department of Teacher Education, Programs in Workforce Education, Dayton, OH 45435. Offers career, technology and vocational education (M Ed, MA); computer/technology education (M Ed, MA); library/media (M Ed, MA); vocational education (M Ed, MA). *Accreditation:* NCATE. *Students:* 5 full-time (3 women), 30 part-time (27 women), 1 international. 17 applicants, 94% accepted. In 2006, 14 degrees awarded. *Degree requirements:* For master's, thesis (for some programs). *Entrance requirements:* For master's, GRE General Test, MAT. Additional exam requirements/recommendations for international students: Required—TOEFL. Application fee: $25. *Financial support:* Available to part-time students. Applicants required to submit FAFSA. *Unit head:* Dr. Stephanie Davis, Associate Dean and Program Advisor, 937-775-2880, Fax: 937-775-3308, E-mail: stephanie.davis@wright.edu. *Application contact:* John Kimble, Associate Director of Graduate Admissions and Records, 937-775-2957, Fax: 937-775-2453, E-mail: john.kimble@wright.edu.

AGNES SCOTT COLLEGE
THE WORLD FOR WOMEN

AGNES SCOTT COLLEGE

Graduate Studies
Master of Arts in Teaching Secondary English

Programs of Study	Agnes Scott College has been preparing teachers through undergraduate elective courses and student-teaching opportunities since 1906. Since 1992, the College has also offered a Master of Arts in Teaching Secondary English program. It is open to men and women with strong academic qualifications who seek certification to teach and who want the benefits of small classes, choice student-teaching placements, and an academic environment that is purposeful yet personal.
	The M.A.T. Secondary English program is a twelve-month course of study that leads to a master's degree and certification for teaching secondary English. The program consists of a three-semester curriculum of English literature and language courses as well as courses and field experience in education. Special features include an emphasis on gender equity, graduate seminars, and a Writing Teachers' Workshop.
Research Facilities	McCain Library has been completely renovated and doubled in size, and access to the Internet is available at every seat. The library contains 221,991 volumes, 18,867 audiovisual items, and 33,125 microforms and receives 15,049 print and electronic periodicals. It also provides a home for the Center for Writing and Speaking. The library holds several noteworthy collections of rare books and manuscripts, including one of the leading Robert Frost collections and the papers of alumna Catherine Marshall LeSourd. Agnes Scott's reciprocal library service gives students direct access to the libraries of eighteen other institutions in the Atlanta-Athens area. Extensive electronic resources are available through the GALILEO project of the University System of Georgia.
Financial Aid	Students studying in the M.A.T. Secondary English program are eligible to receive Federal Stafford Student Loans, GradPLUS, and private student loans. College-administered financial aid is not available for graduate students. Federal loan limits for M.A.T. students are $8500 in subsidized Stafford loans and $12,000 in additional unsubsidized Stafford loans. A student may apply for the GradPLUS loan or a private student loan to cover the remaining cost of education, including living expenses. The Agnes Scott Office of Financial Aid can provide students with information on the amount of eligibility as well as application information.
	M.A.T. students who are Georgia residents may also qualify for the Georgia HOPE Teacher Scholarship Loan Program, which provides loans to students getting a master's degree for teaching in a critical shortage field. The loans are forgiven by teaching in Georgia public school classrooms. Students can apply for these loans online at http://www.GACollege411.org.
Cost of Study	Tuition for the M.A.T. program in 2007–08 is $455 per credit hour. In addition, there are a student activity fee of $175 and a technology fee of $200. The student health insurance fee of $412 is waived if a student has proof of health insurance.
Living and Housing Costs	Two-bedroom apartments are available within walking distance of the campus for $800 to $900 per month. The estimated cost of utilities is $100 to $150 per month.
Student Group	In 2006–07, there were 26 students in the M.A.T. Secondary English program. Students enter the program with a Bachelor of Arts degree or significant preparation in English.
Student Outcomes	The Master of Arts in Teaching Secondary English program has been offered since 1992 and has 182 graduates. The placement rate for graduates seeking teaching positions is 99 percent. Graduates now teach at high schools throughout metro Atlanta.
Location	Agnes Scott's 100-acre wooded campus is located in metropolitan Atlanta and the historic residential community of Decatur. Downtown Atlanta is 6 miles away and is accessible by a rapid-transit rail station two blocks from the campus. Atlanta offers a multitude of opportunities for personal contact with most of the world's cultures and offers entertainment that ranges from rock concerts to the Atlanta Symphony, from local theater to touring Broadway shows, and from recreational parks to major league sports and the world's largest aquarium. It is also home to a presidential library, the High Museum of Art, and eighteen other colleges and universities.
The College and The Program	Agnes Scott has approximately 1,000 undergraduate and graduate students who come from forty states and thirty countries, with 33 percent of the students representing diverse ethnic or cultural backgrounds. Students describe the College as a place where "everyone is working toward something" and where students are challenged by a rigorous academic environment but supported by faculty members who take a personal interest in their success.
	One graduate of the M.A.T. Secondary English program said that Agnes Scott's challenging yet encouraging atmosphere "gives you the formula to find your voice." (Sylvia Martinez '98). Another said that "at Agnes Scott, I acquired the attitude of the 'assumed pursuit of excellence.'"(Al Carson '01).
Applying	To qualify for the program, students must have a Bachelor of Arts degree or significant preparation in English; an undergraduate GPA of at least 3.0 in the major and overall; a passing score on GACE or PRAXIS I; and GRE scores above the 50th percentile in two of the three areas.
	Applicants must submit an official transcript from each college/university attended (if applying during the senior year, it must be sent when the degree is completed); GACE or PRAXIS I scores; GRE scores; three letters of recommendation; a one-page, single-spaced statement of purpose; a writing portfolio with a minimum of two works, including at least one paper from a prior upper-level English course; and a completed application and $35 nonrefundable application fee. An applicant who has an SAT total score of at least 1000 (verbal plus math scores) or minimum ACT score of 43 (obtained by adding the English and math scores) or a GRE total score of at least 1030 (verbal plus quantitative scores) is exempt from submitting GACE or PRAXIS I scores.
	Applications are accepted on a rolling admissions basis, with a final application deadline of April 1. Applicants are notified by May 1. All items should be sent to the Office of Graduate Studies.
Correspondence and Information	Willie Tolliver Jr., Director Doug Talbott, Program Assistant Office of Graduate Studies Agnes Scott College 141 E. College Avenue Decatur, Georgia 30030-3797 Phone: 404-471-5394 800-868-8602 Ext. 5394 (toll-free) E-mail: graduatestudies@agnesscott.edu Web site: http://www.agnesscott.edu

Agnes Scott College

THE FACULTY AND THEIR RESEARCH

Gordon Malcolm Emert Jr., Visiting Assistant Professor of Education; Ph.D. (English education), Virginia. Curriculum development and instructional methods in English education.

Steven R. Guthrie, Professor of English; Ph.D. (English literature), Brown. Medieval literature, history of English, historical linguistics.

Willie Tolliver Jr., Associate Professor of English and Director of Master of Arts in Teaching Secondary English; Ph.D. (English literature), Chicago. African American literature, nineteenth-century American literature, curriculum development.

Rachel Trousdale, Assistant Professor of English; Ph.D. (English literature), Yale. British and American modernism, postmodernism, contemporary poetry.

AGNES SCOTT COLLEGE
THE WORLD FOR WOMEN

AGNES SCOTT COLLEGE

Master of Arts in Teaching Secondary Mathematics and Science

Program of Study	Agnes Scott College offers a Master of Arts in Teaching Secondary Mathematics and Science program. It is open to men and women with strong academic qualifications who seek certification to teach and who want the benefits of small classes, choice student teaching placements, and an academic environment that is purposeful yet personal.
	The Master of Arts in Teaching Secondary Mathematics and Science program is a three-semester, twelve-month course of study that leads to a master's degree and certification for teaching in one of four areas: secondary mathematics, secondary biology, secondary chemistry, or secondary physics.
	The curriculum for mathematics students links mathematical concepts with applications in the sciences and includes a novel internship program that connects mathematics learning to educational theory. In the sciences, students benefit from Agnes Scott's partnership with the Fernbank Science Center, which provides science education for elementary and secondary students in DeKalb County.
Research Facilities	The $36.5-million Science Center, which opened in 2003, has laboratories and computer facilities for research in biology, chemistry, physics, and psychology. These include a nuclear magnetic resonance machine lab; high-end computers for scientific computing, teaching, and research; walk-in controlled environment rooms; a neurophysiology laboratory; and animal physiology workstations. Bradley Observatory has undergone extensive renovation and addition. The Delafield Planetarium has a computer-controlled Zeiss projector, one of only ten in the United States, as well as its 30-inch Beck telescope, one of the largest in the Southeast.
Financial Aid	Students studying in the M.A.T. program are eligible to receive federal Stafford Loans, GradPLUS, and private student loans. College-administered financial aid is not available for graduate students.
	Federal loan limits for M.A.T. students are $8500 in subsidized Stafford Loans and $12,000 in additional unsubsidized Stafford Loans.
	A student may apply for a GradPLUS loan or a private student loan to cover the remaining cost of education, including living expenses. The Agnes Scott office of financial aid provides students with information on the amount of eligibility as well as application information.
	M.A.T. students who are Georgia residents may also qualify for the Georgia HOPE Teacher Scholarship Loan Program, which provides loans to students getting a master's degree for teaching in a critical shortage field. The loans are forgiven by teaching in Georgia public school classrooms. Students can apply for these loans at http://www.GACollege411.org.
Cost of Study	Tuition for the M.A.T. program in 2007–08 is $455 per credit hour. In addition, there are a student activity fee of $175 and a technology fee of $200. The student health insurance fee of $412 is waived if a student has proof of health insurance.
Living and Housing Costs	Two-bedroom apartments are available within walking distance of campus for $800 to $900 per month. Estimated utilities costs are $100–$150 per month.
Student Outcomes	While the M.A.T. in Secondary Mathematics and Science is a new program, the Master of Arts in Teaching Secondary English has been offered since 1992 and has a placement rate of 99 percent for graduates seeking teaching positions.
Location	Agnes Scott's 100-acre wooded campus is located in metropolitan Atlanta and the historic residential community of Decatur. Downtown Atlanta is 6 miles away and is accessible by a rapid-transit rail station two blocks from campus. Atlanta offers a multitude of opportunities for personal contact with most of the world's cultures and offers entertainment that ranges from rock concerts to performances of the Atlanta Symphony; from local theater to touring Broadway shows; from recreational parks to major league sports and the world's largest aquarium. It is also home to a presidential library, the High Museum of Art, and eighteen other colleges and universities.
The College	Agnes Scott has approximately 1,000 undergraduate and graduate students who come from forty states and thirty countries, with 33 percent of the students representing diverse ethnic or cultural backgrounds. Students describe the College as a place where they are challenged by a rigorous academic environment but supported by faculty members who take a personal interest in their success.
Applying	To qualify for the program, students must have a bachelor's degree in or significant preparation in the academic discipline (math, biology, chemistry, or physics); an undergraduate GPA of at least 3.0 in the major and overall; a passing score on the GACE or PRAXIS 1; and GRE scores above the 50th percentile in two of the three areas.
	Applicants must submit an official college transcript from each college/university attended (if applying during the senior year, it must be sent when the degree is completed); GACE Basic Skills Test or PRAXIS I scores; GRE scores; three letters of recommendation; a one-page, single-spaced statement of purpose; and a completed application and $35 nonrefundable application fee. An applicant who has an SAT total score of at least 1000 (verbal plus math scores) or a minimum ACT score of 43 (obtained by adding the English and math scores) or a GRE total score of at least 1030 (verbal plus quantitative scores) is exempt from submitting GACE or PRAXIS I scores.
	Applications are accepted on a rolling admissions basis, with a final application deadline of April 1. Applicants are notified by May 1.
Correspondence and Information	Doug Talbott, Program Assistant Office of Graduate Studies Agnes Scott College 141 E. College Avenue Decatur, Georgia 30030-3797 Phone: 404 471-5394 800 868-8602 Ext. 5394 (toll-free) E-mail: graduatestudies@agnesscott.edu Web site: http://www.agnesscott.edu

Agnes Scott College

THE FACULTY AND THEIR RESEARCH

Victoria Deneroff, Visiting Assistant Professor of Education; Ph.D., UCLA. Science education in urban high schools, inquiry-based middle and high school science curricula.

Lilia Harvey, Associate Professor of Chemistry; Ph.D, Georgia Tech. Organic synthesis and photochemistry.

Myrtle H. Lewin, Professor of Mathematics and Chair; Ph.D., Wisconsin. Historical and cultural aspects of the development of geometry, pedagogy and gender equity issues in teaching mathematics.

Amy J. Lovell, Assistant Professor of Astronomy; Ph.D., Massachusetts Amherst. Chemistry and physics of cometary comae; thermal emission from asteroids, millimeter-wave, and radio.

Karen Thompson, Associate Professor of Biology; Ph.D., Oregon. Differences between male and female insect nervous systems that allow for differences in sexual behavior, significance of the neural mechanisms underlying evolution of specialized behavior.

CLEMSON UNIVERSITY

Master of Agricultural Education

Program of Study

The Master of Agricultural Education is a professional degree program that is designed to enhance the human resource skills in agriculture and education. The flexible program provides a core of planning, delivery, evaluation, and administrative strategies while encouraging specialization in teacher education, adult and extension education, agricultural communications, youth development, or technology transfer.

A minimum of 30 semester hours is required for the professional degree. At least one half of the credit hours in the student's program must come from courses numbered 700 or above. The student's program of study must be approved by his or her advisory committee. Candidates for the degree are required to plan an individual program of study in consultation with the major adviser and graduate committee; complete a minimum of 3 semester hours in adult education, 3 semester hours in research methods, and 3 semester hours in statistics; complete a minimum of 12 semester hours in the major field; and complete a minimum of 6 semester hours in an area of concentration outside the major field.

Research Facilities

Students have access to a research library and research workroom related to projects in agricultural education. Research is primarily conducted through surveys, focus groups, Delphi methods, and case studies. These research activities are conducted on local, state, regional, and national levels. Agricultural education students use the Education Resources Information Center (ERIC) research to review articles in their research interest.

Financial Aid

The department offers two assistantships, which are based on a competitive award and student need. The Federal Stafford Loan is the only form of federal aid available to graduate students through Clemson University's Financial Aid Office. For additional information on graduate financial aid, students should visit http://virtual.clemson.edu/groups/finaid/graduate.htm.

All other forms of assistance for graduate students (assistantships, fellowships, and traineeships) are coordinated through the Graduate School; however, decisions regarding the awarding generally rest solely with the departments.

Cost of Study

Tuition for 2007–08 is $3641 per semester for in-state students and $7285 per semester for nonresidents. Off-campus rates are $330 per hour for in-state students and $660 per hour for nonresidents. Graduate assistants pay a flat fee of $950 per semester and $315 per summer session. Graduate fellows pay South Carolina resident fees.

Living and Housing Costs

On-campus housing is available. For information, students should visit http://www.housing.clemson.edu. The cost of living in Clemson is quite low compared to the national average. Students who choose to live off the campus typically spend $300–$400 per month for rent, depending on location, amenities, roommates, and other factors.

Student Group

Of the approximately 15 students in the program, 56 percent are women, 63 percent attend on a full-time basis, and all are from the United States.

Student Outcomes

Degree recipients hold positions as agriculture teachers, extension agents, agricultural and environmental agency employees, and human resource development specialists in agricultural industry.

Location

Clemson is a small, beautiful college town near the Blue Ridge Mountains and Lake Hartwell in upstate South Carolina. The Upstate is one of the country's fastest-growing areas and is an important part of the I-85 corridor, a multistate area along Interstate 85 that runs from metro Atlanta to Richmond, Virginia, and encompasses Charlotte, North Carolina, and North Carolina's Research Triangle. Atlanta and Charlotte are each a 2-hour drive away. Many financial institutions and other industries have a national headquarters or a major presence in the Upstate, including Wachovia, Bank of America, BMW, Bon Secours St. Francis Health System, Bosch North America, Bowater, Charter Communications, Ernst & Young, Fluor Corporation, IBM, Microsoft, Michelin of North America, and many others.

The University

Clemson is classified by the Carnegie Foundation as an RU/H: Research University (high research activity), a category comprising just 10 percent of all graduate degree–granting universities in America. The University's mission is to fulfill the covenant between its founder and the people of South Carolina to establish a "high seminary of learning" through its responsibilities of teaching, research, and extended public service. The University has identified eight areas of academic emphasis that create collaborations that, in turn, help fulfill the University's mission.

Applying

Applicants may apply on the Web at http://www.grad.clemson.edu/p_apply.html. Applications with a $50 nonrefundable fee should be received no later than five weeks prior to registration. Every required item in support of the application must be on file by that date. Students are advised to contact the department for the deadlines of the program of proposed study.

Correspondence and Information

Tom Dobbins
Graduate Coordinator
225 McAdams Hall
Clemson University
Clemson, South Carolina 29634
Phone: 864-656-3834
Fax: 864-656-5675
E-mail: tdbbns@clemson.edu
Web site: http://virtual.clemson.edu/groups/aged/graduate_overview.htm

Clemson University

THE FACULTY AND THEIR RESEARCH

Thomas R. Dobbins, Associate Professor; Ph.D., Virginia Tech, 1999. Preservice teacher education preparation, burn-out in teachers and teacher educators: cause and effect.

Donnie R. King, Associate Professor; Ph.D., Ohio State, 1990. Biology instruction, agricultural education.

Kevin D. Layfield, Assistant Professor; Ph.D., Penn State, 1998. Agricultural education.

Curtis D. White Sr., Associate Professor; Ph.D., Missouri, 1988. Biology instruction, agricultural education.

Program of Study	The Counselor Education Program at Clemson University offers the Master of Education (M.Ed.) degree for students interested in becoming professional school counselors and student affairs professionals at colleges and universities and working in community mental health agencies. Accredited in 1998 by the Council for Accreditation of Counseling and Related Education Programs (CACREP), a national accrediting agency, this accreditation indicates that the program offers the highest quality in counselor education.
	The program is dedicated to educating and training counselor educators to function in culturally diverse settings. This training utilizes an integrative practitioner-training model emphasizing development, prevention strategies, and enhancement. The programs are designed to provide a challenging yet supportive environment that promotes professional orientation, practice, and self-awareness.
	The curriculum of the Counselor Education Program has a basic core of academic courses that emphasizes theory, professional issues, and growth and development. The curriculum is designed to allow for integrative practice of materials in class, with supervised field experiences. Courses are designed toward continued development of the counselor education and student affairs knowledge base, with the application of this knowledge in self development and practice.
	There are three areas of specialization in the Counselor Education Program, and all are CACREP-approved. These concentration areas are community counseling, school counseling, and student affairs practice (student affairs practice in higher education, student affairs counseling). It is a nonthesis program ranging from 48 to 51 credit hours. The number of hours that applicants may transfer from another institution follows the University guidelines as specified in the catalog. The course must meet the equivalent requirements of a Clemson graduate course and have been taken in the last five years. Courses over five years old are not accepted. The length of study depends on whether a student attends on a full- or part-time basis. For full-time students, the length of study is approximately two years. The program must be completed in six years minus one semester.
	The program also offers some courses at the University Center of Greenville. Generally, these are those courses making up the core curriculum.
	All programs require the successful completion of a comprehensive examination. Upon graduation from this program, students seek jobs as licensed professional counselors, school counselors, or student affairs practitioners.
Research Facilities	Clemson's Community Counseling Clinic (CCC) is the clinical training center for the graduate program in counselor education. Working under the supervision of faculty members, advanced graduate students provide high-quality, short-term, affordable counseling services for individuals, groups, couples, and families in Clemson, South Carolina, and its surrounding communities.
	In addition, graduate students have full access to the University's library system, which contains nearly 2 million books, periodicals, microforms, government publications, and electronic materials, including online access to many of the leading scholarly journals.
Financial Aid	The department does not offer any financial aid. Students enrolled in the student affairs concentration can seek graduate assistantships in the Division of Student Affairs.
Cost of Study	Tuition for 2007–08 is $3641 per semester for in-state students and $7285 per semester for nonresidents. Off-campus rates are $330 per hour for in-state students and $660 per hour for nonresidents. Graduate assistants pay a flat fee of $950 per semester. Graduate fellows pay South Carolina resident fees.
Living and Housing Costs	On-campus housing is available; for information, students should visit http://www.housing.clemson.edu. The cost of living in Clemson is quite low compared to the national average; students who choose to live off-campus typically spend $300–$400 per month for rent, depending on location, amenities, roommates, etc.
Student Group	The program has approximately 150 students. Eighty-three percent are women, 58 percent attend on a full-time basis, and 99 percent are from the United States.
Student Outcomes	Graduates of the Counselor Education program obtain jobs as mental health counselors, school counselors, and student affairs practitioners. Community counseling graduates work in community mental health facilities, drug and alcohol facilities, and private mental health facilities. School counseling graduates work in P–12 schools nationally and throughout the state of South Carolina. Student affairs graduates work in varying functional units at colleges and universities throughout the country.
Location	Clemson is a small, beautiful college town near the Blue Ridge Mountains and Lake Hartwell in upstate South Carolina. The Upstate is one of the country's fastest-growing areas and is an important part of the I-85 corridor, a multistate area along Interstate 85 that runs from metro Atlanta to Richmond, Virginia, and encompasses Charlotte, North Carolina, and North Carolina's Research Triangle. Atlanta and Charlotte are each a two-hour's drive away. Many financial institutions and other industries have national headquarters for a major presence in the Upstate, including Wachovia, Bank of America, BMW, Bon Secours St. Francis Health System, Bosch North America, Bowater, Charter Communications, Ernst and Young, Fluor Corporation, IBM, Microsoft, Michelin of North America, and many others.
The University	Clemson is classified by the Carnegie Foundation as an RU/H: Research University (high research activity), a category comprising just 10 percent of all graduate degree-granting universities in America. The University's mission is to fulfill the covenant between its founder and the people of South Carolina to establish a "high seminary of learning" through its responsibilities of teaching, research, and extended public service. The University has identified eight areas of academic emphasis that create collaborations that, in turn, help fulfill the University's mission.
Applying	The department values diversity, respect for individuals, and the dignity of individuals. Applicants are selected on their ability to succeed academically, personal qualifications that are necessary for functioning as counselors and student affairs professionals, and the appropriateness of their professional goals. Applicants may apply on the Web at http://www.grad.clemson.edu/p_apply.html. Applications require a $50 nonrefundable fee. The application deadline for fall admission is March 1; the deadline for spring admission is October 1. Every required item in support of the application must be on file by that date.
Correspondence and Information	David S. Fleming, Ph.D. Graduate Coordinator Eugene T. Moore School of Education G-01 Tillman Hall Clemson University Clemson, South Carolina 29634-0702 Phone: 864-656-1881 Fax: 864-656-0311 E-mail: dflemin@clemson.edu Web site: http://www.hehd.clemson.edu/schoolofed/index.html

Clemson University

THE FACULTY AND THEIR RESEARCH

Larry Aberthany, Lecturer; M.Ed., Clemson. At-risk youth, group interaction, drug and alcohol education, addictions counseling.

Tony W. Cawthon, Professor; Ph.D., Mississippi State. Student affairs administration, student development theory, multicultural, new professionals.

Kimberly Frazier, Assistant Professor; Ph.D., New Orleans. School counseling, pediatric counseling, self-efficacy in counseling and supervision, culture-centered counseling, ethics.

Pamela A. Havice, Associate Professor; Ph.D., Clemson. Technology, distance education, student affairs administration, multicultural issues, innovative learning environments.

Elaine Hiott, Clinical Faculty; M.Ed., Clemson. Supervision, clinical training.

Jerry Neal, Visiting Assistant Professor; Ed.D., Indiana. Clinical training, supervision.

David Scott, Assistant Professor; Ph.D., North Carolina State. Community counseling, at-risk youth, identity development and career counseling.

Robert I. Urofsky, Assistant Professor; Ph.D., Virginia. School counseling, gender considerations in student development and school counseling, ethics in counseling, counselor education and supervision.

Cheryl B. Warner, Assistant Professor; Ph.D., Georgia. Supervision, multicultural counseling, ethnic identity development, group counseling and skill development.

CLEMSON UNIVERSITY

Master of Education in Reading

Program of Study

There are four paths offered in the Master of Education (M.Ed.) in reading program. The Reading Teacher and Reading Consultant option is offered for students who do not wish to be certified on a supervisory level. It allows students to complete additional literacy course work in lieu of supervisory course work. The Reading Teacher and Reading Consultant with Reading Recovery plan allows reading recovery course work to be used as partial fulfillment of requirements for the master's degree in reading. The Reading Teacher with an Early Literacy emphasis and Reading Consultant plan was developed for those teachers who wish to specialize in early literacy, K–5, but do not wish to be reading recovery trained. The Reading Teacher, Reading Consultant, and Reading Coordinator/Director is the most comprehensive plan in terms of certification.

Core courses that all students must complete include Reading Instruction in the Elementary School, Fundamentals of Basic Reading, Clinical Research in Reading, Organizing and Supervising Reading Programs, Teaching Secondary School Reading, Evaluation and Remediation of Reading Problems, Practicum in Reading, Advanced Educational Psychology, and Educational Tests and Measurements. There is no residency requirement for the M.Ed. in reading program.

Students are involved in two clinical experiences: one semester of evaluation and remediation and one semester of practicum, in which candidates tutor community students who have reading problems.

Research Facilities

The program has a reading clinic equipped with eight iMacs and a variety of software in individual carrels. The facility is set up to facilitate behind-the-glass teaching and feedback. For information on the School's centers and collaboratives, students should visit http://www.hehd.clemson.edu/schoolofed/centers.htm.

Financial Aid

A small number of graduate assistantships are available.

Cost of Study

Tuition for 2007–08 is $3641 per semester for in-state students and $7285 per semester for nonresidents. Off-campus rates are $330 per hour for in-state students and $660 per hour for nonresidents. Graduate assistants pay a flat fee of $950 per semester and $315 per summer session. Graduate fellows pay South Carolina resident fees.

Living and Housing Costs

On-campus housing is available; for information, students should visit http://www.housing.clemson.edu. The cost of living in Clemson is quite low compared to the national average; students who choose to live off campus typically spend $300–$400 per month for rent, depending on location, amenities, roommates, etc.

Student Group

The program has approximately 38 students. All are women and 18 percent participate on a full-time basis.

Student Outcomes

Graduates of the M.Ed. in reading program are prepared for the following, depending on which path they choose: reading teacher, reading consultant, reading coordinator (district administrative position), or reading recovery teacher.

Location

Clemson is a small, beautiful college town near the Blue Ridge Mountains and Lake Hartwell in Upstate South Carolina. The Upstate is one of the country's fastest-growing areas and is an important part of the I-85 corridor, a multistate area along Interstate 85 that runs from metro Atlanta to Richmond, Virginia, and encompasses Charlotte, North Carolina, and North Carolina's Research Triangle. Atlanta and Charlotte are each a 2-hour drive away. Many financial institutions and other industries have national headquarters for a major presence in the Upstate, including Wachovia, Bank of America, BMW, Bon Secours St. Francis Health System, Bosch North America, Bowater, Charter Communications, Ernst & Young, Fluor Corporation, IBM, Microsoft, Michelin of North America, and many others.

The University

Clemson is classified by the Carnegie Foundation as an RU/H: Research University (high research activity), a category comprising just 10 percent of all graduate degree–granting universities in America. The University's mission is to fulfill the covenant between its founder and the people of South Carolina to establish a "high seminary of learning" through its responsibilities of teaching, research, and extended public service. The University has identified eight areas of academic emphasis that create collaborations that, in turn, help fulfill the University's mission.

Applying

Students in these programs are expected to be of high integrity, motivated, and committed to implementing evidence-based instructional and behavioral interventions. Applicants may apply on the Web at http://www.grad.clemson.edu/p_apply.html. Applications with a $50 nonrefundable fee should be received no later than five weeks prior to registration. Every required item in support of the application must be on file by that date. Students are advised to contact the department for the deadlines of the program of proposed study.

Correspondence and Information

David S. Fleming, Ph.D.
Graduate Coordinator
Eugene T. Moore School of Education
G-01 Tillman Hall
Clemson University
Clemson, South Carolina 29634-0702
Phone: 864-656-1881
Fax: 864-656-0311
E-mail: dflemin@clemson.edu
Web site: http://www.hehd.clemson.edu/schoolofed/g-read_po.htm

Clemson University

THE FACULTY AND THEIR RESEARCH

Beatrice Naff Bailey, Professor; Ed.D., Virginia Tech. Curriculum and instruction.
David E. Barrett, Professor; Ph.D., USC. Education psychology.
Wanda Calvert, Clinical Faculty; Ph.D., South Carolina. Elementary education.
Chrystal Dean, Assistant Professor; Ph.D., Vanderbilt. Teaching and learning, math education.
Gail C. Delicio, Associate Professor; Ph.D., Florida State. Education psychology.
Pamela J. Dunston, Associate Professor; Ph.D., Georgia. Reading education.
Elizabeth Edmondson, Assistant Professor; Ph.D., Clemson. Curriculum and instruction.
Lienne C. Federico, Assistant Professor; Ph.D., East Carolina. Educational leadership/English education.
William R. Fisk, Professor and Department Chair; Ph.D., Florida State. School psychology.
Susan King Fullerton, Associate Professor; Ph.D., Maryland. Curriculum and instruction, reading.
Linda Gambrell, Full Professor; Ph.D., Maryland. Curriculum and instruction, reading.
Robert P. Green Jr., Alumni Professor; Ed.D., Virginia. Curriculum and instruction.
Kathy Neal Headley, Professor; Ed.D., Auburn. Reading.
Martha J. Hodge, Associate Professor; Ph.D., Vanderbilt. Special education.
Robert M. Horton, Associate Professor; Ed.D., Cincinnati. Curriculum and instruction.
Larry Brent Igo, Assistant Professor; Ph.D., Nebraska–Lincoln. Educational psychology.
Rebecca Kaminski, Clinical Faculty; Ed.D., Pittsburgh. Instruction and learning.
Antonis Katsiyannis, Professor; Ed.D., William and Mary. Education administration, special education–behavior disorders.
Cheryl Olivia Lane, Assistant Professor; Ph.D., Clemson. Curriculum and instruction.
Charles C. Linnell, Associate Professor; Ed.D., North Carolina State. Industrial arts education.
Jonda Cecole McNair, Assistant Professor; Ph.D., Ohio State. Language, literacy, and culture.
William Paige, Professor; Ph.D., Ohio State. Industrial technology education.
Susan J. Pass, Assistant Professor; Ed.D., Houston. Social studies.
Chris L. Peters, Associate Professor; Ed.D., Georgia. Instructional technology.
Cheryl Poston, Associate Professor; Ed.D., Georgia. Vocational education.
David Paul Reinking, Named Professor; Ph.D., Minnesota, Twin Cities. Reading education.
Paul J. Riccomini, Assistant Professor; Ph.D., Penn State. Special education.
Victoria G. Ridgeway, Associate Professor; Ph.D., Georgia. Reading education.
Suzanne N. Rosenblith, Assistant Professor; Ph.D., Wisconsin–Madison. Educational policy studies.
Joseph Ryan, Assistant Professor; Ph.D., Nebraska–Lincoln. Special education.
Deborah A. Smith, Associate Professor; Ed.D., Tennessee. Physical education.
Pamela M. Stecker, Associate Professor; Ph.D., Vanderbilt. Education and human development.
Dolores A. Stegelin, Professor; Ph.D., Florida. Early childhood development and interdisciplinary research.
Deborah M. Switzer, Professor; Ph.D., Illinois. Educational psychology.
Carol G. Weatherford, Associate Professor; Ed.D., North Carolina State. Occupational education.
Elaine Mumbauer Wiegert, Assistant Professor; Ph.D., Clemson. Curriculum and instruction.
Seal Wilson, Clinical Faculty; Ph.D., Southern Mississippi. Special education.

Davidson Graduate School of Jewish Education

THE JEWISH THEOLOGICAL SEMINARY

William Davidson Graduate School of Jewish Education

Programs of Study

The William Davidson Graduate School of Jewish Education of the Jewish Theological Seminary (JTS) offers Master of Arts (M.A.) and doctoral (Ed.D.) programs in Jewish education. Through its master's program, the Davidson School prepares students to become educators in Jewish educational settings, both formal (day school and synagogue school) and informal (youth groups, camps, Jewish community centers, and adult education programs). The doctoral program prepares students for work in administration, supervision, curriculum design, and research and scholarship in Jewish education. Through a consortium academia agreement, Davidson School students can enroll in courses at Teachers College Columbia University and the Robert F. Wagner Graduate School of Public Service and design individualized programs to fit their educational interests, including nonprofit management, special needs, and early childhood education. The Davidson School is open to men and women without regard to age, race, religion, sexual orientation, or national origin.

Research Facilities

The Library of the Jewish Theological Seminary houses the most complete collection of Judaica in the Western Hemisphere. With more than 340,000 volumes on open shelves, it is ideally suited for the research needs of graduate students. The library's special collection, with more than 30,000 items, affords ample opportunity for original scholarship. All matriculated Davidson School students also benefit from the resources of neighboring Teachers College.

Financial Aid

The M.A. program at the Davidson School offers a significant number of merit-based fellowships. Applicants to the M.A. program may obtain applications for merit-based fellowships directly from the Davidson School Office.

Cost of Study

For the 2006–07 academic year, tuition was $23,660 for full-time Ed.D. study and $18,880 for full-time M.A. study. Part-time students were charged $900 per credit. In addition to tuition, a fee of $375 per semester was charged.

Living and Housing Costs

Rooms and apartments (150 units) are available to single students at a cost of approximately $8000 per academic year. Apartments of various costs are available to married students. The housing application deadline for incoming students is May 12. For more information, students should contact the Office of Residence Life by calling 212-678-8035 or by sending an e-mail to reslife@jtsa.edu.

Student Group

In fall 2005, 146 students were enrolled in the Davidson School. Approximately 68 percent were women. A majority of students receive generous merit-based fellowships. All doctoral students are fully funded during the first two years of residence and full-time course work.

Location

JTS is located on the vibrant Upper West Side of New York City. Its proximity to Columbia University, Union Theological Seminary, and the Manhattan School of Music puts the Davidson School in the heart of a dynamic academic community. Students are encouraged to explore the wealth of cultural activities that New York City offers—from music and dance at Lincoln Center to theater on and off Broadway, from art at the Metropolitan and Whitney museums to the galleries in SoHo and Greenwich Village.

The Seminary

Founded in 1886, the Jewish Theological Seminary is the academic and spiritual center of Conservative Judaism worldwide. In 1904, JTS established the Jewish Museum. JTS's New York campus includes five separate yet integrated schools: the Albert A. List College of Jewish Studies, the Graduate School, the H. L. Miller Cantorial School and College of Jewish Music (formerly the Cantor's Institute and Seminary College of Music), the Rabbinical School, and the William Davidson Graduate School of Jewish Education.

Applying

Applications for admission to degree programs should be made as early as possible. Students are encouraged to complete the application process by March 1 for consideration for fall admission. However, applications are received and reviewed all year. A $50 application fee, official college transcripts, three letters of recommendation (two academic references), and GRE or MAT scores are required. Doctoral applicants must also submit two academic writing samples. To be considered for a merit-based fellowship, it is recommended that candidates apply no later than March 1.

Correspondence and Information

Jamie Beth Schindler, Director of Admissions
William Davidson Graduate School of Jewish Education
The Jewish Theological Seminary
3080 Broadway
New York, New York 10027-4649
Phone: 212-678-8866
E-mail: edschool@jtsa.edu
Web site: http://www.jtsa.edu

The Jewish Theological Seminary

THE FACULTY

Arnold Eisen, Chancellor-Elect.
Michael B. Greenbaum, Vice Chancellor.
William B. Lebeau, Vice Chancellor.
Jack Wertheimer, Provost.
Stephen Garfinkel, Dean of Academic Affairs.

Department of Jewish Education

Barry Holtz, Professor.
Carol Krepon Ingall, Professor.
Adina Ofek, Associate Professor.
Steven M. Brown, Assistant Professor.
Aryeh Davidson, Assistant Professor.
Shira Epstein, Assistant Professor.
Michael B. Greenbaum, Assistant Professor.
Jeffrey S. Kress, Assistant Professor.
Charlotte Abramson, Adjunct Lecturer.
Karen Medwed, Adjunct Lecturer.
Deborah Miller, Adjunct Instructor.

SOUTHERN ILLINOIS UNIVERSITY CARBONDALE

Department of Health Education and Recreation
Health Education

Program of Study

The health education program within the Department of Health Education and Recreation at Southern Illinois University Carbondale (SIUC) is nationally known for its Ph.D. program. In the past five years, doctoral students have received national recognition, such as the American School Health Association's Delbert Oberteuffer Award, the Eta Sigma Gamma National Gamman of the Year Award, and the Social Science Research Council Dissertation Fellowship. Graduates of the program serve in leadership positions in health education and as university faculty members across the country. Faculty members are national leaders in health education and authors of numerous professional articles and books. The department serves as the home of two professional journals, *The Health Educator* and the *International Electronic Journal of Health Education*, as well as the *HEDIR*. Through the student-centered commitment of faculty members, Ph.D. graduates gain a high level of skill in both teaching and research. The department sponsors the Alpha Alpha Chapter of Eta Sigma Gamma, a national health science honorary organization. Faculty members encourage and support the professional development of students through participation and involvement in research projects, workshops, and conferences locally, regionally, and nationally.

Research Facilities

Morris Library at SIUC is a member of several national and local library consortia and other organizations, including the Academic Technology Center, the Association of Research Libraries, the Center for Research Libraries, and the Illinois Library Computer Systems Organization.

The SIUC Safety Center serves as a site for graduate student research and practical experience. Recent projects at the center include a child safety-seat project, a motorcycle rider program, and various research efforts.

Financial Aid

The Department of Health Education and Recreation offers graduate assistantships to graduate students. Graduate assistants have tuition waived during the summer session following two consecutive full semesters of assistantship support. If students continue their degree programs beyond the department limits, they are encouraged to seek assistantships from other sources within the University community.

Cost of Study

In-state graduate tuition is $275 per credit hour in fall 2007. Out-of-state tuition is 2.5 times the in-state tuition rate ($687.50 per credit hour). Graduate students with a graduate assistant appointment of at least 25 percent receive a tuition waiver. Fees vary from $490.11 (1 credit hour) to $1272.45 (12 credit hours).

Living and Housing Costs

For married couples, students with families, and single graduate students, the University has 589 efficiency and one-, two-, and three-bedroom apartments that rent for $460 to $530 per month in 2007–08 (projected rates). Residence halls for single graduate students are also available, as are accessible residence hall rooms and apartments for students with disabilities.

Student Group

Total University enrollment exceeds 21,000, including more than 4,000 graduate students. Men and women come from all fifty states and more than 100 other countries. About 53 percent of the graduate students are women, 23 percent are international, and 13 percent are American minorities. Within the health education graduate program for spring semester 2002, there were a total of 48 doctoral students (18 men and 30 women).

Location

SIUC is 350 miles south of Chicago and 100 miles southeast of St. Louis. Nestled in rolling hills bordered by the Ohio and Mississippi Rivers and enhanced by a mild climate, the area has state parks, national forests and wildlife refuges, and large lakes for outdoor recreation. Much of the area is a part of the 240,000-acre Shawnee National Forest. Cultural offerings include theater, opera, concerts, art exhibits, and cinema. Educational facilities available for the families of students are excellent.

The University

Southern Illinois University Carbondale is a comprehensive public university with a variety of general and professional education programs. The University offers associate, bachelor's, master's, and doctoral degrees as well as the J.D. and M.D. degrees. The University is fully accredited by the North Central Association of Colleges and Schools. The Graduate School has an essential role in the development and coordination of graduate instruction and research programs. The Graduate Council has academic responsibility for determining graduate standards, recommending new graduate programs and research centers, and establishing policies to facilitate the research effort. Southern Illinois University Carbondale is a state-funded university founded in 1869.

Applying

Applications and information should be requested at http://www.hedir.org/forms or at the University Web site. All application materials and information should be returned to the department at the address given in this In-Depth Description. The application deadline is February 15 for summer and fall admission and September 15 for spring admission.

Correspondence and Information

Graduate Coordinator
Department of Health Education and Recreation
Mail Code 4632
Southern Illinois University Carbondale
Carbondale, Illinois 62901-4632
Phone: 618-453-4331 or 2777
E-mail: herec@siu.edu
Web site: http://www.siu.edu/~hedrec

Southern Illinois University Carbondale

THE FACULTY AND THEIR RESEARCH

David A. Birch, Professor and Chair; Ph.D., Penn State, 1990. Comprehensive school health education, coordinated school health promotion, leadership in school health education, parent/family involvement, professional preparation, teaching techniques.

Stephen L. Brown, Assistant Professor; Ph.D., Maryland, 2001. Stress management, mental health, anger, violence, work-site wellness.

Judy C. Drolet, Professor; Ph.D., Oregon, 1982. Human sexuality, sexuality education, mental health, drug education, professional preparation, foundations of health education.

Joyce V. Fetro, Professor; Ph.D., Southern Illinois at Carbondale, 1987. Professional preparation, curriculum development, program planning, death education, substance-use prevention, youth development, program evaluation, research design, marketing and advocacy, program administration/management.

Bart J. Hammig, Assistant Professor; Ph.D., Kansas, 1997. Injury prevention and control, epidemiology, violence, research methods.

Mark J. Kittleson, Professor and Director of Graduate Programs; Ph.D., Akron, 1986. AIDS, program planning, stress management, evaluation, health informatics, biostatistics.

Roberta J. Ogletree, Associate Professor; H.S.D., Indiana, 1991. Foundations of health education, school and college health education, curriculum, women's health, human sexuality education, professional preparation.

Brian M. Rice, Instructor; M.S., Southern Illinois, 1996. First aid and CPR, health and workplace safety, injury control, occupational health and safety, stress management.

Dale O. Ritzel, Professor; Ph.D., Southern Illinois at Carbondale, 1970. Injury control, occupational health and safety, child safety, computer applications, research design.

Kathleen J. Welshimer, Associate Professor; Ph.D., North Carolina at Chapel Hill, 1990. Community organizing, women's and children's health, social-psychological perspectives, community assessment and planning process, risk perception and health communications.

Peggy Wilken, Clinical Assistant Professor; Ph.D., Southern Illinois at Carbondale, 1995. First aid and advanced first-aid concepts, environmental health, sexuality, international health, emotional health and aging.

SOUTHERN ILLINOIS UNIVERSITY CARBONDALE

Department of Workforce Education and Development
Ph.D. Program

Program of Study	The Department of Workforce Education and Development (WED) is one of the largest education, training, and development departments in the United States. According to recent *U.S. News & World Report* ratings, WED has been recognized as among the top ten in the nation. The Department offers programs of study leading to the Master of Science in education and Doctor of Philosophy in education degrees.
	The workforce education and development concentration is a broad, general leadership and professional development degree that serves individuals having knowledge, experience, and interest in career education, career and technical education, public- and private-sector training and development, human resource development, and related technical and professional fields. Even though many students entering the program have a specific occupational area identity (e.g., business education, health careers education, industrial education), the degree is not awarded in a service area specialty.
Research Facilities	Morris Library, named after the late Delyte W. Morris, University President from 1948 to 1970, features an Internet-accessible information network providing entry to library catalogs, abstract and index services, full-text periodical databases, and local and national technological resources (http://www.lib.siu.edu). The library contains more than 2 million volumes, some 12,000 current periodicals and serials, and 3.5 million microforms. Collections of government documents, maps, films and videotapes, and sound recordings are extensive. With the exception of materials in Special Collections, items are arranged on open shelves and available for browsing. The library's public computers provide access to the online catalog and to more than 100 electronic databases, including indexing and abstracting services and the full text of nearly 2,000 journals and newspapers. Many of these resources can also be accessed from personal computers in residence halls, offices, and homes by direct connection with the University computer network or via modem. ILLINET Online provides a circulation system to participating libraries and supports computerized interlibrary loan activity, promoting and enhancing resource sharing statewide.
Financial Aid	Certain research and teaching assistantships and fellowships are available to on-campus students within the Department of Workforce Education and Development, the College of Education and Human Services, and the University. These assistantships and fellowships are limited and very competitive. Federal Stafford Student Loans or Illinois Opportunity Loans may be available for qualified students. Students should complete the Free Application for Federal Student Aid (FAFSA), which determines qualifications for all financial assistance programs.
Cost of Study	In-state graduate tuition is $275 per credit hour in 2007–08. Out-of-state tuition is 2.5 times the in-state tuition rate ($687.50 per credit hour). Graduate students with at least a 25 percent appointment as a graduate assistant receive a tuition waiver. Fees vary from $490.11 (1 credit hour) to $1272.45 (12 credit hours).
Living and Housing Costs	For married couples, students with families, and single graduate students, the University has 690 efficiency and one-, two-, three-, and four-bedroom apartments that rent for $439 to $651 per month in 2007–08 (projected rates). Residence halls for single graduate students are also available, as are accessible residence hall rooms and apartments for students with disabilities.
Student Group	Students are chosen from the best applicants in the United States and around the world. The number of international students enrolled in the Department is one of the highest in the country. In addition to the varied cultures in the Department, there is a significant number of students who have returned to attain their graduate degree after spending a number of years in the workforce. This very diverse group of students forms a strong bond with each other and with the faculty members.
Location	The Carbondale and Jackson County area has an abundance of outdoor as well as indoor activities that can be enjoyed throughout the year. Crab Orchard National Wildlife Refuge, Shawnee National Forest, and Giant City State Park are right in Carbondale's backyard. Carbondale and Southern Illinois University offer a long list of musical, theatrical, and other events that are representative of the diverse community.
The University	Founded in 1869, Southern Illinois University Carbondale (SIUC) maintains more than 100 finely tuned academic programs that lead to associate, baccalaureate, master's, specialist, doctoral, and professional degrees. Fully accredited by the North Central Association of Colleges and Schools, SIUC's faculty-student ratio averages 1:18. SIUC has won the Doctoral/Research University–Extensive distinction from the Carnegie Foundation for the Advancement of Teaching. Only 3.8 percent of colleges and universities in the country have earned that distinction.
Applying	Individuals seeking admission to the doctoral program in workforce education and development must meet all requirements established by the Graduate School, the College of Education and Human Services, and the Department of Workforce Education and Development. Applicants should possess a background of academic and professional experience that provides a foundation for advanced study and research.
	Admission to the WED concentration is determined by a majority vote of the WED graduate faculty based upon the following guidelines and criteria: the nature and quality of previous undergraduate and graduate degrees and course work; a paper prepared by the applicant concerning his or her career goals and how they relate to the doctoral program in workforce education and development; the nature, quality, and variety of previous employment; letters of recommendation relative to personal, professional, and academic competence; professional promise and employment potential of the applicant; Graduate Record Exam (GRE) test scores; a personal interview, if requested by the graduate faculty; and the willingness of a qualified WED graduate faculty member to serve as the applicant's committee chair and dissertation adviser.
Correspondence and Information	Dr. Marcia A. Anderson Director of Graduate Studies Workforce Education and Development Southern Illinois University Carbondale Carbondale, Illinois 62901-4605 Phone: 618-453-3321 E-mail: wed@siu.edu Web site: http://www.wed.siu.edu/Public

Southern Illinois University Carbondale

THE FACULTY

The Department employs more than 40 full-time faculty members, with backgrounds in health, agriculture, technical education, business, family and consumer science, human resource development, and training and development. Workforce Education and Development faculty members present extensive experience in teaching, research, and service and are focused on sharing their expertise with students and providing the scholarly and professional environment necessary for intensive graduate study.

Marcia Anderson, Professor and Director of Graduate Programs in Workforce Education and Development; Ph.D., Southern Illinois, 1975. Worker development, business education, instructional methodology, curriculum development, foundations of work education, women in administration. (E-mail: mandersn@siu.edu)

Clora Mae Baker, Associate Professor; Ph.D., Ohio State, 1989. Teaching methodology, business education, curriculum and instruction, professional development, office administration, qualitative research. (E-mail: cmbaker@siu.edu)

Richard Bortz, Professor; Ph.D., Minnesota, 1967. Instructional systems design, occupational training and curriculum development, organizational and occupational analysis, competency-based education and training, individualized instruction, faculty development and evaluation. (E-mail: bortz@siu.edu)

Jennifer Calvin, Assistant Professor; Ph.D., Ohio State, 2005. Human resource development, international HRD, distance learning, self-regulated learning, change management, impact of culture on learning and work, motivation, communities of practice, professional development. (E-mail: calvin15@siu.edu)

Elizabeth Freeburg, Associate Professor; Ph.D., Southern Illinois Carbondale, 1994. Human performance analysis, behavioral norms, contextual analysis, workplace accommodation, instructional systems design. (E-mail: freeburg@siu.edu)

Barbara Hagler, Assistant Professor; Ph.D., Arizona State, 1991. Business education, improvement of teaching, workforce education foundations, computer technology, distance education, training and human resource development. (E-mail: bhagler@siu.edu)

Phoebe Lenear, Assistant Professor; Ph.D., Illinois at Urbana-Champaign, 1995. Underrepresented minorities in science, technology, engineering, and mathematics fields; e-Mentoring; instructional design and techniques; multimedia technologies; technology education. (E-mail: plenear@siu.edu)

Seburn Pense, Adjunct Professor, Department of Workforce Education and Development, and Assistant Professor, Agricultural Education, Department of Plant, Soil and Agricultural Systems; Ph.D., Oklahoma State, 2002. Agricultural education, science and agricultural literacy, curriculum development, test construction, stakeholder studies, international agriculture, cross-cultural studies. (E-mail: sebpense@siu.edu)

A. R. Putnam, Associate Professor; Ed.D., Oklahoma State, 1978. Industrial education, leadership, human resource development, international education, curriculum and evaluation. (E-mail: bputnam@siu.edu)

Bill Shields, Assistant Professor; M.S., Southern Illinois, 1962. Instructional systems design, methods and techniques of training, training systems management. (E-mail: bshields@siu.edu)

Cynthia Sims, Assistant Professor; Ed.D., Northern Illinois, 2004. Adult education and learning; workforce diversity, power, and privilege; human resource development; service-learning. (E-mail: csims@siu.edu)

Dexter Wakefield, Adjunct Professor, Department Workforce Education and Development, and Assistant Professor, College of Agricultural Sciences; Ph.D., Purdue, 2001. Urban education, multiculturalism, diversity in the workplace, socio-economical issues in America, minorities in agriculture, women in agriculture. (E-mail: wakephd@siu.edu)

John Washburn, Professor; Ed.D., Illinois, 1977. Employment and training, vocational education policy issues and legislation, vocational education research, curriculum development, personnel development, vocational training for special populations. (E-mail: jwash@siu.edu)

Keith Waugh, Associate Professor; Ph.D., Virginia Tech, 1996. Education, training and development, educational research and evaluation, training transfer, group decision processes, person-environment fit. (E-mail: ckwaugh@siu.edu)

STONY BROOK UNIVERSITY, STATE UNIVERSITY OF NEW YORK

Department of Technology and Society
Educational Technology Program

Program of Study

The Department of Technology and Society offers graduate work leading to the Master of Science in technological systems management. The concentration in educational technology is designed for professional educators and educational researchers seeking to understand and innovatively use the computer and World Wide Web technologies that are dramatically changing what, how, where, and when people learn and teach. Students use and assess the latest developments in course software, Web-based learning, educational administration, multimedia equipment, modeling and simulation, virtual reality, and robotics/artificial intelligence and explore how computers and related technologies affect ergonomics, cognition, commerce, and social relations. Emphasis is placed on hands-on design projects and case studies of intriguing new or prospective educational technologies and systems. The program attracts educators, administrators, and information professionals at all levels and venues and people who are interested in pursuing advanced-research careers. The 30-credit program typically may be completed in one year by full-time students and two years by part-time students. All courses are offered in the evening.

An 18-credit Advanced Graduate Certificate in Educational Technology is also available.

Research Facilities

The Department has two advanced computer laboratories available for classroom work and as open laboratories for student projects and explorations. Students also can take advantage of opportunities for collaboration with Stony Brook's powerful resources in engineering and computer science (for example, sensors, communication systems, multimedia development, and miniaturization) and in information systems and psychology.

Financial Aid

Some research and teaching assistantships are available for full-time students. Many companies, government agencies, and national laboratories reimburse tuition costs.

Cost of Study

In 2006–07, full-time tuition at 12 credits for entering in-state residents was $3450 per semester, while out-of-state residents and international students paid $5460. Additional fees for each semester, including (but not limited to) the infirmary, activity, technology, and transportation fee, amount to about $430. International students also pay a service fee of $35 per semester and an orientation fee of $50. Fees for the mandatory Student Health Insurance Plan vary depending on citizenship and employment status.

Living and Housing Costs

For 2006–07, Stony Brook calculated the cost of education excluding tuition, fees, and insurance at $13,520 per year. On-campus apartments range in cost from approximately $316 per month to approximately $1456 per month, depending on the size of the unit and the number of students sharing the space. Off-campus housing options include rooms, houses, and apartments that can be rented from $350 to $2500 per month. Costs including books, food, and transportation may vary depending on academic program and/or personal circumstances.

Student Group

There are 30 matriculated educational technology students, of whom 25 percent are full-time and 75 percent are part-time, within an overall Departmental graduate program of approximately 80 students pursuing concentrations in global operations management, environmental and waste management, or educational technology. Twenty percent of the students come from other countries.

Student Outcomes

Graduates have established a distinguished record in their careers in schools and colleges, academic computing, industrial training, software applications, educational administration, and consulting.

Location

Stony Brook's campus is approximately 50 miles east of Manhattan on the north shore of Long Island. The cultural offerings of New York City and Suffolk County's countryside and seashore are conveniently located nearby. Cold Spring Harbor Laboratory and Brookhaven National Laboratory are easily accessible and have a close relationship with the University.

The University

The University, which was established in 1957, achieved national stature within a generation. Founded at Oyster Bay, Long Island, the school moved to its present location in 1962. Stony Brook has grown to encompass more than 110 buildings on 1,100 acres. There are more than 1,568 faculty members, and the annual budget is more than $805 million. The Graduate Student Organization oversees the spending of the student activity fee for graduate student campus events. International students find the additional four-week Summer Institute in American Living very helpful. The Intensive English Center offers classes in English as a second language. The Career Development Office assists with career planning and has information on full-time employment. Disabled Student Services has a Resource Center that offers placement testing, tutoring, vocational assessment, and psychological counseling. The Counseling Center provides individual, group, family, and marital counseling and psychotherapy. Day-care services are provided in four on-campus facilities. The Writing Center offers tutoring in all phases of writing.

Applying

For domestic students, all application materials to the master's program must be received by March 1 for the summer session, March 15 for the fall semester, and October 1 for the spring semester. For international students, all application materials for the master's program must be received by January 1 for the summer session, March 1 for the fall semester, and September 1 for the spring semester.

Correspondence and Information

Graduate Program Coordinator
Department of Technology and Society
347A Harriman Hall
Stony Brook University, State University of New York
Stony Brook, New York 11794-3760
Phone: 631-632-8765
E-mail: carole.rose@sunysb.edu
Web site: http://www.stonybrook.edu/est

Stony Brook University, State University of New York

THE FACULTY AND THEIR RESEARCH

Senior faculty members are internationally recognized pioneers in technology-society issues, curricular development, educational computing, and educational technologies.

Distinguished Service Professors
David L. Ferguson, Chairperson; Ph.D., Berkeley, 1980. Quantitative methods; computer applications (especially intelligent tutoring systems and decision-support systems); mathematics, science, and engineering education; decision making.
Lester G. Paldy, M.S., Hofstra, 1966. Nuclear arms control, science policy.

Distinguished Teaching Professor
Thomas T. Liao, Emeritus; Ed.D., Columbia, 1971. Computers in education, science and technology education.

Professors
Emil J. Piel, Emeritus; Ed.D., Rutgers, 1960. Decision making, technology-society issues, human-machine systems.
Tian-Lih Teng, Ph.D., Pittsburgh, 1969. Electrical engineering, computer science, management of information systems, electronics commerce.
Marian Visich Jr., Emeritus; Ph.D., Polytechnic of Brooklyn, 1956. Aerospace engineering, technology-society issues.

Associate Professors
Edward Kaplan, Visiting Associate Professor; Ph.D., Pennsylvania, 1973. Environmental systems engineering.
Samuel C. Morris, Visiting Associate Professor; Sc.D., Pittsburgh, 1973. Environmental science, risk analysis.
Sheldon J. Reaven, Graduate Program Director; Ph.D., Berkeley, 1975. Science and technology policy; energy and environmental problems and issues; waste management; recycling and pollution prevention; risk analysis and life-cycle analysis; nuclear, chemical, and biological threats; technology assessment; homeland security.
Lori L. Scarlatos, Ph.D., SUNY at Stony Brook, 1993. Computer-human interaction, multimedia and education, computer graphics.

Assistant Professors
Guodong Sun, Ph.D., Carnegie Mellon, 2000. Energy technology innovation, global climate change, energy and environmental policy, environmental management and regulatory reform in China.
David Tonges, Ph.D., SUNY at Stony Brook, 1998. Technology and environmental impact assessments, solid waste and impacts, alternative energy.

Lecturers
Joanne English Daly, M.S., SUNY at Stony Brook, 1994. Internet technology, computers in learning environments.
Herb Schiller, Emeritus; M.S.M.E., Caltech, 1966; M.S., Polytechnic, 1973. Operations management, manufacturing systems.

TEACHERS COLLEGE COLUMBIA UNIVERSITY

Department of Mathematics, Science, and Technology

Programs of Study

The world has been transformed by achievements in mathematics, science, and technology, and current reforms in education place increasing significance on understanding these fields. The Department of Mathematics, Science, and Technology focuses on issues of educational practice and the related professions in science, technology, mathematics, and cognate human sciences, including the relationships among these disciplines. Specialized programs address the needs of professional practitioners in each of these areas. Students can earn a Master of Arts, Master of Science, Master in Education, Doctor in Education, or Doctor of Philosophy (not available in all specialized programs) degree in communication and education, computing and education, instructional technology and media, mathematics education, or science education. The technology program includes technology's influence on areas such as literacy, teacher education, and culture. The mathematics and science education programs address the preparation of mathematics and science teachers and teacher educators, focusing particularly on the acquisition of scientific and mathematical literacy in order to foster the future development of science and technology, the understanding of environmental sciences, and the link between science and society.

The program in communication, computing, and technology in education provides degrees for students who seek to develop leadership capacities for using information and communication technologies in education across content fields. It includes an initial teacher licensure program at the master's level, leading to certification as a Technology Specialist, K–12. Each program has a unique focus or perspective, but the faculty members share a commitment to the improvement of society through improved scholarly practice in the educating professions and the enhancement of human potential in a broad range of educating institutions, but with a special focus on urban education.

Candidates are required to complete integrative projects that reflect the students' interests or display the specialized skills developed for the degree. Such a project might be a summation of current research and development work or a multimedia instructional application. It is recommended that students take some fieldwork or internships as part of their program.

Research Facilities

The Gottesman Libraries, with more than a million books and materials, is one of the nation's largest and most comprehensive research libraries in education, psychology, and health services. Students also have access to the 5.5 million volumes in the Columbia University library system. Organized research and service activities at Teachers College, in addition to being carried out by individual professors, are conducted through special projects and major institutes.

Data, voice, and video outlets are found in every classroom, office, and residence on the main portion of the campus, and laptops and projectors may be borrowed from Media Services. The Microcomputer Center provides students with PCs and Macintoshes, software, printers, and other peripherals. The center's software library includes PC and Macintosh programs for word processing, Web development, graphics, statistical analysis, and qualitative analysis and databases. The Instructional Media Lab (IML) is a facility in which students and faculty members create rich content for classes, online learning, student teaching, and research. Digital cameras and other equipment are loaned. Workstations allow computer-based full-motion video from camera, VCR, or videodisc to be edited and integrated with animation, digitized voice, and music and to be written to CD, DVD, or tape. IML also provides satellite downlink. Computer classrooms for hands-on instruction include both a PC and a Macintosh room, and the Goodman Family Computer Classroom suite includes a classroom with thirty-two notebook computers on tables that can be reconfigured for varying work groups.

Financial Aid

Each year, Teachers College awards approximately $6 million of its own funds in scholarship and stipend aid and $2 million of endowed funds to new and continuing students. There are no separate scholarship applications; faculty members nominate new students based upon their admission application. Financial assistance is also available through federal aid programs. All students are encouraged to file the FAFSA regardless of eligibility for aid; 51 percent of students receive financial aid.

Cost of Study

For the 2006–07 academic year, tuition was $975 per point, with 12 or more points considered full-time. Fees included the Teachers College, $320; Teachers College research, $320; health service, $356; continuous doctoral advisement registration, $2925; and Ph.D. oral defense, $4319. The tuition deposit was $300. Medical insurance ranged from $553 to $1218.

Living and Housing Costs

Teachers College offers a variety of on-campus housing options that are unique to the area and convenient to the campus. Housing for a single student ranges from $3100 to $8000 per semester, depending upon the type of setting selected. Family housing ranges from $6875 to $8200 per semester. Teachers College has approximately 705 spaces available for single students and 150 apartments for students with families. The buildings are located in the vibrant and historic urban neighborhood of Morningside Heights. Current residence halls are historic buildings similar to other apartment-style buildings that were in New York City in the early 1900s. A new residence hall opened in the fall 2004 semester.

Student Group

There are approximately 5,000 students enrolled at Teachers College. About 77 percent are women, 12 percent are African American, 11 percent are Asian American, and 7 percent are Latino/a. The student body is composed of 13 percent international students from eighty different countries and 87 percent domestic students from all fifty states.

Location

The College is located in the Morningside Heights section of Manhattan's Upper West Side. Home to such venerable New York landmarks as Lincoln Center, the Cathedral of St. John the Divine, Grant's Tomb, Morningside Park, and the Manhattan School of Music, the Upper West Side is bounded by Central Park on the east and the Hudson River on the west. Because the College is located in New York City, students have access to an outstanding array of learning organizations, including museums, libraries, galleries, corporate learning centers, and K–12 schools.

The College and The University

Teachers College was founded in 1887 to provide a new form of schooling for teachers of children from low-income families of New York, one that combined a humanitarian concern to help others with a scientific approach to human development. For more than 100 years, Teachers College has conducted research on the central issues facing education, prepared generations of education leaders, and shaped debate and public policy in education. The College provides programs of study in administration, counseling, curriculum development, and school health care and continues its efforts to strengthen teaching skills, prepare leaders to develop and administer psychological and health-care programs, and develop new teaching software. In 1898, the College became affiliated with Columbia.

Columbia University was founded in 1754 as King's College by royal charter of King George II of England. It is the oldest institution of higher learning in the state of New York and the fifth oldest in the United States. From its beginnings in a schoolhouse in lower Manhattan, the University has grown to encompass two principal campuses: the historic, neoclassical campus in Morningside Heights and the modern Medical Center in Washington Heights. Today, Columbia is one of the top academic and research institutions in the world, conducting research in medicine, science, the arts, and the humanities. It includes three undergraduate schools, thirteen graduate and professional schools, and a school of continuing education. Sixty-four Nobel laureates have taught or studied at Columbia. Each year, the faculty of approximately 4,000 teaches more than 23,000 students from more than 100 countries.

Applying

Teachers College welcomes applicants who wish to pursue graduate study associated with the education, psychological, and health service professions. All applicants receive consideration for admission without regard to race, color, creed, religion, sex, national origin, age, or disability. In order to be considered for scholarships, students must meet the early deadline. Admissions applications received after the early deadlines may be considered on a space-available basis. Certain programs have special application deadlines. The final and early deadline for Ph.D. and all psychology doctoral programs is December 15. The early deadline for Ed.D. programs is January 2, with a final deadline of April 1. The early deadline for master's programs is January 15, with a final deadline of April 15. The early deadline is November 1 for the spring semester. Teachers College requests that applicants collect the required documents for the application process and submit the entire package to the Office of Admission at one time. Admission application deadlines always refer to the date by which the Teachers College Office of Admissions must have received the application components and any other supporting material required by the Department.

Correspondence and Information

Office of Admissions
Teachers College Columbia University
525 West 120th Street, Box 302
New York, New York 10027
Phone: 212-678-3710
Web site: http://www.tc.columbia.edu/discover
http://www.tc.columbia.edu/mst

Teachers College Columbia University

THE FACULTY AND THEIR RESEARCH

Jamsheed Akrami-Ghorveh, Adjunct Associate Professor of Communication and Education; Ed.D., Columbia Teachers College. Cinema as cross-cultural communication, film as art, film as a medium, techniques and aesthetics of video production, film history, writing for radio and television.

O. Roger Anderson, Professor of Natural Sciences and Chair of the Department; Ed.D., Washington (St. Louis). Neurocognitive theory applied to science learning, electron microscopic and physiological ecological studies of eukaryotic microbiota.

John Black, Cleveland E. Dodge Professor of Telecommunications and Education; Ph.D., Stanford. Cognitive and neural network models of understanding, learning, and memory; using cognitive and neural net models to design learning environments; effects of using various technologies on cognition.

Howard R. Budin, Program Director; Ed.D., Columbia Teachers College. Integration of technology into school culture and curriculum; distance learning; using computers for problem solving, collaboration, and democratic deliberation; technology and teacher education.

Thomas Covotsos, Instructor in Science. Urban science education, biology education, middle school science education.

J. Peter Garrity, Adjunct Professor of Mathematics Education; Ed.D., Columbia Teachers College. Mathematics standards, training professional development, curriculum development, information technology, MathCamp.

Alexander Karp, Assistant Professor of Mathematics Education; Ph.D., St. Petersburg State Pedagogical (Russia). Curriculum, teacher training, student achievement level in mathematics, problem solving, history of mathematics education.

Sheila Kieran-Greenbush, Adjunct Assistant Professor of Computing and Education. Computer training, computer programming, curriculum development, Internet resources for education, Web publishing.

Charles Kinzer, Professor of Education; Ph.D., Berkeley. Language, literacy, and technology; computer, multimedia, and future literacies; technology and teacher education; case-based and social aspects of learning in electronic environments.

JoAnne Kleifgen, Associate Professor of Linguistics and Education; Ph.D., Illinois at Urbana-Champaign. Discourse analysis; children's second language and literacy development; computers and communication in schools, communities, and the workplace.

Henry J. Landau, Visiting Professor of Mathematics Education; Ph.D., Harvard. Fourier analysis, moment problems, matrices.

Xiaodong Lin, Associate Professor of Technology and Education; Ph.D., Purdue. Metacognition and problem solving, technology-mediated cultural interactions and their impact on teacher professional development and reflection, Asian education, student domain subject understanding, influence of technology-rich learning environments on lesson development, transcultural collaboration among teachers and students.

Susan Lowes, Adjunct Associate Professor of Computing and Education and Master's Advisor.

Robert McClintock, Sue Ann and John L. Weinberg Professor for the Historical and Philosophical Foundations of Education; Ph.D., Columbia Teachers College. Applications of digital technology to educational reform; interaction of political and educational theory; the city as educator; education as a self-organizing, emergent process.

Ellen B. Meier, Adjunct Assistant Professor of Computing and Education; Ed.D., Columbia Teachers College. Technology integration and school change; technology and teacher education; school leadership and technology; testing, technology, and school reform policies; professional development frameworks for integrating technology.

Felicia M. Moore, Assistant Professor of Science Education; Ph.D., Florida State. Issues of diversity related to pre-service/in-service teacher education and development; curriculum design, focusing on issues of diversity in teaching and assessing science; feminist poststructural thinking in science education and teacher professional development; integration of technology, math, and language arts in science instruction.

Frank A. Moretti, Professor of Communication and Education; Ph.D., Columbia. School-based leadership, digital technology in education, multimedia in education.

Henry Pollak, Visiting Professor of Mathematics; Ph.D., Harvard. Analysis, discrete mathematics, applications of mathematics and their place in mathematics curricula and in teacher education.

Mario Riccobon, Instructor, Instructional Technology and Media. Multimedia management and technical skills programs, computer-based instruction, educational video.

Ann E. Rivet, Assistant Professor of Science Education; Ph.D., Michigan. Science curriculum, inquiry-based learning, urban schools, contextualizing science learning.

Shawna Bu Shell, Instructor, Internship Coordinator, and Master's Advisor. The ways school-provided laptops influence urban student home environments, parental involvement in student education, preparing teachers with specialized methodology to teach in urban environments, integrating technology.

Robin Stern, Adjunct Associate Professor of Communication and Education; Ph.D., NYU. Emotional awareness in corporate and educational settings; renewal work for teachers, school counselors, and administrators; ethical leadership and emotional intelligence.

Robert Taylor, Associate Professor of Computing and Education; Ed.D., Columbia Teachers College. Computer-based technology in education, across the curriculum, and around the world, including its utility for human survival in a balanced ecosystem.

Thane Terrill, Adjunct Associate Professor of Computing and Education; Ed.D., Columbia Teachers College. School-based technology, Web site and multimedia creation, global curriculum, distance learning systems.

Herve Varenne, Professor of Education; Ph.D., Chicago. Culture and communication theory, comparative study of education in and out of school, family structure.

Lalitha Vasudevan, Assistant Professor of Technology and Education; Ph.D., Pennsylvania. Literacies, media, and technologies; youth, race/ethnicity, gender, and urban education; qualitative research, new methodologies, and representation.

Bruce Vogeli, Clifford Brewster Upton Professor of Mathematics Education; Ph.D., Michigan. International and comparative mathematics education, education of the mathematically gifted, curriculum development and evaluation.

Erica Walker, Assistant Professor of Mathematics and Education; Ed.D., Harvard. Racial and gender equity in mathematics education, student persistence in advanced mathematics, mathematics education policy.

VILLANOVA UNIVERSITY

Graduate Program in Counseling and Human Relations

Program of Study

In the Graduate Program in Counseling and Human Relations (CHR) a student can choose one of the following three course concentrations: elementary or secondary school counseling or community counseling. The elementary and secondary school counseling concentrations lead to approval for certification by the Pennsylvania Department of Education, and the community counseling concentration can lead to licensure as a professional counselor with the Bureau of Social Workers, Marriage and Family Therapists, and Professional Counselors. All students take the core program, including electives relating to the area of concentration, and the comprehensive examination, an integral part of the program. They must also demonstrate proficiency in counseling skills during a two-semester internship. A total of 48 credits is required for the degree.

Students have up to six years to complete the program, which begins when they take their first course—transfer or otherwise. Students must take CHR 8605 Laboratory in Counseling Skills and CHR 8655 Laboratory in Group Dynamics within the first 12 hours of graduate work. A thesis is not required but may be done in lieu of 6 credits of elective study.

Research Facilities

The Falvey Memorial Library at Villanova University houses about 600,000 volumes and 3,000 periodicals. An interlibrary loan system operates with the efficiency of e-mail. The library is located in the middle of the campus and includes numerous public-use computer stations that are equipped with sophisticated search engines and data retrieval mechanisms.

Financial Aid

Financial assistance is available, for those who qualify, through a variety of methods. A limited number of full-time graduate assistantships and part-time lab technician positions are available through the department. These positions include tuition remission of either 12 or 6 credits, in addition to a stipend for the full-time positions. Through a local bank, Villanova University has negotiated a student-loan package for which all students may apply. Several scholarships based on academic merit and other factors are available for students. Some provide full tuition. To help with the cost of tuition, Villanova may suggest a number of payment options, including credit card, deferred payment option, and employer tuition reimbursement (if available). Students should contact the Financial Assistance Office at 610-519-6456 for more information.

Students become eligible for financial assistance when they are enrolled for 9 or more credit hours per semester.

Cost of Study

Fees and expenses for graduate students in 2007–08 are $50 for the application fee, $585 per credit for tuition, and $60 per semester for general University fees. Additional tuition and fee information is available by calling the Bursar's Office at 610-519-4258.

Living and Housing Costs

A variety of affordable housing possibilities are available near the Villanova University campus. Housing costs vary in accordance with the option chosen. Room and board for a single graduate student may average about $8000 for a twelve-month period. Villanova University does not provide on-campus housing for graduate students.

Student Group

Students in the graduate CHR program combine a variety of academic backgrounds, professional interests, and personal aims. There are usually about 160 students matriculated in the program, with about one third full-time. The qualities most often mentioned and appreciated among the students are a collegial atmosphere, a high level of intellectual intensity, and practical experience.

Student Outcomes

The Graduate Program in Counseling and Human Relations prepares students to be counselors in school and community mental health agency settings. One track leads to certification as a school counselor through the Pennsylvania Department of Education, while the second track leads to a license in professional counseling through the Bureau of Social Workers, Marriage and Family Therapists, and Professional Counselors. The counseling program is widely recognized both locally and nationally for preparing counselors who know not only what it means to be a counselor but also how to be a professional counselor. Graduates of the program have been readily accepted into many other graduate programs nationwide (e.g., at the Universities of Massachusetts, Connecticut, Colorado, Michigan, and Delaware) and have gone on to distinguish themselves in many counseling programs.

Location

Villanova University is situated on the historic Main Line, in a safe, western suburb of Philadelphia. Villanova is located on Lancaster Avenue (Route 30), 2 minutes from the Blue Route (Route 476) and 5 minutes from the Pennsylvania Turnpike, the Schuylkill Expressway, and Route 202. With ample parking and mass transit stops right on campus grounds, students can travel easily to and from the campus by car, bus, or train.

The University

Villanova University is an institution that is rich in history and Catholic tradition. From its modest beginnings on the country estate of a Revolutionary War officer, the University has seen significant growth in its student population as well as in its position as a leading coeducational institution of higher learning.

Applying

All students interested in graduate studies in counseling and human relations that lead to certification as a school counselor or licensure as a professional counselor must choose the appropriate track prior to admission. Applications for admission are required to include two complete undergraduate transcripts; three letters of recommendation from people who know the candidate personally, professionally, and/or academically; a completed departmental Work Experience and Goals worksheet; and test scores from either the Graduate Record Examinations or the Miller Analogies Test.

Applicants should send the three letters of recommendation, work experience and goals form, and a current resume to Marion Angelini, Department of Education and Human Services, Villanova University, 800 Lancaster Avenue, Villanova, Pennsylvania 19085-1699; they should send the application for admission, the nonrefundable application fee, all official postsecondary transcripts, and the GRE or MAT scores to Graduate Studies in the College of Liberal Arts and Sciences, Villanova University, 800 Lancaster Avenue, Villanova, Pennsylvania 19085-1699. Application forms are available online or from the Office of Graduate Studies. The deadline for receipt of applications for the fall semester is May 1; for the spring semester, November 15. Applications for financial aid are due by April 1.

Correspondence and Information

Department of Education and Human Services
Villanova University
800 Lancaster Avenue
Villanova, Pennsylvania 19085
Phone: 610-519-4620
Fax: 610-519-4623
E-mail: eduhs@villanova.edu
Web site: http://education.villanova.edu

Villanova University

THE FACULTY

Kenneth M. Davis, Associate Professor; Ed.D., Northern Illinois, 1972.
Beverly B. Kahn, Assistant Professor; Ph.D., Temple, 1986.
Krista Malott, Assistant Professor; Ph.D., Northern Colorado, 2005.
Rayna D. Markin, Assistant Professor; Ph.D., Maryland, College Park, 2007.
Michael Mason, Assistant Professor; Ph.D., Oregon State, 1992.
Joan Q. Monnig, Assistant Professor; Ed.D., Massachusetts, 1973.
Robert J. Murray, O.S.A., Assistant Professor and Program Director; Ph.D., Temple, 1995.
Christopher D. Schmidt, Assistant Professor; William and Mary, Ph.D., 2007.

VIRGINIA COMMONWEALTH UNIVERSITY

Program in Art Education

Program of Study
Virginia Commonwealth University (VCU) offers the Master of Art Education (M.A.E.), with two specific tracks. One is for teachers who are already licensed and who wish to deepen their understanding of art education. The second is for people who hold a baccalaureate degree and wish to earn both a master's degree in art education and a teaching license at the same time. The program includes required and elective courses and allows students to pursue their areas of interest. All students are expected to work at a high level of independence, be self-motivated, respect peers and instructors, and participate in the opportunities that the Department of Art Education and the School of the Arts offer. With the assistance of an adviser, the student determines a viable structure for the content and sequence of a program of graduate studies. Such a program can utilize the collective expertise of the art education faculty as well as appropriate community resources. Graduate course work, therefore, could include both on- and off-campus involvement.

Opportunities for personal growth through the M.A.E. program also include the rich resources of other graduate departments in the University, including the visual and performing arts, education (including supervision, administration, and special areas), the natural and social sciences, and the humanities. A thesis or project option may develop from graduate course work or professional involvement. Projects are those endeavors of thesis proportion that do not fit the traditional thesis format. A thesis or project may be explored by descriptive research, historical research, empirical/statistical research, design of learning packages, philosophical study, curriculum development, or action research. In lieu of the thesis, students may elect to complete 6 credit hours of graduate course work in the Department of Art Education. In addition, the student must successfully pass a written and oral examination at the conclusion of all course work. Full-time students who take 9–12 hours per semester and hours in the summer may expect to complete their degree in two years. Students must complete the degree within five years.

Research Facilities
VCU libraries provide a combined capacity of more than 1.7 million volumes and 10,200 periodical titles and an online bibliographic search service accessing hundreds of databases. In addition, the Virginia state and Richmond public libraries are within walking distance of both VCU campuses. Academic Computing provides a variety of microcomputer, minicomputer, and mainframe computing services to support the research and instructional endeavors of its faculty members and students, including consultation, instruction, and computer acquisition.

Well known for presenting the work of nationally and internationally renowned artists, emerging figures, and regional names, the Anderson Gallery at VCU mounts exhibitions that explore currents in contemporary art and design. The Anderson Gallery publishes new writing on contemporary art every year, featuring essays by guest authorities, curators, and gallery faculty members. Catalogues, which combine new scholarship with innovative design, are produced for each major exhibition. The Gallery's publications have received awards from the American Association of Museums (AAM), the Southeastern Museums Conference & Association (SEMC), and design industries, including from the Print Industries of Virginia (PIVA). In addition to presenting important exhibitions, publications, and lecture series, the Anderson Gallery is known for its extensive permanent collection.

Financial Aid
Students may apply for need-based assistance with the University's Financial Aid Office. Current information on financial aid programs, policies, and procedures is available at http://www.vcu.edu/enroll/finaid.

Cost of Study
For full-time study (9–15 credits) in 2007–08, Virginia residents pay tuition and fees of $4452 per semester; nonresidents, $8876 per semester. For part-time study, Virginia residents pay tuition and fees of $465 per credit hour; nonresidents, $954 per credit hour. Some programs require additional fees. On the Medical College of Virginia (MCV) campus, tuition, fees, and other expenses vary in the medicine, pharmacy, nurse anesthesia, dentistry, and School of Allied Health programs.

Living and Housing Costs
Graduate student housing is available on both the MCV campus and the academic campus of Virginia Commonwealth University. Many graduate students live in off-campus housing, which is reasonably priced and readily available in a variety of styles and settings in nearby residential areas or within easy commuting distance. On- and off-campus housing information is available on the Web at http://www.students.vcu.edu/housing.

Student Group
VCU enrolls 30,452 students, 7,611 of whom are graduate students. More than 200 clubs and organizations reflect the diverse social, recreational, educational, political, and religious interests of the student body.

Location
Richmond is Virginia's capital and a major East Coast financial and manufacturing center that offers students a wide range of cultural, educational, and recreational activities. Richmond is located in central Virginia at the intersection of Interstates 95 and 64, 2 hours south of Washington, D.C., and nestled between the Blue Ridge Mountains and the Atlantic Coast. The Richmond region is easily accessible by plane, car, and train. With nearly 1 million residents, the historic city of Richmond combines big-city offerings with small-town hospitality. Applicants are encouraged to explore http://www.visit.richmond.com/ for more information on the city.

The University
VCU is a state-supported coeducational university with a graduate school, a major teaching hospital, and twelve academic and professional units that offer fifty-two undergraduate, twenty-two postbaccalaureate, sixty-five master's, six post-master's certificate, and twenty-nine Ph.D. programs. VCU also offers M.D., D.D.S., D.P.T., and Pharm.D. programs as well as cooperative degree programs with other major Virginia colleges and universities. VCU has one of the largest evening colleges in the United States. The academic campus is located in Richmond's historic Fan District. The health sciences campus and hospital are located 2 miles east in the downtown business district. A University bus service provides free intercampus transportation for faculty members and students. With more than $211 million in annual research funding, the Carnegie Foundation for the Advancement of Teaching ranks Virginia Commonwealth University as one of the nation's top research universities. More than 29,000 undergraduate, certificate, graduate, post-master's, professional, and doctoral students are enrolled in 162 academic programs, forty of which are unique in the commonwealth of Virginia. The faculty members at Virginia Commonwealth University represent the finest American and international graduate institutions and enhance the University's position among the important institutions of higher learning in the United States and the world via their work in the classroom, laboratory, studio, and clinic and in their scholarly publications.

Applying
Admission procedures and program requirements are detailed in the *Graduate Bulletin*. Application deadlines and materials, including the application and the *Graduate Bulletin*, are available online at the Graduate School Web site at http://www.graduate.vcu.edu. Virginia Commonwealth University is an equal opportunity/affirmative action institution providing access to education and employment without regard to age, race, color, national origin, gender, religion, sexual orientation, veteran's status, political affiliation, or disability.

Correspondence and Information
Melanie L. Buffington, Graduate Program Director
Department of Art Education
School of the Arts
812 West Franklin Street
Virginia Commonwealth University
P.O. Box 843084
Richmond, Virginia 23284-3084
Phone: 804-828-3805
Fax: 804-827-0255
E-mail: artedgrad@vcu.edu
Web site: http://www.vcu.edu/arts/arteducation/dept

Virginia Commonwealth University

THE FACULTY AND THEIR RESEARCH

Sarah Branigan, Instructor and Administrative Director; M.A.E., Georgia. Cuban art.

Melanie L. Buffington, Assistant Professor; Ph.D., Ohio State. Museum education, technology in art/museum education, Web 2.0, integrated/interdisciplinary curriculum, preservice teacher preparation, feminist theory and practice.

David Burton, Professor; Ph.D., Penn State. Demographics related to art education, secondary analysis of national (NAEP) research in art education, student art exhibitions.

Min Cho, Assistant Professor; Ph.D., Florida State. Evaluation and teacher training in service-learning, curriculum integration, teacher professional development.

Nancy Lampert, Assistant Professor; Ed.D., William and Mary. Curriculum, technology in art education, critical thinking in the arts.

Pamela G. Taylor, Associate Professor and Chair; Ph.D., Penn State. Service-learning and art foundation, interactive computer technology, inquiry and meaning-based art education, music video and visual culture art education, art education experiences in Cuba, virtual learning portfolios.

Sara Wilson-McKay, Assistant Professor; Ph.D., Penn State. New media theory, social theory, dialogics, action research, collaborative research, preservice teacher training, feminist theory and pedagogy, curriculum development, teaching and learning outcomes.

VIRGINIA COMMONWEALTH UNIVERSITY

Program in Counselor Education

Programs of Study	Virginia Commonwealth University (VCU), through the Department of Counselor Education, prepares counselors with the specialized knowledge and skills required for placement in elementary, middle, and high schools in the Commonwealth of Virginia and throughout the nation. Consistent with this approach are the program goals of graduating students who have knowledge of basic counseling theory and practice, possess competencies in essential counseling services, have the skills necessary to evaluate relevant research, and are committed to evaluating their counseling interventions.

The 48-semester-hour program leads to school counseling licensure in Virginia and preparation for advanced graduate work at the post-master's level. For students who already have a master's degree in education, completion of the 33 credits of program core courses in counseling leads to recommendation for licensure as a school counselor. A written comprehensive examination must be passed successfully at the end of the program. Individuals must meet technology standards approved by the Virginia Board of Education and must supply proof of child-abuse and neglect-recognition training. Individuals who successfully complete the program are eligible for licensure, provisional licensure, or endorsement as a K–12 school counselor.

The Counselor Education Student Networking Association (CESNA) is the department's active student organization whose aim is to develop collegiality and a spirit of professionalism among graduate counselor education students. Relationships established during graduate school provide students with a network of colleagues with whom they may share ideas and resources as they begin their careers as professional school counselors.

The department's nationally recognized counselor-in-residence program allows students to interact with a practicing school counselor who serves a yearlong term as a visiting faculty member in the department. Former counselors-in-residence form a strong cadre of professionals who serve as adjunct instructors in the department when the need arises.

Research Facilities VCU libraries provide a combined capacity of more than 1.7 million volumes and 10,200 periodical titles and an online bibliographic search service accessing hundreds of databases. In addition, the Virginia State and Richmond Public libraries are within walking distance of both VCU campuses. Academic Computing provides a variety of microcomputer, minicomputer, and mainframe computing services to support the research and instructional endeavors of its faculty and students, including consultation, instruction, and computer acquisition.

The School of Education sponsors a variety of centers and institutes that connect students and faculty to the field of practice, including the Center for School Community Collaboration, the Center for Teacher Leadership, the Child Development Center, the Commonwealth Educational Policy Institute (CEPI), the Metropolitan Educational Research Consortium (MERC), the Partnership for People with Disabilities, the Virginia Department of Education's (VDOE) Training & Technical Assistance Center (T/TAC), the Rehabilitation Research and Training Center, the Virginia Adult Learning Resource Center, the Virginia Center for Teaching International Studies, and the Metropolitan Educational Training Alliance (META).

Financial Aid Students may apply for need-based assistance through the University's Financial Aid Office. Current information on financial aid programs, policies, and procedures is available at http://www.vcu.edu/enroll/finaid.

Cost of Study For full-time study (9–15 credits) in 2007–08, Virginia residents pay tuition and fees of $4452 per semester; nonresidents, $8876 per semester. For part-time study, Virginia residents pay tuition and fees of $465 per hour; nonresidents, $954 per hour. Some programs require additional fees. On the Medical College of Virginia (MCV) campus, tuition, fees, and other expenses vary in the medicine, pharmacy, nurse anesthesia, dentistry, and School of Allied Health programs.

Living and Housing Costs Graduate student housing is available on both the MCV campus and the academic campus of Virginia Commonwealth University. Many graduate students live in off-campus housing, which is reasonably priced and readily available in a variety of styles and settings in nearby residential areas or within easy commuting distance. On- and off-campus housing information is available on the Web at http://www.housing.vcu.edu/.

Student Group VCU enrolls 30,452 students, 7,611 of whom are graduate students. More than 200 clubs and organizations reflect the diverse social, recreational, educational, political, and religious interests of the student body.

Location Richmond is Virginia's capital and a major East Coast financial and manufacturing center that offers students a wide range of cultural, educational, and recreational activities. Richmond is located in central Virginia at the intersection of Interstates 95 and 64, 2 hours south of Washington, D.C., and nestled between the Blue Ridge Mountains and the Atlantic coast. The Richmond region is easily accessible by plane, car, and train. With nearly 1 million residents, the historic city of Richmond combines big-city offerings with small-town hospitality. Applicants are encouraged to explore http://www.visit.richmond.com/ for more information on the city.

The University VCU is a state-supported coeducational university with a graduate school, a major teaching hospital, and twelve academic and professional units that offer fifty-two undergraduate, twenty-two postbaccalaureate certificate, sixty-five master's, six post-master's certificate, and twenty-nine Ph.D. programs. VCU also offers M.D., D.D.S., D.P.T., and Pharm.D. programs as well as cooperative degree programs with other major Virginia colleges and universities. VCU has one of the largest evening colleges in the United States. The academic campus is located in Richmond's historic Fan District. The health sciences campus and hospital are located 2 miles east in the downtown business district. A University bus service provides free intercampus transportation for faculty members and students.

With more than $211 million in annual research funding, Virginia Commonwealth University is classified as one of the nation's top research universities by the Carnegie Foundation for the Advancement of Teaching. More than 29,000 undergraduate, certificate, graduate, post-master's, professional, and doctoral students are enrolled in 162 academic programs, forty of which are unique in the commonwealth of Virginia. The faculty members represent the finest American and international graduate institutions and enhance the University's position among the important institutions of higher learning in the United States and the world via their work in the classroom, laboratory, studio, and clinic and in their scholarly publications.

Applying Admission procedures and program requirements are detailed in the *Graduate Bulletin*. Application deadlines and materials, including the application and the *Graduate Bulletin*, are available online at the Graduate School Web site at http://www.graduate.vcu.edu. Virginia Commonwealth University is an equal opportunity/affirmative action institution providing access to education and employment without regard to age, race, color, national origin, gender, religion, sexual orientation, veteran's status, political affiliation, or disability.

Correspondence and Information
Mary Hermann, Director
Department of Counselor Education
School of Education
1015 West Main Street
Virginia Commonwealth University
Richmond, Virginia 23284-2020
Phone: 804-828-2626
Fax: 804-828-1323
E-mail: mahermann @vcu.edu
Web site: http://www.soe.vcu.edu/

Virginia Commonwealth University

THE FACULTY AND THEIR RESEARCH

Donna J. Dockery, Assistant Professor; Ph.D., Virginia. Effective counseling for at-risk and nontraditional students, psychosocial needs of gifted youth, multicultural populations and counseling.

Mary Hermann, Assistant Professor; J.D., Loyola New Orleans, 1995; Ph.D., New Orleans, 2001. School counseling, legal and ethical issues in counseling, gender issues in counseling.

Susan Leone, Associate Professor and Chair; Ed.D., Virginia, 1994. Counseling ethics, group work, counseling history and professionalism.

Catherine Moffett, Affiliate Faculty, Ed.D. School counseling and the promotion of a nurturing academic climate in K–12 schools where achievement gaps are closed and barriers to student learning are removed.

VIRGINIA COMMONWEALTH UNIVERSITY

Department of Music

Program of Study	Virginia Commonwealth University (VCU) offers the Master of Music degree in music education as a three-summer degree course. The program is designed so that the primary course work for the degree is completed in three summers, with a 1-credit online seminar during each fall and spring semester (to monitor student development and to ensure continuous enrollment). Additional time may be required to complete the thesis. The fundamental philosophy of the degree is to assist and enhance the ability of public- and private-school music specialists to teach music effectively to every student. To obtain this goal, music educators are stimulated by current research in music to seek, evaluate, and appropriately implement current ideas and developments in teaching music. Degree candidates complete approximately 9 credit hours each summer for three summers, including courses in general education and teaching pedagogies, as well as specialty courses in choral, instrumental, general, and jazz methods. Summer courses are also open to non-degree-seeking students as workshops.
Research Facilities	VCU libraries provide a combined capacity of more than 1.7 million volumes and 10,200 periodical titles and an online bibliographic search service accessing hundreds of databases. In addition, the Virginia State and Richmond Public libraries are within walking distance of both VCU campuses. Academic Computing provides a variety of microcomputer, minicomputer, and mainframe computing services to support the research and instructional endeavors of its faculty and students, including consultation, instruction, and computer acquisition. The W. E. Singleton Center for the Performing Arts, located at 922 Park Avenue, on the corner of Park Avenue and Harrison Street, houses the 500-seat Sonia Vlahcevic Concert Hall, the administrative offices of the Department of Music, the VCU Music Box Office, large ensemble rehearsal space, classrooms, faculty studios, an organ suite, and percussion practice rooms. The Department of Theatre's Raymond Hodges Theatre is also housed in the Singleton Center, along with that department's administrative offices, the TheatreVCU box office, rehearsal and classroom space, and set-construction areas. The James W. Black Music Center, which underwent renovations in the 2006–07 academic year, is located at 1015 Grove Avenue, directly across from the Singleton Center for the Performing Arts. The 300-seat recital hall provides space for many student recitals as well as ensemble programs. Classrooms and faculty studios, in addition to numerous practice rooms for student use, are in the music center. Formerly Grove Avenue Baptist Church, the building was acquired by the University in 1977 and is part of the University's historic building tour. The building also includes a photography lab and darkroom.
Financial Aid	Students may apply for need-based assistance with the University's Financial Aid Office. Current information on financial aid programs, policies, and procedures is available at http://www.vcu.edu/enroll/finaid.
Cost of Study	For full-time study (9–15 credits) in 2007–08, Virginia residents pay tuition and fees of $4452 per semester; nonresidents, $8876 per semester. For part-time study, Virginia residents pay tuition and fees of $465 per hour; nonresidents, $954 per hour. Some programs require additional fees. On the Medical College of Virginia (MCV) campus, tuition, fees, and other expenses vary in the medicine, pharmacy, nurse anesthesia, dentistry, and School of Allied Health programs.
Living and Housing Costs	Graduate student housing is available on both the MCV campus and the academic campus of Virginia Commonwealth University. Many graduate students live in off-campus housing, which is reasonably priced and readily available in a variety of styles and settings in nearby residential areas or within easy commuting distance. On- and off-campus housing information is available on the Web at http://www.housing.vcu.edu/.
Student Group	VCU enrolls 30,452 students, 7,611 of whom are graduate students. More than 200 clubs and organizations reflect the diverse social, recreational, educational, political, and religious interests of the student body.
Location	Richmond is Virginia's capital and a major East Coast financial and manufacturing center that offers students a wide range of cultural, educational, and recreational activities. Richmond is located in central Virginia at the intersection of Interstates 95 and 64, 2 hours south of Washington, D.C., and nestled between the Blue Ridge Mountains and the Atlantic coast. The Richmond region is easily accessible by plane, car, and train. With nearly 1 million residents, the historic city of Richmond combines big-city offerings with small-town hospitality. Applicants are encouraged to explore http://www.visit.richmond.com/ for more information on the city.
The University	VCU is a state-supported coeducational university with a graduate school, a major teaching hospital, and twelve academic and professional units that offer fifty-two undergraduate, twenty-two postbaccalaureate certificate, sixty-five master's, six post-master's certificate, and twenty-nine Ph.D. programs. VCU also offers M.D., D.D.S., D.P.T., and Pharm.D. programs as well as cooperative degree programs with other major Virginia colleges and universities. VCU has one of the largest evening colleges in the United States. The academic campus is located in Richmond's historic Fan District. The health sciences campus and hospital are located 2 miles east in the downtown business district. A University bus service provides free intercampus transportation for faculty members and students.
	With more than $211 million in annual research funding, Virginia Commonwealth University is classified as one of the nation's top research universities by the Carnegie Foundation for the Advancement of Teaching. More than 29,000 undergraduate, certificate, graduate, post-master's, professional, and doctoral students are enrolled in 162 academic programs, forty of which are unique in the commonwealth of Virginia. The faculty members represent the finest American and international graduate institutions and enhance the University's position among the important institutions of higher learning in the United States and the world via their work in the classroom, laboratory, studio, and clinic and in their scholarly publications.
Applying	Admission procedures and program requirements are detailed in the *Graduate Bulletin*. Application deadlines and materials, including the application and the *Graduate Bulletin*, are available online at the Graduate School Web site at http://www.graduate.vcu.edu. Virginia Commonwealth University is an equal opportunity/affirmative action institution providing access to education and employment without regard to age, race, color, national origin, gender, religion, sexual orientation, veteran's status, political affiliation, or disability.
Correspondence and Information	Linda Johnston School of the Arts Department of Music 922 Park Avenue Virginia Commonwealth University P.O. Box 842004 Richmond, Virginia 23284-2004 Phone: 804-828-1166 E-mail: gradmus@vcu.edu Web site: http://www.pubinfo.vcu.edu/artweb/music/degree/grad.html

Virginia Commonwealth University

THE FACULTY

Departmental faculty members are active in their fields outside of the classroom. In all their student interactions—class work, performance, and applied lessons—this real-world experience is invaluable.

Brass
Rex Richardson, Assistant Professor; M.M., LSU, 2000. Trumpet.
Patrick Smith, Assistant Professor; Ph.D., Florida, 2001. French horn.
Ross Walter, Assistant Professor; D.M.A., LSU, 1996. Low brass.
Robert Ellithorpe, Adjunct. Trombone.
Steven Fenick, Adjunct. Trumpet.

Guitar
John Patykula, Associate Professor and Coordinator; M.A., Virginia Commonwealth, 1982.
Steve Ashby, Adjunct.
Charlie Moeser, Adjunct. Flamenco.
David Robinson, Adjunct.
Kathy Robinson, Adjunct.
David Toussaint, Adjunct.
Andrew Winn, Adjunct.

Jazz Studies
Doug Richards, Professor; M.M., Florida State, 1973. Arranging.
Antonio García, Associate Professor and Director of Jazz Studies; M.M., Rochester, 1985. Trombone.
Rex Richardson, Assistant Professor; M.M., LSU, 2000. Trumpet.
Taylor Barnett, Adjunct. Jazz Orchestra II, trumpet.
Daniel Clarke, Adjunct. Piano.
Victor Dvoskin, Adjunct. Double bass.
Arthur Esposito, Adjunct. Jazz lab.
Michael Ess, Adjunct. Guitar.
George "Skip" Gailes, Adjunct. Saxophone.
Robert Hallahan, Adjunct. Piano.
Bryan Hooten, Adjunct. Small Jazz Ensemble.
J. C. Kuhl, Adjunct. Saxophone.
Tony Martucci, Adjunct. Drum set, percussion.

Music Education
Terry Austin, Professor; Ph.D., Wisconsin–Madison, 1984.
David Greennagel, Assistant Professor and Director of Music Education; Ph.D., Miami, 1994.
Rebecca Tyree, Assistant Professor, Choral Music Education; M.M., Maryland, College Park.

Music History
Doug Richards, Professor; M.M., Florida State, 1973.
Patrick Smith, Assistant Professor; Ph.D., Florida, 2001.
Patrick Carlin, Adjunct.
Kevin Harding, Adjunct.

Music Theory
Sonia Vlahcevic, Professor; Ph.D., Catholic University, 1975.
Bruce Hammel, Associate Professor; D.M.A., Florida State, 1989.
James Wiznerowicz, Assistant Professor; D.M.A., Arizona, 2004.
Taylor Barnett, Adjunct.

Percussion
Kris Keeton, Assistant Professor; M.M., Northwestern, 2003. Percussion.
Mike Boyd, Adjunct. Percussion, drum set.
Tony Martucci, Adjunct. Drum set, percussion.

Piano
Sonia Vlahcevic, Professor; Ph.D., Catholic University, 1975. Piano.
Dmitri Shteinberg, Assistant Professor and Area Coordinator; D.M.A., Manhattan School of Music, 2004.
Laura Candler-White, Adjunct. Piano.
Marta Puig, Adjunct. Piano.
Charles Staples, Adjunct. Piano.
Russell Wilson, Adjunct. Piano.
Ray Breakall, Piano technician.

Strings
Jean Montès, Assistant Professor and Director of Orchestral Studies; Ph.D., Iowa, 2003.
Kelly Ali, Adjunct. Double bass.
Regine Barrau, Adjunct. Violin.
Neal Cary, Adjunct. Cello.
Susanna Klein, Adjunct. Violin.
Tom Lindsay, Adjunct. Violin.
Stephen Schmidt, Adjunct. Violin/viola.

Voice/Opera
L. Wayne Batty, Professor; M.M., Roosevelt, 1949.
Cynthia Donnell, Coordinator and Associate Professor; M.M., North Carolina at Greensboro, 1974.
Melanie Day, Assistant Professor and Opera Theatre Vocal Coach; M.M., Boston University, 1978.
Anne Guthmiller, Adjunct.
Michelle Harman-Gulick, Adjunct.
Jim Smith-Parham, Voice and Vocal Coach and Adjunct.
James Taylor, Adjunct.

Woodwinds
Charles West, Professor and Coordinator of Winds and Percussion; D.M.A., Iowa, 1975. Clarinet.
Bruce Hammel, Associate Professor; D.M.A., Florida State, 1989. Bassoon.
Francile Bilyeu, Assistant Professor; M.M., Tulsa, 1963. Flute.
Susan Davis, Adjunct. Flute.
David Niethamer, Adjunct. Clarinet.
Kevin Piccini, Adjunct. Oboe.
Albert Regni, Adjunct. Saxophone.
James Richmond, Adjunct. Saxophone.

VIRGINIA COMMONWEALTH UNIVERSITY

Program in Reading

Program of Study

Virginia Commonwealth University (VCU) offers the Master of Education (M.Ed.) in reading. For experienced teachers who are prospective reading specialists, the program provides sequential and integrated experiences in areas of the reading curriculum ranging from preschool to adult levels. Students gain an understanding of the developmental and diagnostic processes involved in teaching reading and the language arts and become familiar with the resource and supervisory functions, which are part of the specialist role.

Prior to graduation, students must complete a reading portfolio documenting their work in the program and related work experiences. The M.Ed. in reading is an approved program (K–12) for students who meet Virginia State Department of Education requirements. The reading specialist endorsement also requires completion of three years of teaching in a reading-related field. A cooperative agreement has been established with Virginia State University to permit selected qualified students to complete the M.Ed. in reading program.

Up to 12 credit hours from an approved list may be transferred from the cooperating institution. To obtain the M.Ed. in reading, students must complete at least 36 credits. Students take 9 credits in foundational courses and 15 to 18 credits in the core curriculum. The program also requires a 3-credit research project and at least 9 credits in electives.

Research Facilities

VCU libraries provide a combined capacity of more than 1.7 million volumes, 10,200 periodical titles, and an online bibliographic search service accessing hundreds of databases. In addition, the Virginia state and Richmond public libraries are within walking distance of both VCU campuses. Academic Computing provides a variety of microcomputer, minicomputer, and mainframe computing services to support the research and instructional endeavors of its faculty and students, including consultation, instruction, and computer acquisition.

The School of Education sponsors a variety of centers and institutes that connect students and faculty members to the field of practice, including the Center for School Community Collaboration, the Center for Teacher Leadership, the Child Development Center, the Commonwealth Educational Policy Institute (CEPI), the Metropolitan Educational Research Consortium (MERC), the Partnership for People with Disabilities, the Virginia Department of Education's (VDOE) Training and Technical Assistance Center (T/TAC), the Rehabilitation Research and Training Center, the Virginia Adult Learning Resource Center, the Virginia Center for Teaching International Studies, and the Metropolitan Educational Training Alliance (META).

Financial Aid

Students may apply for need-based assistance through the University's Financial Aid Office. Current information on financial aid programs, policies, and procedures is available at http://www.vcu.edu/enroll/finaid.

Cost of Study

For full-time study (9–15 credits) in 2007–08, Virginia residents pay tuition and fees of $4452 per semester; nonresidents, $8876 per semester. For part-time study, Virginia residents pay tuition and fees of $465 per hour; nonresidents, $954 per hour. Some programs require additional fees. On the Medical College of Virginia (MCV) campus, tuition, fees, and other expenses vary in the medicine, pharmacy, nurse anesthesia, dentistry, and School of Allied Health programs.

Living and Housing Costs

Graduate student housing is available on both the MCV campus and the academic campus of Virginia Commonwealth University. Many graduate students live in off-campus housing, which is reasonably priced and readily available in a variety of styles and settings in nearby residential areas or within easy commuting distance. On- and off-campus housing information is available on the Web at http://www.housing.vcu.edu/.

Student Group

VCU enrolls 30,452 students, 7,611 of whom are graduate students. More than 200 clubs and organizations reflect the diverse social, recreational, educational, political, and religious interests of the student body.

Location

Richmond is Virginia's capital and a major East Coast financial and manufacturing center that offers students a wide range of cultural, educational, and recreational activities. Richmond is located in central Virginia at the intersection of Interstates 95 and 64, 2 hours south of Washington, D.C., and nestled between the Blue Ridge Mountains and the Atlantic coast. The Richmond region is easily accessible by plane, car, and train. With nearly 1 million residents, the historic city of Richmond combines big-city offerings with small-town hospitality. Applicants are encouraged to explore http://www.visit.richmond.com/ for more information on the city.

The University

VCU is a state-supported coeducational university with a graduate school, a major teaching hospital, and twelve academic and professional units that offer fifty-two undergraduate, twenty-two postbaccalaureate certificate, sixty-five master's, six post-master's certificate, and twenty-nine Ph.D. programs. VCU also offers M.D., D.D.S., D.P.T., and Pharm.D. programs as well as cooperative degree programs with other major Virginia colleges and universities. VCU has one of the largest evening colleges in the United States. The academic campus is located in Richmond's historic Fan District. The health sciences campus and hospital are located 2 miles east in the downtown business district. A University bus service provides free intercampus transportation for faculty members and students.

With more than $211 million in annual research funding, Virginia Commonwealth University is classified as one of the nation's top research universities by the Carnegie Foundation for the Advancement of Teaching. More than 29,000 undergraduate, certificate, graduate, post-master's, professional, and doctoral students are enrolled in 162 academic programs, forty of which are unique in the commonwealth of Virginia. The faculty members represent the finest American and international graduate institutions and enhance the University's position among the important institutions of higher learning in the United States and the world via their work in the classroom, laboratory, studio, and clinic and in their scholarly publications.

Applying

Admission procedures and program requirements are detailed in the *Graduate Bulletin*. Application deadlines and materials, including the application and the *Graduate Bulletin,* are available online at the Graduate School Web site at http://www.graduate.vcu.edu. Virginia Commonwealth University is an equal opportunity/affirmative action institution providing access to education and employment without regard to age, race, color, national origin, gender, religion, sexual orientation, veteran's status, political affiliation, or disability.

Correspondence and Information

Michael D. Davis, Chair
Department of Teaching and Learning
School of Education
1015 West Main Street
Virginia Commonwealth University
Richmond, Virginia 23284-2020
Phone: 804-828-1305
Fax: 804-828-1323
E-mail: mddavis@vcu.edu
Web site: http://www.soe.vcu.edu/

Virginia Commonwealth University

THE FACULTY AND THEIR RESEARCH

Nora Alder, Associate Professor; Ed.D., Nevada, 1996. Caring student/teacher relationships and urban schooling and teacher education.

Terry Carter, Assistant Professor; Ph.D., George Washington, 2001. Transformative learning among professionals in the workplace, learning through developmental relationships, including mentoring.

Seonhee Cho, Assistant Professor; Ph.D., Tennessee, 2005. ESL/international students' academic socialization issues that include relationships with peers and teachers, group work, institutional support, and access to academic resources.

Leila Christenbury, Professor; Ed.D., Virginia Tech, 1980. Classroom interaction strategies, specifically questioning; all aspects of young adult literature; the teaching of writing to secondary school students; approaches to teaching and learning in the secondary English classroom.

Michael Davis, Professor and Chair; Ph.D., Illinois, 1975. School change, teacher preparation.

Terry Dozier, Associate Professor and Director of the Center for Teacher Leadership, Ed.D., Promoting and supporting teacher leadership that enhances the quality of teaching and the teaching profession.

Ena Gross, Associate Professor; Ph.D., Georgia State, 1980. Math education.

Jacqueline McDonnough, Assistant Professor; Ph.D., Virginia, 2002. Assessing how pre-service teachers' K-12 science experiences interact with their self-efficacy as future teachers of science.

Tammy Milby, Instructor; M.Ed., Radford, 1995. Struggling readers and writers, teacher quality/professional development practices, low-performing schools.

William Muth, Assistant Professor; Ph.D., George Mason, 2004. Thirdspace and reading components theories, especially as these apply to prison-based family literacy programs and children of incarcerated parents.

Gabriel Reich, Assistant Professor, Ph.D. Social studies teaching and learning, assessment, curriculum.

Joan Rhodes, Assistant Professor; Ph.D., Virginia Commonwealth, 1998. Early literacy development, using hypertext for increasing comprehension, instant messaging and social networking, electronic study skills, emerging and new literacies, assessment and instructional strategies for remediating reading difficulties.

Valerie Robnolt, Assistant Professor; Ph.D., Virginia, 2004. Assessment and instruction of reading comprehension, vocabulary, and fluency; the most effective methods of providing professional development to elementary teachers.

Gary Sarkozi, Assistant Professor; Ph.D., Virginia Commonwealth, 2001. Collecting, analyzing, and evaluating data on activities related to technological integration in the many facets of today's global environment.

Loraine Stewart, Associate Professor; Ed.D., North Carolina at Greensboro, 1991. Examining strategies used by classroom teachers to integrate African American children's literature into the elementary curriculum and the impact this literature has on student achievement.

Doris White, Associate Professor; Ed.D., Illinois, 1971. Multicultural education, urban education, testing and achievement outcomes.

WESTERN MICHIGAN UNIVERSITY

Mallinson Institute for Science Education

Programs of Study

Science education is an interdisciplinary discipline that is devoted to the study and improvement of how people teach and learn science. As an academic discipline, it lies at the intersection between science, education, cognitive psychology, and the history, philosophy, and sociology of science. The George G. Mallinson Institute for Science Education is proud to offer one of the largest faculties of science education specialists in the country.

The Ph.D. in science education is designed for those with a science or science education background who wish to pursue careers as science teachers, science education researchers, curriculum specialists, or professionals in government agencies. The program has three tracks: college science teaching, college science teaching with a discipline-specific research focus, and curriculum and instruction (K–12). Each track provides an understanding of the history of science education and a background in the diverse approaches to educational research. Doctoral candidates are required to complete 72 credit hours, including 15 hours in science education core courses, 24 hours in science core courses, 12 hours in research tools and techniques courses, 6 hours in electives, and 15 hours in a dissertation.

In addition, Western Michigan University (WMU) offers a dual-enrollment program in science education, in which students complete a master's degree program in a particular science (biology, chemistry, geography, geology, or physics) and then a doctoral degree in one of the three tracks listed above.

The Master of Arts in science education is designed for secondary school science teachers who wish to expand their teaching skills as well as for students who are beginning work toward a Ph.D. in science education. Elementary school teachers with a strong science background may qualify for admission. In order to earn the degree, students must complete 30 credit hours, including 9 hours in science education core courses, 15 hours in science core courses, and 6 hours in a thesis or independent research project.

Research Facilities

The Dwight B. Waldo Library forms the nerve center of the entire University community. It contains more than 4.3 million print and electronic items, including more than 2.1 million titles, 9,700 journal subscriptions, and 25,000 tapes and CDs. In addition, the library has a full depository for Michigan state documents and a selective depository for United States government documents. The science reference section contains reference and research sources in biology, chemistry, geology, mathematics, physics, and all areas of medicine and engineering. The science reference desk is also the service point for all current periodicals, newspapers, and the associated microfilm editions of periodicals and newspapers.

Financial Aid

The Institute offers a limited number of graduate assistantships and doctoral associateships each year for full-time graduate students. These positions typically include a stipend, remission of the out-of-state portion of tuition, and, in some cases, remission of all tuition. Students who receive these awards typically teach a section of one of the introductory science courses for prospective teachers, including courses in life, physical, and earth science. Interested students should apply by February 15. Other teaching and research assistantships are available from the University. Students may also borrow under the Federal PLUS or Perkins loan programs or other student loan programs.

Cost of Study

Information about tuition and fees can be found at http://www.wmich.edu/registrar/tuition.

Living and Housing Costs

Information about the cost of on-campus room and board can be found at http://www.wmich.edu/housing. Students living off campus typically pay $400 to $800 per month for a one-bedroom apartment or $500 to $1000 per month for a two bedroom.

Student Group

Students in the program are required to hold undergraduate or graduate degrees in science or science education or have teaching certification. Many of them are also science teachers at the elementary, secondary, or university level. Graduates of the program find employment in science education programs as teachers, curriculum specialists, or researchers.

Location

Kalamazoo, the fifth-largest city in Michigan, is located midway between Chicago and Detroit, a 2½-hour drive from each. Kalamazoo hosts a number of festivals throughout the year as well as theater, music, and ballet performances. Kalamazoo is just 40 minutes from Lake Michigan beaches and only 3 to 4 hours from Michigan's ski country, which is considered the best skiing in the central U.S.

The University

Western Michigan University is a nationally recognized student-centered research university. With an enrollment of more than 26,000, it is one of the fifty largest universities in the nation. Students may choose from more than 250 degree programs and participate in nearly 300 registered student organizations. *U.S. News & World Report* ranks WMU as one of the nation's top 100 public universities.

Applying

Prospective students are required to submit an online application for admission (with a $40 fee) through the Office of Admissions and Orientation (http://www.wmich.edu/admissions/graduate). Applicants should note that the Office of Admissions and Orientation has its own admissions requirements. The Mallinson Institute for Science Education also requires students to submit the following materials directly to the Institute: official transcripts of all previous college work, official GRE scores, a two-page essay describing the student's reasons for entering the program, and three letters of recommendation. For additional information, students should visit http://www.wmich.edu/science.

Correspondence and Information

Mallinson Institute for Science Education
3225 Wood Hall
Western Michigan University
Kalamazoo, Michigan 49008-5444
Phone: 269-387-5398
Fax: 269-387-4998
E-mail: sci-ed@wmich.edu
Web site: http://www.wmich.edu/science/

Western Michigan University

THE FACULTY AND THEIR RESEARCH

William W. Cobern, Professor of Biological Sciences and Science Education and Director of the Mallinson Institute for Science Education; Ph.D., Colorado at Boulder. The role of culture in the teaching and learning of science.

Marcia Fetters, Associate Professor and Interim Assistant Chair of Teaching, Learning, and Leadership; Ph.D., Michigan State. The needs of individuals marginalized from the science education community, science in informal settings, use of toys to teach science concepts.

Herb Fynewever, Assistant Professor of Chemistry; Ph. D., Wisconsin–Madison. How students learn chemistry, how the type and timing of feedback impacts students' learning and how it can be incorporated into homework assignments, peer-to-peer instruction, computer instruction, teacher-student interaction.

Charles Henderson, Assistant Professor of Physics; Ph.D., Minnesota. Educational change, science teachers' beliefs about teaching and learning, student-centered instructional strategies in physics.

Mark Jenness, Senior Researcher and Director of Science and Mathematics Program Improvement; Ed.D., Western Michigan. Evaluation and technical assistance in the areas of science, mathematics, and environmental education.

Heather Petcovic, Assistant Professor of Geological Sciences; Ph.D., Oregon State. A combined approach to understanding how dikes fed lava flows of the Columbia River flood basalts, role of field experience in geoscience education, alternative conceptions in earth sciences, role of informal education programs in promoting scientific literacy in the general public.

David W. Rudge, Associate Professor of Biological Sciences; Ph.D., Pittsburgh. How the history and philosophy of science can be used to inform the teaching of science, H. B. D. Kettlewell's famous experiments on industrial melanism.

David Schuster, Associate Professor of Physics; Ph.D., Witwatersrand (South Africa). Cognition, assessment, teaching and learning in science, educational design, curriculum development, epistemology and inquiry.

Reneé Schwartz, Assistant Professor of Biological Sciences; Ph.D., Oregon State. Developments in learning and teaching of nature of science and scientific inquiry, effective means to utilize authentic scientific experiences to enhance learners' epistemological views of science, scientific inquiry within science classrooms and authentic settings.

Joseph P. Stoltman, Professor of Geography and Science Education; Ph.D., Georgia. Teaching and learning of geography, global change education, spatial analysis of educational reform in Michigan.

WESTMINSTER CHOIR COLLEGE OF RIDER UNIVERSITY

Music Education

Programs of Study	Home of the famous Westminster Symphonic Choir, Westminster Choir College of Rider University integrates music study with professional choral performances conducted in concert with major symphony orchestras. Westminster Choir College offers outstanding music training in a stimulating yet friendly learning environment. Westminster appeals to students who seek excellent musical training and substantial performance experience to become well-rounded career musicians. The College attracts talented musicians from around the world for superb training and practical experience as performers, composers, conductors, teachers, and church musicians.

The choral music experience represents the most distinctive feature of Westminster. Daily rehearsals, supported by intensive musical skills development and by the study of voice and conducting, constitute the foundation of the choral program. At the center of all curricula are the large ensembles: the Chapel Choir and the Symphonic Choir. Smaller ensemble experience is afforded by the Westminster Choir, Westminster Kantorei, Jubilee Singers, Williamson Voices, and the Concert Bell Choir.

The Master of Music (M.M.) degree is offered in music education. The M.M. program reflects the Westminster philosophy that the music educator must be a fully capable musician. Consequently, there is a decided emphasis on performance or composition in the curriculum, with several options available. The professional music education courses are designed primarily to expand and update the techniques of public school music teachers. The Master of Music Education (M.M.E.) is offered and is designed to be completed entirely by means of summer study. Those who enroll for maximum loads normally earn the degree within four summer terms. The M.M.E. program includes education courses, music core courses, choral ensemble performance, and a self-designed focus proposed by the student to the department. The degree culminates in the preparation of the master's thesis.

Other graduate programs are also available at Westminster, including the Master of Music in Sacred Music, Choral Conducting, Voice Pedagogy and Performance, Piano Performance, Organ Performance, Piano Pedagogy and Performance, Piano Accompanying and Coaching, and Composition. The Master of Vocal Pedagogy (M.V.P.) is also offered. Other graduate education programs, as well as graduate business programs, are available on Rider University's campus in Lawrenceville, New Jersey.

Research Facilities
Westminster Choir College's performance facilities include the Bristol Chapel (350 seats), Williamson Hall (100 seats), Scheide Hall (100 seats), and the Playhouse/Opera Theatre (300 seats). Stately Bristol Chapel, housing a 50-rank Aeolian-Skinner organ, a 16-rank Fisk organ, a 14-rank Noack organ, and two 9-foot grand pianos, is a large recital facility for student, faculty, and guest performers. Nestled among the trees, the Playhouse/Opera Theatre offers a stage and two Steinway grand pianos. Beyond Bristol Chapel, Scheide Recital Hall showcases a 44-rank Casavant organ. Westminster offers practice rooms in each of its three residence halls and has more than 120 pianos and twenty-one pipe organs, including practice organs by Flentrop, Holtkamp, Schantz, Moller, and Noack. The Yvonne Theater, located at Rider University's Lawrenceville, New Jersey, campus is also home to performance facilities.

Talbott Library/Learning Center houses 67,000 books, scores, periodicals, and microforms; an electronic piano is provided for in-house score study. The media collection includes more than 25,000 recordings and videos, with facilities for student playback. The library supports the music education curriculum with over 1,000 school-music textbooks, recordings, charts, and other resource materials. The Performance Collection contains approximately 5,300 titles in multiple copies for student study, class assignments, student teaching, and church choirs; a single-copy reference file of approximately 80,000 supplements this collection. Special collections include the Erik Routley Collections of Books and Hymnals, D. DeWitt Wasson Research Collection of Organ Music, and the Organ Historical Society's American Organ Archives.

The library also houses a state-of-the art Music Computing Center with fifteen Kurzweil PC 88 synthesizers, twelve Macintosh eMacs, and three Macintosh G5 computers, all running notation software (Finale) and two sequencers (Garage Band and Digital Performer).

Westminster students may also utilize the comprehensive collections of the Rider University and other local university libraries. Westminster students use the campus academic computing laboratory located in the Talbott Library and additional computer laboratories at Rider.

Voice students use a state-of-the-art voice laboratory, an invaluable resource for vocal pedagogy, for the scientific study of the vocal mechanism and singing. The Piano Department has a fully equipped piano laboratory in which an entire class of students can be instructed simultaneously.

The Westminster Academy is the laboratory school of the Music Education Department and the Westminster Conservatory. Classes are taught in a residency program at John Witherspoon Middle School, located in Princeton, and to home-schooled students at the Westminster Conservatory located on campus. The teaching philosophy at Westminster Academy embraces critical theory, which connects music teaching to the context of social change. Lessons are designed to meet individual learning styles, and the teaching strategies are framed in critical pedagogy. The curriculum seeks to affect transformative learning for both students and their teachers.

Financial Aid
Financial aid is available to qualified graduate students under several state and federal loan programs, including the Federal Stafford Student Loan program. A limited number of graduate assistantship positions are also available. Scholarships have been established through the generosity of benefactors of the College, both individuals and foundations. Scholarship availability varies each year. A complete list of scholarships and awards is available upon request from the Office of Alumni Relations and Development.

Cost of Study
Tuition for 2007–08 is $25,650 per year for full-time graduate study. The part-time rate for graduate study is $930 per credit.

Living and Housing Costs
On-campus room and board in 2007–08 is approximately $9940 per year.

Student Group
Graduate enrollment at Westminster Choir College is approximately 120; 28 percent of the students are men. Graduate students represent twenty-two states and nine countries. Nearly 92 percent pursue their degree full-time. The average age among graduate students is 27.

Location
Located in the culturally rich town of Princeton, New Jersey, Westminster is a 40-minute train ride from the cosmopolitan cultural centers of New York City and Philadelphia, offering Westminster students a wealth of educational and recreational activities. Princeton University, a short walk from Westminster, offers lectures, art exhibits, recitals, and concerts. Through a cooperative agreement, Westminster students may enroll in courses at Princeton University. Near the Westminster campus, the Tony Award–winning McCarter Theatre stages several major productions each year and hosts guest artists and musical performers.

The University and The College
Westminster Choir College of Rider University is a professional college of music with a unique choral emphasis that educates men and women at the undergraduate and graduate levels for careers in church music, education, and performance. Professional training in musical skills, with an emphasis on performance, is complemented by studies in the liberal arts in an atmosphere that encourages individuals in their personal and musical growth and nurtures leadership qualities. All Westminster students perform in professional concerts each year. The 200-voice Westminster Symphonic Choir sings and records on a regular basis with the New York Philharmonic under world-class conductors in Lincoln Center and Carnegie Hall. Originally a pioneer in establishing high standards in church music and choral performance, Westminster maintains the same commitment in its expanded programs. Founded for Christian service, the College welcomes pluralism in religious experience and holds service to all to be ennobling, liberating, and worthy of cultivation.

Westminster's distinguished alumni include world-renowned soprano Laquita Mitchell; Anwar Robinson from *American Idol*; professors at several prestigious national colleges and universities; performers with the Metropolitan Opera, the New York City Opera, and the Chicago Lyric Opera; and leading music ministers and teachers worldwide.

Westminster is accredited by the National Association of Schools of Music (NASM) and the Middle States Association of Colleges and Schools. Its undergraduate music education program is accredited by the National Association of State Directors of Teacher Education and Certification (NASDTEC), which facilitates transferring teaching certificates from participating states, and National Council for Accreditation of Teacher Education (NCATE).

Applying
All applicants must submit a completed graduate application, $50 application fee, a repertoire list, two letters of reference, a personal statement, a resume, and official transcripts from each college or university attended. For applicants whose native language is not English, satisfactory scores on the TOEFL are required. International applicants must have transcripts evaluated by a recognized credential evaluation service.

All applicants must participate in an audition or provide an audition tape. Applicants to the M.M.E. program must also submit a video that shows them conducting or teaching in the classroom, a portfolio, and a proposal for the focus track of study and schedule an interview with the Music Education Department. The application for admission should be submitted by March 1 for fall admission and October 1 for spring admission.

Correspondence and Information
Westminster Choir College of Rider University
101 Walnut Lane
Princeton, New Jersey 08540
Phone: 609-921-7100
Fax: 609-921-2538
E-mail: wccadmission@rider.edu
Web site: http://www.rider.edu/westminster

Westminster Choir College of Rider University

THE FACULTY

Frank Abrahams, Professor and Chair; Ed.D., Temple.
Shelley Beard, Adjunct Instructor; M.M., Indiana Bloomington.
Marie Fosket, Adjunct Instructor; B.A., Montclair State.
Elizabeth Guerriero, Adjunct Instructor; M.M., Denver.
Eric Haltmeier, Adjunct Instructor; B.M., West Virginia.
Joseph Ohrt, Adjunct Professor; Ph.D., South Carolina.
Thomas Parente, Associate Professor; M.A., Rutgers.
Patrick Schmidt, Assistant Professor; M.M., M.M.E., Westminster Choir College.

ACADEMIC AND PROFESSIONAL PROGRAMS IN THE HEALTH-RELATED PROFESSIONS

Section 27
Allied Health

This section contains a directory of institutions offering graduate work in allied health, followed by in-depth entries submitted by institutions that chose to prepare detailed program descriptions. Additional information about programs listed in the directory but not augmented by an in-depth entry may be obtained by writing directly to the dean of a graduate school or chair of a department at the address given in the directory.

For programs offering related work, see also in this book Administration, Instruction, and Theory (Educational Psychology); Dentistry and Dental Sciences; Health Services; Public Health; Special Focus (Education of the Multiply Handicapped); Social Work; and Subject Areas (Counselor Education); in Book 2, Art and Art History (Art Therapy), Family and Consumer Sciences (Gerontology), Performing Arts (Therapies), and Psychology and Counseling; in Book 3, Anatomy, Biophysics, Microbiological Sciences, Pathology and Pathobiology, and Physiology; in Book 4, Physics (Acoustics); and in Book 5, Agricultural Engineering and Bioengineering (Bioengineering), Biomedical Engineering and Biotechnology, and Energy and Power Engineering (Nuclear Engineering).

CONTENTS

Allied Health—General

Alabama State University, School of Graduate Studies, College of Health Sciences, Montgomery, AL 36101-0271. Offers DPT. *Faculty:* 7 full-time (5 women). *Students:* 16 full-time (9 women); includes 10 minority (9 African Americans, 1 Hispanic American). *Entrance requirements:* Additional exam requirements/recommendations for international students: Required—TOEFL (minimum score 500 paper-based; 173 computer-based). *Application deadline:* For fall admission, 7/15 for domestic students; for spring admission, 12/15 for domestic students. Applications are processed on a rolling basis. Application fee: $10. *Expenses:* Tuition, state resident: full-time $1,728; part-time $192 per hour. Tuition, nonresident: full-time $3,456; part-time $334 per hour. *Financial support:* In 2006–07, 4 research assistantships (averaging $9,450 per year) were awarded. *Unit head:* Dr. Denise Chapman, Dean, 334-229-4707, Fax: 334-229-4964, E-mail: dchapman@alasu.edu.

Alderson-Broaddus College, Medical Science Department, Philippi, WV 26416. Offers emergency medical care (MS); rural primary care (MS); surgery (MS). Postbaccalaureate distance learning degree programs offered (minimal on-campus study). *Degree requirements:* For master's, thesis, 2 years of clinical experience. *Entrance requirements:* For master's, National Commission on Certification of Physician Assistants certification or bachelor's degree in related field; full-time clinical employment.

Andrews University, School of Graduate Studies, College of Arts and Sciences, Allied Health Department, Berrien Springs, MI 49104. Offers MSMT. *Accreditation:* APTA.

Arkansas State University, Graduate School, College of Nursing and Health Professions, Program in Health Sciences, Jonesboro, State University, AR 72467. Offers aging studies (Certificate); health sciences (MS); health sciences education (Certificate). Part-time programs available. *Faculty:* 3 full-time (2 women). *Students:* 4 full-time (all women), 10 part-time (7 women); includes 6 minority (all African Americans), 1 international. Average age 32. 10 applicants, 80% accepted, 8 enrolled. *Degree requirements:* For master's, comprehensive exam. *Entrance requirements:* For master's, GRE General Test, Allied Health Professions Admission Test, appropriate bachelor's degree, resumé, writing sample, letters of reference, official transcript. Additional exam requirements/recommendations for international students: Required—TOEFL (minimum score 213 computer-based). *Application deadline:* Applications are processed on a rolling basis. Application fee: $30 ($40 for international students). Electronic applications accepted. *Expenses: Contact institution. Financial support:* Scholarships/grants available. Financial award application deadline: 7/1; financial award applicants required to submit FAFSA. *Unit head:* Chris Hutchinson, Head, 870-972-3073, Fax: 870-972-2004, E-mail: hutch@astate.edu.

Athabasca University, Centre for Nursing and Health Studies, Athabasca, AB T9S 3A3, Canada. Offers advanced nursing practice (MN, Advanced Diploma); generalist (MN); health studies-leadership (MHS). Part-time programs available. Postbaccalaureate distance learning degree programs offered. *Faculty:* 6 full-time (all women), 40 part-time/adjunct (37 women). *Students:* Average age 40. 460 applicants, 81% accepted, 335 enrolled. In 2006, 124 degrees awarded. *Degree requirements:* For master's, comprehensive exam (for some programs), registration (for some programs). *Entrance requirements:* For master's, bachelor's degree in health-related field, 2 years professional health service experience (MHS), bachelor's degree in nursing, 2 years nursing experience (MN), minimum GPA of 3.0 in final 30 credits; for Advanced Diploma, RN license, 2 years health care experience. *Application deadline:* For fall admission, 3/1 for domestic and international students. Application fee: $60. Electronic applications accepted. *Expenses: Contact institution. Unit head:* Dr. Donna Romyn, Director, 780-675-6794, Fax: 780-675-6468, E-mail: dromyn@athabascau.ca. *Application contact:* Lisa Bodnarchuk, Administrative Assistant, 780-675-6381, Fax: 780-675-6468, E-mail: mhs@athabascau.ca.

A.T. Still University of Health Sciences, Arizona School of Health Sciences, Mesa, AZ 85206. Offers advanced occupational therapy (MS); advanced physician assistant (MS); audiology (Au D); human movement (MS); medical informatics (MS); occupational therapy (MS); physical therapy (MS, DPT); physician assistant (MS); sports health care (MS); transitional physical therapy (DPT). *Accreditation:* AOTA (one or more programs are accredited); APTA. Postbaccalaureate distance learning degree programs offered (no on-campus study). *Faculty:* 47 full-time (27 women), 101 part-time/adjunct (60 women). *Students:* 442 full-time (277 women), 732 part-time (579 women); includes 143 minority (38 African Americans, 11 American Indian/Alaska Native, 55 Asian Americans or Pacific Islanders, 39 Hispanic Americans), 4 international. Average age 33. 1,471 applicants, 547 enrolled. In 2006, 104 master's, 432 doctorates awarded. *Degree requirements:* For master's and doctorate, thesis/dissertation (for some programs). *Entrance requirements:* For master's, GRE General Test, minimum GPA of 2.5; for doctorate, GRE, Evaluation of Practicing Audiologists Capabilities (Au D), Physical Therapy Evaluation Tool (DPT), current state licensure, master's degree or equivalent (Au D), minimum GPA of 2.7. *Application deadline:* For fall admission, 2/1 priority date for domestic and international students. Applications are processed on a rolling basis. Application fee: $60. *Expenses: Contact institution. Financial support:* In 2006–07, 382 students received support. Federal Work-Study and scholarships/grants available. Financial award application deadline: 5/1. *Faculty research:* Constraint-induced therapy, scapular motion analysis, shoulder mobility, biomechanics, quadriceps. *Unit head:* Dr. Randy Danielsen, Dean, 480-219-6000, Fax: 480-219-6110, E-mail: rdanielsen@atsu.edu. *Application contact:* Donna Sparks, Associate Director for Admissions, 660-626-2237, Fax: 660-626-2969, E-mail: admissions@atsu.edu.

Barnes-Jewish College of Nursing and Allied Health, Division of Allied Health, St. Louis, MO 63110-1091. Offers dietetic internship (Certificate); education (MSAH); management (MSAH); nutrition (MSAH). Part-time and evening/weekend programs available. *Degree requirements:* For master's, thesis or alternative, registration. *Entrance requirements:* For master's, minimum GPA of 3.0, 2 references, statistics course. Additional exam requirements/recommendations for international students: Required—TOEFL (minimum score 550 paper-based; 213 computer-based).

Baylor University, Graduate School, Academy of Health Sciences, Fort Sam Houston, TX 78234-6100. Offers MHA, MPT, DPT, Dr Sc PT. *Accreditation:* APTA (one or more programs are accredited). *Students:* 150 full-time (49 women); includes 17 minority (7 African Americans, 5 Asian Americans or Pacific Islanders, 5 Hispanic Americans). In 2006, 42 master's, 16 doctorates awarded. *Entrance requirements:* For master's, GRE General Test. *Application deadline:* Applications are processed on a rolling basis. Application fee: $25. *Expenses: Contact institution. Unit head:* Col. Darwin L. Fretwell, Dean, 210-221-8715, Fax: 210-221-7306.

Belmont University, College of Health Sciences, Nashville, TN 37212-3757. Offers MSN, MSOT, DPT, OTD. Part-time programs available. Postbaccalaureate distance learning degree programs offered (minimal on-campus study). *Faculty:* 18 full-time (13 women), 29 part-time/adjunct (22 women). *Students:* 215 full-time (180 women), 10 part-time (9 women); includes 10 minority (9 African Americans, 1 Asian American or Pacific Islander), 2 international. Average age 27. 342 applicants, 42% accepted, 92 enrolled. In 2006, 27 master's, 37 doctorates awarded. *Degree requirements:* For master's, thesis or alternative; for doctorate, thesis/dissertation. *Entrance requirements:* For master's, GRE; for doctorate, 1 year experience as a licensed healthcare professional. Additional exam requirements/recommendations for international students: Required—TOEFL (minimum score 500 paper-based; 173 computer-based). *Application deadline:* Applications are processed on a rolling basis. Application fee: $50. Electronic applications accepted. *Expenses: Contact institution. Financial support:* In 2006–07, 123 students received support, including teaching assistantships with full tuition reimbursements available (averaging $7,020 per year); career-related internships or fieldwork, scholarships/grants, and traineeships also available. Financial award application deadline: 3/1; financial award applicants required to submit FAFSA. *Unit head:* Dr. Debra B. Wollaber, Dean, 615-460-6106, Fax: 615-460-6125, E-mail: wollaberd@mail.belmont.edu. *Application contact:* Dr. Kathryn Baugher, Dean of Enrollment Services, 615-460-6785, Fax: 615-460-5434, E-mail: baugherk@mail.belmont.edu.

Bennington College, Graduate Programs, Program in Allied and Health Sciences, Bennington, VT 05201. Offers Certificate. *Faculty:* 8 full-time (3 women), 1 part-time/adjunct (0 women). *Students:* 11 full-time (3 women); includes 3 minority (2 Asian Americans or Pacific Islanders, 1 Hispanic American). Average age 25. 43 applicants, 47% accepted, 10 enrolled. In 2006, 10 degrees awarded. *Application deadline:* For fall admission, 2/15 priority date for domestic students. Applications are processed on a rolling basis. Application fee: $60. *Expenses: Contact institution.* One-time fee: $75 full-time. Tuition and fees vary according to program. *Financial support:* In 2006–07, 1 student received support. Scholarships/grants available. Financial award application deadline: 4/1; financial award applicants required to submit FAFSA. *Unit head:* Dr. Janet Foley, Chief Health Professions Adviser, 802-440-4463, Fax: 802-440-4461, E-mail: jfoley@bennington.edu. *Application contact:* Ken Himmelman, Dean of Admissions, 802-440-4312, Fax: 802-440-4320, E-mail: admissions@bennington.edu.

Boston University, College of Health and Rehabilitation Sciences—Sargent College, Department of Health Sciences, Boston, MA 02215. Offers applied anatomy and physiology (MS, PhD); nutrition (MS). Part-time programs available. *Faculty:* 11 full-time (9 women), 6 part-time/adjunct (5 women). *Students:* 66 full-time (59 women), 2 part-time (1 woman); includes 8 minority (all Asian Americans or Pacific Islanders), 6 international. Average age 24. 67 applicants, 40% accepted, 20 enrolled.Terminal master's awarded for partial completion of doctoral program. *Degree requirements:* For master's, thesis or alternative; for doctorate, one foreign language, thesis/dissertation, comprehensive exam. *Entrance requirements:* For master's, GRE General Test, minimum GPA of 3.0; for doctorate, GRE General Test. Additional exam requirements/recommendations for international students: Required—TOEFL (minimum score 550 paper-based). *Application deadline:* For fall admission, 3/1 priority date for domestic students; for spring admission, 10/1 for domestic students. Applications are processed on a rolling basis. Application fee: $65. Electronic applications accepted. *Expenses:* Tuition: Full-time $33,330; part-time $1,042 per credit. Required fees: $462; $40. *Financial support:* In 2006–07, 20 fellowships with full tuition reimbursements, 7 research assistantships with full tuition reimbursements, 6 teaching assistantships with full tuition reimbursements were awarded; career-related internships or fieldwork, Federal Work-Study, institutionally sponsored loans, scholarships/grants, and tuition waivers (partial) also available. Support available to part-time students. Financial award application deadline: 4/15. *Faculty research:* Muscle metabolism, body acid-base balance, human performance, diabetes, obesity. *Unit head:* Dr. Kathleen Morgan, Chair, 617-353-7464, E-mail: kmorgan@bu.edu. *Application contact:* Sharon Sankey, Director, Student Services, 617-353-2713, Fax: 617-353-7500, E-mail: ssankey@bu.edu.

Brock University, Faculty of Graduate Studies, Faculty of Applied Health Sciences, St. Catharines, ON L2S 3A1, Canada. Offers M Sc, MA. *Faculty:* 67 full-time (40 women), 4 part-time/adjunct (0 women). *Students:* 75 full-time (50 women), 4 part-time (1 woman). 93 applicants, 55% accepted, 42 enrolled. In 2006, 22 degrees awarded. *Degree requirements:* For master's, thesis. *Entrance requirements:* For master's, honors degree, BA and/or B Sc. Additional exam requirements/recommendations for international students: Required—TOEFL (minimum score 550 paper-based; 213 computer-based; 80 iBT), IELTS (minimum score 7), TWE (minimum score 4). *Application deadline:* For fall admission, 2/15 for domestic students. Application fee: $75. Electronic applications accepted. *Financial support:* Fellowships, research assistantships, teaching assistantships, career-related internships or fieldwork, scholarships/grants, unspecified assistantships, and bursaries available. Support available to part-time students. *Faculty research:* Health and physical activity, aging and health, health advocacy, exercise psychology, community development. *Unit head:* Dr. John Corlett, Dean, 905-688-5550 Ext. 3385, Fax: 905-984-4851, E-mail: john.corlett@brocku.ca. *Application contact:* Michael I. Plyley, Associate Dean, Research and Graduate Studies, 905-688-5550 Ext. 3383, Fax: 905-984-4851, E-mail: mplyley@brocku.ca.

Cleveland State University, College of Graduate Studies, College of Science, Department of Health Sciences, Program in Health Sciences, Cleveland, OH 44115. Offers MS. Part-time and evening/weekend programs available. Postbaccalaureate distance learning degree programs offered (no on-campus study). *Faculty:* 11 full-time (5 women), 1 (woman) part-time/adjunct. *Students:* 2 full-time (1 woman), 43 part-time (34 women); includes 13 minority (10 African Americans, 1 Asian American or Pacific Islander, 2 Hispanic Americans), 4 international. Average age 38. 17 applicants, 47% accepted, 4 enrolled. In 2006, 9 degrees awarded. *Degree requirements:* For master's, thesis, registration. *Application deadline:* For fall admission, 5/15 for international students; for winter admission, 4/1 for international students; for spring admission, 11/1 for international students. *Financial support:* Research assistantships available. *Faculty research:* Assisted technologies, biomechanics, clinical administration, cultural health, gerontology. *Unit head:* Dr. MaryKay Milidonis, Director, 216-687-2447, E-mail: m.milidonis@csuohio.edu.

College Misericordia, College of Health Sciences, Dallas, PA 18612-1098. Offers MSN, MSOT, MSPT, MSSLP, DPT. Part-time and evening/weekend programs available. *Faculty:* 15 full-time (9 women), 11 part-time/adjunct (9 women). *Students:* 62 full-time (50 women), 109 part-time (86 women); includes 3 minority (2 African Americans, 1 Hispanic American). In 2006, 80 degrees awarded. *Entrance requirements:* For master's, GRE General Test or MAT, references. Additional exam requirements/recommendations for international students: Required—TOEFL. *Application deadline:* Applications are processed on a rolling basis. Application fee: $25. Electronic applications accepted. *Expenses:* Tuition: Full-time $19,800; part-time $495 per credit. Required fees: $1,060. *Financial support:* Teaching assistantships, career-related internships or fieldwork, Federal Work-Study, scholarships/grants, traineeships, and tuition waivers (partial) available. Support available to part-time students. Financial award application deadline: 6/30; financial award applicants required to submit FAFSA. *Unit head:* Dr. Ellen McLaughlin, Interim Dean of Health Sciences, 570-674-6399, E-mail: emclaugh@misericordia.edu. *Application contact:* Larree Brown, Coordinator of Part-Time Undergraduate and Graduate Programs, 570-674-6451, Fax: 570-674-6232, E-mail: lbrown@misericordia.edu.

Creighton University, School of Pharmacy and Health Professions, Omaha, NE 68178-0001. Offers Pharm D, MS, DPT, OTD, Pharm D/MS. *Accreditation:* ACPE (one or more programs are accredited). Postbaccalaureate distance learning degree programs offered (no on-campus study). Electronic applications accepted. Expenses: Contact institution. *Faculty research:* Drug synthesis, molecular mechanisms of toxicity, pharmaceutics, health-care systems, biomechanics, ethics.

Dominican College, Division of Allied Health, Orangeburg, NY 10962-1210. Offers MS, DPT. *Unit head:* Sr. Beryl Herdt, Division Director, 845-848-6000, Fax: 845-398-4893, E-mail: beryl.herdt@dc.edu.

Drexel University, College of Nursing and Health Professions, Philadelphia, PA 19104-2875. Offers MA, MFT, MHS, MS, MSN, DPT, PhD, Certificate. *Accreditation:* NLN. Part-time and evening/weekend programs available. Terminal master's awarded for partial completion of doctoral program. *Degree requirements:* For master's, thesis (for some programs), comprehensive exam; for doctorate, thesis/dissertation, qualifying exam. *Entrance requirements:* For doctorate, GRE General Test. Electronic applications accepted.

Duquesne University, John G. Rangos, Sr. School of Health Sciences, Pittsburgh, PA 15282-0001. Offers health management systems (MHMS); occupational therapy (MS); physical therapy (DPT); physician assistant (MPA); speech–language pathology (MS); MBA/MHMS. *Accreditation:* AOTA (one or more programs are accredited); APTA (one or more programs are accredited); ASHA. *Faculty:* 35 full-time (22 women), 24 part-time/adjunct (12 women). *Students:* 261 full-time (229 women), 16 part-time (8 women); includes 11 minority (6 African Americans,

1 American Indian/Alaska Native, 2 Asian Americans or Pacific Islanders, 2 Hispanic Americans), 3 international. Average age 23. 150 applicants, 55% accepted, 41 enrolled. In 2006, 66 master's, 13 doctorates awarded. *Degree requirements:* For doctorate, thesis/dissertation. *Entrance requirements:* For master's, GRE (speech-language pathology), 3 letters of recommendation, minimum GPA of 2.75 (health management systems, occupational therapy), minimum GPA of 3.0 (physical assistant, speech-language pathology); for doctorate, GRE General Test, 3 letters of recommendation, minimum GPA of 3.0, personal interview. Additional exam requirements/recommendations for international students: Required—TOEFL (minimum score 600 paper-based; 250 computer-based). *Application deadline:* For fall admission, 12/1 priority date for domestic students; for winter admission, 5/1 priority date for domestic students. Application fee: $50. Electronic applications accepted. *Expenses: Contact institution.* Tuition and fees vary according to degree level and program. *Financial support:* Federal Work-Study available. *Faculty research:* Neuronal processing, electrical stimulation on peripheral neuropathy, CNS stimulatory and inhibitory signals, behavioral genetic methodologies to development disorders of speech, neurogenic communication disorders. Total annual research expenditures: $66,000. *Unit head:* Dr. Gregory H. Frazer, Dean, 412-396-5303, Fax: 412-396-5554, E-mail: frazer@duq.edu. *Application contact:* Christopher R. Hilf, Recruiter/Academic Advisor, 412-396-5653, Fax: 412-396-5554, E-mail: hilfc@duq.edu.

East Carolina University, Graduate School, School of Allied Health Sciences, Greenville, NC 27858-4353. Offers MPT, MS, MSOT, DPT, PhD. Part-time and evening/weekend programs available. Postbaccalaureate distance learning degree programs offered (no on-campus study). *Faculty:* 58 full-time (29 women). *Students:* 347 full-time (273 women), 55 part-time (49 women); includes 41 minority (25 African Americans, 3 American Indian/Alaska Native, 7 Asian Americans or Pacific Islanders, 6 Hispanic Americans), 4 international. Average age 27. 275 applicants, 14% accepted, 18 enrolled. In 2006, 131 master's, 11 doctorates awarded. *Degree requirements:* For master's, comprehensive exam. *Entrance requirements:* For master's, GRE General Test. Additional exam requirements/recommendations for international students: Required—TOEFL. Application fee: $50. *Financial support:* Research assistantships with partial tuition reimbursements, teaching assistantships with partial tuition reimbursements, career-related internships or fieldwork, Federal Work-Study, and scholarships/grants available. Support available to part-time students. Financial award application deadline: 6/1; financial award applicants required to submit FAFSA. *Faculty research:* Hearing, stuttering, therapeutic activities, ACL injury. *Unit head:* Dr. Stephen Thomas, Dean, 252-744-6010, E-mail: thomass@ecu.edu. *Application contact:* Dean of Graduate School, 252-328-6012, Fax: 252-328-6071, E-mail: gradschool@ecu.edu.

Eastern Kentucky University, The Graduate School, College of Health Sciences, Richmond, KY 40475-3102. Offers MPH, MS, MSN. Part-time programs available. *Faculty:* 48 full-time (39 women), 2 part-time/adjunct (0 women). *Students:* 175 full-time (137 women), 138 part-time (98 women); includes 20 minority (16 African Americans, 2 Asian Americans or Pacific Islanders, 2 Hispanic Americans), 23 international. Average age 30. 179 applicants, 72% accepted, 79 enrolled. *Entrance requirements:* For master's, GRE General Test, minimum GPA of 2.75. Application fee: $30. *Expenses:* Tuition, state resident: full-time $5,610. Tuition, nonresident: full-time $15,910. *Financial support:* Career-related internships or fieldwork and institutionally sponsored loans available. Financial award applicants required to submit CSS PROFILE. *Unit head:* Dr. David D. Gale, Dean, 859-622-1523, Fax: 859-622-1140, E-mail: david.gale@eku.edu.

East Tennessee State University, School of Graduate Studies, College of Public and Allied Health, Johnson City, TN 37614. Offers MPH, MS, MSEH, Au D, DPT, Certificate. Part-time and evening/weekend programs available. *Entrance requirements:* For master's and doctorate, GRE. Additional exam requirements/recommendations for international students: Required—TOEFL (minimum score 550 paper-based; 213 computer-based).

Emory University, School of Medicine, Programs in Allied Health Professions, Atlanta, GA 30322-1100. Offers anesthesiology (MM Sc); anesthesiology/patient monitoring systems (MM Sc); ophthalmic technology (MM Sc); physical therapy (DPT); physician assistant (MM Sc). Postbaccalaureate distance learning degree programs offered. *Faculty:* 27 full-time (16 women), 57 part-time/adjunct (32 women). *Students:* 322 full-time (227 women), 6 part-time (5 women); includes 69 minority (33 African Americans, 4 American Indian/Alaska Native, 28 Asian Americans or Pacific Islanders, 4 Hispanic Americans). Average age 28. 1,149 applicants, 16% accepted, 132 enrolled. In 2006, 80 master's, 21 doctorates awarded. *Entrance requirements:* For master's and doctorate, GRE. *Expenses: Contact institution. Financial support:* In 2006–07, 289 students received support. Federal Work-Study, institutionally sponsored loans, and scholarships/grants available. Support available to part-time students. Financial award application deadline: 2/15; financial award applicants required to submit CSS PROFILE or FAFSA. *Unit head:* Dr. J. Alan Otsuki, Assistant Dean, Office of Medical Education and Student Affairs, 404-727-5655, Fax: 404-727-0045, E-mail: jotsuki@emory.edu. *Application contact:* Roselyn Branch, Associate Director of Registration and Student Affairs, 404-727-5682, Fax: 404-727-0045, E-mail: roselyn.branch@emory.edu.

Ferris State University, College of Allied Health Sciences, Big Rapids, MI 49307. Offers MS. *Expenses:* Tuition, state resident: part-time $355 per credit hour. Tuition, nonresident: part-time $687 per credit hour.

Florida Agricultural and Mechanical University, Division of Graduate Studies, Research, and Continuing Education, School of Allied Health Sciences, Tallahassee, FL 32307-3200. Offers health administration (MS); physical therapy (MPT). *Degree requirements:* For master's, thesis (for some programs). *Entrance requirements:* For master's, GRE General Test or GMAT, minimum GPA of 3.0. Additional exam requirements/recommendations for international students: Required—TOEFL (minimum score 550 paper-based).

Florida Gulf Coast University, College of Health Professions, Fort Myers, FL 33965-6565. Offers MS, MSN. *Accreditation:* AOTA. Part-time and evening/weekend programs available. Postbaccalaureate distance learning degree programs offered (minimal on-campus study). *Faculty:* 42 full-time (35 women), 21 part-time/adjunct (14 women). *Students:* 114 full-time (82 women), 44 part-time (39 women); includes 24 minority (5 African Americans, 2 American Indian/Alaska Native, 4 Asian Americans or Pacific Islanders, 13 Hispanic Americans). Average age 34. 87 applicants, 79% accepted, 46 enrolled. In 2006, 56 degrees awarded. *Degree requirements:* For master's, thesis or alternative. *Entrance requirements:* For master's, GRE General Test or MAT, minimum GPA of 3.0. Additional exam requirements/recommendations for international students: Required—TOEFL (minimum score 550 paper-based; 213 computer-based). *Application deadline:* Applications are processed on a rolling basis. Application fee: $30. Electronic applications accepted. *Expenses:* Tuition, state resident: full-time $4,326. Tuition, nonresident: full-time $18,523. Required fees: $1,211. One-time fee: $5 full-time. *Financial support:* Career-related internships or fieldwork, Federal Work-Study, and institutionally sponsored loans available. *Faculty research:* Gerontology, health care policy, health administration, community-based services. Total annual research expenditures: $344,776. *Unit head:* Dr. Denise Heinemann, Dean, 239-590-7511, Fax: 239-590-7474. *Application contact:* Lynn O'Hare, Administrative Assistant, 239-590-7451, Fax: 239-590-7474, E-mail: lohare@fgcu.edu.

Georgia Southern University, Jack N. Averitt College of Graduate Studies, College of Health and Human Sciences, Statesboro, GA 30460. Offers MS, MSN, Certificate. Part-time and evening/weekend programs available. *Faculty:* 41 full-time (24 women). *Students:* 70 full-time (36 women), 51 part-time (43 women); includes 17 minority (14 African Americans, 2 Asian Americans or Pacific Islanders, 1 Hispanic American), 5 international. Average age 28. 76 applicants, 80% accepted, 46 enrolled. In 2006, 47 degrees awarded. *Degree requirements:* For master's, thesis (for some programs), exams. *Entrance requirements:* For master's, GRE General Test, MAT or GMAT. Additional exam requirements/recommendations for international students: Required—TOEFL (minimum score 550 paper-based; 213 computer-based; 80 iBT). *Application deadline:* For fall admission, 3/1 priority date for domestic students, 3/1 for international students; for spring admission, 10/1 priority date for domestic students, 10/1 for international students. Applications are processed on a rolling basis. Application fee: $50. Electronic applications accepted. *Financial support:* In 2006–07, 100 students received support, including 57 research assistantships with partial tuition reimbursements available (averaging $5,500 per year), teaching assistantships with tuition reimbursements available (averaging $5,500 per year); career-related internships or fieldwork, Federal Work-Study, scholarships/grants, traineeships, tuition waivers (partial), and unspecified assistantships also available. Support available to part-time students. Financial award application deadline: 4/15; financial award applicants required to submit FAFSA. *Unit head:* Dr. Frederick Whitt, Dean, 912-681-5322, Fax: 912-681-5349, E-mail: fwhitt@georgiasouthern.edu. *Application contact:* 912-681-5384, Fax: 912-681-0740, E-mail: gradadmissions@georgiasouthern.edu.

Georgia State University, College of Health and Human Sciences, Atlanta, GA 30303-3083. Offers MPH, MS, MSW, DPT, PhD, Certificate. *Accreditation:* CSWE. Part-time and evening/weekend programs available. *Faculty:* 122. *Students:* 334 full-time (278 women), 197 part-time (183 women); includes 166 minority (129 African Americans, 37 Asian Americans or Pacific Islanders), 26 international. Average age 33. 621 applicants, 41% accepted, 160 enrolled. In 2006, 152 master's, 6 doctorates awarded. *Degree requirements:* For master's, thesis (for some programs); for doctorate, thesis/dissertation, comprehensive exam. *Entrance requirements:* For master's, GRE (some programs accept MAT, GMAT); for doctorate, GRE General Test, RN license, interview. Additional exam requirements/recommendations for international students: Required—TOEFL (minimum score 550 paper-based; 213 computer-based). Application fee: $50. Electronic applications accepted. *Financial support:* In 2006–07, 180 research assistantships with full and partial tuition reimbursements (averaging $3,048 per year) were awarded; fellowships with full tuition reimbursements, teaching assistantships with full tuition reimbursements, career-related internships or fieldwork, Federal Work-Study, institutionally sponsored loans, traineeships, tuition waivers (partial), and unspecified assistantships also available. Support available to part-time students. Financial award application deadline: 4/1; financial award applicants required to submit FAFSA. *Faculty research:* Public health issues, obesity, life-cycle health, substance abuse prevention, women's health. Total annual research expenditures: $2.9 million. *Unit head:* Dr. Susan Kelley, Dean, 404-651-3030, E-mail: skelly@gsu.edu. *Application contact:* 404-651-3064, Fax: 404-651-4871, E-mail: chhs-oaa@gsu.edu.

Grand Valley State University, College of Health Professions, Allendale, MI 49401-9403. Offers MPAS, MS, DPT. *Faculty:* 25 full-time (14 women), 3 part-time/adjunct (2 women). *Students:* 234 full-time (187 women), 18 part-time (17 women); includes 18 minority (5 African Americans, 1 American Indian/Alaska Native, 7 Asian Americans or Pacific Islanders, 5 Hispanic Americans). Average age 25. 250 applicants, 45% accepted, 95 enrolled. In 2006, 74 degrees awarded. *Entrance requirements:* For master's, volunteer work, interview, minimum GPA of 3.0, writing sample; for doctorate, GRE, 50 hours of volunteer work, interview, minimum GPA of 3.0 in last 60 hours, minimum 3.0 in prerequisites, writing sample. Additional exam requirements/recommendations for international students: Required—TOEFL (minimum score 610 paper-based; 253 computer-based). *Application deadline:* For winter admission, 1/15 priority date for domestic and international students. Applications are processed on a rolling basis. Electronic applications accepted. *Expenses:* Tuition, state resident: full-time $5,850; part-time $325 per credit. Tuition, nonresident: full-time $10,800; part-time $600 per credit. Tuition and fees vary according to course load. *Financial support:* In 2006–07, 11 research assistantships with full tuition reimbursements (averaging $8,000 per year) were awarded; career-related internships or fieldwork, Federal Work-Study, institutionally sponsored loans, and scholarships/grants also available. Financial award application deadline: 2/15. *Faculty research:* Skeletal muscle structure, blood platelets, thrombospondin activity, FES exercise for quadriplegics, balance. *Unit head:* Dr. Jane Toot, Dean, 616-331-3356, Fax: 616-331-3350, E-mail: tootj@gvsu.edu. *Application contact:* Darlene Zwart, Student Services Coordinator, 616-331-3958, E-mail: zwartda@gvsu.edu.

Idaho State University, Office of Graduate Studies, Kasiska College of Health Professions, Pocatello, ID 83209. Offers M Coun, MHE, MOT, MPAS, MPH, MS, Au D, DPT, PhD, Certificate, Ed S, Post-Doctoral Certificate, Post-Master's Certificate, Postbaccalaureate Certificate. *Accreditation:* APTA (one or more programs are accredited). Part-time programs available. *Faculty:* 29 full-time (17 women), 1 (woman) part-time/adjunct. *Students:* 355 full-time (227 women), 157 part-time (116 women); includes 20 minority (1 African American, 1 American Indian/Alaska Native, 8 Asian Americans or Pacific Islanders, 10 Hispanic Americans), 14 international. Average age 33. In 2006, 128 master's, 21 doctorates, 5 other advanced degrees awarded. *Degree requirements:* For master's, thesis (for some programs), 8 week externship, comprehensive exam, registration; for doctorate, thesis/dissertation, doctoral internship, 1 year spent in residency at Boise, comprehensive exam, registration; for other advanced degree, thesis, case study, oral exam, comprehensive exam, registration (for some programs). *Entrance requirements:* For master's, GRE General Test, minimum GPA of 3.0, 3 letters of recommendation; for doctorate, GRE General Test, minimum GPA of 3.0, counseling license, professional research, interview; for other advanced degree, GRE General Test or MAT, master's degree in counseling, 3 letters of recommendation, 2 years of work experience. Additional exam requirements/recommendations for international students: Required—TOEFL (minimum score 600 paper-based; 250 computer-based). *Application deadline:* For fall admission, 7/1 for domestic students, 6/1 for international students; for spring admission, 12/1 for domestic students, 11/1 for international students. Applications are processed on a rolling basis. Application fee: $55. *Expenses: Contact institution. Financial support:* In 2006–07, 2 research assistantships with full and partial tuition reimbursements (averaging $11,303 per year), 26 teaching assistantships with full and partial tuition reimbursements (averaging $8,694 per year) were awarded; career-related internships or fieldwork, institutionally sponsored loans, scholarships/grants, traineeships, tuition waivers (full and partial), and unspecified assistantships also available. Support available to part-time students. Financial award application deadline: 1/1. *Faculty research:* Mental health, information technology, dental health, nursing. Total annual research expenditures: $38.7 million. *Unit head:* Dr. Linda Hatzenbuehler, Dean, 208-282-3287, Fax: 208-282-4000, E-mail: hatzlind@isu.edu. *Application contact:* Ellen Combs, Graduate School Technical Records Specialist, 208-282-2150, Fax: 208-282-4847.

Ithaca College, Graduate Studies, School of Health Sciences and Human Performance, Ithaca, NY 14850-7020. Offers MS, DPT. Part-time programs available. *Faculty:* 48 full-time (26 women), 8 part-time/adjunct (all women). *Students:* 242 full-time (196 women), 13 part-time (8 women); includes 10 minority (1 African American, 6 Asian Americans or Pacific Islanders, 3 Hispanic Americans), 7 international. Average age 24. 185 applicants, 42% accepted. In 2006, 116 master's, 47 doctorates awarded. *Degree requirements:* For master's, thesis optional; for doctorate, thesis/dissertation optional. Application fee: $40. *Financial support:* In 2006–07, 219 students received support, including 60 teaching assistantships (averaging $8,124 per year); career-related internships or fieldwork, Federal Work-Study, institutionally sponsored loans, scholarships/grants, and unspecified assistantships also available. Support available to part-time students. Financial award applicants required to submit FAFSA. *Unit head:* Dr. Steven Siconolfi, Dean, 607-274-3237, Fax: 607-274-1137, E-mail: ssiconolfi@ithaca.edu.

Loma Linda University, School of Allied Health Professions, Loma Linda, CA 92350. Offers MHIS, MPT, MS, DPT. *Accreditation:* AOTA; APTA.

Long Island University, C.W. Post Campus, School of Health Professions and Nursing, Brookville, NY 11548-1300. Offers MS, Certificate. Part-time and evening/weekend programs available. Postbaccalaureate distance learning degree programs offered. *Degree requirements:* For master's, thesis. Electronic applications accepted. *Faculty research:* PCR Techniques, breast CA-Mammography Compliance, smoking patterns.

Louisiana State University Health Sciences Center, School of Allied Health Professions, Program in Health Science, New Orleans, LA 70112-2223. Offers clinical concepts (MHS); education (MHS); management administration (MHS). Part-time and evening/weekend programs available. *Degree requirements:* For master's, research project, thesis optional.

Allied Health—General

Louisiana State University Health Sciences Center (continued)
Entrance requirements: For master's, GRE General Test, minimum GPA of 2.5. *Expenses:* Tuition, state resident: full-time $5,868; part-time $722 per credit. Tuition, nonresident: full-time $8,993; part-time $1,104 per credit. *Faculty research:* Healthcare management, stroke, ambulation, neurological gait, early intervention.

Marymount University, School of Health Professions, Arlington, VA 22207-4299. Offers MS, MSN, DPT, Certificate. Part-time and evening/weekend programs available. *Faculty:* 15 full-time (13 women), 6 part-time/adjunct (4 women). *Students:* 64 full-time (55 women), 130 part-time (101 women); includes 56 minority (30 African Americans, 18 Asian Americans or Pacific Islanders, 8 Hispanic Americans), 5 international. Average age 34. 130 applicants, 95% accepted, 78 enrolled. In 2006, 21 master's, 16 doctorates, 2 other advanced degrees awarded. *Entrance requirements:* For master's, GRE, MAT, 2 letters of recommendation, interview, resumé; for doctorate, GRE, 2 letters of recommendation, resumé; for Certificate, interview. Additional exam requirements/recommendations for international students: Required—TOEFL (minimum score 600 paper-based; 250 computer-based). *Application deadline:* Applications are processed on a rolling basis. Application fee: $40. Electronic applications accepted. *Expenses:* Tuition: Full-time $11,160; part-time $620 per credit. Required fees: $113; $630 per credit. *Financial support:* Research assistantships with full and partial tuition reimbursements, career-related internships or fieldwork, scholarships/grants, and unspecified assistantships available. Support available to part-time students. Financial award applicants required to submit FAFSA. *Unit head:* Dr. Tess Cappello, Dean, 703-284-1580, Fax: 703-284-3819, E-mail: tess.cappello@marymount.edu.

Maryville University of Saint Louis, School of Health Professions, St. Louis, MO 63141-7299. Offers MARC, MMT, MOT, MSN, DPT. *Accreditation:* CORE. Part-time and evening/weekend programs available. *Faculty:* 17 full-time (14 women), 11 part-time/adjunct (6 women). *Entrance requirements:* Additional exam requirements/recommendations for international students: Required—TOEFL. *Application deadline:* Applications are processed on a rolling basis. Application fee: $35 ($50 for international students). Electronic applications accepted. *Expenses:* Tuition: Full-time $17,800; part-time $555 per credit. Required fees: $55 per semester. Tuition and fees vary according to degree level and program. *Financial support:* Career-related internships or fieldwork, Federal Work-Study, and campus employment available. Financial award application deadline: 7/31. *Faculty research:* Disability work transition, assessment, reducing work-related musculoskeletal injuries, women's health-AIDS. *Unit head:* Charles Gulas, Dean, 314-529-9625, E-mail: hlthprofessions@maryville.edu. *Application contact:* School of Health Professions—Graduate Programs, 314-529-9523, Fax: 314-529-9139, E-mail: hlthprofessions@maryville.edu.

Medical College of Georgia, School of Allied Health Sciences, Programs in Allied Health Sciences, Augusta, GA 30912. Offers MHS, MPH, MS, DPT. Part-time programs available. Postbaccalaureate distance learning degree programs offered (no on-campus study). *Faculty:* 28 full-time (14 women). *Students:* 36 full-time (24 women), 6 part-time (3 women); includes 10 minority (5 African Americans, 4 Asian Americans or Pacific Islanders, 1 Hispanic American), 3 international. Average age 31. 1 applicant, 0% accepted. In 2006, 7 degrees awarded. *Entrance requirements:* For master's, GRE General Test. Additional exam requirements/recommendations for international students: Required—TOEFL (minimum score 550 paper-based; 213 computer-based). *Application deadline:* Applications are processed on a rolling basis. Application fee: $30. Electronic applications accepted. *Expenses:* Tuition, state resident: full-time $2,293; part-time $192 per credit hour. Tuition, nonresident: full-time $9,169; part-time $765 per credit hour. Required fees: $293 per semester. *Financial support:* Federal Work-Study, institutionally sponsored loans, tuition waivers, and unspecified assistantships available. Support available to part-time students. Financial award application deadline: 5/31; financial award applicants required to submit FAFSA. *Faculty research:* Inflammation, postural control, sensory integration, rehabilitation research, allied health practice, focused educational research. *Application contact:* Dr. Carol Campbell, Associate Dean for Business Operations, 706-721-3436, Fax: 706-721-6067, E-mail: cacampbe@mail.mcg.edu.

Medical University of South Carolina, College of Health Professions, Charleston, SC 29425-0002. Offers MHA, MS, MSR, DHA, DPT. *Accreditation:* CAHME (one or more programs are accredited). Part-time programs available. *Faculty:* 91 full-time (50 women), 6 part-time/adjunct (1 woman). *Students:* 499 full-time (373 women), 38 part-time (26 women); includes 73 minority (45 African Americans, 2 American Indian/Alaska Native, 12 Asian Americans or Pacific Islanders, 14 Hispanic Americans), 8 international. Average age 28. 637 applicants, 44% accepted, 220 enrolled. In 2006, 193 master's, 9 doctorates awarded. *Degree requirements:* For doctorate, thesis/dissertation, comprehensive exam. *Entrance requirements:* For master's, GRE. Additional exam requirements/recommendations for international students: Required—TOEFL (minimum score 600 paper-based; 250 computer-based). Application fee: $75. Electronic applications accepted. *Expenses: Contact institution. Financial support:* In 2006–07, 483 students received support. Career-related internships or fieldwork, Federal Work-Study, scholarships/grants, and tuition waivers (partial) available. Support available to part-time students. Financial award application deadline: 3/15; financial award applicants required to submit FAFSA. *Faculty research:* Spinal cord injury, geriatrics, health economics, health psychology, behavioral medicine. *Unit head:* Dr. Becki A. Trickey, Interim Dean, 843-792-8702, Fax: 843-792-3322, E-mail: trickeyb@musc.edu. *Application contact:* Jennifer R. Bailey, Director of Student Services, 843-792-1601, Fax: 843-792-0253, E-mail: baileyje@musc.edu.

Mercy College, Division of Health Professions, Dobbs Ferry, NY 10522-1189. Offers adult nurse practitioner (MS, AC); communication disorders (MS); nursing (MS), including nursing administration, nursing education; occupational therapy (MS); physical therapy (MS); physician assistant (MPS, MS). *Students:* 264 full-time (200 women), 147 part-time (134 women); includes 152 minority (75 African Americans, 26 Asian Americans or Pacific Islanders, 51 Hispanic Americans), 17 international. Average age 33. In 2006, 109 degrees awarded. Application fee: $62. *Expenses:* Tuition: Part-time $595 per credit. Required fees: $9 per credit. Tuition and fees vary according to program. *Unit head:* Dr. Pat Chute, 914-674-7746, E-mail: pchute@mercy.edu. *Application contact:* Kathleen Jackson, Director of Admissions, 800-Mercy-NY, Fax: 914-674-7382, E-mail: admissions@mercy.edu.

MGH Institute of Health Professions, Graduate Programs, Boston, MA 02129. Offers MS, MSN, DPT, Certificate. Part-time and evening/weekend programs available. Postbaccalaureate distance learning degree programs offered (no on-campus study). *Faculty:* 61 full-time (52 women), 49 part-time/adjunct (31 women). *Students:* 388 full-time (345 women), 305 part-time (240 women); includes 103 minority (27 African Americans, 56 Asian Americans or Pacific Islanders, 20 Hispanic Americans), 1 international. Average age 32. 902 applicants, 53% accepted, 254 enrolled. In 2006, 132 master's, 130 doctorates, 35 other advanced degrees awarded. *Degree requirements:* For master's and doctorate, thesis optional. *Entrance requirements:* For master's, GRE General Test. Additional exam requirements/recommendations for international students: Required—TOEFL (minimum score 550 paper-based; 213 computer-based). *Application deadline:* For fall admission, 1/1 priority date for domestic students, 3/1 for international students; for winter admission, 11/1 priority date for domestic students, 7/1 for international students; for spring admission, 3/1 priority date for domestic students, 11/1 for international students. Application fee: $50. Electronic applications accepted. *Financial support:* In 2006–07, 411 students received support; research assistantships, teaching assistantships, career-related internships or fieldwork, scholarships/grants, traineeships, tuition waivers (partial), and unspecified assistantships available. Support available to part-time students. Financial award application deadline: 3/3; financial award applicants required to submit FAFSA. *Faculty research:* Long-term care, pain mechanisms, communication disorders, patient self-care, disability in the elderly. *Unit head:* Ann W. Caldwell, President, 617-726-8002, Fax: 617-726-3716, E-mail: caldwell.ann@mgh.harvard.edu. *Application contact:* Maureen Rika Judd, Manager of Admissions, 617-726-6069, Fax: 617-726-8010, E-mail: admissions@mghihp.edu.

Midwestern University, Downers Grove Campus, College of Health Sciences, Illinois Campus, Downers Grove, IL 60515-1235. Offers MA, MBS, MMS, MOT, DPT, Psy D. *Accreditation:* AOTA (one or more programs are accredited). *Faculty:* 33 full-time (23 women), 108 part-time/adjunct (24 women). *Students:* 470 full-time (383 women), 3 part-time (1 woman); includes 69 minority (16 African Americans, 39 Asian Americans or Pacific Islanders, 14 Hispanic Americans), 2 international. Average age 25. 921 applicants, 49% accepted, 203 enrolled. In 2006, 74 master's, 23 doctorates awarded. *Entrance requirements:* For master's, GRE General Test. *Application deadline:* Applications are processed on a rolling basis. Application fee: $50. *Expenses: Contact institution. Financial support:* In 2006–07, 229 students received support. Federal Work-Study, institutionally sponsored loans, and scholarships/grants available. Financial award applicants required to submit FAFSA. *Unit head:* Dr. Jacquelyn J. Smith, Dean, 630-515-6388. *Application contact:* Michael Laken, Director of Admissions, 630-515-6148, Fax: 630-971-6086, E-mail: admissil@midwestern.edu.

Midwestern University, Glendale Campus, College of Health Sciences, Arizona Campus, Glendale, AZ 85308. Offers DPM, MA, MBS, MCVS, MHPE, MMS, MOT, MS, Certificate. Part-time programs available. *Faculty:* 26 full-time (11 women), 115 part-time/adjunct (36 women). *Students:* 369 full-time (243 women), 17 part-time (11 women); includes 62 minority (13 African Americans, 4 American Indian/Alaska Native, 26 Asian Americans or Pacific Islanders, 19 Hispanic Americans), 4 international. Average age 28. 806 applicants, 68% accepted, 215 enrolled. In 2006, 84 degrees awarded. *Entrance requirements:* MCAT, DAT, GRE or PCAT, 2 professional letters of recommendation. *Application deadline:* For fall admission, 6/4 for domestic students. Applications are processed on a rolling basis. Application fee: $50. *Expenses: Contact institution. Financial support:* Federal Work-Study available. *Unit head:* Dr. Jacquelyn Smith, Dean, 623-572-3601, Fax: 623-572-3601. *Application contact:* James Walters, Director of Admissions, 888-247-9277, Fax: 623-572-3340, E-mail: admissaz@midwestern.edu.

Minnesota State University Mankato, College of Graduate Studies, College of Allied Health and Nursing, Mankato, MN 56001. Offers MA, MS, MSN, MT, SP. Part-time programs available. *Students:* 101 full-time (73 women), 127 part-time (82 women). Average age 32. In 2006, 66 degrees awarded. *Degree requirements:* For master's, comprehensive exam; for SP, thesis. *Entrance requirements:* For master's, GRE (for some programs), minimum GPA of 3.0 during previous 2 years; for SP, GRE General Test, minimum GPA of 3.0. *Application deadline:* Applications are processed on a rolling basis. Application fee: $40. Electronic applications accepted. *Financial support:* Research assistantships with full tuition reimbursements, teaching assistantships with full tuition reimbursements, career-related internships or fieldwork, Federal Work-Study, institutionally sponsored loans, and unspecified assistantships available. Support available to part-time students. Financial award application deadline: 3/15; financial award applicants required to submit FAFSA. *Unit head:* Dr. Kaye Herth, Dean, 507-389-6315. *Application contact:* 507-389-2321, E-mail: grad@mnsu.edu.

Mountain State University, Graduate Studies, Program in Health Science, Beckley, WV 25802-9003. Offers MHS. Part-time and evening/weekend programs available. Postbaccalaureate distance learning degree programs offered (no on-campus study). *Faculty:* 3 full-time (1 woman), 8 part-time/adjunct (4 women). *Students:* 10 full-time (7 women), 4 part-time (3 women); includes 5 minority (all Asian Americans or Pacific Islanders), 2 international. Average age 34. 20 applicants, 100% accepted, 10 enrolled. In 2006, 1 degree awarded. *Median time to degree:* Master's–2 years full-time, 3 years part-time. *Degree requirements:* For master's, thesis or alternative. *Entrance requirements:* Additional exam requirements/recommendations for international students: Required—TOEFL (minimum score 550 paper-based; 213 computer-based); Recommended—IELTS (minimum score 7). *Application deadline:* For fall admission, 5/31 priority date for domestic and international students. Applications are processed on a rolling basis. Application fee: $25 ($50 for international students). Electronic applications accepted. *Expenses:* Tuition: Full-time $3,660; part-time $305 per credit. Tuition and fees vary according to course load and program. *Financial support:* Federal Work-Study, scholarships/grants, and unspecified assistantships available. Support available to part-time students. Financial award applicants required to submit FAFSA. *Unit head:* Dr. Brian Holloway, Dean of Graduate Studies, 304-929-1438, Fax: 304-929-1637, E-mail: holloway@mountainstate.edu. *Application contact:* Dinah Rock, Coordinator of Graduate Academic Services, 304-929-1588, Fax: 304-929-1637, E-mail: drock@mountainstate.edu.

New Jersey City University, Graduate and Continuing Education, College of Professional Studies, Department of Health Sciences, Jersey City, NJ 07305-1597. Offers community health education (MS); health administration (MS); school health education (MS). Part-time and evening/weekend programs available. *Faculty:* 5. *Students:* Average age 42. In 2006, 25 degrees awarded. *Degree requirements:* For master's, thesis or alternative, internship. *Entrance requirements:* For master's, GRE General Test or MAT. Additional exam requirements/recommendations for international students: Required—TOEFL. *Application deadline:* For fall admission, 8/1 priority date for domestic students; for spring admission, 12/1 for domestic students. Applications are processed on a rolling basis. Application fee: $0. *Expenses:* Tuition, state resident: full-time $7,038; part-time $391 per credit. Tuition, nonresident: full-time $12,510; part-time $695 per credit. Required fees: $65 per credit. *Financial support:* Career-related internships or fieldwork and unspecified assistantships available. *Unit head:* Dr. Lilliam Rosado, Chairperson, 201-200-3461.

Northeastern University, Bouvé College of Health Sciences Graduate School, Boston, MA 02115-5096. Offers Pharm D, MS, MS Ed, PSM, Au D, PhD, CAGS, CAS, MS/MBA. *Accreditation:* ACPE (one or more programs are accredited). Part-time and evening/weekend programs available. *Faculty:* 128 full-time (84 women), 83 part-time/adjunct. *Students:* 923 full-time (740 women), 256 part-time (202 women). 1,624 applicants, 30% accepted. In 2006, 247 master's, 16 doctorates, 25 other advanced degrees awarded. *Degree requirements:* For doctorate, thesis/dissertation, qualifying exam. *Entrance requirements:* For Pharm D, prior admission to undergraduate pharmacy program; for master's and other advanced degree, GRE General Test or MAT; for doctorate, GRE General Test. *Application deadline:* Applications are processed on a rolling basis. Application fee: $50. *Financial support:* In 2006–07, 5 research assistantships with full tuition reimbursements (averaging $15,823 per year), 25 teaching assistantships with full tuition reimbursements were awarded; fellowships, career-related internships or fieldwork, Federal Work-Study, tuition waivers (partial), and administrative assistantships also available. Support available to part-time students. Financial award application deadline: 3/1; financial award applicants required to submit FAFSA. *Faculty research:* Counseling, rehabilitation, biomedical sciences, cardiopulmonary sciences, nursing. *Unit head:* Suzanne B. Greenberg, Director, 617-373-3195, E-mail: s.greenberg@neu.edu. *Application contact:* Margaret Schnabel, Director of Graduate Admissions, 617-373-2708, Fax: 617-373-4704, E-mail: bouvegrad@neu.edu.

Northern Arizona University, Consortium of Professional Schools and Colleges, College of Health Professions, Flagstaff, AZ 86011. Offers MPH, MS, MSN, DPT, Certificate. *Accreditation:* APTA (one or more programs are accredited). Part-time programs available.

Nova Southeastern University, Health Professions Division, College of Allied Health and Nursing, Fort Lauderdale, FL 33314-7796. Offers MH Sc, MMS, MOT, MSN, Au D, DHSc, DPT, OTD, PhD, TDPT. Postbaccalaureate distance learning degree programs offered (minimal on-campus study). *Faculty:* 43 full-time (25 women), 8 part-time/adjunct (4 women). *Students:* 521 full-time (407 women), 379 part-time (278 women); includes 269 minority (119 African Americans, 6 American Indian/Alaska Native, 46 Asian Americans or Pacific Islanders, 98 Hispanic Americans), 14 international. In 2006, 152 master's, 69 doctorates awarded. *Degree requirements:* For master's, thesis/dissertation; for doctorate, thesis/dissertation, comprehensive exam. *Entrance requirements:* For master's and doctorate, GRE General Test. *Application deadline:* Applications are processed on a rolling basis. Application fee: $50. *Expenses: Contact institution. Financial support:* Teaching assistantships, institutionally sponsored loans and unspecified assistantships available. *Unit head:* Dr. Richard Davis, Dean, 954-262-1203, E-mail: redavis@nova.edu. *Application contact:* Marla Frolinger, Admissions Counselor, 954-262-1100, E-mail: marlaf@nova.edu.

Oakland University, Graduate Study and Lifelong Learning, School of Health Sciences, Rochester, MI 48309-4401. Offers MS, MSPT, DPT, Dr Sc PT, Certificate. *Accreditation:* APTA (one or more programs are accredited). *Faculty:* 14 full-time (8 women), 2 part-time/adjunct (1 woman). *Students:* 138 full-time (111 women), 108 part-time (82 women); includes 23 minority (9 African Americans, 12 Asian Americans or Pacific Islanders, 2 Hispanic Americans), 26 international. Average age 28. 238 applicants, 47% accepted, 81 enrolled. In 2006, 8 master's, 27 doctorates, 15 other advanced degrees awarded. *Entrance requirements:* For master's, minimum GPA of 3.0 for unconditional admission; for doctorate, GRE General Test. Additional exam requirements/recommendations for international students: Required—TOEFL (minimum score 550 paper-based; 213 computer-based). *Application deadline:* For fall admission, 10/15 for domestic and international students. Applications are processed on a rolling basis. Application fee: $30. Electronic applications accepted. *Expenses:* Contact institution. *Financial support:* Fellowships, Federal Work-Study, institutionally sponsored loans, and tuition waivers (full) available. Financial award application deadline: 3/1; financial award applicants required to submit FAFSA. *Faculty research:* Community emergency response team preparedness; appropriateness, comprehensiveness, sensitivity, and practicality of outcome measures; assessing effectiveness of innovative intervention program for spinal cord injuries. *Unit head:* Dr. Kenneth R. Hightower, Dean, 248-370-3562, Fax: 248-370-4227, E-mail: hightower@oakland.edu.

The Ohio State University, College of Medicine, School of Allied Medical Professions, Columbus, OH 43210. Offers allied medicine (MS); circulation technology (MS); occupational therapy (MOT); physical therapy (MPT). *Accreditation:* AOTA; APTA. Part-time programs available. *Faculty:* 25 full-time (14 women), 2 part-time/adjunct (1 woman). *Students:* 162 full-time (145 women), 126 part-time (101 women); includes 18 minority (7 African Americans, 1 American Indian/Alaska Native, 7 Asian Americans or Pacific Islanders, 3 Hispanic Americans), 10 international. Average age 27. 27 applicants, 74% accepted, 7 enrolled. In 2006, 82 degrees awarded. *Degree requirements:* For master's, thesis or alternative. *Entrance requirements:* For master's, GRE General Test or minimum GPA of 3.5. Additional exam requirements/recommendations for international students: Required—TOEFL (paper-based 550; computer-based 213) or Michigan English Language Assessment Battery (82). *Application deadline:* For fall admission, 8/15 priority date for domestic students, 7/1 priority date for international students; for winter admission, 12/1 priority date for domestic students, 11/1 priority date for international students; for spring admission, 3/1 priority date for domestic students, 2/1 priority date for international students. Applications are processed on a rolling basis. Application fee: $40 ($50 for international students). Electronic applications accepted. *Expenses:* Tuition, state resident: full-time $9,438. Tuition, nonresident: full-time $22,791. Tuition and fees vary according to course load, campus/location and program. *Financial support:* In 2006–07, 14 students received support; fellowships, research assistantships with full tuition reimbursements available, teaching assistantships with full tuition reimbursements available, traineeships and administrative assistantships available. Financial award application deadline: 3/1. *Faculty research:* Geriatrics, quality assurance, nutrition, interdisciplinary health care. Total annual research expenditures: $596,453. *Unit head:* Deborah S. Larsen, Director, 614-292-5921, Fax: 614-292-0210, E-mail: nichols.3@osu.edu. *Application contact:* 614-292-9444, Fax: 614-292-3895, E-mail: domestic.grad@osu.edu.

Old Dominion University, College of Health Sciences, Norfolk, VA 23529. Offers MPH, MS, MSN, DPT, PhD. Part-time and evening/weekend programs available. Postbaccalaureate distance learning degree programs offered (minimal on-campus study). *Faculty:* 41 full-time (30 women), 10 part-time/adjunct (8 women). *Students:* 220 full-time (174 women), 224 part-time (175 women); includes 69 minority (46 African Americans, 1 American Indian/Alaska Native, 17 Asian Americans or Pacific Islanders, 5 Hispanic Americans), 14 international. Average age 33. 335 applicants, 73% accepted, 110 enrolled. In 2006, 104 master's, 32 doctorates awarded. *Degree requirements:* For doctorate, comprehensive exam. *Entrance requirements:* Additional exam requirements/recommendations for international students: Required—TOEFL. *Application deadline:* Applications are processed on a rolling basis. Application fee: $40. Electronic applications accepted. *Expenses:* Tuition, area resident: Part-time $285 per credit hour. Tuition, nonresident: part-time $715 per credit hour. Required fees: $94 per semester. *Financial support:* In 2006–07, 210 students received support, including 1 fellowship with full tuition reimbursement available (averaging $2,220 per year), 15 research assistantships with tuition reimbursements available (averaging $11,000 per year), 6 teaching assistantships with tuition reimbursements available (averaging $9,000 per year); career-related internships or fieldwork, institutionally sponsored loans, scholarships/grants, traineeships, tuition waivers (partial), and unspecified assistantships also available. Support available to part-time students. Financial award application deadline: 2/15; financial award applicants required to submit FAFSA. *Faculty research:* Health promotion and wellness, health care ethics, health policy, health services, cultural competency. Total annual research expenditures: $360,335. *Unit head:* Dr. Andrew Balas, Dean, 757-683-4960, Fax: 757-683-3674, E-mail: abalas@odu.edu. *Application contact:* Dr. Brenda Stevenson Marshall, Assistant Dean for Education, 757-683-6482, Fax: 757-683-4753, E-mail: bmarshal@odu.edu.

Quinnipiac University, School of Health Sciences, Hamden, CT 06518-1940. Offers MHS, MOT, MS, MSN, DPT, Post Master's Certificate. *Accreditation:* AOTA. *Faculty:* 49 full-time (33 women), 67 part-time/adjunct (38 women). *Students:* 272 full-time (212 women), 105 part-time (96 women); includes 54 minority (14 African Americans, 1 American Indian/Alaska Native, 23 Asian Americans or Pacific Islanders, 16 Hispanic Americans), 8 international. Average age 27. 642 applicants, 35% accepted, 186 enrolled. In 2006, 201 master's, 1 other advanced degree awarded. *Entrance requirements:* Additional exam requirements/recommendations for international students: Required—TOEFL (minimum score 575 paper-based; 233 computer-based; 90 iBT), IELTS (minimum score 7). *Application deadline:* For fall admission, 5/30 priority date for international students; for spring admission, 10/15 priority date for international students. Applications are processed on a rolling basis. Application fee: $45. Electronic applications accepted. *Expenses:* Tuition: Part-time $675 per credit. Required fees: $30 per credit. *Financial support:* Career-related internships or fieldwork, traineeships, tuition waivers (partial), and unspecified assistantships available. Support available to part-time students. Financial award application deadline: 4/15; financial award applicants required to submit FAFSA. *Unit head:* Dr. Edward O'Connor, Dean, 203-582-8710, Fax: 203-582-8706. *Application contact:* 800-462-1944, Fax: 203-582-3443, E-mail: graduate@quinnipiac.edu.

See Close-Up on page 1721.

Regis University, Rueckert-Hartman School for Health Professions, Denver, CO 80221-1099. Offers clinical leadership for physician assistants (MS); health services administration (MS); nursing (MSN); physical therapy (DPT, TDPT). *Faculty:* 3 full-time (all women), 7 part-time/adjunct (4 women). *Students:* 453. In 2006, 55 degrees awarded. *Application deadline:* Applications are processed on a rolling basis. *Expenses:* Contact institution. *Financial support:* Career-related internships or fieldwork and Federal Work-Study available. *Faculty research:* Normal and pathological balance and gait research, normal/pathological upper limb motor control/biomechanics, exercise energy/metabolism research, optical treatment protocols for therapeutic modalities. *Unit head:* Dr. Patricia Ladewig, Academic Dean, 303-458-4174, E-mail: pladewig@regis.edu. *Application contact:* Donna Eastman, Assistant to the Dean, 303-458-4174, Fax: 303-964-5533, E-mail: deastman@regis.edu.

Rosalind Franklin University of Medicine and Science, College of Health Professions, North Chicago, IL 60064-3095. Offers MS, PhD, TDPT. Part-time and evening/weekend programs available. Postbaccalaureate distance learning degree programs offered (minimal on-campus study). Terminal master's awarded for partial completion of doctoral program.

Saint Louis University, Graduate School, Doisy College of Health Sciences, St. Louis, MO 63103-2097. Offers MMS, MOT, MS, MSN, MSN-R, MSPT, DPT, PhD, Certificate. Part-time programs available. *Faculty:* 43 full-time (36 women), 15 part-time/adjunct (13 women). *Students:* 219 full-time (182 women), 30 part-time (27 women); includes 16 minority (4 African Americans, 3 American Indian/Alaska Native, 7 Asian Americans or Pacific Islanders, 2 Hispanic Americans), 2 international. Average age 25. 662 applicants, 12% accepted, 68 enrolled. In 2006, 131 master's, 15 doctorates awarded. *Degree requirements:* For master's, comprehensive exam. *Entrance requirements:* Additional exam requirements/recommendations for international students: Required—TOEFL (minimum score 525 paper-based; 194 computer-based). *Application deadline:* For fall admission, 7/1 for domestic and international students; for spring admission, 11/1 for domestic and international students. Applications are processed on a rolling basis. Application fee: $40. *Expenses:* Tuition: Part-time $800 per credit hour. Required fees: $105 per semester. *Financial support:* In 2006–07, 16 students received support, including 11 research assistantships with full tuition reimbursements available (averaging $12,255 per year), 5 teaching assistantships with full tuition reimbursements available (averaging $12,000 per year); career-related internships or fieldwork, Federal Work-Study, scholarships/grants, traineeships, health care benefits, and unspecified assistantships also available. Support available to part-time students. Financial award application deadline: 6/1; financial award applicants required to submit FAFSA. *Unit head:* Dr. Charlotte Royeen, Dean, 314-977-8501, Fax: 314-977-8503, E-mail: royeencb@slu.edu.

Seton Hall University, School of Graduate Medical Education, Programs in Health Sciences, South Orange, NJ 07079-2697. Offers MS, PhD. Part-time and evening/weekend programs available. *Faculty:* 9 full-time (6 women). *Students:* Average age 33. In 2006, 2 master's, 4 doctorates awarded. Terminal master's awarded for partial completion of doctoral program. *Degree requirements:* For master's, research project; for doctorate, thesis/dissertation, candidacy exam, practicum, research projects, comprehensive exam (for some programs), registration. *Entrance requirements:* For master's, interview, minimum GPA of 3.0, letters of recommendation; for doctorate, GRE (preferred), interview, minimum GPA of 3.0, letters of recommendation. Additional exam requirements/recommendations for international students: Required—TOEFL. *Application deadline:* For fall admission, 4/1 for domestic and international students; for spring admission, 11/1 for domestic and international students. Application fee: $75. Electronic applications accepted. *Financial support:* Traineeships and unspecified assistantships available. *Faculty research:* Movement science, motor learning, dual tasks, clinical decision making, online education, teaching strategies. *Unit head:* Dr. Genevieve Pinto Zipp, Chair, 973-275-2076, Fax: 973-275-2370, E-mail: zippgene@shu.edu. *Application contact:* Deborah Verderosa, Director of Admissions, 973-275-2062, Fax: 973-275-2171, E-mail: gradmeded@shu.edu.

See Close-Up on page 1723.

Shenandoah University, School of Health Professions, Winchester, VA 22601-5195. Offers MS, MSN, DPT, Certificate. *Expenses:* Tuition: Full-time $12,200; part-time $610 per credit. Required fees: $150. Full-time tuition and fees vary according to course load and program. *Application contact:* Information Contact, 540-665-5500, Fax: 540-665-5519.

See Close-Up on page 1733.

South Carolina State University, School of Graduate Studies, Department of Health Sciences, Orangeburg, SC 29117-0001. Offers speech/language pathology (MA). *Accreditation:* ASHA. Part-time and evening/weekend programs available. *Faculty:* 4 full-time (3 women), 3 part-time/adjunct (1 woman). *Students:* 20 full-time (19 women), 37 part-time (35 women); includes 45 minority (44 African Americans, 1 Hispanic American). Average age 31. 38 applicants, 71% accepted, 20 enrolled. In 2006, 9 degrees awarded. *Degree requirements:* For master's, departmental qualifying exam, thesis optional. *Entrance requirements:* For master's, GRE or NTE, minimum GPA of 3.0. *Application deadline:* For fall admission, 6/15 for domestic and international students; for spring admission, 11/1 for domestic and international students. Application fee: $25. Electronic applications accepted. *Expenses:* Tuition, state resident: full-time $7,278. Tuition, nonresident: full-time $14,322. *Financial support:* Career-related internships or fieldwork, Federal Work-Study, and institutionally sponsored loans available. Financial award application deadline: 6/1. *Unit head:* Dr. Gwendolyn Wilson, Interim Chair, 803-536-7063, Fax: 803-536-8593, E-mail: gdwilson@scsu.edu. *Application contact:* Annette Hazzard-Jones, Program Coordinator II, 803-536-8809, Fax: 803-536-8812, E-mail: zs_ahazzard@scsu.edu.

Southwestern Oklahoma State University, College of Professional and Graduate Studies, School of Behavioral Sciences and Education, Specialization in Health Sciences and Microbiology, Weatherford, OK 73096-3098. Offers M Ed.

Temple University, Health Sciences Center and Graduate School, College of Health Professions, Philadelphia, PA 19122-6096. Offers Ed M, MA, MOT, MPH, MS, MSN, DPT, PhD. *Accreditation:* APTA (one or more programs are accredited). Part-time and evening/weekend programs available. Postbaccalaureate distance learning degree programs offered (minimal on-campus study). *Faculty:* 53 full-time (40 women). *Students:* 254 full-time (207 women), 293 part-time (217 women); includes 123 minority (81 African Americans, 30 Asian Americans or Pacific Islanders, 12 Hispanic Americans). Average age 25. 500 applicants, 60% accepted, 165 enrolled. In 2006, 113 master's, 105 doctorates awarded. *Degree requirements:* For doctorate, thesis/dissertation. Application fee: $50. *Expenses:* Tuition, state resident: full-time $12,264; part-time $511 per credit. Tuition, nonresident: full-time $17,904; part-time $746 per credit. Required fees: $84 per course. Tuition and fees vary according to program. *Financial support:* Fellowships, research assistantships, teaching assistantships with full tuition reimbursements, career-related internships or fieldwork, Federal Work-Study, institutionally sponsored loans, traineeships, and tuition waivers (partial) available. Support available to part-time students. Financial award application deadline: 1/15. *Faculty research:* Balance dysfunction, repetitive stress injury, neurobehavioral disorders, bilingual speech-language therapy, smoking cessation. Total annual research expenditures: $2.1 million. *Unit head:* Dr. Ronald T. Brown, Dean, 215-707-4800, Fax: 215-707-7819, E-mail: rtbrown@temple.edu.

See Close-Up on page 1741.

Tennessee State University, The School of Graduate Studies and Research, College of Health Sciences, Nashville, TN 37209-1561. Offers MPT, MS, DPT. *Accreditation:* ASHA (one or more programs are accredited). Part-time and evening/weekend programs available. *Students:* 120 applicants. *Entrance requirements:* For master's, GRE General Test, MAT, minimum GPA of 3.5. *Application deadline:* Applications are processed on a rolling basis. Electronic applications accepted. *Financial support:* Fellowships, research assistantships, teaching assistantships, scholarships/grants available. Financial award application deadline: 3/15. *Faculty research:* Community problems of the elderly, language disorders in children, aphasia, sickle cell disturbances, regional and foreign dialects. Total annual research expenditures: $100,775. *Unit head:* Dr. Kathleen McEnerney, Dean, 615-963-5924, Fax: 615-963-5926, E-mail: kmcenerney@tnstate.edu. *Application contact:* Dr. Harold R. Mitchell, Head, Department of Speech Pathology and Audiology, 615-963-7009, Fax: 615-963-7119, E-mail: hmitchell@tnstate.edu.

Texas Christian University, Harris College of Nursing and Health Sciences, Fort Worth, TX 76129-0002. Offers MS, MSN, MSNA. Part-time and evening/weekend programs available. *Entrance requirements:* For master's, GRE General Test. Additional exam requirements/recommendations for international students: Required—TOEFL. *Application deadline:* For fall admission, 3/1 for domestic students; for spring admission, 12/1 for domestic students. Applications are processed on a rolling basis. Application fee: $0. *Expenses:* Tuition: Part-time $800 per credit hour. *Financial support:* Application deadline: 3/1. *Unit head:* Dr. Paulette Burns, Dean, 817-257-7621.

Texas State University-San Marcos, Graduate School, College of Health Professions, San Marcos, TX 78666. Offers MA, MHA, MS, MSCD, MSPT, MSW. Part-time and evening/weekend programs available. *Faculty:* 34 full-time (21 women), 7 part-time/adjunct (4 women). *Students:* 197 full-time (152 women), 149 part-time (121 women); includes 103 minority (24 African Americans, 1 American Indian/Alaska Native, 13 Asian Americans or Pacific Islanders, 65 Hispanic Americans), 8 international. Average age 30. 174 applicants, 72% accepted, 80 enrolled. In 2006, 146 degrees awarded. *Degree requirements:* For master's, comprehensive exam.

Allied Health—General

Texas State University-San Marcos (continued)
Entrance requirements: For master's, GRE General Test. Additional exam requirements/recommendations for international students: Required—TOEFL. *Application deadline:* For fall admission, 6/15 for domestic students, 6/1 for international students; for spring admission, 10/15 priority date for domestic students, 10/1 for international students. Application fee: $40 ($90 for international students). *Financial support:* In 2006–07, 286 students received support, including 2 research assistantships (averaging $7,668 per year), 26 teaching assistantships (averaging $3,443 per year); fellowships, career-related internships or fieldwork, Federal Work-Study, institutionally sponsored loans, scholarships/grants, and stipends also available. Support available to part-time students. Financial award application deadline: 4/1; financial award applicants required to submit FAFSA. *Unit head:* Dr. Ruth Welborn, Dean, 512-245-3300, Fax: 512-245-3791, E-mail: mw01@txstate.edu. *Application contact:* Dr. J. Michael Willoughby, Dean of Graduate School, 512-245-2581, Fax: 512-245-8365, E-mail: gradcollege@txstate.edu.

Texas Tech University Health Sciences Center, School of Allied Health Sciences, Lubbock, TX 79430. Offers MAT, MOT, MPAS, MPT, MRC, MS, Au D, PhD, Sc D. *Accreditation:* APTA (one or more programs are accredited). *Faculty:* 53 full-time (21 women), 5 part-time/adjunct (all women). *Students:* 494 full-time (364 women), 132 part-time (82 women); includes 144 minority (35 African Americans, 3 American Indian/Alaska Native, 26 Asian Americans or Pacific Islanders, 80 Hispanic Americans), 3 international. Average age 28. In 2006, 47 master's, 11 doctorates awarded. Application fee: $35. Electronic applications accepted. *Financial support:* Fellowships, research assistantships, teaching assistantships, career-related internships or fieldwork, institutionally sponsored loans, scholarships/grants, and tuition waivers (full) available. Financial award application deadline: 9/1; financial award applicants required to submit FAFSA. *Unit head:* Dr. Paul P. Brooke, Dean, 806-743-3223, Fax: 806-743-3249, E-mail: paul.brooke@ttuhsc.edu. *Application contact:* Jeri Moravcik, Assistant Director of Admissions and Student Affairs, 806-743-3220, Fax: 806-743-2994, E-mail: jeri.moravcik@ttuhsc.edu.

Texas Woman's University, Graduate School, College of Health Sciences, Denton, TX 76201. Offers MA, MHA, MOT, MS, DPT, Ed D, PhD. Part-time and evening/weekend programs available. Postbaccalaureate distance learning degree programs offered. *Students:* 825 full-time (737 women), 524 part-time (448 women); includes 343 minority (115 African Americans, 12 American Indian/Alaska Native, 80 Asian Americans or Pacific Islanders, 136 Hispanic Americans), 85 international. Average age 30. In 2006, 333 master's, 24 doctorates awarded. Terminal master's awarded for partial completion of doctoral program. *Degree requirements:* For doctorate, thesis/dissertation, qualifying exam. *Entrance requirements:* Additional exam requirements/recommendations for international students: Required—TOEFL (minimum score 550 paper-based; 213 computer-based; 79 iBT). *Application deadline:* For fall admission, 4/1 for international students; for spring admission, 8/1 for international students. Applications are processed on a rolling basis. Application fee: $30 ($50 for international students). Electronic applications accepted. *Expenses:* Tuition, area resident: Part-time $168 per unit. Tuition, state resident: full-time $4,369. Tuition, nonresident: full-time $9,373; part-time $443 per unit. Required fees: $20 per unit. $177 per term. *Financial support:* In 2006–07, 76 research assistantships (averaging $10,764 per year), 18 teaching assistantships (averaging $10,764 per year) were awarded; career-related internships or fieldwork, Federal Work-Study, institutionally sponsored loans, scholarships/grants, traineeships, health care benefits, tuition waivers (partial), and unspecified assistantships also available. Support available to part-time students. Financial award application deadline: 3/1; financial award applicants required to submit FAFSA. *Faculty research:* Stroke, worksite health and safety, kinematics and kinetics of sports activities, weight management, functional tests for females. *Unit head:* Dr. Jimmy Ishee, Dean, 940-898-2854, Fax: 940-898-2853, E-mail: jishee@twu.edu. *Application contact:* Samuel Wheeler, Coordinator of Graduate Admissions, 940-898-3188, Fax: 940-898-3081, E-mail: wheelersr@twu.edu.

Towson University, Graduate School, Program in Health Science, Towson, MD 21252-0001. Offers MS. Part-time and evening/weekend programs available. *Faculty:* 9 full-time (7 women). *Students:* 13 full-time (11 women), 75 part-time (65 women); includes 29 minority (28 African Americans, 1 Hispanic American), 3 international. 33 applicants, 79% accepted, 14 enrolled. In 2006, 37 degrees awarded. *Degree requirements:* For master's, thesis optional. *Entrance requirements:* For master's, previous course work in health sciences, minimum GPA of 2.75. *Application deadline:* Applications are processed on a rolling basis. Application fee: $50. Electronic applications accepted. *Expenses:* Tuition, state resident: part-time $275 per unit. Tuition, nonresident: part-time $577 per unit. Required fees: $72 per unit. *Financial support:* Federal Work-Study and unspecified assistantships available. Financial award application deadline: 4/1; financial award applicants required to submit FAFSA. *Faculty research:* Issues of the aging, drug and alcohol use prevention, health education, health policy, adolescent/student health. *Unit head:* Dr. Susan Radius, Director, 410-704-4216, Fax: 410-704-4670, E-mail: sradius@towson.edu. *Application contact:* 410-704-2501, Fax: 410-704-4675, E-mail: grads@towson.edu.

University at Buffalo, the State University of New York, Graduate School, School of Public Health and Health Professions, Buffalo, NY 14260. Offers MA, MPH, MS, DPT, PhD, Certificate. Part-time programs available. *Faculty:* 64 full-time (30 women), 43 part-time/adjunct (26 women). *Students:* 283 full-time (168 women), 74 part-time (54 women); includes 46 minority (19 African Americans, 1 American Indian/Alaska Native, 21 Asian Americans or Pacific Islanders, 5 Hispanic Americans), 48 international. Average age 30. 614 applicants, 27% accepted, 117 enrolled. In 2006, 72 master's, 49 doctorates, 7 other advanced degrees awarded. Terminal master's awarded for partial completion of doctoral program. *Degree requirements:* For doctorate, thesis/dissertation, comprehensive exam. *Entrance requirements:* For doctorate, GRE General Test. Additional exam requirements/recommendations for international students: Required—TOEFL (minimum score 250 computer-based). Application fee: $35. Electronic applications accepted. *Financial support:* In 2006–07, 15 fellowships with full tuition reimbursements (averaging $2,500 per year), 3 research assistantships with full tuition reimbursements (averaging $15,000 per year), 18 teaching assistantships with full tuition reimbursements (averaging $8,500 per year) were awarded; career-related internships or fieldwork, Federal Work-Study, institutionally sponsored loans, scholarships/grants, tuition waivers (full and partial), and unspecified assistantships also available. Financial award applicants required to submit FAFSA. *Faculty research:* Public health, epidemiology, rehabilitation, assistive technology, exercise and nutrition science. Total annual research expenditures: $8.9 million. *Unit head:* Dr. Maurizio Trevisan, Dean, 716-829-3434 Ext. 411, Fax: 716-829-2034, E-mail: trevisan@buffalo.edu. *Application contact:* Cassandra F. Walker-Whiteside, Senior Advisor, PHHP Student Advisement and Recruitment Services, 716-829-3434 Ext. 410, Fax: 716-829-2034, E-mail: cfwalker@buffalo.edu.

The University of Alabama at Birmingham, School of Health Professions, Birmingham, AL 35294. Offers MNA, MS, MSHA, DPT, Dr Sc PT, PhD, Certificate. *Accreditation:* AANA/CANAEP (one or more programs are accredited); APTA (one or more programs are accredited); CAHME (one or more programs are accredited). Part-time programs available. *Students:* 632 full-time (439 women), 88 part-time (61 women); includes 107 minority (71 African Americans, 5 American Indian/Alaska Native, 19 Asian Americans or Pacific Islanders, 12 Hispanic Americans), 24 international. Average age 30. 301 applicants, 68% accepted. In 2006, 150 master's, 17 doctorates awarded. *Degree requirements:* For doctorate, thesis/dissertation. Application fee: $35 ($60 for international students). Electronic applications accepted. *Expenses:* Contact institution. Tuition and fees vary according to program. *Financial support:* Fellowships, research assistantships, teaching assistantships, career-related internships or fieldwork, Federal Work-Study, institutionally sponsored loans, scholarships/grants, traineeships, and unspecified assistantships available. Support available to part-time students. *Unit head:* Dr. Harold P. Jones, Dean, 205-934-5149, Fax: 205-934-2412, E-mail: jonesh@uab.edu.

University of Connecticut, Graduate School, School of Allied Health, Field of Allied Health, Storrs, CT 06269. Offers MS. *Faculty:* 17 full-time (7 women). *Students:* 11 full-time (8 women), 6 part-time (4 women). Average age 32. 9 applicants, 78% accepted, 7 enrolled. In 2006, 11 degrees awarded. *Degree requirements:* For master's, comprehensive exam. *Entrance requirements:* Additional exam requirements/recommendations for international students: Required—TOEFL (minimum score 550 paper-based; 213 computer-based). *Application deadline:* For fall admission, 2/1 priority date for domestic and international students; for spring admission, 11/1 for domestic students, 10/1 for international students. Applications are processed on a rolling basis. Application fee: $55. Electronic applications accepted. *Financial support:* In 2006–07, 11 research assistantships with full tuition reimbursements, 2 teaching assistantships with full tuition reimbursements were awarded; fellowships, Federal Work-Study, scholarships/grants, health care benefits, and unspecified assistantships also available. Financial award application deadline: 2/1; financial award applicants required to submit FAFSA. *Unit head:* Thomas Miller, Chairperson, 860-486-2846, Fax: 860-486-5375, E-mail: thomas.miller@uconn.edu. *Application contact:* Susan Gregoire, Graduate Coordinator, 860-486-0015, Fax: 860-486-5375, E-mail: susan.gregoire@uconn.edu.

University of Detroit Mercy, College of Health Professions, Detroit, MI 48221. Offers MS, MSN, Certificate. *Entrance requirements:* For master's, GRE General Test, minimum GPA of 3.0. *Expenses:* Tuition: Full-time $15,750; part-time $875 per credit hour. Required fees: $570. *Faculty research:* Research design, respiratory physiology, AIDS prevention, adolescent health, community, low income health education.

University of Florida, Graduate School, College of Public Health and Health Professions, Gainesville, FL 32611. Offers MHA, MHS, MOT, MPH, Au D, DPT, PhD. *Accreditation:* CAHME (one or more programs are accredited). Part-time programs available. *Faculty:* 63 full-time (34 women), 9 part-time/adjunct (4 women). In 2006, 8 degrees awarded. *Degree requirements:* For doctorate, thesis/dissertation. *Entrance requirements:* For master's, GRE General Test; for doctorate, GRE General Test, minimum GPA of 3.0. Additional exam requirements/recommendations for international students: Required—TOEFL (minimum score 550 paper-based; 213 computer-based). *Application deadline:* Applications are processed on a rolling basis. Application fee: $30. Electronic applications accepted. *Expenses:* Tuition, state resident: full-time $6,827. Tuition, nonresident: full-time $21,951. Required fees: $999. *Financial support:* Fellowships, research assistantships, teaching assistantships, career-related internships or fieldwork, Federal Work-Study, institutionally sponsored loans, and unspecified assistantships available. Support available to part-time students. *Unit head:* Dr. Robert G. Frank, Dean, 352-273-6214, Fax: 352-273-6199, E-mail: rfrank@phhp.ufl.edu. *Application contact:* Dr. Stephanie Hanson, Associate Dean, 352-273-6377, Fax: 352-273-6199, E-mail: shanson@phhp.ufl.edu.

University of Illinois at Chicago, Graduate College, College of Applied Health Sciences, Chicago, IL 60607-7128. Offers MAMS, MS, PhD. *Accreditation:* AOTA. Part-time programs available. *Degree requirements:* For doctorate, thesis/dissertation. *Entrance requirements:* For master's, GRE General Test, minimum GPA of 2.75. Additional exam requirements/recommendations for international students: Required—TOEFL. Electronic applications accepted. *Faculty research:* Care of the elderly, nutritional status for various diseases, immunohematology, computer-aided graphics.

University of Kansas, Graduate Studies Medical Center, School of Allied Health, Lawrence, KS 66045. Offers MA, MOT, MS, Au D, DPT, PhD, Certificate. Part-time programs available. Postbaccalaureate distance learning degree programs offered (minimal on-campus study). *Faculty:* 82 full-time (43 women), 18 part-time/adjunct (17 women). *Students:* 306 full-time (237 women), 43 part-time (30 women); includes 16 minority (5 African Americans, 8 Asian Americans or Pacific Islanders, 3 Hispanic Americans), 9 international. Average age 27. 107 applicants, 79% accepted. In 2006, 80 master's, 14 doctorates, 1 other advanced degree awarded. *Entrance requirements:* Additional exam requirements/recommendations for international students: Required—TOEFL. Application fee: $60. Electronic applications accepted. *Expenses:* Tuition, area resident: Part-time $227 per credit. Tuition, state resident: part-time $543 per credit. Tuition and fees vary according to course load, campus/location, program and reciprocity agreements. *Financial support:* In 2006–07, 260 students received support, including 1 fellowship, 9 teaching assistantships with full tuition reimbursements available (averaging $20,124 per year); health care benefits and unspecified assistantships also available. Financial award applicants required to submit FAFSA. *Faculty research:* Diabetes, obesity, DHA in brain development, enternal nourishment, mapping the inner ear. *Unit head:* Dr. Karen L. Miller, Dean, 913-588-5235, Fax: 913-588-5254, E-mail: kmiller@kumc.edu. *Application contact:* Moffett Ferguson, Student Affairs Coordinator, 913-588-5275, E-mail: mfergus1@kumc.edu.

University of Kentucky, Graduate School, College of Health Sciences, Lexington, KY 40506-0032. Offers MS, MSCD, MSHP, MSPAS, MSPT, MSRMP, DS, PhD. Part-time programs available. *Faculty:* 105 full-time (55 women), 4 part-time/adjunct (2 women). *Students:* 306 full-time (240 women), 26 part-time (24 women); includes 8 minority (4 African Americans, 1 American Indian/Alaska Native, 2 Asian Americans or Pacific Islanders, 1 Hispanic American), 7 international. Average age 28. 149 applicants, 50% accepted, 60 enrolled. In 2006, 143 master's, 3 doctorates awarded. *Degree requirements:* For master's, thesis (for some programs), comprehensive exam. *Entrance requirements:* For master's, GRE General Test, minimum undergraduate GPA of 2.75; for doctorate, GRE General Test, minimum undergraduate GPA of 3.0. Additional exam requirements/recommendations for international students: Required—TOEFL (minimum score 550 paper-based; 213 computer-based). *Application deadline:* For fall admission, 7/17 priority date for domestic students, 2/1 priority date for international students; for spring admission, 12/13 priority date for domestic students, 6/15 priority date for international students. Application fee: $40 ($55 for international students). Electronic applications accepted. *Expenses:* Tuition, state resident: full-time $7,670; part-time $401 per credit hour. Tuition, nonresident: full-time $16,158; part-time $873 per credit hour. *Financial support:* In 2006–07, 9 students received support, including 3 fellowships with full tuition reimbursements available, 5 research assistantships with full tuition reimbursements available (averaging $12,000 per year), 1 teaching assistantship with full tuition reimbursement available (averaging $8,332 per year); career-related internships or fieldwork, Federal Work-Study, institutionally sponsored loans, scholarships/grants, traineeships, health care benefits, tuition waivers (partial), and unspecified assistantships also available. Support available to part-time students. Financial award application deadline: 3/15. *Unit head:* Dr. Lori Gonzalez, Dean, 859-323-1100 Ext. 235, Fax: 859-323-1058, E-mail: lsgonz01@pop.uky.edu. *Application contact:* Dr. Brian Jackson, Senior Associate Dean, 859-257-4667, Fax: 859-257-4676, E-mail: brian.jackson@uky.edu.

University of Massachusetts Lowell, Graduate School, College of Health Professions, Lowell, MA 01854-2881. Offers MS, PhD. *Accreditation:* APTA (one or more programs are accredited). Part-time programs available. *Degree requirements:* For master's, thesis optional; for doctorate, thesis/dissertation. *Entrance requirements:* For master's and doctorate, GRE General Test.

University of Medicine and Dentistry of New Jersey, School of Health Related Professions, Newark, NJ 07107-3001. Offers MPT, MS, DCN, DPT, PhD, Certificate, DMD/MS, MD/MS. *Accreditation:* APTA (one or more programs are accredited); NAACLS. Part-time programs available. *Students:* 326 full-time (252 women), 396 part-time (282 women); includes 217 minority (78 African Americans, 89 Asian Americans or Pacific Islanders, 50 Hispanic Americans), 32 international. Average age 33. 798 applicants, 46% accepted, 276 enrolled. In 2006, 96 master's, 66 doctorates, 14 Certificates awarded. *Degree requirements:* For master's, thesis (for some programs). *Entrance requirements:* For master's, GRE. Additional exam requirements/recommendations for international students: Required—TOEFL. *Application deadline:* Applications are processed on a rolling basis. Application fee: $50. Electronic applications accepted. *Expenses:* Contact institution. *Financial support:* Fellowships, research assistantships, teaching assistantships, Federal Work-Study and institutionally sponsored loans available. Financial award application deadline: 5/1. *Faculty research:* Clinical outcomes. *Unit head:* Dr. David M. Gibson, Dean, 973-972-4276, E-mail: gibson@umdnj.edu. *Application contact:* Brian Lewis, Assistant Dean, 973-972-5454, Fax: 973-972-7463, E-mail: shrpadm@umdnj.edu.

University of Mississippi Medical Center, School of Health Related Professions, Jackson, MS 39216-4505. Offers MOT, MPT. *Accreditation:* AOTA; NAACLS. Part-time programs available. *Faculty:* 26 full-time (21 women). *Students:* 180 full-time (146 women), 29 part-time (21 women); includes 64 minority (59 African Americans, 5 Asian Americans or Pacific Islanders). 67 applicants, 57% accepted, 36 enrolled. In 2006, 25 degrees awarded. *Application deadline:* Applications are processed on a rolling basis. Application fee: $10. *Expenses:* Tuition, state resident: full-time $4,523. Tuition, nonresident: full-time $10,566. *Financial support:* Institutionally sponsored loans and scholarships/grants available. Support available to part-time students. Financial award application deadline: 4/1; financial award applicants required to submit FAFSA. *Unit head:* Dr. Ben L. Mitchell, Dean, 601-984-6300, Fax: 601-984-6344, E-mail: bmitchell@shrp.umsmed.edu.

University of Nebraska Medical Center, School of Allied Health Professions, Omaha, NE 68198. Offers MPAS, MPS, DPT, Certificate. *Accreditation:* APTA (one or more programs are accredited). *Unit head:* Kyle P. Meyer, Associate Dean, 402-559-6680, E-mail: kpmeyer@unmc.edu.

The University of North Carolina at Chapel Hill, School of Medicine and Graduate School, Graduate Programs in Medicine, Department of Allied Health Sciences, Chapel Hill, NC 27599. Offers human movement science (MS, PhD); occupational science (MS, PhD), including occupational science; physical therapy (MPT, MS, DPT), including human movement science (MS), physical therapy (MPT, DPT); rehabilitation counseling and psychology (MS); speech and hearing sciences (MS, Au D, PhD), including audiology (Au D), speech and hearing sciences (MS, PhD). *Accreditation:* APTA (one or more programs are accredited). Postbaccalaureate distance learning degree programs offered. *Faculty:* 38 full-time (30 women), 9 part-time/adjunct (6 women). *Students:* 211 full-time (182 women), 34 part-time (25 women); includes 31 minority (15 African Americans, 2 American Indian/Alaska Native, 10 Asian Americans or Pacific Islanders, 4 Hispanic Americans). Average age 37. 515 applicants, 35% accepted, 130 enrolled. In 2006, 56 master's, 16 doctorates awarded. *Entrance requirements:* For master's, GRE General Test; for doctorate, GRE General Test, minimum GPA of 3.0. Additional exam requirements/recommendations for international students: Required—TOEFL (minimum score 550 paper-based; 79 computer-based), TWE. *Application deadline:* For fall admission, 1/1 for domestic and international students. Application fee: $70. Electronic applications accepted. *Financial support:* In 2006–07, 24 research assistantships with partial tuition reimbursements (averaging $5,468 per year), 6 teaching assistantships were awarded; fellowships with partial tuition reimbursements, career-related internships or fieldwork, Federal Work-Study, institutionally sponsored loans, traineeships, and unspecified assistantships also available. Financial award applicants required to submit FAFSA. Total annual research expenditures: $658,992. *Unit head:* Dr. Lee K. McLean, Chairman, 919-966-9040, Fax: 919-966-8384. *Application contact:* Seletha L. Shaw, Student Services Manager, 919-966-2343, Fax: 919-966-8384, E-mail: slshaw@med.unc.edu.

University of North Florida, College of Health, Jacksonville, FL 32224-2645. Offers MHA, MPH, MPT, MS, MSH, MSN, Certificate. *Accreditation:* CORE. Part-time and evening/weekend programs available. *Faculty:* 38 full-time (28 women). *Students:* 167 full-time (128 women), 86 part-time (68 women); includes 52 minority (25 African Americans, 1 American Indian/Alaska Native, 13 Asian Americans or Pacific Islanders, 13 Hispanic Americans), 12 international. Average age 32. 392 applicants, 41% accepted, 102 enrolled. In 2006, 84 degrees awarded. *Entrance requirements:* For master's, GRE General Test, minimum GPA of 3.0 in last 60 hours. Additional exam requirements/recommendations for international students: Required—TOEFL (minimum score 500 paper-based; 173 computer-based). *Application deadline:* For fall admission, 7/1 priority date for domestic students, 5/1 for international students; for spring admission, 11/1 priority date for domestic students, 10/1 for international students. Applications are processed on a rolling basis. Application fee: $30. Electronic applications accepted. *Expenses:* Tuition, state resident: full-time $4,948; part-time $206 per semester hour. Tuition, nonresident: full-time $19,140; part-time $408 per semester hour. *Financial support:* In 2006–07, 136 students received support, including 14 teaching assistantships (averaging $2,570 per year); research assistantships, career-related internships or fieldwork, Federal Work-Study, scholarships/grants, and tuition waivers (partial) also available. Support available to part-time students. Financial award application deadline: 4/1; financial award applicants required to submit FAFSA. *Faculty research:* Adolescent substance abuse, detection of bacterial agents, spirituality and health, non-vitamin and non-mineral supplements, analyzing ticks and their ability to transfer diseases to humans. Total annual research expenditures: $1.9 million. *Unit head:* Dr. Pamela Chally, Dean, 904-620-2810, E-mail: pchally@unf.edu. *Application contact:* Rachel Broderick, Director of Advising, 904-620-2817, Fax: 904-620-1770, E-mail: rbroderi@unf.edu.

University of Oklahoma Health Sciences Center, College of Medicine, Program in Physician Associate, Oklahoma City, OK 73190. Offers MHS.

University of Oklahoma Health Sciences Center, Graduate College, College of Allied Health, Oklahoma City, OK 73190. Offers MOT, MPT, MS, Au D, PhD, Certificate. *Accreditation:* AOTA; APTA. Part-time programs available. Terminal master's awarded for partial completion of doctoral program. *Degree requirements:* For master's, thesis optional; for doctorate, one foreign language, thesis/dissertation, comprehensive exam. *Entrance requirements:* For master's and doctorate, GRE General Test, 3 letters of recommendation. Additional exam requirements/recommendations for international students: Required—TOEFL.

University of Phoenix–Charlotte Campus, The Artemis School, College of Health and Human Services, Charlotte, NC 28273-3409. Offers health care management (MBA). Evening/weekend programs available. *Faculty:* 1 full-time (0 women), 12 part-time/adjunct (7 women). *Students:* 68 full-time (57 women); includes 35 minority (34 African Americans, 1 Asian American or Pacific Islander), 4 international. In 2006, 12 degrees awarded. *Degree requirements:* For master's, thesis (for some programs), registration. *Entrance requirements:* For master's, minimum undergraduate GPA 2.5, 3 years work experience. Additional exam requirements/recommendations for international students: Required—TOEFL (minimum score 550 paper-based; 213 computer-based; 79 iBT). *Application deadline:* Applications are processed on a rolling basis. Application fee: $45. Electronic applications accepted. *Expenses:* Tuition: Full-time $10,320. Required fees: $760. *Financial support:* Institutionally sponsored loans and scholarships/grants available. Financial award applicants required to submit FAFSA. *Unit head:* Dr. Gil Linne, Dean/Executive Director, 480-557-1757, E-mail: gil.linne@phoenix.edu. *Application contact:* College Chair, 704-504-5409.

University of Phoenix–Las Vegas Campus, The Artemis School, College of Health and Human Services, Las Vegas, NV 89128. Offers marriage, family, and child therapy (MSC); mental health counseling (MSC). *Faculty:* 8 full-time (4 women), 72 part-time/adjunct (37 women). *Students:* 71 full-time (55 women); includes 18 minority (14 African Americans, 1 American Indian/Alaska Native, 3 Hispanic Americans), 2 international. Average age 39. In 2006, 1 degree awarded. *Degree requirements:* For master's, registration. *Entrance requirements:* For master's, minimum undergraduate GPA of 2.5, 3 years of work experience. Additional exam requirements/recommendations for international students: Required—TOEFL (minimum score 550 paper-based; 213 computer-based; 79 iBT). *Application deadline:* Applications are processed on a rolling basis. Application fee: $45. Electronic applications accepted. *Expenses:* Tuition: Full-time $9,576. Required fees: $760. *Financial support:* Institutionally sponsored loans and scholarships/grants available. Financial award applicants required to submit FAFSA. *Unit head:* Dr. Gil Linne, Dean/Executive Director, 480-557-1751, E-mail: gil.linne@phoenix.edu. *Application contact:* Chair, 702-638-7249, Fax: 702-638-8085.

University of Puerto Rico, Medical Sciences Campus, College of Health Related Professions, San Juan, PR 00936-5067. Offers MS, Certificate. Part-time and evening/weekend programs available. *Degree requirements:* For master's, one foreign language. *Entrance requirements:* For master's, EXADEP, interview; for Certificate, Allied Health Professions Admissions Test, minimum GPA of 2.5, interview. *Faculty research:* Infantile autism, aphasia, language problems, toxicology, immunohematology, medical record documentation and quality.

University of St. Francis, College of Nursing and Allied Health, Joliet, IL 60435-6169. Offers nursing (MSN); physician assistant studies (MS). *Accreditation:* AACN. Part-time and evening/weekend programs available. *Faculty:* 10 full-time (8 women), 1 (woman) part-time/adjunct. *Students:* 61 full-time (42 women), 62 part-time (60 women); includes 30 minority (8 African Americans, 1 American Indian/Alaska Native, 8 Asian Americans or Pacific Islanders, 13 Hispanic Americans). Average age 37. 52 applicants, 71% accepted, 22 enrolled. In 2006, 30 degrees awarded. *Degree requirements:* For master's, thesis (for some programs), comprehensive exam (for some programs), registration. *Entrance requirements:* For master's, GRE General Test (MS), minimum GPA of 3.0, 2 years of work experience in clinical nursing, CPR certification, computer competency, 3 letters of recommendation, interview, RN license (MSN); minimum GPA of 2.75, clinical experience (MS). Additional exam requirements/recommendations for international students: Required—TOEFL (minimum score 550 paper-based; 213 computer-based). *Application deadline:* Applications are processed on a rolling basis. Application fee: $30. Electronic applications accepted. *Expenses:* Contact institution. Part-time tuition and fees vary according to campus/location and program. *Financial support:* In 2006–07, 45 students received support. Scholarships/grants, traineeships, tuition waivers (partial), and unspecified assistantships available. Support available to part-time students. Financial award applicants required to submit FAFSA. *Unit head:* Dr. Maria Connolly, Dean, 815-740-3463, Fax: 815-740-4243, E-mail: mconnolly@stfrancis.edu. *Application contact:* Sandra Sloka, Director of Admissions for Graduate and Degree Completion Programs, 800-735-7500, Fax: 815-740-5032, E-mail: ssloka@stfrancis.edu.

University of Saint Francis, Graduate School, Department of Allied Health, Fort Wayne, IN 46808-3994. Offers physician assistant studies (MS). *Accreditation:* ARC-PA. *Faculty:* 5 full-time (3 women), 1 part-time/adjunct (0 women). *Students:* 48 full-time (38 women). Average age 26. In 2006, 6 degrees awarded. *Entrance requirements:* For master's, GRE or MCAT, previous courses in biology, chemistry, and psychology, previous direct patient care. Application fee: $20. *Financial support:* Applicants required to submit FAFSA. *Unit head:* Dr. Nancy Gillespie, Dean, 260-434-3240, Fax: 260-434-7685, E-mail: ngillespie@sf.edu. *Application contact:* James Lashdollar, Admissions Counselor, 260-434-3279, E-mail: jcashdollar@sf.edu.

University of South Alabama, Graduate School, College of Allied Health Professions, Mobile, AL 36688-0002. Offers MHS, MS, Au D, DPT, PhD. *Faculty:* 27 full-time (14 women). *Students:* 278 full-time (234 women), 30 part-time (21 women); includes 20 minority (13 African Americans, 2 American Indian/Alaska Native, 3 Asian Americans or Pacific Islanders, 2 Hispanic Americans), 5 international. 28 applicants, 82% accepted, 18 enrolled. In 2006, 54 master's, 4 doctorates awarded. *Degree requirements:* For master's, externship, thesis optional; for doctorate, thesis/dissertation, clinical internship. *Entrance requirements:* For master's, GRE General Test. *Application deadline:* For fall admission, 9/1 priority date for domestic students. Applications are processed on a rolling basis. Application fee: $25. *Financial support:* Fellowships, research assistantships, career-related internships or fieldwork available. Support available to part-time students. Financial award application deadline: 4/1. *Unit head:* Dr. Richard Talbot, Dean, 251-380-2785.

The University of South Dakota, School of Medicine and Health Sciences and Graduate School, Graduate Programs in Health Sciences, Vermillion, SD 57069-2390. Offers occupational therapy (MS); physical therapy (MS, DPT); physician assistant studies (MS). Part-time programs available. *Faculty:* 15 full-time (9 women), 6 part-time/adjunct (4 women). *Students:* 156 full-time (110 women), 3 part-time (all women); includes 6 minority (1 African American, 2 American Indian/Alaska Native, 3 Asian Americans or Pacific Islanders). Average age 25. 247 applicants, 32% accepted, 71 enrolled. In 2006, 44 degrees awarded. *Entrance requirements:* For master's, GRE General Test, GRE Subject Test. Application fee: $35. *Expenses:* Tuition, state resident: part-time $120 per credit hour. Tuition, nonresident: part-time $355 per credit hour. Required fees: $90 per credit hour. *Financial support:* Research assistantships, teaching assistantships, career-related internships or fieldwork, Federal Work-Study, scholarships/grants, traineeships, and unspecified assistantships available. *Faculty research:* Occupational therapy, physical therapy, vision, pediatrics, geriatrics. Total annual research expenditures: $10,000. *Unit head:* Dr. John Williams, Dean, 605-677-6572, Fax: 605-677-6745, E-mail: jwilliam@usd.edu. *Application contact:* Sheryl Duman, Senior Secretary, 605-677-6572, Fax: 605-677-6745, E-mail: sduman@usd.edu.

The University of Tennessee Health Science Center, College of Allied Health Sciences, Memphis, TN 38163-0002. Offers MCP, MDH, MHIIM, MOT, MSCLS, MSPT, DPT, ScDPT, TDPT. *Accreditation:* AOTA; APTA. Part-time and evening/weekend programs available. Postbaccalaureate distance learning degree programs offered (minimal on-campus study). *Faculty:* 23 full-time (18 women), 23 part-time/adjunct (17 women). *Students:* 197 full-time (141 women), 5 part-time (4 women); includes 43 minority (29 African Americans, 1 American Indian/Alaska Native, 13 Asian Americans or Pacific Islanders). Average age 26. 225 applicants, 57% accepted, 120 enrolled. In 2006, 2 master's, 2 doctorates awarded. Terminal master's awarded for partial completion of doctoral program. *Degree requirements:* For master's, thesis, comprehensive exam, registration; for doctorate, residency. *Entrance requirements:* For master's, GRE (MOT, MSCLS), minimum GPA of 3.0, 3 letters of reference, state license (MDH), national accreditation (MSCLS), GRE if GPA is less than 3.0 (MCP); for doctorate, GRE. Additional exam requirements/recommendations for international students: Required—TOEFL (minimum score 550 paper-based; 213 computer-based; 80 iBT). *Application deadline:* For fall admission, 1/30 priority date for domestic students; for winter admission, 10/1 priority date for domestic students. Application fee: $50. Electronic applications accepted. *Expenses:* Contact institution. *Financial support:* In 2006–07, 2 teaching assistantships were awarded; Federal Work-Study, institutionally sponsored loans, and scholarships/grants also available. Support available to part-time students. Financial award application deadline: 2/15; financial award applicants required to submit FAFSA. *Faculty research:* Gait deviation, muscular dystrophy and strength, hemophilia and exercise, pediatric neurology, self-efficacy. *Unit head:* Dr. William R. Frey, Interim Dean, 901-528-5581, Fax: 901-528-7545, E-mail: wfrey@utmem.edu. *Application contact:* Eunice Taylor, Interim Director, Enrollment Services, 901-448-5560, Fax: 901-448-7772, E-mail: etaylor@utmem.edu.

The University of Texas at El Paso, Graduate School, College of Health Sciences, School of Allied Health, El Paso, TX 79968-0001. Offers MPT, MS.

The University of Texas Medical Branch, School of Allied Health Sciences, Galveston, TX 77555. Offers MOT, MPAS, MPT. *Faculty:* 27 full-time (18 women). *Students:* 311 full-time (243 women), 8 part-time (7 women); includes 90 minority (37 African Americans, 1 American Indian/Alaska Native, 22 Asian Americans or Pacific Islanders, 30 Hispanic Americans), 4 international. Average age 26. 846 applicants, 22% accepted, 172 enrolled. In 2006, 86 degrees awarded. *Degree requirements:* For master's, thesis or alternative. *Entrance requirements:* For master's, GRE, experience in field, minimum GPA of 3.0. Additional exam requirements/recommendations for international students: Required—TOEFL (minimum score 550 paper-based; 212 computer-based). *Application deadline:* For fall admission, 11/1 for domestic students. Applications are processed on a rolling basis. Application fee: $30. Electronic applications accepted. *Financial support:* Career-related internships or fieldwork, Federal Work-Study, institutionally sponsored loans, and scholarships/grants available. Financial award applicants required to submit FAFSA. *Unit head:* Dr. Elizabeth J. Protas, Interim Dean, 409-772-3001, Fax: 409-772-1613, E-mail: ejprotas@utmb.edu. *Application contact:* Raymond Lewis, Associate Dean for Admissions and Student Affairs, 409-772-3030, Fax: 409-747-1624, E-mail: ralewis@utmb.edu.

University of Vermont, Graduate College, College of Nursing and Health Sciences, Burlington, VT 05405. Offers MS, DPT. Part-time programs available. *Students:* 81 (62 women); includes 5 minority (1 African American, 3 Asian Americans or Pacific Islanders, 1 Hispanic American) 1 international. 146 applicants, 52% accepted, 36 enrolled. In 2006, 20 degrees awarded.

Allied Health—General

University of Vermont (continued)
Degree requirements: For master's, thesis. *Entrance requirements:* For master's, GRE General Test. Additional exam requirements/recommendations for international students: Required—TOEFL (minimum score 550 paper-based; 213 computer-based). *Application deadline:* For fall admission, 4/1 priority date for domestic students. Applications are processed on a rolling basis. Application fee: $40. *Expenses:* Tuition, state resident: part-time $434 per credit. Tuition, nonresident: part-time $1,096 per credit. *Financial support:* Fellowships, research assistantships, teaching assistantships, Federal Work-Study available. Financial award application deadline: 3/1. *Unit head:* Dr. Betty Rambur, Dean, 802-656-3860.

University of Wisconsin–Milwaukee, Graduate School, College of Health Sciences, Milwaukee, WI 53201-0413. Offers MS, PhD. Part-time programs available. *Faculty:* 42 full-time (24 women). *Students:* 83 full-time (68 women), 35 part-time (24 women); includes 9 minority (5 African Americans, 3 Asian Americans or Pacific Islanders, 1 Hispanic American), 9 international. Average age 27. 176 applicants, 44% accepted, 28 enrolled. In 2006, 59 degrees awarded. *Application deadline:* For fall admission, 1/1 priority date for domestic students; for spring admission, 9/1 for domestic students. Applications are processed on a rolling basis. Application fee: $45 ($75 for international students). *Expenses: Contact institution.* Tuition and fees vary according to program. *Financial support:* In 2006–07, 6 fellowships, 1 research assistantship, 15 teaching assistantships were awarded; career-related internships or fieldwork, Federal Work-Study, and unspecified assistantships also available. Support available to part-time students. Financial award application deadline: 4/15. *Unit head:* Randall Lambrecht, Dean, 414-229-4712, E-mail: rsl@uwm.edu.

Virginia Commonwealth University, Graduate School, School of Allied Health Professions, Department of Health Administration, Doctoral Program in Health Related Sciences, Richmond, VA 23284-9005. Offers clinical laboratory sciences (PhD); gerontology (PhD); health administration (PhD); nurse anesthesia (PhD); occupational therapy (PhD); physical therapy (PhD); radiation sciences (PhD); rehabilitation leadership (PhD). *Faculty:* 2 full-time (1 woman). *Students:* 4 full-time (all women), 13 part-time (7 women); includes 7 minority (1 African American, 6 Asian Americans or Pacific Islanders), 3 international. In 2006, 2 degrees awarded. *Unit head:* Monica L. White, Director of Student Services, 804-828-3273, Fax: 804-828-8656, E-mail: mlwhite1@vcu.edu.

See Close-Up on page 1745.

Washington University in St. Louis, School of Medicine, Graduate Programs in Medicine, St. Louis, MO 63130-4899. Offers health administration (MHA); occupational therapy (MSOT, OTD); physical therapy (DPT, PhD, PPDPT), including movement science (PhD), physical therapy (DPT, PPDPT). *Students:* 439; includes 62 minority (9 African Americans, 2 American Indian/Alaska Native, 46 Asian Americans or Pacific Islanders, 5 Hispanic Americans), 6 international. In 2006, 209 degrees awarded. *Degree requirements:* For doctorate, thesis/dissertation. *Expenses: Contact institution. Financial support:* Fellowships, research assistantships, career-related internships or fieldwork, Federal Work-Study, and institutionally sponsored loans available. Support available to part-time students. Financial award applicants required to submit FAFSA. *Application contact:* Dr. W. Edwin Dodson, Associate Dean, 314-362-6848, Fax: 314-362-4658, E-mail: wumscoa@msnotes.wustl.edu.

Western University of Health Sciences, College of Allied Health Professions, Pomona, CA 91766-1854. Offers MS, DPT. *Accreditation:* APTA (one or more programs are accredited). *Faculty:* 19 full-time (11 women), 1 (woman) part-time/adjunct. *Students:* 304 full-time (213 women), 44 part-time (25 women); includes 172 minority (15 African Americans, 89 Asian Americans or Pacific Islanders, 68 Hispanic Americans), 2 international. Average age 30. 758 applicants, 35% accepted, 142 enrolled. In 2006, 104 master's, 23 doctorates awarded. *Entrance requirements:* For master's, minimum undergraduate GPA of 2.5, graduate 3.0; for doctorate, GRE General Test, minimum GPA of 2.8, letters of recommendation, interview. *Expenses: Contact institution. Financial support:* Institutionally sponsored loans and scholarships/grants available. Financial award application deadline: 3/2; financial award applicants required to submit FAFSA. *Unit head:* Dr. Stephanie Bowlin, Dean, 909-469-5383. *Application contact:* Audrey Navarro, Information Contact, 909-469-5335, Fax: 909-469-5570, E-mail: admissions@westernu.edu.

Wichita State University, Graduate School, College of Health Professions, Wichita, KS 67260. Offers MPH, MPT, MSN, MSN/MBA. *Accreditation:* APTA (one or more programs are accredited). Part-time programs available. *Entrance requirements:* For master's, GRE. Additional exam requirements/recommendations for international students: Required—TOEFL. Electronic applications accepted.

Anesthesiologist Assistant Studies

Case Western Reserve University, School of Medicine and School of Graduate Studies, Graduate Programs in Medicine, Department of Anesthesiology, Cleveland, OH 44106. Offers MS. *Accreditation:* AANA/CANAEP. *Faculty:* 44 full-time (15 women), 20 part-time/adjunct (8 women). *Students:* 26 full-time (11 women); includes 3 minority (1 African American, 2 Asian Americans or Pacific Islanders), 1 international. Average age 25. 44 applicants, 34% accepted, 15 enrolled. In 2006, 11 degrees awarded. *Degree requirements:* For master's, thesis. *Entrance requirements:* For master's, MCAT. Additional exam requirements/recommendations for international students: Required—TOEFL. *Application deadline:* For fall admission, 10/1 priority date for domestic students. Application fee: $50. Electronic applications accepted. *Financial support:* In 2006–07, 24 students received support; fellowships, research assistantships, teaching assistantships available. Financial award application deadline: 4/30; financial award applicants required to submit FAFSA. *Faculty research:* Metabolism of bioamines, cerebral metabolism, cardiovascular hemodynamics, genetics. *Unit head:* Dr. Howard S. Nearman, Chair, 216-844-7330, Fax: 216-844-3781, E-mail: howard.nearman@utthospitals.org. *Application contact:* Laura Bishop, Education Coordinator, 216-844-8077, Fax: 216-844-7349, E-mail: info@anesthesiaprogram.com.

Emory University, School of Medicine, Programs in Allied Health Professions, Department of Anesthesiology, Atlanta, GA 30322-1100. Offers MM Sc. *Faculty:* 1 (woman) full-time, 9 part-time/adjunct (1 woman). *Students:* 67 full-time (33 women); includes 18 minority (8 African Americans, 1 American Indian/Alaska Native, 7 Asian Americans or Pacific Islanders, 2 Hispanic Americans). Average age 29. 162 applicants, 23% accepted, 37 enrolled. In 2006, 30 degrees awarded. *Entrance requirements:* For master's, GRE General Test or MCAT. Additional exam requirements/recommendations for international students: Required—TOEFL (minimum score 613 paper-based; 257 computer-based). *Application deadline:* For fall admission, 1/1 for domestic and international students. Applications are processed on a rolling basis. Application fee: $60. Electronic applications accepted. *Expenses: Contact institution. Financial support:* In 2006–07, 64 students received support. Institutionally sponsored loans and scholarships/grants available. Financial award application deadline: 4/1; financial award applicants required to submit CSS PROFILE or FAFSA. *Unit head:* Dr. Richard G. Brouillard, Director of Academic Affairs, 404-727-5910, Fax: 404-727-3021. *Application contact:* Jerri J. Elder, Admissions Services Coordinator, 404-727-7125, Fax: 404-727-3021.

South University, Graduate Programs, School of Health Professions, Program in Anesthesiologist Assistant, Savannah, GA 31406-4805. Offers MM Sc.

See Close-Up on page 1735.

Université Laval, Faculty of Medicine, Post-Professional Programs in Medical Studies, Québec, QC G1K 7P4, Canada. Offers anatomy–pathology (DESS); anesthesiology (DESS); cardiology (DESS); care of older people (Diploma); clinical research (DESS); community health (DESS); dermatology (DESS); diagnostic radiology (DESS); emergency medicine (Diploma); family medicine (DESS); general surgery (DESS); geriatrics (DESS); hematology (DESS); internal medicine (DESS); maternal and fetal medicine (Diploma); medical biochemistry (DESS); medical microbiology and infectious diseases (DESS); medical oncology (DESS); nephrology (DESS); neurology (DESS); neurosurgery (DESS); obstetrics and gynecology (DESS); ophthalmology (DESS); orthopedic surgery (DESS); oto-rhino-laryngology (DESS); palliative medicine (Diploma); pediatrics (DESS); plastic surgery (DESS); psychiatry (DESS); pulmonary medicine (DESS); radiology–oncology (DESS); thoracic surgery (DESS); urology (DESS). *Degree requirements:* For other advanced degree, comprehensive exam. *Entrance requirements:* For degree, knowledge of French. Electronic applications accepted.

University of Guelph, Ontario Veterinary College and Graduate Program Services, Graduate Programs in Veterinary Sciences, Department of Clinical Studies, Guelph, ON N1G 2W1, Canada. Offers anesthesiology (M Sc, DV Sc); cardiology (Diploma); clinical studies (Diploma); emergency/critical care (Diploma); medicine (M Sc, DV Sc); neurology (M Sc, DV Sc); ophthalmology (M Sc, DV Sc); surgery (M Sc, DV Sc). *Faculty:* 37. *Students:* 27 (19 women). *Degree requirements:* For master's, thesis/dissertation; for doctorate, thesis/dissertation, comprehensive exam. *Entrance requirements:* Additional exam requirements/recommendations for international students: Required—TOEFL (minimum score 550 paper-based; 213 computer-based), IELTS (minimum score 7). *Application deadline:* For fall admission, 12/6 for domestic students; for winter admission, 10/30 priority date for domestic students; for spring admission, 2/28 priority date for domestic students. Applications are processed on a rolling basis. Application fee: $80. Electronic applications accepted. *Financial support:* Fellowships, research assistantships, teaching assistantships, career-related internships or fieldwork and scholarships/grants available. *Faculty research:* Orthopedics, respirology, oncology, exercise physiology, cardiology. Total annual research expenditures: $1.5 million. *Unit head:* Dr. Dara Allen, Interim Chair, 519-824-4120 Ext. 54001, Fax: 519-767-0311, E-mail: dallen@ouc.uoguelph.ca. *Application contact:* Dr. J. Scott Weese, Graduate Coordinator, 519-824-4120 Ext. 54064, Fax: 519-767-0311, E-mail: jsweese@uoguelph.ca.

Clinical Laboratory Sciences/Medical Technology

Baylor College of Medicine, Graduate School of Biomedical Sciences, Program in Clinical Scientist Training, Houston, TX 77030-3498. Offers MS, PhD. *Faculty:* 44 full-time (11 women). *Students:* 32 full-time (21 women); includes 15 minority (2 African Americans, 10 Asian Americans or Pacific Islanders, 3 Hispanic Americans), 5 international. Average age 38. 12 applicants, 100% accepted, 12 enrolled. In 2006, 1 degree awarded. *Median time to degree:* Master's–1.84 years full-time. *Degree requirements:* For master's, thesis, registration; for doctorate, thesis/dissertation, public defense. *Application deadline:* For fall admission, 2/1 priority date for domestic students. Application fee: $30. Electronic applications accepted. *Financial support:* In 2006–07, 32 fellowships with full tuition reimbursements were awarded; research assistantships with full tuition reimbursements, career-related internships or fieldwork, Federal Work-Study, institutionally sponsored loans, health care benefits, and tuition waivers (full) also available. *Unit head:* Dr. Morey Haymond, Director. *Application contact:* Dr. Olga Watkins, Graduate Program Administrator, 713-798-7132, Fax: 713-798-7119, E-mail: owatkins@bcm.tmc.edu.

The Catholic University of America, School of Arts and Sciences, Department of Biology, Washington, DC 20064. Offers cell and microbial biology (MS, PhD), including cell biology, microbiology; clinical laboratory science (MS, PhD); MSLS/MS. Part-time programs available. *Faculty:* 8 full-time (3 women), 1 (woman) part-time/adjunct. *Students:* 3 full-time (1 woman), 23 part-time (14 women); includes 4 minority (3 African Americans, 1 Asian American or Pacific Islander), 12 international. Average age 31. 33 applicants, 39% accepted, 2 enrolled. In 2006, 5 degrees awarded. Terminal master's awarded for partial completion of doctoral program. *Degree requirements:* For master's, thesis or alternative, comprehensive exam; for doctorate, thesis/dissertation, comprehensive exam. *Entrance requirements:* For master's and doctorate, GRE General Test, GRE Subject Test, 3 letters of recommendation. Additional exam requirements/recommendations for international students: Required—TOEFL (minimum score 580 paper-based; 237 computer-based). *Application deadline:* For fall admission, 2/1 priority date for domestic students; for spring admission, 11/15 priority date for domestic students. Applications are processed on a rolling basis. Application fee: $55. Electronic applications accepted. *Expenses:* Tuition: Full-time $27,700; part-time $1,045 per credit hour. Required fees: $1,290. Part-time tuition and fees vary according to campus/location and program. *Financial support:* Fellowships, research assistantships, teaching assistantships, career-related internships or fieldwork, scholarships/grants, tuition waivers (full and partial), and unspecified assistantships available. Support available to part-time students. Financial award application deadline: 2/1; financial award applicants required to submit FAFSA. *Faculty research:* Cell differentiation, regulation of cell growth, drug resistance, gene cloning and sequencing, developmental biology and neurobiology. *Unit head:* Dr. Venigalla Rao, Chair, 202-319-5267, Fax: 202-319-5721, E-mail: rao@cua.edu.

Duke University, School of Medicine, Clinical Leadership Program, Durham, NC 27708-0586. Offers MHS. In 2006, 5 degrees awarded. *Degree requirements:* For master's, project. *Entrance requirements:* For master's, GRE. *Application deadline:* For fall admission, 5/30 priority date for domestic students. Applications are processed on a rolling basis. Application fee: $100. *Financial support:* In 2006–07, 1 student received support. Application deadline: 5/1; *Unit head:* Michelle J. Lyn, Clinical Associate/Program Director, 919-681-5744, Fax: 919-681-3371, E-mail: lyn00001@mc.duke.edu. *Application contact:* Jessica Kirtley, Administrative Coordinator, 919-681-5744, Fax: 919-681-3371, E-mail: kirte001@mc.duke.edu.

Emory University, School of Medicine, Programs in Allied Health Professions, Atlanta, GA 30322-1100. Offers anesthesiology (MM Sc); anesthesiology/patient monitoring systems (MM Sc); ophthalmic technology (MM Sc); physical therapy (DPT); physician assistant (MM Sc). Postbaccalaureate distance learning degree programs offered. *Faculty:* 27 full-time (16 women), 57 part-time/adjunct (32 women). *Students:* 322 full-time (227 women), 6 part-time (5 women); includes 69 minority (33 African Americans, 4 American Indian/Alaska Native, 28 Asian Americans or Pacific Islanders, 4 Hispanic Americans). Average age 28. 1,149 applicants, 16% accepted, 132 enrolled. In 2006, 80 master's, 21 doctorates awarded. *Entrance requirements:* For master's and doctorate, GRE. *Expenses:* Contact institution. *Financial support:* In 2006–07, 289 students received support. Federal Work-Study, institutionally sponsored loans, and scholarships/grants available. Support available to part-time students. Financial award application deadline: 2/15; financial award applicants required to submit CSS PROFILE or FAFSA. *Unit head:* Dr. J. Alan Otsuki, Assistant Dean, Office of Medical Education and Student Affairs, 404-727-5655, Fax: 404-727-0045, E-mail: jotsuki@emory.edu. *Application contact:* Roselyn Branch, Associate Director of Registration and Student Affairs, 404-727-5682, Fax: 404-727-0045, E-mail: roselyn.branch@emory.edu.

Fairleigh Dickinson University, Metropolitan Campus, University College: Arts, Sciences, and Professional Studies, Henry P. Becton School of Nursing and Allied Health, Program in Medical Technology, Teaneck, NJ 07666-1914. Offers MS. *Students:* Average age 45. 1 applicant, 100% accepted, 0 enrolled. *Application deadline:* Applications are processed on a rolling basis. Application fee: $40. *Unit head:* Dr. Minerva Guttman, Director, Henry P. Becton School of Nursing and Allied Health, 201-692-2000.

Inter American University of Puerto Rico, Metropolitan Campus, Faculty of Science and Technology, Program in Medical Technology, San Juan, PR 00919-1293. Offers administration of laboratories (MS); micromolecular biology (MS). *Accreditation:* NAACLS. Part-time programs available. *Degree requirements:* For master's, comprehensive exam. *Entrance requirements:* For master's, BS in medical technology, minimum GPA of 2.5. Electronic applications accepted.

Long Island University, C.W. Post Campus, School of Health Professions and Nursing, Department of Biomedical Sciences, Program in Clinical Laboratory Management, Brookville, NY 11548-1300. Offers MS. *Accreditation:* NAACLS. Part-time programs available. *Degree requirements:* For master's, thesis. *Entrance requirements:* For master's, minimum GPA of 2.75 in major. Additional exam requirements/recommendations for international students: Required—TOEFL. Electronic applications accepted.

Medical College of Georgia, School of Graduate Studies, Department of Medical Technology, Augusta, GA 30912-1500. Offers MS. *Accreditation:* NAACLS. Part-time programs available. *Faculty:* 3 full-time (all women). *Degree requirements:* For master's, thesis (for some programs). *Entrance requirements:* For master's, GRE General Test. Additional exam requirements/recommendations for international students: Required—TOEFL (minimum score 550 paper-based; 213 computer-based). *Application deadline:* For fall admission, 7/1 for domestic students, 4/15 for international students. Applications are processed on a rolling basis. Application fee: $30. Electronic applications accepted. *Expenses:* Tuition, state resident: full-time $2,293; part-time $192 per credit hour. Tuition, nonresident: full-time $9,169; part-time $765 per credit hour. Required fees: $293 per semester. *Financial support:* Federal Work-Study and institutionally sponsored loans available. Support available to part-time students. Financial award application deadline: 5/31; financial award applicants required to submit FAFSA. *Unit head:* Dr. Elizabeth Kenimer Leibach, Director, 706-721-3046, Fax: 706-721-7631, E-mail: ekenimer@mail.mcg.edu.

Medical College of Wisconsin, Graduate School of Biomedical Sciences, Program in Health Care Technologies, Milwaukee, WI 53226-0509. Offers PhD. *Degree requirements:* For doctorate, thesis/dissertation, registration. *Entrance requirements:* For doctorate, GRE. Additional exam requirements/recommendations for international students: Required—TOEFL.

Michigan State University, The Graduate School, College of Natural Science, Biomedical Laboratory Diagnostics Program, East Lansing, MI 48824. Offers biomedical laboratory operations (MS); clinical laboratory sciences (MS). *Accreditation:* NAACLS. *Faculty:* 3 full-time (1 woman). *Students:* 6 full-time (3 women), 10 part-time (4 women); includes 3 minority (all Hispanic Americans), 4 international. Average age 33. 19 applicants, 26% accepted. In 2006, 5 degrees awarded. *Entrance requirements:* Additional exam requirements/recommendations for international students: Required—TOEFL. Electronic applications accepted. *Expenses:* Tuition, state resident: part-time $346 per credit hour. Tuition, nonresident: part-time $730 per credit hour. Tuition and fees vary according to program. *Financial support:* In 2006–07, 2 fellowships with tuition reimbursements, 3 research assistantships with tuition reimbursements (averaging $11,502 per year), 3 teaching assistantships with tuition reimbursements (averaging $12,582 per year) were awarded. Total annual research expenditures: $138,950. *Unit head:* Dr. Kathryn M. Doig, Director, 517-353-7800, Fax: 517-432-2006, E-mail: doig@msu.edu. *Application contact:* Meg Sowle, Student Records Secretary, 517-353-7800, Fax: 517-432-2006, E-mail: medtech@msu.edu.

Milwaukee School of Engineering, Department of Electrical Engineering and Computer Science, Program in Perfusion, Milwaukee, WI 53202-3109. Offers MS. Part-time and evening/weekend programs available. *Faculty:* 1 full-time (0 women), 3 part-time/adjunct (1 woman). *Students:* 11 full-time (4 women). Average age 33. 11 applicants, 55% accepted, 6 enrolled. In 2006, 7 degrees awarded. *Median time to degree:* Master's–2 years full-time. *Degree requirements:* For master's, thesis. *Entrance requirements:* For master's, GRE General Test or GMAT, BS in an appropriate discipline, undergraduate work in human physiology or anatomy. Additional exam requirements/recommendations for international students: Required—TOEFL (minimum score 550 paper-based; 213 computer-based). Application fee: $30. *Expenses:* Tuition: Part-time $526 per credit. *Financial support:* Career-related internships or fieldwork available. Support available to part-time students. Financial award applicants required to submit FAFSA. *Unit head:* Dr. Ronald Gerrits, Director, 414-277-7561, Fax: 414-277-7494, E-mail: gerrits@msoe.edu. *Application contact:* Julie A. Schuster, Graduate Admissions, 800-332-6763, Fax: 414-277-7475, E-mail: schuster@msoe.edu.

Pontifical Catholic University of Puerto Rico, College of Sciences, Department of Medical Technology, Ponce, PR 00717-0777. Offers Certificate. *Entrance requirements:* For degree, letters of recommendation, interview, minimum GPA of 2.75.

Quinnipiac University, School of Health Sciences, Program for Pathologists' Assistant, Hamden, CT 06518-1940. Offers MHS. *Accreditation:* NAACLS. *Faculty:* 2 full-time (0 women), 3 part-time/adjunct (0 women). *Students:* 35 full-time (24 women); includes 7 minority (1 African American, 4 Asian Americans or Pacific Islanders, 2 Hispanic Americans), 4 international. Average age 28. 78 applicants, 24% accepted, 18 enrolled. In 2006, 17 degrees awarded. *Degree requirements:* For master's, residency. *Entrance requirements:* For master's, interview, BS in biomedical science, minimum GPA of 2.8. Additional exam requirements/recommendations for international students: Required—TOEFL (minimum score 575 paper-based; 233 computer-based; 90 iBT), IELTS (minimum score 7). *Application deadline:* For fall admission, 1/15 for domestic students. Applications are processed on a rolling basis. Application fee: $45. Electronic applications accepted. *Expenses:* Tuition: Part-time $675 per credit. Required fees: $30 per credit. *Financial support:* Career-related internships or fieldwork, tuition waivers (partial), and unspecified assistantships available. Financial award application deadline: 4/15; financial award applicants required to submit FAFSA. *Unit head:* Dr. Kenneth Kaloustian, Director, 203-582-8676, Fax: 203-582-3443, E-mail: ken.kaloustian@quinnipiac.edu. *Application contact:* 800-462-1944, Fax: 203-582-3443, E-mail: graduate@quinnipiac.edu.

See Close-Up on page 1721.

Quinnipiac University, School of Health Sciences, Program in Medical Laboratory Sciences, Hamden, CT 06518-1940. Offers biomedical sciences (MHS); laboratory management (MHS); microbiology (MHS). *Accreditation:* NAACLS. Part-time programs available. *Faculty:* 2 full-time (0 women), 3 part-time/adjunct (2 women). *Students:* 16 full-time (11 women), 29 part-time (24 women); includes 8 minority (2 African Americans, 4 Asian Americans or Pacific Islanders, 2 Hispanic Americans), 2 international. Average age 26. 25 applicants, 88% accepted, 17 enrolled. In 2006, 24 degrees awarded. *Degree requirements:* For master's, thesis optional. *Entrance requirements:* For master's, minimum GPA of 2.75; bachelor's degree in biological, medical, or health sciences. Additional exam requirements/recommendations for international students: Required—TOEFL (minimum score 575 paper-based; 233 computer-based; 90 iBT), IELTS (minimum score 7). *Application deadline:* For fall admission, 7/30 priority date for domestic students, 5/30 priority date for international students; for spring admission, 12/15 priority date for domestic students, 10/15 priority date for international students. Applications are processed on a rolling basis. Application fee: $45. Electronic applications accepted. *Expenses:* Tuition: Part-time $675 per credit. Required fees: $30 per credit. *Financial support:* Tuition waivers (partial) and unspecified assistantships available. Support available to part-time students. Financial award application deadline: 4/15; financial award applicants required to submit FAFSA. *Faculty research:* Microbial physiology, fermentation technology. *Unit head:* Dr. Kenneth Kaloustian, Director, 203-582-8676, Fax: 203-582-3443, E-mail: ken.kaloustian@quinnipiac.edu. *Application contact:* 800-462-1944, Fax: 203-582-3443, E-mail: graduate@quinnipiac.edu.

See Close-Up on page 1721.

Rochester Institute of Technology, Graduate Enrollment Services, College of Science, Department of Medical Sciences, Program in Clinical Chemistry, Rochester, NY 14623-5603. Offers MS. *Students:* 3 full-time (2 women), 5 part-time (3 women); includes 1 minority (Asian American or Pacific Islander), 1 international. 5 applicants, 60% accepted, 2 enrolled. In 2006, 3 degrees awarded. *Entrance requirements:* For master's, minimum GPA of 3.0. Additional exam requirements/recommendations for international students: Required—TOEFL (minimum score 550 paper-based; 213 computer-based; 79 iBT). *Expenses:* Tuition: Full-time $28,491; part-time $800 per credit. Required fees: $201. *Unit head:* Dr. Richard Doolittle, Head, Department of Medical Sciences, 585-475-2978, E-mail: rldsbi@rit.edu.

Rosalind Franklin University of Medicine and Science, College of Health Professions, Department of Clinical Laboratory Sciences, North Chicago, IL 60064-3095. Offers clinical laboratory science (MS); pathologist assistant (MS). Part-time programs available. *Degree requirements:* For master's, thesis (for some programs). *Entrance requirements:* For master's, minimum GPA of 2.8 in science, 2.5 overall. Additional exam requirements/recommendations for international students: Required—TOEFL. *Faculty research:* Clinical microbiology, hematology, and chemistry; pathology.

Rush University, College of Health Sciences, Department of Clinical Laboratory Sciences, Chicago, IL 60612-3832. Offers clinical laboratory management (MS); clinical laboratory science (MS). *Accreditation:* NAACLS. Part-time programs available. *Degree requirements:* For master's, graduate project. *Entrance requirements:* For master's, BS with 16 semester hours of chemistry, 12 semester hours of biology, 3 semester hours of mathematics; interview. Additional exam requirements/recommendations for international students: Required—TOEFL. Electronic applications accepted. *Faculty research:* Hematopoietic disorders, molecular techniques, biochemistry, microbial susceptibility, immunology.

San Francisco State University, Division of Graduate Studies, College of Science and Engineering, Department of Biology, San Francisco, CA 94132-1722. Offers biomedical laboratory science (MS); cell and molecular biology (MS); conservation biology (MS); ecology and systematic biology (MS); marine biology (MS); marine science (MS); microbiology (MS); physiology and behavioral biology (MS). *Entrance requirements:* For master's, minimum GPA of 2.5 in last 60 units. *Application deadline:* For fall admission, 11/30 priority date for domestic students. Applications are processed on a rolling basis. Application fee: $55. *Financial support:* Application deadline: 3/1. *Unit head:* Dr. Michael Goldman. *Application contact:* Dr. Robert Patterson, Coordinator, 415-338-1237, E-mail: patters@sfsu.edu.

State University of New York Upstate Medical University, Program in Medical Technology, Syracuse, NY 13210-2334. Offers MS. *Accreditation:* NAACLS. *Faculty:* 5 full-time, 1 part-time/adjunct. *Students:* 9 full-time (6 women), 3 part-time (all women); includes 7 minority (all African Americans), 2 international. 19 applicants, 79% accepted, 7 enrolled. *Degree requirements:* For master's, thesis. *Entrance requirements:* For master's, GRE General Test, GRE Subject Test, 2 years of medical technology experience. *Application deadline:* For fall admission, 4/1 priority date for domestic students. Applications are processed on a rolling basis. Application fee: $40. *Expenses:* Tuition, state resident: full-time $6,900; part-time $288 per credit. Tuition, nonresident: full-time $10,920; part-time $455 per credit. Required fees: $496. *Financial support:* Federal Work-Study available. Support available to part-time students. Financial award application deadline: 3/1; financial award applicants required to submit FAFSA. *Unit head:* Susan S. Graham, Department Chair, 315-464-4608, E-mail: cls@upstate.edu. *Application contact:* Donna Vavonese, Associate Director of Admissions, 315-464-4570, Fax: 315-464-8867, E-mail: vavonesd@upstate.edu.

Thomas Jefferson University, Jefferson College of Health Professions, Program in Bioscience Technologies, Philadelphia, PA 19107. Offers MS. *Accreditation:* NAACLS. Part-time and evening/weekend programs available. *Faculty:* 4 full-time (3 women), 3 part-time/adjunct (0 women). *Students:* 12 full-time (9 women), 1 (woman) part-time; includes 5 minority (3 African Americans, 2 Asian Americans or Pacific Islanders). Average age 27. 31 applicants, 55% accepted, 13 enrolled. In 2006, 9 degrees awarded. *Degree requirements:* For master's, registration. *Entrance requirements:* For master's, GRE General Test or MAT. Additional exam requirements/recommendations for international students: Required—TOEFL (minimum score 213 computer-based). *Application deadline:* For fall admission, 8/1 priority date for domestic students, 3/1 priority date for international students; for winter admission, 12/1 priority date for domestic students, 6/1 priority date for international students; for spring admission, 4/1 priority date for domestic students. Applications are processed on a rolling basis. Application fee: $50. Electronic applications accepted. *Expenses:* Tuition: Full-time $15,340; part-time $790 per credit. Required fees: $300. *Financial support:* Federal Work-Study and institutionally sponsored loans available. Support available to part-time students. Financial award application deadline: 5/1; financial award applicants required to submit FAFSA. *Faculty research:* Molecular biology of BCR-ABL in chronic myeloid leukemia, diagnostic cytogenetics, ATP binding cassette (ABC), gene family, education outcome studies. Total annual research expenditures: $51,210. *Unit head:* Shirley Greening, Chair, 215-503-8561, Fax: 215-503-2189, E-mail: shirley.greening@jefferson.edu. *Application contact:* Karen A. Jacobs, Director of Admissions and Enrollment Management, 215-503-1040, Fax: 215-503-7241, E-mail: jchp@jefferson.edu.

Universidad de las Américas–Puebla, Division of Graduate Studies, School of Sciences, Program in Clinical Analysis (Biomedicine), Puebla, Mexico. Offers MS. Part-time and evening/weekend programs available. *Degree requirements:* For master's, one foreign language, thesis. *Faculty research:* Clinical techniques, clinical research.

Clinical Laboratory Sciences/Medical Technology

Université de Montréal, Faculty of Medicine and Faculty of Graduate Studies, Graduate Programs in Medicine, Program in Specialized Studies, Montréal, QC H3C 3J7, Canada. Offers anesthesia (DESS); diagnostic radiology (DESS); family medicine (DESS); medical biochemistry (DESS); medical genetics (DESS); medicine (DESS); microbiology and infectious diseases (DESS); nuclear medicine (DESS); obstetrics and gynecology (DESS); ophthalmology (DESS); pediatrics (DESS); psychiatry (DESS); radiology-oncology (DESS); surgery (DESS). *Faculty:* 159 full-time (37 women), 345 part-time/adjunct (102 women). *Entrance requirements:* For degree, proficiency in French. *Application deadline:* For fall admission, 2/1 priority date for domestic students; for winter admission, 11/1 priority date for domestic students; for spring admission, 2/1 priority date for domestic students. Application fee: $30. Electronic applications accepted. *Unit head:* Dr. Pierre Boyle, Vice Dean of Studies, 514-343-6300, Fax: 514-343-5751, E-mail: pierre.boyle@umontreal.ca.

Université de Sherbrooke, Faculty of Medicine and Health Sciences, Graduate Programs in Medicine, Program in Clinical Sciences, Sherbrooke, QC J1K 2R1, Canada. Offers M Sc, PhD. Part-time programs available. *Students:* 39 full-time (23 women), 52 part-time (41 women). Average age 26. 29 applicants, 41% accepted, 12 enrolled. In 2006, 6 master's, 3 doctorates awarded. *Degree requirements:* For master's and doctorate, thesis/dissertation. *Application deadline:* For fall admission, 6/30 for domestic students; for winter admission, 10/31 for domestic students; for spring admission, 2/28 for domestic students. Application fee: $70. Electronic applications accepted. *Unit head:* Dr. Denise St-Cyr Tribble, Director, 819-464-5362, E-mail: denise.stcyr @usherbrooke.ca.

University at Buffalo, the State University of New York, Graduate School, School of Medicine and Biomedical Sciences, Graduate Programs in Medicine and Biomedical Sciences, Department of Biotechnical and Clinical Laboratory Sciences, Buffalo, NY 14260. Offers biotechnology (MS). *Accreditation:* NAACLS. Part-time programs available. *Faculty:* 9 full-time (6 women), 5 part-time/adjunct (3 women). *Students:* 21 full-time (12 women), 2 part-time (1 woman); includes 1 minority (Asian American or Pacific Islander), 13 international. Average age 27. 41 applicants, 34% accepted, 10 enrolled. In 2006, 6 degrees awarded. *Degree requirements:* For master's, thesis, registration. *Entrance requirements:* For master's, GRE General Test, background in biology, chemistry or related field. Additional exam requirements/recommendations for international students: Required—TOEFL (minimum score 233 computer-based). *Application deadline:* For fall admission, 3/1 priority date for domestic students, 2/1 for international students. Applications are processed on a rolling basis. Application fee: $50. Electronic applications accepted. *Financial support:* In 2006–07, 15 students received support, including research assistantships with full and partial tuition reimbursements available (averaging $10,000 per year), 15 teaching assistantships with full tuition reimbursements available (averaging $9,000 per year); Federal Work-Study and unspecified assistantships also available. Financial award application deadline: 3/1. *Faculty research:* Endocrine-immune interaction, tumor immunology, molecular biology, oxidative stress, cell differentiation. Total annual research expenditures: $1.1 million. *Unit head:* Dr. Paul Kostyniak, Chair, 716-829-3630 Ext. 107, Fax: 716-829-3601. *Application contact:* Dr. Stephen T. Koury, Director of Graduate Studies, 716-829-3630 Ext. 111, Fax: 716-829-3601, E-mail: stvkoury@buffalo.edu.

The University of Alabama at Birmingham, School of Health Professions, Department of Diagnostic and Therapeutic Sciences, Program in Clinical Laboratory Science, Birmingham, AL 35294. Offers MS. *Accreditation:* NAACLS. *Students:* 12 full-time (8 women), 6 part-time (4 women); includes 5 minority (all African Americans), 5 international. 8 applicants, 88% accepted. In 2006, 4 degrees awarded. *Degree requirements:* For master's, thesis optional. *Entrance requirements:* For master's, GRE General Test, interview. *Application deadline:* Applications are processed on a rolling basis. Application fee: $35 ($60 for international students). Electronic applications accepted. *Expenses:* Tuition, state resident: part-time $170 per credit hour. Tuition, nonresident: part-time $425 per credit hour. Required fees: $15 per credit hour. $122 per term. Tuition and fees vary according to program. *Financial support:* Application deadline: 4/15. *Faculty research:* Computer enhanced instruction, antiphospholipid antibodies, alternate site testing, technology assessment. *Unit head:* Dr. Edward D. Huechtker, Interim Chair, Department of Diagnostic and Therapeutic Sciences, 205-934-4605.

University of Alberta, Faculty of Medicine and Dentistry and Faculty of Graduate Studies and Research, Graduate Programs in Medicine, Department of Laboratory Medicine and Pathology, Edmonton, AB T6G 2E1, Canada. Offers medical sciences (M Sc, PhD). Part-time programs available. *Faculty:* 8 full-time. *Students:* 8 full-time (4 women), 3 part-time (all women). 25 applicants, 20% accepted. In 2006, 1 master's, 2 doctorates awarded. Terminal master's awarded for partial completion of doctoral program. *Degree requirements:* For master's, thesis; for doctorate, thesis/dissertation, candidacy exam. *Entrance requirements:* For master's and doctorate, 3 letters of recommendation, minimum GPA of 3.0. Additional exam requirements/recommendations for international students: Required—TOEFL. *Application deadline:* For fall admission, 5/15 for international students; for winter admission, 9/15 for international students; for spring admission, 1/15 for international students. Applications are processed on a rolling basis. Application fee: $0. *Financial support:* In 2006–07, 3 fellowships with full tuition reimbursements (averaging $16,000 per year), 6 research assistantships (averaging $12,000 per year), 1 teaching assistantship (averaging $8,000 per year) were awarded; scholarships/grants and unspecified assistantships also available. *Faculty research:* Transplantation, renal pathology, molecular mechanisms of diseases, cryobiology, immunodiagnostics, informatics/cybermedicine, neuroimmunology, microbiology. Total annual research expenditures: $550,000. *Unit head:* Dr. Victor A. Tron, Chair, 780-407-8851, Fax: 780-407-8599, E-mail: vtron@cha.ab.ca. *Application contact:* Dr. Gregory J. Tyrrell, Graduate Coordinator, 780-407-8949, Fax: 780-407-3964, E-mail: g.tyrrell@provlab.ab.ca.

University of Colorado at Denver and Health Sciences Center, Graduate School, Program in Clinical Science, Denver, CO 80217-3364. Offers MS, PhD. *Students:* 2 full-time (both women), 3 part-time (2 women); includes 1 minority (Hispanic American) In 2006, 4 degrees awarded. *Degree requirements:* For doctorate, thesis/dissertation, comprehensive exam. *Entrance requirements:* For master's and doctorate, GRE General Test or MCAT, minimum GPA of 3.0. Additional exam requirements/recommendations for international students: Required—TOEFL (minimum score 550 paper-based; 213 computer-based). *Application deadline:* For fall admission, 1/31 for domestic students. Application fee: $50. *Financial support:* Fellowships, research assistantships, teaching assistantships, Federal Work-Study and institutionally sponsored loans available. Support available to part-time students. Financial award application deadline: 3/15; financial award applicants required to submit FAFSA. *Unit head:* Dr. James Crapo, Director, 303-398-1436. *Application contact:* Lori Stepp, Administrator, 303-398-1657, Fax: 303-270-2249, E-mail: steppl@njc.org.

University of Kentucky, Graduate School, College of Health Sciences, Program in Clinical Sciences, Lexington, KY 40506-0032. Offers MS, DS. *Accreditation:* NAACLS. *Faculty:* 20 full-time (10 women), 2 part-time/adjunct (1 woman). *Students:* 5 full-time (3 women), 3 part-time (2 women); includes 3 minority (all Asian Americans or Pacific Islanders), 4 international. Average age 31. 23 applicants, 30% accepted, 3 enrolled. In 2006, 3 master's, 2 doctorates awarded. *Degree requirements:* For master's, comprehensive exam; for doctorate, thesis/dissertation, comprehensive exam. *Entrance requirements:* For master's, GRE General test, minimum undergraduate GPA of 2.75; for doctorate, GRE General test, minimum undergraduate GPA of 3.0. Additional exam requirements/recommendations for international students: Required—TOEFL (minimum score 550 paper-based; 213 computer-based). *Application deadline:* For fall admission, 7/17 priority date for domestic students, 2/1 priority date for international students; for spring admission, 12/13 priority date for domestic students, 6/15 priority date for international students. Application fee: $40 ($55 for international students). Electronic applications accepted. *Expenses:* Tuition, state resident: full-time $7,670; part-time $401 per credit hour. Tuition, nonresident: full-time $16,158; part-time $873 per credit hour. *Financial support:* In 2006–07, 3 students received support, including 2 research assistantships with full tuition reimbursements available (averaging $16,250 per year), 1 teaching assistantship with full tuition reimbursement available (averaging $8,332 per year); fellowships with full tuition reimbursements available, Federal Work-Study, scholarships/grants, traineeships, health care benefits, tuition waivers (partial), and unspecified assistantships also available. Support available to part-time students. Financial award application deadline: 3/15; financial award applicants required to submit FAFSA. *Unit head:* Dr. Linda Gorman, Director of Graduate Studies, 859-323-1100, Fax: 859-257-2454, E-mail: linda.gorman@uky.edu. *Application contact:* Dr. Brian Jackson, Senior Associate Dean, 859-257-4667, Fax: 859-257-4676, E-mail: brian.jackson@uky.edu.

University of Maryland, Baltimore, Graduate School, Department of Medical and Research Technology, Baltimore, MD 21201. Offers MS. *Accreditation:* NAACLS. Part-time programs available. *Degree requirements:* For master's, thesis or management project. *Entrance requirements:* For master's, GRE General Test, minimum GPA of 3.0. Additional exam requirements/recommendations for international students: Required—TOEFL, TOEFL or IELTS; Recommended—IELTS. Electronic applications accepted. *Faculty research:* Clinical microbiology, immunology, immunohematology, hematology, clinical chemistry, molecular biology.

University of Massachusetts Lowell, Graduate School, College of Health Professions, Department of Clinical Laboratory Studies, Lowell, MA 01854-2881. Offers MS. *Accreditation:* NAACLS. Part-time programs available. *Degree requirements:* For master's, thesis optional. *Entrance requirements:* For master's, GRE General Test. *Faculty research:* Cardiovascular disease, lipoprotein metabolism, micronutrient evaluation, alcohol metabolism, mycobacterial drug resistance.

University of Medicine and Dentistry of New Jersey, School of Health Related Professions, Department of Interdisciplinary Studies, Program in Health Sciences, Newark, NJ 07107-1709. Offers cardiopulmonary sciences (PhD); clinical laboratory sciences (PhD); health sciences (MS); interdisciplinary studies (PhD); nutrition (PhD); physical therapy/movement science (PhD). *Degree requirements:* For doctorate, thesis/dissertation. *Entrance requirements:* For doctorate, interview, writing sample. Additional exam requirements/recommendations for international students: Required—TOEFL. *Application deadline:* For fall admission, 3/1 for domestic students. Applications are processed on a rolling basis. Application fee: $50. Electronic applications accepted. *Unit head:* Dr. Margaret Kildoff, Director, 973-972-4989, Fax: 973-972-7854, E-mail: ms-phd-hs@umdnj.edu.

University of Mississippi Medical Center, School of Graduate Studies in the Health Sciences, Program in Clinical Health Sciences, Jackson, MS 39216-4505. Offers MS, PhD. Part-time programs available. *Faculty:* 8 full-time (2 women), 3 part-time/adjunct (1 woman). *Students:* 27 full-time (21 women), 28 part-time (17 women); includes 18 minority (17 African Americans, 1 Asian American or Pacific Islander). Average age 37. 113 applicants, 58% accepted, 51 enrolled. In 2006, 3 degrees awarded. Terminal master's awarded for partial completion of doctoral program. *Degree requirements:* For master's and doctorate, thesis/dissertation. *Entrance requirements:* For master's and doctorate, GRE, 1 year of clinical experience. Additional exam requirements/recommendations for international students: Required—TOEFL. *Application deadline:* For spring admission, 3/1 for domestic students. Application fee: $10. *Expenses:* Tuition, state resident: full-time $4,523. Tuition, nonresident: full-time $10,566. *Financial support:* Institutionally sponsored loans available. Support available to part-time students. Financial award application deadline: 4/1. *Faculty research:* Clinical outcomes assessment via qualitative measures; health information systems; experimental laboratory evaluation of materials, drugs, hormones, and techniques used in clinical practice. Total annual research expenditures: $141,944. *Unit head:* Dr. David G. Fowler, Director, 601-984-6300, Fax: 601-984-6344, E-mail: dfowler@shrp.umsmed.edu.

University of Nebraska Medical Center, School of Allied Health Professions, Program in Clinical Perfusion Education, Omaha, NE 68198. Offers perfusion science (MPS). *Accreditation:* NAACLS. *Faculty:* 1 full-time (0 women), 37 part-time/adjunct (13 women). *Students:* 6 full-time (4 women); includes 1 minority (African American) Average age 23. 14 applicants, 43% accepted, 6 enrolled. In 2006, 1 degree awarded. *Median time to degree:* Master's–2 years full-time. *Degree requirements:* For master's, thesis, comprehensive exam. *Entrance requirements:* For master's, GRE. *Application deadline:* For fall admission, 1/1 for domestic students. Applications are processed on a rolling basis. Application fee: $45. Electronic applications accepted. *Financial support:* In 2006–07, 1 student received support. Scholarships/grants and tuition waivers (full) available. *Unit head:* David W. Holt, Program Director, 402-559-7227, Fax: 402-559-6455, E-mail: dwholt@unmc.edu. *Application contact:* Cindy L. Skarda, Staff Assistant, 402-559-7227, Fax: 402-559-6455, E-mail: cskarda@unmc.edu.

University of Nebraska Medical Center, School of Allied Health Professions, Program in Cytotechnology, Omaha, NE 68198. Offers Certificate. *Accreditation:* NAACLS. Postbaccalaureate distance learning degree programs offered (minimal on-campus study). *Faculty:* 1 full-time. *Students:* 6 full-time. Average age 30. 11 applicants, 55% accepted. *Application deadline:* For fall admission, 3/1 priority date for domestic and international students. Applications are processed on a rolling basis. Application fee: $40. Electronic applications accepted. *Faculty research:* HPV vaccine. *Unit head:* Dr. Stanley J. Radio, Medical Director, 402-559-7668. *Application contact:* Amber Diane Donnelly, Director, 402-552-2043, Fax: 402-559-9044, E-mail: addonnelly@unmc.edu.

University of North Dakota, School of Medicine and Graduate School, Graduate Programs in Medicine, Department of Clinical Laboratory Science, Grand Forks, ND 58202. Offers MS. *Accreditation:* NAACLS. Postbaccalaureate distance learning degree programs offered (minimal on-campus study). *Faculty:* 4 full-time (2 women). *Students:* 251,717 applicants, 0% accepted, 15 enrolled. In 2006, 9 degrees awarded. *Degree requirements:* For master's, thesis or alternative, comprehensive exam. *Entrance requirements:* For master's, minimum GPA of 3.0. Additional exam requirements/recommendations for international students: Required—TOEFL (minimum score 550 paper-based; 213 computer-based; 79 iBT), IELTS (minimum score 6). *Application deadline:* For fall admission, 2/15 priority date for domestic and international students; for spring admission, 10/15 priority date for domestic and international students. Applications are processed on a rolling basis. Application fee: $35. Electronic applications accepted. *Expenses:* Tuition, state resident: full-time $5,650; part-time $214 per credit. Tuition, nonresident: full-time $14,248; part-time $572 per credit. Required fees: $1,008; $42 per credit. Tuition and fees vary according to reciprocity agreements. *Financial support:* In 2006–07, 4 students received support, including 2 teaching assistantships with full tuition reimbursements available (averaging $12,309 per year); fellowships, Federal Work-Study, institutionally sponsored loans, scholarships/grants, and tuition waivers (full and partial) also available. Support available to part-time students. Financial award application deadline: 3/15. *Unit head:* Prof. Ruth A. Paur, Graduate Director, 701-777-2651, Fax: 701-777-3108, E-mail: ruthpaur@medicine.nodak.edu. *Application contact:* Brenda Halle, Admissions Specialist, 701-777-2947, Fax: 701-777-3619, E-mail: brendahalle@mail.und.edu.

University of Puerto Rico, Medical Sciences Campus, College of Health Related Professions, Program in Clinical Laboratory Science, San Juan, PR 00936-5067. Offers MS. *Accreditation:* NAACLS. Part-time and evening/weekend programs available. *Degree requirements:* For master's, one foreign language, thesis or alternative. *Entrance requirements:* For master's, EXADEP or GRE, minimum GPA of 2.75, bachelor's degree in medical technology, 1 year lab experience, interview. *Faculty research:* Toxicology, virology, biochemistry, immunohematology, nervous system regeneration.

University of Puerto Rico, Medical Sciences Campus, College of Health Related Professions, Program in Cytotechnology, San Juan, PR 00936-5067. Offers Certificate. *Degree requirements:* For Certificate, one foreign language. *Entrance requirements:* For degree, Allied Health Professions Admissions Test, minimum GPA of 2.5, interview.

University of Puerto Rico, Medical Sciences Campus, College of Health Related Professions, Program in Medical Technology, San Juan, PR 00936-5067. Offers Certificate. Part-time programs available. *Degree requirements:* For Certificate, one foreign language. *Entrance requirements:* For degree, Allied Health Professions Admissions Test, bachelor's degree in science, minimum GPA of 2.5.

University of Rhode Island, Graduate School, College of Continuing Education, Program in Clinical Laboratory Sciences, Kingston, RI 02881. Offers MS. *Entrance requirements:* For master's, GRE. *Application deadline:* For fall admission, 4/15 priority date for domestic students. Applications are processed on a rolling basis. Application fee: $35. *Expenses:* Tuition, state resident: full-time $6,032; part-time $335 per credit. Tuition, nonresident: full-time $17,288; part-time $960 per credit. Required fees: $65 per credit. $30 per semester. One-time fee: $80 part-time. *Unit head:* Dr. Gregory Paquette, Director, 401-874-2315.

University of Southern Mississippi, Graduate School, College of Health, Department of Medical Technology, Hattiesburg, MS 39406-0001. Offers MS. *Accreditation:* NAACLS. Part-time programs available. *Faculty:* 4 full-time (all women). *Students:* 4 full-time (3 women), 4 part-time (all women); includes 2 minority (both African Americans) Average age 30. 3 applicants, 67% accepted, 1 enrolled. In 2006, 1 degree awarded. *Degree requirements:* For master's, thesis (for some programs), comprehensive exam, registration. *Entrance requirements:* For master's, GRE General Test, minimum GPA of 2.75. Additional exam requirements/recommendations for international students: Required—TOEFL. *Application deadline:* For fall admission, 3/1 priority date for domestic students, 3/1 for international students. Application fee: $25 ($30 for international students). Electronic applications accepted. *Financial support:* In 2006–07, 2 teaching assistantships with full tuition reimbursements (averaging $2,700 per year) were awarded; research assistantships, Federal Work-Study also available. Financial award application deadline: 3/15. *Faculty research:* Clinical chemistry, clinical microbiology, hematology, clinical management and education, immunohematology. *Unit head:* Dr. Jane Hudson, Chair, 601-266-4908.

The University of Texas Health Science Center at San Antonio, School of Allied Health Sciences, San Antonio, TX 78229-3900. Offers clinical laboratory sciences (MS); dental hygiene (MS); occupational therapy (MOT); physical therapy (MPT); physician assistant studies (MS). *Accreditation:* AOTA; APTA; ARC-PA. *Expenses:* Tuition, state resident: part-time $50 per credit hour. Tuition, nonresident: part-time $325 per credit hour. Required fees: $7.5 per credit hour. $155 per term.

University of the Sacred Heart, Graduate Programs, Department of Natural Sciences, Program in Medical Technology, San Juan, PR 00914-0383. Offers Certificate. *Accreditation:* NAACLS. *Entrance requirements:* For degree, Allied Health Professions Admissions Test, interview.

University of Utah, School of Medicine and The Graduate School, Graduate Programs in Medicine, Department of Pathology, Program in Laboratory Medicine and Biomedical Science, Salt Lake City, UT 84112-1107. Offers MS. Part-time programs available. *Faculty:* 16 full-time (7 women), 1 part-time/adjunct (0 women). *Students:* 18 full-time (7 women), 4 part-time (2 women); includes 4 minority (2 African Americans, 1 American Indian/Alaska Native, 1 Hispanic American). Average age 24. 20 applicants. In 2006, 3 degrees awarded. *Degree requirements:* For master's, thesis, thesis research, comprehensive exam. *Entrance requirements:* For master's, minimum GPA of 3.0 during last 2 years of undergraduate course work, BS in medical laboratory science or related field. Additional exam requirements/recommendations for international students: Required—TOEFL (minimum score 550 paper-based). *Application deadline:* For spring admission, 4/1 priority date for domestic and international students. Applications are processed on a rolling basis. Application fee: $45. *Expenses:* Tuition, state resident: full-time $3,208. Tuition, nonresident: full-time $11,326. Required fees: $608. Tuition and fees vary according to class time and program. *Financial support:* In 2006–07, 4 students received support, including 1 research assistantship (averaging $4,000 per year); teaching assistantships, tuition waivers (partial) and unspecified assistantships also available. Financial award application deadline: 11/30. *Faculty research:* Clinical chemistry, hematology, diagnostic microbiology, immunohematology, cell biology, immunology. *Unit head:* JoAnn P. Fenn, Director of Education, 801-581-3971, Fax: 801-585-2463, E-mail: jfenn@path.utah.edu.

University of Washington, School of Medicine and Graduate School, Graduate Programs in Medicine, Department of Laboratory Medicine, Seattle, WA 98195. Offers MS. *Accreditation:* NAACLS. Part-time programs available. *Degree requirements:* For master's, thesis. *Entrance requirements:* For master's, GRE General Test, medical technology certification or specialist in an area of laboratory medicine.

University of Wisconsin–Milwaukee, Graduate School, College of Health Sciences, Program in Clinical Laboratory Science, Milwaukee, WI 53201-0413. Offers MS. *Accreditation:* NAACLS. Part-time programs available. *Faculty:* 9 full-time (4 women). *Students:* 11 full-time (6 women), 4 part-time (2 women); includes 5 minority (3 African Americans, 1 Asian American or Pacific Islander, 1 Hispanic American), 2 international. 11 applicants, 27% accepted, 1 enrolled. In 2006, 4 degrees awarded. *Entrance requirements:* For master's, GRE General Test. *Application deadline:* For fall admission, 1/1 priority date for domestic students; for spring admission, 9/1 for domestic students. Applications are processed on a rolling basis. Application fee: $45 ($75 for international students). *Expenses:* Tuition, state resident: part-time $510 per credit. Tuition, nonresident: part-time $1,408 per credit. Tuition and fees vary according to program. *Financial support:* In 2006–07, 1 fellowship, 1 research assistantship, 4 teaching assistantships were awarded; career-related internships or fieldwork and unspecified assistantships also available. Support available to part-time students. Financial award application deadline: 4/15. *Unit head:* Robert Burlage, Representative, 414-229-2645, Fax: 414-906-3945, E-mail: burlage@uwm.edu.

Virginia Commonwealth University, Graduate School, School of Allied Health Professions, Department of Clinical Laboratory Sciences, Richmond, VA 23284-9005. Offers MS. *Accreditation:* NAACLS. *Faculty:* 4 full-time (2 women). *Students:* 9 full-time (7 women), 7 part-time (6 women); includes 2 minority (both African Americans) 25 applicants, 20% accepted, 3 enrolled. In 2006, 4 degrees awarded. *Degree requirements:* For master's, one foreign language, thesis. *Entrance requirements:* For master's, GRE General Test, current medical technologist certification. *Application deadline:* For fall admission, 7/1 for domestic students; for spring admission, 11/15 for domestic students. Application fee: $50. *Faculty research:* Educational outcomes assessment, virtual instrumentation development, cost-effective treatment of bacteremia using third generation cephalosporins. *Unit head:* Dr. Theresa Nadder, Chair, 804-828-9469.

See Close-Up on page 1743.

Virginia Commonwealth University, Graduate School, School of Allied Health Professions, Department of Health Administration, Doctoral Program in Health Related Sciences, Richmond, VA 23284-9005. Offers clinical laboratory sciences (PhD); gerontology (PhD); health administration (PhD); nurse anesthesia (PhD); occupational therapy (PhD); physical therapy (PhD); radiation sciences (PhD); rehabilitation leadership (PhD). *Faculty:* 2 full-time (1 woman). *Students:* 4 full-time (all women), 13 part-time (7 women); includes 7 minority (1 African American, 6 Asian Americans or Pacific Islanders), 3 international. In 2006, 2 degrees awarded. *Unit head:* Monica L. White, Director of Student Services, 804-828-3273, Fax: 804-828-8656, E-mail: mlwhite1@vcu.edu.

See Close-Up on page 1745.

Wayne State University, Eugene Applebaum College of Pharmacy and Health Sciences, Department of Fundamental and Applied Sciences, Program in Clinical Laboratory Sciences, Detroit, MI 48202. Offers clinical laboratory science (MS); medical technology (Certificate). *Accreditation:* NAACLS. *Faculty:* 1 full-time (0 women). *Degree requirements:* For master's, thesis optional. *Entrance requirements:* Additional exam requirements/recommendations for international students: Required—TOEFL (minimum score 550 paper-based; 213 computer-based); Recommended—TWE (minimum score 6). *Application deadline:* For fall admission, 6/1 for international students; for winter admission, 10/1 for international students; for spring admission, 2/1 for international students. Applications are processed on a rolling basis. Application fee: $30 ($50 for international students). Electronic applications accepted. *Financial support:* Scholarships/grants available. Support available to part-time students. *Faculty research:* Clinical microbiology, molecular diagnostics, development and evaluation of molecular assays for the diagnosis of infectious diseases. *Unit head:* Carol Watkins, Academic Director, 313-577-5516, Fax: 313-577-5497, E-mail: ad4344@wayne.edu.

Clinical Research

Case Western Reserve University, School of Medicine, Clinical Research Scholars Program, Cleveland, OH 44106. Offers MS.

Duke University, School of Medicine, Clinical Research Program, Durham, NC 27708-0586. Offers MHS. Part-time programs available. *Students:* 8 full-time (3 women), 91 part-time (51 women); includes 35 minority (8 African Americans, 24 Asian Americans or Pacific Islanders, 3 Hispanic Americans). 82 applicants, 96% accepted, 79 enrolled. In 2006, 33 degrees awarded. *Degree requirements:* For master's, research project. *Entrance requirements:* For master's, GRE. *Application deadline:* For fall admission, 5/15 for domestic students. *Expenses:* Contact institution. *Financial support:* In 2006–07, 1 student received support. Institutionally sponsored loans, scholarships/grants, and tuition waivers (full) available. Financial award application deadline: 5/1; financial award applicants required to submit FAFSA. *Unit head:* Dr. Eugene Oddone, Director, 919-681-4560, Fax: 919-681-4569, E-mail: oddon001@mc.duke.edu. *Application contact:* Gail Ladd, Program Coordinator, 919-681-4560, Fax: 919-681-4569, E-mail: ladd0002@mc.duke.edu.

Eastern Michigan University, Graduate School, College of Health and Human Services, School of Health Sciences, Program in Clinical Research Administration, Ypsilanti, MI 48197. Offers MS. Part-time and evening/weekend programs available. Postbaccalaureate distance learning degree programs offered (minimal on-campus study). *Students:* 1 (woman) full-time, 21 part-time (20 women); includes 8 minority (1 African American, 7 Asian Americans or Pacific Islanders), 1 international. Average age 35. In 2006, 3 degrees awarded. *Entrance requirements:* Additional exam requirements/recommendations for international students: Required—TOEFL. *Application deadline:* For fall admission, 5/15 priority date for domestic students, 5/1 priority date for international students; for winter admission, 10/15 priority date for domestic students, 10/1 priority date for international students; for spring admission, 3/15 priority date for domestic students, 3/1 priority date for international students. Applications are processed on a rolling basis. Application fee: $35. *Expenses:* Tuition, state resident: part-time $341 per credit hour. Tuition, nonresident: full-time $16,104; part-time $671 per credit hour. Required fees: $816; $34 per credit hour. $40 per term. One-time fee: $82 full-time. Tuition and fees vary according to course level, course load, degree level and reciprocity agreements. *Financial support:* Fellowships, research assistantships with full tuition reimbursements, teaching assistantships with full tuition reimbursements, career-related internships or fieldwork, Federal Work-Study, institutionally sponsored loans, scholarships/grants, tuition waivers (partial), and unspecified assistantships available. Support available to part-time students. Financial award applicants required to submit FAFSA. *Unit head:* Dr. Elizabeth Francis Connolly, Director, School of Health Sciences, 734-487-4094, Fax: 734-487-4095, E-mail: elizabeth.francis-connolly@emich.edu.

Emory University, Graduate School of Arts and Sciences, Program in Clinical Research, Atlanta, GA 30322-1100. Offers MS. Part-time programs available. *Degree requirements:* For master's, thesis. *Expenses:* Tuition: Full-time $30,246.

The Johns Hopkins University, Bloomberg School of Public Health, Graduate Training Program in Clinical Investigation, Baltimore, MD 21218-2699. Offers MHS, Sc M, PhD. *Faculty:* 18 full-time (4 women), 3 part-time/adjunct (1 woman). *Students:* 18 full-time (13 women), 43 part-time (24 women); includes 20 minority (3 African Americans, 16 Asian Americans or Pacific Islanders, 1 Hispanic American), 7 international. Average age 35. 27 applicants, 70% accepted, 16 enrolled. In 2006, 8 master's, 2 doctorates awarded. *Median time to degree:* Of those who began their doctoral program in fall 1998, 29% received their degree in 8 years or less. *Degree requirements:* For master's and doctorate, thesis/dissertation, comprehensive exam, registration. *Entrance requirements:* For master's and doctorate, 2 letters of recommendation, curriculum vitae, transcripts, statement of purpose. Additional exam requirements/recommendations for international students: Required—TOEFL (minimum score 600 paper-based; 250 computer-based). *Application deadline:* For spring admission, 4/1 for domestic and international students. Applications are processed on a rolling basis. Application fee: $45. Electronic applications accepted. *Expenses:* Tuition: Full-time $32,976. Tuition and fees vary according to degree level and program. *Financial support:* In 2006–07, 58 students received support; fellowships, Federal Work-Study, institutionally sponsored loans, scholarships/grants, and stipends available. Support available to part-time students. Financial award application deadline: 3/15; financial award applicants required to submit FAFSA. *Faculty research:* Ethical issues, biomedical writing, grant writing, epidemiology, biostatistics. *Unit head:* Dr. N. Franklin Adkinson, Director, 410-550-2051, Fax: 410-550-2055, E-mail: fadkinso@jhmi.edu. *Application contact:* Cristina A. DeNardo, Academic Program Manager, 410-502-9734, Fax: 410-502-6966, E-mail: gtpci@jhsph.edu.

Medical University of South Carolina, College of Graduate Studies, Department of Biostatistics, Bioinformatics, and Epidemiology, Program in Clinical Research, Charleston, SC 29425-0002. Offers MS. *Faculty:* 9 full-time (6 women). *Students:* Average age 28. 24 applicants, 92% accepted, 21 enrolled. In 2006, 10 degrees awarded. *Entrance requirements:* Additional exam requirements/recommendations for international students: Required—TOEFL (minimum score 600 paper-based; 250 computer-based). *Application deadline:* For fall admission, 5/21 priority date for domestic and international students. Applications are processed on a rolling basis. Application fee: $75. Electronic applications accepted. *Financial support:* Federal Work-Study and scholarships/grants available. Financial award application deadline: 3/15; financial award applicants required to submit FAFSA. *Unit head:* Dr. Thomas C. Hulsey, Director, 843-792-9907, Fax: 843-876-1126, E-mail: hulseytc@musc.edu.

MGH Institute of Health Professions, Graduate Programs, Program in Clinical Investigation, Boston, MA 02129. Offers MS, Certificate. Part-time and evening/weekend programs available. Postbaccalaureate distance learning degree programs offered. *Faculty:* 3 full-time (1 woman), 26 part-time/adjunct (14 women). *Students:* 3 full-time (2 women), 43 part-time (38 women); includes 16 minority (6 African Americans, 6 Asian Americans or Pacific Islanders, 4 Hispanic Americans). Average age 34. 33 applicants, 100% accepted, 29 enrolled. In 2006, 13 master's, 4 other advanced degrees awarded. *Degree requirements:* For master's, field experience, project. *Entrance requirements:* For master's, GRE General Test. Additional exam requirements/recommendations for international students: Required—TOEFL (minimum score 550 paper-based; 213 computer-based). *Application deadline:* For fall admission, 4/1 for domestic students, 3/1 for international students. Applications are processed on a rolling basis.

Clinical Research

MGH Institute of Health Professions (continued)
Application fee: $50. Electronic applications accepted. *Financial support:* In 2006–07, 17 students received support. Career-related internships or fieldwork, scholarships/grants, tuition waivers (partial), and unspecified assistantships available. Support available to part-time students. Financial award application deadline: 3/3; financial award applicants required to submit FAFSA. *Faculty research:* Management of clinical research studies, outcomes research, operations research in data management and analysis, clinical trials research, genetics of human puberty, HIV/AIDS programs in developing countries. *Unit head:* Paul Boepple, Director, 617-726-5782. *Application contact:* Maureen Rika Judd, Manager of Admissions, 617-726-6069, Fax: 617-726-8010, E-mail: admissions@mghihp.edu.

See Close-Up on page 1963.

Morehouse School of Medicine, Program in Clinical Research, Atlanta, GA 30310-1495. Offers MS. *Degree requirements:* For master's, thesis, registration.

New York University, College of Dentistry, Program in Clinical Research, New York, NY 10012-1019. Offers MS. *Students:* 11 full-time (8 women); includes 10 minority (8 Asian Americans or Pacific Islanders, 2 Hispanic Americans). Average age 34. 11 applicants, 73% accepted, 5 enrolled. In 2006, 10 degrees awarded. *Application deadline:* For fall admission, 6/30 priority date for domestic and international students. Application fee: $100. Electronic applications accepted. *Expenses:* Tuition: Part-time $1,080 per unit. Required fees: $56 per unit. $329 per term. Tuition and fees vary according to program. *Financial support:* Application deadline: 3/1. *Unit head:* Dr. Ralph V. Katz, Chair, 212-998-9550, Fax: 212-995-4436, E-mail: ralph.katz@nyu.edu. *Application contact:* Dr. Anthony M. Palatta, Assistant Dean for Student Affairs and Admissions, 212-998-9918, Fax: 212-995-4240, E-mail: ap16@nyu.edu.

New York University, School of Medicine, New York, NY 10012-1019. Offers clinical investigation (MS); medicine (MD); MD/MA; MD/MPA; MD/MS; MD/PhD. *Accreditation:* LCME/AMA (one or more programs are accredited). *Faculty:* 1,241 full-time (390 women), 318 part-time/adjunct (105 women). *Students:* 984 full-time (509 women); includes 334 minority (58 African Americans, 6 American Indian/Alaska Native, 209 Asian Americans or Pacific Islanders, 61 Hispanic Americans), 83 international. Average age 24. 8,162 applicants, 7% accepted, 201 enrolled. In 2006, 155 MDs, 32 doctorates awarded. *Entrance requirements:* MCAT. Additional exam requirements/recommendations for international students: Required—TOEFL. *Application deadline:* For fall admission, 10/15 for domestic students. Applications are processed on a rolling basis. Application fee: $100. *Expenses: Contact institution.* Tuition and fees vary according to program. *Financial support:* In 2006–07, 486 students received support, including 75 research assistantships (averaging $25,000 per year); fellowships with full tuition reimbursements available, teaching assistantships, Federal Work-Study, institutionally sponsored loans, and health care benefits also available. Financial award application deadline: 7/15; financial award applicants required to submit FAFSA. *Faculty research:* AIDS, cancer, neuroscience, molecular biology. *Unit head:* Dr. Robert M. Glickman, Dean, 212-263-5370, Fax: 212-263-8622. *Application contact:* Dr. Nancy Genieser, Associate Dean, Admissions, 212-263-5290, Fax: 212-263-0720, E-mail: nancy.genieser@nyumc.org.

Northwestern University, The Graduate School, Program in Clinical Investigation, Evanston, IL 60208. Offers MSCI, Certificate. Part-time and evening/weekend programs available. *Faculty research:* Wide range of epidemiologic, clinical and bench research across all medical school departments.

Northwestern University, Northwestern University Feinberg School of Medicine, Department of Clinical Investigation, Evanston, IL 60208. Offers MSCI. Part-time and evening/weekend programs available. *Students:* 9 applicants, 89% accepted, 8 enrolled. In 2006, 16 degrees awarded. *Entrance requirements:* For master's, GRE or MCAT, doctoral degree in healthcare-related field. Additional exam requirements/recommendations for international students: Required—TOEFL. *Application deadline:* For fall admission, 7/1 priority date for domestic students; for winter admission, 10/1 priority date for domestic students; for spring admission, 1/1 priority date for domestic students. Applications are processed on a rolling basis. Application fee: $75. Electronic applications accepted. *Faculty research:* Clinical research. *Unit head:* Lewis J. Smith, Director, 312-503-0501, Fax: 312-503-0555, E-mail: ljsmith@northwestern.edu. *Application contact:* Nancy A. Schelhas, 312-503-5291, Fax: 312-908-9588, E-mail: n-schelhas@northwestern.edu.

Palmer College of Chiropractic, Division of Graduate Studies, Davenport, IA 52803-5287. Offers anatomy (MS); clinical research (MS). *Faculty:* 133 full-time (40 women). *Students:* 8 full-time (3 women), 4 part-time (1 woman). *Degree requirements:* For master's, thesis, comprehensive exam, registration. *Entrance requirements:* For master's, GRE General Test, minimum GPA of 2.5. Additional exam requirements/recommendations for international students: Required—TOEFL. *Application deadline:* For fall admission, 9/1 for domestic students; for spring admission, 5/28 for domestic students. Applications are processed on a rolling basis. Application fee: $50. Electronic applications accepted. *Expenses: Contact institution. Financial support:* In 2006–07, 5 students received support, including teaching assistantships with full and partial tuition reimbursements available (averaging $6,269 per year); research assistantships, Federal Work-Study, institutionally sponsored loans, tuition waivers (full), and stipends also available. Support available to part-time students. Financial award application deadline: 4/1; financial award applicants required to submit FAFSA. *Unit head:* Dr. Jean Murray, Administrator, 563-884-5672, Fax: 563-884-5505, E-mail: jean.murray@palmer.edu. *Application contact:* Dr. Brian McMaster, Assistant Dean, 563-884-5163, Fax: 563-884-5226, E-mail: brian.mcmaster@plamer.edu.

See Close-Up on page 2165.

Texas Tech University Health Sciences Center, School of Nursing, Lubbock, TX 79430. Offers acute care nurse practitioner (MSN, Certificate); administration (MSN); clinical research management (MSN, Certificate); education (MSN); family nurse practitioner (MSN, Certificate); geriatric nurse practitioner (MSN, Certificate); pediatric nurse practitioner (MSN, Certificate). *Accreditation:* AACN. Part-time programs available. Postbaccalaureate distance learning degree programs offered (minimal on-campus study). *Faculty:* 17 full-time (16 women), 5 part-time/adjunct (all women). *Students:* 23 full-time (22 women), 161 part-time (137 women); includes 46 minority (8 African Americans, 2 American Indian/Alaska Native, 6 Asian Americans or Pacific Islanders, 30 Hispanic Americans). Average age 37. 97 applicants, 69% accepted, 67 enrolled. In 2006, 41 degrees awarded. *Degree requirements:* For master's, thesis optional. *Entrance requirements:* For master's, minimum GPA of 3.0, 3 letters of reference, BSN, RN license; for Certificate, minimum GPA of 3.0, 3 letters of reference, RN license. Additional exam requirements/recommendations for international students: Required—TOEFL (minimum score 550 paper-based; 213 computer-based). *Application deadline:* For fall admission, 7/15 priority date for domestic and international students; for spring admission, 11/15 priority date for domestic and international students. Applications are processed on a rolling basis. Application fee: $40. *Financial support:* In 2006–07, 184 students received support. Institutionally sponsored loans, scholarships/grants, and traineeships available. Support available to part-time students. Financial award application deadline: 12/1; financial award applicants required to submit FAFSA. *Faculty research:* Diabetes/obesity, nurse competency, disease management, intervention and measurements, health disparities. Total annual research expenditures: $2.4 million. *Unit head:* Dr. Barbara A. Johnston, Associate Dean for Administrative and Student Affairs, 806-743-3055, Fax: 806-743-1622, E-mail: barbara.johnston@ttuhsc.edu. *Application contact:* Lauren K. Sullivan, Recruiter/Transcultural Coordinator, 806-743-2730 Ext. 309, Fax: 806-743-1622, E-mail: lauren.sullivan@ttuhsc.edu.

Thomas Jefferson University, Jefferson College of Graduate Studies, Program in Clinical Research, Public Health, and Research Management, Philadelphia, PA 19107. Offers Certificate. *Students:* 8 applicants, 100% accepted. *Degree requirements:* For degree, registration. *Entrance requirements:* For degree, GRE General Test (recommended). Additional exam requirements/recommendations for international students: Required—TOEFL (minimum score 213 computer-based). *Application deadline:* For fall admission, 8/1 priority date for domestic students, 3/1 priority date for international students; for winter admission, 12/1 priority date for domestic students, 6/1 priority date for international students; for spring admission, 4/1 priority date for domestic students. Applications are processed on a rolling basis. Application fee: $50. Electronic applications accepted. *Expenses:* Tuition: Full-time $15,340; part-time $790 per credit. Required fees: $300. *Financial support:* In 2006–07, 5 students received support. Federal Work-Study and institutionally sponsored loans available. Support available to part-time students. Financial award applicants required to submit FAFSA. *Faculty research:* Pharmacoeconomics, epidemiology, clinical research, performance improvement, statistics. *Unit head:* Dr. Dennis M. Gross, Associate Dean, 215-503-0156, Fax: 215-503-3433, E-mail: dennis.gross@jefferson.edu. *Application contact:* Eleanor M. Gorman, Assistant Coordinator, Graduate Center Programs, 215-503-5799, Fax: 215-503-3433, E-mail: eleanor.gorman@jefferson.edu.

Touro University International, College of Health Sciences, Program in Health Sciences, Cypress, CA 90630. Offers clinical research administration (MS, Certificate); emergency and disaster management (MS, Certificate); environmental health science (Certificate); health care administration (PhD); health care management (MS), including health informatics; health education (MS, Certificate); health informatics (Certificate); health sciences (PhD); international health (MS); international health: educator or researcher option (PhD); international health: practitioner option (PhD); law and expert witness studies (MS, Certificate); public health (MS); quality assurance (Certificate). Part-time and evening/weekend programs available. Postbaccalaureate distance learning degree programs offered (no on-campus study). In 2006, 322 master's, 21 doctorates awarded. *Degree requirements:* For doctorate, thesis/dissertation, defense of dissertation, comprehensive exam. *Entrance requirements:* For master's, minimum GPA of 3.0; for doctorate, minimum GPA of 3.4, curriculum vitae, course work in research methods or statistics. Additional exam requirements/recommendations for international students: Required—TOEFL (minimum score 550 paper-based). Application fee: $75. *Expenses:* Tuition: Part-time $300 per credit hour. Tuition and fees vary according to course level and program. *Unit head:* Dr. Edith Neumann, Vice President for Academic Affairs, College of Health Sciences, 714-816-0366 Ext. 2030, Fax: 714-226-9844, E-mail: eneumann@tourou.edu.

Tufts University, Sackler School of Graduate Biomedical Sciences, Division of Clinical Care Research, Medford, MA 02155. Offers MS, PhD. Part-time programs available. *Faculty:* 33 full-time (10 women). *Students:* 19 full-time (10 women), 1 part-time; includes 3 minority (all Asian Americans or Pacific Islanders), 3 international. Average age 34. 19 applicants, 47% accepted, 8 enrolled. In 2006, 13 master's, 1 doctorate awarded. Terminal master's awarded for partial completion of doctoral program. *Degree requirements:* For master's and doctorate, thesis/dissertation. *Entrance requirements:* For master's and doctorate, MD or PhD, strong clinical research background. Additional exam requirements/recommendations for international students: Required—TOEFL. *Application deadline:* For fall admission, 1/15 priority date for domestic and international students. Applications are processed on a rolling basis. Application fee: $65. Electronic applications accepted. *Expenses:* Tuition: Full-time $33,672. Tuition and fees vary according to degree level and program. *Financial support:* In 2006–07, 20 fellowships with full tuition reimbursements (averaging $44,000 per year) were awarded. Financial award application deadline: 1/15. *Faculty research:* Clinical study design, mathematical modeling, meta analysis, epidemiologic research, coronary heart disease. *Unit head:* Dr. Harry P. Selker, Program Director, 617-636-5009, Fax: 617-636-8023, E-mail: hselker@lifespan.org. *Application contact:* 617-636-6767, Fax: 617-636-0375, E-mail: sackler-school@tufts.edu.

University of California, Davis, Graduate Studies, Graduate Group in Clinical Research, Davis, CA 95616. Offers MAS. *Degree requirements:* For master's, comprehensive exam. *Entrance requirements:* Additional exam requirements/recommendations for international students: Required—TOEFL (minimum score 550 paper-based; 213 computer-based).

University of California, Los Angeles, School of Medicine and Graduate Division, Graduate Programs in Medicine, Department of Biomathematics, Program in Clinical Research, Los Angeles, CA 90095. Offers MS.

University of California, San Diego, School of Medicine, Program in Clinical Research, La Jolla, CA 92093. Offers MAS.

University of Florida, College of Medicine, Program in Clinical Investigation, Gainesville, FL 32611. Offers clinical investigation (MS); epidemiology (MS); public health (MPH). Part-time programs available. *Faculty:* 40. In 2006, 2 degrees awarded. *Entrance requirements:* For master's, GRE, MD, PhD, DMD/DDS or Pharm D. *Application deadline:* For fall admission, 2/15 priority date for domestic students. Applications are processed on a rolling basis. Application fee: $30. *Expenses:* Tuition, state resident: full-time $6,827. Tuition, nonresident: full-time $21,951. Required fees: $999. *Unit head:* Dr. Marian Limacher, Director, 352-846-1228, E-mail: limacmc@medicine.ufl.edu. *Application contact:* Eve Johnson, Program Assistant, 352-846-1228, Fax: 352-846-1217, E-mail: eve11@ufl.edu.

The University of Iowa, Graduate College, College of Public Health, Department of Epidemiology, Iowa City, IA 52242-1316. Offers clinical investigation (MS); epidemiology (MS, PhD). *Faculty:* 12 full-time, 16 part-time/adjunct. *Students:* 18 full-time (13 women), 33 part-time (19 women); includes 7 minority (1 African American, 5 Asian Americans or Pacific Islanders, 1 Hispanic American), 8 international. 32 applicants, 38% accepted, 5 enrolled. In 2006, 17 master's, 2 doctorates awarded. *Degree requirements:* For master's, exam, thesis optional; for doctorate, thesis/dissertation, comprehensive exam, registration. *Entrance requirements:* For master's and doctorate, GRE General Test, minimum GPA of 3.0. Additional exam requirements/recommendations for international students: Required—TOEFL (minimum score 550 paper-based; 213 computer-based; 81 iBT). *Application deadline:* Applications are processed on a rolling basis. Application fee: $60 ($85 for international students). Electronic applications accepted. *Financial support:* In 2006–07, 19 research assistantships with partial tuition reimbursements, 4 teaching assistantships with partial tuition reimbursements were awarded; fellowships also available. Financial award applicants required to submit FAFSA. *Unit head:* Dr. James C. Torner, Head, 319-384-5001, Fax: 319-384-5004.

University of Louisville, Graduate School, School of Public Health, Program in Clinical Investigation Sciences, Louisville, KY 40292-0001. Offers MS, PhD. *Students:* 6 full-time (3 women), 25 part-time (14 women); includes 6 minority (3 African Americans, 3 Asian Americans or Pacific Islanders), 6 international. Average age 38. In 2006, 34 degrees awarded. *Entrance requirements:* For master's, professional degree or MS in clinical investigation services. *Unit head:* Dr. Susan Muldoon, Head, 502-852-8087, E-mail: susan.muldoon@louisville.edu.

University of Louisville, Graduate School, School of Public Health, Program in Public Health, Louisville, KY 40292-0001. Offers clinical investigation (Certificate); public health (MPH). *Students:* 44 full-time (33 women), 14 part-time (9 women); includes 14 minority (9 African Americans, 3 Asian Americans or Pacific Islanders, 2 Hispanic Americans), 2 international. Average age 29. In 2006, 23 master's, 3 other advanced degrees awarded. *Unit head:* Dr. Robert Jacobs, Head, 502-852-0196, Fax: 502-852-3294, E-mail: rrjaco01@louisville.edu.

University of Maryland, Baltimore, School of Medicine, Department of Epidemiology and Preventive Medicine, Baltimore, MD 21201. Offers biostatistics (MS); clinical research (MS); epidemiology (MS, PhD); gerontology (PhD); molecular epidemiology (PhD); toxicology (MS, PhD); MD/MS; MD/PhD. Part-time programs available. *Degree requirements:* For doctorate, one foreign language, thesis/dissertation, qualifying exam. *Entrance requirements:* For master's and doctorate, GRE General Test, minimum GPA of 3.0. Additional exam requirements/recommendations for international students: Required—TOEFL; Recommended—IELTS. Electronic applications accepted. *Faculty research:* Chronic and infectious disease epidemiology, environmental and occupational health, biostatistics, gerontology.

University of Massachusetts Worcester, Graduate School of Biomedical Sciences, Program in Clinical and Population Health Research, Worcester, MA 01655-0115. Offers PhD. *Faculty:* 46 full-time (18 women). *Entrance requirements:* For doctorate, GRE General Test, master's degree in public health, clinical research, or in one of the social, psychological, physical, or biological sciences, with adequate introductory course work in biostatistics and epidemiology; 3 letters of recommendation. *Application deadline:* For fall admission, 1/15 for domestic students. Application fee: $25 ($50 for international students). *Expenses:* Tuition, state resident: full-time $2,640. Tuition, nonresident: full-time $9,856. Required fees: $3,942. *Financial support:* All full-time graduate students received annual stipend support ($25,740) for the duration of their study available. *Unit head:* Dr. Carole Upshur, Associate Dean, 508-334-7267. *Application contact:* Colleen Corey, Program Coordinator, 508-334-2112.

See Close-Up on page 1821.

University of Michigan, School of Public Health, Interdepartmental Program in Clinical Research Design and Statistical Analysis, Ann Arbor, MI 48109. Offers MS. Offered through the Horace H. Rackham School of Graduate Studies; program admits applicants in odd-numbered calendar years only. Evening/weekend programs available. *Degree requirements:* For master's, comprehensive exam, registration. *Entrance requirements:* For master's, GRE General Test or MCAT. Additional exam requirements/recommendations for international students: Recommended—TOEFL (minimum score 560 paper-based; 220 computer-based). Electronic applications accepted. Expenses: Contact institution. *Faculty research:* Survival analysis, missing data, bayesian inference, health economics, quality of life.

University of Minnesota, Twin Cities Campus, School of Public Health, Major in Clinical Research, Minneapolis, MN 55455-0213. Offers MS. Part-time programs available. *Degree requirements:* For master's, thesis, registration. *Entrance requirements:* For master's, advanced health professional degree. Additional exam requirements/recommendations for international students: Required—TOEFL. Electronic applications accepted. *Expenses:* Tuition, state resident: full-time $9,302; part-time $775 per credit. Tuition, nonresident: full-time $16,400; part-time $1,367 per credit. Full-time tuition and fees vary according to class time, course load, program, reciprocity agreements and student level. *Faculty research:* Osteoporosis prevention; heart disease prevention; role of inflammatory dental disease in the genesis of atherosclerosis; interventional research into AIDS and cancer.

University of Pittsburgh, School of Medicine, Clinical Educator Training Program, Pittsburgh, PA 15260. Offers clinical research (MS, Certificate); medical education (MS); medical research (Certificate). Part-time programs available. Postbaccalaureate distance learning degree programs offered (minimal on-campus study). *Faculty:* 23 full-time (10 women). *Students:* Average age 32. 4 applicants, 100% accepted, 4 enrolled. In 2006, 3 master's, 3 other advanced degrees awarded. *Degree requirements:* For master's, thesis, registration. *Entrance requirements:* For master's and Certificate, GRE, LSAT, MCAT or GMAT (only required of students without previous doctoral level degree). *Application deadline:* For spring admission, 3/1 priority date for domestic and international students. Applications are processed on a rolling basis. Application fee: $0. Electronic applications accepted. *Financial support:* Scholarships/grants and tuition waivers (partial) available. *Faculty research:* Medical education. *Application contact:* Jennifer A. Kush, Coordinator of Student Services, 412-586-9673, Fax: 412-586-9672, E-mail: kushja@upmc.edu.

University of Pittsburgh, School of Medicine, Clinical Research Training Program, Pittsburgh, PA 15260. Offers clinical research (MS, Certificate); medical education (MS, Certificate). Part-time programs available. Postbaccalaureate distance learning degree programs offered (minimal on-campus study). *Faculty:* 46 full-time (16 women). *Students:* Average age 32. 34 applicants, 82% accepted, 28 enrolled. In 2006, 11 master's, 12 Certificates awarded. *Degree requirements:* For master's, thesis, registration. *Entrance requirements:* For master's, GRE, LSAT, MCAT, or GMAT (only required for students without previous doctoral level degree); for Certificate, GRE, LSAT, MCAT, or GMAT (only required of students without previous doctoral level degree). *Application deadline:* For spring admission, 3/1 priority date for domestic and international students. Applications are processed on a rolling basis. Application fee: $0. Electronic applications accepted. *Financial support:* Scholarships/grants and tuition waivers (partial) available. *Faculty research:* Quality of life, mood disorders in children, pediatric palliative care, female pelvic medicines, antibiotic use and racial variations medication use. *Application contact:* Tammy L. Dennis, Coordinator of Student Services, 412-692-2686, Fax: 412-586-9672, E-mail: dennistl@upmc.edu.

University of Virginia, School of Medicine, Department of Public Health Sciences, Program in Health Evaluation Sciences, Charlottesville, VA 22903. Offers clinical investigation and patient-oriented research (MS); informatics in medicine (MS). Part-time programs available. *Students:* 13 full-time (7 women), 7 part-time (4 women); includes 3 minority (all Asian Americans or Pacific Islanders), 2 international. Average age 33. 25 applicants, 92% accepted, 7 enrolled. In 2006, 8 degrees awarded. *Degree requirements:* For master's, thesis (for some programs). *Entrance requirements:* For master's, GRE General Test or MAT. Additional exam requirements/recommendations for international students: Required—TOEFL. Application fee: $60. Electronic applications accepted. *Financial support:* Career-related internships or fieldwork available. Financial award applicants required to submit FAFSA. *Application contact:* Robyn Kells, Coordinator, 434-924-8646, Fax: 434-924-8437, E-mail: ms-hes@virginia.edu.

Vanderbilt University, School of Medicine, Clinical Investigation Program, Nashville, TN 37240-1001. Offers MS. *Students:* 224 applicants, 25% accepted, 35 enrolled. In 2006, 15 master's awarded. *Median time to degree:* Master's–2 years full-time. *Entrance requirements:* Additional exam requirements/recommendations for international students: Required—TOEFL. *Application deadline:* For fall admission, 1/15 for international students. *Expenses:* Tuition: Full-time $24,462. Required fees: $2,515. One-time fee: $30 full-time. Full-time tuition and fees vary according to course load, degree level and program. *Financial support:* In 2006–07, fellowships with full tuition reimbursements (averaging $12,000 per year), research assistantships with full tuition reimbursements (averaging $12,000 per year) were awarded. *Unit head:* Dr. T. Alp Ikizler, Director, 615-322-480, Fax: 615-322-4026. *Application contact:* Susan L. Britt, Coordinator, 615-322-3480, Fax: 615-322-4026, E-mail: susan.britt@mcmail.vanderbilt.edu.

Washington University in St. Louis, School of Medicine, Program in Clinical Investigation, St. Louis, MO 63130-4899. Offers MS. Part-time programs available. *Students:* 16. *Application deadline:* For fall admission, 4/1 for domestic and international students. Application fee: $0. *Unit head:* Dr. Bradley Evanoff, Division Chief—General Medical Sciences, 314-454-8639, Fax: 314-454-5113, E-mail: bevanoff@wustl.edu. *Application contact:* Julie Follman, Program Coordinator, 314-454-8540, Fax: 314-454-8279, E-mail: follman@wustl.edu.

Communication Disorders

Abilene Christian University, Graduate School, College of Education and Human Services, Department of Communication Sciences and Disorders, Abilene, TX 79699-9100. Offers MS. *Accreditation:* ASHA. *Faculty:* 6 part-time/adjunct (5 women). *Students:* 26 full-time (all women), 1 international. 26 applicants, 54% accepted, 9 enrolled. In 2006, 11 degrees awarded. *Degree requirements:* For master's, one foreign language, comprehensive exam. *Entrance requirements:* For master's, GRE General Test. *Application deadline:* For fall admission, 4/1 priority date for domestic students; for spring admission, 11/1 for domestic students. Applications are processed on a rolling basis. Application fee: $40 ($45 for international students). Electronic applications accepted. *Expenses:* Tuition: Full-time $12,504; part-time $521 per hour. Required fees: $700; $34 per hour. *Financial support:* Application deadline: 4/1. *Application contact:* William Horn, Graduate Admissions Counselor, 325-674-2656, Fax: 325-674-6717, E-mail: gradinfo@acu.edu.

Adelphi University, School of Education, Program in Communication Sciences and Disorders, Garden City, NY 11530-0701. Offers audiology (MS, DA); speech-language pathology (MS, DA). *Accreditation:* ASHA. Part-time programs available. *Students:* 161 full-time (158 women), 40 part-time (37 women); includes 15 minority (5 African Americans, 4 Asian Americans or Pacific Islanders, 6 Hispanic Americans). Average age 27. In 2006, 56 degrees awarded. *Degree requirements:* For master's, clinical practice; for doctorate, one foreign language, thesis/dissertation, comprehensive exam. *Entrance requirements:* For master's, GRE General Test and writing exam, 3 letters of recommendation, interview, resumé, 19 credits of prerequisite course work or communications disorders training; for doctorate, GRE General Test, 3 letters of recommendation, interview. Additional exam requirements/recommendations for international students: Required—TOEFL (minimum score 550 paper-based; 213 computer-based). *Application deadline:* For fall admission, 3/1 priority date for domestic students, 3/1 for international students; for spring admission, 10/1 priority date for domestic students, 10/1 for international students. Applications are processed on a rolling basis. Application fee: $50. Electronic applications accepted. *Financial support:* Fellowships, research assistantships with partial tuition reimbursements, teaching assistantships, career-related internships or fieldwork, Federal Work-Study, institutionally sponsored loans, tuition waivers (full), and unspecified assistantships available. Support available to part-time students. Financial award application deadline: 2/15; financial award applicants required to submit FAFSA. *Faculty research:* Pediatric (audiology), child (speech perception with hearing loss), auditory deprivation, fluency, cultural diversity. *Unit head:* Dr. Susan Lederer, Chairperson, 516-877-4781, E-mail: lederer@adelphi.edu. *Application contact:* Christine Murphy, Director of Admissions, 516-877-3050, Fax: 516-877-3039, E-mail: graduateadmissions@adelphi.edu.

Alabama Agricultural and Mechanical University, School of Graduate Studies, School of Education, Department of Counseling and Special Education, Area in Communicative Disorders, Huntsville, AL 35811. Offers M Ed, MS. *Accreditation:* ASHA. Part-time programs available. *Faculty:* 5 full-time (3 women). *Students:* 42 full-time (40 women), 10 part-time (all women); includes 22 minority (all African Americans) In 2006, 7 degrees awarded. *Degree requirements:* For master's, comprehensive exam. *Entrance requirements:* For master's, GRE General Test, minimum GPA of 2.5. *Application deadline:* For fall admission, 5/1 priority date for domestic students. Applications are processed on a rolling basis. Application fee: $25. Electronic applications accepted. *Financial support:* Career-related internships or fieldwork available. Support available to part-time students. Financial award application deadline: 4/1. *Faculty research:* Alternative methods of teaching speech and language to handicapped individuals. *Unit head:* Dr. Terry L. Douglas, Chair, 256-372-5533.

Appalachian State University, Cratis D. Williams Graduate School, College of Education, Department of Language, Reading, and Exceptionalities, Program in Communication Disorders, Boone, NC 28608. Offers MA. Part-time programs available. Postbaccalaureate distance learning degree programs offered. *Students:* 62 full-time (all women); includes 1 minority (American Indian/Alaska Native). 113 applicants, 62% accepted, 34 enrolled. In 2006, 27 degrees awarded. *Degree requirements:* For master's, thesis optional. *Entrance requirements:* For master's, GRE General Test or MAT, minimum GPA of 2.7 in last 60 hours of course work. Additional exam requirements/recommendations for international students: Required—TOEFL (minimum score 550 paper-based; 230 computer-based). *Application deadline:* For fall admission, 2/1 for domestic students, 1/1 for international students; for spring admission, 10/1 for domestic students, 6/1 for international students. Application fee: $50. *Expenses:* Tuition, state resident: full-time $2,600; part-time $127 per hour. Tuition, nonresident: full-time $13,200; part-time $597 per hour. Required fees: $2,000; $546 per term. *Financial support:* Research assistantships, teaching assistantships available. Financial award application deadline: 7/1. *Faculty research:* Clinical service delivery, voice disorders, language disorders, fluency disorders, neurogenic disorders. *Unit head:* Donna Brown, Coordinator, 828-262-2182, Fax: 828-262-6767, E-mail: browndm@appstate.edu.

Arizona State University, Division of Graduate Studies, College of Liberal Arts and Sciences, Division of Natural Sciences and Mathematics, Department of Speech and Hearing Science, Tempe, AZ 85287. Offers audiology (Au D); communication disorders (MS). *Accreditation:* ASHA (one or more programs are accredited). *Degree requirements:* For master's, thesis or alternative, oral and written exams. *Entrance requirements:* For master's, GRE.

Arizona State University, Division of Graduate Studies, College of Liberal Arts and Sciences, Division of Natural Sciences and Mathematics, Interdisciplinary Program in Speech and Hearing Science, Tempe, AZ 85287. Offers PhD.

Arkansas State University, Graduate School, College of Nursing and Health Professions, Program in Communication Disorders, Jonesboro, State University, AR 72467. Offers MCD. *Accreditation:* ASHA. Part-time programs available. *Faculty:* 6 full-time (3 women). *Students:* 35 full-time (all women), 3 part-time (2 women); includes 2 minority (1 African American, 1 Hispanic American). Average age 25. 21 applicants, 76% accepted, 16 enrolled. In 2006, 15 degrees awarded. *Degree requirements:* For master's, thesis or alternative, comprehensive exam. *Entrance requirements:* For master's, GRE General Test, appropriate bachelor's degree, resumé, letters of reference, writing sample, official transcript. Additional exam requirements/recommendations for international students: Required—TOEFL (minimum score 213 computer-based). *Application deadline:* Applications are processed on a rolling basis. Application fee: $30 ($40 for international students). Electronic applications accepted. *Expenses: Contact institution. Financial support:* Scholarships/grants and unspecified assistantships available. Financial award application deadline: 7/1; financial award applicants required to submit FAFSA. *Unit head:* Dr. Richard Neeley, Director, 870-972-3106, Fax: 870-972-3788, E-mail: rneeley@astate.edu.

Armstrong Atlantic State University, School of Graduate Studies, Program in Education, Savannah, GA 31419-1997. Offers adult education (M Ed); early childhood education (M Ed); education (M Ed); elementary education (M Ed); middle grades education (M Ed); secondary education (M Ed), including business education, English education, mathematics education, science education, social science education; special education (M Ed), including behavioral disorders, curriculum and instruction, learning disabilities, speech-language pathology. *Accreditation:* NCATE. Part-time and evening/weekend programs available. Postbaccalaureate distance learning degree programs offered (minimal on-campus study). *Faculty:* 11 full-time (9 women), 13 part-time/adjunct (10 women). *Students:* 50 full-time (42 women), 219 part-time (175 women); includes 71 minority (67 African Americans, 3 Asian Americans or Pacific Islanders, 1 Hispanic American), 6 international. Average age 35. In 2006, 151 degrees awarded. *Degree requirements:* For master's, portfolio. *Entrance requirements:* For master's, GRE General Test or MAT, minimum GPA of 2.5, letters of recommendation. Additional exam requirements/recommendations for international students: Required—TOEFL (minimum score 523 paper-based; 193 computer-based). *Application deadline:* For fall admission, 7/1 priority date for domestic and international students; for spring admission, 11/15 priority date for domestic and international students. Applications are processed on a rolling basis. Application fee: $25. Electronic applications accepted. *Expenses:* Tuition, state resident: full-time

Communication Disorders

Armstrong Atlantic State University (continued)
$2,286; part-time $127 per credit. Tuition, nonresident: full-time $9,144; part-time $508 per credit. One-time fee: $257. *Financial support:* In 2006–07, research assistantships with partial tuition reimbursements (averaging $2,500 per year); career-related internships or fieldwork, Federal Work-Study, scholarships/grants, and unspecified assistantships also available. Support available to part-time students. Financial award applicants required to submit FAFSA. *Unit head:* Dr. Jane McHaney, College of Education Dean, 912-927-5398, Fax: 912-921-7425, E-mail: mchaneia@mail.armstrong.edu.

A.T. Still University of Health Sciences, Arizona School of Health Sciences, Mesa, AZ 85206. Offers advanced occupational therapy (MS); advanced physician assistant (MS); audiology (Au D); human movement (MS); medical informatics (MS); occupational therapy (MS); physical therapy (MS, DPT); physician assistant (MS); sports health care (MS); transitional physical therapy (DPT). *Accreditation:* AOTA (one or more programs are accredited); APTA. Postbaccalaureate distance learning degree programs offered (no on-campus study). *Faculty:* 47 full-time (27 women), 101 part-time/adjunct (60 women). *Students:* 442 full-time (277 women), 732 part-time (579 women); includes 143 minority (38 African Americans, 11 American Indian/Alaska Native, 55 Asian Americans or Pacific Islanders, 39 Hispanic Americans), 4 international. Average age 33. 1,471 applicants, 547 enrolled. In 2006, 104 master's, 432 doctorates awarded. *Degree requirements:* For master's and doctorate, thesis/dissertation (for some programs). *Entrance requirements:* For master's, GRE General Test, minimum GPA of 2.5; for doctorate, GRE, Evaluation of Practicing Audiologists Capabilities (Au D), Physical Therapy Evaluation Tool (DPT), current state licensure, master's degree or equivalent (Au D), minimum GPA of 2.7. *Application deadline:* For fall admission, 2/1 priority date for domestic and international students. Applications are processed on a rolling basis. Application fee: $60. *Expenses: Contact institution. Financial support:* In 2006–07, 382 students received support. Federal Work-Study and scholarships/grants available. Financial award application deadline: 5/1. *Faculty research:* Constraint-induced therapy, scapular motion analysis, shoulder mobility, biomechanics, quadriceps. *Unit head:* Dr. Randy Danielsen, Dean, 480-219-6000, Fax: 480-219-6110, E-mail: rdanielsen@atsu.edu. *Application contact:* Donna Sparks, Associate Director for Admissions, 660-626-2237, Fax: 660-626-2969, E-mail: admissions@atsu.edu.

Auburn University, Graduate School, College of Liberal Arts, Department of Communication Disorders, Auburn University, AL 36849. Offers audiology (MCD, MS, Au D); speech pathology (MCD, MS). *Accreditation:* ASHA (one or more programs are accredited). Part-time programs available. *Faculty:* 9 full-time (5 women). *Students:* 67 full-time (62 women), 11 part-time (10 women); includes 3 minority (1 African American, 2 Asian Americans or Pacific Islanders). Average age 25. 149 applicants, 50% accepted, 38 enrolled. In 2006, 17 degrees awarded. *Degree requirements:* For master's, comprehensive exam (MCD), thesis (MS). *Entrance requirements:* For master's, GRE General Test. *Application deadline:* For fall admission, 7/7 for domestic students; for spring admission, 11/24 for domestic students. Applications are processed on a rolling basis. Application fee: $25 ($50 for international students). Electronic applications accepted. *Expenses:* Tuition, state resident: full-time $5,000. Tuition, nonresident: full-time $15,000. Required fees: $416. Tuition and fees vary according to program. *Financial support:* Research assistantships, teaching assistantships, Federal Work-Study available. Support available to part-time students. Financial award application deadline: 3/15. *Unit head:* Dr. Rebekah Pindzola, Chair, 334-844-9600. *Application contact:* Dr. Joe Pittman, Interim Dean of the Graduate School, 334-844-4700.

Ball State University, Graduate School, College of Sciences and Humanities, Department of Speech Pathology and Audiology, Muncie, IN 47306-1099. Offers MA, Au D. *Accreditation:* ASHA. *Faculty:* 17. *Students:* 91 full-time (85 women), 17 part-time (all women); includes 3 minority (1 African American, 1 American Indian/Alaska Native, 1 Asian American or Pacific Islander), 1 international. Average age 25. 115 applicants, 59% accepted, 31 enrolled. In 2006, 38 master's, 7 doctorates awarded. *Entrance requirements:* For master's, GRE General Test; for doctorate, GRE General Test, interview. Application fee: $25 ($35 for international students). *Financial support:* In 2006–07, 11 teaching assistantships with full tuition reimbursements (averaging $8,968 per year) were awarded; research assistantships with full tuition reimbursements, career-related internships or fieldwork also available. Financial award application deadline: 3/1. *Faculty research:* Adult neurological disorders, stuttering, tinnitus masking, brain stem responses. *Unit head:* Dr. Mary Jo Germani, Chairman, 765-285-8162, Fax: 765-285-5623, E-mail: mgermani@gw.bsu.edu.

Barry University, School of Education, Program in Education for Teachers of Students with Hearing Impairments, Miami Shores, FL 33161-6695. Offers MS. *Unit head:* Dr. Judy Harris-Looby, Director, 305-899-3709, Fax: 305-899-4708, E-mail: jhlooby@mail.barry.edu. *Application contact:* Dave Fletcher, Director of Graduate Admissions, 305-899-3113, Fax: 305-899-2971, E-mail: dfletcher@mail.barry.edu.

Baylor University, Graduate School, College of Arts and Sciences, Department of Communication Sciences and Disorders, Waco, TX 76798. Offers MA, MSCSD. *Accreditation:* ASHA (one or more programs are accredited). *Faculty:* 9 full-time (6 women), 1 (woman) part-time/adjunct. *Students:* 47 full-time (all women), 1 (woman) part-time; includes 8 minority (2 Asian Americans or Pacific Islanders, 6 Hispanic Americans), 2 international. In 2006, 21 degrees awarded. *Entrance requirements:* For master's, GRE General Test. *Application deadline:* Applications are processed on a rolling basis. Application fee: $25. *Expenses: Contact institution. Financial support:* In 2006–07, 25 students received support, including 20 fellowships; Federal Work-Study, institutionally sponsored loans, and tuition waivers (partial) also available. Financial award application deadline: 5/1. *Faculty research:* Nasality, language impairment, stuttering, Spanish speech perception. *Unit head:* Dr. David Garrett, Program Director, 254-710-2567, Fax: 254-710-2590. *Application contact:* Suzanne Keener, Administrative Assistant, 254-710-3588, Fax: 254-710-3870.

Bloomsburg University of Pennsylvania, School of Graduate Studies, College of Professional Studies, School of Education, Department of Exceptionality Programs, Program in Education of the Deaf/Hard of Hearing, Bloomsburg, PA 17815-1301. Offers MS. *Faculty:* 1 full-time (0 women). *Students:* 10 full-time (9 women). Average age 23. 10 applicants, 100% accepted, 9 enrolled. In 2006, 16 degrees awarded. *Entrance requirements:* For master's, PRAXIS, minimum QPA of 3.0. Additional exam requirements/recommendations for international students: Required—TOEFL (minimum score 550 paper-based; 213 computer-based; 79 iBT). *Application deadline:* For fall admission, 3/15 for domestic students. Application fee: $30. Electronic applications accepted. *Expenses:* Tuition, state resident: full-time $6,048; part-time $336 per credit. Tuition, nonresident: full-time $9,678; part-time $538 per credit. Required fees: $1,415. *Financial support:* Unspecified assistantships available. *Faculty research:* Teaching sign language and speech reading through videodisc technology, oral communication skills, sign language. *Unit head:* Dr. Samuel Slike, Coordinator, 570-389-4439, Fax: 570-389-3980, E-mail: sslike@bloomu.edu.

Bloomsburg University of Pennsylvania, School of Graduate Studies, College of Professional Studies, School of Health Sciences, Department of Audiology and Speech Pathology, Program in Audiology, Bloomsburg, PA 17815-1301. Offers Au D. *Accreditation:* ASHA. *Faculty:* 6 full-time (2 women). *Students:* 47 full-time (39 women), 6 part-time (3 women); includes 5 minority (4 African Americans, 1 Asian American or Pacific Islander), 5 international. Average age 28. 17 applicants, 100% accepted, 13 enrolled. In 2006, 7 doctorates awarded. *Entrance requirements:* For doctorate, GRE, 3 letters of recommendation. Additional exam requirements/recommendations for international students: Required—TOEFL. *Application deadline:* For fall admission, 3/1 for domestic students. Application fee: $30. Electronic applications accepted. *Expenses:* Tuition, state resident: full-time $6,048; part-time $336 per credit. Tuition, nonresident: full-time $9,678; part-time $538 per credit. Required fees: $1,415. *Financial support:* Unspecified assistantships available. *Faculty research:* Electrophysiological, industrial, and clinical audiology; hearing aid education; pediatric audiology; auditory processing.

Bloomsburg University of Pennsylvania, School of Graduate Studies, College of Professional Studies, School of Health Sciences, Department of Audiology and Speech Pathology, Program in Speech Pathology, Bloomsburg, PA 17815-1301. Offers MS. *Accreditation:* ASHA. *Faculty:* 5 full-time (3 women). *Students:* 52 full-time (51 women); includes 1 minority (Asian American or Pacific Islander), 3 international. Average age 25. 29 applicants, 100% accepted, 25 enrolled. In 2006, 24 degrees awarded. *Entrance requirements:* For master's, GRE General Test, minimum QPA of 3.0, 3 letters of recommendation. Additional exam requirements/recommendations for international students: Required—TOEFL (minimum score 550 paper-based; 213 computer-based; 79 iBT). *Application deadline:* For fall admission, 2/15 for domestic students. Application fee: $30. Electronic applications accepted. *Expenses:* Tuition, state resident: full-time $6,048; part-time $336 per credit. Tuition, nonresident: full-time $9,678; part-time $538 per credit. Required fees: $1,415. *Financial support:* Unspecified assistantships available. *Faculty research:* Language disorders in children, augmentative communication, neurogenic disorders of speech and language, stuttering, speech science. *Unit head:* Dr. Shaheen Awan, Coordinator, 570-389-4443, Fax: 570-389-5022, E-mail: sawan@bloomu.edu.

Boston University, College of Health and Rehabilitation Sciences—Sargent College, Department of Speech, Language and Hearing Sciences, Boston, MA 02215. Offers audiology (PhD); speech-language pathology (MS, PhD, CAGS). Part-time programs available. *Faculty:* 10 full-time (8 women), 12 part-time/adjunct (5 women). *Students:* 68 full-time (67 women), 5 part-time (all women); includes 4 minority (all Asian Americans or Pacific Islanders), 3 international. Average age 24. 337 applicants, 52% accepted, 40 enrolled. In 2006, 35 degrees awarded. *Median time to degree:* Master's–2 years full-time. *Degree requirements:* For master's, thesis optional; for doctorate, one foreign language, thesis/dissertation, comprehensive exam. *Entrance requirements:* For master's, doctorate, and CAGS, GRE General Test. Additional exam requirements/recommendations for international students: Required—TOEFL (minimum score 550 paper-based). *Application deadline:* For fall admission, 2/1 priority date for domestic students; for spring admission, 10/1 for domestic students. Applications are processed on a rolling basis. Application fee: $65. Electronic applications accepted. *Expenses:* Tuition: Full-time $33,330; part-time $1,042 per credit. Required fees: $462; $40. *Financial support:* In 2006–07, 6 fellowships with full tuition reimbursements, 5 research assistantships with full tuition reimbursements, 5 teaching assistantships with partial tuition reimbursements were awarded; career-related internships or fieldwork, Federal Work-Study, institutionally sponsored loans, scholarships/grants, and tuition waivers (partial) also available. Financial award application deadline: 4/15; financial award applicants required to submit FAFSA. *Faculty research:* Articulation/phonology, fluency, voice and speech science, perception of complex sounds. *Unit head:* Dr. Kristine Strand, Chair, 617-353-3188, E-mail: ksushi@bu.edu. *Application contact:* Sharon Sankey, Director, Student Services, 617-353-2713, Fax: 617-353-7500, E-mail: ssankey@bu.edu.

Bowling Green State University, Graduate College, College of Education and Human Development, School of Education and Intervention Services, Intervention Services Division, Program in Special Education, Bowling Green, OH 43403. Offers assistive technology (M Ed); early childhood intervention (M Ed); gifted education (M Ed); hearing impaired intervention (M Ed); mild/moderate intervention (M Ed); moderate/intensive intervention (M Ed). *Accreditation:* NCATE. Part-time programs available. *Students:* 26 full-time (21 women), 84 part-time (78 women); includes 4 minority (all African Americans) Average age 35. 39 applicants, 87% accepted, 12 enrolled. In 2006, 47 degrees awarded. *Degree requirements:* For master's, thesis or alternative. *Entrance requirements:* For master's, GRE General Test. Additional exam requirements/recommendations for international students: Required—TOEFL. *Application deadline:* For fall admission, 3/1 priority date for domestic students. Applications are processed on a rolling basis. Application fee: $30. Electronic applications accepted. *Expenses:* Tuition, state resident: part-time $535 per hour. Tuition, nonresident: part-time $884 per hour. *Financial support:* In 2006–07, 16 research assistantships with full tuition reimbursements (averaging $5,202 per year) were awarded; teaching assistantships with full tuition reimbursements, Federal Work-Study and unspecified assistantships also available. Financial award applicants required to submit FAFSA. *Faculty research:* Reading and special populations, deafness, early childhood, gifted and talented, behavior disorders. *Application contact:* Dr. Lessie Cochran, Graduate Coordinator, 419-372-7298.

Bowling Green State University, Graduate College, College of Health and Human Services, Department of Communication Disorders, Bowling Green, OH 43403. Offers communication disorders (PhD); speech-language pathology (MS). *Accreditation:* ASHA (one or more programs are accredited). *Faculty:* 14 full-time (5 women), 5 part-time/adjunct (2 women). *Students:* 49 full-time (44 women), 1 part-time; includes 4 minority (2 African Americans, 1 Asian American or Pacific Islander, 1 Hispanic American), 8 international. Average age 26. 117 applicants, 24% accepted, 27 enrolled. In 2006, 22 degrees awarded. *Degree requirements:* For master's, thesis or alternative; for doctorate, thesis/dissertation, foreign language or research tool, comprehensive exam. *Entrance requirements:* For master's, GRE General Test, minimum GPA of 3.0; for doctorate, GRE General Test, minimum GPA of 3.2. Additional exam requirements/recommendations for international students: Required—TOEFL. *Application deadline:* For fall admission, 2/1 for domestic students. Application fee: $30. Electronic applications accepted. *Expenses:* Tuition, state resident: part-time $535 per hour. Tuition, nonresident: part-time $884 per hour. *Financial support:* In 2006–07, 5 research assistantships with full tuition reimbursements (averaging $11,887 per year), 26 teaching assistantships with full tuition reimbursements (averaging $6,052 per year) were awarded; career-related internships or fieldwork, Federal Work-Study, institutionally sponsored loans, and unspecified assistantships also available. Financial award applicants required to submit FAFSA. *Faculty research:* Rehabilitation and mental disorders, forensic rehabilitation, rehabilitation and substance abuse, private rehabilitation and disability management, adjustment to disability. *Unit head:* Dr. Larry Small, Chair, 419-372-6031. *Application contact:* Dr. Lynne Hewitt, Graduate Coordinator, 419-372-7181.

Brigham Young University, Graduate Studies, David O. McKay School of Education, Department of Communication Disorders, Provo, UT 84602-1001. Offers speech-language pathology (MS). *Accreditation:* ASHA. *Faculty:* 10 full-time (4 women), 5 part-time/adjunct (4 women). *Students:* 39 full-time (36 women); includes 1 minority (Asian American or Pacific Islander) 50 applicants, 54% accepted, 18 enrolled. In 2006, 14 degrees awarded. *Degree requirements:* For master's, thesis, exit interview, comprehensive exam. *Entrance requirements:* For master's, GRE General Test, 3 letters of recommendation. Additional exam requirements/recommendations for international students: Required—TOEFL (minimum score 580 paper-based; 237 computer-based). *Application deadline:* For fall admission, 2/1 for domestic and international students. Application fee: $50. Electronic applications accepted. *Financial support:* In 2006–07, 7 research assistantships (averaging $5,000 per year), 13 teaching assistantships (averaging $5,000 per year) were awarded; fellowships, institutionally sponsored loans, scholarships/grants, and tuition waivers (partial) also available. *Faculty research:* Foreign language speech audiometry materials; language sample analysis, language measurement; speech motor control physiology; acrodynamic and kenematic analysis of speech production; and social skills and outcomes of children with language impairment. Total annual research expenditures: $31,742. *Unit head:* Dr. David L. McPherson, Chair, 801-422-6458, Fax: 801-422-0197, E-mail: david_mcpherson@byu.edu. *Application contact:* Kathleen Pierce, Department Secretary, 801-422-4318, Fax: 801-422-0197, E-mail: kathy_pierce@byu.edu.

Brooklyn College of the City University of New York, Division of Graduate Studies, Department of Speech Communication Arts and Sciences, Brooklyn, NY 11210-2889. Offers audiology (Au D); speech (MA, MS Ed); speech and hearing sciences (PhD); speech pathology (MS). The department offers courses at Brooklyn College that are creditable towards the CUNY doctoral degree (with permission of the executive officer of the doctoral program). MS in speech pathology—Fall admissions only, application deadline 2/1. *Accreditation:* ASHA (one or more programs are accredited). Part-time programs available. *Students:* 33 full-time (32 women), 66 part-time (62 women); includes 11 minority (5 African Americans, 1 American Indian/Alaska Native, 3 Asian Americans or Pacific Islanders, 2 Hispanic Americans), 4 international. 276 applicants, 25% accepted, 26 enrolled. In 2006, 37 degrees awarded.

Terminal master's awarded for partial completion of doctoral program. *Degree requirements:* For master's, National Teacher Exam. *Entrance requirements:* For master's, GRE, minimum GPA of 3.0, interview. Additional exam requirements/recommendations for international students: Required—TOEFL. *Application deadline:* For fall admission, 2/1 for domestic and international students. Applications are processed on a rolling basis. Application fee: $125. Electronic applications accepted. *Expenses:* Tuition, state resident: full-time $6,400; part-time $270 per credit. Tuition, nonresident: full-time $12,000; part-time $500 per credit. Required fees: $118 per semester. *Financial support:* Career-related internships or fieldwork, Federal Work-Study, institutionally sponsored loans, scholarships/grants, and traineeships available. Support available to part-time students. Financial award application deadline: 5/1; financial award applicants required to submit FAFSA. *Faculty research:* Language and learning disorders, aphasia, auditory disorders, public and business communication, voice and fluency disorders. *Unit head:* Dr. Timothy Gura, Chairperson, 718-951-5225, Fax: 718-951-4167, E-mail: tgura@brooklyn.cuny.edu. *Application contact:* Karen Alleyne-Pierre, Director of Admissions Services and Enrollment Communications, 718-951-5902, Fax: 718-951-4506, E-mail: grads@brooklyn.cuny.edu.

Buffalo State College, State University of New York, Graduate Studies and Research, Faculty of Applied Science and Education, Department of Speech-Language Pathology, Buffalo, NY 14222-1095. Offers MS Ed. *Accreditation:* ASHA. Part-time and evening/weekend programs available. *Degree requirements:* For master's, thesis or alternative, project. *Entrance requirements:* For master's, minimum GPA of 3.0 in last 60 hours, 22 hours in communication disorders. Additional exam requirements/recommendations for international students: Required—TOEFL (minimum score 550 paper-based; 213 computer-based).

California State University, Chico, Graduate School, College of Communication and Education, Department of Communication Arts and Sciences, Program in Communication Science and Disorders, Chico, CA 95929-0350. Offers MA. *Accreditation:* ASHA. *Students:* 42 full-time (39 women); includes 3 minority (1 Asian American or Pacific Islander, 2 Hispanic Americans), 1 international. Average age 27. 23 applicants, 100% accepted, 18 enrolled. In 2006, 1 degree awarded. *Degree requirements:* For master's, thesis or alternative, oral exam. *Entrance requirements:* For master's, GRE General Test or MAT, 3 letters of recommendation, resumé. Additional exam requirements/recommendations for international students: Required—TOEFL (minimum score 550 paper-based; 213 computer-based). *Application deadline:* For fall admission, 3/1 for domestic and international students; for spring admission, 9/15 for domestic and international students. Applications are processed on a rolling basis. Application fee: $55. Electronic applications accepted. *Financial support:* Teaching assistantships, career-related internships or fieldwork available. *Unit head:* Dr. Patrick McCaffrey, Graduate Coordinator, 530-898-6394.

California State University, East Bay, Academic Programs and Graduate Studies, College of Letters, Arts, and Social Sciences, Department of Communicative Sciences and Disorders, Hayward, CA 94542-3000. Offers speech pathology and audiology (MS). *Accreditation:* ASHA. Part-time programs available. *Faculty:* 6 full-time (5 women). *Students:* 97 full-time (90 women), 14 part-time (all women); includes 25 minority (4 African Americans, 15 Asian Americans or Pacific Islanders, 6 Hispanic Americans), 8 international. Average age 31. 118 applicants, 48% accepted, 39 enrolled. In 2006, 38 degrees awarded. *Degree requirements:* For master's, internship or thesis. *Entrance requirements:* For master's, minimum GPA of 3.0 in last 2 years of course work. Additional exam requirements/recommendations for international students: Required—TOEFL (minimum score 550 paper-based; 213 computer-based). *Application deadline:* For fall admission, 5/31 for domestic students, 4/30 for international students; for winter admission, 9/30 for domestic and international students; for spring admission, 11/30 for international students. Application fee: $55. Electronic applications accepted. *Financial support:* Fellowships, teaching assistantships, career-related internships or fieldwork, Federal Work-Study, institutionally sponsored loans, and scholarships/grants available. Support available to part-time students. Financial award application deadline: 3/2. *Unit head:* Dr. Janet Patterson, Chair, 510-885-3233, Fax: 510-885-2186. *Application contact:* My Huynh, Graduate Prospect Specialist, 510-885-2989, Fax: 510-885-4059, E-mail: my.huynh@csueastbay.edu.

California State University, Fresno, Division of Graduate Studies, College of Health and Human Services, Department of Communicative Disorders, Fresno, CA 93740-8027. Offers communicative disorders (MA), including deaf education, speech/language pathology. *Accreditation:* ASHA. Part-time programs available. *Degree requirements:* For master's, thesis or alternative. *Entrance requirements:* For master's, GRE General Test, minimum GPA of 3.0. Additional exam requirements/recommendations for international students: Required—TOEFL. Electronic applications accepted. *Faculty research:* Disabilities education, technology, writing skills at multiple levels, stuttering treatment.

California State University, Fullerton, Graduate Studies, College of Communications, Department of Human Communications, Fullerton, CA 92834-9480. Offers communicative disorders (MA); speech communication (MA); theory and process (MA). *Accreditation:* ASHA. Part-time programs available. *Students:* 72 full-time (68 women), 37 part-time (31 women); includes 31 minority (2 African Americans, 9 Asian Americans or Pacific Islanders, 20 Hispanic Americans), 5 international. Average age 30. 149 applicants, 28% accepted, 27 enrolled. In 2006, 33 degrees awarded. *Degree requirements:* For master's, thesis or alternative, comprehensive exam. *Entrance requirements:* For master's, minimum GPA of 3.0 in major. Application fee: $55. *Expenses:* Tuition, nonresident: part-time $339 per unit. Required fees: $1,155 per semester. *Financial support:* Teaching assistantships, career-related internships or fieldwork, Federal Work-Study, institutionally sponsored loans, and scholarships/grants available. Support available to part-time students. Financial award application deadline: 3/1. *Faculty research:* Speech therapy. *Unit head:* Dr. Kurt Kitselman, Chair, 714-278-3617.

California State University, Fullerton, Graduate Studies, College of Humanities and Social Sciences, Program in Linguistics, Fullerton, CA 92834-9480. Offers analysis of specific language structures (MA); anthropological linguistics (MA); applied linguistics (MA); communication and semantics (MA); disorders of communication (MA); experimental phonetics (MA). Part-time programs available. *Students:* 9 full-time (5 women), 15 part-time (9 women); includes 8 minority (2 Asian Americans or Pacific Islanders, 6 Hispanic Americans), 6 international. Average age 32. 22 applicants, 59% accepted, 6 enrolled. In 2006, 8 degrees awarded. *Degree requirements:* For master's, one foreign language, thesis or alternative, project. *Entrance requirements:* For master's, minimum GPA of 3.0, undergraduate major in linguistics or related field. Application fee: $55. *Expenses:* Tuition, nonresident: part-time $339 per unit. Required fees: $1,155 per semester. *Financial support:* Career-related internships or fieldwork, Federal Work-Study, institutionally sponsored loans, and scholarships/grants available. Support available to part-time students. Financial award application deadline: 3/1. *Unit head:* Dr. Franz Muller-Gotama, Adviser, 714-278-2441.

California State University, Long Beach, Graduate Studies, College of Health and Human Services, Department of Communicative Disorders, Long Beach, CA 90840. Offers MA. *Accreditation:* ASHA. Part-time programs available. *Faculty:* 7 full-time (6 women), 5 part-time/adjunct (4 women). *Students:* 53 full-time (50 women), 34 part-time (33 women); includes 24 minority (4 African Americans, 11 Asian Americans or Pacific Islanders, 9 Hispanic Americans), 3 international. Average age 30. 167 applicants, 40% accepted, 37 enrolled. In 2006, 19 degrees awarded. *Degree requirements:* For master's, comprehensive exam or thesis. *Entrance requirements:* For master's, minimum GPA of 3.0. *Application deadline:* For fall admission, 7/1 for domestic students; for spring admission, 12/1 for domestic students. Applications are processed on a rolling basis. Application fee: $55. Electronic applications accepted. *Financial support:* Federal Work-Study, institutionally sponsored loans, and scholarships/grants available. Financial award application deadline: 3/2. *Unit head:* Dr. Carolyn Madding, Chair, 562-985-4594, Fax: 562-985-4584, E-mail: madding@csulb.edu. *Application contact:* Dr. Bertty McMicken, Graduate Adviser, 562-985-5282, Fax: 562-985-4584, E-mail: hoarsedoc@aol.com.

California State University, Los Angeles, Graduate Studies, College of Health and Human Services, Department of Communication Disorders, Major in Speech and Hearing Clinic, Los Angeles, CA 90032-8530. Offers MA. *Students:* 1 (woman) full-time. *Degree requirements:* For master's, comprehensive exam. *Entrance requirements:* For master's, undergraduate major in communication disorders or related area, minimum GPA of 2.75 in last 90 units. Additional exam requirements/recommendations for international students: Required—TOEFL. *Application deadline:* For fall admission, 6/30 for domestic students; for spring admission, 2/1 for domestic students. Applications are processed on a rolling basis. Application fee: $55. *Expenses:* Tuition, nonresident: part-time $226 per unit. *Financial support:* Application deadline: 3/1. *Faculty research:* Language acquisition, language disorders, multicultural issues. *Unit head:* Dr. Cari Flint, Head, 323-343-4690.

California State University, Northridge, Graduate Studies, College of Health and Human Development, Department of Communication Disorders and Sciences, Northridge, CA 91330. Offers MS. *Accreditation:* ASHA. *Faculty:* 10 full-time (7 women), 16 part-time/adjunct (13 women). *Students:* 82 full-time (3 women), 40 part-time (3 women); includes 17 minority (3 African Americans, 1 American Indian/Alaska Native, 6 Asian Americans or Pacific Islanders, 7 Hispanic Americans), 1 international. Average age 30. 107 applicants, 30% accepted, 31 enrolled. In 2006, 78 degrees awarded. *Entrance requirements:* For master's, GRE or minimum GPA of 3.5. Additional exam requirements/recommendations for international students: Required—TOEFL. *Application deadline:* For fall admission, 11/30 for domestic students. Application fee: $55. *Expenses:* Tuition, nonresident: full-time $8,136; part-time $4,068 per year. Required fees: $3,624; $1,161 per term. *Financial support:* Application deadline: 3/1. *Faculty research:* Infant stimulation, early intervention program. *Unit head:* Dr. J. Stephen Sinclair, Chair, 818-677-2852. *Application contact:* Dr. Janet T. Reagan, Graduate Coordinator, 818-677-3101.

California State University, Sacramento, Graduate Studies, College of Health and Human Services, Department of Speech Pathology and Audiology, Sacramento, CA 95819-6048. Offers audiology (MS); speech pathology (MS). *Accreditation:* ASHA. *Students:* 83 full-time (75 women), 8 part-time (all women); includes 18 minority (1 African American, 1 American Indian/Alaska Native, 3 Asian Americans or Pacific Islanders, 13 Hispanic Americans), 1 international. Average age 28. 94 applicants, 59% accepted, 33 enrolled. *Degree requirements:* For master's, thesis, writing proficiency exam. *Entrance requirements:* For master's, GRE General Test, appropriate bachelor's degree, minimum GPA of 3.0 in last 2 years of course work. Additional exam requirements/recommendations for international students: Required—TOEFL. *Application deadline:* Applications are processed on a rolling basis. Application fee: $55. Electronic applications accepted. *Financial support:* Career-related internships or fieldwork and Federal Work-Study available. Support available to part-time students. Financial award application deadline: 3/1. *Unit head:* Laureen O'Hanlon, Chair, 916-278-6601, Fax: 916-278-7730.

California University of Pennsylvania, School of Graduate Studies and Research, School of Education, Department of Communication Disorders, California, PA 15419-1394. Offers MS. *Accreditation:* ASHA. Part-time and evening/weekend programs available. *Faculty:* 13 full-time (7 women). *Students:* 23 full-time (21 women), 3 part-time (2 women); includes 1 minority (African American) Average age 29. 44 applicants, 52% accepted. In 2006, 10 degrees awarded. *Median time to degree:* Master's–1.5 years full-time, 2.25 years part-time. *Degree requirements:* For master's, thesis optional. *Entrance requirements:* For master's, GRE General Test, minimum GPA of 3.0, references. Additional exam requirements/recommendations for international students: Required—TOEFL (minimum score 550 paper-based; 213 computer-based; 80 iBT). *Application deadline:* For fall admission, 2/15 priority date for domestic and international students. Applications are processed on a rolling basis. Application fee: $25. Electronic applications accepted. *Expenses:* Tuition, state resident: full-time $6,048; part-time $336 per credit. Tuition, nonresident: full-time $9,678; part-time $538 per credit. Required fees: $1,854; $263 per credit. Full-time tuition and fees vary according to course load, campus/location and program. *Financial support:* Career-related internships or fieldwork, scholarships/grants, traineeships, and unspecified assistantships available. Financial award applicants required to submit FAFSA. *Faculty research:* Normative voice database, communication disorders and health. *Unit head:* Dr. Barbara H. Bonfanti, Chairperson, 724-938-4175, Fax: 724-938-1526, E-mail: bonfanti@cup.edu.

Canisius College, Graduate Division, School of Education and Human Services, Department of Graduate Education, Buffalo, NY 14208-1098. Offers business education (MS); childhood education (MS); college student personnel (MS); differentiated instruction (MS Ed); early childhood education (MS); education administration (MS); education of the deaf and hard of hearing (MS); general education (MS Ed); literacy education (MS Ed); reading education (MS Ed); secondary education (MS); special education (MS). *Accreditation:* NCATE. Part-time and evening/weekend programs available. *Faculty:* 13 full-time (12 women), 74 part-time/adjunct (44 women). *Students:* 377 full-time (267 women), 303 part-time (219 women); includes 43 minority (27 African Americans, 2 American Indian/Alaska Native, 6 Asian Americans or Pacific Islanders, 8 Hispanic Americans), 187 international. Average age 30. In 2006, 296 degrees awarded. Application fee: $25. *Expenses:* Tuition: Part-time $645 per credit hour. Required fees: $19 per credit hour. Tuition and fees vary according to program. *Financial support:* Research assistantships with full tuition reimbursements, career-related internships or fieldwork, institutionally sponsored loans, scholarships/grants, health care benefits, tuition waivers (full and partial), and unspecified assistantships available. *Faculty research:* Autism, Asperger's disease, private higher education, reading strategies. *Unit head:* Rev. Paul Nochelski, Chair of Graduate Education and Leadership, 716-888-3297, Fax: 716-888-3299. *Application contact:* James D. Bagwell, Director of Graduate Recruitment and Admissions, 716-888-2544, Fax: 716-888-3290, E-mail: bagwellj@canisius.edu.

Carlos Albizu University, Graduate Programs in Psychology, San Juan, PR 00901. Offers clinical psychology (MS, PhD, Psy D); general psychology (PhD); industrial/organizational psychology (MS, PhD); speech and language pathology (MS). *Accreditation:* APA (one or more programs are accredited). Part-time and evening/weekend programs available. *Faculty:* 22 full-time (13 women), 61 part-time/adjunct (33 women). *Students:* 603 full-time (515 women), 99 part-time (77 women); all minorities (all Hispanic Americans) Average age 28. 168 applicants, 77% accepted, 124 enrolled. In 2006, 66 master's, 81 doctorates awarded. *Degree requirements:* For master's, one foreign language, thesis, comprehensive exam; for doctorate, one foreign language, thesis/dissertation, written qualifying exams, comprehensive exam. *Entrance requirements:* For master's, GRE General Test or EXADEP, interview, minimum GPA of 3.0; for doctorate, GRE General Test or EXADEP, interview, minimum GPA of 3.0 (industrial/organizational psychology), minimum GPA of 3.25 (clinical psychology). *Application deadline:* For fall admission, 7/19 for domestic and international students; for winter admission, 11/15 for domestic and international students; for spring admission, 4/21 for domestic and international students. Application fee: $75. *Financial support:* In 2006–07, 15 research assistantships, 15 teaching assistantships were awarded; career-related internships or fieldwork, Federal Work-Study, institutionally sponsored loans, scholarships/grants, traineeships, and tuition waivers (partial) also available. Support available to part-time students. Financial award application deadline: 4/21; financial award applicants required to submit FAFSA. *Faculty research:* Psychotherapeutic techniques for Hispanics, psychology of the aged, school dropouts, stress, violence. *Unit head:* Dr. Lourdes Garcia, Chancellor, 787-725-6500 Ext. 34, E-mail: lgarcia@albizu.edu. *Application contact:* Dr. Jaime Veray, Special Assistant to Chancellor, 787-725-6500 Ext. 35, Fax: 787-721-7187, E-mail: jveray@albizu.edu.

Case Western Reserve University, School of Graduate Studies, Department of Communication Sciences, Cleveland, OH 44106. Offers gerontology (Certificate); speech-language pathology (MA, PhD). *Accreditation:* ASHA (one or more programs are accredited). *Faculty:* 5 full-time (4 women), 7 part-time/adjunct (5 women). *Students:* 19 full-time (18 women), 6 part-time (all women), 3 international. Average age 24. 51 applicants, 67% accepted, 11 enrolled. In 2006, 7 master's, 1 doctorate awarded. Terminal master's awarded for partial completion of doctoral program. *Degree requirements:* For master's, thesis optional; for doctorate, thesis/dissertation. *Entrance requirements:* For master's and doctorate, GRE General Test. Additional exam requirements/recommendations for international students: Required—

Communication Disorders

Case Western Reserve University (continued)
TOEFL. *Application deadline:* For fall admission, 3/1 for domestic students. Application fee: $50. *Financial support:* In 2006–07, 19 students received support; research assistantships, career-related internships or fieldwork, Federal Work-Study, scholarships/grants, tuition waivers (partial), and unspecified assistantships available. Financial award application deadline: 3/1; financial award applicants required to submit FAFSA. *Faculty research:* Traumatic brain injury, phonological disorders, child language disorders, communication problems in the aged and Alzheimer's patients, cleft palate, voice disorders. *Unit head:* Stephen E. Haynesworth, Interim Chair, 216-368-2470, Fax: 216-368-6078, E-mail: stephen.haynesworth@case.edu. *Application contact:* Julie Clutter, Assistant, 216-368-2470, Fax: 216-368-6078, E-mail: jac34@case.edu.

Central Michigan University, College of Graduate Studies, The Herbert H. and Grace A. Dow College of Health Professions, Department of Communications Disorders, Program in Audiology, Mount Pleasant, MI 48859. Offers Au D. *Accreditation:* ASHA. *Degree requirements:* For doctorate, thesis/dissertation or alternative, registration. *Entrance requirements:* For doctorate, GRE, interview. Additional exam requirements/recommendations for international students: Required—TOEFL.

Central Michigan University, College of Graduate Studies, The Herbert H. and Grace A. Dow College of Health Professions, Department of Communications Disorders, Program in Speech and Language Pathology, Mount Pleasant, MI 48859. Offers MA. *Accreditation:* ASHA. *Degree requirements:* For master's, thesis or alternative, registration. Expenses: Contact institution. *Faculty research:* Nonvocal persons, speech audiometry, phonological disorders.

Clarion University of Pennsylvania, Office of Research and Graduate Studies, College of Education and Human Services, Department of Communication Sciences and Disorders, Clarion, PA 16214. Offers MS. *Accreditation:* ASHA. Part-time programs available. *Faculty:* 6 full-time (5 women). *Students:* 44 full-time (all women), 16 part-time (all women); includes 1 minority (African American), 1 international. 62 applicants, 31% accepted. In 2006, 27 degrees awarded. *Degree requirements:* For master's, thesis or alternative. *Entrance requirements:* For master's, minimum QPA of 3.0. Additional exam requirements/recommendations for international students: Required—TOEFL (minimum score 573 paper-based; 230 computer-based; 89 iBT). *Application deadline:* For fall admission, 1/31 for domestic and international students. Application fee: $30. Electronic applications accepted. *Expenses:* Tuition, state resident: part-time $336 per credit. Tuition, nonresident: part-time $538 per credit. *Financial support:* In 2006–07, 14 research assistantships with partial tuition reimbursements (averaging $2,001 per year) were awarded; career-related internships or fieldwork also available. Support available to part-time students. Financial award application deadline: 3/1. *Unit head:* Dr. Colleen McAleer, Chair, 814-393-2581, Fax: 814-393-2206, E-mail: cmcaleer@clarion.edu. *Application contact:* Dr. Janis Jarecki-Liu, Graduate Coordinator, 814-393-2445, Fax: 814-393-2206, E-mail: jjareckiliu@clarion.edu.

Cleveland State University, College of Graduate Studies, College of Science, Department of Health Sciences, Program in Speech Pathology and Audiology, Cleveland, OH 44115. Offers MA. *Accreditation:* ASHA. *Faculty:* 4 full-time (2 women). *Students:* 19 full-time (all women), 16 part-time (all women); includes 1 minority (African American) Average age 26. 55 applicants, 67% accepted, 16 enrolled. In 2006, 15 degrees awarded. *Degree requirements:* For master's, thesis optional. *Entrance requirements:* For master's, GRE. Additional exam requirements/recommendations for international students: Required—TOEFL. *Application deadline:* For fall admission, 3/1 priority date for domestic students. Applications are processed on a rolling basis. Application fee: $30. *Financial support:* In 2006–07, 4 research assistantships with full and partial tuition reimbursements (averaging $1,740 per year) were awarded; teaching assistantships with full and partial tuition reimbursements, career-related internships or fieldwork, Federal Work-Study, tuition waivers (full), and unspecified assistantships also available. Financial award application deadline: 3/1. *Faculty research:* Brain stem audiometry, hearing aids, variant dialects, applications of microcomputers, voice disorders. *Unit head:* Dr. Monica Gordon Pershey, Director, 216-687-4534, Fax: 216-687-6993, E-mail: m.pershey@csuohio.edu. *Application contact:* Donna Helwig, Administrative Coordinator to the Chairperson, 216-687-3807, E-mail: d.helwig@csuohio.edu.

College Misericordia, College of Health Sciences, Department of Speech-Language Pathology, Dallas, PA 18612-1098. Offers MSSLP. *Accreditation:* ASHA. *Faculty:* 2 full-time (1 woman), 3 part-time/adjunct (2 women). *Students:* 6 full-time (all women). Average age 22. In 2006, 15 degrees awarded. *Application deadline:* For fall admission, 2/1 priority date for domestic students. Application fee: $25. *Expenses:* Tuition: Full-time $19,800; part-time $495 per credit. Required fees: $1,060. *Financial support:* Scholarships/grants available. Support available to part-time students. Financial award application deadline: 6/30; financial award applicants required to submit FAFSA. *Unit head:* Glen Tellis, Chair, 570-674-6471, E-mail: atellis@misericordia.edu. *Application contact:* Larree Brown, Coordinator of Part-Time Undergraduate and Graduate Programs, 570-674-6451, Fax: 570-674-6232, E-mail: lbrown@misericordia.edu.

The College of New Jersey, Graduate Division, School of Education, Department of Special Education, Language and Literacy, Speech Pathology Program, Ewing, NJ 08628. Offers MA. *Accreditation:* ASHA. Part-time and evening/weekend programs available. *Students:* 17 full-time (all women), 24 part-time (all women); includes 3 minority (1 African American, 2 Hispanic Americans). 129 applicants, 30% accepted. In 2006, 8 degrees awarded. *Degree requirements:* For master's, clinical practicum. *Entrance requirements:* For master's, GRE General Test, minimum GPA of 3.0 in field or 2.75 overall, bachelor's degree in speech pathology. Additional exam requirements/recommendations for international students: Required—TOEFL. *Application deadline:* For fall admission, 4/15 for domestic students; for spring admission, 10/15 for domestic students. Application fee: $50. Electronic applications accepted. *Financial support:* Unspecified assistantships available. Financial award application deadline: 5/1; financial award applicants required to submit FAFSA. *Unit head:* Dr. Jasper Phelps, Coordinator, 609-771-2743. *Application contact:* Susan L. Hydro, Office of Graduate Studies, Assistant Dean, 609-771-2300, Fax: 609-637-5105, E-mail: graduate@tcnj.edu.

The College of New Rochelle, Graduate School, Division of Education, Program in Speech-Language Pathology, New Rochelle, NY 10805-2308. Offers MS. *Faculty:* 2 full-time (both women), 4 part-time/adjunct (3 women). *Students:* Average age 34. In 2006, 11 degrees awarded. *Degree requirements:* For master's, research project. *Entrance requirements:* For master's, interview, minimum GPA of 3.0, teacher hearing handicap certificate, bachelor's degree in speech language pathology. *Application deadline:* For fall admission, 8/1 priority date for domestic students; for spring admission, 4/6 for domestic students. Applications are processed on a rolling basis. Application fee: $35. *Expenses:* Tuition: Part-time $575 per credit. Required fees: $90 per term. *Financial support:* In 2006–07, 1 research assistantship with tuition reimbursement was awarded; scholarships/grants and unspecified assistantships also available. Support available to part-time students. *Unit head:* Dr. Marie Ribarich, Acting Division Head, Division of Education, 914-654-5333, Fax: 914-654-5593, E-mail: mribarich@cnr.edu.

The College of Saint Rose, Graduate Studies, School of Education, Department of Communication Disorders, Albany, NY 12203-1419. Offers MS Ed. *Accreditation:* ASHA. Part-time and evening/weekend programs available. *Degree requirements:* For master's, comprehensive exam or thesis. *Entrance requirements:* For master's, minimum undergraduate GPA of 3.0, on-campus interview, 32 undergraduate credits if undergraduate degree is not in communication disorders. Additional exam requirements/recommendations for international students: Required—TOEFL (minimum score 550 paper-based; 213 computer-based). Electronic applications accepted.

Dalhousie University, Faculty of Graduate Studies, Faculty of Health Professions, School of Human Communication Disorders, Halifax, NS B3H 4R2, Canada. Offers M Sc. *Degree requirements:* For master's, thesis or alternative. *Entrance requirements:* Additional exam requirements/recommendations for international students: Required—TOEFL. Electronic applications accepted. Expenses: Contact institution. *Faculty research:* Audiology, hearing aids, speech and voice disorders, language development and disorders, treatment efficacy.

Duquesne University, John G. Rangos, Sr. School of Health Sciences, Pittsburgh, PA 15282-0001. Offers health management systems (MHMS); occupational therapy (MS); physical therapy (DPT); physician assistant (MPA); speech–language pathology (MS); MBA/MHMS. *Accreditation:* AOTA (one or more programs are accredited); APTA (one or more programs are accredited); ASHA. *Faculty:* 35 full-time (22 women), 24 part-time/adjunct (12 women). *Students:* 261 full-time (229 women), 16 part-time (8 women); includes 11 minority (6 African Americans, 1 American Indian/Alaska Native, 2 Asian Americans or Pacific Islanders, 2 Hispanic Americans), 3 international. Average age 23. 150 applicants, 55% accepted, 41 enrolled. In 2006, 66 master's, 13 doctorates awarded. *Degree requirements:* For doctorate, thesis/dissertation. *Entrance requirements:* For master's, GRE (speech-language pathology), 3 letters of recommendation, minimum GPA of 2.75 (health management systems, occupational therapy), minimum GPA of 3.0 (physical assistant, speech-language pathology); for doctorate, GRE General Test, 3 letters of recommendation, minimum GPA of 3.0, personal interview. Additional exam requirements/recommendations for international students: Required—TOEFL (minimum score 600 paper-based; 250 computer-based). *Application deadline:* For fall admission, 12/1 priority date for domestic students; for winter admission, 5/1 priority date for domestic students. Application fee: $50. Electronic applications accepted. *Expenses: Contact institution.* Tuition and fees vary according to degree level and program. *Financial support:* Federal Work-Study available. *Faculty research:* Neuronal processing, electrical stimulation on peripheral neuropathy, CNS stimulatory and inhibitory signals, behavioral genetic methodologies to development disorders of speech, neurogenic communication disorders. Total annual research expenditures: $66,000. *Unit head:* Dr. Gregory H. Frazer, Dean, 412-396-5303, Fax: 412-396-5554, E-mail: frazer@duq.edu. *Application contact:* Christopher R. Hilf, Recruiter/Academic Advisor, 412-396-5653, Fax: 412-396-5554, E-mail: hilfc@duq.edu.

East Carolina University, Graduate School, School of Allied Health Sciences, Department of Communication Sciences and Disorders, Greenville, NC 27858-4353. Offers communication sciences and disorders (PhD); speech, language and auditory pathology (MS). *Accreditation:* ASHA (one or more programs are accredited). Postbaccalaureate distance learning degree programs offered (no on-campus study). *Students:* 93 full-time (86 women), 41 part-time (37 women); includes 15 minority (9 African Americans, 1 American Indian/Alaska Native, 3 Asian Americans or Pacific Islanders, 2 Hispanic Americans), 2 international. Average age 28. 32 applicants, 6% accepted, 1 enrolled. In 2006, 38 master's, 2 doctorates awarded. *Degree requirements:* For master's, thesis or alternative, comprehensive exam; for doctorate, thesis/dissertation, comprehensive exam. *Entrance requirements:* For master's and doctorate, GRE General Test. Additional exam requirements/recommendations for international students: Required—TOEFL. *Application deadline:* For fall admission, 4/1 for domestic students. Application fee: $50. *Financial support:* In 2006–07, research assistantships with partial tuition reimbursements (averaging $12,000 per year), teaching assistantships with partial tuition reimbursements (averaging $12,000 per year) were awarded; unspecified assistantships also available. Financial award application deadline: 6/1. *Faculty research:* Hearing, language disorders, stuttering, reading disorder. *Unit head:* Dr. Gregg Givens, Chair, 252-744-6099, Fax: 252-328-4470, E-mail: givensg@ecu.edu. *Application contact:* Dean of Graduate School, 252-328-6012, Fax: 252-328-6071, E-mail: gradschool@ecu.edu.

Eastern Illinois University, Graduate School, College of Sciences, Department of Communication Disorders and Sciences, Charleston, IL 61920-3099. Offers MS. *Accreditation:* ASHA. *Faculty:* 10 full-time (6 women). In 2006, 23 degrees awarded. *Degree requirements:* For master's, comprehensive exam. *Application deadline:* For fall admission, 7/31 priority date for domestic students. Applications are processed on a rolling basis. Application fee: $30. *Expenses:* Tuition, state resident: part-time $169 per semester hour. Tuition, nonresident: part-time $508 per semester hour. Required fees: $60 per semester hour. *Financial support:* In 2006–07, 4 research assistantships with tuition reimbursements (averaging $7,200 per year), 5 teaching assistantships with tuition reimbursements (averaging $7,200 per year) were awarded. *Unit head:* Dr. Gail Richard, Chairperson, 217-581-2016, Fax: 217-581-2722, E-mail: gjrichard@eiu.edu. *Application contact:* Dr. Tina Veale, Coordinator, 217-581-2712, Fax: 217-581-7105, E-mail: tkveale@eiu.edu.

Eastern Kentucky University, The Graduate School, College of Education, Department of Special Education, Program in Communication Disorders, Richmond, KY 40475-3102. Offers MA Ed. *Accreditation:* ASHA. *Students:* 33 full-time (all women); includes 1 minority (African American) Average age 25. 51 applicants, 51% accepted, 18 enrolled. *Entrance requirements:* For master's, GRE General Test, minimum GPA of 2.5. Application fee: $30. *Expenses:* Tuition, state resident: full-time $5,610. Tuition, nonresident: full-time $15,910. *Faculty research:* Distance learning, fluency, phonemic awareness, technology, autism. *Application contact:* Dr. Julie Bolling, Coordinator, 859-622-1861, Fax: 859-622-4443, E-mail: julie.bolling@eku.edu.

Eastern Michigan University, Graduate School, College of Education, Department of Special Education, Program in Speech and Language Pathology, Ypsilanti, MI 48197. Offers MA. *Accreditation:* ASHA. Part-time and evening/weekend programs available. Postbaccalaureate distance learning degree programs offered (minimal on-campus study). *Students:* 55 full-time (53 women), 40 part-time (36 women); includes 5 minority (3 African Americans, 2 Hispanic Americans), 3 international. Average age 28. In 2006, 29 degrees awarded. *Entrance requirements:* For master's, GRE General Test. Additional exam requirements/recommendations for international students: Required—TOEFL. *Application deadline:* For fall admission, 5/15 priority date for domestic students, 5/1 priority date for international students; for winter admission, 10/15 priority date for domestic students, 10/1 priority date for international students; for spring admission, 3/15 priority date for domestic students, 3/1 priority date for international students. Applications are processed on a rolling basis. Application fee: $35. *Expenses:* Tuition, state resident: part-time $341 per credit hour. Tuition, nonresident: full-time $16,104; part-time $671 per credit hour. Required fees: $816; $34 per credit hour. $40 per term. One-time fee: $82 full-time. Tuition and fees vary according to course level, course load, degree level and reciprocity agreements. *Financial support:* Fellowships, research assistantships with full tuition reimbursements, teaching assistantships with full tuition reimbursements, career-related internships or fieldwork, Federal Work-Study, institutionally sponsored loans, scholarships/grants, tuition waivers (partial), and unspecified assistantships available. Support available to part-time students. Financial award applicants required to submit FAFSA.

Eastern New Mexico University, Graduate School, College of Liberal Arts and Sciences, Department of Health and Human Services, Portales, NM 88130. Offers speech pathology and audiology (MS). *Accreditation:* ASHA. Part-time programs available. Postbaccalaureate distance learning degree programs offered (minimal on-campus study). *Faculty:* 4 full-time (3 women). *Students:* 9 full-time (7 women), 34 part-time (32 women); includes 18 minority (1 African American, 1 American Indian/Alaska Native, 2 Asian Americans or Pacific Islanders, 14 Hispanic Americans). Average age 43. 29 applicants, 93% accepted. In 2006, 7 degrees awarded. *Degree requirements:* For master's, thesis optional. *Entrance requirements:* For master's, minimum GPA of 2.5. *Application deadline:* For fall admission, 8/20 priority date for domestic students. Applications are processed on a rolling basis. Application fee: $0. Electronic applications accepted. *Expenses:* Tuition, state resident: full-time $2,478; part-time $103 per credit hour. Tuition, nonresident: full-time $8,034; part-time $335 per credit hour. Required fees: $35 per credit hour. *Financial support:* In 2006–07, 12 research assistantships (averaging $8,200 per year) were awarded; fellowships, teaching assistantships, Federal Work-Study also available. Support available to part-time students. Financial award application deadline: 3/1. *Unit head:* Dr. Linda Weems, Graduate Coordinator, 505-562-2700, E-mail: linda.weems@enmu.edu.

Eastern Washington University, Graduate Studies, College of Science, Mathematics and Technology, Department of Communication Disorders, Cheney, WA 99004-2431. Offers MS.

Accreditation: ASHA. *Degree requirements:* For master's, thesis or alternative, comprehensive exam. *Entrance requirements:* For master's, GRE General Test, minimum GPA of 3.0.

East Stroudsburg University of Pennsylvania, Graduate School, School of Health Sciences and Human Performance, Department of Speech Pathology and Audiology, East Stroudsburg, PA 18301-2999. Offers MS. *Accreditation:* ASHA. Part-time and evening/weekend programs available. *Faculty:* 4 full-time (3 women), 2 part-time/adjunct (both women). *Students:* 30 full-time (all women), 13 part-time (all women); includes 5 minority (1 African American, 1 American Indian/Alaska Native, 3 Hispanic Americans). Average age 29. In 2006, 11 degrees awarded. *Degree requirements:* For master's, comprehensive exam. *Entrance requirements:* For master's, GRE General Test, minimum GPA of 2.8, undergraduate background in speech pathology. Additional exam requirements/recommendations for international students: Required—TOEFL (minimum score 560 paper-based; 220 computer-based; 83 iBT). *Application deadline:* For fall admission, 2/1 priority date for domestic and international students; for spring admission, 2/1 for domestic and international students. Applications are processed on a rolling basis. Application fee: $50. *Expenses:* Tuition, state resident: full-time $6,048; part-time $336 per credit. Tuition, nonresident: full-time $9,678; part-time $538 per credit. Required fees: $1,353; $67 per credit. One-time fee: $37 part-time. *Financial support:* In 2006–07, 13 research assistantships with full and partial tuition reimbursements were awarded; Federal Work-Study and institutionally sponsored loans also available. Financial award application deadline: 3/1; financial award applicants required to submit FAFSA. *Faculty research:* Computer-assisted classroom instruction. *Unit head:* Dr. Jane Page, Graduate Coordinator, 570-422-3247, Fax: 570-422-3506, E-mail: jpage@po-box.esu.edu.

East Tennessee State University, School of Graduate Studies, College of Public and Allied Health, Department of Communicative Disorders, Johnson City, TN 37614. Offers audiology (MS, Au D); communicative disorders (MS); special education audiology pre-K-12 (MS); special education speech pathology pre-K-12 (MS); speech pathology (MS). *Accreditation:* ASHA (one or more programs are accredited). Part-time and evening/weekend programs available. *Degree requirements:* For master's, thesis or alternative, comprehensive exam. *Entrance requirements:* For master's, GRE General Test, minimum GPA of 3.0; for doctorate, GRE. Additional exam requirements/recommendations for international students: Required—TOEFL (minimum score 550 paper-based; 213 computer-based). *Faculty research:* Treatment efficacy, hearing aid trials, language development of cleft palate children, phonological processes, neurogenic disorders.

Edinboro University of Pennsylvania, Graduate Studies and Research, School of Liberal Arts, Department of Speech, Language and Hearing, Edinboro, PA 16444. Offers speech language pathology (MA). *Accreditation:* ASHA. Part-time and evening/weekend programs available. *Faculty:* 3 full-time (2 women). *Students:* 43 full-time (40 women); includes 2 minority (1 African American, 1 Hispanic American), 6 international. Average age 26. In 2006, 21 degrees awarded. *Degree requirements:* For master's, thesis or alternative, competency exam. *Entrance requirements:* For master's, GRE or MAT, minimum QPA of 2.5. *Application deadline:* Applications are processed on a rolling basis. Application fee: $30. Electronic applications accepted. *Expenses:* Tuition, state resident: full-time $6,048; part-time $336 per credit. Tuition, nonresident: full-time $9,678; part-time $538 per credit. Required fees: $1,849; $42 per credit. *Financial support:* In 2006–07, 13 research assistantships with full and partial tuition reimbursements (averaging $3,850 per year) were awarded; career-related internships or fieldwork, Federal Work-Study, scholarships/grants, and unspecified assistantships also available. Support available to part-time students. Financial award application deadline: 2/15; financial award applicants required to submit FAFSA. *Unit head:* Dr. Charlotte Molrine, Coordinator, 814-732-2432, Fax: 814-732-2629, E-mail: cmolrine@edinboro.edu. *Application contact:* Dr. R. Scott Baldwin, Dean, 814-732-2752, Fax: 814-732-2268, E-mail: sbaldwin@edinboro.edu.

Elms College, Program in Communication Sciences and Disorders, Chicopee, MA 01013-2839. Offers CAGS. Part-time programs available. *Faculty:* 1 (woman) full-time, 5 part-time/adjunct (3 women). *Students:* Average age 35. 4 applicants, 100% accepted, 3 enrolled. In 2006, 2 degrees awarded. *Entrance requirements:* For degree, minimum GPA of 3.0. *Application deadline:* For fall admission, 7/1 priority date for domestic students; for spring admission, 11/1 priority date for domestic students. Application fee: $30. *Expenses:* Tuition: Full-time $9,180; part-time $510 per credit. Tuition and fees vary according to course load. *Financial support:* Application deadline: 4/15. *Unit head:* Dr. Kathryn James, Chair-CSD Department, 413-265-2253, E-mail: jamesk@elms.edu.

Emerson College, Graduate Studies, School of Communication, Department of Communication Sciences and Disorders, Program in Communication Sciences and Disorders, Boston, MA 02116-4624. Offers speech-language pathology (MS). *Accreditation:* ASHA. *Degree requirements:* For master's, thesis or alternative, comprehensive exam. *Entrance requirements:* For master's, GRE General Test. Additional exam requirements/recommendations for international students: Required—TOEFL. Electronic applications accepted.

See Close-Up on page 1703.

Florida Atlantic University, College of Education, Department of Communication Disorders, Boca Raton, FL 33431-0991. Offers speech-language pathology (MS). *Accreditation:* ASHA. *Faculty:* 5 full-time (3 women), 5 part-time/adjunct (3 women). *Students:* 32 full-time (31 women), 2 part-time (both women); includes 5 minority (2 African Americans, 3 Hispanic Americans). Average age 28. 84 applicants, 58% accepted, 17 enrolled. In 2006, 19 degrees awarded. *Degree requirements:* For master's, thesis optional. *Entrance requirements:* For master's, GRE General Test, minimum undergraduate GPA of 3.0 in last 60 hours of course work or minimum graduate GPA of 3.5. *Application deadline:* For fall admission, 4/1 for domestic students. Application fee: $30. *Expenses:* Tuition, area resident: Full-time $4,394. Tuition, nonresident: full-time $16,441. *Financial support:* Career-related internships or fieldwork available. *Faculty research:* Fluency disorders, auditory processing, child language, adult language and cognition, multicultural speech and language issues. *Unit head:* Dr. Deena Wener, Coordinator, 561-297-2258, Fax: 561-297-2268, E-mail: wener@fau.edu.

Florida International University, College of Nursing and Health Sciences, Department of Communication Sciences and Disorders, Miami, FL 33199. Offers MS. *Accreditation:* ASHA. *Faculty:* 2 full-time (1 woman). *Students:* 53 full-time (52 women), 8 part-time (all women); includes 42 minority (2 African Americans, 40 Hispanic Americans). 59 applicants, 78% accepted, 21 enrolled. In 2006, 19 degrees awarded. *Degree requirements:* For master's, thesis optional. *Entrance requirements:* For master's, GRE General Test. Additional exam requirements/recommendations for international students: Required—TOEFL. Application fee: $25. *Expenses:* Tuition, state resident: part-time $249 per credit hour. Tuition, nonresident: part-time $753 per credit hour. Tuition and fees vary according to program. *Unit head:* Dr. Noma Anderson, Chairperson, 305-348-2873, Fax: 305-348-2740, E-mail: noma.anderson@fiu.edu.

Florida State University, Graduate Studies, College of Communication, Department of Communication Disorders, Tallahassee, FL 32306. Offers communication sciences and disorders (Adv M, MS, PhD). *Accreditation:* ASHA (one or more programs are accredited). Part-time programs available. Postbaccalaureate distance learning degree programs offered (minimal on-campus study). *Faculty:* 17 full-time (14 women), 7 part-time/adjunct (all women). *Students:* 94 full-time (88 women), 2 part-time (both women); includes 25 minority (13 African Americans, 6 Asian Americans or Pacific Islanders, 6 Hispanic Americans). Average age 27. 141 applicants, 46% accepted, 32 enrolled. In 2006, 30 master's, 4 doctorates awarded. *Degree requirements:* For master's, thesis optional; for doctorate, thesis/dissertation. *Entrance requirements:* For master's, GRE General Test, minimum GPA of 3.0; for doctorate, GRE General Test, minimum GPA of 3.0 (undergraduate), 3.5 (graduate). Additional exam requirements/recommendations for international students: Required—TOEFL (minimum score 550 paper-based; 213 computer-based; 80 iBT). *Application deadline:* For fall admission, 2/1 for domestic and international students. Application fee: $30. *Expenses:* Tuition, state resident: full-time $5,822; part-time $243 per credit hour. Tuition, nonresident: full-time $20,976; part-time $874 per credit hour. Tuition and fees vary according to program. *Financial support:* In 2006–07, 52 students received support, including 1 fellowship with full tuition reimbursement available (averaging $16,500 per year), 21 research assistantships with full and partial tuition reimbursements available (averaging $12,750 per year), 16 teaching assistantships with full and partial tuition reimbursements available (averaging $8,100 per year); career-related internships or fieldwork, Federal Work-Study, institutionally sponsored loans, scholarships/grants, tuition waivers (partial), and unspecified assistantships also available. Financial award applicants required to submit FAFSA. *Faculty research:* Autism, neurogenic disorders, early intervention, child language disorders, augmentative communication. Total annual research expenditures: $2.3 million. *Unit head:* Dr. Howard Goldstein, Chairperson, 850-644-6264, Fax: 850-644-8994, E-mail: howard.goldstein@comm.fsu.edu. *Application contact:* Erica A. Lee, Academic Coordinator, 850-644-2253, Fax: 850-644-8994, E-mail: dcd.information@comm.fsu.edu.

Fontbonne University, Graduate Programs, Department of Communication Disorders and Deaf Education, Studies in Early Intervention in Deaf Education, St. Louis, MO 63105-3098. Offers MA. *Faculty:* 3 full-time (all women), 1 (woman) part-time/adjunct. *Students:* 8 full-time (all women), 2 part-time (both women); includes 1 minority (American Indian/Alaska Native). Average age 26. 30 applicants, 33% accepted. In 2006, 11 degrees awarded. *Entrance requirements:* For master's, minimum GPA of 3.0. *Application deadline:* For fall admission, 2/1 for domestic students. Application fee: $25. *Expenses:* Tuition: Full-time $4,890; part-time $489 per credit. Required fees: $160; $76 per credit. Full-time tuition and fees vary according to course load and program. *Financial support:* Application deadline: 4/1; *Unit head:* Dr. Gale Rice, Chair, 314-889-1407, Fax: 314-719-8016, E-mail: grice@fontbonne.edu. *Application contact:* Dr. Susan Lenihan, Director, 314-889-1461, Fax: 314-719-8016, E-mail: slenihan@fontbonne.edu.

Fontbonne University, Graduate Programs, Department of Communication Disorders and Deaf Education, Studies in Speech-Language Pathology, St. Louis, MO 63105-3098. Offers MS. *Faculty:* 6 full-time (5 women), 4 part-time/adjunct (all women). *Students:* 29 full-time (all women), 25 part-time (24 women); includes 2 minority (both African Americans) Average age 27. 70 applicants, 57% accepted. In 2006, 18 degrees awarded. *Entrance requirements:* For master's, minimum GPA of 3.0. *Application deadline:* For fall admission, 2/1 for domestic students. Application fee: $25. *Expenses:* Tuition: Full-time $4,890; part-time $489 per credit. Required fees: $160; $76 per credit. Full-time tuition and fees vary according to course load and program. *Financial support:* Application deadline: 4/1; *Unit head:* Dr. Gale Rice, Chair, 314-889-1407, Fax: 314-719-8016, E-mail: grice@fontbonne.edu. *Application contact:* Dr. Lynne Shields, Director, 314-889-1464, Fax: 314-719-8016, E-mail: lshields@fontbonne.edu.

Fort Hays State University, Graduate School, College of Health and Life Sciences, Department of Communication Disorders, Hays, KS 67601-4099. Offers speech-language pathology (MS). *Accreditation:* ASHA. Part-time programs available. *Faculty:* 4 full-time (2 women). *Students:* 31 full-time (30 women). Average age 28. 25 applicants, 44% accepted. In 2006, 10 degrees awarded. *Degree requirements:* For master's, thesis optional. *Entrance requirements:* For master's, GRE General Test. Additional exam requirements/recommendations for international students: Required—TOEFL (minimum score 550 paper-based; 213 computer-based). *Application deadline:* For fall admission, 3/1 priority date for domestic students. Applications are processed on a rolling basis. Application fee: $35. Electronic applications accepted. *Financial support:* In 2006–07, 3 teaching assistantships (averaging $5,000 per year) were awarded; research assistantships. *Faculty research:* Aural rehabilitation, phonological and articulation skills, middle ear diseases, output capability of stereo cassette units, language development. *Unit head:* Dr. Amy Finch, Chair, 785-628-4496.

Gallaudet University, The Graduate School, School of Communication, Department of Audiology and Speech Language Pathology, Washington, DC 20002-3625. Offers audiology (Au D); speech and language pathology (MS). *Accreditation:* ASHA (one or more programs are accredited). *Degree requirements:* For master's, thesis optional; for doctorate, thesis/dissertation. *Entrance requirements:* For master's, GRE General Test or MAT; for doctorate, GRE General Test or MAT, interview. *Faculty research:* Aural rehabilitation, speech production.

The George Washington University, Columbian College of Arts and Sciences, Department of Speech and Hearing, Washington, DC 20052. Offers speech pathology (MA). *Accreditation:* ASHA. *Degree requirements:* For master's, thesis or alternative, comprehensive exam. *Entrance requirements:* For master's, GRE General Test, interview, minimum GPA of 3.0. Additional exam requirements/recommendations for international students: Required—TOEFL (minimum score 550 paper-based; 213 computer-based). Electronic applications accepted.

Georgia State University, College of Education, Department of Educational Psychology and Special Education, Program in Communication Disorders, Atlanta, GA 30303-3083. Offers M Ed. *Accreditation:* ASHA; NCATE. *Students:* 46 full-time (44 women), 1 (woman) part-time; includes 5 minority (2 African Americans, 3 Asian Americans or Pacific Islanders), 1 international. Average age 26. 57 applicants, 32% accepted. In 2006, 19 degrees awarded. *Degree requirements:* For master's, comprehensive exam. *Entrance requirements:* For master's, GRE General Test, minimum GPA of 2.5. *Application deadline:* For fall admission, 2/15 for domestic students. Application fee: $25. *Financial support:* Research assistantships available. *Faculty research:* Language development, minority students, adult language disorders. *Unit head:* Dr. Ron P. Colarusso, Dean, College of Education, 404-651-2310.

Governors State University, College of Health Professions, Program in Communication Disorders, University Park, IL 60466-0975. Offers MHS. *Accreditation:* ASHA. Part-time and evening/weekend programs available. *Students:* 14 full-time, 90 part-time. Average age 29. *Degree requirements:* For master's, thesis or alternative, practicum, comprehensive exam. *Entrance requirements:* For master's, minimum GPA of 3.3. *Application deadline:* For fall admission, 3/1 priority date for domestic students. Applications are processed on a rolling basis. Application fee: $25. *Expenses:* Tuition, state resident: full-time $4,104; part-time $171 per hour. Tuition, nonresident: part-time $513 per hour. *Financial support:* Research assistantships, career-related internships or fieldwork, Federal Work-Study, institutionally sponsored loans, scholarships/grants, and tuition waivers (full and partial) available. Support available to part-time students. Financial award application deadline: 5/1. *Faculty research:* Speech perception of hearing-impaired, effects of binaural listening, communication assessment of infants, voice characteristics of head-neck cancer patients. *Unit head:* Dr. Sandra A. Mayfield, Coordinator, 708-534-4590, Fax: 708-235-2195, E-mail: s-mayfield@govst.edu.

Graduate School and University Center of the City University of New York, Graduate Studies, Program in Speech and Hearing Sciences, New York, NY 10016-4039. Offers PhD. *Faculty:* 19 full-time (3 women). *Students:* 52 full-time (47 women), 3 part-time (all women); includes 8 minority (1 African American, 3 Asian Americans or Pacific Islanders, 4 Hispanic Americans), 12 international. Average age 37. 14 applicants, 79% accepted, 7 enrolled. In 2006, 2 degrees awarded. *Degree requirements:* For doctorate, one foreign language, thesis/dissertation. *Entrance requirements:* For doctorate, GRE General Test. Additional exam requirements/recommendations for international students: Required—TOEFL. *Application deadline:* For fall admission, 3/1 for domestic students; for spring admission, 11/15 for domestic students. Application fee: $125. Electronic applications accepted. *Financial support:* In 2006–07, 24 fellowships, 1 teaching assistantship were awarded; research assistantships, career-related internships or fieldwork, Federal Work-Study, institutionally sponsored loans, and tuition waivers (full and partial) also available. Financial award application deadline: 2/1; financial award applicants required to submit FAFSA. *Unit head:* Dr. Martin Gitterman, Executive Officer, 212-817-8802, Fax: 212-817-1537.

Hampton University, Graduate College, Program in Communicative Sciences and Disorders, Hampton, VA 23668. Offers MA. *Accreditation:* ASHA. Part-time and evening/weekend programs available. *Entrance requirements:* For master's, GRE General Test. *Faculty research:* Language development, language pathology.

Communication Disorders

Hampton University (continued)

Announcement: The program in communicative sciences and disorders offers graduate training in the specialization of speech-language pathology. Accredited by the American Speech-Language-Hearing Association, the program prepares students to provide speech and language services to children and adults with a variety of communication disorders. Students receive the opportunity for diverse clinical experience in hospital, clinical, and school settings.

Harvard University, Harvard Medical School and Graduate School of Arts and Sciences, Division of Health Sciences and Technology, Speech and Hearing Bioscience and Technology Program, Cambridge, MA 02138. Offers PhD, Sc D. Degrees are offered jointly with Massachusetts Institute of Technology. *Faculty:* 61 full-time (14 women). *Students:* 49 full-time (19 women); includes 13 minority (1 African American, 11 Asian Americans or Pacific Islanders, 1 Hispanic American), 9 international. Average age 28. 21 applicants, 33% accepted, 5 enrolled. In 2006, 12 degrees awarded. *Degree requirements:* For doctorate, thesis/dissertation. *Entrance requirements:* For doctorate, bachelor's degree in engineering or science, previous coursework in differential equations. Additional exam requirements/recommendations for international students: Required—TOEFL. *Application deadline:* For fall admission, 12/15 for domestic and international students. Application fee: $70. Electronic applications accepted. *Expenses: Contact institution.* Full-time tuition and fees vary according to program and student level. *Financial support:* In 2006–07, 35 fellowships with full and partial tuition reimbursements (averaging $50,760 per year), 11 research assistantships with full and partial tuition reimbursements (averaging $43,822 per year), 8 teaching assistantships with full and partial tuition reimbursements (averaging $15,653 per year) were awarded; institutionally sponsored loans, scholarships/grants, traineeships, and unspecified assistantships also available. Financial award application deadline: 1/15. *Faculty research:* Neuroscience audition, physiology, hearing science psychoacoustics, speech communications. *Unit head:* Dr. Louis D. Braida, Director, 617-253-2575, E-mail: braida@mit.edu. *Application contact:* Dr. M. Christian Brown, Co-Chair, Admissions Committee, 617-573-3825, Fax: 617-720-4408, E-mail: mcb@epl.meei.harvard.edu.

See Close-Up on page 1705.

Hofstra University, College of Liberal Arts and Sciences, Department of Speech Language-Hearing Sciences, Hempstead, NY 11549. Offers audiology (MA, Au D); speech-language pathology (MA). *Accreditation:* ASHA (one or more programs are accredited). Part-time programs available. *Faculty:* 7 full-time (4 women), 7 part-time/adjunct (6 women). *Students:* 62 full-time (60 women), 19 part-time (all women); includes 9 minority (2 African Americans, 2 Asian Americans or Pacific Islanders, 5 Hispanic Americans). Average age 26. 209 applicants, 53% accepted, 37 enrolled. In 2006, 37 degrees awarded. Terminal master's awarded for partial completion of doctoral program. *Degree requirements:* For master's, thesis optional; for doctorate, thesis/dissertation, comprehensive exam, registration. *Entrance requirements:* For master's, GRE, 3 letters of recommendation; for doctorate, GRE or master's degree, 3 letters of recommendation. Additional exam requirements/recommendations for international students: Required—TOEFL (minimum score 550 paper-based; 213 computer-based). *Application deadline:* For fall admission, 1/15 priority date for domestic and international students. Application fee: $60. Electronic applications accepted. *Expenses:* Tuition: Full-time $13,320; part-time $740 per credit. Required fees: $930; $155 per term. *Financial support:* In 2006–07, 37 students received support, including 16 fellowships with tuition reimbursements available (averaging $3,870 per year), 2 research assistantships with full and partial tuition reimbursements available (averaging $4,421 per year); career-related internships or fieldwork, Federal Work-Study, scholarships/grants, tuition waivers (full and partial), and unspecified assistantships also available. Financial award applicants required to submit FAFSA. *Faculty research:* Accoustic measures of normal and abnormal voice production, aural rehabilitation of adult speakers with hearing loss, language development in children adopted from foreign countries, efficacy of specific treatment strategies in individuals with aphasia, grammatical markers in second language learners. *Unit head:* Dr. Ronald L. Bloom, Chairperson, 516-463-5308, Fax: 516-463-5260, E-mail: sphrlb@hofstra.edu. *Application contact:* Carol Drummer, Dean of Graduate Admissions, 516-463-4876, Fax: 516-463-4664, E-mail: gradstudent@hofstra.edu.

Howard University, School of Communications, Department of Communication Sciences and Disorders, Washington, DC 20059-0002. Offers communication sciences (PhD); speech pathology (MS). Offered through the Graduate School of Arts and Sciences. *Accreditation:* ASHA (one or more programs are accredited). Part-time programs available. *Degree requirements:* For master's, thesis or alternative, comprehensive exam; for doctorate, one foreign language, thesis/dissertation, comprehensive exam. *Entrance requirements:* For master's, GRE General Test, minimum GPA of 3.2; for doctorate, GRE General Test, minimum GPA of 3.5. Additional exam requirements/recommendations for international students: Required—TOEFL. Electronic applications accepted. *Faculty research:* Multiculturalism, augmentative communication, adult neurological disorders, child language disorders.

Hunter College of the City University of New York, Graduate School, Schools of the Health Professions, Communication Sciences Program, New York, NY 10021-5085. Offers audiology (MS); speech language pathology (MS); teacher of speech and hearing handicapped (MS). *Accreditation:* ASHA. Part-time programs available. *Faculty:* 14 full-time (13 women), 3 part-time/adjunct (2 women). *Students:* 49 full-time (47 women), 2 part-time (1 woman); includes 5 minority (3 African Americans, 2 Hispanic Americans). Average age 28. 360 applicants, 28% accepted, 45 enrolled. In 2006, 46 degrees awarded. *Degree requirements:* For master's, National Teacher Exam, research project. *Entrance requirements:* For master's, GRE, letters of reference. Additional exam requirements/recommendations for international students: Required—TOEFL. *Application deadline:* For fall admission, 4/1 for domestic students, 2/1 for international students; for spring admission, 11/1 for domestic students, 9/1 for international students. Application fee: $125. *Expenses:* Tuition, state resident: part-time $270 per credit. Tuition, nonresident: part-time $500 per credit. Required fees: $45 per semester. *Financial support:* In 2006–07, 12 students received support, including 3 fellowships with partial tuition reimbursements available (averaging $1,000 per year), 6 research assistantships; career-related internships or fieldwork, Federal Work-Study, institutionally sponsored loans, scholarships/grants, and tuition waivers (full and partial) also available. Support available to part-time students. Financial award application deadline: 3/1. *Faculty research:* Aging and communication disorders, fluency, speech science, diagnostic audiology, amplification. Total annual research expenditures: $600,000. *Unit head:* Dr. Dava Waltzman, Director, 212-481-4339, Fax: 212-481-4467, E-mail: dwaltzma@hejira.hunter.cuny.edu. *Application contact:* William Zlata, Director for Graduate Admissions, 212-772-4482, Fax: 212-650-3336, E-mail: admissions@hunter.cuny.edu.

Idaho State University, Office of Graduate Studies, Kasiska College of Health Professions, Department of Communication Sciences and Disorders and Education of the Deaf, Pocatello, ID 83209. Offers audiology (MS, Au D); deaf education (MS); speech language pathology (MS). *Accreditation:* ASHA (one or more programs are accredited). Part-time programs available. Postbaccalaureate distance learning degree programs offered (minimal on-campus study). *Faculty:* 5 full-time (1 woman), 1 (woman) part-time/adjunct. *Students:* 95 full-time (72 women), 16 part-time (13 women); includes 5 minority (4 Asian Americans or Pacific Islanders, 1 Hispanic American), 1 international. Average age 35. In 2006, 35 degrees awarded. *Degree requirements:* For master's and doctorate, externship, thesis optional. *Entrance requirements:* For master's, GRE General Test, minimum GPA of 3.0, 3 letters of recommendation; for doctorate, GRE General Test, minimum GPA of 3.0, 3 letters or recommendation. Additional exam requirements/recommendations for international students: Required—TOEFL (minimum score 600 paper-based; 250 computer-based). *Application deadline:* For fall admission, 7/1 for domestic students, 6/1 for international students; for spring admission, 12/1 for domestic students, 11/1 for international students. Applications are processed on a rolling basis. Application fee: $55. *Financial support:* In 2006–07, 5 teaching assistantships with full and partial tuition reimbursements (averaging $8,694 per year) were awarded; career-related internships or fieldwork, Federal Work-Study, institutionally sponsored loans, scholarships/grants, and unspecified assistantships also available. Financial award application deadline: 1/1. *Faculty research:* Clinical efficacy, voice disorders, closed head injury, phonology, assistive technology. Total annual research expenditures: $497,331. *Unit head:* Joni Loftin, Chairman, 208-282-4196, Fax: 208-282-4571, E-mail: loftjoni@isu.edu. *Application contact:* Ellen Combs, Graduate School Technical Records Specialist, 208-282-2150, Fax: 208-282-4847.

Illinois State University, Graduate School, College of Arts and Sciences, Department of Speech Pathology and Audiology, Normal, IL 61790-2200. Offers MA, MS. *Accreditation:* ASHA. *Faculty:* 7 full-time (6 women). *Students:* 72 full-time (71 women), 22 part-time (all women); includes 6 minority (1 African American, 1 Asian American or Pacific Islander, 4 Hispanic Americans), 1 international. 160 applicants, 39% accepted. In 2006, 36 degrees awarded. *Degree requirements:* For master's, thesis or alternative, 1 term of residency, 2 practica. *Entrance requirements:* For master's, GRE General Test, minimum GPA of 3.0 in last 60 hours. *Application deadline:* Applications are processed on a rolling basis. Application fee: $40. *Expenses:* Tuition, state resident: full-time $3,330; part-time $185 per credit hour. Tuition, nonresident: full-time $6,948; part-time $438 per credit hour. Required fees: $1,259; $52 per credit hour. *Financial support:* In 2006–07, 39 research assistantships (averaging $4,851 per year) were awarded; tuition waivers (full) and unspecified assistantships also available. Financial award application deadline: 4/1. *Unit head:* Dr. Walter Smoski, Chairperson, 309-438-8643.

Indiana State University, School of Graduate Studies, College of Education, Department of Communication Disorders, Terre Haute, IN 47809-1401. Offers speech-language pathology (MA, MS). *Accreditation:* ASHA. Part-time and evening/weekend programs available. *Faculty:* 2 full-time (1 woman), 2 part-time/adjunct (1 woman). *Students:* 25 full-time (23 women), 8 part-time (7 women). Average age 28. 42 applicants, 31% accepted, 12 enrolled. In 2006, 20 degrees awarded. *Degree requirements:* For master's, thesis (for some programs). *Entrance requirements:* For master's, GRE General Test, minimum undergraduate GPA of 2.5. Additional exam requirements/recommendations for international students: Required—TOEFL (minimum score 550 paper-based). *Application deadline:* For fall admission, 7/1 priority date for domestic students; for spring admission, 11/1 priority date for domestic students. Applications are processed on a rolling basis. Application fee: $35. Electronic applications accepted. *Expenses:* Tuition, state resident: part-time $278 per credit. Tuition, nonresident: part-time $552 per credit. *Financial support:* In 2006–07, 6 research assistantships with partial tuition reimbursements (averaging $6,300 per year) were awarded; fellowships, teaching assistantships, institutionally sponsored loans and tuition waivers (partial) also available. Support available to part-time students. Financial award application deadline: 3/1; financial award applicants required to submit FAFSA. *Faculty research:* Vocational/transitional programs, social adjustment, consultation with regular education, microcomputers, stuttering. *Unit head:* Dr. Mark Stimley, Program Director, 812-237-2800.

Indiana University Bloomington, Graduate School, College of Arts and Sciences, Department of Speech and Hearing Sciences, Bloomington, IN 47405-7000. Offers audiology (Au D); auditory sciences (PhD); language sciences (PhD); speech and voice sciences (PhD); speech-language pathology (MA). PhD offered through the University Graduate School. *Accreditation:* ASHA (one or more programs are accredited). *Faculty:* 13 full-time (7 women). *Students:* 94 full-time (89 women), 21 part-time (18 women); includes 3 minority (all Hispanic Americans), 12 international. Average age 26. In 2006, 26 master's, 2 doctorates awarded. Terminal master's awarded for partial completion of doctoral program. *Degree requirements:* For master's, variable foreign language requirement, thesis optional; for doctorate, one foreign language, thesis/dissertation. *Entrance requirements:* For master's and doctorate, GRE General Test. Additional exam requirements/recommendations for international students: Required—TOEFL. *Application deadline:* For fall admission, 1/15 priority date for domestic students, 12/15 for international students; for spring admission, 9/1 priority date for domestic students, 9/1 for international students. Applications are processed on a rolling basis. Application fee: $50 ($60 for international students). Electronic applications accepted. *Expenses:* Tuition, state resident: full-time $5,791; part-time $241 per credit hour. Tuition, nonresident: full-time $16,866; part-time $703 per credit hour. *Financial support:* Fellowships with full tuition reimbursements, research assistantships with full tuition reimbursements, teaching assistantships with full tuition reimbursements, Federal Work-Study and institutionally sponsored loans available. Financial award application deadline: 2/1. *Faculty research:* Speech training, deafness, voice supervision, linguistic analysis, speech reading. *Unit head:* Karen Forrest, Chairperson, 812-855-4156. *Application contact:* Kimberly Elkins, Graduate Secretary, 812-855-4202.

Indiana University of Pennsylvania, School of Graduate Studies and Research, College of Education and Educational Technology, Department of Special Education and Clinical Services, Program in Speech-Language Pathology, Indiana, PA 15705-1087. Offers MS. *Accreditation:* ASHA. *Students:* 34 full-time (33 women); includes 1 minority (African American), 1 international. Average age 23. 71 applicants, 24% accepted. In 2006, 15 degrees awarded. *Degree requirements:* For master's, thesis optional. *Entrance requirements:* For master's, 2 letters of recommendation. Additional exam requirements/recommendations for international students: Required—TOEFL. *Application deadline:* For fall admission, 7/1 priority date for domestic students; for spring admission, 11/1 for domestic students. Applications are processed on a rolling basis. Application fee: $30. *Expenses:* Tuition, state resident: full-time $6,048; part-time $336 per credit. Tuition, nonresident: full-time $9,678; part-time $538 per credit. Required fees: $1,069; $148 per year. *Financial support:* In 2006–07, 7 research assistantships with full and partial tuition reimbursements (averaging $2,495 per year) were awarded; career-related internships or fieldwork and Federal Work-Study also available. Support available to part-time students. Financial award application deadline: 3/15; financial award applicants required to submit FAFSA. *Unit head:* Dr. David Stein, Graduate Coordinator, 724-357-2454, E-mail: dwstein@iup.edu.

Ithaca College, Graduate Studies, School of Health Sciences and Human Performance, Program in Speech-Language and Pathology, Ithaca, NY 14850-7020. Offers speech pathology (MS); teacher of the speech and hearing handicapped (MS). *Accreditation:* ASHA. *Faculty:* 11 full-time (6 women). *Students:* 44 full-time (all women), 3 part-time (all women); includes 2 minority (1 African American, 1 Asian American or Pacific Islander), 3 international. Average age 25. 80 applicants, 24% accepted, 16 enrolled. In 2006, 11 master's awarded. *Degree requirements:* For master's, thesis optional. *Entrance requirements:* For master's, GRE General Test, minimum GPA of 3.0. Additional exam requirements/recommendations for international students: Required—TOEFL (minimum score 550 paper-based; 213 computer-based). *Application deadline:* For fall admission, 2/1 priority date for domestic students; for spring admission, 12/1 for domestic students. Applications are processed on a rolling basis. Application fee: $40. *Financial support:* In 2006–07, 42 students received support, including 18 teaching assistantships (averaging $9,910 per year); career-related internships or fieldwork, Federal Work-Study, institutionally sponsored loans, scholarships/grants, and unspecified assistantships also available. Support available to part-time students. Financial award application deadline: 2/1; financial award applicants required to submit FAFSA. *Faculty research:* Fluency, multi-disciplinary issues, computer applications, child language, speech reception and noise. *Unit head:* Dr. E. Testut, Chairperson, 607-274-3727.

Jackson State University, Graduate School, College of Public Service, Department of Communicative Disorders, Jackson, MS 39217. Offers MS. *Accreditation:* ASHA. *Students:* 10 full-time (all women); includes 6 minority (all African Americans) *Degree requirements:* For master's, comprehensive exam. *Entrance requirements:* For master's, GRE General Test. Additional exam requirements/recommendations for international students: Required—TOEFL. *Application deadline:* For fall admission, 3/1 for domestic students; for spring admission, 10/1 for domestic students. Application fee: $20. *Financial support:* In 2006–07, 5 students received support. Career-related internships or fieldwork, Federal Work-Study, scholarships/grants, tuition waivers (full), and unspecified assistantships available. Support available to part-time students. Financial award application deadline: 3/1; financial award applicants required to submit FAFSA. *Unit head:* Dr. Zenobia Bagli, Chair, 601-432-6717, Fax: 601-432-6844, E-mail: zbagli@ccaix.jsums.edu. *Application contact:* Curtis Gore, Director of Graduate Admissions, 601-979-2455, Fax: 601-974-4325, E-mail: cgore@ccaix.jsums.edu.

James Madison University, College of Graduate and Outreach Programs, College of Integrated Science and Technology, Department of Communication Sciences and Disorders, Program in Audiology, Harrisonburg, VA 22807. Offers Au D. *Accreditation:* ASHA. Part-time programs available. *Students:* 28 full-time (26 women). Average age 27. *Entrance requirements:* For doctorate, 3 letters of recommendation, interview. *Application deadline:* For fall admission, 2/1 for domestic students; for spring admission, 9/1 for domestic students. Application fee: $55. *Expenses:* Tuition, state resident: full-time $6,336; part-time $264 per credit hour. Tuition, nonresident: full-time $17,832; part-time $743 per credit hour. *Financial support:* In 2006–07, 19 students received support, including 1 teaching assistantship with full tuition reimbursement available (averaging $8,167 per year); unspecified assistantships also available. Financial award application deadline: 3/1.

James Madison University, College of Graduate and Outreach Programs, College of Integrated Science and Technology, Department of Communication Sciences and Disorders, Program in Speech-Language Pathology, Harrisonburg, VA 22807. Offers audiology (PhD); clinical audiology (PhD); speech-language pathology (MS, PhD). *Accreditation:* ASHA. Part-time programs available. *Students:* 52 full-time (50 women), 12 part-time (all women); includes 3 minority (1 African American, 1 Asian American or Pacific Islander, 1 Hispanic American). Average age 27. In 2006, 26 master's, 7 doctorates awarded. *Degree requirements:* For master's, thesis. *Entrance requirements:* For master's, GRE General Test, 2 letters of recommendation; for doctorate, GRE, 3 letters of recommendation, interview. Additional exam requirements/recommendations for international students: Required—TOEFL. *Application deadline:* For fall admission, 5/1 priority date for domestic students; for spring admission, 9/1 priority date for domestic students. Applications are processed on a rolling basis. Application fee: $55. Electronic applications accepted. *Expenses:* Tuition, state resident: full-time $6,336; part-time $264 per credit hour. Tuition, nonresident: full-time $17,832; part-time $743 per credit hour. *Financial support:* In 2006–07, 17 students received support. Federal Work-Study and unspecified assistantships available. Financial award application deadline: 3/1; financial award applicants required to submit FAFSA. *Unit head:* Dr. Vicki A. Reed, Academic Unit Head, Department of Communication Sciences and Disorders, 540-568-6440.

Kean University, College of Education, Program in Speech Language Pathology, Union, NJ 07083. Offers MA. *Accreditation:* ASHA. Part-time and evening/weekend programs available. *Faculty:* 8 full-time (6 women). *Students:* 64 full-time (60 women), 39 part-time (all women); includes 20 minority (7 African Americans, 6 Asian Americans or Pacific Islanders, 7 Hispanic Americans). Average age 30. 159 applicants, 44% accepted, 41 enrolled. In 2006, 36 degrees awarded. *Degree requirements:* For master's, thesis, practicum, clinic, comprehensive exam. *Entrance requirements:* For master's, GRE General Test, minimum GPA of 3.2, 3 letters of recommendation, interview. *Application deadline:* For fall admission, 2/1 for domestic students. Application fee: $60 ($150 for international students). Electronic applications accepted. *Expenses:* Tuition, state resident: full-time $8,856; part-time $369 per credit. Tuition, nonresident: full-time $11,256; part-time $469 per credit. *Financial support:* In 2006–07, 12 research assistantships with full tuition reimbursements (averaging $3,217 per year) were awarded; career-related internships or fieldwork and unspecified assistantships also available. *Unit head:* Dr. Barbara D. Glazewski, Program Coordinator, 908-737-5407, E-mail: bglazews@kean.edu. *Application contact:* Joanne Morris, Director of Graduate Admissions, 908-737-3355, Fax: 908-737-3354, E-mail: grad-adm@kean.edu.

Kent State University, Graduate School of Education, Health, and Human Services, School of Speech Pathology and Audiology, Kent, OH 44242-0001. Offers MA, Au D, PhD. *Accreditation:* ASHA. *Faculty:* 19 full-time (13 women). *Students:* 110 full-time (105 women), 7 part-time (all women); includes 7 minority (3 African Americans, 1 American Indian/Alaska Native, 1 Asian American or Pacific Islander, 2 Hispanic Americans), 5 international. Average age 23. 136 applicants, 32% accepted. In 2006, 8 master's, 2 doctorates awarded. *Degree requirements:* For master's, thesis optional; for doctorate, thesis/dissertation. *Entrance requirements:* For master's and doctorate, GRE General Test, minimum GPA of 3.0. Additional exam requirements/recommendations for international students: Required—TOEFL (minimum score 600 paper-based; 250 computer-based). *Application deadline:* For fall admission, 3/1 for domestic students; for spring admission, 10/15 for domestic students. Applications are processed on a rolling basis. Application fee: $30. Electronic applications accepted. *Financial support:* Fellowships with full tuition reimbursements, research assistantships with full tuition reimbursements, teaching assistantships with full tuition reimbursements, career-related internships or fieldwork, Federal Work-Study, scholarships/grants, and tuition waivers (full) available. Financial award application deadline: 3/1. *Faculty research:* Aging, aphasia, voice, electrophysiology, autism. *Unit head:* Dr. Lynne B. Rowan, Director, 330-672-2672, Fax: 330-672-2643, E-mail: lrowan@kent.edu. *Application contact:* Dr. Robert S. Pierce, Coordinator for Graduate Studies, 330-672-2672, Fax: 330-672-2643, E-mail: rpierce@kent.edu.

Lamar University, College of Graduate Studies, College of Fine Arts and Communication, Department of Speech-Language Pathology, Beaumont, TX 77710. Offers audiology (MS, Au D); speech language pathology (MS). *Faculty:* 8 full-time (5 women), 1 (woman) part-time/adjunct. *Students:* 39 full-time (36 women), 4 part-time (all women); includes 13 minority (8 African Americans, 1 American Indian/Alaska Native, 4 Hispanic Americans), 2 international. 53 applicants, 38% accepted, 16 enrolled. *Degree requirements:* For master's, thesis optional; for doctorate, thesis/dissertation. *Entrance requirements:* For master's, GRE general test, minimum GPA 2.5, performance IQ score of 115 required for Deaf students; for doctorate, GRE general test. Additional exam requirements/recommendations for international students: Required—TOEFL. *Application deadline:* For fall admission, 8/1 priority date for domestic students; for spring admission, 12/1 for domestic students. Applications are processed on a rolling basis. Application fee: $25 ($50 for international students). *Expenses:* Tuition, nonresident: part-time $33 per hour. Required fees: $43 per hour. $110 per semester. *Financial support:* Fellowships with tuition reimbursements, teaching assistantships, institutionally sponsored loans available. Support available to part-time students. Financial award application deadline: 4/1. *Application contact:* Debbie Piper, Coordinator of Graduate Admissions, 409-880-8356, Fax: 409-880-8414, E-mail: gradmissions@hal.lamar.edu.

La Salle University, School of Nursing and Health Sciences, Program in Speech-Language-Hearing Science, Philadelphia, PA 19141-1199. Offers MS. *Accreditation:* ASHA.

Lehman College of the City University of New York, Division of Arts and Humanities, Department of Speech–Language–Hearing Sciences, Bronx, NY 10468-1589. Offers speech-language pathology and audiology (MA). *Accreditation:* ASHA. Part-time and evening/weekend programs available. *Degree requirements:* For master's, thesis or alternative.

Lewis & Clark College, Graduate School of Education and Counseling, Department of Education, Program in Special Education, Portland, OR 97219-7899. Offers M Ed. *Accreditation:* NCATE. Part-time and evening/weekend programs available. *Faculty:* 2 full-time (1 woman), 1 (woman) part-time/adjunct. *Students:* Average age 42. 8 applicants, 100% accepted, 4 enrolled. In 2006, 7 degrees awarded. *Entrance requirements:* For master's, minimum GPA of 2.75. Additional exam requirements/recommendations for international students: Required—TOEFL (minimum score 575 paper-based; 233 computer-based). Application fee: $50. Electronic applications accepted. *Expenses:* Tuition: Part-time $610 per semester hour. *Financial support:* In 2006–07, 7 students received support. Career-related internships or fieldwork, Federal Work-Study, institutionally sponsored loans, scholarships/grants, and tuition waivers (partial) available. Support available to part-time students. Financial award applicants required to submit FAFSA. *Unit head:* Christine Moore, Program Coordinator, 503-768-6128, E-mail: cmoore@lclark.edu. *Application contact:* Becky Haas, Director of Admissions, 503-768-6200, Fax: 503-768-6205, E-mail: gseadmit@lclark.edu.

Loma Linda University, School of Allied Health Professions, Department of Speech-Language Pathology and Audiology, Loma Linda, CA 92350. Offers MS. *Accreditation:* ASHA. Part-time programs available. *Degree requirements:* For master's, thesis or alternative. *Entrance requirements:* For master's, GRE General Test.

Long Island University, Brooklyn Campus, Richard L. Conolly College of Liberal Arts and Sciences, Department of Communication Sciences and Disorders, Brooklyn, NY 11201-8423. Offers speech-language pathology (MS). *Accreditation:* ASHA. *Entrance requirements:* For master's, 2 letters of recommendation. Additional exam requirements/recommendations for international students: Required—TOEFL (minimum score 500 paper-based; 173 computer-based). Electronic applications accepted.

Long Island University, C.W. Post Campus, School of Education, Department of Communication Sciences and Disorders, Brookville, NY 11548-1300. Offers speech language pathology (MA). *Accreditation:* ASHA. Part-time and evening/weekend programs available. *Degree requirements:* For master's, comprehensive exam or thesis. *Entrance requirements:* For master's, minimum GPA of 3.0, bachelor's degree in communication sciences and disorders. Electronic applications accepted. *Faculty research:* Aural rehabilitation, spouses' perceptions of speech therapy with their ephasic partners, establish norms associated with swallowing.

Longwood University, Office of Graduate Studies, College of Education and Human Services, Program in Communication Sciences and Disorders, Farmville, VA 23909. Offers MS.

See Close-Up on page 1707.

Louisiana State University and Agricultural and Mechanical College, Graduate School, College of Arts and Sciences, Department of Communication Sciences and Disorders, Baton Rouge, LA 70803. Offers MA, PhD. *Accreditation:* ASHA (one or more programs are accredited). *Faculty:* 12 full-time (10 women), 3 part-time/adjunct (all women). *Students:* 49 full-time (all women), 9 part-time (8 women); includes 10 minority (8 African Americans, 2 Asian Americans or Pacific Islanders), 1 international. Average age 29. 37 applicants, 51% accepted, 4 enrolled. In 2006, 17 master's, 2 doctorates awarded. *Degree requirements:* For doctorate, thesis/dissertation. *Entrance requirements:* For master's and doctorate, GRE General Test, minimum GPA of 3.0. Additional exam requirements/recommendations for international students: Required—TOEFL (minimum score 550 paper-based; 213 computer-based; 79 iBT). *Application deadline:* For fall admission, 1/25 priority date for domestic students, 5/15 for international students; for spring admission, 10/15 for international students. Application fee: $25. Electronic applications accepted. *Financial support:* In 2006–07, 12 students received support, including 3 fellowships with full tuition reimbursements available (averaging $28,197 per year), 5 research assistantships with partial tuition reimbursements available (averaging $12,120 per year), 3 teaching assistantships with partial tuition reimbursements available (averaging $11,167 per year); Federal Work-Study, institutionally sponsored loans, and unspecified assistantships also available. Financial award application deadline: 4/1; financial award applicants required to submit FAFSA. *Faculty research:* Language development, language intervention, aphasia, language of the deaf. Total annual research expenditures: $2,945. *Unit head:* Dr. Paul R. Hoffman, Chair, 225-578-2545, Fax: 225-578-2995, E-mail: cdhoff@lsu.edu. *Application contact:* Dr. Hugh Buckingham, Graduate Adviser, 225-578-6682, Fax: 225-578-6447, E-mail: hbuck@lsu.edu.

Louisiana State University Health Sciences Center, School of Allied Health Professions, Program in Communication Disorders, New Orleans, LA 70112-2223. Offers audiology (MCD); speech pathology (MCD). *Accreditation:* ASHA. *Degree requirements:* For master's, comprehensive exam or thesis. *Entrance requirements:* For master's, GRE General Test, minimum undergraduate GPA of 3.0. *Expenses:* Tuition, state resident: full-time $5,868; part-time $722 per credit. Tuition, nonresident: full-time $8,993; part-time $1,104 per credit. *Faculty research:* Hearing aids, clinical audiology, swallowing respiration, language acquisition, speech science.

Louisiana Tech University, Graduate School, College of Liberal Arts, Department of Speech, Ruston, LA 71272. Offers speech (MA); speech pathology and audiology (MA). *Accreditation:* ASHA. *Degree requirements:* For master's, thesis or alternative. *Entrance requirements:* For master's, GRE General Test.

Loyola College in Maryland, Graduate Programs, College of Arts and Sciences, Department of Speech-Language Pathology and Audiology, Baltimore, MD 21210-2699. Offers MS, CAS. *Accreditation:* ASHA (one or more programs are accredited). Evening/weekend programs available. *Faculty:* 14 full-time (all women), 8 part-time/adjunct (all women). *Students:* 73 full-time (all women); includes 7 minority (2 African Americans, 3 Asian Americans or Pacific Islanders, 2 Hispanic Americans). Average age 25. 184 applicants, 65% accepted, 40 enrolled. In 2006, 40 degrees awarded. *Entrance requirements:* For master's and CAS, GRE General Test, GRE Subject Test (recommended). Additional exam requirements/recommendations for international students: Required—TOEFL (minimum score 550 paper-based; 213 computer-based). *Application deadline:* For fall admission, 2/1 for domestic students. Applications are processed on a rolling basis. Application fee: $50. *Financial support:* Research assistantships available. Financial award applicants required to submit FAFSA. *Unit head:* Kathleen Siren, Chair, 410-617-2000 Ext. 5317. *Application contact:* Scott Greatorex, Director, Graduate Admissions, 410-617-5020, Fax: 410-617-2002, E-mail: graduate@loyola.edu.

Marquette University, Graduate School, College of Health Sciences, Department of Speech Pathology and Audiology, Milwaukee, WI 53201-1881. Offers speech-language pathology (MS). *Accreditation:* ASHA. *Faculty:* 11 full-time (8 women), 4 part-time/adjunct (all women). *Students:* 34 full-time (all women), 22 part-time (20 women); includes 7 minority (1 African American, 1 Asian American or Pacific Islander, 5 Hispanic Americans). Average age 25. In 2006, 31 degrees awarded. *Degree requirements:* For master's, comprehensive exam. *Entrance requirements:* For master's, GRE General Test. Additional exam requirements/recommendations for international students: Required—TOEFL. Application fee: $40. *Financial support:* Research assistantships, teaching assistantships, career-related internships or fieldwork, Federal Work-Study, institutionally sponsored loans, and tuition waivers (full and partial) available. Support available to part-time students. Financial award application deadline: 2/15. *Faculty research:* Language processing in the brain, vocal aging, early language development, birth-to-three intervention, computer applications. *Unit head:* Dr. Kim Halula, Chair, 414-288-9658, Fax: 414-288-3980.

Marshall University, Academic Affairs Division, College of Health Professions, Department of Communication Disorders, Huntington, WV 25755. Offers MA. *Accreditation:* ASHA. *Faculty:* 10 full-time (9 women). *Students:* 53 full-time (51 women), 5 part-time (all women). Average age 26. In 2006, 23 degrees awarded. *Degree requirements:* For master's, thesis optional. *Entrance requirements:* For master's, GRE General Test. Application fee: $40. *Financial support:* Fellowships available. *Unit head:* Kathryn Chezik, Chairperson, 304-696-2979, E-mail: chezik@marshall.edu. *Application contact:* Information Contact, 304-746-1900, Fax: 304-746-1902, E-mail: services@marshall.edu.

Marywood University, Academic Affairs, College of Education and Human Development, Department of Communication Sciences and Disorders, Program in Speech-Language Pathology, Scranton, PA 18509-1598. Offers MS. *Students:* 28 full-time (27 women), 8 part-time (all women). Average age 25. *Degree requirements:* For master's, clinical practicum. *Entrance requirements:* For master's, GRE, minimum undergraduate GPA of 3.0, 2 letters of recommendation, interview. Additional exam requirements/recommendations for international students: Required—TOEFL. *Application deadline:* For fall admission, 4/15 for domestic and international students; for spring admission, 11/15 for domestic and international students. Application fee: $30. *Expenses:* Tuition: Part-time $672 per credit. Tuition and fees vary according to degree level, campus/location and program. *Financial support:* Research assistantships, scholarships/grants available. *Application contact:* 866-279-9663 Ext. 6002, E-mail: grad_inq@marywood.edu.

See Close-Up on page 1709.

Massachusetts Institute of Technology, Whitaker College of Health Sciences and Technology, Harvard-MIT Division of Health Sciences and Technology, Speech and Hearing Bioscience and Technology Program, Cambridge, MA 02139-4307. Offers PhD, Sc D. *Faculty:* 61 full-

Communication Disorders

Massachusetts Institute of Technology (continued)
time (14 women). *Students:* 49 full-time (19 women); includes 13 minority (1 African American, 11 Asian Americans or Pacific Islanders, 1 Hispanic American), 9 international. Average age 28. 21 applicants, 33% accepted, 5 enrolled. In 2006, 12 degrees awarded. *Degree requirements:* For doctorate, thesis/dissertation. *Entrance requirements:* For doctorate, BS in engineering or science, previous coursework in differential equations. Additional exam requirements/recommendations for international students: Required—TOEFL. *Application deadline:* For fall admission, 12/15 for domestic and international students. Application fee: $70. Electronic applications accepted. *Expenses: Contact institution.* Part-time tuition and fees vary according to course load. *Financial support:* In 2006–07, 35 fellowships with full and partial tuition reimbursements (averaging $50,760 per year), 11 research assistantships with full and partial tuition reimbursements (averaging $43,822 per year), 8 teaching assistantships with full and partial tuition reimbursements (averaging $15,653 per year) were awarded; institutionally sponsored loans, scholarships/grants, traineeships, health care benefits, and unspecified assistantships also available. Financial award application deadline: 1/15. *Faculty research:* Neuroscience, auditory physiology, hearing science, psychoacoustics, speech communications. *Unit head:* Dr. Louis D. Braida, Director, 617-253-2575, Fax: 617-258-7354, E-mail: braida@cbgrle.mit.edu. *Application contact:* Dr. M. Christian Brown, Co-Chair, SHS Admissions Committee, 617-573-3875, Fax: 617-720-4408, E-mail: mcb@epl.meei.harvard.edu.

See Close-Up on page 1705.

McGill University, Faculty of Graduate and Postdoctoral Studies, Faculty of Medicine, School of Communication Sciences and Disorders, Montréal, QC H3A 2T5, Canada. Offers communication science and disorders (M Sc); communication sciences and disorders (PhD); speech-language pathology (M Sc A). *Accreditation:* ASHA. *Degree requirements:* For master's, thesis (for some programs); for doctorate, thesis/dissertation. *Entrance requirements:* For master's, minimum GPA of 3.0. Additional exam requirements/recommendations for international students: Required—TOEFL. *Faculty research:* Auditory development, developmental language disorders, speech perception, reading development, language and aging.

Medical University of South Carolina, College of Health Professions, Department of Rehabilitation Sciences, Program in Communication Sciences and Disorders, Charleston, SC 29425-0002. Offers MSR. *Accreditation:* ASHA. *Faculty:* 3 full-time (all women). *Students:* 60 full-time (59 women); includes 4 minority (3 African Americans, 1 Hispanic American), 1 international. Average age 25. 77 applicants, 42% accepted, 26 enrolled. In 2006, 12 degrees awarded. *Degree requirements:* For master's, thesis or alternative, research project. *Entrance requirements:* For master's, GRE General Test, interview, minimum GPA of 3.0, references. Additional exam requirements/recommendations for international students: Required—TOEFL (minimum score 600 paper-based; 250 computer-based). *Application deadline:* For fall admission, 1/15 priority date for domestic and international students. Application fee: $75. Electronic applications accepted. *Financial support:* Federal Work-Study and scholarships/grants available. Support available to part-time students. Financial award application deadline: 3/15; financial award applicants required to submit FAFSA. *Unit head:* Dr. Jennifer Horner, Chair, 843-792-2961, Fax: 843-792-0710, E-mail: hornerj@musc.edu. *Application contact:* Susan Johnson, Student Services Coordinator, 843-792-2961, Fax: 843-792-0710, E-mail: johnsoss@musc.edu.

Mercy College, Division of Health Professions, Program in Communication Disorders, Dobbs Ferry, NY 10522-1189. Offers MS. *Accreditation:* ASHA. *Students:* 59 full-time (58 women), 38 part-time (37 women); includes 29 minority (7 African Americans, 1 Asian American or Pacific Islander, 21 Hispanic Americans), 1 international. Average age 29. In 2006, 26 degrees awarded. *Entrance requirements:* For master's, interview. Application fee: $62. *Expenses:* Tuition: Part-time $595 per credit. Required fees: $9 per credit. Tuition and fees vary according to program. *Unit head:* Dr. Joan Kosta, Director, 914-674-7340, E-mail: jkosta@mercy.edu. *Application contact:* Kathleen Jackson, Director of Admissions, 800-Mercy-NY, Fax: 914-674-7382, E-mail: admissions@mercy.edu.

MGH Institute of Health Professions, Graduate Programs, Program in Communication Sciences and Disorders, Boston, MA 02129. Offers reading (Certificate); speech-language pathology (MS). *Accreditation:* ASHA (one or more programs are accredited). Part-time programs available. *Faculty:* 11 full-time (7 women), 8 part-time/adjunct (6 women). *Students:* 74 full-time (72 women), 26 part-time (24 women); includes 5 minority (1 African American, 3 Asian Americans or Pacific Islanders, 1 Hispanic American). Average age 28. 173 applicants, 57% accepted, 47 enrolled. In 2006, 37 master's, 13 other advanced degrees awarded. *Degree requirements:* For master's, thesis or alternative, research proposal. *Entrance requirements:* For master's, GRE General Test. Additional exam requirements/recommendations for international students: Required—TOEFL (minimum score 550 paper-based; 213 computer-based). *Application deadline:* For fall admission, 1/28 for domestic and international students. Application fee: $50. Electronic applications accepted. *Financial support:* In 2006–07, 68 students received support; research assistantships, teaching assistantships, career-related internships or fieldwork, scholarships/grants, tuition waivers (full and partial), and unspecified assistantships available. Support available to part-time students. Financial award application deadline: 3/3; financial award applicants required to submit FAFSA. *Faculty research:* Children's language disorders, reading, speech disorders, voice disorders, augmentative communication, autism. *Unit head:* Kevin P. Kearns, Director, 617-724-6361, Fax: 617-726-8022, E-mail: kkearns@partners.org. *Application contact:* Maureen Rika Judd, Manager of Admissions, 617-726-6069, Fax: 617-726-8010, E-mail: admissions@mghihp.edu.

See Close-Up on page 1963.

Miami University, Graduate School, College of Arts and Sciences, Department of Speech Pathology and Audiology, Oxford, OH 45056. Offers MA, MS. *Accreditation:* ASHA. Part-time programs available. *Degree requirements:* For master's, thesis (for some programs), final exam. *Entrance requirements:* For master's, GRE, minimum undergraduate GPA of 3.0 during previous 2 years or 2.75 overall. Additional exam requirements/recommendations for international students: Required—TOEFL, TWE. Electronic applications accepted.

Michigan State University, The Graduate School, College of Communication Arts and Sciences, Department of Communicative Sciences and Disorders, East Lansing, MI 48824. Offers MA, PhD. *Accreditation:* ASHA (one or more programs are accredited). *Faculty:* 9 full-time (2 women). *Students:* 43 full-time (42 women), 6 part-time (all women); includes 5 minority (3 African Americans, 2 Hispanic Americans), 2 international. Average age 26. 97 applicants, 30% accepted. In 2006, 23 degrees awarded. *Entrance requirements:* Additional exam requirements/recommendations for international students: Required—TOEFL. Electronic applications accepted. *Expenses:* Tuition, state resident: part-time $346 per credit hour. Tuition, nonresident: part-time $730 per credit hour. Tuition and fees vary according to program. *Financial support:* In 2006–07, 11 fellowships with tuition reimbursements, 1 teaching assistantship with tuition reimbursement (averaging $13,500 per year) were awarded; scholarships/grants also available. Total annual research expenditures: $32,137. *Unit head:* Dr. Michael W. Casby, Chairperson, 517-432-8201, Fax: 517-353-3176, E-mail: casby@msu.edu. *Application contact:* Mary Ann Keilen, Student Affairs Secretary, 517-353-8641, Fax: 517-353-3176, E-mail: keilen@msu.edu.

Minnesota State University Mankato, College of Graduate Studies, College of Allied Health and Nursing, Program in Communication Disorders, Mankato, MN 56001. Offers MS. *Accreditation:* ASHA. Part-time programs available. *Students:* 23 full-time (22 women), 4 part-time (3 women). In 2006, 11 degrees awarded. *Degree requirements:* For master's, thesis or alternative, comprehensive exam. *Entrance requirements:* For master's, GRE General Test, minimum GPA of 3.0 during previous 2 years, references, writing sample. Additional exam requirements/recommendations for international students: Required—TOEFL. *Application deadline:* For fall admission, 2/1 priority date for domestic students; for spring admission, 11/27 for domestic students. Applications are processed on a rolling basis. Application fee: $40. *Financial support:* Research assistantships with full tuition reimbursements, teaching assistantships with full tuition reimbursements, career-related internships or fieldwork, Federal Work-Study, and institutionally sponsored loans available. Support available to part-time students. Financial award application deadline: 3/15. *Faculty research:* Internet/technology issues related to speech-language pathology. *Unit head:* Dr. Patricia Hargrove, Graduate Coordinator, 507-389-1415. *Application contact:* 507-389-2321, E-mail: grad@mnsu.edu.

Minnesota State University Moorhead, Graduate Studies, College of Education and Human Services, Program in Speech-Language Pathology, Moorhead, MN 56563-0002. Offers MS. *Accreditation:* ASHA. *Faculty:* 5 full-time (2 women), 4 part-time/adjunct (2 women). *Students:* 19 full-time (all women), 1 (woman) part-time; includes 1 Hispanic American, 1 international. 64 applicants, 11% accepted. In 2006, 19 degrees awarded. *Degree requirements:* For master's, final oral exam, project or thesis. *Entrance requirements:* For master's, GRE General Test, minimum GPA of 2.75, undergraduate major in speech/language/hearing sciences, 3 letters of recommendation. Additional exam requirements/recommendations for international students: Required—TOEFL (minimum score 550 paper-based; 213 computer-based). *Application deadline:* For fall admission, 2/1 for domestic students, 1/1 for international students. Application fee: $20. Electronic applications accepted. *Financial support:* In 2006–07, 6 research assistantships (averaging $3,000 per year) were awarded; career-related internships or fieldwork, Federal Work-Study, and unspecified assistantships also available. Financial award application deadline: 7/15; financial award applicants required to submit FAFSA. *Unit head:* LaRae McGillivray, Coordinator, 218-477-4639, E-mail: mcgilliv@mnstate.edu.

Minot State University, Graduate School, Program in Communication Disorders, Minot, ND 58707-0002. Offers audiology (MS); speech-language pathology (MS). *Accreditation:* ASHA. *Faculty:* 14 full-time (10 women), 2 part-time/adjunct (both women). *Students:* 29. 42 applicants, 93% accepted, 29 enrolled. In 2006, 25 degrees awarded. *Degree requirements:* For master's, thesis (for some programs), comprehensive exam (for some programs). *Entrance requirements:* For master's, GRE General Test, minimum GPA of 3.0. Additional exam requirements/recommendations for international students: Required—TOEFL. *Application deadline:* For fall admission, 2/15 priority date for domestic students. Application fee: $35. *Financial support:* In 2006–07, 15 students received support, including 5 research assistantships (averaging $1,000 per year), 5 teaching assistantships (averaging $1,000 per year); career-related internships or fieldwork, institutionally sponsored loans, scholarships/grants, traineeships, tuition waivers (partial), and unspecified assistantships also available. Support available to part-time students. Financial award application deadline: 2/5. *Unit head:* Dr. Thomas Linares, Chairperson, 701-858-3031, E-mail: linares@minotstateu.edu. *Application contact:* Brenda Anderson, Administrative Assistant, 701-858-3250, Fax: 701-858-4286, E-mail: brenda.anderson@minotstateu.edu.

Mississippi University for Women, Graduate School, Division of Education and Human Sciences, Columbus, MS 39701-9998. Offers gifted studies (M Ed); instructional management (M Ed); speech/language pathology (MS). *Accreditation:* ASHA; NCATE. Part-time programs available. *Degree requirements:* For master's, thesis optional. *Entrance requirements:* For master's, GRE General Test or NTE (M Ed in gifted education or MS in speech/language pathology), MAT (M Ed in instructional management), minimum QPA of 3.0.

Missouri State University, Graduate College, College of Health and Human Services, Department of Communication Sciences and Disorders, Springfield, MO 65804-0094. Offers audiology (Au D); communication sciences and disorders (MS). *Accreditation:* ASHA (one or more programs are accredited). *Faculty:* 16 full-time (10 women), 1 (woman) part-time/adjunct. *Students:* 74 full-time (68 women), 11 part-time (all women); includes 2 minority (1 American Indian/Alaska Native, 1 Hispanic American), 3 international. Average age 26. 41 applicants, 44% accepted, 14 enrolled. In 2006, 20 master's, 3 doctorates awarded. *Degree requirements:* For master's, thesis or alternative, comprehensive exam. *Entrance requirements:* For master's, GRE General Test, minimum GPA of 3.0. Additional exam requirements/recommendations for international students: Required—TOEFL (minimum score 550 paper-based; 213 computer-based; 79 iBT). *Application deadline:* For fall admission, 2/1 for domestic and international students. Application fee: $35. *Expenses:* Tuition, state resident: full-time $3,582; part-time $199 per credit hour. Tuition, nonresident: full-time $6,984; part-time $199 per credit hour. Required fees: $548. Full-time tuition and fees vary according to course level, course load, program and reciprocity agreements. *Financial support:* In 2006–07, 1 research assistantship with full tuition reimbursement (averaging $6,780 per year) was awarded; teaching assistantships with full tuition reimbursements, career-related internships or fieldwork, Federal Work-Study, scholarships/grants, and unspecified assistantships also available. Support available to part-time students. Financial award application deadline: 3/31; financial award applicants required to submit FAFSA. *Faculty research:* Speech-language pathology, the hearing-impaired and deaf. *Unit head:* Dr. Neil DiSarno, Head, 417-836-5368, Fax: 417-836-4242, E-mail: neildisarno@missouristate.edu.

Montclair State University, The Graduate School, College of Humanities and Social Sciences, Department of Communication Sciences and Disorders, Montclair, NJ 07043-1624. Offers audiology (Sc D); speech/language pathology (MA). *Accreditation:* ASHA (one or more programs are accredited). Part-time and evening/weekend programs available. *Faculty:* 9 full-time (8 women), 5 part-time/adjunct (3 women). *Students:* 96 full-time (87 women), 35 part-time (32 women); includes 20 minority (7 African Americans, 7 Asian Americans or Pacific Islanders, 6 Hispanic Americans), 1 international. 281 applicants, 26% accepted, 45 enrolled. In 2006, 29 master's, 4 doctorates awarded. *Degree requirements:* For master's, thesis (for some programs), comprehensive exam or fieldwork/project, comprehensive exam (for some programs). *Entrance requirements:* For master's, GRE General Test, 2 letters of recommendation; for doctorate, GRE, 2 letters of recommendation. Additional exam requirements/recommendations for international students: Required—TOEFL (minimum score 83 computer-based). *Application deadline:* For fall admission, 3/1 for domestic and international students. Applications are processed on a rolling basis. Application fee: $60. Electronic applications accepted. *Expenses:* Tuition, state resident: part-time $450 per credit. Tuition, nonresident: part-time $682 per credit. Tuition and fees vary according to degree level and program. *Financial support:* In 2006–07, 9 research assistantships with tuition reimbursements were awarded; Federal Work-Study, scholarships/grants, and unspecified assistantships also available. Support available to part-time students. Financial award application deadline: 3/1; financial award applicants required to submit FAFSA. *Unit head:* Dr. Claire Taub, Graduate Adviser, 973-655-7358, E-mail: taubc@mail.montclair.edu.

Murray State University, College of Health Sciences and Human Services, Department of Wellness and Therapeutic Sciences, Program in Speech-Language Pathology, Murray, KY 42071. Offers MS. *Accreditation:* ASHA. Part-time programs available. *Students:* 26 full-time (all women), 46 part-time (all women), 1 international. 30 applicants, 97% accepted. In 2006, 12 degrees awarded. *Degree requirements:* For master's, thesis optional. *Entrance requirements:* For master's, GRE General Test or MAT, minimum GPA of 3.0. Additional exam requirements/recommendations for international students: Required—TOEFL. *Application deadline:* For fall admission, 2/15 for domestic students, 1/15 for international students. Applications are processed on a rolling basis. Application fee: $25. *Financial support:* In 2006–07, 3 teaching assistantships (averaging $3,500 per year) were awarded; research assistantships, Federal Work-Study also available. Financial award application deadline: 4/1. *Unit head:* Dr. Pearl Payne, Graduate Coordinator, 270-809-2674, Fax: 270-809-3963, E-mail: pearl.payne@murraystate.edu.

National University, Academic Affairs, School of Education, Department of Special Education and Technology, La Jolla, CA 92037-1011. Offers deaf and hard of hearing education (MS); educational technology (MS); exceptional student education (MS); special education (MS). Part-time and evening/weekend programs available. Postbaccalaureate distance learning degree programs offered (no on-campus study). *Faculty:* 15 full-time (12 women), 389 part-time/adjunct (232 women). *Students:* 1,039 full-time (706 women), 2,426 part-time (1,549 women); includes 997 minority (337 African Americans, 27 American Indian/Alaska Native, 179 Asian Americans or Pacific Islanders, 454 Hispanic Americans), 19 international. Average age 38.

1,579 applicants, 1481 enrolled. In 2006, 215 degrees awarded. *Degree requirements:* For master's, thesis (for some programs). *Entrance requirements:* For master's, interview, minimum GPA of 2.5. Additional exam requirements/recommendations for international students: Required—TOEFL (minimum score 550 paper-based; 213 computer-based; 80 iBT), IELTS (minimum score 6). *Application deadline:* Applications are processed on a rolling basis. Application fee: $60 ($65 for international students). Electronic applications accepted. *Expenses:* Tuition: Full-time $7,722; part-time $286 per unit. One-time fee: $60. *Financial support:* Career-related internships or fieldwork, institutionally sponsored loans, scholarships/grants, and tuition waivers (partial) available. Support available to part-time students. Financial award application deadline: 6/30; financial award applicants required to submit FAFSA. *Unit head:* Dr. Jane Duckett, Chair, 858-642-8346, Fax: 858-642-8724, E-mail: jduckett@nu.edu. *Application contact:* Dominick Giovanniello, Associate Regional Dean—San Diego, 800-NAT-UNIV, Fax: 858-642-8709, E-mail: dgiovann@nu.edu.

Nazareth College of Rochester, Graduate Studies, Department of Speech-Language Pathology, Communication Sciences and Disorders Program, Rochester, NY 14618-3790. Offers MS. *Accreditation:* ASHA. Part-time programs available. Postbaccalaureate distance learning degree programs offered. *Faculty:* 3 full-time (all women), 7 part-time/adjunct (all women). *Students:* 34 full-time (all women), 28 part-time (27 women); includes 3 minority (1 African American, 2 Asian Americans or Pacific Islanders). Average age 29. 79 applicants, 51% accepted, 16 enrolled. In 2006, 19 degrees awarded. *Degree requirements:* For master's, comprehensive exam. *Entrance requirements:* For master's, GRE General Test, minimum GPA of 3.0. *Application deadline:* For fall admission, 2/1 for domestic students; for spring admission, 10/1 for domestic students. Application fee: $40. *Financial support:* Research assistantships with partial tuition reimbursements available. Financial award application deadline: 3/1. *Unit head:* Lisa Durant-Jones, Director, 585-389-2775, Fax: 585-389-2452, E-mail: ldurant4@naz.edu. *Application contact:* Judith G. Baker, Director, Graduate Admissions, 585-389-2050, Fax: 585-389-2817, E-mail: gradstudies@naz.edu.

New Mexico State University, Graduate School, College of Education, Department of Special Education and Communication Disorders, Las Cruces, NM 88003-8001. Offers special education (MA, Ed D, PhD). *Accreditation:* ASHA (one or more programs are accredited); NCATE. Part-time and evening/weekend programs available. Postbaccalaureate distance learning degree programs offered. *Faculty:* 11 full-time (9 women), 1 (woman) part-time/adjunct. *Students:* 43 full-time (38 women), 106 part-time (82 women); includes 61 minority (3 African Americans, 3 American Indian/Alaska Native, 55 Hispanic Americans), 2 international. Average age 37. 42 applicants, 69% accepted. *Degree requirements:* For master's, thesis or alternative. *Entrance requirements:* For master's, GRE General Test or MAT. *Application deadline:* For fall admission, 3/1 priority date for domestic students. Applications are processed on a rolling basis. Application fee: $30 ($50 for international students). Electronic applications accepted. *Financial support:* In 2006–07, 11 teaching assistantships were awarded; fellowships, research assistantships, career-related internships or fieldwork, Federal Work-Study, and health care benefits also available. Support available to part-time students. Financial award application deadline: 3/1. *Faculty research:* Multicultural special education, multicultural communication disorders, mild disability, school psychology, deaf education, early childhood, bilingual special education. *Unit head:* Dr. Robert Rhodes, Head, 505-646-2402, Fax: 505-646-4234, E-mail: rorhodes@nmsu.edu.

New York Medical College, School of Public Health, Department of Speech-Language Pathology, Valhalla, NY 10595-1691. Offers MS. *Accreditation:* ASHA. *Faculty:* 4 full-time (2 women), 5 part-time/adjunct (3 women). In 2006, 10 degrees awarded. *Degree requirements:* For master's, comprehensive exam, registration. *Entrance requirements:* For master's, GRE General Test, minimum GPA of 3.4. Additional exam requirements/recommendations for international students: Required—TOEFL (minimum score 600 paper-based; 287 computer-based). *Application deadline:* For fall admission, 4/30 for domestic students, 3/30 for international students. Applications are processed on a rolling basis. Application fee: $75. *Financial support:* Application deadline: 6/15; *Faculty research:* AAC, fluency, stroke, pediatric dysphagia. *Unit head:* Dr. Ben C. Watson, Chair, 914-594-4821, Fax: 914-594-4853, E-mail: slp_sph@nymc.edu. *Application contact:* Marian F. McGowan, Information Contact, 914-594-4510, Fax: 914-594-4292, E-mail: sph_admissions@nymc.edu.

See Close-Up on page 1715.

New York University, Steinhardt School of Culture, Education and Human Development, Department of Speech-Language Pathology and Audiology, New York, NY 10012-1019. Offers MA, PhD. *Accreditation:* ASHA. Part-time and evening/weekend programs available. *Faculty:* 9 full-time (8 women), 26 part-time/adjunct (21 women). *Students:* 133 full-time (131 women), 27 part-time (all women); includes 20 minority (9 African Americans, 2 Asian Americans or Pacific Islanders, 9 Hispanic Americans), 4 international. 456 applicants, 41% accepted, 58 enrolled. In 2006, 48 degrees awarded. Terminal master's awarded for partial completion of doctoral program. *Degree requirements:* For master's, thesis (for some programs); for doctorate, thesis/dissertation. *Entrance requirements:* For doctorate, GRE General Test, interview. Additional exam requirements/recommendations for international students: Required—TOEFL. *Application deadline:* For fall admission, 12/15 priority date for domestic and international students; for spring admission, 11/1 for domestic and international students. Applications are processed on a rolling basis. Application fee: $50. *Expenses:* Tuition: Part-time $1,080 per unit. Required fees: $56 per unit. $329 per term. Tuition and fees vary according to program. *Financial support:* Fellowships with full and partial tuition reimbursements, research assistantships with full and partial tuition reimbursements, career-related internships or fieldwork, Federal Work-Study, institutionally sponsored loans, scholarships/grants, tuition waivers (partial), and unspecified assistantships available. Support available to part-time students. Financial award application deadline: 2/1; financial award applicants required to submit FAFSA. *Faculty research:* Evidence-based practice, phonological acquisition, dysphagia, child language acquisition and disorders, neuromotor disorders. *Unit head:* Dr. Celia Stewart, Chairperson, 212-998-5230, Fax: 212-995-4356. *Application contact:* 212-998-5030, Fax: 212-995-4328, E-mail: steinhardt.gradadmissions@nyu.edu.

North Carolina Central University, Division of Academic Affairs, School of Education, Program in Speech Pathology and Audiology, Durham, NC 27707-3129. Offers M Ed. *Accreditation:* ASHA. Part-time and evening/weekend programs available. *Degree requirements:* For master's, thesis or alternative, comprehensive exam. *Entrance requirements:* For master's, GRE, minimum GPA of 3.0 in major, 2.5 overall. Additional exam requirements/recommendations for international students: Required—TOEFL. *Faculty research:* Vocational programs for special needs learners.

Northeastern State University, Graduate College, College of Liberal Arts, Department of Communication Arts, Tahlequah, OK 74464-2399. Offers communication (MA). Part-time and evening/weekend programs available. *Students:* 5 full-time (all women), 12 part-time (8 women); includes 5 minority (1 African American, 4 American Indian/Alaska Native). In 2006, 5 degrees awarded. *Degree requirements:* For master's, comprehensive exam. *Entrance requirements:* For master's, GRE, MAT, minimum GPA of 2.5. Additional exam requirements/recommendations for international students: Required—TOEFL (minimum score 213 computer-based). *Application deadline:* For fall admission, 6/1 priority date for domestic students. Applications are processed on a rolling basis. Application fee: $0 ($25 for international students). Electronic applications accepted. *Financial support:* Teaching assistantships, Federal Work-Study available. Financial award application deadline: 3/1. *Unit head:* Dr. Mike Chanselar, Chair, 918-456-5511 Ext. 3600, Fax: 918-458-2348.

Northeastern State University, Graduate College, College of Science and Health Professions, Department of Speech-Language Pathology, Tahlequah, OK 74464-2399. Offers MS. *Accreditation:* ASHA. Part-time and evening/weekend programs available. *Students:* 30 full-time (28 women), 1 (woman) part-time; includes 9 minority (2 African Americans, 5 American Indian/Alaska Native, 2 Hispanic Americans). In 2006, 13 degrees awarded. *Degree requirements:* For master's, thesis, capstone experience. *Entrance requirements:* For master's, GRE, minimum GPA of 2.75. Additional exam requirements/recommendations for international students: Required—TOEFL (minimum score 213 computer-based). *Application deadline:* For fall admission, 6/1 priority date for domestic students. Applications are processed on a rolling basis. Application fee: $0 ($25 for international students). Electronic applications accepted. *Financial support:* Teaching assistantships, career-related internships or fieldwork and Federal Work-Study available. Financial award application deadline: 3/1. *Unit head:* Dr. Karen Patterson, Chair, 918-456-5111 Ext. 3778, Fax: 918-458-2351.

Northeastern University, Bouvé College of Health Sciences Graduate School, Department of Speech-Language Pathology and Audiology, Boston, MA 02115-5096. Offers audiology (Au D); speech-language pathology (MS). *Accreditation:* ASHA. *Faculty:* 10 full-time (8 women), 7 part-time/adjunct. *Students:* 87 full-time (80 women), 1 (woman) part-time. Average age 25. 224 applicants, 28% accepted. In 2006, 34 master's awarded. *Degree requirements:* For master's, thesis optional. *Entrance requirements:* For master's, GRE General Test or MAT. Additional exam requirements/recommendations for international students: Required—TOEFL. *Application deadline:* For fall admission, 2/15 for domestic students. Application fee: $50. *Financial support:* In 2006–07, 2 teaching assistantships with full tuition reimbursements (averaging $14,690 per year) were awarded; research assistantships with full tuition reimbursements, career-related internships or fieldwork, Federal Work-Study, tuition waivers (partial), and unspecified assistantships also available. Support available to part-time students. Financial award application deadline: 3/1; financial award applicants required to submit FAFSA. *Faculty research:* Psychoacoustics, applied and theoretical aspects of aphasia, developmentally delayed children, hearing impairments. *Unit head:* Dr. Ralf Schlosser, Chairperson, 617-373-3785, Fax: 617-373-8756, E-mail: r.schlosser@neu.edu. *Application contact:* Margaret Schnabel, Director of Graduate Admissions, 617-373-2708, Fax: 617-373-4704, E-mail: bouvegrad@neu.edu.

Northern Arizona University, Consortium of Professional Schools and Colleges, College of Health Professions, Department of Communications Sciences and Disorders, Flagstaff, AZ 86011. Offers MS. *Accreditation:* ASHA. Part-time programs available. *Entrance requirements:* For master's, GRE General Test, minimum GPA of 3.0. *Faculty research:* Meta-analysis of language, laryngeal speech, aphasia.

Northern Illinois University, Graduate School, College of Health and Human Sciences, Department of Communicative Disorders, De Kalb, IL 60115-2854. Offers MA, Au D. *Accreditation:* ASHA (one or more programs are accredited); CORE. *Faculty:* 9 full-time (6 women), 2 part-time/adjunct (1 woman). *Students:* 87 full-time (85 women), 11 part-time (9 women); includes 15 minority (8 African Americans, 1 Asian American or Pacific Islander, 6 Hispanic Americans). Average age 28. 176 applicants, 44% accepted, 45 enrolled. In 2006, 42 degrees awarded. *Degree requirements:* For master's, practicum, thesis optional; for doctorate, practicum, research project. *Entrance requirements:* For master's, GRE General Test, minimum undergraduate GPA of 3.0; for doctorate, GRE General Test, minimum undergraduate GPA of 3.2. Additional exam requirements/recommendations for international students: Required—TOEFL (minimum score 550 paper-based; 213 computer-based). *Application deadline:* For fall admission, 2/1 priority date for domestic students, 5/1 for international students; for spring admission, 9/1 priority date for domestic students, 10/1 for international students. Applications are processed on a rolling basis. Application fee: $30. Electronic applications accepted. *Financial support:* In 2006–07, 3 research assistantships with full tuition reimbursements, 22 teaching assistantships with full tuition reimbursements were awarded; fellowships with full tuition reimbursements, career-related internships or fieldwork, Federal Work-Study, scholarships/grants, tuition waivers (full), and unspecified assistantships also available. Support available to part-time students. Financial award applicants required to submit FAFSA. *Faculty research:* Impact of disability employment, deaf education, American Sign Language, autism, bilingualism. *Unit head:* Dr. Sue Ouellette, Acting Chair, 815-753-1484, Fax: 815-753-9123, E-mail: souellette@niu.edu.

Northern Michigan University, College of Graduate Studies, College of Professional Studies, Department of Communication Disorders, Marquette, MI 49855-5301. Offers MA. Part-time programs available. *Degree requirements:* For master's, thesis or alternative. *Entrance requirements:* For master's, GRE General Test, minimum GPA of 3.0. *Faculty research:* Auditory adaptation, learning disabilities.

Northwestern University, The Graduate School, School of Communication, The Roxelyn and Richard Pepper Department of Communication Sciences and Disorders, Program in Audiology and Hearing Sciences, Evanston, IL 60208. Offers MA, PhD. Admissions and degrees offered through The Graduate School. *Accreditation:* ASHA. Terminal master's awarded for partial completion of doctoral program. *Degree requirements:* For master's, seminar paper, thesis optional; for doctorate, pre-dissertation research project, qualifying exam. *Entrance requirements:* For master's and doctorate, GRE General Test, letters of recommendation. Additional exam requirements/recommendations for international students: Required—TOEFL. *Faculty research:* Auditory physiology, psychoacoustics, auditory evoked potentials, amplification, audiologic assessment and rehabilitation, speech perception, hearing loss and aging.

See Close-Up on page 1717.

Northwestern University, The Graduate School, School of Communication, The Roxelyn and Richard Pepper Department of Communication Sciences and Disorders, Program in Speech and Language Pathology, Evanston, IL 60208. Offers MA, PhD. Admissions and degrees offered through The Graduate School. *Accreditation:* ASHA. Part-time programs available. Terminal master's awarded for partial completion of doctoral program. *Degree requirements:* For master's, thesis optional; for doctorate, 2 pre-dissertation research projects. *Entrance requirements:* For master's and doctorate, GRE General Test, letters of recommendation. Additional exam requirements/recommendations for international students: Required—TOEFL. *Faculty research:* Voice science, language development, acquired neurogenic speech and language, swallowing physiology, acoustics of speech.

See Close-Up on page 1717.

Northwestern University, The Graduate School, School of Communication, The Roxelyn and Richard Pepper Department of Communication Sciences and Disorders, Program in Speech and Language Pathology and Learning Disabilities, Evanston, IL 60208. Offers MA. Admissions and degree offered through The Graduate School. *Accreditation:* ASHA. *Degree requirements:* For master's, seminar paper, thesis optional. *Entrance requirements:* For master's, GRE General Test, letters of recommendation. Additional exam requirements/recommendations for international students: Required—TOEFL. *Faculty research:* Language and cognitive development, phonological and reading development.

See Close-Up on page 1717.

Nova Southeastern University, Fischler School of Education and Human Services, Program in Education, Fort Lauderdale, FL 33314-7796. Offers educational leadership (Ed D); health care education (Ed D); higher education (Ed D); human serviced administration (Ed D); instructional leadership (Ed D); instructional technology distance education (Ed D); organizational leadership (Ed D); special education (Ed D); speech language pathology (Ed D). *Students:* 619 full-time (452 women), 615 part-time (473 women); includes 737 minority (616 African Americans, 2 American Indian/Alaska Native, 14 Asian Americans or Pacific Islanders, 105 Hispanic Americans), 8 international. Average age 38. 480 applicants, 83% accepted, 398 enrolled. *Degree requirements:* For doctorate, thesis/dissertation. *Entrance requirements:* For doctorate, MAT or GRE, master's degree, 2 letters of recommendation, work experience. Additional exam requirements/recommendations for international students: Required—TSE (recommended) with a minimum score of 50; Recommended—TOEFL (minimum score 550 paper-based; 213 computer-based), IELTS (minimum score 6). *Application deadline:* For fall admission, 8/11 priority date for domestic and international students; for winter admission, 12/28 priority date for domestic and international students; for spring admission, 4/22 priority date for domestic and international students. Applications are processed on a rolling basis. Application fee: $50. Electronic applications accepted. *Financial support:* In 2006–07, 2 fellow-

Communication Disorders

Nova Southeastern University (continued)
ships (averaging $9,375 per year) were awarded; scholarships/grants and tuition waivers (full) also available. Support available to part-time students. Financial award application deadline: 1/7; financial award applicants required to submit FAFSA. *Unit head:* Dr. Karen D. Bowser, Associate Dean of Doctoral Programs, 954-262-8500, Fax: 954-262-3912, E-mail: bowserk@nova.edu. *Application contact:* Jennifer Quiñones Nottingham, Dean of Student Affairs, 800-986-3223 Ext. 8624, Fax: 954-262-3911, E-mail: jlquinon@nova.edu.

Nova Southeastern University, Fischler School of Education and Human Services, Programs in Communication Sciences and Disorders, Fort Lauderdale, FL 33314-7796. Offers speech-language pathology (MS, SLPD). *Accreditation:* ASHA. Part-time and evening/weekend programs available. Postbaccalaureate distance learning degree programs offered (minimal on-campus study). *Students:* 21 full-time (20 women), 502 part-time (485 women); includes 136 minority (57 African Americans, 1 American Indian/Alaska Native, 10 Asian Americans or Pacific Islanders, 68 Hispanic Americans), 12 international. Average age 38. 160 applicants, 67% accepted, 107 enrolled. In 2006, 98 master's, 8 doctorates awarded. *Degree requirements:* For master's, practicum; for doctorate, thesis/dissertation, practicum. *Entrance requirements:* For master's, interview, minimum GPA of 3.0, 2 letters of recommendation, background check; for doctorate, GRE or MAT, minimum GPA of 3.2, curriculum vitae, interview, 3 letters of recommendation. Additional exam requirements/recommendations for international students: Recommended—TOEFL (minimum score 550 paper-based; 213 computer-based), IELTS (minimum score 6). *Application deadline:* For fall admission, 8/11 priority date for domestic and international students; for winter admission, 12/28 priority date for domestic students, 12/28 for international students; for spring admission, 4/22 priority date for domestic and international students. Applications are processed on a rolling basis. Application fee: $50. Electronic applications accepted. *Expenses:* Contact institution. *Financial support:* Research assistantships, career-related internships or fieldwork, Federal Work-Study, scholarships/grants, tuition waivers (full), and unspecified assistantships available. Support available to part-time students. Financial award application deadline: 1/7. *Unit head:* Dr. Wren Newman, Associate Dean for Speech Programs, 954-262-7756, Fax: 954-262-3940, E-mail: newmanw@nova.edu. *Application contact:* Jennifer Quiñones Nottingham, Dean of Student Affairs, 800-986-3223 Ext. 8624, Fax: 954-262-3911, E-mail: jlquinon@nova.edu.

Nova Southeastern University, Health Professions Division, College of Allied Health and Nursing, Audiology Department, Fort Lauderdale, FL 33314-7796. Offers Au D. *Accreditation:* ASHA. *Faculty:* 7 full-time (5 women), 6 part-time/adjunct (3 women). *Students:* 30 full-time (29 women), 32 part-time (24 women); includes 13 minority (4 African Americans, 2 Asian Americans or Pacific Islanders, 7 Hispanic Americans). 75 applicants, 27% accepted, 16 enrolled. In 2006, 19 degrees awarded. *Degree requirements:* For doctorate, didactic and clinical competencies. *Entrance requirements:* For doctorate, letters of recommendation. Additional exam requirements/recommendations for international students: Required—TOEFL (minimum score 600 paper-based). *Application deadline:* For winter admission, 3/1 priority date for domestic students. Applications are processed on a rolling basis. Application fee: $50. *Financial support:* In 2006–07, 6 teaching assistantships (averaging $8,400 per year) were awarded. *Faculty research:* Amplification, ethics, professionalism, auditory processing. *Unit head:* Dr. Barry A. Freeman, Chair, 954-262-7717, Fax: 954-262-1181, E-mail: freemanb@nsu.nova.edu.

The Ohio State University, Graduate School, College of Social and Behavioral Sciences, School of Social and Behavioral Science, Department of Speech and Hearing Science, Columbus, OH 43210. Offers MA, Au D, PhD. *Accreditation:* ASHA (one or more programs are accredited). *Faculty:* 30. *Students:* 85 full-time (80 women), 10 part-time (8 women); includes 16 minority (4 African Americans, 1 American Indian/Alaska Native, 6 Asian Americans or Pacific Islanders, 5 Hispanic Americans), 6 international. Average age 26. 216 applicants, 57% accepted, 13 enrolled. In 2006, 28 degrees awarded. *Degree requirements:* For master's, thesis optional; for doctorate, thesis/dissertation. *Entrance requirements:* For master's and doctorate, GRE General Test. Additional exam requirements/recommendations for international students: Required—TOEFL (minimum score 620 paper-based; 260 computer-based). *Application deadline:* For fall admission, 8/15 priority date for domestic students, 7/1 priority date for international students; for winter admission, 12/1 priority date for domestic students, 11/1 priority date for international students; for spring admission, 3/1 priority date for domestic students, 2/1 priority date for international students. Applications are processed on a rolling basis. Application fee: $40 ($50 for international students). Electronic applications accepted. *Expenses:* Tuition, state resident: full-time $9,438. Tuition, nonresident: full-time $22,791. Tuition and fees vary according to course load, campus/location and program. *Financial support:* Fellowships, research assistantships, teaching assistantships, Federal Work-Study and institutionally sponsored loans available. Support available to part-time students. *Unit head:* Lawrence L. Feth, Graduate Studies Committee Chair, 614-292-8207, Fax: 614-292-7504, E-mail: feth.1@osu.edu. *Application contact:* 614-292-9444, Fax: 614-292-3895, E-mail: domestic.grad@osu.edu.

Ohio University, Graduate Studies, College of Health and Human Services, School of Hearing, Speech and Language Sciences, Athens, OH 45701-2979. Offers audiology (Au D); hearing science (PhD); speech language pathology (MA); speech-language science (PhD). *Accreditation:* ASHA (one or more programs are accredited). *Faculty:* 20 full-time (12 women), 10 part-time/adjunct (5 women). *Students:* 69 full-time (62 women), 9 international. Average age 25. 138 applicants, 36% accepted, 29 enrolled. In 2006, 19 master's, 3 doctorates awarded. *Median time to degree:* Of those who began their doctoral program in fall 1998, 83% received their degree in 8 years or less. *Degree requirements:* For master's, thesis optional; for doctorate, thesis/dissertation, comprehensive exam, registration. *Entrance requirements:* For master's, GRE, resumé, tape-recorded speech sample for international students; for doctorate, GRE, tape recorded speech sample for international students. Additional exam requirements/recommendations for international students: Required—TOEFL. *Application deadline:* For fall admission, 2/1 for domestic and international students. Applications are processed on a rolling basis. Application fee: $45. Electronic applications accepted. *Expenses:* Contact institution. *Financial support:* In 2006–07, 60 students received support, including 6 research assistantships with full tuition reimbursements available (averaging $13,600 per year), 3 teaching assistantships with full tuition reimbursements available (averaging $3,700 per year); fellowships with full tuition reimbursements available, career-related internships or fieldwork, Federal Work-Study, institutionally sponsored loans, scholarships/grants, and tuition waivers (full) also available. Financial award application deadline: 2/1. *Faculty research:* Neurogenic communication disorders, speech perception and production, hearing science, swallowing, language disorders. Total annual research expenditures: $350,000. *Unit head:* Dr. M. Brooke Hallowell, Director, 740-593-1407, Fax: 740-593-1356, E-mail: hallowel@ohio.edu. *Application contact:* Teresa M. Tyson-Drummer, Administrative Associate, 740-593-1407, Fax: 740-593-0287, E-mail: tysondr@ohio.edu.

Oklahoma State University, College of Arts and Sciences, Department of Communications Sciences and Disorders, Stillwater, OK 74078. Offers MS. *Accreditation:* ASHA. *Faculty:* 10 full-time (6 women), 4 part-time/adjunct (all women). *Students:* 36 full-time (all women), 2 part-time (both women); includes 3 minority (2 American Indian/Alaska Native, 1 Hispanic American). Average age 24. 35 applicants, 74% accepted, 18 enrolled. In 2006, 10 degrees awarded. *Degree requirements:* For master's, thesis or creative research project. *Entrance requirements:* For master's, GRE, minimum GPA of 3.0. Additional exam requirements/recommendations for international students: Required—TOEFL. *Application deadline:* For fall admission, 7/1 priority date for domestic students, 3/1 priority date for international students; for spring admission, 8/1 priority date for international students. Applications are processed on a rolling basis. Application fee: $40 ($75 for international students). Electronic applications accepted. *Expenses:* Tuition, state resident: part-time $146 per credit hour. Tuition, nonresident: part-time $516 per credit hour. Required fees: $44 per credit hour. Tuition and fees vary according to program. *Financial support:* In 2006–07, 16 teaching assistantships (averaging $3,694 per year) were awarded; research assistantships, career-related internships or fieldwork, Federal Work-Study, scholarships/grants, health care benefits, tuition waivers (partial), and unspecified assistantships also available. Support available to part-time students. Financial award application deadline: 3/1. *Faculty research:* Speech communications. *Unit head:* Dr. Randolph E. Deal, Head, 405-744-6021, Fax: 405-744-8070, E-mail: drandol@okstate.edu.

Old Dominion University, Darden College of Education, Program in Speech-Language Pathology, Norfolk, VA 23529. Offers MS Ed. *Accreditation:* ASHA. *Faculty:* 9 full-time (6 women), 5 part-time/adjunct (all women). *Students:* 35 full-time (all women), 23 part-time (all women); includes 8 minority (6 African Americans, 1 American Indian/Alaska Native, 1 Asian American or Pacific Islander). Average age 26. 94 applicants, 21% accepted. In 2006, 23 degrees awarded. *Degree requirements:* For master's, thesis, written exams, practica, comprehensive exam. *Entrance requirements:* For master's, GRE General Test, minimum GPA of 3.0 in major, 2.8 overall. *Application deadline:* For fall admission, 3/14 for domestic students; for spring admission, 11/1 for domestic students. Applications are processed on a rolling basis. Application fee: $40. Electronic applications accepted. *Expenses:* Tuition, area resident: Part-time $285 per credit hour. Tuition, nonresident: part-time $715 per credit hour. Required fees: $94 per semester. *Financial support:* In 2006–07, 14 students received support, including 10 fellowships (averaging $5,000 per year), 1 teaching assistantship with tuition reimbursement available (averaging $6,000 per year); career-related internships or fieldwork, scholarships/grants, and tuition waivers (partial) also available. Support available to part-time students. Financial award application deadline: 2/15; financial award applicants required to submit CSS PROFILE or FAFSA. *Faculty research:* Childhood language disorders, phonological disorders, stuttering, social dialects, aphasia. *Unit head:* Dr. Nicholas G. Bountress, Graduate Program Director, 757-683-4117, Fax: 757-683-5593, E-mail: splpgpd@odu.edu.

Our Lady of the Lake University of San Antonio, School of Education and Clinical Studies, Program in Communication and Learning Disorders, San Antonio, TX 78207-4689. Offers MA. *Accreditation:* ASHA. Part-time and evening/weekend programs available. *Degree requirements:* For master's, comprehensive clinical practicum, thesis optional. *Entrance requirements:* For master's, GRE General Test or MAT, interview. Additional exam requirements/recommendations for international students: Required—TOEFL. Electronic applications accepted. *Faculty research:* Multicultural issues, neurogenic disorders, neural networks, equivalence learning.

Penn State University Park, Graduate School, College of Health and Human Development, Department of Communication Sciences and Disorders, State College, University Park, PA 16802-1503. Offers MS, PhD. *Accreditation:* ASHA (one or more programs are accredited). *Unit head:* Dr. Gordon W. Blood, Head, 814-865-3177, Fax: 814-863-3759, E-mail: f2x@psu.edu. *Application contact:* Carol Walizer, Information Contact, 814-865-0971, E-mail: cyw2@psu.edu.

See Close-Up on page 1813.

Pennsylvania College of Optometry, Graduate Studies in Vision Impairment and Audiology, Elkins Park, PA 19027-1598. Offers audiology (Au D); education of children and youth with visual and multiple impairments (M Ed, Certificate); low vision rehabilitation (MS, Certificate); orientation and mobility therapy (MS, Certificate); rehabilitation teaching (MS, Certificate); OD/MS. *Accreditation:* ASHA. Part-time programs available. *Entrance requirements:* For master's, GRE or MAT, letters of reference (3), interviews (2). Additional exam requirements/recommendations for international students: Required—TOEFL, TWE. Expenses: Contact institution. *Faculty research:* Knowledge utilization, technology transfer.

Portland State University, Graduate Studies, College of Liberal Arts and Sciences, Department of Speech and Hearing Sciences, Portland, OR 97207-0751. Offers speech-language pathology (MA, MS). *Accreditation:* ASHA (one or more programs are accredited). *Faculty:* 9 full-time (7 women), 2 part-time/adjunct (both women). *Students:* 50 full-time (45 women), 4 part-time (all women); includes 4 minority (all Hispanic Americans), 1 international. Average age 32. 104 applicants, 26% accepted, 23 enrolled. In 2006, 25 degrees awarded. *Degree requirements:* For master's, variable foreign language requirement, thesis or alternative, oral exam. *Entrance requirements:* For master's, GRE General Test, minimum GPA of 3.0 in upper-division course work or 2.75 overall. Additional exam requirements/recommendations for international students: Required—TOEFL (minimum score 550 paper-based; 213 computer-based). *Application deadline:* For fall admission, 2/1 for domestic and international students. Application fee: $50. *Expenses:* Tuition, state resident: full-time $6,426; part-time $238 per credit. Tuition, nonresident: full-time $11,016; part-time $408 per credit. Tuition and fees vary according to course load. *Financial support:* Research assistantships with full tuition reimbursements, teaching assistantships with full tuition reimbursements, career-related internships or fieldwork, Federal Work-Study, and institutionally sponsored loans available. Support available to part-time students. Financial award application deadline: 3/1; financial award applicants required to submit FAFSA. *Faculty research:* Adolescents with clefts, spectral analysis of stuttering, communication in late talkers, speech intelligibility, brainstem response in fitting hearing aids. Total annual research expenditures: $133,364. *Unit head:* Thomas Dolan, Director, 503-725-3533, Fax: 503-725-5385.

Purdue University, Graduate School, College of Liberal Arts, Department of Speech, Language, and Hearing Sciences, West Lafayette, IN 47907. Offers audiology (MS, Au D, PhD); linguistics (MS, PhD); speech and hearing science (MS, PhD); speech-language pathology (MS, PhD). *Accreditation:* ASHA. *Faculty:* 18 full-time (11 women), 2 part-time/adjunct (1 woman). *Students:* 85 full-time (76 women), 4 part-time (2 women); includes 7 minority (4 African Americans, 2 Asian Americans or Pacific Islanders, 1 Hispanic American), 8 international. Average age 26. 198 applicants, 63% accepted, 41 enrolled. In 2006, 30 master's, 2 doctorates awarded. *Degree requirements:* For master's, thesis optional; for doctorate, thesis/dissertation. *Entrance requirements:* For master's and doctorate, GRE. Additional exam requirements/recommendations for international students: Required—TOEFL. *Application deadline:* For fall admission, 3/15 for domestic and international students; for spring admission, 10/15 for domestic and international students. Applications are processed on a rolling basis. Application fee: $55. Electronic applications accepted. *Financial support:* In 2006–07, 8 fellowships with full tuition reimbursements (averaging $16,549 per year), 18 research assistantships with full tuition reimbursements (averaging $14,500 per year), 27 teaching assistantships with full tuition reimbursements (averaging $12,540 per year) were awarded; career-related internships or fieldwork and scholarships/grants also available. Support available to part-time students. Financial award application deadline: 2/1; financial award applicants required to submit FAFSA. *Faculty research:* Psychoacoustics, speech perception, speech physiology, stuttering, child language. *Unit head:* Dr. Robert Novack, Head, 765-494-3788, Fax: 765-494-0771. *Application contact:* Wanda Bailey, Graduate Secretary, 765-494-3786, Fax: 765-494-0771, E-mail: baileywf@purdue.edu.

Queens College of the City University of New York, Division of Graduate Studies, Arts and Humanities Division, Department of Linguistics and Communication Disorders, Program in Speech Pathology, Flushing, NY 11367-1597. Offers MA. *Accreditation:* ASHA. *Faculty:* 9 full-time (6 women). *Students:* 30 full-time (28 women). 141 applicants, 11% accepted, 15 enrolled. In 2006, 13 degrees awarded. *Degree requirements:* For master's, clinical internships, thesis optional. *Entrance requirements:* For master's, GRE General Test, minimum GPA of 3.0. Additional exam requirements/recommendations for international students: Required—TOEFL. *Application deadline:* For fall admission, 2/1 for domestic students. Applications are processed on a rolling basis. Application fee: $125. *Financial support:* Career-related internships or fieldwork, Federal Work-Study, institutionally sponsored loans, and tuition waivers (partial) available. Support available to part-time students. Financial award application deadline: 4/1; financial award applicants required to submit FAFSA. *Unit head:* Sima Gerber, Graduate Adviser, 718-520-2934, E-mail: sima_gerber@qc.edu. *Application contact:* Mario Caruso, Director of Graduate Admissions, 718-997-5200, Fax: 718-997-5193, E-mail: graduate_admissions@qc.edu.

Radford University, Graduate College, Waldron College of Health and Human Services, Department of Communication Science and Disorders, Radford, VA 24142. Offers MA, MS. *Accreditation:* ASHA (one or more programs are accredited). Part-time programs available.

Faculty: 5 full-time (4 women), 1 (woman) part-time/adjunct. *Students:* 63 full-time (all women); includes 9 minority (8 African Americans, 1 Asian American or Pacific Islander). Average age 26. 73 applicants, 78% accepted, 37 enrolled. In 2006, 14 degrees awarded. *Degree requirements:* For master's, thesis (for some programs), comprehensive exam. *Entrance requirements:* For master's, GRE. Additional exam requirements/recommendations for international students: Required—TOEFL. *Application deadline:* For fall admission, 2/1 priority date for domestic students, 4/1 for international students; for spring admission, 10/1 for domestic students, 8/1 for international students. Applications are processed on a rolling basis. Application fee: $40. Electronic applications accepted. *Expenses:* Tuition, state resident: full-time $4,680; part-time $260 per credit hour. Tuition, nonresident: full-time $8,604; part-time $478 per credit hour. *Financial support:* In 2006–07, 46 students received support, including 41 research assistantships with partial tuition reimbursements available (averaging $8,000 per year), teaching assistantships with partial tuition reimbursements available (averaging $8,700 per year); career-related internships or fieldwork, Federal Work-Study, institutionally sponsored loans, scholarships/grants, and unspecified assistantships also available. Financial award application deadline: 3/1; financial award applicants required to submit FAFSA. *Unit head:* Dr. Kenneth M. Cox, Chair, 540-831-7666, Fax: 540-831-6370, E-mail: kcox3@radford.edu.

Rockhurst University, School of Graduate and Professional Studies, Program in Communication Sciences and Disorders, Kansas City, MO 64110-2561. Offers MS. *Accreditation:* ASHA. Part-time and evening/weekend programs available. *Faculty:* 5 full-time (4 women), 2 part-time/adjunct (both women). *Students:* 52 full-time (49 women), 23 part-time (21 women); includes 3 minority (all Hispanic Americans) Average age 28. 83 applicants, 66% accepted, 22 enrolled. In 2006, 14 degrees awarded. *Entrance requirements:* For master's, GRE General Test, interview, minimum GPA of 3.0, letters of recommendation. Additional exam requirements/recommendations for international students: Required—TOEFL (minimum score 550 paper-based). *Application deadline:* Applications are processed on a rolling basis. Application fee: $25. *Expenses:* Tuition: Full-time $9,810; part-time $6,540 per year. Required fees: $400 per term. *Financial support:* Career-related internships or fieldwork, institutionally sponsored loans, and unspecified assistantships available. Financial award applicants required to submit FAFSA. *Faculty research:* Bioacoustics, physiology, applied speech science, pediatric nutrition/dysphagia, communication/cognition. *Unit head:* Dr. Dennis Ingrisano, Chair, 816-501-4742, Fax: 816-501-4169, E-mail: dennis.ingrisano@rockhurst.edu. *Application contact:* Michele Huiatt, Director of Graduate Recruitment Admission, 816-501-3490, Fax: 816-501-4241, E-mail: michele.huiatt@rockhurst.edu.

Rush University, College of Health Sciences, Department of Communication Disorders and Sciences, Chicago, IL 60612-3832. Offers audiology (Au D); speech-language pathology (MS). *Accreditation:* ASHA (one or more programs are accredited). Part-time programs available. *Degree requirements:* For master's, thesis optional; for doctorate, investigative project. *Entrance requirements:* For master's and doctorate, GRE General Test, minimum GPA of 3.0. Additional exam requirements/recommendations for international students: Required—TOEFL. Electronic applications accepted. Expenses: Contact institution. *Faculty research:* Electrostimulation of subthalamic nucleus, sensory feedback in speech modulation, sentence complexity in children's writing, velopharyngeal function, adult neurology.

St. Cloud State University, School of Graduate Studies, College of Fine Arts and Humanities, Department of Communication Sciences and Disorders, St. Cloud, MN 56301-4498. Offers MS. *Accreditation:* ASHA. *Faculty:* 5 full-time (4 women), 1 (woman) part-time/adjunct. *Students:* 24 full-time (23 women), 8 part-time (7 women), 2 international. 35 applicants, 57% accepted. In 2006, 15 degrees awarded. *Degree requirements:* For master's, thesis or alternative, comprehensive exam (for some programs). *Entrance requirements:* For master's, GRE General Test, minimum GPA of 2.75. Additional exam requirements/recommendations for international students: Required—MELAB; Recommended—TOEFL (minimum score 550 paper-based; 213 computer-based), IELTS (minimum score 7). *Application deadline:* For fall admission, 2/1 for domestic and international students. Application fee: $35. Electronic applications accepted. *Financial support:* Federal Work-Study, scholarships/grants, and unspecified assistantships available. Financial award application deadline: 3/1. *Unit head:* Dr. Monica Devens, Chairperson, 320-308-4173, E-mail: mcdevers@stcloudstate.edu. *Application contact:* Linda Lou Krueger, School of Graduate Studies, 320-308-2113, Fax: 320-308-5371, E-mail: lekrueger@stcloudstate.edu.

Saint Louis University, Graduate School, College of Public Service and Graduate School, Department of Communication Sciences and Disorders, St. Louis, MO 63103-2097. Offers MA, MA-R. *Accreditation:* ASHA (one or more programs are accredited). Part-time programs available. *Faculty:* 7 full-time (4 women), 4 part-time/adjunct (all women). *Students:* 46 full-time (all women), 2 part-time (both women); includes 7 minority (3 African Americans, 1 Asian American or Pacific Islander, 3 Hispanic Americans). Average age 24. 89 applicants, 65% accepted, 18 enrolled. In 2006, 15 degrees awarded. *Degree requirements:* For master's, thesis (for some programs), comprehensive oral and written exams. *Entrance requirements:* For master's, GRE General Test, letters of recommendation, resumé. Additional exam requirements/recommendations for international students: Required—TOEFL (minimum score 525 paper-based; 194 computer-based). *Application deadline:* For fall admission, 2/1 priority date for domestic students, 2/1 for international students; for spring admission, 11/1 for domestic and international students. Application fee: $40. *Expenses:* Tuition: Part-time $800 per credit hour. Required fees: $105 per semester. *Financial support:* In 2006–07, 39 students received support, including 1 research assistantship (averaging $16,400 per year), 10 teaching assistantships with full tuition reimbursements available (averaging $10,500 per year); Federal Work-Study, scholarships/grants, traineeships, health care benefits, tuition waivers, and unspecified assistantships also available. Support available to part-time students. Financial award application deadline: 6/1; financial award applicants required to submit FAFSA. *Faculty research:* Communication disorders in culturally and linguistically diverse populations, bilingual and biliteracy (Hispanic) assessment and intervention, disability study-specific to World Health Organization classifications, early intervention in communication disorders, voice of the head and neck involved patient. Total annual research expenditures: $5,000. *Unit head:* Dr. Travis T Threats, Chairperson, 314-977-3175, Fax: 314-977-3360, E-mail: threatst@slu.edu. *Application contact:* Gary Behrman, Associate Dean of the Graduate School, 314-977-3827, E-mail: behrmang@slu.edu.

Saint Xavier University, Graduate Studies, School of Arts and Sciences, Department of Speech-Language Pathology, Chicago, IL 60655-3105. Offers MS. *Accreditation:* ASHA. *Faculty:* 8. *Students:* 45 full-time (44 women), 17 part-time (all women); includes 3 minority (1 Asian American or Pacific Islander, 2 Hispanic Americans). Average age 26. *Entrance requirements:* For master's, GRE General Test, minimum GPA of 3.0, undergraduate course work in speech. *Application deadline:* For fall admission, 3/1 for domestic students. Application fee: $35. *Expenses: Contact institution. Financial support:* Career-related internships or fieldwork available. Support available to part-time students. Financial award applicants required to submit FAFSA. *Unit head:* Dr. Michael Flahive, Graduate Director, 773-298-3566, Fax: 773-779-9061, E-mail: flahive@sxu.edu. *Application contact:* Beth Gierach, Managing Director of Admission, 773-298-3053, Fax: 773-298-3076, E-mail: gierach@sxu.edu.

San Diego State University, Graduate and Research Affairs, College of Health and Human Services, Department of Speech, Language, and Hearing Sciences, San Diego, CA 92182. Offers audiology (Au D); communicative disorders (MA); language and communicative disorders (PhD). *Accreditation:* ASHA (one or more programs are accredited). Part-time programs available. *Students:* 69 full-time (66 women), 16 part-time (12 women); includes 13 minority (1 American Indian/Alaska Native, 3 Asian Americans or Pacific Islanders, 9 Hispanic Americans), 7 international. Average age 29. 262 applicants, 31% accepted, 27 enrolled. In 2006, 38 degrees awarded. *Degree requirements:* For master's, thesis (for some programs), comprehensive exam (for some programs); for doctorate, thesis/dissertation. *Entrance requirements:* For master's and doctorate, GRE General Test. Additional exam requirements/recommendations for international students: Required—TOEFL. *Application deadline:* For fall admission, 2/1 for domestic and international students. Application fee: $55. Electronic applications accepted. *Financial support:* In 2006–07, 49 teaching assistantships were awarded; fellowships, research assistantships, career-related internships or fieldwork and unspecified assistantships also available. Financial award applicants required to submit FAFSA. *Faculty research:* Brain/behavior relationships in language development, grammatical processing and language disorders, interdisciplinary training of bilingual speech pathologists. Total annual research expenditures: $1.2 million. *Unit head:* Beverly Wulfeck, Interim Director, 619-594-7108, Fax: 619-594-7109, E-mail: bwulfeck@mail.sdsu.edu. *Application contact:* Elizabeth Allen, Graduate Adviser, 619-594-6663, Fax: 619-594-7109, E-mail: eallen@mail.sdsu.edu.

San Francisco State University, Division of Graduate Studies, College of Education, Department of Special Education, Program in Communicative Disorders, San Francisco, CA 94132-1722. Offers MS. *Accreditation:* ASHA. Part-time programs available. *Students:* 80 (70 women). *Entrance requirements:* For master's, minimum GPA of 2.5 in last 60 units. *Application deadline:* For fall admission, 11/30 priority date for domestic students. Applications are processed on a rolling basis. Application fee: $55. *Financial support:* Application deadline: 3/1. *Unit head:* Dr. Minnie Graham, Coordinator, 415-338-7656, E-mail: mgraham@sfsu.edu.

San Jose State University, Graduate Studies and Research, College of Education, Department of Communicative Disorders and Sciences, San Jose, CA 95192-0001. Offers speech pathology (MA). *Accreditation:* ASHA. Evening/weekend programs available. *Students:* 115 full-time (111 women), 5 part-time (all women); includes 45 minority (3 African Americans, 1 American Indian/Alaska Native, 19 Asian Americans or Pacific Islanders, 22 Hispanic Americans), 3 international. Average age 30. 98 applicants, 67% accepted, 45 enrolled. In 2006, 24 degrees awarded. *Entrance requirements:* For master's, MAT. *Application deadline:* For fall admission, 6/29 for domestic students; for spring admission, 11/30 for domestic students. Applications are processed on a rolling basis. Application fee: $59. Electronic applications accepted. *Financial support:* Career-related internships or fieldwork available. Financial award applicants required to submit FAFSA. *Unit head:* Gloria Weddington, Chair, 408-924-3688, Fax: 408-924-3641.

Seton Hall University, School of Graduate Medical Education, Program in Speech-Language Pathology, South Orange, NJ 07079-2697. Offers MS. *Accreditation:* ASHA. *Faculty:* 7 full-time (4 women), 5 part-time/adjunct (3 women). *Students:* 45 full-time (all women); includes 4 minority (3 Asian Americans or Pacific Islanders, 1 Hispanic American), 1 international. Average age 25. 104 applicants, 34% accepted, 22 enrolled. In 2006, 24 degrees awarded. *Entrance requirements:* For master's, GRE, bachelor's degree, clinical experience; minimum GPA of 3.0, undergraduate preprofessional coursework in communication sciences and disorders. *Application deadline:* For fall admission, 3/1 priority date for domestic students. Applications are processed on a rolling basis. Application fee: $75. Electronic applications accepted. *Financial support:* In 2006–07, 1 student received support, including 1 research assistantship with partial tuition reimbursement available (averaging $4,000 per year); unspecified assistantships and student technology assistantships also available. *Faculty research:* Child language disorders, motor speech control, voice disorders, dysphagia, early intervention/teaming. *Unit head:* Dr. Robert F. Orlikoff, Chair, 973-275-2825, Fax: 973-275-2370, E-mail: gradmeded@shu.edu. *Application contact:* Deborah Verderosa, Director of Admissions, 973-275-2062, Fax: 973-275-2171, E-mail: gradmeded@shu.edu.

See Close-Up on page 1731.

South Carolina State University, School of Graduate Studies, Department of Health Sciences, Orangeburg, SC 29117-0001. Offers speech/language pathology (MA). *Accreditation:* ASHA. Part-time and evening/weekend programs available. *Faculty:* 4 full-time (3 women), 3 part-time/adjunct (1 woman). *Students:* 20 full-time (19 women), 37 part-time (35 women); includes 45 minority (44 African Americans, 1 Hispanic American). Average age 31. 38 applicants, 71% accepted, 20 enrolled. In 2006, 9 degrees awarded. *Degree requirements:* For master's, departmental qualifying exam, thesis optional. *Entrance requirements:* For master's, GRE or NTE, minimum GPA of 3.0. *Application deadline:* For fall admission, 6/15 for domestic and international students; for spring admission, 11/1 for domestic and international students. Application fee: $25. Electronic applications accepted. *Expenses:* Tuition, state resident: full-time $7,278. Tuition, nonresident: full-time $14,322. *Financial support:* Career-related internships or fieldwork, Federal Work-Study, and institutionally sponsored loans available. Financial award application deadline: 6/1. *Unit head:* Dr. Gwendolyn Wilson, Interim Chair, 803-536-7063, Fax: 803-536-8593, E-mail: gdwilson@scsu.edu. *Application contact:* Annette Hazzard-Jones, Program Coordinator II, 803-536-8809, Fax: 803-536-8812, E-mail: zs_ahazzard@scsu.edu.

Southeastern Louisiana University, College of Nursing and Health Sciences, Department of Communication Sciences and Disorders, Hammond, LA 70402. Offers MS. *Accreditation:* ASHA; NCATE. *Faculty:* 5 full-time (4 women). *Students:* 37 full-time (35 women), 28 part-time (27 women); includes 4 minority (all African Americans), 1 international. Average age 28. 27 applicants, 100% accepted, 19 enrolled. In 2006, 32 degrees awarded. *Degree requirements:* For master's, thesis optional. *Entrance requirements:* For master's, GRE General Test, 3 letters of reference, minimum GPA of 2.5. Additional exam requirements/recommendations for international students: Required—TOEFL (minimum score 500 paper-based; 173 computer-based). *Application deadline:* For fall admission, 7/15 priority date for domestic students, 6/1 priority date for international students; for spring admission, 12/1 priority date for domestic students, 10/1 priority date for international students. Applications are processed on a rolling basis. Application fee: $20 ($30 for international students). Electronic applications accepted. *Expenses:* Tuition, state resident: full-time $2,216; part-time $123 per credit. Tuition, nonresident: full-time $6,212; part-time $345 per credit. Required fees: $986; $55 per credit. Part-time tuition and fees vary according to course load. *Financial support:* Federal Work-Study, institutionally sponsored loans, scholarships/grants, unspecified assistantships, and administrative assistantships available. Support available to part-time students. Financial award application deadline: 5/1; financial award applicants required to submit FAFSA. *Faculty research:* Conversation in standard and communication disordered, autism, language disorders and literacy, acoustic characteristics of American English, educational needs of children with cochlear implants. *Unit head:* Dr. Paula Currie, Department Head, 985-549-2214, Fax: 985-549-5030, E-mail: pcurrie@selu.edu. *Application contact:* Sandra Meyers, Graduate Admissions Analyst, 985-549-2066, Fax: 985-549-5632, E-mail: admissions@selu.edu.

Southeast Missouri State University, School of Graduate Studies, Department of Communication Disorders, Cape Girardeau, MO 63701-4799. Offers MA. *Accreditation:* ASHA. *Faculty:* 6 full-time (5 women). *Students:* 26 full-time (all women), 4 part-time (all women), 1 international. Average age 25. 29 applicants, 55% accepted. In 2006, 13 degrees awarded. *Degree requirements:* For master's, thesis or alternative, comprehensive exam. *Entrance requirements:* For master's, GRE, minimum undergraduate GPA of 3.0. Additional exam requirements/recommendations for international students: Required—TOEFL (minimum score 550 paper-based; 213 computer-based). *Application deadline:* For fall admission, 3/1 for domestic and international students. Applications are processed on a rolling basis. Application fee: $20 ($100 for international students). *Financial support:* In 2006–07, 24 students received support, including 11 research assistantships with full tuition reimbursements available (averaging $7,100 per year); career-related internships or fieldwork and unspecified assistantships also available. Financial award applicants required to submit FAFSA. *Unit head:* Dr. Sakina Drummond, Chairperson, 573-651-2155, E-mail: ssdrummond@semo.edu. *Application contact:* Marsha L. Arant, Senior Administrative Assistant, Office of Graduate Studies, 573-651-2192, Fax: 573-651-2001, E-mail: marant@semo.edu.

Southern Connecticut State University, School of Graduate Studies, School of Health and Human Services, Department of Communication Disorders, New Haven, CT 06515-1355. Offers audiology (MS); speech pathology (MS). *Accreditation:* ASHA. Part-time programs available. *Faculty:* 12 full-time, 2 part-time/adjunct. *Students:* 115 full-time (113 women), 14 part-time (13 women); includes 19 minority (7 African Americans, 12 Hispanic Americans), 1 international. 147 applicants, 26% accepted, 37 enrolled. In 2006, 38 degrees awarded. *Degree requirements:* For master's, thesis or alternative, clinical experience. *Entrance*

Communication Disorders

Southern Connecticut State University (continued)
requirements: For master's, GRE, interview, minimum QPA of 3.0. *Application deadline:* For fall admission, 3/1 for domestic students. Application fee: $50. Electronic applications accepted. *Financial support:* Career-related internships or fieldwork available. Financial award application deadline: 4/15; financial award applicants required to submit FAFSA. *Unit head:* Dr. James Dempsey, Chairperson, 203-392-5962, Fax: 203-392-5968, E-mail: dempsey@southernct.edu. *Application contact:* Dr. Deborah Weiss, Graduate Coordinator, 203-392-6615, Fax: 203-392-5968, E-mail: weissd1@southernct.edu.

Southern Illinois University Carbondale, Graduate School, College of Education, Rehabilitation Institute, Department of Communication Disorders and Sciences, Carbondale, IL 62901-4701. Offers MS. *Accreditation:* ASHA. *Faculty:* 4 full-time (2 women). *Students:* 31 full-time (all women), 12 part-time (all women); includes 3 minority (2 African Americans, 1 Asian American or Pacific Islander), 2 international. Average age 29. 83 applicants, 12% accepted, 0 enrolled. In 2006, 17 degrees awarded. *Degree requirements:* For master's, thesis. *Entrance requirements:* For master's, GRE, minimum GPA of 3.0. Additional exam requirements/recommendations for international students: Required—TOEFL. *Application deadline:* For fall admission, 2/1 for domestic students. Application fee: $20. *Financial support:* In 2006–07, 17 students received support, including 1 fellowship with full tuition reimbursement available, 7 research assistantships with full tuition reimbursements available; teaching assistantships with full tuition reimbursements available, career-related internships or fieldwork, Federal Work-Study, institutionally sponsored loans, tuition waivers (full), and unspecified assistantships also available. *Faculty research:* Neurolinguistics, language processing, child language, fluency, phonology. *Application contact:* Mary Falaster, Administrative Clerk, 618-453-8274, E-mail: mfalast@siu.edu.

Southern Illinois University Edwardsville, Graduate Studies and Research, School of Education, Department of Special Education and Communication Disorders, Program in Speech Language Pathology, Edwardsville, IL 62026-0001. Offers MS. *Accreditation:* ASHA. Part-time and evening/weekend programs available. *Students:* 52 full-time (49 women); includes 2 minority (1 Asian American or Pacific Islander, 1 Hispanic American). Average age 33. 86 applicants, 33% accepted. In 2006, 23 degrees awarded. *Degree requirements:* For master's, thesis or alternative, final exam. *Entrance requirements:* For master's, GRE, minimum GPA of 3.0. Additional exam requirements/recommendations for international students: Required—TOEFL. *Application deadline:* For fall admission, 2/1 for domestic and international students. Application fee: $30. Electronic applications accepted. *Financial support:* Fellowships with full tuition reimbursements, research assistantships, teaching assistantships with full tuition reimbursements, career-related internships or fieldwork, Federal Work-Study, institutionally sponsored loans, traineeships, and unspecified assistantships available. Support available to part-time students. Financial award application deadline: 3/1; financial award applicants required to submit FAFSA.

State University of New York at Fredonia, Graduate Studies, Department of Speech Pathology and Audiology, Fredonia, NY 14063-1136. Offers MS, MS Ed. *Accreditation:* ASHA. Part-time and evening/weekend programs available. *Faculty:* 7 full-time (5 women), 2 part-time/adjunct (both women). *Students:* 54 full-time (52 women); includes 3 minority (1 Asian American or Pacific Islander, 2 Hispanic Americans). Average age 25. In 2006, 30 degrees awarded. *Degree requirements:* For master's, clinical practice, thesis optional. *Application deadline:* For fall admission, 8/5 for domestic students; for spring admission, 12/1 for domestic students. Application fee: $50. *Expenses:* Tuition, state resident: full-time $6,900; part-time $288 per credit hour. Tuition, nonresident: full-time $10,920; part-time $455 per credit hour. Required fees: $1,132; $47 per credit hour. *Financial support:* In 2006–07, 7 teaching assistantships with partial tuition reimbursements (averaging $3,250 per year) were awarded; research assistantships, career-related internships or fieldwork and tuition waivers (full and partial) also available. Support available to part-time students. Financial award application deadline: 3/15. *Unit head:* Dr. Kim Tillery, Chair, 716-673-4617, E-mail: kimberly.tillery@fredonia.edu.

State University of New York at New Paltz, Graduate School, Faculty of Liberal Arts and Sciences, Department of Communication Disorders, New Paltz, NY 12561. Offers MS. *Accreditation:* ASHA. Part-time and evening/weekend programs available. *Faculty:* 9 full-time (all women), 6 part-time/adjunct (4 women). *Students:* 43 full-time (42 women), 22 part-time (all women); includes 5 minority (1 African American, 4 Hispanic Americans), 1 international. Average age 32. In 2006, 19 degrees awarded. *Degree requirements:* For master's, thesis, comprehensive exam. *Entrance requirements:* For master's, GRE General Test or MAT, minimum GPA of 3.0. Additional exam requirements/recommendations for international students: Required—TOEFL (minimum score 550 paper-based; 213 computer-based; 80 iBT). *Application deadline:* For fall admission, 3/1 for domestic and international students. Application fee: $50. Electronic applications accepted. *Expenses:* Tuition, state resident: full-time $6,900; part-time $288 per credit hour. Tuition, nonresident: full-time $10,920; part-time $455 per credit hour. *Financial support:* In 2006–07, 5 students received support, including 3 teaching assistantships with partial tuition reimbursements available (averaging $5,000 per year); Federal Work-Study, institutionally sponsored loans, scholarships/grants, health care benefits, and unspecified assistantships also available. *Unit head:* Dr. Stella Turk, Chairman, 845-257-3600. *Application contact:* Dr. Elizabeth Hester, Coordinator, 845-257-3465.

State University of New York at Plattsburgh, Division of Education, Health, and Human Services, Department of Communication Disorders, Plattsburgh, NY 12901-2681. Offers speech-language pathology (MA). *Accreditation:* ASHA. Part-time programs available. *Faculty:* 11 full-time (7 women), 8 part-time/adjunct (all women). *Students:* 26 full-time (25 women), 2 part-time (both women); includes 1 minority (Asian American or Pacific Islander), 6 international. Average age 28. 48 applicants, 42% accepted, 16 enrolled. In 2006, 12 degrees awarded. *Degree requirements:* For master's, National Teacher Exam, thesis optional. *Entrance requirements:* For master's, GRE General Test, minimum GPA of 3.0. *Application deadline:* For fall admission, 3/1 for domestic students. Applications are processed on a rolling basis. Application fee: $50. *Expenses:* Tuition, state resident: full-time $6,900; part-time $288 per credit hour. Tuition, nonresident: full-time $10,920; part-time $455 per credit hour. *Financial support:* In 2006–07, 23 students received support. Career-related internships or fieldwork and Federal Work-Study available. Support available to part-time students. Financial award application deadline: 4/15; financial award applicants required to submit FAFSA. *Faculty research:* Ototoxins and noise effects on hearing, language impairment in Alzheimer's disease, attitudes on stuttering, diagnostic audiology. *Unit head:* Dr. Patrick Coppens, Chair, 518-564-5178, Fax: 518-564-4069. *Application contact:* Dr. R. Wacker, Information Contact, 518-564-2170, E-mail: wackerrl@splava.cc.plattsburgh.edu.

State University of New York College at Geneseo, Graduate Studies, Department of Communicative Disorders and Sciences, Geneseo, NY 14454-1401. Offers MA. *Accreditation:* ASHA. *Faculty:* 5 full-time (2 women), 2 part-time/adjunct (1 woman). *Students:* 38 full-time (all women), 7 part-time (6 women); includes 1 minority (Hispanic American), 1 international. Average age 24. 76 applicants, 51% accepted, 18 enrolled. In 2006, 24 degrees awarded. *Degree requirements:* For master's, thesis optional. *Entrance requirements:* For master's, GRE General Test. Additional exam requirements/recommendations for international students: Required—TOEFL. *Application deadline:* For fall admission, 2/1 for domestic and international students; for spring admission, 10/1 for domestic students. Applications are processed on a rolling basis. Application fee: $50. *Financial support:* Fellowships, research assistantships, teaching assistantships, career-related internships or fieldwork, institutionally sponsored loans, and unspecified assistantships available. Financial award application deadline: 4/1; financial award applicants required to submit FAFSA. *Faculty research:* Stuttering in young children. *Unit head:* Dr. Linda House, Chairperson, 585-245-5328, Fax: 585-245-5434, E-mail: house@geneseo.edu. *Application contact:* Dr. Robert E. Owens, Professor, 585-245-5131, Fax: 585-245-5434, E-mail: owens@geneseo.edu.

Stephen F. Austin State University, Graduate School, College of Education, Department of Human Services, Nacogdoches, TX 75962. Offers counseling (MA); school psychology (MA); special education (M Ed); speech pathology (MS). *Accreditation:* ACA (one or more programs are accredited); ASHA (one or more programs are accredited); CORE; NCATE. *Degree requirements:* For master's, thesis (for some programs), comprehensive exam. *Entrance requirements:* For master's, GRE General Test, minimum GPA of 2.8. Additional exam requirements/recommendations for international students: Required—TOEFL.

Syracuse University, Graduate School, College of Arts and Sciences, Department of Communication Sciences and Disorders, Program in Audiology, Syracuse, NY 13244. Offers Au D, PhD. Part-time programs available. *Students:* 13 full-time (11 women), 1 (woman) part-time, 2 international. 16 applicants, 69% accepted, 6 enrolled. *Degree requirements:* For doctorate, thesis/dissertation. *Entrance requirements:* For doctorate, GRE General Test. *Application deadline:* For fall admission, 1/15 priority date for domestic students. Applications are processed on a rolling basis. Application fee: $65. Electronic applications accepted. *Expenses:* Tuition: Full-time $16,920; part-time $940 per credit hour. Required fees: $930; $930 per year. *Application contact:* Information Contact, 315-443-9615.

Syracuse University, Graduate School, College of Arts and Sciences, Department of Communication Sciences and Disorders, Program in Speech Language Pathology, Syracuse, NY 13244. Offers MS, PhD. Program offers New York State teacher certification. Part-time programs available. *Students:* 40 full-time (39 women), 10 part-time (all women); includes 5 minority (2 African Americans, 3 Asian Americans or Pacific Islanders), 4 international. 63 applicants, 68% accepted, 13 enrolled. *Degree requirements:* For master's, thesis or alternative; for doctorate, thesis/dissertation. *Entrance requirements:* For master's and doctorate, GRE. Additional exam requirements/recommendations for international students: Required—TOEFL. *Application deadline:* For fall admission, 2/1 priority date for domestic students. Applications are processed on a rolling basis. Application fee: $65. Electronic applications accepted. *Expenses:* Tuition: Full-time $16,920; part-time $940 per credit hour. Required fees: $930; $930 per year. *Application contact:* Information Contact, 315-443-9615.

Teachers College Columbia University, Graduate Faculty of Education, Department of Biobehavioral Studies, Program in Speech-Language Pathology, New York, NY 10027-6696. Offers Ed M, MS, Ed D, PhD. *Accreditation:* ASHA. *Faculty:* 5 full-time (3 women). *Students:* 96 full-time (90 women), 34 part-time (31 women); includes 29 minority (5 African Americans, 10 Asian Americans or Pacific Islanders, 14 Hispanic Americans), 12 international. Average age 29. 435 applicants, 24% accepted, 48 enrolled. In 2006, 50 master's, 3 doctorates awarded. Terminal master's awarded for partial completion of doctoral program. *Degree requirements:* For doctorate, thesis/dissertation. *Application deadline:* For fall admission, 2/1 priority date for domestic students. Application fee: $65. *Expenses:* Tuition: Full-time $23,400; part-time $975 per credit. Required fees: $320 per term. *Financial support:* Fellowships, teaching assistantships, career-related internships or fieldwork, Federal Work-Study, institutionally sponsored loans, and tuition waivers (full and partial) available. Support available to part-time students. Financial award application deadline: 2/1. *Faculty research:* Neuropathology of speech, stuttering, language disorders in children and adults, motor speech. *Application contact:* Debbie Lesperance, Assistant Director of Admission, 212-678-3710, Fax: 212-678-4171.

See Close-Up on page 1739.

Teachers College Columbia University, Graduate Faculty of Education, Department of Health and Behavioral Studies, Program in Hearing Impairment, New York, NY 10027-6696. Offers MA, Ed D. *Faculty:* 1 full-time (0 women), 2 part-time/adjunct. *Students:* 20 full-time (all women), 20 part-time (16 women); includes 7 minority (1 African American, 1 American Indian/Alaska Native, 4 Asian Americans or Pacific Islanders, 1 Hispanic American), 1 international. Average age 26. 21 applicants, 90% accepted, 12 enrolled. In 2006, 16 degrees awarded. *Degree requirements:* For doctorate, thesis/dissertation. *Application deadline:* For fall admission, 5/15 for domestic students; for spring admission, 12/1 for domestic students. Application fee: $65. *Expenses:* Tuition: Full-time $23,400; part-time $975 per credit. Required fees: $320 per term. *Financial support:* Fellowships, career-related internships or fieldwork, Federal Work-Study, institutionally sponsored loans, and tuition waivers (full and partial) available. Support available to part-time students. Financial award application deadline: 2/1. *Faculty research:* Language development, reading/writing, cognitive abilities, text analysis, auditory streaming. *Application contact:* Peter Shon, Assistant Director of Admission, 212-678-3305, Fax: 212-678-4171, E-mail: shon@exchange.tc.columbia.edu.

See Close-Up on page 1129.

Teachers College Columbia University, Graduate Faculty of Education, Department of Health and Behavioral Studies, Program in Teaching of Sign Language, New York, NY 10027-6696. Offers MA. *Accreditation:* NCATE. *Students:* 5 full-time (4 women), 17 part-time (14 women); includes 3 minority (2 African Americans, 1 Asian American or Pacific Islander). Average age 33. 17 applicants, 65% accepted, 9 enrolled. In 2006, 6 degrees awarded. Application fee: $65. *Expenses:* Tuition: Full-time $23,400; part-time $975 per credit. Required fees: $320 per term. *Application contact:* Peter Shon, Assistant Director of Admission, 212-678-3305, Fax: 212-678-4171, E-mail: shon@exchange.tc.columbia.edu.

See Close-Up on page 1129.

Temple University, Health Sciences Center and Graduate School, College of Health Professions, Department of Communication Sciences, Program in Speech-Language-Hearing, Philadelphia, PA 19122-6096. Offers MA. *Students:* 47 full-time (44 women), 15 part-time (all women). In 2006, 21 degrees awarded. *Entrance requirements:* For master's, GRE General Test, minimum GPA of 3.0. Additional exam requirements/recommendations for international students: Required—TOEFL (minimum score 550 paper-based; 213 computer-based; 79 iBT). *Application deadline:* For fall admission, 2/1 for domestic students, 12/15 for international students. Application fee: $50. Electronic applications accepted. *Expenses:* Tuition, state resident: full-time $12,264; part-time $511 per credit. Tuition, nonresident: full-time $17,904; part-time $746 per credit. Required fees: $84 per course. Tuition and fees vary according to program. *Financial support:* Teaching assistantships with full tuition reimbursements available. Financial award application deadline: 1/15; financial award applicants required to submit FAFSA.

Tennessee State University, The School of Graduate Studies and Research, College of Health Sciences, Department of Speech Pathology and Audiology, Nashville, TN 37209-1561. Offers speech and hearing science (MS). Part-time programs available. Postbaccalaureate distance learning degree programs offered (minimal on-campus study). *Faculty:* 9 full-time (5 women), 1 (woman) part-time/adjunct. *Students:* 50 full-time (48 women), 32 part-time (31 women); includes 22 minority (18 African Americans, 2 American Indian/Alaska Native, 2 Hispanic Americans). Average age 24. 132 applicants, 42% accepted, 46 enrolled. In 2006, 21 degrees awarded. *Degree requirements:* For master's, thesis optional. *Entrance requirements:* For master's, GRE General Test, MAT, minimum GPA of 3.5. Additional exam requirements/recommendations for international students: Required—TOEFL. *Application deadline:* For fall admission, 3/15 for domestic and international students. Application fee: $25. *Financial support:* Fellowships with tuition reimbursements, research assistantships with tuition reimbursements, teaching assistantships with tuition reimbursements, scholarships/grants, traineeships, and unspecified assistantships available. Support available to part-time students. Financial award application deadline: 3/15; financial award applicants required to submit FAFSA. *Faculty research:* Auditory dunction to sickle cell disease, assessment and management of dysphagia, early intervention language disorders, multicultural diversity. Total annual research expenditures: $100,775. *Unit head:* Dr. Harold R. Mitchell, Head, Department of Speech Pathology and Audiology, 615-963-7009, Fax: 615-963-7119, E-mail: hmitchell@tnstate.edu.

Texas A&M University–Kingsville, College of Graduate Studies, College of Arts and Sciences, Department of Communication, Kingsville, TX 78363. Offers MS. *Accreditation:* ASHA. *Degree requirements:* For master's, thesis or alternative, comprehensive exam. *Entrance requirements:* For master's, GRE General Test. Additional exam requirements/recommendations for international students: Required—TOEFL.

Texas Christian University, Harris College of Nursing and Health Sciences, Department of Communication Sciences and Disorders, Fort Worth, TX 76129-0002. Offers speech-language pathology (MS). *Accreditation:* ASHA. Part-time and evening/weekend programs available. *Degree requirements:* For master's, comprehensive exam. *Entrance requirements:* For master's, GRE General Test, previous course work in speech-language pathology. Additional exam requirements/recommendations for international students: Required—TOEFL. *Application deadline:* For fall admission, 3/1 for domestic students; for spring admission, 12/1 for domestic students. Applications are processed on a rolling basis. Application fee: $0. *Expenses:* Tuition: Part-time $800 per credit hour. *Financial support:* Unspecified assistantships available. Financial award application deadline: 3/1. *Unit head:* Dr. Bill Ryan, Chairperson, 817-257-7621, E-mail: b.ryan@tcu.edu.

Texas State University-San Marcos, Graduate School, College of Health Professions, Department of Communication Disorders, San Marcos, TX 78666. Offers MA, MSCD. *Accreditation:* ASHA (one or more programs are accredited). Part-time programs available. *Faculty:* 5 full-time (4 women). *Students:* 34 full-time (32 women), 13 part-time (all women); includes 12 minority (1 African American, 1 Asian American or Pacific Islander, 10 Hispanic Americans). Average age 25. 77 applicants, 47% accepted, 22 enrolled. In 2006, 16 degrees awarded. *Degree requirements:* For master's, thesis (for some programs), practicum, comprehensive exam. *Entrance requirements:* For master's, GRE General Test, minimum GPA of 3.0 in communications disorders, 2.75 in last 60 hours of course work; 25 hours of observation. Additional exam requirements/recommendations for international students: Required—TOEFL. *Application deadline:* For fall admission, 3/1 for domestic and international students. Application fee: $40 ($90 for international students). *Financial support:* In 2006–07, 37 students received support, including 8 teaching assistantships (averaging $1,428 per year); fellowships, research assistantships, career-related internships or fieldwork, Federal Work-Study, institutionally sponsored loans, and scholarships/grants also available. Support available to part-time students. Financial award application deadline: 4/1; financial award applicants required to submit FAFSA. *Faculty research:* Stuttering, aphasia, neurogenic disorders, child language, autism. *Unit head:* Dr. Maria Pianna Gonzales, Chair, 512-245-2330, Fax: 512-245-2029, E-mail: mg29@txstate.edu.

Texas Tech University Health Sciences Center, School of Allied Health Sciences, Program in Speech, Language and Hearing Sciences, Lubbock, TX 79430. Offers MS, Au D, PhD. *Accreditation:* ASHA (one or more programs are accredited). *Faculty:* 14 full-time (10 women), 3 part-time/adjunct (all women). *Students:* 78 full-time (75 women), 8 part-time (all women); includes 11 minority (3 Asian Americans or Pacific Islanders, 8 Hispanic Americans), 1 international. Average age 28. 115 applicants, 35% accepted, 40 enrolled. In 2006, 18 master's, 7 doctorates awarded. *Degree requirements:* For master's, thesis optional; for doctorate, thesis/dissertation, comprehensive exam. *Entrance requirements:* For master's, GRE General Test, GRE Writing Test. Additional exam requirements/recommendations for international students: Required—TOEFL. *Application deadline:* For fall admission, 2/1 for domestic students, 4/30 for international students; for winter admission, 9/30 for international students; for spring admission, 11/30 for international students. Application fee: $35. Electronic applications accepted. *Financial support:* In 2006–07, 15 students received support, including 6 research assistantships, 5 teaching assistantships; career-related internships or fieldwork, institutionally sponsored loans, and scholarships/grants also available. Financial award application deadline: 9/1; financial award applicants required to submit FAFSA. *Faculty research:* Craniofacial anomalies, evoked potentials, neurolinguistics, language simulations, vocal fold burns. Total annual research expenditures: $150,000. *Unit head:* Dr. Rajinder Koul, Chairperson, 806-743-5660 Ext. 227, Fax: 806-742-0907, E-mail: rajinder.koul@ttuhsc.edu. *Application contact:* Lindsay Roberts, Director of Admissions and Student Affairs, 806-743-3220, Fax: 806-743-3249, E-mail: lindsay.roberts@ttuhsc.edu.

Texas Woman's University, Graduate School, College of Health Sciences, Department of Communication Sciences and Disorders, Denton, TX 76201. Offers education of the deaf (MS); speech-language pathology (MS). *Accreditation:* ASHA. Part-time programs available. Postbaccalaureate distance learning degree programs offered (no on-campus study). *Students:* 218 full-time (215 women), 54 part-time (50 women); includes 78 minority (18 African Americans, 4 American Indian/Alaska Native, 5 Asian Americans or Pacific Islanders, 51 Hispanic Americans), 1 international. Average age 31. In 2006, 42 degrees awarded. *Degree requirements:* For master's, thesis, comprehensive exam. *Entrance requirements:* For master's, GRE General Test, minimum GPA of 3.0, interview, 2 letters of reference. Additional exam requirements/recommendations for international students: Required—TOEFL (minimum score 550 paper-based; 213 computer-based; 79 iBT). *Application deadline:* For fall admission, 4/1 for international students; for spring admission, 8/1 for international students. Applications are processed on a rolling basis. Application fee: $30 ($50 for international students). Electronic applications accepted. *Expenses:* Tuition, area resident: Part-time $168 per unit. Tuition, state resident: full-time $4,369. Tuition, nonresident: full-time $9,373; part-time $443 per unit. Required fees: $20 per unit. $177 per term. *Financial support:* In 2006–07, 9 research assistantships (averaging $9,468 per year), teaching assistantships (averaging $9,468 per year) were awarded; career-related internships or fieldwork, Federal Work-Study, institutionally sponsored loans, scholarships/grants, traineeships, health care benefits, and unspecified assistantships also available. Support available to part-time students. Financial award application deadline: 3/1; financial award applicants required to submit FAFSA. *Faculty research:* Stroke, language assessment auditory processing and relationship between speech and language, effectiveness of distance education learning. *Unit head:* Dr. Alfred H. White, Chair, 940-898-2025, Fax: 940-898-2070, E-mail: awhite@twu.edu. *Application contact:* Samuel Wheeler, Coordinator of Graduate Admissions, 940-898-3188, Fax: 940-898-3081, E-mail: wheelersr@twu.edu.

Towson University, Graduate School, Program in Audiology, Towson, MD 21252-0001. Offers Au D. *Accreditation:* ASHA. *Faculty:* 5 full-time (4 women), 6 part-time/adjunct (4 women). *Students:* 41 full-time (37 women), 3 part-time (all women); includes 4 minority (3 African Americans, 1 Hispanic American). 31 applicants, 71% accepted, 9 enrolled. In 2006, 9 degrees awarded. *Entrance requirements:* For doctorate, GRE, 3 letters of recommendation, minimum GPA of 3.0. Additional exam requirements/recommendations for international students: Required—TOEFL (minimum score 600 paper-based). *Application deadline:* For fall admission, 2/1 for domestic students. Application fee: $50. Electronic applications accepted. *Expenses:* Tuition, state resident: part-time $275 per unit. Tuition, nonresident: part-time $577 per unit. Required fees: $72 per unit. *Financial support:* In 2006–07, 4 fellowships with tuition reimbursements, 1 research assistantship with tuition reimbursement were awarded; traineeships, tuition waivers (partial), and unspecified assistantships also available. Financial award application deadline: 4/1; financial award applicants required to submit FAFSA. *Faculty research:* Auditory processing, cortical potentials, otoacoustic emissions, electrophysiology, cochlear implants. *Unit head:* Dr. Diana Emanuel, Graduate Program Director, 410-704-2417, Fax: 410-704-4131, E-mail: demanuel@towson.edu. *Application contact:* 410-704-2501, Fax: 410-704-4675, E-mail: grads@towson.edu.

Towson University, Graduate School, Program in Speech-Language Pathology, Towson, MD 21252-0001. Offers MS. *Accreditation:* ASHA. *Faculty:* 9 full-time (7 women), 2 part-time/adjunct (both women). *Students:* 81 full-time (80 women), 5 part-time (4 women); includes 9 minority (5 African Americans, 1 Asian American or Pacific Islander, 3 Hispanic Americans), 1 international. 132 applicants, 62% accepted, 36 enrolled. In 2006, 50 degrees awarded. *Degree requirements:* For master's, thesis (for some programs), exam, comprehensive exam. *Entrance requirements:* For master's, minimum GPA of 3.0 in major, undergraduate course-work in speech-language pathology. Additional exam requirements/recommendations for international students: Required—TOEFL (minimum score 600 paper-based). *Application deadline:* For fall admission, 1/15 for domestic students. Application fee: $50. Electronic applications accepted. *Expenses:* Tuition, state resident: part-time $275 per unit. Tuition, nonresident: part-time $577 per unit. Required fees: $72 per unit. *Financial support:* In 2006–07, 7 students received support. Federal Work-Study and unspecified assistantships available. Financial award application deadline: 4/1; financial award applicants required to submit FAFSA. *Faculty research:* Oral-literate issues, narratives, localization in noise, cross-language assessment, temporal processing of speech. *Unit head:* Dr. Celia Bassich, Graduate Program Director, 410-704-2449, Fax: 410-704-4131, E-mail: cbassich@towson.edu. *Application contact:* The Graduate School, 410-704-2449, Fax: 410-704-4675, E-mail: grads@towson.edu.

Truman State University, Graduate School, Division of Human Potential and Performance, Program in Communication Disorders, Kirksville, MO 63501-4221. Offers MA. *Accreditation:* ASHA. *Degree requirements:* For master's, thesis optional. *Entrance requirements:* For master's, GRE General Test, minimum GPA of 3.0. Additional exam requirements/recommendations for international students: Required—TOEFL (minimum score 550 paper-based; 213 computer-based). Electronic applications accepted.

Université de Montréal, Faculty of Medicine and Faculty of Graduate Studies, Graduate Programs in Medicine, School of Speech Therapy and Audiology, Montréal, QC H3C 3J7, Canada. Offers speech therapy (DESS); speech-language pathology and audiology (MOA). *Faculty:* 12 full-time (7 women), 6 part-time/adjunct (5 women). *Students:* 128 full-time (124 women), 134 part-time (131 women). 93 applicants, 67% accepted, 62 enrolled. In 2006, 68 master's, 1 other advanced degree awarded. *Degree requirements:* For master's, thesis. *Entrance requirements:* For master's, B Sc in speech-language pathology and audiology, proficiency in French. *Application deadline:* For fall admission, 2/1 for domestic students. Application fee: $30. Electronic applications accepted. *Faculty research:* Aphasia in adults, dysarthria, speech and hearing-impaired children, noise-induced hearing impairment, computerized audiometry. *Unit head:* Louise Getty, Director, 514-343-7458, Fax: 514-343-2115. *Application contact:* Renee Beland, Graduate Director, 514-343-7022.

Université Laval, Faculty of Medicine, Graduate Programs in Medicine, Program in Speech Therapy, Québec, QC G1K 7P4, Canada. Offers M Sc. *Entrance requirements:* For master's, knowledge of French, interview. Electronic applications accepted.

University at Buffalo, the State University of New York, Graduate School, College of Arts and Sciences, Department of Communicative Disorders, Buffalo, NY 14260. Offers audiology (Au D); communicative disorders and sciences (MA, PhD). *Accreditation:* ASHA (one or more programs are accredited). *Faculty:* 20 full-time (14 women), 2 part-time/adjunct (1 woman). *Students:* 116 full-time (109 women), 6 part-time (4 women); includes 8 minority (3 African Americans, 1 American Indian/Alaska Native, 3 Asian Americans or Pacific Islanders, 1 Hispanic American), 22 international. 194 applicants, 37% accepted, 38 enrolled. In 2006, 33 master's, 7 doctorates awarded. *Median time to degree:* Of those who began their doctoral program in fall 1998, 100% received their degree in 8 years or less. *Degree requirements:* For master's, thesis or alternative, exam; for doctorate, thesis/dissertation, exams. *Entrance requirements:* For master's and doctorate, GRE General Test, minimum GPA of 3.0. Additional exam requirements/recommendations for international students: Required—TOEFL (minimum score 550 paper-based; 213 computer-based; 79 iBT). *Application deadline:* For fall admission, 1/15 priority date for domestic and international students. Application fee: $35. Electronic applications accepted. *Financial support:* In 2006–07, 22 students received support, including 3 fellowships with full tuition reimbursements available (averaging $3,000 per year), 19 teaching assistantships with full tuition reimbursements available (averaging $6,464 per year); career-related internships or fieldwork, Federal Work-Study, institutionally sponsored loans, scholarships/grants, health care benefits, tuition waivers (partial), and unspecified assistantships also available. Financial award applicants required to submit FAFSA. *Faculty research:* Hearing and speech science, child and adult language disorders, augmentative communication, cochlear implants, tinitis. Total annual research expenditures: $2.7 million. *Unit head:* Dr. Elaine T. Stathopoulos, Chairperson, 716-829-2797 Ext. 625, Fax: 716-829-3979, E-mail: stathop@acsu.buffalo.edu. *Application contact:* Linda L. Mehwert, Graduate Admissions Coordinator, 716-829-2797 Ext. 603, Fax: 716-829-3979, E-mail: lmehwert@buffalo.edu.

The University of Akron, Graduate School, College of Fine and Applied Arts, School of Speech-Language Pathology and Audiology, Program in Audiology, Akron, OH 44325. Offers Au D. *Accreditation:* ASHA. *Students:* 36 full-time (33 women); includes 3 minority (2 African Americans, 1 Asian American or Pacific Islander), 2 international. Average age 25. 26 applicants, 62% accepted, 10 enrolled. In 2006, 10 degrees awarded. *Degree requirements:* For doctorate, 2000 clock hours of clinical experience, academic and competency-based exams. *Entrance requirements:* For doctorate, GRE, minimum GPA of 2.75, letters of recommendation. Additional exam requirements/recommendations for international students: Required—TOEFL (minimum score 550 paper-based; 213 computer-based; 79 iBT). *Application deadline:* For fall admission, 2/15 for domestic students. Applications are processed on a rolling basis. Application fee: $30 ($40 for international students). Electronic applications accepted. *Expenses:* Tuition, state resident: full-time $6,164; part-time $342 per credit. Tuition, nonresident: full-time $10,575; part-time $588 per credit. Required fees: $806; $43 per credit. $12 per term. Tuition and fees vary according to course load, degree level and program. *Unit head:* Dr. Sharon Lesner, Coordinator, 330-972-6118, E-mail: lesner@uakron.edu.

The University of Akron, Graduate School, College of Fine and Applied Arts, School of Speech-Language Pathology and Audiology, Program in Speech-Language Pathology, Akron, OH 44325. Offers MA. *Accreditation:* ASHA. *Students:* 63 full-time (62 women), 1 (woman) part-time; includes 6 minority (3 African Americans, 1 Asian American or Pacific Islander, 2 Hispanic Americans). Average age 26. 101 applicants, 50% accepted, 33 enrolled. In 2006, 30 degrees awarded. *Entrance requirements:* For master's, GRE, minimum GPA of 3.0, letters of recommendation, resumé. Additional exam requirements/recommendations for international students: Required—TOEFL (minimum score 550 paper-based; 213 computer-based; 79 iBT). *Application deadline:* For fall admission, 2/15 for domestic students. Applications are processed on a rolling basis. Application fee: $30 ($40 for international students). Electronic applications accepted. *Expenses:* Tuition, state resident: full-time $6,164; part-time $342 per credit. Tuition, nonresident: full-time $10,575; part-time $588 per credit. Required fees: $806; $43 per credit. $12 per term. Tuition and fees vary according to course load, degree level and program. *Unit head:* Dr. Yvonne Gillette, Coordinator, 330-972-6115, E-mail: ygillette@uakron.edu.

The University of Alabama, Graduate School, College of Arts and Sciences, Department of Communicative Disorders, Tuscaloosa, AL 35487. Offers MS. *Accreditation:* ASHA. *Faculty:* 4 full-time (all women), 2 part-time/adjunct (both women). *Students:* 33 full-time (31 women), 24 part-time (23 women); includes 7 African Americans, 1 Hispanic American, 2 international. Average age 23. 71 applicants, 66% accepted, 31 enrolled. In 2006, 28 degrees awarded. *Median time to degree:* Master's–4.4 years full-time. *Degree requirements:* For master's, thesis optional. *Entrance requirements:* For master's, MAT or GRE. Additional exam requirements/recommendations for international students: Required—TOEFL, Must pass English grammar and articulation in department. *Application deadline:* For spring admission, 2/1 for domestic and international students. Applications are processed on a rolling basis. Electronic applications accepted. *Financial support:* In 2006–07, 13 students received support, including 10 research assistantships (averaging $7,000 per year); career-related internships or fieldwork, Federal Work-Study, scholarships/grants, traineeships, health care benefits, and unspecified assistantships also available. Financial award application deadline: 7/14. *Faculty research:* Aphasia, aging, hearing loss, child language, literacy, multiculture, voice, swallowing, pedagogy. *Unit head:* Dr. Karen F. Steckol, Professor, Chair and Clinic Director, 205-348-7131, Fax: 205-348-1845, E-mail: ksteckol@bama.ua.edu.

University of Alberta, Faculty of Graduate Studies and Research, Department of Speech Pathology and Audiology, Edmonton, AB T6G 2E1, Canada. Offers speech pathology and audiology (PhD); speech-language pathology (M Sc). *Faculty:* 7 full-time (5 women), 2 part-time/adjunct (both women). *Students:* 61 full-time (59 women), 17 part-time (all women). Average age 26. 175 applicants, 21% accepted. In 2006, 36 degrees awarded. *Degree requirements:* For master's, thesis (for some programs), clinical practicum (MSLP). *Entrance requirements:* For master's, GRE, minimum GPA of 6.5 on a 9.0 scale. Additional exam requirements/recommendations for international students: Required—TOEFL. *Application deadline:* For fall admission, 2/15 for domestic students. Application fee: $60. *Financial support:* Research assistantships, teaching assistantships, career-related internships or fieldwork, institutionally sponsored loans, and scholarships/grants available. *Faculty research:* Clinical

Communication Disorders

University of Alberta (continued)

education, hearing conservation, motor speech disorders, child language, voice resonance. *Unit head:* Dr. Karen Pollock, Chair, 780-492-0840, Fax: 403-492-9333, E-mail: karen.pollock@ualberta.ca. *Application contact:* Anita Moore, Administrative Assistant, 403-492-0840, Fax: 403-492-9333, E-mail: mscslp.info@rehabmed.ualberta.ca.

The University of Arizona, Graduate College, College of Science, Department of Speech and Hearing Sciences, Tucson, AZ 85721. Offers MS, Au D, PhD. *Accreditation:* ASHA (one or more programs are accredited). *Faculty:* 20 full-time (13 women), 5 part-time/adjunct (all women). *Students:* 65 full-time (58 women), 18 part-time (15 women); includes 7 minority (4 Asian Americans or Pacific Islanders, 3 Hispanic Americans), 4 international. Average age 29. 129 applicants, 21% accepted, 22 enrolled. In 2006, 27 master's, 3 doctorates awarded. *Degree requirements:* For master's, thesis optional. *Entrance requirements:* For master's and doctorate, GRE General Test, minimum GPA of 3.0. Additional exam requirements/recommendations for international students: Required—TOEFL. *Application deadline:* For fall admission, 2/1 for domestic students; for spring admission, 10/1 for domestic students. Applications are processed on a rolling basis. Application fee: $50. *Financial support:* In 2006–07, 3 fellowships with tuition reimbursements, 2 research assistantships with full tuition reimbursements (averaging $5,356 per year), 16 teaching assistantships with full tuition reimbursements (averaging $5,356 per year) were awarded; career-related internships or fieldwork, Federal Work-Study, institutionally sponsored loans, scholarships/grants, health care benefits, tuition waivers (full and partial), and unspecified assistantships also available. Financial award application deadline: 2/1. *Faculty research:* Alzheimer's disease, speech motor control, auditory-evoked potentials, analyzing pathological speech. Total annual research expenditures: $1.1 million. *Unit head:* Dr. Elena Plante, Head, 520-621-1644, Fax: 520-621-9901, E-mail: eplante@email.arizona.edu. *Application contact:* Pamela Adams, Information Contact, 520-621-1192, Fax: 520-621-9901, E-mail: adamsp@email.arizona.edu.

University of Arkansas, Graduate School, College of Education and Health Professions, Department of Rehabilitation, Human Resources and Communication Disorders, Program in Communication Disorders, Fayetteville, AR 72701-1201. Offers MS. *Accreditation:* ASHA. Part-time programs available. *Students:* 36 full-time (35 women), 3 part-time (2 women); includes 4 minority (1 African American, 2 American Indian/Alaska Native, 1 Hispanic American). 11 applicants, 36% accepted. In 2006, 10 degrees awarded. *Degree requirements:* For master's, 8 week externship, thesis optional. *Entrance requirements:* For master's, GRE General Test. Application fee: $40 ($50 for international students). *Financial support:* In 2006–07, 1 fellowship was awarded; research assistantships, teaching assistantships, career-related internships or fieldwork and Federal Work-Study also available. Support available to part-time students. Financial award application deadline: 4/1; financial award applicants required to submit FAFSA. *Unit head:* Barbara Shadden, Head, 479-575-4917, E-mail: bshadde@uark.edu.

University of Arkansas for Medical Sciences, Graduate School, Program in Communicative Disorders, Little Rock, AR 72205-7199. Offers MS, PhD. *Accreditation:* ASHA. Part-time programs available. *Faculty:* 9 full-time (4 women), 2 part-time/adjunct (1 woman). *Students:* 42 full-time, 5 part-time. *Degree requirements:* For master's, thesis or alternative. *Entrance requirements:* For master's, GRE General Test. Application fee: $0. *Financial support:* Research assistantships available. Support available to part-time students. *Unit head:* Dr. Thomas Guyette, Chair, 501-569-3155. *Application contact:* Terri Hutton, Graduate Program Coordinator, 501-569-3155, E-mail: huttonterrij@uams.edu.

The University of British Columbia, Faculty of Medicine, School of Audiology and Speech Sciences, Vancouver, BC V6T 1Z1, Canada. Offers M Sc, PhD. *Accreditation:* ASHA. *Faculty:* 9 full-time (6 women), 9 part-time/adjunct (8 women). *Students:* 63 full-time (57 women). Average age 27. 162 applicants, 19% accepted, 30 enrolled. In 2006, 26 degrees awarded. *Median time to degree:* Master's–2 years full-time. *Degree requirements:* For master's, thesis or alternative, externship; for doctorate, thesis/dissertation, comprehensive exam. *Entrance requirements:* Additional exam requirements/recommendations for international students: Required—TOEFL (minimum score 600 paper-based; 250 computer-based; 100 iBT). *Application deadline:* For fall admission, 2/28 for domestic and international students. Applications are processed on a rolling basis. Application fee: $90 Canadian dollars ($150 Canadian dollars for international students). Electronic applications accepted. *Financial support:* In 2006–07, 13 students received support, including 3 fellowships with full tuition reimbursements available (averaging $18,000 per year), 4 research assistantships; teaching assistantships, career-related internships or fieldwork, Federal Work-Study, institutionally sponsored loans, scholarships/grants, tuition waivers (full and partial), and unspecified assistantships also available. Financial award application deadline: 1/15. *Faculty research:* Language development, experimental phonetics, linguistic aphasiology, amplification, auditory physiology. Total annual research expenditures: $214,008. *Unit head:* Dr. Valter Ciocca, Director, 604-822-2266, Fax: 604-822-6569, E-mail: director@audiospeech.ubc.ca. *Application contact:* Sue Bryant, Graduate Program Assistant, 604-822-5591, Fax: 604-822-6569, E-mail: inquiry@audiospeech.ubc.ca.

University of California, San Diego, Office of Graduate Studies, Interdisciplinary Program in Language and Communicative Disorders, La Jolla, CA 92093. Offers PhD. *Accreditation:* ASHA. Electronic applications accepted.

University of California, San Diego, School of Medicine, Program in Audiology, La Jolla, CA 92093. Offers Au D.

University of Central Arkansas, Graduate School, College of Health and Behavioral Sciences, Department of Speech-Language Pathology, Conway, AR 72035-0001. Offers MS. *Accreditation:* ASHA. *Faculty:* 8 full-time (4 women), 3 part-time/adjunct (2 women). *Students:* 79 full-time (78 women), 13 part-time (all women); includes 8 minority (6 African Americans, 1 American Indian/Alaska Native, 1 Asian American or Pacific Islander). 43 applicants, 100% accepted, 43 enrolled. In 2006, 33 degrees awarded. *Degree requirements:* For master's, portfolio, internship, thesis optional. *Entrance requirements:* For master's, GRE General Test, NTE, minimum GPA of 2.7. Additional exam requirements/recommendations for international students: Required—TOEFL (minimum score 550 paper-based; 213 computer-based). *Application deadline:* For fall admission, 3/1 priority date for domestic students; for spring admission, 10/1 for domestic students. Applications are processed on a rolling basis. Application fee: $25 ($40 for international students). *Expenses: Contact institution.* One-time fee: $65 part-time. *Financial support:* In 2006–07, 3 research assistantships with full and partial tuition reimbursements (averaging $4,000 per year), 3 teaching assistantships (averaging $3,000 per year) were awarded; career-related internships or fieldwork, Federal Work-Study, scholarships/grants, traineeships, and unspecified assistantships also available. Financial award application deadline: 2/15; financial award applicants required to submit FAFSA. *Unit head:* Dr. John Lowe, Chairperson, 501-450-3176, Fax: 501-450-5474, E-mail: jlowe@uca.edu. *Application contact:* Sharon Ross, Graduate Advisor, 501-450-5489, Fax: 501-450-5474, E-mail: sharonr@uca.edu.

University of Central Florida, College of Education, Doctoral Program in Education, Orlando, FL 32816. Offers communication sciences and disorders (PhD); counselor education (PhD); curriculum and instruction (PhD); elementary education (PhD); exceptional education (PhD); hospitality education (PhD); instructional technology (PhD); mathematics education (PhD). *Students:* 86 full-time (63 women), 9 part-time (4 women); includes 21 minority (15 African Americans, 2 Asian Americans or Pacific Islanders, 4 Hispanic Americans), 19 international. Average age 39. In 2006, 16 degrees awarded. Application fee: $30. Electronic applications accepted. *Expenses:* Tuition, state resident: full-time $6,167; part-time $257 per credit hour. Tuition, nonresident: full-time $22,790; part-time $950 per credit hour. *Financial support:* In 2006–07, 44 fellowships with partial tuition reimbursements (averaging $3,700 per year), 54 research assistantships with partial tuition reimbursements (averaging $7,000 per year), 9 teaching assistantships with partial tuition reimbursements (averaging $7,000 per year) were awarded.

University of Central Florida, College of Health and Public Affairs, Department of Communication Sciences and Disorders, Orlando, FL 32816. Offers child language disorders (Certificate); communication sciences and disorders (MA); medical speech-language pathology (Certificate); multicultural/multilingual speech-language pathology (Certificate). *Accreditation:* ASHA (one or more programs are accredited). Part-time and evening/weekend programs available. *Faculty:* 24 full-time (17 women), 16 part-time/adjunct (14 women). *Students:* 172 full-time (166 women), 28 part-time (all women); includes 42 minority (13 African Americans, 6 Asian Americans or Pacific Islanders, 23 Hispanic Americans). Average age 26. In 2006, 71 master's awarded. *Degree requirements:* For master's, thesis or alternative, NESPH exam or comprehensive exam. *Entrance requirements:* For master's, GRE General Test, minimum GPA of 3.0 in last 60 hours. Additional exam requirements/recommendations for international students: Required—TOEFL. *Application deadline:* For fall admission, 4/1 for domestic students; for spring admission, 11/1 for domestic students. Electronic applications accepted. *Expenses:* Tuition, state resident: full-time $6,167; part-time $257 per credit hour. Tuition, nonresident: full-time $22,790; part-time $950 per credit hour. *Financial support:* In 2006–07, 5 fellowships with partial tuition reimbursements (averaging $3,100 per year), 20 research assistantships with partial tuition reimbursements (averaging $3,600 per year), 5 teaching assistantships with partial tuition reimbursements (averaging $6,000 per year) were awarded; career-related internships or fieldwork, Federal Work-Study, institutionally sponsored loans, and unspecified assistantships also available. Financial award application deadline: 3/1; financial award applicants required to submit FAFSA. *Unit head:* Dr. Jane Lieberman, Chair, 407-249-4798, E-mail: jlieberm@mail.ucf.edu. *Application contact:* Dr. Linda I. Rosa-Lugo, Coordinator, 407-384-4798, E-mail: lrosa@mail.ucf.edu.

University of Central Missouri, The Graduate School, College of Health and Human Services, Department of Communication Disorders, Warrensburg, MO 64093. Offers speech pathology and audiology (MS). Part-time programs available. *Faculty:* 9 full-time (5 women). *Students:* 36 full-time (35 women), 8 part-time (7 women); includes 1 minority (African American) Average age 26. 22 applicants, 91% accepted, 11 enrolled. In 2006, 13 degrees awarded. *Degree requirements:* For master's, project, research paper, or thesis; observation (25 hours); clinical practicum (350 hours); National Examination in Speech Pathology and Audiology (NESPA) exam. *Entrance requirements:* For master's, GRE, minimum GPA of 3.0, clinical practicum. Additional exam requirements/recommendations for international students: Required—TOEFL (minimum score 500 paper-based; 173 computer-based). *Application deadline:* For fall admission, 6/1 priority date for domestic students, 5/1 priority date for international students; for spring admission, 10/1 priority date for domestic students, 10/1 for international students. Applications are processed on a rolling basis. Application fee: $30 ($50 for international students). *Expenses:* Tuition, state resident: full-time $5,448; part-time $227 per credit hour. Tuition, nonresident: full-time $10,896; part-time $454 per credit hour. Required fees: $336; $14 per credit hour. *Financial support:* In 2006–07, 14 students received support; teaching assistantships with partial tuition reimbursements available, Federal Work-Study, scholarships/grants, unspecified assistantships, and administrative and laboratory assistantships available. Support available to part-time students. Financial award application deadline: 3/1; financial award applicants required to submit FAFSA. *Faculty research:* Computer applications, audiology, and noise-induced hearing loss; speech intelligibility in noise for individuals with dysarthia; effectiveness of contrastive treatment approaches for phonological disorders; language development, bilingual development and pragmatic linguistic disorder; clinical supervision models. *Unit head:* Dr. Carl Harlan, Chair, 660-543-4606, Fax: 660-543-4918, E-mail: harlan@ucmo.edu.

University of Central Oklahoma, College of Graduate Studies and Research, College of Education, Department of Curriculum and Instruction, Program in Speech-Language Pathology, Edmond, OK 73034-5209. Offers M Ed. *Accreditation:* ASHA. Part-time programs available. *Entrance requirements:* For master's, GRE General Test. Additional exam requirements/recommendations for international students: Required—TOEFL (minimum score 550 paper-based; 213 computer-based). Electronic applications accepted.

University of Cincinnati, Division of Research and Advanced Studies, College of Allied Health Sciences, Department of Communication Sciences and Disorders, Cincinnati, OH 45221. Offers MA, Au D, PhD. *Accreditation:* ASHA (one or more programs are accredited). *Degree requirements:* For master's, thesis optional; for doctorate, thesis/dissertation, comprehensive exam. *Entrance requirements:* For master's and doctorate, GRE General Test, minimum GPA of 3.0. Additional exam requirements/recommendations for international students: Required—TOEFL (minimum score 600 paper-based; 250 computer-based). Electronic applications accepted. *Faculty research:* Neurogenic speech and language disorders, speech science, linguistics, swallowing disorders, speech-language pathology.

University of Cincinnati, Division of Research and Advanced Studies, College of Education, Criminal Justice, and Human Services, Division of Teacher Education, Cincinnati, OH 45221. Offers curriculum and instruction (M Ed, Ed D); deaf studies (Certificate); early childhood education (M Ed); middle childhood education (M Ed); postsecondary literacy instruction (Certificate); reading/literacy (M Ed, Ed D); secondary education (M Ed); special education (M Ed, Ed D); teaching English as a second language (M Ed, Ed D, Certificate); teaching science (MS). Part-time programs available. *Degree requirements:* For doctorate, thesis/dissertation. *Entrance requirements:* For master's, GRE General Test. *Application deadline:* For fall admission, 2/1 for domestic students. Application fee: $30. Electronic applications accepted. *Financial support:* Fellowships, career-related internships or fieldwork, tuition waivers (partial), and unspecified assistantships available. *Unit head:* David Naylor, Student Contact, 513-556-3563, Fax: 513-556-2483, E-mail: david.naylor@uc.edu. *Application contact:* Dr. Richard Kretschmer, Graduate Program Director, 513-556-4547, Fax: 513-556-1001, E-mail: richard.kretschmer@uc.edu.

University of Colorado at Boulder, Graduate School, College of Arts and Sciences, Department of Speech, Language and Hearing Sciences, Boulder, CO 80309. Offers audiology (Au D, PhD); clinical research and practice in audiology (PhD); speech, language and hearing science (MA); speech-language pathology (MA, PhD); speech-language-hearing sciences (PhD). *Accreditation:* ASHA (one or more programs are accredited). *Faculty:* 9 full-time (6 women). *Students:* 104 full-time (98 women), 5 part-time (4 women); includes 7 minority (1 African American, 1 Asian American or Pacific Islander, 5 Hispanic Americans), 3 international. Average age 29. 90 applicants, 98% accepted. In 2006, 27 master's, 4 doctorates awarded. Terminal master's awarded for partial completion of doctoral program. *Degree requirements:* For master's, thesis or alternative, comprehensive exam; for doctorate, one foreign language, thesis/dissertation. *Entrance requirements:* For master's, GRE General Test, minimum undergraduate GPA of 3.25; for doctorate, GRE General Test. *Application deadline:* For fall admission, 2/1 priority date for domestic students, 2/1 for international students. Applications are processed on a rolling basis. Application fee: $50 ($60 for international students). *Financial support:* In 2006–07, 31 fellowships (averaging $5,104 per year), 3 research assistantships (averaging $11,454 per year), 10 teaching assistantships (averaging $10,355 per year) were awarded; tuition waivers (full) also available. Financial award application deadline: 2/1. *Faculty research:* Speech-language pathology. Total annual research expenditures: $2.1 million. *Unit head:* John Hausen, Chair, 303-492-3065, Fax: 303-492-3274, E-mail: john.hansen@colorado.edu. *Application contact:* Kathleen Exman, Graduate Program Assistant, 303-492-6445, Fax: 303-492-3274, E-mail: slhsgrad@colorado.edu.

University of Connecticut, Graduate School, College of Liberal Arts and Sciences, Department of Communication Sciences, Storrs, CT 06269. Offers communication sciences (MA, Au D, PhD), including audiology (Au D, PhD), communication processes (MA), communication processes and marketing communication (PhD), speech-language pathology (MA, PhD); Au D/PhD. *Accreditation:* ASHA (one or more programs are accredited). *Faculty:* 25 full-time (11 women). *Students:* 97 full-time (70 women), 6 part-time (3 women); includes 7 minority (4 African Americans, 2 Asian Americans or Pacific Islanders, 1 Hispanic American), 14 international. Average age 26. 275 applicants, 48% accepted, 76 enrolled. In 2006, 22 master's, 8 doctorates awarded. Terminal master's awarded for partial completion of doctoral program. *Degree requirements:* For master's, comprehensive exam; for doctorate, thesis/dissertation. *Entrance* *requirements:* For master's and doctorate, GRE General Test. Additional exam requirements/recommendations for international students: Required—TOEFL (minimum score 550 paper-based; 213 computer-based). *Application deadline:* For fall admission, 2/1 priority date for domestic and international students; for spring admission, 11/1 for domestic students, 10/1 for international students. Applications are processed on a rolling basis. Application fee: $55. Electronic applications accepted. *Financial support:* In 2006–07, 15 research assistantships with full tuition reimbursements, 29 teaching assistantships with full tuition reimbursements were awarded; fellowships, Federal Work-Study, scholarships/grants, health care benefits, and unspecified assistantships also available. Financial award application deadline: 2/1; financial award applicants required to submit FAFSA. *Unit head:* Carl A. Coelho, Chair, 860-486-2628. *Application contact:* Sue Kiss, Administrative Assistant, 860-486-2628, Fax: 860-486-5422, E-mail: comsci3@uconnvm.edu.

University of Connecticut, Graduate School, College of Liberal Arts and Sciences, Department of Communication Sciences, Field of Communication Sciences, Program in Audiology, Storrs, CT 06269. Offers Au D, PhD, Au D/PhD. *Accreditation:* ASHA. *Faculty:* 5 full-time (4 women). *Students:* 15 full-time (all women); includes 2 minority (both African Americans) Average age 23. 55 applicants, 71% accepted, 15 enrolled. In 2006, 2 degrees awarded. *Financial support:* In 2006–07, 4 teaching assistantships were awarded. *Application contact:* Sue Kiss, Administrative Assistant, 860-486-2628, Fax: 860-486-5422, E-mail: comsci3@uconnvm.edu.

University of Connecticut, Graduate School, College of Liberal Arts and Sciences, Department of Communication Sciences, Field of Communication Sciences, Program in Speech-Language Pathology, Storrs, CT 06269. Offers MA, PhD. *Accreditation:* ASHA. *Faculty:* 11 full-time (5 women). *Students:* 44 full-time (41 women), 1 (woman) part-time; includes 8 minority (7 Asian Americans or Pacific Islanders, 1 Hispanic American). Average age 25. 130 applicants, 50% accepted, 38 enrolled. In 2006, 16 degrees awarded. Terminal master's awarded for partial completion of doctoral program. *Degree requirements:* For master's, thesis optional; for doctorate, thesis/dissertation. *Entrance requirements:* For master's and doctorate, GRE General Test. Additional exam requirements/recommendations for international students: Required—TOEFL (minimum score 550 paper-based; 213 computer-based). *Application deadline:* For fall admission, 2/1 priority date for domestic and international students; for spring admission, 11/1 for domestic students, 10/1 for international students. Applications are processed on a rolling basis. Application fee: $55. Electronic applications accepted. *Financial support:* Fellowships, research assistantships with full tuition reimbursements, teaching assistantships with full tuition reimbursements, Federal Work-Study, scholarships/grants, health care benefits, and unspecified assistantships available. Financial award application deadline: 2/1; financial award applicants required to submit FAFSA. *Application contact:* Sue Kiss, Administrative Assistant, 860-486-2628, Fax: 860-486-5422, E-mail: comsci3@uconnvm.edu.

University of Florida, Graduate School, College of Liberal Arts and Sciences, Department of Communication Sciences and Disorders, Gainesville, FL 32611. Offers MA, Au D, PhD. *Accreditation:* ASHA (one or more programs are accredited). *Faculty:* 11 full-time (6 women), 2 part-time/adjunct (both women). *Students:* 204 (184 women); includes 27 minority (8 African Americans, 1 American Indian/Alaska Native, 8 Asian Americans or Pacific Islanders, 10 Hispanic Americans) 11 international. In 2006, 28 master's, 58 doctorates awarded. *Degree requirements:* For master's, thesis optional; for doctorate, variable foreign language requirement, thesis/dissertation. *Entrance requirements:* For master's and doctorate, GRE General Test, minimum GPA of 3.0. Additional exam requirements/recommendations for international students: Required—TOEFL (minimum score 550 paper-based; 213 computer-based). *Application deadline:* For fall admission, 6/1 priority date for domestic students. Applications are processed on a rolling basis. Application fee: $30. Electronic applications accepted. *Expenses:* Tuition, state resident: full-time $6,827. Tuition, nonresident: full-time $21,951. Required fees: $999. *Financial support:* In 2006–07, 6 research assistantships (averaging $10,459 per year) were awarded; fellowships, teaching assistantships, career-related internships or fieldwork and unspecified assistantships also available. *Faculty research:* Phonetic science, cochlear implant, dyslexia, auditory development, voice. *Unit head:* Christine Sapienza, Chair, 352-392-2046 Ext. 233. *Application contact:* Dr. Scott Griffiths, Graduate Coordinator, On-Campus Program, 352-392-2113 Ext. 258, Fax: 352-846-0243, E-mail: sgriff@csd.ufl.edu.

University of Florida, Graduate School, College of Public Health and Health Professions and College of Liberal Arts and Sciences, Program in Audiology, Gainesville, FL 32611. Offers Au D. *Accreditation:* ASHA. Postbaccalaureate distance learning degree programs offered. *Faculty:* 7 full-time (5 women). *Students:* 122 (110 women); includes 13 minority (4 African Americans, 1 American Indian/Alaska Native, 5 Asian Americans or Pacific Islanders, 3 Hispanic Americans) 4 international. In 2006, 61 degrees awarded. *Entrance requirements:* For doctorate, GRE General Test, minimum GPA of 3.0. Additional exam requirements/recommendations for international students: Required—TOEFL (minimum score 550 paper-based; 213 computer-based). *Application deadline:* Applications are processed on a rolling basis. Application fee: $30. Electronic applications accepted. *Expenses:* Tuition, state resident: full-time $6,827. Tuition, nonresident: full-time $21,951. Required fees: $999. *Financial support:* In 2006–07, 9 research assistantships (averaging $8,444 per year), 2 teaching assistantships (averaging $7,871 per year) were awarded. *Unit head:* Dr. Alice E. Holmes, Director, 866-479-6160, E-mail: aholmes@phhp.ufl.edu. *Application contact:* Dr. Scott Griffiths, Graduate Coordinator, On-Campus Program, 352-392-2113 Ext. 258, Fax: 352-846-0243, E-mail: sgriff@csd.ufl.edu.

University of Georgia, Graduate School, College of Education, Department of Communication Sciences and Special Education, Athens, GA 30602. Offers M Ed, MA, Ed D, PhD, Ed S. *Accreditation:* ASHA (one or more programs are accredited). *Faculty:* 17 full-time (6 women). *Students:* 88 full-time (82 women), 73 part-time (65 women); includes 15 minority (8 African Americans, 4 Asian Americans or Pacific Islanders, 3 Hispanic Americans), 7 international. Average age 24. 191 applicants, 51% accepted, 47 enrolled. In 2006, 45 master's, 4 doctorates, 5 other advanced degrees awarded. Terminal master's awarded for partial completion of doctoral program. *Degree requirements:* For master's, thesis (for some programs), comprehensive exam (for some programs); for doctorate, thesis/dissertation. *Entrance requirements:* For master's, doctorate, and Ed S, GRE General Test. Additional exam requirements/recommendations for international students: Required—TOEFL. *Application deadline:* For fall admission, 7/1 priority date for domestic students; for spring admission, 11/15 for domestic students. Application fee: $50. Electronic applications accepted. *Financial support:* Fellowships, research assistantships, teaching assistantships, unspecified assistantships available. *Unit head:* Dr. Anne C. Bothe, Head, 706-542-0436, Fax: 706-542-5348, E-mail: abothe@uga.edu. *Application contact:* Dr. Anne C. Bothe, Graduate Coordinator, 706-542-0436, Fax: 706-542-5348, E-mail: abothe@coe.uga.edu.

University of Hawaii at Manoa, John A. Burns School of Medicine and Graduate Division, Graduate Programs in Biomedical Sciences, Division of Speech Pathology and Audiology, Honolulu, HI 96816. Offers MS. *Accreditation:* ASHA. *Faculty:* 5 full-time (2 women). *Students:* 20 full-time (all women), 4 part-time (all women); includes 14 minority (all Asian Americans or Pacific Islanders), 1 international. Average age 29. 48 applicants, 38% accepted, 10 enrolled. In 2006, 15 degrees awarded. *Degree requirements:* For master's, thesis optional. *Entrance requirements:* For master's, GRE General Test, minimum GPA of 3.0. Additional exam requirements/recommendations for international students: Required—TOEFL (minimum score 580 paper-based; 237 computer-based; 92 iBT). *Application deadline:* For fall admission, 3/1 for domestic and international students; for spring admission, 9/1 for domestic and international students. Application fee: $50. *Financial support:* In 2006–07, 10 students received support, including 1 research assistantship (averaging $16,176 per year); career-related internships or fieldwork, Federal Work-Study, institutionally sponsored loans, and tuition waivers (full and partial) also available. Support available to part-time students. *Faculty research:* Emerging language (child phonology and special populations), central auditory function, developmental phonology, processing in the aging. *Application contact:* James Yates, 808-956-5483, Fax: 808-956-5482.

University of Houston, College of Liberal Arts and Social Sciences, Department of Communication Disorders, Houston, TX 77204. Offers speech language pathology (MA). *Accreditation:* ASHA. Part-time programs available. *Faculty:* 4 full-time (all women), 9 part-time/adjunct (all women). *Students:* 65 full-time (61 women), 5 part-time (all women); includes 23 minority (10 African Americans, 1 Asian American or Pacific Islander, 12 Hispanic Americans), 1 international. Average age 28. 80 applicants, 35% accepted, 22 enrolled. In 2006, 24 degrees awarded. *Degree requirements:* For master's, comprehensive exam. *Entrance requirements:* For master's, GRE General Test, minimum GPA of 3.0 in last 60 hours, course work in communication disorders. *Application deadline:* For fall admission, 2/1 priority date for domestic students; for winter admission, 10/1 for domestic students. Applications are processed on a rolling basis. Application fee: $25 ($75 for international students). *Expenses:* Tuition, state resident: full-time $5,429; part-time $226 per credit. Tuition, nonresident: full-time $12,029; part-time $501 per credit. Required fees: $2,454. *Financial support:* Fellowships with full tuition reimbursements, research assistantships with full tuition reimbursements, teaching assistantships with full tuition reimbursements, career-related internships or fieldwork, Federal Work-Study, institutionally sponsored loans, scholarships/grants, health care benefits, and unspecified assistantships available. Support available to part-time students. Financial award application deadline: 3/10. *Faculty research:* Stuttering, voice disorders, language disorders, phonological processing, cognition. *Unit head:* Lynn Maher, Chairperson, 713-743-2896, Fax: 713-743-2926, E-mail: lmmaher@uh.edu. *Application contact:* Holly Chermack, Graduate Coordinator, 713-743-2897, Fax: 713-743-2926, E-mail: hchermack@bayou.uh.edu.

University of Illinois at Urbana–Champaign, Graduate College, College of Applied Health Studies, Department of Speech and Hearing Science, Champaign, IL 61820. Offers MA, Au D, PhD. *Accreditation:* ASHA (one or more programs are accredited). *Faculty:* 13 full-time (7 women), 1 part-time/adjunct (0 women). *Students:* 67 full-time (65 women), 2 part-time (both women); includes 6 minority (4 African Americans, 1 Asian American or Pacific Islander, 1 Hispanic American), 9 international. 160 applicants, 16% accepted, 15 enrolled. In 2006, 23 master's, 5 doctorates awarded. *Degree requirements:* For doctorate, thesis/dissertation. *Entrance requirements:* For master's, GRE General Test, minimum GPA of 3.0. *Application deadline:* For fall admission, 1/16 for domestic students. Applications are processed on a rolling basis. Application fee: $50 ($60 for international students). Electronic applications accepted. *Financial support:* In 2006–07, 22 fellowships, 20 research assistantships, 20 teaching assistantships were awarded; tuition waivers (full and partial) also available. Financial award application deadline: 2/15. *Unit head:* Ron D. Chambers, Head, 217-333-2230, Fax: 217-244-2235, E-mail: rdc@uiuc.edu. *Application contact:* Joyce Woodworth, Administrative Aide, 217-244-2537, Fax: 217-244-2235, E-mail: jwoodwor@uiuc.edu.

The University of Iowa, Graduate College, College of Liberal Arts and Sciences, Department of Speech Pathology and Audiology, Program in Professional Speech Pathology and Audiology, Iowa City, IA 52242-1316. Offers MA, Au D. *Accreditation:* ASHA. *Students:* 58 full-time (50 women), 2 part-time (both women); includes 2 minority (1 African American, 1 Asian American or Pacific Islander), 3 international. 156 applicants, 48% accepted, 26 enrolled. In 2006, 17 master's, 2 doctorates awarded. *Degree requirements:* For master's, exam, thesis optional; for doctorate, practicum. *Entrance requirements:* For master's and doctorate, GRE General Test, minimum GPA of 3.0. Additional exam requirements/recommendations for international students: Required—TOEFL (minimum score 550 paper-based; 213 computer-based; 81 iBT). *Application deadline:* For fall admission, 1/15 for domestic and international students. Application fee: $60 ($85 for international students). Electronic applications accepted. *Financial support:* In 2006–07, 17 research assistantships with partial tuition reimbursements, 6 teaching assistantships with partial tuition reimbursements were awarded; fellowships also available. Financial award applicants required to submit FAFSA. *Unit head:* Paul Abbas, Chair, Department of Speech Pathology and Audiology, 319-335-8733, Fax: 319-335-8851.

The University of Iowa, Graduate College, College of Liberal Arts and Sciences, Department of Speech Pathology and Audiology, Program in Speech and Hearing Science, Iowa City, IA 52242-1316. Offers PhD. *Students:* 23 full-time (19 women), 11 part-time (8 women); includes 4 minority (1 African American, 1 Asian American or Pacific Islander, 2 Hispanic Americans), 12 international. 14 applicants, 29% accepted, 3 enrolled. In 2006, 4 degrees awarded. *Degree requirements:* For doctorate, thesis/dissertation, comprehensive exam, registration. *Entrance requirements:* For doctorate, GRE General Test, minimum GPA of 3.0. Additional exam requirements/recommendations for international students: Required—TOEFL (minimum score 550 paper-based; 213 computer-based; 81 iBT). *Application deadline:* For fall admission, 1/15 for domestic and international students; for spring admission, 10/1 for domestic students. Application fee: $60 ($85 for international students). Electronic applications accepted. *Financial support:* In 2006–07, 1 fellowship, 11 research assistantships with partial tuition reimbursements, 10 teaching assistantships with partial tuition reimbursements were awarded. Financial award applicants required to submit FAFSA. *Unit head:* Paul Abbas, Chair, Department of Speech Pathology and Audiology, 319-335-8733, Fax: 319-335-8851.

University of Kansas, Graduate Studies, College of Liberal Arts and Sciences, Department of Speech-Language-Hearing: Sciences and Disorders, Lawrence, KS 66045. Offers audiology (PhD); speech-language pathology (MA, PhD). Offered jointly with the Department of Hearing and Speech at the Kansas City campus. *Accreditation:* ASHA. Part-time programs available. *Faculty:* 14 full-time, 1 part-time/adjunct. *Students:* 77 full-time (72 women), 16 part-time (11 women); includes 8 minority (2 African Americans, 2 American Indian/Alaska Native, 4 Hispanic Americans), 6 international. Average age 28. 85 applicants, 59% accepted. In 2006, 23 master's, 2 doctorates awarded. *Degree requirements:* For master's, thesis optional; for doctorate, thesis/dissertation, comprehensive exam, registration. *Entrance requirements:* For master's and doctorate, GRE General Test, MAT, minimum GPA of 3.0. Additional exam requirements/recommendations for international students: Required—TOEFL. *Application deadline:* For fall admission, 1/15 for domestic and international students; for spring admission, 10/1 for domestic and international students. Application fee: $55 ($60 for international students). Electronic applications accepted. *Expenses:* Tuition, area resident: Part-time $227 per credit. Tuition, state resident: part-time $543 per credit. Tuition and fees vary according to course load, campus/location, program and reciprocity agreements. *Financial support:* Fellowships with full tuition reimbursements, research assistantships, teaching assistantships with full and partial tuition reimbursements, career-related internships or fieldwork, Federal Work-Study, and institutionally sponsored loans available. Support available to part-time students. Financial award application deadline: 3/1; financial award applicants required to submit FAFSA. *Faculty research:* Reading disorders, language acquisition, auditory electrophysiology, genetics of language, phonological development. *Unit head:* Hugh W. Catts, Chair, 785-864-0630, Fax: 785-864-3974, E-mail: catts@ku.edu. *Application contact:* Wanda Lowe, Administrative Professional, 785-864-0634, E-mail: wlowe@ku.edu.

University of Kansas, Graduate Studies Medical Center, Intercampus Program in Communicative Disorders, Lawrence, KS 66045. Offers audiology (MA, Au D, PhD); speech-language pathology (MA, PhD). *Faculty:* 16 full-time (4 women), 8 part-time/adjunct (7 women). *Students:* 21 full-time (17 women), 5 part-time (2 women); includes 1 minority (African American), 2 international. Average age 29. 106 applicants, 73% accepted, 22 enrolled. In 2006, 4 master's, 3 doctorates awarded. *Median time to degree:* Master's–1.82 years full-time, 6.35 years part-time; doctorate–6.75 years part-time. Of those who began their doctoral program in fall 1998, 25% received their degree in 8 years or less. *Application deadline:* For fall admission, 1/15 for domestic students; for spring admission, 10/1 for domestic students. Application fee: $45. *Expenses:* Tuition, area resident: Part-time $227 per credit. Tuition, state resident: part-time $543 per credit. Tuition and fees vary according to course load, campus/location, program and reciprocity agreements. *Financial support:* In 2006–07, 1 fellowship with partial tuition reimbursement (averaging $14,000 per year) was awarded; research assistantships with partial tuition reimbursements, teaching assistantships with partial tuition reimbursements, scholarships/grants, traineeships, and unspecified assistantships also available. *Faculty research:* Child language development, diagnosis and treatment of language disorders; newborn/pediatric hearing testing and treatment of hearing loss in children; voice disorders; auditory physiology and applied electrophysiology; diagnosis and treatment for adult speech and

Communication Disorders

University of Kansas (continued)
language disorders. *Unit head:* Dr. John A. Ferraro, Chair, 913-588-5937, Fax: 913-588-5923, E-mail: jferraro@kumc.edu. *Application contact:* Diane Wright-Cook, Coordinator, 913-588-5937, Fax: 913-588-5923, E-mail: dswright@kumc.edu.

University of Kentucky, Graduate School, College of Health Sciences, Program in Communication Disorders, Lexington, KY 40506-0032. Offers MSCD. *Accreditation:* ASHA. *Faculty:* 21 full-time (12 women). *Students:* 43 full-time (42 women). Average age 25. 8 applicants, 13% accepted, 1 enrolled. In 2006, 20 degrees awarded. *Degree requirements:* For master's, comprehensive exam. *Entrance requirements:* For master's, GRE General Test, minimum undergraduate GPA of 2.75. Additional exam requirements/recommendations for international students: Required—TOEFL (minimum score 550 paper-based; 213 computer-based). *Application deadline:* For fall admission, 7/17 priority date for domestic students, 2/1 priority date for international students; for spring admission, 12/13 priority date for domestic students, 6/15 priority date for international students. Application fee: $40 ($55 for international students). Electronic applications accepted. *Expenses:* Tuition, state resident: full-time $7,670; part-time $401 per credit hour. Tuition, nonresident: full-time $16,158; part-time $873 per credit hour. *Financial support:* In 2006–07, 3 students received support, including 2 fellowships with full tuition reimbursements available, research assistantships with full tuition reimbursements available (averaging $6,000 per year); teaching assistantships with full tuition reimbursements available, Federal Work-Study, scholarships/grants, traineeships, health care benefits, tuition waivers (partial), and unspecified assistantships also available. Support available to part-time students. Financial award application deadline: 3/15. *Faculty research:* Swallowing disorders, infant speech development, child language intervention, augmentative communication. *Unit head:* Dr. Jodelle Deem, Director of Graduate Studies, 859-323-1100, Fax: 859-323-8957, E-mail: jfdeem1@pop.uky.edu. *Application contact:* Dr. Brian Jackson, Senior Associate Dean, 859-257-4667, Fax: 859-257-4676, E-mail: brian.jackson@uky.edu.

University of Louisiana at Lafayette, Graduate School, College of Liberal Arts, Department of Communicative Disorders, Lafayette, LA 70504. Offers MS, PhD. *Accreditation:* ASHA (one or more programs are accredited). *Faculty:* 10 full-time (6 women). *Students:* 51 full-time (46 women), 6 part-time (all women); includes 10 minority (6 African Americans, 1 Asian American or Pacific Islander, 3 Hispanic Americans), 4 international. Average age 29. 78 applicants, 40% accepted, 15 enrolled. In 2006, 23 master's, 1 doctorate awarded. *Degree requirements:* For master's, thesis or alternative, registration. *Entrance requirements:* For master's, GRE General Test, minimum GPA of 2.75. Additional exam requirements/recommendations for international students: Required—TOEFL (minimum score 550 paper-based; 213 computer-based). *Application deadline:* For fall admission, 5/15 for domestic and international students; for spring admission, 10/1 for domestic and international students. Application fee: $25 ($30 for international students). *Expenses:* Tuition, state resident: full-time $3,247; part-time $93 per credit hour. Tuition, nonresident: full-time $9,427; part-time $350 per credit hour. *Financial support:* In 2006–07, 3 fellowships with full tuition reimbursements (averaging $14,850 per year), 10 research assistantships with full tuition reimbursements (averaging $8,950 per year) were awarded; teaching assistantships, Federal Work-Study and unspecified assistantships also available. Financial award application deadline: 5/1. *Unit head:* Dr. Martin J. Ball, Head, 337-482-6721, Fax: 337-482-6195, E-mail: mjball@louisiana.edu. *Application contact:* Dr. John Tetnowski, Coordinator, 337-482-6869, Fax: 337-482-6195, E-mail: tetnowski@louisiana.edu.

University of Louisiana at Monroe, Graduate Studies and Research, College of Health Sciences, Department of Communicative Disorders, Monroe, LA 71209-0001. Offers MS. *Accreditation:* ASHA. *Faculty:* 8 full-time (all women). *Students:* 35 full-time (33 women), 4 part-time (all women); includes 5 minority (all African Americans), 1 international. Average age 27. In 2006, 18 degrees awarded. *Degree requirements:* For master's, thesis optional. *Entrance requirements:* For master's, GRE General Test, minimum GPA of 2.5 or GRE General Test. *Application deadline:* For fall admission, 3/1 priority date for domestic students; for spring admission, 10/1 for domestic students. Application fee: $20 ($30 for international students). *Expenses:* Tuition, state resident: part-time $124 per credit hour. Tuition, nonresident: part-time $124 per credit hour. *Financial support:* Research assistantships, teaching assistantships, career-related internships or fieldwork, Federal Work-Study, and unspecified assistantships available. Financial award application deadline: 4/1. *Faculty research:* Child language, stuttering, multicultural issues, ethics. *Unit head:* Dr. Judy Fellows, Interim Head, 318-342-1392, Fax: 318-342-1687, E-mail: fellows@ulm.edu.

University of Louisville, School of Medicine, Department of Surgery, Division of Communicative Disorders, Program in Audiology, Louisville, KY 40292-0001. Offers Au D. *Accreditation:* ASHA. *Students:* 36 full-time (29 women); includes 2 minority (both African Americans), 1 international. Average age 27. In 2006, 9 degrees awarded.

University of Louisville, School of Medicine, Department of Surgery, Division of Communicative Disorders, Program in Communicative Disorders, Louisville, KY 40292-0001. Offers MS. *Accreditation:* ASHA. *Students:* 53 full-time (all women), 3 part-time (all women), 1 international. Average age 28. In 2006, 18 degrees awarded. *Degree requirements:* For master's, certification, thesis optional. *Entrance requirements:* For master's, GRE General Test, minimum GPA of 3.0. *Application deadline:* For fall admission, 1/15 for domestic students. Application fee: $50. *Financial support:* Research assistantships, career-related internships or fieldwork, institutionally sponsored loans, and scholarships/grants available. Financial award application deadline: 4/30. *Unit head:* Dr. David R. Cunningham, Director, 502-852-5274, Fax: 502-852-0865, E-mail: drcunn01@gwise.louisville.edu.

University of Maine, Graduate School, College of Liberal Arts and Sciences, Department of Communication Sciences and Disorders, Orono, ME 04469. Offers MA. *Accreditation:* ASHA. *Faculty:* 8. *Students:* 32 full-time (31 women), 5 part-time (all women); includes 1 minority (African American), 2 international. Average age 29. 46 applicants, 59% accepted, 14 enrolled. In 2006, 27 degrees awarded. *Entrance requirements:* For master's, GRE General Test. Additional exam requirements/recommendations for international students: Required—TOEFL. *Application deadline:* For fall admission, 2/1 priority date for domestic students. Applications are processed on a rolling basis. Application fee: $50. Electronic applications accepted. *Financial support:* In 2006–07, 2 research assistantships with full tuition reimbursements (averaging $10,000 per year) were awarded; fellowships, teaching assistantships, career-related internships or fieldwork, Federal Work-Study, institutionally sponsored loans, and tuition waivers (full and partial) also available. Support available to part-time students. Financial award application deadline: 3/1. *Faculty research:* Interpersonal communication between supervisor and supervised, clinicians and clients; language and voice impairments; children's pragmatics. *Unit head:* Dr. Nancy Hall, Chair, 207-581-2006, Fax: 207-581-1953. *Application contact:* Scott G. Delcourt, Associate Dean of the Graduate School, 207-581-3219, Fax: 207-581-3232, E-mail: graduate@maine.edu.

University of Maryland, College Park, Graduate Studies, College of Behavioral and Social Sciences, Department of Hearing and Speech Sciences, College Park, MD 20742. Offers audiology (MA, PhD); hearing and speech sciences (Au D); language pathology (MA, PhD); neuroscience (PhD); speech (MA, PhD). *Accreditation:* ASHA (one or more programs are accredited). *Faculty:* 18 full-time (all women), 13 part-time/adjunct (9 women). *Students:* 71 full-time (70 women), 24 part-time (all women); includes 14 minority (5 African Americans, 3 Asian Americans or Pacific Islanders, 6 Hispanic Americans), 3 international. 207 applicants, 43% accepted, 27 enrolled. In 2006, 13 master's, 1 doctorate awarded. *Degree requirements:* For master's, thesis optional; for doctorate, thesis/dissertation, written and oral exams. *Entrance requirements:* For master's, GRE General Test, minimum GPA of 3.5, 3 letters of recommendation; for doctorate, GRE General Test, minimum GPA of 3.5. Additional exam requirements/recommendations for international students: Required—TOEFL. *Application deadline:* For fall admission, 2/1 for domestic and international students. Applications are processed on a rolling basis. Application fee: $60. Electronic applications accepted. *Financial support:* In 2006–07, 1 fellowship with full tuition reimbursement (averaging $6,660 per year), 2 research assistantships (averaging $14,371 per year), 19 teaching assistantships with tuition reimbursements (averaging $13,951 per year) were awarded; career-related internships or fieldwork, Federal Work-Study, and scholarships/grants also available. Support available to part-time students. Financial award applicants required to submit FAFSA. *Faculty research:* Speech perception, language acquisition, bilingualism, hearing loss. Total annual research expenditures: $512,784. *Unit head:* Dr. Nan B. Ratner, Chair, 301-405-4217, Fax: 301-314-2023, E-mail: nratner@umd.edu. *Application contact:* Dean of Graduate School, 301-405-4190, Fax: 301-314-9305.

University of Maryland, College Park, National Institutes of Health Sponsored Programs, Graduate Program in Sensory and Communication Neuroscience, College Park, MD 20742. Offers audiology (PhD); language pathology (PhD); neuroscience (PhD); speech (PhD). *Degree requirements:* For doctorate, thesis/dissertation, written and oral examinations. *Entrance requirements:* For doctorate, GRE General Test, minimum GPA of 3.5. Additional exam requirements/recommendations for international students: Required—TOEFL. Electronic applications accepted. *Faculty research:* Speech, perception, language acquisition, bilingualism, hearing loss.

University of Massachusetts Amherst, Graduate School, School of Public Health and Health Sciences, Department of Communication Disorders, Amherst, MA 01003. Offers MA, PhD. *Accreditation:* ASHA (one or more programs are accredited). Part-time programs available. *Faculty:* 10 full-time (8 women). *Students:* 58 full-time (50 women), 5 part-time (all women); includes 4 minority (1 African American, 1 Asian American or Pacific Islander, 2 Hispanic Americans), 4 international. Average age 28. 160 applicants, 56% accepted, 31 enrolled. In 2006, 21 master's, 1 doctorate awarded. *Degree requirements:* For master's, thesis optional; for doctorate, thesis/dissertation. *Entrance requirements:* For master's and doctorate, GRE General Test. Additional exam requirements/recommendations for international students: Required—TOEFL (minimum score 530 paper-based; 197 computer-based). *Application deadline:* For fall admission, 2/1 priority date for domestic and international students; for spring admission, 10/1 for domestic and international students. Applications are processed on a rolling basis. Application fee: $40 ($65 for international students). Electronic applications accepted. *Expenses:* Tuition, state resident: full-time $2,640; part-time $110 per credit. Tuition, nonresident: full-time $9,936; part-time $414 per credit. Required fees: $8,969; $3,129 per term. One-time fee: $257 full-time. Tuition and fees vary according to class time, course load, campus/location and reciprocity agreements. *Financial support:* In 2006–07, 8 research assistantships with full tuition reimbursements (averaging $6,962 per year), 8 teaching assistantships with full tuition reimbursements (averaging $6,566 per year) were awarded; fellowships with full tuition reimbursements, career-related internships or fieldwork, Federal Work-Study, scholarships/grants, traineeships, and unspecified assistantships also available. Support available to part-time students. Financial award application deadline: 2/1. *Unit head:* Dr. Jane Baran, Head, 413-545-0131, Fax: 413-545-1264, E-mail: baran@comdis.umass.edu.

University of Memphis, Graduate School, School of Audiology and Speech-Language Pathology, Memphis, TN 38152. Offers MA, Au D, PhD. *Accreditation:* ASHA. Part-time programs available. *Faculty:* 28 full-time (17 women), 2 part-time/adjunct (both women). *Students:* 50 full-time (43 women), 6 part-time (all women); includes 5 minority (4 African Americans, 1 Hispanic American), 3 international. Average age 27. In 2006, 17 master's, 2 doctorates awarded. Terminal master's awarded for partial completion of doctoral program. *Degree requirements:* For master's, thesis or alternative, comprehensive exam; for doctorate, thesis/dissertation, qualifying exam. *Entrance requirements:* For master's, GRE General Test or MAT, minimum GPA of 3.0; for doctorate, GRE General Test, minimum GPA of 3.5. *Application deadline:* For fall admission, 2/1 for domestic students. Application fee: $25 ($50 for international students). *Financial support:* Research assistantships available. *Faculty research:* Hearing aid characteristic selection, language acquisition, speech disorders, characteristics of the aging voice, hearing science. Total annual research expenditures: $602,566. *Unit head:* Dr. Maurice Mendel, Dean, 901-678-5800. *Application contact:* Dr. David J. Wark, Coordinator of Graduate Studies, 901-678-5800.

University of Minnesota, Duluth, Graduate School, College of Education and Human Service Professions, Department of Communication Sciences and Disorders, Duluth, MN 55812-2496. Offers MA. *Accreditation:* ASHA. Part-time programs available. *Faculty:* 6 full-time (4 women), 3 part-time/adjunct (all women). *Students:* 29 full-time (28 women). Average age 25. 56 applicants, 50% accepted, 20 enrolled. In 2006, 15 degrees awarded. *Degree requirements:* For master's, research project, oral exam. *Entrance requirements:* For master's, minimum GPA of 3.0, undergraduate degree in communication sciences and disorders. Additional exam requirements/recommendations for international students: Required—TOEFL (minimum score 550 paper-based; 213 computer-based). *Application deadline:* For fall admission, 2/1 for domestic students. Application fee: $55 ($75 for international students). *Financial support:* In 2006–07, 28 students received support; fellowships with full and partial tuition reimbursements available, career-related internships or fieldwork, Federal Work-Study, institutionally sponsored loans, and tuition waivers (full and partial) available. Financial award application deadline: 2/1. *Faculty research:* Clinical supervision, augmentative communication, speech understanding, fluency, developmental apraxia of speech. Total annual research expenditures: $1,000. *Unit head:* Dr. Faith Loven, Director of Graduate Studies, 218-726-8204, Fax: 218-726-8693, E-mail: floven@d.umn.edu.

University of Minnesota, Twin Cities Campus, Graduate School, College of Liberal Arts, Department of Speech-Language-Hearing Sciences, Minneapolis, MN 55455. Offers audiology (Au D); speech-language pathology (MA); speech-language-hearing sciences (PhD). *Accreditation:* ASHA (one or more programs are accredited). *Faculty:* 15 full-time (10 women), 11 part-time/adjunct (5 women). *Students:* 122 full-time (114 women); includes 13 minority (2 African Americans, 2 American Indian/Alaska Native, 8 Asian Americans or Pacific Islanders, 1 Hispanic American). Average age 24. 207 applicants, 43% accepted, 36 enrolled. In 2006, 45 master's, 4 doctorates awarded. Terminal master's awarded for partial completion of doctoral program. *Degree requirements:* For master's, thesis, 375 client contact hours; for doctorate, thesis/dissertation, comprehensive exam, registration. *Entrance requirements:* For master's and doctorate, GRE General Test, minimum GPA of 3.0. Additional exam requirements/recommendations for international students: Required—TOEFL. *Application deadline:* For fall admission, 1/1 for domestic and international students. Application fee: $55 ($75 for international students). Electronic applications accepted. *Expenses:* Tuition, state resident: full-time $9,302; part-time $775 per credit. Tuition, nonresident: full-time $16,400; part-time $1,367 per credit. Full-time tuition and fees vary according to class time, course load, program, reciprocity agreements and student level. *Financial support:* In 2006–07, 1 fellowship with full tuition reimbursement (averaging $16,500 per year), 6 research assistantships with full and partial tuition reimbursements, 12 teaching assistantships with full and partial tuition reimbursements were awarded; Federal Work-Study, health care benefits, tuition waivers (partial), and unspecified assistantships also available. Financial award application deadline: 2/1; financial award applicants required to submit CSS PROFILE. *Faculty research:* Normal and disordered child phonology, specific language impairment, bilingual and multicultural aspects of language, TBI, AAC. Total annual research expenditures: $500,000. *Unit head:* Jennifer Windsor, Chair, 612-626-2016, Fax: 612-624-7586, E-mail: windsor@umn.edu. *Application contact:* Mary Kennedy, Director of Graduate Studies, 612-624-3322, Fax: 612-624-7586, E-mail: slhsgrad@umn.edu.

University of Mississippi, Graduate School, School of Applied Sciences, Department of Communicative Disorders, Oxford, University, MS 38677. Offers MS. *Accreditation:* ASHA. *Faculty:* 7 full-time (6 women), 5 part-time/adjunct (4 women). *Students:* 42 full-time (all women), 4 part-time (all women); includes 10 minority (9 African Americans, 1 Asian American or Pacific Islander), 1 international. In 2006, 14 degrees awarded. *Entrance requirements:* For master's, GRE General Test, minimum GPA of 3.0. Additional exam requirements/recommendations for international students: Required—TOEFL. *Application deadline:* For fall admission, 2/1 for domestic students; for spring admission, 10/1 for domestic students. Applications are processed on a rolling basis. Application fee: $25. Electronic applications accepted. *Expenses:* Tuition, state resident: full-time $4,602; part-time $256 per credit hour. Tuition, nonresident: full-time $10,566; part-time $587 per credit hour. *Financial support:* Scholarships/

grants available. Financial award application deadline: 3/1; financial award applicants required to submit FAFSA. *Unit head:* Dr. Carolyn Wiles Higdon, Chair, 662-915-7652, Fax: 662-915-5717, E-mail: chigdon@olemiss.edu.

University of Missouri–Columbia, School of Health Professions, Program in Communication Science and Disorders, Columbia, MO 65211. Offers MHS. *Accreditation:* ASHA. *Faculty:* 8 full-time (6 women). *Students:* 28 full-time (27 women), 5 part-time (all women); includes 2 minority (1 Asian American or Pacific Islander, 1 Hispanic American), 1 international. In 2006, 11 degrees awarded. *Entrance requirements:* For master's, GRE General Test, minimum GPA of 3.0. Additional exam requirements/recommendations for international students: Required—TOEFL (minimum score 600 paper-based; 250 computer-based; 100 iBT). *Application deadline:* For fall admission, 2/15 priority date for domestic students. Applications are processed on a rolling basis. Application fee: $45 ($60 for international students). *Financial support:* Research assistantships, teaching assistantships, institutionally sponsored loans available. *Unit head:* Dr. Barbara McLay, Director of Graduate Studies, 573-882-8409, E-mail: mclayb@missouri.edu.

University of Montevallo, College of Arts and Sciences, Department of Speech Pathology and Audiology, Montevallo, AL 35115. Offers MS. *Accreditation:* ASHA. *Degree requirements:* For master's, comprehensive exam. *Entrance requirements:* For master's, GRE General Test, MAT, minimum GPA of 2.5 or 2.7 in last 60 hours. Additional exam requirements/recommendations for international students: Required—TOEFL (minimum score 550 paper-based).

University of Nebraska at Kearney, College of Graduate Study, College of Education, Department of Communication Disorders, Kearney, NE 68849-0001. Offers speech pathology (MS Ed). *Accreditation:* ASHA. Part-time programs available. *Faculty:* 3 full-time (2 women). *Students:* 25 full-time (23 women), 5 part-time (all women); includes 1 minority (Hispanic American), 4 international. 25 applicants, 72% accepted. In 2006, 10 degrees awarded. *Entrance requirements:* For master's, GRE General Test. *Application deadline:* For fall admission, 2/1 for domestic and international students; for spring admission, 8/1 for domestic and international students. Application fee: $45. Electronic applications accepted. *Expenses:* Tuition, state resident: part-time $161 per hour. Tuition, nonresident: part-time $332 per hour. Required fees: $57 per hour. *Financial support:* In 2006–07, 2 research assistantships with full tuition reimbursements (averaging $8,200 per year), 2 teaching assistantships (averaging $8,200 per year) were awarded; career-related internships or fieldwork and unspecified assistantships also available. Support available to part-time students. Financial award application deadline: 3/1; financial award applicants required to submit FAFSA. *Faculty research:* Neurogenic, communication disorders in adults, phonological development and disorders, orofacial anomalies, audiologic rehabilitation of the elderly. *Unit head:* Dr. Lawrence Hilton, Chair, 308-856-8300, Fax: 308-865-8397, E-mail: hiltonlm@unk.edu.

University of Nebraska at Omaha, Graduate Studies and Research, College of Education, Department of Special Education and Communication Disorders, Omaha, NE 68182. Offers special education (MS); speech-language pathology (MA, MS). *Accreditation:* ASHA (one or more programs are accredited); NCATE. Part-time and evening/weekend programs available. *Faculty:* 9 full-time (7 women). *Students:* 20 full-time (all women), 67 part-time (57 women); includes 2 minority (1 African American, 1 Asian American or Pacific Islander). Average age 30. 63 applicants, 70% accepted, 18 enrolled. In 2006, 41 degrees awarded. *Degree requirements:* For master's, thesis (for some programs), comprehensive exam. *Entrance requirements:* For master's, GRE General Test or MAT, minimum GPA of 3.0. Additional exam requirements/recommendations for international students: Required—TOEFL (minimum score 500 paper-based; 173 computer-based; 61 iBT). *Application deadline:* For fall admission, 2/1 for domestic students; for spring admission, 9/1 for domestic students. Applications are processed on a rolling basis. Application fee: $45. Electronic applications accepted. *Financial support:* In 2006–07, 69 students received support; fellowships, research assistantships with tuition reimbursements available, career-related internships or fieldwork, Federal Work-Study, institutionally sponsored loans, scholarships/grants, tuition waivers (partial), and unspecified assistantships available. Support available to part-time students. Financial award application deadline: 3/1; financial award applicants required to submit FAFSA. *Unit head:* Dr. Mary Friehe, Chairperson, 402-554-2201.

University of Nebraska–Lincoln, Graduate College, College of Education and Human Services, Department of Special Education and Communication Disorders, Program in Speech-Language Pathology and Audiology, Lincoln, NE 68588. Offers MS. *Accreditation:* ASHA. *Degree requirements:* For master's, thesis optional. *Entrance requirements:* For master's, GRE. Additional exam requirements/recommendations for international students: Required—TOEFL (minimum score 500 paper-based; 173 computer-based). Electronic applications accepted.

University of Nevada, Reno, School of Medicine and Graduate School, Graduate Programs in Medicine, Department of Speech Pathology and Audiology, Reno, NV 89557. Offers speech pathology (PhD); speech pathology and audiology (MS). *Accreditation:* ASHA (one or more programs are accredited). *Faculty:* 5. *Students:* 33 full-time (31 women); includes 3 minority (1 Asian American or Pacific Islander, 2 Hispanic Americans), 1 international. Average age 27. 24 applicants, 79% accepted, 16 enrolled. In 2006, 20 degrees awarded. *Degree requirements:* For master's, thesis optional; for doctorate, thesis/dissertation. *Entrance requirements:* For master's, GRE General Test, minimum GPA of 2.75; for doctorate, GRE General Test, minimum GPA of 3.0. Additional exam requirements/recommendations for international students: Required—TOEFL. *Application deadline:* For fall admission, 3/1 priority date for domestic students. Applications are processed on a rolling basis. Application fee: $60 ($95 for international students). *Financial support:* In 2006–07, 3 research assistantships, 1 teaching assistantship were awarded; fellowships also available. Financial award application deadline: 3/1. *Faculty research:* Language impairment in children, voice disorders, stuttering. *Unit head:* Dr. Kerry Lewis, Graduate Program Director, 775-784-4887, E-mail: klewis@med.unr.edu.

University of New Hampshire, Graduate School, School of Health and Human Services, Department of Communication Sciences and Disorders, Durham, NH 03824. Offers early childhood intervention (MS); language and literature disabilities (MS). *Accreditation:* ASHA. Part-time programs available. *Faculty:* 10 full-time. *Students:* 43 full-time (all women), 6 part-time (5 women); includes 1 minority (African American) Average age 35. 80 applicants, 60% accepted, 22 enrolled. In 2006, 26 degrees awarded. *Degree requirements:* For master's, thesis or alternative. *Entrance requirements:* For master's, GRE General Test or MAT. Additional exam requirements/recommendations for international students: Required—TOEFL (minimum score 550 paper-based; 213 computer-based). *Application deadline:* For fall admission, 4/1 priority date for domestic students, 4/1 for international students. Applications are processed on a rolling basis. Application fee: $60. Electronic applications accepted. *Expenses:* Tuition, state resident: full-time $8,540; part-time $474 per credit hour. Tuition, nonresident: full-time $20,990; part-time $862 per credit hour. Required fees: $1,343; $356 per term. Tuition and fees vary according to course load, program and reciprocity agreements. *Financial support:* In 2006–07, 1 research assistantship, 6 teaching assistantships were awarded; fellowships, career-related internships or fieldwork, Federal Work-Study, scholarships/grants, and tuition waivers (full and partial) also available. Support available to part-time students. Financial award application deadline: 2/15. *Faculty research:* Speech pathology. *Unit head:* Dr. Stephen Calculator, Chairperson, 603-862-3836. *Application contact:* Maria Russell, Administrative Assistant, 603-862-0144, E-mail: communication.disorders@unh.edu.

University of New Mexico, Graduate School, College of Arts and Sciences, Department of Speech and Hearing Sciences, Albuquerque, NM 87131-2039. Offers MS. *Accreditation:* ASHA. *Faculty:* 4 full-time (all women), 2 part-time/adjunct (1 woman). *Students:* 51 full-time (49 women), 10 part-time (9 women); includes 26 minority (1 African American, 1 American Indian/Alaska Native, 1 Asian American or Pacific Islander, 23 Hispanic Americans), 1 international. Average age 32. 70 applicants, 43% accepted, 22 enrolled. In 2006, 25 degrees awarded. *Degree requirements:* For master's, thesis optional. *Entrance requirements:* For master's, GRE General Test, minimum GPA of 3.2 during previous 2 years. Additional exam requirements/recommendations for international students: Required—TOEFL. *Application deadline:* For fall admission, 2/15 for domestic students; for spring admission, 9/15 for domestic students. Application fee: $50. Electronic applications accepted. *Financial support:* In 2006–07, 37 students received support, including 10 research assistantships with partial tuition reimbursements available (averaging $6,100 per year); career-related internships or fieldwork, Federal Work-Study, scholarships/grants, health care benefits, and unspecified assistantships also available. Financial award application deadline: 2/15; financial award applicants required to submit FAFSA. *Faculty research:* AAC, child language assessment, speech perception, swallowing disorders, cultural influences on language acquisition. Total annual research expenditures: $99,569. *Unit head:* Dr. Philip S. Dale, Chair, 505-277-4453, Fax: 505-277-0968, E-mail: dalep@unm.edu. *Application contact:* Maria C. Pearson, Administrative Assistant, 505-277-4453, Fax: 505-277-0968.

The University of North Carolina at Chapel Hill, School of Medicine and Graduate School, Graduate Programs in Medicine, Chapel Hill, NC 27599. Offers allied health sciences (MPT, MS, Au D, DPT, PhD), including human movement science (MS, PhD), occupational science (MS, PhD), physical therapy (MPT, MS, DPT), rehabilitation counseling and psychology (MS), speech and hearing sciences (MS, Au D, PhD); biochemistry and biophysics (MS, PhD); biomedical engineering (MS, PhD); cell and developmental biology (PhD); cell and molecular physiology (PhD); genetics and molecular biology (PhD); microbiology and immunology (MS, PhD), including immunology, microbiology; neurobiology (PhD); pathology and laboratory medicine (PhD), including experimental pathology; pharmacology (PhD); MD/PhD. Post-baccalaureate distance learning degree programs offered. *Faculty:* 470 full-time (156 women), 101 part-time/adjunct (17 women). *Students:* 730 full-time (447 women), 36 part-time (27 women); includes 110 minority (43 African Americans, 6 American Indian/Alaska Native, 48 Asian Americans or Pacific Islanders, 13 Hispanic Americans), 79 international. In 2006, 73 master's, 62 doctorates awarded. Terminal master's awarded for partial completion of doctoral program. *Degree requirements:* For master's, comprehensive exam; for doctorate, thesis/dissertation. *Application deadline:* Applications are processed on a rolling basis. Application fee: $65. Electronic applications accepted. *Expenses: Contact institution. Financial support:* In 2006–07, 77 fellowships with full and partial tuition reimbursements, 309 research assistantships with full tuition reimbursements, 23 teaching assistantships with full tuition reimbursements were awarded; career-related internships or fieldwork, Federal Work-Study, institutionally sponsored loans, traineeships, tuition waivers (full and partial), and unspecified assistantships also available. Support available to part-time students. Financial award applicants required to submit FAFSA. *Unit head:* Dr. William I. Roper, Dean, 919-966-4161, Fax: 919-966-6354.

The University of North Carolina at Chapel Hill, School of Medicine and Graduate School, Graduate Programs in Medicine, Department of Allied Health Sciences, Division of Speech and Hearing Sciences, Chapel Hill, NC 27599. Offers audiology (Au D); speech and hearing sciences (MS, PhD). *Accreditation:* ASHA (one or more programs are accredited). Post-baccalaureate distance learning degree programs offered (no on-campus study). *Faculty:* 12 full-time (11 women), 9 part-time/adjunct (5 women). *Students:* 66 full-time (61 women), 1 (woman) part-time; includes 9 minority (5 African Americans, 1 Asian American or Pacific Islander, 3 Hispanic Americans). Average age 32. 168 applicants, 32% accepted, 34 enrolled. In 2006, 22 degrees awarded. *Degree requirements:* For master's, thesis optional; for doctorate, thesis/dissertation, comprehensive exam. *Entrance requirements:* For master's, GRE General Test, minimum GPA of 3.0; for doctorate, GRE, minimum GPA of 3.0. Additional exam requirements/recommendations for international students: Required—TOEFL (minimum score 550 paper-based; 79 computer-based). *Application deadline:* For fall admission, 1/1 for domestic and international students. Application fee: $70. Electronic applications accepted. *Financial support:* In 2006–07, 26 students received support, including 7 fellowships with full tuition reimbursements available (averaging $13,000 per year), 15 research assistantships with partial tuition reimbursements available (averaging $5,389 per year), 1 teaching assistantship (averaging $2,667 per year); career-related internships or fieldwork, Federal Work-Study, scholarships/grants, traineeships, health care benefits, and unspecified assistantships also available. Financial award application deadline: 1/1. *Faculty research:* Child language and literacy, family participation in early intervention, child and adult hearing loss and treatment, vocal characteristics of African-American speakers and aging populations, adult apraxia of speech. Total annual research expenditures: $67,044. *Unit head:* Dr. Jackson Roush, Director, 919-966-9467, Fax: 919-966-0100, E-mail: jroush@med.unc.edu. *Application contact:* Ina Diana, Admission Assistant, 919-966-1007, Fax: 919-966-0100.

The University of North Carolina at Greensboro, Graduate School, School of Health and Human Performance, Department of Communication Sciences and Disorders, Greensboro, NC 27412-5001. Offers speech language pathology (PhD); speech pathology and audiology (MA). *Accreditation:* ASHA. *Faculty:* 8 full-time (6 women), 11 part-time/adjunct (9 women). *Students:* 58 full-time (52 women); includes 12 minority (8 African Americans, 2 Asian Americans or Pacific Islanders, 2 Hispanic Americans). 141 applicants, 28% accepted. *Degree requirements:* For master's, thesis or alternative. *Entrance requirements:* For master's, GRE General Test. Additional exam requirements/recommendations for international students: Required—TOEFL. *Application deadline:* For fall admission, 2/15 for domestic students. Application fee: $45. Electronic applications accepted. *Expenses:* Tuition, state resident: full-time $2,692. Tuition, nonresident: full-time $13,742. *Financial support:* Fellowships with full tuition reimbursements, research assistantships with full tuition reimbursements, teaching assistantships with full tuition reimbursements, career-related internships or fieldwork, Federal Work-Study, scholarships/grants, and traineeships available. Support available to part-time students. *Unit head:* Dr. Celia R. Hooper, Head, 336-334-5184, Fax: 336-334-4475, E-mail: chooper@uncg.edu. *Application contact:* Michelle Harkleroad, Director of Graduate Admissions, 336-334-4884, Fax: 336-334-4424, E-mail: mbharkle@uncg.edu.

University of North Dakota, Graduate School, College of Arts and Sciences, Department of Communication Disorders and Speech-Language Pathology, Grand Forks, ND 58202. Offers communication sciences and disorders (PhD); speech-language pathology (MS). *Accreditation:* ASHA (one or more programs are accredited). Part-time programs available. *Faculty:* 6 full-time (1 woman). *Students:* 40 full-time (all women), 12 part-time (11 women); includes 1 Asian American or Pacific Islander, 22 international. 57 applicants, 14% accepted, 7 enrolled. In 2006, 20 degrees awarded. *Median time to degree:* Master's–2 years full-time. *Degree requirements:* For master's, thesis or alternative, comprehensive exam; for doctorate, thesis/dissertation, final exam, comprehensive exam. *Entrance requirements:* For master's and doctorate, GRE General Test, minimum GPA of 3.0. Additional exam requirements/recommendations for international students: Required—TOEFL (minimum score 550 paper-based; 213 computer-based; 79 iBT), IELTS (minimum score 6). *Application deadline:* For fall admission, 2/15 for domestic and international students. Application fee: $35. Electronic applications accepted. *Expenses:* Tuition, state resident: full-time $5,650; part-time $214 per credit. Tuition, nonresident: full-time $14,248; part-time $572 per credit. Required fees: $1,008; $42 per credit. Tuition and fees vary according to reciprocity agreements. *Financial support:* In 2006–07, 13 students received support, including 3 research assistantships with full tuition reimbursements available, 3 teaching assistantships with full tuition reimbursements available (averaging $10,413 per year); fellowships, Federal Work-Study, institutionally sponsored loans, scholarships/grants, health care benefits, tuition waivers (full and partial), and unspecified assistantships also available. Support available to part-time students. Financial award application deadline: 3/15; financial award applicants required to submit FAFSA. *Faculty research:* Mass communications, journalism, community law, international communications, cultural studies. *Unit head:* Dr. Kevin Fire, Graduate Director, 701-777-3232, Fax: 701-777-4578, E-mail: kevin_fire@und.nodak.edu. *Application contact:* Staci Wells, Admissions Associate, 701-777-2945, Fax: 701-777-3619, E-mail: gradschool@mail.und.nodak.edu.

University of Northern Colorado, Graduate School, College of Natural and Health Sciences, School of Human Sciences, Program in Audiology and Speech Language Sciences, Greeley, CO 80639. Offers audiology (Au D); speech language pathology (MA). *Accreditation:* ASHA (one or more programs are accredited). Part-time and evening/weekend programs available. Post-

Communication Disorders

University of Northern Colorado (continued)

baccalaureate distance learning degree programs offered (no on-campus study). *Faculty:* 7 full-time (all women). *Students:* 63 full-time (61 women), 1 (woman) part-time; includes 4 minority (2 Asian Americans or Pacific Islanders, 2 Hispanic Americans). Average age 26. 109 applicants, 39% accepted, 19 enrolled. In 2006, 23 master's, 7 doctorates awarded. *Degree requirements:* For master's, thesis or alternative, comprehensive exam; for doctorate, thesis/dissertation, comprehensive exam. *Entrance requirements:* For master's and doctorate, GRE General Test. *Application deadline:* Applications are processed on a rolling basis. Application fee: $50 ($60 for international students). Electronic applications accepted. *Expenses:* Tuition, state resident: full-time $5,118; part-time $213 per credit hour. Tuition, nonresident: full-time $14,832; part-time $618 per credit hour. Required fees: $674; $34 per credit hour. *Financial support:* In 2006–07, 62 students received support, including 7 fellowships (averaging $1,000 per year), 7 research assistantships (averaging $9,623 per year); teaching assistantships, unspecified assistantships also available. Financial award application deadline: 3/1; financial award applicants required to submit FAFSA. *Unit head:* Dr. Kathleen Fahey, Chairperson, 970-351-2734.

University of Northern Iowa, Graduate College, College of Humanities and Fine Arts, Department of Communicative Disorders, Cedar Falls, IA 50614. Offers audiology (MA); speech pathology (MA). *Accreditation:* ASHA. Part-time and evening/weekend programs available. *Faculty:* 9 full-time (4 women), 1 part-time/adjunct (0 women). *Students:* 48 full-time (all women), 1 (woman) part-time; includes 5 minority (4 African Americans, 1 Asian American or Pacific Islander), 1 international. 55 applicants, 53% accepted, 15 enrolled. In 2006, 18 degrees awarded. *Entrance requirements:* For master's, GRE. Additional exam requirements/recommendations for international students: Required—TOEFL (minimum score 500 paper-based; 180 computer-based; 61 iBT). *Application deadline:* For fall admission, 8/1 priority date for domestic students. Applications are processed on a rolling basis. Application fee: $30 ($50 for international students). *Expenses:* Tuition, state resident: full-time $5,936. Tuition, nonresident: full-time $14,074. *Financial support:* Career-related internships or fieldwork, Federal Work-Study, scholarships/grants, and tuition waivers (full and partial) available. Financial award application deadline: 2/1. *Unit head:* Dr. Clifford L. Highnam, Head, 319-273-2217, Fax: 319-273-6384, E-mail: clifford.highnam@uni.edu.

University of North Texas, Robert B. Toulouse School of Graduate Studies, College of Arts and Sciences, Department of Speech and Hearing Sciences, Denton, TX 76203. Offers audiology (Au D); speech-language pathology (MA, MS). *Accreditation:* ASHA. Part-time programs available. *Faculty:* 11 full-time (8 women). *Students:* 85 full-time (78 women), 7 part-time (6 women); includes 20 minority (4 African Americans, 1 American Indian/Alaska Native, 4 Asian Americans or Pacific Islanders, 11 Hispanic Americans), 2 international. Average age 25. 157 applicants, 80% accepted, 31 enrolled. In 2006, 21 degrees awarded. *Degree requirements:* For master's, internship, thesis optional. *Entrance requirements:* For master's, GRE General Test, minimum GPA of 3.0 in major, 2.8 overall; 15 hours of course work in communication disorders. *Application deadline:* For fall admission, 2/15 for domestic students; for spring admission, 10/1 for domestic students. Application fee: $50 ($75 for international students). *Expenses:* Tuition, state resident: full-time $3,573; part-time $198 per credit. Tuition, nonresident: full-time $8,577; part-time $476 per credit. Required fees: $1,258; $126 per credit. One-time fee: $150 full-time. Tuition and fees vary according to course load. *Financial support:* Fellowships, research assistantships, teaching assistantships, career-related internships or fieldwork, Federal Work-Study, institutionally sponsored loans, and unspecified assistantships available. Financial award application deadline: 3/15. *Faculty research:* Communication disorders in aging, voice disorders, language development, speech perception, brain mapping. Total annual research expenditures: $90,000. *Unit head:* Dr. Jeffrey A. Cokely, Chair, 940-565-2481, Fax: 940-565-4058, E-mail: cokely@unt.edu. *Application contact:* Dr. Maria Jimenez-Castro, Graduate Adviser, 940-565-7367, Fax: 940-565-4058, E-mail: mjimenez@unt.edu.

University of Oklahoma Health Sciences Center, Graduate College, College of Allied Health, Department of Communication Sciences and Disorders, Oklahoma City, OK 73190. Offers audiology (MS, Au D, PhD); communication sciences and disorders (Certificate); education of the deaf (MS); speech-language pathology (MS, PhD). *Accreditation:* ASHA (one or more programs are accredited). Part-time programs available. Terminal master's awarded for partial completion of doctoral program. *Degree requirements:* For master's, thesis optional; for doctorate, one foreign language, thesis/dissertation, comprehensive exam. *Entrance requirements:* For master's and doctorate, GRE General Test, 3 letters of recommendation. Additional exam requirements/recommendations for international students: Required—TOEFL (minimum score 550 paper-based). *Faculty research:* Event-related potentials, cleft palate, fluency disorders, language disorders, hearing and speech science.

University of Ottawa, Faculty of Graduate and Postdoctoral Studies, Faculty of Health Sciences, School of Rehabilitation Sciences, Ottawa, ON K1N 6N5, Canada. Offers audiology (M Sc); orthophony (M Sc). Part-time and evening/weekend programs available. *Entrance requirements:* For master's, honors degree or equivalent, minimum B average. Electronic applications accepted.

University of Pittsburgh, School of Health and Rehabilitation Sciences, Department of Communication Science and Disorders, Pittsburgh, PA 15260. Offers MA, MS, Au D, CScD, PhD. *Accreditation:* ASHA (one or more programs are accredited). *Faculty:* 16 full-time (11 women), 1 part-time/adjunct (0 women). *Students:* 117 full-time (109 women), 15 part-time (13 women); includes 5 minority (4 African Americans, 1 Asian American or Pacific Islander), 10 international. Average age 27. 166 applicants, 64% accepted, 40 enrolled. In 2006, 27 master's, 11 doctorates awarded. *Median time to degree:* Of those who began their doctoral program in fall 1998, 9% received their degree in 8 years or less. *Degree requirements:* For master's, thesis (for some programs), comprehensive exam; for doctorate, thesis/dissertation, comprehensive exam. *Entrance requirements:* For master's and doctorate, GRE General Test. Additional exam requirements/recommendations for international students: Required—TOEFL, IELTS. *Application deadline:* For fall admission, 3/15 for domestic students; for spring admission, 3/15 priority date for domestic students. Applications are processed on a rolling basis. Application fee: $50. Electronic applications accepted. *Expenses:* Contact institution. *Financial support:* In 2006–07, 9 research assistantships with partial tuition reimbursements (averaging $18,258 per year), 1 teaching assistantship with full tuition reimbursement (averaging $14,560 per year) were awarded; fellowships, career-related internships or fieldwork, Federal Work-Study, institutionally sponsored loans, scholarships/grants, and traineeships also available. Financial award application deadline: 3/20; financial award applicants required to submit FAFSA. *Faculty research:* Pediatric and geriatric neurogenic speech and language, pediatric hearing disorders, hearing aids, language development, speech motor control. Total annual research expenditures: $1.1 million. *Unit head:* Malcolm R. McNeil, Chairman, 412-383-6541, Fax: 412-383-6555, E-mail: mcneil@pitt.edu. *Application contact:* Theresa Niecgorski, Admissions Secretary, 412-383-6540, Fax: 412-383-6555, E-mail: thn49@pitt.edu.

University of Puerto Rico, Medical Sciences Campus, College of Health Related Professions, Program in Audiology, San Juan, PR 00936-5067. Offers MS. *Accreditation:* ASHA. *Degree requirements:* For master's, one foreign language, thesis or alternative, comprehensive exam. *Entrance requirements:* For master's, EXADEP, minimum GPA of 2.5, interview, fluency in Spanish. *Faculty research:* Hearing, auditory brainstem responses, otoacoustic emissions.

University of Puerto Rico, Medical Sciences Campus, College of Health Related Professions, Program in Speech-Language Pathology, San Juan, PR 00936-5067. Offers MS. *Accreditation:* ASHA. *Degree requirements:* For master's, one foreign language, thesis or alternative, comprehensive exam. *Entrance requirements:* For master's, EXADEP, interview; previous course work in linguistics, statistics, human development, and basic concepts in speech-language pathology; minimum GPA of 2.5. *Faculty research:* Aphasia, autism, language, aphasia, assistive technology.

University of Redlands, College of Arts and Sciences, Department of Communicative Disorders, Redlands, CA 92373-0999. Offers MS. *Accreditation:* ASHA. *Faculty:* 8 full-time (5 women), 6 part-time/adjunct (4 women). *Students:* 46 full-time (45 women), 2 part-time (both women); includes 5 minority (2 Asian Americans or Pacific Islanders, 3 Hispanic Americans), 1 international. Average age 23. In 2006, 22 degrees awarded. *Degree requirements:* For master's, final exam. *Entrance requirements:* For master's, GMAT or GRE, minimum GPA of 3.0, 3 letters of recommendation. Additional exam requirements/recommendations for international students: Required—TOEFL (minimum score 550 paper-based; 213 computer-based). *Application deadline:* For fall admission, 2/15 priority date for domestic students. Applications are processed on a rolling basis. Application fee: $40. Electronic applications accepted. *Expenses:* Contact institution. *Financial support:* In 2006–07, 5 fellowships with partial tuition reimbursements, 3 research assistantships with partial tuition reimbursements (averaging $2,000 per year) were awarded; career-related internships or fieldwork, scholarships/grants, and unspecified assistantships also available. Financial award application deadline: 3/2; financial award applicants required to submit FAFSA. *Faculty research:* Neuropathy. *Unit head:* Dr. Chris Walker, Chairman, 909-793-2121, Fax: 909-335-5192, E-mail: christopher_walker@redlands.edu. *Application contact:* Christine Mee, Administrative Assistant, 909-793-2121, Fax: 909-335-5192, E-mail: christine_mee@redlands.edu.

University of Rhode Island, Graduate School, College of Human Science and Services, Department of Communicative Disorders, Kingston, RI 02881. Offers audiology (Au D); speech-language pathology (MS). *Accreditation:* ASHA (one or more programs are accredited). *Entrance requirements:* For master's, MAT or GRE. *Application deadline:* For fall admission, 4/15 priority date for domestic students; for spring admission, 11/15 for domestic students. Applications are processed on a rolling basis. Application fee: $35. *Expenses:* Tuition, state resident: full-time $6,032; part-time $335 per credit. Tuition, nonresident: full-time $17,288; part-time $960 per credit. Required fees: $65 per credit. $30 per semester. One-time fee: $80 part-time. *Unit head:* Dr. Jay Singer, Chair, 401-874-4742.

University of South Alabama, Graduate School, College of Allied Health Professions, Department of Speech Pathology and Audiology, Mobile, AL 36688-0002. Offers audiology (Au D); communication sciences and disorders (PhD); speech and hearing sciences (MS). *Accreditation:* ASHA. *Faculty:* 9 full-time (6 women). *Students:* 76 full-time (71 women); includes 5 minority (3 African Americans, 1 Asian American or Pacific Islander, 1 Hispanic American), 2 international. 23 applicants, 96% accepted. In 2006, 10 master's, 4 doctorates awarded. *Degree requirements:* For master's, externship, thesis optional; for doctorate, thesis/dissertation, clinical internship. *Entrance requirements:* For master's, GRE General Test. *Application deadline:* For fall admission, 9/1 priority date for domestic students. Applications are processed on a rolling basis. Application fee: $25. *Financial support:* Fellowships, research assistantships, career-related internships or fieldwork available. Support available to part-time students. Financial award application deadline: 4/1. *Faculty research:* Computer applications to speech and hearing science, telecommunications and clinical research in articulation and languages. *Unit head:* Dr. Paul Dagenais, Acting Chair, 251-380-2600.

University of South Carolina, The Graduate School, Arnold School of Public Health, Department of Communication Sciences and Disorders, Columbia, SC 29208. Offers MCD, MSP, PhD. *Accreditation:* ASHA (one or more programs are accredited). Postbaccalaureate distance learning degree programs offered. *Degree requirements:* For master's and doctorate, thesis/dissertation, comprehensive exam. *Entrance requirements:* For master's, GRE General Test, minimum GPA of 3.0; for doctorate, GRE General Test, master's degree in audiology or speech pathology. Electronic applications accepted. *Faculty research:* Noise-induced hearing loss, recurrent laryngeal nerve regeneration, cleft palate, child language-phonology, epidemiology of craniofacial anomalies.

The University of South Dakota, Graduate School, College of Arts and Sciences, Department of Communication Disorders, Vermillion, SD 57069-2390. Offers audiology (Au D); communications disorders (MA); speech-language pathology (MA). *Accreditation:* ASHA (one or more programs are accredited). Part-time programs available. *Faculty:* 12 full-time (10 women). *Students:* 48 full-time (47 women). In 2006, 21 degrees awarded. *Degree requirements:* For master's, comprehensive exam; for doctorate, thesis/dissertation, comprehensive exam. *Entrance requirements:* For master's, GRE General Test, minimum GPA of 3.0. Additional exam requirements/recommendations for international students: Required—TOEFL (minimum score 550 paper-based; 213 computer-based; 79 iBT). *Application deadline:* For fall admission, 2/1 for domestic students; for spring admission, 10/15 for domestic students. Application fee: $35. Electronic applications accepted. *Expenses:* Tuition, state resident: part-time $120 per credit hour. Tuition, nonresident: part-time $355 per credit hour. Required fees: $90 per credit hour. *Financial support:* In 2006–07, 2 research assistantships with partial tuition reimbursements (averaging $4,626 per year), 10 teaching assistantships with partial tuition reimbursements (averaging $4,626 per year) were awarded; career-related internships or fieldwork, Federal Work-Study, scholarships/grants, and unspecified assistantships also available. Support available to part-time students. Financial award application deadline: 5/1; financial award applicants required to submit FAFSA. *Faculty research:* Craniofacial anomalies, central auditory processing, phonological disorders. *Unit head:* Dr. Teri Bellis, Chair, 605-677-5474, Fax: 605-677-5767, E-mail: dcom@usd.edu.

University of Southern Mississippi, Graduate School, College of Health, Department of Speech and Hearing Sciences, Hattiesburg, MS 39406-0001. Offers MA, MS, Au D. *Accreditation:* ASHA (one or more programs are accredited). *Faculty:* 10 full-time (2 women). *Students:* 47 full-time (all women), 1 part-time; includes 3 minority (all African Americans), 1 international. Average age 24. 89 applicants, 49% accepted, 24 enrolled. In 2006, 19 degrees awarded. *Degree requirements:* For master's, thesis or alternative, comprehensive exam; for doctorate, thesis/dissertation, comprehensive exam. *Entrance requirements:* For master's, GRE General Test, minimum GPA of 3.0 in field of study, 2.75 in last 2 years; for doctorate, GRE General Test, minimum GPA of 3.5. Additional exam requirements/recommendations for international students: Required—TOEFL. *Application deadline:* For fall admission, 3/1 for domestic and international students. Application fee: $25 ($30 for international students). Electronic applications accepted. *Financial support:* In 2006–07, 6 research assistantships with full and partial tuition reimbursements (averaging $6,666 per year) were awarded; teaching assistantships with full and partial tuition reimbursements, career-related internships or fieldwork, Federal Work-Study, institutionally sponsored loans, and tuition waivers (full) also available. Financial award application deadline: 3/15. *Faculty research:* Voice disorders, auditory-evoked responses, acoustic analysis of speech, child language, parent-child interaction. *Unit head:* Dr. Brett Kemker, Interim Chair, 601-266-5216.

University of South Florida, Graduate School, College of Arts and Sciences, Department of Communication Sciences and Disorders, Tampa, FL 33620-9951. Offers PhD. *Accreditation:* ASHA. Part-time and evening/weekend programs available. Postbaccalaureate distance learning degree programs offered (minimal on-campus study). *Faculty:* 29 full-time (23 women), 11 part-time/adjunct (8 women). *Students:* 132 full-time (127 women), 52 part-time (49 women); includes 44 minority (12 African Americans, 12 Asian Americans or Pacific Islanders, 20 Hispanic Americans), 1 international. 255 applicants, 53% accepted, 83 enrolled. In 2006, 11 doctorates awarded. *Application deadline:* For fall admission, 12/1 for domestic students. Application fee: $30. Electronic applications accepted. *Financial support:* Career-related internships or fieldwork, scholarships/grants, and unspecified assistantships available. Financial award application deadline: 6/30. *Faculty research:* Speech perception, motor speech, neurogenic communication disorder, oncology, speech acoustics. Total annual research expenditures: $468,333. *Unit head:* Dr. Arthur Guilford, Information Contact, 813-974-2006, Fax: 813-974-0822, E-mail: jharring@chuma1.cas.usf.edu. *Application contact:* Dr. Elaine Silliman, Information Contact, 813-974-9780, Fax: 813-974-0822, E-mail: silliman@chuma1.cas.usf.edu.

The University of Tennessee, Graduate School, College of Arts and Sciences, Department of Audiology and Speech Pathology, Program in Audiology, Knoxville, TN 37996. Offers MA.

Accreditation: ASHA. *Students:* 39 (36 women); includes 1 Asian American or Pacific Islander, 1 Hispanic American 2 international. In 2006, 20 master's awarded. *Degree requirements:* For master's, thesis or alternative. *Entrance requirements:* For master's, GRE General Test, minimum GPA of 2.7. Additional exam requirements/recommendations for international students: Required—TOEFL. *Application deadline:* For fall admission, 2/1 priority date for domestic students. Applications are processed on a rolling basis. Application fee: $35. Electronic applications accepted. *Expenses:* Tuition, state resident: full-time $5,574. Tuition, nonresident: full-time $16,840. Required fees: $792. *Financial support:* Application deadline: 2/1; *Unit head:* Dr. Stephen Handel, Interim Head, Department of Audiology and Speech Pathology, 865-974-5019, Fax: 865-974-1539, E-mail: shandel@utk.edu.

The University of Tennessee, Graduate School, College of Arts and Sciences, Department of Audiology and Speech Pathology, Program in Speech and Hearing Science, Knoxville, TN 37996. Offers audiology (PhD); hearing science (PhD); speech and language pathology (PhD); speech and language science (PhD). *Accreditation:* ASHA. *Students:* 13 (11 women) 7 international. In 2006, 1 degree awarded. *Degree requirements:* For doctorate, thesis/dissertation. *Entrance requirements:* For doctorate, GRE General Test, minimum GPA of 2.7. Additional exam requirements/recommendations for international students: Required—TOEFL. *Application deadline:* For fall admission, 2/1 priority date for domestic students. Applications are processed on a rolling basis. Application fee: $35. Electronic applications accepted. *Expenses:* Tuition, state resident: full-time $5,574. Tuition, nonresident: full-time $16,840. Required fees: $792. *Financial support:* Application deadline: 2/1; *Unit head:* Dr. Stephen Handel, Interim Head, Department of Audiology and Speech Pathology, 865-974-5019, Fax: 865-974-1539, E-mail: shandel@utk.edu.

The University of Tennessee, Graduate School, College of Arts and Sciences, Department of Audiology and Speech Pathology, Program in Speech Pathology, Knoxville, TN 37996. Offers MA. *Accreditation:* ASHA. *Students:* 53 (46 women) 3 international. In 2006, 18 degrees awarded. *Degree requirements:* For master's, thesis or alternative. *Entrance requirements:* For master's, GRE General Test, minimum GPA of 2.7. Additional exam requirements/recommendations for international students: Required—TOEFL. *Application deadline:* For fall admission, 2/1 priority date for domestic students. Applications are processed on a rolling basis. Application fee: $35. Electronic applications accepted. *Expenses:* Tuition, state resident: full-time $5,574. Tuition, nonresident: full-time $16,840. Required fees: $792. *Financial support:* Application deadline: 2/1; *Unit head:* Dr. Stephen Handel, Interim Head, Department of Audiology and Speech Pathology, 865-974-5019, Fax: 865-974-1539, E-mail: shandel@utk.edu.

The University of Tennessee, Graduate School, College of Education, Health and Human Sciences, Program in Education, Knoxville, TN 37996. Offers art education (MS); counseling education (PhD); cultural studies in education (PhD); curriculum (MS, Ed S); curriculum, educational research and evaluation (Ed D, PhD); early childhood education (PhD); early childhood special education (MS); education of deaf and hard of hearing (MS); educational administration and policy studies (Ed D, PhD); educational administration and supervision (Ed S); educational psychology (Ed D, PhD); elementary education (MS, Ed S); elementary teaching (MS); English education (MS, Ed S); exercise science (PhD); foreign language/ESL education (MS, Ed S); instructional technology (MS, Ed D, PhD, Ed S); literacy, language and ESL education (PhD); literacy, language education, and ESL education (Ed D); mathematics education (MS, Ed S); modified and comprehensive special education (MS); reading education (MS, Ed S); school counseling (Ed S); school psychology (PhD, Ed S); science education (MS, Ed S); secondary teaching (MS); social foundations (MS); social science education (MS, Ed S); socio-cultural foundations of sports and education (PhD); special education (Ed S); teacher education (Ed D, PhD). *Accreditation:* NCATE. Part-time and evening/weekend programs available. *Students:* 529 (401 women); includes 39 minority (23 African Americans, 2 American Indian/Alaska Native, 9 Asian Americans or Pacific Islanders, 5 Hispanic Americans) 34 international. 420 applicants, 50% accepted. In 2006, 258 master's, 28 doctorates awarded. *Degree requirements:* For master's and Ed S, thesis optional; for doctorate, variable foreign language requirement, thesis/dissertation. *Entrance requirements:* For master's, minimum GPA of 2.7; for doctorate and Ed S, GRE General Test, minimum GPA of 2.7. Additional exam requirements/recommendations for international students: Required—TOEFL. *Application deadline:* For fall admission, 2/1 priority date for domestic students. Applications are processed on a rolling basis. Application fee: $35. Electronic applications accepted. *Expenses:* Tuition, state resident: full-time $5,574. Tuition, nonresident: full-time $16,840. Required fees: $792. *Financial support:* In 2006–07, 4 fellowships, 9 teaching assistantships were awarded; career-related internships or fieldwork, Federal Work-Study, institutionally sponsored loans, and unspecified assistantships also available. Financial award application deadline: 2/1; financial award applicants required to submit FAFSA. *Unit head:* Dr. Lester Knight, Head, 865-974-0907, Fax: 865-974-8718, E-mail: lknight@utk.edu.

The University of Texas at Austin, Graduate School, College of Communication, Department of Communication Sciences and Disorders, Austin, TX 78712-1111. Offers MA, PhD. *Accreditation:* ASHA (one or more programs are accredited). *Entrance requirements:* For master's and doctorate, GRE General Test.

The University of Texas at Dallas, School of Behavioral and Brain Sciences, Program in Audiology, Richardson, TX 75083-0688. Offers Au D. *Accreditation:* ASHA. *Faculty:* 9 full-time (3 women), 1 part-time/adjunct (0 women). *Students:* 24 full-time (21 women), 7 part-time (all women); includes 4 minority (1 African American, 3 Hispanic Americans). Average age 25. 53 applicants, 23% accepted, 8 enrolled. In 2006, 8 degrees awarded. *Degree requirements:* For doctorate, thesis/dissertation. *Entrance requirements:* Additional exam requirements/recommendations for international students: Required—TOEFL (minimum score 550 paper-based; 213 computer-based). *Application deadline:* For fall admission, 7/15 for domestic students; for spring admission, 11/15 for domestic students. Applications are processed on a rolling basis. Application fee: $50 ($100 for international students). Electronic applications accepted. *Financial support:* Fellowships, research assistantships, teaching assistantships, Federal Work-Study available. Support available to part-time students. Financial award application deadline: 4/30; financial award applicants required to submit FAFSA. *Faculty research:* Cochlear implants, auditory electrophysiology, psychoacoustics. *Unit head:* Dr. Linda Thibodeau, Head, 972-883-2425, Fax: 972-883-2491, E-mail: thib@utdallas.edu. *Application contact:* Dr. Robert D. Stillman, Head, 972-883-3106, Fax: 972-883-3022, E-mail: stillman@utdallas.edu.

The University of Texas at Dallas, School of Behavioral and Brain Sciences, Program in Communication Disorders, Richardson, TX 75083-0688. Offers MS. *Accreditation:* ASHA. Part-time and evening/weekend programs available. *Faculty:* 12 full-time (9 women), 1 part-time/adjunct (0 women). *Students:* 164 full-time (161 women), 5 part-time (all women); includes 19 minority (4 African Americans, 3 Asian Americans or Pacific Islanders, 12 Hispanic Americans), 2 international. Average age 25. 254 applicants, 44% accepted, 72 enrolled. In 2006, 103 degrees awarded. *Degree requirements:* For master's, thesis optional. *Entrance requirements:* For master's, GRE General Test, minimum GPA of 3.0. Additional exam requirements/recommendations for international students: Required—TOEFL (minimum score 550 paper-based; 213 computer-based). *Application deadline:* For fall admission, 7/15 for domestic students; for spring admission, 11/15 for domestic students. Applications are processed on a rolling basis. Application fee: $50 ($100 for international students). Electronic applications accepted. *Financial support:* In 2006–07, 5 research assistantships with tuition reimbursements (averaging $11,137 per year), 2 teaching assistantships with tuition reimbursements (averaging $9,558 per year) were awarded; fellowships with tuition reimbursements, Federal Work-Study also available. Support available to part-time students. Financial award application deadline: 4/30; financial award applicants required to submit FAFSA. *Faculty research:* Brain mapping, evoked potentials, speech production, child language, aphasia. *Unit head:* Dr. Robert D. Stillman, Head, 972-883-3106, Fax: 972-883-3022, E-mail: stillman@utdallas.edu.

The University of Texas at El Paso, Graduate School, College of Health Sciences, School of Allied Health, Program in Speech Language Pathology, El Paso, TX 79968-0001. Offers MS. *Accreditation:* ASHA. *Degree requirements:* For master's, 250 clock hours of supervised practicum, thesis optional. *Entrance requirements:* For master's, GRE General Test, minimum GPA of 3.0 in undergraduate major. Additional exam requirements/recommendations for international students: Required—TOEFL. Electronic applications accepted. *Faculty research:* Cleft palate, bilingual language disorders, clinical supervision, hearing loss.

The University of Texas–Pan American, College of Health Sciences and Human Services, Department of Communication Sciences and Disorders, Edinburg, TX 78541-2999. Offers MS. *Accreditation:* ASHA. Part-time programs available. *Faculty:* 6 full-time (5 women), 1 (woman) part-time/adjunct. *Students:* 31 full-time (30 women), 11 part-time (all women); includes 41 minority (all Hispanic Americans) Average age 24. 57 applicants, 33% accepted, 19 enrolled. In 2006, 40 degrees awarded. *Degree requirements:* For master's, NESPA exam, thesis optional. *Entrance requirements:* For master's, GRE General Test, minimum GPA of 3.0 in major, 3 letters of recommendation, resumé. Additional exam requirements/recommendations for international students: Required—TOEFL (minimum score 550 paper-based). Application fee: $35. *Expenses:* Tuition, state resident: full-time $2,577; part-time $143 per credit hour. Tuition, nonresident: full-time $7,527; part-time $418 per credit hour. Required fees: $561. *Financial support:* In 2006–07, 2 research assistantships (averaging $3,000 per year), 3 teaching assistantships (averaging $2,740 per year) were awarded; career-related internships or fieldwork, Federal Work-Study, institutionally sponsored loans, and scholarships/grants also available. Financial award application deadline: 9/1; financial award applicants required to submit FAFSA. *Faculty research:* Bilingual/bicultural language development/disorders, elementary-age language disorders, voice disorders. Total annual research expenditures: $7,000. *Unit head:* Dr. Janice A. Maville, Professor and Interim Chair, 956-316-3491, Fax: 956-318-5238, E-mail: jmaville@utpa.edu.

University of the District of Columbia, College of Arts and Sciences, Department of Language and Communication Disorders, Program in Speech and Language Pathology, Washington, DC 20008-1175. Offers MS. *Accreditation:* ASHA. Part-time programs available. *Students:* 16 full-time (14 women), 8 part-time (all women); includes 12 minority (11 African Americans, 1 Hispanic American). Average age 30. 37 applicants, 81% accepted, 19 enrolled. In 2006, 15 degrees awarded. *Degree requirements:* For master's, thesis optional. *Entrance requirements:* For master's, GRE General Test, writing proficiency exam. *Application deadline:* For fall admission, 6/15 priority date for domestic students; for spring admission, 11/1 for domestic students. Applications are processed on a rolling basis. Application fee: $20. *Financial support:* Fellowships, research assistantships available. Financial award application deadline: 6/10. *Faculty research:* Child language, dialect variation, English as a second language. *Application contact:* LaVerne Hill Flannigan, Director of Admission, 202-274-6069.

University of the Pacific, School of Pharmacy and Health Sciences, Department of Speech-Language Pathology, Stockton, CA 95211-0197. Offers MS. *Accreditation:* ASHA. *Faculty:* 9 full-time (5 women), 8 part-time/adjunct (all women). *Students:* 43 full-time (39 women), 4 part-time (all women); includes 10 minority (1 American Indian/Alaska Native, 6 Asian Americans or Pacific Islanders, 3 Hispanic Americans). Average age 27. 86 applicants, 45% accepted, 21 enrolled. In 2006, 23 degrees awarded. *Entrance requirements:* For master's, GRE General Test. Additional exam requirements/recommendations for international students: Required—TOEFL (minimum score 475 paper-based; 150 computer-based). *Application deadline:* For fall admission, 2/1 for domestic students. Application fee: $75. *Expenses:* Tuition: Full-time $26,920. Required fees: $430. Tuition and fees vary according to course load. *Financial support:* Institutionally sponsored loans available. Support available to part-time students. Financial award application deadline: 2/1; financial award applicants required to submit FAFSA. *Unit head:* Dr. Robert Hanyak, Chairman, 209-946-3223, E-mail: rhanyak@pacific.edu.

The University of Toledo, College of Graduate Studies, College of Health Science and Human Service, Division of Human Services, Toledo, OH 43606-3390. Offers counselor education and school psychology (MA, PhD, Ed S), including counselor education, guidance/counselor education (PhD), school psychology (MA, Ed S); criminal justice (MA, Certificate), including criminal justice (MA), juvenile justice (Certificate), severe behavioral spectrum (Certificate); health education (PhD); kinesiology (MSX, PhD), including exercise science; public health and rehabilitative services (MA, MPH), including public health (MPH), speech language pathology (MA); recreation and leisure (MA); social work (MS); speech-language pathology (MA). *Students:* 398 full-time (319 women), 270 part-time (194 women); includes 78 minority (60 African Americans, 8 Asian Americans or Pacific Islanders, 10 Hispanic Americans), 23 international. 641 applicants, 51% accepted, 246 enrolled.Application fee: $45. *Unit head:* Dr. Jerome M. Sulivan, Dean, College of Health Science and Human Service, 419-530-4180.

The University of Toledo, College of Graduate Studies, College of Health Science and Human Service, Division of Human Services, Department of Public Health and Rehabilitative Services, Speech-Language Pathology Program, Toledo, OH 43606-3390. Offers MA. *Accreditation:* ASHA. *Students:* 36 full-time (all women), 2 part-time (both women). Average age 24. 49 applicants, 55% accepted, 23 enrolled. In 2006, 9 degrees awarded. *Application deadline:* For fall admission, 3/1 priority date for domestic students. Application fee: $45. *Financial support:* Research assistantships with full tuition reimbursements available. *Unit head:* Dr. Ruth Kucharewski, Chair, 419-530-2762, E-mail: rkuchar@utnet.utoledo.edu. *Application contact:* Bernie Spiegel, Information Contact, E-mail: bspiegel@utnet.utoledo.edu.

University of Toronto, School of Graduate Studies, Life Sciences Division, Department of Speech-Language Pathology, Toronto, ON M5S 1A1, Canada. Offers M Sc, MH Sc, PhD. Part-time programs available. *Degree requirements:* For master's, thesis (for some programs), clinical internship (MH Sc), oral thesis defense (M Sc); for doctorate, thesis/dissertation, oral thesis defense, comprehensive exam. *Entrance requirements:* For master's, minimum B+ average in last 2 years (MH Sc), B average in final year (M Sc); volunteer/work experience in a clinical setting (MH Sc); for doctorate, previous research experience or thesis, resumé, 3 writing samples, 3 letters of recommendation. Additional exam requirements/recommendations for international students: Recommended—TWE.

University of Tulsa, Graduate School, College of Arts and Sciences, Program in Speech-Language Pathology, Tulsa, OK 74104-3189. Offers MS. *Accreditation:* ASHA. Part-time programs available. *Faculty:* 8 full-time (all women). *Students:* 21 full-time (20 women), 1 (woman) part-time; includes 2 minority (1 American Indian/Alaska Native, 1 Asian American or Pacific Islander). Average age 25. 24 applicants, 71% accepted, 7 enrolled. In 2006, 7 degrees awarded. *Median time to degree:* Master's–2 years full-time. *Degree requirements:* For master's, thesis optional. *Entrance requirements:* For master's, GRE General Test. Additional exam requirements/recommendations for international students: Required—TOEFL. *Application deadline:* For fall admission, 2/1 priority date for domestic students. Applications are processed on a rolling basis. Application fee: $4. Electronic applications accepted. *Expenses:* Tuition: Full-time $13,338; part-time $741 per credit hour. *Financial support:* In 2006–07, 10 students received support, including 10 teaching assistantships with full and partial tuition reimbursements available (averaging $10,300 per year); fellowships, research assistantships with full tuition reimbursements available, career-related internships or fieldwork, Federal Work-Study, scholarships/grants, traineeships, tuition waivers (full and partial), and unspecified assistantships also available. Support available to part-time students. Financial award application deadline: 2/1; financial award applicants required to submit FAFSA. *Faculty research:* Speech-language pathology in handicapped preschool children, stuttering, aphasia, language development, neurogenic communication disorders. *Unit head:* Dr. Paula Cadogan, Chairperson, 918-631-2897, Fax: 918-631-3668, E-mail: paula-cadogan@utulsa.edu. *Application contact:* Mary Moody, Adviser, 918-631-2914, E-mail: grad@utulsa.edu.

University of Utah, The Graduate School, College of Health, Department of Communication Sciences and Disorders, Salt Lake City, UT 84112-1107. Offers audiology (Au D); speech-language pathology (MA, MS, PhD). *Accreditation:* ASHA (one or more programs are accredited). *Faculty:* 12 full-time (6 women), 5 part-time/adjunct (4 women). *Students:* 66 full-time (53 women), 12 part-time (7 women); includes 3 minority (2 Asian Americans or Pacific Islanders, 1 Hispanic American), 2 international. Average age 28. 103 applicants, 66% accepted, 42

Communication Disorders

University of Utah (continued)

enrolled. In 2006, 23 master's, 1 doctorate awarded. *Median time to degree:* Of those who began their doctoral program in fall 1998, 100% received their degree in 8 years or less. *Degree requirements:* For master's, thesis or alternative, written exam; for doctorate, thesis/dissertation, written and oral exams. *Entrance requirements:* For master's and doctorate, GRE General Test, minimum GPA of 3.0. Additional exam requirements/recommendations for international students: Required—TOEFL (minimum score 500 paper-based; 173 computer-based), TSE. *Application deadline:* For fall admission, 2/15 priority date for domestic and international students; for spring admission, 11/1 priority date for domestic and international students. Application fee: $45 ($65 for international students). Electronic applications accepted. *Expenses: Contact institution.* Tuition and fees vary according to class time and program. *Financial support:* Research assistantships with partial tuition reimbursements, teaching assistantships with partial tuition reimbursements, career-related internships or fieldwork and tuition waivers (partial) available. Financial award application deadline: 2/15; financial award applicants required to submit FAFSA. *Faculty research:* Motor speech disorders, fluency disorders, language disorders, pediatric audiology, speech and hearing science. Total annual research expenditures: $74,703. *Unit head:* Dr. Bruce L. Smith, Chairman, 801-585-6783, Fax: 801-581-7955, E-mail: bruce.smith@hsc.utah.edu. *Application contact:* Angelina Harder, Executive Secretary, 801-585-6725, Fax: 801-581-7955, E-mail: angelina.harder@hsc.utah.edu.

University of Virginia, Curry School of Education, Department of Human Services, Program in Communication Disorders, Charlottesville, VA 22903. Offers M Ed. *Accreditation:* ASHA. *Students:* 60 full-time (all women); includes 6 minority (2 African Americans, 3 Asian Americans or Pacific Islanders, 1 Hispanic American), 1 international. Average age 25. 96 applicants, 69% accepted, 23 enrolled. In 2006, 29 degrees awarded. *Degree requirements:* For master's, thesis (for some programs), comprehensive exam (for some programs). *Entrance requirements:* For master's, GRE General Test. Additional exam requirements/recommendations for international students: Required—TOEFL (minimum score 600 paper-based; 250 computer-based). *Application deadline:* Applications are processed on a rolling basis. Application fee: $60. *Financial support:* Fellowships with tuition reimbursements available. Financial award applicants required to submit FAFSA. *Application contact:* Vincent Reyes, Student Enrollment Coordinator, 434-924-6354, E-mail: vjr2y@virginia.edu.

University of Washington, Graduate School, College of Arts and Sciences, Department of Speech and Hearing Sciences, Seattle, WA 98195. Offers MS, PhD. *Accreditation:* ASHA (one or more programs are accredited). *Degree requirements:* For master's, thesis or alternative, comprehensive exam; for doctorate, thesis/dissertation. *Entrance requirements:* For master's and doctorate, GRE, minimum GPA of 3.0. Additional exam requirements/recommendations for international students: Required—TOEFL. Electronic applications accepted. *Faculty research:* Treatment of communication disorders across the life span, speech physiology, auditory perception, behavioral and physiologic audiology.

The University of Western Ontario, Faculty of Graduate Studies, Biosciences Division, School of Communication Sciences and Disorders, London, ON N6A 5B8, Canada. Offers audiology (M Cl Sc, M Sc); speech-language pathology (M Cl Sc, M Sc). *Faculty:* 14 full-time (6 women), 1 (woman) part-time/adjunct. *Students:* 117 full-time (112 women). 225 applicants, 18% accepted. In 2006, 45 degrees awarded. *Degree requirements:* For master's, thesis (for some programs), supervised clinical practicum. *Entrance requirements:* For master's, 14 hours volunteer experience in field of study, minimum B average during last 2 years, previous course work in developmental psychology and statistics, 4-year honors degree. Additional exam requirements/recommendations for international students: Required—TOEFL (minimum score 620 paper-based; 260 computer-based). *Application deadline:* For fall admission, 1/15 for domestic students. *Financial support:* In 2006–07, 21 teaching assistantships were awarded; research assistantships, Federal Work-Study also available. Financial award application deadline: 4/1. *Faculty research:* Child language, voice, neurogenics; auditory function, stuttering. *Unit head:* Dr. Ronald C. Watson, Acting Director, 519-661-2111 Ext. 88227, Fax: 519-850-2369, E-mail: ronwatso@uwo.ca. *Application contact:* Dr. R. E. Martin, Graduate Chair, 519-661-2111 Ext. 88921, Fax: 519-850-2369, E-mail: remartin@uwo.ca.

University of West Georgia, Graduate School, College of Education, Department of Special Education and Speech-Language Pathology, Program in Speech-Language Pathology, Carrollton, GA 30118. Offers M Ed. *Accreditation:* ASHA. Part-time and evening/weekend programs available. *Students:* 29 full-time (all women), 14 part-time (all women); includes 9 minority (8 African Americans, 1 Hispanic American). Average age 22. In 2006, 18 degrees awarded. *Degree requirements:* For master's, one foreign language, comprehensive exam. *Entrance requirements:* For master's, GRE General Test, minimum GPA of 3.0, interview, 3 letters of recommendation. *Application deadline:* For fall admission, 8/1 priority date for domestic students; for spring admission, 12/18 for domestic students. Application fee: $20. Electronic applications accepted. *Expenses:* Tuition, state resident: full-time $2,286; part-time $127 per credit. Tuition, nonresident: full-time $9,144; part-time $508 per credit. Required fees: $494; $27 per credit. $121 per semester. *Financial support:* In 2006–07, 2 research assistantships with full tuition reimbursements (averaging $6,000 per year) were awarded; career-related internships or fieldwork, scholarships/grants, and unspecified assistantships also available. Support available to part-time students. Financial award applicants required to submit FAFSA. *Faculty research:* Dialect variations, literature based intervention, comparing norm referred and criterion referred testing. *Application contact:* Dr. Charles W. Clark, Chair, 678-839-6508, E-mail: cclark@westga.edu.

University of Wisconsin–Eau Claire, College of Education and Human Sciences, Program in Communication Sciences and Disorders, Eau Claire, WI 54702-4004. Offers MS. *Accreditation:* ASHA. *Faculty:* 6 full-time (4 women). *Students:* 33 full-time (32 women); includes 1 minority (Hispanic American), 2 international. Average age 24. 93 applicants, 17% accepted, 16 enrolled. In 2006, 15 degrees awarded. *Degree requirements:* For master's, thesis optional. *Entrance requirements:* For master's, Wisconsin residency, minimum GPA of 3.3 in communication disorders, minimum GPA of 2.75 overall or minimum GPA of 2.9 during previous 2 years. *Application deadline:* For fall admission, 3/1 for domestic students. Applications are processed on a rolling basis. Application fee: $45. *Expenses:* Tuition, state resident: full-time $6,533; part-time $363 per credit. Tuition, nonresident: full-time $17,143; part-time $952 per credit. Tuition and fees vary according to program and reciprocity agreements. *Financial support:* In 2006–07, 31 students received support, including 5 teaching assistantships (averaging $3,890 per year); career-related internships or fieldwork and Federal Work-Study also available. Financial award application deadline: 3/1; financial award applicants required to submit FAFSA. *Unit head:* Dr. Kristine Retherford, Chair, 715-836-4905, Fax: 715-836-4846, E-mail: retherk@uwec.edu.

University of Wisconsin–Madison, Graduate School, College of Letters and Science, Department of Communicative Disorders, Madison, WI 53706-1380. Offers MS, PhD. *Accreditation:* ASHA (one or more programs are accredited). *Degree requirements:* For doctorate, thesis/dissertation. *Entrance requirements:* For master's and doctorate, GRE. Electronic applications accepted. *Faculty research:* Language disorders in children and adults, disorders of speech production, intelligibility, fluency, hearing impairment, deafness.

University of Wisconsin–Milwaukee, Graduate School, College of Health Sciences, Department of Communication Sciences and Disorders, Milwaukee, WI 53201-0413. Offers MS. *Accreditation:* ASHA. Part-time programs available. *Faculty:* 5 full-time (4 women). *Students:* 45 full-time (all women), 3 part-time (all women); includes 2 minority (both African Americans), 2 international. 106 applicants, 44% accepted, 14 enrolled. In 2006, 24 degrees awarded. *Degree requirements:* For master's, thesis or alternative. *Application deadline:* For fall admission, 1/1 priority date for domestic students; for spring admission, 9/1 for domestic students. Applications are processed on a rolling basis. Application fee: $45 ($75 for international students). *Expenses:* Tuition, state resident: part-time $510 per credit. Tuition, nonresident: part-time $1,408 per credit. Tuition and fees vary according to program. *Financial support:* In 2006–07, 1 fellowship, 1 teaching assistantship were awarded; research assistantships, career-related internships or fieldwork and unspecified assistantships also available. Support available to part-time students. Financial award application deadline: 4/15. *Unit head:* Carol Seery, Representative, 414-229-4263, Fax: 414-906-3910, E-mail: cseery@uwm.edu.

University of Wisconsin–River Falls, Outreach and Graduate Studies, College of Education and Professional Studies, Department of Communicative Disorders, River Falls, WI 54022-5001. Offers communicative disorders (MS); secondary education-communicative disorders (MSE). *Accreditation:* ASHA (one or more programs are accredited). Part-time programs available. *Degree requirements:* For master's, comprehensive exam. *Entrance requirements:* For master's, minimum GPA of 2.75, 3 letters of reference. *Faculty research:* SHRG, voice, language, audiology.

University of Wisconsin–Stevens Point, College of Professional Studies, School of Communicative Disorders, Stevens Point, WI 54481-3897. Offers MS, Au D. *Accreditation:* ASHA (one or more programs are accredited). *Faculty:* 11 full-time (8 women). *Students:* 50 full-time (all women), 4 part-time (all women); includes 3 minority (1 African American, 1 American Indian/Alaska Native, 1 Asian American or Pacific Islander), 1 international. In 2006, 29 degrees awarded. *Degree requirements:* For master's, clinical semester and capstone project, thesis optional; for doctorate, capstone project and full-time clinical externship. *Entrance requirements:* For master's, completion of specific course contents and practicum experiences at the undergraduate level. *Application deadline:* For fall admission, 1/10 for domestic students. Application fee: $45. *Expenses:* Tuition, state resident: full-time $5,910; part-time $328 per credit. Tuition, nonresident: full-time $16,520; part-time $918 per credit. Required fees: $756; $73 per credit. *Financial support:* Research assistantships, teaching assistantships, Federal Work-Study and unspecified assistantships available. Financial award application deadline: 5/1; financial award applicants required to submit FAFSA. *Unit head:* Dr. Gary Cumley, Head, 715-346-4699, Fax: 715-346-2157, E-mail: gcumley@uwsp.edu. *Application contact:* Leslie Plonsker, Information Contact, 715-346-2328, Fax: 715-346-2157, E-mail: lplonske@uwsp.edu.

University of Wisconsin–Whitewater, School of Graduate Studies, College of Education, Program in Communicative Disorders, Whitewater, WI 53190-1790. Offers MS. *Accreditation:* ASHA. Part-time and evening/weekend programs available. Postbaccalaureate distance learning degree programs offered (no on-campus study). *Students:* 32 full-time (all women), 2 part-time (both women); includes 3 minority (2 Asian Americans or Pacific Islanders, 1 Hispanic American). Average age 27. 74 applicants, 31% accepted, 10 enrolled. In 2006, 15 degrees awarded. *Degree requirements:* For master's, thesis or alternative, comprehensive exam. *Entrance requirements:* For master's, 2 letters of recommendation. Additional exam requirements/recommendations for international students: Required—TOEFL (minimum score 550 paper-based; 213 computer-based). *Application deadline:* For fall admission, 2/1 for domestic and international students. Applications are processed on a rolling basis. Application fee: $45. Electronic applications accepted. *Expenses:* Tuition, state resident: full-time $3,311. Tuition, nonresident: full-time $8,616. Required fees: $368 per credit. *Financial support:* Research assistantships, Federal Work-Study, unspecified assistantships, and out-of-state fee waivers available. Support available to part-time students. Financial award application deadline: 3/15; financial award applicants required to submit FAFSA. *Faculty research:* Occupational hearing conservation. *Unit head:* Dr. Scott Bradley, Coordinator, 262-472-5202, Fax: 262-472-5210, E-mail: bradleys@uww.edu. *Application contact:* Sally A. Lange, School of Graduate Studies, 262-472-1006, Fax: 262-472-5027, E-mail: gradschl@uww.edu.

University of Wyoming, Graduate School, College of Health Sciences, Division of Communication Disorders, Program in Neuroscience, Laramie, WY 82070. Offers audiology (PhD). *Accreditation:* ASHA. Part-time programs available. *Faculty:* 5 full-time (3 women). *Students:* 11 full-time (7 women); includes 1 minority (African American), 3 international. Average age 29. *Entrance requirements:* Additional exam requirements/recommendations for international students: Required—TOEFL. Application fee: $50. *Financial support:* In 2006–07, 1 student received support, including 1 research assistantship with partial tuition reimbursement available (averaging $10,384 per year); Federal Work-Study, institutionally sponsored loans, and scholarships/grants also available. Financial award application deadline: 2/15. *Faculty research:* Audiometric techniques with infants, applications of insert earphones, auditory evoked potentials and neurodevelopment. *Application contact:* Claoma T. Woodall, Office Associate, Senior, 307-766-6427, Fax: 307-766-5584, E-mail: woodall@uwyo.edu.

University of Wyoming, Graduate School, College of Health Sciences, Division of Communication Disorders, Program in Speech-Language Pathology, Laramie, WY 82070. Offers MS. *Accreditation:* ASHA. Part-time programs available. Postbaccalaureate distance learning degree programs offered (minimal on-campus study). *Faculty:* 8 full-time (6 women). *Students:* 26 full-time (all women), 21 part-time (18 women); includes 1 minority (Hispanic American), 2 international. Average age 29. 79 applicants, 32% accepted. In 2006, 6 degrees awarded. *Entrance requirements:* For master's, GRE General Test, minimum GPA of 3.0. Additional exam requirements/recommendations for international students: Required—TOEFL. *Application deadline:* For fall admission, 2/15 for domestic students; for spring admission, 11/1 for domestic students. Application fee: $50. *Financial support:* In 2006–07, 8 students received support, including 8 research assistantships with partial tuition reimbursements available (averaging $5,031 per year); Federal Work-Study, scholarships/grants, and tuition waivers (partial) also available. Financial award application deadline: 2/15. *Faculty research:* Intervention approaches for school age children with language disorders, multiple sclerosis, voice, effect of aging on voicing durations, cleft palate. Total annual research expenditures: $5,000. *Application contact:* Claoma T. Woodall, Office Associate, Senior, 307-766-6427, Fax: 307-766-5584, E-mail: woodall@uwyo.edu.

Utah State University, School of Graduate Studies, College of Education and Human Services, Department of Communicative Disorders and Deaf Education, Logan, UT 84322. Offers audiology (Au D, Ed S); communication disorders and deaf education (M Ed); communicative disorders and deaf education (MA, MS). *Accreditation:* ASHA (one or more programs are accredited). Evening/weekend programs available. Postbaccalaureate distance learning degree programs offered (minimal on-campus study). *Faculty:* 14 full-time (8 women), 6 part-time/adjunct (5 women). *Students:* 244 full-time (157 women), 44 part-time (38 women), 28 international. Average age 28. 79 applicants, 67% accepted, 34 enrolled. In 2006, 20 master's, 5 doctorates awarded. *Degree requirements:* For master's, thesis optional; for Ed S, thesis or alternative. *Entrance requirements:* For master's, GRE General Test, minimum GPA of 3.0, 3 recommendations; for doctorate, GRE General Test, interview, minimum GPA of 3.25. Additional exam requirements/recommendations for international students: Required—TOEFL. *Application deadline:* For fall admission, 1/1 for domestic and international students. Application fee: $50 ($60 for international students). *Expenses: Contact institution. Financial support:* In 2006–07, 32 students received support, including 6 fellowships with full tuition reimbursements available (averaging $3,000 per year), 1 research assistantship (averaging $3,000 per year), 3 teaching assistantships (averaging $3,000 per year); career-related internships or fieldwork, Federal Work-Study, institutionally sponsored loans, scholarships/grants, tuition waivers (full and partial), unspecified assistantships, and stipends also available. Support available to part-time students. Financial award application deadline: 2/1. *Faculty research:* Parent-infant intervention with hearing-impaired infants, voice disorders, language development and disorders, oto-accoustic emissions, deaf or hard-of-hearing infants. Total annual research expenditures: $3.6 million. *Unit head:* Dr. Beth R. Foley, Head, 435-797-3924, Fax: 435-797-0221, E-mail: beth.foley@usu.edu. *Application contact:* Prof. Dee R. Child, Assistant Head and Adviser, 435-797-2318, Fax: 435-797-0221, E-mail: deec@cc.usu.edu.

Valdosta State University, Graduate School, College of Education, Department of Special Education and Communication Disorders, Valdosta, GA 31698. Offers communication disorders (M Ed); special education (M Ed, Ed S). *Accreditation:* ASHA (one or more programs are accredited); NCATE. Part-time and evening/weekend programs available. *Degree requirements:* For master's, thesis (for some programs), comprehensive written and/or oral exams; for Ed S, thesis. *Entrance requirements:* For master's, GRE General Test or MAT, minimum GPA of 2.5; for Ed S, GRE General Test or MAT, minimum GPA of 3.0. Additional exam requirements/recommendations for international students: Required—TOEFL (minimum score 523 paper-based; 193 computer-based). Electronic applications accepted.

Vanderbilt University, School of Medicine, Department of Hearing and Speech Sciences, Nashville, TN 37240-1001. Offers audiology (Au D, PhD); education of the deaf (MED); hearing and speech sciences (MS); speech-language-pathology (MS). *Faculty:* 25 full-time (10 women), 7 part-time/adjunct (5 women). *Students:* 98 full-time (85 women); includes 7 minority (1 African American, 4 Asian Americans or Pacific Islanders, 2 Hispanic Americans). Average age 28. 224 applicants, 25% accepted, 35 enrolled. In 2006, 15 master's, 10 doctorates awarded. *Median time to degree:* Master's–2 years full-time; doctorate–4 years full-time. *Degree requirements:* For master's, thesis optional; for doctorate, thesis/dissertation, final and qualifying exams. *Entrance requirements:* For master's and doctorate, GRE General Test. Additional exam requirements/recommendations for international students: Required—TOEFL. *Application deadline:* For fall admission, 1/15 for domestic and international students. Electronic applications accepted. *Expenses:* Tuition: Full-time $24,462. Required fees: $2,515. One-time fee: $30 full-time. Full-time tuition and fees vary according to course load, degree level and program. *Financial support:* In 2006–07, fellowships with full tuition reimbursements (averaging $12,000 per year), research assistantships with full tuition reimbursements (averaging $12,000 per year) were awarded; career-related internships or fieldwork, institutionally sponsored loans, and tuition waivers (full and partial) also available. Financial award application deadline: 1/15. *Faculty research:* Audiology, speech-language pathology, child language. *Unit head:* Dr. Fred H. Bess, Chair, 615-936-5000, Fax: 615-936-5014, E-mail: fred.h.bess@vanderbilt.edu. *Application contact:* Edward G. Conture, Director of Graduate Studies, 615-936-5103, Fax: 615-936-5013, E-mail: edward.g.conture@vanderbilt.edu.

Washington State University Spokane, Graduate Programs, Program in Speech and Hearing Sciences, Spokane, WA 99210-1495. Offers MA. *Faculty:* 10. *Students:* 48 full-time (47 women), 6 part-time (all women); includes 9 minority (2 American Indian/Alaska Native, 2 Asian Americans or Pacific Islanders, 5 Hispanic Americans, 7 international. Average age 27. 91 applicants, 26% accepted, 16 enrolled. *Degree requirements:* For master's, thesis (for some programs), comprehensive exam, registration. *Entrance requirements:* For master's, GRE, minimum GPA of 3.0, 3 letters of recommendation. Additional exam requirements/recommendations for international students: Required—TOEFL (minimum score 550 paper-based; 213 computer-based). *Application deadline:* For fall admission, 2/1 for domestic students, 3/1 for international students; for spring admission, 9/1 for domestic students, 7/1 for international students. Application fee: $50. *Expenses:* Tuition, state resident: full-time $7,066. Tuition, nonresident: full-time $17,204. Tuition and fees vary according to program. *Financial support:* In 2006–07, 36 students received support, including 8 fellowships (averaging $4,351 per year), 5 teaching assistantships with full and partial tuition reimbursements available (averaging $13,056 per year); research assistantships with full and partial tuition reimbursements available, Federal Work-Study, scholarships/grants, health care benefits, tuition waivers (partial), and unspecified assistantships also available. *Faculty research:* Central auditory processing disorders, articulation, cleft palate. *Unit head:* Dr. Chuck Madison, Director, 509-358-7602, E-mail: madisonc@wsu.edu. *Application contact:* Graduate School Admissions, 800-GRADWSU, Fax: 509-335-1949, E-mail: gradsch@wsu.edu.

Washington University in St. Louis, School of Medicine, Program in Audiology and Communication Sciences, St Louis, MO 63110. Offers audiology (Au D); deaf education (MS); speech and hearing sciences (PhD). *Accreditation:* ASHA (one or more programs are accredited). *Faculty:* 22 full-time (12 women), 18 part-time/adjunct (12 women). *Students:* 64 full-time (all women), 7 part-time (6 women); includes 5 minority (2 African Americans, 2 Asian Americans or Pacific Islanders, 1 Hispanic American), 1 international. Average age 24. 111 applicants, 23% accepted, 26 enrolled. In 2006, 12 master's, 8 doctorates awarded. Terminal master's awarded for partial completion of doctoral program. *Median time to degree:* Master's–2 years full-time; doctorate–4 years full-time. Of those who began their doctoral program in fall 1998, 100% received their degree in 8 years or less. *Degree requirements:* For master's, thesis, independent study project, oral exam, comprehensive exam, registration; for doctorate, thesis/dissertation, capstone project, oral exam, comprehensive exam, registration. *Entrance requirements:* For master's, GRE General Test, minimum B average in undergraduate course work; for doctorate, GRE General Test, minimum B average. Additional exam requirements/recommendations for international students: Required—TOEFL (minimum score 600 paper-based; 250 computer-based). *Application deadline:* For fall admission, 2/15 for domestic and international students. Application fee: $50 ($75 for international students). *Expenses:* Contact institution. *Financial support:* In 2006–07, 64 students received support, including 64 fellowships (averaging $15,000 per year); career-related internships or fieldwork, institutionally sponsored loans, scholarships/grants, health care benefits, tuition waivers (partial), and unspecified assistantships also available. Support available to part-time students. Financial award application deadline: 2/15; financial award applicants required to submit FAFSA. *Faculty research:* Sensory aids, noise, speech perception, biological deafness, audiology. *Unit head:* Dr. William W. Clark, Program Director, 314-747-0104, Fax: 314-747-0105, E-mail: clarkw@wustl.edu. *Application contact:* Elizabeth A. Elliott, Graduate Program Coordinator, 314-747-0104, Fax: 314-747-0105, E-mail: elliottb@wustl.edu.

Wayne State University, College of Liberal Arts and Sciences, Department of Communications Disorders and Sciences, Detroit, MI 48202. Offers audiology (MA, MS, Au D, PhD); communication disorders and science (MA, PhD); speech-language pathology (MA, PhD). *Accreditation:* ASHA (one or more programs are accredited). *Faculty:* 21 full-time (13 women). *Students:* 89 full-time (84 women), 12 part-time (8 women); includes 7 minority (5 African Americans, 2 Asian Americans or Pacific Islanders), 21 international. Average age 28. 127 applicants, 36% accepted, 38 enrolled. In 2006, 30 master's, 7 doctorates awarded. *Degree requirements:* For doctorate, thesis/dissertation. *Entrance requirements:* For master's and doctorate, GRE. Additional exam requirements/recommendations for international students: Required—TOEFL (minimum score 550 paper-based; 213 computer-based); Recommended—TWE (minimum score 6). *Application deadline:* For fall admission, 7/1 for domestic students, 6/1 for international students; for winter admission, 10/1 for international students; for spring admission, 2/1 for international students. Applications are processed on a rolling basis. Application fee: $30 ($50 for international students). Electronic applications accepted. *Financial support:* In 2006–07, 4 students received support, including 1 research assistantship with tuition reimbursement available (averaging $12,500 per year); fellowships with tuition reimbursements available, teaching assistantships, career-related internships or fieldwork also available. Support available to part-time students. Financial award application deadline: 2/1. *Faculty research:* Language disorders in children and adults, speech perception and production, neuroimaging of speech and language, literacy in high risk populations hearing assessment and hearing loss prevention. Total annual research expenditures: $197,875. *Unit head:* Alex Johnson, Chair, 313-577-3339, E-mail: aa3925@wayne.edu. *Application contact:* Kristine Sbaschnig, Graduate Director, 313-577-6293, E-mail: ad4458@wayne.edu.

West Chester University of Pennsylvania, Graduate Studies, School of Health Sciences, Department of Communicative Disorders, West Chester, PA 19383. Offers MA. *Accreditation:* ASHA. Part-time and evening/weekend programs available. Postbaccalaureate distance learning degree programs offered (minimal on-campus study). *Students:* 51 full-time (all women), 46 part-time (45 women); includes 1 Hispanic American, 1 international. Average age 28. 154 applicants, 44% accepted, 32 enrolled. In 2006, 25 degrees awarded. *Degree requirements:* For master's, thesis optional. *Entrance requirements:* For master's, MAT or GRE. *Application deadline:* For fall admission, 4/15 priority date for domestic students; for spring admission, 10/15 for domestic students. Applications are processed on a rolling basis. Application fee: $35. *Financial support:* In 2006–07, 10 research assistantships with full tuition reimbursements (averaging $5,000 per year) were awarded; unspecified assistantships also available. Support available to part-time students. Financial award application deadline: 2/15; financial award applicants required to submit FAFSA. *Faculty research:* Identification/interaction with students with communicative disorders. *Unit head:* Dr. Michael Weiss, Chair, 610-436-3447, E-mail: mweiss@wcupa.edu.

Western Carolina University, Graduate School, College of Education and Allied Professions, Department of Human Services, Program in Communication Disorders, Cullowhee, NC 28723. Offers MS. *Accreditation:* ASHA. Part-time and evening/weekend programs available. *Degree requirements:* For master's, thesis optional. *Entrance requirements:* For master's, GRE General Test. Additional exam requirements/recommendations for international students: Required—TOEFL (minimum score 550 paper-based; 213 computer-based).

Western Illinois University, School of Graduate Studies, College of Fine Arts and Communication, Department of Communication Sciences and Disorders, Macomb, IL 61455-1390. Offers MS. *Accreditation:* ASHA. Part-time programs available. *Students:* 51 full-time (all women); includes 2 minority (1 African American, 1 Hispanic American), 3 international. Average age 24. 102 applicants, 31% accepted. In 2006, 18 degrees awarded. *Degree requirements:* For master's, thesis or alternative, comprehensive exam. *Entrance requirements:* For master's, minimum GPA of 3.0. Additional exam requirements/recommendations for international students: Required—TOEFL (minimum score 550 paper-based; 213 computer-based; 80 iBT). *Application deadline:* Applications are processed on a rolling basis. Application fee: $30. Electronic applications accepted. *Expenses:* Tuition, state resident: part-time $200 per credit hour. Tuition, nonresident: part-time $400 per credit hour. *Financial support:* In 2006–07, 20 students received support, including 20 research assistantships with full tuition reimbursements available (averaging $6,568 per year). Financial award applicants required to submit FAFSA. *Unit head:* Dr. Maureen Marx, Chairperson, 309-298-1955. *Application contact:* Dr. Barbara Baily, Director of Graduate Studies/Associate Provost, 309-298-1806, Fax: 309-298-2345, E-mail: grad-office@wiu.edu.

Western Kentucky University, Graduate Studies, College of Health and Human Services, Department of Communication Disorders, Bowling Green, KY 42101. Offers MS. *Accreditation:* ASHA. Part-time and evening/weekend programs available. Postbaccalaureate distance learning degree programs offered (no on-campus study). *Faculty:* 6 full-time (3 women), 1 part-time/adjunct (0 women). *Students:* 59 full-time (58 women), 82 part-time (80 women); includes 41 minority (21 African Americans, 4 Asian Americans or Pacific Islanders, 16 Hispanic Americans). Average age 31. 75 applicants, 15% accepted, 6 enrolled. In 2006, 66 degrees awarded. *Degree requirements:* For master's, written exam. *Entrance requirements:* For master's, GRE General Test, 3 letters of recommendation. Additional exam requirements/recommendations for international students: Required—TOEFL (minimum score 555 paper-based; 213 computer-based; 79 iBT). *Application deadline:* For fall admission, 2/15 for domestic students, 4/1 for international students; for spring admission, 11/1 for domestic students, 9/1 for international students. Applications are processed on a rolling basis. Application fee: $35. *Expenses:* Tuition, state resident: full-time $6,520; part-time $226 per hour. Tuition, nonresident: full-time $7,140; part-time $357 per hour. International tuition: $15,820 full-time. *Financial support:* In 2006–07, 1 student received support, including 1 research assistantship with partial tuition reimbursement available (averaging $9,500 per year); career-related internships or fieldwork, Federal Work-Study, institutionally sponsored loans, tuition waivers (partial), and unspecified assistantships also available. Support available to part-time students. Financial award application deadline: 4/1; financial award applicants required to submit FAFSA. *Unit head:* Dr. Joseph E Etienne, Department Head, 270-745-4303, E-mail: joseph.etienne@wku.edu.

Western Michigan University, Graduate College, College of Health and Human Services, Department of Speech Pathology and Audiology, Kalamazoo, MI 49008-5202. Offers audiology (MA); speech pathology (MA). *Accreditation:* ASHA. *Degree requirements:* For master's, clinical practicum, thesis optional. *Entrance requirements:* For master's, GRE General Test.

Western Washington University, Graduate School, College of Humanities and Social Sciences, Department of Communication Sciences and Disorders, Bellingham, WA 98225-5996. Offers MA. *Accreditation:* ASHA. Part-time programs available. *Faculty:* 6. *Students:* 42 full-time (39 women), 7 part-time (all women); includes 1 minority (Asian American or Pacific Islander), 3 international. 80 applicants, 55% accepted, 24 enrolled. In 2006, 27 degrees awarded. *Degree requirements:* For master's, thesis optional. *Entrance requirements:* For master's, GRE General Test, minimum GPA of 3.0 in last 60 semester hours or last 90 quarter hours. Additional exam requirements/recommendations for international students: Required—TOEFL (minimum score 567 paper-based; 227 computer-based). *Application deadline:* For fall admission, 2/1 for domestic students. Application fee: $50. *Expenses:* Tuition, state resident: full-time $6,609; part-time $199 per credit. Tuition, nonresident: full-time $16,845; part-time $540 per credit. *Financial support:* In 2006–07, 8 teaching assistantships with partial tuition reimbursements (averaging $9,339 per year) were awarded; career-related internships or fieldwork, Federal Work-Study, institutionally sponsored loans, scholarships/grants, tuition waivers (partial), and unspecified assistantships also available. Support available to part-time students. Financial award application deadline: 2/15; financial award applicants required to submit FAFSA. *Faculty research:* Autism, stroke and stroke perception, aural rehabilitation and cochlear implants, paradoxical vocal fold motion, auditory processing and Alzheimer's disease. *Unit head:* Dr. Barbara Mathers-Schmidt, Chair, 360-650-3885, E-mail: barbara.mathers-schmidt@wwu.edu. *Application contact:* Dr. Lina Zeine, Graduate Adviser, 360-650-3178.

West Texas A&M University, College of Fine Arts and Humanities, Department of Art, Communication, and Theater, Program in Communication Disorders, Canyon, TX 79016-0001. Offers MS. *Accreditation:* ASHA. Part-time programs available. *Degree requirements:* For master's, thesis optional. *Entrance requirements:* For master's, GRE General Test, minimum B average in all clinical courses, liability insurance, first aid card, immunizations. Additional exam requirements/recommendations for international students: Required—TOEFL (minimum score 550 paper-based).

West Virginia University, College of Human Resources and Education, Department of Speech Pathology and Audiology, Morgantown, WV 26506. Offers audiology (Au D); speech-language pathology (MS). *Accreditation:* ASHA. *Faculty:* 12 full-time (8 women), 1 (woman) part-time/adjunct. *Students:* 65 full-time (64 women), 2 part-time (1 woman); includes 2 minority (1 African American, 1 Hispanic American), 1 international. Average age 25. 120 applicants, 44% accepted. In 2006, 31 degrees awarded. *Degree requirements:* For master's, PRAXIS, thesis optional; for doctorate, thesis/dissertation or alternative, PRAXIS. *Entrance requirements:* For master's, GRE General Test, minimum GPA of 3.0 Letter of recommendation; for doctorate, GRE General Test, Letters of recommendation. Additional exam requirements/recommendations for international students: Required—TOEFL. *Application deadline:* For fall admission, 2/15 for domestic students. Application fee: $45. Electronic applications accepted. *Expenses:* Tuition, state resident: full-time $4,926; part-time $276 per credit hour. Tuition, nonresident: full-time $14,278; part-time $796 per credit hour. Tuition and fees vary according to program. *Financial support:* In 2006–07, 60 students received support, including 3 research assistantships with full tuition reimbursements available (averaging $8,264 per year), 4 teaching assistantships with full tuition reimbursements available (averaging $8,264 per year); career-related internships or fieldwork, Federal Work-Study, institutionally sponsored loans, and tuition waivers (full and partial) also available. Financial award application deadline: 3/1; financial award applicants required to submit FAFSA. *Faculty research:* Speech perception, language disorders in children, auditory skills, fluency disorders, phonological disorders in children. Total annual research expenditures: $41,141. *Unit head:* Dr. Lynn R. Cartwright, Chair, 304-293-2377 Ext. 1840, Fax: 304-293-7565, E-mail: lynn.cartwright@mail.wvu.edu. *Application contact:* Kelly C. Johnson, Administrative Secretary, 304-293-6817, Fax: 304-293-7565, E-mail: kelly.johnson@mail.wvu.edu.

Wichita State University, Graduate School, College of Education, Department of Communicative Disorders and Sciences, Wichita, KS 67260. Offers communications sciences (MA, PhD). *Accreditation:* ASHA (one or more programs are accredited). *Degree requirements:* For master's, comprehensive exam; for doctorate, one foreign language, thesis/dissertation. *Entrance requirements:* For master's, GRE General Test, minimum GPA of 2.75; for doctorate, GRE General Test, appropriate master's degree. Additional exam requirements/recommendations for international students: Required—TOEFL. *Faculty research:* Language, hearing disabilities.

Communication Disorders

William Paterson University of New Jersey, College of Science and Health, Department of Communication Disorders, Wayne, NJ 07470-8420. Offers speech pathology (MS). *Accreditation:* ASHA. Part-time and evening/weekend programs available. *Students:* 39 full-time (38 women), 29 part-time (28 women); includes 5 minority (1 African American, 1 Asian American or Pacific Islander, 3 Hispanic Americans). *Degree requirements:* For master's, 250 hours of clinical experience, thesis optional. *Entrance requirements:* For master's, GRE General Test, MAT, minimum GPA of 2.75. *Application deadline:* For fall admission, 3/1 for domestic students. Applications are processed on a rolling basis. Application fee: $50. Electronic applications accepted. *Financial support:* Research assistantships with tuition reimbursements, career-related internships or fieldwork and unspecified assistantships available. Support available to part-time students. Financial award application deadline: 4/1; financial award applicants required to submit FAFSA. *Faculty research:* Language development, methodological studies, language disorders, phonological disorders, speech and hearing science. *Unit head:* Dr. Jennifer Ryan Hsu, Graduate Coordinator, 973-720-2208. *Application contact:* Danielle Liautaud, Director, 973-720-3579, Fax: 973-720-2035, E-mail: liautaudd@wpunj.edu.

Worcester State College, Graduate Studies, Program in Speech-Language Pathology, Worcester, MA 01602-2597. Offers MS. *Accreditation:* ASHA. Part-time and evening/weekend programs available. *Students:* 46 full-time (44 women), 39 part-time (all women); includes 1 minority (Asian American or Pacific Islander), 1 international. Average age 28. 133 applicants, 30% accepted, 28 enrolled. In 2006, 34 degrees awarded. *Degree requirements:* For master's, thesis, national licensing exam, comprehensive exam. *Entrance requirements:* For master's, GRE General Test or MAT, 15 credits of course work in human communication. Additional exam requirements/recommendations for international students: Required—TOEFL (minimum score 550 paper-based; 213 computer-based). *Application deadline:* For fall admission, 3/1 for domestic and international students. Application fee: $30. *Expenses:* Contact institution. *Financial support:* In 2006–07, 4 research assistantships (averaging $4,400 per year) were awarded; career-related internships or fieldwork, Federal Work-Study, institutionally sponsored loans, scholarships/grants, and unspecified assistantships also available. Support available to part-time students. Financial award application deadline: 3/1; financial award applicants required to submit FAFSA. *Faculty research:* Hearing threshold norms, language learning disabilities. *Unit head:* Dr. Maryann Power, Coordinator, 508-929-8629, Fax: 508-929-8475, E-mail: mpower@worcester.edu. *Application contact:* Nicole Brown, Assistant Dean of Graduate and Continuing Education, 508-929-8787, Fax: 508-929-8100, E-mail: nbrown@worcester.edu.

Dental Hygiene

Boston University, Goldman School of Dental Medicine, Graduate Programs in Dentistry, Boston, MA 02215. Offers advanced general dentistry (CAGS); dental public health (MS, MSD, D Sc D, CAGS); dentistry (DMD); endodontics (MSD, D Sc D, CAGS); implantology (CAGS); operative dentistry (MSD, D Sc D, CAGS); oral and maxillofacial surgery (MSD, D Sc D, CAGS); oral biology (MSD, D Sc, D Sc D, PhD); orthodontics (MSD, D Sc D, CAGS); pediatric dentistry (MSD, D Sc D, CAGS); periodontology (MSD, D Sc D, CAGS); prosthodontics (MSD, D Sc D, CAGS). *Students:* 152 full-time (62 women); includes 13 minority (1 African American, 11 Asian Americans or Pacific Islanders, 1 Hispanic American), 75 international. Average age 29. In 2006, 224 first professional degrees, 22 master's, 10 doctorates, 63 other advanced degrees awarded. *Degree requirements:* For master's and doctorate, thesis/dissertation; for CAGS, thesis (for some programs). *Entrance requirements:* For DMD, DAT, minimum GPA of 3.0; for CAGS, dental degree. *Application deadline:* For fall admission, 5/1 for domestic students. Applications are processed on a rolling basis. Application fee: $60. *Expenses:* Contact institution. *Financial support:* Career-related internships or fieldwork and institutionally sponsored loans available. Financial award application deadline: 4/15; financial award applicants required to submit CSS PROFILE or FAFSA. *Faculty research:* Defensive mechanisms, bone-cell regulation, protein biochemistry, molecular biology, biomaterials. *Application contact:* 617-638-4787, Fax: 617-638-4798.

See Close-Up on page 2179.

Dalhousie University, Faculty of Dentistry, Program in Dental Hygiene, Halifax, NS B3H 4R2, Canada. Offers Diploma. *Entrance requirements:* For degree, course work in biology, psychology, sociology, writing. Additional exam requirements/recommendations for international students: Required—TWE (minimum score 5), Michigan English Language Assessment Battery, TOEFL (580 paper-based; 237 computer-based) or IELTS (7 paper-based).

Idaho State University, Office of Graduate Studies, Kasiska College of Health Professions, Department of Dental Sciences, Pocatello, ID 83209. Offers advanced general dentistry (Post-Doctoral Certificate); dental hygiene (MS). Postbaccalaureate distance learning degree programs offered (minimal on-campus study). *Faculty:* 6 full-time (all women). *Students:* 18 full-time (5 women), 21 part-time (all women); includes 3 minority (1 Asian American or Pacific Islander, 2 Hispanic Americans), 1 international. Average age 27. In 2006, 4 degrees awarded. *Degree requirements:* For master's, thesis, one year sequences, practicum, comprehensive exam, registration; for Post-Doctoral Certificate, 1 year residency, thesis optional. *Entrance requirements:* For master's, GRE and/or MAT, minimum GPA of 3.0 in upper division undergraduate courses, current dental hygiene license, 2 letters of recommendation; for Post-Doctoral Certificate, DAT. Additional exam requirements/recommendations for international students: Required—TOEFL (minimum score 600 paper-based; 213 computer-based). *Application deadline:* For fall admission, 7/1 for domestic students, 6/1 for international students; for spring admission, 12/1 for domestic students, 11/1 for international students. Applications are processed on a rolling basis. Application fee: $55. *Expenses:* Contact institution. *Financial support:* In 2006–07, 1 teaching assistantship with full and partial tuition reimbursement (averaging $8,694 per year) was awarded. Financial award application deadline: 1/1. *Unit head:* Dr. Brian Crawford, Chair, 208-282-5275, Fax: 208-282-5834, E-mail: crawbri3@isu.edu. *Application contact:* Ellen Combs, Graduate School Technical Records Specialist, 208-282-2150, Fax: 208-282-4847.

Medical College of Georgia, School of Graduate Studies, Department of Dental Hygiene, Augusta, GA 30912-1500. Offers MS. Part-time programs available. *Faculty:* 2 full-time (both women). *Degree requirements:* For master's, thesis. *Entrance requirements:* For master's, GRE General Test. Additional exam requirements/recommendations for international students: Required—TOEFL (minimum score 550 paper-based; 213 computer-based). *Application deadline:* For fall admission, 7/1 for domestic students; for spring admission, 4/15 for domestic students. Applications are processed on a rolling basis. Application fee: $30. *Expenses:* Tuition, state resident: full-time $2,293; part-time $192 per credit hour. Tuition, nonresident: full-time $9,169; part-time $765 per credit hour. Required fees: $293 per semester. *Financial support:* Available to part-time students. Application deadline: 5/31; *Unit head:* Marie A. Collins, Chair/Assistant Professor, 706-721-2938, Fax: 706-721-8857, E-mail: mcollins@mail.mcg.edu.

Old Dominion University, College of Health Sciences, Program in Dental Hygiene, Norfolk, VA 23529. Offers MS. *Accreditation:* ADA. Part-time programs available. *Faculty:* 8 full-time (all women). *Students:* 3 full-time (all women), 12 part-time (all women); includes 2 minority (1 Asian American or Pacific Islander, 1 Hispanic American). Average age 34. 6 applicants, 67% accepted, 3 enrolled. In 2006, 4 degrees awarded. *Median time to degree:* Master's–1.5 years full-time, 4 years part-time. *Degree requirements:* For master's, pass writing proficiency exam, thesis optional. *Entrance requirements:* For master's, Dental Hygiene National Board Exam (for U.S. educated dental hygienists) and for Canadian educated dental hygienist, BS or certificate in dental hygiene or related area, minimum GPA of 2.8 (3.0 in major), letters of recommendation, self-evaluation essay on career goals. Additional exam requirements/recommendations for international students: Required—TOEFL (minimum score 550 paper-based; 213 computer-based). *Application deadline:* For fall admission, 7/1 for domestic students, 4/15 for international students; for spring admission, 12/1 for domestic students, 10/1 for international students. Applications are processed on a rolling basis. Application fee: $40. Electronic applications accepted. *Expenses:* Tuition, area resident: Part-time $285 per credit hour. Tuition, nonresident: part-time $715 per credit hour. Required fees: $94 per semester. *Financial support:* In 2006–07, 4 students received support, including 3 teaching assistantships with tuition reimbursements available (averaging $6,000 per year); fellowships, research assistantships, career-related internships or fieldwork, scholarships/grants, tuition waivers (partial), and unspecified assistantships also available. Support available to part-time students. Financial award application deadline: 2/15; financial award applicants required to submit CSS PROFILE or FAFSA. *Faculty research:* Clinical dental hygiene practice, dental hygiene client health behaviors, dental hygiene education interventions, oral product testing. Total annual research expenditures: $14,586. *Unit head:* Prof. Michele L. Darby, Graduate Program Director, 757-683-5232, Fax: 757-683-5329, E-mail: mdarby@odu.edu.

Texas A&M Health Science Center, Baylor College of Dentistry, Graduate Division, Department of Dental Hygiene, College Station, TX 77840. Offers MS. Part-time programs available. *Degree requirements:* For master's, thesis (for some programs). *Entrance requirements:* For master's, GRE General Test, National Dental Hygiene Board Exam, minimum GPA of 3.0 in dental hygiene course work, 2.7 overall. *Faculty research:* Assessment of outcomes, dental materials, educational research, HIV patients, underserved patient populations, handicapped patients.

Université de Montréal, Faculty of Graduate Studies, Faculty of Dental Medicine and Faculty of Graduate Studies, Graduate Programs in Dentistry, Montréal, QC H3C 3J7, Canada. Offers multidisciplinary residency (Certificate); oral and dental sciences (M Sc); orthodontics (M Sc); pediatric dentistry (M Sc); prosthodontics rehabilitation (M Sc); stomatology residency (Certificate). *Application deadline:* For fall admission, 10/1 for domestic students. Application fee: $30. Electronic applications accepted. *Unit head:* Arlette Kolta, Associate Dean for Research, 514-343-7112, Fax: 514-343-2233.

University of Alberta, Faculty of Medicine and Dentistry, Department of Dentistry, Program in Dental Hygiene, Edmonton, AB T6G 2E1, Canada. Offers Diploma. *Faculty:* 7 full-time (all women), 26 part-time/adjunct. *Students:* 84 full-time (83 women). 154 applicants, 32% accepted, 42 enrolled. *Application deadline:* For fall admission, 11/1 for domestic students. Application fee: $75. Electronic applications accepted. *Unit head:* Dr. Sharon Compton, Director, 780-492-4479, Fax: 780-492-8552. *Application contact:* Melanie Grams, Administrative Assistant, 780-492-1319, Fax: 780-492-7536, E-mail: melanie.grams@ualberta.ca.

University of Maryland, Baltimore, Graduate School, Graduate Programs in Dentistry, Department of Dental Hygiene, Baltimore, MD 21201. Offers MS. *Degree requirements:* For master's, thesis or alternative. *Entrance requirements:* For master's, GRE General Test, minimum GPA of 3.0. Additional exam requirements/recommendations for international students: Required—TOEFL, TOEFL or IELTS; Recommended—IELTS. Electronic applications accepted. *Faculty research:* Dental hygiene education, health care management, health system theory and policy development, hospital dental hygiene, clinical practice.

University of Missouri–Kansas City, School of Dentistry, Kansas City, MO 64110-2499. Offers advanced education in dentistry (Graduate Dental Certificate); dental hygiene education (MS); dental specialties (Graduate Dental Certificate); dentistry (DDS); diagnostic sciences (Graduate Dental Certificate); oral and maxillofacial surgery (Graduate Dental Certificate); oral biology (MS, PhD); orthodontics and dentofacial orthopedics (Graduate Dental Certificate); pediatric dentistry (Graduate Dental Certificate); periodontics (Graduate Dental Certificate); prosthodontics (Graduate Dental Certificate). *Accreditation:* ADA (one or more programs are accredited). *Faculty:* 102 full-time (36 women), 77 part-time/adjunct (22 women). *Students:* 424 full-time (155 women), 34 part-time (27 women); includes 60 minority (10 African Americans, 2 American Indian/Alaska Native, 38 Asian Americans or Pacific Islanders, 10 Hispanic Americans), 12 international. Average age 27. 687 applicants, 17% accepted, 110 enrolled. In 2006, 92 DDSs, 25 other advanced degrees awarded. *Degree requirements:* For master's and doctorate, thesis/dissertation. *Entrance requirements:* For DDS, DAT; for master's, DAT, letters of evaluation, personal interview; for Graduate Dental Certificate, DDS. Additional exam requirements/recommendations for international students: Required—TOEFL. Application fee: $35 ($50 for international students). *Expenses:* Contact institution. *Financial support:* In 2006–07, 8 fellowships (averaging $42,540 per year), 28 research assistantships (averaging $21,670 per year) were awarded; career-related internships or fieldwork, Federal Work-Study, institutionally sponsored loans, and tuition waivers (full and partial) also available. Support available to part-time students. Financial award applicants required to submit FAFSA. *Faculty research:* Biomaterials, dental use of lasers, effectiveness of periodontal treatments, temporomandibular joint dysfunction. Total annual research expenditures: $3 million. *Unit head:* Dr. Michael Reed, Dean, 816-235-2010, E-mail: reedm@umkc.edu. *Application contact:* 816-235-2080.

University of New Mexico, School of Medicine, Program in Dental Hygiene, Albuquerque, NM 87131-2039. Offers MS.

The University of Texas Health Science Center at San Antonio, School of Allied Health Sciences, San Antonio, TX 78229-3900. Offers clinical laboratory sciences (MS); dental hygiene (MS); occupational therapy (MOT); physical therapy (MPT); physician assistant studies (MS). *Accreditation:* AOTA; APTA; ARC-PA. *Expenses:* Tuition, state resident: part-time $50 per credit hour. Tuition, nonresident: part-time $325 per credit hour. Required fees: $7.5 per credit hour. $155 per term.

Emergency Medical Services

Alderson-Broaddus College, Medical Science Department, Philippi, WV 26416. Offers emergency medical care (MS); rural primary care (MS); surgery (MS). Postbaccalaureate distance learning degree programs offered (minimal on-campus study). *Degree requirements:* For master's, thesis, 2 years of clinical experience. *Entrance requirements:* For master's, National Commission on Certification of Physician Assistants certification or bachelor's degree in related field; full-time clinical employment.

Drexel University, College of Nursing and Health Professions, Emergency and Public Safety Services Program, Philadelphia, PA 19104-2875. Offers MS. Part-time and evening/weekend programs available. *Degree requirements:* For master's, comprehensive exam. *Entrance requirements:* For master's, GRE General Test, minimum GPA of 2.75.

The George Washington University, School of Public Health and Health Services, Department of Prevention and Community Health, Washington, DC 20052. Offers community-oriented primary care (MPH); health promotion (MPH); maternal and child health (MPH); public health and emergency management (Certificate). *Accreditation:* CEPH. *Entrance requirements:* For master's, GRE or GMAT, 2 letters of recommendation, resumé. Additional exam requirements/recommendations for international students: Required—TOEFL.

Oklahoma State University, College of Arts and Sciences, Department of Political Science, Stillwater, OK 74078. Offers fire and emergency management administration (MS); political science (MA). *Faculty:* 20 full-time (5 women), 2 part-time/adjunct (0 women). *Students:* 29 full-time (13 women), 41 part-time (13 women); includes 17 minority (7 African Americans, 7 American Indian/Alaska Native, 1 Asian American or Pacific Islander, 2 Hispanic Americans), 1 international. Average age 33. 49 applicants, 65% accepted, 19 enrolled. In 2006, 12 degrees awarded. *Degree requirements:* For master's, thesis or creative component. *Entrance requirements:* For master's, GRE. Additional exam requirements/recommendations for international students: Required—TOEFL. *Application deadline:* For fall admission, 6/1 priority date for domestic students, 3/1 priority date for international students; for spring admission, 8/1 priority date for international students. Applications are processed on a rolling basis. Application fee: $40 ($75 for international students). Electronic applications accepted. *Expenses:* Tuition, state resident: part-time $146 per credit hour. Tuition, nonresident: part-time $516 per credit hour. Required fees: $44 per credit hour. Tuition and fees vary according to program. *Financial support:* In 2006–07, 3 research assistantships (averaging $10,976 per year), 10 teaching assistantships (averaging $9,325 per year) were awarded; Federal Work-Study, scholarships/grants, health care benefits, tuition waivers (partial), and unspecified assistantships also available. Support available to part-time students. Financial award application deadline: 3/1. *Faculty research:* Fire and emergency management, environmental dispute resolution, voting and elections, women and politics, urban politics. *Unit head:* Dr. James Scott, Head, 405-744-5572, Fax: 405-744-6534.

San Diego State University, Graduate and Research Affairs, College of Health and Human Services, Graduate School of Public Health, San Diego, CA 92182. Offers environmental health (MPH); epidemiology (MPH, PhD), including biostatistics (MPH); global emergency preparedness and response (MS); health behavior (PhD); health promotion (MPH); health services administration (MPH); toxicology (MS); MSW/MPH. *Accreditation:* ABET (one or more programs are accredited); CAHME (one or more programs are accredited); CEPH (one or more programs are accredited). Part-time programs available. *Degree requirements:* For master's, thesis (for some programs), comprehensive exam (for some programs); for doctorate, thesis/dissertation. *Entrance requirements:* For master's, GMAT (health services administration MPH), GRE General Test; for doctorate, GRE General Test. Additional exam requirements/recommendations for international students: Required—TOEFL. *Faculty research:* Evaluation of tobacco, AIDS prevalence and prevention, mammography, infant death project, Alzheimer's in elderly Chinese.

Université Laval, Faculty of Medicine, Post-Professional Programs in Medical Studies, Québec, QC G1K 7P4, Canada. Offers anatomy–pathology (DESS); anesthesiology (DESS); cardiology (DESS); care of older people (Diploma); clinical research (DESS); community health (DESS); dermatology (DESS); diagnostic radiology (DESS); emergency medicine (Diploma); family medicine (DESS); general surgery (DESS); geriatrics (DESS); hematology (DESS); internal medicine (DESS); maternal and fetal medicine (Diploma); medical biochemistry (DESS); medical microbiology and infectious diseases (DESS); medical oncology (DESS); nephrology (DESS); neurology (DESS); neurosurgery (DESS); obstetrics and gynecology (DESS); ophthalmology (DESS); orthopedic surgery (DESS); oto-rhino-laryngology (DESS); palliative medicine (Diploma); pediatrics (DESS); plastic surgery (DESS); psychiatry (DESS); pulmonary medicine (DESS); radiology–oncology (DESS); thoracic surgery (DESS); urology (DESS). *Degree requirements:* For other advanced degree, comprehensive exam. *Entrance requirements:* For degree, knowledge of French. Electronic applications accepted.

Occupational Therapy

Alvernia College, Graduate and Continuing Studies, Department of Occupational Therapy, Reading, PA 19607-1799. Offers MSOT. *Accreditation:* AOTA. Part-time and evening/weekend programs available. *Degree requirements:* For master's, thesis optional. Electronic applications accepted.

American International College, School of Health Sciences, Program in Occupational Therapy, Springfield, MA 01109-3189. Offers MSOT. *Accreditation:* AOTA. *Faculty:* 5 full-time (all women). *Students:* 8 full-time (all women), 4 part-time (all women); includes 3 minority (all African Americans) Average age 32. In 2006, 2 degrees awarded. *Degree requirements:* For master's, thesis (for some programs), comprehensive exam, registration. *Entrance requirements:* Additional exam requirements/recommendations for international students: Required—TOEFL. *Application deadline:* For fall admission, 7/1 priority date for domestic and international students; for spring admission, 12/1 priority date for domestic and international students. Applications are processed on a rolling basis. Application fee: $50. Electronic applications accepted. *Expenses: Contact institution. Financial support:* Career-related internships or fieldwork, Federal Work-Study, and unspecified assistantships available. Support available to part-time students. Financial award application deadline: 4/1; financial award applicants required to submit FAFSA. *Unit head:* Cathy Dow-Royer, Director, 413-205-3262, Fax: 413-205-3943, E-mail: cathy.dowroyer@aic.edu. *Application contact:* Keshawn Dodds, Associate Director of Graduate Admissions, 413-205-3549, Fax: 413-205-3911, E-mail: keshawn.dodds@aic.edu.

A.T. Still University of Health Sciences, Arizona School of Health Sciences, Mesa, AZ 85206. Offers advanced occupational therapy (MS); advanced physician assistant (MS); audiology (Au D); human movement (MS); medical informatics (MS); occupational therapy (MS); physical therapy (MS, DPT); physician assistant (MS); sports health care (MS); transitional physical therapy (DPT). *Accreditation:* AOTA (one or more programs are accredited); APTA. Postbaccalaureate distance learning degree programs offered (no on-campus study). *Faculty:* 47 full-time (27 women), 101 part-time/adjunct (60 women). *Students:* 442 full-time (277 women), 732 part-time (579 women); includes 143 minority (38 African Americans, 11 American Indian/Alaska Native, 55 Asian Americans or Pacific Islanders, 39 Hispanic Americans), 4 international. Average age 33. 1,471 applicants, 547 enrolled. In 2006, 104 master's, 432 doctorates awarded. *Degree requirements:* For master's and doctorate, thesis/dissertation (for some programs). *Entrance requirements:* For master's, GRE General Test, minimum GPA of 2.5; for doctorate, GRE, Evaluation of Practicing Audiologists Capabilities (Au D), Physical Therapy Evaluation Tool (DPT), current state licensure, master's degree or equivalent (Au D), minimum GPA of 2.7. *Application deadline:* For fall admission, 2/1 priority date for domestic and international students. Applications are processed on a rolling basis. Application fee: $60. *Expenses: Contact institution. Financial support:* In 2006–07, 382 students received support. Federal Work-Study and scholarships/grants available. Financial award application deadline: 5/1. *Faculty research:* Constraint-induced therapy, scapular motion analysis, shoulder mobility, biomechanics, quadriceps. *Unit head:* Dr. Randy Danielsen, Dean, 480-219-6000, Fax: 480-219-6110, E-mail: rdanielsen@atsu.edu. *Application contact:* Donna Sparks, Associate Director for Admissions, 660-626-2237, Fax: 660-626-2969, E-mail: admissions@atsu.edu.

Barry University, School of Natural and Health Sciences, Program in Occupational Therapy, Miami Shores, FL 33161-6695. Offers MS. *Accreditation:* AOTA. *Students:* 50 full-time (40 women), 23 part-time (18 women); includes 32 minority (12 African Americans, 2 Asian Americans or Pacific Islanders, 18 Hispanic Americans), 2 international. 71 applicants, 44% accepted, 31 enrolled. In 2006, 23 degrees awarded. *Application deadline:* Applications are processed on a rolling basis. Application fee: $30. Electronic applications accepted. *Unit head:* Dr. Douglas Mitchell, Director, 305-899-3213, Fax: 305-899-2958, E-mail: dmitchell@mail.barry.edu. *Application contact:* Jocelyn Goulet, Director, Health Services Admissions Operation, 305-899-3541, Fax: 305-899-3232, E-mail: jgoulet@mail.barry.edu.

Bay Path College, Program in Occupational Therapy, Longmeadow, MA 01106-2292. Offers MOT, MS. *Accreditation:* AOTA. Part-time and evening/weekend programs available. *Entrance requirements:* Additional exam requirements/recommendations for international students: Recommended—TOEFL (minimum score 500 paper-based). Electronic applications accepted.

Belmont University, College of Health Sciences, School of Occupational Therapy, Nashville, TN 37212-3757. Offers MSOT, OTD. *Accreditation:* AOTA. Evening/weekend programs available. *Faculty:* 8 full-time (7 women), 11 part-time/adjunct (9 women). *Students:* 112 full-time (98 women), 1 part-time; includes 9 minority (8 African Americans, 1 Asian American or Pacific Islander). Average age 29. 158 applicants, 46% accepted, 52 enrolled. In 2006, 24 master's, 9 doctorates awarded. *Degree requirements:* For master's, thesis or alternative, 6 months of supervised clinical work; for doctorate, thesis/dissertation, 6 months of supervised clinical work. *Entrance requirements:* For master's, GRE General Test, MAT, 50-100 observation hours, 1 year experience as licensed healthcare professional; for doctorate, GRE, MAT, 50û100 observation hours. Additional exam requirements/recommendations for international students: Required—TOEFL (minimum score 500 paper-based; 173 computer-based). *Application deadline:* For fall admission, 3/31 priority date for domestic students. Applications are processed on a rolling basis. Application fee: $50. Electronic applications accepted. *Expenses: Contact institution. Financial support:* Application deadline: 3/1; *Faculty research:* Gerontology, applied kinesiology, rehabilitation outcomes, pediatrics. *Unit head:* Dr. Ruth Ford, Associate Dean, 615-460-6700, Fax: 615-460-6475, E-mail: fordr@mail.belmont.edu. *Application contact:* Vicki Bourne, Program Assistant, 615-460-6705, Fax: 615-460-6475, E-mail: bournev@mail.belmont.edu.

Boston University, College of Health and Rehabilitation Sciences—Sargent College, Department of Occupational Therapy and Rehabilitation Counseling, Boston, MA 02215. Offers occupational therapy (MS, MSOT); rehabilitation sciences (D Sc). *Accreditation:* AOTA (one or more programs are accredited); CORE. Part-time programs available. Postbaccalaureate distance learning degree programs offered (minimal on-campus study). *Faculty:* 12 full-time (all women), 2 part-time/adjunct (both women). *Students:* 104 full-time (99 women), 74 part-time (69 women); includes 18 minority (2 African Americans, 13 Asian Americans or Pacific Islanders, 3 Hispanic Americans), 6 international. Average age 28. 85 applicants, 74% accepted, 25 enrolled. In 2006, 42 master's, 4 doctorates awarded. *Median time to degree:* Of those who began their doctoral program in fall 1998, 100% received their degree in 8 years or less. *Degree requirements:* For master's, full-time internship, thesis optional; for doctorate, thesis/dissertation. *Entrance requirements:* For master's, minimum GPA of 3.0; BS in occupational therapy; for doctorate, GRE General Test. Additional exam requirements/recommendations for international students: Required—TOEFL (minimum score 550 paper-based; 213 computer-based), TWE (minimum score 5). *Application deadline:* For fall admission, 2/15 priority date for domestic and international students. Applications are processed on a rolling basis. Application fee: $60. Electronic applications accepted. *Expenses:* Tuition: Full-time $33,330; part-time $1,042 per credit. Required fees: $462; $40. *Financial support:* In 2006–07, 1 research assistantship with full tuition reimbursement, 1 teaching assistantship with full tuition reimbursement (averaging $15,000 per year) were awarded; career-related internships or fieldwork, Federal Work-Study, institutionally sponsored loans, scholarships/grants, and tuition waivers (partial) also available. Financial award application deadline: 4/15; financial award applicants required to submit FAFSA. *Faculty research:* Sensory integration, outcomes measurement, impact of Parkinson's disease, families of people with autism. Total annual research expenditures: $283,380. *Unit head:* Dr. Wendy J. Coster, Department Chair, 617-353-2727, Fax: 617-353-2926, E-mail: wjcoster@bu.edu. *Application contact:* Sharon Sankey, Director, Student Services, 617-353-2713, Fax: 617-353-7500, E-mail: ssankey@bu.edu.

Brenau University, Graduate Programs, School of Health and Science, Gainesville, GA 30501. Offers family nurse practitioner (MS); nurse educator (MS); occupational therapy (MS); psychology (MS). *Accreditation:* AOTA; NLN. Part-time and evening/weekend programs available. *Faculty:* 21 full-time (18 women), 5 part-time/adjunct (2 women). *Students:* 56 full-time (52 women), 36 part-time (35 women); includes 22 minority (18 African Americans, 1 American Indian/Alaska Native, 2 Asian Americans or Pacific Islanders, 1 Hispanic American), 1 international. Average age 31. 76 applicants, 51% accepted, 28 enrolled. In 2006, 40 degrees awarded. *Degree requirements:* For master's, clinical practicum hours. *Entrance requirements:* For master's, GRE General Test or MAT. Additional exam requirements/recommendations for international students: Required—TOEFL (minimum score 550 paper-based). *Application deadline:* Applications are processed on a rolling basis. Application fee: $30. *Expenses: Contact institution. Financial support:* In 2006–07, 14 students received support. Scholarships/grants available. Support available to part-time students. Financial award application deadline: 7/15; financial award applicants required to submit FAFSA. *Faculty research:* Cultural competency, family violence. *Unit head:* Dr. Gale Starich, Dean, 777-718-5305, Fax: 770-297-5929, E-mail: gstarich@brenau.edu. *Application contact:* Nathan Goss, Admissions Coordinator, 770-534-6162, Fax: 770-538-4701, E-mail: ngoss@brenau.edu.

California State University, Dominguez Hills, College of Health and Human Services, Program in Occupational Therapy, Carson, CA 90747-0001. Offers MS. *Accreditation:* AOTA. *Faculty:* 4 full-time (3 women), 8 part-time/adjunct (5 women). *Students:* 46 full-time (34 women), 1 (woman) part-time; includes 22 minority (5 African Americans, 11 Asian Americans or Pacific Islanders, 6 Hispanic Americans). Average age 33. 1 applicant, 0% accepted.

Occupational Therapy

California State University, Dominguez Hills (continued)

Degree requirements: For master's, comprehensive exam. *Entrance requirements:* For master's, GRE. Additional exam requirements/recommendations for international students: Required—TOEFL, TWE. *Application deadline:* For fall admission, 9/15 priority date for domestic students. Electronic applications accepted. *Expenses:* Tuition, nonresident: part-time $339 per unit. Required fees: $1,148 per term. Tuition and fees vary according to program. *Faculty research:* Child school functioning, assessment, lifespan occupational development, low vision occupational therapy intervention. *Unit head:* Dr. Mitchell T. Maki, Dean, College of Health and Human Services, 301-243-2046, E-mail: mmaki@csudh.edu.

Chatham University, Program in Occupational Therapy, Pittsburgh, PA 15232-2826. Offers MOT, OTD. *Accreditation:* AOTA. *Students:* 28 full-time (27 women). Average age 34. 25 applicants, 52% accepted, 13 enrolled. In 2006, 9 degrees awarded. *Entrance requirements:* For master's and doctorate, recommendation letter, community service, volunteer service. Additional exam requirements/recommendations for international students: Required—TOEFL (minimum score 600 paper-based; 250 computer-based; 100 iBT); Recommended—IELTS (minimum score 7). *Application deadline:* For fall admission, 5/1 priority date for domestic and international students. Applications are processed on a rolling basis. Application fee: $45. Electronic applications accepted. *Unit head:* Dr. Joyce Salls, Director, 412-365-1177, E-mail: salls@chatham.edu. *Application contact:* Office of Graduate Admissions, 412-365-1825, Fax: 412-365-1609, E-mail: admissions@chatham.edu.

Cleveland State University, College of Graduate Studies, College of Science, Department of Health Sciences, Program in Occupational Therapy, Cleveland, OH 44115. Offers MOT. *Accreditation:* AOTA. *Faculty:* 6 full-time (4 women), 3 part-time/adjunct (all women). *Students:* 87 full-time (75 women), 40 part-time (31 women); includes 17 minority (12 African Americans, 3 Asian Americans or Pacific Islanders, 2 Hispanic Americans), 3 international. Average age 28. 30 applicants, 100% accepted, 25 enrolled. In 2006, 6 degrees awarded. *Degree requirements:* For master's, registration. *Entrance requirements:* Additional exam requirements/recommendations for international students: Required—TOEFL (minimum score 550 paper-based; 220 computer-based). *Application deadline:* For winter admission, 3/15 priority date for domestic and international students. Applications are processed on a rolling basis. Application fee: $55. Electronic applications accepted. *Financial support:* In 2006–07, 7 students received support, including research assistantships with full tuition reimbursements available (averaging $13,540 per year). Financial award application deadline: 4/1. *Faculty research:* Pediatrics, psychology, daily living, exercise physiology, neuromuscular disorders. Total annual research expenditures: $225,000. *Unit head:* Dr. Glenn D. Goodman, Director, 216-687-2493, Fax: 216-687-9316, E-mail: g.goodman@csuohio.edu. *Application contact:* Karen J. Bradley, Secretary, 216-687-3567, Fax: 216-687-9316, E-mail: k.bradley@csuohio.edu.

College Misericordia, College of Health Sciences, Program in Occupational Therapy, Dallas, PA 18612-1098. Offers MSOT. *Accreditation:* AOTA. *Faculty:* 4 full-time (2 women), 3 part-time/adjunct (all women). *Students:* 14 full-time (13 women), 2 part-time (both women). Average age 23. In 2006, 34 degrees awarded. *Application deadline:* Applications are processed on a rolling basis. Application fee: $25. Electronic applications accepted. *Expenses:* Tuition: Full-time $19,800; part-time $495 per credit. Required fees: $1,060. *Financial support:* Teaching assistantships, career-related internships or fieldwork and scholarships/grants available. Support available to part-time students. Financial award application deadline: 6/30; financial award applicants required to submit FAFSA. *Application contact:* Larree Brown, Coordinator of Part-Time Undergraduate and Graduate Programs, 570-674-6451, Fax: 570-674-6232, E-mail: lbrown@misericordia.edu.

College of St. Catherine, Graduate Programs, Program in Occupational Therapy, St. Paul, MN 55105-1789. Offers MA. *Accreditation:* AOTA. Part-time and evening/weekend programs available. *Degree requirements:* For master's, thesis. *Entrance requirements:* For master's, GRE, minimum GPA of 3.0. Additional exam requirements/recommendations for international students: Required—Michigan English Language Assessment Battery or TOEFL.

See Close-Up on page 1699.

The College of St. Scholastica, Graduate Studies, Department of Occupational Therapy, Duluth, MN 55811-4199. Offers MA. *Accreditation:* AOTA. Part-time programs available. *Faculty:* 3 full-time (2 women), 4 part-time/adjunct (3 women). *Students:* 27 full-time (25 women), 1 (woman) part-time. Average age 23. 20 applicants, 85% accepted, 16 enrolled. In 2006, 9 degrees awarded. *Degree requirements:* For master's, thesis. *Entrance requirements:* For master's, interview, minimum GPA of 2.7. Additional exam requirements/recommendations for international students: Required—TOEFL (minimum score 550 paper-based; 213 computer-based; 79 iBT). *Application deadline:* For fall admission, 11/15 for domestic and international students. Applications are processed on a rolling basis. Application fee: $50. Electronic applications accepted. *Financial support:* In 2006–07, 25 students received support, including 1 teaching assistantship (averaging $1,450 per year); Federal Work-Study and scholarships/grants also available. Support available to part-time students. Financial award applicants required to submit FAFSA. *Faculty research:* Gerontology, occupational therapy administration, neurorehabilitation, occupational therapy in nontraditional settings, clinical fieldwork issues. *Unit head:* Dr. Carolyn Dorfman, Director, 218-723-6697, Fax: 218-723-6290, E-mail: cdorfman@css.edu. *Application contact:* Tonya J. Roth, Graduate Recruitment Counselor, 218-723-6285, Fax: 218-733-2275, E-mail: gradstudies@css.edu.

Colorado State University, Graduate School, College of Applied Human Sciences, Department of Occupational Therapy, Fort Collins, CO 80523-0015. Offers MS. *Accreditation:* AOTA. *Faculty:* 7 full-time (5 women). *Students:* 148 full-time (140 women), 13 part-time (10 women); includes 10 minority (1 American Indian/Alaska Native, 3 Asian Americans or Pacific Islanders, 6 Hispanic Americans), 6 international. Average age 27. 148 applicants, 44% accepted, 45 enrolled. In 2006, 51 degrees awarded. *Degree requirements:* For master's, group research project or thesis, 24 weeks of full-time field work. *Entrance requirements:* For master's, GRE, minimum GPA of 3.0, 3 letters of reference, resumé, experience with people who have disabilities. Additional exam requirements/recommendations for international students: Required—TOEFL (minimum score 550 paper-based; 240 computer-based; 94 iBT). *Application deadline:* For fall admission, 2/1 priority date for domestic and international students; for spring admission, 2/1 priority date for international students. Application fee: $50. *Expenses:* Tuition, state resident: full-time $4,248; part-time $236 per credit. Tuition, nonresident: full-time $15,642; part-time $869 per credit. Required fees: $66 per credit. Tuition and fees vary according to program. *Financial support:* In 2006–07, 39 students received support, including 12 fellowships with partial tuition reimbursements available (averaging $1,500 per year), 2 teaching assistantships with partial tuition reimbursements available (averaging $5,750 per year); research assistantships, Federal Work-Study, scholarships/grants, and traineeships also available. Support available to part-time students. Financial award application deadline: 4/30. *Faculty research:* Geriatrics, school-based service, traumatic brain injury, neurorehabilitation, neurobehavioral development. Total annual research expenditures: $655,931. *Unit head:* Dr. Lise Youngblade, Head, 970-491-5558, Fax: 970-491-6920, E-mail: lise.youngblade@colostate.edu. *Application contact:* Linda McDowell, Admissions Coordinator, 970-491-6253, Fax: 970-491-6290, E-mail: otinfo@cahs.colostate.edu.

Columbia University, College of Physicians and Surgeons, Programs in Occupational Therapy, New York, NY 10032. Offers movement science (Ed D), including occupational therapy; occupational therapy (professional) (MS); occupational therapy administration or education (post-professional) (MS); MPH/MS. *Accreditation:* AOTA. *Faculty:* 9 full-time (8 women), 6 part-time/adjunct (4 women). *Students:* 114 full-time (106 women), 6 part-time (all women); includes 28 minority (5 African Americans, 17 Asian Americans or Pacific Islanders, 6 Hispanic Americans), 5 international. Average age 26. In 2006, 47 degrees awarded. *Degree requirements:* For master's, project, 6 months of fieldwork, thesis for post-professional students; for doctorate, thesis/dissertation, comprehensive exam. *Entrance requirements:* For master's, undergraduate course work in anatomy, physiology, statistics, psychology, social sciences, humanities, English composition; NBCOT eligibility; for doctorate, NBCOT certified. Additional exam requirements/recommendations for international students: Required—TOEFL (minimum score 250 computer-based), TWE (minimum score 4). *Application deadline:* For fall admission, 12/31 for domestic and international students. Application fee: $75. Electronic applications accepted. *Expenses:* *Contact institution.* *Financial support:* In 2006–07, 80 students received support. Career-related internships or fieldwork, Federal Work-Study, institutionally sponsored loans, and scholarships/grants available. Financial award application deadline: 4/15; financial award applicants required to submit FAFSA. *Faculty research:* Community mental health, developmental tasks of late life, infant play, cognition, obesity, motor learning. Total annual research expenditures: $30,000. *Unit head:* Dr. Janet Falk-Kessler, Director, 212-305-5267, Fax: 212-305-4569, E-mail: jf6@columbia.edu. *Application contact:* Marilyn Harper, Administrative Assistant, 212-305-5267, Fax: 212-305-4569, E-mail: mh15@columbia.edu.

Concordia University Wisconsin, Graduate Programs, School of Health and Human Services, Program in Occupational Therapy, Mequon, WI 53097-2402. Offers MOT. *Accreditation:* AOTA. *Faculty:* 6 full-time (4 women), 2 part-time/adjunct (1 woman). *Students:* 61 (54 women). In 2006, 5 degrees awarded. *Degree requirements:* For master's, thesis or alternative, comprehensive exam. *Entrance requirements:* Additional exam requirements/recommendations for international students: Required—TOEFL. Application fee: $35 ($125 for international students). *Financial support:* Application deadline: 8/1. *Unit head:* Dr. Linda Samuel, Interim Director, 262-243-4469, E-mail: linda.samuel@cuw.edu. *Application contact:* Graduate Admissions, 262-243-4248, Fax: 262-243-4428.

Creighton University, School of Pharmacy and Health Professions, Program in Occupational Therapy, Omaha, NE 68178-0001. Offers OTD. *Accreditation:* AOTA. Postbaccalaureate distance learning degree programs offered (minimal on-campus study). Electronic applications accepted. *Expenses:* Tuition: Part-time $595 per credit hour. Required fees: $38 per semester. *Faculty research:* Ethics, health care systems.

Dalhousie University, Faculty of Graduate Studies, Faculty of Health Professions, School of Occupational Therapy, Halifax, NS B3H 4R2, Canada. Offers M Sc. Part-time and evening/weekend programs available. Postbaccalaureate distance learning degree programs offered (no on-campus study). *Degree requirements:* For master's, thesis. Electronic applications accepted. *Faculty research:* Gender, health systems, design, geriatrics power and empowerment.

Dominican College, Division of Allied Health, Department of Occupational Therapy, Orangeburg, NY 10962-1210. Offers MS. Students enter program as undergraduates. *Accreditation:* AOTA. Part-time and evening/weekend programs available. *Faculty:* 4 full-time (all women), 10 part-time/adjunct (8 women). *Students:* 47 full-time (all women), 84 part-time (58 women); includes 37 minority (18 African Americans, 8 Asian Americans or Pacific Islanders, 11 Hispanic Americans). Average age 39. In 2006, 17 degrees awarded. *Degree requirements:* For master's, 2 clinical affiliations. *Entrance requirements:* For master's, minimum GPA of 3.0, writing sample, 3 letters of recommendation. Additional exam requirements/recommendations for international students: Required—TOEFL (minimum score 550 paper-based; 213 computer-based). *Application deadline:* Applications are processed on a rolling basis. Application fee: $50. *Financial support:* Applicants required to submit FAFSA. *Unit head:* Dr. Sandra Countee, Program Director, 845-848-7900 Ext. 1219, Fax: 845-398-4893, E-mail: sandra.countee@dc.edu. *Application contact:* Director of Admissions, 845-848-7900, Fax: 845-365-3150, E-mail: admissions@dc.edu.

Dominican University of California, Graduate Programs, School of Arts and Sciences, Program in Occupational Therapy, San Rafael, CA 94901-2298. Offers MS. *Accreditation:* AOTA. Part-time programs available. *Degree requirements:* For master's, thesis, registration. *Entrance requirements:* For master's, minimum GPA of 3.0, clinical experience, course work in nursing research course and statistics, CPR certification, professional liability and malpractice insurance, interview. Additional exam requirements/recommendations for international students: Required—TOEFL (minimum score 550 paper-based; 213 computer-based). Electronic applications accepted.

Duquesne University, John G. Rangos, Sr. School of Health Sciences, Pittsburgh, PA 15282-0001. Offers health management systems (MHMS); occupational therapy (MS); physical therapy (DPT); physician assistant (MPA); speech–language pathology (MS); MBA/MHMS. *Accreditation:* AOTA (one or more programs are accredited); APTA (one or more programs are accredited); ASHA. *Faculty:* 35 full-time (22 women), 24 part-time/adjunct (12 women). *Students:* 261 full-time (229 women), 16 part-time (8 women); includes 11 minority (6 African Americans, 1 American Indian/Alaska Native, 2 Asian Americans or Pacific Islanders, 2 Hispanic Americans), 3 international. Average age 23. 150 applicants, 55% accepted, 41 enrolled. In 2006, 66 master's, 13 doctorates awarded. *Degree requirements:* For doctorate, thesis/dissertation. *Entrance requirements:* For master's, GRE (speech-language pathology), 3 letters of recommendation, minimum GPA of 2.75 (health management systems, occupational therapy), minimum GPA of 3.0 (physical assistant, speech-language pathology); for doctorate, GRE General Test, 3 letters of recommendation, minimum GPA of 3.0, personal interview. Additional exam requirements/recommendations for international students: Required—TOEFL (minimum score 600 paper-based; 250 computer-based). *Application deadline:* For fall admission, 12/1 priority date for domestic students; for winter admission, 5/1 priority date for domestic students. Application fee: $50. Electronic applications accepted. *Expenses:* *Contact institution.* Tuition and fees vary according to degree level and program. *Financial support:* Federal Work-Study available. *Faculty research:* Neuronal processing, electrical stimulation on peripheral neuropathy, CNS stimulatory and inhibitory signals, behavioral genetic methodologies to development disorders of speech, neurogenic communication disorders. Total annual research expenditures: $66,000. *Unit head:* Dr. Gregory H. Frazer, Dean, 412-396-5303, Fax: 412-396-5554, E-mail: frazer@duq.edu. *Application contact:* Christopher R. Hilf, Recruiter/Academic Advisor, 412-396-5653, Fax: 412-396-5554, E-mail: hilfc@duq.edu.

D'Youville College, Occupational Therapy Department, Buffalo, NY 14201-1084. Offers MS. *Accreditation:* AOTA. *Faculty:* 7 full-time (all women), 3 part-time/adjunct (2 women). *Students:* 75 full-time (66 women), 38 part-time (33 women); includes 5 minority (2 African Americans, 2 American Indian/Alaska Native, 1 Hispanic American), 30 international. Average age 25. 88 applicants, 53% accepted, 20 enrolled. In 2006, 19 degrees awarded. *Degree requirements:* For master's, thesis optional. *Entrance requirements:* Additional exam requirements/recommendations for international students: Required—TOEFL (minimum score 500 paper-based; 173 computer-based). *Application deadline:* For fall admission, 5/1 priority date for international students; for spring admission, 9/1 priority date for international students. Applications are processed on a rolling basis. Application fee: $25. Electronic applications accepted. *Faculty research:* Learning styles, range of motion in the elderly, hospice care, culture, health. *Unit head:* Dr. Merlene Gingher, Chair, 716-829-7624, Fax: 716-829-8137. *Application contact:* Linda Fisher, Graduate Admissions Director, 716-829-8400, Fax: 716-829-7900, E-mail: graduateadmissions@dyc.edu.

East Carolina University, Graduate School, School of Allied Health Sciences, Department of Occupational Therapy, Greenville, NC 27858-4353. Offers MSOT. *Accreditation:* AOTA. Part-time programs available. Postbaccalaureate distance learning degree programs offered (minimal on-campus study). *Students:* 38 full-time (36 women), 3 part-time (all women); includes 2 minority (both African Americans) Average age 24. 36 applicants, 78% accepted. In 2006, 12 degrees awarded. *Degree requirements:* For master's, thesis or research project. *Entrance requirements:* For master's, GRE General Test. Additional exam requirements/recommendations for international students: Required—TOEFL. *Application deadline:* For fall admission, 6/1 for domestic students. Applications are processed on a rolling basis. Application fee: $50. Electronic applications accepted. *Financial support:* In 2006–07, 2 research assistantships were awarded; career-related internships or fieldwork and Federal Work-Study also available. Financial award application deadline: 6/1; financial award applicants required to submit FAFSA. *Faculty research:* Quality of life, assistive technology, environmental contributions, modifications of occupation to health, therapeutic activities. *Unit head:* Dr. Anne Dickerson, Chair, 252-744-6190, Fax: 252-328-4470, E-mail: dickersona@ecu.edu. *Application contact:* Dean of Graduate School, 252-328-6012, Fax: 252-328-6071, E-mail: gradschool@ecu.edu.

East Carolina University, Graduate School, School of Allied Health Sciences, Program in Rehabilitation Studies, Greenville, NC 27858-4353. Offers rehabilitation counseling (MS); substance abuse and clinical counseling (MS); vocational evaluation (MS). *Accreditation:* CORE. Part-time and evening/weekend programs available. *Students:* 61 full-time (45 women), 10 part-time (8 women); includes 9 minority (8 African Americans, 1 American Indian/Alaska Native), 2 international. Average age 31. 22 applicants, 14% accepted, 3 enrolled. In 2006, 21 degrees awarded. *Degree requirements:* For master's, thesis or alternative, internship, comprehensive exam. *Entrance requirements:* For master's, GRE General Test or MAT. Additional exam requirements/recommendations for international students: Required—TOEFL. *Application deadline:* For fall admission, 3/1 priority date for domestic students; for spring admission, 10/1 priority date for domestic students. Applications are processed on a rolling basis. Application fee: $50. *Financial support:* Research assistantships with partial tuition reimbursements, teaching assistantships with partial tuition reimbursements, Federal Work-Study and scholarships/grants available. Support available to part-time students. Financial award application deadline: 3/1. *Unit head:* Dr. Paul Alston, Chair, 252-744-6290, Fax: 252-328-0725, E-mail: alstonp@ecu.edu. *Application contact:* Dean of Graduate School, 252-328-6012, Fax: 252-328-6071, E-mail: gradschool@ecu.edu.

Eastern Kentucky University, The Graduate School, College of Health Sciences, Department of Occupational Therapy, Richmond, KY 40475-3102. Offers MS. *Accreditation:* AOTA. Part-time programs available. *Faculty:* 13 full-time (all women). *Students:* 82 full-time (78 women), 2 part-time (both women); includes 2 minority (both African Americans) Average age 25. 89 applicants, 4% accepted, 1 enrolled. In 2006, 43 degrees awarded. *Degree requirements:* For master's, thesis optional. *Entrance requirements:* For master's, GRE General Test, minimum GPA of 3.0. *Application deadline:* For fall admission, 6/1 for domestic students. Application fee: $35. *Expenses:* Tuition, state resident: full-time $5,610. Tuition, nonresident: full-time $15,910. *Financial support:* Career-related internships or fieldwork, institutionally sponsored loans, and unspecified assistantships available. Financial award applicants required to submit CSS PROFILE. *Faculty research:* Rehabilitation, pediatrics, leadership issues. *Unit head:* Dr. Colleen Schneck, Chair, 859-622-3300, Fax: 859-622-1601.

Eastern Michigan University, Graduate School, College of Health and Human Services, School of Health Sciences, Program in Occupational Therapy, Ypsilanti, MI 48197. Offers MOT, MS. Part-time and evening/weekend programs available. Postbaccalaureate distance learning degree programs offered (minimal on-campus study). *Students:* 48 full-time (43 women), 39 part-time (34 women); includes 18 minority (13 African Americans, 3 Asian Americans or Pacific Islanders, 2 Hispanic Americans). Average age 28. In 2006, 24 degrees awarded. *Entrance requirements:* Additional exam requirements/recommendations for international students: Required—TOEFL. *Application deadline:* For fall admission, 5/15 priority date for domestic students, 5/1 priority date for international students; for winter admission, 10/15 priority date for domestic students, 10/1 priority date for international students; for spring admission, 3/15 priority date for domestic students, 3/1 priority date for international students. Applications are processed on a rolling basis. Application fee: $35. *Expenses:* Tuition, state resident: part-time $341 per credit hour. Tuition, nonresident: full-time $16,104; part-time $671 per credit hour. Required fees: $816; $34 per credit hour. $40 per term. One-time fee: $82 full-time. Tuition and fees vary according to course level, course load, degree level and reciprocity agreements. *Financial support:* Fellowships, research assistantships with full tuition reimbursements, teaching assistantships with full tuition reimbursements, career-related internships or fieldwork, Federal Work-Study, institutionally sponsored loans, scholarships/grants, tuition waivers (partial), and unspecified assistantships available. Support available to part-time students. Financial award applicants required to submit FAFSA. *Unit head:* Dr. Elizabeth Francis Connolly, Director, School of Health Sciences, 734-487-4094, Fax: 734-487-4095, E-mail: elizabeth.francis-connolly@emich.edu.

Eastern Washington University, Graduate Studies, College of Science, Mathematics and Technology, Program in Occupational Therapy, Cheney, WA 99004-2431. Offers MOT. *Accreditation:* AOTA. *Degree requirements:* For master's, comprehensive exam.

Florida Gulf Coast University, College of Health Professions, Department of Occupational Therapy, Fort Myers, FL 33965-6565. Offers MS. *Faculty:* 42 full-time (35 women), 21 part-time/adjunct (14 women). *Students:* 10 full-time (9 women), 14 part-time (13 women); includes 4 minority (1 African American, 3 Hispanic Americans). Average age 30. 21 applicants, 86% accepted, 14 enrolled. In 2006, 2 degrees awarded. *Entrance requirements:* For master's, GRE General Test, MAT, minimum GPA 3.0. Additional exam requirements/recommendations for international students: Required—TOEFL (minimum score 550 paper-based; 213 computer-based). *Application deadline:* For fall admission, 2/15 for domestic students; for spring admission, 6/1 for domestic students. Applications are processed on a rolling basis. Application fee: $30. Electronic applications accepted. *Expenses:* Tuition, state resident: full-time $4,326. Tuition, nonresident: full-time $18,523. Required fees: $1,211. One-time fee: $5 full-time. *Unit head:* Tina Gelpi, Head, 239-590-7551, Fax: 239-590-7474, E-mail: tgelpi@fgcu.edu.

Florida International University, College of Nursing and Health Sciences, Department of Occupational Therapy, Miami, FL 33199. Offers MS. *Accreditation:* AOTA. Part-time programs available. *Faculty:* 5 full-time (4 women). *Students:* 63 full-time (57 women), 20 part-time (17 women); includes 60 minority (14 African Americans, 3 Asian Americans or Pacific Islanders, 43 Hispanic Americans), 3 international. Average age 29. 36 applicants, 86% accepted, 22 enrolled. In 2006, 23 degrees awarded. *Degree requirements:* For master's, thesis. *Entrance requirements:* For master's, GRE General Test, minimum GPA of 3.0. Additional exam requirements/recommendations for international students: Required—TOEFL. *Application deadline:* For fall admission, 4/1 priority date for domestic students; for spring admission, 10/1 for domestic students. Applications are processed on a rolling basis. Application fee: $25. *Expenses:* Tuition, state resident: part-time $249 per credit hour. Tuition, nonresident: part-time $753 per credit hour. Tuition and fees vary according to program. *Financial support:* Fellowships, research assistantships, teaching assistantships, career-related internships or fieldwork, Federal Work-Study, and institutionally sponsored loans available. *Unit head:* Dr. Patricia Scott, Chairperson, 305-348-3105, Fax: 305-348-1240, E-mail: patricia_j.scott@fiu.edu.

Gannon University, School of Graduate Studies, College of Sciences, Engineering, and Health Sciences, School of Health Sciences, Program in Occupational Therapy, Erie, PA 16541-0001. Offers MS. Offered as five-year program. *Accreditation:* AOTA. *Students:* 18 full-time (17 women). Average age 22. 4 applicants, 50% accepted, 1 enrolled. In 2006, 13 degrees awarded. *Degree requirements:* For master's, thesis. *Entrance requirements:* Additional exam requirements/recommendations for international students: Required—TOEFL (minimum score 500 paper-based; 173 computer-based). Application fee: $25. *Expenses:* Tuition: Full-time $12,240; part-time $680 per credit. Required fees: $496; $16 per credit. Tuition and fees vary according to course load, degree level, campus/location and program. *Financial support:* Career-related internships or fieldwork available. Support available to part-time students. Financial award application deadline: 7/1; financial award applicants required to submit FAFSA. *Unit head:* Jeff Boss, Director, 814-871-5670, E-mail: boss001@gannon.edu. *Application contact:* Debra Meszaros, Director of Graduate Recruitment, 814-871-5819, Fax: 814-871-5827, E-mail: cfal@gannon.edu.

Gannon University, School of Graduate Studies, College of Sciences, Engineering, and Health Sciences, School of Sciences, Program in Environmental and Occupational Science and Health, Erie, PA 16541-0001. Offers Certificate. *Students:* Average age 52. 1 applicant, 100% accepted, 1 enrolled. *Entrance requirements:* Additional exam requirements/recommendations for international students: Required—TOEFL (minimum score 500 paper-based; 173 computer-based). *Application deadline:* Applications are processed on a rolling basis. Application fee: $25. *Expenses:* Tuition: Full-time $12,240; part-time $680 per credit. Required fees: $496; $16 per credit. Tuition and fees vary according to course load, degree level, campus/location and program. *Financial support:* Application deadline: 7/1. *Unit head:* Dr. Harry Diz, Chair, 814-871-7633, E-mail: diz001@gannon.edu. *Application contact:* Debra Meszaros, Director of Graduate Recruitment, 814-871-5819, Fax: 814-871-5827, E-mail: cfal@gannon.edu.

Governors State University, College of Health Professions, Program in Occupational Therapy, University Park, IL 60466-0975. Offers MOT. *Accreditation:* AOTA. *Students:* 47 full-time, 8 part-time. Average age 30. *Degree requirements:* For master's, thesis or alternative. *Entrance requirements:* For master's, minimum GPA of 3.0 in field, 2.75 overall. *Application deadline:* For fall admission, 4/30 priority date for domestic students. Application fee: $25. *Expenses:* Tuition, state resident: full-time $4,104; part-time $171 per hour. Tuition, nonresident: part-time $513 per hour. *Financial support:* Application deadline: 5/1. *Unit head:* Dr. Catherine Brady, Coordinator, 708-534-5000 Ext. 5489.

Grand Valley State University, College of Health Professions, Occupational Therapy Program, Allendale, MI 49401-9403. Offers MS. *Accreditation:* AOTA. *Faculty:* 5 full-time (4 women). *Students:* 37 full-time (all women), 15 part-time (all women). Average age 26. 31 applicants, 68% accepted, 18 enrolled. In 2006, 5 degrees awarded. *Degree requirements:* For master's, thesis or alternative, fieldwork, project. *Entrance requirements:* For master's, interview, volunteer work, writing sample. Additional exam requirements/recommendations for international students: Required—TOEFL (minimum score 610 paper-based; 253 computer-based). *Application deadline:* For winter admission, 1/15 priority date for domestic students. Applications are processed on a rolling basis. Application fee: $30. Electronic applications accepted. *Expenses:* Tuition, state resident: full-time $5,850; part-time $325 per credit. Tuition, nonresident: full-time $10,800; part-time $600 per credit. Tuition and fees vary according to course load. *Financial support:* In 2006–07, 2 research assistantships with full and partial tuition reimbursements (averaging $8,000 per year) were awarded; unspecified assistantships also available. Financial award application deadline: 2/15. *Faculty research:* Teaching/learning methods, continuing professional education, clinical reasoning, geriatrics, performing artists. *Unit head:* Dr. Nancy Powell, Director, 616-331-3356, Fax: 616-331-3350, E-mail: powelln@gvsu.edu. *Application contact:* Darlene Zwart, Student Services Coordinator, 616-331-3958, E-mail: zwartda@gvsu.edu.

Idaho State University, Office of Graduate Studies, Kasiska College of Health Professions, Department of Physical and Occupational Therapy, Program in Occupational Therapy, Pocatello, ID 83209. Offers MOT. *Accreditation:* AOTA. *Faculty:* 1 (woman) full-time. *Students:* 19 full-time (14 women). Average age 27. In 2006, 5 degrees awarded. *Degree requirements:* For master's, thesis, oral and written exam, comprehensive exam, registration. *Entrance requirements:* For master's, GRE General Test, minimum GPA of 3.0, 80 hours in 2 practice settings of occupational therapy. Additional exam requirements/recommendations for international students: Required—TOEFL (minimum score 600 paper-based; 213 computer-based). *Application deadline:* For fall admission, 7/1 for domestic students, 6/1 for international students; for spring admission, 12/1 for domestic students, 11/1 for international students. Applications are processed on a rolling basis. Application fee: $55. *Expenses:* Contact institution. *Financial support:* In 2006–07, teaching assistantships with full and partial tuition reimbursements (averaging $8,694 per year); career-related internships or fieldwork, Federal Work-Study, institutionally sponsored loans, and tuition waivers (full and partial) also available. Support available to part-time students. Financial award application deadline: 1/1. *Faculty research:* Human movement, health care.

Indiana University–Purdue University Indianapolis, Indiana University School of Medicine, School of Health and Rehabilitation Sciences, Indianapolis, IN 46202-2896. Offers health sciences education (MS); nutrition and dietetics (MS); occupational therapy (MS); physical therapy (DPT). Part-time and evening/weekend programs available. *Faculty:* 8 full-time (5 women). *Students:* 180 full-time (149 women), 35 part-time (21 women); includes 17 minority (6 African Americans, 7 Asian Americans or Pacific Islanders, 4 Hispanic Americans), 3 international. Average age 27. In 2006, 9 master's, 32 doctorates awarded. *Degree requirements:* For master's, thesis (for some programs). *Entrance requirements:* For master's, GRE General Test, minimum GPA of 3.0. Additional exam requirements/recommendations for international students: Required—TOEFL. *Application deadline:* For fall admission, 1/15 priority date for domestic students; for spring admission, 10/15 for domestic students. Application fee: $50 ($60 for international students). *Expenses:* Tuition, state resident: full-time $5,437; part-time $227 per credit hour. Tuition, nonresident: full-time $15,694; part-time $654 per credit hour. Required fees: $620. Tuition and fees vary according to course load, campus/location and program. *Financial support:* Fellowships, research assistantships, teaching assistantships, Federal Work-Study, institutionally sponsored loans, and scholarships/grants available. Support available to part-time students. Financial award applicants required to submit FAFSA. *Unit head:* Dr. Mark S. Sothmann, Dean of the School of Allied Health Sciences, 317-274-4702, E-mail: msothman@iupui.edu.

Ithaca College, Graduate Studies, School of Health Sciences and Human Performance, Program in Occupational Therapy, Ithaca, NY 14850-7020. Offers MS. Students enter the program as freshmen. *Accreditation:* AOTA. *Faculty:* 4 full-time (all women), 4 part-time/adjunct (all women). *Students:* 21 full-time (all women). Average age 22. In 2006, 22 degrees awarded. *Degree requirements:* For master's, clinical fieldwork, thesis optional. *Financial support:* In 2006–07, 20 students received support. Career-related internships or fieldwork, Federal Work-Study, institutionally sponsored loans, and scholarships/grants available. Support available to part-time students. Financial award applicants required to submit FAFSA. *Faculty research:* Development of clinical reasoning in occupational therapy, upper extremity dexterity and neuromotor control, aging and human occupations, occupational therapy for preschool and school-aged children, musician rehabilitation. *Unit head:* Dr. Diane Long, Graduate Chairperson, 607-274-3093.

James Madison University, College of Graduate and Outreach Programs, College of Integrated Science and Technology, Department of Health Sciences, Program in Occupational Therapy, Harrisonburg, VA 22807. Offers MOT. *Accreditation:* AOTA. Part-time programs available. *Students:* 23 full-time (21 women). Average age 27. *Entrance requirements:* For master's, GRE General Test, GRE Subject Test, 3 reference forms, evidence of one instructional experience, documentation of competency in computer technology and info seeking skills. *Application deadline:* For fall admission, 2/1 priority date for domestic students; for spring admission, 9/1 priority date for domestic students. Application fee: $55. *Expenses:* Tuition, state resident: full-time $6,336; part-time $264 per credit hour. Tuition, nonresident: full-time $17,832; part-time $743 per credit hour. *Financial support:* Application deadline: 3/1. *Unit head:* Dr. Jeff Loveland, Coordinator, 540-568-2399.

Kean University, College of Natural, Applied and Health Sciences, Program in Occupational Therapy, Union, NJ 07083. Offers MS. *Accreditation:* AOTA. Part-time and evening/weekend programs available. *Faculty:* 3 full-time (all women). *Students:* 60 full-time (54 women), 1 (woman) part-time; includes 8 minority (2 African Americans, 4 Asian Americans or Pacific Islanders, 2 Hispanic Americans). Average age 25. 83 applicants, 55% accepted, 26 enrolled. In 2006, 8 degrees awarded. *Degree requirements:* For master's, 6 months of field work, final project. *Entrance requirements:* For master's, minimum GPA of 3.0, 3 letters of recommendation, interview. *Application deadline:* For fall admission, 2/1 for domestic students. Application fee: $60 ($150 for international students). *Expenses:* Tuition, state resident: full-time $8,856; part-time $369 per credit. Tuition, nonresident: full-time $11,256; part-time $469 per credit. *Financial support:* In 2006–07, 12 research assistantships with full tuition reimbursements (averaging $3,217 per year) were awarded. *Unit head:* Dr. Lynne Richard, Program Coordinator, 908-737-3384, E-mail: lynricha@kean.edu. *Application contact:* Joanne Morris, Director of Graduate Admissions, 908-737-3355, Fax: 908-737-3354, E-mail: grad-adm@kean.edu.

Keuka College, Program in Occupational Therapy, Keuka Park, NY 14478-0098. Offers MS. *Accreditation:* AOTA. *Faculty:* 5 full-time (3 women). *Students:* 12 full-time (10 women).

Occupational Therapy

Keuka College (continued)

Average age 23. 12 applicants, 100% accepted. In 2006, 16 degrees awarded. *Degree requirements:* For master's, thesis or alternative, clinical internships. *Entrance requirements:* For master's, minimum GPA of 3.0, BS in occupational therapy at Keuka College. Additional exam requirements/recommendations for international students: Required—TOEFL (minimum score 550 paper-based; 213 computer-based). *Application deadline:* For fall admission, 8/15 priority date for domestic students; for winter admission, 12/15 priority date for domestic students; for spring admission, 4/15 priority date for domestic students. Applications are processed on a rolling basis. Application fee: $30. *Expenses: Contact institution. Unit head:* Dr. Vicki Smith, Associate Professor and Chair, 315-279-5666, Fax: 315-279-5439, E-mail: vlsmith@mail.keuka.edu.

Maryville University of Saint Louis, School of Health Professions, Occupational Therapy Program, St. Louis, MO 63141-7299. Offers MOT. *Accreditation:* AOTA. *Application deadline:* Applications are processed on a rolling basis. Application fee: $20. Electronic applications accepted. *Expenses:* Tuition: Full-time $17,800; part-time $555 per credit. Required fees: $55 per semester. Tuition and fees vary according to degree level and program. *Financial support:* Career-related internships or fieldwork, Federal Work-Study, and campus employment available. Financial award application deadline: 7/31. *Faculty research:* Older driver safety rehabilitation options, adaptive equipment and training remediation, injured workers disability interventions. *Unit head:* Dr. Paula Bohr, Director, 314-529-9682, Fax: 314-529-9139, E-mail: pbohr@maryville.edu. *Application contact:* 314-529-9350, Fax: 314-529-9927, E-mail: admissions@maryville.edu.

McMaster University, Faculty of Health Sciences, Professional Program in Occupational Therapy, Hamilton, ON L8S 4M2, Canada. Offers M Sc. *Students:* 118 full-time. In 2006, 48 degrees awarded. *Degree requirements:* For master's, coursework, fieldwork and independent research project. *Entrance requirements:* For master's, minimum B average over last 60 undergraduate units. Additional exam requirements/recommendations for international students: Required—TOEFL (minimum score 600 paper-based; 250 computer-based). Application fee: $225 ($250 for international students). *Unit head:* Prof. Deborah Stewart, Assistant Dean, 905-525-9140 Ext. 27803. *Application contact:* Dr. Mary Law, Associate Dean, 905-525-9140 Ext. 22867, Fax: 905-524-0069.

Medical College of Georgia, School of Allied Health Sciences, Programs in Allied Health Sciences, Department of Occupational Therapy, Augusta, GA 30912-1500. Offers MHS, MS. *Accreditation:* AOTA. Part-time programs available. *Faculty:* 6 full-time (5 women). *Students:* 93 full-time (80 women); includes 17 minority (13 African Americans, 2 Asian Americans or Pacific Islanders, 2 Hispanic Americans). Average age 29. 58 applicants, 45% accepted, 21 enrolled. In 2006, 35 degrees awarded. *Degree requirements:* For master's, thesis. *Entrance requirements:* For master's, GRE General Test. Additional exam requirements/recommendations for international students: Required—TOEFL (minimum score 550 paper-based; 213 computer-based; 79 iBT). *Application deadline:* For fall admission, 2/15 for domestic students. Applications are processed on a rolling basis. Application fee: $30. Electronic applications accepted. *Expenses:* Tuition, state resident: full-time $2,293; part-time $192 per credit hour. Tuition, nonresident: full-time $9,169; part-time $765 per credit hour. Required fees: $293 per semester. *Financial support:* Federal Work-Study and institutionally sponsored loans available. Support available to part-time students. Financial award application deadline: 5/31; financial award applicants required to submit FAFSA. *Unit head:* Dr. Kathy Bradley, Chair and Associate Professor, 706-721-3641, Fax: 706-721-9718, E-mail: kbradley@mail.mcg.edu.

Medical University of South Carolina, College of Health Professions, Department of Rehabilitation Sciences, Program in Occupational Therapy, Charleston, SC 29425-0002. Offers MSR. *Accreditation:* AOTA. *Faculty:* 4 full-time (3 women), 3 part-time/adjunct (1 woman). *Students:* 76 full-time (70 women); includes 4 minority (2 African Americans, 1 Asian American or Pacific Islander, 1 Hispanic American). Average age 25. 48 applicants, 60% accepted, 27 enrolled. In 2006, 29 degrees awarded. *Degree requirements:* For master's, thesis or alternative, research project. *Entrance requirements:* For master's, GRE General Test, interview, minimum GPA of 3.0, references. Additional exam requirements/recommendations for international students: Required—TOEFL (minimum score 600 paper-based; 250 computer-based). *Application deadline:* For fall admission, 1/15 priority date for domestic and international students; for spring admission, 11/1 for international students. Application fee: $75. Electronic applications accepted. *Financial support:* Federal Work-Study and scholarships/grants available. Support available to part-time students. Financial award application deadline: 3/15; financial award applicants required to submit FAFSA. *Unit head:* Dr. Maralynne Mitcham, Director, 843-792-9734, Fax: 843-792-0710, E-mail: mitchamm@musc.edu. *Application contact:* Susan Johnson, Student Services Coordinator, 843-792-2961, Fax: 843-792-0710, E-mail: johnsoss@musc.edu.

Mercy College, Division of Health Professions, Program in Occupational Therapy, Dobbs Ferry, NY 10522-1189. Offers MS. *Accreditation:* AOTA. Evening/weekend programs available. *Students:* 63 full-time (53 women), 21 part-time (19 women); includes 40 minority (22 African Americans, 7 Asian Americans or Pacific Islanders, 11 Hispanic Americans). Average age 32. In 2006, 21 degrees awarded. *Degree requirements:* For master's, thesis, fieldwork. *Entrance requirements:* For master's, minimum GPA of 3.0, interview. Additional exam requirements/recommendations for international students: Required—TOEFL. *Application deadline:* For fall admission, 11/15 for domestic students. Application fee: $62. *Expenses:* Tuition: Part-time $595 per credit. Required fees: $9 per credit. Tuition and fees vary according to program. *Financial support:* Career-related internships or fieldwork, Federal Work-Study, and institutionally sponsored loans available. Financial award applicants required to submit FAFSA. *Faculty research:* Occupational therapy intervention, outcomes and assessment. *Unit head:* Joan Toglia, Director, 914-674-7815 Ext. 600, Fax: 914-674-7840, E-mail: otprogram@mercy.edu. *Application contact:* Kathleen Jackson, Director of Admissions, 800-Mercy-NY, Fax: 914-674-7382, E-mail: admissions@mercy.edu.

Midwestern University, Downers Grove Campus, College of Health Sciences, Illinois Campus, Program in Occupational Therapy, Downers Grove, IL 60515-1235. Offers MOT. *Accreditation:* AOTA. *Faculty:* 7 full-time (6 women). *Students:* 75 full-time (72 women); includes 9 minority (3 African Americans, 3 Asian Americans or Pacific Islanders, 3 Hispanic Americans). Average age 25. 61 applicants, 79% accepted, 25 enrolled. In 2006, 13 degrees awarded. *Entrance requirements:* For master's, GRE General Test. *Application deadline:* Applications are processed on a rolling basis. Application fee: $50. *Expenses: Contact institution. Financial support:* Federal Work-Study and scholarships/grants available. Financial award applicants required to submit FAFSA. *Unit head:* Kimberly A Bryze, Director, 630-515-7226, E-mail: kbryze@midwestern.edu. *Application contact:* Michael Laken, Director of Admissions, 630-515-6148, Fax: 630-971-6086, E-mail: admissil@midwestern.edu.

Announcement: Midwestern University is committed to educating the health-care team of the new century. The University administers the Chicago College of Osteopathic Medicine, the Chicago College of Pharmacy, the College of Health Sciences, the Arizona College of Osteopathic Medicine, and the College of Pharmacy–Glendale. The Occupational Therapy Program offers the Master of Occupational Therapy (MOT) degree at both the Downers Grove and Glendale campuses. Focusing on holistic health care, the program includes collaborative learning between OT students and other health professions students. The curriculum is designed to prepare entry-level practitioners to provide expanded occupational therapy services in large, small, traditional, and nontraditional community and clinical practice settings that require independent judgment, leadership, and self-directed practice. Contact the Office of Admissions, Midwestern University, 800-458-6253 (Downers Grove campus); 888-247-9277 (Glendale campus); e-mail: admissil@midwestern.edu (Downers Grove campus); admissaz@midwestern.edu (Glendale campus); WWW: http://www.midwestern.edu.

Midwestern University, Glendale Campus, College of Health Sciences, Arizona Campus, Program in Occupational Therapy, Glendale, AZ 85308. Offers MOT. *Accreditation:* AOTA.

Faculty: 4 full-time (all women), 3 part-time/adjunct (all women). *Students:* 41 full-time (37 women); includes 6 minority (1 African American, 3 Asian Americans or Pacific Islanders, 2 Hispanic Americans). Average age 26. 25 applicants, 84% accepted, 15 enrolled. In 2006, 5 degrees awarded. *Entrance requirements:* For master's, GRE. *Application deadline:* Applications are processed on a rolling basis. Application fee: $50. *Expenses: Contact institution. Unit head:* Christine R. Merchant, Director, 623-572-3638, E-mail: cmerch@midwestern.edu. *Application contact:* James Walters, Director of Admissions, 888-247-9277, Fax: 623-572-3340, E-mail: admissaz@midwestern.edu.

Milligan College, Program in Occupational Therapy, Milligan College, TN 37682. Offers MSOT. *Accreditation:* AOTA. *Faculty:* 5 full-time (3 women), 2 part-time/adjunct (1 woman). *Students:* 44 full-time (38 women), 3 part-time (all women). Average age 28. 40 applicants, 80% accepted, 26 enrolled. In 2006, 21 degrees awarded. *Degree requirements:* For master's, thesis. *Entrance requirements:* For master's, GRE. Additional exam requirements/recommendations for international students: Required—TOEFL (minimum score 550 paper-based; 213 computer-based; 80 iBT). *Application deadline:* For spring admission, 4/1 priority date for domestic and international students. Applications are processed on a rolling basis. Application fee: $30. Electronic applications accepted. *Expenses: Contact institution.* Tuition and fees vary according to course load and program. *Financial support:* In 2006–07, 1 teaching assistantship (averaging $6,000 per year) was awarded; career-related internships or fieldwork and institutionally sponsored loans also available. Financial award application deadline: 4/15; financial award applicants required to submit FAFSA. *Faculty research:* Handwriting, creativity, leadership in rehabilitation, workforce shortages in occupational therapy, evidence-based practice in industrial rehabilitation. *Unit head:* Jeff Snodgrass, Program Director and Associate Professor, 423-975-8010, Fax: 423-975-8019, E-mail: jsnodgrass@milligan.edu. *Application contact:* Claire Marr, Office Manager and Admissions Representative, 423-975-8010, Fax: 423-975-8019, E-mail: cmarr@milligan.edu.

Mount Mary College, Graduate Programs, Program in Occupational Therapy, Milwaukee, WI 53222-4597. Offers MS. *Accreditation:* AOTA. Part-time and evening/weekend programs available. *Faculty:* 2 full-time (both women), 4 part-time/adjunct (all women). *Students:* 16 full-time (all women), 14 part-time (all women); includes 3 minority (2 African Americans, 1 Hispanic American). Average age 30. 27 applicants, 78% accepted, 17 enrolled. In 2006, 18 degrees awarded. *Degree requirements:* For master's, thesis or alternative, professional development portfolio, comprehensive exam. *Entrance requirements:* For master's, minimum GPA of 2.75, occupational therapy license, 1 year of work experience. Additional exam requirements/recommendations for international students: Required—TOEFL (minimum score 500 paper-based; 173 computer-based). *Application deadline:* For fall admission, 10/15 priority date for domestic and international students; for spring admission, 3/15 for domestic and international students. Application fee: $35 ($75 for international students). *Expenses:* Tuition: Part-time $490 per credit. Required fees: $48 per term. Tuition and fees vary according to course load and program. *Financial support:* Career-related internships or fieldwork available. Support available to part-time students. Financial award application deadline: 5/1; financial award applicants required to submit FAFSA. *Faculty research:* Clinical reasoning, occupational science, sensory integration. *Unit head:* Dr. Jane Olson, Director, 414-258-4810 Ext. 348, E-mail: olsonj@mtmary.edu.

New York Institute of Technology, Graduate Division, School of Allied Health and Life Sciences, Program in Occupational Therapy, Old Westbury, NY 11568-8000. Offers MS. *Accreditation:* AOTA. *Students:* 34 full-time (28 women), 3 part-time (all women); includes 13 minority (6 African Americans, 5 Asian Americans or Pacific Islanders, 2 Hispanic Americans), 1 international. Average age 29. 30 applicants, 73% accepted, 2 enrolled. In 2006, 9 degrees awarded. *Degree requirements:* For master's, thesis. *Entrance requirements:* For master's, minimum GPA of 2.0 in science or mathematics, 2.5 overall; 100 hours of supervised volunteer work; interview; 2 professional letters of recommendation. Additional exam requirements/recommendations for international students: Required—TOEFL (minimum score 550 paper-based; 213 computer-based). *Application deadline:* For fall admission, 7/1 priority date for domestic students; for spring admission, 12/1 priority date for domestic students. Applications are processed on a rolling basis. Application fee: $50. Electronic applications accepted. *Expenses:* Tuition: Full-time $16,800; part-time $700 per credit. *Financial support:* Research assistantships with partial tuition reimbursements available. Financial award applicants required to submit FAFSA. *Unit head:* Hermine Plotnick, Chair, 516-686-3738, Fax: 516-686-3795, E-mail: hplotnic@nyit.edu. *Application contact:* Jacquelyn Nealon, Dean of Admissions and Financial Aid, 516-686-7925, Fax: 516-686-7613, E-mail: jnealon@nyit.edu.

New York University, Steinhardt School of Culture, Education and Human Development, Department of Occupational Therapy, New York, NY 10012-1019. Offers advanced occupational therapy (MA); occupational therapy (MA, MS, DPS, PhD). *Accreditation:* AOTA (one or more programs are accredited). Part-time and evening/weekend programs available. *Faculty:* 9 full-time (7 women), 8 part-time/adjunct (7 women). *Students:* 159 full-time (150 women), 29 part-time (26 women); includes 28 minority (5 African Americans, 16 Asian Americans or Pacific Islanders, 7 Hispanic Americans), 20 international. 253 applicants, 64% accepted, 60 enrolled. In 2006, 49 master's, 3 doctorates awarded. Terminal master's awarded for partial completion of doctoral program. *Degree requirements:* For master's, thesis (for some programs), project; for doctorate, thesis/dissertation. *Entrance requirements:* For doctorate, GRE General Test, interview. Additional exam requirements/recommendations for international students: Required—TOEFL. *Application deadline:* For fall admission, 12/15 priority date for domestic and international students; for spring admission, 11/1 for domestic and international students. Applications are processed on a rolling basis. Application fee: $50. *Expenses:* Tuition: Part-time $1,080 per unit. Required fees: $56 per unit. $329 per term. Tuition and fees vary according to program. *Financial support:* Fellowships with full and partial tuition reimbursements, teaching assistantships with full and partial tuition reimbursements, career-related internships or fieldwork, Federal Work-Study, scholarships/grants, traineeships, tuition waivers (partial), and unspecified assistantships available. Support available to part-time students. Financial award application deadline: 2/1; financial award applicants required to submit FAFSA. *Faculty research:* Pediatrics, assistive rehabilitation technology, adaptive computer technology for children with disabilities, cognitive bases of adult disablement, upper limb rehabilitation. *Unit head:* Dr. Jim Hinojosa, Chairperson, 212-998-5825, Fax: 212-995-4044. *Application contact:* 212-998-5030, Fax: 212-995-4328, E-mail: steinhardt.gradadmissions@nyu.edu.

Nova Southeastern University, Health Professions Division, College of Allied Health and Nursing, Department of Occupational Therapy, Fort Lauderdale, FL 33314-7796. Offers MOT, OTD, PhD. *Accreditation:* AOTA (one or more programs are accredited). Postbaccalaureate distance learning degree programs offered. *Faculty:* 11 full-time (9 women), 6 part-time/adjunct (3 women). *Students:* 69 full-time (63 women), 41 part-time (38 women); includes 29 minority (12 African Americans, 4 Asian Americans or Pacific Islanders, 13 Hispanic Americans), 1 international. Average age 27. 96 applicants, 75% accepted, 47 enrolled. In 2006, 19 master's, 3 doctorates awarded. *Median time to degree:* Of those who began their doctoral program in fall 1998, 100% received their degree in 8 years or less. *Degree requirements:* For master's, thesis or alternative; for doctorate, thesis/dissertation (for some programs), comprehensive exam (for some programs), registration. *Entrance requirements:* For master's and doctorate, GRE General Test. *Application deadline:* Applications are processed on a rolling basis. Application fee: $50. Electronic applications accepted. *Financial support:* Federal Work-Study and institutionally sponsored loans available. *Faculty research:* Older adult falls prevention, sensory integration, diabetes, autism, literacy. *Unit head:* Dr. Sandee M. Dunbar, Chair, 954-262-1243, Fax: 954-262-2290, E-mail: sdunbar@nova.edu. *Application contact:* Corinne Kessler, Admissions Counselor, 954-262-1110, Fax: 954-262-2282, E-mail: kcorinne@nsu.nova.edu.

The Ohio State University, College of Medicine, School of Allied Medical Professions, Program in Occupational Therapy, Columbus, OH 43210. Offers MOT. *Accreditation:* AOTA. *Students:* 63 full-time (61 women), 27 part-time (23 women); includes 9 minority (4 African Americans, 2 Asian Americans or Pacific Islanders, 3 Hispanic Americans), 3 international.

Average age 26. In 2006, 27 degrees awarded. *Entrance requirements:* For master's, GRE General Test. Additional exam requirements/recommendations for international students: Required—TOEFL (paper-based 550; computer-based 213) or Michigan English Language Assessment Battery (82). *Application deadline:* For fall admission, 8/15 priority date for domestic students, 7/1 priority date for international students; for winter admission, 12/1 priority date for domestic students, 11/1 priority date for international students; for spring admission, 3/1 priority date for domestic students, 2/1 priority date for international students. Applications are processed on a rolling basis. Application fee: $40 ($50 for international students). Electronic applications accepted. *Expenses:* Tuition, state resident: full-time $9,438. Tuition, nonresident: full-time $22,791. Tuition and fees vary according to course load, campus/location and program. *Unit head:* Dr. Jane D. Case-Smith, Director, 614-292-5824, Fax: 614-292-0210, E-mail: case-smith.1@osu.edu. *Application contact:* 614-292-9444, Fax: 614-292-3895, E-mail: domestic.grad@osu.edu.

Pacific University, School of Occupational Therapy, Forest Grove, OR 97116-1797. Offers MOT. *Accreditation:* AOTA. *Faculty:* 6 full-time (4 women), 4 part-time/adjunct (all women). *Students:* 64 full-time (57 women), 1 (woman) part-time; includes 8 minority (5 Asian Americans or Pacific Islanders, 3 Hispanic Americans). Average age 27. 55 applicants, 58% accepted, 22 enrolled. In 2006, 17 degrees awarded. *Degree requirements:* For master's, research project, professional project. *Application deadline:* For fall admission, 12/1 priority date for domestic students. Applications are processed on a rolling basis. Application fee: $55. Electronic applications accepted. *Expenses: Contact institution. Financial support:* In 2006–07, 65 students received support; fellowships, research assistantships, teaching assistantships, career-related internships or fieldwork, Federal Work-Study, and scholarships/grants available. Support available to part-time students. Financial award applicants required to submit FAFSA. *Faculty research:* Cultural competency development, disability policy, scholarship of teaching and learning, driver rehabilitation and older adult visual perception, neurorehabilitation and motor learning. Total annual research expenditures: $3,500. *Unit head:* Dr. John A. White, Director, 503-352-7355, Fax: 503-352-2980, E-mail: whiteja@pacificu.edu. *Application contact:* Jon-Erik Larsen, Director of Graduate and Professional Admissions, 503-352-2900, Fax: 503-352-2975, E-mail: admissions@pacificu.edu.

Philadelphia University, School of Science and Health, Program in Occupational Therapy, Philadelphia, PA 19144-5497. Offers MS. *Accreditation:* AOTA. Evening/weekend programs available. *Faculty:* 3 full-time (all women), 3 part-time/adjunct (all women). *Students:* 42 full-time (34 women), 13 part-time (12 women); includes 1 African American. 77 applicants, 62% accepted, 29 enrolled. In 2006, 14 degrees awarded. *Degree requirements:* For master's, practicum. *Entrance requirements:* For master's, GRE or MAT. Additional exam requirements/recommendations for international students: Required—TOEFL (minimum score 550 paper-based; 213 computer-based; 79 iBT). *Application deadline:* For fall admission, 2/15 priority date for domestic students. Applications are processed on a rolling basis. Application fee: $35. Electronic applications accepted. *Financial support:* In 2006–07, research assistantships with partial tuition reimbursements (averaging $2,000 per year); career-related internships or fieldwork, Federal Work-Study, and unspecified assistantships also available. Financial award applicants required to submit FAFSA. *Unit head:* Catherine Verrier Piersol, Director, 215-951-6853, Fax: 215-951-2615, E-mail: piersolc@philau.edu. *Application contact:* Jack A. Klett, Director of Graduate Admissions, 215-951-2943, Fax: 215-951-2907, E-mail: gradadm@philau.edu.

Quinnipiac University, School of Health Sciences, Program in Occupational Therapy, Hamden, CT 06518-1940. Offers MOT. Students are admitted to the program as undergraduates. *Faculty:* 10 full-time (all women), 26 part-time/adjunct (21 women). *Students:* 58 full-time (53 women); includes 8 minority (3 Asian Americans or Pacific Islanders, 5 Hispanic Americans). Average age 21. 36 applicants, 100% accepted, 36 enrolled. In 2006, 20 degrees awarded. *Median time to degree:* Master's–1.5 years full-time. *Entrance requirements:* Additional exam requirements/recommendations for international students: Required—TOEFL (minimum score 575 paper-based; 233 computer-based; 90 iBT). *Expenses:* Tuition: Part-time $675 per credit. Required fees: $30 per credit. *Financial support:* Scholarships/grants and unspecified assistantships available. Financial award application deadline: 4/15. *Unit head:* Kimberly Hartmann, Chairperson, 203-582-8679, E-mail: kim.hartmann@quinnipiac.edu. *Application contact:* 800-462-1944, E-mail: admissions@quinnipiac.edu.

The Richard Stockton College of New Jersey, Graduate Programs, Program in Occupational Therapy, Pomona, NJ 08240-0195. Offers MSOT. *Accreditation:* AOTA. *Faculty:* 7 full-time (all women). *Students:* 40 full-time (39 women), 18 part-time (16 women); includes 2 minority (both Hispanic Americans) Average age 33. In 2006, 12 degrees awarded. *Degree requirements:* For master's, fieldwork, research project. *Entrance requirements:* For master's, minimum GPA of 3.0, 120 hours of work, volunteer or community service. *Application deadline:* For fall admission, 4/1 for domestic students. Application fee: $50. *Expenses:* Tuition, state resident: full-time $9,746. Tuition, nonresident: full-time $14,462. Required fees: $2,340. *Financial support:* Career-related internships or fieldwork and scholarships/grants available. Support available to part-time students. Financial award application deadline: 3/1. *Faculty research:* Home health based occupational therapy for women with HIV/AIDS. *Unit head:* Dr. Victoria Scindler, Program Director, 609-652-6018, E-mail: msot@stockton.edu. *Application contact:* Alison Henry, Associate Director of Admissions, 609-652-4261, Fax: 609-626-5541, E-mail: admissions@stockston.edu.

Rockhurst University, School of Graduate and Professional Studies, Program in Occupational Therapy, Kansas City, MO 64110-2561. Offers MOT. *Accreditation:* AOTA. Part-time programs available. *Faculty:* 5 full-time (all women), 2 part-time/adjunct (both women). *Students:* 28 full-time (24 women), 2 part-time (both women); includes 7 minority (4 African Americans, 1 American Indian/Alaska Native, 2 Hispanic Americans). Average age 26. 50 applicants, 60% accepted, 23 enrolled. In 2006, 28 degrees awarded. *Entrance requirements:* For master's, minimum GPA of 3.0. *Application deadline:* For fall admission, 1/15 priority date for domestic students. Applications are processed on a rolling basis. Application fee: $25. Electronic applications accepted. *Expenses:* Tuition: Full-time $9,810; part-time $6,540 per year. Required fees: $400 per term. *Financial support:* In 2006–07, 5 research assistantships, 10 teaching assistantships were awarded; career-related internships or fieldwork, institutionally sponsored loans, and unspecified assistantships also available. Financial award application deadline: 4/1; financial award applicants required to submit FAFSA. *Faculty research:* Problem-based learning, cognitive rehabilitation behavioral state in infants and children, adult neurological defects and prosthetics. *Unit head:* Dr. Kris Vacek, Chair, 816-501-4635, Fax: 816-501-4643, E-mail: kris.vacek@rockhurst.edu. *Application contact:* Jyll Kafer, Director of Graduate Recruitment Admission, 816-501-4097, Fax: 816-501-4241, E-mail: jyll.kafer@rockhurst.edu.

Rush University, College of Health Sciences, Department of Occupational Therapy, Chicago, IL 60612-3832. Offers MS. *Accreditation:* AOTA. *Degree requirements:* For master's, thesis optional. *Entrance requirements:* For master's, GRE General Test. Electronic applications accepted. *Faculty research:* Intervention and practice strategies in the stroke population and the impact of evidenced based interventions.

Sacred Heart University, Graduate Studies, College of Education and Health Professions, Program in Occupational Therapy, Fairfield, CT 06825-1000. Offers MSOT. *Accreditation:* AOTA. *Faculty:* 5 full-time (all women), 15 part-time/adjunct (13 women). *Students:* 17 full-time (16 women), 15 part-time (all women), 2 international. Average age 27. 38 applicants, 92% accepted, 20 enrolled. In 2006, 18 degrees awarded. *Entrance requirements:* For master's, minimum GPA of 3.0. Additional exam requirements/recommendations for international students: Required—TOEFL (minimum score 550 paper-based; 213 computer-based). *Application deadline:* For fall admission, 1/15 priority date for domestic students. Applications are processed on a rolling basis. Application fee: $50 ($100 for international students). Electronic applications accepted. *Expenses: Contact institution. Financial support:* Career-related internships or fieldwork, institutionally sponsored loans, and unspecified assistantships available. Support available to part-time students. Financial award applicants required to submit FAFSA. *Unit head:* Dr. Jody Bortone, Director, 203-396-8023, Fax: 203-365-7508, E-mail: gradstudies@sacredheart.edu. *Application contact:* Kathy Dilks, Assistant Dean of Graduate Admissions, Health Professions, 203-396-8259, Fax: 203-365-4732, E-mail: gradstudies@sacredheart.edu.

Sage Graduate School, Graduate School, Division of Health and Rehabilitation Sciences, Program in Occupational Therapy, Troy, NY 12180-4115. Offers MS. *Accreditation:* AOTA. Part-time and evening/weekend programs available. *Faculty:* 8 full-time (all women), 3 part-time/adjunct (all women). *Students:* 28 full-time (26 women), 12 part-time (11 women); includes 2 minority (1 African American, 1 Asian American or Pacific Islander). Average age 26. 16 applicants, 81% accepted, 11 enrolled. In 2006, 7 degrees awarded. *Application deadline:* Applications are processed on a rolling basis. Application fee: $40. *Expenses:* Tuition: Full-time $9,270; part-time $515 per credit hour. *Financial support:* Career-related internships or fieldwork, scholarships/grants, and unspecified assistantships available. Support available to part-time students. *Unit head:* Wendy Krupnick, Director of Occupational Therapy Program, 518-244-2056, E-mail: krupnw@sage.edu. *Application contact:* Shannon K. Easton, Director of Graduate and Adult Admission, 518-244-2443, Fax: 518-244-6880, E-mail: sgsadm@sage.edu.

Saginaw Valley State University, Crystal M. Lange College of Nursing and Health Sciences, Program in Occupational Therapy, University Center, MI 48710. Offers MSOT. *Accreditation:* AOTA. *Faculty:* 6 full-time (4 women). *Students:* 24 full-time (23 women). Average age 23. 1 applicant, 0% accepted. *Expenses:* Tuition, state resident: full-time $7,225; part-time $301 per credit hour. Tuition, nonresident: full-time $13,888; part-time $579 per credit hour. Required fees: $330; $14 per credit hour. Tuition and fees vary according to course load. *Unit head:* Dr. Margaret Flatt, Assistant Dean, 989-964-4130, Fax: 989-964-4024, E-mail: flatt@svsu.edu.

St. Ambrose University, College of Education and Health Sciences, Program in Occupational Therapy, Davenport, IA 52803-2898. Offers MOT. *Accreditation:* AOTA. *Faculty:* 8 full-time (7 women), 5 part-time/adjunct (3 women). *Students:* 42 full-time (39 women). Average age 26. 30 applicants, 97% accepted, 29 enrolled. In 2006, 25 degrees awarded. *Degree requirements:* For master's, board exams. *Entrance requirements:* For master's, 50 hours of volunteer experience in 2 occupational therapy settings, minimum GPA of 2.7, essay or interview on campus, 3 letters of reference. Additional exam requirements/recommendations for international students: Required—TOEFL. *Application deadline:* For fall admission, 1/31 for domestic students. Application fee: $25. Electronic applications accepted. *Financial support:* In 2006–07, 6 students received support, including 2 research assistantships with partial tuition reimbursements available (averaging $4,000 per year); career-related internships or fieldwork, Federal Work-Study, scholarships/grants, tuition waivers (partial), and unspecified assistantships also available. Financial award application deadline: 8/15; financial award applicants required to submit FAFSA. *Unit head:* Phyllis Wenthe, Director, 563-333-6276, Fax: 563-333-6243, E-mail: pwenthe@saunix.sau.edu. *Application contact:* Elizabeth Berridge, Director of Graduate Student Recruitment, 563-333-6271, Fax: 563-333-6268, E-mail: berridgeelizabethb@sau.edu.

Saint Francis University, Department of Occupational Therapy, Loretto, PA 15940-0600. Offers MOT. *Accreditation:* AOTA. *Faculty:* 5 full-time (3 women). *Students:* 11 full-time (9 women). Average age 22. 11 applicants, 100% accepted, 11 enrolled. In 2006, 19 degrees awarded. *Degree requirements:* For master's, one foreign language, thesis. *Expenses:* Tuition: Part-time $661 per credit. Tuition and fees vary according to program. *Faculty research:* Retention, technology, work injury, distance learning. *Unit head:* Dr. Donald Walkovich, Chair, 814-472-3899, Fax: 814-472-3950, E-mail: dwalkovich@francis.edu.

Saint Louis University, Graduate School, Doisy College of Health Sciences, Department of Occupational Science and Occupational Therapy, St. Louis, MO 63103-2097. Offers MOT. *Accreditation:* AOTA. *Faculty:* 11 full-time (all women), 6 part-time/adjunct (all women). *Students:* 43 full-time (41 women); includes 1 minority (African American) Average age 24. 28 applicants, 68% accepted, 14 enrolled. In 2006, 22 degrees awarded. *Degree requirements:* For master's, project. *Entrance requirements:* Additional exam requirements/recommendations for international students: Required—TOEFL (minimum score 525 paper-based; 194 computer-based). *Application deadline:* For fall admission, 7/1 for domestic and international students; for spring admission, 11/1 for domestic and international students. Application fee: $40. *Expenses:* Tuition: Part-time $800 per credit hour. Required fees: $105 per semester. *Financial support:* In 2006–07, 1 student received support. Federal Work-Study, scholarships/grants, health care benefits, and unspecified assistantships available. Support available to part-time students. *Faculty research:* Autism spectrum and Asperger's disease, early intervention with children of homeless families, disability awareness program development of developing countries, environmental adaptations and universal design for persons who are disabled and/or aging, physical activity models for persons with dementia. Total annual research expenditures: $3,000. *Unit head:* Dr. Karen Barney, Chairperson, 314-577-8514, Fax: 314-977-5415, E-mail: barneykf@slu.edu.

Salem State College, Graduate School, Program in Occupational Therapy, Salem, MA 01970-5353. Offers MS. *Accreditation:* AOTA. Part-time and evening/weekend programs available. *Students:* Average age 39.Application fee: $35. *Unit head:* Jean MacLachlan, Coordinator, 978-542-6075, E-mail: jmaclachlan@salemstate.edu.

Samuel Merritt College, Department of Occupational Therapy, Oakland, CA 94609-3108. Offers MOT. *Accreditation:* AOTA. *Degree requirements:* For master's, project. *Entrance requirements:* For master's, GRE General Test, minimum GPA of 2.6 in science, 2.8 overall; 40-70 hours of volunteer or professional occupational therapy experience; interview. Additional exam requirements/recommendations for international students: Required—TOEFL. Expenses: Contact institution.

San Jose State University, Graduate Studies and Research, College of Applied Sciences and Arts, Department of Occupational Therapy, San Jose, CA 95192-0001. Offers MS. *Accreditation:* AOTA. *Students:* 88 full-time (84 women), 2 part-time (both women); includes 23 minority (1 African American, 13 Asian Americans or Pacific Islanders, 9 Hispanic Americans). Average age 28. 171 applicants, 64% accepted, 68 enrolled. In 2006, 48 degrees awarded. *Degree requirements:* For master's, thesis or alternative. *Entrance requirements:* For master's, GRE, minimum GPA of 3.0. *Application deadline:* For fall admission, 6/29 for domestic students; for spring admission, 11/30 for domestic students. Applications are processed on a rolling basis. Application fee: $59. Electronic applications accepted. *Financial support:* Career-related internships or fieldwork, Federal Work-Study, and institutionally sponsored loans available. Financial award applicants required to submit FAFSA. *Faculty research:* Generic occupational therapy, psychosocial rehabilitation, physical rehabilitation, organizational development, occupational performance. *Unit head:* Marti Southam, Chair, 408-924-3070, Fax: 408-924-3088.

Seton Hall University, School of Graduate Medical Education, Program in Occupational Therapy, South Orange, NJ 07079-2697. Offers MS. *Accreditation:* AOTA. *Faculty:* 5 full-time (4 women), 15 part-time/adjunct (11 women). *Students:* 41 full-time (38 women), 1 (woman) part-time. Average age 28. 55 applicants, 87% accepted, 13 enrolled. In 2006, 14 degrees awarded. *Entrance requirements:* For master's, health care experience, minimum GPA of 3.0, 50 hours of occupational therapy volunteer work, pre-requisite courses. Additional exam requirements/recommendations for international students: Required—TOEFL. *Application deadline:* For fall admission, 2/15 for domestic and international students. Applications are processed on a rolling basis. Application fee: $75. Electronic applications accepted. *Financial support:* In 2006–07, 3 students received support, including 3 teaching assistantships with partial tuition reimbursements available (averaging $1,000 per year). *Faculty research:* Occupational genesis, occupational technology, pediatric OT, community practice, families of children with special needs; family routines; complementary medicine and wellness. *Unit head:* Dr. Ruth Segal, Chair, 973-761-7145, Fax: 973-275-2370. *Application contact:* Deborah Verderosa, Director of Admissions, 973-275-2062, Fax: 973-275-2171, E-mail: gradmeded@shu.edu.

See Close-Up on page 1725.

Occupational Therapy

Shenandoah University, School of Health Professions, Division of Occupational Therapy, Winchester, VA 22601-5195. Offers MS. *Accreditation:* AOTA. *Faculty:* 3 full-time (all women), 2 part-time/adjunct (both women). *Students:* 30 full-time (28 women), 20 part-time (19 women). Average age 26. 25 applicants, 52% accepted, 11 enrolled. In 2006, 20 degrees awarded. *Degree requirements:* For master's, fieldwork. *Entrance requirements:* For master's, 24 hours of clinical exposure, 2 references, writing sample, minimum GPA of 3.0. Additional exam requirements/recommendations for international students: Required—TOEFL (minimum score 527 paper-based; 197 computer-based; 71 iBT). *Application deadline:* For fall admission, 7/1 for domestic students. Applications are processed on a rolling basis. Application fee: $30. Electronic applications accepted. *Expenses: Contact institution.* Full-time tuition and fees vary according to course load and program. *Financial support:* In 2006–07, 40 students received support. Institutionally sponsored loans, scholarships/grants, and ACT and FED loans available. Support available to part-time students. Financial award application deadline: 3/15; financial award applicants required to submit FAFSA. *Faculty research:* Evaluation of community programs; elder care—home care, guardianship, competence; sensory processing in autism, community life of Iraqi veterans. *Unit head:* Dr. Deborah Maar, Director, 540-665-5542, Fax: 540-665-5564, E-mail: dmaar@su.edu. *Application contact:* David Anthony, Dean of Admissions, 540-665-4581, Fax: 540-665-4627, E-mail: admit@su.edu.

Spalding University, Graduate Studies, College of Health and Natural Sciences, Auerbach School of Occupational Therapy, Louisville, KY 40203-2188. Offers occupational therapy (advanced-level) (MS); occupational therapy (entry-level) (MS). *Accreditation:* AOTA. *Degree requirements:* For master's, project. *Entrance requirements:* For master's, interview, letters of recommendation. Additional exam requirements/recommendations for international students: Required—TOEFL. Electronic applications accepted. *Faculty research:* High-risk youth, community-dwelling older adults, assistive technology, mother-infant relationships, community accessibility.

Springfield College, Graduate Programs, Program in Occupational Therapy, Springfield, MA 01109-3797. Offers M Ed, MS, CAS. *Accreditation:* AOTA (one or more programs are accredited). Part-time programs available. *Faculty:* 5 full-time (all women), 1 (woman) part-time/adjunct. *Students:* 70; includes 2 minority (1 Asian American or Pacific Islander, 1 Hispanic American), 1 international. Average age 27. 44 applicants, 89% accepted, 29 enrolled. In 2006, 13 degrees awarded. *Degree requirements:* For master's and CAS, research project. *Entrance requirements:* For master's, interview. Additional exam requirements/recommendations for international students: Required—TOEFL (minimum score 550 paper-based; 213 computer-based). *Application deadline:* For fall admission, 1/15 for domestic students; for winter admission, 11/1 for domestic students; for spring admission, 11/1 for domestic students. Applications are processed on a rolling basis. Application fee: $50. Electronic applications accepted. *Expenses:* Tuition: Full-time $12,222; part-time $679 per credit. Required fees: $25; $25 per year. One-time fee: $25 full-time. *Financial support:* In 2006–07, 4 teaching assistantships with partial tuition reimbursements were awarded; fellowships with partial tuition reimbursements, career-related internships or fieldwork, Federal Work-Study, institutionally sponsored loans, and tuition waivers (full and partial) also available. Financial award application deadline: 3/1. *Faculty research:* Gerontology, parental stress, assistive technology, learning disabilities. *Unit head:* Katherine Post, Director, 413-748-3785, Fax: 413-748-3796, E-mail: kpost@spfdcol.edu. *Application contact:* Donald James Shaw, Director of Graduate Admissions, 413-748-3060, Fax: 413-748-3069, E-mail: donald_shaw_jr@spfldcol.edu.

Stony Brook University, State University of New York, Stony Brook University Medical Center, Health Sciences Center, School of Health Technology and Management, Stony Brook, NY 11794. Offers community health (Advanced Certificate); health care management (Advanced Certificate); health care policy and management (MS); occupational therapy (MS); physical therapy (MS, DPT). *Accreditation:* APTA. Part-time programs available. *Faculty:* 26 full-time (15 women), 21 part-time/adjunct (12 women). *Students:* 198 full-time (147 women), 130 part-time (89 women); includes 87 minority (29 African Americans, 1 American Indian/Alaska Native, 37 Asian Americans or Pacific Islanders, 20 Hispanic Americans), 4 international. 907 applicants, 25% accepted. In 2006, 33 master's, 106 doctorates, 15 other advanced degrees awarded. *Degree requirements:* For master's, thesis. *Entrance requirements:* For master's, GRE General Test, minimum GPA of 3.0, work experience in field. *Application deadline:* For fall admission, 1/15 for domestic students. Application fee: $60. *Expenses:* Tuition, state resident: full-time $6,900; part-time $288 per credit. Tuition, nonresident: full-time $10,920; part-time $455 per credit. *Financial support:* In 2006–07, 1 fellowship was awarded; career-related internships or fieldwork, Federal Work-Study, and institutionally sponsored loans also available. Financial award application deadline: 3/15. *Faculty research:* Health promotion and disease prevention. Total annual research expenditures: $527,101. *Unit head:* Dr. Craig A. Lehmann, Dean, 631-444-2251, Fax: 631-444-7621. *Application contact:* Alan Leiken, Associate Dean for Graduate Studies, 631-444-3240, Fax: 631-444-7621.

Temple University, Health Sciences Center and Graduate School, College of Health Professions, Department of Occupational Therapy, Philadelphia, PA 19122-6096. Offers MOT, MS. *Accreditation:* AOTA. Part-time programs available. *Faculty:* 9 full-time (7 women). *Students:* 47 full-time (45 women), 32 part-time (27 women); includes 11 minority (7 African Americans, 4 Asian Americans or Pacific Islanders), 1 international. 77 applicants, 61% accepted, 26 enrolled. In 2006, 9 degrees awarded. *Degree requirements:* For master's, thesis, comprehensive exam (for some programs). *Entrance requirements:* For master's, GRE General Test or MAT, minimum GPA of 3.0, interview. Additional exam requirements/recommendations for international students: Required—TOEFL (minimum score 550 paper-based; 213 computer-based; 79 iBT). *Application deadline:* For fall admission, 8/1 for domestic students, 12/15 for international students; for spring admission, 12/1 for domestic students, 8/1 for international students. Applications are processed on a rolling basis. Application fee: $50. Electronic applications accepted. *Expenses: Contact institution.* Tuition and fees vary according to program. *Financial support:* Research assistantships, teaching assistantships with full tuition reimbursements, career-related internships or fieldwork, Federal Work-Study, and institutionally sponsored loans available. Financial award application deadline: 1/15; financial award applicants required to submit FAFSA. *Faculty research:* Pediatrics, elderly, sensory integration, education, participation. Total annual research expenditures: $150,000. *Unit head:* Dr. Moya Kinnealey, Chair, 215-707-4813, Fax: 215-707-7656, E-mail: moya.kinnealey@temple.edu.

See Close-Up on page 1741.

Texas Tech University Health Sciences Center, School of Allied Health Sciences, Program in Occupational Therapy, Lubbock, TX 79430. Offers MOT. *Accreditation:* AOTA. *Faculty:* 5 full-time (3 women). *Students:* 91 full-time (81 women); includes 5 African Americans, 13 Hispanic Americans. Average age 24. 74 applicants, 47% accepted, 35 enrolled. In 2006, 28 degrees awarded. *Entrance requirements:* Additional exam requirements/recommendations for international students: Required—TOEFL. *Application deadline:* For fall admission, 10/15 priority date for domestic students; for spring admission, 2/1 priority date for domestic students. Application fee: $35. Electronic applications accepted. *Financial support:* Career-related internships or fieldwork, institutionally sponsored loans, and scholarships/grants available. Financial award application deadline: 9/1; financial award applicants required to submit FAFSA. *Unit head:* Dr. Steve Sawyer, Chair, 806-743-3226, Fax: 806-743-3249, E-mail: steve.sawyer@ttuhsc.edu. *Application contact:* Jeri Moravcik, Assistant Director of Admissions and Student Affairs, 806-743-3220, Fax: 806-743-2994, E-mail: jeri.moravcik@ttuhsc.edu.

Texas Woman's University, Graduate School, College of Health Sciences, School of Occupational Therapy, Denton, TX 76201. Offers MA, MOT, PhD. *Accreditation:* AOTA (one or more programs are accredited). Part-time and evening/weekend programs available. Post-baccalaureate distance learning degree programs offered. *Students:* 223 full-time (211 women), 77 part-time (66 women); includes 74 minority (31 African Americans, 3 American Indian/Alaska Native, 16 Asian Americans or Pacific Islanders, 24 Hispanic Americans), 9 international. Average age 31. In 2006, 79 master's, 4 doctorates awarded. *Degree requirements:* For master's, thesis/dissertation; for doctorate, thesis/dissertation, comprehensive exam. *Entrance requirements:* For master's, GRE General Test, minimum GPA of 3.0, certification in occupational therapy, interview, OTR certification may be required; for doctorate, GRE General Test, minimum GPA of 3.0, interview, 3 letters of reference, certification in occupational therapy or related field, master's degree in occupational therapy or related field. Additional exam requirements/recommendations for international students: Required—TOEFL (minimum score 550 paper-based; 213 computer-based; 79 iBT). *Application deadline:* For fall admission, 4/1 for international students; for spring admission, 8/1 for international students. Applications are processed on a rolling basis. Application fee: $100. Electronic applications accepted. *Expenses:* Tuition, area resident: Part-time $168 per unit. Tuition, state resident: full-time $4,369. Tuition, nonresident: full-time $9,373; part-time $443 per unit. Required fees: $20 per unit. $177 per term. *Financial support:* In 2006–07, 5 research assistantships (averaging $10,206 per year), 1 teaching assistantship (averaging $10,206 per year) were awarded; career-related internships or fieldwork, Federal Work-Study, institutionally sponsored loans, scholarships/grants, traineeships, health care benefits, and unspecified assistantships also available. Support available to part-time students. Financial award application deadline: 3/1; financial award applicants required to submit FAFSA. *Faculty research:* Quality of life/wellness, Alzheimer's disease, hand rehabilitation, psychosocial dysfunction, adaptation/chronic disability. *Unit head:* Dr. Sally Schultz, Director, 940-898-2803, Fax: 940-898-2806, E-mail: sschultz@twu.edu. *Application contact:* Samuel Wheeler, Coordinator of Graduate Admissions, 940-898-3188, Fax: 940-898-3081, E-mail: wheelersr@twu.edu.

Thomas Jefferson University, Jefferson College of Health Professions, Program in Occupational Therapy, Philadelphia, PA 19107. Offers MS. *Accreditation:* AOTA. Part-time programs available. *Faculty:* 9 full-time (8 women), 3 part-time/adjunct (2 women). *Students:* 62 full-time (59 women), 4 part-time (all women); includes 5 minority (3 African Americans, 2 Hispanic Americans). Average age 25. 86 applicants, 81% accepted, 66 enrolled. In 2006, 37 degrees awarded. *Degree requirements:* For master's, thesis (for some programs), registration. *Entrance requirements:* For master's, GRE General Test or MAT. Additional exam requirements/recommendations for international students: Required—TOEFL (minimum score 213 computer-based). *Application deadline:* For fall admission, 3/1 priority date for domestic and international students. Applications are processed on a rolling basis. Application fee: $50. Electronic applications accepted. *Expenses: Contact institution. Financial support:* Fellowships with tuition reimbursements, research assistantships, Federal Work-Study, institutionally sponsored loans, and traineeships available. Support available to part-time students. Financial award application deadline: 5/1; financial award applicants required to submit FAFSA. *Faculty research:* Functional outcomes in traumatic brain injury, clinical reasoning in therapist/patient interactions, gerontology, sensory integration in pediatrics, effective intervention for homeless. Total annual research expenditures: $3.5 million. *Unit head:* Dr. Roseann Schaaf, Graduate Director, 215-503-9609, Fax: 215-503-0376, E-mail: roseann.schaaf@jefferson.edu. *Application contact:* Karen A. Jacobs, Director of Admissions and Enrollment Management, 215-503-1040, Fax: 215-503-7241, E-mail: jchp@jefferson.edu.

Touro College, Barry Z. Levine School of Health Sciences, Occupational Therapy Program, New York, NY 10010. Offers MS. *Accreditation:* AOTA. *Entrance requirements:* For master's, interview, minimum GPA of 2.8.

Towson University, Graduate School, Program in Occupational Therapy, Towson, MD 21252-0001. Offers MS. *Accreditation:* AOTA. Part-time and evening/weekend programs available. *Faculty:* 14 full-time (all women), 2 part-time/adjunct (both women). *Students:* 103 full-time (96 women), 25 part-time (23 women); includes 22 minority (16 African Americans, 4 Asian Americans or Pacific Islanders, 2 Hispanic Americans), 3 international. 52 applicants, 79% accepted, 30 enrolled. In 2006, 39 degrees awarded. *Degree requirements:* For master's, exam, thesis optional. *Entrance requirements:* For master's, minimum GPA of 3.0. *Application deadline:* For spring admission, 8/1 for domestic students. Applications are processed on a rolling basis. Application fee: $50. *Expenses:* Tuition, state resident: part-time $275 per unit. Tuition, nonresident: part-time $577 per unit. Required fees: $72 per unit. *Financial support:* In 2006–07, teaching assistantships (averaging $2,000 per year); Federal Work-Study and unspecified assistantships also available. Financial award application deadline: 4/1; financial award applicants required to submit FAFSA. *Faculty research:* Issues of the aging, training caregivers, hand function in children, family studies, community programs/collaboration. *Unit head:* Sonia Lawson, Graduate Program Director, 410-704-2313, Fax: 410-704-2322, E-mail: slawson@towson.edu. *Application contact:* 410-704-2501, Fax: 410-704-4675, E-mail: grads@towson.edu.

Tufts University, Graduate School of Arts and Sciences, Department of Occupational Therapy, Medford, MA 02155. Offers MA, MS, OTD. *Accreditation:* AOTA. *Faculty:* 6 full-time, 8 part-time/adjunct. *Students:* 108 (105 women); includes 9 minority (2 African Americans, 6 Asian Americans or Pacific Islanders, 1 Hispanic American) 7 international. 101 applicants, 80% accepted, 43 enrolled. In 2006, 31 master's, 3 doctorates awarded. *Degree requirements:* For master's, thesis (for some programs). *Entrance requirements:* For master's, GRE General Test. Additional exam requirements/recommendations for international students: Required—TOEFL (minimum score 550 paper-based; 213 computer-based; 80 iBT). *Application deadline:* For fall admission, 2/15 for domestic students, 12/30 for international students; for spring admission, 10/15 for domestic students, 9/15 for international students. Applications are processed on a rolling basis. Application fee: $70. Electronic applications accepted. *Expenses: Contact institution.* Tuition and fees vary according to degree level and program. *Financial support:* Teaching assistantships with partial tuition reimbursements, career-related internships or fieldwork, Federal Work-Study, scholarships/grants, and tuition waivers (partial) available. Support available to part-time students. Financial award application deadline: 2/15; financial award applicants required to submit FAFSA. *Unit head:* Sharan Schwartzberg, Chair, 617-627-3720.

Tufts University, Graduate School of Arts and Sciences, Graduate Certificate Programs, Advanced Professional Study in Occupational Therapy Program, Medford, MA 02155. Offers Certificate. Part-time and evening/weekend programs available. *Students:* Average age 35. 4 applicants, 100% accepted, 4 enrolled. *Application deadline:* For fall admission, 8/15 priority date for domestic students; for spring admission, 12/12 priority date for domestic students. Applications are processed on a rolling basis. Application fee: $65. Electronic applications accepted. *Expenses: Contact institution.* Tuition and fees vary according to degree level and program. *Financial support:* Career-related internships or fieldwork available. Support available to part-time students. Financial award application deadline: 5/1; financial award applicants required to submit FAFSA. *Application contact:* Angela Foss, Program Administrator, 617-627-3395, Fax: 617-627-3016, E-mail: gradschool@ase.tufts.edu.

University at Buffalo, the State University of New York, Graduate School, School of Public Health and Health Professions, Department of Rehabilitation Science, Program in Occupational Therapy, Buffalo, NY 14260. Offers MS. *Accreditation:* AOTA. *Students:* 24 full-time (all women), 3 part-time (all women); includes 3 minority (2 African Americans, 1 Hispanic American), 4 international. Average age 23. 10 applicants, 80% accepted, 3 enrolled. In 2006, 23 degrees awarded. *Degree requirements:* For master's, thesis, project. *Entrance requirements:* For master's, GRE, BS in occupational therapy. Additional exam requirements/recommendations for international students: Required—TOEFL (minimum score 550 paper-based; 213 computer-based; 79 iBT). *Application deadline:* For fall admission, 6/1 priority date for domestic students, 4/1 for international students; for spring admission, 11/1 priority date for domestic students, 9/1 for international students. Application fee: $35. Electronic applications accepted. *Financial support:* In 2006–07, 6 students received support, including 3 teaching assistantships with partial tuition reimbursements available (averaging $6,023 per year); unspecified assistantships also available. Financial award application deadline: 3/1; financial award applicants required to submit FAFSA. *Faculty research:* Sensory integration, assistive technology, aging and technology, transition for students with emotional/behavioral problems. Total annual research expenditures: $489,000. *Unit head:* Dr. Susan Nochajski, Graduate Program Director, 716-829-3141 Ext. 133, Fax: 716-829-3217, E-mail: nochajsk@buffalo.edu. *Application contact:*

Dr. Susan Nochajski, Graduate Program Director, 716-829-3141 Ext. 133, Fax: 716-829-3217, E-mail: nochajsk@buffalo.edu.

The University of Alabama at Birmingham, School of Health Professions, Department of Occupational Therapy, Programs in Occupational Therapy, Birmingham, AL 35294. Offers MS. *Students:* 84 full-time (80 women), 10 part-time (9 women); includes 19 minority (15 African Americans, 1 American Indian/Alaska Native, 1 Asian American or Pacific Islander, 2 Hispanic Americans). 46 applicants, 78% accepted. In 2006, 23 degrees awarded. *Expenses:* Tuition, state resident: part-time $170 per credit hour. Tuition, nonresident: part-time $425 per credit hour. Required fees: $15 per credit hour. $122 per term. Tuition and fees vary according to program. *Unit head:* Dr. Penelope Moyers, Chair, Department of Occupational Therapy, 205-934-3568, Fax: 205-934-0402, E-mail: pmoyers@uab.edu.

University of Alberta, Faculty of Graduate Studies and Research, Department of Occupational Therapy, Edmonton, AB T6G 2E1, Canada. Offers M Sc, PhD. Part-time programs available. *Faculty:* 13 full-time (10 women). *Students:* 3 full-time (2 women), 8 part-time (5 women). Average age 28. 4 applicants, 25% accepted. In 2006, 3 degrees awarded. *Degree requirements:* For master's, thesis. *Entrance requirements:* For master's, bachelor's degree in occupational therapy, minimum GPA of 6.9 on a 9.0 scale. Additional exam requirements/recommendations for international students: Required—TOEFL. *Application deadline:* For fall admission, 5/15 for domestic students, 3/15 for international students; for winter admission, 10/15 for domestic students, 7/15 for international students. Applications are processed on a rolling basis. Application fee: $0. Electronic applications accepted. *Financial support:* In 2006–07, 1 research assistantship (averaging $2,721 per year), 1 teaching assistantship (averaging $2,535 per year) were awarded; career-related internships or fieldwork, institutionally sponsored loans, and scholarships/grants also available. Financial award application deadline: 1/1. *Faculty research:* Work evaluation, pediatrics, geriatrics, program evaluation, community-based rehabilitation. *Unit head:* L. Liu, Graduate Program Coordinator, 780-492-1595, Fax: 780-492-1626. *Application contact:* Angela Libutti, Administrative Assistant, Graduate Studies, 780-492-1595, Fax: 780-492-1626, E-mail: mscot.info@rehabmed.ualberta.ca.

University of Central Arkansas, Graduate School, College of Health and Behavioral Sciences, Department of Occupational Therapy, Conway, AR 72035-0001. Offers MS. *Accreditation:* AOTA. *Faculty:* 6 full-time (5 women), 1 (woman) part-time/adjunct. *Students:* 28 full-time (23 women), 7 part-time (all women). 20 applicants, 100% accepted, 20 enrolled. In 2006, 39 degrees awarded. *Degree requirements:* For master's, internship, thesis optional. *Entrance requirements:* For master's, GRE General Test, minimum GPA of 2.7. Additional exam requirements/recommendations for international students: Required—TOEFL (minimum score 550 paper-based; 213 computer-based). *Application deadline:* For fall admission, 3/1 priority date for domestic students; for spring admission, 10/1 for domestic students. Applications are processed on a rolling basis. Application fee: $25 ($40 for international students). *Expenses: Contact institution.* One-time fee: $65 part-time. *Financial support:* In 2006–07, 6 research assistantships (averaging $2,200 per year) were awarded; Federal Work-Study, scholarships/grants, and unspecified assistantships also available. Financial award application deadline: 2/15; financial award applicants required to submit FAFSA. *Unit head:* Dr. Linda Musselman, Chair, 501-450-3192, Fax: 501-450-5503, E-mail: lindam@uca.edu. *Application contact:* Nanette Fitzhugh, Administrative Assistant, 501-450-5063, Fax: 501-450-5678, E-mail: fitzhugh@uca.edu.

The University of Findlay, Graduate and Professional Studies, College of Health Professions, Program in Occupational Therapy, Findlay, OH 45840-3653. Offers MOT. *Accreditation:* AOTA. Part-time and evening/weekend programs available. *Students:* 33 full-time (28 women), 8 part-time (7 women); includes 1 minority (Asian American or Pacific Islander), 1 international. Average age 35. 17 applicants, 100% accepted, 17 enrolled. In 2006, 29 degrees awarded. *Entrance requirements:* For master's, 50 hours of observation, 3 letters of recommendation. Additional exam requirements/recommendations for international students: Required—TOEFL (minimum score 550 paper-based). *Application deadline:* Applications are processed on a rolling basis. Application fee: $25. Electronic applications accepted. *Financial support:* In 2006–07, 8 students received support, including 2 teaching assistantships with full tuition reimbursements available (averaging $6,000 per year); unspecified assistantships also available. Financial award application deadline: 4/1; financial award applicants required to submit FAFSA. *Unit head:* Cynthia Goodwin, Director, 419-434-6936, Fax: 419-434-4822.

University of Florida, Graduate School, College of Public Health and Health Professions, Department of Occupational Therapy, Gainesville, FL 32611. Offers MHS, MOT. *Accreditation:* AOTA. Postbaccalaureate distance learning degree programs offered. *Faculty:* 4 full-time (2 women), 3 part-time/adjunct (2 women). *Students:* 122 (113 women); includes 7 minority (all Hispanic Americans) 1 international. In 2006, 56 master's awarded. *Degree requirements:* For master's, research project. *Entrance requirements:* For master's, GRE General Test, minimum GPA of 3.0. Additional exam requirements/recommendations for international students: Required—TOEFL (minimum score 550 paper-based; 213 computer-based). *Application deadline:* For fall admission, 2/15 for domestic students; for spring admission, 10/15 for domestic students. Application fee: $30. Electronic applications accepted. *Expenses:* Tuition, state resident: full-time $6,827. Tuition, nonresident: full-time $21,951. Required fees: $999. *Financial support:* In 2006–07, 9 research assistantships (averaging $11,494 per year) were awarded; fellowships, teaching assistantships, career-related internships or fieldwork, institutionally sponsored loans, and unspecified assistantships also available. Support available to part-time students. *Faculty research:* Occupational therapy related to ergonomics, body image, pediatrics, HIV, and hand therapy. *Unit head:* Dr. William C. Mann, Chair, 352-273-6135, Fax: 352-273-6042, E-mail: wmann@phhp.ufl.edu. *Application contact:* Dr. Craig Velozo, Associate Chair, 352-273-6135, Fax: 352-273-6042, E-mail: cvelozo@phhp.ufl.edu.

University of Illinois at Chicago, Graduate College, College of Applied Health Sciences, Program in Occupational Therapy, Chicago, IL 60607-7128. Offers MS. *Accreditation:* AOTA. Part-time programs available. *Degree requirements:* For master's, thesis. *Entrance requirements:* For master's, GRE General Test, minimum GPA of 2.75, previous course work in statistics. Additional exam requirements/recommendations for international students: Required—TOEFL. Electronic applications accepted. *Faculty research:* Sensory integration, perception, play, treatment efficacy, instrument development.

University of Indianapolis, Graduate Programs, School of Occupational Therapy, Indianapolis, IN 46227-3697. Offers MHS, MOT, DHS. *Accreditation:* AOTA. Part-time and evening/weekend programs available. *Faculty:* 8 full-time (7 women), 7 part-time/adjunct (5 women). *Students:* 57 full-time (55 women), 112 part-time (102 women); includes 6 minority (1 African American, 3 Asian Americans or Pacific Islanders, 2 Hispanic Americans). Average age 27. In 2006, 41 degrees awarded. *Degree requirements:* For master's, thesis. *Entrance requirements:* For master's, minimum GPA of 3.0, interview; for doctorate, minimum GPA of 3.3, BA/BS or MAIMS from OT Program, current state license, currently in practice as OT or have 1000 hours of practice in last 5 years. Additional exam requirements/recommendations for international students: Required—TOEFL (minimum score 550 paper-based; 237 computer-based; 92 iBT), TWE (minimum score 5). *Application deadline:* For fall admission, 11/1 for domestic students, 2/1 for international students. Application fee: $55. *Expenses: Contact institution. Financial support:* Career-related internships or fieldwork, Federal Work-Study, tuition waivers (full and partial), and unspecified assistantships available. Financial award application deadline: 5/1; financial award applicants required to submit FAFSA. *Unit head:* Dr. Mary Huer, Dean of Health Sciences, 317-788-3500, Fax: 317-788-3542, E-mail: huerm@ulndy.edu. *Application contact:* Jerry Lowery, Admissons Counselor, 317-788-3457, Fax: 317-788-3542, E-mail: loweryj@uindy.edu.

University of Kansas, Graduate Studies Medical Center, School of Allied Health, Department of Occupational Therapy Education, Lawrence, KS 66045. Offers occupational therapy (MOT, MS); therapeutic science (PhD). *Accreditation:* AOTA. Part-time programs available. *Faculty:* 12 full-time (10 women), 4 part-time/adjunct (all women). *Students:* 62 full-time (60 women), 9 part-time (all women); includes 4 minority (2 Asian Americans or Pacific Islanders, 2 Hispanic Americans), 2 international. Average age 27. 17 applicants, 71% accepted, 11 enrolled. In 2006, 31 degrees awarded. *Median time to degree:* Master's–1.75 years full-time, 3.75 years part-time. *Degree requirements:* For doctorate, thesis/dissertation, oral defense, comprehensive exam. *Entrance requirements:* For master's, 1 year of experience in a field related to disability; for doctorate, 24 hours of master's level research. *Application deadline:* For fall admission, 4/1 for international students. Application fee: $60. Electronic applications accepted. *Expenses:* Tuition, area resident: Part-time $227 per credit. Tuition, state resident: part-time $543 per credit. Tuition and fees vary according to course load, campus/location, program and reciprocity agreements. *Financial support:* In 2006–07, 3 students received support, including 3 teaching assistantships with full and partial tuition reimbursements available (averaging $41,288 per year); research assistantships with partial tuition reimbursements available. *Faculty research:* The impact of sensory processing in everyday life; brain activity in various disorders and conditions; home and work modifications; cognition, executive function and problem solving in everyday life; best practices in serving children, families and schools. *Unit head:* Dr. Winifred W. Dunn, Chair, 913-588-7195, Fax: 913-588-4568, E-mail: wdunn@kumc.edu. *Application contact:* Dr. Laura Neely, Admission Officer, 913-588-7174, Fax: 913-588-4568, E-mail: lneely@kumc.edu.

University of Mary, Department of Occupational Therapy, Bismarck, ND 58504-9652. Offers MS. *Accreditation:* AOTA. Postbaccalaureate distance learning degree programs offered (minimal on-campus study). In 2006, 10 degrees awarded. *Degree requirements:* For master's, thesis or alternative, practicum. *Entrance requirements:* For master's, ACT or equivalent, minimum GPA of 2.75, 48 hours of volunteer experience. *Application deadline:* For spring admission, 1/15 priority date for domestic and international students. Applications are processed on a rolling basis. Electronic applications accepted. *Expenses: Contact institution. Financial support:* In 2006–07, 2 teaching assistantships with full tuition reimbursements (averaging $2,500 per year) were awarded; career-related internships or fieldwork, Federal Work-Study, institutionally sponsored loans, scholarships/grants, and unspecified assistantships also available. Support available to part-time students. Financial award applicants required to submit FAFSA. *Faculty research:* Safe homes for well elderly, occupation and spirituality, professional development in the spiritual domain, case method instruction, ergonomics, assistive technology. Total annual research expenditures: $4,000. *Unit head:* Janeene Sibla, Program Director, 701-255-7500, Fax: 701-255-7687. *Application contact:* Geri Toineeta, Program Secretary, 701-355-8216.

University of Mississippi Medical Center, School of Health Related Professions, Department of Occupational Therapy, Jackson, MS 39216-4505. Offers MOT. *Accreditation:* AOTA. *Faculty:* 10 full-time (9 women). *Students:* 51 full-time (47 women); includes 11 minority (all African Americans) 55 applicants, 60% accepted, 33 enrolled. *Application deadline:* For fall admission, 1/30 for domestic students. Application fee: $10. *Expenses:* Tuition, state resident: full-time $4,523. Tuition, nonresident: full-time $10,566. *Financial support:* Application deadline: 3/31; *Unit head:* Bette A. Groat, Chairman, 601-984-6350, E-mail: bgroat@shrp.umsmed.edu.

University of Missouri–Columbia, School of Health Professions, Program in Occupational Therapy, Columbia, MO 65211. Offers MOT. *Accreditation:* AOTA. *Faculty:* 3 full-time (2 women), 1 (woman) part-time/adjunct. *Students:* 16 full-time (all women); includes 2 minority (both African Americans) *Entrance requirements:* Additional exam requirements/recommendations for international students: Required—TOEFL (minimum score 500 paper-based; 173 computer-based). Application fee: $45 ($60 for international students). *Unit head:* Dr. Guy L. McCormack, Department Chair, 573-882-3988, E-mail: muot@health.missouri.edu.

University of New England, College of Health Professions, Program in Occupational Therapy, Biddeford, ME 04005-9526. Offers occupational therapy (MS); post professional occupational therapy (MS). *Accreditation:* AOTA. *Faculty:* 10 full-time (8 women), 2 part-time/adjunct (1 woman). *Students:* 12 full-time (11 women), 4 part-time (all women). Average age 27. 15 applicants, 93% accepted, 13 enrolled. In 2006, 22 degrees awarded. *Degree requirements:* For master's, research project. *Entrance requirements:* For master's, minimum undergraduate GPA of 3.0, 1 level II clinical. *Application deadline:* Applications are processed on a rolling basis. Application fee: $40. *Expenses: Contact institution. Financial support:* Application deadline: 5/1; *Faculty research:* Aging and cognition, neurobehavioral basis of motor control, post breast surgery syndrome, sensory modulation, ergonomics. *Unit head:* Regi Robrett, Director, 207-283-0170 Ext. 2233, Fax: 207-602-5963, E-mail: rrobnett@une.edu. *Application contact:* Peggy Warden, Assistant Dean of Graduate Admissions, 207-221-4225, Fax: 207-221-4898, E-mail: admissions@une.edu.

University of New Hampshire, Graduate School, School of Health and Human Services, Department of Occupational Therapy, Durham, NH 03824. Offers MS. Degree offered in professional and post-professional tracks. *Accreditation:* AOTA. Part-time programs available. *Faculty:* 7 full-time. *Students:* 68 full-time (63 women), 14 part-time (11 women). Average age 36. 48 applicants, 88% accepted, 36 enrolled. In 2006, 42 degrees awarded. *Degree requirements:* For master's, thesis or alternative. *Entrance requirements:* For master's, GRE General Test, current certification as an OTR from the American Occupational Therapy Board or World Federation of Occupational Therapy. Additional exam requirements/recommendations for international students: Required—TOEFL (minimum score 550 paper-based; 213 computer-based). *Application deadline:* For fall admission, 4/1 for domestic and international students; for winter admission, 12/1 for domestic students. Applications are processed on a rolling basis. Application fee: $60. Electronic applications accepted. *Expenses:* Tuition, state resident: full-time $8,540; part-time $474 per credit hour. Tuition, nonresident: full-time $20,990; part-time $862 per credit hour. Required fees: $1,343; $356 per term. Tuition and fees vary according to course load, program and reciprocity agreements. *Financial support:* In 2006–07, 1 fellowship was awarded; research assistantships, teaching assistantships, career-related internships or fieldwork, Federal Work-Study, and scholarships/grants also available. Support available to part-time students. Financial award application deadline: 2/15. *Unit head:* Dr. Elizabeth Crepeau, Chairperson, 603-862-3420, E-mail: ecrepeau@cisunix.unh.edu. *Application contact:* Alice Vosburg, Administrative Assistant, 603-862-2168, E-mail: ot.dept@unh.edu.

University of New Mexico, School of Medicine, Program in Occupational Therapy, Albuquerque, NM 87131-5196. Offers MOT. *Accreditation:* AOTA. Part-time programs available. *Degree requirements:* For master's, thesis, clinical fieldwork. *Entrance requirements:* For master's, interview, writing sample, volunteer experience, additional application fee. Additional exam requirements/recommendations for international students: Required—TOEFL. Electronic applications accepted. *Faculty research:* Gait analysis.

The University of North Carolina at Chapel Hill, School of Medicine and Graduate School, Graduate Programs in Medicine, Chapel Hill, NC 27599. Offers allied health sciences (MPT, MS, Au D, DPT, PhD), including human movement science (MS, PhD), occupational science (MS, PhD), physical therapy (MPT, MS, DPT), rehabilitation counseling and psychology (MS), speech and hearing sciences (MS, Au D, PhD); biochemistry and biophysics (MS, PhD); biomedical engineering (MS, PhD); cell and developmental biology (PhD); cell and molecular physiology (PhD); genetics and molecular biology (PhD); microbiology and immunology (MS, PhD), including immunology, microbiology; neurobiology (PhD); pathology and laboratory medicine (PhD), including experimental pathology; pharmacology (PhD); MD/PhD. Postbaccalaureate distance learning degree programs offered. *Faculty:* 470 full-time (156 women), 101 part-time/adjunct (17 women). *Students:* 730 full-time (447 women), 36 part-time (27 women); includes 110 minority (43 African Americans, 6 American Indian/Alaska Native, 48 Asian Americans or Pacific Islanders, 13 Hispanic Americans), 79 international. In 2006, 73 master's, 62 doctorates awarded. Terminal master's awarded for partial completion of doctoral program. *Degree requirements:* For master's, comprehensive exam; for doctorate, thesis/dissertation. *Application deadline:* Applications are processed on a rolling basis. Application fee: $65. Electronic applications accepted. *Expenses: Contact institution. Financial support:* In 2006–07, 77 fellowships with full and partial tuition reimbursements, 309 research assistantships with full tuition reimbursements, 23 teaching assistantships with full tuition reimbursements were awarded; career-related internships or fieldwork, Federal Work-Study, institutionally sponsored loans, traineeships, tuition waivers (full and partial), and unspecified assistantships

Occupational Therapy

The University of North Carolina at Chapel Hill (continued)
also available. Support available to part-time students. Financial award applicants required to submit FAFSA. *Unit head:* Dr. William I. Roper, Dean, 919-966-4161, Fax: 919-966-6354.

The University of North Carolina at Chapel Hill, School of Medicine and Graduate School, Graduate Programs in Medicine, Department of Allied Health Sciences, Division of Occupational Science, Chapel Hill, NC 27599. Offers occupational science (MS, PhD). *Accreditation:* AOTA. *Faculty:* 10 full-time (all women), 2 part-time/adjunct (both women). *Students:* 39 full-time (36 women); includes 3 minority (1 African American, 1 American Indian/Alaska Native, 1 Asian American or Pacific Islander). Average age 24. 58 applicants, 48% accepted, 23 enrolled. In 2006, 16 degrees awarded. *Degree requirements:* For master's, collaborative research project, thesis optional; for doctorate, thesis/dissertation. *Entrance requirements:* For master's, GRE General Test; for doctorate, GRE, master's degree in occupational therapy, relevant social behavioral sciences or health field. Additional exam requirements/recommendations for international students: Required—TOEFL (minimum score 550 paper-based; 79 computer-based). *Application deadline:* For fall admission, 1/1 for domestic and international students. Application fee: $70. Electronic applications accepted. *Financial support:* In 2006–07, 35 students received support, including 1 fellowship with full tuition reimbursement available (averaging $6,000 per year), 1 research assistantship (averaging $7,215 per year); traineeships and unspecified assistantships also available. Financial award application deadline: 1/1; financial award applicants required to submit FAFSA. *Faculty research:* Parents and infants in co-occupations, psychosocial dysfunction, predictors of autism, factors influencing the occupation of primates, factors influencing occupations of people with dementia, occupational development of young children. Total annual research expenditures: $46,081. *Unit head:* Cathy Nielson, Director, 919-966-2452, Fax: 919-966-9007, E-mail: cnielson@med.unc.edu. *Application contact:* Jenny Womack, Admissions Co-Chair, 919-843-4463, Fax: 919-966-9007, E-mail: jwomack@med.unc.edu.

University of North Dakota, School of Medicine and Graduate School, Graduate Programs in Medicine, Department of Occupational Therapy, Grand Forks, ND 58202. Offers MOT. *Accreditation:* AOTA. *Faculty:* 8 full-time (all women). *Students:* 34 full-time (31 women), 29 part-time (23 women); includes 2 minority (1 Asian American or Pacific Islander, 1 Hispanic American), 1 international. In 2006, 32 degrees awarded. *Entrance requirements:* For master's, letter of reference; volunteer or work experience, preferably from health-related field; interview; minimum GPA of 2.7. Additional exam requirements/recommendations for international students: Required—TOEFL (minimum score 550 paper-based; 213 computer-based; 79 iBT), IELTS (minimum score 6). *Application deadline:* For fall admission, 1/4 for domestic students. Application fee: $35. *Expenses:* Tuition, state resident: full-time $5,650; part-time $214 per credit. Tuition, nonresident: full-time $14,248; part-time $572 per credit. Required fees: $1,008; $42 per credit. Tuition and fees vary according to reciprocity agreements. *Unit head:* Janet Jedlicka, Chairperson, 701-777-2017, Fax: 701-777-2212. *Application contact:* Brenda Halle, Admissions Specialist, 701-777-2947, Fax: 701-777-3619, E-mail: brendahalle@mail.und.edu.

University of Oklahoma Health Sciences Center, Graduate College, College of Allied Health, Department of Occupational Therapy, Oklahoma City, OK 73190. Offers MOT. *Accreditation:* AOTA.

University of Pittsburgh, School of Health and Rehabilitation Sciences, Department of Occupational Therapy, Pittsburgh, PA 15260. Offers MOT. *Accreditation:* AOTA. *Faculty:* 7 full-time (all women). *Students:* 78 full-time (73 women), 2 part-time (1 woman); includes 5 minority (4 African Americans, 1 Asian American or Pacific Islander), 2 international. Average age 27. 58 applicants, 95% accepted, 35 enrolled. In 2006, 29 degrees awarded. *Degree requirements:* For master's, registration. *Entrance requirements:* For master's, GRE General Test, volunteer experience. Additional exam requirements/recommendations for international students: Required—TOEFL (minimum score 550 paper-based; 213 computer-based; 80 iBT), IELTS (minimum score 7). *Application deadline:* Applications are processed on a rolling basis. Application fee: $50. Electronic applications accepted. *Expenses:* Contact institution. *Financial support:* In 2006–07, 1 fellowship (averaging $15,398 per year) was awarded; research assistantships, teaching assistantships, Federal Work-Study also available. Total annual research expenditures: $396,783. *Unit head:* Dr. Joan Rogers, Chairperson, 412-383-6620, Fax: 412-383-6613, E-mail: admissions@shrs.pitt.edu. *Application contact:* Shameem Gangjee, Director of Admissions, 412-383-6558, Fax: 412-383-6535, E-mail: admissions@shrs.pitt.edu.

University of Pittsburgh, School of Health and Rehabilitation Sciences, Program in Health and Rehabilitation Sciences, Pittsburgh, PA 15260. Offers dietetics (MS); health and rehabilitation sciences (MS), including clinical dietetics, coordinated with dietetics, health care supervision and management, health information systems, occupational therapy, physical therapy, rehabilitation counseling, rehabilitation science and technology, sports medicine; wellness and human performance (MS). *Accreditation:* APTA. Part-time and evening/weekend programs available. *Faculty:* 40 full-time (23 women), 3 part-time/adjunct (2 women). *Students:* 93 full-time (67 women), 54 part-time (35 women); includes 31 minority (12 African Americans, 18 Asian Americans or Pacific Islanders, 1 Hispanic American), 15 international. Average age 30. 122 applicants, 82% accepted, 64 enrolled. In 2006, 28 degrees awarded. *Entrance requirements:* For master's, minimum GPA of 3.0. Additional exam requirements/recommendations for international students: Required—TOEFL, IELTS. *Application deadline:* Applications are processed on a rolling basis. Application fee: $50. Electronic applications accepted. *Financial support:* In 2006–07, 11 research assistantships with full tuition reimbursements (averaging $16,918 per year) were awarded; teaching assistantships, Federal Work-Study, institutionally sponsored loans, traineeships, and unspecified assistantships also available. Support available to part-time students. Financial award applicants required to submit FAFSA. *Faculty research:* Assistive technology, seating and wheeled mobility, cellular neurophysiology, low back syndrome, augmentative communication. Total annual research expenditures: $953,246. *Application contact:* Shameem Gangjee, Director of Admissions, 412-383-6558, Fax: 412-383-6535, E-mail: admissions@shrs.pitt.edu.

University of Puget Sound, Graduate Studies, School of Occupational Therapy and Physical Therapy, Program in Occupational Therapy, Tacoma, WA 98416. Offers MOT, MSOT. *Accreditation:* AOTA. *Faculty:* 6 full-time (4 women), 4 part-time/adjunct (all women). *Students:* 49 full-time (47 women), 22 part-time (21 women); includes 12 minority (2 African Americans, 9 Asian Americans or Pacific Islanders, 1 Hispanic American), 1 international. Average age 28. 75 applicants, 83% accepted, 25 enrolled. In 2006, 23 degrees awarded. *Median time to degree:* Master's–2.5 years full-time. *Degree requirements:* For master's, thesis (for some programs), publishable paper. *Entrance requirements:* For master's, GRE General Test, minimum GPA of 3.0. Additional exam requirements/recommendations for international students: Required—TOEFL (minimum score 550 paper-based; 213 computer-based; 80 iBT). *Application deadline:* For fall admission, 1/15 priority date for domestic and international students. Applications are processed on a rolling basis. Application fee: $65. Electronic applications accepted. *Expenses:* Tuition: Full-time $26,390. Tuition and fees vary according to course load. *Financial support:* In 2006–07, 28 students received support, including 16 fellowships (averaging $8,000 per year); career-related internships or fieldwork and scholarships/grants also available. Support available to part-time students. Financial award application deadline: 3/31; financial award applicants required to submit FAFSA. *Faculty research:* Scope of practice for school-based occupational therapy, family occupational adaptation to schizophrenia, clinical decision making, low vision adaptation, assistive technology. Total annual research expenditures: $3,000. *Unit head:* Dr. George S. Tomlin, Director, 253-879-3522, Fax: 253-879-2933, E-mail: tomlin@ups.edu. *Application contact:* Dr. George H. Mills, Vice President for Enrollment, 253-879-3211, Fax: 253-879-3993, E-mail: admission@ups.edu.

University of St. Augustine for Health Sciences, Graduate Programs, Division of Occupational Therapy, St. Augustine, FL 32086. Offers MOT, OTD. *Accreditation:* AOTA. *Entrance requirements:* For master's, GRE General Test.

The University of Scranton, Graduate School, Program in Occupational Therapy, Scranton, PA 18510. Offers MS. *Accreditation:* AOTA. *Faculty:* 6 full-time (5 women). *Students:* 13 full-time (all women), 4 part-time (all women); includes 1 minority (Asian American or Pacific Islander) Average age 23. 16 applicants, 94% accepted. In 2006, 13 degrees awarded. *Degree requirements:* For master's, thesis, capstone experience. *Entrance requirements:* For master's, minimum GPA of 2.75. Additional exam requirements/recommendations for international students: Required—TOEFL (minimum score 500 paper-based; 173 computer-based), IELTS (minimum score 6). *Application deadline:* Applications are processed on a rolling basis. Application fee: $50. *Expenses:* Tuition: Part-time $684 per credit. Required fees: $25 per term. *Financial support:* In 2006–07, 2 students received support, including 2 teaching assistantships with full tuition reimbursements available (averaging $6,600 per year); career-related internships or fieldwork, Federal Work-Study, and unspecified assistantships also available. Support available to part-time students. Financial award application deadline: 3/1. *Unit head:* Dr. Marlene Morgan, Director, 570-941-5789, Fax: 570-941-4380.

University of South Alabama, Graduate School, College of Allied Health Professions, Department of Occupational Therapy, Mobile, AL 36688-0002. Offers MS. *Accreditation:* AOTA. *Faculty:* 3 full-time (all women). *Students:* 45 full-time (42 women); includes 5 minority (all African Americans), 1 international. In 2006, 10 degrees awarded. *Unit head:* Dr. Marjorie Scaffa, Chair, 251-434-3939.

The University of South Dakota, School of Medicine and Health Sciences and Graduate School, Graduate Programs in Health Sciences, Department of Occupational Therapy, Vermillion, SD 57069-2390. Offers MS. *Accreditation:* AOTA. Part-time programs available. *Faculty:* 5 full-time (4 women). *Students:* 41 full-time (33 women), 3 part-time (all women); includes 1 minority (American Indian/Alaska Native). Average age 25. 39 applicants, 85% accepted, 25 enrolled. In 2006, 8 degrees awarded. *Degree requirements:* For master's, 6 months of supervised fieldwork, thesis optional. *Entrance requirements:* For master's, courses in human anatomy, human physiology, general psychology, abnormal psychology, lifespan development, statistics. Additional exam requirements/recommendations for international students: Required—TOEFL (minimum score 550 paper-based; 213 computer-based). *Application deadline:* For fall admission, 11/1 priority date for domestic and international students. Applications are processed on a rolling basis. Application fee: $35. *Expenses:* Contact institution. *Financial support:* In 2006–07, 12 students received support, including 10 research assistantships with partial tuition reimbursements available; teaching assistantships with partial tuition reimbursements available, scholarships/grants and traineeships also available. Financial award application deadline: 3/1. *Faculty research:* Low vision in youth and adults, agricultural/rural, health, childhood obesity, adolescent mental health, elder health and well being. *Unit head:* Barbara L. Brockevelt, Chairperson, 605-677-5600, Fax: 605-677-6581, E-mail: bbrockev@usd.edu. *Application contact:* Connie Twedt, Program Assistant, 605-677-5600, Fax: 605-677-6581, E-mail: usdot@usd.edu.

University of Southern California, Graduate School, Independent Health Professions, Department of Occupational Therapy, Program in Occupational Science, Los Angeles, CA 90089. Offers PhD. *Students:* 15 full-time (8 women), 8 part-time (7 women); includes 3 minority (1 African American, 1 Asian American or Pacific Islander, 1 Hispanic American), 2 international. In 2006, 4 degrees awarded. *Degree requirements:* For doctorate, thesis/dissertation. *Entrance requirements:* For doctorate, GRE General Test. *Application deadline:* For fall admission, 12/1 priority date for domestic students. Application fee: $85. *Expenses:* Tuition: Full-time $33,314; part-time $1,121 per credit. Required fees: $522. Full-time tuition and fees vary according to program. *Financial support:* In 2006–07, research assistantships with partial tuition reimbursements (averaging $18,500 per year), teaching assistantships with partial tuition reimbursements (averaging $18,500 per year) were awarded; fellowships, Federal Work-Study, institutionally sponsored loans, and scholarships/grants also available. Support available to part-time students. Financial award application deadline: 2/15; financial award applicants required to submit FAFSA.

University of Southern California, Graduate School, Independent Health Professions, Department of Occupational Therapy, Program in Occupational Therapy, Los Angeles, CA 90089. Offers MA, OTD. *Accreditation:* AOTA. *Students:* 221 full-time (210 women), 7 part-time (6 women); includes 91 minority (8 African Americans, 2 American Indian/Alaska Native, 60 Asian Americans or Pacific Islanders, 21 Hispanic Americans), 19 international. In 2006, 84 master's, 15 doctorates awarded. *Degree requirements:* For master's, comprehensive exam or thesis. *Entrance requirements:* For master's, GRE General Test. *Application deadline:* For fall admission, 12/1 priority date for domestic students. Applications are processed on a rolling basis. Application fee: $85. *Expenses:* Tuition: Full-time $33,314; part-time $1,121 per credit. Required fees: $522. Full-time tuition and fees vary according to program. *Financial support:* In 2006–07, research assistantships with partial tuition reimbursements (averaging $18,500 per year), teaching assistantships with partial tuition reimbursements (averaging $18,500 per year) were awarded; fellowships, Federal Work-Study, institutionally sponsored loans, and scholarships/grants also available. Support available to part-time students. Financial award application deadline: 2/15; financial award applicants required to submit FAFSA.

University of Southern Indiana, Graduate Studies, College of Nursing and Health Professions, Program in Occupational Therapy, Evansville, IN 47712-3590. Offers MSOT. *Accreditation:* AOTA. Part-time programs available. Postbaccalaureate distance learning degree programs offered (minimal on-campus study). *Faculty:* 5 full-time (4 women). *Students:* 20 full-time (16 women), 3 part-time (all women), 1 international. Average age 30. 3 applicants, 67% accepted, 1 enrolled. In 2006, 28 degrees awarded. *Entrance requirements:* Additional exam requirements/recommendations for international students: Required—TOEFL (minimum score 500 paper-based; 173 computer-based). *Application deadline:* For fall admission, 8/15 priority date for domestic students, 3/1 priority date for international students. Applications are processed on a rolling basis. Application fee: $25. *Expenses:* Tuition, state resident: full-time $3,888; part-time $216 per credit hour. Tuition, nonresident: full-time $7,688; part-time $426 per credit hour. Required fees: $220; $23 per term. Tuition and fees vary according to course load and reciprocity agreements. *Financial support:* In 2006–07, 17 students received support. Federal Work-Study, scholarships/grants, tuition waivers (full and partial), and unspecified assistantships available. Financial award application deadline: 3/1; financial award applicants required to submit FAFSA. *Unit head:* Dr. Barbara Williams, Director, 812-461-5396, E-mail: bjwilliams4@usi.edu.

University of Southern Maine, Program in Occupational Therapy, Lewiston, ME 04240. Offers MOT. *Accreditation:* AOTA. Part-time programs available. *Degree requirements:* For master's, fieldwork, original research. *Entrance requirements:* For master's, minimum GPA of 3.0, writing sample, interview, reference letters, job shadow observation. Electronic applications accepted. *Expenses:* Tuition, state resident: full-time $4,860; part-time $270 per credit hour. Tuition, nonresident: full-time $13,572; part-time $754 per credit hour. Required fees: $222 per semester. Tuition and fees vary according to course load. *Faculty research:* Multicultural curricula, cultural competence, parents responses to fussy infants, chronic pain.

The University of Texas Health Science Center at San Antonio, School of Allied Health Sciences, San Antonio, TX 78229-3900. Offers clinical laboratory sciences (MS); dental hygiene (MS); occupational therapy (MOT); physical therapy (MPT); physician assistant studies (MS). *Accreditation:* AOTA; APTA; ARC-PA. *Expenses:* Tuition, state resident: part-time $50 per credit hour. Tuition, nonresident: part-time $325 per credit hour. Required fees: $7.5 per credit hour. $155 per term.

The University of Texas Medical Branch, School of Allied Health Sciences, Department of Occupational Therapy, Galveston, TX 77555. Offers MOT. *Accreditation:* AOTA. *Faculty:* 4 full-time (all women), 3 part-time/adjunct (1 woman). *Students:* 73 full-time (60 women); includes 31 minority (14 African Americans, 10 Asian Americans or Pacific Islanders, 7 Hispanic Americans), 1 international. Average age 27. In 2006, 10 degrees awarded. *Entrance requirements:* For master's, MAT, 20 volunteer hours, telephone interview, 2 references. Application fee: $30. *Financial support:* In 2006–07, fellowships (averaging $23,000 per year), research assistantships with full tuition reimbursements (averaging $23,000 per year) were awarded. Financial award applicants required to submit FAFSA. *Unit head:* Dr. Gretchen Stone, Chair and Associate Professor, 409-772-3061, Fax: 409-747-1615, E-mail: gestone@utmb.edu. *Application contact:* Sharon G. McEachern, Special Programs Coordinator II, 409-772-3062, Fax: 409-747-1615, E-mail: smceache@utmb.edu.

The University of Texas–Pan American, College of Health Sciences and Human Services, Department of Occupational Therapy, Edinburg, TX 78541-2999. Offers MS. *Accreditation:* AOTA. Evening/weekend programs available. *Faculty:* 6 full-time (all women). *Students:* 35 full-time (24 women); includes 33 minority (1 African American, 32 Hispanic Americans). 67 applicants, 37% accepted, 25 enrolled. In 2006, 16 degrees awarded. *Entrance requirements:* For master's, Health Occupations Aptitude Examination. *Application deadline:* For fall admission, 5/31 for domestic students; for winter admission, 11/1 priority date for domestic students. Application fee: $35. *Expenses:* Tuition, state resident: full-time $2,577; part-time $143 per credit hour. Tuition, nonresident: full-time $7,527; part-time $418 per credit hour. Required fees: $561. *Financial support:* Fellowships, research assistantships, teaching assistantships, career-related internships or fieldwork, Federal Work-Study, institutionally sponsored loans, scholarships/grants, traineeships, and unspecified assistantships available. *Faculty research:* Parenting of handicapped children, effects of healing touch on student stress, impact of RGV culture on women's roles. *Unit head:* Judith E. Bowen, Chair, 956-381-2474, Fax: 956-381-2476, E-mail: jebowen@panam.edu. *Application contact:* Dr. Theresa Pfeifer, Chair of Admissions Committee, 956-381-2475, Fax: 956-381-2476, E-mail: tapfeifer@utpa.edu.

The University of Toledo, College of Graduate Studies, College of Health Science and Human Service, Division of Health, Program in Occupational Therapy, Toledo, OH 43606-3390. Offers MOT, OTD. *Accreditation:* AOTA. *Faculty:* 6 full-time, 4 part-time/adjunct. *Students:* 49 full-time (45 women), 12 part-time (4 women); includes 3 minority (1 African American, 1 Asian American or Pacific Islander, 1 Hispanic American). Average age 25. 32 applicants, 88% accepted, 21 enrolled. In 2006, 17 degrees awarded. *Degree requirements:* For master's, scholarly project. *Entrance requirements:* For master's, GRE General Test, interview, minimum undergraduate GPA of 3.0, writing sample. *Application deadline:* For fall admission, 4/1 for domestic students. Applications are processed on a rolling basis. Application fee: $45. *Expenses: Contact institution. Financial support:* Federal Work-Study, institutionally sponsored loans, and scholarships/grants available. Financial award applicants required to submit FAFSA. *Faculty research:* Therapeutic occupation, pediatric neuroscience, grief/loss, motor control. Total annual research expenditures: $2,453. *Unit head:* Dr. Barbara Kopp-Miller, Chair, 419-530-4630. *Application contact:* Andrea Jacobs, Student Contact, 419-530-4636.

University of Utah, The Graduate School, College of Health, Division of Occupational Therapy, Salt Lake City, UT 84112-1107. Offers MOT. *Accreditation:* AOTA. *Faculty:* 7 full-time (all women), 34 part-time/adjunct (22 women). *Students:* 50 full-time (41 women); includes 1 minority (Asian American or Pacific Islander) Average age 29. 26 applicants, 92% accepted, 18 enrolled. In 2006, 23 degrees awarded. *Degree requirements:* For master's, thesis or alternative, project. *Entrance requirements:* For master's, GRE General Test. Additional exam requirements/recommendations for international students: Required—TOEFL (minimum score 575 paper-based; 233 computer-based). *Application deadline:* For fall admission, 1/15 for domestic students. Application fee: $75. *Expenses: Contact institution.* Tuition and fees vary according to class time and program. *Financial support:* In 2006–07, 7 students received support, including research assistantships with full tuition reimbursements available (averaging $10,000 per year); career-related internships or fieldwork, Federal Work-Study, institutionally sponsored loans, scholarships/grants, and unspecified assistantships also available. Financial award application deadline: 2/15; financial award applicants required to submit FAFSA. *Faculty research:* Community-based practice, occupational science, obesity, refugee, resilience. Total annual research expenditures: $5,000. *Unit head:* Dr. JoAnne Wright, Chairperson, 801-585-9135, Fax: 801-585-1001, E-mail: joanne.wright@hsc.utah.edu. *Application contact:* Kelly C. Brown, Academic Advisor, 801-585-0555, Fax: 801-585-1001, E-mail: kelly.brown@hsc.utah.edu.

University of Washington, School of Medicine and Graduate School, Graduate Programs in Medicine, Department of Rehabilitation Medicine, Seattle, WA 98195. Offers occupational therapy (MOT); physical therapy (DPT); rehabilitation science (PhD). *Faculty:* 56. *Students:* 175. Average age 30. In 2006, 25 master's, 30 doctorates awarded. *Median time to degree:* Master's–2 years full-time; doctorate–3 years full-time. *Degree requirements:* For doctorate, thesis/dissertation (for some programs), comprehensive exam (for some programs). *Entrance requirements:* Additional exam requirements/recommendations for international students: Required—TOEFL. Application fee: $45. *Faculty research:* Pediatric topics, balance, brain injury, spinal cord injury, pain, assistive technology. *Unit head:* Dr. Peter C. Esselman, Professor and Chair, 206-543-3600, Fax: 206-685-3244, E-mail: esselman@u.washington.edu. *Application contact:* Dr. Jean Deitz, Graduate Program Coordinator, 206-598-5396, Fax: 206-685-3244, E-mail: deitz@u.washington.edu.

The University of Western Ontario, Faculty of Graduate Studies, Biosciences Division, School of Occupational Therapy, London, ON N6A 5B8, Canada. Offers M Sc. Part-time programs available. *Faculty:* 11 full-time (10 women), 1 part-time/adjunct (0 women). *Students:* Average age 35. 9 applicants, 44% accepted, 3 enrolled. In 2006, 2 degrees awarded. *Degree requirements:* For master's, thesis. *Entrance requirements:* For master's, Canadian BA in occupational therapy or equivalent, minimum B+ average in last 2 years of 4 year degree. Additional exam requirements/recommendations for international students: Required—TOEFL (minimum score 570 paper-based; 250 computer-based). *Application deadline:* For fall admission, 2/15 priority date for domestic students. Application fee: $50 Canadian dollars. *Financial support:* Scholarships/grants available. Financial award application deadline: 4/1. *Faculty research:* Human occupation, clumsy children, biomechanics, learning disabilities, ergonomics. *Unit head:* Prof. Thelma Sumsion, Director, 519-661-2175 Ext. 86291, Fax: 519-661-3894, E-mail: tsumsion@uwo.ca. *Application contact:* Dr. C. Lee, Graduate Chair, 519-661-2111 Ext. 88958, Fax: 519-661-3894, E-mail: cjlee@uwo.ca.

University of Wisconsin–La Crosse, Office of University Graduate Studies, College of Science and Health, Department of Health Professions, Program in Occupational Therapy, La Crosse, WI 54601-3742. Offers MS. *Accreditation:* AOTA. *Students:* 36 full-time (33 women). Average age 23. 27 applicants, 93% accepted, 12 enrolled. *Degree requirements:* For master's, 6 month clinical internship. *Entrance requirements:* For master's, minimum GPA of 3.0, job shadowing. *Faculty research:* Handwriting interventions, kinematic analysis of movement. *Application contact:* Kathryn Kiefer, Associate Director of Admissions, 608-785-8939, E-mail: admissions@uwlax.edu.

University of Wisconsin–Madison, Graduate School, School of Education, Department of Kinesiology, Occupational Therapy Program, Madison, WI 53706-1380. Offers MS, PhD. *Degree requirements:* For doctorate, thesis/dissertation. Application fee: $45. *Financial support:* Fellowships with full tuition reimbursements, research assistantships with full tuition reimbursements, teaching assistantships with full tuition reimbursements, traineeships and project assistantships available. *Unit head:* Dr. Marty Schneider, Occupational Therapy Program Coordinator, 608-262-2936, E-mail: schneider@education.wisc.edu. *Application contact:* Diane Harlowe, Admissions Coordinator, 608-265-2223, Fax: 608-262-1639, E-mail: otadmissions@education.wisc.edu.

University of Wisconsin–Milwaukee, Graduate School, College of Health Sciences, Department of Occupational Therapy, Milwaukee, WI 53201-0413. Offers MS. *Accreditation:* AOTA. *Faculty:* 9 full-time (6 women). *Students:* 7 full-time (6 women), 3 part-time (all women), 1 international. 17 applicants, 53% accepted, 2 enrolled. In 2006, 21 degrees awarded. *Degree requirements:* For master's, thesis or alternative. *Application deadline:* For fall admission, 1/1 priority date for domestic students; for spring admission, 9/1 for domestic students. Applications are processed on a rolling basis. Application fee: $45 ($75 for international students). *Expenses:* Tuition, state resident: part-time $510 per credit. Tuition, nonresident: part-time $1,408 per credit. Tuition and fees vary according to program. *Financial support:* In 2006–07, 1 fellowship was awarded; research assistantships, teaching assistantships, unspecified assistantships also available. Support available to part-time students. Financial award application deadline: 4/15. *Unit head:* Virginia Stoffel, Representative, 414-229-4713, Fax: 414-229-5100, E-mail: stoffelv@uwm.edu.

Utica College, Program in Occupational Therapy, Utica, NY 13502-4892. Offers MS. *Accreditation:* AOTA. Part-time and evening/weekend programs available. *Faculty:* 7 full-time (all women). *Students:* 30 full-time (26 women); includes 2 minority (1 African American, 1 Asian American or Pacific Islander). 17 applicants, 100% accepted, 17 enrolled. In 2006, 4 degrees awarded. *Degree requirements:* For master's, thesis. *Entrance requirements:* For master's, physical health exam, CPR certification, 60 hours of volunteer experience, minimum GPA of 3.0. Additional exam requirements/recommendations for international students: Required—TOEFL (minimum score 550 paper-based; 213 computer-based). *Application deadline:* Applications are processed on a rolling basis. Application fee: $50. Electronic applications accepted. *Expenses: Contact institution. Financial support:* In 2006–07, 30 students received support. Career-related internships or fieldwork, scholarships/grants, tuition waivers (partial), and unspecified assistantships available. Support available to part-time students. Financial award application deadline: 3/15; financial award applicants required to submit FAFSA. *Unit head:* Sally Townsend, Director, Occupational Therapy Program, 315-792-3239, E-mail: stownsend@utica.edu. *Application contact:* John D. Rowe, Director of Graduate Admissions, 315-792-3824, Fax: 315-792-3003, E-mail: jrowe@utica.edu.

Virginia Commonwealth University, Graduate School, School of Allied Health Professions, Department of Health Administration, Doctoral Program in Health Related Sciences, Richmond, VA 23284-9005. Offers clinical laboratory sciences (PhD); gerontology (PhD); health administration (PhD); nurse anesthesia (PhD); occupational therapy (PhD); physical therapy (PhD); radiation sciences (PhD); rehabilitation leadership (PhD). *Faculty:* 2 full-time (1 woman). *Students:* 4 full-time (all women), 13 part-time (7 women); includes 7 minority (1 African American, 6 Asian Americans or Pacific Islanders), 3 international. In 2006, 2 degrees awarded. *Unit head:* Monica L. White, Director of Student Services, 804-828-3273, Fax: 804-828-8656, E-mail: mlwhite1@vcu.edu.

See Close-Up on page 1745.

Virginia Commonwealth University, Graduate School, School of Allied Health Professions, Department of Occupational Therapy, Richmond, VA 23284-9005. Offers MS, MSOT. *Accreditation:* AOTA (one or more programs are accredited). *Faculty:* 7 full-time (6 women). *Students:* 69 full-time (64 women), 11 part-time (10 women); includes 11 minority (8 African Americans, 1 American Indian/Alaska Native, 1 Asian American or Pacific Islander, 1 Hispanic American), 1 international. 8 applicants, 100% accepted, 7 enrolled. In 2006, 12 degrees awarded. *Degree requirements:* For master's, fieldwork. *Entrance requirements:* For master's, GRE General Test. *Application deadline:* For fall admission, 2/1 for domestic students. Application fee: $50. *Faculty research:* Children with complex care needs, instrument development, carpal tunnel syndrome, development of oral-motor feeding programs, school system practice. *Unit head:* Dr. Sandra H. Cash, Director, 804-828-3645, Fax: 804-828-0782, E-mail: shcash@vcu.edu.

See Close-Up on page 1747.

Washington University in St. Louis, School of Medicine, Graduate Programs in Medicine, Program in Occupational Therapy, St. Louis, MO 63130-4899. Offers MSOT, OTD. *Accreditation:* AOTA. *Faculty:* 18 full-time (14 women). *Students:* 163 full-time (153 women); includes 21 minority (5 African Americans, 1 American Indian/Alaska Native, 15 Asian Americans or Pacific Islanders), 4 international. Average age 23. 168 applicants, 58% accepted, 60 enrolled. In 2006, 23 master's, 12 doctorates awarded. Terminal master's awarded for partial completion of doctoral program. *Degree requirements:* For master's, complete fieldwork 1 and 2 experiences; for doctorate, complete fieldwork 1, 2, and 3 experiences. *Entrance requirements:* For master's, GRE General Test, bachelor's degree in another field or enrollment in an affiliated 3/2 institution; for doctorate, GRE General Test, bachelor's degree in another field or enrollment in an affiliated institution. Additional exam requirements/recommendations for international students: Required—TOEFL (minimum score 250 computer-based), TWE (minimum score 5). *Application deadline:* For fall admission, 1/31 priority date for domestic and international students. Applications are processed on a rolling basis. Application fee: $55. Electronic applications accepted. *Financial support:* In 2006–07, 10 research assistantships with partial tuition reimbursements (averaging $4,000 per year), 12 teaching assistantships with partial tuition reimbursements (averaging $3,750 per year) were awarded; Federal Work-Study, scholarships/grants, and health care benefits also available. Support available to part-time students. Financial award application deadline: 1/31; financial award applicants required to submit FAFSA. *Faculty research:* Brain injury, ergonomics, work performance, caregiving, quality of life. Total annual research expenditures: $1.8 million. *Unit head:* Dr. Carolyn Baum, Director, 314-286-1600 Ext. 1619, Fax: 314-286-1601, E-mail: wuotinfo@wustl.edu. *Application contact:* Elaine Halley, Recruitment Manager, 314-286-1600 Ext. 1617, Fax: 314-286-1601, E-mail: wuotinfo@wustl.edu.

Wayne State University, Eugene Applebaum College of Pharmacy and Health Sciences, Department of Health Care Sciences, Program in Occupational Therapy, Detroit, MI 48202. Offers MOT, MS. *Accreditation:* AOTA. Part-time programs available. *Faculty:* 2 full-time (both women), 3 part-time/adjunct (all women). *Students:* 16 full-time (all women), 2 part-time (both women); includes 4 minority (3 African Americans, 1 Asian American or Pacific Islander), 5 international. Average age 27. 8 applicants, 25% accepted, 0 enrolled. In 2006, 20 degrees awarded. *Degree requirements:* For master's, thesis optional. *Entrance requirements:* Additional exam requirements/recommendations for international students: Required—TOEFL (minimum score 550 paper-based; 213 computer-based); Recommended—TWE (minimum score 6). *Application deadline:* For fall admission, 7/1 for domestic students, 6/1 for international students; for winter admission, 10/1 for international students; for spring admission, 3/15 for domestic students, 2/1 for international students. Applications are processed on a rolling basis. Application fee: $30 ($50 for international students). Electronic applications accepted. *Financial support:* Research assistantships with tuition reimbursements, teaching assistantships, career-related internships or fieldwork and scholarships/grants available. Support available to part-time students. *Faculty research:* Assistive technology, education and fieldwork innovation, gerontology, motor control, rehabilitation outcomes. *Unit head:* Joseph Pellerito, Program Director, 313-577-5880, Fax: 313-577-5822, E-mail: ah2668@wayne.edu.

Western Michigan University, Graduate College, College of Health and Human Services, Department of Occupational Therapy, Kalamazoo, MI 49008-5202. Offers MS. *Accreditation:* AOTA. *Entrance requirements:* For master's, GRE General Test.

West Virginia University, School of Medicine, Graduate Programs in Human Performance and Applied Exercise Science, Program in Occupational Therapy, Morgantown, WV 26506. Offers MOT. Students enter program as undergraduates. *Accreditation:* AOTA. Post-baccalaureate distance learning degree programs offered. *Degree requirements:* For master's, clinical rotation. Expenses: Contact institution. Tuition and fees vary according to program.

Winston-Salem State University, Department of Occupational Therapy, Winston-Salem, NC 27110-0003. Offers MS. *Accreditation:* AOTA. *Faculty:* 5 full-time (all women). *Students:* 18 full-time (14 women); includes 8 minority (7 African Americans, 1 American Indian/Alaska Native). Average age 22. 22 applicants, 68% accepted, 15 enrolled. *Degree requirements:* For master's, registration. *Entrance requirements:* For master's, GRE, 3 letters of recommendation (one from a licensed occupational therapist where volunteer or work experiences were performed; the other two from former professors or persons acquainted with academic potential); writing sample . Additional exam requirements/recommendations for international students: Required—TOEFL. *Application deadline:* For fall admission, 3/15 for domestic and international students. Applications are processed on a rolling basis. Application fee: $40. Electronic applications accepted. *Expenses:* Tuition, state resident: full-time $2,010. Tuition, nonresident: full-time $10,502. Tuition and fees vary according to course load. *Financial*

Occupational Therapy

Winston-Salem State University (continued)
support: In 2006–07, 15 students received support; research assistantships, teaching assistantships, career-related internships or fieldwork, institutionally sponsored loans, scholarships/grants, and tuition waivers (partial) available. *Faculty research:* Assistive technology, environmental adaptations, comprehensive performance evaluations. Total annual research expenditures: $320,322. *Unit head:* Dr. Dorothy P. Bethea, Chair and Associate Professor, 336-750-3172, Fax: 336-750-3173, E-mail: betheadp@wssu.edu. *Application contact:* 336-750-2102, Fax: 336-750-3042, E-mail: graduate@wssu.edu.

Worcester State College, Graduate Studies, Program in Occupational Therapy, Worcester, MA 01602-2597. Offers MOT. *Accreditation:* AOTA. *Students:* 23 full-time (all women), 1 (woman) part-time, 1 international. Average age 29. 34 applicants, 97% accepted, 17 enrolled. In 2006, 18 degrees awarded. *Degree requirements:* For master's, thesis optional. *Entrance requirements:* For master's, GRE General Test or MAT, minimum undergraduate GPA of 3.2. Additional exam requirements/recommendations for international students: Required—TOEFL (minimum score 550 paper-based; 213 computer-based). *Application deadline:* For fall admission, 3/15 priority date for domestic students. Application fee: $30. *Expenses:* Contact institution. *Financial support:* In 2006–07, 3 research assistantships with full tuition reimbursements (averaging $4,267 per year) were awarded; career-related internships or fieldwork, Federal Work-Study, institutionally sponsored loans, scholarships/grants, and unspecified assistantships also available. Support available to part-time students. Financial award application deadline: 3/1; financial award applicants required to submit FAFSA. *Unit head:* Dr. Andrea Bilics, Coordinator, 508-929-8895, Fax: 508-929-8178, E-mail: abilics@worcester.edu. *Application contact:* Nicole Brown, Assistant Dean of Continuing Education, 508-929-8787, Fax: 508-929-8100, E-mail: nbrown@worcester.edu.

Xavier University, College of Social Sciences, Health and Education, Occupational Therapy Program, Cincinnati, OH 45207. Offers MOT. *Accreditation:* AOTA. *Faculty:* 5 full-time (all women). *Students:* 18 full-time (17 women). Average age 30. 19 applicants, 89% accepted, 17 enrolled. In 2006, 2 degrees awarded. *Degree requirements:* For master's, thesis or alternative, research project. *Entrance requirements:* For master's, GRE, minimum GPA of 2.8, volunteer hours. Additional exam requirements/recommendations for international students: Required—TOEFL. *Application deadline:* For fall admission, 8/1 for domestic and international students. *Expenses:* Tuition: Part-time $462 per credit hour. Part-time tuition and fees vary according to degree level, campus/location and program. *Financial support:* Applicants required to submit FAFSA. *Faculty research:* Occupation ethics, technology, mentoring, professional behavior. *Unit head:* Dr. Carol Scheerer, Chair, 513-745-3310, Fax: 513-745-3261, E-mail: scheerer@xavier.edu. *Application contact:* Jo Plunkett, Program Assistant, 513-745-3360, Fax: 513-745-1048, E-mail: xugrad@xavier.edu.

Physical Therapy

Alabama State University, School of Graduate Studies, College of Health Sciences, Department of Physical Therapy, Montgomery, AL 36101-0271. Offers DPT. *Accreditation:* APTA. *Faculty:* 7 full-time (5 women). *Students:* 16 full-time (9 women); includes 10 minority (9 African Americans, 1 Hispanic American). Terminal master's awarded for partial completion of doctoral program. *Entrance requirements:* Additional exam requirements/recommendations for international students: Required—TOEFL (minimum score 500 paper-based; 173 computer-based). *Application deadline:* For fall admission, 7/15 for domestic students; for spring admission, 12/15 for domestic students. Applications are processed on a rolling basis. Application fee: $10. *Expenses:* Tuition, state resident: full-time $1,728; part-time $192 per hour. Tuition, nonresident: full-time $3,456; part-time $334 per hour. *Financial support:* In 2006–07, 4 research assistantships (averaging $9,450 per year) were awarded.

American International College, School of Health Sciences, Program in Physical Therapy, Springfield, MA 01109-3189. Offers MPT, DPT. *Accreditation:* APTA. *Faculty:* 7 full-time (5 women). *Students:* 38 full-time (23 women); includes 4 minority (2 African Americans, 1 Asian American or Pacific Islander, 1 Hispanic American), 2 international. Average age 27. In 2006, 11 degrees awarded. *Degree requirements:* For master's, thesis (for some programs), comprehensive exam, registration. *Entrance requirements:* For master's, minimum GPA of 3.2, writing sample. Additional exam requirements/recommendations for international students: Required—TOEFL. *Application deadline:* For fall admission, 7/1 priority date for domestic and international students; for spring admission, 12/1 priority date for domestic and international students. Applications are processed on a rolling basis. Application fee: $50. *Expenses:* Contact institution. *Financial support:* Career-related internships or fieldwork available. Support available to part-time students. Financial award application deadline: 4/1; financial award applicants required to submit FAFSA. *Unit head:* Dr. Edward Swanson, Director, 413-205-3320, Fax: 413-205-3943, E-mail: edward.swanson@aic.edu. *Application contact:* Keshawn Dodds, Associate Director of Graduate Admissions, 413-205-3549, Fax: 413-205-3911, E-mail: keshawn.dodds@aic.edu.

Andrews University, School of Graduate Studies, College of Arts and Sciences, Department of Physical Therapy, Postprofessional Physical Therapy Program, Berrien Springs, MI 49104. Offers Dr Sc PT, TDPT. *Accreditation:* APTA. *Students:* 45 full-time (21 women), 15 part-time (8 women); includes 8 minority (2 African Americans, 6 Asian Americans or Pacific Islanders), 8 international. Average age 32. *Application deadline:* For fall admission, 12/1 priority date for domestic students. Applications are processed on a rolling basis. Application fee: $40. *Expenses:* Contact institution. *Financial support:* Federal Work-Study, institutionally sponsored loans, and scholarships/grants available. Financial award application deadline: 9/1; financial award applicants required to submit FAFSA. *Faculty research:* Home health patient profile, clinical education, breeding success of marine birds, trends in home health care for physical therapy, patient motivation in acute rehabilitation. *Unit head:* Kathy Berglund, Director of Professional Programs, 269-471-6076, Fax: 269-471-2866, E-mail: berglund@andrews.edu.

Angelo State University, College of Graduate Studies, College of Sciences, Department of Physical Therapy, San Angelo, TX 76909. Offers MPT. *Accreditation:* APTA. *Faculty:* 6 full-time (4 women). *Students:* 39 full-time (29 women), 17 part-time (11 women); includes 12 minority (2 African Americans, 1 American Indian/Alaska Native, 2 Asian Americans or Pacific Islanders, 7 Hispanic Americans), 1 international. Average age 25. 42 applicants, 45% accepted, 19 enrolled. In 2006, 18 degrees awarded. *Degree requirements:* For master's, 3 clinical placements. *Entrance requirements:* For master's, GRE General Test, interview, minimum undergraduate GPA of 3.0 in all prerequisite courses. Additional exam requirements/recommendations for international students: Required—TOEFL or IELTS. *Application deadline:* For fall admission, 4/28 priority date for domestic students, 3/15 for international students. Applications are processed on a rolling basis. Application fee: $40 ($50 for international students). Electronic applications accepted. *Expenses:* Tuition, state resident: full-time $2,340; part-time $130 per hour. Tuition, nonresident: full-time $7,290; part-time $405 per hour. Required fees: $906; $56 per hour. *Financial support:* In 2006–07, 50 students received support. Scholarships/grants available. Financial award application deadline: 3/1; financial award applicants required to submit FAFSA. *Faculty research:* Women and lipoproteins, international distance education, quadriceps femoris and the VMO, ergonomics, children and obesity. *Unit head:* Dr. Scott Hasson, Department Head, 325-942-2581 Ext. 278, E-mail: ptdept@angelo.edu. *Application contact:* Mark W. Pape, Chair, 325-942-2545 Ext. 232, E-mail: mark.pape@angelo.edu.

Arcadia University, Graduate Studies, Department of Physical Therapy, Glenside, PA 19038-3295. Offers DPT. *Accreditation:* APTA. *Faculty:* 6 full-time (4 women), 20 part-time/adjunct (15 women). *Students:* 143 full-time (104 women), 28 part-time (23 women); includes 10 minority (3 African Americans, 5 Asian Americans or Pacific Islanders, 2 Hispanic Americans), 1 international. In 2006, 41 degrees awarded. *Application deadline:* For fall admission, 1/31 for domestic students. Application fee: $50. *Expenses:* Contact institution. *Financial support:* In 2006–07, 15 students received support. Career-related internships or fieldwork, tuition waivers (partial), and unspecified assistantships available. *Unit head:* Dr. Rebecca L. Craik, Chair, 215-572-2143. *Application contact:* 215-572-2910, Fax: 215-572-4049, E-mail: admiss@arcadia.edu.

Arkansas State University, Graduate School, College of Nursing and Health Professions, Program in Physical Therapy, Jonesboro, State University, AR 72467. Offers MPT. *Accreditation:* APTA. Part-time programs available. *Faculty:* 1 full-time (0 women), 1 (woman) part-time/adjunct. *Students:* 16 full-time (11 women), 31 part-time (21 women); includes 2 minority (1 African American, 1 Asian American or Pacific Islander), 1 international. Average age 27. 20 applicants, 75% accepted, 15 enrolled. *Degree requirements:* For master's, comprehensive exam. *Entrance requirements:* For master's, GRE General Test, Allied Health Profession Admissions Test, appropriate bachelor's degree, letters of reference, resumé, official transcript. Additional exam requirements/recommendations for international students: Required—TOEFL (minimum score 213 computer-based). *Application deadline:* Applications are processed on a rolling basis. Application fee: $30 ($40 for international students). Electronic applications accepted. *Expenses:* Contact institution. *Financial support:* Scholarships/grants available. Financial award application deadline: 7/1; financial award applicants required to submit FAFSA. *Unit head:* Dr. James Farris, Director, 870-972-3591, Fax: 870-972-3652, E-mail: jfarris@astate.edu.

Armstrong Atlantic State University, School of Graduate Studies, Program in Physical Therapy, Savannah, GA 31419-1997. Offers MSPT. *Accreditation:* APTA. *Faculty:* 4 full-time (2 women). *Students:* 54 full-time (46 women); includes 3 minority (2 African Americans, 1 Asian American or Pacific Islander), 2 international. Average age 26. In 2006, 11 degrees awarded. *Degree requirements:* For master's, thesis, oral presentation. *Entrance requirements:* For master's, GRE General Test, minimum GPA of 2.75; course work in general chemistry, physics, anatomy, physiology, statistics; letters of recommendation, bachelor's degree. Additional exam requirements/recommendations for international students: Required—TOEFL (minimum score 523 paper-based; 193 computer-based). *Application deadline:* For fall admission, 1/15 for domestic students. Applications are processed on a rolling basis. Application fee: $25. Electronic applications accepted. *Expenses:* Tuition, state resident: full-time $2,286; part-time $127 per credit. Tuition, nonresident: full-time $9,144; part-time $508 per credit. One-time fee: $257. *Financial support:* In 2006–07, research assistantships with partial tuition reimbursements (averaging $2,500 per year); career-related internships or fieldwork, scholarships/grants, and unspecified assistantships also available. Financial award applicants required to submit FAFSA. *Faculty research:* Exercise modalities, physical agents, magnetic therapy, leadership development, perception of physical therapists. *Unit head:* Dr. David A. Lake, Department Head, 912-921-2327, Fax: 912-921-5838, E-mail: lakedavi@mail.armstrong.edu.

A.T. Still University of Health Sciences, Arizona School of Health Sciences, Mesa, AZ 85206. Offers advanced occupational therapy (MS); advanced physician assistant (MS); audiology (Au D); human movement (MS); medical informatics (MS); occupational therapy (MS); physical therapy (MS, DPT); physician assistant (MS); sports health care (MS); transitional physical therapy (DPT). *Accreditation:* AOTA (one or more programs are accredited); APTA. Postbaccalaureate distance learning degree programs offered (no on-campus study). *Faculty:* 47 full-time (27 women), 101 part-time/adjunct (60 women). *Students:* 442 full-time (277 women), 732 part-time (579 women); includes 143 minority (38 African Americans, 11 American Indian/Alaska Native, 55 Asian Americans or Pacific Islanders, 39 Hispanic Americans), 4 international. Average age 33. 1,471 applicants, 547 enrolled. In 2006, 104 master's, 432 doctorates awarded. *Degree requirements:* For master's and doctorate, thesis/dissertation (for some programs). *Entrance requirements:* For master's, GRE General Test, minimum GPA of 2.5; for doctorate, GRE, Evaluation of Practicing Audiologists Capabilities (Au D), Physical Therapy Evaluation Tool (DPT), current state licensure, master's degree or equivalent (Au D), minimum GPA of 2.7. *Application deadline:* For fall admission, 2/1 priority date for domestic and international students. Applications are processed on a rolling basis. Application fee: $60. *Expenses:* Contact institution. *Financial support:* In 2006–07, 382 students received support. Federal Work-Study and scholarships/grants available. Financial award application deadline: 5/1. *Faculty research:* Constraint-induced therapy, scapular motion analysis, shoulder mobility, biomechanics, quadriceps. *Unit head:* Dr. Randy Danielsen, Dean, 480-219-6000, Fax: 480-219-6110, E-mail: rdanielsen@atsu.edu. *Application contact:* Donna Sparks, Associate Director for Admissions, 660-626-2237, Fax: 660-626-2969, E-mail: admissions@atsu.edu.

Azusa Pacific University, School of Behavioral and Applied Sciences, Department of Physical Therapy, Azusa, CA 91702-7000. Offers entry-level (DPT); transitional (DPT). *Accreditation:* APTA. Part-time and evening/weekend programs available. Postbaccalaureate distance learning degree programs offered. *Faculty:* 7 full-time (3 women). *Students:* 50 full-time (28 women); includes 15 minority (2 African Americans, 6 Asian Americans or Pacific Islanders, 7 Hispanic Americans). 46 applicants, 76% accepted, 26 enrolled. In 2006, 12 degrees awarded. *Degree requirements:* For doctorate, thesis/dissertation. *Entrance requirements:* For doctorate, GRE General Test. Additional exam requirements/recommendations for international students: Required—TOEFL (minimum score 600 paper-based; 250 computer-based). *Application deadline:* For fall admission, 11/15 for domestic and international students. Applications are processed on a rolling basis. Application fee: $45 ($65 for international students). Electronic applications accepted. *Expenses:* Contact institution. *Financial support:* Career-related internships or fieldwork available. Financial award applicants required to submit FAFSA. *Faculty research:* FES and spinal cord injury, electromyogram and muscle pathology, thermal regulation and body composition. *Unit head:* Dr. Michael Laymon, Chair, 626-815-5020, Fax: 626-815-5017, E-mail: mlaymon@apu.edu. *Application contact:* Anel Herrera, Administrative Manager, 626-815-5014, Fax: 626-815-5017, E-mail: aherrera@apu.edu.

Baylor University, Graduate School, Academy of Health Sciences, Program in Physical Therapy, Fort Sam Houston, TX 78234. Offers MPT, DPT. Offered jointly with the U.S. Army. *Accreditation:* APTA. *Students:* 70 full-time (30 women); includes 8 minority (3 African Americans, 2 Asian Americans or Pacific Islanders, 3 Hispanic Americans). In 2006, 16 degrees awarded. *Degree requirements:* For master's, research paper. *Entrance requirements:* For master's, GRE General Test. *Application deadline:* For fall admission, 2/1 for domestic students. Applications are processed on a rolling basis. Application fee: $25. *Faculty research:* Effect of electrical stimulation on normal and immobilized muscle, effects of inversion traction. *Unit head:* Lt. Col. Timothy Flynn, Director, 210-221-5187, Fax: 210-221-7585, E-mail: timothy.flynn@cen.amedd.army.mil. *Application contact:* Gail Dreitzler, Class Advisor, 210-221-8410, E-mail: gail.dreitzler@cen.amedd.army.mil.

Baylor University, Graduate School, Academy of Health Sciences, Program in Physical Therapy, Brooke Army Medical Center, Fort Sam Houston, TX 78234-6200. Offers Dr Sc PT. Offered jointly with the U.S. Army. *Students:* 4 full-time (2 women). In 2006, 4 degrees awarded.

Degree requirements: For doctorate, project, paper. *Entrance requirements:* For doctorate, GRE General Test. *Unit head:* Maj. Daniel G. Rendeiro, Director, 210-916-4074, E-mail: daniel.rendeiro@cen.amedd.army.mil.

Baylor University, Graduate School, Academy of Health Sciences, Program in Physical Therapy, U.S. Army Military Academy, West Point, NY 76798. Offers Dr Sc PT. Offered jointly with the U.S. Army. *Accreditation:* APTA. *Students:* 3 full-time (0 women). In 2006, 4 degrees awarded. *Unit head:* Lt. Col. Josef Moore, Director, 845-938-3324 Ext. 688, Fax: 845-938-5053, E-mail: josef.moore@mercury.westpoint.amedd.army.mil.

Bellarmine University, Donna and Allan Lansing School of Nursing and Health Sciences, Louisville, KY 40205-0671. Offers nursing administration (MSN); nursing education (MSN); physical therapy (DPT). *Accreditation:* AACN; APTA. *Faculty:* 15 full-time (11 women), 8 part-time/adjunct (7 women). *Students:* 112 full-time (87 women), 70 part-time (66 women); includes 12 minority (7 African Americans, 4 Asian Americans or Pacific Islanders, 1 Hispanic American), 1 international. Average age 31. In 2006, 44 degrees awarded. *Degree requirements:* For doctorate, comprehensive exam. *Entrance requirements:* For master's, GRE General Test, minimum undergraduate GPA of 2.75, RN license; for doctorate, minimum prerequisites course-work GPA of 2.75, 2.5 overall; 25 hours of documented service in physical therapy; physical ability to perform tasks of a physical therapist. Additional exam requirements/recommendations for international students: Required—TOEFL (minimum score 550 paper-based; 213 computer-based; 80 iBT). *Application deadline:* For fall admission, 10/15 priority date for domestic students. Applications are processed on a rolling basis. Application fee: $25. Electronic applications accepted. *Expenses: Contact institution.* Tuition and fees vary according to program. *Financial support:* Career-related internships or fieldwork and scholarships/grants available. *Faculty research:* Pain, empathy, leadership styles, control. *Unit head:* Dr. Susan H. Davis, Dean, 800-274-4723 Ext. 8217, E-mail: sdavis@bellarmine.edu. *Application contact:* Julie Armstrong-Binnix, Health Science Recruiter, 800-274-4723 Ext. 8364, E-mail: julieab@bellarmine.edu.

Belmont University, College of Health Sciences, School of Physical Therapy, Nashville, TN 37212-3757. Offers DPT. *Accreditation:* APTA. *Faculty:* 9 full-time (5 women), 15 part-time/adjunct (10 women). *Students:* 99 full-time (78 women); includes 3 minority (2 African Americans, 1 Asian American or Pacific Islander), 1 international. Average age 25. 168 applicants, 35% accepted, 35 enrolled. In 2006, 28 degrees awarded. *Median time to degree:* Doctorate–3 years full-time. *Degree requirements:* For doctorate, registration. *Entrance requirements:* For doctorate, GRE General Test, minimum GPA of 3.0, 50 observation hours. Additional exam requirements/recommendations for international students: Required—TOEFL (minimum score 500 paper-based; 173 computer-based). *Application deadline:* For fall admission, 8/31 priority date for domestic and international students. Applications are processed on a rolling basis. Application fee: $50. Electronic applications accepted. *Expenses: Contact institution. Financial support:* In 2006–07, 74 students received support. Scholarships/grants available. Financial award applicants required to submit FAFSA. *Faculty research:* Clinical electrophysiology, orthopedic injuries in shoulders and knees, biochemical analysis of softball pitchers. *Unit head:* Dr. John S. Halle, Associate Dean, 615-460-6727, Fax: 615-460-6729, E-mail: hallej@mail.belmont.edu. *Application contact:* Lucy Baltimore, Program Assistant, 615-460-6726, Fax: 615-460-6729, E-mail: baltimorel@mail.belmont.edu.

Boston University, College of Health and Rehabilitation Sciences—Sargent College, Department of Physical Therapy and Athletic Training, Boston, MA 02215. Offers physical therapy (DPT); rehabilitation sciences (D Sc). *Accreditation:* APTA (one or more programs are accredited). Postbaccalaureate distance learning degree programs offered (minimal on-campus study). *Faculty:* 15 full-time (11 women), 22 part-time/adjunct (15 women). *Students:* 117 full-time (96 women), 185 part-time (128 women); includes 32 minority (3 African Americans, 18 Asian Americans or Pacific Islanders, 11 Hispanic Americans), 5 international. Average age 32. 185 applicants, 56% accepted, 33 enrolled. In 2006, 212 doctorates awarded. *Degree requirements:* For doctorate, thesis/dissertation (for some programs). *Entrance requirements:* For doctorate, GRE General Test, master's degree. Additional exam requirements/recommendations for international students: Required—TOEFL (minimum score 550 paper-based). *Application deadline:* For fall admission, 1/5 for domestic students. Applications are processed on a rolling basis. Application fee: $70. Electronic applications accepted. *Expenses:* Tuition: Full-time $33,330; part-time $1,042 per credit. Required fees: $462; $40. *Financial support:* In 2006–07, 3 research assistantships with full tuition reimbursements, 10 teaching assistantships with full tuition reimbursements were awarded; career-related internships or fieldwork, Federal Work-Study, institutionally sponsored loans, scholarships/grants, and tuition waivers (partial) also available. Financial award application deadline: 4/15. *Faculty research:* EMG, gait, infant assessment, motor control, orthopedics. *Unit head:* Dr. Julie Keysor, Chairman, 617-353-2735, E-mail: jkeysor@bu.edu. *Application contact:* Sharon Sankey, Director, Student Services, 617-353-2713, Fax: 617-353-7500, E-mail: ssankey@bu.edu.

Bradley University, Graduate School, College of Education and Health Sciences, Department of Physical Therapy and Health Science, Peoria, IL 61625-0002. Offers physical therapy (DPT). *Accreditation:* APTA. *Students:* 40 full-time (33 women). *Entrance requirements:* For doctorate, GRE, 2 letters of recommendation. Additional exam requirements/recommendations for international students: Required—TOEFL (minimum score 600 paper-based; 250 computer-based). *Application deadline:* Applications are processed on a rolling basis. Application fee: $40 ($50 for international students). *Expenses: Contact institution. Financial support:* Scholarships/grants, tuition waivers (partial), and unspecified assistantships available. Financial award application deadline: 4/1. *Unit head:* Dr. Mary Jo Mays, Chairperson, 309-677-3489, E-mail: jun@bradley.edu. *Application contact:* Dr. Andrew J. Strubhar, Information Contact, 309-677-2856, E-mail: ajs@bradley.edu.

California State University, Fresno, Division of Graduate Studies, College of Health and Human Services, Department of Physical Therapy, Fresno, CA 93740-8027. Offers MPT. *Accreditation:* APTA. *Degree requirements:* For master's, comprehensive exam. *Entrance requirements:* For master's, GRE General Test, minimum GPA of 3.0. Additional exam requirements/recommendations for international students: Required—TOEFL. Electronic applications accepted. *Faculty research:* Dance, occupational health, ethics.

California State University, Long Beach, Graduate Studies, College of Health and Human Services, Department of Physical Therapy, Long Beach, CA 90840. Offers MPT. *Accreditation:* APTA. *Faculty:* 9 full-time (5 women), 8 part-time/adjunct (5 women). *Students:* 100 full-time (56 women), 4 part-time (3 women); includes 32 minority (1 African American, 20 Asian Americans or Pacific Islanders, 11 Hispanic Americans), 1 international. Average age 28. 96 applicants, 59% accepted, 40 enrolled. In 2006, 18 degrees awarded. *Degree requirements:* For master's, thesis. *Entrance requirements:* For master's, GRE General Test. *Application deadline:* For fall admission, 7/1 for domestic students; for spring admission, 12/1 for domestic students. Applications are processed on a rolling basis. Application fee: $55. Electronic applications accepted. *Financial support:* Federal Work-Study, institutionally sponsored loans, and scholarships/grants available. Financial award application deadline: 3/2; financial award applicants required to submit FAFSA. *Unit head:* Dr. Kay Cerny, Chair, 562-985-4072, Fax: 562-985-4069, E-mail: kcerny@csulb.edu. *Application contact:* Information Contact, 562-985-4072, Fax: 562-985-4069.

California State University, Northridge, Graduate Studies, College of Health and Human Development, Department of Physical Therapy, Northridge, CA 91330. Offers MPT. *Accreditation:* APTA. *Faculty:* 7 full-time (6 women), 9 part-time/adjunct (6 women). *Students:* 91 full-time (28 women), 1 part-time; includes 28 minority (1 African American, 1 American Indian/Alaska Native, 16 Asian Americans or Pacific Islanders, 10 Hispanic Americans), 2 international. Average age 27. 90 applicants, 46% accepted, 39 enrolled. In 2006, 26 degrees awarded. *Entrance requirements:* For master's, GRE General Test or minimum GPA of 3.0. Additional exam requirements/recommendations for international students: Required—TOEFL. *Application deadline:* For fall admission, 11/30 for domestic students. Application fee: $55. *Expenses:* Tuition, nonresident: full-time $8,136; part-time $4,068 per year. Required fees: $3,624; $1,161 per term. *Financial support:* Application deadline: 3/1. *Unit head:* Dr. Janen Beling, Chair, 818-677-2203.

Carroll College, Program in Physical Therapy, Waukesha, WI 53186-5593. Offers MPT, DPT. *Accreditation:* APTA. *Faculty:* 5 full-time (2 women), 1 part-time/adjunct (0 women). *Students:* 47 full-time (39 women); includes 1 minority (Hispanic American) Average age 25. 48 applicants, 69% accepted, 32 enrolled. *Degree requirements:* For master's, thesis (for some programs). *Entrance requirements:* For master's, GRE General Test, recommendations, clinical observation. Additional exam requirements/recommendations for international students: Required—TOEFL. *Application deadline:* For fall admission, 7/14 for domestic students. Applications are processed on a rolling basis. Application fee: $25. *Expenses: Contact institution.* Part-time tuition and fees vary according to program. *Financial support:* In 2006–07, 35 students received support, including fellowships (averaging $3,000 per year). Support available to part-time students. Financial award application deadline: 3/15; financial award applicants required to submit FAFSA. *Faculty research:* Physical therapy education, geriatrics, neural control of movement, wellness and prevention in apparently healthy individuals with disease and disability. *Unit head:* Dr. Jane F. Hopp, Dean, Natural and Health Sciences, 262-524-7294, E-mail: jhopp@cc.edu. *Application contact:* Jennifer L. Wells-Sperry, Director of Graduate Admission, 262-524-7357, Fax: 262-951-3037, E-mail: jwells@cc.edu.

Central Michigan University, College of Graduate Studies, The Herbert H. and Grace A. Dow College of Health Professions, School of Rehabilitation and Medical Sciences, Mount Pleasant, MI 48859. Offers physical therapy (DPT); physician assistant (MS). *Accreditation:* APTA; ARC-PA. *Degree requirements:* For master's, thesis or alternative, comprehensive exam (for some programs), registration.

Chapman University, Graduate Studies, Wilkinson College of Letters and Sciences, Department of Physical Therapy, Orange, CA 92866. Offers DPT. *Accreditation:* APTA. *Faculty:* 9 full-time (8 women), 3 part-time/adjunct (1 woman). *Students:* 86 full-time (62 women), 43 part-time (31 women); includes 10 minority (8 Asian Americans or Pacific Islanders, 2 Hispanic Americans), 2 international. Average age 25. 204 applicants, 50% accepted, 50 enrolled. In 2006, 34 degrees awarded. *Degree requirements:* For doctorate, comprehensive exam, registration. *Entrance requirements:* For doctorate, GRE General Test, minimum undergraduate GPA of 3.0. Additional exam requirements/recommendations for international students: Required—TOEFL (minimum score 550 paper-based). *Application deadline:* For fall admission, 12/5 priority date for domestic and international students. Application fee: $65. Electronic applications accepted. *Expenses: Contact institution. Financial support:* In 2006–07, 30 students received support, including 9 fellowships (averaging $2,259 per year); Federal Work-Study also available. Financial award application deadline: 6/30; financial award applicants required to submit FAFSA. *Unit head:* Dr. Venita Lovelace-Chandler, Chair, 714-997-6755, E-mail: lovelacech@chapman.edu. *Application contact:* Saundra Hoover, Director of Graduate Admissions, 714-997-6786, E-mail: shoover@chapman.edu.

Chatham University, Program in Physical Therapy, Pittsburgh, PA 15232-2826. Offers DPT, TDPT. *Accreditation:* APTA. Part-time and evening/weekend programs available. *Students:* 66 full-time (48 women), 37 part-time (14 women). Average age 29. 86 applicants, 67% accepted, 44 enrolled. In 2006, 28 degrees awarded. *Degree requirements:* For doctorate, thesis/dissertation, clinical research project. *Entrance requirements:* For doctorate, GRE, community service, interview, minimum GPA of 3.0, writing sample, volunteer work experience. Additional exam requirements/recommendations for international students: Required—TOEFL (minimum score 600 paper-based; 250 computer-based; 100 iBT); Recommended—IELTS (minimum score 7), TWE (minimum score 5). *Application deadline:* For fall admission, 1/5 priority date for domestic students. Applications are processed on a rolling basis. Application fee: $45. Electronic applications accepted. *Financial support:* Career-related internships or fieldwork available. Financial award applicants required to submit FAFSA. *Faculty research:* Stroke rehabilitation, pediatric physical therapy, psychological issues of health. *Unit head:* Dr. Patricia Downey, Director, 412-365-1199, Fax: 412-365-1505, E-mail: downey@chatham.edu. *Application contact:* 412-365-1825, Fax: 412-365-1609, E-mail: admissions@chatham.edu.

Clarke College, Physical Therapy Program, Dubuque, IA 52001-3198. Offers MSPT. Freshman-entry master's degree program; entry to the MSPT is determined after junior year of the BS program. *Accreditation:* APTA. *Entrance requirements:* For master's, minimum GPA of 3.0, 16-24 hours of clinical experience in 3 different areas. *Faculty research:* Qualitative research, occupational health, discontinuous anaerobic studies, low back dysfunction.

Clarkson University, Graduate School, Center for Health Science, Department of Physical Therapy, Potsdam, NY 13699. Offers MPT, DPT. *Accreditation:* APTA. *Faculty:* 6 full-time (4 women), 2 part-time/adjunct (both women). *Students:* 26 full-time (19 women), 2 part-time (1 woman). Average age 26. 17 applicants, 82% accepted, 12 enrolled. In 2006, 4 degrees awarded. *Entrance requirements:* For master's, GRE. Additional exam requirements/recommendations for international students: Required—TOEFL. *Application deadline:* For fall admission, 5/15 priority date for domestic students; for spring admission, 10/15 priority date for domestic students. Application fee: $25 ($35 for international students). Electronic applications accepted. *Expenses:* Tuition: Full-time $22,776; part-time $949 per credit. Required fees: $215. *Financial support:* In 2006–07, 28 students received support. Tuition waivers (partial) available. *Faculty research:* Membrane transport, community based health, gerontology, muscle structure or function, fibromyalgia. Total annual research expenditures: $18,848.

Cleveland State University, College of Graduate Studies, College of Science, Department of Health Sciences, Program in Physical Therapy, Cleveland, OH 44115. Offers DPT. *Accreditation:* APTA. *Faculty:* 5 full-time (3 women), 7 part-time/adjunct (5 women). *Students:* 43 full-time (30 women). Average age 27. 6 applicants, 0% accepted. *Entrance requirements:* Additional exam requirements/recommendations for international students: Required—TOEFL (minimum score 550 paper-based; 220 computer-based). *Application deadline:* For spring admission, 11/2 for domestic and international students. Applications are processed on a rolling basis. Application fee: $30. Electronic applications accepted. *Financial support:* In 2006–07, 8 students received support, including 4 research assistantships with partial tuition reimbursements available (averaging $5,220 per year), teaching assistantships with partial tuition reimbursements available (averaging $1,740 per year). *Faculty research:* Biomechanics, exercise physiology, motor control, neurological disorders, physical dysfunctions. *Unit head:* Dr. M. Ann Reinthal, Director, 216-687-3576, Fax: 216-687-9316, E-mail: a.karas@csuohio.edu.

College Misericordia, College of Health Sciences, Program in Physical Therapy, Dallas, PA 18612-1098. Offers MSPT, DPT. *Accreditation:* APTA. *Faculty:* 6 full-time (3 women), 2 part-time/adjunct (1 woman). *Students:* 42 full-time (31 women), 67 part-time (47 women); includes 2 minority (1 African American, 1 Hispanic American). Average age 26. In 2006, 28 degrees awarded. *Degree requirements:* For master's, thesis optional. *Entrance requirements:* For master's, GRE General Test or MAT. *Application deadline:* For fall admission, 12/15 priority date for domestic students. Applications are processed on a rolling basis. Application fee: $25. Electronic applications accepted. *Expenses:* Tuition: Full-time $19,800; part-time $495 per credit. Required fees: $1,060. *Financial support:* Teaching assistantships, career-related internships or fieldwork, scholarships/grants, and tuition waivers (partial) available. Support available to part-time students. Financial award application deadline: 6/30; financial award applicants required to submit FAFSA. *Faculty research:* Wound care, computer-assisted instruction, instruction in applied physiology, isokinetics, prosthetics. *Unit head:* Dr. Susan Barker, Department Chair, 570-674-6422, E-mail: sbarker@misericordia.edu. *Application contact:* Larree Brown, Coordinator of Part-Time Undergraduate and Graduate Programs, 570-674-6451, Fax: 570-674-6232, E-mail: lbrown@misericordia.edu.

College of Mount St. Joseph, Physical Therapy Program, Cincinnati, OH 45233-1670. Offers MPT, DPT. *Accreditation:* APTA. *Faculty:* 8 full-time (all women), 1 (woman) part-time/adjunct. *Students:* 52 full-time (38 women), 6 part-time (4 women), 2 international. Average age 24. 46 applicants, 85% accepted, 23 enrolled. In 2006, 24 degrees awarded. *Degree requirements:* For master's, registration; for doctorate, clinical internship. *Entrance requirements:*

Physical Therapy

College of Mount St. Joseph (continued)
For doctorate, GRE, minimum GPA of 3.0, prerequisite coursework in sciences, humanities, social sciences, and statistics, 80 observation hours. Additional exam requirements/recommendations for international students: Required—TOEFL (minimum score 560 paper-based; 220 computer-based). *Application deadline:* For spring admission, 9/1 priority date for domestic and international students. Application fee: $50. Electronic applications accepted. *Expenses: Contact institution. Financial support:* In 2006–07, 24 students received support. Career-related internships or fieldwork, Federal Work-Study, and scholarships/grants available. Support available to part-time students. Financial award application deadline: 6/1; financial award applicants required to submit FAFSA. *Faculty research:* Utilizing technology in learning, neurobiology, assessment of student learning, critical thinking. *Unit head:* Dr. Darla Vale, Chair, Health Sciences Department, 513-244-4322, Fax: 513-451-2547, E-mail: darla_vale@mail.msj.edu. *Application contact:* Marilyn Hoskins, Assistant Director of Admissions for Graduate Recruitment, 513-244-4723, Fax: 513-244-4629, E-mail: marilyn_hoskins@mail.msg.edu.

College of St. Catherine, Graduate Programs, Program in Physical Therapy, St. Paul, MN 55105-1789. Offers MPT, DPT. Offered at Minneapolis campus only. *Accreditation:* APTA. *Degree requirements:* For master's, research project. *Entrance requirements:* For master's, MAT, minimum GPA of 3.0. Additional exam requirements/recommendations for international students: Required—Michigan English Language Assessment Battery or TOEFL.

See Close-Up on page 1701.

The College of St. Scholastica, Graduate Studies, Department of Physical Therapy, Duluth, MN 55811-4199. Offers DPT. *Accreditation:* APTA. *Faculty:* 8 full-time (6 women). *Students:* 46 full-time (37 women), 29 part-time (22 women); includes 4 minority (1 American Indian/Alaska Native, 2 Asian Americans or Pacific Islanders, 1 Hispanic American). Average age 23. 67 applicants, 63% accepted, 42 enrolled. *Entrance requirements:* For doctorate, GRE, minimum GPA of 3.0, interview. Additional exam requirements/recommendations for international students: Required—TOEFL (minimum score 550 paper-based; 213 computer-based; 79 iBT). *Application deadline:* For fall admission, 11/15 for domestic and international students. Applications are processed on a rolling basis. Application fee: $50. Electronic applications accepted. *Financial support:* In 2006–07, 69 students received support, including 5 teaching assistantships (averaging $759 per year); Federal Work-Study and scholarships/grants also available. Support available to part-time students. Financial award applicants required to submit FAFSA. *Faculty research:* Postural control, reliability and validity of spinal assessment tools, biomechanics of golf swing and low back pain, gait assessment and treatment, ethical issues. *Unit head:* Dr. Denise Wise, Director, 218-723-6523, E-mail: dwise@css.edu. *Application contact:* Tonya J. Roth, Graduate Recruitment Counselor, 218-723-6285, Fax: 218-733-2275, E-mail: gradstudies@css.edu.

Columbia University, College of Physicians and Surgeons, Program in Physical Therapy, New York, NY 10032. Offers DPT. *Accreditation:* APTA. *Faculty:* 10 full-time (7 women), 15 part-time/adjunct (6 women). *Students:* 104 full-time; includes 31 minority (2 African Americans, 24 Asian Americans or Pacific Islanders, 5 Hispanic Americans). Average age 27. 160 applicants, 56% accepted, 48 enrolled. *Degree requirements:* For doctorate, fieldwork, capstone project. *Entrance requirements:* For doctorate, GRE General Test, undergraduate course work in biology, chemistry, physics, psychology, statistics and humanities. Additional exam requirements/recommendations for international students: Required—TOEFL. *Application deadline:* For fall admission, 12/15 priority date for domestic and international students; for winter admission, 2/1 priority date for domestic and international students. Applications are processed on a rolling basis. Application fee: $100. Electronic applications accepted. *Expenses: Contact institution. Financial support:* In 2006–07, 48 students received support. Career-related internships or fieldwork, Federal Work-Study, institutionally sponsored loans, scholarships/grants, and tuition waivers (partial) available. Financial award application deadline: 4/15; financial award applicants required to submit FAFSA. *Faculty research:* Motor control, motion analysis, back assessment, recovery of function following neurological injury, women's health. Total annual research expenditures: $300,000. *Unit head:* Dr. Risa Granick, Director, 212-305-6907, Fax: 212-305-4569, E-mail: rg2135@columbia.edu. *Application contact:* Cynthia Worthington, Admissions Coordinator, 212-305-0470, Fax: 212-305-4569, E-mail: cw75@columbia.edu.

Concordia University Wisconsin, Graduate Programs, School of Health and Human Services, Program in Physical Therapy, Mequon, WI 53097-2402. Offers MSPT, DPT. *Accreditation:* APTA. *Faculty:* 5 part-time/adjunct (2 women). *Students:* 122 (94 women). In 2006, 2 master's, 20 doctorates awarded. *Degree requirements:* For master's, thesis or alternative, comprehensive exam. *Entrance requirements:* Additional exam requirements/recommendations for international students: Required—TOEFL. *Application deadline:* For fall admission, 3/1 for domestic students. Application fee: $50 ($125 for international students). *Expenses: Contact institution. Financial support:* Application deadline: 8/1. *Unit head:* Dr. Teresa Steffen, Director, 262-243-4280, E-mail: teresa.steffen@cuw.edu.

Creighton University, School of Pharmacy and Health Professions, Program in Physical Therapy, Omaha, NE 68178-0001. Offers DPT. *Accreditation:* APTA. *Entrance requirements:* For doctorate, GRE. Electronic applications accepted. *Expenses:* Tuition: Part-time $595 per credit hour. Required fees: $38 per semester.

Daemen College, Department of Physical Therapy, Amherst, NY 14226-3592. Offers DPT, TDPT. *Accreditation:* APTA. Part-time programs available. *Faculty:* 8 full-time (5 women), 3 part-time/adjunct (1 woman). *Students:* 52 full-time (40 women), 36 part-time (22 women); includes 6 minority (1 African American, 3 Asian Americans or Pacific Islanders, 2 Hispanic Americans), 6 international. Average age 31. 64 applicants, 55% accepted, 29 enrolled. *Entrance requirements:* For doctorate, bachelor's degree in physical therapy, state registration. Additional exam requirements/recommendations for international students: Required—TOEFL (minimum score 500 paper-based; 173 computer-based). *Application deadline:* For fall admission, 3/1 priority date for domestic and international students; for spring admission, 10/1 priority date for domestic and international students. Applications are processed on a rolling basis. Application fee: $25. Electronic applications accepted. *Expenses:* Tuition: Full-time $11,700; part-time $650 per credit hour. Required fees: $15 per credit hour. Tuition and fees vary according to course load. *Financial support:* In 2006–07, 16 students received support; teaching assistantships, Federal Work-Study, institutionally sponsored loans, and scholarships/grants available. Support available to part-time students. Financial award application deadline: 2/15; financial award applicants required to submit FAFSA. *Faculty research:* Athletic injuries, myofacial pain syndrome, electrical stimulation and tissue healing, lumbar spine dysfunction, temporomandibular joint syndrome. *Unit head:* Dr. Sharon L. Held, Chair, 716-839-8344, Fax: 716-839-8537, E-mail: sheld@daemen.edu. *Application contact:* Karl Shallowhorn, Associate Director of Graduate Admissions, 716-839-8225, Fax: 716-839-8229, E-mail: kshallow@daemen.edu.

Des Moines University, College of Health Sciences, Program in Physical Therapy, Des Moines, IA 50312-4104. Offers DPT. *Accreditation:* APTA. *Faculty:* 8 full-time (6 women). *Students:* 130 full-time (89 women); includes 5 minority (1 American Indian/Alaska Native, 1 Asian American or Pacific Islander, 3 Hispanic Americans), 1 international. Average age 24. 211 applicants, 43% accepted, 50 enrolled. *Entrance requirements:* Additional exam requirements/recommendations for international students: Required—TOEFL. *Application deadline:* For fall admission, 1/31 priority date for domestic students. Applications are processed on a rolling basis. Application fee: $25. Electronic applications accepted. *Expenses: Contact institution. Financial support:* In 2006–07, 9 students received support. Career-related internships or fieldwork, institutionally sponsored loans, scholarships/grants, and university employment available. Support available to part-time students. Financial award application deadline: 4/15; financial award applicants required to submit FAFSA. *Unit head:* Traci Bush, Director, 515-271-1432, E-mail: traci.bush@dmu.edu. *Application contact:* Josh Kvinlaug-Lewis, Admissions Coordinator, 515-271-7854, Fax: 515-271-7145, E-mail: paadmit@dmu.edu.

Dominican College, Division of Allied Health, Department of Physical Therapy, Orangeburg, NY 10962-1210. Offers MS, DPT. *Accreditation:* APTA. Part-time and evening/weekend programs available. *Faculty:* 4 full-time (3 women), 6 part-time/adjunct (3 women). *Students:* 41 full-time (24 women), 15 part-time (11 women); includes 18 minority (6 African Americans, 8 Asian Americans or Pacific Islanders, 4 Hispanic Americans). Average age 33. In 2006, 2 master's, 8 doctorates awarded. *Degree requirements:* For master's, 3 clinical affiliations. *Entrance requirements:* For master's, minimum GPA of 3.0. Additional exam requirements/recommendations for international students: Required—TOEFL (minimum score 550 paper-based; 213 computer-based). *Application deadline:* Applications are processed on a rolling basis. Application fee: $50. *Financial support:* Applicants required to submit FAFSA. *Unit head:* Dr. Michael Gallucci, Program Director, 845-848-6048, Fax: 845-398-4893. *Application contact:* Director of Admissions, 845-848-7900, Fax: 845-365-3150, E-mail: admissions@dc.edu.

Drexel University, College of Nursing and Health Professions, Department of Rehabilitation Sciences, Philadelphia, PA 19104-2875. Offers hand/upper quarter rehabilitation (MHS, MS, PhD); movement science (MHS, MS, PhD); orthopedics (MHS, MS, PhD); pediatrics (MHS, MS, PhD); physical therapy (DPT, Certificate). *Accreditation:* APTA. Part-time programs available. Terminal master's awarded for partial completion of doctoral program. *Degree requirements:* For master's, comprehensive exam; for doctorate, thesis/dissertation, qualifying exam. *Entrance requirements:* For master's and doctorate, GRE General Test.

Duke University, School of Medicine, Physical Therapy Division, Durham, NC 27708-0586. Offers DPT. *Accreditation:* APTA. *Faculty:* 5 full-time (0 women), 2 part-time/adjunct (0 women). *Students:* 144 full-time (125 women); includes 14 minority (4 African Americans, 1 American Indian/Alaska Native, 7 Asian Americans or Pacific Islanders, 2 Hispanic Americans). 180 applicants, 36% accepted, 63 enrolled. In 2006, 32 degrees awarded. *Degree requirements:* For doctorate, scholarly project. *Entrance requirements:* For doctorate, GRE, previous course work in anatomy, physiology, biological sciences, chemistry, physics, psychology, and statistics. Additional exam requirements/recommendations for international students: Required—TOEFL. *Application deadline:* For fall admission, 12/1 priority date for domestic and international students. Applications are processed on a rolling basis. Application fee: $75. Electronic applications accepted. *Expenses: Contact institution. Financial support:* In 2006–07, 120 students received support. Federal Work-Study, institutionally sponsored loans, and scholarships/grants available. Financial award application deadline: 5/1; financial award applicants required to submit FAFSA. *Faculty research:* Geriatrics, visual plasticity, educational outcomes, orthopaedics, neurology. *Unit head:* Dr. Jan K. Richardson, Professor of the Practice/Division Chief, 919-684-6020, Fax: 919-668-3024, E-mail: richa052@mc.duke.edu. *Application contact:* Anita Aiken, Admissions Coordinator, 919-668-5206, Fax: 919-688-3024, E-mail: anita.aiken@duke.edu.

Duquesne University, John G. Rangos, Sr. School of Health Sciences, Pittsburgh, PA 15282-0001. Offers health management systems (MHMS); occupational therapy (MS); physical therapy (DPT); physician assistant (MPA); speech-language pathology (MS); MBA/MHMS. *Accreditation:* AOTA (one or more programs are accredited); APTA (one or more programs are accredited); ASHA. *Faculty:* 35 full-time (22 women), 24 part-time/adjunct (12 women). *Students:* 261 full-time (229 women), 16 part-time (8 women); includes 11 minority (6 African Americans, 1 American Indian/Alaska Native, 2 Asian Americans or Pacific Islanders, 2 Hispanic Americans), 3 international. Average age 23. 150 applicants, 55% accepted, 41 enrolled. In 2006, 66 master's, 13 doctorates awarded. *Degree requirements:* For doctorate, thesis/dissertation. *Entrance requirements:* For master's, GRE (speech-language pathology), 3 letters of recommendation, minimum GPA of 2.75 (health management systems, occupational therapy), minimum GPA of 3.0 (physical assistant, speech-language pathology); for doctorate, GRE General Test, 3 letters of recommendation, minimum GPA of 3.0, personal interview. Additional exam requirements/recommendations for international students: Required—TOEFL (minimum score 600 paper-based; 250 computer-based). *Application deadline:* For fall admission, 12/1 priority date for domestic students; for winter admission, 5/1 priority date for domestic students. Application fee: $50. Electronic applications accepted. *Expenses: Contact institution.* Tuition and fees vary according to degree level and program. *Financial support:* Federal Work-Study available. *Faculty research:* Neuronal processing, electrical stimulation on peripheral neuropathy, CNS stimulatory and inhibitory signals, behavioral genetic methodologies to development disorders of speech, neurogenic communication disorders. Total annual research expenditures: $66,000. *Unit head:* Dr. Gregory H. Frazer, Dean, 412-396-5303, Fax: 412-396-5554, E-mail: frazer@duq.edu. *Application contact:* Christopher R. Hilf, Recruiter/Academic Advisor, 412-396-5653, Fax: 412-396-5554, E-mail: hilfc@duq.edu.

D'Youville College, Department of Physical Therapy, Buffalo, NY 14201-1084. Offers advanced orthopedic physical therapy (Certificate); manual physical therapy (Certificate); physical therapy (MPT, MS, DPT). *Accreditation:* APTA. Part-time programs available. *Faculty:* 9 full-time (5 women), 5 part-time/adjunct (1 woman). *Students:* 73 full-time (37 women), 16 part-time (6 women); includes 7 minority (2 African Americans, 3 Asian Americans or Pacific Islanders, 2 Hispanic Americans), 58 international. Average age 27. 27 applicants, 37% accepted, 7 enrolled. In 2006, 59 master's awarded. *Degree requirements:* For master's, project or thesis. *Entrance requirements:* Additional exam requirements/recommendations for international students: Required—TOEFL (minimum score 500 paper-based; 173 computer-based). *Application deadline:* For fall admission, 5/1 priority date for international students; for spring admission, 9/1 priority date for international students. Applications are processed on a rolling basis. Application fee: $25. Electronic applications accepted. *Financial support:* Federal Work-Study and scholarships/grants available. Support available to part-time students. Financial award application deadline: 3/1; financial award applicants required to submit FAFSA. *Faculty research:* Therapeutic effects of Tai Chi, selected topics in orthopedics. *Unit head:* Dr. Lynn Rivers, Chair, 716-829-7708 Ext. 7708, Fax: 716-829-8137, E-mail: riversl@dyc.edu. *Application contact:* Linda Fisher, Graduate Admissions Director, 716-829-8400, Fax: 716-829-7900, E-mail: graduateadmissions@dyc.edu.

East Carolina University, Graduate School, School of Allied Health Sciences, Department of Physical Therapy, Greenville, NC 27858-4353. Offers MPT, DPT. *Accreditation:* APTA. *Students:* 68 full-time (44 women), 1 (woman) part-time; includes 6 minority (2 African Americans, 1 American Indian/Alaska Native, 1 Asian American or Pacific Islander, 2 Hispanic Americans). Average age 24. 32 applicants, 34% accepted, 9 enrolled. In 2006, 33 master's, 9 doctorates awarded. *Degree requirements:* For master's, comprehensive exam. *Entrance requirements:* For master's, GRE General Test. Additional exam requirements/recommendations for international students: Required—TOEFL. *Application deadline:* For fall admission, 1/15 for domestic students. Application fee: $50. *Financial support:* Application deadline: 6/1. *Faculty research:* Diabetes and obesity, diabetic foot, ACL injury. *Unit head:* Dr. Denis Brunt, Chair, 252-744-6238, Fax: 252-328-4354, E-mail: bruntd@ecu.edu.

Eastern Washington University, Graduate Studies, College of Science, Mathematics and Technology, Program in Physical Therapy, Cheney, WA 99004-2431. Offers DPT. *Accreditation:* APTA. *Degree requirements:* For doctorate, thesis/dissertation or final project. *Entrance requirements:* For doctorate, GRE General Test, minimum GPA of 3.0, 75 hours of experience, 3 letters of recommendation.

East Tennessee State University, School of Graduate Studies, College of Public and Allied Health, Department of Physical Therapy, Johnson City, TN 37614. Offers DPT. *Accreditation:* APTA. *Entrance requirements:* Additional exam requirements/recommendations for international students: Required—TOEFL (minimum score 550 paper-based; 213 computer-based). *Faculty research:* Adult developmental delay, vestibular dysfunction, iontophoresis, musculoskeletal dysfunction, educational technology.

Elon University, Program in Physical Therapy, Elon, NC 27244-2010. Offers DPT. *Accreditation:* APTA. *Faculty:* 12 full-time (9 women), 9 part-time/adjunct (6 women). *Students:* 117 full-time (81 women); includes 8 minority (5 African Americans, 1 Asian American or Pacific Islander, 2 Hispanic Americans). Average age 23. 188 applicants, 28% accepted, 38 enrolled. In 2006, 37 degrees awarded. *Entrance requirements:* For doctorate, GRE General Test. Additional exam requirements/recommendations for international students: Required—TOEFL (minimum score 550 paper-based; 213 computer-based; 79 iBT). *Application deadline:* For winter admission, 12/1 priority date for domestic students. Applications are processed on a rolling basis. Application fee: $50. Electronic applications accepted. *Expenses: Contact institution. Financial support:* In 2006–07, 8 students received support. Federal Work-Study and scholarships/grants available. Support available to part-time students. Financial award application deadline: 10/1; financial award applicants required to submit FAFSA. *Faculty research:* Neural dynamics, orthopedic clinical outcomes, falls in the elderly, exercise response in children with neurological impairment, instructional technology. *Unit head:* Dr. Elizabeth A. Rogers, Chair, 336-278-6400, Fax: 336-278-6414, E-mail: rogers@elon.edu. *Application contact:* Art Fadde, Director of Graduate Admissions, 800-334-8448 Ext. 3, Fax: 336-278-7699, E-mail: afadde@elon.edu.

Emory University, School of Medicine, Programs in Allied Health Professions, Physical Therapy Program, Atlanta, GA 30322-1100. Offers DPT. *Accreditation:* APTA. *Faculty:* 17 full-time (11 women), 41 part-time/adjunct (26 women). *Students:* 101 full-time (87 women), 5 part-time (4 women); includes 15 minority (7 African Americans, 1 American Indian/Alaska Native, 7 Asian Americans or Pacific Islanders). Average age 25. 172 applicants, 41% accepted, 42 enrolled. In 2006, 21 degrees awarded. *Entrance requirements:* For doctorate, GRE General Test. *Application deadline:* For fall admission, 10/1 priority date for domestic and international students. Applications are processed on a rolling basis. Application fee: $60. Electronic applications accepted. *Expenses: Contact institution. Financial support:* In 2006–07, 84 students received support. Institutionally sponsored loans and scholarships/grants available. Financial award application deadline: 4/1; financial award applicants required to submit FAFSA. *Faculty research:* Constraint induced recovery in stroke exercise in patients with vestibular hypofunction, immune response to exercise in aging, functional electrical stimulation and spinal cord injury. *Unit head:* Dr. Susan J. Herdman, Director, 404-712-5683, Fax: 404-712-4130, E-mail: pt_admissions@learnlink.emory.edu. *Application contact:* Monica George-Komi, Admission Coordinator, 404-712-5657, Fax: 404-712-4130, E-mail: mgeorg2@emory.edu.

Florida Agricultural and Mechanical University, Division of Graduate Studies, Research, and Continuing Education, School of Allied Health Sciences, Division of Physical Therapy, Tallahassee, FL 32307-3200. Offers MPT. *Accreditation:* APTA. *Entrance requirements:* For master's, GRE General Test or GMAT, minimum GPA of 3.0. Additional exam requirements/recommendations for international students: Required—TOEFL.

Florida Gulf Coast University, College of Health Professions, Department of Physical Therapy, Fort Myers, FL 33965-6565. Offers MS. *Accreditation:* APTA. Part-time programs available. Postbaccalaureate distance learning degree programs offered (minimal on-campus study). *Faculty:* 42 full-time (35 women), 21 part-time/adjunct (14 women). *Students:* 26 full-time (15 women), 14 part-time (11 women); includes 6 minority (1 Asian American or Pacific Islander, 5 Hispanic Americans). Average age 30. 43 applicants, 70% accepted, 14 enrolled. In 2006, 10 degrees awarded. *Degree requirements:* For master's, thesis or alternative. *Entrance requirements:* For master's, GRE General Test or MAT, minimum GPA of 3.0. Additional exam requirements/recommendations for international students: Required—TOEFL (minimum score 550 paper-based; 213 computer-based). *Application deadline:* For fall admission, 1/15 priority date for domestic students. Applications are processed on a rolling basis. Application fee: $30. Electronic applications accepted. *Expenses:* Tuition, state resident: full-time $4,326. Tuition, nonresident: full-time $18,523. Required fees: $1,211. One-time fee: $5 full-time. *Financial support:* Career-related internships or fieldwork, Federal Work-Study, and institutionally sponsored loans available. *Faculty research:* Physical therapy practice and education. *Unit head:* Ellen K. Williamson, Chair, 239-590-7531, Fax: 239-590-7474, E-mail: ekwill@fgcu.edu.

Florida International University, College of Nursing and Health Sciences, Department of Physical Therapy, Miami, FL 33199. Offers MS. *Accreditation:* APTA. Part-time programs available. *Faculty:* 7 full-time (4 women). *Students:* 127 full-time (86 women), 12 part-time (all women); includes 97 minority (19 African Americans, 1 American Indian/Alaska Native, 8 Asian Americans or Pacific Islanders, 69 Hispanic Americans), 3 international. Average age 28. 89 applicants, 60% accepted, 37 enrolled. In 2006, 44 degrees awarded. *Degree requirements:* For master's, thesis. *Entrance requirements:* For master's, GRE General Test, minimum GPA of 3.0, physical therapy license. Additional exam requirements/recommendations for international students: Required—TOEFL. *Application deadline:* For fall admission, 4/1 priority date for domestic students; for spring admission, 10/1 for domestic students. Applications are processed on a rolling basis. Application fee: $25. *Expenses:* Tuition, state resident: part-time $249 per credit hour. Tuition, nonresident: part-time $753 per credit hour. Tuition and fees vary according to program. *Faculty research:* Isokinetic test results and gait abnormalities after knee arthroscopy. *Unit head:* Dr. Leonard Elbaum, Chairperson, 305-348-3113, Fax: 305-348-1240, E-mail: leonard.elbaum@fiu.edu.

Franklin Pierce University, Graduate Studies, Rindge, NH 03461-0060. Offers information technology management (MS); leadership (MBA); physical therapy (MS). *Accreditation:* APTA. Part-time and evening/weekend programs available. *Entrance requirements:* For master's, minimum GPA of 2.5. Additional exam requirements/recommendations for international students: Required—TOEFL (minimum score 550 paper-based; 195 computer-based). Electronic applications accepted.

Gannon University, School of Graduate Studies, College of Sciences, Engineering, and Health Sciences, School of Health Sciences, Program in Physical Therapy, Erie, PA 16541-0001. Offers DPT. *Accreditation:* APTA. *Students:* 88 full-time (61 women), 2 part-time (both women), 9 international. Average age 25. 92 applicants, 77% accepted, 39 enrolled. In 2006, 16 doctorates awarded. *Entrance requirements:* Additional exam requirements/recommendations for international students: Required—TOEFL (minimum score 500 paper-based; 173 computer-based). *Application deadline:* For fall admission, 10/15 for domestic students. Application fee: $50. *Expenses: Contact institution.* Tuition and fees vary according to course load, degree level, campus/location and program. *Financial support:* Available to part-time students. Application deadline: 7/1; *Unit head:* Kristine Legters, Chair, 814-871-5641, E-mail: legters001@gannon.edu. *Application contact:* Debra Meszaros, Director of Graduate Recruitment, 814-871-5819, Fax: 814-871-5827, E-mail: cfal@gannon.edu.

The George Washington University, School of Medicine and Health Sciences, Health Sciences Programs, Program in Physical Therapy, Washington, DC 20052. Offers DPT. *Accreditation:* APTA. *Entrance requirements:* Additional exam requirements/recommendations for international students: Required—TOEFL (minimum score 550 paper-based; 213 computer-based).

Georgia State University, College of Health and Human Sciences, School of Health Professions, Division of Physical Therapy, Atlanta, GA 30303-3083. Offers DPT. *Accreditation:* APTA. *Faculty:* 9 full-time (6 women), 1 (woman) part-time/adjunct. *Students:* 105 full-time (80 women); includes 17 minority (11 African Americans, 6 Asian Americans or Pacific Islanders), 4 international. Average age 27. 211 applicants, 33% accepted, 44 enrolled. *Entrance requirements:* Additional exam requirements/recommendations for international students: Required—TOEFL (minimum score 550 paper-based; 213 computer-based). *Application deadline:* For fall admission, 1/10 priority date for domestic students. Applications are processed on a rolling basis. Application fee: $50. Electronic applications accepted. *Expenses: Contact institution. Financial support:* In 2006–07, research assistantships with full and partial tuition reimbursements (averaging $3,108 per year); Federal Work-Study, institutionally sponsored loans, scholarships/grants, tuition waivers (partial), and unspecified assistantships also available. Support available to part-time students. Financial award application deadline: 4/1; financial award applicants required to submit FAFSA. *Faculty research:* Transcranial magnetic stimulation, wheelchair transfer, foot health, wheelchair propulsion, physical activity in adult day care. Total annual research expenditures: $22,533. *Unit head:* Dr. Leslie F Taylor, Chair, 404-651-3091, E-mail: ltaylor@gsu.edu. *Application contact:* Leigh Walling, Senior Academic Adviser, 404-651-3064, Fax: 404-651-4871, E-mail: lwalling@gsu.edu.

Governors State University, College of Health Professions, Program in Physical Therapy, University Park, IL 60466-0975. Offers MPT, DPT. *Accreditation:* APTA. *Students:* 58 full-time, 10 part-time. Average age 29. *Degree requirements:* For master's, thesis or alternative. *Entrance requirements:* For master's, minimum GPA of 3.0 in field, 2.75 overall. *Application deadline:* For fall admission, 1/31 priority date for domestic students. Application fee: $25. *Expenses:* Tuition, state resident: full-time $4,104; part-time $171 per hour. Tuition, nonresident: part-time $513 per hour. *Financial support:* Application deadline: 5/1. *Unit head:* Dr. Russell Carter, Co-Coordinator, 708-534-5000 Ext. 7291.

Grand Valley State University, College of Health Professions, Physical Therapy Program, Allendale, MI 49401-9403. Offers MS, DPT. *Accreditation:* APTA. *Faculty:* 11 full-time (6 women), 2 part-time/adjunct (1 woman). *Students:* 113 full-time (85 women); includes 7 minority (3 African Americans, 4 Hispanic Americans). Average age 24. 138 applicants, 36% accepted, 41 enrolled. In 2006, 42 degrees awarded. *Degree requirements:* For master's, thesis optional. *Entrance requirements:* For master's, minimum GPA of 3.0 in most recent 60 hours and in prerequisites, 50 hours of volunteer work; for doctorate, GRE, minimum GPA of 3.0 in most recent 60 hours and in prerequisites, 50 hours of volunteer work, interview, writing sample. Additional exam requirements/recommendations for international students: Required—TOEFL (minimum score 610 paper-based; 253 computer-based). *Application deadline:* For winter admission, 1/15 priority date for domestic and international students. Applications are processed on a rolling basis. Application fee: $30. Electronic applications accepted. *Expenses:* Tuition, state resident: full-time $5,850; part-time $325 per credit. Tuition, nonresident: full-time $10,800; part-time $600 per credit. Tuition and fees vary according to course load. *Financial support:* In 2006–07, 6 research assistantships with full and partial tuition reimbursements (averaging $8,000 per year) were awarded; career-related internships or fieldwork, Federal Work-Study, institutionally sponsored loans, and unspecified assistantships also available. Financial award application deadline: 2/15. *Faculty research:* Balance deficits, motion analysis, nutritional knowledge of female athletes, trust in athletic performance, spinal functions dysfunction. *Unit head:* Dr. John Peck, Director, 616-331-3356, Fax: 616-331-3350, E-mail: peckj@gvsu.edu. *Application contact:* Darlene Zwart, Student Services Coordinator, 616-331-3958, E-mail: zwartda@gvsu.edu.

Hampton University, Graduate College, Program in Physical Therapy, Hampton, VA 23668. Offers DPT. *Accreditation:* APTA. *Degree requirements:* For doctorate, thesis/dissertation, oral defense, qualifying exam. *Entrance requirements:* For doctorate, GRE General Test, minimum GPA of 3.0 or master's degree in physics or related field.

Hardin-Simmons University, Graduate School, Holland School of Sciences and Mathematics, Doctoral Program in Physical Therapy, Abilene, TX 79698-0001. Offers DPT. *Accreditation:* APTA. *Faculty:* 8 full-time (4 women), 2 part-time/adjunct (1 woman). *Students:* 78 full-time (54 women); includes 7 minority (1 African American, 1 Asian American or Pacific Islander, 5 Hispanic Americans). Average age 25. 106 applicants, 26% accepted, 26 enrolled. *Entrance requirements:* Additional exam requirements/recommendations for international students: Required—TOEFL (minimum score 500 paper-based; 213 computer-based). *Application deadline:* For fall admission, 9/1 priority date for domestic and international students; for spring admission, 2/1 for domestic and international students. Applications are processed on a rolling basis. Application fee: $50 ($100 for international students). *Expenses: Contact institution.* One-time fee: $50. Tuition and fees vary according to course load and degree level. *Financial support:* In 2006–07, 65 students received support. Scholarships/grants available. Financial award application deadline: 3/1; financial award applicants required to submit FAFSA. *Faculty research:* Neuraltension testing, strength of Special Olympians, health promotion for seniors, Vastus Medialis recruitment, spirituality. *Application contact:* Dr. Janelle K. O'Connell, Department Head, 325-670-5860, Fax: 325-670-5868, E-mail: joconnel@hsutx.edu.

Humboldt State University, Graduate Studies, College of Professional Studies, Department of Kinesiology, Arcata, CA 95521-8299. Offers athletic training education (MS); exercise science/wellness management (MS); pre-physical therapy (MS); teaching/coaching (MS). *Students:* 10 full-time (5 women), 5 part-time (1 woman); includes 4 minority (1 African American, 3 Asian Americans or Pacific Islanders). Average age 31. 15 applicants, 73% accepted, 6 enrolled. In 2006, 3 degrees awarded. *Degree requirements:* For master's, thesis or alternative. *Entrance requirements:* For master's, GMAT, minimum GPA of 2.5. Additional exam requirements/recommendations for international students: Required—TOEFL. *Application deadline:* Applications are processed on a rolling basis. Application fee: $55. *Financial support:* Teaching assistantships, career-related internships or fieldwork, Federal Work-Study, and institutionally sponsored loans available. Financial award application deadline: 3/1; financial award applicants required to submit FAFSA. *Faculty research:* Human performance, adapted physical education, physical therapy. *Unit head:* Dr. Sue MacConnie, Chair, 707-826-4536, Fax: 707-826-5451, E-mail: sem1@humboldt.edu. *Application contact:* Dr. Kathy Munoz, Coordinator, 707-826-3840, Fax: 707-826-5451, E-mail: kdm1@humboldt.edu.

Hunter College of the City University of New York, Graduate School, Schools of the Health Professions, Program in Physical Therapy, New York, NY 10021-5085. Offers MPT. *Accreditation:* APTA. *Faculty:* 4 full-time (1 woman), 1 (woman) part-time/adjunct. *Students:* 77 full-time (60 women); includes 12 minority (2 African Americans, 7 Asian Americans or Pacific Islanders, 3 Hispanic Americans). Average age 29. In 2006, 37 degrees awarded. *Entrance requirements:* For master's, 2 semesters of course work in biology, physics, chemistry, and psychology; 1 semester of mathematics, statistics, and English composition; CPR certification; minimum GPA of 3.0; documented clinical experience of at least 75 hours under the supervision of a licensed physical therapist, with a minimum of 50 hours in a hospital-based setting. Additional exam requirements/recommendations for international students: Required—TOEFL. *Application deadline:* For fall admission, 4/1 for domestic students, 2/1 for international students; for spring admission, 11/1 for domestic students, 9/1 for international students. Applications are processed on a rolling basis. Application fee: $125. *Expenses:* Tuition, state resident: part-time $270 per credit. Tuition, nonresident: part-time $500 per credit. Required fees: $45 per semester. *Financial support:* Career-related internships or fieldwork and Federal Work-Study available. *Faculty research:* Kinematic analysis, Parkinson's disease, gait dysfunction, electrotherapy, brain neurotransmitters. Total annual research expenditures: $11,745. *Unit head:* Dr. Gary Krasilovsky, Associate Professor and Director, 212-481-7556, E-mail: gkrasilo@hunter.cuny.edu. *Application contact:* William Zlata, Director for Graduate Admissions, 212-772-4482, Fax: 212-650-3336, E-mail: admissions@hunter.cuny.edu.

Husson College, Graduate Studies Division, Program in Physical Therapy, Bangor, ME 04401-2999. Offers MSPT. Freshman-entry master's degree program. *Accreditation:* APTA. Part-time and evening/weekend programs available. *Degree requirements:* For master's, thesis optional.

Idaho State University, Office of Graduate Studies, Kasiska College of Health Professions, Department of Physical and Occupational Therapy, Program in Physical Therapy, Pocatello, ID 83209. Offers DPT. *Accreditation:* APTA. *Faculty:* 4 full-time (2 women). *Students:* 54 full-time (29 women), 12 part-time (3 women); includes 1 minority (Hispanic American), 2 international. Average age 29. In 2006, 16 degrees awarded. *Degree requirements:* For doctorate, thesis/dissertation, oral and written exam, comprehensive exam, registration. *Entrance requirements:* For doctorate, GRE General Test, minimum GPA of 3.0, 80 hours in 2 practice settings of physical therapy. Additional exam requirements/recommendations for international students: Required—TOEFL (minimum score 600 paper-based; 213 computer-based). *Application deadline:* For fall admission, 7/1 for domestic students, 6/1 for international students; for spring admission, 12/1 for domestic students, 11/1 for international students. Applications are processed on a rolling basis. Application fee: $55. *Expenses: Contact institution. Financial support:* In 2006–07, teaching assistantships with full and partial tuition reimbursements (averaging $8,694 per year); career-related internships or fieldwork, Federal Work-Study, institutionally sponsored loans, scholarships/grants, and tuition waivers (full) also available. Support available to part-time students. Financial award application deadline: 1/1. *Faculty research:* Cardiovascular/pulmonary balance, neural plasticity, orthopedics, geriatrics, hypertension. Total annual research

Physical Therapy

Idaho State University (continued)
expenditures: $38,000. *Application contact:* Ellen Combs, Graduate School Technical Records Specialist, 208-282-2150, Fax: 208-282-4847.

Indiana University–Purdue University Indianapolis, Indiana University School of Medicine, School of Health and Rehabilitation Sciences, Indianapolis, IN 46202-2896. Offers health sciences education (MS); nutrition and dietetics (MS); occupational therapy (MS); physical therapy (DPT). Part-time and evening/weekend programs available. *Faculty:* 8 full-time (5 women). *Students:* 180 full-time (149 women), 35 part-time (21 women); includes 17 minority (6 African Americans, 7 Asian Americans or Pacific Islanders, 4 Hispanic Americans), 3 international. Average age 27. In 2006, 9 master's, 32 doctorates awarded. *Degree requirements:* For master's, thesis (for some programs). *Entrance requirements:* For master's, GRE General Test, minimum GPA of 3.0. Additional exam requirements/recommendations for international students: Required—TOEFL. *Application deadline:* For fall admission, 1/15 priority date for domestic students; for spring admission, 10/15 for domestic students. Application fee: $50 ($60 for international students). *Expenses:* Tuition, state resident: full-time $5,437; part-time $227 per credit hour. Tuition, nonresident: full-time $15,694; part-time $654 per credit hour. Required fees: $620. Tuition and fees vary according to course load, campus/location and program. *Financial support:* Fellowships, research assistantships, teaching assistantships, Federal Work-Study, institutionally sponsored loans, and scholarships/grants available. Support available to part-time students. Financial award applicants required to submit FAFSA. *Unit head:* Dr. Mark S. Sothmann, Dean of the School of Allied Health Sciences, 317-274-4702, E-mail: msothman@iupui.edu.

Ithaca College, Graduate Studies, School of Health Sciences and Human Performance, Program in Physical Therapy, Ithaca, NY 14850-7020. Offers DPT. Students enter the program as freshmen. *Accreditation:* APTA. *Faculty:* 8 full-time (5 women), 4 part-time/adjunct (all women). *Students:* 129 full-time (101 women), 1 part-time; includes 8 minority (5 Asian Americans or Pacific Islanders, 3 Hispanic Americans). Average age 23. In 2006, 47 doctorates awarded. *Degree requirements:* For doctorate, thesis/dissertation optional. *Financial support:* In 2006–07, 105 students received support. Career-related internships or fieldwork, Federal Work-Study, institutionally sponsored loans, and scholarships/grants available. Support available to part-time students. Financial award applicants required to submit FAFSA. *Unit head:* Michael Pagliarulo, Graduate Chairperson, 585-274-1328 Ext. 13.

Langston University, School of Physical Therapy, Langston, OK 73050-0907. Offers DPT. *Accreditation:* APTA.

Loma Linda University, School of Allied Health Professions, Department of Physical Therapy, Loma Linda, CA 92350. Offers MPT, DPT. *Accreditation:* APTA.

Long Island University, Brooklyn Campus, School of Health Professions, Division of Physical Therapy, Brooklyn, NY 11201-8423. Offers DPT, TDPT. *Accreditation:* APTA. Part-time and evening/weekend programs available. *Entrance requirements:* Additional exam requirements/recommendations for international students: Required—TOEFL (minimum score 500 paper-based; 173 computer-based). Electronic applications accepted.

Louisiana State University Health Sciences Center, School of Allied Health Professions, Department of Physical Therapy, New Orleans, LA 70112-2223. Offers MPT. *Accreditation:* APTA. *Degree requirements:* For master's, thesis optional. *Entrance requirements:* For master's, GRE General Test, 60 hours experience in physical therapy, minimum GPA of 3.0. *Expenses:* Tuition, state resident: full-time $5,868; part-time $722 per credit. Tuition, nonresident: full-time $8,993; part-time $1,104 per credit. *Faculty research:* Wound healing, spinal cord injury, pain management, geriatrics, muscle physiology, muscle damage, motor control, balance.

Marquette University, Graduate School, College of Health Sciences, Department of Physical Therapy, Milwaukee, WI 53201-1881. Offers DPT. *Accreditation:* APTA. *Faculty:* 10 full-time (5 women), 21 part-time/adjunct (11 women). *Students:* 63 full-time (48 women); includes 7 minority (1 Asian American or Pacific Islander, 6 Hispanic Americans), 1 international. Average age 24. In 2006, 68 degrees awarded. *Entrance requirements:* Additional exam requirements/recommendations for international students: Required—TOEFL. Application fee: $40. *Financial support:* Application deadline: 2/15. *Unit head:* Dr. Lawrence G. Pan, Chair, 414-288-7161, Fax: 414-288-5987.

Marymount University, School of Health Professions, Program in Physical Therapy, Arlington, VA 22207-4299. Offers DPT. *Accreditation:* APTA. *Faculty:* 6 full-time (5 women), 4 part-time/adjunct (2 women). *Students:* 53 full-time (47 women), 74 part-time (47 women); includes 27 minority (10 African Americans, 12 Asian Americans or Pacific Islanders, 5 Hispanic Americans), 3 international. Average age 32. 98 applicants, 93% accepted, 58 enrolled. In 2006, 16 degrees awarded. *Degree requirements:* For doctorate, thesis/dissertation. *Entrance requirements:* For doctorate, GRE, 40 hours of clinical work experience, interview, 2 letters of recommendation, resumé, PT license. Additional exam requirements/recommendations for international students: Required—TOEFL (minimum score 600 paper-based; 250 computer-based). *Application deadline:* For fall admission, 12/15 priority date for domestic students. Application fee: $40. *Expenses:* Contact institution. *Financial support:* Research assistantships with full tuition reimbursements, career-related internships or fieldwork, scholarships/grants, and unspecified assistantships available. Financial award applicants required to submit FAFSA. *Unit head:* Dr. Rita Wong, Chair, 703-284-5982, Fax: 703-284-3819, E-mail: rita.wong@marymount.edu.

Maryville University of Saint Louis, School of Health Professions, Physical Therapy Program, St. Louis, MO 63141-7299. Offers DPT. *Accreditation:* APTA. *Application deadline:* Applications are processed on a rolling basis. Application fee: $20. Electronic applications accepted. *Expenses:* Tuition: Full-time $17,800; part-time $555 per credit. Required fees: $55 per semester. Tuition and fees vary according to degree level and program. *Financial support:* Career-related internships or fieldwork, Federal Work-Study, and campus employment available. Financial award application deadline: 7/31. *Faculty research:* Memory and exercise. *Unit head:* Dr. Judy Woehrle, Director, 314-529-9514, Fax: 314-529-7495, E-mail: jwoehrle@maryville.edu. *Application contact:* 314-529-9350, Fax: 314-529-9927, E-mail: admissions@maryville.edu.

Mayo School of Health Sciences, Program in Physical Therapy, Rochester, MN 55905. Offers DPT. *Accreditation:* APTA. *Faculty:* 5 full-time (0 women), 2 part-time/adjunct (both women). *Students:* 66 full-time (47 women); includes 3 minority (all Asian Americans or Pacific Islanders) Average age 25. 54 applicants, 39% accepted. *Entrance requirements:* Additional exam requirements/recommendations for international students: Required—TOEFL. *Application deadline:* For winter admission, 1/15 for domestic students. Applications are processed on a rolling basis. Application fee: $50. Electronic applications accepted. *Financial support:* Scholarships/grants available. Financial award applicants required to submit FAFSA. *Unit head:* Dr. John Hollman, Director, 507-284-8487. *Application contact:* Carol Cooper, Secretary, 507-284-2054, E-mail: cooper.carol@mayo.edu.

McMaster University, Faculty of Health Sciences, Professional Program in Physiotherapy, Hamilton, ON L8S 4M2, Canada. Offers M Sc. *Students:* 116 full-time. In 2006, 47 degrees awarded. *Degree requirements:* For master's, clinical placements, independent research project. *Entrance requirements:* For master's, minimum B average over last 60 undergraduate units. Additional exam requirements/recommendations for international students: Required—TOEFL (minimum score 600 paper-based; 250 computer-based). Application fee: $225 ($250 for international students). *Unit head:* Dr. Laurie Wishart, Assistant Dean, 905-525-9140 Ext. 22685. *Application contact:* Dr. Mary Law, Associate Dean, 905-525-9140 Ext. 22867, Fax: 905-524-0069.

Medical College of Georgia, School of Allied Health Sciences, Programs in Allied Health Sciences, Department of Physical Therapy, Augusta, GA 30912-1500. Offers MS, DPT. *Accreditation:* APTA (one or more programs are accredited). Part-time programs available. Postbaccalaureate distance learning degree programs offered (no on-campus study). *Faculty:* 3 full-time (0 women). *Students:* 139 full-time (109 women); includes 20 minority (12 African Americans, 5 Asian Americans or Pacific Islanders, 3 Hispanic Americans). Average age 27. In 2006, 37 degrees awarded. *Degree requirements:* For doctorate, acute experience and rehabilitation experience. *Entrance requirements:* For doctorate, GRE. Additional exam requirements/recommendations for international students: Required—TOEFL (minimum score 550 paper-based; 213 computer-based; 79 iBT). *Application deadline:* For fall admission, 3/15 for domestic students. Applications are processed on a rolling basis. Application fee: $30. Electronic applications accepted. *Expenses:* Tuition, state resident: full-time $2,293; part-time $192 per credit hour. Tuition, nonresident: full-time $9,169; part-time $765 per credit hour. Required fees: $293 per semester. *Financial support:* Federal Work-Study and institutionally sponsored loans available. Support available to part-time students. Financial award application deadline: 5/31; financial award applicants required to submit FAFSA. *Unit head:* Dr. Douglas E. Keskula, Chair and Associate Professor, 706-721-2141, Fax: 706-721-3209, E-mail: dkeskula@mail.mcg.edu.

Medical University of South Carolina, College of Health Professions, Department of Rehabilitation Sciences, Program in Physical Therapy, Charleston, SC 29425-0002. Offers DPT. *Accreditation:* APTA. Postbaccalaureate distance learning degree programs offered (minimal on-campus study). *Faculty:* 7 full-time (4 women), 2 part-time/adjunct (1 woman). *Students:* 53 full-time (45 women); includes 6 minority (3 African Americans, 3 Asian Americans or Pacific Islanders). Average age 25. 109 applicants, 54% accepted, 52 enrolled. *Entrance requirements:* For doctorate, GRE, references, minimum GPA of 3.0, volunteer hours. Additional exam requirements/recommendations for international students: Required—TOEFL (minimum score 600 paper-based; 250 computer-based). *Application deadline:* For fall admission, 1/15 priority date for domestic and international students. Application fee: $75. Electronic applications accepted. *Financial support:* Federal Work-Study available. Support available to part-time students. Financial award application deadline: 3/15; financial award applicants required to submit FAFSA. *Unit head:* Dr. Kathleen Cegles, Director, 843-792-9345, Fax: 843-792-0710, E-mail: cegles@musc.edu. *Application contact:* Susan Johnson, Student Services Coordinator, 843-792-2961, Fax: 843-792-0710, E-mail: johnsoss@musc.edu.

Mercy College, Division of Health Professions, Program in Physical Therapy, Dobbs Ferry, NY 10522-1189. Offers MS. *Accreditation:* APTA. Evening/weekend programs available. *Students:* 62 full-time (27 women), 21 part-time (14 women); includes 35 minority (13 African Americans, 7 Asian Americans or Pacific Islanders, 15 Hispanic Americans), 1 international. Average age 35. In 2006, 16 degrees awarded. *Degree requirements:* For master's, thesis or alternative. *Entrance requirements:* For master's, minimum GPA of 3.0 in final 30 credits of course work, interview, letters of reference. *Application deadline:* For fall admission, 1/15 for domestic students. Application fee: $62. *Expenses:* Tuition: Part-time $595 per credit. Required fees: $9 per credit. Tuition and fees vary according to program. *Financial support:* Teaching assistantships available. *Faculty research:* Functional outcomes, wound management, cardiopulmonary rehabilitation, academic predictors of success. *Unit head:* Dr. Claudia B. Fenderson, Director, 914-674-7828, Fax: 914-674-7840, E-mail: ptprogram@mercy.edu. *Application contact:* Kathleen Jackson, Director of Admissions, 800-Mercy-NY, Fax: 914-674-7382, E-mail: admissions@mercy.edu.

MGH Institute of Health Professions, Graduate Programs, Post-Professional Program in Physical Therapy, Boston, MA 02129. Offers MS, DPT, Certificate. Part-time and evening/weekend programs available. *Faculty:* 16 full-time (15 women), 3 part-time/adjunct (all women). *Students:* 7 full-time (5 women), 151 part-time (110 women); includes 29 minority (5 African Americans, 21 Asian Americans or Pacific Islanders, 3 Hispanic Americans). Average age 36. 69 applicants, 91% accepted, 43 enrolled. In 2006, 5 master's, 99 doctorates, 4 other advanced degrees awarded. *Degree requirements:* For master's, thesis, clinical preceptorship. *Entrance requirements:* For master's, GRE General Test, graduation from an approved program in physical therapy, 1 year of work experience as a physical therapist. Additional exam requirements/recommendations for international students: Required—TOEFL (minimum score 550 paper-based; 213 computer-based). *Application deadline:* For fall admission, 7/1 priority date for domestic students, 3/1 for international students; for winter admission, 11/1 priority date for domestic students, 7/1 for international students; for spring admission, 3/1 priority date for domestic students, 11/1 for international students. Applications are processed on a rolling basis. Application fee: $50. Electronic applications accepted. *Financial support:* In 2006–07, 1 student received support. Career-related internships or fieldwork, scholarships/grants, tuition waivers (partial), and unspecified assistantships available. Support available to part-time students. Financial award application deadline: 3/3; financial award applicants required to submit FAFSA. *Faculty research:* Disability in the elderly; gait, balance and posture; cardiac rehabilitation; relationship of impairment to disability; effect of muscle strengthening in the elderly. *Unit head:* Dr. Leslie G. Portney, Director, 617-726-3170, Fax: 617-724-6321, E-mail: lportney@mghihp.edu. *Application contact:* Maureen Rika Judd, Manager of Admissions, 617-726-6069, Fax: 617-726-8010, E-mail: admissions@mghihp.edu.

See Close-Up on page 1963.

MGH Institute of Health Professions, Graduate Programs, Professional Program in Physical Therapy, Boston, MA 02129. Offers DPT. *Accreditation:* APTA. *Faculty:* 16 full-time (15 women), 5 part-time/adjunct (3 women). *Students:* 83 full-time (68 women), 31 part-time (27 women); includes 14 minority (2 African Americans, 8 Asian Americans or Pacific Islanders, 4 Hispanic Americans). Average age 26. 116 applicants, 67% accepted, 47 enrolled. In 2006, 31 degrees awarded. *Degree requirements:* For doctorate, thesis/dissertation or alternative, research project. *Entrance requirements:* For doctorate, GRE General Test, interview. Additional exam requirements/recommendations for international students: Required—TOEFL (minimum score 550 paper-based; 213 computer-based). *Application deadline:* For spring admission, 12/31 for domestic students, 11/1 for international students. Application fee: $50. Electronic applications accepted. *Financial support:* In 2006–07, 93 students received support; research assistantships, teaching assistantships, career-related internships or fieldwork, scholarships/grants, tuition waivers (full and partial), and unspecified assistantships available. Support available to part-time students. Financial award application deadline: 3/3; financial award applicants required to submit FAFSA. *Faculty research:* Disability in the elderly; gait, balance, and posture; cardiac rehabilitation; relationship of impairment to disability. *Unit head:* Dr. Leslie G. Portney, Director, 617-726-3170, Fax: 617-724-6321, E-mail: lportney@mghihp.edu. *Application contact:* Maureen Rika Judd, Manager of Admissions, 617-726-6069, Fax: 617-726-8010, E-mail: admissions@mghihp.edu.

See Close-Up on page 1963.

Midwestern University, Downers Grove Campus, College of Health Sciences, Illinois Campus, Program in Physical Therapy, Downers Grove, IL 60515-1235. Offers DPT. *Accreditation:* APTA. *Faculty:* 9 full-time (6 women), 4 part-time/adjunct (3 women). *Students:* 120 full-time (93 women), 2 part-time; includes 13 minority (1 African American, 10 Asian Americans or Pacific Islanders, 2 Hispanic Americans), 1 international. Average age 24. 157 applicants, 76% accepted, 43 enrolled. In 2006, 23 doctorates awarded. *Entrance requirements:* For doctorate, GRE General Test. *Application deadline:* Applications are processed on a rolling basis. Application fee: $50. *Expenses:* Contact institution. *Financial support:* In 2006–07, 87 students received support. Federal Work-Study available. *Unit head:* Donna Cech, Director, 630-515-7221, E-mail: dcechx@midwestern.edu. *Application contact:* Michael Laken, Director of Admissions, 630-515-6148, Fax: 630-971-6086, E-mail: admissil@midwestern.edu.

Announcement: Midwestern University is committed to educating the health-care team of the new century. The University administers the Chicago College of Osteopathic Medicine, the Chicago College of Pharmacy, the College of Health Sciences, the Arizona College of Osteopathic Medicine, and the College of Pharmacy–Glendale. The University operates campuses in Downers Grove, Illinois, and in Glendale, Arizona. The Physical Therapy Program offers the Doctor of Physical Therapy (DPT) degree on the Downers Grove campus. The 32-month program includes classroom interaction—often with students in other programs, such as occupational therapy, providing students with valuable perspectives—and 33 weeks of full-time clinical experience under the supervision of licensed physical therapists in diverse hospital and clinical settings. Contact the Office of Admissions, Midwestern University, 555 31st Street, Downers Grove, IL 60515; 800-458-6253; e-mail: admissil@midwestern.edu; WWW: http://www.midwestern.edu.

Missouri State University, Graduate College, College of Health and Human Services, Department of Physical Therapy, Springfield, MO 65804-0094. Offers MPT. *Accreditation:* APTA. *Faculty:* 6 full-time (3 women), 6 part-time/adjunct (2 women). *Students:* 71 full-time (48 women); includes 4 minority (3 American Indian/Alaska Native, 1 Asian American or Pacific Islander), 3 international. Average age 25. 55 applicants, 45% accepted, 20 enrolled. In 2006, 10 degrees awarded. *Degree requirements:* For master's, thesis or alternative, comprehensive exam. *Entrance requirements:* For master's, GRE General Test, minimum GPA of 3.0. Additional exam requirements/recommendations for international students: Required—TOEFL (minimum score 550 paper-based; 213 computer-based; 79 iBT). *Application deadline:* For fall admission, 1/15 for domestic students. Application fee: $35. *Expenses:* Tuition, state resident: full-time $3,582; part-time $199 per credit hour. Tuition, nonresident: full-time $6,984; part-time $199 per credit hour. Required fees: $548. Full-time tuition and fees vary according to course level, course load, program and reciprocity agreements. *Financial support:* Research assistantships with full tuition reimbursements, teaching assistantships with full tuition reimbursements, Federal Work-Study and unspecified assistantships available. Financial award application deadline: 3/31; financial award applicants required to submit FAFSA. *Unit head:* Dr. Akinniran Oladehin, Head, 417-836-8728, E-mail: physicaltherapy@missouristate.edu.

Mount St. Mary's College, Graduate Division, Department of Physical Therapy, Los Angeles, CA 90007. Offers DPT. *Accreditation:* APTA. *Faculty:* 3 full-time (all women), 4 part-time/adjunct (all women). *Students:* 74 full-time (48 women); includes 26 minority (2 African Americans, 15 Asian Americans or Pacific Islanders, 9 Hispanic Americans). Average age 26. In 2006, 3 degrees awarded. *Entrance requirements:* For doctorate, GRE General Test, minimum GPA of 3.0. Additional exam requirements/recommendations for international students: Required—TOEFL. *Application deadline:* For fall admission, 12/1 priority date for domestic students. Application fee: $75. *Expenses:* Contact institution. *Financial support:* Application deadline: 3/15; *Unit head:* Dr. Deborah Lowe, Chair, 213-477-2601, Fax: 213-477-2609, E-mail: dlowe@msmc.la.edu. *Application contact:* 213-477-2676, E-mail: dptinfo@msmc.la.edu.

Nazareth College of Rochester, Graduate Studies, Department of Physical Therapy, Doctoral Program in Physical Therapy, Rochester, NY 14618-3790. Offers DPT. *Faculty:* 10 full-time (7 women). *Students:* 8 full-time (6 women); includes 2 minority (1 Asian American or Pacific Islander, 1 Hispanic American). Average age 28. 12 applicants, 100% accepted, 8 enrolled. *Entrance requirements:* For doctorate, minimum GPA of 3.0. *Application deadline:* For fall admission, 2/1 for domestic students. Application fee: $40. *Financial support:* Research assistantships with partial tuition reimbursements available. Financial award application deadline: 3/1; financial award applicants required to submit FAFSA. *Application contact:* Judith G. Baker, Director, Graduate Admissions, 585-389-2050, Fax: 585-389-2817, E-mail: gradstudies@naz.edu.

Nazareth College of Rochester, Graduate Studies, Department of Physical Therapy, Master's Program in Physical Therapy, Rochester, NY 14618-3790. Offers MS. *Accreditation:* APTA. *Faculty:* 10 full-time (7 women). *Students:* 26 full-time (19 women); includes 1 minority (Asian American or Pacific Islander) In 2006, 12 degrees awarded. *Entrance requirements:* For master's, minimum GPA of 3.0. Application fee: $0. *Financial support:* Research assistantships with partial tuition reimbursements available. Financial award application deadline: 3/1; financial award applicants required to submit FAFSA. *Application contact:* Judith G. Baker, Director, Graduate Admissions, 585-389-2050, Fax: 585-389-2817, E-mail: gradstudies@naz.edu.

Neumann College, Program in Physical Therapy, Aston, PA 19014-1298. Offers MS, DPT. *Accreditation:* APTA. Evening/weekend programs available. *Faculty:* 5 full-time (3 women), 10 part-time/adjunct (8 women). *Students:* 69 full-time (42 women), 19 part-time (10 women); includes 14 minority (3 African Americans, 6 Asian Americans or Pacific Islanders, 5 Hispanic Americans). Average age 30. 96 applicants, 47% accepted, 35 enrolled. In 2006, 19 degrees awarded. *Entrance requirements:* Additional exam requirements/recommendations for international students: Required—TOEFL. *Application deadline:* For fall admission, 12/1 for domestic students. Application fee: $50. *Expenses:* Contact institution. *Financial support:* Available to part-time students. Application deadline: 3/15; *Unit head:* Dr. Robert Post, Director, 610-558-5233, Fax: 610-459-1370, E-mail: postr@neumann.edu. *Application contact:* Louise Bank, Assistant Director of Admissions, Graduate and Evening Programs, 610-558-5604, Fax: 610-459-1370, E-mail: bankl@neumann.edu.

New York Institute of Technology, Graduate Division, School of Allied Health and Life Sciences, Program in Physical Therapy, Old Westbury, NY 11568-8000. Offers MS, DPT. *Accreditation:* APTA. *Students:* 126 full-time (68 women), 3 part-time (1 woman); includes 30 minority (6 African Americans, 18 Asian Americans or Pacific Islanders, 6 Hispanic Americans), 7 international. Average age 27. 108 applicants, 64% accepted, 0 enrolled. In 2006, 30 degrees awarded. *Degree requirements:* For master's, thesis. *Entrance requirements:* For master's, minimum GPA of 3.0, interview, 100 hours of volunteer work, 2 letters of recommendation. Additional exam requirements/recommendations for international students: Required—TOEFL (minimum score 550 paper-based; 213 computer-based). *Application deadline:* For fall admission, 7/1 priority date for domestic students; for spring admission, 12/1 priority date for domestic students. Application fee: $50. *Expenses:* Tuition: Full-time $16,800; part-time $700 per credit. *Financial support:* Research assistantships with partial tuition reimbursements available. Financial award applicants required to submit FAFSA. *Unit head:* Dr. Peter Douris, Chair, 516-686-7696, E-mail: pdouns@nyit.edu. *Application contact:* Jacquelyn Nealon, Dean of Admissions and Financial Aid, 516-686-7925, Fax: 516-686-7613, E-mail: jnealon@nyit.edu.

New York Medical College, School of Public Health, Department of Physical Therapy, Valhalla, NY 10595-1691. Offers DPT. *Accreditation:* APTA. *Faculty:* 6 full-time (3 women), 23 part-time/adjunct (14 women). *Students:* Average age 27. 133 applicants, 44% accepted. In 2006, 46 degrees awarded. *Degree requirements:* For doctorate, comprehensive exam, registration. *Entrance requirements:* For doctorate, GRE General Test, minimum GPA of 3.0. Additional exam requirements/recommendations for international students: Required—TOEFL (minimum score 600 paper-based; 250 computer-based). *Application deadline:* Applications are processed on a rolling basis. Application fee: $75. *Expenses:* Contact institution. *Financial support:* Application deadline: 4/30; *Faculty research:* Neurobehavioral studies, biomechanical analysis at shoulder and knee, prediction of falls in elderly. *Unit head:* Dr. Michael Majsak, Chair, 914-594-4917, Fax: 914-594-4292, E-mail: michael_majsak@nymc.edu. *Application contact:* Marian F. McGowan, Information Contact, 914-594-4510, Fax: 914-594-4292, E-mail: sph_admissions@nymc.edu.

See Close-Up on page 1713.

New York University, Steinhardt School of Culture, Education and Human Development, Department of Physical Therapy, New York, NY 10012-1019. Offers physical therapists pathokinesiology (MA); physical therapy (DPT); practicing physical therapist (DPT); research in physical therapy (PhD). *Accreditation:* APTA (one or more programs are accredited). Part-time and evening/weekend programs available. *Faculty:* 10 full-time (5 women), 6 part-time/adjunct (1 woman). *Students:* 89 full-time (70 women), 9 part-time (5 women); includes 24 minority (6 African Americans, 1 American Indian/Alaska Native, 12 Asian Americans or Pacific Islanders, 5 Hispanic Americans), 12 international. 135 applicants, 68% accepted, 37 enrolled. In 2006, 11 master's, 22 doctorates awarded. Terminal master's awarded for partial completion of doctoral program. *Degree requirements:* For master's, thesis (for some programs); for doctorate, thesis/dissertation. *Entrance requirements:* For master's, physical therapy certificate; for doctorate, GRE General Test, interview, physical therapy certificate. Additional exam requirements/recommendations for international students: Required—TOEFL. *Application deadline:* For fall admission, 12/15 priority date for domestic and international students; for spring admission, 11/1 for domestic and international students. Applications are processed on a rolling basis. Application fee: $50. *Expenses:* Tuition: Part-time $1,080 per unit. Required fees: $56 per unit. $329 per term. Tuition and fees vary according to program. *Financial support:* Fellowships with full and partial tuition reimbursements, research assistantships with full and partial tuition reimbursements, career-related internships or fieldwork, Federal Work-Study, scholarships/grants, tuition waivers (partial), and unspecified assistantships available. Support available to part-time students. Financial award application deadline: 2/1; financial award applicants required to submit FAFSA. *Faculty research:* Motor learning and control, neuromuscular disorders, biomechanics and ergonomics, movement analysis, exercise physiology. *Unit head:* Dr. Wen K. Ling, Chairperson, 212-998-9400, Fax: 212-995-4190. *Application contact:* 212-998-5030, Fax: 212-995-4328, E-mail: steinhardt.gradadmissions@nyu.edu.

Northern Arizona University, Consortium of Professional Schools and Colleges, College of Health Professions, Department of Physical Therapy, Flagstaff, AZ 86011. Offers DPT. Program accepts only Arizona residents. *Accreditation:* APTA. Expenses: Contact institution.

Northern Illinois University, Graduate School, College of Health and Human Sciences, School of Allied Health Professions, De Kalb, IL 60115-2854. Offers physical therapy (MPT); public health (MPH). Admission to MPT program as undergraduate only. *Accreditation:* APTA; CEPH. Part-time programs available. *Faculty:* 9 full-time (6 women). *Students:* 72 full-time (53 women), 31 part-time (26 women); includes 17 minority (8 African Americans, 7 Asian Americans or Pacific Islanders, 2 Hispanic Americans), 30 international. Average age 27. 186 applicants, 55% accepted, 17 enrolled. In 2006, 56 degrees awarded. *Degree requirements:* For master's, internship, research paper in public health, thesis optional. *Entrance requirements:* For master's, GRE General Test, minimum GPA of 2.75. Additional exam requirements/recommendations for international students: Required—TOEFL (minimum score 550 paper-based; 213 computer-based). *Application deadline:* For fall admission, 6/1 for domestic students, 5/1 for international students; for spring admission, 11/1 for domestic students, 10/1 for international students. Applications are processed on a rolling basis. Application fee: $30. Electronic applications accepted. *Financial support:* In 2006–07, 18 research assistantships with full tuition reimbursements were awarded; fellowships with full tuition reimbursements, teaching assistantships with full tuition reimbursements, career-related internships or fieldwork, Federal Work-Study, scholarships/grants, tuition waivers (full), and unspecified assistantships also available. Support available to part-time students. Financial award applicants required to submit FAFSA. *Faculty research:* Stroke rehabilitation, radon exposure prevention, environmental causes of cancer, body image in young girls. *Unit head:* Interim Chair, 815-753-6329, Fax: 815-753-0720.

North Georgia College & State University, Graduate Studies, Department of Physical Therapy, Dahlonega, GA 30597. Offers DPT. *Accreditation:* APTA. *Faculty:* 9 full-time (5 women). *Students:* 47. Average age 32. 49 applicants, 51% accepted. *Entrance requirements:* For doctorate, interview. *Application deadline:* Applications are processed on a rolling basis. Application fee: $25. Electronic applications accepted. *Expenses:* Tuition, state resident: full-time $3,044; part-time $127 per credit hour. Tuition, nonresident: full-time $12,172; part-time $508 per credit hour. Required fees: $892; $458 per semester. *Financial support:* Available to part-time students. Application deadline: 5/1. *Faculty research:* Ergonomics, spinal mobility measurements, electrophysiology, orthopedic physical therapy. *Unit head:* Dr. Robert Laird, Chair, 706-864-1480, Fax: 706-864-1493, E-mail: rlaird@ngcsu.edu. *Application contact:* Dr. Donna A. Gessell, Director of Graduate Studies and External Programs, 706-864-1528, Fax: 706-867-2795, E-mail: dgessell@ngcsu.edu.

Northwestern University, Northwestern University Feinberg School of Medicine, Department of Physical Therapy and Human Movement Sciences, Chicago, IL 60611-2814. Offers DPT. *Accreditation:* APTA. *Faculty:* 15 full-time (8 women), 6 part-time/adjunct (4 women). *Students:* 182 full-time (161 women); includes 24 minority (7 African Americans, 12 Asian Americans or Pacific Islanders, 5 Hispanic Americans), 1 international. Average age 24. 297 applicants, 40% accepted, 65 enrolled. In 2006, 61 degrees awarded. *Degree requirements:* For doctorate, synthesis project. *Entrance requirements:* For doctorate, GRE General Test, minimum GPA of 2.75 in required course work. Additional exam requirements/recommendations for international students: Required—TOEFL (minimum score 265 computer-based). *Application deadline:* For fall admission, 11/1 for domestic students. Application fee: $50. Electronic applications accepted. *Expenses:* Contact institution. *Financial support:* In 2006–07, 150 students received support. Institutionally sponsored loans and scholarships/grants available. Financial award applicants required to submit FAFSA. *Faculty research:* Neuromuscular control, student performance, clinical outcomes. Total annual research expenditures: $2.5 million. *Unit head:* Dr. Julius Dewald, Associate Professor and Chair, 312-908-6788, Fax: 312-908-0741, E-mail: j-dewald@northwestern.edu. *Application contact:* Lynn Rogers, Manager of Admissions and Student Records, 312-908-6781, Fax: 312-908-0741, E-mail: lcr-mpt@northwestern.edu.

Nova Southeastern University, Health Professions Division, College of Allied Health and Nursing, Department of Physical Therapy, Fort Lauderdale, FL 33314-7796. Offers DPT, PhD, TDPT. *Accreditation:* APTA. Part-time programs available. Postbaccalaureate distance learning degree programs offered (minimal on-campus study). *Faculty:* 13 full-time (9 women), 9 part-time/adjunct (5 women). *Students:* 117 full-time (88 women), 65 part-time (45 women); includes 65 minority (27 African Americans, 1 American Indian/Alaska Native, 14 Asian Americans or Pacific Islanders, 23 Hispanic Americans), 11 international. Average age 25. 121 applicants, 37% accepted, 45 enrolled. In 2006, 14 doctorates awarded. *Degree requirements:* For doctorate, thesis/dissertation, comprehensive exam. *Entrance requirements:* For doctorate, GRE General Test. Additional exam requirements/recommendations for international students: Required—TOEFL. *Application deadline:* For spring admission, 2/1 priority date for domestic students. Applications are processed on a rolling basis. Application fee: $50. *Expenses:* Contact institution. *Faculty research:* Therapeutic exercise. *Unit head:* Dr. Stanley H. Wilson, Associate Professor and Chair, 954-262-1266, Fax: 954-262-1783, E-mail: swilson@nsu.nova.edu. *Application contact:* Ada Santiago, Admissions Counselor, 954-262-1110, Fax: 954-262-2282, E-mail: asantiago@nova.edu.

Oakland University, Graduate Study and Lifelong Learning, School of Health Sciences, Program in Physical Therapy, Rochester, MI 48309-4401. Offers neurological rehabilitation (Certificate); orthopedic manual physical therapy (Certificate); orthopedic physical therapy (Certificate); pediatric rehabilitation (Certificate); physical therapy (MSPT, DPT, Dr Sc PT); teaching and learning for rehabilitation professionals (Certificate). *Accreditation:* APTA. *Faculty:* 10 full-time (8 women), 1 (woman) part-time/adjunct. *Students:* 117 full-time (98 women), 77 part-time (59 women); includes 23 minority (9 African Americans, 12 Asian Americans or Pacific Islanders, 2 Hispanic Americans), 20 international. Average age 27. 205 applicants, 39% accepted, 56 enrolled. In 2006, 4 master's, 27 doctorates, 13 Certificates awarded. *Degree requirements:* For master's, thesis (for some programs). *Entrance requirements:* For master's, acceptance in the 2-year preparatory post-baccalaureate program, minimum GPA of 3.0; for doctorate, GRE General Test. Additional exam requirements/recommendations for international students: Required—TOEFL (minimum score 550 paper-based; 213 computer-based). *Application deadline:* For fall admission, 10/15 for domestic and international students. Application fee: $35. *Expenses:* Contact institution. *Financial support:* Federal Work-Study, institutionally sponsored loans, and tuition waivers (full) available. Financial award application deadline: 3/1; financial award applicants required to submit FAFSA. *Unit head:* Dr. Kristine A. Thompson, Program Director, 248-370-4041, E-mail: marcoux@oakland.edu.

The Ohio State University, College of Medicine, School of Allied Medical Professions, Program in Physical Therapy, Columbus, OH 43210. Offers MPT. *Accreditation:* APTA. *Students:* 81 full-time (69 women), 35 part-time (24 women); includes 5 minority (1 African American, 4 Asian Americans or Pacific Islanders). Average age 24. 1 applicant, 0% accepted. In 2006, 36 degrees awarded. *Entrance requirements:* For master's, GRE General Test. Additional exam requirements/recommendations for international students: Required—TOEFL (paper-based 550; computer-based 213) or Michigan English Language Assessment Bat-

Physical Therapy

The Ohio State University (continued)

tery (82). *Application deadline:* For fall admission, 8/15 priority date for domestic students, 7/1 priority date for international students; for winter admission, 12/1 priority date for domestic students, 11/1 priority date for international students; for spring admission, 3/1 priority date for domestic students, 2/1 priority date for international students. Applications are processed on a rolling basis. Application fee: $40 ($50 for international students). Electronic applications accepted. *Expenses:* Tuition, state resident: full-time $9,438. Tuition, nonresident: full-time $22,791. Tuition and fees vary according to course load, campus/location and program. *Unit head:* Deborah Heiss, Interim Director, 614-292-5921, Fax: 614-292-0210, E-mail: heiss.8@osu.edu. *Application contact:* 614-292-9444, Fax: 614-292-3895, E-mail: domestic.grad@osu.edu.

Ohio University, Graduate Studies, College of Health and Human Services, School of Physical Therapy, Athens, OH 45701-2979. Offers DPT. *Accreditation:* APTA. *Faculty:* 6 full-time (2 women), 1 (woman) part-time/adjunct. *Students:* 72 full-time (51 women); includes 4 minority (2 African Americans, 1 Asian American or Pacific Islander, 1 Hispanic American), 2 international. 86 applicants, 43% accepted. *Entrance requirements:* Additional exam requirements/recommendations for international students: Required—TOEFL. Application fee: $45. *Financial support:* In 2006–07, 26 students received support, including 3 research assistantships with full tuition reimbursements available, 2 teaching assistantships with full tuition reimbursements available (averaging $7,416 per year); Federal Work-Study, institutionally sponsored loans, scholarships/grants, tuition waivers (full), and unspecified assistantships also available. Financial award application deadline: 3/15. *Faculty research:* Motor control, muscle architecture, postural control, morphonetrics, sensory integration. *Unit head:* Dr. Averell S. Overby, Director, 740-593-1224, Fax: 740-593-0292, E-mail: overby@ohio.edu. *Application contact:* Rhonda Gibson, Senior Secretary, 740-593-1224, Fax: 740-593-0292, E-mail: gibson@ohio.edu.

Old Dominion University, College of Health Sciences, Program in Physical Therapy, Norfolk, VA 23529. Offers DPT. *Accreditation:* APTA. *Faculty:* 8 full-time (6 women), 6 part-time/adjunct (4 women). *Students:* 95 full-time (74 women), 8 part-time (7 women); includes 12 minority (9 African Americans, 1 Asian American or Pacific Islander, 2 Hispanic Americans), 3 international. Average age 25. 170 applicants, 48% accepted, 49 enrolled. In 2006, 30 degrees awarded. *Degree requirements:* For doctorate, thesis/dissertation or alternative, clinical internships, research project, comprehensive exam, registration. *Entrance requirements:* For doctorate, GRE, 3 letters of recommendation, 80 hours volunteer experience. Additional exam requirements/recommendations for international students: Required—TOEFL. *Application deadline:* For fall admission, 12/1 for domestic and international students. Applications are processed on a rolling basis. Application fee: $40. *Expenses:* Contact institution. *Financial support:* In 2006–07, 1 fellowship (averaging $15,000 per year), 1 research assistantship with partial tuition reimbursement (averaging $7,500 per year), 2 teaching assistantships (averaging $5,000 per year) were awarded; career-related internships or fieldwork also available. Financial award applicants required to submit FAFSA. *Faculty research:* Virtual reality and rehabilitation, rehabilitation foramputes, electromyography, dance medicine, biomechanics. Total annual research expenditures: $5,000. *Unit head:* Dr. Martha Walker, Graduate Program Director, 757-683-4519, Fax: 757-683-4410, E-mail: ptgpd@odu.edu.

Pacific University, School of Physical Therapy, Forest Grove, OR 97116-1797. Offers entry level (DPT); post-professional (DPT). *Accreditation:* APTA. *Faculty:* 11 full-time (7 women), 2 part-time/adjunct (0 women). *Students:* 116 full-time (82 women), 13 part-time (11 women); includes 12 minority (9 Asian Americans or Pacific Islanders, 3 Hispanic Americans). Average age 28. 278 applicants, 25% accepted, 38 enrolled. In 2006, 41 degrees awarded. *Degree requirements:* For doctorate, evidence-based capstone project thesis. *Entrance requirements:* For doctorate, 100 hours of volunteer/observational hours, minimum cumulative GPA of 3.0, prerequisite courses with a C grade or better, minimum GPA of 2.5 in science/statistics. Additional exam requirements/recommendations for international students: Required—TOEFL (minimum score 600 paper-based; 105 computer-based). *Application deadline:* For fall admission, 12/1 for domestic and international students. Application fee: $25. Electronic applications accepted. *Expenses:* Contact institution. *Financial support:* In 2006–07, 108 students received support, including 1 fellowship (averaging $3,000 per year); research assistantships, teaching assistantships, career-related internships or fieldwork, Federal Work-Study, and scholarships/grants also available. Financial award application deadline: 5/1; financial award applicants required to submit FAFSA. *Faculty research:* Balance disorders, geriatrics, orthopedic treatment outcomes, obesity, women's health. *Unit head:* Dr. Richard Rutt, Director, 503-352-7377, E-mail: ruttra@pacificu.edu. *Application contact:* Stephanie Krusemark, Assistant Director of Graduate and Professional Admissions, 503-352-2900, Fax: 503-352-2975, E-mail: admissions@pacificcu.edu.

Quinnipiac University, School of Health Sciences, Program in Physical Therapy, Hamden, CT 06518-1940. Offers DPT. Entry-level 6½ year program. *Accreditation:* APTA. *Faculty:* 11 full-time (8 women), 11 part-time/adjunct (3 women). *Students:* 31 full-time (25 women); includes 2 minority (1 Asian American or Pacific Islander, 1 Hispanic American). Average age 21. 26 applicants, 100% accepted, 26 enrolled. *Degree requirements:* For doctorate, capstone research project. *Entrance requirements:* For doctorate, successful completion of undergraduate degree requirements from Quinnipiac: BS in health science studies with minor in biology. *Expenses:* Tuition: Part-time $675 per credit. Required fees: $30 per credit. *Financial support:* Scholarships/grants, tuition waivers (partial), and unspecified assistantships available. Financial award application deadline: 4/15; financial award applicants required to submit FAFSA. *Unit head:* Donald Kowalsky, Chairperson, 203-582-8681, E-mail: donald.kowalsky@quinnipiac.edu. *Application contact:* 800-462-1944, Fax: 203-582-8901, E-mail: graduate@quinnipiac.edu.

Regis University, Rueckert-Hartman School for Health Professions, Program in Physical Therapy, Denver, CO 80221-1099. Offers DPT, TDPT. Offered at Northwest Denver Campus. *Accreditation:* APTA. *Faculty:* 9 full-time (5 women), 31 part-time/adjunct (18 women). *Students:* 290 full-time. Average age 26. 150 applicants, 50% accepted. In 2006, 13 degrees awarded. *Degree requirements:* For doctorate, clinical hours, research project. *Entrance requirements:* For doctorate, GRE General Test. *Application deadline:* For spring admission, 1/5 priority date for domestic students. Application fee: $75. *Financial support:* In 2006–07, 66 students received support, including 3 research assistantships (averaging $4,000 per year), 3 teaching assistantships (averaging $4,000 per year); Federal Work-Study and scholarships/grants also available. Financial award applicants required to submit FAFSA. *Faculty research:* Motor control, performance, stressor to motor performance, biomechanics of throwing, neuroscience. *Unit head:* Dr. Barbara Tschoepe, Director, 303-458-4152, Fax: 303-964-5474, E-mail: btschoep@regis.edu. *Application contact:* Kim Frisch, Director of Admissions, 303-458-4344, Fax: 303-964-5400, E-mail: kfrisch@regis.edu.

The Richard Stockton College of New Jersey, Graduate Programs, Program in Physical Therapy, Pomona, NJ 08240-0195. Offers MPT, DPT. *Accreditation:* APTA. *Faculty:* 7 full-time (6 women), 4 part-time/adjunct (3 women). *Students:* 31 full-time (25 women), 1 (woman) part-time; includes 1 minority (Hispanic American) Average age 29. 200 applicants. In 2006, 31 degrees awarded. *Degree requirements:* For master's, clinical rotation, project. *Application deadline:* For fall admission, 1/8 priority date for domestic students. Applications are processed on a rolling basis. Application fee: $50. *Expenses:* Tuition, state resident: full-time $9,746. Tuition, nonresident: full-time $14,462. Required fees: $2,340. *Financial support:* Career-related internships or fieldwork, Federal Work-Study, and scholarships/grants available. Support available to part-time students. Financial award application deadline: 3/1; financial award applicants required to submit FAFSA. *Faculty research:* Spinal flexibility in the well elderly, use of traditional Chinese medicine concepts in physical therapy, computerized vs. traditional study in human gross anatomy. *Unit head:* Bess Kathrins, Program Director, 609-652-4638, E-mail: bess.kathrins@stockton.edu. *Application contact:* Alison Henry, Associate Director of Admissions, 609-652-4261, Fax: 609-626-5541, E-mail: admissions@stockton.edu.

Rockhurst University, School of Graduate and Professional Studies, Program in Physical Therapy, Kansas City, MO 64110-2561. Offers DPT. *Accreditation:* APTA. *Faculty:* 10 full-time (5 women), 1 (woman) part-time/adjunct. *Students:* 99 full-time (75 women), 3 part-time (all women); includes 5 minority (1 African American, 4 Hispanic Americans), 1 international. Average age 25. 169 applicants, 38% accepted, 40 enrolled. *Entrance requirements:* For doctorate, 3 letters of recommendation, interview, minimum GPA of 3.0, physical therapy experience. *Application deadline:* For fall admission, 1/2 priority date for domestic students. Applications are processed on a rolling basis. Application fee: $25. Electronic applications accepted. *Expenses:* Tuition: Full-time $9,810; part-time $6,540 per year. Required fees: $400 per term. *Financial support:* In 2006–07, 5 research assistantships, 10 teaching assistantships were awarded; career-related internships or fieldwork, institutionally sponsored loans, and unspecified assistantships also available. Financial award application deadline: 4/1; financial award applicants required to submit FAFSA. *Faculty research:* Clinical decision making, geriatrics, balance in persons with neurological disorders, physical rehabilitation following total joint replacement, clinical education. *Unit head:* Dr. Brian McKiernan, Chair, 816-501-4059, Fax: 816-501-4169, E-mail: brian.mckiernan@rockhurst.edu. *Application contact:* Jyll Kafer, Director of Graduate Recruitment Admission, 816-501-4097, Fax: 816-501-4241, E-mail: jyll.kafer@rockhurst.edu.

Rosalind Franklin University of Medicine and Science, College of Health Professions, Department of Physical Therapy, North Chicago, IL 60064-3095. Offers MS, TDPT. *Accreditation:* APTA. Part-time programs available. Postbaccalaureate distance learning degree programs offered (no on-campus study). *Degree requirements:* For master's, thesis. *Entrance requirements:* For master's, minimum GPA of 2.8, physical therapy license. *Faculty research:* Faculty research productivity, measurement, recruitment and retention, orthopedic dysfunction, spinal malfunction.

Rutgers, The State University of New Jersey, Camden, Graduate School of Arts and Sciences, Program in Physical Therapy, Camden, NJ 08102-1401. Offers MPT. *Accreditation:* APTA. *Faculty:* 7 full-time (3 women). *Students:* 25 full-time (18 women); includes 6 minority (1 African American, 3 Asian Americans or Pacific Islanders, 2 Hispanic Americans). Average age 27. 14 applicants, 0% accepted. In 2006, 8 degrees awarded. *Degree requirements:* For master's, internships, master's project. *Entrance requirements:* For master's, GRE General Test, physical therapy experience. *Application deadline:* For fall admission, 12/1 priority date for domestic students. Applications are processed on a rolling basis. Application fee: $20. Electronic applications accepted. *Financial support:* In 2006–07, 5 fellowships (averaging $200 per year) were awarded; career-related internships or fieldwork, Federal Work-Study, and institutionally sponsored loans also available. Financial award application deadline: 3/15; financial award applicants required to submit FAFSA. *Faculty research:* Clinical education, migrant workers, biomechanical constraints on motor control, high intensity strength training and the elderly, posture and ergonomics. *Unit head:* Marie Koval Nardone, Director, 856-566-6456, Fax: 856-566-6458, E-mail: mptgradm@umdnj.edu. *Application contact:* Joanne Olivera, Coordinator, 856-225-6104, Fax: 856-225-6498, E-mail: olivera@camuga.rutgers.edu.

Sacred Heart University, Graduate Studies, College of Education and Health Professions, Faculty of Physical Therapy, Fairfield, CT 06825-1000. Offers DPT. *Accreditation:* APTA. *Faculty:* 9 full-time (5 women). *Students:* 81 full-time (57 women), 12 part-time (7 women); includes 1 African American, 4 Asian Americans or Pacific Islanders, 3 Hispanic Americans, 1 international. Average age 25. 89 applicants, 84% accepted, 48 enrolled. *Entrance requirements:* Additional exam requirements/recommendations for international students: Required—TOEFL (minimum score 550 paper-based; 213 computer-based). *Application deadline:* For fall admission, 1/15 priority date for domestic students. Applications are processed on a rolling basis. Application fee: $50 ($100 for international students). Electronic applications accepted. *Expenses:* Contact institution. Full-time tuition and fees vary according to degree level and program. *Financial support:* Career-related internships or fieldwork, institutionally sponsored loans, and unspecified assistantships available. Support available to part-time students. Financial award applicants required to submit FAFSA. *Unit head:* Dr. Michael Emery, Director, 203-365-7656. *Application contact:* Kathy Dilks, Assistant Dean of Graduate Admissions, Health Professions, 203-396-8259, Fax: 203-365-4732, E-mail: gradstudies@sacredheart.edu.

Sage Graduate School, Graduate School, Division of Health and Rehabilitation Sciences, Program in Physical Therapy, Troy, NY 12180-4115. Offers PhD. *Accreditation:* APTA. *Faculty:* 8 full-time (7 women), 5 part-time/adjunct (all women). *Students:* 48 full-time (37 women), 40 part-time (29 women); includes 2 minority (1 African American, 1 Hispanic American). Average age 29. 24 applicants, 92% accepted, 20 enrolled. In 2006, 37 degrees awarded. *Entrance requirements:* Additional exam requirements/recommendations for international students: Required—TOEFL (minimum score 550 paper-based; 213 computer-based). *Application deadline:* Applications are processed on a rolling basis. Application fee: $40. *Expenses:* Tuition: Full-time $9,270; part-time $515 per credit hour. *Financial support:* Career-related internships or fieldwork, scholarships/grants, and unspecified assistantships available. Support available to part-time students. Financial award application deadline: 3/1; financial award applicants required to submit FAFSA. *Unit head:* Marjane Selleck, Chair, 518-244-2060. *Application contact:* Shannon K. Easton, Director of Graduate and Adult Admission, 518-244-2443, Fax: 518-244-6880, E-mail: sgsadm@sage.edu.

St. Ambrose University, College of Education and Health Sciences, Department of Physical Therapy, Davenport, IA 52803-2898. Offers DPT. *Accreditation:* APTA. *Faculty:* 8 full-time (3 women), 1 (woman) part-time/adjunct. *Students:* 65 full-time (48 women), 22 part-time (16 women); includes 2 minority (both Hispanic Americans), 1 international. Average age 27. 31 applicants, 97% accepted, 22 enrolled. In 2006, 34 degrees awarded. *Degree requirements:* For doctorate, board exams. *Entrance requirements:* For doctorate, GRE, interview. Additional exam requirements/recommendations for international students: Required—TOEFL. *Application deadline:* For fall admission, 1/15 priority date for domestic students. Application fee: $25. *Financial support:* In 2006–07, 9 research assistantships with partial tuition reimbursements (averaging $3,600 per year) were awarded; career-related internships or fieldwork, tuition waivers (partial), and unspecified assistantships also available. Financial award application deadline: 3/15; financial award applicants required to submit FAFSA. *Faculty research:* Human motor control, orthopedic physical therapy, cardiopulmonary physical therapy, kinesiology/biomechanics. *Unit head:* Dr. Sandra Cassady, Director, 563-333-6409, Fax: 563-333-6410, E-mail: scassady@sau.edu. *Application contact:* Elizabeth Berridge, Director of Graduate Student Recruitment, 563-333-6271, Fax: 563-333-6268, E-mail: berridgeelizabethb@sau.edu.

Saint Francis University, Department of Physical Therapy, Loretto, PA 15940-0600. Offers DPT. *Accreditation:* APTA. *Faculty:* 8 full-time (5 women), 1 part-time/adjunct (0 women). *Students:* 55 full-time (39 women); includes 3 minority (1 African American, 2 Asian Americans or Pacific Islanders). Average age 24. 30 applicants, 63% accepted, 10 enrolled. In 2006, 16 degrees awarded. *Median time to degree:* Doctorate–3 years full-time. *Entrance requirements:* For doctorate, minimum QPA of 3.0, 80 hours of clinical experience. Additional exam requirements/recommendations for international students: Required—TOEFL. *Application deadline:* For winter admission, 1/15 for domestic and international students. Application fee: $30. Electronic applications accepted. *Expenses:* Tuition: Part-time $661 per credit. Tuition and fees vary according to program. *Financial support:* In 2006–07, 8 students received support, including 8 teaching assistantships with partial tuition reimbursements available; career-related internships or fieldwork also available. *Faculty research:* Ergonomics, geriatrics, collaborative learning, energy expenditure, teaching and learning. *Unit head:* Dr. Patricia I. Fitzgerald, Interim Department Chair/Associate Professor, 814-472-3199, Fax: 814-472-3140, E-mail: pfitzgerald@francis.edu.

Saint Louis University, Graduate School, Doisy College of Health Sciences, Department of Physical Therapy, St. Louis, MO 63103-2097. Offers MSPT, DPT. Students enter MSPT program as freshmen. *Accreditation:* APTA. Part-time programs available. *Faculty:* 17 full-time (13 women). *Students:* 108 full-time (85 women), 30 part-time (27 women); includes 9 minority (2 African Americans, 2 American Indian/Alaska Native, 3 Asian Americans or Pacific Islanders, 2 Hispanic Americans), 2 international. Average age 25. 26 applicants, 96% accepted, 20 enrolled. In 2006, 73 master's, 15 doctorates awarded. *Entrance requirements:* Additional exam requirements/recommendations for international students: Required—TOEFL (minimum score 525 paper-based; 194 computer-based). *Application deadline:* For fall admission, 7/1 for domestic and international students; for spring admission, 11/1 for domestic and international students. Applications are processed on a rolling basis. Application fee: $40. *Expenses:* Tuition: Part-time $800 per credit hour. Required fees: $105 per semester. *Financial support:* In 2006–07, 11 students received support. Career-related internships or fieldwork, Federal Work-Study, scholarships/grants, traineeships, health care benefits, and unspecified assistantships available. Support available to part-time students. Financial award application deadline: 6/1; financial award applicants required to submit FAFSA. *Faculty research:* Patellofemoral pain and associated risk factors; prevalence of disordered eating in physical therapy students; effects of selected interventions for children with cerebral palsy on gait and posture: hippotherapy, ankle strengthening, supported treadmill training, spirituality in physical therapy/patient care, risk factors for exercise-related leg pain in running athletes. *Unit head:* Dr. Mark Reinking, Chairperson, 314-577-8505, E-mail: reinking@slu.edu.

Samuel Merritt College, Department of Physical Therapy, Oakland, CA 94609-3108. Offers MPT, MSPT. *Accreditation:* APTA. *Entrance requirements:* For master's, GRE General Test, minimum GPA of 2.6 in science, 2.8 overall in last 60 hours (MPT); minimum GPA of 3.0 in physical therapy (MSPT); related work experience; interview. Additional exam requirements/recommendations for international students: Required—TOEFL. Expenses: Contact institution. *Faculty research:* Human movement, motor control, falls prevention in the elderly.

San Francisco State University, Division of Graduate Studies, College of Health and Human Services, Program in Physical Therapy, San Francisco, CA 94132-1722. Offers MS, DPT, Dr Sc PT. *Faculty:* 9 full-time (all women), 4 part-time/adjunct (3 women). *Students:* 59 full-time (49 women). In 2006, 32 degrees awarded. *Degree requirements:* For master's, comprehensive exam; for doctorate, thesis/dissertation. *Entrance requirements:* For master's, GRE, minimum GPA of 3.0, 150 hours of work experience; for doctorate, GRE, physical therapy license, minimum GPA of 3.0. *Application deadline:* For fall admission, 11/1 for domestic students. Application fee: $55. *Financial support:* Career-related internships or fieldwork and institutionally sponsored loans available. *Faculty research:* Balance disorders, movement disorders, gait, psychological issues in disability. *Unit head:* Dr. Linda Wanek, Director, 415-338-2001, E-mail: lwanek@sfsu.edu. *Application contact:* Lillie Wong, Academic Coordinator, 415-476-3147, E-mail: gppt@sfsu.edu.

Seton Hall University, School of Graduate Medical Education, Program in Physical Therapy, South Orange, NJ 07079-2697. Offers professional physical therapy (DPT). *Accreditation:* APTA. *Faculty:* 7 full-time (5 women), 16 part-time/adjunct (9 women). *Students:* 88 full-time (65 women); includes 18 minority (6 African Americans, 8 Asian Americans or Pacific Islanders, 4 Hispanic Americans). Average age 22. 91 applicants, 38% accepted, 24 enrolled. In 2006, 18 degrees awarded. *Degree requirements:* For doctorate, research project. *Entrance requirements:* Additional exam requirements/recommendations for international students: Required—TOEFL. *Application deadline:* For fall admission, 11/15 priority date for domestic and international students; for spring admission, 2/15 for domestic and international students. Applications are processed on a rolling basis. Application fee: $75. Electronic applications accepted. *Financial support:* In 2006–07, 6 students received support. Federal Work-Study and unspecified assistantships available. *Faculty research:* Electrical stimulation, motor learning. *Unit head:* Dr. Doreen Stiskal, Acting Chair, Department of Physical Therapy, 973-275-2051, Fax: 973-275-2370. *Application contact:* Deborah Verderosa, Director of Admissions, 973-275-2062, Fax: 973-275-2171, E-mail: gradmeded@shu.edu.

See Close-Up on page 1727.

Shenandoah University, School of Health Professions, Division of Physical Therapy, Winchester, VA 22601-5195. Offers physical therapy and non-traditional physical therapy (DPT). *Accreditation:* APTA. Part-time programs available. Postbaccalaureate distance learning degree programs offered. *Faculty:* 7 full-time (4 women), 4 part-time/adjunct (2 women). *Students:* 104 full-time (86 women), 78 part-time (50 women); includes 1 minority (African American), 5 international. Average age 32. 235 applicants, 66% accepted, 95 enrolled. In 2006, 46 degrees awarded. *Entrance requirements:* For doctorate, GRE General Test, minimum GPA of 2.8, 3 letters of recommendation. Additional exam requirements/recommendations for international students: Required—TOEFL (minimum score 527 paper-based; 197 computer-based; 71 iBT). *Application deadline:* For fall admission, 3/31 for domestic students. Applications are processed on a rolling basis. Application fee: $30. Electronic applications accepted. *Expenses: Contact institution.* Full-time tuition and fees vary according to course load and program. *Financial support:* In 2006–07, 74 students received support. Institutionally sponsored loans and scholarships/grants available. Support available to part-time students. Financial award application deadline: 3/15; financial award applicants required to submit FAFSA. *Faculty research:* Efficacy of aquatic therapy, domestic violence education in physical therapy, elector myography; gender, ethnicity and pain; extra cellular matrix remodeling. *Unit head:* Dr. Rose A. Schmieg, Director, 540-665-5534, Fax: 540-545-7387, E-mail: rschmieg@su.edu. *Application contact:* David Anthony, Dean of Admissions, 540-665-4581, Fax: 540-665-4627, E-mail: admit@su.edu.

Simmons College, School for Health Studies, Program in Physical Therapy, Boston, MA 02115. Offers DPT. *Accreditation:* APTA. Postbaccalaureate distance learning degree programs offered (no on-campus study). *Faculty:* 5 full-time (all women), 20 part-time/adjunct (17 women). *Students:* 39 full-time (33 women), 126 part-time (103 women); includes 17 minority (6 African Americans, 7 Asian Americans or Pacific Islanders, 4 Hispanic Americans), 1 international. Average age 25. 60 applicants, 55% accepted, 7 enrolled. In 2006, 124 degrees awarded. *Degree requirements:* For doctorate, registration. *Entrance requirements:* For doctorate, GRE, courses in biology, chemistry, exercise physiology, physics, psychology, statistics, anatomy, and physiology. Additional exam requirements/recommendations for international students: Required—TOEFL. *Application deadline:* Applications are processed on a rolling basis. Application fee: $100. Electronic applications accepted. *Expenses: Contact institution. Financial support:* Fellowships, research assistantships with partial tuition reimbursements, teaching assistantships with partial tuition reimbursements, Federal Work-Study, institutionally sponsored loans, scholarships/grants, and unspecified assistantships available. Support available to part-time students. Financial award application deadline: 3/1; financial award applicants required to submit FAFSA. *Faculty research:* Cardiopulmonary rehabilitation, manual physical therapy techniques, early child development of motor skills, spinal impairments and rheumatoid arthritis. *Unit head:* Dr. Shelley Goodgold, Interim Department Chair, 617-521-2635, Fax: 617-521-3032, E-mail: sgoodgold@simmons.edu. *Application contact:* Staff Assistant, 617-521-2650, Fax: 617-521-3137, E-mail: gshsadm@simmons.edu.

Slippery Rock University of Pennsylvania, Graduate Studies (Recruitment), College of Health, Environment, and Science, School of Physical Therapy, Slippery Rock, PA 16057-1383. Offers DPT. *Accreditation:* APTA. *Degree requirements:* For doctorate, thesis/dissertation (for some programs), clinical residency, comprehensive exam (for some programs). *Entrance requirements:* For doctorate, GRE General Test, minimum GPA of 2.75. Additional exam requirements/recommendations for international students: Required—TOEFL (minimum score 550 paper-based; 213 computer-based). *Application deadline:* For fall admission, 7/1 priority date for domestic and international students; for spring admission, 11/1 priority date for domestic and international students. Applications are processed on a rolling basis. Application fee: $35. Electronic applications accepted. *Expenses: Contact institution. Financial support:* Career-related internships or fieldwork, Federal Work-Study, scholarships/grants, and unspecified assistantships available. Financial award application deadline: 5/1. *Unit head:* Dr. Carol Martin-Elkins, Graduate Coordinator, 724-738-2080, Fax: 724-738-2113, E-mail: carol.martin-elkins@sru.edu. *Application contact:* April Longwell, Interim Director of Graduate Studies, 724-738-2051 Ext. 2116, Fax: 724-738-2146, E-mail: graduate.studies@sru.edu.

Southwest Baptist University, Graduate Studies, Program in Physical Therapy, Bolivar, MO 65613-2597. Offers DPT. *Accreditation:* APTA. *Degree requirements:* For doctorate, 3-4 clinical education experiences. *Entrance requirements:* Additional exam requirements/recommendations for international students: Required—TOEFL (minimum score 550 paper-based; 213 computer-based). Expenses: Contact institution. *Faculty research:* Balance and falls prevention, distance and web based learning, foot and ankle intervention, pediatrics, musculoskeletal management.

Springfield College, Graduate Programs, Program in Physical Therapy, Springfield, MA 01109-3797. Offers MS. *Accreditation:* APTA. *Faculty:* 8 full-time (6 women), 14 part-time/adjunct (11 women). *Students:* 41 full-time. Average age 24. 23 applicants, 48% accepted, 6 enrolled. In 2006, 22 degrees awarded. *Degree requirements:* For master's, research project. *Entrance requirements:* For master's, GRE General Test, interview, minimum GPA of 3.0. Additional exam requirements/recommendations for international students: Required—TOEFL (minimum score 550 paper-based; 213 computer-based). *Application deadline:* For fall admission, 12/1 for domestic students; for winter admission, 11/1 for domestic students; for spring admission, 11/1 for domestic students. Applications are processed on a rolling basis. Application fee: $50. Electronic applications accepted. *Expenses:* Tuition: Full-time $12,222; part-time $679 per credit. Required fees: $25; $25 per year. One-time fee: $25 full-time. *Financial support:* In 2006–07, 2 teaching assistantships with partial tuition reimbursements were awarded; fellowships with partial tuition reimbursements, career-related internships or fieldwork, Federal Work-Study, institutionally sponsored loans, and tuition waivers (full and partial) also available. Financial award application deadline: 3/1. *Faculty research:* Technology in physical therapy, ergonomics, professional issues, orthopedics, clinical education. *Unit head:* Dr. Linda Tsoumas, Director, 413-748-3369, Fax: 413-748-3371, E-mail: ltsoumas@spfldcol.edu. *Application contact:* Donald James Shaw, Director of Graduate Admissions, 413-748-3060, Fax: 413-748-3069, E-mail: donald_shaw_jr@spfldcol.edu.

State University of New York Upstate Medical University, Department of Physical Therapy, Syracuse, NY 13210-2334. Offers DPT. *Accreditation:* APTA. Part-time and evening/weekend programs available. Postbaccalaureate distance learning degree programs offered (minimal on-campus study). *Faculty:* 9 full-time (5 women), 5 part-time/adjunct (2 women). *Students:* 67 full-time (49 women), 40 part-time (26 women); includes 5 minority (2 African Americans, 1 Asian American or Pacific Islander, 2 Hispanic Americans), 2 international. Average age 27. 130 applicants, 59% accepted, 60 enrolled. In 2006, 17 degrees awarded. *Application deadline:* For fall admission, 1/15 for domestic students. Applications are processed on a rolling basis. Application fee: $30. *Expenses:* Tuition, state resident: full-time $6,900; part-time $288 per credit. Tuition, nonresident: full-time $10,920; part-time $455 per credit. Required fees: $496. *Financial support:* In 2006–07, 52 students received support. Federal Work-Study and scholarships/grants available. Support available to part-time students. Financial award application deadline: 3/1; financial award applicants required to submit FAFSA. *Unit head:* Dr. Susan Miller, Interim Chair, 315-464-5101, Fax: 315-464-4608. *Application contact:* Donna Vavonese, Associate Director of Admissions, 315-464-4570, Fax: 315-464-8867, E-mail: vavonesd@upstate.edu.

Stony Brook University, State University of New York, Stony Brook University Medical Center, Health Sciences Center, School of Health Technology and Management, Stony Brook, NY 11794. Offers community health (Advanced Certificate); health care management (Advanced Certificate); health care policy and management (MS); occupational therapy (MS); physical therapy (MS, DPT). *Accreditation:* APTA. Part-time programs available. *Faculty:* 26 full-time (15 women), 21 part-time/adjunct (12 women). *Students:* 198 full-time (147 women), 130 part-time (89 women); includes 87 minority (29 African Americans, 1 American Indian/Alaska Native, 37 Asian Americans or Pacific Islanders, 20 Hispanic Americans), 4 international. 907 applicants, 25% accepted. In 2006, 33 master's, 106 doctorates, 15 other advanced degrees awarded. *Degree requirements:* For master's, thesis. *Entrance requirements:* For master's, GRE General Test, minimum GPA of 3.0, work experience in field. *Application deadline:* For fall admission, 1/15 for domestic students. Application fee: $60. *Expenses:* Tuition, state resident: full-time $6,900; part-time $288 per credit. Tuition, nonresident: full-time $10,920; part-time $455 per credit. *Financial support:* In 2006–07, 1 fellowship was awarded; career-related internships or fieldwork, Federal Work-Study, and institutionally sponsored loans also available. Financial award application deadline: 3/15. *Faculty research:* Health promotion and disease prevention. Total annual research expenditures: $527,101. *Unit head:* Dr. Craig A. Lehmann, Dean, 631-444-2251, Fax: 631-444-7621. *Application contact:* Alan Leiken, Associate Dean for Graduate Studies, 631-444-3240, Fax: 631-444-7621.

Temple University, Health Sciences Center and Graduate School, College of Health Professions, Department of Physical Therapy, Philadelphia, PA 19122-6096. Offers DPT, PhD. *Accreditation:* APTA (one or more programs are accredited). Part-time and evening/weekend programs available. *Faculty:* 11 full-time (9 women). *Students:* 128 full-time (97 women), 87 part-time (51 women); includes 53 minority (32 African Americans, 17 Asian Americans or Pacific Islanders, 4 Hispanic Americans), 4 international. 200 applicants, 40% accepted, 76 enrolled. *Degree requirements:* For doctorate, thesis/dissertation. *Entrance requirements:* For doctorate, GRE General Test, interview. Additional exam requirements/recommendations for international students: Required—TOEFL (minimum score 550 paper-based; 213 computer-based; 79 iBT). *Application deadline:* For fall admission, 4/1 for domestic students, 12/15 for international students. Application fee: $50. Electronic applications accepted. *Expenses:* Tuition, state resident: full-time $12,264; part-time $511 per credit. Tuition, nonresident: full-time $17,904; part-time $746 per credit. Required fees: $84 per course. Tuition and fees vary according to program. *Financial support:* Career-related internships or fieldwork and institutionally sponsored loans available. Support available to part-time students. Financial award application deadline: 1/15; financial award applicants required to submit FAFSA. *Faculty research:* Balance dysfunction, biomechanics, development, qualitative research, developmental neuroscience, health services. Total annual research expenditures: $300,000. *Unit head:* Dr. Emily A. Keshner, Chair, 215-707-4815, Fax: 215-707-7500, E-mail: ekeshner@temple.edu.

See Close-Up on page 1741.

Tennessee State University, The School of Graduate Studies and Research, College of Health Sciences, Department of Physical Therapy, Nashville, TN 37209-1561. Offers MPT, DPT. *Accreditation:* APTA. Part-time programs available. Postbaccalaureate distance learning degree programs offered (minimal on-campus study). *Faculty:* 8 full-time (4 women), 1 (woman) part-time/adjunct. *Students:* 55 full-time (35 women); includes 27 minority (26 African Americans, 1 Hispanic American). Average age 25. 50 applicants, 54% accepted, 27 enrolled. In 2006, 4 degrees awarded. *Degree requirements:* For master's, thesis optional. *Entrance requirements:* For master's, GRE General Test, MAT. *Application deadline:* For fall admission, 1/15 for domestic and international students. Application fee: $25. *Financial support:* In 2006–07, 2 research assistantships with tuition reimbursements were awarded; fellowships with tuition reimbursements, teaching assistantships with tuition reimbursements, scholarships/grants, traineeships, and unspecified assistantships also available. Support available to part-time students. Financial award applicants required to submit FAFSA. *Faculty research:* Evidence-Based Research Clinical Research Case Studies/Reports Qualitative Research Education Assessment Total knee anthroplasty; Ergonomics; Childhood obesity. *Unit head:* Dr. Rosalyn Pitt, Department Head, 615-963-5944, Fax: 615-963-5935, E-mail: rpitt@tnstate.edu.

Texas State University-San Marcos, Graduate School, College of Health Professions, Department of Physical Therapy, San Marcos, TX 78666. Offers MSPT. Applicants accepted in summer only. *Accreditation:* APTA. *Faculty:* 8 full-time (6 women), 1 (woman) part-time/adjunct. *Students:* 57 full-time (38 women), 27 part-time (16 women); includes 22 minority (2 African Americans, 4 Asian Americans or Pacific Islanders, 16 Hispanic Americans), 4 international. Average age 27. 209 applicants, 23% accepted, 37 enrolled. In 2006, 30 degrees awarded. *Degree requirements:* For master's, thesis optional. *Entrance requirements:* For master's, GRE General Test, minimum GPA of 3.0 in last 60 hours of course work. Additional exam requirements/recommendations for international students: Required—TOEFL.

Physical Therapy

Texas State University-San Marcos (continued)
Application deadline: For fall admission, 10/15 for domestic students. Application fee: $65 ($115 for international students). *Financial support:* In 2006–07, 72 students received support, including 8 teaching assistantships (averaging $2,103 per year); research assistantships, career-related internships or fieldwork, Federal Work-Study, and institutionally sponsored loans also available. Support available to part-time students. Financial award application deadline: 4/1; financial award applicants required to submit FAFSA. *Faculty research:* Exercise, gait training, wellness. *Unit head:* Dr. Barbara Sanders, Chair, 512-245-8351, Fax: 512-245-8736, E-mail: bs04@txstate.edu.

Texas Tech University Health Sciences Center, School of Allied Health Sciences, Program in Physical Therapy, Lubbock, TX 79430. Offers MPT, Sc D. *Accreditation:* APTA. *Faculty:* 18 full-time (5 women). *Students:* 154 full-time (88 women), 55 part-time (27 women); includes 32 minority (5 African Americans, 7 Asian Americans or Pacific Islanders, 20 Hispanic Americans), 1 international. Average age 27. 198 applicants, 37% accepted, 74 enrolled. In 2006, 48 master's, 4 doctorates awarded. *Entrance requirements:* Additional exam requirements/recommendations for international students: Required—TOEFL. *Application deadline:* For fall admission, 10/15 priority date for domestic students; for winter admission, 2/1 priority date for domestic students. Application fee: $35. Electronic applications accepted. *Financial support:* Career-related internships or fieldwork, institutionally sponsored loans, and scholarships/grants available. Financial award application deadline: 9/1; financial award applicants required to submit FAFSA. *Faculty research:* Closed chain proprioception; effects of unloading; retrospective studies including ACL, hippotherapy, orthopedic/sports medicine injuries. *Unit head:* Dr. Steve Sawyer, Chair, 806-743-3226, Fax: 806-743-3249, E-mail: steve.sawyer@ttuhsc.edu. *Application contact:* Jeri Moravcik, Assistant Director of Admissions and Student Affairs, 806-743-3220, Fax: 806-743-2994, E-mail: jeri.moravcik@ttuhsc.edu.

Texas Woman's University, Graduate School, College of Health Sciences, School of Physical Therapy, Denton, TX 76201. Offers physical therapy (MS, DPT, PhD), including clinical level (MS, PhD), entry level (MS). *Accreditation:* APTA (one or more programs are accredited). Part-time and evening/weekend programs available. *Students:* 186 full-time (160 women), 80 part-time (66 women); includes 42 minority (6 African Americans, 2 American Indian/Alaska Native, 17 Asian Americans or Pacific Islanders, 17 Hispanic Americans), 7 international. Average age 27. In 2006, 92 master's, 7 doctorates awarded. *Degree requirements:* For master's and doctorate, thesis/dissertation. *Entrance requirements:* For master's, GRE General Test (for entry level), resumé, 2 letters of recommendation; for doctorate, interview, resumé, eligibility for Texas Physical Therapy license, 2 letters of recommendation. Additional exam requirements/recommendations for international students: Required—TOEFL (minimum score 550 paper-based; 213 computer-based; 79 iBT). *Application deadline:* For fall admission, 4/1 for international students; for spring admission, 8/1 for international students. Applications are processed on a rolling basis. Application fee: $100. Electronic applications accepted. *Expenses:* Tuition, area resident: Part-time $168 per unit. Tuition, state resident: full-time $4,369. Tuition, nonresident: full-time $9,373; part-time $443 per unit. Required fees: $20 per unit. $177 per term. *Financial support:* In 2006–07, 4 research assistantships (averaging $10,206 per year), teaching assistantships (averaging $10,206 per year) were awarded; career-related internships or fieldwork, Federal Work-Study, institutionally sponsored loans, scholarships/grants, traineeships, health care benefits, and unspecified assistantships also available. Support available to part-time students. Financial award application deadline: 3/1; financial award applicants required to submit FAFSA. *Faculty research:* Functional test for females, shoulder rehabilitation, electrophysiologic evaluation, stroke rehabilitation, osteoporosis and exercise. *Unit head:* Dr. Sharon Olson, Director, 713-794-2090, Fax: 713-794-2071, E-mail: solson@twu.edu. *Application contact:* Samuel Wheeler, Coordinator of Graduate Admissions, 940-898-3188, Fax: 940-898-3081, E-mail: wheelersr@twu.edu.

Thomas Jefferson University, Jefferson College of Health Professions, Program in Physical Therapy, Philadelphia, PA 19107. Offers MS, DPT. *Accreditation:* APTA. *Faculty:* 7 full-time (3 women), 1 (woman) part-time/adjunct. *Students:* 33 full-time (29 women), 2 part-time (1 woman); includes 5 minority (2 African Americans, 3 Hispanic Americans). 152 applicants, 32% accepted, 35 enrolled. In 2006, 41 degrees awarded. *Degree requirements:* For master's, thesis or alternative, registration. *Entrance requirements:* For master's, minimum GPA of 3.0. Additional exam requirements/recommendations for international students: Required—TOEFL (minimum score 213 computer-based). *Application deadline:* For fall admission, 3/1 priority date for domestic and international students. Applications are processed on a rolling basis. Application fee: $50. Electronic applications accepted. *Expenses: Contact institution. Financial support:* Federal Work-Study and institutionally sponsored loans available. Support available to part-time students. Financial award application deadline: 5/1; financial award applicants required to submit FAFSA. *Faculty research:* Gait and motion analysis, motor control and learning, single motor unit discharge in human muscle, musculoskeletal injuries, cancer rehabilitation. *Unit head:* Dr. Penny Kroll, Director, 215-503-8961, Fax: 215-503-3499, E-mail: penny.kroll@jefferson.edu. *Application contact:* Karen A. Jacobs, Director of Admissions and Enrollment Management, 215-503-1040, Fax: 215-503-7241, E-mail: jchp@jefferson.edu.

Touro College, Barry Z. Levine School of Health Sciences, Physical Therapy Program, New York, NY 10010. Offers MS. *Accreditation:* APTA. *Degree requirements:* For master's, thesis, community service project. *Entrance requirements:* For master's, interview, minimum GPA of 2.8, 100 hours of physical therapy work experience.

Université de Montréal, Faculty of Medicine and Faculty of Graduate Studies, Graduate Programs in Medicine, Program in Specialized Studies, Montréal, QC H3C 3J7, Canada. Offers anesthesia (DESS); diagnostic radiology (DESS); family medicine (DESS); medical biochemistry (DESS); medical genetics (DESS); medicine (DESS); microbiology and infectious diseases (DESS); nuclear medicine (DESS); obstetrics and gynecology (DESS); ophthalmology (DESS); pediatrics (DESS); psychiatry (DESS); radiology-oncology (DESS); surgery (DESS). *Faculty:* 159 full-time (37 women), 345 part-time/adjunct (102 women). *Entrance requirements:* For degree, proficiency in French. *Application deadline:* For fall admission, 2/1 priority date for domestic students; for winter admission, 11/1 priority date for domestic students; for spring admission, 2/1 priority date for domestic students. Application fee: $30. Electronic applications accepted. *Unit head:* Dr. Pierre Boyle, Vice Dean of Studies, 514-343-6300, Fax: 514-343-5751, E-mail: pierre.boyle@umontreal.ca.

University at Buffalo, the State University of New York, Graduate School, School of Public Health and Health Professions, Department of Rehabilitation Science, Program in Physical Therapy, Buffalo, NY 14260. Offers DPT. *Accreditation:* APTA. *Students:* 126 full-time (71 women), 1 part-time; includes 20 minority (9 African Americans, 1 American Indian/Alaska Native, 9 Asian Americans or Pacific Islanders, 1 Hispanic American), 2 international. 131 applicants, 35% accepted, 44 enrolled. In 2006, 39 degrees awarded. *Entrance requirements:* For doctorate, GRE. Additional exam requirements/recommendations for international students: Required—TOEFL. *Application deadline:* For fall admission, 12/1 for domestic and international students. Application fee: $35. Electronic applications accepted. *Financial support:* Career-related internships or fieldwork and Federal Work-Study available. *Faculty research:* Biomechanics of gait and balance, balance retraining, electrotherapy for inflammation, physical therapy education outcomes. *Unit head:* Dr. Louise Gilchrist, Program Director, 716-829-3141 Ext. 191, Fax: 716-829-3217, E-mail: lag@acsu.buffalo.edu. *Application contact:* Dr. Louise Gilchrist, Program Director, 716-829-3141 Ext. 191, Fax: 716-829-3217, E-mail: lag@acsu.buffalo.edu.

The University of Alabama at Birmingham, School of Health Professions, Department of Physical Therapy, Birmingham, AL 35294. Offers DPT, Dr Sc PT. *Accreditation:* APTA. *Students:* 101 full-time (84 women), 8 part-time (7 women); includes 13 minority (10 African Americans, 1 Asian American or Pacific Islander, 2 Hispanic Americans), 1 international. 3 applicants, 33% accepted. In 2006, 10 degrees awarded. *Application deadline:* For winter admission, 1/15 for domestic students. Application fee: $35 ($60 for international students). Electronic applications accepted. *Expenses:* Tuition, state resident: part-time $170 per credit hour. Tuition, nonresident: part-time $425 per credit hour. Required fees: $15 per credit hour. $122 per term. Tuition and fees vary according to program. *Financial support:* In 2006–07, 2 fellowships with tuition reimbursements (averaging $6,000 per year), 10 research assistantships were awarded; career-related internships or fieldwork, Federal Work-Study, and institutionally sponsored loans also available. Financial award application deadline: 11/15. *Faculty research:* Geriatrics, exercise physiology, aquatic therapy, industrial rehabilitation, outcome measurement. Total annual research expenditures: $44,538. *Unit head:* Dr. Sharon E. Shaw, Chair, 205-934-3566, Fax: 205-934-3566, E-mail: sshaw@uab.edu. *Application contact:* Geeta Chhabra, Assistant, 205-934-3566, Fax: 205-975-7787, E-mail: gchhabra@uab.edu.

University of Alberta, Faculty of Graduate Studies and Research, Department of Physical Therapy, Edmonton, AB T6G 2E1, Canada. Offers M Sc, PhD. Part-time programs available. *Faculty:* 12 full-time (6 women). *Students:* 7 full-time (5 women), 6 part-time (4 women). Average age 28. 10 applicants, 50% accepted. In 2006, 2 degrees awarded. *Degree requirements:* For master's, thesis. *Entrance requirements:* For master's, bachelor's degree in physical therapy, minimum GPA of 6.5 on a 9.0 scale. Additional exam requirements/recommendations for international students: Required—TOEFL. *Application deadline:* For fall admission, 3/1 for domestic and international students; for winter admission, 7/1 for domestic and international students. Applications are processed on a rolling basis. Application fee: $0. Electronic applications accepted. *Financial support:* In 2006–07, 2 research assistantships, 2 teaching assistantships were awarded; scholarships/grants also available. Financial award application deadline: 1/1. *Faculty research:* Spinal disorders, musculoskeletal disorders, ergonomics, sports therapy, motor development, cardiac rehabilitation/therapeutic exercise. *Unit head:* Dr. J. Yang, Graduate Program Coordinator, 780-492-1595, Fax: 780-492-1626. *Application contact:* Angela Libutti, Administrative Assistant, Graduate Studies, 780-492-1595, Fax: 780-492-1626, E-mail: mscpt.info@rehabmed.ualberta.ca.

University of California, San Francisco, Graduate Division, Program in Physical Therapy, San Francisco, CA 94143. Offers MS, DPT, DPTSc. *Accreditation:* APTA. *Faculty:* 13 full-time (11 women), 1 (woman) part-time/adjunct. *Students:* 41 full-time (33 women); includes 11 minority (1 American Indian/Alaska Native, 8 Asian Americans or Pacific Islanders, 2 Hispanic Americans). In 2006, 31 degrees awarded. *Entrance requirements:* For master's, GRE General Test. Application fee: $40. *Financial support:* Institutionally sponsored loans available. Financial award application deadline: 1/10. *Unit head:* Dr. Nancy Byl, Director, 415-502-0494, E-mail: byln@ptrehab.ucsf.edu. *Application contact:* Lillie Wong, Program Assistant, 415-476-3147, Fax: 415-502-0523, E-mail: wongl@prehab.vcsf.edu.

University of Central Arkansas, Graduate School, College of Health and Behavioral Sciences, Department of Physical Therapy, Conway, AR 72035-0001. Offers DPT, PhD. *Accreditation:* APTA. *Faculty:* 18 full-time (10 women), 1 part-time/adjunct (0 women). *Students:* 136 full-time (93 women), 11 part-time (7 women); includes 16 minority (11 African Americans, 1 American Indian/Alaska Native, 2 Asian Americans or Pacific Islanders, 2 Hispanic Americans), 2 international. 50 applicants, 100% accepted, 50 enrolled. In 2006, 27 doctorates awarded. *Degree requirements:* For doctorate, thesis/dissertation, comprehensive exam. *Entrance requirements:* Additional exam requirements/recommendations for international students: Required—TOEFL (minimum score 550 paper-based; 213 computer-based). *Application deadline:* For fall admission, 3/1 priority date for domestic students; for spring admission, 10/1 for domestic students. Applications are processed on a rolling basis. Application fee: $25 ($40 for international students). *Expenses: Contact institution.* One-time fee: $65 part-time. *Financial support:* In 2006–07, 4 research assistantships with partial tuition reimbursements (averaging $6,000 per year) were awarded; Federal Work-Study, scholarships/grants, and unspecified assistantships also available. Financial award application deadline: 2/15; financial award applicants required to submit FAFSA. *Unit head:* Dr. Nancy Reese, Chairperson, 501-450-3611, Fax: 501-450-5822, E-mail: nancyr@uca.edu. *Application contact:* Nanette Fitzhugh, Administrative Assistant, 501-450-5063, Fax: 501-450-5678, E-mail: fitzhugh@uca.edu.

University of Central Florida, College of Health and Public Affairs, Department of Health Professions, Program in Physical Therapy, Orlando, FL 32816. Offers MS. *Accreditation:* APTA. *Students:* 63 full-time (47 women), 1 (woman) part-time; includes 11 minority (3 African Americans, 2 Asian Americans or Pacific Islanders, 6 Hispanic Americans). Average age 27. 93 applicants, 57% accepted, 29 enrolled. In 2006, 23 degrees awarded. Application fee: $30. Electronic applications accepted. *Expenses:* Tuition, state resident: full-time $6,167; part-time $257 per credit hour. Tuition, nonresident: full-time $22,790; part-time $950 per credit hour. *Financial support:* In 2006–07, 3 fellowships with tuition reimbursements (averaging $5,000 per year), 7 research assistantships (averaging $6,600 per year) were awarded; teaching assistantships with tuition reimbursements, career-related internships or fieldwork, institutionally sponsored loans, scholarships/grants, tuition waivers (partial), and unspecified assistantships also available. *Unit head:* Dr. Gerald V. Smith, Coordinator, 407-823-3470, Fax: 407-823-3464, E-mail: gesmith@mail.ucf.edu.

University of Colorado at Denver and Health Sciences Center, School of Medicine, Child Health Associate/Physician Assistant Program, Denver, CO 80217-3364. Offers pediatrics (MPAS). *Accreditation:* ARC-PA. *Students:* 79 full-time (63 women); includes 5 minority (4 Asian Americans or Pacific Islanders, 1 Hispanic American). Average age 28. 135 applicants, 30% accepted, 35 enrolled. In 2006, 22 degrees awarded. *Entrance requirements:* For master's, GRE General Test, minimum GPA of 2.8, 3 letters of recommendation. Additional exam requirements/recommendations for international students: Required—TOEFL (minimum score 550 paper-based; 213 computer-based). *Application deadline:* For fall admission, 10/15 for domestic students. Application fee: $85. *Expenses: Contact institution. Financial support:* Career-related internships or fieldwork, Federal Work-Study, and institutionally sponsored loans available. Support available to part-time students. Financial award application deadline: 3/15; financial award applicants required to submit FAFSA. *Unit head:* Dr. Anita Glicken, Interim Director, 303-315-7963. *Application contact:* Janice Chapman, Admissions and Course Support, 303-724-1340, E-mail: chapa-info@uchsc.edu.

University of Colorado at Denver and Health Sciences Center, School of Medicine, Program in Physical Therapy, Denver, CO 80217-3364. Offers DPT. *Accreditation:* APTA. *Students:* 125 full-time (105 women), 10 part-time (8 women); includes 9 minority (4 Asian Americans or Pacific Islanders, 5 Hispanic Americans), 4 international. Average age 27. 80 applicants, 81% accepted, 48 enrolled. *Entrance requirements:* For doctorate, GRE, minimum GPA of 3.0, 3 letters of reference, CPR Certification, 45 hours of field work. Additional exam requirements/recommendations for international students: Required—TOEFL (minimum score 550 paper-based; 213 computer-based). *Application deadline:* For spring admission, 12/15 for domestic students. Application fee: $50. *Financial support:* Research assistantships, teaching assistantships, Federal Work-Study and scholarships/grants available. Financial award application deadline: 3/15; financial award applicants required to submit FAFSA. *Faculty research:* Interventions for early and mid-stages of Parkinson's Disease, physical therapy for individuals with recurrent lower back pain. *Unit head:* Margaret Schenkman, Director, 303-372-9375, E-mail: margaret.schenkman@uchsc.edu. *Application contact:* Betti Krapfl, Admissions Advisor, 313-372-9144, Fax: 303-372-9016, E-mail: betti.krapfl@uchsc.edu.

University of Connecticut, Graduate School, School of Allied Health, Field of Physical Therapy, Storrs, CT 06269. Offers MS. *Accreditation:* APTA. *Faculty:* 18 full-time (7 women). *Students:* 28 full-time (17 women); includes 4 minority (1 African American, 2 Asian Americans or Pacific Islanders, 1 Hispanic American). Average age 23. 30 applicants, 97% accepted, 28 enrolled. In 2006, 31 degrees awarded. *Degree requirements:* For master's, comprehensive exam. *Entrance requirements:* Additional exam requirements/recommendations for international students: Required—TOEFL (minimum score 550 paper-based; 213 computer-based). *Application deadline:* For fall admission, 2/1 priority date for domestic and international students; for spring admission, 11/1 for domestic students, 10/1 for international students. Applications are processed on a rolling basis. Application fee: $55. Electronic applications accepted. *Financial support:* Research assistantships, Federal Work-Study available. Financial award application deadline: 2/1; financial award applicants required to submit FAFSA. *Unit head:* Scott Hasson,

Head, 860-486-0019, Fax: 860-486-1588, E-mail: scott.hasson@uconn.edu. *Application contact:* Dale Dubina, Assistant, 860-486-0049, Fax: 860-486-1588, E-mail: dale.dubina@uconn.edu.

University of Delaware, College of Arts and Sciences, Department of Physical Therapy, Newark, DE 19716. Offers DPT. *Accreditation:* APTA. *Degree requirements:* For doctorate, registration. *Entrance requirements:* For doctorate, GRE, 100 hours clinical experience, 3 letters of recommendation. Additional exam requirements/recommendations for international students: Required—TOEFL (minimum score 550 paper-based; 213 computer-based). Electronic applications accepted. *Faculty research:* Movement sciences, applied physiology, physical rehabilitation.

The University of Findlay, Graduate and Professional Studies, College of Health Professions, Program in Physical Therapy, Findlay, OH 45840-3653. Offers MPT. *Accreditation:* APTA. Part-time and evening/weekend programs available. *Students:* 87 full-time (49 women); includes 2 minority (1 African American, 1 Hispanic American), 2 international. Average age 35. 18 applicants, 100% accepted, 18 enrolled. In 2006, 37 degrees awarded. *Entrance requirements:* For master's, 2 letters of recommendation, 100 hours of observation. Additional exam requirements/recommendations for international students: Required—TOEFL (minimum score 550 paper-based). *Application deadline:* For fall admission, 7/15 for domestic and international students. Applications are processed on a rolling basis. Application fee: $25. Electronic applications accepted. *Financial support:* In 2006–07, 1 teaching assistantship (averaging $6,000 per year) was awarded; tuition waivers (full and partial) also available. *Unit head:* Dr. Robert Frampton, Director, 419-434-6752, Fax: 419-434-4822, E-mail: frampton@findlay.edu.

University of Florida, Graduate School, College of Public Health and Health Professions, Department of Physical Therapy, Gainesville, FL 32611. Offers DPT. *Accreditation:* APTA. *Faculty:* 7 full-time (3 women), 2 part-time/adjunct (1 woman). *Students:* 110 (82 women); includes 21 minority (2 African Americans, 7 Asian Americans or Pacific Islanders, 12 Hispanic Americans) 2 international. *Entrance requirements:* Additional exam requirements/recommendations for international students: Required—TOEFL (minimum score 515 paper-based; 213 computer-based). *Application deadline:* For fall admission, 6/1 priority date for domestic students; for spring admission, 2/15 priority date for domestic students. Applications are processed on a rolling basis. Application fee: $30. Electronic applications accepted. *Expenses:* Tuition, state resident: full-time $6,827. Tuition, nonresident: full-time $21,951. Required fees: $999. *Financial support:* In 2006–07, 1 research assistantship (averaging $11,543 per year) was awarded; fellowships, teaching assistantships, career-related internships or fieldwork also available. *Faculty research:* Exercise physiology, motor control, rehabilitation, geriatrics. *Unit head:* Dr. Krista Vandenborne, Chair, 352-273-6116, Fax: 352-273-6109, E-mail: kvandenb@phhp.ufl.edu. *Application contact:* Dr. Jane Day, Assistant Chair, 352-273-6085, Fax: 352-273-6109, E-mail: jday@phhp.ufl.edu.

University of Hartford, College of Education, Nursing, and Health Professions, Program in Physical Therapy, West Hartford, CT 06117-1599. Offers MSPT, DPT. *Accreditation:* APTA. *Faculty:* 7 full-time (5 women), 4 part-time/adjunct (3 women). *Students:* 33 full-time (27 women), 23 part-time (18 women); includes 7 minority (4 African Americans, 3 Hispanic Americans), 4 international. Average age 25. 5 applicants, 60% accepted, 3 enrolled. In 2006, 22 degrees awarded. *Entrance requirements:* For master's, GRE, 3 letters of recommendation. Additional exam requirements/recommendations for international students: Required—TOEFL (minimum score 550 paper-based; 213 computer-based). *Application deadline:* For fall admission, 2/1 for domestic students. Application fee: $40 ($55 for international students). *Expenses:* Tuition: Part-time $515 per credit. Required fees: $200 per term. *Financial support:* In 2006–07, 1 research assistantship (averaging $9,000 per year) was awarded; teaching assistantships. Financial award application deadline: 6/1; financial award applicants required to submit FAFSA. *Unit head:* Dr. Catherine Certo, Director, 860-768-5367, E-mail: certo@mail.hartford.edu. *Application contact:* Reneé Murphy, Assistant Director of Graduate Admissions, 860-768-4371, Fax: 860-768-5160, E-mail: gettoknow@hartford.edu.

University of Illinois at Chicago, Graduate College, College of Applied Health Sciences, Physical Therapy Program, Chicago, IL 60607-7128. Offers MS. *Accreditation:* APTA. *Degree requirements:* For master's, thesis. *Entrance requirements:* For master's, GRE General Test, minimum GPA of 2.75. Additional exam requirements/recommendations for international students: Required—TOEFL. Electronic applications accepted.

University of Indianapolis, Graduate Programs, Krannert School of Physical Therapy, Indianapolis, IN 46227-3697. Offers MHS, DHS, DPT, TDPT. *Accreditation:* APTA (one or more programs are accredited). Part-time and evening/weekend programs available. *Faculty:* 11 full-time (4 women), 6 part-time/adjunct (5 women). *Students:* 139 full-time (117 women), 107 part-time (73 women); includes 9 minority (5 African Americans, 4 Asian Americans or Pacific Islanders), 39 international. Average age 27. In 2006, 36 master's, 52 doctorates awarded. *Entrance requirements:* For doctorate, GRE General Test (DPT), minimum GPA of 3.0 (DPT), 3 letters of recommendation (for physical therapist). Additional exam requirements/recommendations for international students: Required—TOEFL (minimum score 250 computer-based; 100 iBT), TWE (minimum score 5). *Application deadline:* For fall admission, 10/12 for domestic students. Application fee: $50. Electronic applications accepted. *Expenses: Contact institution. Financial support:* Teaching assistantships, career-related internships or fieldwork, Federal Work-Study, scholarships/grants, tuition waivers (full and partial), and unspecified assistantships available. Financial award application deadline: 5/1; financial award applicants required to submit FAFSA. *Faculty research:* Patella positioning, reaction time, allocation of physical therapy resources. *Unit head:* Dr. Mary Huer, Dean of Health Sciences, 317-788-3500, Fax: 317-788-3542, E-mail: huerm@uIndy.edu. *Application contact:* Kelly Wilson, Admissions Counselor, 317-788-4909, Fax: 317-788-3542, E-mail: kwilson@uindy.edu.

The University of Iowa, Roy J. and Lucille A. Carver College of Medicine and Graduate College, Graduate Programs in Medicine, Graduate Program in Physical Therapy and Rehabilitation Science, Iowa City, IA 52242-1316. Offers physical therapy (DPT); rehabilitation science (PhD). *Accreditation:* APTA (one or more programs are accredited). *Faculty:* 7 full-time (3 women), 8 part-time/adjunct (0 women). *Students:* 116 full-time (77 women), 8 part-time (6 women); includes 2 minority (both Hispanic Americans), 11 international. Average age 24. 99 applicants, 40% accepted, 36 enrolled. In 2006, 3 doctorates awarded. *Degree requirements:* For doctorate, thesis/dissertation (for some programs). *Entrance requirements:* For doctorate, GRE, Physical Therapist Degree. Additional exam requirements/recommendations for international students: Required—TOEFL (minimum score 250 computer-based; 100 iBT). *Application deadline:* For fall admission, 1/1 for domestic students. Application fee: $50 ($75 for international students). Electronic applications accepted. *Expenses: Contact institution. Financial support:* In 2006–07, 94 students received support, including 2 research assistantships with partial tuition reimbursements available (averaging $19,537 per year), 4 teaching assistantships with partial tuition reimbursements available (averaging $19,537 per year); fellowships with partial tuition reimbursements available, Federal Work-Study, institutionally sponsored loans, scholarships/grants, health care benefits, and unspecified assistantships also available. Support available to part-time students. Financial award application deadline: 1/1; financial award applicants required to submit FAFSA. *Faculty research:* Muscle fatigue, motor control, pain mechanisms, body composition, sports medicine, occupational safety, neuromuscular physiology. Total annual research expenditures: $351,848. *Unit head:* Dr. Richard K. Shields, Director, 319-335-9791, Fax: 319-335-9707, E-mail: physical-therapy@uiowa.edu.

University of Kansas, Graduate Studies Medical Center, School of Allied Health, Department of Physical Therapy and Rehabilitation Science, Lawrence, KS 66045. Offers MS, DPT, PhD. *Accreditation:* APTA. *Faculty:* 16 full-time (10 women), 4 part-time/adjunct (all women). *Students:* 119 full-time (92 women), 22 part-time (12 women); includes 5 minority (2 African Americans, 3 Asian Americans or Pacific Islanders), 4 international. Average age 26. 160 applicants, 39% accepted, 58 enrolled. In 2006, 11 degrees awarded. *Median time to degree:* Doctorate–1.65 years full-time, 4.35 years part-time. *Degree requirements:* For master's, research project with paper. *Entrance requirements:* For master's and doctorate, GRE General Test, minimum GPA of 3.0. Additional exam requirements/recommendations for international students: Required—TOEFL. *Application deadline:* For fall admission, 12/1 for domestic students. Application fee: $60. Electronic applications accepted. *Expenses:* Tuition, area resident: Part-time $227 per credit. Tuition, state resident: part-time $543 per credit. Tuition and fees vary according to course load, campus/location, program and reciprocity agreements. *Financial support:* Research assistantships with tuition reimbursements, teaching assistantships with full and partial tuition reimbursements, career-related internships or fieldwork, Federal Work-Study, institutionally sponsored loans, and scholarships/grants available. Financial award application deadline: 3/30; financial award applicants required to submit FAFSA. *Faculty research:* Stroke rehabilitation and the effects on balance and coordination; deep brain stimulation and Parkinson's Disease; peripheral neuropathies, pain and the effects of exercise; islet transplants for Type 1 diabetes; cardiac disease associated with diabetes. *Unit head:* Dr. Lisa Stehno-Bittel, Chair, 913-588-6733, Fax: 913-588-4568, E-mail: lbittel@kumc.edu. *Application contact:* Molly Smalley, Admission's Coordinator, 913-588-6799, Fax: 913-588-4568, E-mail: msmalley@kumc.edu.

University of Kentucky, Graduate School, College of Health Sciences, Program in Physical Therapy, Lexington, KY 40506-0032. Offers MSPT. *Accreditation:* APTA. *Faculty:* 21 full-time (12 women). *Students:* 126 full-time (92 women); includes 4 minority (2 African Americans, 1 American Indian/Alaska Native, 1 Hispanic American), 2 international. Average age 25. 52 applicants, 85% accepted, 38 enrolled. In 2006, 55 degrees awarded. *Degree requirements:* For master's, thesis optional. *Entrance requirements:* For master's, GRE General Test, minimum undergraduate GPA of 2.75, U.S. physical therapist license. Additional exam requirements/recommendations for international students: Required—TOEFL (minimum score 550 paper-based; 213 computer-based). *Application deadline:* For fall admission, 7/17 priority date for domestic students, 2/1 priority date for international students; for spring admission, 12/13 priority date for domestic students, 6/15 priority date for international students. Application fee: $40 ($55 for international students). Electronic applications accepted. *Expenses:* Tuition, state resident: full-time $7,670; part-time $401 per credit hour. Tuition, nonresident: full-time $16,158; part-time $873 per credit hour. *Financial support:* In 2006–07, 1 student received support, including 1 fellowship with full tuition reimbursement available; research assistantships with full tuition reimbursements available, teaching assistantships with full tuition reimbursements available, Federal Work-Study, scholarships/grants, traineeships, health care benefits, tuition waivers (partial), and unspecified assistantships also available. Support available to part-time students. Financial award application deadline: 3/15. *Faculty research:* Orthopedics, biomechanics, electrophysiological stimulation, neural plasticity, brain damage and mechanism. Total annual research expenditures: $35,000. *Unit head:* Dr. Arthur J. Nitz, Director of Graduate Studies, 859-323-1100, Fax: 859-323-6003, E-mail: ajnitz1@pop.uky.edu. *Application contact:* Dr. Brian Jackson, Senior Associate Dean, 859-257-4667, Fax: 859-257-4676, E-mail: brian.jackson@uky.edu.

University of Mary, Department of Physical Therapy, Bismarck, ND 58504-9652. Offers DPT. Applications must be requested in writing. *Accreditation:* APTA. *Students:* 78 full-time (56 women). 40 applicants, 75% accepted, 29 enrolled. *Degree requirements:* For doctorate, professional paper. *Entrance requirements:* For doctorate, minimum GPA of 3.0 in core requirements, 40 hours of paid/volunteer experience. Additional exam requirements/recommendations for international students: Required—TOEFL. *Application deadline:* For fall admission, 1/1 priority date for domestic students; for spring admission, 3/1 priority date for domestic students. Applications are processed on a rolling basis. Application fee: $0. Electronic applications accepted. *Expenses: Contact institution. Financial support:* In 2006–07, teaching assistantships with partial tuition reimbursements (averaging $2,500 per year); career-related internships or fieldwork also available. Financial award applicants required to submit FAFSA. *Faculty research:* Proprioception, falls and elderly, clinical biomechanics, admission predictors, electromyography and muscle performance, wellness. *Unit head:* Joellen Marie Roller, Program Director, 701-355-8053, Fax: 701-255-7687, E-mail: rollerj@umary.edu.

University of Maryland, Baltimore, School of Medicine, Graduate Program in Life Sciences, Department of Physical Therapy and Rehabilitation Science, Baltimore, MD 21201. Offers physical rehabilitation science (PhD); physical therapy (DPT, DS). *Accreditation:* APTA. Postbaccalaureate distance learning degree programs offered. *Degree requirements:* For doctorate, thesis/dissertation, registration. *Entrance requirements:* For doctorate, GRE General Test. Additional exam requirements/recommendations for international students: Required—TOEFL; Recommended—IELTS.

University of Maryland Eastern Shore, Graduate Programs, Department of Physical Therapy, Princess Anne, MD 21853-1299. Offers DPT. *Accreditation:* APTA. *Faculty:* 8 full-time (3 women), 2 part-time/adjunct (0 women). *Students:* 52 full-time (36 women); includes 25 minority (21 African Americans, 2 Asian Americans or Pacific Islanders, 2 Hispanic Americans). Average age 24. 121 applicants, 50% accepted, 26 enrolled. In 2006, 15 degrees awarded. *Degree requirements:* For doctorate, thesis/dissertation, clinical practicum, research project. *Entrance requirements:* For doctorate, minimum GPA of 3.0, course work in science and mathematics, interview, knowledge of the physical therapy field. Additional exam requirements/recommendations for international students: Required—TOEFL (minimum score 213 computer-based). *Application deadline:* For fall admission, 1/1 for domestic and international students. Application fee: $30. Electronic applications accepted. *Financial support:* In 2006–07, 6 students received support, including 4 teaching assistantships (averaging $18,000 per year); career-related internships or fieldwork, scholarships/grants, and unspecified assistantships also available. Financial award application deadline: 3/1; financial award applicants required to submit FAFSA. *Faculty research:* Allied health projects. Total annual research expenditures: $119,478. *Unit head:* Dr. Raymond Blakely, Chair, 410-651-6310, Fax: 410-651-6259, E-mail: rblakely@umes.edu.

University of Massachusetts Lowell, Graduate School, College of Health Professions, Department of Physical Therapy, Lowell, MA 01854-2881. Offers advanced practice (MS); physical therapy (MS). *Accreditation:* APTA. *Degree requirements:* For master's, thesis optional. *Entrance requirements:* For master's, GRE General Test. *Faculty research:* Orthopedics, pediatrics, electrophysiology, cardiopulmonary, neurology.

University of Medicine and Dentistry of New Jersey, School of Health Related Professions, Department of Developmental and Rehabilitative Sciences, Program in Physical Therapy (Entry Level) –Newark, Newark, NJ 07107-3001. Offers DPT. *Accreditation:* APTA. *Entrance requirements:* Additional exam requirements/recommendations for international students: Required—TOEFL. *Application deadline:* For fall admission, 12/1 priority date for domestic students. Applications are processed on a rolling basis. Application fee: $50. Electronic applications accepted. *Unit head:* Dr. Alma S. Merians, Chairperson, Department of Developmental and Rehabilitative Sciences, 973-972-5272, Fax: 973-972-3717, E-mail: merians@umdnj.edu.

University of Medicine and Dentistry of New Jersey, School of Health Related Professions, Department of Developmental and Rehabilitative Sciences, Program in Physical Therapy (Post-Professional Level) –Newark, Newark, NJ 07107-1709. Offers DPT. *Accreditation:* APTA. *Entrance requirements:* Additional exam requirements/recommendations for international students: Required—TOEFL. *Application deadline:* For fall admission, 7/1 for domestic students; for spring admission, 11/1 for domestic students. Applications are processed on a rolling basis. Application fee: $50. Electronic applications accepted. *Unit head:* Dr. Ellen C. Ross, Director, 973-972-2372, Fax: 973-972-3717, E-mail: rossec@umdnj.edu.

University of Medicine and Dentistry of New Jersey, School of Health Related Professions, Department of Developmental and Rehabilitative Sciences, Program in Physical Therapy–Stratford, Stratford, NJ 08084. Offers MPT. *Accreditation:* APTA. *Entrance requirements:* For master's, GRE General Test, related work or volunteer experience. Additional exam requirements/recommendations for international students: Required—TOEFL. *Application deadline:* For fall admission, 12/15 priority date for domestic students. Applications are processed on a rolling basis. Application fee: $50. Electronic applications accepted. *Unit head:* Marie Koval Nardone, Director, 856-566-6456, Fax: 856-566-6458, E-mail: mptgradm@umdnj.edu.

Physical Therapy

University of Medicine and Dentistry of New Jersey, School of Health Related Professions, Department of Interdisciplinary Studies, Program in Health Sciences, Newark, NJ 07107-1709. Offers cardiopulmonary sciences (PhD); clinical laboratory sciences (PhD); health sciences (MS); interdisciplinary studies (PhD); nutrition (PhD); physical therapy/movement science (PhD). *Degree requirements:* For doctorate, thesis/dissertation. *Entrance requirements:* For doctorate, interview, writing sample. Additional exam requirements/recommendations for international students: Required—TOEFL. *Application deadline:* For fall admission, 3/1 for domestic students. Applications are processed on a rolling basis. Application fee: $50. Electronic applications accepted. *Unit head:* Dr. Margaret Kildoff, Director, 973-972-4989, Fax: 973-972-7854, E-mail: ms-phd-hs@umdnj.edu.

University of Miami, Graduate School, Miller School of Medicine, Graduate Programs in Medicine, Department of Physical Therapy, Coral Gables, FL 33124. Offers DPT, PhD. *Accreditation:* APTA (one or more programs are accredited). *Faculty:* 15 full-time (9 women), 3 part-time/adjunct (2 women). *Students:* 127 full-time (84 women); includes 29 minority (5 African Americans, 2 American Indian/Alaska Native, 7 Asian Americans or Pacific Islanders, 15 Hispanic Americans), 4 international. Average age 26. 250 applicants, 40% accepted. In 2006, 29 degrees awarded. *Degree requirements:* For doctorate, thesis/dissertation, comprehensive exam. *Entrance requirements:* For doctorate, GRE General Test. Additional exam requirements/recommendations for international students: Required—TOEFL. *Application deadline:* For winter admission, 1/5 for domestic and international students. Applications are processed on a rolling basis. Application fee: $65. Electronic applications accepted. *Expenses: Contact institution. Financial support:* In 2006–07, 98 students received support, including 20 research assistantships with full tuition reimbursements available, 24 teaching assistantships with partial tuition reimbursements available; career-related internships or fieldwork, Federal Work-Study, institutionally sponsored loans, scholarships/grants, unspecified assistantships, and stipends also available. Financial award application deadline: 3/1; financial award applicants required to submit FAFSA. *Faculty research:* Central pattern generators in SCI balance and vestibular function in children, amputee rehabilitation. Total annual research expenditures: $400,000. *Unit head:* Dr. Sherrill Hayes, Professor and Chair, 305-284-4535, E-mail: physicaltherapy@miami.edu. *Application contact:* Jean Fowler, Admissions Coordinator, 305-284-4535, Fax: 305-284-6128, E-mail: phsyicaltherapy@miami.edu.

University of Michigan–Flint, School of Health Professions and Studies, Program in Physical Therapy, Flint, MI 48502-1950. Offers DPT. *Accreditation:* APTA. Part-time programs available. *Faculty:* 5 full-time (4 women). *Students:* 60 full-time (44 women), 38 part-time (28 women); includes 28 minority (17 African Americans, 8 Asian Americans or Pacific Islanders, 3 Hispanic Americans), 2 international. Average age 26. 91 applicants, 68% accepted, 21 enrolled. *Entrance requirements:* Additional exam requirements/recommendations for international students: Required—TOEFL (minimum score 550 paper-based; 220 computer-based), IELTS (minimum score 7). *Application deadline:* For fall admission, 8/1 priority date for domestic students, 3/1 priority date for international students; for winter admission, 11/15 priority date for domestic students, 7/1 priority date for international students; for spring admission, 3/15 priority date for domestic students, 11/1 priority date for international students. Applications are processed on a rolling basis. Application fee: $55. Electronic applications accepted. *Expenses: Contact institution.* Full-time tuition and fees vary according to degree level and program. Part-time tuition and fees vary according to course load and degree level. *Financial support:* Career-related internships or fieldwork, Federal Work-Study, and scholarships/grants available. Support available to part-time students. Financial award applicants required to submit FAFSA. *Faculty research:* Cumulative trauma disorders, oncology rehabilitation, neurological rehabilitation, musculoskeletal rehabilitation, cardiopulmonary rehabilitation. Total annual research expenditures: $282,025. *Unit head:* Dr. Donna Fry, Interim Director, 810-762-3373, E-mail: donnafry@umflint.edu. *Application contact:* Reva Kidd, Administrative Assistant, 810-762-3373, Fax: 810-766-6668, E-mail: rpeariso@umflint.edu.

University of Minnesota, Twin Cities Campus, Medical School and Graduate School, Graduate Programs in Medicine, Program in Physical Therapy, Minneapolis, MN 55455-0213. Offers DPT. *Accreditation:* APTA. *Faculty:* 12 full-time (8 women). *Students:* 114 full-time (87 women); includes 2 minority (both Hispanic Americans) Average age 25. 141 applicants, 49% accepted, 50 enrolled. In 2006, 31 degrees awarded. *Median time to degree:* Doctorate–3 years full-time. Of those who began their doctoral program in fall 1998, 100% received their degree in 8 years or less. *Entrance requirements:* For doctorate, GRE. Additional exam requirements/recommendations for international students: Required—TOEFL (minimum score 79 iBT). *Application deadline:* Applications are processed on a rolling basis. Application fee: $0. Electronic applications accepted. *Expenses: Contact institution. Financial support:* In 2006–07, 100 students received support. Scholarships/grants and tuition waivers (partial) available. Financial award applicants required to submit FAFSA. *Faculty research:* Aging, stroke, ergonomics, muscle, balance. Total annual research expenditures: $300,000. *Unit head:* Dr. James R. Carey, Director, 612-626-5517, Fax: 612-625-4274, E-mail: carey007@maroon.tc.umn.edu. *Application contact:* Dr. Richard DiFabio, Professor, 612-626-2746, Fax: 612-625-7192, E-mail: difab001@maroon.tc.umn.edu.

University of Mississippi Medical Center, School of Health Related Professions, Department of Physical Therapy, Jackson, MS 39216-4505. Offers MPT. *Accreditation:* APTA. *Faculty:* 13 full-time (9 women). *Students:* 99 full-time (62 women), 19 part-time (11 women); includes 7 minority (5 African Americans, 1 American Indian/Alaska Native, 1 Asian American or Pacific Islander). 67 applicants, 57% accepted, 36 enrolled. In 2006, 25 degrees awarded. *Application deadline:* For fall admission, 9/3 priority date for domestic students; for winter admission, 12/1 for domestic students. Applications are processed on a rolling basis. Application fee: $10. *Expenses:* Tuition, state resident: full-time $4,523. Tuition, nonresident: full-time $10,566. *Financial support:* Scholarships/grants available. Financial award application deadline: 4/1; financial award applicants required to submit FAFSA. *Faculty research:* Pain, acupressure, seating, patient satisfaction, physical therapy educational issues. *Unit head:* Neva E. Greenwald, Chair, 601-984-6330, Fax: 601-984-6344, E-mail: ngreenwald@shrp.umsmed.edu. *Application contact:* Ruth M. Burgess, Assistant Professor, 601-984-6356, Fax: 601-815-1715, E-mail: rburgess@shrp.umsmed.edu.

University of Missouri–Columbia, School of Health Professions, Program in Physical Therapy, Columbia, MO 65211. Offers MPT. *Accreditation:* APTA. *Faculty:* 8 full-time (6 women). *Students:* 45 full-time (35 women), 1 part-time. In 2006, 34 degrees awarded. *Entrance requirements:* For master's, GRE General Test, minimum GPA of 3.0. Additional exam requirements/recommendations for international students: Required—TOEFL (minimum score 600 paper-based; 250 computer-based; 100 iBT). *Application deadline:* Applications are processed on a rolling basis. Application fee: $45 ($60 for international students). *Financial support:* Research assistantships, teaching assistantships, institutionally sponsored loans available. *Unit head:* Dr. Marian Minor, Director of Graduate Studies, 573-882-1579, E-mail: minorm@missouri.edu.

The University of Montana, School of Physical Therapy and Rehabilitation Science, Missoula, MT 59812-0002. Offers physical therapy (DPT). *Accreditation:* APTA. *Degree requirements:* For doctorate, professional paper. *Entrance requirements:* For doctorate, GRE General Test. Additional exam requirements/recommendations for international students: Required—TOEFL. Electronic applications accepted. Expenses: Contact institution. *Faculty research:* Muscle stiffness, fitness with a disability, psychosocial aspects of disability, clinical learning, motion analysis.

University of Nebraska Medical Center, School of Allied Health Professions, Division of Physical Therapy Education, Omaha, NE 68198. Offers DPT. *Accreditation:* APTA. *Faculty:* 9 full-time (4 women), 2 part-time/adjunct (both women). *Students:* 121 full-time (87 women); includes 6 minority (2 African Americans, 1 American Indian/Alaska Native, 2 Asian Americans or Pacific Islanders, 1 Hispanic American). Average age 25. 143 applicants, 29% accepted. *Entrance requirements:* For doctorate, GRE General Test. Additional exam requirements/recommendations for international students: Required—TOEFL. *Application deadline:* For fall admission, 11/15 for domestic students. Application fee: $45. Electronic applications accepted. *Financial support:* Applicants required to submit FAFSA. *Faculty research:* Aquatics effects on MS, balance control-age, performance in physical therapy with COPD, wheelchair use in nursing homes, human activity profile. Total annual research expenditures: $30,000. *Unit head:* Dr. Patricia A. Hageman, Director, 402-559-4259. *Application contact:* Rita Parks-Agnew, Administrative Assistant and Admissions Coordinator, 402-559-4259, E-mail: rparks@unmc.edu.

University of Nevada, Las Vegas, Graduate College, Division of Health Sciences, Department of Physical Therapy, Las Vegas, NV 89154-9900. Offers MS, DPT. *Accreditation:* APTA. *Faculty:* 7 full-time (2 women), 3 part-time/adjunct (all women). *Students:* 59 full-time (32 women); includes 5 minority (1 African American, 4 Asian Americans or Pacific Islanders). 4 applicants, 0% accepted. In 2006, 3 degrees awarded. *Degree requirements:* For master's, comprehensive exam. *Entrance requirements:* For master's, GRE General Test, minimum GPA of 2.75. Additional exam requirements/recommendations for international students: Required—TOEFL (minimum score 550 paper-based; 213 computer-based; 80 iBT). *Application deadline:* For fall admission, 1/31 for domestic and international students. Application fee: $60 ($75 for international students). Electronic applications accepted. *Financial support:* In 2006–07, 7 research assistantships with partial tuition reimbursements (averaging $12,000 per year), 1 teaching assistantship with partial tuition reimbursement (averaging $12,000 per year) were awarded; career-related internships or fieldwork, Federal Work-Study, institutionally sponsored loans, scholarships/grants, health care benefits, and unspecified assistantships also available. Support available to part-time students. *Unit head:* Dr. J. Wesley McWhorter, Interim Chair, 702-895-3003. *Application contact:* Graduate College Admissions Evaluator, 702-895-3320, E-mail: gradcollege@unlv.edu.

University of New England, College of Health Professions, Program in Physical Therapy, Biddeford, ME 04005-9526. Offers physical therapy (DPT); post professional physical therapy (DPT). *Accreditation:* APTA. *Faculty:* 6 full-time (2 women), 7 part-time/adjunct (4 women). *Students:* 52 full-time (35 women), 18 part-time (14 women); includes 3 minority (2 Asian Americans or Pacific Islanders, 1 Hispanic American), 2 international. Average age 29. 109 applicants, 52% accepted, 42 enrolled. *Entrance requirements:* Additional exam requirements/recommendations for international students: Required—TOEFL. *Application deadline:* For fall admission, 2/1 for domestic students. Applications are processed on a rolling basis. Application fee: $40. Electronic applications accepted. *Expenses: Contact institution. Financial support:* In 2006–07, 3 students received support. Scholarships/grants available. Financial award application deadline: 5/1; financial award applicants required to submit FAFSA. *Faculty research:* Biomechanics, motor control, clinical education, functional outcomes, health policy. *Unit head:* Michael Sheldon, Director, 207-283-0170 Ext. 4591, E-mail: msheldon@une.edu. *Application contact:* Peggy Warden, Assistant Dean of Graduate Admissions, 207-221-4225, Fax: 207-221-4898, E-mail: admissions@une.edu.

University of New Mexico, School of Medicine, Program in Physical Therapy, Albuquerque, NM 87131-2039. Offers MPT. *Accreditation:* APTA. *Degree requirements:* For master's, thesis or alternative, comprehensive exam. *Entrance requirements:* For master's, GRE General Test, GRE writing assessment test, interview, minimum GPA of 3.0, additional application fee. Additional exam requirements/recommendations for international students: Required—TOEFL (minimum score 580 paper-based; 237 computer-based). *Faculty research:* Gait analysis, motion analysis, balance, articular cartilage, quality of life.

The University of North Carolina at Chapel Hill, School of Medicine and Graduate School, Graduate Programs in Medicine, Chapel Hill, NC 27599. Offers allied health sciences (MPT, MS, Au D, DPT, PhD), including human movement science (MS, PhD), occupational science (MS, PhD), physical therapy (MPT, MS, DPT), rehabilitation counseling and psychology (MS), speech and hearing sciences (MS, Au D, PhD); biochemistry and biophysics (MS, PhD); biomedical engineering (MS, PhD); cell and developmental biology (PhD); cell and molecular physiology (PhD); genetics and molecular biology (PhD); microbiology and immunology (MS, PhD), including immunology, microbiology; neurobiology (PhD); pathology and laboratory medicine (PhD), including experimental pathology; pharmacology (PhD); MD/PhD. Post-baccalaureate distance learning degree programs offered. *Faculty:* 470 full-time (156 women), 101 part-time/adjunct (17 women). *Students:* 730 full-time (447 women), 36 part-time (27 women); includes 110 minority (43 African Americans, 6 American Indian/Alaska Native, 48 Asian Americans or Pacific Islanders, 13 Hispanic Americans), 79 international. In 2006, 73 master's, 62 doctorates awarded. Terminal master's awarded for partial completion of doctoral program. *Degree requirements:* For master's, comprehensive exam; for doctorate, thesis/dissertation. *Application deadline:* Applications are processed on a rolling basis. Application fee: $65. Electronic applications accepted. *Expenses: Contact institution. Financial support:* In 2006–07, 77 fellowships with full and partial tuition reimbursements, 309 research assistantships with full tuition reimbursements, 23 teaching assistantships with full tuition reimbursements were awarded; career-related internships or fieldwork, Federal Work-Study, institutionally sponsored loans, traineeships, tuition waivers (full and partial), and unspecified assistantships also available. Support available to part-time students. Financial award applicants required to submit FAFSA. *Unit head:* Dr. William I. Roper, Dean, 919-966-4161, Fax: 919-966-6354.

The University of North Carolina at Chapel Hill, School of Medicine and Graduate School, Graduate Programs in Medicine, Department of Allied Health Sciences, Program in Physical Therapy, Chapel Hill, NC 27599. Offers human movement science (MS); physical therapy (MPT, DPT). *Accreditation:* APTA. Part-time and evening/weekend programs available. Post-baccalaureate distance learning degree programs offered (no on-campus study). *Faculty:* 14 full-time (10 women), 3 part-time/adjunct (2 women). *Students:* 57 full-time (47 women), 32 part-time (24 women); includes 10 minority (6 African Americans, 1 American Indian/Alaska Native, 3 Asian Americans or Pacific Islanders). Average age 43. 189 applicants, 39% accepted, 54 enrolled. In 2006, 16 master's, 15 doctorates awarded. *Degree requirements:* For master's, thesis/dissertation or alternative, comprehensive exam; for doctorate, thesis/dissertation or alternative. *Entrance requirements:* For master's, GRE General Test, minimum GPA of 3.0, prerequisite coursework, experience with physical therapy; for doctorate, physical therapy license. Additional exam requirements/recommendations for international students: Required—TOEFL (minimum score 550 paper-based; 79 computer-based). *Application deadline:* For fall admission, 11/1 for domestic and international students. Application fee: $70. Electronic applications accepted. *Financial support:* In 2006–07, 49 students received support, including 2 fellowships with tuition reimbursements available (averaging $9,000 per year); research assistantships with tuition reimbursements available, career-related internships or fieldwork and institutionally sponsored loans also available. Financial award application deadline: 11/1; financial award applicants required to submit FAFSA. *Faculty research:* Traumatic brain injury, quality of life after heart and/or lung transplant, cultural diversity, life care planning, rehabilitation education and supervision. Total annual research expenditures: $253,511. *Unit head:* Dr. Darlene K. Sekerak, Associate Professor and Director, 919-843-8660, Fax: 919-966-3678, E-mail: darlene_sekerak@med.unc.edu. *Application contact:* William C. Smithson, Registrar, 919-966-4708, Fax: 919-966-3678, E-mail: willsmit@med.unc.edu.

University of North Dakota, School of Medicine and Graduate School, Graduate Programs in Medicine, Department of Physical Therapy, Grand Forks, ND 58202. Offers MPT, DPT. *Accreditation:* APTA. *Faculty:* 11 full-time (7 women). *Students:* 101 full-time (71 women), 49 part-time (32 women); includes 17 minority (2 African Americans, 5 American Indian/Alaska Native, 8 Asian Americans or Pacific Islanders, 2 Hispanic Americans), 3 international. 12 applicants, 100% accepted, 12 enrolled. *Degree requirements:* For master's, thesis or alternative, comprehensive exam. *Entrance requirements:* For master's and doctorate, minimum GPA of 3.0, pre-physical therapy program. *Application deadline:* For fall admission, 2/15 priority date for domestic students. Application fee: $35. *Expenses:* Tuition, state resident: full-time $5,650; part-time $214 per credit. Tuition, nonresident: full-time $14,248; part-time $572 per credit. Required fees: $1,008; $42 per credit. Tuition and fees vary according to reciprocity agreements. *Financial support:* In 2006–07, 1 student received support; fellowships, research assistantships, teaching assistantships, tuition waivers (partial) available. *Faculty research:*

Practice-based program. *Unit head:* Dr. Tom M. Mohr, Chairperson, 701-777-3862, Fax: 701-777-4199, E-mail: tommohr@medicine.nodak.edu. *Application contact:* Brenda Halle, Admissions Specialist, 701-777-2947, Fax: 701-777-3619, E-mail: brendahalle@mail.und.edu.

University of North Florida, College of Health, Department of Athletic Training and Physical Therapy, Jacksonville, FL 32224-2645. Offers physical therapy (MPT). *Accreditation:* APTA. Part-time and evening/weekend programs available. *Faculty:* 5 full-time (1 woman). *Students:* 48 full-time (35 women); includes 7 minority (6 African Americans, 1 Hispanic American). Average age 27. 157 applicants, 31% accepted, 25 enrolled. In 2006, 24 degrees awarded. *Degree requirements:* For master's, internship. *Entrance requirements:* For master's, GRE General Test, minimum GPA of 3.0 in last 60 hours, volunteer/observation experience. Additional exam requirements/recommendations for international students: Required—TOEFL (minimum score 500 paper-based; 173 computer-based). *Application deadline:* For fall admission, 4/15 for domestic and international students. Application fee: $30. Electronic applications accepted. *Expenses:* Tuition, state resident: full-time $4,948; part-time $206 per semester hour. Tuition, nonresident: full-time $19,140; part-time $408 per semester hour. *Financial support:* In 2006–07, 39 students received support, including 3 teaching assistantships (averaging $1,205 per year); career-related internships or fieldwork, Federal Work-Study, scholarships/grants, and tuition waivers (partial) also available. Support available to part-time students. Financial award application deadline: 4/1; financial award applicants required to submit FAFSA. *Faculty research:* Clinical outcomes related to orthopedic physical therapy interventions, instructional multimedia in physical therapy education, effect of functional electrical stimulation orthostatic hypotension in acute complete spinal cord injury individuals. *Unit head:* Dr. Rusty Smith, Interim Chair, 904-620-2841, E-mail: arsmith@unf.edu.

University of Oklahoma Health Sciences Center, Graduate College, College of Allied Health, Department of Physical Therapy, Oklahoma City, OK 73190. Offers MPT. *Accreditation:* APTA.

University of Pittsburgh, School of Health and Rehabilitation Sciences, Department of Physical Therapy, Pittsburgh, PA 15260. Offers DPT. *Accreditation:* APTA. *Faculty:* 13 full-time (8 women). *Students:* 129 full-time (88 women); includes 6 minority (1 African American, 1 American Indian/Alaska Native, 4 Asian Americans or Pacific Islanders), 1 international. Average age 25. 181 applicants, 50% accepted, 45 enrolled. In 2006, 34 degrees awarded. *Degree requirements:* For doctorate, clinical practice. *Entrance requirements:* For doctorate, GRE, volunteer work in physical therapy. Additional exam requirements/recommendations for international students: Required—TOEFL (minimum score 550 paper-based; 213 computer-based; 80 iBT), IELTS (minimum score 7). *Application deadline:* For fall admission, 1/31 for domestic students. Applications are processed on a rolling basis. Application fee: $50. Electronic applications accepted. *Expenses:* Contact institution. *Financial support:* Federal Work-Study, scholarships/grants, and traineeships available. Support available to part-time students. Financial award applicants required to submit FAFSA. *Faculty research:* Biomechanics, neuromuscular system, sports medicine, movement analysis, validity/outcomes of clinical procedures. Total annual research expenditures: $689,572. *Unit head:* Dr. Anthony Delitto, Chairman, 412-383-6630, Fax: 412-383-6629, E-mail: delitto@pitt.edu. *Application contact:* Shameem Gangjee, Director of Admissions, 412-383-6558, Fax: 412-383-6535, E-mail: admissions@shrs.pitt.edu.

University of Pittsburgh, School of Health and Rehabilitation Sciences, Program in Health and Rehabilitation Sciences, Pittsburgh, PA 15260. Offers dietetics (MS); health and rehabilitation sciences (MS), including clinical dietetics, coordinated with dietetics, health care supervision and management, health information systems, occupational therapy, physical therapy, rehabilitation counseling, rehabilitation science and technology, sports medicine; wellness and human performance (MS). *Accreditation:* APTA. Part-time and evening/weekend programs available. *Faculty:* 40 full-time (23 women), 3 part-time/adjunct (2 women). *Students:* 93 full-time (67 women), 54 part-time (35 women); includes 31 minority (12 African Americans, 18 Asian Americans or Pacific Islanders, 1 Hispanic American), 15 international. Average age 30. 122 applicants, 82% accepted, 64 enrolled. In 2006, 28 degrees awarded. *Entrance requirements:* For master's, minimum GPA of 3.0. Additional exam requirements/recommendations for international students: Required—TOEFL, IELTS. *Application deadline:* Applications are processed on a rolling basis. Application fee: $50. Electronic applications accepted. *Financial support:* In 2006–07, 11 research assistantships with full tuition reimbursements (averaging $16,918 per year) were awarded; teaching assistantships, Federal Work-Study, institutionally sponsored loans, traineeships, and unspecified assistantships also available. Support available to part-time students. Financial award applicants required to submit FAFSA. *Faculty research:* Assistive technology, seating and wheeled mobility, cellular neurophysiology, low back syndrome, augmentative communication. Total annual research expenditures: $953,246. *Application contact:* Shameem Gangjee, Director of Admissions, 412-383-6558, Fax: 412-383-6535, E-mail: admissions@shrs.pitt.edu.

University of Puerto Rico, Medical Sciences Campus, College of Health Related Professions, Program in Physical Therapy, San Juan, PR 00936-5067. Offers MS. *Accreditation:* APTA. Part-time and evening/weekend programs available. *Degree requirements:* For master's, one foreign language, thesis. *Entrance requirements:* For master's, EXADEP, minimum GPA of 2.8, interview, first aid training and CPR certification.

University of Puget Sound, Graduate Studies, School of Occupational Therapy and Physical Therapy, Program in Physical Therapy, Tacoma, WA 98416. Offers DPT. *Accreditation:* APTA. *Faculty:* 5 full-time (4 women), 23 part-time/adjunct (18 women). *Students:* 94 full-time (71 women), 7 part-time (5 women); includes 22 minority (2 African Americans, 4 American Indian/Alaska Native, 15 Asian Americans or Pacific Islanders, 1 Hispanic American), 1 international. Average age 26. 201 applicants, 49% accepted, 33 enrolled. In 2006, 48 degrees awarded. *Median time to degree:* Doctorate–3 years full-time. *Degree requirements:* For doctorate, thesis/dissertation or alternative, comprehensive exam. *Entrance requirements:* For doctorate, GRE General Test, minimum GPA of 3.0. Additional exam requirements/recommendations for international students: Required—TOEFL (minimum score 550 paper-based; 213 computer-based; 80 iBT). *Application deadline:* For fall admission, 1/5 priority date for domestic and international students. Applications are processed on a rolling basis. Application fee: $65. Electronic applications accepted. *Expenses:* Tuition: Full-time $26,390. Tuition and fees vary according to course load. *Financial support:* In 2006–07, 28 students received support, including 18 fellowships (averaging $7,112 per year); career-related internships or fieldwork and scholarships/grants also available. Support available to part-time students. Financial award application deadline: 3/31; financial award applicants required to submit FAFSA. *Faculty research:* Manual therapy, performance injuries in musicians, oncologic physical therapy, pediatric physical therapy and pain management. Total annual research expenditures: $1.3 million. *Unit head:* Dr. Kathleen Hummel-Berry, Director, 253-879-3531, Fax: 253-879-2933, E-mail: hummel@ups.edu. *Application contact:* Dr. George H. Mills, Vice President for Enrollment, 253-879-3211, Fax: 253-879-3993, E-mail: admission@ups.edu.

University of Rhode Island, Graduate School, College of Human Science and Services, Department of Kinesiology, Physical Therapy Program, Kingston, RI 02881. Offers DPT. *Accreditation:* APTA. *Application deadline:* For fall admission, 4/15 priority date for domestic students; for spring admission, 11/15 for domestic students. Applications are processed on a rolling basis. Application fee: $35. *Expenses:* Tuition, state resident: full-time $6,032; part-time $335 per credit. Tuition, nonresident: full-time $17,288; part-time $960 per credit. Required fees: $65 per credit. $30 per semester. One-time fee: $80 part-time. *Unit head:* Dr. Beth Marcoux, Director, 401-874-5001.

University of St. Augustine for Health Sciences, Graduate Programs, Division of Advanced Studies, St. Augustine, FL 32086. Offers MH Sc, DH Sc, TDPT. Part-time programs available. Postbaccalaureate distance learning degree programs offered (minimal on-campus study). *Entrance requirements:* For master's, GRE General Test, BS in physical therapy or equivalent; for doctorate, GRE General Test, master's degree in related field. Additional exam requirements/recommendations for international students: Required—TOEFL.

University of St. Augustine for Health Sciences, Graduate Programs, Division of Entry-Level Physical Therapy, St. Augustine, FL 32086. Offers DPT. *Accreditation:* APTA.

University of St. Augustine for Health Sciences, Graduate Programs, Division of Physical Therapy, St. Augustine, FL 32086. Offers DPT, Certificate. *Accreditation:* APTA. *Entrance requirements:* Additional exam requirements/recommendations for international students: Required—TOEFL.

The University of Scranton, Graduate School, Department of Physical Therapy, Scranton, PA 18510. Offers MPT, DPT. *Accreditation:* APTA. Part-time programs available. Postbaccalaureate distance learning degree programs offered (no on-campus study). *Faculty:* 7 full-time (3 women). *Students:* 42 full-time (29 women), 58 part-time (41 women); includes 3 minority (1 Asian American or Pacific Islander, 2 Hispanic Americans), 1 international. Average age 28. 73 applicants, 100% accepted. In 2006, 26 master's, 21 doctorates awarded. *Degree requirements:* For master's, thesis (for some programs), capstone experience. *Entrance requirements:* For master's, minimum GPA of 3.0; for doctorate, physical therapist license. Additional exam requirements/recommendations for international students: Required—TOEFL (minimum score 500 paper-based; 173 computer-based), IELTS (minimum score 6). *Application deadline:* Applications are processed on a rolling basis. Application fee: $50. *Expenses:* Tuition: Part-time $684 per credit. Required fees: $25 per term. *Financial support:* In 2006–07, 2 students received support, including 2 teaching assistantships (averaging $4,400 per year); career-related internships or fieldwork, Federal Work-Study, and unspecified assistantships also available. Support available to part-time students. Financial award application deadline: 3/1. *Unit head:* Dr. John P. Sanko, Chair, 570-941-7934, Fax: 570-941-7940, E-mail: sankoi1@scranton.edu.

University of South Alabama, Graduate School, College of Allied Health Professions, Department of Physical Therapy, Mobile, AL 36688-0002. Offers DPT, PhD. *Accreditation:* APTA. *Faculty:* 7 full-time (1 woman). *Students:* 91 full-time (65 women), 29 part-time (20 women); includes 9 minority (5 African Americans, 1 American Indian/Alaska Native, 2 Asian Americans or Pacific Islanders, 1 Hispanic American), 2 international. 5 applicants, 20% accepted, 1 enrolled. *Application deadline:* For fall admission, 9/1 priority date for domestic students. Applications are processed on a rolling basis. Application fee: $25. *Financial support:* Application deadline: 4/1. *Unit head:* Dr. Dennis Fell, Chair, 251-434-3575.

The University of South Dakota, School of Medicine and Health Sciences and Graduate School, Graduate Programs in Health Sciences, Department of Physical Therapy, Vermillion, SD 57069-2390. Offers MS, DPT. *Accreditation:* APTA. *Faculty:* 7 full-time (3 women), 5 part-time/adjunct (4 women). *Students:* 54 full-time (33 women); includes 1 minority (Asian American or Pacific Islander) Average age 24. 40 applicants, 65% accepted, 26 enrolled. In 2006, 15 degrees awarded. *Entrance requirements:* For doctorate, GRE General Test. Additional exam requirements/recommendations for international students: Required—TOEFL. *Application deadline:* For spring admission, 5/31 for domestic students. Applications are processed on a rolling basis. Application fee: $35. *Expenses:* Contact institution. *Financial support:* Scholarships/grants available. *Faculty research:* Physical therapy, knee rehabilitation, pediatric intervention, wound care, motion analysis. Total annual research expenditures: $15,000. *Unit head:* Lana Svien, Chairperson, 605-677-5915, Fax: 605-677-6529, E-mail: lsvien@usd.edu. *Application contact:* Tammy Goetz, Information Contact, 605-677-5915, Fax: 605-677-6529.

University of Southern California, Graduate School, Independent Health Professions, Department of Biokinesiology and Physical Therapy, Program in Physical Therapy, Los Angeles, CA 90089. Offers MS, DPT. *Accreditation:* APTA (one or more programs are accredited). *Students:* 271 full-time (196 women), 12 part-time (9 women); includes 118 minority (9 African Americans, 2 American Indian/Alaska Native, 86 Asian Americans or Pacific Islanders, 21 Hispanic Americans), 5 international. 192 applicants, 70% accepted. In 2006, 79 doctorates awarded. *Degree requirements:* For doctorate, thesis/dissertation. *Entrance requirements:* For master's and doctorate, GRE General Test. *Application deadline:* For fall admission, 12/1 priority date for domestic students. Application fee: $85. *Expenses:* Tuition: Full-time $33,314; part-time $1,121 per credit. Required fees: $522. Full-time tuition and fees vary according to program. *Financial support:* In 2006–07, research assistantships (averaging $18,500 per year), teaching assistantships (averaging $18,500 per year) were awarded; fellowships, Federal Work-Study, institutionally sponsored loans, and scholarships/grants also available. Support available to part-time students. Financial award application deadline: 2/15; financial award applicants required to submit FAFSA.

University of South Florida, College of Medicine, School of Physical Therapy, Tampa, FL 33620-9951. Offers MS. *Accreditation:* APTA. *Faculty:* 1 (woman) full-time. *Students:* 53 full-time (40 women), 1 (woman) part-time; includes 15 minority (5 African Americans, 2 Asian Americans or Pacific Islanders, 8 Hispanic Americans). 33 applicants, 100% accepted, 33 enrolled. In 2006, 1 degree awarded. *Entrance requirements:* For master's, GRE General Test, minimum GPA of 3.0 in last 60 hours of coursework. Additional exam requirements/recommendations for international students: Required—TOEFL (minimum score 600 paper-based; 250 computer-based). *Application deadline:* For fall admission, 9/1 for domestic students, 2/1 for international students. Application fee: $30. *Financial support:* Applicants required to submit FAFSA. Total annual research expenditures: $448,933. *Unit head:* Dr. William S. Quillen, Associate Dean/Director, 813-974-8870, Fax: 813-974-8915, E-mail: dpt@hsc.usf.edu. *Application contact:* Robin Hudson, Administration Service Coordinator, 813-974-8870, Fax: 813-974-8915, E-mail: dpt@hsc.usf.edu.

The University of Tennessee at Chattanooga, Graduate School, College of Health, Education and Professional Studies, Department of Physical Therapy, Chattanooga, TN 37403-2598. Offers DPT. *Accreditation:* APTA. *Faculty:* 7 full-time (4 women). *Students:* 64 full-time (45 women); includes 2 minority (1 African American, 1 Asian American or Pacific Islander), 1 international. Average age 24. 75 applicants, 13% accepted, 3 enrolled. In 2006, 26 degrees awarded. *Degree requirements:* For doctorate, qualifying exams. *Entrance requirements:* For doctorate, interview, minimum GPA of 3.0 in science and overall. *Application deadline:* For fall admission, 8/1 priority date for domestic students; for spring admission, 12/1 priority date for domestic students. Applications are processed on a rolling basis. Application fee: $30. *Expenses:* Tuition, state resident: full-time $5,434; part-time $339 per hour. Tuition, nonresident: full-time $14,830; part-time $861 per hour. Required fees: $940; $178 per hour. *Financial support:* Application deadline: 4/1; *Faculty research:* Diabetes and round management; disabilities; animal physical therapy and rehabilitation; orthopedics. Total annual research expenditures: $6,474. *Unit head:* Dr. David Levine, Head, 423-425-5240, Fax: 423-425-2215. *Application contact:* Dr. Deborah E. Arfken, Dean of Graduate Studies, 423-425-4666, Fax: 423-425-5223, E-mail: deborah-arfken@utc.edu.

The University of Tennessee Health Science Center, College of Allied Health Sciences, Memphis, TN 38163-0002. Offers MCP, MDH, MHIIM, MOT, MSCLS, MSPT, DPT, ScDPT, TDPT. *Accreditation:* AOTA; APTA. Part-time and evening/weekend programs available. Postbaccalaureate distance learning degree programs offered (minimal on-campus study). *Faculty:* 23 full-time (18 women), 23 part-time/adjunct (17 women). *Students:* 197 full-time (141 women), 5 part-time (4 women); includes 43 minority (29 African Americans, 1 American Indian/Alaska Native, 13 Asian Americans or Pacific Islanders). Average age 26. 225 applicants, 57% accepted, 120 enrolled. In 2006, 2 master's, 2 doctorates awarded. Terminal master's awarded for partial completion of doctoral program. *Degree requirements:* For master's, thesis, comprehensive exam, registration; for doctorate, residency. *Entrance requirements:* For master's, GRE (MOT, MSCLS), minimum GPA of 3.0, 3 letters of reference, state license (MDH), national accreditation (MSCLS), GRE if GPA is less than 3.0 (MCP); for doctorate, GRE. Additional exam requirements/recommendations for international students: Required—TOEFL (minimum score 550 paper-based; 213 computer-based; 80 iBT). *Application deadline:* For fall admission, 1/30 priority date for domestic students; for winter admission, 10/1 priority date for domestic students. Application fee: $50. Electronic applications accepted. *Expenses:* Contact institution. *Financial support:* In 2006–07, 2 teaching assistantships were awarded; Federal Work-Study, institutionally sponsored loans, and scholarships/grants also available. Support

Physical Therapy

The University of Tennessee Health Science Center (continued)
available to part-time students. Financial award application deadline: 2/15; financial award applicants required to submit FAFSA. *Faculty research:* Gait deviation, muscular dystrophy and strength, hemophilia and exercise, pediatric neurology, self-efficacy. *Unit head:* Dr. William R. Frey, Interim Dean, 901-528-5581, Fax: 901-528-7545, E-mail: wfrey@utmem.edu. *Application contact:* Eunice Taylor, Interim Director, Enrollment Services, 901-448-5560, Fax: 901-448-7772, E-mail: etaylor@utmem.edu.

The University of Texas at El Paso, Graduate School, College of Health Sciences, School of Allied Health, Program in Physical Therapy, El Paso, TX 79968-0001. Offers MPT. *Accreditation:* APTA. *Entrance requirements:* For master's, GRE General Test. Additional exam requirements/recommendations for international students: Required—TOEFL. Electronic applications accepted.

The University of Texas Health Science Center at San Antonio, School of Allied Health Sciences, San Antonio, TX 78229-3900. Offers clinical laboratory sciences (MS); dental hygiene (MS); occupational therapy (MOT); physical therapy (MPT); physician assistant studies (MS). *Accreditation:* AOTA; APTA; ARC-PA. *Expenses:* Tuition, state resident: part-time $50 per credit hour. Tuition, nonresident: part-time $325 per credit hour. Required fees: $7.5 per credit hour. $155 per term.

The University of Texas Medical Branch, School of Allied Health Sciences, Department of Physical Therapy, Galveston, TX 77555. Offers MPT. *Accreditation:* APTA. *Faculty:* 10 full-time (6 women), 4 part-time/adjunct (3 women). *Students:* 96 full-time (67 women); includes 23 minority (12 African Americans, 7 Asian Americans or Pacific Islanders, 4 Hispanic Americans). Average age 26. 249 applicants, 46 enrolled. In 2006, 38 degrees awarded. *Degree requirements:* For master's, thesis or alternative. *Entrance requirements:* For master's, GRE, documentation of 40 hours' experience. *Application deadline:* For fall admission, 11/1 for domestic and international students. Applications are processed on a rolling basis. Application fee: $30. Electronic applications accepted. *Financial support:* Federal Work-Study, institutionally sponsored loans, and scholarships/grants available. Financial award applicants required to submit FAFSA. *Faculty research:* Muscle metabolism; balance; cardiopulmonary responses to exercise; joint function (cervical); head stability. *Unit head:* Dr. Carolyn J. Utsey, Acting Chair, 409-772-9497, Fax: 409-772-3014, E-mail: cutsey@utmb.edu. *Application contact:* Dr. Helen L. Rogers, Director of Admissions, 409-772-9496, Fax: 409-747-1613, E-mail: dwise@utmb.edu.

The University of Texas Southwestern Medical Center at Dallas, Southwestern Allied Health Sciences School, Physical Therapy Program, Dallas, TX 75390. Offers MPT. *Accreditation:* APTA. *Students:* 76 full-time (64 women); includes 9 minority (1 African American, 2 Asian Americans or Pacific Islanders, 6 Hispanic Americans), 2 international. Average age 24. 187 applicants, 26% accepted, 37 enrolled. In 2006, 32 degrees awarded. *Entrance requirements:* For master's, GRE, minimum GPA of 3.0. Additional exam requirements/recommendations for international students: Required—TOEFL (minimum score 600 paper-based; 220 computer-based). *Application deadline:* For spring admission, 9/1 priority date for domestic students. Application fee: $10. Electronic applications accepted. *Expenses:* Tuition, state resident: part-time $120 per semester hour. Tuition, nonresident: part-time $395 per semester hour. Required fees: $42 per semester hour. Tuition and fees vary according to program. *Financial support:* Application deadline: 3/1; *Unit head:* Dr. Patricia Winchester, Chair, 214-648-1551, Fax: 214-648-1511, E-mail: patricia.winchester@utsouthwestern.edu. *Application contact:* Billy Crawford, Education Coordinator, 214-648-1566, Fax: 214-648-1511, E-mail: billy.crawford@utsouthwestern.edu.

University of the Pacific, School of Pharmacy and Health Sciences, Department of Physical Therapy, Stockton, CA 95211-0197. Offers MS, DPT. *Accreditation:* APTA. *Faculty:* 7 full-time (5 women), 6 part-time/adjunct (5 women). *Students:* 67 full-time (44 women), 2 part-time (1 woman); includes 18 minority (1 American Indian/Alaska Native, 13 Asian Americans or Pacific Islanders, 4 Hispanic Americans). Average age 25. 135 applicants, 44% accepted, 36 enrolled. In 2006, 32 degrees awarded. *Entrance requirements:* For master's, GRE General Test, minimum GPA of 3.0. Additional exam requirements/recommendations for international students: Required—TOEFL (minimum score 475 paper-based; 150 computer-based). *Application deadline:* For fall admission, 1/4 for domestic students. Application fee: $75. *Expenses:* Tuition: Full-time $26,920. Required fees: $430. Tuition and fees vary according to course load. *Financial support:* Federal Work-Study available. Financial award application deadline: 3/1; financial award applicants required to submit FAFSA. *Unit head:* Dr. Cathy Peterson, Chair, 209-946-2947, Fax: 209-946-2410.

University of the Sciences in Philadelphia, College of Graduate Studies, Transitional Doctor of Physical Therapy Program, Philadelphia, PA 19104-4495. Offers DPT. *Accreditation:* APTA. Part-time and evening/weekend programs available. Postbaccalaureate distance learning degree programs offered (no on-campus study). *Faculty:* 8 full-time (6 women). *Students:* Average age 30. 12 applicants, 100% accepted, 10 enrolled.Application fee: $0. *Expenses:* Tuition: Part-time $1,058 per credit. Tuition and fees vary according to program. *Faculty research:* Orthopedic and neurologic physical therapy, motor control and orthotic evaluation, effects of electrical stimulation on wound healing, ethics. Total annual research expenditures: $2,000. *Unit head:* Dr. Susan Wainwright, Director, 215-596-8849, Fax: 215-596-3121, E-mail: s.wainwr@usip.edu. *Application contact:* Lorraine Cella, Assistant to Dean of Graduate Studies, 215-596-8926, E-mail: l.cella@usip.edu.

The University of Toledo, College of Graduate Studies, College of Health Science and Human Service, Division of Health, Program in Physical Therapy, Toledo, OH 43606-3390. Offers MS, DPT. *Accreditation:* APTA. *Students:* 51 full-time (39 women), 22 part-time (16 women); includes 2 minority (1 African American, 1 Asian American or Pacific Islander). 48 applicants, 75% accepted, 29 enrolled.*Application contact:* Liz Henderson, Student Contact, 419-383-3518, E-mail: lhenderson@utoledo.edu.

The University of Toledo, College of Graduate Studies, College of Medicine, Program in Orthopedic Science, Toledo, OH 43606-3390. Offers MS. *Students:* 1 applicant, 100% accepted, 0 enrolled. *Degree requirements:* For master's, thesis, qualifying exam. *Entrance requirements:* For master's, GRE General Test, minimum undergraduate GPA of 3.0.

University of Utah, The Graduate School, College of Health, Division of Physical Therapy, Salt Lake City, UT 84112-1107. Offers DPT, PPDPT. *Accreditation:* APTA. *Faculty:* 11 full-time (6 women), 3 part-time/adjunct (1 woman). *Students:* 122 full-time (55 women), 4 part-time (all women); includes 7 minority (1 African American, 1 Asian American or Pacific Islander, 5 Hispanic Americans), 2 international. Average age 28. 110 applicants, 47% accepted, 41 enrolled. In 2006, 41 degrees awarded. *Median time to degree:* Of those who began their doctoral program in fall 1998, 99% received their degree in 8 years or less. *Degree requirements:* For doctorate, clinical project. *Entrance requirements:* For doctorate, minimum GPA of 3.0, volunteer work. Additional exam requirements/recommendations for international students: Required—TOEFL (minimum score 575 paper-based; 233 computer-based). *Application deadline:* For fall admission, 11/8 priority date for domestic students. Applications are processed on a rolling basis. Application fee: $75. *Expenses:* Contact institution. Tuition and fees vary according to class time and program. *Financial support:* In 2006–07, 20 students received support. Federal Work-Study, institutionally sponsored loans, and scholarships/grants available. Financial award application deadline: 9/30; financial award applicants required to submit FAFSA. *Faculty research:* Rehabilitation and Parkinson's Disease, motor control and musculoskeletal dysfunction, burs/wound care, rehabilitation and multiple sclerosis, cancer. Total annual research expenditures: $183,414. *Unit head:* Dr. R. Scott Ward, Chair, 801-581-8681, Fax: 801-585-5629, E-mail: scott.ward@hsc.utah.edu. *Application contact:* Joyce Bawden, Advisor, 801-585-3122, Fax: 801-585-5629, E-mail: joyce.bawden@hsc.utah.edu.

University of Vermont, Graduate College, College of Nursing and Health Sciences, Program in Physical Therapy, Burlington, VT 05405. Offers DPT. *Accreditation:* APTA. *Students:* 39 (23 women); includes 1 minority (Hispanic American) 1 international. 69 applicants, 67% accepted, 12 enrolled. *Entrance requirements:* For doctorate, GRE General Test. Additional exam requirements/recommendations for international students: Required—TOEFL (minimum score 550 paper-based; 213 computer-based). *Application deadline:* For fall admission, 1/15 priority date for domestic students. Applications are processed on a rolling basis. Application fee: $40. Electronic applications accepted. *Expenses:* Tuition, state resident: part-time $434 per credit. Tuition, nonresident: part-time $1,096 per credit. *Financial support:* Fellowships, research assistantships, teaching assistantships, Federal Work-Study available. Financial award application deadline: 3/1. *Unit head:* Dr. Diane Jette, Coordinator, 802-656-3252.

University of Washington, School of Medicine and Graduate School, Graduate Programs in Medicine, Department of Rehabilitation Medicine, Seattle, WA 98195. Offers occupational therapy (MOT); physical therapy (DPT); rehabilitation science (PhD). *Faculty:* 56. *Students:* 175. Average age 30. In 2006, 25 master's, 30 doctorates awarded. *Median time to degree:* Master's–2 years full-time; doctorate–3 years full-time. *Degree requirements:* For doctorate, thesis/dissertation (for some programs), comprehensive exam (for some programs). *Entrance requirements:* Additional exam requirements/recommendations for international students: Required—TOEFL. Application fee: $45. *Faculty research:* Pediatric topics, balance, brain injury, spinal cord injury, pain, assistive technology. *Unit head:* Dr. Peter C. Esselman, Professor and Chair, 206-543-3600, Fax: 206-685-3244, E-mail: esselman@u.washington.edu. *Application contact:* Dr. Jean Deitz, Graduate Program Coordinator, 206-598-5396, Fax: 206-685-3244, E-mail: deitz@u.washington.edu.

The University of Western Ontario, Faculty of Graduate Studies, Biosciences Division, School of Physical Therapy, London, ON N6A 5B8, Canada. Offers M Sc, MPT. *Accreditation:* APTA. Part-time programs available. *Faculty:* 5 full-time (3 women). *Students:* 6 full-time (3 women), 7 part-time (6 women). Average age 27. In 2006, 1 degree awarded. *Degree requirements:* For master's, thesis. *Entrance requirements:* For master's, B Sc in physical therapy. Additional exam requirements/recommendations for international students: Required—TOEFL. *Application deadline:* For fall admission, 8/15 for domestic students, 2/15 for international students; for winter admission, 12/15 for domestic students; for spring admission, 4/15 for domestic students. Applications are processed on a rolling basis. Application fee: $0. *Financial support:* In 2006–07, 1 fellowship with tuition reimbursement (averaging $20,000 per year), 3 teaching assistantships (averaging $9,900 per year) were awarded; scholarships/grants also available. Financial award application deadline: 4/1. *Faculty research:* Muscle strength, wound healing, motor control, respiratory physiology, exercise physiology. *Unit head:* Dr. S. Jayne Garland, Director, 519-661-2111 Ext. 88946, Fax: 519-661-3866. *Application contact:* Dr. D. Lucy, Graduate Secretary, 519-661-2111 Ext. 88843, Fax: 519-661-3866.

University of Wisconsin–La Crosse, Office of University Graduate Studies, College of Science and Health, Department of Health Professions, Program in Physical Therapy, La Crosse, WI 54601-3742. Offers MSPT, DPT. *Accreditation:* APTA. *Students:* 85 full-time (60 women), 42 part-time (30 women); includes 4 minority (2 American Indian/Alaska Native, 2 Asian Americans or Pacific Islanders). Average age 24. 125 applicants, 41% accepted, 43 enrolled. In 2006, 40 degrees awarded. *Entrance requirements:* Additional exam requirements/recommendations for international students: Required—TOEFL (minimum score 550 paper-based; 213 computer-based). Application fee: $45. *Financial support:* In 2006–07, 5 research assistantships with partial tuition reimbursements (averaging $4,921 per year) were awarded; career-related internships or fieldwork, scholarships/grants, traineeships, health care benefits, unspecified assistantships, and grant/contract-funded assistantships also available. Financial award application deadline: 11/1. *Unit head:* Dr. Michele Thorman, Director, 608-785-8466, E-mail: thorman.mich@uwlax.edu. *Application contact:* Kathryn Kiefer, Associate Director of Admissions, 608-785-8939, E-mail: admissions@uwlax.edu.

Utica College, Department of Physical Therapy, Utica, NY 13502-4892. Offers DPT, TDPT. *Accreditation:* APTA. *Faculty:* 8 full-time (4 women). *Students:* 43 full-time (32 women), 66 part-time (46 women); includes 6 minority (2 African Americans, 1 American Indian/Alaska Native, 2 Asian Americans or Pacific Islanders, 1 Hispanic American), 1 international. 45 applicants, 89% accepted, 34 enrolled. In 2006, 27 degrees awarded. *Degree requirements:* For doctorate, thesis/dissertation (for some programs), comprehensive exam. *Entrance requirements:* For doctorate, GRE, MCAT, DAT or OPT, BS, minimum GPA of 3.0. Additional exam requirements/recommendations for international students: Required—TOEFL (minimum score 550 paper-based; 213 computer-based). *Application deadline:* Applications are processed on a rolling basis. Application fee: $50. Electronic applications accepted. *Expenses:* Contact institution. *Financial support:* In 2006–07, 42 students received support. Career-related internships or fieldwork, scholarships/grants, tuition waivers (partial), and unspecified assistantships available. Support available to part-time students. Financial award application deadline: 3/15. *Unit head:* Dr. Dale Scalise-Smith, Director of Physical Therapy, 315-792-3376, E-mail: dscalise-smith@utica.edu. *Application contact:* John D. Rowe, Director of Graduate Admissions, 315-792-3824, Fax: 315-792-3003, E-mail: jrowe@utica.edu.

Virginia Commonwealth University, Graduate School, School of Allied Health Professions, Department of Physical Therapy, Richmond, VA 23284-9005. Offers advanced physical therapy (MS); anatomy and neurobiology (PhD); entry-level physical therapy (MS); physiology (PhD). *Accreditation:* APTA (one or more programs are accredited). *Faculty:* 13 full-time (9 women). *Students:* 148 full-time (113 women), 104 part-time (76 women); includes 24 minority (13 African Americans, 1 American Indian/Alaska Native, 7 Asian Americans or Pacific Islanders, 3 Hispanic Americans). 23 applicants, 87% accepted, 15 enrolled. In 2006, 3 master's, 54 doctorates awarded. *Degree requirements:* For doctorate, thesis/dissertation. *Entrance requirements:* For master's and doctorate, GRE General Test. *Application deadline:* For fall admission, 2/15 priority date for domestic students. Application fee: $50. *Financial support:* Fellowships available. *Faculty research:* Eye movement, bilabyrinthectomy on ferret muscle fiber typing, neck disability index, cost-effective care, training effect on muscle. *Unit head:* Dr. Thomas P. Mayhew, Chair, 804-828-0223, Fax: 804-828-8111, E-mail: tpmayhew@vcu.edu.

See Close-Up on page 1749.

Virginia Commonwealth University, Medical College of Virginia-Professional Programs, School of Medicine and Graduate Programs, School of Medicine Graduate Programs, Department of Anatomy and Neurobiology, Richmond, VA 23284-9005. Offers anatomy (MS, PhD); anatomy and physical therapy (PhD); neuroscience (MS, PhD). *Faculty:* 29 full-time (5 women). *Students:* 52 full-time (19 women), 4 part-time (2 women); includes 6 minority (2 African Americans, 1 American Indian/Alaska Native, 3 Asian Americans or Pacific Islanders), 7 international. 110 applicants, 38% accepted, 25 enrolled. In 2006, 3 master's, 3 doctorates awarded. *Degree requirements:* For master's, thesis; for doctorate, thesis/dissertation, comprehensive oral and written exams. *Entrance requirements:* For master's, DAT, GRE General Test, or MCAT; for doctorate, DAT, GRE General Test, MCAT. *Application deadline:* For fall admission, 2/15 priority date for domestic students. Application fee: $50. *Financial support:* Fellowships available. *Unit head:* Dr. John T. Povlishock, Chair, 804-828-9623, Fax: 804-828-9477, E-mail: jtpovlis@vcu.edu. *Application contact:* Dr. George R. Leichnetz, Director, Graduate Programs in Anatomy and Neurobiology, 804-828-9512, Fax: 804-828-9477, E-mail: grleichn@vcu.edu.

See Close-Up on page 1745.

Walsh University, Graduate Programs, Program in Physical Therapy, North Canton, OH 44720-3396. Offers M Sc. *Accreditation:* APTA. *Faculty:* 6 full-time (5 women). *Students:* 39 full-time (27 women); includes 1 minority (African American) Average age 24. 40 applicants, 63% accepted, 19 enrolled. In 2006, 11 degrees awarded. *Degree requirements:* For master's, research project, 3 clinical placements. *Entrance requirements:* For master's, GRE General Test, previous course work in anatomy, physiology, chemistry, statistics, psychology, biology, and physics; minimum GPA of 3.0. Additional exam requirements/recommendations for international students: Required—TOEFL (minimum score 500 paper-based; 173 computer-based). *Application deadline:* For fall admission, 5/1 for domestic students. Applications are processed on a rolling basis. Application fee: $25. Electronic applications accepted. *Expenses:*

Contact institution. Financial support: In 2006–07, 21 students received support, including 2 research assistantships with partial tuition reimbursements available (averaging $3,664 per year); tuition waivers (partial) and unspecified assistantships also available. Financial award application deadline: 12/31. *Faculty research:* Motor control (inter-limb coordination), post-stroke neural rehabilitation, exercise intervention (Tai Chi for osteoarthritis), direct access to physical therapy services, clinical education for physical therapists. *Unit head:* Dr. Susan Bemis, Chair, 330-490-7362, E-mail: sbemis@walsh.edu. *Application contact:* Brett D. Freshour, Vice President of Enrollment Management, 330-490-7286, Fax: 330-490-7165, E-mail: bfreshour@walsh.edu.

Washington University in St. Louis, School of Medicine, Graduate Programs in Medicine, Program in Physical Therapy, St. Louis, MO 63130-4899. Offers movement science (PhD); physical therapy (DPT, PPDPT). *Accreditation:* APTA (one or more programs are accredited). Part-time and evening/weekend programs available. Postbaccalaureate distance learning degree programs offered. *Faculty:* 31 full-time (24 women), 14 part-time/adjunct (4 women). *Students:* 196 full-time (162 women), 56 part-time (35 women); includes 37 minority (4 African Americans, 1 American Indian/Alaska Native, 28 Asian Americans or Pacific Islanders, 4 Hispanic Americans). Average age 24. 201 applicants, 76% accepted, 77 enrolled. In 2006, 65 degrees awarded. *Degree requirements:* For doctorate, thesis/dissertation (for some programs). *Entrance requirements:* For doctorate, GRE, sample of written work (PhD); for PPDPT, GRE, professional degree in physical therapy, clinical experience. Additional exam requirements/recommendations for international students: Required—TOEFL (minimum score 600 paper-based; 250 computer-based; 100 iBT), TWE (minimum score 5). *Application deadline:* For fall admission, 11/15 priority date for domestic and international students; for winter admission, 3/1 priority date for domestic and international students; for spring admission, 3/31 for domestic and international students. Applications are processed on a rolling basis. Electronic applications accepted. *Expenses: Contact institution. Financial support:* In 2006–07, 187 students received support, including 3 fellowships with tuition reimbursements available (averaging $17,000 per year), 7 research assistantships (averaging $4,000 per year); Federal Work-Study, institutionally sponsored loans, and scholarships/grants also available. Support available to part-time students. Financial award application deadline: 3/1; financial award applicants required to submit CSS PROFILE or FAFSA. *Faculty research:* Movement and movement dysfunction. Total annual research expenditures: $1.2 million. *Unit head:* Dr. Susan S. Deusinger, Director, 314-286-1400, Fax: 314-286-1410. *Application contact:* Sarah J. Rands, Admissions and Student Affairs Coordinator, 314-286-1402, Fax: 314-286-1410, E-mail: rands@wustl.edu.

Wayne State University, Eugene Applebaum College of Pharmacy and Health Sciences, Department of Health Care Sciences, Program in Physical Therapy, Detroit, MI 48202. Offers MPT. *Accreditation:* APTA. *Faculty:* 7 full-time (6 women), 2 part-time/adjunct (0 women). *Students:* Average age 26. 45 applicants, 84% accepted. In 2006, 25 degrees awarded. *Entrance requirements:* Additional exam requirements/recommendations for international students: Required—TOEFL (minimum score 550 paper-based; 213 computer-based); Recommended—TWE (minimum score 6). *Application deadline:* For fall admission, 6/1 for international students; for winter admission, 10/1 for international students; for spring admission, 2/1 for international students. Applications are processed on a rolling basis. Application fee: $30 ($50 for international students). Electronic applications accepted. *Unit head:* Susan Talley, Academic Director, 313-577-1432, Fax: 313-577-8685, E-mail: ac1563@wayne.edu.

Western Carolina University, Graduate School, College of Applied Science, Department of Physical Therapy, Cullowhee, NC 28723. Offers MPT. *Accreditation:* APTA. *Degree requirements:* For master's, comprehensive exam. *Entrance requirements:* For master's, GRE General Test. Additional exam requirements/recommendations for international students: Required—TOEFL (minimum score 550 paper-based; 213 computer-based).

Western University of Health Sciences, College of Allied Health Professions, Program in Physical Therapy, Pomona, CA 91766-1854. Offers DPT. *Accreditation:* APTA. *Faculty:* 7 full-time (5 women), 1 (woman) part-time/adjunct. *Students:* 91 full-time (66 women), 36 part-time (19 women); includes 59 minority (6 African Americans, 34 Asian Americans or Pacific Islanders, 19 Hispanic Americans), 1 international. Average age 30. 157 applicants, 71% accepted, 44 enrolled. In 2006, 23 degrees awarded. *Entrance requirements:* For doctorate, GRE General Test, minimum GPA of 2.8, letters of recommendation, interview. *Application deadline:* For fall admission, 12/1 priority date for domestic students. Applications are processed on a rolling basis. Application fee: $60. *Expenses: Contact institution. Financial support:* Institutionally sponsored loans, scholarships/grants, and Veterans Educational Benefits available. Financial award application deadline: 3/2; financial award applicants required to submit FAFSA. *Unit head:* Georgeanne Vlad, Chair, 909-469-5215, Fax: 909-469-5692, E-mail: gvlad@westernu.edu. *Application contact:* Natalie Salaiz, Information Contact, 909-469-5335, E-mail: admissions@westernu.edu.

West Virginia University, School of Medicine, Graduate Programs in Human Performance and Applied Exercise Science, Division of Physical Therapy, Morgantown, WV 26506. Offers MPT. Students enter program as undergraduates. *Accreditation:* APTA. Evening/weekend programs available. Postbaccalaureate distance learning degree programs offered (minimal on-campus study). *Degree requirements:* For master's, clinical rotation. Expenses: Contact institution. Tuition and fees vary according to program.

Wheeling Jesuit University, Department of Physical Therapy, Wheeling, WV 26003-6295. Offers DPT. *Accreditation:* APTA. Postbaccalaureate distance learning degree programs offered (no on-campus study). *Faculty:* 5 full-time (1 woman), 7 part-time/adjunct (2 women). *Students:* 63 full-time (38 women); includes 7 minority (3 African Americans, 1 American Indian/Alaska Native, 2 Asian Americans or Pacific Islanders, 1 Hispanic American). Average age 23. 66 applicants, 48% accepted, 32 enrolled. In 2006, 29 degrees awarded. *Degree requirements:* For doctorate, thesis/dissertation, comprehensive exam. *Entrance requirements:* For doctorate, GRE, minimum GPA of 3.0. Additional exam requirements/recommendations for international students: Required—TOEFL (minimum score 600 paper-based; 250 computer-based). *Application deadline:* For fall admission, 1/15 priority date for domestic and international students. Applications are processed on a rolling basis. Application fee: $25. Electronic applications accepted. *Expenses: Contact institution.* One-time fee: $380 full-time. Full-time tuition and fees vary according to course load, degree level and program. *Financial support:* Unspecified assistantships available. Financial award application deadline: 8/1; financial award applicants required to submit FAFSA. *Faculty research:* Problem-based learning versus traditional education outcomes, anterior cruciate ligament injuries in women athletes, prevention of disease and wellness, pediatrics. *Unit head:* Dr. Luis G. Vargas, Director, 504-243-2432, Fax: 504-243-2042.

Wichita State University, Graduate School, College of Health Professions, Department of Physical Therapy, Wichita, KS 67260. Offers MPT. *Accreditation:* APTA. *Entrance requirements:* For master's, GRE, minimum GPA of 3.0. Additional exam requirements/recommendations for international students: Required—TOEFL. Electronic applications accepted.

Widener University, School of Human Service Professions, Institute for Physical Therapy Education, Chester, PA 19013-5792. Offers MS, DPT. *Accreditation:* APTA. *Degree requirements:* For master's, thesis. *Entrance requirements:* For master's, GRE. Expenses: Contact institution. *Faculty research:* Social support, aquatics, children and adults with movement dysfunction, physical therapy modalities.

Winston-Salem State University, Department of Physical Therapy, Winston-Salem, NC 27110-0003. Offers MPT. *Accreditation:* APTA. *Faculty:* 7 full-time (5 women), 7 part-time/adjunct (2 women). *Students:* 56 full-time (40 women); includes 19 minority (16 African Americans, 1 Asian American or Pacific Islander, 2 Hispanic Americans). 60 applicants, 43% accepted, 26 enrolled. In 2006, 18 degrees awarded. *Degree requirements:* For master's, registration. *Entrance requirements:* For master's, GRE, 3 letters of recommendations. *Application deadline:* For fall admission, 1/31 for domestic and international students. Applications are processed on a rolling basis. Application fee: $40. Electronic applications accepted. *Expenses:* Tuition, state resident: full-time $2,010. Tuition, nonresident: full-time $10,502. Tuition and fees vary according to course load. *Financial support:* In 2006–07, 26 students received support, including 7 teaching assistantships (averaging $2,500 per year); career-related internships or fieldwork, institutionally sponsored loans, scholarships/grants, and tuition waivers (partial) also available. *Faculty research:* Tissue healing; neuroimaging with functional recovery; visual, proprioceptive and vestibular sensor inputs roles. *Unit head:* Dr. Teresa Conner-Kerr, Chair and Professor, 336-750-2193, Fax: 336-750-2192, E-mail: connerkerr@wssu.edu. *Application contact:* School of Graduate Studies and Research, 336-750-2102, Fax: 336-750-3042, E-mail: graduate@wssu.edu.

Youngstown State University, Graduate School, College of Health and Human Services, Department of Physical Therapy, Youngstown, OH 44555-0001. Offers MPT. *Accreditation:* APTA. *Entrance requirements:* For master's, GRE, minimum GPA of 3.0. Additional exam requirements/recommendations for international students: Required—TOEFL.

Physician Assistant Studies

Albany Medical College, Center for Physician Assistant Studies, Albany, NY 12208-3479. Offers MS. *Accreditation:* ARC-PA. *Faculty:* 9 full-time (5 women), 3 part-time/adjunct (1 woman). *Students:* 63 full-time (48 women); includes 1 minority (Asian American or Pacific Islander) Average age 32. 363 applicants, 12% accepted, 30 enrolled. In 2006, 25 degrees awarded. *Median time to degree:* Master's–2.33 years full-time. *Degree requirements:* For master's, thesis, comprehensive exam. *Entrance requirements:* For master's, GRE. Additional exam requirements/recommendations for international students: Required—TOEFL. *Application deadline:* For winter admission, 11/1 for domestic and international students. Applications are processed on a rolling basis. Application fee: $50. *Expenses: Contact institution. Financial support:* In 2006–07, 4 students received support. Scholarships/grants available. Financial award application deadline: 10/1; financial award applicants required to submit FAFSA. *Faculty research:* Genetics, education, informatics. *Unit head:* Dr. David F. Irvine, Director, 518-262-5251, Fax: 518-262-6698, E-mail: irvined@mail.amc.edu. *Application contact:* Rosalyn Green, Secretary, 518-262-5251, E-mail: greenr@mail.amc.edu.

A.T. Still University of Health Sciences, Arizona School of Health Sciences, Mesa, AZ 85206. Offers advanced occupational therapy (MS); advanced physician assistant (MS); audiology (Au D); human movement (MS); medical informatics (MS); occupational therapy (MS); physical therapy (MS, DPT); physician assistant (MS); sports health care (MS); transitional physical therapy (DPT). *Accreditation:* AOTA (one or more programs are accredited); APTA. Postbaccalaureate distance learning degree programs offered (no on-campus study). *Faculty:* 47 full-time (27 women), 101 part-time/adjunct (60 women). *Students:* 442 full-time (277 women), 732 part-time (579 women); includes 143 minority (38 African Americans, 11 American Indian/Alaska Native, 55 Asian Americans or Pacific Islanders, 39 Hispanic Americans), 4 international. Average age 33. 1,471 applicants, 547 enrolled. In 2006, 104 master's, 432 doctorates awarded. *Degree requirements:* For master's and doctorate, thesis/dissertation (for some programs). *Entrance requirements:* For master's, GRE General Test, minimum GPA of 2.5; for doctorate, GRE, Evaluation of Practicing Audiologists Capabilities (Au D), Physical Therapy Evaluation Tool (DPT), current state licensure, master's degree or equivalent (Au D), minimum GPA of 2.7. *Application deadline:* For fall admission, 2/1 priority date for domestic and international students. Applications are processed on a rolling basis. Application fee: $60. *Expenses: Contact institution. Financial support:* In 2006–07, 382 students received support. Federal Work-Study and scholarships/grants available. Financial award application deadline: 5/1. *Faculty research:* Constraint-induced therapy, scapular motion analysis, shoulder mobility, biomechanics, quadriceps. *Unit head:* Dr. Randy Danielsen, Dean, 480-219-6000, Fax: 480-219-6110, E-mail: rdanielsen@atsu.edu. *Application contact:* Donna Sparks, Associate Director for Admissions, 660-626-2237, Fax: 660-626-2969, E-mail: admissions@atsu.edu.

Augsburg College, Program in Physicians Assistant Studies, Minneapolis, MN 55454-1351. Offers MS. *Accreditation:* ARC-PA. *Faculty:* 7 full-time (6 women), 1 part-time/adjunct (0 women). *Students:* 85 full-time (69 women); includes 8 minority (1 African American, 7 Asian Americans or Pacific Islanders). Average age 29. 130 applicants, 22% accepted, 28 enrolled. In 2006, 25 degrees awarded. *Application deadline:* For spring admission, 10/1 for domestic students. Application fee: $20. *Expenses:* Tuition: Full-time $10,584; part-time $1,764 per course. Required fees: $300; $35 per course. Tuition and fees vary according to program. *Financial support:* In 2006–07, 26 students received support. Application deadline: 8/1; *Unit head:* Dawn B. Ludwig, Director, 612-330-1331, Fax: 612-330-1757, E-mail: ludwig@augsburg.edu. *Application contact:* Carrie Benton, Information Contact, 612-330-1039, Fax: 612-330-1757, E-mail: paprog@augsburg.edu.

Barry University, School of Graduate Medical Sciences, Physician Assistant Program, Miami Shores, FL 33161-6695. Offers MCMS. *Accreditation:* ARC-PA. *Students:* 178 full-time (135 women), 2 part-time (1 woman); includes 50 minority (14 African Americans, 2 American Indian/Alaska Native, 8 Asian Americans or Pacific Islanders, 26 Hispanic Americans), 6 international. 567 applicants, 13% accepted, 69 enrolled. In 2006, 48 degrees awarded. *Entrance requirements:* For master's, GRE General Test. *Application deadline:* For fall admission, 2/1 for domestic students. Applications are processed on a rolling basis. Application fee: $30. Electronic applications accepted. *Financial support:* Applicants required to submit FAFSA. *Unit head:* Dr. Doreen Parkhurst, Program Director, 305-899-4065, Fax: 305-899-3253, E-mail: dparkhurst@mail.barry.edu. *Application contact:* Marc A. Weiner, Director of Graduate and Medical Sciences Admissions and Marketing, 305-899-3130, Fax: 305-899-3253, E-mail: mweiner@mail.barry.edu.

Baylor College of Medicine, School of Allied Health Sciences, Physician Assistant Program, Houston, TX 77030-3498. Offers MS. *Accreditation:* ARC-PA. *Faculty:* 5 full-time (4 women), 4 part-time/adjunct (2 women). *Students:* 96 full-time (79 women); includes 19 minority (5 African Americans, 1 American Indian/Alaska Native, 9 Asian Americans or Pacific Islanders, 4 Hispanic Americans). Average age 28. 574 applicants, 8% accepted, 35 enrolled. In 2006, 27 master's awarded. *Degree requirements:* For master's, thesis. *Entrance requirements:* For master's, GRE General Test. *Application deadline:* For fall admission, 10/1 for domestic students. Applications are processed on a rolling basis. Application fee: $0. Electronic applications accepted. *Expenses: Contact institution. Financial support:* In 2006–07, 70 students received support. Career-related internships or fieldwork, Federal Work-Study, institutionally sponsored loans, and scholarships/grants available. Financial award application deadline: 5/11; financial award applicants required to submit FAFSA. *Faculty research:* Breastfeeding, PA studies, multiculturalism, alcoholism prevention, women's health. *Unit head:* Carl E. Fasser,

Physician Assistant Studies

Baylor College of Medicine (continued)
Director, 713-798-5405, Fax: 713-798-6128, E-mail: cfasser@bcm.tmc.edu. *Application contact:* Dr. Lloyd H. Michael, Senior Associate Dean of the Medical School, 713-798-4842, Fax: 713-798-5563, E-mail: lmichael@bcm.edu.

Butler University, College of Pharmacy, Indianapolis, IN 46208-3485. Offers pharmaceutical science (Pharm D, MS); physician assistance studies (MS). *Accreditation:* ACPE (one or more programs are accredited). Part-time and evening/weekend programs available. *Faculty:* 34 full-time (17 women), 9 part-time/adjunct (7 women). *Students:* 369 full-time (275 women), 9 part-time (7 women); includes 26 minority (7 African Americans, 1 American Indian/Alaska Native, 17 Asian Americans or Pacific Islanders, 1 Hispanic American), 9 international. Average age 24. 135 applicants, 82% accepted, 87 enrolled. In 2006, 84 degrees awarded. *Degree requirements:* For master's, research paper or thesis. *Application deadline:* For fall admission, 8/1 priority date for domestic students; for spring admission, 12/15 for domestic students. Applications are processed on a rolling basis. Application fee: $35. Electronic applications accepted. *Expenses:* Contact institution. Tuition and fees vary according to program. *Financial support:* Applicants required to submit FAFSA. *Faculty research:* Anti-seizure drugs, casein kinase inhibitors, speech recognition interface for prescribing drugs, pharmacoeconomics. Total annual research expenditures: $92,000. *Unit head:* Dr. Mary Andritz, Dean, 317-940-9451, Fax: 317-940-6172, E-mail: mandritz@butler.edu. *Application contact:* Dr. Kent VanTyle, Professor, 317-940-9580, E-mail: kvantyle@butler.edu.

California State University, Dominguez Hills, College of Health and Human Services, Division of Health Sciences, Carson, CA 90747-0001. Offers gerontology (MA); health sciences (MS). Part-time programs available. *Faculty:* 1 (woman) full-time, 3 part-time/adjunct (all women). *Students:* 7 full-time (5 women), 19 part-time (16 women); includes 16 minority (9 African Americans, 7 Hispanic Americans), 1 international. Average age 39. 14 applicants, 71% accepted, 5 enrolled. In 2006, 4 degrees awarded. *Degree requirements:* For master's, comprehensive exam. *Entrance requirements:* Additional exam requirements/recommendations for international students: Required—TOEFL, TWE. *Application deadline:* For fall admission, 8/15 priority date for domestic students. Applications are processed on a rolling basis. Electronic applications accepted. *Expenses:* Tuition, nonresident: part-time $339 per unit. Required fees: $1,148 per term. Tuition and fees vary according to program. *Faculty research:* International health, health promotion and disease prevention, public health. *Unit head:* Dr. Mitchell T. Maki, Dean, College of Health and Human Services, 301-243-2046, E-mail: mmaki@csudh.edu.

Central Michigan University, College of Graduate Studies, The Herbert H. and Grace A. Dow College of Health Professions, School of Rehabilitation and Medical Sciences, Mount Pleasant, MI 48859. Offers physical therapy (DPT); physician assistant (MS). *Accreditation:* APTA; ARC-PA. *Degree requirements:* For master's, thesis or alternative, comprehensive exam (for some programs), registration.

Chatham University, Program in Physician Assistant Studies, Pittsburgh, PA 15232-2826. Offers MPAS. *Accreditation:* ARC-PA. *Students:* 97 full-time (86 women), 1 (woman) part-time. Average age 25. 295 applicants, 19% accepted, 55 enrolled. In 2006, 42 degrees awarded. *Degree requirements:* For master's, thesis, clinical experience, research project. *Entrance requirements:* For master's, community service, interview, minimum GPA of 3.0, health science work or shadowing, volunteer work experience. Additional exam requirements/recommendations for international students: Required—TOEFL (minimum score 600 paper-based; 250 computer-based; 100 iBT); Recommended—IELTS (minimum score 7), TWE (minimum score 5). *Application deadline:* For fall admission, 1/15 priority date for domestic students. Applications are processed on a rolling basis. Application fee: $45. Electronic applications accepted. *Financial support:* Career-related internships or fieldwork available. Financial award applicants required to submit FAFSA. *Faculty research:* Public health, developmental disabilities, complimentary and alternative medicine, toxicology, education methods. *Unit head:* Luis Ramos, Director, 412-365-1314, Fax: 412-365-1213, E-mail: lramos@chatham.edu. *Application contact:* 412-365-1825, Fax: 412-365-1609, E-mail: admissions@chatham.edu.

Daemen College, Physician Assistant Department, Amherst, NY 14226-3592. Offers MS. *Accreditation:* ARC-PA. *Faculty:* 3 full-time (0 women). *Students:* 62 full-time (49 women); includes 4 minority (2 African Americans, 1 Asian American or Pacific Islander, 1 Hispanic American). Average age 26. 185 applicants, 19% accepted, 8 enrolled. In 2006, 21 degrees awarded. *Degree requirements:* For master's, registration. *Entrance requirements:* For master's, 120 hours of employment or volunteer work providing direct patient care. Additional exam requirements/recommendations for international students: Required—TOEFL (minimum score 500 paper-based; 173 computer-based). *Application deadline:* For fall admission, 3/1 priority date for domestic and international students; for spring admission, 10/1 priority date for domestic and international students. Applications are processed on a rolling basis. Application fee: $25. Electronic applications accepted. *Expenses:* Tuition: Full-time $11,700; part-time $650 per credit hour. Required fees: $15 per credit hour. Tuition and fees vary according to course load. *Financial support:* Federal Work-Study and institutionally sponsored loans available. Financial award application deadline: 2/15; financial award applicants required to submit FAFSA. *Unit head:* Gregg L. Shutts, Director, 716-839-8316, Fax: 716-839-8252, E-mail: shutts@daemen.edu. *Application contact:* Karl Shallowhorn, Associate Director of Graduate Admissions, 716-839-8225, Fax: 716-839-8229, E-mail: kshallow@daemen.edu.

DeSales University, Graduate Division, Program in Physician Assistant Studies, Center Valley, PA 18034-9568. Offers MSPAS. *Accreditation:* ARC-PA. *Faculty:* 6 full-time. *Students:* 40 full-time. Average age 25. 205 applicants, 28% accepted. In 2006, 34 degrees awarded. *Degree requirements:* For master's, comprehensive exam. *Entrance requirements:* For master's, GRE General Test, health care experience. Additional exam requirements/recommendations for international students: Required—TOEFL (minimum score 610 paper-based). *Application deadline:* For fall admission, 1/15 priority date for domestic students. Applications are processed on a rolling basis. Electronic applications accepted. *Expenses:* Contact institution. *Financial support:* Institutionally sponsored loans and scholarships/grants available. Support available to part-time students. Financial award application deadline: 2/28; financial award applicants required to submit FAFSA. *Faculty research:* Antibiotic usage, intestinal cystitis, postpartum depression. *Unit head:* Christine Bruce, Director, 610-282-1100 Ext. 1474, Fax: 610-282-1893, E-mail: christine.bruce@desales.edu. *Application contact:* Linda Schroeder, Program Secretary, 610-282-1100 Ext. 1415, Fax: 610-282-1893, E-mail: linda.schroeder@desales.edu.

Des Moines University, College of Health Sciences, Physician Assistant Program, Des Moines, IA 50312-4104. Offers MS. *Accreditation:* ARC-PA. *Faculty:* 6 full-time (2 women). *Students:* 78 full-time (62 women); includes 1 minority (Asian American or Pacific Islander) Average age 25. 311 applicants, 17% accepted, 40 enrolled. In 2006, 36 degrees awarded. *Degree requirements:* For master's, research project. *Entrance requirements:* For master's, GRE, interview, minimum GPA of 2.8, related work experience. *Application deadline:* For fall admission, 12/31 for domestic students. Applications are processed on a rolling basis. Application fee: $0. Electronic applications accepted. *Expenses:* Contact institution. *Financial support:* In 2006–07, 8 students received support. Career-related internships or fieldwork, institutionally sponsored loans, scholarships/grants, and university employment available. Support available to part-time students. Financial award application deadline: 4/1; financial award applicants required to submit FAFSA. *Unit head:* Jolene Kelly, Director, 515-271-1685, E-mail: jolene.kelly@dmu.edu. *Application contact:* Josh Kvinlaug-Lewis, Admissions Coordinator, 515-271-7864, Fax: 515-271-7145, E-mail: paadmit@dmu.edu.

Drexel University, College of Nursing and Health Professions, Program in Advanced Physician Assistant Studies, Philadelphia, PA 19104-2875. Offers MHS. *Accreditation:* ARC-PA. Electronic applications accepted.

Duke University, School of Medicine, Physician Assistant Program, Durham, NC 27708-0586. Offers MHS. *Accreditation:* ARC-PA. *Faculty:* 9 full-time (7 women), 3 part-time/adjunct (1 woman). *Students:* 108 full-time (85 women); includes 27 minority (13 African Americans, 1 American Indian/Alaska Native, 9 Asian Americans or Pacific Islanders, 4 Hispanic Americans). Average age 28. 380 applicants, 15% accepted, 56 enrolled. In 2006, 41 degrees awarded. *Entrance requirements:* For master's, GRE, minimum of 5 courses in biological sciences with courses in anatomy, physiology and microbiology, 8 undergraduate hours in chemistry and statistics, patient care experience. *Application deadline:* For fall admission, 10/1 for domestic students. Application fee: $0. Electronic applications accepted. *Expenses:* Contact institution. *Financial support:* In 2006–07, 97 students received support. Institutionally sponsored loans and scholarships/grants available. Financial award application deadline: 5/1; financial award applicants required to submit FAFSA. *Unit head:* Patricia M. Dieter, Director/Assistant Clinical Professor, 919-681-3161, Fax: 919-681-9666, E-mail: patricia.dieter@duke.edu. *Application contact:* Wendy Z. Elwell, Program Coordinator, 919-681-3154, Fax: 919-681-9666, E-mail: wendy.elwell@duke.edu.

Duquesne University, John G. Rangos, Sr. School of Health Sciences, Pittsburgh, PA 15282-0001. Offers health management systems (MHMS); occupational therapy (MS); physical therapy (DPT); physician assistant (MPA); speech–language pathology (MS); MBA/MHMS. *Accreditation:* AOTA (one or more programs are accredited); APTA (one or more programs are accredited); ASHA. *Faculty:* 35 full-time (22 women), 24 part-time/adjunct (12 women). *Students:* 261 full-time (229 women), 16 part-time (8 women); includes 11 minority (6 African Americans, 1 American Indian/Alaska Native, 2 Asian Americans or Pacific Islanders, 2 Hispanic Americans), 3 international. Average age 23. 150 applicants, 55% accepted, 41 enrolled. In 2006, 66 master's, 13 doctorates awarded. *Degree requirements:* For doctorate, thesis/dissertation. *Entrance requirements:* For master's, GRE (speech-language pathology), 3 letters of recommendation, minimum GPA of 2.75 (health management systems, occupational therapy), minimum GPA of 3.0 (physical assistant, speech-language pathology); for doctorate, GRE General Test, 3 letters of recommendation, minimum GPA of 3.0, personal interview. Additional exam requirements/recommendations for international students: Required—TOEFL (minimum score 600 paper-based; 250 computer-based). *Application deadline:* For fall admission, 12/1 priority date for domestic students; for winter admission, 5/1 priority date for domestic students. Application fee: $50. Electronic applications accepted. *Expenses:* Contact institution. Tuition and fees vary according to degree level and program. *Financial support:* Federal Work-Study available. *Faculty research:* Neuronal processing, electrical stimulation on peripheral neuropathy, CNS stimulatory and inhibitory signals, behavioral genetic methodologies to development disorders of speech, neurogenic communication disorders. Total annual research expenditures: $66,000. *Unit head:* Dr. Gregory H. Frazer, Dean, 412-396-5303, Fax: 412-396-5554, E-mail: frazer@duq.edu. *Application contact:* Christopher R. Hilf, Recruiter/Academic Advisor, 412-396-5653, Fax: 412-396-5554, E-mail: hilfc@duq.edu.

D'Youville College, Physician Assistant Department, Buffalo, NY 14201-1084. Offers MS. *Accreditation:* ARC-PA. *Faculty:* 5 full-time (3 women). *Students:* 76 full-time (54 women), 4 part-time (all women); includes 7 minority (3 African Americans, 2 Asian Americans or Pacific Islanders, 2 Hispanic Americans), 6 international. Average age 26. 162 applicants, 23% accepted, 24 enrolled. *Entrance requirements:* Additional exam requirements/recommendations for international students: Required—TOEFL (minimum score 500 paper-based; 173 computer-based). *Application deadline:* For fall admission, 5/1 priority date for international students; for spring admission, 9/1 priority date for international students. Applications are processed on a rolling basis. Application fee: $25. Electronic applications accepted. *Unit head:* Maureen F. Finney, Chair, 716-829-7730, E-mail: finneym@dyc.edu. *Application contact:* Linda Fisher, Graduate Admissions Director, 716-829-8400, Fax: 716-829-7900, E-mail: graduateadmissions@dyc.edu.

East Carolina University, Graduate School, School of Allied Health Sciences, Department of Physician Assistant Studies, Greenville, NC 27858-4353. Offers MS. *Accreditation:* ARC-PA. *Students:* 87 full-time (62 women); includes 9 minority (4 African Americans, 3 Asian Americans or Pacific Islanders, 2 Hispanic Americans). Average age 27. 48 applicants, 92% accepted. In 2006, 27 degrees awarded. Application fee: $50. *Unit head:* Larry Dennis, Director, 252-744-1100, E-mail: dennisl@ecu.edu. *Application contact:* Dean of Graduate School, 252-328-6012, Fax: 252-328-6071, E-mail: gradschool@ecu.edu.

Eastern Virginia Medical School, Master of Physician Assistant Program, Norfolk, VA 23501-1980. Offers MPA. *Accreditation:* ARC-PA. *Faculty:* 7 full-time (3 women). *Students:* 97. 403 applicants, 14% accepted, 51 enrolled. In 2006, 33 degrees awarded. *Entrance requirements:* For master's, GRE. Additional exam requirements/recommendations for international students: Required—TOEFL. *Application deadline:* For winter admission, 6/1 for domestic students. Applications are processed on a rolling basis. Application fee: $50. Electronic applications accepted. *Expenses:* Contact institution. *Financial support:* In 2006–07, 97 students received support. Applicants required to submit FAFSA. *Unit head:* Dr. Thomas Parish, Director, 757-446-7126, Fax: 757-446-7403, E-mail: parishtg@evms.edu. *Application contact:* Rose Mwayungu, Director of Health Professions Enrollment, 757-446-7158, Fax: 757-446-8915, E-mail: mwayunra@evms.edu.

Emory University, School of Medicine, Programs in Allied Health Professions, Physician Assistant Program, Atlanta, GA 30322-1100. Offers MM Sc. *Accreditation:* ARC-PA. Post-baccalaureate distance learning degree programs offered (minimal on-campus study). *Faculty:* 8 full-time (4 women), 3 part-time/adjunct (2 women). *Students:* 151 full-time (106 women), 1 (woman) part-time; includes 36 minority (18 African Americans, 2 American Indian/Alaska Native, 14 Asian Americans or Pacific Islanders, 2 Hispanic Americans). Average age 28. 775 applicants, 9% accepted, 51 enrolled. In 2006, 50 degrees awarded. *Median time to degree:* Master's–2.33 years full-time, 3.33 years part-time. *Entrance requirements:* For master's, GRE General Test. Additional exam requirements/recommendations for international students: Required—TOEFL (minimum score 250 computer-based). *Application deadline:* For fall admission, 10/1 for domestic and international students. Applications are processed on a rolling basis. Application fee: $30. Electronic applications accepted. *Expenses:* Contact institution. *Financial support:* In 2006–07, 138 students received support. Institutionally sponsored loans and scholarships/grants available. Financial award application deadline: 4/1; financial award applicants required to submit FAFSA. *Faculty research:* Cultural competency in medical education, farmworker health, computer-assisted learning, physician assistants in primary care, geriatric functional assessment. *Unit head:* Virginia Joslin, Director, 404-727-7827, Fax: 404-727-7836, E-mail: vjoslin@learnlink.emory.edu. *Application contact:* Kaye Johnson, Assistant Director of Admissions, 404-727-7857, Fax: 404-727-7836, E-mail: ljohn07@learnlink.emory.edu.

Gannon University, School of Graduate Studies, College of Sciences, Engineering, and Health Sciences, School of Health Sciences, Program in Physician Assistant, Erie, PA 16541-0001. Offers MPAS. Program requires five years to complete. *Accreditation:* ARC-PA. *Students:* 41 full-time (35 women), 1 part-time, 1 international. Average age 23. 42 applicants, 31% accepted, 7 enrolled. In 2006, 40 degrees awarded. *Degree requirements:* For master's, thesis. *Entrance requirements:* Additional exam requirements/recommendations for international students: Required—TOEFL (minimum score 500 paper-based; 173 computer-based). Application fee: $25. *Expenses:* Tuition: Full-time $12,240; part-time $680 per credit. Required fees: $496; $16 per credit. Tuition and fees vary according to course load, degree level, campus/location and program. *Financial support:* Application deadline: 7/1; *Unit head:* Michele Roth-Kauffman, Chair, 814-871-5643, E-mail: rothkauf001@gannon.edu. *Application contact:* Debra Meszaros, Director of Graduate Recruitment, 814-871-5819, Fax: 814-871-5827, E-mail: cfal@gannon.edu.

The George Washington University, School of Medicine and Health Sciences, Health Sciences Programs, Physician Assistant Program, Washington, DC 20052. Offers MSHS, MSHS/MPH. *Accreditation:* ARC-PA. *Entrance requirements:* For master's, GRE General Test, BA/BS with clinical experience. Electronic applications accepted.

Grand Valley State University, College of Health Professions, Physician Assistant Studies Program, Allendale, MI 49401-9403. Offers MPAS. *Accreditation:* ARC-PA. *Faculty:* 6 full-time (2 women), 6 part-time/adjunct (3 women). *Students:* 90 full-time (70 women); includes 5 minority (2 African Americans, 2 Asian Americans or Pacific Islanders, 1 Hispanic American). Average age 25. 92 applicants, 33% accepted, 30 enrolled. In 2006, 28 degrees awarded. *Degree requirements:* For master's, thesis, clinical rotations, project. *Entrance requirements:* For master's, interview, 250 hours of health care experience. Additional exam requirements/recommendations for international students: Required—TOEFL (minimum score 610 paper-based; 253 computer-based). *Application deadline:* For fall admission, 11/1 for domestic and international students. Application fee: $30. Electronic applications accepted. *Expenses:* Tuition, state resident: full-time $5,850; part-time $325 per credit. Tuition, nonresident: full-time $10,800; part-time $600 per credit. Tuition and fees vary according to course load. *Financial support:* In 2006–07, 1 research assistantship (averaging $8,000 per year) was awarded; institutionally sponsored loans also available. Financial award application deadline: 2/15. *Faculty research:* Women's health, pain management, PA practice issues, hematology/hemostasis, patient education. *Unit head:* Wallace Boeve, Director, 616-331-3356, Fax: 616-331-5999, E-mail: boevew@gvsu.edu. *Application contact:* Darlene Zwart, Student Services Coordinator, 616-331-3958, E-mail: zwartdo@gvsu.edu.

Harding University, College of Sciences, Searcy, AR 72149-0001. Offers physician assistant studies (MS). *Faculty:* 4 full-time (1 woman), 3 part-time/adjunct (1 woman). *Students:* 40 full-time (30 women); includes 3 minority (2 African Americans, 1 Asian American or Pacific Islander). Average age 27. 112 applicants, 21% accepted, 24 enrolled. *Entrance requirements:* For master's, GRE. *Application deadline:* For fall admission, 11/1 for domestic students. Applications are processed on a rolling basis. Electronic applications accepted. *Expenses:* Tuition: Part-time $455 per semester hour. Required fees: $20 per semester hour. Tuition and fees vary according to course load. *Financial support:* In 2006–07, 40 students received support. Institutionally sponsored loans and scholarships/grants available. Financial award applicants required to submit FAFSA. *Unit head:* Michael Murphy, Director, 501-279-5642, E-mail: mmurphy1@harding.edu.

Idaho State University, Office of Graduate Studies, Kasiska College of Health Professions, Program in Physician Assistant Studies, Pocatello, ID 83209. Offers MPAS. *Accreditation:* ARC-PA. *Faculty:* 1 full-time (0 women). *Students:* 60 full-time (36 women); includes 2 minority (both Hispanic Americans) Average age 29. In 2006, 29 degrees awarded. *Degree requirements:* For master's, thesis (for some programs), portfolio, clinical year, oral case presentation, comprehensive exam, registration. *Entrance requirements:* For master's, GRE General Test, minimum GPA of 3.0, letters of reference. Additional exam requirements/recommendations for international students: Required—TOEFL (minimum score 500 paper-based; 213 computer-based). *Application deadline:* For fall admission, 1/15 for domestic and international students. Application fee: $55. *Expenses: Contact institution. Financial support:* In 2006–07, teaching assistantships with full and partial tuition reimbursements (averaging $8,694 per year); career-related internships or fieldwork, Federal Work-Study, scholarships/grants, tuition waivers, and unspecified assistantships also available. Support available to part-time students. Financial award application deadline: 1/1. Total annual research expenditures: $169,665. *Unit head:* Dr. John M. Schroeder, Director, 208-282-4726, Fax: 208-282-4969, E-mail: schrjohn@isu.edu. *Application contact:* Ellen Combs, Graduate School Technical Records Specialist, 208-282-2150, Fax: 208-282-4847.

James Madison University, College of Graduate and Outreach Programs, College of Integrated Science and Technology, Department of Health Sciences, Program in Physician Assistant Studies, Harrisonburg, VA 22807. Offers MPAS. *Accreditation:* ARC-PA. Part-time programs available. *Students:* 32 full-time (25 women), 1 (woman) part-time; includes 5 minority (1 African American, 3 Asian Americans or Pacific Islanders, 1 Hispanic American). Average age 27. In 2006, 13 degrees awarded. *Entrance requirements:* For master's, GRE General Test. *Application deadline:* For fall admission, 5/1 priority date for domestic students; for spring admission, 9/1 priority date for domestic students. Application fee: $55. *Expenses:* Tuition, state resident: full-time $6,336; part-time $264 per credit hour. Tuition, nonresident: full-time $17,832; part-time $743 per credit hour. *Financial support:* Application deadline: 3/1; *Unit head:* James Hammond, Coordinator, 540-568-2395.

King's College, Program in Physician Assistant Studies, Wilkes-Barre, PA 18711-0801. Offers MSPAS. *Accreditation:* ARC-PA. *Faculty:* 6 full-time (5 women), 6 part-time/adjunct (4 women). *Students:* 64 full-time (55 women); includes 4 minority (3 African Americans, 1 Hispanic American), 1 international. Average age 25. 265 applicants, 24% accepted, 41 enrolled. In 2006, 34 degrees awarded. *Degree requirements:* For master's, thesis. *Entrance requirements:* For master's, GRE. Additional exam requirements/recommendations for international students: Required—TOEFL (minimum score 600 paper-based; 250 computer-based). *Application deadline:* For fall admission, 11/1 priority date for domestic and international students. Application fee: $30. Electronic applications accepted. *Expenses:* Tuition: Full-time $26,598; part-time $625 per credit. Required fees: $900. *Unit head:* Dr. Elizabeth S. Lott, Director of Graduate Programs, 570-208-5991, Fax: 570-825-9049, E-mail: eslott@kings.edu.

Le Moyne College, Department of Physician Assistant Studies, Syracuse, NY 13214. Offers MS. *Accreditation:* ARC-PA. *Faculty:* 7 full-time (5 women), 8 part-time/adjunct (3 women). *Students:* 87 full-time (64 women), 1 part-time; includes 15 minority (4 African Americans, 7 Asian Americans or Pacific Islanders, 4 Hispanic Americans). Average age 28. 236 applicants, 21% accepted, 37 enrolled. In 2006, 20 degrees awarded. *Entrance requirements:* For master's, minimum GPA of 3.0, patient contact, interview, writing sample, 2 letters of recommendation. Additional exam requirements/recommendations for international students: Required—TOEFL (minimum score 550 paper-based; 213 computer-based). *Application deadline:* For fall admission, 10/1 for domestic and international students. Electronic applications accepted. *Expenses: Contact institution.* Tuition and fees vary according to program. *Financial support:* In 2006–07, 83 students received support. Applicants required to submit FAFSA. *Faculty research:* Cultural competence, educational outcomes, HIV Aids. *Unit head:* Dr. Linda G. Allison, Professor and Chair of Department of Physician Assistant Studies, 315-445-4745, Fax: 315-445-4602, E-mail: allisolg@lemoyne.edu. *Application contact:* Kristen P. Trapasso, Director of Graduate Admission, 315-445-4265, Fax: 315-445-6027, E-mail: trapaskp@lemoyne.edu.

Lock Haven University of Pennsylvania, Office of Graduate Studies, Department of Health Science, Lock Haven, PA 17745-2390. Offers physician assistant in rural primary care (MHS). *Accreditation:* ARC-PA. *Entrance requirements:* For master's, minimum undergraduate GPA of 3.0. Additional exam requirements/recommendations for international students: Required—TOEFL. Electronic applications accepted.

Loma Linda University, School of Allied Health Professions, Department of Physician Assistant, Loma Linda, CA 92350. Offers MS. *Accreditation:* ARC-PA.

Marietta College, Program in Physician Assistant Studies, Marietta, OH 45750-4000. Offers MS. *Accreditation:* ARC-PA. *Faculty:* 3 full-time (2 women), 1 part-time/adjunct (0 women). *Students:* 43 full-time (28 women), 1 (woman) part-time. Average age 25. *Unit head:* Dr. Gloria M. Stewart, Director, 740-370-4458.

Marquette University, Graduate School, College of Health Sciences, Department of Physician Assistant Studies, Milwaukee, WI 53201-1881. Offers MS. Students enter the program as undergraduates. *Accreditation:* ARC-PA. *Faculty:* 6 full-time (3 women), 1 (woman) part-time/adjunct. *Students:* 51 full-time (39 women), 2 part-time (both women); includes 5 minority (1 African American, 1 Asian American or Pacific Islander, 3 Hispanic Americans). Average age 28. In 2006, 34 degrees awarded. *Entrance requirements:* Additional exam requirements/recommendations for international students: Required—TOEFL. Application fee: $40. *Financial support:* Application deadline: 2/15. *Unit head:* Timothy Gengembre, Chair, 414-288-5688, Fax: 414-288-7951.

Marywood University, Academic Affairs, College of Health and Human Services, Department of Physician Assistant Studies, Clinical Physician Assistant Track, Scranton, PA 18509-1598. Offers MS. *Expenses:* Tuition: Part-time $672 per credit. Tuition and fees vary according to degree level, campus/location and program. *Unit head:* Dr. Karen E. Arscott, Director, Department of Physician Assistant Studies, 570-348-6298, E-mail: arscott@es.marywood.edu.

Marywood University, Academic Affairs, College of Health and Human Services, Department of Physician Assistant Studies, Physician Assistant Studies Program, Scranton, PA 18509-1598. Offers MS. *Students:* 41 full-time (29 women); includes 3 minority (1 African American, 2 Asian Americans or Pacific Islanders), 1 international. Average age 29. *Expenses:* Tuition: Part-time $672 per credit. Tuition and fees vary according to degree level, campus/location and program. *Unit head:* Dr. Karen E. Arscott, Director, Department of Physician Assistant Studies, 570-348-6298, E-mail: arscott@es.marywood.edu.

Medical College of Georgia, School of Graduate Studies, Department of Physician Assistant, Augusta, GA 30912. Offers MPA, MS. *Accreditation:* ARC-PA. Part-time programs available. *Faculty:* 8 full-time (2 women). *Students:* Average age 35. In 2006, 1 degree awarded. *Degree requirements:* For master's, thesis or alternative. *Entrance requirements:* For master's, GRE General Test. Additional exam requirements/recommendations for international students: Required—TOEFL (minimum score 550 paper-based; 213 computer-based), TWE. *Application deadline:* For fall admission, 10/15 for domestic students. Applications are processed on a rolling basis. Application fee: $30. Electronic applications accepted. *Expenses:* Tuition, state resident: full-time $2,293; part-time $192 per credit hour. Tuition, nonresident: full-time $9,169; part-time $765 per credit hour. Required fees: $293 per semester. *Financial support:* In 2006–07, 1 research assistantship with partial tuition reimbursement (averaging $20,782 per year) was awarded; Federal Work-Study and institutionally sponsored loans also available. Support available to part-time students. Financial award application deadline: 5/31; financial award applicants required to submit FAFSA. *Unit head:* Dr. Bonnie Dadig, Chair/Program Director, 706-721-3246, Fax: 706-721-3990, E-mail: bdadig@mail.mcg.edu.

Medical University of South Carolina, College of Health Professions, Department of Clinical Services, Physician Assistant Program, Charleston, SC 29425-0002. Offers MS. *Accreditation:* ARC-PA. *Faculty:* 6 full-time (2 women), 2 part-time/adjunct (1 woman). *Students:* 113 full-time (93 women), 3 part-time (all women); includes 17 minority (8 African Americans, 1 Asian American or Pacific Islander, 8 Hispanic Americans). Average age 27. 208 applicants, 29% accepted, 59 enrolled. *Degree requirements:* For master's, clinical clerkship, research project. *Entrance requirements:* For master's, GRE General Test, interview, minimum GPA of 3.0, 3 references. Additional exam requirements/recommendations for international students: Required—TOEFL (minimum score 600 paper-based; 250 computer-based). *Application deadline:* For fall admission, 12/1 for domestic and international students. Application fee: $75. Electronic applications accepted. *Financial support:* Federal Work-Study available. Financial award application deadline: 3/15; financial award applicants required to submit FAFSA. *Unit head:* Dr. Reamer L. Bushardt, Program Director, 843-792-9570, Fax: 843-792-0506, E-mail: busharr@musc.edu. *Application contact:* Marguerite Rodgers, Student Services Coordinator, 843-792-3789, Fax: 843-792-0506, E-mail: rodgersm@musc.edu.

Mercy College, Division of Health Professions, Program in Physician Assistant, Dobbs Ferry, NY 10522-1189. Offers MPS, MS. *Accreditation:* ARC-PA. Evening/weekend programs available. *Students:* 62 full-time (54 women), 1 (woman) part-time; includes 12 minority (5 African Americans, 5 Asian Americans or Pacific Islanders, 2 Hispanic Americans), 1 international. Average age 26. In 2006, 24 degrees awarded. *Degree requirements:* For master's, project. *Entrance requirements:* For master's, interview, minimum GPA of 3.0, volunteer experience in community-based or medical service (strongly recommended). Additional exam requirements/recommendations for international students: Required—TOEFL. *Application deadline:* For spring admission, 12/1 for domestic students. Application fee: $62. *Expenses:* Tuition: Part-time $595 per credit. Required fees: $9 per credit. Tuition and fees vary according to program. *Unit head:* Theresa Horvath, Director, 914-674-7635, Fax: 718-239-7831, E-mail: paprogram@mercy.edu. *Application contact:* Kathleen Jackson, Director of Admissions, 800-Mercy-NY, Fax: 914-674-7382, E-mail: admissions@mercy.edu.

Methodist University, School of Graduate Studies, Fayetteville, NC 28311-1498. Offers business administration (MBA); justice administration (MJA); physician assistant studies (MPA).

Midwestern University, Downers Grove Campus, College of Health Sciences, Illinois Campus, Program in Physician Assistant Studies, Downers Grove, IL 60515-1235. Offers MMS. *Accreditation:* ARC-PA. *Faculty:* 9 full-time (6 women), 89 part-time/adjunct (17 women). *Students:* 170 full-time (143 women); includes 15 minority (13 Asian Americans or Pacific Islanders, 2 Hispanic Americans). Average age 26. 552 applicants, 32% accepted, 85 enrolled. In 2006, 51 degrees awarded. *Entrance requirements:* For master's, GRE General Test. *Application deadline:* Applications are processed on a rolling basis. Application fee: $50. *Expenses: Contact institution. Financial support:* In 2006–07, 65 students received support. Federal Work-Study available. *Unit head:* Dr. Lisa Wallace, Director, 630-515-7404. *Application contact:* Michael Laken, Director of Admissions, 630-515-6148, Fax: 630-971-6086, E-mail: admissil@midwestern.edu.

Announcement: Midwestern University is committed to educating the health-care team of the new century. The University administers the Chicago College of Osteopathic Medicine, the Chicago College of Pharmacy, the College of Health Sciences, the Arizona College of Osteopathic Medicine, and the College of Pharmacy–Glendale. The University operates campuses in Downers Grove, Illinois, and in Glendale, Arizona. The Physician Assistant Program offers a 27-month Master of Medical Sciences (MMS) degree in physician assistant studies at both the Downers Grove and Glendale campuses. The program also offers a master's completion track for licensed PAs who already have a bachelor's degree. In addition to comprehensive basic science and clinical experiences, many PA students become involved in community service projects, further enhancing their perspectives on the PA's role in health care. Contact the Office of Admissions, Midwestern University; 800-458-6253 (Downers Grove campus), 888-247-9277 (Glendale campus); e-mail: admissil@midwestern.edu (Downers Grove campus), admissaz@midwestern.edu (Glendale campus); WWW: http://www.midwestern.edu.

Midwestern University, Glendale Campus, College of Health Sciences, Arizona Campus, Program in Physician Assistant Studies, Glendale, AZ 85308. Offers MMS. *Accreditation:* ARC-PA. *Faculty:* 2 part-time/adjunct (0 women). *Students:* 165 full-time (128 women), 2 part-time (1 woman); includes 10 minority (1 African American, 1 Asian American or Pacific Islander, 8 Hispanic Americans). Average age 26. 443 applicants, 35% accepted, 85 enrolled. In 2006, 57 degrees awarded. *Entrance requirements:* For master's, GRE. *Application deadline:* Applications are processed on a rolling basis. Application fee: $50. *Expenses: Contact institution. Financial support:* Applicants required to submit FAFSA. *Unit head:* Kevin Lohenry, Director, 623-572-3611. *Application contact:* James Walters, Director of Admissions, 888-247-9277, Fax: 623-572-3340, E-mail: admissaz@midwestern.edu.

Missouri State University, Graduate College, College of Health and Human Services, Department of Physician Assistant Studies, Springfield, MO 65804-0094. Offers MS. *Accreditation:* ARC-PA. *Faculty:* 2 full-time (0 women), 32 part-time/adjunct (6 women). *Students:* 45 full-time (33 women). Average age 29. 1 applicant, 0% accepted. In 2006, 22 degrees awarded. *Degree requirements:* For master's, thesis or alternative, comprehensive exam. *Entrance requirements:* For master's, GRE General Test, minimum GPA of 3.0. Additional exam requirements/recommendations for international students: Required—TOEFL (minimum score 550 paper-based; 213 computer-based; 79 iBT). *Application deadline:* For spring admission, 7/22 for domestic students. Application fee: $35. *Expenses:* Tuition, state resident: full-time $3,582; part-time $199 per credit hour. Tuition, nonresident: full-time $6,984; part-time $199 per credit hour. Required fees: $548. Full-time tuition and fees vary according to course level, course load, program and reciprocity agreements. *Financial support:* Application deadline: 3/31; *Unit head:* Dr. Steven Dodge, Head, 417-836-6151, Fax: 417-836-6406, E-mail: physicianasststudies@missouristate.edu.

Mountain State University, Graduate Studies, Physician Assistant Program, Beckley, WV 25802-9003. Offers MSPA. Admittance in junior year only. *Accreditation:* ARC-PA. *Faculty:*

Physician Assistant Studies

Mountain State University (continued)
5 full-time (3 women), 16 part-time/adjunct (4 women). *Students:* 86 full-time (57 women), 4 part-time (3 women); includes 5 minority (3 African Americans, 1 American Indian/Alaska Native, 1 Asian American or Pacific Islander), 2 international. Average age 27. 125 applicants, 29% accepted, 36 enrolled. In 2006, 29 degrees awarded. *Median time to degree:* Master's–2 years full-time, 3 years part-time. *Degree requirements:* For master's, thesis or alternative, comprehensive exam. *Entrance requirements:* Additional exam requirements/recommendations for international students: Required—TOEFL (minimum score 550 paper-based; 213 computer-based); Recommended—IELTS (minimum score 7). *Application deadline:* For fall admission, 5/31 priority date for domestic and international students. Applications are processed on a rolling basis. Application fee: $25 ($50 for international students). Electronic applications accepted. *Expenses:* Contact institution. Tuition and fees vary according to course load and program. *Financial support:* In 2006–07, 7 research assistantships (averaging $1,200 per year) were awarded; career-related internships or fieldwork, Federal Work-Study, scholarships/grants, and unspecified assistantships also available. Support available to part-time students. Financial award application deadline: 3/1; financial award applicants required to submit FAFSA. *Unit head:* Dr. Patsy Haslam, Dean of School of Health Science, 304-929-1327, Fax: 304-256-5571, E-mail: phaslam@mountainstate.edu. *Application contact:* Debra Campbell, Graduate Program Director for Masters Physician Assistant, 304-929-1451, Fax: 304-256-5571, E-mail: bcampbell@mountainside.edu.

See Close-Up on page 1711.

New York Institute of Technology, Graduate Division, School of Allied Health and Life Sciences, Program in Physician Assistant, Old Westbury, NY 11568-8000. Offers MS. *Accreditation:* ARC-PA. *Students:* 53 full-time (43 women); includes 6 minority (1 African American, 1 Asian American or Pacific Islander, 4 Hispanic Americans). 70 applicants, 51% accepted, 16 enrolled. *Degree requirements:* For master's, thesis. *Entrance requirements:* For master's, minimum GPA of 3.0, interview, 100 hours of volunteer work, 2 letters of recommendation. Additional exam requirements/recommendations for international students: Required—TOEFL (minimum score 550 paper-based; 213 computer-based). *Application deadline:* For fall admission, 7/1 priority date for domestic students; for spring admission, 12/1 priority date for domestic students. Application fee: $50. *Expenses:* Tuition: Full-time $16,800; part-time $700 per credit. *Financial support:* Research assistantships with partial tuition reimbursements available. Financial award applicants required to submit FAFSA. *Unit head:* Salvatori Barese, Chair, 516-686-3804, E-mail: sbarese@nyit.edu. *Application contact:* Jacquelyn Nealon, Dean of Admissions and Financial Aid, 516-686-7925, Fax: 516-686-7613, E-mail: jnealon@nyit.edu.

Northeastern University, Bouvé College of Health Sciences Graduate School, School of Health Professions, Physician Assistant Program, Boston, MA 02115-5096. Offers MS. *Accreditation:* ARC-PA. *Faculty:* 3 full-time (2 women), 138 part-time/adjunct (54 women). *Students:* 69 full-time (50 women); includes 8 minority (1 African American, 1 American Indian/Alaska Native, 5 Asian Americans or Pacific Islanders, 1 Hispanic American). Average age 26. 220 applicants, 19% accepted, 34 enrolled. In 2006, 31 degrees awarded. *Degree requirements:* For master's, registration. *Entrance requirements:* For master's, minimum undergraduate GPA of 3.0; 2 semesters of biology in addition to 1 lab; 2 semesters of chemistry in addition to 1 lab; coursework in anatomy, physiology, and statistics with minimum B average in each; 2,000 hours of hands-on patient care experience. Additional exam requirements/recommendations for international students: Required—TOEFL (minimum score 600 paper-based; 250 computer-based; 100 iBT). *Application deadline:* For fall admission, 11/1 for domestic students. Application fee: $50. *Expenses:* Contact institution. *Financial support:* In 2006–07, 63 students received support. Federal Work-Study and institutionally sponsored loans available. Financial award application deadline: 3/1; financial award applicants required to submit FAFSA. *Faculty research:* Education and training, reimbursement. *Unit head:* Dr. Rosann M Ippolito, Program Director, 617-373-3195, E-mail: r.ippolito@neu.edu. *Application contact:* Carol G. Goldberg, Director of PA Program Admissions, 617-373-3195, E-mail: c.goldberg@neu.edu.

Nova Southeastern University, Health Professions Division, College of Allied Health and Nursing, Department of Physician Assistant Studies, Fort Lauderdale, FL 33314-7796. Offers medical science/physician assistant (MMS). Students enter program as undergraduates. *Accreditation:* ARC-PA. *Faculty:* 15 full-time (4 women), 1 part-time/adjunct (0 women). *Students:* 252 full-time (199 women), 4 part-time (all women); includes 57 minority (10 African Americans, 3 American Indian/Alaska Native, 12 Asian Americans or Pacific Islanders, 32 Hispanic Americans). 764 applicants, 17% accepted, 90 enrolled. In 2006, 88 degrees awarded. *Entrance requirements:* For master's, GRE, minimum GPA of 2.9. *Application deadline:* Applications are processed on a rolling basis. Application fee: $170. Electronic applications accepted. *Expenses:* Contact institution. *Financial support:* In 2006–07, 85 students received support. *Unit head:* Bill Marquardt, Chair and Program Director, 954-262-1252, E-mail: marquard@nsu.nova.edu. *Application contact:* Judy Dickman, Admissions Counselor, 954-262-1109, E-mail: dickman@nsu.nova.edu.

Pacific University, School of Physician Assistant Studies, Forest Grove, OR 97116-1797. Offers MHS, MS. *Accreditation:* ARC-PA. *Faculty:* 8 full-time (4 women), 2 part-time/adjunct (0 women). *Students:* 82 full-time (53 women), 4 part-time (1 woman); includes 11 minority (4 African Americans, 2 Asian Americans or Pacific Islanders, 5 Hispanic Americans). Average age 31. 542 applicants, 12% accepted, 42 enrolled. In 2006, 44 degrees awarded. *Degree requirements:* For master's, thesis, clinical grad project, comprehensive exam. *Entrance requirements:* For master's, minimum of 1000 hours of direct clinical patient care, prerequisite coursework with a C grade or higher minimum science. Additional exam requirements/recommendations for international students: Required—TOEFL (minimum score 600 paper-based; 105 computer-based). *Application deadline:* For fall admission, 10/20 for domestic and international students. Application fee: $55. *Expenses:* Contact institution. *Financial support:* In 2006–07, 80 students received support; fellowships, research assistantships, teaching assistantships, career-related internships or fieldwork and Federal Work-Study available. Financial award applicants required to submit FAFSA. *Faculty research:* International clinical education, evidence based medicine impact of discrimination on health. *Unit head:* Randy Randolph, Director, 503-352-2898, Fax: 503-359-2977, E-mail: pa@pacificu.edu. *Application contact:* Stephanie Krusemark, Assistant Director of Graduate and Professional Admissions, 503-352-2900, Fax: 503-352-2975, E-mail: admissions@pacificu.edu.

Philadelphia College of Osteopathic Medicine, Graduate and Professional Programs, Physician Assistant Program, Philadelphia, PA 19131-1694. Offers health sciences (MS). *Accreditation:* ARC-PA. *Faculty:* 7 full-time (4 women), 42 part-time/adjunct (12 women). *Students:* 114 full-time (93 women); includes 28 minority (6 African Americans, 17 Asian Americans or Pacific Islanders, 5 Hispanic Americans). Average age 26. 773 applicants, 10% accepted, 54 enrolled. In 2006, 45 degrees awarded. *Degree requirements:* For master's, thesis, registration. *Entrance requirements:* For master's, minimum GPA of 3.0; course work in biology, chemistry, health science, math, social science; 200 hours patient contact. *Application deadline:* For fall admission, 12/1 for domestic students. *Unit head:* Dr. John M. Cavenagh, Chair, 215-871-6772, Fax: 215-871-6702, E-mail: johnca@pcom.edu. *Application contact:* Carol A. Fox, Associate Vice President for Enrollment Management, 215-871-6700, Fax: 215-871-6719, E-mail: carolf@pcom.edu.

See Close-Up on page 1719.

Philadelphia University, School of Science and Health, Program in Physician Assistant Studies, Philadelphia, PA 19144-5497. Offers MS. *Accreditation:* ARC-PA. *Faculty:* 7 full-time (3 women). *Students:* 50 full-time (44 women), 1 (woman) part-time. 484 applicants, 24% accepted, 35 enrolled. *Entrance requirements:* For master's, MCAT, GRE, or MAT. Additional exam requirements/recommendations for international students: Required—TOEFL (minimum score 550 paper-based; 213 computer-based; 79 iBT). *Application deadline:* For fall admission, 12/15 for domestic students. Application fee: $35. *Financial support:* Career-related internships or fieldwork, Federal Work-Study, and unspecified assistantships available. Financial award applicants required to submit FAFSA. *Unit head:* Michael Rackover, Director, 215-951-2908, Fax: 215-951-2526, E-mail: rackoverm@philau.edu. *Application contact:* Jack A. Klett, Director of Graduate Admissions, 215-951-2943, Fax: 215-951-2907, E-mail: gradadm@philau.edu.

Quinnipiac University, School of Health Sciences, Program for Pathologists' Assistant, Hamden, CT 06518-1940. Offers MHS. *Accreditation:* NAACLS. *Faculty:* 2 full-time (0 women), 3 part-time/adjunct (0 women). *Students:* 35 full-time (24 women); includes 7 minority (1 African American, 4 Asian Americans or Pacific Islanders, 2 Hispanic Americans), 4 international. Average age 28. 78 applicants, 24% accepted, 18 enrolled. In 2006, 17 degrees awarded. *Degree requirements:* For master's, residency. *Entrance requirements:* For master's, interview, BS in biomedical science, minimum GPA of 2.8. Additional exam requirements/recommendations for international students: Required—TOEFL (minimum score 575 paper-based; 233 computer-based; 90 iBT), IELTS (minimum score 7). *Application deadline:* For fall admission, 1/15 for domestic students. Applications are processed on a rolling basis. Application fee: $45. Electronic applications accepted. *Expenses:* Tuition: Part-time $675 per credit. Required fees: $30 per credit. *Financial support:* Career-related internships or fieldwork, tuition waivers (partial), and unspecified assistantships available. Financial award application deadline: 4/15; financial award applicants required to submit FAFSA. *Unit head:* Dr. Kenneth Kaloustian, Director, 203-582-8676, Fax: 203-582-3443, E-mail: ken.kaloustian@quinnipiac.edu. *Application contact:* 800-462-1944, Fax: 203-582-3443, E-mail: graduate@quinnipiac.edu.

See Close-Up on page 1721.

Quinnipiac University, School of Health Sciences, Program for Physician Assistant, Hamden, CT 06518-1940. Offers MHS. *Accreditation:* ARC-PA. *Faculty:* 8 full-time (5 women), 7 part-time/adjunct (3 women). *Students:* 98 full-time (70 women); includes 9 minority (1 American Indian/Alaska Native, 5 Asian Americans or Pacific Islanders, 3 Hispanic Americans). Average age 27. 405 applicants, 19% accepted, 51 enrolled. In 2006, 52 degrees awarded. *Median time to degree:* Master's–2 years full-time. *Degree requirements:* For master's, comprehensive exam. *Entrance requirements:* For master's, minimum GPA of 3.0; course work in biological, physical, and behavioral sciences; interviews; 2000 hours direct patient care experience. *Application deadline:* For fall admission, 10/15 for domestic students. Application fee: $45. *Expenses:* Tuition: Part-time $675 per credit. Required fees: $30 per credit. *Financial support:* Career-related internships or fieldwork, tuition waivers (partial), and unspecified assistantships available. Financial award application deadline: 4/15; financial award applicants required to submit FAFSA. *Unit head:* Cynthia Booth-Lord, Director, 203-582-5297, Fax: 203-582-8706, E-mail: cynthia.lord@quinnipiac.edu. *Application contact:* Scott Farber, E-mail: graduate@quinnipiac.edu.

See Close-Up on page 1721.

Regis University, Rueckert-Hartman School for Health Professions, Denver, CO 80221-1099. Offers clinical leadership for physician assistants (MS); health services administration (MS); nursing (MSN); physical therapy (DPT, TDPT). *Faculty:* 3 full-time (all women), 7 part-time/adjunct (4 women). *Students:* 453. In 2006, 55 degrees awarded. *Application deadline:* Applications are processed on a rolling basis. *Expenses:* Contact institution. *Financial support:* Career-related internships or fieldwork and Federal Work-Study available. *Faculty research:* Normal and pathological balance and gait research, normal/pathological upper limb motor control/biomechanics, exercise energy/metabolism research, optical treatment protocols for therapeutic modalities. *Unit head:* Dr. Patricia Ladewig, Academic Dean, 303-458-4174, E-mail: pladewig@regis.edu. *Application contact:* Donna Eastman, Assistant to the Dean, 303-458-4174, Fax: 303-964-5533, E-mail: deastman@regis.edu.

Rosalind Franklin University of Medicine and Science, College of Health Professions, Department of Physician Assistant, North Chicago, IL 60064-3095. Offers MS. *Accreditation:* ARC-PA. *Degree requirements:* For master's, thesis. *Entrance requirements:* For master's, Critical Thinking Exam, GRE, writing sample. Electronic applications accepted. *Faculty research:* Problem-based learning, testing in interview for future success, learning by case review via computer.

Saint Francis University, Department of Physician Assistant Sciences, Loretto, PA 15940-0600. Offers health science (MHS); medical science (MMS); physician assistant sciences (MPAS). *Accreditation:* ARC-PA. *Faculty:* 10 full-time (8 women), 3 part-time/adjunct (0 women). *Students:* 109 full-time (78 women), 2 part-time (1 woman); includes 9 minority (3 African Americans, 6 Asian Americans or Pacific Islanders). Average age 25. 403 applicants, 16% accepted, 26 enrolled. In 2006, 50 degrees awarded. *Entrance requirements:* For master's, interview. Additional exam requirements/recommendations for international students: Required—TOEFL. *Application deadline:* For fall admission, 11/1 for domestic and international students. Applications are processed on a rolling basis. Application fee: $160. Electronic applications accepted. *Expenses:* Tuition: Part-time $661 per credit. Tuition and fees vary according to program. *Financial support:* Applicants required to submit FAFSA. *Unit head:* Donna L. Yeisley, Chair, 814-472-3130, Fax: 814-472-3137, E-mail: dyeisley@francis.edu. *Application contact:* Marie S. Link, Director of Research, 814-472-3138, Fax: 814-472-3137, E-mail: mslpa1@mail.francis.edu.

Saint Louis University, Graduate School, Doisy College of Health Sciences, Department of Physician Assistant Education, St. Louis, MO 63103-2097. Offers MMS. *Accreditation:* ARC-PA. Part-time programs available. *Faculty:* 5 full-time (all women), 6 part-time/adjunct (4 women). *Students:* 68 full-time (56 women); includes 6 minority (1 African American, 1 American Indian/Alaska Native, 4 Asian Americans or Pacific Islanders). Average age 26. 608 applicants, 6% accepted, 34 enrolled. In 2006, 30 degrees awarded. *Entrance requirements:* Additional exam requirements/recommendations for international students: Required—TOEFL (minimum score 525 paper-based; 194 computer-based). *Application deadline:* For fall admission, 12/1 for domestic and international students. Applications are processed on a rolling basis. Application fee: $40. Electronic applications accepted. *Expenses:* Tuition: Part-time $800 per credit hour. Required fees: $105 per semester. *Financial support:* In 2006–07, 3 students received support. Federal Work-Study, scholarships/grants, traineeships, and unspecified assistantships available. Support available to part-time students. Financial award application deadline: 6/1; financial award applicants required to submit FAFSA. *Faculty research:* Professionalism, evidence based teaching and practice, inter-rater reliability of evaluation process, use of standardized simulated patients in clinical training. Total annual research expenditures: $5,000. *Unit head:* Dr. Dana Sayre-Stanhope, Chairperson, 314-977-8521, Fax: 314-977-8649, E-mail: sayreds@slu.edu.

Samuel Merritt College, Department of Physician Assistant Studies, Oakland, CA 94609-3108. Offers MPA. *Accreditation:* ARC-PA. *Entrance requirements:* For master's, health care experience, minimum GPA of 3.0, previous course work in statistics.

Seton Hall University, School of Graduate Medical Education, Physician Assistant Program, South Orange, NJ 07079-2697. Offers MS. *Accreditation:* ARC-PA. *Faculty:* 5 full-time (2 women), 25 part-time/adjunct (4 women). *Students:* 77 full-time (64 women); includes 20 minority (3 African Americans, 1 American Indian/Alaska Native, 13 Asian Americans or Pacific Islanders, 3 Hispanic Americans). Average age 26. 85 applicants, 49% accepted, 30 enrolled. In 2006, 22 degrees awarded. *Median time to degree:* Master's–3 years full-time. *Entrance requirements:* For master's, GRE, health care experience, interview, minimum GPA of 3.0. Additional exam requirements/recommendations for international students: Required—TOEFL. *Application deadline:* For fall admission, 11/15 priority date for domestic students; for winter admission, 4/15 for domestic students. Applications are processed on a rolling basis. Application fee: $75. Electronic applications accepted. *Financial support:* In 2006–07, 2 teaching assistantships with partial tuition reimbursements (averaging $1,000 per year) were awarded; Federal Work-Study, institutionally sponsored loans, scholarships/grants, and unspecified assistantships also available. *Unit head:* Prof. Joseph L. Monaco, Interim Program Director,

973-275-2596, Fax: 973-275-2370, E-mail: gradmeded@shu.edu. *Application contact:* Deborah Ann Verderosa, Office of Graduate Medical Education, 973-275-2062, Fax: 973-275-2370, E-mail: gradmeded@shu.edu.

See Close-Up on page 1729.

Seton Hill University, Program in Physician Assistant, Greensburg, PA 15601. Offers MS. *Accreditation:* ARC-PA. *Faculty:* 5 full-time (3 women), 6 part-time/adjunct (3 women). *Students:* 22 full-time (18 women); includes 5 minority (2 African Americans, 2 American Indian/Alaska Native, 1 Asian American or Pacific Islander). Average age 29. 285 applicants, 12% accepted, 22 enrolled. In 2006, 18 degrees awarded. *Entrance requirements:* For master's, minimum GPA of 3.0, 23 credits of prerequisite coursework, 350 hours of experience in healthcare setting, interview. Additional exam requirements/recommendations for international students: Required—TOEFL (minimum score 600 paper-based; 250 computer-based). *Application deadline:* For spring admission, 3/1 for domestic and international students. Application fee: $110. Electronic applications accepted. *Expenses: Contact institution. Financial support:* Application deadline: 8/15; *Faculty research:* Underserved populations, women's health, healthcare for elderly. *Unit head:* Cathy Shallenberger, Director, 724-838-2455, Fax: 724-838-7843, E-mail: shallenberger@setonhill.edu. *Application contact:* Christine Schaeffer, Director of Graduate and Adult Studies, 724-838-4283, Fax: 724-830-1891, E-mail: schaeffer@setonhill.edu.

Shenandoah University, School of Health Professions, Division of Physician Assistant Studies, Winchester, VA 22601-5195. Offers MS. *Accreditation:* ARC-PA. *Faculty:* 5 full-time (2 women). *Students:* 94 full-time (82 women), 2 part-time (both women); includes 1 minority (Asian American or Pacific Islander) Average age 28. 332 applicants, 19% accepted, 37 enrolled. In 2006, 23 degrees awarded. *Degree requirements:* For master's, project. *Entrance requirements:* For master's, GRE General Test, minimum GPA of 3.0, 3 letters of reference, medical terminology proficiency. Additional exam requirements/recommendations for international students: Required—TOEFL (minimum score 527 paper-based; 197 computer-based; 71 iBT). *Application deadline:* For fall admission, 2/1 for domestic students. Applications are processed on a rolling basis. Application fee: $30. Electronic applications accepted. *Expenses: Contact institution.* Full-time tuition and fees vary according to course load and program. *Financial support:* In 2006–07, 68 students received support. Institutionally sponsored loans and scholarships/grants available. Support available to part-time students. Financial award application deadline: 3/15; financial award applicants required to submit FAFSA. *Faculty research:* Educational outcomes, women's health, epidemiology professional leadership. Total annual research expenditures: $84,000. *Unit head:* Anthony A. Miller, Director, 540-545-7257, Fax: 540-542-6210, E-mail: amiller@su.edu. *Application contact:* David Anthony, Dean of Admissions, 540-665-4581, Fax: 540-665-4627, E-mail: admit@su.edu.

South University, Graduate Programs, School of Health Professions, Program in Physician Assistant Studies, Savannah, GA 31406-4805. Offers MS. *Accreditation:* ARC-PA. *Entrance requirements:* For master's, GRE General Test, minimum GPA of 2.6 overall, 3.0 in science courses; 3 letters of reference; minimum of 32 credit hours of science. Additional exam requirements/recommendations for international students: Required—TOEFL (minimum score 600 paper-based; 250 computer-based).

See Close-Up on page 1737.

Springfield College, Graduate Programs, Program in Physician Assistant Studies, Springfield, MA 01109-3797. Offers MS. *Accreditation:* ARC-PA. *Faculty:* 4 full-time (2 women), 100 part-time/adjunct. *Students:* 36 full-time. Average age 28. 45 applicants, 2% accepted, 1 enrolled. In 2006, 25 degrees awarded. *Entrance requirements:* Additional exam requirements/recommendations for international students: Required—TOEFL (minimum score 550 paper-based; 213 computer-based). *Application deadline:* For spring admission, 6/15 for domestic and international students. Application fee: $50. Electronic applications accepted. *Expenses:* Tuition: Full-time $12,222; part-time $679 per credit. Required fees: $25; $25 per year. One-time fee: $25 full-time. *Financial support:* Federal Work-Study and scholarships/grants available. Financial award application deadline: 3/1; financial award applicants required to submit FAFSA. *Unit head:* Dr. Jennifer Hixon, Director, 413-748-3541, Fax: 413-748-3595, E-mail: jhixon@spfldcol.edu.

Texas Tech University Health Sciences Center, School of Allied Health Sciences, Program in Physician Assistant Studies, Lubbock, TX 79430. Offers MPAS. *Accreditation:* ARC-PA. *Faculty:* 6 full-time (2 women). *Students:* 93 full-time (67 women); includes 27 minority (1 African American, 1 American Indian/Alaska Native, 10 Asian Americans or Pacific Islanders, 15 Hispanic Americans). Average age 28. 665 applicants, 8% accepted, 52 enrolled. In 2006, 40 degrees awarded. *Entrance requirements:* Additional exam requirements/recommendations for international students: Required—TOEFL. *Application deadline:* For fall admission, 12/1 for domestic students. Application fee: $35. Electronic applications accepted. *Financial support:* Career-related internships or fieldwork, institutionally sponsored loans, and scholarships/grants available. Financial award applicants required to submit FAFSA. *Unit head:* Dr. Hal Larsen, Chair, 806-743-3223, E-mail: hal.larsen@ttuhsc.edu. *Application contact:* Jeri Moravcik, Assistant Director of Admissions and Student Affairs, 806-743-3220, Fax: 806-743-2994, E-mail: jeri.moravcik@ttuhsc.edu.

Touro University College of Osteopathic Medicine, Professional Program, Vallejo, CA 94592. Offers education (MA); osteopathic medicine (DO); pharmacy (Pharm D); physician assistant studies (MS); public health (MPH). *Accreditation:* AOsA; ARC-PA. *Faculty:* 61 full-time (26 women), 30 part-time/adjunct (16 women). *Students:* 950 full-time (579 women); includes 354 minority (39 African Americans, 5 American Indian/Alaska Native, 258 Asian Americans or Pacific Islanders, 52 Hispanic Americans). Average age 26. 2,113 applicants, 13% accepted, 269 enrolled. In 2006, 109 first professional degrees, 43 master's awarded. *Median time to degree:* Of those who began their doctoral program in fall 1998, 98% received their degree in 8 years or less. *Entrance requirements:* For first professional degree and master's, BS/BA. *Application deadline:* For fall admission, 6/1 for domestic students. Applications are processed on a rolling basis. Application fee: $100. Electronic applications accepted. *Financial support:* In 2006–07, 3 fellowships (averaging $3,000 per year) were awarded. *Faculty research:* Diabetes, heart disease. *Application contact:* Steve Davis, Admissions Counselor, 707-638-5527, Fax: 707-638-5270, E-mail: sdavis@touro.edu.

Towson University, Graduate School, Program in Physician Assistant Studies, Towson, MD 21252-0001. Offers MS. *Accreditation:* ARC-PA. *Faculty:* 4 full-time (2 women), 6 part-time/adjunct (0 women). *Students:* 60 full-time (44 women); includes 6 minority (1 African American, 2 Asian Americans or Pacific Islanders, 3 Hispanic Americans). 1 applicant, 0% accepted. In 2006, 33 degrees awarded. *Entrance requirements:* Additional exam requirements/recommendations for international students: Required—TOEFL. Application fee: $50. *Expenses: Contact institution. Financial support:* Application deadline: 4/1; *Unit head:* Marcie Weinstein, Graduate Program Director, 410-704-4049, E-mail: mweinstein@towson.edu. *Application contact:* Central Application Service for Physician Assistants, 240-497-1895.

Trevecca Nazarene University, Graduate Division, Division of Natural and Applied Sciences, Major in Physician Assistant, Nashville, TN 37210-2877. Offers MS. *Accreditation:* ARC-PA. *Faculty:* 6 full-time (3 women), 6 part-time/adjunct (4 women). *Students:* 66 full-time (49 women); includes 1 minority (African American) Average age 26. In 2006, 32 degrees awarded. *Degree requirements:* For master's, professional assessment, qualifying exam. *Entrance requirements:* For master's, GRE General Test, health care experience, minimum GPA of 3.25, 3 letters of recommendation, reference. Additional exam requirements/recommendations for international students: Required—TOEFL (minimum score 500 paper-based; 173 computer-based). *Application deadline:* For fall admission, 11/1 for domestic students. Application fee: $45. *Expenses: Contact institution.* Tuition and fees vary according to degree level and program. *Financial support:* Applicants required to submit FAFSA. *Application contact:* Admissions Coordinator, 615-248-1621, Fax: 615-248-1622, E-mail: admissions_pa@trevecca.edu.

Union College, Program in Physician Assistant Studies, Lincoln, NE 68506-4300. Offers MPAS. *Accreditation:* ARC-PA.

The University of Alabama at Birmingham, School of Health Professions, Department of Critical Care, Physician Assistant Studies, Birmingham, AL 35294. Offers MS. *Accreditation:* ARC-PA. *Students:* 61 full-time (43 women); includes 10 minority (4 African Americans, 1 American Indian/Alaska Native, 3 Asian Americans or Pacific Islanders, 2 Hispanic Americans). 31 applicants, 100% accepted. *Expenses:* Tuition, state resident: part-time $170 per credit hour. Tuition, nonresident: part-time $425 per credit hour. Required fees: $15 per credit hour. $122 per term. Tuition and fees vary according to program. *Unit head:* Dr. Edward D. Huechtker, Chair, Department of Critical Care, 205-934-4605.

University of Colorado at Denver and Health Sciences Center, School of Medicine, Child Health Associate/Physician Assistant Program, Denver, CO 80217-3364. Offers pediatrics (MPAS). *Accreditation:* ARC-PA. *Students:* 79 full-time (63 women); includes 5 minority (4 Asian Americans or Pacific Islanders, 1 Hispanic American). Average age 28. 135 applicants, 30% accepted, 35 enrolled. In 2006, 22 degrees awarded. *Entrance requirements:* For master's, GRE General Test, minimum GPA of 2.8, 3 letters of recommendation. Additional exam requirements/recommendations for international students: Required—TOEFL (minimum score 550 paper-based; 213 computer-based). *Application deadline:* For fall admission, 10/15 for domestic students. Application fee: $85. *Expenses: Contact institution. Financial support:* Career-related internships or fieldwork, Federal Work-Study, and institutionally sponsored loans available. Support available to part-time students. Financial award application deadline: 3/15; financial award applicants required to submit FAFSA. *Unit head:* Dr. Anita Glicken, Interim Director, 303-315-7963. *Application contact:* Janice Chapman, Admissions and Course Support, 303-724-1340, E-mail: chapa-info@uchsc.edu.

University of Detroit Mercy, College of Health Professions, Physician Assistant Program, Detroit, MI 48221. Offers MS. *Accreditation:* ARC-PA. *Degree requirements:* For master's, thesis or alternative. *Entrance requirements:* For master's, GRE General Test, minimum GPA of 3.0. Expenses: Contact institution. *Faculty research:* Substance abuse prevention, international health care, public health.

University of Florida, College of Medicine, Program in Physician Assistant, Gainesville, FL 32611. Offers MPAS. *Accreditation:* ARC-PA. *Faculty:* 3 full-time (1 woman). *Students:* 120 full-time (81 women); includes 28 minority (7 African Americans, 4 Asian Americans or Pacific Islanders, 17 Hispanic Americans). Average age 28. 581 applicants, 14% accepted, 60 enrolled. In 2006, 60 degrees awarded. *Entrance requirements:* For master's, GRE General Test, interview. *Application deadline:* For fall admission, 10/1 for domestic students. Application fee: $30. Electronic applications accepted. *Expenses:* Tuition, state resident: full-time $6,827. Tuition, nonresident: full-time $21,951. Required fees: $999. *Financial support:* In 2006–07, 102 students received support. Scholarships/grants available. Financial award application deadline: 4/1; financial award applicants required to submit FAFSA. *Unit head:* Wayne D. Bottom, Assistant Dean/Director, 352-265-7955, Fax: 352-265-7996, E-mail: bottow@medicine.ufl.edu. *Application contact:* Joan C. Crisman, Admissions Adviser, 352-265-7955, Fax: 352-265-7996, E-mail: crismj@medicine.ufl.edu.

The University of Iowa, Roy J. and Lucille A. Carver College of Medicine and Graduate College, Graduate Programs in Medicine, Program in Physician Assistant, Iowa City, IA 52242-1316. Offers MPAS. *Accreditation:* ARC-PA. *Faculty:* 4 full-time (1 woman). *Students:* 50 full-time (36 women); includes 5 minority (1 African American, 2 Asian Americans or Pacific Islanders, 2 Hispanic Americans). Average age 25. 367 applicants, 7% accepted, 25 enrolled. In 2006, 23 degrees awarded. *Degree requirements:* For master's, comprehensive clinical exam. *Entrance requirements:* For master's, GRE General Test, health care/research experience. *Application deadline:* For spring admission, 11/15 for domestic students. Applications are processed on a rolling basis. Application fee: $60. Electronic applications accepted. *Financial support:* In 2006–07, 43 students received support. Institutionally sponsored loans and scholarships/grants available. Financial award application deadline: 3/1; financial award applicants required to submit FAFSA. *Unit head:* Dr. David P. Asprey, Director, 319-335-8922, Fax: 319-335-8923, E-mail: david-asprey@uiowa.edu. *Application contact:* Janet L. Steenlage, Program Assistant, 319-353-5956, Fax: 319-335-8923, E-mail: janet-steenlage@uiowa.edu.

University of Kentucky, Graduate School, College of Health Sciences, Program in Physician Assistant Studies, Lexington, KY 40506-0032. Offers MSPAS. *Accreditation:* ARC-PA. *Faculty:* 18 full-time (9 women), 2 part-time/adjunct (1 woman). *Students:* 106 full-time (88 women), 1 (woman) part-time; includes 3 minority (2 African Americans, 1 Asian American or Pacific Islander). Average age 28. 2 applicants, 50% accepted, 1 enrolled. In 2006, 57 degrees awarded. *Degree requirements:* For master's, comprehensive exam. *Entrance requirements:* For master's, GRE General test, minimum undergraduate GPA of 2.75. Additional exam requirements/recommendations for international students: Required—TOEFL (minimum score 550 paper-based; 213 computer-based). *Application deadline:* For fall admission, 7/17 priority date for domestic students, 2/1 priority date for international students; for spring admission, 12/13 priority date for domestic students, 6/15 priority date for international students. Application fee: $40 ($55 for international students). Electronic applications accepted. *Expenses:* Tuition, state resident: full-time $7,670; part-time $401 per credit hour. Tuition, nonresident: full-time $16,158; part-time $873 per credit hour. *Financial support:* In 2006–07, 1 student received support, including 1 fellowship with full tuition reimbursement available; research assistantships with full tuition reimbursements available, teaching assistantships with full tuition reimbursements available, Federal Work-Study, scholarships/grants, traineeships, health care benefits, tuition waivers (partial), and unspecified assistantships also available. Support available to part-time students. Financial award application deadline: 3/15; financial award applicants required to submit FAFSA. *Unit head:* Dr. Gerry A. Gairola, Director of Graduate Studies, 859-323-1100, Fax: 859-257-2454, E-mail: gagair01@pop.uky.edu. *Application contact:* Dr. Brian Jackson, Senior Associate Dean, 859-257-4667, Fax: 859-257-4676, E-mail: brian.jackson@uky.edu.

University of Medicine and Dentistry of New Jersey, School of Health Related Professions, Department of Primary Care, Physician Assistant Program–Piscataway, Piscataway, NJ 08854-5635. Offers MS. *Accreditation:* ARC-PA. *Degree requirements:* For master's, internship. *Entrance requirements:* For master's, interview, minimum GPA of 3.0. Additional exam requirements/recommendations for international students: Required—TOEFL. *Application deadline:* For fall admission, 3/15 for domestic students; for spring admission, 11/1 for domestic students. Applications are processed on a rolling basis. Application fee: $50. Electronic applications accepted. *Unit head:* Ruth Fixelle, Director, 732-235-4444, E-mail: fixellru@umdnj.edu. *Application contact:* Information Contact, 732-235-4444, Fax: 732-235-4820.

University of Nebraska Medical Center, School of Allied Health Professions, Division of Physician Assistant Education, Omaha, NE 68198. Offers MPAS. *Accreditation:* ARC-PA. *Faculty:* 5 full-time (1 woman), 300 part-time/adjunct (75 women). *Students:* 118 full-time (99 women); includes 3 minority (1 African American, 1 Asian American or Pacific Islander, 1 Hispanic American). Average age 25. 282 applicants, 16% accepted, 40 enrolled. In 2006, 40 degrees awarded. *Degree requirements:* For master's, research paper. *Entrance requirements:* For master's, GRE General Test, 16 undergraduate hours of course work in both biology and chemistry, 3 undergraduate hours of course work in math, 6 undergraduate hours of course work in English, 9 undergraduate hours of course work in psychology, minimum GPA of 2.8. Additional exam requirements/recommendations for international students: Required—TOEFL (minimum score 600 paper-based; 250 computer-based). *Application deadline:* For fall admission, 11/1 for domestic students. Application fee: $120. *Financial support:* In 2006–07, 114 students received support. Institutionally sponsored loans and scholarships/grants available. Financial award applicants required to submit FAFSA. *Faculty research:* Substance abuse, mental health, women's health, geriatrics. *Unit head:* Dr. James E. Somers, Director, 402-559-9495. *Application contact:* Diane K. Landon, Information Contact, 402-559-2232, Fax: 402-559-5356, E-mail: dklandon@unmc.edu.

Physician Assistant Studies

University of New England, College of Health Professions, Program in Physician Assistant, Biddeford, ME 04005-9526. Offers MS. *Accreditation:* ARC-PA. *Faculty:* 6 full-time (3 women), 20 part-time/adjunct (6 women). *Students:* 84 full-time (57 women); includes 6 minority (1 Asian American or Pacific Islander, 5 Hispanic Americans). Average age 30. 494 applicants, 15% accepted, 47 enrolled. In 2006, 48 degrees awarded. *Degree requirements:* For master's, 12 month rotations. *Entrance requirements:* For master's, minimum GPA of 2.5. Additional exam requirements/recommendations for international students: Required—TOEFL. *Application deadline:* For fall admission, 11/1 for domestic students. Applications are processed on a rolling basis. Application fee: $40. *Expenses:* Contact institution. *Financial support:* In 2006–07, 4 students received support. Scholarships/grants available. Financial award application deadline: 5/1; financial award applicants required to submit FAFSA. *Unit head:* Erich Andrew Fogg, Director, 207-797-7688 Ext. 4527, Fax: 207-221-4711, E-mail: efogg@une.edu. *Application contact:* Peggy Warden, Assistant Dean of Graduate Admissions, 207-221-4225, Fax: 207-221-4898, E-mail: admissions@une.edu.

University of North Dakota, School of Medicine and Graduate School, Graduate Programs in Medicine, Physician Assistant Program, Grand Forks, ND 58202. Offers MPAS. *Accreditation:* ARC-PA. *Faculty:* 6 full-time (all women). *Students:* 25 full-time (20 women), 34 part-time (21 women); includes 2 American Indian/Alaska Native, 1 Asian American or Pacific Islander. 31 applicants, 100% accepted, 30 enrolled. In 2006, 23 degrees awarded. *Entrance requirements:* For master's, current RN licensure, minimum of 4 years of clinical experience, current ACLS certification, interview, letters of recommendation. *Application deadline:* For fall admission, 2/15 priority date for domestic students. Application fee: $35. *Expenses:* Tuition, state resident: full-time $5,650; part-time $214 per credit. Tuition, nonresident: full-time $14,248; part-time $572 per credit. Required fees: $1,008; $42 per credit. Tuition and fees vary according to reciprocity agreements. *Unit head:* Prof. Mary Ann Laxon, Director, 701-777-2344. *Application contact:* Brenda Halle, Admissions Specialist, 701-777-2947, Fax: 701-777-3619, E-mail: brendahalle@mail.und.edu.

University of North Texas Health Science Center at Fort Worth, Texas College of Osteopathic Medicine, Program in Physician Assistant Studies, Fort Worth, TX 76107-2699. Offers MPAS. *Accreditation:* ARC-PA. *Degree requirements:* For master's, thesis or alternative, research paper. *Entrance requirements:* For master's, minimum GPA of 2.85. *Faculty research:* Impact of mid-level providers on medical treatment, curriculum development, pain in geriatric patients, biopsychosocial risk factors.

University of St. Francis, College of Nursing and Allied Health, Joliet, IL 60435-6169. Offers nursing (MSN); physician assistant studies (MS). *Accreditation:* AACN. Part-time and evening/weekend programs available. *Faculty:* 10 full-time (8 women), 1 (woman) part-time/adjunct. *Students:* 61 full-time (42 women), 62 part-time (60 women); includes 30 minority (8 African Americans, 1 American Indian/Alaska Native, 8 Asian Americans or Pacific Islanders, 13 Hispanic Americans). Average age 37. 52 applicants, 71% accepted, 22 enrolled. In 2006, 30 degrees awarded. *Degree requirements:* For master's, thesis (for some programs), comprehensive exam (for some programs), registration. *Entrance requirements:* For master's, GRE General Test (MS), minimum GPA of 3.0, 2 years of work experience in clinical nursing, CPR certification, computer competency, 3 letters of recommendation, interview, RN license (MSN); minimum GPA of 2.75, clinical experience (MS). Additional exam requirements/recommendations for international students: Required—TOEFL (minimum score 550 paper-based; 213 computer-based). *Application deadline:* Applications are processed on a rolling basis. Application fee: $30. Electronic applications accepted. *Expenses:* Contact institution. Part-time tuition and fees vary according to campus/location and program. *Financial support:* In 2006–07, 45 students received support. Scholarships/grants, traineeships, tuition waivers (partial), and unspecified assistantships available. Support available to part-time students. Financial award applicants required to submit FAFSA. *Unit head:* Dr. Maria Connolly, Dean, 815-740-3463, Fax: 815-740-4243, E-mail: mconnolly@stfrancis.edu. *Application contact:* Sandra Sloka, Director of Admissions for Graduate and Degree Completion Programs, 800-735-7500, Fax: 815-740-5032, E-mail: ssloka@stfrancis.edu.

University of Saint Francis, Graduate School, Department of Allied Health, Fort Wayne, IN 46808-3994. Offers physician assistant studies (MS). *Accreditation:* ARC-PA. *Faculty:* 5 full-time (3 women), 1 part-time/adjunct (0 women). *Students:* 48 full-time (38 women). Average age 26. In 2006, 6 degrees awarded. *Entrance requirements:* For master's, GRE or MCAT, previous courses in biology, chemistry, and psychology, previous direct patient care. Application fee: $20. *Financial support:* Applicants required to submit FAFSA. *Unit head:* Dr. Nancy Gillespie, Dean, 260-434-3240, Fax: 260-434-7685, E-mail: ngillespie@sf.edu. *Application contact:* James Lashdollar, Admissions Counselor, 260-434-3279, E-mail: jcashdollar@sf.edu.

University of South Alabama, Graduate School, College of Allied Health Professions, Department of Physician Assistant Studies, Mobile, AL 36688-0002. Offers MHS. *Accreditation:* ARC-PA. *Faculty:* 5 full-time (2 women). *Students:* 66 full-time (56 women); includes 1 minority (American Indian/Alaska Native). In 2006, 34 degrees awarded. *Degree requirements:* For master's, externship, thesis optional. *Entrance requirements:* For master's, GRE General Test. *Application deadline:* For fall admission, 9/1 priority date for domestic students. Applications are processed on a rolling basis. Application fee: $25. *Financial support:* Application deadline: 4/1. *Unit head:* Richard Nenstiel, Chair, 251-434-3641, Fax: 251-434-3646.

The University of South Dakota, School of Medicine and Health Sciences and Graduate School, Graduate Programs in Health Sciences, Department of Physician Assistant Studies, Vermillion, SD 57069-2390. Offers MS. *Accreditation:* ARC-PA. *Faculty:* 3 full-time (2 women), 1 part-time/adjunct (0 women). *Students:* 61 full-time (44 women); includes 4 minority (1 African American, 1 American Indian/Alaska Native, 2 Asian Americans or Pacific Islanders). Average age 27. 168 applicants, 12% accepted, 20 enrolled. In 2006, 21 degrees awarded. *Entrance requirements:* Additional exam requirements/recommendations for international students: Required—TOEFL (minimum score 550 paper-based; 213 computer-based). *Application deadline:* For spring admission, 10/1 for domestic and international students. Application fee: $150. Electronic applications accepted. *Expenses:* Contact institution. *Financial support:* In 2006–07, 61 students received support. Scholarships/grants available. Financial award application deadline: 3/15; financial award applicants required to submit FAFSA. *Faculty research:* Neuroscience, teaching techniques in physician assistant education. *Unit head:* Wade A. Nilson, Chair, 605-677-6573, Fax: 605-677-6569, E-mail: wnilson@usd.edu. *Application contact:* Janet Fulk, Program Assistant, 605-677-6719, E-mail: jfulk@usd.edu.

University of Southern California, Keck School of Medicine and Graduate School, Graduate Programs in Medicine, Primary Care Physician Assistant Program, Los Angeles, CA 90089. Offers MPAP. *Accreditation:* ARC-PA. *Faculty:* 4 full-time (3 women), 2 part-time/adjunct (both women). *Students:* 120 full-time (82 women); includes 59 minority (6 African Americans, 25 Asian Americans or Pacific Islanders, 28 Hispanic Americans). Average age 27. 485 applicants, 17% accepted, 35 enrolled. In 2006, 32 degrees awarded. *Degree requirements:* For master's, clinical training. *Entrance requirements:* For master's, GRE or MCAT. Additional exam requirements/recommendations for international students: Required—TOEFL (minimum score 200 computer-based). *Application deadline:* For fall admission, 12/1 for domestic and international students. Applications are processed on a rolling basis. Application fee: $35. *Expenses:* Contact institution. Full-time tuition and fees vary according to program. *Financial support:* In 2006–07, 114 students received support. Institutionally sponsored loans and scholarships/grants available. Financial award application deadline: 2/24; financial award applicants required to submit FAFSA. *Unit head:* Dr. Rosslyn Byous, Program Associate Director, 626-457-4262, Fax: 626-457-4245, E-mail: byous@usc.edu. *Application contact:* Steve Arbuckle, Director of Admission and Student Services, 626-457-4269, Fax: 626-457-4272, E-mail: arbuckle@usc.edu.

The University of Texas Health Science Center at San Antonio, School of Allied Health Sciences, San Antonio, TX 78229-3900. Offers clinical laboratory sciences (MS); dental hygiene (MS); occupational therapy (MOT); physical therapy (MPT); physician assistant studies (MS). *Accreditation:* AOTA; APTA; ARC-PA. *Expenses:* Tuition, state resident: part-time $50 per credit hour. Tuition, nonresident: part-time $325 per credit hour. Required fees: $7.5 per credit hour. $155 per term.

The University of Texas Medical Branch, School of Allied Health Sciences, Department of Physician Assistant Studies, Galveston, TX 77555. Offers MPAS. *Accreditation:* ARC-PA. *Faculty:* 7 full-time (4 women), 27 part-time/adjunct (8 women). *Students:* 105 full-time (89 women), 3 part-time (all women); includes 18 minority (3 African Americans, 4 Asian Americans or Pacific Islanders, 11 Hispanic Americans). Average age 26. In 2006, 46 degrees awarded. *Entrance requirements:* For master's, GRE, interview. Electronic applications accepted. *Financial support:* Applicants required to submit FAFSA. *Unit head:* Dr. Richard Rahr, Chair, 409-772-3047, Fax: 409-772-9710, E-mail: rrahr@utmb.edu. *Application contact:* Karen S. Stephenson, Admissions Coordinator, 409-772-9564, Fax: 409-772-9710, E-mail: kstephen@utmb.edu.

The University of Texas Southwestern Medical Center at Dallas, Southwestern Allied Health Sciences School, Physician Assistant Studies Program, Dallas, TX 75390. Offers MPAS. *Accreditation:* ARC-PA. *Students:* 110 full-time (87 women), 1 part-time; includes 33 minority (5 African Americans, 1 American Indian/Alaska Native, 15 Asian Americans or Pacific Islanders, 12 Hispanic Americans). Average age 27. 567 applicants, 8% accepted, 35 enrolled. In 2006, 32 degrees awarded. *Entrance requirements:* For master's, GRE, minimum GPA of 3.0. *Application deadline:* For spring admission, 10/1 for domestic students. Electronic applications accepted. *Expenses:* Tuition, state resident: part-time $120 per semester hour. Tuition, nonresident: part-time $395 per semester hour. Required fees: $42 per semester hour. Tuition and fees vary according to program. *Financial support:* Application deadline: 3/1; *Unit head:* Dr. Eugene Jones, Chair, 214-648-1701, Fax: 214-648-1003, E-mail: pa.sahss@utsouthwestern.edu. *Application contact:* Isela Perez, Education Coordinator, 214-648-1701, Fax: 214-648-1003, E-mail: isela.perez@utsouthwestern.edu.

The University of Toledo, College of Graduate Studies, College of Health Science and Human Service, Division of Health, Physician Assistant Studies Program, Toledo, OH 43606-3390. Offers MSBS. *Accreditation:* ARC-PA. *Faculty:* 3 full-time, 1 part-time/adjunct. *Students:* 60 full-time (49 women), 27 part-time (20 women); includes 8 minority (5 African Americans, 2 Asian Americans or Pacific Islanders, 1 Hispanic American). Average age 25. 245 applicants, 18% accepted, 32 enrolled. In 2006, 9 degrees awarded. *Degree requirements:* For master's, scholarly project. *Entrance requirements:* For master's, GRE, interview, minimum undergraduate GPA of 3.0, writing sample. *Application deadline:* For fall admission, 2/15 for domestic students. Application fee: $45. *Expenses:* Contact institution. *Financial support:* Federal Work-Study, institutionally sponsored loans, and scholarships/grants available. Financial award applicants required to submit FAFSA. *Unit head:* Patricia Hogue, Director, 419-383-4807, E-mail: phogue@utoledo.edu. *Application contact:* Kristi Hayes, Secretary, 419-383-5408, E-mail: khayes@utoledo.edu.

University of Utah, School of Medicine and The Graduate School, Graduate Programs in Medicine, Department of Family and Preventive Medicine, Utah Physician Assistant Program, Salt Lake City, UT 84112-1107. Offers MPAS. *Accreditation:* ARC-PA. *Faculty:* 8 full-time (3 women), 11 part-time/adjunct (5 women). *Students:* 72 full-time (36 women); includes 10 minority (1 African American, 3 American Indian/Alaska Native, 4 Asian Americans or Pacific Islanders, 2 Hispanic Americans). Average age 29. 479 applicants, 8% accepted, 36 enrolled. In 2006, 34 degrees awarded. *Median time to degree:* Master's–2 years full-time. *Degree requirements:* For master's, thesis or alternative, comprehensive exam. *Entrance requirements:* Additional exam requirements/recommendations for international students: Required—TOEFL (minimum score 550 paper-based). *Application deadline:* For fall admission, 10/1 for domestic students. Electronic applications accepted. *Expenses:* Contact institution. *Financial support:* Scholarships/grants available. *Faculty research:* Physical assistant education, evidence-based medicine, technology and education, international medicine education. Total annual research expenditures: $150,000. *Unit head:* Dr. Donald M. Pedersen, Director, 801-585-7426, Fax: 801-581-5807, E-mail: dpedersen@upap.utah.edu. *Application contact:* Doris Dalton, Admissions Coordinator, 801-581-7766, Fax: 801-581-5807, E-mail: admissions@upap.utah.edu.

University of Wisconsin–La Crosse, Office of University Graduate Studies, College of Science and Health, Department of Health Professions, Program in Physician Assistant Studies, La Crosse, WI 54601-3742. Offers MS. *Accreditation:* ARC-PA. *Students:* 26 full-time (22 women); includes 3 minority (1 African American, 1 Asian American or Pacific Islander, 1 Hispanic American). Average age 27. 187 applicants, 7% accepted, 14 enrolled. In 2006, 12 degrees awarded. *Degree requirements:* For master's, comprehensive exam. *Entrance requirements:* For master's, GRE, minimum GPA of 3.0 overall and in science. Additional exam requirements/recommendations for international students: Required—TOEFL (minimum score 550 paper-based; 213 computer-based). *Application deadline:* For fall admission, 9/1 for domestic students. *Unit head:* Dr. Edward Malone, Director, 608-785-8470, E-mail: malone.edwa@uwlax.edu. *Application contact:* Kathryn Kiefer, Associate Director of Admissions, 608-785-8939, E-mail: admissions@uwlax.edu.

Wagner College, Division of Graduate Studies, Department of Biological Sciences, Program in Advanced Physician Assistant Studies, Staten Island, NY 10301-4495. Offers MS. *Accreditation:* ARC-PA. Part-time programs available. *Faculty:* 5 full-time (all women), 3 part-time/adjunct (all women). *Students:* 11 full-time (10 women), 6 part-time (4 women); includes 5 minority (2 African Americans, 1 Asian American or Pacific Islander, 2 Hispanic Americans). 9 applicants, 67% accepted, 6 enrolled. In 2006, 13 degrees awarded. *Degree requirements:* For master's, thesis, comprehensive exam. *Entrance requirements:* For master's, minimum GPA of 3.0; bachelor's degree in one of the biological sciences, chemistry or physician assistant studies; physician assistant certification. Additional exam requirements/recommendations for international students: Required—TOEFL (minimum score 550 paper-based; 217 computer-based). *Application deadline:* For fall admission, 8/1 priority date for domestic students, 6/30 priority date for international students; for spring admission, 12/10 for domestic students, 11/15 for international students. Applications are processed on a rolling basis. Application fee: $50 ($85 for international students). *Expenses:* Tuition: Full-time $15,120; part-time $840 per credit. *Financial support:* Fellowships, career-related internships or fieldwork, Federal Work-Study, and unspecified assistantships available. Financial award applicants required to submit FAFSA. *Unit head:* Nora Lowy, Director, 718-390-4610. *Application contact:* Susan Rosenberg, Office of Graduate Studies, 718-390-3106, Fax: 718-390-3456, E-mail: graduate@wagner.edu.

Wayne State University, Eugene Applebaum College of Pharmacy and Health Sciences, Department of Health Care Sciences, Program in Physician Assistant Studies, Detroit, MI 48202. Offers MS. *Accreditation:* ARC-PA. *Faculty:* 5 full-time (0 women), 1 part-time/adjunct (0 women). *Students:* 87 full-time (75 women); includes 6 minority (2 African Americans, 2 Asian Americans or Pacific Islanders, 2 Hispanic Americans). Average age 26. 6 applicants, 17% accepted, 0 enrolled. In 2006, 48 degrees awarded. *Entrance requirements:* For master's, GRE General Test, minimum GPA of 3.0, course work in science, 500 hours of work experience in health services. Additional exam requirements/recommendations for international students: Required—TOEFL (minimum score 550 paper-based; 213 computer-based); Recommended—TWE (minimum score 6). *Application deadline:* For fall admission, 10/1 for domestic students, 6/1 for international students; for winter admission, 10/1 for international students; for spring admission, 2/1 for international students. Applications are processed on a rolling basis. Application fee: $30 ($50 for international students). Electronic applications accepted. *Financial support:* Career-related internships or fieldwork available. Financial award applicants required to submit FAFSA. *Faculty research:* Medical treatment outcomes, learning and performance evaluation, service-learning research. *Unit head:* Stephanie Gilkey, Academic Director, 313-577-9666, Fax: 313-577-5467, E-mail: ab4703@wayne.edu. *Application contact:* James Frick, Graduate Director, 313-577-3954, E-mail: aa3573@wayne.edu.

Western Michigan University, Graduate College, College of Health and Human Services, Department of Physician Assistant, Kalamazoo, MI 49008-5202. Offers MS. *Accreditation:* ARC-PA. Part-time programs available.

Western University of Health Sciences, College of Allied Health Professions, Program in Physician Assistant Studies, Pomona, CA 91766-1854. Offers MS. *Accreditation:* ARC-PA. *Faculty:* 10 full-time (5 women). *Students:* 193 full-time (135 women); includes 102 minority (8 African Americans, 47 Asian Americans or Pacific Islanders, 47 Hispanic Americans). Average age 29. 576 applicants, 24% accepted, 95 enrolled. In 2006, 97 degrees awarded. *Entrance requirements:* For master's, minimum GPA of 2.5, letters of recommendation, interview. *Application deadline:* For fall admission, 11/15 for domestic students; for spring admission, 3/1 for domestic students. Application fee: $50. *Expenses:* Contact institution. *Financial support:* Institutionally sponsored loans, scholarships/grants, and Veterans Educational Benefits available. Financial award application deadline: 3/2; financial award applicants required to submit FAFSA. *Unit head:* Roy Guizado, Chair, 909-469-5445, Fax: 909-469-5407. *Application contact:* Audrey Navarro, Information Contact, 909-469-5335, Fax: 909-469-5570, E-mail: admissions@westernu.edu.

Yale University, School of Medicine, Physician Associate Program, New Haven, CT 06520. Offers MM Sc. *Accreditation:* ARC-PA. *Faculty:* 4 full-time (3 women), 17 part-time/adjunct (7 women). *Students:* 63 full-time (42 women); includes 4 minority (2 Asian Americans or Pacific Islanders, 2 Hispanic Americans), 1 international. Average age 26. 515 applicants, 8% accepted, 32 enrolled. In 2006, 29 degrees awarded. *Entrance requirements:* For master's, GRE General Test. Additional exam requirements/recommendations for international students: Required—TOEFL. *Application deadline:* For fall admission, 9/1 for domestic and international students. Application fee: $0. Electronic applications accepted. *Expenses:* Contact institution. *Financial support:* In 2006–07, 34 students received support. Institutionally sponsored loans and scholarships/grants available. Financial award application deadline: 5/1; financial award applicants required to submit CSS PROFILE or FAFSA. *Faculty research:* Correlation of GRE scores and program performance, relationship of PA programs and pharmaceutical companies, initial practice patterns of physician assistants with emergency medicine experience. Total annual research expenditures: $10,000. *Unit head:* Mary Warner, Director/Assistant Dean, 203-785-2860, Fax: 203-785-3601, E-mail: mary.warner@yale.edu. *Application contact:* Eric E. Lederer, Assistant Director for Student Affairs, 203-785-2860, Fax: 203-785-3601, E-mail: eric.lederer@yale.edu.

Rehabilitation Sciences

Boston University, College of Health and Rehabilitation Sciences—Sargent College, Department of Physical Therapy and Athletic Training, Boston, MA 02215. Offers physical therapy (DPT); rehabilitation sciences (D Sc). *Accreditation:* APTA (one or more programs are accredited). Postbaccalaureate distance learning degree programs offered (minimal on-campus study). *Faculty:* 15 full-time (11 women), 22 part-time/adjunct (15 women). *Students:* 117 full-time (96 women), 185 part-time (128 women); includes 32 minority (3 African Americans, 18 Asian Americans or Pacific Islanders, 11 Hispanic Americans), 5 international. Average age 32. 185 applicants, 56% accepted, 33 enrolled. In 2006, 212 doctorates awarded. *Degree requirements:* For doctorate, thesis/dissertation (for some programs). *Entrance requirements:* For doctorate, GRE General Test, master's degree. Additional exam requirements/recommendations for international students: Required—TOEFL (minimum score 550 paper-based). *Application deadline:* For fall admission, 1/5 for domestic students. Applications are processed on a rolling basis. Application fee: $70. Electronic applications accepted. *Expenses:* Tuition: Full-time $33,330; part-time $1,042 per credit. Required fees: $462; $40. *Financial support:* In 2006–07, 3 research assistantships with full tuition reimbursements, 10 teaching assistantships with full tuition reimbursements were awarded; career-related internships or fieldwork, Federal Work-Study, institutionally sponsored loans, scholarships/grants, and tuition waivers (partial) also available. Financial award application deadline: 4/15. *Faculty research:* EMG, gait, infant assessment, motor control, orthopedics. *Unit head:* Dr. Julie Keysor, Chairman, 617-353-2735, E-mail: jkeysor@bu.edu. *Application contact:* Sharon Sankey, Director, Student Services, 617-353-2713, Fax: 617-353-7500, E-mail: ssankey@bu.edu.

California University of Pennsylvania, School of Graduate Studies and Research, School of Education, Department of Athletic Training, Program in Exercise Science and Health Promotion, California, PA 15419-1394. Offers fitness and wellness (MS); performance enhancement and injury prevention (MS); rehabilitation sciences (MS); sport management (MS); sport psychology (MS). Part-time and evening/weekend programs available. Postbaccalaureate distance learning degree programs offered (no on-campus study). *Faculty:* 34 full-time (15 women), 7 part-time/adjunct (0 women). *Students:* 382 full-time (167 women), 44 part-time (15 women); includes 68 minority (35 African Americans, 2 American Indian/Alaska Native, 17 Asian Americans or Pacific Islanders, 14 Hispanic Americans). Average age 31. In 2006, 176 degrees awarded. *Median time to degree:* Master's–1.5 years full-time, 2.25 years part-time. *Degree requirements:* For master's, thesis optional. *Entrance requirements:* For master's, minimum QPA of 3.0. Additional exam requirements/recommendations for international students: Required—TOEFL (minimum score 550 paper-based; 213 computer-based; 80 iBT). *Application deadline:* For fall admission, 8/1 priority date for domestic and international students; for winter admission, 12/1 priority date for domestic and international students; for spring admission, 5/1 priority date for domestic and international students. Applications are processed on a rolling basis. Application fee: $25. Electronic applications accepted. *Expenses:* Contact institution. *Financial support:* Career-related internships or fieldwork, scholarships/grants, and unspecified assistantships available. Financial award applicants required to submit FAFSA. *Faculty research:* Reducing obesity in children, sport performance, creating unique biomechanical assessment techniques, Web-based training for fitness professionals, Webcams. Total annual research expenditures: $25,000. *Unit head:* Prof. Barry McGlumphy, Graduate Coordinator, 724-938-1694, Fax: 724-938-4342, E-mail: mcglumphy@cup.edu.

Canisius College, Graduate Division, School of Education and Human Services, Department of Health and Human Performance, Buffalo, NY 14208-1098. Offers MS. Part-time and evening/weekend programs available. *Faculty:* 4 full-time (0 women), 3 part-time/adjunct (1 woman). *Students:* 9 full-time (6 women), 7 part-time (all women). Average age 24. 12 applicants, 75% accepted, 6 enrolled. In 2006, 5 degrees awarded. *Degree requirements:* For master's, thesis, project internship. Application fee: $25. *Expenses:* Tuition: Part-time $645 per credit hour. Required fees: $19 per credit hour. Tuition and fees vary according to program. *Financial support:* In 2006–07, 9 students received support, including 1 teaching assistantship with tuition reimbursement available (averaging $6,000 per year); career-related internships or fieldwork, institutionally sponsored loans, health care benefits, and unspecified assistantships also available. *Faculty research:* Delayed onset of muscle soreness, exercising muscle blood flow, aging. Total annual research expenditures: $13,000. *Unit head:* Dr. Peter M. Koehneke, Chair, 716-888-2954, E-mail: koehneke@canisius.edu.

Central Michigan University, College of Graduate Studies, The Herbert H. and Grace A. Dow College of Health Professions, School of Rehabilitation and Medical Sciences, Mount Pleasant, MI 48859. Offers physical therapy (DPT); physician assistant (MS). *Accreditation:* APTA; ARC-PA. *Degree requirements:* For master's, thesis or alternative, comprehensive exam (for some programs), registration.

Clarion University of Pennsylvania, Office of Research and Graduate Studies, College of Education and Human Services, Department of Special Education and Rehabilitative Sciences, Program in Rehabilitative Sciences, Clarion, PA 16214. Offers MS. *Faculty:* 11 full-time (5 women). *Students:* 10 full-time (5 women), 30 part-time (23 women); includes 1 minority (Hispanic American) 19 applicants, 89% accepted. In 2006, 21 degrees awarded. *Degree requirements:* For master's, thesis or alternative. *Entrance requirements:* For master's, GRE General Test or MAT, minimum QPA of 3.0. Additional exam requirements/recommendations for international students: Required—TOEFL (minimum score 550 paper-based; 213 computer-based; 80 iBT). *Application deadline:* For fall admission, 8/1 priority date for domestic students, 4/15 priority date for international students; for spring admission, 12/1 priority date for domestic students, 9/15 priority date for international students. Applications are processed on a rolling basis. Application fee: $30. Electronic applications accepted. *Expenses:* Tuition, state resident: part-time $336 per credit. Tuition, nonresident: part-time $538 per credit. *Financial support:* In 2006–07, 2 research assistantships (averaging $2,001 per year) were awarded. *Application contact:* Dr. Mark Kilwein, Graduate Program Coordinator, 814-393-2486, Fax: 814-393-1951, E-mail: mkilwein@clarion.edu.

Concordia University Wisconsin, Graduate Programs, School of Health and Human Services, Program in Rehabilitation Science, Mequon, WI 53097-2402. Offers MSRS. *Students:* 10 (6 women).

Drake University, School of Education, Department of Leadership, Counseling and Adult Development, Program in Rehabilitation, Des Moines, IA 50311-4516. Offers rehabilitation administration (MS); rehabilitation counseling (MS); rehabilitation placement (MS). Part-time and evening/weekend programs available. *Faculty:* 10 full-time (3 women), 28 part-time/adjunct (16 women). *Students:* 17 applicants, 53% accepted. In 2006, 4 degrees awarded. *Degree requirements:* For master's, thesis (for some programs), internships (for some programs), comprehensive exam, registration. *Entrance requirements:* For master's, GRE General Test, MAT or Drake SOE writing assessment, resumé, 2 letters of recommendation. Additional exam requirements/recommendations for international students: Required—TOEFL (minimum score 550 paper-based; 213 computer-based). *Application deadline:* For fall admission, 7/1 priority date for domestic students, 6/1 priority date for international students; for spring admission, 11/1 priority date for domestic students, 10/1 priority date for international students. Applications are processed on a rolling basis. Application fee: $25. Electronic applications accepted. *Financial support:* Career-related internships or fieldwork available. Support available to part-time students. *Faculty research:* Counseling and rehabilitation, behavioral supports, inquiry-based science methods, teacher quality enhancement. Total annual research expenditures: $1.5 million. *Unit head:* Dr. Matt Bruinekool, Advisor, 515-271-4507, E-mail: matt.bruinekool@drake.edu. *Application contact:* Ann J. Martin, Graduate Coordinator, 515-271-2034, Fax: 515-271-2831, E-mail: ann.martin@drake.edu.

East Carolina University, Graduate School, School of Allied Health Sciences, Program in Rehabilitation Studies, Greenville, NC 27858-4353. Offers rehabilitation counseling (MS); substance abuse and clinical counseling (MS); vocational evaluation (MS). *Accreditation:* CORE. Part-time and evening/weekend programs available. *Students:* 61 full-time (45 women), 10 part-time (8 women); includes 9 minority (8 African Americans, 1 American Indian/Alaska Native), 2 international. Average age 31. 22 applicants, 14% accepted, 3 enrolled. In 2006, 21 degrees awarded. *Degree requirements:* For master's, thesis or alternative, internship, comprehensive exam. *Entrance requirements:* For master's, GRE General Test or MAT. Additional exam requirements/recommendations for international students: Required—TOEFL. *Application deadline:* For fall admission, 3/1 priority date for domestic students; for spring admission, 10/1 priority date for domestic students. Applications are processed on a rolling basis. Application fee: $50. *Financial support:* Research assistantships with partial tuition reimbursements, teaching assistantships with partial tuition reimbursements, Federal Work-Study and scholarships/grants available. Support available to part-time students. Financial award application deadline: 3/1. *Unit head:* Dr. Paul Alston, Chair, 252-744-6290, Fax: 252-328-0725, E-mail: alstonp@ecu.edu. *Application contact:* Dean of Graduate School, 252-328-6012, Fax: 252-328-6071, E-mail: gradschool@ecu.edu.

East Stroudsburg University of Pennsylvania, Graduate School, School of Health Sciences and Human Performance, Department of Exercise Science, East Stroudsburg, PA 18301-2999. Offers cardiac rehabilitation and exercise science (MS). Part-time and evening/weekend programs available. *Faculty:* 4 full-time (1 woman), 1 part-time/adjunct (0 women). *Students:* 25 full-time (16 women), 6 part-time (2 women); includes 1 minority (African American), 4 international. Average age 28. In 2006, 32 degrees awarded. *Degree requirements:* For master's, comprehensive exam. *Entrance requirements:* Additional exam requirements/recommendations for international students: Required—TOEFL (minimum score 560 paper-based; 220 computer-based; 83 iBT). *Application deadline:* For fall admission, 7/31 priority date for domestic students, 5/1 priority date for international students; for spring admission, 11/30 for domestic students, 10/1 for international students. Applications are processed on a rolling basis. Application fee: $50. *Expenses:* Tuition, state resident: full-time $6,048; part-time $336 per credit. Tuition, nonresident: full-time $9,678; part-time $538 per credit. Required fees: $1,353; $67 per credit. One-time fee: $37 part-time. *Financial support:* In 2006–07, 19 research assistantships with full and partial tuition reimbursements were awarded; Federal Work-Study and institutionally sponsored loans also available. Financial award application deadline: 3/1. *Unit head:* Dr. Shala Davis, Graduate Coordinator, 570-422-3302, Fax: 570-422-3616, E-mail: sdavis@po-box.esu.edu.

Indiana University–Purdue University Indianapolis, Indiana University School of Medicine, School of Health and Rehabilitation Sciences, Indianapolis, IN 46202-2896. Offers health sciences education (MS); nutrition and dietetics (MS); occupational therapy (MS); physical therapy (DPT). Part-time and evening/weekend programs available. *Faculty:* 8 full-time (5 women). *Students:* 180 full-time (149 women), 35 part-time (21 women); includes 17 minority (6 African Americans, 7 Asian Americans or Pacific Islanders, 4 Hispanic Americans), 3 international. Average age 27. In 2006, 9 master's, 32 doctorates awarded. *Degree requirements:* For master's, thesis (for some programs). *Entrance requirements:* For master's, GRE General Test, minimum GPA of 3.0. Additional exam requirements/recommendations for international students: Required—TOEFL. *Application deadline:* For fall admission, 1/15 priority date for domestic students; for spring admission, 10/15 for domestic students. Application fee: $50 ($60 for international students). *Expenses:* Tuition, state resident: full-time $5,437; part-time $227 per credit hour. Tuition, nonresident: full-time $15,694; part-time $654 per credit hour. Required fees: $620. Tuition and fees vary according to course load, campus/location and program. *Financial support:* Fellowships, research assistantships, teaching assistantships, Federal Work-Study, institutionally sponsored loans, and scholarships/grants available. Support available to part-time students. Financial award applicants required to submit FAFSA. *Unit head:* Dr. Mark S. Sothmann, Dean of the School of Allied Health Sciences, 317-274-4702, E-mail: msothman@iupui.edu.

McGill University, Faculty of Graduate and Postdoctoral Studies, Faculty of Medicine, School of Physical and Occupational Therapy, Montréal, QC H3A 2T5, Canada. Offers rehabilitation science (M Sc, PhD). Terminal master's awarded for partial completion of doctoral program. *Degree requirements:* For master's and doctorate, thesis/dissertation. *Entrance requirements:* For master's, GRE General Test, B Sc in related discipline, minimum GPA of 3.0; for doctorate, M Sc in related discipline. Additional exam requirements/recommendations for international students: Required—TOEFL. *Faculty research:* Exercise and aging, biomechanics, spinal cord injury, spasticity, health outcome measures.

Rehabilitation Sciences

McMaster University, Faculty of Health Sciences and School of Graduate Studies, Program in Rehabilitation Science (course-based), Hamilton, ON L8S 4M2, Canada. Offers M Sc. Part-time programs available. *Degree requirements:* For master's, online courses and scholarly paper. *Entrance requirements:* For master's, minimum B+ average in final year of a 4-year undergraduate health professional program or other relevant program. Additional exam requirements/recommendations for international students: Required—TOEFL (minimum score 600 paper-based; 250 computer-based). *Application deadline:* For fall admission, 9/15 for domestic students; for spring admission, 5/1 for domestic students. Application fee: $90. *Unit head:* Dr. Joyce Tryssenaar, Coordinator, 905-524-0669. *Application contact:* Dr. Carl Richards, Associate Dean, 905-525-9140 Ext. 22982, Fax: 905-546-1129.

McMaster University, Faculty of Health Sciences and School of Graduate Studies, Program in Rehabilitation Science (Thesis Option), Hamilton, ON L8S 4M2, Canada. Offers M Sc, PhD. Part-time programs available. *Students:* 12 full-time, 18 part-time. In 2006, 5 degrees awarded. *Degree requirements:* For master's, thesis. *Entrance requirements:* For master's, minimum B+ average in final year of a 4-year undergraduate health professional program or other relevant program. Additional exam requirements/recommendations for international students: Required—TOEFL (minimum score 600 paper-based; 250 computer-based). *Application deadline:* For fall admission, 2/28 for domestic students. Application fee: $90. *Financial support:* Teaching assistantships available. *Unit head:* Dr. Seanne Wilkins, Coordinator, 905-525-9140 Ext.27839. *Application contact:* Dr. Carl Richards, Associate Dean, 905-525-9140 Ext. 22983, Fax: 905-546-1129.

Medical University of South Carolina, College of Health Professions, Department of Rehabilitation Sciences, Charleston, SC 29425-0002. Offers communication sciences and disorders (MSR); occupational therapy (MSR); physical therapy (DPT). Postbaccalaureate distance learning degree programs offered (minimal on-campus study). *Faculty:* 14 full-time (10 women), 5 part-time/adjunct (2 women). *Students:* 189 full-time (174 women); includes 14 minority (8 African Americans, 4 Asian Americans or Pacific Islanders, 2 Hispanic Americans), 1 international. Average age 25. In 2006, 90 degrees awarded. *Degree requirements:* For master's, thesis or alternative, research project. *Entrance requirements:* For master's, GRE General Test, interview, minimum GPA of 3.0. Additional exam requirements/recommendations for international students: Required—TOEFL (minimum score 600 paper-based; 250 computer-based). Electronic applications accepted. *Financial support:* Federal Work-Study and scholarships/grants available. Support available to part-time students. Financial award application deadline: 3/15; financial award applicants required to submit FAFSA. *Faculty research:* Spinal cord injury, long term care residence, geriatric education, learning strategies, fatigue during cancer treatments. Total annual research expenditures: $629,415. *Unit head:* Dr. Jennifer Horner, Chair, 843-792-2961, Fax: 843-792-0710, E-mail: hornerj@musc.edu. *Application contact:* Susan Johnson, Student Services Coordinator, 843-792-2961, Fax: 843-792-0710, E-mail: johnsoss@musc.edu.

Northwestern Health Sciences University, School of Massage Therapy, Bloomington, MN 55431-1599. Offers Professional Certificate.

Pennsylvania College of Optometry, Graduate Studies in Vision Impairment and Audiology, Elkins Park, PA 19027-1598. Offers audiology (Au D); education of children and youth with visual and multiple impairments (M Ed, Certificate); low vision rehabilitation (MS, Certificate); orientation and mobility therapy (MS, Certificate); rehabilitation teaching (MS, Certificate); OD/MS. *Accreditation:* ASHA. Part-time programs available. *Entrance requirements:* For master's, GRE or MAT, letters of reference (3), interviews (2). Additional exam requirements/recommendations for international students: Required—TOEFL, TWE. Expenses: Contact institution. *Faculty research:* Knowledge utilization, technology transfer.

Queen's University at Kingston, School of Graduate Studies and Research, Faculty of Health Sciences, School of Rehabilitation Therapy, Kingston, ON K7L 3N6, Canada. Offers M Sc, PhD. Part-time programs available. *Degree requirements:* For master's, thesis/dissertation; for doctorate, thesis/dissertation, comprehensive exam. *Entrance requirements:* Additional exam requirements/recommendations for international students: Required—TOEFL. *Faculty research:* Disability, community, motor performance, rehabilitation, treatment efficiency.

Queen's University at Kingston, School of Graduate Studies and Research, School of Physical and Health Education, Kingston, ON K7L 3N6, Canada. Offers applied exercise science (PhD); biomechanics/ergonomics (M Sc); exercise physiology rehabilitation (M Sc); social psychology of sport and exercise rehabilitation (MA); sociology of sport (MA). Part-time programs available. *Degree requirements:* For master's, thesis (for some programs); for doctorate, thesis/dissertation, comprehensive exam. *Entrance requirements:* For master's and doctorate, minimum B+ average. Additional exam requirements/recommendations for international students: Required—TOEFL. Electronic applications accepted. *Faculty research:* Expert performance ergonomics, obesity research, pregnancy and exercise, gender and sport participation.

University at Buffalo, the State University of New York, Graduate School, School of Public Health and Health Professions, Department of Rehabilitation Science, Buffalo, NY 14260. Offers assistive and rehabilitation technology (Certificate); occupational therapy (MS); physical therapy (DPT). *Faculty:* 21 full-time (15 women), 14 part-time/adjunct (9 women). *Students:* 156 full-time (99 women), 8 part-time (6 women); includes 23 minority (11 African Americans, 1 American Indian/Alaska Native, 9 Asian Americans or Pacific Islanders, 2 Hispanic Americans), 10 international. Average age 30. 8 applicants, 38% accepted, 2 enrolled. In 2006, 23 master's, 41 doctorates, 7 other advanced degrees awarded. *Degree requirements:* For doctorate, thesis/dissertation, comprehensive exam. *Entrance requirements:* For master's, BS in occupational therapy; for doctorate, GRE General Test. Additional exam requirements/recommendations for international students: Required—TOEFL (minimum score 550 paper-based; 213 computer-based). Application fee: $35. Electronic applications accepted. *Financial support:* In 2006–07, 2 research assistantships with full and partial tuition reimbursements (averaging $15,000 per year), 2 teaching assistantships with full and partial tuition reimbursements (averaging $11,198 per year) were awarded; scholarships/grants and unspecified assistantships also available. *Faculty research:* Communicative disorders, nursing, occupational therapy, physical therapy, exercise physiology. Total annual research expenditures: $489,000. *Unit head:* Dr. Robert Birkard, Chair, 716-829-3141 Ext. 120, Fax: 716-829-2317, E-mail: rfb@buffalo.edu. *Application contact:* Dr. Robert Birkard, Chair, 716-829-3141 Ext. 120, Fax: 716-829-2317, E-mail: rfb@buffalo.edu.

The University of Alabama at Birmingham, School of Health Professions, Department of Occupational Therapy, Program in Low Vision Rehabilitation, Birmingham, AL 35294. Offers Certificate. *Expenses:* Tuition, state resident: part-time $170 per credit hour. Tuition, nonresident: part-time $425 per credit hour. Required fees: $15 per credit hour. $122 per term. Tuition and fees vary according to program. *Unit head:* Mary Warren, Head, 205-934-3568, E-mail: warrenm@uab.edu. *Application contact:* Elaine Satterfield, Admissions Secretary, 205-934-3568, E-mail: satterfe@uab.edu.

University of Alberta, Faculty of Graduate Studies and Research, Faculty of Rehabilitation Medicine, Edmonton, AB T6G 2E1, Canada. Offers PhD. *Faculty:* 28 full-time (17 women). *Students:* 11 full-time (6 women), 4 part-time (2 women). Average age 32. 10 applicants, 50% accepted, 5 enrolled. In 2006, 2 degrees awarded. *Degree requirements:* For doctorate, thesis/dissertation. *Entrance requirements:* For doctorate, GRE, minimum GPA of 7.0 on a 9.0 scale. Additional exam requirements/recommendations for international students: Required—TOEFL. *Application deadline:* For fall admission, 3/1 for domestic and international students; for winter admission, 7/1 for domestic and international students. Applications are processed on a rolling basis. Application fee: $0. Electronic applications accepted. *Financial support:* In 2006–07, 1 fellowship (averaging $16,000 per year), 7 research assistantships (averaging $2,721 per year), 1 teaching assistantship (averaging $2,535 per year) were awarded; institutionally sponsored loans, scholarships/grants, and traineeships also available. Financial award application deadline: 1/1. *Faculty research:* Musculoskeletal disorders, neuromotor control, exercise physiology, motor speech disorders, assistive technologies, cardiac rehabilitation/therapeutic exercise. *Unit head:* Dr. P. Hagler, Associate Dean, 780-492-1595, Fax: 780-492-1626, E-mail: paul.hagler@ualberta.ca. *Application contact:* Angela Libutti, Administrative Assistant, Graduate Studies, 780-492-1595, Fax: 780-492-1626, E-mail: thesis.info@rehabmed.ualberta.ca.

The University of British Columbia, Faculty of Medicine, School of Rehabilitation Sciences, Vancouver, BC V6T 1Z1, Canada. Offers M Sc, MOT, MPT, MRSc, PhD. *Faculty:* 16 full-time (15 women), 7 part-time/adjunct (5 women). *Students:* 186 full-time (155 women). Average age 30. 311 applicants, 27% accepted, 85 enrolled. In 2006, 2 master's, 1 doctorate awarded. *Degree requirements:* For master's, thesis/dissertation, registration; for doctorate, thesis/dissertation, comprehensive exam, registration. *Entrance requirements:* For master's, minimum B+ average; for doctorate, minimum B+ average, master's degree. Additional exam requirements/recommendations for international students: Required—TOEFL (minimum score 600 paper-based; 250 computer-based), GRE. *Application deadline:* For fall admission, 2/1 priority date for domestic and international students; for winter admission, 7/1 priority date for domestic and international students. Application fee: $90 Canadian dollars ($150 Canadian dollars for international students). Electronic applications accepted. *Financial support:* In 2006–07, 25 students received support, including 1 fellowship with partial tuition reimbursement available (averaging $16,000 per year), 2 research assistantships, 3 teaching assistantships (averaging $5,000 per year); Federal Work-Study, institutionally sponsored loans, scholarships/grants, and tuition waivers (full and partial) also available. *Faculty research:* Disability, rehabilitation and society, exercise science and rehabilitation, neurorehabilitation and motor control. *Unit head:* Dr. Brenda Loveridge, Interim Director, 604-822-7414, Fax: 604-822-7624. *Application contact:* Jacqueline G. Chin, Student Services Program Assistant, 604-822-7050, Fax: 604-822-7624, E-mail: jachin@interchange.ubc.ca.

University of Cincinnati, Division of Research and Advanced Studies, College of Allied Health Sciences, Department of Rehabilitation Science, Cincinnati, OH 45221. Offers DPT. *Accreditation:* APTA. *Faculty:* 9 full-time (7 women), 2 part-time/adjunct (0 women). *Students:* 38 full-time (30 women); includes 3 minority (2 African Americans, 1 Hispanic American). 50 applicants, 50% accepted, 20 enrolled. *Entrance requirements:* For doctorate, GRE General Test, bachelor's degree with minimum GPA of 3.0, 50 hours volunteer/work in physical therapy setting. Additional exam requirements/recommendations for international students: Required—TOEFL. *Application deadline:* For fall admission, 1/11 for domestic and international students. Application fee: $40. Electronic applications accepted. *Financial support:* In 2006–07, 4 research assistantships with partial tuition reimbursements (averaging $6,000 per year), 5 teaching assistantships with partial tuition reimbursements (averaging $6,000 per year) were awarded; tuition waivers (partial) also available. *Faculty research:* Biomechanics, sports-related injuries, motor learning, stroke rehabilitation. *Unit head:* Dr. Lizanne Mulligan, Graduate Program Director, 513-558-7482, E-mail: mulligea@uc.edu. *Application contact:* Beth Bextermueller, Program Coordinator, 513-558-7455, Fax: 513-558-7474, E-mail: beth.bextermueller@uc.edu.

University of Florida, Graduate School, College of Public Health and Health Professions, Program in Rehabilitation Science, Gainesville, FL 32611. Offers PhD. *Faculty:* 26. *Degree requirements:* For doctorate, thesis/dissertation. *Entrance requirements:* For doctorate, GRE General Test, minimum GPA of 3.0. Additional exam requirements/recommendations for international students: Required—TOEFL (minimum score 550 paper-based; 213 computer-based). *Application deadline:* Applications are processed on a rolling basis. Application fee: $30. Electronic applications accepted. *Expenses:* Tuition, state resident: full-time $6,827. Tuition, nonresident: full-time $21,951. Required fees: $999. *Financial support:* In 2006–07, 12 research assistantships (averaging $11,538 per year) were awarded; teaching assistantships. *Unit head:* Dr. William C. Mann, Director, 352-273-6883, Fax: 352-273-6588, E-mail: wmann@phhp.ufl.edu. *Application contact:* Dr. Margaret Odom, Program Assistant, 352-273-6098, Fax: 352-273-6588, E-mail: modom@phhp.ufl.edu.

The University of Iowa, Roy J. and Lucille A. Carver College of Medicine and Graduate College, Graduate Programs in Medicine, Graduate Program in Physical Therapy and Rehabilitation Science, Iowa City, IA 52242-1316. Offers physical therapy (DPT); rehabilitation science (PhD). *Accreditation:* APTA (one or more programs are accredited). *Faculty:* 7 full-time (3 women), 8 part-time/adjunct (0 women). *Students:* 116 full-time (77 women), 8 part-time (6 women); includes 2 minority (both Hispanic Americans), 11 international. Average age 24. 99 applicants, 40% accepted, 36 enrolled. In 2006, 3 doctorates awarded. *Degree requirements:* For doctorate, thesis/dissertation (for some programs). *Entrance requirements:* For doctorate, GRE, Physical Therapist Degree. Additional exam requirements/recommendations for international students: Required—TOEFL (minimum score 250 computer-based; 100 iBT). *Application deadline:* For fall admission, 1/1 for domestic students. Application fee: $50 ($75 for international students). Electronic applications accepted. *Expenses:* Contact institution. *Financial support:* In 2006–07, 94 students received support, including 2 research assistantships with partial tuition reimbursements available (averaging $19,537 per year), 4 teaching assistantships with partial tuition reimbursements available (averaging $19,537 per year); fellowships with partial tuition reimbursements available, Federal Work-Study, institutionally sponsored loans, scholarships/grants, health care benefits, and unspecified assistantships also available. Support available to part-time students. Financial award application deadline: 1/1; financial award applicants required to submit FAFSA. *Faculty research:* Muscle fatigue, motor control, pain mechanisms, body composition, sports medicine, occupational safety, neuromuscular physiology. Total annual research expenditures: $351,848. *Unit head:* Dr. Richard K. Shields, Director, 319-335-9791, Fax: 319-335-9707, E-mail: physical-therapy@uiowa.edu.

University of Kansas, Graduate Studies Medical Center, School of Allied Health, Department of Occupational Therapy Education, Lawrence, KS 66045. Offers occupational therapy (MOT, MS); therapeutic science (PhD). *Accreditation:* AOTA. Part-time programs available. *Faculty:* 12 full-time (10 women), 4 part-time/adjunct (all women). *Students:* 62 full-time (60 women), 9 part-time (all women); includes 4 minority (2 Asian Americans or Pacific Islanders, 2 Hispanic Americans), 2 international. Average age 27. 17 applicants, 71% accepted, 11 enrolled. In 2006, 31 degrees awarded. *Median time to degree:* Master's–1.75 years full-time, 3.75 years part-time. *Degree requirements:* For doctorate, thesis/dissertation, oral defense, comprehensive exam. *Entrance requirements:* For master's, 1 year of experience in a field related to disability; for doctorate, 24 hours of master's level research. *Application deadline:* For fall admission, 4/1 for international students. Application fee: $60. Electronic applications accepted. *Expenses:* Tuition, area resident: Part-time $227 per credit. Tuition, state resident: part-time $543 per credit. Tuition and fees vary according to course load, campus/location, program and reciprocity agreements. *Financial support:* In 2006–07, 3 students received support, including 3 teaching assistantships with full and partial tuition reimbursements available (averaging $41,288 per year); research assistantships with partial tuition reimbursements available. *Faculty research:* The impact of sensory processing in everyday life; brain activity in various disorders and conditions; home and work modifications; cognition, executive function and problem solving in everyday life; best practices in serving children, families and schools. *Unit head:* Dr. Winifred W. Dunn, Chair, 913-588-7195, Fax: 913-588-4568, E-mail: wdunn@kumc.edu. *Application contact:* Dr. Laura Neely, Admission Officer, 913-588-7174, Fax: 913-588-4568, E-mail: lneely@kumc.edu.

University of Kentucky, Graduate School, College of Health Sciences, Program in Rehabilitation Sciences, Lexington, KY 40506-0032. Offers PhD. *Accreditation:* AOTA. *Faculty:* 22 full-time (12 women). *Students:* 12 full-time (8 women), 19 part-time (18 women), 1 international. Average age 41. 15 applicants, 67% accepted, 9 enrolled. In 2006, 1 degree awarded. *Degree requirements:* For doctorate, thesis/dissertation, comprehensive exam. *Entrance requirements:* For doctorate, GRE General test, minimum undergraduate GPA of 2.75. Additional exam requirements/recommendations for international students: Required—TOEFL (minimum score 550 paper-based; 213 computer-based). *Application deadline:* For fall admission, 7/17 priority date for domestic students, 2/1 priority date for international students; for spring admission, 12/13 priority date for domestic students, 6/15 priority date for international students. Application fee: $40 ($55 for international students). Electronic applications accepted. *Expenses:* Tuition, state resident: full-time $7,670; part-time $401 per credit hour. Tuition, nonresident:

full-time $16,158; part-time $873 per credit hour. *Financial support:* In 2006–07, 2 students received support, including 2 research assistantships with full tuition reimbursements available (averaging $9,364 per year); fellowships with full tuition reimbursements available, teaching assistantships with full tuition reimbursements available, Federal Work-Study, scholarships/grants, traineeships, health care benefits, tuition waivers (partial), and unspecified assistantships also available. Support available to part-time students. Financial award application deadline: 3/15; financial award applicants required to submit FAFSA. *Unit head:* Dr. Jodelle Deem, Director of Graduate Studies, 859-323-1100, Fax: 859-323-8957, E-mail: jfdeem1@pop.uky.edu. *Application contact:* Dr. Brian Jackson, Senior Associate Dean, 859-257-4667, Fax: 859-257-4676, E-mail: brian.jackson@uky.edu.

University of Manitoba, Faculty of Medicine and Faculty of Graduate Studies, Graduate Programs in Medicine, Department of Medical Rehabilitation, Winnipeg, MB R3T 2N2, Canada. Offers rehabilitation (M Sc). Part-time programs available. *Faculty research:* Understanding of human dynamics, motor control and neurological dysfunction, exercise physiology, functional motion of the upper extremity and effects of musculoskeletal disorders.

University of Maryland, Baltimore, School of Medicine, Graduate Program in Life Sciences, Department of Physical Therapy and Rehabilitation Science, Baltimore, MD 21201. Offers physical rehabilitation science (PhD); physical therapy (DPT, DS). *Accreditation:* APTA. Postbaccalaureate distance learning degree programs offered. *Degree requirements:* For doctorate, thesis/dissertation, registration. *Entrance requirements:* For doctorate, GRE General Test. Additional exam requirements/recommendations for international students: Required—TOEFL; Recommended—IELTS.

University of Maryland Eastern Shore, Graduate Programs, Department of Rehabilitation Services, Princess Anne, MD 21853-1299. Offers rehabilitation counseling (MS). *Accreditation:* CORE. Part-time and evening/weekend programs available. *Faculty:* 4 full-time (2 women), 4 part-time/adjunct (2 women). *Students:* 17 full-time (11 women), 11 part-time (9 women); includes 22 minority (21 African Americans, 1 Hispanic American), 2 international. Average age 23. 28 applicants, 61% accepted, 14 enrolled. In 2006, 11 degrees awarded. *Degree requirements:* For master's, internship. *Entrance requirements:* For master's, interview. Additional exam requirements/recommendations for international students: Required—TOEFL (minimum score 213 computer-based). *Application deadline:* For fall admission, 5/1 priority date for domestic and international students. Application fee: $30. Electronic applications accepted. *Financial support:* In 2006–07, 6 students received support, including 3 research assistantships with full tuition reimbursements available (averaging $13,000 per year); scholarships/grants and unspecified assistantships also available. Financial award application deadline:3/1. *Faculty research:* Long-term rehabilitation training. Total annual research expenditures: $149,062. *Unit head:* Dr. William Talley, Chair, 410-651-6261, Fax: 410-651-6736, E-mail: wbtalley@umes.edu. *Application contact:* Dr. MaryAnn Rahimi, Coordinator, 410-651-6514, Fax: 410-651-6736, E-mail: merahimi@umes.edu.

University of Northern Iowa, Graduate College, College of Education, School of Health, Physical Education, and Leisure Services, Cedar Falls, IA 50614. Offers community health education (Ed D); health education (MA, Ed D); leisure services (MA, Ed D), including leisure services (Ed D), program administration (MA), youth/human services administration (MA); physical education (MA), including physical education, scientific basis of physical education, teaching/coaching; rehabilitation studies (Ed D). Part-time and evening/weekend programs available. *Faculty:* 34 full-time (17 women). *Students:* 98 full-time (49 women), 31 part-time (17 women); includes 21 minority (18 African Americans, 3 Hispanic Americans), 23 international. 94 applicants, 74% accepted, 59 enrolled. In 2006, 35 degrees awarded. *Degree requirements:* For master's, thesis or alternative, comprehensive exam; for doctorate, thesis/dissertation. *Entrance requirements:* For master's, minimum GPA of 3.5, 3 years of educational experience; for doctorate, GRE. Additional exam requirements/recommendations for international students: Required—TOEFL (minimum score 500 paper-based; 180 computer-based; 61 iBT). *Application deadline:* Applications are processed on a rolling basis. Application fee: $30 ($50 for international students). *Expenses:* Tuition, state resident: full-time $5,936. Tuition, nonresident: full-time $14,074. *Financial support:* Career-related internships or fieldwork, Federal Work-Study, institutionally sponsored loans, scholarships/grants, tuition waivers (full and partial), and unspecified assistantships available. Support available to part-time students. Financial award application deadline: 2/1. *Unit head:* Dr. Christopher R. Edginton, Director, 319-273-2840, Fax: 319-273-5958, E-mail: christopher.edginton@uni.edu.

University of North Texas, Robert B. Toulouse School of Graduate Studies, College of Public Affairs and Community Service, Center for Rehabilitation Studies, Denton, TX 76203. Offers rehabilitation counseling (MS); rehabilitation studies (MS); vocational evaluation (MS); work adjustment services (MS). *Accreditation:* CORE. Part-time programs available. *Students:* 1 (woman) full-time, 2 part-time (1 woman); includes 2 minority (both African Americans), 1 international. Average age 35. *Degree requirements:* For master's, thesis optional. *Entrance requirements:* For master's, GRE General Test. Additional exam requirements/recommendations for international students: Recommended—TOEFL (minimum score 550 paper-based; 213 computer-based). *Application deadline:* For fall admission, 7/15 for domestic students; for spring admission, 12/1 for domestic students. Applications are processed on a rolling basis. Application fee: $50 ($75 for international students). *Expenses:* Tuition, state resident: full-time $3,573; part-time $198 per credit. Tuition, nonresident: full-time $8,577; part-time $476 per credit. Required fees: $1,258; $126 per credit. One-time fee: $150 full-time. Tuition and fees vary according to course load. *Financial support:* Career-related internships or fieldwork, Federal Work-Study, institutionally sponsored loans, and scholarships/grants available. Financial award application deadline: 4/1. *Faculty research:* Biofeedback, job placement and development, adjustment services for handicapped. Total annual research expenditures: $55,000. *Unit head:* Dr. Paul Leung, Chair, 940-565-2488, Fax: 940-565-3960, E-mail: pleung@scs.unt.edu.

University of Oklahoma Health Sciences Center, Graduate College, College of Allied Health, Department of Rehabilitation Sciences, Oklahoma City, OK 73190. Offers MS. *Degree requirements:* For master's, thesis optional. *Entrance requirements:* For master's, GRE General Test, 2 years clinical experience, 3 letters of reference. Additional exam requirements/recommendations for international students: Required—TOEFL (minimum score 550 paper-based).

University of Ottawa, Faculty of Graduate and Postdoctoral Studies, Faculty of Health Sciences, School of Rehabilitation Sciences, Ottawa, ON K1N 6N5, Canada. Offers audiology (M Sc); orthophony (M Sc). Part-time and evening/weekend programs available. *Entrance requirements:* For master's, honors degree or equivalent, minimum B average. Electronic applications accepted.

University of Pittsburgh, School of Health and Rehabilitation Sciences, Department of Rehabilitation Science and Technology, Pittsburgh, PA 15260. Offers assistive rehabilitation technology (Certificate). *Students:* 10 full-time (7 women), 6 part-time (all women), 2 international. Average age 37. *Financial support:* Applicants required to submit FAFSA.

University of Pittsburgh, School of Health and Rehabilitation Sciences, Program in Health and Rehabilitation Sciences, Pittsburgh, PA 15260. Offers dietetics (MS); health and rehabilitation sciences (MS), including clinical dietetics, coordinated with dietetics, health care supervision and management, health information systems, occupational therapy, physical therapy, rehabilitation counseling, rehabilitation science and technology, sports medicine; wellness and human performance (MS). *Accreditation:* APTA. Part-time and evening/weekend programs available. *Faculty:* 40 full-time (23 women), 3 part-time/adjunct (2 women). *Students:* 93 full-time (67 women), 54 part-time (35 women); includes 31 minority (12 African Americans, 18 Asian Americans or Pacific Islanders, 1 Hispanic American), 15 international. Average age 30. 122

applicants, 82% accepted, 64 enrolled. In 2006, 28 degrees awarded. *Entrance requirements:* For master's, minimum GPA of 3.0. Additional exam requirements/recommendations for international students: Required—TOEFL, IELTS. *Application deadline:* Applications are processed on a rolling basis. Application fee: $50. Electronic applications accepted. *Financial support:* In 2006–07, 11 research assistantships with full tuition reimbursements (averaging $16,918 per year) were awarded; teaching assistantships, Federal Work-Study, institutionally sponsored loans, traineeships, and unspecified assistantships also available. Support available to part-time students. Financial award applicants required to submit FAFSA. *Faculty research:* Assistive technology, seating and wheeled mobility, cellular neurophysiology, low back syndrome, augmentative communication. Total annual research expenditures: $953,246. *Application contact:* Shameem Gangjee, Director of Admissions, 412-383-6558, Fax: 412-383-6535, E-mail: admissions@shrs.pitt.edu.

University of Pittsburgh, School of Health and Rehabilitation Sciences, Program in Rehabilitation Science, Pittsburgh, PA 15260. Offers PhD. Part-time programs available. *Faculty:* 40 full-time (23 women), 3 part-time/adjunct (2 women). *Students:* 35 full-time (18 women), 16 part-time (9 women); includes 1 minority (Asian American or Pacific Islander), 21 international. Average age 34. 28 applicants, 57% accepted, 10 enrolled. In 2006, 5 degrees awarded. *Entrance requirements:* For doctorate, GRE. Additional exam requirements/recommendations for international students: Required—TOEFL, IELTS. *Application deadline:* Applications are processed on a rolling basis. Application fee: $50. Electronic applications accepted. *Financial support:* In 2006–07, 15 research assistantships with full and partial tuition reimbursements (averaging $24,380 per year) were awarded. Total annual research expenditures: $5.2 million. *Unit head:* Dr. George Carvell, Associate Dean of Graduate Studies, 412-383-6639, Fax: 412-383-6629, E-mail: gcarvell@pitt.edu. *Application contact:* Shameem Gangjee, Director of Admissions, 412-383-6558, Fax: 412-383-6535, E-mail: admissions@shrs.pitt.edu.

University of South Carolina, School of Medicine and The Graduate School, Graduate Programs in Medicine, Program in Rehabilitation Counseling, Columbia, SC 29208. Offers psychiatric rehabilitation (Certificate); rehabilitation counseling (MRC). *Accreditation:* CORE. Part-time and evening/weekend programs available. *Degree requirements:* For master's, internship, practicum. *Entrance requirements:* For master's and Certificate, GRE General Test or GMAT. Electronic applications accepted. Expenses: Contact institution. *Faculty research:* Quality of life, alcohol dependency, technology for disabled, psychiatric rehabilitation, women with disabilities.

University of Toronto, School of Graduate Studies, Life Sciences Division, Department of Rehabilitation Science, Toronto, ON M5S 1A1, Canada. Offers M Sc. *Degree requirements:* For master's, thesis. *Entrance requirements:* For master's, B Sc or equivalent; specialization in occupational therapy, physical therapy, or a related field; minimum B+ average in final 2 years.

University of Washington, School of Medicine and Graduate School, Graduate Programs in Medicine, Department of Rehabilitation Medicine, Seattle, WA 98195. Offers occupational therapy (MOT); physical therapy (DPT); rehabilitation science (PhD). *Faculty:* 56. *Students:* 175. Average age 30. In 2006, 25 master's, 30 doctorates awarded. *Median time to degree:* Master's–2 years full-time; doctorate–3 years full-time. *Degree requirements:* For doctorate, thesis/dissertation (for some programs), comprehensive exam (for some programs). *Entrance requirements:* Additional exam requirements/recommendations for international students: Required—TOEFL. Application fee: $45. *Faculty research:* Pediatric topics, balance, brain injury, spinal cord injury, pain, assistive technology. *Unit head:* Dr. Peter C. Esselman, Professor and Chair, 206-543-3600, Fax: 206-685-3244, E-mail: esselman@u.washington.edu. *Application contact:* Dr. Jean Deitz, Graduate Program Coordinator, 206-598-5396, Fax: 206-685-3244, E-mail: deitz@u.washington.edu.

University of Wisconsin–La Crosse, Office of University Graduate Studies, College of Science and Health, Department of Exercise and Sport Science, Program in Clinical Exercise Physiology, La Crosse, WI 54601-3742. Offers MS. *Students:* 16 full-time (12 women), 3 part-time (1 woman); includes 1 minority (Hispanic American), 2 international. Average age 26. 31 applicants, 52% accepted, 15 enrolled. In 2006, 13 degrees awarded. *Degree requirements:* For master's, thesis optional. *Entrance requirements:* Additional exam requirements/recommendations for international students: Required—TOEFL (minimum score 550 paper-based; 213 computer-based). *Application deadline:* For fall admission, 2/1 for domestic and international students; for spring admission, 10/1 for domestic and international students. Application fee: $45. *Financial support:* In 2006–07, 6 research assistantships (averaging $5,601 per year) were awarded; career-related internships or fieldwork, Federal Work-Study, institutionally sponsored loans, health care benefits, tuition waivers (full and partial), and unspecified assistantships also available. Financial award application deadline: 2/1; financial award applicants required to submit FAFSA. *Faculty research:* Cardiovascular physiology, wellness, risk factors for heart disease, obesity, exercise adherence. *Unit head:* Dr. John Porcari, Director, 608-785-8684, Fax: 608-785-8686, E-mail: porcari.john@uwlax.edu. *Application contact:* Kathryn Kiefer, Associate Director of Admissions, 608-785-8939, E-mail: admissions@uwlax.edu.

University of Wisconsin–Madison, Graduate School, School of Education, Department of Kinesiology, Therapeutic Science Program, Madison, WI 53706-1380. Offers MS. *Accreditation:* AOTA. *Entrance requirements:* For master's, GRE General Test. Application fee: $38. *Financial support:* Fellowships with full tuition reimbursements, research assistantships with full tuition reimbursements, teaching assistantships with full tuition reimbursements, traineeships and project assistantships available. *Unit head:* Dr. Li Li Ji, Chair, Department of Kinesiology, 608-262-0048.

Virginia Commonwealth University, Graduate School, School of Education, Department of Health and Human Performance, Richmond, VA 23284-9005. Offers athletic training (MS); exercise science (MS); rehabilitation and movement science (PhD); teacher education (MS). *Faculty:* 7 full-time (2 women). *Students:* 13 full-time (8 women), 28 part-time (17 women); includes 3 minority (2 African Americans, 1 American Indian/Alaska Native), 1 international. 8 applicants, 100% accepted, 8 enrolled. *Entrance requirements:* For master's, GRE General Test or MAT. *Application deadline:* For fall admission, 5/15 for domestic students; for spring admission, 11/15 for domestic students. Applications are processed on a rolling basis. Application fee: $50. *Financial support:* Career-related internships or fieldwork, Federal Work-Study, and institutionally sponsored loans available. Support available to part-time students. Financial award application deadline: 3/1. *Unit head:* Dr. Edmund Acevedo, Chair, 804-828-1948, Fax: 804-828-1946, E-mail: eoacevedo@vcu.edu. *Application contact:* Dr. Michael D. Davis, Director, Graduate Studies, 804-828-6530, Fax: 804-827-0676, E-mail: mddavis@vcu.edu.

See Close-Ups on pages 1751, 2333, and 2331.

Wayne State University, School of Medicine, Graduate Programs in Medicine, Department of Physical Medicine and Rehabilitation, Detroit, MI 48202. Offers rehabilitation science administration (Certificate); rehabilitation sciences (MS). *Students:* 1 applicant, 0% accepted. *Entrance requirements:* For master's, MD or DO. Additional exam requirements/recommendations for international students: Required—TOEFL (minimum score 550 paper-based; 213 computer-based); Recommended—TWE (minimum score 6). *Application deadline:* For fall admission, 6/1 for international students; for winter admission, 10/1 for international students; for spring admission, 2/1 for international students. Applications are processed on a rolling basis. Application fee: $30 ($50 for international students). Electronic applications accepted. *Faculty research:* Traumatic brain injury, biomechanics, spinal cord injury, spasticity, pediatric rehabilitation. Total annual research expenditures: $68,870. *Unit head:* Jay Meythaler, Chair, 313-966-0444, Fax: 313-745-1063, E-mail: av1259@wayne.edu. *Application contact:* Marilyn Wayland, Graduate Director, 313-745-9880, E-mail: ac8450@wayne.edu.

THE COLLEGE OF
ST. CATHERINE

COLLEGE OF ST. CATHERINE

Department of Occupational Therapy

Programs of Study

The Master of Arts in Occupational Therapy (M.A.O.T.) program provides excellent entry-level and post-professional education in occupational therapy based on an occupational science and liberal arts foundation. It prepares students for advanced occupational therapy roles and leadership in existing and emerging areas of practice. The M.A.O.T. program offers two tracks of graduate courses to both women and men. One track is available to those who wish to complete the academic requirements necessary for certification (entry-level); the other is for credentialed occupational therapists interested in graduate studies (post-professional). The program is available in a traditional weekday format as well as a weekend format.

The M.A.O.T. program focuses on the development of advanced occupational therapy practice and leadership roles. These roles require acquisition and integration of multiple skills in order to solve complex problems and work effectively in the rapidly changing health, community, and educational systems. The following themes are woven throughout the curriculum: communication, management and supervision, collaboration, technology, ethics and leadership development, critical thinking, theory application, health-pathology continuum, client-centered practice, human occupation across the life span, service delivery and innovation, inquiry, and research. The curriculum develops students' skills and knowledge for each theme and reinforces the reciprocal nature of information between practice and education.

Entry-level students are generally expected to complete the 72-credit program in sequence within three years of initial enrollment. The entry-level program is offered in both day and weekend formats. The 36-credit program for post-professional students is offered only in the weekend format. Post-professional students must complete all courses and the thesis requirement within five years of initial enrollment.

The entry-level curriculum includes four level-I fieldwork experiences (100 hours) and two full-time, three-month level II fieldwork experiences, with the option of a third level II fieldwork experience in a specialty area.

All academic, thesis, and fieldwork requirements must be completed in order to be eligible for the National Board for Certification in Occupational Therapy (NBCOT) national certification examination. Graduation from the M.A.O.T. program and passing the examination are both necessary to be certified as a registered occupational therapist (OTR).

Research Facilities

The College participates in Cooperating Libraries in Consortium (CLIC), which comprises facilities of fifty-two libraries on the Minnesota State University's online catalog system. CLIC puts more than 1 million volumes and a subscription list of 5,000 periodicals at students' disposal. Numerous online research services are available. The library is also linked to the Twin Cities Biomedical Consortium, allowing access to thirty-two health-related libraries. Complete library and computing services are available on both the Minneapolis and St. Paul campuses.

Financial Aid

Graduate students may apply for financial assistance in the form of state and federal loan programs, grants, scholarships, and work-study programs. Loans are the most common source of aid. All students seeking aid must submit a Free Application for Federal Student Aid (FAFSA). More information is available from the Office for Financial Aid (651-690-6540 or 800-945-4599 Ext. 6540; e-mail: finaid@stkate.edu).

Cost of Study

Tuition for the M.A.O.T. program in 2007–08 is $642 per credit.

Living and Housing Costs

Campus housing is available to graduate students on a space-available basis. For rates and other details, students can visit the Web site at http://www.stkate.edu/residence life.

Student Group

Students in the M.A.O.T. program represent a diverse range of ages and life experiences. Eighty to 90 percent of entering students are women. Recent classes have been approximately 85 percent entry-level students, both recent baccalaureate graduates and people entering OT from careers in other fields. Two-thirds of M.A.O.T. graduate students are enrolled in the day format program.

Location

The occupational therapy program is located on the College's St. Paul campus in an attractive, well-kept, residential neighborhood. The Twin Cities area, nationally known for the arts and cultural activities, also has hundreds of parks and lakes that provide year-round recreational opportunities.

The College

The College of St. Catherine is a Catholic college founded in 1905 by the Sisters of St. Joseph of Carondelet. Occupational therapy has been part of the curriculum since 1945. The College encourages the development of leadership skills and fosters the intellectual, personal, and spiritual growth of all students. The College offers bachelor's degrees to women and associate and graduate degrees to men and women. Total enrollment is more than 5,400; graduate program enrollment is 1,400. The College is accredited by the Higher Learning Commission and is a member of the North Central Association of Colleges and Schools. The occupational therapy graduate curriculum is fully accredited by the Accreditation Council for Occupational Therapy Education (ACOTE) of the American Occupational Therapy Association.

Applying

Required application materials include an application with $25 fee, official transcripts from each postsecondary school attended, three clinical recommendation forms, and a summary of volunteer and work experiences. A minimum cumulative GPA of 3.0 on a 4.0 scale and a minimum prerequisite supporting work GPA of 2.75 on a 4.0 scale is expected. The GRE is not required. Prerequisite course work for the entry-level program is anatomy and physiology I and II, general psychology, life span developmental psychology, abnormal psychology, medical terminology, and statistics. Applications received by February 1 are given priority consideration.

Correspondence and Information

Office of Graduate Admission #4027
College of St. Catherine
2004 Randolph Avenue
St. Paul, Minnesota 55105-1794
Phone: 651-690-6933
      800-945-4599 Ext. 6933 (toll-free)
Fax: 651-690-6549
E-mail: graduate_study@stkate.edu
Web site: http://www.stkate.edu/graduatestudy

College of St. Catherine

THE FACULTY AND THEIR RESEARCH

The Master of Arts in Occupational Therapy program is taught by outstanding faculty members who bring the latest developments in the profession to the classroom. They are recognized locally and nationally for their contributions to the profession in the areas of teaching, research, publication, innovative practice ideas, and leadership. Faculty members represent all areas of specialization, including mental health, occupational science, physical disabilities, community health, pediatrics, geriatrics, administration, and education.

Julie Bass Haugen, Professor, Chair, and M.A.O.T. Program Director; Ph.D., Minnesota; OTR, FAOTA. Motor behavior, occupation and health, qualitative and quantitative research methods.

Linda Buxell, Assistant Professor and Level II Fieldwork Coordinator; M.A., USC; OTR/L. Holistic health, sensory integration, and occupational science.

John Fleming, Assistant Professor; M.O.T., Western Michigan; OTR/L. Academic and fieldwork education, gerontology, community practice, qualitative research methods.

Nancy Flinn, Assistant Professor; M.A., Minnesota; OTR/L. Task-oriented approach to motor behavior problems, constraint-induced therapy, emerging educational technologies.

Jyothi Gupta, Assistant Professor; Ph.D., Windsor; OTR/L, OT(C). Work and productivity, aging and mental health, spirituality and culture, interdisciplinary work, community partnerships.

Kristi Haertl, Assistant Professor; M.S., Cardinal Stritch; OTR/L. Psychosocial and community practice, the efficacy of sensory integration treatment, holistic health, qualitative research designs.

Amy Heinz, Instructor and Level I Fieldwork Coordinator; M.A., St. Catherine; OTR.

Mary Lou Henderson, Associate Professor and Director of the Occupational Science Program; M.S., Kansas; OTR/L. Occupational science, pediatrics, student learning, teaching.

Merri Lee Henderson, Assistant Professor and Level II Fieldwork Coordinator; M.S., Wisconsin; OTR/L. Fieldwork.

David Luedke, Associate Professor; M.A., Minnesota.

Kathleen Matuska, Associate Professor; M.P.H., Minnesota; OTR/L. Educational programs for individuals with multiple sclerosis, community wellness programs for senior citizens.

Barbara O'Keefe, Assistant Professor; M.S., Mankato State; OTR/L, CRC. Case management for workers' compensation, ergonomics and worksite evaluations and accommodations.

Karen M. Sames, Associate Professor; M.B.A., St. Thomas; OTR/L. Cost-effectiveness of services, reimbursement issues, occupation-based practice, ethics in practice, alternative teaching models.

Sharon Stoffel, Associate Professor; M.A., St. Mary's (Minnesota); OTR/L, FAOTA. Aging, environmental design, applied ethics, occupational storying, community-based well elder programs.

Catherine N. Sullivan, Assistant Professor; Ph.D., Minnesota; OTR/L. Spatially coordinated behavior, wheelchair locomotion, spatial cognition, biomechanics, ergonomics, driving.

Dawn Torine-Micko, Assistant Professor; M.A., St. Catherine; OTR/L. Early childhood intervention, assistive technology and school systems, service dogs, pet therapy.

THE COLLEGE OF
ST. CATHERINE

COLLEGE OF ST. CATHERINE

Department of Physical Therapy

Programs of Study	The College of St. Catherine's Doctor of Physical Therapy (D.P.T.) degree program is a thirty-three-month, full-time, day-scheduled program. It focuses on clinical decision-making skills and on the application of research principles to everyday clinical practice. The D.P.T. degree is an entry-level clinical doctorate that prepares graduates for autonomous, evidence-based clinical practice in complex environments.
	Clinical learning and practice are integrated throughout the innovative curriculum. The program includes forty weeks of full-time clinical experience as well as many part-time clinical experiences over the three years. In addition to course work in general clinical education, rehabilitation, out-patient PT, research, and ethics and leadership, some required courses are acute care, long-term care, home care, complex trauma, pediatrics, and an amputee clinic. Course material is organized around clinical cases and practice settings, with each setting presented through five streams: medical and behavioral science; practice environment; examination, evaluation, and diagnosis; plan of care, intervention, and outcomes; and health-care administration. The complexity of concepts and cases in each setting increases as the curriculum progresses. During the last two years of the program, students complete a research project.
	The Department's teaching methods support the curriculum. Courses are taught by teams of faculty members with expertise in basic and clinical sciences who utilize a variety of instructional methods including lecture, supervised skills laboratory sessions, group discussion/inquiry, community visits, case-study learning, student presentations, independent study, writing-intensive components, on-site clinical learning, and problem-based tutorials. Service learning and learning experiences designed to facilitate cultural competence are an integral part of the curriculum.
	Students have many opportunities to work with faculty members on research projects and to pursue their own research interests. Faculty members and students regularly present at regional and national physical therapy conferences.
Research Facilities	The physical therapy program has four on-site laboratories as well as access to numerous clinical sites throughout the area. The library is linked to the Twin Cities Biomedical Consortium, allowing access to thirty-two health-related libraries. The College participates in Cooperating Libraries in Consortium (CLIC), which comprises facilities from fifty-two libraries in the Minnesota State University's online catalog system. CLIC puts more than 1 million volumes and a subscription list of 5,000 periodicals at students' disposal. Numerous online research services are also available. Complete library and computing services are available on both the Minneapolis and St. Paul campuses.
Financial Aid	Graduate students may apply for financial assistance in the form of state and federal loan programs, grants, scholarships, and work-study programs. Loans are the most common source of aid. All students seeking aid must submit a Free Application for Federal Student Aid (FAFSA). More information is available from the Office for Financial Aid (651-690-6540 or 800-945-4599 Ext. 6540; e-mail: finaid@stkate.edu).
Cost of Study	Tuition for the D.P.T. program in 2007–08 is $10,044.
Living and Housing Costs	Campus housing is available to D.P.T. graduate students on a space-available basis. For rates and other details, students can visit the Web site at http://www.stkate.edu/residencelife.
Student Group	Up to 28 D.P.T. students are admitted each year; all are full-time. Generally, 80 percent of the students are women. Students in the D.P.T. program represent a diverse range of ages and life experiences. Most entering students are recent baccalaureate graduates, although each recent class has included students entering physical therapy from careers in other fields.
Location	The Department of Physical Therapy overlooks the Mississippi River on the College's Minneapolis campus in the vibrant, collegiate Cedar-Riverside neighborhood. The wooded St. Paul campus, with its new Student Center, is easily accessible by freeway; shuttle buses run between campuses. The Twin Cities area, nationally known for the arts and cultural activities, also has hundreds of area parks and lakes providing year-round recreational opportunities.
The College	The College of St. Catherine is a Catholic college founded in 1905 by the Sisters of St. Joseph of Carondelet. Physical therapy has been part of the curriculum for more than thirty years. The College encourages the development of leadership skills and fosters the intellectual, personal, and spiritual growth of all students. The College offers bachelor's degrees for women and associate and graduate degrees for men and women. Total enrollment is more than 5,400; graduate program enrollment is 1,400. The College is accredited by the Higher Learning Commission and is a member of the North Central Association of Colleges and Schools. The Doctor of Physical Therapy program is accredited by the Commission on Accreditation in Physical Therapy Education (CAPTE).
Applying	Applicants are evaluated on the basis of their overall academic record (cumulative and prerequisite grade point averages), clinical recommendations, GRE scores, personal statement, and leadership and health-care related experiences. Required materials include an application plus a $25 fee, personal statement, official transcripts from all postsecondary institutions, two clinical experience references (at least one from a physical therapist), and GRE scores. A minimum cumulative grade point average of 3.0 on a 4.0 scale is expected. The application deadline is January 20. Later applications may be considered on a space-available basis. Decision notification is in late February.
Correspondence and Information	Office of Graduate Admission #4027 College of St. Catherine 2004 Randolph Avenue St. Paul, Minnesota 55105-1794 Phone: 651-690-6933 800-945-4599 Ext. 6933 (toll-free) Fax: 651-690-6549 E-mail: graduate_study@stkate.edu Web site: http://www.stkate.edu/graduatestudy

College of St. Catherine

THE FACULTY AND THEIR RESEARCH

Cort Cieminski, Assistant Professor; M.S., Boise State; PT, ATC/R, CSCS. Flexibility measurement issues, shoulder biomechanics and fitness testing.

Megan Dowdal-Osborn, Assistant Professor; M.P.T., St. Catherine; PT. Vestibular/balance issues and neurologic intervention.

Kristen Gerlach, Assistant Professor; Ph.D., SUNY at Buffalo; PT. Risk factors for injury in female runners and women's health.

Laura Gilchrist, Assistant Professor; Ph.D., Minnesota; PT. Cancer pain, chronic pain.

Jyothi Gupta, Assistant Professor; Ph.D., Windsor; OTR/L, OT(C). Work and productivity, aging and mental health, spirituality and culture, interdisciplinary work, community partnerships.

Mary Sue Ingram, Assistant Professor; Ph.D., Minnesota. Spinal cord injuries and electrical simulation.

Susan Klappa, Assistant Professor; M.P.T., St. Catherine; PT. Peripheral neuropathy and diabetes, lumbopelvic influences on patellofemoral pain and aquatic therapy.

Paul Niemuth, Assistant Professor; D.Sc., Rocky Mountain University of Health Professions; PT, OCS, ATC/R. Orthopedic physical therapy, sports medicine, running injuries, hip joint.

John Schmitt, Assistant Professor; Ph.D., Minnesota; PT. Measurement of rehabilitation outcomes, risk factors for musculoskeletal injuries.

Debra Selheim, Associate Professor; Ph.D., Minnesota; PT. How learning occurs; educational factors that affect how students approach learning.

Mary Weddle, Assistant Professor and Director of Clinical Education; M.F.A., Iowa; M.S.P.T., Beaver. Beliefs held by geriatric women related to exercise, Tai Chi.

EMERSON COLLEGE

School of Communication
Master of Science in Speech Communication Sciences and Disorders

Program of Study	For more than sixty years, Emerson has been a pioneer in communication sciences and disorders, earning a reputation for excellence in clinical preparation. Fully accredited by the American Speech-Language-Hearing Association (ASHA), the Master of Science in Speech Communication Sciences and Disorders (M.S.Sp.) Program prepares students to be critical thinkers and innovative clinicians and helps to build the foundation for a successful career in one of the fastest-growing fields in the country.
	Emerson offers the academic and clinical resources of a large research university within a small college setting. Course work and clinical experiences, as well as Emerson's faculty and state-of-the-art facilities, enable students to develop the skills to assess and treat a broad range of communication disorders in pediatric, school age, adult, and geriatric populations.
	For more information about Emerson's Master of Science in Speech Communication Sciences and Disorders Program, students should visit http://admission.emerson.edu/admission/graduate/academics/csd.cfm.
Research Facilities	The Emerson College library has more than 200,000 volumes, 20,000 journals (paper and electronic), 8,000 e-books, 10,000 nonprint materials, and 10,000 microforms in its collection that focuses on communication studies and the performing arts. Through membership in the Fenway Consortium, graduate students have access to more than 2 million volumes. Computer-assisted reference services provide bibliographic databases through Dialog, BRS, and other online services. The Online Computer Library Center is used for student research support.
	M.S.Sp. degree candidates gain valuable hands-on experience in the Media Services Center, which provides students with access to approximately 2,400 films, videos, laser discs, and DVDs. The center is home to audio, video, and multimedia production facilities; a video studio; and several nonlinear editing suites comparable to those of any television studio in a major U.S. city.
Financial Aid	Emerson College offers several financial assistance programs that make graduate education possible: merit-based awards (domestic and international applicants), low-interest federal loans (domestic applicants only), Federal Work-Study (domestic applicants only), private loans (domestic and international applicants), Student Employment (domestic and international applicants), and alternative payment plans (domestic and international applicants). For detailed information, prospective students should visit the Office of Student Financial Services Web site at http://www.emerson.edu/financial_services/info-grad.cfm.
Cost of Study	Tuition for the 2007–08 academic year is $840 per credit hour. Other fees vary and may apply.
Living and Housing Costs	Though on-campus housing is not available for its graduate students, the Emerson College Office of Off-Campus Student Services (http://www.emerson.edu/offcampus_housing/) offers assistance in finding housing, including local apartment listings, realtor lists, temporary accommodations, search tips, pertinent neighborhood information, a roommate networking service, and more. Costs for housing are comparable to those of rental properties available in larger East Coast cities.
Student Group	More than 950 graduate students representing forty-five states and sixty countries are enrolled in Emerson programs.
Student Outcomes	Emerson graduates work in many different settings, including schools, hospitals, rehabilitation facilities, nursing homes, in private practice, and as consultants.
Location	Situated in the heart of downtown Boston, Emerson offers access to the vast resources of a city that is home to the nation's finest educational institutions and an international hub of culture, media production, writing, publishing, communication, commerce, and medical innovation. Boston is a career launching pad for Emerson's students, many of whom intern or work at world-renowned organizations throughout the city. Emerson students from around the country and the world absorb the city's unique blend of local and global culture, and many find that Boston is an education in itself.
The College	Emerson College, founded in 1880 by Charles Wesley Emerson, has expanded upon its original mission of promoting the study of oratory and the performing arts by offering some of the nation's most distinctive graduate programs in communication.
Applying	Emerson's graduate programs welcome applicants from across the United States and around the world. Admission is competitive and selective. The College is looking for students whose academic and professional backgrounds, communication skills, and passion for the field meet the demands of their chosen program and promise a successful career.
	The application deadline is February 15 for domestic and international applicants. Applications that are not complete by the final deadline are not reviewed be the admission committee. Applicants are responsible for ensuring the completion of their application. Application fees are nonrefundable; application forms and supporting materials become the property of the Office of Graduate Admission once they are sent to the office and are not returned.
	All application materials, with the exception of GRE test scores, must be submitted together in one package to ensure timely review. A complete application includes the application form (students may apply online or they may download the PDF version), the application fee ($60 for domestic applicants; $75 for international applicants), official transcripts from all colleges/universities previously attended, three sealed letters of recommendation (by persons best able to assess academic and professional qualifications, including motivation, goals, and clinical potential), GRE test scores, an essay, and a professional resume.
	Applicants whose native language is not English must provide evidence of English proficiency by submitting official TOEFL or IELTS test results. (Students from India and the Philippines are considered nonnative English speakers and are required to take the TOEFL.) Emerson College's school code for the TOEFL is 3367; no department code is needed. The minimum TOEFL score is 550 on the paper-based test (213 on the computer-based test or 80 on the Internet-based test). The minimum IELTS score is 6.5. Applicants who do not meet this requirement will not be reviewed for admission. For more information about these tests, students should visit http://www.toefl.org or http://www.ielts.org.
	Decisions are made on complete applications within six eight weeks. Deadlines for merit-based and federal aid applications for fall are February 15 and April 1, respectively. Students seeking additional information about financing their graduate education should visit http://www.emerson.edu/financial_services/info-grad.cfm/.
Correspondence and Information	Office of Graduate Admission Emerson College 120 Boylston Street Boston, Massachusetts 02116-4624 Phone: 617-824-8610 Fax: 617-824-8614 E-mail: gradapp@emerson.edu Web site: http://admission.emerson.edu/admission/graduate

Emerson College

THE FACULTY AND THEIR RESEARCH

Cynthia L. Bartlett, Graduate Program Director, Associate Professor of Communication Sciences and Disorders, and Coordinator for Educator Preparation; Ph.D., Pittsburgh; CCC (Speech-Language Pathology), ASHA. Teacher, lecturer, author, researcher, and specialist in adult neurogenic communicative disorders, Dr. Bartlett has authored or co-authored articles in *Brain and Language, Aphasiology,* and the *Journal of Speech Language Pathology and Audiology* as well as several book chapters. More than fifteen years of hospital and medical center clinical experience provide the impetus for her ongoing interests in speech, language, and communicative difficulties in adults with acquired brain damage.

Amit Bajaj, Assistant Professor of Communication Sciences and Disorders; Ph.D., Wichita State; CCC (Speech-Language Pathology), ASHA. Teacher, researcher, and author, Dr. Bajaj's areas of expertise are fluency disorders and speech science. He has published in the area of fluency disorders in the *Journal of Fluency Disorders* and *Proceedings of the Fifth Oxford Dysfluency Conference,* and in the area of epistemological beliefs in the *Journal of Educational Psychology.* He has presented papers at national and international venues in areas that include fluency disorders, multicultural issues, and use of technology.

Anthony S. Bashir, Professor of Communication Sciences and Disorders and Coordinator, Academic Support Services and Disability Services; Ph.D., Northwestern; CCC (Speech-Language Pathology) and Fellow, ASHA. Dr. Bashir is a teacher, lecturer, and author in the areas of learning disabilities and language disorders. He has also been chairperson of the ASHA Joint Committee on Learning Disabilities and is the author of numerous articles.

Lynn M. Conners, Clinical Instructor in Communication Sciences and Disorders; M.S.Sp., Emerson; CCC (Speech-Language Pathology), ASHA. A Certified Early Intervention Specialist (CEIS), experienced clinician, and supervisor, Ms. Conners supervises graduate student clinicians participating in the Thayer Lindsley Family Centered Program for young children who are deaf and hard of hearing and their families and in the Robbins Center for Speech, Language, and Hearing.

Laura Glufling-Tham, Clinical Instructor in Communication Sciences and Disorders; M.S., Northeastern; CCC (Speech-Language Pathology), ASHA. An experienced clinical supervisor and teacher, Ms. Glufling-Tham has many years of clinical experience working with adults with cognitive-communicative disorders, including aphasia, apraxia of speech, dysarthria, cognitive-linguistic impairments, and dysphagia.

Jacqueline Weis Liebergott, Professor of Communication Sciences and Disorders and President of Emerson College; Ph.D., Pittsburgh; CCC (Speech-Language Pathology), ASHA. Dr. Liebergott has extensive experience in the field of language disorders in children. Her research has included a longitudinal investigation of full-term and at-risk infants and a follow-up study of the relationship between early language development and academic success in normal and at-risk children.

Seton Lindsay, Clinical Instructor in Communication Sciences and Disorders; M.S.Sp. Emerson. CCC (Speech-Language Pathology), ASHA. An experienced clinician, lecturer, and clinical supervisor, Ms. Lindsay specializes in work with young children who have a variety of developmental communication disorders. She has worked clinically on multidisciplinary teams evaluating and treating children with developmental disorders.

Shelly Lipschultz, Clinical Instructor in Communication Sciences and Disorders; M.S., Wisconsin–Madison; CCC (Speech-Language Pathology), ASHA. Clinical supervisor, teacher, and consultant in speech-language disorders, Ms. Lipschultz has developed videotapes and test protocols for the informal assessment of cognitive and language abilities of young children, developmentally delayed adults, and nonspeaking persons.

Amy B. Litwack, Clinical Instructor in Communication Sciences and Disorders and Clinical Outreach Coordinator; M.S., Boston University. CCC (Speech-Language Pathology), ASHA. An experienced clinical supervisor and teacher, Ms. Litwack has many years of clinical experience working with adults with cognitive-communicative disorders including aphasia, apraxia of speech, dysarthria, cognitive-communicative impairments, and dysphagia. She supervises graduate student clinicians in the department's Program for Acquired Communication Disorders.

David M. Luterman, Professor Emeritus of Communication Sciences and Disorders and Founding Director of the Thayer Lindsley Family-Centered Program for Hearing-Impaired Children (1960); D.Ed., Penn State; CCC (Audiology) and Fellow, ASHA. Dr. Luterman is a well-known teacher, researcher, author, consultant, and lecturer. He is a specialist in the hearing-impaired and in counseling. His books include *Counseling the Communicatively Disordered and their Families, Deafness in Perspective, Deafness in the Family, When your Child is Deaf, In the Shadows: Living and Coping with a Loved One's Chronic Illness, The Young Deaf Child,* and *Early Childhood Deafness* (with Ellen Kurtzer-White). Dr. Luterman has presented many lectures and symposia around the world.

David Lowell Maxwell, Professor of Communication Sciences and Disorders; Ph.D., Southern Illinois; CCC (Speech-Language Pathology), ASHA. Teacher, researcher, consultant, and lecturer, with expertise in stuttering, orofacial malformations, and neurogenic disorders of speech and language, Dr. Maxwell has held appointments and consultancies at Boston University Medical School, Tufts New England Medical School, Eunice Kennedy Shriver Center, Massachusetts General Hospital, Douglas Thom Clinic, and numerous public schools and rehabilitation agencies throughout New England. He is the co-author (with Dr. Eiki Satake) of *Research and Statistical Methods in Communication Disorders* and *Theory of Probability for Clinical Diagnostic Testing.* His current research interests are the role of temporal information processing in speech and language, working memory operations in oral language, and the use of probability statistics to improve the accuracy of diagnostic testing.

Betsy C. Micucci, Clinical Instructor of Communication Sciences and Disorders; M.S., Emerson; CCC (Speech-Language Pathology), ASHA. Clinical supervisor, teacher, consultant, and early-intervention specialist, Ms. Micucci coordinates the early intervention curriculum that prepares students for early intervention certification. Ms. Micucci was Associate Director and Speech-Language Pathology Department Head at the Eunice Kennedy Shriver Center University Affiliated Program in Waltham, Massachusetts, prior to coming to Emerson College.

Maria Mody, Associate Professor of Communication Sciences and Disorders; Ph.D., CUNY Graduate Center; CCC (Speech-Language Pathology), ASHA. Researcher, lecturer, teacher, and author in areas relating to the behavioral and neural bases of reading and language disorders in children, Dr. Mody has used behavioral observations, electromagnetic recordings, and metabolic methods to study performance of typical and clinical populations with a variety of developmental disorders. She has lectured widely in these areas in the U.S. and abroad and has published in such journals as the *Journal of the Acoustic Society of America, Phonetica, Journal of Experimental Child Psychology, Clinical Linguistics and Phonetics,* and *Journal of Learning Disabilities.*

Mark Parker, Assistant Professor of Communication Sciences and Disorders; Ph.D., LSU Health Sciences Center. Audiologist, lecturer, and researcher in the application of stem cell technology to the treatment of hearing loss, Dr. Parker has published in the *Journal of Neuroscience Research, Audiology and Neuro-Otology, Experimental Neurology,* and *Drug Discovery Today.* He also holds the position of Associate Research Scientist in the Department of Otology and Laryngology at Harvard Medical School, Children's Hospital, Laboratory of Cellular and Molecular Hearing Research.

Marie-Kay Rimshaw, Clinical Instructor in Communication Sciences and Disorders; M.S., Wisconsin–Stevens Point; CCC (Speech-Language Pathology), ASHA. Clinical supervisor, consultant, and teacher, Ms. Rimshaw has developed residential communication programs for adults with Alzheimer's disease, and she specializes in child language disorders. Ms. Rimshaw has provided clinical instruction and supervision for graduate students in the Midwest, and prior to joining the Emerson faculty, she was the manager of the HealthSouth Braintree Rehabilitation Network Clinic in Chestnut Hill, Massachusetts.

Sandra Cohn Thau, Director of Clinical Education and Program Director for Teacher Education; M.A., Northwestern; CCC (Speech-Language Pathology), ASHA. Clinical supervisor, teacher, and consultant in speech-language disorders, Ms. Thau was the former coordinator of student training and the Rehabilitation Coordinator at the Kennedy Memorial Hospital (now Franciscan Children's Hospital) in Boston.

Krista M. Wilkinson, Associate Professor of Communication Sciences and Disorders; Ph.D., Georgia State. Researcher, teacher, author, and lecturer, Dr. Wilkinson has authored or co-authored more than twenty articles in such publications as the *Journal of Speech and Hearing Research, Augmentative and Alternative Communication, American Journal on Mental Retardation, Journal of Child Language,* and *Journal of Experimental Child Psychology.* Dr. Wilkinson has lectured extensively to professional organizations and has served as instructor for an ASHA online professional development workshop. Her federally funded research interests are in the area of language acquisition and use in typically and non-typically developing children, including mechanisms of vocabulary acquisition, referential use, and gender differences in the use of language among youths with mental retardation. Dr. Wilkinson also retains an affiliation with the Eunice Kennedy Shriver Center.

HARVARD UNIVERSITY/
MASSACHUSETTS INSTITUTE OF TECHNOLOGY
Division of Health Sciences and Technology
Speech and Hearing Bioscience and Technology Program

Program of Study	A four-plus-year curriculum leads to a Ph.D. in speech and hearing bioscience and technology awarded by Massachusetts Institute of Technology (MIT). This doctoral program is designed to develop research scientists who can apply the concepts and methods of the physical and biological sciences to basic and clinical problems in speech and hearing through innovative research. To meet this goal, the program combines a rigorous course curriculum in quantitative methods for studying speech and hearing with broad exposure to issues, including clinical diagnosis and treatment. The interdisciplinary nature of the program is illustrated by the diversity of interests of its faculty of about 60, which is drawn from about ten different departments at Harvard and MIT.
	The first two to three years are devoted principally to course work in the anatomical, acoustical, physiological, perceptual, and cognitive basics and to clinical approaches to speech and hearing problems. Early introduction of key concepts in acoustics, anatomy, and physiology provides a solid base from which to pursue individual research interests. Students work with research advisers to develop a thorough understanding of basic concepts and tools in their fields of concentration. While students have considerable flexibility in changing their areas of concentration as their educational horizons expand, on admission to the program students should indicate their interests. Throughout the program, special attention is paid to teaching scientific values and discussing issues of integrity and scholarly practice.
	Students must master core material in the field of speech and hearing that spans many traditional disciplines. Mastery of this core material is tested in the written part of the General Examination. Students must also plan a concentration, a program of course work and research in one of five focus areas consisting of physiology and neuroscience, perception, signal and system analysis, speech and language, and speech pathology. The focus area forms the basis for the oral portion of the General Examination.
	Active participation in research begins as early as the summer following the first year. By the end of the second year, students should have identified an area of professional interest. A research project is then chosen that forms the basis of a Ph.D. thesis and demonstrates the ability to do original research. Thesis research can be done at MIT, Harvard, or at one of the teaching hospitals.
Research Facilities	The resources available for research training include laboratories at MIT, Harvard University (including Harvard Medical School), and Harvard-affiliated hospitals. Students have free access to the libraries and other educational and recreational resources of both universities.
Financial Aid	The Division of Health Sciences and Technology (HST), primarily through an NIH training grant, provides full support for the students enrolled in this program provided they are citizens or permanent residents of the U.S. This includes a stipend of approximately $23,268 per year. This support continues through three years of study, after which support comes from the research laboratories where students conduct their Ph.D. research.
Cost of Study	Tuition and fees for this program were $35,040 for the 2006–07 academic year. Tuition is covered by training grants and research assistantships for U.S. citizens and permanent residents. Foreign applicants must guarantee that provisions have been made for their support if they wish to be considered.
Living and Housing Costs	Living expenses, including room, meals, and miscellaneous expenses, average $2000 per month for single students and slightly more for married students. Single graduate students at MIT may live in one of five graduate residences. Married graduate students at MIT may live at Westgate or Eastgate graduate apartments. Many graduate students live in apartments and houses in the surrounding communities.
Student Group	The Speech and Hearing Bioscience and Technology Program (SHBT) enrolled 49 students in 2006–07, including 19 women.
Student Outcomes	The breadth of the program qualifies its graduates for a wide range of careers in basic and applied research in industry, universities, hospitals, or government laboratories concerned with biological and man-made communications systems. Specific areas include basic research on the neural, physiological, and perceptual processes that underlie communication by speech and hearing; speech recognition systems that couple acoustic input to computer systems; analysis of central nervous system behavior to determine neural abnormalities in people with speech-processing disorders; development of measures of environments (conference room, airport terminal, open spaces) that provide specifications for effective voice communication; and design of speech production and hearing prostheses to alleviate pathological conditions.
Location	Harvard and MIT are located in Cambridge, Massachusetts, just across the Charles River from Boston.
The Institutions and The Division	Harvard is the oldest college in the United States, founded in 1636. MIT, founded in 1861 as a private, endowed institution committed to the extension of knowledge through teaching and research, has grown to be one of the foremost research universities in the world.
	The HST Division, established in 1977, formalized a major collaborative effort in the health sciences that began in 1970. This effort, designed to focus science and technology on human needs, draws on the complementary strengths of the two institutions.
Applying	Applicants to the program should have a bachelor's degree in physical science, biology, psychology, linguistics, communicative sciences and disorders, engineering, or computer science, with strong analytical skills. Course work in the first year assumes familiarity with calculus, college-level physics, probability and statistics, and biology. Students are accepted based on interests, academic background, intellectual capacity, curiosity, motivation, energy, and character. While GRE scores are desirable, they are not required. Applicants should note the program's emphasis on broad-based research education rather than on clinical or narrowly focused technical training. For additional information, students should contact Dr. M. Christian Brown, Chairman of the SHBT Admissions Committee, via e-mail at mcb@epl.meei.harvard.edu.
	Applicants can apply online by going to http://web.mit.edu/admissions/ or by downloading a PDF version of the MIT graduate application at http://web.mit.edu/admissions/www/graduate/applications/download.html. For "department," applicants should list "HST" and use "SHBT" under "interdisciplinary program." All applicants should also be sure to check HST's admissions Web page at http://hst.mit.edu/admissions/public for up-to-date information on admissions processes. Students should submit their applications and supporting documentation by December 15. It is the student's responsibility to ensure that all materials are received.
Correspondence and Information	Dr. Martha L. Gray Co-Director, Division of HST Room E25-519 Massachusetts Institute of Technology Cambridge, Massachusetts 02139 Phone: 617-258-8974 Web site: http://web.mit.edu/shbt Dr. Louis D. Braida Program Director Room 36-747 Massachusetts Institute of Technology Cambridge, Massachusetts 02139 Phone: 617-253-2575

Harvard University/Massachusetts Institute of Technology

THE FACULTY AND THEIR RESEARCH

Research facilities include sites at MIT, the Harvard Medical School, and several of the Harvard-affiliated teaching hospitals. Collaborative work with other local universities is possible by special arrangement. The key to the abbreviations in each faculty member's entry is BWH: Brigham and Women's Hospital; BU: Boston University; CH: Children's Hospital; HMS: Harvard Medical School; HU: Harvard University; MEEI: Massachusetts Eye and Ear Infirmary; MGH: Massachusetts General Hospital; MIT: Massachusetts Institute of Technology; and Tufts: Tufts University.

Joe C. Adams, Ph.D.; HMS, MEEI. Cochlear homeostasis.
Louis D. Braida, Ph.D.; MIT. Psychoacoustics, aids for the deaf.
M. Christian Brown, Ph.D.; HMS, MEEI. Auditory physiology.
David N. Caplan, M.D., Ph.D.; HMS, MGH. Neurological bases of language.
Peter Cariani, Ph.D.; Tufts. Temporal coding and music perception.
H. Steven Colburn, Ph.D.; BU. Binaural auditory psychophysics.
David P. Corey, Ph.D.; HMS. Cell and molecular biology of the ear.
Suzanne Corkin, Ph.D.; MIT, MGH. Brain and cognitive functions.
Douglas A. Cotanche, Ph.D.; HMS, CH. Hair cell regeneration.
Bertrand Delgutte, Ph.D.; MIT, MEEI. Auditory neuroscience and perception.
Nathaniel I. Durlach, Ph.D.; MIT. Man-machine interactions.
Ruth-Anne Eatock, Ph.D.; HMS, MEEI. Sensory transduction in the inner ear.
Donald K. Eddington, Ph.D.; MIT, MEEI. Cochlear implants.
Albert Edge, Ph.D.; HMS, MEEI. Inner ear cell regeneration.
Ramon A. Franco, M.D.; HMS, MEEI. Laryngology, head and neck surgery.
Dennis M. Freeman, Ph.D.; MIT. Auditory mechanisms in the ear.
Barbara C. Fullerton, Ph.D.; HMS, MEEI. Auditory neuroanatomy.
Anne Giersch, Ph.D.; BWH. Human deafness genetics.
James R. Glass, Ph.D.; MIT. Speech processing for human-machine interaction.
David Gow, Ph.D.; HMS, MGH. Spoken word recognition.
Julie E. Greenberg, Ph.D.; MIT. Signal processing for hearing aids.
Frank Guenther, Ph.D.; BU, MIT. Motor control of speech production.
John J. Guinan, Ph.D.; MEEI, HMS. Cochlear physiology and auditory reflexes.
Christopher F. Halpin, Ph.D.; HMS, MEEI. Audiology.
Kenneth Hancock, Ph.D.; HMS, MEEI. Auditory neuroscience.
Marc D. Hauser, Ph.D.; HU. Neuroethology of primate vocal communication.
James Heaton, Ph.D.; HMS, MGH. Voice and speech production.
Barbara S. Herrmann, Ph.D.; HMS, MEEI. Evoked responses in audiology.
Robert E. Hillman, Ph.D.; HMS, MGH. Vocal function and voice testing.
Kevin P. Kearns, Ph.D.; MGH. Aphasia, speech pathology.
James B. Kobler, Ph.D.; HMS, MGH. Neuroscience of speaking and swallowing.
Sharon Kujawa, Ph.D.; MEEI. Audiology, human deafness genetics.
Robert A. Levine, M.D.; HMS, MEEI. Auditory neurology.
Richard Lewis, M.D.; HMS, MEEI. Vestibular and oculomotor systems.
M. Charles Liberman, Ph.D.; HMS, MEEI. Auditory physiology.
Michael J. McKenna, M.D.; HMS, MEEI. Otolaryngology.
Jennifer R. Melcher, Ph.D.; MEEI, HMS. Noninvasive imaging of the central auditory system.
Saumil N. Merchant, M.D.; HMS, MEEI. Otology.
Daniel Merfeld, Ph.D.; MEEI. Neural processing of motion cues.
Maria Mody, Ph.D.; HU, MGH. Neurobiological correlates of language.
Cynthia Morton, Ph.D.; HMS, BWH. Cytogenetics.
Joseph B. Nadol Jr., M.D.; HMS, MEEI. Otology and laryngology.
Joseph S. Perkell, D.M.D., Ph.D.; MIT, BU. Speech production.
Thomas Quatieri, Ph.D.; MIT. Digital speech processing.
Steven D. Rauch, Ph.D.; MEEI. Hearing and balance disorders.
Charlotte M. Reed, Ph.D.; MIT. Auditory psychophysics, aids for the deaf.
Bruce Rosen, Ph.D.; HMS, MGH. Magnetic resonance imaging, functional neuroimaging.
John J. Rosowski, Ph.D.; HMS, MEEI. Physiological acoustics, comparative audition.
William F. Sewell, Ph.D.; HMS, MEEI. Auditory neuropharmacology.
Howard C. Shane, Ph.D.; HMS, CH. Assistive devices for the multihandicapped.
Stefanie Shattuck-Hufnagel, Ph.D.; MIT. Speech and language.
Christopher A. Shera, Ph.D.; HMS, MEEI. Cochlear physiology and otoacoustic emissions.
Barbara Shinn-Cunningham, Ph.D.; BU. Binaural hearing.
Janet Slifka, Ph.D.; MIT. Speech production and lexical access.
Kenneth N. Stevens, Sc.D.; MIT. Speech and language communication.
Conrad Wall, Ph.D.; MEEI. Vestibular function and interactions in vision.
Patrick Wolfe, Ph.D.; HU. Signal processing, auditory perception.
Steven M. Zeitels, M.D.; MHS, MGH. Phonosurgery, voice disorders.
Victor W. Zue, Ph.D.; MIT. Spoken language systems.
Lionel Zupan, Ph.D.; MEEI. Vestibular physiology.
George Zweig, Ph.D.; MIT. Computational analysis of inner-ear mechanics.

LONGWOOD UNIVERSITY

Program in Communication Sciences and Disorders

Program of Study

The 48-credit-hour Master of Science in Communication Sciences and Disorders Program provides in-depth course work and practicum experiences designed to provide students a scholarly foundation and expertise in areas of articulation-phonology, infant and child language disorders, voice disorders, craniofacial anomalies, motor-speech disorders, stuttering, aural rehabilitation, dysphagia, and aphasia. Advanced training involves practicum experiences with a diverse population of adults and children in clinical and school settings.

The Master of Science is the entry-level degree for employment as a speech-language pathologist and prepares students for the remediation of communication disorders. The program prepares students to meet the requirements for the American-Speech-Language Hearing Association (ASHA) Certificate of Clinical Competence (CCC) in Speech-Language Pathology, Commonwealth of Virginia Professional Licensure, and Virginia Department of Education Teacher Licensure, with endorsement in speech and language disorders. All students are required to participate in the Longwood University Speech-Language Clinic Program.

To meet ASHA-accreditation requirements, all students must complete a minimum of 325 hours of supervised clinical experience at the graduate level and a minimum of 400 hours, including 25 observation hours, from the combined undergraduate and graduate programs. The 400 hours includes experience in the evaluation and treatment of children and adults and with a variety of types and severities of disorders of speech, language, and hearing. Completion of at least 30 graduate clinic hours is required in the Longwood University Speech-Language Clinic prior to off-campus practicum placement. Students must complete a minimum of two off-campus practicum experiences that are approved by the Communication Sciences and Disorders Department.

Students take the Praxis II National Exam in Speech-Language Pathology near the conclusion of their graduate program. Speech-language pathologists seeking public school employment in the Commonwealth of Virginia are required to earn teacher licensure. Passing scores on Praxis I or an equivalent SAT score are required.

Research Facilities

The Communication Sciences and Disorders Program is located in Longwood's Hull Building, which houses one of eleven academic computing labs on campus. Most courses are taught or supplemented by Blackboard, which provides access to class resources via the Internet (http://blackboard.longwood.edu). Sona-Speech, spectrographic equipment used for treating a broad range of speech and voice problems, is available in the Speech and Language Center as well as for use in speech science class. Video recording equipment is installed in each therapy room at the Speech and Language Center to record sessions for supervisor and student review. Students use audiometers for conducting hearing screenings.

The Greenwood Library, located near the center of the campus offers 245,000 cataloged titles and currently subscribes to 1,475 journals. Some 700,000 microform units and sound and video recordings supplement the book and journal collections. The library also provides access to the holdings of other libraries through its interlibrary loan service. Library collections can be accessed through an online catalog from any point on the campus wireless network or the Internet. Forty-eight workstations in the library information commons provide Internet access and a variety of reference services, including REFWorks, a bibliographic organizer linked to online databases, and Microsoft Word.

Financial Aid

Scholarships, grants, loans, and work-study programs are available. Students can obtain more information online at http://www.longwood.edu/financialaid/. The Communication Disorders Foundation of Virginia (CDF) provides two scholarships annually to graduate students in Virginia in speech-language pathology or audiology. The Jason Foundation plans to offer a scholarship to second-year master's students in communication sciences and disorders at Longwood University who are interested in working with individuals with brain injury. Additional scholarship opportunities are posted online as they become available.

Cost of Study

In 2006–07, tuition and fees were $281 per credit hour for in-state students and $607 per credit hour for out-of-state residents.

Living and Housing Costs

On-campus housing is not provided to graduate students. Convenient off-campus housing is available.

Student Group

There are about 600 students enrolled in Longwood University's graduate programs.

Location

Longwood's central Virginia location offers beauty, recreation, shopping, nightlife, and convenience. Farmville is a dynamic two-college town (Hampden-Sydney College is also located there) that has a hometown appeal. Students enjoy historic sites, theater, trendy restaurants, the great outdoors, numerous stores, and quaint shops—all without the congestion or high prices of a big city. Three state parks are within 30 minutes of the campus, where students can enjoy outdoor activities. Cabins and campground facilities are also available. Longwood is approximately 1 hour from Charlottesville, Lynchburg, and Richmond. King's Dominion amusement park and Wintergreen ski resort are within 2 hours. Colonial Williamsburg, Busch Gardens theme park, Water Country USA, and the Blue Ridge Mountains are 2 hours away. Virginia Beach and Washington, D.C., are within a 3-hour drive. Farmville weather is generally favorable year-round. Occasionally, a moderate amount of snowfall sends students to the hills for a day of sledding and skiing.

The University

Longwood University has educated Virginia undergraduates since 1839 and graduate students since 1955. It is dedicated to the development of citizen leaders who are prepared to make positive contributions to the common good of society. Building upon its strong foundation in the liberal arts and sciences, Longwood provides an environment in which exceptional teaching fosters student learning, scholarship, and achievement. Longwood's job placement rate is more than 90 percent. For the ninth straight year, Longwood has been listed in "Universities–Master's (South): Top Schools" by *U.S. News & World Report*.

Applying

Applicants must have an undergraduate degree in communication or in an unrelated discipline. Applicants must also have completed the speech-language pathology prerequisites, including Anatomy and Physiology of the Speech and Hearing Mechanisms, Phonetics (Transcription), Speech Science, Introduction to Audiology and Hearing Science, Language Development Across the Lifespan, Phonology and Language Disorders, Introduction to Clinical Practice, and Neurology of Human Communication. The minimum undergraduate GPA is 3.0.

Students must submit the completed application, the $40 nonrefundable application fee, official transcripts, scores from the General Test of the GRE, a personal essay (500-word minimum) in which the reasons for seeking graduate education are discussed, and two letters of recommendation. Applications are due by February 1 for consideration for the fall semester. Applicants are notified of a decision no later than March 15 and must accept the offer by submitting a deposit by April 15.

Correspondence and Information

Dr. Lissa Power-deFur, Program Coordinator
Program in Communication Sciences and Disorders
Hull Building, Room 260
Longwood University
Farmville, Virginia 23909
Phone: 434-395-2369
E-mail: powerdefurea@longwood.edu
Web site: http://www.longwood.edu/cehs/graduatecsds/index.htm

Longwood University

THE FACULTY AND THEIR RESEARCH

At Longwood University, great teaching is the highest faculty priority. It is a fact that attracts and retains some of the best professors in their fields. The College of Education and Human Services prides itself on the fact that many of the nation's best educators and administrators, social workers, therapeutic recreation specialists, exercise scientists, speech and language therapists, library media specialists, and school/community counselors have come from this college. Faculty members offer easy accessibility and a caring attitude as they mentor students and support their academic success. All instructors are experts in their fields and in their classrooms. The faculty members and clinical supervisors in the Program in Communication Sciences and Disorders provide a uniquely supportive environment for students. Faculty members are committed to providing students highly relevant training in a vibrant learning community while meeting individual student needs. Each faculty member has established office hours for individual consultation with students.

Peggy C. Agee, Instructor of Communication Sciences; M.Ed., Virginia; CCC-SLP. Autism and literacy.

Gayle H. Daly, Instructor of Communication Sciences; M.S., James Madison; CCC-SLP. Language disorders in children and adolescents.

Carol C. Dudding, Assistant Professor of Communication Sciences and Disorders; Ph.D., Virginia; CCC-SLP. Adult neuro-disorders, dysphagia and technology.

Elizabeth A. Power-deFur, Associate Professor of Education and Chair, Department of Education, Special Education, Social Work, and Communication Disorders; Ph.D., Virginia; CCC-SLP/A. School services, aural rehabilitation.

MARYWOOD UNIVERSITY

Department of Communication Sciences and Disorders
Master's Program in Speech-Language Pathology

Programs of Study

Speech-language pathologists serve individuals who have communication deficits and/or swallowing difficulties. Work settings include hospitals, schools, clinics, rehabilitation centers, and nursing homes. The study of speech-language pathology emphasizes the normal aspects of human communication as well as the etiological, social-emotional, cognitive, and education factors associated with disorders of language, articulation-phonology, voice, fluency, swallowing, and hearing.

In order to become a certified speech-language pathologist, students must earn a master's degree, pass the national examination in speech-language pathology, and complete a clinical fellowship experience. Once students are certified and also meet state licensure requirements, they are eligible to work with individuals who have communication deficits and/or swallowing difficulties across the life span.

Marywood University offers a five-year program leading to a Master of Science degree in speech-language pathology. The program is accredited by the Council on Academic Accreditation of the American Speech-Language-Hearing Association. During the Preprofessional Phase (undergraduate; years 1–3) of the program, students take classes to meet the liberal arts core requirements and also complete courses in basic human communication processes that prepare them for application and admittance to the Professional Phase (graduate; years 4–5) of the program. This phase concentrates on course work in various communication disorders across the life span and provides clinical experiences through which students learn to apply knowledge and skills to children and adults who have various speech-language-swallowing disorders. An option to pursue teacher certification is also offered.

The faculty is dedicated to providing students with a high-quality education and opportunities to integrate theory and research into clinical practice. Its mission is to provide a supportive environment in which students prepare for entry-level professional clinical practice.

Research Facilities

The Department of Communication Sciences and Disorders (CSD) is housed in the William G. McGowan Center for Graduate and Professional Studies and is part of the College of Education and Human Development. This state-of-the-art facility offers a concentrated base for classrooms, computer labs, the student clinical preparation room, and the Speech-Language-Hearing Clinic. The clinic has eight therapy rooms and two diagnostic rooms, all of which have audiovisual monitoring capabilities for parents, caregivers, and clinical supervisors. Students also have access to an Assistive Technology Lab, which has the latest adaptive equipment that prepares them to implement a Universal Design for Learning.

The Learning Resources Center houses the library and media center. The library collection consists of more than 217,290 bound volumes, 881 print journal titles, and more than 44,300 nonprint items. Numerous electronic full-text and indexing/abstracting databases are accessible on campus through networked workstations and remotely from a student's home or office computer.

Financial Aid

Assistantships, scholarships, and loans are available to graduate students. Students enrolled in at least 6 credits per semester can borrow under the Federal Stafford Student Loan program. Information is available from the financial aid office.

Cost of Study

Tuition for 2007–08 is $695 per credit. General fees are $850 per year full-time and $280 per semester part-time.

Living and Housing Costs

The Office of Student Affairs maintains a listing of private off-campus rooms and apartments. Rents off campus are less than in major metropolitan areas.

Student Group

There are approximately 40 full-time graduate students who are enrolled in the Professional Phase (graduate level) of the five-year program. They come from many states, including Pennsylvania, New York, Massachusetts, Connecticut, New Jersey, Maryland, and Florida.

Location

Marywood University is situated in a suburban section of Scranton, a city of about 75,000. It is located a little more than 100 miles from New York City to the east and Philadelphia to the south. It is served by the Wilkes-Barre–Scranton International Airport and is easily accessible by a network of interstate highways. The Pocono Mountains resort areas and several beautiful lakes can be reached within 45 minutes or less. Montage Mountain ski area is 15 minutes away.

The University

Marywood University, established in 1915, is an independent, comprehensive Catholic university, owned and sponsored by the Congregation of Sisters, Servants of the Immaculate Heart of Mary. Graduate studies were inaugurated in 1921.

Applying

Prospective students applying to the Professional Phase of the program should have an undergraduate degree in communication sciences and disorders or in speech-language pathology or the equivalent undergraduate course sequence, with a minimum GPA of 3.0 overall. Undergraduate course work should include basic human communication processes, the basic sciences, mathematics, and social science. Students must submit the completed application; the $30 application fee; GRE scores; the personal essay questions, included with the application; and two letters of recommendation from individuals who can attest to the student's potential for success in graduate school. Applicants may be required to complete a personal or phone interview at the discretion of the Graduate Program Director and/or the CSD Chairperson. Preference is given to applicants who can attend the program full-time and take the full complement of courses offered within the context of a cohort model. Typically, students are admitted in the fall. Spring semester admissions are made on a case-by-case basis. Part-time students are also admitted on a case-by-case basis and are expected to carry a minimum of 9 credits per semester.

Correspondence and Information

Dr. Mona R. Griffer
Department of Communication Sciences and Disorders
College of Education and Human Development
Marywood University
2300 Adams Avenue
Scranton, Pennsylvania 18509-1598
Phone: 570-348-6299
E-mail: commsci@marywood.edu
Web site: http://www.marywood.edu/departments/commsci/SLP.stm

Marywood University

THE FACULTY AND THEIR RESEARCH

Janet Bisset, Chair, Department of Communication Sciences and Disorders; Ph.D., Memphis. Adult neurogenics.

Cynthia Fadden-Herron, Clinical Audiologist; Au.D., Florida. Audiological assessment and management of pediatric patients, the difficult-to-test and special needs populations.

Mona R. Griffer, Associate Professor and Director, Master's Program in Speech-Language Pathology; Ed.D., Nova Southeastern. Family-centered early intervention service delivery, pediatric language development and disorders, pediatric oral-motor/feeding development and deficits, the supervisory process.

Renee S. Jourdanais, Clinical Supervisor; M.S., Nazareth; CCC/SLP. Individuals with cleft palate/craniofacial anomalies, hearing impairment, the stroke population.

Mary Margaret Mazzaccaro, Clinical Supervisor; M.S., Florida State; CCC/SLP. Early intervention, the geriatric populations.

Andrea M. Novak, Clinic Director; M.A., Edinboro; CCC/SLP. Adult neurogenics, swallowing disorders.

Vijay Ramachandra, Assistant Professor; Ph.D. candidate, Bowling Green State. Relationships between brain, cognition, and language.

Sheri Skrutski, Clinical Audiologist; Au.D., Florida. Pediatric and geriatric diagnostic and rehabilitative areas of audiology.

Mountain State University™

MOUNTAIN STATE UNIVERSITY

Physician Assistant Program

Program of Study

Over 4,000 new physician assistants (PAs) are needed each year across the United States. PAs are well-recognized and valued members of the modern health-care team—professionals licensed to practice medicine under the direction and responsible supervision of a physician.

PAs provide a broad range of diagnostic and therapeutic services. They take patient histories, conduct physical exams, diagnose and treat illnesses, counsel on preventive care, order and interpret tests, and assist in surgery. In most states, including West Virginia, physician assistants can write prescriptions.

PAs are educated in the medical model. They take many of the same core courses as medical students, but their overall formal education path is much shorter. At MSU, physician assistants receive two years of broad education in medicine, starting with classroom and laboratory instruction in the basic medical and behavioral sciences. In the third year, clinical rotations in internal medicine, family medicine, surgery, pediatrics, obstetrics and gynecology, emergency medicine, and geriatric medicine offer practical training and experience to the PA student. Upon completion of the program, students are prepared to take the PANCE (Physician Assistant National Certification Exam). MSU's pass rate for first-time test takers of the PANCE is exceptional (94.3 percent in 2006).

Unlike most master's degree programs, the MSU PA Program does not require students to have a bachelor's degree to gain admission to the program. It is an entry-level master's program that includes both prerequisite studies at the undergraduate level and graduate-level professional studies. The program is offered at the Beckley campus; undergraduate prerequisite studies may be completed through distance learning.

Mountain State University's Physician Assistant Program maintains continuing accreditation by the Accreditation Review Commission on Education for the Physician Assistant, Inc. (ARC-PA).

Research Facilities

Learning resources for graduate and undergraduate students include multimedia classrooms, computer laboratories, computer-assisted instruction, nursing and health assessment labs, and laboratories for the basic sciences. The Robert C. Byrd Learning Resource Center includes a student-centered library and media center. The collection comprises more than 95,000 titles, supplemented both by interlibrary loan and by extensive electronic resources, including ProQuest, CINAL (Cumulative Index to Nursing and Allied Health Literature), SIRS (Social Issues Resources Index), EBSCOhost, WESTLAW, Wilson Web, Newsbank, and Medline. The newly created Technology Zone includes state-of-the-art telecommunication links, technology equipment, high-speed access and software, and a 3-D immersion module.

Financial Aid

Eligible graduate students may qualify for Federal Stafford Student Loans. Prospective students must submit the Free Application for Federal Student Aid (FAFSA) for determination of eligibility. Most graduate students receive some sort of financial assistance.

Cost of Study

Tuition for 2006–07 was $375 per credit hour. Payment plans are available. Additional fees are charged for graduation, thesis review, and thesis binding.

Living and Housing Costs

Many affordable housing opportunities are available in the neighborhoods surrounding the campus and in other nearby areas, which range from suburban to rural. Monthly rents average $300 to $600. Graduate students may also live in the residence hall on campus. Residence hall fees for 2006–07 were $1405 per semester for double occupancy and $2100 per semester for a private room. Students living on campus are required to purchase one of the University's meal plans.

Student Group

Mountain State University serves more than 6,000 students a year. Graduate enrollment and programming have grown steadily since the University's first graduate program was launched in 1998. Students in the Physician Assistant Program range in age from 20 to 50, and 60 percent are women.

Student Outcomes

Recent MSU graduates report starting salaries between $68,517 and $71,004. Most graduates are working in West Virginia as primary health providers, although MSU PA graduates can be found throughout the U.S. working in family practice, surgery, orthopedics, psychiatry, emergency medicine, nephrology, pediatrics, internal medicine, cardiology, and dermatology.

Location

Mountain State University's main campus is located near downtown Beckley, West Virginia, a small city that serves as a regional center for business, health care, education, and tourism in the heart of the southern West Virginia mountains. The Beckley area offers the excitement of city life, the quiet of a small town, and a wealth of recreational and cultural opportunities. Nearby recreational opportunities include whitewater rafting on the famed New and Gauley Rivers, skiing, hiking, biking, climbing and rappelling, and other outdoor pursuits. Beckley is an hour's drive from the state capital of Charleston and just a few hours from Pittsburgh; Washington, D.C.; and other eastern metropolitan areas.

The University

For more than seventy years, Mountain State University has been a leader in overcoming barriers to higher education and in offering academic programs that combine a liberal arts foundation with career-oriented studies. The University features innovative programming, flexible learning arrangements, well-qualified and deeply committed faculty members, and outstanding student services, all in a relaxed atmosphere.

Graduate degree programs are offered through the University's School of Graduate Studies, some in conjunction with the School of Extended and Distance Education.

Applying

Admission to the professional program is limited and competitive, with class capacities mandated by accreditation guidelines. Applications are accepted on a rolling admissions basis. Unlike most master's degree programs, the MSU PA program does not require applicants to have a bachelor's degree to gain admission to the program.

Correspondence and Information

Mountain State University Information Center
Box 9003
Mountain State University
Beckley, West Virginia 25802-9003
Phone: 304-929-INFO (4636)
    866-FOR-MSU1 (367-6781; toll-free)
Web site: http://www.mountainstate.edu

Mountain State University

THE FULL-TIME GRADUATE FACULTY

Debra Campbell, M.H.S., PA-C; Program Director. Family medicine, gastroenterology, nephrology.
Melissa Lilly, M.S.P.A., PA-C; Clinical Coordinator. General internal medicine, family/rural medicine and rehabilitative health care, gastroenterology.
Michael McMillion, M.S.P.A., PA-C. Family/rural medicine.
Jennifer Pack, M.S.P.A., PA-C; Academic Coordinator. Family/rural medicine, emergency medicine.

NEW YORK MEDICAL COLLEGE

School of Public Health
Program in Physical Therapy

Program of Study

The Program in Physical Therapy is a three-year, entry-level Doctor of Physical Therapy (D.P.T.) degree program that is fully accredited by the Commission on Accreditation of the American Physical Therapy Association (CAPTE) and approved by the New York State Department of Education. The program admits students for full-time study each June.

The primary purpose of the program is to prepare competent and caring physical therapists who are capable of clinical leadership in a variety of settings and who are prepared to adapt to changes in the health-care system. In addition, the program is dedicated to serving as an educational resource for individuals and institutions in the region, conducting clinical research, and generating scholarship that contributes to the evidence upon which physical therapy is based. A predominant mission of the program is to instill within its graduates an appreciation of community service, particularly the importance of addressing the health-care needs of underserved populations.

A major feature of the program is an innovative problem-based learning format that helps students translate their knowledge of foundational sciences into clinical practice. The curriculum includes traditional lecture and laboratory sessions, problem-based learning tutorials and laboratories, hands-on practice labs with clients, visits to area clinics and hospitals, and full-time clinical education experiences. It is the integration of course work in the sciences, clinical-skills labs, and more than nine months of clinical education that results in the success of its graduates. The School is very proud that last year's graduates had a first-time passing rate on the National Licensure Exam of 93 percent, far above the average for New York State (74 percent) and the entire nation (83 percent).

Research Facilities

Research facilities include the Alumni Computer Laboratory and the recently expanded Health Sciences Library (HSL). The HSL maintains a collection of approximately 200,000 volumes and 10,454 journals, of which many are available online. The HSL online catalog contains a master list of books, journals, media, and equipment owned by the library and is available on campus and also electronically off site. A full array of reference and information services are also provided.

The Program in Physical Therapy also has two well-equipped physical therapy laboratories for teaching and research. Instruction in anatomy, the basis for physical therapy, involves small-group cadaver dissection under the supervision of School of Medicine faculty members in the state-of-the-art laboratory of the Department of Cell Biology and Anatomy.

Financial Aid

Financial aid is available. Students are encouraged to talk to staff members in Student Financial Planning, who can help them to determine their needs and to apply for appropriate aid packages. In addition, a number of Dean's Scholarships are available for students with outstanding admissions credentials for the first year of study.

Cost of Study

For 2006–07, tuition was $23,500. Annual fees totaled $370. Health insurance, if purchased through the College, is an additional cost.

Living and Housing Costs

On-campus housing is available on a limited basis for single and married students, with priority given to first-year students. The 2006–07 housing charges for single students ranged from $505 to $675 per month. Charges for unfurnished apartments vary based on size and location. Assistance in obtaining off-campus housing is available from the Office of Student Housing.

Student Group

There are 1,660 students enrolled at New York Medical College; 760 are in the School of Medicine (M.D. degree program), 500 in the School of Public Health (doctoral degrees, Master of Public Health, and Master of Science degrees), and 250 are in the Graduate School of Basic Medical Sciences (doctoral and Master of Science degrees).

Location

New York Medical College is located on a lovely 565-acre campus shared with Westchester Medical Center in Valhalla, New York. Its suburban site in the center of Westchester County is approximately 20 miles north of New York City. There are ample educational and cultural opportunities available in the New York metropolitan area. In addition, the school is 20 miles from the Hudson Highlands, the Appalachian Trail, and Bear Mountain Park and 35 miles from the beaches of Long Island Sound and the Atlantic Ocean.

The College

Founded in 1860, New York Medical College has a strong history of involvement in medical and health education and in training, research, and professional and community service. It is chartered as a health sciences university by the Regents of the State of New York and is a member of the Middle States Association of Colleges and Secondary Schools. The mission of New York Medical College is carried out through three schools: the School of Medicine, the Graduate School of Basic Medical Sciences, and the School of Public Health.

Applying

There is an online application module available at http://www.nymc.edu/sph/programs/pt. In addition, the application packet may be downloaded from the Web site. Application packages and information about prerequisites are also available from the Office of Admissions of the School of Public Health. A nonrefundable fee of $75 must accompany each application. Scores on the Graduate Record Examinations (GRE) are required. Applicants whose native language is not English are required to obtain a minimum TOEFL score of 600 on the paper-based test, 250 on the computer-based test, or 100 on the Internet-based test. Admission decisions are made without regard to race, color, national origin, religion, sex, or handicap.

Correspondence and Information

Marian McGowan
Assistant Dean for Admissions
School of Public Health
New York Medical College
Valhalla, New York 10595
Phone: 914-594-4510
        888-336-NYMC (toll-free)
Fax: 914-594-4292
E-mail: sph_admissions@nymc.edu
Web site: http://www.nymc.edu/sph/PT

New York Medical College

THE FACULTY

Peter Anello, Clinical Instructor: B.S., SUNY Downstate Medical Center; PT.

David Asprinio, Associate Professor of Clinical Public Health; M.D., Vermont. Orthopedic Residency, Brown; Trauma Fellowship, Hospital for Special Surgery/Cornell; Spine Fellowship, Maryland.

Amy Bialek, Clinical Instructor; M.S., New York Medical College.

Jeffrey A. Bonneville, Visiting Lecturer; M.D., University of Health Sciences Antigua (West Indies).

Jennifer Brennan, Clinical Instructor; B.S., Vermont; PT.

Kendra Miller Cocciardi, Clinical Instructor; D.P.T., SUNY at Stony Brook; PT.

Catherine Culliton, Visiting Lecturer; M.P.A., Pace; PT.

Catherine L. Curtis, Assistant Professor; Ed.D., Columbia Teachers College; PT.

Lori Quinn Dannheim, Senior Lecturer; M.A., Ed.M., Ed.D., Columbia; PT.

Robert D'Elia, Clinical Instructor; M.S., Iona; M.S., New York Medical College; PT.

Janet P. Dolot, Assistant Professor; D.P.T., Simmons; PT.

Elizabeth A. Dominick, Clinical Instructor; D.P.T., Boston University; PT.

Caron Du Bois, Clinical Instructor; M.S., Columbia; PT.

Susan V. Duff, Clinical Instructor; M.P.T., Hahnemann; M.A., Ed.D., Columbia Teachers College; PT., OTR/L, CHT.

Todd Edelson, Clinical Instructor; D.P.T., MGH Institute of Health Professions; DipMDT.

Jody Feld, Clinical Instructor; D.P.T., Stony Brook, SUNY; PT, NCS.

Robin Fillhart, Clinical Instructor; M.S., LIU; PT.

Julie Fineman, Clinical Instructor; Ed.M., Columbia Teachers College; PT.

William H. Frishman, Professor of Clinical Public Health; M.D., Boston University.

Linda Gray, Clinical Instructor; Ph.D., NYU.

Ivan Hernandez, Clinical Instructor; D.P.T., NYU.

Steven Lichtman, Visiting Lecturer; Ed.D., Columbia Teachers College.

Jessica Magro, Clinical Instructor; M.S., New York Medical College; PT.

Michael J. Majsak, Associate Professor and Department Chair; Ed.D., Columbia Teachers College; PT.

Agnes McConlogue, Clinical Instructor; M.A., Touro; PT.

Daniel L. Millrood, Clinical Assistant Professor; Ed.M., Columbia; PT.

Roger Muzii, Clinical Instructor; Ph.D., Columbia; PT.

Stuart A. Newman, Professor of Clinical Public Health; Ph.D., Chicago.

Lauralynn O'Halloran, Clinical Instructor; M.A., NYU; PT.

Daniel F. Peters, Assistant Professor of Physical Therapy and of Speech Language Pathology; M.D., New York Medical College; FACS.

Stephen J. Peterson, Professor of Clinical Public Health; M.D., Cebu Doctors' College of Medicine (Philippines); FACP.

Matthew A. Pravetz, OFM, Associate Professor of Clinical Public Health; M.Div., Seton Hall; Ph.D., New York Medical College.

Michael A. Priore, Clinical Instructor; M.S., New York Medical College; PT.

Jennifer Raponi, Clinical Instructor; M.S., New York Medical College; PT.

Sheila Reed, Clinical Instructor; M.S.P.T., Miami (Florida); PT.

Phil Reppert, Clinical Instructor; M.Ed., CUNY, Queens; PT, ATP.

Meryle H. Richman, Clinical Instructor; M.S., LIU; PT, CST.

Julie Rosenberg, Clinical Instructor; M.A., Columbia; M.S., Mercy; PT.

Tushar Shah, Assistant Professor of Clinical Public Health; M.B.B.S., M.D., Gujarat University (India).

Sansor C. Sharma, Professor of Clinical Public Health; Ph.D., Edinburgh (Scotland).

Steven W. Srebnik, Clinical Instructor; M.S., Boston University; PT, CHT.

Carl Thompson, Associate Professor of Clinical Public Health; Ph.D., Virginia.

Tamara Weinstein, Clinical Instructor; M.S., LIU; PT.

Dawn Wicker, Clinical Instructor; B.S., Quinnipiac.

Thomas Willson, Clinical Instructor; M.S., New York Medical College; PT.

PHYSICAL THERAPY RESEARCH ACTIVITIES

The effects of cognitive retraining on patients who have undergone coronary artery bypass graft surgery.

The effects of exercise training on heart variability and the correlation with changes in right heart echocardiography in patients with chronic obstructive pulmonary disease.

Transfer of training among exercise types.

A multicenter trial for stage 1b cardiac rehabilitation.

Community-based strategies of physical therapy education.

Motor control and motor learning in patients with Parkinson's disease.

Falls risk assessments for the elderly.

Dance screening and injuries in collegiate dancers..

Fecal incontinence in the elderly.

Formal evaluation of change in curriculum to improve analysis skills in PT students.

Clinical issues in geriatrics.

Outcomes of patients with bilateral versus unilateral total knee replacement.

NEW YORK MEDICAL COLLEGE

School of Public Health
Program in Speech-Language Pathology

Program of Study

New York Medical College offers a medically-oriented, two-year Speech-Language Pathology (SLP) Program resulting in a Master of Science (M.S.) degree. It admits students each September. The program prepares skilled clinicians, who are committed to excellence, in the delivery of speech-language pathology services in health-care facilities and other professional settings. The program operates in an academic health-center environment in which medically oriented education and training is enriched by the integration of resources from the Schools of Public Health, Basic Medical Sciences, and Medicine, as well as the clinical resources of the Speech and Hearing Center of the Westchester Institute for Human Development (WIHD). Faculty members and students use state-of-the-art clinical and technological resources to advance the field of speech-language pathology through original research and innovative care. Completion of the program leads to qualification for licensure and credentials necessary for entry into the profession.

The Speech-Language Pathology Program is approved by the New York State Education Department and is fully accredited by the Council on Academic Accreditation of the American Speech-Language-Hearing Association (ASHA).

Research Facilities

Research facilities include the Alumni Computer Laboratory and the recently expanded Health Sciences Library (HSL), which maintains a collection of more than 198,025 volumes and 10,454 journals, many of which are available online. The HSL online catalog contains a master list of books, journals, media, and equipment owned by the library and is available on campus and also electronically off-site. A full array of reference and information services is also provided.

The department's Voice and Speech Clinical Research Laboratory, housed at the Speech and Hearing Center at WIHD, is the program's primary research facility for studies of normal and disordered speech and voice production. The laboratory is equipped to make acoustic, kinematic, aerodynamic, and myoelectric measurements related to voice and speech, as well as to conduct video endoscopic evaluations of the vocal tract and larynx. The department also uses the facilities of the Assistive Technology Center at WIHD for teaching and research.

Financial Aid

Financial aid is available. Students are encouraged to talk to staff members in Student Financial Planning who can help them to determine their needs and to apply for appropriate aid packages.

Cost of Study

For 2006–07, the tuition was $23,500. Annual fees totaled $270. Health insurance purchased through the College is separate.

Living and Housing Costs

On-campus housing is available on a limited basis for single and married students. The 2006–07 housing charges for single students ranged from $505 to $675 per month. Charges for unfurnished apartments vary based on size and location. Assistance in obtaining off-campus housing is available from the Office of Student Housing.

Student Group

The Speech-Language Pathology Program is a full-time program requiring two years (five semesters) of study.

Location

New York Medical College is located on a 565-acre campus shared with Westchester Medical Center in Valhalla, New York. Its suburban site in the center of Westchester County is approximately 20 miles north of New York City. There are ample educational, recreational, and cultural opportunities available locally and in the New York metropolitan area.

The College

Founded in 1860, New York Medical College has a strong history of involvement in medical and health education and in training, research, and professional and community service. It is chartered as a health sciences university by the Regents of the State of New York and is a member of the Middle States Association of Colleges and Secondary Schools. The mission of New York Medical College is carried out through three schools: the School of Medicine, the Graduate School of Basic Medical Sciences, and the School of Public Health.

Applying

There is an online application module available at http://www.nymc.edu/sph/programs/slp. In addition, the application packet may be downloaded from the Web site. Application packages and information about prerequisites are also available from the Office of Admissions of the School of Public Health. A nonrefundable fee of $75 must accompany each application. Applicants whose native language is not English are required to obtain a minimum TOEFL score of 660 on the paper-based test, 287 on the computer-based test, or 117 on the Internet-based test. Admission decisions are made without regard to race, color, national origin, religion, sex, or handicap.

Correspondence and Information

Dr. Ben Watson, Department Chair, SLP
School of Public Health
New York Medical College
Valhalla, New York 10595
Phone: 914-594-4239
         888-336-NYMC (toll-free)
Fax: 914-594-4292
E-mail: slp_sph@nymc.edu
Web site: http://www.nymc.edu/slp

Marian F. McGowan, Assistant Dean for Admissions
School of Public Health
New York Medical College
Valhalla, New York 10595
Phone: 914-594-4510
         888-336-NYMC (toll-free)
E-mail: sph_admissions@nymc.edu

New York Medical College

THE FACULTY

The program has 4 full-time faculty members, as well as a number of part-time and clinical faculty members. Clinicians in the community teach clinical courses and supervise clinical practicums. Faculty members from the School of Medicine and the Graduate School of Basic Medical Sciences teach the gross anatomy course. Faculty members from other programs in the School of Public Health teach courses in research and public health.

Regina Albinus, Clinical Instructor; M.S.Ed., SUNY at New Paltz; CCC-A.
Renee Angelo, Clinical Instructor; M.S., Columbia Teachers College; CCC-A.
Michael Cunningham, Clinical Instructor; M.S., Long Island; M.S., New York Medical College; CCC-SLP.
William Fitzgibbon, Lecturer; Au.D., Florida.
Kathleen Franklin, Associate Professor of Clinical Speech-Language Pathology and of Public Health Practice, Disability and Human Development; Ph.D., Nebraska–Lincoln.
Shelley Hirsch, Lecturer; M.A., St. Johns.
Kathleen Kaiser, Clinical Instructor; M.S., Columbia Teachers College; CCC-SLP.
Jenny Koshy, Clinical Instructor; M.A., Hofstra; CCC-A.
Andrea Kriniske, Lecturer; M.A., NYU; CCC-SLP.
Barbara J. Leader, Senior Lecturer; M.S., CUNY, Hunter; CCC-SLP.
Etoile M. LeBlanc, Lecturer; M.S., Columbia Teachers College.
Susan Levin, Clinical Instructor; M.S., Boston University; CCC-SLP.
Lisa Maniscalco, Clinical Instructor; M.S., Adelphi; CCC-SLP.
Maureen McGee, Clinical Instructor; M.S., Columbia Teachers College; CCC-A.
Erin McMurrer, Clinical Instructor; M.S., Loyola; CCC-SLP.
Noreen Moynihan, Clinical Instructor; M.S., New York Medical College; CCC-SLP.
Christina M. Pipala, Lecturer; M.S., Ithaca.
Barbara Posen, Clinical Instructor; M.S., CUNY, Hunter; CCC-A.
Paula J. Prata, Lecturer; M.S., Long Island; CCC-SLP.
Joanne A. Sanchez, Clinical Instructor; M.S., Columbia Teachers College; CCC-SLP.
Mindy Schmelzer, Lecturer; Au.D., Pennsylvania School of Optometry.
Aimee Seiderer, Lecturer; M.S., Columbia.
Shirley Tennyson, Clinical Instructor; Ed.M., Columbia; CCC-SLP.
Chandler Thompson, Lecturer; D.M.A., Michigan State; M.S., New York Medical College.
Lisa Velella, Clinical Instructor; M.A., St. John's.
Robert A. Violin, Associate Professor of Speech-Language Pathology; Ph.D., CUNY Graduate Center.
Ben Watson, Professor of Speech-Language Pathology and Chair; Ph.D., Connecticut.

Research Activities

Speech production in normal aged speakers.
Correlates of fluent and dysfluent speech production in adult stutterers.
Survey of speech-language pathologists who work within hospice organizations.
Development of literacy skills in individuals with severe disabilities who use augmentative and alternative communication services.
The effects of voice output communication aids (VOCAs) on the interaction patterns of individuals with autism.
Assessment of residents of a local agency for appropriate AAC interventions and training of staff members on the use of the AAC interventions.
The development of protocols or guidelines for developing protocols for the efficient and functionally effective use of biofeedback in the context of motor learning theory.

NORTHWESTERN UNIVERSITY

The Roxelyn and Richard Pepper Department of Communication Sciences and Disorders
Programs in Audiology and Hearing Sciences, Learning Disabilities,
and Speech and Language Pathology

Programs of Study

The Department of Communication Sciences and Disorders offers graduate study in audiology and hearing sciences, learning disabilities, and speech and language pathology at the M.A. and Ph.D. degree levels. A combined M.A. degree in speech and language pathology and learning disabilities and an Au.D. degree in clinical audiology are available. Opportunities for postdoctoral study exist across all areas.

Normal/developmental aspects of communication and learning are covered, along with courses on disorders of articulation, language, hearing, learning, swallowing, memory, fluency, attention, perception, voice, symbolization, and other related topics. Clinical/educational setting practice is provided on site and in area schools, hospitals, clinics, rehabilitation agencies, and industrial and private practice locations. Courses at the M.A. level may lead to professional certification and/or preparation for advanced study in the field and in related areas. Study in the Au.D. degree program meets academic and clinical requirements for independent practice in audiology. Programs of study at the Ph.D. level include courses taken within the Department as well as other departments (e.g., neuroscience, bioengineering, linguistics, psychology, cognitive science, medicine, physiology, and others) and are tailored to an individual's experience and interest in basic or applied/clinical research. Independent study and research are encouraged, and small-group seminars are offered. Courses, laboratory work, and field activities offer opportunities to learn research methods and use scientific instrumentation. Doctoral students have opportunities for supervised research and teaching. Students are prepared for careers as speech and language pathologists, clinical audiologists, learning disabilities specialists, teacher-investigators, and researchers. Graduates are employed in schools; hospitals; rehabilitation centers and clinics; special education centers; industry; local, state, and federal agencies; universities; research centers; private medical, educational, and clinical facilities; and other settings.

Faculty teaching and research interest areas are identified in the Department Faculty and Their Research section of this description. Further information is available on the Department's Web site at http://www.communication.northwestern.edu/csd/.

Research Facilities

The Department maintains research laboratories that study how speech sounds are generated, speech sound characteristics in different languages, and the relationship between speech sounds and linguistic units; how speech elements are processed, interpreted, and decoded into linguistic units; speech synthesis, speech and voice recognition, and speech coding; electromyographic signals from speech muscles; electroencephalographic signals from the brain; speech articulator and laryngeal system activity; swallow behavior; word-finding deficits in children; language abilities in children; language processing in bilinguals and language and memory using eye-tracking, functional neuroimaging techniques, and narrative analysis; sentence processing in aphasic persons using functional magnetic resonance imaging techniques; verb structure in aphasia; language decline in dementia; perceptual, orthographic, phonological, semantic, and syntactic processes in development of oral language and reading; development and disorders of written language; cognitive, linguistic, and academic problems of adults with learning disabilities; cognitive processing in children; acoustic properties of speech signals; psychological and social effects of hearing loss in aging adults; molecular, cellular, physiological, and psychological bases of audition; and function of normal and abnormal auditory systems. Additional information about these laboratories and others can be found on the Department's Web site.

Financial Aid

The Graduate School and University provide fellowships and scholarships; the Department selects fellowship and scholarship awardees and also recommends the awarding of teaching assistantships. In addition, principal investigators may provide financial assistance for a limited number of students. Students seeking loans must apply to a financial aid officer in the Graduate School.

Cost of Study

Tuition in 2007–08 is $11,688 per quarter. This cost is reduced to $3896 per quarter for Ph.D. students who are admitted to candidacy. Reduced tuition is available to Au.D. students; prospective students should contact the Au.D. program assistant for further information.

Living and Housing Costs

The University has a limited number of living units for single and married students on the Evanston and Chicago campuses. Many students find satisfactory accommodations in private homes and in apartments near the campuses; rents vary widely.

Student Group

An average of 40 students begin master's study in speech and language pathology each fall, and up to 10 new students begin master's study in learning disabilities. At the doctoral level, approximately 10 students begin study in the Au.D. degree program and about 7 new students begin study in the Ph.D. degree program. Students from within the disciplines and from other disciplines are encouraged to apply for graduate study. There are approximately 13,000 full-time students enrolled on the Evanston and Chicago campuses annually; approximately 40 percent are in graduate and professional programs.

Location

The main campus of the University is located in Evanston on the shore of Lake Michigan. The Chicago campus, about 12 miles south of Evanston, is also on the lakeshore near the center of the business district, one of Chicago's most attractive areas. An immense variety of cultural, social, and recreational activities can be found on and near each campus.

The University

Northwestern University, one of the nation's largest private universities, was founded in 1851. The College of Arts and Sciences (Weinberg); the Technological Institute (McCormick); the Schools of Education and Social Policy, Journalism, Music, and Communication; and the Graduate School of Management (Kellogg) are located on the Evanston campus. The Medical and Law Schools are located on the Chicago campus. There is a continuing expansion of facilities and programs, much of it in science and medicine, which will continue during the next ten years thanks to a vigorous program of financial contributions.

Applying

Applications are sought from highly qualified students from many fields. The Department typically admits students to begin in the fall quarter. Application deadlines are as follows: December 31, Ph.D. Program in Communication Sciences and Disorders, and February 1, M.A. Programs in Speech and Language Pathology and Learning Disabilities, the Joint M.A. in Speech and Language Pathology and Learning Disabilities, and the Au.D. Clinical Doctorate Program. Applicants to the Au.D. program should submit a paper application (available at http://www.communication.northwestern.edu/csd/programs/graduate/phdaud/), transcripts, and letters of recommendation to the Doctor of Audiology Program, 2240 Campus Drive, Evanston, Illinois 60208-3540. GRE scores should be submitted to Institution Code 1565. Applicants to programs other than the Au.D. should submit an online application, available at http://www.northwestern.edu/graduate; GRE scores to Institution Code 1565; and transcripts to the graduate application coordinator. Letters of recommendation may either be submitted as part of the online application or via mail, also to the graduate application coordinator.

Correspondence and Information

Graduate Application Coordinator
Department of Communication Sciences
  and Disorders
2240 Campus Drive
Evanston, Illinois 60208-3540
Phone: 847-491-5073
E-mail: ccoy@northwestern.edu
Web site: http://www.communication.
  northwestern.edu

Au.D. Program Assistant
Department of Communication Sciences
  and Disorders
2240 Campus Drive
Evanston, Illinois 60208-3540
Phone: 847-491-4541
E-mail: s-erler@northwestern.edu
Web site: http://www.communication.
  northwestern.edu

Graduate Admissions
The Graduate School
Northwestern University
Evanston, Illinois 60208
Phone: 847-491-7265

Northwestern University

THE DEPARTMENT FACULTY AND THEIR RESEARCH

Amy Booth, Ph.D., Pittsburgh. Cognitive development, infancy, learning, memory and social cognition.
James Booth, Ph.D., Maryland. Neural bases of the development of language, reading, and attention.
Mary Ann Cheatham, Ph.D., Northwestern. Cochlear physiology and functional genomics.
Peter Dallos, Ph.D., Northwestern. Biophysics and physiology of the cochlea.
Sumit Dhar, Ph.D., Purdue. Applied auditory physiology.
Kimberly Fisher, Ph.D., Oklahoma. Voice disorders, physiology of the larynx.
Dean C. Garstecki, Ph.D., Illinois at Urbana-Champaign. Hearing loss and aging.
Nina Kraus, Ph.D., Northwestern. Neurobiology of speech and music.
Charles R. Larson, Chairman; Ph.D., Washington (Seattle). Voice physiology.
Jerilyn Ann Logemann, Ph.D., Northwestern. Structural anomalies of the vocal tract, dysphagia.
Viorica Marian, Ph.D., Cornell. Psycholinguistics, bilingualism, memory and language.
Jessica Maye, Ph.D., Rochester. Language acquisition, psycholinguistics, developmental phonetics/phonology.
Barbara Roa Pauloski, Ph.D., Northwestern. Voice, speech, and swallowing.
Claus-Peter Richter, M.D., Ph.D., Frankfurt (Germany). Physiology of the cochlea.
Mario A. Ruggero, Ph.D., Chicago. Biophysics and physiology of the middle and inner ears.
Jonathan Siegel, Ph.D., Washington (St. Louis). Biophysics and physiology of the cochlea.
Cynthia Thompson, Ph.D., Kansas. Neurological disorders of language and cognition.
Catherine Warrier, Ph.D., McGill. Lateralization of auditory processes.
Patrick Wong, Ph.D., Texas at Austin. Functional neuroanatomy of speech perception.
Beverly Wright, Ph.D., Texas at Austin. Perceptual learning, auditory perception in individuals, psychoacoustics.
Dongsun Yim, Ph.D., Minnesota. Child language disorders.
Steven Zecker, Ph.D., Wayne State. Auditory processing and learning.
Jing Zheng, Ph.D., Michigan State. Molecular and cellular biology of the cochlea.

Lecturers and Clinical Faculty
Frances Block, M.A., Northwestern. Supervision, language disorders in older children.
Kathy L. Harper, M.A., Northwestern. Early literacy.
Kristen Larsen, M.A., Northwestern. Dysphagia, neurological speech and language disorders in adults.
Paula McGuire, Ph.D., Northwestern. Articulatory/phonological development and disorders.
Susan Mulhern, M.A., Northwestern. Articulation and language problems in children.
Jane Rankin, Ph.D., Colorado. Parenting and communication, adolescent self-consciousness.
Sharon Veis, M.A., Northwestern. Swallowing disorders, language disorders after neurosurgery.
Anna Wagner, M.A., Northwestern. Language, literacy, and learning disabilities.

Adjunct Faculty
Joanne Bregman, Ph.D., Northwestern. High-risk infants and their families.
Martha Burns, Ph.D., Northwestern. Aphasia and adult neurological disorders.
Leora Cherney, Ph.D., Northwestern. Aphasia and neurological disorders.
Dawn B. Koch, Ph.D., Northwestern. Cochlear implantation.
Harold Pelzer, M.D., Northwestern. Treatment for head and neck cancer.

Emeritus Faculty
Elaine Brown-Grant, M.A., Northwestern. Clinical supervision.
Gerald Canter, Ph.D., Northwestern. Neurology of speech and language.
Hilda Fisher, Ph.D., LSU. Vocal physiology and pathologies.
Doris J. Johnson, Ph.D., Northwestern. Relationship between auditory disorders and higher levels of learning.
David Rutherford, Ph.D., Northwestern. Speech perception and production, word retrieval skills.
Laura Ann Wilber, Ph.D., Northwestern. Pediatric audiology, audiologic instrumentation.

PHILADELPHIA COLLEGE OF OSTEOPATHIC MEDICINE
Physician Assistant Program

Program of Study

The Physician Assistant (PA) Program is a twenty-six-month program that leads to a Master of Science degree in health sciences. Students are prepared for clinical practice, using a variety of learning strategies: formal lectures, practical laboratory classes, clinical education, and clinical research. Students develop patient communication skills and advanced clinical problem-solving skills in addition to acquiring technical proficiency in areas related to professional practice. Graduates of the program develop and implement clinical treatment plans with their supervising physician. The program is highly intensive. Most of the program is provided by physicians in order to ensure that patient-care functions provided by the Physician Assistant Program graduates are of the highest quality.

There also exists a five-year cooperative program between the University of the Sciences in Philadelphia (USP) and Philadelphia College of Osteopathic Medicine (PCOM). The program consists of two distinct phases: the preprofessional phase and the professional phase. After successful completion of the fourth year, students earn a B.S. in health science from USP and an M.S. from PCOM after completion of the fifth year. The B.S. degree does not qualify the student as a PA. Students must complete the entire professional phase of the program (years four and five) and obtain an M.S. from PCOM to become eligible to be certified as a PA. PCOM has the ultimate responsibility for granting the M.S. degree.

This unique program, which offers an undergraduate program at USP and the professional PA graduate program at PCOM, provides students with the ability to positively affect the lives of their patients, their families, their employers, and their communities. Students become lifelong learners, developing a baseline of analytic and critical thinking skills that prepare them for the challenges of caring for the entire patient, young or old, from the emergency room to the operating room.

Research Facilities

PCOM's library features both a well-developed collection of medical journals and texts and new capabilities for access to online medical references and Internet searching in a facility that provides individual student stations, Internet terminals, advanced audiovisual resources, and a large student computer lab.

Financial Aid

The Financial Aid Office at PCOM offers financial assistance to students through the Federal Stafford Student Loans program, institutional grants, and various alternative private loan programs.

Cost of Study

In 2006–07, the direct costs of attending PCOM (including tuition, fees, required health insurance, books, and supplies) averaged approximately $30,460 per year.

Living and Housing Costs

Students live off campus within the Philadelphia metropolitan and suburban areas, as there is no on-campus housing. Room and board costs vary by each student's individual preferences.

Student Group

Admission to the PA Program is competitive and selective. The College looks for academically and socially well-rounded individuals who are committed to caring for patients. The class of 2008 matriculates with 54 students, 42 women and 12 men, ranging in age from 21 to 47. Twenty-one are residents of Pennsylvania.

Location

Philadelphia College of Osteopathic Medicine is the second largest of twenty-three osteopathic colleges in the United States, with campuses in both Philadelphia and suburban Atlanta. The PA studies program is offered only on the Philadelphia campus, which is located in a suburban setting on City Avenue, minutes away from Fairmount Park, Philadelphia's historic district, art museums, theaters, restaurants, and professional sports complexes. PCOM's renovated facilities include two large lecture halls, small classrooms, labs for teaching and research, and a state-of-the-art library.

The College

PCOM, chartered in 1899, enrolls approximately 1,700 students in its various programs and is committed to educating community-responsive, primary-care–oriented physicians and physician assistants to practice medicine in the twenty-first century. Supported by the latest in medical and educational technology, PCOM emphasizes treating the whole person, not merely the symptoms. The Department of Physician Assistant Studies coordinates the PA Program between USP and PCOM and offers an early hands-on medical education experience during the professional phase. Students have a committed, professional, humanistic faculty who are leaders in the osteopathic and physician assistant national health-care community. The PA Program provides a thorough foundation in health-care delivery that focuses on comprehensive, humanistic health care.

Applying

Selection for the Physician Assistant Program is very competitive. Applicants must complete a baccalaureate degree from an accredited college or university in the United States, Canada, or the United Kingdom with a minimum GPA of 2.8 (on a 4.0 scale), document 200 hours of experience in volunteer or employment related to the health-care industry, and fulfill the following course requirements: five semesters of biology, three semesters of chemistry, one semester of physics or another health related science, two semesters of mathematics, and three semesters of social science courses. All requirements must have been completed within the last ten years, unless the applicant has completed an advanced degree or has extensive experience in the field of patient care. Selected applicants are invited to interview on campus. Applications and deadline information are available online at http://www.caspaonline.org.

Correspondence and Information

Office of Admissions
Philadelphia College of Osteopathic Medicine
4170 City Avenue
Philadelphia, Pennsylvania 19131
Phone: 215-871-6700
      800-999-6998 (toll-free)
Fax: 215-871-6719
E-mail: paadmissions@pcom.edu
Web site: http://www.pcom.edu

Philadelphia College of Osteopathic Medicine

THE FACULTY AND THEIR RESEARCH

Full-Time Faculty

Marie Bensulock, M.S., UMDNJ; PA-C. Women's health, pediatrics.
John Cavenagh, Ph.D., Yale; PA-C. Emergency medicine.
Marilyn DiFeliciantonio, M.L.S., Hahnemann; PA-C. Hematology, oncology.
Paul Krajewski, M.S., Philadelphia College of Osteopathic Medicine; PA-C. Orthopedic surgery, emergency medicine.
Laura Molloy, M.M.S., Saint Francis (Pennsylvania); PA-C. Family medicine, women's health.
Christine Mount, M.S., University of Medicine and Dentistry of New Jersey; PA-C. Neurology, emergency medicine, trauma.
Dan Scott, M.S., Philadelphia University; PA-C. Cardiology, emergency medicine.

Adjunct Faculty

Patrick Auth, M.S., Hahnemann; PA-C. Emergency medicine and orthopedics.
Shawn Boyle, Pharm.D., University of the Sciences in Philadelphia. Pharmacology.
Patrick Coughlin, Ph.D., Cincinnati. Anatomy.
Robert Cuzzolino, Ed.D., Temple. Academic policy.
Daniel DuPont, D.O., Philadelphia College of Osteopathic Medicine. Pulmonology.
Leonard Finkelstein, D.O., Philadelphia College of Osteopathic Medicine. Surgery and urology.
Matthew Hay, M.S., Philadelphia College of Osteopathic Medicine; PA-C. General surgery.
Melissa Hoffman, M.S., Philadelphia College of Osteopathic Medicine; PA-C. General surgery.
Saul Jeck, D.O., Philadelphia College of Osteopathic Medicine; FACOOG. Obstetrics and gynecology.
Michael Kennedy, Ph.D., Rochester. Human physiology.
Colleen Maguire, M.H.S., Hahnemann; PA-C. Obstetrics and gynecology, emergency medicine.
John Manzella, D.O., NYIT. Internal medicine.
Burton Mark, D.O., Kirksville College of Osteopathic Medicine. Psychiatry.
Gregory McDonald, D.O., Philadelphia College of Osteopathic Medicine. Pathology.
Tracy Offerdahl, Pharm.D., Temple. Pharmacy.
Richard Pascucci, D.O., Philadelphia College of Osteopathic Medicine; FACOI. Rheumatology.
Margaret Reinhart, M.M.A., M.T., Penn State; ASCP. Laboratory diagnostics.
Amanda Stoll, M.S., Philadelphia College of Osteopathic Medicine; PA-C. Dermatology.
Rosemary Vickers, D.O., Philadelphia College of Osteopathic Medicine. Pediatrics.

QUINNIPIAC UNIVERSITY

School of Health Sciences

Programs of Study

The School of Health Sciences is committed to developing professionals through comprehensive, career-oriented programs. The person-to-person nature of a Quinnipiac education sets it apart as one of the Northeast's premier education centers for health professionals. The entire staff at the School of Health Sciences takes the time to help each student plan a graduate program best suited to his or her interests, strengths, and career goals. Students are guided by expert faculty members who are current with the latest techniques, technologies, and research in their specialties. Many are also practitioners and consultants in their respective fields. The personal touch is also evident in the School of Health Sciences' extensive internship and field work programs. Through the University's affiliations with nearly 1,000 hospitals and health-care facilities nationwide, students develop interpersonal skills and apply their classroom work in real-life settings with on-site mentors.

The School of Health Sciences offers the following graduate degree programs: Master of Health Science (M.H.S.) in medical laboratory sciences; M.S. in molecular and cell biology; Master of Science in Nursing (M.S.N.) with adult nurse practitioner, family nurse practitioner, and forensic nurse clinical specialist tracks; pathologists' assistant (M.H.S.); and physician assistant (M.H.S.). Post-master's certificates are offered in the adult nurse practitioner, family nurse practitioner, and forensic nurse clinical specialist tracks.

Research Facilities

Students in the School's graduate programs utilize a wide array of scientific and professional facilities. The state-of-the-art Clinical Skills Laboratory contains physical examination tables and sophisticated computer programs and models for teaching and to enable nursing students to practice diagnostic and physical assessment skills. Two critical-care units duplicate their hospital counterparts. The Nursing Computer Laboratory houses software for skills practice. Computer-assisted programs provide simulated health assessment and physical examination situations for students to experience, assess, and evaluate. A training laboratory for pathologists' assistant students contains various types of microscopes critical to the training of the students and a range of equipment used for preparing tissues for diagnosis, such as microtome, cryo/cut microtome, a dual/camera B42 microscope, a fluorescent microscope with camera, eight-head microscopes (housed at Veteran's Hospital), incubators, and spectrophotometers. Specialized facilities for the Physician Assistant Program include a physical diagnosis lab with eighteen physical exam tables and a PA CD server that includes a program that students use to practice their clinical skills as well as test-prep software for the PA certification test. Laboratories utilized by students in the Molecular and Cell Biology and Medical Laboratory Sciences/Biomedical Sciences Programs contain all the equipment used in professional research laboratories, including ultracentrifuges, spectrophotometers, a Kodak imaging station, electron microscopes, and quantitative PCR, HPLC, and immunoflourescence imaging equipment. Echlin Health Sciences Center houses classrooms designed for clinical practice in the health sciences and extensive computer and robotics equipment as well as lecture halls and seminar rooms. All of the classrooms are wired, so that the faculty members can utilize the Internet, specialized computer programs, and the library databases and resources in their classes.

The University also provides an impressive collection of health science resources. Arnold Bernhard Library, one of the most technologically advanced centers for electronic information and learning resources anywhere in the country, houses a vast Health Science Center section that contains texts and journals as well as citations and abstracts to health-care articles and a national citation database of scholarly articles in the health sciences. Students also have access to scores of online databases and resources, including Basic Biosis, *Biochemical Journal*, Biological Sciences from Cambridge Scientific Abstracts, CINAHL, FirstSearch, Harrison's Online Medical Clinic, Health Reference Center, *Journal of Chemical Education, Journal of Chemical Investigation,* Medline, National Science Digital Library, *New England Journal of Medicine,* Proquest Direct, PubMed, Science Direct, and Stat Ref. Off-campus e-mail users have full access to the University's computer network.

Financial Aid

Several avenues are available to help students fund their education. Students may be eligible for Federal Stafford Student Loans. Physician assistant students receive a reduction in tuition during their clinical year.

Cost of Study

Tuition in 2006–07 was $625 per credit hour. In addition, student fees were $275 per semester for full-time students and $30 per credit for part-time students.

Living and Housing Costs

On-campus housing is available during the summer. Privately owned housing is available near the campus. For more information concerning off-campus housing, interested students should contact the Office of Residential Life or visit the University's Web site.

Student Group

The School of Health Sciences enrolls 336 full-time and 99 part-time students, 349 of whom are women.

Location

The University is located on a beautiful campus in Hamden, Connecticut, a suburb of New Haven. It is approximately 30 minutes from Hartford, 90 minutes from New York City, and 2 hours from Boston.

The University

Quinnipiac University is nationally recognized as one of the leading centers for higher learning in the Northeast and is consistently ranked among the best master's-level universities in the north in *U.S. News & World Report's* Guide to America's Best Colleges. All programs have integrated computer technology into academic and campus life, and Quinnipiac has been recognized in *Yahoo! Internet Life* for its achievements in technology. In 2006, Quinnipiac was ranked ninth in *PC Magazine's* 2007 Top Wired Colleges.

The University enrolls about 5,000 undergraduate and 1,800 graduate students and offers a full range of undergraduate and graduate programs through the School of Health Sciences, the School of Communications, the School of Business, the College of Liberal Arts, and the School of Law.

Applying

In general, applicants should have a bachelor's degree from an accredited institution, with a minimum GPA of 3.0. Students should submit the completed application, the application fee, and official transcripts. International students must also submit TOEFL scores. Other requirements may include letters of recommendation, professional licensure, and an interview. Specific application requirements and deadlines are available online. Students should check the Web site for more information.

Correspondence and Information

Office of Graduate Admissions
Quinnipiac University
275 Mount Carmel Avenue
Hamden, Connecticut 06518
Phone: 203-582-8672
      800-462-1944 (toll-free)
Fax: 203-582-3443
E-mail: graduate@quinnipiac.edu
Web site: http://www.quinnipiac.edu

Quinnipiac University

THE FACULTY AND THEIR RESEARCH

GRADUATE NURSING PROGRAMS

Full-Time Faculty

Jeanne LeVasseur, Professor and Director of the Graduate Nursing Program; Ph.D., Connecticut; RN, APRN, FNP, ANP. Women's health, the art of nursing, combat nursing.

Mary Helming, Assistant Professor; M.S.N., Yale; APRN, BC, FNP.

Laima M. Karosas, Associate Professor; Ph.D., Connecticut; APRN, FNP, ANP. International health care.

Barbara A. Moynihan, Professor; M.S.N., Southern Connecticut State; Ph.D., Connecticut; APRN, BC. Forensic nursing, psychotherapy.

Lynn C. Price, Associate Professor; J.D., George Washington; M.P.H./M.S.N., Yale; FNP. Health policy analysis.

Janice Thompson, Professor; Ph.D., Adelphi; APRN.

MEDICAL LABORATORY SCIENCES/BIOMEDICAL SCIENCES PROGRAM

Full-Time Faculty

Thomas Brady, Ph.D., Connecticut. Clinical pathology.

Deborah Clark, Ph.D., Cornell. Biochemistry.

Lisa Cuchara, Ph.D., Albany Medical College. Immunohematology, pathogenic microbiology, transplantation immunology.

Charlotte Hammond, Ph.D., Connecticut. Molecular biology.

Kenneth Kaloustian, Ph.D., New Hampshire. Physiology and endocrinology.

Edward O'Connor, Ph.D., Albany Medical College. Neuropharmacology.

Dennis Richardson, Ph.D., Nebraska–Lincoln. Parasitology.

Gene Wong, Ph.D., Alberta. Developmental biology.

Adjunct Faculty

Kenneth Carley, Dr.Ph., Alabama. Epidemiology.

Janet Emanuel, Ph.D., Yale. Human genetics.

John Howe, Ph.D., California, Davis. Molecular pathology.

Edward McDonough, M.D., New York Medical College. Forensic pathology.

Lena Prisco, Ph.D., Connecticut. Molecular biology.

Thomas Tinghitella, Ph.D., Notre Dame. Microbiology.

MOLECULAR AND CELL BIOLOGY PROGRAM

Full-time Faculty

Thomas Brady, Ph.D., Connecticut. Clinical pathology.

Deborah Clark, Ph.D., Cornell. Biochemistry.

Charlotte Hammond, Ph.D., Connecticut Health Center. Molecular biology.

Kenneth Kaloustian, Ph.D., New Hampshire. Physiology and endocrinology.

Edward O'Connor, Ph.D., Albany Medical College. Neuropharmacology.

Gene Wong, Ph.D., Alberta. Developmental biology.

Adjunct Faculty

Kenneth Carley, Dr.P.H., Alabama. Epidemiology.

Janet Emanuel, Ph.D., Yale. Human genetics.

John Howe, M.D., Yale.

Edward McDonough, M.D., New York Medical College. Forensic pathology.

Lena Prisco, Ph.D., Connecticut. Molecular biology.

Thomas Tinghitella, Ph.D., Notre Dame. Microbiology.

PATHOLOGISTS' ASSISTANT PROGRAM

Full-Time Faculty

Irwin Beitch, Ph.D., Richmond. Histology/histochemistry.

Tania Blyth, M.H.S., Quinnipiac. Biomedical sciences.

Thomas Brady, Ph.D., Connecticut. Clinical pathology.

Lisa Cuchara, Ph.D., Albany Medical College. Microbiology/immunology.

William Hennessy, B.S., Montclair State; RT, (R)(M). Radiology.

Kenneth Kaloustian, Ph.D., New Hampshire. Physiology and endocrinology.

Edward Tantorski, M.P.H., Yale. Physical therapy.

Gene Wong, Ph.D., Alberta. Developmental biology.

Adjunct Faculty

Steven Bilodeau, M.H.S., Quinnipiac; PA. Pathologists' assistant.

Nelson Gelfman, M.D., Pennsylvania.

Leo Kelly, M.H.S., Quinnipiac; PA. Pathologists' assistant.

Edward McDonough, M.D., New York Medical College. Forensic pathology.

Erika Sembler, M.H.S., Quinnipiac; PA. Pathologists' assistant.

PHYSICIAN ASSISTANT PROGRAM

Full-Time Faculty

Lisa Barratt, M.S., Saint Joseph (Connecticut); PA, Yale; PA-C. Surgical critical care.

Dawn Colomb-Lippa, PA, M.H.S., Quinnipiac; PA-C. Orthopedics.

William Kohlhepp, PA, Rutgers; M.H.A., Quinnipiac; PA-C. Occupational medicine.

Cynthia Booth Lord, PA, Yale; M.H.S., Quinnipiac; PA-C. Family medicine.

John McNab, PA, M.H.S., Duke. Transplant surgery.

Terry O'Donnell, PA, M.H.S., Quinnipiac. Allergy and asthma.

Cindy Rossi, PA, Yale; M.H.S., Quinnipiac. Allergy and asthma.

Adjunct Faculty

Robert Ackroyd, Pathologist Assistant; M.H.S., Quinnipiac. Pathology.

Thomas Brady, Chair, Department of Biomedical Sciences; Ph.D., Connecticut. Clinical pathology.

Kenneth Carley, Epidemiologist, AIDS Surveillance Unit, Connecticut Department of Public Health; Ph.D., Alabama. Epidemiology.

Bernard Clark, Director of Non-Invasive Cardiology, Director of the Outpatient Adult Cardiology Unit, and faculty member, Department of Medicine, Saint Francis Hospital and Medical Center; M.D., George Washington. Cardiology.

Timothy Ferrarotti, M.H.S., Quinnipiac; PA-C. Emergency medicine.

Ellen R. Fischbein, M.D., SUNY at Buffalo. Psychiatry.

Jill Fitzgerald, Pharmacy Clinical Coordinator, Clinical Supervisor, and staff pharmacist, Department of Pharmacy Services, Midstate Medial Center; Pharm.D., North Carolina. Pharmacology.

Peter Juergensen, Metabolism Associate, Nephrology and Endocrinology Department, Yale New Haven Hospital and the Hospital of St. Raphael; PA, Yale.

Kenneth Kaloustian, Chairman, Department of Medical Laboratory Sciences; Ph.D., New Hampshire. Physiology and endocrinology.

Shanta Elizabeth Kapadia, Associate Research Scientist and Lecturer, Yale University School of Medicine; M.B.B.S., M.Surg., Christian Medical College (India). Anatomy.

Michael Nabel, Professor, Department of Mathematics; Ph.D., NYU. Biostatistics.

Judy Nunes, Neurosurgical Physician Assistant, Hospital of Saint Raphael; PA, Yale. Neurology.

Marilyn E. Olsen, M.H.S., Quinnipiac; PA-C. Nephrology.

Edward Louis Osborn, M.D., Connecticut. Ophthalmology.

Brian Peck, Attending Physician, Waterbury Hospital, and Assistant Clinical Professor, Yale University School of Medicine; M.D., Virginia Commonwealth. Rheumatology.

John Pike, Physician Assistant, Cardiac Surgery Service, Saint Francis Hospital and Medical Center; PA, Fairfax. Surgery.

Richard Pope, Physician Assistant, Arthritis Center of Connecticut; PA, SUNY at Stony Brook. Rheumatology.

Stanley Rothman, Professor and Chairman, Department of Mathematics; Ph.D., Wisconsin. Mathematics.

Ronald Rozett, Medical Director, Physician Assistant Program, and Director, Master of Health Administration Program; M.D., Harvard. Internal medicine.

Peter Sandor, PA, M.H.S., Quinnipiac. Surgical ICU.

John Smagula, PA, Kentucky; RT. Radiology.

Donald A. Solimini, Physician Assistant, Pediatrics, Level II Special Care Nursery, New Britain General Hospital; M.H.A., Quinnipiac; PA-C. Pediatrics.

Michael Therrien, Director of Clinical Cardiology and Outcomes Management, Hoffman Heart Institute of Connecticut, Saint Francis Hospital and Medical Center; M.M.M., Carnegie Mellon; M.D., Connecticut; CPE. Cardiology.

Laura Troidle, Physician Assistant, Metabolism Associates; PA, Yale. Nephrology.

SETON HALL UNIVERSITY

School of Graduate Medical Education
Post-Professional Health Sciences Programs

Programs of Study

The School of Graduate Medical Education at Seton Hall University offers Doctor of Philosophy (Ph.D.) in the Health Sciences and Master of Science (M.S.) in the Health Sciences Programs. Both programs are distinguished by their interdisciplinary approach to graduate study. Their fundamental design is a model of professional education that is broadly based on a flexible core curriculum in the health sciences with specialization that permits practicing professionals to assume leadership roles as advanced practitioners, health-care managers, researchers, and health-profession educators. Innovative scheduling allows for full- and part-time studies.

Three areas of specialization are offered in each degree program. For the master's program, the areas are health professions leadership, movement science, and athletic training. The three tracks offered in the Ph.D. program are health professions leadership, movement science, and speech-language pathology.

The health professions leadership specialization track is designed to provide education for those health-care professionals seeking leadership roles in a variety of health-care settings. As such, the leadership track prepares these individuals to design and evaluate methodologies for the delivery of high-quality, cost-effective, and integrated health-care services and health professions education programs; to apply the theories and functions of health-care management, strategies planning, finance, budgeting, and marketing in the design and delivery of health-care services and health professions education programs; to influence health-care policies and regulations that affect the delivery of health care and the education of health professionals; and to utilize tools for managing health-care and educational information. The course work can be combined with independent study in order to design a program of study that provides an even closer match for the individual's interests and professional goals. Supervised research and teaching experiences further supplement this comprehensive and rigorous training program.

The goal of the concentration in movement science is to develop a coherent view of theory, clinical practice, and research in motor learning and control. Study is directed at both normal and dysfunctional movement. In-depth mentored model of study in the areas of pediatric rehabilitation, adult neuromuscular rehabilitation, or adult orthopedic rehabilitation can be pursued in attempt to complement the foundational movement science curriculum, and supervised teaching and research experiences round out the program.

The specialization track in speech-language pathology offers a flexible program of advanced study tailored to address the individual needs of students with a primary interest that can range from basic research in speech, voice, or language science to applied research and/or clinical applications related to speech and language disorders.

The specialization in athletic training offered at the master's level enables students to advance athletic training within the health-care system to better serve clients, the profession, and the community as clinicians, educators, administrators, and researchers.

The Master of Science in Health Sciences Program requires the completion of 39 credits: 6 credits of core courses, 18 credits of specialization courses, and 12 credits of research courses. After completing 21 credits (including at least 9 credits in their specialization and the research methods course), students may register for a research project course in which they demonstrate comprehensive knowledge of research design and other core components. It is expected that each student share their completed research project in a journal article, symposium presentation, and formal integrated paper and/or poster presentation. The research project must be completed within two years of completing course work.

The Ph.D. in Health Sciences Program is committed to the enhancement of knowledge by assisting students in the development of basic research skills; the investigation of research questions in the clinical arena, health-care services, or health professions education environment; and the acquisition and distribution of new information to society. It requires the completion of 60 to 66 credits beyond the master's degree or 48 credits beyond the D.P.T. or professional doctoral degree (90 to 93 for baccalaureate-prepared students). All students are required to complete a minimum of 9 credits of core courses, 3 credits of practicum/teaching experience, 30 credits of specialization courses, 9 credits of research courses, 12 credits of dissertation, and 3 credits of electives (if appropriate). A student may combine this course work with independent study to tailor the program to meet his or her interests and goals. The program is further enhanced by supervised research and teaching experiences and participation in research forums, seminars, practicums, and research projects.

Research Facilities

The libraries at Seton Hall and within the School of Graduate Medical Education contain numerous publications, periodicals, journals, and databases for students in the Health Sciences Program.

Financial Aid

Nearly 90 percent of the students who entered Seton Hall last year received some form of financial aid. Graduate assistantships are available for tuition remission and a small stipend, and there are teaching, research, and administrative positions throughout the University. Loans are available to students enrolled in at least 6 credits per semester.

Cost of Study

Tuition in 2007–08 is $826 per credit. University fees are $105 per semester for full-time students and $85 for part-time students. Additional fees are required for technology, parking, and use of the Recreation Center.

Living and Housing Costs

Limited housing space is available for graduate students at Ora Manor Apartments, approximately 1 mile from campus. Seton Hall provides shuttle service to campus during the academic year; public transportation is also available. In addition, South Orange residents rent space to students. Off-campus listings are available through the Department of Housing and Residence Life.

Student Group

The program is designed for practicing health professionals interested in pursuing advanced education.

Location

Seton Hall is located 14 miles southwest of New York City on 58 green acres in South Orange, New Jersey. It lies at the foot of South Mountain, the first elevation west of New York. South Orange's Main Street is home to several area businesses and the Montrose Park Historic District, a residential neighborhood rich with history.

The School

Seton Hall University's School of Graduate Medical Education was established in 1987 to prepare health-care professionals to assume leadership roles. Residency programs offer training for physicians and dentists in specialty and subspecialty areas. Continuing education updates practicing professionals on recent advances in the diagnosis and management of medical and physical disorders. Innovative graduate programs provide enhanced knowledge through flexible and diverse curricula. The School was the first in New Jersey to offer a clinical doctoral program and Master of Science in occupational therapy and athletic training programs.

Applying

Admission to the programs requires a bachelor's degree (students admitted to the Ph.D. program with a baccalaureate must complete additional credits). A minimum GPA of 3.0; a completed application; two letters of recommendation, preferably from current or previous employers; official transcripts from previous schools; a personal interview; a curriculum vitae or resume; and a statement of goals and research interests are required and GREs are preferred. Applications are accepted throughout the academic year for the master's program. The application deadline is April 1 for fall admission and November 1 for spring admission to the Ph.D. program.

Correspondence and Information

Graduate Programs in Health Sciences
School of Graduate Medical Education, McQuaid Hall
Seton Hall University
400 South Orange Avenue
South Orange, New Jersey 07079
Phone: 973-275-2076
Fax: 973-275-2370
E-mail: gradmeded@shu.edu
Web site: http://www.shu.edu/academics/gradmeded/post-professional-programs.cfm

Seton Hall University

THE FACULTY AND THEIR RESEARCH

Genevieve Pinto Zipp, Chair; Ed.D., PT. Dual task, motor control/postural and clinical decision making, administration, curriculum design (learning styles/mind mapping).

Venu Balasubramanian, Ph.D. Speech-language pathology.

Lee Cabell, Ph.D. Motor control and learning, biomechanics.

Terry Cahill, Ph.D. Leadership and health-care finance and management.

Nina Capone, Ph.D. Speech-language pathology.

Mary Ann Clark, Ed.D., PT. Administration.

Vikram N. Dayalu, Ph.D. Speech-language pathology.

Debra Deluca, J.D. Legal issues in health care, pharmacology.

Diana Glendinning, Ph.D., PT. Parkinson's disease.

John Mitchell, Ph.D. Ethics and health sciences.

Valerie Olson, Ph.D., PT. Learning styles, clinical decision making, curriculum design, administration.

Robert Orlikoff, Ph.D. Speech-language pathology.

Howard James Phillips, Ph.D., PT. Orthopedics.

Brian Shulman, Ph.D., CCC-SLP, ASHA Fellow. Speech-language pathology.

Susan Simpkins, Ed.D., PT. Dual task, motor control and learning across the life span, postural control and balance issues.

Thomas Sowa, Ph.D. Integrating technology and curriculum.

Doreen Stiskal, Ph.D., PT. Dual task, arthritis investigations, orthopedics.

SETON HALL UNIVERSITY

School of Graduate Medical Education
Occupational Therapy Program

Program of Study

The Occupational Therapy Program offered by the School of Graduate Medical Education at Seton Hall University is an entry-level Master of Science in Occupational Therapy.

Occupational therapy (OT) promotes wellness through everyday activities (occupations). The profession helps people of all ages overcome challenges to participation in their daily lives by developing the living skills necessary for independence and satisfaction. OT services typically include customized treatment programs to improve one's ability to perform daily activities, comprehensive home and job site evaluations with adaptation recommendations, performance skills assessments and treatment, adaptive equipment recommendations and usage training, and guidance to family members and caregivers.

The M.S. in Occupational Therapy program in the School of Graduate Medical Education is a professional program that prepares graduates for certification and state licensure as entry-level practitioners in the field.

The M.S. in Occupational Therapy program is accredited by the Accreditation Council for Occupational Therapy Education (http://www.aota.org/Educate/Schools.aspx) of the American Occupational Therapy Association, 4720 Montgomery Lane, P.O. Box 31220, Bethesda, MD 20824-1220. The six-semester, 84-credit program offers a unique blend of experiential and academic experiences with a community and entrepreneurship model. Through this dynamic interplay, students are well-prepared to begin professional practice as entry-level occupational therapists.

The program is distinguished by its integration of theory with application of skills and a focus on knowledge of and sensitivity to culturally diverse populations. The School's prime location allows exposure to diverse and challenging OT practice settings such as hospitals, rehabilitation centers, public and specialty schools, and private practices in the New Jersey and New York metropolitan area as well as out of state. While most programs provide only two fieldwork (clinical) experiences, Seton Hall's M.S. in Occupational Therapy program provides experiences equivalent to approximately nine months of full-time clinical work.

Foundation courses are "cross-program," meaning students gain an appreciation from their peers in other health professions, including athletic training and physical therapy, and learn from distinguished, interdisciplinary faculty members. Weekly clinical experiences are integrated with courses in psychosocial practice, rehabilitation, and pediatrics. Students also have the opportunity to complete fieldwork in an advanced area of practice such as hand therapy or early intervention.

Servant leadership plays an important role in the program. Students reach out to the local community and develop a business plan for the OT practice. This opportunity allows students to experience entrepreneurship and leadership in addition to traditional OT practice. Some students choose to implement their plan upon graduation. Graduates of the program quickly move to leadership roles in the OT field.

Program graduates are eligible to take the National Certification Examination for the Occupational Therapist. The program boasts a 100 percent job placement rating. A majority of the program's graduates practice in pediatrics, mainly in the school system, while others are employed in nursing homes, hospitals, rehabilitation centers, private clinics and home care, and hand therapy.

Research Facilities

The libraries at Seton Hall and within the School of Graduate Medical Education contain numerous publications, periodicals, journals, and databases for students in the Occupational Therapy Program.

Financial Aid

Nearly 90 percent of the students who entered Seton Hall last year received some form of financial aid. Graduate assistantships are available for tuition remission and a small stipend, and there are teaching, research, and administrative positions throughout the University. Loans are available to students enrolled in at least 6 credits per semester, though some require full-time study.

Cost of Study

Tuition for the 2007–08 academic year is $826 per credit. University fees are $105 per semester for full-time students and $85 for part-time students. Additional fees are required for technology, parking, and use of the Recreation Center.

**Living and
Housing Costs**

Limited housing space is available for graduate students at Ora Manor Apartments, approximately 1 mile from campus. Seton Hall provides a shuttle service to campus during the academic year; public transportation is also available. In addition, South Orange residents rent space to students. Off-campus listings are available through the Department of Housing and Residence Life.

Student Group

Students in the program represent diverse interests and backgrounds. They include individuals who are seeking professional graduate education directly following graduation from undergraduate programs, individuals who decided to change their careers, and seniors who took pre–occupational therapy classes as undergraduates at Seton Hall University. Students come from diverse ethnic and cultural backgrounds.

Location

Seton Hall is located 14 miles southwest of New York City on 58 green acres in South Orange, New Jersey. It lies at the foot of South Mountain, the first elevation west of New York. South Orange's Main Street is home to several area businesses and the Montrose Park Historic District, a residential neighborhood rich with history.

The School

The School of Graduate Medical Education, established in 1987, is a graduate professional school within the University structure utilizing a multi-institutional/integrated approach to graduate education. In recent years, the School expanded its mission and direction to include the graduate education of health-care providers other than physicians and dentists. In response to the changing health-care needs of society, the School of Graduate Medical Education seeks to utilize community and University resources to establish a nationally recognized educational center for health professionals. The School's innovative approach provides students with effective tools for becoming leaders in today's health-care arena.

Applying

Admission into the professional Occupational Therapy Program requires a bachelor's degree; a cumulative GPA of 3.0 or better; course work in human anatomy and physiology, psychology, and other related subjects; and three letters of recommendation, at least one of which must be from an OTR. The application deadline is February 15. After the deadline, applications continue to be accepted until the class is filled.

**Correspondence
and Information**

Master of Science in Occupational Therapy
School of Graduate Medical Education, McQuaid Hall
Seton Hall University
400 South Orange Avenue
South Orange, New Jersey 07079
Phone: 973-761-7145
Fax: 973-275-2370
E-mail: gradmeded@shu.edu
Web site: http://www.shu.edu/academics/gradmeded/ms-occupational-therapy/

Seton Hall University

THE FACULTY

Catherine N. Colucci, M.A., OTR; Director of Clinical Education.
Robert Faraci, Ph.D., OTR; Associate Professor.
Meryl M. Picard, M.S.W., OTR; Assistant Professor.
Ruth Segal, Ph.D., OTR; Professor and Chair.
Elizabeth M. Torcivia, M.P.A., Ph.D., OTR; Assistant Professor.

SETON HALL UNIVERSITY

School of Graduate Medical Education
Doctor of Physical Therapy Program

Program of Study

The School of Graduate Medical Education offers an entry-level Doctor of Physical Therapy (D.P.T.) professional program that prepares physical therapists to assume leadership roles in rehabilitation services, prevention, and health-maintenance programs as well as in professional and community organizations. Graduates are prepared to develop health-care policy and appropriate standards to ensure availability, accessibility, and excellence in the delivery of physical therapy services.

The entry-level Doctor of Physical Therapy (D.P.T.) program is a four-year, 120-credit program that includes academic courses and clinical practicums in physical therapy. Course work includes foundation sciences, professional practice, physical therapy, clinical management, medical management, critical inquiry, and clinical experience. Students take internships in their second, third, and fourth years and embark on research projects beginning in their second year. Students develop the skills they need to perform as entry-level practitioners and to grow and adapt to the rapid changes in health-care delivery. Graduates are thoroughly prepared for the Physical Therapy Licensure Examination.

Research Facilities

Research projects conducted in the Functional Human Performance Laboratory focus on the neuromusculoskeletal processes underlying human movement and function. The laboratory is equipped with state-of-the-art instrumentation and software for conducting sophisticated movement analysis across the life span, including gait and posture studies. The lab is currently equipped to conduct research utilizing kinematics, kinetics, EMG, isokinetics, and physiological and balance measurement tools.

Financial Aid

Nearly 90 percent of the students who entered Seton Hall last year received some form of financial aid. Graduate assistantships are available for tuition remission and a small stipend, and there are teaching, research, and administrative positions throughout the University. Loans are available to students enrolled in at least 6 credits per semester, though some require full-time study.

Cost of Study

Tuition for the 2007–08 academic year is $826 per credit. University fees are $105 per semester for full-time students. Additional fees are required for technology, parking, and use of the Recreation Center.

Living and Housing Costs

Limited housing space is available for graduate students at Ora Manor Apartments, approximately 1 mile from campus. Seton Hall provides a shuttle service to campus during the academic year; public transportation is also available. In addition, South Orange residents rent space to students. Off-campus listings are available through the Department of Housing and Residence Life.

Student Group

Many students in the entry-level professional program are seeking the training necessary to assume leadership positions in the health-care arena and to influence the development of policy and standard setting in physical therapy practice.

Location

Seton Hall is located 14 miles southwest of New York City on 58 green acres in South Orange, New Jersey, at the foot of South Mountain, which is the first elevation west of New York. South Orange's Main Street is home to several area businesses and the Montrose Park Historic District, a residential neighborhood rich in history.

The School

The School of Graduate Medical Education, established in 1987, is a graduate professional school within the University structure utilizing a multi-institutional/integrated approach to graduate education. In recent years, the School expanded its mission and direction to include the graduate education of health-care providers other than physicians and dentists. In response to the changing health-care needs of society, the School of Graduate Medical Education seeks to utilize community and University resources to establish a nationally recognized educational center for health professionals. The School's innovative approach provides students with effective tools for becoming leaders in today's health-care arena.

Applying

The following are required for entry into the D.P.T. program: a baccalaureate degree from an accredited institution, a preferred cumulative grade point average (GPA) of 3.0 on a 4.0 scale, 50 hours of clinical observation, official transcripts from all colleges and universities attended, three letters of recommendation (one from a licensed physical therapist who also may have been a supervisor for the clinical observation and two letters from personal or professional sources), scores of the Graduate Record Examinations (GRE) taken within past five years, and the completion of applicant essay question. International students must submit a TOEFL score of at least 550 (paper-based).

Applicants must also complete the following prerequisite courses with an acceptable average and with a grade of C or better: human anatomy and physiology (8 credits), chemistry (8 credits), physics (8 credits), social sciences (9 credits), college math or statistics (3 credits), and English/communications (6 credits). All prerequisite science courses must include a laboratory, and all prerequisite courses must have been completed no longer than ten years prior to the application date. Students with incomplete prerequisites may apply, but they must state how they plan to satisfy the prerequisites by the end of the spring/summer semester prior to the start of the program.

Students must read, understand, meet, and sign the Essential Functions of the School of Graduate Medical Education and the DPT program upon acceptance into the program. Qualified students are admitted without regard to race, color, religion, age, disability, natural origin, sexual orientation, ancestry, or gender.

The application deadline is February 15; however, early review is November 15.

Correspondence and Information

Doctor of Physical Therapy Program
School of Graduate Medical Education, McQuaid Hall
Seton Hall University
400 South Orange Avenue
South Orange, New Jersey 07079
Phone: 973-275-2051
Fax: 973-275-2171
E-mail: gradmeded@shu.edu
Web site: http://www.shu.edu/academics/gradmeded/doctor-physical-therapy/

Seton Hall University

THE FACULTY

Doreen M. Stiskal, Chair, Doctor of Physical Therapy Program; Ph.D., PT.
Mary Alexander, D.P.T., PT, PCS.
Irene DeMasi, Director of Clinical Education, Doctor of Physical Therapy Program; D.P.T., PT.
Diana Glendinning, Ph.D.
Catherine Maher, D.P.T., PT, GCS.
H. James Phillips, Ph.D., PT, OCS, ATC, FAAOMPT.
Kim Poulsen, Director of Clinical Education, Doctor of Physical Therapy Program; D.P.T., PT.
Genevieve Pinto Zipp, Ed.D., PT.

Support Faculty

Carolyn Goeckel, Chair, Athletic Training; M.A., ATC.
Vicci Hill-Lombardi, Ed.D., ATC.
John J. Mitchell Jr., Ph.D.
Mary Murray, Director of Clinical Education, Athletic Training; M.A., ATC.
Thomas Sowa, Ph.D.

SCHOOL OF GRADUATE MEDICAL EDUCATION
SETON HALL UNIVERSITY

SETON HALL UNIVERSITY

School of Graduate Medical Education
Master of Science in Physician Assistant Program

Program of Study	Physician assistants (PAs) are highly educated clinicians who provide patient services with the supervision of a licensed physician. Since the 1990s, the demand for PA services has outpaced the supply of PA graduates. In an effort to alleviate this shortage, Seton Hall University School of Graduate Medical Education (SGME) has established a physician assistant studies program. The Master of Science in Physician Assistant (M.S.P.A.) Program is designed to develop health-care practitioners who practice with physicians within the health-care community in a variety of settings; possess a broad base of knowledge with which to serve patients of all ages; critically appraise health science literature and apply the appropriate principles and procedures to the recognition, evaluation, interpretation, and understanding of current trends; and demonstrate knowledge and sensitivity to culturally diverse populations and their attitudes toward health and illness. This 96-credit, three-year professional program includes courses specific to physician assistant practice that are intended not only to provide students with the technical skills necessary to perform as entry-level practitioners but also to enable them to grow and adapt to the rapid changes in the professions and the health-care delivery system.
	In the first year, students take classes in human anatomy, human physiology, health maintenance and education, clinical medicine, psychiatry, pharmacology, clinical therapeutics, neuroscience, pathophysiology, and clinical and diagnostic methods. No advanced placements, transfer credit, or credit for experiential learning is granted. The program recommends that students do not engage in outside employment during the academic year.
Research Facilities	The University Libraries have notable resources, including extensive holdings of nearly 600,000 book volumes, 1,127 current periodical subscriptions, back-files of more than 6,500 serial titles, electronic access to full-text articles in more than 25,000 journals, a broad selection of indexing and abstracting services in both digital and print formats, various microform collections, music CDs, and audiovisual aids. The University Libraries are a selective depository for U.S. federal, state of New Jersey, and U.N. publications. Depository status provides exclusive access to thousands of publications in electronic or print formats. For added bibliographic access and document delivery, the University Libraries participate in consortia such as PALCI, VALE, and the international OCLC. It provides more than 5,000 interlibrary loans free of charge. A majority of periodical interlibrary loans are delivered through e-mail.
Financial Aid	Nearly 90 percent of students receive some form of financial aid. Graduate assistantships are available for tuition remission and a small stipend, and there are teaching, research, and administrative positions throughout the University. Loans are available to students enrolled in at least 6 credits per semester.
Cost of Study	Tuition in 2007–08 is $826 per credit. University fees are $105 per semester for full-time students; the technology fee per semester for full-time students is $200. Additional fees are required for parking and for use of the Recreation Center.
Living and Housing Costs	Limited housing space is available for graduate students at Ora Manor Apartments, approximately 1 mile from campus. Seton Hall provides a shuttle service to campus during the academic year; public transportation is also available. In addition, South Orange residents rent space to students. Off-campus listings are available through the Department of Housing and Residence Life.
Student Group	The program is composed of practicing health professionals interested in pursuing advanced education.
Location	Seton Hall is located 14 miles southwest of New York City on 58 green acres in South Orange, New Jersey. It lies at the foot of South Mountain, the first elevation west of New York. South Orange's Main Street is home to several area businesses and the Montrose Park Historic District, a residential neighborhood rich with history.
The University and The School	Seton Hall is a major Catholic university. In a diverse and collaborative environment, the University focuses on academic and ethical development. Seton Hall students are prepared to be leaders in their professional and community lives in a global society and are challenged by an outstanding faculty, an evolving technologically advanced setting, and values-centered curricula.
	Seton Hall University's School of Graduate Medical Education was established in 1987 to prepare health-care professionals to assume leadership roles. Residency programs offer training for physicians and dentists in specialty and subspecialty areas. Continuing education updates practicing professionals on recent advances in the diagnosis and management of medical and physical disorders. Innovative graduate programs provide enhanced knowledge through flexible and diverse curricula. The School was the first in New Jersey to offer a clinical doctoral program and Master of Science in occupational therapy and athletic training programs. Seton Hall's Physician Assistant Program is fully accredited by the Accreditation Review Commission on Education for the Physician Assistant (ARC-PA). The Physician Assistant Student Society of Seton Hall University (PASSSHU) is active with philanthropic activities in conjunction with the American Academy of Physician Assistants.
Applying	Applicants should have a baccalaureate degree from an accredited institution, with a GPA of at least 3.0. Prerequisite courses include human anatomy and physiology (8 credits), microbiology (4 credits), chemistry (8 credits), precalculus (3 credits), general biology (4 credits), and psychology (3 credits). Students must submit the completed application, the $75 application fee, official transcripts of all colleges and universities attended, GRE scores, and three letters of recommendation. International students must also submit TOEFL scores. A minimum of 100 hours of health-care experience is required. A personal interview is required. The application deadline is April 15.
Correspondence and Information	Joann Codella, Secretary Master of Science in Physician Assistant Program School of Graduate Medical Education, McQuaid Hall Seton Hall University 400 South Orange Avenue South Orange, New Jersey 07079 Phone: 973-275-2596 Fax: 973-275-2370 E-mail: codelljo@shu.edu Web site: http://www.shu.edu/academics/gradmeded/ms-physician-assistant/

Seton Hall University

THE FACULTY

Carol Biscardi, Assistant Professor and Chair; M.S., St. John's; PA-C.
Gary J. Bouchard, Ph.D., Seton Hall; PA-C.
Christopher Hanifin, Instructor; M.S.P.A., Seton Hall; PA-C.
Ellen D. Mandel, Assistant Professor; M.S., University of Medicine and Dentistry of New Jersey; M.P.A., Seton Hall; PA-C, RD, CDE.
Joseph L. Monaco, Assistant Professor; M.S.J., Seton Hall; PA-C.
Denise Rizzolo, M.S., Seton Hall; PA-C.
Mona Sedrak, Ph.D., Walden; PA-C.

SETON HALL UNIVERSITY

School of Graduate Medical Education
Speech-Language Pathology Program

Programs of Study

The Master of Science in Speech-Language Pathology Program prepares speech-language pathologists (SLPs) with the knowledge, skill, and judgment to advance the art and science of their professional practice. SLPs are professionals who evaluate and treat speech, voice, language, and oral motor problems. SLPs work with children and adults who cannot make speech sounds or cannot make them clearly, have impaired speech rhythm and fluency, and have difficulty understanding or producing language. They also work with people who have eating and swallowing disorders. Speech and language problems may result from hearing loss, injury, cerebral palsy, stroke, cleft palate, or mental retardation. Using special instruments, as well as written and oral tests, SLPs determine the nature of these impairments and devise strategies for treatment.

This 65-credit, five-semester program includes academic course work and clinical practica that prepare graduates to critically analyze and convey information to patients, colleagues, and other professionals as well as to adapt to the rapid changes in the profession and in the health-care service-delivery system.

The Master of Science in Speech-Language Pathology Program received full accreditation for an eight-year period by the Council on Academic Accreditation (CAA) of the American Speech-Language-Hearing Association (ASHA) effective May 1, 2006 through April 30, 2014. In order for an individual to be eligible to apply for national certification with ASHA, a student must initiate and complete course work and clinical practicum at a CAA-accredited institution.

Research Facilities

Three on-campus labs—the Developmental Language and Cognition Laboratory, the Clinical Speech and Voice Laboratory, and the Sensory-Motor Integration Laboratory—are used by faculty and students to study normal and disordered child language acquisition, speech motor control, speech and voice acoustics, and adult language and cognition. Current research efforts include investigation of the cognitive skills that underlie the speech and language development; the relationship between semantic learning and lexical expression; the role of auditory, visual, and audio-visual feedback in speech production and comprehension; and the role of imitation and action observation on speech production.

Financial Aid

Almost 90 percent of the students who entered Seton Hall last year received some form of financial aid. Graduate assistantships are available for tuition remission and a small stipend. Teaching, research, and administrative positions are available throughout the University.

Cost of Study

Tuition for the 2007–08 academic year is $826 per credit. University fees are $105 per semester for full-time students. Additional fees are required for technology, parking, and use of the Recreation Center.

Living and Housing Costs

Seton Hall University does not provide on-campus housing for graduate students. There are numerous apartments available in South Orange and many residents rent space to students. The University provides local shuttle bus service to campus during the academic year. Off-campus listings are available through the Department of Housing and Residence Life.

Student Group

The Department of Speech-Language Pathology supports a local chapter of the National Student Speech-Language-Hearing Association (NSSLHA), organized and run by members of the graduate student body under the advisement of a member of the faculty.

Location

Seton Hall is located 14 miles southwest of New York City on 58 green acres in South Orange, New Jersey. It lies at the foot of South Mountain, the first elevation west of New York. South Orange's Main Street is home to several area businesses and the Montrose Park Historic District, a residential neighborhood rich with history.

The School

The School of Graduate Medical Education, established in 1987, is a graduate professional school within the University structure utilizing a multi-institutional/integrated approach to graduate education. In recent years, the School expanded its mission and direction to include the graduate education of health-care providers other than physicians and dentists. In response to the changing health-care needs of society, the School of Graduate Medical Education seeks to utilize community and University resources to establish a nationally recognized educational center for health professionals. The School's innovative approach provides students with effective tools for becoming leaders in today's health-care arena.

Applying

Admission to the program requires a bachelor's degree in speech and hearing sciences or communication disorders or a degree in another field with the required preparatory course work; an overall GPA of at least 3.0; an essay; GRE scores received within the past five years; and three letters of recommendation. The application deadline is March 1. A personal interview is required of all applicants being considered for admission.

Correspondence and Information

Speech-Language Pathology Program
School of Graduate Medical Education, Alfieri Hall
Seton Hall University
400 South Orange Avenue
South Orange, New Jersey 07079
Phone: 973-275-2825
Fax: 973-275-2171
E-mail: gradmeded@shu.edu
Web site: http://www.shu.edu/academics/gradmeded/ms-speech-language-pathology/

Seton Hall University

THE FACULTY

Robert F. Orlikoff, Ph.D., CCC-SLP; Professor of Speech-Language Pathology and Chair.
Venugopal Balasubramanian, Ph.D., CCC-SLP; Associate Professor of Speech-Language Pathology.
Nina C. Capone, Ph.D., CCC-SLP; Associate Professor of Speech-Language Pathology.
Theresa A. Cardillo, M.A., CCC-SLP; Director of Clinical Education.
Vikram N. Dayalu, Ph.D., CCC-SLP; Associate Professor of Speech-Language Pathology.
Patricia Remshifski, M.S., CCC-SLP; Director of Clinical Education.
Brian B. Shulman, Ph.D., CCC-SLP, ASHA Fellow, BRS-CL; Professor of Speech-Language Pathology and Acting Dean.
Deborah Welling, Au.D., CCC-A/FAAA; Associate Professor of Speech-Language Pathology.

SHENANDOAH UNIVERSITY

School of Health Professions

Programs of Study	The School of Health Professions at Shenandoah University, located on the campus of Winchester Medical Center in Winchester, Virginia, offers graduate programs in athletic training, nursing, occupational therapy, physical therapy, and physician assistant studies.
	The athletic training program offers students a combination of hands-on clinical training, classroom instruction, clinical research, and distance-based education. Clinical field experiences are available on campus and in collegiate and professional sports settings. Resources and the curriculum are created to meet the standards for accreditation from the Commission on Accreditation of Allied Health Education Programs. In this entry-level master's program, students are prepared to take the certification examination given by the National Athletic Trainers' Association Board of Certification. This is not an advanced master's degree program for the certified professional.
	The college offers a dual-degree Master of Science in athletic training and doctorate in physical therapy program. The program is dedicated to training educated physical therapists and athletic trainers who are reflective practitioners who provide effective, evidence-based, compassionate care for the prevention, diagnosis, and treatment of movement dysfunction.
	The Division of Physical Therapy offers a fully accredited entry-level professional program that provides the academic study and clinical experience required by the American Physical Therapy Association (APTA) for work as a physical therapist. Through this program, students earn a Doctor of Physical Therapy (D.P.T.) degree. The program begins in late August and extends for three years, with graduation in August of the third year. Interspersed throughout the program are approximately eight months of clinical experiences in more than 250 clinical sites, including full-time clinical affiliations in a variety of practice settings. Students are required to complete a minimum of 97 semester hours of course work over the three years of full-time study and may take elective courses in their third year.
	Shenandoah University has a rich history of meeting the need for nurses educated at the associate and baccalaureate levels. It is now prepared to meet the need for nurses educated at advanced levels by offering a graduate nursing program. Students selected for the Master of Science in Nursing (M.S.N.) program find themselves in a clinically based curriculum that facilitates their professional development as scholars capable of providing safe and innovative advanced care. The program offers a Master of Science in Nursing with three specialty tracks: health systems management, family nurse practitioner studies, and nurse midwifery.
	The master's program in occupational therapy is dynamic, emphasizing practical and active learning. Students participate in small-group learning sessions throughout the curriculum, discussing actual clients and solving real clinical questions. The program prepares students to practice client-centered occupational therapy and facilitate positive changes in health and participation within individuals, environments, and social systems. Shenandoah University's graduate occupational therapy curriculum is nationally recognized for its problem-based and social learning models. Students learn from each other, faculty members, clinicians, and clients in the community. Opportunities for students include service learning, interactive lectures, experiential learning, and clinical case groups.
	The physician assistant studies program is one of the newest educational programs at Shenandoah University. This accredited, seven-semester, twenty-seven-month graduate-level program leading to a master's degree offers brand-new, state-of-the-art classrooms and labs with modern computer technology and experienced faculty members with national reputations in the physician assistant profession. The program is located on the campus of the Winchester Medical Center, a 408-bed regional referral hospital, which is part of Valley Health System. The charter physician assistant studies class of 16 students was accepted in fall 2001.
Research Facilities	The library collections of Shenandoah University are housed in two facilities. The Alson H. Smith, Jr. Library is the main library facility for the University. The branch Health Sciences Library is located in the Health Professions Building on the grounds of the Winchester Medical Center. Current total holdings number more than 275,000 items, including 123,000 books and bound journals, 13,000 recordings, 16,000 scores, 1,500 videotapes, and 115,000 ERIC documents.
Financial Aid	Financial aid is available to qualified graduate students through subsidized and unsubsidized federal student loans worth up to $18,500 per year. The Virginia Tuition Assistance Grant is available to first-time graduate students for two to four years, depending upon qualifications and program of study. Alternative types of loans are also available when federal and state loans have been fulfilled. Graduate assistantships and tuition discounts are also available to students who qualify.
Cost of Study	For the 2007–08 academic year, the master's programs in athletic training, occupational therapy, physical therapy, and physician assistant studies are $640 per credit. The doctoral program in nontraditional pharmacy and the transitional-doctoral program in physical therapy are also $520 per credit, as are all other graduate programs.
Living and Housing Costs	Room and board range from $2650 to $3775 per semester for on-campus housing. Off-campus housing is also available; prices are within the standard range for medium-sized East Coast cities.
Student Group	Students enrolled in the programs offered through the School of Health Professions attend Shenandoah University to become highly trained in all aspects of their desired professions, leading to rewarding careers in the health sciences. Nearly all students in these programs have undergraduate degrees and training in their majors and have proven themselves during that training and/or in professional work as intelligent, capable health-care practitioners interested in expanding their knowledge base, improving their skills, and advancing in their profession.
Location	Founded in 1744, Winchester, Virginia, is the oldest city west of the Blue Ridge Mountains in the state. Located approximately 70 miles west of Washington, D.C., at the northern entrance of the Shenandoah Valley, it encompasses 9.3 square miles and is the medical, commercial, industrial, and agricultural center for the region. The city has a population of 23,000 and continues to preserve its important role in America's history as the home of General Stonewall Jackson's military headquarters and the location of George Washington's office in the mid-1700s.
The University and The School	Founded in 1875, Shenandoah University offers a creative combination of educational opportunities through programs in the arts and sciences, business, health professions, and the performing arts. The University offers associate, bachelor's, master's, and doctoral degrees in programs throughout the curricula. Shenandoah University continues its voluntary affiliation with the United Methodist Church while continuing to renew its mission in light of a broad contemporary understanding of Judeo-Christian principles. It offers voluntary worship services and service projects as well as other opportunities for spiritual enrichment, fulfilling the religious needs of a diverse student body. The School of Health Professions is located on the campus of Winchester Medical Center in Winchester, Virginia.
Applying	Each program has varying academic requirements, but generally, a minimum GPA of 2.8 on a 4.0 scale is required for consideration for admission. SAT or GRE scores are viewed on a competitive basis. Letters of reference and a completed essay are required. The University has a rolling admissions procedure.
Correspondence and Information	Admissions Office Shenandoah University 1460 University Drive Winchester, Virginia 22601 Phone: 540-665-4581 800-432-2266 (toll-free) E-mail: admit@su.edu Web site: http://www.su.edu/academic/healthprof.asp

Shenandoah University

THE FACULTY

Division of Athletic Training
Rose A. Schmieg, Assistant Professor and Director, Division of Athletic Training; Ph.D., University of St. Augustine for Health Sciences.
Michael Powers, Assistant Professor; Ph.D., Virginia.

Division of Nursing and Respiratory Care
Sheila Sparks Ralph, Professor and Director, Division of Nursing and Respiratory Care; D.N.Sc., Catholic University.
K. Joy Buck, Assistant Professor; Ph.D. candidate, Virginia.
Elizabeth Courts, Assistant Professor; M.S.N., Virginia Commonwealth.
Janice DuBrueler, Assistant Professor; Ph.D. candidate, Catholic University.
Cheryl Dumont, Adjunct Clinical Instructor; M.S., Delaware.
Juliana Fehr, Associate Professor, Midwifery; Ph.D., George Mason.
Kathryn Ganske, Assistant Professor; Ph.D., Virginia.
Patricia B. Krauskopf, Assistant Professor; Ph.D. candidate, Virginia.
Patricia Kropp, Adjunct Clinical Instructor; M.S.N., Catholic University.
Sharon K. Mailey, Professor and Associate Director; Ph.D., North Carolina.
Jennifer Matthews, Adjunct Associate Professor; Ph.D., George Mason.
Vickie Morley, Adjunct Assistant Professor; M.S.N., Texas Medical Branch.
Martha Morrow, Associate Professor; D.N.Sc., George Mason.
Marian Newton, Associate Professor; Ph.D., Nebraska Medical Center.
Kathleen Quarles, Adjunct Clinical Instructor; M.S.N., George Mason.
Maureen Quinn, Professor; Ph.D., NYU.
Sherlyn Shaughnessy, Adjunct Clinical Instructor; M.B.A., Shenandoah; M.S.N., Virginia.
Wanida P. Wanant, Associate Professor; D.N.Sc., Catholic University.
Pamela Webber, Professor; Ph.D., George Mason.
Helen Zebarth, Assistant Professor; M.Ed., Boston University.

Division of Occupational Therapy
Deborah Marr, Associate Professor and Director, Division of Occupational Therapy; Sc.D., Boston University.
Mary Corcoran, Professor; Ph.D., Pennsylvania.
Leslie B. Davidson, Assistant Professor; Ph.D. candidate, Virginia Tech.
Susan Lin, Assistant Professor; Sc.D., Boston University.
Orit Simhoni, Assistant Professor; Ph.D., Nova Southeastern.
Yvonne Russell Teske, Associate Professor; Ph.D., Michigan.

Division of Physical Therapy
Rose A. Schmieg, Assistant Professor and Director, Division of Physical Therapy; Ph.D., University of St. Augustine for Health Science.
Karen Abraham-Justice, Assistant Professor; Ph.D., East Carolina.
Andrea Fergus, Assistant Professor and Associate Director; Ph.D., Virginia.
Sheri Hale, Assistant Professor; Ph.D., Penn State.
D. Michael McKeough, Associate Professor; Ed.D., Columbia.
Edward C. Schrank, Assistant Professor; D.Sc. candidate, Rocky Mountain.
Todd Telemeco, Instructor; Ph.D. candidate, Virginia Commonwealth.
Melissa Wolff-Burke, Assistant Professor; Ed.D., Tennessee, Knoxville.

Division of Physician Assistant Studies
Anthony A. Miller, Associate Professor and Director, Division of Physician Assistant Studies; Ph.D. candidate, Toledo.
Rachel A. Carlson, Assistant Professor; M.S., Medical College of Ohio.
William Dalton, Assistant Professor and Clinical Coordinator, M.S.Ed., Duquesne; PA-C.
Raymond L. Eifel, Assistant Professor; M.S., George Williams.
Brenda Kaminski, Assistant Professor; M.P.H., George Washington; PA-C.
James C. Laidlaw, Adjunct Associate Professor; M.D., Michigan.
Rebecca Redman, Adjunct Assistant Professor; Pharm.D., Maryland, Baltimore.

SOUTH UNIVERSITY

Savannah Campus
Anesthesiologist Assistant Program

Program of Study

The Master of Medical Science (M.M.Sc.) Anesthesiologist Assistant (AA) Program is designed to provide classroom, laboratory, and clinical experiences that prepare graduates to deliver anesthesia care to patients of all ages and severities of illness for the full spectrum of surgical procedures. As one of the Southeast's premier providers of health-professions education, the AA program at South University has already established a reputation for attracting some of the nation's top students.

A career as an AA offers both challenges and rewards, and the University's program emphasizes both classroom and practical learning. In addition to the experienced faculty members, students have access to some of the most advanced learning tools in the country. The school maintains a fully equipped mock operating room and student lab where students obtain experience that prepares them for clinical rotations and, ultimately, a full-time position as a member of an anesthesia care team.

In the first year of this intensive twenty-eight-month program curriculum, students are focused on the scientific foundations of anesthesia practice through classroom simulation, laboratory work, and clinical experience. As the year progresses, the amount of time that students spend at clinical sites steadily increases. The senior year comprises full-time clinical experience in four-week blocks, plus weekly senior seminar meetings in which students deliver presentations on various topics related to anesthesia care, sharing best practices from their experiences across the country. A minimum of 2,700 hours of clinical experience is required delivering anesthesia in various settings while incorporating a comprehensive span of surgical procedures performed on patients. Students have the opportunity to complete their clinical rotations at some of the nation's most prominent health-care institutions, ranging from major hospitals to regional health-care centers.

Research Facilities

Facilities for the Anesthesiologist Assistant Program include a sophisticated mock operating room with SimMan, a lifelike simulator that provides students with the opportunity to practice real-world scenarios before stepping into a hospital. A unique fully equipped anesthesia learning laboratory was built specifically for the program and features the latest in industry technology and equipment.

The campus library, constructed in 2007, provides comfortable study space for students, wireless Internet capabilities for laptop network connectivity, a computer lab, and reference and interlibrary loan services. The open-stack book collection includes access to reference, reserve, and circulating materials, along with tutorial aides and program-specific resources for class assignments. The periodical collection also supports the curricula by way of authoritative journals in both print and electronic formats. The adjoining research center, which is furnished with ten computer workstations, offers students access to the Internet, online database services such as the MEDLINE office suite, tutorials, and class-support software.

Financial Aid

A wide range of financial aid options is available to students who qualify. The Savannah campus of South University offers access to federal and state aid, including grants, loans, and work-study programs. Eligible students may apply for veterans' educational benefits and are encouraged to investigate the availability of grants and scholarships through community resources. As a first step, students should complete the Free Application for Federal Student Aid (FAFSA). Students may apply electronically at http://www.fafsa.ed.gov or at the campus Student Financial Services Department. Applications should be submitted promptly to receive consideration for the maximum amount of aid.

Cost of Study

Tuition information for the Anesthesiologist Assistant Program may be obtained by contacting the School of Pharmacy via the South University Web site at http://www.southuniversity.edu.

Living and Housing Costs

South University offers school-sponsored student housing at its Savannah, Georgia, campus in conjunction with several local apartment complexes. Due to the full-time nature of the program, Anesthesiologist Assistant Program students typically live in rental homes, town homes, or apartments in the Savannah area. More information is available by contacting the Director of Student Housing at 912-201-8000.

Student Group

The Savannah campus of South University has a diverse student body enrolled in both day and evening classes.

Location

Located on the south side of the historic city of Savannah, the Atlantic Ocean and recreational amenities of Tybee Island, with their beaches and numerous outdoor activities, are just a short drive away. In addition, the campus is located just a short drive from Hilton Head Island and Charleston, South Carolina.

The University

South University is accredited as a Level V institution by the Commission on Colleges, Southern Association of Colleges and Schools (SACS; 1866 Southern Lane, Decatur, Georgia 30033-4097; phone: 404-679-4501), to award associate, bachelor's, master's, and doctoral degrees. The Anesthesiologist Assistant Program is accredited by the Commission for Accreditation of Allied Health Education Programs (CAAHEP; 1361 Park Street, Clearwater, Florida 33756; phone: 727-210-2350).

Applying

Students are accepted into the Anesthesiologist Assistant Program once each year, with classes beginning in June and commencement taking place in mid-September of the following year. Entrance into the program is gained through a formal application review and assessment of the applicant's potential for professional and academic achievement. Prospective students must complete premedicine course work at a regionally accredited U.S. college or university, as described on the program's Web site. The admissions process requires official transcripts from all colleges and universities attended, scores from the Graduate Record Examinations (GRE) or the Medical College Admission Test (MCAT) that are not more than five years old, three letters of recommendation, proof of at least 8 hours spent with an anesthesiologist or anesthetist in an operating room, and a summary of an article published in a current anesthesia journal. For the GRE, the program must receive official score reports directly from the Educational Testing Service. The code for South University is 5157. For the MCAT, the program must receive official score reports directly from the Medical College Admission Testing service.

Correspondence and Information

Applications for admission to the South University Anesthesiologist Assistant Program are available by contacting:

Anesthesiologist Assistant Program
South University
709 Mall Boulevard
Savannah, Georgia 31406-4805

Phone: 912-201-8083
Fax: 912-201-8070
E-mail: aaprograminfo@southuniversity.edu
Web site: http://www.southuniversity.edu/aa

South University

THE FACULTY

One of the most outstanding aspects of South University's Anesthesiologist Assistant Program is the dedication of the faculty members and their ability to cultivate a supportive learning environment. Faculty members are committed to their roles as mentors, teachers, and colearners. They are also dedicated to the training of students who can assume positions of leadership within the field of anesthesiology. A current list of program faculty members is available at the South University Web site (http://www.southuniversity.edu/aa).

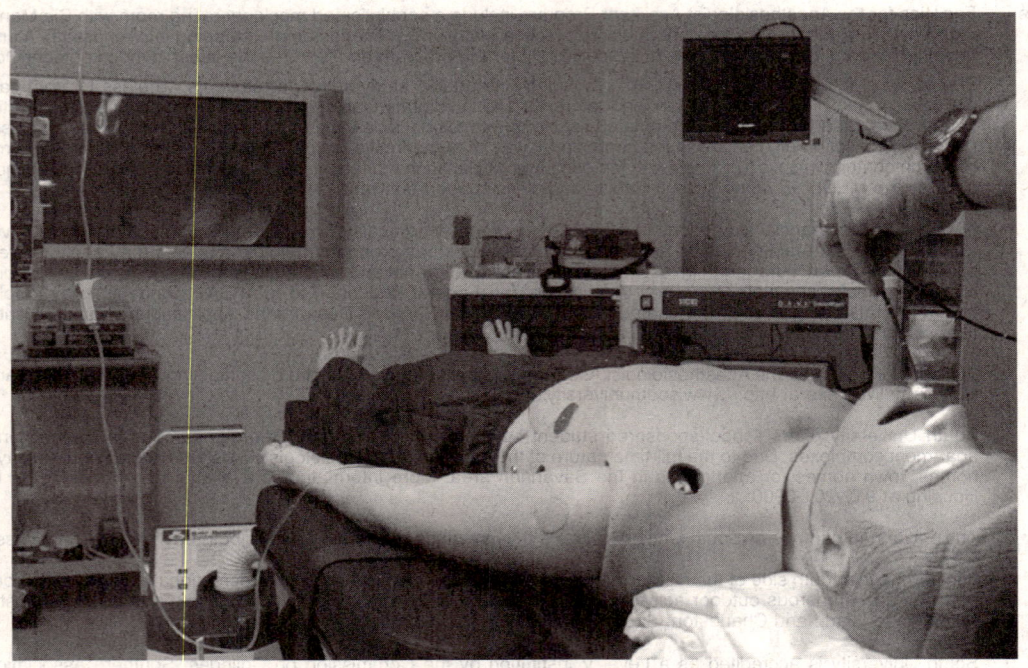

One of the main features of South University's Anesthesiologist Assistant Program is its mock operating room. Modeled after actual operating rooms, the room is complete with current anesthesia equipment and SimMan, a model patient that is used to simulate real-life scenarios.

SouthUniversity℠

SOUTH UNIVERSITY

Savannah Campus
School of Health Professions
Physician Assistant Studies Program

Program of Study

The Master of Science in Physician Assistant Studies (M.S.P.A.) degree program at South University is an intensive twenty-seven-month curriculum structured around full-time course work. With students applying from across the country through the national Central Application Service for Physician Assistants (CASPA) system, South University routinely attracts students who have received their undergraduate educations at major public universities. The program focuses on the study of pathology, physiology, epidemiology, pharmacology, diagnosis, management, and treatment. Students learn in small groups with on-site laboratories where individualized attention is delivered by faculty members who have a variety of both professional and teaching experience.

Within the first months of the program, students begin to gain clinical experience in emergency medicine, surgical procedures, life support, internal medicine, and office practices. Program graduates are qualified to take the National Commission on the Certification of Physician Assistants (NCCPA) exam.

Once certified, graduates are prepared to work in internal medicine and family practice or specialty areas such as OB/GYN, pediatrics, surgery, orthopedics, postoperative care, cardiology, or many other specialties. In these areas, graduates may examine and treat patients, order and interpret lab results and X-rays, make diagnoses, prescribe medications, and take medical histories. They also may treat minor injuries, counsel patients, and carry out therapy instructions.

Research Facilities

The Physician Assistant (PA) Program is housed in the School of Health Professions building at its campus in historic Savannah, Georgia. The campus features dedicated PA classrooms and lab facilities. The University recently opened a new on-campus library, more than doubling its previous library space. The new facility features comfortable study space for students, wireless Internet capabilities for laptop network connectivity, separate computer labs, and reference and interlibrary loan services.

Financial Aid

A wide range of financial aid options is available to students who qualify. The Savannah campus of South University offers access to federal and state programs, including grants, loans, and work-study programs. Eligible students may apply for veterans' educational benefits and are encouraged to investigate the availability of grants and scholarships through community resources. As a first step, students should complete the Free Application for Federal Student Aid (FAFSA). Students may apply electronically at http://www.fafsa.ed.gov or with the campus Director of Student Financial Services. Applications should be submitted promptly to receive consideration for the maximum amount of aid.

Cost of Study

Tuition information for the Physician Assistant Studies Program may be obtained by contacting Physician Assistant Studies Program Admissions at South University's Savannah campus.

Living and Housing Costs

South University offers a variety of school-sponsored student housing options at its Savannah, Georgia, campus in conjunction with local apartment complexes. Due to the full-time nature of the program, PA students typically live in rental homes or apartments in the Savannah area. More information is available by contacting the Director of Student Housing at 912-201-8000.

Student Group

The Savannah campus of South University has a diverse student body enrolled in both day and evening classes. Students are primarily commuters who live within 50 miles of the city.

Location

Located on the south side of the historic city of Savannah, the campus is situated on 9 acres of land. It is convenient to the city's bustling midtown section and a full range of educational and cultural activities. The Atlantic Ocean and recreational amenities of Tybee Island, including beaches and numerous outdoor activities, are just a short drive away. In addition, the campus is located just a short drive from Hilton Head Island and Charleston, South Carolina.

The Program

Accreditation for South University's Physician Assistant Studies Program has been granted by the Accreditation Review Commission on Education for the Physician Assistant Programs (ARC-PA). The program is also a member of the Association of Physician Assistant Programs, the national organization representing physician assistant education programs. South University is accredited by the Commission on Colleges, Southern Association of Colleges and Schools (1866 Southern Lane, Decatur, Georgia 30033-4097; phone: 404-679-4501) to award associate, bachelor's, master's, and doctoral degrees.

Applying

Students are accepted into the Master of Science in Physician Assistant Studies degree program on an annual basis. Candidates may choose to qualify for early admission or general admission. Entrance into the program is gained through a formal application review and interview process. Acceptance is competitive and based on the admission committee's evaluation of the applicant's academic background (completed bachelor's degree with overall minimum GPA of 2.6 and recommended science GPA of 3.0 or better), personal motivation, and ability to be self-supporting throughout the rigors of the program. No transfer credit is accepted for this program. The South University Physician Assistant Studies Program utilizes CASPA (http://www.caspaonline.org); students who wish to do so, may apply online through CASPA. In addition to application through CASPA, prospective students must also complete a supplemental application. This application is available online at http://www.southuniversity.edu/pa or by contacting the physician assistant department.

The South University Physician Assistant Studies program is accepting applications for the class beginning January 2008. All applications for this class must be complete by September 1, 2007.

Correspondence and Information

Applications for admission to the South University Master of Science in Physician Assistant Studies degree program are available by contacting:

Physician Assistant Studies Program
South University
709 Mall Boulevard
Savannah, Georgia 31406-4805
Phone: 912-201-8025
        866-629-2901 (toll-free)
Fax: 912-201-8070
E-mail: paprogram@southuniversity.edu
Web site: http://www.southuniversity.edu/pa

South University

THE FACULTY

One of the most outstanding aspects of South University's Physician Assistant Studies Program is the dedication of the faculty members and their ability to cultivate a supportive learning environment. Faculty members are committed to their roles as mentors, teachers, and colearners. They are also dedicated to the training of students who can assume positions of leadership within the medical field. A current list of program faculty members is available in the South University catalog, which is located on the South University Web site (http://www.southuniversity.edu/pa).

South University PA students celebrate the completion of their first year of study and the beginning of clinical rotations.

TEACHERS COLLEGE COLUMBIA UNIVERSITY

Department of Biobehavioral Sciences

Programs of Study

The Department of Biobehavioral Sciences at Teachers College Columbia University offers programs that derive educational and clinical applications from an understanding of the biological processes underlying human communication and movement and their disorders. An understanding of the normal biobehavioral processes is applied to clinical practice. The scientific knowledge obtained from studying each of these specialized fields is used to enhance the educational, adaptive, and communicative capabilities of individuals with normal and impaired abilities across the life span.

Students may earn a Master of Arts (M.A.), Master of Science (M.S.), Master of Education (M.Ed.), Doctor of Education (Ed.D.), or Doctor of Philosophy (Ph.D.) in one of the following fields of study: movement sciences and education, physical education, neuroscience and education, or speech-language pathology and audiology. As these professionals often work in interdisciplinary teams, the Department facilitates opportunities for students to interact across professional boundaries. Requirements are 32 points for M.A. and M.S. degree programs, 75 points for the Ph.D., 60 points for the Ed.M., and 90 points for the Ed.D. Master's programs can be completed in twelve to eighteen months of full-time study or two to three years of part-time study. A culminating project is required, which may involve a scholarly review of research and theory or a basic or applied research report. Ed.D. and Ph.D. programs include course work that focuses on research methods and require participation in research experiences to demonstrate competence as well as the successful completion of a dissertation.

Research Facilities

The Department maintains clinics and laboratories to support the teaching and research components of the programs, including the Edward D. Mysak Speech and Hearing Center and laboratories in applied physiology, motor learning and control, kinematic analysis, infant development, language, cognition, and neuroscience. The Edward D. Mysak Speech and Hearing Center offers a range of diagnostic and therapeutic services to individuals of all ages with mild to severe communication disorders. Qualified students assist in the provision of these services under the direct supervision of the faculty and staff members. Laboratories in language, cognition, and neuroscience investigate the cognitive and neural underpinnings of language development and processing in normal and impaired populations. Current projects include EEG, MEG, fMRI, and eye-tracking studies of linguistic processing in infant through adult populations; investigations of the neural basis of motor control, movement science disorders, and hand functions and cerebral palsy; and the development and test of new rehabilitation strategies. The physical education laboratory has a variety of video and computer analysis equipment for conducting research in physical education. Current projects in physical education pedagogy include examining the interrelationships of student and teacher process variables with student attitudes toward physical education for both urban and suburban schools, and investigation of issues related to testing and assessment in physical education.

The Gottesman Libraries, with more than a million books and materials, is one of the nation's largest and most comprehensive research libraries in education, psychology, and health services. Students have access to the 5.5 million volumes in the Columbia University library system. Data, voice, and video outlets are found in every classroom, office, and residence on the main portion of the campus, and laptops and projectors may be borrowed from Media Services. The Microcomputer Center provides students with PCs and Macs, software, printers, and other peripherals. The Instructional Media Lab (IML) is a facility in which students and faculty members create rich content for classes, online learning, student teaching, and research. Computer classrooms for hands-on instruction include both a PC and a Macintosh room, and the Goodman Family Computer Classroom suite includes a classroom equipped with thirty-two notebook computers on tables that can be reconfigured to accommodate varying work-group sizes.

Financial Aid

Each year, Teachers College awards approximately $6 million of its own funds in scholarship and stipend aid and $2 million of endowed funds to new and continuing students. There are no separate scholarship applications. Faculty members nominate new students for these scholarships based upon their admission application. Financial assistance is also available through federal aid programs. All students are encouraged to file a Free Application for Federal Student Aid (FAFSA), regardless of eligibility for federal aid. Fifty-one percent of students receive financial aid.

Cost of Study

For the 2006–07 academic year, tuition was $975 per point, with 12 or more points considered full-time. Fees included the Teachers College, $320; Teachers College research, $320; health service, $356; continuous doctoral advisement registration, $2925; and Ph.D. oral defense, $4319. The tuition deposit was $300. Medical insurance ranged from $553 to $1218.

Living and Housing Costs

Teachers College offers a variety of on-campus housing options that are unique to the area and convenient to the campus. Housing for a single student ranges from $3100 to $8000 per semester, depending on the type of setting selected. Family housing ranges from $6875 to $8200 per semester. Teachers College has approximately 705 spaces available for single students and 150 apartments for students with families. The buildings are located in the vibrant and historic urban neighborhood of Morningside Heights. Current residence halls are historic buildings similar to other apartment-style buildings that were in New York City in the early 1900s. A new residence hall opened in the fall 2004 semester.

Student Group

There are approximately 5,000 students enrolled at Teachers College. Of those, 77 percent are female and 23 percent are male; 12 percent are African American, 11 percent Asian American, and 7 percent are Latino/a. The student body comprises 13 percent international students from eighty different countries, and 87 percent domestic students, from fifty different states.

Location

The College is located in the Morningside Heights section of Manhattan's Upper West Side, which is home to such venerable New York landmarks as Lincoln Center, the Cathedral of St. John the Divine, Grant's Tomb, Morningside Park, and the Manhattan School of Music. The Upper West Side is bounded by Central Park on the east and the Hudson River on the west. Located in New York City, students have access to an outstanding array of learning organizations, including museums, libraries, galleries, corporate learning centers, and K–12 schools.

The College and The University

Teachers College was founded in 1887 to provide a new form of schooling for teachers of children from low-income families of New York, one that combined a humanitarian concern to help others with a scientific approach to human development. For more than 100 years, Teachers College has conducted research on the central issues facing education, prepared generations of education leaders, and shaped debate and public policy in education. The College provides programs of study in administration, counseling, curriculum development, and school health care and continues its efforts to strengthen teaching skills, prepare leaders to develop and administer psychological and health-care programs, and develop new teaching software. In 1898, the College became affiliated with Columbia.

Columbia University was founded in 1754 as King's College by royal charter of King George II of England. It is the oldest institution of higher learning in the state of New York and the fifth-oldest in the United States. From its beginnings in a schoolhouse in lower Manhattan, the University has grown to encompass two principal campuses: the historic, neoclassical campus in Morningside Heights and the modern Medical Center in Washington Heights. Today, Columbia is one of the top academic and research institutions in the world, conducting research in medicine, science, the arts, and the humanities. It includes three undergraduate schools, thirteen graduate and professional schools, and a school of continuing education. Sixty-four Nobel laureates have taught or studied at Columbia. Each year, the faculty of approximately 4,000 teaches more than 23,000 students from more than 150 countries.

Applying

Teachers College welcomes applicants who wish to pursue graduate study associated with the education, psychological, and health service professions. All applicants receive consideration for admission without regard to race, color, creed, religion, sex, national origin, age, or disability. In order to be considered for scholarships, students must meet the priority deadline. Admissions applications received after the priority deadlines may be considered on a space available basis. Certain programs have special application deadlines. The final and early deadline for Ph.D. and all psychology doctoral programs is December 15. The early deadline for Ed.D. programs is January 2, with a final deadline of April 1. The early deadline for master's programs is January 15, with a final deadline of April 15. For applicants wishing to start in the spring semester, the early deadline is November 1. Teachers College requests that applicants collect the required documents for the application process and submit the entire package to the Office of Admission at one time. Admission application deadlines always refer to the date by which the Teachers College Office of Admissions must have received the application components and any other supporting material required by the Department. For more information as well as an online application, prospective students should visit http://www.tc.columbia.edu/admissions.

Correspondence and Information

Office of Admissions
Teachers College Columbia University
525 West 120th Street, Box 302
New York, New York 10027

Phone: 212-678-3710
Web site: http://www.tc.columbia.edu/discover
http://www.tc.columbia/bbs

Teachers College Columbia University

THE FACULTY AND THEIR RESEARCH

John H. Saxman, Professor of Speech and Language Pathology and Department Chair; Ph.D., Purdue. Communication disorders, phonatory behaviors across the life-span, experimental phonetics.

Mark Budde, Adjunct Associate Professor of Speech and Language Pathology; Ed.D., Columbia.

Cynthia Cohen, Instructor; M.S., Teachers College, Columbia.

Catherine Crowley, Adjunct Assistant Professor of Speech and Language Pathology; J.D., Rutgers, Newark. Children and adolescents from homes with linguistic and sociolinguistic differences, impact of language socialization practices on those children.

Ronald DeMeersman, Professor of Applied Physiology and Education; Ph.D., Indiana. Modulators of autonomic outflow, effects of aerobic improvements on autonomic and blood pressure regulation, noninvasive assessment of physiologic data.

Karen Froud, Assistant Professor of Speech and Language Pathology; Ph.D., University College (London). Behavioral and neural responses to linguistic stimuli in normal and damaged adult brains, aphasia, schizophrenia, brain imaging (EEG and MEG).

Antoinette Gentile, Professor of Psychology and Education; Ph.D., SUNY at Stony Brook. Motor learning and development, neuromotor control processes, rehabilitative strategies.

Andrew Gordon, Associate Professor of Movement Sciences and Education; Ph.D., Karolinska Institute (Sweden). Use of sensory information during the learning and control of well-learned manual skills (sensorimotor control), biological basis of hand impairments in populations with movement disorders.

Peter Gordon, Associate Professor of Speech and Language Pathology; Ph.D., MIT. Language acquisition and processing, developmental neuroscience of language and cognition, cross-cultural studies of numerical cognition and linguistic knowledge.

Terry Kaminski, Adjunct Assistant Professor of Movement Sciences; Ed.D., Columbia.

Carol Kaufman, Adjunct Assistant Professor of Speech and Language Pathology; Ed.D., Columbia.

Erika Levy, Assistant Professor of Speech and Language Pathology; Ph.D., CUNY Graduate Center. Cross-language speech production and perception, second-language speech learning, multilingualism.

Steven Lichtman, Adjunct Assistant Professor of Movement Sciences; Ed.D., Columbia.

Andrew McDonough, Adjunct Assistant Professor of Movement Sciences; Ed.D., Columbia.

Michael McMahon, Adjunct Assistant Professor of Speech and Language Pathology; Ph.D., Hawaii.

Thomas Murray, Adjunct Professor of Speech and Language Pathology; Ph.D., Florida.

Roger Muzii, Adjunct Assistant Professor of Movement Sciences; Ph.D., Columbia.

Jo Ann Nicholas, Adjunct Associate Professor of Speech and Language Pathology and Director of the Edward D. Mysak Speech and Hearing Clinic; Ed.D., Columbia.

Honor O'Malley, Associate Professor of Audiology; Ph.D., Purdue. Function of the normal ear, psychoacoustics and auditory physiology, intraoperative monitoring of hearing during neurotologic surgery.

Lorraine Ramig, Adjunct Professor of Speech and Language Pathology; Ph.D., Purdue.

Susan Schwager, Adjunct Professor of Education; Ed.D., Columbia Teachers College. Physical education pedagogy.

Justine Sheppard, Adjunct Associate Professor of Speech and Language Pathology; Ph.D., Columbia.

Stephen Silverman, Professor of Education; Ed.D., Massachusetts Amherst. Physical education pedagogy, research methods.

Jaclyn Spitzer, Adjunct Professor of Speech and Language Pathology; Ed.D., Columbia.

Ronald Tikofsky, Adjunct Professor of Speech and Language Pathology; Ph.D., Utah.

Carol Tompkins, Instructor; M.S., Teachers College, Columbia.

Karin Wexler, Adjunct Associate Professor of Speech and Language Pathology; Ph.D., Columbia.

Lesley Wolk, Adjunct Associate Professor of Speech and Language Pathology; Ph.D., Syracuse.

Adrienne Zion, Honorary Professor of Movement Sciences; Ed.D., Columbia.

TEMPLE UNIVERSITY

College of Health Professions

Programs of Study
Temple University College of Health Professions (CHP) offers entry-level and advanced professional programs in communication sciences, health-information management, kinesiology, nursing, occupational therapy, physical therapy, public health, and therapeutic recreation. Bachelor's degree programs are offered in communication sciences, health-information management, kinesiology, nursing, public health, and therapeutic recreation. Advanced master's and doctoral programs offer certified or licensed health professionals the opportunity to augment and extend their basic preparation by acquiring in-depth knowledge and expertise in specialty areas and developing education and management skills necessary for leadership roles in their professions. Communication Sciences offers a Ph.D. program with concentration areas of speech-language pathology and speech science and Master of Arts (M.A.) degrees in speech-language pathology and linguistics. The Department of Kinesiology offers M.Ed. and Ph.D. degrees, specializing in the behavioral sciences (concentrations in curriculum and instruction and psychology of human movement) and somatic sciences (concentrations in athletic training and exercise physiology). It prepares entry- and advanced-level health-care providers, practitioners, and teachers who advance the applications of health behaviors (e.g. physical activity, good decision making in health behaviors, and the relationship between the two) as well as research scholars who work in academic institutions and research centers. The master's program of the Department of Nursing prepares experienced nurses to be nurse practitioners, clinical nurse specialists, and nurse educators. The certificate program for nurse educators is open only to M.S.N.–prepared nurses. The nurse practitioner program prepares baccalaureate-prepared nurses to be either adult nurse practitioners, family nurse practitioners, or pediatric nurse practitioners. It is also open to master's-prepared clinical specialists who wish to earn a certificate and qualify for national certification as a nurse practitioner. The clinical nurse specialist track prepares graduates for roles in psychiatric/mental-health nursing. The Department of Occupational Therapy offers a Master of Occupational Therapy (M.O.T.) degree that prepares students with baccalaureate degrees in other disciplines to become registered occupational therapists. An advanced Master of Science (M.S.) degree is also offered, which prepares experienced occupational therapists to take on leadership positions in research, clinical practice, clinical education, and administration. The doctor of physical therapy (D.P.T.) program of the Department of Physical Therapy is a three-year entry-level degree program, and the Ph.D. in physical therapy prepares researchers and academicians for the discipline. The department also offers an online program for practicing clinicians to transition to the D.P.T. The Department of Public Health offers several master's programs designed for emerging and experienced professionals to obtain leadership positions in health promotion and epidemiologic research, health policy, and program administration. Offered are the Master of Public Health (M.P.H.) in community health education with dual-degree options with medicine, osteopathic medicine, podiatric medicine, or social work; Master of Science (M.S.) degrees in epidemiology and environmental health with M.B.A. dual-degree options, and a Master of Education with emphasis on school health and health counseling. The Department of Therapeutic Recreation offers a master's program (Ed.M.) for students with baccalaureate degrees in other disciplines who wish to become certified recreation therapists. The master's program is also designed for experienced recreation therapists who wish to advance their knowledge and skills as clinicians or administrators. The Departments of Therapeutic Recreation and Public Health offer a Ph.D. program in health studies with specialized areas of study in public health (environmental health, health communication, or health education) and therapeutic recreation.

Research Facilities
Mentored by Temple faculty members, graduate students have the opportunity to be involved in research and service activities in a variety of related health facilities in the Philadelphia area. The Department of Kinesiology has a Biokinetics Research Laboratory with five divisions: athletic training, exercise physiology, exercise and sport psychology, curriculum and instruction, and motor development. The Department of Physical Therapy has a motion analysis lab, a qualitative research analysis lab, an animal behavior lab, and a cellular biology lab. The Department of Nursing manages the Temple Health Connection, a community-based health center in North Philadelphia. The Department of Communication Sciences maintains a speech-language-hearing center, bilingual center, and the Center for Cognitive Neurosciences. The Department of Occupational Therapy maintains a neuromuscular function lab and a life skills laboratory. The Department of Public Health maintains four research centers focusing on health behaviors, Asian health, emergency preparedness, and women's health.

Financial Aid
Financial assistance is supplemental to the student's or family's financial resources. Graduate students are eligible to apply for both University fellowships and CHP teaching/research graduate assistantships, externships, internships, or tuition scholarships.

Cost of Study
In-state graduate tuition for 2006–07 was $532 per credit hour. Out-of-state tuition for 2006–07 was $777 per credit hour. Each program has specific course fees in addition to University-wide student fees.

Living and Housing Costs
Students live in apartments and houses in the surrounding area.

Student Group
CHP enrolls approximately 650 graduate students. A majority of these students are enrolled full-time in the doctoral program in physical therapy and the entry-level master's programs in occupational therapy and communication sciences.

Location
Philadelphia is rich in tradition and is one of the world's most respected centers for education, health care, and the arts. Convenient to Center City Philadelphia by public transportation, the Departments of Communication Sciences, Kinesiology, Therapeutic Recreation, and Public Health are located on Temple University's main campus, whereas the Departments of Health Information Management, Nursing, Occupational Therapy, and Physical Therapy are located 2 miles north at the University's Health Sciences Center.

The University and The College
Temple University is a state-related public university, located about 2 miles from Center City Philadelphia. Composed of seventeen schools and colleges, the University offers a wide range of specialized programs and degrees. The College of Health Professions was established in 1966 at Temple University's Health Sciences Center to meet a critical national need for increasing numbers of educated, highly skilled health-care professionals. Over thirty-five years, the College has become one of the leading centers of comprehensive health-care education in the nation, with six undergraduate programs and seven graduate programs.

CHP programs share library, classroom, and computer learning facilities and other scholarly services with the College of Education, Department of Psychology, and Schools of Dentistry, Medicine, Pharmacy, and Podiatry as well as other academic and clinical units. Its presence on two campuses provides a rich experience for students as they interact with professionals from a variety of disciplines.

Applying
Applicants must submit a graduate application form with three letters of reference, a personal statement, and results of the General Test of the Graduate Record Examinations. The Miller Analogies Test is accepted for the programs in kinesiology (master's only), nursing, occupational therapy, and therapeutic recreation. Application deadlines are as follows: D.P.T. program, January 15; Ph.D. in physical therapy, April 1; M.O.T., March 15; communication sciences, February 1 for the M.A. and March 1 for the Ph.D.; M.Ed. and Ph.D. in kinesiology, January 15; public health, February 15 for fall admission and October 15 for spring admission; therapeutic recreation, June 1 for fall admission and October 15 for spring admission; and Ph.D. in health studies (therapeutic recreation or public health), January 15. Applications for advanced master's and certificate programs are accepted at any time.

Correspondence and Information
College of Health Professions
Temple University
3307 North Broad Street
Philadelphia, Pennsylvania 19140
Phone: 215-707-4800
Fax: 215-707-7819
Web site: http://www.temple.edu/CHP

Temple University

THE FACULTY

Administration
Ronald T. Brown, Ph.D., Dean.
Donna Weiss, Ph.D., Associate Dean, Academic and Student Affairs.
Jane Kurz, Ph.D., Associate Dean, Faculty Affairs.

Department of Communication Sciences
Brian A. Goldstein, Acting Chair; Ph.D., Temple; CCC/SLP. Normal and disordered phonology, development of Spanish phonology.
Beth Levine, Director of Clinical Education and Clinical Services; M.S., Boston University.
Reinhardt J. Heuer, Ph.D., Oregon; CCC/SLP. Voice, dysphagia.
Aquiles Iglesias, Ph.D., Iowa; CCC/SLP. Speech and language services in multicultural populations.
Camilla Keach, Ph.D., Massachusetts. Theoretical linguistics, syntax.
Rena A. Krakow, Ph.D., Yale. Speech motor control, speech acoustics and perception.
Nadine Martin, Ph.D., Temple. Adult language disorders, cognitive neuroscience.
Barbara Mastriano, Ph.D., Temple; CCC/SLP. Adult neurological disorders, communication and aging, child language disorders.
Brian McHugh, Ph.D., UCLA. Phonology.
Gary Milsark, Ph.D., MIT. Linguistics, psycholinguistics, language acquisition.
Kim Sabourin, M.A., Maryland, College Park. Clinical supervision.
Doris Fallon Snyder, M.A., Temple; CCC/SLP-A. Diagnostic and rehabilitative audiology, child language disorders.

Department of Health Information Management
Laurinda B. Harman, Chair; Ph.D., Fielding Graduate University; RHIA. Ethics and health information systems.
Cathy A. Flite, M.Ed., Widener; RHIA. Electronic health record and human resource management.
Margaret M. Foley, Ph.D., Temple; RHIA, CCS. Birth certificate data quality, ICD-9-CM data quality assessment and clinical vocabularies.
Karen McBride, M.S., Philadelphia University; RHIA. Clinical affiliations.
Mary E. Morton, M.L.I.S., LSU; RHIA. Medical informatics, electronic health record, user acceptance of clinical information systems.

Department of Kinesiology
Michael Sitler, Chair; Ed.D., NYU; ATC. Evidence-based athletic training and sports medicine.
Michael D. Brown, Ph.D., Maryland, College Park. Roles of exercise and genes and their interaction on peripheral vascular and renal function in hypertensive individuals, role of genes and exercise on oxidative stress.
Jeffrey Gehris, Ph.D., Temple. Department of Kinesiology PHETE Program.
Zebulon V. Kendrick, Ph.D., Temple. Cellular, biochemical, and physiological adaptations of exercise physiology.
Joseph Libonati, Ph.D., Temple. Cardiac hypertrophy with exercise training and hypertension, left ventricular diastolic function and ischemia/reperfusion performance in cardiac and skeletal muscle.
Melissa A. Napolitano, Ph.D., Duke. Physical activity adoption and maintenance, obesity and behavioral weight control, smoking cessation, use of technology in interventions and women's health.
William Oddou, Ph.D., Oregon State. Exercise science, exercise programming for members of special populations.
Marcella V. Ridenour, Ph.D., Purdue. Motor behavior.
Thomas Rooney, Ph.D., Temple. Effects of circadian-rhythm dysfunction on human performance, methicillin-resistant *staphylococcus aureus* awareness in athletes, use of new technology to support distance learning.
Michael L. Sachs, Ph.D., Florida State. Exercise and sport psychology, especially motivation and adherence and addiction to exercise.
Mayra C. Santiago, Ph.D., Minnesota. Promotion of health via exercise/physical activity in persons with physical disabilities.
John Susko, B.S., Temple. Standards, efficacy, and/or interdisciplinary issues related to physical activity, education, and/or curriculum and instruction.
Ricky Swalm, Ph.D., Temple. Learning styles of kinesiology students and identifying congruent styles between teaching and learning to enhance development.
Ryan Tierney, Ph.D., Temple. Dynamic stabilization of the head and neck to prevent injury.
Vanessa R. Yingling, Ph.D., Waterloo. Role of endocrine status, nutrition and exercise in the development of peak bone strength.

Department of Nursing
Jill B. Derstine, Chair; Ph.D., Temple; RN, FAAN. Rehabilitation, community interventions in rehab, international nursing.
Diane C. Adler, Ph.D., Pennsylvania; RN, FAAN. Experience and caring needs of mechanically ventilated patients.
Pamela J. Bender, M.S.N., Villanova; CRNP. Psychiatric mental health nursing across the lifespan, with special interest in ADA and ADHA; nursing leadership; health assessment; advanced practice psychiatric nursing and family nurse practitioner.
Kathleen D. Black, D.N.Sc., Widener; RNC. Maternal and child health, high-risk obstetrics, pregnancy-induced hypertension.
Catherine Curley, M.S.N., West Chester; RN. Community nursing, obesity in children.
Carol E. Dakin, Ph.D., Pennsylvania; RN. Teaching effectiveness, measurement, and documentation; stress management in students.
Susan B. Dickey, Ph.D., Pennsylvania; RNC. Ethicolegal aspects of pediatric and adolescent health care, health policy.
Patricia DiGiacomo, M.S.N., Temple. Maternal child care, leadership.
Patricia Dillion, D.N.Sc., Widener. Physical assessment, teaching models, using simulation as an alternative teaching method.
Evelyn Dogbey, M.S.N., Temple; CRNP. Medical-surgical nursing, adult health nursing, compassion fatigue.
Elaine L. Gross, M.S.N., Villanova; RN. Developmental disabilities, medication administration training for unlicensed personnel, distance education.
Felicia J. Haskins, M.S.N., Widener. Adult health nursing, community health.
Barbara Hughes, M.S.N., Pennsylvania; RN. Critical thinking, predictors of success in RN and B.S.N. students.
Patricia Hentz, Ed.D., Columbia; CS, PMH, NP-BC. Family therapy, stress and coping, ethics.
Anne-Marie Kiehne, Ph.D., Temple; RN. Role of intercessory prayer in the maintenance and restoration of health.
Jane M. Kurz, Ph.D., Delaware; RN. Stress and coping, transplants (heart and lung), families.
Rita J. Lourie, M.S.N., M.P.H., Texas; RN. Disease prevention and health care to the underserved, especially lead poisoning and breastfeeding; health promotion.
Kathleen Mahoney, Ph.D., M.S.N., NYU; CRNP. Perception of health of partner in spouses with chronic illness.
Lori Martin-Plank, M.S.P.H., M.S.N., Pennsylvania; APRN. Community, adult, and pediatrics; caring for diverse populations, with particular interest in the Hispanic client/family.
Kim A. Noble, M.S.N., Widener; RN. Critical-care nursing, use of technology as a teaching strategy, characteristics of the learner.
Ann Linguiti Pron, M.S.N., Pennsylvania; CRNP. Pediatric primary care, immunizations, nurse practitioner practice issues.
Nancy L. Rothman, Ed.D., Temple; RN. Testing community-based prevention/intervention strategies.
Karen Moore Schaefer, D.N.Sc., Catholic University. Women with chronic illness, with special emphasis on fibromyalgia; Levine's conservatory model.
Elizabeth Westgard, M.S.N., Drexel. Using technology to facilitate clinical practice, critical care nursing.
Dolores M. Zygmont, Ph.D., Temple; RN. Development of professional expertise in critical-care nurses, leadership (emotional intelligence), adult learning.

Department of Occupational Therapy
Moya Kinnealey, Chair; Ph.D., Temple; OTR/L. Sensory integration, clinical descriptions, outcome studies in both children and adults.
Ruth S. Farber, Ph.D., Temple; OTR/L. Career development of women across the family life cycle, family-centered care and parenting with a disability.
Michael J. Gerg, M.S., Temple. Ergonomics in disabled and nondisabled populations.
Kristie P. Koenig, Ph.D., Temple; OTR/L. Sensory processing deficits in children and their effect on adaptability and temperament, predictors of student success transitioning from classroom to clinic.
Linda L. Levy, M.A., Temple; OTR/L. Gerontology, geriatrics psychological adaptation and aging, cognitive capacity related to functional outcome, falling, clinical reasoning.
C. Tom North, M.B.A., Ph.D., Temple; OTR/L. Stability of self-efficacy in clinical depression.
Elizabeth Pfeiffer, Ph.D., Nova Southeastern; OTR/L. Sensory processing, adaptive behavior and anxiety/depression in people with autistic spectrum disorder.
Donna Weiss, Ph.D., Temple; OTR/L. Group process, teaching/learning environments, clinical reasoning, faculty development.

Department of Physical Therapy
Emily A. Keshner, Professor and Chair; Ed.D., Columbia; PT. Sensory integration of postural control of healthy and clinical populations, neurophysiologic and mechanical mechanisms underlying postural control.
Robert Gabriel, Clinical Associate Professor and Assistant Chair; M.B.A., Ph.D., St. Louis; PT. Muscle physiology and performance, spinal modeling, assessment of student performance.
Mary F. Barbe, Ph.D., Wake Forest. Plasticity in the central nervous system during development and after injury.
Ann E. Barr, Ph.D., NYU; PT. Modeling of repetitive strain injuries.
Laurita M. Hack, Ph.D., Pennsylvania; PT. Health services.
Margery Lockhard, Ph.D., Hahnemann; PT. Joint structure and integrity, instructional design.
Stephanie Muth, M.P.T., Thomas Jefferson. Rehabilitation.
Roberta A. Newton, Ph.D., Virginia Commonwealth; PT. Prediction of falls in older adults, balance abilities in select populations.
Kim A. Nixon-Cave, Ph.D., Temple; PT. Pediatric development and cultural influences.
Mary Sinnott, M.Ed., Temple; PT. Cardiopulmonary care, health systems organization.
James Stephens, Ph.D., Temple; PT. Motor learning, neurological intervention.
Ann F. VanSant, Ph.D., Wisconsin–Madison; PT. Life span motor development in functional motor tasks.
Kristin von Nieda, M.Ed., Temple; PT. Instructional design, prevention.

Department of Public Health
Alice Hausman, Chair; Ph.D., M.P.H., SUNY at Binghamton. Program planning and evaluation, violence prevention, evidence-based practice.
Sarah B. Bass, Ph.D., M.P.H., Temple. Program planning, human sexuality, health communication.
Bradley Collins, Ph.D., SUNY at Binghamton. Health psychology, maternal and child health, smoking cessation, health behavior, obesity.
Nikki Franke, Ed.D., Temple. Urban health issues, community health programs.
Judith Gold, Sc.D., Massachusetts Lowell. Epidemiology, biological modeling, office ergonomics, computer use in youth.
Thomas F. Gordon, Ph.D., Michigan State. Health communication, mind-body medicine, research methodology.
Clara Haignere, Ph.D., M.P.H., Denver; CHES. Adolescent health, HIV/AIDS, health behavior theories, international public health, Costa Rican summer-abroad program.
Alexandra Hanlon, Ph.D., Temple. Nonlinear mixed effects modeling, oncology, survival analysis.
Jennifer Ibrahim, Ph.D., Berkley; M.P.H. Massachusetts Amherst. Health policy, tobacco control.
Stephen Lepore, Ph.D., California, Irvine. Psycho-oncology, cancer prevention and control, social disparities in health, evidence-based behavioral medicine, social relations, stress, educational and behavioral interventions for promoting health.
Grace Ma, Ph.D., M.P.H., Oklahoma; CHES. Addiction and substance abuse prevention, transcultural health care, cancer prevention and control.
Deborah Nelson, Ph.D., Pittsburgh. Epidemiology, maternal and child health, women's health.
Robert M. Patterson, Sc.D., Harvard; CIH. Environmental and occupational health.
Sheryl Burt Ruzek, M.P.H., Berkeley; Ph.D., California, Davis. Women's health, maternal-child health, health policy, risk communication.
Brenda Seals, Ph.D., M.P.H., Iowa. Mental health epidemiology, applied public health.
Jay Segal, Ph.D., Ohio State. Health counseling, stress management, human sexuality.

Department of Therapeutic Recreation
John W. Shank, Chair; Ed.D., Boston University; CTRS. Social-psychological aspects of health, leisure, and disability; stress and coping; ethics.
Rosangela Boyd, Ph.D., Clemson; CTRS. Aging, developmental disabilities, multiculturalism, assistive technology.
Catherine Coyle, Ph.D., Temple; CTRS. Theory, health, and wellness; psychosocial aspects of health, leisure, and disability; therapeutic recreation in special education.
Adam Davey, Ph.D., Pennsylvania. Adult psychosocial adjustment, care networks, extreme longevity, statistical methods.
Yoshitaka Iwasaki, Ph.D., Waterloo. Diversity and health, stress/trauma and coping/healing, quality of life and leisure, community-based participatory action research with and for nondominant population groups (e.g., indigenous individuals, people with disability).
Susanne Lesnik-Emas, Ed.D., Temple; CTRS. Rehabilitation and community re-entry, dementia care, caregiving for persons with disabilities and chronic illness, advocacy and ethics.
Rhonda Nelson, Ed.M., Temple; CTRS. Gerontology, alternative/complementary therapies, assistive technology, recreation modalities and facilitation techniques.
Barbara Wilhite, Ed.D., Georgia; CTRS. Aging, developmental disabilities, sport and disability, experiential education, theory.

VIRGINIA COMMONWEALTH UNIVERSITY

Clinical Laboratory Sciences

Programs of Study

To accommodate the educational needs of students from a variety of academic backgrounds, the Department of Clinical Laboratory Sciences (CLS) at Virginia Commonwealth University (VCU) offers a Master of Science in clinical laboratory sciences with three tracks—advanced, categorical, and accelerated. Students holding a baccalaureate degree in clinical laboratory sciences/medical technology and generalist certification by the National Credentialing Agency for Laboratory Personnel, Inc., or the Board of Registry of the American Society for Clinical Pathologists are eligible for the advanced master's track. Candidates may specialize and complete a project or thesis in clinical chemistry, hematology, microbiology, immunohematology, immunology, or molecular diagnostics. In addition to the basic science requirement, each student chooses an area of secondary emphasis in biomedical research, education, management, or business. The categorical master's track is designed for students with a baccalaureate degree in biology or chemistry. This track provides specialized study, including a clinical practicum, in clinical chemistry, hematology, microbiology, or immunohematology. A project or thesis is required. Upon completion of the curriculum, students are eligible to take a national certification examination in the area in which they performed their concentrated study. The accelerated master's track integrates undergraduate and graduate course work and leads to the awarding of a B.S. and an M.S. degree simultaneously. Upon completion of the curriculum, students are eligible to take the national certification examinations for a CLS/MT generalist.

A Ph.D. program in health-related sciences with a track in clinical laboratory sciences is also offered. Structured as a four-year course of study, the program is intended to meet the national critical need for allied health professionals who are prepared at the doctoral level in the areas of teaching, research, and administration. The program curriculum consists of a total of 51 credit hours (18 credits of common interdisciplinary core courses, 12 credits of research methods core courses, 9 credits of specialty track courses, and 12 credits of dissertation research).

Research Facilities

VCU libraries provide a combined capacity of more than 1.7 million volumes and 10,200 periodical titles and an online bibliographic search service accessing hundreds of databases. In addition, the Virginia state and Richmond public libraries are within walking distance of both VCU campuses. Academic Computing provides a variety of microcomputer, minicomputer, and mainframe computing services to support the research and instructional endeavors of its faculty members and students, including consultation, instruction, and computer acquisition.

Financial Aid

Students may apply for need-based assistance with the University's Financial Aid Office. Current information on financial aid programs, policies, and procedures is available at http://www.vcu.edu/enroll/finaid.

Cost of Study

For full-time study (9–15 credits) in 2007–08, Virginia residents pay tuition and fees of $4452 per semester; nonresidents, $8876 per semester. For part-time study, Virginia residents pay tuition and fees of $465 per credit hour; nonresidents, $954 per credit hour. Some programs require additional fees. On the Medical College of Virginia (MCV) campus, tuition, fees, and other expenses vary in the medicine, pharmacy, nurse anesthesia, dentistry, and School of Allied Health programs.

Living and Housing Costs

Graduate student housing is available on both the MCV campus and the academic campus of Virginia Commonwealth University. Many graduate students live in off-campus housing, which is reasonably priced and readily available in a variety of styles and settings in nearby residential areas or within easy commuting distance. On- and off-campus housing information is available on the Web at http://www.students.vcu.edu/housing.

Student Group

VCU enrolls 30,452 students, 7,611 of whom are graduate students. More than 200 clubs and organizations reflect the diverse social, recreational, educational, political, and religious interests of the student body.

Location

Richmond is Virginia's capital and a major East Coast financial and manufacturing center that offers students a wide range of cultural, educational, and recreational activities. Richmond is located in central Virginia at the intersection of Interstates 95 and 64, 2 hours south of Washington, D.C., and nestled between the Blue Ridge Mountains and the Atlantic Coast. The Richmond region is easily accessible by plane, car, and train. With nearly 1 million residents, the historic city of Richmond combines big-city offerings with small-town hospitality. Applicants are encouraged to explore http://www.visit.richmond.com/ for more information on the city.

The University

VCU is a state-supported coeducational university with a graduate school, a major teaching hospital, and twelve academic and professional units that offer fifty-two undergraduate, twenty-two postbaccalaureate certificate, sixty-five master's, six post-master's certificate, and twenty-nine Ph.D. programs. VCU also offers M.D., D.D.S., D.P.T., and Pharm.D. programs as well as cooperative degree programs with other major Virginia colleges and universities. VCU has one of the largest evening colleges in the United States. The academic campus is located in Richmond's historic Fan District. The health sciences campus and hospital are located 2 miles east in the downtown business district. A University bus service provides free intercampus transportation for faculty members and students.

With more than $211 million in annual research funding, the Carnegie Foundation for the Advancement of Teaching ranks Virginia Commonwealth University as one of the nation's top research universities. More than 29,000 undergraduate, certificate, graduate, post-master's, professional, and doctoral students are enrolled in 162 academic programs, forty of which are unique in the commonwealth of Virginia. The faculty members at Virginia Commonwealth University represent the finest American and international graduate institutions and enhance the University's position among the important institutions of higher learning in the United States and the world via their work in the classroom, laboratory, studio, and clinic and in their scholarly publications.

Applying

Admission procedures and program requirements are detailed in the *Graduate Bulletin*. Application deadlines and materials, including the application and the *Graduate Bulletin*, are available online at the Graduate School Web site at http://www.graduate.vcu.edu. Virginia Commonwealth University is an equal opportunity/affirmative action institution providing access to education and employment without regard to age, race, color, national origin, gender, religion, sexual orientation, veteran's status, political affiliation, or disability.

Correspondence and Information

Teresa S. Nadder, Chairman
Department of Clinical Laboratory Sciences
School of Allied Health Professions
Virginia Commonwealth University
301 College Street
P.O. Box 980583
Richmond, Virginia 23298-0583
Phone: 804-828-9469
Fax: 804-828-1911
E-mail: tsnadder@vcu.edu
Web site: http://www.sahp.vcu.edu/cls/

Virginia Commonwealth University

THE FACULTY AND THEIR RESEARCH

Linda Beck, Assistant Professor of Hematology; Ph.D., Virginia Commonwealth, 1995; MT(ASCP). Cellular biology/hematology.

William J. Korzun, Associate Professor of Clinical Chemistry–Instrumentation; Ph.D., Virginia Commonwealth, 1988; DABCC, MT(ASCP). Homocysteine metabolism.

Teresa S. Nadder, Associate Professor and Chairman; Ph.D., Virginia Commonwealth, 1998; CLS(NCA), MT(ASCP). Assessment of the major and general education outcomes, curriculum design, and the genetic effects of attention deficit hyperactivity disorder (ADHD).

Katherine A. Prentice, Assistant Professor and Clinical Coordinator; M.A., Central Michigan, 1977; MT(ASCP). Clinical practicums, education/management.

Ronald R. Sauer, Associate Professor of Microbiology; M.A., California, Davis, 1972; SM(NRM), SM(ASCP). Environmental air sampling and the diagnosis of sick building syndrome.

VIRGINIA COMMONWEALTH UNIVERSITY

School of Allied Health Professions
Ph.D. in Health-Related Sciences

Programs of Study

Virginia Commonwealth University (VCU) offers the Ph.D. in Health-Related Sciences Program, designed mainly as a distance-learning program, with the cooperation and commitment of the nine departments of the School of Allied Professions—Clinical Laboratory Sciences, Gerontology, Health Administration, Nurse Anesthesia, Occupational Therapy, Patient Counseling, Physical Therapy, Radiation Sciences, and Rehabilitation Counseling. Structured as a four-year course of study, the program is intended to meet the national critical need for allied health professionals who are prepared at the doctoral level in the areas of teaching, research, and administration. This doctoral program emphasizes both an interdisciplinary and multimedia focus, drawing from resources across the University.

The program curriculum consists of a total of 51 credit hours (18 credits of common interdisciplinary core courses, 12 credits of research methods core courses, 9 hours of specialty track courses, and 12 hours of dissertation research). Over the course of study, students spend periods on campus ranging from seven to fourteen days each during June/July and early January, attending lectures and seminars and interacting with each other and faculty members. During the off-campus component of each semester, students pursue their studies employing a variety of innovative educational technologies (e.g., computer conferencing, computer-aided instruction, videotape packages, and programmed instructional material), in addition to assigned readings and the completion of various assignments and projects. Students spend the first 2½ years (comprising five 6-month semesters) completing course work. Two written comprehensive examinations are administered, one for the common interdisciplinary core and one for the research methods core. The final year and a half (or longer) is spent developing the doctoral dissertation. Studies should be based on a formal theoretical or conceptually explicit framework for investigating a question or testing a hypothesis relevant to the allied health field.

Research Facilities

VCU libraries provide a combined capacity of more than 1.7 million volumes and 10,200 periodical titles and an online bibliographic search service accessing hundreds of databases. In addition, the Virginia State and Richmond Public Libraries are within walking distance of both VCU campuses. Academic Computing provides a variety of microcomputer, minicomputer, and mainframe computing services to support the research and instructional endeavors of the faculty and students, including consultation, instruction, and computer acquisition.

Financial Aid

Students may apply for need-based assistance with the University's Financial Aid Office. Current information on financial aid programs, policies, and procedures is available at http://www.vcu.edu/enroll/finaid.

Cost of Study

For full-time study (9–15 credits) in 2007–08, Virginia residents pay tuition and fees of $4452 per semester; nonresidents, $8876 per semester. For part-time study, Virginia residents pay tuition and fees of $465 per hour; nonresidents, $954 per hour. Some programs require additional fees. On the Medical College of Virginia (MCV) campus, tuition, fees, and other expenses vary in the medicine, pharmacy, nurse anesthesia, dentistry, and School of Allied Health programs.

Living and Housing Costs

Graduate student housing is available on both the MCV campus and the academic campus of Virginia Commonwealth University. Many graduate students live in off-campus housing, which is reasonably priced and readily available in a variety of styles and settings in nearby residential areas or within easy commuting distance. On- and off-campus housing information is available on the Web at http://www.housing.vcu.edu/.

Student Group

VCU enrolls 30,452 students, 7,611 of whom are graduate students. More than 200 clubs and organizations reflect the diverse social, recreational, educational, political, and religious interests of the student body.

Location

Richmond is Virginia's capital and a major East Coast financial and manufacturing center that offers students a wide range of cultural, educational, and recreational activities. Richmond is located in central Virginia at the intersection of Interstates 95 and 64, 2 hours south of Washington, D.C., and nestled between the Blue Ridge Mountains and the Atlantic coast. The Richmond region is easily accessible by plane, car, and train. With nearly 1 million residents, the historic city of Richmond combines big-city offerings with small-town hospitality. Applicants are encouraged to explore http://www.visit.richmond.com/ for more information on the city.

The University

VCU is a state-supported coeducational university with a graduate school, a major teaching hospital, and twelve academic and professional units that offer fifty-two undergraduate, twenty-two postbaccalaureate certificate, sixty-five master's, six post-master's certificate, and twenty-nine Ph.D. programs. VCU also offers M.D., D.D.S., D.P.T., O.T.D., D.N.A.P., and Pharm.D. programs as well as cooperative degree programs with other major Virginia colleges and universities. VCU has one of the largest evening colleges in the United States. The academic campus is located in Richmond's historic Fan District. The health sciences campus and hospital are located 2 miles east in the downtown business district. A University bus service provides free intercampus transportation for faculty members and students.

With more than $211 million in annual research funding, Virginia Commonwealth University is classified as one of the nation's top research universities by the Carnegie Foundation for the Advancement of Teaching. More than 29,000 undergraduate, certificate, graduate, post-master's, professional, and doctoral students are enrolled in 162 academic programs, forty of which are unique in the commonwealth of Virginia. The faculty members represent the finest American and international graduate institutions and enhance the University's position among the important institutions of higher learning in the United States and the world via their work in the classroom, laboratory, studio, and clinic and in their scholarly publications.

Applying

Admission procedures and program requirements are detailed in the *Graduate Bulletin*. Application deadlines and materials, including the application and the *Graduate Bulletin*, are available online at the Graduate School Web site at http://www.graduate.vcu.edu. Virginia Commonwealth University is an equal opportunity/affirmative action institution providing access to education and employment without regard to age, race, color, national origin, gender, religion, sexual orientation, veteran's status, political affiliation, or disability.

Correspondence and Information

Monica L. White, Director of Student Services
Virginia Commonwealth University
1200 East Broad Street
P.O. Box 980233
Richmond, Virginia 23298
Phone: 804-828-7247
Fax: 804-828-8656
E-mail: mlwhite1@vcu.edu
Web site: http://www.sahp.vcu.edu/aboutphd.htm

Virginia Commonwealth University

THE FACULTY

CLINICAL LABORATORY SCIENCES
Linda Beck, Assistant Professor of Hematology; Ph.D., Virginia Commonwealth; MT(ASCP).
William J. Korzun, Associate Professor of Clinical Chemistry–Instrumentation; Ph.D., Virginia Commonwealth; DABCC, MT(ASCP).
Teresa S. Nadder, Associate Professor and Chairman; Ph.D., Virginia Commonwealth; CLS(NCA), MT(ASCP).

GERONTOLOGY
J. James Cotter, Associate Professor, Assistant Dean for Distance Education, and Director of the Doctoral Program in Health Related Sciences; Ph.D., Virginia Commonwealth.
Kimberly Taylor, Assistant Professor; Ph.D., Virginia.
Ayn Welleford, Associate Professor, Chair, and Associate Director of the Virginia Geriatric Education Center; Ph.D., Virginia Commonwealth.

HEALTH ADMINISTRATION
Gloria J. Bazzoli, Bon Secours Professor of Health Administration; Ph.D., Cornell.
Cathy J. Bradley, Professor; Ph.D., North Carolina.
Dolores G. Clement, Professor; Dr.P.H., Berkeley.
Jan P. Clement, Professor; Ph.D., North Carolina.
Kelly J. Devers, Associate Professor; Ph.D., Northwestern.
Robert E. Hurley, Professor; Ph.D., North Carolina.
Roice D. Luke, Professor; Ph.D., Michigan.
Michael J. McCue, Professor; D.B.A., Kentucky.
Stephen S. Mick, Arthur Graham Glasgow Professor and Chair; Ph.D., Yale.
Yasar A. Ozcan, Professor; Ph.D., Virginia Commonwealth.
Ramesh K. Shukla, Professor; Ph.D., Wisconsin–Madison.
Kenneth R. White, Charles P. Cardwell, Jr., Professor; Ph.D., Virginia Commonwealth; FACHE.

NURSE ANESTHESIA
Chuck Biddle, Professor and Director of Research; Ph.D., Missouri; CRNA. Patient safety.
Cecil Drain, Dean of the School of Allied Health Professions; Ph.D., Texas A&M; CRNA, FAAN. Post-anesthesia nursing.
Michael D. Fallacaro, Professor and Chair; D.N.S., SUNY at Buffalo; CRNA.
William Hartland, Associate Professor and Director of Education; Ph.D., Virginia Commonwealth; CRNA.
Elizabeth Monti-Seibert, Director of Doctoral Education; Ph.D., South Carolina; CRNA.

OCCUPATIONAL THERAPY
Marie Anzalone, Assistant Professor; Sc.D., Boston University; OTR, FAOTA.
Al Copolillo, Associate Professor; Ph.D., Illinois at Chicago; OTR/L.
Tony Gentry, Assistant Professor; Ph.D., Virginia; OTR/L.
Shelly J. Lane, Professor and Chairman; Ph.D., Texas Health Science Center at San Antonio; OTR, FAOTA.
Stacey Reynolds, Assistant Professor; Ph.D., Virginia Commonwealth.
Jayne T. Shepherd, Associate Professor and Director, Post-Professional Program; M.S., Virginia Commonwealth; OTR/L, FAOTA.
Dianne F. Simons, Assistant Professor; Ph.D., Virginia Commonwealth; OTR/L.
Jodi L. Teitelman, Associate Professor; Ph.D., Virginia Commonwealth.

PHYSICAL THERAPY
Ross Arena, Associate Professor; Ph.D., Virginia Commonwealth; PT, FACSM, FAACVPR.
Dixie H. Bowman, Assistant Professor; Ed.D., Nova Southeastern; D.P.T., Virginia Commonwealth; PT.
Stacey Dusing, Assistant Professor; Ph.D., North Carolina at Chapel Hill; PT.
Sheryl Finucane, Assistant Professor and Coordinator of Graduate Education; Ph.D., Virginia Commonwealth; PT.
Dianne V. Jewell, Assistant Professor; Ph.D., Virginia Commonwealth; PT, CCS, FAACVPR.
Thomas P. Mayhew, Associate Professor and Department Chair; Ph.D., Virginia Commonwealth; PT.
Lori Michener, Associate Professor; Ph.D., Hahnemann; PT, ATC, SCS.
Peter Pidcoe, Associate Professor; Ph.D., Illinois at Chicago; PT.
Daniel Riddle, Otto D. Payton Professor and Assistant Department Chair; Ph.D., Virginia Commonwealth; PT, FAPTA.
Mary Snyder Shall, Associate Professor; Ph.D., Virginia Commonwealth; PT.
Lisa Donegan Shoaf, Assistant Professor and Director of Clinical Education; Ph.D., Virginia Commonwealth; PT.

RADIATION SCIENCES
Terri Fauber, Associate Professor; Ed.D., William & Mary.
Jeffrey Legg, Assistant Professor and Department Chair; Ph.D., Virginia Commonwealth.

REHABILITATION LEADERSHIP
Amy Armstrong, Assistant Professor; Ph.D., Virginia Commonwealth; CRC.
Allen Lewis, Assistant Professor and Interim Chair; Ph.D., Virginia Commonwealth.
Brian McMahon, Professor; Ph.D., Wisconsin–Madison; CRC, NCC, CCM.
Christine Reid, Professor; Ph.D., IIT; CRC.
Christopher Wagner, Associate Professor; Ph.D., Virginia Commonwealth; CRC.
Steven West, Assistant Professor; Ph.D., Texas Tech; CRC.

VIRGINIA COMMONWEALTH UNIVERSITY

Department of Occupational Therapy

Programs of Study	Virginia Commonwealth University (VCU) offers a certificate program and three degrees, as well as a doctoral concentration, in occupational therapy. The Master of Science in Occupational Therapy (M.S.O.T.), a professional entry-level degree program, is designed for students who wish to become occupational therapists and who have at least 90 credits toward an undergraduate degree. This program includes academic courses, a research project, and fieldwork experiences. Interested students may pursue an additional Certificate in Aging Studies, offered in conjunction with the Department of Gerontology, Gerontology Education Center. Requirements include 9 credits of core gerontology courses and 8 credits of electives consistent with the study of aging. Students who want to complete the Certificate in Aging Studies in addition to the M.S.O.T. take a total of 41 credits.
	A postprofessional Master of Science and a postprofessional Occupational Therapy Doctorate (O.T.D.) are available for registered occupational therapists. The former degree program emphasizes advanced clinical problem solving and abstract reasoning, with pediatric, geriatric, or neurorehabilitation concentrations. The program is for highly motivated learners interested in developing research skills and providing theory and evidence-based practice. The curriculum requires 33 credit hours, including a thesis, and is designed for part-time students. The goal of the O.T.D. program is to prepare B.S. or M.S. occupational therapists for leadership positions in health, education, and community services. Students gain advanced knowledge in occupation and theoretical foundations of occupational therapy, research processes, scientific foundations for practice, and leadership theories and implementation. This curriculum includes 43–55 credit hours and culminates in a capstone leadership project in lieu of a thesis or a dissertation. Both postprofessional degrees are also offered in a distance learning format, using either the Internet or video format.
	Students can earn a Ph.D. in health-related sciences, with a concentration in occupational therapy, through the School of Allied Health Professions. Structured as a four-year course of study, the program is intended to meet the national critical need for allied health professionals who are prepared at the doctoral level in the areas of teaching, research, and administration. The program curriculum consists of a total of 51 credit hours (18 credits of common interdisciplinary core courses, 12 credits of research methods core courses, 9 credits of specialty track courses, and 12 credits of dissertation research).
Research Facilities	VCU libraries provide a combined capacity of more than 1.7 million volumes and 10,200 periodical titles and an online bibliographic search service accessing hundreds of databases. In addition, the Virginia state and Richmond public libraries are within walking distance of both VCU campuses. Academic Computing provides a variety of microcomputer, minicomputer, and mainframe computing services to support the research and instructional endeavors of its faculty members and students, including consultation, instruction, and computer acquisition. The Sensory Processing and Stress Evaluation (SPASE) Lab at VCU, one of only six such centers nationwide, studies sensory-processing disorders (SPD) and how best to treat children with this disorder.
Financial Aid	Some scholarships are available. Students may apply for need-based assistance with the University's Financial Aid Office. Current information on financial aid programs, policies, and procedures is available at http://www.vcu.edu/enroll/finaid.
Cost of Study	For full-time study (9–15 credits) in 2007–08, Virginia residents pay tuition and fees of $4452 per semester; nonresidents, $8876 per semester. For part-time study, Virginia residents pay tuition and fees of $465 per credit hour; nonresidents, $954 per credit hour. Some programs require additional fees. On the Medical College of Virginia (MCV) campus, tuition, fees, and other expenses vary in the medicine, pharmacy, nurse anesthesia, dentistry, and School of Allied Health programs.
Living and Housing Costs	Graduate student housing is available on both the MCV campus and the academic campus of Virginia Commonwealth University. Many graduate students live in off-campus housing, which is reasonably priced and readily available in a variety of styles and settings in nearby residential areas or within easy commuting distance. On- and off-campus housing information is available on the Web at http://www.students.vcu.edu/housing.
Student Group	VCU enrolls 30,452 students, 7,611 of whom are graduate students. More than 200 clubs and organizations reflect the diverse social, recreational, educational, political, and religious interests of the student body.
Location	Richmond is Virginia's capital and a major East Coast financial and manufacturing center that offers students a wide range of cultural, educational, and recreational activities. Richmond is located in central Virginia at the intersection of Interstates 95 and 64, 2 hours south of Washington, D.C., and nestled between the Blue Ridge Mountains and the Atlantic Coast. The Richmond region is easily accessible by plane, car, and train. With nearly 1 million residents, the historic city of Richmond combines big-city offerings with small-town hospitality. Applicants are encouraged to explore http://www.visit.richmond.com/ for more information on the city.
The University	VCU is a state-supported coeducational university with a graduate school, a major teaching hospital, and twelve academic and professional units that offer fifty-two undergraduate, twenty-two postbaccalaureate certificate, sixty-five master's, six post-master's certificate, and twenty-nine Ph.D. programs. VCU also offers M.D., D.D.S., D.P.T., and Pharm.D. programs as well as cooperative degree programs with other major Virginia colleges and universities. VCU has one of the largest evening colleges in the United States. The academic campus is located in Richmond's historic Fan District. The health sciences campus and hospital are located 2 miles east in the downtown business district. A University bus service provides free intercampus transportation for faculty members and students.
	With more than $211 million in annual research funding, the Carnegie Foundation for the Advancement of Teaching ranks Virginia Commonwealth University as one of the nation's top research universities. More than 29,000 undergraduate, certificate, graduate, post-master's, professional, and doctoral students are enrolled in 162 academic programs, forty of which are unique in the commonwealth of Virginia. The faculty members at Virginia Commonwealth University represent the finest American and international graduate institutions and enhance the University's position among the important institutions of higher learning in the United States and the world via their work in the classroom, laboratory, studio, and clinic and in their scholarly publications.
Applying	Admission procedures and program requirements are detailed in the *Graduate Bulletin*. Application deadlines and materials, including the application and the *Graduate Bulletin,* are available online at the Graduate School Web site at http://www.graduate.vcu.edu. Virginia Commonwealth University is an equal opportunity/affirmative action institution providing access to education and employment without regard to age, race, color, national origin, gender, religion, sexual orientation, veteran's status, political affiliation, or disability.
Correspondence and Information	Sandra H. Cash Department of Occupational Therapy School of Allied Health Professions Virginia Commonwealth University 1000 East Marshall Street P.O. Box 980008 Richmond, Virginia 23298-0008 Phone: 804-828-2219 Fax: 804-828-0782 E-mail: scasj@vcu.edu Web site: http://www.sahp.vcu.edu/occu/programs.htm

Virginia Commonwealth University

THE FACULTY AND THEIR RESEARCH

Marie Anzalone, Assistant Professor; Sc.D., Boston University; OTR, FAOTA. Mother-child interaction during play, goodness of fit between parents and children with regulatory or sensory-processing disorders, efficacy of sensory integration intervention with children who have autism.

Sandra H. Cash, Associate Professor, Assistant Chair, and Director, Entry-Level Master's Program; M.S., Virginia Commonwealth, 1973; OTR/L. Assistive-device use and admission criteria.

Al Copolillo, Associate Professor; Ph.D., Illinois at Chicago, 1997; OTR/L. Outcomes of occupational therapy interventions for older adults with low vision.

Tony Gentry, Assistant Professor; Ph.D., Virginia; OTR/L. Neurological rehabilitation and assistive technology for cognition.

Shelly J. Lane, Professor and Chairman; Ph.D., Texas Health Science Center at San Antonio, 1984; OTR, FAOTA. Infants at risk for developmental delay and learning disabilities, neuroscience applications to occupational therapy.

Stacey Reynolds, Assistant Professor; M.S., Gannon, 2001. Physiologic stress reactivity patterns in children with sensory modulation dysfunction.

Jayne T. Shepherd, Associate Professor and Director, Post-Professional Program; M.S., Virginia Commonwealth, 1981; OTR/L, FAOTA. School-based therapy, assistive technology in pediatrics, ADL and IADL skills, adolescent transition services from school to community, play.

Dianne F. Simons, Assistant Professor; Ph.D., Virginia, 1985; OTR/L. Occupation-based practice, design and assessment of Web-based instruction and learning, fostering resiliency in adolescents through engagement in occupation.

Jodi L. Teitelman, Associate Professor; Ph.D., Virginia Commonwealth, 1983. Persons with Alzheimer's disease and their family caregivers.

CLINICAL FACULTY

Francis Atherton	Marjorie S. Elliot	Cathy Jones	Carrie Reid-Russell
Fiona Bessey-Bushnell	Annette Ernst	Lynn Kitchens	William C. Schmidt
Teresa Bowers	Laura Evans	Jo Lawler	Geraldine N. Seeber
Susan M. Broyles	Carol Granger	Anne McDonnell	Sheila Z. Selznick
Mary D. Bullock	Judith D. Hanshaw	Robin McNeny	Kate Smitherman
Patricia Cooper	Sarah Hopkins	Sheril Lynne Michel	Carolyn Velletri
Jean C. Dise	Susan B. Howard	Lori L. Phillipo	Page Wilhoite
Andrea Earle	Carole K. Ivey		

VIRGINIA COMMONWEALTH UNIVERSITY

Department of Physical Therapy

Programs of Study
Virginia Commonwealth University (VCU) offers a three-year degree program leading to a Doctor of Physical Therapy (D.P.T.). The professional track prepares students for entry into the profession by teaching them to evaluate and manage patients with physical therapy problems effectively and in accordance with ethical principles. The program provides students with strategies to continually define and meet their own educational needs in order to keep skills and knowledge current throughout their professional careers. The Department also offers a transitional track leading to the Doctor of Physical Therapy (t-DPT). The t-DPT program is designed for practicing clinicians and offers a didactic augmentation of clinicians' professional education to meet current and future expectations for physical therapy practice. The t-DPT program provides practicing therapists with a mechanism to attain degree parity with more-recently trained therapists who hold the professional D.P.T. by addressing the key differences between their professional baccalaureate or master's degree physical therapy education and the current professional D.P.T. degree education. The curriculum is designed for practicing clinicians to complete through part-time, largely distance-based study in one to three years.

The Department of Physical Therapy, in cooperation with the Department of Anatomy and Neurobiology and the Department of Physiology of the School of Medicine, offers two doctoral-training programs to qualified physical therapists—one in anatomy/physical therapy and one in physiology/physical therapy. The Department also works with other schools to offer additional doctoral programs, such as in rehabilitation and movement science and in health-related sciences. Although each program is unique in specific goals, these programs prepare physical therapy academicians who can contribute to the understanding and application of therapeutic procedures through basic and applied research and who can teach both clinical and didactic physical therapy on all academic levels.

Research Facilities
Multiple on-site labs at VCU allow faculty members and students to conduct research across a wide spectrum of clinically relevant topics. The Clinical Cardiopulmonary Exercise Testing Laboratory contains two SensorMedics ventilatory-expired gas systems, a Cardiosoft twelve-lead ECG system, a fully automated Tango exercise blood pressure system, and a SensorMedics treadmill and a lower-extremity ergometer.

The 1,200-square-foot Musculoskeletal Biomechanics and Motor Control Laboratory participates in collaborative research in the fields of motor control, biomechanics, and human performance, giving students an opportunity to use tools in evaluating human movement. The Sensorimotor Development Research Center is a complex of laboratories established to provide research at various stages, ranging from basic animal experiments to application to human studies. In the animal behavior lab, high-definition digital video cameras are set up to film animals performing righting tasks, climbing on inclined planes, and balancing tasks. The animal surgery laboratory features a specialized surgical table designed to hold anesthetized animals in a stereotaxic frame during acute experiments for in vivo stimulation of neurons at the nucleus or nerve and measuring the contractile characteristics of spinal-nerve-innervated muscles or cranial-nerve-innervated muscles. The 400-pound granite tabletop can be "floated" to minimize the effect of floor vibration when measuring the forces of single motor units. Surgical lighting is available to optimize visualization. Physiologic data from strain gauge and differential amplifiers table are converted to digital media and recorded using PowerLab software.

In the histology laboratory, muscle, bone, or connective tissue are collected from animals and stored in a negative-70-degree freezer. The laboratory is outfitted with an exhaust hood, an autoclave, cabinets, a refrigerator, centrifuges, freezers, and wet-lab counters and sinks.

Financial Aid
Students may apply for need-based assistance with the University's Financial Aid Office. Current information on financial aid programs, policies, and procedures is available at http://www.vcu.edu/enroll/finaid.

Cost of Study
For full-time study (9–15 credits) in 2007–08, Virginia residents pay tuition and fees of $4452 per semester; nonresidents, $8876 per semester. For part-time study, Virginia residents pay tuition and fees of $465 per hour; nonresidents, $954 per hour. Some programs require additional fees. On the Medical College of Virginia (MCV) campus, tuition, fees, and other expenses vary in the medicine, pharmacy, nurse anesthesia, dentistry, and School of Allied Health programs.

Living and Housing Costs
Graduate student housing is available on both the MCV campus and the academic campus of Virginia Commonwealth University. Many graduate students live in off-campus housing, which is reasonably priced and readily available in a variety of styles and settings in nearby residential areas or within easy commuting distance. On- and off-campus housing information is available on the Web at http://www.housing.vcu.edu/.

Student Group
VCU enrolls 30,452 students, 7,611 of whom are graduate students. More than 200 clubs and organizations reflect the diverse social, recreational, educational, political, and religious interests of the student body.

Location
Richmond is Virginia's capital and a major East Coast financial and manufacturing center that offers students a wide range of cultural, educational, and recreational activities. Richmond is located in central Virginia at the intersection of Interstates 95 and 64, 2 hours south of Washington, D.C., and nestled between the Blue Ridge Mountains and the Atlantic coast. The Richmond region is easily accessible by plane, car, and train. With nearly 1 million residents, the historic city of Richmond combines big-city offerings with small-town hospitality. Applicants are encouraged to explore http://www.visit.richmond.com/ for more information on the city.

The University
VCU is a state-supported coeducational university with a graduate school, a major teaching hospital, and twelve academic and professional units that offer fifty-two undergraduate, twenty-two postbaccalaureate certificate, sixty-five master's, six post-master's certificate, and twenty-nine Ph.D. programs. VCU also offers M.D., D.D.S., D.P.T., and Pharm.D. programs as well as cooperative degree programs with other major Virginia colleges and universities. VCU has one of the largest evening colleges in the United States. The academic campus is located in Richmond's historic Fan District. The health sciences campus and hospital are located 2 miles east in the downtown business district. A University bus service provides free intercampus transportation for faculty members and students. With more than $211 million in annual research funding, Virginia Commonwealth University is classified as one of the nation's top research universities by the Carnegie Foundation for the Advancement of Teaching. More than 29,000 undergraduate, certificate, graduate, post-master's, professional, and doctoral students are enrolled in 162 academic programs, forty of which are unique in the commonwealth of Virginia. The faculty members represent the finest American and international graduate institutions and enhance the University's position among the important institutions of higher learning in the United States and the world via their work in the classroom, laboratory, studio, and clinic and in their scholarly publications.

Applying
Admission procedures and program requirements are detailed in the *Graduate Bulletin*. Application deadlines and materials, including the application and the *Graduate Bulletin*, are available online at the Graduate School Web site at http://www.graduate.vcu.edu. Virginia Commonwealth University is an equal opportunity/affirmative action institution providing access to education and employment without regard to age, race, color, national origin, gender, religion, sexual orientation, veteran's status, political affiliation, or disability.

Correspondence and Information
Laura S. Spittle, D.P.T. Admissions Coordinator
Department of Physical Therapy
School of Allied Health Professions
Virginia Commonwealth University
1200 East Broad Street
P.O. Box 980224
Richmond, Virginia 23298-0224
Phone: 804-828-0234
Fax: 804-828-8111
E-mail: lsspittl@vcu.edu
Web site: http://www.vcu.edu/pt/index.html

Virginia Commonwealth University

THE FACULTY AND THEIR RESEARCH

Ross Arena, Associate Professor; Ph.D., Virginia Commonwealth; PT, FACSM, FAACVPR. Cardiopulmonary physical therapy and exercise physiology, prognostic significance of cardiopulmonary exercise testing in patients with heart failure.

Dixie H. Bowman, Assistant Professor; Ed.D., Nova Southeastern; D.P.T., Virginia Commonwealth; PT. Assessment, professional development, excellence in teaching and learning.

Stacey Dusing, Assistant Professor; Ph.D., North Carolina at Chapel Hill; PT. Pediatrics, including developmental disability; impact of prematurity on motor development; motor development in children with lysosomal storage disorders.

Sheryl Finucane, Assistant Professor and Coordinator of Graduate Education; Ph.D., Virginia Commonwealth; PT. Microanatomy, musculoskeletal tissue healing and adaptation to exercise.

Cheryl Ford-Smith, Associate Professor; D.P.T., Virginia Commonwealth; PT, NCS. Rehabilitation, prosthetics, and orthotics; fall prevention in the elderly; reliability of balance-evaluation tools; treatment intervention for balance; vestibular rehabilitation.

Dianne V. Jewell, Assistant Professor; Ph.D., Virginia Commonwealth; PT, CCS, FAACVPR. Cardiovascular and pulmonary co-morbidities in rehabilitation populations; primary physical therapy care of patients without health insurance; physical therapy practice variation in the management of patients with cardiovascular, pulmonary, or orthopaedic impairments.

Thomas P. Mayhew, Associate Professor and Department Chair; Ph.D., Virginia Commonwealth; PT. Gross anatomy, measurements of muscular and functional performance in pediatric and adult patients with neuromuscular disease, muscular adaptation to exercise.

Lori Michener, Associate Professor; Ph.D., Hahnemann; PT, ATC, SCS. Shoulder movement, orthopedic physical therapy; three-dimensional measurement of glenohumeral and scapular kinematics; subacromial impingement syndrome; assessment of functional limitations and disability in patients with shoulder and/or cervical dysfunctions; assessment of treatment outcomes in orthopedic and sports physical therapy.

Peter Pidcoe, Associate Professor; Ph.D., Illinois at Chicago; PT. Biomechanics, kinesiology; biomechanics, and motor control aspects of human motion in sports medicine, pediatrics, and elite-performance settings; quantitative assessment and design of therapeutic interventions in orthopedic treatment settings; design and construction of specialized research equipment.

Daniel Riddle, Otto D. Payton Professor and Assistant Department Chair; Ph.D., Virginia Commonwealth; PT, FAPTA. Measurement and assessment: reliability and validity of measurements in orthopedic physical therapy, assessment of treatment outcomes in orthopedic physical therapy; low back pain; foot and ankle.

Mary Snyder Shall, Associate Professor; Ph.D., Virginia Commonwealth; PT. Neuroanatomy, motor control, fine motor control, extraocular motor units, compartmentalization of skeletal muscle, vestibular afferent input to extraocular, spinal-cord-innervated muscles.

Lisa Donegan Shoaf, Assistant Professor and Director of Clinical Education; Ph.D., Virginia Commonwealth; PT. Professional issues, clinical education models, low back pain, sports medicine.

Karen Sparrow, Director of the Transitional D.P.T. Program; Ph.D., Virginia Commonwealth; PT. Connective tissue healing, technology in education.

Emma Wheeler, Assistant Professor and Director of Admissions; D.P.T., Virginia Commonwealth; PT. Geriatrics, therapeutic modalities.

VIRGINIA COMMONWEALTH UNIVERSITY

Ph.D. in Rehabilitation and Movement Science

Programs of Study

Virginia Commonwealth University (VCU) offers the Ph.D. in rehabilitation and movement science. This degree program is an interdisciplinary one that was developed through a collaborative partnership of the Departments of Health and Human Performance, Physical Therapy, and Physical Medicine and Rehabilitation. The program prepares applied scientists capable of approaching multifaceted health care, preventive medicine, and rehabilitation initiatives from an integrative rather than competitive perspective and to prepare graduates to assume leadership positions in higher-education teaching, research, and management within rehabilitation and movement science. There are two program tracks—exercise physiology and neuromusculoskeletal dynamics. The exercise physiology track prepares individuals to teach, conduct research, and direct external funding initiatives in the areas of exercise physiology, cardiopulmonary rehabilitation, and physiology, particularly in areas associated with metabolic and chronic disease states. The neuromusculoskeletal dynamics track prepares individuals for teaching, research, and clinical initiatives associated with the identification and rehabilitation of movement disorders.

The Ph.D. requires a minimum of 30 credit hours of course work, 3 credit hours of clinical laboratory rotations, 3 credit hours of professional development course work, and 12 credit hours of dissertation research. Course work is interdisciplinary in nature and includes options in biostatistics, the basic life sciences, epidemiology, and other relevant areas. In addition, students conduct a substantial original investigation under the direction of a primary adviser and advisory committee. The doctoral degree must be obtained within seven years of matriculation. Full-time students usually satisfy all requirements within four to five years. Part-time students may take the full seven years to complete all courses and the research project.

Research Facilities

A wide range of study opportunities are available with core and affiliate faculty members using state-of-the-art equipment in six laboratories.

VCU libraries provide a combined capacity of more than 1.7 million volumes and 10,200 periodical titles and an online bibliographic search service accessing hundreds of databases. In addition, the Virginia State and Richmond Public Libraries are within walking distance of both VCU campuses. Academic Computing provides a variety of microcomputer, minicomputer, and mainframe computing services to support the research and instructional endeavors of the faculty and students, including consultation, instruction, and computer acquisition.

Financial Aid

Students may apply for need-based assistance with the University's Financial Aid Office. Current information on financial aid programs, policies, and procedures is available at http://www.vcu.edu/enroll/finaid.

Cost of Study

For full-time study (9–15 credits) in 2007–08, Virginia residents pay tuition and fees of $4452 per semester; nonresidents, $8876 per semester. For part-time study, Virginia residents pay tuition and fees of $465 per hour; nonresidents, $954 per hour. Some programs require additional fees. On the Medical College of Virginia (MCV) campus, tuition, fees, and other expenses vary in the medicine, pharmacy, nurse anesthesia, dentistry, and School of Allied Health programs.

Living and Housing Costs

Graduate student housing is available on both the MCV campus and the academic campus of Virginia Commonwealth University. Many graduate students live in off-campus housing, which is reasonably priced and readily available in a variety of styles and settings in nearby residential areas or within easy commuting distance. On- and off-campus housing information is available on the Web at http://www.housing.vcu.edu/.

Student Group

VCU enrolls 30,452 students, 7,611 of whom are graduate students. More than 200 clubs and organizations reflect the diverse social, recreational, educational, political, and religious interests of the student body.

Location

Richmond is Virginia's capital and a major East Coast financial and manufacturing center that offers students a wide range of cultural, educational, and recreational activities. Richmond is located in central Virginia at the intersection of Interstates 95 and 64, 2 hours south of Washington, D.C., and nestled between the Blue Ridge Mountains and the Atlantic coast. The Richmond region is easily accessible by plane, car, and train. With nearly 1 million residents, the historic city of Richmond combines big-city offerings with small-town hospitality. Applicants are encouraged to explore http://www.visit.richmond.com/ for more information on the city.

The University

VCU is a state-supported coeducational university with a graduate school, a major teaching hospital, and twelve academic and professional units that offer fifty-two undergraduate, twenty-two postbaccalaureate certificate, sixty-five master's, six post-master's certificate, and twenty-nine Ph.D. programs. VCU also offers M.D., D.D.S., D.P.T., and Pharm.D. programs as well as cooperative degree programs with other major Virginia colleges and universities. VCU has one of the largest evening colleges in the United States. The academic campus is located in Richmond's historic Fan District. The health sciences campus and hospital are located 2 miles east in the downtown business district. A University bus service provides free intercampus transportation for faculty members and students.

With more than $211 million in annual research funding, Virginia Commonwealth University is classified as one of the nation's top research universities by the Carnegie Foundation for the Advancement of Teaching. More than 29,000 undergraduate, certificate, graduate, post-master's, professional, and doctoral students are enrolled in 162 academic programs, forty of which are unique in the commonwealth of Virginia. The faculty members represent the finest American and international graduate institutions and enhance the University's position among the important institutions of higher learning in the United States and the world via their work in the classroom, laboratory, studio, and clinic and in their scholarly publications.

Applying

Admission procedures and program requirements are detailed in the *Graduate Bulletin*. Application deadlines and materials, including the application and the *Graduate Bulletin*, are available online at the Graduate School Web site at http://www.graduate.vcu.edu. Virginia Commonwealth University is an equal opportunity/affirmative action institution providing access to education and employment without regard to age, race, color, national origin, gender, religion, sexual orientation, veteran's status, political affiliation, or disability.

Correspondence and Information

Brent Arnold, Director
School of Education
Virginia Commonwealth University
1015 West Main Street
P.O. Box 842020
Richmond, Virginia 23284-2020
Phone: 804-828-1948
Fax: 804-828-1946
E-mail: barnold@vcu.edu
Web site: http://www.soe.vcu.edu/apply/phd_studies/phd_rehabmsci.html

Virginia Commonwealth University

THE FACULTY AND THEIR RESEARCH

HEALTH AND HUMAN PERFORMANCE

Edmund Acevedo, Professor and Chair; Ph.D., North Carolina at Greensboro. Impact of stress and fitness level on an individual's health.

Brent Arnold, Associate Professor; Ph.D., Virginia. Proprioceptive loss in functional ankle instability, ability to perceive force and its relationship to joint stability, impairments in balance and movement following lower-extremity injury.

Ted Conway, Professor and Associate Dean, Research Services; Ph.D. Optimization of an accurate elastic and time-dependent load-deformation relationship for biological tissues to develop a more robust human joint mechanics model; inclusion of underrepresented groups in science, technology, engineering, and math education.

Ronald Evans, Assistant Professor; Ph.D., Auburn. Skeletal and myocardial alterations associated with myocardial volume overload and chronic heart failure, lactate transport and metabolism, physical activity and obesity in children and adolescents, role of physical activity in successful weight loss following gastric bypass surgery.

Scott Ross, Assistant Professor; Ph.D., North Carolina at Chapel Hill. Effects of functional ankle instability on postural stability, effects of functional ankle instability on time to stabilization measures following single-leg jump landings, improving postural stability with balance training exercises and stochastic resonance.

Beverly Warren, Dean and Professor; Ed.D., Alabama; Ph.D., Auburn; FACSM. Impact of physical activity on weight loss and weight maintenance in weight-challenged populations, environmental influences on obesity treatment and prevention strategies for decreasing childhood obesity.

PHYSICAL MEDICINE AND REHABILTATION

David Cifu, Professor; M.D., Boston University. Geriatrics and stroke, brain injury, spinal cord injury, orthopedic rehabilitation.

Jeffery Ericksen, Associate Professor; M.D., Miami. Inpatient rehabilitation and holistic approaches to musculoskeletal pain syndromes in the outpatient setting.

David Hess, Associate Professor; Ph.D., Nova Southeastern. Long-term psychosocial outcomes of cancer survivors.

Jeffrey Kreutzer, Professor; Ph.D., Bowling Green State. Traumatic brain injury and rehabilitation.

J. Patrick McGowan, Assistant Professor; M.D., Virginia Commonwealth.

William McKinley, Professor; M.D., Albany Medical College. Spinal-cord injury and pain assessment.

Michelle Meade, Associate Professor; Ph.D., Ohio. Health disparities, employment and community reintegration after spinal-cord injury, self-management, and health behaviors and obesity after spinal-cord injury.

Eugenio Monasterio, Assistant Professor; M.D., Ponce School of Medicine.

Janet Niemeier, Associate Professor; Ph.D., Virginia Commonwealth.

Abu Qutubuddin, Assistant Professor, M.D.

William Walker, Associate Professor; M.D., Virginia Commonwealth. Spine pain, occupational injuries, electrodiagnostics, neurorehabilitation.

Paul Wehman, Professor and Chair; Ph.D., Wisconsin–Madison. Transition from school to adulthood, special education as it relates to young adulthood.

PHYSICAL THERAPY

Dixie H. Bowman, Assistant Professor; Ed.D., Nova Southeastern; D.P.T., Virginia Commonwealth; PT. Assessment, professional development, excellence in teaching and learning.

Sheryl Finucane, Assistant Professor and Coordinator of Graduate Education; Ph.D., Virginia Commonwealth; PT. Microanatomy, musculoskeletal tissue healing and adaptation to exercise.

Lori Michener, Associate Professor; Ph.D., Hahnemann; PT, ATC, SCS. Shoulder movement, orthopedic physical therapy; three-dimensional measurement of glenohumeral and scapular kinematics; subacromial impingement syndrome; assessment of functional limitations and disability in patients with shoulder and/or cervical dysfunctions; assessment of treatment outcomes in orthopedic and sports physical therapy.

Peter Pidcoe, Associate Professor; Ph.D., Illinois at Chicago; PT. Biomechanics, kinesiology; biomechanics, and motor control aspects of human motion in sports medicine, pediatrics, and elite-performance settings; quantitative assessment and design of therapeutic interventions in orthopedic treatment settings; design and construction of specialized research equipment.

Section 28
Health Sciences

This section contains a directory of institutions offering graduate work in health sciences, followed by in-depth entries submitted by institutions that chose to prepare detailed program descriptions. Additional information about programs listed in the directory but not augmented by an in-depth entry may be obtained by writing directly to the dean of a graduate school or chair of a department at the address given in the directory.

For programs offering related work, see also in this book Dentistry and Dental Sciences, Health Services, Medicine, Nursing, and Public Health; in Book 3, Biological and Biomedical Sciences and Biophysics (Radiation Biology); in Book 4, Physics; and in Book 5, Agricultural Engineering and Bioengineering (Bioengineering), Biomedical Engineering and Biotechnology, and Energy and Power Engineering (Nuclear Engineering).

CONTENTS

Program Directories

Announcements

Close-Ups

See also:

Health Physics/Radiological Health

Bloomsburg University of Pennsylvania, School of Graduate Studies, College of Science and Technology, Department of Biological and Allied Health Sciences, Radiologist Assistant Program, Bloomsburg, PA 17815-1301. Offers MS. *Faculty:* 19 full-time (5 women). *Students:* 6 full-time (3 women), 1 (woman) part-time; includes 2 minority (both African Americans), 1 international. Average age 34. 7 applicants, 86% accepted. *Entrance requirements:* For master's, ARRT certificate and regis in radiography receptor agreement, curriculum vitae, 3 letters of recommendation. Additional exam requirements/recommendations for international students: Required—TOEFL (minimum score 550 paper-based; 213 computer-based; 79 iBT). *Expenses:* Tuition, state resident: full-time $6,048; part-time $336 per credit. Tuition, nonresident: full-time $9,678; part-time $538 per credit. Required fees: $1,415. *Unit head:* Christine Mehlbaum, Unit Head, 570-389-4527, E-mail: cmelbau@bloomu.edu.

Drexel University, College of Medicine, Biomedical Graduate Programs, Program in Radiation Oncology, Philadelphia, PA 19104-2875. Offers radiation (MS); radiation biology (MS); radiation physics (PhD); radiation science (PhD); radiopharmaceutical science (MS, PhD). Part-time programs available. Terminal master's awarded for partial completion of doctoral program. *Degree requirements:* For master's, thesis, comprehensive exam; for doctorate, one foreign language, thesis/dissertation, qualifying exam. *Entrance requirements:* For master's, GRE General Test, minimum GPA of 2.75; for doctorate, GRE General Test, minimum GPA of 3.0. Additional exam requirements/recommendations for international students: Required—TOEFL. Electronic applications accepted. *Faculty research:* Improved cancer therapy by linear accelerators and internal, sealed radiation sources; algorithms for improved superminicomputer-assisted radiation therapy simulation and tumor imaging; molecular and cellular mechanisms of radiation damage.

Emory University, Graduate School of Arts and Sciences, Department of Physics, Atlanta, GA 30322-1100. Offers biophysics (PhD); condensed matter physics (PhD); non-linear physics (PhD); radiological physics (PhD); soft condensed matter physics (PhD); solid-state physics (PhD); statistical physics (PhD); MS/PhD. *Degree requirements:* For doctorate, thesis/dissertation, qualifier proposal (PhD). *Entrance requirements:* For doctorate, GRE General Test, minimum GPA of 3.0. Additional exam requirements/recommendations for international students: Required—TOEFL (minimum score 600 paper-based). Electronic applications accepted. *Expenses:* Tuition: Full-time $30,246. *Faculty research:* Experimental studies of the structure and function of metalloproteins, soft condensed matter, granular materials, biophotonics and fluorescence correlation spectroscopy, single molecule studies of DNA-protein systems.

Georgetown University, Graduate School of Arts and Sciences, Programs in Biomedical Sciences, Department of Health Physics, Washington, DC 20057. Offers health physics (MS); radiobiology (MS). *Degree requirements:* For master's, thesis. *Entrance requirements:* Additional exam requirements/recommendations for international students: Required—TOEFL.

Georgia Institute of Technology, Graduate Studies and Research, College of Engineering, George W. Woodruff School of Mechanical Engineering, Nuclear and Radiological Engineering and Medical Physics Programs, Atlanta, GA 30332-0001. Offers medical physics (MS); nuclear and radiological engineering (MSNE, PhD). Part-time programs available. Postbaccalaureate distance learning degree programs offered (no on-campus study). Terminal master's awarded for partial completion of doctoral program. *Degree requirements:* For master's, thesis optional; for doctorate, thesis/dissertation, comprehensive exam. *Entrance requirements:* For master's and doctorate, GRE General Test, minimum GPA of 3.0. Additional exam requirements/recommendations for international students: Required—TOEFL (minimum score 580 paper-based; 240 computer-based). *Faculty research:* Reactor physics, nuclear materials, plasma physics, radiation detection, radiological assessment.

Illinois Institute of Technology, Graduate College, College of Science and Letters, Department of Biological, Chemical and Physical Sciences, Physics Division, Chicago, IL 60616-3793. Offers health physics (MHP); physics (MS, PhD). Part-time programs available. Postbaccalaureate distance learning degree programs offered. *Faculty:* 15 full-time (1 woman), 4 part-time/adjunct (1 woman). *Students:* 12 full-time (1 woman), 51 part-time (15 women); includes 7 minority (1 African American, 1 American Indian/Alaska Native, 3 Asian Americans or Pacific Islanders, 2 Hispanic Americans), 15 international. Average age 33. 73 applicants, 49% accepted, 7 enrolled. In 2006, 8 degrees awarded. Terminal master's awarded for partial completion of doctoral program. *Degree requirements:* For master's, thesis (for some programs), comprehensive exam; for doctorate, thesis/dissertation, comprehensive exam. *Entrance requirements:* For master's and doctorate, GRE General Test, minimum undergraduate GPA of 3.0. Additional exam requirements/recommendations for international students: Required—TOEFL (minimum score 550 paper-based; 213 computer-based). *Application deadline:* For fall admission, 5/1 for domestic and international students; for spring admission, 10/15 for domestic and international students. Applications are processed on a rolling basis. Application fee: $40. Electronic applications accepted. *Expenses:* Tuition: Full-time $13,086; part-time $727 per credit. Required fees: $7 per credit. $235 per term. Tuition and fees vary according to class time, course level, course load, program and student level. *Financial support:* In 2006–07, 12 research assistantships with full tuition reimbursements (averaging $17,000 per year), 10 teaching assistantships with full tuition reimbursements (averaging $15,000 per year) were awarded; fellowships, Federal Work-Study, institutionally sponsored loans, scholarships/grants, health care benefits, and unspecified assistantships also available. Support available to part-time students. Financial award applicants required to submit FAFSA. *Faculty research:* Elementary particle physics, accelerator physics, synchrotron radiation, research on materials and biological systems, XANES and XAFS, computational simulation of membranes. Total annual research expenditures: $2 million. *Unit head:* Dr. Howard A. Rubin, Associate Chair, Professor, 312-567-3395, Fax: 312-567-3494, E-mail: rubin@iit.edu. *Application contact:* Morgan Frederick, Assistant Director of Graduate Communications, 866-472-3448, Fax: 312-567-3138, E-mail: inquiry.grad@iit.edu.

McGill University, Faculty of Graduate and Postdoctoral Studies, Faculty of Medicine, Medical Radiation Physics Unit, Montréal, QC H3A 2T5, Canada. Offers M Sc, PhD. *Degree requirements:* For master's and doctorate, thesis/dissertation. *Entrance requirements:* For master's, B Sc in physics, minimum GPA of 3.0. Additional exam requirements/recommendations for international students: Required—TOEFL. *Faculty research:* Radiation dosimetry, biodegradable polymers, stereotactic radiosurgery, brachytherapy, functional MR brain imaging.

McMaster University, School of Graduate Studies, Faculty of Science, Department of Medical Physics and Applied Radiation Sciences, Hamilton, ON L8S 4M2, Canada. Offers health and radiation physics (M Sc); medical physics (M Sc, PhD). Part-time programs available. *Faculty:* 13 full-time, 7 part-time/adjunct. *Students:* 33 full-time, 6 part-time. 3 applicants, 0% accepted. *Degree requirements:* For master's, thesis or alternative. *Entrance requirements:* For master's, minimum B+ average. Additional exam requirements/recommendations for international students: Required—TOEFL (minimum score 550 paper-based; 213 computer-based). *Application deadline:* For fall admission, 3/31 priority date for domestic students. Applications are processed on a rolling basis. Application fee: $90. *Financial support:* In 2006–07, teaching assistantships (averaging $8,440 per year); scholarships/grants also available. *Faculty research:* Imaging, toxicology, dosimetry, body composition, medical lasers. Total annual research expenditures: $800,000. *Unit head:* Dr. Fiona McNeill, Chair, 905-525-9140 Ext. 26891, Fax: 905-522-5982, E-mail: fmcneill@mcmaster.ca. *Application contact:* Wendy Malarek, Administrator, 905-525-9140 Ext. 24182, Fax: 905-522-5982, E-mail: malarek@mcmaster.ca.

Medical College of Georgia, School of Graduate Studies, Department of Radiologic Sciences, Augusta, GA 30912. Offers MS. Part-time programs available. *Faculty:* 4 full-time (0 women). *Entrance requirements:* For master's, GRE General Test. Additional exam requirements/recommendations for international students: Required—TOEFL (minimum score 550 paper-based; 213 computer-based). *Application deadline:* For fall admission, 6/30 priority date for domestic students. Applications are processed on a rolling basis. Application fee: $30. Electronic applications accepted. *Expenses:* Tuition, state resident: full-time $2,293; part-time $192 per credit hour. Tuition, nonresident: full-time $9,169; part-time $765 per credit hour. Required fees: $293 per semester. *Financial support:* Federal Work-Study, institutionally sponsored loans, and unspecified assistantships available. Support available to part-time students. Financial award application deadline: 5/31; financial award applicants required to submit FAFSA. *Unit head:* Dr. Gregory Passmore, Chair and Associate Professor, 706-721-3691, Fax: 706-721-8293, E-mail: gpassmor@mail.mcg.edu.

Midwestern State University, Graduate Studies, College of Health Sciences and Human Services, Program in Radiology, Wichita Falls, TX 76308. Offers radiologic administration (MSR); radiologic education (MSR); radiologic sciences (MSR); radiologist assistant (MSR). Part-time and evening/weekend programs available. Postbaccalaureate distance learning degree programs offered (minimal on-campus study). *Faculty:* 4 full-time (2 women). *Students:* 1 (woman) full-time, 62 part-time (44 women); includes 15 minority (6 African Americans, 4 American Indian/Alaska Native, 2 Asian Americans or Pacific Islanders, 3 Hispanic Americans), 1 international. Average age 38. 24 applicants, 88% accepted, 17 enrolled. In 2006, 21 degrees awarded. *Degree requirements:* For master's, thesis optional. *Entrance requirements:* For master's, GRE General Test, MAT or GMAT, credentials in one of the medical imaging modalities or radiation therapy, one year's experience, three letters of recommendation from past and/or present educators and employers. Additional exam requirements/recommendations for international students: Required—TOEFL (minimum score 550 paper-based; 213 computer-based). *Application deadline:* For fall admission, 7/1 for domestic students, 4/1 for international students; for spring admission, 11/1 for domestic students, 8/1 for international students. Applications are processed on a rolling basis. Application fee: $35 ($50 for international students). Electronic applications accepted. *Financial support:* In 2006–07, 63 students received support. Career-related internships or fieldwork, Federal Work-Study, institutionally sponsored loans, scholarships/grants, tuition waivers (partial), and unspecified assistantships available. Support available to part-time students. Financial award application deadline: 5/1; financial award applicants required to submit FAFSA. *Unit head:* Dr. Nadia Bugg, Chair, 940-397-4571, Fax: 940-397-4513, E-mail: nadia.bugg@mwsu.edu.

New York Chiropractic College, Program in Diagnostic Imaging, Seneca Falls, NY 13148-0800. Offers MS. *Faculty:* 1 full-time (0 women), 6 part-time/adjunct (2 women). *Students:* 3 applicants, 33% accepted, 1 enrolled. *Entrance requirements:* For master's, DC degree. *Expenses:* Tuition: Full-time $14,960. Required fees: $680. *Financial support:* Applicants required to submit FAFSA. *Unit head:* Dr. John Taylor, Director of Program of Diagnostic Imaging, E-mail: jtaylor@nycc.edu.

Oregon State University, Graduate School, College of Engineering, Department of Nuclear Engineering and Radiation Health Physics, Corvallis, OR 97331. Offers nuclear engineering (MS, PhD); radiation health physics (MS, PhD). Part-time programs available. *Faculty:* 8 full-time (1 woman). *Students:* 34 full-time (7 women), 21 part-time (6 women); includes 4 minority (1 African American, 3 Hispanic Americans), 6 international. Average age 31. 51 applicants, 61% accepted, 12 enrolled. In 2006, 5 master's, 2 doctorates awarded. Terminal master's awarded for partial completion of doctoral program. *Degree requirements:* For master's and doctorate, thesis/dissertation. *Entrance requirements:* For master's and doctorate, GRE General Test, minimum GPA of 3.0 in last 90 hours. Additional exam requirements/recommendations for international students: Required—TOEFL (minimum score 550 paper-based; 213 computer-based). *Application deadline:* For fall admission, 6/15 for domestic students. Applications are processed on a rolling basis. Application fee: $50. *Financial support:* In 2006–07, 3 fellowships with full tuition reimbursements (averaging $16,650 per year), 14 research assistantships with partial tuition reimbursements (averaging $12,627 per year), 6 teaching assistantships with full tuition reimbursements (averaging $12,627 per year) were awarded; institutionally sponsored loans also available. Support available to part-time students. Financial award application deadline: 2/1. *Faculty research:* Reactor thermal hydraulics and safety, applications of radiation and nuclear techniques, computational methods development, environmental transport of radioactive materials. Total annual research expenditures: $2.5 million. *Unit head:* Dr. Jose N. Reyes, Head, 541-737-2343, Fax: 541-737-0480, E-mail: reyes@ne.oregonstate.edu. *Application contact:* Dr. Qiao Wu, Coordinator, 541-737-7066, Fax: 541-737-0480, E-mail: nuc_engr@ne.orst.edu.

San Diego State University, Graduate and Research Affairs, College of Sciences, Department of Physics, Program in Radiological Physics, San Diego, CA 92182. Offers MS. Part-time programs available. *Students:* 1 applicant, 0% accepted. In 2006, 1 degree awarded. *Degree requirements:* For master's, oral or written exam, thesis optional. *Entrance requirements:* For master's, GRE General Test, GRE Subject Test (physics), 2 letters of recommendation. Additional exam requirements/recommendations for international students: Required—TOEFL. *Application deadline:* For fall admission, 2/1 for domestic students, 2/1 priority date for international students; for spring admission, 11/1 for domestic students, 10/1 priority date for international students. Applications are processed on a rolling basis. Application fee: $55. Electronic applications accepted. *Financial support:* Career-related internships or fieldwork and unspecified assistantships available. Financial award applicants required to submit FAFSA. *Faculty research:* Computational radiological physics, medical physics. *Application contact:* Calvin Johnson, Graduate Advisor, 619-594-1284, Fax: 619-594-5485, E-mail: cjohnson@sciences.sdsu.edu.

Texas A&M University, College of Engineering, Department of Nuclear Engineering, College Station, TX 77843. Offers health physics (MS); nuclear engineering (M Eng, MS, PhD). *Faculty:* 11 full-time (1 woman), 6 part-time/adjunct (0 women). *Students:* 90 full-time (20 women), 19 part-time (5 women); includes 12 minority (2 African Americans, 2 Asian Americans or Pacific Islanders, 8 Hispanic Americans), 29 international. Average age 28. 74 applicants, 59% accepted, 31 enrolled. In 2006, 15 master's, 1 doctorate awarded. *Degree requirements:* For master's, thesis or alternative; for doctorate, thesis/dissertation, departmental qualifying exams. *Entrance requirements:* For master's and doctorate, GRE General Test, 3 letters of recommendation. Additional exam requirements/recommendations for international students: Required—TOEFL. *Application deadline:* For fall admission, 3/1 for domestic and international students; for spring admission, 8/1 for domestic and international students. Applications are processed on a rolling basis. Application fee: $50 ($75 for international students). Electronic applications accepted. *Expenses:* Tuition, state resident: full-time $4,697. Tuition, nonresident: full-time $11,297. Required fees: $2,272. *Financial support:* Fellowships, research assistantships, career-related internships or fieldwork, scholarships/grants, and unspecified assistantships available. Financial award application deadline: 4/1; financial award applicants required to submit FAFSA. *Faculty research:* Accelerators, aerosols, computational transport, fission, fusion. Total annual research expenditures: $4.2 million. *Unit head:* Dr. William Burchill, Head, 979-845-4161. *Application contact:* Dr. Marvin L. Adams, Graduate Coordinator, 979-845-7090.

Université de Montréal, Faculty of Medicine and Faculty of Graduate Studies, Graduate Programs in Medicine, Program in Specialized Studies, Montréal, QC H3C 3J7, Canada. Offers anesthesia (DESS); diagnostic radiology (DESS); family medicine (DESS); medical biochemistry (DESS); medical genetics (DESS); medicine (DESS); microbiology and infectious diseases (DESS); nuclear medicine (DESS); obstetrics and gynecology (DESS); ophthalmology (DESS); pediatrics (DESS); psychiatry (DESS); radiology-oncology (DESS); surgery (DESS). *Faculty:* 159 full-time (37 women), 345 part-time/adjunct (102 women). *Entrance requirements:* For degree, proficiency in French. *Application deadline:* For fall admission, 2/1 priority date for domestic students; for winter admission, 11/1 priority date for domestic students; for spring admission, 2/1 priority date for domestic students. Application fee: $30. Electronic applications accepted. *Unit head:* Dr. Pierre Boyle, Vice Dean of Studies, 514-343-6300, Fax: 514-343-5751, E-mail: pierre.boyle@umontreal.ca.

Université Laval, Faculty of Medicine, Post-Professional Programs in Medical Studies, Québec, QC G1K 7P4, Canada. Offers anatomy–pathology (DESS); anesthesiology (DESS); cardiology (DESS); care of older people (Diploma); clinical research (DESS); community health (DESS); dermatology (DESS); diagnostic radiology (DESS); emergency medicine (Diploma); family medicine (DESS); general surgery (DESS); geriatrics (DESS); hematology (DESS); internal medicine (DESS); maternal and fetal medicine (Diploma); medical biochemistry (DESS); medical microbiology and infectious diseases (DESS); medical oncology (DESS); nephrology (DESS); neurology (DESS); neurosurgery (DESS); obstetrics and gynecology (DESS); ophthalmology (DESS); orthopedic surgery (DESS); oto-rhino-laryngology (DESS); palliative medicine (Diploma); pediatrics (DESS); plastic surgery (DESS); psychiatry (DESS); pulmonary medicine (DESS); radiology–oncology (DESS); thoracic surgery (DESS); urology (DESS). *Degree requirements:* For other advanced degree, comprehensive exam. *Entrance requirements:* For degree, knowledge of French. Electronic applications accepted.

University of Alberta, Faculty of Medicine and Dentistry and Faculty of Graduate Studies and Research, Graduate Programs in Medicine, Department of Radiology and Diagnostic Imaging, Edmonton, AB T6G 2E1, Canada. Offers medical sciences (PhD); radiology and diagnostic imaging (M Sc). *Faculty:* 2 part-time/adjunct (0 women). *Students:* 2 full-time (0 women); includes 1 minority (Asian American or Pacific Islander) Average age 25. 50 applicants, 2% accepted. In 2006, 1 degree awarded. Terminal master's awarded for partial completion of doctoral program. *Degree requirements:* For master's and doctorate, thesis/dissertation. *Entrance requirements:* For master's, minimum GPA of 6.5 on a 9.0 scale; for doctorate, M Sc. *Application deadline:* For fall admission, 4/1 priority date for domestic students; for winter admission, 7/1 priority date for domestic students. Application fee: $60. *Financial support:* In 2006–07, 2 fellowships, 1 research assistantship, 1 teaching assistantship were awarded; career-related internships or fieldwork also available. Financial award application deadline: 3/31. *Faculty research:* Spectroscopic attenuation correction, nuclear medicine technology, monoclonal antibody labeling, bone mineral analysis using ultrasound. Total annual research expenditures: $325,000. *Unit head:* Dr. Robert Lambert, Academic Chair, 780-407-6907, Fax: 780-407-1202, E-mail: rglambert@cha.ab.ca. *Application contact:* Dr. L. J. Filipow, Graduate Coordinator, 780-407-6907, Fax: 780-407-1202, E-mail: filipow@shaw.ca.

University of Cincinnati, Division of Research and Advanced Studies, College of Engineering, Department of Mechanical, Industrial and Nuclear Engineering, Program in Health Physics, Cincinnati, OH 45221. Offers MS. *Degree requirements:* For master's, thesis or alternative. *Entrance requirements:* For master's, GRE General Test. Additional exam requirements/recommendations for international students: Required—TOEFL (minimum score 575 paper-based; 233 computer-based). Electronic applications accepted.

University of Cincinnati, Division of Research and Advanced Studies, College of Medicine, Graduate Programs in Biomedical Sciences, Department of Radiological Sciences, Cincinnati, OH 45267. Offers medical physics (MS). Part-time programs available. *Degree requirements:* For master's, project. *Entrance requirements:* For master's, GRE General Test. Additional exam requirements/recommendations for international students: Required—TOEFL (minimum score 575 paper-based). Electronic applications accepted. *Faculty research:* Radiation oncology, radiologic imaging, dosimetry, radiation biology, radiation therapy.

University of Illinois at Urbana–Champaign, Graduate College, College of Engineering, Department of Nuclear, Plasma, and Radiological Engineering, Champaign, IL 61820. Offers health physics (MS, PhD); nuclear engineering (MS, PhD). *Faculty:* 10 full-time (0 women), 2 part-time/adjunct (0 women). *Students:* 59 full-time (10 women), 4 part-time (2 women); includes 4 minority (1 African American, 3 Asian Americans or Pacific Islanders), 35 international. 69 applicants, 41% accepted, 14 enrolled. In 2006, 11 master's, 4 doctorates awarded. *Degree requirements:* For master's and doctorate, thesis/dissertation. *Application deadline:* For fall admission, 3/1 priority date for domestic students. Applications are processed on a rolling basis. Application fee: $50 ($60 for international students). Electronic applications accepted. *Financial support:* In 2006–07, 7 fellowships, 44 research assistantships, 14 teaching assistantships were awarded. Financial award application deadline: 2/15. *Unit head:* James F. Stubbins, Head, 217-333-6474, Fax: 217-333-3906, E-mail: jstubbin@uiuc.edu. *Application contact:* Becky Meline, Admissions and Records Officer I, 217-333-3598, Fax: 217-333-3906, E-mail: bmeline@uiuc.edu.

University of Kentucky, Graduate School, College of Health Sciences, Program in Radiation Sciences, Lexington, KY 40506-0032. Offers health physics (MSHP); radiological medical physics (MSRMP). Offered in cooperation with Graduate Programs in Medicine. Part-time programs available. *Faculty:* 3 full-time (0 women). *Students:* 14 full-time (7 women), 3 part-time (all women); includes 1 minority (Asian American or Pacific Islander) Average age 28. 49 applicants, 24% accepted, 8 enrolled. In 2006, 8 degrees awarded. *Degree requirements:* For master's, thesis, comprehensive exam. *Entrance requirements:* For master's, GRE General Test, minimum undergraduate GPA of 2.75. Additional exam requirements/recommendations for international students: Required—TOEFL (minimum score 550 paper-based; 213 computer-based). *Application deadline:* For fall admission, 7/17 priority date for domestic students, 2/1 priority date for international students; for spring admission, 12/13 priority date for domestic students, 6/15 priority date for international students. Application fee: $40 ($55 for international students). Electronic applications accepted. *Expenses:* Tuition, state resident: full-time $7,670; part-time $401 per credit hour. Tuition, nonresident: full-time $16,158; part-time $873 per credit hour. *Financial support:* Fellowships with full tuition reimbursements, research assistantships with full tuition reimbursements, teaching assistantships with full tuition reimbursements, Federal Work-Study, institutionally sponsored loans, scholarships/grants, traineeships, health care benefits, tuition waivers (partial), and unspecified assistantships available. Support available to part-time students. Financial award application deadline: 3/15; financial award applicants required to submit FAFSA. *Faculty research:* Dosimetry, manpower studies, diagnostic imaging physics, shielding. *Unit head:* Dr. Ralph Christensen, Director of Graduate Studies, 859-323-1100, Fax: 859-257-2454, E-mail: rcchri1@pop.uky.edu. *Application contact:* Dr. Brian Jackson, Senior Associate Dean, 859-257-4667, Fax: 859-257-4676, E-mail: brian.jackson@uky.edu.

University of Massachusetts Lowell, Graduate School, College of Arts and Sciences, Department of Physics and Applied Physics, Program in Radiological Sciences and Protection, Lowell, MA 01854-2881. Offers MS, PhD. Terminal master's awarded for partial completion of doctoral program. *Degree requirements:* For master's, one foreign language, thesis; for doctorate, 2 foreign languages, thesis/dissertation. *Entrance requirements:* For master's and doctorate, GRE General Test. Electronic applications accepted.

University of Medicine and Dentistry of New Jersey, School of Health Related Professions, Department of Medical Imaging Sciences, Newark, NJ 07107-1709. Offers radiologist assistant (MS). *Entrance requirements:* Additional exam requirements/recommendations for international students: Required—TOEFL. *Application deadline:* For fall admission, 5/1 for domestic students. Applications are processed on a rolling basis. Application fee: $50. Electronic applications accepted. *Unit head:* Gladys Montane, Chairperson, 973-972-8528, E-mail: raprgm@umdnj.edu.

University of Michigan, Horace H. Rackham School of Graduate Studies, College of Engineering, Department of Nuclear Engineering and Radiological Sciences, Ann Arbor, MI 48109. Offers nuclear engineering (Nuc E); nuclear engineering and radiological sciences (MSE, PhD); nuclear science (MS, PhD). Terminal master's awarded for partial completion of doctoral program. *Degree requirements:* For master's, thesis optional; for doctorate, thesis/dissertation, oral defense of dissertation, preliminary exams. *Entrance requirements:* For master's and doctorate, GRE General Test. Additional exam requirements/recommendations for international students: Required—TOEFL (minimum score 560 paper-based; 220 computer-based). Electronic applications accepted. *Faculty research:* Fission systems and radiation transport, materials, plasma and fusion, radiation measurements and imaging, radiation safety.

University of Missouri–Columbia, Graduate School, College of Engineering, Nuclear Science and Engineering Institute, Columbia, MO 65211. Offers nuclear power engineering (MS, PhD), including health physics (MS), medical physics (MS), nuclear power engineering (MS). *Faculty:* 5 full-time (0 women). *Students:* 47 full-time (10 women), 6 part-time (2 women); includes 12 minority (1 African American, 4 Asian Americans or Pacific Islanders, 7 Hispanic Americans), 13 international. In 2006, 3 master's, 5 doctorates awarded. *Degree requirements:* For master's, research project; for doctorate, thesis/dissertation. *Entrance requirements:* For master's and doctorate, GRE General Test. Additional exam requirements/recommendations for international students: Required—TOEFL (minimum score 500 paper-based; 173 computer-based). *Application deadline:* For fall admission, 3/15 priority date for domestic students. Application fee: $45 ($60 for international students). *Financial support:* Fellowships, research assistantships, teaching assistantships, institutionally sponsored loans available. *Unit head:* Dr. Tushar Ghosh, Director of Graduate Studies, 573-882-9736, E-mail: ghosht@missouri.edu.

University of Missouri–Columbia, School of Health Professions, Program in Cardiopulmonary and Diagnostic Sciences, Columbia, MO 65211. Offers diagnostic medical ultrasound (MHS). *Faculty:* 7 full-time (5 women), 1 (woman) part-time/adjunct. *Students:* 7 full-time (5 women), 1 (woman) part-time; includes 2 minority (1 African American, 1 Asian American or Pacific Islander), 1 international. In 2006, 8 degrees awarded. *Entrance requirements:* Additional exam requirements/recommendations for international students: Required—TOEFL (minimum score 500 paper-based; 173 computer-based). Application fee: $45 ($60 for international students). *Unit head:* Dr. Moses Hdeib, Director, 573-884-2994, E-mail: hdeibm@health.missouri.edu.

University of Nevada, Las Vegas, Graduate College, Division of Health Sciences, Department of Health Physics, Las Vegas, NV 89154-9900. Offers MS. *Accreditation:* ABET. Part-time programs available. *Faculty:* 7 full-time (2 women), 4 part-time/adjunct (2 women). *Students:* 9 full-time (3 women), 3 part-time (1 woman); includes 1 minority (Asian American or Pacific Islander), 3 international. 4 applicants, 100% accepted, 2 enrolled. In 2006, 4 degrees awarded. *Degree requirements:* For master's, professional paper, oral exam, thesis optional. *Entrance requirements:* For master's, GRE General Test, minimum GPA of 3.0. Additional exam requirements/recommendations for international students: Required—TOEFL (minimum score 550 paper-based; 213 computer-based; 80 iBT). *Application deadline:* For fall admission, 6/15 for domestic students, 5/1 for international students; for spring admission, 11/15 for domestic students, 10/1 for international students. Application fee: $60 ($75 for international students). Electronic applications accepted. *Financial support:* In 2006–07, 4 research assistantships with partial tuition reimbursements (averaging $10,000 per year) were awarded; teaching assistantships with partial tuition reimbursements, career-related internships or fieldwork, Federal Work-Study, institutionally sponsored loans, scholarships/grants, health care benefits, and unspecified assistantships also available. Support available to part-time students. Financial award application deadline: 3/1. *Unit head:* Dr. Steen Madsen, Chair, 702-895-3299. *Application contact:* Graduate College Admissions Evaluator, 702-895-3320, Fax: 702-895-4180, E-mail: gradcollege@unlv.edu.

University of Oklahoma Health Sciences Center, College of Medicine and Graduate College, Graduate Programs in Medicine, Department of Radiological Sciences, Oklahoma City, OK 73190. Offers medical radiation physics (MS, PhD), including diagnostic radiology, nuclear medicine, radiation therapy, ultrasound. Part-time programs available. Terminal master's awarded for partial completion of doctoral program. *Degree requirements:* For master's and doctorate, thesis/dissertation. *Entrance requirements:* For master's, GRE General Test; for doctorate, GRE General Test, 3 letters of recommendation. Additional exam requirements/recommendations for international students: Required—TOEFL. *Faculty research:* Monte Carlo applications in radiation therapy, observer performed studies in diagnostic radiology, error analysis in gated cardiac nuclear medicine studies, nuclear medicine absorbed fraction determinations.

The University of Toledo, College of Graduate Studies, College of Medicine, Department of Radiation Oncology, Toledo, OH 43606-3390. Offers medical physics (MS). Part-time programs available. *Faculty:* 2 full-time (0 women), 1 part-time/adjunct (0 women). *Students:* 6 full-time (1 woman), 7 part-time; includes 2 minority (both Asian Americans or Pacific Islanders), 2 international. Average age 33. 19 applicants, 58% accepted, 8 enrolled. *Degree requirements:* For master's, thesis, qualifying exam. *Entrance requirements:* For master's, GRE General Test, minimum undergraduate GPA of 3.0. Application fee: $45. *Financial support:* Federal Work-Study and institutionally sponsored loans available. Financial award applicants required to submit FAFSA. *Faculty research:* 3-D treatment planning, stereotactic radiosurgery. *Unit head:* Dr. Ishmael Persai, Program Director, 419-383-4117, Fax: 419-383-6140, E-mail: mcogradschool@mco.edu. *Application contact:* Joann Braatz, Secretary, 419-383-4117, Fax: 419-383-6140, E-mail: mcogradschool@mco.edu.

The University of Toledo, College of Graduate Studies, College of Medicine, Department of Radiology, Toledo, OH 43606-3390. Offers MS. Part-time programs available. *Students:* Average age 35. In 2006, 1 degree awarded. *Degree requirements:* For master's, thesis, qualifying exam. *Entrance requirements:* For master's, GRE General Test, minimum undergraduate GPA of 3.0. Application fee: $45. *Financial support:* Federal Work-Study and institutionally sponsored loans available. Financial award applicants required to submit FAFSA. *Faculty research:* Radiation dosimetry, digital image processing, mathematical modeling, magnetic resonance imaging. *Unit head:* Dr. Lee Woldenberg, Chairman, 419-383-4117. *Application contact:* Joann Braatz, Secretary, 419-383-4117, Fax: 419-383-6140, E-mail: mcogradschool@mco.edu.

Virginia Commonwealth University, Graduate School, School of Allied Health Professions, Department of Health Administration, Doctoral Program in Health Related Sciences, Richmond, VA 23284-9005. Offers clinical laboratory sciences (PhD); gerontology (PhD); health administration (PhD); nurse anesthesia (PhD); occupational therapy (PhD); physical therapy (PhD); radiation sciences (PhD); rehabilitation leadership (PhD). *Faculty:* 2 full-time (1 woman). *Students:* 4 full-time (all women), 13 part-time (7 women); includes 7 minority (1 African American, 6 Asian Americans or Pacific Islanders), 3 international. In 2006, 2 degrees awarded. *Unit head:* Monica L. White, Director of Student Services, 804-828-3273, Fax: 804-828-8656, E-mail: mlwhite1@vcu.edu.

See Close-Up on page 1745.

Wayne State University, School of Medicine, Graduate Programs in Medicine, Department of Radiation Oncology, Detroit, MI 48202. Offers medical physics (PhD); radiological physics (MS). Part-time and evening/weekend programs available. *Faculty:* 14 full-time (0 women), 2 part-time/adjunct (0 women). *Students:* 25 applicants, 52% accepted, 10 enrolled. In 2006, 12 degrees awarded. Terminal master's awarded for partial completion of doctoral program. *Degree requirements:* For master's, thesis, essay, exit exam; for doctorate, thesis/dissertation, qualifying exam. *Entrance requirements:* For master's, GRE General Test, BS in physics or related area; for doctorate, GRE General Test, GRE Subject Test, BS in physics or related area. Additional exam requirements/recommendations for international students: Required—TOEFL (minimum score 550 paper-based; 213 computer-based); Recommended—TWE (minimum score 6). *Application deadline:* For fall admission, 1/15 for domestic students, 6/1 for international students; for winter admission, 10/1 for international students; for spring admission, 2/1 for international students. Applications are processed on a rolling basis. Application fee: $30 ($50 for international students). Electronic applications accepted. *Financial support:* In 2006–07, 1 fellowship (averaging $38,000 per year), 2 research assistantships (averaging $20,175 per year) were awarded; teaching assistantships, career-related internships or fieldwork also available. Support available to part-time students. Financial award application deadline: 1/15. *Faculty research:* Radiotherapy physics, hyperthermia, magnetic resonance imaging and spectroscopy, clinical ultrasound, x-ray physics. Total annual research expenditures:

Health Physics/Radiological Health

Wayne State University (continued)
$474,509. *Unit head:* Andrew Turrisi, Chair, 313-966-2774, Fax: 313-745-2314, E-mail: ar9642@wayne.edu. *Application contact:* Michael Joiner, Professor, 313-745-2489, E-mail: joinerm@kci.wayne.edu.

Wayne State University, School of Medicine, Graduate Programs in Medicine, Department of Radiology, Detroit, MI 48202. Offers medical physics (PhD); radiological physics (MS). Part-time and evening/weekend programs available. *Faculty:* 4 full-time (0 women), 1 part-time/adjunct (0 women). *Students:* 27 full-time (8 women), 4 part-time (2 women); includes 4 minority (all Asian Americans or Pacific Islanders), 12 international. Average age 31. 21 applicants, 86% accepted, 6 enrolled. In 2006, 12 degrees awarded. *Degree requirements:* For master's, essay, exam; for doctorate, thesis/dissertation. *Entrance requirements:* For master's, GRE General Test, BS in physics or related area; for doctorate, GRE. Additional exam requirements/recommendations for international students: Required—TOEFL (minimum score 550 paper-based; 213 computer-based); Recommended—TWE (minimum score 6). *Application deadline:* For fall admission, 4/1 for domestic students, 6/1 for international students; for winter admission, 10/1 for international students; for spring admission, 2/1 for international students. Applications are processed on a rolling basis. Application fee: $30 ($50 for international students). Electronic applications accepted. *Financial support:* In 2006–07, 1 fellowship with tuition reimbursement (averaging $38,760 per year), 3 research assistantships with tuition reimbursements (averaging $20,200 per year) were awarded; teaching assistantships, career-related internships or fieldwork also available. Support available to part-time students. Financial award application deadline: 3/1. *Faculty research:* Radiotherapy and imaging physics, hyperthermia, magnetic resonance imaging and spectroscopy, clinical ultrasound, lasers in medicine. Total annual research expenditures: $48,000. *Unit head:* Wilbur Smith, Chair, 313-745-3430, Fax: 313-577-8600, E-mail: aj0262@wayne.edu. *Application contact:* Jay Burmeister, Graduate Director, 313-745-2483, E-mail: burmeist@med.wayne.edu.

Medical Imaging

MGH Institute of Health Professions, Graduate Programs, Program in Medical Imaging, Boston, MA 02129. Offers Certificate. Postbaccalaureate distance learning degree programs offered (minimal on-campus study). *Faculty:* 2 full-time (1 woman), 1 (woman) part-time/adjunct. *Students:* 13 full-time (10 women), 11 part-time (6 women); includes 3 minority (1 African American, 1 Asian American or Pacific Islander, 1 Hispanic American). Average age 39. 41 applicants, 39% accepted, 13 enrolled. In 2006, 11 degrees awarded. *Entrance requirements:* Additional exam requirements/recommendations for international students: Required—TOEFL (minimum score 550 paper-based; 213 computer-based). *Application deadline:* For fall admission, 4/15 for domestic students, 3/1 for international students. Application fee: $50. Electronic applications accepted. *Financial support:* In 2006–07, 20 students received support. Application deadline: 3/3; *Unit head:* Richard Terrass, Director, 617-726-0781. *Application contact:* Maureen Rika Judd, Manager of Admissions, 617-726-6069, Fax: 617-726-8010, E-mail: admissions@mghihp.edu.

University of Cincinnati, Division of Research and Advanced Studies, College of Engineering, Department of Biomedical Engineering, Cincinnati, OH 45221. Offers bioinformatics (PhD); biomechanics (PhD); medical imaging (PhD); tissue engineering (PhD). Part-time programs available. *Degree requirements:* For doctorate, one foreign language, thesis/dissertation. *Entrance requirements:* For doctorate, GRE General Test. Additional exam requirements/recommendations for international students: Required—TOEFL (minimum score 600 paper-based; 250 computer-based).

University of Florida, College of Medicine, Department of Biochemistry and Molecular Biology, Gainesville, FL 32611. Offers biochemistry and molecular biology (MS, PhD); imaging science and technology (MS, PhD). *Faculty:* 28 full-time (7 women). In 2006, 2 degrees awarded. *Degree requirements:* For doctorate, thesis/dissertation. *Entrance requirements:* For doctorate, GRE General Test, minimum GPA of 3.0. Additional exam recuirements/recommendations for international students: Required—TOEFL. *Application deadline:* For fall admission, 2/15 for domestic students. Applications are processed on a rolling basis. Application fee: $30. Electronic applications accepted. *Expenses:* Tuition, state resident: full-time $6,827. Tuition, nonresident: full-time $21,951. Required fees: $999. *Financial support:* In 2006–07, 27 research assistantships with full tuition reimbursements (averaging $25,612 per year) were awarded; fellowships with full tuition reimbursements, traineeships and unspecified assistantships also available. Financial award application deadline: 3/1. *Faculty research:* Gene expression, metabolic regulation, structural biology, enzyme mechanism, membrane transporters. *Unit head:* Dr. James Flanegan, Director, 352-392-0688, E-mail: flanegan@ufl.edu. *Application contact:* Dr. Wayne McCormack, Program Director, 352-392-7413, Fax: 352-846-3466, E-mail: idp@ufl.edu.

University of Southern California, Graduate School, Viterbi School of Engineering, Department of Biomedical Engineering, Program in Medical Imaging and Imaging Informatics, Los Angeles, CA 90089. Offers MS. *Students:* 5 full-time (2 women), 7 part-time (1 woman); includes 6 minority (all Asian Americans or Pacific Islanders), 5 international. In 2006, 7 degrees awarded. *Degree requirements:* For master's, thesis. *Entrance requirements:* For master's, GRE General Test, GRE Subject Test. *Application deadline:* For fall admission, 12/1 priority date for domestic students. Application fee: $85. *Expenses:* Tuition: Full-time $33,314; part-time $1,121 per credit. Required fees: $522. Full-time tuition and fees vary according to program. *Financial support:* In 2006–07, research assistantships (averaging $18,500 per year), teaching assistantships (averaging $18,500 per year) were awarded. Financial award application deadline: 2/15.

Medical Physics

Cleveland State University, College of Graduate Studies, College of Science, Department of Physics, Cleveland, OH 44115. Offers applied optics (MS); condensed matter physics (MS); medical physics (MS). Part-time and evening/weekend programs available. *Faculty:* 5 full-time (1 woman), 3 part-time/adjunct (0 women). *Students:* 3 full-time (1 woman), 16 part-time (6 women); includes 4 minority (2 African Americans, 1 American Indian/Alaska Native, 1 Hispanic American), 1 international. Average age 31. 14 applicants, 43% accepted, 5 enrolled. In 2006, 3 degrees awarded. *Entrance requirements:* For master's, undergraduate degree in engineering, physics, chemistry or mathematics. Additional exam requirements/recommendations for international students: Required—TOEFL (minimum score 525 paper-based; 197 computer-based), GRE. *Application deadline:* For fall admission, 7/15 priority date for domestic and international students. Applications are processed on a rolling basis. Application fee: $30. Electronic applications accepted. *Financial support:* In 2006–07, 1 research assistantship with full and partial tuition reimbursement (averaging $5,666 per year) was awarded; fellowships with tuition reimbursements, teaching assistantships, tuition waivers (full) also available. *Faculty research:* Statistical physics, experimental solid-state physics, theoretical optics, macromolecular crystallography, experimental optics. Total annual research expenditures: $350,000. *Unit head:* Dr. Miron Kaufman, Chairperson, 216-687-2436, Fax: 216-523-7268, E-mail: m.kaufman@csuohio.edu. *Application contact:* Dr. James A. Lock, Director, 216-687-2420, Fax: 216-523-7268, E-mail: j.lock@csuohio.edu.

Columbia University, Fu Foundation School of Engineering and Applied Science, Department of Applied Physics and Applied Mathematics, New York, NY 10027. Offers applied mathematics (MS, PhD); applied physics (MS, Eng Sc D, PhD); applied physics and applied mathematics (Engr); materials science and engineering (MS, Eng Sc D, PhD); medical physics (MS). Part-time programs available. Postbaccalaureate distance learning degree programs offered (no on-campus study). *Faculty:* 19 full-time (1 woman), 13 part-time/adjunct (1 woman). *Students:* 95 full-time (24 women), 36 part-time (8 women); includes 14 minority (1 American Indian/Alaska Native, 10 Asian Americans or Pacific Islanders, 3 Hispanic Americans), 45 international. Average age 24. 300 applicants, 21% accepted, 34 enrolled. In 2006, 33 master's, 16 doctorates awarded. Terminal master's awarded for partial completion of doctoral program. *Degree requirements:* For master's, comprehensive exam; for doctorate, thesis/dissertation, qualifying exam. *Entrance requirements:* For master's and doctorate, GRE General Test, GRE Subject Test (strongly recommended). Additional exam requirements/recommendations for international students: Required—TOEFL. *Application deadline:* For fall admission, 12/15 priority date for domestic and international students; for spring admission, 10/1 priority date for domestic and international students. Applications are processed on a rolling basis. Application fee: $45. Electronic applications accepted. *Financial support:* In 2006–07, 5 fellowships with full tuition reimbursements (averaging $30,000 per year), 60 research assistantships with full tuition reimbursements (averaging $26,750 per year), 16 teaching assistantships with full tuition reimbursements (averaging $26,750 per year) were awarded; Federal Work-Study, scholarships/grants, and unspecified assistantships also available. Financial award application deadline: 12/15; financial award applicants required to submit FAFSA. *Faculty research:* Plasma physics, applied mathematics, solid-state and optical physics, laser physics, atmospheric, climate and earth science. *Unit head:* Dr. Irving P. Herman, Professor and Chairman, 212-854-4950, E-mail: seasinfo@apam@columbia.edu. *Application contact:* Ria Miranda, Department Administrator, 212-854-4458, Fax: 212-854-8257, E-mail: seasinfo.apam@columbia.edu.

Columbia University, Mailman School of Public Health, Division of Environmental Health Sciences, Program in Medical Physics/Health Physics, New York, NY 10027. Offers public health (MPH, Dr PH), including health, medical physics. Part-time programs available. *Degree requirements:* For doctorate, thesis/dissertation. *Entrance requirements:* For master's, GRE General Test, bachelor's degree in physics, engineering, or mathematics; for doctorate, GRE General Test, bachelor's degree in physics, engineering, or mathematics; MPH or equivalent (Dr PH). *Application deadline:* For spring admission, 10/1 for domestic students. Applications are processed on a rolling basis. Application fee: $60. *Financial support:* Career-related internships or fieldwork and Federal Work-Study available. Support available to part-time students. Financial award application deadline: 3/15; financial award applicants required to submit FAFSA. *Faculty research:* Health effects of radiation and other physical agents. *Unit head:* Dr. Cheng Shie Wuu, Professor of Clinical Radiation Oncology and Public Health, 212-305-3464, Fax: 212-305-4012.

Drexel University, College of Medicine, Biomedical Graduate Programs, Program in Radiation Oncology, Philadelphia, PA 19104-2875. Offers radiation (MS); radiation biology (MS); radiation physics (PhD); radiation science (PhD); radiopharmaceutical science (MS, PhD). Part-time programs available. Terminal master's awarded for partial completion of doctoral program. *Degree requirements:* For master's, thesis, comprehensive exam; for doctorate, one foreign language, thesis/dissertation, qualifying exam. *Entrance requirements:* For master's, GRE General Test, minimum GPA of 2.75; for doctorate, GRE General Test, minimum GPA of 3.0. Additional exam requirements/recommendations for international students: Required—TOEFL. Electronic applications accepted. *Faculty research:* Improved cancer therapy by linear accelerators and internal, sealed radiation sources; algorithms for improved superminicomputer-assisted radiation therapy simulation and tumor imaging; molecular and cellular mechanisms of radiation damage.

East Carolina University, Graduate School, Thomas Harriot College of Arts and Sciences, Department of Physics, Greenville, NC 27858-4353. Offers applied and biomedical physics (MS); medical physics (MS); physics (PhD). Part-time programs available. *Faculty:* 19 full-time (2 women). *Students:* 23 full-time (8 women), 14 part-time (1 woman); includes 2 minority (both African Americans), 9 international. Average age 30. 11 applicants, 36% accepted, 4 enrolled. In 2006, 8 degrees awarded. *Degree requirements:* For master's, one foreign language, comprehensive exam. *Entrance requirements:* For master's, GRE General Test. Additional exam requirements/recommendations for international students: Required—TOEFL. *Application deadline:* Applications are processed on a rolling basis. Application fee: $50. *Financial support:* Research assistantships with partial tuition reimbursements, teaching assistantships with partial tuition reimbursements, Federal Work-Study available. Support available to part-time students. Financial award application deadline: 6/1. *Unit head:* Dr. John Sutherland, Chair, 252-328-6737, Fax: 252-328-6314, E-mail: sutherlandj@ecu.edu. *Application contact:* Dean of Graduate School, 252-328-6012, Fax: 252-328-6071, E-mail: gradschool@ecu.edu.

Georgia Institute of Technology, Graduate Studies and Research, College of Engineering, George W. Woodruff School of Mechanical Engineering, Nuclear and Radiological Engineering and Medical Physics Programs, Atlanta, GA 30332-0001. Offers medical physics (MS); nuclear and radiological engineering (MSNE, PhD). Part-time programs available. Postbaccalaureate distance learning degree programs offered (no on-campus study). Terminal master's awarded for partial completion of doctoral program. *Degree requirements:* For master's, thesis optional; for doctorate, thesis/dissertation, comprehensive exam. *Entrance requirements:* For master's and doctorate, GRE General Test, minimum GPA of 3.0. Additional exam requirements/recommendations for international students: Required—TOEFL (minimum score 580 paper-based; 240 computer-based). *Faculty research:* Reactor physics, nuclear materials, plasma physics, radiation detection, radiological assessment.

Harvard University, Graduate School of Arts and Sciences, Department of Physics, Cambridge, MA 02138. Offers experimental physics (PhD); medical engineering/medical physics (PhD), including applied physics, engineering sciences, physics; theoretical physics (PhD). *Students:* 174. *Degree requirements:* For doctorate, thesis/dissertation, final exams, laboratory experience. *Entrance requirements:* For doctorate, GRE General Test, GRE Subject Test. Additional exam requirements/recommendations for international students: Required—TOEFL. *Application deadline:* For fall admission, 12/14 for domestic students. Application fee: $60. *Expenses:* Tuition: Full-time $30,275. Full-time tuition and fees vary according to program and student level. *Financial support:* Fellowships, research assistantships, teaching assistantships, career-related internships or fieldwork, Federal Work-Study, and institutionally sponsored loans available. Financial award application deadline: 12/30. *Faculty research:* Particle physics, condensed matter physics, atomic physics. *Unit head:* Sheila Ferguson, Administrator, 617-495-4327. *Application contact:* Office of Admissions and Financial Aid, 617-495-5315.

Harvard University, Harvard Medical School and Graduate School of Arts and Sciences, Division of Health Sciences and Technology and Department of Physics and School of Engineering and Applied Sciences, Program in Medical Engineering/Medical Physics, Cambridge, MA 02138. Offers medical engineering (PhD); medical engineering/medical physics (Sc D); medical physics (PhD). *Students:* 126 full-time (33 women); includes 45 minority (5 African Americans, 1 American Indian/Alaska Native, 31 Asian Americans or Pacific Islanders, 8 Hispanic Americans), 31 international. Average age 27. 294 applicants, 9% accepted, 20 enrolled. In 2006, 10 degrees awarded. *Degree requirements:* For doctorate, thesis/dissertation, oral and written qualifying exams. *Entrance requirements:* For doctorate, GRE (only if required by joint department), bachelor's degree in engineering or science. *Application deadline:* For fall admission, 12/15 for domestic and international students. Application fee: $70. *Expenses: Contact institution.* Full-time tuition and fees vary according to program and student level. *Financial support:* In 2006–07, 61 fellowships with full and partial tuition reimbursements (averaging $57,898 per year), 46 research assistantships with full tuition reimbursements (averaging $43,300 per year), 11 teaching assistantships with full tuition reimbursements (averaging $16,010 per year) were awarded; career-related internships or fieldwork, institutionally sponsored loans, traineeships, health care benefits, and unspecified assistantships also available. Financial award application deadline: 1/15; financial award applicants required to submit FAFSA. *Faculty research:* Regenerative biomedical technologies; biomedical imaging and optics; biophysics; systems physiology; bioinstrumentation; biomedical informatics/integrative genomics. *Unit head:* Dr. Martha Gray, Director, 617-253-2307. *Application contact:* Catherine Modica, Admissions Coordinator, 617-253-2307, Fax: 617-253-6692, E-mail: cmodica@mit.edu.

Massachusetts Institute of Technology, Whitaker College of Health Sciences and Technology, Harvard-MIT Division of Health Sciences and Technology, Medical Engineering/Medical Physics Program, Cambridge, MA 02139-4307. Offers medical engineering (PhD); medical engineering and medical physics (Sc D); medical physics (PhD). *Students:* 126 full-time (33 women); includes 45 minority (5 African Americans, 1 American Indian/Alaska Native, 31 Asian Americans or Pacific Islanders, 8 Hispanic Americans), 31 international. Average age 27. 294 applicants, 9% accepted, 20 enrolled. In 2006, 10 degrees awarded. *Degree requirements:* For doctorate, thesis/dissertation, oral and written departmental qualifying exams. *Entrance requirements:* For doctorate, GRE (only if reported by joint department), bachelor's degree in engineering or science. *Application deadline:* For fall admission, 12/15 for domestic and international students. Application fee: $70. Electronic applications accepted. *Expenses: Contact institution.* Part-time tuition and fees vary according to course load. *Financial support:* In 2006–07, 61 fellowships with full and partial tuition reimbursements (averaging $57,898 per year), 46 research assistantships with full and partial tuition reimbursements (averaging $43,300 per year), 11 teaching assistantships with full and partial tuition reimbursements (averaging $16,010 per year) were awarded; career-related internships or fieldwork, institutionally sponsored loans, traineeships, health care benefits, and unspecified assistantships also available. Financial award application deadline: 1/15. *Faculty research:* Regenerative biomedical technologies, biomedical imaging and optics, biophysics, systems physiology, bioinstrumentation, biomedical informatics/integrative genomics. *Unit head:* Dr. Martha L. Gray, Director, E-mail: mgray@mit.edu. *Application contact:* Catherine A. Modica, Admissions Coordinator, 617-253-2307, Fax: 617-253-6692, E-mail: cmodica@mit.edu.

McGill University, Faculty of Graduate and Postdoctoral Studies, Faculty of Medicine, Medical Radiation Physics Unit, Montréal, QC H3A 2T5, Canada. Offers M Sc, PhD. *Degree requirements:* For master's and doctorate, thesis/dissertation. *Entrance requirements:* For master's, B Sc in physics, minimum GPA of 3.0. Additional exam requirements/recommendations for international students: Required—TOEFL. *Faculty research:* Radiation dosimetry, biodegradable polymers, stereotactic radiosurgery, brachytherapy, functional MR brain imaging.

McMaster University, School of Graduate Studies, Faculty of Science, Department of Medical Physics and Applied Radiation Sciences, Hamilton, ON L8S 4M2, Canada. Offers health and radiation physics (M Sc); medical physics (M Sc, PhD). Part-time programs available. *Faculty:* 13 full-time, 7 part-time/adjunct. *Students:* 33 full-time, 6 part-time. 3 applicants, 0% accepted. *Degree requirements:* For master's, thesis or alternative. *Entrance requirements:* For master's, minimum B+ average. Additional exam requirements/recommendations for international students: Required—TOEFL (minimum score 550 paper-based; 213 computer-based). *Application deadline:* For fall admission, 3/31 priority date for domestic students. Applications are processed on a rolling basis. Application fee: $90. *Financial support:* In 2006–07, teaching assistantships (averaging $8,440 per year); scholarships/grants also available. *Faculty research:* Imaging, toxicology, dosimetry, body composition, medical lasers. Total annual research expenditures: $800,000. *Unit head:* Dr. Fiona McNeill, Chair, 905-525-9140 Ext. 26891, Fax: 905-522-5982, E-mail: fmcneill@mcmaster.ca. *Application contact:* Wendy Malarek, Administrator, 905-525-9140 Ext. 24182, Fax: 905-522-5982, E-mail: malarek@mcmaster.ca.

Oakland University, Graduate Study and Lifelong Learning, College of Arts and Sciences, Department of Physics, Rochester, MI 48309-4401. Offers medical physics (PhD); physics (MS). *Faculty:* 4 full-time (0 women). *Students:* 17 full-time (6 women), 6 part-time (5 women); includes 2 minority (both Asian Americans or Pacific Islanders), 9 international. Average age 33. 16 applicants, 88% accepted, 8 enrolled. In 2006, 1 degree awarded. *Degree requirements:* For doctorate, thesis/dissertation. *Entrance requirements:* For master's, minimum GPA of 3.0 for unconditional admission; for doctorate, GRE Subject Test, GRE General Test, minimum GPA of 3.0 for unconditional admission. Additional exam requirements/recommendations for international students: Required—TOEFL (minimum score 550 paper-based; 213 computer-based). *Application deadline:* For fall admission, 7/15 priority date for domestic students, 5/1 priority date for international students; for winter admission, 12/1 priority date for domestic students, 9/1 priority date for international students; for spring admission, 3/15 priority date for domestic students. Applications are processed on a rolling basis. Application fee: $35. Electronic applications accepted. *Expenses: Contact institution.* *Financial support:* Fellowships, career-related internships or fieldwork, Federal Work-Study, institutionally sponsored loans, and tuition waivers (full) available. Financial award application deadline: 3/1; financial award applicants required to submit FAFSA. *Faculty research:* Quantitative molecular imagings of articular cartilage, multifunctional ferrite-ferroelectric layered structures for microwave and millimeter wave devices, magnoelectric materials for antenna structures. *Unit head:* Dr. Andrei N. Slavin, Chair, 248-370-3416, Fax: 248-370-3401, E-mail: slavin@oakland.edu.

Rosalind Franklin University of Medicine and Science, College of Health Professions, Department of Medical Radiation Physics, North Chicago, IL 60064-3095. Offers MS, PhD. Terminal master's awarded for partial completion of doctoral program. *Degree requirements:* For doctorate, thesis/dissertation. *Entrance requirements:* For master's, GRE General Test; for doctorate, GRE General Test, MS in physics. Additional exam requirements/recommendations for international students: Required—TOEFL, TWE. Expenses: Contact institution.

Rush University, Graduate College, Division of Medical Physics, Chicago, IL 60612-3832. Offers MS, PhD. Terminal master's awarded for partial completion of doctoral program. *Degree requirements:* For master's, thesis, qualifying exam; for doctorate, thesis/dissertation, preliminary

and qualifying exams. *Entrance requirements:* For master's, GRE General Test, BS in physics or physical science; for doctorate, GRE General Test, GRE Subject Test. Additional exam requirements/recommendations for international students: Required—TOEFL. Electronic applications accepted. *Faculty research:* Radiation therapy treatment planning, dosimetry, diagnostic radiology and nuclear imaging.

Stony Brook University, State University of New York, Graduate School, College of Engineering and Applied Sciences, Department of Biomedical Engineering, Program in Medical Physics, Stony Brook, NY 11794. Offers PhD. *Expenses:* Tuition, state resident: full-time $6,900; part-time $288 per credit. Tuition, nonresident: full-time $10,920; part-time $455 per credit.

Announcement: In the treatment of diseases and the discovery of new cures and new methodology for diagnosis, physics goes hand-in-hand with medicine. This concentration, in conjunction with the biomedical engineering program, integrates these theories seamlessly. Students involved in study and research in this concentration are on the front line in the quest to advance human life.

See Close-Up on page 1761.

University of Alberta, Faculty of Graduate Studies and Research, Department of Physics, Edmonton, AB T6G 2E1, Canada. Offers astrophysics (M Sc, PhD); condensed matter (M Sc, PhD); geophysics (M Sc, PhD); medical physics (M Sc, PhD); subatomic physics (M Sc, PhD). *Faculty:* 36 full-time (3 women), 7 part-time/adjunct (0 women). *Students:* 56 full-time (6 women), 16 part-time (2 women), 25 international. 85 applicants, 35% accepted. In 2006, 7 master's, 10 doctorates awarded. *Degree requirements:* For master's and doctorate, thesis/dissertation. *Entrance requirements:* For master's and doctorate, minimum GPA of 7.0 on a 9.0 scale. Additional exam requirements/recommendations for international students: Required—TOEFL. *Application deadline:* For fall admission, 2/15 priority date for domestic students. Applications are processed on a rolling basis. *Financial support:* In 2006–07, 6 fellowships with partial tuition reimbursements, 40 teaching assistantships were awarded; research assistantships, career-related internships or fieldwork, institutionally sponsored loans, and scholarships/grants also available. Financial award application deadline: 2/15. *Faculty research:* Cosmology, astroparticle physics, high-intermediate energy, magnetism, superconductivity. Total annual research expenditures: $3.1 million. *Unit head:* Dr. R. Marchand, Associate Chair, 780-492-1072, E-mail: assoc-chair@phys.ualberta.ca. *Application contact:* Lynn Chandler, Program Advisor, 780-492-1072, Fax: 780-492-0714, E-mail: grad.program@phys.ualberta.ca.

University of California, Los Angeles, School of Medicine and Graduate Division, Graduate Programs in Medicine, Program in Biomedical Physics, Los Angeles, CA 90095. Offers MS, PhD. *Degree requirements:* For master's, comprehensive exam or thesis; for doctorate, thesis/dissertation, oral and written qualifying exams. *Entrance requirements:* For master's and doctorate, GRE General Test. Additional exam requirements/recommendations for international students: Required—TOEFL.

University of Central Arkansas, Graduate School, College of Health and Behavioral Sciences, Department of Health Sciences, Conway, AR 72035-0001. Offers health education (MS); health systems (MS). *Faculty:* 9 full-time (5 women), 1 part-time/adjunct (0 women). *Students:* 7 full-time (5 women), 15 part-time (10 women); includes 8 minority (5 African Americans, 1 American Indian/Alaska Native, 2 Asian Americans or Pacific Islanders), 1 international. 7 applicants, 100% accepted, 7 enrolled. In 2006, 7 degrees awarded. *Degree requirements:* For master's, thesis optional. *Entrance requirements:* For master's, GRE General Test, minimum GPA of 2.7. Additional exam requirements/recommendations for international students: Required—TOEFL (minimum score 550 paper-based; 213 computer-based). *Application deadline:* For fall admission, 3/1 priority date for domestic students; for spring admission, 10/1 for domestic students. Applications are processed on a rolling basis. Application fee: $25 ($40 for international students). *Expenses:* Tuition, state resident: full-time $4,194; part-time $233 per semester. Tuition, nonresident: full-time $5,963; part-time $429 per semester. International tuition: $6,162 full-time. Required fees: $65; $23 per semester. One-time fee: $65 part-time. *Financial support:* In 2006–07, 4 research assistantships (averaging $5,700 per year) were awarded; Federal Work-Study, scholarships/grants, tuition waivers (partial), and unspecified assistantships also available. Financial award application deadline: 2/15; financial award applicants required to submit FAFSA. *Unit head:* Emogene Fox, Chairperson, 501-450-5508, Fax: 501-450-5515, E-mail: emogenef@uca.edu. *Application contact:* Nanette Fitzhugh, Administrative Assistant, 501-450-5063, Fax: 501-450-5678, E-mail: fitzhugh@uca.edu.

University of Chicago, Division of the Biological Sciences and Pritzker School of Medicine, Graduate Program in Medical Physics, Chicago, IL 60637-1513. Offers PhD. *Faculty:* 28 full-time (2 women), 2 part-time/adjunct (0 women). *Students:* 29 full-time (7 women); includes 5 minority (4 Asian Americans or Pacific Islanders, 1 Hispanic American), 15 international. Average age 29. 32 applicants, 22% accepted, 3 enrolled. In 2006, 5 degrees awarded. *Degree requirements:* For doctorate, thesis/dissertation, comprehensive qualifying exams. *Entrance requirements:* For doctorate, GRE General Test, GRE Subject Test (physics). Additional exam requirements/recommendations for international students: Required—TOEFL. *Application deadline:* For fall admission, 12/28 priority date for domestic and international students. Application fee: $55. Electronic applications accepted. *Expenses:* Tuition: Full-time $34,920. Required fees: $612. One-time fee: $35 full-time. Full-time tuition and fees vary according to course load, degree level and program. *Financial support:* In 2006–07, 29 students received support, including fellowships with full tuition reimbursements available (averaging $26,893 per year), research assistantships with full tuition reimbursements available (averaging $26,893 per year); institutionally sponsored loans, scholarships/grants, traineeships, and health care benefits also available. Financial award applicants required to submit FAFSA. *Faculty research:* Medical imaging, radiation therapy, computer vision, computer-aided diagnosis. Total annual research expenditures: $5 million. *Unit head:* Dr. Maryellen L. Giger, Chair, 773-702-6778, Fax: 773-702-0371, E-mail: m-giger@uchicago.edu. *Application contact:* Tarnisha Smith, Student Affairs Administrator, 773-702-6154, Fax: 773-702-0371, E-mail: tsmith@radiology.bsd.uchicago.edu.

See Close-Up on page 1763.

University of Cincinnati, Division of Research and Advanced Studies, College of Medicine, Graduate Programs in Biomedical Sciences, Department of Radiological Sciences, Cincinnati, OH 45267. Offers medical physics (MS). Part-time programs available. *Degree requirements:* For master's, project. *Entrance requirements:* For master's, GRE General Test. Additional exam requirements/recommendations for international students: Required—TOEFL (minimum score 575 paper-based). Electronic applications accepted. *Faculty research:* Radiation oncology, radiologic imaging, dosimetry, radiation biology, radiation therapy.

University of Colorado at Boulder, Graduate School, College of Arts and Sciences, Department of Physics, Boulder, CO 80309. Offers chemical physics (PhD); geophysics (PhD); liquid crystal science and technology (PhD); mathematical physics (PhD); medical physics (PhD); optical sciences and engineering (PhD); physics (MS, PhD). *Faculty:* 41 full-time (4 women). *Students:* 175 full-time (31 women), 43 part-time (9 women); includes 11 minority (2 African Americans, 2 American Indian/Alaska Native, 5 Asian Americans or Pacific Islanders, 2 Hispanic Americans), 61 international. Average age 27. 45 applicants, 100% accepted. In 2006, 10 master's, 18 doctorates awarded. Terminal master's awarded for partial completion of doctoral program. *Degree requirements:* For master's, thesis or alternative, comprehensive exam; for doctorate, thesis/dissertation, comprehensive exam. *Entrance requirements:* For master's and doctorate, GRE General Test, GRE Subject Test, minimum undergraduate GPA of 3.0. Additional exam requirements/recommendations for international students: Required—TOEFL. *Application deadline:* For fall admission, 1/15 priority date for domestic students, 1/15 for international students. Applications are processed on a rolling basis. Application fee: $50 ($60 for international students). Electronic applications accepted. *Financial support:* In 2006–07, 49 fellowships with full tuition reimbursements (averaging $11,469 per year), 142 research assistantships with full tuition reimbursements (averaging $16,064 per year), 39 teaching

Medical Physics

University of Colorado at Boulder (continued)
assistantships with full tuition reimbursements (averaging $13,569 per year) were awarded; scholarships/grants also available. Financial award application deadline: 1/15. *Faculty research:* Atomic and molecular physics, nuclear physics, condensed matter, elementary particle physics, laser or optical physics, plasma physics, geophysics, OSEP, astrophysics and chemical physics. Total annual research expenditures: $25.2 million. *Unit head:* John Cumalat, Chair, 303-492-6952, Fax: 303-492-3352, E-mail: jcumalat@pizero.colorado.edu. *Application contact:* Graduate Program Assistant, 303-492-6954, Fax: 303-492-3352, E-mail: phys@colorado.edu.

University of Kentucky, Graduate School, College of Health Sciences, Program in Radiation Sciences, Lexington, KY 40506-0032. Offers health physics (MSHP); radiological medical physics (MSRMP). Offered in cooperation with Graduate Programs in Medicine. Part-time programs available. *Faculty:* 3 full-time (0 women). *Students:* 14 full-time (7 women), 3 part-time (all women); includes 1 minority (Asian American or Pacific Islander) Average age 28. 49 applicants, 24% accepted, 8 enrolled. In 2006, 8 degrees awarded. *Degree requirements:* For master's, thesis, comprehensive exam. *Entrance requirements:* For master's, GRE General Test, minimum undergraduate GPA of 2.75. Additional exam requirements/recommendations for international students: Required—TOEFL (minimum score 550 paper-based; 213 computer-based). *Application deadline:* For fall admission, 7/17 priority date for domestic students, 2/1 priority date for international students; for spring admission, 12/13 priority date for domestic students, 6/15 priority date for international students. Application fee: $40 ($55 for international students). Electronic applications accepted. *Expenses:* Tuition, state resident: full-time $7,670; part-time $401 per credit hour. Tuition, nonresident: full-time $16,158; part-time $873 per credit hour. *Financial support:* Fellowships with full tuition reimbursements, research assistantships with full tuition reimbursements, teaching assistantships with full tuition reimbursements, Federal Work-Study, institutionally sponsored loans, scholarships/grants, traineeships, health care benefits, tuition waivers (partial), and unspecified assistantships available. Support available to part-time students. Financial award application deadline: 3/15; financial award applicants required to submit FAFSA. *Faculty research:* Dosimetry, manpower studies, diagnostic imaging physics, shielding. *Unit head:* Dr. Ralph Christensen, Director of Graduate Studies, 859-323-1100, Fax: 859-257-2454, E-mail: rcchri1@pop.uky.edu. *Application contact:* Dr. Brian Jackson, Senior Associate Dean, 859-257-4667, Fax: 859-257-4676, E-mail: brian.jackson@uky.edu.

University of Massachusetts Worcester, Graduate School of Biomedical Sciences, Program in Biomedical Engineering and Medical Physics, Worcester, MA 01655-0115. Offers PhD. *Faculty:* 11 full-time (2 women). *Degree requirements:* For doctorate, thesis/dissertation. *Entrance requirements:* For doctorate, GRE General Test. Additional exam requirements/recommendations for international students: Required—TOEFL (minimum score 600 paper-based; 250 computer-based). *Application deadline:* For fall admission, 12/15 for domestic and international students. Applications are processed on a rolling basis. Application fee: $25 ($50 for international students). *Expenses:* Tuition, state resident: full-time $2,640. Tuition, nonresident: full-time $9,856. Required fees: $3,942. *Financial support:* In 2006–07, research assistantships with full tuition reimbursements (averaging $25,235 per year); unspecified assistantships also available. *Faculty research:* Tissue engineering, imaging, bioinstrumentation. *Unit head:* Dr. Peter Grigg, Director, 508-856-2457.

University of Minnesota, Twin Cities Campus, Graduate School, Program in Biophysical Sciences and Medical Physics, Minneapolis, MN 55455-0213. Offers MS, PhD. Part-time programs available. *Degree requirements:* For master's, research paper, oral exam, thesis optional; for doctorate, thesis/dissertation, oral/written preliminary exam, oral final exam. *Expenses:* Tuition, state resident: full-time $9,302; part-time $775 per credit. Tuition, nonresident: full-time $16,400; part-time $1,367 per credit. Full-time tuition and fees vary according to class time, course load, program, reciprocity agreements and student level. *Faculty research:* Theoretical biophysics, radiological physics, cellular and molecular biophysics.

Announcement: This interdisciplinary program provides research training and experience in biophysics, medical imaging, magnetic resonance imaging and spectroscopy, radiobiology, and radiation therapy physics. Thirty-one faculty members from 11 departments provide diverse opportunities for multidisciplinary research. A strong undergraduate physics background is desirable. Limited financial aid is available.

See Close-Up on page 1765.

University of Missouri–Columbia, Graduate School, College of Engineering, Nuclear Science and Engineering Institute, Columbia, MO 65211. Offers nuclear power engineering (MS, PhD), including health physics (MS), medical physics (MS), nuclear power engineering (MS). *Faculty:* 5 full-time (0 women). *Students:* 47 full-time (10 women), 6 part-time (2 women); includes 12 minority (1 African American, 4 Asian Americans or Pacific Islanders, 7 Hispanic Americans), 13 international. In 2006, 3 master's, 5 doctorates awarded. *Degree requirements:* For master's, research project; for doctorate, thesis/dissertation. *Entrance requirements:* For master's and doctorate, GRE General Test. Additional exam requirements/recommendations for international students: Required—TOEFL (minimum score 500 paper-based; 173 computer-based). *Application deadline:* For fall admission, 3/15 priority date for domestic students. Application fee: $45 ($60 for international students). *Financial support:* Fellowships, research assistantships, teaching assistantships, institutionally sponsored loans available. *Unit head:* Dr. Tushar Ghosh, Director of Graduate Studies, 573-882-9736, E-mail: ghosht@missouri.edu.

University of Oklahoma Health Sciences Center, College of Medicine and Graduate College, Graduate Programs in Medicine, Department of Radiological Sciences, Oklahoma City, OK 73190. Offers medical radiation physics (MS, PhD), including diagnostic radiology, nuclear medicine, radiation therapy, ultrasound. Part-time programs available. Terminal master's awarded for partial completion of doctoral program. *Degree requirements:* For master's and doctorate, thesis/dissertation. *Entrance requirements:* For master's, GRE General Test; for doctorate, GRE General Test, 3 letters of recommendation. Additional exam requirements/recommendations for international students: Required—TOEFL. *Faculty research:* Monte Carlo applications in radiation therapy, observer performed studies in diagnostic radiology, error analysis in gated cardiac nuclear medicine studies, nuclear medicine absorbed fraction determinations.

University of Pennsylvania, School of Arts and Sciences, Graduate Group in Physics and Astronomy, Philadelphia, PA 19104. Offers medical physics (MS); physics (PhD). Part-time programs available. *Degree requirements:* For doctorate, thesis/dissertation, oral, preliminary, and final exams. *Entrance requirements:* For doctorate, GRE General Test, GRE Subject Test (recommended). Additional exam requirements/recommendations for international students: Required—TOEFL. Electronic applications accepted. *Faculty research:* Astrophysics, condensed matter experiment, condensed matter theory, particle experiment, particle theory.

The University of Texas Health Science Center at Houston, Graduate School of Biomedical Sciences, Program in Medical Physics, Houston, TX 77225-0036. Offers MS, PhD, MD/PhD. *Faculty:* 43 full-time (3 women). *Students:* 34 full-time (11 women); includes 3 minority (1 African American, 1 Asian American or Pacific Islander, 1 Hispanic American), 6 international. Average age 25. 70 applicants, 10% accepted, 5 enrolled. In 2006, 7 master's, 2 doctorates awarded. *Degree requirements:* For master's and doctorate, thesis/dissertation. *Entrance requirements:* For master's and doctorate, GRE General Test. Additional exam requirements/recommendations for international students: Required—TOEFL, TWE. *Application deadline:* For fall admission, 1/15 priority date for domestic students; for spring admission, 11/1 for domestic students. Applications are processed on a rolling basis. Application fee: $10. Electronic applications accepted. *Financial support:* Fellowships with full tuition reimbursements, research assistantships with full tuition reimbursements, teaching assistantships, institutionally sponsored loans, scholarships/grants, and health care benefits available. Financial award application deadline: 1/15. *Faculty research:* Image-guided therapy (radiation, surgical, and thermal); motion mitigation in radiation therapy; functional imaging applications to treatment planning and early assessment of therapy; photon, proton, and brachytherapy dosimetry and treatment plan optimization; intensity modulated radiation therapy (IMRT) and stereotactic radiosurgery. *Unit head:* Dr. Edward F. Jackson, Director, 713-745-0559, Fax: 713-745-0581, E-mail: ejackson@mdanderson.org. *Application contact:* Dr. Victoria P. Knutson, Assistant Dean of Admissions, 713-500-9860, Fax: 713-500-9877, E-mail: victoria.p.knutson@uth.tmc.edu.

The University of Texas Health Science Center at San Antonio, Graduate School of Biomedical Sciences, Radiological Sciences Graduate Program, San Antonio, TX 78229-3900. Offers MS, PhD. *Faculty:* 35 full-time (7 women), 32 part-time/adjunct (5 women). *Students:* 51 full-time (20 women), 5 part-time (1 woman); includes 9 minority (1 African American, 2 Asian Americans or Pacific Islanders, 6 Hispanic Americans), 24 international. 34 applicants, 38% accepted, 8 enrolled. In 2006, 2 master's, 5 doctorates awarded. *Median time to degree:* Of those who began their doctoral program in fall 1998, 22% received their degree in 8 years or less. *Entrance requirements:* Additional exam requirements/recommendations for international students: Required—TOEFL (minimum score 550 paper-based; 213 computer-based). *Application deadline:* For fall admission, 3/1 for domestic and international students. Applications are processed on a rolling basis. Application fee: $10. Electronic applications accepted. *Expenses:* Tuition, state resident: part-time $50 per credit hour. Tuition, nonresident: part-time $325 per credit hour. Required fees: $7.5 per credit hour. $155 per term. *Financial support:* In 2006–07, teaching assistantships (averaging $24,783 per year). *Unit head:* Dr. Geoffrey Clarke, Chair, Committee on Graduate Studies, 210-567-5550, Fax: 210-567-5541, E-mail: clarkeg@uthscsa.edu. *Application contact:* Loretta M. Edwards, Academic Coordinator, 210-567-5550, Fax: 210-567-5541, E-mail: edwards@uthscsa.edu.

The University of Toledo, College of Graduate Studies, College of Medicine, Department of Radiation Oncology, Program in Medical Physics, Toledo, OH 43606-3390. Offers MS. *Application contact:* Joann Braatz, Secretary, 419-383-4117, Fax: 419-383-6140, E-mail: mcogradschool@mco.edu.

University of Victoria, Faculty of Graduate Studies, Faculty of Science, Department of Physics and Astronomy, Victoria, BC V8W 2Y2, Canada. Offers astronomy and astrophysics (M Sc, PhD); condensed matter physics (M Sc, PhD); experimental particle physics (M Sc, PhD); medical physics (M Sc, PhD); ocean physics (PhD); ocean physics and geophysics (M Sc); theoretical physics (M Sc, PhD). *Degree requirements:* For master's, thesis, registration; for doctorate, thesis/dissertation, candidacy exam, comprehensive exam, registration. *Entrance requirements:* For master's and doctorate, GRE. Additional exam requirements/recommendations for international students: Required—TOEFL (minimum score 575 paper-based; 233 computer-based), IELTS (minimum score 7). Electronic applications accepted. *Faculty research:* Old stellar populations; observational cosmology and large scale structure; cp violation; atlas.

University of Wisconsin–Madison, School of Medicine and Public Health and Graduate School, Graduate Programs in Medicine, Department of Medical Physics, Madison, WI 53706-1380. Offers health physics (MS); medical physics (MS, PhD). Part-time programs available. *Faculty:* 26 full-time (1 woman), 12 part-time/adjunct (0 women). *Students:* 112 full-time (30 women); includes 8 minority (1 African American, 3 Asian Americans or Pacific Islanders, 4 Hispanic Americans), 33 international. Average age 27. 164 applicants, 23% accepted, 21 enrolled. In 2006, 26 master's, 10 doctorates awarded. Terminal master's awarded for partial completion of doctoral program. *Median time to degree:* Of those who began their doctoral program in fall 1998, 100% received their degree in 8 years or less. *Degree requirements:* For master's, comprehensive exam, registration; for doctorate, thesis/dissertation, comprehensive exam, registration. *Entrance requirements:* For master's and doctorate, GRE General Test, GRE Subject Test (physics), minimum GPA of 3.0. Additional exam requirements/recommendations for international students: Required—TOEFL. *Application deadline:* For fall admission, 1/1 priority date for domestic students, 12/15 for international students. Application fee: $45. Electronic applications accepted. *Financial support:* In 2006–07, 92 students received support, including 4 fellowships with full tuition reimbursements available (averaging $18,480 per year), 84 research assistantships with full tuition reimbursements available (averaging $18,480 per year), 4 teaching assistantships with full tuition reimbursements available (averaging $1,875 per year); traineeships also available. Financial award application deadline: 12/15. *Faculty research:* Biomagnetism: imaging and physiology, medical imaging processing, radiation therapy and radiation physics. Total annual research expenditures: $4.5 million. *Unit head:* Dr. James A. Zagzebski, Chair, 608-262-2171, Fax: 608-262-2413, E-mail: jazagzeb@wisc.edu. *Application contact:* Debra A. Torgerson, Graduate Coordinator, 608-265-6504, Fax: 608-262-2413, E-mail: datorger@wisc.edu.

Vanderbilt University, School of Medicine, Program in Medical Physics, Nashville, TN 37240-1001. Offers MS. Part-time programs available. *Faculty:* 9 full-time (0 women), 3 part-time/adjunct (1 woman). *Students:* 20. 80 applicants, 15% accepted, 10 enrolled. In 2006, 8 degrees awarded. *Entrance requirements:* For master's, GRE General Test. Additional exam requirements/recommendations for international students: Required—TOEFL. *Application deadline:* For fall admission, 1/31 for domestic and international students. Application fee: $40. Electronic applications accepted. *Expenses:* Tuition: Full-time $24,462. Required fees: $2,515. One-time fee: $30 full-time. Full-time tuition and fees vary according to course load, degree level and program. *Financial support:* In 2006–07, 16 students received support. Institutionally sponsored loans and tuition waivers (partial) available. *Faculty research:* MRI Imaging, PET Imaging, Nuclear Medicine Dosimetry, Monte Carlo Dosimetry Protons. *Unit head:* Charles W. Coffey, Director, 615-322-2555, E-mail: charles.w.coffey@vanderbilt.edu. *Application contact:* Volker E. Oberacker, Director of Graduate Studies, 615-322-2774, Fax: 615-343-7263, E-mail: volker.e.oberacker@vanderbilt.edu.

Virginia Commonwealth University, Graduate School, College of Humanities and Sciences, Department of Physics, Richmond, VA 23284-9005. Offers applied physics (MS); medical physics (MS, PhD); physics (MS). Part-time programs available. *Faculty:* 8 full-time (3 women). *Students:* 21 full-time (5 women), 3 part-time; includes 1 minority (African American), 5 international. 38 applicants, 39% accepted. In 2006, 5 degrees awarded. *Degree requirements:* For master's, thesis optional. *Entrance requirements:* For master's, GRE. *Application deadline:* For fall admission, 8/1 for domestic students; for spring admission, 12/1 for domestic students. Applications are processed on a rolling basis. Application fee: $50. *Financial support:* Fellowships, teaching assistantships, Federal Work-Study, institutionally sponsored loans, and tuition waivers (full and partial) available. Support available to part-time students. *Faculty research:* Condensed-matter theory and experimentation, electronic instrumentation, relativity. *Unit head:* Dr. Robert H. Gowdy, Chair, 804-828-1821, Fax: 804-828-7073, E-mail: rhgowdy@vcu.edu. *Application contact:* Dr. Alison Baski, Graduate Program Director, 804-828-8295, Fax: 804-828-7073, E-mail: aabaski@vcu.edu.

See Close-Up on page 1767.

Wayne State University, School of Medicine, Graduate Programs in Medicine, Department of Radiation Oncology, Detroit, MI 48202. Offers medical physics (PhD); radiological physics (MS). Part-time and evening/weekend programs available. *Faculty:* 14 full-time (0 women), 2 part-time/adjunct (0 women). *Students:* 25 applicants, 52% accepted, 10 enrolled. In 2006, 12 degrees awarded. Terminal master's awarded for partial completion of doctoral program. *Degree requirements:* For master's, thesis, essay, exit exam; for doctorate, thesis/dissertation, qualifying exam. *Entrance requirements:* For master's, GRE General Test, BS in physics or related area; for doctorate, GRE General Test, GRE Subject Test, BS in physics or related area. Additional exam requirements/recommendations for international students: Required—TOEFL (minimum score 550 paper-based; 213 computer-based); Recommended—TWE (minimum score 6). *Application deadline:* For fall admission, 1/15 for domestic students, 6/1 for international students; for winter admission, 10/1 for international students; for spring admission, 2/1 for international students. Applications are processed on a rolling basis. Application fee: $30 ($50 for international students). Electronic applications accepted. *Financial support:* In 2006–07, 1 fellowship (averaging $38,000 per year), 2 research assistantships (averaging $20,175 per year) were awarded; teaching assistantships, career-related internships or fieldwork also available. Support available to part-time students. Financial award application deadline: 1/15. *Faculty research:* Radiotherapy physics, hyperthermia, magnetic resonance imaging and spectroscopy, clinical ultrasound, x-ray physics. Total annual research expenditures: $474,509. *Unit head:* Andrew Turrisi, Chair, 313-966-2774, Fax: 313-745-2314, E-mail: ar9642@ wayne.edu. *Application contact:* Michael Joiner, Professor, 313-745-2489, E-mail: joinerm@ kci.wayne.edu.

Wayne State University, School of Medicine, Graduate Programs in Medicine, Department of Radiology, Detroit, MI 48202. Offers medical physics (PhD); radiological physics (MS). Part-time and evening/weekend programs available. *Faculty:* 4 full-time (0 women), 1 part-time/ adjunct (0 women). *Students:* 27 full-time (8 women), 4 part-time (2 women); includes 4 minority (all Asian Americans or Pacific Islanders), 12 international. Average age 31. 21 applicants, 86% accepted, 6 enrolled. In 2006, 12 degrees awarded. *Degree requirements:* For master's, essay, exam; for doctorate, thesis/dissertation. *Entrance requirements:* For master's, GRE General Test, BS in physics or related area; for doctorate, GRE. Additional exam requirements/recommendations for international students: Required—TOEFL (minimum score 550 paper-based; 213 computer-based); Recommended—TWE (minimum score 6). *Application deadline:* For fall admission, 4/1 for domestic students, 6/1 for international students; for winter admission, 10/1 for international students; for spring admission, 2/1 for international students. Applications are processed on a rolling basis. Application fee: $30 ($50 for international students). Electronic applications accepted. *Financial support:* In 2006–07, 1 fellow-ship with tuition reimbursement (averaging $38,760 per year), 3 research assistantships with tuition reimbursements (averaging $20,200 per year) were awarded; teaching assistantships, career-related internships or fieldwork also available. Support available to part-time students. Financial award application deadline: 3/1. *Faculty research:* Radiotherapy and imaging physics, hyperthermia, magnetic resonance imaging and spectroscopy, clinical ultrasound, lasers in medicine. Total annual research expenditures: $48,000. *Unit head:* Wilbur Smith, Chair, 313-745-3430, Fax: 313-577-8600, E-mail: aj0262@wayne.edu. *Application contact:* Jay Burmeister, Graduate Director, 313-745-2483, E-mail: burmeist@med.wayne.edu.

Wright State University, School of Graduate Studies, College of Science and Mathematics, Department of Physics, Program in Physics, Dayton, OH 45435. Offers geophysics (MS); medical physics (MS). Part-time and evening/weekend programs available. *Students:* 4 full-time (0 women), 2 part-time; includes 1 minority (African American) Average age 34. 3 applicants, 100% accepted. *Degree requirements:* For master's, thesis. *Entrance requirements:* Additional exam requirements/recommendations for international students: Required—TOEFL. *Application deadline:* For fall admission, 3/1 priority date for domestic students. Applications are processed on a rolling basis. Application fee: $25. *Financial support:* Fellowships, research assistantships, teaching assistantships, Federal Work-Study, institutionally sponsored loans, and tuition waivers (full and partial) available. Support available to part-time students. Financial award application deadline: 3/1; financial award applicants required to submit FAFSA. *Faculty research:* Solid-state physics, optics, geophysics.

STATE UNIVERSITY OF NEW YORK

STONY BROOK

THE GRADUATE SCHOOL

STONY BROOK UNIVERSITY, STATE UNIVERSITY OF NEW YORK

Department of Biomedical Engineering
Programs in Medical Physics

Programs of Study

In conjunction with the School of Medicine, the Department of Biomedical Engineering offers both the Master of Science in biomedical engineering (BME) with a concentration in medical physics and the Ph.D. in biomedical engineering with a concentration in medical physics.

Thirty graduate credits are required to earn the Master of Science in BME/medical physics. Thirteen to 17 credits must consist of the six core BME courses, including four pertaining to medical physics. The student has the option of earning the Master of Science degree in BME on either a thesis or nonthesis track. If nonthesis, the student undertakes elective graduate course work to complete the 30 credits. In the thesis option, the student must complete at least 6 credits of thesis research and submit and defend a written thesis. An overall grade point average of at least 3.0 out of 4.0 must be maintained.

A minimum of 15 graduate credits beyond the master's in BME level are required for completion of the Doctor of Philosophy degree in BME/medical physics. There are no course requirements per se, though certain courses may be required to fill any gaps in the student's knowledge. Following completion of a qualifying exam, an independent basic research program is undertaken. One semester of teaching practicum must be satisfactorily performed. Completion of this research program culminates in the submission and oral defense of a dissertation. The University requires at least two consecutive semesters of full-time graduate study. All requirements for the Ph.D. must be completed within seven years after completing 24 credits of graduate study.

Research Facilities

Ongoing biomedical research and development, combined with exceptional facilities at the University and Brookhaven National Laboratories, have helped distinguish Stony Brook as a superb resource for education and research in both the engineering and health sciences. Stony Brook not only offers some of the best facilities in the field, but also provides students with exceptional access to them. The U.S. Department of Energy's Brookhaven National Laboratory creates and operates major facilities available to university, industrial, and government personnel for basic and applied research in physical, biomedical, and environmental sciences and in selected energy technologies. The Center for Biotechnology was established in 1983 as a cooperative research and development partnership between universities, private industry, and New York State. Its goal has been to capitalize on the resources of New York's medical biotechnology research for the purpose of fueling economic development in New York State. The University also houses the Magnetic Resonance Research Laboratory. Several other laboratories involved in medical imaging, polymer structure, musculoskeletal, and other research are available.

Financial Aid

Fellowship stipends and tuition waivers are available for select students. Distribution of these awards is based on GRE test scores, undergraduate performance, professional experience, and research/career objectives as outlined in a personal statement. Inquiries for graduate information, applications, and catalogs are welcomed. Financial aid is also available in the form of research assistantships. The majority of students are supported by assistantships (which include health insurance coverage) offered both by the Department of Biomedical Engineering and by individual faculty members' research grants. Student loans are also available.

Cost of Study

In 2006–07, full-time tuition at 12 credits for entering in-state residents was $3450 per semester, while out-of-state residents and international students paid $5460. Additional fees for each semester, including (but not limited to) the infirmary, activity, technology, and transportation fee, amount to about $430. International students also pay a service fee of $35 per semester and an orientation fee of $50. Fees for the mandatory Student Health Insurance Plan vary depending on citizenship and employment status.

Living and Housing Costs

For 2006–07, Stony Brook calculated the cost of education excluding tuition, fees, and insurance at $13,520 per year. On-campus apartments range in cost from approximately $316 per month to approximately $1456 per month, depending on the size of the unit and the number of students sharing the space. Off-campus housing options include rooms, houses, and apartments that can be rented from $350 to $2500 per month. Costs including books, food, and transportation may vary depending on academic program and/or personal circumstances.

Location

Stony Brook's campus is approximately 50 miles east of Manhattan on the north shore of Long Island. The cultural offerings of New York City and Suffolk County's countryside and seashore are conveniently located nearby. Cold Spring Harbor Laboratory and Brookhaven National Laboratory are easily accessible from, and have close relationships with, the University.

The University

The University, established in 1957, achieved national stature within a generation. Founded at Oyster Bay, Long Island, the school moved to its present location in 1962. Stony Brook has grown to encompass more than 110 buildings on 1,100 acres. There are more than 1,570 faculty members, and the annual budget is more than $805 million. The Graduate Student Organization oversees the spending of the student activity fee for graduate student campus events. International students find the additional four-week Summer Institute in American Living very helpful. The Intensive English Center offers classes in English as a second language. The Career Development Office assists with career planning and has information on permanent full-time employment. Disabled Student Services has a Resource Center that offers placement testing, tutoring, vocational assessment, and psychological counseling. The Counseling Center provides individual, group, family, and marital counseling and psychotherapy. Day-care services are provided in four on-campus facilities. The Writing Center offers tutoring in all phases of writing.

Applying

Certain minimum entrance requirements are set by the State University of New York in order for applicants to be admitted to the Graduate School to pursue graduate studies in biomedical engineering. To be considered for admission, all students must complete and submit an online application or an official graduate application form downloaded from the Web, a letter of introduction describing the student's educational and career goals, three letters of recommendation, and two official copies of all previous college transcripts. Transcripts of both undergraduate and graduate work must be submitted. If a student attended a junior college and these credits are not listed on the senior college transcript with grades, a separate junior college transcript is required. If transcripts are in a foreign language, certified English translations are required in addition to the original documents. Scores from the Graduate Record Examinations (GRE) General Test are also required; some programs also require the advanced test. To be admitted to the Graduate School, an applicant must have the preparation and ability that, in the judgment of the program and the Graduate School, are sufficient to enable him or her to progress satisfactorily in a degree or certificate program. An equivalent to a United States bachelor's degree is required, with a minimum overall grade point average (GPA) of 2.75 on a 4.0 scale; the student must present evidence that such a degree will be awarded by the time he or she begins graduate work. Admission into the degree-granting programs in biomedical engineering typically requires a GPA considerably higher than the minimum required by the Graduate School itself.

Correspondence and Information

Anne Marie Dusatko, Administrative Secretary
Department of Biomedical Engineering
HSC T18, Rm. 030
Stony Brook University, State University of New York
Stony Brook, New York 11794-8181

Phone: 631-444-2303
Fax: 631-444-6646
E-mail: ann.dusatko@sunysb.edu
Web site: http://bme.sunysb.edu/bme/grad/degree.html

Stony Brook University, State University of New York

THE FACULTY AND THEIR RESEARCH

Helen Benveniste, Ph.D. Exploring, characterizing, and understanding diagnostic MR contrast parameters suitable to visualize neural pathology.

Terry Button, Ph.D. Radiology, imaging modulation.

F. Avraham Dilmanian, Ph.D. Radiation therapy and medical imaging.

Yu-Shin Ding, Ph.D. Development of new methodologies to synthesize short half-lived radiopharmaceuticals and applying them towards investigation of biochemical transformations.

Joanna Fowler, Ph.D. Nuclear medicine, biochemical effects of drugs on the brain.

James W. Goldfarb, Ph.D. Application of magnetic resonance imaging (MRI) to the cardiovascular system, particularly in the area of myocardial function and blood vessels.

Rita Goldstein, Ph.D. Neuroimaging, cognitive neuroscience, neurobiological changes in brain chemistry.

Wei Huang, Ph.D. Magnetic resonance spectroscopy.

Chris Jacobsen, Ph.D. High-resolution X-ray imaging.

Kathryn Kolsky, Ph.D. Development and production of radioisotopes using the BLIP facility, a high-energy charged particle accelerator.

Jerome Z. Liang, Ph.D. Medical imaging hardware.

Jean Logan, Ph.D. Kinetic modeling of data from PET experiments.

Lisa Miller, Ph.D. Study of chemical makeup of tissue in disease, using high-resolution infrared and X-ray imaging and Brookhaven National Synchrotron Light Source.

Michiko Miura, Ph.D. PET, SPECT, and MRI of drug delivery processes.

Klaus Mueller, Ph.D. Computer graphics, visualization, medical imaging.

Nand Relan, Ph.D. Use of radionuclides for medical imaging.

Nathaniel Reicheck, M.D. Cardiac MRI, cardiac mechanics and remodeling.

David J. Schlyer, Ph.D. Positron emission tomography.

Peter K. Thanos, Ph.D. Gene therapy and dopaminergic mechanisms of alcohol and drug abuse.

Paul Vaska, Ph.D. All aspects of advancing the instrumentation for positron emission tomography.

Mark Wagshul, Ph.D. Utilizing MRI techniques for better understanding, diagnosing, and treatment of disease.

Yi Wang, Ph.D. Tissue contrast, artifact suppression, and MRI sequence design related to fast cardiac imaging; myocardium perfusion on ischemic heart.

Keith Welsh, Ph.D. Clinical medical physics, radiation oncology.

Wei Zhao, Ph.D. Development of novel detector concept and new clinical applications for early detection of cancer.

Zhong Zhong, Ph.D. Medical imaging and diagnosis using monochromatic X-rays, X-ray phase contrast, and X-ray optics.

THE UNIVERSITY OF CHICAGO

Pritzker School of Medicine
Division of the Biological Sciences
Graduate Program in Medical Physics

Programs of Study

The Department of Radiology and the Department of Radiation and Cellular Oncology offer a joint program leading to an M.S. or a Ph.D. degree in medical physics. These training programs prepare graduates for research careers in academic institutions, national laboratories, hospitals, and private industry. The first year of study is devoted to course work in the areas of basic interactions of radiation with matter, physics of radiation therapy, nuclear medicine, diagnostic X-ray radiology and computed tomography, magnetic resonance imaging, ultrasound, and health physics. During that year, students are also introduced to research methods. At the end of the first year, qualifying/comprehensive examinations are given. Second-year courses include elective subjects and research courses. Thesis research completes the requirements for the advanced degree. Students are encouraged and are given support to present their results at national meetings. The M.S. degree is only granted as a terminal degree or as a transitional degree en route to the Ph.D. Two years of residency are required, during which students may elect specialized training directed toward either research or clinical-support applications of physics in radiology or radiation oncology.

Research Facilities

As leading research facilities, the Departments of Radiology and of Radiation and Cellular Oncology are equipped for state-of-the-art research in medical physics. Advanced imaging equipment in the Department of Radiology includes 40- and 64-slice helical CT scanners, magnetic resonance imagers, electron paramagnetic resonance imagers, computed-radiography systems, digital chest and mammography systems, PET/CT scanners, advanced SPECT scanners, and ultrasound scanners. The Department of Radiation and Cellular Oncology operates ten linear accelerators, multileaf collimators, on-board imagers, and electronic portal imagers. The Department of Radiology has a large number of systems for molecular imaging, including a micro-CT, a panel-based micro-PET, an ultrahigh-resolution micro-SPECT, optical imagers, a high-field micro-MRI, and an electron paramagnet resonance imager. The varied and numerous computers in the departments are linked with a high-speed network. There are also several specialized image processing computers and high-power computer clusters.

Financial Aid

Most graduate students in the department receive full support and tuition remission from various faculty research grants and University funds. This financial aid is available to candidates on a competitive basis. Stipends are approximately $25,000 and also cover tuition and health fees. In some cases, support is restricted to citizens and permanent residents of the United States.

Cost of Study

In 2006–07, full-time tuition was approximately $40,244 for three quarters. Tuition is usually waived for students if a proper arrangement for a research assistantship is established. Additional mandatory fees of approximately $594 per quarter include health insurance and activities fees.

Living and Housing Costs

Living expenses for a single student are approximately $16,000 per year. Housing information can be obtained through the Graduate Student Assignment Office, the University of Chicago, 824 East 58th Street, Chicago, Illinois 60637.

Student Group

In spring 2007, there are 33 graduate students (6 women and 27 men) in the program. All receive financial assistance. Five new graduate students have been accepted for admission with financial aid for fall 2007.

Student Outcomes

Since 1992, there have been 42 doctoral graduates from the programs. More than 20 of the graduates have academic positions at institutions such as the Universities of Chicago, California at San Francisco, Michigan, MIT, and Stanford, as well as at the Mayo Clinics. Some of these involve a combination of clinical service and research, while the others are purely academic positions. Several graduates are working in industry with medical imaging companies.

Location

The University of Chicago is located in an urban setting in Hyde Park, a culturally rich and ethnically diverse neighborhood adjacent to Lake Michigan, 7 miles south of downtown Chicago. The city has numerous theaters, museums, and restaurants that are easily accessible by public transportation. The University of Chicago operates a shuttle service on campus.

The University

Since its inception in 1892, the University of Chicago has been one of the premier educational institutions in the world. The Pritzker School of Medicine is part of the Division of the Biological Sciences, which offers opportunities for interdisciplinary research and collaboration between the basic sciences and clinical staff members. As a result, the University of Chicago is recognized internationally for its innovative and advanced research in the life sciences.

Applying

Application forms may be obtained from the address listed in this description. The application form, all undergraduate and graduate school transcripts (official copies), and three letters of recommendation must be submitted by the second week of January for admission in the following autumn. Students are also required to provide official reports of scores on the GRE General Test and Subject Test scores in physics. International students whose native language is not English are required to submit an official report of a TOEFL score that is no more than five years old. A minimum score of 600 (paper based) or 250 (computer based) is required to be considered for admission. The program encourages applications from women and minority students. While the program grants both M.S. and Ph.D. degrees, the training is designed for individuals who seek a Ph.D. in medical physics. As a result, students seeking only an M.S. degree are discouraged from applying.

Correspondence and Information

Maryellen Giger, Ph.D.
Director, Committee on Medical Physics
The University of Chicago
5841 South Maryland Avenue, MC-2026
Chicago, Illinois 60637
Phone: 773-702-6778
Fax: 773-702-0371
E-mail: m-giger@uchicago.edu
Web site: http://www.uchicago.edu

The University of Chicago

THE FACULTY AND THEIR RESEARCH

S. G. Armato, Associate Professor; Ph.D., Chicago, 1997.
C. T. Chen, Associate Professor; Ph.D., Chicago, 1986.
K. Doi, Professor; Ph.D., Waseda (Japan), 1969.
M. L. Giger, Professor; Ph.D., Chicago, 1985.
H. J. Halpern, Professor; Ph.D., Wisconsin, 1976; M.D., Miami (Florida), 1980.
Y. Jiang, Associate Professor; Ph.D., Chicago, 1997.
C.-M. Kao, Assistant Professor; Ph.D., Chicago, 1997.
G. S. Karczmar, Professor; Ph.D., Berkeley, 1984.
P. LaRiviére, Assistant Professor; Ph.D., Chicago, 2000.
D. N. Levin, Emeritus Professor; Ph.D., Harvard, 1970; M.D., Chicago, 1981.
A. E. Lujan, Assistant Professor; Ph.D., Michigan, 1999.
C. E. Metz, Professor; Ph.D., Pennsylvania, 1969.
R. M. Nishikawa, Associate Professor; Ph.D., Toronto, 1990.
B. C. O'Brien-Penney, Associate Professor; Ph.D., Worcester Polytechnic, 1979.
X. Pan, Professor; Ph.D., Chicago, 1991.
C. A. Pelizzari, Associate Professor; Ph.D., Michigan, 1974.
C. S. Reft, Assistant Professor; Ph.D., Pittsburgh, 1973.
J. C. Roeske, Associate Professor; Ph.D., Chicago, 1992.

CURRENT RESEARCH PROJECTS

X-RAY IMAGING

Image feature analysis (using artificial neural networks, wavelet transforms, etc.) and computer-aided diagnosis in digital radiography
Chest radiography: detection of lung nodules and pneumothoraces, classification of normal and abnormal lungs with interstitial disease, quantification of abnormal heart size, image registration for temporal subtraction, correlation of chest radiographs with radioisotope images, detection of asymmetries and CP angle blunting
Mammography: detection of breast masses and clustered microcalcifications, diagnosis of breast lesions, assessment of cancer risk
Mangiography: automated vessel size measurements in DSA and coronary arteriography, automated tracking and characterization of the vessel tree in DSA and coronary arteriography, determination and rendering of 3-D vascular structures from two or more views
Angiography: segmentation, description and rendering of aorta and its branches
Musculoskeletal radiology: quantification of osteoporosis and bone strength
Detection of lung nodules, temporal subtraction, 3-D visualization, detection of abnormalities in chest CT
Clinical impact of digital radiography: effect of image compression on detection of abnormalities in chest radiographs, development and evaluation of picture archiving and communications systems (PACS), improvements in diagnostic image quality using density correction and unsharp masking
Tomosynthesis for breast imaging: imaging physics, system evaluation, data base, CAD for tomosynthesis breast imaging
Advanced computed tomography: image reconstruction, analysis, evaluation, and applications
Relationship between image quality and the accuracy of image-analysis techniques

MAGNETIC RESONANCE IMAGING (MRI)

Functional MR imaging of the brain
Analysis of dynamic MR images of brain and cerebrospinal fluid pulsations
Development and application of MR for measurement of tumor blood flow, metabolism, and response to therapy
Computer-assisted electroencephalography using 3-D multimodality images of the brain
New algorithms for constrained MR image acquisition and reconstruction
Development of new targeted MR contrast agents
Computerized analyses of lesions in MR images of the breast

NUCLEAR MEDICINE

Instrumentation: development of advanced PET and miniature gamma camera
Physics: investigation of photon attenuation, scattered radiation, spatial blurring, and noise properties in PET and SPECT
Image reconstruction and processing: development of novel methods for reconstruction of 2-D and 3-D tomographic images, development of statistical methods for image reconstruction and processing, development of methods for 3-D image visualization
Radiopharmaceuticals: PET radiopharmaceuticals for the study of flow, metabolism, and neurotransmitter-receptor systems, SPECT radiopharmaceuticals for neurotransmitter-receptor systems
Functional imaging: drug interactions with enzyme receptors and neuroreceptors, neurotransmitter-receptor interactions, brain mapping

COMPUTED TOMOGRAPHY (CT)

Physics in modern computed tomography
Image reconstruction in cone-beam computed tomography
Microcomputed tomography
Tomosynthesis for breast imaging
Phase-contrast computed tomography

ULTRASOUND IMAGING

Ultrasound imaging physics
Tomographic ultrasound imaging
Ultrasound image processing and analysis

RADIATION ONCOLOGY

Development of advanced computerized radiotherapy treatment-planning tools
Computer techniques for multimodality image registration and visualization
Imaging and oxymetry of tumor physiology with low-frequency electron paramagnetic resonance (EPR)
Dosimetry for radioimmunotherapy
Free-radical toxicity via spin trapping and genetic engineering
Applications of computer vision in radiotherapy treatment delivery
High-quality volume rendering from 3-D medical image datasets
Biological modeling of tumor control and normal tissue complication
Intensity-modulated radiotherapy and inverse plan optimization
Monte Carlo simulation of radiation transport
Radiation-induced gene therapy
Analysis of biological images
Stereotactic methods

OBJECTIVE EVALUATION OF DIAGNOSTIC PERFORMANCE

Development and applications of receiver operating characteristic (ROC) analysis
Methodology for optimal utilization of diagnostic tests

UNIVERSITY
OF MINNESOTA

UNIVERSITY OF MINNESOTA

Graduate Program in Biophysical Sciences and Medical Physics

Programs of Study

The Graduate Program in Biophysical Sciences and Medical Physics is interdisciplinary, with faculty members having primary appointments in departments that include radiology, physics, engineering, computer science, physiology, dentistry, genetics, and biochemistry. Programs lead to the M.S. and Ph.D. degrees. Students concentrate in research areas that include molecular biophysics, medical imaging, magnetic resonance imaging and spectroscopy, radiobiology, radiation therapy physics, and mathematical biophysics and computation. A limited number of students prepare for employment as hospital-based medical physicists through a program that includes opportunities for course work, laboratories, and directed study to provide experience in areas such as purchase specification, acceptance testing, quality assurance, and radiation safety. The majority of students prepare for research careers.

Candidates for the M.S. degree may pursue either thesis or nonthesis plans of study. The thesis plan is considered suitable for students with full-time employment if their thesis can be related to their work assignments. The nonthesis plan is more suitable for students planning to work in government or hospital settings where technical knowledge is more germane than research experience. Students in the nonthesis plan perform a research project under the direction of a faculty member and present the work to their faculty committee in an oral exam.

Candidates for the Ph.D. take preliminary written exams at the end of the first year of study or as soon as possible after completing the core course sequence—topics in physics for medicine and biology. An oral preliminary exam focuses on the plan for thesis research and the student's grasp of related information and is taken by the fall of the third year of full-time registration or its equivalent.

The program reports to the Basic Science Policy and Review Council of the Graduate School and receives a small amount of funding in the form of block grants from the Graduate School. However, graduate student support is almost exclusively obtained through grants and contracts held by the faculty members.

Research Facilities

Students have access to personal computers and workstations as well as the facilities of the Minnesota Supercomputer Institute. Separate research facilities exist for the Center for Magnetic Resonance Research, the Center for Immunotherapy, Radiobiology, Radiation Therapy, Diagnostic Radiology, and the School of Dentistry.

Financial Aid

The majority of students receive some sort of financial aid, typically a 50-percent-time research assistantship with full tuition waiver. The sources of funds are NIH awards, departmental grants and contracts, and Graduate School block grants. For details on need-based awards, students should contact the Office of Student Financial Aid, 210 Fraser Hall, University of Minnesota, 106 Pleasant Street, SE, Minneapolis, Minnesota 55455-0422 (phone: 612-624-1665). Applications as early as January for the following fall quarter are encouraged.

Cost of Study

Tuition per semester for full-time students (6–14 semester credits) was $4374 for residents and $7924 for nonresidents in 2005–06. On average, tuition increases about 5 percent annually and is usually determined in July. A per-semester student services fee covers basic outpatient health care, student organization fees, and the student newspaper.

Living and Housing Costs

The cost of living is comparable to that of other Midwestern urban areas. The University offers dormitory housing for single and married graduate students. Information about housing in the Twin Cities area may be obtained from University of Minnesota Housing Services, Comstock Hall–East, 210 Delaware Street Southeast, Minneapolis, Minnesota 55455-0307.

Student Group

The graduate program typically has 20–25 students. One to 5 are M.S. students and the rest are Ph.D. students. In recent years, 23 percent have been women and 31 percent have been international students. Four to 6 new students are admitted each year. The total Graduate School enrollment is 9,000 students in 170 fields of study.

Location

The Graduate School of the University of Minnesota is located on the banks of the Mississippi River in the Twin Cities of Minneapolis (the largest city in Minnesota) and St. Paul (the state capital). The Twin Cities area, with a population of 2.3 million, provides an unusual combination of the personal and the cosmopolitan. It is home to the Tyrone Guthrie Theatre and the St. Paul Chamber orchestra, as well as a rich array of locally cherished theater, music, and arts organizations. It is also a thriving center of commerce, with major corporate headquarters in electronics and computers, food processing, retailing, and transportation. The area consistently ranks near the top on quality-of-life and residential satisfaction ratings, thanks in part to an extensive park system that covers 12,500 acres and includes more than 200 lakes. Residents may also drive a few hours north to the Boundary Waters Canoe Area Wilderness, one of the most unsullied wilderness areas in the nation.

The University and The Program

The University of Minnesota awarded its first Ph.D. in 1888. The biophysical sciences program, dating back to the early 1950s, is administered by the Graduate School of the University of Minnesota but involves collaborative teaching and research efforts from the Medical School. The program offers opportunities for interdisciplinary research and collaboration among clinical faculty members from the Fairview University Hospital, basic sciences departments, engineering, statistics, and computer science. Faculty members and students interact in Hospital, Medical School, and Graduate School projects. The Hospital and Medical School are internationally known for programs in bone marrow transplant, artificial organ development, and functional neurological imaging.

Applying

Applicants are required to possess strong backgrounds in physics and math with some course work in chemistry, biology or anatomy, and physiology. GRE General Test scores and three letters of recommendation are required to apply. International applicants must receive TOEFL scores above 550. Applicants are encouraged to submit materials early for fall consideration.

Correspondence and Information

E. Russell Ritenour
Department of Radiology, Box 292 UMHC
University of Minnesota School of Medicine
420 Delaware Street, SE
Minneapolis, Minnesota 55455
Phone: 612-626-0131
Fax: 612-626-1951
E-mail: riten001@tc.umn.edu
Web site: http://www.drad.umn.edu/faculty/geise/BPHY2.htm

University of Minnesota

THE FACULTY AND THEIR RESEARCH

Dwight L. Anderson, Ph.D. Structure and assembly of bacterial viruses.

Vincent Barnett, Ph.D. Correlation of mechanical response and molecular dynamics of muscle proteins, studies of the biochemical and physiological interaction of myosin and actin and the elasticity of titin. Techniques include electron paramagnetic resonance spectroscopy (EPR), measurement of muscle stiffness, and force generation.

Victor A. Bloomfield, Ph.D. Ion-induced transition in DNA, hydrodynamic theory, quasi-electric light scattering, dynamics of concentrated biopolymer solutions.

Bianca M. Conti-Fine, M.D. Neurobiochemistry and neuropharmacology.

Ralph DeLong, Ph.D. Robotics as applied to reproducing mandibular movement, three-dimensional digitalization of anatomic structures and computer graphics, wear of dental materials and oral anatomic structures, computer modeling of the masticatory system.

William H. Douglas, Ph.D. Robotics as applied to reproducing mandibular movement, three-dimensional digitalization of anatomic structures and computer graphics, wear of dental materials and oral anatomic structures, computer modeling of masticatory system.

Stanley M. Finkelstein, Ph.D. Hemodynamic impedance properties of peripheral vasculature, respiratory and cardiovascular simulation, monitoring of long-term care for chronic diseases, biomedical signal processing.

John E. Foker, M.D., Ph.D. Myocardial metabolism.

Michael G. Garwood, Ph.D. Magnetic resonance imaging and spectroscopy methods, the design of improved radio frequency pulses, pulse sequences to localize spectroscopic signals to specific tissues or organs of interest, fast imaging, application of these methods to investigate brain tumor metabolism in animals and humans.

Richard A. Geise, Ph.D. Radiation dose determination, particularly bone dosimetry from high-dose interventional procedures; evaluation of radiologic equipment performance, particularly mammography and computer tomography systems; dosimetry and performance evaluation of shock wave lithotripters, particularly by measurement of cavitation.

Bruce J. Gerbi, Ph.D. Ionization chamber response characteristics in high-energy proton and electron beams, electron contamination determination in high-energy proton beams, deposition of radiation dose for obliquely incident photon beams.

Rolf Gruetter, Ph.D. Study of biochemical pathways and physiology using NMR spectroscopy (MRI); interdisciplinary approaches to study regulation of metabolism in health and disease, such as combining MRS with PET, MRS with functional anatomic imaging, and MRS with molecular biology/gene therapy.

Bruce Hammer, Ph.D. Nuclear magnetic resonance imaging and spectroscopy.

Bruce E. Hasselquist, Ph.D. Computer modeling of imaging in nuclear medicine, including the effects of attenuation and scatter in single photon emission computed tomography; simultaneous dual isotope imaging in nuclear medicine.

Patrick Higgins, Ph.D. Radiation dosimetry, basic mechanisms of radiation interaction with matter using measurements and computer models, quantification of dose distributions in tissues against biological or clinical endpoints, thermal dosimetry and heat transport modeling for hyperthermia.

Russell K. Hobbie, Ph.D. Radiological physics.

James Holte, Ph.D. Technologies that support the delivery of high-quality health care at lower costs, including instrumentation, biological system modeling, and the creation of readily searchable database structures; flow of information, material, and people in the medical enterprise, using sensors, signal analysis, information capture, and storage (real-time measurement and long-term archiving).

Xiaoping Hu, Ph.D. Acquisition, reconstruction, processing, and visualization of medical imaging data and application of medical imaging techniques, with emphasis on magnetic resonance imaging and spectroscopy.

Michael Jerosch-Herold, Ph.D. Magnetic resonance imaging methods for functional evaluation of tissues or organs, in particular the heart; magnetic resonance perfusion imaging; tracer kinetic modeling for quantification of tissue blood flow; image processing for evaluation of heart function; application of MRI methods to experimental models of coronary artery disease.

Faiz M. Khan, Ph.D. Dosimetry of electron and photon beams radiotherapy treatment planning, portal electron imaging.

Seong-Gi Kim, Ph.D. Mapping the development and plasticity of the columnar organization in the mammalian cortex; development and application of columnar-resolution fMRI methods and their verification using single-unit and optical-imaging techniques.

Jeih-San Liow, Ph.D. Optimization of data acquisition, image reconstruction/processing, compartmental modeling and statistical analysis techniques for quantitative positron emission tomography (PET).

Merle K. Loken, M.D., Ph.D. Development and evaluation of radiopharmaceutical and instrumentation (including use of computers) for establishing new procedures in the practice of nuclear medicine.

Rex E. Lovrien, Ph.D. Enzymology, calorimetry, thermochemistry of biochemical reactions, development of new legends and methods for separations, protection, confirmation control, cocrystallization of proteins.

Robert Margolis, Ph.D. Biophysics of the middle ear: measuring the impedance in the ear canal of human and animal subjects with normal auditory function and with various ear pathologies; inner ear electrophysiology: auditory-evoked potentials that originate in the inner ear and auditory neural pathway.

Scott M. O'Grady, Ph.D. Mechanisms and regulation of electrolyte transport across epithelial tissues, role of electroneutral cotransport and exchange mechanisms in vectorial salt and water transport in epithelia, regulation of cell volume and intracellular pH.

Richard E. Poppele, Ph.D. Mammalian muscle spindles, mechanical properties of muscle, the nature of the transduction mechanism, encoding of muscle receptor information within the central nervous system.

Kelly Rehm, Ph.D. Digital image processing and evaluation; analysis and visualization of three-dimensional brain image volumes acquired by PET, MRI, and fMRI.

Stephen J. Riederer, Ph.D. The physics and engineering of diagnostic medical imaging systems, especially magnetic resonance imaging (MRI); high-speed MR image acquisition and reconstruction, vascular MRI and MR angiography, compensation for motion during MR image acquisition.

E. Russell Ritenour, Ph.D. Performance evaluation of radiologic imaging systems, specific absorption rate calculation for magnetic resonance imaging (MRI), ultrasound-induced mutation in mammalian cells, ultrasound dosimetry.

Andreas Rosenberg, Ph.D. Dynamics of protein structure, studies by methods such as fluorescence quenching and isotope exchange kinetics, structure-function relationships in red-cell cytoskeleton, studies by partial reconstruction of membrane structures.

Chang W. Song, Ph.D. Biological effects of radiation, vascular function in tumors and normal tissues, radiosensitization and radioprotection, microelectrode method to measure tissue pH and p02, ion transport through the cell membrane.

Arthur E. Stillman, M.D., Ph.D. Proton magnetic resonance spectroscopy of the brain for following treatment effects, functional magnetic resonance imaging of the brain for therapy planning.

Stephen Strother, Ph.D. Medical imaging, particularly positron emission tomography (PET) and magnetic resonance imaging (MRI), with emphasis on parameter estimation, optimal model selection, and artificial neural networks for functional activation studies of the brain.

David D. Thomas, Ph.D. Spectroscopic studies of molecular dynamics in energy transducing ATPase of muscle; myosin, actin, muscle fibers, sarcoplasmic reticulum, calcium transport, ATPase; electron paramagnetic resonance (EPR), phosphorescence, fluorescence.

Kamil Ugurbil, Ph.D. Development of magnetic resonance methods and their applications in vivo for obtaining physiological, functional, anatomical, and biochemical information noninvasively; functional mapping in the human brain; cardiac bioenergetics.

Warren J. Warwick, Ph.D. New models of the function of the lung, noninvasive measurements of physiologic functions, integration of computer technology in the practice of medicine, mucous transport in the airway, water balance in the lungs, total body water and body composition analysis, allometric effects seen in physiologic tests during growth.

Clare K. Woodward, Ph.D. Protein structure and dynamics, protein folding, construction and physical-chemical characterization of protein variants produced by site-directed mutagenesis, NMR, hydrogen exchange, colorimetry, protein engineering, computer-based molecular modeling of proteins, molecular graphics of proteins.

VIRGINIA COMMONWEALTH UNIVERSITY

Programs in Medical Physics

Programs of Study	Virginia Commonwealth University (VCU) offers master's and doctoral degrees in medical physics through the VCU Department of Physics in conjunction with the Departments of Radiation Oncology and Radiology at the VCU Medical Center. Although the graduate program officially matriculated its first students in fall 2004, the Medical Physics Division has been active in teaching, clinical service, and research roles at VCU since the early 1970s. Faculty members from the Department of Physics provide students with a solid foundation in fundamental physics, and students receive didactic, clinical, and research training in the physics of medical imaging and in radiation therapy from faculty members from the Departments of Radiology and Radiation Oncology, respectively. Students also receive training in advanced health physics and advanced didactic training in radiation biology from leading experts in the field.
	The M.S. program is designed to ensure students are suited to work as clinical medical physicists through course work and practical clinical training in physics as it is applied to the diagnosis and treatment of human diseases. Required course work provides training in radiation dosimetry, radiation biology, radiation therapy, imaging, and health physics.
	The Ph.D. program is designed to establish the researchers of tomorrow in medical physics. The Ph.D. program offers students course work and research training in physics as it is applied to the diagnosis and treatment of human diseases. Research interests include functional imaging using PET and NMR, CT image artifact removal and deformation, intensity-modulated radiation therapy, radiation therapy dose calculations, 4-D radiation therapy, and brachytherapy dose calculations.
Research Facilities	VCU libraries provide a combined capacity of more than 1.7 million volumes, 10,200 periodical titles, and an online bibliographic search service accessing hundreds of databases.
	The Molecular Imaging Center supports clinical and investigational positron emission tomography (PET) imaging, a medical cyclotron, PET imaging of experimental animals, and a state-of-the-art magnetic resonance imaging system with 3.0 Tesla high-strength magnetic fields.
	Designated as a Cancer Center by the National Cancer Institute, the VCU Massey Cancer Center is dedicated to basic-science research to advance the scientific community's knowledge about cancer treatment and prevention. These efforts are supported by a group of shared resources that include facilities for biostatistics, flow cytometry, histopathology, hybridoma and cell culture, molecular biology, nucleic acids, structural biology, transgenic mice, and virus vector.
Financial Aid	All Ph.D. students are funded by the program through either a research or teaching assistantship. M.S. students are not directly supported by the program but may be able to secure other means of financial aid. Students may apply for need-based assistance with the University's Financial Aid Office. Graduate research assistantships are occasionally available through research programs in the department. Students can find current information on financial aid programs, policies, and procedures at http://www.vcu.edu/enroll/finaid.
Cost of Study	For full-time study (9–15 credits) in 2007–08, Virginia residents pay tuition and fees of $4452 per semester; nonresidents, $8876 per semester. For part-time study, Virginia residents pay tuition and fees of $465 per hour; nonresidents, $954 per hour. Some programs require additional fees. On the Medical College of Virginia (MCV) campus, tuition, fees, and other expenses vary in the medicine, pharmacy, nurse anesthesia, dentistry, and School of Allied Health programs.
Living and Housing Costs	Graduate student housing is available on both the MCV campus and the academic campus of Virginia Commonwealth University. Many graduate students live in off-campus housing, which is reasonably priced and readily available in a variety of styles and settings in nearby residential areas or within easy commuting distance. On- and off-campus housing information is available on the Web at http://www.housing.vcu.edu/.
Student Group	VCU enrolls 30,452 students, 7,611 of whom are graduate students. More than 200 clubs and organizations reflect the diverse social, recreational, educational, political, and religious interests of the student body.
Location	Richmond is Virginia's capital and a major East Coast financial and manufacturing center that offers students a wide range of cultural, educational, and recreational activities. Richmond is located in central Virginia at the intersection of Interstates 95 and 64, 2 hours south of Washington, D.C., and nestled between the Blue Ridge Mountains and the Atlantic coast. The Richmond region is easily accessible by plane, car, and train. With nearly 1 million residents, the historic city of Richmond combines big-city offerings with small-town hospitality. Applicants are encouraged to explore http://www.visit.richmond.com/ for more information on the city.
The University	VCU is a state-supported coeducational university with a graduate school, a major teaching hospital, and twelve academic and professional units that offer fifty-two undergraduate, twenty-two postbaccalaureate certificate, sixty-five master's, six post-master's certificate, and twenty-nine Ph.D. programs. VCU also offers M.D., D.D.S., D.P.T., and Pharm.D. programs as well as cooperative degree programs with other major Virginia colleges and universities. VCU has one of the largest evening colleges in the United States. The academic campus is located in Richmond's historic Fan District. The health sciences campus and hospital are located 2 miles east in the downtown business district. A University bus service provides free intercampus transportation for faculty members and students.
	With more than $211 million in annual research funding, Virginia Commonwealth University is classified as one of the nation's top research universities by the Carnegie Foundation for the Advancement of Teaching. More than 29,000 undergraduate, certificate, graduate, post-master's, professional, and doctoral students are enrolled in 162 academic programs, forty of which are unique in the commonwealth of Virginia. The faculty members represent the finest American and international graduate institutions and enhance the University's position among the important institutions of higher learning in the United States and the world via their work in the classroom, laboratory, studio, and clinic and in their scholarly publications.
Applying	Admission procedures and program requirements are detailed in the *Graduate Bulletin.* Application deadlines and materials, including the application and the *Graduate Bulletin,* are available online at the Graduate School Web site at http://www.graduate.vcu.edu/. Virginia Commonwealth University is an equal opportunity/affirmative action institution providing access to education and employment without regard to age, race, color, national origin, gender, religion, sexual orientation, veteran's status, political affiliation, or disability.
Correspondence and Information	Dr. Jeffrey Siebers, Director Medical Physics Graduate Program Virginia Commonwealth University Richmond, Virginia 23284-3051 Phone: 804-828-7780 E-mail: medphys@vcu.edu Web site: http://www.medicalphysics.vcu.edu/

Virginia Commonwealth University

THE FACULTY AND THEIR RESEARCH

Department of Physics

David Ameen, Assistant Professor; Ph.D., Virginia Commonwealth, 2000.

Alison A. Baski, Associate Professor; Ph.D., Stanford, 1991. Structural and electronic properties of semiconductor surfaces using scanning microscopy techniques.

Marilyn F. Bishop, Associate Professor; Ph.D., California, Irvine, 1976. Charge density waves, superconductivity, biopolymers.

Robert H. Gowdy, Associate Professor; Ph.D., Yale, 1968. General relativity and cosmology, physics education.

Purusottam Jena, Professor; Ph.D., California, 1970. Theory of electronic structure of metals and alloys; semiconductors, intermetallic compounds, and insulators; defect complexes; hydrogen in metals; small atomic clusters.

Shiv. N. Khanna, Professor; Ph.D., Delhi, 1976. Theoretical solid-state physics, electronic structure of amorphous metals and alloys, atomic clusters, quantum Hall effect.

Durig Lewis, Assistant Professor; Ph.D., London, 1993. K–12 education.

Martin Muñoz, Assistant Professor; Ph.D., Campinas (Brazil), 1996. Optical properties of semiconductors, materials, and devices.

V. Adam Niculescu, Associate Professor; Ph.D., Bucharest, 1971. Magnetic, electrical, and structural properties of metals and alloys; production and characterization of amorphous and metal alloys; physics education.

Mikhail Reshchikov, Assistant Professor; Ph.D., Kalinin Polytechnic (Russia), 1989. Point defects in semiconductors, optical properties of wide-bandgap semiconductors.

Chhanda Samanta, Honorary Affiliate Graduate Faculty; Ph.D., Maryland, College Park, 1981. Nuclear physics, radioactive ion beam, theory and experiment.

James M. Sullivan, Assistant Professor; Ph.D., Tennessee-Knoxville, 2001. Theoretical solid-state physics, electronic structure of DNA modified surfaces, theory of ferromagnetic semiconductors and scanning tunneling microscopy.

Gregory B. Tait, Associate Professor of Electrical Engineering and Physics; Ph.D., Johns Hopkins, 1991. Heterostructure semiconductor devices and nonlinear microwave circuits.

Pat Woodworth, Instructor; M.S., Virginia Commonwealth, 2000. K–12 education.

Department of Radiology

Timmerie Cohen, Assistant Professor; B.S., Virginia Commonwealth, 1997.

Mark Crosthwaite, Associate Professor; M.Ed., Louisville, 1989.

Terri Fauber, Associate Professor; Ed.D., William & Mary, 1996.

Millard Justice, Assistant Professor; M.S., Virginia Tech, 2004.

Jeffrey Legg, Assistant Professor and Department Chair; Ph.D., Virginia Commonwealth.

Elizabeth Meixner, Assistant Professor; M.Ed., Virginia Commonwealth, 1981.

Paul Riley, Assistant Professor; B.S., Virginia Commonwealth, 1995.

Department of Radiation Oncology

Olubunmi Abayomi, Associate Professor; M.D., Lagos (Nigeria). Gynecological malignancies, head and neck cancers, general radiation oncology, delayed effects of irradiation.

Anthony Addesa, Assistant Professor; M.D., Hahnemann, 1990. Tumors of the central nervous system, stereotactic radiosurgery, image-guided radiotherapy, prostate brachytherapy.

Mitchell Anscher, Chairman; M.D., Virginia Commonwealth, 1981. Prevention and treatment of normal tissue injury after cancer therapy.

Douglas Arthur, Associate Professor; M.D., Wake Forest, 1989. Brachytherapy, management of breast and genitourinary malignancies, soft tissue malignancies.

Christopher L. Bartee, Research Associate. Intensity-modulated radiotherapy, electronic portal imaging, respiratory gating.

Stanley Benedict, Associate Professor; Ph.D., UCLA, 1992. Radiobiological dosimetry of continuous and intermittent irradiation delivery in stereotactic radiotherapy.

Michael Chang, Assistant Professor; M.D., Thomas Jefferson, 1997. Use of stereotactic radiotherapy in the treatment of central nervous system, thoracic, and breast malignancies; IMRT for prostate cancers.

Theodore Chung, Associate Professor; M.D., Ph.D., Maryland, 1991. Developing novel approaches to cancer treatment through identification of molecular events that regulate cancer growth, death, and progression; clinical application of gene therapy.

Laurie Cuttino, Assistant Professor; M.D., Virginia Commonwealth. Partial breast irradiation, novel aplications of IMRT for breast cancer, radiobiological modeling.

Nesrin Dogan, Associate Professor; Ph.D., Michigan, 1993. Intensity-modulated radiotherapy delivery techniques, quality assurance, optimization, Monte Carlo treatment planning.

Mirek Fatyga, Assistant Professor; Ph.D., Indiana, 1986. Software development for radiation therapy, applications of radiobiology to treatment planning.

Paul Graves, Assistant Professor; Ph.D., Indiana, 1995. How RNA silencing is regulated in response to extracellular or intracellular cues.

Michael Hagan, Professor; Ph.D., Illinois at Urbana-Champaign, 1978; M.D., Baylor College of Medicine, 1989. Improving cancer control through radiation treatment.

Christopher Johnson, Associate Professor; M.D., Virginia Commonwealth, 1981. Alternative schedules of radiation therapy for treatment of malignancies of the head and neck.

Ross Mikkelsen, Professor; Ph.D., California, Santa Barbara, 1973. Mechanisms by which cells sense radiation and metabolically produced reactive oxygen and how resulting signals are amplified and translated into cellular responses; growth factor signaling and cellular response to radiation, with specific emphasis on how the early reactive oxygen/nitrogen signal activates growth factor receptor regulated pro-proliferative and anti-apoptotic signaling.

Monica Morris, Associate Professor; M.D., Baylor College of Medicine, 1993. Radiation late effects, factors influencing individual differences in radiosensitivity.

Martin Murphy, Associate Professor; Ph.D., Chicago, 1980. Developing fast, automatic image-guided procedures for planning and delivering radiation treatments via both external beams and brachytherapy.

Tony Mustain, Assistant Professor; M.B.A., Virginia Commonwealth, 1984. Operational and financial management, strategic development of the radiation oncology practice.

Nirmal Sakthi, Instructor; M.S., East Carolina, 2000. Patient immobilization techniques, optimization of beam parameters for intensity-modulated radiation therapy.

Habeeb Saleh, Assistant Professor; Ph.D., Texas A&M, 1995. Image-guided radiation therapy, cranial/extracranial stereotactic radiotherapy, quality assurance.

Jeffrey Siebers, Associate Professor; Ph.D., Wisconsin, 1990. Achieving accurate dose evaluation for three-dimensional conformal radiation therapy (3DCRT); intensity-modulated radiation therapy (IMRT), particularly using Monte Carlo transport simulation of therapy treatment systems.

Shiyu Song, Assistant Professor; M.D., Qingdao (China), 1983; Ph.D., Wisconsin, 1999. Application of new technology such as IMRT and combined therapies in the management of head and neck cancer.

Lisa-Marie Sturla, Assistant Professor; Ph.D., Leeds, 1999. Elucidation of mechanisms of tumor cell resistance to ionizing radiation mediated by the epidermal growth factor receptor.

Dorin A. Todor, Assistant Professor; Ph.D., Old Dominion. Intraoperative assessment of LDR implants, automatic tracking of markers in EPID images for lung treatments, real-time imaging techniques for HDR breast catheter implants.

Kristoffer Valerie, Professor; Ph.D., Royal Institute of Technology (Sweden), 1986. DNA double-strand break (DSB) repair, radiation-induced signaling, developing novel approaches for sensitizing tumor cells to radiation.

Jeffrey Williamson, Professor; Ph.D., Minnesota, 1982. Modeling distortion and movement of internal organs due to brachytherapy applicator insertion, tumor regression, and changes in patient position.

Yan Wu, Instructor; M.S., Tianjin, 1985; M.S., Southampton, 1993. Delivery techniques of intensity-modulated radiotherapy, optimization, signal processing and neural networks.

Adly Yacoub, Instructor; Ph.D., National Institute of Research (France), 1987. The molecular mechanisms of tumor radioresistance, what determines the central decision of cells: whether to die or not to die.

Hualiang Zhong, Assistant Professor; Ph.D., Western Ontario, 2000. IMRT dose optimization incorporating tissue motion uncertainty, modeling distortion and movement of internal organs due to brachytherapy dose delivery, applying 3-D elastograpy in tumor detection and evaluation during radiation treatment trials.

Section 29
Health Services

This section contains a directory of institutions offering graduate work in health services, followed by in-depth entries submitted by institutions that chose to prepare detailed program descriptions. Additional information about programs listed in the directory but not augmented by an in-depth entry may be obtained by writing directly to the dean of a graduate school or chair of a department at the address given in the directory.

For programs offering related work, see also in this book Allied Health, Business Administration and Management, Nursing, and Public Health.

CONTENTS

Health Services Management and Hospital Administration

Alaska Pacific University, Graduate Programs, Business Administration Department, Program in Business Administration, Anchorage, AK 99508-4672. Offers business administration (MBA); global finance (MBA); health services administration (MBA). Part-time and evening/weekend programs available. *Faculty:* 6 full-time (3 women), 4 part-time/adjunct (1 woman). *Students:* 5 full-time (3 women), 46 part-time (25 women); includes 16 minority (2 African Americans, 11 American Indian/Alaska Native, 3 Asian Americans or Pacific Islanders), 1 international. Average age 37. In 2006, 11 degrees awarded. *Degree requirements:* For master's, capstone course. *Entrance requirements:* For master's, GMAT or GRE, minimum GPA of 3.0. *Application deadline:* For fall admission, 4/1 priority date for domestic students; for spring admission, 12/15 for domestic students. Applications are processed on a rolling basis. Application fee: $25. *Expenses:* Tuition: Part-time $550 per credit hour. Required fees: $100 per semester. Tuition and fees vary according to program. *Financial support:* In 2006–07, fellowships (averaging $6,300 per year), 6 research assistantships (averaging $4,112 per year) were awarded; career-related internships or fieldwork and Federal Work-Study also available. Support available to part-time students. Financial award application deadline: 4/15. *Unit head:* Dr. Tracy Stewart, Director, 907-564-8358, Fax: 907-562-4276, E-mail: tstewart@alaskapacific.edu.

Albany State University, College of Arts and Sciences, Department of History, Political Science and Public Administration, Albany, GA 31705-2717. Offers community and economic development (MPA); criminal justice (MPA); fiscal management (MPA); general management (MPA); health administration and policy (MPA); human resources management (MPA); public policy (MPA); water resource management and policy (MPA). *Accreditation:* NASPAA. Part-time programs available. *Degree requirements:* For master's, thesis, comprehensive exam. *Entrance requirements:* For master's, GRE General Test, minimum GPA of 2.5. Electronic applications accepted. *Faculty research:* Transportation, urban affairs, political economy.

American InterContinental University Online, Program in Business Administration, Hoffman Estates, IL 60192. Offers accounting and finance (MBA); healthcare management (MBA); human resource management (MBA); international business (MBA); management (MBA); marketing (MBA); operations management (MBA); organizational psychology and development (MBA); project management (MBA). Evening/weekend programs available. Postbaccalaureate distance learning degree programs offered (no on-campus study). *Entrance requirements:* Additional exam requirements/recommendations for international students: Required—TOEFL (minimum score 550 paper-based; 213 computer-based). *Application deadline:* Applications are processed on a rolling basis. Application fee: $50. Electronic applications accepted. *Financial support:* Institutionally sponsored loans and scholarships/grants available. Financial award applicants required to submit FAFSA. *Unit head:* Kerri J Holloway, Vice President of Academic Affairs, 847-851-5000 Ext. 15399, Fax: 847-586-6309, E-mail: kholloway@aivonline.edu. *Application contact:* 877-701-3800, E-mail: info@aiuonline.edu.

American Sentinel University, Graduate Programs, Englewood, CO 80112. Offers business administration (MBA); business intelligence (MS); computer science (MSCS); health information management (MS); healthcare (MBA); information systems (MSIS); nursing (MSN). Part-time and evening/weekend programs available. Postbaccalaureate distance learning degree programs offered (no on-campus study). *Faculty:* 40. *Students:* 400. Average age 36. In 2006, 47 degrees awarded. *Entrance requirements:* Additional exam requirements/recommendations for international students: Required—TOEFL (minimum score 600 paper-based; 215 computer-based). *Application deadline:* Applications are processed on a rolling basis. Application fee: $50. Electronic applications accepted. *Unit head:* Janette D. Marshall, Registrar, 800-729-2427 Ext. 2211, Fax: 205-326-3822, E-mail: jan.marshall@americansentinel.edu. *Application contact:* Natalie A. Nixon, Director of Admissions, 800-729-2427, Fax: 205-328-2229, E-mail: natalie.nixon@americansentinel.edu.

Andrew Jackson University, Brian Tracy College of Business and Entrepreneurship, Birmingham, AL 35244. Offers entrepreneurship (MBA); finance (MBA); health services management (MBA); hospitality and tourism management (MBA); human resource management (MBA); international business (MBA); management (MBA); marketing (MBA). Part-time and evening/weekend programs available. Postbaccalaureate distance learning degree programs offered (no on-campus study). *Faculty:* 13 part-time/adjunct (1 woman). *Students:* Average age 40. In 2006, 6 degrees awarded. *Entrance requirements:* For master's, course work in calculus, statistics. Additional exam requirements/recommendations for international students: Required—TOEFL (minimum score 550 paper-based; 213 computer-based). *Application deadline:* Applications are processed on a rolling basis. Application fee: $75. *Expenses:* Tuition: Part-time $705 per course. *Application contact:* Betty Howell, Director of Student Affairs, 205-871-9288 Ext. 108, Fax: 205-871-9294, E-mail: bhowell@aju.edu.

Aquinas Institute of Theology, Graduate and Professional Programs, St. Louis, MO 63108. Offers health care mission (MAHCM); ministry (M Div); pastoral care (Certificate); pastoral ministry (MAPM); pastoral studies (MAPS); preaching (D Min); spiritual direction (Certificate); theology (M Div, MA); M Div/MA; MAPS/MSW. *Accreditation:* ATS (one or more programs are accredited). Part-time and evening/weekend programs available. Postbaccalaureate distance learning degree programs offered (minimal on-campus study). *Degree requirements:* For master's, one foreign language, comprehensive exam, thesis or major paper; for doctorate, thesis/dissertation. *Entrance requirements:* For M Div and master's, MAT; for doctorate, 3 years of ministerial experience, 6 hours of graduate course work in homiletics, M Div or the equivalent, minimum GPA of 3.0. Additional exam requirements/recommendations for international students: Required—TOEFL. *Faculty research:* Theology of preaching, hermeneutics, lay ecclesial ministry, pastoral and practical theology.

Argosy University, Atlanta Campus, College of Business, Atlanta, GA 30328. Offers accounting (DBA); customized professional concentration (MBA, DBA); finance (MBA); healthcare administration (MBA); information systems (DBA); information systems management (MBA); international business (MBA, DBA); management (MBA, DBA); marketing (MBA, DBA). Part-time programs available. *Students:* 53 full-time (38 women), 35 part-time (28 women); includes 73 minority (66 African Americans, 3 Asian Americans or Pacific Islanders, 4 Hispanic Americans). *Degree requirements:* For master's, comprehensive exam (for some programs), registration; for doctorate, thesis/dissertation, comprehensive exam, registration. *Entrance requirements:* For master's, minimum undergraduate GPA of 3.0; for doctorate, master's degree, minimum GPA of 3.0. Additional exam requirements/recommendations for international students: Required—TOEFL. *Application deadline:* For fall admission, 7/1 priority date for domestic students, 6/1 for international students; for spring admission, 11/1 priority date for domestic students, 10/1 for international students. Applications are processed on a rolling basis. Application fee: $50. Electronic applications accepted. *Financial support:* Applicants required to submit FAFSA. *Unit head:* Dr. Robert A. Berg, Department Chair, 770-407-1042, E-mail: rberg@argosy.edu. *Application contact:* Christa Holton, Director of Admissions, 770-671-1200 Ext. 1014, Fax: 770-671-9050, E-mail: cholton@argosy.edu.

See Close-Up on page 207.

Argosy University, Chicago Campus, College of Business, Chicago, IL 60603. Offers accounting (DBA); customized professional concentration (MBA, DBA); finance (MBA); healthcare administration (MBA); information systems (DBA); information systems management (MBA); international business (MBA, DBA); management (MBA, DBA); marketing (MBA, DBA). Part-time and evening/weekend programs available. *Faculty:* 2 full-time (both women), 4 part-time/adjunct (3 women). *Students:* 52 full-time (30 women), 18 part-time (7 women); includes 37 minority (24 African Americans, 7 Asian Americans or Pacific Islanders, 6 Hispanic Americans). Average age 37. 32 applicants, 81% accepted, 25 enrolled. In 2006, 9 master's, 2 doctorates awarded. *Entrance requirements:* For master's and doctorate, minimum GPA of 3.0. Additional exam requirements/recommendations for international students: Required—TOEFL (minimum score 550 paper-based; 213 computer-based). *Application deadline:* For fall admission, 2/28 for domestic and international students; for spring admission, 10/30 for domestic and international students. Applications are processed on a rolling basis. Application fee: $50. Electronic applications accepted. *Financial support:* In 2006–07, 3 students received support. Scholarships/grants available. Financial award application deadline: 4/1. *Unit head:* Dr. Cynthia Scarlett, Associate Head, 800-626-4123, Fax: 212-727-7750, E-mail: cscarlett@argosy.edu. *Application contact:* Ashley Delaney, Director of Admissions, 800-626-4123, Fax: 312-777-7750, E-mail: argosyadmissions@argosy.edu.

See Close-Up on page 209.

Argosy University, Chicago Campus, College of Health Sciences, Chicago, IL 60603. Offers health services management (MS).

Argosy University, Denver Campus, College of Business, Denver, CO 80203. Offers accounting (DBA); customized professional concentraion (DBA); customized professional concentration (MBA); finance (MBA); healthcare administration (MBA); information systems (DBA); information systems management (MBA); international business (MBA, DBA); management (MBA, MSM, DBA); marketing (MBA, DBA).

See Close-Up on page 213.

Argosy University, Hawai'i Campus, College of Business, Honolulu, HI 96813. Offers accounting (DBA); customized professional concentration (MBA, DBA); finance (MBA, Certificate); healthcare administration (MBA, Certificate); information systems (DBA); information systems management (MBA, Certificate); international business (MBA, DBA, Certificate); management (MBA, DBA); marketing (MBA, DBA, Certificate). Evening/weekend programs available. *Faculty:* 12 part-time/adjunct (2 women). *Students:* 3 full-time (2 women), 1 part-time; includes 2 minority (1 Asian American or Pacific Islander, 1 Hispanic American). 6 applicants, 67% accepted, 3 enrolled. *Degree requirements:* For master's, capstone project. *Entrance requirements:* For master's, minimum GPA of 3.0 in last 60 hours. Additional exam requirements/recommendations for international students: Required—TOEFL (minimum score 550 paper-based; 213 computer-based). *Application deadline:* For fall admission, 1/15 priority date for domestic students; for spring admission, 10/15 for domestic students. Applications are processed on a rolling basis. Application fee: $50. *Financial support:* Teaching assistantships, Federal Work-Study and scholarships/grants available. Support available to part-time students. *Unit head:* Lisa Parker, Interim Chair, College of Business and Information Technology, 888-323-2777, Fax: 808-536-5505, E-mail: lparker@argosy.edu. *Application contact:* Cherie Andrade, Director of Admissions, 888-323-2777, Fax: 808-536-5505, E-mail: candrade@argosy.edu.

See Close-Up on page 215.

Argosy University, Inland Empire Campus, College of Business, San Bernardino, CA 92408. Offers accounting (DBA); customized professional concentration (MBA, DBA); finance (MBA); healthcare administration (MBA); information systems (DBA); information systems management (MBA); international business (MBA, DBA); management (DBA); mangement (MBA); marketing (MBA, DBA).

See Close-Up on page 217.

Argosy University, Orange County Campus, College of Business, Santa Ana, CA 92704. Offers accounting (DBA, Adv C); customized professional concentration (MBA, DBA); finance (MBA, Certificate); healthcare administration (MBA, Certificate); information systems (DBA, Adv C); information systems management (MBA); international business (MBA, DBA, Adv C, Certificate); management (MBA, MSM, DBA, EDBA); mangement (Adv C); marketing (MBA, DBA, Adv C, Certificate); organizational leadership (Ed D); public administration (MBA, Certificate). Part-time and evening/weekend programs available. *Faculty:* 4 full-time (1 woman), 20 part-time/adjunct (7 women). *Students:* 163 full-time (64 women), 41 part-time (16 women). Average age 42. 72 applicants, 51 enrolled. In 2006, 6 master's, 23 doctorates awarded. *Degree requirements:* For doctorate, thesis/dissertation, preliminary and final dissertation defense, comprehensive exam. *Entrance requirements:* For master's, minimum GPA of 3.0 in final 2 years of course work, 3 letters of recommendation, resumé; for doctorate, minimum GPA of 3.0 in graduate study, 3 letters of recommendation, resumé. Additional exam requirements/recommendations for international students: Required—TOEFL. *Application deadline:* Applications are processed on a rolling basis. Application fee: $50. Electronic applications accepted. *Financial support:* Federal Work-Study, institutionally sponsored loans, and scholarships/grants available. Support available to part-time students. Financial award applicants required to submit FAFSA. *Faculty research:* Crisis management, leadership in organizations, finance, business systems. *Unit head:* Dr. Ray London, Dean, 800-716-9598, Fax: 714-437-1284, E-mail: auocadmissions@argosy.edu. *Application contact:* Mark Betz, Director of Admissions, 800-716-9598, Fax: 714-437-1697, E-mail: mbetz@argosy.edu.

See Close-Up on page 221.

Argosy University, Phoenix Campus, College of Business, Phoenix, AZ 85021. Offers accounting (DBA); customized professional concentration (MBA, DBA); finance (MBA); healthcare administration (MBA); information systems (DBA); information systems management (MBA); international business (MBA, DBA); management (MBA, DBA); marketing (MBA, DBA). Part-time and evening/weekend programs available. *Faculty:* 1 full-time (0 women). *Students:* 7 full-time (4 women); includes 2 minority (1 African American, 1 Hispanic American). *Entrance requirements:* For doctorate, master's degree. Additional exam requirements/recommendations for international students: Required—TOEFL (minimum score 550 paper-based; 213 computer-based). Application fee: $50. *Financial support:* In 2006–07, 2 students received support. Federal Work-Study, institutionally sponsored loans, and scholarships/grants available. Support available to part-time students. Financial award applicants required to submit FAFSA. *Unit head:* Dr. Gary Berg, Program Chair, 866-216-2777, Fax: 602-216-2601. *Application contact:* Andy Hughes, Director of Admissions, 866-216-2777 Ext. 3110, Fax: 602-216-2601, E-mail: ahughes@argosyu.edu.

See Close-Up on page 223.

Argosy University, San Francisco Bay Area Campus, College of Business, Point Richmond, CA 94804-3547. Offers accounting (DBA); corporate compliance (MBA); customized professional concentration (MBA, DBA); finance (MBA); healthcare administration (MBA); information systems (DBA); information systems management (MBA); international business (MBA, DBA); management (MBA, MSM, DBA); marketing (MBA, DBA). Part-time and evening/weekend programs available. *Faculty:* 2 full-time (0 women), 9 part-time/adjunct (0 women). *Students:* 29 full-time (8 women), 9 part-time (2 women); includes 30 minority (5 African Americans, 24 Asian Americans or Pacific Islanders, 1 Hispanic American). 21 applicants, 76% accepted, 13 enrolled. In 2006, 3 master's, 2 doctorates awarded. *Degree requirements:* For master's, capstone project; for doctorate, thesis/dissertation, comprehensive exam, registration. *Entrance requirements:* For master's, minimum GPA of 3.0; for doctorate, MBA or minimum GPA of 3.0. Additional exam requirements/recommendations for international students: Required—TOEFL (minimum score 550 paper-based; 213 computer-based). *Application deadline:* For fall admission, 7/1 priority date for domestic and international students; for winter admission, 11/1 priority date for domestic and international students; for spring admission, 4/1 priority date for domestic and international students. Applications are processed on a rolling basis. Application fee: $50. Electronic applications accepted. *Financial support:* Federal Work-Study and scholarships/grants available. Support available to part-time students. Financial award applicants required to submit FAFSA. *Unit head:* Dr. Anthony Martinez, Department Chair, Business and Information Technology, 866-215-0277, Fax: 510-215-0299, E-mail: amartinez@argosy.edu. *Application contact:* John Vincent Stofan, Director of Admissions, 866-215-2727 Ext. 205, Fax: 510-215-0299, E-mail: jstofan@argosyu.edu.

See Close-Up on page 227.

Argosy University, Santa Monica Campus, College of Business, Santa Monica, CA 90405. Offers accounting (DBA); customized professional concentration (MBA, DBA); finance (MBA); healthcare administration (MBA); information systems (DBA); information systems management (MBA); international business (MBA, DBA); management (MBA, MS, MSM, DBA); marketing (MBA, DBA).

See Close-Up on page 229.

Argosy University, Sarasota Campus, College of Business, Sarasota, FL 34235-8246. Offers accounting (DBA, Adv C); customized professional concentration (MBA, DBA); finance (MBA, Certificate); healtcare administration (Certificate); healthcare administration (MBA); information systems (DBA, Adv C); information systems management (MBA, Certificate); international business (MBA, DBA, Adv C, Certificate); management (MBA, MSM, DBA); mangement (Adv C); marketing (MBA, DBA, Adv C, Certificate). Part-time and evening/weekend programs available. Postbaccalaureate distance learning degree programs offered (minimal on-campus study). *Faculty:* 6 full-time (3 women), 13 part-time/adjunct (5 women). *Students:* 71 applicants, 92% accepted, 64 enrolled. In 2006, 7 master's, 30 doctorates awarded. *Degree requirements:* For doctorate, thesis/dissertation, comprehensive exam. *Entrance requirements:* For master's, minimum GPA of 3.0; for doctorate, minimum undergraduate GPA of 3.0. Additional exam requirements/recommendations for international students: Required—TOEFL. *Application deadline:* Applications are processed on a rolling basis. Application fee: $50. Electronic applications accepted. *Financial support:* Federal Work-Study and scholarships/grants available. Support available to part-time students. Financial award application deadline: 4/1; financial award applicants required to submit FAFSA. *Unit head:* Dr. Kathleen Cornett, Dean, 800-331-5995, Fax: 941-379-9464, E-mail: kcornett@argosy.edu. *Application contact:* Admissions Representative, 800-331-5995 Ext. 221, Fax: 941-379-5964.

See Close-Up on page 231.

Argosy University, Schaumburg Campus, College of Business, Schaumburg, IL 60173-5403. Offers accounting (DBA, Adv C); corporate compliance (MBA); customized professional concentration (MBA, DBA); finance (MBA, Certificate); healthcare administration (MBA, Certificate); information systems (DBA, Adv C); information systems management (MBA, Certificate); international business (MBA, DBA, Adv C, Certificate); management (MBA, DBA, Adv C, Certificate); marketing (MBA, DBA, Adv C, Certificate). Part-time and evening/weekend programs available. *Faculty:* 1 (woman) full-time, 7 part-time/adjunct (0 women). *Students:* 36 full-time, 23 part-time. 13 applicants, 69% accepted, 9 enrolled. In 2006, 5 master's, 4 doctorates awarded. *Degree requirements:* For doctorate, thesis/dissertation, comprehensive exam. *Entrance requirements:* For master's and doctorate, minimum GPA of 3.0. Additional exam requirements/recommendations for international students: Required—TOEFL. *Application deadline:* For fall admission, 3/15 priority date for domestic and international students; for spring admission, 10/15 priority date for domestic and international students. Applications are processed on a rolling basis. Application fee: $50. Electronic applications accepted. *Expenses: Contact institution. Financial support:* Federal Work-Study and scholarships/grants available. *Unit head:* Dr. Harriet Kandelman, Dean, 866-290-2777, Fax: 847-548-6159, E-mail: agrosyadmissions@argosy.edu. *Application contact:* Jamal Scott, Director of Admissions, 847-598-6159, Fax: 630-598-6191, E-mail: jscott@argosy.edu.

See Close-Up on page 233.

Argosy University, Seattle Campus, College of Business, Seattle, WA 98121. Offers accounting (DBA); customized professional concentration (MBA, DBA); finance (MBA); healthcare administration (MBA); information systems (DBA); information systems management (MBA); international business (MBA, DBA); management (MSM, DBA); mangement (MBA); marketing (MBA, DBA). Part-time and evening/weekend programs available. *Students:* 1 applicant, 100% accepted, 1 enrolled. In 2006, 1 degree awarded. *Degree requirements:* For master's, capstone experience; for doctorate, thesis/dissertation, comprehensive exam (for some programs). *Entrance requirements:* For master's, minimum GPA of 3.0 in last 2 years or cumulative of 2.7; for doctorate, minimum GPA of 3.0. Additional exam requirements/recommendations for international students: Required—TOEFL (minimum score 550 paper-based; 213 computer-based). *Application deadline:* For fall admission, 4/15 priority date for domestic students, 4/15 for international students; for winter admission, 10/15 priority date for domestic students. Applications are processed on a rolling basis. Application fee: $50. Electronic applications accepted. *Expenses: Contact institution. Financial support:* Federal Work-Study and unspecified assistantships available. Support available to part-time students. Financial award applicants required to submit FAFSA. *Unit head:* Dr. Kylene Quinn, Chair, 206-393-3543, Fax: 206-283-5777, E-mail: kquinn@argosy.edu. *Application contact:* Heather Simpson, Director of Admissions, 866-283-4500, Fax: 206-283-5777, E-mail: hsimpson@argosy.edu.

See Close-Up on page 235.

Argosy University, Tampa Campus, College of Business, Tampa, FL 33614. Offers accounting (DBA); customized professional concentration (MBA, DBA); finance (MBA, Certificate); healthcare administration (MBA, Certificate); information systems (DBA); information systems management (MBA); international business (MBA, DBA, Certificate); management (MBA, MSM, DBA); marketing (MBA, DBA, Certificate); public administration (MBA). *Entrance requirements:* For doctorate, minimum GPA of 3.0. *Unit head:* Dr. Andrew Ghillyer, Dean, 813-393-5270, E-mail: aghillyer@argosy.edu.

See Close-Up on page 237.

Argosy University, Twin Cities Campus, College of Business, Eagan, MN 55121. Offers accounting (DBA); corporate compliance (MBA); customized professional certification (DBA); customized professional concentration (MBA); finance (MBA); healthcare administration (MBA); information systems (DBA); information systems management (MBA); international business (MBA, DBA); management (MBA, MSM, DBA, EDBA); marketing (MBA, DBA). Part-time and evening/weekend programs available. *Faculty:* 1 (woman) full-time, 20 part-time/adjunct (6 women). *Students:* 47 full-time (23 women), 20 part-time (11 women); includes 21 minority (10 African Americans, 1 American Indian/Alaska Native, 9 Asian Americans or Pacific Islanders, 1 Hispanic American). Average age 39. 72 applicants, 76% accepted, 45 enrolled. In 2006, 6 degrees awarded. *Degree requirements:* For doctorate, thesis/dissertation, comprehensive exam. *Entrance requirements:* For master's, 3 letters of recommendation, bachelor's degree in a related field, minimum undergraduate GPA of 3.0, resumé; for doctorate, 3 letters of recommendation, master's degree in a related field, minimum GPA of 3.0, resumé. Additional exam requirements/recommendations for international students: Required—TOEFL (minimum score 550 paper-based; 213 computer-based). *Application deadline:* For fall admission, 5/15 priority date for domestic students, 5/15 for international students; for spring admission, 10/15 priority date for domestic students, 10/15 for international students. Applications are processed on a rolling basis. Application fee: $50. Electronic applications accepted. *Financial support:* In 2006–07, 3 fellowships with partial tuition reimbursements, 3 teaching assistantships with partial tuition reimbursements were awarded; Federal Work-Study and scholarships/grants also available. Financial award applicants required to submit FAFSA. *Unit head:* Dr. Paula King, Department Head, 651-846-3377, E-mail: pking@argosy.edu. *Application contact:* Jennifer Radke, 2nd Director of Graduate Admissions, 651-846-3300, Fax: 651-994-7954, E-mail: tcadmissions@argosy.edu.

See Close-Up on page 239.

Argosy University, Twin Cities Campus, College of Health Sciences, Eagan, MN 55121. Offers health services management (MS).

Argosy University, Washington DC Campus, College of Business, Arlington, VA 22209. Offers accounting (DBA); customized professional concentration (MBA, DBA); finance (MBA); healthcare administration (MBA); information systems (DBA); information systems management (MBA); international business (MBA, DBA); international business marketing (Graduate Certificate); management (MBA, DBA); marketing (MBA, DBA). *Faculty:* 1 full-time (0 women), 5 part-time/adjunct (2 women). *Students:* 5 full-time (4 women), 4 part-time (1 woman); includes 4 minority (3 African Americans, 1 Asian American or Pacific Islander). 21 applicants, 86% accepted. *Degree requirements:* For master's, thesis (for some programs), comprehensive exam (for some programs); for doctorate, thesis/dissertation, comprehensive exam. *Entrance requirements:* For master's and doctorate, minimum GPA of 3.0. Additional exam requirements/recommendations for international students: Required—TOEFL (minimum score 550 paper-based; 213 computer-based). *Application deadline:* For fall admission, 6/15 priority date for domestic students; for spring admission, 10/15 priority date for domestic students. Application fee: $50. *Financial support:* Federal Work-Study and scholarships/grants available. Financial award applicants required to submit FAFSA. *Unit head:* Dr. Colleen Logan, Academic Affairs Officer, 866-703-2777, Fax: 703-521-5850, E-mail: dcadmissions@argosy.edu. *Application contact:* Emily Peck, Director of Admissions, 866-703-2777 Ext. 5851, Fax: 703-526-5850, E-mail: dcadmissions@argosy.edu.

See Close-Up on page 241.

Arizona State University, Division of Graduate Studies, W.P. Carey School of Business, School of Health Management and Policy, Tempe, AZ 85287. Offers MHSM, MPH, MBA/MHSM. *Accreditation:* CAHME. *Entrance requirements:* For master's, GMAT.

Armstrong Atlantic State University, School of Graduate Studies, Program in Health Science, Savannah, GA 31419-1997. Offers health services administration (MHSA); public health (MPH). *Accreditation:* CAHME; CEPH. Part-time and evening/weekend programs available. Postbaccalaureate distance learning degree programs offered (no on-campus study). *Faculty:* 4 full-time (0 women), 3 part-time/adjunct (0 women). *Students:* 30 full-time (22 women), 72 part-time (51 women); includes 37 minority (33 African Americans, 1 American Indian/Alaska Native, 1 Asian American or Pacific Islander, 2 Hispanic Americans), 6 international. Average age 34. In 2006, 23 degrees awarded. *Degree requirements:* For master's, internship, thesis optional. *Entrance requirements:* For master's, GMAT or GRE General Test, MAT, minimum GPA of 2.6. Additional exam requirements/recommendations for international students: Required—TOEFL (minimum score 523 paper-based; 193 computer-based). *Application deadline:* For fall admission, 7/1 priority date for domestic and international students; for spring admission, 11/15 priority date for domestic and international students. Applications are processed on a rolling basis. Application fee: $25. Electronic applications accepted. *Expenses:* Tuition, state resident: full-time $2,286; part-time $127 per credit. Tuition, nonresident: full-time $9,144; part-time $508 per credit. One-time fee: $257. *Financial support:* In 2006–07, research assistantships with partial tuition reimbursements (averaging $2,500 per year); career-related internships or fieldwork, Federal Work-Study, scholarships/grants, tuition waivers (full), and unspecified assistantships also available. Support available to part-time students. Financial award applicants required to submit FAFSA. *Faculty research:* Health administration, community health, health education. *Unit head:* Dr. James Streater, Department Head, 912-921-7346, Fax: 912-921-7350, E-mail: mssm@mail.armstrong.edu.

A.T. Still University of Health Sciences, School of Health Management, Kirksville, MO 63501. Offers geriatric healthcare (MGH); health administration (MHA); health education (DH Ed, MH Ed); public health (MPH). Part-time and evening/weekend programs available. Postbaccalaureate distance learning degree programs offered (no on-campus study). *Faculty:* 1 full-time (0 women), 45 part-time/adjunct (17 women). *Students:* 18 full-time (14 women), 194 part-time (130 women); includes 39 minority (20 African Americans, 8 American Indian/Alaska Native, 9 Asian Americans or Pacific Islanders, 2 Hispanic Americans). Average age 34. In 2006, 75 degrees awarded. *Degree requirements:* For master's, thesis (for some programs), capstone project. *Entrance requirements:* For master's, minimum GPA of 2.5, bachelor's degree or equivalent from U.S. institution. Additional exam requirements/recommendations for international students: Required—TOEFL (minimum score 500 paper-based; 222 computer-based). *Application deadline:* For fall admission, 8/27 for domestic students, 8/4 for international students; for winter admission, 10/25 for domestic students, 11/26 for international students; for spring admission, 2/10 for domestic students, 3/17 for international students. Applications are processed on a rolling basis. Electronic applications accepted. *Expenses: Contact institution. Financial support:* Application deadline: 5/1; *Unit head:* Dr. Jon Persavich, Dean, 660-626-2820, Fax: 660-626-2826, E-mail: jpersavich@atsu.edu. *Application contact:* Donna Sparks, Associate Director for Admissions, 660-626-2237, Fax: 660-626-2969, E-mail: admissions@atsu.edu.

Avila University, School of Business, Kansas City, MO 64145-1698. Offers accounting (MBA); finance (MBA); general management (MBA); health care administration (MBA); international business (MBA); management information systems (MBA); marketing (MBA). Part-time and evening/weekend programs available. *Faculty:* 8 full-time (4 women), 17 part-time/adjunct (4 women). *Students:* 31 full-time (19 women), 165 part-time (96 women); includes 18 minority (14 African Americans, 1 American Indian/Alaska Native, 3 Hispanic Americans), 16 international. Average age 32. 77 applicants, 81% accepted, 62 enrolled. In 2006, 54 degrees awarded. *Degree requirements:* For master's, capstone course. *Entrance requirements:* For master's, GMAT, minimum GPA of 3.0. Additional exam requirements/recommendations for international students: Required—TOEFL (minimum score 550 paper-based). *Application deadline:* For fall admission, 7/30 priority date for domestic students; for winter admission, 11/30 priority date for domestic students; for spring admission, 2/28 priority date for domestic students. Applications are processed on a rolling basis. Application fee: $20. Electronic applications accepted. *Expenses:* Tuition: Full-time $7,470; part-time $415 per credit. *Financial support:* In 2006–07, 78 students received support. Career-related internships or fieldwork available. Support available to part-time students. Financial award applicants required to submit FAFSA. *Faculty research:* Leadership characteristics, financial hedging, group dynamics. *Unit head:* Dr. Richard Woodall, Dean, 816-501-3798, Fax: 816-501-2463. *Application contact:* JoAnna Giffin, MBA Admissions Director, 816-501-3601, Fax: 816-501-2463, E-mail: joanna.giffin@avila.edu.

Baker College Center for Graduate Studies, Programs in Business, Flint, MI 48507-9843. Offers accounting (MBA); computer information systems (MBA); finance (MBA); general business (MBA); health and recreation services management (MBA); health care management (MBA); human resource management (MBA); industrial management (MBA); international business (MBA); leadership (MBA); marketing (MBA). MBA in health and recreation services management enrollment limited to international students. Part-time and evening/weekend programs available. *Faculty:* 15 full-time (6 women), 425 part-time/adjunct (200 women). *Students:* 370 full-time (190 women), 1,060 part-time (560 women); includes 372 minority (205 African Americans, 27 American Indian/Alaska Native, 66 Asian Americans or Pacific Islanders, 74 Hispanic Americans), 30 international. Average age 38. 780 applicants, 85% accepted, 567 enrolled. In 2006, 202 degrees awarded. *Degree requirements:* For master's, portfolio. *Entrance requirements:* For master's, 3 years of work experience, minimum undergraduate GPA of 2.5, writing sample, letters of recommendation. Additional exam requirements/recommendations for international students: Required—TOEFL (minimum score 550 paper-based; 213 computer-based). *Application deadline:* For fall admission, 8/6 priority date for domestic students; for winter admission, 12/15 priority date for domestic students; for spring admission, 2/15 priority date for domestic students. Applications are processed on a rolling basis. Application fee: $25. Electronic applications accepted. *Expenses:* Tuition: Full-time $7,200; part-time $300 per credit hour. *Financial support:* In 2006–07, 410 students received support. Scholarships/grants available. Support available to part-time students. Financial award applicants required to submit FAFSA. *Unit head:* Dr. Michael Heberling, President, 800-469-

Health Services Management and Hospital Administration

Baker College Center for Graduate Studies (continued)
3165, Fax: 810-766-4399, E-mail: heberling@baker.edu. *Application contact:* Chuck J. Gurden, Vice President for Graduate and Online Admissions, 800-469-3165, Fax: 810-766-2051, E-mail: chuck@baker.edu.

Baldwin-Wallace College, Graduate Programs, Division of Business Administration, Program in Health Care Executive Management, Berea, OH 44017-2088. Offers MBA. Part-time and evening/weekend programs available. *Students:* 32 full-time (18 women), 8 part-time (7 women); includes 3 minority (1 African American, 1 American Indian/Alaska Native, 1 Asian American or Pacific Islander), 1 international. Average age 37. 13 applicants, 92% accepted, 10 enrolled. In 2006, 15 degrees awarded. *Entrance requirements:* For master's, interview, work experience. *Application deadline:* For fall admission, 7/23 priority date for domestic students; for spring admission, 12/10 priority date for domestic students. Applications are processed on a rolling basis. Application fee: $25. Electronic applications accepted. *Expenses:* Tuition: Part-time $760 per credit hour. Tuition and fees vary according to program. *Financial support:* Applicants required to submit FAFSA. *Unit head:* Tom Campanella, Director of Health Care Executive MBA, 440-826-3818, Fax: 440-826-3868, E-mail: tcampane@bw.edu. *Application contact:* Barbara McClelland, Graduate Business Coordinator, Executive and Executive Health Care MBA, 440-826-2064, Fax: 440-826-3868, E-mail: bmcclell@bw.edu.

Barnes-Jewish College of Nursing and Allied Health, Division of Allied Health, St. Louis, MO 63110-1091. Offers dietetic internship (Certificate); education (MSAH); management (MSAH); nutrition (MSAH). Part-time and evening/weekend programs available. *Degree requirements:* For master's, thesis or alternative, registration. *Entrance requirements:* For master's, minimum GPA of 3.0, 2 references, statistics course. Additional exam requirements/recommendations for international students: Required—TOEFL (minimum score 550 paper-based; 213 computer-based).

Barnes-Jewish College of Nursing and Allied Health, Division of Nursing, St. Louis, MO 63110-1091. Offers adult nurse practitioner (MSN); education (MSN); gerontology nurse practitioner (MSN); holistics (MSN); management/administration (MSN); neonatal nurse practitioner (MSN); oncology (MSN). *Accreditation:* AACN; AANA/CANAEP. Part-time and evening/weekend programs available. *Degree requirements:* For master's, thesis or alternative, registration. *Entrance requirements:* For master's, minimum GPA of 3.0, 2 references, statistics course. Additional exam requirements/recommendations for international students: Required—TOEFL (minimum score 550 paper-based; 213 computer-based).

Barry University, Andreas School of Business, Graduate Certificate Programs, Miami Shores, FL 33161-6695. Offers finance (Certificate); health services administration (Certificate); international business (Certificate); management (Certificate); management information systems (Certificate); marketing (Certificate). *Application contact:* Dave Fletcher, Director of Graduate Admissions, 305-899-3113, Fax: 305-899-2971, E-mail: dfletcher@mail.barry.edu.

Barry University, School of Natural and Health Sciences, Graduate Certificate Programs, Miami Shores, FL 33161-6695. Offers health care leadership (Certificate); health care planning and informatics (Certificate); histotechnology (Certificate); long term care management (Certificate); medical group practice management (Certificate); quality improvement and outcomes management (Certificate). *Unit head:* Dr. Alan S. Whiteman, Director, 305-899-3237, Fax: 305-899-3543, E-mail: awhiteman@mail.barry.edu. *Application contact:* Jocelyn Goulet, Director, Health Services Admissions Operation, 305-899-3541, Fax: 305-899-3232, E-mail: jgoulet@mail.barry.edu.

Barry University, School of Natural and Health Sciences, Program in Health Services Administration, Miami Shores, FL 33161-6695. Offers MS. Part-time and evening/weekend programs available. *Students:* 13 full-time (11 women), 69 part-time (49 women); includes 55 minority (9 African Americans, 2 Asian Americans or Pacific Islanders, 44 Hispanic Americans), 3 international. 140 applicants, 25% accepted, 28 enrolled. In 2006, 33 degrees awarded. *Degree requirements:* For master's, comprehensive exam. *Entrance requirements:* For master's, GMAT or GRE General Test, 2 years of experience in the health field, minimum GPA of 3.0, 1 semester of course work in computer applications or the equivalent (business). *Application deadline:* Applications are processed on a rolling basis. Application fee: $30. Electronic applications accepted. *Financial support:* Applicants required to submit FAFSA. *Unit head:* Dr. Alan S. Whiteman, Director, 305-899-3237, Fax: 305-899-3543, E-mail: awhiteman@mail.barry.edu. *Application contact:* Jocelyn Goulet, Director, Health Services Admissions Operation, 305-899-3541, Fax: 305-899-3232, E-mail: jgoulet@mail.barry.edu.

Baylor University, Graduate School, Academy of Health Sciences, Program in Health Care Administration, Fort Sam Houston, TX 78234. Offers MHA. Offered jointly with the U.S. Army. *Accreditation:* CAHME. *Students:* 80 full-time (19 women); includes 9 minority (4 African Americans, 3 Asian Americans or Pacific Islanders, 2 Hispanic Americans). In 2006, 42 degrees awarded. *Entrance requirements:* For master's, GRE General Test. *Application deadline:* For fall admission, 6/15 for domestic students. Applications are processed on a rolling basis. Application fee: $25. *Faculty research:* Data quality, public health policy, organizational behavior, AIDS. *Unit head:* Cmdr. Dan Dominguez, Director, 210-221-6935 Ext. 6443, E-mail: daniel.dominguez@cen.amedd.army.mil. *Application contact:* Renee Pryor, Program Administrator, 210-221-6443, Fax: 210-221-6010.

Bellevue University, Graduate School, Program in Health Care Administration, Bellevue, NE 68005-3098. Offers MS. Postbaccalaureate distance learning degree programs offered.

See Close-Up on page 1801.

Bernard M. Baruch College of the City University of New York, Zicklin School of Business, Zicklin Executive Programs, Baruch/Mt. Sinai Program in Health Care Administration, New York, NY 10010-5585. Offers MBA. *Accreditation:* CAHME. Part-time and evening/weekend programs available. *Faculty:* 8 full-time (3 women), 5 part-time/adjunct (2 women). *Students:* Average age 32. 81 applicants, 35% accepted, 25 enrolled. In 2006, 32 degrees awarded. *Entrance requirements:* For master's, GMAT, personal interview, work experience in health care. Additional exam requirements/recommendations for international students: Required—TOEFL. *Application deadline:* For fall admission, 6/30 for domestic students. Applications are processed on a rolling basis. Application fee: $125. Electronic applications accepted. *Expenses:* Contact institution. *Faculty research:* Economics of reproductive health, multivariate point estimation. *Unit head:* Robert Stolinsky, Director, 646-312-3100, Fax: 646-312-3104, E-mail: robert_stolinsky@baruch.cuny.edu. *Application contact:* Robert Stolinsky, Director, 646-312-3100, Fax: 646-312-3104, E-mail: robert_stolinsky@baruch.cuny.edu.

Boston University, School of Management, Master of Business Administration Program, Boston, MA 02215. Offers advanced accounting (Certificate); general management (MBA); healthcare management (MBA); public and nonprofit management (MBA); JD/MBA; MBA/MA; MBA/MPH; MBA/MS; MBA/MSIS; MS/MBA. Part-time and evening/weekend programs available. *Faculty:* 104 full-time (21 women). *Students:* 299 full-time (114 women), 487 part-time (190 women); includes 124 minority (12 African Americans, 2 American Indian/Alaska Native, 94 Asian Americans or Pacific Islanders, 16 Hispanic Americans), 143 international. Average age 26. 1,482 applicants, 42% accepted, 300 enrolled. In 2006, 342 degrees awarded. *Entrance requirements:* For master's, GMAT. *Application deadline:* For fall admission, 5/1 for domestic students. Applications are processed on a rolling basis. Application fee: $125. Electronic applications accepted. *Expenses:* Tuition: Full-time $33,330; part-time $1,042 per credit. Required fees: $462; $40. *Financial support:* Career-related internships or fieldwork, Federal Work-Study, institutionally sponsored loans, and tuition waivers (partial) available. Support available to part-time students. Financial award applicants required to submit FAFSA. *Unit head:* Dr. John Chalykoff, Associate Dean, Academic Program, 617-353-4157, Fax: 617-353-5003, E-mail: chalykof@bu.edu. *Application contact:* Hayden Estrada, Assistant Dean, Admissions, 617-353-2670, Fax: 617-353-7368, E-mail: mba@bu.edu.

Boston University, School of Public Health, Health Law, Bioethics and Human Rights Department, Boston, MA 02215. Offers MPH. *Students:* 16 full-time (13 women), 18 part-time (13 women); includes 4 minority (3 Asian Americans or Pacific Islanders, 1 Hispanic American), 3 international. Average age 25. *Entrance requirements:* For master's, GRE General Test. Additional exam requirements/recommendations for international students: Required—TOEFL or IELTS. *Application deadline:* For fall admission, 2/1 for domestic students; for spring admission, 10/15 for domestic students. Applications are processed on a rolling basis. Application fee: $95. Electronic applications accepted. *Expenses:* Tuition: Full-time $33,330; part-time $1,042 per credit. Required fees: $462; $40. *Financial support:* Career-related internships or fieldwork, Federal Work-Study, institutionally sponsored loans, scholarships/grants, and tuition waivers (partial) available. Support available to part-time students. *Unit head:* Prof. George Annas, Chair, 617-638-4626. *Application contact:* LePhan Quan, Assistant Director of Admissions, 617-638-4640, Fax: 617-638-5299, E-mail: asksph@bu.edu.

Boston University, School of Public Health, Health Policy and Management Department, Boston, MA 02215. Offers M Sc, MPH, D Sc. *Accreditation:* CAHME. *Students:* 32 full-time (25 women), 48 part-time (37 women); includes 22 minority (7 African Americans, 14 Asian Americans or Pacific Islanders, 1 Hispanic American), 6 international. Average age 26. *Entrance requirements:* For master's, GRE General Test. Additional exam requirements/recommendations for international students: Required—TOEFL or IELTS. *Application deadline:* For fall admission, 2/1 for domestic students; for spring admission, 10/15 for domestic students. Applications are processed on a rolling basis. Application fee: $95. Electronic applications accepted. *Expenses:* Tuition: Full-time $33,330; part-time $1,042 per credit. Required fees: $462; $40. *Financial support:* Career-related internships or fieldwork, Federal Work-Study, institutionally sponsored loans, scholarships/grants, and tuition waivers (partial) available. Support available to part-time students. *Unit head:* Dr. Gary Young, Chair, 617-638-5042, E-mail: hlthserv@bu.edu. *Application contact:* LePhan Quan, Assistant Director of Admissions, 617-638-4640, Fax: 617-638-5299, E-mail: asksph@bu.edu.

Brandeis University, The Heller School for Social Policy and Management, Program in Human Services, Waltham, MA 02454-9110. Offers child, youth, and family services (MBA); health care administration (MBA); human services (MBA); MBA/MA. Part-time and evening/weekend programs available. *Degree requirements:* For master's, team consulting project. *Entrance requirements:* For master's, GMAT. Additional exam requirements/recommendations for international students: Required—TOEFL (minimum score 600 paper-based). Electronic applications accepted. Expenses: Contact institution. *Faculty research:* Health care, child and family, elder and disabled services, general human services.

See Close-Up on page 247.

Brandeis University, The Heller School for Social Policy and Management, Program in Sustainable International Development, Waltham, MA 02454-9110. Offers international development (MA); international health policy and management (MS); sustainable development (MA). *Degree requirements:* For master's, 2nd-year fieldwork or internship. *Entrance requirements:* Additional exam requirements/recommendations for international students: Required—TOEFL. Electronic applications accepted. Expenses: Contact institution. *Faculty research:* Water resource management, human rights, biosphere management, rural development, public policy and governance.

Brenau University, Graduate Programs, School of Business and Mass Communication, Gainesville, GA 30501. Offers accounting (MBA); healthcare management (MBA); leadership development (MBA); management (MBA); organizational development (MS). Part-time and evening/weekend programs available. Postbaccalaureate distance learning degree programs offered (no on-campus study). *Faculty:* 12 full-time (6 women), 16 part-time/adjunct (5 women). *Students:* 49 full-time (32 women), 148 part-time (89 women); includes 52 minority (45 African Americans, 2 Asian Americans or Pacific Islanders, 5 Hispanic Americans), 2 international. Average age 35. 222 applicants, 55% accepted, 111 enrolled. In 2006, 64 degrees awarded. *Degree requirements:* For master's, thesis (for some programs). *Entrance requirements:* For master's, GMAT, GRE General Test, or MAT, minimum undergraduate GPA of 3.0, faculty interview. Additional exam requirements/recommendations for international students: Required—TOEFL (minimum score 550 paper-based). *Application deadline:* Applications are processed on a rolling basis. Application fee: $30. Electronic applications accepted. *Expenses:* Contact institution. *Financial support:* Career-related internships or fieldwork available. Financial award application deadline: 7/15; financial award applicants required to submit FAFSA. *Faculty research:* International business, women in management entrepreneurship, simulations in business, Internet/online teaching in business, managerial leadership. *Unit head:* Dr. Bill Haney, Dean, 770-538-4707, Fax: 770-537-4701, E-mail: whaney@brenau.edu. *Application contact:* Nathan Goss, Admissions Coordinator, 770-534-6162, Fax: 770-538-4701, E-mail: ngoss@brenau.edu.

Brooklyn College of the City University of New York, Division of Graduate Studies, Department of Health and Nutrition Science, Program in Public Health, Brooklyn, NY 11210-2889. Offers community health (MPH); health care management (MPH); health care policy and administration (MPH). *Accreditation:* CEPH. *Students:* 3 full-time (2 women), 49 part-time (35 women); includes 27 minority (18 African Americans, 5 Asian Americans or Pacific Islanders, 4 Hispanic Americans), 7 international. 45 applicants, 71% accepted, 11 enrolled. In 2006, 5 degrees awarded. *Entrance requirements:* For master's, GRE, 2 letters of recommendation, essay. *Application deadline:* For fall admission, 3/1 priority date for domestic students, 2/1 priority date for international students; for spring admission, 11/1 priority date for domestic students, 10/1 priority date for international students. Applications are processed on a rolling basis. Application fee: $125. Electronic applications accepted. *Expenses:* Tuition, state resident: full-time $6,400; part-time $270 per credit. Tuition, nonresident: full-time $12,000; part-time $500 per credit. Required fees: $118 per semester. *Financial support:* Application deadline: 5/1. *Unit head:* Dr. Jean Grassman, Graduate Deputy Chairperson, 718-951-5026, Fax: 718-951-4670, E-mail: grassman@brooklyn.cuny.edu. *Application contact:* Karen Alleyne-Pierre, Director of Admissions Services and Enrollment Communications, 718-951-5902, Fax: 718-951-4506, E-mail: grads@brooklyn.cuny.edu.

California College for Health Sciences, Program in Business Administration in Healthcare, Salt Lake City, UT 84107. Offers healthcare administration (MBA). Part-time and evening/weekend programs available. Postbaccalaureate distance learning degree programs offered (no on-campus study). *Degree requirements:* For master's, fieldwork/internship.

California College for Health Sciences, Program in Healthcare Administration, Salt Lake City, UT 84107. Offers MSHCA. Part-time and evening/weekend programs available. Postbaccalaureate distance learning degree programs offered (no on-campus study). *Degree requirements:* For master's, fieldwork, internship. *Entrance requirements:* For master's, previous course work in psychology.

California College for Health Sciences, Program in Health Services, Salt Lake City, UT 84107. Offers community health (MSHS); wellness promotion (MSHS). Part-time and evening/weekend programs available. Postbaccalaureate distance learning degree programs offered (no on-campus study). *Degree requirements:* For master's, fieldwork, internship, final project (wellness promotion). *Entrance requirements:* For master's, previous course work in psychology.

California Lutheran University, Graduate Studies, School of Business, Thousand Oaks, CA 91360-2787. Offers finance (MBA); healthcare management (MBA); international business (MBA); management information systems (MBA); marketing (MBA); organizational behavior (MBA); small business/entrepreneurship (MBA). Evening/weekend programs available. *Entrance requirements:* For master's, GMAT, interview, minimum GPA of 3.0. Expenses: Contact institution.

California State University, Bakersfield, Division of Graduate Studies and Research, School of Business and Public Administration, Program in Health Care Management, Bakersfield, CA 93311-1022. Offers MSA. *Faculty:* 3 full-time (1 woman), 3 part-time/adjunct (1 woman).

Students: Average age 28. 4 applicants, 100% accepted. In 2006, 13 degrees awarded. *Entrance requirements:* For master's, GRE. *Application deadline:* Applications are processed on a rolling basis. Application fee: $55. *Unit head:* Dr. Thomas Martinez, Head, 661-654-6542, Fax: 661-664-2438.

California State University, Chico, Graduate School, College of Behavioral and Social Sciences, Department of Political Science, Program in Public Administration, Chico, CA 95929-0722. Offers health administration (MPA); local government management (MPA); public administration (MPA). *Accreditation:* NASPAA. *Students:* 13 full-time (7 women), 24 part-time (11 women); includes 8 minority (1 African American, 2 American Indian/Alaska Native, 1 Asian American or Pacific Islander, 4 Hispanic Americans), 1 international. Average age 32. 22 applicants, 95% accepted, 10 enrolled. In 2006, 6 degrees awarded. *Degree requirements:* For master's, thesis or alternative, oral exam. *Entrance requirements:* For master's, 2 letters of recommendation. Additional exam requirements/recommendations for international students: Required—TOEFL (minimum score 550 paper-based; 213 computer-based). *Application deadline:* For fall admission, 3/1 for domestic and international students; for spring admission, 9/15 for domestic and international students. Applications are processed on a rolling basis. Application fee: $55. Electronic applications accepted. *Financial support:* Fellowships, career-related internships or fieldwork available. *Unit head:* Dr. Donna Kemp, Graduate Coordinator, 530-898-5734.

California State University, East Bay, Academic Programs and Graduate Studies, College of Letters, Arts, and Social Sciences, Department of Public Affairs and Administration, Hayward, CA 94542-3000. Offers health care administration (MS); public administration (MPA). *Accreditation:* NASPAA. Part-time and evening/weekend programs available. *Faculty:* 6 full-time (1 woman), 10 part-time/adjunct (2 women). *Students:* 41 full-time (31 women), 219 part-time (164 women); includes 142 minority (70 African Americans, 41 Asian Americans or Pacific Islanders, 31 Hispanic Americans), 19 international. Average age 35. 149 applicants, 70% accepted, 75 enrolled. In 2006, 104 degrees awarded. *Degree requirements:* For master's, comprehensive exam or thesis. *Entrance requirements:* For master's, minimum GPA of 3.0. Additional exam requirements/recommendations for international students: Required—TOEFL (minimum score 550 paper-based; 213 computer-based). *Application deadline:* For fall admission, 5/31 for domestic students, 4/30 for international students; for winter admission, 9/30 for domestic and international students; for spring admission, 12/31 for domestic students, 11/30 for international students. Applications are processed on a rolling basis. Application fee: $55. Electronic applications accepted. *Financial support:* Fellowships, teaching assistantships, career-related internships or fieldwork, Federal Work-Study, institutionally sponsored loans, and scholarships/grants available. Support available to part-time students. Financial award application deadline: 3/2. *Unit head:* Dr. Jay Umeh, 510-885-3282, Fax: 510-885-3726. *Application contact:* My Huynh, Graduate Prospect Specialist, 510-885-2989, Fax: 510-885-4059, E-mail: my.huynh@csueastbay.edu.

California State University, Fresno, Division of Graduate Studies, College of Health and Human Services, Department of Public Health, Fresno, CA 93740-8027. Offers environmental/occupational health (MPH); health administration (MPH); health promotion (MPH). *Accreditation:* CEPH. Part-time and evening/weekend programs available. *Degree requirements:* For master's, thesis or alternative. *Entrance requirements:* For master's, GRE General Test, minimum GPA of 2.5. Additional exam requirements/recommendations for international students: Required—TOEFL. Electronic applications accepted. *Faculty research:* Foster parent training, geriatrics, tobacco control.

California State University, Long Beach, Graduate Studies, College of Health and Human Services, Department of Nursing, Long Beach, CA 90840. Offers nursing (MS); nursing-health care administration (MS). *Accreditation:* AACN. Part-time programs available. *Faculty:* 32 full-time (30 women), 25 part-time/adjunct (19 women). *Students:* 101 full-time (92 women), 119 part-time (114 women); includes 127 minority (28 African Americans, 2 American Indian/Alaska Native, 59 Asian Americans or Pacific Islanders, 38 Hispanic Americans), 2 international. Average age 37. 138 applicants, 79% accepted, 89 enrolled. In 2006, 73 degrees awarded. *Degree requirements:* For master's, thesis optional. *Entrance requirements:* For master's, minimum GPA of 3.0. *Application deadline:* For fall admission, 7/1 for domestic students; for spring admission, 12/1 for domestic students. Applications are processed on a rolling basis. Application fee: $55. Electronic applications accepted. *Financial support:* Federal Work-Study, institutionally sponsored loans, and scholarships/grants available. Financial award application deadline: 3/2. *Faculty research:* Newborns of drug-dependent mothers, abuse of residents in nursing homes, interventions in care of Alzheimer's patients. *Unit head:* Dr. Loucine Huckabay, Director, 562-985-4463, Fax: 562-985-2382, E-mail: huckabay@csulb.edu. *Application contact:* Dr. Bonnie Kellogg, Graduate Coordinator, 562-985-8243, Fax: 562-985-2382, E-mail: bkellogg@csulb.edu.

California State University, Long Beach, Graduate Studies, College of Health and Human Services, Program in Health Care Administration, Long Beach, CA 90840. Offers health care administration (MS, Certificate). *Accreditation:* CAHME. Part-time programs available. *Faculty:* 3 full-time (1 woman), 15 part-time/adjunct (6 women). *Students:* 11 full-time (5 women), 53 part-time (36 women); includes 13 minority (4 African Americans, 3 Asian Americans or Pacific Islanders, 6 Hispanic Americans), 2 international. Average age 35. 57 applicants, 74% accepted, 38 enrolled. In 2006, 10 degrees awarded. *Degree requirements:* For master's, comprehensive exam or thesis. *Entrance requirements:* For master's, minimum GPA of 3.0. *Application deadline:* For fall admission, 7/1 for domestic students; for spring admission, 12/1 for domestic students. Applications are processed on a rolling basis. Application fee: $55. Electronic applications accepted. *Financial support:* Federal Work-Study, institutionally sponsored loans, and scholarships/grants available. Financial award application deadline: 3/2. *Faculty research:* Long-term care, Immigration Reform Act and health care, physician reimbursement. *Unit head:* Dr. Tony Sinay, Director, 562-985-5694, Fax: 562-985-8886, E-mail: tsinay@csulb.edu. *Application contact:* Information Contact, 562-985-5694, Fax: 562-985-8886.

California State University, Los Angeles, Graduate Studies, College of Business and Economics, Program in Health Care Management, Los Angeles, CA 90032-8530. Offers MS. Part-time and evening/weekend programs available. *Students:* 2 full-time (1 woman), 39 part-time (26 women); includes 21 minority (5 African Americans, 10 Asian Americans or Pacific Islanders, 6 Hispanic Americans), 5 international. In 2006, 7 degrees awarded. *Degree requirements:* For master's, comprehensive exam. *Entrance requirements:* For master's, GMAT, minimum GPA of 2.5 during previous 2 years of course work. Additional exam requirements/recommendations for international students: Required—TOEFL. *Application deadline:* For fall admission, 6/30 for domestic students; for spring admission, 11/30 for domestic students. Applications are processed on a rolling basis. Application fee: $55. *Expenses:* Tuition, nonresident: part-time $226 per unit. *Financial support:* In 2006–07, 7 students received support. Career-related internships or fieldwork and Federal Work-Study available. Support available to part-time students. Financial award application deadline: 3/1. *Unit head:* Dr. Steve McGuire, Coordinator, 323-343-2890, Fax: 323-343-6461.

California State University, Northridge, Graduate Studies, College of Health and Human Development, Department of Health Sciences, Northridge, CA 91330. Offers health administration (MS); health education (MPH). *Accreditation:* CEPH. *Faculty:* 18 full-time (11 women), 32 part-time/adjunct (18 women). *Students:* 69 full-time (16 women), 64 part-time (22 women); includes 58 minority (18 African Americans, 20 Asian Americans or Pacific Islanders, 20 Hispanic Americans), 14 international. Average age 31. 127 applicants, 52% accepted, 39 enrolled. In 2006, 39 degrees awarded. *Entrance requirements:* For master's, GRE General Test or minimum GPA of 3.0. Additional exam requirements/recommendations for international students: Required—TOEFL. *Application deadline:* For fall admission, 11/30 for domestic students. Application fee: $55. *Expenses:* Tuition, nonresident: full-time $8,136; part-time $4,068 per year. Required fees: $3,624; $1,161 per term. *Financial support:* Teaching assistantships available. Financial award application deadline: 3/1. *Faculty research:* Labor market needs assessment, health education products, dental hygiene, independent practice prototype. *Unit head:* Dr. Brian Malec, Chair, 818-677-3101. *Application contact:* Dr. Janet T. Reagan, Graduate Coordinator, 818-677-3101.

California State University, San Bernardino, Graduate Studies, College of Natural Sciences, Program in Health Services Administration, San Bernardino, CA 92407-2397. Offers MS. *Faculty:* 5 full-time (2 women). *Students:* 22 full-time (17 women), 4 part-time (2 women); includes 15 minority (8 African Americans, 1 American Indian/Alaska Native, 3 Asian Americans or Pacific Islanders, 3 Hispanic Americans), 1 international. Average age 29. 23 applicants, 52% accepted, 6 enrolled. In 2006, 7 degrees awarded. *Degree requirements:* For master's, thesis or alternative. *Application deadline:* For fall admission, 8/31 priority date for domestic students. Application fee: $55. *Financial support:* Fellowships, research assistantships, teaching assistantships available. *Faculty research:* Smoking and health, oral hygiene, menopause, health services research. *Unit head:* Dr. Cynthia Paxton, Chair, 909-537-5339, Fax: 909-537-7037, E-mail: cpaxton@csusb.edu.

Capella University, School of Business and Technology, Minneapolis, MN 55402. Offers accounting (MBA), including system design and programming; business (Certificate), including human resource management (MS, PhD, Certificate), information technology management (MS, PhD, Certificate), leadership (MBA, MS, PhD, Certificate); finance (MBA); general business (MBA); health care management (MBA); information technology (MS, Certificate), including general information technology (MS), information security, network architecture and design (MS), professional projects management (Certificate), project management and leadership (MS), system design and development (MS),); information technology management (MBA); marketing (MBA); organization and management (MBA, MS, PhD), including general business (PhD), general organization and management (MBA, MS), human resource management (MS, PhD, Certificate), information technology management (MS, PhD, Certificate), leadership (MBA, MS, PhD, Certificate); project management (MBA). Part-time and evening/weekend programs available. Postbaccalaureate distance learning degree programs offered (minimal on-campus study). Terminal master's awarded for partial completion of doctoral program. *Degree requirements:* For master's, integrative project, thesis optional; for doctorate, thesis/dissertation, comprehensive exam, registration. *Entrance requirements:* Additional exam requirements/recommendations for international students: Required—TOEFL (minimum score 550 paper-based; 213 computer-based), TWE (minimum score 4). Electronic applications accepted. *Faculty research:* Business policies: strategic, corporate, and financial management; interplay of technological, organizational and social change.

Capella University, School of Human Services, Minneapolis, MN 55402. Offers addictions counseling (Certificate); counseling studies (MS, PhD); criminal justice (MS, PhD, Certificate); diversity studies (Certificate); general human services (MS, PhD); health care administration (MS, PhD, Certificate); management of nonprofit agencies (MS, PhD, Certificate); marital, couple and family counseling/therapy (MS); marriage and family services (Certificate); mental health counseling (MS); professional counseling (Certificate); social and community services (MS, PhD, Certificate). Part-time and evening/weekend programs available. Postbaccalaureate distance learning degree programs offered (minimal on-campus study). Terminal master's awarded for partial completion of doctoral program. *Degree requirements:* For master's, integrative project, thesis optional; for doctorate, thesis/dissertation, comprehensive exam, registration. *Entrance requirements:* Additional exam requirements/recommendations for international students: Required—TOEFL (minimum score 550 paper-based; 213 computer-based), TWE (minimum score 4). Electronic applications accepted. *Faculty research:* Compulsive and addictive behaviors, substance abuse, assessment of psychopathology and neuropsychology.

Cardean University, MBA Program, Chicago, IL 60606-7204. Offers accounting and information systems (MBA); e-commerce (MBA); finance (MBA); global management (MBA); health care administration (MBA); human resources management (MBA); leadership (MBA); management of information systems (MBA); management of technology (MBA); marketing (MBA); professional accounting (MBA); project management (MBA); risk management (MBA); strategy and economics (MBA). Part-time and evening/weekend programs available. Postbaccalaureate distance learning degree programs offered (no on-campus study). *Entrance requirements:* Additional exam requirements/recommendations for international students: Required—TOEFL (minimum score 550 paper-based; 213 computer-based).

Cardinal Stritch University, College of Business and Management, Programs in Management for Adults, Milwaukee, WI 53217-3985. Offers business administration (MBA); financial services (MS); health care executives (MBA); management (MS). Part-time and evening/weekend programs available.

Carnegie Mellon University, H. John Heinz III School of Public Policy and Management, Program in Health Care Policy and Management, Pittsburgh, PA 15213-3891. Offers MSHCPM. Part-time and evening/weekend programs available. *Degree requirements:* For master's, internship. Electronic applications accepted.

See Close-Up on page 1803.

Carnegie Mellon University, H. John Heinz III School of Public Policy and Management, Program in Medical Management, Pittsburgh, PA 15213-3891. Offers MMM.

Case Western Reserve University, School of Medicine and School of Graduate Studies, Graduate Programs in Medicine, Department of Epidemiology and Biostatistics, Cleveland, OH 44106. Offers biostatistics (MS, PhD); epidemiology (MS, PhD); genetic and molecular epidemiology (MS, PhD); health policy (MS, PhD); public health (MPH). Part-time programs available. *Faculty:* 34 full-time (19 women), 55 part-time/adjunct (14 women). *Students:* 122 full-time (71 women), 65 part-time (30 women); includes 73 minority (24 African Americans, 3 American Indian/Alaska Native, 40 Asian Americans or Pacific Islanders, 6 Hispanic Americans). Average age 32. 166 applicants, 78% accepted, 54 enrolled. In 2006, 22 master's, 8 doctorates awarded. Terminal master's awarded for partial completion of doctoral program. *Median time to degree:* Of those who began their doctoral program in fall 1998, 90% received their degree in 8 years or less. *Degree requirements:* For master's, thesis (for some programs), comprehensive exam; for doctorate, thesis/dissertation, comprehensive exam. *Entrance requirements:* For master's, GRE General Test (MCAT may be substituted), 3 recommendations; for doctorate, GRE General Test, 3 recommendations. Additional exam requirements/recommendations for international students: Required—TOEFL (minimum score 550 paper-based; 213 computer-based). *Application deadline:* For fall admission, 2/1 priority date for domestic and international students; for winter admission, 10/1 priority date for domestic students. Applications are processed on a rolling basis. Application fee: $50. Electronic applications accepted. *Financial support:* In 2006–07, 60 students received support, including 14 fellowships with full and partial tuition reimbursements available (averaging $20,772 per year), 38 research assistantships with full and partial tuition reimbursements available (averaging $20,772 per year); teaching assistantships with full and partial tuition reimbursements available, career-related internships or fieldwork, scholarships/grants, traineeships, tuition waivers (full and partial), and unspecified assistantships also available. Support available to part-time students. Financial award application deadline: 2/1. *Faculty research:* Ecologic studies of cancer incidence, statistical modeling, health policy, statistical methods in human genetics. Total annual research expenditures: $12.7 million. *Unit head:* Dr. Alfred A. Rimm, Chairman, 216-368-3197, Fax: 216-368-3970, E-mail: aar2@po.cwru.edu. *Application contact:* Alicia M Boscarello, Graduate Student Coordinator, 216-368-5957, Fax: 216-368-3970, E-mail: amb62@case.edu.

Central Michigan University, Central Michigan University Off-Campus Programs, Program in Administration, Mount Pleasant, MI 48859. Offers acquisitions administration (MSA, Certificate); general administration (MSA, Certificate); health services administration (MSA, Certificate); human resources administration (MSA, Certificate); information resource management (MSA, Certificate); international administration (MSA, Certificate); leadership (MSA, Certificate); public administration (MSA, Certificate); software engineering administration (MSA, Certificate); vehicle design and manufacturing administration (MSA, Certificate). Part-time and evening/weekend

Health Services Management and Hospital Administration

Central Michigan University (continued)

programs available. Postbaccalaureate distance learning degree programs offered (no on-campus study). *Students:* Average age 38. *Entrance requirements:* For master's, minimum GPA of 2.7 in major. *Application deadline:* Applications are processed on a rolling basis. Application fee: $50. Electronic applications accepted. *Financial support:* Scholarships/grants available. Support available to part-time students. Financial award applicants required to submit FAFSA. *Unit head:* Dr. Peter G. Ross, Director, 989-774-6525, Fax: 989-774-2575, E-mail: ross1pg@cmich.edu. *Application contact:* 877-268-4636, E-mail: cmuoffcampus@cmich.edu.

Central Michigan University, Central Michigan University Off-Campus Programs, Program in Health Administration, Mount Pleasant, MI 48859. Offers DHA. Part-time and evening/weekend programs available. Postbaccalaureate distance learning degree programs offered (minimal on-campus study). *Faculty:* 8 part-time/adjunct. *Students:* 45 applicants, 60% accepted, 25 enrolled.Electronic applications accepted. *Financial support:* Scholarships/grants available. Support available to part-time students. Financial award applicants required to submit FAFSA. *Unit head:* Dr. Michael Kennedy, Director, 989-774-1640, E-mail: kenne1m@cmich.edu. *Application contact:* Off-Campus Programs Call Center, E-mail: cmuoffcampus@cmich.edu.

Central Michigan University, College of Graduate Studies, Program in Administration, Mount Pleasant, MI 48859. Offers general administration (MSA); health services administration (MSA); hospitality and tourism administration (MSA); human resource administration (MSA); information resource administration (MSA); international administration (MSA); leadership (MSA); organizational communications (MSA); public administration (MSA); recreation and park administration (MSA); software engineering (MSA); sports administration (MSA). *Accreditation:* AACSB. *Degree requirements:* For master's, thesis or alternative. *Entrance requirements:* For master's, minimum undergraduate GPA of 2.5.

See Close-Up on page 253.

Charleston Southern University, Program in Business, Charleston, SC 29423-8087. Offers accounting (MBA); finance (MBA); health care administration (MBA); information systems (MBA); organizational development (MBA). Part-time and evening/weekend programs available. *Degree requirements:* For master's, thesis optional. *Entrance requirements:* For master's, GMAT. *Faculty research:* Economic forecasting.

Clark University, Graduate School, Graduate School of Management, Business Administration Program, Worcester, MA 01610-1477. Offers accounting (MBA); finance (MBA); global business (MBA); health care management (MBA); management (MBA); management of information technology (MBA); marketing (MBA). *Accreditation:* AACSB. Part-time and evening/weekend programs available. *Students:* 122 full-time (64 women), 113 part-time (42 women); includes 18 minority (3 African Americans, 9 Asian Americans or Pacific Islanders, 6 Hispanic Americans), 115 international. Average age 29. 235 applicants, 78% accepted, 80 enrolled. In 2006, 109 degrees awarded. *Degree requirements:* For master's, thesis optional. *Application deadline:* For fall admission, 6/1 priority date for domestic students; for spring admission, 12/1 priority date for domestic students. Applications are processed on a rolling basis. Application fee: $50. Electronic applications accepted. *Financial support:* In 2006–07, research assistantships with partial tuition reimbursements (averaging $6,000 per year), teaching assistantships with partial tuition reimbursements (averaging $6,000 per year) were awarded; fellowships with full and partial tuition reimbursements, career-related internships or fieldwork, Federal Work-Study, institutionally sponsored loans, and tuition waivers (partial) also available. Support available to part-time students. Financial award application deadline: 5/31. *Faculty research:* Organizational development, accounting, marketing, finance, human resource management. *Application contact:* Patricia Tollo, Admissions Director, 508-793-7406, Fax: 508-793-8822, E-mail: clarkmba@clarku.edu.

See Close-Up on page 257.

Clayton State University, School of Graduate Studies, Program in Health Administration, Morrow, GA 30260-0285. Offers MHA.

Cleveland State University, College of Graduate Studies, Nance College of Business Administration, MBA Programs, Cleveland, OH 44115. Offers business statistics (MBA); finance (MBA); health care administration (MBA); marketing (MBA); operations management (MBA); JD/MBA; MSN/MBA. *Accreditation:* AACSB. Part-time and evening/weekend programs available. *Faculty:* 21 full-time (5 women), 10 part-time/adjunct (1 woman). *Students:* 276 full-time (119 women), 623 part-time (279 women); includes 120 minority (74 African Americans, 3 American Indian/Alaska Native, 32 Asian Americans or Pacific Islanders, 11 Hispanic Americans), 108 international. Average age 28. 530 applicants, 51% accepted, 146 enrolled. In 2006, 308 degrees awarded. *Entrance requirements:* For master's, GMAT or GRE. Additional exam requirements/recommendations for international students: Required—TOEFL (minimum score 525 paper-based; 197 computer-based). *Application deadline:* For fall admission, 7/15 priority date for domestic students, 5/15 for international students; for spring admission, 12/15 priority date for domestic students, 11/1 for international students. Applications are processed on a rolling basis. Application fee: $30. *Financial support:* In 2006–07, 45 research assistantships with full and partial tuition reimbursements (averaging $6,960 per year), 1 teaching assistantship with full and partial tuition reimbursement (averaging $7,800 per year) were awarded; tuition waivers (full) and unspecified assistantships also available. Financial award application deadline: 5/17; financial award applicants required to submit FAFSA. Total annual research expenditures: $63,645. *Unit head:* Bruce Gottschalk, Associate Dean, 216-687-3730, Fax: 216-687-5311, E-mail: cbacsu@csuohio.edu. *Application contact:* Patricia Hite, Director, Academic Program Support, 216-687-6925, Fax: 216-687-6888, E-mail: p.hite@csuohio.edu.

College of Saint Elizabeth, Department of Health Professions and Related Sciences, Morristown, NJ 07960-6989. Offers health care management (MS). Part-time and evening/weekend programs available. *Faculty:* 1 (woman) full-time, 3 part-time/adjunct (1 woman). *Students:* Average age 41. In 2006, 7 degrees awarded. *Degree requirements:* For master's, culminating experience, thesis optional. *Entrance requirements:* For master's, minimum GPA of 3.0. *Application deadline:* Applications are processed on a rolling basis. Application fee: $35. Electronic applications accepted. *Financial support:* Career-related internships or fieldwork, tuition waivers (partial), and unspecified assistantships available. Support available to part-time students. Financial award application deadline: 3/15; financial award applicants required to submit FAFSA. *Faculty research:* Consumer protection in health care. *Unit head:* Linda Hunter, Director of the Graduate Program in Health Care Management, 973-290-4040, Fax: 973-290-4167, E-mail: lhunter@cse.edu. *Application contact:* Michael Szarek, Director of Enrollment Management, 973-290-4112, Fax: 973-290-4167, E-mail: mszarek@cse.edu.

Colorado Technical University Sioux Falls Campus, Programs in Business Administration and Management, Sioux Falls, SD 57108. Offers business administration (MBA); business management (MSM); health science management (MSM); human resources management (MSM); information technology (MSM); organizational leadership (MSM); project management (MBA); technology management (MBA). Evening/weekend programs available. *Degree requirements:* For master's, thesis optional. *Entrance requirements:* For master's, minimum 2 years work experience, resumé.

Columbia Southern University, MBA Program, Orange Beach, AL 36561. Offers electronic business and technology (MBA); healthcare management (MBA); human resources management (MBA); international management (MBA); marketing (MBA); project management (MBA); public administration (MBA); sport management (MBA). Part-time and evening/weekend programs available. Postbaccalaureate distance learning degree programs offered (no on-campus study). *Entrance requirements:* Additional exam requirements/recommendations for international students: Required—TOEFL. Electronic applications accepted.

Columbia University, Mailman School of Public Health, Division of Health Policy and Management, New York, NY 10032. Offers Exec MPH, MPH. Evening/weekend programs available. *Students:* 245. In 2006, 102 degrees awarded. *Degree requirements:* For master's, thesis optional. *Entrance requirements:* For master's, GRE General Test. *Application deadline:* For fall admission, 2/1 for domestic students; for spring admission, 10/1 for domestic students. Application fee: $60. Electronic applications accepted. *Financial support:* Research assistantships, teaching assistantships, career-related internships or fieldwork and Federal Work-Study available. Support available to part-time students. Financial award application deadline: 2/1; financial award applicants required to submit FAFSA. *Faculty research:* Health care reform, health care cost containment, improving quality of health care, assessment of health care technology. *Unit head:* Sherry Glied, Head, 212-305-3924, Fax: 212-305-3405. *Application contact:* June Saunders, Associate Director of Admissions, 212-305-3927, Fax: 212-342-4861, E-mail: ph-admit@columbia.edu.

Concordia University, School of Graduate Studies, John Molson School of Business, Montréal, QC H3G 1M8, Canada. Offers administration (M Sc, Diploma); aviation management (Certificate, Diploma); business administration (MBA, UA Undergraduate Associate, PhD), including international aviation (UA Undergraduate Associate); chartered accountancy (Diploma); community organizational development (Certificate); event management and fundraising (Certificate); executive business administration (EMBA); investment management (Diploma); investment management option (MBA); management accounting (Certificate); management of healthcare organizations (Certificate); sport administration (Diploma). *Accreditation:* AACSB. Part-time and evening/weekend programs available. *Students:* 447 full-time (174 women), 448 part-time (206 women). 925 applicants, 59% accepted, 319 enrolled. In 2006, 183 master's, 6 doctorates, 62 other advanced degrees awarded. *Degree requirements:* For master's, one foreign language, thesis (for some programs), research project; for doctorate, one foreign language, thesis/dissertation; for other advanced degree, one foreign language. *Entrance requirements:* For master's and doctorate, GMAT. Additional exam requirements/recommendations for international students: Required—TOEFL. Application fee: $50. *Expenses:* Contact institution. *Financial support:* Fellowships, career-related internships or fieldwork available. *Faculty research:* General business, capital markets, international business. *Unit head:* Dr. Jerry Tomberlin, Dean, 514-848-2424 Ext. 2700, Fax: 514-848-4502. *Application contact:* Dr. Michel Magnan, Associate Dean, Graduate Programs, 514-848-2424 Ext. 4145, Fax: 514-848-4208.

Concordia University Wisconsin, Graduate Programs, School of Business and Legal Studies, MBA Program, Mequon, WI 53097-2402. Offers finance (MBA); health care administration (MBA); human resource management (MBA); international business (MBA); international business-English/Chinese (MBA); management (MBA); management information services (MBA); managerial communications (MBA); marketing (MBA); public administration (MBA); risk management (MBA). Postbaccalaureate distance learning degree programs offered (minimal on-campus study). *Students:* 504 (249 women). In 2006, 110 degrees awarded. *Degree requirements:* For master's, thesis or alternative, comprehensive exam. *Entrance requirements:* Additional exam requirements/recommendations for international students: Required—TOEFL. *Application deadline:* For fall admission, 8/1 priority date for domestic students; for spring admission, 1/15 for domestic students. Applications are processed on a rolling basis. Application fee: $50. *Expenses:* Contact institution. *Financial support:* Application deadline: 8/1. *Unit head:* Dr. David Borst, Director, 262-243-4298, Fax: 262-243-4428, E-mail: david.borst@cuw.edu.

Cornell University, Graduate School, Graduate Fields of Human Ecology, Field of Policy Analysis and Management, Ithaca, NY 14853-0001. Offers consumer policy (PhD); evaluation (PhD); family and social welfare policy (PhD); health administration (MHA); health management and policy (PhD). *Faculty:* 33 full-time (14 women). *Students:* 54 full-time (30 women); includes 12 minority (3 African Americans, 6 Asian Americans or Pacific Islanders, 3 Hispanic Americans), 15 international. Average age 28. 69 applicants, 35% accepted, 16 enrolled. In 2006, 17 master's, 3 doctorates awarded. *Degree requirements:* For master's and doctorate, thesis/dissertation, registration. *Entrance requirements:* For master's, GRE General Test or GMAT, 2 letters of recommendation; for doctorate, GRE General Test, 2 letters of recommendation. Additional exam requirements/recommendations for international students: Required—TOEFL (minimum score 550 paper-based; 213 computer-based). *Application deadline:* For fall admission, 1/15 for domestic students. Application fee: $60. Electronic applications accepted. *Expenses:* Tuition: Full-time $32,800. Full-time tuition and fees vary according to program. *Financial support:* In 2006–07, 33 students received support, including 6 fellowships with full and partial tuition reimbursements available, 12 research assistantships with full and partial tuition reimbursements available, 15 teaching assistantships with full and partial tuition reimbursements available; institutionally sponsored loans, scholarships/grants, health care benefits, tuition waivers (full and partial), and unspecified assistantships also available. Financial award applicants required to submit FAFSA. *Faculty research:* Health policy, family policy, social welfare policy, program evaluation, consumer policy. *Unit head:* Director of Graduate Studies, 607-255-7772. *Application contact:* Graduate Field Assistant, 607-255-7772, Fax: 607-255-4071, E-mail: pam_phd@cornell.edu.

Dalhousie University, Faculty of Graduate Studies, Faculty of Health Professions, School of Health Services Administration, Halifax, NS B3H 4R2, Canada. Offers MHSA, LL B/MHSA, MN/MHSA. *Accreditation:* CAHME. Part-time programs available. *Entrance requirements:* For master's, GMAT. Additional exam requirements/recommendations for international students: Required—TOEFL. Expenses: Contact institution. *Faculty research:* Hospital, nursing, long-term, public, and community health administration; government administration in health areas.

Dallas Baptist University, Graduate School of Business, Business Administration Program, Dallas, TX 75211-9299. Offers accounting (MBA); business communication (MBA); conflict resolution management (MBA); e-business (MBA); entrepreneurship (MBA); finance (MBA); health care management (MBA); international business (MBA); management (MBA); management information systems (MBA); marketing (MBA); project management (MBA); technology and engineering management (MBA). *Accreditation:* ACBSP. Part-time and evening/weekend programs available. Postbaccalaureate distance learning degree programs offered (no on-campus study). *Faculty:* 49 full-time (21 women), 112 part-time/adjunct (46 women). *Students:* 103 full-time, 318 part-time. 226 applicants, 38% accepted. In 2006, 124 degrees awarded. *Entrance requirements:* For master's, GMAT, minimum GPA of 3.0. Additional exam requirements/recommendations for international students: Required—TOEFL. *Application deadline:* Applications are processed on a rolling basis. Application fee: $25. Electronic applications accepted. *Expenses:* Tuition: Full-time $8,370; part-time $465 per credit hour. Required fees: $465 per credit hour. *Financial support:* Career-related internships or fieldwork, Federal Work-Study, institutionally sponsored loans, scholarships/grants, and tuition waivers (full and partial) available. Support available to part-time students. *Faculty research:* Sports management, services marketing, retailing, strategic management, financial planning/investments. *Unit head:* Dr. Sandra S. Reid, Director, 214-333-5244, Fax: 214-333-5293, E-mail: graduate@dbu.edu. *Application contact:* Kit P. Montgomery, Director of Graduate Programs, 214-333-5242, Fax: 214-333-5579, E-mail: graduate@dbu.edu.

Dallas Baptist University, Graduate School of Business, Management Program, Dallas, TX 75211-9299. Offers business communication (MA); conflict resolution management (MA); general management (MA); health care management (MA); human resource management (MA). Part-time and evening/weekend programs available. Postbaccalaureate distance learning degree programs offered (no on-campus study). *Faculty:* 49 full-time (21 women), 112 part-time/adjunct (46 women). *Students:* 46 full-time, 194 part-time. 96 applicants. In 2006, 77 degrees awarded. *Entrance requirements:* For master's, minimum GPA of 3.0. Additional exam requirements/recommendations for international students: Required—TOEFL. *Application deadline:* Applications are processed on a rolling basis. Application fee: $25. Electronic applications accepted. *Expenses:* Tuition: Full-time $8,370; part-time $465 per credit hour. Required fees: $465 per credit hour. *Financial support:* Federal Work-Study, institutionally sponsored loans, scholarships/grants, and tuition waivers (full and partial) available. Support available to part-time students. *Faculty research:* Organizational behavior, conflict personalities. *Unit head:* Connie F. Throne, Director of Organizational Management Program, 214-333-5244,

Fax: 214-333-5579, E-mail: graduate@dbu.edu. *Application contact:* Kit P. Montgomery, Director of Graduate Programs, 214-333-5242, Fax: 214-333-5579, E-mail: graduate@dbu.edu.

Davenport University, Sneden Graduate School, Warren, MI 48092-5209. Offers accounting (MBA); commerce (MBA); finance (MBA); health care management (MBA); human resources management (MBA); management (MBA). *Entrance requirements:* For master's, minimum undergraduate GPA of 2.7.

Davenport University, Sneden Graduate School, Dearborn, MI 48126-3799. Offers accounting (MBA); e-business (MBA); finance (MBA); global business (MBA); health care management (MBA); human resources management (MBA); management (MBA); marketing (MBA). Part-time and evening/weekend programs available. Postbaccalaureate distance learning degree programs offered (no on-campus study). *Entrance requirements:* For master's, minimum GPA of 2.7, previous course work in accounting and statistics. *Faculty research:* Accounting, international accounting, social and environmental accounting, finance.

DePaul University, Charles H. Kellstadt Graduate School of Business, Department of Management, Chicago, IL 60604-2287. Offers entrepreneurship (MBA); health sector management (MBA); human resource management (MBA, MSHR); leadership/change management (MBA); management planning and strategy (MBA); operations management (MBA). Part-time and evening/weekend programs available. *Faculty:* 36 full-time (7 women), 35 part-time/adjunct (16 women). *Students:* 173 full-time (71 women), 134 part-time (61 women); includes 60 minority (12 African Americans, 34 Asian Americans or Pacific Islanders, 14 Hispanic Americans), 13 international. Average age 31. In 2006, 112 degrees awarded. *Entrance requirements:* For master's, GMAT, GRE (MSHR), 2 letters of recommendation, resumé. Additional exam requirements/recommendations for international students: Required—TOEFL (minimum score 550 paper-based; 213 computer-based). *Application deadline:* For fall admission, 7/1 for domestic students; for winter admission, 10/1 for domestic students; for spring admission, 2/1 for domestic students. Applications are processed on a rolling basis. Application fee: $60. Electronic applications accepted. *Financial support:* Research assistantships available. Financial award application deadline: 4/1. *Faculty research:* Growth management, creativity and innovation, quality management and business process design, entrepreneurship. *Application contact:* Christopher E. Kinsella, Director of Cohort MBA Programs, 312-362-8810, Fax: 312-362-6677, E-mail: kgsb@depaul.edu.

DePaul University, School of Public Service, Chicago, IL 60604-2287. Offers financial administration management (Certificate); health administration (Certificate); health law and policy (MS); international public services (MS); metropolitan planning (Certificate); public administration (MS); public service management (MS), including association management, fundraising and philanthropy, healthcare administration, higher education administration, metropolitan planning, non-profit administration, public administration, public policy; public services (Certificate); JD/MS; MA/MS. Part-time and evening/weekend programs available. Postbaccalaureate distance learning degree programs offered (minimal on-campus study). *Faculty:* 11 full-time (2 women), 19 part-time/adjunct (16 women). *Students:* 195 full-time (146 women), 132 part-time (89 women); includes 114 minority (58 African Americans, 1 American Indian/Alaska Native, 27 Asian Americans or Pacific Islanders, 28 Hispanic Americans). 140 applicants, 96% accepted, 96 enrolled. In 2006, 89 degrees awarded. *Degree requirements:* For master's, thesis or integrative seminar. *Entrance requirements:* For master's, minimum GPA of 2.7. Additional exam requirements/recommendations for international students: Required—TOEFL (minimum score 550 paper-based; 213 computer-based; 80 iBT), IELTS (minimum score 7). *Application deadline:* Applications are processed on a rolling basis. Application fee: $25. Electronic applications accepted. *Financial support:* In 2006–07, 28 students received support, including 3 research assistantships with full tuition reimbursements available (averaging $7,000 per year); career-related internships or fieldwork, Federal Work-Study, institutionally sponsored loans, scholarships/grants, and tuition waivers (partial) also available. Support available to part-time students. Financial award application deadline: 7/1; financial award applicants required to submit FAFSA. *Faculty research:* Government financing, transportation, leadership, health care, volunteerism and organizational behavior, non-profit organizations. Total annual research expenditures: $20,000. *Unit head:* Dr. J. Patrick Murphy, Director, 312-362-5608, Fax: 312-362-5506, E-mail: jpmurphy@depaul.edu. *Application contact:* Megan B. Balderston, Director of Admissions and Marketing, 312-362-5565, Fax: 312-362-5506, E-mail: pubserv@depaul.edu.

Des Moines University, College of Health Sciences, Program in Healthcare Administration, Des Moines, IA 50312-4104. Offers MHA. Part-time and evening/weekend programs available. *Faculty:* 1 (woman) full-time, 2 part-time/adjunct (0 women). *Students:* 27 full-time (17 women), 12 part-time (11 women). 31 applicants, 97% accepted, 30 enrolled. In 2006, 10 degrees awarded. *Entrance requirements:* For master's, minimum GPA of 3.0. Additional exam requirements/recommendations for international students: Required—TOEFL (minimum score 600 paper-based). *Application deadline:* For fall admission, 8/25 priority date for domestic and international students; for winter admission, 1/5 priority date for domestic and international students; for spring admission, 5/1 priority date for domestic and international students. Applications are processed on a rolling basis. Application fee: $35. *Expenses:* Contact institution. *Financial support:* In 2006–07, 1 student received support. Career-related internships or fieldwork, institutionally sponsored loans, scholarships/grants, and university employment available. Support available to part-time students. Financial award applicants required to submit FAFSA. *Faculty research:* Quality improvement, rural sociology, women's health, health promotion, patient education. *Unit head:* Dr. Carla Stebbins, Director, 515-271-1497. *Application contact:* Lisa Vroegh, Admissions Coordinator, 515-271-1364, Fax: 515-271-7162, E-mail: hmadmit@dmu.edu.

Duke University, Fuqua School of Business, Concentration in Health Sector Management for Full-Time Programs, Durham, NC 27708-0586. Offers Certificate. Program must be taken while pursuing MBA. *Accreditation:* CAHME. *Faculty:* 7 full-time (1 woman), 7 part-time/adjunct (0 women). *Students:* 134 full-time (40 women). Average age 29. 259 applicants, 51% accepted, 73 enrolled. *Entrance requirements:* Additional exam requirements/recommendations for international students: Required—TOEFL. *Application deadline:* Applications are processed on a rolling basis. Application fee: $185. Electronic applications accepted. *Financial support:* In 2006–07, 17 students received support. Scholarships/grants available. Financial award application deadline: 3/1. *Faculty research:* Health information technology, venture capital in health care, new business development, impact of genetics on practice of medicine, economics of the pharmaceutical innovation. *Unit head:* Kevin Schulman, Director, 919-660-7989, Fax: 919-660-7843, E-mail: hsm@fuqua.duke.edu. *Application contact:* Liz Riley Hargrove, Assistant Dean and Director of Admissions, 919-660-7705, Fax: 919-681-8026, E-mail: admissions-info@fuqua.duke.edu.

Duke University, Fuqua School of Business, Concentration in Health Sector Management for Weekend and Global Programs, Durham, NC 27708-0586. Offers Certificate. Program must be taken while pursuibg WEMBA or GEMBA. *Faculty:* 7 full-time (1 woman), 7 part-time/adjunct (0 women). *Students:* 93 full-time (22 women). Average age 32.*Unit head:* Kevin Schulman, Director, 919-660-7989, Fax: 919-660-7843, E-mail: hsm@fuqua.duke.edu. *Application contact:* Dan McCleary, Director of EMBA Admissions, 919-60-8002, Fax: 919-681-8026, E-mail: admissions-info@fuqua.duke.edu.

Duquesne University, John G. Rangos, Sr. School of Health Sciences, Pittsburgh, PA 15282-0001. Offers health management systems (MHMS); occupational therapy (MS); physical therapy (DPT); physician assistant (MPA); speech-language pathology (MS); MBA/MHMS. *Accreditation:* AOTA (one or more programs are accredited); APTA (one or more programs are accredited); ASHA. *Faculty:* 35 full-time (22 women), 24 part-time/adjunct (12 women). *Students:* 261 full-time (229 women), 16 part-time (8 women); includes 11 minority (6 African Americans, 1 American Indian/Alaska Native, 2 Asian Americans or Pacific Islanders, 2 Hispanic Americans), 3 international. Average age 23. 150 applicants, 55% accepted, 41 enrolled. In 2006, 66 master's, 13 doctorates awarded. *Degree requirements:* For doctorate, thesis/dissertation. *Entrance requirements:* For master's, GRE (speech-language pathology), 3 letters of recommendation, minimum GPA of 2.75 (health management systems, occupational therapy), minimum GPA of 3.0 (physical assistant, speech-language pathology); for doctorate, GRE General Test, 3 letters of recommendation, minimum GPA of 3.0, personal interview. Additional exam requirements/recommendations for international students: Required—TOEFL (minimum score 600 paper-based; 250 computer-based). *Application deadline:* For fall admission, 12/1 priority date for domestic students; for winter admission, 5/1 priority date for domestic students. Application fee: $50. Electronic applications accepted. *Expenses:* Contact institution. Tuition and fees vary according to degree level and program. *Financial support:* Federal Work-Study available. *Faculty research:* Neuronal processing, electrical stimulation on peripheral neuropathy, CNS stimulatory and inhibitory signals, behavioral genetic methodologies to development disorders of speech, neurogenic communication disorders. Total annual research expenditures: $66,000. *Unit head:* Dr. Gregory H. Frazer, Dean, 412-396-5303, Fax: 412-396-5554, E-mail: frazer@duq.edu. *Application contact:* Christopher R. Hilf, Recruiter/Academic Advisor, 412-396-5653, Fax: 412-396-5554, E-mail: hilfc@duq.edu.

D'Youville College, Department of Health Services Administration, Buffalo, NY 14201-1084. Offers clinical research associate (Certificate); health services administration (MS, Certificate); long term care administration (Certificate). Part-time and evening/weekend programs available. *Faculty:* 4 full-time (3 women), 3 part-time/adjunct (1 woman). *Students:* 12 full-time (7 women), 54 part-time (38 women); includes 8 minority (all African Americans), 17 international. Average age 37. 40 applicants, 70% accepted, 17 enrolled. In 2006, 7 master's, 1 other advanced degree awarded. *Degree requirements:* For master's, project or thesis. *Entrance requirements:* For master's, minimum GPA of 3.0 in major. Additional exam requirements/recommendations for international students: Required—TOEFL (minimum score 500 paper-based; 173 computer-based). *Application deadline:* For fall admission, 5/1 priority date for international students; for spring admission, 9/1 priority date for international students. Applications are processed on a rolling basis. Application fee: $25. Electronic applications accepted. *Financial support:* In 2006–07, 1 research assistantship with partial tuition reimbursement (averaging $3,000 per year) was awarded; career-related internships or fieldwork, Federal Work-Study, and scholarships/grants also available. Support available to part-time students. Financial award application deadline: 3/1; financial award applicants required to submit FAFSA. *Faculty research:* Outcomes research in rehabilitation medicine, cost/benefit analysis prospective payment systems. *Unit head:* Dr. Walter Iwanenko, Chair, 716-829-7612, Fax: 716-829-8184. *Application contact:* Linda Fisher, Graduate Admissions Director, 716-829-8400, Fax: 716-829-7900, E-mail: graduateadmissions@dyc.edu.

Eastern Kentucky University, The Graduate School, College of Arts and Sciences, Department of Government, Program in General Public Administration, Richmond, KY 40475-3102. Offers community development (MPA); community health administration (MPA); general public administration (MPA). *Accreditation:* NASPAA. Part-time and evening/weekend programs available. *Students:* 17 full-time (10 women), 30 part-time (15 women); includes 5 minority (4 African Americans, 1 American Indian/Alaska Native), 4 international. Average age 31. 23 applicants, 83% accepted, 11 enrolled. In 2006, 12 degrees awarded. *Entrance requirements:* For master's, GRE General Test, minimum GPA of 2.5. Application fee: $30. *Expenses:* Tuition, state resident: full-time $5,610. Tuition, nonresident: full-time $15,910. *Unit head:* Dr. Sara Zeigler, Chair, Department of Government, 859-622-5931.

East Tennessee State University, School of Graduate Studies, College of Business and Technology, Department of Management and Marketing, Johnson City, TN 37614. Offers business administration (MBA, Certificate); health care management (Certificate). Part-time and evening/weekend programs available. *Degree requirements:* For master's, comprehensive exam. *Entrance requirements:* For master's, GMAT, minimum GPA of 2.5. Additional exam requirements/recommendations for international students: Required—TOEFL (minimum score 550 paper-based; 213 computer-based).

East Tennessee State University, School of Graduate Studies, College of Nursing, Johnson City, TN 37614. Offers advanced nursing practice (Post Master's Certificate); health care management (Certificate); nursing (MSN, DSN). *Accreditation:* AACN. Part-time programs available. *Degree requirements:* For master's, thesis optional. *Entrance requirements:* For master's, GRE General Test, minimum GPA of 3.0, bachelor's degree in nursing, current RN license. Additional exam requirements/recommendations for international students: Required—TOEFL (minimum score 550 paper-based; 213 computer-based). *Faculty research:* Rural primary care, health care for the homeless, community health problems across the lifespan, nursing education research, school health services.

East Tennessee State University, School of Graduate Studies, College of Public and Allied Health, Department of Public Health, Johnson City, TN 37614. Offers community health (MPH); epidemiology (Certificate); gerontology (Certificate); health care management (Certificate); public health (MPH); public health administration (MPH). *Accreditation:* CEPH. Part-time programs available. *Degree requirements:* For master's, thesis optional. *Entrance requirements:* For master's, GRE General Test, 2 years of community health experience. Additional exam requirements/recommendations for international students: Required—TOEFL (minimum score 550 paper-based; 213 computer-based). *Faculty research:* Rural health issues, youth and adolescent health, health of the elderly, environmental epidemiology, spatial analysis of data.

Emory University, Rollins School of Public Health, Department of Health Policy and Management, Atlanta, GA 30322-1100. Offers health outcomes management (MPH); health policy (MPH); health policy research (MSPH); health services management (MPH); health services research and health policy (PhD). Part-time programs available. *Students:* 105 full-time (83 women), 3 part-time (2 women). Average age 27. 169 applicants, 88% accepted, 61 enrolled. In 2006, 54 degrees awarded. *Degree requirements:* For master's, practicum, capstone course, thesis optional. *Entrance requirements:* For master's, GRE General Test. Additional exam requirements/recommendations for international students: Required—TOEFL (minimum score 550 paper-based; 215 computer-based). *Application deadline:* For fall admission, 1/5 priority date for domestic and international students. Application fee: $75. Electronic applications accepted. *Expenses:* Tuition: Full-time $30,246. *Financial support:* Fellowships with full and partial tuition reimbursements, career-related internships or fieldwork, Federal Work-Study, institutionally sponsored loans, and scholarships/grants available. Support available to part-time students. Financial award application deadline: 1/5. *Faculty research:* U.S. health policy and financing, healthcare organization and financing. *Unit head:* David H Howard, Director of Graduate Studies, 404-727-3487, Fax: 404-727-9198, E-mail: david.howard@emory.edu. *Application contact:* Kathy Wollenzien, Director, Academic Programs, 404-724-5701, Fax: 404-727-9198, E-mail: kwollen@sph.emory.edu.

Emory University, Rollins School of Public Health, Program in Career Public Health, Atlanta, GA 30322-1100. Offers applied epidemiology (MPH); outcomes option (MPH); prevention (MPH). Part-time and evening/weekend programs available. Postbaccalaureate distance learning degree programs offered (minimal on-campus study). *Students:* 11 full-time (10 women), 101 part-time (69 women). Average age 40. 69 applicants, 68% accepted, 37 enrolled. In 2006, 18 degrees awarded. *Degree requirements:* For master's, thesis, practicum. *Entrance requirements:* Additional exam requirements/recommendations for international students: Required—TOEFL (minimum score 550 paper-based; 213 computer-based). *Application deadline:* For fall admission, 1/5 priority date for domestic students, 1/5 for international students. Applications are processed on a rolling basis. Application fee: $75. Electronic applications accepted. *Expenses:* Tuition: Full-time $30,246. *Financial support:* Fellowships with full and partial tuition reimbursements, career-related internships or fieldwork, institutionally sponsored loans, and scholarships/grants available. Support available to part-time students. Financial award application deadline: 1/5. *Unit head:* Dr. Iris Smith, Director, 404-727-2925, Fax: 404-727-3996, E-mail: ismith@sph.emory.edu. *Application contact:* Robie Freeman Burks, Assistant Director of Academic Programs, 404-727-8739, Fax: 404-727-8768, E-mail: rfreem2@sph.emory.edu.

Health Services Management and Hospital Administration

Fairfield University, School of Nursing, Fairfield, CT 06824-5195. Offers adult nurse practitioner (MSN, PMC); family nurse practitioner (MSN, PMC); healthcare management (MSN); nurse anesthesia (MSN); psychiatric nurse practitioner (MSN, PMC). *Accreditation:* AACN; AANA/CANAEP. Part-time programs available. *Faculty:* 13 full-time (12 women), 2 part-time/adjunct (both women). *Students:* 3 full-time (all women), 39 part-time (all women); includes 5 minority (2 African Americans, 3 Asian Americans or Pacific Islanders). Average age 42. 23 applicants, 30% accepted, 3 enrolled. In 2006, 9 degrees awarded. *Degree requirements:* For master's, capstone project. *Entrance requirements:* For master's, MAT or GRE, minimum QPA of 3.0, RN license, resumé, 2 recommendations; for PMC, 1 year of work experience as a registered nurse. Additional exam requirements/recommendations for international students: Required—TOEFL (minimum score 550 paper-based; 213 computer-based; 79 iBT). *Application deadline:* For fall admission, 4/1 priority date for domestic students, 6/15 priority date for international students; for spring admission, 11/1 priority date for domestic students, 10/15 priority date for international students. Applications are processed on a rolling basis. Application fee: $55. *Expenses:* Contact institution. *Financial support:* Traineeships available. Financial award applicants required to submit FAFSA. *Faculty research:* Critical care, nursing outcomes, care of older adults, leadership, community health. *Unit head:* Dr. Jeanne M. Novotny, Dean, 203-254-4000 Ext. 2701, Fax: 203-254-4126, E-mail: jnovotny@mail.fairfield.edu. *Application contact:* Marianne Gumpper, Director of Graduate and Continuing Studies Admissions, 203-254-4184, Fax: 203-254-4073, E-mail: gradadmis@mail.fairfield.edu.

Fairleigh Dickinson University, Metropolitan Campus, Silberman College of Business, Center for Healthcare Management Studies, Program in Management for Health System Executives, Teaneck, NJ 07666-1914. Offers MBA. *Students:* 10 full-time (6 women), 2 part-time (1 woman). Average age 38. 2 applicants, 50% accepted, 0 enrolled. In 2006, 7 degrees awarded. *Application deadline:* Applications are processed on a rolling basis. *Unit head:* Dr. Peter Caliguari, Director, Center for Healthcare Management Studies, 201-692-2000.

Florida Atlantic University, College of Business, Department of Industry Studies, Boca Raton, FL 33431-0991. Offers business administration (MBA); health administration (MHA). *Faculty:* 8 full-time (2 women), 3 part-time/adjunct (0 women). *Students:* 8 full-time (7 women), 23 part-time (16 women); includes 9 minority (2 African Americans, 3 Asian Americans or Pacific Islanders, 4 Hispanic Americans), 4 international. Average age 31. 31 applicants, 48% accepted, 11 enrolled. In 2006, 35 degrees awarded. *Degree requirements:* For master's, registration. *Entrance requirements:* For master's, GMAT or GRE, minimum GPA of 3.0 in last 60 hours of course work. Additional exam requirements/recommendations for international students: Required—TOEFL (minimum score 600 paper-based; 250 computer-based). *Application deadline:* For fall admission, 7/1 for domestic students, 1/15 for international students; for spring admission, 11/1 for domestic students, 8/15 for international students. Applications are processed on a rolling basis. Application fee: $30. Electronic applications accepted. *Expenses:* Tuition, area resident: Full-time $4,394. Tuition, nonresident: full-time $16,441. *Financial support:* Research assistantships with full tuition reimbursements, career-related internships or fieldwork, tuition waivers (partial), and unspecified assistantships available. *Faculty research:* Sports administration, healthcare, policy, finance, real estate, senior living. *Unit head:* Dr. Carl Riegel, Chair, 561-297-0656, E-mail: criegel@fau.edu. *Application contact:* Dr. Robert Hays, Director, Health Administration, 561-297-3198, E-mail: rhays@fau.edu.

Florida International University, College of Nursing and Health Sciences, Department of Health Services Administration, Miami, FL 33199. Offers MHSA. *Accreditation:* CAHME. Part-time and evening/weekend programs available. *Faculty:* 1 (woman) full-time. *Students:* 14 full-time (12 women), 25 part-time (22 women); includes 31 minority (12 African Americans, 2 American Indian/Alaska Native, 2 Asian Americans or Pacific Islanders, 15 Hispanic Americans), 3 international. Average age 31. 31 applicants, 68% accepted, 6 enrolled. In 2006, 23 degrees awarded. *Entrance requirements:* For master's, GRE General Test, interview, minimum GPA of 3.0. Additional exam requirements/recommendations for international students: Required—TOEFL. *Application deadline:* For fall admission, 4/1 priority date for domestic students; for spring admission, 10/1 for domestic students. Applications are processed on a rolling basis. Application fee: $25. *Expenses:* Tuition, state resident: part-time $249 per credit hour. Tuition, nonresident: part-time $753 per credit hour. Tuition and fees vary according to program. *Unit head:* Dr. Gloria Deckard, Head, 305-348-0429, Fax: 305-348-5848, E-mail: gloria.deckard@fiu.edu.

Framingham State College, Division of Graduate and Continuing Education, Program in Health Care Administration, Framingham, MA 01701-9101. Offers MA. Part-time and evening/weekend programs available. *Faculty:* 2 full-time, 4 part-time/adjunct. *Students:* 35. In 2006, 8 degrees awarded. *Unit head:* Dr. George Jarnis, Coordinator, 508-626-4824, Fax: 508-626-4030, E-mail: gjarnis@frc.mass.edu. *Application contact:* 508-626-4550, Fax: 508-626-4030, E-mail: dgce@frc.mass.edu.

Francis Marion University, Graduate Programs, School of Business, Florence, SC 29501-0547. Offers business (MBA); health management (MBA). *Accreditation:* AACSB. Part-time and evening/weekend programs available. *Faculty:* 16 full-time (2 women). *Students:* 7 full-time (5 women), 49 part-time (24 women); includes 11 minority (8 African Americans, 1 Asian American or Pacific Islander, 2 Hispanic Americans), 1 international. Average age 31. 32 applicants, 100% accepted, 13 enrolled. In 2006, 18 degrees awarded. *Degree requirements:* For master's, comprehensive exam. *Entrance requirements:* For master's, GMAT. *Application deadline:* For fall admission, 4/15 priority date for domestic students; for spring admission, 10/15 priority date for domestic students. Applications are processed on a rolling basis. Application fee: $30. *Expenses:* Tuition, state resident: full-time $6,527; part-time $326 per credit hour. Tuition, nonresident: full-time $13,054; part-time $653 per credit hour. Required fees: $185; $5 per credit hour. $45 per term. *Financial support:* In 2006–07, 2 research assistantships (averaging $3,000 per year) were awarded; unspecified assistantships also available. Support available to part-time students. Financial award application deadline: 3/1; financial award applicants required to submit FAFSA. *Faculty research:* Ethics, directions of MBA, international business, regional economics, environmental issues. *Unit head:* Dr. M. Barry O'Brien, Dean, 843-661-1419, Fax: 843-661-1432, E-mail: mbobrien@fmarion.edu.

Friends University, Graduate School, Division of Business, Technology, and Leadership, Program in Health Care Leadership, Wichita, KS 67213. Offers MHCL. Evening/weekend programs available. *Students:* 54 full-time. *Entrance requirements:* Additional exam requirements/recommendations for international students: Required—TOEFL (minimum score 560 paper-based; 220 computer-based). *Application deadline:* For fall admission, 6/1 priority date for domestic students, 5/1 priority date for international students; for spring admission, 11/1 priority date for domestic students, 10/1 priority date for international students. *Unit head:* Donna Ehrlich, Director, 800-794-6945 Ext. 5646.

The George Washington University, School of Medicine and Health Sciences, Health Sciences Programs, Washington, DC 20052. Offers adult nurse practitioner (MSN, Post Master's Certificate); advanced family nurse practitioner (Post Master's Certificate); clinical practice management (MSHS); clinical research administration (MSHS); clinical research administration for nurses (MSN); emergency services management (MSHS); end-of-life care (MSHS, MSN); family nurse practitioner (MSN); immunohematology (MSHS); nursing leadership and management (MSN); oral biology (MSHS); physical therapy (DPT); physician assistant (MSHS); MSHS/MPH. Postbaccalaureate distance learning degree programs offered (no on-campus study). *Entrance requirements:* Additional exam requirements/recommendations for international students: Required—TOEFL (minimum score 550 paper-based; 213 computer-based). Expenses: Contact institution.

The George Washington University, School of Public Health and Health Services, Department of Health Policy, Washington, DC 20052. Offers MPH, MS. *Degree requirements:* For master's, case study or special project. *Entrance requirements:* For master's, GMAT, GRE General Test, or MCAT. Additional exam requirements/recommendations for international students: Required—TOEFL.

The George Washington University, School of Public Health and Health Services, Department of Health Services Management and Leadership, Washington, DC 20052. Offers health management and leadership (MHSA); health policy (MHSA); health services administration (Specialist); public health management (MPH). *Accreditation:* CAHME (one or more programs are accredited). *Degree requirements:* For master's, internship or residency. *Entrance requirements:* For master's, GMAT or GRE; for Specialist, GMAT or GRE, master's degree in related field. Additional exam requirements/recommendations for international students: Required—TOEFL. *Faculty research:* Hospital administration, ambulatory health care, social gerontology, health care financing, health care ethics.

The George Washington University, School of Public Health and Health Services, Doctoral Program in Public Health, Washington, DC 20052. Offers environmental and occupational health (Dr PH); health behavior (Dr PH); health policy (Dr PH). *Accreditation:* CEPH. *Faculty research:* Community organization, tele-medicine, long-term care, financing for vulnerable populations, quantitative analysis in public health policy.

Georgia Institute of Technology, Graduate Studies and Research, College of Engineering, School of Industrial and Systems Engineering, Program in Health Systems, Atlanta, GA 30332-0001. Offers MSHS. *Entrance requirements:* For master's, GRE General Test, minimum GPA of 3.0. Additional exam requirements/recommendations for international students: Required—TOEFL. Electronic applications accepted. *Faculty research:* Emergency medical services, health development planning, health services evaluations.

Georgia Southern University, Jack N. Averitt College of Graduate Studies, Jiann-Ping Hsu College of Public Health, Program in Health Services Administration, Statesboro, GA 30460. Offers MHSA. Part-time programs available. *Students:* 10 full-time (7 women), 3 part-time (2 women); includes 6 minority (5 African Americans, 1 Asian American or Pacific Islander), 1 international. Average age 28. 7 applicants, 43% accepted, 2 enrolled. In 2006, 2 degrees awarded. *Degree requirements:* For master's, managerial residency in health service or thesis, thesis optional. *Entrance requirements:* For master's, GRE General Test, GMAT, minimum GPA of 2.75, resumé. Additional exam requirements/recommendations for international students: Required—TOEFL (minimum score 550 paper-based; 213 computer-based). *Application deadline:* For fall admission, 3/1 priority date for domestic students, 3/1 for international students; for spring admission, 10/1 priority date for domestic students, 10/1 for international students. Applications are processed on a rolling basis. Application fee: $50. Electronic applications accepted. *Financial support:* In 2006–07, 8 students received support, including research assistantships with partial tuition reimbursements available (averaging $5,500 per year), teaching assistantships with partial tuition reimbursements available (averaging $5,500 per year); career-related internships or fieldwork, Federal Work-Study, scholarships/grants, tuition waivers (partial), and unspecified assistantships also available. Support available to part-time students. Financial award applicants required to submit FAFSA. *Unit head:* Dr. Gerald Ledlaw, Coordinator, 912-681-0713, E-mail: gledlaw@georgiasouthern.edu. *Application contact:* 912-681-5384, Fax: 912-681-0740, E-mail: gradadmissions@georgiasouthern.edu.

Georgia State University, J. Mack Robinson College of Business, Institute of Health Administration, Atlanta, GA 30303-3083. Offers MBA, MHA, MSHA. *Accreditation:* CAHME. *Faculty:* 5 full-time (2 women). *Students:* 27 full-time (13 women), 38 part-time (18 women); includes 12 minority (6 African Americans, 6 Asian Americans or Pacific Islanders), 5 international. Average age 30. 20 applicants, 45% accepted, 6 enrolled. In 2006, 21 degrees awarded. *Entrance requirements:* For master's, GMAT. Additional exam requirements/recommendations for international students: Required—TOEFL (minimum score 610 paper-based; 255 computer-based; 101 iBT). *Application deadline:* For fall admission, 5/1 for domestic students, 2/1 for international students; for spring admission, 10/15 for domestic students, 5/1 for international students. Applications are processed on a rolling basis. Application fee: $50. Electronic applications accepted. *Financial support:* Career-related internships or fieldwork and tuition waivers (partial) available. Support available to part-time students. Financial award applicants required to submit FAFSA. *Unit head:* Dr. Andrew T. Sumner, Director, 404-651-2637, Fax: 404-651-1230.

Governors State University, College of Health Professions, Program in Health Administration, University Park, IL 60466-0975. Offers MHA. *Accreditation:* CAHME. *Students:* 9 full-time, 76 part-time. Average age 35. *Degree requirements:* For master's, field experience or internship. *Entrance requirements:* For master's, minimum GPA of 3.0 in last 60 hours of undergraduate course work or 9 hours of graduate course work. *Application deadline:* For fall admission, 7/15 priority date for domestic students; for spring admission, 11/10 for domestic students. Applications are processed on a rolling basis. Application fee: $25. *Expenses:* Tuition, state resident: full-time $4,104; part-time $171 per hour. Tuition, nonresident: part-time $513 per hour. *Financial support:* Research assistantships, career-related internships or fieldwork, Federal Work-Study, institutionally sponsored loans, scholarships/grants, and tuition waivers (full and partial) available. Financial award application deadline: 5/1. *Unit head:* Dr. Ralph Bell, Head.

Grand Valley State University, College of Community and Public Service, School of Public and Nonprofit Administration, Program in Health Administration, Allendale, MI 49401-9403. Offers MHA. Part-time and evening/weekend programs available. *Faculty:* 6 full-time (2 women), 3 part-time/adjunct (1 woman). *Students:* 17 full-time (10 women), 28 part-time (18 women); includes 10 minority (5 African Americans, 1 American Indian/Alaska Native, 3 Asian Americans or Pacific Islanders, 1 Hispanic American). Average age 32. 28 applicants, 89% accepted, 17 enrolled. In 2006, 3 degrees awarded. *Entrance requirements:* Additional exam requirements/recommendations for international students: Required—TOEFL. *Application deadline:* For fall admission, 5/1 priority date for domestic students; for winter admission, 11/1 priority date for domestic students. Applications are processed on a rolling basis. Application fee: $30. Electronic applications accepted. *Expenses:* Tuition, state resident: full-time $5,850; part-time $325 per credit. Tuition, nonresident: full-time $10,800; part-time $600 per credit. Tuition and fees vary according to course load. *Financial support:* In 2006–07, 10 students received support, including 10 research assistantships with full and partial tuition reimbursements available (averaging $8,000 per year). Financial award application deadline: 5/1. *Faculty research:* Long-term care and aging, Medicare and Medicaid finance and administration, health economics. *Unit head:* Dr. Mark Hoffman, Director, School of Public and Nonprofit Administration, 616-331-6575, Fax: 616-331-7120, E-mail: hoffman@gvsu.edu.

Grand Valley State University, Kirkhof College of Nursing, Allendale, MI 49401-9403. Offers advanced practice (MSN); case management (MSN); nursing administration (MSN); nursing education (MSN); MSN/MBA. *Accreditation:* AACN. Part-time programs available. *Faculty:* 17 full-time (all women), 1 (woman) part-time/adjunct. *Students:* 3 full-time (all women), 46 part-time (42 women); includes 4 minority (1 African American, 1 Asian American or Pacific Islander, 2 Hispanic Americans). Average age 35. 15 applicants, 67% accepted, 8 enrolled. In 2006, 20 degrees awarded. *Degree requirements:* For master's, thesis optional. *Entrance requirements:* For master's, GRE, minimum GPA of 3.0 in upper-division course work, course work in statistics, Michigan RN license. Additional exam requirements/recommendations for international students: Required—TOEFL. *Application deadline:* For fall admission, 3/15 priority date for domestic students. Applications are processed on a rolling basis. Application fee: $30. Electronic applications accepted. *Expenses:* Tuition, state resident: full-time $5,850; part-time $325 per credit. Tuition, nonresident: full-time $10,800; part-time $600 per credit. Tuition and fees vary according to course load. *Financial support:* In 2006–07, 7 research assistantships with full and partial tuition reimbursements (averaging $8,000 per year) were awarded; career-related internships or fieldwork, Federal Work-Study, institutionally sponsored loans, and traineeships also available. Financial award application deadline: 2/15. *Faculty research:* Multigenerational health promotion, chronic disease prevention, end-of-life issues; nursing workload, family caregiver health. Total annual research expenditures: $36,000. *Unit head:* Dr. Phyllis Gendler, Dean, 616-331-7161, Fax: 616-331-7362, E-mail: gendlerp@gvsu.

edu. *Application contact:* Dr. Jean Martin, Director of Graduate Programs, 616-331-7167, Fax: 616-331-7362, E-mail: martinj@gvsu.edu.

Harvard University, Business School, Doctoral Programs in Management, Boston, MA 02163. Offers business administration (DBA); business economics (PhD); health policy management (PhD); information and technology management (PhD); organizational behavior (PhD). *Degree requirements:* For doctorate, thesis/dissertation, comprehensive exam (for some programs). *Entrance requirements:* For doctorate, GRE General Test or GMAT. Additional exam requirements/recommendations for international students: Required—TOEFL. *Expenses:* Tuition: Full-time $30,275. Full-time tuition and fees vary according to program and student level.

Harvard University, Graduate School of Arts and Sciences, Committee on Higher Degrees in Health Policy, Cambridge, MA 02138. Offers PhD. *Students:* 40 full-time (26 women). 64 applicants, 20% accepted. In 2006, 5 degrees awarded. *Degree requirements:* For doctorate, thesis/dissertation. *Entrance requirements:* For doctorate, GMAT, GRE General Test, or MCAT. Additional exam requirements/recommendations for international students: Required—TOEFL. *Application deadline:* For fall admission, 12/30 for domestic students. Application fee: $60. *Expenses:* Tuition: Full-time $30,275. Full-time tuition and fees vary according to program and student level. *Financial support:* Fellowships, research assistantships, teaching assistantships, career-related internships or fieldwork and Federal Work-Study available. Financial award application deadline: 12/30; financial award applicants required to submit FAFSA. *Unit head:* Joan Curhan, Program Director, 617-495-1357. *Application contact:* Office of Admissions and Financial Aid, 617-495-5315.

Harvard University, School of Public Health, Department of Health Policy and Management, Boston, MA 02115-6096. Offers health policy (PhD); health policy and management (SM, SD). Part-time programs available. *Degree requirements:* For doctorate, thesis/dissertation, qualifying exam. *Entrance requirements:* For master's and doctorate, GRE. Additional exam requirements/recommendations for international students: Required—TOEFL (minimum score 560 paper-based; 220 computer-based); Recommended—IELTS (minimum score 7). *Expenses:* Tuition: Full-time $30,275. Full-time tuition and fees vary according to program and student level. *Faculty research:* Environmental science and risk management.

Hofstra University, Frank G. Zarb School of Business, Department of Management, Entrepreneurship and General Management, Hempstead, NY 11549. Offers health services management (MBA); human resource management (MS, Advanced Certificate); management (EMBA, MBA), including business administration (EMBA); quality management (MBA). Part-time and evening/weekend programs available. *Faculty:* 8 full-time (2 women), 1 part-time/adjunct (0 women). *Students:* 46 full-time (19 women), 238 part-time (114 women); includes 55 minority (20 African Americans, 25 Asian Americans or Pacific Islanders, 10 Hispanic Americans), 9 international. Average age 32. 183 applicants, 90% accepted, 117 enrolled. In 2006, 17 master's, 3 other advanced degrees awarded. *Degree requirements:* For master's, thesis optional. *Entrance requirements:* For master's, GMAT, 2 letters of recommendation, resumé, essay. Additional exam requirements/recommendations for international students: Required—TOEFL (minimum score 550 paper-based; 213 computer-based). *Application deadline:* Applications are processed on a rolling basis. Application fee: $60. Electronic applications accepted. *Expenses:* Tuition: Full-time $13,320; part-time $740 per credit. Required fees: $930; $155 per term. *Financial support:* In 2006–07, 25 students received support, including 17 fellowships with tuition reimbursements available (averaging $5,367 per year), 3 research assistantships with full and partial tuition reimbursements available (averaging $7,232 per year); tuition waivers (full and partial) and unspecified assistantships also available. Financial award applicants required to submit FAFSA. *Faculty research:* Business/personal ethics, stakeholders, whistle blowing and national/global labor practices; family business, entrepreneurship (for & non-profit); competition, innovation; risk taking, problem solving; and supple chain management, scheduling and health care industry. Total annual research expenditures: $24,000. *Unit head:* Dr. Mamdouh I. Farid, Chairperson, 516-463-5735, Fax: 516-463-4834, E-mail: mgbmif@hofstra.edu. *Application contact:* Carol Drummer, Dean of Graduate Admissions, 516-463-4876, Fax: 516-463-4664, E-mail: gradstudent@hofstra.edu.

Hofstra University, School of Education and Allied Human Services, Department of Health Professions and Family Studies, Program in Health Administration, Hempstead, NY 11549. Offers MHA. Part-time programs available. *Students:* 31 full-time (22 women), 40 part-time (30 women); includes 30 minority (23 African Americans, 5 Asian Americans or Pacific Islanders, 2 Hispanic Americans), 2 international. Average age 32. 51 applicants, 98% accepted, 29 enrolled. In 2006, 28 degrees awarded. *Degree requirements:* For master's, HADM 300. *Entrance requirements:* For master's, interview, 2 letters of recommendation, essay. Additional exam requirements/recommendations for international students: Required—TOEFL (minimum score 550 paper-based; 213 computer-based). *Application deadline:* Applications are processed on a rolling basis. Application fee: $60. Electronic applications accepted. *Expenses:* Tuition: Full-time $13,320; part-time $740 per credit. Required fees: $930; $155 per term. *Financial support:* In 2006–07, 16 students received support, including 4 fellowships with tuition reimbursements available (averaging $3,750 per year), 2 research assistantships with full and partial tuition reimbursements available (averaging $5,500 per year); career-related internships or fieldwork, scholarships/grants, tuition waivers (full and partial), and unspecified assistantships also available. Support available to part-time students. Financial award applicants required to submit FAFSA. *Faculty research:* Health care policy, managed care, health care law, health and leadership, health care management. *Unit head:* Prof. Lauren B. Mangino, Program Director, 516-463-5224. *Application contact:* Carol Drummer, Dean of Graduate Admissions, 516-463-4876, Fax: 516-463-4664, E-mail: gradstudent@hofstra.edu.

Houston Baptist University, College of Business and Economics, Program in Health Administration, Houston, TX 77074-3298. Offers MSHA. Part-time and evening/weekend programs available. *Degree requirements:* For master's, registration. *Entrance requirements:* For master's, GMAT, minimum GPA of 2.5. Additional exam requirements/recommendations for international students: Required—TOEFL (minimum score 550 paper-based; 213 computer-based).

Illinois Institute of Technology, Stuart School of Business, Program in Business Administration, Chicago, IL 60616-3793. Offers entrepreneurship (MBA); financial management (MBA); financial markets (MBA); healthcare management (MBA); information technology management (MBA); international business (MBA); management science (MBA); marketing (MBA); operations, quality, and technology management (MBA); strategic management of organizations (MBA); sustainable enterprise (MBA); JD/MBA; MBA/MS. *Accreditation:* AACSB. Part-time and evening/weekend programs available. *Faculty:* 13 full-time (1 woman), 9 part-time/adjunct (0 women). *Students:* 74 full-time (29 women), 42 part-time (16 women); includes 17 minority (5 African Americans, 11 Asian Americans or Pacific Islanders, 1 Hispanic American), 74 international. Average age 29. 247 applicants, 70% accepted, 51 enrolled. In 2006, 45 degrees awarded. *Entrance requirements:* For master's, GMAT. Additional exam requirements/recommendations for international students: Required—TOEFL (minimum score 600 paper-based; 250 computer-based). *Application deadline:* For fall admission, 8/15 priority date for domestic students, 7/1 for international students; for winter admission, 11/1 priority date for domestic students, 10/1 for international students; for spring admission, 1/1 priority date for domestic students, 1/1 for international students. Applications are processed on a rolling basis. Application fee: $75. Electronic applications accepted. *Expenses: Contact institution.* Tuition and fees vary according to class time, course level, course load, program and student level. *Financial support:* Career-related internships or fieldwork, Federal Work-Study, institutionally sponsored loans, scholarships/grants, traineeships, health care benefits, tuition waivers, and unspecified assistantships available. Support available to part-time students. Financial award applicants required to submit FAFSA. *Faculty research:* Knowledge management, healthcare management, sustainability in supply chain. *Unit head:* Dr. George P. Nassos, Interim Director, 312-906-6543, Fax: 312-906-6549, E-mail: george.nassos@iit.edu. *Application contact:* Brian Jansen, Director of Graduate Admissions, 312-906-6521, Fax: 312-906-6549, E-mail: admission@stuart.iit.edu.

Indiana University Northwest, School of Public and Environmental Affairs, Gary, IN 46408-1197. Offers criminal justice (MPA); environmental affairs (Certificate); health services administration (MPA); human services administration (MPA); nonprofit management (Certificate); public administration (MPA); public management (MPA, Certificate). *Accreditation:* NASPAA (one or more programs are accredited). Part-time programs available. *Faculty:* 5 full-time (3 women). *Students:* 16 full-time (12 women), 118 part-time (92 women); includes 89 minority (76 African Americans, 1 Asian American or Pacific Islander, 12 Hispanic Americans). Average age 39. In 2006, 30 master's, 31 other advanced degrees awarded. *Degree requirements:* For master's, registration. *Entrance requirements:* For master's, GRE General Test or GMAT, letters of recommendation. *Application deadline:* For fall admission, 8/15 priority date for domestic students. Applications are processed on a rolling basis. Application fee: $25. *Expenses:* Tuition, state resident: full-time $4,332; part-time $181 per credit hour. Tuition, nonresident: full-time $10,081; part-time $420 per credit hour. Tuition and fees vary according to course load, campus/location and program. *Financial support:* Career-related internships or fieldwork, Federal Work-Study, and tuition waivers (partial) available. Support available to part-time students. Financial award application deadline: 3/1. *Faculty research:* Employment in income security policies, evidence in criminal justice, equal employment law, social welfare policy and welfare reform, public finance in developing countries. *Unit head:* Karen Evans, Interim Assistant Dean/Division Director, 219-980-6695, Fax: 219-980-6737. *Application contact:* Sandra Hall Smith, Secretary, 219-980-6695, Fax: 219-980-6737, E-mail: shsmith@iun.edu.

Indiana University–Purdue University Indianapolis, School of Public and Environmental Affairs, Indianapolis, IN 46202-2896. Offers health administration (MHA); public affairs (MPA), including criminal justice, environmental management, nonprofit management, policy analysis, public management; JD/MHA; MBA/MHA; MSN/MHA. *Accreditation:* CAHME (one or more programs are accredited). Part-time and evening/weekend programs available. *Faculty:* 17 full-time (6 women). *Students:* 83 full-time (56 women), 290 part-time (129 women); includes 50 minority (26 African Americans, 2 American Indian/Alaska Native, 17 Asian Americans or Pacific Islanders, 5 Hispanic Americans), 6 international. Average age 35. In 2006, 77 master's awarded. *Entrance requirements:* For master's, GRE General Test, minimum GPA of 3.0 (preferred). Additional exam requirements/recommendations for international students: Required—TOEFL. *Application deadline:* For fall admission, 7/15 priority date for domestic students; for spring admission, 11/15 for domestic students. Applications are processed on a rolling basis. Application fee: $50 ($60 for international students). *Expenses:* Tuition, state resident: full-time $5,437; part-time $227 per credit hour. Tuition, nonresident: full-time $15,694; part-time $654 per credit hour. Required fees: $620. Tuition and fees vary according to course load, campus/location and program. *Financial support:* Fellowships with full and partial tuition reimbursements, research assistantships with full and partial tuition reimbursements, career-related internships or fieldwork, Federal Work-Study, institutionally sponsored loans, and scholarships/grants available. Support available to part-time students. Financial award application deadline: 3/1. *Faculty research:* Economic development, water and air quality, ethics, financing, organization design and structure. Total annual research expenditures: $1.9 million. *Unit head:* Dr. Greg Lindsey, Associate Dean, 317-274-4656, Fax: 317-274-5153. *Application contact:* 317-274-4656, Fax: 317-274-5153, E-mail: speainfo@speanet.iupui.edu.

Indiana University South Bend, School of Public and Environmental Affairs, South Bend, IN 46634-7111. Offers health systems administration and policy (MPA); health systems management (Certificate); nonprofit management (Certificate); public and community services administration and policy (MPA); public management (Certificate); urban affairs (Certificate). *Accreditation:* NASPAA. Part-time and evening/weekend programs available. *Faculty:* 4 full-time (1 woman). *Students:* 11 full-time (7 women), 36 part-time (29 women); includes 8 minority (5 African Americans, 1 Asian American or Pacific Islander, 2 Hispanic Americans), 3 international. Average age 34. In 2006, 27 degrees awarded. *Entrance requirements:* For master's, GRE General Test, minimum undergraduate GPA of 2.5. *Application deadline:* For fall admission, 7/1 priority date for domestic students; for spring admission, 11/1 for domestic students. Applications are processed on a rolling basis. *Expenses:* Tuition, state resident: full-time $4,450; part-time $185 per credit hour. Tuition, nonresident: full-time $10,954; part-time $456 per credit hour. Tuition and fees vary according to course load, campus/location and program. *Financial support:* Fellowships, research assistantships, career-related internships or fieldwork, Federal Work-Study, and institutionally sponsored loans available. Support available to part-time students. Financial award application deadline: 3/1; financial award applicants required to submit FAFSA. *Unit head:* Leda M. Hall, Dean, 574-520-4803.

Indiana Wesleyan University, College of Adult and Professional Studies, Program in Business Administration, Marion, IN 46953-4974. Offers accounting (MBA); applied management (MBA); health care management (MBA). Evening/weekend programs available. Post-baccalaureate distance learning degree programs offered (no on-campus study). *Faculty:* 13 full-time (1 woman), 162 part-time/adjunct (31 women). *Students:* 1,163 full-time. Average age 34. In 2006, 792 degrees awarded. *Degree requirements:* For master's, applied management project. *Entrance requirements:* For master's, minimum GPA of 2.5, related 3 years full time work experience, math/statistics (3 hours or proficiency exam). Additional exam requirements/recommendations for international students: Required—TOEFL (minimum score 550 paper-based; 213 computer-based). *Application deadline:* Applications are processed on a rolling basis. Application fee: $25. Electronic applications accepted. *Expenses:* Tuition: Full-time $16,000; part-time $400 per credit. Required fees: $3,000. Tuition and fees vary according to degree level, campus/location and program. *Financial support:* Applicants required to submit FAFSA. *Unit head:* Dr. Jim Kraai, Director, 765-677-2882, Fax: 765-677-2023, E-mail: jim.kraai@indwes.edu. *Application contact:* Kris Douglas, Marketing Manager, 800-234-5327, Fax: 765-674-8028, E-mail: kris.douglas@apollogrp.org.

Institute of Public Administration, Programs in Public Administration, Dublin, Ireland. Offers healthcare management (MA); local government management (MA); public management (MA, Diploma).

Iona College, School of Arts and Science, Program in Health Service Administration, New Rochelle, NY 10801-1890. Offers MS, Certificate. Part-time and evening/weekend programs available. *Faculty:* 3 full-time (2 women), 4 part-time/adjunct (2 women). *Students:* 7 full-time (6 women), 52 part-time (44 women); includes 22 minority (12 African Americans, 1 Asian American or Pacific Islander, 9 Hispanic Americans). Average age 39. 20 applicants, 75% accepted, 12 enrolled. In 2006, 18 master's, 2 other advanced degrees awarded. *Degree requirements:* For master's, thesis or alternative. *Entrance requirements:* For master's, minimum undergraduate GPA of 2.75. Additional exam requirements/recommendations for international students: Required—TOEFL (minimum score 550 paper-based; 213 computer-based). *Application deadline:* Applications are processed on a rolling basis. Application fee: $50. Electronic applications accepted. *Expenses:* Tuition: Part-time $665 per credit. Required fees: $150 per term. *Financial support:* Career-related internships or fieldwork and unspecified assistantships available. Support available to part-time students. *Faculty research:* Changing professional roles, clinical protocols. *Unit head:* Vincent Maher, Chair, 914-633-2192, E-mail: vmaher@iona.edu. *Application contact:* Veronica Jarek-Prinz, Graduate Admissions, 914-633-2289, Fax: 914-633-2012, E-mail: vjarekprinz@iona.edu.

The Johns Hopkins University, Bloomberg School of Public Health, Department of Health Policy and Management, Baltimore, MD 21205-1996. Offers health and public policy (PhD); health care management and leadership (Dr PH); health finance and management (MHS); health policy (MHS); health services research (PhD). *Accreditation:* CAHME (one or more programs are accredited). Part-time programs available. *Faculty:* 54 full-time (29 women), 142 part-time/adjunct (55 women). *Students:* 128 full-time (92 women), 52 part-time (17 women); includes 42 minority (17 African Americans, 2 American Indian/Alaska Native, 20 Asian Americans or Pacific Islanders, 3 Hispanic Americans), 47 international. Average age 29. 196 applicants, 52% accepted, 45 enrolled. In 2006, 24 master's, 20 doctorates awarded. *Median time to degree:* Of those who began their doctoral program in fall 1998, 94% received their degree in 8 years or less. *Degree requirements:* For master's, internship; for doctorate, thesis/dissertation, 1 year full-time residency, oral and written exams, comprehensive exam, registration. *Entrance*

Health Services Management and Hospital Administration

The Johns Hopkins University (continued)
requirements: For master's, GRE General Test/GMAT, 3 letters of recommendation, curriculum vitae; for doctorate, GRE General Test, 3 letters of recommendation, curriculum vitae. Additional exam requirements/recommendations for international students: Required—TOEFL (minimum score 600 paper-based; 250 computer-based). *Application deadline:* For fall admission, 12/1 for domestic and international students. Application fee: $45. Electronic applications accepted. *Expenses:* Tuition: Full-time $32,976. Tuition and fees vary according to degree level and program. *Financial support:* In 2006–07, 180 students received support, including 2 fellowships (averaging $43,856 per year); Federal Work-Study, institutionally sponsored loans, scholarships/grants, traineeships, and stipends also available. Support available to part-time students. Financial award application deadline: 3/15; financial award applicants required to submit FAFSA. *Faculty research:* Quality of care and health outcomes, health care finance and technology, vulnerable populations, injury prevention, health policy. Total annual research expenditures: $22.8 million. *Unit head:* Dr. Ellen J. MacKenzie, Chairman, 410-955-3625. *Application contact:* Mary Sewell, Coordinator, 410-955-2488, Fax: 410-614-9152, E-mail: msewell@jhsph.edu.

The Johns Hopkins University, Bloomberg School of Public Health, Department of International Health, Baltimore, MD 21218-2699. Offers disease prevention and control (MHS, PhD); health systems (MHS, PhD); human nutrition (MHS, PhD); international health (Dr PH); social and behavioral interventions (MHS, PhD). *Faculty:* 119 full-time (63 women), 170 part-time/adjunct (55 women). *Students:* 197 full-time (159 women), 7 part-time (4 women); includes 36 minority (4 African Americans, 1 American Indian/Alaska Native, 25 Asian Americans or Pacific Islanders, 6 Hispanic Americans), 58 international. Average age 27. 376 applicants, 46% accepted, 68 enrolled. In 2006, 39 master's, 19 doctorates awarded. *Median time to degree:* Of those who began their doctoral program in fall 1998, 63% received their degree in 8 years or less. *Degree requirements:* For master's, thesis (for some programs), internship, comprehensive exam, registration; for doctorate, thesis/dissertation, 1 year full-time residency, oral and written exams, comprehensive exam, registration. *Entrance requirements:* For master's, GRE General Test or MCAT, 3 letters of recommendation, resumé; for doctorate, GRE General Test, 3 letters of recommendation, resumé. Additional exam requirements/recommendations for international students: Required—TOEFL (minimum score 600 paper-based; 280 computer-based). *Application deadline:* For fall admission, 1/2 priority date for domestic and international students. Applications are processed on a rolling basis. Application fee: $45. Electronic applications accepted. *Expenses:* Tuition: Full-time $32,976. Tuition and fees vary according to degree level and program. *Financial support:* In 2006–07, 203 students received support, including 9 fellowships (averaging $32,000 per year); Federal Work-Study, institutionally sponsored loans, scholarships/grants, traineeships, and stipends also available. Support available to part-time students. Financial award application deadline: 3/15; financial award applicants required to submit FAFSA. *Faculty research:* Nutrition, infectious diseases, health systems, economics, humanitarian emergencies. Total annual research expenditures: $62 million. *Unit head:* Dr. Robert E. Black, Chairman, 410-955-3934, Fax: 410-955-7159, E-mail: rblack@jhsph.edu. *Application contact:* Jennifer Shaffer, Academic Program Administrator, 410-955-3734, Fax: 410-955-7159, E-mail: jshaffer@jhsph.edu.

The Johns Hopkins University, Carey Business School, Business of Health Program, Baltimore, MD 21218-2699. Offers business of medicine (Certificate); business of nursing (Certificate); leadership and management in the life sciences (MBA, Certificate); medical services management (MBA); MBA/MPH; MBA/MS; MBA/MSN. Part-time and evening/weekend programs available. *Students:* 31 full-time (17 women), 207 part-time (93 women); includes 50 minority (20 African Americans, 26 Asian Americans or Pacific Islanders, 4 Hispanic Americans), 6 international. Average age 38. 222 applicants, 90% accepted, 168 enrolled. In 2006, 40 master's, 66 other advanced degrees awarded. *Degree requirements:* For master's, project. *Entrance requirements:* For master's, GMAT or GRE, minimum GPA of 3.0, resumé, work experience, two letters of recommendation; for Certificate, minimum GPA of 3.0, resumé, work experience, two letters of recommendation. Additional exam requirements/recommendations for international students: Required—TOEFL (minimum score 600 paper-based; 250 computer-based; 100 iBT). *Application deadline:* For fall admission, 5/1 for international students; for spring admission, 10/15 for international students. Applications are processed on a rolling basis. Application fee: $60. *Expenses:* Tuition: Full-time $32,976. Tuition and fees vary according to degree level and program. *Financial support:* Scholarships/grants available. Support available to part-time students. Financial award application deadline: 6/1; financial award applicants required to submit FAFSA. *Unit head:* Dr. Doug Hough, Chair, 410-516-2324, Fax: 410-516-2033, E-mail: douglas.hough@jhu.edu. *Application contact:* Robin Reed, Senior Academic Coordinator, 800-gotojhu, Fax: 410-872-1251, E-mail: onestop.admissions@jhu.edu.

Jones International University, Graduate School of Business Administration, Centennial, CO 80112. Offers accounting (MBA); business communication (MABC); entrepreneurship (MABC, MBA); finance (MBA); global enterprise management (MBA); health care management (MBA); information security management (MBA); information technology management (MBA); leadership and influence (MABC); leading the customer-driven organization (MABC); negotiation and conflict management (MBA); project management (MABC, MBA). Program only offered online. Part-time and evening/weekend programs available. Postbaccalaureate distance learning degree programs offered (no on-campus study). *Degree requirements:* For master's, capstone project. *Entrance requirements:* For master's, minimum cumulative GPA of 2.5. Additional exam requirements/recommendations for international students: Recommended—TOEFL (minimum score 550 paper-based; 213 computer-based). Electronic applications accepted.

Kean University, College of Business and Public Administration, Program in Public Administration, Union, NJ 07083. Offers criminal justice (MPA); environmental management (MPA); health services administration (MPA); non-profit management (MPA); public administration (MPA). *Accreditation:* NASPAA. Part-time and evening/weekend programs available. *Faculty:* 7 full-time (4 women). *Students:* 78 full-time (52 women), 101 part-time (62 women); includes 118 minority (84 African Americans, 9 Asian Americans or Pacific Islanders, 25 Hispanic Americans), 13 international. Average age 32. 76 applicants, 83% accepted, 40 enrolled. In 2006, 50 degrees awarded. *Degree requirements:* For master's, thesis, internship, research seminar. *Entrance requirements:* For master's, 2 letters of recommendation, interview. *Application deadline:* For fall admission, 5/1 for domestic students; for spring admission, 11/1 for domestic students. Application fee: $60 ($150 for international students). Electronic applications accepted. *Expenses:* Tuition, state resident: full-time $8,856; part-time $369 per credit. Tuition, nonresident: full-time $11,256; part-time $469 per credit. Required fees: $1,125; $94 per credit. *Financial support:* In 2006–07, 18 research assistantships with full tuition reimbursements (averaging $3,217 per year) were awarded; career-related internships or fieldwork, institutionally sponsored loans, and unspecified assistantships also available. Financial award application deadline: 5/1. *Faculty research:* Fiscal impact of New Federalism, New Jersey state and local government, computer application in public management. *Unit head:* Dr. Craig P. Donovan, Program Coordinator, 908-737-4307, E-mail: cpdonova@kean.edu. *Application contact:* Joanne Morris, Director of Graduate Admissions, 908-737-3355, Fax: 908-737-3354, E-mail: grad-adm@kean.edu.

Kennesaw State University, College of Health and Human Services, Program in Advanced Care Management and Leadership, Kennesaw, GA 30144-5591. Offers MSN. Part-time and evening/weekend programs available. *Students:* 7 full-time (all women); includes 3 minority (2 African Americans, 1 Asian American or Pacific Islander). Average age 36. 10 applicants, 80% accepted, 5 enrolled. In 2006, 6 degrees awarded. *Entrance requirements:* For master's, GRE General Test, minimum GPA of 3.0, 3 years experience, RN license. Additional exam requirements/recommendations for international students: Required—TOEFL (minimum score 550 paper-based; 213 computer-based; 80 iBT), IELTS (minimum score 6). *Application deadline:* For fall admission, 5/31 for domestic and international students. Application fee: $50. Electronic applications accepted. *Expenses:* Tuition, state resident: full-time $3,044; part-time $127 per semester hour. Tuition, nonresident: full-time $12,172; part-time $508 per semester hour. Required fees: $353 per semester. Full-time tuition and fees vary according to campus/location and program. *Financial support:* In 2006–07, research assistantships with tuition reimbursements (averaging $4,000 per year); unspecified assistantships also available. *Unit head:* Dr. B. Regina Dorman, Director, 770-423-6172, Fax: 770-423-6627, E-mail: gdorman@kennesaw.edu. *Application contact:* Vilma Marquez, Admissions Counselor, 770-420-4377, Fax: 770-423-6885, E-mail: ksugrad@kennesaw.edu.

King's College, William G. McGowan School of Business, Wilkes-Barre, PA 18711-0801. Offers health care administration (MS). *Accreditation:* AACSB; CAHME. Part-time and evening/weekend programs available. *Faculty:* 4 full-time (1 woman), 1 part-time/adjunct (0 women). *Students:* Average age 35. In 2006, 6 degrees awarded. *Entrance requirements:* Additional exam requirements/recommendations for international students: Required—TOEFL (minimum score 600 paper-based; 250 computer-based). *Application deadline:* For fall admission, 7/31 priority date for domestic students; for spring admission, 12/1 priority date for domestic students. Applications are processed on a rolling basis. Application fee: $35. *Expenses:* Tuition: Full-time $26,598; part-time $625 per credit. Required fees: $900. *Unit head:* Dr. John J. Ryan, Director, 570-208-5932, Fax: 570-826-5989, E-mail: jjryan@kings.edu. *Application contact:* Dr. Elizabeth S. Lott, Director of Graduate Programs, 570-208-5991, Fax: 570-825-9049, E-mail: eslott@kings.edu.

Lake Erie College, Division of Management Studies, Painesville, OH 44077-3389. Offers general management (MBA); management healthcare administration (MBA). Part-time and evening/weekend programs available. *Faculty:* 6 full-time (2 women), 4 part-time/adjunct (1 woman). *Students:* Average age 33. 40 applicants, 98% accepted, 29 enrolled. In 2006, 22 degrees awarded. *Entrance requirements:* For master's, GMAT, resumé, references. Additional exam requirements/recommendations for international students: Required—TOEFL (minimum score 590 paper-based). *Application deadline:* For fall admission, 8/1 priority date for domestic students, 6/1 for international students; for spring admission, 12/15 for domestic students, 10/1 for international students. Applications are processed on a rolling basis. Application fee: $25 ($50 for international students). Electronic applications accepted. *Expenses:* Tuition: Part-time $595 per credit hour. Required fees: $45 per credit hour. *Financial support:* Career-related internships or fieldwork available. Financial award applicants required to submit FAFSA. *Faculty research:* Organizational effectiveness. *Unit head:* Prof. Robert Trebar, Associate Dean, 440-375-7115, Fax: 440-375-7005, E-mail: rtrebar@lec.edu. *Application contact:* Admissions Office, 440-375-7050, Fax: 440-375-7005, E-mail: admissions@lec.edu.

Lamar University, College of Graduate Studies, College of Business, Beaumont, TX 77710. Offers accounting (MBA); experiential business and Entrepreneurship (MBA); financial management (MBA); healthcare administration (MBA); information systems (MBA); management (MBA). *Accreditation:* AACSB. Part-time and evening/weekend programs available. *Faculty:* 20 full-time (8 women), 2 part-time/adjunct (1 woman). *Students:* 55 full-time (27 women), 45 part-time (20 women); includes 17 minority (9 African Americans, 4 Asian Americans or Pacific Islanders, 4 Hispanic Americans), 14 international. Average age 29. 131 applicants, 34% accepted, 29 enrolled. In 2006, 29 degrees awarded. *Degree requirements:* For master's, thesis optional. *Entrance requirements:* For master's, GMAT. Additional exam requirements/recommendations for international students: Required—TOEFL (minimum score 525 paper-based; 197 computer-based). *Application deadline:* For fall admission, 3/15 priority date for domestic students; for spring admission, 10/1 priority date for domestic students. Applications are processed on a rolling basis. Application fee: $25 ($50 for international students). *Expenses:* Tuition, nonresident: part-time $33 per hour. Required fees: $43 per hour. $110 per semester. *Financial support:* In 2006–07, 12 students received support, including 4 research assistantships with partial tuition reimbursements available; fellowships with tuition reimbursements available, career-related internships or fieldwork, Federal Work-Study, institutionally sponsored loans, scholarships/grants, and tuition waivers (partial) also available. Support available to part-time students. Financial award application deadline: 4/1; financial award applicants required to submit FAFSA. *Faculty research:* Marketing, finance, quantitative methods, MIS, legal, environmental. Total annual research expenditures: $26,000. *Unit head:* Dr. Enrique R. Venta, Dean, 409-880-8604, Fax: 409-880-8088, E-mail: henry.venta@lamar.edu. *Application contact:* Dr. Brad Mayer, Professor and Associate Dean, 409-880-2383, Fax: 409-880-8605, E-mail: bradley.mayer@lamar.edu.

Lindenwood University, Graduate Programs, Programs in Individualized Education, St. Charles, MO 63301-1695. Offers administration (MSA); business administration (MBA); communications (MA); criminal justice and administration (MS); gerontology (MA); health management (MS); human resource management (MS); management (MSA); marketing (MSA); writing (MFA). Part-time and evening/weekend programs available. *Faculty:* 18 full-time (9 women), 50 part-time/adjunct (25 women). *Students:* 595 full-time (348 women), 55 part-time (37 women); includes 176 minority (163 African Americans, 1 American Indian/Alaska Native, 5 Asian Americans or Pacific Islanders, 7 Hispanic Americans), 10 international. Average age 34. In 2006, 303 degrees awarded. *Degree requirements:* For master's, thesis. *Entrance requirements:* For master's, interview, minimum GPA of 3.0. Additional exam requirements/recommendations for international students: Required—TOEFL. *Application deadline:* For fall admission, 9/30 priority date for domestic and international students; for winter admission, 12/30 priority date for domestic and international students; for spring admission, 3/30 priority date for domestic and international students. Applications are processed on a rolling basis. Application fee: $30 ($100 for international students). *Expenses:* Tuition: Part-time $340 per credit hour. Tuition and fees vary according to course level, course load, degree level and program. *Financial support:* Career-related internships or fieldwork, institutionally sponsored loans, tuition waivers (partial), and unspecified assistantships available. Financial award application deadline: 6/30; financial award applicants required to submit FAFSA. *Unit head:* Dan Kemper, Dean of LCIE, 636-916-9125, E-mail: dkemper@lindenwood.edu. *Application contact:* Brett Barger, Dean, Adult, Corporate and Graduate Admissions, 636-949-4934, Fax: 636-949-4109, E-mail: adultadmissions@lindenwood.edu.

Lipscomb University, MBA Program, Nashville, TN 37204-3951. Offers accounting (MBA); business administration (general) (MBA); conflict management (MBA); financial services (MBA); healthcare management (MBA); leadership (MBA); nonprofit management (MBA). *Accreditation:* ACBSP. Part-time and evening/weekend programs available. *Faculty:* 11 full-time (3 women), 6 part-time/adjunct (0 women). *Students:* 18 full-time (6 women), 50 part-time (23 women); includes 5 minority (4 African Americans, 1 American Indian/Alaska Native), 2 international. Average age 30. 48 applicants, 73% accepted, 27 enrolled. In 2006, 30 degrees awarded. *Median time to degree:* Master's–1 year full-time, 2.3 years part-time. *Entrance requirements:* For master's, GMAT, interview, 2 references, resumé. Additional exam requirements/recommendations for international students: Required—TOEFL (minimum score 570 paper-based; 230 computer-based). *Application deadline:* For fall admission, 7/1 for domestic students, 2/1 for international students; for winter admission, 12/1 for domestic students, 6/1 for international students. Applications are processed on a rolling basis. Application fee: $50 ($75 for international students). Electronic applications accepted. *Expenses:* Contact institution. *Financial support:* In 2006–07, 25 students received support. Career-related internships or fieldwork, Federal Work-Study, scholarships/grants, tuition waivers (partial), and unspecified assistantships available. Support available to part-time students. Financial award application deadline: 7/1; financial award applicants required to submit FAFSA. *Faculty research:* Impact of spirituality on organization commitment; leadership; psychological empowerment; training. *Unit head:* Dr. Steven K. Yoho, Associate Dean of Graduate Business Studies, 615-966-1833, Fax: 615-966-1818, E-mail: steven.yoho@lipscomb.edu. *Application contact:* Jackie Cash, MBA Assistant, 615-966-1833, Fax: 615-966-1818, E-mail: jackie.cash@lipscomb.edu.

Loma Linda University, School of Public Health, Programs in Health Administration, Loma Linda, CA 92350. Offers MHA, MPH. *Entrance requirements:* For master's, GMAT (MHA). Additional exam requirements/recommendations for international students: Required—Michigan Test of English Language Proficiency or TOEFL.

Long Island University, Brooklyn Campus, School of Health Professions, Department of Community Health, Brooklyn, NY 11201-8423. Offers community mental health (MS); family health (MS); health management (MS). Part-time and evening/weekend programs available. *Entrance requirements:* For master's, 2 letters of recommendation. Additional exam requirements/recommendations for international students: Required—TOEFL (minimum score 500 paper-based; 173 computer-based). Electronic applications accepted.

Long Island University, C.W. Post Campus, College of Management, School of Public Service, Department of Health Care and Public Administration, Brookville, NY 11548-1300. Offers gerontology (Certificate); health care administration (MPA); health care administration/gerontology (MPA); nonprofit management (MPA, Certificate); public administration (MPA). *Accreditation:* NASPAA (one or more programs are accredited). Part-time and evening/weekend programs available. *Degree requirements:* For master's, thesis. *Entrance requirements:* For master's, GMAT, minimum GPA of 2.5; for Certificate, minimum GPA of 2.5. Electronic applications accepted. *Faculty research:* Critical issues in sexuality, social work in religious communities, gerontological social work.

Long Island University, Rockland Graduate Campus, Graduate School, Program in Health Administration, Orangeburg, NY 10962. Offers financial management (MPA); gerontology (Advanced Certificate); health administration (MPA); health services management (MPA); long term care administration (MPA); medical practice management (MPA); nonprofit management (MPA, Advanced Certificate). *Entrance requirements:* For master's, GRE General Test.

Louisiana State University in Shreveport, College of Business Administration, Shreveport, LA 71115-2399. Offers healthcare (MBA). *Accreditation:* AACSB. Part-time and evening/weekend programs available. *Entrance requirements:* For master's, GMAT. Additional exam requirements/recommendations for international students: Required—TOEFL (minimum score 550 paper-based; 213 computer-based). *Faculty research:* Real estate, organizational behavior, finance, operations research, information systems technology.

Louisiana State University in Shreveport, College of Liberal Arts, Program in Health Administration, Shreveport, LA 71115-2399. Offers MHA. Part-time programs available. *Faculty:* 4 full-time (0 women), 3 part-time/adjunct (2 women). *Students:* 4 full-time (all women), 13 part-time (6 women); includes 1 African American, 2 Asian Americans or Pacific Islanders. 5 applicants, 100% accepted, 2 enrolled. In 2006, 3 degrees awarded. *Degree requirements:* For master's, thesis, master-level project. *Entrance requirements:* For master's, GRE or GMAT. Additional exam requirements/recommendations for international students: Required—TOEFL (minimum score 550 paper-based; 213 computer-based). *Application deadline:* For fall admission, 6/30 for domestic and international students; for spring admission, 11/30 for domestic and international students. Applications are processed on a rolling basis. Application fee: $10 ($20 for international students). *Financial support:* In 2006–07, 3 students received support, including 3 research assistantships with full tuition reimbursements available (averaging $3,200 per year). *Faculty research:* Healthcare marketing, law and ethics, leadership. *Unit head:* Dr. John L Fortenberry, Director, 318-795-4208, Fax: 318-797-5358, E-mail: jfortenberry@lsus.edu.

Loyola University Chicago, Graduate School, Marcella Niehoff School of Nursing, Health Systems Management Program, Chicago, IL 60611-2196. Offers MSN, MSN/MBA. Part-time and evening/weekend programs available. *Students:* 3 full-time (all women), 20 part-time (all women). Average age 36. 20 applicants, 90% accepted. In 2006, 10 degrees awarded. *Degree requirements:* For master's, comprehensive exam or oral thesis defense. *Application deadline:* Applications are processed on a rolling basis. Application fee: $40. Electronic applications accepted. *Financial support:* Teaching assistantships, traineeships and unspecified assistantships available. Financial award application deadline: 3/1. *Faculty research:* Patient classification systems, career/job mobility. *Unit head:* Dr. Ida Androwich, Dean, 773-508-3255, E-mail: iandrow@luc.edu. *Application contact:* Dr. Vicki A. Keough, Associate Professor, 708-216-3582, Fax: 708-216-9555, E-mail: vkeough@luc.edu.

Loyola University New Orleans, City College, Program in Nursing, New Orleans, LA 70118-6195. Offers family nurse practitioner (MSN); health care systems management (MSN). *Accreditation:* NLN. Postbaccalaureate distance learning degree programs offered. *Degree requirements:* For master's, 700 hours of clinical practice. *Entrance requirements:* For master's, GRE, BSN, Louisiana nursing license, 1 year of work experience in clinical nursing, minimum undergraduate GPA of 2.8, interview. Additional exam requirements/recommendations for international students: Required—TOEFL (minimum score 550 paper-based; 213 computer-based). *Faculty research:* Increasing compliance with treatment, patient satisfaction with care provided by nurse practitioners.

Madonna University, Program in Health Services, Livonia, MI 48150-1173. Offers MSHS. Part-time programs available. *Faculty:* 2 full-time (both women), 5 part-time/adjunct (0 women). *Students:* Average age 38. 2 applicants, 50% accepted. In 2006, 2 degrees awarded. *Degree requirements:* For master's, thesis or alternative. *Entrance requirements:* For master's, GRE General Test or minimum GPA of 3.25. Additional exam requirements/recommendations for international students: Required—TOEFL, TWE. *Application deadline:* For fall admission, 8/1 priority date for domestic students; for winter admission, 12/1 priority date for domestic students; for spring admission, 4/1 priority date for domestic students. Applications are processed on a rolling basis. Application fee: $25 ($200 for international students). Electronic applications accepted. *Financial support:* Institutionally sponsored loans and scholarships/grants available. Support available to part-time students. *Unit head:* Dr. Ted Biermann, Dean, 734-432-5515, E-mail: tbiermann@madonna.edu. *Application contact:* Sandra Kellums, Coordinator of Graduate Admissions and Records, 734-432-5667, Fax: 734-432-5862, E-mail: skellum@madonna.edu.

Marshall University, Academic Affairs Division, Lewis College of Business, Graduate School of Management, Program in Health Care Administration, Huntington, WV 25755. Offers MS. Part-time and evening/weekend programs available. *Students:* 79 full-time (54 women), 23 part-time (13 women); includes 7 minority (3 African Americans, 2 American Indian/Alaska Native, 1 Asian American or Pacific Islander, 1 Hispanic American), 3 international. Average age 30. In 2006, 40 degrees awarded. *Degree requirements:* For master's, comprehensive assessment. *Entrance requirements:* For master's, GMAT or GRE General Test. *Application deadline:* Applications are processed on a rolling basis. Application fee: $40. *Financial support:* Career-related internships or fieldwork and tuition waivers (full) available. Support available to part-time students. Financial award applicants required to submit FAFSA. *Application contact:* Information Contact, 304-746-1900, Fax: 304-746-1902, E-mail: services@marshall.edu.

Marymount University, School of Business Administration, Program in Health Care Management, Arlington, VA 22207-4299. Offers MS. *Accreditation:* CAHME. Part-time and evening/weekend programs available. *Students:* 12 full-time (6 women), 15 part-time (10 women); includes 11 minority (9 African Americans, 1 Asian American or Pacific Islander, 1 Hispanic American), 3 international. Average age 35. 38 applicants, 100% accepted, 7 enrolled. In 2006, 10 degrees awarded. *Degree requirements:* For master's, thesis or alternative. *Entrance requirements:* For master's, GMAT or GRE General Test, resumé. Additional exam requirements/recommendations for international students: Required—TOEFL (minimum score 600 paper-based; 250 computer-based). *Application deadline:* Applications are processed on a rolling basis. Application fee: $40. Electronic applications accepted. *Expenses:* Tuition: Full-time $11,160; part-time $620 per credit. Required fees: $113; $630 per credit. *Financial support:* Research assistantships with full tuition reimbursements, career-related internships or fieldwork, scholarships/grants, and unspecified assistantships available. Support available to part-time students. Financial award applicants required to submit FAFSA. *Unit head:* Dr. Kristie Stover, Director, 703-284-5922, Fax: 703-527-3830, E-mail: kristie.stover@marymount.edu.

Marywood University, Academic Affairs, College of Health and Human Services, Department of Nursing and Public Administration, Program in Health Services Administration, Scranton, PA 18509-1598. Offers long-term care management (MHSA); managed care (MHSA). Part-time and evening/weekend programs available. *Students:* 2 full-time (both women), 13 part-time (11 women). Average age 39. 2 applicants, 100% accepted. In 2006, 3 degrees awarded. *Degree requirements:* For master's, thesis or alternative, internship/practicum. *Entrance requirements:* Additional exam requirements/recommendations for international students: Required—TOEFL (minimum score 550 paper-based; 213 computer-based). *Application deadline:* For fall admission, 4/15 priority date for domestic and international students; for spring admission, 11/15 priority date for domestic and international students. Applications are processed on a rolling basis. Application fee: $30. Electronic applications accepted. *Expenses:* Tuition: Part-time $672 per credit. Tuition and fees vary according to degree level, campus/location and program. *Financial support:* Research assistantships with tuition reimbursements, career-related internships or fieldwork, scholarships/grants, tuition waivers (partial), and unspecified assistantships available. Support available to part-time students. Financial award application deadline: 2/15; financial award applicants required to submit FAFSA. *Application contact:* Dr. Deborah M. Flynn, Coordinator of Graduate Advising (Enrollment Management), 570-348-6211, E-mail: flynn@ac.marywood.edu.

Massachusetts College of Pharmacy and Health Sciences, Graduate Studies, Program in Drug Regulatory Affairs and Health Policy, Boston, MA 02115-5896. Offers MS. Part-time and evening/weekend programs available. *Degree requirements:* For master's, thesis, oral defense of thesis. *Entrance requirements:* For master's, GRE General Test, minimum QPA of 3.0. Additional exam requirements/recommendations for international students: Required—TOEFL (minimum score 550 paper-based). *Faculty research:* Epidemiology, drug policy, drug regulation, ethics.

McGill University, Faculty of Graduate and Postdoctoral Studies, Faculty of Medicine, Departments of Epidemiology and Biostatistics, and Occupational Health, Montréal, QC H3A 2T5, Canada. Offers community health (M Sc); environmental health (M Sc); epidemiology and biostatistics (M Sc, PhD, Diploma); health care evaluation (M Sc); medical statistics (M Sc); occupational health (M Sc). *Accreditation:* CEPH (one or more programs are accredited). *Degree requirements:* For master's, thesis optional; for doctorate, thesis/dissertation. *Entrance requirements:* For master's, GRE, minimum GPA of 3.0; for doctorate, GRE. *Faculty research:* Chronic and infectious disease epidemiology, health services research, pharmacoepidemiology.

Medical University of South Carolina, College of Health Professions, Department of Health Administration and Policy, Doctoral Program in Health Administration, Charleston, SC 29425-0002. Offers DHA. *Faculty:* 14 full-time (7 women), 1 part-time/adjunct (0 women). *Students:* 38 full-time (16 women); includes 1 minority (Asian American or Pacific Islander), 3 international. Average age 40. 31 applicants, 65% accepted, 12 enrolled. *Degree requirements:* For doctorate, thesis/dissertation, comprehensive exam. *Entrance requirements:* For doctorate, experience in health care, interview, master's degree in relevant field, resumé, 3 references. Additional exam requirements/recommendations for international students: Required—TOEFL (minimum score 600 paper-based; 250 computer-based). *Application deadline:* For fall admission, 8/15 for domestic and international students. Applications are processed on a rolling basis. Application fee: $75. *Financial support:* Application deadline: 3/15; *Unit head:* Dr. James S. Zoller, Program Director, 843-792-3849, Fax: 843-792-3327, E-mail: zollerjs@musc.edu. *Application contact:* Ann Brown, Student and Alumni Manager, 843-792-2115, Fax: 843-792-3327, E-mail: brownah@musc.edu.

Medical University of South Carolina, College of Health Professions, Department of Health Administration and Policy, Program in Health Administration-Executive, Charleston, SC 29425-0002. Offers MHA. Part-time programs available. Postbaccalaureate distance learning degree programs offered (no on-campus study). *Faculty:* 14 full-time (7 women), 1 part-time/adjunct (0 women). *Students:* 11 full-time (3 women), 27 part-time (18 women); includes 3 minority (2 African Americans, 1 Hispanic American), 1 international. Average age 37. 21 applicants, 86% accepted, 18 enrolled. In 2006, 9 degrees awarded. *Degree requirements:* For master's, 20 hours of community service. *Entrance requirements:* For master's, GRE General Test or GMAT, minimum GPA of 3.0. Additional exam requirements/recommendations for international students: Required—TOEFL (minimum score 600 paper-based; 250 computer-based). *Application deadline:* For fall admission, 2/1 priority date for domestic and international students; for spring admission, 11/15 priority date for domestic and international students. Application fee: $75. Electronic applications accepted. *Financial support:* Federal Work-Study and scholarships/grants available. Support available to part-time students. Financial award application deadline: 3/15; financial award applicants required to submit FAFSA. *Faculty research:* Computer-based patient records, Internet use in health care, health information networks, continuous quality improvement, organizational behavior. *Unit head:* Dr. Andrea W. White, Program Director, 843-792-4493, Fax: 843-792-3327, E-mail: whiteand@musc.edu. *Application contact:* Ann Brown, Student and Alumni Manager, 843-792-2115, Fax: 843-792-3327, E-mail: brownah@musc.edu.

Medical University of South Carolina, College of Health Professions, Department of Health Administration and Policy, Program in Health Administration-Residential, Charleston, SC 29425-0002. Offers MHA. *Accreditation:* CAHME. Part-time programs available. Postbaccalaureate distance learning degree programs offered (minimal on-campus study). *Faculty:* 14 full-time (7 women), 1 part-time/adjunct (0 women). *Students:* 47 full-time (25 women), 4 part-time (all women); includes 10 minority (9 African Americans, 1 Hispanic American), 2 international. Average age 26. 50 applicants, 56% accepted, 20 enrolled. In 2006, 28 degrees awarded. *Degree requirements:* For master's, 20 hours of community service, internship or field project. *Entrance requirements:* For master's, GRE General Test, GMAT, minimum GPA of 3.0, 3 references, interview. Additional exam requirements/recommendations for international students: Required—TOEFL (minimum score 550 paper-based; 213 computer-based). *Application deadline:* For fall admission, 3/1 priority date for domestic and international students. Application fee: $75. *Financial support:* Federal Work-Study and scholarships/grants available. Support available to part-time students. Financial award application deadline: 3/15; financial award applicants required to submit FAFSA. *Unit head:* Dr. Andrea W. White, Program Director, 843-792-4493, Fax: 843-792-3327, E-mail: whiteand@musc.edu. *Application contact:* Ann Brown, Student and Alumni Manager, 843-792-2115, Fax: 843-792-3327, E-mail: brownah@musc.edu.

Meharry Medical College, School of Graduate Studies, Division of Community Health Sciences, Nashville, TN 37208-9989. Offers general preventive medicine (MSPH); health services administration (MSPH); occupational medicine (MSPH); public health administration (MSPH). Part-time and evening/weekend programs available. *Degree requirements:* For master's, thesis, externship. *Entrance requirements:* For master's, GRE General Test, GMAT. Expenses: Contact institution. *Faculty research:* Policy and management, health care financing, health education and promotion.

Mercy College, Division of Social and Behavioral Sciences, Program in Health Services Management, Dobbs Ferry, NY 10522-1189. Offers MPA, MS, Certificate. *Students:* 4 full-time (all women), 23 part-time (19 women); includes 13 minority (7 African Americans, 1 Asian American or Pacific Islander, 5 Hispanic Americans), 1 international. Average age 38. In 2006, 13 degrees awarded. *Entrance requirements:* For master's, interview, letters of recommendation, minimum undergraduate GPA of 3.0. Application fee: $37. *Expenses:* Tuition: Part-time $595 per credit. Required fees: $9 per credit. Tuition and fees vary according to program. *Unit head:* Dr. Mary C. Kraetzer, Program Director, 914-674-7341, E-mail: mkraetzer@mercy.edu. *Application contact:* Kathleen Jackson, Director of Admissions, 800-Mercy-NY, Fax: 914-674-7382, E-mail: admissions@mercy.edu.

Middle Tennessee State University, College of Graduate Studies, College of Liberal Arts, Department of Sociology and Anthropology, Program in Health Care Management, Murfreesboro, TN 37132. Offers Graduate Certificate. *Students:* 7 full-time (4 women); includes 5 minority (all African Americans) *Entrance requirements:* Additional exam requirements/recommendations for international students: Required—TOEFL (minimum score 525 paper-based; 195 computer-based). *Financial support:* Application deadline: 5/1. *Unit head:* Dr. Ronald Aday, Head, 615-898-2693.

Midwestern State University, Graduate Studies, College of Business Administration, Wichita Falls, TX 76308. Offers business administration (MBA); health services administration (MBA).

Health Services Management and Hospital Administration

Midwestern State University (continued)

Accreditation: ACBSP. Part-time and evening/weekend programs available. *Faculty:* 13 full-time (1 woman). *Students:* 21 full-time (12 women), 35 part-time (12 women); includes 6 minority (2 African Americans, 4 Hispanic Americans), 19 international. Average age 30. 19 applicants, 68% accepted, 12 enrolled. In 2006, 15 degrees awarded. *Degree requirements:* For master's, thesis optional. *Entrance requirements:* For master's, GMAT. Additional exam requirements/recommendations for international students: Required—TOEFL (minimum score 550 paper-based; 213 computer-based). *Application deadline:* For fall admission, 7/1 for domestic students, 4/1 for international students; for spring admission, 11/1 for domestic students, 8/1 for international students. Applications are processed on a rolling basis. Application fee: $35 ($50 for international students). Electronic applications accepted. *Financial support:* In 2006–07, 34 students received support, including 2 teaching assistantships with partial tuition reimbursements available (averaging $7,766 per year); career-related internships or fieldwork, Federal Work-Study, institutionally sponsored loans, tuition waivers (partial), and unspecified assistantships also available. Support available to part-time students. Financial award application deadline: 5/1; financial award applicants required to submit FAFSA. *Faculty research:* Small business management, health care personnel administration, Pacific Rim trade, AIDS in the workplace, technology transfer. *Unit head:* Anthony Chelte, Dean, 940-397-4088, Fax: 940-397-4280, E-mail: anthony.chelte@mwsu.edu. *Application contact:* Dr. David Wierschem, Graduate Coordinator, 940-397-6260, Fax: 940-397-4280, E-mail: david.wierschem@mwsu.edu.

Midwestern State University, Graduate Studies, College of Health Sciences and Human Services, Nursing Program, Wichita Falls, TX 76308. Offers family nurse practitioner (MSN); health services administration (MSN); nurse educator (MSN). *Accreditation:* AACN. Part-time and evening/weekend programs available. *Faculty:* 8 full-time (all women), 2 part-time/adjunct (both women). *Students:* 12 full-time (10 women), 49 part-time (40 women); includes 8 minority (1 African American, 2 American Indian/Alaska Native, 1 Asian American or Pacific Islander, 4 Hispanic Americans), 3 international. Average age 39. 19 applicants, 84% accepted, 12 enrolled. In 2006, 10 degrees awarded. *Degree requirements:* For master's, thesis optional. *Entrance requirements:* For master's, GRE General Test or MAT. Additional exam requirements/recommendations for international students: Required—TOEFL (minimum score 550 paper-based; 213 computer-based). *Application deadline:* For fall admission, 7/1 for domestic students, 4/1 for international students; for spring admission, 11/1 for domestic students, 8/1 for international students. Applications are processed on a rolling basis. Application fee: $35 ($50 for international students). Electronic applications accepted. *Financial support:* In 2006–07, 58 students received support, including 1 teaching assistantship with partial tuition reimbursement available (averaging $7,500 per year); career-related internships or fieldwork, Federal Work-Study, institutionally sponsored loans, scholarships/grants, tuition waivers (partial), and unspecified assistantships also available. Support available to part-time students. Financial award application deadline: 5/1; financial award applicants required to submit FAFSA. *Unit head:* Dr. Melissa Ford, Chair, 940-397-4601, Fax: 940-397-4513, E-mail: melissa.ford@mwsu.edu. *Application contact:* 800-842-1922, Fax: 940-397-4672, E-mail: admissions@mwsu.edu.

Midwestern State University, Graduate Studies, College of Health Sciences and Human Services, Program in Health Services and Public Administration, Wichita Falls, TX 76308. Offers health services administration (MHA); public administration (MPA); public administration (administrative justice) (MPA); public administration (health services administration) with certificate (MPA); public administration (health services) (MPA). Part-time and evening/weekend programs available. *Faculty:* 4 full-time (1 woman), 2 part-time/adjunct (1 woman). *Students:* 12 full-time (3 women), 38 part-time (19 women); includes 5 minority (3 African Americans, 2 Hispanic Americans), 9 international. Average age 35. 23 applicants, 78% accepted, 12 enrolled. In 2006, 8 degrees awarded. *Degree requirements:* For master's, thesis, comprehensive exam. *Entrance requirements:* For master's, GRE. Additional exam requirements/recommendations for international students: Required—TOEFL (minimum score 550 paper-based; 213 computer-based). *Application deadline:* For fall admission, 7/1 for domestic students, 4/1 for international students; for spring admission, 11/1 for domestic students, 8/1 for international students. Applications are processed on a rolling basis. Application fee: $35 ($50 for international students). Electronic applications accepted. *Financial support:* In 2006–07, 42 students received support, including 2 teaching assistantships with partial tuition reimbursements available (averaging $7,125 per year); career-related internships or fieldwork, Federal Work-Study, institutionally sponsored loans, scholarships/grants, tuition waivers (partial), and unspecified assistantships also available. Support available to part-time students. Financial award application deadline: 5/1; financial award applicants required to submit FAFSA. *Unit head:* Dr. Kirk Harlow, Acting Chair, 940-397-4745, Fax: 940-397-6291, E-mail: kirk.harlow@mwsu.edu. *Application contact:* 800-842-1922, Fax: 940-397-4672, E-mail: admissions@mwsu.edu.

Mississippi College, Graduate School, Program in Health Services Administration, Clinton, MS 39058. Offers MHSA. Part-time programs available. *Faculty:* 4 part-time/adjunct (1 woman). *Students:* 7 full-time (4 women), 39 part-time (33 women); includes 35 minority (all African Americans), 2 international. Average age 31. In 2006, 22 degrees awarded. *Degree requirements:* For master's, comprehensive exam. *Entrance requirements:* For master's, GRE General Test, minimum GPA of 2.5. Additional exam requirements/recommendations for international students: Recommended—IELTS. *Application deadline:* For fall admission, 8/15 priority date for domestic students. Applications are processed on a rolling basis. Application fee: $25. Electronic applications accepted. *Expenses:* Tuition: Full-time $7,290; part-time $405 per hour. Required fees: $150 per term. Tuition and fees vary according to campus/location and program. *Financial support:* Career-related internships or fieldwork, Federal Work-Study, and unspecified assistantships available. Support available to part-time students. Financial award application deadline: 4/1; financial award applicants required to submit FAFSA. *Unit head:* Jeannie Lane, Adviser, 601-925-3891, Fax: 601-925-3889, E-mail: jlane@mc.edu.

Missouri State University, Graduate College, College of Business Administration, Department of Management, Springfield, MO 65804-0094. Offers health administration (MHA). Part-time and evening/weekend programs available. *Faculty:* 12 full-time (4 women). *Students:* 20 full-time (13 women), 21 part-time (9 women), 11 international. Average age 29. 54 applicants, 35% accepted, 16 enrolled. In 2006, 5 degrees awarded. *Degree requirements:* For master's, thesis optional. *Entrance requirements:* For master's, GMAT or GRE, minimum GPA of 2.75. Additional exam requirements/recommendations for international students: Required—TOEFL (minimum score 550 paper-based; 213 computer-based; 79 iBT), IELTS (minimum score 6). *Application deadline:* For fall admission, 7/20 priority date for domestic students; for spring admission, 12/20 priority date for domestic students. Application fee: $35. *Expenses:* Tuition, state resident: full-time $3,582; part-time $199 per credit hour. Tuition, nonresident: full-time $6,984; part-time $199 per credit hour. Required fees: $548. Full-time tuition and fees vary according to course level, course load, program and reciprocity agreements. *Financial support:* Teaching assistantships with full tuition reimbursements, career-related internships or fieldwork, institutionally sponsored loans, scholarships/grants, tuition waivers, and unspecified assistantships available. Support available to part-time students. Financial award application deadline: 3/31; financial award applicants required to submit FAFSA. *Unit head:* Dr. Barry Wisdom, Department Head, 417-836-5415, E-mail: barrywisdom@missouristate.edu. *Application contact:* Dr. Robert Lunn, MHA Program Director, 417-836-5647, E-mail: robertlunn@missouristate.edu.

Monmouth University, Graduate School, School of Business Administration, West Long Branch, NJ 07764-1898. Offers accounting (MBA); business administration (MBA); health care management (MBA, Certificate). *Accreditation:* AACSB. Part-time and evening/weekend programs available. *Faculty:* 30 full-time (11 women), 3 part-time/adjunct (1 woman). *Students:* 36 full-time (18 women), 198 part-time (88 women); includes 22 minority (9 African Americans, 1 American Indian/Alaska Native, 6 Asian Americans or Pacific Islanders, 6 Hispanic Americans), 12 international. Average age 30. 123 applicants, 89% accepted, 54 enrolled. In 2006, 74 degrees awarded. *Degree requirements:* For master's, capstone course. *Entrance requirements:* For master's, GMAT, minimum GPA of 3.0 in major, 2.75 overall. Additional exam requirements/recommendations for international students: Required—TOEFL (minimum score 550 paper-based; 213 computer-based; 79 iBT), IELTS (minimum score 5), MELAB 77, Cambridge A, B, C. *Application deadline:* For fall admission, 7/15 priority date for domestic students, 6/1 for international students; for spring admission, 11/15 priority date for domestic students, 11/1 for international students. Applications are processed on a rolling basis. Application fee: $50. Electronic applications accepted. *Expenses:* Tuition: Full-time $12,780; part-time $710 per credit. Required fees: $628; $314 per term. *Financial support:* In 2006–07, 126 fellowships (averaging $1,459 per year), 12 research assistantships (averaging $8,362 per year) were awarded; career-related internships or fieldwork, scholarships/grants, tuition waivers (partial), and unspecified assistantships also available. Support available to part-time students. Financial award application deadline: 3/1; financial award applicants required to submit FAFSA. *Faculty research:* Information technology and marketing, behavioral research in accounting, human resources, management of technology. *Unit head:* Donald Smith, Program Director, 732-571-7536, Fax: 732-263-5517, E-mail: dsmith@monmouth.edu. *Application contact:* Kevin Roane, Director, Office of Graduate Admission, 732-571-3452, Fax: 732-263-5123, E-mail: gradadm@monmouth.edu.

Montana State University–Billings, College of Allied Health Professions, Department of Health Administration, Billings, MT 59101-0298. Offers MHA. Postbaccalaureate distance learning degree programs offered (minimal on-campus study). *Students:* 13. 7 applicants, 100% accepted, 7 enrolled. *Degree requirements:* For master's, thesis or professional paper and/or field experience, thesis optional. *Entrance requirements:* For master's, GRE General Test or GMAT, minimum undergraduate GPA of 3.0, graduate 3.25; 3 years' clinical or administrative experience in health care delivery or 5 years' experience in business or industry management. *Application deadline:* For fall admission, 4/20 for domestic students. Applications are processed on a rolling basis. Application fee: $40. *Expenses:* Tuition, state resident: full-time $4,599. Tuition, nonresident: full-time $10,786. *Financial support:* Career-related internships or fieldwork, Federal Work-Study, institutionally sponsored loans, scholarships/grants, tuition waivers (partial), and unspecified assistantships available. Support available to part-time students. Financial award application deadline: 5/1; financial award applicants required to submit FAFSA. *Unit head:* Dr. Sheila McGinnis, Program Director, 406-896-5840, E-mail: smcginnis@msubillings.edu. *Application contact:* David M. Sullivan, Graduate Studies Counselor, 406-657-2053, Fax: 406-657-2299, E-mail: dsullivan@msubillings.edu.

Mount Aloysius College, Program in Health and Human Services Administration, Cresson, PA 16630-1999. Offers MS.

National University, Academic Affairs, School of Health and Human Services, Department of Health Sciences, La Jolla, CA 92037-1011. Offers health care administration (MS). Part-time and evening/weekend programs available. Postbaccalaureate distance learning degree programs offered. *Faculty:* 2 full-time (0 women), 1 (woman) part-time/adjunct. *Students:* 6 full-time (5 women), 8 part-time (3 women); includes 6 minority (2 African Americans, 4 Hispanic Americans). Average age 33. 16 applicants. *Degree requirements:* For master's, thesis. *Entrance requirements:* For master's, interview, minimum GPA of 2.5. Additional exam requirements/recommendations for international students: Required—TOEFL (minimum score 550 paper-based; 213 computer-based; 80 iBT). Application fee: $60 ($65 for international students). *Expenses:* Tuition: Full-time $7,722; part-time $286 per unit. One-time fee: $60. *Financial support:* Career-related internships or fieldwork, institutionally sponsored loans, and scholarships/grants available. Support available to part-time students. Financial award application deadline: 6/30; financial award applicants required to submit FAFSA. *Unit head:* Dr. Bart Chapman, Chair, 858-642-8391, Fax: 858-642-8781, E-mail: bchapman@nu.edu. *Application contact:* Dominick Giovanniello, Associate Regional Dean—San Diego, 800-NAT-UNIV, Fax: 858-642-8709, E-mail: dgiovann@nu.edu.

Nebraska Methodist College, Program in Medical Group Administration, Omaha, NE 68114. Offers MS. *Expenses:* Tuition: Part-time $486 per credit hour. Required fees: $25 per credit hour. Full-time tuition and fees vary according to program. *Unit head:* Sarah Bonney, Program Director, 402-354-7200, Fax: 402-354-7020. *Application contact:* Deann Sterner, Director of Admissions, 402-354-7200, Fax: 402-354-7020, E-mail: admissions@methodistcollege.edu.

New England College, Program in Management, Henniker, NH 03242-3293. Offers healthcare administration (MS); nonprofit leadership (MS); organizational leadership (MS). Part-time and evening/weekend programs available. *Degree requirements:* For master's, independent research project. Electronic applications accepted.

New Jersey City University, Graduate and Continuing Education, College of Professional Studies, Department of Health Sciences, Jersey City, NJ 07305-1597. Offers community health education (MS); health administration (MS); school health education (MS). Part-time and evening/weekend programs available. *Faculty:* 5. *Students:* Average age 42. In 2006, 25 degrees awarded. *Degree requirements:* For master's, thesis or alternative, internship. *Entrance requirements:* For master's, GRE General Test or MAT. Additional exam requirements/recommendations for international students: Required—TOEFL. *Application deadline:* For fall admission, 8/1 priority date for domestic students; for spring admission, 12/1 for domestic students. Applications are processed on a rolling basis. Application fee: $0. *Expenses:* Tuition, state resident: full-time $7,038; part-time $391 per credit. Tuition, nonresident: full-time $12,510; part-time $695 per credit. Required fees: $65 per credit. *Financial support:* Career-related internships or fieldwork and unspecified assistantships available. *Unit head:* Dr. Lilliam Rosado, Chairperson, 201-200-3461.

The New School: A University, Milano The New School for Management and Urban Policy, Program in Health Services Management and Policy, New York, NY 10011. Offers health services management and policy (MS); medical group practice management (Adv C). Part-time and evening/weekend programs available. *Students:* 15 full-time (11 women), 37 part-time (30 women). Average age 36. In 2006, 18 degrees awarded. *Degree requirements:* For master's, thesis. *Entrance requirements:* For master's, interview. *Application deadline:* For fall admission, 8/1 priority date for domestic students; for winter admission, 1/15 priority date for domestic students. Applications are processed on a rolling basis. Application fee: $50. *Financial support:* Research assistantships, Federal Work-Study, scholarships/grants, and tuition waivers (full and partial) available. Support available to part-time students. Financial award application deadline: 3/1; financial award applicants required to submit FAFSA. *Faculty research:* Health care economics. *Unit head:* Dr. Alex F. Schwartz, Chair, 212-229-5400 Ext. 1415, Fax: 212-229-5404, E-mail: schwartz@newschool.edu. *Application contact:* Peter King, Director of Admissions, 212-229-5400, Fax: 212-229-5354, E-mail: kingp@newschool.edu.

See Close-Up on page 1809.

New York Institute of Technology, Ellis College, Old Westbury, NY 11568. Offers accounting and information systems (MBA); e-commerce (MBA); finance (MBA); global management (MBA); healthcare administration (MBA); human resources management (MBA); leadership (MBA); management of information systems (MBA); management of technology (MBA); marketing (MBA); professional accounting (MBA); project management (MBA); risk management (MBA); strategy and economics (MBA). Ellis College is a collaboration between New York Institute of Technology and UNext online learning company. Part-time and evening/weekend programs available. Postbaccalaureate distance learning degree programs offered (no on-campus study). *Entrance requirements:* For master's, interview. Additional exam requirements/recommendations for international students: Required—TOEFL (minimum score 550 paper-based; 213 computer-based). Electronic applications accepted. *Expenses:* Tuition: Full-time $16,800; part-time $700 per credit.

New York Medical College, School of Public Health, Department of Health Policy and Management, Valhalla, NY 10595-1691. Offers MPH. Part-time and evening/weekend programs available. In 2006, 17 degrees awarded. *Degree requirements:* For master's, thesis, registration. *Entrance requirements:* For master's, minimum GPA of 3.0; work experience.

Additional exam requirements/recommendations for international students: Required—TOEFL (minimum score 600 paper-based; 250 computer-based). *Application deadline:* For fall admission, 8/1 priority date for domestic students, 5/15 for international students; for spring admission, 12/1 priority date for domestic students, 10/15 for international students. Applications are processed on a rolling basis. Application fee: $35 ($60 for international students). Electronic applications accepted. *Financial support:* Career-related internships or fieldwork, Federal Work-Study, and institutionally sponsored loans available. Financial award application deadline: 6/15; financial award applicants required to submit FAFSA. *Unit head:* Annette Choolfaian, Chair, 914-594-4250, Fax: 914-594-4292, E-mail: annette@nymc.edu. *Application contact:* Marian F. McGowan, Information Contact, 914-594-4510, Fax: 914-594-4292, E-mail: sph_admissions@nymc.edu.

See Close-Ups on pages 1811 and 2043.

New York University, Robert F. Wagner Graduate School of Public Service, Program in Health Policy and Management, New York, NY 10012-1019. Offers health finance (MPA); health policy analysis (MPA); health policy and management (Advanced Certificate); health services management (MPA); international health (MPA); MBA/MPA; MD/MPA. *Accreditation:* CAHME (one or more programs are accredited). Part-time and evening/weekend programs available. *Faculty:* 8 full-time (3 women), 8 part-time/adjunct (6 women). *Students:* 63 full-time (44 women), 97 part-time (76 women); includes 53 minority (14 African Americans, 25 Asian Americans or Pacific Islanders, 14 Hispanic Americans), 15 international. Average age 28. 186 applicants, 52% accepted, 41 enrolled. In 2006, 64 degrees awarded. *Degree requirements:* For master's, thesis or alternative, residency (internship) or capstone/end event. *Entrance requirements:* For master's, minimum undergraduate GPA of 3.0. Additional exam requirements/recommendations for international students: Required—TOEFL (minimum score 600 paper-based; 250 computer-based), TWE (minimum score 4). *Application deadline:* For fall admission, 6/1 for domestic students, 1/15 for international students; for spring admission, 11/15 for domestic students, 10/1 for international students. Applications are processed on a rolling basis. Application fee: $70. Electronic applications accepted. *Expenses:* Contact institution. Tuition and fees vary according to program. *Financial support:* In 2006–07, 29 fellowships (averaging $10,160 per year), 2 research assistantships with full and partial tuition reimbursements (averaging $15,000 per year) were awarded; career-related internships or fieldwork, Federal Work-Study, institutionally sponsored loans, scholarships/grants, health care benefits, and unspecified assistantships also available. Support available to part-time students. Financial award application deadline: 1/15; financial award applicants required to submit FAFSA. *Unit head:* Prof. Anthony Kovner, Director, 212-998-7440, Fax: 212-995-4162. *Application contact:* Bethany Godsoe, Assistant Dean, Enrollment and Student Services, 212-998-7414, Fax: 212-995-4164, E-mail: wagner.admissions@nyu.edu.

Northeastern University, College of Arts and Sciences, Department of Political Science, Program in Public Administration, Boston, MA 02115-5096. Offers development administration (MPA); health administration and policy (MPA); state and local government (MPA). *Accreditation:* NASPAA. Part-time and evening/weekend programs available. *Faculty:* 8 full-time (0 women), 8 part-time/adjunct (1 woman). *Students:* 24 full-time (10 women), 17 part-time (10 women). Average age 32. In 2006, 16 degrees awarded. *Degree requirements:* For master's, thesis optional. *Entrance requirements:* For master's, GRE General Test. Additional exam requirements/recommendations for international students: Required—TOEFL. *Application deadline:* For fall admission, 2/1 priority date for domestic students, 5/1 for international students. Applications are processed on a rolling basis. Application fee: $50. *Financial support:* Research assistantships with tuition reimbursements, teaching assistantships with tuition reimbursements, career-related internships or fieldwork, Federal Work-Study, tuition waivers (full and partial), and unspecified assistantships available. Support available to part-time students. Financial award application deadline: 2/1; financial award applicants required to submit FAFSA. *Faculty research:* National health care, Third World development, leadership and ethics, science and technology, budgeting. *Unit head:* Dr. Christopher Bosso, Graduate Coordinator, 617-373-2796, Fax: 617-373-5311, E-mail: gradpolisci@neu.edu. *Application contact:* Brynn Thompson, Graduate Programs Assistant, 617-373-4404, Fax: 617-373-5311, E-mail: gradpolisci@neu.edu.

Northwest Missouri State University, Graduate School, Melvin and Valorie Booth College of Business and Professional Studies, Program In Health Management, Maryville, MO 64468-6001. Offers MBA. Part-time programs available. *Faculty:* 15 full-time (2 women). *Students:* 1 full-time (0 women), 1 part-time. 5 applicants, 40% accepted, 1 enrolled. *Degree requirements:* For master's, comprehensive exam. *Entrance requirements:* For master's, GMAT, minimum GPA of 2.5. Additional exam requirements/recommendations for international students: Required—TOEFL (minimum score 550 paper-based; 213 computer-based). *Application deadline:* For fall admission, 7/1 for domestic and international students; for spring admission, 12/1 for domestic students, 11/15 for international students. Applications are processed on a rolling basis. Application fee: $0 ($50 for international students). Electronic applications accepted. *Financial support:* Application deadline: 3/1; *Unit head:* Dr. Mark Jelavich, Director, 660-562-1763. *Application contact:* Dr. Frances Shipley, Dean of Graduate School, 660-562-1145, Fax: 660-562-1096, E-mail: gradsch@nwmissouri.edu.

OGI School of Science & Engineering at Oregon Health & Science University, Graduate Studies, Department of Management in Science and Technology, Beaverton, OR 97006-8921. Offers health care management (Certificate); management in science and technology (MS, Certificate). Part-time and evening/weekend programs available. *Faculty:* 3 full-time (1 woman), 39 part-time/adjunct (15 women). *Students:* Average age 38. 8 applicants, 38% accepted, 2 enrolled. In 2006, 26 master's, 10 other advanced degrees awarded. *Degree requirements:* For master's, thesis, registration. *Entrance requirements:* For master's, 2 years of work experience. Additional exam requirements/recommendations for international students: Recommended—TOEFL (minimum score 625 paper-based; 263 computer-based). *Application deadline:* Applications are processed on a rolling basis. Application fee: $65. Electronic applications accepted. *Expenses:* Tuition, nonresident: full-time $22,760; part-time $625 per credit. Required fees: $65 per term. *Financial support:* Tuition waivers (partial) available. *Unit head:* Jim Huntzicker, Head, 503-748-3075. *Application contact:* Shelly Charles, Enrollment Manager, 503-748-1335, Fax: 503-748-1285, E-mail: charles@ohsu.edu.

The Ohio State University, College of Public Health, Program in Health Services Management and Policy, Columbus, OH 43210. Offers MHA. *Students:* 42 full-time (26 women), 19 part-time (10 women); includes 13 minority (8 African Americans, 3 Asian Americans or Pacific Islanders, 2 Hispanic Americans), 3 international. Average age 27. 63 applicants, 73% accepted, 20 enrolled. In 2006, 25 degrees awarded. *Entrance requirements:* For master's, GRE or GMAT. Additional exam requirements/recommendations for international students: Required—TOEFL (minimum score 577 paper-based; 233 computer-based). *Application deadline:* Applications are processed on a rolling basis. Application fee: $40 ($50 for international students). Electronic applications accepted. *Expenses:* Tuition, state resident: full-time $9,438. Tuition, nonresident: full-time $22,791. Tuition and fees vary according to course load, campus/location and program. *Unit head:* Sharon B. Schweikhart, Graduate Studies Committee Chair, 614-292-9708, Fax: 614-292-3572, E-mail: schweikhart.1@osu.edu. *Application contact:* Graduate Admissions, 614-292-9994, Fax: 614-292-3985, E-mail: domestic.grad@osu.edu.

Ohio University, Graduate Studies, College of Health and Human Services, School of Health Sciences, Athens, OH 45701-2979. Offers MHA, MPH. Part-time programs available. Postbaccalaureate distance learning degree programs offered. *Faculty:* 9 full-time (3 women), 3 part-time/adjunct (all women). *Students:* 6 full-time (5 women), 3 part-time (all women); includes 1 minority (African American), 2 international. 35 applicants, 71% accepted, 8 enrolled. In 2006, 6 degrees awarded. *Degree requirements:* For master's, internship. *Entrance requirements:* For master's, GMAT, GRE General Test, previous course work in accounting, management, and statistics. Additional exam requirements/recommendations for international students: Required—TOEFL (minimum score 550 paper-based; 213 computer-based). *Application deadline:* For fall admission, 6/1 for domestic students. Applications are processed on a rolling basis. Application fee: $45. *Financial support:* In 2006–07, 4 students received support, including 4 research assistantships (averaging $7,200 per year), teaching assistantships (averaging $7,200 per year); career-related internships or fieldwork, Federal Work-Study, and institutionally sponsored loans also available. Financial award application deadline: 6/1. *Faculty research:* Health care management, health policy, managed care, long term care administration. *Unit head:* Matthew Adeyanju, Director, 740-593-1849, Fax: 740-593-0555, E-mail: adeyanju@ohio.edu. *Application contact:* Douglas Bolon, Graduate Coordinator, Master of Health Administration Program, 740-593-0750, Fax: 740-593-0555, E-mail: bolon@ohio.edu.

Oklahoma City University, Meinders School of Business, Program in Business Administration, Oklahoma City, OK 73106-1402. Offers finance (MBA); health administration (MBA); information technology (MBA); integrated marketing communications (MBA); international business (MBA); marketing (MBA); JD/MBA. *Accreditation:* ACBSP. Part-time and evening/weekend programs available. *Faculty:* 30 full-time (7 women), 24 part-time/adjunct (5 women). *Students:* 291 full-time (112 women), 186 part-time (68 women); includes 57 minority (27 African Americans, 9 American Indian/Alaska Native, 12 Asian Americans or Pacific Islanders, 9 Hispanic Americans), 218 international. Average age 27. In 2006, 341 degrees awarded. *Degree requirements:* For master's, comprehensive exam. *Entrance requirements:* For master's, minimum GPA of 2.5. Additional exam requirements/recommendations for international students: Required—TOEFL (minimum score 510 paper-based). *Application deadline:* For fall admission, 8/22 for domestic students; for spring admission, 1/15 for domestic students. Applications are processed on a rolling basis. Application fee: $30 ($70 for international students). *Financial support:* Fellowships with partial tuition reimbursements, career-related internships or fieldwork, Federal Work-Study, institutionally sponsored loans, and tuition waivers (partial) available. Support available to part-time students. Financial award application deadline: 8/1. *Faculty research:* Management information systems, international business strategies. *Unit head:* Dr. Mahmood Shandiz, Head, 405-208-5130, Fax: 405-208-5098, E-mail: mshandiz@okcu.edu. *Application contact:* Leslie McKenzie, Director, Graduate Admissions, 800-633-7242, Fax: 405-208-5356, E-mail: gadmissions@okcu.edu.

Oklahoma State University, Graduate College, Interdisciplinary Program in Natural and Applied Sciences, Interdisciplinary Program in Health Care Administration, Stillwater, OK 74078. Offers MS. *Expenses:* Tuition, state resident: part-time $146 per credit hour. Tuition, nonresident: part-time $516 per credit hour. Required fees: $44 per credit hour. Tuition and fees vary according to program. *Unit head:* Dr. Leigh Goodson, Program Director, 918-561-8312.

Old Dominion University, College of Health Sciences, Program in Community Health and Environmental Health, Norfolk, VA 23529. Offers community health professions (MS); environmental health (MS); health care administration (MS); long-term care administration (MS); wellness and promotion (MS). Part-time and evening/weekend programs available. Postbaccalaureate distance learning degree programs offered (no on-campus study). *Faculty:* 5 full-time (4 women), 5 part-time/adjunct (1 woman). *Students:* 10 full-time (7 women), 33 part-time (24 women); includes 6 minority (5 African Americans, 1 Asian American or Pacific Islander), 8 international. Average age 33. 32 applicants, 88% accepted, 15 enrolled. In 2006, 19 degrees awarded. *Degree requirements:* For master's, oral exam, written exam, thesis optional. *Entrance requirements:* For master's, GRE General Test, minimum GPA of 2.75. Additional exam requirements/recommendations for international students: Required—TOEFL. *Application deadline:* For fall admission, 8/1 priority date for domestic students, 7/1 priority date for international students; for winter admission, 11/1 priority date for domestic students, 10/1 priority date for international students; for spring admission, 4/1 priority date for domestic students, 3/1 priority date for international students. Applications are processed on a rolling basis. Application fee: $40. Electronic applications accepted. *Expenses:* Tuition, area resident: Part-time $285 per credit hour. Tuition, nonresident: part-time $715 per credit hour. Required fees: $94 per semester. *Financial support:* In 2006–07, 5 research assistantships with tuition reimbursements (averaging $14,000 per year) were awarded; career-related internships or fieldwork, institutionally sponsored loans, scholarships/grants, and tuition waivers (partial) also available. Support available to part-time students. Financial award applicants required to submit FAFSA. *Faculty research:* Toxicology, domestic violence, health policy and planning, environmental hazards, obesity, substance abuse, minority health spirituality, women's health. Total annual research expenditures: $150,133. *Unit head:* Dr. Clare Houseman, Chair, 757-683-4259, Fax: 757-683-4410, E-mail: chpgdd@odu.edu.

Oregon State University, Graduate School, College of Health and Human Sciences, Department of Public Health, Program in Health Management and Policy, Corvallis, OR 97331. Offers MS. Application fee: $50. *Unit head:* Dr. Leonard H. Friedman, Coordinator, 541-737-2323.

Our Lady of the Lake University of San Antonio, School of Business, San Antonio, TX 78207-4689. Offers general (MBA), including finance, international business, management; health care management (MBA). *Accreditation:* ACBSP. Part-time and evening/weekend programs available. *Degree requirements:* For master's, thesis optional. *Entrance requirements:* For master's, GMAT, GRE General Test, or MAT. Electronic applications accepted. *Faculty research:* International marketing, employee benefits, decision process.

Pace University, Dyson College of Arts and Sciences, Department of Public Administration, New York, NY 10038. Offers government management (MPA); health care administration (MPA); nonprofit management (MPA); JD/MPA. Offered at White Plains, NY location only. Part-time and evening/weekend programs available. *Faculty:* 4 full-time, 6 part-time/adjunct. *Students:* 31 full-time (19 women), 79 part-time (48 women); includes 45 minority (30 African Americans, 5 Asian Americans or Pacific Islanders, 10 Hispanic Americans), 4 international. Average age 34. 69 applicants, 74% accepted, 27 enrolled. In 2006, 38 degrees awarded. *Degree requirements:* For master's, capstone project. *Entrance requirements:* For master's, GRE General Test. *Application deadline:* For fall admission, 8/1 priority date for domestic students; for spring admission, 12/1 priority date for domestic students. Applications are processed on a rolling basis. Application fee: $65. Electronic applications accepted. *Expenses:* Tuition: Part-time $890 per credit. *Financial support:* Research assistantships, career-related internships or fieldwork, Federal Work-Study, and tuition waivers (partial) available. Support available to part-time students. Financial award applicants required to submit FAFSA. *Unit head:* Dr. Joseph Ryan, Chairperson, 914-422-4303. *Application contact:* Joanna Broda, Director of Admissions, 914-422-4283, Fax: 914-422-4287, E-mail: gradwp@pace.edu.

Park University, College of Graduate and Professional Studies, Kansas City, MO 54105. Offers adult education (M Ed); at-risk students (M Ed); disaster and emergency management (MPA); educational administration (M Ed); entrepreneurship (MBA); general business (MBA); general education (M Ed); government/business relations (MPA); healthcare/services management (MBA, MPA); international business (MBA); K-12 certification (MAT); management information systems (MBA); management of information systems (MPA); middle school certification (MAT); multi-cultural education (M Ed); nonprofit management (MPA); public management (MPA); school law (M Ed); secondary school certification (MAT); special education (M Ed). Part-time and evening/weekend programs available. Postbaccalaureate distance learning degree programs offered (no on-campus study). *Degree requirements:* For master's, thesis (for some programs), comprehensive exam, registration. *Entrance requirements:* For master's, GRE, GMAT, teacher certification (M Ed). Additional exam requirements/recommendations for international students: Required—TOEFL (minimum score 550 paper-based). Electronic applications accepted. *Faculty research:* Literacy, leadership, brain based research, multicultural education, diversity.

Penn State Great Valley, Graduate Studies, Management Division, Malvern, PA 19355-1488. Offers biotechnology and health industry management (MBA); business administration (MBA); finance (M Fin); leadership development (MLD); new venture and entrepreneurial studies (MBA);).

Health Services Management and Hospital Administration

Penn State Harrisburg, Graduate School, School of Public Affairs, Middletown, PA 17057-4898. Offers criminal justice (MA); health administration (MHA); public administration (MPA); public affairs (PhD); MPA/JD. *Expenses:* Tuition, state resident: full-time $13,224; part-time $551 per credit. Tuition, nonresident: full-time $18,652; part-time $777 per credit. Required fees: $84 per semester. *Unit head:* Dr. Steven A. Peterson, Professor of Politics, 717-948-6058, E-mail: sap12@psu.edu.

Penn State University Park, Graduate School, College of Health and Human Development, Department of Health Policy and Administration, State College, University Park, PA 16802-1503. Offers MHA, MS, PhD, MBA/MHA. *Accreditation:* CAHME. *Unit head:* Dr. Dennis G. Shea, Head, 814-863-5421, Fax: 814-863-7402, E-mail: dgs4@psu.edu.

See Close-Up on page 1813.

Pfeiffer University, Program in Health Administration, Misenheimer, NC 28109-0960. Offers MHA, MBA/MHA. *Faculty:* 5 full-time (1 woman), 10 part-time/adjunct (2 women). *Students:* 71 full-time (54 women), 299 part-time (238 women); includes 149 minority (138 African Americans, 1 American Indian/Alaska Native, 5 Asian Americans or Pacific Islanders, 5 Hispanic Americans), 3 international. Average age 38. In 2006, 81 degrees awarded. *Expenses:* Tuition: Part-time $380 per semester hour. Tuition and fees vary according to campus/location. *Financial support:* Applicants required to submit FAFSA. *Unit head:* Dr. Joel Vickers, Director, 204-521-9116 Ext. 228.

Philadelphia University, School of Business Administration, Program in Business Administration, Philadelphia, PA 19144-5497. Offers business administration (MBA); finance (MBA); health care management (MBA); international business (MBA); marketing (MBA); MBA/MS. Part-time and evening/weekend programs available. Postbaccalaureate distance learning degree programs offered (no on-campus study). *Faculty:* 10 full-time (2 women), 8 part-time/adjunct (0 women). *Students:* 43 full-time (24 women), 87 part-time (45 women); includes 3 Asian Americans or Pacific Islanders. 154 applicants, 56% accepted, 37 enrolled. In 2006, 85 degrees awarded. *Entrance requirements:* For master's, GMAT. Additional exam requirements/recommendations for international students: Required—TOEFL (minimum score 550 paper-based; 213 computer-based; 79 iBT). *Application deadline:* Applications are processed on a rolling basis. Application fee: $35. *Financial support:* In 2006–07, research assistantships with full tuition reimbursements (averaging $2,500 per year); career-related internships or fieldwork, Federal Work-Study, scholarships/grants, and unspecified assistantships also available. Support available to part-time students. Financial award applicants required to submit FAFSA. *Unit head:* MarySheila McDonald, Assistant Dean for Graduate Programs, 215-951-2950, Fax: 215-951-2653, E-mail: mcdonaldm@philau.edu. *Application contact:* Jack A. Klett, Director of Graduate Admissions, 215-951-2943, Fax: 215-951-2907, E-mail: gradadm@philau.edu.

Portland State University, Graduate Studies, College of Urban and Public Affairs, Program in Health Studies, Portland, OR 97207-0751. Offers health administration (MPA); health administration and policy (MPH). Part-time and evening/weekend programs available. *Faculty:* 12 full-time (8 women), 8 part-time/adjunct (6 women). *Students:* 35 full-time (30 women), 28 part-time (25 women); includes 8 minority (1 Asian American or Pacific Islander, 7 Hispanic Americans), 5 international. Average age 32. 70 applicants, 83% accepted, 32 enrolled. In 2006, 20 degrees awarded. *Degree requirements:* For master's, internship (MPA), practicum (MPH). *Entrance requirements:* For master's, minimum GPA of 3.0 in upper-division course work or 2.75 overall, resumé, 3 recommendation forms. Additional exam requirements/recommendations for international students: Required—TOEFL (minimum score 550 paper-based; 213 computer-based). *Application deadline:* For fall admission, 4/1 for domestic students, 3/1 for international students; for spring admission, 11/1 for domestic and international students. Application fee: $50. *Expenses:* Tuition, state resident: full-time $6,426; part-time $238 per credit. Tuition, nonresident: full-time $11,016; part-time $408 per credit. Tuition and fees vary according to course load. *Financial support:* Fellowships, research assistantships, teaching assistantships, career-related internships or fieldwork, Federal Work-Study, and institutionally sponsored loans available. Support available to part-time students. Financial award application deadline: 3/1; financial award applicants required to submit FAFSA. Total annual research expenditures: $268,773. *Application contact:* Rod Johnson, Admissions Officer, 503-725-4044, Fax: 503-725-5199, E-mail: rod@pdx.edu.

Portland State University, Graduate Studies, College of Urban and Public Affairs, School of Community Health, Portland, OR 97207-0751. Offers gerontology (Certificate); health education (MA, MS); health education and health promotion (MPH); health studies (MPA, MPH), including health administration and policy. *Accreditation:* CEPH. Part-time programs available. *Faculty:* 13 full-time (9 women), 8 part-time/adjunct (6 women). *Students:* 36 full-time (30 women), 34 part-time (27 women); includes 9 minority (1 African American, 1 Asian American or Pacific Islander, 7 Hispanic Americans), 5 international. Average age 32. 73 applicants, 84% accepted, 34 enrolled. In 2006, 20 degrees awarded. *Degree requirements:* For master's, oral and written exams. *Entrance requirements:* For master's, GRE General Test, 3 letters of recommendation. Additional exam requirements/recommendations for international students: Required—TOEFL (minimum score 550 paper-based; 213 computer-based). *Application deadline:* For fall admission, 2/1 for domestic and international students. Application fee: $50. *Expenses:* Tuition, state resident: full-time $6,426; part-time $238 per credit. Tuition, nonresident: full-time $11,016; part-time $408 per credit. Tuition and fees vary according to course load. *Financial support:* In 2006–07, 4 research assistantships with full tuition reimbursements (averaging $7,286 per year) were awarded; fellowships, teaching assistantships, career-related internships or fieldwork, Federal Work-Study, scholarships/grants, and unspecified assistantships also available. Support available to part-time students. Financial award application deadline: 3/1; financial award applicants required to submit FAFSA. Total annual research expenditures: $766,046. *Unit head:* Carlos J. Crespo, Interim Director, 503-725-5102, Fax: 503-725-5100. *Application contact:* Elizabeth Bull, Assistant to the Director, 503-725-4592, Fax: 503-725-5100, E-mail: bulle@pdx.edu.

Quinnipiac University, School of Business, Program in Health Care Management, Hamden, CT 06518-1940. Offers MBA, JD/MBA. Part-time and evening/weekend programs available. *Faculty:* 3 full-time (2 women), 3 part-time/adjunct (1 woman). *Students:* 3 full-time (2 women), 3 part-time (1 woman); includes 2 minority (both Asian Americans or Pacific Islanders) Average age 27. 10 applicants, 60% accepted, 6 enrolled. *Degree requirements:* For master's, thesis or alternative, internship. *Entrance requirements:* For master's, GMAT, minimum GPA of 3.0. Additional exam requirements/recommendations for international students: Required—TOEFL (minimum score 575 paper-based; 233 computer-based; 90 iBT), IELTS (minimum score 7). *Application deadline:* For fall admission, 7/30 priority date for domestic students, 5/30 priority date for international students; for spring admission, 12/15 priority date for domestic students, 10/15 priority date for international students. Applications are processed on a rolling basis. Application fee: $45. Electronic applications accepted. *Expenses:* Tuition: Part-time $675 per credit. Required fees: $30 per credit. *Financial support:* Career-related internships or fieldwork, tuition waivers (partial), and unspecified assistantships available. Support available to part-time students. Financial award application deadline: 4/15; financial award applicants required to submit FAFSA. *Faculty research:* Health care financing, health policy, health care marketing, health economics, health care management information systems. *Unit head:* Dr. Ronald Rozett, Director, 203-582-8249, Fax: 203-582-8664, E-mail: ronald.rozett@quinnipiac.edu. *Application contact:* 800-462-1944, Fax: 203-582-3443, E-mail: graduate@quinnipiac.edu.

See Close-Up on page 311.

Regent University, Graduate School, Robertson School of Government, Virginia Beach, VA 23464-9800. Offers health care policy and administration (MA); international politics (MA); law and public policy (MA); political leadership and management (MA); political management (MA); public administration (MA); public policy (MA); terrorism and homeland defense (MA); world economies and political development (MA); JD/MA; M Div/MA; M Ed/MA; MBA/MA. Part-time programs available. *Faculty:* 7 full-time (2 women), 7 part-time/adjunct (0 women). *Students:* 73 full-time (48 women), 78 part-time (40 women); includes 42 minority (28 African Americans, 5 Asian Americans or Pacific Islanders, 9 Hispanic Americans), 3 international. Average age 31. 189 applicants, 51% accepted, 63 enrolled. In 2006, 31 degrees awarded. *Degree requirements:* For master's, internship, thesis optional. *Entrance requirements:* For master's, GRE General Test or LSAT, minimum undergraduate GPA of 2.75, writing sample, resumé, interview, references. Additional exam requirements/recommendations for international students: Required—TOEFL (minimum score 577 paper-based; 233 computer-based). *Application deadline:* For fall admission, 5/1 priority date for domestic students; for spring admission, 11/1 priority date for domestic students. Applications are processed on a rolling basis. Application fee: $50. Electronic applications accepted. *Expenses:* Contact institution. *Financial support:* In 2006–07, 151 students received support. Scholarships/grants and unspecified assistantships available. Support available to part-time students. Financial award application deadline: 9/1; financial award applicants required to submit FAFSA. *Faculty research:* Education reform, political character issues, social capital concerns, administrative ethics, biblical law and public policy. *Unit head:* Dr. Charles W. Dunn, Dean, 757-226-4322, Fax: 757-226-4643, E-mail: cwdunn@regent.edu. *Application contact:* Althea Bishard, Registrar and Executive Director of Enrollment and Academic Services, 800-373-5504, Fax: 757-226-4381, E-mail: admissions@regent.edu.

Regis University, Rueckert-Hartman School for Health Professions, Denver, CO 80221-1099. Offers clinical leadership for physician assistants (MS); health services administration (MS); nursing (MSN); physical therapy (DPT, TDPT). *Faculty:* 3 full-time (all women), 7 part-time/adjunct (4 women). *Students:* 453. In 2006, 55 degrees awarded. *Application deadline:* Applications are processed on a rolling basis. *Expenses:* Contact institution. *Financial support:* Career-related internships or fieldwork and Federal Work-Study available. *Faculty research:* Normal and pathological balance and gait research, normal/pathological upper limb motor control/biomechanics, exercise energy/metabolism research, optical treatment protocols for therapeutic modalities. *Unit head:* Dr. Patricia Ladewig, Academic Dean, 303-458-4174, E-mail: pladewig@regis.edu. *Application contact:* Donna Eastman, Assistant to the Dean, 303-458-4174, Fax: 303-964-5533, E-mail: deastman@regis.edu.

Roberts Wesleyan College, Division of Adult Professional Studies, Rochester, NY 14624-1997. Offers health administration (MS). Evening/weekend programs available. *Faculty:* 2 full-time (0 women), 9 part-time/adjunct (5 women). *Students:* 57 full-time (28 women). Average age 34. In 2006, 26 degrees awarded. *Degree requirements:* For master's, thesis or alternative. *Entrance requirements:* For master's, minimum GPA of 3.0, verifiable work experience or recommendation. *Application deadline:* Applications are processed on a rolling basis. Application fee: $35. *Financial support:* In 2006–07, 15 students received support. Applicants required to submit FAFSA. *Faculty research:* Small business entrepreneurship, church management. *Unit head:* Dr. William Walence, Chair, 585-594-6210. *Application contact:* Cheryl Johnson, Program Coordinator, 585-594-6452, E-mail: johnson_cheryl@roberts.edu.

Rochester Institute of Technology, Graduate Enrollment Services, College of Applied Science and Technology, Department of Hospitality and Service Management, Program in Health Systems Administration, Rochester, NY 14623-5603. Offers health systems administration (MS); health systems-finance (AC); integrated health systems (AC). *Students:* 4 full-time (2 women), 32 part-time (21 women); includes 5 minority (1 African American, 1 American Indian/Alaska Native, 3 Asian Americans or Pacific Islanders), 3 international. 24 applicants, 63% accepted, 7 enrolled. In 2006, 12 degrees awarded. *Entrance requirements:* For master's, minimum GPA of 3.0; for AC, GRE, minimum GPA of 3.0. Additional exam requirements/recommendations for international students: Required—TOEFL. *Application deadline:* For fall admission, 3/1 priority date for domestic students. Applications are processed on a rolling basis. Application fee: $50. *Expenses:* Tuition: Full-time $28,491; part-time $800 per credit. Required fees: $201. *Unit head:* Linda Underhill, Chair, 585-475-7359, E-mail: lmuism@rit.edu.

Rosalind Franklin University of Medicine and Science, College of Health Professions, Department of Healthcare Management, North Chicago, IL 60064-3095. Offers healthcare management (MS); healthcare risk management (MS); physician assistant studies (MS). Part-time programs available. Postbaccalaureate distance learning degree programs offered (minimal on-campus study). *Degree requirements:* For master's, thesis. *Entrance requirements:* For master's, minimum GPA of 2.8, risk management experience, professional certificate or license. *Faculty research:* Impact on medical malpractice claims, quantifying impact on claim activity and hospital finances, impact of risk management activities on reducing claims.

Rush University, College of Health Sciences, Department of Health Systems Management, Chicago, IL 60612-3832. Offers MS, DHSc. *Accreditation:* CAHME. Part-time and evening/weekend programs available. *Degree requirements:* For master's and doctorate, thesis/dissertation. *Entrance requirements:* For master's, GMAT or GRE General Test, previous undergraduate course work in accounting and statistics; for doctorate, GRE General Test, master's degree preferably in a health discipline. Additional exam requirements/recommendations for international students: Required—TOEFL. Electronic applications accepted. *Faculty research:* Organizational performance, occupational health, quality of care indicators, leadership development, entrepreneurship, health insurance and disability, managed care.

Rutgers, The State University of New Jersey, Newark, Graduate School, Program in Public Administration, Newark, NJ 07102. Offers health care administration (MPA); human resources administration (MPA); public administration (PhD); public management (MPA); public policy analysis (MPA); urban systems and issues (MPA). *Accreditation:* NASPAA (one or more programs are accredited). Part-time and evening/weekend programs available. *Faculty:* 12 full-time (4 women). *Students:* 66 full-time (39 women), 202 part-time (114 women); includes 154 minority (93 African Americans, 1 American Indian/Alaska Native, 36 Asian Americans or Pacific Islanders, 24 Hispanic Americans). 252 applicants, 60% accepted, 71 enrolled. In 2006, 57 master's, 8 doctorates awarded. *Degree requirements:* For master's, thesis or alternative, comprehensive exam; for doctorate, thesis/dissertation. *Entrance requirements:* For master's, GRE, minimum undergraduate B average; for doctorate, GRE, MPA, minimum B average. *Application deadline:* For fall admission, 7/1 priority date for domestic students; for spring admission, 12/1 for domestic students. Applications are processed on a rolling basis. Application fee: $50. Electronic applications accepted. *Financial support:* In 2006–07, 5 fellowships with full tuition reimbursements (averaging $18,000 per year), 2 research assistantships (averaging $18,347 per year), 11 teaching assistantships with full tuition reimbursements (averaging $18,347 per year) were awarded; career-related internships or fieldwork also available. Support available to part-time students. Financial award application deadline: 3/1. *Faculty research:* Government finance, municipal and state government, public productivity. *Unit head:* Dr. Marc Holzer, Chairman and Director, 973-353-5093 Ext. 23, E-mail: mholzer@andromeda.rutgers.edu. *Application contact:* Gail Daniels, Contact, 201-973-5093 Ext. 11, E-mail: gaild@andromeda.rutgers.edu.

Sage Graduate School, Graduate School, Division of Management, Communications and Legal Studies, Program in Health Services Administration, Troy, NY 12180-4115. Offers gerontology (MS); health education (MS); management (MS). Part-time and evening/weekend programs available. *Faculty:* 3 full-time (1 woman), 4 part-time/adjunct (2 women). *Students:* 1 (woman) full-time, 13 part-time (11 women). Average age 32. 8 applicants, 100% accepted, 8 enrolled. In 2006, 5 degrees awarded. *Entrance requirements:* For master's, minimum GPA of 2.75. Additional exam requirements/recommendations for international students: Required—TOEFL (minimum score 550 paper-based; 213 computer-based). Application fee: $40. *Expenses:* Tuition: Full-time $9,270; part-time $515 per credit hour. *Financial support:* Career-related internships or fieldwork, scholarships/grants, and unspecified assistantships available. Support available to part-time students. Financial award application deadline: 3/1; financial award applicants required to submit FAFSA. *Application contact:* Shannon K. Easton, Director of Graduate and Adult Admission, 518-244-2443, Fax: 518-244-6880, E-mail: sgsadm@sage.edu.

St. Ambrose University, College of Business, Program in Business Administration, Davenport, IA 52803-2898. Offers business administration (DBA); health care (MBA); human resources (MBA). *Accreditation:* ACBSP. Part-time and evening/weekend programs available. *Faculty:* 29 full-time (4 women), 24 part-time/adjunct (5 women). *Students:* 99 full-time (47 women), 352 part-time (164 women); includes 48 minority (28 African Americans, 6 Asian Americans or Pacific Islanders, 14 Hispanic Americans), 16 international. Average age 35. 201 applicants, 84% accepted, 112 enrolled. In 2006, 119 master's, 5 doctorates awarded. *Degree requirements:* For master's, thesis or alternative, capstone seminar, comprehensive exam (for some programs), registration; for doctorate, thesis/dissertation, oral and written exams, comprehensive exam, registration. *Entrance requirements:* For master's, GMAT; for doctorate, GMAT, master's degree. Additional exam requirements/recommendations for international students: Required—TOEFL. *Application deadline:* For fall admission, 8/15 priority date for domestic students; for winter admission, 12/15 for domestic students; for spring admission, 1/1 for domestic students. Applications are processed on a rolling basis. Application fee: $25. Electronic applications accepted. *Expenses:* Contact institution. *Financial support:* In 2006–07, 338 students received support, including 8 research assistantships with partial tuition reimbursements available; career-related internships or fieldwork, scholarships/grants, tuition waivers (partial), and unspecified assistantships also available. Support available to part-time students. Financial award application deadline: 3/15; financial award applicants required to submit FAFSA. *Unit head:* Allison S. Ambrose, Director of MBA Academic Services, 563-333-6155, Fax: 563-333-6243, E-mail: ambroseallisons@sau.edu. *Application contact:* Elizabeth Berridge, Director of Graduate Student Recruitment, 563-333-6271, Fax: 563-333-6268, E-mail: berridgeelizabethb@sau.edu.

Saint Joseph's College of Maine, Program in Health Services Administration, Standish, ME 04084-5263. Offers MHSA. Degree program is external; available only by correspondence and online. Part-time programs available. Postbaccalaureate distance learning degree programs offered (minimal on-campus study). *Faculty:* 3 full-time (2 women), 15 part-time/adjunct (8 women). *Students:* Average age 43. 93 applicants, 94% accepted, 82 enrolled. In 2006, 35 degrees awarded. *Degree requirements:* For master's, summer residency. *Entrance requirements:* For master's, 2 years of health-related experience. *Application deadline:* Applications are processed on a rolling basis. Application fee: $50. Electronic applications accepted. *Expenses:* Tuition: Part-time $350 per credit. *Financial support:* Institutionally sponsored loans available. Support available to part-time students. *Faculty research:* Health care organization, policy, and management; long-term care. *Unit head:* John Pratt, Interim Director, 207-893-7981, Fax: 207-893-7987. *Application contact:* 800-752-4723, Fax: 207-892-7480, E-mail: info@sjcme.edu.

St. Joseph's College, Suffolk Campus, Program in Management, Patchogue, NY 11772-2399. Offers health care (AC); health care management (MS); human resource management (AC); human resources management (MS); organizational management (MS).

Saint Joseph's University, College of Arts and Sciences, Department of Health Services, Philadelphia, PA 19131-1395. Offers health administration (MS); health education (MS); nurse anesthesia (MS). Evening/weekend programs available. *Faculty:* 5 full-time (2 women), 12 part-time/adjunct (6 women). *Students:* 45 full-time (27 women), 147 part-time (107 women); includes 51 minority (45 African Americans, 3 Asian Americans or Pacific Islanders, 3 Hispanic Americans), 9 international. Average age 34. In 2006, 62 degrees awarded. *Entrance requirements:* For master's, 2 letters of recommendation. Additional exam requirements/recommendations for international students: Required—TOEFL. *Application deadline:* For fall admission, 7/15 for domestic students. Application fee: $35. *Financial support:* Fellowships, career-related internships or fieldwork available. *Unit head:* Dr. John Newhouse, Chair, 610-660-1578.

Saint Joseph's University, Erivan K. Haub School of Business, Professional MBA Program, Program in Health and Medical Services Administration, Philadelphia, PA 19131-1395. Offers MBA, DO/MBA. Part-time and evening/weekend programs available. *Students:* 4 full-time (2 women), 14 part-time (6 women); includes 6 minority (4 African Americans, 2 Hispanic Americans). Average age 30. In 2006, 7 degrees awarded. *Entrance requirements:* For master's, GMAT, 2 letters of recommendation, resumé. Additional exam requirements/recommendations for international students: Required—TOEFL. *Application deadline:* For fall admission, 7/15 priority date for domestic students, 4/15 for international students; for spring admission, 11/15 priority date for domestic students, 10/15 for international students. Applications are processed on a rolling basis. Application fee: $35. *Financial support:* Fellowships, research assistantships, unspecified assistantships available. Financial award application deadline: 5/1. *Unit head:* Dr. David B. White, Unit Head, 610-660-1582.

Saint Louis University, Graduate School, School of Public Health and Graduate School, Department of Health Management and Policy, St. Louis, MO 63103-2097. Offers health administration (MHA); public health studies (PhD). *Accreditation:* CAHME. Part-time programs available. *Faculty:* 11 full-time (4 women), 15 part-time/adjunct (0 women). *Students:* 33 full-time (17 women), 8 part-time (6 women); includes 11 minority (8 African Americans, 3 Asian Americans or Pacific Islanders), 2 international. Average age 29. 79 applicants, 68% accepted, 17 enrolled. In 2006, 28 master's, 3 doctorates awarded. *Degree requirements:* For master's, internship. *Entrance requirements:* For master's, GMAT or GRE General Test, LSAT, MCAT, letters of recommendation, resumé. Additional exam requirements/recommendations for international students: Required—TOEFL (minimum score 525 paper-based; 194 computer-based). *Application deadline:* For fall admission, 7/1 for domestic students, 5/1 for international students; for spring admission, 11/1 for domestic students. Applications are processed on a rolling basis. Application fee: $40. *Expenses:* Tuition: Part-time $800 per credit hour. Required fees: $105 per semester. *Financial support:* In 2006–07, 17 students received support. Federal Work-Study, scholarships/grants, traineeships, health care benefits, and unspecified assistantships available. Support available to part-time students. Financial award application deadline: 6/1; financial award applicants required to submit FAFSA. *Faculty research:* Management of HIV/AIDS, rural health services, prevention of asthma, genetics and health services use, health insurance and access to care. *Unit head:* Dr. Richard S. Kurz, Chairperson, 314-977-8111, Fax: 314-977-8150, E-mail: kurzrs@slu.edu. *Application contact:* Gary Behrman, Associate Dean of the Graduate School, 314-977-3827, E-mail: behrmang@slu.edu.

Saint Mary's University of Minnesota, School of Graduate and Professional Programs, Program in Health and Human Services Administration, Winona, MN 55987-1399. Offers MA. *Unit head:* Susan McGovern, Director, 612-728-5109, Fax: 612-728-5121, E-mail: smcgover@smumn.edu.

St. Thomas University, School of Graduate Studies, Department of Management, Miami Gardens, FL 33054-6459. Offers accounting (MBA); general management (MSM, Certificate); health management (MBA, MSM, Certificate); human resource management (MBA, MSM, Certificate); international business (MBA, MIB, MSM, Certificate); justice administration (MSM, Certificate); management accounting (MSM, Certificate); public management (MSM, Certificate). Part-time and evening/weekend programs available. *Degree requirements:* For master's, comprehensive exam. *Entrance requirements:* For master's, interview, minimum GPA of 3.0 or GMAT. Additional exam requirements/recommendations for international students: Required—TOEFL. Electronic applications accepted.

Saint Xavier University, Graduate Studies, Graham School of Management, Chicago, IL 60655-3105. Offers e-commerce (MBA); employee health benefits (Certificate); finance (MBA, MS); financial analysis and investments (MBA); financial planning (MBA, Certificate); financial trading and practice (MBA, Certificate); generalist/administration (MBA); health administration (MBA, MS); managed care (Certificate); management (MBA, MS); marketing (MBA); public and non-profit management (MBA); public health (MPH); service management (MBA); training and performance management (MBA); MBA/MS. *Accreditation:* ACBSP. Part-time and evening/weekend programs available. *Faculty:* 27. *Students:* 67 full-time (32 women), 291 part-time (152 women). Average age 35. In 2006, 61 degrees awarded. *Entrance requirements:* For master's, GMAT, minimum GPA of 3.0, 2 years of work experience. *Application deadline:* For fall admission, 8/15 for domestic students. Applications are processed on a rolling basis. Application fee: $35. Electronic applications accepted. *Expenses:* Contact institution. *Financial support:* Career-related internships or fieldwork available. Support available to part-time students. Financial award applicants required to submit FAFSA. *Unit head:* Dr. John Eber, Dean, 773-298-3601, Fax: 773-298-3601, E-mail: eber@sxu.edu. *Application contact:* Beth Gierach, Managing Director of Admission, 773-298-3053, Fax: 773-298-3076, E-mail: gierach@sxu.edu.

Salve Regina University, Graduate Studies, Program in Health Services Administration, Newport, RI 02840-4192. Offers MS, Certificate. Part-time and evening/weekend programs available. Postbaccalaureate distance learning degree programs offered. *Faculty:* 1 (woman) full-time, 4 part-time/adjunct (1 woman). *Students:* 5 full-time (1 woman), 53 part-time (45 women). Average age 41. 23 applicants, 87% accepted, 18 enrolled. In 2006, 12 master's, 1 other advanced degree awarded. *Degree requirements:* For master's, internship. *Entrance requirements:* For master's, GMAT, GRE General Test, or MAT, health care work experience or 400 internship hours. Additional exam requirements/recommendations for international students: Required—TOEFL or IELTS. *Application deadline:* For fall admission, 3/15 priority date for domestic and international students; for spring admission, 9/15 priority date for domestic and international students. Applications are processed on a rolling basis. Application fee: $50. Electronic applications accepted. *Financial support:* Career-related internships or fieldwork and Federal Work-Study available. Support available to part-time students. Financial award application deadline: 3/1. *Unit head:* Dr. Joan Chapdelaine, Director, 401-341-3190, Fax: 401-341-2993, E-mail: chapdelj@salve.edu. *Application contact:* Karen E. Johnson, Graduate Admissions Counselor, 401-341-2153, Fax: 401-341-2973, E-mail: johnsonke@salve.edu.

San Diego State University, Graduate and Research Affairs, College of Health and Human Services, Graduate School of Public Health, San Diego, CA 92182. Offers environmental health (MPH); epidemiology (MPH, PhD), including biostatistics (MPH); global emergency preparedness and response (MS); health behavior (PhD); health promotion (MPH); health services administration (MPH); toxicology (MS); MSW/MPH. *Accreditation:* ABET (one or more programs are accredited); CAHME (one or more programs are accredited); CEPH (one or more programs are accredited). Part-time programs available. *Degree requirements:* For master's, thesis (for some programs), comprehensive exam (for some programs); for doctorate, thesis/dissertation. *Entrance requirements:* For master's, GMAT (health services administration MPH), GRE General Test; for doctorate, GRE General Test. Additional exam requirements/recommendations for international students: Required—TOEFL. *Faculty research:* Evaluation of tobacco, AIDS prevalence and prevention, mammography, infant death project, Alzheimer's in elderly Chinese.

Seton Hall University, College of Arts and Sciences, Department of Public and Healthcare Administration, South Orange, NJ 07079-2697. Offers arts administration (MPA); health policy and management (MPA); healthcare administration (MHA); nonprofit organization management (MPA); public service: leadership, governance, and policy (MPA). *Accreditation:* NASPAA. Part-time and evening/weekend programs available. Postbaccalaureate distance learning degree programs offered (minimal on-campus study). *Degree requirements:* For master's, research project. Electronic applications accepted.

See Close-Up on page 1815.

Seton Hall University, College of Nursing, Department of Graduate Nursing, Health Systems Administration Program, South Orange, NJ 07079-2697. Offers MSN. *Accreditation:* AACSB. Part-time programs available. *Degree requirements:* For master's, research project. *Entrance requirements:* For master's, GRE General Test or MAT, BSN.

Seton Hall University, Stillman School of Business, Programs in Business Administration, South Orange, NJ 07079-2697. Offers accounting (MBA); finance (MBA); financial markets, institutions and instruments (MBA); healthcare management (MBA); information systems (MBA); international business (MBA); management (MBA); marketing (MBA); pharmaceutical management (MBA); sport management (MBA). Part-time and evening/weekend programs available. *Faculty:* 57 full-time (13 women), 30 part-time/adjunct (3 women). *Students:* 57 full-time (16 women), 180 part-time (57 women); includes 9 African Americans, 10 Asian Americans or Pacific Islanders, 7 Hispanic Americans. Average age 29. 195 applicants, 47% accepted, 48 enrolled. In 2006, 144 degrees awarded. *Median time to degree:* Master's–1.6 years full-time, 2.3 years part-time. *Degree requirements:* For master's, 20 hours of community service (Social Responsibility Project). *Entrance requirements:* For master's, GMAT, minimum GPA of 2.75. Additional exam requirements/recommendations for international students: Required—TOEFL (minimum score 550 paper-based; 213 computer-based). *Application deadline:* For fall admission, 6/1 priority date for domestic students; for spring admission, 11/1 priority date for domestic students. Applications are processed on a rolling basis. Application fee: $75 ($100 for international students). Electronic applications accepted. *Financial support:* In 2006–07, 40 students received support, including research assistantships with full and partial tuition reimbursements available (averaging $5,400 per year); career-related internships or fieldwork, Federal Work-Study, scholarships/grants, and unspecified assistantships also available. Support available to part-time students. Financial award application deadline: 6/1; financial award applicants required to submit FAFSA. *Faculty research:* Financial, hedge funds, international business, legal issues, disclosure and branding. *Unit head:* Dr. Joyce A. Strawser, Associate Dean for Undergraduate and MBA Curricula, 973-761-9225, Fax: 973-761-9217, E-mail: strawsjo@shu.edu. *Application contact:* Catherine Bianchi, Director of Graduate Admissions, 973-761-9220, Fax: 973-761-9208, E-mail: biancha@shu.edu.

Shenandoah University, Byrd School of Business, Winchester, VA 22601-5195. Offers business administration (MBA); health care management (Certificate); information systems and computer technology (Certificate). *Accreditation:* AACSB. Part-time and evening/weekend programs available. *Faculty:* 11 full-time (2 women), 1 part-time/adjunct (0 women). *Students:* 23 full-time (9 women), 10 part-time (3 women); includes 1 minority (Asian American or Pacific Islander), 7 international. Average age 29. 27 applicants, 59% accepted, 12 enrolled. In 2006, 23 degrees awarded. *Entrance requirements:* For master's, GMAT or GRE, 2 letters of recommendation, resumé. Additional exam requirements/recommendations for international students: Required—TOEFL (minimum score 527 paper-based; 197 computer-based; 71 iBT). *Application deadline:* Applications are processed on a rolling basis. Application fee: $30. Electronic applications accepted. *Expenses:* Tuition: Full-time $12,200; part-time $610 per credit. Required fees: $150. Full-time tuition and fees vary according to course load and program. *Financial support:* In 2006–07, 28 students received support, including 4 fellowships with partial tuition reimbursements available (averaging $1,518 per year), 8 teaching assistantships with partial tuition reimbursements available (averaging $4,278 per year); career-related internships or fieldwork, institutionally sponsored loans, and unspecified assistantships also available. Support available to part-time students. Financial award application deadline: 3/15; financial award applicants required to submit FAFSA. *Faculty research:* Business and economics, marketing. *Unit head:* Dr. Randy Boxx, Dean, 540-665-4572, Fax: 540-665-5437, E-mail: rboxx@su.edu. *Application contact:* David Anthony, Dean of Admissions, 540-665-4581, Fax: 540-665-4627, E-mail: admit@su.edu.

See Close-Up on page 321.

Simmons College, School for Health Studies, Program in Health Care Administration, Boston, MA 02115. Offers MHA, CAGS. *Accreditation:* CAHME (one or more programs are accredited). Part-time and evening/weekend programs available. *Faculty:* 13. *Students:* 5 full-time (all women), 37 part-time (31 women); includes 5 minority (1 African American, 1 American Indian/Alaska Native, 2 Asian Americans or Pacific Islanders, 1 Hispanic American), 1 international. Average age 32. 20 applicants, 80% accepted. In 2006, 10 degrees awarded. *Degree requirements:* For master's, thesis, fieldwork. *Entrance requirements:* For master's, GMAT or GRE. Additional exam requirements/recommendations for international students: Required—TOEFL (minimum score 550 paper-based; 230 computer-based). *Application deadline:* For fall admission, 6/1 for domestic and international students; for spring admission,

Health Services Management and Hospital Administration

Simmons College (continued)
12/1 for domestic students. Applications are processed on a rolling basis. Application fee: $50. Electronic applications accepted. *Expenses:* Contact institution. *Financial support:* Fellowships, research assistantships with tuition reimbursements, teaching assistantships with tuition reimbursements, career-related internships or fieldwork, institutionally sponsored loans, traineeships, and unspecified assistantships available. Support available to part-time students. Financial award application deadline: 3/1; financial award applicants required to submit FAFSA. *Faculty research:* International science/technology policies, middle managers in health care organizations, biotechnology and pharmaceuticals, labor relations in health care, women CEO's in health care organizations. Total annual research expenditures: $130,000. *Unit head:* Dr. John M. Lowe, Director, 617-521-2375, Fax: 617-521-3046, E-mail: john.lowe@simmons.edu. *Application contact:* Vilma Torres, Administrative Assistant, 617-521-2654, Fax: 617-521-3137, E-mail: shs@simmons.edu.

Southeastern University, College of Graduate Studies, Program in Health Services Administration, Washington, DC 20024-2788. Offers MPA. Part-time and evening/weekend programs available. *Entrance requirements:* Additional exam requirements/recommendations for international students: Required—TOEFL.

Southeast Missouri State University, School of Graduate Studies, Harrison College of Business, Cape Girardeau, MO 63701-4799. Offers accounting (MBA); environmental management (MBA); finance (MBA); general management (MBA); health administration (MBA); industrial management (MBA); international business (MBA). *Accreditation:* AACSB. Part-time and evening/weekend programs available. Postbaccalaureate distance learning degree programs offered (no on-campus study). *Faculty:* 33 full-time (10 women). *Students:* 35 full-time (18 women), 40 part-time (24 women); includes 5 minority (2 African Americans, 3 Asian Americans or Pacific Islanders), 9 international. Average age 27. 35 applicants, 86% accepted. In 2006, 23 degrees awarded. *Degree requirements:* For master's, applied research project. *Entrance requirements:* For master's, GMAT, minimum undergraduate GPA of 2.5. Additional exam requirements/recommendations for international students: Required—TOEFL (minimum score 550 paper-based; 213 computer-based). *Application deadline:* For fall admission, 8/1 for domestic students, 4/1 for international students; for spring admission, 11/21 for domestic students, 10/1 for international students. Applications are processed on a rolling basis. Application fee: $20 ($100 for international students). *Financial support:* In 2006–07, 54 students received support, including 31 research assistantships with full tuition reimbursements available (averaging $7,100 per year); career-related internships or fieldwork and unspecified assistantships also available. Financial award applicants required to submit FAFSA. *Unit head:* Dr. Kenneth Heischmidt, Director MBA Program, 573-651-2912, Fax: 573-651-5032, E-mail: kheischmidt@semo.edu. *Application contact:* Marsha L. Arant, Senior Administrative Assistant, Office of Graduate Studies, 573-651-2192, Fax: 573-651-2001, E-mail: marant@semo.edu.

Southern Adventist University, School of Business and Management, Collegedale, TN 37315-0370. Offers accounting (MBA); administration (MS); financial services (MFS); health care administration (MBA); human resource management (MBA); management (MBA); marketing (MBA). Part-time and evening/weekend programs available. Postbaccalaureate distance learning degree programs offered (no on-campus study). *Faculty:* 7 full-time (0 women), 2 part-time/adjunct (1 woman). *Students:* 18 full-time (8 women), 66 part-time (37 women); includes 15 minority (6 African Americans, 7 Asian Americans or Pacific Islanders, 2 Hispanic Americans). Average age 35. 32 applicants, 84% accepted, 24 enrolled. In 2006, 11 degrees awarded. *Entrance requirements:* For master's, GMAT. Additional exam requirements/recommendations for international students: Required—TOEFL. *Application deadline:* For fall admission, 8/1 priority date for domestic students, 7/1 for international students; for winter admission, 12/1 priority date for domestic students, 11/1 for international students; for spring admission, 4/1 priority date for domestic students, 3/1 for international students. Applications are processed on a rolling basis. Application fee: $25. Electronic applications accepted. *Financial support:* In 2006–07, 32 students received support. Scholarships/grants available. Financial award application deadline: 9/1; financial award applicants required to submit FAFSA. *Unit head:* Dr. Don Van Ornam, Dean, 423-236-2750, Fax: 423-236-1527, E-mail: dvanorna@southern.edu. *Application contact:* Linda Wilhelm, Admissions Coordinator, 423-236-2751, Fax: 423-236-1527, E-mail: sbm@southern.edu.

Southwest Baptist University, Graduate Studies, Program in Business, Bolivar, MO 65613-2597. Offers business administration (MBA); health administration (MBA). *Accreditation:* ACBSP. Part-time and evening/weekend programs available. *Degree requirements:* For master's, comprehensive exam. *Entrance requirements:* For master's, interviews, minimum GPA of 2.75. Additional exam requirements/recommendations for international students: Required—TOEFL (minimum score 550 paper-based; 213 computer-based).

Springfield College, Graduate Programs, Program in Health Care Management, Springfield, MA 01109-3797. Offers MS. Part-time and evening/weekend programs available. *Faculty:* 7 full-time (4 women), 2 part-time/adjunct (both women). *Students:* 4. Average age 32. 4 applicants, 100% accepted, 4 enrolled. *Degree requirements:* For master's, comprehensive exam. *Entrance requirements:* Additional exam requirements/recommendations for international students: Required—TOEFL (minimum score 550 paper-based; 213 computer-based). *Application deadline:* For fall admission, 1/15 for domestic students; for winter admission, 11/1 for domestic students; for spring admission, 12/1 for domestic students. Applications are processed on a rolling basis. Application fee: $50. Electronic applications accepted. *Expenses:* Tuition: Full-time $12,222; part-time $679 per credit. Required fees: $25; $25 per year. One-time fee: $25 full-time. *Financial support:* Fellowships with partial tuition reimbursements, career-related internships or fieldwork, Federal Work-Study, and institutionally sponsored loans available. Financial award application deadline: 3/1; financial award applicants required to submit FAFSA. *Unit head:* Dr. John Doyle, Director, 413-748-3199, Fax: 413-748-3452. *Application contact:* Donald James Shaw, Director of Graduate Admissions, 413-748-3060, Fax: 413-748-3069, E-mail: donald_shaw_jr@spfldcol.edu.

State University of New York at Binghamton, Graduate School, School of Management, Program in Business Administration, Binghamton, NY 13902-6000. Offers business administration (MBA, PhD); health care professional executive (MBA). *Accreditation:* AACSB. *Students:* 234 full-time (89 women), 30 part-time (11 women); includes 14 minority (3 African Americans, 11 Asian Americans or Pacific Islanders), 123 international. Average age 29. 449 applicants, 51% accepted. In 2006, 101 master's, 2 doctorates awarded. *Degree requirements:* For doctorate, thesis/dissertation. *Entrance requirements:* For master's and doctorate, GMAT. Additional exam requirements/recommendations for international students: Required—TOEFL. *Application deadline:* For fall admission, 4/15 priority date for domestic students, 1/15 priority date for international students; for spring admission, 11/1 for domestic students, 10/1 priority date for international students. Applications are processed on a rolling basis. Application fee: $60. Electronic applications accepted. *Financial support:* In 2006–07, 39 students received support, including 1 fellowship with full tuition reimbursement available (averaging $8,700 per year), 34 teaching assistantships with full tuition reimbursements available (averaging $7,302 per year); research assistantships, career-related internships or fieldwork, Federal Work-Study, institutionally sponsored loans, tuition waivers (full and partial), and unspecified assistantships also available. Support available to part-time students. Financial award application deadline: 2/15. *Unit head:* George Bobinski, Associate Dean, 607-777-2315, E-mail: gbobins@binghamton.edu.

State University of New York Institute of Technology, School of Business, Program in Health Services Administration, Utica, NY 13504-3050. Offers MS. Part-time and evening/weekend programs available. Postbaccalaureate distance learning degree programs offered (no on-campus study). *Faculty:* 4 full-time (2 women), 1 part-time/adjunct (0 women). *Students:* 13 full-time (7 women), 27 part-time (18 women); includes 5 African Americans, 2 Asian Americans or Pacific Islanders, 1 Hispanic American, 2 international. *Degree requirements:* For master's, capstone or project. *Entrance requirements:* For master's, GMAT or GRE, minimum GPA of 3.0. Additional exam requirements/recommendations for international students: Required—TOEFL (minimum score 550 paper-based; 213 computer-based). *Application deadline:* For fall admission, 6/15 priority date for domestic students. Applications are processed on a rolling basis. Application fee: $50. *Expenses:* Tuition, state resident: full-time $3,452; part-time $288 per credit hour. Tuition, nonresident: full-time $10,920; part-time $455 per credit hour. Required fees: $927; $38 per credit hour. *Financial support:* In 2006–07, 1 research assistantship (averaging $7,500 per year) was awarded; career-related internships or fieldwork, Federal Work-Study, scholarships/grants, health care benefits, and unspecified assistantships also available. Financial award application deadline: 6/1; financial award applicants required to submit FAFSA. *Faculty research:* Institutional utilization, health policy, health finance. Total annual research expenditures: $1,000. *Unit head:* Gary Scherzer, Program Director, 315-792-7393, Fax: 315-793-7138, E-mail: fgds@sunyit.edu. *Application contact:* Marybeth Lyons, Director of Admissions, 315-792-7500, Fax: 315-792-7837, E-mail: smbl@sunyit.edu.

Stephens College, Division of Graduate and Continuing Studies, Program in Health Information Administration, Columbia, MO 65215-0002. Offers Postbaccalaureate Certificate. Part-time programs available. Postbaccalaureate distance learning degree programs offered (minimal on-campus study). *Students:* Average age 41. *Entrance requirements:* Additional exam requirements/recommendations for international students: Required—TOEFL (minimum score 213 computer-based). *Application deadline:* Applications are processed on a rolling basis. Application fee: $25. Electronic applications accepted. *Unit head:* Darla Branda, Director, Health Information Administration, 800-388-7579, E-mail: bclimer@stephens.edu. *Application contact:* Mellodie Wilson, Associate Director, 800-388-7579, E-mail: online@stephens.edu.

Stony Brook University, State University of New York, Stony Brook University Medical Center, Health Sciences Center, School of Health Technology and Management, Stony Brook, NY 11794. Offers community health (Advanced Certificate); health care management (Advanced Certificate); health care policy and management (MS); occupational therapy (MS); physical therapy (MS, DPT). *Accreditation:* APTA. Part-time programs available. *Faculty:* 26 full-time (15 women), 21 part-time/adjunct (12 women). *Students:* 198 full-time (147 women), 130 part-time (89 women); includes 87 minority (29 African Americans, 1 American Indian/Alaska Native, 37 Asian Americans or Pacific Islanders, 20 Hispanic Americans), 4 international. 907 applicants, 25% accepted. In 2006, 33 master's, 106 doctorates, 15 other advanced degrees awarded. *Degree requirements:* For master's, thesis. *Entrance requirements:* For master's, GRE General Test, minimum GPA of 3.0, work experience in field. *Application deadline:* For fall admission, 1/15 for domestic students. Application fee: $60. *Expenses:* Tuition, state resident: full-time $6,900; part-time $288 per credit. Tuition, nonresident: full-time $10,920; part-time $455 per credit. *Financial support:* In 2006–07, 1 fellowship was awarded; career-related internships or fieldwork, Federal Work-Study, and institutionally sponsored loans also available. Financial award application deadline: 3/15. *Faculty research:* Health promotion and disease prevention. Total annual research expenditures: $527,101. *Unit head:* Dr. Craig A. Lehmann, Dean, 631-444-2251, Fax: 631-444-7621. *Application contact:* Alan Leiken, Associate Dean for Graduate Studies, 631-444-3240, Fax: 631-444-7621.

Suffolk University, Sawyer Business School, Department of Public Administration, Boston, MA 02108-2770. Offers disability studies (MPA); health administration (MPA); nonprofit management (MPA); public administration (CASPA); public finance and human resources (MPA); state and local government (MPA); JD/MPA; MPA/MS. *Accreditation:* NASPAA (one or more programs are accredited). Part-time and evening/weekend programs available. *Faculty:* 11 full-time (4 women), 7 part-time/adjunct (4 women). *Students:* 40 full-time (25 women), 123 part-time (80 women); includes 22 minority (12 African Americans, 4 Asian Americans or Pacific Islanders, 6 Hispanic Americans), 9 international. Average age 31. 103 applicants, 87% accepted, 48 enrolled. In 2006, 65 degrees awarded. *Entrance requirements:* Additional exam requirements/recommendations for international students: Required—TOEFL (minimum score 550 paper-based; 213 computer-based; 80 iBT). *Application deadline:* For fall admission, 6/15 priority date for domestic students, 6/15 for international students; for spring admission, 11/1 priority date for domestic students, 11/1 for international students. Applications are processed on a rolling basis. Application fee: $50. Electronic applications accepted. *Expenses:* Contact institution. *Financial support:* In 2006–07, 55 fellowships with full and partial tuition reimbursements (averaging $8,817 per year) were awarded; career-related internships or fieldwork and Federal Work-Study also available. Support available to part-time students. Financial award application deadline: 4/1; financial award applicants required to submit FAFSA. *Faculty research:* Local government, health care, federal policy, mental health, HIV/AIDS. Total annual research expenditures: $200,000. *Unit head:* Dr. Rick Beinecke, Chair, 617-573-8062, E-mail: rbeineck@suffolk.edu. *Application contact:* Judith Reynolds, Director of Graduate Admissions, 617-573-8302, Fax: 617-523-0116, E-mail: grad.admission@suffolk.edu.

Suffolk University, Sawyer Business School, Program in Health Administration, Boston, MA 02108-2770. Offers MBAH, MHA. Part-time and evening/weekend programs available. *Faculty:* 5 full-time (2 women), 3 part-time/adjunct (2 women). *Students:* 3 full-time (2 women), 27 part-time (20 women); includes 1 African American, 2 Asian Americans or Pacific Islanders, 1 Hispanic American, 2 international. Average age 32. 23 applicants, 83% accepted, 15 enrolled. In 2006, 22 degrees awarded. *Entrance requirements:* Additional exam requirements/recommendations for international students: Required—TOEFL (minimum score 550 paper-based; 213 computer-based; 80 iBT). *Application deadline:* For fall admission, 6/15 priority date for domestic students, 6/15 for international students; for spring admission, 11/1 priority date for domestic students, 11/1 for international students. Applications are processed on a rolling basis. Application fee: $50. Electronic applications accepted. *Expenses:* Contact institution. *Financial support:* In 2006–07, 12 students received support, including 12 fellowships with full and partial tuition reimbursements available (averaging $9,675 per year); career-related internships or fieldwork, Federal Work-Study, and institutionally sponsored loans also available. Support available to part-time students. Financial award application deadline: 4/1; financial award applicants required to submit FAFSA. *Faculty research:* Mental health, federal policy, health care. *Unit head:* Dr. Rick Beinecke, Chair, 617-573-8062, E-mail: rbeineck@suffolk.edu. *Application contact:* Judith Reynolds, Director of Graduate Admissions, 617-573-8302, Fax: 617-523-0116, E-mail: grad.admission@suffolk.edu.

Syracuse University, Graduate School, Maxwell School of Citizenship and Public Affairs, Program in Health Services Management and Policy, Syracuse, NY 13244. Offers CAS. Part-time and evening/weekend programs available. *Students:* 9 applicants, 100% accepted, 6 enrolled. *Entrance requirements:* Additional exam requirements/recommendations for international students: Required—TOEFL. Application fee: $65. Electronic applications accepted. *Expenses:* Tuition: Full-time $16,920; part-time $940 per credit hour. Required fees: $930; $930 per year. *Unit head:* Dr. Thomas Dennison, 315-443-9215, Fax: 315-443-9721, E-mail: thdennis@syr.edu.

Temple University, Graduate School, Fox School of Business and Management, Doctoral Programs in Business, Philadelphia, PA 19122-6096. Offers accounting (PhD); economics (PhD); finance (PhD); general and strategic management (PhD); healthcare management (PhD); human resource administration (PhD); international business administration (PhD); management information systems (PhD); management science/operations research (PhD); marketing (PhD); risk, insurance, and health-care management (PhD); statistics (PhD); tourism (PhD). *Accreditation:* AACSB. *Entrance requirements:* For doctorate, GRE General Test, minimum GPA of 3.0, master's degree. Additional exam requirements/recommendations for international students: Required—TOEFL. *Expenses:* Tuition, state resident: full-time $12,264; part-time $511 per credit. Tuition, nonresident: full-time $17,904; part-time $746 per credit. Required fees: $84 per course. Tuition and fees vary according to program.

Temple University, Graduate School, Fox School of Business and Management, Masters Programs in Business, MBA Programs, Philadelphia, PA 19122-6096. Offers accounting (MBA); business administration (EMBA, MBA); e-business (MBA); economics (MBA); finance (MBA); general and strategic management (MBA); healthcare management (MBA); human resource administration (MBA); international business (IMBA); management information systems (MBA); management science/operations management (MBA); marketing (MBA); risk management and insurance (MBA); statistics (MBA). EMBA offered in Philadelphia, PA and Tokyo, Japan. *Accreditation:* AACSB. *Entrance requirements:* For master's, GMAT, minimum undergraduate GPA of 3.0. Additional exam requirements/recommendations for international students: Required—TOEFL. *Expenses:* Tuition, state resident: full-time $12,264; part-time $511 per credit. Tuition, nonresident: full-time $17,904; part-time $746 per credit. Required fees: $84 per course. Tuition and fees vary according to program.

Temple University, Graduate School, Fox School of Business and Management, Masters Programs in Business, MS Programs, Philadelphia, PA 19122-6096. Offers accounting and financial management (MS); actuarial science (MS); e-business (MS); finance (MS); healthcare financial management (MS); human resource administration (MS); management information systems (MS); management science/operations management (MS); marketing (MS); statistics (MS). *Accreditation:* AACSB. *Entrance requirements:* For master's, GRE General Test, minimum undergraduate GPA of 3.0. Additional exam requirements/recommendations for international students: Required—TOEFL. *Expenses:* Tuition, state resident: full-time $12,264; part-time $511 per credit. Tuition, nonresident: full-time $17,904; part-time $746 per credit. Required fees: $84 per course. Tuition and fees vary according to program.

Texas A&M Health Science Center, School of Rural Public Health, College Station, TX 77843-1266. Offers environmental/occupational health (MPH); epidemiology/biostatistics (MPH); health policy/management (MPH); social and behavioral health (MPH). *Accreditation:* CEPH. Part-time programs available. Postbaccalaureate distance learning degree programs offered (no on-campus study). *Faculty:* 16 full-time (7 women), 4 part-time/adjunct (1 woman). *Students:* 43 full-time (27 women), 118 part-time (76 women); includes 63 minority (13 African Americans, 13 Asian Americans or Pacific Islanders, 37 Hispanic Americans), 1 international. Average age 32. 162 applicants, 83% accepted, 118 enrolled. In 2006, 10 degrees awarded. *Degree requirements:* For master's, thesis optional. *Entrance requirements:* For master's, GRE General Test, minimum undergraduate GPA of 3.0. *Application deadline:* For fall admission, 8/27 for domestic students; for spring admission, 1/14 for domestic students. Applications are processed on a rolling basis. Application fee: $35 ($75 for international students). Electronic applications accepted. *Financial support:* In 2006–07, research assistantships (averaging $10,800 per year). *Faculty research:* Tobacco cessation, youth health risk. Total annual research expenditures: $1.7 million. *Unit head:* Dr. Ciro V. Sumaya, Dean. *Application contact:* Dr. James Robinson, Professor/Special Advisor to the Dean, 409-845-2387, Fax: 409-862-8371, E-mail: jrobinson@medicine.tamu.edu.

Texas A&M University–Corpus Christi, Graduate Studies and Research, College of Business, Corpus Christi, TX 78412-5503. Offers accounting (M Acc); health care administration (MBA); international business (MBA). *Accreditation:* AACSB. Part-time and evening/weekend programs available. *Degree requirements:* For master's, thesis (for some programs), comprehensive exam, registration. *Entrance requirements:* For master's, GMAT. Additional exam requirements/recommendations for international students: Required—TOEFL. Electronic applications accepted.

Texas A&M University–Corpus Christi, Graduate Studies and Research, College of Nursing and Health Sciences, Corpus Christi, TX 78412-5503. Offers clinical nurse specialist (MSN); family nurse practitioner (MSN); health care administration (MSN); leadership in nursing systems (MSN). *Accreditation:* AACN. Part-time and evening/weekend programs available. *Degree requirements:* For master's, thesis (for some programs), comprehensive exam, registration. *Entrance requirements:* For master's, GRE General Test. Additional exam requirements/recommendations for international students: Required—TOEFL. Electronic applications accepted.

Texas State University-San Marcos, Graduate School, College of Health Professions, Department of Health Administration, San Marcos, TX 78666. Offers healthcare administration (MHA). *Accreditation:* CAHME. Part-time and evening/weekend programs available. *Faculty:* 6 full-time (2 women). *Students:* 35 full-time (19 women), 21 part-time (16 women); includes 10 minority (1 African American, 4 Asian Americans or Pacific Islanders, 5 Hispanic Americans), 2 international. Average age 30. 24 applicants, 88% accepted, 14 enrolled. In 2006, 28 degrees awarded. *Degree requirements:* For master's, committee review, thesis optional. *Entrance requirements:* For master's, GRE General Test, minimum GPA of 2.75 in last 60 hours of course work. Additional exam requirements/recommendations for international students: Required—TOEFL. *Application deadline:* For fall admission, 6/15 priority date for domestic students, 6/1 for international students; for spring admission, 10/15 priority date for domestic students, 10/1 for international students. Applications are processed on a rolling basis. Application fee: $40 ($90 for international students). *Financial support:* In 2006–07, 41 students received support, including 1 research assistantship (averaging $6,570 per year), 5 teaching assistantships (averaging $7,210 per year); career-related internships or fieldwork, Federal Work-Study, institutionally sponsored loans, and stipends also available. Support available to part-time students. Financial award application deadline: 4/1; financial award applicants required to submit FAFSA. *Faculty research:* Managerial ethics, health care financial management, health services delivery in rural areas, health services delivery in medically underserved areas, telemedicine. *Unit head:* Dr. Oren Renick, Chair, 512-245-3556, Fax: 512-245-8712, E-mail: cr13@txstate.edu. *Application contact:* Dr. J. Michael Willoughby, Dean of Graduate School, 512-245-2581, Fax: 512-245-8365, E-mail: gradcollege@txstate.edu.

Texas State University-San Marcos, Graduate School, College of Health Professions, Department of Health Services and Research, Program in Healthcare Human Resources, San Marcos, TX 78666. Offers MS. *Accreditation:* CAHME. Part-time and evening/weekend programs available. *Faculty:* 1 full-time (0 women), 1 part-time/adjunct (0 women). *Students:* 5 full-time (4 women), 8 part-time (all women); includes 2 African Americans, 1 Asian American or Pacific Islander, 2 Hispanic Americans, 1 international. Average age 34. 4 applicants, 75% accepted, 3 enrolled. In 2006, 8 degrees awarded. *Degree requirements:* For master's, committee review. *Entrance requirements:* For master's, GRE General Test, minimum GPA of 2.75 in last 60 hours of course work. Additional exam requirements/recommendations for international students: Required—TOEFL. *Application deadline:* For fall admission, 6/15 priority date for domestic students, 6/1 for international students; for spring admission, 10/15 priority date for domestic students, 10/1 for international students. Applications are processed on a rolling basis. Application fee: $40 ($90 for international students). *Financial support:* In 2006–07, 10 students received support; research assistantships, teaching assistantships, career-related internships or fieldwork, Federal Work-Study, and institutionally sponsored loans available. Support available to part-time students. Financial award application deadline: 4/1; financial award applicants required to submit FAFSA. *Faculty research:* Human resource development, health institutions. *Unit head:* Dr. Oren Renick, Chair, 512-245-3556, Fax: 512-245-8712, E-mail: cr13@txstate.edu.

Texas Tech University, Jerry S. Rawls College of Business Administration, Area of Information Systems and Quantitative Sciences, Lubbock, TX 79409. Offers business statistics (MS, PhD); health organization management (MS); management information systems (MS, PhD); production and operations management (MS, PhD). Part-time programs available. *Faculty:* 15 full-time (0 women). *Students:* 18 full-time (6 women), 6 part-time (1 woman); includes 2 minority (1 African American, 1 Hispanic American), 11 international. Average age 31. 32 applicants, 53% accepted, 11 enrolled. In 2006, 13 master's, 5 doctorates awarded. Terminal master's awarded for partial completion of doctoral program. *Degree requirements:* For master's, comprehensive exam or capstone course; for doctorate, thesis/dissertation, qualifying exams. *Entrance requirements:* For master's and doctorate, GMAT, holistic profile of academic credentials. Additional exam requirements/recommendations for international students: Required—TOEFL (minimum score 550 paper-based; 213 computer-based; 79 iBT). *Application deadline:* For fall admission, 7/1 priority date for domestic students, 3/1 priority date for international students; for spring admission, 11/1 priority date for domestic students, 9/1 priority date for international students. Applications are processed on a rolling basis. Application fee: $50 ($60 for international students). Electronic applications accepted. *Expenses:* Tuition, state resident: full-time $4,440. Tuition, nonresident: full-time $11,040. Required fees: $2,136. *Financial support:* In 2006–07, 2 research assistantships (averaging $8,000 per year), 9 teaching assistantships (averaging $16,930 per year) were awarded; Federal Work-Study, scholarships/grants, and unspecified assistantships also available. *Faculty research:* Database management systems, systems management and engineering, expert systems and adaptive knowledge-based sciences, statistical analysis and design. *Unit head:* Dr. James Hoffman, Area Coordinator, 806-742-3192, Fax: 806-742-3958, E-mail: james.hoffman@ttu.edu. *Application contact:* Cynthia D. Barnes, Director, Graduate Services Center, 806-742-3184, Fax: 806-742-3958, E-mail: ba_grad@ttu.edu.

Texas Tech University, Jerry S. Rawls College of Business Administration, Programs in Business Administration, Lubbock, TX 79409. Offers agricultural business (MBA); entrepreneurship (MBA); finance (MBA); general business (MBA); health organization management (MBA); international business (MBA); management and leadership skills (MBA); management information systems (MBA); marketing (MBA); statistics (MBA); JD/MBA; MBA/M Arch; MBA/MA; MBA/MD; MBA/MS. Part-time and evening/weekend programs available. *Students:* 65 full-time (16 women), 347 part-time (121 women); includes 74 minority (5 African Americans, 5 American Indian/Alaska Native, 24 Asian Americans or Pacific Islanders, 40 Hispanic Americans), 24 international. Average age 25. 382 applicants, 82% accepted, 244 enrolled. In 2006, 150 degrees awarded. *Degree requirements:* For master's, capstone course. *Entrance requirements:* For master's, GMAT, holistic review of academic credentials. Additional exam requirements/recommendations for international students: Required—TOEFL (minimum score 550 paper-based; 213 computer-based; 79 iBT). *Application deadline:* For fall admission, 7/1 priority date for domestic students, 3/1 priority date for international students; for spring admission, 11/1 priority date for domestic students, 9/1 priority date for international students. Applications are processed on a rolling basis. Application fee: $50 ($60 for international students). Electronic applications accepted. *Expenses:* Tuition, state resident: full-time $4,440. Tuition, nonresident: full-time $11,040. Required fees: $2,136. *Financial support:* In 2006–07, 36 research assistantships (averaging $8,000 per year) were awarded; teaching assistantships, career-related internships or fieldwork, Federal Work-Study, scholarships/grants, health care benefits, and unspecified assistantships also available. Support available to part-time students. Financial award applicants required to submit FAFSA. *Unit head:* Dr. W. Jay Conover, Director, 806-742-1546, Fax: 806-742-3958, E-mail: jay.conover@ttu.edu. *Application contact:* Cynthia D. Barnes, Director, Graduate Services Center, 806-742-3184, Fax: 806-742-3958, E-mail: ba_grad@ttu.edu.

Texas Tech University Health Sciences Center, School of Allied Health Sciences, Program in Clinical Practice Management, Lubbock, TX 79430. Offers MS. *Accreditation:* CORE. Part-time programs available. *Faculty:* 3 full-time (0 women). *Students:* 3 full-time (2 women), 17 part-time (15 women); includes 8 minority (3 African Americans, 1 American Indian/Alaska Native, 2 Asian Americans or Pacific Islanders, 2 Hispanic Americans). Average age 28. 15 applicants, 67% accepted, 10 enrolled. In 2006, 14 degrees awarded. *Entrance requirements:* Additional exam requirements/recommendations for international students: Required—TOEFL. *Application deadline:* For fall admission, 8/1 for domestic students; for spring admission, 12/1 for domestic students. Applications are processed on a rolling basis. Application fee: $35. Electronic applications accepted. *Financial support:* Institutionally sponsored loans available. *Unit head:* Dr. Robin Satterwhite, Chair, 806-743-2263, Fax: 806-743-3249, E-mail: robin.satterwhite@ttuhsc.edu. *Application contact:* Jeri Moravcik, Assistant Director of Admissions and Student Affairs, 806-743-3220, Fax: 806-743-2994, E-mail: jeri.moravcik@ttuhsc.edu.

Texas Wesleyan University, Graduate Programs, Programs in Business Administration, Fort Worth, TX 76105-1536. Offers business administration (MBA); geriatrics (MSHA); health administration (MSHA); public health (MSHA). *Accreditation:* ACBSP. Part-time and evening/weekend programs available. *Faculty:* 13 full-time (3 women), 4 part-time/adjunct (1 woman). *Students:* 15 full-time (7 women), 42 part-time (30 women); includes 27 minority (14 African Americans, 1 American Indian/Alaska Native, 4 Asian Americans or Pacific Islanders, 8 Hispanic Americans). Average age 31. In 2006, 18 degrees awarded. *Degree requirements:* For master's, capstone course. *Entrance requirements:* For master's, GMAT, minimum GPA of 3.0 in final 60 hours of undergraduate course work, 2.75 overall. *Application deadline:* Applications are processed on a rolling basis. Application fee: $30 ($50 for international students). Electronic applications accepted. *Expenses: Contact institution.* Tuition and fees vary according to program. *Financial support:* Federal Work-Study, scholarships/grants, and tuition waivers (full and partial) available. Support available to part-time students. Financial award application deadline: 3/15; financial award applicants required to submit FAFSA. *Unit head:* Dr. Charles Little, Director, 817-531-6500, Fax: 817-531-6585.

Texas Woman's University, Graduate School, College of Health Sciences, Program in Health Care Administration-Houston Center, Denton, TX 76201. Offers MHA. *Accreditation:* CAHME. Part-time and evening/weekend programs available. *Students:* 43 full-time (34 women), 75 part-time (60 women); includes 65 minority (28 African Americans, 2 American Indian/Alaska Native, 25 Asian Americans or Pacific Islanders, 10 Hispanic Americans), 8 international. Average age 33. In 2006, 22 degrees awarded. *Degree requirements:* For master's, thesis or alternative, comprehensive exam. *Entrance requirements:* For master's, GMAT or GRE, interview, resumé, 3 letters of reference. Additional exam requirements/recommendations for international students: Required—TOEFL (minimum score 550 paper-based; 213 computer-based; 79 iBT). *Application deadline:* For fall admission, 4/1 for international students; for spring admission, 8/1 for international students. Applications are processed on a rolling basis. Application fee: $30 ($50 for international students). Electronic applications accepted. *Expenses:* Tuition, area resident: Part-time $168 per unit. Tuition, state resident: full-time $4,369. Tuition, nonresident: full-time $9,373; part-time $443 per unit. Required fees: $20 per unit. $177 per term. *Financial support:* In 2006–07, 1 research assistantship (averaging $9,288 per year), teaching assistantships (averaging $9,288 per year) were awarded; career-related internships or fieldwork, Federal Work-Study, institutionally sponsored loans, scholarships/grants, traineeships, health care benefits, and unspecified assistantships also available. Support available to part-time students. Financial award application deadline: 3/1; financial award applicants required to submit FAFSA. *Faculty research:* Organizational culture, medical errors, ethical analysis in health care, leadership and professional development, strategic management. *Unit head:* Dr. Kelley Moseley, Program Director, 713-794-2061, Fax: 713-794-2350, E-mail: kmoseley@twu.edu. *Application contact:* Samuel Wheeler, Coordinator of Graduate Admissions, 940-898-3188, Fax: 940-898-3081, E-mail: wheelersr@twu.edu.

Texas Woman's University, Graduate School, College of Nursing, Denton, TX 76201. Offers adult health nurse practitioner (MS); health systems management (MS); nursing (MS); nursing education (MS); nursing science (PhD). *Accreditation:* AACN. Part-time programs available. Postbaccalaureate distance learning degree programs offered. *Students:* 41 full-time (38 women), 512 part-time (490 women); includes 211 minority (121 African Americans, 2 American Indian/Alaska Native, 64 Asian Americans or Pacific Islanders, 24 Hispanic Americans), 9 international. Average age 41. In 2006, 129 master's, 16 doctorates awarded. *Degree requirements:* For master's, thesis or alternative; for doctorate, thesis/dissertation, comprehensive exam. *Entrance requirements:* For master's, GRE or MAT, minimum GPA of 3.0, RN license, BS in nursing; for doctorate, GRE or MAT, MS in nursing, minimum GPA of 3.5, RN license, coursework in statistics, graduate research, 2 letters of reference. Additional exam requirements/recommendations for international students: Required—TOEFL (minimum score 550 paper-based; 213 computer-based; 79 iBT). *Application deadline:* For fall admission, 4/1 for international students; for spring admission, 8/1 for international students. Applications are processed on a rolling basis. Application fee: $30 ($50 for international students). Electronic applications accepted. *Expenses:* Tuition, area resident: Part-time $168 per unit. Tuition, state resident: full-time $4,369. Tuition, nonresident: full-time $9,373; part-time $443 per unit. Required fees: $20 per unit. $177 per term. *Financial support:* In 2006–07, 11 research assistantships (averaging $11,232 per year), 3 teaching assistantships (averaging $11,232 per year) were awarded; career-related internships or fieldwork, Federal Work-Study, institutionally sponsored loans, scholarships/grants, traineeships, health care benefits, and unspecified assistantships also available. Support available to part-time students. Financial award application deadline: 3/1; financial award applicants required to submit FAFSA. *Faculty research:*

Health Services Management and Hospital Administration

Texas Woman's University (continued)
Health of women across the life span, child health issues, self-care and heart failure, smoking cessation, timing of labor and delivery. *Unit head:* Dr. Marcia Hern, Dean, 940-898-2401, Fax: 940-898-2437, E-mail: mhern@twu.edu. *Application contact:* Samuel Wheeler, Coordinator of Graduate Admissions, 940-898-3188, Fax: 940-898-3081, E-mail: wheelersr@twu.edu.

Touro College, Barry Z. Levine School of Health Sciences, Health Information Management Program, New York, NY 10010. Offers Certificate. *Entrance requirements:* For degree, minimum GPA of 2.5. Expenses: Contact institution.

Touro University International, College of Health Sciences, Cypress, CA 90630. Offers MS, PhD, Certificate. Part-time and evening/weekend programs available. Postbaccalaureate distance learning degree programs offered (no on-campus study). In 2006, 322 master's, 21 doctorates awarded. *Entrance requirements:* For master's, minimum GPA of 3.0; for doctorate, minimum GPA of 3.4. Additional exam requirements/recommendations for international students: Required—TOEFL (minimum score 550 paper-based). Application fee: $75. *Expenses:* Tuition: Part-time $300 per credit hour. Tuition and fees vary according to course level and program. *Unit head:* Dr. Edith Neumann, Vice President for Academic Affairs, 714-816-0366 Ext. 2030, Fax: 714-226-9844, E-mail: eneumann@tourou.edu.

Towson University, Graduate School, Program in Clinician-Administrator Transition, Towson, MD 21252-0001. Offers Certificate. *Students:* 3 applicants, 67% accepted, 1 enrolled. In 2006, 2 degrees awarded. *Entrance requirements:* For degree, minimum GPA of 3.0; bachelor's or master's degree in a clinical field; licensure, licensure eligibility, or certificate in a clinical field. *Application deadline:* Applications are processed on a rolling basis. Application fee: $50. Electronic applications accepted. *Expenses:* Tuition, state resident: part-time $275 per unit. Tuition, nonresident: part-time $577 per unit. Required fees: $72 per unit. *Financial support:* Application deadline: 4/1. *Unit head:* Marcie Weinstein, Graduate Program Director, 410-704-4049, E-mail: mweinstein@towson.edu. *Application contact:* 410-704-2501, Fax: 410-704-4675, E-mail: grads@towson.edu.

Trinity University, Department of Health Care Administration, San Antonio, TX 78212-7200. Offers MS. *Accreditation:* CAHME. Part-time programs available. Postbaccalaureate distance learning degree programs offered (minimal on-campus study). *Faculty:* 5 full-time (1 woman), 5 part-time/adjunct (1 woman). *Students:* 50 full-time (26 women), 50 part-time (20 women); includes 23 minority (8 African Americans, 7 Asian Americans or Pacific Islanders, 8 Hispanic Americans), 2 international. Average age 28. In 2006, 27 degrees awarded. *Degree requirements:* For master's, research projects. *Entrance requirements:* For master's, GMAT, GRE General Test, previous course work in accounting, economics, and statistics. *Application deadline:* For fall admission, 6/1 priority date for domestic students. Applications are processed on a rolling basis. Application fee: $30. *Financial support:* In 2006–07, 9 research assistantships (averaging $9,500 per year) were awarded; career-related internships or fieldwork, institutionally sponsored loans, traineeships, and unspecified assistantships also available. Financial award application deadline: 4/1. *Unit head:* Dr. Mary E. Stefl, Chair, 210-999-8424, Fax: 210-999-8108, E-mail: mstefl@trinity.edu. *Application contact:* Sharon Hubenak, Director of Recruiting and Residencies, 210-999-8107, Fax: 210-999-8108, E-mail: shubenak@trinity.edu.

See Close-Up on page 1817.

Tulane University, School of Public Health and Tropical Medicine, Department of Health Systems Management, New Orleans, LA 70118-5669. Offers MHA, MMM, MPH, PhD, Sc D, JD/MHA, MD/MPH. *Accreditation:* CAHME (one or more programs are accredited). *Faculty:* 16 full-time (6 women), 5 part-time/adjunct (2 women). *Students:* 119 full-time (74 women), 51 part-time (30 women). *Degree requirements:* For doctorate, thesis/dissertation, comprehensive exam. *Entrance requirements:* For master's, GMAT, GRE General Test; for doctorate, GRE General Test. Additional exam requirements/recommendations for international students: Required—TOEFL. *Application deadline:* For fall admission, 4/15 priority date for domestic and international students; for spring admission, 10/15 priority date for domestic and international students. Applications are processed on a rolling basis. Application fee: $40. Electronic applications accepted. *Financial support:* Fellowships with tuition reimbursements, Federal Work-Study, scholarships/grants, traineeships, and tuition waivers (partial) available. Support available to part-time students. Financial award application deadline: 4/15. *Faculty research:* Health policy, organizational governance, international health administration. *Unit head:* Dr. Claudia Campbell, Chair, 504-588-5428. *Application contact:* Clarissa Koederitz, Senior Program Coordinator, 504-588-5429, E-mail: clar@tulane.edu.

Union Graduate College, Center for Bioethics and Clinical Leadership, Program in Clinical Leadership in Health Management, Schenectady, NY 12308-3107. Offers MS. Part-time and evening/weekend programs available. *Students:* 68 full-time (39 women); includes 30 minority (all Asian Americans or Pacific Islanders) Average age 20. 339 applicants, 19% accepted, 20 enrolled. In 2006, 10 degrees awarded. *Degree requirements:* For master's, capstone course. *Entrance requirements:* For master's, MCAT or GMAT, letters of recommendation. Additional exam requirements/recommendations for international students: Required—TOEFL (minimum score 550 paper-based; 213 computer-based). *Application deadline:* For spring admission, 5/1 for domestic students. Application fee: $60. *Expenses:* Contact institution. *Financial support:* Federal Work-Study, scholarships/grants, health care benefits, and tuition waivers (partial) available. Support available to part-time students. Financial award applicants required to submit FAFSA. *Application contact:* Rhonda Sheehan, Director of Graduate Admissions Registrar, 518-388-6238, Fax: 518-388-6686, E-mail: sheehanr@union.edu.

Union Graduate College, School of Management, Program in Health Systems Administration, Schenectady, NY 12308-3107. Offers MBA, Certificate. *Accreditation:* CAHME (one or more programs are accredited). Part-time and evening/weekend programs available. *Students:* 17 full-time (11 women), 22 part-time (11 women); includes 1 African American, 7 Asian Americans or Pacific Islanders, 3 international. Average age 30. 15 applicants, 80% accepted, 10 enrolled. In 2006, 13 degrees awarded. *Degree requirements:* For master's, internships, capstone course. *Entrance requirements:* For master's, GMAT, minimum GPA of 3.0. Additional exam requirements/recommendations for international students: Required—TOEFL (minimum score 550 paper-based; 213 computer-based). *Application deadline:* Applications are processed on a rolling basis. Application fee: $60. *Financial support:* Research assistantships, career-related internships or fieldwork, Federal Work-Study, scholarships/grants, health care benefits, and tuition waivers (partial) available. Support available to part-time students. Financial award applicants required to submit FAFSA. *Unit head:* Dr. Martin A. Strosberg, Co-Chair, 518-388-6299, E-mail: strasbem@union.edu. *Application contact:* Rhonda Sheehan, Director of Graduate Admissions Registrar, 518-388-6238, Fax: 518-388-6686, E-mail: sheehanr@union.edu.

Universidad de Ciencias Medicas, Graduate Programs, San Jose, Costa Rica. Offers health of administration (MHA); medical and surgery (MD); pharmacy (Pharm D). Part-time programs available. *Faculty:* 36 full-time (11 women), 250 part-time/adjunct (66 women). *Students:* 1,224 full-time (791 women); includes 1,131 Hispanic Americans. Average age 21. 403 applicants, 100% accepted, 293 enrolled. *Median time to degree:* Of those who began their doctoral program in fall 1998, 40% received their degree in 8 years or less. *Entrance requirements:* For first professional degree, admissions test; for master's, MD or bachelors degree. *Application deadline:* For winter admission, 1/6 priority date for domestic and international students; for spring admission, 7/6 priority date for domestic and international students. *Financial support:* In 2006–07, 150 students received support. Institutionally sponsored loans and scholarships/grants available. Financial award application deadline: 10/1; financial award applicants required to submit FAFSA. *Unit head:* Dr. Misael Chinchilla, President of Academic Affairs, 506-296-3944 Ext. 147, Fax: 506-231-4368, E-mail: chinchillacm@ucimed.com. *Application contact:* Lic. Karol Córdoba, Assistant of Program of International, 506-296-3944 Ext. 158, Fax: 506-290-6116, E-mail: cordobaak@ucimed.com.

Universidad de Iberoamerica, Graduate School, San Jose, Costa Rica. Offers clinical psychology (M Psych); educational psychology (M Psych); hospital and health services management (MHA); intensive care nursing (MN); medicine (MD). *Entrance requirements:* For master's, 2 letters of recommendation, interview.

Universidad Nacional Pedro Henriquez Urena, Graduate School, Santo Domingo, Dominican Republic. Offers accounting and auditing (M Acct); animal production (M Agr); business administration (MBA, PhD); Caribbean tropical architecture (M Arch); conservation of monuments and cultural goods (M Arch); economics (M Econ); education (PhD); environmental engineering (MEE); horticulture (M Agr); hospital administration (PhD); humanities (PhD); international relations (MPS); management of natural resources (MNRM); project management (M Man, MPM); public administration (MPS); sanitary engineering (ME); social science (PhD); veterinary medicine (DVM).

Université de Montréal, Faculty of Medicine and Faculty of Graduate Studies, Graduate Programs in Medicine, Department of Health Administration, Montréal, QC H3C 3J7, Canada. Offers M Sc, DESS. *Accreditation:* CAHME. *Faculty:* 18 full-time (8 women), 18 part-time/adjunct (5 women). *Students:* 78 full-time (48 women), 44 part-time (34 women). 75 applicants, 21% accepted, 9 enrolled. In 2006, 20 master's, 8 other advanced degrees awarded. *Degree requirements:* For master's, thesis. *Entrance requirements:* For master's, proficiency in French. *Application deadline:* For fall admission, 2/1 priority date for domestic students; for winter admission, 11/1 priority date for domestic students; for spring admission, 2/1 priority date for domestic students. Applications are processed on a rolling basis. Application fee: $30. Electronic applications accepted. *Financial support:* Career-related internships or fieldwork and institutionally sponsored loans available. *Unit head:* Renaldo N. Battista, Chairperson, 514-343-5631, Fax: 514-343-2448.

University at Albany, State University of New York, School of Public Health, Department of Health Policy, Management, and Behavior, Albany, NY 12222-0001. Offers MS. *Students:* 4 full-time (1 woman), 5 part-time (4 women). Average age 31. In 2006, 2 degrees awarded. *Degree requirements:* For master's, thesis. *Entrance requirements:* For master's, GRE General Test. Additional exam requirements/recommendations for international students: Required—TOEFL (minimum score 550 paper-based; 213 computer-based). *Application deadline:* For fall admission, 4/1 for domestic students, 5/1 for international students; for spring admission, 11/30 for domestic students, 11/1 for international students. Applications are processed on a rolling basis. Application fee: $75. Electronic applications accepted. *Expenses:* Tuition, state resident: full-time $6,900; part-time $288 per credit. Tuition, nonresident: full-time $10,920; part-time $455 per credit. Required fees: $1,139. *Financial support:* Application deadline: 4/1. *Unit head:* Dr. Edward Hannan, Chair, 518-402-0333.

The University of Akron, Graduate School, College of Business Administration, Department of Management, Program in Management-Health Services Administration, Akron, OH 44325. Offers MSM. *Students:* 5 full-time (all women), 4 part-time (all women), 2 international. Average age 32. 4 applicants, 25% accepted, 1 enrolled. In 2006, 1 degree awarded. *Entrance requirements:* Additional exam requirements/recommendations for international students: Required—TOEFL (minimum score 550 paper-based; 213 computer-based; 79 iBT). *Application deadline:* Applications are processed on a rolling basis. Electronic applications accepted. *Expenses:* Tuition, state resident: full-time $6,164; part-time $342 per credit. Tuition, nonresident: full-time $10,575; part-time $588 per credit. Required fees: $806; $43 per credit. $12 per term. Tuition and fees vary according to course load, degree level and program. *Application contact:* Dr. James Divoky, Director of Graduate Business Programs, 330-972-7043, Fax: 330-972-6588, E-mail: jdivoky@uakron.edu.

The University of Alabama at Birmingham, School of Health Professions, Department of Health Services Administration, Program in Administration-Health Services, Birmingham, AL 35294. Offers PhD. *Students:* 10 full-time (8 women), 20 part-time (4 women); includes 9 minority (8 African Americans, 1 American Indian/Alaska Native), 7 international. 15 applicants, 47% accepted. In 2006, 6 degrees awarded. *Degree requirements:* For doctorate, thesis/dissertation. *Entrance requirements:* For doctorate, GMAT or GRE General Test. *Application deadline:* For fall admission, 4/15 priority date for domestic students. Application fee: $35 ($60 for international students). Electronic applications accepted. *Expenses:* Tuition, state resident: part-time $170 per credit hour. Tuition, nonresident: part-time $425 per credit hour. Required fees: $15 per credit hour. $122 per term. Tuition and fees vary according to program. *Financial support:* In 2006–07, 11 students received support, including 4 fellowships, 6 research assistantships, 1 teaching assistantship; career-related internships or fieldwork, institutionally sponsored loans, and unspecified assistantships also available. Financial award application deadline: 4/15. *Faculty research:* Healthcare strategic management, marketing, and organization studies. Total annual research expenditures: $1.5 million. *Unit head:* Dr. Samuel R. Hernandez, Co-Director, 205-934-1649, Fax: 205-975-6608, E-mail: hernande@uab.edu.

The University of Alabama at Birmingham, School of Health Professions, Department of Health Services Administration, Program in Health Administration, Birmingham, AL 35294. Offers MSHA. *Accreditation:* CAHME. *Students:* 112 full-time (42 women), 1 part-time; includes 16 minority (10 African Americans, 4 Asian Americans or Pacific Islanders, 2 Hispanic Americans). 90 applicants, 59% accepted. In 2006, 47 degrees awarded. *Degree requirements:* For master's, administrative residency. *Entrance requirements:* For master's, GMAT, GRE General Test, minimum GPA of 3.0 in final 60 hours of undergraduate course work. *Application deadline:* Applications are processed on a rolling basis. Application fee: $35 ($60 for international students). Electronic applications accepted. *Expenses:* Tuition, state resident: part-time $170 per credit hour. Tuition, nonresident: part-time $425 per credit hour. Required fees: $15 per credit hour. $122 per term. Tuition and fees vary according to program. *Financial support:* In 2006–07, 45 students received support. Career-related internships or fieldwork, Federal Work-Study, scholarships/grants, and traineeships available. Financial award application deadline: 5/1. *Unit head:* Dr. Stephen J. O'Connor, Director, 205-934-1735, E-mail: sjo@uab.edu.

The University of Alabama at Birmingham, School of Public Health, Department of Health Care Organization and Policy, Birmingham, AL 35294. Offers MPH, MSPH. *Degree requirements:* For master's, fieldwork, research project. *Entrance requirements:* For master's, GRE General Test or MAT. *Application deadline:* Applications are processed on a rolling basis. Application fee: $35 ($60 for international students). Electronic applications accepted. *Expenses:* Tuition, state resident: part-time $170 per credit hour. Tuition, nonresident: part-time $425 per credit hour. Required fees: $15 per credit hour. $122 per term. Tuition and fees vary according to program. *Financial support:* Career-related internships or fieldwork available. *Faculty research:* Public health administration and policy, health education, maternal and child health. *Unit head:* Dr. Peter M. Ginter, Chair, 205-935-8970, E-mail: pginter@uab.edu. *Application contact:* Nancy O. Pinson, Coordinator of Student Admissions, 205-934-4993, Fax: 205-975-5484.

University of Alberta, School of Public Health, Department of Public Health Sciences, Edmonton, AB T6G 2E1, Canada. Offers clinical epidemiology (M Sc, MPH); environmental and occupational health (MPH); environmental health sciences (M Sc); epidemiology (M Sc); global health (M Sc, MPH); health policy and management (MPH); health policy research (M Sc); health technology assessment (MPH); occupational health (M Sc); population health (M Sc); public health leadership (MPH); public health sciences (PhD); quantitative methods (MPH). *Accreditation:* CEPH (one or more programs are accredited). *Faculty:* 24 full-time (5 women), 59 part-time/adjunct (13 women). *Students:* 49 full-time, 49 part-time. 81 applicants, 31% accepted. In 2006, 28 degrees awarded. Terminal master's awarded for partial completion of doctoral program. *Degree requirements:* For master's, thesis (for some programs); for doctorate, thesis/dissertation. *Entrance requirements:* For master's, GMAT or GRE General Test. Additional exam requirements/recommendations for international students: Required—TOEFL (paper-based 550; computer-based 213) or IELTS (paper-based 6). *Application deadline:* For fall admission, 3/15 for domestic students, 7/1 for international students; for winter admission, 11/1 for international students; for spring admission, 3/1 for international students. Applications are processed on a rolling basis. Application fee: $0. Electronic applications accepted. *Financial* *support:* In 2006–07, 11 students received support, including 6 research assistantships with tuition reimbursements available (averaging $2,200 per year); fellowships, teaching assistantships, career-related internships or fieldwork and tuition waivers (partial) also available. Financial award application deadline: 2/1. *Faculty research:* Biostatistics, health promotion and socio-behavioral health science. Total annual research expenditures: $5.7 million. *Unit head:* L. Duncan Saunders, Acting Chair, 780-492-6814, Fax: 780-492-0364. *Application contact:* Felicity R. Hey, Graduate Programs Administrator, 780-492-6407, Fax: 780-492-0364, E-mail: felicity.hey@ualberta.ca.

University of Arkansas at Little Rock, Graduate School, College of Professional Studies, Department of Health Services Administration, Little Rock, AR 72204-1099. Offers MHSA. Part-time and evening/weekend programs available. *Degree requirements:* For master's, directed study or residency. *Entrance requirements:* For master's, GMAT or GRE General Test, interview, minimum GPA of 2.75.

University of Baltimore, Graduate School, The Yale Gordon College of Liberal Arts, School of Public Affairs, Program in Health Systems Management, Baltimore, MD 21201-5779. Offers MS. Part-time and evening/weekend programs available. *Faculty:* 4 full-time (2 women), 9 part-time/adjunct (5 women). *Students:* 16 full-time (14 women), 40 part-time (29 women); includes 37 minority (34 African Americans, 1 American Indian/Alaska Native, 1 Asian American or Pacific Islander, 1 Hispanic American), 2 international. Average age 36. 17 applicants, 76% accepted, 7 enrolled. In 2006, 44 degrees awarded. *Entrance requirements:* For master's, minimum undergraduate GPA of 3.0. Additional exam requirements/recommendations for international students: Required—TOEFL (minimum score 550 paper-based; 213 computer-based). *Application deadline:* For fall admission, 6/1 for domestic students; for spring admission, 12/1 for domestic students. Application fee: $45. *Expenses:* Tuition, state resident: full-time $5,322; part-time $591 per credit. Tuition, nonresident: full-time $7,527; part-time $830 per credit. *Unit head:* Dr. John Callhan, Director, 410-837-6089, E-mail: jcallhan@ubalt.edu. *Application contact:* Dean Dreibelbis, Assistant Director, Office of Graduate Admissions, 410-837-6565, Fax: 410-837-4793, E-mail: gradadmissions@ubalt.edu.

The University of British Columbia, Faculty of Medicine, Department of Health Care and Epidemiology, Vancouver, BC V6T 1W5, Canada. Offers clinical epidemiology (MH Sc); community health (MH Sc); epidemiology/clinical epidemiology (M Sc, PhD); health administration (MHA); health services research (M Sc, PhD); occupational and environmental health (M Sc, PhD); occupational health (MH Sc). *Accreditation:* CEPH (one or more programs are accredited). Part-time programs available. *Faculty:* 27 full-time (7 women). *Students:* 27 full-time (4 women), 10 part-time (2 women). Average age 31. 91 applicants, 30% accepted. In 2006, 14 master's, 1 doctorate awarded. *Degree requirements:* For master's and doctorate, thesis/dissertation. *Entrance requirements:* For master's, GRE General Test, MD or equivalent (MH Sc); for doctorate, work experience. *Application deadline:* For fall admission, 3/31 for domestic students. Applications are processed on a rolling basis. Application fee: $65. Electronic applications accepted. *Financial support:* In 2006–07, 7 students received support, including 1 fellowship; career-related internships or fieldwork also available. *Faculty research:* AIDS, public health, environmental toxicology, infectious diseases, health evaluation, epidemiology. Total annual research expenditures: $4.8 million. *Unit head:* M. T. Schechter, Head, 604-822-3910, Fax: 604-822-4994, E-mail: martin.schechter@ubc.ca. *Application contact:* Laurel Slaney, Program Assistant, 604-822-5405, Fax: 604-822-4994, E-mail: laurel.slaney@ubc.ca.

University of California, Berkeley, Graduate Division, School of Public Health, Division of Health Policy and Management, Berkeley, CA 94720-1500. Offers MPH, MBA/MPH, MCP/MPH, MPP/MPH. *Accreditation:* CAHME; CEPH. *Degree requirements:* For master's, comprehensive exam. *Entrance requirements:* For master's, GRE General Test, minimum GPA of 3.0. *Application deadline:* Applications are processed on a rolling basis. Application fee: $60 ($80 for international students). *Financial support:* Fellowships, research assistantships, teaching assistantships, Federal Work-Study and unspecified assistantships available. *Unit head:* James C. Robinson, Professor, 510-642-0564. *Application contact:* Greta Gebhardt, Administrative Assistant, 510-642-4578, Fax: 510-643-6981, E-mail: gretag@uclink.berkeley.edu.

University of California, Berkeley, Graduate Division, School of Public Health, Group in Health Services and Policy Analysis, Berkeley, CA 94720-1500. Offers PhD. *Degree requirements:* For doctorate, thesis/dissertation, qualifying exam. *Entrance requirements:* For doctorate, GRE General Test, minimum GPA of 3.0. *Application deadline:* For fall admission, 12/1 for domestic students. Applications are processed on a rolling basis. Application fee: $60 ($80 for international students). *Financial support:* Fellowships, research assistantships, teaching assistantships, unspecified assistantships available. *Unit head:* William Dow, Chair, 510-643-5439, E-mail: wdow@berkeley.edu. *Application contact:* Dion Shimatsu-ong, Graduate Assistant for Admission, 510-643-8571, Fax: 510-643-6981, E-mail: hspa_phd@berkeley.edu.

University of California, Los Angeles, Graduate Division, School of Public Health, Department of Health Services, Los Angeles, CA 90095. Offers MS, PhD. *Degree requirements:* For master's, comprehensive exam or thesis; for doctorate, thesis/dissertation, oral and written qualifying exams. *Entrance requirements:* For master's, GRE General Test, minimum GPA of 3.0; for doctorate, GRE General Test, minimum undergraduate GPA of 3.0. Electronic applications accepted.

University of California, San Diego, School of Medicine, Program in Leadership in Healthcare Organizations, La Jolla, CA 92093. Offers MAS.

University of Central Florida, College of Health and Public Affairs, Department of Health Professions, Program in Health Services Administration, Orlando, FL 32816. Offers MS, Certificate. *Accreditation:* CAHME. Part-time and evening/weekend programs available. *Students:* 34 full-time (26 women), 77 part-time (54 women); includes 29 minority (16 African Americans, 8 Asian Americans or Pacific Islanders, 5 Hispanic Americans), 4 international. In 2006, 52 master's awarded. *Degree requirements:* For master's, thesis or alternative, research report, comprehensive exam. *Entrance requirements:* For master's, GRE General Test. Additional exam requirements/recommendations for international students: Required—TOEFL. *Application deadline:* For fall admission, 7/15 for domestic students; for spring admission, 10/1 for domestic students. Application fee: $30. Electronic applications accepted. *Expenses:* Tuition, state resident: full-time $6,167; part-time $257 per credit hour. Tuition, nonresident: full-time $22,790; part-time $950 per credit hour. *Financial support:* In 2006–07, 1 fellowship with partial tuition reimbursement (averaging $5,000 per year), 14 research assistantships with partial tuition reimbursements (averaging $4,000 per year) were awarded; teaching assistantships with partial tuition reimbursements, career-related internships or fieldwork, Federal Work-Study, institutionally sponsored loans, and unspecified assistantships also available. Financial award application deadline: 3/1; financial award applicants required to submit FAFSA. *Application contact:* Dr. Dawn M. Oetjen, Coordinator, 407-823-2359, E-mail: doetjen@mail.ucf.edu.

University of Colorado at Colorado Springs, Graduate School, Graduate School of Business Administration, Colorado Springs, CO 80933-7150. Offers accounting (MBA); finance (MBA); general health care administration (MBA); information systems (MBA); international business management (MBA); marketing (MBA); service management/technology management (MBA). *Accreditation:* AACSB. Part-time and evening/weekend programs available. *Faculty:* 15 full-time (4 women), 4 part-time/adjunct (0 women). *Students:* 158 full-time (70 women), 290 part-time (87 women); includes 48 minority (11 African Americans, 1 American Indian/Alaska Native, 20 Asian Americans or Pacific Islanders, 16 Hispanic Americans), 7 international. Average age 33. 158 applicants, 75% accepted, 51 enrolled. In 2006, 119 degrees awarded. *Entrance requirements:* For master's, GMAT. *Application deadline:* For fall admission, 6/1 for domestic students; for spring admission, 11/1 for domestic students. Application fee: $60 ($75 for international students). *Expenses:* Contact institution. Tuition and fees vary according to course load, campus/location and program. *Financial support:* Career-related internships or fieldwork, Federal Work-Study, and institutionally sponsored loans available. Support available to part-time students. Financial award applicants required to submit FAFSA. *Faculty research:* Quality financial reporting, investments and corporate governance, group support systems, environmental and project management, customer relationship management. Total annual research expenditures: $99,250. *Unit head:* Dr. Venkateshwar Reddy, Dean, 719-262-3113, Fax: 719-262-3494, E-mail: vreddy@uccs.edu. *Application contact:* Amy DeLourenco, MBA Program Director, 719-262-3408, Fax: 719-262-3100, E-mail: busadvsr@uccs.edu.

University of Colorado at Denver and Health Sciences Center, Business School, Executive MBA Program in Health Administration, Denver, CO 80248-0006. Offers health administration (MBA); pharmaceutical management (MBA). *Accreditation:* CAHME. Evening/weekend programs available. Postbaccalaureate distance learning degree programs offered (minimal on-campus study). *Faculty:* 3 full-time (1 woman). *Students:* 30 full-time (14 women), 25 part-time (12 women); includes 5 minority (2 African Americans, 1 Asian American or Pacific Islander, 2 Hispanic Americans), 2 international. 21 applicants, 76% accepted, 13 enrolled. In 2006, 3 degrees awarded. *Entrance requirements:* For master's, 3 years clinical or management experience in health care field. Additional exam requirements/recommendations for international students: Required—TOEFL. *Application deadline:* For fall admission, 4/15 priority date for domestic students. Applications are processed on a rolling basis. Application fee: $50. Electronic applications accepted. *Expenses:* Contact institution. *Financial support:* Institutionally sponsored loans and scholarships/grants available. Financial award application deadline: 4/1. *Unit head:* W. Scott Guthrie, Director, 303-623-1888, Fax: 800-623-5778, E-mail: scott_guthrie@cudenver.edu. *Application contact:* Peter Taffe, Program Manager, 303-623-1888, Fax: 303-623-6228, E-mail: peter_taffe@cudenver.edu.

University of Colorado at Denver and Health Sciences Center, Business School, Program in Health Administration, Denver, CO 80217-3364. Offers MS. *Accreditation:* CAHME. Part-time and evening/weekend programs available. *Faculty:* 3 full-time (1 woman). *Students:* Average age 34. 14 applicants, 43% accepted, 0 enrolled. In 2006, 3 degrees awarded. *Entrance requirements:* For master's, GMAT. Additional exam requirements/recommendations for international students: Required—TOEFL (minimum score 525 paper-based; 197 computer-based). *Application deadline:* For fall admission, 6/1 for domestic students, 3/15 for international students; for spring admission, 11/1 priority date for domestic students, 10/1 for international students. Applications are processed on a rolling basis. Application fee: $50 ($75 for international students). Electronic applications accepted. *Financial support:* Federal Work-Study, institutionally sponsored loans, and traineeships available. Support available to part-time students. Financial award application deadline: 4/1; financial award applicants required to submit FAFSA. *Faculty research:* Cost containment, financial management, governance, rural health-care delivery systems. *Unit head:* Errol Biggs, Director, 303-556-5845, Fax: 303-556-5899, E-mail: errolbriggs@aol.com. *Application contact:* Shelly Townley, Admissions Coordinator, 303-556-5956, Fax: 303-556-5904, E-mail: shelly.townley@cudenver.edu.

University of Connecticut, Graduate School, School of Business, Storrs, CT 06269. Offers accounting (MS, PhD); business administration (Exec MBA, MBA, PhD); finance (PhD); health care management and insurance studies (MBA); management (PhD); management consulting (MBA); marketing (PhD); marketing intelligence (MBA); MA/MBA; MBA/MSW. *Accreditation:* AACSB. *Faculty:* 70 full-time (14 women). *Students:* 378 full-time (126 women), 852 part-time (322 women); includes 154 minority (43 African Americans, 5 American Indian/Alaska Native, 71 Asian Americans or Pacific Islanders, 35 Hispanic Americans), 171 international. Average age 30. 632 applicants, 72% accepted, 452 enrolled. In 2006, 413 master's, 9 doctorates awarded. *Degree requirements:* For master's, comprehensive exam; for doctorate, thesis/dissertation. *Entrance requirements:* For master's and doctorate, GMAT. Additional exam requirements/recommendations for international students: Required—TOEFL (minimum score 550 paper-based; 213 computer-based). *Application deadline:* For fall admission, 2/1 priority date for domestic and international students; for spring admission, 11/1 for domestic students, 10/1 for international students. Applications are processed on a rolling basis. Electronic applications accepted. *Financial support:* In 2006–07, 107 research assistantships with full tuition reimbursements, 4 teaching assistantships with full tuition reimbursements were awarded; fellowships, career-related internships or fieldwork, Federal Work-Study, scholarships/grants, health care benefits, and unspecified assistantships also available. Financial award application deadline: 2/1; financial award applicants required to submit FAFSA. *Unit head:* William Curt Hunter, Dean, 860-486-2317, Fax: 860-846-0889, E-mail: william.hunter@uconn.edu. *Application contact:* Richard Dino, Admissions Chairperson, 860-486-4483, E-mail: rich.dino@uconn.edu.

See Close-Up on page 343.

University of Dallas, Graduate School of Management, Irving, TX 75062-4736. Offers accounting (MBA, MS); business management (MBA); corporate finance (MBA, MM); engineering management (MBA, MM); entrepreneurship (MBA, MM); financial services (MBA, MM); global business (MBA, MM); health services management (MBA, MM); human resource management (MBA, MM, MS); information assurance (MBA, MM, MS); information technology (MBA, MM, MS); information technology service management (MBA); IT service management (MS); marketing (MM); marketing management (MBA); not-for-profit management (MBA); organization development (MBA); project management (MBA, MM); sports and entertainment management (MBA, MM); strategic leadership (MBA); supply chain management (MBA); supply chain management and market logistics (MM); telecommunications management (MBA, MM). *Accreditation:* ACBSP. Part-time and evening/weekend programs available. Postbaccalaureate distance learning degree programs offered (no on-campus study). *Faculty:* 26 full-time (5 women), 85 part-time/adjunct (18 women). *Students:* 227 full-time (98 women), 1,160 part-time (446 women); includes 473 minority (209 African Americans, 3 American Indian/Alaska Native, 143 Asian Americans or Pacific Islanders, 118 Hispanic Americans), 224 international. Average age 34. 556 applicants, 86% accepted, 291 enrolled. In 2006, 476 degrees awarded. *Entrance requirements:* Additional exam requirements/recommendations for international students: Required—TOEFL. *Application deadline:* Applications are processed on a rolling basis. Application fee: $50. Electronic applications accepted. *Expenses:* Contact institution. *Financial support:* In 2006–07, 468 students received support. Scholarships/grants and unspecified assistantships available. Financial award application deadline: 2/15; financial award applicants required to submit FAFSA. *Unit head:* Dr. J. Lee Whittington, Dean, 972-721-5230. *Application contact:* Sarah Stivison, Director of Graduate Admissions, 972-721-5198, Fax: 972-721-4009, E-mail: admiss@gsm.udallas.edu.

University of Detroit Mercy, College of Health Professions, Program in Health Services Administration, Detroit, MI 48221. Offers MS. *Degree requirements:* For master's, thesis. *Entrance requirements:* For master's, GRE General Test, minimum GPA of 3.0. *Expenses:* Tuition: Full-time $15,750; part-time $875 per credit hour. Required fees: $570. *Faculty research:* Health systems issues, organizational theory.

University of Detroit Mercy, College of Health Professions, Program in Health Systems Management, Detroit, MI 48221. Offers MSN. *Expenses:* Tuition: Full-time $15,750; part-time $875 per credit hour. Required fees: $570.

University of Evansville, College of Education and Health Sciences, Department of Nursing and Health Sciences, Evansville, IN 47722. Offers health services administration (MS). Part-time and evening/weekend programs available. *Faculty:* 1 full-time (0 women), 4 part-time/adjunct (1 woman). *Students:* 1 full-time (0 women), 9 part-time (7 women), 1 international. Average age 42. 2 applicants, 100% accepted, 1 enrolled. In 2006, 11 degrees awarded. *Median time to degree:* Master's–1.5 years full-time, 2.75 years part-time. *Entrance requirements:* For master's, GRE or GMAT, 2 letters of reference, interview. Additional exam requirements/recommendations for international students: Required—TOEFL (minimum score 500 paper-based). *Application deadline:* For fall admission, 7/1 priority date for domestic and international students; for spring admission, 10/1 priority date for domestic students. Applications are processed on a rolling basis. Application fee: $20 ($50 for international students). *Expenses:* Contact institution. Tuition and fees vary according to course load and program. *Financial support:* In 2006–07, 2 students received support. Career-related internships or fieldwork

Health Services Management and Hospital Administration

University of Evansville (continued)
available. Support available to part-time students. Financial award application deadline: 7/1; financial award applicants required to submit FAFSA. *Unit head:* Dr. Amy Hall, Department Chair, 812-488-2343, Fax: 812-488-2717, E-mail: ah169@evansville.edu. *Application contact:* Dr. William Stroube, Director, Health Services Administration Program, 812-488-2343, Fax: 812-488-2717, E-mail: hsa@evansville.edu.

University of Florida, College of Pharmacy and Graduate School, Graduate Programs in Pharmacy, Department of Pharmacy Health Care Administration, Gainesville, FL 32611. Offers MSP, PhD. Part-time programs available. *Faculty:* 8 full-time (5 women), 1 part-time/adjunct (0 women). *Students:* 29 (14 women); includes 7 minority (4 African Americans, 3 Hispanic Americans) 12 international. Average age 31. In 2006, 2 master's, 2 doctorates awarded. *Degree requirements:* For doctorate, thesis/dissertation. *Entrance requirements:* For master's, minimum GPA of 3.0; for doctorate, GRE General Test, minimum GPA of 3.0. Additional exam requirements/recommendations for international students: Required—TOEFL. *Application deadline:* For fall admission, 3/1 priority date for domestic students. Applications are processed on a rolling basis. Application fee: $30. Electronic applications accepted. *Expenses:* Tuition, state resident: full-time $6,827. Tuition, nonresident: full-time $21,951. Required fees: $999. *Financial support:* In 2006–07, 14 teaching assistantships (averaging $22,029 per year) were awarded; fellowships, research assistantships, tuition waivers (full) also available. Financial award application deadline: 2/1. *Faculty research:* Pharmaceutical care, drug use systems, drug-related morbidity, pharmacy law. *Unit head:* Dr. Richard Segal, Chair, 352-273-6268, Fax: 352-273-6270, E-mail: segal@cop.health.ufl.edu. *Application contact:* Dr. Carole Kimberlin, Graduate Coordinator, 352-273-6263, Fax: 352-273-6270, E-mail: kimber@cop.ufl.edu.

University of Florida, Graduate School, College of Public Health and Health Professions, Department of Health Services Research, Management and Policy, Gainesville, FL 32611. Offers health administration (MHA); health services research (PhD). *Accreditation:* CAHME. Part-time programs available. *Faculty:* 13 full-time (7 women), 2 part-time/adjunct (1 woman). *Students:* 55 (27 women); includes 17 minority (8 African Americans, 2 Asian Americans or Pacific Islanders, 7 Hispanic Americans) 6 international. In 2006, 33 master's, 3 doctorates awarded. *Entrance requirements:* For master's, GRE General Test, minimum GPA of 3.0. Additional exam requirements/recommendations for international students: Required—TOEFL (minimum score 550 paper-based; 213 computer-based). *Application deadline:* For fall admission, 4/1 for domestic students. Applications are processed on a rolling basis. Application fee: $30. Electronic applications accepted. *Expenses:* Tuition, state resident: full-time $6,827. Tuition, nonresident: full-time $21,951. Required fees: $999. *Financial support:* In 2006–07, 6 research assistantships (averaging $9,461 per year) were awarded; fellowships, teaching assistantships, career-related internships or fieldwork and unspecified assistantships also available. *Faculty research:* Hospital profitability, indigent care, rural health care systems, AIDS education, managed care, outcomes. *Unit head:* Dr. R. Paul Duncan, Chair, 352-273-6073, Fax: 352-273-6075, E-mail: pduncan@phhp.ufl.edu. *Application contact:* Barbara Ross, Student Services Coordinator, 352-273-6074, Fax: 352-273-6075, E-mail: bross@phhp.ufl.edu.

See Close-Up on page 1819.

University of Florida, Graduate School, Warrington College of Business Administration, Programs in Business Administration, Gainesville, FL 32611. Offers accounting (MBA); arts administration (MBA); business strategy and public policy (MBA); competitive strategy (MBA); decision and information sciences (MBA); electronic commerce (MBA); finance (MBA); general business (MBA); global management (MBA); Graham-Buffett security analysis (MBA); health administration (MBA); human resources management (MBA); international studies (MBA); Latin American business (MBA); management (MBA); marketing (MBA); sports administration (MBA); JD/MBA; MBA/MS; MBA/PhD; MBA/Pharm D; MD/MBA. *Accreditation:* AACSB. Part-time and evening/weekend programs available. Postbaccalaureate distance learning degree programs offered. *Faculty:* 14. *Students:* 950 (282 women); includes 189 minority (31 African Americans, 2 American Indian/Alaska Native, 66 Asian Americans or Pacific Islanders, 90 Hispanic Americans) 56 international. In 2006, 481 degrees awarded. *Entrance requirements:* For master's, GMAT, minimum GPA of 3.0, interview. Additional exam requirements/recommendations for international students: Required—TOEFL (minimum score 550 paper-based; 213 computer-based). *Application deadline:* For fall admission, 4/15 for domestic students; for winter admission, 10/15 priority date for domestic students; for spring admission, 2/15 for domestic students. Applications are processed on a rolling basis. Application fee: $30. Electronic applications accepted. *Expenses:* Tuition, state resident: full-time $6,827. Tuition, nonresident: full-time $21,951. Required fees: $999. *Financial support:* Fellowships, research assistantships, teaching assistantships, career-related internships or fieldwork, scholarships/grants, and unspecified assistantships available. Support available to part-time students. Financial award application deadline: 2/15; financial award applicants required to submit FAFSA. *Faculty research:* Accounting, finance, insurance, management, real estate and urban analysis marketing. *Unit head:* Alex Sevilla, Director, 352-392-7992 Ext. 1206. *Application contact:* Patrick Foran, Associate Director of Admissions, 352-392-7992 Ext. 282, Fax: 352-392-8791, E-mail: patrick.foran@cba.ufl.edu.

University of Houston–Clear Lake, School of Business, Program in Healthcare Administration, Houston, TX 77058-1098. Offers MHA, MHA/MBA. *Students:* 101 full-time, 68 part-time; includes 62 minority (16 African Americans, 1 American Indian/Alaska Native, 37 Asian Americans or Pacific Islanders, 8 Hispanic Americans), 29 international. 152 applicants, 54% accepted, 48 enrolled. In 2006, 38 degrees awarded. *Degree requirements:* For master's, thesis optional. *Entrance requirements:* For master's, GMAT. Additional exam requirements/recommendations for international students: Required—TOEFL (minimum score 550 paper-based; 213 computer-based). *Unit head:* Dr. Ashish Chandra, Professor, 832-842-2031.

University of Illinois at Chicago, Graduate College, School of Public Health, Program in Health Policy Administration, Chicago, IL 60607-7128. Offers MPH, MS, Dr PH, PhD. Part-time programs available. Terminal master's awarded for partial completion of doctoral program. *Degree requirements:* For master's, thesis, field practicum; for doctorate, thesis/dissertation, independent research, internship. *Entrance requirements:* For master's and doctorate, GRE General Test, minimum GPA of 2.75. Additional exam requirements/recommendations for international students: Required—TOEFL. Electronic applications accepted.

The University of Iowa, Graduate College, College of Public Health, Department of Health Management and Policy, Iowa City, IA 52242-1316. Offers MHA, PhD, JD/MHA, MBA/MHA, MHA/MA, MHA/MS. *Accreditation:* CAHME (one or more programs are accredited). *Faculty:* 8 full-time, 8 part-time/adjunct. *Students:* 49 full-time (28 women), 10 part-time (5 women); includes 8 minority (2 African Americans, 1 American Indian/Alaska Native, 3 Asian Americans or Pacific Islanders, 2 Hispanic Americans), 6 international. 88 applicants, 27% accepted, 17 enrolled. In 2006, 27 master's, 1 doctorate awarded. *Degree requirements:* For master's, registration; for doctorate, thesis/dissertation, comprehensive exam, registration. *Entrance requirements:* For master's, GRE General Test (GMAT/MCAT/DAT/LSAT/TCAT may be substituted), minimum GPA of 3.0; for doctorate, GRE General Test, minimum GPA of 3.0. Additional exam requirements/recommendations for international students: Required—TOEFL (minimum score 600 paper-based; 250 computer-based; 100 iBT). *Application deadline:* For fall admission, 5/1 priority date for domestic students. Applications are processed on a rolling basis. Application fee: $60 ($85 for international students). Electronic applications accepted. *Expenses:* Contact institution. *Financial support:* In 2006–07, 1 fellowship, 44 research assistantships with partial tuition reimbursements, 8 teaching assistantships with partial tuition reimbursements were awarded. Financial award applicants required to submit FAFSA. *Unit head:* Dr. Berry Greene, Interim Head, 319-384-5135, Fax: 319-384-5125.

University of Kansas, Graduate Studies Medical Center, Department of Health Policy and Management, Lawrence, KS 66045. Offers MHSA, JD/MHSA, MHSA/MS. *Accreditation:* CAHME. Part-time programs available. *Faculty:* 7 full-time (3 women), 1 part-time/adjunct (0 women). *Students:* 31 full-time (19 women), 18 part-time (11 women); includes 13 minority (5 African Americans, 1 American Indian/Alaska Native, 4 Asian Americans or Pacific Islanders, 3 Hispanic Americans), 2 international. Average age 31. 31 applicants, 16% accepted. In 2006, 16 degrees awarded. *Median time to degree:* Master's–1.09 years full-time, 1.57 years part-time. *Entrance requirements:* For master's, GMAT, GRE General Test. Additional exam requirements/recommendations for international students: Required—TOEFL. *Application deadline:* For fall admission, 4/15 for domestic students. Application fee: $35. *Expenses:* Tuition, area resident: Part-time $227 per credit. Tuition, state resident: part-time $543 per credit. Tuition and fees vary according to course load, campus/location, program and reciprocity agreements. *Financial support:* In 2006–07, 4 students received support; fellowships, research assistantships, teaching assistantships, career-related internships or fieldwork and scholarships/grants available. Support available to part-time students. Financial award applicants required to submit FAFSA. *Faculty research:* Economic analysis of long-term care facilities, healthcare workforce supply and demand, the impact of disaster preparedness on individuals with developmental disabilities, policy analysis and readiness for biological outbreaks, gender issues in health roles and functions. *Unit head:* Michael R. Bleich, Chair, 913-588-2908, Fax: 913-588-8890, E-mail: mbleich@kumc.edu. *Application contact:* Adam S. Keener, Student Services Manager, 913-588-3763, Fax: 913-588-8236, E-mail: akeener2@kumc.edu.

University of Kentucky, Graduate School, Program in Health Administration, Lexington, KY 40506-0032. Offers MHA. *Accreditation:* CAHME. *Faculty:* 11 full-time (3 women), 4 part-time/adjunct (1 woman). *Students:* 26 full-time (14 women), 20 part-time (11 women); includes 7 minority (5 African Americans, 1 Asian American or Pacific Islander, 1 Hispanic American), 2 international. Average age 29. 63 applicants, 57% accepted, 20 enrolled. In 2006, 15 degrees awarded. *Degree requirements:* For master's, comprehensive exam. *Entrance requirements:* For master's, GRE General test, minimum undergraduate GPA of 2.75. Additional exam requirements/recommendations for international students: Required—TOEFL (minimum score 550 paper-based; 213 computer-based). *Application deadline:* For fall admission, 7/17 priority date for domestic students, 2/1 priority date for international students; for spring admission, 12/13 priority date for domestic students, 6/15 priority date for international students. Application fee: $40 ($55 for international students). Electronic applications accepted. *Expenses:* Tuition, state resident: full-time $7,670; part-time $401 per credit hour. Tuition, nonresident: full-time $16,158; part-time $873 per credit hour. *Financial support:* In 2006–07, 2 students received support, including 1 fellowship with full tuition reimbursement available (averaging $7,500 per year), 1 research assistantship with full tuition reimbursement available (averaging $9,000 per year); teaching assistantships with full tuition reimbursements available, Federal Work-Study, scholarships/grants, traineeships, health care benefits, tuition waivers (partial), and unspecified assistantships also available. Support available to part-time students. Financial award application deadline: 3/15; financial award applicants required to submit FAFSA. *Faculty research:* Health economy, health finance, health policy. *Unit head:* Dr. Sarah Wackerbarth, Director of Graduate Studies, 859-257-5145, Fax: 859-323-1937, E-mail: sbwack0@uky.edu. *Application contact:* Dr. Brian Jackson, Senior Associate Dean, 859-257-4667, Fax: 859-257-4676, E-mail: brian.jackson@uky.edu.

University of La Verne, College of Business and Public Management, Graduate Programs in Business Administration, La Verne, CA 91750-4443. Offers accounting (MBA); business (MBIT); executive management (MBA-EP); finance (MBA, MBA-EP); health services management (MBA); information technology (MBA, MBA-EP); international business (MBA, MBA-EP); leadership (MBA-EP); managed care (MBA); management (MBA, MBA-EP); marketing (MBA, MBA-EP). Part-time and evening/weekend programs available. *Faculty:* 15 full-time (7 women), 13 part-time/adjunct (7 women). *Students:* 277 full-time (133 women), 112 part-time (64 women); includes 144 minority (32 African Americans, 3 American Indian/Alaska Native, 70 Asian Americans or Pacific Islanders, 39 Hispanic Americans), 160 international. Average age 30. In 2006, 142 degrees awarded. *Entrance requirements:* For master's, minimum undergraduate GPA of 3.0, 2 letters of recommendation, resumé. Additional exam requirements/recommendations for international students: Required—TOEFL (minimum score 550 paper-based; 213 computer-based). *Application deadline:* Applications are processed on a rolling basis. Application fee: $50. *Expenses:* Contact institution. *Financial support:* Career-related internships or fieldwork, institutionally sponsored loans, and scholarships/grants available. Financial award application deadline: 3/2; financial award applicants required to submit FAFSA. *Unit head:* Dr. Ibrahim Helou, Chairperson, 909-593-3511 Ext. 4211, Fax: 909-392-2704, E-mail: heloua@ulv.edu. *Application contact:* Dr. Julius Walecki, Marketing Director, 909-593-3511 Ext. 4192, Fax: 909-392-2704, E-mail: cbpm@ulv.edu.

University of La Verne, College of Business and Public Management, Program in Gerontology, La Verne, CA 91750-4443. Offers business administration (MS); counseling (MS); gerontology (Certificate); gerontology administration (MS); health services management (MS); public administration (MS). Part-time programs available. *Faculty:* 7 full-time (2 women), 8 part-time/adjunct (4 women). *Students:* 7 full-time (all women), 21 part-time (20 women); includes 16 minority (7 African Americans, 1 American Indian/Alaska Native, 2 Asian Americans or Pacific Islanders, 6 Hispanic Americans). Average age 45. In 2006, 12 degrees awarded. *Entrance requirements:* For master's, minimum GPA of 2.5. Additional exam requirements/recommendations for international students: Required—TOEFL (minimum score 550 paper-based; 213 computer-based). *Application deadline:* Applications are processed on a rolling basis. Application fee: $50. *Expenses:* Contact institution. *Financial support:* Institutionally sponsored loans available. Financial award application deadline: 3/2; financial award applicants required to submit FAFSA. *Unit head:* Joan Branin, Chairperson, 909-593-3511 Ext. 4247, E-mail: braninj@ulv.edu. *Application contact:* Jo Nell Baker, Director, Graduate Admissions and Academic Services, 909-593-3511 Ext. 4244, Fax: 909-392-2761, E-mail: gradadmt@ulv.edu.

University of La Verne, College of Business and Public Management, Program in Health Administration, La Verne, CA 91750-4443. Offers financial management (MHA); health administration (MHA); human resources (MHA); information management (MHA); leadership and management (MHA); managed care (MHA); marketing and business development (MHA). Part-time programs available. *Faculty:* 7 full-time (2 women), 8 part-time/adjunct (4 women). *Students:* 13 full-time (9 women), 20 part-time (14 women); includes 19 minority (5 African Americans, 6 Asian Americans or Pacific Islanders, 8 Hispanic Americans). Average age 39. In 2006, 18 degrees awarded. *Entrance requirements:* For master's, minimum undergraduate GPA of 2.5, 3 letters of reference, curriculum vitae or resumé, writing sample. Additional exam requirements/recommendations for international students: Required—TOEFL (minimum score 550 paper-based; 213 computer-based). *Application deadline:* Applications are processed on a rolling basis. Application fee: $50. *Expenses:* Contact institution. *Financial support:* Application deadline: 3/2; *Unit head:* Joan Branin, Chairperson, 909-593-3511 Ext. 4247, E-mail: braninj@ulv.edu. *Application contact:* Jo Nell Baker, Director, Graduate Admissions and Academic Services, 909-593-3511 Ext. 4244, Fax: 909-392-2761, E-mail: gradadmt@ulv.edu.

University of La Verne, Regional Campus Administration, Graduate Programs, Central Coast/Vandenberg Air Force Base Campuses, La Verne, CA 91750-4443. Offers business (MBA-EP), including health services management, information technology; health administration (MHA); leadership and management (MS). *Faculty:* 6 part-time/adjunct (0 women). *Students:* 14 full-time (5 women), 20 part-time (8 women); includes 7 minority (1 African American, 1 American Indian/Alaska Native, 5 Hispanic Americans). Average age 38. In 2006, 11 degrees awarded. *Entrance requirements:* For master's, 2 letters of recommendation, resumé. *Application deadline:* Applications are processed on a rolling basis. Application fee: $50. *Expenses:* Contact institution. *Financial support:* Institutionally sponsored loans available. Financial award application deadline: 3/2; financial award applicants required to submit FAFSA. *Unit head:* Kitt Vincent, Director, Central Coast Campus, 805-542-9690 Ext. 321, Fax: 805-542-9735, E-mail: vincentk@ulv.edu.

University of La Verne, Regional Campus Administration, Graduate Programs, High Desert Campus, Victorville, CA 91750-4443. Offers business (MBA-EP); health administration (MHA); leadership and management (MS). *Faculty:* 2 part-time/adjunct (0 women). *Students:* 1 full-time (0 women), 13 part-time (7 women); includes 8 minority (5 African Americans, 1 American Indian/Alaska Native, 2 Hispanic Americans). Average age 41. In 2006, 1 degree awarded. *Entrance requirements:* For master's, 2 letters of recommendation, resumé. *Application deadline:* Applications are processed on a rolling basis. Application fee: $50. *Expenses: Contact institution. Financial support:* Application deadline: 3/2; *Unit head:* Teresa Anderson, Director, 760-843-0086, Fax: 760-843-9505, E-mail: tanderson7@ulv.edu.

University of La Verne, Regional Campus Administration, Graduate Programs, Inland Empire Campus, Ranche Cucamonga, CA 91750-4443. Offers business (MBA-EP), including health services management, information technology, management, marketing; health administration (MHA); leadership and management (MS). *Faculty:* 2 full-time (1 woman), 8 part-time/adjunct (2 women). *Students:* 21 full-time (16 women), 32 part-time (18 women); includes 29 minority (13 African Americans, 1 American Indian/Alaska Native, 4 Asian Americans or Pacific Islanders, 11 Hispanic Americans). Average age 37. In 2006, 17 degrees awarded. *Entrance requirements:* For master's, 2 letters of recommendation, resumé. *Application deadline:* Applications are processed on a rolling basis. Application fee: $50. *Expenses: Contact institution. Financial support:* Institutionally sponsored loans available. Financial award application deadline: 3/2; financial award applicants required to submit FAFSA. *Unit head:* Jerry Ford, Director, 909-484-3858 Ext. 228, Fax: 909-484-9469, E-mail: fordj@ulv.edu.

University of La Verne, Regional Campus Administration, Graduate Programs, Kern County Campus, Bakersfield, CA 93301. Offers business (MBA-EP), including information technology, management, marketing; health administration (MHA); leadership and management (MS). *Faculty:* 4 part-time/adjunct (2 women). *Students:* 2 full-time (1 woman), 7 part-time (4 women); includes 2 minority (1 African American, 1 Hispanic American). Average age 37. In 2006, 4 degrees awarded. *Entrance requirements:* For master's, 2 letters of recommendation, resumé. *Application deadline:* Applications are processed on a rolling basis. Application fee: $50. *Expenses: Contact institution. Financial support:* Institutionally sponsored loans available. Financial award application deadline: 3/2; financial award applicants required to submit FAFSA. *Unit head:* Val Garcia, 661-328-1430, E-mail: vgarcia6@ulv.edu.

University of La Verne, Regional Campus Administration, Graduate Programs, Orange County Campus, Garden Grove, CA 92840. Offers business (MBA-EP), including health services management, information technology, management, marketing, supply chain management; health administration (MHA); leadership and management (MS); public administration (MPA). *Faculty:* 4 full-time (1 woman), 3 part-time/adjunct (1 woman). *Students:* 19 full-time (8 women), 64 part-time (29 women); includes 37 minority (4 African Americans, 2 American Indian/Alaska Native, 15 Asian Americans or Pacific Islanders, 16 Hispanic Americans). Average age 41. In 2006, 18 degrees awarded. *Entrance requirements:* For master's, 2 letters of recommendation, resumé. *Application deadline:* Applications are processed on a rolling basis. Application fee: $50. *Expenses: Contact institution. Financial support:* Institutionally sponsored loans available. Financial award application deadline: 3/2; financial award applicants required to submit FAFSA. *Unit head:* Pamela Bergovoy, Director, 714-534-4860, Fax: 714-534-4865, E-mail: bergovoy@ulv.edu.

University of La Verne, Regional Campus Administration, Graduate Programs, San Fernando Valley Campus, Burbank, CA 91505. Offers business (MBA-EP), including health services management, information technology, management, marketing; health administration (MHA); leadership and management (MS). *Faculty:* 3 full-time (2 women), 6 part-time/adjunct (2 women). *Students:* 24 full-time (12 women), 57 part-time (31 women); includes 42 minority (12 African Americans, 1 American Indian/Alaska Native, 9 Asian Americans or Pacific Islanders, 20 Hispanic Americans), 1 international. Average age 39. In 2006, 45 degrees awarded. *Entrance requirements:* For master's, 2 letters of recommendation, resumé. *Application deadline:* Applications are processed on a rolling basis. Application fee: $50. *Expenses: Contact institution. Financial support:* Institutionally sponsored loans available. Financial award application deadline: 3/2; financial award applicants required to submit FAFSA. *Unit head:* Nelly Kazman, Director, 818-846-4008 Ext. 26, Fax: 818-566-1047, E-mail: kazmann@ulv.edu.

University of La Verne, Regional Campus Administration, Graduate Programs, Ventura County/Point Mugu Naval Air Station Campuses, La Verne, CA 91750-4443. Offers business (MBA-EP), including health services management, information technology, management, marketing; business organizational management (MS); health administration (MHA); leadership and management (MS). *Faculty:* 2 full-time (0 women), 8 part-time/adjunct (1 woman). *Students:* 22 full-time (7 women), 29 part-time (16 women); includes 19 minority (4 African Americans, 7 Asian Americans or Pacific Islanders, 8 Hispanic Americans). Average age 40. In 2006, 26 degrees awarded. *Entrance requirements:* For master's, 2 letters of recommendation, resumé. Application fee: $50. *Expenses: Contact institution. Financial support:* Institutionally sponsored loans available. Financial award application deadline: 3/2; financial award applicants required to submit FAFSA. *Unit head:* Janet Meyer, Director, Ventura Campus, 805-981-8030 Ext. 225, Fax: 805-981-8033, E-mail: jmeyer2@ulv.edu.

University of Louisiana at Lafayette, Graduate School, College of Business Administration, Lafayette, LA 70504. Offers business administration (MBA); health care administration (MBA); health care certification (MBA). *Accreditation:* AACSB. Part-time programs available. *Faculty:* 34 full-time (11 women). *Students:* 68 full-time (28 women), 106 part-time (55 women); includes 18 minority (8 African Americans, 3 American Indian/Alaska Native, 3 Asian Americans or Pacific Islanders, 4 Hispanic Americans), 17 international. Average age 28. 122 applicants, 43% accepted, 38 enrolled. In 2006, 63 degrees awarded. *Entrance requirements:* For master's, GMAT, minimum GPA of 2.75. *Application deadline:* For fall admission, 5/15 for domestic and international students; for spring admission, 10/1 for domestic and international students. Application fee: $25 ($30 for international students). *Expenses:* Tuition, state resident: full-time $3,247; part-time $93 per credit hour. Tuition, nonresident: full-time $9,427; part-time $350 per credit hour. *Financial support:* In 2006–07, 15 research assistantships with full tuition reimbursements (averaging $5,500 per year) were awarded; Federal Work-Study, tuition waivers (full), and unspecified assistantships also available. Support available to part-time students. Financial award application deadline: 5/1. *Unit head:* Ellen Cook, Acting Dean, 337-482-6491, Fax: 337-482-5883, E-mail: edcook@louisiana.edu. *Application contact:* Dr. P. Robert Viguerie, Director, MBA, 337-482-6119, Fax: 337-482-5883, E-mail: mbadirector@louisiana.edu.

University of Maryland, Baltimore County, Graduate School, College of Arts, Humanities and Social Sciences, Department of Emergency Health Services, Baltimore, MD 21250. Offers administration, planning, and policy (MS); education (MS); emergency health services (MS); preventive medicine and epidemiology (MS). Part-time and evening/weekend programs available. Postbaccalaureate distance learning degree programs offered (no on-campus study). *Faculty:* 4 full-time (0 women), 7 part-time/adjunct (1 woman). *Students:* 3 full-time (2 women), 32 part-time (12 women); includes 3 African Americans, 1 American Indian/Alaska Native, 3 Hispanic Americans. Average age 33. 22 applicants, 59% accepted, 11 enrolled. In 2006, 9 degrees awarded. *Median time to degree:* Master's–2.3 years full-time, 5 years part-time. *Degree requirements:* For master's, thesis (for some programs), comprehensive exam. *Entrance requirements:* For master's, GRE General Test, minimum GPA of 3.0. Additional exam requirements/recommendations for international students: Required—TOEFL (minimum score 550 paper-based; 213 computer-based; 80 iBT). *Application deadline:* For fall admission, 7/1 for domestic students. Applications are processed on a rolling basis. Application fee: $45. *Expenses:* Tuition, state resident: part-time $412 per credit hour. Tuition, nonresident: part-time $681 per credit hour. Required fees: $91 per credit hour. One-time fee: $75 part-time. *Financial support:* In 2006–07, fellowships with tuition reimbursements (averaging $55,000 per year), research assistantships with tuition reimbursements (averaging $21,000 per year) were awarded; teaching assistantships, career-related internships or fieldwork, Federal Work-Study, health care benefits, and unspecified assistantships also available. Financial award application deadline: 5/30; financial award applicants required to submit FAFSA. *Faculty research:* EMS management, disaster health services, emergency management. Total annual research expenditures: $500,000. *Unit head:* Dr. Bruce Walz, Chairman, 410-455-3223. *Application contact:* Dr. Rick Bissell, Program Director, 410-455-3776, Fax: 410-455-3045, E-mail: bissell@umbc.edu.

University of Maryland University College, Graduate School of Management and Technology, Program in Health Care Administration, Adelphi, MD 20783. Offers MS, Certificate. Part-time and evening/weekend programs available. Postbaccalaureate distance learning degree programs offered (no on-campus study). *Students:* 5 full-time (2 women), 368 part-time (289 women); includes 190 minority (160 African Americans, 1 American Indian/Alaska Native, 12 Asian Americans or Pacific Islanders, 17 Hispanic Americans), 3 international. Average age 36. 96 applicants, 100% accepted, 66 enrolled. In 2006, 79 master's, 1 other advanced degree awarded. *Degree requirements:* For master's, thesis or alternative. *Application deadline:* Applications are processed on a rolling basis. Application fee: $50. Electronic applications accepted. *Financial support:* Federal Work-Study and scholarships/grants available. Support available to part-time students. Financial award application deadline: 6/1; financial award applicants required to submit FAFSA. *Unit head:* Dr. Kathleen Edwards, Head, 301-985-7200, Fax: 301-985-4611, E-mail: kedwards@umuc.edu. *Application contact:* Coordinator, Graduate Admissions, 301-985-7155, Fax: 301-985-7175, E-mail: gradinfo@umuc.edu.

University of Massachusetts Boston, Office of Graduate Studies, John W. McCormack Graduate School of Policy Studies, Program in Gerontology, Boston, MA 02125-3393. Offers gerontology (MS, PhD, Certificate); gerontology research (MA); management in aging services (MA). Part-time programs available. *Students:* 6 full-time (5 women), 26 part-time (25 women). Average age 40. 22 applicants, 55% accepted, 4 enrolled. In 2006, 7 master's, 2 doctorates awarded. *Median time to degree:* Master's–2 years full-time; doctorate–6 years full-time. *Degree requirements:* For doctorate, thesis/dissertation, comprehensive exam. *Entrance requirements:* For doctorate, GRE General Test, minimum GPA of 3.0. *Application deadline:* For fall admission, 2/1 for domestic students. Application fee: $40 ($50 for international students). *Expenses:* Tuition, state resident: full-time $2,590; part-time $301 per credit. Tuition, nonresident: full-time $9,758; part-time $427 per credit. One-time fee: $495 full-time. *Financial support:* In 2006–07, 8 research assistantships with full tuition reimbursements (averaging $13,000 per year), 4 teaching assistantships with full tuition reimbursements (averaging $8,500 per year) were awarded; career-related internships or fieldwork, Federal Work-Study, and unspecified assistantships also available. Support available to part-time students. Financial award application deadline: 3/1; financial award applicants required to submit FAFSA. *Faculty research:* Aging with a chronic disability, pension policy and social security system, elderly minorities, health services research, living arrangements. *Unit head:* Dr. Ellen Bruce, Director, 617-287-7300, E-mail: ellen.bruce@umb.edu. *Application contact:* Peggy Roldan, Graduate Admissions Coordinator, 617-287-6400, Fax: 617-287-6236, E-mail: bos.gadm@dpc.umassp.edu.

University of Massachusetts Lowell, Graduate School, College of Health Professions, Department of Health Services Administration, Lowell, MA 01854-2881. Offers MS. Part-time programs available. *Degree requirements:* For master's, thesis optional. *Entrance requirements:* For master's, GRE General Test. *Faculty research:* Alzheimer's disease, total quality management systems, information systems, market analysis.

University of Medicine and Dentistry of New Jersey, School of Health Related Professions, Department of Interdisciplinary Studies, Program in Health Systems, Newark, NJ 07107-1709. Offers MS. *Entrance requirements:* For master's, minimum GPA of 2.75. Additional exam requirements/recommendations for international students: Required—TOEFL. *Application deadline:* For fall admission, 5/15 for domestic students; for spring admission, 10/1 for domestic students. Applications are processed on a rolling basis. Application fee: $50. Electronic applications accepted. *Unit head:* Dr. Ann W. Tucker, Chairperson, Department of Interdisciplinary Studies, 856-566-6434, Fax: 856-566-6458, E-mail: tuckeraw@umdnj.edu.

University of Memphis, Graduate School, College of Arts and Sciences, School of Urban Affairs and Public Policy, Division of Health Administration, Memphis, TN 38152. Offers MHA. *Accreditation:* CAHME. *Faculty:* 3 full-time (1 woman), 4 part-time/adjunct (2 women). *Students:* 19 full-time (9 women), 12 part-time (8 women); includes 8 minority (3 African Americans, 4 Asian Americans or Pacific Islanders, 1 Hispanic American), 2 international. Average age 24. 18 applicants, 67% accepted. In 2006, 14 degrees awarded. *Degree requirements:* For master's, thesis or alternative, internship, comprehensive exam. *Entrance requirements:* For master's, GRE General Test or GMAT, minimum GPA of 3.0. *Application deadline:* For fall admission, 8/1 for domestic students; for spring admission, 12/1 for domestic students. Applications are processed on a rolling basis. Application fee: $25 ($50 for international students). *Faculty research:* Health insurance reform, health promotion/disease prevention, physician executives, healthcare access. *Unit head:* Dr. Lutchmie Narine, Director, 901-678-5552, Fax: 901-678-2981, E-mail: lnarine@memphis.edu.

University of Michigan, School of Public Health, Department of Health Management and Policy, Ann Arbor, MI 48109. Offers health management and policy (MHSA, MPH); health services organization and policy (PhD); JD/MHSA; MD/MPH; MHSA/MBA; MHSA/MNA; MHSA/MPP; MHSA/MSIOE; MPH/JD; MPH/MPP. PhD offered through the Horace H. Rackham School of Graduate Studies. *Accreditation:* CAHME (one or more programs are accredited). Part-time and evening/weekend programs available. *Degree requirements:* For doctorate, thesis/dissertation, oral defense of dissertation, preliminary exam. *Entrance requirements:* For master's, GMAT, GRE General Test; for doctorate, GRE General Test. Additional exam requirements/recommendations for international students: Required—TOEFL. Electronic applications accepted. *Faculty research:* Economics, long term care and aging, women's health, healthcare finance, understanding organization.

University of Minnesota, Twin Cities Campus, Carlson School of Management, Carlson Full-time MBA Program, Minneapolis, MN 55455-0213. Offers accounting (MBA); entrepreneurship (MBA); finance (MBA); healthcare management (MBA); information and decision sciences (MBA); international business (MBA); marketing and logistics management (MBA); operations and management science (MBA); strategic management and organization (MBA); supply chain management (MBA); JD/MBA; MD/MBA; MHA/MBA. *Accreditation:* AACSB. *Faculty:* 125 full-time (27 women), 120 part-time/adjunct. *Students:* 218 full-time (70 women); includes 18 minority (4 African Americans, 1 American Indian/Alaska Native, 10 Asian Americans or Pacific Islanders, 3 Hispanic Americans), 86 international. Average age 28. 418 applicants, 53% accepted, 124 enrolled. In 2006, 105 degrees awarded. *Median time to degree:* Master's–2 years full-time. *Entrance requirements:* For master's, GMAT. Additional exam requirements/recommendations for international students: Required—TOEFL (minimum score 580 paper-based; 240 computer-based), IELTS. *Application deadline:* For fall admission, 4/15 for domestic students, 2/15 for international students. Application fee: $60 ($90 for international students). Electronic applications accepted. *Expenses: Contact institution.* Full-time tuition and fees vary according to class time, course load, program, reciprocity agreements and student level. *Financial support:* In 2006–07, 131 students received support, including 127 fellowships with full and partial tuition reimbursements available (averaging $20,000 per year); research assistantships with partial tuition reimbursements available, teaching assistantships with partial tuition reimbursements available, career-related internships or fieldwork, Federal Work-Study, institutionally sponsored loans, scholarships/grants, health care benefits, tuition waivers (full and partial), and unspecified assistantships also available. Support available to part-time students. Financial award application deadline: 2/15; financial award applicants required to submit FAFSA. *Faculty research:* IT, strategy, marketing, finance, quality management. *Unit head:* Kathryn J. Carlson, MBA Programs and Executive Education, 612-624-2039, Fax: 612-625-1012, E-mail: fulltimeembainfo@csom.umn.edu. *Application contact:* Jeffrey Bieganek, Director, Admissions and Business Development, MBA Programs and Executive Education, 612-625-6558, Fax: 612-625-1012, E-mail: full-timembainfo@csom.umn.edu.

University of Minnesota, Twin Cities Campus, Graduate School, Program in Health Informatics, Minneapolis, MN 55455-0213. Offers MHI, MS, PhD, MD/MHI. Part-time programs available. *Faculty:* 19 full-time (6 women), 8 part-time/adjunct (1 woman). *Students:* 47 full-time (21 women), 8 part-time (3 women); includes 26 minority (2 African Americans, 24 Asian Americans or Pacific Islanders). Average age 34. 26 applicants, 81% accepted, 17 enrolled. In 2006, 3 master's, 1 doctorate awarded. *Median time to degree:* Master's–4 years full-time; doctorate–5 years full-time. *Degree requirements:* For master's, thesis or alternative;

Health Services Management and Hospital Administration

University of Minnesota, Twin Cities Campus (continued)
for doctorate, thesis/dissertation. *Entrance requirements:* For master's and doctorate, GRE General Test, previous course work in life sciences, programming, differential equations. Additional exam requirements/recommendations for international students: Required—TOEFL (minimum score 550 paper-based; 237 computer-based). *Application deadline:* For fall admission, 6/15 for domestic and international students; for winter admission, 10/15 for domestic and international students; for spring admission, 3/15 for domestic and international students. Applications are processed on a rolling basis. Application fee: $75. Electronic applications accepted. *Expenses:* Tuition, state resident: full-time $9,302; part-time $775 per credit. Tuition, nonresident: full-time $16,400; part-time $1,367 per credit. Full-time tuition and fees vary according to class time, course load, program, reciprocity agreements and student level. *Financial support:* In 2006–07, 26 students received support, including 9 fellowships with full tuition reimbursements available (averaging $39,785 per year), 16 research assistantships with full and partial tuition reimbursements available (averaging $16,598 per year), 1 teaching assistantship with full and partial tuition reimbursement available (averaging $16,598 per year); Federal Work-Study, scholarships/grants, traineeships, and tuition waivers (full and partial) also available. Financial award application deadline: 1/15. *Faculty research:* Medical decision making, physiological control systems, population studies, clinical information systems, telemedicine. Total annual research expenditures: $1.4 million. *Unit head:* Dr. Stuart Speedie, Director of Graduate Studies, 612-625-8440, Fax: 612-625-7166, E-mail: speed002@umn.edu. *Application contact:* Doreen Gruebele, Executive Administrative Specialist, 612-625-8440, Fax: 612-625-7166, E-mail: doreen@umn.edu.

University of Minnesota, Twin Cities Campus, School of Public Health, Department of Healthcare Management, Minneapolis, MN 55455-0213. Offers MHA. *Accreditation:* AACSB; CAHME. Part-time and evening/weekend programs available. Postbaccalaureate distance learning degree programs offered (minimal on-campus study). *Entrance requirements:* For master's, GMAT or GRE General Test, minimum GPA of 3.0. Additional exam requirements/recommendations for international students: Required—TOEFL (minimum score 580 paper-based). Electronic applications accepted. Expenses: Contact institution. Full-time tuition and fees vary according to class time, course load, program, reciprocity agreements and student level. *Faculty research:* Managed care, physician payment, structure and performance of healthcare systems, long-term care.

Announcement: Minnesota's MHA has earned a national reputation for excellence in educating leaders for the health-care industry. A strong curriculum, blending advanced management theory with practical experience in health-care settings, draws upon the rich resources of a dynamic and innovative health-care community in Minneapolis–St. Paul. Paid residency, personal coaching, individualized placement, dual degrees, ranked 2nd in the nation.

See Close-Up on page 1823.

University of Minnesota, Twin Cities Campus, School of Public Health, Major in Health Services Research, Policy, and Administration, Minneapolis, MN 55455-0213. Offers MS, PhD, JD/MS, JD/PhD, MD/PhD, MPP/MS. Part-time programs available. Terminal master's awarded for partial completion of doctoral program. *Degree requirements:* For master's, thesis, internship, final oral exam; for doctorate, thesis/dissertation, teaching experience, written preliminary exam, final oral exam. *Entrance requirements:* For master's, GRE General Test, course work in mathematics; for doctorate, GRE General Test, prerequisite courses in calculus, statistics and microeconomics. Additional exam requirements/recommendations for international students: Required—TOEFL (minimum score 600 paper-based; 250 computer-based). *Expenses:* Tuition, state resident: full-time $9,302; part-time $775 per credit. Tuition, nonresident: full-time $16,400; part-time $1,367 per credit. Full-time tuition and fees vary according to class time, course load, program, reciprocity agreements and student level. *Faculty research:* Outcomes, economics and statistics, sociology, health care management.

University of Minnesota, Twin Cities Campus, School of Public Health, Major in Public Health Administration and Policy, Minneapolis, MN 55455-0213. Offers MPH, MPH/JD, MPH/MSN. Part-time programs available. *Degree requirements:* For master's, thesis, field experience. *Entrance requirements:* For master's, GRE General Test. Additional exam requirements/recommendations for international students: Required—TOEFL. Electronic applications accepted. *Expenses:* Tuition, state resident: full-time $9,302; part-time $775 per credit. Tuition, nonresident: full-time $16,400; part-time $1,367 per credit. Full-time tuition and fees vary according to class time, course load, program, reciprocity agreements and student level. *Faculty research:* Community health service organizations, nursing services, dental services, the elderly, insurance coverage.

University of Missouri–Columbia, Graduate School, Department of Health Management and Informatics, Columbia, MO 65211. Offers health administration (MHA); health informatics (MHA); health services management (MHA). *Accreditation:* CAHME. Part-time programs available. *Faculty:* 15 full-time (4 women), 1 (woman) part-time/adjunct. *Students:* 75 full-time (42 women), 23 part-time (11 women); includes 15 minority (10 African Americans, 2 Asian Americans or Pacific Islanders, 3 Hispanic Americans), 26 international. In 2006, 12 degrees awarded. *Entrance requirements:* For master's, GRE General Test or GMAT, minimum GPA of 3.0. Additional exam requirements/recommendations for international students: Required—TOEFL (minimum score 500 paper-based; 173 computer-based). Application fee: $45 ($60 for international students). *Financial support:* Fellowships, research assistantships, teaching assistantships, institutionally sponsored loans available. *Unit head:* Dr. Robert DeGraaff, Director of Graduate Studies, 573-882-1783, E-mail: degraaffr@missouri.edu.

University of Missouri–St. Louis, Graduate School, Program in Gerontology, St. Louis, MO 63121. Offers gerontology (MS, Certificate); long term care administration (Certificate). Part-time and evening/weekend programs available. *Faculty:* 10 full-time (4 women), 7 part-time/adjunct (all women). *Students:* 5 full-time (4 women), 16 part-time (12 women); includes 4 minority (3 African Americans, 1 Asian American or Pacific Islander), 1 international. Average age 39. In 2006, 4 degrees awarded. *Entrance requirements:* For master's, 3 letters of recommendation. Additional exam requirements/recommendations for international students: Required—TOEFL (minimum score 550 paper-based; 213 computer-based). *Application deadline:* For fall admission, 7/15 priority date for domestic students; for spring admission, 12/15 priority date for domestic students. Applications are processed on a rolling basis. Application fee: $35 ($40 for international students). Electronic applications accepted. *Expenses:* Tuition, state resident: part-time $332 per credit hour. Tuition, nonresident: part-time $770 per credit hour. *Financial support:* Research assistantships with full tuition reimbursements, teaching assistantships with full tuition reimbursements, career-related internships or fieldwork and Federal Work-Study available. *Faculty research:* Health care policy, social support and stress, retirement policy health behavior, ethnic differences in aging. *Unit head:* Diane O'Brien, Director, 314-516-5421, E-mail: obriendia@umsl.edu. *Application contact:* 314-516-5458, Fax: 314-516-6996, E-mail: gradadm@umsl.edu.

University of Missouri–St. Louis, Graduate School, Program in Public Policy Administration, St. Louis, MO 63121. Offers health policy (MPPA); local government management (MPPA); managing human resources and organization (MPPA); nonprofit organization management (MPPA); nonprofit organization management and leadership (Certificate); policy research and analysis (MPPA); public sector human resources management (MPPA). *Accreditation:* NASPAA. Part-time and evening/weekend programs available. *Faculty:* 8 full-time (5 women), 5 part-time/adjunct (1 woman). *Students:* 21 full-time (13 women), 61 part-time (35 women); includes 22 minority (18 African Americans, 1 American Indian/Alaska Native, 2 Asian Americans or Pacific Islanders, 1 Hispanic American), 4 international. Average age 34. In 2006, 22 degrees awarded. *Entrance requirements:* For master's, 3 letters of recommendation. Additional exam requirements/recommendations for international students: Required—TOEFL (minimum score 550 paper-based; 213 computer-based). *Application deadline:* For fall admission, 7/15 priority date for domestic students; for spring admission, 12/15 priority date for domestic students. Applications are processed on a rolling basis. Application fee: $35 ($40 for international students). Electronic applications accepted. *Expenses:* Tuition, state resident: part-time $332 per credit hour. Tuition, nonresident: part-time $770 per credit hour. *Financial support:* In 2006–07, 2 research assistantships with full tuition reimbursements (averaging $14,100 per year) were awarded; teaching assistantships with partial tuition reimbursements, career-related internships or fieldwork also available. *Faculty research:* Urban policy, public finance, evaluation. *Unit head:* Brady Baybeck, Director, 314-516-5145, Fax: 314-516-5210, E-mail: baybeck@umsl.edu. *Application contact:* 314-516-5458, Fax: 314-516-6996, E-mail: gradadm@umsl.edu.

University of New Hampshire, Graduate School, School of Health and Human Services, Department of Health Management and Policy, Durham, NH 03824. Offers public health: ecology (MPH); public health: nursing (MPH); public health: policy and management (MPH). *Accreditation:* CEPH. Part-time and evening/weekend programs available. *Faculty:* 9 full-time. *Students:* 16 full-time (14 women), 34 part-time (25 women); includes 3 minority (1 African American, 1 Asian American or Pacific Islander, 1 Hispanic American). Average age 29. 29 applicants, 90% accepted, 14 enrolled. In 2006, 15 degrees awarded. *Entrance requirements:* For master's, GMAT or GRE General Test. Additional exam requirements/recommendations for international students: Required—TOEFL (minimum score 550 paper-based; 213 computer-based). *Application deadline:* For fall admission, 4/1 priority date for domestic students, 4/1 for international students. Applications are processed on a rolling basis. Application fee: $60. Electronic applications accepted. *Expenses: Contact institution.* Tuition and fees vary according to course load, program and reciprocity agreements. *Financial support:* In 2006–07, 1 fellowship was awarded; research assistantships, teaching assistantships, scholarships/grants also available. Financial award application deadline: 2/15. *Unit head:* Dr. John Seavey, Chairperson, 603-862-3414. *Application contact:* Chris Hamann, Administrative Assistant, 603-862-2733, E-mail: masterof.publichealth@unh.edu.

University of New Haven, Graduate School, School of Business, Program in Business Administration, West Haven, CT 06516-1916. Offers accounting (MBA); business policy and strategy (MBA); finance (MBA); health care management (MBA); human resources management (MBA); international business (MBA); marketing (MBA); public relations (MBA); sports management (MBA); technology management (MBA); MBA/MPA; MBA/MSIE. Part-time and evening/weekend programs available. *Degree requirements:* For master's, thesis or alternative. *Entrance requirements:* For master's, GMAT.

University of New Haven, Graduate School, School of Business, Program in Health Care Administration, West Haven, CT 06516-1916. Offers MS. *Degree requirements:* For master's, thesis or alternative.

University of New Haven, Graduate School, School of Business, Program in Public Administration, West Haven, CT 06516-1916. Offers health care management (MPA); personnel and labor relations (MPA); MBA/MPA. Part-time and evening/weekend programs available. *Degree requirements:* For master's, thesis or alternative.

University of New Orleans, Graduate School, College of Business Administration, Program in Health Care Management, New Orleans, LA 70148. Offers MS. *Students:* 54 (37 women). Average age 33. In 2006, 32 degrees awarded. *Degree requirements:* For master's, thesis optional. *Entrance requirements:* For master's, GRE or GMAT. Additional exam requirements/recommendations for international students: Required—TOEFL (minimum score 550 paper-based; 213 computer-based). *Application deadline:* For fall admission, 7/1 priority date for domestic students, 6/1 for international students; for spring admission, 11/15 priority date for domestic students, 10/1 for international students. Applications are processed on a rolling basis. Application fee: $40. Electronic applications accepted. *Financial support:* Application deadline: 5/15; *Unit head:* Dr. Walter Lane, Chairperson, 504-280-7145, Fax: 504-280-6397, E-mail: wlane@uno.edu. *Application contact:* Dr. Paul Hensel, Associate Dean, 504-280-6954, Fax: 504-280-6693, E-mail: phensel@uno.edu.

The University of North Carolina at Chapel Hill, Graduate School, School of Public Health, Department of Health Policy and Administration, Chapel Hill, NC 27599. Offers MHA, MPH, MSPH, Dr PH, PhD, DDS/MPH, JD/MPH, MBA/MHA, MD/MPH, MHA/MBA, MHA/MSIS, MHA/MSLS. *Accreditation:* CAHME (one or more programs are accredited). Part-time programs available. Postbaccalaureate distance learning degree programs offered (minimal on-campus study). *Faculty:* 33 full-time (12 women), 65 part-time/adjunct. *Students:* 305 full-time (195 women); includes 50 minority (26 African Americans, 1 American Indian/Alaska Native, 13 Asian Americans or Pacific Islanders, 10 Hispanic Americans), 30 international. Average age 28. 405 applicants, 40% accepted, 103 enrolled. In 2006, 113 master's, 7 doctorates awarded. *Median time to degree:* Of those who began their doctoral program in fall 1998, 100% received their degree in 8 years or less. *Degree requirements:* For master's, capstone course or master's paper; for doctorate, thesis/dissertation, comprehensive exam, registration. *Entrance requirements:* For master's and doctorate, GRE General Test, minimum GPA of 3.0. Additional exam requirements/recommendations for international students: Required—TOEFL. *Application deadline:* For fall admission, 1/1 priority date for domestic and international students. Applications are processed on a rolling basis. Application fee: $70. Electronic applications accepted. *Financial support:* In 2006–07, 2 fellowships with full and partial tuition reimbursements (averaging $37,607 per year), 12 research assistantships with full and partial tuition reimbursements (averaging $11,104 per year), 38 teaching assistantships with full and partial tuition reimbursements (averaging $8,791 per year) were awarded; career-related internships or fieldwork, Federal Work-Study, institutionally sponsored loans, scholarships/grants, health care benefits, and unspecified assistantships also available. Financial award application deadline: 1/1; financial award applicants required to submit FAFSA. *Faculty research:* Organizational behavior; human resource management in healthcare; health services finance; mental health economics, service, and research; strategic planning and marketing. *Unit head:* Dr. Peggy Leatt, Chair, 919-843-2748, Fax: 919-966-6961, E-mail: leatt@email.unc.edu. *Application contact:* Cara Doyle, Student Services Manager, 919-966-7391, Fax: 919-966-6961, E-mail: doylec@email.unc.edu.

The University of North Carolina at Charlotte, Graduate School, College of Health and Human Services, Department of Health Behavior and Administration, Charlotte, NC 28223-0001. Offers health behavior and administration (MHA); public health (MSPH). *Faculty:* 10 full-time (5 women), 5 part-time/adjunct (2 women). *Students:* 40 full-time (26 women), 14 part-time (10 women); includes 14 minority (9 African Americans, 5 Asian Americans or Pacific Islanders), 12 international. Average age 30. 44 applicants, 93% accepted, 15 enrolled. In 2006, 16 degrees awarded. *Degree requirements:* For master's, thesis or comprehensive exam. *Entrance requirements:* For master's, GRE or MAT (public health), GRE or GMAT (health administration), minimum GPA of 3.0 during previous 2 years, 2.75 overall. Additional exam requirements/recommendations for international students: Required—TOEFL (minimum score 557 paper-based; 220 computer-based). *Application deadline:* For fall admission, 7/1 for domestic students, 5/1 for international students; for spring admission, 11/1 for domestic students, 10/1 for international students. Applications are processed on a rolling basis. Application fee: $55. Electronic applications accepted. *Expenses:* Tuition, state resident: full-time $2,719; part-time $170 per credit. Tuition, nonresident: full-time $12,926; part-time $808 per credit. Required fees: $1,555. *Financial support:* In 2006–07, 3 research assistantships (averaging $7,940 per year) were awarded; fellowships, teaching assistantships, career-related internships or fieldwork, Federal Work-Study, institutionally sponsored loans, scholarships/grants, and unspecified assistantships also available. Support available to part-time students. Financial award application deadline: 4/1; financial award applicants required to submit FAFSA. *Faculty research:* Pediatric asthma self-management, reproductive epidemiology, social aspects of injury prevention, chronic illness self-care, competency-based professional education. Total annual research expenditures: $561,332. *Unit head:* Dr. Andrew R. Harver, Chair, 704-687-2957, Fax: 704-687-6122, E-mail: arharver@email.uncc.edu. *Application contact:* Kathy B. Giddings, Director of Graduate Admissions, 704-687-3366, Fax: 704-687-3279, E-mail: gradadm@email.uncc.edu.

University of North Florida, College of Health, Department of Public Health, Jacksonville, FL 32224-2645. Offers community health (MPH); geriatric management (MSH); health administration (MHA); health behavior research and evaluation (Certificate); nutrition (MSH); rehabilitation counseling (MS). *Accreditation:* CORE. Part-time and evening/weekend programs available. *Faculty:* 21 full-time (16 women). *Students:* 78 full-time (60 women), 54 part-time (40 women); includes 31 minority (16 African Americans, 7 Asian Americans or Pacific Islanders, 8 Hispanic Americans), 10 international. Average age 32. 136 applicants, 47% accepted, 38 enrolled. In 2006, 50 degrees awarded. *Degree requirements:* For master's, thesis optional. *Entrance requirements:* For master's, GRE General Test (MSH, MS, MPH), GMAT or GRE General Test (MHA), minimum GPA of 3.0 in last 60 hours. Additional exam requirements/recommendations for international students: Required—TOEFL (minimum score 500 paper-based; 173 computer-based). *Application deadline:* For fall admission, 7/1 priority date for domestic students, 5/1 for international students; for spring admission, 11/10 priority date for domestic students, 10/1 for international students. Applications are processed on a rolling basis. Application fee: $30. Electronic applications accepted. *Expenses:* Tuition, state resident: full-time $4,948; part-time $206 per semester hour. Tuition, nonresident: full-time $19,140; part-time $408 per semester hour. *Financial support:* In 2006–07, 64 students received support, including 11 teaching assistantships (averaging $2,942 per year); research assistantships, career-related internships or fieldwork, Federal Work-Study, scholarships/grants, and tuition waivers (partial) also available. Support available to part-time students. Financial award application deadline: 4/1; financial award applicants required to submit FAFSA. *Faculty research:* Dietary supplements; alcohol, tobacco, and other drug use prevention; turnover among health professionals; aging; psychosocial aspects of disabilities. Total annual research expenditures: $438,597. *Unit head:* Dr. Judith Perkin, Chair, 904-620-2840, Fax: 904-620-2848, E-mail: jperkin@unf.edu. *Application contact:* Rachel Broderick, Director of Advising, 904-620-2817, Fax: 904-620-1770, E-mail: rbroderi@unf.edu.

University of North Texas Health Science Center at Fort Worth, School of Public Health, Fort Worth, TX 76107-2699. Offers biostatistics (MPH); community health (MPH); disease control and prevention (Dr PH); environmental health (MPH); epidemiology (MPH); health behavior (MPH); health policy and management (MPH, Dr PH); DO/MPH; MA/MPH; MS/MPH; PhD/MPH. *Accreditation:* CEPH. Part-time and evening/weekend programs available. *Degree requirements:* For master's, thesis or alternative, supervised internship; for doctorate, thesis/dissertation, supervised internship. *Entrance requirements:* For master's, GRE General Test. Additional exam requirements/recommendations for international students: Required—TOEFL. Electronic applications accepted.

University of Oklahoma Health Sciences Center, Graduate College, College of Public Health, Department of Health Administration and Policy, Oklahoma City, OK 73190. Offers MHA, MPH, MS, Dr PH, PhD, JD/MPH, MBA/MPH. *Accreditation:* CAHME. Part-time programs available. *Degree requirements:* For master's, thesis (for some programs), comprehensive exam; for doctorate, 2 foreign languages, thesis/dissertation, comprehensive exam. *Entrance requirements:* For master's, 3 letters of recommendation, resumé; for doctorate, GRE General Test, letters of recommendation. Additional exam requirements/recommendations for international students: Required—TOEFL (minimum score 570 paper-based; 230 computer-based). *Faculty research:* Public health administration, health institutions management, public policy and the aged, injury control.

University of Ottawa, Faculty of Graduate and Postdoctoral Studies, School of Management, Health Administration Program, Ottawa, ON K1N 6N5, Canada. Offers MHA. Part-time programs available. *Degree requirements:* For master's, residency, thesis optional. *Entrance requirements:* For master's, GMAT, bachelor's degree or equivalent, minimum B average. Additional exam requirements/recommendations for international students: Recommended—TOEFL (minimum score 237 computer-based). Electronic applications accepted.

University of Pennsylvania, Wharton School, Health Care Systems Department, Philadelphia, PA 19104. Offers AM, MBA, PhD. *Accreditation:* CAHME (one or more programs are accredited). *Degree requirements:* For doctorate, thesis/dissertation, comprehensive exam. *Entrance requirements:* For master's, GMAT; for doctorate, GMAT or GRE. Electronic applications accepted. *Faculty research:* Health economics, health policy, health care management, health insurance and financing.

University of Phoenix–Atlanta Campus, The Artemis School, College of Health and Human Services, Sandy Springs, GA 30350-4153. Offers health care management (MBA). Evening/weekend programs available. *Faculty:* 9 full-time (5 women), 56 part-time/adjunct (24 women). *Students:* 52 full-time (38 women); includes 28 minority (26 African Americans, 2 Asian Americans or Pacific Islanders). In 2006, 26 degrees awarded. *Degree requirements:* For master's, thesis (for some programs), registration. *Entrance requirements:* For master's, minimum undergraduate GPA of 2.5, 3 years of work experience. Additional exam requirements/recommendations for international students: Required—TOEFL (minimum score 550 paper-based; 213 computer-based; 79 iBT). *Application deadline:* Applications are processed on a rolling basis. Application fee: $45. Electronic applications accepted. *Expenses:* Tuition: Full-time $10,560. Required fees: $760. *Financial support:* Institutionally sponsored loans and scholarships/grants available. Financial award applicants required to submit FAFSA. *Unit head:* Dr. Gil Linne, Dean/Executive Director, 480-557-1221, E-mail: gil.linne@phoenix.edu.

University of Phoenix–Augusta Campus, College of Health and Human Services, Augusta, GA 30909-4583. Offers health administration (MHA); health care management (MBA); nursing (MSN); MSN/MHA.

University of Phoenix–Austin Campus, College of Health and Human Services, Austin, TX 78759. Offers health administration (MHA); health care management (MBA).

University of Phoenix–Bay Area Campus, The Artemis School, College of Health and Human Services, Pleasanton, CA 94588-3677. Offers administration of justice and security (MS); family nurse practitioner (MSN); health care management (MBA); marriage, family and child therapy (MSC). Evening/weekend programs available. *Faculty:* 19 full-time (8 women), 184 part-time/adjunct (85 women). *Students:* 58 full-time (51 women); includes 22 minority (6 African Americans, 12 Asian Americans or Pacific Islanders, 4 Hispanic Americans), 6 international. Average age 42. In 2006, 13 degrees awarded. *Degree requirements:* For master's, thesis (for some programs), registration. *Entrance requirements:* For master's, minimum undergraduate GPA of 2.5, 3 years of work experience, RN license. Additional exam requirements/recommendations for international students: Required—TOEFL (minimum score 550 paper-based; 213 computer-based; 79 iBT). *Application deadline:* Applications are processed on a rolling basis. Application fee: $45. Electronic applications accepted. *Expenses:* Tuition: Full-time $12,648. Required fees: $760. *Financial support:* Institutionally sponsored loans and scholarships/grants available. Financial award applicants required to submit FAFSA. *Unit head:* Dr. Gil Linne, Dean/Executive Director, 480-557-1751, E-mail: gil.linne@phoenix.edu. *Application contact:* Chair, 877-416-4100.

University of Phoenix–Central Florida Campus, The Artemis School, College of Health and Human Services, Maitland, FL 32751-7057. Offers health administration (MHA); health and human services (MSN); health care management (MBA). Evening/weekend programs available. *Faculty:* 24 full-time (17 women), 46 part-time/adjunct (27 women). *Students:* 49 full-time (46 women); includes 15 minority (8 African Americans, 2 Asian Americans or Pacific Islanders, 5 Hispanic Americans), 7 international. Average age 44. In 2006, 43 degrees awarded. *Degree requirements:* For master's, thesis (for some programs), registration. *Entrance requirements:* For master's, minimum undergraduate GPA of 2.5, 3 years work experience, RN license. Additional exam requirements/recommendations for international students: Required—TOEFL (minimum score 550 paper-based; 213 computer-based; 79 iBT). *Application deadline:* Applications are processed on a rolling basis. Application fee: $45. Electronic applications accepted. *Expenses:* Tuition: Full-time $9,450. Required fees: $760. *Financial support:* Institutionally sponsored loans and scholarships/grants available. Financial award applicants required to submit FAFSA. *Unit head:* Dr. Gil Linne, Dean/Executive Director, 480-557-1751, E-mail: gil.linne@phoenix.edu. *Application contact:* Chair, 407-667-0525, Fax: 407-667-0560.

University of Phoenix–Central Valley Campus, College of Health and Human Services, Fresno, CA 93720. Offers health care management (MBA); nursing (MSN).

University of Phoenix–Chattanooga Campus, College of Health and Human Services, Chattanooga, TN 37421-3707. Offers health care management (MBA).

University of Phoenix–Cheyenne Campus, College of Health and Human Services, Cheyenne, WY 82009. Offers health administration (MHA); health care education (MSN); health care management (MBA); nursing (MSN); MSN/MBA; MSN/MHA.

University of Phoenix–Cincinnati Campus, The Artemis School, College of Health and Human Services, West Chester, OH 45069-4875. Offers health care management (MBA). Evening/weekend programs available. *Degree requirements:* For master's, thesis (for some programs), registration. *Entrance requirements:* For master's, minimum undergraduate GPA of 2.5, 3 years of work experience. Additional exam requirements/recommendations for international students: Required—TOEFL (minimum score 550 paper-based; 79 iBT). *Application deadline:* Applications are processed on a rolling basis. Application fee: $45. Electronic applications accepted. *Expenses:* Tuition: Full-time $11,832. Required fees: $760. *Financial support:* Institutionally sponsored loans and scholarships/grants available. Financial award applicants required to submit FAFSA. *Unit head:* Dr. Gil Linne, Dean/Executive Director, 480-557-1221, E-mail: gil.linne@phoenix.edu. *Application contact:* College Chair, 573-772-9600.

University of Phoenix–Cleveland Campus, The Artemis School, College of Health and Human Services, Independence, OH 44131-2194. Offers administration of justice and security (MS); health care management (MBA); nursing (MSN); psychology (MS). Evening/weekend programs available. *Faculty:* 3 full-time (0 women), 24 part-time/adjunct (18 women). *Students:* 23 full-time (all women); includes 9 minority (all African Americans), 3 international. Average age 47. In 2006, 3 degrees awarded. *Degree requirements:* For master's, thesis (for some programs), registration. *Entrance requirements:* For master's, minimum undergraduate GPA of 2.5, 3 years of work experience. Additional exam requirements/recommendations for international students: Required—TOEFL (minimum score 550 paper-based; 213 computer-based; 79 iBT). *Application deadline:* Applications are processed on a rolling basis. Application fee: $45. Electronic applications accepted. *Expenses:* Tuition: Full-time $11,608. Required fees: $760. *Financial support:* Institutionally sponsored loans and scholarships/grants available. Financial award applicants required to submit FAFSA. *Unit head:* Dr. Gil Linne, Dean/Executive Director, 480-557-1751, E-mail: gil.linne@phoenix.edu. *Application contact:* Campus College Chair, 216-447-8807.

University of Phoenix–Columbus Georgia Campus, The Artemis School, College of Health and Human Services, Columbus, GA 31904-6321. Offers health care management (MBA). *Faculty:* 11 full-time (4 women), 25 part-time/adjunct (12 women). *Students:* 7 full-time (5 women); includes 3 minority (2 African Americans, 1 Hispanic American). Average age 38. In 2006, 10 master's awarded. *Degree requirements:* For master's, thesis (for some programs), registration. *Entrance requirements:* For master's, minimum undergraduate GPA of 2.5, 3 years of work experience. Additional exam requirements/recommendations for international students: Required—TOEFL (minimum score 550 paper-based; 213 computer-based; 79 iBT). *Application deadline:* Applications are processed on a rolling basis. Application fee: $45. Electronic applications accepted. *Expenses:* Tuition: Full-time $10,200. Required fees: $760. *Financial support:* Institutionally sponsored loans and scholarships/grants available. Financial award applicants required to submit FAFSA. *Unit head:* Dr. Gil Linne Linne, Dean/Executive Director, 480-557-1751, E-mail: gil.linne@phoenix.edu.

University of Phoenix–Columbus Ohio Campus, The Artemis School, College of Health and Human Services, Columbus, OH 43240-4032. Offers health care management (MBA). Evening/weekend programs available. *Degree requirements:* For master's, thesis (for some programs), registration. *Entrance requirements:* For master's, minimum undergraduate GPA of 2.5, 3 years work experience. Additional exam requirements/recommendations for international students: Required—TOEFL (minimum score 550 paper-based; 213 computer-based; 79 iBT). *Application deadline:* Applications are processed on a rolling basis. Application fee: $45. Electronic applications accepted. *Expenses:* Tuition: Full-time $11,832. Required fees: $760. *Financial support:* Institutionally sponsored loans and scholarships/grants available. Financial award applicants required to submit FAFSA. *Unit head:* Dr. Gil Linne, Dean/Executive Director, 480-557-1221, E-mail: gil.linne@phoenix.edu. *Application contact:* College Chair, 614-433-0095.

University of Phoenix–Dallas Campus, The Artemis School, College of Health and Human Services, Dallas, TX 75251-2009. Offers health care management (MBA). *Faculty:* 6 part-time/adjunct (1 woman). *Students:* 32 full-time (22 women); includes 14 minority (11 African Americans, 3 Hispanic Americans), 3 international. Average age 37. In 2006, 11 degrees awarded. *Degree requirements:* For master's, thesis (for some programs), registration. *Entrance requirements:* For master's, minimum undergraduate GPA of 2.5, 3 years of work experience. Additional exam requirements/recommendations for international students: Required—TOEFL (minimum score 550 paper-based; 213 computer-based; 79 iBT). *Application deadline:* Applications are processed on a rolling basis. Application fee: $45. Electronic applications accepted. *Expenses:* Tuition: Full-time $11,832. Required fees: $760. *Financial support:* Institutionally sponsored loans and scholarships/grants available. *Unit head:* Dr. Gil Linne, Dean/Executive Director, 480-557-1221, E-mail: gil.linne@phoenix.edu. *Application contact:* Chair, 972-385-1055, Fax: 972-385-1700.

University of Phoenix–Denver Campus, The Artemis School, College of Health and Human Services, Lone Tree, CO 80124-5453. Offers community counseling (MSC); health care management (MBA); marriage, family and child therapy (MSC); nursing (MSN). Evening/weekend programs available. *Faculty:* 17 full-time (7 women), 126 part-time/adjunct (62 women). *Students:* 147 full-time (114 women); includes 18 minority (9 African Americans, 1 American Indian/Alaska Native, 1 Asian American or Pacific Islander, 7 Hispanic Americans), 16 international. Average age 39. In 2006, 34 master's awarded. *Degree requirements:* For master's, thesis (for some programs), registration. *Entrance requirements:* For master's, minimum undergraduate GPA of 2.5, 3 years work experience, RN license. Additional exam requirements/recommendations for international students: Required—TOEFL (minimum score 550 paper-based; 213 computer-based; 79 iBT). *Application deadline:* Applications are processed on a rolling basis. Application fee: $45. Electronic applications accepted. *Expenses:* Tuition: Full-time $10,032. Required fees: $760. *Financial support:* Institutionally sponsored loans and scholarships/grants available. Financial award applicants required to submit FAFSA. *Unit head:* Dr. Gil Linne, Dean/Executive Director, 480-557-1751, E-mail: gil.linne@phoenix.edu. *Application contact:* Chair, 303-694-9093, Fax: 303-662-0911.

University of Phoenix–Des Moines Campus, College of Health and Human Services, Des Moines, IA 50266. Offers health care management (MBA).

University of Phoenix–Detroit Campus, College of Health and Human Services, Southfield, MI 48076. Offers family nurse practitioner (MSN); health administration (MHA); health care management (MBA); nursing (MSN); MSN/MBA.

University of Phoenix–Eastern Washington Campus, The Artemis School, College of Health and Human Services, Spokane Valley, WA 99212-2531. Offers health care management (MBA). Evening/weekend programs available. *Faculty:* 4 full-time (1 woman), 19 part-time/adjunct (5 women). *Students:* 1 full-time (0 women). Average age 27. *Degree requirements:* For master's, thesis (for some programs), registration. *Entrance requirements:* For master's, minimum undergraduate GPA of 2.5, 3 years of work experience. Additional exam requirements/recommendations for international students: Required—TOEFL (minimum score 550 paper-based; 213 computer-based; 79 iBT). *Application deadline:* Applications are processed on a rolling basis. Application fee: $45. Electronic applications accepted. *Expenses:* Tuition: Full-time $9,120. Required fees: $760. *Financial support:* Institutionally sponsored loans and

Health Services Management and Hospital Administration

University of Phoenix–Eastern Washington Campus (continued)
scholarships/grants available. Financial award applicants required to submit FAFSA. *Unit head:* Dr. Gil Linne, Dean/Executive Director, 480-557-1251, E-mail: gil.linne@phoenix.edu.

University of Phoenix–Fort Lauderdale Campus, The Artemis School, College of Health and Human Services, Fort Lauderdale, FL 33309. Offers health administration (MHA); health care education (MSN); health care management (MBA); nursing (MSN); MSN/MBA. Evening/weekend programs available. *Faculty:* 22 full-time (10 women), 56 part-time/adjunct (28 women). *Students:* 197 full-time (173 women); includes 73 minority (60 African Americans, 2 Asian Americans or Pacific Islanders, 11 Hispanic Americans), 33 international. Average age 43. In 2006, 52 degrees awarded. *Degree requirements:* For master's, thesis (for some programs), registration. *Entrance requirements:* For master's, minimum undergraduate GPA of 2.5, 3 years work experience, RN license. Additional exam requirements/recommendations for international students: Required—TOEFL (minimum score 550 paper-based; 213 computer-based; 79 iBT). *Application deadline:* Applications are processed on a rolling basis. Application fee: $45. Electronic applications accepted. *Expenses:* Tuition: Full-time $9,450. Required fees: $760. *Financial support:* Institutionally sponsored loans and scholarships/grants available. Financial award applicants required to submit FAFSA. *Unit head:* Dr. Gil Linne, Dean/Executive Director, 480-557-1751, E-mail: gil.linne@phoenix.edu. *Application contact:* 954-382-5303, Fax: 954-382-5303.

University of Phoenix–Harrisburg Campus, College of Health and Human Services, Harrisburg, PA 17112. Offers health administration (MHA); health care management (MBA); nursing (MSN); nursing/health care education (MSN); MSN/MBA; MSN/MHA.

University of Phoenix–Hawaii Campus, The Artemis School, College of Health and Human Services, Honolulu, HI 96813-4317. Offers administration of justice and security (MS); community counseling (MSC); family nurse practitioner (MSN); health administration (MHA); health care management (MBA); marriage, family and child therapy (MSC); nursing (MSN); psychology (MS). Evening/weekend programs available. *Faculty:* 20 full-time (12 women), 84 part-time/adjunct (46 women). *Students:* 47 full-time (36 women); includes 20 minority (2 African Americans, 15 Asian Americans or Pacific Islanders, 3 Hispanic Americans), 9 international. Average age 41. In 2006, 13 degrees awarded. *Degree requirements:* For master's, thesis (for some programs), registration. *Entrance requirements:* For master's, minimum undergraduate GPA of 2.5, 3 years of work experience, RN license. Additional exam requirements/recommendations for international students: Required—TOEFL (minimum score 550 paper-based; 213 computer-based; 79 iBT). *Application deadline:* Applications are processed on a rolling basis. Application fee: $45. Electronic applications accepted. *Expenses:* Tuition: Full-time $11,520. Required fees: $760. *Financial support:* Institutionally sponsored loans and scholarships/grants available. Financial award applicants required to submit FAFSA. *Unit head:* Dr. Gil Linne, Dean/Executive Director, 480-557-1751, E-mail: gil.linne@phoenix.edu. *Application contact:* Chair, 808-536-2686, Fax: 808-536-3848.

University of Phoenix–Houston Campus, The Artemis School, College of Health and Human Services, Houston, TX 77079-2004. Offers health care management (MBA). *Faculty:* 2 full-time (1 woman), 13 part-time/adjunct (0 women). *Students:* 110 full-time (87 women); includes 60 minority (42 African Americans, 6 Asian Americans or Pacific Islanders, 12 Hispanic Americans), 5 international. Average age 37. In 2006, 22 degrees awarded. *Degree requirements:* For master's, thesis (for some programs), registration. *Entrance requirements:* For master's, minimum undergraduate GPA of 2.5, 3 years of work experience. Additional exam requirements/recommendations for international students: Required—TOEFL (minimum score 550 paper-based; 213 computer-based; 79 iBT). *Application deadline:* Applications are processed on a rolling basis. Application fee: $45. Electronic applications accepted. *Expenses:* Tuition: Full-time $11,832. Required fees: $760. *Financial support:* Institutionally sponsored loans and scholarships/grants available. *Unit head:* Dr. Gil Linne, Dean/Executive Director, 480-557-1751, E-mail: gil.linne@phoenix.edu. *Application contact:* Campus College Chair, 913-465-9966, Fax: 713-465-2628.

University of Phoenix–Idaho Campus, The Artemis School, College of Health and Human Services, Meridian, ID 83642-3014. Offers health administration (MHA); health care management (MBA); psychology (MS). Evening/weekend programs available. *Faculty:* 4 full-time (1 woman), 22 part-time/adjunct (4 women). *Degree requirements:* For master's, thesis (for some programs), registration. *Entrance requirements:* For master's, minimum undergraduate GPA of 2.5, 3 years of work experience. Additional exam requirements/recommendations for international students: Required—TOEFL (minimum score 550 paper-based; 213 computer-based). *Application deadline:* Applications are processed on a rolling basis. Application fee: $45. Electronic applications accepted. *Expenses:* Tuition: Full-time $9,104. *Financial support:* Institutionally sponsored loans and scholarships/grants available. *Unit head:* Dr. Gil Linne, Dean/Executive Director, 480-557-1751, E-mail: gil.linne@phoenix.edu. *Application contact:* College Chair, 208-888-1505, Fax: 208-888-4775.

University of Phoenix–Indianapolis Campus, The Artemis School, College of Health and Human Services, Indianapolis, IN 46250-932. Offers administration of justice and security (MS); health administration (MHA); health care management (MBA); nursing (MSN); psychology (MS). Evening/weekend programs available. *Faculty:* 1 full-time (0 women), 10 part-time/adjunct (4 women). *Students:* 1 (woman) full-time; minority (African American) Average age 38. In 2006, 2 degrees awarded. *Degree requirements:* For master's, thesis, registration (for some programs). *Entrance requirements:* For master's, 3 years work experience, minimum undergraduate GPA of 2.5. Additional exam requirements/recommendations for international students: Required—TOEFL (minimum score 500 paper-based; 213 computer-based). *Application deadline:* Applications are processed on a rolling basis. Application fee: $45. Electronic applications accepted. *Expenses:* Tuition: Full-time $10,320. Required fees: $760. *Financial support:* Institutionally sponsored loans and scholarships/grants available. Financial award applicants required to submit FAFSA. *Unit head:* Dr. Gil Linne, Dean/Executive Director, 480-557-1751, E-mail: gil.linne@phoenix.edu.

University of Phoenix–Jersey City Campus, College of Health and Human Services, Jersey City, NJ 07310. Offers health care management (MBA).

University of Phoenix–Kansas City Campus, The Artemis School, College of Health and Human Services, Kansas City, MO 64131-4517. Offers administration of justice and security (MS); community counseling (MSC); health administration (MHA); health care management (MBA); nursing (MSN). Evening/weekend programs available. *Faculty:* 4 full-time (0 women), 16 part-time/adjunct (7 women). *Students:* 16 full-time (15 women); includes 1 minority (African American), 5 international. Average age 44. In 2006, 2 degrees awarded. *Degree requirements:* For master's, thesis (for some programs), registration. *Entrance requirements:* For master's, 3 years work experience, minimum undergraduate GPA or 2.5. Additional exam requirements/recommendations for international students: Required—TOEFL (minimum score 550 paper-based; 213 computer-based). Application fee: $45. *Expenses:* Tuition: Full-time $11,064. Required fees: $760. *Financial support:* Institutionally sponsored loans and scholarships/grants available. *Unit head:* Dr. Gil Linne, Dean/Executive Director, 480-557-1751, E-mail: gil.linne@phoenix.edu. *Application contact:* Chair, 816-943-9600, Fax: 816-943-6675.

University of Phoenix–Louisiana Campus, The Artemis School, College of Health and Human Services, Metairie, LA 70001-2082. Offers administration of justice and security (MS); health care management (MBA); nursing (MSN); psychology (MS); MSN/MBA. Evening/weekend programs available. *Faculty:* 2 full-time (both women), 52 part-time/adjunct (32 women). *Students:* 29 full-time (23 women); includes 14 minority (13 African Americans, 1 Asian American or Pacific Islander), 2 international. Average age 34. In 2006, 17 degrees awarded. *Degree requirements:* For master's, thesis (for some programs), registration. *Entrance requirements:* For master's, minimum undergraduate GPA of 2.5, 3 years work experience, RN license. Additional exam requirements/recommendations for international students: Required—TOEFL (minimum score 550 paper-based; 213 computer-based; 79 iBT). *Application deadline:* Applications are processed on a rolling basis. Application fee: $45. Electronic applications accepted. *Expenses:* Tuition: Full-time $11,832. Required fees: $760. *Financial support:* Institutionally sponsored loans and scholarships/grants available. Financial award applicants required to submit FAFSA. *Unit head:* Dr. Gil Linne, Dean/Executive Director, 480-557-1751, E-mail: gil.linne@phoenix.edu. *Application contact:* Chair, 504-461-8852, Fax: 504-464-6373.

University of Phoenix–Louisville Campus, College of Health and Human Services, Louisville, KY 40223-3839. Offers health care management (MBA).

University of Phoenix–Madison Campus, College of Health and Human Services, Madison, WI 53718-2416. Offers health care management (MBA).

University of Phoenix–Memphis Campus, College of Health and Human Services, Cordova, TN 38018. Offers health administration (MHA); health care management (MBA).

University of Phoenix–Metro Detroit Campus, The Artemis School, College of Health and Human Services, Southfield, MI 48076. Offers health care management (MBA); nursing (MSN); MSN/MBA-HCM. Evening/weekend programs available. *Faculty:* 13 full-time (8 women), 83 part-time/adjunct (50 women). *Students:* 211 full-time (190 women); includes 95 minority (92 African Americans, 2 Asian Americans or Pacific Islanders, 1 Hispanic American), 5 international. Average age 40. In 2006, 57 master's awarded. *Degree requirements:* For master's, thesis (for some programs), registration. *Entrance requirements:* For master's, minimum undergraduate GPA of 2.5, 3 years of work experience, RN license. Additional exam requirements/recommendations for international students: Required—TOEFL (minimum score 550 paper-based; 213 computer-based; 79 iBT). *Application deadline:* Applications are processed on a rolling basis. Application fee: $45. Electronic applications accepted. *Expenses:* Tuition: Full-time $12,168. Required fees: $760. *Financial support:* Institutionally sponsored loans and scholarships/grants available. Financial award applicants required to submit FAFSA. *Unit head:* Dr. Gil Linne, Dean/Executive Director, 480-557-1751, E-mail: gil.linne@phoenix.edu. *Application contact:* Chair, 800-834-2438, Fax: 248-267-0147.

University of Phoenix–Minneapolis/St. Louis Park Campus, College of Health and Human Services, St. Louis Park, MN 55426. Offers family nurse practitioner (MSN); health care management (MBA); nursing (MSN).

University of Phoenix–Nashville Campus, The Artemis School, College of Health and Human Services, Nashville, TN 37214-5048. Offers health administration (MHA); health care management (MBA). Evening/weekend programs available. *Faculty:* 3 full-time (0 women), 18 part-time/adjunct (7 women). *Students:* 52 full-time (37 women); includes 21 minority (19 African Americans, 1 American Indian/Alaska Native, 1 Asian American or Pacific Islander), 1 international. Average age 38. In 2006, 37 degrees awarded. *Degree requirements:* For master's, thesis (for some programs), registration. *Entrance requirements:* For master's, minimum undergraduate GPA of 2.5, 3 years of work experience. Additional exam requirements/recommendations for international students: Required—TOEFL (minimum score 550 paper-based; 213 computer-based). *Application deadline:* Applications are processed on a rolling basis. Application fee: $45. Electronic applications accepted. *Expenses:* Tuition: Full-time $10,104. Required fees: $760. *Financial support:* Institutionally sponsored loans and scholarships/grants available. Financial award applicants required to submit FAFSA. *Unit head:* Dr. Gil Linne, Dean/Executive Director, 480-559-1751, E-mail: gil.linne@phoenix.edu. *Application contact:* Chair, 615-872-0188.

University of Phoenix–New Mexico Campus, The Artemis School, College of Health and Human Services, Albuquerque, NM 87109-4645. Offers health care management (MBA); marriage and family therapy (MSC). Evening/weekend programs available. *Faculty:* 19 full-time (12 women), 135 part-time/adjunct (75 women). *Students:* 217 full-time (156 women); includes 93 minority (9 African Americans, 4 American Indian/Alaska Native, 4 Asian Americans or Pacific Islanders, 76 Hispanic Americans), 17 international. Average age 39. In 2006, 40 degrees awarded. *Degree requirements:* For master's, thesis (for some programs), registration. *Entrance requirements:* For master's, minimum undergraduate GPA of 2.5, 3 years of work experience, RN license. Additional exam requirements/recommendations for international students: Required—TOEFL (minimum score 550 paper-based; 213 computer-based; 79 iBT). *Application deadline:* Applications are processed on a rolling basis. Application fee: $45. Electronic applications accepted. *Expenses:* Tuition: Full-time $9,005. Required fees: $760. *Financial support:* Institutionally sponsored loans and scholarships/grants available. Financial award applicants required to submit FAFSA. *Unit head:* Dr. Gil Linne, Dean/Executive Director, 480-557-1751, E-mail: gil.linne@phoenix.edu. *Application contact:* Campus College Chair-Nursing, 505-821-4800, Fax: 505-821-5551.

University of Phoenix—Northern Nevada Campus, College of Health and Human Services, Reno, NV 89511. Offers health administration (MHA); health care management (MBA); nursing (MSN); nursing/health care education (MSN); MSN/MBA; MSN/MHA.

University of Phoenix–Northern Virginia Campus, College of Health and Human Services, Reston, VA 20190. Offers health administration (MHA); health care management (MBA); nursing (MSN).

University of Phoenix–North Florida Campus, The Artemis School, College of Health and Human Services, Jacksonville, FL 32216-0959. Offers health administration (MHA); health care education (MSN); health care management (MBA); nursing (MSN); MSN/MBA. Evening/weekend programs available. *Faculty:* 13 full-time (10 women), 58 part-time/adjunct (42 women). *Students:* 69 full-time (52 women); includes 33 minority (26 African Americans, 5 Asian Americans or Pacific Islanders, 2 Hispanic Americans), 7 international. Average age 41. In 2006, 15 master's awarded. *Degree requirements:* For master's, thesis (for some programs), registration. *Entrance requirements:* For master's, minimum undergraduate GPA of 2.5, 3 years work experience, RN license. Additional exam requirements/recommendations for international students: Required—TOEFL (minimum score 550 paper-based; 213 computer-based; 79 iBT). *Application deadline:* Applications are processed on a rolling basis. Application fee: $45. Electronic applications accepted. *Financial support:* Institutionally sponsored loans and scholarships/grants available. Financial award applicants required to submit FAFSA. *Unit head:* Dr. Gil Linne, Dean, 480-557-1751, E-mail: gil.linne@phoenix.edu. *Application contact:* Chair, 904-636-6645, Fax: 904-636-0998.

University of Phoenix–Northwest Arkansas Campus, College of Health and Human Services, Rogers, AR 72756-9615. Offers health administration (MHA); health care education (MSN); health care management (MBA); nursing (MSN); MSN/MBA.

University of Phoenix–Northwest Indiana, College of Health and Human Services, Merrillville, IN 46410. Offers health administration (MHA); nursing (MSN); nursing/health care education (MSN); MSN/MBA; MSN/MHA.

University of Phoenix–Omaha Campus, College of Health and Human Services, Omaha, NE 68154-5240. Offers health administration (MHA); health care management (MBA).

University of Phoenix Online Campus, The Artemis School, College of Health and Human Services, Phoenix, AZ 85034-7209. Offers administration of justice and security (MS); health care administration (MHA); health care management (MBA, MSN); nurse practitioner (MSN); nursing (MSN); nursing education (MSN); psychology (MS); MSN/MBA-HCM; MSN/MHA. *Accreditation:* AACN. Evening/weekend programs available. *Faculty:* 10 full-time (9 women), 1,743 part-time/adjunct (1,042 women). *Students:* 8,196 full-time (6,937 women); includes 1,916 minority (1,301 African Americans, 56 American Indian/Alaska Native, 268 Asian Americans or Pacific Islanders, 291 Hispanic Americans), 849 international. Average age 40. In 2006, 6,951 master's awarded. *Degree requirements:* For master's, thesis (for some programs), registration. *Entrance requirements:* For master's, 3 years of work experience, minimum undergraduate GPA of 2.5, RN license. Additional exam requirements/recommendations for international students: Required—TOEFL (minimum score 550 paper-based; 213 computer-based; 79 iBT). *Application deadline:* Applications are processed on a rolling basis. Application fee: $45. Electronic applications accepted. *Expenses:* Tuition: Full-time $12,664. Required fees: $760. *Financial support:* Institutionally sponsored loans and scholarships/grants available. Financial award applicants required to submit FAFSA. *Unit head:* Dr. Gil Linne, Dean/Executive Director, 480-552-1751, E-mail: gil.linne@phoenix.edu. *Application contact:* Dr. Gil Linne, Dean/Executive Director, 480-552-1751, E-mail: gil.linne@phoenix.edu.

University of Phoenix Online Campus, School of Advanced Studies, Phoenix, AZ 85034-7209. Offers business administration (DBA); education (Ed D); health administration (DHA); organizational management (DM). Evening/weekend programs available. *Faculty:* 36 full-time (13 women), 551 part-time/adjunct (224 women). *Students:* 4,544 full-time (2,756 women); includes 1,550 minority (1,136 African Americans, 32 American Indian/Alaska Native, 152 Asian Americans or Pacific Islanders, 230 Hispanic Americans), 378 international. Average age 44. In 2006, 210 degrees awarded. *Degree requirements:* For doctorate, thesis/dissertation. *Entrance requirements:* For doctorate, 3 letters of recommendation, minimum master's GPA of 3.0, 3 years professional work experience. Additional exam requirements/recommendations for international students: Required—TOEFL (minimum score 550 paper-based; 213 computer-based; 79 iBT). *Application deadline:* Applications are processed on a rolling basis. Application fee: $45. Electronic applications accepted. *Expenses:* Tuition: Full-time $12,664. Required fees: $760. *Financial support:* Institutionally sponsored loans and scholarships/grants available. Financial award applicants required to submit FAFSA. *Unit head:* Dr. Dawn Iwamoto, Dean/Executive Director, 480-557-3228, E-mail: dawn.iwamoto@phoenix.edu. *Application contact:* Information Contact, 800-697-8223.

University of Phoenix–Oregon Campus, The Artemis School, College of Health and Human Services, Tigard, OR 97223. Offers administration of justice and security (MS); health administration (MHA); health care management (MBA); nursing (MSN); psychology (MS); MSN/MBA. Evening/weekend programs available. *Faculty:* 9 full-time (4 women), 53 part-time/adjunct (25 women). *Students:* 2 full-time (1 woman), (both international). Average age 36. *Degree requirements:* For master's, thesis (for some programs), registration. *Entrance requirements:* For master's, minimum undergraduate GPA of 2.5, 3 years of work experience, current RN license (nursing). Additional exam requirements/recommendations for international students: Required—TOEFL (minimum score 550 paper-based; 213 computer-based; 79 iBT). *Application deadline:* Applications are processed on a rolling basis. Application fee: $45. Electronic applications accepted. *Expenses:* Tuition: Full-time $10,200. Required fees: $760. *Financial support:* Institutionally sponsored loans and scholarships/grants available. *Unit head:* Dr. Gil Linne, Dean/Executive Director, 480-557-1221, E-mail: gil.linne@phoenix.edu. *Application contact:* College Chair, 503-403-1250.

University of Phoenix–Philadelphia Campus, The Artemis School, College of Health and Human Services, Wayne, PA 19087-2121. Offers health care management (MBA). Evening/weekend programs available. *Faculty:* 2 full-time (0 women), 12 part-time/adjunct (4 women). *Students:* 37 full-time (30 women); includes 20 minority (16 African Americans, 1 American Indian/Alaska Native, 2 Asian Americans or Pacific Islanders, 1 Hispanic American), 5 international. Average age 36. In 2006, 8 degrees awarded. *Degree requirements:* For master's, thesis (for some programs), registration. *Entrance requirements:* For master's, minimum undergraduate GPA of 2.5, 3 years work experience. Additional exam requirements/recommendations for international students: Required—TOEFL (minimum score 550 paper-based; 213 computer-based; 79 iBT). *Application deadline:* Applications are processed on a rolling basis. Application fee: $45. Electronic applications accepted. *Expenses:* Tuition: Full-time $13,560. Required fees: $760. *Financial support:* Institutionally sponsored loans and scholarships/grants available. *Unit head:* Dr. Gil Linne, Dean/Executive Director, 480-557-1751, E-mail: gin.linne@phoenix.edu.

University of Phoenix–Phoenix Campus, The Artemis School, College of Health and Human Services, Phoenix, AZ 85040-1958. Offers community counseling (MSC); family nurse practitioner (MSN); health care management (MBA); nurse practitioner (Certificate); nursing (MSN); nursing health care education (Certificate). Evening/weekend programs available. *Faculty:* 45 full-time (20 women), 510 part-time/adjunct (308 women). *Students:* 493 full-time (420 women); includes 79 minority (17 African Americans, 4 American Indian/Alaska Native, 20 Asian Americans or Pacific Islanders, 38 Hispanic Americans), 12 international. Average age 38. In 2006, 166 degrees awarded. *Degree requirements:* For master's, thesis (for some programs), registration. *Entrance requirements:* For master's, 3 years of work experience in field, minimum undergraduate GPA of 2.5, RN license. Additional exam requirements/recommendations for international students: Required—TOEFL (minimum score 550 paper-based; 213 computer-based; 79 iBT). *Application deadline:* Applications are processed on a rolling basis. Application fee: $45. Electronic applications accepted. *Financial support:* Institutionally sponsored loans and scholarships/grants available. Financial award applicants required to submit FAFSA. *Unit head:* Dr. Gil Linne, Dean/Executive Director, 480-557-1751, E-mail: gil.linne@phoenix.edu. *Application contact:* Chair, 480-804-7400, Fax: 480-557-2320.

University of Phoenix–Pittsburgh Campus, The Artemis School, College of Health and Human Services, Pittsburgh, PA 15276. Offers administration of justice and security (MS); health administration (MHA); health care management (MBA); nursing (MSN); nursing education (MSN); psychology (MS); MSN/MBA; MSN/MHA. Evening/weekend programs available. *Faculty:* 2 full-time (0 women), 10 part-time/adjunct (1 woman). *Students:* 11 full-time (8 women); includes 3 minority (all African Americans) Average age 36. In 2006, 1 degree awarded. *Degree requirements:* For master's, thesis (for some programs), registration. *Entrance requirements:* For master's, minimum undergraduate GPA of 2.5, 3 years work experience, current RN license (nursing). Additional exam requirements/recommendations for international students: Required—TOEFL (minimum score 550 paper-based; 213 computer-based; 79 iBT). *Application deadline:* Applications are processed on a rolling basis. Application fee: $45. Electronic applications accepted. *Expenses:* Tuition: Full-time $13,560. Required fees: $760. *Financial support:* Institutionally sponsored loans and scholarships/grants available. *Unit head:* Dr. Gil Linne, Dean/Executive Director, 480-557-1751, E-mail: gil.linne@phoenix.edu.

University of Phoenix–Puerto Rico Campus, The Artemis School, College of Health and Human Services, Guaynabo, PR 00968. Offers marriage, family and child therapy (MSC); mental health counseling (MSC). Evening/weekend programs available. *Faculty:* 4 full-time (3 women), 20 part-time/adjunct (14 women). *Students:* 160 full-time (122 women); includes 84 minority (all Hispanic Americans), 4 international. Average age 35. In 2006, 67 degrees awarded. *Degree requirements:* For master's, thesis (for some programs), registration. *Entrance requirements:* For master's, Counselor Preparation Comprehensive Examination, minimum undergraduate GPA of 2.5, 3 years work experience. Additional exam requirements/recommendations for international students: Required—TOEFL (minimum score 550 paper-based; 213 computer-based; 79 iBT). *Application deadline:* Applications are processed on a rolling basis. Application fee: $45. Electronic applications accepted. *Expenses:* Tuition: Full-time $5,816. Required fees: $760. *Financial support:* Institutionally sponsored loans and scholarships/grants available. Financial award applicants required to submit FAFSA. *Unit head:* Dr. Gil Linne, Dean/Executive Director, 480-557-1074, E-mail: gil.linne@phoenix.edu. *Application contact:* Chair, 787-731-5400, Fax: 787-731-1510.

University of Phoenix–Raleigh Campus, College of Health and Human Services, Raleigh, NC 27606. Offers health care management (MBA).

University of Phoenix–Renton Learning Center, College of Health and Human Services, Renton, WA 98005. Offers health administration (MHA); health care education (MSN); health care management (MBA); nursing (MSN); MSN/MBA; MSN/MHA.

University of Phoenix–Richmond Campus, The Artemis School, College of Health and Human Services, Richmond, VA 23230. Offers administration of justice and security (MS); health administration (MHA); health care management (MBA); nursing (MSN); psychology (MS). Evening/weekend programs available. *Faculty:* 4 part-time/adjunct (1 woman). *Students:* 2 full-time (1 woman); includes 1 minority (African American) Average age 38. *Degree requirements:* For master's, thesis (for some programs), registration. *Entrance requirements:* For master's, minimum undergraduate GPA of 2.5, 3 years work experience, current RN license for nursing programs. Additional exam requirements/recommendations for international students: Required—TOEFL (minimum score 500 paper-based; 213 computer-based; 79 iBT). *Application deadline:* Applications are processed on a rolling basis. Application fee: $45. Electronic applications accepted. *Financial support:* Institutionally sponsored loans and scholarships/grants available. Financial award applicants required to submit FAFSA. *Unit head:* Dr. Gil Linne, Dean/Executive Director, 480-557-1751, E-mail: gil.linne@phoenix.edu. *Application contact:* Chair, 804-288-3390.

University of Phoenix–Sacramento Valley Campus, The Artemis School, College of Health and Human Services, Sacramento, CA 95833-3632. Offers administration of justice and security (MS); family nurse practitioner (MSN); health care management (MBA); marriage, family and child counseling (MSC); nursing (MSN); nursing education (MSN). Evening/weekend programs available. *Faculty:* 36 full-time (27 women), 270 part-time/adjunct (121 women). *Students:* 330 full-time (266 women); includes 73 minority (38 African Americans, 2 American Indian/Alaska Native, 16 Asian Americans or Pacific Islanders, 17 Hispanic Americans), 29 international. Average age 40. In 2006, 82 degrees awarded. *Degree requirements:* For master's, thesis (for some programs), registration. *Entrance requirements:* For master's, RN license, minimum undergraduate GPA of 2.5, 3 years work experience. Additional exam requirements/recommendations for international students: Required—TOEFL (minimum score 550 paper-based; 213 computer-based; 79 iBT). *Application deadline:* Applications are processed on a rolling basis. Application fee: $45. Electronic applications accepted. *Expenses:* Tuition: Full-time $12,024. Required fees: $760. *Financial support:* Institutionally sponsored loans and scholarships/grants available. Financial award applicants required to submit FAFSA. *Unit head:* Dr. Gil Linne, Dean/Executive Director, 480-557-1757, E-mail: gil.linne@phoenix.edu. *Application contact:* College Chair, 916-923-2107, Fax: 916-923-3914.

University of Phoenix–St. Louis Campus, The Artemis School, College of Health and Human Services, St. Louis, MO 63043-4828. Offers health care management (MBA). Evening/weekend programs available. *Faculty:* 10 part-time/adjunct (1 woman). *Students:* 1 full-time (0 women). *Degree requirements:* For master's, thesis (for some programs), registration. *Entrance requirements:* For master's, minimum undergraduate GPA of 2.5, 3 years work experience. Additional exam requirements/recommendations for international students: Required—TOEFL (minimum score 550 paper-based; 213 computer-based; 79 iBT). *Application deadline:* Applications are processed on a rolling basis. Application fee: $45. Electronic applications accepted. *Expenses:* Tuition: Full-time $11,832. Required fees: $762. *Financial support:* Institutionally sponsored loans and scholarships/grants available. *Unit head:* Dr. Gil Linne, Dean/Executive Director, 480-557-1751, E-mail: gin.linne@phoenix.edu. *Application contact:* College Chair, 314-298-9755.

University of Phoenix–San Antonio Campus, College of Health and Human Services, San Antonio, TX 78230. Offers health administration (MHA); health care management (MBA).

University of Phoenix–Savannah Campus, College of Health and Human Services, Savannah, GA 31405-7400. Offers health administration (MHA); health care management (MBA); nursing (MSN); nursing/health care education (MSN); MSN/MBA; MSN/MHA.

University of Phoenix–Southern Arizona Campus, The Artemis School, College of Health and Human Services, Tucson, AZ 85712-2732. Offers administration of justice and security (MS); family nurse practitioner (Certificate); health administration (MHA); marriage, family and child therapy (MSC); nursing (MSN). Evening/weekend programs available. *Faculty:* 24 full-time (17 women), 212 part-time/adjunct (127 women). *Students:* 192 full-time (158 women); includes 38 minority (16 African Americans, 3 Asian Americans or Pacific Islanders, 19 Hispanic Americans), 16 international. In 2006, 34 degrees awarded. *Degree requirements:* For master's, thesis (for some programs), registration. *Entrance requirements:* For master's, minimum undergraduate GPA of 2.5, 3 years of work experience, RN license. Additional exam requirements/recommendations for international students: Required—TOEFL (minimum score 550 paper-based; 213 computer-based; 79 iBT). *Application deadline:* Applications are processed on a rolling basis. Application fee: $45. Electronic applications accepted. *Expenses:* Tuition: Full-time $8,669. Required fees: $760. *Financial support:* Institutionally sponsored loans and scholarships/grants available. Financial award applicants required to submit FAFSA. *Unit head:* Dr. Gil Linne, Dean/Executive Director, 480-557-1757, E-mail: gil.linne@phoenix.edu. *Application contact:* Campus College Chair, 520-881-6512, Fax: 520-795-6177.

University of Phoenix–Southern California Campus, The Artemis School, College of Health and Human Services, Costa Mesa, CA 92626. Offers family nurse practitioner (MSN, Certificate); health care education (MSN); health care management (MBA); marriage, family and child therapy (MSC); nursing (MSN). Evening/weekend programs available. *Faculty:* 53 full-time (32 women), 456 part-time/adjunct (240 women). *Students:* 623 full-time (524 women); includes 237 minority (98 African Americans, 2 American Indian/Alaska Native, 62 Asian Americans or Pacific Islanders, 75 Hispanic Americans), 59 international. Average age 40. In 2006, 113 degrees awarded. *Degree requirements:* For master's, thesis (for some programs), registration. *Entrance requirements:* For master's, minimum undergraduate GPA of 2.5, 3 years work experience, RN license. Additional exam requirements/recommendations for international students: Required—TOEFL (minimum score 550 paper-based; 213 computer-based; 79 iBT). *Application deadline:* Applications are processed on a rolling basis. Application fee: $45. Electronic applications accepted. *Expenses:* Tuition: Full-time $13,512. Required fees: $760. *Financial support:* Institutionally sponsored loans and scholarships/grants available. Financial award applicants required to submit FAFSA. *Unit head:* Dr. Gil Linne, Dean/Executive Director, 480-557-1751, E-mail: gil.linne@phoenix.edu. *Application contact:* Campus College Chair, 714-398-1878, Fax: 714-378-5856.

University of Phoenix–Southern Colorado Campus, The Artemis School, College of Health and Human Services, Colorado Springs, CO 80919-2335. Offers community counseling (MSC); health care management (MBA); marriage, family and child therapy (MSC); nursing (MSN). Evening/weekend programs available. *Faculty:* 2 full-time (both women), 100 part-time/adjunct (37 women). *Students:* 76 full-time (52 women); includes 10 minority (3 African Americans, 2 American Indian/Alaska Native, 5 Hispanic Americans). Average age 38. In 2006, 20 degrees awarded. *Degree requirements:* For master's, thesis (for some programs), registration. *Entrance requirements:* For master's, minimum undergraduate GPA of 2.5, 3 years of work experience, RN license. Additional exam requirements/recommendations for international students: Required—TOEFL (minimum score 550 paper-based; 213 computer-based; 79 iBT). *Application deadline:* Applications are processed on a rolling basis. Application fee: $45. Electronic applications accepted. *Expenses:* Tuition: Full-time $10,291. Required fees: $760. *Financial support:* Institutionally sponsored loans and scholarships/grants available. Financial award applicants required to submit FAFSA. *Unit head:* Dr. Gil Linne, Dean/Executive Director, 480-557-1751, E-mail: gil.linne@phoenix.edu. *Application contact:* Chair, 719-599-5282, Fax: 719-599-7973.

University of Phoenix–Springfield Campus, College of Health and Human Services, Springfield, MO 65804-7211. Offers administration/health care management (MSN); health administration (MHA); health care management (MBA); nursing (MSN); MSN/MBA; MSN/MHA.

University of Phoenix–Vancouver Campus, The Artemis School, College of Health and Human Services, Burnaby, BC V5C 6G9, Canada. Offers health care management (MBA). Evening/weekend programs available. *Students:* 2 full-time (0 women). Average age 36. *Degree requirements:* For master's, thesis (for some programs), registration. *Entrance requirements:* For master's, minimum undergraduate GPA of 2.5, 3 years work experience. Additional exam requirements/recommendations for international students: Required—TOEFL (minimum score 550 paper-based; 213 computer-based; 79 iBT). *Application deadline:* Applications are processed on a rolling basis. Application fee: $45. Electronic applications accepted. *Expenses:* Tuition: Full-time $12,840. Required fees: $760. *Financial support:* Institutionally

Health Services Management and Hospital Administration

University of Phoenix–Vancouver Campus (continued)
sponsored loans available. *Unit head:* Dr. Gil Linne, Dean/Executive Director, 480-557-1751, E-mail: gil.linne@phoenix.edu.

University of Phoenix–Washington Campus, The Artemis School, College of Health and Human Services, Seattle, WA 98188-7500. Offers health care management (MBA). Evening/weekend programs available. *Faculty:* 1 full-time (0 women), 35 part-time/adjunct (17 women). *Students:* 20 full-time (16 women); includes 8 minority (4 African Americans, 3 Asian Americans or Pacific Islanders, 1 Hispanic American), 1 international. Average age 37. *Degree requirements:* For master's, thesis (for some programs), registration. *Entrance requirements:* For master's, minimum undergraduate GPA of 2.5, 3 years of work experience. Additional exam requirements/recommendations for international students: Required—TOEFL (minimum score 550 paper-based; 213 computer-based; 79 iBT). *Application deadline:* Applications are processed on a rolling basis. Application fee: $45. Electronic applications accepted. *Expenses:* Tuition: Full-time $10,200. Required fees: $760. *Financial support:* Institutionally sponsored loans and scholarships/grants available. *Unit head:* Dr. Gil Linne, Dean/Executive Director, 480-557-1221, E-mail: gil.linne@phoenix.edu. *Application contact:* College Chair, 206-268-5800, Fax: 206-241-8848.

University of Phoenix–West Florida Campus, The Artemis School, College of Health and Human Services, Temple Terrace, FL 33637. Offers health administration (MHA); health care education (MSN); health care management (MBA); MSN/MBA. Evening/weekend programs available. Postbaccalaureate distance learning degree programs offered. *Faculty:* 19 full-time (12 women), 56 part-time/adjunct (31 women). *Students:* 87 full-time (79 women); includes 21 minority (12 African Americans, 1 Asian American or Pacific Islander, 8 Hispanic Americans), 10 international. Average age 45. In 2006, 18 degrees awarded. *Degree requirements:* For master's, thesis (for some programs), registration. *Entrance requirements:* For master's, minimum undergraduate GPA of 2.5, RN license, 3 years work experience. Additional exam requirements/recommendations for international students: Required—TOEFL (minimum score 550 paper-based; 213 computer-based; 79 iBT). *Application deadline:* Applications are processed on a rolling basis. Application fee: $45. Electronic applications accepted. *Expenses:* Tuition: Full-time $9,450. Required fees: $760. *Financial support:* Institutionally sponsored loans and scholarships/grants available. Financial award applicants required to submit FAFSA. *Unit head:* Dr. Gil Linne, Dean, 480-557-1751, E-mail: gil.linne@phoenix.edu. *Application contact:* Chair, 813-626-7911, Fax: 813-977-1449.

University of Phoenix–West Michigan Campus, The Artemis School, College of Health and Human Services, Walker, MI 49544. Offers health care management (MBA); nursing (MSN). Evening/weekend programs available. *Faculty:* 9 full-time (3 women), 49 part-time/adjunct (28 women). *Students:* 40 full-time (35 women); includes 8 minority (6 African Americans, 2 Hispanic Americans), 3 international. Average age 39. In 2006, 7 master's awarded. *Degree requirements:* For master's, thesis (for some programs), registration. *Entrance requirements:* For master's, minimum undergraduate GPA of 2.5, 3 years work experience, RN license. Additional exam requirements/recommendations for international students: Required—TOEFL (minimum score 550 paper-based; 213 computer-based; 79 iBT). *Application deadline:* Applications are processed on a rolling basis. Application fee: $45. Electronic applications accepted. *Expenses:* Tuition: Full-time $12,043. Required fees: $760. *Financial support:* Institutionally sponsored loans and scholarships/grants available. Financial award applicants required to submit FAFSA. *Unit head:* Dr. Gil Linne, Dean/Executive Director, 480-557-1751, E-mail: gil.linne@phoenix.edu. *Application contact:* Chair, 888-345-9699, Fax: 616-794-5300.

University of Phoenix–Wisconsin Campus, The Artemis School, College of Health and Human Services, Brookfield, WI 53045-6608. Offers MSN/MBA-HCM. Evening/weekend programs available. *Faculty:* 8 part-time/adjunct (6 women). *Students:* 2 full-time (1 woman). Average age 48. *Entrance requirements:* Additional exam requirements/recommendations for international students: Required—TOEFL (minimum score 550 paper-based; 213 computer-based; 79 iBT). *Application deadline:* Applications are processed on a rolling basis. Application fee: $45. Electronic applications accepted. *Expenses:* Tuition: Full-time $10,944. Required fees: $760. *Financial support:* Institutionally sponsored loans and scholarships/grants available. Financial award applicants required to submit FAFSA. *Unit head:* Dr. Gil Linne, Dean/Executive Director, 480-557-1751, E-mail: gin.linne@phoenix.edu.

University of Pittsburgh, Graduate School of Public Health, Department of Behavioral and Community Health Sciences, Pittsburgh, PA 15260. Offers behavioral and community health sciences (MPH, Dr PH); lesbian, gay, bisexual and transgender health and wellness (Certificate); minority health and health disparities (Certificate); program evaluation (Certificate); public health and aging (Certificate); public health preparedness (Certificate); MID/MPH; MPH/MPA; MPH/MSW; MPH/PhD. *Accreditation:* CAHME (one or more programs are accredited). Part-time programs available. *Faculty:* 20 full-time (9 women), 17 part-time/adjunct (8 women). *Students:* 48 full-time (39 women), 33 part-time (27 women); includes 21 minority (14 African Americans, 1 American Indian/Alaska Native, 5 Asian Americans or Pacific Islanders, 1 Hispanic American), 3 international. Average age 31. 125 applicants, 62% accepted, 28 enrolled. In 2006, 24 master's, 2 doctorates awarded. *Median time to degree:* Of those who began their doctoral program in fall 1998, 100% received their degree in 8 years or less. *Degree requirements:* For master's, thesis; for doctorate, thesis/dissertation, preliminary exams, comprehensive exam. *Entrance requirements:* For master's and Certificate, GRE; for doctorate, GRE, master's degree in public health or related field. Additional exam requirements/recommendations for international students: Required—TOEFL (minimum score 550 paper-based; 213 computer-based). *Application deadline:* For fall admission, 5/1 priority date for domestic students, 4/1 for international students; for winter admission, 9/1 for international students; for spring admission, 10/1 priority date for domestic students, 2/1 for international students. Applications are processed on a rolling basis. Application fee: $50 ($60 for international students). Electronic applications accepted. *Financial support:* In 2006–07, 20 students received support, including 14 research assistantships with tuition reimbursements available, 6 teaching assistantships with tuition reimbursements available; career-related internships or fieldwork, scholarships/grants, and unspecified assistantships also available. Support available to part-time students. *Faculty research:* Maternal and child health, program evaluation, community-based participatory research, minority health and health disparities, aging. Total annual research expenditures: $1.3 million. *Unit head:* Dr. Robert M. Goodman, Chairman, 412-624-3100, Fax: 412-624-5510, E-mail: rmg16@pitt.edu. *Application contact:* Natalie C Arnold, Recruitment and Academic Affairs Administrator, 412-624-3107, Fax: 412-624-5510, E-mail: narnold@pi.edu.

University of Pittsburgh, Graduate School of Public Health, Department of Health Policy and Management, Pittsburgh, PA 15260. Offers MHA, MPH, JD/MPH. *Accreditation:* CAHME. Part-time programs available. *Faculty:* 14 full-time (7 women), 12 part-time/adjunct (5 women). *Students:* 29 full-time (20 women), 13 part-time (8 women); includes 10 minority (4 African Americans, 5 Asian Americans or Pacific Islanders, 1 Hispanic American), 3 international. Average age 27. 80 applicants, 65% accepted, 18 enrolled. In 2006, 7 degrees awarded. *Degree requirements:* For master's, essay. *Entrance requirements:* For master's, GRE, 3 credits of course work in mathematics, 3 credits of course work in biology, 6 credits of course work in social sciences. Additional exam requirements/recommendations for international students: Required—TOEFL (minimum score 550 paper-based; 213 computer-based; 80 iBT). *Application deadline:* For fall admission, 4/30 priority date for domestic students, 4/1 for international students; for winter admission, 9/1 for international students; for spring admission, 10/30 priority date for domestic students, 2/1 for international students. Applications are processed on a rolling basis. Application fee: $50 ($60 for international students). Electronic applications accepted. *Financial support:* In 2006–07, 7 students received support, including 5 research assistantships with full tuition reimbursements available (averaging $20,333 per year), 2 teaching assistantships with tuition reimbursements available; career-related internships or fieldwork, scholarships/grants, and unspecified assistantships also available. Financial award applicants required to submit FAFSA. *Faculty research:* Health care financing/insurance, long-term care, health policy, health law, nursing homes. Total annual research expenditures: $637,031. *Unit head:* Dr. Judith R. Lave, Chair, 412-624-0898, Fax: 412-624-3146, E-mail: lave@vms.cis.pitt.edu. *Application contact:* Donna Schultz, Administrative Assistant, 412-624-3123, Fax: 412-624-3146, E-mail: dschultz@pitt.edu.

University of Pittsburgh, School of Health and Rehabilitation Sciences, Program in Health and Rehabilitation Sciences, Pittsburgh, PA 15260. Offers dietetics (MS); health and rehabilitation sciences (MS), including clinical dietetics, coordinated with dietetics, health care supervision and management, health information systems, occupational therapy, physical therapy, rehabilitation counseling, rehabilitation science and technology, sports medicine; wellness and human performance (MS). *Accreditation:* APTA. Part-time and evening/weekend programs available. *Faculty:* 40 full-time (23 women), 3 part-time/adjunct (2 women). *Students:* 93 full-time (67 women), 54 part-time (35 women); includes 31 minority (12 African Americans, 18 Asian Americans or Pacific Islanders, 1 Hispanic American), 15 international. Average age 30. 122 applicants, 82% accepted, 64 enrolled. In 2006, 28 degrees awarded. *Entrance requirements:* For master's, minimum GPA of 3.0. Additional exam requirements/recommendations for international students: Required—TOEFL, IELTS. *Application deadline:* Applications are processed on a rolling basis. Application fee: $50. Electronic applications accepted. *Financial support:* In 2006–07, 11 research assistantships with full tuition reimbursements (averaging $16,918 per year) were awarded; teaching assistantships, Federal Work-Study, institutionally sponsored loans, traineeships, and unspecified assistantships also available. Support available to part-time students. Financial award applicants required to submit FAFSA. *Faculty research:* Assistive technology, seating and wheeled mobility, cellular neurophysiology, low back syndrome, augmentative communication. Total annual research expenditures: $953,246. *Application contact:* Shameem Gangjee, Director of Admissions, 412-383-6558, Fax: 412-383-6535, E-mail: admissions@shrs.pitt.edu.

University of Puerto Rico, Medical Sciences Campus, Graduate School of Public Health, Department of Health Services Administration, Program in Health Services Administration, San Juan, PR 00936-5067. Offers MHSA. *Accreditation:* CAHME. Part-time programs available. *Faculty:* 6 full-time (3 women). *Students:* 55 (31 women). 48 applicants, 50% accepted. In 2006, 11 degrees awarded. *Degree requirements:* For master's, thesis. *Entrance requirements:* For master's, GRE, previous course work in accounting, statistics, economics, algebra, and managerial finance. *Application deadline:* For fall admission, 3/15 for domestic students. Application fee: $20. *Financial support:* Career-related internships or fieldwork and Federal Work-Study available. Financial award application deadline: 4/30. *Unit head:* Dr. José Capriles, Coordinator, 787-758-2525 Ext. 1440, Fax: 787-759-6719, E-mail: jcapriles@rcm.upr.edu. *Application contact:* Prof. Mayra E. Santiago-Vargas, Counselor, 787-756-5244, Fax: 787-759-6719, E-mail: msantiago@rcm.upr.edu.

University of St. Francis, College of Professional Studies, Joliet, IL 60435-6169. Offers health services administration (MS); training and development (MS). Part-time and evening/weekend programs available. Postbaccalaureate distance learning degree programs offered (no on-campus study). *Faculty:* 4 full-time (1 woman), 36 part-time/adjunct (19 women). *Students:* 95 full-time (78 women), 623 part-time (545 women); includes 98 minority (67 African Americans, 2 American Indian/Alaska Native, 13 Asian Americans or Pacific Islanders, 16 Hispanic Americans), 1 international. Average age 44. 215 applicants, 83% accepted, 136 enrolled. In 2006, 272 degrees awarded. *Degree requirements:* For master's, thesis (for some programs), comprehensive exam (for some programs), registration. *Entrance requirements:* For master's, minimum GPA of 2.75, 2 letters of recommendation, computer competency, 2 years of work experience. Additional exam requirements/recommendations for international students: Required—TOEFL (minimum score 550 paper-based; 213 computer-based). *Application deadline:* Applications are processed on a rolling basis. Application fee: $30. Electronic applications accepted. *Expenses:* Contact institution. Part-time tuition and fees vary according to campus/location and program. *Financial support:* In 2006–07, 163 students received support. Tuition waivers (partial) available. Support available to part-time students. Financial award applicants required to submit FAFSA. *Unit head:* Dr. Michael LaRocco, Dean, 815-740-3452, Fax: 815-774-2920, E-mail: mlarocco@stfrancis.edu. *Application contact:* Sandra Sloka, Director of Admissions for Graduate and Degree Completion Programs, 800-735-7500, Fax: 815-740-5032, E-mail: ssloka@stfrancis.edu.

University of St. Thomas, Graduate Studies, Opus College of Business, Health Care UST MBA Program, St. Paul, MN 55105-1096. Offers MBA. *Accreditation:* CAHME. Part-time and evening/weekend programs available. Postbaccalaureate distance learning degree programs offered (minimal on-campus study). *Faculty:* 3 full-time (1 woman), 5 part-time/adjunct (1 woman). *Students:* Average age 35. 18 applicants, 89% accepted, 12 enrolled. In 2006, 16 degrees awarded. *Degree requirements:* For master's, thesis. *Entrance requirements:* For master's, GMAT, minimum 5-7 years of work experience in health care. Additional exam requirements/recommendations for international students: Required—TOEFL. *Application deadline:* For fall admission, 4/1 priority date for domestic students. Applications are processed on a rolling basis. Application fee: $75. *Expenses:* Contact institution. *Financial support:* Fellowships, research assistantships, career-related internships or fieldwork, institutionally sponsored loans, and scholarships/grants available. Support available to part-time students. Financial award application deadline: 7/1; financial award applicants required to submit FAFSA. *Unit head:* Dr. Jack Militello, Director, 651-962-4128, Fax: 651-962-4129. *Application contact:* Alice M. Nulsen, Program Services Manager, 651-962-4128, Fax: 651-962-4129, E-mail: amnulsen@stthomas.edu.

University of San Francisco, College of Professional Studies, Program in Public Administration, Concentration in Health Services Administration, San Francisco, CA 94117-1080. Offers MPA. Part-time and evening/weekend programs available. *Faculty:* 1 full-time (0 women), 1 (woman) part-time/adjunct. *Students:* 48 full-time (35 women); includes 20 minority (8 African Americans, 8 Asian Americans or Pacific Islanders, 4 Hispanic Americans), 3 international. Average age 38. 31 applicants, 97% accepted, 22 enrolled. In 2006, 24 degrees awarded. *Degree requirements:* For master's, thesis optional. *Entrance requirements:* For master's, minimum GPA of 3.0. Application fee: $55 ($65 for international students). *Expenses:* Tuition: Full-time $17,370; part-time $965 per unit. Tuition and fees vary according to degree level, campus/location and program. *Financial support:* In 2006–07, 39 students received support. Application deadline: 3/2; *Application contact:* 415-422-6000.

University of Saskatchewan, College of Graduate Studies and Research, College of Commerce, Program in Business Administration, Saskatoon, SK S7N 5A2, Canada. Offers agribusiness management (MBA); biotechnology management (MBA); health services management (MBA); indigenous management (MBA); international business management (MBA).

The University of Scranton, Graduate School, Department of Health Administration and Human Resources, Program in Health Administration, Scranton, PA 18510. Offers MHA. *Accreditation:* CAHME. Part-time and evening/weekend programs available. *Students:* 19 full-time (10 women), 9 part-time (7 women); includes 7 minority (1 African American, 6 Asian Americans or Pacific Islanders), 3 international. Average age 29. 21 applicants, 95% accepted. In 2006, 17 degrees awarded. *Degree requirements:* For master's, capstone experience. *Entrance requirements:* For master's, minimum GPA of 2.75. Additional exam requirements/recommendations for international students: Required—TOEFL (minimum score 550 paper-based; 173 computer-based), IELTS (minimum score 6). *Application deadline:* For fall admission, 4/15 priority date for domestic students. Applications are processed on a rolling basis. Application fee: $50. *Expenses:* Tuition: Part-time $684 per credit. Required fees: $25 per term. *Financial support:* Fellowships, teaching assistantships, career-related internships or fieldwork and unspecified assistantships available. Financial award application deadline: 3/1. *Unit head:* Dr. Peter C. Olden, Director, 570-941-4242, Fax: 570-941-4201, E-mail: oldenp1@scranton.edu.

University of South Carolina, The Graduate School, Arnold School of Public Health, Department of Health Services Policy and Management, Columbia, SC 29208. Offers MHA, MPH, Dr PH, PhD, MPH/MSN, MSW/MPH. *Accreditation:* CAHME (one or more programs are accredited). *Degree requirements:* For master's, thesis or alternative, internship (MHA), comprehensive exam; for doctorate, thesis/dissertation, comprehensive exam. *Entrance requirements:* For master's, GMAT (MHA), GRE General Test (MPH); for doctorate, GRE General Test. Additional exam requirements/recommendations for international students: Required—TOEFL (minimum score 570 paper-based; 230 computer-based). Electronic applications accepted. *Faculty research:* Health systems management, evaluation, and planning; forecast applications in health care; Medicaid process to health care services.

University of Southern California, Graduate School, School of Policy, Planning and Development, Program in Health Administration, Los Angeles, CA 90089. Offers MHA, MHA/MS. *Accreditation:* CAHME. *Students:* 64 full-time (38 women), 56 part-time (37 women); includes 64 minority (13 African Americans, 1 American Indian/Alaska Native, 31 Asian Americans or Pacific Islanders, 19 Hispanic Americans), 8 international. In 2006, 32 degrees awarded. *Entrance requirements:* For master's, GRE General Test. *Application deadline:* For fall admission, 12/1 priority date for domestic students. Application fee: $85. *Expenses:* Tuition: Full-time $33,314; part-time $1,121 per credit. Required fees: $522. Full-time tuition and fees vary according to program. *Financial support:* In 2006–07, research assistantships (averaging $18,500 per year), teaching assistantships (averaging $18,500 per year) were awarded; fellowships, Federal Work-Study, institutionally sponsored loans, and scholarships/grants also available. Support available to part-time students. Financial award application deadline: 2/15; financial award applicants required to submit FAFSA. *Unit head:* Dr. LaVonna Lewis, Director, 213-740-6842, E-mail: sppd@usc.edu.

University of Southern Indiana, Graduate Studies, College of Nursing and Health Professions, Program in Health Administration, Evansville, IN 47712-3590. Offers MHA. Part-time programs available. Postbaccalaureate distance learning degree programs offered (minimal on-campus study). *Faculty:* 1 full-time (0 women). *Students:* Average age 36. 7 applicants, 100% accepted, 6 enrolled. In 2006, 9 degrees awarded. *Entrance requirements:* For master's, GRE or GMAT, minimum GPA of 3.0. Additional exam requirements/recommendations for international students: Required—TOEFL (minimum score 500 paper-based; 173 computer-based). *Application deadline:* For fall admission, 6/1 for domestic students, 1/1 priority date for international students. Applications are processed on a rolling basis. Application fee: $25. Electronic applications accepted. *Expenses:* Tuition, state resident: full-time $3,888; part-time $216 per credit hour. Tuition, nonresident: full-time $7,688; part-time $426 per credit hour. Required fees: $220; $23 per term. Tuition and fees vary according to course load and reciprocity agreements. *Financial support:* In 2006–07, 6 students received support. Federal Work-Study, scholarships/grants, tuition waivers (full and partial), and unspecified assistantships available. Financial award application deadline: 3/1; financial award applicants required to submit FAFSA. *Unit head:* Dr. Kevin Valadares, Director, 812-461-5277, E-mail: kvaladar@usi.edu.

University of Southern Maine, Edmund S. Muskie School of Public Service, Program in Health Policy and Management, Portland, ME 04104-9300. Offers MS, Certificate, JD/MS. *Accreditation:* CAHME. Part-time and evening/weekend programs available. Postbaccalaureate distance learning degree programs offered (minimal on-campus study). *Degree requirements:* For master's, thesis, capstone project, field experience. *Entrance requirements:* For master's, GRE General Test. Additional exam requirements/recommendations for international students: Required—TOEFL. Electronic applications accepted. *Expenses:* Tuition, state resident: full-time $4,860; part-time $270 per credit hour. Tuition, nonresident: full-time $13,572; part-time $754 per credit hour. Required fees: $222 per semester. Tuition and fees vary according to course load. *Faculty research:* Health care, child welfare, social services, aging, substance abuse, health policy.

University of Southern Mississippi, Graduate School, College of Health, Department of Community Health Sciences, Hattiesburg, MS 39406-0001. Offers epidemiology and biostatistics (MPH); health education (MPH); health policy/administration (MPH); occupational/environmental health (MPH); public health nutrition (MPH). *Accreditation:* CEPH. Part-time and evening/weekend programs available. *Faculty:* 10 full-time (3 women). *Students:* 53 full-time (32 women), 13 part-time (10 women); includes 25 minority (24 African Americans, 1 Asian American or Pacific Islander), 15 international. Average age 30. 114 applicants, 84% accepted, 35 enrolled. In 2006, 27 degrees awarded. *Degree requirements:* For master's, thesis (for some programs), comprehensive exam, registration. *Entrance requirements:* For master's, GRE General Test, minimum GPA of 2.75 in last 60 hours. Additional exam requirements/recommendations for international students: Required—TOEFL. *Application deadline:* For fall admission, 3/1 for domestic and international students. Applications are processed on a rolling basis. Application fee: $25 ($30 for international students). *Financial support:* In 2006–07, 9 research assistantships with full tuition reimbursements (averaging $5,906 per year) were awarded; teaching assistantships with full tuition reimbursements, career-related internships or fieldwork and Federal Work-Study also available. Financial award application deadline: 3/15. *Faculty research:* Rural health care delivery, school health, nutrition of pregnant teens, risk factor reduction, sexually transmitted diseases. *Unit head:* Dr. James McGuire, Chair, 601-266-5437, Fax: 601-266-5043.

University of South Florida, Graduate School, College of Public Health, Department of Health Policy and Management, Tampa, FL 33620-9951. Offers MHA, MPH, MSPH, PhD. Part-time and evening/weekend programs available. *Faculty:* 7 full-time (2 women), 3 part-time/adjunct (1 woman). *Students:* 42 full-time (25 women), 39 part-time (23 women); includes 27 minority (12 African Americans, 9 Asian Americans or Pacific Islanders, 6 Hispanic Americans), 8 international. Average age 31. 45 applicants, 69% accepted, 12 enrolled. In 2006, 20 degrees awarded. *Median time to degree:* Master's–1.62 years full-time, 3.15 years part-time. *Degree requirements:* For master's, thesis (for some programs), comprehensive exam; for doctorate, thesis/dissertation, comprehensive exam. *Entrance requirements:* For master's, GRE General Test or GMAT, minimum GPA of 3.0 in upper-level course work; for doctorate, GRE General Test, minimum GPA of 3.0 in upper-level course work. Additional exam requirements/recommendations for international students: Required—TOEFL (minimum score 550 paper-based; 213 computer-based; 79 iBT). *Application deadline:* For fall admission, 6/1 for domestic students, 1/2 for international students; for spring admission, 10/15 for domestic students, 7/1 for international students. Applications are processed on a rolling basis. Application fee: $30. Electronic applications accepted. *Financial support:* In 2006–07, 1 fellowship with full tuition reimbursement (averaging $7,500 per year), 5 research assistantships with full and partial tuition reimbursements (averaging $2,917 per year), 5 teaching assistantships (averaging $3,456 per year) were awarded; career-related internships or fieldwork, Federal Work-Study, institutionally sponsored loans, scholarships/grants, traineeships, and unspecified assistantships also available. Support available to part-time students. Financial award applicants required to submit FAFSA. *Faculty research:* Tracking community health, inpatient care, discharge policies, stroke education, leadership practices. Total annual research expenditures: $14,096. *Unit head:* Dr. Barbara L. Orban, Chairperson, 813-974-7701, Fax: 813-974-6741. *Application contact:* Michelle Robinson, Academic Advisor, 813-974-6665, Fax: 813-974-8121, E-mail: mrobinso@health.usf.edu.

The University of Tennessee, Graduate School, College of Education, Health and Human Sciences, Program in Public Health, Knoxville, TN 37996. Offers community health education (MPH); gerontology (MPH); health planning/administration (MPH); MS/MPH. *Accreditation:* CEPH. *Students:* 42 (36 women); includes 3 minority (2 African Americans, 1 Hispanic American) 3 international. 48 applicants, 54% accepted. In 2006, 34 degrees awarded. *Degree requirements:* For master's, thesis optional. *Entrance requirements:* For master's, minimum GPA of 2.7. Additional exam requirements/recommendations for international students: Required—TOEFL. *Application deadline:* For fall admission, 2/1 priority date for domestic students. Applications are processed on a rolling basis. Application fee: $35. Electronic applications accepted. *Expenses:* Tuition, state resident: full-time $5,574. Tuition, nonresident: full-time $16,840. Required fees: $792. *Financial support:* Application deadline: 2/1; *Unit head:* Dr. Charles B. Hamilton, Graduate Representative, 865-974-6674, E-mail: cbhamilton@utk.edu.

The University of Texas at Arlington, Graduate School, College of Business Administration, Program in Health Care Administration, Arlington, TX 76019. Offers MS. Part-time and evening/weekend programs available. In 2006, 25 degrees awarded. *Entrance requirements:* For master's, GRE General Test or GMAT, minimum GPA of 3.0. Additional exam requirements/recommendations for international students: Required—TOEFL (minimum score 550 paper-based; 213 computer-based). *Application deadline:* For fall admission, 6/16 for domestic students. Application fee: $35 ($50 for international students). *Expenses:* Tuition, state resident: full-time $5,528. Tuition, nonresident: full-time $10,478. International tuition: $10,608 full-time. *Financial support:* In 2006–07, 1 fellowship (averaging $1,000 per year) was awarded. Financial award application deadline: 6/1; financial award applicants required to submit FAFSA. *Application contact:* Dr. Mike West, Assistant Dean, 817-272-1287, Fax: 817-272-5799, E-mail: mpwest@uta.edu.

The University of Texas at Dallas, School of Management, Program in Management and Administrative Sciences, Richardson, TX 75083-0688. Offers information technology and management (MS); management and administrative science (MS); medical management (MS). *Accreditation:* AACSB. Part-time and evening/weekend programs available. *Faculty:* 53 full-time (8 women), 4 part-time/adjunct (1 woman). *Students:* 67 full-time (25 women), 127 part-time (53 women); includes 46 minority (12 African Americans, 1 American Indian/Alaska Native, 27 Asian Americans or Pacific Islanders, 6 Hispanic Americans), 86 international. Average age 31. 140 applicants, 89% accepted, 74 enrolled. In 2006, 73 degrees awarded. *Degree requirements:* For master's, thesis optional. *Entrance requirements:* For master's, GMAT. Additional exam requirements/recommendations for international students: Required—TOEFL (minimum score 550 paper-based; 213 computer-based). *Application deadline:* Applications are processed on a rolling basis. Application fee: $50 ($100 for international students). Electronic applications accepted. *Financial support:* In 2006–07, 1 research assistantship with tuition reimbursement (averaging $9,000 per year), 22 teaching assistantships with tuition reimbursements (averaging $13,457 per year) were awarded; fellowships, career-related internships or fieldwork, Federal Work-Study, institutionally sponsored loans, and scholarships/grants also available. Support available to part-time students. Financial award application deadline: 4/30; financial award applicants required to submit FAFSA. *Faculty research:* Integrated and detailed knowledge of functional areas of management, as well as analytical tools for effective appraisal and decision making. *Unit head:* Dr. Diane McNulty, Associate Dean and College Master, 972-883-2705, Fax: 972-883-2799, E-mail: dmcnulty@utdallas.edu. *Application contact:* David B. Ritchey, Director of Advising, 972-883-2701, Fax: 972-883-6425, E-mail: davidr@utdallas.edu.

See Close-Up on page 365.

The University of Texas at Tyler, Graduate Studies, College of Business and Technology, Tyler, TX 75799-0001. Offers business administration (MBA); general management (MBA); health care track (MBA); human resource development and technology (MS), including human resource development, industrial distribution, industrial safety, industrial technology, instructional technology, technology systems; MSN/MBA. *Accreditation:* AACSB. Part-time and evening/weekend programs available. Postbaccalaureate distance learning degree programs offered (no on-campus study). *Entrance requirements:* Additional exam requirements/recommendations for international students: Required—TOEFL (minimum score 215 computer-based). Electronic applications accepted. *Expenses:* Tuition, state resident: part-time $50 per credit hour. Tuition, nonresident: part-time $328 per credit hour. Required fees: $107 per credit hour. $426 per term. *Faculty research:* Business ethics, financial policy, policy and strategy, economic multipliers, tax policy.

University of the Sciences in Philadelphia, College of Graduate Studies, Program in Health Policy, Philadelphia, PA 19104-4495. Offers MS, PhD. Part-time and evening/weekend programs available. *Faculty:* 9 full-time (4 women), 9 part-time/adjunct (4 women). *Students:* 4 full-time (2 women), 32 part-time (21 women); includes 2 minority (1 African American, 1 Hispanic American), 1 international. Average age 40. In 2006, 5 master's, 1 doctorate awarded. *Degree requirements:* For doctorate, thesis/dissertation, comprehensive exam. *Entrance requirements:* For master's and doctorate, GRE General Test. Additional exam requirements/recommendations for international students: Required—TOEFL, TWE. *Application deadline:* For fall admission, 6/1 for domestic students, 5/1 for international students; for winter admission, 12/1 for domestic students, 10/1 for international students; for spring admission, 3/1 for international students. Applications are processed on a rolling basis. Application fee: $50. *Expenses:* Tuition: Part-time $1,058 per credit. Tuition and fees vary according to program. *Financial support:* In 2006–07, 1 student received support. Tuition waivers (partial) and unspecified assistantships available. Support available to part-time students. Financial award application deadline: 5/1. *Faculty research:* Managed care, pharmacoeconomics, health law and regulation, rehabilitation, genetic technologies. Total annual research expenditures: $167,599. *Unit head:* Dr. Robert I. Field, Director, 215-596-7618, Fax: 215-596-7614, E-mail: r.field@usip.edu. *Application contact:* Joyce D'Angelo, Administrative Assistant, 215-596-8937, E-mail: j.dangel@usip.edu.

See Close-Up on page 2253.

The University of Toledo, College of Graduate Studies, College of Arts and Sciences, Department of Political Science and Public Administration, Program in Public Administration, Toledo, OH 43606-3390. Offers health care policy (MPA); municipal administration (MPA); public administration (MPA). *Accreditation:* NASPAA. *Students:* 5 full-time (3 women), 16 part-time (10 women); includes 2 minority (both African Americans), 1 international. Average age 31. 17 applicants, 76% accepted, 7 enrolled. In 2006, 3 master's awarded. *Degree requirements:* For master's, internship. *Entrance requirements:* For master's, GRE General Test, minimum GPA of 3.0. *Application deadline:* For fall admission, 8/1 priority date for domestic students. Applications are processed on a rolling basis. Application fee: $45. Electronic applications accepted. *Financial support:* Research assistantships, teaching assistantships available. Financial award application deadline: 4/1. *Faculty research:* Economic development, health administration, personnel, budgeting, urban administration. *Application contact:* Dr. Hugh Hinton, Director, 419-530-2385, E-mail: hugh.hinton@utoledo.edu.

University of Virginia, School of Medicine, Department of Public Health Sciences, Charlottesville, VA 22903. Offers health evaluation sciences (MS), including clinical investigation and patient-oriented research, informatics in medicine; public health (MPH). Part-time programs available. *Students:* 30 full-time (18 women), 11 part-time (6 women); includes 11 minority (5 African Americans, 6 Asian Americans or Pacific Islanders), 2 international. Average age 33. 78 applicants, 62% accepted, 30 enrolled. In 2006, 8 degrees awarded. *Entrance requirements:* For master's, GRE General Test or MCAT. Additional exam requirements/recommendations for international students: Required—TOEFL. *Application deadline:* Applications are processed on a rolling basis. Application fee: $60. Electronic applications accepted. *Financial support:* Career-related internships or fieldwork available. Financial award applicants required to submit FAFSA. *Unit head:* William A. Knaus, Director, 434-924-8430, Fax: 434-924-8437. *Application contact:* Robyn Kells, Coordinator, 434-924-8646, Fax: 434-924-8437, E-mail: ms-hes@virginia.edu.

University of Washington, Graduate School, School of Public Health and Community Medicine, Department of Health Services, Graduate Program in Health Services Administration, Seattle, WA 98195. Offers EMHA, MHA, MHA/MBA, MHA/MD, MHA/MPA. *Accreditation:* CAHME. *Degree requirements:* For master's, capstone project. *Entrance requirements:* For master's, GRE General Test or GMAT preferred, MCAT accepted, minimum GPA of 3.0. Additional exam requirements/recommendations for international students: Required—TOEFL (minimum score 580 paper-based; 237 computer-based). *Faculty research:* Managed care, interorganizational analysis, quality assurance, cost and outcomes of health care, management development.

University of Wisconsin–Oshkosh, The School of Graduate Studies, College of Letters and Science, Department of Public Administration, Oshkosh, WI 54901. Offers general agency (MPA); health care (MPA). Part-time and evening/weekend programs available. *Degree*

Health Services Management and Hospital Administration

University of Wisconsin–Oshkosh (continued)

requirements: For master's, thesis or alternative, registration. *Entrance requirements:* For master's, public service-related experience, resumé, sample of written work. Additional exam requirements/recommendations for international students: Required—TOEFL (minimum score 550 paper-based; 213 computer-based). Electronic applications accepted. *Faculty research:* Drug policy, local government state revenues and expenditures, health care regulation.

Villanova University, College of Nursing, Villanova, PA 19085-1690. Offers adult nurse practitioner (MSN, Post Master's Certificate); clinical case management (MSN, Post Master's Certificate); geriatric nurse practitioner (MSN, Post Master's Certificate); health care administration (MSN); nurse anesthetist (MSN, Post Master's Certificate); nursing (PhD); nursing education (MSN, Post Master's Certificate); pediatric nurse practitioner (MSN, Post Master's Certificate). *Accreditation:* AACN; AANA/CANAEP; NLN. Part-time programs available. Post-baccalaureate distance learning degree programs offered (minimal on-campus study). *Faculty:* 14 full-time (all women), 2 part-time/adjunct (both women). *Students:* 41 full-time (27 women), 164 part-time (128 women); includes 17 minority (8 African Americans, 1 American Indian/Alaska Native, 8 Asian Americans or Pacific Islanders), 6 international. Average age 31. 137 applicants, 50% accepted, 48 enrolled. In 2006, 47 degrees awarded. *Median time to degree:* Master's–2 years full-time, 5 years part-time. *Degree requirements:* For master's, independent study project; for doctorate, thesis/dissertation, comprehensive exam. *Entrance requirements:* For master's, GRE or MAT, BSN, 1 year of recent nursing experience, physical assessment, course work in statistics; for doctorate, GRE. Additional exam requirements/recommendations for international students: Required—TOEFL. *Application deadline:* For fall admission, 7/1 priority date for domestic students, 7/1 for international students; for spring admission, 12/1 priority date for domestic students, 12/1 for international students. Applications are processed on a rolling basis. Application fee: $50. *Expenses:* Contact institution. *Financial support:* In 2006–07, 50 students received support, including 4 teaching assistantships with full tuition reimbursements available (averaging $12,165 per year); institutionally sponsored loans, scholarships/grants, traineeships, and tuition waivers (full) also available. Financial award application deadline: 3/1; financial award applicants required to submit FAFSA. *Faculty research:* Genetics, ethics, cognitive development of students, women with disabilities, nursing leadership. *Unit head:* Dr. Marguerite K. Schlag, Assistant Dean and Director, Graduate Program, 610-519-4907, Fax: 610-519-7650, E-mail: marguerite.schlag@villanova.edu.

Virginia Commonwealth University, Graduate School, School of Allied Health Professions, Department of Health Administration, Doctoral Program in Health Related Sciences, Richmond, VA 23284-9005. Offers clinical laboratory sciences (PhD); gerontology (PhD); health administration (PhD); nurse anesthesia (PhD); occupational therapy (PhD); physical therapy (PhD); radiation sciences (PhD); rehabilitation leadership (PhD). *Faculty:* 2 full-time (1 woman). *Students:* 4 full-time (all women), 13 part-time (7 women); includes 7 minority (1 African American, 6 Asian Americans or Pacific Islanders), 3 international. In 2006, 2 degrees awarded. *Unit head:* Monica L. White, Director of Student Services, 804-828-3273, Fax: 804-828-8656, E-mail: mlwhite1@vcu.edu.

See Close-Up on page 1745.

Virginia Commonwealth University, Graduate School, School of Allied Health Professions, Department of Health Administration, Doctoral Program in Health Services Organization and Research, Richmond, VA 23298-0203. Offers PhD. *Students:* 1 (woman) full-time, 1 international. In 2006, 4 degrees awarded. *Degree requirements:* For doctorate, thesis/dissertation, residency. *Entrance requirements:* For doctorate, GMAT or GRE General Test. *Application deadline:* For fall admission, 4/15 priority date for domestic students. Application fee: $50. *Unit head:* Dr. Michael J. McCue, Director, 804-828-1893, Fax: 804-828-1894, E-mail: mjmccue@vcu.edu. *Application contact:* Information Contact, 804-828-5520, Fax: 804-828-1894, E-mail: bdeshazo@hsc.vcu.edu.

See Close-Ups on pages 1825 and 1827.

Virginia Commonwealth University, Graduate School, School of Allied Health Professions, Department of Health Administration, Master's Program in Health Administration, Richmond, VA 23298-0203. Offers MHA, JD/MHA, MD/MHA. *Accreditation:* CAHME. *Students:* 48 full-time (22 women), 23 part-time (17 women); includes 16 minority (9 African Americans, 7 Asian Americans or Pacific Islanders). In 2006, 14 degrees awarded. *Degree requirements:* For master's, residency. *Entrance requirements:* For master's, GMAT or GRE General Test, course work in accounting, economics, and statistics. *Application deadline:* For fall admission, 3/15 priority date for domestic students. Application fee: $50. *Unit head:* Dr. Stephen S. Mick, Chair, 804-828-5221, E-mail: micks@vcu.edu. *Application contact:* Information Contact, 804-828-0719, Fax: 804-828-1894, E-mail: shavasy@hsc.vcu.edu.

See Close-Up on page 1825.

Virginia Commonwealth University, Graduate School, School of Allied Health Professions, Department of Health Administration, Professional Online Master's Program in Health Administration, Richmond, VA 23298-0203. Offers MSHA. *Accreditation:* CAHME. *Students:* 29 full-time (17 women), 16 part-time (8 women); includes 7 minority (4 African Americans, 2 Asian Americans or Pacific Islanders, 1 Hispanic American), 1 international. In 2006, 46 degrees awarded. *Degree requirements:* For master's, residency. *Entrance requirements:* For master's, GMAT or GRE General Test. *Application deadline:* For fall admission, 3/15 for domestic students. Application fee: $50. *Unit head:* Dr. Jan P. Clement, Director, 804-828-0719, Fax: 804-828-8194, E-mail: jpclemen@vcu.edu. *Application contact:* Information Contact, 804-828-0719, Fax: 804-828-7799, E-mail: cwwells@hsc.vcu.edu.

See Close-Up on page 1825.

Wagner College, Division of Graduate Studies, Department of Business Administration, Program in Health Care Administration, Staten Island, NY 10301-4495. Offers MBA. *Faculty:* 1 (woman) full-time. *Students:* 2 full-time (1 woman), 1 (woman) part-time. In 2006, 2 degrees awarded. *Degree requirements:* For master's, thesis optional. *Entrance requirements:* For master's, GMAT, minimum GPA of 2.6. Additional exam requirements/recommendations for international students: Required—TOEFL (minimum score 550 paper-based; 217 computer-based). *Application deadline:* For fall admission, 8/1 priority date for domestic students, 6/30 priority date for international students; for spring admission, 12/10 priority date for domestic students, 11/15 for international students. Applications are processed on a rolling basis. Application fee: $50 ($85 for international students). *Expenses:* Tuition: Full-time $15,120; part-time $840 per credit. *Financial support:* Fellowships, unspecified assistantships available. Financial award applicants required to submit FAFSA. *Application contact:* Susan Rosenberg, Office of Graduate Studies, 718-390-3106, Fax: 718-390-3456, E-mail: graduate@wagner.edu.

Walden University, Graduate Programs, School of Health and Human Services, Minneapolis, MN 55401. Offers health services (PhD); human services (PhD); nursing (MS); public health (MPH, PhD). Part-time and evening/weekend programs available. Postbaccalaureate distance learning degree programs offered (minimal on-campus study). *Faculty:* 100. *Students:* 2,383 full-time (2,074 women), 1,082 part-time (876 women); includes 840 minority (662 African Americans, 18 American Indian/Alaska Native, 83 Asian Americans or Pacific Islanders, 77 Hispanic Americans), 24 international. Average age 42. 1,164 applicants, 85% accepted, 813 enrolled. In 2006, 212 master's, 30 doctorates awarded. *Degree requirements:* For master's, thesis (for some programs); for doctorate, thesis/dissertation. *Entrance requirements:* For master's, minimum GPA of 3.0; for doctorate, 3 years of professional experience, master's degree. Additional exam requirements/recommendations for inter-

national students: Required—TOEFL (minimum score 550 paper-based; 213 computer-based), IELTS (minimum score 7). *Application deadline:* For fall admission, 8/15 priority date for domestic and international students; for winter admission, 11/15 priority date for domestic and international students; for spring admission, 12/15 priority date for domestic and international students. Applications are processed on a rolling basis. Application fee: $50. Electronic applications accepted. *Financial support:* Fellowships with partial tuition reimbursements, tuition waivers (partial) available. Support available to part-time students. Financial award applicants required to submit FAFSA. *Unit head:* Dr. Gary J. Burkholder, Dean, 800-925-3368, Fax: 612-338-5092. *Application contact:* 866-4-WALDEN, Fax: 410-843-8780, E-mail: request@waldenu.edu.

Washington State University, Graduate School, College of Pharmacy, Department of Health Policy and Administration, Pullman, WA 99164. Offers MHPA. *Application fee:* $50. *Expenses:* Tuition, state resident: full-time $7,066. Tuition, nonresident: full-time $17,204. *Unit head:* Winsor Schmidt, Chair.

Washington State University Spokane, Graduate Programs, Program in Health Policy and Administration, Spokane, WA 99210-1495. Offers MHPA. *Accreditation:* CAHME. Part-time and evening/weekend programs available. *Faculty:* 7 full-time (2 women), 7 part-time/adjunct (4 women). *Students:* 31 full-time (12 women), 8 part-time (6 women); includes 5 minority (1 African American, 1 American Indian/Alaska Native, 2 Asian Americans or Pacific Islanders, 1 Hispanic American), 4 international. Average age 35. 39 applicants, 46% accepted, 13 enrolled. *Degree requirements:* For master's, thesis (for some programs), oral exam, comprehensive exam (for some programs). *Entrance requirements:* For master's, GRE General Test or GMAT, minimum GPA of 3.0, 3 letters of recommendation. Additional exam requirements/recommendations for international students: Required—TOEFL (paper-based 550; computer-based 213) or IELTS (paper-based 7). *Application deadline:* For fall admission, 5/1 priority date for domestic students, 3/1 for international students; for spring admission, 9/1 priority date for domestic students, 7/1 for international students. Application fee: $50. *Expenses:* Tuition, state resident: full-time $7,066. Tuition, nonresident: full-time $17,204. Tuition and fees vary according to program. *Financial support:* In 2006–07, 27 students received support, including 5 fellowships (averaging $6,301 per year), 5 research assistantships with full and partial tuition reimbursements available (averaging $13,917 per year); teaching assistantships, career-related internships or fieldwork also available. Support available to part-time students. Financial award application deadline: 4/1. Total annual research expenditures: $728,061. *Unit head:* Winsor C. Schmidt, Chair, 509-358-7981, E-mail: schmidtw@wsu.edu. *Application contact:* Graduate School Admissions, 800-GRADWSU, Fax: 509-335-1949, E-mail: gradsch@wsu.edu.

Washington University in St. Louis, School of Medicine, Graduate Programs in Medicine, Health Administration Program, St. Louis, MO 63130-4899. Offers MHA. The Health Administration Program is not accepting applications. It will be discontinued in 2008. *Accreditation:* CAHME. *Faculty:* 3 full-time (1 woman), 14 part-time/adjunct (4 women). *Students:* 47 full-time (21 women); includes 16 minority (7 African Americans, 7 Asian Americans or Pacific Islanders, 2 Hispanic Americans), 7 international. Average age 25. 66 applicants, 64% accepted, 29 enrolled. In 2006, 19 degrees awarded. *Entrance requirements:* For master's, GMAT or GRE General Test, 1 semester of course work in basic accounting, minimum GPA of 3.0. Additional exam requirements/recommendations for international students: Required—TOEFL (minimum score 550 paper-based; 213 computer-based). *Application deadline:* For fall admission, 4/30 priority date for international students. Applications are processed on a rolling basis. Application fee: $30 ($50 for international students). Electronic applications accepted. *Financial support:* Institutionally sponsored loans, scholarships/grants, and health care benefits available. Support available to part-time students. Financial award application deadline: 5/1; financial award applicants required to submit FAFSA. *Faculty research:* Economics, cost effectiveness, and epidemiological analyses, especially with respect to organ transplantation. *Unit head:* Dr. Stuart B. Boxerman, Director, 314-362-4277, Fax: 314-362-3265, E-mail: stuart@wubios.wustl.edu. *Application contact:* Marilyn A. Hummert, Coordinator of Financial and Student Services, 314-362-3274, Fax: 314-362-3265, E-mail: marilyn@wubios.wustl.edu.

Wayland Baptist University, Graduate Programs, Programs in Business Administration/Management, Plainview, TX 79072-6998. Offers general business (MBA); health care administration (MBA); human resource management (MBA); international management (MBA); management (MA, MBA), including human resource management (MA), organization management (MA); management information systems (MBA). Part-time and evening/weekend programs available. Postbaccalaureate distance learning degree programs offered (no on-campus study). *Faculty:* 3 full-time (0 women). *Students:* 1 full-time (0 women), 7 part-time (2 women); includes 1 minority (Hispanic American). Average age 28. 1 applicant, 100% accepted, 1 enrolled. In 2006, 2 degrees awarded. *Degree requirements:* For master's, capstone course. *Entrance requirements:* For master's, GMAT, GRE or MAT. Additional exam requirements/recommendations for international students: Required—TOEFL (minimum score 500 paper-based; 173 computer-based). *Application deadline:* Applications are processed on a rolling basis. Application fee: $35. *Expenses:* Tuition: Full-time $6,120; part-time $340 per credit hour. Required fees: $50 per term. *Financial support:* Federal Work-Study, institutionally sponsored loans, and scholarships/grants available. Support available to part-time students. Financial award application deadline: 5/1; financial award applicants required to submit FAFSA. *Unit head:* Dr. Otto Schacht, Chairman, 806-291-1020, Fax: 806-291-1957.

Weber State University, College of Health Professions, Program of Health Administration, Ogden, UT 84408-1001. Offers MHA. *Faculty:* 4 full-time (0 women), 6 part-time/adjunct (1 woman). *Students:* 23 full-time (6 women), 8 part-time (4 women). Average age 39. 38 applicants, 82% accepted, 31 enrolled. *Entrance requirements:* For master's, GMAT or GRE. Additional exam requirements/recommendations for international students: Required—TOEFL. *Application deadline:* For fall admission, 3/1 for domestic students. Applications are processed on a rolling basis. Application fee: $30 ($45 for international students). *Expenses:* Tuition, state resident: full-time $3,950; part-time $203 per semester. Tuition, nonresident: full-time $10,371; part-time $518 per semester. Required fees: $544; $24 per semester. Tuition and fees vary according to course load and program. *Unit head:* Dr. Lloyd R. Burton, Chair, 801-626-7005, Fax: 801-626-6475, E-mail: lburton1@weber.edu. *Application contact:* Shari A. Love, Secretary II, 801-626-7242, Fax: 801-626-6475, E-mail: slove@weber.edu.

Webster University, School of Business and Technology, Department of Business, St. Louis, MO 63119-3194. Offers business (MA); business and organizational security management (MBA); computer resources and information management (MBA); environmental management (MBA); finance (MA, MBA); health services management (MBA); human resources development (MBA); human resources management (MBA); international business (MA, MBA); management and leadership (MBA); marketing (MBA); procurement and acquisitions management (MBA); telecommunications management (MBA). Part-time and evening/weekend programs available. Postbaccalaureate distance learning degree programs offered (no on-campus study). *Students:* 1,205 full-time (629 women), 4,197 part-time (2,153 women); includes 2,005 minority (1,467 African Americans, 29 American Indian/Alaska Native, 212 Asian Americans or Pacific Islanders, 297 Hispanic Americans), 485 international. Average age 33. *Application deadline:* Applications are processed on a rolling basis. Application fee: $25 ($50 for international students). *Expenses:* Tuition: Full-time $8,820; part-time $490 per credit. Tuition and fees vary according to degree level, campus/location and program. *Financial support:* Federal Work-Study available. Support available to part-time students. Financial award application deadline: 4/1; financial award applicants required to submit FAFSA. *Unit head:* Bradford Scott, Chair, 314-961-2260 Ext. 7574, Fax: 314-968-7077, E-mail: buschair@webster.edu. *Application contact:* Director of Graduate and Evening Student Admissions, Fax: 314-968-7116, E-mail: gadmit@webster.edu.

Webster University, School of Business and Technology, Department of Management, St. Louis, MO 63119-3194. Offers business and organizational security management (MA); computer resources and information management (MA); environmental management (MS); health care management (MA); health services management (MA); human resources development (MA); human resources management (MA); management (DM); management and leadership (MA); marketing (MA); procurement and acquisitions management (MA); public administration (MA); quality management (MA); space systems operations management (MS); telecommunications management (MA). Part-time and evening/weekend programs available. Postbaccalaureate distance learning degree programs offered (no on-campus study). *Students:* 1,396 full-time (746 women), 4,727 part-time (2,579 women); includes 3,065 minority (2,374 African Americans, 45 American Indian/Alaska Native, 158 Asian Americans or Pacific Islanders, 488 Hispanic Americans), 128 international. Average age 37. In 2006, 9 degrees awarded. *Degree requirements:* For doctorate, thesis/dissertation, written exam. *Entrance requirements:* For doctorate, GMAT, 3 years of work experience, MBA. *Application deadline:* Applications are processed on a rolling basis. Application fee: $25 ($50 for international students). *Expenses:* Tuition: Full-time $8,820; part-time $490 per credit. Tuition and fees vary according to degree level, campus/location and program. *Financial support:* Federal Work-Study available. Support available to part-time students. Financial award application deadline: 4/1; financial award applicants required to submit FAFSA. *Unit head:* Jeffrey Haldeman, Chair, 314-961-2660 Ext. 7552, Fax: 314-968-7077, E-mail: mgtchair@webster.edu. *Application contact:* Director of Graduate and Evening Student Admissions, Fax: 314-968-7116, E-mail: gadmit@webster.edu.

West Chester University of Pennsylvania, Graduate Studies, School of Business and Public Affairs, Program in Administration, West Chester, PA 19383. Offers health services (MSA); human research management (MSA); individualized (MSA); leadership for women (MSA); long-term care (MSA); public administration (MSA); regional planning (MSA); sport and athletic training (MSA); training and development (MSA). Part-time and evening/weekend programs available. *Students:* 3 full-time (all women), 4 part-time (1 woman); includes 1 minority (African American) Average age 31. 20 applicants, 90% accepted. In 2006, 31 degrees awarded. *Degree requirements:* For master's, comprehensive exam. *Entrance requirements:* For master's, GMAT, GRE General Test, or MAT, interview, minimum GPA of 3.0. *Application deadline:* For fall admission, 4/15 priority date for domestic students; for spring admission, 10/15 for domestic students. Applications are processed on a rolling basis. Application fee: $35. *Financial support:* In 2006–07, research assistantships with full tuition reimbursements (averaging $5,000 per year); career-related internships or fieldwork and unspecified assistantships also available. Support available to part-time students. Financial award application deadline: 2/15; financial award applicants required to submit FAFSA. *Unit head:* Dr. Duane Milne, Director, 610-436-2448, E-mail: dmilne@wcupa.edu.

West Chester University of Pennsylvania, Graduate Studies, School of Health Sciences, Department of Health, West Chester, PA 19383. Offers emergency preparedness (Certificate); environmental health (MS); gerontology (MS); health care administration (Certificate); health services (MSA); integrative health (Certificate); public health (MPH, MS); school health (M Ed). Part-time and evening/weekend programs available. *Students:* 35 full-time (27 women), 65 part-time (50 women); includes 19 African Americans, 1 Asian American or Pacific Islander, 9 international. Average age 34. 58 applicants, 98% accepted, 30 enrolled. In 2006, 36 degrees awarded. *Degree requirements:* For master's, thesis (for some programs), comprehensive exam. *Entrance requirements:* For master's, GRE. *Application deadline:* For fall admission, 4/15 priority date for domestic students; for spring admission, 10/15 for domestic students. Applications are processed on a rolling basis. Application fee: $35. *Financial support:* In 2006–07, 9 research assistantships with full tuition reimbursements (averaging $5,000 per year) were awarded; unspecified assistantships also available. Support available to part-time students. Financial award application deadline: 2/15; financial award applicants required to submit FAFSA. *Faculty research:* HIV/AIDS education, teacher preparation, water quality. *Unit head:* Dr. Roger Mustalish, Chair, 610-436-2931, E-mail: rmustalish@wcupa.edu. *Application contact:* Dr. Bethann Cinelli, Graduate Coordinator, 610-436-2267, E-mail: bcinelli@wcupa.edu.

Western Carolina University, Graduate School, College of Applied Science, Department of Health Sciences, Cullowhee, NC 28723. Offers MHS. Part-time and evening/weekend programs available. *Degree requirements:* For master's, thesis optional. *Entrance requirements:* For master's, GRE General Test. Additional exam requirements/recommendations for international students: Required—TOEFL (minimum score 550 paper-based; 213 computer-based).

Western Connecticut State University, Division of Graduate Studies, Ancell School of Business, Program in Health Administration, Danbury, CT 06810-6885. Offers MHA. Part-time and evening/weekend programs available. *Faculty:* 12 full-time (3 women), 1 part-time/adjunct (0 women). *Students:* 2 full-time (0 women), 22 part-time (12 women); includes 4 minority (3 African Americans, 1 Hispanic American), 1 international. Average age 43. In 2006, 19 degrees awarded. *Entrance requirements:* For master's, GMAT, GRE, or MAT, minimum GPA of 2.5. *Application deadline:* For fall admission, 8/1 priority date for domestic students. Applications are processed on a rolling basis. Application fee: $40. *Financial support:* Fellowships, career-related internships or fieldwork available. Support available to part-time students. Financial award application deadline: 5/1; financial award applicants required to submit FAFSA. *Unit head:* Dr. Neil Dworkin, Assistant Professor, 203-837-8475. *Application contact:* Chris Shankle, Associate Director of Graduate Admissions, 203-837-8244, Fax: 203-837-8338, E-mail: shanklec@wcsu.edu.

Western Illinois University, School of Graduate Studies, College of Education and Human Services, Department of Health Sciences, Macomb, IL 61455-1390. Offers health education (MS); health services administration (Certificate). *Accreditation:* NCATE. Part-time programs available. *Students:* 23 full-time (16 women), 34 part-time (30 women); includes 2 minority (1 African American, 1 Hispanic American), 4 international. Average age 32. 33 applicants, 88% accepted. In 2006, 15 degrees awarded. *Degree requirements:* For master's, thesis or alternative, comprehensive exam. *Entrance requirements:* For master's, minimum GPA of 2.75. Additional exam requirements/recommendations for international students: Required—TOEFL (minimum score 550 paper-based; 213 computer-based; 80 iBT). *Application deadline:* Applications are processed on a rolling basis. Application fee: $30. Electronic applications accepted. *Expenses:* Tuition, state resident: part-time $200 per credit hour. Tuition, nonresident: part-time $400 per credit hour. *Financial support:* In 2006–07, 10 students received support, including 10 research assistantships with full tuition reimbursements available (averaging $6,568 per year). Financial award applicants required to submit FAFSA. *Unit head:* Dr. Diane Hamilton-Hancock, Chairperson, 309-298-1076. *Application contact:* Dr. Barbara Baily, Director of Graduate Studies/Associate Provost, 309-298-1806, Fax: 309-298-2345, E-mail: grad-office@wiu.edu.

Western Kentucky University, Graduate Studies, College of Health and Human Services, Department of Public Health, Bowling Green, KY 42101. Offers healthcare administration (MHA); public health (MPH). *Accreditation:* CEPH. Part-time and evening/weekend programs available. *Faculty:* 13 full-time (4 women), 4 part-time/adjunct (2 women). *Students:* 89 full-time (33 women), 45 part-time (23 women); includes 14 minority (10 African Americans, 2 Asian Americans or Pacific Islanders, 2 Hispanic Americans), 88 international. Average age 28. 170 applicants, 38% accepted, 32 enrolled. In 2006, 32 degrees awarded. *Degree requirements:* For master's, thesis or alternative, comprehensive exam. *Entrance requirements:* For master's, GRE General Test, minimum GPA of 2.75. Additional exam requirements/recommendations for international students: Required—TOEFL (minimum score 555 paper-based; 213 computer-based; 79 iBT). *Application deadline:* For fall admission, 7/1 priority date for domestic students, 4/1 for international students; for spring admission, 11/1 for domestic students, 9/1 for international students. Applications are processed on a rolling basis. Application fee: $35. *Expenses:* Tuition, state resident: full-time $6,520; part-time $226 per hour. Tuition, nonresident: full-time $7,140; part-time $357 per hour. International tuition: $15,820 full-time. *Financial support:* In 2006–07, 10 research assistantships with partial tuition reimbursements (averaging $9,500 per year) were awarded; career-related internships or fieldwork, Federal Work-Study, institutionally sponsored loans, tuition waivers (partial), unspecified assistantships, and service awards also available. Support available to part-time students. Financial award application deadline: 4/1; financial award applicants required to submit FAFSA. *Faculty research:* Health education training, driver traffic safety, community readiness, occupational injuries, local health departments. Total annual research expenditures: $88,907. *Unit head:* Dr. David Dunn, Interim Head, 270-745-6395, Fax: 270-745-4437, E-mail: david.dunn@wku.edu.

Widener University, School of Business Administration, Program in Health and Medical Services Administration, Chester, PA 19013-5792. Offers MBA, MHA, MD/MBA, MD/MHA, Psy D/MBA, Psy D/MHA. *Accreditation:* CAHME (one or more programs are accredited). Part-time and evening/weekend programs available. *Degree requirements:* For master's, clerkship, residency. *Entrance requirements:* For master's, GMAT, interview, minimum GPA of 2.5. Electronic applications accepted. *Faculty research:* Cost containment in health care, reimbursement of hospitals, strategic behavior.

Widener University, School of Human Service Professions, Institute for Graduate Clinical Psychology, Program in Clinical Psychology and Health and Medical Services Administration, Chester, PA 19013-5792. Offers Psy D/MBA, Psy D/MHA. *Accreditation:* APA (one or more programs are accredited); CAHME. Electronic applications accepted. *Faculty research:* Psychosocial competence, family systems, medical care systems and financing.

William Woods University, Graduate and Adult Studies, Fulton, MO 65251-1098. Offers administration (M Ed, Ed S); agribusiness (MBA); curriculum/instruction (M Ed); health management (MBA); human services (MBA); instructional leadership (Ed S). Evening/weekend programs available. *Faculty:* 38 full-time (14 women), 174 part-time/adjunct (50 women). *Students:* 1,944 full-time (1,230 women); includes 71 minority (43 African Americans, 16 American Indian/Alaska Native, 7 Asian Americans or Pacific Islanders, 5 Hispanic Americans), 41 international. 824 applicants, 86% accepted, 631 enrolled. In 2006, 919 master's, 112 other advanced degrees awarded. *Median time to degree:* Master's–1.5 years full-time; Ed S–1.5 years full-time. *Degree requirements:* For master's, capstone course (MBA), action research (M Ed); for Ed S, field experience. *Entrance requirements:* For master's, 2 recommendations, resumé, BA/BS; teaching certification (M Ed); course work in economics and accounting (MBA); for Ed S, M Ed, 2 letters of recommendation, resumé, teaching certification. Additional exam requirements/recommendations for international students: Required—TOEFL (minimum score 550 paper-based). *Application deadline:* Applications are processed on a rolling basis. Application fee: $25. Electronic applications accepted. *Expenses:* Tuition: Part-time $255 per credit hour. Tuition and fees vary according to program. *Financial support:* Institutionally sponsored loans available. Financial award applicants required to submit FAFSA. *Unit head:* Sean Siebert, Dean of Graduate and Adult Studies Enrollment Services, 573-592-4383, Fax: 573-592-1164. *Application contact:* Linda Rembish, Administrative Assistant, 800-995-3199, Fax: 573-592-1164, E-mail: cgas@williamwoods.edu.

Wilmington College, Division of Business, New Castle, DE 19720-6491. Offers business administration (MBA); finance (MBA); health care administration (MBA, MS); human resource management (MS); management (MS); management information systems (MBA); organizational leadership (MS); public administration (MS); transportation and logistics (MBA, MS). Part-time and evening/weekend programs available. *Faculty:* 3 full-time (0 women). *Students:* 230 full-time (138 women), 432 part-time (274 women); includes 109 minority (98 African Americans, 1 American Indian/Alaska Native, 3 Asian Americans or Pacific Islanders, 7 Hispanic Americans). Average age 34. 229 applicants, 100% accepted, 156 enrolled. In 2006, 273 degrees awarded. *Entrance requirements:* Additional exam requirements/recommendations for international students: Required—TOEFL (minimum score 500 paper-based; 173 computer-based). *Application deadline:* Applications are processed on a rolling basis. Application fee: $25. *Financial support:* Applicants required to submit FAFSA. *Unit head:* Dr. Robert Edelson, Chair, 302-295-1147, Fax: 302-328-7021, E-mail: robert.e.edelson@wilmcoll.edu. *Application contact:* Chris Ferguson, Director of Admissions and Financial Aid, 302-328-9407 Ext. 256, Fax: 302-328-5164, E-mail: inquire@wilmcoll.edu.

Worcester State College, Graduate Studies, Program in Health Care Administration, Worcester, MA 01602-2597. Offers MS. *Students:* Average age 38. 20 applicants, 75% accepted, 7 enrolled. In 2006, 7 degrees awarded. *Degree requirements:* For master's, thesis optional. *Entrance requirements:* For master's, MAT and GRE. Additional exam requirements/recommendations for international students: Required—TOEFL (minimum score 550 paper-based; 213 computer-based). Application fee: $30. *Expenses:* Tuition, state resident: full-time $4,518; part-time $251 per credit hour. Tuition, nonresident: full-time $4,518; part-time $251 per credit hour. *Unit head:* Robert Shafner, Coordinator, 508-929-8739, Fax: 508-929-8175, E-mail: rshafner@worcester.edu. *Application contact:* Nicole Brown, Assistant Dean of Graduate and Continuing Education, 508-929-8787, Fax: 508-929-8100, E-mail: nbrown@worcester.edu.

Wright State University, School of Graduate Studies, Raj Soin College of Business, Department of Management, Dayton, OH 45435. Offers flexible business (MBA); health care management (MBA); international business (MBA); management, innovation and change (MBA); project management (MBA); supply chain management (MBA); MBA/MS. *Students:* 47 full-time (22 women), 154 part-time (63 women). Average age 31. 40 applicants, 90% accepted. In 2006, 71 degrees awarded. *Entrance requirements:* For master's, GMAT, minimum AACSB index of 1000. Additional exam requirements/recommendations for international students: Required—TOEFL. Application fee: $25. *Financial support:* Fellowships, research assistantships, teaching assistantships, unspecified assistantships available. Support available to part-time students. Financial award applicants required to submit FAFSA. *Unit head:* Dr. Riad Ajami, Chair, 937-775-2375, Fax: 937-775-3545, E-mail: riad.ajami@wright.edu. *Application contact:* Michael Evans, Director of MBA Programs, 937-775-2437, Fax: 937-775-3545, E-mail: michael.evans@wright.edu.

Xavier University, College of Social Sciences, Health and Education, Program in Health Services Administration, Cincinnati, OH 45207. Offers MHSA, MBA/MHSA. *Accreditation:* CAHME. Part-time and evening/weekend programs available. *Faculty:* 6 full-time (2 women), 7 part-time/adjunct (1 woman). *Students:* 45 full-time (23 women), 45 part-time (23 women); includes 21 minority (13 African Americans, 6 Asian Americans or Pacific Islanders, 2 Hispanic Americans). Average age 27. 65 applicants, 43% accepted, 27 enrolled. In 2006, 31 degrees awarded. *Median time to degree:* Master's–2.25 years full-time, 3 years part-time. *Degree requirements:* For master's, thesis, administrative residency, project. *Entrance requirements:* For master's, GMAT or GRE, minimum undergraduate GPA of 3.0, interview. Additional exam requirements/recommendations for international students: Required—TOEFL (minimum score 550 paper-based; 213 computer-based). *Application deadline:* For fall admission, 7/15 priority date for domestic students. Applications are processed on a rolling basis. Application fee: $35. Electronic applications accepted. *Expenses:* Tuition: Part-time $462 per credit hour. Part-time tuition and fees vary according to degree level, campus/location and program. *Financial support:* Career-related internships or fieldwork, scholarships/grants, unspecified assistantships, and residency stipends available. Financial award application deadline: 5/1; financial award applicants required to submit FAFSA. *Faculty research:* Early hospital admission and quality, ethical foundations for leadership, physician work force planning, utilization issues for stroke patients. *Unit head:* Dr. Ida Critelli Schick, Director, 513-745-

Health Services Management and Hospital Administration

Xavier University (continued)
3716, Fax: 513-745-4301, E-mail: schicki@xavier.edu. *Application contact:* Christina Swift, Coordinator for Recruitment and Promotion, 513-745-3687, Fax: 513-745-4301.

See Close-Up on page 1829.

Yale University, School of Medicine, School of Public Health, Division of Health Policy and Administration, New Haven, CT 06520. Offers MPH, PhD. PhD offered through the Graduate School. *Accreditation:* CAHME. Part-time programs available. *Faculty:* 14 full-time (7 women), 11 part-time/adjunct (4 women). *Students:* Average age 26. In 2006, 32 master's, 3 doctorates awarded. *Degree requirements:* For master's, thesis, internship. *Entrance requirements:* For master's, GMAT, GRE, or MCAT, previous undergraduate course work in mathematics and science. Additional exam requirements/recommendations for international students: Required—TOEFL. *Application deadline:* For fall admission, 1/15 for domestic and international students. Electronic applications accepted. *Financial support:* Career-related internships or fieldwork, Federal Work-Study, institutionally sponsored loans, and scholarships/grants available. Support available to part-time students. Financial award application deadline: 3/1; financial award applicants required to submit FAFSA. *Faculty research:* Health politics, policy, and regulation; mental health and substance abuse; consumer choice and decision making; determinants of clinical decision making. *Unit head:* Dr. Jody L. Sindelar, Division Head, 203-785-2854, Fax: 203-785-6287, E-mail: jody.sindelar@yale.edu. *Application contact:* Jacqui Comshaw, Director of Admissions, 203-785-2844, Fax: 203-785-4845, E-mail: eph.admissions@yale.edu.

See Close-Up on page 2073.

Youngstown State University, Graduate School, College of Health and Human Services, Department of Health Professions, Youngstown, OH 44555-0001. Offers health and human services (MHHS); public health (MPH). *Accreditation:* NAACLS. Part-time and evening/weekend programs available. *Degree requirements:* For master's, thesis optional. *Entrance requirements:* For master's, GRE General Test, minimum GPA of 3.0. Additional exam requirements/recommendations for international students: Required—TOEFL. *Faculty research:* Drug prevention, multiskilling in health care, organizational behavior, health care management, health behaviors, research management.

Health Services Research

Arizona State University, Division of Graduate Studies, W.P. Carey School of Business, Program in Business Administration, Tempe, AZ 85287. Offers accountancy (PhD); business administration (MBA); finance (PhD); health services research (PhD); information management (PhD); management (PhD); marketing (PhD); supply chain management (PhD); JD/MBA; MBA/M Arch; MBA/MHSM. MBA/MIM offered jointly with Thunderbird, The American Graduate School of International Management and Groupe Ecole Supéieure de Commerce, Toulouse, France. *Accreditation:* AACSB. *Degree requirements:* For master's, thesis optional; for doctorate, thesis/dissertation. *Entrance requirements:* For master's, GMAT.

Brown University, Graduate School, Division of Biology and Medicine, Department of Community Health, Program in Health Services Research, Providence, RI 02912. Offers MS, PhD.

Clarkson University, Graduate School, Center for Health Science, Department of Basic Science, Potsdam, NY 13699. Offers MS. Part-time and evening/weekend programs available. *Students:* 1 (woman) full-time. Average age 53.Application fee: $25 ($35 for international students). *Expenses:* Tuition: Full-time $22,776; part-time $949 per credit. Required fees: $215. *Faculty research:* Health science, environmental health.

Cornell University, Joan and Sanford I. Weill Medical College and Graduate School of Medical Sciences, Weill Graduate School of Medical Sciences, Program in Clinical Epidemiology and Health Services Research, New York, NY 10021. Offers MS. *Faculty:* 17 full-time (6 women), 3 part-time/adjunct (0 women). *Students:* 14 full-time (9 women); includes 6 minority (2 African Americans, 2 Asian Americans or Pacific Islanders, 2 Hispanic Americans), 1 international. 2 applicants, 100% accepted, 2 enrolled. In 2006, 6 degrees awarded. *Degree requirements:* For master's, thesis. *Entrance requirements:* For master's, 3 years of work experience, MD or RN certificate. *Application deadline:* For fall admission, 12/15 for domestic students. Application fee: $60. *Financial support:* Scholarships/grants available. *Unit head:* Dr. Carol Mancuso, Director. *Application contact:* Susan Toro, Administrator, 212-746-1607.

Dartmouth College, School of Arts and Sciences, Center for the Evaluative Clinical Sciences, Hanover, NH 03755. Offers evaluative clinical sciences (MS, PhD); public health (MPH). Part-time programs available. *Faculty:* 26 full-time (12 women), 10 part-time/adjunct (9 women). *Students:* 35 full-time (20 women), 27 part-time (15 women); includes 6 minority (5 Asian Americans or Pacific Islanders, 1 Hispanic American), 4 international. Average age 36. 68 applicants, 69% accepted, 22 enrolled. In 2006, 10 master's, 3 doctorates awarded. *Degree requirements:* For master's, research project or practicum; for doctorate, thesis/dissertation. *Entrance requirements:* For master's and doctorate, GRE or MCAT, 3 letters of recommendation. Additional exam requirements/recommendations for international students: Required—TOEFL. *Application deadline:* For fall admission, 1/15 for domestic students. Applications are processed on a rolling basis. Application fee: $50. *Expenses:* Tuition: Full-time $33,297. *Financial support:* In 2006–07, fellowships with tuition reimbursements (averaging $21,000 per year); research assistantships, teaching assistantships with tuition reimbursements, institutionally sponsored loans and scholarships/grants also available. Financial award application deadline: 6/1; financial award applicants required to submit FAFSA. *Faculty research:* Prevention and treatment of cardiovascular diseases, health care cost containment, variation of delivery of care, health care improvement, decision evaluation. Total annual research expenditures: $71.3 million. *Unit head:* Dr. Gerald T. O'Connor, Director, 603-650-1782. *Application contact:* Susan M. Benson, Academic Programs Director, 603-650-1782, Fax: 603-650-1900, E-mail: ecs@dartmouth.edu.

Announcement: The MPH degree is designed for individuals who wish to research and improve the delivery and practice of public health care. This unique public health degree program will provide graduates with the academic knowledge and skill sets to make an impact in public health-care practice and evidence-based public health research.

See Close-Up on page 1805.

Emory University, Rollins School of Public Health, Department of Health Policy and Management, Atlanta, GA 30322-1100. Offers health outcomes management (MPH); health policy (MPH); health policy research (MSPH); health services management (MPH); health services research and health policy (PhD). Part-time programs available. *Students:* 105 full-time (83 women), 3 part-time (2 women). Average age 27. 169 applicants, 88% accepted, 61 enrolled. In 2006, 54 degrees awarded. *Degree requirements:* For master's, practicum, capstone course, thesis optional. *Entrance requirements:* For master's, GRE General Test. Additional exam requirements/recommendations for international students: Required—TOEFL (minimum score 550 paper-based; 215 computer-based). *Application deadline:* For fall admission, 1/5 priority date for domestic and international students. Application fee: $75. Electronic applications accepted. *Expenses:* Tuition: Full-time $30,246. *Financial support:* Fellowships with full and partial tuition reimbursements, career-related internships or fieldwork, Federal Work-Study, institutionally sponsored loans, and scholarships/grants available. Support available to part-time students. Financial award application deadline: 1/5. *Faculty research:* U.S. health policy and financing, healthcare organization and financing. *Unit head:* David H Howard, Director of Graduate Studies, 404-727-3487, Fax: 404-727-9198, E-mail: david.howard@emory.edu. *Application contact:* Kathy Wollenzien, Director, Academic Programs, 404-724-5701, Fax: 404-727-9198, E-mail: kwollen@sph.emory.edu.

Florida State University, Graduate Studies, College of Social Sciences, Interdisciplinary Social Health Sciences Programs, Tallahassee, FL 32306. Offers MHPR, MPA, MPH, MS, MPA/MS. *Faculty:* 5 full-time (2 women), 1 part-time/adjunct (0 women). *Students:* 13 full-time (9 women), 20 part-time (17 women); includes 16 minority (15 African Americans, 1 Hispanic American). Average age 25. 55 applicants, 56% accepted, 14 enrolled. In 2006, 4 degrees awarded. *Degree requirements:* For master's, internship, research paper. *Entrance requirements:* For master's, GRE General Test, minimum GPA of 3.0. *Application deadline:* For fall admission, 3/15 priority date for domestic students; for winter admission, 9/15 priority date for domestic students. Applications are processed on a rolling basis. Application fee: $30. Electronic applications accepted. *Expenses:* Tuition, state resident: full-time $5,822; part-time $243 per credit hour. Tuition, nonresident: full-time $20,976; part-time $874 per credit hour. Tuition and fees vary according to program. *Financial support:* In 2006–07, 1 student received support, including 1 fellowship with tuition reimbursement available (averaging $15,000 per year), research assistantships with full tuition reimbursements available (averaging $11,000 per year). Financial award application deadline: 3/15. *Faculty research:* Health behavior surveillance, long term care policy, long term care evaluation, HMO's, Medicaid. Total annual research expenditures: $1 million. *Unit head:* Dr. William G. Weissert, Director, 850-644-4418, Fax: 850-644-1367, E-mail: wweisser@fsu.edu.

The George Washington University, School of Medicine and Health Sciences, Health Sciences Programs, Washington, DC 20052. Offers adult nurse practitioner (MSN, Post Master's Certificate); advanced family nurse practitioner (Post Master's Certificate); clinical practice management (MSHS); clinical research administration (MSHS); clinical research administration for nurses (MSN); emergency services management (MSHS); end-of-life care (MSHS, MSN); family nurse practitioner (MSN); immunohematology (MSHS); nursing leadership and management (MSN); oral biology (MSHS); physical therapy (DPT); physician assistant (MSHS); MSHS/MPH. Postbaccalaureate distance learning degree programs offered (no on-campus study). *Entrance requirements:* Additional exam requirements/recommendations for international students: Required—TOEFL (minimum score 550 paper-based; 213 computer-based). Expenses: Contact institution.

The Johns Hopkins University, Bloomberg School of Public Health, Department of Health Policy and Management, Baltimore, MD 21205-1996. Offers health and public policy (PhD); health care management and leadership (Dr PH); health finance and management (MHS); health policy (MHS); health services research (PhD). *Accreditation:* CAHME (one or more programs are accredited). Part-time programs available. *Faculty:* 54 full-time (29 women), 142 part-time/adjunct (55 women). *Students:* 128 full-time (92 women), 52 part-time (17 women); includes 42 minority (17 African Americans, 2 American Indian/Alaska Native, 20 Asian Americans or Pacific Islanders, 3 Hispanic Americans), 47 international. Average age 29. 196 applicants, 52% accepted, 45 enrolled. In 2006, 24 master's, 20 doctorates awarded. *Median time to degree:* Of those who began their doctoral program in fall 1998, 94% received their degree in 8 years or less. *Degree requirements:* For master's, internship; for doctorate, thesis/dissertation, 1 year full-time residency, oral and written exams, comprehensive exam, registration. *Entrance requirements:* For master's, GRE General Test/GMAT, 3 letters of recommendation, curriculum vitae; for doctorate, GRE General Test, 3 letters of recommendation, curriculum vitae. Additional exam requirements/recommendations for international students: Required—TOEFL (minimum score 600 paper-based; 250 computer-based). *Application deadline:* For fall admission, 12/1 for domestic and international students. Application fee: $45. Electronic applications accepted. *Expenses:* Tuition: Full-time $32,976. Tuition and fees vary according to degree level and program. *Financial support:* In 2006–07, 180 students received support, including 2 fellowships (averaging $43,856 per year); Federal Work-Study, institutionally sponsored loans, scholarships/grants, traineeships, and stipends also available. Support available to part-time students. Financial award application deadline: 3/15; financial award applicants required to submit FAFSA. *Faculty research:* Quality of care and health outcomes, health care finance and technology, vulnerable populations, injury prevention, health policy. Total annual research expenditures: $22.8 million. *Unit head:* Dr. Ellen J. MacKenzie, Chairman, 410-955-3625. *Application contact:* Mary Sewell, Coordinator, 410-955-2488, Fax: 410-614-9152, E-mail: msewell@jhsph.edu.

Lehigh University, College of Business and Economics, Bethlehem, PA 18015-3094. Offers accounting (MS), including accounting and information analysis; business administration (MBA); economics (MS, PhD), including economics, health and bio-pharmaceutical economics (MS); entrepreneurship (Certificate); finance (MS), including analytical finance, finance; organizational leadership (Certificate); project management (Certificate); supply chain management (Certificate); MBA/E; MBA/M Ed. *Accreditation:* AACSB. Part-time and evening/weekend programs available. Postbaccalaureate distance learning degree programs offered (minimal on-campus study). *Faculty:* 64 full-time (14 women), 12 part-time/adjunct (0 women). *Students:* 87 full-time (25 women), 219 part-time (60 women); includes 34 minority (9 African Americans, 22 Asian Americans or Pacific Islanders, 3 Hispanic Americans), 56 international. 371 applicants, 69% accepted, 151 enrolled. In 2006, 103 master's, 2 doctorates awarded. Terminal master's awarded for partial completion of doctoral program. *Degree requirements:* For master's, thesis optional; for doctorate, thesis/dissertation, proposal defense, comprehensive exam. *Entrance requirements:* For master's, GMAT, GRE General Test; for doctorate, GMAT or GRE General Test. Additional exam requirements/recommendations for international students: Required—TOEFL (minimum score 600 paper-based; 250 computer-based). *Application deadline:* For fall admission, 7/15 for domestic students, 5/1 for international students; for spring admission, 12/1 for domestic and international students. Applications are processed on a rolling basis. Application fee: $60. Electronic applications accepted. *Expenses:* Contact institution. *Financial support:* In 2006–07, 2 fellowships with full tuition reimbursements (averaging $13,200 per year), 8 research assistantships with full and partial tuition reimbursements (averaging $1,000 per year), 13 teaching assistantships with full tuition reimbursements (averaging $13,200 per year) were awarded; career-related internships or fieldwork, scholarships/grants, health care benefits, tuition waivers (full and partial), and unspecified assistantships also available. Support available to part-time students. Financial award application deadline: 1/15. *Faculty research:* Public finance, energy, investments, activity-based costing, management information systems. *Unit head:* Michael G. Kolchin, Graduate Business Programs, 610-758-4450, Fax: 610-758-5283, E-mail: mgk1@lehigh.edu. *Application contact:* Mary- Theresa Taglang, Director of Graduate Programs, 610-758-5285, Fax: 610-758-5283, E-mail: mtt4@lehigh.edu.

See Close-Ups on pages 283, 285, and 1807.

McMaster University, Faculty of Health Sciences and School of Graduate Studies, Program in Health Research Methodology (course-based), Hamilton, ON L8S 4M2, Canada. Offers M Sc. Part-time programs available. *Students:* 11 full-time, 34 part-time. In 2006, 12 degrees awarded. *Degree requirements:* For master's, research internship, scholarly paper courses. *Entrance requirements:* For master's, 4 year honors degree, minimum B+ average in last year of course work. Additional exam requirements/recommendations for international students: Required—TOEFL (minimum score 580 paper-based; 237 computer-based). *Application deadline:* For fall admission, 11/1 for domestic students. Application fee: $90. *Financial support:* Teaching assistantships available. *Unit head:* Dr. Kathy Bennett, Coordinator, 905-525-9140 Ext. 26236. *Application contact:* Dr. Carl Richards, Associate Dean, 905-525-9140 Ext. 27718, Fax: 905-546-1129.

McMaster University, Faculty of Health Sciences and School of Graduate Studies, Program in Health Research Methodology (thesis), Hamilton, ON L8S 4M2, Canada. Offers M Sc, PhD. Part-time programs available. *Students:* 61 full-time, 46 part-time. In 2006, 5 master's, 7 doctorates awarded. *Degree requirements:* For master's, thesis/dissertation; for doctorate, thesis/dissertation, comprehensive exam. *Entrance requirements:* For master's, honors degree, minimum B+ average in last year of undergraduate course work; for doctorate, M Sc, minimum B+ average. Additional exam requirements/recommendations for international students: Required—TOEFL (minimum score 580 paper-based; 237 computer-based; 92 iBT). *Application deadline:* For fall admission, 11/1 for domestic students; for winter admission, 2/28 for domestic students. Application fee: $90. *Financial support:* Teaching assistantships available. *Unit head:* Dr. Kathy Bennett, Coordinator, 905-525-9140 Ext. 22218. *Application contact:* Dr. Carl Richards, Associate Dean, 905-525-9140 Ext. 22983, Fax: 905-546-1129.

Old Dominion University, College of Health Sciences, Program in Health Services Research, Norfolk, VA 23529. Offers PhD. Evening/weekend programs available. *Faculty:* 2 full-time (both women), 15 part-time/adjunct (10 women). *Students:* 5 full-time (all women), 21 part-time (14 women); includes 11 minority (9 African Americans, 2 Asian Americans or Pacific Islanders), 3 international. Average age 43. 11 applicants, 82% accepted, 7 enrolled. In 2006, 2 degrees awarded. *Median time to degree:* Of those who began their doctoral program in fall 1998, 38% received their degree in 8 years or less. *Degree requirements:* For doctorate, thesis/dissertation, comprehensive exam. *Entrance requirements:* For doctorate, GRE, minimum GPA of 3.25, master's degree. Additional exam requirements/recommendations for international students: Required—TOEFL (minimum score 550 paper-based). *Application deadline:* For fall admission, 7/1 for domestic students, 6/1 for international students; for winter admission, 11/1 for domestic students, 10/1 for international students; for spring admission, 4/1 for domestic students, 3/1 for international students. Applications are processed on a rolling basis. Application fee: $40. Electronic applications accepted. *Expenses:* Tuition, area resident: Part-time $285 per credit hour. Tuition, nonresident: part-time $715 per credit hour. Required fees: $94 per semester. *Financial support:* In 2006–07, 8 students received support, including 4 fellowships with full tuition reimbursements available (averaging $15,000 per year), 3 research assistantships with tuition reimbursements available (averaging $15,000 per year), 1 teaching assistantship with tuition reimbursement available (averaging $15,000 per year); career-related internships or fieldwork, scholarships/grants, and tuition waivers (partial) also available. Financial award applicants required to submit FAFSA. *Faculty research:* Access to health services, health outcomes, women's health, domestic violence, health policy, health policy and planning, economics of obesity, substance abuse. Total annual research expenditures:$150,133. *Unit head:* Dr. Stacey Plichta, Graduate Program Director, 757-683-4989, Fax: 757-683-6333, E-mail: splichta@odu.edu.

Penn State Hershey Medical Center, College of Medicine, Graduate School Programs in the Biomedical Sciences, Graduate Program in Health Evaluation Sciences, Hershey, PA 17033-2360. Offers MS. Part-time programs available. *Students:* 1 full-time (0 women), 8 part-time (4 women); includes 3 minority (2 Asian Americans or Pacific Islanders, 1 Hispanic American), 2 international. Average age 27. *Median time to degree:* Of those who began their doctoral program in fall 1998, 100% received their degree in 8 years or less. *Degree requirements:* For master's, thesis or alternative, registration. *Entrance requirements:* For master's, MCAT, GRE General Test. Additional exam requirements/recommendations for international students: Required—TOEFL (minimum score 550 paper-based). *Application deadline:* For fall admission, 2/1 priority date for domestic and international students. Applications are processed on a rolling basis. Application fee: $45. Electronic applications accepted. *Financial support:* Fellowships with full tuition reimbursements, Federal Work-Study, scholarships/grants, and health care benefits available. Financial award applicants required to submit FAFSA. *Faculty research:* Clinical trials, statistical methods in genetic epidemiology, genetic factors in nicotine dependence and dementia syndromes, health economics, cancer. *Unit head:* Dr. David Mauger, Chair, 717-531-7178, Fax: 717-531-5779, E-mail: hes-grad-hmc@psu.edu. *Application contact:* Mardi Sawyer, Program Administrator, 717-531-7178, Fax: 717-531-5779, E-mail: hes-grad-hmc@psu.edu.

Stanford University, School of Medicine, Graduate Programs in Medicine, Division of Health Services Research, Stanford, CA 94305-9991. Offers MS. Division accepts internal applicants only. *Degree requirements:* For master's, thesis. Electronic applications accepted. *Faculty research:* Cost and quality of life in cardiovascular disease, technology assessment, physician decision making.

Texas State University-San Marcos, Graduate School, College of Health Professions, Department of Health Services and Research, Program in Health Services Research, San Marcos, TX 78666. Offers MS. Part-time and evening/weekend programs available. *Faculty:* 1 full-time (0 women), 1 (woman) part-time/adjunct. *Students:* 10 full-time (5 women), 8 part-time (6 women); includes 4 minority (2 Asian Americans or Pacific Islanders, 2 Hispanic Americans), 1 international. Average age 31. 5 applicants, 100% accepted, 3 enrolled. In 2006, 20 degrees awarded. *Degree requirements:* For master's, committee review. *Entrance requirements:* For master's, GRE General Test, minimum GPA of 2.75 in last 60 hours of course work. Additional exam requirements/recommendations for international students: Required—TOEFL. *Application deadline:* For fall admission, 6/15 priority date for domestic students, 6/1 for international students; for spring admission, 10/15 priority date for domestic students, 10/1 for international students. Applications are processed on a rolling basis. Application fee: $40 ($90 for international students). *Financial support:* In 2006–07, 7 students received support, including 2 teaching assistantships (averaging $5,076 per year); research assistantships, career-related internships or fieldwork, Federal Work-Study, and institutionally sponsored loans also available. Support available to part-time students. Financial award application deadline: 4/1; financial award applicants required to submit FAFSA. *Faculty research:* Computer applications, quantitative management science technology, philosophy and methodology of research, evaluation. *Unit head:* Dr. Oren Renick, Graduate Advisor, 512-245-3556, Fax: 512-245-8712, E-mail: cr13@txstate.edu.

Thomas Jefferson University, Jefferson College of Graduate Studies, Program in Clinical Research, Public Health, and Research Management, Philadelphia, PA 19107. Offers Certificate. *Students:* 8 applicants, 100% accepted. *Degree requirements:* For degree, registration. *Entrance requirements:* For degree, GRE General Test (recommended). Additional exam requirements/recommendations for international students: Required—TOEFL (minimum score 213 computer-based). *Application deadline:* For fall admission, 8/1 priority date for domestic students, 3/1 priority date for international students; for winter admission, 12/1 priority date for domestic students, 6/1 priority date for international students; for spring admission, 4/1 priority date for domestic students. Applications are processed on a rolling basis. Application fee: $50. Electronic applications accepted. *Expenses:* Tuition: Full-time $15,340; part-time $790 per credit. Required fees: $300. *Financial support:* In 2006–07, 5 students received support. Federal Work-Study and institutionally sponsored loans available. Support available to part-time students. Financial award applicants required to submit FAFSA. *Faculty research:* Pharmacoeconomics, epidemiology, clinical research, performance improvement, statistics. *Unit head:* Dr. Dennis M. Gross, Associate Dean, 215-503-0156, Fax: 215-503-3433, E-mail: dennis.gross@jefferson.edu. *Application contact:* Eleanor M. Gorman, Assistant Coordinator, Graduate Center Programs, 215-503-5799, Fax: 215-503-3433, E-mail: eleanor.gorman@jefferson.edu.

University of Alberta, School of Public Health, Department of Public Health Sciences, Edmonton, AB T6G 2E1, Canada. Offers clinical epidemiology (M Sc, MPH); environmental and occupational health (MPH); environmental health sciences (M Sc); epidemiology (M Sc); global health (M Sc, MPH); health policy and management (MPH); health policy research (M Sc); health technology assessment (MPH); occupational health (M Sc); population health (M Sc); public health leadership (MPH); public health sciences (PhD); quantitative methods (MPH). *Accreditation:* CEPH (one or more programs are accredited). *Faculty:* 24 full-time (5 women), 59 part-time/adjunct (13 women). *Students:* 49 full-time, 49 part-time. 81 applicants, 31% accepted. In 2006, 28 degrees awarded. Terminal master's awarded for partial completion of doctoral program. *Degree requirements:* For master's, thesis (for some programs); for doctorate, thesis/dissertation. *Entrance requirements:* For master's, GMAT or GRE General Test. Additional exam requirements/recommendations for international students: Required—TOEFL (paper-based 550; computer-based 213) or IELTS (paper-based 6). *Application deadline:* For fall admission, 3/15 for domestic students, 7/1 for international students; for winter admission, 11/1 for international students; for spring admission, 3/1 for international students. Applications are processed on a rolling basis. Application fee: $0. Electronic applications accepted. *Financial support:* In 2006–07, 11 students received support, including 6 research assistantships with tuition reimbursements available (averaging $2,200 per year); fellowships, teaching assistantships, career-related internships or fieldwork and tuition waivers (partial) also available. Financial award application deadline: 2/1. *Faculty research:* Biostatistics, health promotion and socio-behavioral health science. Total annual research expenditures: $5.7 million. *Unit head:* L. Duncan Saunders, Acting Chair, 780-492-6814, Fax: 780-492-0364. *Application contact:* Felicity R. Hey, Graduate Programs Administrator, 780-492-6407, Fax: 780-492-0364, E-mail: felicity.hey@ualberta.ca.

The University of British Columbia, Faculty of Medicine, Department of Health Care and Epidemiology, Vancouver, BC V6T 1W5, Canada. Offers clinical epidemiology (MH Sc); community health (MH Sc); epidemiology/clinical epidemiology (M Sc, PhD); health administration (MHA); health services research (M Sc, PhD); occupational and environmental health (M Sc, PhD); occupational health (MH Sc). *Accreditation:* CEPH (one or more programs are accredited). Part-time programs available. *Faculty:* 27 full-time (7 women). *Students:* 27 full-time (4 women), 10 part-time (2 women). Average age 31. 91 applicants, 30% accepted. In 2006, 14 master's, 1 doctorate awarded. *Degree requirements:* For master's and doctorate, thesis/dissertation. *Entrance requirements:* For master's, GRE General Test, MD or equivalent (MH Sc); for doctorate, work experience. *Application deadline:* For fall admission, 3/31 for domestic students. Applications are processed on a rolling basis. Application fee: $65. Electronic applications accepted. *Financial support:* In 2006–07, 7 students received support, including 1 fellowship; career-related internships or fieldwork also available. *Faculty research:* AIDS, public health, environmental toxicology, infectious diseases, health evaluation, epidemiology. Total annual research expenditures: $4.8 million. *Unit head:* M. T. Schechter, Head, 604-822-3910, Fax: 604-822-4994, E-mail: martin.schechter@ubc.ca. *Application contact:* Laurel Slaney, Program Assistant, 604-822-5405, Fax: 604-822-4994, E-mail: laurel.slaney@ubc.ca.

University of Florida, Graduate School, College of Public Health and Health Professions, Department of Health Services Research, Management and Policy, Gainesville, FL 32611. Offers health administration (MHA); health services research (PhD). *Accreditation:* CAHME. Part-time programs available. *Faculty:* 13 full-time (7 women), 2 part-time/adjunct (1 woman). *Students:* 55 (27 women); includes 17 minority (8 African Americans, 2 Asian Americans or Pacific Islanders, 7 Hispanic Americans) 6 international. In 2006, 33 master's, 3 doctorates awarded. *Entrance requirements:* For master's, GRE General Test, minimum GPA of 3.0. Additional exam requirements/recommendations for international students: Required—TOEFL (minimum score 550 paper-based; 213 computer-based). *Application deadline:* For fall admission, 4/1 for domestic students. Applications are processed on a rolling basis. Application fee: $30. Electronic applications accepted. *Expenses:* Tuition, state resident: full-time $6,827. Tuition, nonresident: full-time $21,951. Required fees: $999. *Financial support:* In 2006–07, 6 research assistantships (averaging $9,461 per year) were awarded; fellowships, teaching assistantships, career-related internships or fieldwork and unspecified assistantships also available. *Faculty research:* Hospital profitability, indigent care, rural health care systems, AIDS education, managed care, outcomes. *Unit head:* Dr. R. Paul Duncan, Chair, 352-273-6073, Fax: 352-273-6075, E-mail: pduncan@phhp.ufl.edu. *Application contact:* Barbara Ross, Student Services Coordinator, 352-273-6074, Fax: 352-273-6075, E-mail: bross@phhp.ufl.edu.

See Close-Up on page 1819.

University of La Verne, College of Business and Public Management, Program in Health Administration, La Verne, CA 91750-4443. Offers financial management (MHA); health administration (MHA); human resources (MHA); information management (MHA); leadership and management (MHA); managed care (MHA); marketing and business development (MHA). Part-time programs available. *Faculty:* 7 full-time (2 women), 8 part-time/adjunct (4 women). *Students:* 13 full-time (9 women), 20 part-time (14 women); includes 19 minority (5 African Americans, 6 Asian Americans or Pacific Islanders, 8 Hispanic Americans). Average age 39. In 2006, 18 degrees awarded. *Entrance requirements:* For master's, minimum undergraduate GPA of 2.5, 3 letters of reference, curriculum vitae or resumé, writing sample. Additional exam requirements/recommendations for international students: Required—TOEFL (minimum score 550 paper-based; 213 computer-based). *Application deadline:* Applications are processed on a rolling basis. Application fee: $50. *Expenses: Contact institution. Financial support:* Application deadline: 3/2; *Unit head:* Joan Branin, Chairperson, 909-593-3511 Ext. 4247, E-mail: braninj@ulv.edu. *Application contact:* Jo Nell Baker, Director, Graduate Admissions and Academic Services, 909-593-3511 Ext. 4244, Fax: 909-392-2761, E-mail: gradadmt@ulv.edu.

University of Maryland, Baltimore, Graduate School, Graduate Programs in Pharmacy, Department of Pharmaceutical Health Service Research, Baltimore, MD 21201. Offers epidemiology (MS); pharmacy administration (PhD); Pharm D/PhD. Part-time programs available. *Faculty:* 14 full-time (8 women). *Students:* 21 full-time (10 women), 5 part-time (1 woman); includes 3 minority (2 African Americans, 1 Hispanic American), 20 international. Average age 26. 39 applicants, 15% accepted, 5 enrolled. In 2006, 2 degrees awarded. *Degree requirements:* For doctorate, thesis/dissertation, comprehensive exam. *Entrance requirements:* For doctorate, GRE General Test. Additional exam requirements/recommendations for international students: Required—TOEFL (minimum score 550 paper-based; 215 computer-based), IELTS. *Application deadline:* For fall admission, 7/1 for domestic students, 1/15 for international students; for winter admission, 12/1 for domestic students, 5/1 for international students. Applications are processed on a rolling basis. Application fee: $125. *Financial support:* In 2006–07, 1 fellowship with tuition reimbursement (averaging $20,000 per year), 4 research assistantships with full tuition reimbursements (averaging $21,772 per year), 4 teaching assistantships with full tuition reimbursements (averaging $21,772 per year) were awarded; career-related internships or fieldwork, scholarships/grants, traineeships, and unspecified assistantships also available. Financial award application deadline: 2/15; financial award applicants required to submit FAFSA. *Faculty research:* Pharmacoeconomics, outcomes research, public health policy, drug therapy and aging. Total annual research expenditures: $1.5 million. *Unit head:* Diane Kaufman, Administrative Director, 410-706-3555, E-mail: dkaufman@rx.umaryland.edu. *Application contact:* Tracie Jones, Graduate Coordinator, 410-706-7613, Fax: 410-706-5394, E-mail: tjones@umaryland.edu.

University of Massachusetts Worcester, Graduate School of Biomedical Sciences, Program in Clinical and Population Health Research, Worcester, MA 01655-0115. Offers PhD. *Faculty:*

Health Services Research

University of Massachusetts Worcester (continued)
46 full-time (18 women). *Entrance requirements:* For doctorate, GRE General Test, master's degree in public health, clinical research, or in one of the social, psychological, physical, or biological sciences, with adequate introductory course work in biostatistics and epidemiology; 3 letters of recommendation. *Application deadline:* For fall admission, 1/15 for domestic students. Application fee: $25 ($50 for international students). *Expenses:* Tuition, state resident: full-time $2,640. Tuition, nonresident: full-time $9,856. Required fees: $3,942. *Financial support:* All full-time graduate students received annual stipend support ($25,740) for the duration of their study available. *Unit head:* Dr. Carole Upshur, Associate Dean, 508-334-7267. *Application contact:* Colleen Corey, Program Coordinator, 508-334-2112.

See Close-Up on page 1821.

University of Minnesota, Twin Cities Campus, School of Public Health, Major in Health Services Research, Policy, and Administration, Minneapolis, MN 55455-0213. Offers MS, PhD, JD/MS, JD/PhD, MD/PhD, MPP/MS. Part-time programs available. Terminal master's awarded for partial completion of doctoral program. *Degree requirements:* For master's, thesis, internship, final oral exam; for doctorate, thesis/dissertation, teaching experience, written preliminary exam, final oral exam. *Entrance requirements:* For master's, GRE General Test, course work in mathematics; for doctorate, GRE General Test, prerequisite courses in calculus, statistics and microeconomics. Additional exam requirements/recommendations for international students: Required—TOEFL (minimum score 600 paper-based; 250 computer-based). *Expenses:* Tuition, state resident: full-time $9,302; part-time $775 per credit. Tuition, nonresident: full-time $16,400; part-time $1,367 per credit. Full-time tuition and fees vary according to class time, course load, program, reciprocity agreements and student level. *Faculty research:* Outcomes, economics and statistics, sociology, health care management.

University of New Brunswick Fredericton, School of Graduate Studies, Applied Health Services Research Program, Fredericton, NB E3B 5A3, Canada. Offers MA. *Students:* 3 full-time (all women), 2 part-time (both women). In 2006, 1 degree awarded. *Degree requirements:* For master's, thesis. *Entrance requirements:* For master's, BA. Application fee: $50 Canadian dollars. *Unit head:* Dr. Edmund Biden, Associate Dean of Graduate Studies, 506-458-7154, Fax: 506-453-4817, E-mail: biden@unb.ca. *Application contact:* Janet Amurault, Graduate Secretary, 506-458-7558, Fax: 506-453-4817, E-mail: jamiraul@unb.ca.

The University of North Carolina at Charlotte, Graduate School, College of Health and Human Services, Program in Health Services Research, Charlotte, NC 28223-0001. Offers PhD. *Students:* 9 full-time (8 women), 3 part-time (all women); includes 1 African American, 1 international. Average age 36. 9 applicants, 78% accepted, 7 enrolled. *Entrance requirements:* For doctorate, GRE. Additional exam requirements/recommendations for international students: Required—TOEFL (minimum score 557 paper-based; 220 computer-based). *Application deadline:* For fall admission, 7/1 for domestic students, 5/1 for international students; for spring admission, 11/1 for domestic students, 10/1 for international students. Application fee: $55. *Expenses:* Tuition, state resident: full-time $2,719; part-time $170 per credit. Tuition, nonresident: full-time $12,926; part-time $808 per credit. Required fees: $1,555. *Financial support:* Career-related internships or fieldwork, Federal Work-Study, institutionally sponsored loans, scholarships/grants, traineeships, and unspecified assistantships available. Support available to part-time students. Financial award application deadline: 4/1; financial award applicants required to submit FAFSA. *Unit head:* Dr. David R. Longford, Director, 704-687-4661. *Application contact:* Kathy B. Giddings, Director of Graduate Admissions, 704-687-3366, Fax: 704-687-3279, E-mail: gradadm@email.uncc.edu.

University of North Florida, College of Health, Department of Public Health, Jacksonville, FL 32224-2645. Offers community health (MPH); geriatric management (MSH); health administration (MHA); health behavior research and evaluation (Certificate); nutrition (MSH); rehabilitation counseling (MS). *Accreditation:* CORE. Part-time and evening/weekend programs available. *Faculty:* 21 full-time (16 women). *Students:* 78 full-time (60 women), 54 part-time (40 women); includes 31 minority (16 African Americans, 7 Asian Americans or Pacific Islanders, 8 Hispanic Americans), 10 international. Average age 32. 136 applicants, 47% accepted, 38 enrolled. In 2006, 50 degrees awarded. *Degree requirements:* For master's, thesis optional. *Entrance requirements:* For master's, GRE General Test (MSH, MS, MPH), GMAT or GRE General Test (MHA), minimum GPA of 3.0 in last 60 hours. Additional exam requirements/recommendations for international students: Required—TOEFL (minimum score 500 paper-based; 173 computer-based). *Application deadline:* For fall admission, 7/1 priority date for domestic students, 5/1 for international students; for spring admission, 11/10 priority date for domestic students, 10/1 for international students. Applications are processed on a rolling basis. Application fee: $30. Electronic applications accepted. *Expenses:* Tuition, state resident: full-time $4,948; part-time $206 per semester hour. Tuition, nonresident: full-time $19,140; part-time $408 per semester hour. *Financial support:* In 2006–07, 64 students received support, including 11 teaching assistantships (averaging $2,942 per year); research assistantships, career-related internships or fieldwork, Federal Work-Study, scholarships/grants, and tuition waivers (partial) also available. Support available to part-time students. Financial award application deadline: 4/1; financial award applicants required to submit FAFSA. *Faculty research:* Dietary supplements; alcohol, tobacco, and other drug use prevention; turnover among health professionals; aging; psychosocial aspects of disabilities. Total annual research expenditures: $438,597. *Unit head:* Dr. Judith Perkin, Chair, 904-620-2840, Fax: 904-620-2848, E-mail: jperkin@unf.edu. *Application contact:* Rachel Broderick, Director of Advising, 904-620-2817, Fax: 904-620-1770, E-mail: rbroderi@unf.edu.

University of Ottawa, Faculty of Graduate and Postdoctoral Studies, Interdisciplinary Programs, Ottawa, ON K1N 6N5, Canada. Offers e-business (Certificate); e-commerce (Certificate); finance (Certificate); health services and policies research (Diploma); population health (PhD); population health risk assessment and management (Certificate); public management and governance (Certificate); systems science (Certificate).

University of Puerto Rico, Medical Sciences Campus, Graduate School of Public Health, Department of Health Services Administration, Program in Evaluation Research of Health Systems, San Juan, PR 00936-5067. Offers MS. Part-time programs available. *Students:* 35 (28 women) 1 international. 24 applicants, 54% accepted. In 2006, 1 degree awarded. *Degree requirements:* For master's, thesis. *Entrance requirements:* For master's, GRE, previous course work in algebra and statistics. *Application deadline:* For fall admission, 3/15 for domestic students. Application fee: $20. *Expenses:* Contact institution. *Financial support:* Research assistantships, teaching assistantships, career-related internships or fieldwork, Federal Work-Study, and institutionally sponsored loans available. Financial award application deadline: 4/30. *Unit head:* Dr. Mildred Vera, Coordinator, 787-758-2525 Ext. 1422, Fax: 787-759-6719, E-mail: mvera@rcm.upr.edu. *Application contact:* Prof. Mayra E. Santiago-Vargas, Counselor, 787-756-5244, Fax: 787-759-6719, E-mail: msantiago@rcm.upr.edu.

University of Rochester, School of Medicine and Dentistry, Graduate Programs in Medicine and Dentistry, Department of Community and Preventive Medicine, Program in Health Services Research and Policy, Rochester, NY 14627-0250. Offers PhD, MPH/PhD. *Degree requirements:* For doctorate, thesis/dissertation, qualifying exam. *Entrance requirements:* For doctorate, GRE General Test.

University of Southern California, Keck School of Medicine and Graduate School, Graduate Programs in Medicine, Department of Preventive Medicine, Program in Health Behavior Research, Los Angeles, CA 90089. Offers PhD. *Faculty:* 22 full-time (13 women), 1 (woman) part-time/adjunct. *Students:* 30 full-time (24 women); includes 15 minority (3 African Americans, 1 American Indian/Alaska Native, 6 Asian Americans or Pacific Islanders, 5 Hispanic Americans), 3 international. Average age 32. 63 applicants, 14% accepted, 6 enrolled. In 2006, 2 degrees awarded. *Median time to degree:* Doctorate–4.5 years full-time. Of those who began their doctoral program in fall 1998, 100% received their degree in 8 years or less. *Degree requirements:* For doctorate, thesis/dissertation, comprehensive exam, registration. *Entrance requirements:* For doctorate, GRE General Test, minimum GPA of 3.0. Additional exam requirements/recommendations for international students: Required—TOEFL (minimum score 600 paper-based; 250 computer-based). *Application deadline:* For fall admission, 2/1 priority date for domestic students, 2/1 for international students. Application fee: $85. Electronic applications accepted. *Expenses:* Tuition: Full-time $33,314; part-time $1,121 per credit. Required fees: $522. Full-time tuition and fees vary according to program. *Financial support:* In 2006–07, 9 fellowships with full tuition reimbursements (averaging $20,861 per year), 18 research assistantships with full tuition reimbursements (averaging $20,861 per year), 1 teaching assistantship with full tuition reimbursement (averaging $20,861 per year) were awarded; institutionally sponsored loans, scholarships/grants, traineeships, health care benefits, tuition waivers (full), and unspecified assistantships also available. Financial award application deadline: 2/1. *Faculty research:* Substance abuse prevention; cancer and heart disease prevention; health promotion; obesity prevention; behavioral, social, environmental and genetic risks for disease. Total annual research expenditures: $13.4 million. *Unit head:* Dr. C. Anderson Johnson, Director, 626-457-4065, Fax: 323-457-4012, E-mail: carljohn@hsc.usc.edu. *Application contact:* Marny Barovich, Academic Affairs Coordinator, 626-457-6648, Fax: 626-457-4012, E-mail: barovich@hsc.usc.edu.

University of Virginia, School of Medicine, Department of Public Health Sciences, Charlottesville, VA 22903. Offers health evaluation sciences (MS), including clinical investigation and patient-oriented research, informatics in medicine; public health (MPH). Part-time programs available. *Students:* 30 full-time (18 women), 11 part-time (6 women); includes 11 minority (5 African Americans, 6 Asian Americans or Pacific Islanders), 2 international. Average age 33. 78 applicants, 62% accepted, 30 enrolled. In 2006, 8 degrees awarded. *Entrance requirements:* For master's, GRE General Test or MCAT. Additional exam requirements/recommendations for international students: Required—TOEFL. *Application deadline:* Applications are processed on a rolling basis. Application fee: $60. Electronic applications accepted. *Financial support:* Career-related internships or fieldwork available. Financial award applicants required to submit FAFSA. *Unit head:* William A. Knaus, Director, 434-924-8430, Fax: 434-924-8437. *Application contact:* Robyn Kells, Coordinator, 434-924-8646, Fax: 434-924-8437, E-mail: ms-hes@virginia.edu.

University of Washington, Graduate School, School of Public Health and Community Medicine, Department of Health Services, Seattle, WA 98195. Offers health services (MS, PhD); health services administration (MHA); health services administration and planning (EMHA); public health (MPH); MHA/MBA; MHA/MD; MHA/MPA; MPH/MAIS; MPH/MN; MPH/MPA; MPH/MS; MPH/MSW. Part-time and evening/weekend programs available. Postbaccalaureate distance learning degree programs offered (minimal on-campus study). Terminal master's awarded for partial completion of doctoral program. *Degree requirements:* For master's, thesis, practicum (MPH); for doctorate, thesis/dissertation, comprehensive exam, registration. *Entrance requirements:* For master's, GRE General Test, minimum GPA of 3.0; for doctorate, GRE General Test. Additional exam requirements/recommendations for international students: Required—TOEFL. *Faculty research:* Health promotion and disease prevention, maternal and child health, international health, health services research design, program evaluation.

Virginia Commonwealth University, Graduate School, School of Allied Health Professions, Department of Health Administration, Doctoral Program in Health Services Organization and Research, Richmond, VA 23298-0203. Offers PhD. *Students:* 1 (woman) full-time, 1 international. In 2006, 4 degrees awarded. *Degree requirements:* For doctorate, thesis/dissertation, residency. *Entrance requirements:* For doctorate, GMAT or GRE General Test. *Application deadline:* For fall admission, 4/15 priority date for domestic students. Application fee: $50. *Unit head:* Dr. Michael J. McCue, Director, 804-828-1893, Fax: 804-828-1894, E-mail: mjmccue@vcu.edu. *Application contact:* Information Contact, 804-828-5520, Fax: 804-828-1894, E-mail: bdeshazo@hsc.vcu.edu.

See Close-Ups on pages 1825 and 1827.

Wake Forest University, School of Medicine and Graduate School, Graduate Programs in Medicine, Program in Clinical Epidemiology and Health Services Research, Winston-Salem, NC 27109. Offers MS. *Degree requirements:* For master's, thesis. *Entrance requirements:* For master's, GRE General Test. Additional exam requirements/recommendations for international students: Required—TOEFL. *Faculty research:* Research methodologies, statistical methods, measurement of health outcomes. health economics.

BELLEVUE UNIVERSITY

Master of Healthcare Administration
Master of Science in Human Services

Programs of Study

The Master of Healthcare Administration (M.H.A.) program is offered online, providing health-care professionals an opportunity to study the various areas of planning, organizing, leading, and controlling as they provide administrative guidance to others within their health-related organization. The program is designed to give students the ability to analyze the various knowledge and skill areas that are needed to be effective in a rapidly changing environment. The external influences that impact health-care organizations are examined, with the intent to better manage the internal operations as various team members collaborate in their efforts to create the optimum quality of care for consumers. The degree is a 39-credit-hour program that culminates in a 3-credit-hour capstone project, as well as a professional practicum. It is offered in an accelerated, cohort format, which allows students to move through the program with the same class, completing it in eighteen months.

The Master of Science in Human Services program offers two options: a 36-credit-hour option in Individual and Community Services and an expanded 48-credit-hour Mental Health Counseling option. The Individual and Community Services option is designed for students whose main goal is to obtain a general master's degree with emphasis on preparation for direct and administrative service roles rather than therapy or counseling roles. It includes all necessary courses to enable a graduate to apply for provisional licensure as a mental health professional. Additional courses in chemical dependency counseling taken as electives or a specialized internship make it possible for students in this option to meet Nebraska Certified Provisional Alcohol/Drug Abuse Counselor (CPADAC) standards. The expanded Mental Health Counseling option prepares students for increasing career opportunities in therapy and counseling. It includes enhanced clinical course work and increased internship requirements. Graduates of this option gain a strong foundation in clinical assessment and treatment topics. They also benefit from a recommended, supervised experience of 450 contact hours in preparation for application for the Nebraska Department of Health and Human Services Provisionally Licensed Mental Health Practitioner (PLMHP) and/or CPADAC. Students are also well prepared for further graduate education in the area of human services. The program is offered in the classroom only.

Research Facilities

Renovated in 2002, the Freeman/Lozier Library houses a collection of approximately 105,000 volumes, 5,200 current periodical subscriptions, the Integrated Media Center, and collaborative learning/study areas. The Integrated Media Center provides student access to computerized and Web-based resources, along with the training facilities to educate students on how to effectively use these resources. Bellevue University and its professional librarians provide the academic services necessary to support and maintain high-quality undergraduate, graduate, and online education. Access to the library's entire collection is available electronically through an online catalog (iLink) along with nine other Nebraska Independent Library Collections. Online access to information is provided free of charge to all students and faculty members of Bellevue University through various database providers, such as ProQuest Direct, EBSCOhost, LexisNexis Academic Universe, OCLC, and netLibrary.

Additional online services and resources available are Virtual Reference Librarian (VRL), where students can converse directly with reference librarians online in real time; ERes, which allows the library to maintain an electronic reserve system; Periodicals Holdings List A–Z, which serves as a comprehensive list of the library's electronic and print titles; NoodleBib, a Web application that allows students to create and edit MLA and APA style source lists; and Turnitin.com, recognized worldwide as the standard in online plagiarism prevention.

Financial Aid

Financial assistance is available from the federal and state government, the University, and private sources and includes scholarships, work-study programs, and student loans. Scholarships do not have to be repaid. Student loans must be repaid. In general, all U.S. citizens and eligible noncitizens enrolled in an approved degree program may apply for financial aid. For additional information, students should call 402-293-3762.

Cost of Study

Tuition for 2006–07 was $340 per credit hour. For example, tuition for the 43-credit-hour cohort online M.H.A. program was $14,620, excluding books and fees.

Living and Housing Costs

Student housing is available for graduate students. Students who are interested can obtain more information by calling 402-557-7415.

Student Group

The total University enrollment for fall 2006 was 6,808, with 1,482 students registered in graduate programs. The majority of the graduate students are studying full-time in evening and online classes.

The University

Bellevue University is one of Nebraska's largest fully accredited independent colleges. Programs serve the needs of nearly 7,000 students annually and cater to working adult students as well as traditional undergraduates. Benefits include accelerated degree-completion programs, online programs, an online library, cooperative credit transfer agreements, and flexible corporate partnerships.

Applying

To apply, students should submit the application online or by mail, pay the fees, and submit transcripts for evaluation. Admissions counselors work with students to complete the official admissions process. An individualized plan is completed for each student, defining the requirements needed to achieve their degree goal.

Correspondence and Information

Admissions
Bellevue University
1000 Galvin Road South
Bellevue, Nebraska 68005
Phone: 402-293-2000
      800-756-7920 (toll-free)
E-mail: info@bellevue.edu
Web site: http://www.bellevue.edu

Bellevue University

THE FACULTY

The Bellevue University full-time and adjunct faculty consists of 246 men and 152 women teaching students from freshman to graduate level. The student-faculty ratio is 22:1. For most classes and programs, Bellevue University employs adjunct faculty members who are professionals in their respective fields. Faculty members are screened to ensure that each is current on issues and technology.

Carnegie Mellon

CARNEGIE MELLON UNIVERSITY

H. John Heinz III School of Public Policy and Management
Master of Science in Health Care Policy and Management

Programs of Study

The Master of Science in Health Care Policy and Management (M.S.H.C.P.M.) program prepares students by offering a curriculum that emphasizes economics, finance, information systems, and management within the contexts of health care; access to premier faculty and research centers; a student-centric environment that promotes learning; and a degree that can be completed in one calendar year of intensive full-time study. The curriculum provides a unique combination of course work that teaches students to think strategically about the economic, political, and financial environment in which health care is delivered; provides students with an understanding of how to manage and lead organizations; and equips students with the technical and analytic tools—including information technologies—that help them work more efficiently and effectively. Students begin the program in the fall semester and must fulfill a total of 180 units with a cumulative QPA of 3.0, finish the core curriculum, and complete Systems Synthesis, a group capstone project, during the third semester of study.

The 2½-year M.S.H.C.P.M./M.B.A. dual-degree program educates students whose professional careers require an understanding of the interface between the private- and public-sectors and the health-care industry. Students begin at the Tepper School of Business, take 162 units of required core courses, and must meet all M.B.A. requirements, such as management game, core electives, concentrations, and breadth. Students are required to take 108 units of course work at the Heinz School. Dual-degree students begin the program in the fall semester.

Research Facilities

The Heinz School has an international reputation for the quality of its research. The School's interdisciplinary environment creates exciting opportunities for collaboration and produces a breadth of research work not typically found in schools of comparable size. The faculty and research centers consistently receive funding support from government agencies, foundations, and corporate partners, including the National Science Foundation; the Heinz Endowments; the Mellon Foundation; the U.S. Departments of Defense, Commerce, Health and Human Services, and Housing and Urban Development; the Sloan Foundation; and the National Institute of Justice. Research centers include the Center for Behavioral Decision Research (CBDR), the National Consortium on Violence Research (NCOVR), the Center for Economic Development (CED), the Center for Arts Management and Technology (CAMT), the Arts and Cultural Observatory (ACO), the Center for Computational Analysis of Social and Organizational Systems (CASOS), the Software Industry Center, the Sustainable Computing Consortium (SCC), and the Institute for the Study of Information Technology and Society (InSITeS).

Financial Aid

Some scholarships are awarded annually to students committed to the health-care field. Scholarship awards range from $6000 to full tuition per semester. Fulbright Scholars are eligible for half-tuition scholarships. Alumni scholarships are awarded based on public-interest work experience. Scholarships of at least $6000 per semester are awarded to Coro Fellows, returned Peace Corps volunteers, and Teach for America alumni. A limited number of Regional Leaders Scholarships are awarded to incoming full-time students who have demonstrated a commitment to the Pittsburgh community. Other merit scholarships are available, and eligible students may borrow up to $18,500 under the Federal Stafford Student Loan Programs. Federal Perkins Loans are also available.

Cost of Study

In the 2007–08 academic year, full-time tuition is $17,300 per semester. Other expenses include $1000 annually for health insurance and $200 per semester in miscellaneous fees. Students can also expect to spend approximately $460 per semester on books and supplies.

Living and Housing Costs

A wide range of affordable housing options are available close to the Carnegie Mellon campus. Housing costs in Pittsburgh are typically lower than those in other urban settings. Room and board for a single graduate student average around $5600 per semester. Carnegie Mellon does not provide housing for graduate students.

Student Group

The fall 2006–07 incoming classes included 39 students, of whom 14 are international (from Denmark, Greece, China, Canada, Korea, India, and Taiwan). Most students have at least one year of work experience before entering the program; 26 percent have a business/management background, while 36 percent have a science/medical background.

Student Outcomes

Graduates are employed by health-care organizations in the nonprofit, public, private, and consulting sectors and hold a variety of professional and management positions.

Location

Carnegie Mellon is located in Oakland, a cultural center of Pittsburgh, Pennsylvania, on a 90-acre campus adjacent to Schenley Park, the city's largest park. The campus is conveniently located for easy access to many cultural and sporting events and is only 4 miles from the downtown business and cultural district. Pittsburgh is the thirteenth-largest metropolitan area in the United States. The city has good public transportation, diverse cultural attractions, and three professional sports teams. New York City, Philadelphia, Toronto, and Washington, D.C., are all within driving distance. Many recreational facilities, including ski areas and state parks, are located nearby.

The University and The School

Carnegie Mellon was first established in 1900 as the Carnegie Technical School through a gift from Andrew Carnegie. In 1912, the name of the school was changed to Carnegie Institute of Technology. Mellon Institute, founded in 1913 by A. W. and R. B. Mellon, merged with Carnegie Institute of Technology in 1967 to become Carnegie Mellon University. The University has an enrollment of about 8,500, approximately 3,300 of whom are engaged in graduate study. Rated one of the country's top public policy schools by *U.S. News & World Report*, the Heinz School advances public interest through research and education. By strategically integrating expertise in policy, management, and information technology, the faculty focuses on critical public issues, including arts management, crime and violence, health care, information systems and technology, and public policy.

Applying

Candidates must have an undergraduate degree from an accredited university in the United States or its equivalent abroad, and they should have taken at least one college-level course in statistics. Students must submit the online application form (including essay and resume), official transcripts from all colleges and universities attended, and three letters of recommendation. The GRE or GMAT is required of applicants to the M.S.H.C.P.M. program. The GMAT is required of all M.S.H.C.P.M./M.B.A. applicants. The TOEFL or the IELTS is required of all applicants whose native language is not English. The early decision deadline is December 1; applicants are notified by January 15 and must respond to the offer of admission no later than January 31. February 1 is the final application deadline, but if the class is not full, the program continues to accept applications until all spaces are filled.

Correspondence and Information

Laura Synnott, Executive Director of Health Care Programs
H. John Heinz III School of Public Policy and Management
Carnegie Mellon University
5000 Forbes Avenue
Pittsburgh, Pennsylvania 15213-3890
Phone: 412-268-2164
E-mail: hnzadmit@andrew.cmu.edu
Web site: http://www.heinz.cmu.edu/hcpm/

Carnegie Mellon University

THE FACULTY

The H. John Heinz III School of Public Policy and Management includes the following faculty members.

Alessandro Acquisti, Assistant Professor of Information Technology and Public Policy.
Ashish Arora, Professor of Economics and Public Policy.
Linda C. Babcock, James M. Walton Professor of Economics.
Joseph Balestreire, Adjunct Associate Professor in Health Systems.
Edward Barr, Associate Teaching Professor.
James Bente, Adjunct Faculty.
Mary Gail Biebel, Adjunct Faculty.
Alfred Blumstein, Erik S. Jonsson University Professor of Urban Systems and Operations Research.
Silvia Borzutzky, Teaching Professor.
Barbara Carryer, Adjunct Professor of Entrepreneurship.
Jonathan P. Caulkins, Professor of Operations Research and Public Policy.
Karen B. Clay, Visiting Assistant Professor of History and Public Policy.
Jeffrey Cooper, Adjunct Faculty.
Michael L. DeKay, Assistant Professor of Engineering, Public Policy, and Decision Sciences.
George T. Duncan, Professor of Statistics.
Dennis Epple, Thomas Lord Professor of Economics.
Penny S. Ferreira, Distinguished Service Professor of Environmental and Policy Law.
Aloysius Gallagher, Adjunct Associate Professor of Human Resource Management
Martin S. Gaynor, E. J. Barone Professor of Economics and Health Policy.
Mark Giaquinto, Adjunct Faculty.
Wilpen L. Gorr, Professor of Public Policy and Information Systems.
Michael P. Johnson, Associate Professor of Management Science and Urban Affairs.
Chris Kowalsky, Adjunct Faculty.
David M. Krackhardt, Professor of Organizations and Public Policy.
Ramayya Krishnan, William W. and Ruth F. Cooper Professor of Management Science and Information Systems.
Kristen S. Kurland, Associate Teaching Professor.
Lester B. Lave, James Higgins Professor of Economics and Finance, Professor of Urban and Public Affairs, and Professor of Engineering and Public Policy.
Peter Madsen, Senior Lecturer in Ethics and Public Policy.
Irene McFadden, Adjunct Faculty.
Barbara Mistick, Distinguished Service Professor of Entrepreneurship and Public Policy.
Daniel Nagin, Teresa and H. John Heinz III Professor of Public Policy.
Eric Nyberg, Assistant Professor of Computer Science and Public Policy.
Rema Padman, Professor of Operations Research and Information Management.
Denise M. Rousseau, H. J. Heinz II Professor of Organizational Behavior.
Rosanne Saunders, Adjunct Associate Professor of Health Management.
Kathleen Smith, Associate Teaching Professor.
Michael D. Smith, Assistant Professor of Information Technology.
Wayne D. Smouse, Adjunct Faculty.
Melvin Stephens, Assistant Professor of Economics.
Shelby Stewman, Professor of Sociology and Demography.
Robert P. Strauss, Professor of Economics and Public Policy.
Laura Synnott, Associate Teaching Professor.
Joel Tarr, Richard S. Caliguiri Professor of Urban and Environmental History and Policy.
Lowell J. Taylor, Professor of Economics and Public Policy.
Andrew Thurman, Adjunct Faculty.
Brian To, Adjunct Professor of Management.
K. Craig Trout, Adjunct Faculty.
William B. Vogt, Assistant Professor of Economics.
Victor Weedn, Principal Research Scientist.

DARTMOUTH COLLEGE

The Dartmouth Institute for Health Policy and Clinical Practice

Programs of Study

The following graduate degrees are offered through the Dartmouth Institute for Health Policy and Clinical Practice (TDI): Master of Science (M.S.), Master of Public Health (M.P.H.), and Doctor of Philosophy (Ph.D.). These degree programs (as well as a postdoctoral program) are geared toward physicians, health-care administrators, health policy makers, and others interested in the areas of health policy and clinical practice and their application to current issues in the public health and health-care systems. The M.S. and M.P.H. programs are twelve months in length for students enrolled full-time. Part-time students can complete the program in two or three years. To qualify for graduation, M.P.H. and M.S. students must complete 56 credits and all required courses. While the overarching program provides skills in the areas of outcomes research and health-care improvement, M.S. students have the option to select concentrations in the areas of either clinical/health services research or health-care leadership.

Research Facilities

The majority of TDI faculty members have offices in Centerra Park, located between Dartmouth College in Hanover, New Hampshire, and Dartmouth-Hitchcock Medical Center in Lebanon, New Hampshire. TDI classrooms are also located in Centerra Park. In addition, TDI maintains close affiliations with the clinical services at both the White River Junction Veterans Affairs Medical Center and the Dartmouth-Hitchcock Medical Center, as well as with other research groups at Dartmouth. These include faculty members in the Departments of Community and Family Medicine, Medicine, Surgery, Radiology, Psychiatry, Psychology, and Economics. In addition, the C. Everett Koop Institute, the Center for Aging, the Norris Cotton Cancer Center, and the Psychiatric Research Center offer faculty support.

Financial Aid

The Financial Aid Office of Dartmouth assists students who require financial aid to apply for loans. For more information on loans, prospective students should call 603-646-2451 or write to the Financial Aid Office, Dartmouth College, 6024 McNutt Hall, Hanover, New Hampshire 03755.

Cost of Study

Tuition is charged at the same rate as other graduate programs at Dartmouth. For 2007–08, full-time tuition is $46,620 for four terms ($11,655 per term). In addition, health insurance for students is required and may be purchased for dependents. Students must purchase their own books, materials, and laptop computer.

Living and Housing Costs

Information on rental properties in the Hanover area is available through the Dartmouth Rental Housing Office in Hanover at 603-646-2170. Graduate students may also apply for graduate student housing through the same office. Early application is important. General rental information is available on the Internet at http://www.dartmouthre.com. Local furnished apartments rent for an average of $650 to $750 per month. Students (married, with families, and single) have access to unfurnished apartments owned by Dartmouth that rent for $500 to $700 per month.

Student Group

Total graduate student enrollment at Dartmouth is nearly 1,400 students. Undergraduate enrollment is approximately 4,100. There are currently 130 M.S., M.P.H., and Ph.D. students in the health policy and clinical practice program. The student population is a mix of approximately 30 percent physicians, 40 percent individuals who have recently completed their undergraduate work and have limited working experience, and 30 percent professionals actively involved in health care.

Location

Dartmouth College is located in Hanover, New Hampshire, a small New England town on the Connecticut River between the White Mountains of New Hampshire and the Green Mountains of Vermont. Hanover is about 2½ hours by car from Boston and 3½ hours from Montreal. Combining the advantages of a rural setting with the resources of an Ivy League college, Hanover offers a spectacular array of outdoor activities, including Alpine and Nordic skiing, rock climbing, hiking, canoeing, sailing, and riding. In addition, a varied and active cultural life is centered on the Hopkins Center for the Creative and Performing Arts.

The Institute

The Dartmouth Institute for Health Policy and Clinical Practice (formerly the Center for the Evaluative Clinical Sciences) was established at the Dartmouth Medical School in 1989. TDI is the locus for a diverse group of scientists and clinician-scholars interested in evaluating such fundamental issues in medicine as how well medical procedures actually work, how to improve the quality of medical and surgical care, how health-care resources are distributed and used, and how patients value medical interventions and their consequences. The mission of TDI is to measure, organize, and improve health and health care. Current work within the TDI includes studies of patients' decisions when confronted with complex and uncertain medical choices, the processes and potential biases in the diagnosis and treatment of disease, the distribution of health-care resources across hospital market areas, issues in the delivery and payment of care to geriatric patients, the impact of managed care on patient outcomes and costs, and methods to continually improve patient outcomes and satisfaction with care.

Applying

Applicants without graduate or professional degrees must submit scores from the Graduate Record Examinations (GRE) or the Medical College Admissions Test (MCAT). GRE and MCAT information is available from ETS at 609-771-7670. Applications to TDI are completed through an online application process, where applicants self-manage their files. The online application is available at http://ecs.dartmouth.edu/pages/info/applying.htm. Through the admissions process, applicants are asked to provide a written statement expressing their interest in the areas of health policy and clinical practice and what their goals are within these areas. In addition, three letters of reference and all transcripts are required. The application fee is $50. Admissions are made on a rolling basis; TDI accepts applications on a space-available basis until April 1. It is the long-standing policy of Dartmouth College to actively support equality of opportunity for all persons regardless of race or ethnic background, and no student shall be denied admission or be otherwise discriminated against because of race, color, sex, religion, national or ethnic origin, or handicap. The College's equal opportunity program aims to provide encouragement to women and members of minority groups to apply to the graduate programs.

Correspondence and Information

Office of Educational Programs
The Dartmouth Institute for Health Policy and Clinical Practice
30 Lafayette Street, 1st Floor
Lebanon, New Hampshire 03766
Phone: 603-653-3268
Fax: 603-653-3266
E-mail: ecs.educational.programs@dartmouth.edu
Web site: http://ecs.dartmouth.edu

Dartmouth College

THE FACULTY AND THEIR RESEARCH

Paul B. Batalden, M.D. Health-care process improvement and leadership development.

Ethan Berke, M.D., M.P.H. Use of medical geography in understanding issues of public health, aging, activity, obesity.

Bernard F. Cole, Ph.D. Development and application of statistical methods for incorporating quality-of-life considerations in the evaluation of cancer treatments.

Samuel Finlayson, M.D. Further exploration of the choice between laparoscopic surgery and medical therapy for gastroesophageal reflux disease (GERD) from several perspectives, including economics, preference-based decision making, and quality of life.

Elliott S. Fisher, M.D., M.P.H. Uses of administrative databases for epidemiological and clinical research.

Ann Barry Flood, Ph.D. Theory and policy implications of professional and organizational factors that influence the efficiency and outcomes of health care.

David Goodman, M.D. Development of novel methods for measuring physician resources and understanding the relationship between regional physician capacity, population risks, and health outcomes.

Jiang Gui, Ph.D. Development of statistical, probabilistic, and computational methods for genetic and genomic data analysis.

Nathaniel Jones III, Ph.D., M.B.A. Policy and economic implications of various methods of health-care financing and health system reforms.

Margaret R. Karagas, Ph.D. Environmental health and public health, biologic mechanisms and prevention of cancer.

Robin Larson, M.D., M.P.H. Health outcomes research.

Donald S. Likosky, Ph.D. Redesigning cardiac surgery to prevent neurological injury.

Hilary Llewellyn-Thomas, Ph.D. Assessment of patient health status and shared decision-making applications.

Todd MacKenzie, Ph.D. Survival/time-to-event analysis, diabetes.

Sharon McDonnell, M.D., M.P.H. Public health, epidemiology, chronic disease prevention.

Robert K. McLellan, M.D., M.P.H. Environmental health issues, occupational medicine.

Nancy Morden, M.D., M.P.H. Prescription benefits design, prescription drug utilization, pharmacoeconomics.

Carolyn J. Murray, M.D., M.P.H. Occupational health and public health.

Eugene C. Nelson, M.P.H., D.Sc. Improvement of health-care delivery systems and the measurement of clinical processes in relationship to health outcomes, satisfaction, and total cost.

Gerald T. O'Connor, Ph.D., D.Sc. Prevention and treatment of cardiovascular diseases, uses of epidemiology in clinical medicine, assessing medical and surgical treatment outcomes.

Rosemary A. Orgren, Ph.D. Health professions education; providers of primary, geriatric, and gerontological public health care.

Lisa M. Schwartz, M.D. Medical decision making and risk communication.

Mark E. Splaine, M.D. Accelerating quality measurement and improvement.

Anna N. A. Tosteson, Sc.D. Decision analytic modeling, economic evaluation, and statistical methods for diagnostic technology assessment.

William B. Weeks, M.D., M.B.A. Patient safety, quality improvement, and business aspects of medicine.

H. Gilbert Welch, M.D., M.P.H. Early detection efforts and problems, fundamental effects of advancing time of diagnosis.

John E. Wennberg, M.D., M.P.H. Population-based rates for the utilization and distribution of health-care services, Dartmouth Atlas of Health Care.

Steve Woloshin, M.D. Medical decision making and risk communication.

Michael Zubkoff, Ph.D. Measurement of variations in the process, outcomes, and costs of medical care for chronic disease patients treated in different systems of care and by different medical specialties.

LEHIGH UNIVERSITY

College of Business and Economics
Master of Science in Health and Bio-Pharmaceutical Economics

Programs of Study
Government agencies, health insurers, health-care providers, biotechnology firms, and pharmaceutical manufacturers have become increasingly interested in the cost effectiveness of new drugs, therapies, diagnostic procedures, and medical equipment. The Master of Science (M.S.) in Health and Bio-Pharmaceutical Economics Program at Lehigh University prepares students to carry out sophisticated cost effectiveness and cost-benefit analyses for organizations such as those within the health-care sector.

The program focuses on outcomes assessment and the role of economics in the field of health care. Designed for individuals with a strong science or bioengineering background, the program offers the analytical skills to carry out sophisticated studies of the benefits and costs associated with new drugs, medical therapies, and diagnostic procedures; to perform critical analyses in support of strategic marketing decisions; and to minimize risk and uncertainty in research and development (R&D) project portfolios.

This one-year, 30-credit-hour program offers individuals with a strong science, premed, or bioengineering background the skills needed for pharmaco-economic studies, strategic marketing research, and financial analysis in health-related industries. The core curriculum focuses on both economic analysis and health-care-sector analysis. Electives may include business and economic courses, seminar-style courses taught by industry executives, independent study, or a thesis option.

Research Facilities
The College of Business and Economics (CBE) has a number of centers and institutes to provide greater research and academic opportunities for students and faculty members, which complement the scholarly activities of academic departments. Research centers and institutes include the E-Collaboration Research Center, the Iacocca Institute, the Martindale Center for the Study of Private Enterprise, the Murray H. Goodman Center for Real Estate Studies, the Musser Center for Entrepreneurship, the Rauch Center for Business Communication, the Small Business Development Center, and the Center for Value Chain Research.

Financial Aid
Financial aid is ordinarily available only for regular, full-time graduate students. Teaching assistantships, research assistantships, graduate assistantships, fellowships, and scholarships are academic awards made by individual academic departments. Several graduate assistantships unrelated to a particular area of study can be obtained by applying to the administrative offices. International students are also encouraged to apply for funding to outside sponsoring agencies and/or home governments.

Cost of Study
Tuition for the 2007–08 academic year is $630 per credit hour, or $1890 per 3-credit course. Part-time students may take up to 8 credit hours per semester and 5 credit hours in each summer session. Full-time students may enroll in up to 9 credit hours of course work per semester and 6 credit hours in each summer session. The average full-time student enrolls in 9 credit hours per semester.

Living and Housing Costs
Rental rates for on-campus graduate student apartments range from $470 per month plus utilities for an efficiency apartment to $625 per month plus utilities for a three-bedroom apartment.

Student Group
Students pursuing a degree in heath and biopharmaceutical engineering come from diverse backgrounds in the life sciences field. Chemistry and biology majors as well as doctors and pharmacists make up the class profile.

Location
Lehigh's picturesque 1,600-acre wooded campus is actually built into the side of what is affectionately known as "Old South Mountain" in historic Bethlehem, Pennsylvania. A little more than an hour's car ride from Philadelphia or New York City, Lehigh is located within the thriving economic and cultural corridor of the eastern United States.

The University and The College
Graduate study at Lehigh University revolves around a commitment to excellence in teaching and research that dates back to 1882, when the University first began awarding graduate degrees. Today, Lehigh graduate students across the University's four colleges enjoy the benefits of the institution's reputation as one of the most selective national universities in the country, including its state-of-the-art laboratories and research centers, well-equipped libraries, and vast technology resources.

Lehigh's College of Business and Economics offers its graduate students a cutting-edge curriculum, which is designed to mirror business functions and decision making from the perspective of the firm as a whole. CBE graduates acquire the skills and abilities that are required of future leaders in an ever-changing business environment. Academic excellence, an outstanding faculty, and outstanding student body offer full- and part-time students an intellectually stimulating environment.

Applying
In order to undertake master's-level work in health and biopharmaceutical economics, a student must have an undergraduate degree with a major in the life sciences or a related field (such as chemistry, premed, chemical engineering, or bioengineering). Applicants are expected to have competed two courses in calculus, a course in statistics, and courses in both principles and intermediate microeconomics. Applicants lacking one or more of these background prerequisites may still be admitted to the program; however, courses taken to remedy background deficiencies do not count toward the required minimum credit hours for the degree.

Application for admission is made to the Graduate Programs Office in the College of Business and Economics. In addition to an essay, transcripts, a resume, and two academic letters of recommendation, all applicants are required to submit scores for the Graduate Management Admission Test (GMAT) or the Graduate Record Examinations (GRE) aptitude test. Successful applicants generally score in the top quarter on the quantitative portion of either exam. International students are required to score at least 600 on the Test of English as a Foreign Language (TOEFL) proficiency examination. An application fee of $65, which may not be waived or deferred, is required. A CBE faculty admissions committee reviews all applications and bases its decision upon the applicant's academic abilities, motivation, maturity, and potential to complete graduate studies successfully.

Correspondence and Information
Corinn McBride
Director of Recruitment and Admissions
College of Business and Economics
Lehigh University
621 Taylor Street
Bethlehem, Pennsylvania 18015
Phone: 610-758-5280
Fax: 610-758-5283
E-mail: mbaadmissions@lehigh.edu
Web site: http://www3.lehigh.edu/business/cbemshbp.asp

Lehigh University

THE FACULTY AND THEIR RESEARCH

Mark R. Adams, Professor of Practice, Business Minor Program; M.B.A., Pittsburgh; J.D., Baltimore; CFA, CPA. Accounting, corporate reporting, finance, capital evaluations and investments.

Anne-Marie Anderson, Assistant Professor of Finance; M.B.A., Tulsa, 1998; Ph.D., Arizona, 2003. Corporate restructuring, mergers and acquisitions, valuation.

J. Richard Aronson, William L. Clayton Professor of Business and Economics and Director, Martindale Center for the Study of Private Enterprise; Ph.D., Clark, 1964. Tax and expenditure analysis, pension funds, municipal bond analysis, fiscal federalism.

Richard W. Barsness, Professor Emeritus; Ph.D., Minnesota, 1963. International business, corporate strategy in the airline industry.

John W. Bonge, Professor Emeritus; Ph.D., Northwestern, 1968. Business strategy and entrepreneurship.

Paul R. Brown, Professor of Accounting and Dean, College of Business and Economics; Ph.D., Texas at Austin. Financial statement analysis, FASB/SEC policy analysis, international reporting and analysis, earnings measurement and management, managing earnings expectations.

Stephen J. Buell, Professor; Ph.D., Lehigh, 1977. High-yield bonds, corporate bankruptcy.

Franklin J. Carter, Assistant Professor of Marketing; Ph.D., Carnegie Mellon, 1997. Business-to-business marketing, sales force management, diffusion of innovation.

Ravi Chitturi, Assistant Professor of Marketing; M.B.A., 1996, Ph.D., 2003, Texas at Austin. Technology and innovation, design and consumer emotions, brand value and marketing strategy.

Shin-Yi Chou, Assistant Professor of Economics; Ph.D., Duke, 1999. Health economics.

Karen M. Collins, Associate Professor; Ph.D., Virginia Tech, 1988. Behavioral dimensions of public accounting practice (including stress, turnover, and upward mobility of women), ethnic diversity.

James A. Dearden, Professor; Ph.D., Penn State, 1987. Game theory, marketing science, institution design, microeconomics.

Mary E. Deily, Associate Professor; Ph.D., Harvard, 1985. Industrial organization, exit behavior, industries in transition.

Dale F. Falcinelli, Swartley Professor of Finance, Professor of Practice in Marketing and Management, and Chairman, vSeries Corporate Entrepreneurship; M.A., Lehigh, 1972. Contemporary marketing, business management policies, entrepreneurship, strategic business analysis.

Robert C. Giambatista, Assistant Professor of Management; Ph.D., Wisconsin–Madison, 1999. Leadership, groups, decision making, diversity.

Paul Gordon, Professor of Practice; M.B.A., Wisconsin–Madison; CPA. Financial accounting.

James A. Greenleaf, Associate Professor; Ph.D., NYU, 1973. Portfolio management, derivative instruments, international investments, quantitative applications to investments.

Frank Gunter, Associate Professor; Ph.D., Johns Hopkins, 1985. Economies of Colombia, Iraq, China, and Latvia; capital flight; customs; unions.

Parveen P. Gupta, Frank L. McGee Professor of Accounting; Ph.D., Penn State, 1987. Process redesign through reengineering and benchmarking within manufacturing and service organizations; assessment of business risks and controls within the value chain; business valuation; financial analysis, corporate governance, and internal auditing.

Reetika Gupta, Assistant Professor of Marketing: Ph.D., CUNY, Baruch. Complexity in interactive consumption environments, consumer learning of new products.

James A. Hall, Associate Professor; Ph.D., Oklahoma State, 1979. Systems design, internal control of systems, computer systems auditing.

Thomas J. Hyclak, Professor; Ph.D., Notre Dame, 1976. Labor market developments in transition economies, urban economic development.

Arthur E. King, Professor; Ph.D., Ohio State, 1976. Applied econometrics, comparative economics, economics of Central Europe.

Richard J. Kish, Professor; Ph.D., Florida, 1988. Fixed-income securities, efficient markets, international mergers.

Michael G. Kolchin, Professor; D.B.A., Indiana, 1980. Comparative buying processes, purchasing education and training, purchasing effectiveness, supply chain management optimization.

Nevena T. Koukova, Assistant Professor of Marketing; Ph.D., Maryland, 2005. Pricing of digital products, bundling and unbundling of electronic content, and behavioral aspects of bundling; marketing strategy; consumer analysis; marketing research; principles of marketing; services marketing.

Robert Kuchta, Professor of Practice; M.S., NJIT, 1982. Marketing as a business.

James A. Largay, Professor; Ph.D., Cornell, 1971. Cash flow reporting, intercorporate investments, derivative financial investments.

James M. Maskulka, Associate Professor; D.B.A., Kent State, 1984. Marketing communications, branding, media.

Teresa McCarthy, Assistant Professor of Supply Chain Management; Ph.D., Tennessee, 2003. Role of marketing in demand management, demand planning and demand forecasting, market orientation and supply chain orientation, collaboration forecasting and sales force forecasting management, e-commerce demand management.

Judith A. McDonald, Associate Professor; Ph.D., Princeton, 1986. United States–Canada economic relations, external debt and tropical deforestation issues, pay equity, gender differences in starting salaries.

Matthew A. Melone, Associate Professor; J.D., Pennsylvania, 1993. Taxation, law and accounting, real estate law, partnership and LLC taxation.

Erin Moore, Assistant Professor of Accounting; Ph.D., Massachusetts, 2006; CPA. Earnings restatements, firm valuation.

Vincent G. Munley, Professor; Ph.D., SUNY at Binghamton, 1979. Political economy of state and local government finances.

David H. Myers, Professor of Practice; Ph.D., Washington (Seattle), 2001. Conditional performance measurement of mutual funds; pension funds, portfolio strategies, Japanese equity markets, international investing, stochastic programming applications for asset/liability management.

George A. Nation III, Professor; J.D., Villanova, 1983. Commercial lending law topics, environmental liability for lenders, promissory notes, guaranty and surety law, product liability.

Nandkumar Nayar, Professor and Hans Baer Chair in Finance; Ph.D., Iowa, 1988. Investment banking and financing methods, derivative securities, working capital management, tax issues, game theory modeling.

Anthony P. O'Brien, Professor; Ph.D., Berkeley, 1986. Business history, economic history, microeconomics.

John W. Paul, Professor; Ph.D., Lehigh, 1978. Audits of small businesses, audits of information systems, statistical sampling in auditing, cost allocation, activity-based costing.

Catherine M. Ridings, Assistant Professor; Ph.D., Drexel, 2000. Virtual communities, trust, e-commerce, management of technical personnel.

Heibatollah Sami, Eugene and Sue Mercy Professor of Accounting; Ph.D., Louisiana State, 1984. Impact of accounting information on capital markets, international accounting, auditing.

Michael D. Santoro, Associate Professor; Ph.D., Rutgers, 1998. Organizational strategy, entrepreneurship and intrapreneurship, sources of technological innovation, role of industry-university collaboration in advancing new technologies.

Theodore W. Schlie, Associate Professor; Ph.D., Northwestern, 1973. Advanced manufacturing and competitive strategy, globalization of industrial research and development, international competitiveness.

Susan A. Sherer, Kenan Professor of Information Technology Management, Business Information Systems Program Director, and Co-director for the Center for Value Chain Research; Ph.D., Pennsylvania, 1988. Software failure risk, management of software development, manufacturing networks, interorganizational information systems, strategic information systems, IT investment management.

Kenneth P. Sinclair, Professor and Accounting Department Chairman; Ph.D., Massachusetts, 1972. Performance evaluation, human resource accounting, case studies in managerial accounting.

K. Sivakumar, Arthur Tauck Professor of International Marketing and Logistics and Professor and Chairperson of Marketing; Ph.D., Syracuse, 1992. Pricing, international marketing, innovation management.

Quingjiu (Tom) Tao, Assistant Professor of Management; Ph.D., Pittsburgh, 2004. Strategic alliance in emerging market environments, institutions and firm behavior, first mover advantage in international market entry.

Larry W. Taylor, Professor; Ph.D., North Carolina, 1984. Specification testing for economic models, finite-sample issues in econometrics, econometric methodology, macroeconomic modeling, qualitative dependent variables.

Stephen F. Thode, Associate Professor and Director, Goodman Center for Real Estate Studies; D.B.A., Indiana, 1980. New mortgage products, mortgage pricing, affordable housing financing, taxation of real estate investments, real option pricing.

Robert J. Thornton, Charles W. MacFarlane Professor of Economics and Program Director; Ph.D., Illinois, 1970. Unionism and collective bargaining, public employment, labor market discrimination, forensic economics.

Robert J. Trent, Associate Professor and Program Director, Supply Chain Management Program; Ph.D., Michigan State, 1993. Cross-functional teams in purchasing.

Geraldo M. Vasconcellos, Allen DuBois Professor of Finance and Economics and Director, Business Minor Program; Ph.D., Illinois at Urbana-Champaign, 1986. Cross-border mergers and acquisitions foreign direct investment, international financial markets, privatizations, financial structure and development.

Todd A. Watkins, Associate Professor; Ph.D., Harvard, 1986. Technology and industrial policy, economics and management of innovation, defense and optoelectronics industries.

Samuel C. Weaver, Swartley Professor of Finance; Ph.D., Lehigh, 1985. Value-based management, performance metrics, capital evaluation, cost of capital, mergers and acquisitions.

Wenlong Weng, Assistant Professor; Ph.D., Stanford, 2001. Managerial economics, planning and decision making under uncertainty, real options, financial risk measurement and management.

Yuliang (Oliver) Yao, Assistant Professor of Business Information Systems; M.B.A., Rensselaer, 1997; Ph.D., Maryland, 2002. Supply chain management, electronic commerce, technology issues in supply chains, logistics modeling/simulation.

THE NEW SCHOOL
A UNIVERSITY

THE NEW SCHOOL: A UNIVERSITY

Milano The New School for Management and Urban Policy
Program in Health Services Management and Policy

Program of Study

The Master of Science in Health Services Management and Policy program prepares students for leadership roles in the rapidly changing health-care industry. Students acquire new skills in gathering, interpreting, and presenting many types of contextual and issue-related data relevant to the health-care environment. The program is built on a base of applied policy and professional practice that encourages flexibility and openness to new health service needs and client diversity. Students learn to manage and lead within a professional environment and to assess, initiate, and facilitate change. Degree candidates gain the knowledge and skills required to improve the performance of the health-care system, become immediate agents of change within their organizations, and map a career path in line with the pace of the industry.

Building on a foundation of core courses, the program strengthens students' understanding of the fundamental aspects of the health-care sector while sharpening their analytic and decision-making skills. Degree candidates also attain expertise in doing original research and in professional writing and business planning. Students new to the field or career changers effectively jump-start their careers and gain practical experience through a field internship requirement.

To fulfill the required 42 credits, students structure a program comprising three components: a required schoolwide core of 12 credits, a required program core of 12 credits, and 18 credits of elective courses.

Research Facilities

The Center for New York City Affairs is a nonpartisan institute dedicated to advancing innovative public policies that strengthen neighborhoods, support families, and reduce urban poverty. Tools include rigorous analysis, research, candid public dialogue with stakeholders and opinion leaders, and strategic planning with government officials, nonprofit practitioners, and community residents. The center's original applied research and public seminars examine the politics of community change in local and state government and identify critical problems facing urban families and communities. The center's public programs offer community leaders and other participants the opportunity to meet powerful players in and around government and to learn about the context, the influential organizations, and other aspects of the policymaking landscape in New York City and urban America.

Financial Aid

Milano offers financial aid packages in the form of scholarships, fellowships, and loans. Financial aid awards are decided on a first-come, first-served basis, and applicants are encouraged to apply early to receive priority consideration. Financial aid award decisions are made after students are accepted at Milano. Applicants interested in obtaining financial aid should submit the Free Application for Federal Student Aid (FAFSA) or the Renewal Application for Federal Student Aid. More information is available from the Office of Financial Services at 212-229-8930.

Cost of Study

Tuition in 2006–07 was $1032 per credit, and fees were approximately $200 each term.

Living and Housing Costs

The University Housing Office maintains a comprehensive resource center with apartment listings. University-run apartments and residence halls are also available. The cost of housing, food, transportation, books, and living expenses averages $17,000 annually. For more information, students should go online to http://www.newschool.edu/studentservices.

Student Group

There are 112 students in the program; 21 attend on a full-time basis. Of these students, 87 are women, 55 are members of underrepresented groups, and 11 are international students.

Location

The New School's location in New York City gives students access to an abundance of resources. Students are encouraged to take advantage of the city's many museums, performance venues, and other cultural institutions, which are only a walk or a subway ride away. An extension of the classroom, the city also offers excellent professional and networking opportunities, and some classes require that students work with outside businesses to complete assignments—giving them unparalleled real-world experience. Internships and apprenticeships with leading New York City companies and organizations in every field are also available, and many students have moved on from internships to successful careers with those companies and organizations upon graduation.

The University and The School

The New School pioneered the idea of lifelong university-level education for adults. It was created for teachers and students from different backgrounds who were willing to take risks for their intellectual and political beliefs. Milano The New School for Management and Urban Policy trains leaders for the nonprofit, public, and private sectors with a measurable difference. The faculty blends theory with practice and progressive analysis with hands-on activism. Milano students work on local and global issues that affect organizations and urban communities—in New York City and around the world. The New School is accredited by the Commission on Higher Education of the Middle States Association of Colleges and Schools. A privately supported institution, The New School is chartered as a university by the Regents of the State of New York.

Applying

Students must submit the completed application form, the $50 application fee, official transcripts from all postsecondary institutions attended, a 300-word essay explaining their professional goals, two letters of recommendation, and a resume. Applications are reviewed on a rolling admissions basis. Although there is no specific deadline, applicants are strongly encouraged to apply by March 1 for the fall semester and by October 1 for the spring semester in order to take full advantage of financial aid and housing opportunities.

Correspondence and Information

Program in Health Services Management and Policy
Milano The New School for Management and Urban Policy
The New School
72 Fifth Avenue, 3rd Floor
New York, New York 10011
Phone: 212-229-5400
Fax: 212-229-5354
E-mail: milanoadmissions@newschool.edu
Web site: http://www.milano.newschool.edu

The New School: A University

THE FACULTY AND THEIR RESEARCH

Warren Balinsky, Associate Professor and Chair of Health Services Management; Ph.D., Case Western Reserve. Home health care and the applications of planning, development, marketing, and research to health services management and policy. Dr. Balinsky has written two books on home care; he has also written articles on various aspects of emergency preparedness, health care of the elderly, health-care reimbursement, health status indices, home care, pediatric health care, and the unequal distribution of medical personnel within the health-care system.

Robert Beauregard, Professor; Ph.D., Cornell. Urbanization in the United States, with particular focus on industrial urban decline after World War II and current problems posed by growth and decline in cities. Dr. Beauregard is currently working on *Writing Urban Theory,* a series of essays, and *Why Cities Endure,* a book investigating why some cities prosper while others do not. Dr. Beauregard teaches courses on the political economy of the city, urban redevelopment, neighborhood change, social theory, and research design.

Howard Berliner, Professor of Health Services Management and Director of Ph.D. in Public and Urban Policy Program; Sc.D., Johns Hopkins. Needs of vulnerable populations and access to health services for the uninsured. Dr. Berliner is the author of seven books, most recently *The Health Marketplace: New York City 1990–2010* with Ginzberg et al. He has also written numerous articles and reviews on health policy in academic and professional journals. Dr. Berliner served for two years as the assistant state health commissioner for New Jersey.

John Clinton, Visiting Assistant Professor; Ph.D., Fordham. Interprofessional collaboration. Dr. Clinton has served as corporation senior consultant on social responsibility at MetLife, senior vice president of the LightHouse for the Blind, and an administrator at NYU, Fordham University, and Hartwick College. He has been a consultant to foundations, nonprofit organizations, corporations, and higher education institutions.

Dennis Derryck, Professor of Professional Practice; Ph.D., Fordham. Innovative policies and strategies affecting the economic sustainability of nonprofit organizations. Dr. Derryck has held leadership positions in organizations involved in community economic development, operations and fiscal management, and research and policy analysis. He currently serves as chair of WE ACT for Environmental Justice and is vice chair of SoBro, the South Bronx Overall Economic Development Corporation.

Elizabeth Dickey, Professor; Ed.D., Massachusetts Amherst. Organizational behavior and leadership, with a psychosocial emphasis. Dr. Dickey is a developmental clinical psychologist. Between 1991 and 2005, she served as dean and then provost of The New School.

Peter Eisinger, Henry Cohen Professor; Ph.D., Yale. Urban politics and policy, state and local economic development, U.S. politics, state politics, federalism. Author of *Toward an End to Hunger in America.*

Alec Ian Gershberg, Associate Professor; Ph.D., Pennsylvania. School governance, education finance, decentralization in the developing world and in the United States, immigrant students in public schools in New York and California. Dr. Gershberg has conducted extensive research on Latin America—particularly Mexico, Nicaragua, and Ecuador—as well as on Egypt, Romania, and sub-Saharan Africa. He has been a frequent consultant to the World Bank, the Inter-American Development Bank, and the Urban Institute. Dr. Gershberg is the lead author of *Beyond Bilingual Education: New Immigrants and Public School Policies in California.*

Martin Greller, Professor and Associate Dean for Academic Affairs; Ph.D., Yale. Factors associated with career continuity for older workers, feedback systems in organizations as tools for increasing organizational effectiveness. Recent projects include an assessment of training needs for entry-level peace officers and a review of pay equity issues for a legislative body.

Darrick Hamilton, Assistant Professor; Ph.D., North Carolina at Chapel Hill. Ethnic and racial disparities in wealth, home ownership, and labor markets. Dr. Hamilton's articles can be found in *African American Research Perspectives, American Economics Review, Applied Economics Letters, Challenge: The Magazine of Economic Affairs, Journal of Economic Psychology, Review of Black Political Economy, Social Science Quarterly, Southern Economics Journal,* and *Transforming Anthropology.*

David Howell, Professor; Ph.D., New School. Labor markets at the local, national, and international levels. Recent publications have examined the effects of immigration on the economic status of foreign and native-born workers in New York City, the nature of recent changes in skill requirements and the determinants of relative wage trends in the United States, and the extent to which labor market institutions and social policy explain patterns of unemployment in Europe and the United States. Dr. Howell is the editor of *Fighting Unemployment: The Limits of Free Market Orthodoxy.*

Mark Lipton, Professor of Management and Chair of Management; Ph.D., Massachusetts Amherst. Management, leadership, organizational strategy. Author of *Guiding Growth: How Vision Keeps Companies on Course.* Dr. Lipton's research and opinions on management and strategy have appeared in *Executive Excellence, Harvard Business Review, The Journal of Management Consulting, Optimize, Organization Development Journal,* and *Sloan Management Review,* among others.

Edwin Melendez, Professor; Ph.D., Massachusetts Amherst. Economics. Dr. Melendez was director of the Mauricio Gastón Institute for Latino Community Development and Public Policy at the University of Massachusetts Boston (1992–98) and director of the Community Development Research Center at the Milano Graduate School (1999–2004). He has worked as a consultant on employment, economic development, job creation, and small business for numerous government, community, and philanthropic foundations. Dr. Melendez has managed more than thirty-five research, outreach, and demonstration projects and supervised or collaborated with more than 60 researchers in projects that resulted in several books, special issues of academic journals, and other publications.

Aida Rodriguez, Professor of Professional Practice; Ph.D., Massachusetts. Leadership and effective management in the nonprofit sector. Formerly deputy director of the Equal Opportunity Division of the Rockefeller Foundation, Dr. Rodriguez now serves on various nonprofit boards, including One Economy, Inc.; Alliance for Nonprofit Management; and the Association for Public Policy Analysis and Management. Dr. Rodriguez is an adviser on philanthropic initiatives in the United States and in Latin America, including the Funders' Collaborative for Strong Latino Communities.

Bryna Sanger, Professor; Ph.D., Brandeis. Public policy and management, changes in service delivery and management systems induced by welfare reform in states and localities around the country. Former dean of the Robert J. Milano Graduate School of Management and Urban Policy, Dr. Sanger has worked in a wide range of policy and management areas, including city service delivery, welfare reform, leadership, innovation, and performance management. She recently led a research effort with the National Civic League on the experiences of cities that have developed exemplary performance measurement systems and that report to and engage citizens in their efforts. Her most recent book on this topic is entitled *The Welfare Marketplace: Privatization and Welfare Reform.*

Alex F. Schwartz, Associate Professor, Chair of Department of Urban Policy Analysis and Management, and Senior Research Associate, Community Development Research Center; Ph.D., Rutgers. Housing and community development, including affordable housing programs, community reinvestment, and community development corporations. Dr. Schwartz's most recent publication is *Housing Policy in the United States.* His research has also appeared in such journals as *Cityscape, Economic Development Quarterly, International Journal of Urban and Regional Research,* and the *Journal of Urban Affairs.*

Lisa J. Servon, Associate Professor and Associate Director of Community Development Research Center; Ph.D., Berkeley. Urban poverty, community development, economic development, gender issues. Dr. Servon recently coedited *Gender and Planning: A Reader* (with Susan Fainstein), which covers a range of planning and development fields, including transportation, land use, history, gender, housing, social justice, environmental design, race, and economic and community development. The book was selected as one of the Top 10 Books for 2006 by Planetizen, a public-interest information exchange for the urban planning, design, and development community.

Nidhi Srinivas, Assistant Professor of Nonprofit Management; Ph.D., McGill. Civil society, specifically management of nongovernmental organizations, and the transfer and transformation of management knowledge. Dr. Srinivas teaches courses on nonprofit management, international development, and strategic decision making. Courses he has developed include Managing Institutions for Development (part of the core curriculum in the graduate program in international affairs) and Civil Society and South Asia.

Antonin Wagner, Visiting Professor; Ph.D., Fribourg (Switzerland). Economics. From 1996 to 2000, Dr. Wagner was president of the International Society for Third Sector Research, the leading scholarly institution in the nonprofit field. He has served as a consultant on social security–related issues to the Swiss Federal Statistical Office and the World Bank in Washington. He is a member of the editorial board of several international journals and has published widely in English, German, and French on the welfare state and civil society.

Tatiana Wah, Assistant Professor; Ph.D., Rutgers. Regional and local economic development planning and developing nations, with a particular focus on small developing nations' economies. Dr. Wah's recent work is on transnational expatriate (immigrant) recovery and engagement programs of developing countries, particularly Haiti. She has been involved in community development work in the New York African American and Caribbean communities as a consultant, nonprofit administrator, and activist/advocate.

Mary R. Watson, Assistant Professor; Ph.D., Vanderbilt. Contemporary human capital issues in organizations, with particular emphasis on the social impact of labor market discontinuities. Dr. Watson teaches courses on management and organization behavior, human resources, social impact management, and globalization. She has a strong interest in cultural, racial, ethnic, and gender inequalities in the workplace and society. Dr. Watson's upcoming book (with Dr. Rikki Abzug), tentatively titled *Human Resources in Social Purpose Organizations,* is scheduled to be published by Jossey-Bass in 2007.

Part-Time Faculty
The part-time faculty members of Milano The New School for Management and Urban Policy are high-level executives and managers in the institutions and agencies for which they work and the organizations for which they volunteer. They bring to the classroom valuable insight into current management and policy issues from both their personal experience and relevant curriculum. For a current listing of part-time faculty members, students should visit the Faculty page of the Milano Web site at http://www.milano.newschool.edu.

NEW YORK MEDICAL COLLEGE

Health Policy and Management Program

Program of Study	The School of Public Health is a member of the Association of Schools of Public Health (ASPH). The Department of Health Policy and Management in the School of Public Health at New York Medical College (NYMC) offers a Master of Public Health (M.P.H.) degree in health policy and management. The department, in conjunction with the Center for Disaster Medicine of the School of Public Health, also offers a concentration and a graduate certificate in emergency preparedness. Graduate certificates in managed care and management of long-term-care facilities are also offered.
	Classes are offered in the late afternoon or early evening, Monday through Thursday, and students may be full- or part-time. Some Saturday and online courses are also available. An individual may apply as a matriculated student or take courses on a nonmatriculated basis for up to 9 credits.
	The public policy, administrative, and technological complexities in health-care systems today require managers and policy makers to have a broad-based education. The courses leading to the degree in health policy and management are designed to provide the students with an understanding of the business, programmatic, planning, and policy areas of health care. The program prepares students for careers in a wide range of health services and research settings.
	The M.P.H. degree is a 46-credit program, which includes a 1-credit practicum. Courses include Health Care in the U.S., Introduction to Biostatistics, Introduction to Epidemiology, Health Economics, Behavior and Social Factors in Public Health, Environmental Influences on Human Health, Law and Health, Financial Administration of Health Delivery Systems, Managing Health Care, and Organizational Theory. A 3-credit capstone course or a 3-credit thesis is also required. All students who are pursuing the M.P.H. degree are required to show evidence of computer literacy through the successful completion of the Computer Literacy Competency project during their first semester; a 1-credit course is available to students who desire formal instruction in computer skills.
	Students accepted into the School of Medicine may also apply to the M.P.H. program, providing an opportunity to pursue both degrees simultaneously. The degree can be completed within the four years of medical school, or the student may elect to take five years to complete both programs.
Research Facilities	The Health Sciences Library (HSL) maintains a collection of more than 200,000 volumes and 10,454 journals. Many of these periodicals are available through the library's homepage on the Web at http://library.nymc.edu. The HSL online catalog is the master list of books, journals, media, and equipment owned by the library and is available online and electronically off-site. The library serves all faculty and staff members, residents, and students of NYMC with a complete set of information resources and services. It also houses a 20-person classroom, a nine-workstation PC lab, two small-group study rooms, and study space for students.
Financial Aid	The College's Financial Aid Office helps those students who qualify for federal financial aid programs to obtain need-based and non-need-based loans, grants, and external scholarships. The College also offers work-study opportunities of up to 20 hours per week for students who qualify.
Cost of Study	Costs for 2006–07 were as follows for a full-time (12 credits) student: tuition, $645 per credit; entrance fee, $100; network access and student activity fees, $10; books and supplies, $1752; and miscellaneous expenses, $3024. There are also health insurance and graduation fees.
Living and Housing Costs	Students can choose from a variety of on-campus and off-campus housing arrangements. On-campus yearly costs include approximately $3746 for food and $7746 for housing. Off-campus students pay approximately $12,000 for housing, $1200 for utilities, and $1400 for transportation.
Student Group	There are 1,660 students enrolled at New York Medical College; 760 are in the School of Medicine (M.D. degree program), 500 in the School of Public Health (doctoral, Master of Public Health, and Master of Science degrees), and 250 are in the Graduate School of Basic Medical Sciences (doctoral and Master of Science degrees). Students in the Health Policy and Management Program come from a wide range of educational and employment backgrounds. Consistent with the quantitative tracks of epidemiology and biostatistics, the College attracts students with recent baccalaureate degrees in the areas of biomedical sciences, computer sciences, or information systems. Students also come to the program with backgrounds as medical students, health-care professionals, and administrators in the health-care sector and information technology field.
Location	Located in the picturesque Hudson Valley of Westchester County in New York State, New York Medical College offers students unmatched scenic beauty on the East Coast with quick access to New York City, one of the most famous cities in the U.S., if not the entire world. New York City is home to Broadway theater, numerous art galleries and museums, professional sports franchises, and unmatched shopping, restaurant, and entertainment opportunities as well as dozens of medical facilities focusing on patient care and research.
The College	New York Medical College awards advanced degrees to students who are preparing for careers in medicine, science, and the health professions. The College has 1,350 full-time faculty members and 1,450 part-time and voluntary faculty members who teach, conduct research, and provide patient care at twenty-eight hospital affiliates. The extensive network of affiliated hospitals includes large urban medical centers, small suburban hospitals, and technologically advanced, regional tertiary-care facilities. Students in the College's various advanced degree programs are afforded a breadth of learning opportunities and experiences that is unparalleled in the nation.
Applying	Applicants must have a minimum cumulative GPA of 3.0 from their undergraduate studies. Students with a GPA of less than 3.0 may enter as nonmatriculants. Nonmatriculants may file for matriculant status after they have successfully completed 9 graduate credits with a minimum GPA of 3.0.
	Application for matriculation must be completed well in advance of registration. Applications for the fall term must be received by August 1; for the spring term, by December 1; and for the summer term, by May 1. The deadlines for international students are May 15 (fall), October 15 (spring), and March 15 (summer).
	To enroll, applicants must submit the following materials: a completed application form; a nonrefundable $50 application fee ($100 for international students); official transcripts for all postsecondary course work sent directly to the Assistant Dean for Admissions for the School of Public Health; two completed recommendation forms; a personal statement of approximately 250 words; and proof of immunization against measles, mumps, and rubella. International students must submit a TOEFL score of at least 600 (paper-based exam), 250 (computer-based exam), or 100 (Internet-based exam).
Correspondence and Information	Marian F. McGowan, Assistant Dean for Admissions School of Public Health Room 316 New York Medical College Valhalla, New York 10595 Phone: 914-594-4510 E-mail: Sph_admissions@nymc.edu Web site: http://www.nymc.edu/sph	Annette Choolfaian, Professor and Chair Department of Health Policy and Management School of Public Health New York Medical College Valhalla, New York 10595 Phone: 914-594-4250 E-mail: annette@nymc.edu

New York Medical College

THE FACULTY

Lawerence W. Bassett, Visiting Lecturer; M.B.A., NYU.
Joyce M. Bove, Visiting Lecturer; M.P.A., Indiana.
Peter Brown, Visiting Lecturer; M.B.A., Iona; M.A., Manhattan.
Norman R. Cates, Senior Lecturer; Ph.D., Fordham.
Lydia V. Cavieux, Senior Lecturer; M.P.A., NYU.
C. Gene Cayten, Professor of Clinical Public Health; M.D., New York Medical College; M.P.H., Yale.
Annette Choolfaian, Professor of Public Health Practice and Chair, Department of Health Policy and Management; B.S.N., Bridgeport; M.P.A., NYU; RN.
Gerald Culliton, Senior Lecturer; M.P.A., Pace.
Gail A. Currie, Senior Lecturer; M.S., USC.
Deborah D'Agostino, Visiting Lecturer; M.P.H., Columbia.
Barbara DeCesare, Lecturer; J.D., Case Western Reserve; M.P.H., Yale; RN.
Garrett T. Doering, Lecturer; M.S., Maryland.
Theresa Haviland, Lecturer; M.P.H., New York Medical College.
Katherine Kavasilas Iaconetti, Senior Lecturer; Ph.D., Walden.
Harvey Jolt, Visiting Lecturer; Ph.D., NYU; FACHE.
George J. Kehayas, Senior Lecturer; J.D., Fordham.
Jeanne Marie Kiss, Lecturer; Ph.D., NYU.
Raymond T. LaManna, Lecturer; M.A., Columbia Teachers College; M.S., Fordham; M.Div., St. Joseph's Seminary.
Eliot J. Lazar, Senior Lecturer; M.D., SUNY Upstate Medical Center; M.B.A., NYU.
Joan Liman, Lecturer; M.D., M.P.H., New York Medical College.
David S. Markenson, Associate Professor and Director, Center for Disaster Medicine.; M.D., Albert Einstein College of Medicine.
Louis Martir, Visiting Lecturer; M.S., Iona.
John A. McClung, Associate Professor of Clinical Public Health; M.D., New York Medical College.
Patrick J. Montana, Senior Lecturer; M.S., LIU; M.B.A., Cincinnati; Ph.D., NYU.
James J. O'Brien, Associate Professor; Ph.D., Fordham.
Daniel Gerard O'Hare, S.J., Senior Lecturer; M.A., Fordham; M.Div., Loyola; Ph.D., Fordham.
Kobi Peleg, Distinguished Lecturer; M.P.H., Uniformed Services University of the Health Sciences; Ph.D., Ben Gurion (Israel).
Scot Phelps, Lecturer; J.D., Brooklyn Law; M.P.H., Yale.
Michael J. Reilly, Assistant Professor and Assistant Director, Center for Disaster Medicine; M.P.H., Yale.
Gerard D. Robilotti, Distinguished Lecturer; M.S., Columbia.
Thomas Saccardi, Senior Lecturer; M.B.A., St. John's; M.Ph., Ph.D., CUNY; FACHE.
Jose R. Sanchez, Visiting Lecturer; M.S., Adelphi; LMSW, ACSW.
Joel Seligman, Visiting Lecturer; M.B.A., M.P.H., Columbia.
Inez Madeline Sieben, Lecturer; M.P.H., Boston University.
Carol J. Spizzirri, Visiting Lecturer; B.S.N., Mount Scenario; RN.
Jeffrey S. Stier, Senior Lecturer; M.D., Maryland.
Richard K. Stone, Professor of Clinical Public Health; M.D., New York Medical College.
Denise Caspler Tahara, Assistant Professor; M.B.A., M.Phil., Ph.D., NYU.
Lita M. Talbot, Lecturer; M.S., Columbia.
Theodore Tully Jr., Visiting Lecturer; B.A., Iona; AEMT-P.
Deborah Viola, Assistant Professor; M.B.A., Fairleigh Dickinson; Ph.D., CUNY.
Kurt Lee Weinmann, Senior Lecturer; J.D., Cornell.
Arthur E. Weintraub, Visiting Lecturer; M.P.A., NYU.
Jane Woolley, Senior Lecturer; Ed.D., Columbia.
Douglas York, Lecturer; M.P.H., New York Medical College; Ph.D., Pace.

PENN STATE UNIVERSITY PARK

College of Health and Human Development

Programs of Study

Penn State's College of Health and Human Development is the first to combine the study of health and the prevention of illness with the study of human development throughout the life span. Graduate degrees are available in nine programs: Biobehavioral Health; Communication Sciences and Disorders; Health Policy and Administration; Hospitality Management; Human Development and Family Studies; Kinesiology; Nursing; Nutrition; and Recreation, Park and Tourism Management.

The College has many distinguished faculty members who are carrying out research on a wide range of issues, such as child language development, family dynamics and youth development, cardiovascular disease, diabetes, vitamin metabolism, aging, leisure behavior, health-care cost containment and quality improvement, exercise, genetic basis of behavior, role of attitudes and education in treating AIDS, and effects of day care on children's development.

Research Facilities

The College has several research centers, clinics, institutes, and laboratories, including the Prevention Research Center for the Promotion of Human Development, the Center for Developmental and Health Genetics, the Methodology Center, the Center for Human Development and Family Research in Diverse Contexts, the Gerontology Center, the General Clinical Research Center, the Center for Health Care and Policy Research, and the Center for Childhood Obesity Research. Among the University's other major resources are libraries and computer centers for instruction and research.

Financial Aid

Financial support other than loans is provided for 64 percent of the College's full-time students and 41 percent of its part-time students. Students may apply for grants, loans, fellowships, scholarships, assistantships, veterans' benefits, traineeships, instructorships, resident assistant positions, and work-study positions. Teaching and research assistantships offer students a stipend and a grant-in-aid for tuition. Employment is also possible at the University and in the community. Financial aid application deadlines vary, but in general it is best to apply by February 1 for the next academic year. Information can be obtained from each department or from the Graduate School Information Center, Penn State University, 113 Kern Graduate Building, University Park, Pennsylvania 16802-3300.

Cost of Study

Tuition for 12 or more credits during the 2006–07 academic year was $6612 per semester for Pennsylvania residents and $12,032 for nonresidents. Tuition for fewer than 12 credits per semester was $551 per credit for residents and $1003 for nonresidents. Students were also charged a $202 computer fee and a $57 activity fee.

Living and Housing Costs

The cost of living at the University Park Campus and in surrounding areas is moderate. The University offers on-campus apartments as well as dormitory rooms. Dormitory residents may purchase meal plans ranging in price from about $1500 to $2000 per semester. On-campus housing rates range from about $605 to $1000 per month. For those who prefer off-campus housing, private homes and apartment complexes in the area offer accommodations at a wide range of prices.

Student Group

Approximately 400 graduate students are enrolled in the College; 73 percent are women, 25 percent are international, and 10 percent belong to minority groups.

Student Outcomes

Graduates enter such diverse fields as rehabilitation; work-site health promotion; public- and private-sector human services, including academic research and teaching; employee assistance programs; health-care administration; nursing specialties; park and recreation planning; nutrition science and education; physiology; consulting; research; education; speech-language pathology; and audiology. The College helps prepare students for research, teaching, managerial, and policy roles in a variety of settings, including the health-care field, government agencies, universities, foundations, and large and small corporations. Graduates work in hospitals, rehabilitation centers, long-term-care facilities, or research laboratories. Other employers include human service agencies, health organizations, insurance companies, the food and pharmaceutical industries, restaurants, hotels, resorts, and parks.

Location

State College, in the middle of an area of more than 100,000 residents, is the major cultural center of central Pennsylvania. The town has a collegiate atmosphere and is within a 5-hour drive of New York; Washington, D.C.; and Philadelphia. There is bus and air commuting service to all major cities. The University and the community sponsor cultural, athletic, professional, and scholarly events. There are excellent recreational opportunities on campus and in the surrounding open countryside and mountain forests.

The University and The College

Founded in 1855, Penn State is Pennsylvania's land-grant university. It is a major research institution and a member of the Association of American Universities. The University enrolls approximately 10,500 graduate students. Most of the graduate programs are offered at the University Park Campus.

The College of Health and Human Development was the first in the country to take a comprehensive approach to the health, development, and well-being of individuals and families. Several of its programs are among the oldest of their type and are consistently ranked among the nation's best. Many of its faculty members are internationally renowned.

Applying

For admission to a graduate program, applicants must have a baccalaureate degree and must submit transcripts of all prior college work. Applicants also must meet department requirements for course work in specific fields and for the minimum grade point average. Most departments also require letters of recommendation, a statement of the applicant's research and career interests, and scores from the Graduate Record Examinations or an approved equivalent test.

Correspondence and Information

Karl M. Newell, Associate Dean for Research and Graduate Education
201 Henderson Building
Penn State University
University Park, Pennsylvania 16802-2426
Phone: 814-863-7519
E-mail: healthhd@psu.edu
Web site: http://www.hhdev.psu.edu/

Penn State University Park

GRADUATE PROGRAMS AND PROGRAM HEADS

GRADUATE PROGRAMS OF THE COLLEGE OF HEALTH AND HUMAN DEVELOPMENT

Biobehavioral Health (Ph.D.): John Graham, Professor-in-Charge of the Graduate Program; 315 Health and Human Development Building East (814-863-7256). This program helps prepare students to focus on how biological, behavioral, sociocultural, and environmental variables interact to influence health in individuals as well as groups. Because the level of health often is a product of variables that interact, understanding effective interventions may require combinations of biological, behavioral, sociocultural, and environmental strategies. Scholars and professionals who can bring this integrated perspective to their work are needed in research, teaching, and policy roles in a variety of settings, including the health-care field, research laboratories, government agencies, universities, and medical schools. Web site: http://bbh.hhdev.psu.edu/grads/index.html.

Communication Sciences and Disorders (M.S., Ph.D.): Dr. Adele Miccio, Professor-in-Charge of the Graduate Program; 122 Moore Building (814-865-0971). The program prepares professionals to work with people who have a communication disorder. Program requirements emphasize a clinical research approach to speech-language pathology and audiology. The M.S. program is accredited by the Educational Standards Board, and the Speech and Hearing Clinic is accredited by the Professional Service Board of the American Speech-Language-Hearing Association. Settings for student training and research include therapy and diagnostic services in the in-house Speech and Hearing Clinic and laboratories in speech science, audiology, speech-language pathology, assistive devices (technology transfer), and environmental acoustics. Most M.S. graduates take positions in health-related settings such as clinics, hospitals, and rehabilitation centers; others work in schools. Ph.D. graduates work in universities, hospitals, and rehabilitation centers. A growing number of graduates enter private practice. Web site: http://cmdis.hhdev.psu.edu/grad/index.html.

Health Policy and Administration (M.H.A., M.S., Ph.D.): Dr. Dennis Scanlon, Professor-in-Charge of the Graduate Program; 116 Henderson Building (814-863-2859). The M.H.A. is accredited by the Commission on Accreditation in Health Management Education, with a requirement of 49 credits, including an intervening summer course and internship experience. The M.H.A. degree program prepares students for management positions in hospitals, health systems, multigroup practices, nursing homes, managed-care organizations, health insurance companies, consulting firms, and government health organizations. The M.S. and Ph.D. provide training in health services research, emphasizing aging and long-term care, quality improvement in health systems and health-care organizations, health disparities in children, youths and families, and demography and population health outcomes. Web site: http://www.hhdev.psu.edu/hpa/prospect/grad/index.html.

Hospitality Management (M.S., Ph.D.): Dr. Anna Mattila, Professor-in-Charge of the Graduate Program; 201 Mateer Building (814-865-1853). This program prepares students for executive, research, or educational roles in the hospitality industry or academic institutions. The program emphasizes the design and management of services related to providing lodging and food in both the private and public sectors. The M.S. and Ph.D. degrees in hotel, restaurant, and institutional management are focused on conceptual and research issues in the field of hospitality management. Students entering the program are expected to have at least two years of experience in a relevant field. Web site: http://www.hhdev.psu.edu/shm/grad/index.html.

Human Development and Family Studies (Ph.D.): Dr. Douglas Teti, Professor-in-Charge of the Graduate Program; 211 Henderson Building South (814-863-8001). Students in this interdisciplinary program are trained to design and conduct research that advances knowledge about individual and family development. Interventions that promote healthy development are an additional focus of research. The program takes a life-span perspective on development in infancy, childhood, adolescence, adulthood, and old age. Understanding the familial, cultural, and community context of development is integral to this perspective. Ph.D. graduates of the program are research scientists, educators, and administrators of agencies and programs. HDFS faculty members are affiliated with five centers that promote research and graduate training: the Prevention Research Center for the Promotion of Human Development, Child Development Laboratory, Gerontology Center, Methodology Center, and Center for Human Development and Family Research in Diverse Contexts. Web site: http://www.hhdev.psu.edu/hdfs/grad.

Kinesiology (M.S., Ph.D.): Dr. John Challis, Professor-in-Charge of the Graduate Program; 266 Recreation Building (814-863-0842; kinesgrad@psu.edu). The program offers seven areas of specialization: athletic training and sports medicine, biomechanics, exercise physiology, history and philosophy of sport, motor control, pedagogy of physical activity and health, and psychology of movement and sport. All areas stress research and the completion of a scholarly thesis under the direction of a faculty adviser. Graduates pursue careers in academia and private industry. Web site: http://hhdev.psu.edu/kines/grad/index.html.

Nursing (M.S., Ph.D.): Dr. Janice Penrod, Professor-in-Charge of the Graduate Program; 203 Health and Human Development East Building (814-863-2211). The M.S. degree program of the School of Nursing has two options that prepare nurses for advanced practice as nurse practitioners and clinical nurse specialists. All options can be completed in four semesters of full-time study or as individually planned in part-time study. A post-master's certificate program is available for preparation as a family nurse practitioner. The program combines advanced knowledge and nursing research with input from a rich multidisciplinary environment and emphasizes advanced practice in rural and medically underserved communities. Graduates serve in hospitals, clinics, and community and other health-care-delivery settings. The doctoral program is designed to develop clinical scholars, faculty, and researchers. Web site: http://www.hhdev.psu.edu/nurs/grad/index.html.

Nutritional Sciences (M.S., Ph.D.): Dr. John Beard, Professor-in-Charge of Graduate Program; 126 Henderson Building South (814-865-3448). The M.S. degree in nutrition has an emphasis in public health. The Ph.D. program is promoting and developing leaders in nutrition. Research facilities include nutritional biochemical laboratories in the College of Health and Human Development, the College of Agricultural Sciences, and the General Clinical Research Center. Collaboration with faculty members in the College of Medicine also provides additional opportunities for clinical research. Graduates of the program work in the food, fitness, and pharmaceutical industries; on government and community-based projects; and in teaching and research. Web site: http://nutrition.hhdev.psu.edu/grad/index.html.

Recreation, Park and Tourism Management (M.S., Ph.D.): Dr. Harry Zinn, Professor-in-Charge of the Graduate Program; 201 Mateer Building (814-865-1852). This program prepares students for careers in administration, research, and teaching. Students work in the community, including public park and recreation systems, voluntary agencies, and private commercial enterprises; in therapeutic settings; and in park planning, interpretive services, outdoor education, and outdoor recreation. The program emphasizes research in leisure behavior, with concentration on field application and innovative approaches and practices in recreation and leisure services. Recreation, Park and Tourism Management is affiliated with the Shaver's Creek Environmental Center. Web site: http://hhdev.psu.edu/rptm/grad/index.html.

SETON HALL UNIVERSITY

Department of Public and Healthcare Administration

Programs of Study

The Department of Public and Healthcare Administration (DPHA) offers two graduate degree programs, the Master of Healthcare Administration (M.H.A.) and the Master of Public Administration (M.P.A.). Each degree program requires 39 credits and is tailored to the working adult student, with classes offered in the late afternoons and evenings, on Saturday mornings, online, and in four-day compressed courses available over two weekends. Courses are offered year-round, including during three separate summer sessions. Upon completion of the M.H.A. degree, students accept positions in a variety of health-care institutions, such as hospitals, nursing homes, and other health-care-related institutions.

The M.H.A. curriculum is similar to that of the M.P.A. with the health-care concentration, but it requires extra courses in health-care finance and management. Generally, health-care students who are committed to working for health-care providers (hospitals, long-term-care facilities, physician practices, and ambulatory-care facilities) enroll in this degree program, although both health-care administration degrees lead to a variety of management opportunities with health-care organizations.

The Department of Public and Healthcare Administration, in conjunction with Seton Hall's School of Diplomacy, offers a 60-credit degree program leading to a joint M.P.A./M.A. in diplomacy degree. The Department also offers 15-credit certificate programs in health-care administration, arts administration, and nonprofit management. Students completing any of the certificate programs may elect to apply the credits toward either the M.P.A. or M.H.A. degrees if they wish to continue their education.

Research Facilities

The Center for Public Service conducts applied public policy research and provides technical assistance to community-based organizations through its Nonprofit Sector Research Institute. Students are given opportunities to participate in research projects and gain hands-on management experience through a number of academic and technical assistance programs.

The Walsh Library, a state-of-the-art 155,000-square-foot building, houses 500,000 titles, 1,875 current periodicals, and an extensive collection of microform and other nonprint items that include videotapes, CD-ROM music, and other electronic media. Fahy Hall has twenty-eight classrooms, two TV studios, a Macintosh and IBM graphics lab, two classroom amphitheaters, and language and statistics labs. McNulty Hall has well-equipped science labs. The College of Nursing Building contains a multipurpose practice-demonstration room, with twelve hospital beds, an amphitheater, an independent study area, and a computer laboratory. Completed in 1997, Jubilee Hall, a six-story facility with 126,000 square feet of academic space, features high-tech classrooms with computer and multimedia capabilities and the Center for Securities Trading and Analysis, commonly referred to as the Trading Room.

Financial Aid

The DPHA has a limited number of graduate assistantships both within the Department and throughout the University, which cover tuition costs and provide a modest stipend in exchange for 20 hours of work per week. Students interested in graduate assistant positions should complete an online application at http://www.shu.edu/applying/graduate/grad-finaid.cfm. Students interested in other financial aid options should visit the same Web site for more information.

In addition, through an arrangement with the VA New Jersey Health Care system, the Department offers the Healthcare Administration Residency Program, a two-year residency that provides students whose interests or career objectives are in health-care administration the opportunity for study supplemented by work experiences in health-care administration. Interested applicants accepted into the M.H.A. program are referred to the VA for an interview. Those who are selected by the Department and the VA work 20 hours per week for the VA Hospital, two blocks from campus, and receive support in the form of a stipend plus tuition reimbursement.

Cost of Study

Tuition is $826 per credit. Fees total about $300 a semester.

Living and Housing Costs

Seton Hall maintains a limited supply of housing to accommodate graduate students. On-campus room and board total about $9000 per year. Housing and living costs in South Orange and surrounding towns are comparable to most suburban cities, with studio and one-bedroom apartments renting for $650 to $900 per month.

Student Group

Typical M.P.A. and M.H.A. students have some work experience, although the programs do accept students straight from undergraduate programs. The Department also sponsors a student chapter of Upsilon Phi Delta, the honorary society for health-care administrators.

Location

Seton Hall is located on 58 acres in the village of South Orange, New Jersey, a suburban residential area 14 miles southwest of New York City. The town center is a 10-minute walk from the campus and features bookstores, coffee shops, and restaurants. The heart of midtown Manhattan is about 25 minutes away by train; students can take advantage of everything this exciting city has to offer while still living in a suburban area.

The University and The Department

Founded in 1856, Seton Hall is a private coeducational Catholic institution—the nation's oldest diocesan institution of higher education in the United States. With a total enrollment of about 10,000, including approximately 4,500 graduate students, the University comprises nine colleges and schools. Seton Hall is accredited by the Middle States Association of Colleges and Schools. The University has offered the M.P.A. degree since 1980, six years before the establishment of the Center for Public Service and thirteen years before the Department of Public Administration came into existence. The Center for Public Service was established in 1986 to house the M.P.A. program, conduct applied public policy research, and initiate training programs for the public and nonprofit sectors. In 1993, the Department of Public Administration was formed, and, five years later, the Center for Public Service and Department of Public Administration began offering the M.H.A. degree. To show the added emphasis on health care, the Department later changed its name to the Department of Public and Healthcare Administration.

The Center for Public Service houses a chapter of Pi Alpha Alpha, the National Honor Society of Public Administration, and student chapters of the American College of Healthcare Executives (ACHE) and the American Society for Public Administration (ASPA).

Applying

Applicants must submit a completed application, the $50 application fee, official transcripts from all colleges and universities attended, a current resume, three letters of recommendation, and scores from the GRE, GMAT, or LSAT. Professionals with five or more years of work experience do not need to provide standardized test scores. Applications are accepted throughout the year, and admissions decisions are made on a rolling basis.

The DPHA, at its discretion, may accept up to 6 graduate degree credits from another accredited university. The credits must be in courses consistent with both the content and standards of the M.P.A. or M.H.A. degrees. Students wishing to transfer credits should speak directly to the Department chair.

Correspondence and Information

Dr. Naomi Wish, Chair
Department of Public and Healthcare Administration
Jubilee Hall, 5th Floor
Seton Hall University
400 South Orange Avenue
South Orange, New Jersey 07079
Phone: 973-761-9510
Fax: 973-275-2463
E-mail: artsci@shu.edu
    gdpha@shu.edu
Web site: http://www.shu.edu/academics/artsci/graduate-public-health-admin-programs.cfm

Seton Hall University

THE FACULTY AND THEIR RESEARCH

Full-time Faculty

Paul Cavanagh, Assistant Professor; M.S.W., Ph.D., Columbia. Dr. Cavanagh is a professional social worker with extensive experience working with children and adults with a developmental disability. He has worked as an advocacy caseworker and has been the director of a Medicaid Day Treatment program. In addition, Dr. Cavanagh was the Executive Director of an AmeriCorps affiliate program for five years. His dissertation examined the labor choices of mother's with a child with a severe developmental disability. His current research is examining the availability and use of child care for children with severe developmental disabilities.

Philip S. DiSalvio, Associate Professor and Academic Director, Online M.H.A. Program; Ed.D., Harvard. Management, finance, strategic planning, ethics. Former Robert Wood Johnson Faculty Fellow in Healthcare Finance. Consulting and advising extensively in the health-care industry in management development, leadership, and strategic planning, Dr. DiSalvio has served as speaker, seminar leader, and facilitator for numerous health-care organizations and is a Faculty Associate for the American College of Health Care Executives. Author of *Managing Computers in Health Care* and *Managing Computers in Healthcare: A Self-Directed Series for Healthcare Executives.*

Jonathan Engel, Associate Professor; M.B.A., Ph.D., Yale. Research methods, health systems and policy, historical evolution of U.S. health and social welfare policy, managerial decision making. Dr. Engel is the author of *Doctors and Reformers: Discussion and Debate on Health Policy, 1925–1950* and *Poor People's Medicine: Medicaid and U.S. Charity Care Since 1960.* He is currently completing the manuscript of his third book, *The Epidemic: A History of Aids,* which examines the political and scientific responses to the AIDS crisis since its inception in 1980.

Matthew Hale, Assistant Professor; Ph.D., USC. Politics and the Internet, local involvement in political processes. Since 1998, Dr. Hale has worked with the Norman Lear Center Local News Archive on projects analyzing local television news coverage of election campaigns. Dr. Hale has written extensively on the adoption and use of Web pages by municipalities and neighborhood groups and is currently exploring how the media cover nonprofit organizations.

Anne M. Hewitt, Assistant Professor and Director, Seton Center for Community Health; Ph.D., Temple. Community health development and assessment, health literacy, worksite health. Former American Lung Association Principal Investigator. Author of articles in *American Journal of Health Studies* and *Journal of Occupational Medicine.* Dr. Hewitt also provides program evaluation assistance to various state and local organizations as well as nonprofit agencies and health-care institutions.

Amadu Jacky Kaba, Assistant Professor; Ph.D., Seton Hall. Higher education leadership, management and policy. Author of articles in *Education Policy Analysis Archives, Journal of African American Studies,* and *Journal of Black Studies.*

Naomi Bailin Wish, Professor, Department Chair, and Director, Center for Public Service; Ph.D., Rutgers. Policy analysis, program evaluation, quantitative methods. Author of articles in *Public Administration Review, International Journal of Public Administration, American Journal of Economics and Sociology,* and the *Municipal Yearbook.*

Part-time Faculty

Sandra Bograd, Adjunct Instructor in Healthcare Law.
Mary Jo Buchanan, Adjunct Instructor in Nonprofit Finance.
Barkley Calkins, Adjunct Instructor in Nonprofit Management and Project Coordinator for NSRI.
Renee Carniol, Adjunct Instructor in Healthcare Management.
Vincent Farinella, Adjunct Instructor in Healthcare Management.
Abe Kasbo, Adjunct Instructor in Healthcare Management and Marketing.
Emily Marcelli, Adjunct Instructor in Healthcare Management.
Alan Negreann, Adjunct Instructor in Public Sector Financial Management.
Mareta Wester, Adjunct Instructor in Arts Administration.
Audrey Winkler, Adjunct Instructor in Nonprofit Management.

TRINITY UNIVERSITY

Department of Health Care Administration

Programs of Study

Trinity University offers two graduate programs leading to an M.S. in health-care administration. The faculty has designed the curriculum to provide the theoretical knowledge and practical skills necessary for leadership in health-care organizations and institutions, focusing on the interpersonal and organizational skills that facilitate critical thinking in the analysis and resolution of problems that are particular to the complex and competitive field of health-care management.

The On-Campus Program prepares students, through varied and comprehensive courses in health-care administration and the administrative residency, to make sound, informed professional decisions at the highest levels of the field. The full-time program consists of 54 semester hours: 48 hours of on-campus courses (usually requiring sixteen months—four semesters—for completion) and a stipend-supported residency carrying 6 hours of academic credit (usually completed in an additional twelve months). The administrative residency offers students the opportunity to balance administrative experience and education by applying theories and techniques learned through course work in a carefully selected health-care system setting. Students are guided in their residencies by an on-site experienced health-care administrator and by a faculty member from the Department of Health Care Administration.

The Department also offers an Executive Program, which recognizes both the desire for further education among individuals currently working in health-care management positions and the importance and value of practical experience to professional education. This program is designed for individuals currently holding responsible positions in a health-care setting who are searching for a part-time distance learning experience. The core curriculum includes fourteen courses, totaling 42 semester hours of graduate credit. Each semester begins with a three- to four-day intensive on-campus session, followed by written assignments and regular telephone conferences. The Executive Program usually takes two years to complete.

Research Facilities

The Elizabeth Coates Maddux Library affords ample resources and space for graduate study. The growing holdings number more than 1 million volumes of books and bound periodicals, in addition to microfilm collections, government documents, and audiovisual materials, and include a comprehensive collection in health-care administration. Graduate students also have access to specialized research collections in San Antonio and, through the interlibrary loan program, to facilities at such nearby institutions as the University of Texas at Austin and the University of Texas Health Science Center at San Antonio.

Trinity's Computer Center provides excellent support for graduate course work and research. The center houses network servers and student labs.

Financial Aid

Trinity University's financial aid and business offices facilitate student applications for loans and deferred-payment plans. The Department offers graduate assistantships to students enrolled in the On-Campus Program through University endowment funds. Most financial aid determinations are made on the basis of scholarship, financial need, and available funds. Executive Program students are encouraged to inquire about educational reimbursement that may be available through their current employer.

Cost of Study

The 2007–08 tuition is $1036 per semester hour, or $12,432 per semester, for full-time students. The technology fee for graduate students is $112.50 per semester.

Living and Housing Costs

Most graduate students live within a short driving distance of the campus. While the responsibility for securing housing rests with the student, the University Housing Office offers assistance whenever possible. Living expenses average $10,000 per year for a single student.

Student Group

The On-Campus Program can admit approximately 30 students, while the Executive Program can admit 20 students. The 2006–07 mean age for on-campus students was 24; 50 percent were women. Students enter this program with a variety of undergraduate degrees and health-care experience. The Executive Program attracts older students—the mean age was 37—from a wide range of geographical locations and health-care management positions. The Department's active Alumni Association provides a support base and network for program graduates.

Student Outcomes

Trinity graduates have been highly successful at securing jobs at appropriate levels for their backgrounds. Many of Trinity's health-care administration program graduates begin their careers in operational management positions. Examples of job placements for recent graduates include hospitals, hospital systems, long-term-care organizations, managed-care organizations, medical group practice management, insurance organizations, and consulting firms.

Location

The San Antonio community is Texas's most historic metropolitan area and the nation's eighth-largest city. Its warm semitropical climate and historic charm have attracted many growth industries, including biomedical research. The Alamo, which is surrounded by downtown skyscrapers, stands near the popular San Antonio River Walk. In addition, the Gulf Coast beach, Texas Hill Country, and the colorful country of Mexico are only a short drive from Trinity's campus.

The University and The Department

Trinity is a private, highly selective institution that emphasizes undergraduate liberal arts and select M.S. programs in professional fields. The University was founded in 1869, but the Skyline Campus is 53 years old.

The graduate program in health-care administration admitted its first class in 1965. There are more than 1,700 alumni of the program. The Department has been accredited by the Commission on Accreditation of Healthcare Management Education (CAHME), formerly known as the Accrediting Commission on Education for Health Services Administration (ACEHSA), since 1969.

Applying

All applicants must have a bachelor's degree from an accredited college or university. The degree may be in any undergraduate major. Applicants are required to take either the GRE General Test or the GMAT. A graduate degree can obviate the need to submit scores from either test. Applicants are evaluated on the basis of transcripts, standardized test scores, letters of recommendation, a resume, a statement of purpose, and a required personal interview. Prerequisite courses for the On-Campus Program include 3 hours of undergraduate credit in each of the fields of accounting, economics, and statistics. For the Executive Program, the applicant must have a basic knowledge of these areas and a competency in computer spreadsheet applications. Application for the fall should be made by June 1. Earlier applications for admission and Departmental financial aid are given priority.

Correspondence and Information

Department of Health Care Administration
Trinity University
One Trinity Place
HCAD #58
San Antonio, Texas 78212-7200
Phone: 210-999-8107
Fax: 210-999-8108
E-mail: hca@trinity.edu
Web site: http://www.trinity.edu/departments/healthcare

Trinity University

THE FACULTY AND THEIR RESEARCH

Amer A. Kaissi, Assistant Professor; Ph.D., Minnesota. Patient safety and quality of care, teamwork in health-care high-risk areas, organizational culture and structure, medical group practices.

William C. McCaughrin, Associate Professor; Ph.D., Michigan. Organization theory and its uses in health services research, quality, access and multiculturalism, community health analysis, health policy.

Jody R. Rogers, Visiting Professor; Ph.D., Minnesota; FACHE. Strategic management and planning, organizational effectiveness, health-care leadership.

Edward J. Schumacher, Associate Professor; Ph.D., Florida State. Health-care labor markets, empirical analysis of unions, labor market for workers with disabilities, hospital competition and technology investments.

Ted R. Sparling, Associate Professor; Dr.P.H., Texas. Management theory, strategic planning, human resource management, health-care ethics, managed care, rural health.

Mary E. Stefl, Professor and Department Chair; Ph.D., Cincinnati. Former Chair, Accrediting Commission on Education for Health Services Administration. Former Chair, Board of Directors of the Association of University Programs in Health Administration. Career paths in health-care executives, community needs analysis and planning, civic engagement in health administration curriculum.

UNIVERSITY OF FLORIDA

Department of Health Services Research, Management and Policy

Programs of Study

The Department of Health Services Research, Management and Policy offers the Master of Health Administration (M.H.A.). The program provides a high-quality educational experience that prepares well-qualified and motivated individuals to become managers and leaders of health-related organizations. The program features a comprehensive sequence of courses and seminars that are designed to allow students to develop a powerful set of analytical skills and knowledge about health-care delivery, organization, and financing. The program also allows students to apply their skills and knowledge to integrated problem-solving exercises through a summer internship program.

In the M.H.A. program, students complete four semesters of course work over a two-year period, with an internship in the summer between the first and second years. Students must successfully complete a minimum of 61 credit hours.

In addition to the M.H.A. program, the Department of Health Services Research, Management and Policy also offers a Ph.D. program in health services research. More information on these programs can be received by contacting the Department of Health Services Research, Management and Policy.

Research Facilities

Students have access to superior research facilities and institutions. The Department of Health Services Research, Management and Policy, College of Public Health and Health Professions, is part of the University of Florida (UF) Health Science Center. The Health Science Center is a major academic medical teaching referral center with more than 1,300 faculty members and research funding that exceeds $90 million annually. The Health Science Center also houses the Colleges of Dentistry, Medicine, Nursing, Pharmacy, and Veterinary Medicine, as well as the Communicore, which is a common teaching, laboratory, lecture theater, library, and computer facility used by all academic programs.

Financial Aid

Aside from loans, the most common types of graduate student aid are health administration graduate assistantships and traineeship awards. Minority scholarships, fellowships, and summer programs are also available.

Cost of Study

Because the University of Florida is a public institution, it is able to offer one of the most affordable graduate M.H.A. programs in the country, even for non-Florida residents. In 2007, tuition for graduate students is $284.44 per credit hour for Florida residents and $914.63 per credit hour for nonresidents. Students in the M.H.A. program register for 13 to 15 credit hours per semester.

Living and Housing Costs

A variety of on-campus and off-campus housing options are available. Average living expenses in Gainesville for a two-semester academic year are $4200 for off-campus housing, $2420 for meals, $470 for transportation, and $691 for health insurance and other personal expenses.

Student Group

The University of Florida has a total student enrollment of about 45,000, of whom about 25 percent are graduate students. Typically, the M.H.A. program admits 20–25 students per year. The student population in the Department of Health Services Research, Management and Policy is diverse; students vary widely in age, background, experience, race, ethnicity, and culture. The program actively and successfully recruits high-quality students from all backgrounds.

Location

The University of Florida is located in Gainesville, Florida, midway between the Atlantic Ocean and the Gulf of Mexico. It is within 2 hours of such well-known recreational sites as Cedar Key, St. Augustine, Walt Disney World, and the Kennedy Space Center. The city combines natural beauty with opportunities for a variety of recreational and cultural activities. The local area has lakes, rivers, and springs as well as excellent biking and hiking routes. Museums, theaters, and concert facilities provide diverse cultural events.

The University

The University of Florida is a public institution that was founded in 1853. The campus stretches west from downtown Gainesville toward acres of scenic and rural Alachua County. The University has an ongoing commitment to the excellence of its health-related programs, as demonstrated by the success of the University of Florida Health Science Center. Students benefit from the overall excellence in research and teaching at the University of Florida. In addition, UF has one of the top collegiate athletic programs in the country.

Applying

Students are admitted only in the fall semester of each year. Applications are due by April 1 for admission the following August. Applications are evaluated based on Graduate Record Examination (GRE) or Graduate Management Admission Test (GMAT) scores, undergraduate grades, three letters of recommendation, a current resume, commitment to a career in health administration, and evidence of prior volunteer or work experience. Applications from members of minority groups are especially encouraged. Applicants from non-English-speaking countries should provide evidence of competence in English on the Test of English as a Foreign Language (TOEFL).

Correspondence and Information

Department of Health Services Research, Management and Policy
College of Public Health and Health Professions
University of Florida
P.O. Box 100195
Gainesville, Florida 32610-0195
Phone: 352-273-6073
Fax: 352-273-6075
Web site: http://www.phhp.ufl.edu/has

University of Florida

THE FACULTY AND THEIR RESEARCH

Neale R. Chumbler, Ph.D., Assistant Professor. Access to care, health-service utilization of older adults with stroke and dementia, assessments of outcomes of care.

R. Paul Duncan, Ph.D., Professor and Chair. Access to various forms of health and medical care, risk adjustment methodologies for pricing health-care coverage, dental-care utilization, survey of health insurance coverage, provider services organizations.

Louis C. Gapenski, Ph.D., Professor. Health-care finance, riskiness of alternative reimbursement methods. Dr. Gapenski is the author of widely used health-care finance and corporate finance textbooks.

Allyson Hall, Ph.D., Research Associate Professor. Medicaid, access to care, health insurance coverage, vulnerable populations, the health-care safety net.

Jeffrey S. Harman, Ph.D., Assistant Professor. Mental health economics, with access to mental health services, role of social and economic factors on utilization of mental health services.

Christy Harris Lemak, Ph.D., Associate Professor. Research on organizations that serve vulnerable populations, evaluation of community collaboratives, management and strategy.

Niccie L. McKay, Ph.D., Associate Professor. Nursing home cost analysis and rural hospital closures, efficiency differences among hospitals, financing of rehabilitation hospital industry.

Robert Weech-Maldonado, M.B.A., Ph.D., Associate Professor. Impact of organizational factors on access, quality, and costs of care for vulnerable populations, particularly the elderly and racial/ethnic minorities.

Zhou Yang, Ph.D., Assistant Professor. Health economics, aging and disability, Medicare and Medicaid policy, long-term care, pharmaceutical economics.

Amy K. Yarbrough, Ph.D., Assistant Professor. Executive selection practices and strategic orientation in acute-care hospitals, collaborative behaviors of health-care organizations, technology acceptance among physicians.

UNIVERSITY OF MASSACHUSETTS WORCESTER

University of Massachusetts Medical School
Clinical & Population Health Research

Program of Study	The Clinical & Population Health Research (CPHR) program, the newest program track in the Graduate School of Biomedical Sciences at the University of Massachusetts Medical School (UMMS) in Worcester, addresses the national need to move health research from the laboratory to the bedside and from individual patients and health-care sites to systems of care. The program emphasizes research skills and provides students with the necessary tools to conduct research on health-care access, screening, treatment, quality, and outcomes.
	A coherent core curriculum is based on appropriate statistical, epidemiologic, and research methods as well as an understanding of the contextual issues of health and health care. Students must complete 90 credits in order to earn the Ph.D. degree. Students are expected to complete three different lab/research project rotations during their first year of study. This lab work culminates in the selection of a research placement for writing a qualifying paper and then a dissertation proposal. Students complete their dissertation research with their selected mentor.
	In addition to the core curriculum and lab rotations, the program requires three electives, which are chosen from among a wide array of special topics, and the demonstration of teaching skills in a research seminar or course-lecture format. During the second year, there are required courses on research ethics and scientific writing as well as a dissertation seminar. The program typically takes four years to complete.
	UMMS is accredited by the Liaison Committee on Medical Education and the New England Association of Schools and Colleges.
Research Facilities	The Clinical & Population Health Research program builds on the significant array of clinical departments and special centers and institutes addressing a range of specific health-care needs providing outstanding access to diverse resources, including:
	Commonwealth Medicine and affiliated centers: Center for Health Policy and Research, Center for Health Care Financing, Shriver Center/Center for Developmental Disability Evaluation and Research, Office of Community Programs, AHEC Network.
	Department of Family Medicine and Community Health
	Department of Medicine: Division of Cardiovascular Medicine, Division of Preventive and Behavioral Medicine
	Department of Orthopedics
	Department of Pediatrics
	Department of Psychiatry and affiliated centers: Clubhouse Research, Center for Mental Health Services Research
	Center for Outcomes Research
	Meyers Primary Care Institute
	Myelodysplastic Syndromes (MDS) Center at UMass Memorial Health Care
Financial Aid	Entering full-time students are eligible for graduate assistantships, which carry an annual stipend of $26,500 (2007–08). Financial support is available in the form of a research assistantship once a thesis adviser is identified, which continues the annual stipend. Students may also apply for and receive stipend support from external funding agencies. Domestic students may also borrow up to $8500 in subsidized Stafford loans or $18,500 in unsubsidized loans.
Cost of Study	All full-time students are supported with assistantships and full tuition waivers. Student health, dental, and disability insurance is provided by the School. Students' costs include books, fees (limited), software, and parking permit. Students are also required to have a laptop computer that meets UMMS specifications (cost may be included in student loan).
Living and Housing Costs	There are no on-campus housing facilities for graduate students, but off-campus housing is available. Students can expect to spend $800 to $1100 per month for a two-bedroom apartment or $500 to $800 per month for a one-bedroom unit. Annual parking passes are available for $80. Local public transportation is also available.
Student Group	The students in the program come from varying ethnic and socioeconomic backgrounds. All have clinical research experience in one of the social, psychological, physical, or biological sciences and have completed course work in biostatistics and epidemiology.
Student Outcomes	The program develops researchers with strong core competencies in statistics, epidemiology, and research methodologies applicable to clinical trials and population health studies and has a specific emphasis on public-sector issues and vulnerable populations. Students are prepared to conduct investigator-initiated clinical and health-services research and applied research in clinical and public-sector health services delivery systems.
Location	Located in the heart of the commonwealth, Worcester is the third-largest city in New England and is 40 miles west of Boston. Worcester and the surrounding towns offer a wide range of educational, cultural, and recreational activities. Skiing and hiking areas and numerous ponds and rivers are located in the Worcester region, as are many other educational institutions, including Worcester Polytechnic Institute, Assumption College, Clark University, and Holy Cross College. The beaches of Cape Cod and Rhode Island as well as the ski areas of Vermont, New Hampshire, and Maine are within easy driving distance of the campus.
The Medical School	The University of Massachusetts Medical School is an integral part of the state university system, which consists of four other campuses in Lowell, Dartmouth, Amherst, and Boston. It was founded in 1962 to meet the health-care needs of residents of the commonwealth. Today, it serves 800 students in nursing, medicine, and biomedical sciences. It is consistently ranked in the top 10 percent of the nation's 125 medical schools by *U.S. News & World Report*, and, in 2004, federal and private research grants and contracts rose to more than $167 million—making it one of the fastest-growing research institutions in the United States.
Applying	Applicants are expected to have a master's degree in public health, clinical research, or in one of the social, psychological, physical, or biological sciences, with adequate introductory course work in biostatistics and epidemiology and some clinical research experience. Admission to the program requires the completion of the online application, official transcripts from all colleges previously attended, official GRE scores, three letters of recommendation, and a $25 application fee for Massachusetts residents ($50 for nonresidents). All application materials must be received by January 15, but applicants are encouraged to submit their materials prior to that date.
Correspondence and Information	CPHR Program Admissions–Rm. S1-824 Graduate School of Biomedical Sciences University of Massachusetts Medical School 55 Lake Avenue, North Worcester, Massachusetts 01655 Phone: 508-334-2112 E-mail: cphr@umassmed.edu Web site: http://www.umassmed.edu/cphr

University of Massachusetts Worcester

THE FACULTY AND THEIR RESEARCH

Students should visit the program's Web site for the most up-to-date information on the more than 40 program faculty members and their research interests:
http://www.umassmed.edu/cphr/faculty/index.aspx

UNIVERSITY OF MINNESOTA

Program in Healthcare Management

Program of Study

Students choose the University of Minnesota program because of its strengths in four key areas: its national reputation for excellence in health-care education; its innovative curriculum that blends advanced management theory with current issues in health care and practical experience; the diversity and quality of job and fellowship placements available to its graduates; and its alumni network, the largest of its kind in the country, which actively supports the program's activities. Students in the Minnesota program also benefit greatly from its location in the dynamic health-care community of the Minneapolis–St. Paul area, which provides students with access to organizations pioneering the health-care systems of tomorrow.

The Minnesota Master of Healthcare Administration (M.H.A.) program is a professional management program designed to prepare students for executive and leadership positions in health-care organizations and corporations. The curriculum consists of two academic years (eighteen months) of classroom preparation and a three-month administrative residency between the two years. The first year provides students with an orientation to health care, management theory, and important health-care organizations and corporations. The second phase of the curriculum, the summer residency and clerkship, gives students a chance to apply theory to actual health-care organizations. During the second year of the program, students complete advanced required course work, a management project, and electives in an area of concentration. Students may concentrate in a wide variety of areas including finance, marketing, management information systems, long-term care, and e-commerce.

For the required residency, students are placed in health-care organizations throughout the country. After graduation, students may accept positions or fellowships.

A dual M.H.A./M.B.A. degree and a part-time option for working professionals are available.

Research Facilities

Diehl Hall, one of fourteen libraries on campus, subscribes to more than 3,300 periodicals and has more than 300,000 bound volumes. The University maintains numerous computer facilities that are available for instruction, training, and use by graduate students. In addition, the computer laboratory, specifically for use by graduate students in the Carlson School of Management, contains personal computers linked to the main University computer system.

Financial Aid

The program offers many awards and scholarships that have been established by alumni and friends of the program. These are based upon promise of early achievement and academic performance.

The University of Minnesota Alumni Association has developed an educational trust fund that makes $4000 available for every M.H.A. student to borrow once he or she has successfully completed the first semester of study. Students may also work within the Department of Healthcare Management as research assistants.

Cost of Study

Full-time graduate tuition for residents in 2007–08 is approximately $15,000 annually. Resident tuition applies to students from Minnesota, North Dakota, South Dakota, Wisconsin, and Manitoba. Nonresident tuition is approximately $23,000 annually. Fees and mandatory health insurance cost approximately $1500 per semester.

Living and Housing Costs

Room and board expenses for a single student are about $750 per month. Married students should expect to pay about $1200 per month, plus $150 per month for each child.

Student Group

Twenty-five students from throughout the United States enter the program each fall. Most have some health-care and/or management experience. Ages range from 22 to 35. About half of the students are women. Students have had a wide range of undergraduate majors.

Location

Minneapolis and St. Paul make up an attractive metropolitan area of 2 million people. The University of Minnesota benefits from access to a health-care community that leads the nation in the development of new ideas in health-care organization. The metropolitan area is also known for outstanding cultural and recreational activities, parks, and lakes.

The Program

The University of Minnesota Program in Healthcare Management is one of the nation's first academic programs in health administration. Since its beginning, the Minnesota program has been widely recognized for its leadership in the field, for its academic excellence, and for the quality and success of its graduates. The Alumni Association, the country's largest health administration alumni group, provides financial support to the program and its students and conducts a placement service for students and graduates. The program is housed in the state-of-the-art Carlson School of Management.

Applying

The M.H.A. program accepts students to enter in the fall semester for twenty-one months of full-time study. Admission to the program is selective. Although academic ability is a principal criterion, experience and aptitude are given serious consideration.

Applicants to the M.H.A. program must hold a baccalaureate degree from an accredited institution. Course work in accounting, statistics, and microeconomics is recommended. Applicants must submit scores on the General Test of the GRE or on the GMAT. It is recommended that M.H.A. applications be submitted as early as January, although they will be accepted through March, for entrance the following fall. The program publishes a separate admissions brochure and application form, which applicants are encouraged to request.

Correspondence and Information

Program in Healthcare Management
3-140 Carlson School of Management
University of Minnesota
Minneapolis, Minnesota 55455
Phone: 612-624-8818
　　　877-MHA-UofM (toll-free)
Fax: 612-624-8804
E-mail: mnerney@csom.umn.edu
Web site: http://www.CarlsonSchool.umn.edu/MHA

University of Minnesota

THE FACULTY

Jean Abraham, Assistant Professor; Ph.D. (health-care economics), Carnegie Mellon.
Arif Altaf, Lecturer; M.H.A., Minnesota.
Mary Baich, Instructor; M.H.A. (health-care administration), Minnesota.
James Begun, Professor and Department Chair; Ph.D. (sociology), North Carolina.
Jon B. Christianson, Professor; Ph.D. (economics), Wisconsin.
Robert Connor, Associate Professor; Ph.D. (health-care finance), Pennsylvania (Wharton).
Doug Cropper, Lecturer; M.H.A., Minnesota.
N. Tor Dahl, Lecturer; M.B.A. (health-care economics), Norwegian School of Economics.
Bright Dornblaser, Associate Professor; M.H.A. (problem solving), Minnesota.
Marie Dotseth, Lecturer; M.H.A. (health-care policy), Minnesota.
Mark Enger, Lecturer; M.H.A., Minnesota.
David Feinwachs, Instructor; J.D., Ph.D. (health-care law), Minnesota.
Michael Finch, Senior Lecturer; Ph.D. (sociology), Minnesota.
Walter Flynn, Adjunct Instructor; M.B.A. (human resources), Xavier.
Leslie Grant, Associate Professor; Ph.D. (human development and aging), California, San Francisco.
Gregory W. Hart, Instructor; M.H.A., Minnesota.
Jena Hausmann, Lecturer; M.H.A., Minnesota.
William Henry, Lecturer; M.H.A., Minnesota.
Steve G. Hillestad, Instructor; M.A. (health administration), M.A. (public affairs), Wisconsin.
Steve Housch, Lecturer; M.H.A., Minnesota.
George O. Johnson, Emeritus Professor; Ph.D. (hospital administration), Minnesota.
Robert Kaufman, Lecturer; M.H.A., Minnesota.
Geoffrey L. Kaufmann, Instructor; M.A. (health-care management), Chicago.
Venetia Kudrle, Lecturer; M.H.A., Minnesota.
Stuart Laird, Lecturer; M.H.A., Minnesota.
Patrick Langan, Instructor; M.B.A. (human resources), St. Thomas (Minnesota).
Shari Levy, Lecturer; M.H.A., Minnesota.
Theodor J. Litman, Emeritus Professor; Ph.D. (sociology), Minnesota.
Mara Melum, Lecturer; M.P.A. (strategy), Syracuse.
Richard Norling, Instructor; M.H.A. (health-care administration), Minnesota.
Steve Parente, Assistant Professor; Ph.D. (health-care finance), Johns Hopkins.
Kimberly Pederson, Lecturer; M.B.A. (health-care finance), Minnesota.
David PeKarna, Adjunct Instructor; M.H.A. (health-care administration), Minnesota.
Sandra Potthoff, Associate Professor and Program Director; Ph.D. (operations research), Wisconsin.
John Reiling, Lecturer; M.H.A. (health-care administration), Minnesota; M.A. (teaching), St. Thomas (Minnesota).
James A. Rice, Lecturer; M.H.A. (international health care), Minnesota.
William Riley, Instructor; Ph.D. (health-care finance), Minnesota.
Roger Upson, Adjunct Instructor; Ph.D. (finance), Michigan.
Margaret Van Bree, Adjunct Assistant Professor; M.H.A., Dr.P.H. (health systems management), Tulane.
Vernon E. Weckwerth, Professor and Coordinator, Alternative Studies Program; Ph.D. (biometry), Minnesota.
Mary Ellen Wells, Lecturer; M.H.A., Minnesota.
Stan Williams, Lecturer; Ph.D., Minnesota.
Helen Yates, Instructor; M.A. (public administration), Harvard.

VIRGINIA COMMONWEALTH UNIVERSITY

School of Allied Health Professions
Department of Health Administration

Programs of Study

Virginia Commonwealth University (VCU) is the home of five excellent graduate programs in health services administration. Four master's degree programs are designed to prepare individuals for executive positions in health service organizations: the Master of Health Administration (M.H.A.) degree program; the Professional M.S.H.A. Program–Online leading to the degree of Master of Science in Health Administration; a dual-degree program leading to the M.H.A. and Juris Doctor (J.D.) degrees; and a dual-degree program leading to the M.H.A. and Doctor of Medicine (M.D.) degrees. The fifth graduate degree program offered by the Department of Health Administration is a Ph.D. degree in health services organization and research.

The M.H.A. degree program is a full-time program completed in four semesters of on-campus study followed by a paid, one-year administrative residency. The Professional M.S.H.A. Program–Online is oriented to individuals working full-time, residing anywhere in the United States, who seek graduate management education for continued career development. Utilizing a distance learning model, self-motivated, mature, and experienced professionals interact with faculty members and classmates using state-of-the-art Internet technology throughout a twenty-two-month course of study, which includes six one-week on-campus sessions on the VCU Medical Center campus. Part-time options for the M.S.H.A. program are also available. The dual M.H.A./J.D. degree program, conducted in cooperation with the Schools of Law at the University of Richmond and Washington and Lee University, allows students to complete the dual-degree requirements in 4 to 4½ years. The M.H.A./M.D. degree program is conducted in cooperation with the VCU School of Medicine and allows students to complete both the M.H.A. and M.D. degrees in five years.

The Ph.D. degree program prepares individuals for positions as faculty members, researchers, policy analysts, and top-level staff members in complex health organizations. The Ph.D. course work can be completed in two years of full-time study (on-campus), exclusive of dissertation requirements.

Research Facilities

The David G. Williamson Jr. Institute for Health Studies of the Department of Health Administration provides both a financial and structural framework for the research activities of faculty members and students. The department is well equipped with computer technology and has excellent access to relevant databases on which significant and valuable health services research is conducted.

Financial Aid

Students are eligible for limited scholarships and traineeships offered through the School of Allied Health Professions and the Department of Health Administration. In addition, the department offers some employment assistance and some facilitation for opportunities for students to work with faculty members, area alumni, and many other organizations in part-time and summer employment opportunities. During the third year of the M.H.A. program (the administrative residency), students are paid by their sponsoring organization.

Cost of Study

For the 2006–07 academic year, full-time tuition and fees for the M.H.A. and Ph.D. programs were $8321 for Virginia residents and $17,562 for non-Virginia residents. The Professional M.S.H.A. Program–Online was $11,003 for Virginia residents and $20,244 for non-Virginia residents.

Living and Housing Costs

University-sponsored housing includes dormitories located on campus and a number of apartments for married students. Average expenses for on-campus housing are approximately $2000 per semester. Many options for off-campus housing are available throughout the city and surrounding areas, some accessible to campus via public transportation. Off-campus housing ranges from $500 to more than $1000 per month and is available within easy travel distances of the VCU Medical Center Campus.

Student Group

Approximately 30 students are admitted annually to the M.H.A. (including M.H.A./J.D. and M.H.A./M.D. programs) and 25 to the Professional M.S.H.A. Program–Online. The Ph.D. program admits, on average, 6 students each year. A master's degree is required for admission to the Ph.D. program. While experience in health services is desirable for admission to the graduate programs, it is not a requirement for the M.H.A. or Ph.D. programs. The M.S.H.A. program requires five years of professional experience in a health-related field. International students and students from diverse cultural backgrounds are represented in each of the graduate programs.

Student Outcomes

The demand for professionally prepared health services executives, educators, and researchers remains high. Alumni/ae of the master's-level graduate programs hold leadership positions in hospitals, nursing homes, integrated health systems, managed care organizations, health insurance companies, and management consulting firms. Ph.D. graduates hold positions as university faculty members, health services researchers, and policy analysts.

Location

Richmond, the capital of Virginia, is located along the scenic James River and, with a metropolitan population approaching 1 million, offers a wide variety of cultural and leisure opportunities, including museums, art galleries, stage and music performances, and sports events. Colonial Williamsburg, Jamestown, and Yorktown are nearby, and Richmond is a 2-hour drive from beautiful Atlantic coast beaches, the scenic Blue Ridge Mountains, and Washington, D.C. The blend of tradition, economic development, affordable living, temperate climate, and geographic location provides an attractive environment in which to live and work.

The University

Virginia Commonwealth University is the largest urban institution of higher education in Virginia. Approximately 3,780 students are on the VCU Medical Center Campus, and overall University enrollment is 30,381. VCU's Department of Health Administration ranked fifth in the 2004 *U.S. News & World Report*'s Health Disciplines: Health Services Administration (Master's). The M.H.A. program (founded in 1949) was one of the first programs of its kind in the United States. The Department of Health Administration has produced almost 2,100 graduates who have been leaders in the advancement of the profession of health administration and management. The M.S.H.A. program, founded in 1988, was one of the first distance learning programs to use the Internet for course delivery.

Applying

Admission to the graduate programs is competitive and is granted on a rolling basis; therefore, applicants are encouraged to apply early. All applications for the M.H.A. program must be received by March 1 and applications for the M.S.H.A. and doctoral programs are due April 1 for enrollment consideration for the class matriculating the next fall semester. Students applying for admission to a dual-degree program must apply to and be accepted by both the Department of Health Administration and the department or school sponsoring the second degree.

Correspondence and Information

Director, Graduate Program in Health
   Administration (M.H.A.)
Department of Health Administration
Virginia Commonwealth University
P.O. Box 980203
Richmond, Virginia 23298-0203
Phone: 804-828-0719
Fax: 804-828-1894
E-mail: shavasy@vcu.edu
Web site: http://www.had.vcu.edu

Director, Professional M.S.H.A. Program–
   Online
Department of Health Administration
Virginia Commonwealth University
P.O. Box 980203
Richmond, Virginia 23298-0203
Phone: 804-828-7799
Fax: 804-828-1894
E-mail: cwwells@vcu.edu
Web site: http://www.had.vcu.edu

Director, Ph.D. Program
Department of Health Administration
Virginia Commonwealth University
P.O. Box 980203
Richmond, Virginia 23298-0203
Phone: 804-828-5220
Fax: 804-828-1894
E-mail: bdeshazo@vcu.edu
Web site: http://www.had.vcu.edu

Virginia Commonwealth University

THE FACULTY AND THEIR RESEARCH

Thomas C. Barker, Professor and Dean Emeritus, School of Allied Health Professions; Ph.D. (hospital and health administration), Iowa, 1963. Health policy, long-term care, ethics in health care and health manpower education, distribution and utilization.

Gloria J. Bazzoli, Professor; Ph.D., Cornell, 1981. Health economics, health plan organization and financing, reimbursement systems, safety net organizations.

Cathy J. Bradley, Professor; Ph.D. (health policy and administration), North Carolina, 1994. Health economists, health outcomes with regard to cancer and its treatment; joint appointment with the Massey Cancer Center, VCU Medical Center.

Dolores G. Clement, Professor and Director of the Professional M.S.H.A. Program–Online; Dr.P.H. (health policy and administration), Berkeley, 1988. Health-care policy, the management of information for complex health-care organizations, and international health care; examination of patterns of diffusion, growth, and survival among alternative health-care organizations; satisfaction and access to care in Medicare-risk contract HMOs; and the use of alternative payment strategies by Medicare.

Jan P. Clement, Professor; Ph.D. (health policy and administration), North Carolina, 1986. Financial strategy for health-care firms, the financial behavior of managers of not-for-profit firms, and financial evaluation techniques; empirical research on cost-shifting, uncompensated care, and corporate strategy.

Kelly J. Devers, Associate Professor; Ph.D. (sociology), Northwestern, 1994. Health-care organization and policy; provider organization, competition, and impacts; qualitative and mixed research methods.

Mark L. Diana, Instructor; Ph.D. (health services organization and research), Virginia Commonwealth, 2006. Information systems and performance.

Shirley Rogers Gibson, Adjunct Instructor; M.S.H.A., Virginia Commonwealth, 1990; RN. Professional development, leadership, nursing administration.

Robert E. Hurley, Associate Professor; Ph.D. (health policy and administration), North Carolina, 1988. Alternative delivery and financing systems, Medicaid reform, the application of organization theory to health services organizations.

Roice D. Luke, Professor; Ph.D. (medical-care organization, health economics), Michigan, 1976. Strategic management and health-care policy; the structures of local markets and the strategic behaviors of local hospital systems.

Michael J. McCue, Professor and Director of Ph.D. Program; D.B.A. (finance), Kentucky, 1985. Health-care finance and performance of multihospital systems; the financial and operating performance of system-affiliated psychiatric and rehabilitative hospitals.

Stephen S. Mick, Arthur Graham Glasgow Professor and Chair of the Department of Health Administration; Ph.D. (sociology), Yale, 1973. Medical care organization, health-care workforce, rural health care, comparative national systems.

Yasar A. Ozcan, Professor; Ph.D. (health administrative sciences), Virginia Commonwealth, 1988. Mathematical modeling applications in health care, health-care information systems, general statistical applications; health systems productivity, technical efficiency, financial efficiency, and effectiveness for health-care providers.

Ramesh K. Shukla, Professor and Director, David G. Williamson Jr. Institute for Health Studies; Ph.D. (systems engineering), Wisconsin–Madison, 1977. Workforce utilization and productivity, decision support systems, and hospital information systems; evaluating various strategies for improving productivity without reducing quality of care or employee satisfaction; assessing and separating the effects of people, structures, and systems on nursing performance and productivity.

Karen N. Swisher, Professor; J.D., Richmond, 1981. Medical law, medical sociology, business policy, and bioethics.

Kenneth R. White, Charles P. Cardwell Jr. Professor (also with VCU School of Nursing) and Director, Graduate Program in Health Administration (M.H.A.); Ph.D. (health services organization and research), Virginia Commonwealth, 1996. Organizational theory and design, behavior of Catholic health-care organizations, the strategic direction of health administration.

Larry J. Williams, University Professor; Ph.D. (organizational behavior), Indiana. Organizational psychology and behavior, human resources management.

OTHER UNIVERSITY FACULTY MEMBERS WITH JOINT APPOINTMENTS

Tilahun Adera, Professor, Ph.D.
Robert Cohen, Professor, Ph.D.
Anthony J. DeLellis, Associate Professor, Ed.D.
Donald C. H. Gehring, Assistant Professor, J.D.
Jack O. Lanier, Professor, Dr.P.H.
Paul E. Mazmanian, Professor, Ph.D.
Michael A. Pyles, Assistant Professor, Ph.D.
Sheldon M. Retchin, Professor, M.D.
Karen M. Sanders, Professor, M.D.
Thomas J. Smith, Professor, M.D.
Wally R. Smith, Associate Professor, M.D.
David S. Wilkinson, Professor, M.D., Ph.D.

VIRGINIA COMMONWEALTH UNIVERSITY

Department of Health Administration
Ph.D. in Health Services Organization and Research

Program of Study

Virginia Commonwealth University (VCU) offers a Ph.D. in Health Services Organization and Research, a challenging 57-credit program that prepares individuals for positions as faculty members, researchers, policy analysts, and top-level staffers in complex health organizations. Students learn to apply research methods and scientific knowledge drawn from the behavioral and managerial sciences to the study of health organizations, services, and systems.

Courses are distributed across four areas—foundations of health services organization and research (9 credit hours), health services organization theory (12 credit hours), health services research methods (18 credit hours), and an area of specialization (9 credit hours). Students take two written comprehensive examinations, which cover health services organization theory and health services research methods. Areas of specialization are drawn from elective courses and from independent study with faculty members in their areas of expertise, such as long-term care, mental health services, managed care, quality management, and international health. The course work is sequenced so that it can be completed in two years of full-time on-site study (exclusive of dissertation credits). In addition, 9 credit hours of dissertation credit are required. Students orally defend a written dissertation proposal before their dissertation committee. Subsequently, they write and orally defend the completed dissertation.

Research Facilities

The VCU Health Systems (MCV Campus), one of the largest teaching hospitals in the nation, and other clinical facilities of the VCU Medical Center are readily accessible to the Department's students and faculty members. In addition, the Department has clinical affiliations and close working relationships with a large number of health-care organizations and agencies in Virginia and throughout the United States. The organizations and agencies are used extensively as clinical facilities in the Department's educational programs.

VCU libraries provide a combined capacity of more than 1.7 million volumes and 10,200 periodical titles and an online bibliographic search service accessing hundreds of databases. In addition, the Virginia State and Richmond Public Libraries are within walking distance of both VCU campuses. Academic Computing provides a variety of microcomputer, minicomputer, and mainframe computing services to support the research and instructional endeavors of the faculty and students, including consultation, instruction, and computer acquisition.

Financial Aid

Students may apply for need-based assistance with the University's Financial Aid Office. Current information on financial aid programs, policies, and procedures is available at http://www.vcu.edu/enroll/finaid.

Cost of Study

For full-time study (9–15 credits) in 2007–08, Virginia residents pay tuition and fees of $4452 per semester; nonresidents, $8876 per semester. For part-time study, Virginia residents pay tuition and fees of $465 per hour; nonresidents, $954 per hour. Some programs require additional fees. On the Medical College of Virginia (MCV) campus, tuition, fees, and other expenses vary in the medicine, pharmacy, nurse anesthesia, dentistry, and School of Allied Health programs.

Living and Housing Costs

Graduate student housing is available on both the MCV campus and the Monroe Park campus of Virginia Commonwealth University. Many graduate students live in off-campus housing, which is reasonably priced and readily available in a variety of styles and settings in nearby residential areas or within easy commuting distance. On- and off-campus housing information is available on the Web at http://www.housing.vcu.edu/.

Student Group

VCU enrolls 30,452 students, 7,611 of whom are graduate students. More than 200 clubs and organizations reflect the diverse social, recreational, educational, political, and religious interests of the student body.

Location

Richmond is Virginia's capital and a major East Coast financial and manufacturing center that offers students a wide range of cultural, educational, and recreational activities. Richmond is located in central Virginia at the intersection of Interstates 95 and 64, 2 hours south of Washington, D.C., and nestled between the Blue Ridge Mountains and the Atlantic coast. The Richmond region is easily accessible by plane, car, and train. With nearly 1 million residents, the historic city of Richmond combines big-city offerings with small-town hospitality. Applicants are encouraged to explore http://www.visit.richmond.com/ for more information on the city.

The University

VCU is a state-supported, coeducational university with a graduate school, a major teaching hospital, and twelve academic and professional units that offer fifty-two undergraduate, twenty-two postbaccalaureate certificate, sixty-five master's, six post-master's certificate, and twenty-nine Ph.D. programs. VCU also offers M.D., D.D.S., D.P.T., and Pharm.D. programs as well as cooperative degree programs with other major Virginia colleges and universities. VCU has one of the largest evening colleges in the United States. The Monroe Park campus is located in Richmond's historic Fan District. The health sciences campus and hospital (MVC campus) are located 2 miles east in the downtown business district. A University bus service provides free intercampus transportation for faculty members and students.

With more than $211 million in annual research funding, Virginia Commonwealth University is classified as one of the nation's top research universities by the Carnegie Foundation for the Advancement of Teaching. More than 29,000 undergraduate, certificate, graduate, post-master's, professional, and doctoral students are enrolled in 162 academic programs, forty of which are unique in the commonwealth of Virginia. The faculty members represent the finest American and international graduate institutions and enhance the University's position among the important institutions of higher learning in the United States and the world via their work in the classroom, laboratory, studio, and clinic and in their scholarly publications.

Applying

Admission procedures and program requirements are detailed in the *Graduate Bulletin*. Application deadlines and materials, including the application and the *Graduate Bulletin*, are available online at the Graduate School Web site at http://www.graduate.vcu.edu. Virginia Commonwealth University is an equal opportunity/affirmative action institution providing access to education and employment without regard to age, race, color, national origin, gender, religion, sexual orientation, veteran's status, political affiliation, or disability.

Correspondence and Information

Beverly DeShazo, Coordinator
Ph.D. in Health Services Organization and Research Program
Department of Health Administration
School of Allied Health Professions
Virginia Commonwealth University
1008 East Clay Street
Richmond, Virginia 23298
Phone: 804-828-5220
E-mail: bdeshazo@vcu.edu
Web site: http://www.had.vcu.edu/programs/phd

Virginia Commonwealth University

THE FACULTY AND THEIR RESEARCH

Gloria J. Bazzoli, Bon Secours Professor of Health Administration; Ph.D., Cornell. U.S. hospital operations and the functioning of hospital markets.
The influence of health policy and market factors on the hospital safety net. *Health Services Res.* 41:1159–80, 2006. With Lindrooth, Kang, and Hasnain-Wynia.

Cathy J. Bradley, Professor; Ph.D., North Carolina. Labor market outcomes associated with chronic disease, health insurance policy, health-care disparities and inequalities in health, methodology development for cost-effectiveness analysis.
Medicaid, Medicare, and the Michigan Tumor Registry: A linkage strategy. *Med. Decis. Making*, July 19, 2007. With Given, Luo, Roberts, Copeland, and Virnig.

Dolores G. Clement, Professor; Dr.P.H., Berkeley. Medicare managed care, understanding charity care, evaluation of distance-learning programs.
Are consumers reshaping hospitals? Complementary and alternative medicine in U.S. hospitals, 1999–2003. *Health Care Manage. Rev.* 31(2):1–10, 2006. With J. Clement, Chen, Burke, and Zazzali.

Jan P. Clement, Professor; Ph.D., North Carolina, 1986. Financial performance of hospital firms, strategic alliances, subsidiaries of larger firms.
Does the patient's payer matter in hospital patient safety? A study of urban hospitals. *Med. Care* 45(2), 2007. With Lindrooth, Chukmaitov, and Chen.

Kelly J. Devers, Associate Professor; Ph.D., Northwestern. Hospitals' and medical groups' response to changing market and policy forces and their impact on cost and quality and patient safety.
Qualitative data analysis for health services research: Developing taxonomy, themes, and theory. *Health Serv. Res.* January 24, 2007. With Bradley and Curry.

Shirley Gibson, Director of Professional Development; M.S.H.A., Virginia Commonwealth.

Robert E. Hurley, Professor; Ph.D., North Carolina. Public-sector initiatives and reform strategies.
Geography and destiny: Local market perspectives on regional Medicare advantage plans. *Health Affairs* 24(4):1014–21, 2005. With Strunk and Grossman.

Roice D. Luke, Professor; Ph.D., Michigan. Local health-care systems, networks, and markets.
Taxonomy of health networks and systems: A reassessment. *Health Serv. Res.* 41(3,1):618–28, 2006.

Michael J. McCue, Professor; D.B.A., Kentucky. Health-care corporate finance, financial evaluation of health-care providers and health plans.
A market, operation, and mission assessment of large rural for-profit hospitals with positive cash flow. *J. Rural Health* 23(1):10–6, 2007.

Stephen S. Mick, Arthur Graham Glasgow Professor and Chair; Ph.D., Yale. The health-care workforce (particularly international medical graduates, or IMGs), rural health care, and the relation between health-care resources, use of services, and health status.
The contribution of organization theory to nursing health services research. *Nurs. Outlook* 53(6):317–23, 2005. With Mark.

Yasar A. Ozcan, Professor; Ph.D., Virginia Commonwealth. Creating benchmarks for physicians and other health-care providers using data envelopment analysis (DEA).
Longitudinal analysis of efficiency in multiple output dialysis markets. *Health Care Manag. Sci.* 7(4):253–61, 2004. With Ozgen.

Ramesh K. Shukla, Professor; Ph.D., Wisconsin–Madison. Assessing and separating the effects of people, structures, and systems on manpower performance and productivity in nursing services.

Karen N. Swisher, Professor; J.D., Richmond. Medical malpractice, bioethics, managed care, employment law, and risk management.

Kenneth R. White, Charles P. Cardwell, Jr., Professor; Ph.D., Virginia Commonwealth; FACHE. Nonprofit health-care organizations, Catholic hospital ownership, and organizational identity; the strategic direction of the health professions, particularly nursing and health administration; hospital response to provision of end-of-life care; hospital design and hospital history.
Health-care professionals. In *Introduction to Health Services*, 6th ed., eds. Williams and Torrens. Albany, NY: Delmar Press, 2007. With Mick.

XAVIER UNIVERSITY

College of Social Sciences
Graduate Program in Health Services Administration

Program of Study

The Graduate Program in Health Services Administration (GPHSA) awards a Master of Health Services Administration (M.H.S.A.) degree. Established in 1958, the Graduate Program has a strong tradition of success and is accredited by the Commission on Accreditation of Healthcare Management Education (CAHME).

The program's academic work and administrative residency prepare qualified individuals with the specific knowledge and experience required to achieve high-level management positions and success in today's rapidly changing health-care field. Critical to this success is the understanding of patient, community, governmental, clinical, and ethical influences on health-care management decision making. The program of study develops a strong foundation of business management skills, then further enhances the student's ability to succeed in the health-care field through course work in areas such as applied epidemiology, population-based planning, clinical outcomes management, ethical decision making, health-policy analysis, physician relations, managed care, integrated health delivery systems, and provider payment strategies.

Students may pursue an M.H.S.A./M.B.A. dual degree by completing one to two additional semesters of M.B.A. graduate course work. The Graduate Program also offers a concentration in long-term care administration. After completing an administrative residency under the preceptorship of a licensed nursing home administrator, the student may sit for the State of Ohio licensure exam.

The traditional full-time program involves sixteen months of academic study on campus, followed by an eight- to twelve-month full-time administrative residency in a health-care facility under the supervision of a preceptor. The part-time program for health-care professionals consists of nine semesters of academic study along with directed field experiences completed at their places of employment.

Research Facilities

Affiliations with the Greater Cincinnati Health Council, the Southern Ohio Health Services Network, and the Public Health Department provide opportunities for faculty members and students to work cooperatively with a variety of health professionals in addressing vital operational and policy issues. There are more than 130 health-care organizations in greater Cincinnati, ranging from large integrated delivery systems and medical centers to rural health networks, managed-care institutions, group practices, consulting firms, long-term-care facilities, and insurance companies. The program has collaborative relationships with many of these organizations, and these provide additional opportunities for the Graduate Program to conduct applied health-care research.

The McDonald Memorial Library collection at Xavier University numbers more than 350,000 books and periodicals and 600,000 pieces of microfilm and microfiche. The library receives more than 1,500 subscriptions to periodicals, including a comprehensive listing for the GPHSA. Electronic resources include computerized indexes and online research services. Xavier University provides state-of-the-art computer-related services and Internet access.

Financial Aid

Students are eligible to apply for graduate assistantships, university and program scholarships, professional association and minority scholarships and grants, deferred tuition payment plans, and loan funds. Students typically receive stipends from their preceptor organizations during the administrative residency. Administrative stipends in recent years averaged more than $3000 per month.

The Graduate Program's relationship with health services organizations throughout the greater Cincinnati area often results in part-time paid research assistantships or internships. These informal arrangements provide students with financial assistance while they gain valuable health-care work experience.

Cost of Study

The 2006–07 tuition fees are $515 per credit hour. The student should also budget approximately $600 per semester for textbooks and other fees. The stipend students receive during the administrative residency typically helps offset the total cost of the academic portion of the degree.

Living and Housing Costs

Graduate students live off-campus throughout the Cincinnati area. Living expenses average $1000 per month. This estimate may vary depending on the personal requirements of the individual student. Information about off-campus housing can be obtained by contacting Commuter Services at 513-745-3824.

Student Group

The Graduate Program's first-year student body consists of approximately 25 full-time students and 8 part-time students. The class is typically split equally between men and women, with an average age of 24 for the full-time students and 29 for the evening students.

The students are highly motivated and share a deep sense of social responsibility. Strong interpersonal, communication, and creative problem-solving skills; work experience; community involvement; and personal commitment are characteristics of the Xavier GPHSA student.

Student Outcomes

Upon graduation, students obtain managerial leadership positions in a variety of health-care organizations, including integrated delivery systems; managed care and insurance companies; medical group practices; long-term care facilities; governmental health, policy, and regulatory agencies; and consulting firms.

More than 75 percent of recent graduates were offered a position in the same organization where they did their residency. Half of the students took positions within a hospital or medical center setting, with the rest going into managed care, group practice, long-term care, and consulting.

Location

Cincinnati has been rated as one of the nation's most livable cities. Xavier University, a 10-minute drive from downtown, is ideally situated with easy access to Cincinnati's many attractions. The city offers unlimited dining, recreation, entertainment, and cultural activities.

The University and The Program

Xavier University, a private Jesuit institution established in 1831, and the Graduate Program in Health Services Administration are nationally recognized for preparing individuals who serve as models of values-based leaders and managers within their organizations, their professions, and their communities.

GPHSA alumni have a national reputation for leadership excellence in health services administration. Individual alumni have been recognized with such prestigious honors as the American College of Healthcare Executives' Young Administrator of the Year award. With more than 1,600 members, the Graduate Program Alumni Association provides strong support to students, including scholarship funding, a mentoring program, and career assistance after graduation.

Applying

A bachelor's degree from an accredited school is required of all applicants. Typically, applicants are considered academically qualified for acceptance into the Graduate Program if their cumulative undergraduate GPA is 3.0 or above and their GMAT or GRE quantitative score is in at least the 20th percentile and their verbal score is in at least the 50th percentile. Two completed recommendation forms, a resume, a $35 application fee, transcripts from all undergraduate institutions attended, and a statement of intent must be included with the application. A formal interview is required before the final selection. Preference is given to students with strong academic backgrounds and health-related work experience.

Correspondence and Information

Graduate Program in Health Services Administration
Xavier University
3800 Victory Parkway
Cincinnati, Ohio 45207-7331
Phone: 513-745-3687
      800-344-4698 Ext. 3687 (toll-free)
Fax: 513-745-4301
E-mail: xumhsa@xavier.edu
Web site: http://www.xu.edu/mhsa

Xavier University

THE FACULTY AND THEIR RESEARCH

Ida Critelli Schick, Professor and Chair/Director; Ph.D. (philosophy), Marquette; M.S. (health planning and administration), Cincinnati. Privacy and confidentiality of information in an electronic environment, success factors of ethics committees in health care, ethical issues in managed-care organizations and ethical foundations of leadership.

Lin Guo, Associate Professor; Ph.D. (industrial engineering), Cincinnati. Early hospital readmission and quality, success factors of ethics committees in health care, avoidable hospital conditions, utilization issues for stroke patients, ergonomic assessment of nurses.

Edmond Hooker, Assistant Professor; M.D., Eastern Virginia Medical School. Health-care quality and clinical emergency medicine.

D. Patrick Redmon, Associate Professor; Ph.D. (economics), Michigan State. Health-care financing for hospitals.

Thomas J. Ruthemeyer, Assistant Professor; M.B.A., Xavier; CPA. Management accounting, corporate finance, financial management of health-care organizations.

Visiting Faculty and Their Courses

Karen E. Kent, Visiting Assistant Professor; M.S. (health systems), Rush. Managerial concepts, strategic management and marketing, integrative seminar.

Adjunct Faculty and Their Courses

Yousuf Ahmad, Vice President, Clinical Informatics, Mercy Health Partners of Western Ohio; Ph.D. (public health), Kentucky; M.B.A., M.H.S.A., Xavier. Health-care services in the United States, information systems for health-care services.

Alan R. Bayowski, Vice President, Corporate Development and Communications, Southwestern Ohio Senior Services, Inc.; M.S. (gerontological studies), Miami (Ohio). Administration of agencies serving the aged.

Michael Connelly, President and CEO, Catholic Health Care Partners; J.D., DePaul; M.A. (health services administration), Wisconsin. Health-care legal aspects.

Terry R. Frech, Director, Network Management, Anthem, Inc.; M.Ed. (health), Youngstown State. Health insurance systems and concepts.

William M. Freedman, Partner, Dinsmore & Shohl LLP; J.D., Harvard. Health-care legal aspects.

George F. Gordon, M.Ed., Xavier; M.B.A., Cincinnati; LPC. Health-care workforce strategies.

Judy Hayes, Executive Director, PriMed; M.B.A., Xavier; M.S.N., Evansville. Medical group practice management.

Michael W. Hawkins, Partner, Dinsmore & Shohl LLP; J.D., Kentucky. Conflict resolution and mediation.

Mark A. Wellinghoff, Executive Director, Carespring, Inc.; M.S. (community health/planning administration), Cincinnati. Administration of institutions serving the aged.

Emeritus Faculty

Albert A. Bocklet, Associate Professor; Ph.D., (adult education), Arizona State. Quality of care and the application of neural network technologies to clinical and managerial decision making.

Jack G. Reamy, Associate Professor; Ph.D. (management and policy sciences), Texas. Physician workforce planning, with a focus on current reforms in Central and Eastern Europe.

Executives-in-Residence

Terry White, Executive-in-Residence; Retired President/Chief Executive Officer, MetroHealth System, Cleveland; former President/Chief Executive Officer, University Hospital, Cincinnati; LFACHE.

L. Thomas Wilburn, Senior Executive-in-Residence; Retired President/Chief Executive Officer, TriHealth; former President/Chief Executive Officer, Bethesda Hospital, Inc.; former President/Chief Executive Officer, Bethesda, Inc.; former Vice President/Chief Operating Officer, Community Hospital, Indianapolis.

Section 30
Nursing

This section contains a directory of institutions offering graduate work in nursing, followed by in-depth entries submitted by institutions that chose to prepare detailed program descriptions. Additional information about programs listed in the directory but not augmented by an in-depth entry may be obtained by writing directly to the dean of a graduate school or chair of a department at the address given in the directory.

For programs offering related work, see also in this book Health Services and Public Health and in Book 2, Family and Consumer Sciences (Gerontology).

CONTENTS

Program Directories

Announcements

Close-Ups

Nursing—General

Abilene Christian University, Graduate School, School of Nursing, Abilene, TX 79699-9100. Offers MSN. *Accreditation:* AACN. *Faculty:* 5 part-time/adjunct (all women). *Students:* 4 full-time (3 women), 7 part-time (6 women); includes 1 minority (Hispanic American) 11 applicants, 64% accepted, 7 enrolled. In 2006, 7 degrees awarded. *Entrance requirements:* For master's, GRE General Test. *Application deadline:* For fall admission, 4/1 priority date for domestic students; for spring admission, 11/1 for domestic students. Applications are processed on a rolling basis. Application fee: $40 ($45 for international students). Electronic applications accepted. *Expenses:* Tuition: Full-time $12,504; part-time $521 per hour. Required fees: $700; $34 per hour. *Financial support:* Application deadline: 4/1. *Unit head:* Dr. Jan Noles, Dean, 325-671-2399. *Application contact:* William Horn, Graduate Admissions Counselor, 325-674-2656, Fax: 325-674-6717, E-mail: gradinfo@acu.edu.

Adelphi University, School of Nursing, Garden City, NY 11530-0701. Offers MS, PhD, Certificate. *Accreditation:* AACN. Part-time and evening/weekend programs available. *Faculty:* 27 full-time (24 women). *Students:* 5 full-time (all women), 171 part-time (161 women); includes 56 minority (33 African Americans, 1 American Indian/Alaska Native, 17 Asian Americans or Pacific Islanders, 5 Hispanic Americans). Average age 44. 94 applicants, 48% accepted, 45 enrolled. In 2006, 31 master's, 5 other advanced degrees awarded. *Degree requirements:* For master's, thesis or alternative. *Entrance requirements:* For master's, BSN, clinical experience, 1 course in basic statistics, minimum GPA of 3.0, 2 letters of recommendation, resumé or curriculum vitae; for doctorate, GRE, licensure as RN in New York, professional writing sample (scholarly writing), 3 letters of recommendation, resumé or curriculum vitae; for Certificate, MSN. Additional exam requirements/recommendations for international students: Required—TOEFL (minimum score 550 paper-based; 213 computer-based). *Application deadline:* For fall admission, 3/15 for domestic students. Application fee: $50. Electronic applications accepted. *Financial support:* In 2006–07, 1 research assistantship with full and partial tuition reimbursement (averaging $1,180 per year), 3 teaching assistantships (averaging $7,800 per year) were awarded; career-related internships or fieldwork, unspecified assistantships, and graduate achievement awards also available. Support available to part-time students. Financial award application deadline: 2/15; financial award applicants required to submit FAFSA. *Faculty research:* Social practices in healthcare, bereavement, family grief, historiography, gerontology. *Unit head:* Dr. Patrick Coonan, Dean, 516-877-4511, E-mail: coonan@adelphi.edu. *Application contact:* Christine Murphy, Director of Admissions, 516-877-3050, Fax: 516-877-3039, E-mail: graduateadmissions@adelphi.edu.

See Close-Up on page 1945.

Albany State University, College of Health Professions, Albany, GA 31705-2717. Offers nursing (MS). *Accreditation:* NLN. Part-time programs available. *Degree requirements:* For master's, thesis, comprehensive exam. *Entrance requirements:* For master's, GRE General Test or MAT, BSN; current Georgia RN license; minimum GPA of 3.0; previous course work in health assessment, nursing research, pathophysiology, and statistics. Electronic applications accepted.

Alcorn State University, School of Graduate Studies, School of Nursing, Natchez, MS 39122-8399. Offers rural nursing (MSN). *Accreditation:* NLN. *Faculty:* 3 full-time (all women), 2 part-time/adjunct (both women). *Students:* 25 full-time (22 women), 17 part-time (15 women); includes 22 minority (all African Americans) In 2006, 18 degrees awarded. *Application deadline:* For fall admission, 7/15 priority date for domestic students; for spring admission, 11/25 for domestic students. Applications are processed on a rolling basis. Application fee: $0 ($10 for international students). *Unit head:* Dr. Mary Hill, Dean, 601-304-4304.

Allen College, Program in Nursing, Waterloo, IA 50703. Offers acute care nurse practitioner (MSN); family nurse practitioner (MSN); health education (MSN); leadership in health care delivery (MSN). *Accreditation:* AACN; NLN. Part-time and evening/weekend programs available. *Faculty:* 2 full-time (both women), 4 part-time/adjunct (all women). *Students:* 19 full-time (17 women), 42 part-time (39 women). Average age 37. 62 applicants, 94% accepted, 46 enrolled. In 2006, 3 degrees awarded. *Degree requirements:* For master's, thesis optional. *Entrance requirements:* For master's, minimum GPA of 3.0. Additional exam requirements/recommendations for international students: Required—TOEFL (minimum score 550 paper-based). *Application deadline:* For fall admission, 7/15 priority date for domestic students; for spring admission, 12/1 priority date for domestic students. Applications are processed on a rolling basis. Application fee: $50. Electronic applications accepted. *Expenses:* Tuition: Full-time $9,824; part-time $562 per credit hour. Required fees: $481. One-time fee: $220 part-time. Tuition and fees vary according to course load. *Financial support:* In 2006–07, 58 students received support, including 1 teaching assistantship (averaging $10,116 per year); institutionally sponsored loans, scholarships/grants, and traineeships also available. Support available to part-time students. Financial award application deadline: 8/15; financial award applicants required to submit FAFSA. *Faculty research:* Pain and aged, congestive heart failure. *Unit head:* Nancy Kramer, Chair, 319-226-2040, Fax: 319-226-2070, E-mail: kramerna@ihs.org.

Alverno College, School of Nursing, Milwaukee, WI 53234-3922. Offers MSN. Part-time and evening/weekend programs available. *Faculty:* 1 (woman) full-time, 6 part-time/adjunct (all women). *Students:* 18 full-time (16 women), 13 part-time (all women); includes 4 minority (1 African American, 1 American Indian/Alaska Native, 1 Asian American or Pacific Islander, 1 Hispanic American). Average age 35. 23 applicants, 65% accepted, 9 enrolled. *Degree requirements:* For master's, 500 clinical hours-capstone. *Entrance requirements:* For master's, BSN, current license. Additional exam requirements/recommendations for international students: Required—TOEFL. *Application deadline:* For fall admission, 8/1 priority date for domestic students; for spring admission, 12/25 priority date for domestic students. Applications are processed on a rolling basis. Application fee: $20. Electronic applications accepted. *Expenses:* Contact institution. Tuition and fees vary according to program. *Financial support:* In 2006–07, 21 students received support. Federal Work-Study available. Support available to part-time students. Financial award application deadline: 4/15. *Faculty research:* Impact of stroke on sexuality, children's asthma management factors affecting baccalaureate student success. *Unit head:* Julie Millenbruch, Program Director, Fax: 414-382-6354, E-mail: julie.millenbruch@alverno.edu. *Application contact:* Carolyn Wise, Graduate Recruiter, 800-933-3401, Fax: 414-382-6354, E-mail: carolyn.wise@alverno.edu.

American International College, School of Health Sciences, Department of Nursing, Springfield, MA 01109-3189. Offers MSN. *Students:* 1 (woman) full-time, 8 part-time (all women). Average age 45. *Entrance requirements:* Additional exam requirements/recommendations for international students: Required—TOEFL. Application fee: $50. *Expenses:* Tuition: Part-time $585 per semester hour. Required fees: $100 per year. Full-time tuition and fees vary according to program. *Unit head:* Dr. Anne Glanovsky, Chair, 413-205-3514, Fax: 413-205-3514, E-mail: anne.glanovsky@aic.edu. *Application contact:* Keshawn Dodds, Associate Director of Graduate Admissions, 413-205-3549, Fax: 413-205-3911, E-mail: keshawn.dodds@aic.edu.

American Sentinel University, Graduate Programs, Englewood, CO 80112. Offers business administration (MBA); business intelligence (MS); computer science (MSCS); health information management (MS); healthcare (MBA); information systems (MSIS); nursing (MSN). Part-time and evening/weekend programs available. Postbaccalaureate distance learning degree programs offered (no on-campus study). *Faculty:* 40. *Students:* 400. Average age 36. In 2006, 47 degrees awarded. *Entrance requirements:* Additional exam requirements/recommendations for international students: Required—TOEFL (minimum score 600 paper-based; 215 computer-based). *Application deadline:* Applications are processed on a rolling basis. Application fee: $50. Electronic applications accepted. *Unit head:* Janette D. Marshall, Registrar, 800-729-2427 Ext. 2211, Fax: 205-326-3822, E-mail: jan.marshall@americansentinel.edu. *Application contact:* Natalie A. Nixon, Director of Admissions, 800-729-2427, Fax: 205-328-2229, E-mail: natalie.nixon@americansentinel.edu.

American University of Beirut, Graduate Programs, School of Nursing, Beirut, Lebanon. Offers MSN. Part-time programs available. *Faculty:* 5 full-time (4 women). *Students:* 4 full-time (3 women), 32 part-time (28 women). Average age 27. 20 applicants, 65% accepted, 9 enrolled. In 2006, 3 degrees awarded. *Entrance requirements:* For master's, GRE, letter of recommendation. Additional exam requirements/recommendations for international students: Required—TOEFL (minimum score 600 paper-based; 250 computer-based; 100 iBT), IELTS (minimum score 8). *Application deadline:* For fall admission, 4/30 for domestic and international students; for spring admission, 11/1 for domestic and international students. Application fee: $50. *Financial support:* In 2006–07, 1 student received support. Career-related internships or fieldwork, institutionally sponsored loans, scholarships/grants, health care benefits, and unspecified assistantships available. Financial award application deadline: 2/2. *Faculty research:* Pain management and palliative care, stress and post-traumatic stress disorder, health benefits and chronic illness, health promotion and community interventions. Total annual research expenditures: $59,200. *Unit head:* Dr. Huda Huijer Abu-Saad, Director of School of Nursing, 961-1374374 Ext. 5952, Fax: 961-1744476, E-mail: hh35@aub.edu.lb. *Application contact:* Dr. Salim Kanaan, Director of Admissions Office, 961-1-374374 Ext. 2592, Fax: 961-1-750775, E-mail: admissions@aub.edu.lb.

Andrews University, School of Graduate Studies, College of Arts and Sciences, Department of Nursing, Berrien Springs, MI 49104. Offers MS. *Accreditation:* NLN. Part-time and evening/weekend programs available. *Degree requirements:* For master's, thesis. *Entrance requirements:* For master's, minimum GPA of 2.5, 1 year of nursing experience, RN license. *Faculty research:* Theory for nursing, salary equitability.

Arizona State University, Division of Graduate Studies, College of Nursing, Tempe, AZ 85287. Offers MS, MS/MHSM. *Accreditation:* AACN. *Degree requirements:* For master's, thesis, oral and written exams. *Entrance requirements:* For master's, GRE.

Arkansas State University, Graduate School, College of Nursing and Health Professions, Department of Nursing, Jonesboro, State University, AR 72467. Offers aging studies (Certificate); nurse anesthesia (MSN); nursing (MSN). *Accreditation:* AANA/CANAEP (one or more programs are accredited); NLN. Part-time programs available. *Faculty:* 8 full-time (7 women), 3 part-time/adjunct (all women). *Students:* 63 full-time (28 women), 110 part-time (73 women); includes 27 minority (22 African Americans, 1 Asian American or Pacific Islander, 4 Hispanic Americans). Average age 33. 89 applicants, 72% accepted, 64 enrolled. In 2006, 55 degrees awarded. *Degree requirements:* For master's, thesis or alternative, comprehensive exam. *Entrance requirements:* For master's, GRE General Test or MAT, appropriate bachelor's degree, current Arkansas nursing license, CPR certification, acceptable immunization status, physical examination, professional liability insurance, official transcript. Additional exam requirements/recommendations for international students: Required—TOEFL (minimum score 213 computer-based). *Application deadline:* Applications are processed on a rolling basis. Application fee: $30 ($40 for international students). Electronic applications accepted. *Expenses:* Contact institution. *Financial support:* Career-related internships or fieldwork, scholarships/grants, and unspecified assistantships available. Financial award application deadline: 7/1; financial award applicants required to submit FAFSA.

Armstrong Atlantic State University, School of Graduate Studies, Program in Nursing, Savannah, GA 31419-1997. Offers MSN. *Accreditation:* AACN. Part-time and evening/weekend programs available. *Faculty:* 4 full-time (all women). *Students:* 14 full-time (13 women), 32 part-time (29 women); includes 13 minority (11 African Americans, 2 Asian Americans or Pacific Islanders), 3 international. Average age 40. In 2006, 17 degrees awarded. *Degree requirements:* For master's, project, thesis optional. *Entrance requirements:* For master's, GRE General Test or MAT, minimum GPA of 2.5, letter of recommendation, Georgia RN license, BS nursing, letter of intent, etc.. Additional exam requirements/recommendations for international students: Required—TOEFL (minimum score 523 paper-based; 193 computer-based). *Application deadline:* For fall admission, 7/1 priority date for domestic and international students; for spring admission, 11/15 priority date for domestic and international students. Applications are processed on a rolling basis. Application fee: $25. Electronic applications accepted. *Expenses:* Tuition, state resident: full-time $2,286; part-time $127 per credit. Tuition, nonresident: full-time $9,144; part-time $508 per credit. One-time fee: $257. *Financial support:* In 2006–07, research assistantships with partial tuition reimbursements (averaging $2,500 per year); Federal Work-Study, scholarships/grants, and unspecified assistantships also available. Support available to part-time students. Financial award applicants required to submit FAFSA. *Faculty research:* Osteoporosis, cancer, tai chi, heart disease. *Unit head:* Dr. Camille Stern, Department Head, 912-921-5311, Fax: 912-920-6579, E-mail: nure@mail.armstrong.edu. *Application contact:* Dr. Anita Nivens, Graduate Coordinator, 912-921-5724, Fax: 912-920-6579, E-mail: nivensan@mail.armstrong.edu.

Athabasca University, Centre for Nursing and Health Studies, Athabasca, AB T9S 3A3, Canada. Offers advanced nursing practice (MN, Advanced Diploma); generalist (MN); health studies-leadership (MHS). Part-time programs available. Postbaccalaureate distance learning degree programs offered. *Faculty:* 6 full-time (all women), 40 part-time/adjunct (37 women). *Students:* Average age 40. 460 applicants, 81% accepted, 335 enrolled. In 2006, 124 degrees awarded. *Degree requirements:* For master's, comprehensive exam (for some programs), registration (for some programs). *Entrance requirements:* For master's, bachelor's degree in health-related field, 2 years professional health service experience (MHS), bachelor's degree in nursing, 2 years nursing experience (MN), minimum GPA of 3.0 in final 30 credits; for Advanced Diploma, RN license, 2 years health care experience. *Application deadline:* For fall admission, 3/1 for domestic and international students. Application fee: $60. Electronic applications accepted. *Expenses:* Contact institution. *Unit head:* Dr. Donna Romyn, Director, 780-675-6794, Fax: 780-675-6468, E-mail: dromyn@athabascau.ca. *Application contact:* Lisa Bodnarchuk, Administrative Assistant, 780-675-6381, Fax: 780-675-6468, E-mail: mhs@athabascau.ca.

Augsburg College, Program in Transcultural Community Health Nursing, Minneapolis, MN 55454-1351. Offers MA. *Accreditation:* AACN. *Faculty:* 2 full-time (both women). *Students:* 6 full-time (all women), 43 part-time (42 women); includes 2 minority (both African Americans), 1 international. Average age 45. 120 applicants, 18% accepted, 20 enrolled. In 2006, 8 degrees awarded. *Degree requirements:* For master's, thesis or alternative. *Application deadline:* For fall admission, 8/1 for domestic students; for winter admission, 12/4 for domestic students; for spring admission, 3/9 for domestic students. Application fee: $35. *Expenses:* Tuition: Full-time $10,584; part-time $1,764 per course. Required fees: $300; $35 per course. Tuition and fees vary according to program. *Financial support:* In 2006–07, 5 students received support. Application deadline: 8/1; *Unit head:* Dr. Cheryl J. Leuning, Director, 612-330-1214, E-mail: leuning@augsburg.edu. *Application contact:* Sharon Wade, Coordinator, 612-330-1209, E-mail: wades@augsburg.edu.

Augustana College, Program in Advanced Nursing Practice in Emerging Health Systems, Sioux Falls, SD 57197. Offers community health nursing (MA). *Accreditation:* AACN. Part-time programs available. Postbaccalaureate distance learning degree programs offered (minimal on-campus study). *Degree requirements:* For master's, portfolio, oral exam, paper. *Entrance requirements:* For master's, current licensure, minimum GPA of 3.0, previous course work in statistics, bachelor's degree in nursing. Additional exam requirements/recommendations for international students: Required—TOEFL. *Faculty research:* HIV infected persons, nursing theory development, nursing workforce development.

Austin Peay State University, College of Graduate Studies, College of Professional Programs and Social Sciences, School of Nursing, Clarksville, TN 37044. Offers MS. Part-time programs available. Postbaccalaureate distance learning degree programs offered. *Faculty:* 1 (woman) full-time. *Students:* 2 full-time (both women), 27 part-time (26 women); includes 9 minority (6 African Americans, 1 Asian American or Pacific Islander, 2 Hispanic Americans). Average age 37. In 2006, 1 degree awarded. *Entrance requirements:* For master's, GRE

General Test, minimum GPA of 3.0, RN license eligibility, 3 letters of recommendation. Additional exam requirements/recommendations for international students: Required—TOEFL (minimum score 600 paper-based). *Application deadline:* For fall admission, 7/31 priority date for domestic students; for spring admission, 12/17 priority date for domestic students. Applications are processed on a rolling basis. Application fee: $25. Electronic applications accepted. *Expenses:* Tuition, state resident: full-time $5,138; part-time $272 per credit hour. Tuition, nonresident: full-time $14,832; part-time $693 per credit hour. Required fees: $1,009. *Financial support:* Career-related internships or fieldwork, Federal Work-Study, institutionally sponsored loans, and scholarships/grants available. Support available to part-time students. *Unit head:* Dr. Francisca Ann Farrar, Director, 931-221-7737, Fax: 931-221-6490, E-mail: farrarf@apsu.edu. *Application contact:* Dr. Doris Davenport, Associate Professor, 931-221-7467, Fax: 931-221-7595, E-mail: davenportd@apsu.edu.

Azusa Pacific University, School of Nursing, Azusa, CA 91702-7000. Offers nursing (MSN); nursing education (PhD). *Accreditation:* AACN. Part-time and evening/weekend programs available. *Faculty:* 12 full-time (11 women). *Students:* 56 full-time (49 women), 100 part-time (96 women); includes 73 minority (12 African Americans, 1 American Indian/Alaska Native, 33 Asian Americans or Pacific Islanders, 27 Hispanic Americans), 5 international. In 2006, 16 degrees awarded. *Degree requirements:* For master's, thesis optional. *Entrance requirements:* For master's, BSN. *Application deadline:* Applications are processed on a rolling basis. Application fee: $45 ($65 for international students). *Expenses:* Tuition: Part-time $475 per credit. *Financial support:* Teaching assistantships, scholarships/grants, traineeships, and unspecified assistantships available. Support available to part-time students. Financial award application deadline: 10/15. *Faculty research:* Family adaptation to illness and crisis, bioethical issues in nursing, self-care activities, quality of life issues, home health. Total annual research expenditures: $177,950. *Unit head:* Dr. Aja Lesh, Interim Dean/Professor, 626-815-5386, E-mail: alesh@apu.edu. *Application contact:* Barb Barthelmess, Graduate Program Secretary, 626-815-5391, Fax: 626-815-5414.

Ball State University, Graduate School, College of Applied Science and Technology, School of Nursing, Muncie, IN 47306-1099. Offers MS. *Accreditation:* AACN. Part-time programs available. *Faculty:* 13. *Students:* 3 full-time (all women), 249 part-time (232 women); includes 13 minority (6 African Americans, 2 American Indian/Alaska Native, 1 Asian American or Pacific Islander, 4 Hispanic Americans), 2 international. Average age 42. 74 applicants, 72% accepted, 43 enrolled. In 2006, 40 degrees awarded. *Entrance requirements:* For master's, bachelor's degree in nursing, minimum GPA of 2.8 in upper-level course work, interview, resumé. Application fee: $25 ($35 for international students). *Financial support:* In 2006–07, 2 teaching assistantships with full tuition reimbursements (averaging $9,586 per year) were awarded; research assistantships, career-related internships or fieldwork also available. Financial award application deadline: 3/1. *Unit head:* Dr. Linda Siktberg, Director, 765-285-5570, Fax: 765-285-2169.

Barnes-Jewish College of Nursing and Allied Health, Division of Nursing, St. Louis, MO 63110-1091. Offers adult nurse practitioner (MSN); education (MSN); gerontology nurse practitioner (MSN); holistics (MSN); management/administration (MSN); neonatal nurse practitioner (MSN); oncology (MSN). *Accreditation:* AACN; AANA/CANAEP. Part-time and evening/weekend programs available. *Degree requirements:* For master's, thesis or alternative, registration. *Entrance requirements:* For master's, minimum GPA of 3.0, 2 references, statistics course. Additional exam requirements/recommendations for international students: Required—TOEFL (minimum score 550 paper-based; 213 computer-based).

Barry University, School of Nursing, Miami Shores, FL 33161-6695. Offers MSN, PhD, Certificate, MSN/MBA. Part-time and evening/weekend programs available. *Faculty:* 28. *Students:* 36 full-time (33 women), 204 part-time (174 women); includes 128 minority (44 African Americans, 7 Asian Americans or Pacific Islanders, 77 Hispanic Americans), 2 international. Average age 41. In 2006, 63 master's, 6 doctorates awarded. *Degree requirements:* For master's, research project or thesis; for doctorate, thesis/dissertation. *Entrance requirements:* For master's, GRE General Test or MAT, BSN, minimum GPA of 3.0, course work in statistics and research, Florida RN license; for doctorate, GRE General Test or MAT, minimum GPA of 3.3, MSN. *Application deadline:* For fall admission, 5/1 priority date for domestic students. Applications are processed on a rolling basis. Application fee: $30. Electronic applications accepted. *Financial support:* In 2006–07, 3 research assistantships (averaging $5,000 per year), 3 teaching assistantships (averaging $5,000 per year) were awarded; scholarships/grants and tuition waivers (full) also available. Financial award application deadline: 5/1; financial award applicants required to submit FAFSA. *Faculty research:* Adult education, nurse practitioner, stress reduction in pregnancy, prevention of cardiac problems, in children, level of school age children. *Unit head:* Dr. Pegge L. Bell, Dean, 305-899-3840, Fax: 305-899-3831, E-mail: pbell@mail.barry.edu. *Application contact:* Dave Fletcher, Director of Graduate Admissions, 305-899-3113, Fax: 305-899-2971, E-mail: dfletcher@mail.barry.edu.

Baylor University, Graduate School, Louise Herrington School of Nursing, Dallas, TX 75246. Offers family nurse practitioner (MSN); neonatal nurse practitioner (MSN); nursing administration and management (MSN). *Accreditation:* AACN. *Students:* 10 full-time (all women), 27 part-time (26 women); includes 6 minority (1 African American, 1 Asian American or Pacific Islander, 4 Hispanic Americans), 1 international. In 2006, 13 degrees awarded. *Entrance requirements:* For master's, GRE General Test. *Application deadline:* For fall admission, 8/1 for domestic students; for spring admission, 12/1 for domestic students. Applications are processed on a rolling basis. Application fee: $25. *Unit head:* Dr. Pauline Johnson, Graduate Program Director, 214-820-3361, Fax: 214-818-8692, E-mail: pauline_johnson@baylor.edu. *Application contact:* Suzanne Keener, Administrative Assistant, 254-710-3588, Fax: 254-710-3870.

Bellarmine University, Donna and Allan Lansing School of Nursing and Health Sciences, Louisville, KY 40205-0671. Offers nursing administration (MSN); nursing education (MSN); physical therapy (DPT). *Accreditation:* AACN; APTA. *Faculty:* 15 full-time (11 women), 8 part-time/adjunct (7 women). *Students:* 112 full-time (87 women), 70 part-time (66 women); includes 12 minority (7 African Americans, 4 Asian Americans or Pacific Islanders, 1 Hispanic American), 1 international. Average age 31. In 2006, 44 degrees awarded. *Degree requirements:* For doctorate, comprehensive exam. *Entrance requirements:* For master's, GRE General Test, minimum undergraduate GPA of 2.75, RN license; for doctorate, minimum prerequisites coursework GPA of 2.75, 2.5 overall; 25 hours of documented service in physical therapy; physical ability to perform tasks of a physical therapist. Additional exam requirements/recommendations for international students: Required—TOEFL (minimum score 550 paper-based; 213 computer-based; 80 iBT). *Application deadline:* For fall admission, 10/15 priority date for domestic students. Applications are processed on a rolling basis. Application fee: $25. Electronic applications accepted. *Expenses:* Contact institution. Tuition and fees vary according to program. *Financial support:* Career-related internships or fieldwork and scholarships/grants available. *Faculty research:* Pain, empathy, leadership styles, control. *Unit head:* Dr. Susan H. Davis, Dean, 800-274-4723 Ext. 8217, E-mail: sdavis@bellarmine.edu. *Application contact:* Julie Armstrong-Binnix, Health Science Recruiter, 800-274-4723 Ext. 8364, E-mail: julieab@bellarmine.edu.

Belmont University, College of Health Sciences, School of Nursing, Nashville, TN 37212-3757. Offers MSN. *Accreditation:* AACN. Part-time programs available. *Faculty:* 1 (woman) full-time, 3 part-time/adjunct (all women). *Students:* 4 full-time (all women), 8 part-time (all women). Average age 30. 16 applicants, 94% accepted, 5 enrolled. In 2006, 3 degrees awarded. *Degree requirements:* For master's, comprehensive exam, registration. *Entrance requirements:* For master's, GRE, BSN, minimum GPA of 3.0. Additional exam requirements/recommendations for international students: Required—TOEFL (minimum score 550 paper-based; 213 computer-based). *Application deadline:* For fall admission, 8/1 for domestic students; for spring admission, 10/15 priority date for domestic students. Applications are processed on a rolling basis. Application fee: $50. Electronic applications accepted. *Expenses:* Contact institution. *Financial support:* In 2006–07, 6 students received support. Scholarships/grants and traineeships available. Financial award application deadline: 3/1; financial award applicants required to submit FAFSA. *Faculty research:* Postpartum postoperative care, adherence/compliance behavior in chronic illness, women's health in primary care. *Unit head:* Dr. Leslie J. Higgins, Director, Graduate Program, 615-460-6027, Fax: 615-460-5644, E-mail: higginsl@mail.belmont.edu. *Application contact:* Cathy Hendon, Admissions Coordinator, 615-460-6107, Fax: 615-460-6125, E-mail: hendonc@mail.belmont.edu.

Bethel College, Division of Graduate Studies, Program in Nursing, Mishawaka, IN 46545-5591. Offers MSN. *Faculty:* 5 part-time/adjunct (all women). *Students:* 1 (woman) full-time, 30 part-time (27 women); includes 4 minority (2 African Americans, 2 Hispanic Americans). 18 applicants, 94% accepted, 15 enrolled. *Entrance requirements:* Additional exam requirements/recommendations for international students: Required—TOEFL (minimum score 540 paper-based; 207 computer-based). Application fee: $25. *Expenses:* Tuition: Full-time $5,940; part-time $330 per credit hour. *Unit head:* Karon Schwartz, Graduate Nursing Program Director, 574-257-3382, E-mail: schwark@bethelcollege.edu. *Application contact:* Karon Schwartz, Graduate Nursing Program Director, 574-257-3382, E-mail: schwark@bethelcollege.edu.

Bethel University, Graduate School, Department of Nursing, St. Paul, MN 55112-6999. Offers Christian health ministry (MA); healthcare leadership (MA); nursing education (MA, Certificate). *Accreditation:* AACN. *Faculty:* 12 full-time (10 women). *Students:* 44 full-time (all women), 10 part-time (8 women); includes 2 minority (1 African American, 1 Hispanic American). Average age 41. In 2006, 7 master's, 2 other advanced degrees awarded. *Degree requirements:* For master's, thesis, internship, comprehensive exam. *Entrance requirements:* For master's, MAT, interview, minimum GPA of 3.0, RN experience, BSN, letters of reference, course work in statistics. Additional exam requirements/recommendations for international students: Required—TOEFL (minimum score 550 paper-based; 213 computer-based). *Application deadline:* For fall admission, 3/20 priority date for domestic students. Application fee: $25. Electronic applications accepted. *Expenses:* Tuition: Part-time $395 per credit. Tuition and fees vary according to program. *Financial support:* Institutionally sponsored loans and scholarships/grants available. *Unit head:* Dr. Mary P. Reuland, Director, 651-638-6189, Fax: 651-635-8604, E-mail: reumar@bethel.edu. *Application contact:* Karen Akslen, Graduate Admissions Adviser, 651-635-8011, Fax: 651-635-1464, E-mail: k-akslen@bethel.edu.

Bloomsburg University of Pennsylvania, School of Graduate Studies, College of Professional Studies, School of Health Sciences, Department of Nursing, Bloomsburg, PA 17815-1301. Offers adult and family nurse practitioner (MSN); adult health and illness (MSN); community health (MSN); nursing (MSN); nursing administration (MSN). *Accreditation:* AACN. *Faculty:* 11 full-time (all women). *Students:* 9 full-time (all women), 27 part-time (24 women). Average age 36. 10 applicants, 100% accepted, 5 enrolled. In 2006, 6 degrees awarded. *Degree requirements:* For master's, thesis. *Entrance requirements:* For master's, minimum QPA of 3.0. Additional exam requirements/recommendations for international students: Required—TOEFL. *Application deadline:* Applications are processed on a rolling basis. Application fee: $30. Electronic applications accepted. *Expenses:* Tuition, state resident: full-time $6,048; part-time $336 per credit. Tuition, nonresident: full-time $9,678; part-time $538 per credit. Required fees: $1,415. *Financial support:* Unspecified assistantships available. *Faculty research:* Cardiopulmonary nursing, cancer topics, women's health. *Application contact:* Dr. Michelle Ficca, Coordinator, 570-389-4615, Fax: 570-389-5008, E-mail: mficca@bloomu.edu.

Boston College, William F. Connell School of Nursing, Chestnut Hill, MA 02467-3800. Offers adult health nursing (MS); community health nursing (MS); family health (MS); gerontology (MS); maternal/child health nursing (MS), including pediatric and women's health; nurse anesthesia (MS); nursing (PhD); psychiatric-mental health nursing (MS); MBA/MS; MS/MA; MS/PhD. *Accreditation:* AACN; AANA/CANAEP (one or more programs are accredited). Part-time programs available. *Faculty:* 46 full-time (44 women), 34 part-time/adjunct (all women). *Students:* 155 full-time (137 women), 56 part-time (54 women); includes 10 minority (4 African Americans, 5 Asian Americans or Pacific Islanders, 1 Hispanic American), 6 international. Average age 34. 276 applicants, 47% accepted, 67 enrolled. In 2006, 61 master's, 4 doctorates awarded. *Median time to degree:* Of those who began their doctoral program in fall 1998, 100% received their degree in 8 years or less. *Degree requirements:* For master's, research project; for doctorate, thesis/dissertation, computer literacy exam or foreign language, comprehensive exam. *Entrance requirements:* For master's, GRE General Test, bachelor's degree in nursing; for doctorate, GRE General Test, master's degree in nursing. Additional exam requirements/recommendations for international students: Required—TOEFL (minimum score 550 paper-based; 213 computer-based). *Application deadline:* For fall admission, 10/15 for domestic and international students; for spring admission, 3/15 for domestic and international students. Application fee: $40. Electronic applications accepted. *Financial support:* In 2006–07, 104 students received support, including 15 fellowships with partial tuition reimbursements available (averaging $10,045 per year), 3 research assistantships (averaging $10,000 per year), 4 teaching assistantships (averaging $12,548 per year); Federal Work-Study, institutionally sponsored loans, scholarships/grants, traineeships, and tuition waivers (partial) also available. Support available to part-time students. Financial award application deadline: 3/1; financial award applicants required to submit FAFSA. *Faculty research:* Ethics, reduction of risk behaviors, support during chronic illness, violence, gerontology. Total annual research expenditures: $1.1 million. *Unit head:* Dr. Barbara Hazard, Dean, 617-552-4251, Fax: 617-552-0931, E-mail: barbara.munro@bc.edu. *Application contact:* Zanifer John-Bayard, Graduate Programs Assistant, 617-552-4059, Fax: 617-552-0745, E-mail: johnza@bc.edu.

Bowie State University, Graduate Programs, Department of Nursing, Bowie, MD 20715-9465. Offers administration of nursing services (MS); family nurse practitioner (MS); nursing education (MS). *Accreditation:* NLN. Part-time programs available. *Faculty:* 7 full-time (4 women), 14 part-time/adjunct (9 women). *Students:* 9 full-time (all women), 9 part-time (8 women); includes 15 minority (all African Americans) Average age 42. 8 applicants, 88% accepted, 4 enrolled. In 2006, 7 degrees awarded. *Degree requirements:* For master's, thesis, research paper, comprehensive exam. *Entrance requirements:* For master's, minimum GPA of 2.5. *Application deadline:* For fall admission, 5/15 for domestic students. Applications are processed on a rolling basis. Application fee: $40. Electronic applications accepted. *Expenses:* Tuition, state resident: full-time $7,344; part-time $306 per credit. Tuition, nonresident: full-time $14,304; part-time $396 per credit. Required fees: $1,078; $77 per credit. $539 per term. One-time fee: $40. *Financial support:* Institutionally sponsored loans and traineeships available. Financial award application deadline: 4/1. *Faculty research:* Minority health, women's health, gerontology, leadership management. *Unit head:* Dr. Bonita Jenkins, Acting Chairperson, 301-860-3210, E-mail: mccaskill@bowiestate.edu. *Application contact:* Angela Issac, Information Contact.

Bradley University, Graduate School, College of Education and Health Sciences, Department of Nursing, Peoria, IL 61625-0002. Offers nurse administered anesthesia (MSN); nursing administration (MSN). *Accreditation:* AANA/CANAEP; NLN. Part-time and evening/weekend programs available. *Students:* 3 full-time (0 women), 47 part-time (29 women); includes 6 minority (1 African American, 1 American Indian/Alaska Native, 4 Asian Americans or Pacific Islanders). 16 applicants, 19% accepted, 3 enrolled. In 2006, 24 degrees awarded. *Degree requirements:* For master's, thesis optional. *Entrance requirements:* For master's, GRE General Test or MAT, interview, Illinois RN license, advanced cardiac life support certification, pediatric advanced life support certification, 3 letters of recommendation. Additional exam requirements/recommendations for international students: Required—TOEFL (minimum score 550 paper-based; 213 computer-based; 79 iBT). *Application deadline:* For fall admission, 5/15 priority date for domestic and international students; for spring admission, 10/15 priority date for domestic and international students. Applications are processed on a rolling basis. Application fee: $40 ($50 for international students). *Financial support:* Research assistantships, scholarships/grants, tuition waivers (partial), and unspecified assistantships available. Financial award application deadline: 4/1. *Unit head:* Dr. Francesca Armmer, Chairperson, 309-677-2528, E-mail: faa@bradley.edu.

Nursing—General

Briar Cliff University, Program in Nursing, Sioux City, IA 51104-0100. Offers MSN. *Accreditation:* NLN. Part-time and evening/weekend programs available. Expenses: Contact institution.

Brigham Young University, Graduate Studies, College of Nursing, Provo, UT 84602-1001. Offers family nurse practitioner (MS). *Accreditation:* AACN. *Faculty:* 26 full-time (24 women). *Students:* 12 full-time (10 women), 15 part-time (12 women); includes 3 minority (2 Asian Americans or Pacific Islanders, 1 Hispanic American). Average age 25. 28 applicants, 54% accepted, 15 enrolled. In 2006, 9 degrees awarded. *Degree requirements:* For master's, thesis. *Entrance requirements:* For master's, GRE, minimum GPA of 3.0 in last 60 hours, interview, BS in nursing, pathophysiology class within undergraduate program, course work in basic statistics. Additional exam requirements/recommendations for international students: Required—TOEFL. *Application deadline:* For spring admission, 12/1 for domestic students. Applications are processed on a rolling basis. Application fee: $50. Electronic applications accepted. *Financial support:* In 2006–07, 21 students received support, including 2 research assistantships with full and partial tuition reimbursements available (averaging $10,000 per year), 3 teaching assistantships with full and partial tuition reimbursements available (averaging $10,000 per year); institutionally sponsored loans, scholarships/grants, tuition waivers (full), and unspecified assistantships also available. Support available to part-time students. Financial award application deadline: 2/1; financial award applicants required to submit FAFSA. *Faculty research:* Cardiovascular risk factors, stroke patients, nutrition, stress among children, family response to life-threatening illness. Total annual research expenditures: $1,200. *Unit head:* Dr. Mary Williams, Interim Dean, 801-422-5626, Fax: 801-422-0536, E-mail: mary_williams@byu.edu.

See Close-Up on page 1947.

California State University, Bakersfield, Division of Graduate Studies and Research, School of Natural Sciences and Mathematics, Program in Nursing, Bakersfield, CA 93311-1022. Offers MS. *Accreditation:* AACN. *Degree requirements:* For master's, thesis, cognate in business. *Entrance requirements:* For master's, MAT, BSN from NLN-accredited program. *Faculty research:* AIDS, gerontological nursing, cultural health beliefs.

California State University, Chico, Graduate School, College of Natural Sciences, School of Nursing, Chico, CA 95929-0200. Offers MS. *Accreditation:* AACN. Postbaccalaureate distance learning degree programs offered. *Faculty:* 13 full-time (all women), 5 part-time/adjunct (all women). *Students:* Average age 44. 21 applicants, 100% accepted, 19 enrolled. In 2006, 2 degrees awarded. *Degree requirements:* For master's, thesis, oral exam. *Entrance requirements:* For master's, GRE or MAT, previous course work in statistics, California nursing license. Additional exam requirements/recommendations for international students: Required—TOEFL (minimum score 550 paper-based; 213 computer-based). *Application deadline:* For fall admission, 3/1 for domestic and international students. Applications are processed on a rolling basis. Application fee: $55. Electronic applications accepted. *Financial support:* Career-related internships or fieldwork available. *Unit head:* Dr. Sherry D. Fox, Director, 530-898-5891. *Application contact:* Dr. Irene Morgan, Graduate Coordinator, 530-898-6207.

California State University, Dominguez Hills, College of Health and Human Services, Program in Nursing, Carson, CA 90747-0001. Offers MSN. *Accreditation:* AACN. Part-time programs available. Postbaccalaureate distance learning degree programs offered. *Faculty:* 14 full-time (13 women), 17 part-time/adjunct (15 women). *Students:* 73 full-time (61 women), 314 part-time (294 women); includes 151 minority (59 African Americans, 2 American Indian/Alaska Native, 57 Asian Americans or Pacific Islanders, 33 Hispanic Americans), 1 international. Average age 43. 138 applicants, 92% accepted, 86 enrolled. In 2006, 35 degrees awarded. *Degree requirements:* For master's, comprehensive exam. *Entrance requirements:* For master's, minimum GPA of 2.5, 3.0 in prior coursework in statistics, research, pathophysiology and assessment. Additional exam requirements/recommendations for international students: Required—TOEFL. *Application deadline:* For fall admission, 6/1 for domestic students; for spring admission, 11/1 for domestic students. Applications are processed on a rolling basis. Application fee: $55. Electronic applications accepted. *Expenses:* Tuition, nonresident: part-time $339 per unit. Required fees: $1,148 per term. Tuition and fees vary according to program. *Faculty research:* AIDS/HIV, health promotion, elderly. *Unit head:* Dr. Carole Shea, Chair, 310-243-2050, E-mail: cshea@csudh.edu. *Application contact:* 310-243-2060.

California State University, Fresno, Division of Graduate Studies, College of Health and Human Services, Department of Nursing, Fresno, CA 93740-8027. Offers nursing (MS), including clinical specialty, primary care nurse practitioner. *Accreditation:* AACN. Part-time and evening/weekend programs available. *Degree requirements:* For master's, thesis or alternative. *Entrance requirements:* For master's, GRE General Test, 1 year of clinical practice, previous course work in statistics, BSN, minimum GPA of 3.0 in nursing. Additional exam requirements/recommendations for international students: Required—TOEFL. Electronic applications accepted. *Faculty research:* Training grant, HIV assessment.

California State University, Fullerton, Graduate Studies, College of Health and Human Development, Department of Nursing, Fullerton, CA 92834-9480. Offers MS. *Accreditation:* AACN; AANA/CANAEP. Part-time programs available. *Students:* 115 full-time (73 women), 134 part-time (124 women); includes 109 minority (8 African Americans, 58 Asian Americans or Pacific Islanders, 43 Hispanic Americans), 3 international. Average age 34. 318 applicants, 64% accepted, 147 enrolled. In 2006, 59 degrees awarded. Application fee: $55. *Expenses:* Tuition, nonresident: part-time $339 per unit. Required fees: $1,155 per semester. *Financial support:* Career-related internships or fieldwork, Federal Work-Study, institutionally sponsored loans, scholarships/grants, and traineeships available. Support available to part-time students. *Unit head:* Dr. Paula Herberg, Chair, 714-278-5570.

California State University, Long Beach, Graduate Studies, College of Health and Human Services, Department of Nursing, Long Beach, CA 90840. Offers nursing (MS); nursing-health care administration (MS). *Accreditation:* AACN. Part-time programs available. *Faculty:* 32 full-time (30 women), 25 part-time/adjunct (19 women). *Students:* 101 full-time (92 women), 119 part-time (114 women); includes 127 minority (28 African Americans, 2 American Indian/Alaska Native, 59 Asian Americans or Pacific Islanders, 38 Hispanic Americans), 2 international. Average age 37. 138 applicants, 79% accepted, 89 enrolled. In 2006, 73 degrees awarded. *Degree requirements:* For master's, thesis optional. *Entrance requirements:* For master's, minimum GPA of 3.0. *Application deadline:* For fall admission, 7/1 for domestic students; for spring admission, 12/1 for domestic students. Applications are processed on a rolling basis. Application fee: $55. Electronic applications accepted. *Financial support:* Federal Work-Study, institutionally sponsored loans, and scholarships/grants available. Financial award application deadline: 3/2. *Faculty research:* Newborns of drug-dependent mothers, abuse of residents in nursing homes, interventions in care of Alzheimer's patients. *Unit head:* Dr. Loucine Huckabay, Director, 562-985-4463, Fax: 562-985-2382, E-mail: huckabay@csulb.edu. *Application contact:* Dr. Bonnie Kellogg, Graduate Coordinator, 562-985-8243, Fax: 562-985-2382, E-mail: bkellogg@csulb.edu.

California State University, Los Angeles, Graduate Studies, College of Health and Human Services, School of Nursing, Los Angeles, CA 90032-8530. Offers health science (MA); nursing (MS). *Accreditation:* NLN. Part-time and evening/weekend programs available. *Faculty:* 9 full-time (8 women), 7 part-time/adjunct (all women). *Students:* 80 full-time (68 women), 175 part-time (153 women); includes 157 minority (18 African Americans, 1 American Indian/Alaska Native, 97 Asian Americans or Pacific Islanders, 41 Hispanic Americans), 4 international. In 2006, 31 degrees awarded. *Degree requirements:* For master's, project or thesis. *Entrance requirements:* For master's, minimum GPA of 3.0 in nursing, course work in nursing and statistics. Additional exam requirements/recommendations for international students: Required—TOEFL. *Application deadline:* For fall admission, 6/30 for domestic students; for spring admission, 2/1 for domestic students. Applications are processed on a rolling basis. Application fee: $55. *Expenses:* Tuition, nonresident: part-time $226 per unit. *Financial support:* Federal Work-Study available. Support available to part-time students. Financial award application deadline: 3/1. *Faculty research:* Family stress, geripsychiatric nursing, self-care counseling, holistic nursing, adult health. *Unit head:* Dr. Pat Chin, Acting Chair, 323-343-4700, Fax: 323-343-6454.

California State University, Sacramento, Graduate Studies, College of Health and Human Services, Division of Nursing, Sacramento, CA 95819-6048. Offers MS. *Accreditation:* AACN. Part-time programs available. *Students:* 69 full-time (61 women), 92 part-time (83 women); includes 38 minority (5 African Americans, 1 American Indian/Alaska Native, 21 Asian Americans or Pacific Islanders, 11 Hispanic Americans), 3 international. Average age 39. 214 applicants, 57% accepted, 61 enrolled. *Degree requirements:* For master's, thesis or alternative, writing proficiency exam. *Entrance requirements:* For master's, GRE, bachelor's degree in nursing, minimum GPA of 3.0. Additional exam requirements/recommendations for international students: Required—TOEFL. *Application deadline:* Applications are processed on a rolling basis. Application fee: $55. Electronic applications accepted. *Financial support:* Research assistantships, teaching assistantships, career-related internships or fieldwork and Federal Work-Study available. Support available to part-time students. Financial award application deadline: 3/1. *Unit head:* Dr. Ann Stoltz, Chair, 916-278-6525, Fax: 916-278-6311.

California State University, San Bernardino, Graduate Studies, College of Natural Sciences, Program in Nursing, San Bernardino, CA 92407-2397. Offers MS. *Faculty:* 16 full-time, 7 part-time/adjunct. *Students:* 7 full-time (all women), 2 part-time (both women); includes 1 minority (Asian American or Pacific Islander) Average age 47. 8 applicants, 38% accepted, 1 enrolled. In 2006, 11 degrees awarded. Application fee: $55. *Unit head:* Dr. Marcia Raines, Chair, 909-537-5380, Fax: 909-537-7089, E-mail: mraines@csusb.edu.

Capital University, School of Nursing, Columbus, OH 43209-2394. Offers administration (MSN); legal studies (MSN); theological studies (MSN); JD/MSN; MBA/MSN; MSN/MTS. *Accreditation:* AACN. Part-time and evening/weekend programs available. *Faculty:* 11 full-time (all women), 2 part-time/adjunct (both women). *Students:* 16 full-time (15 women), 72 part-time (67 women); includes 5 minority (4 African Americans, 1 Asian American or Pacific Islander), 8 international. Average age 41. 20 applicants, 90% accepted, 18 enrolled. In 2006, 14 degrees awarded. *Degree requirements:* For master's, thesis or alternative, registration. *Entrance requirements:* For master's, BSN, current RN license, minimum GPA of 3.0, undergraduate courses in statistics and research. Additional exam requirements/recommendations for international students: Required—TOEFL (minimum score 550 paper-based). *Application deadline:* For fall admission, 3/30 priority date for domestic and international students; for spring admission, 9/30 priority date for domestic and international students. Applications are processed on a rolling basis. Application fee: $25. *Expenses: Contact institution.* Part-time tuition and fees vary according to program. *Financial support:* In 2006–07, 2 students received support. Career-related internships or fieldwork and traineeships available. Financial award applicants required to submit FAFSA. *Faculty research:* Bereavement, wellness/health promotion, emergency cardiac care, critical thinking, complementary and alternative healthcare. *Unit head:* Dr. Elaine F. Haynes, Dean and Professor, 614-236-6703, Fax: 614-236-6157, E-mail: ehaynes@capital.edu. *Application contact:* Dr. Jill D Steuer, Professor and Director of the MSN Program, 614-236-6393, Fax: 614-236-6157, E-mail: jsteuer@capital.edu.

Cardinal Stritch University, College of Nursing, Milwaukee, WI 53217-3985. Offers MSN. *Accreditation:* AACN. Part-time and evening/weekend programs available. *Degree requirements:* For master's, thesis. *Entrance requirements:* For master's, interview, minimum GPA of 3.0, RN license, portfolio, formal paper, letters of recommendation (3). Expenses: Contact institution.

Announcement: The Ruth S. Coleman College of Nursing has provided innovative, distinctive nursing programs for more than a decade, with more than 1,000 graduates providing high-quality nursing care to patients. Stritch features small classes, flexible scheduling, and lots of one-on-one instruction. In addition, Stritch offers the full range of nursing programs, from associate through master's degrees. For more information, visit www.stritch.edu/nursing or call 800-347-8822, ext. 4042.

Carlow University, School of Nursing, Pittsburgh, PA 15213-3165. Offers home health advanced practice nursing (MSN, PMC); nursing case management/leadership (MSN); nursing leadership (MSN). *Accreditation:* AACN. Part-time and evening/weekend programs available. Postbaccalaureate distance learning degree programs offered (minimal on-campus study). *Degree requirements:* For master's, thesis or alternative. *Entrance requirements:* For master's, GRE General Test, 1 year of professional experience, BSN, interview, minimum GPA of 3.0, Pennsylvania RN license, previous graduate course work in statistics, resumé, 3 letters of recommendation; for PMC, MSN. Additional exam requirements/recommendations for international students: Required—TOEFL (minimum score 550 paper-based; 213 computer-based). Electronic applications accepted. *Faculty research:* Research utilization, community and home health, medically underserved.

Carson-Newman College, Department of Nursing, Jefferson City, TN 37760. Offers family nurse practitioner (MSN). *Accreditation:* AACN. *Faculty:* 2 full-time (both women), 10 part-time/adjunct (9 women). *Students:* 21 full-time (18 women), 11 part-time (all women); includes 1 African American. Average age 32. In 2006, 6 degrees awarded. *Application deadline:* For fall admission, 7/15 priority date for domestic students. Applications are processed on a rolling basis. Application fee: $50. *Expenses:* Tuition: Part-time $270 per credit hour. *Unit head:* Dr. Patricia Kraft, Dean and Chair, 865-471-3426.

Case Western Reserve University, Frances Payne Bolton School of Nursing, Doctoral Program in Nursing, Cleveland, OH 44106. Offers PhD. *Faculty:* 33 full-time (all women), 2 part-time/adjunct (both women). *Students:* 20 full-time (18 women), 43 part-time (37 women); includes 7 minority (5 African Americans, 1 Asian American or Pacific Islander, 1 Hispanic American), 25 international. Average age 40. 19 applicants, 79% accepted, 4 enrolled. In 2006, 22 degrees awarded. *Degree requirements:* For doctorate, thesis/dissertation. *Entrance requirements:* For doctorate, GRE General Test. *Application deadline:* For fall admission, 3/1 priority date for domestic students. Applications are processed on a rolling basis. Application fee: $25. *Financial support:* In 2006–07, 7 research assistantships, 3 teaching assistantships (averaging $1,800 per year) were awarded; institutionally sponsored loans, scholarships/grants, and tuition waivers (partial) also available. Support available to part-time students. Financial award application deadline: 6/30; financial award applicants required to submit FAFSA. *Faculty research:* Acute care nursing, parent-child gerontology, information systems, clinical decisions. *Unit head:* Dr. Jaclene Zavszniewski, Associate Dean for Doctoral Education, 216-368-3612, E-mail: jaz@case.edu. *Application contact:* Peter Taylor, Recruitment and Retention Specialist, 216-368-0349, Fax: 216-368-0124, E-mail: peter.taylor@case.edu.

Case Western Reserve University, Frances Payne Bolton School of Nursing, Doctor of Nursing Practice Program, Cleveland, OH 44106. Offers acute care nurse practitioner (DNP); adult nurse practitioner (DNP); family nurse practitioner (DNP); gerontological nurse practitioner (DNP); graduate entry/pre-licensure option (DNP); medical-surgical nursing (DNP); midwifery/family nursing (DNP); neonatal nurse practitioner (DNP); pediatric nurse practitioner (DNP); post-licensure option (DNP); psychiatric mental health nurse practitioner (DNP); women's health nurse practitioner (DNP). Graduate entry option allows baccalaureate-prepared college graduates from non-nursing backgrounds to earn certificate and MSN in addition to ND. *Students:* 125 full-time (109 women), 308 part-time (290 women); includes 47 minority (21 African Americans, 1 American Indian/Alaska Native, 18 Asian Americans or Pacific Islanders, 7 Hispanic Americans), 7 international. 190 applicants, 70% accepted, 80 enrolled. In 2006, 35 degrees awarded. Terminal master's awarded for partial completion of doctoral program. *Degree requirements:* For doctorate, thesis/dissertation. *Entrance requirements:* For doctorate, GRE General Test or MAT. *Application deadline:* For fall admission, 6/1 priority date for domestic students. Applications are processed on a rolling basis. Application fee: $75. *Financial support:* In 2006–07, 6 students received support, including 1 teaching assistantship; research assistantships, Federal Work-Study, institutionally sponsored loans, and tuition waivers (partial) also available. Support available to part-time students. Financial award application deadline:

6/30; financial award applicants required to submit FAFSA. *Faculty research:* Clinical nursing, acute care, gerontology, mental health, critical care. *Unit head:* Dr. Georgia Narsavage, Director, 216-368-6304, Fax: 216-368-3542, E-mail: gln2@cwru.edu. *Application contact:* Peter Taylor, Recruitment and Retention Specialist, 216-368-0349, Fax: 216-368-0124, E-mail: peter.taylor@case.edu.

Case Western Reserve University, Frances Payne Bolton School of Nursing, Master's Programs in Nursing, Cleveland, OH 44106. Offers community health nursing (MSN); medical-surgical nursing (MSN); nurse anesthesia (MSN); nurse midwifery (MSN); nurse practitioner (MSN), including acute care cardiovascular nursing, acute care nurse practitioner, acute care/flight nurse, adult nurse practitioner, family nurse practitioner, gerontological nurse practitioner, neonatal nurse practitioner, pediatric nurse practitioner, psychiatric-mental health nurse practitioner, women's health nurse practitioner; nursing informatics (MSN). *Accreditation:* NLN. Part-time programs available. Postbaccalaureate distance learning degree programs offered (minimal on-campus study). *Faculty:* 54 full-time (50 women), 5 part-time/adjunct (3 women). *Students:* 42 full-time (30 women), 107 part-time (95 women); includes 28 minority (12 African Americans, 11 Asian Americans or Pacific Islanders, 5 Hispanic Americans), 7 international. Average age 35. 181 applicants, 43% accepted, 48 enrolled. In 2006, 75 degrees awarded. *Degree requirements:* For master's, thesis optional. *Entrance requirements:* For master's, GRE General Test or MAT. *Application deadline:* Applications are processed on a rolling basis. Application fee: $75. *Financial support:* In 2006–07, 7 teaching assistantships with tuition reimbursements were awarded; fellowships, research assistantships, institutionally sponsored loans, traineeships, and tuition waivers (partial) also available. Support available to part-time students. Financial award application deadline: 6/30. *Faculty research:* Preterm skin contact effects on electrophysiologic sleep, intergenerational caregiving to at risk youth, maintaining exercise in cardiac rehabilitation, left ventricular function and duration of mechanical ventilation. *Unit head:* Dr. Carol Savrin, Director, 216-368-6304, Fax: 215-368-3542, E-mail: cls18@case.edu. *Application contact:* Peter Taylor, Recruitment and Retention Specialist, 216-368-0349, Fax: 216-368-0124, E-mail: peter.taylor@case.edu.

Case Western Reserve University, Frances Payne Bolton School of Nursing and Department of Anthropology, Nursing/Anthropology Program, Cleveland, OH 44106. Offers MSN/MA. *Application deadline:* Applications are processed on a rolling basis. Application fee: $75. *Financial support:* Fellowships, research assistantships, teaching assistantships available. Financial award application deadline: 6/30. *Unit head:* Dr. Carol Savrin, Head, 216-368-6304, Fax: 215-368-3542, E-mail: cls18@case.edu. *Application contact:* Peter Taylor, Recruitment and Retention Specialist, 216-368-0349, Fax: 216-368-0124, E-mail: peter.taylor@case.edu.

Case Western Reserve University, Frances Payne Bolton School of Nursing, Nursing/Bioethics Program, Cleveland, OH 44106. Offers MSN/MA. *Application deadline:* Applications are processed on a rolling basis. Application fee: $75. *Financial support:* Fellowships, research assistantships, teaching assistantships available. Financial award application deadline: 6/30. *Unit head:* Dr. Barbara Daly, Head, 216-368-5994, E-mail: barbara.daly@case.edu. *Application contact:* Peter Taylor, Recruitment and Retention Specialist, 216-368-0349, Fax: 216-368-0124, E-mail: peter.taylor@case.edu.

Case Western Reserve University, Frances Payne Bolton School of Nursing, Nursing/Public Health Program, Cleveland, OH 44106. Offers MSN/MPH. Application fee: $75. *Unit head:* Dr. Deborah Lindell, Head, 216-368-3740, E-mail: dxl41@case.edu. *Application contact:* Peter Taylor, Recruitment and Retention Specialist, 216-368-0349, Fax: 216-368-0124, E-mail: peter.taylor@case.edu.

The Catholic University of America, School of Nursing, Washington, DC 20064. Offers advanced practice nursing (MSN), including administration of nursing service, adult nurse practitioner, education, family nurse practitioner, geriatric nurse practitioner, pediatric nurse practitioner, psychiatric-mental health, school health nurse practitioner; clinical nursing (DN Sc). *Accreditation:* AACN; NLN. Part-time programs available. *Faculty:* 17 full-time (all women), 19 part-time/adjunct (18 women). *Students:* 27 full-time (25 women), 58 part-time (57 women); includes 31 minority (20 African Americans, 6 Asian Americans or Pacific Islanders, 5 Hispanic Americans), 6 international. Average age 43. 38 applicants, 76% accepted, 15 enrolled. In 2006, 15 master's, 7 doctorates awarded. *Degree requirements:* For master's, thesis optional; for doctorate, thesis/dissertation, comprehensive exam. *Entrance requirements:* For master's, GRE General Test or MAT, 3 letters of recommendation, BA in nursing, RN registration; for doctorate, GRE General Test, 3 letters of recommendation, BA in nursing, RN registration. Additional exam requirements/recommendations for international students: Required—TOEFL (minimum score 550 paper-based; 213 computer-based). *Application deadline:* For fall admission, 2/1 priority date for domestic students; for spring admission, 11/15 priority date for domestic students. Applications are processed on a rolling basis. Application fee: $55. Electronic applications accepted. *Expenses:* Tuition: Full-time $27,700; part-time $1,045 per credit hour. Required fees: $1,290. Part-time tuition and fees vary according to campus/location and program. *Financial support:* Research assistantships, teaching assistantships, career-related internships or fieldwork, Federal Work-Study, scholarships/grants, tuition waivers (full and partial), and unspecified assistantships available. Support available to part-time students. Financial award application deadline: 2/1; financial award applicants required to submit FAFSA. *Faculty research:* Outcome research–readmission of home health care patients with congestive heart failure, spirituality of chronic illness, minority multigravidos utilization of prenatal care. *Unit head:* Dr. Nalini Jairath, Dean, 202-319-5403, Fax: 202-319-6485, E-mail: jairath@cua.edu.

Chatham University, Program in Nursing, Pittsburgh, PA 15232-2826. Offers MSN, DNP. *Students:* 5 full-time (all women). Average age 45. *Entrance requirements:* For master's and doctorate, RN license. Additional exam requirements/recommendations for international students: Required—TOEFL (minimum score 600 paper-based; 250 computer-based; 100 iBT); Recommended—IELTS (minimum score 7). *Application deadline:* For fall admission, 5/1 priority date for domestic students. Applications are processed on a rolling basis. Electronic applications accepted. *Unit head:* Dr. Carol Patton, Director, 412-365-2726, E-mail: cpatton@chatham.edu. *Application contact:* Office of Graduate Admissions, 412-365-1825, Fax: 412-365-1609, E-mail: admissions@chatham.edu.

Clarion University of Pennsylvania, Office of Research and Graduate Studies, School of Nursing, Program in Nursing, Clarion, PA 16214. Offers MSN. *Accreditation:* NLN. *Faculty:* 4 full-time (all women). *Students:* 1 (woman) full-time, 53 part-time (44 women); includes 1 minority (African American) 44 applicants, 82% accepted. In 2006, 25 degrees awarded. *Degree requirements:* For master's, thesis, comprehensive exam. *Entrance requirements:* For master's, minimum QPA of 2.75. Additional exam requirements/recommendations for international students: Required—TOEFL (minimum score 550 paper-based; 213 computer-based; 80 iBT). *Application deadline:* For fall admission, 6/1 for domestic students, 4/15 priority date for international students; for spring admission, 11/1 for domestic students, 9/15 priority date for international students. Application fee: $30. *Expenses:* Tuition, state resident: part-time $336 per credit. Tuition, nonresident: part-time $538 per credit. *Financial support:* In 2006–07, 1 research assistantship with full tuition reimbursement (averaging $4,002 per year) was awarded. Financial award application deadline: 3/1. *Unit head:* Dr. Debbie Ciesielka, Graduate Coordinator, 412-578-7277, E-mail: dciesielka@clarion.edu.

Clarke College, Department of Nursing and Health, Dubuque, IA 52001-3198. Offers administration of nursing systems (MSN); advanced practice nursing (MSN); education (MSN); family nurse practitioner (MSN, PMC). *Accreditation:* AACN. Part-time programs available. *Entrance requirements:* For master's, GRE General Test or MAT, BSN, minimum GPA of 3.0. Electronic applications accepted. *Faculty research:* Narrative pedagogy, ethics, end-of-life care, pedagogy, family systems.

Clarkson College, Graduate Programs, Department of Nursing, Omaha, NE 68131-2739. Offers administration (MSN); education (MSN); family nurse practitioner (MSN). *Accreditation:* NLN. Part-time and evening/weekend programs available. Postbaccalaureate distance learning degree programs offered (minimal on-campus study). *Degree requirements:* For master's, on-campus skills assessment (family nurse practitioner), comprehensive exam or thesis. *Entrance requirements:* For master's, minimum GPA of 3.0, 2 references, resumé. Additional exam requirements/recommendations for international students: Required—TOEFL (minimum score 600 paper-based; 250 computer-based). Electronic applications accepted.

Clayton State University, School of Graduate Studies, Program in Nursing, Morrow, GA 30260-0285. Offers MSN.

Clemson University, Graduate School, College of Health, Education, and Human Development, School of Nursing, Clemson, SC 29634. Offers MS. *Accreditation:* AACN. Part-time programs available. Postbaccalaureate distance learning degree programs offered. *Faculty:* 19 full-time (all women). *Students:* 28 full-time (27 women), 54 part-time (52 women); includes 13 minority (9 African Americans, 1 American Indian/Alaska Native, 1 Asian American or Pacific Islander, 2 Hispanic Americans). Average age 37. 21 applicants, 100% accepted, 11 enrolled. In 2006, 21 degrees awarded. *Degree requirements:* For master's, thesis or alternative. *Entrance requirements:* For master's, GRE General Test, RN license. Additional exam requirements/recommendations for international students: Required—TOEFL. *Application deadline:* For fall admission, 6/1 for domestic students; for spring admission, 12/1 for domestic students. Application fee: $50. Electronic applications accepted. *Expenses:* Tuition, state resident: full-time $8,812; part-time $450 per hour. Tuition, nonresident: full-time $18,036; part-time $760 per hour. Required fees: $474; $5 per term. *Financial support:* Fellowships, research assistantships, teaching assistantships, career-related internships or fieldwork and traineeships available. Financial award applicants required to submit FAFSA. *Faculty research:* Risk behaviors and chronic risk-taking in early adolescents, stress in older caregivers, home care of elderly, cancer awareness, pain. Total annual research expenditures: $19,547. *Unit head:* Dr. Pat Smart, Director, 864-656-5528, Fax: 864-656-5488, E-mail: townsep@clemson.edu. *Application contact:* Rosanne Pruitt, Coordinator, 864-656-5528, Fax: 864-656-5488, E-mail: prosan@clemson.edu.

See Close-Up on page 1949.

Cleveland State University, College of Graduate Studies, College of Education and Human Services, School of Nursing, Cleveland, OH 44115. Offers clinical nursing leader (MSN); forensic nursing (MSN); population health nursing (MSN); MSN/MBA. *Accreditation:* AACN. Part-time programs available. *Faculty:* 8 full-time (all women). *Students:* Average age 44. In 2006, 1 degree awarded. *Degree requirements:* For master's, thesis or alternative, portfolio, population health project. *Entrance requirements:* For master's, RN license, BSN, course work in statistics. Additional exam requirements/recommendations for international students: Required—TOEFL (minimum score 525 paper-based; 197 computer-based), IELTS (minimum score 6). *Application deadline:* For fall admission, 5/1 priority date for domestic students. Applications are processed on a rolling basis. Application fee: $30. Electronic applications accepted. *Financial support:* In 2006–07, 3 students received support. Tuition waivers (full) and unspecified assistantships available. Support available to part-time students. Financial award application deadline: 3/1; financial award applicants required to submit FAFSA. *Faculty research:* Diabetes management, African-American elders medication compliance, risk in home visiting, suffering, COPD and stress. Total annual research expenditures: $204,029. *Unit head:* Dr. Noreen C. Frisch, Director, 216-523-7237, Fax: 216-687-3556, E-mail: n.frisch@csuohio.edu. *Application contact:* Dr. Sharon Radzyminski, Director, Graduate Nursing Program, 216-687-3558, Fax: 216-687-3556, E-mail: s.radzyminski@csuohio.edu.

College Misericordia, College of Health Sciences, Department of Nursing, Dallas, PA 18612-1098. Offers MSN. *Accreditation:* AACN. Part-time and evening/weekend programs available. *Faculty:* 3 full-time (all women), 3 part-time/adjunct (all women). *Students:* Average age 38. In 2006, 3 degrees awarded. *Degree requirements:* For master's, practicum, thesis optional. *Entrance requirements:* For master's, GRE General Test or MAT, interview, minimum GPA of 2.5, physical assessment, course work in statistics. *Application deadline:* For fall admission, 8/7 priority date for domestic students; for spring admission, 1/3 for domestic students. Applications are processed on a rolling basis. Application fee: $25. Electronic applications accepted. *Expenses:* Contact institution. *Financial support:* Teaching assistantships, career-related internships or fieldwork, scholarships/grants, traineeships, tuition waivers (partial), and unspecified assistantships available. Support available to part-time students. Financial award application deadline: 6/30. *Faculty research:* Quality of life, maternal-child, spirituality, critical thinking, adult health. *Unit head:* Dr. Cheryl Fuller, Coordinator of Graduate Nursing, 570-674-6219, E-mail: cfuller@misericordia.edu. *Application contact:* Larree Brown, Coordinator of Part-Time Undergraduate and Graduate Programs, 570-674-6451, Fax: 570-674-6232, E-mail: lbrown@misericordia.edu.

College of Mount St. Joseph, Master of Nursing Program, Cincinnati, OH 45233-1670. Offers MN. *Faculty:* 6 full-time (5 women), 1 (woman) part-time/adjunct. *Students:* 24 full-time (19 women); includes 7 minority (all African Americans), 1 international. Average age 32. 40 applicants, 88% accepted, 24 enrolled. In 2006, 24 degrees awarded. *Degree requirements:* For master's, evidence-based project. *Entrance requirements:* For master's, GRE or minimum GPA of 3.0; interview; course work in chemistry, anatomy, physiology, microbiology, psychology, sociology, statistics, life span development, and nutrition; non-nursing bachelor's degree. Additional exam requirements/recommendations for international students: Required—TOEFL (minimum score 560 paper-based; 220 computer-based). *Application deadline:* Applications are processed on a rolling basis. Application fee: $50. Electronic applications accepted. *Expenses:* Contact institution. *Financial support:* Career-related internships or fieldwork available. Financial award application deadline: 6/1; financial award applicants required to submit FAFSA. *Faculty research:* Utilizing technology in learning, assessment of student learning, critical thinking. *Unit head:* Dr. Darla Vale, Chair, Health Sciences Department, 513-244-4322, Fax: 513-451-2547, E-mail: darla_vale@mail.msj.edu. *Application contact:* Marilyn Hoskins, Assistant Director of Admissions for Graduate Recruitment, 513-244-4723, Fax: 513-244-4629, E-mail: marilyn_hoskins@mail.msg.edu.

College of Mount Saint Vincent, School of Professional and Continuing Studies, Department of Nursing, Riverdale, NY 10471-1093. Offers adult nurse practitioner (MSN, PMC); family nurse practitioner (MSN, PMC); nurse educator (PMC); nursing administration (MSN); nursing for the adult and aged (MSN). *Accreditation:* AACN. Part-time programs available. *Faculty:* 2 full-time (1 woman), 6 part-time/adjunct (all women). *Students:* 1 (woman) full-time, 67 part-time (59 women); includes 43 minority (21 African Americans, 16 Asian Americans or Pacific Islanders, 6 Hispanic Americans). Average age 37. In 2006, 16 degrees awarded. *Degree requirements:* For master's, registration. *Entrance requirements:* For master's, BSN, interview, RN license, minimum GPA of 3.0, letters of reference. Additional exam requirements/recommendations for international students: Required—TOEFL. *Application deadline:* For fall admission, 6/1 for domestic and international students; for spring admission, 11/1 for domestic students, 10/1 for international students. Applications are processed on a rolling basis. Application fee: $50. *Expenses:* Contact institution. *Financial support:* Career-related internships or fieldwork available. Financial award application deadline: 6/1; financial award applicants required to submit FAFSA. *Unit head:* Carol Vicino, Director, 718-405-3354, Fax: 718-405-3286.

The College of New Jersey, Graduate Division, School of Nursing, Health and Exercise Science, Ewing, NJ 08628. Offers M Ed, MAT, MSN, Certificate. *Accreditation:* AACN. Part-time and evening/weekend programs available. *Faculty:* 3. *Students:* 6 applicants, 100% accepted. In 2006, 10 degrees awarded. *Degree requirements:* For master's, comprehensive exam. *Entrance requirements:* For master's, GRE General Test, minimum GPA of 3.0 in field or 2.75 overall. Additional exam requirements/recommendations for international students: Required—TOEFL. *Application deadline:* For fall admission, 3/15 for domestic students. Application fee: $60. Electronic applications accepted. *Financial support:* Unspecified assistantships available. Financial award application deadline: 5/1; financial award applicants required to submit FAFSA. *Unit head:* Dr. Susan Bakewell-Sachs, Dean, 609-771-2541, Fax: 609-637-5159. *Application contact:* Susan L. Hydro, Office of Graduate Studies, Assistant Dean, 609-771-2300, Fax: 609-637-5105, E-mail: graduate@tcnj.edu.

Nursing—General

The College of New Rochelle, Graduate School, Program in Nursing, New Rochelle, NY 10805-2308. Offers acute care nurse practitioner (MS, Certificate); clinical specialist in holistic nursing (MS, Certificate); family nurse practitioner (MS, Certificate); nursing and health care management (MS); nursing education (Certificate). *Accreditation:* AACN. Part-time programs available. *Faculty:* 7 full-time (6 women), 3 part-time/adjunct (all women). *Students:* Average age 44. In 2006, 23 degrees awarded. *Degree requirements:* For master's, registration. *Entrance requirements:* For master's, GRE General Test or MAT, BSN, malpractice insurance, minimum GPA of 3.0, RN license. *Application deadline:* For fall admission, 9/1 priority date for domestic students; for spring admission, 1/15 priority date for domestic students. Applications are processed on a rolling basis. Application fee: $30. *Expenses: Contact institution. Financial support:* Traineeships available. Support available to part-time students. Financial award application deadline: 8/15. *Faculty research:* Holistic modalities, academic success variables. *Unit head:* Dr. Mary Alice Donius, Dean, 914-654-5804, Fax: 914-654-5994.

College of St. Catherine, Graduate Programs, Program in Nursing, St. Paul, MN 55105-1789. Offers MA. *Accreditation:* NLN. Part-time and evening/weekend programs available. *Degree requirements:* For master's, thesis. *Entrance requirements:* For master's, GRE General Test, bachelor's degree in nursing, current nursing license, 2 years of recent clinical practice. Additional exam requirements/recommendations for international students: Required—TOEFL.

The College of St. Scholastica, Graduate Studies, Department of Nursing, Duluth, MN 55811-4199. Offers MA, PMC. *Accreditation:* AACN. Part-time programs available. *Faculty:* 9 full-time (8 women), 5 part-time/adjunct (all women). *Students:* 80 full-time (75 women), 28 part-time (26 women); includes 6 minority (1 African American, 2 American Indian/Alaska Native, 2 Asian Americans or Pacific Islanders, 1 Hispanic American), 3 international. Average age 38. 55 applicants, 82% accepted, 39 enrolled. In 2006, 19 degrees awarded. *Degree requirements:* For master's, thesis. *Entrance requirements:* For master's, GRE General Test or MAT, bachelor's degree in nursing, interview, RN license, minimum GPA of 3.0. Additional exam requirements/recommendations for international students: Required—TOEFL (minimum score 550 paper-based; 213 computer-based; 79 iBT). *Application deadline:* For fall admission, 3/15 priority date for domestic students, 3/15 for international students. Applications are processed on a rolling basis. Application fee: $50. Electronic applications accepted. *Financial support:* In 2006–07, 89 students received support. Scholarships/grants and traineeships available. Support available to part-time students. Financial award applicants required to submit FAFSA. *Faculty research:* Critical thinking and professional development, social organization of responsibility, rural health HIV/AIDS prevention, web-based instruction in nursing. *Unit head:* Carleen Maynard, Director, 218-723-6452, Fax: 218-723-6472. *Application contact:* Tonya J. Roth, Graduate Recruitment Counselor, 218-723-6285, Fax: 218-733-2275, E-mail: gradstudies@css.edu.

College of Staten Island of the City University of New York, Graduate Programs, Department of Nursing, Staten Island, NY 10314-6600. Offers adult health nursing (MS, 6th Year Certificate); gerontological nursing (MS, 6th Year Certificate). *Accreditation:* NLN. Part-time and evening/weekend programs available. *Students:* 1 (woman) full-time, 39 part-time (38 women); includes 14 minority (7 African Americans, 6 Asian Americans or Pacific Islanders, 1 Hispanic American), 1 international. Average age 39. 11 applicants, 82% accepted, 9 enrolled. In 2006, 5 degrees awarded. *Degree requirements:* For master's, 42 credits with 500 supervised hours, thesis optional; for 6th Year Certificate, 12-21 credits with 500 supervised hours. *Entrance requirements:* For master's, minimum undergraduate GPA of 3.0 in nursing courses, New York RN license, 2 professional references, specific undergraduate courses; for 6th Year Certificate, master's degree in nursing for post masters advanced certificate. Additional exam requirements/recommendations for international students: Required—TOEFL (minimum score 550 paper-based; 213 computer-based; 79 iBT). *Application deadline:* Applications are processed on a rolling basis. Application fee: $125. *Expenses:* Tuition, state resident: full-time $6,400; part-time $270 per credit. Tuition, nonresident: part-time $500 per credit. Required fees: $53 per semester. *Financial support:* In 2006–07, 1 student received support. Traineeships available. Financial award applicants required to submit FAFSA. *Faculty research:* Students perceptions concerning factors restricting or supporting retention, quality of life among breast cancer survivors. *Unit head:* Dr. Mary O'Donnell, Chairperson, 718-982-3822, Fax: 718-982-4124, E-mail: nursingmasters@mail.csi.cuny.edu. *Application contact:* Emmanuel Esperance, Deputy Director of Office of Recruitment and Admissions, 718-982-2190, Fax: 718-982-2500, E-mail: admissions@mail.csi.cuny.edu.

Columbia University, School of Nursing, New York, NY 10032. Offers MS, DN Sc, DrNP, Adv C, MBA/MS, MPH/MS. *Accreditation:* AACN. Part-time programs available. *Faculty:* 80. *Students:* 173 full-time (159 women), 248 part-time (233 women); includes 82 minority (22 African Americans, 1 American Indian/Alaska Native, 35 Asian Americans or Pacific Islanders, 24 Hispanic Americans). Average age 31. 248 applicants, 100% accepted, 101 enrolled. In 2006, 175 master's, 11 doctorates, 7 other advanced degrees awarded. *Degree requirements:* For doctorate, thesis/dissertation. *Entrance requirements:* For master's, GRE General Test, BSN, 1 year of clinical experience (preferred); for doctorate, GRE General Test, MSN; course work in statistics, research, and theory. Additional exam requirements/recommendations for international students: Required—TOEFL. *Application deadline:* Applications are processed on a rolling basis. Electronic applications accepted. *Expenses: Contact institution. Financial support:* Research assistantships, teaching assistantships, Federal Work-Study and institutionally sponsored loans available. Support available to part-time students. Financial award applicants required to submit FAFSA. *Faculty research:* HIV/AIDS, health promotion/disease prevention, health policies, advanced practice, urban health. *Unit head:* Dr. Mary O'Neil Mundinger, Dean, 212-305-3582. *Application contact:* Judy Wolfe, Director of Admissions, 800-899-8895, E-mail: nursing@columbia.edu.

See Close-Up on page 1951.

Concordia University Wisconsin, Graduate Programs, School of Health and Human Services, Program in Nursing, Mequon, WI 53097-2402. Offers family nurse practitioner (MSN); geriatric nurse practitioner (MSN); nurse educator (MSN). *Accreditation:* AACN. Postbaccalaureate distance learning degree programs offered (minimal on-campus study). *Faculty:* 2 full-time (1 woman), 5 part-time/adjunct (all women). *Students:* 217 (199 women). Average age 29. In 2006, 37 degrees awarded. *Degree requirements:* For master's, thesis or alternative, comprehensive exam. *Entrance requirements:* Additional exam requirements/recommendations for international students: Required—TOEFL. *Application deadline:* For fall admission, 8/1 priority date for domestic students. Applications are processed on a rolling basis. Application fee: $35. *Expenses: Contact institution. Financial support:* Application deadline: 8/1. *Unit head:* Dr. Ruth Gresley, Director, 262-243-4452, E-mail: ruth.gresley@cuw.edu.

Coppin State University, Division of Graduate Studies, Helene Fuld School of Nursing, Baltimore, MD 21216-3698. Offers family nurse practitioner (PMC); nursing (MSN). *Accreditation:* NLN. Part-time and evening/weekend programs available. *Faculty:* 4 full-time (all women), 5 part-time/adjunct (4 women). *Students:* 25 full-time (23 women), 5 part-time (all women); includes 26 minority (all African Americans), 2 international. Average age 36. 20 applicants, 85% accepted, 13 enrolled. In 2006, 15 degrees awarded. *Degree requirements:* For master's, thesis, clinical internship, comprehensive exam, registration. *Entrance requirements:* For master's, GRE, bachelor's degree in nursing, interview, minimum GPA of 3.0, RN license. Additional exam requirements/recommendations for international students: Required—TOEFL (minimum score 550 paper-based). *Application deadline:* For fall admission, 5/30 for domestic students. Applications are processed on a rolling basis. Application fee: $45. *Financial support:* Career-related internships or fieldwork, Federal Work-Study, institutionally sponsored loans, and scholarships/grants available. Support available to part-time students. Financial award application deadline: 6/30; financial award applicants required to submit FAFSA. *Unit head:* Dr. Marcella Copes, Dean, 410-951-3991, Fax: 410-462-3032, E-mail: mcopes@coppin.edu.

Creighton University, School of Nursing, Omaha, NE 68178-0001. Offers MS. *Accreditation:* AACN. Part-time programs available. Postbaccalaureate distance learning degree programs offered (minimal on-campus study). *Faculty:* 16 full-time (all women), 1 (woman) part-time/adjunct. *Students:* 35 full-time (31 women), 35 part-time (32 women); includes 4 minority (1 African American, 1 Asian American or Pacific Islander, 2 Hispanic Americans). Average age 35. 33 applicants, 91% accepted, 27 enrolled. In 2006, 24 degrees awarded. *Median time to degree:* Master's–2 years full-time, 4 years part-time. *Degree requirements:* For master's, capstone project, thesis optional. *Entrance requirements:* For master's, BSN, minimum GPA of 3.0, RN license. Additional exam requirements/recommendations for international students: Required—TOEFL (minimum score 600 paper-based; 250 computer-based; 100 iBT). *Application deadline:* For fall admission, 3/15 priority date for domestic and international students; for spring admission, 10/15 priority date for domestic and international students. Applications are processed on a rolling basis. Application fee: $40. Electronic applications accepted. *Expenses:* Tuition: Part-time $595 per credit hour. Required fees: $38 per semester. *Financial support:* Career-related internships or fieldwork, Federal Work-Study, institutionally sponsored loans, and traineeships available. Financial award applicants required to submit FAFSA. *Faculty research:* Hereditary cancer family adaptation, osteoporosis prevention, partnering with high-risk clients, obesity prevention in children, participatory action research with a Native American tribe, evaluation of simulated clinical experiences. *Unit head:* Dr. Eleanor V. Howell, Dean, 402-280-2004, Fax: 402-280-2045, E-mail: howell@creighton.edu. *Application contact:* Dr. Mary Kunes-Connell, Associate Dean for Academic and Clinical Affairs, 402-280-2024, Fax: 402-280-2045, E-mail: mkc@creighton.edu.

Daemen College, Department of Nursing, Amherst, NY 14226-3592. Offers adult nurse practitioner (MS, Certificate); nursing executive leadership (MS); palliative care nursing (MS, Certificate). *Accreditation:* NLN. Part-time programs available. *Faculty:* 2 full-time (both women), 2 part-time/adjunct (both women). *Students:* 13 full-time (12 women), 63 part-time (59 women); includes 12 minority (10 African Americans, 1 Asian American or Pacific Islander, 1 Hispanic American), 3 international. Average age 41. 36 applicants, 58% accepted, 18 enrolled. In 2006, 9 degrees awarded. *Degree requirements:* For master's, thesis or alternative. *Entrance requirements:* For master's, 1 year medical/surgical experiences, minimum GPA of 3.25, state nursing license and registration, 1 course in statistics. Additional exam requirements/recommendations for international students: Required—TOEFL (minimum score 500 paper-based; 173 computer-based). *Application deadline:* For fall admission, 3/1 priority date for domestic and international students; for spring admission, 10/1 priority date for domestic and international students. Applications are processed on a rolling basis. Application fee: $25. Electronic applications accepted. *Expenses:* Tuition: Full-time $11,700; part-time $650 per credit hour. Required fees: $15 per credit hour. Tuition and fees vary according to course load. *Financial support:* Institutionally sponsored loans and scholarships/grants available. Financial award application deadline: 2/15; financial award applicants required to submit FAFSA. *Faculty research:* Professional stress, client behavior, drug therapy, treatment modalities and pulmonary cancers, chemical dependency. *Unit head:* Dr. Mary Lou Rusin, Chair, 716-839-8387, Fax: 716-839-8403, E-mail: mrusin@daemen.edu. *Application contact:* Karl Shallowhorn, Associate Director of Graduate Admissions, 716-839-8225, Fax: 716-839-8229, E-mail: kshallow@daemen.edu.

Dalhousie University, Faculty of Graduate Studies, Faculty of Health Professions, School of Nursing, Halifax, NS B3H 4R2, Canada. Offers MN, MN/MHSA. Part-time programs available. Postbaccalaureate distance learning degree programs offered (minimal on-campus study). *Degree requirements:* For master's, thesis optional. *Entrance requirements:* For master's, GRE General Test, minimum GPA of 3.0. Additional exam requirements/recommendations for international students: Required—TOEFL. *Faculty research:* Coping, social support, health promotion, aging, feminist studies.

Delta State University, Graduate Programs, School of Nursing, Cleveland, MS 38733-0001. Offers MSN. *Accreditation:* AACN. Part-time programs available. *Faculty:* 3 full-time (all women), 2 part-time/adjunct (1 woman). *Students:* 35 full-time (all women), 26 part-time (23 women); includes 20 minority (all African Americans) Average age 41. In 2006, 15 degrees awarded. *Degree requirements:* For master's, thesis optional. *Entrance requirements:* For master's, GRE General Test. *Application deadline:* For fall admission, 8/1 priority date for domestic students; for spring admission, 12/1 priority date for domestic students. Applications are processed on a rolling basis. Application fee: $0. Electronic applications accepted. *Financial support:* Research assistantships, career-related internships or fieldwork, Federal Work-Study, and institutionally sponsored loans available. Financial award application deadline: 6/1. *Unit head:* Dr. Lizabeth Carlson, Dean, 662-846-4268, Fax: 662-846-4267, E-mail: lcarlson@deltastate.edu.

DePaul University, College of Liberal Arts and Sciences, Department of Nursing, Chicago, IL 60604-2287. Offers advanced practice nursing (MS); masters entry into nursing practice (MS); nurse anesthesia (MS). MS in nurse anesthesia offered jointly with Ravenswood Hospital Medical Center. *Accreditation:* AACN; AANA/CANAEP. *Faculty:* 13 full-time (10 women), 10 part-time/adjunct (all women). *Students:* 128 full-time (107 women), 36 part-time (31 women); includes 43 minority (19 African Americans, 2 American Indian/Alaska Native, 16 Asian Americans or Pacific Islanders, 6 Hispanic Americans), 2 international. Average age 39. 80 applicants, 100% accepted. In 2006, 9 master's awarded. *Degree requirements:* For master's, thesis optional. *Entrance requirements:* For master's, GRE, BSN, minimum GPA of 2.85, RN license. Application fee: $25. *Financial support:* In 2006–07, 5 fellowships (averaging $2,000 per year) were awarded; traineeships also available. *Faculty research:* Children's health, women's health, health promotion. *Unit head:* Dr. Susan Poslusny, Chair, 773-325-7280, Fax: 773-325-7282, E-mail: sposlusn@wppost.depaul.edu. *Application contact:* Christine Werdrick, Coordinator of Student Academic Services and Department Operations, 773-325-7280, Fax: 773-325-7282, E-mail: cwerdric@depaul.edu.

DeSales University, Graduate Division, Programs in Nursing, Center Valley, PA 18034-9568. Offers adult advanced practice nurse specialist (MSN); family nurse practitioner (MSN); nurse educator (MSN); MSN/MBA. *Accreditation:* NLN. Part-time and evening/weekend programs available. In 2006, 9 degrees awarded. *Degree requirements:* For master's, thesis optional. *Entrance requirements:* For master's, GRE General Test, MAT, minimum B average in undergraduate course work, health assessment course or equivalent, course work in statistics. *Application deadline:* For spring admission, 3/15 for domestic students. Applications are processed on a rolling basis. Application fee: $35. *Expenses: Contact institution. Financial support:* In 2006–07, 1 student received support. Unspecified assistantships available. Support available to part-time students. Financial award applicants required to submit FAFSA. *Faculty research:* Women's health, theory validation, needs of homeless, behavior risk evaluation, wound healing. *Unit head:* Dr. Carol Gullo Mest, Director, 610-282-1100 Ext. 1394, Fax: 610-282-2254, E-mail: carol.mest@desales.edu. *Application contact:* Megan Szivos, Secretary for MSN Program, 610-282-1100 Ext. 1664, Fax: 610-282-2254, E-mail: megan.szivos@desales.edu.

Dominican College, Division of Nursing, Department of Nursing, Orangeburg, NY 10962-1210. Offers family nurse practitioner (MSN). *Accreditation:* AACN. Part-time and evening/weekend programs available. *Faculty:* 6. *Students:* 6 full-time (all women), 31 part-time (26 women); includes 18 minority (8 African Americans, 6 Asian Americans or Pacific Islanders, 4 Hispanic Americans). Average age 40. In 2006, 5 degrees awarded. *Entrance requirements:* For master's, bachelor's degree in nursing, minimum GPA of 3.0, RN license, 1 year of nursing experience, 3 letters of recommendation. Additional exam requirements/recommendations for international students: Required—TOEFL (minimum score 550 paper-based; 213 computer-based). *Application deadline:* Applications are processed on a rolling basis. Application fee: $50. *Financial support:* Applicants required to submit FAFSA. *Unit head:* Lynn Weissman, Program Director, 845-848-6026, Fax: 845-398-4891, E-mail: lynn.weissman@dc.edu. *Application contact:* Director of Admissions, 845-848-7900, Fax: 845-365-3150, E-mail: admissions@dc.edu.

Dominican University of California, Graduate Programs, School of Arts and Sciences, Program in Nursing, San Rafael, CA 94901-2298. Offers geriatric and nurse educator (MS); integrated health practices (MS). *Accreditation:* AACN. Part-time and evening/weekend programs available. *Degree requirements:* For master's, thesis, registration. *Entrance* *requirements:* For master's, minimum GPA of 3.0, clinical experience, course work in nursing research and statistics, CPR certification, professional liability and malpractice insurance, interview. Additional exam requirements/recommendations for international students: Required—TOEFL (minimum score 550 paper-based; 213 computer-based). Electronic applications accepted.

Drexel University, College of Nursing and Health Professions, Graduate Nursing Program, Philadelphia, PA 19104-2875. Offers MSN. *Accreditation:* AACN; NLN. Electronic applications accepted.

Duke University, School of Nursing, Program in Nursing, Durham, NC 27708-0586. Offers PhD. *Faculty:* 31 full-time (27 women). *Students:* 5 full-time (4 women); includes 1 African American, 1 American Indian/Alaska Native, 1 Asian American or Pacific Islander. 22 applicants, 23% accepted, 5 enrolled. *Degree requirements:* For doctorate, thesis/dissertation, comprehensive exam, registration. *Entrance requirements:* For doctorate, GRE General Test. Additional exam requirements/recommendations for international students: Required—TOEFL (minimum score 550 paper-based; 213 computer-based; 83 iBT), IELTS (minimum score 7). *Application deadline:* For fall admission, 12/31 for domestic and international students. Application fee: $75. Electronic applications accepted. *Financial support:* In 2006–07, 5 fellowships (averaging $17,000 per year) were awarded; institutionally sponsored loans, scholarships/grants, and health care benefits also available. *Faculty research:* Nursing management practices, adolescents and families undergoing intense treatments, psychosocial and chronic disease. Total annual research expenditures: $3.5 million. *Unit head:* Ruth A. Anderson, Director of Graduate Studies, 919-668-4599, Fax: 919-681-8899, E-mail: nursingphd@mc.duke.edu. *Application contact:* Revonda P. Huppert, Program Coordinator, 919-668-4797, Fax: 919-681-8899, E-mail: huppert@duke.edu.

Duquesne University, School of Nursing, Doctoral Program in Nursing, Pittsburgh, PA 15282-0001. Offers PhD. Part-time and evening/weekend programs available. Postbaccalaureate distance learning degree programs offered (minimal on-campus study). *Faculty:* 12 full-time (11 women), 1 part-time/adjunct (0 women). *Students:* 25 full-time (21 women), 40 part-time (37 women); includes 5 minority (3 African Americans, 1 American Indian/Alaska Native, 1 Asian American or Pacific Islander). 23 applicants, 43% accepted, 10 enrolled. In 2006, 10 degrees awarded. *Degree requirements:* For doctorate, thesis/dissertation, preliminary exam. *Entrance requirements:* For doctorate, GRE General Test, bachelor's degree in nursing, master's degree in nursing with pre-requisite in nursing theory research methods, 6 graduate credits in statistics. Additional exam requirements/recommendations for international students: Required—TOEFL (minimum score 550 paper-based; 250 computer-based). *Application deadline:* For fall admission, 2/1 for domestic and international students. Application fee: $50. *Expenses:* *Contact institution.* Tuition and fees vary according to degree level and program. *Financial support:* In 2006–07, 9 students received support, including 4 research assistantships with tuition reimbursements available (averaging $1,600 per year); teaching assistantships with partial tuition reimbursements available, institutionally sponsored loans, traineeships, and unspecified assistantships also available. Financial award application deadline: 8/20; financial award applicants required to submit FAFSA. *Faculty research:* Vulnerable underserved populations, ethics, health disparities, community based, forensics. *Unit head:* Dr. Joan Such Lockhart, Professor and Associate Dean of Academic Affairs, 412-396-6540, Fax: 412-396-1821, E-mail: lockhart@duq.edu. *Application contact:* Susan Hardner, Nurse Recruiter, 412-396-4945, Fax: 412-396-6346, E-mail: nursing@duq.edu.

Duquesne University, School of Nursing, Master's Program in Nursing, Pittsburgh, PA 15282-0001. Offers acute care nursing (Post-Master's Certificate); acute care nursing specialist (MSN); family nurse practitioner (MSN, Post-Master's Certificate); forensic nursing (MSN, Post-Master's Certificate); nursing administration (MSN, Post-Master's Certificate); nursing education (MSN, Post-Master's Certificate); psychiatric/mental health nursing (MSN, Post-Master's Certificate); MSN/MBA. *Accreditation:* AACN. Part-time and evening/weekend programs available. Postbaccalaureate distance learning degree programs offered (minimal on-campus study). *Faculty:* 20 full-time (19 women), 4 part-time/adjunct (all women). *Students:* 73 full-time (70 women), 83 part-time (79 women); includes 11 minority (4 African Americans, 3 American Indian/Alaska Native, 1 Asian American or Pacific Islander, 3 Hispanic Americans). 72 applicants, 75% accepted, 49 enrolled. In 2006, 20 master's, 11 other advanced degrees awarded. *Degree requirements:* For master's, culminating paper. *Entrance requirements:* For master's, MAT or GRE, 1 year of work experience, bachelor's degree in nursing, undergraduate course work in statistics, health assessment course (family nurse practitioner, nursing education, acute care clinical nurse specialist). *Application deadline:* For fall admission, 4/1 for domestic and international students; for spring admission, 11/1 for domestic and international students. Applications are processed on a rolling basis. Application fee: $50. *Expenses:* *Contact institution.* Tuition and fees vary according to degree level and program. *Financial support:* In 2006–07, 10 students received support, including 9 research assistantships with partial tuition reimbursements available (averaging $1,600 per year), 1 teaching assistantship with partial tuition reimbursement available (averaging $1,600 per year); fellowships with partial tuition reimbursements available, institutionally sponsored loans, scholarships/grants, traineeships, and tuition waivers (partial) also available. Financial award application deadline: 8/20. *Faculty research:* Depression, culture, vulnerable populations, ethics, health disparities, community based. Total annual research expenditures: $377,400. *Unit head:* Dr. Joan Such Lockhart, Professor and Associate Dean of Academic Affairs, 412-396-6540, Fax: 412-396-1821, E-mail: lockhart@duq.edu. *Application contact:* Susan Hardner, Nurse Recruiter, 412-396-4945, Fax: 412-396-6346, E-mail: nursing@duq.edu.

D'Youville College, Department of Nursing, Buffalo, NY 14201-1084. Offers community health nursing/education (MSN); community health nursing/high risk parents and children (MSN); community health nursing/management (MSN); family nurse practitioner (MS); nursing and health-related professions (Certificate); nursing with clinical focus choice (MSN). *Accreditation:* AACN. Part-time and evening/weekend programs available. *Faculty:* 26 full-time (all women), 7 part-time/adjunct (6 women). *Students:* 77 full-time (72 women), 101 part-time (95 women); includes 17 minority (12 African Americans, 1 American Indian/Alaska Native, 4 Hispanic Americans), 89 international. Average age 36. 177 applicants, 58% accepted, 37 enrolled. In 2006, 41 master's, 2 other advanced degrees awarded. *Degree requirements:* For master's, membership on board of community agency, publishable paper, thesis optional. *Entrance requirements:* For master's, BS in nursing, minimum GPA of 3.0, course work in statistics and computers. Additional exam requirements/recommendations for international students: Required—TOEFL (minimum score 500 paper-based; 173 computer-based). *Application deadline:* For fall admission, 5/1 priority date for international students; for spring admission, 9/1 priority date for international students. Applications are processed on a rolling basis. Application fee: $25. Electronic applications accepted. *Financial support:* In 2006–07, 1 research assistantship with partial tuition reimbursement (averaging $3,000 per year) was awarded; Federal Work-Study and scholarships/grants also available. Support available to part-time students. Financial award application deadline: 3/1; financial award applicants required to submit FAFSA. *Faculty research:* Nursing curriculum, nursing theory-testing, wellness research, communication and socialization patterns. *Unit head:* Dr. Verna Kieffer, Chair, 716-829-7613, Fax: 716-829-8159. *Application contact:* Linda Fisher, Graduate Admissions Director, 716-829-8400, Fax: 716-829-7900, E-mail: graduateadmissions@dyc.edu.

See Close-Up on page 1953.

East Carolina University, Graduate School, School of Nursing, Greenville, NC 27858-4353. Offers MSN, PhD. *Accreditation:* AANA/CANAEP (one or more programs are accredited); ACNM/DOA (one or more programs are accredited); NLN. Part-time programs available. *Faculty:* 31 full-time (27 women). *Students:* 122 full-time (112 women), 254 part-time (230 women); includes 47 minority (39 African Americans, 3 American Indian/Alaska Native, 3 Asian Americans or Pacific Islanders, 2 Hispanic Americans), 2 international. Average age 36. 79 applicants, 27% accepted, 20 enrolled. In 2006, 56 master's, 4 doctorates awarded. *Degree requirements:* For master's, thesis optional. *Entrance requirements:* For master's, GRE General Test or MAT, bachelor's degree in nursing, professional license, minimum B average in nursing. *Application deadline:* For fall admission, 6/1 priority date for domestic students. Applications are processed on a rolling basis. Application fee: $50. *Financial support:* Research assistantships with partial tuition reimbursements, teaching assistantships with partial tuition reimbursements, Federal Work-Study available. Support available to part-time students. Financial award application deadline: 6/1. *Unit head:* Dr. Sylvia Brown, Interim Dean, 252-744-6427, Fax: 252-328-4300. *Application contact:* Dean of Graduate School, 252-328-6012, Fax: 252-328-6071, E-mail: gradschool@ecu.edu.

Eastern Kentucky University, The Graduate School, College of Health Sciences, Department of Nursing, Richmond, KY 40475-3102. Offers rural community health care (MSN); rural health family nurse practitioner (MSN). *Accreditation:* AACN. *Faculty:* 15 full-time (14 women), 1 part-time/adjunct (0 women). *Students:* 24 full-time (all women), 75 part-time (65 women). Average age 37. 71 applicants, 41% accepted, 27 enrolled. In 2006, 33 degrees awarded. *Entrance requirements:* For master's, GRE General Test, minimum GPA of 2.75. Application fee: $35. *Expenses:* Tuition, state resident: full-time $5,610. Tuition, nonresident: full-time $15,910. *Unit head:* Dr. Deborah Whitehouse, Chair, 859-622-1956, Fax: 859-622-1972.

Eastern Washington University, Graduate Studies, Intercollegiate College of Nursing, Cheney, WA 99004-2431. Offers MN. *Degree requirements:* For master's, thesis, comprehensive exam. *Entrance requirements:* For master's, GRE General Test, minimum GPA of 3.0.

East Tennessee State University, School of Graduate Studies, College of Nursing, Johnson City, TN 37614. Offers advanced nursing practice (Post Master's Certificate); health care management (Certificate); nursing (MSN, DSN). *Accreditation:* AACN. Part-time programs available. *Degree requirements:* For master's, thesis optional. *Entrance requirements:* For master's, GRE General Test, minimum GPA of 3.0, bachelor's degree in nursing, current RN license. Additional exam requirements/recommendations for international students: Required—TOEFL (minimum score 550 paper-based; 213 computer-based). *Faculty research:* Rural primary care, health care for the homeless, community health problems across the lifespan, nursing education research, school health services.

Edgewood College, Program in Nursing, Madison, WI 53711-1997. Offers MS. *Accreditation:* AACN. *Students:* 1 (woman) full-time, 35 part-time (30 women), 1 international. Average age 41. In 2006, 11 degrees awarded. *Degree requirements:* For master's, practicum, research project. *Entrance requirements:* For master's, minimum GPA of 3.0. Additional exam requirements/recommendations for international students: Required—TOEFL. *Application deadline:* For fall admission, 8/24 priority date for domestic students, 8/1 for international students; for spring admission, 1/10 priority date for domestic students, 10/1 for international students. Applications are processed on a rolling basis. Application fee: $25. Electronic applications accepted. *Unit head:* Dr. Margaret Noreuil, Chair, 608-663-2820, Fax: 608-663-3291, E-mail: mnoreuil@edgewood.edu. *Application contact:* Paula O'Malley, Graduate Student Admissions Counselor, 608-663-2282, Fax: 608-663-3291, E-mail: gradprograms@edgewood.edu.

Edinboro University of Pennsylvania, Graduate Studies and Research, School of Science, Management and Technology, Department of Nursing, Edinboro, PA 16444. Offers family nurse practitioner (MSN). *Accreditation:* NLN. Part-time and evening/weekend programs available. *Faculty:* 1 (woman) full-time. *Students:* Average age 41. *Degree requirements:* For master's, thesis, competency exam. *Entrance requirements:* For master's, GRE or MAT, minimum QPA of 2.5. *Application deadline:* Applications are processed on a rolling basis. Application fee: $30. Electronic applications accepted. *Expenses:* Tuition, state resident: full-time $6,048; part-time $336 per credit. Tuition, nonresident: full-time $9,678; part-time $538 per credit. Required fees: $1,849; $42 per credit. *Financial support:* In 2006–07, 1 research assistantship with full and partial tuition reimbursement (averaging $3,850 per year) was awarded; career-related internships or fieldwork, Federal Work-Study, scholarships/grants, and unspecified assistantships also available. Support available to part-time students. Financial award application deadline: 2/15; financial award applicants required to submit FAFSA. *Unit head:* Ellen Pfadt, Acting Chairperson, 814-732-1128, Fax: 814-732-2536, E-mail: epfadt@edinboro.edu. *Application contact:* Dr. R. Scott Baldwin, Dean, 814-732-2752, Fax: 814-732-2268, E-mail: sbaldwin@edinboro.edu.

Elmhurst College, Graduate Programs, Program in Nursing, Elmhurst, IL 60126-3296. Offers MSN. *Accreditation:* AACN. Part-time and evening/weekend programs available. *Faculty:* 2 full-time (both women). *Students:* Average age 43. 15 applicants, 73% accepted, 10 enrolled. *Entrance requirements:* For master's, 3 recommendations. Additional exam requirements/recommendations for international students: Required—TOEFL (minimum score 550 paper-based; 213 computer-based). *Application deadline:* Applications are processed on a rolling basis. Application fee: $25. Electronic applications accepted. *Expenses:* Tuition: Part-time $781 per hour. Required fees: $75 per hour. Part-time tuition and fees vary according to course load and student level. *Financial support:* In 2006–07, 3 students received support. Federal Work-Study and scholarships/grants available. Support available to part-time students. Financial award application deadline: 6/1; financial award applicants required to submit FAFSA. *Application contact:* Elizabeth D. Kuebler, Director of Adult and Graduate Admission, 630-617-3069, Fax: 630-617-5501, E-mail: betsyk@elmhurst.edu.

Emory University, Graduate School of Arts and Sciences, Program in Nursing, Atlanta, GA 30322-1100. Offers PhD. *Accreditation:* AACN. *Degree requirements:* For doctorate, thesis/dissertation, comprehensive exam, registration. *Entrance requirements:* For doctorate, GRE General Test. Additional exam requirements/recommendations for international students: Required—TOEFL. Electronic applications accepted. *Expenses:* Tuition: Full-time $30,246. *Faculty research:* Symptoms, self management, care-giving, biobehavioral approaches, women's health.

Emory University, Nell Hodgson Woodruff School of Nursing, Atlanta, GA 30322-1100. Offers adult and elder health advanced practice nursing (MSN), including acute and critical care, adult nurse practitioner, gerontology, oncology; emergency nurse practitioner (MSN); family nurse practitioner (MSN); family nurse-midwife (MSN); leadership in healthcare (MSN); nurse midwifery (MSN); nursing administration (MSN); pediatric advanced nursing practice (MSN); public health nursing (MSN); women's health nurse practitioner (MSN); MSN/MPH. *Accreditation:* AACN; ACNM/DOA (one or more programs are accredited). Part-time programs available. *Entrance requirements:* For master's, GRE General Test or MAT, minimum GPA of 3.0, BS in nursing, RN license and additional course work, 3 letters of recommendation. Additional exam requirements/recommendations for international students: Required—TOEFL (minimum score 600 paper-based; 250 computer-based). Electronic applications accepted. Expenses: Contact institution. *Faculty research:* Older adult falls and injuries, minority health issues, cardiac symptoms amd quality of life, bio-ethics and decision making, menopausal issues.

See Close-Up on page 1955.

Excelsior College, School of Nursing, Albany, NY 12203-5159. Offers clinical systems management (MS); nursing (MS). *Accreditation:* NLN. Part-time and evening/weekend programs available. Postbaccalaureate distance learning degree programs offered (no on-campus study). *Faculty:* 3 full-time (all women), 21 part-time/adjunct (19 women). *Students:* 16 full-time (12 women), 116 part-time (96 women); includes 20 minority (11 African Americans, 1 American Indian/Alaska Native, 5 Asian Americans or Pacific Islanders, 3 Hispanic Americans). Average age 45. 53 applicants, 92% accepted, 48 enrolled. In 2006, 8 degrees awarded. *Entrance requirements:* For master's, RN license. *Application deadline:* Applications are processed on a rolling basis. Application fee: $100. Electronic applications accepted. *Expenses:* Tuition: Part-time $365 per credit hour. *Financial support:* In 2006–07, 20 students received support. Scholarships/grants and traineeships available. Support available to part-time students. Financial award application deadline: 8/26. *Faculty research:* Leadership development, test anxiety, use of technology in online learning. *Unit head:* Dr. Patricia Ann Edwards, Director, Graduate Program in Nursing/Associate Dean, 518-464-8500, Fax: 518-464-8777, E-mail: msn@excelsior.

Nursing—General

Excelsior College (continued)

edu. *Application contact:* Christine McIlwraith, Graduate Advisor, 518-464-8500, Fax: 518-464-8777, E-mail: nursingmasters@excelsior.edu.

Fairfield University, School of Nursing, Fairfield, CT 06824-5195. Offers adult nurse practitioner (MSN, PMC); family nurse practitioner (MSN, PMC); healthcare management (MSN); nurse anesthesia (MSN); psychiatric nurse practitioner (MSN, PMC). *Accreditation:* AACN; AANA/CANAEP. Part-time programs available. *Faculty:* 13 full-time (12 women), 2 part-time/adjunct (both women). *Students:* 3 full-time (all women), 39 part-time (all women); includes 5 minority (2 African Americans, 3 Asian Americans or Pacific Islanders). Average age 42. 23 applicants, 30% accepted, 3 enrolled. In 2006, 9 degrees awarded. *Degree requirements:* For master's, capstone project. *Entrance requirements:* For master's, MAT or GRE, minimum QPA of 3.0, RN license, resumé, 2 recommendations; for PMC, 1 year of work experience as a registered nurse. Additional exam requirements/recommendations for international students: Required—TOEFL (minimum score 550 paper-based; 213 computer-based; 79 iBT). *Application deadline:* For fall admission, 4/1 priority date for domestic students, 6/15 priority date for international students; for spring admission, 11/1 priority date for domestic students, 10/15 priority date for international students. Applications are processed on a rolling basis. Application fee: $55. *Expenses:* Contact institution. *Financial support:* Traineeships available. Financial award applicants required to submit FAFSA. *Faculty research:* Critical care, nursing outcomes, care of older adults, leadership, community health. *Unit head:* Dr. Jeanne M. Novotny, Dean, 203-254-4000 Ext. 2701, Fax: 203-254-4126, E-mail: jnovotny@mail.fairfield.edu. *Application contact:* Marianne Gumpper, Director of Graduate and Continuing Studies Admissions, 203-254-4184, Fax: 203-254-4073, E-mail: gradadmis@mail.fairfield.edu.

Fairleigh Dickinson University, Metropolitan Campus, University College: Arts, Sciences, and Professional Studies, Henry P. Becton School of Nursing and Allied Health, Program in Nursing, Teaneck, NJ 07666-1914. Offers MSN, Certificate. *Accreditation:* AACN. *Students:* Average age 43. 33 applicants, 82% accepted, 19 enrolled. In 2006, 11 degrees awarded. *Application deadline:* Applications are processed on a rolling basis. Application fee: $40. *Unit head:* Dr. Minerva Guttman, Director, Henry P. Becton School of Nursing and Allied Health, 201-692-2000.

Felician College, Program in Advanced Practice Nursing, Lodi, NJ 07644-2117. Offers adult nurse practitioner (MSN, PMC); family nurse practitioner (MSN, PMC); school nurse/teacher of health education (Certificate). *Accreditation:* AACN. Part-time and evening/weekend programs available. Postbaccalaureate distance learning degree programs offered (no on-campus study). *Students:* 29 applicants, 90% accepted, 24 enrolled. *Degree requirements:* For master's, scholarly project. *Entrance requirements:* For master's, BS in nursing or equivalent, minimum GPA of 3.0, 2 letters of recommendation, RN license; for other advanced degree, RN license, minimum GPA of 2.75. Additional exam requirements/recommendations for international students: Recommended—TOEFL (minimum score 550 paper-based; 213 computer-based). *Application deadline:* Applications are processed on a rolling basis. Application fee: $40. *Expenses:* Tuition: Part-time $675 per credit. Tuition and fees vary according to program. *Financial support:* In 2006–07, 10 students received support. Traineeships available. Financial award applicants required to submit FAFSA. *Faculty research:* Anxiety and fear, curriculum innovation, health promotion. *Unit head:* Dr. Muriel Shore, Dean, Division of Health Sciences, 201-559-6030, E-mail: shorem@inet.felician.edu. *Application contact:* Wendy Lin-Cook, Director of Adult and Graduate Admission, 201-559-6077, Fax: 201-559-6138, E-mail: adultandgraduate@felician.edu.

See Close-Up on page 1957.

Ferris State University, College of Allied Health Sciences, School of Nursing, Big Rapids, MI 49307. Offers nursing (MS); nursing administration (MS); nursing education (MS); nursing informatics (MS). Part-time and evening/weekend programs available. Postbaccalaureate distance learning degree programs offered (minimal on-campus study). *Faculty:* 2 full-time (1 woman). *Students:* Average age 39. 22 applicants, 100% accepted, 22 enrolled. In 2006, 2 degrees awarded. *Median time to degree:* Master's–3 years part-time. *Degree requirements:* For master's, thesis, practicum, comprehensive exam. *Entrance requirements:* For master's, BS in nursing, writing sample, letters of reference, 2 years clinical experience. Additional exam requirements/recommendations for international students: Required—TOEFL (minimum score 550 paper-based). *Application deadline:* For fall admission, 8/26 for domestic students; for winter admission, 12/16 for domestic students. Applications are processed on a rolling basis. Application fee: $30. Electronic applications accepted. *Expenses:* Tuition, state resident: part-time $355 per credit hour. Tuition, nonresident: part-time $687 per credit hour. *Financial support:* In 2006–07, 3 students received support. Scholarships/grants available. *Faculty research:* Nursing education-minority student focus student attitudes toward aging. *Unit head:* Dr. Julie A. Coon, Director, 231-591-2267, Fax: 231-591-2325, E-mail: coonj@ferris.edu.

Florida Agricultural and Mechanical University, Division of Graduate Studies, Research, and Continuing Education, School of Nursing, Tallahassee, FL 32307-3200. Offers MS. *Accreditation:* NLN. *Entrance requirements:* Additional exam requirements/recommendations for international students: Required—TOEFL.

Florida Atlantic University, College of Nursing, Boca Raton, FL 33431-0991. Offers MS, DNS, Post Master's Certificate. *Accreditation:* AACN. Part-time programs available. *Faculty:* 20 full-time (19 women), 13 part-time/adjunct (10 women). *Students:* 76 full-time (72 women), 213 part-time (197 women); includes 107 minority (63 African Americans, 15 Asian Americans or Pacific Islanders, 29 Hispanic Americans), 4 international. Average age 40. 134 applicants, 60% accepted, 72 enrolled. In 2006, 81 master's, 4 doctorates awarded. *Degree requirements:* For master's, thesis or alternative; for doctorate, thesis/dissertation, comprehensive exam. *Entrance requirements:* For master's, GRE General Test, bachelor's degree in nursing, Florida RN license, minimum GPA of 3.0; for doctorate, GRE General Test, curriculum vitae, Florida RN license, minimum GPA of 3.5, MS in nursing. *Application deadline:* For fall admission, 6/2 for domestic students; for spring admission, 10/20 for domestic students. Applications are processed on a rolling basis. Application fee: $30. *Expenses:* Tuition, area resident: Full-time $4,394. Tuition, nonresident: full-time $16,441. *Financial support:* In 2006–07, 62 students received support, including 11 research assistantships with partial tuition reimbursements available, 6 teaching assistantships with partial tuition reimbursements available; career-related internships or fieldwork, Federal Work-Study, institutionally sponsored loans, scholarships/grants, and traineeships also available. Support available to part-time students. *Faculty research:* Econometrics of nurse-patient relationship, Alzheimer's disease, community-based programs, falls, self-healing. *Unit head:* Dr. Anne Boykin, Dean, 561-297-3206, Fax: 561-297-3687, E-mail: boykina@acc.fau.edu. *Application contact:* Dr. Lynne M. Dunphy, Graduate Coordinator, 561-297-3261, Fax: 561-297-0088, E-mail: ldunphy@fau.edu.

Florida Gulf Coast University, College of Health Professions, School of Nursing, Fort Myers, FL 33965-6565. Offers MSN. *Accreditation:* AACN; AANA/CANAEP. Part-time programs available. *Faculty:* 42 full-time (35 women), 21 part-time/adjunct (14 women). *Students:* 50 full-time (35 women), 10 part-time (all women); includes 9 minority (3 African Americans, 2 American Indian/Alaska Native, 3 Asian Americans or Pacific Islanders, 1 Hispanic American). Average age 36. 16 applicants, 88% accepted, 12 enrolled. In 2006, 41 degrees awarded. *Degree requirements:* For master's, thesis or alternative. *Entrance requirements:* For master's, GRE General Test, MAT, minimum GPA of 3.0. Additional exam requirements/recommendations for international students: Required—TOEFL (minimum score 550 paper-based; 213 computer-based). *Application deadline:* For fall admission, 4/15 priority date for domestic students; for spring admission, 8/1 for domestic students. Applications are processed on a rolling basis. Application fee: $30. Electronic applications accepted. *Expenses:* Tuition, state resident: full-time $4,326. Tuition, nonresident: full-time $18,523. Required fees: $1,211. One-time fee: $5 full-time. *Faculty research:* Gerontology, community health, ethical and legal aspects of health care, critical care. *Unit head:* Dr. Peg Gray-Vickrey, Interim Director, 239-590-1094, Fax: 239-590-7474, E-mail: mgrayvic@fgcu.edu.

Florida International University, College of Nursing and Health Sciences, School of Nursing, Miami, FL 33199. Offers MSN, PhD. *Accreditation:* AANA/CANAEP; NLN. Part-time programs available. *Faculty:* 30 full-time (25 women), 2 part-time/adjunct (1 woman). *Students:* 119 full-time (79 women), 109 part-time (83 women); includes 152 minority (45 African Americans, 19 Asian Americans or Pacific Islanders, 88 Hispanic Americans). Average age 38. 157 applicants, 28% accepted, 31 enrolled. In 2006, 69 degrees awarded. *Degree requirements:* For master's, thesis. *Entrance requirements:* For master's, GRE General Test, bachelor's degree in nursing, minimum GPA of 3.0. Additional exam requirements/recommendations for international students: Required—TOEFL. *Application deadline:* For fall admission, 4/1 priority date for domestic students; for spring admission, 10/1 for domestic students. Applications are processed on a rolling basis. Application fee: $25. *Expenses:* Tuition, state resident: part-time $249 per credit hour. Tuition, nonresident: part-time $753 per credit hour. Tuition and fees vary according to program. *Faculty research:* Adult health nursing. *Unit head:* Dr. Divina Grossman, Dean, 305-919-5301, Fax: 305-919-5395, E-mail: divina.grossman@fiu.edu.

See Close-Up on page 1959.

Florida Southern College, Program in Nursing, Lakeland, FL 33801-5698. Offers MSN. *Accreditation:* AACN. Part-time and evening/weekend programs available. *Faculty:* 5 full-time (all women). *Students:* Average age 43. 16 applicants, 75% accepted, 11 enrolled. In 2006, 11 degrees awarded. *Entrance requirements:* For master's, Florida RN license. Additional exam requirements/recommendations for international students: Required—TOEFL (minimum score 550 paper-based). *Application deadline:* For fall admission, 6/1 for domestic students; for spring admission, 11/1 for domestic students. Applications are processed on a rolling basis. Application fee: $30. *Expenses:* Tuition: Part-time $250 per credit hour. Required fees: $10 per term. Tuition and fees vary according to program. *Financial support:* In 2006–07, 10 students received support. Scholarships/grants and traineeships available. Support available to part-time students. *Faculty research:* End of life care, dementia, health promotion. *Unit head:* Dr. Mavra E. Kear, Program Coordinator, 863-680-4310, Fax: 863-680-3872, E-mail: mkear@flsouthern.edu. *Application contact:* Craig Story, Evening Program Director, 863-680-6276, Fax: 863-680-4205, E-mail: cstory@flsouthern.edu.

Florida State University, Graduate Studies, College of Nursing, Tallahassee, FL 32306. Offers family nurse practitioner (MSN, Certificate); nurse educator (MSN, Certificate); pediatric nurse practitioner (MSN, Certificate). *Accreditation:* AACN. Part-time programs available. Postbaccalaureate distance learning degree programs offered (no on-campus study). *Faculty:* 10 full-time (9 women), 1 part-time/adjunct (0 women). *Students:* 10 full-time (all women), 75 part-time (69 women); includes 16 minority (10 African Americans, 2 Asian Americans or Pacific Islanders, 4 Hispanic Americans). Average age 39. 43 applicants, 81% accepted, 32 enrolled. In 2006, 13 master's, 9 other advanced degrees awarded. *Degree requirements:* For master's, Research Project (optional), thesis optional. *Entrance requirements:* For master's, GRE General Test, minimum GPA of 3.0, BSN, Florida RN license. Additional exam requirements/recommendations for international students: Required—TOEFL (minimum score 550 paper-based). *Application deadline:* For fall admission, 7/1 for domestic students; for spring admission, 10/15 for domestic students. Applications are processed on a rolling basis. Application fee: $30. Electronic applications accepted. *Expenses:* Tuition, state resident: full-time $5,822; part-time $243 per credit hour. Tuition, nonresident: full-time $20,976; part-time $874 per credit hour. Tuition and fees vary according to program. *Financial support:* In 2006–07, 25 students received support, including 1 fellowship with partial tuition reimbursement available (averaging $6,300 per year), 3 research assistantships with partial tuition reimbursements available (averaging $3,000 per year), 13 teaching assistantships with partial tuition reimbursements available (averaging $3,000 per year); career-related internships or fieldwork, Federal Work-Study, institutionally sponsored loans, traineeships, and tuition waivers (partial) also available. Financial award application deadline: 4/15; financial award applicants required to submit FAFSA. *Faculty research:* Distance learning, gerontology, health promotion, educational strategies, rehabilitation of brain injured patients. *Unit head:* Dr. Katherine P. Mason, Dean, 850-644-5417, Fax: 850-644-7660, E-mail: kmason@mailer.fsu.edu. *Application contact:* Eddie Page, Graduate Program Coordinator, 850-644-5638, Fax: 850-645-7321, E-mail: epage@fsu.edu.

Fort Hays State University, Graduate School, College of Health and Life Sciences, Department of Nursing, Hays, KS 67601-4099. Offers MSN. *Accreditation:* AACN. *Faculty:* 6 full-time (all women). *Students:* 3 full-time (2 women), 62 part-time (60 women); includes 1 minority (Asian American or Pacific Islander) Average age 29. 17 applicants, 100% accepted. In 2006, 15 degrees awarded. *Degree requirements:* For master's, thesis optional. *Entrance requirements:* For master's, GRE General Test or MAT. Additional exam requirements/recommendations for international students: Required—TOEFL (minimum score 550 paper-based; 213 computer-based). *Application deadline:* For fall admission, 7/1 priority date for domestic students. Applications are processed on a rolling basis. Application fee: $35. Electronic applications accepted. *Financial support:* In 2006–07, 1 teaching assistantship (averaging $5,000 per year) was awarded; research assistantships. *Unit head:* Dr. Liane Connelly, Chair, 785-628-4511.

Franciscan University of Steubenville, Graduate Programs, Department of Nursing, Steubenville, OH 43952-1763. Offers MSN. *Accreditation:* NLN. Part-time and evening/weekend programs available. *Degree requirements:* For master's, thesis. *Entrance requirements:* For master's, GRE General Test, MAT.

Frontier School of Midwifery and Family Nursing, Graduate Programs, Hyden, KY 41749. Offers community-based family nurse practitioner (MSN, Post Master's Certificate); community-based nurse-midwifery education (MSN, Post Master's Certificate); community-based women[0092]s health care nurse practitioner (MSN, Post Master's Certificate). *Accreditation:* ACNM; NLN.

Gannon University, School of Graduate Studies, College of Sciences, Engineering, and Health Sciences, School of Health Sciences, Program in Nursing, Erie, PA 16541-0001. Offers anesthesia (MSN); business administration (MSN); case management (MSN); medical-surgical nursing (MSN); nurse anesthesia (Certificate); nursing rural practitioner (MSN). *Accreditation:* AACN; AANA/CANAEP (one or more programs are accredited). Part-time and evening/weekend programs available. *Students:* 15 full-time (5 women), 44 part-time (37 women). Average age 35. 8 applicants, 88% accepted, 5 enrolled. In 2006, 14 master's, 2 other advanced degrees awarded. *Degree requirements:* For master's, thesis. *Entrance requirements:* For master's, GRE General Test, MAT, bachelor's degree from a NLN-approved nursing program, interview, Pennsylvania RN license. Additional exam requirements/recommendations for international students: Required—TOEFL (minimum score 500 paper-based; 173 computer-based). *Application deadline:* For fall admission, 4/15 for domestic students. Application fee: $25. *Expenses:* Tuition: Full-time $12,240; part-time $680 per credit. Required fees: $496; $16 per credit. Tuition and fees vary according to course load, degree level, campus/location and program. *Financial support:* Career-related internships or fieldwork and traineeships available. Support available to part-time students. Financial award application deadline: 7/1; financial award applicants required to submit FAFSA. *Unit head:* Dr. Sharon Thompson, Interim Director, 814-871-5345, E-mail: thompson001@gannon.edu. *Application contact:* Debra Meszaros, Director of Graduate Recruitment, 814-871-5819, Fax: 814-871-5827, E-mail: cfal@gannon.edu.

Gardner-Webb University, Graduate School, Program in Nursing, Boiling Springs, NC 28017. Offers MSN, PMC. *Accreditation:* NLN. *Faculty:* 2 full-time (both women), 2 part-time/adjunct (both women). *Students:* 3 full-time (all women), 66 part-time (63 women); includes 11 minority (10 African Americans, 1 Asian American or Pacific Islander). In 2006, 30 degrees awarded. *Expenses:* Tuition: Full-time $3,144; part-time $262 per hour. *Unit head:* Dr. Gayle B. Price, Dean, Graduate School, 704-406-4723, Fax: 704-406-4329, E-mail: gradschool@gardner-webb.edu.

George Mason University, College of Health and Human Services, Fairfax, VA 22030. Offers advanced clinical nursing (MSN); nurse practitioner (MSN); nursing (MSN, PhD); nursing administration (MSN); nursing education (Certificate); nursing educator (MSN); social work (MSW). *Accreditation:* AACN. *Faculty:* 69 full-time (55 women), 75 part-time/adjunct (66 women). *Students:* 98 full-time (81 women), 301 part-time (260 women); includes 121 minority (60 African Americans, 45 Asian Americans or Pacific Islanders, 16 Hispanic Americans), 27 international. Average age 39. 326 applicants, 61% accepted, 121 enrolled. In 2006, 89 master's, 7 doctorates, 11 other advanced degrees awarded. *Degree requirements:* For doctorate, thesis/dissertation, oral/written exams. *Entrance requirements:* For master's, RN license, minimum GPA of 3.0 in last 60 hours of course work; for doctorate, MAT, 3 years of nursing experience, master's degree, minimum GPA of 3.25, professional liability insurance. *Application deadline:* For fall admission, 5/1 for domestic students; for spring admission, 11/1 for domestic students. Application fee: $60 ($75 for international students). Electronic applications accepted. *Expenses:* Tuition, state resident: full-time $5,724; part-time $238 per credit. Tuition, nonresident: full-time $16,896; part-time $704 per credit. Required fees: $1,656; $69 per credit. *Financial support:* Fellowships, research assistantships, teaching assistantships, tuition waivers (partial) available. Support available to part-time students. Financial award application deadline: 3/1; financial award applicants required to submit FAFSA. *Unit head:* Dr. Shirley S. Travis, Dean, 703-993-1918. *Application contact:* Dr. James D. Vail, Associate Dean, Graduate Programs and Research, 703-993-1947, Fax: 703-993-1942, E-mail: nursinfo@gmu.edu.

Georgetown University, Graduate School of Arts and Sciences, School of Nursing and Health Studies, Washington, DC 20057. Offers nursing (MS). *Accreditation:* AACN; AANA/CANAEP; ACNM/DOA. *Degree requirements:* For master's, thesis optional. *Entrance requirements:* For master's, GRE General Test or MAT, bachelor's degree in nursing from NLN-accredited school, minimum undergraduate GPA of 3.0. Additional exam requirements/recommendations for international students: Required—TOEFL.

Georgia College & State University, Graduate School, School of Health Sciences, Department of Nursing, Milledgeville, GA 31061. Offers MSN, MSN/MBA. *Accreditation:* NLN. Part-time programs available. *Degree requirements:* For master's, thesis optional. *Entrance requirements:* For master's, GMAT, GRE General Test, or MAT, bachelor's degree in nursing, RN license. Additional exam requirements/recommendations for international students: Required—TOEFL. Electronic applications accepted. *Expenses:* Tuition, state resident: full-time $3,222; part-time $179 per credit hour. Tuition, nonresident: full-time $12,870; part-time $715 per credit hour. Required fees: $391 per semester. Tuition and fees vary according to course load.

Georgia Southern University, Jack N. Averitt College of Graduate Studies, College of Health and Human Sciences, School of Nursing, Statesboro, GA 30460. Offers rural community health nurse practitioner (MSN); rural community health nurse specialist (Certificate); rural family nurse practitioner (MSN, Certificate); women's health nurse practitioner (MSN, Certificate). *Accreditation:* AACN. Part-time programs available. Postbaccalaureate distance learning degree programs offered. *Faculty:* 13 full-time (all women). *Students:* 6 full-time (all women), 40 part-time (38 women); includes 6 minority (all African Americans) Average age 34. 14 applicants, 100% accepted. In 2006, 15 degrees awarded. *Degree requirements:* For master's, thesis optional. *Entrance requirements:* For master's, GRE General Test or MAT, minimum GPA of 3.0, Georgia nursing license, 2 years of clinical experience, CPR certification; for Certificate, MSN. Additional exam requirements/recommendations for international students: Required—TOEFL (minimum score 550 paper-based; 213 computer-based; 80 iBT). *Application deadline:* For fall admission, 3/1 priority date for domestic students, 3/1 for international students; for spring admission, 10/1 priority date for domestic students, 10/1 for international students. Applications are processed on a rolling basis. Application fee: $50. Electronic applications accepted. *Financial support:* In 2006–07, 35 students received support, including research assistantships with partial tuition reimbursements available (averaging $5,500 per year), teaching assistantships with partial tuition reimbursements available (averaging $5,500 per year); career-related internships or fieldwork, Federal Work-Study, scholarships/grants, traineeships, tuition waivers (partial), and unspecified assistantships also available. Support available to part-time students. Financial award application deadline: 4/15; financial award applicants required to submit FAFSA. *Faculty research:* Caring, HIV disease, qualitative health research, health policy, rural nursing. Total annual research expenditures: $189,915. *Unit head:* Dr. Jean Bartels, Chair, 912-681-5479, Fax: 912-681-0536, E-mail: jbartels@georgiasouthern.edu. *Application contact:* 912-681-5384, Fax: 912-681-0740, E-mail: gradadmissionss@georgiasouthern.edu.

Georgia State University, College of Health and Human Sciences, School of Nursing, Atlanta, GA 30303-3083. Offers adult health (MS); child health (MS); family nurse practitioner (MS); health promotion, protection and restoration (PhD); nursing (Certificate); perinatal/women's health (MS); psychiatric/mental health (MS). *Accreditation:* AACN. Part-time and evening/weekend programs available. *Faculty:* 35 full-time (all women), 1 (woman) part-time/adjunct. *Students:* 72 full-time (66 women), 128 part-time (123 women); includes 75 minority (61 African Americans, 9 Asian Americans or Pacific Islanders, 5 Hispanic Americans), 2 international. Average age 37. 70 applicants, 54% accepted, 30 enrolled. In 2006, 39 master's, 6 doctorates awarded. *Degree requirements:* For master's, research activity; for doctorate, thesis/dissertation, comprehensive exam. *Entrance requirements:* For master's, MAT (preferred) or GRE, interview, RN license; for doctorate, GRE General Test. Additional exam requirements/recommendations for international students: Required—TOEFL (minimum score 550 paper-based; 213 computer-based). *Application deadline:* For fall admission, 3/1 priority date for domestic students; for spring admission, 10/1 priority date for domestic students. Applications are processed on a rolling basis. Application fee: $50. Electronic applications accepted. *Expenses:* Contact institution. *Financial support:* In 2006–07, research assistantships with full and partial tuition reimbursements (averaging $3,108 per year); fellowships with full tuition reimbursements, teaching assistantships, Federal Work-Study, institutionally sponsored loans, scholarships/grants, traineeships, and tuition waivers (partial) also available. Support available to part-time students. Financial award application deadline: 4/1; financial award applicants required to submit FAFSA. *Faculty research:* Breast cancer prevention, sexually compulsive behaviors, health risks in minority youth, asthma treatment strategies, adolescent alcohol-related issues. Total annual research expenditures: $221,691. *Unit head:* Dr. Barbara Woodring, Director, 404-651-3040. *Application contact:* Barbara Smith, Admissions Counselor II, 404-651-3834, Fax: 404-651-4871, E-mail: bbsmith@gsu.edu.

Gonzaga University, School of Professional Studies, Department of Nursing, Spokane, WA 99258. Offers MSN. *Accreditation:* AACN. *Students:* 19 full-time (18 women), 136 part-time (122 women); includes 8 minority (6 Asian Americans or Pacific Islanders, 2 Hispanic Americans). Average age 42. In 2006, 44 degrees awarded. *Entrance requirements:* For master's, MAT, minimum B average in undergraduate course work. Additional exam requirements/recommendations for international students: Required—TOEFL. *Application deadline:* For fall admission, 7/20 priority date for domestic students; for spring admission, 11/1 for domestic students. Applications are processed on a rolling basis. Application fee: $40. *Expenses:* Tuition: Full-time $10,620; part-time $590 per credit. *Financial support:* Application deadline: 3/1. *Unit head:* Mary Sue Gorski, 509-328-4220 Ext. 3587. *Application contact:* Dr. Joseph Albert, Contact, 509-328-4220 Ext. 3564.

Governors State University, College of Health Professions, Program in Nursing, University Park, IL 60466-0975. Offers MSN. *Accreditation:* NLN. *Students:* 10 full-time, 80 part-time. Average age 35. *Degree requirements:* For master's, thesis or alternative, practicum, comprehensive exam. *Entrance requirements:* For master's, GRE General Test, minimum GPA of 3.0 in upper-division nursing course work, 2.5 overall; BSN verification of AAS or employment as registered nurse; Illinois licensure; BSN from NLN-accredited institution. *Application deadline:* For fall admission, 7/15 priority date for domestic students; for spring admission, 11/10 for domestic students. Applications are processed on a rolling basis. Application fee: $25. *Expenses:* Tuition, state resident: full-time $4,104; part-time $171 per hour. Tuition, nonresident: part-time $513 per hour. *Financial support:* Research assistantships, career-related internships or fieldwork, Federal Work-Study, institutionally sponsored loans, and tuition waivers (full and partial) available. Support available to part-time students. Financial award application deadline: 5/1. *Unit head:* Dr. Catherine Tymkow, Coordinator.

Graceland University, School of Nursing, Independence, MO 64050-3434. Offers family nurse practitioner (MSN, PMC); health care administration (MSN, PMC); nurse educator (MSN, PMC). Part-time programs available. Postbaccalaureate distance learning degree programs offered (minimal on-campus study). *Faculty:* 11 full-time (all women), 5 part-time/adjunct (all women). *Students:* 94 full-time (93 women), 123 part-time (102 women); includes 16 minority (10 African Americans, 4 Asian Americans or Pacific Islanders, 2 Hispanic Americans). Average age 44. 123 applicants, 90% accepted, 105 enrolled. In 2006, 42 master's, 2 other advanced degrees awarded. *Median time to degree:* Master's–2.5 years full-time, 4 years part-time. *Degree requirements:* For master's, thesis optional. *Entrance requirements:* For master's, BSN from nationally accredited program, portfolio, RN license, minimum GPA of 3.0. *Application deadline:* For fall admission, 6/1 priority date for domestic students; for winter admission, 10/1 priority date for domestic students; for spring admission, 3/1 priority date for domestic students. Applications are processed on a rolling basis. Application fee: $50. Electronic applications accepted. *Expenses:* Contact institution. *Financial support:* In 2006–07, 3 students received support. Institutionally sponsored loans and traineeships available. Support available to part-time students. Financial award applicants required to submit FAFSA. *Faculty research:* International nursing, family care-giving, health promotion. *Unit head:* Dr. Kathryn A Ballou, Dean, 800-833-0524 Ext. 4201, Fax: 816-833-2990, E-mail: kaballou@graceland.edu. *Application contact:* John D. Koehler, Manager of Recruiting, 816-833-0524 Ext. 4804, Fax: 816-833-2990, E-mail: jkoehler@graceland.edu.

Grambling State University, School of Graduate Studies and Research, College of Professional Studies, School of Nursing, Grambling, LA 71245. Offers family nurse practitioner (MSN, PMC); nurse educator (MSN). *Accreditation:* NLN. Part-time programs available. *Faculty:* 4 full-time (all women), 4 part-time/adjunct (2 women). *Students:* 26 full-time (21 women), 24 part-time (20 women); includes 27 minority (26 African Americans, 1 Asian American or Pacific Islander). Average age 38. In 2006, 13 degrees awarded. *Degree requirements:* For master's, thesis (for some programs), comprehensive exam (for some programs). *Entrance requirements:* For master's, GRE, minimum GPA of 3.0 on last degree, interview, 2 years experience as RN. Additional exam requirements/recommendations for international students: Required—TOEFL. *Application deadline:* For fall admission, 7/1 for domestic students; for spring admission, 12/1 for domestic students. Application fee: $20 ($30 for international students). *Expenses:* Tuition, state resident: full-time $2,232; part-time $124 per credit hour. Tuition, nonresident: full-time $7,582; part-time $124 per credit hour. Required fees: $1,127. *Financial support:* In 2006–07, 25 students received support. Application deadline: 5/31. *Unit head:* Dr. Rhonda Hensley, Director, 318-274-2897, Fax: 318-274-3491, E-mail: hensleyr@gram.edu.

Grand Valley State University, Kirkhof College of Nursing, Allendale, MI 49401-9403. Offers advanced practice (MSN); case management (MSN); nursing administration (MSN); nursing education (MSN); MSN/MBA. *Accreditation:* AACN. Part-time programs available. *Faculty:* 17 full-time (all women), 1 (woman) part-time/adjunct. *Students:* 3 full-time (all women), 46 part-time (42 women); includes 4 minority (1 African American, 1 Asian American or Pacific Islander, 2 Hispanic Americans). Average age 35. 15 applicants, 67% accepted, 8 enrolled. In 2006, 20 degrees awarded. *Degree requirements:* For master's, thesis optional. *Entrance requirements:* For master's, GRE, minimum GPA of 3.0 in upper-division course work, course work in statistics, Michigan RN license. Additional exam requirements/recommendations for international students: Required—TOEFL. *Application deadline:* For fall admission, 3/15 priority date for domestic students. Applications are processed on a rolling basis. Application fee: $30. Electronic applications accepted. *Expenses:* Tuition, state resident: full-time $5,850; part-time $325 per credit. Tuition, nonresident: full-time $10,800; part-time $600 per credit. Tuition and fees vary according to course load. *Financial support:* In 2006–07, 7 research assistantships with full and partial tuition reimbursements (averaging $8,000 per year) were awarded; career-related internships or fieldwork, Federal Work-Study, institutionally sponsored loans, and traineeships also available. Financial award application deadline: 2/15. *Faculty research:* Multigenerational health promotion, chronic disease prevention, end-of-life issues; nursing workload, family caregiver health. Total annual research expenditures: $36,000. *Unit head:* Dr. Phyllis Gendler, Dean, 616-331-7161, Fax: 616-331-7362, E-mail: gendlerp@gvsu.edu. *Application contact:* Dr. Jean Martin, Director of Graduate Programs, 616-331-7167, Fax: 616-331-7362, E-mail: martinj@gvsu.edu.

Gwynedd-Mercy College, School of Nursing, Gwynedd Valley, PA 19437-0901. Offers clinical nurse specialist (MSN), including gerontology, oncology, pediatrics; nurse practitioner (MSN), including adult health, pediatric health. *Accreditation:* NLN. *Faculty:* 5 full-time (all women), 3 part-time/adjunct (2 women). *Students:* 7 full-time (5 women), 38 part-time (35 women); includes 3 minority (1 African American, 1 Asian American or Pacific Islander, 1 Hispanic American). Average age 41. 18 applicants, 89% accepted, 11 enrolled. In 2006, 5 degrees awarded. *Degree requirements:* For master's, thesis optional. *Entrance requirements:* For master's, GRE General Test or MAT, 2 years of experience, physical assessment, course work in statistics, BSN from an NLNAC accredited program, 2 letters of recommendation, personal interview. Additional exam requirements/recommendations for international students: Required—TOEFL (minimum score 575 paper-based). *Application deadline:* For fall admission, 8/1 priority date for domestic students; for winter admission, 12/1 priority date for domestic students. Applications are processed on a rolling basis. Application fee: $25. Electronic applications accepted. *Expenses:* Contact institution. *Financial support:* In 2006–07, 21 students received support. Scholarships/grants, traineeships, and unspecified assistantships available. Financial award application deadline: 8/30. *Faculty research:* Critical thinking, primary care, domestic violence, multiculturalism, nursing centers. *Unit head:* Dr. Andrea D. Hollingsworth, Dean, 215-646-7300 Ext. 539, Fax: 215-641-5517, E-mail: hollingsworth.a@gmc.edu. *Application contact:* Dr. Barbara A. Jones, Director, 215-646-7300 Ext. 407, Fax: 215-641-5564, E-mail: jones.b@gmc.edu.

Hampton University, Graduate College, Department of Nursing, Hampton, VA 23668. Offers MS. *Accreditation:* AACN; NLN. Part-time and evening/weekend programs available. *Degree requirements:* For master's, thesis optional. *Entrance requirements:* For master's, GRE General Test. *Faculty research:* Curriculum development, physical and mental assessment.

Hardin-Simmons University, Graduate School, School of Nursing, Abilene, TX 79698-0001. Offers advanced healthcare delivery (MSN); family nurse practitioner (MSN). *Accreditation:* AACN. Part-time programs available. *Faculty:* 5 full-time (all women). *Students:* 1 full-time (0 women), 8 part-time (6 women). Average age 39. 5 applicants, 100% accepted, 3 enrolled. In 2006, 2 degrees awarded. *Degree requirements:* For master's, thesis or alternative, comprehensive exam. *Entrance requirements:* For master's, GRE, minimum undergraduate GPA of 3.0 in major, 2.8 overall; interview; upper-level course work in statistics; CPR certification; letters of recommendation. Additional exam requirements/recommendations for international students: Required—TOEFL (minimum score 550 paper-based; 213 computer-based). *Application deadline:* For fall admission, 8/15 priority date for domestic students; for spring admission, 1/5 priority date for domestic students. Applications are processed on a rolling basis. Application fee: $50 ($100 for international students). *Expenses:* Contact institution. One-time fee: $50. Tuition and fees vary according to course load and degree level. *Financial support:* In 2006–07, 8 students received support. Career-related internships or fieldwork and scholarships/grants available. Support available to part-time students. Financial award application deadline: 6/30; financial award applicants required to submit FAFSA. *Faculty research:* Child abuse, alternative medicine, pediatric chronic disease, health promotion. *Unit head:* Dr. Janet Noles, Dean, 325-672-2441, Fax: 325-670-1564, E-mail: jnoles@hsutx.edu. *Application contact:* Dr. Gary Stanlake, Dean of Graduate Studies, 325-670-1298, Fax: 325-670-1564, E-mail: gradoff@hsutx.edu.

Nursing—General

Hawai'i Pacific University, School of Nursing, Honolulu, HI 96813. Offers community clinical nurse specialist (MSN); community clinical nurse specialist educator option (MSN); family nurse practitioner (MSN). *Accreditation:* NLN. Part-time and evening/weekend programs available. *Faculty:* 11 full-time (all women), 1 part-time/adjunct (0 women). *Students:* 26 full-time (23 women), 10 part-time (all women); includes 18 minority (2 African Americans, 1 American Indian/Alaska Native, 13 Asian Americans or Pacific Islanders, 2 Hispanic Americans). Average age 35. 22 applicants, 77% accepted, 13 enrolled. In 2006, 10 degrees awarded. *Degree requirements:* For master's, practicum, professional paper. *Entrance requirements:* For master's, bachelor's degree in nursing, minimum GPA of 3.0. Additional exam requirements/recommendations for international students: Recommended—TOEFL (minimum score 550 paper-based; 213 computer-based), TWE (minimum score 5). *Application deadline:* Applications are processed on a rolling basis. Application fee: $50. Electronic applications accepted. *Expenses:* Tuition: Full-time $10,080; part-time $560 per credit. *Financial support:* In 2006–07, 20 students received support. Career-related internships or fieldwork, Federal Work-Study, scholarships/grants, and traineeships available. Support available to part-time students. Financial award application deadline: 3/1; financial award applicants required to submit FAFSA. *Faculty research:* Hawaiian elders, traditional healing and nursing center. *Unit head:* Dr. Patricia Langotsuka, Interim Dean, 808-236-5812, Fax: 808-236-5818, E-mail: potsuka@hpu.edu. *Application contact:* Danny Lam, Assistant Director of Graduate Admissions, 808-544-1135, Fax: 808-544-0280, E-mail: graduate@hpu.edu.

See Close-Up on page 1961.

Holy Family University, Graduate School, School of Nursing, Philadelphia, PA 19114-2094. Offers MSN. *Accreditation:* AACN. Part-time and evening/weekend programs available. *Degree requirements:* For master's, thesis or alternative, registration. *Entrance requirements:* For master's, bachelor's degree in nursing; RN license; minimum GPA of 3.0, letters of reference (2).

Holy Names University, Graduate Division, Department of Nursing, Oakland, CA 94619-1699. Offers community health nursing/case manager (MS); family nurse practitioner (MS). *Accreditation:* AACN. Part-time and evening/weekend programs available. *Faculty:* 1 (woman) full-time, 7 part-time/adjunct (all women). *Students:* 73 full-time (68 women), 22 part-time (20 women); includes 45 minority (22 African Americans, 1 American Indian/Alaska Native, 13 Asian Americans or Pacific Islanders, 9 Hispanic Americans). Average age 44. 52 applicants, 65% accepted, 26 enrolled. In 2006, 10 master's awarded. *Entrance requirements:* For master's, bachelor's degree in nursing or related field, California RN license or eligibility, minimum GPA of 3.0, previous course work in research or statistics. Additional exam requirements/recommendations for international students: Required—TOEFL. *Application deadline:* For fall admission, 8/1 priority date for domestic students; for spring admission, 12/1 priority date for domestic students. Applications are processed on a rolling basis. Application fee: $50. *Expenses:* Tuition: Full-time $10,800; part-time $600 per unit. Required fees: $240; $120 per term. *Financial support:* In 2006–07, 36 students received support. Scholarships/grants available. Support available to part-time students. Financial award application deadline: 3/2; financial award applicants required to submit FAFSA. *Faculty research:* Women's reproductive health, gerontology, attitudes about aging, schizophrenic families, international health issues. *Unit head:* Dr. Fay Bower, Program Director, 510-436-1127. *Application contact:* 800-430-1351, Fax: 510-436-1325, E-mail: admissions@hnu.edu.

Howard University, College of Pharmacy, Nursing and Allied Health Sciences, Division of Nursing, Washington, DC 20059-0002. Offers nurse practitioner (Certificate); primary family health nursing (MSN). *Accreditation:* AACN. Part-time programs available. *Faculty:* 3 full-time (all women), 6 part-time/adjunct (all women). *Students:* 23 full-time (20 women), 5 part-time (all women); includes 26 minority (23 African Americans, 1 American Indian/Alaska Native, 1 Asian American or Pacific Islander, 1 Hispanic American). Average age 36. 15 applicants, 73% accepted. In 2006, 1 master's, 1 other advanced degree awarded. *Median time to degree:* Master's–4 years part-time. *Degree requirements:* For master's, thesis optional. *Entrance requirements:* For master's, RN license, minimum GPA of 3.0, BS in nursing. *Application deadline:* For fall admission, 4/1 priority date for domestic students; for spring admission, 11/1 for domestic students. Applications are processed on a rolling basis. Application fee: $45. *Financial support:* In 2006–07, teaching assistantships (averaging $16,000 per year); career-related internships or fieldwork, institutionally sponsored loans, and scholarships/grants also available. Financial award application deadline: 4/1. *Faculty research:* Urinary incontinence, breast cancer prevention, depression in the elderly, adolescent pregnancy. *Unit head:* Dr. Mamie C. Montague, Associate Dean (Interim), 202-806-7456, Fax: 202-806-5958, E-mail: mmontague@howard.edu. *Application contact:* Dr. Mamie C. Montague, Chair, Graduate Program, 202-806-7460, Fax: 202-806-5958, E-mail: mmontague@howard.edu.

Hunter College of the City University of New York, Graduate School, Schools of the Health Professions, Hunter-Bellevue School of Nursing, New York, NY 10021-5085. Offers MS, AC, MS/MPH. *Accreditation:* AACN. Part-time programs available. *Faculty:* 24 full-time (21 women), 21 part-time/adjunct (19 women). *Students:* 12 full-time (2 women), 179 part-time (164 women); includes 77 minority (44 African Americans, 20 Asian Americans or Pacific Islanders, 13 Hispanic Americans). Average age 37. 50 applicants, 100% accepted, 39 enrolled. In 2006, 39 master's, 1 other advanced degree awarded. *Degree requirements:* For master's, practicum, portfolio. *Entrance requirements:* For master's, BSN, minimum GPA of 3.0, New York RN license, course work in basic statistics, resumé; for AC, MSN, minimum GPA of 3.0. Additional exam requirements/recommendations for international students: Required—TOEFL. *Application deadline:* For fall admission, 4/1 for domestic students; for spring admission, 11/1 for domestic students. Applications are processed on a rolling basis. Application fee: $125. *Expenses:* Tuition, state resident: part-time $270 per credit. Tuition, nonresident: part-time $500 per credit. Required fees: $45 per semester. *Financial support:* In 2006–07, 9 students received support. Federal Work-Study, scholarships/grants, traineeships, and tuition waivers (partial) available. Support available to part-time students. Financial award application deadline: 5/1; financial award applicants required to submit FAFSA. *Faculty research:* Aging, high-risk mothers and babies, adolescent health, care of HIV/AIDS clients, critical care nursing. *Unit head:* Dr. Audra Ridikas, Director, 212-481-7596, Fax: 212-481-5078, E-mail: aridikas@hunter.cuny.edu. *Application contact:* William Zlata, Director for Graduate Admissions, 212-772-4482, Fax: 212-650-3336, E-mail: admissions@hunter.cuny.edu.

Husson College, Graduate Studies Division, Program in Nursing, Bangor, ME 04401-2999. Offers family nurse practitioner (MSN); nursing (MSN); psychiatric nursing (MSN). *Accreditation:* AACN. *Entrance requirements:* For master's, MAT, BSN. Expenses: Contact institution.

Idaho State University, Office of Graduate Studies, Kasiska College of Health Professions, Department of Nursing, Pocatello, ID 83209. Offers MS, Post-Master's Certificate. *Accreditation:* AACN. Part-time programs available. *Faculty:* 4 full-time (all women), 1 (woman) part-time/adjunct. *Students:* 26 full-time (23 women), 37 part-time (33 women); includes 2 minority (both Asian Americans or Pacific Islanders) Average age 38. In 2006, 22 master's, 1 other advanced degree awarded. *Degree requirements:* For master's, thesis optional; for Post-Master's Certificate, thesis optional. *Entrance requirements:* For master's, GRE General Test, interview, 3 letters of reference, active RN license; for Post-Master's Certificate, GRE General Test, 3 letters of reference, practicum or nursing license. Additional exam requirements/recommendations for international students: Required—TOEFL (minimum score 600 paper-based; 213 computer-based). *Application deadline:* For fall admission, 7/1 for domestic students, 6/1 for international students; for spring admission, 12/1 for domestic students, 11/1 for international students. Applications are processed on a rolling basis. Application fee: $55. *Financial support:* In 2006–07, 3 teaching assistantships with full and partial tuition reimbursements (averaging $8,694 per year) were awarded; career-related internships or fieldwork, Federal Work-Study, scholarships/grants, traineeships, and unspecified assistantships also available. Support available to part-time students. Financial award application deadline: 1/1. *Faculty research:* Health promotions, health of homeless, exercise and elderly, student stress, midwifery. Total annual research expenditures: $371,792. *Unit head:* Dr. Carol Ashton, Chair, 208-282-2443, Fax: 208-282-4476, E-mail: ashtcaro@isu.edu. *Application contact:* Ellen Combs, Graduate School Technical Records Specialist, 208-282-2150, Fax: 208-282-4847.

Illinois State University, Graduate School, Mennonite College of Nursing, Normal, IL 61790. Offers family nurse practitioner (PMC); nursing (MSN). *Accreditation:* AACN. *Faculty:* 7 full-time (all women). *Students:* 17 full-time (16 women), 21 part-time (18 women); includes 3 minority (1 African American, 2 Asian Americans or Pacific Islanders), 1 international. 11 applicants, 100% accepted. In 2006, 13 master's, 1 other advanced degree awarded. Application fee: $40. *Expenses:* Tuition, state resident: full-time $3,330; part-time $185 per credit hour. Tuition, nonresident: full-time $6,948; part-time $438 per credit hour. Required fees: $1,259; $52 per credit hour. *Financial support:* In 2006–07, 4 research assistantships (averaging $6,694 per year) were awarded. *Faculty research:* Expanding the teaching-nursing home culture in the state of Illinois, advanced education nursing traineeship program, collaborative doctoral program-caring for older adults. Total annual research expenditures: $757,962. *Unit head:* Nancy Ridenour, Dean, 309-438-7400, Fax: 309-438-2620.

Immaculata University, College of Graduate Studies, Department of Nursing, Immaculata, PA 19345. Offers MSN. *Accreditation:* AACN. *Students:* 12 applicants, 75% accepted, 9 enrolled. *Entrance requirements:* For master's, MAT or GRE, BSN. Additional exam requirements/recommendations for international students: Required—TOEFL. *Application deadline:* Applications are processed on a rolling basis. Application fee: $35. *Unit head:* Dr. Jean Klein, Director of Graduate Nursing, 610-647-4400 Ext. 3306, Fax: 610-993-8550, E-mail: jklein@immaculata.edu. *Application contact:* 610-647-4400 Ext. 3211, Fax: 610-993-8550, E-mail: graduate@immaculata.edu.

Indiana State University, School of Graduate Studies, College of Nursing, Terre Haute, IN 47809-1401. Offers MS. *Accreditation:* NLN. Part-time programs available. *Faculty:* 6 full-time (all women), 5 part-time/adjunct (all women). *Students:* 37 full-time (34 women), 123 part-time (111 women); includes 25 minority (14 African Americans, 2 American Indian/Alaska Native, 4 Asian Americans or Pacific Islanders, 5 Hispanic Americans), 2 international. Average age 38. 101 applicants, 97% accepted, 76 enrolled. In 2006, 10 degrees awarded. *Degree requirements:* For master's, thesis or alternative. *Entrance requirements:* For master's, BSN, RN license, minimum undergraduate GPA of 3.0. *Application deadline:* For fall admission, 7/1 priority date for domestic students; for spring admission, 11/1 priority date for domestic students. Applications are processed on a rolling basis. Application fee: $35. Electronic applications accepted. *Expenses:* Tuition, state resident: part-time $278 per credit. Tuition, nonresident: part-time $552 per credit. *Financial support:* In 2006–07, 3 research assistantships with partial tuition reimbursements (averaging $6,300 per year) were awarded; teaching assistantships with partial tuition reimbursements, career-related internships or fieldwork and Federal Work-Study also available. Support available to part-time students. Financial award application deadline: 3/1; financial award applicants required to submit FAFSA. *Faculty research:* Nursing faculty-student interactions, clinical evaluation, program evaluation, sexual dysfunction, faculty attitudes. *Unit head:* Dr. Esther Acree, Interim Dean, 812-237-3683.

Indiana University of Pennsylvania, School of Graduate Studies and Research, College of Health and Human Services, Department of Nursing and Allied Health, Program in Nursing, Indiana, PA 15705-1087. Offers MS. *Accreditation:* AACN. Part-time programs available. *Faculty:* 3 full-time (2 women), 2 part-time/adjunct (both women). *Students:* 20 full-time (18 women), 49 part-time (47 women); includes 1 minority (African American) Average age 41. 46 applicants, 78% accepted. In 2006, 21 degrees awarded. *Degree requirements:* For master's, thesis optional. *Entrance requirements:* For master's, 2 letters of recommendation. Additional exam requirements/recommendations for international students: Required—TOEFL. *Application deadline:* For fall admission, 7/1 priority date for domestic students; for spring admission, 11/1 for domestic students. Applications are processed on a rolling basis. Application fee: $30. *Expenses:* Tuition, state resident: full-time $6,048; part-time $336 per credit. Tuition, nonresident: full-time $9,678; part-time $538 per credit. Required fees: $1,069; $148 per year. *Financial support:* In 2006–07, 6 research assistantships with full and partial tuition reimbursements (averaging $2,495 per year) were awarded; Federal Work-Study also available. Support available to part-time students. Financial award application deadline: 3/15; financial award applicants required to submit FAFSA. *Unit head:* Dr. Nashat Zuraikat, Graduate Coordinator, 724-357-3262, E-mail: zuraikat@iup.edu.

Indiana University–Purdue University Fort Wayne, School of Health Sciences, Department of Nursing, Fort Wayne, IN 46805-1499. Offers nursing administration (MS, Certificate). Part-time programs available. *Faculty:* 9 full-time (all women). *Students:* Average age 47. 9 applicants, 100% accepted, 5 enrolled. In 2006, 2 degrees awarded. *Entrance requirements:* For master's, GRE Writing Test, BS in nursing, eligibility for Indiana RN license, minimum GPA of 3.0. Additional exam requirements/recommendations for international students: Required—TOEFL (minimum score 600 paper-based; 260 computer-based). *Application deadline:* For fall admission, 8/1 priority date for domestic students; for spring admission, 12/1 for domestic students. Application fee: $55. Electronic applications accepted. *Expenses:* Tuition, state resident: full-time $4,039; part-time $224 per credit. Tuition, nonresident: full-time $9,220; part-time $512 per credit. Required fees: $429; $24 per credit. Tuition and fees vary according to course load. *Financial support:* Scholarships/grants available. Support available to part-time students. Financial award application deadline: 3/1; financial award applicants required to submit FAFSA. Total annual research expenditures: $333,000. *Unit head:* Dr. Carol Sternberger, Chair, 260-481-6816, Fax: 260-481-5707, E-mail: sternber@ipfw.edu.

Indiana University–Purdue University Indianapolis, School of Nursing, Indianapolis, IN 46202-2896. Offers acute care nurse practitioner (MSN); adult health clinical nurse specialist (MSN); adult health nursing (MSN), including adult clinical nurse specialist; adult nurse practitioner (MSN); adult psychiatric/mental health nursing (MSN); child psychiatric/mental health nursing (MSN); community health nursing (MSN); family nurse practitioner (MSN); neonatal nurse practitioner (MSN); nursing science (PhD); pediatric clinical nurse specialist (MSN); women's health nurse practitioner (MSN); MSN/MPA; MSN/MPH. *Accreditation:* AACN; NLN (one or more programs are accredited). Part-time programs available. *Faculty:* 45 full-time (44 women), 1 (woman) part-time/adjunct. *Students:* 52 full-time (51 women), 415 part-time (396 women); includes 27 minority (16 African Americans, 3 Asian Americans or Pacific Islanders, 8 Hispanic Americans), 4 international. Average age 38. In 2006, 106 master's, 3 doctorates awarded. Terminal master's awarded for partial completion of doctoral program. *Degree requirements:* For master's and doctorate, thesis/dissertation. *Entrance requirements:* For master's, GRE General Test, minimum GPA of 3.0, RN license; for doctorate, GRE General Test, minimum GPA of 3.5, MSN, RN license. Additional exam requirements/recommendations for international students: Required—TOEFL. *Application deadline:* For fall admission, 2/15 for domestic students; for spring admission, 9/15 for domestic students. Application fee: $50 ($60 for international students). *Expenses:* Tuition, state resident: full-time $5,437; part-time $227 per credit hour. Tuition, nonresident: full-time $15,694; part-time $654 per credit hour. Required fees: $620. Tuition and fees vary according to course load, campus/location and program. *Financial support:* In 2006–07, 93 students received support; fellowships with full tuition reimbursements available, research assistantships with full tuition reimbursements available, teaching assistantships with full tuition reimbursements available, Federal Work-Study, institutionally sponsored loans, scholarships/grants, and tuition waivers (full) available. Support available to part-time students. Financial award application deadline: 5/1. *Faculty research:* Chronic illness, cancer, health services research, family health. Total annual research expenditures: $3 million. *Unit head:* Associate Dean for Graduate Programs, 317-274-2806, E-mail: nursing@iupui.edu. *Application contact:* Martez Plummer, Assistant Dean for Student Affairs, 317-274-2806, E-mail: mplummer@iupui.edu.

Indiana Wesleyan University, College of Graduate Studies, Division of Nursing, Marion, IN 46953-4974. Offers community health nursing (MS); nursing (Post Master's Certificate); nursing administration (MS); nursing education (MS); primary care nursing (MS). *Accreditation:* AACN. Part-time and evening/weekend programs available. *Faculty:* 2 full-time (both women), 6 part-time/adjunct (3 women). *Students:* 312 full-time (296 women), 8 part-time (4 women);

includes 45 minority (41 African Americans, 2 Asian Americans or Pacific Islanders, 2 Hispanic Americans). Average age 40. In 2006, 87 degrees awarded. *Degree requirements:* For master's, thesis. *Entrance requirements:* For master's, GRE, RN license, 1 year of related experience, graduate statistics course. *Application deadline:* For fall admission, 7/31 priority date for domestic students; for winter admission, 11/15 priority date for domestic students; for spring admission, 4/15 priority date for domestic students. Electronic applications accepted. *Expenses: Contact institution.* Tuition and fees vary according to degree level, campus/location and program. *Financial support:* In 2006–07, 15 fellowships were awarded; career-related internships or fieldwork, scholarships/grants, and traineeships also available. Support available to part-time students. Financial award application deadline: 3/15. *Faculty research:* Primary health care with international emphasis, international nursing. *Unit head:* Pam Giles, Director, 765-677-1716, E-mail: gradnurse@indwes.edu. *Application contact:* David McMillan, Assistant Director of Enrollment Management, 765-677-2688, E-mail: david.mcmillan@indwes.edu.

Inter American University of Puerto Rico, Arecibo Campus, Program in Nursing, Arecibo, PR 00614-4050. Offers community nursing (MS); primary care nursing (MS). *Entrance requirements:* For master's, EXADEP or GRE or MAT, 2 letters of recommendation, bachelor's degree in nursing, minimum GPA of 2.5 in last 60 credits, minimum 1 year nursing experience, nursing license.

Jacksonville State University, College of Graduate Studies and Continuing Education, College of Nursing, Jacksonville, AL 36265-1602. Offers MSN. *Accreditation:* AACN. *Faculty:* 2 full-time (both women). In 2006, 10 degrees awarded. *Entrance requirements:* For master's, GRE General Test or MAT. *Application deadline:* Applications are processed on a rolling basis. Application fee: $20. Electronic applications accepted. *Expenses:* Tuition, state resident: full-time $5,400; part-time $225 per credit hour. Tuition, nonresident: full-time $10,800; part-time $450 per credit hour. One-time fee: $20 full-time. *Financial support:* In 2006–07, 3 teaching assistantships with tuition reimbursements were awarded. Financial award application deadline: 4/1. *Unit head:* Dr. Sarah Latham, Dean, 256-782-5431.

Jacksonville University, College of Arts and Sciences, School of Nursing, Jacksonville, FL 32211-3394. Offers MSN. *Accreditation:* AACN. Part-time programs available. *Degree requirements:* For master's, thesis. *Entrance requirements:* For master's, GRE General Test, BS in nursing from an accredited program, course work in statistics within last 5 years, Florida nursing license. Additional exam requirements/recommendations for international students: Required—TOEFL (minimum score 550 paper-based). Expenses: Contact institution.

James Madison University, College of Graduate and Outreach Programs, College of Integrated Science and Technology, Department of Nursing, Harrisonburg, VA 22807. Offers MSN. *Accreditation:* AACN. *Faculty:* 5 full-time (all women). *Students:* 10 full-time (9 women), 7 part-time (all women). Average age 27. In 2006, 4 degrees awarded. *Entrance requirements:* For master's, GRE General Test. *Application deadline:* For fall admission, 4/1 priority date for domestic students; for spring admission, 9/1 priority date for domestic students. Application fee: $55. *Expenses:* Tuition, state resident: full-time $6,336; part-time $264 per credit hour. Tuition, nonresident: full-time $17,832; part-time $743 per credit hour. *Financial support:* In 2006–07, 1 student received support. Unspecified assistantships available. Financial award application deadline: 3/1; financial award applicants required to submit FAFSA. *Unit head:* Dr. Merle E. Mast, Academic Unit Head, 540-568-6314.

Jefferson College of Health Sciences, Program in Nursing, Roanoke, VA 24031-3186. Offers nursing education (MSN); nursing management (MSN). *Accreditation:* AACN.

The Johns Hopkins University, School of Nursing, Baltimore, MD 21218-2699. Offers MSN, PhD, Certificate, MSN/MBA, MSN/MPH. *Accreditation:* AACN; NLN (one or more programs are accredited). Part-time programs available. *Faculty:* 33 full-time (26 women), 7 part-time/adjunct (6 women). *Students:* 79 full-time (74 women), 174 part-time (166 women); includes 71 minority (18 African Americans, 5 American Indian/Alaska Native, 42 Asian Americans or Pacific Islanders, 6 Hispanic Americans), 1 international. Average age 30. 287 applicants, 84% accepted, 105 enrolled. In 2006, 47 master's, 3 doctorates awarded. *Degree requirements:* For master's, portfolio or scholarly project, thesis optional; for doctorate, thesis/dissertation. *Entrance requirements:* For master's, GRE, interview, minimum GPA of 3.0, BSN, RN license; for doctorate, GRE, interview, minimum GPA of 3.0, resumé, RN license, writing sample; for Certificate, interview, minimum GPA of 3.0, MSN, resumé, RN license. Additional exam requirements/recommendations for international students: Required—TOEFL (minimum score 550 paper-based; 230 computer-based). *Application deadline:* For fall admission, 3/1 priority date for domestic and international students; for winter admission, 7/1 priority date for domestic and international students; for spring admission, 7/1 priority date for domestic and international students. Applications are processed on a rolling basis. Application fee: $75. *Expenses: Contact institution.* Tuition and fees vary according to degree level and program. *Financial support:* In 2006–07, 37 students received support, including 6 fellowships with partial tuition reimbursements available (averaging $23,272 per year); research assistantships with full tuition reimbursements available, teaching assistantships with full tuition reimbursements available, career-related internships or fieldwork, Federal Work-Study, institutionally sponsored loans, scholarships/grants, traineeships, and tuition waivers (partial) also available. Support available to part-time students. Financial award application deadline: 3/15; financial award applicants required to submit FAFSA. *Faculty research:* Hypertension, violence, cardiovascular risk symptom management, symptom management, health disparities. Total annual research expenditures: $6.1 million. *Unit head:* Dr. Martha N. Hill, Dean, 410-955-7544, Fax: 410-955-4890, E-mail: mnhill@son.jhmi.edu. *Application contact:* Mary O'Rourke, Director of Admissions/Student Services, 410-955-7548, Fax: 410-614-7086, E-mail: orourke@son.jhmi.edu.

Kean University, College of Natural, Applied and Health Sciences, Program in Nursing, Union, NJ 07083. Offers clinical management (MSN); community health (MSN). *Accreditation:* NLN. Part-time and evening/weekend programs available. *Faculty:* 7 full-time (all women). *Students:* 5 full-time (4 women), 62 part-time (57 women); includes 42 minority (26 African Americans, 12 Asian Americans or Pacific Islanders, 4 Hispanic Americans). Average age 43. 29 applicants, 93% accepted, 19 enrolled. In 2006, 23 degrees awarded. *Degree requirements:* For master's, thesis or alternative, clinical field experience. *Entrance requirements:* For master's, BS in nursing, RN license, 2 letters of recommendation, interview. *Application deadline:* For fall admission, 5/1 for domestic students; for spring admission, 11/1 for domestic students. Application fee: $60 ($150 for international students). *Expenses:* Tuition, state resident: full-time $8,856; part-time $369 per credit. Tuition, nonresident: full-time $11,256; part-time $469 per credit. *Financial support:* Research assistantships with full tuition reimbursements available. *Unit head:* Dr. Estelle A. Pisani, Program Coordinator, 908-737-3386, E-mail: episani@kean.edu. *Application contact:* Joanne Morris, Director of Graduate Admissions, 908-737-3355, Fax: 908-737-3354, E-mail: grad-adm@kean.edu.

Kean University, College of Natural, Applied and Health Sciences, Program in Nursing and Public Administration, Union, NJ 07083. Offers MSN/MPA. *Accreditation:* NLN. Part-time and evening/weekend programs available. *Faculty:* 7 full-time (all women). *Students:* 2 full-time (both women), 16 part-time (13 women); includes 14 minority (12 African Americans, 2 Hispanic Americans), 1 international. Average age 41. 7 applicants, 100% accepted, 2 enrolled. *Application deadline:* For fall admission, 5/1 for domestic students. Application fee: $60 ($150 for international students). Electronic applications accepted. *Expenses:* Tuition, state resident: full-time $8,856; part-time $369 per credit. Tuition, nonresident: full-time $11,256; part-time $469 per credit. *Financial support:* In 2006–07, 1 research assistantship with full tuition reimbursement (averaging $3,217 per year) was awarded. *Unit head:* Dr. Estelle A. Pisani, Program Coordinator, 908-737-3386, E-mail: episani@kean.edu. *Application contact:* Joanne Morris, Director of Graduate Admissions, 908-737-3355, Fax: 908-737-3354, E-mail: grad-adm@kean.edu.

Kennesaw State University, College of Health and Human Services, Program in Primary Care Nurse Practitioner, Kennesaw, GA 30144-5591. Offers MSN. *Accreditation:* AACN. Part-time and evening/weekend programs available. *Faculty:* 7 full-time (6 women), 15 part-time/adjunct (10 women). *Students:* 56 full-time (53 women), 13 part-time (11 women); includes 15 minority (13 African Americans, 2 Hispanic Americans), 1 international. Average age 38. 104 applicants, 42% accepted, 40 enrolled. In 2006, 36 degrees awarded. *Entrance requirements:* For master's, GRE General Test, minimum GPA of 2.5, RN license, 3 years of professional experience. Additional exam requirements/recommendations for international students: Required—TOEFL (minimum score 550 paper-based; 213 computer-based). *Application deadline:* For fall admission, 5/31 for domestic students. Application fee: $50. Electronic applications accepted. *Expenses:* Tuition, state resident: full-time $3,044; part-time $127 per semester hour. Tuition, nonresident: full-time $12,172; part-time $508 per semester hour. Required fees: $353 per semester. Full-time tuition and fees vary according to campus/location and program. *Financial support:* In 2006–07, 2 research assistantships with full tuition reimbursements (averaging $15,000 per year) were awarded; Federal Work-Study and unspecified assistantships also available. Support available to part-time students. Financial award application deadline: 6/15; financial award applicants required to submit FAFSA. *Unit head:* Dr. B. Regina Dorman, Director, 770-423-6172, Fax: 770-423-6627, E-mail: gdorman@kennesaw.edu. *Application contact:* Vilma Marquez, Admissions Counselor, 770-420-4377, Fax: 770-423-6885, E-mail: ksugrad@kennesaw.edu.

Kent State University, College of Nursing, Kent, OH 44242-0001. Offers clinical nursing (MSN), including nursing of the adult (medical/surgical nursing), psychiatric mental health nursing; nursing (PhD); nursing administration (MSN); nursing education (MSN); parent-child nursing (MSN). *Accreditation:* NLN. Part-time programs available. *Degree requirements:* For master's, thesis optional; for doctorate, thesis/dissertation, comprehensive exam, registration. *Entrance requirements:* For master's, GRE if undergraduate GPA is less than 3.0, minimum GPA of 2.75; for doctorate, GRE, MSN. Additional exam requirements/recommendations for international students: Required—TOEFL. Electronic applications accepted. Expenses: Contact institution. *Faculty research:* Women and violence, methodological specialties, osteoporosis in women, new caregivers and the elderly.

Lamar University, College of Graduate Studies, College of Arts and Sciences, Department of Nursing, Beaumont, TX 77710. Offers nursing administration online (MSN); nursing education online (MSN); MSN/MBA. *Accreditation:* NLN. Part-time and evening/weekend programs available. *Faculty:* 10 full-time (all women). *Students:* 2 full-time (0 women), 7 part-time (4 women). Average age 42. 10 applicants, 40% accepted, 2 enrolled. In 2006, 2 master's awarded. *Median time to degree:* Of those who began their doctoral program in fall 1998, 100% received their degree in 8 years or less. *Degree requirements:* For master's, practicum project presentation, evidence-based project. *Entrance requirements:* For master's, GRE General Test, MAT, criminal background check, RN license, NLN-accredited BSN, college course work in graduate statistics in past 5 years, letters of recommendation, minimum undergraduate GPA of 3.0. Additional exam requirements/recommendations for international students: Required—TOEFL, MAT. *Application deadline:* For fall admission, 8/1 priority date for domestic students; for spring admission, 12/1 priority date for domestic students. Applications are processed on a rolling basis. Application fee: $25 ($50 for international students). *Expenses:* Tuition, nonresident: part-time $33 per hour. Required fees: $43 per hour. $110 per semester. *Financial support:* In 2006–07, 3 students received support, including 2 teaching assistantships (averaging $24,000 per year); scholarships/grants and traineeships also available. Financial award application deadline: 4/1. *Faculty research:* Student retention, theory, caregiving, on-line course and research. Total annual research expenditures: $6,000. *Unit head:* Dr. Nancy Blume, Director of Graduate Nursing Studies, 409-880-8820, Fax: 409-880-8698, E-mail: nancy.blume@lamar.edu. *Application contact:* Shelly R. Belk, Administrative Associate, 409-880-7720.

La Roche College, School of Graduate Studies, Program in Nursing, Pittsburgh, PA 15237-5898. Offers family nurse practitioner (MSN); nursing management (MSN). *Accreditation:* AANA/CANAEP; NLN. Part-time and evening/weekend programs available. *Faculty:* 2 full-time (both women), 1 part-time/adjunct (0 women). *Students:* Average age 46. *Median time to degree:* Master's–2 years full-time, 4 years part-time. *Degree requirements:* For master's, internship, practicum, thesis optional. *Entrance requirements:* For master's, GRE General Test, BSN, nursing license, work experience. *Application deadline:* For fall admission, 8/15 priority date for domestic students; for spring admission, 12/15 priority date for domestic students. Applications are processed on a rolling basis. Application fee: $50. Electronic applications accepted. *Expenses: Contact institution. Financial support:* Application deadline: 3/31; *Faculty research:* Patient education, perception. *Unit head:* Dr. Rosemary McCarthy, Division Chair, 412-536-1173, Fax: 412-536-1175, E-mail: mccartr1@laroche.edu. *Application contact:* Hope Schiffgens, Director of Admissions for Graduate and Continuing Education, 412-536-1266, Fax: 412-536-1283, E-mail: schombh1@laroche.edu.

La Salle University, School of Nursing and Health Sciences, Philadelphia, PA 19141-1199. Offers adult health and illness, clinical nurse specialist (MSN); gerontology (Certificate); nursing administration (MSN); nursing education (Certificate); nursing informatics (Certificate); primary care of adults-nurse practitioner (MSN); public health nursing (MSN); school nursing (Certificate); speech-language-hearing science (MS); wound, ostomy and continence nursing (Certificate); wound, ostomy, and continence nursing (MSN); MSN/MBA. *Accreditation:* AACN. Part-time programs available. Postbaccalaureate distance learning degree programs offered (minimal on-campus study). *Entrance requirements:* For master's, GRE or MAT, 1 year of professional work experience, BSN, Pennsylvania RN license. Expenses: Contact institution. *Faculty research:* Medication errors, wound care, metacognition, education of RN students.

Lehman College of the City University of New York, Division of Natural and Social Sciences, Department of Nursing, Bronx, NY 10468-1589. Offers adult health nursing (MS); nursing of older adults (MS); parent-child nursing (MS); pediatric nurse practitioner (MS). *Accreditation:* AACN. Part-time and evening/weekend programs available. *Entrance requirements:* For master's, bachelor's degree in nursing, New York RN license.

Le Moyne College, Department of Nursing, Syracuse, NY 13214. Offers MS. Part-time and evening/weekend programs available. *Faculty:* 1 (woman) full-time, 3 part-time/adjunct (2 women). *Students:* 13 applicants, 69% accepted, 9 enrolled. *Entrance requirements:* For master's, interview, minimum GPA of 3.0, NY RN license, 2 letters of recommendation, writing sample. Additional exam requirements/recommendations for international students: Required—TOEFL (minimum score 550 paper-based; 213 computer-based). *Application deadline:* Applications are processed on a rolling basis. Application fee: $50. *Expenses: Contact institution. Financial support:* Available to part-time students. Applicants required to submit FAFSA. *Faculty research:* Patient education. *Unit head:* Dr. Susan B. Bastable, Professor and Chair of Department of Nursing, 315-445-5435, Fax: 315-445-4602, E-mail: bastabsb@lemoyne.edu. *Application contact:* Kristen P. Trapasso, Director of Graduate Admission, 315-445-4265, Fax: 315-445-6027, E-mail: trapaskp@lemoyne.edu.

Lewis University, College of Nursing and Health Professions, Program in Nursing, Romeoville, IL 60446. Offers case management (MSN); nursing administration (MSN); nursing education (MSN); MSN/MBA. *Accreditation:* AACN. Part-time and evening/weekend programs available. *Degree requirements:* For master's, clinical practicum. *Entrance requirements:* For master's, GRE General Test, GRE Subject Test, minimum undergraduate GPA of 2.75, degree in nursing, RN license, letter of recommendation, interview, resumé or curriculum vitae. Additional exam requirements/recommendations for international students: Required—TOEFL (minimum score 550 paper-based; 213 computer-based). Electronic applications accepted. *Faculty research:* Cancer prevention, phenomenological methods, public policy analysis.

Liberty University, College of Arts and Sciences, Lynchburg, VA 24502. Offers counseling (MA); nursing (MSN); pastoral care and counseling (PhD); professional counseling (PhD). *Accreditation:* AACN. Part-time programs available. Postbaccalaureate distance learning degree programs offered (minimal on-campus study). *Faculty:* 13 full-time (2 women), 54 part-time/adjunct (15 women). *Students:* 205 full-time (146 women), 947 part-time (718 women); includes 302 minority (255 African Americans, 5 American Indian/Alaska Native, 11 Asian Americans or Pacific Islanders, 31 Hispanic Americans), 34 international. Average age 36. 1,480 applicants,

Nursing—General

Liberty University (continued)
88% accepted, 553 enrolled. In 2006, 201 master's, 5 doctorates awarded. *Degree requirements:* For master's, comprehensive exam (for some programs); for doctorate, thesis/dissertation, comprehensive exam. *Entrance requirements:* For master's, GRE General Test (MSN), minimum undergraduate GPA of 3.0; for doctorate, GRE General Test, minimum master's GPA of 3.25. Additional exam requirements/recommendations for international students: Required—TOEFL (minimum score 600 paper-based; 250 computer-based). *Application deadline:* For fall admission, 6/1 priority date for domestic students; for spring admission, 11/1 priority date for domestic students. Applications are processed on a rolling basis. Application fee: $35. Electronic applications accepted. *Financial support:* In 2006–07, 817 students received support, including 9 teaching assistantships with tuition reimbursements available; Federal Work-Study also available. *Faculty research:* God concept and adult attachment, building marital strength, image of God and gender, breastfeeding behavior among adolescent mothers, osteoporosis. *Unit head:* Dr. Ronald E. Hawkins, Dean, 434-592-4030, Fax: 434-522-0416, E-mail: rehawkin@liberty.edu. *Application contact:* Kyle A Falce, Director of Graduate Admissions, 800-424-9596, Fax: 800-628-7977, E-mail: gradadmissions@liberty.edu.

Lincoln Memorial University, School of Nursing and Allied Health, Harrogate, TN 37752-1901. Offers nursing (MSN). *Faculty:* 4 full-time (all women). *Students:* 10 full-time (all women); includes 1 minority (African American) *Unit head:* Dr. Mary Modorin, Dean, 423-869-6319, Fax: 423-869-6244, E-mail: maryanne.moderin@lmunet.edu.

Loma Linda University, Department of Graduate Nursing, Loma Linda, CA 92350. Offers adult and aging family nursing (MS); growing family nursing (MS); nursing administration (MS, Certificate). *Accreditation:* AACN. Part-time programs available. *Degree requirements:* For master's, thesis or alternative. *Entrance requirements:* For master's, GRE General Test.

Long Island University, Brooklyn Campus, School of Nursing, Brooklyn, NY 11201-8423. Offers MS, Certificate. *Accreditation:* AACN. *Entrance requirements:* For master's, New York RN license, 2 letters of recommendation. Additional exam requirements/recommendations for international students: Required—TOEFL (minimum score 500 paper-based; 173 computer-based). Electronic applications accepted.

Long Island University, C.W. Post Campus, School of Health Professions and Nursing, Department of Nursing, Brookville, NY 11548-1300. Offers clinical nurse specialist (MS); family nurse practitioner (MS, Certificate). *Accreditation:* AACN. Part-time and evening/weekend programs available. *Degree requirements:* For master's, thesis. *Entrance requirements:* For master's, minimum GPA of 3.0 in major, bachelor's degree in nursing, NYS registered nurse, interview. Electronic applications accepted. *Faculty research:* Lactation/breast cancer, early discharge in maternity.

Louisiana State University Health Sciences Center, School of Nursing, New Orleans, LA 70112-2223. Offers adult health and illness (MN); adult health and nursing (DNS); neonatal nurse practitioner (MN); nursing (MN); nursing service administration (MN, DNS); parent-child health nursing (MN); primary care nurse practitioner (MN); psychiatric/community mental health nursing (MN, DNS); public health/community health nursing (MN, DNS). *Accreditation:* AACN; AANA/CANAEP (one or more programs are accredited). Part-time programs available. *Degree requirements:* For master's, thesis optional; for doctorate, thesis/dissertation. *Entrance requirements:* For master's, GRE General Test, MAT, minimum GPA of 3.0; for doctorate, GRE General Test, minimum GPA of 3.5. Additional exam requirements/recommendations for international students: Required—TOEFL. *Expenses:* Tuition, state resident: full-time $5,868; part-time $722 per credit. Tuition, nonresident: full-time $8,993; part-time $1,104 per credit. *Faculty research:* Advanced clinical practice, nursing education, health, social support, nursing administration.

Loyola University Chicago, Graduate School, Marcella Niehoff School of Nursing, Chicago, IL 60611-2196. Offers acute care clinical nurse specialist (MSN); acute care nurse practitioner (MSN); adult clinical nurse specialist (MSN); adult nurse practitioner (MSN); cardiovascular health and disease management clinical nurse specialist (MSN); emergency nurse practitioner (MSN); family nurse practitioner (MSN); health systems management (MSN); nursing (PhD); oncology clinical nurse specialist (MSN); population-based infection control and environmental safety (MSN); women's health nurse practitioner (MSN); M Div/MSN; MSN/MBA. *Accreditation:* AACN. Part-time and evening/weekend programs available. *Faculty:* 26 full-time (25 women), 58 part-time/adjunct (50 women). *Students:* 60 full-time (54 women), 227 part-time (213 women); includes 48 minority (13 African Americans, 23 Asian Americans or Pacific Islanders, 12 Hispanic Americans), 1 international. Average age 32. 31 applicants, 45% accepted. In 2006, 33 master's, 8 doctorates awarded. Terminal master's awarded for partial completion of doctoral program. *Degree requirements:* For master's, comprehensive exam; for doctorate, thesis/dissertation, preliminary exam. *Entrance requirements:* For master's, BSN, minimum GPA of 3.0, Illinois RN license, 3 letters of recommendation, 1 year experience in area of specialty prior to clinical; for doctorate, GRE General Test, BSN, minimum GPA of 3.0, professional license. Additional exam requirements/recommendations for international students: Required—TOEFL (minimum score 650 paper-based; 280 computer-based). *Application deadline:* For fall admission, 8/1 priority date for domestic and international students; for spring admission, 12/1 priority date for domestic and international students. Applications are processed on a rolling basis. Application fee: $40. Electronic applications accepted. *Expenses:* Contact institution. *Financial support:* In 2006–07, 10 students received support, including 1 fellowship with tuition reimbursement available, 4 research assistantships with tuition reimbursements available, 1 teaching assistantship with tuition reimbursement available; career-related internships or fieldwork, Federal Work-Study, institutionally sponsored loans, traineeships, and unspecified assistantships also available. Support available to part-time students. Financial award applicants required to submit FAFSA. *Faculty research:* Immunology, women and heart disease, PNI, diabetes, cardiovascular disease. *Unit head:* Dr. Ida Androwich, Dean, 773-508-3255, E-mail: iandrow@luc.edu. *Application contact:* Dr. Vicki A. Keough, Associate Professor, 708-216-3582, Fax: 708-216-9555, E-mail: vkeough@luc.edu.

Loyola University New Orleans, City College, Program in Nursing, New Orleans, LA 70118-6195. Offers family nurse practitioner (MSN); health care systems management (MSN). *Accreditation:* NLN. Postbaccalaureate distance learning degree programs offered. *Degree requirements:* For master's, 700 hours of clinical practice. *Entrance requirements:* For master's, GRE, BSN, Louisiana nursing license, 1 year of work experience in clinical nursing, minimum undergraduate GPA of 2.8, interview. Additional exam requirements/recommendations for international students: Required—TOEFL (minimum score 550 paper-based; 213 computer-based). *Faculty research:* Increasing compliance with treatment, patient satisfaction with care provided by nurse practitioners.

Madonna University, Program in Nursing, Livonia, MI 48150-1173. Offers adult health: chronic health conditions (MSN); adult nurse practitioner (MSN); nursing administration (MSN); MSN/MSBA. *Accreditation:* AACN. Part-time programs available. *Faculty:* 3 full-time (all women). *Students:* 12 full-time (all women), 82 part-time (80 women); includes 9 minority (5 African Americans, 3 Asian Americans or Pacific Islanders, 1 Hispanic American), 3 international. Average age 40. 20 applicants, 50% accepted. In 2006, 10 degrees awarded. *Degree requirements:* For master's, thesis or alternative. *Entrance requirements:* For master's, GRE General Test, Michigan nursing license. *Application deadline:* For fall admission, 8/1 priority date for domestic students; for winter admission, 12/1 priority date for domestic students; for spring admission, 4/1 priority date for domestic students. Applications are processed on a rolling basis. Application fee: $25 ($200 for international students). Electronic applications accepted. *Financial support:* Career-related internships or fieldwork, Federal Work-Study, institutionally sponsored loans, and scholarships/grants available. Support available to part-time students. *Faculty research:* Coping, caring. *Unit head:* Dr. Nancy O'Connor, Chairperson, 734-432-5461, Fax: 734-432-5463, E-mail: noconnor@madonna.edu. *Application contact:* Sandra Kellums, Coordinator of Graduate Admissions and Records, 734-432-5667, Fax: 734-432-5862, E-mail: skellum@madonna.edu.

Malone College, School of Nursing, Graduate Program in Nursing, Canton, OH 44709-3897. Offers clinical nurse specialist (MSN); family nurse practitioner (MSN). *Accreditation:* AACN. Evening/weekend programs available. *Faculty:* 6 full-time (all women), 8 part-time/adjunct (7 women). *Students:* Average age 35. In 2006, 9 degrees awarded. *Degree requirements:* For master's, thesis. *Entrance requirements:* For master's, minimum GPA of 3.0 from BSN program, interview. *Application deadline:* For fall admission, 5/31 for international students. Applications are processed on a rolling basis. Application fee: $25. *Expenses:* Contact institution. *Financial support:* Tuition waivers (partial) available. Support available to part-time students. Financial award application deadline: 6/30. *Faculty research:* Compassion: teaching/observing/providing issues/needs of migrant populations, psychosocial care of patients close to death, the process of reconstitution, newborn health concerns in Mali, West Africa. *Unit head:* Dr. Karen R. Gehrling, Director, 330-471-8163, Fax: 330-471-8407, E-mail: kgerhling@malone.edu. *Application contact:* Dr. David Kleffman, Recruiter, 330-471-8447, Fax: 330-471-8343, E-mail: dkleffman@malone.edu.

Mansfield University of Pennsylvania, Graduate Studies, Program in Nursing, Mansfield, PA 16933. Offers MSN. *Accreditation:* NLN. Part-time and evening/weekend programs available. Postbaccalaureate distance learning degree programs offered. *Faculty:* 1 (woman) full-time, 2 part-time/adjunct (both women). *Students:* Average age 42. 25 applicants, 56% accepted, 7 enrolled. *Degree requirements:* For master's, thesis optional. *Entrance requirements:* For master's, minimum GPA of 3.0. Additional exam requirements/recommendations for international students: Required—TOEFL (minimum score 550 paper-based; 220 computer-based). *Application deadline:* For fall admission, 8/1 priority date for domestic students, 6/1 priority date for international students; for spring admission, 11/1 priority date for domestic students, 9/1 priority date for international students. Applications are processed on a rolling basis. Application fee: $25. Electronic applications accepted. *Expenses:* Tuition, state resident: part-time $336 per credit. Tuition, nonresident: part-time $538 per credit. Tuition and fees vary according to course load and reciprocity agreements. *Financial support:* Unspecified assistantships available. *Faculty research:* Women's health, gyniatrics, art therapy, nursing empowerment. *Unit head:* Dr. Janeen Sheehe, Chairperson, 570-662-4522, E-mail: jsheehe@mansfield.edu. *Application contact:* Judi Brayer, Assistant Director of Enrollment Management/Graduate Admissions, 570-662-4818, Fax: 570-662-4121, E-mail: jbrayer@mansfield.edu.

Marian College of Fond du Lac, School of Nursing, Fond du Lac, WI 54935-4699. Offers adult nurse practitioner (MSN); nurse educator (MSN). *Accreditation:* AACN. Part-time and evening/weekend programs available. *Faculty:* 4 full-time (3 women), 4 part-time/adjunct (2 women). *Students:* 13 full-time (all women), 15 part-time (all women); includes 1 minority (American Indian/Alaska Native). Average age 37. 9 applicants, 100% accepted, 9 enrolled. In 2006, 16 degrees awarded. *Degree requirements:* For master's, thesis, 675 clinical practicum hours. *Entrance requirements:* For master's, 3 letters of professional recommendation, undergraduate work in nursing research, statistics, health assessment. Additional exam requirements/recommendations for international students: Required—TOEFL (minimum score 525 paper-based). *Application deadline:* Applications are processed on a rolling basis. Application fee: $50. Electronic applications accepted. *Expenses:* Contact institution. *Financial support:* In 2006–07, 19 students received support. Institutionally sponsored loans and scholarships/grants available. Support available to part-time students. Financial award application deadline: 3/1; financial award applicants required to submit FAFSA. *Unit head:* Dr. James C. McCann, Dean, School of Nursing, 920-923-8094, Fax: 920-923-8770, E-mail: jcmccann70@mariancollege.edu. *Application contact:* Dr. Lea Monahan, Director, 920-923-7608, Fax: 920-923-8770, E-mail: lmonahan@mariancollege.edu.

Marquette University, Graduate School, College of Nursing, Milwaukee, WI 53201-1881. Offers adult nurse practitioner (Certificate); advanced practice nursing (MSN), including adult, children, neonatal nurse practitioner, nurse-midwifery, older adult; gerontological nurse practitioner (Certificate); neonatal nurse practitioner (Certificate); nurse-midwifery (Certificate); nursing (PhD); pediatric nurse practitioner (Certificate). *Accreditation:* AACN. Part-time and evening/weekend programs available. *Faculty:* 29 full-time (27 women), 39 part-time/adjunct (37 women). *Students:* 104 full-time (98 women), 122 part-time (114 women); includes 18 minority (5 African Americans, 2 American Indian/Alaska Native, 4 Asian Americans or Pacific Islanders, 7 Hispanic Americans), 2 international. Average age 34. 122 applicants, 79% accepted, 73 enrolled. In 2006, 46 degrees awarded. *Degree requirements:* For master's, thesis or alternative, comprehensive exam. *Entrance requirements:* For master's, GRE General Test, BSN, Wisconsin RN license. Additional exam requirements/recommendations for international students: Required—TOEFL. Application fee: $40. *Financial support:* In 2006–07, 6 research assistantships, 1 teaching assistantship were awarded; career-related internships or fieldwork, Federal Work-Study, institutionally sponsored loans, scholarships/grants, and tuition waivers (full and partial) also available. Support available to part-time students. Financial award application deadline: 2/15. *Faculty research:* Psychosocial adjustment to chronic illness, gerontology, reminiscence, health policy: uninsured and access, hospital care delivery systems. Total annual research expenditures: $1.1 million. *Unit head:* Dr. Lea Acord, Dean, 414-288-3812, Fax: 414-288-1578. *Application contact:* Dr. Judy Miller, Director of Graduate Studies, 414-288-3810, Fax: 414-288-1578.

Marshall University, Academic Affairs Division, College of Health Professions, Department of Nursing, Huntington, WV 25755. Offers MSN. *Faculty:* 15 full-time (14 women), 2 part-time/adjunct (1 woman). *Students:* 11 full-time (all women), 98 part-time (95 women). Average age 37. In 2006, 27 degrees awarded. *Entrance requirements:* For master's, GRE General Test. Application fee: $40. *Unit head:* Dr. Sandra Marra, Chairperson, 304-696-2639, E-mail: scott@marshall.edu. *Application contact:* Information Contact, 304-746-1900, Fax: 304-746-1902, E-mail: services@marshall.edu.

Marymount University, School of Health Professions, Program in Nursing, Arlington, VA 22207-4299. Offers family nurse practitioner (MSN, Certificate); nursing administration (MSN, Certificate); nursing education (MSN, Certificate); RN to MSN (MSN). *Accreditation:* AACN; NLN. Part-time and evening/weekend programs available. *Faculty:* 7 full-time (all women), 1 (woman) part-time/adjunct. *Students:* 4 full-time (3 women), 36 part-time (35 women); includes 23 minority (15 African Americans, 5 Asian Americans or Pacific Islanders, 3 Hispanic Americans), 1 international. Average age 42. 17 applicants, 100% accepted, 10 enrolled. In 2006, 13 master's, 2 other advanced degrees awarded. *Degree requirements:* For master's, comprehensive exam. *Entrance requirements:* For master's, 2 letters of recommendation, interview, RN license, resumé; for Certificate, interview. *Application deadline:* Applications are processed on a rolling basis. Application fee: $40. Electronic applications accepted. *Expenses:* Tuition: Full-time $11,160; part-time $620 per credit. Required fees: $113; $630 per credit. *Financial support:* Research assistantships with partial tuition reimbursements, career-related internships or fieldwork, scholarships/grants, and unspecified assistantships available. Support available to part-time students. Financial award applicants required to submit FAFSA. *Unit head:* Dr. Susan Bidwell, Chair, 703-284-1593, Fax: 703-284-3819, E-mail: susan.bidwell@marymount.edu.

Maryville University of Saint Louis, School of Health Professions, Nursing Program, St. Louis, MO 63141-7299. Offers MSN. *Accreditation:* AACN. *Students:* 15 full-time (14 women), 75 part-time (70 women); includes 5 African Americans, 1 Asian American or Pacific Islander, 2 Hispanic Americans. Average age 38. 24 applicants, 96% accepted, 21 enrolled. In 2006, 6 degrees awarded. *Degree requirements:* For master's, research project. *Entrance requirements:* For master's, BSN, current licensure. Additional exam requirements/recommendations for international students: Required—TOEFL (minimum score 550 paper-based). *Application deadline:* Applications are processed on a rolling basis. Application fee: $35 ($50 for international students). Electronic applications accepted. *Expenses:* Tuition: Full-time $17,800; part-time $555 per credit. Required fees: $55 per semester. Tuition and fees vary according to degree level and program. *Financial support:* Federal Work-Study and campus employment available. Support available to part-time students. Financial award application deadline: 7/31. *Unit head:* Dr. Mary Curtis, Director, 314-529-9478, Fax: 314-529-9139.

McGill University, Faculty of Graduate and Postdoctoral Studies, Faculty of Medicine, School of Nursing, Montréal, QC H3A 2T5, Canada. Offers nurse practitioner (Graduate Diploma); nursing (M Sc A, PhD). Part-time programs available. *Degree requirements:* For doctorate, thesis/dissertation. *Entrance requirements:* For master's, GRE General Test, minimum GPA of 3.0; for doctorate, GRE General Test. Additional exam requirements/recommendations for international students: Required—TOEFL. *Faculty research:* Pain, maternal-child nursing, women's health, children in hospitals, elderly.

McKendree College, Graduate Programs, Lebanon, IL 62254-1299. Offers business administration (MBA); counseling (MA); education (M Ed); nursing (MSN).

McMaster University, Faculty of Health Sciences and School of Graduate Studies, Program in Nursing (course-based), Hamilton, ON L8S 4M2, Canada. Offers M Sc. *Students:* 6 full-time. In 2006, 6 degrees awarded. *Degree requirements:* For master's, scholarly paper. *Entrance requirements:* For master's, 4 year honors BSCN, minimum B+ average in last 60 units. Additional exam requirements/recommendations for international students: Required—TOEFL (minimum score 580 paper-based; 237 computer-based; 92 iBT). *Application deadline:* For winter admission, 1/31 for domestic students. Application fee: $90. *Financial support:* Teaching assistantships available. *Unit head:* Dr. Margaret Black, Coordinator, 905-525-9140 Ext. 22259. *Application contact:* Dr. Carl Richards, Associate Dean, 905-525-9140, Fax: 905-546-1129.

McMaster University, Faculty of Health Sciences and School of Graduate Studies, Program in Nursing (thesis), Hamilton, ON L8S 4M2, Canada. Offers M Sc, PhD. *Students:* 69 full-time, 2 part-time. In 2006, 10 master's, 2 doctorates awarded. *Degree requirements:* For master's, thesis/dissertation; for doctorate, thesis/dissertation, comprehensive exam. *Entrance requirements:* For master's, honors B Sc N, B+ average in last 60 units; for doctorate, M Sc, minimum B+ average. Additional exam requirements/recommendations for international students: Required—TOEFL (minimum score 580 paper-based; 237 computer-based; 92 iBT). *Application deadline:* For winter admission, 1/31 for domestic students. Application fee: $90. *Financial support:* Teaching assistantships available. *Unit head:* Dr. Margaret Black, Coordinator, 905-525-9140 Ext. 22259. *Application contact:* Dr. Carl Richards, Associate Dean, 905-525-9140 Ext. 22983, Fax: 905-546-1129.

McNeese State University, Graduate School, College of Nursing, Lake Charles, LA 70609. Offers MSN. *Accreditation:* NLN. *Faculty:* 4 full-time (all women), 1 (woman) part-time/adjunct. *Students:* 16 full-time (11 women), 42 part-time (37 women); includes 7 minority (all African Americans) In 2006, 14 degrees awarded. *Degree requirements:* For master's, comprehensive exam. *Entrance requirements:* For master's, GRE, minimum 1 year clinical practice as RN. *Application deadline:* For fall admission, 5/15 priority date for domestic students. Applications are processed on a rolling basis. Application fee: $20 ($30 for international students). *Expenses:* Tuition, area resident: Full-time $2,226; part-time $193 per hour. Required fees: $919; $106 per hour. *Financial support:* Application deadline: 5/1. *Unit head:* Dr. Peggy L. Wolfe, Dean, 337-475-5820, Fax: 337-475-5924, E-mail: pwolfe@mcneese.edu.

Medical College of Georgia, School of Graduate Studies, Programs in Nursing, Augusta, GA 30912-1500. Offers adult nursing (MSN); community health nursing (MSN); mental health nursing (MSN); nurse practitioner (MSN); nursing (DNP, PhD); nursing anesthesia (MSN); parent-child nursing (MSN). *Accreditation:* AACN; AANA/CANAEP. Part-time programs available. *Faculty:* 18 full-time (16 women), 1 part-time/adjunct (0 women). *Students:* 95 full-time (76 women), 42 part-time (37 women); includes 24 minority (20 African Americans, 4 Asian Americans or Pacific Islanders). Average age 37. 156 applicants, 35% accepted, 24 enrolled. In 2006, 28 master's, 10 doctorates awarded. *Degree requirements:* For master's, thesis (for some programs); for doctorate, thesis/dissertation. *Entrance requirements:* For master's, GRE General Test, MAT; for doctorate, GRE General Test. Additional exam requirements/recommendations for international students: Required—TOEFL (minimum score 550 paper-based; 213 computer-based). *Application deadline:* For fall admission, 7/1 for domestic students, 4/15 for international students. Applications are processed on a rolling basis. Application fee: $30. Electronic applications accepted. *Expenses:* Tuition, state resident: full-time $2,293; part-time $192 per credit hour. Tuition, nonresident: full-time $9,169; part-time $765 per credit hour. Required fees: $293 per semester. *Financial support:* In 2006–07, 78 students received support, including 9 research assistantships with partial tuition reimbursements available (averaging $23,000 per year); Federal Work-Study, institutionally sponsored loans, traineeships, tuition waivers, and unspecified assistantships also available. Support available to part-time students. Financial award application deadline: 5/31; financial award applicants required to submit FAFSA. *Unit head:* Dr. Lucy Marion, Dean, 706-721-6258, Fax: 706-721-8169, E-mail: lumarion@mail.mcg.edu.

Medical University of South Carolina, College of Nursing, Program in Nursing, Charleston, SC 29425-0002. Offers PhD. *Accreditation:* AACN. Part-time programs available. Postbaccalaureate distance learning degree programs offered (minimal on-campus study). *Faculty:* 17 full-time (16 women). *Students:* 2 full-time (1 woman), 21 part-time (19 women); includes 3 minority (all African Americans) Average age 28. 6 applicants, 67% accepted, 4 enrolled. In 2006, 4 degrees awarded. *Degree requirements:* For doctorate, thesis/dissertation, mentored teaching and research seminar, comprehensive exam. *Entrance requirements:* For doctorate, GRE General Test, interview, minimum GPA of 3.5, BSN, RN license, curriculum vitae. Additional exam requirements/recommendations for international students: Required—TOEFL (minimum score 600 paper-based; 250 computer-based). *Application deadline:* For fall admission, 2/1 priority date for domestic and international students. Applications are processed on a rolling basis. Application fee: $75. Electronic applications accepted. *Financial support:* Federal Work-Study and scholarships/grants available. Financial award application deadline: 3/15; financial award applicants required to submit FAFSA. *Unit head:* Gail A. Barbosa, Director, 843-792-3815. *Application contact:* Erika M. Jenkins, Administrative Coordinator, 843-792-3815, Fax: 843-792-9285, E-mail: jenkinse@musc.edu.

Memorial University of Newfoundland, School of Graduate Studies, School of Nursing, St. John's, NL A1C 5S7, Canada. Offers MN, PMD. Part-time programs available. *Degree requirements:* For master's, thesis optional; for PMD, clinical placement. *Entrance requirements:* For master's, bachelor's degree in nursing, 1 year experience in nursing practice, practicing license; for PMD, 2 years clinical nursing experience, practicing license (Canada) or proof of registration as a practicing nurse (international), letter from a health care agency guaranteeing clinical placement. Electronic applications accepted. *Faculty research:* Women's health, infant feeding practices, nursing management, care of the elderly, children's health.

Mercer University, Graduate Studies, Cecil B. Day Campus, Georgia Baptist College of Nursing, Macon, GA 31207-0003. Offers nurse education (Certificate); nursing (MSN). *Accreditation:* AACN. Part-time programs available. *Faculty:* 13 full-time (12 women). *Students:* 8 full-time (all women), 5 part-time (all women); includes 4 minority (all African Americans) Average age 39. 5 applicants, 100% accepted, 4 enrolled. In 2006, 8 degrees awarded. *Degree requirements:* For master's, thesis (for some programs), registration. *Entrance requirements:* For master's, MAT or GRE, bachelor's degree from an accredited nursing program, registered GA nursing license. Additional exam requirements/recommendations for international students: Required—TOEFL (minimum score 80 iBT). *Application deadline:* For fall admission, 7/1 for domestic students, 4/15 for international students; for spring admission, 12/1 for domestic students. Applications are processed on a rolling basis. Application fee: $50. *Expenses:* Contact institution. *Financial support:* In 2006–07, 13 students received support. Institutionally sponsored loans, scholarships/grants, and traineeships available. Support available to part-time students. Financial award applicants required to submit FAFSA. *Faculty research:* Osteoporosis, honor system, women and alcoholism, nursing assessment measures. *Unit head:* Dr. Susan S. Gunby, Dean/Professor, 678-547-6799, Fax: 678-547-6796, E-mail: nursing@mercer.edu. *Application contact:* Lynn Vines, Director of Admissions, 678-547-6700, Fax: 678-547-6794, E-mail: nursing@mercer.edu.

Mercy College, Division of Health Professions, Program in Nursing, Dobbs Ferry, NY 10522-1189. Offers nursing administration (MS); nursing education (MS). *Accreditation:* AACN. Part-time programs available. *Students:* 18 full-time (8 women), 65 part-time (62 women); includes 36 minority (28 African Americans, 6 Asian Americans or Pacific Islanders, 2 Hispanic Americans), 14 international. Average age 41. In 2006, 15 degrees awarded. *Degree requirements:* For master's, comprehensive project. *Entrance requirements:* For master's, GRE General Test or MAT, BSN, minimum GPA of 3.0, 2 letters of reference, interview, US RN registration. *Application deadline:* For fall admission, 8/15 priority date for domestic students; for spring admission, 2/15 for domestic students. Applications are processed on a rolling basis. Application fee: $62. *Expenses:* Tuition: Part-time $595 per credit. Required fees: $9 per credit. Tuition and fees vary according to program. *Financial support:* Career-related internships or fieldwork, Federal Work-Study, and institutionally sponsored loans available. Support available to part-time students. *Faculty research:* Program evaluation, cost and home care, children of alcoholic parents, clinical decision making. *Unit head:* Dr. Mary McGuiness, Director, Nursing Programs, 914-674-7863 Ext. 551, E-mail: mmcguiness@mercy.edu. *Application contact:* Kathleen Jackson, Director of Admissions, 800-Mercy-NY, Fax: 914-674-7382, E-mail: admissions@mercy.edu.

Metropolitan State University, School of Nursing, St. Paul, MN 55106-5000. Offers MSN. *Accreditation:* AACN. Part-time programs available. *Degree requirements:* For master's, thesis or alternative. *Entrance requirements:* For master's, GRE General Test or MAT, minimum GPA of 3.0, RN license. *Faculty research:* Women's health, gerontology.

MGH Institute of Health Professions, Graduate Programs, Program in Nursing, Boston, MA 02129. Offers advanced practice nursing (MSN); gerontological nursing (MSN); pediatric nursing (MSN); psychiatric nursing (MSN); teaching and learning for health care education (Certificate); women's health nursing (MSN). *Accreditation:* NLN (one or more programs are accredited). *Faculty:* 29 full-time (28 women), 9 part-time/adjunct (7 women). *Students:* 208 full-time (188 women), 43 part-time (35 women); includes 36 minority (12 African Americans, 17 Asian Americans or Pacific Islanders, 7 Hispanic Americans), 1 international. Average age 29. 302 applicants, 62% accepted, 101 enrolled. In 2006, 77 master's, 3 other advanced degrees awarded. *Degree requirements:* For master's, thesis or alternative. *Entrance requirements:* For master's, GRE General Test, minimum GPA of 3.0. Additional exam requirements/recommendations for international students: Required—TOEFL (minimum score 550 paper-based; 213 computer-based). *Application deadline:* For fall admission, 1/10 for domestic and international students. Application fee: $50. Electronic applications accepted. *Financial support:* In 2006–07, 212 students received support, including 1 research assistantship (averaging $1,200 per year), 2 teaching assistantships (averaging $1,200 per year); career-related internships or fieldwork, scholarships/grants, traineeships, tuition waivers (full and partial), and unspecified assistantships also available. Support available to part-time students. Financial award application deadline: 3/3; financial award applicants required to submit FAFSA. *Faculty research:* Biobehavioral nursing, HIV/AIDS, gerontological nursing, women's health, vulnerable populations, health systems . *Unit head:* Margery Chisholm, Director, 617-724-0480, Fax: 617-726-8022, E-mail: mchisholm@mghihp.edu. *Application contact:* Maureen Rika Judd, Manager of Admissions, 617-726-6069, Fax: 617-726-8010, E-mail: admissions@mghihp.edu.

See Close-Up on page 1963.

Michigan State University, The Graduate School, College of Nursing, East Lansing, MI 48824. Offers MSN, PhD. *Accreditation:* AACN. Part-time programs available. Postbaccalaureate distance learning degree programs offered (no on-campus study). *Faculty:* 22 full-time (19 women). *Students:* 35 full-time (31 women), 156 part-time (146 women); includes 14 minority (8 African Americans, 1 American Indian/Alaska Native, 2 Asian Americans or Pacific Islanders, 3 Hispanic Americans), 1 international. Average age 39. 134 applicants, 70% accepted. In 2006, 24 master's, 1 doctorate awarded. *Entrance requirements:* Additional exam requirements/recommendations for international students: Required—TOEFL (minimum score 580 paper-based; 213 computer-based), Michigan State University ELT (85), Michigan ELAB (83). *Application deadline:* For fall admission, 11/1 priority date for domestic students. Application fee: $50. Electronic applications accepted. *Expenses:* Tuition, state resident: part-time $346 per credit hour. Tuition, nonresident: part-time $730 per credit hour. Tuition and fees vary according to program. *Financial support:* In 2006–07, 42 fellowships with tuition reimbursements, 5 research assistantships with tuition reimbursements (averaging $12,839 per year) were awarded. *Faculty research:* Hormone replacement therapy, end of life research, human-animal bond, chronic disease, family home care for cancer. Total annual research expenditures: $1.5 million. *Unit head:* Dr. Mary Mundt, Dean, 517-355-6527, Fax: 517-353-9553, E-mail: mary.mundt@msu.edu. *Application contact:* Tiffany Tewel, Secretary for Student Affairs, 517-353-4827, Fax: 517-353-9553, E-mail: nurse@hc.msu.edu.

Middle Tennessee State University, College of Graduate Studies, College of Basic and Applied Sciences, School of Nursing, Murfreesboro, TN 37132. Offers MSN. Part-time and evening/weekend programs available. Postbaccalaureate distance learning degree programs offered. *Faculty:* 12 full-time (11 women), 1 part-time/adjunct (0 women). *Students:* Average age 38. 7 applicants, 100% accepted. *Entrance requirements:* Additional exam requirements/recommendations for international students: Required—TOEFL (minimum score 525 paper-based; 195 computer-based). *Application deadline:* For fall admission, 8/1 priority date for domestic students. Applications are processed on a rolling basis. Application fee: $25. Electronic applications accepted. *Financial support:* Application deadline: 5/1. *Unit head:* Dr. Lynn Parsons, Director, 615-898-5340.

Midwestern State University, Graduate Studies, College of Health Sciences and Human Services, Nursing Program, Wichita Falls, TX 76308. Offers family nurse practitioner (MSN); health services administration (MSN); nurse educator (MSN). *Accreditation:* AACN. Part-time and evening/weekend programs available. *Faculty:* 8 full-time (all women), 2 part-time/adjunct (both women). *Students:* 12 full-time (10 women), 49 part-time (40 women); includes 8 minority (1 African American, 2 American Indian/Alaska Native, 1 Asian American or Pacific Islander, 4 Hispanic Americans), 3 international. Average age 39. 19 applicants, 84% accepted, 12 enrolled. In 2006, 10 degrees awarded. *Degree requirements:* For master's, thesis optional. *Entrance requirements:* For master's, GRE General Test or MAT. Additional exam requirements/recommendations for international students: Required—TOEFL (minimum score 550 paper-based; 213 computer-based). *Application deadline:* For fall admission, 7/1 for domestic students, 4/1 for international students; for spring admission, 11/1 for domestic students, 8/1 for international students. Applications are processed on a rolling basis. Application fee: $35 ($50 for international students). Electronic applications accepted. *Financial support:* In 2006–07, 58 students received support, including 1 teaching assistantship with partial tuition reimbursement available (averaging $7,500 per year); career-related internships or fieldwork, Federal Work-Study, institutionally sponsored loans, scholarships/grants, tuition waivers (partial), and unspecified assistantships also available. Support available to part-time students. Financial award application deadline: 5/1; financial award applicants required to submit FAFSA. *Unit head:* Dr. Melissa Ford, Chair, 940-397-4601, Fax: 940-397-4513, E-mail: melissa.ford@mwsu.edu. *Application contact:* 800-842-1922, Fax: 940-397-4672, E-mail: admissions@mwsu.edu.

Millersville University of Pennsylvania, Graduate School, School of Science and Mathematics, Department of Nursing, Millersville, PA 17551-0302. Offers MSN. *Accreditation:* NLN. Part-time and evening/weekend programs available. *Faculty:* 5 full-time (all women), 4 part-time/adjunct (3 women). *Students:* 1 (woman) full-time, 33 part-time (29 women); includes 2 minority (1 American Indian/Alaska Native, 1 Asian American or Pacific Islander). Average age 40. 8 applicants, 88% accepted, 7 enrolled. In 2006, 11 degrees awarded. *Degree requirements:* For master's, scholarly project, clinical internship. *Entrance requirements:* For master's, GRE or MAT, BSN, minimum GPA of 3.0, RN license, 1 year of clinical experience, interview, undergraduate course work in statistics and health assessment, 3 letters of reference, resumé, computer literacy. Additional exam requirements/recommendations for international students: Required—TOEFL (minimum score 500 paper-based; 183 computer-based). *Application deadline:* For fall admission, 3/1 for domestic students; for spring admission, 10/1 for domestic

Nursing—General

Millersville University of Pennsylvania (continued)
students. Applications are processed on a rolling basis. Application fee: $35. *Expenses:* Tuition, state resident: full-time $6,048; part-time $336 per credit. Tuition, nonresident: full-time $9,678; part-time $538 per credit. Required fees: $1,244. Tuition and fees vary according to course load. *Financial support:* In 2006–07, 1 student received support, including 1 research assistantship with full tuition reimbursement available (averaging $4,250 per year); Federal Work-Study, institutionally sponsored loans, and unspecified assistantships also available. Support available to part-time students. Financial award application deadline: 3/15; financial award applicants required to submit FAFSA. *Faculty research:* Pediatric obesity, women and heart disease, geriatrics, school nursing, school-age youth. *Unit head:* Dr. Deborah T. Castellucci, Chair, 717-872-3410, Fax: 717-872-3985, E-mail: deborah.castellucci@millersville.edu. *Application contact:* Dr. Victor S. DeSantis, Dean of Graduate Studies, 717-872-3099, Fax: 717-871-2022, E-mail: victor.desantis@millersville.edu.

Minnesota State University Mankato, College of Graduate Studies, College of Allied Health and Nursing, Department of Nursing, Mankato, MN 56001. Offers family nursing (MSN), including clinical nurse specialist, educator, family nurse practitioner, manager; managed care (MSN), including clinical nurse specialist, educator, family nurse practitioner, manager. *Accreditation:* AACN; NLN. *Students:* 12 full-time (all women), 34 part-time (32 women). Average age 39. In 2006, 15 degrees awarded. *Degree requirements:* For master's, internships, research project or thesis. *Entrance requirements:* For master's, GRE General Test or on-campus essay, minimum GPA of 3.0 during previous 2 years, BSN or equivalent references. Additional exam requirements/recommendations for international students: Required—TOEFL. *Application deadline:* For fall admission, 1/15 priority date for domestic students; for spring admission, 11/27 for domestic students. Applications are processed on a rolling basis. Application fee: $40. Electronic applications accepted. *Financial support:* Research assistantships with full tuition reimbursements, teaching assistantships with full tuition reimbursements available. Financial award application deadline: 3/15; financial award applicants required to submit FAFSA. *Faculty research:* Psychosocial nursing, computers in nursing, family adaptation. *Unit head:* Dr. Sonja Meiers, Graduate Coordinator, 507-389-1725. *Application contact:* Collaborative MSN Program Admissions, 507-389-6022.

Minnesota State University Moorhead, Graduate Studies, College of Education and Human Services, Moorhead, MN 56563-0002. Offers counseling and student affairs (MS); curriculum and instruction (MS); educational leadership (MS, Ed S); nursing (MS); reading (MS); special education (MS); speech-language pathology (MS). *Accreditation:* NCATE. Part-time and evening/weekend programs available. *Faculty:* 18 full-time (11 women), 25 part-time/adjunct (13 women). *Students:* 45 full-time (42 women), 167 part-time (130 women); includes 4 minority (2 American Indian/Alaska Native, 2 Hispanic Americans), 4 international. 154 applicants, 56% accepted. In 2006, 60 degrees awarded. *Degree requirements:* For master's, final oral exam, project or thesis. *Entrance requirements:* Additional exam requirements/recommendations for international students: Required—TOEFL. *Application deadline:* For fall admission, 4/15 priority date for domestic students; for spring admission, 11/1 priority date for domestic students. Applications are processed on a rolling basis. Application fee: $20. Electronic applications accepted. *Financial support:* Career-related internships or fieldwork, Federal Work-Study, and unspecified assistantships available. Financial award application deadline: 7/15; financial award applicants required to submit FAFSA. *Unit head:* Dr. Michael Parsons, Dean of Education and Human Services, 218-477-2096. *Application contact:* Karla Wenger, Graduate Studies Office, 218-477-2344, Fax: 218-477-2482, E-mail: wengerk@mnstate.edu.

Mississippi University for Women, Graduate School, Division of Nursing, Columbus, MS 39701-9998. Offers MSN, Certificate. *Accreditation:* AACN. Part-time programs available. *Degree requirements:* For master's, thesis, comprehensive exam. *Entrance requirements:* For master's, GRE General Test, bachelor's degree in nursing, previous course work in statistics, proficiency in English.

Missouri State University, Graduate College, College of Health and Human Services, Department of Nursing, Springfield, MO 65804-0094. Offers MSN. *Accreditation:* AACN. *Faculty:* 5 full-time (4 women), 2 part-time/adjunct (both women). *Students:* 14 full-time (12 women), 13 part-time (12 women). Average age 39. 4 applicants, 75% accepted, 2 enrolled. In 2006, 7 degrees awarded. *Degree requirements:* For master's, thesis or alternative, comprehensive exam. *Entrance requirements:* For master's, GRE General Test, minimum GPA of 3.0, RN license. Additional exam requirements/recommendations for international students: Required—TOEFL (minimum score 550 paper-based; 213 computer-based; 79 iBT). *Application deadline:* For fall admission, 7/20 priority date for domestic students; for spring admission, 12/20 priority date for domestic students. Applications are processed on a rolling basis. Application fee: $35. Electronic applications accepted. *Expenses:* Tuition, state resident: full-time $3,582; part-time $199 per credit hour. Tuition, nonresident: full-time $6,984; part-time $199 per credit hour. Required fees: $548. Full-time tuition and fees vary according to course level, course load, program and reciprocity agreements. *Financial support:* In 2006–07, research assistantships with full tuition reimbursements (averaging $6,575 per year), 2 teaching assistantships with full tuition reimbursements (averaging $6,780 per year) were awarded; Federal Work-Study and unspecified assistantships also available. Financial award application deadline: 3/31; financial award applicants required to submit FAFSA. *Unit head:* Dr. Kathryn Hope, Head, 417-836-5310, Fax: 417-836-5484, E-mail: nursing@missouristate.edu.

Molloy College, Department of Nursing, Rockville Centre, NY 11571-5002. Offers adult nurse practitioner (Advanced Certificate); clinical nurse specialist: adult health (Advanced Certificate); family nurse practitioner (Advanced Certificate); nurse practitioner psychiatry (Advanced Certificate); nursing (MS); nursing administration (Advanced Certificate); nursing administration with informatics (Advanced Certificate); nursing education (Advanced Certificate); nursing informatics (Advanced Certificate); pediatric nurse practitioner (Advanced Certificate). *Accreditation:* AACN. Part-time and evening/weekend programs available. *Degree requirements:* For master's, thesis optional. *Entrance requirements:* For master's, 3 letters of reference, BS in nursing, minimum undergraduate GPA of 3.0; for Advanced Certificate, 3 letters of reference, master's degree in nursing. *Faculty research:* Hardiness and aging, alcoholism, current ethics, breast cancer, nurse role perception.

Monmouth University, Graduate School, The Marjorie K. Unterberg School of Nursing and Health Studies, West Long Branch, NJ 07764-1898. Offers advanced practice nursing (Post-Master's Certificate); nursing (MSN); school nursing (Certificate); substance awareness coordinator (Certificate). *Accreditation:* AACN. Part-time and evening/weekend programs available. *Faculty:* 10 full-time (all women), 1 part-time/adjunct (0 women). *Students:* 5 full-time (4 women), 189 part-time (186 women); includes 26 minority (9 African Americans, 13 Asian Americans or Pacific Islanders, 4 Hispanic Americans). Average age 43. 94 applicants, 100% accepted, 44 enrolled. In 2006, 38 degrees awarded. *Entrance requirements:* For master's, GRE General Test, RN license, 1 year of work experience, minimum undergraduate GPA of 2.75. Additional exam requirements/recommendations for international students: Required—TOEFL (minimum score 550 paper-based; 213 computer-based; 79 iBT), IELTS (minimum score 5), MELAB 77, Cambridge A, B, C. *Application deadline:* For fall admission, 7/15 priority date for domestic students, 6/1 for international students; for spring admission, 11/15 priority date for domestic students, 11/1 for international students. Applications are processed on a rolling basis. Application fee: $50. Electronic applications accepted. *Expenses:* Tuition: Full-time $12,780; part-time $710 per credit. Required fees: $628; $314 per term. *Financial support:* In 2006–07, 136 fellowships (averaging $1,053 per year), 4 research assistantships (averaging $3,483 per year) were awarded; career-related internships or fieldwork, scholarships/grants, tuition waivers (partial), and unspecified assistantships also available. Support available to part-time students. Financial award application deadline: 3/1; financial award applicants required to submit FAFSA. *Faculty research:* Relationship of undergraduate GPA and GRE to succeed in a graduate nursing program. *Unit head:* Dr. Janet Mahoney, Director, 732-571-3443, Fax: 732-263-5131, E-mail: jmahoney@monmouth.edu. *Application contact:* Kevin Roane, Director, Office of Graduate Admission, 732-571-3452, Fax: 732-263-5123, E-mail: gradadm@monmouth.edu.

Mountain State University, Graduate Studies, Program in Nursing, Beckley, WV 25802-9003. Offers administration/education (MSN); family nurse practitioner (MSN); nurse anesthesia (MSN); registered nurse anesthetist (Certificate). *Accreditation:* AANA/CANAEP; NLN. Part-time programs available. Postbaccalaureate distance learning degree programs offered (minimal on-campus study). *Faculty:* 6 full-time (4 women), 14 part-time/adjunct (7 women). *Students:* 80 full-time (64 women), 10 part-time (all women); includes 1 minority (African American) Average age 37. 29 applicants, 100% accepted, 17 enrolled. In 2006, 4 degrees awarded. *Median time to degree:* Master's–2 years full-time, 3 years part-time. *Degree requirements:* For master's, thesis or alternative, comprehensive exam. *Entrance requirements:* For master's, GRE. Additional exam requirements/recommendations for international students: Required—TOEFL (minimum score 550 paper-based; 213 computer-based); Recommended—IELTS (minimum score 7). *Application deadline:* For spring admission, 6/30 for domestic and international students. Applications are processed on a rolling basis. Application fee: $25 ($50 for international students). Electronic applications accepted. *Expenses:* Contact institution. Tuition and fees vary according to course load and program. *Financial support:* In 2006–07, 2 research assistantships (averaging $1,200 per year) were awarded; Federal Work-Study, scholarships/grants, and unspecified assistantships also available. Support available to part-time students. Financial award applicants required to submit FAFSA. *Unit head:* Dr. Jessica Sharp, Senior Academic Officer for Graduate Nursing, 304-929-1425, Fax: 304-929-1601, E-mail: jsharp@mountainstate.edu. *Application contact:* Melody Tilley, Program Specialist, 304-929-1576, Fax: 304-929-1601, E-mail: mtilley@mountainstate.edu.

See Close-Up on page 1965.

Mount Carmel College of Nursing, College of Nursing, Columbus, OH 43222. Offers adult health (MS); nursing education (MS). Part-time programs available. *Entrance requirements:* For master's, letters of recommendation, current resumé, baccalaureate degree in nursing, current Ohio RN license, cumulative GPA of 3.0. Additional exam requirements/recommendations for international students: Required—TOEFL (minimum score 550 paper-based).

See Close-Up on page 1967.

Mount Saint Mary College, Division of Nursing, Newburgh, NY 12550-3494. Offers adult nurse practitioner (MS), including nursing education, nursing management; clinical nurse specialist-adult health (MS), including nursing education, nursing management. *Accreditation:* AACN. Part-time and evening/weekend programs available. *Faculty:* 3 full-time (2 women), 1 (woman) part-time/adjunct. *Students:* 1 (woman) full-time, 28 part-time (26 women); includes 3 minority (2 African Americans, 1 Asian American or Pacific Islander). Average age 42. 12 applicants, 100% accepted, 10 enrolled. In 2006, 6 degrees awarded. *Degree requirements:* For master's, research utilization project. *Entrance requirements:* For master's, BSN, minimum GPA of 3.0, RN license. *Application deadline:* For fall admission, 6/3 priority date for domestic students; for spring admission, 10/31 priority date for domestic students. Applications are processed on a rolling basis. Application fee: $35. *Expenses:* Tuition: Full-time $11,880; part-time $660 per credit. *Financial support:* Unspecified assistantships and nursing lab assistant available. Financial award application deadline: 3/15; financial award applicants required to submit FAFSA. *Unit head:* Dr. Karen Baldwin, Coordinator, 845-569-3512, Fax: 845-562-6762, E-mail: baldwin@msmc.edu.

Mount St. Mary's College, Graduate Division, Program in Nursing, Los Angeles, CA 90049-1599. Offers MS. *Accreditation:* AACN. *Students:* 32 full-time (29 women), 9 part-time (8 women); includes 25 minority (7 African Americans, 6 Asian Americans or Pacific Islanders, 12 Hispanic Americans). Average age 43. In 2006, 24 degrees awarded. *Expenses:* Tuition: Part-time $630 per unit. *Unit head:* Dr. Marsha Sato, Chair, 310-954-4231. *Application contact:* Tom Hoener, Director, Graduate Recruitment, 213-477-2800, Fax: 213-477-2519, E-mail: thoener@msmc.la.edu.

Murray State University, College of Health Sciences and Human Services, Program in Nursing, Murray, KY 42071. Offers clinical nurse specialist (MSN); family nurse practitioner (MSN); nurse anesthesia (MSN). *Accreditation:* AACN; AANA/CANAEP. *Faculty:* 8 full-time (7 women). *Students:* 37 full-time (30 women), 7 part-time (6 women); includes 2 minority (1 African American, 1 Hispanic American). 85 applicants, 35% accepted, 21 enrolled. In 2006, 22 degrees awarded. *Degree requirements:* For master's, research project. *Entrance requirements:* For master's, GRE General Test, BSN, interview, RN licensure. Additional exam requirements/recommendations for international students: Required—TOEFL (minimum score 550 paper-based). *Application deadline:* For fall admission, 3/1 for domestic students, 4/15 for international students. Application fee: $30. *Financial support:* Traineeships available. Financial award application deadline: 4/1. *Faculty research:* Fibromyalgis, primary care, rural health. *Unit head:* Dr. Nancey E. M. France, Graduate Coordinator and Professor, 270-809-6671, Fax: 270-809-6662, E-mail: nancey.france@murraystate.edu.

Nazareth College of Rochester, Graduate Studies, Department of Nursing, Rochester, NY 14618-3790. Offers gerontological nurse practitioner (MS). *Accreditation:* AACN. Part-time programs available. *Faculty:* 3 full-time (all women), 1 (woman) part-time/adjunct. *Students:* 1 (woman) full-time, 19 part-time (18 women); includes 5 minority (3 African Americans, 1 American Indian/Alaska Native, 1 Asian American or Pacific Islander). 2 applicants, 100% accepted, 2 enrolled. *Entrance requirements:* For master's, minimum GPA of 3.0. *Application deadline:* For fall admission, 8/1 priority date for domestic students; for spring admission, 11/1 for domestic students. Applications are processed on a rolling basis. Application fee: $40. *Financial support:* Research assistantships with partial tuition reimbursements, career-related internships or fieldwork available. Support available to part-time students. Financial award application deadline: 3/1; financial award applicants required to submit FAFSA. *Unit head:* Dr. Marie O'Toole, Chairperson, 585-389-2712, Fax: 585-389-2452, E-mail: mooole3@naz.edu. *Application contact:* Judith G. Baker, Director, Graduate Admissions, 585-389-2050, Fax: 585-389-2817, E-mail: gradstudies@naz.edu.

Nebraska Methodist College, Program in Nursing, Omaha, NE 68114. Offers MSN. *Accreditation:* AACN. Evening/weekend programs available. Postbaccalaureate distance learning degree programs offered (minimal on-campus study). *Faculty:* 7 full-time (all women), 3 part-time/adjunct (all women). *Students:* 40 full-time (all women); includes 2 minority (1 African American, 1 Asian American or Pacific Islander). Average age 41. 25 applicants, 84% accepted, 17 enrolled. In 2006, 14 degrees awarded. *Degree requirements:* For master's, thesis. *Entrance requirements:* For master's, interview. Additional exam requirements/recommendations for international students: Required—TOEFL (minimum score 550 paper-based; 213 computer-based; 80 iBT). *Application deadline:* For spring admission, 11/1 for domestic and international students. Applications are processed on a rolling basis. Application fee: $25. *Expenses:* Tuition: Part-time $486 per credit hour. Required fees: $25 per credit hour. Full-time tuition and fees vary according to program. *Financial support:* In 2006–07, 13 students received support; research assistantships with full and partial tuition reimbursements available, scholarships/grants available. Support available to part-time students. Financial award applicants required to submit FAFSA. *Faculty research:* Spirituality, student outcomes, service learning, leadership and administration, women's issues. *Unit head:* Linda Foley, Program Chair, 402-354-7050, Fax: 402-354-7020, E-mail: linda.foley@methodistcollege.edu. *Application contact:* Deann Sterner, Director of Admissions, 402-354-7200, Fax: 402-354-7020, E-mail: admissions@methodistcollege.edu.

Nebraska Wesleyan University, University College, Program in Nursing, Lincoln, NE 68504-2796. Offers MSN. *Accreditation:* NLN. Part-time programs available. *Faculty:* 4 full-time (3 women), 6 part-time/adjunct (all women). *Students:* 20 full-time (all women), 36 part-time (34 women); includes 5 minority (1 African American, 2 American Indian/Alaska Native, 2 Hispanic Americans). Average age 39. In 2006, 20 degrees awarded. *Expenses:* Tuition: Part-time $290 per credit. *Unit head:* Dr. Jeri L. Brandt, Director of Nursing Program, 402-465-2336, E-mail: jlb@nebrwesleyan.edu.

Neumann College, Program in Nursing and Health Sciences, Aston, PA 19014-1298. Offers MS. *Accreditation:* NLN. Part-time programs available. *Faculty:* 5 full-time (4 women), 1 part-time/

adjunct (0 women). *Students:* 1 full-time (0 women), 27 part-time (26 women); includes 2 minority (1 African American, 1 Hispanic American). Average age 44. 10 applicants, 100% accepted, 8 enrolled. In 2006, 3 degrees awarded. *Entrance requirements:* For master's, GRE or MAT. Additional exam requirements/recommendations for international students: Required—TOEFL. *Application deadline:* Applications are processed on a rolling basis. Application fee: $50. *Expenses: Contact institution. Financial support:* Available to part-time students. Application deadline: 3/15; *Unit head:* Dr. Kathleen Hoover, Dean, Division of Nursing and Health Services, 610-558-5561, Fax: 610-459-1370. *Application contact:* Louise Bank, Assistant Director of Admissions, Graduate and Evening Programs, 610-558-5604, Fax: 610-459-1370, E-mail: bankl@neumann.edu.

New Jersey City University, Graduate and Continuing Education, College of Professional Studies, Department of Nursing, Jersey City, NJ 07305-1597. Offers holistic nursing (MSN); urban health (MSN). Part-time and evening/weekend programs available. *Faculty:* 1. *Students:* Average age 57. In 2006, 1 degree awarded. *Application deadline:* For fall admission, 8/1 priority date for domestic students; for spring admission, 12/1 for domestic students. Applications are processed on a rolling basis. Application fee: $0. *Expenses:* Tuition, state resident: full-time $7,038; part-time $391 per credit. Tuition, nonresident: full-time $12,510; part-time $695 per credit. Required fees: $65 per credit. *Unit head:* Dr. Gloria Boseman, Chair, 201-200-3157, E-mail: gboseman@njcu.edu.

New Mexico State University, Graduate School, College of Health and Social Services, School of Nursing, Las Cruces, NM 88003-8001. Offers community/public health (MSN); medical-surgical (adult health) (MSN); psychiatric/mental health (MSN). *Accreditation:* AACN. Part-time programs available. Postbaccalaureate distance learning degree programs offered (minimal on-campus study). *Faculty:* 12 full-time (all women), 5 part-time/adjunct (4 women). *Students:* 27 full-time (24 women), 25 part-time (all women); includes 13 minority (1 African American, 12 Hispanic Americans), 1 international. Average age 45. 24 applicants, 83% accepted. In 2006, 14 degrees awarded. *Degree requirements:* For master's, clinical practice, RN licensure, thesis optional. *Entrance requirements:* For master's, BSN, minimum GPA of 3.0, course work in statistics, 3 letters of reference, writing sample. Additional exam requirements/recommendations for international students: Required—NCLEX. *Application deadline:* For fall admission, 3/1 priority date for domestic students; for spring admission, 10/1 priority date for domestic students. Applications are processed on a rolling basis. Application fee: $30 ($50 for international students). Electronic applications accepted. *Financial support:* In 2006–07, 2 teaching assistantships were awarded; fellowships, research assistantships, career-related internships or fieldwork, Federal Work-Study, scholarships/grants, traineeships, and health care benefits also available. Financial award application deadline: 3/1. *Faculty research:* Advanced practice nursing, evidence-based nursing practice, health policy, community outreach, clinical judgment. *Unit head:* Dr. Esperanza V. Joyce, Director, 505-646-3812, Fax: 505-646-2167, E-mail: evjoyce@nmsu.edu. *Application contact:* Dr. Mary Hoke, Associate Director for Graduate Studies, 505-646-3812, Fax: 505-646-2167, E-mail: mhoke@nmsu.edu.

New York University, College of Dentistry, College of Nursing, New York, NY 10012-1019. Offers MS, PhD, Advanced Certificate, MS/MS. *Accreditation:* AACN. Part-time and evening/weekend programs available. *Faculty:* 30 full-time (all women). *Students:* 16 full-time (all women), 468 part-time (432 women); includes 172 minority (74 African Americans, 77 Asian Americans or Pacific Islanders, 21 Hispanic Americans). 177 applicants, 85% accepted, 123 enrolled. In 2006, 100 master's, 10 doctorates, 7 other advanced degrees awarded. Terminal master's awarded for partial completion of doctoral program. *Degree requirements:* For master's, thesis (for some programs); for doctorate, thesis/dissertation. *Entrance requirements:* For master's, BS in nursing, AS in nursing with another BS/BA degree; for doctorate, GRE General Test, interview; for Advanced Certificate, master's degree. Additional exam requirements/recommendations for international students: Required—TOEFL. *Application deadline:* Applications are processed on a rolling basis. Application fee: $65. *Expenses:* Tuition: Part-time $1,080 per unit. Required fees: $56 per unit. $329 per term. Tuition and fees vary according to program. *Financial support:* In 2006–07, 2 research assistantships with full and partial tuition reimbursements were awarded; fellowships with full and partial tuition reimbursements, career-related internships or fieldwork, Federal Work-Study, institutionally sponsored loans, scholarships/grants, and tuition waivers (partial) also available. Support available to part-time students. Financial award application deadline: 2/1; financial award applicants required to submit FAFSA. *Faculty research:* Gerontology, geriatric nursing, breast cancer, Alzheimer's disease, diabetes, bioethics, AIDS care, uses of technology in nursing. *Unit head:* Dr. Terry Fulmer, Dean, College of Nursing, 212-998-5303, Fax: 212-995-3143. *Application contact:* Amy Knowles, Assistant Dean for Student Affairs and Admissions, 212-998-5333, Fax: 212-995-4302, E-mail: ak96@nyu.edu.

North Dakota State University, The Graduate School, College of Pharmacy, Nursing and Allied Sciences, Graduate Nursing Program, Fargo, ND 58105. Offers MS, DNP. *Accreditation:* AACN. Part-time programs available. Postbaccalaureate distance learning degree programs offered (minimal on-campus study). *Faculty:* 1 full-time (0 women), 5 part-time/adjunct (all women). *Students:* 10 full-time (8 women), 17 part-time (15 women). Average age 35. 12 applicants, 100% accepted, 11 enrolled. In 2006, 1 master's, 1 doctorate awarded. *Median time to degree:* Master's–2.5 years part-time; doctorate–2.5 years full-time. *Degree requirements:* For master's and doctorate, thesis/dissertation or alternative, oral defense. *Entrance requirements:* For master's, bachelor's degree with nursing major, minimum GPA of 3.0 in nursing courses, RN license; for doctorate, bachelor's or master's degree with a nursing major, minimum GPA of 3.0 in nursing courses, RN license. Additional exam requirements/recommendations for international students: Required—TOEFL, IELTS. *Application deadline:* For fall admission, 7/15 priority date for domestic students; for winter admission, 2/1 priority date for domestic students; for spring admission, 11/15 priority date for domestic students. Applications are processed on a rolling basis. Application fee: $45 ($60 for international students). Electronic applications accepted. *Expenses: Contact institution. Financial support:* In 2006–07, 1 research assistantship with full tuition reimbursement (averaging $1,600 per year), 6 teaching assistantships with full tuition reimbursements (averaging $4,668 per year) were awarded; traineeships and unspecified assistantships also available. Financial award application deadline: 8/15; financial award applicants required to submit CSS PROFILE or FAFSA. *Faculty research:* Prevention of farmers' hearing loss, breast cancer in Native American women, colon cancer, quality improvement in a wellness center. Total annual research expenditures: $142,500. *Unit head:* Dr. Mary Margaret Mooney, Chair, 701-231-7395, Fax: 701-231-7606, E-mail: mary.mooney@ndsu.edu.

Northeastern University, Bouvé College of Health Sciences Graduate School, School of Nursing, Boston, MA 02115-5096. Offers MS, PhD, CAS, MS/MBA. *Accreditation:* AACN. Part-time programs available. *Faculty:* 30 full-time (29 women), 30 part-time/adjunct. *Students:* 152 full-time (127 women), 91 part-time (78 women). Average age 38. 300 applicants, 25% accepted. In 2006, 58 degrees awarded. *Degree requirements:* For doctorate, thesis/dissertation. *Entrance requirements:* For master's, GRE General Test, minimum GPA of 3.0, previous course work in statistics, 1-2 years of nursing experience, RN license; for CAS, MS in nursing. Additional exam requirements/recommendations for international students: Required—TOEFL. *Application deadline:* Applications are processed on a rolling basis. Application fee: $50. *Financial support:* In 2006–07, 34 students received support, including 2 research assistantships with full tuition reimbursements available (averaging $13,546 per year), 7 teaching assistantships with full tuition reimbursements available (averaging $13,546 per year); fellowships, career-related internships or fieldwork, institutionally sponsored loans, tuition waivers (full and partial), and unspecified assistantships also available. Support available to part-time students. Financial award application deadline: 7/1; financial award applicants required to submit FAFSA. *Faculty research:* Community-based health care delivery, coping and adaptation, functional disability in the elderly, psychological trauma. *Unit head:* Dr. Nancy Hoffart, Dean, 617-373-3649, Fax: 617-373-8675, E-mail: n.hoffart@neu.edu. *Application contact:* Margaret Schnabel, Director of Graduate Admissions, 617-373-2708, Fax: 617-373-4704, E-mail: bouvegrad@neu.edu.

Northern Arizona University, Consortium of Professional Schools and Colleges, College of Health Professions, School of Nursing, Flagstaff, AZ 86011. Offers case management (Certificate); nursing (MSN). *Accreditation:* AACN. *Degree requirements:* For master's, project or thesis. *Entrance requirements:* For master's, GRE General Test, minimum GPA of 3.0.

Northern Illinois University, Graduate School, College of Health and Human Sciences, School of Nursing, De Kalb, IL 60115-2854. Offers MS. *Accreditation:* AACN. Part-time programs available. *Faculty:* 12 full-time (11 women), 1 (woman) part-time/adjunct. *Students:* 10 full-time (all women), 133 part-time (130 women); includes 26 minority (9 African Americans, 1 American Indian/Alaska Native, 9 Asian Americans or Pacific Islanders, 7 Hispanic Americans). Average age 39. 44 applicants, 77% accepted, 25 enrolled. In 2006, 28 degrees awarded. *Degree requirements:* For master's, internship, thesis optional. *Entrance requirements:* For master's, minimum GPA of 3.0 in last 60 hours, BA in nursing, nursing license. Additional exam requirements/recommendations for international students: Required—TOEFL (minimum score 550 paper-based; 213 computer-based). *Application deadline:* For fall admission, 6/1 for domestic students, 5/1 for international students; for spring admission, 11/1 for domestic students, 10/1 for international students. Applications are processed on a rolling basis. Application fee: $30. Electronic applications accepted. *Financial support:* In 2006–07, 16 research assistantships with full tuition reimbursements, 2 teaching assistantships with full tuition reimbursements were awarded; fellowships with full tuition reimbursements, career-related internships or fieldwork, Federal Work-Study, scholarships/grants, tuition waivers (full), and unspecified assistantships also available. Support available to part-time students. Financial award applicants required to submit FAFSA. *Faculty research:* Neonatal intensive care, stress and coping, refugee and immigrant issues, older adults, autoimmune disorders. *Unit head:* Dr. Brigid Lusk, Chair, 815-753-0663, Fax: 815-753-0814, E-mail: blusk@niu.edu.

Northern Kentucky University, Office of Graduate Programs, School of Nursing and Health Professions, Program in Nursing, Highland Heights, KY 41099. Offers MSN, Post-Master's Certificate. *Accreditation:* NLN. Part-time and evening/weekend programs available. Postbaccalaureate distance learning degree programs offered (no on-campus study). *Faculty:* 10 full-time (all women), 7 part-time/adjunct (6 women). *Students:* 25 full-time (24 women), 111 part-time (105 women); includes 6 minority (2 African Americans, 4 Asian Americans or Pacific Islanders). Average age 37. 58 applicants, 83% accepted, 42 enrolled. In 2006, 30 degrees awarded. *Degree requirements:* For master's, investigative project. *Entrance requirements:* For master's, GRE (if GPA is below 3.5), minimum GPA of 3.0. Additional exam requirements/recommendations for international students: Required—TOEFL (minimum score 550 paper-based; 213 computer-based; 79 iBT), Michigan (must be taken at NKU). *Application deadline:* For fall admission, 8/1 priority date for domestic students, 6/1 priority date for international students; for spring admission, 12/1 priority date for domestic students, 10/1 priority date for international students. Applications are processed on a rolling basis. Application fee: $30. Electronic applications accepted. *Expenses:* Tuition, state resident: full-time $5,274; part-time $293 per hour. Tuition, nonresident: full-time $10,314; part-time $573 per hour. Tuition and fees vary according to course load, program and reciprocity agreements. *Financial support:* In 2006–07, 48 students received support. Traineeships and unspecified assistantships available. *Faculty research:* Nursing outcomes, disease management, clinical, prevention, health promotion. *Unit head:* Dr. Denise Robinson, Program Director, 859-572-5178, Fax: 859-572-6098, E-mail: robinson@nku.edu.

Northern Michigan University, College of Graduate Studies, College of Professional Studies, Department of Nursing, Marquette, MI 49855-5301. Offers MSN. *Accreditation:* AACN. Part-time and evening/weekend programs available. *Degree requirements:* For master's, thesis or alternative. *Entrance requirements:* For master's, GRE General Test, minimum GPA of 3.0.

North Park University, School of Nursing, Chicago, IL 60625-4895. Offers MS, MBA/MS. *Accreditation:* AACN. Part-time and evening/weekend programs available. *Degree requirements:* For master's, thesis. *Entrance requirements:* For master's, GMAT, MAT. *Faculty research:* Aging, consultation roles, critical thinking skills, family breakdown, science of caring.

Northwestern State University of Louisiana, Graduate Studies and Research, College of Nursing, Shreveport, LA 71101-4653. Offers MSN. *Accreditation:* AACN. Part-time programs available. *Faculty:* 9 full-time (all women), 5 part-time/adjunct (all women). *Students:* 27 full-time (23 women), 106 part-time (99 women); includes 17 minority (16 African Americans, 1 Hispanic American). Average age 36. In 2006, 27 degrees awarded. *Degree requirements:* For master's, thesis or alternative, comprehensive exam, registration. *Entrance requirements:* For master's, GRE General Test, 6 months of clinical nursing experience, BS in nursing, minimum GPA of 3.0. *Application deadline:* For fall admission, 8/1 priority date for domestic students; for spring admission, 1/10 for domestic students. Applications are processed on a rolling basis. Application fee: $20 ($30 for international students). *Financial support:* Career-related internships or fieldwork and Federal Work-Study available. Support available to part-time students. Financial award application deadline: 7/15. *Unit head:* Dr. Norann Planchock, Director, 318-677-3100, Fax: 318-676-7887, E-mail: planchockn@alpha.nsula.edu. *Application contact:* Dr. Steven G. Horton, Associate Provost/Dean, Graduate Studies, Research, and Information Systems, 318-357-5851, Fax: 318-357-5019, E-mail: grad_school@nsula.edu.

Nova Southeastern University, Health Professions Division, College of Allied Health and Nursing, Department of Nursing, Fort Lauderdale, FL 33314-7796. Offers MSN. *Accreditation:* AACN. Part-time and evening/weekend programs available. Postbaccalaureate distance learning degree programs offered (no on-campus study). *Faculty:* 4 full-time (all women). *Students:* 3 full-time (all women), 35 part-time (all women); includes 12 minority (11 African Americans, 1 Asian American or Pacific Islander). *Entrance requirements:* For master's, minimum GPA of 3.0, RN, BSN. *Application deadline:* Applications are processed on a rolling basis. Electronic applications accepted. *Faculty research:* Nursing education, curriculum, clinical research, interdisciplinary research. *Unit head:* Dr. Diane Whitehead, Professor. *Application contact:* Dr. Jean Davis, Application Contact, 954-262-7300, E-mail: djean@nsu.nova.edu.

Oakland University, Graduate Study and Lifelong Learning, School of Nursing, Rochester, MI 48309-4401. Offers MSN, DNP, Certificate. *Accreditation:* AACN. Part-time and evening/weekend programs available. *Faculty:* 16 full-time (13 women), 1 part-time/adjunct (0 women). *Students:* 68 full-time (57 women), 124 part-time (110 women); includes 28 minority (16 African Americans, 1 American Indian/Alaska Native, 7 Asian Americans or Pacific Islanders, 4 Hispanic Americans), 2 international. Average age 37. 185 applicants, 43% accepted, 52 enrolled. In 2006, 39 master's, 1 other advanced degree awarded. *Entrance requirements:* For master's, GRE General Test, minimum GPA of 3.0 for unconditional admission. Application fee: $35. Electronic applications accepted. *Expenses:* Tuition, state resident: full-time $9,936; part-time $414 per credit. Tuition, nonresident: full-time $17,202; part-time $716 per credit. *Financial support:* Federal Work-Study, institutionally sponsored loans, and tuition waivers (full) available. Financial award application deadline: 3/1; financial award applicants required to submit FAFSA. *Faculty research:* Accelerated Health Care Career Training Initiative. Total annual research expenditures: $42,565. *Unit head:* Dr. Linda Thompson, Dean, 248-370-4081, Fax: 248-370-4279. *Application contact:* Mary Bray, Graduate Program Coordinator, 248-370-4482.

See Close-Up on page 1969.

The Ohio State University, Graduate School, College of Nursing, Columbus, OH 43210. Offers MS, PhD. *Accreditation:* AACN; ACNM/DOA. Part-time programs available. *Faculty:* 31. *Students:* 174 full-time (160 women), 103 part-time (96 women); includes 34 minority (19 African Americans, 5 American Indian/Alaska Native, 8 Asian Americans or Pacific Islanders, 2 Hispanic Americans), 4 international. Average age 32. 203 applicants, 54% accepted, 18 enrolled. In 2006, 69 master's, 2 doctorates awarded. *Degree requirements:* For master's, thesis optional; for doctorate, thesis/dissertation. *Entrance requirements:* For master's and doctorate, GRE General Test. Additional exam requirements/recommendations for international students: Required—TOEFL (minimum score 600 paper-based; 250 computer-based). *Application deadline:* For fall admission, 8/15 priority date for domestic students, 7/1

Nursing—General

The Ohio State University (continued)
priority date for international students; for winter admission, 12/1 priority date for domestic students, 11/1 priority date for international students; for spring admission, 3/1 priority date for domestic students, 2/1 priority date for international students. Applications are processed on a rolling basis. Application fee: $40 ($50 for international students). Electronic applications accepted. *Expenses:* Tuition, state resident: full-time $9,438. Tuition, nonresident: full-time $22,791. Tuition and fees vary according to course load, campus/location and program. *Financial support:* Fellowships, research assistantships, teaching assistantships, Federal Work-Study, institutionally sponsored loans, and unspecified assistantships available. Support available to part-time students. *Unit head:* Dr. Elizabeth R. Lenz, Dean, 614-292-8900, Fax: 614-292-4535, E-mail: lenz.23@osu.edu. *Application contact:* 614-292-9444, Fax: 614-292-3895, E-mail: domestic.grad@osu.edu.

The Ohio State University at Marion, Graduate Programs, Marion, OH 43302-5695. Offers early childhood education (pre-K to grade 3) (M Ed); integrated teaching and learning (MA); middle childhood education (grades 4-9) (M Ed); nursing (MS, PhD); social work (MSW); MS/PhD. *Students:* 63 full-time (56 women), 43 part-time (41 women); includes 2 minority (both African Americans), 1 international. Average age 32. *Degree requirements:* For master's, thesis (for some programs), comprehensive exam (for some programs). *Entrance requirements:* For master's and doctorate, GRE, minimum undergraduate GPA of 3.0. Additional exam requirements/recommendations for international students: Required—TOEFL, IELTS or Michigan English Language Assessment Battery. *Application deadline:* For fall admission, 8/15 priority date for domestic students, 7/1 priority date for international students; for winter admission, 12/1 priority date for domestic students, 11/1 priority date for international students; for spring admission, 3/1 priority date for domestic students, 2/1 priority date for international students. Applications are processed on a rolling basis. Application fee: $40 ($50 for international students). Electronic applications accepted. *Expenses:* Tuition, state resident: full-time $8,919. Tuition, nonresident: full-time $22,272. Tuition and fees vary according to course load, campus/location and program. *Unit head:* Gregory S. Rose, Dean/Director, 740-389-6786 Ext. 6218, E-mail: rose.9@osu.edu. *Application contact:* Graduate Admissions, 614-292-9444, Fax: 614-292-3895, E-mail: domestic.grad@osu.edu.

Oklahoma City University, Kramer School of Nursing, Oklahoma City, OK 73106-1402. Offers MSN. *Students:* 7 full-time (all women), 17 part-time (14 women); all minorities (3 African Americans, 3 American Indian/Alaska Native, 1 Asian American or Pacific Islander, 17 Hispanic Americans). Average age 47. 15 applicants, 93% accepted. In 2006, 2 degrees awarded. *Degree requirements:* For master's, thesis. *Entrance requirements:* For master's, registered nurse licensure, minimum undergraduate GPA of 3.0, BSN from nationally accredited nursing program, completion of courses in health assessment and statistics. Additional exam requirements/recommendations for international students: Required—TOEFL (minimum score 550 paper-based). *Expenses:* Tuition: Full-time $12,780; part-time $710 per hour. Required fees: $89 per hour. *Unit head:* Dr. Marvel L. Williamson, Dean, 405-208-5900, Fax: 405-208-5914, E-mail: mwilliamson@okcu.edu. *Application contact:* Dr. Susan Barnes, Director, MSN Program, 405-208-5917, Fax: 405-208-5914, E-mail: sbarnes@okcu.edu.

Old Dominion University, College of Health Sciences, Program in Nursing, Norfolk, VA 23529. Offers MSN. *Accreditation:* AACN; AANA/CANAEP. Part-time programs available. Postbaccalaureate distance learning degree programs offered (no on-campus study). *Faculty:* 9 full-time (7 women), 20 part-time/adjunct (17 women). *Students:* 105 full-time (84 women), 98 part-time (95 women); includes 25 minority (13 African Americans, 1 American Indian/Alaska Native, 9 Asian Americans or Pacific Islanders, 2 Hispanic Americans). Average age 37. 119 applicants, 94% accepted, 100 enrolled. In 2006, 74 degrees awarded. *Median time to degree:* Master's–2 years full-time, 3 years part-time. *Degree requirements:* For master's, comprehensive exam. *Entrance requirements:* For master's, GRE or MAT, BSN; minimum GPA of 3.0 in nursing, 2.8 overall. Additional exam requirements/recommendations for international students: Required—TOEFL. *Application deadline:* For fall admission, 6/1 for domestic students. Applications are processed on a rolling basis. Application fee: $40. Electronic applications accepted. *Expenses:* Tuition, area resident: Part-time $285 per credit hour. Tuition, nonresident: part-time $715 per credit hour. Required fees: $94 per semester. *Financial support:* In 2006–07, 43 students received support, including 2 research assistantships with tuition reimbursements available (averaging $5,249 per year); teaching assistantships, career-related internships or fieldwork, scholarships/grants, traineeships, and tuition waivers (partial) also available. Support available to part-time students. Financial award application deadline: 2/15; financial award applicants required to submit FAFSA. *Faculty research:* Health and culture, cardiovascular health, transition of military families, genetics, cultural diversity. Total annual research expenditures: $231,117. *Unit head:* Dr. Laurel Garzon, Graduate Program Director, 757-683-5250, Fax: 757-683-5253, E-mail: nursgpd@odu.edu.

Oregon Health & Science University, School of Nursing, Portland, OR 97239-3098. Offers MPH, MS, PhD, Post Master's Certificate. *Accreditation:* AACN; ACNM/DOA (one or more programs are accredited). Part-time programs available. *Degree requirements:* For master's, thesis optional; for doctorate, thesis/dissertation. *Entrance requirements:* For master's, GRE General Test, bachelor's degree in nursing, minimum undergraduate GPA of 3.0, previous course work in statistics; for doctorate, GRE General Test, master's degree in nursing; minimum undergraduate GPA of 3.0, 3.5 graduate; for Post Master's Certificate, master's degree in nursing. Electronic applications accepted. Expenses: Contact institution. *Faculty research:* Nursing care of older persons; families in health, illness, and transition; family caregiving; end of life care/decision making; mother-infant interactions; pregnancy outcomes; enteral feeding; psychoactive drugs in long-term care.

Otterbein College, Department of Nursing, Westerville, OH 43081. Offers adult nurse practitioner (MSN, Certificate); clinical nurse leader (MSN); family nurse practitioner (MSN, Certificate); nurse service administration (MSN). *Accreditation:* AACN; NLN. Part-time and evening/weekend programs available. Postbaccalaureate distance learning degree programs offered (minimal on-campus study). *Students:* 7 full-time, 118 part-time; includes 5 minority (4 African Americans, 1 Hispanic American). Average age 40. 47 applicants, 94% accepted, 33 enrolled. In 2006, 37 degrees awarded. *Degree requirements:* For master's, thesis (for some programs), comprehensive exam (for some programs). *Entrance requirements:* For master's and Certificate, official transcripts, 2 reference forms, essay, resumé. Additional exam requirements/recommendations for international students: Required—TOEFL (minimum score 550 paper-based; 213 computer-based; 79 iBT). *Application deadline:* For fall admission, 8/10 priority date for domestic students, 7/10 for international students; for winter admission, 12/7 priority date for domestic students, 11/7 for international students; for spring admission, 2/28 priority date for domestic students, 1/31 for international students. Applications are processed on a rolling basis. *Expenses:* Tuition: Full-time $7,560; part-time $315 per credit. Tuition and fees vary according to program. *Financial support:* Traineeships available. Support available to part-time students. Financial award applicants required to submit FAFSA. *Faculty research:* Patient education, women's health, trauma curriculum development, administration. *Unit head:* Dr. Barbara Schaffner, Chair, 614-823-1735, Fax: 614-823-3131, E-mail: bschaffner@otterbein.edu. *Application contact:* Vicki Miller, Administrative Assistant, Office of Graduate Programs, 614-823-3210, Fax: 614-823-3208, E-mail: grad@otterbein.edu.

Pace University, Lienhard School of Nursing, New York, NY 10038. Offers MS, Advanced Certificate. *Accreditation:* AACN. Part-time and evening/weekend programs available. *Faculty:* 2 full-time (both women). *Students:* 20 full-time (19 women), 171 part-time (156 women); includes 96 minority (55 African Americans, 1 American Indian/Alaska Native, 27 Asian Americans or Pacific Islanders, 13 Hispanic Americans), 5 international. Average age 37. 84 applicants, 93% accepted, 43 enrolled. In 2006, 38 master's, 2 other advanced degrees awarded. *Degree requirements:* For master's, thesis. *Entrance requirements:* For master's, GRE General Test or MAT, RN license; for Advanced Certificate, RN license, completion of 2nd degree in nursing. *Application deadline:* For fall admission, 7/31 priority date for domestic students; for spring admission, 11/30 for domestic students. Applications are processed on a rolling basis. Application fee: $65. Electronic applications accepted. *Expenses:* Contact institution. *Financial support:* Research assistantships, career-related internships or fieldwork, Federal Work-Study, and tuition waivers (partial) available. Support available to part-time students. Financial award applicants required to submit FAFSA. *Unit head:* Dr. Harriet Feldman, Dean, 914-773-3341. *Application contact:* Joanna Broda, Director of Admissions, 212-346-1652, Fax: 212-346-1585, E-mail: gradnyc@pace.edu.

See Close-Up on page 1971.

Pacific Lutheran University, Division of Graduate Studies, School of Nursing, Tacoma, WA 98447. Offers MSN. *Accreditation:* AACN. Part-time and evening/weekend programs available. *Faculty:* 4 full-time (3 women), 3 part-time/adjunct (1 woman). *Students:* 69 full-time (62 women), 2 part-time (both women); includes 4 minority (1 African American, 2 Asian Americans or Pacific Islanders, 1 Hispanic American), 1 international. Average age 34. 63 applicants, 56% accepted, 24 enrolled. In 2006, 30 degrees awarded. *Degree requirements:* For master's, thesis or alternative, registration. *Entrance requirements:* For master's, GRE General Test, minimum undergraduate GPA of 3.0. Additional exam requirements/recommendations for international students: Required—TOEFL (minimum score 550 paper-based; 213 computer-based). *Application deadline:* For fall admission, 4/1 priority date for domestic students. Applications are processed on a rolling basis. Application fee: $40. *Expenses:* Tuition: Full-time $17,544. Part-time tuition and fees vary according to program. *Financial support:* In 2006–07, 4 students received support, including 1 fellowship (averaging $2,500 per year); Federal Work-Study, scholarships/grants, and unspecified assistantships also available. Financial award application deadline: 3/1. *Unit head:* Dr. Terry Miller, Dean and Graduate Program Director, 253-535-7672, Fax: 253-535-7590, E-mail: millertw@plu.edu. *Application contact:* Linda DuBay, Senior Office Assistant, 253-535-7151, Fax: 253-536-5136, E-mail: admissions@plu.edu.

Penn State University Park, Graduate School, College of Health and Human Development, School of Nursing, State College, University Park, PA 16802-1503. Offers MS, PhD. *Accreditation:* AACN; NLN. *Unit head:* Dr. Paula F. Milone-Nuzzo, Director, 814-863-0245, E-mail: pxm36@psu.edu. *Application contact:* Information Contact, E-mail: nursgrad@psu.edu.

See Close-Up on page 1813.

Pittsburg State University, Graduate School, College of Arts and Sciences, Department of Nursing, Pittsburg, KS 66762. Offers MSN. *Accreditation:* AACN. *Students:* 25. *Entrance requirements:* For master's, GRE General Test. Application fee: $35 ($60 for international students). *Expenses:* Tuition, state resident: full-time $2,144; part-time $181 per credit hour. Tuition, nonresident: full-time $5,273; part-time $442 per credit hour. Tuition and fees vary according to course load and campus/location. *Unit head:* Dr. Mary Carol Pomatto, Chairperson, 620-235-4432. *Application contact:* Jamie Vanderbeck, Assistant Director, 620-235-4223, Fax: 620-235-4219, E-mail: jvanderb@pittstate.edu.

Point Loma Nazarene University, Graduate Studies, Program in Nursing, San Diego, CA 92106-2899. Offers MSN. *Accreditation:* AACN. *Faculty:* 9 full-time (8 women). *Students:* 15 full-time (14 women), 5 part-time (all women); includes 7 minority (2 African Americans, 1 American Indian/Alaska Native, 1 Asian American or Pacific Islander, 3 Hispanic Americans). Average age 45. *Entrance requirements:* For master's, MAT, BS in nursing, interview, minimum GPA of 3.0, RN license. *Application deadline:* Applications are processed on a rolling basis. Application fee: $30. *Unit head:* Barbara Taylor, Dean, 619-849-2766.

Pontifical Catholic University of Puerto Rico, College of Sciences, Department of Nursing, Ponce, PR 00717-0777. Offers medical-surgical nursing (MS); mental health and psychiatric nursing (MS). *Accreditation:* NLN. Part-time and evening/weekend programs available. *Degree requirements:* For master's, thesis, clinical research paper, comprehensive exam (for some programs), registration. *Entrance requirements:* For master's, GRE General Test, 2 letters of recommendation, interview, minimum GPA of 2.5. Electronic applications accepted.

Prairie View A&M University, Graduate School, College of Nursing, Houston, TX 77030. Offers family nurse practitioner (MSN); nursing administration (MSN); nursing education (MSN). *Accreditation:* AACN; NLN. Part-time programs available. *Faculty:* 3 full-time (all women), 4 part-time/adjunct (3 women). *Students:* 18 full-time (16 women), 59 part-time (51 women); includes 71 minority (62 African Americans, 5 Asian Americans or Pacific Islanders, 4 Hispanic Americans). Average age 38. 37 applicants, 100% accepted, 32 enrolled. In 2006, 7 degrees awarded. *Median time to degree:* Master's–1.5 years full-time, 2.5 years part-time. *Degree requirements:* For master's, thesis, comprehensive exam. *Entrance requirements:* For master's, MAT or GRE, BS in nursing; 2 years of experience as a registered nurse; 1 course each in statistics, basic health and assessment. *Application deadline:* For fall admission, 6/1 priority date for domestic students; for spring admission, 11/1 priority date for domestic students. Applications are processed on a rolling basis. Application fee: $50. *Financial support:* In 2006–07, 17 students received support. Career-related internships or fieldwork, Federal Work-Study, institutionally sponsored loans, scholarships/grants, and traineeships available. Support available to part-time students. Financial award application deadline: 4/1; financial award applicants required to submit FAFSA. *Faculty research:* Software development and violence prevention, health promotion and prevention. Total annual research expenditures: $350,000. *Unit head:* Dr. Betty N. Adams, Dean, 713-797-7009, Fax: 713-797-7013, E-mail: bnadams@pvamu.edu. *Application contact:* Dr. Pamela C. Willson, Associate Professor, 713-797-7011, Fax: 713-797-7012, E-mail: pcwillson@pvamu.edu.

Purdue University Calumet, Graduate School, School of Nursing, Hammond, IN 46323-2094. Offers MS. *Accreditation:* NLN. Part-time programs available. Postbaccalaureate distance learning degree programs offered (minimal on-campus study). *Entrance requirements:* For master's, BSN, minimum B average. Additional exam requirements/recommendations for international students: Required—TOEFL. Electronic applications accepted. *Faculty research:* Adult health, cardiovascular and pulmonary nursing.

Queen's University at Kingston, School of Graduate Studies and Research, Faculty of Health Sciences, School of Nursing, Kingston, ON K7L 3N6, Canada. Offers M Sc. *Degree requirements:* For master's, thesis. *Entrance requirements:* For master's, RN license. Additional exam requirements/recommendations for international students: Required—TOEFL. *Faculty research:* Women and children's health, health and chronic illness.

Queens University of Charlotte, Hayworth College, Division of Nursing, Charlotte, NC 28274-0002. Offers nursing management (MSN). *Accreditation:* AACN. *Faculty:* 2 full-time (both women), 3 part-time/adjunct (all women). *Students:* 2 full-time (both women), 17 part-time (13 women); includes 6 minority (all African Americans) Average age 27. 11 applicants, 82% accepted, 9 enrolled. In 2006, 10 degrees awarded. *Degree requirements:* For master's, research project. *Entrance requirements:* For master's, minimum GPA of 3.0. Additional exam requirements/recommendations for international students: Required—TOEFL. *Application deadline:* Applications are processed on a rolling basis. Application fee: $40. Electronic applications accepted. *Expenses:* Contact institution. *Unit head:* Dr. William K. Cody, Chair, 704-337-2542. *Application contact:* Holly Boyd, Director of Admissions, 704-337-2574, Fax: 704-337-2415.

Radford University, Graduate College, Waldron College of Health and Human Services, School of Nursing, Radford, VA 24142. Offers MSN. *Accreditation:* AACN. Part-time programs available. Postbaccalaureate distance learning degree programs offered (minimal on-campus study). *Faculty:* 5 full-time (all women), 2 part-time/adjunct (both women). *Students:* 8 full-time (7 women), 18 part-time (all women); includes 1 minority (African American) Average age 40. 9 applicants, 78% accepted, 2 enrolled. In 2006, 10 degrees awarded. *Degree requirements:* For master's, thesis optional. *Entrance requirements:* For master's, GRE or MAT. Additional exam requirements/recommendations for international students: Required—TOEFL. *Application deadline:* For fall admission, 3/1 priority date for domestic students, 4/1 for international students; for spring admission, 10/1 for domestic students, 8/1 for international students. Applications are processed on a rolling basis. Application fee: $40. Electronic applications accepted. *Expenses:* Tuition, state resident: full-time $4,680; part-time $260 per credit hour. Tuition, nonresident: full-time $8,604; part-time $478 per credit hour. *Financial support:* In 2006–07, 9 students received support, including 8 research assistantships with partial tuition reimbursements available (averaging $8,000 per year), teaching assistantships with partial tuition reimbursements available (averaging $8,700 per year); career-related internships or fieldwork, Federal Work-Study, institutionally sponsored loans, scholarships/grants, and unspecified assistantships also available. Financial award application deadline: 3/1; financial award applicants required to submit FAFSA. *Unit head:* Dr. Marcella J. Griggs, Director, 540-831-7700, Fax: 540-831-6299, E-mail: mgriggs@radford.edu.

Regis College, Department of Nursing, Weston, MA 02493. Offers nurse educator (Certificate); nurse practitioner (Certificate); nursing (MS). *Accreditation:* NLN. Part-time and evening/weekend programs available. *Faculty:* 14 full-time (13 women), 18 part-time/adjunct (15 women). *Students:* 157 full-time (142 women), 176 part-time (166 women); includes 49 minority (35 African Americans, 1 American Indian/Alaska Native, 9 Asian Americans or Pacific Islanders, 4 Hispanic Americans). Average age 36. 167 applicants, 83% accepted, 139 enrolled. In 2006, 45 master's, 13 other advanced degrees awarded. *Degree requirements:* For master's, thesis. *Entrance requirements:* For master's, GRE General Test or MAT, minimum GPA of 3.0. *Application deadline:* Applications are processed on a rolling basis. Application fee: $50. Electronic applications accepted. *Expenses:* Tuition: Full-time $23,680; part-time $665 per credit hour. *Financial support:* In 2006–07, 31 students received support, including 8 research assistantships (averaging $35,000 per year); Federal Work-Study, scholarships/grants, traineeships, and unspecified assistantships also available. Support available to part-time students. Financial award applicants required to submit FAFSA. *Faculty research:* Health policy, education, aging, job satisfaction, psychiatric nursing, critical thinking. *Unit head:* Dr. Antoinette Hays, Dean, School of Nursing and Health Professions, 781-768-7091, Fax: 781-768-8339, E-mail: antoinette.hays@regiscollege.edu.

Regis University, Rueckert-Hartman School for Health Professions, Program in Nursing, Denver, CO 80221-1099. Offers MSN. Offered at Northwest Denver Campus. *Accreditation:* AACN. Part-time programs available. Postbaccalaureate distance learning degree programs offered. *Faculty:* 13 full-time (12 women), 54 part-time/adjunct (45 women). *Students:* 49. In 2006, 16 degrees awarded. *Degree requirements:* For master's, thesis or alternative, final project. *Entrance requirements:* For master's, MAT, BS in nursing, current Colorado RN, 2 years of nursing experience. *Application deadline:* For fall admission, 1/15 for domestic students; for spring admission, 9/15 for domestic students. Applications are processed on a rolling basis. Application fee: $75. *Financial support:* Career-related internships or fieldwork available. *Unit head:* Dr. Candace Gearing Berardinelli, Director, 303-458-4232, E-mail: cberardi@regis.edu. *Application contact:* Admissions Counselor, 303-458-4344, E-mail: shcp@regis.edu.

Research College of Nursing, Nursing Program, Kansas City, MO 64132. Offers executive nurse practitioner (MSN); family nurse practitioner (MSN); nursing education (MSN). *Accreditation:* AACN. Part-time programs available. Postbaccalaureate distance learning degree programs offered (no on-campus study). *Faculty:* 11 full-time (all women). *Students:* Average age 30. In 2006, 6 degrees awarded. *Degree requirements:* For master's, research project. *Entrance requirements:* For master's, minimum GPA of 3.0, interview, 3 letters of recommendation. Additional exam requirements/recommendations for international students: Required—TOEFL (minimum score 550 paper-based; 213 computer-based), TWE. *Application deadline:* For spring admission, 10/1 priority date for domestic students. Applications are processed on a rolling basis. Application fee: $50. *Expenses:* Tuition: Part-time $350 per credit hour. *Financial support:* Applicants required to submit FAFSA. *Unit head:* Dr. Nancy O. De Basio, President and Dean, 816-995-2815, Fax: 816-995-2817, E-mail: nancy.debasio@researchcollege.edu. *Application contact:* Leslie Ann Mendenhall, Director of Transfer and Graduate Recruitment, 816-995-2820, Fax: 816-995-2813, E-mail: leslie.mendenhall@researchcollege.edu.

Rhode Island College, School of Graduate Studies, School of Nursing, Providence, RI 02908-1991. Offers MSN. *Expenses:* Tuition, state resident: part-time $244 per credit. Tuition, nonresident: part-time $512 per credit. Required fees: $12 per credit. $66 per term. Tuition and fees vary according to degree level, program and reciprocity agreements. *Financial support:* Federal Work-Study, scholarships/grants, health care benefits, and unspecified assistantships available. Support available to part-time students. Financial award application deadline: 5/15; financial award applicants required to submit FAFSA. *Unit head:* Dr. Jane Williams, Interim Director, 401-456-8013, Fax: 401-456-8206, E-mail: jwilliams@ric.edu.

The Richard Stockton College of New Jersey, Graduate Programs, Program in Nursing, Pomona, NJ 08240-0195. Offers MSN. *Accreditation:* AACN. Part-time programs available. *Faculty:* 8 full-time (6 women). *Students:* 4 full-time (3 women), 20 part-time (18 women); includes 2 minority (1 African American, 1 Asian American or Pacific Islander). Average age 43. In 2006, 8 degrees awarded. *Degree requirements:* For master's, 300 clinical hours. *Entrance requirements:* For master's, GRE General Test, CPR certification, minimum GPA of 3.0, RN license. *Application deadline:* For fall admission, 6/1 for domestic students. Applications are processed on a rolling basis. Application fee: $50. *Expenses:* Tuition, state resident: full-time $9,746. Tuition, nonresident: full-time $14,462. Required fees: $2,340. *Financial support:* Career-related internships or fieldwork and Federal Work-Study available. Support available to part-time students. Financial award application deadline: 3/1; financial award applicants required to submit FAFSA. *Faculty research:* Psychoneuroimmunology, relationship of nutrition and disease, mental health as affected by chronic disease states, home care for elderly relatives. *Unit head:* Cheryle Eisele, Program Director, 609-652-4496, E-mail: cheryl.eisele@stockton.edu. *Application contact:* Alison Henry, Associate Director of Admissions, 609-652-4261, Fax: 609-626-5541, E-mail: admissions@stockston.edu.

Rivier College, School of Graduate Studies, Department of Nursing and Health Sciences, Nashua, NH 03060-5086. Offers family nurse practitioner (MS); nursing education (MS). *Accreditation:* NLN. Part-time and evening/weekend programs available. *Faculty:* 5 full-time (4 women), 2 part-time/adjunct (0 women). *Students:* 6 full-time (all women), 28 part-time (27 women); includes 1 minority (Asian American or Pacific Islander) Average age 41. In 2006, 18 degrees awarded. *Degree requirements:* For master's, registration. *Entrance requirements:* For master's, GRE, MAT. *Application deadline:* Applications are processed on a rolling basis. Application fee: $25. Electronic applications accepted. *Financial support:* Available to part-time students. Application deadline: 2/1; *Unit head:* Dr. Paula Williams, Head, 603-897-8529. *Application contact:* Diane Monahan, Director of Graduate Admissions, 603-897-8129, Fax: 603-897-8810, E-mail: gradadm@rivier.edu.

Robert Morris University, Graduate Studies, School of Nursing, Moon Township, PA 15108-1189. Offers MS. *Accreditation:* AACN. Part-time and evening/weekend programs available. *Faculty:* 2 full-time (both women). *Students:* Average age 38. 17 applicants, 82% accepted, 10 enrolled. In 2006, 8 degrees awarded. *Entrance requirements:* For master's, letters of recommendation. Additional exam requirements/recommendations for international students: Required—TOEFL (minimum score 550 paper-based; 213 computer-based). *Application deadline:* For fall admission, 7/1 priority date for domestic and international students; for spring admission, 11/1 priority date for domestic and international students. Applications are processed on a rolling basis. Application fee: $35. Electronic applications accepted. *Expenses: Contact institution.* Part-time tuition and fees vary according to degree level and program. *Financial support:* Federal Work-Study, institutionally sponsored loans, and unspecified assistantships available. Financial award application deadline: 5/1; financial award applicants required to submit FAFSA. *Unit head:* Dr. Lynda J. Davidson, Dean, 412-269-3859, Fax: 412-262-8494, E-mail: davidsonl@rmu.edu. *Application contact:* Kellie L. Laurenzi, Assistant Dean, Enrollment Services, 412-262-8235, Fax: 412-299-2425, E-mail: laurenzi@rmu.edu.

Roberts Wesleyan College, Division of Nursing, Rochester, NY 14624-1997. Offers nursing administration (MSN); nursing education (MSN). *Faculty:* 13 full-time (all women), 6 part-time/adjunct (4 women). *Entrance requirements:* For master's, minimum GPA of 3.0; BS in nursing; interview; RN license; resumé; course work in statistics and health assessment. Additional exam requirements/recommendations for international students: Required—TOEFL. *Unit head:* Dr. Susanne M. Mohnkern, Chair, 585-594-6000, E-mail: mohnkerns@roberts.edu. *Application contact:* Yvonne Strong, Admissions Coordinator, 585-594-6388, E-mail: strong_yvonne@roberts.edu.

Rush University, College of Nursing, Chicago, IL 60612-3832. Offers MSN, DN Sc, DNP, Post-Master's Certificate. *Accreditation:* AACN; AANA/CANAEP (one or more programs are accredited). Part-time programs available. Postbaccalaureate distance learning degree programs offered (minimal on-campus study). *Faculty:* 42 full-time (40 women), 31 part-time/adjunct (29 women). *Students:* 66 full-time (54 women), 239 part-time (225 women); includes 41 minority (15 African Americans, 9 Asian Americans or Pacific Islanders, 17 Hispanic Americans). Average age 34. 197 applicants, 83% accepted, 153 enrolled. In 2006, 57 master's, 13 doctorates awarded. Terminal master's awarded for partial completion of doctoral program. *Degree requirements:* For master's, capstone project; for doctorate, thesis/dissertation, DNP leadership project. *Entrance requirements:* For master's, GRE General Test (waived if nursing GPA is greater than 3.0 or cumulative GPA is greater than 3.25, interview; for doctorate, GRE General Test, interview, course work in statistics (DN Sc). Additional exam requirements/recommendations for international students: Required—TOEFL, TWE. *Application deadline:* For fall admission, 7/1 for domestic students; for winter admission, 11/1 for domestic students; for spring admission, 1/15 for domestic students. Applications are processed on a rolling basis. Application fee: $40. Electronic applications accepted. *Financial support:* In 2006–07, 237 students received support, including 6 teaching assistantships with partial tuition reimbursements available (averaging $22,000 per year); fellowships, research assistantships, Federal Work-Study, institutionally sponsored loans, scholarships/grants, and traineeships also available. Support available to part-time students. Financial award application deadline: 4/15; financial award applicants required to submit FAFSA. *Faculty research:* Parenting intervention, immigrant mental health, caregiver interventions, immune function, cardiac risk reduction. Total annual research expenditures: $3.3 million. *Unit head:* Dr. Melanie Dreher, Dean, 312-942-7117, Fax: 312-942-3043. *Application contact:* Hicela Castruita Woods, Director, College Admissions Services, 312-942-7100, Fax: 312-942-2219, E-mail: hicela_castruita@rush.edu.

Rutgers, The State University of New Jersey, Newark, Graduate School, Program in Nursing, Newark, NJ 07102. Offers nursing (MS), including acute care of adults and aged, advanced practice in pediatric nursing, advanced practice with childbearing families, community health nursing, family nurse practitioner, primary care of adults and aged, psychiatric/mental health nursing. *Accreditation:* AACN. Part-time programs available. *Faculty:* 33 full-time (32 women). *Students:* 11 full-time (all women), 186 part-time (175 women); includes 70 minority (28 African Americans, 30 Asian Americans or Pacific Islanders, 12 Hispanic Americans). 255 applicants, 58% accepted, 72 enrolled. In 2006, 40 master's awarded. *Degree requirements:* For master's, comprehensive exam. *Entrance requirements:* For master's, GRE General Test, RN license, minimum B average, BS in nursing. Additional exam requirements/recommendations for international students: Required—TOEFL. *Application deadline:* For fall admission, 2/15 for domestic students; for spring admission, 12/1 for domestic students. Applications are processed on a rolling basis. Application fee: $50. Electronic applications accepted. *Financial support:* In 2006–07, 3 fellowships (averaging $8,000 per year) were awarded; teaching assistantships with full tuition reimbursements, career-related internships or fieldwork, Federal Work-Study, institutionally sponsored loans, scholarships/grants, traineeships, and tuition waivers (full and partial) also available. Financial award application deadline: 4/15. *Faculty research:* HIV/AIDS, quality of life—MS and breast cancer, sleep patterns of cardiac patients. *Unit head:* Dr. Wendy Nehring, Program Director, 973-353-5293 Ext. 606, Fax: 973-353-1277, E-mail: nehring@nightingale.rutgers.edu. *Application contact:* Dr. Linda Scheetz, Associate Dean for Student Life and Services, 973-353-5060 Ext. 611, Fax: 973-353-1277, E-mail: lscheetz@andromeda.rutgers.edu.

Sacred Heart University, Graduate Studies, College of Education and Health Professions, Faculty of Nursing, Fairfield, CT 06825-1000. Offers clinical nurse leader (MSN); family nurse practitioner (MSN); patient care services administration (MSN); MSN/MBA. *Accreditation:* AACN. Part-time and evening/weekend programs available. Postbaccalaureate distance learning degree programs offered (minimal on-campus study). *Faculty:* 12 full-time (all women). *Students:* 6 full-time (all women), 64 part-time (59 women); includes 11 minority (7 African Americans, 1 Asian American or Pacific Islander, 3 Hispanic Americans). Average age 39. 34 applicants, 94% accepted, 26 enrolled. In 2006, 10 degrees awarded. *Entrance requirements:* For master's, BSN, minimum GPA of 3.0. Additional exam requirements/recommendations for international students: Required—TOEFL (minimum score 550 paper-based; 213 computer-based). *Application deadline:* Applications are processed on a rolling basis. Application fee: $50 ($100 for international students). Electronic applications accepted. *Expenses: Contact institution.* Full-time tuition and fees vary according to degree level and program. *Financial support:* Career-related internships or fieldwork, institutionally sponsored loans, and unspecified assistantships available. Support available to part-time students. Financial award applicants required to submit FAFSA. *Unit head:* Dr. Dori Sullivan, Director, Graduate Program in Nursing, 203-371-7715. *Application contact:* Kathy Dilks, Assistant Dean of Graduate Admissions, Health Professions, 203-396-8259, Fax: 203-365-4732, E-mail: gradstudies@sacredheart.edu.

Sage Graduate School, Graduate School, Division of Nursing, Troy, NY 12180-4115. Offers adult health (MS); adult nurse practitioner (MS, Post Master's Certificate); community health (MS); family nurse practitioner (MS, Post Master's Certificate); nursing (Post Master's Certificate); nursing-medical surgical (MS); psychiatric mental health nurse practitioner (MS), including psychiatric mental health; MBA/MS. *Accreditation:* AACN. Part-time and evening/weekend programs available. *Faculty:* 8 full-time (all women), 3 part-time/adjunct (all women). *Students:* 38 full-time (34 women), 63 part-time (60 women); includes 9 minority (4 African Americans, 1 American Indian/Alaska Native, 3 Asian Americans or Pacific Islanders, 1 Hispanic American). Average age 40. 67 applicants, 79% accepted, 31 enrolled. In 2006, 39 master's, 11 other advanced degrees awarded. *Degree requirements:* For master's, thesis or alternative. *Entrance requirements:* For master's, BS in nursing, minimum GPA of 2.75. Additional exam requirements/recommendations for international students: Required—TOEFL (minimum score 550 paper-based; 213 computer-based). *Application deadline:* Applications are processed on a rolling basis. Application fee: $40. *Expenses:* Tuition: Full-time $9,270; part-time $515 per credit hour. *Financial support:* Career-related internships or fieldwork, scholarships/grants, and unspecified assistantships available. Support available to part-time students. Financial award application deadline: 3/1; financial award applicants required to submit FAFSA. *Unit head:* Dr. Glenda Kelman, Chair, 518-244-2001, E-mail: kelmag@sage.edu. *Application contact:* Shannon K. Easton, Director of Graduate and Adult Admission, 518-244-2443, Fax: 518-244-6880, E-mail: sgsadm@sage.edu.

Saginaw Valley State University, Crystal M. Lange College of Nursing and Health Sciences, Program in Nursing, University Center, MI 48710. Offers MSN. *Accreditation:* AACN. *Students:* 1 applicant, 100% accepted, 0 enrolled. *Expenses:* Tuition, state resident: full-time $7,225; part-time $301 per credit hour. Tuition, nonresident: full-time $13,888; part-time $579 per credit hour. Required fees: $330; $14 per credit hour. Tuition and fees vary according to course load. *Unit head:* Dr. Margaret Flatt, Assistant Dean, 989-964-4130, Fax: 989-964-4024, E-mail: flatt@svsu.edu.

St. Ambrose University, College of Education and Health Sciences, Program in Nursing, Davenport, IA 52803-2898. Offers MSN. Part-time and evening/weekend programs available. *Faculty:* 1 (woman) full-time, 1 (woman) part-time/adjunct. *Students:* 11 full-time (all women), 26 part-time (all women); includes 1 Hispanic American. Average age 45. 15 applicants, 67% accepted, 9 enrolled. *Entrance requirements:* Additional exam requirements/recommendations for international students: Required—TOEFL. *Application deadline:* Applications are processed on a rolling basis. Application fee: $25. Electronic applications accepted. *Financial support:* In 2006–07, 37 students received support. Career-related internships or fieldwork, tuition waivers (partial), and unspecified assistantships available. Support available to part-time students. *Unit*

Nursing—General

St. Ambrose University (continued)
head: Dr. Delores Hilden, Director, 563-333-6076, Fax: 563-333-6063. *Application contact:* Elizabeth Berridge, Director Graduate Studies Recruitment, 563-333-6271, Fax: 563-333-6268, E-mail: berridgeelizabethb@sau.edu.

Saint Joseph College, Graduate Division, Department of Nursing, West Hartford, CT 06117-2700. Offers family health nurse practitioner (MS); family health nursing (MS); nursing (Post Master's Certificate); psychiatric/mental health nursing (MS). *Accreditation:* AACN. Part-time and evening/weekend programs available. *Degree requirements:* For master's and Post Master's Certificate, thesis. *Entrance requirements:* For master's, GRE General Test or MAT, 2 letters of recommendation; for Post Master's Certificate, MAT, master's degree in nursing, minimum GPA of 3.0. Additional exam requirements/recommendations for international students: Required—NCLEX. Electronic applications accepted. *Faculty research:* Reproductive health and substance abuse, problem-based learning, role of clinical faculty, students' international studies experience.

St. Joseph's College, New York, Graduate Programs, Program in Nursing, Brooklyn, NY 11205-3688. Offers MS.

See Close-Up on page 1973.

Saint Joseph's College of Maine, Department of Nursing, Standish, ME 04084-5263. Offers nursing (MS); nursing administration and leadership (Certificate); nursing and health care education (Certificate). MS degree offered only through faculty-directed independent study. *Accreditation:* AACN. Part-time programs available. Postbaccalaureate distance learning degree programs offered (minimal on-campus study). *Faculty:* 2 full-time (both women), 8 part-time/adjunct (all women). *Students:* Average age 43. 65 applicants, 91% accepted, 54 enrolled. In 2006, 26 degrees awarded. *Degree requirements:* For master's, summer residency. *Entrance requirements:* For master's, MAT. *Application deadline:* Applications are processed on a rolling basis. Application fee: $50. Electronic applications accepted. *Expenses:* Tuition: Part-time $350 per credit. *Financial support:* Institutionally sponsored loans available. Support available to part-time students. *Unit head:* Dr. Margaret Hourigan, Chair, 207-893-7970, Fax: 207-892-7423, E-mail: mhourigan@sjcme.edu. *Application contact:* 800-752-4723, Fax: 207-892-7480, E-mail: info@sjcme.edu.

St. Joseph's College, Suffolk Campus, Program in Nursing, Patchogue, NY 11772-2399. Offers MS.

Saint Louis University, Graduate School, Doisy College of Health Sciences, School of Nursing, St. Louis, MO 63104. Offers MSN, MSN-R, PhD, Certificate. *Accreditation:* AACN. Part-time programs available. Postbaccalaureate distance learning degree programs offered (minimal on-campus study). *Faculty:* 37 full-time (36 women), 26 part-time/adjunct (25 women). *Students:* 55 full-time (51 women), 235 part-time (215 women); includes 33 minority (19 African Americans, 3 American Indian/Alaska Native, 7 Asian Americans or Pacific Islanders, 4 Hispanic Americans), 9 international. Average age 36. 156 applicants, 83% accepted, 88 enrolled. In 2006, 38 master's, 4 doctorates, 21 other advanced degrees awarded. *Degree requirements:* For master's, thesis optional; for doctorate, thesis/dissertation, preliminary exams, comprehensive exam, registration. *Entrance requirements:* For master's, letters of recommendation, resumé; for doctorate, GRE General Test, letters of recommendation, resumé. Additional exam requirements/recommendations for international students: Required—TOEFL (minimum score 525 paper-based; 194 computer-based). *Application deadline:* For fall admission, 7/1 for domestic and international students; for spring admission, 11/1 for domestic and international students. Applications are processed on a rolling basis. Application fee: $40. *Expenses:* Tuition: Part-time $800 per credit hour. Required fees: $105 per semester. *Financial support:* In 2006–07, 64 students received support, including 2 research assistantships (averaging $10,250 per year), 5 teaching assistantships with full tuition reimbursements available (averaging $11,000 per year); Federal Work-Study, scholarships/grants, traineeships, health care benefits, tuition waivers, and unspecified assistantships also available. Support available to part-time students. Financial award application deadline: 6/1; financial award applicants required to submit FAFSA. *Faculty research:* Sensory enhancement in the elderly, fall prevention in elderly, tube feeding replacement and gastroenerology, patient outcomes, exercise behavior in the older adult. Total annual research expenditures: $1 million. *Unit head:* Dr. Teri A. Murray, Director, 314-977-8900, Fax: 314-977-8949, E-mail: tmurray4@slu.edu. *Application contact:* Gary Behrman, Associate Dean of the Graduate School, 314-977-3827, E-mail: behrmang@slu.edu.

Saint Peter's College, Nursing Program, Jersey City, NJ 07306-5997. Offers MSN. *Accreditation:* AACN. Part-time and evening/weekend programs available. *Entrance requirements:* For master's, GRE or MAT. *Faculty research:* Battered women's perceptions of the emergency department experience, quality outcomes.

Saint Xavier University, Graduate Studies, School of Nursing, Chicago, IL 60655-3105. Offers adult health clinical nurse specialist (MS); family nurse practitioner (MS, PMC); leadership in community health nursing (MS); psychiatric-mental health clinical nurse specialist (MS); psychiatric-mental health clinical specialist (PMC); MBA/MS. *Accreditation:* AACN. Part-time and evening/weekend programs available. *Faculty:* 11. *Students:* 20 full-time (14 women), 120 part-time (113 women). Average age 40. In 2006, 36 degrees awarded. *Entrance requirements:* For master's, GRE General Test or MAT, minimum GPA of 3.0, RN license. *Application deadline:* For fall admission, 2/15 for domestic students; for spring admission, 9/15 for domestic students. Applications are processed on a rolling basis. Application fee: $35. *Financial support:* Available to part-time students. Applicants required to submit FAFSA. *Unit head:* Beth Gierach, Managing Director of Admission, 773-298-3053, Fax: 773-298-3076, E-mail: gierach@sxu.edu.

Salem State College, Graduate School, Program in Nursing, Salem, MA 01970-5353. Offers advanced practice in rehabilitation (MSN); direct entry nursing (MSN); nursing (MSN, MBA/MSN); MBA/MSN. *Accreditation:* AACN; NLN. Part-time and evening/weekend programs available. *Faculty:* 5 full-time (all women). *Students:* 19 full-time (17 women), 49 part-time (all women); includes 8 minority (6 African Americans, 1 Asian American or Pacific Islander, 1 Hispanic American), 1 international. Average age 40. In 2006, 14 degrees awarded. *Entrance requirements:* For master's, GRE General Test, MAT. *Application deadline:* Applications are processed on a rolling basis. Application fee: $35. *Unit head:* Kathleen Skrabat, Coordinator, 978-542-6646, Fax: 978-542-7215, E-mail: kskrabat@salemstate.edu.

Salisbury University, Graduate Division, Program in Nursing, Salisbury, MD 21801-6837. Offers MS. *Accreditation:* AACN. Part-time programs available. *Faculty:* 3 full-time (all women), 2 part-time/adjunct (both women). *Students:* 2 full-time (both women), 15 part-time (all women). Average age 36. 8 applicants, 100% accepted, 8 enrolled. In 2006, 7 degrees awarded. *Degree requirements:* For master's, thesis or capstone project. *Entrance requirements:* For master's, minimum GPA of 3.0, interview, resumé, CPR certification, proof of immunizations. Additional exam requirements/recommendations for international students: Required—TOEFL (minimum score 550 paper-based; 213 computer-based). *Application deadline:* For fall admission, 2/15 for domestic students; for spring admission, 10/15 for domestic students. Applications are processed on a rolling basis. Application fee: $45. Electronic applications accepted. *Expenses:* Tuition, state resident: part-time $260 per credit hour. Tuition, nonresident: part-time $546 per credit hour. Required fees: $52 per credit hour. *Financial support:* Career-related internships or fieldwork, scholarships/grants, and unspecified assistantships available. Support available to part-time students. Financial award applicants required to submit FAFSA. *Faculty research:* Female health and maternity, adolescent health, family health, school health. *Unit head:* Dr. Karin E. Johnson, Director, 410-543-6411, Fax: 410-548-3313, E-mail: kejohnson@salisbury.edu. *Application contact:* Eleanor W. Morris, Administrative Assistant II, 410-543-6401, Fax: 410-548-3313, E-mail: ewmorris@salisbury.edu.

Samford University, Ida V. Moffett School of Nursing, Birmingham, AL 35229-0002. Offers MSN, MSNA, MBA/MSN. *Accreditation:* AACN; AANA/CANAEP (one or more programs are accredited). Part-time programs available. *Faculty:* 8 full-time (all women). *Students:* 84 full-time (62 women), 21 part-time (15 women); includes 8 minority (6 African Americans, 2 Asian Americans or Pacific Islanders). Average age 33. 112 applicants, 62% accepted, 38 enrolled. In 2006, 32 degrees awarded. *Entrance requirements:* For master's, GRE General Test or MAT, Alabama RN license, BSN from an NLN-accredited school, minimum GPA of 3.0. Additional exam requirements/recommendations for international students: Required—TOEFL (minimum score 550 paper-based; 213 computer-based). *Application deadline:* For spring admission, 1/2 for domestic students. Applications are processed on a rolling basis. Application fee: $25. *Expenses: Contact institution.* One-time fee: $25 part-time. Full-time tuition and fees vary according to program and student level. *Financial support:* In 2006–07, 20 students received support. Career-related internships or fieldwork, Federal Work-Study, and institutionally sponsored loans available. Financial award application deadline: 3/1; financial award applicants required to submit FAFSA. *Faculty research:* Cultural self efficiency, health seeking behaviors, central hemodynamics in women undergoing cesarean section with regional anesthesia, health status of migrant farm workers. *Unit head:* Dr. Nena F. Sanders, Dean, 205-726-2629, E-mail: nfsander@samford.edu. *Application contact:* Stacy W. Miner, Graduate Admissions and Alumni Administrator, 205-726-2047, Fax: 205-870-4179, E-mail: sewaldre@samford.edu.

Samuel Merritt College, School of Nursing, Oakland, CA 94609-3108. Offers case management (MSN); family nurse practitioner (MSN, Certificate); nurse anesthetist (MSN, Certificate); nursing (MSN). *Accreditation:* AACN; AANA/CANAEP (one or more programs are accredited). Part-time and evening/weekend programs available. *Degree requirements:* For master's, thesis or alternative. *Entrance requirements:* For master's, minimum GPA of 2.5 in science, 3.0 overall; previous course work in statistics; current RN license. Additional exam requirements/recommendations for international students: Required—TOEFL. *Faculty research:* Gerontology, community health, maternal-child health, sexually transmitted diseases, substance abuse, oncology.

San Diego State University, Graduate and Research Affairs, College of Health and Human Services, School of Nursing, San Diego, CA 92182. Offers MS. *Accreditation:* AACN; ACNM/DOA. Part-time and evening/weekend programs available. *Students:* 53 full-time (48 women), 42 part-time (37 women); includes 10 minority (7 Asian Americans or Pacific Islanders, 3 Hispanic Americans). Average age 31. 46 applicants, 72% accepted, 12 enrolled. In 2006, 35 degrees awarded. *Entrance requirements:* For master's, GRE General Test, previous course work in statistics and physical assessment, 3 letters of recommendation, California RN license. Additional exam requirements/recommendations for international students: Required—TOEFL. *Application deadline:* For fall admission, 1/15 for domestic and international students; for spring admission, 11/1 for domestic students, 10/1 for international students. Applications are processed on a rolling basis. Application fee: $55. Electronic applications accepted. *Financial support:* Career-related internships or fieldwork, scholarships/grants, traineeships, and unspecified assistantships available. Financial award applicants required to submit FAFSA. *Faculty research:* Health promotion, nursing systems and leadership, maternal-child nursing, advanced practice nursing, child oral health. Total annual research expenditures: $887,445. *Unit head:* Catherine Todero, Director, 619-594-6504, Fax: 619-594-3765. *Application contact:* Sue Hadley, Graduate Advisor, 619-594-2770, Fax: 619-594-2765, E-mail: shadley@mail.sdsu.edu.

San Francisco State University, Division of Graduate Studies, College of Health and Human Services, School of Nursing, San Francisco, CA 94132-1722. Offers case management (MS), including long-term care, primary care/family nurse practitioner; nursing administration (MS); nursing education (MS). *Accreditation:* AACN. Part-time programs available. *Faculty:* 12 full-time (10 women). *Students:* Average age 32. In 2006, 28 degrees awarded. *Degree requirements:* For master's, thesis. *Entrance requirements:* For master's, minimum GPA of 3.0. *Application deadline:* For fall admission, 11/30 priority date for domestic students; for spring admission, 5/31 for domestic students. Applications are processed on a rolling basis. Application fee: $55. *Financial support:* In 2006–07, 35 students received support, including 35 fellowships; career-related internships or fieldwork also available. Financial award application deadline: 3/1. *Faculty research:* Nursing case management and clinical outcomes, outcome of undergraduate and graduate education in nursing, patient education strategies and learning outcomes. Total annual research expenditures: $25,000. *Unit head:* Dr. Karen Johnson-Brennan, Interim Director, 415-338-1801, Fax: 415-338-0555. *Application contact:* Dr. Frank McLaughlin, Graduate Coordinator, 415-338-1802, E-mail: femc@sfsu.edu.

San Jose State University, Graduate Studies and Research, College of Applied Sciences and Arts, School of Nursing, San Jose, CA 95192-0001. Offers gerontology nurse practitioner (MS); nursing (Certificate); nursing administration (MS); nursing education (MS). *Accreditation:* AACN. Part-time and evening/weekend programs available. *Students:* 15 full-time (13 women), 70 part-time (66 women); includes 30 minority (2 African Americans, 21 Asian Americans or Pacific Islanders, 7 Hispanic Americans). Average age 41. 73 applicants, 70% accepted, 15 enrolled. In 2006, 34 degrees awarded. *Degree requirements:* For master's, thesis. *Entrance requirements:* For master's, BS in nursing, RN license. *Application deadline:* For fall admission, 6/29 for domestic students; for spring admission, 11/30 for domestic students. Applications are processed on a rolling basis. Application fee: $59. Electronic applications accepted. *Financial support:* Career-related internships or fieldwork, institutionally sponsored loans, and scholarships/grants available. Support available to part-time students. Financial award applicants required to submit FAFSA. *Faculty research:* Nurse-managed clinics, computers in nursing. *Unit head:* Jayne Cohen, Director, 408-924-3131, Fax: 408-924-3135. *Application contact:* Dr. Phyllis Connolly, Graduate Coordinator, 408-924-3144.

Seattle Pacific University, Graduate School, School of Health Sciences, Seattle, WA 98119-1997. Offers MSN, Certificate. *Accreditation:* AACN. Part-time and evening/weekend programs available. *Faculty:* 2 full-time (both women). *Students:* 17 applicants, 71% accepted, 8 enrolled. In 2006, 15 degrees awarded. *Degree requirements:* For master's, thesis, internships; for Certificate, internships. *Entrance requirements:* For master's, GRE General Test, BS or BSN from NLN-accredited program, interview, Washington RN license; for Certificate, MSN, minimum GPA of 3.5. *Application deadline:* For fall admission, 9/1 priority date for domestic students. Applications are processed on a rolling basis. Application fee: $50. *Expenses: Contact institution.* *Financial support:* In 2006–07, 2 teaching assistantships were awarded; career-related internships or fieldwork and traineeships also available. Financial award applicants required to submit FAFSA. *Faculty research:* Health promotion, intercultural/international education, empathy/spiritual care, social policy, critical care/quality of life. *Unit head:* Dr. Lucille Kelley, Dean, 206-281-2608, Fax: 206-281-2767, E-mail: lkelley@spu.edu. *Application contact:* Dr. Donna J. Allis, Director, 206-281-2649, Fax: 206-281-2767, E-mail: dallis@spu.edu.

Seattle University, College of Nursing, Program in Nursing, Seattle, WA 98122-1090. Offers leadership in community nursing (MSN), including program development, spirituality and health; primary care nurse practitioner (MSN), including family nurse practitioner, psychiatric mental health nurse practitioner. *Students:* 6 full-time (all women), 8 part-time (7 women); includes 2 African Americans. Average age 40. *Application contact:* Janet Shandley, Associate Dean of Graduate Admissions, 206-296-5900, Fax: 206-298-5656, E-mail: grad_admissions@seattleu.edu.

Seton Hall University, College of Nursing, South Orange, NJ 07079-2697. Offers MA, MSN, PhD, MSN/MA. *Accreditation:* AACN. Part-time programs available. *Degree requirements:* For master's, research project; for doctorate, thesis/dissertation. *Entrance requirements:* For master's, GRE or MAT, BSN; for doctorate, GRE, master's degree in nursing. Additional exam requirements/recommendations for international students: Required—TOEFL. Electronic applications accepted. *Faculty research:* Parent/child, adult, and gerontological nursing; breast cancer; families of children with HIV; parish nursing.

Shenandoah University, School of Health Professions, Division of Nursing, Winchester, VA 22601-5195. Offers family nurse practitioner (Certificate); nurse-midwifery (Certificate);

nursing (MSN); psychiatric mental health nurse practitioner (Certificate). *Accreditation:* AACN; ACNM/DOA. Part-time programs available. *Faculty:* 9 full-time (all women), 2 part-time/adjunct (both women). *Students:* 5 full-time (all women), 19 part-time (18 women). Average age 37. 40 applicants, 78% accepted, 19 enrolled. In 2006, 11 master's, 4 other advanced degrees awarded. *Degree requirements:* For master's, research project. *Entrance requirements:* For master's, GRE General Test, previous course work in statistics, community nursing, and physical assessment; RN license; minimum undergraduate GPA of 2.8; appropriate clinical experience; curriculum vitae; for Certificate, MSN, minimum GPA of 3.0. Additional exam requirements/recommendations for international students: Required—TOEFL (minimum score 527 paper-based; 197 computer-based; 71 iBT). *Application deadline:* For fall admission, 6/15 priority date for domestic and international students. Applications are processed on a rolling basis. Application fee: $30. Electronic applications accepted. *Expenses:* Tuition: Full-time $12,200; part-time $610 per credit. Required fees: $150. Full-time tuition and fees vary according to course load and program. *Financial support:* In 2006–07, 21 students received support, including 3 fellowships with partial tuition reimbursements available (averaging $1,500 per year), 2 teaching assistantships with partial tuition reimbursements available (averaging $3,482 per year); institutionally sponsored loans and scholarships/grants also available. Support available to part-time students. Financial award application deadline: 3/15; financial award applicants required to submit FAFSA. *Faculty research:* Nurse caring behaviors, end of life issues, women's health, gerontology, nursing diagnosis. Total annual research expenditures: $80,000. *Unit head:* Dr. Sheila Ralph, Director, 540-678-4381, Fax: 540-665-5519, E-mail: ssparks@su.edu. *Application contact:* David Anthony, Dean of Admissions, 540-665-4581, Fax: 540-665-4627, E-mail: admit@su.edu.

Simmons College, School for Health Studies, Program in Primary Health Care Nursing, Boston, MA 02115. Offers health professions education (PhD); primary health care nursing (MS, CAGS). *Accreditation:* AACN. Part-time programs available. *Faculty:* 8 full-time (7 women), 2 part-time/adjunct (both women). *Students:* 74 full-time (65 women), 84 part-time (81 women); includes 16 minority (4 African Americans, 10 Asian Americans or Pacific Islanders, 2 Hispanic Americans). Average age 30. 194 applicants, 61% accepted, 61 enrolled. In 2006, 30 master's, 1 other advanced degree awarded. *Median time to degree:* 2 years part-time. *Degree requirements:* For master's, thesis/dissertation, registration; for doctorate, thesis/dissertation, comprehensive exam, registration. *Entrance requirements:* For master's, GRE, courses in statistics and health assessment; for CAGS, previous coursework in microbiology, statistics, developmental psychology, organic and inorganic chemistry. Additional exam requirements/recommendations for international students: Required—TOEFL (minimum score 550 paper-based; 230 computer-based). *Application deadline:* For fall admission, 6/1 for domestic and international students; for winter admission, 11/1 for domestic and international students; for spring admission, 11/1 for domestic and international students. Applications are processed on a rolling basis. Application fee: $50. Electronic applications accepted. *Expenses:* Contact institution. *Financial support:* In 2006–07, 10 fellowships with partial tuition reimbursements were awarded; research assistantships, teaching assistantships, institutionally sponsored loans, scholarships/grants, and traineeships also available. Financial award application deadline: 3/1; financial award applicants required to submit FAFSA. *Faculty research:* Nursing leadership and mentoring, gerontology/home care, nurse practitioner in occupational health, adolescent pregnancy, developmental disabilities. Total annual research expenditures: $392,500. *Unit head:* Dr. Judy A. Beal, Chairperson, 617-521-2139, Fax: 617-521-3045, E-mail: judy.beal@simmons.edu. *Application contact:* Vilma Torres, Administrative Assistant, 617-521-2654, Fax: 617-521-3137, E-mail: shs@simmons.edu.

Slippery Rock University of Pennsylvania, Graduate Studies (Recruitment), College of Health, Environment, and Science, Department of Nursing, Slippery Rock, PA 16057-1383. Offers MSN. *Accreditation:* NLN. Part-time and evening/weekend programs available. Postbaccalaureate distance learning degree programs offered (minimal on-campus study). *Degree requirements:* For master's, thesis, comprehensive exam. *Entrance requirements:* For master's, minimum QPA of 2.75. Electronic applications accepted. *Expenses:* Tuition, state resident: part-time $336 per credit. Tuition, nonresident: part-time $538 per credit. Required fees: $84 per credit. $37 per semester. *Faculty research:* Sexually transmitted disease prevention, chronic illnesses, decision making, health promotion, evidence based practice.

South Dakota State University, Graduate School, College of Nursing, Brookings, SD 57007. Offers MS, PhD. *Accreditation:* AACN. Part-time and evening/weekend programs available. Postbaccalaureate distance learning degree programs offered. *Faculty:* 20 full-time (18 women). *Students:* 6 full-time (all women), 168 part-time (162 women); includes 5 minority (1 African American, 2 American Indian/Alaska Native, 1 Asian American or Pacific Islander, 1 Hispanic American). 15 applicants, 93% accepted. In 2006, 26 degrees awarded. *Degree requirements:* For master's, thesis (for some programs), oral exam, comprehensive exam. *Entrance requirements:* For master's, registered nurse; for doctorate, registered nurse with MS. Additional exam requirements/recommendations for international students: Required—TOEFL (minimum score 600 paper-based; 220 computer-based). *Application deadline:* For fall admission, 3/1 priority date for domestic students. Application fee: $15. *Expenses:* Contact institution. *Financial support:* In 2006–07, 2 fellowships, 1 research assistantship, 3 teaching assistantships were awarded; career-related internships or fieldwork, Federal Work-Study, scholarships/grants, and unspecified assistantships also available. *Faculty research:* Rural health, aging, health promotion, Native American health, woman's health, underserved populations, quality of life. *Unit head:* Dr. Sandra J. Bunkers, Department Head, Graduate Nursing, 605-688-4114, Fax: 605-688-5827. *Application contact:* LeAnn K. Nelson, Senior Secretary, 605-688-4114, Fax: 605-688-5827, E-mail: leann.nelson@sdstate.edu.

Southeastern Louisiana University, College of Nursing and Health Sciences, School of Nursing, Hammond, LA 70402. Offers MSN. Part-time programs available. *Faculty:* 11 full-time (all women). *Students:* 13 full-time (10 women), 60 part-time (52 women); includes 6 minority (5 African Americans, 1 Hispanic American), 1 international. Average age 36. 29 applicants, 100% accepted, 24 enrolled. In 2006, 6 degrees awarded. *Degree requirements:* For master's, thesis optional. *Entrance requirements:* For master's, GRE General Test, 1 year experience in clinical practice, minimum GPA of 2.7, physical assessment, bachelor's degree in nursing. Additional exam requirements/recommendations for international students: Required—TOEFL (minimum score 500 paper-based; 173 computer-based). *Application deadline:* For fall admission, 7/15 priority date for domestic students, 6/1 priority date for international students; for spring admission, 12/1 priority date for domestic students, 10/1 priority date for international students. Applications are processed on a rolling basis. Application fee: $20 ($30 for international students). Electronic applications accepted. *Expenses:* Tuition, state resident: full-time $2,216; part-time $123 per credit. Tuition, nonresident: full-time $6,212; part-time $345 per credit. Required fees: $986; $55 per credit. Part-time tuition and fees vary according to course load. *Financial support:* Career-related internships or fieldwork, Federal Work-Study, institutionally sponsored loans, scholarships/grants, unspecified assistantships, and administrative assistantship available. Support available to part-time students. Financial award application deadline: 5/1; financial award applicants required to submit FAFSA. *Faculty research:* Healthy farm families-intervention outcomes, motivational interviewing in client teaching, migrant worker health, novice to expert in the nursing faculty role, effectiveness and satisfaction with distance learning. Total annual research expenditures: $65,187. *Unit head:* Dr. Barbara Moffett, Director, 985-549-2156, Fax: 985-549-2869, E-mail: bmoffett@selu.edu. *Application contact:* Sandra Meyers, Graduate Admissions Analyst, 985-549-2066, Fax: 985-549-5632, E-mail: admissions@selu.edu.

Southeast Missouri State University, School of Graduate Studies, Department of Nursing, Cape Girardeau, MO 63701-4799. Offers MSN. *Accreditation:* AACN. Part-time programs available. *Faculty:* 13 full-time (all women). *Students:* 10 full-time (9 women), 36 part-time (33 women); includes 2 minority (1 American Indian/Alaska Native, 1 Asian American or Pacific Islander). Average age 38. 23 applicants, 96% accepted. In 2006, 12 degrees awarded. *Degree requirements:* For master's, thesis. *Entrance requirements:* For master's, minimum GPA of 3.0, Missouri nursing license, clinical experience, CPR certification, RSN or equivalent, professional liability insurance. Additional exam requirements/recommendations for international students: Required—TOEFL (minimum score 550 paper-based; 213 computer-based). *Application deadline:* For fall admission, 8/1 for domestic students, 4/1 for international students; for spring admission, 11/21 for domestic students, 10/1 for international students. Applications are processed on a rolling basis. Application fee: $20 ($100 for international students). Electronic applications accepted. *Financial support:* In 2006–07, 25 students received support, including 6 teaching assistantships with full tuition reimbursements available (averaging $7,100 per year); career-related internships or fieldwork and unspecified assistantships also available. Financial award applicants required to submit FAFSA. *Unit head:* Dr. Gloria Green, Interim Chair, 573-651-5154, E-mail: gjgreen@semo.edu. *Application contact:* Marsha L. Arant, Senior Administrative Assistant, Office of Graduate Studies, 573-651-2192, Fax: 573-651-2001, E-mail: marant@semo.edu.

Southern Adventist University, School of Nursing, Collegedale, TN 37315-0370. Offers adult nurse practitioner (MSN); family nurse practitioner (MSN); nurse educator (MSN); MSN/MSBA. *Accreditation:* NLN. Part-time programs available. *Faculty:* 1 (woman) full-time, 5 part-time/adjunct (all women). *Students:* 45 full-time (41 women), 17 part-time (14 women); includes 5 minority (2 African Americans, 2 Asian Americans or Pacific Islanders, 1 Hispanic American). Average age 35. 40 applicants, 95% accepted, 31 enrolled. In 2006, 20 degrees awarded. *Degree requirements:* For master's, thesis or project. *Entrance requirements:* For master's, RN license. Additional exam requirements/recommendations for international students: Required—TOEFL (minimum score 600 paper-based). *Application deadline:* For fall admission, 7/1 for domestic and international students; for winter admission, 12/1 for domestic and international students. Applications are processed on a rolling basis. Application fee: $25. Electronic applications accepted. *Financial support:* In 2006–07, 1 teaching assistantship with partial tuition reimbursement (averaging $5,000 per year) was awarded. *Faculty research:* Pain management, ethics, corporate wellness, caring spirituality, stress. *Unit head:* Dr. Barbara James, Dean, 423-236-2940, Fax: 423-236-1940, E-mail: bjames@southern.edu. *Application contact:* Diane Proffitt, Enrollment Counselor, 423-236-2941, Fax: 423-236-1940, E-mail: dproffitt@southern.edu.

Southern Connecticut State University, School of Graduate Studies, School of Health and Human Services, Department of Nursing, New Haven, CT 06515-1355. Offers nursing administration (MSN); nursing education (MSN). *Accreditation:* AACN; AANA/CANAEP. Part-time and evening/weekend programs available. *Faculty:* 6 full-time, 1 part-time/adjunct. *Students:* 2 full-time (both women), 29 part-time (27 women); includes 4 minority (3 African Americans, 1 Hispanic American). 15 applicants, 93% accepted, 10 enrolled. In 2006, 14 degrees awarded. *Degree requirements:* For master's, thesis. *Entrance requirements:* For master's, GRE, MAT, interview, minimum QPA of 2.8, RN license, minimum 1 year of professional nursing experience. *Application deadline:* For fall admission, 7/15 priority date for domestic students. Applications are processed on a rolling basis. Application fee: $50. Electronic applications accepted. *Financial support:* Application deadline: 4/15; *Unit head:* Dr. Cesarina Thompson, Chairperson, 203-392-6487, Fax: 203-392-6493, E-mail: thompson_c@southernct.edu. *Application contact:* Dr. Eileen Crutchlow, Graduate Coordinator, 203-392-6489, Fax: 203-392-6493, E-mail: crutchlow1@southernct.edu.

Southern Illinois University Edwardsville, Graduate Studies and Research, School of Nursing, Edwardsville, IL 62026-0001. Offers MS, Post-Master's Certificate. *Accreditation:* AACN. *Faculty:* 26 full-time (24 women). *Students:* 72 full-time (53 women), 136 part-time (125 women); includes 16 minority (8 African Americans, 1 American Indian/Alaska Native, 5 Asian Americans or Pacific Islanders, 2 Hispanic Americans). Average age 33. 94 applicants, 32% accepted. In 2006, 35 master's, 3 other advanced degrees awarded. *Degree requirements:* For master's, thesis or alternative, final exam, comprehensive exam, registration. *Entrance requirements:* For master's, appropriate bachelor's degree, RN license. Additional exam requirements/recommendations for international students: Required—TOEFL. *Application deadline:* For fall admission, 1/1 for domestic and international students. Application fee: $30. Electronic applications accepted. *Financial support:* In 2006–07, 2 fellowships with full tuition reimbursements, 1 research assistantship were awarded; teaching assistantships, career-related internships or fieldwork, Federal Work-Study, institutionally sponsored loans, scholarships/grants, traineeships, and unspecified assistantships also available. Support available to part-time students. Financial award application deadline: 3/1; financial award applicants required to submit FAFSA. *Unit head:* Dr. Marcia Maurer, Dean, 618-650-3959, E-mail: mamaure@siue.edu. *Application contact:* Dr. Jacquelyn Clement, Director, 618-650-3923, E-mail: jclemen@siue.edu.

Southern Nazarene University, Graduate College, School of Nursing, Bethany, OK 73008. Offers nursing education (MS); nursing leadership (MS). *Accreditation:* AACN. Part-time and evening/weekend programs available. *Students:* 30. In 2006, 14 degrees awarded. *Expenses:* Tuition: Part-time $507 per credit. *Unit head:* Dr. Carol Dorough, Dean, 405-491-6365, E-mail: cdorough@snu.edu.

Southern University and Agricultural and Mechanical College, School of Nursing, Baton Rouge, LA 70813. Offers educator/administrator (PhD); family health nursing (MSN); family nurse practitioner (Post Master's Certificate); geriatric nurse practitioner/gerontology (PhD). *Accreditation:* AACN; NLN. Part-time programs available. *Degree requirements:* For master's and doctorate, thesis/dissertation, comprehensive exam. *Entrance requirements:* For master's, GRE General Test, BSN, minimum GPA of 2.7; for doctorate, GRE General Test; for Post Master's Certificate, MSN. Additional exam requirements/recommendations for international students: Required—TOEFL (minimum score 525 paper-based; 193 computer-based). *Faculty research:* Health promotions, vulnerable populations, (community-based) cardiovascular participating research, health disparities chronic diseases, care of the elderly.

Spalding University, Graduate Studies, College of Health and Natural Sciences, School of Nursing, Louisville, KY 40203-2188. Offers adult nurse practitioner (MSN); family nurse practitioner (MSN); leadership in nursing and healthcare (MSN); pediatric nurse practitioner (MSN). *Accreditation:* AACN. Part-time and evening/weekend programs available. *Degree requirements:* For master's, thesis, comprehensive exam (for some programs). *Entrance requirements:* For master's, GRE General Test, BSN or bachelor's degree and RN licensure. *Faculty research:* Nurse educational administration, gerontology, bioterrorism, healthcare ethics, leadership.

Spring Hill College, Graduate Programs, Program in Nursing, Mobile, AL 36608-1791. Offers clinical nurse leader (MSN). *Accreditation:* AACN. Part-time and evening/weekend programs available. Postbaccalaureate distance learning degree programs offered (no on-campus study). *Faculty:* 3 full-time (all women). *Students:* 9 full-time (8 women), 7 part-time (6 women); includes 8 minority (6 African Americans, 2 Hispanic Americans). Average age 42. *Entrance requirements:* For master's, GRE or MAT, RN with minimum of 1 year clinical experience or BSN with minimum 3.0 GPA; also must be working in a clinical setting or have access to a healthcare facility for clinical integration and research. Additional exam requirements/recommendations for international students: Required—TOEFL (minimum score 550 paper-based; 213 computer-based). *Application deadline:* Applications are processed on a rolling basis. Application fee: $25. Electronic applications accepted. *Expenses:* Contact institution. *Financial support:* In 2006–07, 10 students received support. Scholarships/grants available. Support available to part-time students. Financial award applicants required to submit FAFSA. *Unit head:* Dr. Carol M. Harrison, Chair of Nursing Division, 251-380-4492, Fax: 251-460-4495, E-mail: charrison@shc.edu. *Application contact:* Joyce Genz, Dean of Life Long Learning and Director of Graduate Programs, 251-380-3094, Fax: 251-460-2190, E-mail: grad@shc.edu.

State University of New York at Binghamton, Graduate School, Decker School of Nursing, Binghamton, NY 13902-6000. Offers MS, PhD, Certificate. *Accreditation:* AACN. Part-time and evening/weekend programs available. *Faculty:* 30 full-time (28 women), 9 part-time/adjunct (8 women). *Students:* 44 full-time (39 women), 36 part-time (35 women); includes 4 minority (3 African Americans, 1 Asian American or Pacific Islander), 6 international. Average age 40. 33 applicants, 97% accepted. In 2006, 24 master's, 4 doctorates, 5 Certificates awarded. *Degree requirements:* For master's, thesis/dissertation, comprehensive exam; for doctorate, thesis/dissertation. *Entrance requirements:* For master's, GRE General Test. Additional exam

Nursing—General

State University of New York at Binghamton (continued)

requirements/recommendations for international students: Required—TOEFL. *Application deadline:* For fall admission, 4/15 priority date for domestic students, 1/15 priority date for international students; for spring admission, 11/1 for domestic students, 10/1 priority date for international students. Applications are processed on a rolling basis. Electronic applications accepted. *Financial support:* In 2006–07, 43 students received support, including 7 fellowships with partial tuition reimbursements available (averaging $7,743 per year), 3 research assistantships with full tuition reimbursements available (averaging $7,233 per year), 12 teaching assistantships with full tuition reimbursements available (averaging $6,325 per year); career-related internships or fieldwork, Federal Work-Study, institutionally sponsored loans, traineeships, tuition waivers (full and partial), and unspecified assistantships also available. Support available to part-time students. Financial award application deadline: 2/15. *Unit head:* Dr. Joyce Ferrario, Dean, 607-777-2311, Fax: 607-777-4440, E-mail: jferrari@binghamton.edu. *Application contact:* Theresa Grabo, Director of Graduate Studies, 607-777-6163, Fax: 607-777-4440, E-mail: tgrabo@binghamton.edu.

State University of New York at New Paltz, Graduate School, Faculty of Liberal Arts and Sciences, Department of Nursing, New Paltz, NY 12561. Offers clinical nurse specialist adult health (CAS); gerontological nursing (MS). *Accreditation:* AACN. Part-time and evening/weekend programs available. *Faculty:* 6 full-time (all women), 2 part-time/adjunct (1 woman). *Students:* Average age 45. In 2006, 3 degrees awarded. *Entrance requirements:* For master's, minimum GPA of 3.0. Additional exam requirements/recommendations for international students: Required—TOEFL (minimum score 550 paper-based; 213 computer-based; 80 iBT). *Application deadline:* For fall admission, 5/15 priority date for domestic students, 5/15 for international students; for spring admission, 11/15 priority date for domestic students, 11/15 for international students. Applications are processed on a rolling basis. Application fee: $50. Electronic applications accepted. *Expenses:* Tuition, state resident: full-time $6,900; part-time $288 per credit hour. Tuition, nonresident: full-time $10,920; part-time $455 per credit hour. *Unit head:* Dr. Eleanor Richards, Chair, 845-257-2922.

State University of New York Downstate Medical Center, College of Nursing, Graduate Program in Nursing, Brooklyn, NY 11203-2098. Offers nurse anesthesia (MS); nurse practitioner (MS, Post Master's Certificate); nursing (MS). *Accreditation:* AACN. Part-time programs available. *Degree requirements:* For master's, clinical research project, thesis optional. *Entrance requirements:* For master's, GRE, BSN; minimum GPA of 3.0; previous undergraduate course work in statistics, health assessment, and nursing research; RN license; for Post Master's Certificate, BSN; minimum GPA of 3.0; RN license; previous undergraduate course work in statistics, health assessment, and nursing research. *Expenses:* Tuition, state resident: full-time $6,900; part-time $288 per credit. Tuition, nonresident: full-time $10,920; part-time $455 per credit. Required fees: $100; $20 per credit. $50 per semester. Tuition and fees vary according to course load. *Faculty research:* AIDS, continuity of care, case management, self-care.

State University of New York Institute of Technology, School of Nursing and Health Systems, Utica, NY 13504-3050. Offers adult nurse practitioner (MS, CAS); family nurse practitioner (MS, CAS); gerontological nurse practitioner (MS, CAS); nursing administration (MS, CAS); nursing education (MS, CAS). *Accreditation:* AACN. Part-time programs available. *Faculty:* 9 full-time (all women), 5 part-time/adjunct (4 women). *Students:* 21 full-time (20 women), 38 part-time (36 women), 1 international. *Degree requirements:* For master's, thesis or project. *Entrance requirements:* For master's, GRE General Test if undergraduate GPA is lower than 3.3, minimum GPA of 3.0 in last 30 hours of undergraduate course work, bachelor's degree in nursing, 1 year of professional experience, RN license, interview, 2 letters of recommendation. Additional exam requirements/recommendations for international students: Required—TOEFL (minimum score 550 paper-based; 213 computer-based). *Application deadline:* For fall admission, 6/15 priority date for domestic students. Applications are processed on a rolling basis. Application fee: $50. *Expenses:* Tuition, state resident: full-time $3,452; part-time $288 per credit hour. Tuition, nonresident: full-time $10,920; part-time $455 per credit hour. Required fees: $927; $38 per credit hour. *Financial support:* Federal Work-Study, scholarships/grants, traineeships, and unspecified assistantships available. Financial award applicants required to submit FAFSA. *Faculty research:* Evidence-based practice, gerontological health issues, nursing informatics, nursing education, healthcare in minority populations. *Unit head:* Dr. Esther Bankert, Dean, 315-792-7295, Fax: 315-792-7555, E-mail: esther.bankert@sunyit.edu. *Application contact:* Marybeth Lyons, Director of Admissions, 315-792-7500, Fax: 315-792-7837, E-mail: smbl@sunyit.edu.

State University of New York Upstate Medical University, College of Nursing, Syracuse, NY 13210-2334. Offers nurse practitioner (Post Master's Certificate); nursing (MS). *Accreditation:* AACN. Part-time programs available. *Faculty:* 9 full-time (all women), 5 part-time/adjunct (4 women). *Students:* 29 full-time (all women), 62 part-time (56 women); includes 7 minority (4 African Americans, 3 Hispanic Americans). Average age 39. 41 applicants, 95% accepted, 29 enrolled. In 2006, 18 master's, 8 other advanced degrees awarded. *Degree requirements:* For master's, thesis or alternative. *Entrance requirements:* For master's, 3 years of work experience. *Application deadline:* For fall admission, 3/15 priority date for domestic and international students. Applications are processed on a rolling basis. Application fee: $40. Electronic applications accepted. *Expenses:* Tuition, state resident: full-time $6,900; part-time $288 per credit. Tuition, nonresident: full-time $10,920; part-time $455 per credit. Required fees: $496. *Financial support:* Federal Work-Study, institutionally sponsored loans, scholarships/grants, and traineeships available. Support available to part-time students. Financial award application deadline: 3/1; financial award applicants required to submit FAFSA. *Unit head:* Dr. Elvira Szigeti, Dean, 315-464-4276, Fax: 315-464-5168. *Application contact:* Donna Vavonese, Associate Director of Admissions, 315-464-4570, Fax: 315-464-8867, E-mail: vavonesd@upstate.edu.

Stony Brook University, State University of New York, Stony Brook University Medical Center, Health Sciences Center, School of Nursing, Stony Brook, NY 11794. Offers MS, Certificate. *Accreditation:* AACN; ACNM/DOA. Postbaccalaureate distance learning degree programs offered. *Faculty:* 30 full-time (29 women), 18 part-time/adjunct (16 women). *Students:* 60 full-time (57 women), 397 part-time (367 women); includes 96 minority (48 African Americans, 1 American Indian/Alaska Native, 25 Asian Americans or Pacific Islanders, 22 Hispanic Americans), 4 international. Average age 30. 285 applicants, 75% accepted. In 2006, 169 master's, 40 other advanced degrees awarded. *Degree requirements:* For master's, thesis. *Entrance requirements:* For master's, BSN, minimum GPA of 3.0, course work in statistics. *Application deadline:* For fall admission, 1/15 for domestic students. Application fee: $60. *Expenses:* Tuition, state resident: full-time $6,900; part-time $288 per credit. Tuition, nonresident: full-time $10,920; part-time $455 per credit. *Financial support:* Fellowships, research assistantships, teaching assistantships, career-related internships or fieldwork, Federal Work-Study, institutionally sponsored loans, and traineeships available. Financial award application deadline: 3/15. Total annual research expenditures: $663,558. *Unit head:* Dr. Lenora McClean, Dean, 631-444-3200, Fax: 631-444-6628, E-mail: lenora.mcclean@stonybrook.edu.

Temple University, Health Sciences Center and Graduate School, College of Health Professions, Department of Nursing, Philadelphia, PA 19122-6096. Offers MSN. *Accreditation:* AACN. Part-time programs available. *Faculty:* 11 full-time (all women). *Students:* 16 full-time (11 women), 56 part-time (47 women); includes 20 minority (11 African Americans, 6 Asian Americans or Pacific Islanders, 3 Hispanic Americans). 33 applicants, 42% accepted, 14 enrolled. In 2006, 19 degrees awarded. *Degree requirements:* For master's, thesis or research project. *Entrance requirements:* For master's, GRE General Test, current RN license, interview. Additional exam requirements/recommendations for international students: Required—TOEFL (minimum score 550 paper-based; 213 computer-based; 79 iBT). *Application deadline:* For fall admission, 8/15 priority date for domestic students, 12/15 for international students; for spring admission, 12/15 for domestic students, 8/1 for international students. Applications are processed on a rolling basis. Application fee: $50. Electronic applications accepted. *Expenses:* Tuition, state resident: full-time $12,264; part-time $511 per credit. Tuition, nonresident: full-time $17,904; part-time $746 per credit. Required fees: $84 per course. Tuition and fees vary according to program. *Financial support:* Teaching assistantships with full tuition reimbursements, career-related internships or fieldwork, institutionally sponsored loans, and traineeships available. Support available to part-time students. Financial award application deadline: 1/15; financial award applicants required to submit FAFSA. *Faculty research:* Osteoporosis, sensory deprivation in elderly, child abuse, attitudes towards AIDS, management styles. Total annual research expenditures: $958,778. *Unit head:* Dr. Jill Derstine, Chair, 215-707-4688, Fax: 215-707-3758, E-mail: jderst01@temple.edu.

See Close-Up on page 1741.

Tennessee State University, The School of Graduate Studies and Research, School of Nursing, Nashville, TN 37209-1561. Offers family nurse practitioner (MSN); holistic nursing (MSN); nursing administration (MSN); nursing education (MSN); nursing informatics (MSN). *Accreditation:* NLN. *Faculty:* 6 full-time (5 women). *Students:* 32 full-time (18 women), 71 part-time (69 women); includes 32 minority (29 African Americans, 2 Asian Americans or Pacific Islanders, 1 Hispanic American), 1 international. Average age 37. 78 applicants, 49% accepted, 30 enrolled. In 2006, 7 degrees awarded. *Entrance requirements:* For master's, GRE General Test or MAT, BSN, current RN license, minimum GPA of 3.0. *Application deadline:* Applications are processed on a rolling basis. *Financial support:* In 2006–07, research assistantships (averaging $5,500 per year), 2 teaching assistantships (averaging $5,500 per year) were awarded. *Unit head:* Dr. Bernadeen Fleming, Interim Dean, 615-963-7106, Fax: 615-963-5049, E-mail: dfleming@tnstate.edu.

Tennessee Technological University, School of Nursing, Cookeville, TN 38505. Offers MSN. *Students:* 4 full-time (all women), 25 part-time (22 women); includes 2 minority (both African Americans) 14 applicants, 64% accepted, 7 enrolled.Application fee: $25 ($30 for international students). *Expenses:* Tuition, state resident: full-time $8,748; part-time $319 per hour. Tuition, nonresident: full-time $23,524; part-time $740 per hour. *Unit head:* Dr. Shelia Green, Interim Dean, 931-372-3203, Fax: 931-372-6244, E-mail: sgreen@tntech.edu. *Application contact:* Dr. Francis Otuonye, Associate Vice President for Research and Graduate Studies, 931-372-3233.

Texas A&M International University, Office of Graduate Studies and Research, School of Nursing, Laredo, TX 78041-1900. Offers MSN. *Faculty:* 3 full-time (all women), 1 (woman) part-time/adjunct. *Students:* 1 full-time (0 women), 25 part-time (16 women); includes 25 minority (all Hispanic Americans) Average age 53. 12 applicants, 92% accepted, 9 enrolled. Application fee: $25. *Expenses:* Tuition, state resident: full-time $1,580. Tuition, nonresident: full-time $5,432. Required fees: $3,808. *Financial support:* In 2006–07, 14 students received support. *Unit head:* Dr. Susan Walker, Director, 956-326-2574, E-mail: swalker@tamiu.edu. *Application contact:* Rosie Espinoza, Director, Office of Admissions, 956-326-2200, Fax: 956-326-2269, E-mail: enroll@tamiu.edu.

Texas A&M University–Corpus Christi, Graduate Studies and Research, College of Nursing and Health Sciences, Corpus Christi, TX 78412-5503. Offers clinical nurse specialist (MSN); family nurse practitioner (MSN); health care administration (MSN); leadership in nursing systems (MSN). *Accreditation:* AACN. Part-time and evening/weekend programs available. *Degree requirements:* For master's, thesis (for some programs), comprehensive exam, registration. *Entrance requirements:* For master's, GRE General Test. Additional exam requirements/recommendations for international students: Required—TOEFL. Electronic applications accepted.

Texas Christian University, Harris College of Nursing and Health Sciences, Program in Nursing, Fort Worth, TX 76129-0002. Offers adult nursing (MSN). *Accreditation:* AACN; AANA/CANAEP. *Entrance requirements:* For master's, GRE General Test or MAT, 3 letters of reference, 2 years course work experience in nursing, current nursing licensure. Additional exam requirements/recommendations for international students: Required—TOEFL. Application fee: $0. *Expenses:* Tuition: Part-time $800 per credit hour. *Financial support:* Application deadline: 3/1. *Unit head:* Marinda Allender, Director of Student Affairs, 817-257-7650. *Application contact:* Dr. Kathleen Baldwin, Director of Graduate Studies, 817-257-6756, E-mail: k.baldwin@tcu.edu.

Texas Tech University Health Sciences Center, School of Nursing, Lubbock, TX 79430. Offers acute care nurse practitioner (MSN, Certificate); administration (MSN); clinical research management (MSN, Certificate); education (MSN); family nurse practitioner (MSN, Certificate); geriatric nurse practitioner (MSN, Certificate); pediatric nurse practitioner (MSN, Certificate). *Accreditation:* AACN. Part-time programs available. Postbaccalaureate distance learning degree programs offered (minimal on-campus study). *Faculty:* 17 full-time (16 women), 5 part-time/adjunct (all women). *Students:* 23 full-time (22 women), 161 part-time (137 women); includes 46 minority (8 African Americans, 2 American Indian/Alaska Native, 6 Asian Americans or Pacific Islanders, 30 Hispanic Americans). Average age 37. 97 applicants, 69% accepted, 67 enrolled. In 2006, 41 degrees awarded. *Degree requirements:* For master's, thesis optional. *Entrance requirements:* For master's, minimum GPA of 3.0, 3 letters of reference, BSN, RN license; for Certificate, minimum GPA of 3.0, 3 letters of reference, RN license. Additional exam requirements/recommendations for international students: Required—TOEFL (minimum score 550 paper-based; 213 computer-based). *Application deadline:* For fall admission, 7/15 priority date for domestic and international students; for spring admission, 11/15 priority date for domestic and international students. Applications are processed on a rolling basis. Application fee: $40. *Financial support:* In 2006–07, 184 students received support. Institutionally sponsored loans, scholarships/grants, and traineeships available. Support available to part-time students. Financial award application deadline: 12/1; financial award applicants required to submit FAFSA. *Faculty research:* Diabetes/obesity, nurse competency, disease management, intervention and measurements, health disparities. Total annual research expenditures: $2.4 million. *Unit head:* Dr. Barbara A. Johnston, Associate Dean for Administrative and Student Affairs, 806-743-3055, Fax: 806-743-1622, E-mail: barbara.johnston@ttuhsc.edu. *Application contact:* Lauren K. Sullivan, Recruiter/Transcultural Coordinator, 806-743-2730 Ext. 309, Fax: 806-743-1622, E-mail: lauren.sullivan@ttuhsc.edu.

Texas Woman's University, Graduate School, College of Nursing, Denton, TX 76201. Offers adult health nurse practitioner (MS); health systems management (MS); nursing (MS); nursing education (MS); nursing science (PhD). *Accreditation:* AACN. Part-time programs available. Postbaccalaureate distance learning degree programs offered. *Students:* 41 full-time (38 women), 512 part-time (490 women); includes 211 minority (121 African Americans, 2 American Indian/Alaska Native, 64 Asian Americans or Pacific Islanders, 24 Hispanic Americans), 9 international. Average age 41. In 2006, 129 master's, 16 doctorates awarded. *Degree requirements:* For master's, thesis or alternative; for doctorate, thesis/dissertation, comprehensive exam. *Entrance requirements:* For master's, GRE or MAT, minimum GPA of 3.0, RN license, BS in nursing; for doctorate, GRE or MAT, MS in nursing, minimum GPA of 3.5, RN license, coursework in statistics, graduate research, 2 letters of reference. Additional exam requirements/recommendations for international students: Required—TOEFL (minimum score 550 paper-based; 213 computer-based; 79 iBT). *Application deadline:* For fall admission, 4/1 for international students; for spring admission, 8/1 for international students. Applications are processed on a rolling basis. Application fee: $30 ($50 for international students). Electronic applications accepted. *Expenses:* Tuition, area resident: Part-time $168 per unit. Tuition, state resident: full-time $4,369. Tuition, nonresident: full-time $9,373; part-time $443 per unit. Required fees: $20 per unit. $177 per term. *Financial support:* In 2006–07, 11 research assistantships (averaging $11,232 per year), 3 teaching assistantships (averaging $11,232 per year) were awarded; career-related internships or fieldwork, Federal Work-Study, institutionally sponsored loans, scholarships/grants, traineeships, health care benefits, and unspecified assistantships also available. Support available to part-time students. Financial award application deadline: 3/1; financial award applicants required to submit FAFSA. *Faculty research:* Health of women across the life span, child health issues, self-care and heart failure, smoking cessation, timing of labor and delivery. *Unit head:* Dr. Marcia Hern, Dean, 940-898-2401, Fax:

940-898-2437, E-mail: mhern@twu.edu. *Application contact:* Samuel Wheeler, Coordinator of Graduate Admissions, 940-898-3188, Fax: 940-898-3081, E-mail: wheelersr@twu.edu.

Thomas Edison State College, School of Nursing, Trenton, NJ 08608-1176. Offers MSN. Part-time programs available. Postbaccalaureate distance learning degree programs offered (no on-campus study). *Students:* Average age 36. 11 applicants, 1 enrolled. *Entrance requirements:* For master's, BSN. Additional exam requirements/recommendations for international students: Required—TOEFL (minimum score 550 paper-based; 213 computer-based). *Application deadline:* For fall admission, 8/15 for domestic and international students; for winter admission, 11/15 for domestic and international students; for spring admission, 2/15 for domestic and international students. Application fee: $75. *Expenses:* Tuition, nonresident: part-time $422 per credit. Part-time tuition and fees vary according to program. *Financial support:* Applicants required to submit FAFSA. *Application contact:* Renee San Giacomo, Director of Admissions, 888-442-8372, Fax: 609-984-8447, E-mail: admissions@tesc.edu.

Thomas Jefferson University, Jefferson College of Health Professions, Program in Nursing, Philadelphia, PA 19107. Offers MS. *Accreditation:* AACN. Part-time programs available. Postbaccalaureate distance learning degree programs offered (no on-campus study). *Faculty:* 8 full-time (7 women), 2 part-time/adjunct (both women). *Students:* 15 full-time (11 women), 87 part-time (82 women); includes 37 minority (24 African Americans, 10 Asian Americans or Pacific Islanders, 3 Hispanic Americans). Average age 33. 50 applicants, 80% accepted, 10 enrolled. In 2006, 41 degrees awarded. *Degree requirements:* For master's, registration. *Entrance requirements:* For master's, GRE or MAT, BSN or equivalent, CPR certification, professional RN license, previous undergraduate course work in statistics and nursing research, minimum GPA of 3.0. Additional exam requirements/recommendations for international students: Required—TOEFL (minimum score 213 computer-based). *Application deadline:* For fall admission, 3/1 priority date for domestic and international students. Applications are processed on a rolling basis. Application fee: $50. Electronic applications accepted. *Expenses: Contact institution. Financial support:* In 2006–07, 49 students received support; fellowships with tuition reimbursements available, research assistantships, Federal Work-Study, institutionally sponsored loans, and scholarships/grants available. Support available to part-time students. Financial award application deadline: 5/1; financial award applicants required to submit FAFSA. *Faculty research:* Interdisciplinary primary care, women and HIV, health promotion and disease prevention, psychosocial impact of disability, ethical decision making. Total annual research expenditures: $498,070. *Unit head:* Dr. Mary Bowen, Graduate Director, 215-503-6057, Fax: 215-503-0376, E-mail: mary.bowen@jefferson.edu. *Application contact:* Karen A. Jacobs, Director of Admissions and Enrollment Management, 215-503-1040, Fax: 215-503-7241, E-mail: jchp@jefferson.edu.

See Close-Up on page 1975.

Thomas University, Department of Nursing, Thomasville, GA 31792-7499. Offers MSN. Part-time programs available. *Faculty:* 3 full-time (all women). *Students:* 11 full-time (all women); includes 2 minority (1 African American, 1 Asian American or Pacific Islander). *Entrance requirements:* For master's, resumé, 3 academic/professional references. Additional exam requirements/recommendations for international students: Required—TOEFL (minimum score 600 paper-based; 250 computer-based). *Application deadline:* For fall admission, 8/1 priority date for domestic students, 6/1 for international students; for spring admission, 12/1 priority date for domestic students, 10/1 for international students. Applications are processed on a rolling basis. Application fee: $50 ($125 for international students). Electronic applications accepted. *Expenses:* Tuition: Part-time $376 per credit. Required fees: $130 per semester. *Financial support:* Applicants required to submit FAFSA. *Unit head:* Sue Otto, Assistant Professor and Interim Chair Nursing, 229-226-1621 Ext. 154, Fax: 229-226-1653, E-mail: sotto@thomasu.edu. *Application contact:* Acrienne Diggs, Assistant Director of Admissions, 229-226-1621 Ext. 127, Fax: 229-227-6919, E-mail: adiggs@thomasu.edu.

Towson University, Graduate School, Program in Nursing, Towson, MD 21252-0001. Offers MS, Certificate. *Accreditation:* AACN. Part-time programs available. *Faculty:* 8 full-time (all women), 2 part-time/adjunct (1 woman). *Students:* 2 full-time (both women), 59 part-time (54 women); includes 20 minority (17 African Americans, 1 American Indian/Alaska Native, 1 Asian American or Pacific Islander, 1 Hispanic American). Average age 39. 17 applicants, 76% accepted, 8 enrolled. In 2006, 10 master's, 18 other advanced degrees awarded. *Degree requirements:* For master's, thesis optional. *Entrance requirements:* For master's, minimum GPA of 3.0, copy of current nursing license, bachelor's degree in nursing, curriculum vitae; for Certificate, minimum GPA of 3.0, copy of current nursing license, curriculum vitae, bachelor's degree in nursing. *Application deadline:* Applications are processed on a rolling basis. Application fee: $50. Electronic applications accepted. *Expenses:* Tuition, state resident: part-time $275 per unit. Tuition, nonresident: part-time $577 per unit. Required fees: $72 per unit. *Financial support:* Application deadline: 4/1. *Faculty research:* End of life care, caring, health policy, parish nursing. *Unit head:* Marilyn Tuls Halstead, Graduate Program Director, 410-704-4204. *Application contact:* 410-704-2501, Fax: 410-704-4675, E-mail: grads@towson.edu.

Troy University, Graduate School, College of Health and Human Services, Program in Nursing, Troy, AL 36082. Offers MSN. *Accreditation:* NLN. Part-time and evening/weekend programs available. *Students:* 30 full-time (28 women), 78 part-time (69 women); includes 44 minority (43 African Americans, 1 American Indian/Alaska Native). Average age 37. In 2006, 18 degrees awarded. *Degree requirements:* For master's, thesis optional. *Entrance requirements:* For master's, minimum GPA of 2.5, BSN. Additional exam requirements/recommendations for international students: Required—TOEFL (minimum score 523 paper-based; 200 computer-based). *Application deadline:* Applications are processed on a rolling basis. Application fee: $50. Electronic applications accepted. *Expenses:* Tuition, state resident: full-time $4,368; part-time $182 per hour. Tuition, nonresident: full-time $8,736; part-time $364 per hour. Required fees: $50 per term. *Financial support:* Available to part-time students. Applicants required to submit FAFSA. *Unit head:* Dr. Geraldine Allen, Director, 334-241-8656, Fax: 334-241-8656, E-mail: gallen@troy.edu. *Application contact:* Brenda K. Campbell, Director of Graduate Admissions, 334-670-3178, Fax: 334-670-3733, E-mail: bcamp@troy.edu.

Uniformed Services University of the Health Sciences, Graduate School of Nursing, Bethesda, MD 20814. Offers nurse anesthesia (MSN); nurse practitioner (MSN); perioperative clinical nurse specialty (MSN). Available to military officers only. *Accreditation:* AACN; NLN. Postbaccalaureate distance learning degree programs offered (no on-campus study). *Degree requirements:* For master's, thesis or alternative. *Entrance requirements:* For master's, GRE General Test, MAT, BSN, clinical experience, minimum GPA of 3.0, previous course work in science. Electronic applications accepted. *Faculty research:* Prenatal care, military health care, military readiness, distance learning.

Union University, School of Nursing, Jackson, TN 38305-3697. Offers nurse anesthetist (PMC); nursing education (MSN, PMC). *Accreditation:* AACN; AANA/CANAEP. *Faculty:* 15 full-time (14 women), 3 part-time/adjunct (2 women). *Students:* 47 full-time (36 women); includes 12 minority (10 African Americans, 1 American Indian/Alaska Native, 1 Asian American or Pacific Islander). Average age 38. 12 applicants, 100% accepted, 12 enrolled. In 2006, 9 degrees awarded. *Degree requirements:* For master's, thesis or alternative, registration. *Entrance requirements:* For master's, GRE, 3 letters of reference, bachelor's degree in nursing, minimum GPA of 3.0. Additional exam requirements/recommendations for international students: Required—TOEFL (minimum score 560 paper-based; 220 computer-based). *Application deadline:* For fall admission, 8/1 priority date for domestic students, 8/1 for international students. Application fee: $25. Electronic applications accepted. *Financial support:* Traineeships available. Financial award applicants required to submit FAFSA. *Faculty research:* Children's health, occupational rehabilitation, informatics, health promotion. *Unit head:* Dr. Tim Smith, Dean, 731-661-5200, Fax: 731-661-5504. *Application contact:* Elsie Cressman, Coordinator of MSN Programs, 731-661-5120, Fax: 731-661-5504, E-mail: ecressman@uu.edu.

Université de Montréal, Faculty of Graduate Studies, Faculty of Nursing, Montréal, QC H3C 3J7, Canada. Offers M Sc, PhD, DESS. Part-time programs available. *Faculty:* 27 full-time (21 women), 22 part-time/adjunct (20 women). *Students:* 126 full-time (115 women), 164 part-time (149 women). 218 applicants, 64% accepted, 121 enrolled. In 2006, 35 master's, 2 doctorates, 8 other advanced degrees awarded. *Degree requirements:* For master's, one foreign language, thesis optional; for doctorate, thesis/dissertation, general exam; for DESS, one foreign language. *Entrance requirements:* For master's, doctorate, and DESS, proficiency in French. *Application deadline:* For fall admission, 2/1 priority date for domestic students; for winter admission, 11/1 priority date for domestic students; for spring admission, 2/1 priority date for domestic students. Applications are processed on a rolling basis. Application fee: $30. Electronic applications accepted. *Financial support:* Fellowships, research assistantships, teaching assistantships, career-related internships or fieldwork, Federal Work-Study, and institutionally sponsored loans available. *Faculty research:* Mental and physical care of chronic patients, care of the hospitalized aged, cancer nursing, home care of caregivers, AIDS patients. *Unit head:* Céline Goulet, Dean, 514-343-6436, Fax: 514-343-2306. *Application contact:* Francine Gratton, Vice Dean of Studies, 514-343-5835, Fax: 514-343-2306, E-mail: francine.gratton@umontreal.ca.

Université du Québec à Rimouski, Graduate Programs, Program in Nursing Studies, Rimouski, QC G5L 3A1, Canada. Offers M Sc, Diploma. *Students:* 1 full-time, 11 part-time. Application fee: $50. *Unit head:* Guy Belanger, Director, 418-724-1475, Fax: 418-724-1525, E-mail: guy_belanger@uqar.qc.ca. *Application contact:* Marc Berube, Office of Admission, 418-724-1433, Fax: 418-724-1525, E-mail: marc_berube@uqar.qc.ca.

Université du Québec à Trois-Rivières, Graduate Programs, Program in Nursing Sciences, Trois-Rivières, QC G9A 5H7, Canada. Offers M Sc, DESS. Part-time programs available.

Université du Québec en Outaouais, Graduate Programs, Program in Nursing, Gatineau, QC J8X 3X7, Canada. Offers M Sc, Diploma. *Students:* 6 full-time, 20 part-time, 2 international. *Application deadline:* For fall admission, 6/1 priority date for domestic students, 3/1 for international students; for winter admission, 8/1 priority date for domestic students, 10/1 for international students. Application fee: $30. *Unit head:* Judith Lapierre, Director, 819-595-3900 Ext. 2267, Fax: 819-595-2384, E-mail: judith.lapierre@uqo.edu. *Application contact:* Registrar's Office, 819-773-1850, Fax: 819-773-1835, E-mail: registraire@ugo.ca.

Université Laval, Faculty of Nursing, Programs in Nursing, Québec, QC G1K 7P4, Canada. Offers M Sc, Diploma. *Degree requirements:* For master's, thesis (for some programs). *Entrance requirements:* For master's, French exam, knowledge of English; for Diploma, knowledge of French. Electronic applications accepted.

University at Buffalo, the State University of New York, Graduate School, School of Nursing, Buffalo, NY 14260. Offers acute care nurse practitioner (MS, Certificate); adult health nursing (MS, Certificate); child health nursing (MS); family nurse practitioner (Certificate); family nursing (MS); geriatric nurse practitioner (MS, Certificate); maternal and women's health nurse practitioner (Certificate); maternal and women's health nursing (MS); nurse anesthetist (MS); nursing (PhD); nursing education (Certificate); pediatric nurse practitioner (Certificate); psychiatric/mental health nurse practitioner (Certificate); psychiatric/mental health nursing (MS). *Accreditation:* AACN; AANA/CANAEP (one or more programs are accredited). Part-time programs available. Postbaccalaureate distance learning degree programs offered. *Faculty:* 38 full-time (34 women), 15 part-time/adjunct (14 women). *Students:* 131 full-time (108 women), 64 part-time (61 women); includes 29 minority (11 African Americans, 9 Asian Americans or Pacific Islanders, 9 Hispanic Americans), 20 international. Average age 28. 346 applicants, 25% accepted, 51 enrolled. In 2006, 49 master's, 3 doctorates, 6 other advanced degrees awarded. Terminal master's awarded for partial completion of doctoral program. *Degree requirements:* For master's, comprehensive exams or project; for doctorate, thesis/dissertation, comprehensive exam. *Entrance requirements:* For master's, GRE General Test (if overall GPA is below 3.0), interview, minimum GPA of 3.0, RN license, 3 references; for doctorate, GRE General Test, minimum GPA of 3.25, RN license, BS or MS in nursing, 3 references, writing sample; for Certificate, interview, minimum GPA of 3.0 or GRE General Test, RN license, MS in nursing. Additional exam requirements/recommendations for international students: Required—TOEFL (minimum score 550 paper-based; 213 computer-based; 79 iBT), IELTS (minimum score 7). *Application deadline:* For fall admission, 6/1 priority date for domestic students, 3/1 priority date for international students; for spring admission, 11/1 for domestic students, 9/15 priority date for international students. Applications are processed on a rolling basis. Application fee: $50. Electronic applications accepted. *Financial support:* In 2006–07, 78 students received support, including 13 fellowships with full tuition reimbursements available (averaging $7,220 per year), 10 research assistantships with tuition reimbursements available (averaging $17,881 per year), 23 teaching assistantships with full tuition reimbursements available (averaging $11,245 per year); Federal Work-Study, scholarships/grants, traineeships, health care benefits, and unspecified assistantships also available. Financial award application deadline: 3/15; financial award applicants required to submit FAFSA. *Faculty research:* Oncology symptom management, end of life decision making, changing behaviors using the transtheoretical model, addictions, nursing workforce. Total annual research expenditures: $1.7 million. *Unit head:* Dr. Jean K. Brown, Dean, Interim, 716-829-2533, Fax: 716-829-2566, E-mail: jebrown@buffalo.edu. *Application contact:* Dr. Elaine R. Cusker, Assistant Dean, 716-829-2537, Fax: 716-829-2021, E-mail: ecusker@buffalo.edu.

The University of Akron, Graduate School, College of Nursing, Akron, OH 44325. Offers nursing (MSN, PhD); public health (MPH). *Accreditation:* AACN; AANA/CANAEP (one or more programs are accredited). Part-time programs available. *Faculty:* 22 full-time (all women), 17 part-time/adjunct (15 women). *Students:* 67 full-time (53 women), 167 part-time (139 women); includes 24 minority (16 African Americans, 8 Asian Americans or Pacific Islanders), 1 international. Average age 36. 67 applicants, 81% accepted, 40 enrolled. In 2006, 60 master's, 1 doctorate awarded. *Degree requirements:* For master's, thesis optional (MSN), capstone project (MPH); for doctorate, one foreign language, thesis/dissertation, qualifying exam. *Entrance requirements:* For master's, GRE or MAT, minimum GPA of 3.0, interview, license (MSN), minimum GPA of 2.75 (MPH), letters of recommendation; for doctorate, GRE, minimum GPA of 3.0, MSN, licensure or eligibility for licensure, writing sample, letters of recommendation, interview. Additional exam requirements/recommendations for international students: Required—TOEFL (minimum score 550 paper-based; 213 computer-based; 79 iBT). *Application deadline:* For fall admission, 8/15 for domestic students. Applications are processed on a rolling basis. Application fee: $30 ($40 for international students). Electronic applications accepted. *Expenses:* Tuition, state resident: full-time $6,164; part-time $342 per credit. Tuition, nonresident: full-time $10,575; part-time $588 per credit. Required fees: $806; $43 per credit. $12 per term. Tuition and fees vary according to course load, degree level and program. *Financial support:* In 2006–07, 15 fellowships with full tuition reimbursements, 14 research assistantships with full tuition reimbursements, 12 teaching assistantships with full tuition reimbursements were awarded; career-related internships or fieldwork, Federal Work-Study, and tuition waivers (full) also available. *Faculty research:* Health promotion and chronic disease prevention; mental health and psychosocial resilience; gerontological health, trauma and violence; gut oxygenation during shock and trauma. Total annual research expenditures: $295,321. *Unit head:* Dr. Margaret Wineman, Interim Dean, 330-972-7551, E-mail: wineman@uakron.edu.

The University of Alabama, Graduate School, Capstone College of Nursing, Tuscaloosa, AL 35487. Offers MSN, MSN/Ed D. *Accreditation:* AACN. Part-time and evening/weekend programs available. *Faculty:* 15 full-time (14 women). *Students:* 1 (woman) full-time, 56 part-time (53 women); includes 16 African Americans. Average age 39. 39 applicants, 72% accepted, 23 enrolled. In 2006, 16 degrees awarded. *Median time to degree:* Master's–2 years part-time. *Degree requirements:* For master's, registration. *Entrance requirements:* For master's, GRE (if GPA is below 3.0), BSN, RN licensure, minimum GPA of 3.0. *Application deadline:* For fall admission, 6/1 priority date for domestic students. Application fee: $25. *Financial support:* In 2006–07, 4 students received support, including 2 fellowships with full tuition reimbursements available (averaging $14,000 per year); scholarships/grants and traineeships also available. Financial award application deadline: 4/1. *Faculty research:* Diabetes education, childhood asthma, HIV/AIDS prevention and care, breast cancer in rural minority women, nursing labor cost, nursing case management. Total annual research expenditures:

Nursing—General

The University of Alabama (continued)

$1,434. *Unit head:* Dr. Sara E. Barger, Dean, 205-348-1040, Fax: 205-348-5559, E-mail: sbarger@bama.ua.edu. *Application contact:* Dr. Marietta Stanton, Director, Undergraduate Program, 205-348-1020, Fax: 205-348-5559, E-mail: mstanton@bama.ua.edu.

The University of Alabama at Birmingham, School of Nursing, Birmingham, AL 35294. Offers MSN, PhD. *Accreditation:* AACN. *Students:* 75 full-time (71 women), 241 part-time (227 women); includes 56 minority (49 African Americans, 1 American Indian/Alaska Native, 5 Asian Americans or Pacific Islanders, 1 Hispanic American), 7 international. Average age 37. 107 applicants, 94% accepted. In 2006, 62 master's, 7 doctorates awarded. Terminal master's awarded for partial completion of doctoral program. *Degree requirements:* For doctorate, thesis/dissertation, research mentorship experience. *Entrance requirements:* For master's, GRE General Test, BS in nursing, interview; for doctorate, GRE General Test, computer literacy, course work in statistics, interview, minimum GPA of 3.0, MS in nursing. Additional exam requirements/recommendations for international students: Required—TOEFL. *Application deadline:* Applications are processed on a rolling basis. Application fee: $35 ($60 for international students). Electronic applications accepted. *Expenses: Contact institution.* Tuition and fees vary according to program. *Financial support:* In 2006–07, 3 fellowships (averaging $12,833 per year), 1 research assistantship, teaching assistantships (averaging $6,760 per year) were awarded; Federal Work-Study also available. Support available to part-time students. *Unit head:* Dr. Doreen C. Harper, Dean, 205-934-5360, E-mail: dcharper@uab.edu. *Application contact:* Dr. Lynda L. Harrison, Associate for Graduate Studies, 205-934-6787.

The University of Alabama in Huntsville, School of Graduate Studies, College of Nursing, Huntsville, AL 35899. Offers family nurse practitioner (Certificate); nursing (MSN). *Accreditation:* AACN. Part-time and evening/weekend programs available. Postbaccalaureate distance learning degree programs offered. *Faculty:* 11 full-time (10 women), 8 part-time/adjunct (5 women). *Students:* 54 full-time (53 women), 79 part-time (72 women); includes 22 minority (13 African Americans, 5 American Indian/Alaska Native, 4 Hispanic Americans). Average age 36. 94 applicants, 93% accepted, 70 enrolled. In 2006, 44 master's, 12 other advanced degrees awarded. *Degree requirements:* For master's, thesis or alternative, oral and written exams, comprehensive exam, registration. *Entrance requirements:* For master's, MAT or GRE, Alabama RN license, BSN, minimum GPA of 3.0. Additional exam requirements/recommendations for international students: Required—TOEFL (minimum score 500 paper-based; 173 computer-based). *Application deadline:* For fall admission, 5/30 priority date for domestic students, 2/28 priority date for international students; for spring admission, 10/10 priority date for domestic students, 7/10 priority date for international students. Applications are processed on a rolling basis. Application fee: $40. *Expenses:* Tuition, state resident: full-time $6,072; part-time $253 per credit hour. Tuition, nonresident: full-time $12,476; part-time $519 per credit hour. *Financial support:* In 2006–07, 61 students received support, including 54 fellowships with full and partial tuition reimbursements available (averaging $1,937 per year), 7 teaching assistantships with full and partial tuition reimbursements available (averaging $6,540 per year); research assistantships, career-related internships or fieldwork, Federal Work-Study, institutionally sponsored loans, scholarships/grants, traineeships, health care benefits, and unspecified assistantships also available. Support available to part-time students. Financial award application deadline: 4/1; financial award applicants required to submit FAFSA. *Faculty research:* Home health care, gerontology, pediatric nursing, family nurse practitioner, adult acute care administration. Total annual research expenditures: $19,540. *Unit head:* Dr. Fay Raines, Dean, 256-824-6345, Fax: 256-824-6026, E-mail: rainesc@email.uah.edu. *Application contact:* Lavan Wilson, Director of Student Affairs, 256-824-6742, Fax: 256-824-6026, E-mail: wilsonol@email.uah.edu.

University of Alaska Anchorage, College of Health and Social Welfare, School of Nursing, Anchorage, AK 99508-8060. Offers family nurse practitioner (Certificate); nursing (MS); nursing education (Certificate); psychiatric nurse practitioner (Certificate). *Accreditation:* NLN. Part-time and evening/weekend programs available. *Students:* 10 full-time (all women), 38 part-time (34 women); includes 6 minority (3 African Americans, 2 American Indian/Alaska Native, 1 Hispanic American). 15 applicants, 27% accepted. In 2006, 12 degrees awarded. *Degree requirements:* For master's, individual project. *Entrance requirements:* For master's, GRE or MAT, BS in nursing, interview, minimum GPA of 3.0, RN license, 1 year of part-time or 6 months of full-time clinical experience. Additional exam requirements/recommendations for international students: Required—TOEFL (minimum score 550 paper-based; 213 computer-based). *Application deadline:* For fall admission, 3/1 for domestic students; for spring admission, 11/1 for domestic students. Application fee: $45. *Expenses:* Tuition, state resident: part-time $268 per credit. Tuition, nonresident: part-time $547 per credit. Required fees: $124 per semester. Tuition and fees vary according to reciprocity agreements and student level. *Financial support:* Teaching assistantships, career-related internships or fieldwork, Federal Work-Study, and health care benefits available. Support available to part-time students. Financial award application deadline: 4/1; financial award applicants required to submit FAFSA. *Unit head:* Dr. Jean Ballantyne, Director, 907-786-4571, Fax: 907-786-4558. *Application contact:* Marie Samson, Coordinator of Student Affairs, 907-786-4561.

University of Alberta, Faculty of Graduate Studies and Research, Faculty of Nursing, Edmonton, AB T6G 2E1, Canada. Offers MN, PhD. Part-time programs available. *Faculty:* 58 full-time (all women), 1 part-time/adjunct (0 women). *Students:* 39 full-time (37 women), 154 part-time (149 women). 48 applicants, 88% accepted, 40 enrolled. In 2006, 13 master's, 6 doctorates awarded. *Degree requirements:* For master's, clinical practice, thesis optional; for doctorate, thesis/dissertation. *Entrance requirements:* For master's, B Sc N, 1 year of clinical nursing experience in specialty area; for doctorate, MN. Additional exam requirements/recommendations for international students: Required—TOEFL (minimum score 550 paper-based; 213 computer-based). *Application deadline:* For fall admission, 6/1 for domestic and international students; for winter admission, 10/1 for domestic and international students; for spring admission, 2/1 for domestic and international students. Applications are processed on a rolling basis. *Financial support:* In 2006–07, 12 fellowships with partial tuition reimbursements (averaging $23,868 per year), 27 research assistantships with partial tuition reimbursements (averaging $6,186 per year), 12 teaching assistantships with partial tuition reimbursements (averaging $2,365 per year) were awarded; institutionally sponsored loans and scholarships/grants also available. *Faculty research:* Symptom management, healthy human development, health policy, teaching excellence and information. Total annual research expenditures: $3.2 million. *Unit head:* Dr. M. Allen, Associate Dean, 780-492-4338, Fax: 780-492-2551. *Application contact:* Elaine Carswell, Administrative Assistant, 403-492-4567, Fax: 403-492-2551, E-mail: graduate@nurs.ualberta.ca.

The University of Arizona, Graduate College, College of Nursing, Tucson, AZ 85721. Offers MS, DNP, PhD. *Accreditation:* AACN. Part-time programs available. Postbaccalaureate distance learning degree programs offered (minimal on-campus study). *Faculty:* 28 full-time (all women), 4 part-time/adjunct (3 women). *Students:* 71 full-time (65 women), 81 part-time (72 women); includes 22 minority (2 African Americans, 3 American Indian/Alaska Native, 8 Asian Americans or Pacific Islanders, 9 Hispanic Americans), 15 international. Average age 42. 72 applicants, 63% accepted, 34 enrolled. In 2006, 21 master's, 11 doctorates awarded. Terminal master's awarded for partial completion of doctoral program. *Median time to degree:* Of those who began their doctoral program in fall 1998, 43% received their degree in 8 years or less. *Degree requirements:* For master's, thesis optional; for doctorate, thesis/dissertation, comprehensive exam, registration. *Entrance requirements:* For master's, GRE General Test, Arizona RN license, BSN; for doctorate, GRE General Test (not required for applicants with a master's degree), BSN or MS in nursing. Additional exam requirements/recommendations for international students: Required—TOEFL (minimum score 550 paper-based; 213 computer-based). *Application deadline:* For fall admission, 1/15 for domestic students, 12/1 for international students. Application fee: $50. Electronic applications accepted. *Expenses: Contact institution.* *Financial support:* In 2006–07, 76 students received support, including 22 fellowships (averaging $1,136 per year), 16 research assistantships with partial tuition reimbursements available (averaging $15,000 per year), 2 teaching assistantships with partial tuition reimbursements available (averaging $15,000 per year); career-related internships or fieldwork, institutionally sponsored loans, scholarships/grants, traineeships, and tuition waivers (full) also available. Financial award application deadline: 6/1. *Faculty research:* Vulnerable populations, injury mechanisms and biobehavioral responses, health care systems, informatics, rural health. Total annual research expenditures: $4.8 million. *Unit head:* Dr. Marjorie A. Isenberg, Dean, 520-626-6152, Fax: 520-626-6424, E-mail: misenberg@nursing.arizona.edu. *Application contact:* Vickie L. Radoye, Assistant Dean, Student Affairs, 520-626-3808, Fax: 520-626-6424, E-mail: vradoye@nursing.arizona.edu.

University of Arkansas, Graduate School, College of Education and Health Professions, Program in Nursing, Fayetteville, AR 72701-1201. Offers MSN. *Accreditation:* AACN. *Students:* 4 full-time (all women), 4 part-time (3 women); includes 1 minority (African American) 7 applicants, 43% accepted.Application fee: $40 ($50 for international students). *Financial support:* Fellowships, research assistantships, teaching assistantships available. *Unit head:* Dr. Thomas A. Kippenbrock, Director of Nursing, 479-575-3904, Fax: 479-575-3218, E-mail: tkippen@uark.edu.

University of Arkansas for Medical Sciences, Graduate School, College of Nursing, Little Rock, AR 72205-7199. Offers MN Sc, PhD. *Accreditation:* AACN. Part-time programs available. *Faculty:* 26 full-time (23 women), 8 part-time/adjunct (7 women). *Students:* 19 full-time, 198 part-time. *Entrance requirements:* For master's, MAT. Application fee: $0. *Financial support:* Career-related internships or fieldwork and traineeships available. Support available to part-time students. *Unit head:* Dr. Claudia P. Barone, Dean, 501-686-5374. *Application contact:* Dr. Elaine Souder, Information Contact, 501-296-1893.

The University of British Columbia, Faculty of Graduate Studies, Faculty of Applied Science, School of Nursing, Vancouver, BC V6T 1Z1, Canada. Offers MSN, PhD. Part-time programs available. *Faculty:* 28 full-time (27 women), 35 part-time/adjunct (all women). *Students:* 147 full-time (138 women), 121 part-time (110 women). Average age 40. 112 applicants, 63% accepted, 58 enrolled. In 2006, 34 degrees awarded. *Degree requirements:* For master's, essay or thesis; for doctorate, thesis/dissertation, comprehensive exam. *Entrance requirements:* For master's, GRE, bachelor's degree in nursing; for doctorate, GRE, master's degree in nursing. Additional exam requirements/recommendations for international students: Required—TOEFL. *Application deadline:* For fall admission, 1/31 for domestic students, 12/15 for international students; for winter admission, 5/31 for international students; for spring admission, 6/30 for domestic students. Application fee: $90 ($150 for international students). Electronic applications accepted. *Financial support:* In 2006–07, 4 fellowships (averaging $8,000 per year), 14 research assistantships (averaging $800 per year), 3 teaching assistantships were awarded. *Faculty research:* Women and children, aging, critical care, cross-cultural. Total annual research expenditures: $712,000. *Unit head:* Dr. Sally Thorne, Professor and Director, 604-822-7748, Fax: 604-822-7466, E-mail: thorne@nursing.ubc.ca. *Application contact:* Peggy Faulkner, Graduate Admissions, 604-822-7446, Fax: 604-822-7466, E-mail: peggy@nursing.ubc.ca.

University of Calgary, Faculty of Graduate Studies, Faculty of Nursing, Calgary, AB T2N 1N4, Canada. Offers MN, PhD, PMD. Part-time programs available. *Faculty:* 46 full-time (44 women), 215 part-time/adjunct (201 women). *Students:* 86 full-time (81 women), 31 part-time (30 women). Average age 30. 53 applicants, 81% accepted, 33 enrolled. In 2006, 24 master's, 5 doctorates, 5 other advanced degrees awarded. *Degree requirements:* For master's, thesis (for some programs), comprehensive exam (for some programs); for doctorate, thesis/dissertation. *Entrance requirements:* For master's, 2 years of clinical experience, nursing registration; for doctorate, nursing registration; for PMD, 3 years of clinical experience, nursing registration. Additional exam requirements/recommendations for international students: Required—TOEFL (minimum score 600 paper-based; 250 computer-based). *Application deadline:* For fall admission, 2/1 for domestic and international students. Application fee: $100 ($130 for international students). Electronic applications accepted. *Expenses: Contact institution.* *Financial support:* In 2006–07, 23 students received support, including 8 fellowships (averaging $21,375 per year), 14 teaching assistantships (averaging $6,786 per year); institutionally sponsored loans, scholarships/grants, health care benefits, and unspecified assistantships also available. Support available to part-time students. *Faculty research:* Adult health, family systems, community health, women's health, perinatal child health. *Unit head:* Dr. Carol Ewashen, Associate Dean, Graduate Programs, 403-220-6259, Fax: 403-284-4803. *Application contact:* Pat Jolly, Graduate Programs Administrator, 403-220-7288, Fax: 403-284-4803, E-mail: pjolly@ucalgary.ca.

University of California, Los Angeles, Graduate Division, School of Nursing, Los Angeles, CA 90095. Offers MSN, PhD, MBA/MSN, MD/PhD. *Accreditation:* AACN. *Degree requirements:* For master's, comprehensive exam; for doctorate, thesis/dissertation, oral and written qualifying exams. *Entrance requirements:* For master's, Commission on Graduates of Foreign Nursing Schools Exam, minimum GPA of 3.0, bachelor's degree in nursing; for doctorate, GRE General Test, Commission on Graduates of Foreign Nursing Schools exam, minimum undergraduate GPA of 3.0, bachelor's degree in nursing. Additional exam requirements/recommendations for international students: Required—TOEFL. Electronic applications accepted. *Faculty research:* AIDS, adolescents, gerontology, homeless, activity/mobility.

University of California, San Francisco, Graduate Division, School of Nursing, Program in Nursing, San Francisco, CA 94143. Offers MS, PhD. *Accreditation:* AACN; ACNM/DOA (one or more programs are accredited). *Students:* 591 full-time (529 women), 10 part-time (8 women); includes 163 minority (28 African Americans, 4 American Indian/Alaska Native, 92 Asian Americans or Pacific Islanders, 39 Hispanic Americans), 17 international. *Degree requirements:* For master's, thesis or alternative, comprehensive exam; for doctorate, thesis/dissertation. *Entrance requirements:* For master's and doctorate, GRE General Test. *Application deadline:* For fall admission, 3/1 for domestic students. Application fee: $40. *Expenses: Contact institution.* *Financial support:* Fellowships, Federal Work-Study available. Support available to part-time students. Financial award application deadline: 1/10. *Application contact:* Jeff Kilmer, Director, Office of Student and Curricular Affairs, 415-476-0600, E-mail: jeff.kilmer@nursing.ucsf.edu.

University of Central Arkansas, Graduate School, College of Health and Behavioral Sciences, Department of Nursing, Conway, AR 72035-0001. Offers clinical nurse specialist (MSN); nurse practitioner (MSN). *Accreditation:* AACN. *Faculty:* 8 full-time (all women). *Students:* 8 full-time (all women), 54 part-time (46 women); includes 8 minority (6 African Americans, 1 American Indian/Alaska Native, 1 Asian American or Pacific Islander), 1 international. 5 applicants, 100% accepted, 5 enrolled. In 2006, 8 degrees awarded. *Degree requirements:* For master's, clinicals, thesis optional. *Entrance requirements:* For master's, GRE General Test, minimum GPA of 2.7. Additional exam requirements/recommendations for international students: Required—TOEFL (minimum score 550 paper-based; 213 computer-based). *Application deadline:* For fall admission, 3/1 priority date for domestic students; for spring admission, 10/1 for domestic students. Applications are processed on a rolling basis. Application fee: $25 ($40 for international students). *Expenses: Contact institution.* One-time fee: $65 part-time. *Financial support:* Federal Work-Study, traineeships, and unspecified assistantships available. Financial award application deadline: 2/15; financial award applicants required to submit FAFSA. Total annual research expenditures: $216,643. *Unit head:* Dr. Barbara Williams, Chairperson, 501-450-3119, Fax: 501-450-5503, E-mail: barbaraw@uca.edu. *Application contact:* Nanette Fitzhugh, Administrative Assistant, 501-450-5063, Fax: 501-450-5678, E-mail: fitzhugh@uca.edu.

University of Central Florida, College of Health and Public Affairs, College of Nursing, Orlando, FL 32816. Offers adult practitioner (Post-Master's Certificate); family practitioner (Post-Master's Certificate); nursing (DNP, PhD); nursing education (Post-Master's Certificate); pediatric practitioner (Post-Master's Certificate). *Accreditation:* AACN. Part-time and evening/weekend programs available. *Faculty:* 35 full-time (32 women), 28 part-time/adjunct (25 women). *Students:* 84 full-time (75 women), 167 part-time (154 women); includes 41 minority (11 African Americans, 1 American Indian/Alaska Native, 8 Asian Americans or Pacific Islanders, 21 Hispanic Americans), 2 international. Average age 38. In 2006, 30 Post-Master's Certificates awarded. *Entrance requirements:* Additional exam requirements/recommendations for international students: Required—TOEFL. *Application deadline:* For fall admission, 2/15 for domestic students; for spring admission, 9/15 for domestic students. Application fee: $30. Electronic applications accepted. *Expenses:* Tuition, state resident: full-time $6,167; part-time $257 per credit hour. Tuition, nonresident: full-time $22,790; part-time $950 per credit hour. *Financial support:* In 2006–07, 35 fellowships with partial tuition reimbursements (averaging $1,550 per year), 9 research assistantships with partial tuition reimbursements (averaging $4,500 per year), 3 teaching assistantships with partial tuition reimbursements (averaging $15,400 per year) were awarded; career-related internships or fieldwork, Federal Work-Study, institutionally sponsored loans, traineeships, and unspecified assistantships also available. Financial award application deadline: 3/1; financial award applicants required to submit FAFSA. *Unit head:* Dr. Jean D. Leuner, Dean, College of Nursing, 407-823-5496, Fax: 407-823-5675, E-mail: jleuner@mail.ucf.edu.

University of Central Missouri, The Graduate School, College of Health and Human Services, Department of Nursing, Warrensburg, MO 64093. Offers rural family nursing (MS). *Accreditation:* AACN. Part-time programs available. *Faculty:* 16 full-time (all women). *Students:* 6 full-time (4 women), 40 part-time (37 women); includes 2 minority (both African Americans) Average age 42. 16 applicants, 88% accepted, 10 enrolled. In 2006, 7 degrees awarded. *Degree requirements:* For master's, thesis or research project, internship, clinical practica, capstone clinical. *Entrance requirements:* For master's, interview, 1 year of post-baccalaureate nursing experience, minimum GPA of 3.0. Additional exam requirements/recommendations for international students: Required—TOEFL (minimum score 500 paper-based; 173 computer-based). *Application deadline:* For fall admission, 6/1 priority date for domestic students, 5/1 priority date for international students; for spring admission, 10/1 priority date for domestic students, 10/1 for international students. Applications are processed on a rolling basis. Application fee: $30 ($50 for international students). *Expenses:* Tuition, state resident: full-time $5,448; part-time $227 per credit hour. Tuition, nonresident: full-time $10,896; part-time $454 per credit hour. Required fees: $336; $14 per credit hour. *Financial support:* In 2006–07, 2 students received support. Federal Work-Study and scholarships/grants available. Support available to part-time students. Financial award application deadline: 3/1; financial award applicants required to submit FAFSA. *Faculty research:* Rural health and rural nursing, family nursing, geriatrics, wellness and health promotion, leadership. Total annual research expenditures: $59,183. *Unit head:* Dr. Julie Clawson, Chair, 660-543-4775, Fax: 660-543-8304, E-mail: clawson@ucmo.edu.

University of Cincinnati, Graduate School, College of Nursing, Cincinnati, OH 45221-0038. Offers clinical nurse specialist (MSN), including adult health, community health, neonatal, nursing administration, occupational health, pediatric health, psychiatric nursing, women's health; nurse anesthesia (MSN); nurse midwifery (MSN); nurse practitioner (MSN), including acute care, ambulatory care, family, family/psychiatric, women's health; nursing (PhD); MBA/MSN. *Accreditation:* AACN; AANA/CANAEP (one or more programs are accredited); ACNM/DOA. Part-time programs available. Postbaccalaureate distance learning degree programs offered (no on-campus study). *Faculty:* 41 full-time (39 women), 16 part-time/adjunct (15 women). *Students:* 159 full-time (125 women), 149 part-time (145 women); includes 40 minority (22 African Americans, 1 American Indian/Alaska Native, 16 Asian Americans or Pacific Islanders, 1 Hispanic American). Average age 34. 385 applicants, 49% accepted, 132 enrolled. In 2006, 77 master's, 5 doctorates awarded. Terminal master's awarded for partial completion of doctoral program. *Median time to degree:* Of those who began their doctoral program in fall 1998, 55% received their degree in 8 years or less. *Degree requirements:* For master's, thesis or alternative, registration; for doctorate, thesis/dissertation, comprehensive exam, registration. *Entrance requirements:* For master's and doctorate, GRE General Test. Additional exam requirements/recommendations for international students: Required—TOEFL (minimum score 520 paper-based; 190 computer-based). *Application deadline:* For fall admission, 7/26 priority date for domestic and international students. Applications are processed on a rolling basis. Application fee: $40. Electronic applications accepted. *Financial support:* In 2006–07, 164 students received support, including 7 fellowships with full tuition reimbursements available (averaging $13,571 per year), research assistantships with full tuition reimbursements available (averaging $12,000 per year), 8 teaching assistantships with full tuition reimbursements available (averaging $12,000 per year); career-related internships or fieldwork, scholarships/grants, traineeships, tuition waivers (partial), and unspecified assistantships also available. Support available to part-time students. Financial award application deadline: 5/1; financial award applicants required to submit FAFSA. *Faculty research:* Substance abuse, injury and violence, symptom management. Total annual research expenditures: $1.3 million. *Unit head:* Dr. Andrea R. Lindell, Dean, 513-558-5330, Fax: 513-558-9030, E-mail: andrea.lindell@uc.edu. *Application contact:* Loren Carter, Program Coordinator, 513-558-5072, Fax: 513-558-7523, E-mail: loren.carter@uc.edu.

University of Colorado at Colorado Springs, Graduate School, Beth-El College of Nursing, Colorado Springs, CO 80933-7150. Offers adult health nurse practitioner and clinical specialist (MSN); family practitioner (MSN), including community clinical specialist, forensic clinical specialist, holistic clinical specialist; gerontology (MSN); neonatal nurse practitioner and clinical specialist (MSN); nursing administration (MSN); women nurse practitioner (MSN). *Accreditation:* AACN. Part-time programs available. Postbaccalaureate distance learning degree programs offered (minimal on-campus study). *Faculty:* 10 full-time (7 women), 14 part-time/adjunct (7 women). *Students:* 84 full-time (77 women), 53 part-time (52 women); includes 22 minority (6 African Americans, 3 American Indian/Alaska Native, 2 Asian Americans or Pacific Islanders, 11 Hispanic Americans). Average age 37. 54 applicants, 85% accepted, 30 enrolled. In 2006, 36 degrees awarded. *Degree requirements:* For master's, thesis optional; for doctorate, capstone project. *Entrance requirements:* For master's, GRE General Test or MAT, BSN, minimum GPA of 3.0, unrestricted RN license; for doctorate, interview; active RN license; MA; minimum GPA of 3.3; National Certification as NP, CNS, or CNS; portfolio. Additional exam requirements/recommendations for international students: Required—TOEFL. *Application deadline:* For fall admission, 6/1 priority date for domestic students; for spring admission, 11/15 for domestic students. Application fee: $60 ($75 for international students). Electronic applications accepted. *Expenses: Contact institution.* Tuition and fees vary according to course load, campus/location and program. *Financial support:* Fellowships, career-related internships or fieldwork, Federal Work-Study, and institutionally sponsored loans available. Support available to part-time students. *Faculty research:* Women's health, uncertainty, empowerment, family experience in chronic illness. Total annual research expenditures: $260,389. *Unit head:* Dr. Carole Schoffstall, Dean, 719-262-4418, Fax: 719-262-4416, E-mail: cschoffs@uccs.edu.

University of Colorado at Denver and Health Sciences Center, School of Nursing, Programs in Nursing, Denver, CO 80217-3364. Offers MS, PhD, Post Master's Certificate. *Accreditation:* AACN; NLN. Postbaccalaureate distance learning degree programs offered. *Students:* 249 full-time (238 women), 63 part-time (57 women); includes 32 minority (6 African Americans, 4 American Indian/Alaska Native, 12 Asian Americans or Pacific Islanders, 10 Hispanic Americans), 5 international. Average age 36. 267 applicants, 72% accepted, 177 enrolled. In 2006, 69 master's, 6 doctorates awarded. *Degree requirements:* For doctorate, thesis/dissertation, comprehensive exam. *Entrance requirements:* For master's, GRE General Test, minimum GPA of 3.0, current Colorado RN license; for doctorate, GRE General Test, minimum GPA of 3.0, portfolio, resumé or curriculum vitae. Additional exam requirements/recommendations for international students: Required—TOEFL (minimum score 550 paper-based; 213 computer-based). *Application deadline:* For fall admission, 12/1 for domestic students. Application fee: $50. Electronic applications accepted. *Financial support:* Career-related internships or fieldwork, Federal Work-Study, and institutionally sponsored loans available. Support available to part-time students. Financial award application deadline: 3/15; financial award applicants required to submit FAFSA. *Unit head:* Dr. Kathy Magilvy, Assistant Dean, 303-315-4324.

University of Connecticut, Graduate School, School of Nursing, Field of Nursing, Storrs, CT 06269. Offers adult acute care (Post-Master's Certificate); adult primary care (Post-Master's Certificate); community health (Post-Master's Certificate); neonatal acute care (Post-Master's Certificate); nursing (MS, PhD); patient care services and systems administration (Post-Master's Certificate); psychiatric mental health (Post-Master's Certificate). *Accreditation:* AACN. *Faculty:* 20 full-time (18 women). *Students:* 38 full-time (33 women), 70 part-time (65 women); includes 17 minority (3 African Americans, 10 Asian Americans or Pacific Islanders, 4 Hispanic Americans), 1 international. Average age 37. 64 applicants, 69% accepted, 44 enrolled. In 2006, 25 master's, 7 doctorates, 1 other advanced degree awarded. *Degree requirements:* For master's, comprehensive exam; for doctorate, thesis/dissertation. *Entrance requirements:* Additional exam requirements/recommendations for international students: Required—TOEFL (minimum score 550 paper-based; 213 computer-based). *Application deadline:* For fall admission, 2/1 priority date for domestic and international students; for spring admission, 11/1 for domestic students, 10/1 for international students. Applications are processed on a rolling basis. Application fee: $55. Electronic applications accepted. *Financial support:* In 2006–07, 4 research assistantships with full tuition reimbursements, 13 teaching assistantships with full tuition reimbursements were awarded; fellowships, Federal Work-Study, scholarships/grants, health care benefits, and unspecified assistantships also available. Financial award application deadline: 2/1; financial award applicants required to submit FAFSA. *Unit head:* E. Carol Polifroni, Chairperson, 860-486-0511, Fax: 860-486-0001, E-mail: polifron@uconn.edu. *Application contact:* Lisa Mazzola, Academic Advisor Coordinator, 860-486-1973, E-mail: lisa.mazzola@uconn.edu.

University of Delaware, College of Health Sciences, School of Nursing, Newark, DE 19716. Offers adult nurse practitioner (MSN, PMC); cardiopulmonary clinical nurse specialist (MSN, PMC); cardiopulmonary clinical nurse specialist/adult nurse practitioner (MSN, PMC); family nurse practitioner (MSN, PMC); gerontology clinical nurse specialist (MSN, PMC); gerontology clinical nurse specialist geriatric nurse practitioner (PMC); gerontology clinical nurse specialist/geriatric nurse practitioner (MSN); health services administration (MSN, PMC); nursing of children clinical nurse specialist (MSN, PMC); nursing of children clinical nurse specialist/pediatric nurse practitioner (MSN, PMC); oncology/immune deficiency clinical nurse specialist (MSN, PMC); oncology/immune deficiency clinical nurse specialist/adult nurse practitioner (MSN, PMC); perinatal/women's health clinical nurse specialist (MSN, PMC); perinatal/women's health clinical nurse specialist/women's health nurse practitioner (MSN, PMC); psychiatric nursing clinical nurse specialist (MSN, PMC). *Accreditation:* AACN; NLN (one or more programs are accredited). Part-time and evening/weekend programs available. Postbaccalaureate distance learning degree programs offered (minimal on-campus study). *Degree requirements:* For master's, thesis optional. *Entrance requirements:* For master's, BSN, interview, RN license. Electronic applications accepted. *Faculty research:* Marriage and chronic illness, health promotion, congestive heart failure patient outcomes, school nursing, diabetes in children.

University of Evansville, College of Education and Health Sciences, Department of Nursing and Health Sciences, Evansville, IN 47722. Offers health services administration (MS). Part-time and evening/weekend programs available. *Faculty:* 1 full-time (0 women), 4 part-time/adjunct (1 woman). *Students:* 1 full-time (0 women), 9 part-time (7 women), 1 international. Average age 42. 2 applicants, 100% accepted, 1 enrolled. In 2006, 11 degrees awarded. *Median time to degree:* Master's–1.5 years full-time, 2.75 years part-time. *Entrance requirements:* For master's, GRE or GMAT, 2 letters of reference, interview. Additional exam requirements/recommendations for international students: Required—TOEFL (minimum score 500 paper-based). *Application deadline:* For fall admission, 7/1 priority date for domestic and international students; for spring admission, 10/1 priority date for domestic students. Applications are processed on a rolling basis. Application fee: $20 ($50 for international students). *Expenses: Contact institution.* Tuition and fees vary according to course load and program. *Financial support:* In 2006–07, 2 students received support. Career-related internships or fieldwork available. Support available to part-time students. Financial award application deadline: 7/1; financial award applicants required to submit FAFSA. *Unit head:* Dr. Amy Hall, Department Chair, 812-488-2343, Fax: 812-488-2717, E-mail: ah169@evansville.edu. *Application contact:* Dr. William Stroube, Director, Health Services Administration Program, 812-488-2343, Fax: 812-488-2717, E-mail: hsa@evansville.edu.

University of Florida, Graduate School, College of Nursing, Gainesville, FL 32611. Offers nursing (MSN); nursing sciences (PhD). *Accreditation:* AACN; ACNM/DOA (one or more programs are accredited). Part-time programs available. *Faculty:* 28 full-time (26 women). *Students:* 285 (264 women); includes 39 minority (12 African Americans, 3 American Indian/Alaska Native, 8 Asian Americans or Pacific Islanders, 16 Hispanic Americans). Average age 35. In 2006, 75 master's, 5 doctorates awarded. *Degree requirements:* For master's, thesis optional; for doctorate, thesis/dissertation. *Entrance requirements:* For master's and doctorate, GRE General Test, minimum GPA of 3.0. Additional exam requirements/recommendations for international students: Required—TOEFL (minimum score 550 paper-based; 213 computer-based). *Application deadline:* For fall admission, 3/1 priority date for domestic students. Applications are processed on a rolling basis. Application fee: $30. Electronic applications accepted. *Expenses:* Tuition, state resident: full-time $6,827. Tuition, nonresident: full-time $21,951. Required fees: $999. *Financial support:* In 2006–07, 2 research assistantships with partial tuition reimbursements (averaging $16,352 per year), 1 teaching assistantship with partial tuition reimbursement (averaging $24,904 per year) were awarded; fellowships with partial tuition reimbursements, career-related internships or fieldwork and Federal Work-Study also available. Support available to part-time students. *Faculty research:* Wellness in the elderly, women's health, sleep patterns, immune competence, hypertension. *Unit head:* Dr. Kathleen A. Long, Dean, 352-273-6324, Fax: 352-273-6505, E-mail: longka@nursing.ufl.edu. *Application contact:* Dr. Karin Polifko-Harris, Associate Dean, 352-273-6331, Fax: 352-273-6440, E-mail: kpolifko@nursing.ufl.edu.

University of Hartford, College of Education, Nursing, and Health Professions, Program in Nursing, West Hartford, CT 06117-1599. Offers community/public health nursing (MSN); nursing education (MSN); nursing management (MSN). *Accreditation:* AACN. Part-time and evening/weekend programs available. *Faculty:* 6 full-time (all women), 2 part-time/adjunct (both women). *Students:* 1 (woman) full-time, 170 part-time (163 women); includes 12 minority (5 African Americans, 1 American Indian/Alaska Native, 6 Hispanic Americans). Average age 43. 60 applicants, 97% accepted, 54 enrolled. In 2006, 46 degrees awarded. *Degree requirements:* For master's, research project. *Entrance requirements:* For master's, BSN, Connecticut RN license. Additional exam requirements/recommendations for international students: Required—TOEFL (minimum score 550 paper-based; 213 computer-based). *Application deadline:* For fall admission, 4/15 priority date for domestic students; for spring admission, 12/1 for domestic students. Application fee: $40 ($55 for international students). Electronic applications accepted. *Expenses: Contact institution. Financial support:* Teaching assistantships, Federal Work-Study available. Support available to part-time students. Financial award application deadline: 6/1; financial award applicants required to submit FAFSA. *Faculty research:* Child development, women in doctoral study, applying feminist theory in teaching methods, near death experience, grandmothers as primary care providers. *Unit head:* Mary Beth Mathews, Chair, 860-768-4217, Fax: 860-768-5346, E-mail: mbmathews@hartford.edu. *Application contact:* Marlene Hall, Assistant Dean, 860-768-5116, E-mail: mhall@hartford.edu.

University of Hawaii at Manoa, Graduate Division, College of Health Sciences and Social Welfare, School of Nursing and Dental Hygiene, Honolulu, HI 96822. Offers clinical nurse specialist (MS), including adult health, community mental health; nurse practitioner (MS), including adult health, community mental health, family nurse practitioner; nursing (PhD, Graduate Certificate); nursing administration (MS). *Accreditation:* AACN; NLN (one or more programs are accredited). *Faculty:* 32 full-time (29 women), 1 (woman) part-time/adjunct. *Students:* 30 full-time (28 women), 94 part-time (83 women); includes 10 minority (3 African Americans, 1 American Indian/Alaska Native, 2 Asian Americans or Pacific Islanders, 4 Hispanic Americans), 2 international. 119 applicants, 53% accepted, 54 enrolled. In 2006, 12 master's, 4 doctorates awarded. *Median time to degree:* Of those who began their doctoral program in fall 1998, 57% received their degree in 8 years or less. *Degree requirements:* For master's, thesis optional; for doctorate, thesis/dissertation, comprehensive exam. *Entrance requirements:* For master's, Hawaii RN license. Additional exam requirements/recommendations for international students: Required—TOEFL (minimum score 580 paper-based; 237 computer-based; 92 iBT). *Application deadline:* For fall admission, 3/1 for domestic and international

Nursing—General

University of Hawaii at Manoa (continued)
students. Application fee: $50. *Financial support:* In 2006–07, 1 teaching assistantship (averaging $13,296 per year) was awarded. Total annual research expenditures: $3.1 million.

University of Illinois at Chicago, Graduate College, College of Nursing, Chicago, IL 60607-7128. Offers MS, PhD, MBA/MS, MPH/MS. *Accreditation:* AACN. Part-time programs available. *Degree requirements:* For master's, thesis or alternative; for doctorate, thesis/dissertation. *Entrance requirements:* For master's and doctorate, GRE General Test, minimum GPA of 2.75. Additional exam requirements/recommendations for international students: Required—TOEFL. Electronic applications accepted. Expenses: Contact institution.

University of Indianapolis, Graduate Programs, School of Nursing, Indianapolis, IN 46227-3697. Offers family practice (post-RN) (MSN); gerontological nurse practitioner (MSN); nurse-midwifery (MSN); nursing (MSN); nursing administration (MSN); nursing education (MSN); MBA/MSN. *Accreditation:* AACN; ACNM. *Faculty:* 7 full-time (all women), 3 part-time/adjunct (all women). *Students:* 9 full-time (all women), 121 part-time (115 women); includes 17 minority (16 African Americans, 1 Asian American or Pacific Islander). Average age 41. In 2006, 7 degrees awarded. *Entrance requirements:* For master's, minimum GPA of 3.0, interview, letters of recommendation, resumé, IN nursing license, 1 year professional practice. Additional exam requirements/recommendations for international students: Required—TOEFL (minimum score 550 paper-based; 213 computer-based). *Application deadline:* For fall admission, 8/1 for domestic students; for winter admission, 12/15 for domestic students; for spring admission, 4/15 for domestic students. Applications are processed on a rolling basis. Application fee: $50. *Financial support:* Federal Work-Study available. *Unit head:* Dr. Sharon Isaac, Dean, 317-788-3207, E-mail: isaac@uindy.edu. *Application contact:* T.C. Crum, 317-788-2128, Fax: 317-788-3542, E-mail: tcrum@uindy.edu.

The University of Iowa, Graduate College, College of Nursing, Iowa City, IA 52242-1316. Offers MSN, PhD, MBA/MSN, MSN/MPH. *Accreditation:* AACN; AANA/CANAEP (one or more programs are accredited). *Faculty:* 31 full-time, 103 part-time/adjunct. *Students:* 76 full-time (63 women), 128 part-time (121 women); includes 7 minority (2 African Americans, 1 American Indian/Alaska Native, 3 Asian Americans or Pacific Islanders, 1 Hispanic American), 17 international. 78 applicants, 88% accepted, 53 enrolled. In 2006, 48 master's, 9 doctorates awarded. *Degree requirements:* For master's, portfolio, project, thesis optional; for doctorate, thesis/dissertation, comprehensive exam, registration. *Entrance requirements:* For master's, minimum GPA of 3.0; for doctorate, GRE General Test, minimum GPA of 3.0. Additional exam requirements/recommendations for international students: Required—TOEFL (minimum score 550 paper-based; 213 computer-based; 81 iBT). Application fee: $60 ($85 for international students). Electronic applications accepted. *Expenses: Contact institution. Financial support:* In 2006–07, 21 fellowships, 29 research assistantships with partial tuition reimbursements, 24 teaching assistantships with partial tuition reimbursements were awarded. Financial award applicants required to submit FAFSA. *Unit head:* Martha Craft-Rosenberg, Interim Dean, 319-335-7009, Fax: 319-335-9990.

University of Kansas, Graduate Studies Medical Center, School of Nursing, Kansas City, KS 66160. Offers nurse educator (PMC); nurse midwife (PMC); nursing (MS, PhD); psychiatric/mental health nurse practitioner (PMC). *Accreditation:* AACN; ACNM/DOA. Part-time programs available. Postbaccalaureate distance learning degree programs offered (minimal on-campus study). *Faculty:* 53 full-time (50 women), 3 part-time/adjunct (all women). *Students:* 63 full-time (59 women), 200 part-time (190 women); includes 37 minority (16 African Americans, 3 American Indian/Alaska Native, 12 Asian Americans or Pacific Islanders, 6 Hispanic Americans), 4 international. Average age 38. 88 applicants, 82% accepted, 62 enrolled. In 2006, 39 master's, 5 doctorates awarded. Terminal master's awarded for partial completion of doctoral program. *Median time to degree:* Master's–2.05 years full-time, 2.95 years part-time; doctorate–3.26 years part-time. Of those who began their doctoral program in fall 1998, 66% received their degree in 8 years or less. *Degree requirements:* For master's, general oral exam, thesis optional; for doctorate, one foreign language, thesis/dissertation, comprehensive oral and written exam. *Entrance requirements:* For master's, GRE General Test, bachelor's degree in nursing, minimum GPA of 3.0, RN license, 1 year of clinical experience; for doctorate, GRE General Test, master's degree in nursing, minimum GPA of 3.5. Additional exam requirements/recommendations for international students: Required—TOEFL. *Application deadline:* For fall admission, 4/1 for domestic students; for winter admission, 7/1 for domestic students; for spring admission, 9/1 for domestic students. Application fee: $50. *Expenses:* Tuition, area resident: Part-time $227 per credit. Tuition, state resident: part-time $543 per credit. Tuition and fees vary according to course load, campus/location, program and reciprocity agreements. *Financial support:* In 2006–07, 106 students received support, including 7 research assistantships (averaging $19,000 per year), 23 teaching assistantships with full and partial tuition reimbursements available (averaging $19,000 per year); traineeships also available. Financial award application deadline: 7/7. *Faculty research:* Breastfeeding practices of teen mothers, prevention of pressure ulcers, caregiving of families of patients using technology in the home, self care talk intervention partnership between caregivers of stroke survivors and nurses, smoking cessation. *Unit head:* Dr. Karen L. Miller, Dean, 913-588-1604, Fax: 913-588-1660, E-mail: kmiller@kumc.edu. *Application contact:* Dr. Rita K. Clifford, Associate Dean, Student Affairs, 913-588-1619, Fax: 913-588-1615, E-mail: rcliffor@kumc.edu.

University of Kentucky, Graduate School, Graduate School Programs in the College of Nursing, Program in Nursing, Lexington, KY 40506-0032. Offers MSN, PhD. *Accreditation:* AACN. *Faculty:* 24 full-time (23 women), 3 part-time/adjunct (2 women). *Students:* 72 full-time (66 women), 131 part-time (121 women); includes 6 minority (all African Americans), 8 international. Average age 38. 113 applicants, 59% accepted, 53 enrolled. In 2006, 35 master's, 7 doctorates awarded. *Median time to degree:* Of those who began their doctoral program in fall 1998, 69% received their degree in 8 years or less. *Degree requirements:* For master's, research project, thesis optional; for doctorate, thesis/dissertation, comprehensive exam. *Entrance requirements:* For master's, GRE General test, minimum undergraduate GPA of 2.75; for doctorate, GRE General Test, minimum undergraduate GPA of 2.75, graduate work GPA of 3.0. Additional exam requirements/recommendations for international students: Required—TOEFL (minimum score 550 paper-based; 213 computer-based). *Application deadline:* For fall admission, 7/17 priority date for domestic students, 2/1 priority date for international students; for spring admission, 12/13 priority date for domestic students, 6/15 priority date for international students. Application fee: $40 ($55 for international students). Electronic applications accepted. *Expenses:* Tuition, state resident: full-time $7,670; part-time $401 per credit hour. Tuition, nonresident: full-time $16,158; part-time $873 per credit hour. *Financial support:* In 2006–07, 2 fellowships with full tuition reimbursements (averaging $3,958 per year), 13 research assistantships with full tuition reimbursements (averaging $10,000 per year), 5 teaching assistantships with full tuition reimbursements (averaging $8,160 per year) were awarded; Federal Work-Study, scholarships/grants, traineeships, health care benefits, tuition waivers (partial), and unspecified assistantships also available. Support available to part-time students. Financial award application deadline: 3/15; financial award applicants required to submit FAFSA. *Unit head:* Dr. Patricia Howard, Director of Graduate Studies, 859-323-6332, Fax: 859-323-1057. *Application contact:* Dr. Brian Jackson, Senior Associate Dean, 859-257-4667, Fax: 859-257-4676, E-mail: brian.jackson@uky.edu.

University of Lethbridge, School of Graduate Studies, Lethbridge, AB T1K 3M4, Canada. Offers accounting (MScM); addictions counseling (M Sc); agricultural biotechnology (M Sc); agricultural studies (M Sc, MA); anthropology (MA); archaeology (MA); art (MA); biochemistry (M Sc); biological sciences (M Sc); biomolecular science (PhD); biosystems and biodiversity (PhD); Canadian studies (MA); chemistry (M Sc); computer science (M Sc); computer science and geographical information science (M Sc); counseling psychology (M Ed); dramatic arts (MA); earth, space, and physical science (PhD); economics (MA); educational leadership (M Ed); English (MA); environmental science (M Sc); evolution and behavior (PhD); exercise science (M Sc); finance (MScM); French (MA); French/German (MA); French/Spanish (MA); general education (M Ed); general management (MScM); geography (M Sc, MA); German (MA); health sciences (M Sc, MA); history (MA); human resource management and labour relations (MScM); individualized multidisciplinary (M Sc, MA); information systems (MScM); international management (MScM); kinesiology (M Sc, MA); management (M Sc, MA); marketing (MScM); mathematics (M Sc); music (MA); Native American studies (MA); neuroscience (M Sc, PhD); new media (MA); nursing (M Sc); philosophy (MA); physics (M Sc); policy and strategy (MScM); political science (MA); psychology (M Sc, MA); religious studies (MA); sociology (MA); theoretical and computational science (PhD); urban and regional studies (MA). Part-time and evening/weekend programs available. *Students:* 200 full-time, 90 part-time. In 2006, 105 master's, 3 doctorates awarded. *Degree requirements:* For doctorate, thesis/dissertation, comprehensive exam. *Entrance requirements:* For master's, GMAT (M Sc management), bachelor's degree in related field, minimum GPA of 3.0 during previous 20 graded semester courses, 2 years teaching or related experience (M Ed); for doctorate, master's degree, minimum graduate GPA of 3.5. Additional exam requirements/recommendations for international students: Required—TOEFL. Application fee: $60 Canadian dollars. *Financial support:* Fellowships, research assistantships, teaching assistantships, scholarships/grants, health care benefits, and unspecified assistantships available. *Faculty research:* Movement and brain plasticity, gibberellin physiology, photosynthesis, carbon cycling, molecular properties of main-group ring components. *Unit head:* Dr. Jo-Anne Fiske, Interim Dean, 403-329-2121, Fax: 403-329-2097. *Application contact:* Kathy Schrage, Administrative Assistant, Office of the Academic Vice President, 403-329-2121, Fax: 403-329-2097, E-mail: inquiries@uleth.ca.

University of Louisiana at Lafayette, Graduate School, College of Nursing, Lafayette, LA 70504. Offers MSN. *Accreditation:* NLN. *Faculty:* 11 full-time (all women), 1 (woman) part-time/adjunct. *Students:* 13 full-time (10 women), 50 part-time (41 women); includes 9 minority (8 African Americans, 1 American Indian/Alaska Native). Average age 37. 30 applicants, 37% accepted, 10 enrolled. In 2006, 17 degrees awarded. *Degree requirements:* For master's, thesis or alternative, registration. *Entrance requirements:* For master's, GRE General Test, minimum GPA of 2.75. Additional exam requirements/recommendations for international students: Required—TOEFL (minimum score 550 paper-based; 213 computer-based). *Application deadline:* For fall admission, 5/15 for domestic and international students; for spring admission, 10/1 for domestic students. Applications are processed on a rolling basis. Application fee: $25 ($30 for international students). Electronic applications accepted. *Expenses:* Tuition, state resident: full-time $3,247; part-time $93 per credit hour. Tuition, nonresident: full-time $9,427; part-time $350 per credit hour. *Financial support:* Fellowships with full tuition reimbursements available. *Unit head:* Dr. Gail Poirrier, Dean, 337-482-6808, Fax: 337-482-5649, E-mail: jdc6124@louisiana.edu. *Application contact:* Dr. Carolyn P. Delahoussaye, Graduate Coordinator, 337-482-5617, Fax: 337-482-5649, E-mail: cgp6303@louisiana.edu.

University of Louisville, Graduate School, School of Nursing, Louisville, KY 40292-0001. Offers MSN, PhD. *Accreditation:* AACN. Part-time programs available. *Faculty:* 30 full-time (28 women), 18 part-time/adjunct (all women). *Students:* 38 full-time (36 women), 54 part-time (49 women); includes 9 minority (7 African Americans, 1 Asian American or Pacific Islander, 1 Hispanic American). Average age 34. In 2006, 23 degrees awarded. *Degree requirements:* For master's, thesis (for some programs). *Entrance requirements:* For master's, GRE General Test, bachelor's degree in nursing, minimum GPA of 3.0, RN license. *Application deadline:* For fall admission, 5/1 priority date for domestic students; for spring admission, 10/1 priority date for domestic students. Applications are processed on a rolling basis. Application fee: $50. *Financial support:* In 2006–07, 10 teaching assistantships were awarded; institutionally sponsored loans, scholarships/grants, and traineeships also available. Financial award application deadline: 4/15; financial award applicants required to submit FAFSA. *Faculty research:* Maternal-child/family stress after pregnancy loss, postpartum depression, access to healthcare (underserved populations), quality of life issues, physical activity (impact on chronic/acute conditions). *Unit head:* Dr. Cynthia A. McCurren, Interim Dean, 502-852-8300, Fax: 502-852-5044, E-mail: camccu01@gwise.louisville.edu.

University of Maine, Graduate School, College of Business, Public Policy and Health, School of Nursing, Orono, ME 04469. Offers MS, CAS. *Accreditation:* AACN. *Faculty:* 4. *Students:* 7 full-time (5 women), 11 part-time (all women). Average age 40. 5 applicants, 80% accepted, 4 enrolled. In 2006, 8 master's awarded. *Entrance requirements:* For master's, GRE General Test. Additional exam requirements/recommendations for international students: Required—TOEFL. *Application deadline:* Applications are processed on a rolling basis. Application fee: $50. Electronic applications accepted. *Financial support:* Career-related internships or fieldwork, Federal Work-Study, institutionally sponsored loans, and tuition waivers (full and partial) available. Support available to part-time students. Financial award application deadline: 3/1. *Unit head:* Dr. Therese Shipps, Director, 207-581-2599, Fax: 207-581-2585. *Application contact:* Scott G. Delcourt, Associate Dean of the Graduate School, 207-581-3219, Fax: 207-581-3232, E-mail: graduate@maine.edu.

University of Manitoba, Faculty of Graduate Studies, Faculty of Nursing, Winnipeg, MB R3T 2N2, Canada. Offers MN. *Degree requirements:* For master's, thesis.

University of Mary, Division of Nursing, Bismarck, ND 58504-9652. Offers family nurse practitioner (MSN); nurse management (MSN); nursing educator (MSN). *Accreditation:* AACN. Part-time and evening/weekend programs available. Postbaccalaureate distance learning degree programs offered (minimal on-campus study). *Faculty:* 2 full-time (both women), 8 part-time/adjunct (5 women). *Students:* 28 full-time (27 women), 22 part-time (all women); includes 2 minority (1 African American, 1 Hispanic American), 1 international. Average age 32. 32 applicants, 66% accepted, 19 enrolled. In 2006, 26 degrees awarded. *Degree requirements:* For master's, thesis (for some programs), internship (family nurse practitioner), practice teaching, comprehensive exam. *Entrance requirements:* For master's, minimum GPA of 3.0 in nursing, interview, letters of recommendation. *Application deadline:* For fall admission, 4/15 priority date for domestic students. Applications are processed on a rolling basis. Application fee: $40. Electronic applications accepted. *Financial support:* In 2006–07, 14 fellowships with partial tuition reimbursements, 3 teaching assistantships with partial tuition reimbursements were awarded; institutionally sponsored loans also available. Support available to part-time students. Financial award application deadline: 7/1. *Faculty research:* Gerontology issues, rural nursing, health policy, primary care, women's health. *Unit head:* Glenda Reemts, Director, 701-255-7500 Ext. 8041, Fax: 701-255-7687. *Application contact:* Traci L. Schell, Secretary, 701-355-8016, Fax: 701-255-7687, E-mail: tschell@umary.edu.

University of Maryland, Baltimore, Graduate School, School of Nursing, Doctoral Program in Nursing, Baltimore, MD 21201. Offers direct nursing (PhD); indirect nursing (PhD). *Degree requirements:* For doctorate, thesis/dissertation. *Entrance requirements:* For doctorate, GRE General Test, minimum GPA of 3.0, MS in nursing. Additional exam requirements/recommendations for international students: Required—TOEFL; Recommended—IELTS. Electronic applications accepted.

University of Maryland, Baltimore, Graduate School, School of Nursing, Master's Program in Nursing, Baltimore, MD 21201. Offers community health nursing (MS); gerontological nursing (MS); maternal-child nursing (MS); medical-surgical nursing (MS); nurse-midwifery education (MS); nursing administration (MS); nursing education (MS); nursing health policy (MS); primary care nursing (MS); psychiatric nursing (MS); MS/MBA. *Accreditation:* AANA/CANAEP; ACNM/DOA; NLN (one or more programs are accredited). Part-time programs available. *Degree requirements:* For master's, thesis or alternative, comprehensive exam (for some programs). *Entrance requirements:* For master's, GRE General Test, minimum GPA of 2.75, course work in statistics, BS in nursing. Additional exam requirements/recommendations for international students: Required—TOEFL, TOEFL or IELTS; Recommended—IELTS. Electronic applications accepted.

University of Massachusetts Amherst, Graduate School, School of Nursing, Amherst, MA 01003. Offers MS, PhD, MS/MPH. *Accreditation:* AACN. Part-time programs available. *Faculty:* 23 full-time (all women). *Students:* 25 full-time (24 women), 59 part-time (58 women); includes 12 minority (6 African Americans, 1 Asian American or Pacific Islander, 5 Hispanic Americans),

3 international. Average age 43. 59 applicants, 85% accepted, 39 enrolled. In 2006, 10 master's, 1 doctorate awarded. *Degree requirements:* For master's, thesis optional; for doctorate, thesis/dissertation. *Entrance requirements:* For master's, GRE General Test, RN licensure, minimum GPA of 3.0, course work in statistics and physical assessment, interview, 2 letters of recommendation, scholarly writing sample. Additional exam requirements/recommendations for international students: Required—TOEFL (minimum score 530 paper-based; 197 computer-based). *Application deadline:* For fall admission, 2/1 priority date for domestic and international students; for spring admission, 10/1 for domestic and international students. Applications are processed on a rolling basis. Application fee: $40 ($65 for international students). Electronic applications accepted. *Expenses:* Tuition, state resident: full-time $2,640; part-time $110 per credit. Tuition, nonresident: full-time $9,936; part-time $414 per credit. Required fees: $8,969; $3,129 per term. One-time fee: $257 full-time. Tuition and fees vary according to class time, course load, campus/location and reciprocity agreements. *Financial support:* In 2006–07, 27 fellowships with full tuition reimbursements (averaging $404 per year), 3 research assistantships with full tuition reimbursements (averaging $1,877 per year), 29 teaching assistantships with full tuition reimbursements (averaging $8,587 per year) were awarded; career-related internships or fieldwork, Federal Work-Study, scholarships/grants, traineeships, tuition waivers (full), and unspecified assistantships also available. Support available to part-time students. Financial award application deadline: 2/1. *Faculty research:* Health of older adults and their caretakers, mental health of individuals and families, health of children and adolescents, power and decision making, transcultural health. *Unit head:* Dr. Eileen T. Breslin, Dean, 413-545-6883, Fax: 413-545-0086, E-mail: breslin@nursing.umass.edu. *Application contact:* Information Contact, 413-545-5096, Fax: 413-577-2550.

University of Massachusetts Boston, Office of Graduate Studies, College of Nursing and Health Sciences, Boston, MA 02125-3393. Offers MS, PhD, MS/MBA. *Accreditation:* AACN. Part-time and evening/weekend programs available. *Students:* 52 full-time (47 women), 104 part-time (100 women); includes 26 minority (16 African Americans, 10 Asian Americans or Pacific Islanders), 2 international. Average age 38. 113 applicants, 72% accepted, 73 enrolled. In 2006, 24 master's, 4 doctorates awarded. *Median time to degree:* Doctorate–4 years full-time. *Degree requirements:* For master's, comprehensive exam; for doctorate, thesis/dissertation, comprehensive exam. *Entrance requirements:* For master's, minimum GPA of 2.75; for doctorate, GRE General Test, master's degree, minimum GPA of 3.3. *Application deadline:* For fall admission, 3/1 priority date for domestic students; for spring admission, 11/1 for domestic students. Application fee: $25. *Expenses:* Tuition, state resident: full-time $2,590; part-time $301 per credit. Tuition, nonresident: full-time $9,758; part-time $427 per credit. One-time fee: $495 full-time. *Financial support:* In 2006–07, 3 research assistantships with full tuition reimbursements (averaging $13,000 per year), 13 teaching assistantships with full tuition reimbursements (averaging $13,000 per year) were awarded; career-related internships or fieldwork, Federal Work-Study, and unspecified assistantships also available. Support available to part-time students. Financial award application deadline: 3/1; financial award applicants required to submit FAFSA. *Faculty research:* Domestic abuse and pregnancy, health policy and home health care, caregiving burdens of families, the chronically ill, health care delivery models and their impact on outcomes, health promotion and disease prevention among the elderly. *Unit head:* Dr. Greer Glazer, Dean, 617-287-7500. *Application contact:* Peggy Roldan, Graduate Admissions Coordinator, 617-287-6400, Fax: 617-287-6236, E-mail: bos.gadm@dpc.umassp.edu.

University of Massachusetts Lowell, Graduate School, College of Health Professions, Department of Nursing, Lowell, MA 01854-2881. Offers administration of nursing services (PhD), including health promotion; family and community health nursing (MS); gerontological nursing (MS); occupational health nursing (MS), including adult psychiatric nursing, occupational health nursing. *Accreditation:* AACN. *Degree requirements:* For master's, thesis optional; for doctorate, thesis/dissertation. *Entrance requirements:* For master's and doctorate, GRE General Test. *Faculty research:* Gerontology, women's health issues, long-term care, alcoholism, health promotion.

University of Massachusetts Worcester, Graduate School of Nursing, Worcester, MA 01655-0115. Offers adult acute/critical care nurse practitioner (MS, Certificate); adult ambulatory/community care nurse practitioner (MS, Certificate); gerontological nurse practitioner (Certificate); nurse educator (MS, Certificate); nursing (PhD). *Accreditation:* AACN. Part-time programs available. *Faculty:* 39. *Students:* 46 full-time (43 women), 6 part-time (2 women); includes 5 minority (2 African Americans, 2 Asian Americans or Pacific Islanders, 1 Hispanic American). Average age 38. 42 applicants, 71% accepted. In 2006, 26 master's, 2 doctorates, 6 other advanced degrees awarded. *Degree requirements:* For doctorate, thesis/dissertation. *Entrance requirements:* For master's, GRE General Test, BSN, previous course work in statistics; for Certificate, master's degree. *Application deadline:* For fall admission, 3/15 for domestic students. Applications are processed on a rolling basis. Application fee: $40 ($60 for international students). *Expenses:* Tuition, state resident: full-time $2,640. Tuition, nonresident: full-time $9,856. Required fees: $3,942. *Financial support:* In 2006–07, 4 students received support. Scholarships/grants and traineeships available. Support available to part-time students. Financial award application deadline: 3/22; financial award applicants required to submit FAFSA. *Faculty research:* Premature menopause with cancer treatment, quality of life and cancer, complementary therapies, psychoneuroimmunology, patient outcomes/outcomes research. *Unit head:* Dr. Janet Hale, Associate Dean, 508-856-5661, Fax: 508-856-6552. *Application contact:* Larry Shattuck, Director of Recruitment and Retention, 508-856-5801, Fax: 508-856-6552.

University of Medicine and Dentistry of New Jersey, School of Nursing, Newark, NJ 07107-1709. Offers adult health (MSN); adult occupational health (MSN); advanced practice nursing (MSN, Post Master's Certificate); family nurse practitioner (MSN); nurse anesthesia (MSN); nursing (MSN); nursing education (MSN, Post Master's Certificate); nursing informatics (MSN); urban health (PhD); women's health practitioner (MSN). *Accreditation:* AANA/CANAEP; NLN (one or more programs are accredited). Part-time programs available. *Students:* 93 full-time (82 women), 307 part-time (274 women); includes 195 minority (92 African Americans, 1 American Indian/Alaska Native, 69 Asian Americans or Pacific Islanders, 33 Hispanic Americans), 1 international. Average age 39. 472 applicants, 63% accepted, 203 enrolled. In 2006, 57 master's, 6 other advanced degrees awarded. *Entrance requirements:* For master's, GRE, RN license; basic life support, statistics, and health assessment experience. Additional exam requirements/recommendations for international students: Required—TOEFL. *Application deadline:* Applications are processed on a rolling basis. Application fee: $50. Electronic applications accepted. *Expenses:* Contact institution. *Financial support:* Teaching assistantships, institutionally sponsored loans and scholarships/grants available. Support available to part-time students. Financial award application deadline: 5/1. *Faculty research:* HIV/AIDS, diabetes education, learned helplessness, nursing science, psychoeducation. *Unit head:* Dr. Susan Salmond, Interim Dean, 973-972-9239, Fax: 973-972-3225, E-mail: salmonsu@umdnj.edu.

University of Miami, Graduate School, School of Nursing and Health Studies, Coral Gables, FL 33124. Offers acute care (MSN), including acute care nurse practitioner, nurse anesthesia; community health (MSN); nursing (PhD); primary care (MSN), including adult nurse practitioner, family nurse practitioner, nurse midwifery, psychiatric/mental health nursing, women's health practitioner. *Accreditation:* AACN; AANA/CANAEP; ACNM/DOA (one or more programs are accredited). Part-time programs available. *Faculty:* 10 full-time (8 women), 1 (woman) part-time/adjunct. *Students:* 33 full-time (24 women), 27 part-time (24 women); includes 28 minority (7 African Americans, 5 Asian Americans or Pacific Islanders, 16 Hispanic Americans), 2 international. Average age 34. 108 applicants, 48% accepted, 30 enrolled. In 2006, 15 master's, 1 doctorate awarded. *Degree requirements:* For master's, thesis optional; for doctorate, thesis/dissertation. *Entrance requirements:* For master's, GRE General Test, BSN, minimum GPA of 3.0, Florida RN license; for doctorate, GRE General Test, BSN or MSN, minimum GPA of 3.0. Additional exam requirements/recommendations for international students: Required—TOEFL (minimum score 550 paper-based; 213 computer-based). *Application deadline:* For fall admission, 4/30 priority date for domestic students; for spring admission, 11/1 priority date for domestic students. Applications are processed on a rolling basis. Application fee: $50. Electronic applications accepted. *Financial support:* In 2006–07, 12 students received support, including 3 research assistantships with tuition reimbursements available (averaging $9,000 per year), 5 teaching assistantships with tuition reimbursements available (averaging $9,000 per year); fellowships, Federal Work-Study, institutionally sponsored loans, scholarships/grants, and unspecified assistantships also available. Support available to part-time students. Financial award application deadline: 3/1; financial award applicants required to submit FAFSA. *Faculty research:* Transcultural nursing, exercise and depression in Alzheimer's disease, infectious diseases/HIV–AIDS, postpartum depression, outcomes assessment. Total annual research expenditures: $31.9 million. *Unit head:* Dr. Nilda Peragallo, Dean, 305-284-2107, Fax: 305-667-3787, E-mail: nperagallo@miami.edu. *Application contact:* Anne Stabb, Graduate Advisor, 305-284-2533, Fax: 305-284-4827, E-mail: astabb@miami.edu.

University of Michigan, Horace H. Rackham School of Graduate Studies, School of Nursing, Ann Arbor, MI 48109. Offers MS, PhD, Post Master's Certificate, MBA/MS, MHSA/MS, MS/MS. *Accreditation:* AACN; ACNM/DOA (one or more programs are accredited). Part-time programs available. Postbaccalaureate distance learning degree programs offered (minimal on-campus study). Terminal master's awarded for partial completion of doctoral program. *Degree requirements:* For master's, registration; for doctorate, thesis/dissertation, oral defense of dissertation, preliminary exam. *Entrance requirements:* For master's, GRE General Test, minimum B average; for doctorate, GRE General Test, nursing license, minimum B average, 2 original papers. Electronic applications accepted. *Faculty research:* Preparation of clinical nurse researchers, biobehavior, women's health, health promotion, substance abuse, psychobiology of menopause, fertility, obesity, health care systems.

University of Michigan–Flint, School of Health Professions and Studies, Program in Nursing, Flint, MI 48502-1950. Offers MSN. *Accreditation:* AACN. Part-time programs available. *Faculty:* 4 full-time (all women), 3 part-time/adjunct (2 women). *Students:* 2 full-time (both women), 37 part-time (36 women); includes 5 minority (3 African Americans, 2 Asian Americans or Pacific Islanders). Average age 39. 27 applicants, 70% accepted, 16 enrolled. In 2006, 8 degrees awarded. *Degree requirements:* For master's, thesis. *Entrance requirements:* Additional exam requirements/recommendations for international students: Required—TOEFL (minimum score 550 paper-based; 220 computer-based), IELTS (minimum score 7). *Application deadline:* For fall admission, 8/1 priority date for domestic students, 3/1 priority date for international students; for winter admission, 11/15 priority date for domestic students, 7/1 priority date for international students; for spring admission, 3/15 priority date for domestic students, 11/1 priority date for international students. Applications are processed on a rolling basis. Application fee: $55. Electronic applications accepted. *Expenses:* Contact institution. *Financial support:* In 2006–07, 24 students received support. Federal Work-Study and scholarships/grants available. *Faculty research:* Family system stress, self breast exam, family roads evaluation, causal model testing for psychosocial development, basic needs. *Unit head:* Dr. Marge Andrews, Director, 810-762-3420, Fax: 810-766-6851, E-mail: mmandrew@umflint.edu. *Application contact:* Bradley T. Maki, Director of Graduate Admissions, 810-762-3171, Fax: 810-766-6789, E-mail: bmaki@umflint.edu.

University of Minnesota, Twin Cities Campus, Graduate School, School of Nursing, Minneapolis, MN 55455-0213. Offers MN, MS, DNP, PhD. *Accreditation:* AACN; AANA/CANAEP; ACNM/DOA (one or more programs are accredited). Part-time programs available. Postbaccalaureate distance learning degree programs offered (minimal on-campus study). *Faculty:* 58 full-time (56 women), 22 part-time/adjunct (20 women). *Students:* 167 full-time (152 women), 183 part-time (166 women); includes 28 minority (9 African Americans, 3 American Indian/Alaska Native, 8 Asian Americans or Pacific Islanders, 8 Hispanic Americans). Average age 37. 220 applicants, 76% accepted. In 2006, 87 master's, 7 doctorates awarded. Terminal master's awarded for partial completion of doctoral program. *Degree requirements:* For master's, final oral exam, project or thesis; for doctorate, thesis/dissertation. *Entrance requirements:* For master's and doctorate, GRE General Test. Additional exam requirements/recommendations for international students: Required—TOEFL (minimum score 586 paper-based; 240 computer-based). Application fee: $55 ($75 for international students). *Expenses:* Contact institution. *Financial support:* Fellowships, research assistantships, teaching assistantships, career-related internships or fieldwork and traineeships available. Financial award applicants required to submit FAFSA. *Faculty research:* Child and family health promotion, nursing research on elders. *Unit head:* Dr. Connie Delaney, Dean, 612-624-5959, Fax: 612-626-2359. *Application contact:* Information Contact, 612-624-4454, Fax: 612-624-3174, E-mail: nurseoss@umn.edu.

University of Mississippi Medical Center, School of Graduate Studies in the Health Sciences, Program in Nursing, Jackson, MS 39216-4505. Offers MSN, PhD. *Accreditation:* AACN. Part-time and evening/weekend programs available. *Faculty:* 21 full-time (19 women), 2 part-time/adjunct (1 woman). *Students:* 113 full-time (101 women), 13 part-time (11 women); includes 34 minority (31 African Americans, 2 Asian Americans or Pacific Islanders, 1 Hispanic American). Average age 35. 31 applicants, 81% accepted, 15 enrolled. In 2006, 25 master's, 3 doctorates awarded. *Degree requirements:* For master's, thesis optional; for doctorate, thesis/dissertation, publishable paper, comprehensive exam. *Entrance requirements:* For master's, GRE, 1 year of clinical experience, RN license; for doctorate, GRE, RN license, professional nursing experience, master's degree. *Application deadline:* Applications are processed on a rolling basis. Application fee: $10. Electronic applications accepted. *Expenses:* Contact institution. *Financial support:* Institutionally sponsored loans and traineeships available. Support available to part-time students. Financial award application deadline: 4/1. *Faculty research:* Quality of life, neuroscience nursing, adult learning, gerontology, child birthing/parenting education. Total annual research expenditures: $200,000. *Unit head:* Dr. Kaye Bender, Dean, School of Nursing, 601-984-6200. *Application contact:* Dr. Rowena Elliott, Director of Student Affairs, 601-984-6252, E-mail: relliott@son.umsmed.edu.

University of Missouri–Columbia, Graduate School, Sinclair School of Nursing, Columbia, MO 65211. Offers MS, PhD. *Accreditation:* AACN. Part-time programs available. *Faculty:* 23 full-time (21 women). *Students:* 59 full-time (52 women), 149 part-time (144 women); includes 16 minority (8 African Americans, 5 American Indian/Alaska Native, 2 Asian Americans or Pacific Islanders, 1 Hispanic American), 4 international. In 2006, 28 master's, 4 doctorates awarded. *Degree requirements:* For master's, thesis, non-thesis, or practicum; oral exam; for doctorate, thesis/dissertation. *Entrance requirements:* For master's, GRE General Test, BSN, minimum GPA of 3.0 during last 60 hours, nursing license. Additional exam requirements/recommendations for international students: Required—TOEFL (minimum score 550 paper-based; 213 computer-based; 79 iBT). *Application deadline:* For fall admission, 2/1 priority date for domestic students. Applications are processed on a rolling basis. Application fee: $45 ($60 for international students). *Financial support:* Fellowships, research assistantships, teaching assistantships, career-related internships or fieldwork, institutionally sponsored loans, traineeships, and tuition waivers (full) available. *Faculty research:* Pain, stepfamilies, chemotherapy-related nausea and vomiting, stress management, self-care deficit theory. *Unit head:* Dr. Roxanne W. McDaniel, Director of Graduate Studies, 573-882-0257, E-mail: mcdanielr@missouri.edu.

University of Missouri–Kansas City, School of Nursing, Kansas City, MO 64110-2499. Offers adult clinical nurse specialist (MSN), including adult nurse practitioner, women's health nurse practitioner; family nurse practitioner (MSN); neonatal nurse practitioner (MSN); nurse educator (MSN); nurse executive (MSN); nursing (PhD); pediatric nurse practitioner (MSN). *Accreditation:* AACN. Part-time programs available. Postbaccalaureate distance learning degree programs offered (minimal on-campus study). *Faculty:* 31 full-time (26 women), 32 part-time/adjunct (31 women). *Students:* 36 full-time (all women), 213 part-time (202 women); includes 23 minority (6 African Americans, 2 American Indian/Alaska Native, 6 Asian Americans or Pacific Islanders, 9 Hispanic Americans). Average age 36. 121 applicants, 72% accepted, 71 enrolled. In 2006, 69 master's, 1 doctorate awarded. *Median time to degree:* Of those who began their doctoral program in fall 1998, 60% received their degree in 8 years or less. *Degree requirements:* For master's, thesis or alternative. *Entrance requirements:* For master's, minimum undergraduate GPA of 3.2; for doctorate, GRE, 3 letters of reference, interview and original essay by invitation. Additional exam requirements/recommendations for international students:

Nursing—General

University of Missouri–Kansas City (continued)

Required—TOEFL (minimum score 550 paper-based). *Application deadline:* For fall admission, 2/1 priority date for domestic students; for spring admission, 9/15 priority date for domestic students. Application fee: $25. *Expenses:* Tuition, state resident: full-time $4,975; part-time $276 per credit. Tuition, nonresident: full-time $12,847; part-time $713 per credit. Required fees: $595; $595 per year. *Financial support:* In 2006–07, 30 students received support, including 6 research assistantships (averaging $3,450 per year), 7 teaching assistantships with partial tuition reimbursements available (averaging $12,650 per year); fellowships, career-related internships or fieldwork, Federal Work-Study, institutionally sponsored loans, and tuition waivers (full and partial) also available. Support available to part-time students. Financial award application deadline: 6/30; financial award applicants required to submit FAFSA. *Faculty research:* Geriatrics/gerontology, children's pain, neonatology, Alzheimer's care, cancer caregivers. Total annual research expenditures: $1 million. *Unit head:* Dr. Lora Lacey-Haun, Dean, 816-235-1700, Fax: 816-235-1701, E-mail: lacey-haunc@umkc.edu. *Application contact:* Leah Wilder, Coordinator for Admissions and Recruitment, 816-235-5768, Fax: 816-235-1701, E-mail: wilderl@umkc.edu.

University of Missouri–St. Louis, College of Nursing, St. Louis, MO 63121. Offers nurse practitioner (Certificate); nursing (MSN, PhD). *Accreditation:* AACN. *Faculty:* 11 full-time (all women), 2 part-time/adjunct (both women). *Students:* 22 full-time (19 women), 154 part-time (152 women); includes 23 minority (17 African Americans, 3 Asian Americans or Pacific Islanders, 3 Hispanic Americans), 1 international. Average age 36. In 2006, 39 master's, 6 doctorates awarded. *Degree requirements:* For doctorate, thesis/dissertation. *Entrance requirements:* For master's, supplemental application, statement of purpose; for doctorate, GRE General Test, 2 letters of recommendation. Additional exam requirements/recommendations for international students: Required—TOEFL (minimum score 550 paper-based; 213 computer-based). *Application deadline:* For fall admission, 4/1 for domestic students; for winter admission, 10/30 for domestic students; for spring admission, 7/1 for domestic students. Applications are processed on a rolling basis. Application fee: $35 ($40 for international students). Electronic applications accepted. *Expenses:* Tuition, state resident: part-time $332 per credit hour. Tuition, nonresident: part-time $770 per credit hour. *Financial support:* In 2006–07, 2 research assistantships with full and partial tuition reimbursements (averaging $11,520 per year) were awarded; teaching assistantships with full and partial tuition reimbursements. *Faculty research:* Health promotion and restoration, family disruption, violence abuse, battered women, health survey methods. *Unit head:* Dean Juliann Sebastian, Dean, 314-516-6066. *Application contact:* 314-516-5458, Fax: 314-516-6996, E-mail: gradadm@umsl.edu.

University of Mobile, Graduate Programs, Program in Nursing, Mobile, AL 36613. Offers MSN. *Accreditation:* AACN. Part-time and evening/weekend programs available. *Faculty:* 11 part-time/adjunct (10 women). *Students:* 25 (22 women); includes 4 minority (3 African Americans, 1 Hispanic American). Average age 36. In 2006, 11 degrees awarded. *Degree requirements:* For master's, thesis or alternative, comprehensive exam. *Entrance requirements:* For master's, GMAT, GRE General Test, or MAT. Additional exam requirements/recommendations for international students: Required—TOEFL. *Application deadline:* For fall admission, 8/3 priority date for domestic students; for spring admission, 12/23 for domestic students. Applications are processed on a rolling basis. Application fee: $40 ($50 for international students). *Expenses:* Tuition: Part-time $340 per hour. Required fees: $121 per term. Tuition and fees vary according to course load. *Financial support:* Federal Work-Study available. Support available to part-time students. Financial award application deadline: 8/1. *Faculty research:* Nursing management, transcultural nursing, spiritual aspects, educational expectations. *Unit head:* Dr. Elizabeth Flanagan, Dean, School of Nursing, 251-442-2227, Fax: 251-442-2520, E-mail: elizabethflanagan@free.umobile.edu. *Application contact:* Dr. Kaye F. Brown, Associate Vice President for Academic Affairs, 251-442-2289, Fax: 251-442-2523, E-mail: kayeb@mail.umobile.edu.

University of Nebraska Medical Center, Graduate Studies, Graduate Program in Nursing, Omaha, NE 68198. Offers MSN, PhD. *Accreditation:* AACN. Part-time programs available. Postbaccalaureate distance learning degree programs offered. *Faculty:* 55 full-time (all women). *Students:* 70 full-time (67 women), 239 part-time (231 women); includes 21 minority (10 African Americans, 2 American Indian/Alaska Native, 4 Asian Americans or Pacific Islanders, 5 Hispanic Americans), 3 international. Average age 35. 138 applicants, 81% accepted, 98 enrolled. In 2006, 60 master's, 6 doctorates awarded. *Median time to degree:* Of those who began their doctoral program in fall 1998, 100% received their degree in 8 years or less. *Degree requirements:* For master's, research project or thesis; for doctorate, thesis/dissertation, comprehensive exam, registration. *Entrance requirements:* For master's, minimum GPA of 3.0; for doctorate, GRE General Test, minimum GPA of 3.2. Additional exam requirements/recommendations for international students: Required—TOEFL (minimum score 550 paper-based; 213 computer-based). *Application deadline:* For fall admission, 5/1 priority date for domestic students, 4/1 for international students; for spring admission, 10/1 for domestic students, 8/1 for international students. Applications are processed on a rolling basis. Application fee: $45. Electronic applications accepted. *Expenses:* Contact institution. *Financial support:* In 2006–07, 120 students received support, including 24 fellowships (averaging $4,500 per year), 7 research assistantships (averaging $6,000 per year), 21 teaching assistantships with tuition reimbursements available (averaging $6,000 per year); institutionally sponsored loans, scholarships/grants, traineeships, and unspecified assistantships also available. Support available to part-time students. Financial award application deadline: 2/1; financial award applicants required to submit FAFSA. *Faculty research:* Health promotion, sleep and fatigue in cancer patients, symptoms management in cardiovascular disease, prevention of osteoporosis in breast cancer survivors. Total annual research expenditures: $4.5 million. *Unit head:* Dr. Sarah A. Thompson, Associate Dean for Academic Programs, 402-559-4286, E-mail: sathompson@unmc.edu.

University of Nevada, Las Vegas, Graduate College, Division of Health Sciences, School of Nursing, Las Vegas, NV 89154-9900. Offers family nurse practitioner (MS, Post-Master's Certificate); nursing (PhD); nursing education (MS, Post-Master's Certificate); pediatric nurse practitioner (MS). *Accreditation:* NLN. Part-time programs available. *Faculty:* 21 full-time (all women), 6 part-time/adjunct (all women). *Students:* 74 full-time (59 women), 66 part-time (61 women); includes 24 minority (2 African Americans, 15 Asian Americans or Pacific Islanders, 7 Hispanic Americans), 46 international. 190 applicants, 66% accepted, 107 enrolled. In 2006, 11 degrees awarded. *Degree requirements:* For master's, research project, thesis optional. *Entrance requirements:* For master's, GRE General Test, minimum GPA of 3.0 during previous 2 years, minimum overall GPA of 2.75. Additional exam requirements/recommendations for international students: Required—TOEFL (minimum score 550 paper-based; 213 computer-based; 80 iBT). *Application deadline:* For fall admission, 3/15 for domestic and international students. Application fee: $60 ($75 for international students). Electronic applications accepted. *Financial support:* In 2006–07, 7 research assistantships with partial tuition reimbursements (averaging $10,000 per year) were awarded; career-related internships or fieldwork, Federal Work-Study, institutionally sponsored loans, scholarships/grants, health care benefits, and unspecified assistantships also available. Support available to part-time students. Financial award application deadline: 3/1. *Unit head:* Dr. Carolyn Yucha, Dean, 702-895-3415. *Application contact:* Graduate College Admissions Evaluator, 702-895-3320, Fax: 702-895-4180, E-mail: gradcollege@unlv.edu.

University of Nevada, Reno, Graduate School, College of Health and Human Sciences, Orvis School of Nursing, Reno, NV 89557. Offers MSN. *Accreditation:* AACN. *Faculty:* 7. *Students:* 21 full-time (20 women), 20 part-time (19 women); includes 2 minority (1 Asian American or Pacific Islander, 1 Hispanic American). Average age 41. 16 applicants, 81% accepted, 10 enrolled. In 2006, 10 degrees awarded. *Degree requirements:* For master's, thesis optional. *Entrance requirements:* For master's, GRE General Test or MAT, minimum GPA of 3.0 in bachelor degree from accredited school. Additional exam requirements/recommendations for international students: Required—TOEFL. *Application deadline:* For fall admission, 3/1 priority date for domestic students. Applications are processed on a rolling basis. Application fee: $60 ($95 for international students). *Financial support:* In 2006–07, 3 research assistantships were awarded; teaching assistantships. Financial award application deadline: 3/1. *Unit head:* Dr. Alice Running, Graduate Program Director, 775-682-7148.

University of New Brunswick Fredericton, School of Graduate Studies, Faculty of Nursing, Fredericton, NB E3B 5A3, Canada. Offers advance nurse practitioner (MN); nursing (MN). *Faculty:* 30 full-time (all women). *Students:* 6 full-time (all women), 48 part-time (all women). In 2006, 9 degrees awarded. *Entrance requirements:* For master's, undergraduate coursework in statistics and nursing research, GPA of 3.3 or better, registration as a nurse in New Brunswick (or eligible), statement of professional and research interests and career goals. Application fee: $50 Canadian dollars. *Financial support:* In 2006–07, 5 research assistantships, 4 teaching assistantships were awarded; fellowships also available. *Unit head:* Gad Storr, Director of Graduate Studies, 506-458-7643, Fax: 506-447-3057. *Application contact:* Francis Perry, Graduate Secretary, 506-451-6844, Fax: 506-447-3057, E-mail: fperry@unb.ca.

University of New Hampshire, Graduate School, School of Health and Human Services, Department of Nursing, Durham, NH 03824. Offers MS. *Accreditation:* AACN. Part-time programs available. *Faculty:* 12 full-time. *Students:* 45 full-time (42 women), 67 part-time (63 women); includes 3 minority (1 African American, 2 Asian Americans or Pacific Islanders), 2 international. Average age 36. 27 applicants, 93% accepted, 17 enrolled. In 2006, 48 degrees awarded. *Degree requirements:* For master's, thesis or alternative. *Entrance requirements:* For master's, GRE General Test or MAT. Additional exam requirements/recommendations for international students: Required—TOEFL (minimum score 550 paper-based; 213 computer-based). *Application deadline:* For fall admission, 4/1 priority date for domestic students, 4/1 for international students; for winter admission, 12/1 for domestic students. Applications are processed on a rolling basis. Application fee: $50. Electronic applications accepted. *Expenses:* Tuition, state resident: full-time $8,540; part-time $474 per credit hour. Tuition, nonresident: full-time $20,990; part-time $862 per credit hour. Required fees: $1,343; $356 per term. Tuition and fees vary according to course load, program and reciprocity agreements. *Financial support:* In 2006–07, 6 fellowships, 2 teaching assistantships were awarded; research assistantships, Federal Work-Study, scholarships/grants, and tuition waivers (full and partial) also available. Financial award application deadline: 2/15. *Faculty research:* Adult health, nursing administration, family nurse practitioner. *Unit head:* Dr. Lynette Ament, Chairperson, 603-862-2390. *Application contact:* Jane Dufresne, Administrative Assistant, 603-862-2299, E-mail: nursing.department@unh.edu.

University of New Mexico, Graduate School, College of Nursing, Albuquerque, NM 87131-2039. Offers MSN, PhD, MSN/MA. *Accreditation:* AACN; ACNM/DOA (one or more programs are accredited). Part-time programs available. Postbaccalaureate distance learning degree programs offered. *Faculty:* 44 full-time (39 women), 9 part-time/adjunct (all women). *Students:* 66 full-time (63 women), 147 part-time (136 women); includes 53 minority (5 African Americans, 8 American Indian/Alaska Native, 2 Asian Americans or Pacific Islanders, 38 Hispanic Americans), 2 international. Average age 42. 119 applicants, 57% accepted, 55 enrolled. In 2006, 39 master's awarded. *Degree requirements:* For master's, thesis optional; for doctorate, thesis/dissertation, registration. *Entrance requirements:* For master's, GRE General Test, minimum GPA of 3.0, course work in statistics recommended, interview for some concentrations, BSN or RN with BA with petition; for doctorate, interview, minimum GPA of 3.0, writing sample, MSN or BSN with MA with petition. Additional exam requirements/recommendations for international students: Required—TOEFL. Application fee: $50. Electronic applications accepted. *Financial support:* In 2006–07, 64 students received support, including 1 research assistantship (averaging $3,000 per year), 9 teaching assistantships with partial tuition reimbursements available (averaging $5,800 per year); scholarships/grants, traineeships, and tuition waivers (full) also available. Financial award application deadline: 3/1; financial award applicants required to submit FAFSA. *Faculty research:* Women's and children's health, dysphnea, medically fragile children, pregnancy prevention in teens, Lupus. Total annual research expenditures: $948,246. *Unit head:* Dr. Robin Meize-Grochowski, Senior Associate Dean of Academic Affairs, 505-272-8327, Fax: 505-272-3970, E-mail: rmeize@salud.unm.edu. *Application contact:* Elizabeth Rowe, Student Program Advisor, 505-272-4223, Fax: 505-272-3970, E-mail: erowe@unm.edu.

University of North Alabama, College of Nursing, Florence, AL 35632-0001. Offers MSN. *Accreditation:* AACN. *Faculty:* 1 (woman) part-time/adjunct. *Expenses:* Tuition, state resident: full-time $4,080. Tuition, nonresident: full-time $8,160. Required fees: $764. *Unit head:* Dr. Birdie Bailey, Dean, 256-765-4984, E-mail: bibailey@una.edu. *Application contact:* Dr. Sue Wilson, Dean of Enrollment Management, 256-765-4316, Fax: 256-765-4349, E-mail: sjwilson@una.edu.

The University of North Carolina at Chapel Hill, School of Nursing, Chapel Hill, NC 27599. Offers nursing (MSN, PhD). *Accreditation:* AACN; NLN (one or more programs are accredited). Part-time programs available. *Degree requirements:* For master's, thesis, comprehensive exam; for doctorate, thesis/dissertation, 3 exams. *Entrance requirements:* For master's and doctorate, GRE General Test. *Faculty research:* Chronic illness, parenting, cardiovascular health in children, elderly, HIV-AIDS.

The University of North Carolina at Charlotte, Graduate School, College of Health and Human Services, School of Nursing, Charlotte, NC 28223-0001. Offers MSN. *Accreditation:* AACN. *Faculty:* 16 full-time (14 women), 4 part-time/adjunct (3 women). *Students:* 62 full-time (52 women), 104 part-time (95 women); includes 14 minority (8 African Americans, 1 Asian American or Pacific Islander, 5 Hispanic Americans), 1 international. Average age 34. 108 applicants, 52% accepted, 46 enrolled. In 2006, 62 degrees awarded. *Entrance requirements:* For master's, GRE General Test, minimum GPA of 3.0 in undergraduate major. Additional exam requirements/recommendations for international students: Required—TOEFL (minimum score 570 paper-based; 220 computer-based). *Application deadline:* For fall admission, 7/15 for domestic students, 5/1 for international students; for spring admission, 11/15 for domestic students, 10/1 for international students. Application fee: $55. *Expenses:* Tuition, state resident: full-time $2,719; part-time $170 per credit. Tuition, nonresident: full-time $12,926; part-time $808 per credit. Required fees: $1,555. *Financial support:* In 2006–07, 2 research assistantships (averaging $1,204 per year), 2 teaching assistantships (averaging $4,032 per year) were awarded; fellowships, career-related internships or fieldwork, Federal Work-Study, institutionally sponsored loans, scholarships/grants, traineeships, and unspecified assistantships also available. Support available to part-time students. Financial award application deadline: 4/1; financial award applicants required to submit FAFSA. *Unit head:* Dr. Lucille L. Travis, Director, 704-687-7952, Fax: 704-687-6017. *Application contact:* Kathy B. Giddings, Director of Graduate Admissions, 704-687-3366, Fax: 704-687-3279, E-mail: gradadm@email.uncc.edu.

The University of North Carolina at Greensboro, Graduate School, School of Nursing, Greensboro, NC 27412-5001. Offers adult clinical nurse specialist (MSN, PMC); adult/gerontological nurse practitioner (MSN, PMC); nurse anesthesia (MSN, PMC); nursing (PhD); nursing administration (MSN); nursing education (MSN); MSN/MBA. *Accreditation:* AACN; AANA/CANAEP; NLN. *Faculty:* 24 full-time (23 women), 27 part-time/adjunct (22 women). *Students:* 231 full-time (197 women), 98 part-time (83 women); includes 56 minority (41 African Americans, 3 American Indian/Alaska Native, 9 Asian Americans or Pacific Islanders, 3 Hispanic Americans). 206 applicants, 59% accepted. *Degree requirements:* For master's, thesis or alternative. *Entrance requirements:* For master's, GRE General Test or MAT, BSN, clinical experience, liability insurance, RN license; for PMC, liability insurance, MSN, RN license. Additional exam requirements/recommendations for international students: Required—TOEFL. Application fee: $45. Electronic applications accepted. *Expenses:* Tuition, state resident: full-time $2,692. Tuition, nonresident: full-time $13,742. *Financial support:* Research assistantships with full tuition reimbursements, career-related internships or fieldwork, Federal Work-Study, scholarships/grants, and traineeships available. Support available to part-time students. *Unit head:* Dr. Lynne Pearcey, Dean, 336-334-5177, Fax: 336-334-3628, E-mail: l_pearce@uncg.edu. *Application contact:* Michelle Harkleroad, Director of Graduate Admissions, 336-334-4884, Fax: 336-334-4424, E-mail: mbharkle@uncg.edu.

The University of North Carolina Wilmington, School of Nursing, Wilmington, NC 28403-3297. Offers MSN. *Accreditation:* AACN; NLN. *Faculty:* 9 full-time (all women), 1 (woman) part-time/adjunct. *Students:* 11 full-time (9 women), 9 part-time (8 women); includes 1 minority (American Indian/Alaska Native). Average age 34. 25 applicants, 88% accepted, 16 enrolled. In 2006, 9 degrees awarded. *Degree requirements:* For master's, thesis or master's project. *Entrance requirements:* For master's, GRE General Test, bachelor's degree in nursing. *Application deadline:* For fall admission, 3/1 for domestic students. Applications are processed on a rolling basis. Application fee: $45. Electronic applications accepted. *Financial support:* In 2006–07, 2 teaching assistantships were awarded. Financial award application deadline: 3/15. *Unit head:* Dr. Virginia W. Adams, Dean, 910-962-7410, E-mail: adamsv@uncw.edu. *Application contact:* Dr. Robert D. Roer, Dean, Graduate School, 910-962-4117, Fax: 910-962-3787, E-mail: roer@uncw.edu.

University of North Dakota, Graduate School, College of Nursing, Grand Forks, ND 58202. Offers MS, PhD. *Accreditation:* AACN; AANA/CANAEP (one or more programs are accredited). Part-time programs available. Postbaccalaureate distance learning degree programs offered (minimal on-campus study). *Faculty:* 18 full-time (all women). *Students:* 61 full-time (45 women), 51 part-time (45 women); includes 8 American Indian/Alaska Native, 25 international. 92 applicants, 46% accepted, 39 enrolled. *Degree requirements:* For master's, thesis or alternative. *Entrance requirements:* For master's, minimum GPA of 3.0; for doctorate, GRE or MAT, minimum GPA of 3.0. Additional exam requirements/recommendations for international students: Required—TOEFL (minimum score 550 paper-based; 213 computer-based; 79 iBT), IELTS (minimum score 6). *Application deadline:* For fall admission, 12/1 for domestic and international students. Application fee: $35. Electronic applications accepted. *Expenses:* Tuition, state resident: full-time $5,650; part-time $214 per credit. Tuition, nonresident: full-time $14,248; part-time $572 per credit. Required fees: $1,008; $42 per credit. Tuition and fees vary according to reciprocity agreements. *Financial support:* In 2006–07, 4 research assistantships (averaging $10,498 per year), 7 teaching assistantships with full tuition reimbursements (averaging $10,669 per year) were awarded; fellowships, Federal Work-Study, institutionally sponsored loans, scholarships/grants, traineeships, and tuition waivers (full and partial) also available. Support available to part-time students. Financial award application deadline: 3/15; financial award applicants required to submit FAFSA. *Faculty research:* Adult health, anesthesia, rural health, health administration, family nurse practitioner. Total annual research expenditures: $904,692. *Unit head:* Dr. Chandice Covington, Dean, 701-777-4555, Fax: 701-777-4096, E-mail: chandicecovington@mail.und.edu. *Application contact:* Brenda Halle, Admissions Specialist, 701-777-2947, Fax: 701-777-3619, E-mail: brendahalle@mail.und.edu.

University of Northern Colorado, Graduate School, College of Natural and Health Sciences, School of Nursing, Greeley, CO 80639. Offers clinical nurse specialist in chronic illness (MS); family nurse practitioner (MS); nursing education (MS, PhD). *Accreditation:* AACN. Postbaccalaureate distance learning degree programs offered. *Faculty:* 12 full-time (all women). *Students:* 58 full-time (57 women), 20 part-time (19 women); includes 6 minority (2 American Indian/Alaska Native, 4 Hispanic Americans). Average age 40. 63 applicants, 68% accepted, 21 enrolled. In 2006, 21 degrees awarded. *Degree requirements:* For master's, thesis or alternative, comprehensive exam; for doctorate, thesis/dissertation, comprehensive exam. *Entrance requirements:* For master's and doctorate, GRE General Test, minimum GPA of 3.0 in last 60 hours, BS in nursing, 2 letters of recommendation. *Application deadline:* Applications are processed on a rolling basis. Application fee: $50 ($60 for international students). Electronic applications accepted. *Expenses:* Tuition, state resident: full-time $5,118; part-time $213 per credit hour. Tuition, nonresident: full-time $14,832; part-time $618 per credit hour. Required fees: $674; $34 per credit hour. *Financial support:* In 2006–07, 47 students received support, including 4 fellowships (averaging $1,006 per year), 3 research assistantships (averaging $7,108 per year), 2 teaching assistantships (averaging $4,832 per year); unspecified assistantships also available. Financial award application deadline: 3/1; financial award applicants required to submit FAFSA. *Unit head:* Dr. Diane Peters, Interim Co-Director, 970-351-2293, Fax: 970-351-1707.

University of North Florida, College of Health, School of Nursing, Jacksonville, FL 32224-2645. Offers advanced practice nursing (MSN); primary care nurse practitioner (Certificate). *Accreditation:* AACN. *Faculty:* 12 full-time (11 women). *Students:* 36 full-time (28 women), 29 part-time (25 women); includes 11 minority (3 African Americans, 1 American Indian/Alaska Native, 3 Asian Americans or Pacific Islanders, 4 Hispanic Americans), 2 international. Average age 35. 104 applicants, 45% accepted, 39 enrolled. In 2006, 11 degrees awarded. *Degree requirements:* For master's, thesis optional. *Entrance requirements:* For master's, GRE General Test, minimum GPA of 3.0 in last 60 hours of course work, BSN, clinical experience, resumé. Additional exam requirements/recommendations for international students: Required—TOEFL (minimum score 500 paper-based; 173 computer-based). *Application deadline:* For fall admission, 5/1 for domestic and international students. Applications are processed on a rolling basis. Application fee: $30. Electronic applications accepted. *Expenses:* Tuition, state resident: full-time $4,948; part-time $206 per semester hour. Tuition, nonresident: full-time $19,140; part-time $408 per semester hour. *Financial support:* In 2006–07, 33 students received support; research assistantships available. Financial award application deadline: 4/1; financial award applicants required to submit FAFSA. *Faculty research:* Teen pregnancy, diabetes, ethical decision making, family caregivers. Total annual research expenditures: $1.4 million. *Unit head:* Dr. Lilia Loriz, Director, 904-620-2684, E-mail: lloriz@unf.edu.

University of Oklahoma Health Sciences Center, Graduate College, College of Nursing, Oklahoma City, OK 73190. Offers MS, MS/MBA. *Accreditation:* NLN. Part-time programs available. *Degree requirements:* For master's, thesis optional. *Entrance requirements:* For master's, 3 letters of recommendation, Oklahoma RN license, statistics course, research methods, computer course or completion of a computer literacy test. *Faculty research:* Parenting and Native Americans, elderly reminiscence, diabetes in Native Americans.

University of Ottawa, Faculty of Graduate and Postdoctoral Studies, Faculty of Health Sciences, School of Nursing, Ottawa, ON K1N 6N5, Canada. Offers nurse practitioner (Certificate); nursing (M Sc, PhD); nursing/primary health care (M Sc). Part-time and evening/weekend programs available. *Degree requirements:* For master's, thesis or alternative. *Entrance requirements:* For master's, honors degree or equivalent, minimum B average. Electronic applications accepted. *Faculty research:* Decision making in nursing, evaluating complete nursing interventions.

University of Pennsylvania, School of Nursing, Philadelphia, PA 19104. Offers MSN, PhD, Certificate, MBA/MSN, MBA/PhD, MSN/PhD. *Accreditation:* AACN; AANA/CANAEP. Part-time programs available. Postbaccalaureate distance learning degree programs offered. Terminal master's awarded for partial completion of doctoral program. *Degree requirements:* For doctorate, thesis/dissertation. *Entrance requirements:* For master's, GMAT (MBA/MSN), GRE General Test, BSN, minimum GPA of 3.0; for doctorate, GMAT (MBA/PhD), GRE General Test, BSN or MSN, minimum GPA of 3.0. Additional exam requirements/recommendations for international students: Required—TOEFL. Expenses: Contact institution. *Faculty research:* Nursing and patient outcomes research.

University of Phoenix–Atlanta Campus, The Artemis School, College of Health and Human Services, Sandy Springs, GA 30350-4153. Offers health care management (MBA). Evening/weekend programs available. *Faculty:* 9 full-time (5 women), 56 part-time/adjunct (24 women). *Students:* 52 full-time (38 women); includes 28 minority (26 African Americans, 2 Asian Americans or Pacific Islanders). In 2006, 26 degrees awarded. *Degree requirements:* For master's, thesis (for some programs), registration. *Entrance requirements:* For master's, minimum undergraduate GPA of 2.5, 3 years of work experience. Additional exam requirements/recommendations for international students: Required—TOEFL (minimum score 550 paper-based; 213 computer-based; 79 iBT). *Application deadline:* Applications are processed on a rolling basis. Application fee: $45. Electronic applications accepted. *Expenses:* Tuition: Full-time $10,560. Required fees: $760. *Financial support:* Institutionally sponsored loans and scholarships/grants available. Financial award applicants required to submit FAFSA. *Unit head:* Dr. Gil Linne, Dean/Executive Director, 480-557-1221, E-mail: gil.linne@phoenix.edu.

University of Phoenix–Augusta Campus, College of Health and Human Services, Augusta, GA 30909-4583. Offers health administration (MHA); health care management (MBA); nursing (MSN); MSN/MHA.

University of Phoenix–Central Florida Campus, The Artemis School, College of Health and Human Services, Maitland, FL 32751-7057. Offers health administration (MHA); health and human services (MSN); health care management (MBA). Evening/weekend programs available. *Faculty:* 24 full-time (17 women), 46 part-time/adjunct (27 women). *Students:* 49 full-time (46 women); includes 15 minority (8 African Americans, 2 Asian Americans or Pacific Islanders, 5 Hispanic Americans), 7 international. Average age 44. In 2006, 43 degrees awarded. *Degree requirements:* For master's, thesis (for some programs), registration. *Entrance requirements:* For master's, minimum undergraduate GPA of 2.5, 3 years work experience, RN license. Additional exam requirements/recommendations for international students: Required—TOEFL (minimum score 550 paper-based; 213 computer-based; 79 iBT). *Application deadline:* Applications are processed on a rolling basis. Application fee: $45. Electronic applications accepted. *Expenses:* Tuition: Full-time $9,450. Required fees: $760. *Financial support:* Institutionally sponsored loans and scholarships/grants available. Financial award applicants required to submit FAFSA. *Unit head:* Dr. Gil Linne, Dean/Executive Director, 480-557-1751, E-mail: gil.linne@phoenix.edu. *Application contact:* Chair, 407-667-0525, Fax: 407-667-0560.

University of Phoenix–Central Valley Campus, College of Health and Human Services, Fresno, CA 93720. Offers health care management (MBA); nursing (MSN).

University of Phoenix–Charlotte Campus, The Artemis School, College of Health and Human Services, Charlotte, NC 28273-3409. Offers health care management (MBA). Evening/weekend programs available. *Faculty:* 1 full-time (0 women), 12 part-time/adjunct (7 women). *Students:* 68 full-time (57 women); includes 35 minority (34 African Americans, 1 Asian American or Pacific Islander), 4 international. In 2006, 12 degrees awarded. *Degree requirements:* For master's, thesis (for some programs), registration. *Entrance requirements:* For master's, minimum undergraduate GPA 2.5, 3 years work experience. Additional exam requirements/recommendations for international students: Required—TOEFL (minimum score 550 paper-based; 213 computer-based; 79 iBT). *Application deadline:* Applications are processed on a rolling basis. Application fee: $45. Electronic applications accepted. *Expenses:* Tuition: Full-time $10,320. Required fees: $760. *Financial support:* Institutionally sponsored loans and scholarships/grants available. Financial award applicants required to submit FAFSA. *Unit head:* Dr. Gil Linne, Dean/Executive Director, 480-557-1757, E-mail: gil.linne@phoenix.edu. *Application contact:* College Chair, 704-504-5409.

University of Phoenix–Cheyenne Campus, College of Health and Human Services, Cheyenne, WY 82009. Offers health administration (MHA); health care education (MSN); health care management (MBA); nursing (MSN); MSN/MBA; MSN/MHA.

University of Phoenix–Cleveland Campus, The Artemis School, College of Health and Human Services, Independence, OH 44131-2194. Offers administration of justice and security (MS); health care management (MBA); nursing (MSN); psychology (MS). Evening/weekend programs available. *Faculty:* 3 full-time (0 women), 24 part-time/adjunct (18 women). *Students:* 23 full-time (all women); includes 9 minority (all African Americans), 3 international. Average age 47. In 2006, 3 degrees awarded. *Degree requirements:* For master's, thesis (for some programs), registration. *Entrance requirements:* For master's, minimum undergraduate GPA of 2.5, 3 years of work experience. Additional exam requirements/recommendations for international students: Required—TOEFL (minimum score 550 paper-based; 213 computer-based; 79 iBT). *Application deadline:* Applications are processed on a rolling basis. Application fee: $45. Electronic applications accepted. *Expenses:* Tuition: Full-time $11,608. Required fees: $760. *Financial support:* Institutionally sponsored loans and scholarships/grants available. Financial award applicants required to submit FAFSA. *Unit head:* Dr. Gil Linne, Dean/Executive Director, 480-557-1751, E-mail: gil.linne@phoenix.edu. *Application contact:* Campus College Chair, 216-447-8807.

University of Phoenix–Denver Campus, The Artemis School, College of Health and Human Services, Lone Tree, CO 80124-5453. Offers community counseling (MSC); health care management (MBA); marriage, family and child therapy (MSC); nursing (MSN). Evening/weekend programs available. *Faculty:* 17 full-time (7 women), 126 part-time/adjunct (62 women). *Students:* 147 full-time (114 women); includes 18 minority (9 African Americans, 1 American Indian/Alaska Native, 1 Asian American or Pacific Islander, 7 Hispanic Americans), 16 international. Average age 39. In 2006, 34 master's awarded. *Degree requirements:* For master's, thesis (for some programs), registration. *Entrance requirements:* For master's, minimum undergraduate GPA of 2.5, 3 years work experience, RN license. Additional exam requirements/recommendations for international students: Required—TOEFL (minimum score 550 paper-based; 213 computer-based; 79 iBT). *Application deadline:* Applications are processed on a rolling basis. Application fee: $45. Electronic applications accepted. *Expenses:* Tuition: Full-time $10,032. Required fees: $760. *Financial support:* Institutionally sponsored loans and scholarships/grants available. Financial award applicants required to submit FAFSA. *Unit head:* Dr. Gil Linne, Dean/Executive Director, 480-557-1751, E-mail: gil.linne@phoenix.edu. *Application contact:* Chair, 303-694-9093, Fax: 303-662-0911.

University of Phoenix–Detroit Campus, College of Health and Human Services, Southfield, MI 48076. Offers family nurse practitioner (MSN); health administration (MHA); health care management (MBA); nursing (MSN); MSN/MBA.

University of Phoenix–Fort Lauderdale Campus, The Artemis School, College of Health and Human Services, Fort Lauderdale, FL 33309. Offers health administration (MHA); health care education (MSN); health care management (MBA); nursing (MSN); MSN/MBA. Evening/weekend programs available. *Faculty:* 22 full-time (10 women), 56 part-time/adjunct (28 women). *Students:* 197 full-time (173 women); includes 73 minority (60 African Americans, 2 Asian Americans or Pacific Islanders, 11 Hispanic Americans), 33 international. Average age 43. In 2006, 52 degrees awarded. *Degree requirements:* For master's, thesis (for some programs), registration. *Entrance requirements:* For master's, minimum undergraduate GPA of 2.5, 3 years work experience, RN license. Additional exam requirements/recommendations for international students: Required—TOEFL (minimum score 550 paper-based; 213 computer-based; 79 iBT). *Application deadline:* Applications are processed on a rolling basis. Application fee: $45. Electronic applications accepted. *Expenses:* Tuition: Full-time $9,450. Required fees: $760. *Financial support:* Institutionally sponsored loans and scholarships/grants available. Financial award applicants required to submit FAFSA. *Unit head:* Dr. Gil Linne, Dean/Executive Director, 480-557-1751, E-mail: gil.linne@phoenix.edu. *Application contact:* 954-382-5303, Fax: 954-382-5303.

University of Phoenix–Harrisburg Campus, College of Health and Human Services, Harrisburg, PA 17112. Offers health administration (MHA); health care management (MBA); nursing (MSN); nursing/health care education (MSN); MSN/MBA; MSN/MHA.

University of Phoenix–Hawaii Campus, The Artemis School, College of Health and Human Services, Honolulu, HI 96813-4317. Offers administration of justice and security (MS); community counseling (MSC); family nurse practitioner (MSN); health administration (MHA); health care management (MBA); marriage, family and child therapy (MSC); nursing (MSN); psychology (MS). Evening/weekend programs available. *Faculty:* 20 full-time (12 women), 84 part-time/adjunct (46 women). *Students:* 47 full-time (36 women); includes 20 minority (2 African Americans, 15 Asian Americans or Pacific Islanders, 3 Hispanic Americans), 9 international. Average age 41. In 2006, 13 degrees awarded. *Degree requirements:* For master's, thesis (for some programs), registration. *Entrance requirements:* For master's, minimum undergraduate GPA of 2.5, 3 years of work experience, RN license. Additional exam requirements/recommendations for international students: Required—TOEFL (minimum score 550 paper-based; 213 computer-based; 79 iBT). *Application deadline:* Applications are processed on a rolling basis. Application fee: $45. Electronic applications accepted. *Expenses:* Tuition: Full-time $11,520. Required fees: $760. *Financial support:* Institutionally sponsored loans and

Nursing—General

University of Phoenix–Hawaii Campus (continued)
scholarships/grants available. Financial award applicants required to submit FAFSA. *Unit head:* Dr. Gil Linne, Dean/Executive Director, 480-557-1751, E-mail: gil.linne@phoenix.edu. *Application contact:* Chair, 808-536-2686, Fax: 808-536-3848.

University of Phoenix–Indianapolis Campus, The Artemis School, College of Health and Human Services, Indianapolis, IN 46250-932. Offers administration of justice and security (MS); health administration (MHA); health care management (MBA); nursing (MSN); psychology (MS). Evening/weekend programs available. *Faculty:* 1 full-time (0 women), 10 part-time/adjunct (4 women). *Students:* 1 (woman) full-time; minority (African American) Average age 38. In 2006, 2 degrees awarded. *Degree requirements:* For master's, thesis, registration (for some programs). *Entrance requirements:* For master's, 3 years work experience, minimum undergraduate GPA of 2.5. Additional exam requirements/recommendations for international students: Required—TOEFL (minimum score 500 paper-based; 213 computer-based). *Application deadline:* Applications are processed on a rolling basis. Application fee: $45. Electronic applications accepted. *Expenses:* Tuition: Full-time $10,320. Required fees: $760. *Financial support:* Institutionally sponsored loans and scholarships/grants available. Financial award applicants required to submit FAFSA. *Unit head:* Dr. Gil Linne, Dean/Executive Director, 480-557-1751, E-mail: gil.linne@phoenix.edu.

University of Phoenix–Kansas City Campus, The Artemis School, College of Health and Human Services, Kansas City, MO 64131-4517. Offers administration of justice and security (MS); community counseling (MSC); health administration (MHA); health care management (MBA); nursing (MSN). Evening/weekend programs available. *Faculty:* 4 full-time (0 women), 16 part-time/adjunct (7 women). *Students:* 16 full-time (15 women); includes 1 minority (African American), 5 international. Average age 44. In 2006, 2 degrees awarded. *Degree requirements:* For master's, thesis (for some programs), registration. *Entrance requirements:* For master's, 3 years work experience, minimum undergraduate GPA or 2.5. Additional exam requirements/recommendations for international students: Required—TOEFL (minimum score 550 paper-based; 213 computer-based). Application fee: $45. *Expenses:* Tuition: Full-time $11,064. Required fees: $760. *Financial support:* Institutionally sponsored loans and scholarships/grants available. *Unit head:* Dr. Gil Linne, Dean/Executive Director, 480-557-1751, E-mail: gil.linne@phoenix.edu. *Application contact:* Chair, 816-943-9600, Fax: 816-943-6675.

University of Phoenix–Louisiana Campus, The Artemis School, College of Health and Human Services, Metairie, LA 70001-2082. Offers administration of justice and security (MS); health care management (MBA); nursing (MSN); psychology (MS); MSN/MBA. Evening/weekend programs available. *Faculty:* 2 full-time (both women), 52 part-time/adjunct (32 women). *Students:* 29 full-time (23 women); includes 14 minority (13 African Americans, 1 Asian American or Pacific Islander), 2 international. Average age 34. In 2006, 17 degrees awarded. *Degree requirements:* For master's, thesis (for some programs), registration. *Entrance requirements:* For master's, minimum undergraduate GPA of 2.5, 3 years work experience, RN license. Additional exam requirements/recommendations for international students: Required—TOEFL (minimum score 550 paper-based; 213 computer-based; 79 iBT). *Application deadline:* Applications are processed on a rolling basis. Application fee: $45. Electronic applications accepted. *Expenses:* Tuition: Full-time $11,832. Required fees: $760. *Financial support:* Institutionally sponsored loans and scholarships/grants available. Financial award applicants required to submit FAFSA. *Unit head:* Dr. Gil Linne, Dean/Executive Director, 480-557-1751, E-mail: gil.linne@phoenix.edu. *Application contact:* Chair, 504-461-8852, Fax: 504-464-6373.

University of Phoenix–Maryland Campus, The Artemis School, College of Health and Human Services, Columbia, MD 21045-5424. Offers administration of justice and security (MS); nursing (MSN); nursing education (MSN); psychology (MS); MSN/MBA; MSN/MHA. Evening/weekend programs available. *Faculty:* 8 part-time/adjunct (7 women). *Students:* 1 (woman) full-time; minority (African American) Average age 27. *Degree requirements:* For master's, thesis (for some programs), registration. *Entrance requirements:* For master's, minimum undergraduate GPA of 2.5, 3 years work experience. Additional exam requirements/recommendations for international students: Required—TOEFL (minimum score 550 paper-based; 213 computer-based; 79 iBT). *Application deadline:* Applications are processed on a rolling basis. Application fee: $45. Electronic applications accepted. *Expenses:* Tuition: Full-time $13,200. Required fees: $760. *Financial support:* Institutionally sponsored loans and scholarships/grants available. Financial award applicants required to submit FAFSA. *Unit head:* Dr. Gil Linne, Dean/Executive Director, 480-557-1751, E-mail: gil.line@phoenix.com. *Application contact:* Campus Chair, 410-872-9001.

University of Phoenix–Metro Detroit Campus, The Artemis School, College of Health and Human Services, Southfield, MI 48076. Offers health care management (MBA); nursing (MSN); MSN/MBA-HCM. Evening/weekend programs available. *Faculty:* 13 full-time (8 women), 83 part-time/adjunct (50 women). *Students:* 211 full-time (190 women); includes 95 minority (92 African Americans, 2 Asian Americans or Pacific Islanders, 1 Hispanic American), 5 international. Average age 40. In 2006, 57 master's awarded. *Degree requirements:* For master's, thesis (for some programs), registration. *Entrance requirements:* For master's, minimum undergraduate GPA of 2.5, 3 years of work experience, RN license. Additional exam requirements/recommendations for international students: Required—TOEFL (minimum score 550 paper-based; 213 computer-based; 79 iBT). *Application deadline:* Applications are processed on a rolling basis. Application fee: $45. Electronic applications accepted. *Expenses:* Tuition: Full-time $12,168. Required fees: $760. *Financial support:* Institutionally sponsored loans and scholarships/grants available. Financial award applicants required to submit FAFSA. *Unit head:* Dr. Gil Linne, Dean/Executive Director, 480-557-1751, E-mail: gil.linne@phoenix.edu. *Application contact:* Chair, 800-834-2438, Fax: 248-267-0147.

University of Phoenix–Minneapolis/St. Louis Park Campus, College of Health and Human Services, St. Louis Park, MN 55426. Offers family nurse practitioner (MSN); health care management (MBA); nursing (MSN).

University of Phoenix–New Mexico Campus, The Artemis School, College of Health and Human Services, Albuquerque, NM 87109-4645. Offers health care management (MBA); marriage and family therapy (MSC). Evening/weekend programs available. *Faculty:* 19 full-time (12 women), 135 part-time/adjunct (75 women). *Students:* 217 full-time (156 women); includes 93 minority (9 African Americans, 4 American Indian/Alaska Native, 4 Asian Americans or Pacific Islanders, 76 Hispanic Americans), 17 international. Average age 39. In 2006, 40 degrees awarded. *Degree requirements:* For master's, thesis (for some programs), registration. *Entrance requirements:* For master's, minimum undergraduate GPA of 2.5, 3 years of work experience, RN license. Additional exam requirements/recommendations for international students: Required—TOEFL (minimum score 550 paper-based; 213 computer-based; 79 iBT). *Application deadline:* Applications are processed on a rolling basis. Application fee: $45. Electronic applications accepted. *Expenses:* Tuition: Full-time $9,005. Required fees: $760. *Financial support:* Institutionally sponsored loans and scholarships/grants available. Financial award applicants required to submit FAFSA. *Unit head:* Dr. Gil Linne, Dean/Executive Director, 480-557-1751, E-mail: gil.linne@phoenix.edu. *Application contact:* Campus College Chair-Nursing, 505-821-4800, Fax: 505-821-5551.

University of Phoenix—Northern Nevada Campus, College of Health and Human Services, Reno, NV 89511. Offers health administration (MHA); health care management (MBA); nursing (MSN); nursing/health care education (MSN); MSN/MBA; MSN/MHA.

University of Phoenix–Northern Virginia Campus, College of Health and Human Services, Reston, VA 20190. Offers health administration (MHA); health care management (MBA); nursing (MSN).

University of Phoenix–North Florida Campus, The Artemis School, College of Health and Human Services, Jacksonville, FL 32216-0959. Offers health administration (MHA); health care education (MSN); health care management (MBA); nursing (MSN); MSN/MBA. Evening/weekend programs available. *Faculty:* 13 full-time (10 women), 58 part-time/adjunct (42 women). *Students:* 69 full-time (52 women); includes 33 minority (26 African Americans, 5 Asian Americans or Pacific Islanders, 2 Hispanic Americans), 7 international. Average age 41. In 2006, 15 master's awarded. *Degree requirements:* For master's, thesis (for some programs), registration. *Entrance requirements:* For master's, minimum undergraduate GPA of 2.5, 3 years work experience, RN license. Additional exam requirements/recommendations for international students: Required—TOEFL (minimum score 550 paper-based; 213 computer-based; 79 iBT). *Application deadline:* Applications are processed on a rolling basis. Application fee: $45. Electronic applications accepted. *Financial support:* Institutionally sponsored loans and scholarships/grants available. Financial award applicants required to submit FAFSA. *Unit head:* Dr. Gil Linne, Dean, 480-557-1751, E-mail: gil.linne@phoenix.edu. *Application contact:* Chair, 904-636-6645, Fax: 904-636-0998.

University of Phoenix–Northwest Arkansas Campus, College of Health and Human Services, Rogers, AR 72756-9615. Offers health administration (MHA); health care education (MSN); health care management (MBA); nursing (MSN); MSN/MBA.

University of Phoenix–Northwest Indiana, College of Health and Human Services, Merrillville, IN 46410. Offers health administration (MHA); nursing (MSN); nursing/health care education (MSN); MSN/MBA; MSN/MHA.

University of Phoenix Online Campus, The Artemis School, College of Health and Human Services, Phoenix, AZ 85034-7209. Offers administration of justice and security (MS); health care administration (MHA); health care management (MBA, MSN); nurse practitioner (MSN); nursing (MSN); nursing education (MSN); psychology (MS); MSN/MBA-HCM; MSN/MHA. *Accreditation:* AACN. Evening/weekend programs available. *Faculty:* 10 full-time (9 women), 1,743 part-time/adjunct (1,042 women). *Students:* 8,196 full-time (6,937 women); includes 1,916 minority (1,301 African Americans, 56 American Indian/Alaska Native, 268 Asian Americans or Pacific Islanders, 291 Hispanic Americans), 849 international. Average age 40. In 2006, 6,951 master's awarded. *Degree requirements:* For master's, thesis (for some programs), registration. *Entrance requirements:* For master's, 3 years of work experience, minimum undergraduate GPA of 2.5, RN license. Additional exam requirements/recommendations for international students: Required—TOEFL (minimum score 550 paper-based; 213 computer-based; 79 iBT). *Application deadline:* Applications are processed on a rolling basis. Application fee: $45. Electronic applications accepted. *Expenses:* Tuition: Full-time $12,664. Required fees: $760. *Financial support:* Institutionally sponsored loans and scholarships/grants available. Financial award applicants required to submit FAFSA. *Unit head:* Dr. Gil Linne, Dean/Executive Director, 480-552-1751, E-mail: gil.linne@phoenix.edu. *Application contact:* Dr. Gil Linne, Dean/Executive Director, 480-552-1751, E-mail: gil.linne@phoenix.edu.

University of Phoenix–Phoenix Campus, The Artemis School, College of Health and Human Services, Phoenix, AZ 85040-1958. Offers community counseling (MSC); family nurse practitioner (MSN); health care management (MBA); nurse practitioner (Certificate); nursing (MSN); nursing health care education (Certificate). Evening/weekend programs available. *Faculty:* 45 full-time (20 women), 510 part-time/adjunct (308 women). *Students:* 493 full-time (420 women); includes 79 minority (17 African Americans, 4 American Indian/Alaska Native, 20 Asian Americans or Pacific Islanders, 38 Hispanic Americans), 12 international. Average age 38. In 2006, 166 degrees awarded. *Degree requirements:* For master's, thesis (for some programs), registration. *Entrance requirements:* For master's, 3 years of work experience in field, minimum undergraduate GPA of 2.5, RN license. Additional exam requirements/recommendations for international students: Required—TOEFL (minimum score 550 paper-based; 213 computer-based; 79 iBT). *Application deadline:* Applications are processed on a rolling basis. Application fee: $45. Electronic applications accepted. *Financial support:* Institutionally sponsored loans and scholarships/grants available. Financial award applicants required to submit FAFSA. *Unit head:* Dr. Gil Linne, Dean/Executive Director, 480-557-1751, E-mail: gil.linne@phoenix.edu. *Application contact:* Chair, 480-804-7400, Fax: 480-557-2320.

University of Phoenix–Renton Learning Center, College of Health and Human Services, Renton, WA 98005. Offers health administration (MHA); health care education (MSN); health care management (MBA); nursing (MSN); MSN/MBA; MSN/MHA.

University of Phoenix–Richmond Campus, The Artemis School, College of Health and Human Services, Richmond, VA 23230. Offers administration of justice and security (MS); health administration (MHA); health care management (MBA); nursing (MSN); psychology (MS). Evening/weekend programs available. *Faculty:* 4 part-time/adjunct (1 woman). *Students:* 2 full-time (1 woman); includes 1 minority (African American) Average age 38. *Degree requirements:* For master's, thesis (for some programs), registration. *Entrance requirements:* For master's, minimum undergraduate GPA of 2.5, 3 years work experience, current RN license for nursing programs. Additional exam requirements/recommendations for international students: Required—TOEFL (minimum score 500 paper-based; 213 computer-based; 79 iBT). *Application deadline:* Applications are processed on a rolling basis. Application fee: $45. Electronic applications accepted. *Financial support:* Institutionally sponsored loans and scholarships/grants available. Financial award applicants required to submit FAFSA. *Unit head:* Dr. Gil Linne, Dean/Executive Director, 480-557-1751, E-mail: gil.linne@phoenix.edu. *Application contact:* Chair, 804-288-3390.

University of Phoenix–Sacramento Valley Campus, The Artemis School, College of Health and Human Services, Sacramento, CA 95833-3632. Offers administration of justice and security (MS); family nurse practitioner (MSN); health care management (MBA); marriage, family and child counseling (MSC); nursing (MSN); nursing education (MSN). Evening/weekend programs available. *Faculty:* 36 full-time (27 women), 270 part-time/adjunct (121 women). *Students:* 330 full-time (266 women); includes 73 minority (38 African Americans, 2 American Indian/Alaska Native, 16 Asian Americans or Pacific Islanders, 17 Hispanic Americans), 29 international. Average age 40. In 2006, 82 degrees awarded. *Degree requirements:* For master's, thesis (for some programs), registration. *Entrance requirements:* For master's, RN license, minimum undergraduate GPA of 2.5, 3 years work experience. Additional exam requirements/recommendations for international students: Required—TOEFL (minimum score 550 paper-based; 213 computer-based; 79 iBT). *Application deadline:* Applications are processed on a rolling basis. Application fee: $45. Electronic applications accepted. *Expenses:* Tuition: Full-time $12,024. Required fees: $760. *Financial support:* Institutionally sponsored loans and scholarships/grants available. Financial award applicants required to submit FAFSA. *Unit head:* Dr. Gil Linne, Dean/Executive Director, 480-557-1757, E-mail: gil.linne@phoenix.edu. *Application contact:* College Chair, 916-923-2107, Fax: 916-923-3914.

University of Phoenix–San Diego Campus, The Artemis School, College of Health and Human Services, San Diego, CA 92123. Offers administration of justice and security (MS); marriage, family and child counseling (MSC); marriage, family and child therapy (MSC); nursing (MSN); MSN/MBA. Evening/weekend programs available. *Faculty:* 32 full-time (20 women), 160 part-time/adjunct (66 women). *Students:* 281 full-time (225 women); includes 75 minority (20 African Americans, 1 American Indian/Alaska Native, 21 Asian Americans or Pacific Islanders, 33 Hispanic Americans), 15 international. Average age 37. In 2006, 81 degrees awarded. *Degree requirements:* For master's, thesis (for some programs), registration. *Entrance requirements:* For master's, minimum undergraduate GPA of 2.5, 3 years work experience, RN license. Additional exam requirements/recommendations for international students: Required—TOEFL (minimum score 550 paper-based; 213 computer-based; 79 iBT). *Application deadline:* Applications are processed on a rolling basis. Application fee: $45. Electronic applications accepted. *Expenses:* Tuition: Full-time $11,419. Required fees: $760. *Financial support:* Institutionally sponsored loans and scholarships/grants available. Financial award applicants required to submit FAFSA. *Unit head:* Dr. Gil Linne, Dean/Executive Director, 480-557-1751, E-mail: gil.linne@phoenix.edu. *Application contact:* Campus College Chair, 888-UOP-INFO, Fax: 858-509-4399.

University of Phoenix–Savannah Campus, College of Health and Human Services, Savannah, GA 31405-7400. Offers health administration (MHA); health care management (MBA); nursing (MSN); nursing/health care education (MSN); MSN/MBA; MSN/MHA.

University of Phoenix–Southern California Campus, The Artemis School, College of Health and Human Services, Costa Mesa, CA 92626. Offers family nurse practitioner (MSN, Certificate); health care education (MSN); health care management (MBA); marriage, family and child therapy (MSC); nursing (MSN). Evening/weekend programs available. *Faculty:* 53 full-time (32 women), 456 part-time/adjunct (240 women). *Students:* 623 full-time (524 women); includes 237 minority (98 African Americans, 2 American Indian/Alaska Native, 62 Asian Americans or Pacific Islanders, 75 Hispanic Americans), 59 international. Average age 40. In 2006, 113 degrees awarded. *Degree requirements:* For master's, thesis (for some programs), registration. *Entrance requirements:* For master's, minimum undergraduate GPA of 2.5, 3 years work experience, RN license. Additional exam requirements/recommendations for international students: Required—TOEFL (minimum score 550 paper-based; 213 computer-based; 79 iBT). *Application deadline:* Applications are processed on a rolling basis. Application fee: $45. Electronic applications accepted. *Expenses:* Tuition: Full-time $13,512. Required fees: $760. *Financial support:* Institutionally sponsored loans and scholarships/grants available. Financial award applicants required to submit FAFSA. *Unit head:* Dr. Gil Linne, Dean/Executive Director, 480-557-1751, E-mail: gil.linne@phoenix.edu. *Application contact:* Campus College Chair, 714-398-1878, Fax: 714-378-5856.

University of Phoenix–Southern Colorado Campus, The Artemis School, College of Health and Human Services, Colorado Springs, CO 80919-2335. Offers community counseling (MSC); health care management (MBA); marriage, family and child therapy (MSC); nursing (MSN). Evening/weekend programs available. *Faculty:* 2 full-time (both women), 100 part-time/adjunct (37 women). *Students:* 76 full-time (52 women); includes 10 minority (3 African Americans, 2 American Indian/Alaska Native, 5 Hispanic Americans). Average age 38. In 2006, 20 degrees awarded. *Degree requirements:* For master's, thesis (for some programs), registration. *Entrance requirements:* For master's, minimum undergraduate GPA of 2.5, 3 years of work experience, RN license. Additional exam requirements/recommendations for international students: Required—TOEFL (minimum score 550 paper-based; 213 computer-based; 79 iBT). *Application deadline:* Applications are processed on a rolling basis. Application fee: $45. Electronic applications accepted. *Expenses:* Tuition: Full-time $10,291. Required fees: $760. *Financial support:* Institutionally sponsored loans and scholarships/grants available. Financial award applicants required to submit FAFSA. *Unit head:* Dr. Gil Linne, Dean/Executive Director, 480-557-1751, E-mail: gil.linne@phoenix.edu. *Application contact:* Chair, 719-599-5282, Fax: 719-599-7973.

University of Phoenix–Springfield Campus, College of Health and Human Services, Springfield, MO 65804-7211. Offers administration/health care management (MSN); health administration (MHA); health care management (MBA); nursing (MSN); MSN/MBA; MSN/MHA.

University of Phoenix–Utah Campus, The Artemis School, College of Health and Human Services, Salt Lake City, UT 84123-4617. Offers business administration healthcare (MSN); mental health counseling (MSC); nursing (MSN). Evening/weekend programs available. *Faculty:* 25 full-time (8 women), 105 part-time/adjunct (46 women). *Students:* 381 full-time (264 women); includes 20 minority (2 African Americans, 1 American Indian/Alaska Native, 8 Asian Americans or Pacific Islanders, 9 Hispanic Americans), 9 international. Average age 38. In 2006, 59 degrees awarded. *Degree requirements:* For master's, thesis (for some programs), registration. *Entrance requirements:* For master's, minimum undergraduate GPA of 2.5, 3 years work experience, RN license. Additional exam requirements/recommendations for international students: Required—TOEFL (minimum score 550 paper-based; 213 computer-based; 79 iBT). *Application deadline:* Applications are processed on a rolling basis. Application fee: $45. Electronic applications accepted. *Expenses:* Tuition: Full-time $9,104. Required fees: $760. *Financial support:* Institutionally sponsored loans and scholarships/grants available. Financial award applicants required to submit FAFSA. *Unit head:* Dr. Gil Linne, Dean/Executive Director, 480-557-1751, E-mail: gil.linne@phoenix.edu. *Application contact:* Chair, 801-263-1444, Fax: 801-269-9766.

University of Phoenix–Vancouver Campus, The Artemis School, College of Health and Human Services, Burnaby, BC V5C 6G9, Canada. Offers health care management (MBA). Evening/weekend programs available. *Students:* 2 full-time (0 women). Average age 36. *Degree requirements:* For master's, thesis (for some programs), registration. *Entrance requirements:* For master's, minimum undergraduate GPA of 2.5, 3 years work experience. Additional exam requirements/recommendations for international students: Required—TOEFL (minimum score 550 paper-based; 213 computer-based; 79 iBT). *Application deadline:* Applications are processed on a rolling basis. Application fee: $45. Electronic applications accepted. *Expenses:* Tuition: Full-time $12,840. Required fees: $760. *Financial support:* Institutionally sponsored loans available. *Unit head:* Dr. Gil Linne, Dean/Executive Director, 480-557-1751, E-mail: gil.linne@phoenix.edu.

University of Phoenix–West Florida Campus, The Artemis School, College of Health and Human Services, Temple Terrace, FL 33637. Offers health administration (MHA); health care education (MSN); health care management (MBA); MSN/MBA. Evening/weekend programs available. Postbaccalaureate distance learning degree programs offered. *Faculty:* 19 full-time (12 women), 56 part-time/adjunct (31 women). *Students:* 87 full-time (79 women); includes 21 minority (12 African Americans, 1 Asian American or Pacific Islander, 8 Hispanic Americans), 10 international. Average age 45. In 2006, 18 degrees awarded. *Degree requirements:* For master's, thesis (for some programs), registration. *Entrance requirements:* For master's, minimum undergraduate GPA of 2.5, RN license, 3 years work experience. Additional exam requirements/recommendations for international students: Required—TOEFL (minimum score 550 paper-based; 213 computer-based; 79 iBT). *Application deadline:* Applications are processed on a rolling basis. Application fee: $45. Electronic applications accepted. *Expenses:* Tuition: Full-time $9,450. Required fees: $760. *Financial support:* Institutionally sponsored loans and scholarships/grants available. Financial award applicants required to submit FAFSA. *Unit head:* Dr. Gil Linne, Dean, 480-557-1751, E-mail: gil.linne@phoenix.edu. *Application contact:* Chair, 813-626-7911, Fax: 813-977-1449.

University of Phoenix–West Michigan Campus, The Artemis School, College of Health and Human Services, Walker, MI 49544. Offers health care management (MBA); nursing (MSN). Evening/weekend programs available. *Faculty:* 9 full-time (3 women), 49 part-time/adjunct (28 women). *Students:* 40 full-time (35 women); includes 8 minority (6 African Americans, 2 Hispanic Americans), 3 international. Average age 39. In 2006, 7 master's awarded. *Degree requirements:* For master's, thesis (for some programs), registration. *Entrance requirements:* For master's, minimum undergraduate GPA of 2.5, 3 years work experience, RN license. Additional exam requirements/recommendations for international students: Required—TOEFL (minimum score 550 paper-based; 213 computer-based; 79 iBT). *Application deadline:* Applications are processed on a rolling basis. Application fee: $45. Electronic applications accepted. *Expenses:* Tuition: Full-time $12,043. Required fees: $760. *Financial support:* Institutionally sponsored loans and scholarships/grants available. Financial award applicants required to submit FAFSA. *Unit head:* Dr. Gil Linne, Dean/Executive Director, 480-557-1751, E-mail: gil.linne@phoenix.edu. *Application contact:* Chair, 888-345-9699, Fax: 616-784-5300.

University of Pittsburgh, School of Nursing, Pittsburgh, PA 15260. Offers MSN, DNP, PhD. *Accreditation:* AACN. Part-time programs available. *Faculty:* 53 full-time (47 women), 4 part-time/adjunct (all women). *Students:* 168 full-time (127 women), 175 part-time (161 women); includes 26 minority (13 African Americans, 10 Asian Americans or Pacific Islanders, 3 Hispanic Americans). Average age 38. 197 applicants, 38% accepted, 70 enrolled. In 2006, 99 master's, 3 doctorates awarded. *Degree requirements:* For master's, thesis optional; for doctorate, thesis/dissertation, comprehensive exam. *Entrance requirements:* For master's, GRE or MAT, BSN, RN license, 1-3 years nursing experience, letters of recommendation, resumé, course work in statistics; for doctorate, GRE, BSN, RN license, course work in statistics resumé, letters of recommendation. Additional exam requirements/recommendations for international students: Required—TOEFL (minimum score 550 paper-based; 213 computer-based; 80 iBT). *Application deadline:* Applications are processed on a rolling basis. Application fee: $50. Electronic applications accepted. *Expenses: Contact institution. Financial support:* In 2006–07, 26 students received support, including 21 research assistantships with full and partial tuition reimbursements available (averaging $17,145 per year), 3 teaching assistantships with full and partial tuition reimbursements available (averaging $20,993 per year); institutionally sponsored loans, scholarships/grants, traineeships, health care benefits, and unspecified assistantships also available. Support available to part-time students. Financial award application deadline: 7/1; financial award applicants required to submit FAFSA. *Faculty research:* Healthcare outcomes, basic science, chronic disorders, critical care, adolescent health, women's health. Total annual research expenditures: $5.5 million. *Unit head:* Dr. Jacqueline Dunbar-Jacob, Dean, 412-624-7838, Fax: 412-624-2401, E-mail: dunbar@pitt.edu. *Application contact:* Laurie Lapsley, Administrator of Graduate Student Services, 412-624-9670, Fax: 412-624-2409, E-mail: lapsleyl@pitt.edu.

University of Portland, Graduate School, School of Nursing, Portland, OR 97203-5798. Offers MS. *Accreditation:* AACN. Part-time and evening/weekend programs available. Postbaccalaureate distance learning degree programs offered (minimal on-campus study). *Faculty:* 11 full-time (10 women). *Students:* 28 full-time, 17 part-time. *Entrance requirements:* For master's, GRE General Test or MAT, Oregon RN license, BSN, course work in statistics, resumé, 3 letters of recommendation. Additional exam requirements/recommendations for international students: Required—TOEFL (minimum score 550 paper-based; 80 iBT). *Application deadline:* Applications are processed on a rolling basis. Application fee: $50. *Expenses:* Contact institution. Tuition and fees vary according to program. *Financial support:* Fellowships, research assistantships, Federal Work-Study and scholarships/grants available. Support available to part-time students. Financial award application deadline: 3/1; financial award applicants required to submit FAFSA. *Unit head:* Dr. Terry Misener, Dean, 503-943-7211, Fax: 503-943-7399, E-mail: misener@up.edu. *Application contact:* Dr. Joanne Warner, Associate Dean, 503-943-7211, E-mail: warner@up.edu.

University of Puerto Rico, Medical Sciences Campus, School of Nursing, San Juan, PR 00936-5067. Offers anesthesia (MSN); clinical specialist (MSN); family nurse practitioner (MSN); nurse administrator (MSN); nursing education (MSN). *Accreditation:* AACN; AANA/CANAEP. Part-time and evening/weekend programs available. *Faculty:* 12 full-time (11 women), 3 part-time/adjunct (2 women). *Students:* 115 full-time (all women), 13 part-time (9 women); includes 123 minority (all Hispanic Americans), 3 international. 70 applicants, 71% accepted. In 2006, 40 degrees awarded. *Degree requirements:* For master's, one foreign language. *Entrance requirements:* For master's, GRE or EXADEP, interview, Puerto Rico RN license or professional license for international students, general and specific point average, article analysis. *Application deadline:* For spring admission, 4/30 priority date for domestic and international students. Applications are processed on a rolling basis. Application fee: $33. Electronic applications accepted. *Financial support:* In 2006–07, research assistantships with full tuition reimbursements (averaging $28,175 per year), teaching assistantships with full tuition reimbursements (averaging $48,965 per year) were awarded; Federal Work-Study, traineeships, tuition waivers (full), and unspecified assistantships also available. Financial award application deadline: 6/30. *Faculty research:* HIV, health disparities, teen violence, women and violence, neurological disorders. *Unit head:* Dr. Suane E. Sánchez, Dean, 787-758-2525 Ext. 2100, Fax: 787-281-0721, E-mail: sesanchez@rcm.upr.edu. *Application contact:* Dr. Angelica Y. Matos, Director Graduate Department, 787-758-2525, Fax: 787-281-0721.

University of Rhode Island, Graduate School, College of Nursing, Kingston, RI 02881. Offers administration (MS); clinical specialist in gerontology (MS); clinical specialist in psychiatric/mental health (MS); family nurse practitioner (MS); nurse midwifery (MS); nursing (PhD); nursing education (MS). *Accreditation:* AACN; ACNM/DOA (one or more programs are accredited). In 2006, 34 master's, 5 doctorates awarded. *Application deadline:* For fall admission, 4/15 for domestic students. Application fee: $35. *Expenses:* Tuition, state resident: full-time $6,032; part-time $335 per credit. Tuition, nonresident: full-time $17,288; part-time $960 per credit. Required fees: $65 per credit. $30 per semester. One-time fee: $80 part-time. *Unit head:* Dayle Joseph, Dean, 401-874-2766.

University of Rochester, School of Nursing, Rochester, NY 14642. Offers MS, PhD, Certificate. *Accreditation:* NLN (one or more programs are accredited). Part-time programs available. *Faculty:* 29 full-time (26 women), 19 part-time/adjunct (17 women). *Students:* 44 full-time (37 women), 145 part-time (127 women); includes 29 minority (16 African Americans, 1 American Indian/Alaska Native, 7 Asian Americans or Pacific Islanders, 5 Hispanic Americans), 2 international. Average age 38. 33 applicants, 73% accepted, 23 enrolled. In 2006, 50 master's, 1 doctorate awarded. Terminal master's awarded for partial completion of doctoral program. *Degree requirements:* For master's, comprehensive exam or thesis; for doctorate, thesis/dissertation. *Entrance requirements:* For master's, BS in nursing, minimum GPA of 3.0, course work in statistics; for doctorate, GRE General Test, MS in nursing, minimum GPA of 3.5; for Certificate, MS in nursing. Additional exam requirements/recommendations for international students: Recommended—TOEFL (minimum score 560 paper-based; 230 computer-based). *Application deadline:* For fall admission, 11/1 priority date for domestic and international students. Application fee: $25. *Financial support:* In 2006–07, 13 fellowships with full and partial tuition reimbursements (averaging $13,900 per year), 4 research assistantships (averaging $10,000 per year), 3 teaching assistantships with full and partial tuition reimbursements (averaging $2,800 per year) were awarded; scholarships/grants, traineeships, tuition waivers (partial), and unspecified assistantships also available. Support available to part-time students. Financial award application deadline: 6/30. *Faculty research:* Clinical research in aging, managing asthma in children, interventions to improve outcomes in critically ill children and their mothers, nurse home visitation studies, medical device evaluation and critical care clinical studies. Total annual research expenditures: $3.2 million. *Unit head:* Dr. Patricia Chiverton, Dean, 585-275-5451, Fax: 585-273-1268, E-mail: patricia_chiverton@urmc.rochester.edu. *Application contact:* Elaine Andolina, Director of Admissions, 585-275-2375, Fax: 585-756-8299, E-mail: elaine_andolina@urmc.rochester.edu.

University of St. Francis, College of Nursing and Allied Health, Joliet, IL 60435-6169. Offers nursing (MSN); physician assistant studies (MS). *Accreditation:* AACN. Part-time and evening/weekend programs available. *Faculty:* 10 full-time (8 women), 1 (woman) part-time/adjunct. *Students:* 61 full-time (42 women), 62 part-time (60 women); includes 30 minority (8 African Americans, 1 American Indian/Alaska Native, 8 Asian Americans or Pacific Islanders, 13 Hispanic Americans). Average age 37. 52 applicants, 77% accepted, 22 enrolled. In 2006, 30 degrees awarded. *Degree requirements:* For master's, thesis (for some programs), comprehensive exam (for some programs), registration. *Entrance requirements:* For master's, GRE General Test (MS), minimum GPA of 3.0, 2 years of work experience in clinical nursing, CPR certification, computer competency, 3 letters of recommendation, interview, RN license (MSN); minimum GPA of 2.75, clinical experience (MS). Additional exam requirements/recommendations for international students: Required—TOEFL (minimum score 550 paper-based; 213 computer-based). *Application deadline:* Applications are processed on a rolling basis. Application fee: $30. Electronic applications accepted. *Expenses: Contact institution.* Part-time tuition and fees vary according to campus/location and program. *Financial support:* In 2006–07, 45 students received support. Scholarships/grants, traineeships, tuition waivers (partial), and unspecified assistantships available. Support available to part-time students. Financial award applicants required to submit FAFSA. *Unit head:* Dr. Maria Connolly, Dean, 815-740-3463, Fax: 815-740-4243, E-mail: mconnolly@stfrancis.edu. *Application contact:* Sandra Sloka, Director of Admissions for Graduate and Degree Completion Programs, 800-735-7500, Fax: 815-740-5032, E-mail: ssloka@stfrancis.edu.

University of Saint Francis, Graduate School, Department of Nursing, Fort Wayne, IN 46808-3994. Offers MSN. *Accreditation:* AACN. Part-time and evening/weekend programs available. Postbaccalaureate distance learning degree programs offered (no on-campus study). *Faculty:* 7 full-time (6 women), 5 part-time/adjunct (all women). *Students:* 4 full-time (all women), 33 part-time (30 women); includes 1 minority (Asian American or Pacific Islander) Average age 42. 9 applicants, 67% accepted. In 2006, 6 degrees awarded. *Degree requirements:* For master's, research project. *Entrance requirements:* For master's, GRE, minimum GPA of 3.2,

Nursing—General

University of Saint Francis (continued)
Indiana RN license. *Application deadline:* For fall admission, 7/1 priority date for domestic students; for spring admission, 11/1 priority date for domestic students. Applications are processed on a rolling basis. Application fee: $20. *Financial support:* In 2006–07, 19 students received support. Federal Work-Study and unspecified assistantships available. Financial award applicants required to submit FAFSA. *Unit head:* Dr. Nancy Gillespie, Dean, 260-434-3240, Fax: 260-434-7685, E-mail: ngillespie@sf.edu. *Application contact:* James Lashdollar, Admissions Counselor, 260-434-3279, E-mail: jcashdollar@sf.edu.

University of San Diego, Hahn School of Nursing and Health Sciences, San Diego, CA 92110-2492. Offers accelerated nursing (for RNs only) (MSN); adult clinical nurse specialist (MSN, Post Master's Certificate); adult nurse practitioner (MSN, Post Master's Certificate); clinical nursing (MSN); entry-level nursing (for non-RNs) (MSN); executive nurse leader (MSN); family nurse practitioner (MSN, Post Master's Certificate); nursing science (PhD); pediatric nurse practitioner (MSN, Post Master's Certificate). *Accreditation:* AACN. Part-time and evening/weekend programs available. *Faculty:* 13 full-time (12 women), 33 part-time/adjunct (all women). *Students:* 103 full-time (85 women), 138 part-time (131 women); includes 58 minority (7 African Americans, 3 American Indian/Alaska Native, 26 Asian Americans or Pacific Islanders, 22 Hispanic Americans), 4 international. Average age 37. 261 applicants, 54% accepted, 87 enrolled. In 2006, 35 master's, 19 doctorates awarded. *Degree requirements:* For doctorate, thesis/dissertation, residency. *Entrance requirements:* For master's, GRE General Test (for entry-level nursing), BSN and current California RN licensure (for all programs except entry-level nursing); minimum GPA of 3.0; for doctorate, GRE General Test, minimum GPA of 3.5, MSN, current California RN licensure. Additional exam requirements/recommendations for international students: Required—TOEFL, TWE. *Application deadline:* Applications are processed on a rolling basis. Application fee: $45. Electronic applications accepted. *Financial support:* Scholarships/grants and traineeships available. Support available to part-time students. Financial award application deadline: 4/1; financial award applicants required to submit FAFSA. *Faculty research:* Health promotion, decision making, psychogeriatric nursing, historical nursing, leadership behavior. *Unit head:* Dr. Sally Hardin, Dean, 619-260-4550, Fax: 619-260-6814. *Application contact:* Stephen Pultz, Director of Admissions, 619-260-4524, Fax: 619-260-4158, E-mail: grads@sandiego.edu.

See Close-Up on page 1977.

University of San Francisco, School of Nursing, San Francisco, CA 94117-1080. Offers advanced practice nursing-nurse practitioner and clinical nurse specialist (MSN), including adult health nursing; nursing administration (MSN); MSN/MBA; MSN/MPA; MSN/MSIS. *Accreditation:* AACN. Part-time programs available. *Faculty:* 6 full-time (5 women), 10 part-time/adjunct (9 women). *Students:* 126 full-time (106 women), 11 part-time (10 women); includes 46 minority (3 African Americans, 36 Asian Americans or Pacific Islanders, 7 Hispanic Americans), 5 international. Average age 31. 219 applicants, 65% accepted, 47 enrolled. In 2006, 53 degrees awarded. *Entrance requirements:* For master's, minimum GPA of 3.0. *Application deadline:* Applications are processed on a rolling basis. Application fee: $40. *Expenses:* Tuition: Full-time $17,370; part-time $965 per unit. Tuition and fees vary according to degree level, campus/location and program. *Financial support:* In 2006–07, 114 students received support. Institutionally sponsored loans available. Financial award application deadline: 3/2. *Faculty research:* Direct patient/client care, providers of health care. *Unit head:* Dr. Judith Karshmer, Dean, 415-422-6681, Fax: 415-422-6877, E-mail: nursing@usfca.edu.

University of Saskatchewan, College of Graduate Studies and Research, College of Nursing, Saskatoon, SK S7N 5E5, Canada. Offers MN. Part-time programs available. *Degree requirements:* For master's, registration. *Entrance requirements:* Additional exam requirements/recommendations for international students: Required—TOEFL.

The University of Scranton, Graduate School, Department of Nursing, Scranton, PA 18510. Offers adult health nursing (MSN); family nurse practitioner (MSN, PMC); nurse anesthesia (MSN, PMC). Applicants accepted in odd-numbered years only. *Accreditation:* AACN; AANA/CANAEP. Part-time and evening/weekend programs available. *Faculty:* 13 full-time (all women), 2 part-time/adjunct (both women). *Students:* 44 full-time (29 women), 30 part-time (27 women); includes 5 minority (1 African American, 2 Asian Americans or Pacific Islanders, 2 Hispanic Americans). Average age 36. 63 applicants, 68% accepted. In 2006, 19 degrees awarded. *Degree requirements:* For master's, thesis (for some programs), capstone experience. *Entrance requirements:* For master's, BSN, minimum GPA of 3.0, Pennsylvania RN license. Additional exam requirements/recommendations for international students: Required—TOEFL (minimum score 500 paper-based; 173 computer-based), IELTS (minimum score 6). *Application deadline:* For fall admission, 9/1 for domestic students. Applications are processed on a rolling basis. Application fee: $50. *Expenses:* Tuition: Part-time $684 per credit. Required fees: $25 per term. *Financial support:* In 2006–07, 7 teaching assistantships with full and partial tuition reimbursements (averaging $4,085 per year) were awarded; career-related internships or fieldwork, Federal Work-Study, and unspecified assistantships also available. Support available to part-time students. Financial award application deadline: 3/1. *Faculty research:* Home care, doctoral education, health care of women and children, pain, health promotion and adolescence. *Unit head:* Dr. Patricia Harrington, Chair, 570-941-7673, Fax: 570-941-4201, E-mail: harringtonp1@scranton.edu. *Application contact:* Dr. Mary Jane Hanson, Director, 570-941-4060, Fax: 570-941-4201, E-mail: hansonm2@scranton.edu.

University of South Alabama, Graduate School, College of Nursing, Mobile, AL 36688-0002. Offers adult health nursing (MSN); community/mental health nursing (MSN); maternal/child nursing (MSN); nursing (DSN). *Accreditation:* AACN. *Faculty:* 25 full-time (23 women), 8 part-time/adjunct (all women). *Students:* 661 full-time (602 women), 127 part-time (108 women); includes 160 minority (123 African Americans, 6 American Indian/Alaska Native, 19 Asian Americans or Pacific Islanders, 12 Hispanic Americans), 1 international. In 2006, 166 degrees awarded. *Unit head:* Dr. Debra C. Davis, Dean, 251-434-3414.

University of South Carolina, The Graduate School, College of Nursing, Columbia, SC 29208. Offers advanced practice clinical nursing (MSN, Certificate), including acute care nurse practitioner, advanced practice clinical nursing (MSN); advanced practice nursing in primary care (MSN, Certificate); advanced practice nursing in psychiatric mental health (MSN, Certificate); clinical nursing (MSN), including acute care clinical specialist, acute care nurse practitioner (MSN, Certificate), women's health nurse practitioner; community mental health and psychiatric health nursing (MSN), including psychiatric/mental health nurse practitioner, psychiatric/mental health specialist; health nursing (MSN), including adult nurse practitioner, community/public health clinical nurse specialist, family nurse practitioner, pediatric nurse practitioner; nursing administration (MSN); nursing practice (DNP); nursing science (PhD); MPH/MSN. *Accreditation:* AACN. Part-time programs available. *Degree requirements:* For master's, thesis or alternative, comprehensive exam; for doctorate, thesis/dissertation or alternative, computer language, dissertation (PhD); research utilization project (DNP), comprehensive exam. *Entrance requirements:* For master's, GRE General Test, MAT, BS in nursing, RN license; for doctorate, GRE General Test, BSN or master's degree in nursing, previous course work in nursing theory and statistics, RN license; for Certificate, MSN. Additional exam requirements/recommendations for international students: Required—TOEFL (minimum score 570 paper-based; 230 computer-based). Electronic applications accepted. Expenses: Contact institution. *Faculty research:* Modeling theory and nursing paradigms, health promoting behaviors, violence against women, rural diabetes nursing, infant health outcomes.

University of Southern Indiana, Graduate Studies, College of Nursing and Health Professions, Program in Nursing, Evansville, IN 47712-3590. Offers MSN. Part-time programs available. Postbaccalaureate distance learning degree programs offered (minimal on-campus study). *Faculty:* 9 full-time (all women), 1 (woman) part-time/adjunct. *Students:* 8 full-time (all women), 183 part-time (167 women); includes 5 minority (2 African Americans, 1 American Indian/Alaska Native, 2 Asian Americans or Pacific Islanders). Average age 40. 52 applicants, 96% accepted, 35 enrolled. In 2006, 50 degrees awarded. *Entrance requirements:* For master's, minimum GPA of 3.0, licensure or eligibility for licensure in Indiana, 1 year or 2000 hours of clinical practice, bachelor's degree in nursing from accredited school. Additional exam requirements/recommendations for international students: Required—TOEFL (minimum score 550 paper-based; 213 computer-based). *Application deadline:* For fall admission, 2/1 for domestic students, 1/1 priority date for international students. Applications are processed on a rolling basis. Application fee: $25. *Expenses:* Tuition, state resident: full-time $3,888; part-time $216 per credit hour. Tuition, nonresident: full-time $7,688; part-time $426 per credit hour. Required fees: $220; $23 per term. Tuition and fees vary according to course load and reciprocity agreements. *Financial support:* In 2006–07, 76 students received support. Federal Work-Study, scholarships/grants, tuition waivers (full and partial), and unspecified assistantships available. Financial award application deadline: 3/1; financial award applicants required to submit FAFSA. *Unit head:* Dr. Ann H. White, Director, 812-465-1154, E-mail: awhite@usi.edu.

University of Southern Maine, College of Nursing and Health Professions, Portland, ME 04104-9300. Offers adult health nursing (PMC); clinical nurse leader (MS); clinical nurse specialist psychiatric-mental health nursing (MS); family nursing (PMC); medical/surgical nursing (MS); nurse practitioner adult health nursing (MS); nurse practitioner family nursing (MS); nurse practitioner psychiatric/mental health nursing (MS); psychiatric-mental health nursing (PMC); MBA/MSN. *Accreditation:* AACN. Part-time programs available. *Faculty:* 13 full-time (all women), 5 part-time/adjunct (4 women). *Students:* 55 full-time (53 women), 52 part-time (50 women); includes 6 minority (all Asian Americans or Pacific Islanders) Average age 36. 88 applicants, 93% accepted, 57 enrolled. In 2006, 25 degrees awarded. *Degree requirements:* For master's, thesis optional. *Entrance requirements:* For master's, GRE General Test or MAT, minimum GPA of 3.0. Additional exam requirements/recommendations for international students: Required—TOEFL (minimum score 550 paper-based; 213 computer-based). *Application deadline:* Applications are processed on a rolling basis. Application fee: $50. Electronic applications accepted. *Expenses:* Tuition, state resident: full-time $4,860; part-time $270 per credit hour. Tuition, nonresident: full-time $13,572; part-time $754 per credit hour. Required fees: $222 per semester. Tuition and fees vary according to course load. *Financial support:* In 2006–07, 14 students received support, including 5 research assistantships with tuition reimbursements available (averaging $3,375 per year), 7 teaching assistantships with tuition reimbursements available (averaging $3,375 per year); career-related internships or fieldwork, Federal Work-Study, scholarships/grants, traineeships, tuition waivers (full and partial), and unspecified assistantships also available. Support available to part-time students. Financial award application deadline: 2/15; financial award applicants required to submit FAFSA. *Faculty research:* Women's health, nursing history, weight control, community services, substance abuse. *Unit head:* Susan Sepples, Director of Nursing Program, 207-780-4505, Fax: 207-228-8177, E-mail: sepples@usm.maine.edu. *Application contact:* Mary Sloan, Director of Graduate Admissions, 207-780-4386, Fax: 207-780-4969, E-mail: gradstudies@usm.maine.edu.

University of Southern Mississippi, Graduate School, College of Health, School of Nursing, Hattiesburg, MS 39406-0001. Offers adult health nursing (MSN); community health nursing (MSN); ethics (PhD); family nurse practitioner (MSN); leadership (PhD); nursing service administration (MSN); policy analysis (PhD); psychiatric nursing (MSN). *Accreditation:* AACN. Part-time and evening/weekend programs available. *Faculty:* 14 full-time (all women). *Students:* 39 full-time (31 women), 69 part-time (62 women); includes 18 minority (15 African Americans, 1 Asian American or Pacific Islander, 2 Hispanic Americans), 1 international. Average age 39. 46 applicants, 50% accepted, 17 enrolled. In 2006, 36 master's, 6 doctorates awarded. *Degree requirements:* For master's, thesis optional; for doctorate, thesis/dissertation, comprehensive exam, registration. *Entrance requirements:* For master's, GRE General Test, minimum GPA of 2.75, nursing license, BS in nursing; for doctorate, GRE General Test, master's degree in nursing, minimum GPA of 3.5. Additional exam requirements/recommendations for international students: Required—TOEFL. *Application deadline:* For fall admission, 3/15 priority date for domestic students, 5/1 for international students. Applications are processed on a rolling basis. Application fee: $25 ($30 for international students). Electronic applications accepted. *Financial support:* In 2006–07, 1 research assistantship with full tuition reimbursement (averaging $10,125 per year), 1 teaching assistantship (averaging $10,125 per year) were awarded; Federal Work-Study and traineeships also available. Financial award application deadline: 3/15. *Faculty research:* Gerontology, caregivers, HIV, bereavement, pain, nursing leadership. *Unit head:* Dr. Katherine Nugent, Director and Associate Dean, 601-266-5500, Fax: 601-266-5927. *Application contact:* Dr. Anne Brock, Graduate Coordinator, 601-266-5500, Fax: 601-266-5927.

University of South Florida, Graduate School, College of Nursing, Tampa, FL 33620-9951. Offers MS, PhD. *Accreditation:* AACN; NLN (one or more programs are accredited). Part-time programs available. *Faculty:* 41 full-time (36 women), 10 part-time/adjunct (8 women). *Students:* 122 full-time (110 women), 206 part-time (186 women); includes 58 minority (30 African Americans, 1 American Indian/Alaska Native, 9 Asian Americans or Pacific Islanders, 18 Hispanic Americans), 1 international. Average age 33. 13 applicants, 100% accepted, 13 enrolled. In 2006, 58 master's, 3 doctorates awarded. *Degree requirements:* For master's, thesis optional; for doctorate, thesis/dissertation. *Entrance requirements:* For master's and doctorate, GRE General Test. *Application deadline:* For fall admission, 6/1 for domestic students, 6/15 for international students; for spring admission, 10/15 for domestic and international students. Applications are processed on a rolling basis. Application fee: $30. *Financial support:* Federal Work-Study, institutionally sponsored loans, scholarships/grants, traineeships, tuition waivers (partial), and unspecified assistantships available. Financial award application deadline: 2/1; financial award applicants required to submit FAFSA. *Faculty research:* Aging, oncology, substance abuse, domestic violence, acute and chronic illness, women's health issues. Total annual research expenditures: $2.8 million. *Unit head:* Dr. Patricia A. Burns, Dean, 813-974-7813, Fax: 813-974-5418, E-mail: pburns@hsc.usf.edu. *Application contact:* Carl H. Storck, Director of Student Affairs, 813-974-7513, Fax: 813-974-3118, E-mail: cstorck@hsc.usf.edu.

See Close-Up on page 1979.

The University of Tampa, Nursing Program, Tampa, FL 33606-1490. Offers adult nurse practitioner (MSN); family nurse practitioner (MSN); nursing administration (MSN); nursing education (MSN). *Accreditation:* NLN. Part-time and evening/weekend programs available. *Faculty:* 5 full-time (all women), 10 part-time/adjunct (9 women). *Students:* 3 full-time (all women), 67 part-time (63 women); includes 2 minority (both African Americans), 1 international. Average age 40. 46 applicants, 61% accepted, 18 enrolled. In 2006, 29 degrees awarded. *Degree requirements:* For master's, oral exam, practicum, thesis optional. *Entrance requirements:* For master's, GRE General Test, minimum GPA of 3.0, RN license. *Application deadline:* For fall admission, 8/20 priority date for domestic students. Applications are processed on a rolling basis. Application fee: $40. Electronic applications accepted. *Expenses:* Tuition: Part-time $426 per credit hour. Required fees: $35 per year. *Financial support:* In 2006–07, 2 students received support, including 2 research assistantships with tuition reimbursements available (averaging $1,500 per year); career-related internships or fieldwork and unspecified assistantships also available. Support available to part-time students. Financial award applicants required to submit FAFSA. *Faculty research:* Domestic violence (assessment in emergency departments, changing demographics), transcultural health assessment, priorities in maintaining autonomy of elderly. *Unit head:* Dr. Nancy Ross, Director, 813-253-6223, Fax: 813-258-7214, E-mail: nross@ut.edu. *Application contact:* Barbara P. Strickler, Vice President for Enrollment, 888-646-2738, Fax: 813-258-7398, E-mail: admissions@ut.edu.

The University of Tennessee, Graduate School, College of Nursing, Knoxville, TN 37996. Offers MSN, PhD. *Accreditation:* AACN; AANA/CANAEP. Part-time programs available. *Faculty:* 41 full-time (38 women). *Students:* 115 full-time (96 women), 62 part-time (55 women). In 2006, 57 master's, 5 doctorates awarded. *Degree requirements:* For master's, thesis or alternative; for doctorate, thesis/dissertation. *Entrance requirements:* For master's and doctorate, GRE General Test, minimum GPA of 2.7. Additional exam requirements/recommendations for international students: Required—TOEFL. *Application deadline:* For fall admission, 2/1 priority date for domestic students. Applications are processed on a rolling basis. Application fee: $35. Electronic applications accepted. *Expenses:* Tuition, state resident: full-time $5,574. Tuition, nonresident: full-time $16,840. Required fees: $792. *Financial support:* In 2006–07, 3 fellowships, 1 research assistantship were awarded; teaching assistantships, Federal Work-Study, institutionally sponsored loans, and unspecified assistantships also available. Financial award application deadline: 2/1; financial award applicants required to submit FAFSA. *Unit head:* Dr. Joan L. Creasia, Dean, 865-974-4151, Fax: 865-974-3569, E-mail: jcreasia@utk.edu. *Application contact:* Dr. Martha Alligood, Graduate Representative, 865-974-7606, E-mail: stuservices@cn.gw.utk.edu.

The University of Tennessee at Chattanooga, Graduate School, College of Health, Education and Professional Studies, School of Nursing, Chattanooga, TN 37403-2598. Offers administration (MSN); adult health (MSN); education (MSN); family nurse practitioner (MSN); nurse anesthesia (MSN). *Accreditation:* AACN; AANA/CANAEP. *Faculty:* 13 full-time (all women). *Students:* 40 full-time (32 women), 47 part-time (41 women); includes 9 minority (1 African American, 2 American Indian/Alaska Native, 4 Asian Americans or Pacific Islanders, 2 Hispanic Americans). Average age 34. 14 applicants, 71% accepted, 2 enrolled. In 2006, 29 degrees awarded. *Degree requirements:* For master's, qualifying exams. *Entrance requirements:* For master's, GRE General Test, MAT, BSN, minimum GPA of 3.0, eligibility for Tennessee RN license. *Application deadline:* For fall admission, 8/1 priority date for domestic students; for spring admission, 12/1 priority date for domestic students. Applications are processed on a rolling basis. Application fee: $30. *Expenses:* Tuition, state resident: full-time $5,434; part-time $339 per hour. Tuition, nonresident: full-time $14,830; part-time $861 per hour. Required fees: $940; $178 per hour. *Financial support:* Application deadline: 4/1; *Faculty research:* Diabetes in women; health care for elderly; alternative medicine; hypertension; nurse anesthesia. Total annual research expenditures: $357,538. *Unit head:* Dr. Kay R. Lindgren, Head, 423-425-4646, Fax: 423-425-4668, E-mail: kay-lindgren@utc.edu. *Application contact:* Dr. Deborah E. Arfken, Dean of Graduate Studies, 423-425-4666, Fax: 423-425-5223, E-mail: deborah-arfken@utc.edu.

The University of Tennessee Health Science Center, College of Graduate Health Sciences and College of Nursing, PhD Program in Nursing, Memphis, TN 38163-0002. Offers PhD. Part-time programs available. *Faculty:* 10 full-time (9 women), 1 (woman) part-time/adjunct. *Students:* 28 full-time (all women), 2 part-time (both women); includes 12 minority (11 African Americans, 1 Asian American or Pacific Islander). Average age 38. 10 applicants, 70% accepted, 7 enrolled. In 2006, 3 degrees awarded. *Degree requirements:* For doctorate, thesis/dissertation, oral and written preliminary and comprehensive exams. *Entrance requirements:* For doctorate, GRE General Test, minimum GPA of 3.0. Additional exam requirements/recommendations for international students: Required—TOEFL. *Application deadline:* For fall admission, 2/1 for domestic and international students. Application fee: $0. Electronic applications accepted. *Expenses:* Tuition, state resident: full-time $8,267. Tuition, nonresident: full-time $20,747. Required fees: $60. One-time fee: $55 full-time. *Financial support:* In 2006–07, 1 fellowship, 3 research assistantships, 4 teaching assistantships were awarded; institutionally sponsored loans, traineeships, tuition waivers (full), and unspecified assistantships also available. Financial award application deadline: 2/28; financial award applicants required to submit FAFSA. *Faculty research:* Obesity in children, genetic markers in transplantation, relative caregivers, quality of life, renal transplantation. Total annual research expenditures: $407,000. *Unit head:* Dr. Donna Hathaway, Dean, 901-448-6135, Fax: 901-448-4121, E-mail: dhathaway@utmem.edu. *Application contact:* Sahar A. Khalifa, Counselor, Enrollment Services, 901-448-4854, E-mail: skhalifa@utmem.edu.

The University of Tennessee Health Science Center, College of Nursing, Memphis, TN 38163-0002. Offers MSN, DNP, PhD. *Accreditation:* AACN; AANA/CANAEP. Postbaccalaureate distance learning degree programs offered (minimal on-campus study). *Faculty:* 19 full-time (17 women), 8 part-time/adjunct (5 women). *Students:* 240 full-time (197 women), 1 (woman) part-time; includes 53 minority (47 African Americans, 1 Asian American or Pacific Islander, 5 Hispanic Americans). Average age 29. 225 applicants, 43% accepted, 79 enrolled. In 2006, 31 master's, 5 doctorates awarded. *Degree requirements:* For master's and doctorate, thesis/dissertation. *Entrance requirements:* For master's, GRE General Test, BSN, minimum GPA of 3.0; for doctorate, minimum GPA of 3.0. Additional exam requirements/recommendations for international students: Required—TOEFL. *Application deadline:* For fall admission, 2/1 for domestic students; for winter admission, 9/1 for domestic students. Application fee: $50. Electronic applications accepted. *Expenses:* Contact institution. One-time fee: $55 full-time. *Financial support:* In 2006–07, 44 students received support; fellowships with partial tuition reimbursements available, teaching assistantships, Federal Work-Study, institutionally sponsored loans, scholarships/grants, and traineeships available. Support available to part-time students. Financial award application deadline: 2/28; financial award applicants required to submit FAFSA. *Unit head:* Dr. Donna Hathaway, Dean, 901-448-6135, Fax: 901-448-4121, E-mail: dhathaway@utmem.edu. *Application contact:* Eunice Taylor, Interim Director, Enrollment Services, 901-448-5560, Fax: 901-448-7772, E-mail: etaylor@utmem.edu.

The University of Texas at Arlington, Graduate School, School of Nursing, Arlington, TX 76019. Offers administration/supervision of nursing (MSN); nurse practitioner (MSN); nursing science (PhD); teaching of nursing (MSN). *Accreditation:* AACN. Part-time and evening/weekend programs available. *Faculty:* 22 full-time (21 women), 11 part-time/adjunct (10 women). *Students:* 52 full-time (50 women), 334 part-time (310 women); includes 86 minority (37 African Americans, 6 American Indian/Alaska Native, 24 Asian Americans or Pacific Islanders, 19 Hispanic Americans), 18 international. Average age 37. 178 applicants, 96% accepted, 117 enrolled. In 2006, 30 degrees awarded. *Degree requirements:* For master's, comprehensive exam, thesis or master's completion project; for doctorate, thesis/dissertation, diagnostic exam after 18 hours. *Entrance requirements:* For master's, GRE General Test, minimum GPA of 3.0, Texas nursing license, minimum C in undergraduate statistics course, physical assessment course within last 3 years; for doctorate, GRE General Test, minimum undergraduate, graduate and statistics GPA of 3.0; Texas RN license; interview; 3 letters of reference. Additional exam requirements/recommendations for international students: Required—TOEFL (minimum score 550 paper-based; 213 computer-based). *Application deadline:* For fall admission, 6/16 for domestic students. Applications are processed on a rolling basis. Application fee: $35 ($50 for international students). *Expenses:* Tuition, state resident: full-time $5,528. Tuition, nonresident: full-time $10,478. International tuition: $10,608 full-time. *Financial support:* In 2006–07, 37 students received support, including 24 fellowships with partial tuition reimbursements available (averaging $3,000 per year), 6 research assistantships (averaging $7,992 per year), 7 teaching assistantships (averaging $10,080 per year); career-related internships or fieldwork and traineeships also available. Financial award application deadline: 6/1; financial award applicants required to submit FAFSA. *Unit head:* Dr. Elizabeth C. Poster, Dean, 817-272-2776, Fax: 817-272-5006, E-mail: poster@uta.edu. *Application contact:* Dr. Susan Grove, Graduate Adviser, 817-272-2776, Fax: 817-272-5006, E-mail: grove@uta.edu.

The University of Texas at Austin, Graduate School, School of Nursing, Austin, TX 78712-1111. Offers MSN, PhD. *Accreditation:* AACN. Part-time programs available. *Degree requirements:* For master's, thesis optional; for doctorate, thesis/dissertation. *Entrance requirements:* For master's and doctorate, GRE General Test. Additional exam requirements/recommendations for international students: Required—TOEFL (minimum score 550 paper-based; 213 computer-based). Electronic applications accepted. *Faculty research:* Chronic illness management, memory and aging, health promotion, women's health, adolescent health.

The University of Texas at El Paso, Graduate School, College of Health Sciences, School of Nursing, El Paso, TX 79968-0001. Offers community health (MSN); community health/family nurse practitioner (MSN); nurse midwifery (MSN); nursing administration (MSN); nursing-clinical (MSN); post master's nursing (MSN); women's health care (MSN). *Accreditation:* AACN. *Degree requirements:* For master's, thesis optional. *Entrance requirements:* For master's, GRE General Test or MAT, BSN, minimum GPA of 3.0, previous course work in statistics. Additional exam requirements/recommendations for international students: Required—TOEFL. Electronic applications accepted.

The University of Texas at Tyler, College of Nursing and Health Sciences, Program in Nursing, Tyler, TX 75799-0001. Offers nurse practitioner (MSN); nursing administration (MSN); nursing education (MSN); MSN/MBA. *Accreditation:* AACN. Part-time and evening/weekend programs available. Postbaccalaureate distance learning degree programs offered (no on-campus study). *Faculty:* 14 full-time (13 women), 4 part-time/adjunct (3 women). *Students:* 13 full-time (11 women), 134 part-time (122 women); includes 25 minority (16 African Americans, 2 American Indian/Alaska Native, 2 Asian Americans or Pacific Islanders, 5 Hispanic Americans). Average age 39. 37 applicants, 32 enrolled. In 2006, 15 degrees awarded. *Degree requirements:* For master's, thesis (for some programs), comprehensive exam (for some programs). *Entrance requirements:* For master's, GRE General Test or MAT, GMAT, minimum undergraduate GPA of 3.0, course work in statistics, RN license, BSN. *Application deadline:* For fall admission, 3/1 priority date for domestic students; for spring admission, 10/1 priority date for domestic students. Applications are processed on a rolling basis. Application fee: $0. Electronic applications accepted. *Expenses:* Tuition, state resident: part-time $50 per credit hour. Tuition, nonresident: part-time $328 per credit hour. Required fees: $107 per credit hour. $426 per term. *Financial support:* In 2006–07, 15 students received support, including 12 fellowships, 3 research assistantships (averaging $2,200 per year); institutionally sponsored loans and scholarships/grants also available. Financial award application deadline: 8/1; financial award applicants required to submit FAFSA. *Faculty research:* Psychosocial adjustment, aging, support/commitment of caregivers, psychological abuse and violence, hope/hopelessness, professional values, end of life cave, suicidology, clinical supervision, workforce retention and issues, global health issues. *Unit head:* Dr. Susan Yarbrough, Assistant Dean, 903-566-1220, E-mail: syarbrou@mail.uttyl.edu. *Application contact:* Bonnie Purser, Office of Graduate Studies, 903-566-7142, Fax: 903-566-7068, E-mail: bpurser@uttyler.edu.

The University of Texas Health Science Center at Houston, School of Nursing, Houston, TX 77225-0036. Offers MSN, DNP, DSN, MSN/MPH. *Accreditation:* AACN; AANA/CANAEP. Part-time programs available. *Faculty:* 76 full-time (69 women), 25 part-time/adjunct (23 women). *Students:* 225 full-time (125 women), 188 part-time (169 women); includes 113 minority (47 African Americans, 2 American Indian/Alaska Native, 34 Asian Americans or Pacific Islanders, 30 Hispanic Americans), 11 international. Average age 41. 308 applicants, 38% accepted, 94 enrolled. In 2006, 124 master's, 9 doctorates awarded. *Degree requirements:* For master's, thesis, research project, or clinical project; for doctorate, thesis/dissertation. *Entrance requirements:* For master's, GRE or MAT, BSN, Texas RN license, related work experience, interview, writing sample; for doctorate, GRE, interview, Texas RN license, portfolio, masters degree. Additional exam requirements/recommendations for international students: Required—TOEFL (minimum score 550 paper-based; 213 computer-based; 79 iBT). *Application deadline:* For fall admission, 5/1 priority date for domestic students. Applications are processed on a rolling basis. Application fee: $30. Electronic applications accepted. *Financial support:* In 2006–07, 101 students received support; research assistantships with tuition reimbursements available, teaching assistantships with tuition reimbursements available, institutionally sponsored loans, scholarships/grants, traineeships, and tuition waivers (full) available. Support available to part-time students. *Faculty research:* Malnutrition in institutionalized elderly, defining nursing, sensitive outcome measures, substance abuse in mothers during pregnancy, psychoeducational intervention among caregivers of stroke patients. Total annual research expenditures: $150,000. *Unit head:* Dr. Patricia Starck, Dean, 713-500-2100, Fax: 713-500-2107. *Application contact:* Laurie G. Rutherford, Student Affairs, 713-500-2101, Fax: 713-500-2107, E-mail: laurie.g.rutherford@uth.tmc.edu.

The University of Texas Health Science Center at San Antonio, Graduate School of Biomedical Sciences, School of Nursing, San Antonio, TX 78229-3900. Offers MSN, PhD. *Accreditation:* AACN. Part-time programs available. *Faculty:* 36 full-time (all women), 2 part-time/adjunct (0 women). *Students:* 40 full-time (32 women), 197 part-time (171 women); includes 91 minority (21 African Americans, 10 Asian Americans or Pacific Islanders, 60 Hispanic Americans). Average age 40. 116 applicants, 53% accepted, 45 enrolled. In 2006, 58 master's, 2 doctorates awarded. Terminal master's awarded for partial completion of doctoral program. *Median time to degree:* Master's–2 years full-time, 3 years part-time; doctorate–3.5 years full-time, 5 years part-time. Of those who began their doctoral program in fall 1998, 80% received their degree in 8 years or less. *Degree requirements:* For master's, thesis/dissertation, registration; for doctorate, thesis/dissertation, comprehensive exam, registration. *Entrance requirements:* For master's, minimum GPA of 3.0, work experience, personal interview; for doctorate, GRE, MAT, minimum GPA of 3.0, personal interview. *Application deadline:* For fall admission, 2/1 for domestic students; for spring admission, 9/1 for domestic students. Application fee: $45. *Expenses:* Tuition, state resident: part-time $50 per credit hour. Tuition, nonresident: part-time $325 per credit hour. Required fees: $7.5 per credit hour. $155 per term. *Financial support:* In 2006–07, 37 students received support; research assistantships, teaching assistantships, institutionally sponsored loans and scholarships/grants available. Financial award application deadline: 4/1. *Faculty research:* Pain, wound healing, organizational structure, aging, AIDS. *Unit head:* Dr. Robin Froman, Dean, 210-567-5800, E-mail: froman@uthscsa.edu. *Application contact:* Dr. Beverly Robinson, Associate Dean for Graduate Nursing Program and Director of Doctoral Studies, 210-567-5815, Fax: 210-567-3813, E-mail: robinsonb@uthscsa.edu.

The University of Texas Medical Branch, Graduate School of Biomedical Sciences, Doctoral Program in Nursing, Galveston, TX 77555. Offers PhD. *Faculty:* 10 full-time (9 women). *Students:* 20 full-time (17 women), 23 part-time (21 women); includes 16 minority (8 African Americans, 1 American Indian/Alaska Native, 4 Asian Americans or Pacific Islanders, 3 Hispanic Americans). Average age 48. 16 applicants, 69% accepted, 11 enrolled. In 2006, 5 degrees awarded. *Degree requirements:* For doctorate, thesis/dissertation, comprehensive exam, registration. *Entrance requirements:* For doctorate, GRE General Test, minimum GPA of 3.0, BSN and MSN or equivalent advanced degree, 2 writing samples, 3 letters of reference, curriculum vitae or resumé. Additional exam requirements/recommendations for international students: Required—TOEFL (minimum score 550 paper-based; 213 computer-based). *Application deadline:* For fall admission, 3/1 for domestic students, 3/1 priority date for international students. Applications are processed on a rolling basis. Application fee: $30 ($75 for international students). Electronic applications accepted. *Financial support:* In 2006–07, 2 teaching assistantships (averaging $25,000 per year) were awarded; scholarships/grants and unspecified assistantships also available. Financial award applicants required to submit FAFSA. *Unit head:* Dr. Alice T. Hill, Director, 409-772-8251, Fax: 409-747-1550, E-mail: ahill@utmb.edu. *Application contact:* Anita T. Padilla, Administrative Secretary, 409-747-1528, Fax: 409-747-1550, E-mail: apadilla@utmb.edu.

The University of Texas Medical Branch, School of Nursing, Master's Program in Nursing, Galveston, TX 77555. Offers MSN. *Students:* 38 full-time (32 women), 167 part-time (151 women); includes 40 minority (20 African Americans, 20 Hispanic Americans). Average age 40. In 2006, 50 degrees awarded. *Entrance requirements:* For master's, GRE General Test or MAT, minimum BSN GPA of 3.0, 3 references, interview, 1 year nursing experience. Additional exam requirements/recommendations for international students: Required—TOEFL (minimum score 550 paper-based). *Unit head:* Dr. Christine A. Boodley, Associate Director, 404-772-8310, Fax: 404-772-8323, E-mail: cbray@utmb.edu. *Application contact:* Maria D. Castro, Special Programs Coordinator I, 409-747-1548, Fax: 409-747-1522, E-mail: mdcastro@utmb.edu.

The University of Texas–Pan American, College of Health Sciences and Human Services, Department of Nursing, Edinburg, TX 78541-2999. Offers adult health nursing (MSN); family nurse practitioner (MSN); pediatric nurse practitioner (MSN). *Accreditation:* AACN. Part-time and evening/weekend programs available. *Faculty:* 8 full-time (7 women). *Students:* 19 applicants, 100% accepted, 19 enrolled. In 2006, 22 degrees awarded. *Median time to degree:* Master's–3 years part-time. *Degree requirements:* For master's, thesis optional. *Entrance requirements:* For master's, Texas RN licensure, undergraduate physical assessment courses. Additional exam requirements/recommendations for international students: Required—TOEFL (minimum score 550 paper-based). *Application deadline:* Applications are processed on a rolling basis. Application fee: $35. Electronic applications accepted. *Expenses:* Contact institution.

Nursing—General

The University of Texas–Pan American (continued)
Financial support: In 2006–07, 15 students received support. Scholarships/grants and traineeships available. *Faculty research:* Health promotion, adolescent pregnancy, herbal and nontraditional approaches, healing touch stress. Total annual research expenditures: $5,000. *Unit head:* Dr. Carolina G. Huerta, Chair, 956-381-3495, Fax: 956-381-2384, E-mail: chuerta@panam.edu. *Application contact:* Dr. Janice A. Maville, Professor and Interim Chair, 956-316-3491, Fax: 956-318-5238, E-mail: jmaville@utpa.edu.

University of the Incarnate Word, School of Graduate Studies and Research, School of Nursing and Health Professions, Program in Nursing, San Antonio, TX 78209-6397. Offers MSN. *Accreditation:* AACN. Part-time and evening/weekend programs available. *Students:* 5 full-time (4 women), 39 part-time (35 women); includes 24 minority (7 African Americans, 1 American Indian/Alaska Native, 3 Asian Americans or Pacific Islanders, 13 Hispanic Americans). Average age 42. In 2006, 18 degrees awarded. *Degree requirements:* For master's, comprehensive exam or thesis. *Entrance requirements:* For master's, GRE General Test, minimum GPA of 3.0. Additional exam requirements/recommendations for international students: Required—TOEFL. *Application deadline:* For fall admission, 8/15 priority date for domestic students; for spring admission, 12/31 for domestic students. Applications are processed on a rolling basis. Application fee: $20. *Expenses:* Tuition: Part-time $570 per credit hour. Required fees: $54 per credit hour. One-time fee: $195 part-time. Tuition and fees vary according to degree level. *Financial support:* Federal Work-Study, scholarships/grants, and traineeships available. Support available to part-time students. Financial award application deadline: 3/1. *Faculty research:* Learning styles, epilepsy, menopausal women, addictive behavior, adolescent pregnancy. *Unit head:* Dr. Sandra Strickland, Chairman, 210-829-3988, Fax: 210-829-3174, E-mail: strickla@uiwtx.edu. *Application contact:* Andrea Cyterski-Acosta, Dean of Enrollment, 210-829-6005, Fax: 210-829-3921, E-mail: cyterski@uiwtx.edu.

The University of Toledo, College of Graduate Studies, College of Nursing, Toledo, OH 43606-3390. Offers advanced practice nursing (MSN), including clinical nurse specialist, family nurse practitioner. *Accreditation:* AACN. Part-time programs available. *Faculty:* 29 full-time. *Students:* 64 full-time (58 women), 151 part-time (144 women); includes 13 minority (10 African Americans, 1 Asian American or Pacific Islander, 2 Hispanic Americans), 4 international. Average age 38. 129 applicants, 75% accepted, 87 enrolled. In 2006, 36 master's, 4 other advanced degrees awarded. *Degree requirements:* For master's, thesis or scholarly project. *Entrance requirements:* For master's, GRE General Test, BS in nursing, minimum undergraduate GPA of 3.0. *Application deadline:* For fall admission, 5/1 for domestic students; for spring admission, 9/1 for domestic students. Application fee: $45. *Expenses:* Contact institution. *Financial support:* Federal Work-Study, institutionally sponsored loans, and scholarships/grants available. *Faculty research:* Sexuality issues, prenatal testing, health care of homeless, nursing education, chronic/acute pain, eating disorders, low birth weight infants. Total annual research expenditures: $399,038. *Unit head:* Dr. Jeri Millstead, Dean, 419-383-5858, Fax: 419-383-6140, E-mail: mcogradschool@mco.edu. *Application contact:* Dr. Janet Robinson, Associate Dean, 419-383-5820, E-mail: jrobinson@mco.edu.

University of Toronto, School of Graduate Studies, Life Sciences Division, Department of Nursing Science, Toronto, ON M5S 1A1, Canada. Offers MN, PhD, Certificate, Diploma, MBA/MN. Part-time programs available. *Degree requirements:* For doctorate, thesis/dissertation, departmental and final oral exam/thesis defense. *Entrance requirements:* For master's, B Sc N or equivalent, minimum B average in next-to-final year, resumé, (MN), 3 letters of reference (MN); for doctorate, minimum B+ average, master's degree in nursing or a related area, resumé, 2 letters of recommendation. Expenses: Contact institution.

University of Utah, The Graduate School, College of Nursing, Program in Nursing, Salt Lake City, UT 84112-1107. Offers MS, PhD. Part-time programs available. *Faculty:* 51 full-time (46 women), 15 part-time/adjunct (13 women). *Students:* 100 full-time (90 women), 120 part-time (104 women); includes 17 minority (1 African American, 1 American Indian/Alaska Native, 7 Asian Americans or Pacific Islanders, 8 Hispanic Americans), 2 international. Average age 37. 119 applicants, 62% accepted, 60 enrolled. In 2006, 78 master's, 3 doctorates awarded. *Median time to degree:* Of those who began their doctoral program in fall 1998, 50% received their degree in 8 years or less. *Degree requirements:* For master's, thesis or project; for doctorate, thesis/dissertation. *Entrance requirements:* For master's, GRE General Test, Utah RN license; for doctorate, GRE General Test, interview, Utah RN license. Additional exam requirements/recommendations for international students: Required—TOEFL (minimum score 500 paper-based; 173 computer-based). *Application deadline:* For fall admission, 7/1 for domestic students. Application fee: $45 ($65 for international students). *Expenses:* Contact institution. Tuition and fees vary according to class time and program. *Financial support:* In 2006–07, 32 fellowships (averaging $7,250 per year), 13 teaching assistantships (averaging $9,000 per year) were awarded. Financial award application deadline: 3/15. *Faculty research:* Psysocial, physiological, first child. Total annual research expenditures: $1.9 million. *Application contact:* Carrie Radmall, Manager, 801-581-8798, Fax: 801-581-4642, E-mail: carrie.radmall@nurs.utah.edu.

University of Vermont, Graduate College, College of Nursing and Health Sciences, Department of Nursing, Burlington, VT 05405. Offers MS. *Accreditation:* AACN. *Students:* 42 (39 women); includes 4 minority (1 African American, 3 Asian Americans or Pacific Islanders). 77 applicants, 39% accepted, 24 enrolled. In 2006, 7 degrees awarded. *Entrance requirements:* For master's, GRE General Test. Additional exam requirements/recommendations for international students: Required—TOEFL (minimum score 550 paper-based; 213 computer-based). *Application deadline:* For fall admission, 4/1 priority date for domestic students. Applications are processed on a rolling basis. Application fee: $40. *Expenses:* Tuition, state resident: part-time $434 per credit. Tuition, nonresident: part-time $1,096 per credit. *Financial support:* Application deadline: 3/1. *Unit head:* Dr. Gregg Newschwander, Chair, 802-656-3860.

University of Victoria, Faculty of Graduate Studies, Faculty of Human and Social Development, School of Nursing, Victoria, BC V8W 2Y2, Canada. Offers advanced nursing practice; (leadership option) (MN); advanced nursing practice; (nurse practitioner option) (MN); policy and practice (MN). PhD offered by special arrangement. Part-time programs available. Post-baccalaureate distance learning degree programs offered (no on-campus study). *Entrance requirements:* Additional exam requirements/recommendations for international students: Required—TOEFL (minimum score 575 paper-based; 233 computer-based), IELTS (minimum score 7). Electronic applications accepted.

University of Virginia, School of Nursing, Charlottesville, VA 22903. Offers MSN, PhD, MSN/MBA. *Accreditation:* AACN. *Students:* 30 full-time (28 women), 5 part-time (all women); includes 5 minority (2 African Americans, 2 Asian Americans or Pacific Islanders, 1 Hispanic American). Average age 41. 23 applicants, 57% accepted, 10 enrolled. In 2006, 8 degrees awarded. *Degree requirements:* For doctorate, thesis/dissertation, oral final, comprehensive exam. *Entrance requirements:* For master's, GRE General Test, MAT; for doctorate, GRE General Test. *Application deadline:* For fall admission, 2/1 for domestic students. Applications are processed on a rolling basis. Application fee: $60. Electronic applications accepted. *Expenses:* Contact institution. *Financial support:* Fellowships, research assistantships, teaching assistantships, Federal Work-Study and scholarships/grants available. Financial award application deadline: 3/1; financial award applicants required to submit FAFSA. *Unit head:* B. Jeanette Lancaster, Dean, 434-924-0141. *Application contact:* Clay Hysell, Assistant Dean for Graduate Student Services, 434-924-0141, E-mail: nur-osa@virginia.edu.

University of Washington, Graduate School, School of Nursing, Seattle, WA 98195. Offers MN, MS, PhD, MHA/MN, MN/MPH. *Accreditation:* AACN; ACNM/DOA (one or more programs are accredited). Part-time programs available. *Degree requirements:* For master's, thesis (for some programs); for doctorate, thesis/dissertation. *Entrance requirements:* For master's, GRE, minimum GPA of 3.0, resumé; for doctorate, GRE, minimum GPA of 3.0. Additional exam requirements/recommendations for international students: Required—TOEFL. *Faculty research:* High risk youth, pain management, women's health, oncology, sleep.

University of Washington, Bothell, Program in Nursing, Bothell, WA 98011-8246. Offers MA. *Faculty:* 8 full-time (all women), 3 part-time/adjunct (2 women). *Students:* Average age 47. 37 applicants, 78% accepted, 22 enrolled. In 2006, 12 degrees awarded. *Degree requirements:* For master's, thesis. *Entrance requirements:* For master's, GRE General Test. Additional exam requirements/recommendations for international students: Required—TOEFL. *Application deadline:* For fall admission, 3/1 priority date for domestic students. Applications are processed on a rolling basis. Application fee: $45. Electronic applications accepted. *Financial support:* Federal Work-Study and unspecified assistantships available. *Faculty research:* Human development, ethics, community health, gerontology, administration. *Unit head:* Prof. Mary Baroni, Nursing Program Director, 425-352-3543, Fax: 425-352-3237, E-mail: mbaroni@uwb.edu. *Application contact:* Judy Lynn, Administrative Coordinator, 425-352-5376, Fax: 425-352-3237, E-mail: jlynn@uwb.edu.

The University of Western Ontario, Faculty of Graduate Studies, Health Sciences Division, School of Nursing, London, ON N6A 5B8, Canada. Offers M Sc N, PhD. Part-time programs available. *Faculty:* 9 full-time (8 women), 2 part-time/adjunct (both women). *Students:* 19 full-time (18 women), 13 part-time (12 women). 23 applicants, 65% accepted, 9 enrolled. *Degree requirements:* For master's and doctorate, thesis/dissertation. *Application deadline:* For fall admission, 2/1 for domestic students. Application fee: $50. *Financial support:* In 2006–07, 15 students received support, including 5 research assistantships (averaging $7,500 per year), 10 teaching assistantships (averaging $8,900 per year). Financial award application deadline: 4/1. *Faculty research:* Empowerment, self-efficacy, family health, community health, gerontology. Total annual research expenditures: $402,600. *Unit head:* Dr. Mary-Anne Andrusyszyn, Acting Director, 519-661-6590, E-mail: maandrus@uwo.ca. *Application contact:* Dolly Goldenberg, Graduate Chair, 519-661-2111 Ext. 83409, Fax: 519-850-2514, E-mail: nursweb@uwo.ca.

University of West Georgia, Graduate School, College of Arts and Sciences, Department of Nursing, Carrollton, GA 30118. Offers MSN. *Accreditation:* AACN. Part-time programs available. *Faculty:* 8 full-time (all women). *Students:* 8 full-time (all women), 18 part-time (all women); includes 3 minority (all African Americans) Average age 36. 10 applicants, 100% accepted, 10 enrolled. In 2006, 5 degrees awarded. *Degree requirements:* For master's, thesis or alternative, comprehensive exam. *Entrance requirements:* For master's, GRE or MAT, BSN degree, Georgia RN license, 1 year nursing practice. *Application deadline:* For fall admission, 6/1 for domestic and international students. Application fee: $20. *Expenses:* Tuition, state resident: full-time $2,286; part-time $127 per credit. Tuition, nonresident: full-time $9,144; part-time $508 per credit. Required fees: $494; $27 per credit. $121 per semester. *Financial support:* In 2006–07, 13 students received support, including fellowships (averaging $7,857 per year), 1 research assistantship with full tuition reimbursement available (averaging $6,000 per year); institutionally sponsored loans also available. Financial award application deadline: 1/2; financial award applicants required to submit FAFSA. *Faculty research:* Caring in nursing education, pain assessment in older adults, pain outcomes. Total annual research expenditures: $3,000. *Unit head:* Dr. Kathryn Mary Grams, Chair, 678-839-6552, Fax: 678-839-6553, E-mail: kgrams@westga.edu. *Application contact:* Dr. Charles W. Clark, Chair, 678-839-6508, E-mail: cclark@westga.edu.

University of Windsor, Faculty of Graduate Studies and Research, Faculty of Nursing, Windsor, ON N9B 3P4, Canada. Offers M Sc, MN. *Degree requirements:* For master's, thesis or alternative. *Entrance requirements:* For master's, minimum B average, certificate of competence (nurse registration). Additional exam requirements/recommendations for international students: Required—TOEFL (minimum score 560 paper-based; 220 computer-based). Electronic applications accepted.

University of Wisconsin–Eau Claire, College of Nursing and Health Sciences, Program in Nursing, Eau Claire, WI 54702-4004. Offers MSN. *Faculty:* 15 full-time (all women), 2 part-time/adjunct (both women). *Students:* 20 full-time (all women), 47 part-time (45 women). Average age 35. 33 applicants, 94% accepted, 7 enrolled. In 2006, 15 degrees awarded. *Expenses:* Tuition, state resident: full-time $6,533; part-time $363 per credit. Tuition, nonresident: full-time $17,143; part-time $952 per credit. Tuition and fees vary according to program and reciprocity agreements. *Financial support:* In 2006–07, 31 students received support. *Unit head:* Dr. Elaine Wendt, Dean, College of Nursing and Health Sciences, 715-836-5287, Fax: 715-836-5925, E-mail: wendtle@uwec.edu.

University of Wisconsin–Madison, School of Nursing, Madison, WI 53792-2455. Offers MS, PhD, MS/MPH. *Accreditation:* AACN. Part-time programs available. Postbaccalaureate distance learning degree programs offered (no on-campus study). *Faculty:* 23 full-time (all women). *Students:* 58 full-time (all women), 145 part-time (136 women); includes 8 minority (1 African American, 1 American Indian/Alaska Native, 3 Asian Americans or Pacific Islanders, 3 Hispanic Americans). Average age 37. 79 applicants, 73% accepted, 43 enrolled. In 2006, 44 master's, 3 doctorates awarded. *Median time to degree:* Master's–2 years full-time; doctorate–3.5 years full-time. Of those who began their doctoral program in fall 1998, 100% received their degree in 8 years or less. *Degree requirements:* For master's, research practicum; for doctorate, thesis/dissertation, comprehensive exam. *Entrance requirements:* For master's, GRE General Test, 1 year professional experience recommended, BS in nursing from accredited program, course work in statistics during previous 5 years, minimum GPA 3.0 last 60 credits, professional nursing license; for doctorate, GRE General Test, 2 samples of scholarly written work, BS in nursing from an accredited program, minimum undergraduate GPA of 3.0 in last 60 credits. Additional exam requirements/recommendations for international students: Required—TOEFL (minimum score 550 paper-based; 213 computer-based). *Application deadline:* For fall admission, 3/1 priority date for domestic students; for spring admission, 10/1 priority date for domestic students. Application fee: $45. Electronic applications accepted. *Financial support:* In 2006–07, 88 students received support, including 10 fellowships with tuition reimbursements available (averaging $20,000 per year), 10 research assistantships with tuition reimbursements available (averaging $19,000 per year), 7 teaching assistantships with tuition reimbursements available (averaging $13,000 per year); career-related internships or fieldwork, Federal Work-Study, institutionally sponsored loans, scholarships/grants, traineeships, health care benefits, and unspecified assistantships also available. Support available to part-time students. Financial award application deadline: 6/1. *Faculty research:* Nursing informatics to promote self-care and disease management skills among patients and caregivers; quality of care to frail, vulnerable, and chronically ill populations; study of health-related and health-seeking behaviors; eliminating health disparities. Total annual research expenditures: $2.2 million. *Unit head:* Dr. Katharyn A. May, Dean, 608-263-5155, Fax: 608-263-5323, E-mail: kamay@wisc.edu. *Application contact:* Marcia L. Voss, Master's Program Coordinator, 608-263-5258, Fax: 608-263-5332, E-mail: mlvoss@wisc.edu.

University of Wisconsin–Milwaukee, Graduate School, College of Nursing, Milwaukee, WI 53201-0413. Offers MS, PhD, Certificate. *Accreditation:* AACN. Part-time programs available. *Faculty:* 36 full-time (35 women). *Students:* 121 full-time (109 women), 122 part-time (117 women); includes 29 minority (16 African Americans, 1 American Indian/Alaska Native, 6 Asian Americans or Pacific Islanders, 6 Hispanic Americans), 6 international. Average age 39. 110 applicants, 45% accepted, 39 enrolled. In 2006, 37 master's, 7 doctorates awarded. *Degree requirements:* For master's and doctorate, thesis/dissertation. *Entrance requirements:* For master's, GRE General Test or MAT. *Application deadline:* For fall admission, 1/1 priority date for domestic students; for spring admission, 9/1 for domestic students. Applications are processed on a rolling basis. Application fee: $45 ($75 for international students). *Expenses:* Tuition, state resident: part-time $510 per credit. Tuition, nonresident: part-time $1,408 per credit. Tuition and fees vary according to program. *Financial support:* In 2006–07, 11 teaching assistantships were awarded; fellowships, research assistantships, career-related internships or fieldwork, Federal Work-Study, and unspecified assistantships also available. Support available to part-time students. Financial award application deadline: 4/15. *Unit head:* Karen Morin, Representative, 414-229-5474, Fax: 414-229-6474. *Application contact:* Ellen K. Murphy, Representative, 414-229-5468.

University of Wisconsin–Oshkosh, The School of Graduate Studies, College of Nursing, Oshkosh, WI 54901. Offers adult health and illness (MSN); family nurse practitioner (MSN). *Accreditation:* AACN. Part-time programs available. *Degree requirements:* For master's, thesis or alternative, clinical paper. *Entrance requirements:* For master's, RN license, BSN, previous course work in statistics and health assessment, minimum undergraduate GPA of 3.0, letters of recommendation. Additional exam requirements/recommendations for international students: Required—TOEFL (minimum score 550 paper-based; 213 computer-based). Electronic applications accepted. *Faculty research:* Adult health and illness, nurse practitioners practice, health care service, advanced practitioner roles, natural alternative complementary healthcare.

University of Wyoming, Graduate School, College of Health Sciences, Fay W. Whitney School of Nursing, Laramie, WY 82070. Offers MS. *Accreditation:* AACN. Part-time programs available. Postbaccalaureate distance learning degree programs offered (no on-campus study). *Faculty:* 10 full-time (all women). *Students:* 15 full-time (12 women), 78 part-time (68 women); includes 2 minority (1 African American, 1 Hispanic American). Average age 42. 61 applicants, 56% accepted. In 2006, 21 degrees awarded. *Degree requirements:* For master's, thesis. *Entrance requirements:* For master's, GRE General Test, BSN from NLN-accredited school, minimum GPA of 3.0. *Application deadline:* For fall admission, 11/1 priority date for domestic students; for spring admission, 2/1 priority date for domestic students. Application fee: $50. *Financial support:* In 2006–07, 4 students received support, including research assistantships with full tuition reimbursements available (averaging $10,062 per year), teaching assistantships with full tuition reimbursements available (averaging $10,062 per year); career-related internships or fieldwork, institutionally sponsored loans, scholarships/grants, traineeships, and unspecified assistantships also available. Support available to part-time students. Financial award application deadline: 2/1. *Faculty research:* Support systems for the elderly, fetal alcohol syndrome, teen pregnancy, rehabilitation with chronic mental illness, global peace building among women. Total annual research expenditures: $444,522. *Unit head:* Dr. Pamela N. Clarke, Dean and Professor, 307-766-6569, Fax: 307-766-4294, E-mail: pclarke@uwyo.edu. *Application contact:* Debbie Shoefelt, Credentials Analyst / Academic Advisor, 307-766-4292, Fax: 307-766-4294, E-mail: shoefelt@uwyo.edu.

Ursuline College, School of Graduate Studies, Program in Nursing, Pepper Pike, OH 44124-4398. Offers MSN. *Accreditation:* AACN. Part-time programs available. *Faculty:* 3 full-time (all women), 5 part-time/adjunct (4 women). *Students:* Average age 40. 24 applicants, 100% accepted, 24 enrolled. In 2006, 23 degrees awarded. *Degree requirements:* For master's, comprehensive exam. *Entrance requirements:* For master's, minimum undergraduate GPA of 3.0, bachelor's degree in nursing, eligibility for or current Ohio RN license. Additional exam requirements/recommendations for international students: Required—TOEFL (minimum score 500 paper-based; 173 computer-based). *Application deadline:* For fall admission, 8/1 priority date for domestic students. Applications are processed on a rolling basis. Application fee: $25. *Expenses:* Tuition: Full-time $12,078; part-time $671 per credit hour. Required fees: $60 per semester. *Financial support:* In 2006–07, 36 students received support. Federal Work-Study available. Financial award application deadline: 3/1. *Unit head:* Director, 440-449-3425, Fax: 440-449-4267.

Valdosta State University, Graduate School, College of Nursing, Valdosta, GA 31698. Offers MSN. *Accreditation:* AACN. Part-time programs available. *Degree requirements:* For master's, thesis (for some programs), comprehensive written and/or oral exams. *Entrance requirements:* For master's, GRE General Test, minimum GPA of 2.8. Additional exam requirements/recommendations for international students: Required—TOEFL (minimum score 523 paper-based; 193 computer-based). Electronic applications accepted. *Faculty research:* Nutrition, children's health beliefs, alternative treatment modalities, job satisfaction, leadership.

Valparaiso University, Graduate Division, College of Nursing, Valparaiso, IN 46383. Offers management (Certificate); nursing (MSN, Post-Master's Certificate); MBA/MSN. *Accreditation:* AACN. Part-time and evening/weekend programs available. *Faculty:* 5 part-time/adjunct (all women). *Students:* 18 full-time (16 women), 25 part-time (24 women); includes 3 minority (2 African Americans, 1 Hispanic American). Average age 40. In 2006, 16 master's, 7 other advanced degrees awarded. *Entrance requirements:* For master's, minimum GPA of 3.0, undergraduate major in nursing. Additional exam requirements/recommendations for international students: Required—TOEFL (minimum score 550 paper-based; 213 computer-based). *Application deadline:* Applications are processed on a rolling basis. Application fee: $30 ($50 for international students). Electronic applications accepted. *Expenses:* Contact institution. Tuition and fees vary according to program. *Financial support:* Scholarships/grants available. Support available to part-time students. Financial award applicants required to submit FAFSA. *Unit head:* Dr. Janet Brown, Dean, 219-464-5289, Fax: 219-464-5425, E-mail: janet.brown@valpo.edu.

Vanderbilt University, Graduate School, Program in Nursing Science, Nashville, TN 37240-1001. Offers PhD. *Faculty:* 11 full-time (8 women). *Students:* 20 full-time (18 women); includes 1 minority (African American), 1 international. 24 applicants, 46% accepted, 7 enrolled. In 2006, 2 degrees awarded. *Degree requirements:* For doctorate, thesis/dissertation, final and qualifying exams. *Entrance requirements:* For doctorate, GRE General Test. *Application deadline:* For fall admission, 1/15 for domestic and international students. Application fee: $0. Electronic applications accepted. *Expenses:* Tuition: Full-time $24,462. Required fees: $2,515. One-time fee: $30 full-time. Full-time tuition and fees vary according to course load, degree level and program. *Financial support:* Research assistantships with full tuition reimbursements, teaching assistantships with full tuition reimbursements, career-related internships or fieldwork and tuition waivers (full and partial) available. Financial award application deadline: 1/15. *Faculty research:* Adaptation to chronic illness/conditions, health problems related to stress and coping, vulnerable childbearing and child rearing families. *Unit head:* Melanie Lutenbacher, Director, 615-322-3800, Fax: 615-343-8204, E-mail: melanie.lutenbacher@vanderbilt.edu.

Vanderbilt University, School of Nursing, Nashville, TN 37235. Offers adult acute care nurse practitioner (MSN); adult health nurse practitioner/forensic (MSN); adult nurse practitioner/cardiovascular disease management and prevention (MSN); adult nurse practitioner/palliative care (MSN); clinical management (clinical nurse leader/specialist) (MSN); family nurse practitioner (MSN); gerontology nurse practitioner (MSN); health systems management (MSN); neonatal nurse practitioner (MSN); nurse midwifery (MSN); nursing informatics (MSN); nursing science (PhD); pediatric acute care nurse practitioner (MSN); pediatric primary care nurse practitioner (MSN); psychiatric-mental health nurse practitioner (MSN); women's health nurse practitioner (MSN); MBA/MSN; MSN/MTS; MSN/PhD. *Accreditation:* ACNM/DOA; NLN (one or more programs are accredited). Part-time and evening/weekend programs available. Postbaccalaureate distance learning degree programs offered (minimal on-campus study). *Faculty:* 95 full-time (83 women), 432 part-time/adjunct (314 women). *Students:* 371 full-time (325 women), 206 part-time (180 women); includes 59 minority (38 African Americans, 2 American Indian/Alaska Native, 7 Asian Americans or Pacific Islanders, 12 Hispanic Americans). Average age 27. 611 applicants, 55% accepted, 308 enrolled. In 2006, 256 master's, 2 doctorates awarded. *Degree requirements:* For doctorate, thesis/dissertation. *Entrance requirements:* For master's, GRE, interview; for doctorate, GRE, interview, 3 letters of recommendation. Additional exam requirements/recommendations for international students: Required—TOEFL. *Application deadline:* For fall admission, 12/1 priority date for domestic and international students. Applications are processed on a rolling basis. Application fee: $50. *Expenses:* Contact institution. *Financial support:* In 2006–07, 404 students received support, including 5 research assistantships (averaging $8,000 per year); Federal Work-Study, institutionally sponsored loans, and unspecified assistantships also available. Support available to part-time students. Financial award application deadline: 3/15; financial award applicants required to submit CSS PROFILE or FAFSA. *Faculty research:* Lymphedema post cancer treatment, palliative care and bereavement, patient safety and quality of care, health care workforce issues, symptom management including pain and fatigue. Total annual research expenditures: $1.1 million. *Unit head:* Dr. Colleen Conway-Welch, Dean, 615-343-8776, Fax: 615-343-7711, E-mail: colleen.conway-welch@vanderbilt.edu. *Application contact:* Cheryl Feldner, Assistant Director of Admissions, 615-322-3800, Fax: 615-343-0333, E-mail: cheryl.feldner@vanderbilt.edu.

Villanova University, College of Nursing, Villanova, PA 19085-1690. Offers adult nurse practitioner (MSN, Post Master's Certificate); clinical case management (MSN, Post Master's Certificate); geriatric nurse practitioner (MSN, Post Master's Certificate); health care administration (MSN); nurse anesthetist (MSN, Post Master's Certificate); nursing (PhD); nursing education (MSN, Post Master's Certificate); pediatric nurse practitioner (MSN, Post Master's Certificate). *Accreditation:* AACN; AANA/CANAEP; NLN. Part-time programs available. Postbaccalaureate distance learning degree programs offered (minimal on-campus study). *Faculty:* 14 full-time (all women), 2 part-time/adjunct (both women). *Students:* 41 full-time (27 women), 164 part-time (128 women); includes 17 minority (8 African Americans, 1 American Indian/Alaska Native, 8 Asian Americans or Pacific Islanders), 6 international. Average age 31. 137 applicants, 50% accepted, 48 enrolled. In 2006, 47 degrees awarded. *Median time to degree:* Master's–2 years full-time, 5 years part-time. *Degree requirements:* For master's, independent study project; for doctorate, thesis/dissertation, comprehensive exam. *Entrance requirements:* For master's, GRE or MAT, BSN, 1 year of recent nursing experience, physical assessment, course work in statistics; for doctorate, GRE. Additional exam requirements/recommendations for international students: Required—TOEFL. *Application deadline:* For fall admission, 7/1 priority date for domestic students, 7/1 for international students; for spring admission, 12/1 priority date for domestic students, 12/1 for international students. Applications are processed on a rolling basis. Application fee: $50. *Expenses:* Contact institution. *Financial support:* In 2006–07, 50 students received support, including 4 teaching assistantships with full tuition reimbursements available (averaging $12,165 per year); institutionally sponsored loans, scholarships/grants, traineeships, and tuition waivers (full) also available. Financial award application deadline: 3/1; financial award applicants required to submit FAFSA. *Faculty research:* Genetics, ethics, cognitive development of students, women with disabilities, nursing leadership. *Unit head:* Dr. Marguerite K. Schlag, Assistant Dean and Director, Graduate Program, 610-519-4907, Fax: 610-519-7650, E-mail: marguerite.schlag@villanova.edu.

Announcement: The College offers a 45-credit master's program to prepare adult, pediatric, and geriatric nurse practitioners; nurse anesthetists; nurse educators; and health-care administrators. The 51-credit PhD program prepares teacher-scholars for rewarding careers in academic and research positions within nursing higher education.

Virginia Commonwealth University, Graduate School, School of Nursing, Richmond, VA 23284-9005. Offers adult health nursing (MS); child health nursing (MS); family health nursing (MS); health system (PhD); immunocompetence (PhD); nurse practitioner (MS, Certificate); nursing administration (MS), including clinical nurse manager, nurse executive; psychiatric-mental health nursing (MS); risk and resilience (PhD); women's health nursing (MS). *Accreditation:* NLN (one or more programs are accredited). Part-time and evening/weekend programs available. *Faculty:* 23 full-time (21 women). *Students:* 131 full-time (125 women), 137 part-time (129 women); includes 33 minority (19 African Americans, 11 Asian Americans or Pacific Islanders, 3 Hispanic Americans), 12 international. 110 applicants, 82% accepted, 66 enrolled. In 2006, 57 master's, 1 doctorate, 3 other advanced degrees awarded. *Degree requirements:* For master's, thesis optional; for doctorate, thesis/dissertation. *Entrance requirements:* For master's, GRE General Test, BSN, minimum GPA of 2.8; for doctorate, GRE General Test. *Application deadline:* For fall admission, 2/1 priority date for domestic students. Application fee: $50. *Financial support:* Fellowships, research assistantships, teaching assistantships, career-related internships or fieldwork and institutionally sponsored loans available. *Unit head:* Dr. Nancy F. Langston, Dean, 804-828-5174, Fax: 804-828-7743, E-mail: nflangst@vcu.edu. *Application contact:* Susan Lipp, Admissions Counselor, 804-828-5171, Fax: 804-828-7743, E-mail: slipp@vcu.edu.

See Close-Up on page 1983.

Viterbo University, Graduate Program in Nursing, La Crosse, WI 54601-4797. Offers MSN. *Accreditation:* AACN. Part-time programs available. Postbaccalaureate distance learning degree programs offered (minimal on-campus study). *Faculty:* 5 full-time, 5 part-time/adjunct. *Students:* 53 full-time (52 women), 17 part-time (all women); includes 1 minority (Asian American or Pacific Islander) Average age 37. In 2006, 15 degrees awarded. *Entrance requirements:* For master's, GRE General Test or MAT, bachelor's degree in nursing, minimum GPA of 3.0, RN license. *Application deadline:* For spring admission, 2/1 priority date for domestic students. Applications are processed on a rolling basis. Application fee: $25. *Expenses:* Contact institution. *Financial support:* In 2006–07, 8 students received support. Institutionally sponsored loans, scholarships/grants, and traineeships available. Financial award application deadline: 6/1; financial award applicants required to submit FAFSA. *Unit head:* Dr. Bonnie Nesbitt, Director, 608-796-3688, Fax: 608-796-3668, E-mail: bjnesbitt@viterbo.edu. *Application contact:* 608-796-3671.

Wagner College, Division of Graduate Studies, Department of Nursing, Program in Nursing, Staten Island, NY 10301-4495. Offers MS. *Accreditation:* NLN. Part-time and evening/weekend programs available. *Faculty:* 5 full-time (all women), 3 part-time/adjunct (all women). *Students:* 5 full-time (all women), 63 part-time (58 women); includes 13 minority (6 African Americans, 5 Asian Americans or Pacific Islanders, 2 Hispanic Americans). 14 applicants, 93% accepted, 11 enrolled. In 2006, 14 degrees awarded. *Degree requirements:* For master's, thesis optional. *Entrance requirements:* For master's, BS in nursing, current clinical experience, minimum GPA of 2.75. *Application deadline:* For fall admission, 8/1 priority date for domestic students; for spring admission, 12/10 for domestic students. Applications are processed on a rolling basis. Application fee: $50 ($80 for international students). *Expenses:* Tuition: Full-time $15,120; part-time $840 per credit. *Financial support:* Fellowships, traineeships and unspecified assistantships available. Financial award applicants required to submit FAFSA. *Application contact:* 718-390-3411.

Walden University, Graduate Programs, School of Health and Human Services, Minneapolis, MN 55401. Offers health services (PhD); human services (PhD); nursing (MS); public health (MPH, PhD). Part-time and evening/weekend programs available. Postbaccalaureate distance learning degree programs offered (minimal on-campus study). *Faculty:* 100. *Students:* 2,383 full-time (2,074 women), 1,082 part-time (876 women); includes 840 minority (662 African Americans, 18 American Indian/Alaska Native, 83 Asian Americans or Pacific Islanders, 77 Hispanic Americans), 24 international. Average age 42. 1,164 applicants, 85% accepted, 813 enrolled. In 2006, 212 master's, 30 doctorates awarded. *Degree requirements:* For master's, thesis (for some programs); for doctorate, thesis/dissertation. *Entrance requirements:* For master's, minimum GPA of 3.0; for doctorate, 3 years of professional experience, master's degree. Additional exam requirements/recommendations for international students: Required—TOEFL (minimum score 550 paper-based; 213 computer-based), IELTS (minimum score 7). *Application deadline:* For fall admission, 8/15 priority date for domestic and international students; for winter admission, 11/15 priority date for domestic and international students; for spring admission, 12/15 priority date for domestic and international students. Applications are processed on a rolling basis. Application fee: $50. Electronic applications accepted. *Financial support:* Fellowships with partial tuition reimbursements, tuition waivers (partial) available. Support available to part-time students. Financial award applicants required to submit FAFSA. *Unit head:* Dr. Gary J. Burkholder, Dean, 800-925-3368, Fax: 612-338-5092. *Application contact:* 866-4-WALDEN, Fax: 410-843-8780, E-mail: request@waldenu.edu.

Washington State University Spokane, Graduate Programs, Intercollegiate College of Nursing, Spokane, WA 99210-1495. Offers MN. *Faculty:* 64. *Students:* 26 full-time (21 women), 36 part-time (35 women); includes 6 minority (3 American Indian/Alaska Native, 1 Asian American or Pacific Islander, 2 Hispanic Americans). 45 applicants, 64% accepted, 22 enrolled. *Degree requirements:* For master's, thesis (for some programs), oral exam, research project, comprehensive exam (for some programs). *Entrance requirements:* For master's, minimum GPA of 3.0, Washington state RN license, physical assessment skills, course work in statistics, recommendations, written interview (nurse practitioner). *Application deadline:* For fall admission, 1/15 for domestic students; for spring admission, 8/5 for domestic students. Application fee: $50. *Expenses:* Tuition, state resident: full-time $7,066. Tuition, nonresident: full-

Nursing—General

Washington State University Spokane (continued)
time $17,204. Tuition and fees vary according to program. *Financial support:* In 2006–07, 62 students received support, including 11 fellowships (averaging $4,407 per year), 12 teaching assistantships with tuition reimbursements available (averaging $17,350 per year). *Faculty research:* Cardiovascular and type 2 diabetes in children, evaluation of strategies to increase physical activity in sedentary people. Total annual research expenditures: $1.2 million. *Unit head:* Dr. Patricia Butterfield, Dean, 509-324-7360, Fax: 509-858-7336. *Application contact:* Graduate School Admissions, 800-GRADWSU, Fax: 509-335-1949, E-mail: gradsch@wsu.edu.

Washington State University Tri-Cities, Graduate Programs, Intercollegiate College of Nursing, Richland, WA 99352-1671. Offers MN. Part-time programs available. Postbaccalaureate distance learning degree programs offered (minimal on-campus study). *Faculty:* 10. *Students:* 11 full-time (all women), 15 part-time (11 women); includes 1 minority (Hispanic American) 6 applicants, 100% accepted, 3 enrolled. *Degree requirements:* For master's, thesis (for some programs), oral exam, research project, comprehensive exam (for some programs). *Entrance requirements:* For master's, current Washington state RN license, minimum cumulative GPA of 2.5, minimum GPA of 2.0 in each nursing course. *Application deadline:* For fall admission, 1/15 for domestic students, 3/1 for international students; for spring admission, 8/5 for domestic students, 7/1 for international students. Application fee: $50. *Expenses:* Tuition, state resident: full-time $7,066. Tuition, nonresident: full-time $17,204. *Financial support:* In 2006–07, 24 students received support, including 5 fellowships (averaging $4,050 per year), 3 teaching assistantships with tuition reimbursements available (averaging $13,056 per year). *Unit head:* Lorrie Dawson, Unit Head, 509-372-7000, Fax: 509-372-7354. *Application contact:* Graduate School Admissions, 800-GRADWSU, Fax: 509-335-1949, E-mail: gradsch@wsu.edu.

Washington State University Vancouver, Graduate Programs, Intercollegiate College of Nursing, Vancouver, WA 98686. Offers MN. *Faculty:* 20. *Students:* 11 full-time (10 women), 76 part-time (72 women); includes 5 minority (1 American Indian/Alaska Native, 1 Asian American or Pacific Islander, 3 Hispanic Americans). 44 applicants, 68% accepted, 14 enrolled. *Degree requirements:* For master's, thesis (for some programs), research project, comprehensive exam (for some programs). *Entrance requirements:* For master's, Washington RN license, minimum GPA of 3.0. Additional exam requirements/recommendations for international students: Required—TOEFL. *Application deadline:* For fall admission, 2/1 for domestic and international students; for spring admission, 10/1 for domestic students, 7/1 for international students. Applications are processed on a rolling basis. Application fee: $50. Electronic applications accepted. *Expenses:* Tuition, state resident: full-time $7,066. Tuition, nonresident: full-time $17,204. *Financial support:* In 2006–07, 52 students received support, including 8 fellowships with tuition reimbursements available (averaging $5,437 per year), 2 teaching assistantships with tuition reimbursements available (averaging $17,360 per year). *Faculty research:* Cultural competence in nursing, prescribing controlled substances by Advanced Registered Nurse Practitioners, Decreasing health disparities, workforce diversity. Total annual research expenditures: $86,529. *Unit head:* Dr. Dawn Doutrich, Interim Academic Director, 360-546-9752, Fax: 360-546-9038.

Wayne State University, College of Nursing, Program in Nursing, Detroit, MI 48202. Offers PhD. Part-time programs available. *Students:* 32 full-time (30 women), 14 part-time (all women); includes 9 minority (8 African Americans, 1 Hispanic American), 6 international. Average age 46. 12 applicants, 50% accepted, 5 enrolled. In 2006, 5 degrees awarded. *Degree requirements:* For doctorate, thesis/dissertation. *Entrance requirements:* For doctorate, GRE General Test, minimum GPA of 3.3. Additional exam requirements/recommendations for international students: Required—TOEFL (minimum score 550 paper-based; 213 computer-based); Recommended—TWE (minimum score 6). *Application deadline:* For fall admission, 2/15 for domestic students, 6/1 for international students; for winter admission, 10/1 for international students; for spring admission, 2/1 for international students. Application fee: $30 ($50 for international students). Electronic applications accepted. *Financial support:* In 2006–07, 18 students received support; fellowships, research assistantships, institutionally sponsored loans and scholarships/grants available. Support available to part-time students. Financial award application deadline: 7/1. *Faculty research:* Self-care, transcultural care, adaptation to acute and chronic illness, urban health and health care systems. *Application contact:* Associate Dean, 313-577-4138.

Webster University, College of Arts and Sciences, Department of Nursing, St. Louis, MO 63119-3194. Offers MSN. *Accreditation:* NLN. *Students:* 1 (woman) full-time, 72 part-time (68 women); includes 12 minority (8 African Americans, 3 Asian Americans or Pacific Islanders, 1 Hispanic American), 1 international. Average age 45. In 2006, 24 degrees awarded. *Entrance requirements:* For master's, 1 year of clinical experience, BSN, interview, minimum C+ average in statistics and physical assessment, minimum GPA of 3.0, RN license. *Application deadline:* Applications are processed on a rolling basis. Application fee: $25 ($50 for international students). *Expenses:* Tuition: Full-time $8,820; part-time $490 per credit. Tuition and fees vary according to degree level, campus/location and program. *Financial support:* Federal Work-Study available. Support available to part-time students. Financial award application deadline: 4/1; financial award applicants required to submit FAFSA. *Faculty research:* Health teaching. *Unit head:* Susan Heady, Chair, 314-968-7176, Fax: 314-963-6101, E-mail: schappan@webster.edu. *Application contact:* Director of Graduate and Evening Student Admissions, Fax: 314-968-7116, E-mail: gadmit@webste.edu.

Wesley College, Nursing Program, Dover, DE 19901-3875. Offers MSN. *Accreditation:* NLN. Part-time and evening/weekend programs available. *Faculty:* 4 full-time (3 women). *Students:* 14 full-time (all women), 44 part-time (42 women); includes 15 minority (13 African Americans, 2 Hispanic Americans). Average age 36. 70 applicants, 86% accepted, 40 enrolled. In 2006, 14 degrees awarded. *Degree requirements:* For master's, portfolio, thesis optional. *Entrance requirements:* For master's, GRE or MAT. *Application deadline:* Applications are processed on a rolling basis. Application fee: $25. Electronic applications accepted. *Expenses:* Tuition: Full-time $6,120; part-time $340 per credit. Required fees: $60; $60 per year. *Financial support:* Traineeships available. Financial award applicants required to submit FAFSA. *Faculty research:* Childhood obesity, organizational behavior, health promotion and wellness. *Unit head:* G. R. Myers, Director of Graduate Admissions, 302-736-2343, E-mail: myersgr@wesley.edu. *Application contact:* Marie Cusick, Coordinator of Graduate and Evening Programs, 302-736-2352, E-mail: cusickma@wesley.edu.

West Chester University of Pennsylvania, Graduate Studies, School of Health Sciences, Department of Nursing, West Chester, PA 19383. Offers nursing (MSN); nursing education (MSN). *Accreditation:* AACN. Part-time and evening/weekend programs available. *Students:* 10 full-time (9 women), 40 part-time (all women); includes 2 African Americans. Average age 42. 19 applicants, 100% accepted, 15 enrolled. In 2006, 12 degrees awarded. *Degree requirements:* For master's, thesis optional. *Entrance requirements:* For master's, GRE General Test or MAT, RN license. *Application deadline:* For fall admission, 4/15 priority date for domestic students; for spring admission, 10/15 for domestic students. Applications are processed on a rolling basis. Application fee: $35. *Financial support:* In 2006–07, research assistantships with full tuition reimbursements (averaging $5,000 per year); unspecified assistantships also available. Support available to part-time students. Financial award application deadline: 2/15; financial award applicants required to submit FAFSA. *Faculty research:* Violence against women. *Unit head:* Dr. Ann Coghlan Stowe, Chair, 610-436-2331, E-mail: astowe@wcupa.edu.

Western Carolina University, Graduate School, College of Applied Science, Department of Nursing, Cullowhee, NC 28723. Offers MSN. *Accreditation:* AACN. Part-time and evening/weekend programs available. *Degree requirements:* For master's, thesis optional. *Entrance requirements:* For master's, GRE General Test. Additional exam requirements/recommendations for international students: Required—TOEFL (minimum score 550 paper-based; 213 computer-based).

Western Connecticut State University, Division of Graduate Studies, School of Professional Studies, Nursing Department, Danbury, CT 06810-6885. Offers adult nurse practitioner (MSN); clinical nurse specialist (MSN). *Accreditation:* AACN. Part-time and evening/weekend programs available. *Faculty:* 6 full-time (5 women), 1 part-time/adjunct (0 women). *Students:* Average age 42. In 2006, 11 degrees awarded. *Degree requirements:* For master's, thesis or research project. *Entrance requirements:* For master's, MAT, bachelor's degree in nursing, minimum GPA of 3.0, previous course work in statistics and nursing research, RN license. *Application deadline:* For fall admission, 8/1 priority date for domestic students. Applications are processed on a rolling basis. Application fee: $40. *Financial support:* Career-related internships or fieldwork available. Support available to part-time students. Financial award application deadline: 5/1; financial award applicants required to submit FAFSA. *Unit head:* Dr. Patricia Z. Lund, Professor, 203-837-8567. *Application contact:* Chris Shankle, Associate Director of Graduate Admissions, 203-837-8244, Fax: 203-837-8338, E-mail: shanklec@wcsu.edu.

See Close-Up on page 1985.

Western Kentucky University, Graduate Studies, College of Health and Human Services, Department of Nursing, Bowling Green, KY 42101. Offers MSN. *Accreditation:* AACN. Part-time and evening/weekend programs available. *Faculty:* 6 full-time (all women). *Students:* 27 full-time (26 women), 45 part-time (44 women); includes 6 minority (3 African Americans, 1 American Indian/Alaska Native, 1 Asian American or Pacific Islander, 1 Hispanic American). Average age 38. 17 applicants, 65% accepted, 9 enrolled. In 2006, 31 degrees awarded. *Degree requirements:* For master's, thesis optional. *Entrance requirements:* For master's, GRE General Test, minimum GPA of 2.75. Additional exam requirements/recommendations for international students: Required—TOEFL (minimum score 555 paper-based; 213 computer-based; 79 iBT). *Application deadline:* For fall admission, 8/1 priority date for domestic students, 4/1 for international students; for spring admission, 4/14 for domestic students, 9/1 for international students. Applications are processed on a rolling basis. Application fee: $35. *Expenses:* Tuition, state resident: full-time $6,520; part-time $226 per hour. Tuition, nonresident: full-time $7,140; part-time $357 per hour. International tuition: $15,820 full-time. *Financial support:* In 2006–07, 3 students received support; research assistantships with partial tuition reimbursements available, teaching assistantships with partial tuition reimbursements available, Federal Work-Study, institutionally sponsored loans, traineeships, tuition waivers (partial), and unspecified assistantships available. Support available to part-time students. Financial award application deadline: 4/1; financial award applicants required to submit FAFSA. *Faculty research:* Folic acid, disease and injury prevention, rural mobile health, mental health issues. *Unit head:* Dr. Donna Blackburn, Head, 270-745-3391, Fax: 270-745-3392, E-mail: donna.blackburn@wku.edu.

Western University of Health Sciences, College of Graduate Nursing, Pomona, CA 91766-1854. Offers family nurse practitioner (MSN). *Accreditation:* AACN. Part-time and evening/weekend programs available. Postbaccalaureate distance learning degree programs offered. *Faculty:* 8 full-time (all women), 9 part-time/adjunct (7 women). *Students:* 149 full-time (129 women), 7 part-time (all women); includes 83 minority (7 African Americans, 56 Asian Americans or Pacific Islanders, 20 Hispanic Americans), 1 international. Average age 33. 163 applicants, 48% accepted, 67 enrolled. In 2006, 13 degrees awarded. *Degree requirements:* For master's, culminating project. *Entrance requirements:* For master's, GRE General Test, BSN or bachelor's degree in related field, certificate nurse practitioner, minimum GPA of 3.0, interview, letters of recommendation. Additional exam requirements/recommendations for international students: Required—TOEFL. *Application deadline:* For fall admission, 3/1 priority date for domestic students. Applications are processed on a rolling basis. Application fee: $60. *Expenses:* Contact institution. *Financial support:* Institutionally sponsored loans, scholarships/grants, and Veterans Educational Benefits available. Financial award application deadline: 3/2; financial award applicants required to submit FAFSA. *Unit head:* Karen J. Hanford, Dean, 909-469-5243, Fax: 909-469-5521, E-mail: khanford@westernu.edu. *Application contact:* Audrey Navarro, Information Contact, 909-469-5335, Fax: 909-469-5570, E-mail: admissions@westernu.edu.

Westminster College, School of Nursing and Health Sciences, Salt Lake City, UT 84105-3697. Offers family nurse practitioner (MSN); nurse anesthesia (MSNA); nursing (MSN); nursing education (MSN). *Accreditation:* AACN; AANA/CANAEP. Part-time and evening/weekend programs available. *Faculty:* 9 full-time (8 women). *Students:* 44 full-time (31 women), 13 part-time (9 women); includes 4 minority (1 African American, 2 Asian Americans or Pacific Islanders, 1 Hispanic American), 1 international. Average age 39. 57 applicants, 65% accepted, 32 enrolled. In 2006, 5 degrees awarded. *Degree requirements:* For master's, project or thesis. *Entrance requirements:* For master's, resumé, Utah RN license in good standing, minimum GPA of 3.0, 3 letters of recommendation, proof of completed BSN from accredited nursing school, proof of clear state and federal background check, drug test results, personal interview. Additional exam requirements/recommendations for international students: Required—TOEFL (minimum score 550 paper-based; 213 computer-based). *Application deadline:* For fall admission, 8/1 priority date for domestic students. Applications are processed on a rolling basis. Application fee: $40. Electronic applications accepted. *Financial support:* In 2006–07, 39 students received support. Career-related internships or fieldwork and tuition remissions available. Support available to part-time students. Financial award applicants required to submit FAFSA. *Faculty research:* Learning styles assessment, curriculum simulation, self-esteem and learning success. *Unit head:* Dr. Jean Dyer, Dean, 801-832-2168, Fax: 801-832-3110, E-mail: jdyer@westminstercollege.edu. *Application contact:* Joel Bauman, Vice President of Enrollment Services, 801-832-2200, Fax: 801-832-3101, E-mail: admission@westminstercollege.edu.

West Texas A&M University, College of Agriculture, Nursing, and Natural Sciences, Division of Nursing, Canyon, TX 79016-0001. Offers MSN. *Accreditation:* AACN. Part-time programs available. Postbaccalaureate distance learning degree programs offered (minimal on-campus study). *Degree requirements:* For master's, thesis optional. *Entrance requirements:* For master's, GRE General Test, bachelor's degree in nursing, minimum GPA of 3.0 in last 60 hours. Additional exam requirements/recommendations for international students: Required—TOEFL (minimum score 550 paper-based). Electronic applications accepted. *Faculty research:* Family-focused nursing, nursing traineeship, professional nursing.

West Virginia University, School of Nursing, Morgantown, WV 26506. Offers nurse practitioner (Certificate); nursing (MSN, PhD). *Accreditation:* AACN. Part-time programs available. Postbaccalaureate distance learning degree programs offered (minimal on-campus study). *Faculty:* 40 full-time (38 women), 15 part-time/adjunct (all women). *Students:* 47 full-time (46 women), 89 part-time (85 women); includes 1 minority (African American) Average age 36. 121 applicants, 74% accepted, 72 enrolled. In 2006, 20 degrees awarded. *Degree requirements:* For master's, thesis or alternative; for doctorate, thesis/dissertation, comprehensive exam. *Entrance requirements:* For master's, minimum GPA of 3.0, current U.S. RN license, BSN, course work in statistics and physical assessment; for doctorate, GRE General Test, minimum graduate GPA of 3.0, minimum grade of B in graduate statistics course work. Additional exam requirements/recommendations for international students: Required—TOEFL. *Application deadline:* For fall admission, 6/1 for domestic students. Application fee: $45. Electronic applications accepted. *Expenses:* Contact institution. Tuition and fees vary according to program. *Financial support:* In 2006–07, 89 students received support, including 1 teaching assistantship; institutionally sponsored loans, tuition waivers (partial), and graduate administrative assistantships also available. Financial award application deadline: 2/1; financial award applicants required to submit FAFSA. *Faculty research:* Rural primary health/health promotion, parent/child/women's health, cardiovascular risk reduction, complementary health modalities, breast cancer detection-care. Total annual research expenditures: $1.2 million. *Unit head:* Dr. E. Jane Martin, Dean, 304-293-4831, Fax: 304-293-6826, E-mail: ejmartin@hsc.wvu.edu. *Application contact:* Dr. Mary Jane Smith, Associate Dean for Graduate Programs, 304-293-4298, Fax: 304-293-2546, E-mail: mjsmith@hsc.wvu.edu.

Wheeling Jesuit University, Department of Nursing, Wheeling, WV 26003-6295. Offers MSN. *Accreditation:* AACN. Part-time and evening/weekend programs available. Postbaccalaureate distance learning degree programs offered (minimal on-campus study). *Faculty:* 3 full-time (all women), 1 (woman) part-time/adjunct. *Students:* 12 full-time (10 women), 62 part-time (59 women); includes 2 minority (1 African American, 1 Hispanic American). Average age 42. 28 applicants, 96% accepted, 21 enrolled. In 2006, 11 degrees awarded. *Degree requirements:* For master's, thesis (for some programs). *Entrance requirements:* For master's, GRE General Test, BSN, minimum GPA of 3.0, course work in research and statistics, US nursing license. Additional exam requirements/recommendations for international students: Required—TOEFL (minimum score 600 paper-based; 250 computer-based; 80 iBT). *Application deadline:* For fall admission, 8/1 priority date for domestic students; for spring admission, 12/15 priority date for domestic students. Applications are processed on a rolling basis. Application fee: $25. Electronic applications accepted. *Expenses:* Tuition: Full-time $8,910; part-time $405 per credit hour. Required fees: $105 per semester. One-time fee: $380 full-time. Full-time tuition and fees vary according to course load, degree level and program. *Financial support:* Federal Work-Study, scholarships/grants, and unspecified assistantships available. Financial award application deadline: 8/1; financial award applicants required to submit FAFSA. *Faculty research:* Low income and uninsured women, public policy, spirituality and aging, delivery of online education, quality of life, heart failure. *Unit head:* Dr. Rose M. Kutlenios, Chair, 304-243-2227, Fax: 304-243-4441, E-mail: rosekut@wju.edu. *Application contact:* Becky Forney, Associate Dean of Adult Education, 304-243-2250, Fax: 304-243-4441, E-mail: bforney@wju.edu.

Wichita State University, Graduate School, College of Health Professions, School of Nursing, Wichita, KS 67260. Offers clinical nurse specialist (MSN); nurse midwifery (MSN); nurse practitioner (MSN); nursing and health care systems administration (MSN); MSN/MBA. *Accreditation:* AACN. Part-time programs available. *Degree requirements:* For master's, thesis optional. *Entrance requirements:* For master's, GRE, BSN, minimum undergraduate GPA of 2.75. Additional exam requirements/recommendations for international students: Required—TOEFL. Electronic applications accepted. *Faculty research:* Adolescent pregnancy, alcoholism, arthritis and chronic disease, health practices of elderly, diabetes.

Widener University, School of Nursing, Chester, PA 19013-5792. Offers MSN, DN Sc, PMC. *Accreditation:* AACN; NLN (one or more programs are accredited). Part-time and evening/weekend programs available. *Degree requirements:* For doctorate, thesis/dissertation. *Entrance requirements:* For master's, GRE General Test, BSN, undergraduate course in statistics; for doctorate, GRE General Test, MSN, undergraduate course in statistics. Electronic applications accepted. Expenses: Contact institution. *Faculty research:* Women's health leadership, nursing education, research utilization, program evaluation, health promotion.

Wilkes University, Graduate Studies and Continued Learning, Nesbitt College of Pharmacy and Nursing, Department of Nursing, Wilkes-Barre, PA 18766-0002. Offers MSN. *Accreditation:* AACN. Part-time and evening/weekend programs available. *Students:* 27 full-time (18 women), 12 part-time (11 women); includes 8 minority (6 African Americans, 2 Asian Americans or Pacific Islanders). Average age 34. In 2006, 15 degrees awarded. *Entrance requirements:* For master's, GRE General Test, MAT. Additional exam requirements/recommendations for international students: Required—TOEFL (minimum score 500 paper-based; 173 computer-based). *Application deadline:* Applications are processed on a rolling basis. Application fee: $40. *Financial support:* Federal Work-Study and unspecified assistantships available. Financial award application deadline: 3/1; financial award applicants required to submit FAFSA. *Unit head:* Dr. Mary Ann Merrigan, Chair, 570-408-4070, Fax: 570-408-7807, E-mail: maryann.merrigan@wilkes.edu. *Application contact:* Kathleen Houlihan, Director of Graduate Studies, 570-408-3235, Fax: 570-408-7846, E-mail: kathleen.houlihan@wilkes.edu.

William Carey University, Graduate Studies, School of Nursing, Hattiesburg, MS 39401-5499. Offers MSN. Part-time programs available. *Faculty:* 5 full-time (all women), 2 part-time/adjunct (both women). *Students:* 13 full-time (all women), 4 part-time (all women); includes 4 minority (all African Americans) 15 applicants, 12 enrolled. In 2006, 8 degrees awarded. *Degree requirements:* For master's, thesis or alternative. *Entrance requirements:* For master's, GRE, minimum GPA of 3.0, RN license. Additional exam requirements/recommendations for international students: Required—TOEFL (minimum score 500 paper-based; 213 computer-based). *Application deadline:* For fall admission, 8/7 for domestic and international students; for winter admission, 10/30 for domestic and international students; for spring admission, 2/12 for domestic and international students. Application fee: $25. *Expenses:* Tuition: Full-time $5,040; part-time $240 per credit hour. Tuition and fees vary according to course load. *Financial support:* In 2006–07, 16 students received support. Federal Work-Study and scholarships/grants available. Support available to part-time students. Financial award applicants required to submit FAFSA. *Unit head:* Dr. Mary Stewart, Dean, 601-318-6147, Fax: 601-318-6446, E-mail: mary.stewart@wmcarey.edu. *Application contact:* Jason Douglas, Clerical Assistant, Graduate Admissions, 601-318-6774, Fax: 601-318-6765, E-mail: jason.douglas@wmcarey.edu.

William Paterson University of New Jersey, College of Science and Health, Department of Nursing, Wayne, NJ 07470-8420. Offers MSN. *Accreditation:* AACN. Part-time and evening/weekend programs available. *Students:* 5 full-time (all women), 34 part-time (all women); includes 6 minority (1 African American, 3 Asian Americans or Pacific Islanders, 2 Hispanic Americans). *Entrance requirements:* For master's, GRE General Test, minimum GPA of 2.75. *Application deadline:* Applications are processed on a rolling basis. Application fee: $50. Electronic applications accepted. *Financial support:* Research assistantships with tuition reimbursements, unspecified assistantships available. Financial award application deadline:4/1. *Unit head:* Dr. Kem Louie, Program Director, 973-720-3215. *Application contact:* Danielle Liautaud, Director, 973-720-3579, Fax: 973-720-2035, E-mail: liautaudd@wpunj.edu.

Wilmington College, Division of Nursing, New Castle, DE 19720-6491. Offers adult nurse practitioner (MSN); family nurse practitioner (MSN); gerontology (MSN); leadership (MSN); nursing (MSN); women's nurse practitioner (MSN). *Accreditation:* AACN; NLN. Part-time programs available. *Students:* 30 full-time (28 women), 195 part-time (176 women); includes 24 minority (19 African Americans, 3 Asian Americans or Pacific Islanders, 2 Hispanic Americans). Average age 39. 54 applicants, 100% accepted, 48 enrolled. In 2006, 58 degrees awarded. *Degree requirements:* For master's, thesis. *Entrance requirements:* For master's, BSN, RN license, interview, 3 letters of recommendation. Additional exam requirements/recommendations for international students: Required—TOEFL (minimum score 500 paper-based; 173 computer-based). *Application deadline:* For fall admission, 3/31 priority date for domestic students. Applications are processed on a rolling basis. Application fee: $25. *Financial support:* In 2006–07, 28 fellowships with tuition reimbursements (averaging $2,200 per year) were awarded; traineeships also available. Financial award applicants required to submit FAFSA. *Faculty research:* Outcomes assessment, student writing ability. *Unit head:* Dr. Mary Letitia Gallagher, Chair, 302-328-9401 Ext. 161, Fax: 302-328-7081, E-mail: tgall@wilmcoll.edu. *Application contact:* Chris Ferguson, Director of Admissions and Financial Aid, 302-328-9407 Ext. 256, Fax: 302-328-5164, E-mail: inquire@wilmcoll.edu.

Winona State University, Graduate Studies, College of Nursing and Health Sciences, Winona, MN 55987-5838. Offers adult nurse practitioner (MS); clinical nurse specialist (MS); family

nurse practitioner (MS); nurse administrator (MS); nurse educator (MS). *Accreditation:* AACN. Part-time programs available. *Faculty:* 10 full-time (all women). *Students:* 70 applicants, 57% accepted, 32 enrolled. In 2006, 32 master's awarded. *Degree requirements:* For master's, thesis. *Application deadline:* For fall admission, 2/1 for domestic students. Application fee: $20. *Financial support:* In 2006–07, 3 research assistantships with partial tuition reimbursements (averaging $6,000 per year) were awarded; Federal Work-Study, traineeships, and unspecified assistantships also available. Support available to part-time students. Financial award applicants required to submit FAFSA. *Unit head:* Dr. Timothy Gaspar, Graduate Director, 507-457-5122, E-mail: tgaspar@winona.msus.edu.

Winston-Salem State University, Program in Nursing, Winston-Salem, NC 27110-0003. Offers MSN. *Accreditation:* AACN. Part-time and evening/weekend programs available. Post-baccalaureate distance learning degree programs offered. *Faculty:* 11 full-time (10 women). *Students:* 52 full-time (46 women), 31 part-time (26 women); includes 47 minority (41 African Americans, 3 Asian Americans or Pacific Islanders, 3 Hispanic Americans). 57 applicants, 42% accepted, 24 enrolled. In 2006, 11 degrees awarded. *Degree requirements:* For master's, registration. *Entrance requirements:* For master's, GRE, MAT, resumé, NC or state compact license, 3 letters of recommendation. *Application deadline:* For fall admission, 7/15 for domestic and international students; for spring admission, 11/15 for domestic and international students. Applications are processed on a rolling basis. Application fee: $40. Electronic applications accepted. *Expenses:* Tuition, state resident: full-time $2,010. Tuition, nonresident: full-time $10,502. Tuition and fees vary according to course load. *Financial support:* In 2006–07, 24 students received support, including 2 research assistantships (averaging $5,000 per year), 1 teaching assistantship (averaging $2,500 per year); career-related internships or fieldwork, institutionally sponsored loans, scholarships/grants, traineeships, and tuition waivers (partial) also available. *Faculty research:* Elimination of health care disparities. Total annual research expenditures: $174,598. *Unit head:* Dr. Gohar Karami, Chair, 336-750-3278, Fax: 336-750-2568, E-mail: karamig@wssu.edu. *Application contact:* Graduate Studies and Research, 336-750-2102, Fax: 336-750-3042, E-mail: graduate@wssu.edu.

Wright State University, School of Graduate Studies, College of Nursing and Health, Program in Nursing, Dayton, OH 45435. Offers acute care nurse practitioner (MS); administration of nursing and health care systems (MS); adult health (MS); child and adolescent health (MS); community health (MS); family nurse practitioner (MS); nurse practitioner (MS); school nurse (MS); MBA/MS. *Accreditation:* AACN. Part-time and evening/weekend programs available. *Students:* 46 full-time (45 women), 124 part-time (117 women); includes 16 minority (13 African Americans, 1 Asian American or Pacific Islander, 2 Hispanic Americans). Average age 39. 45 applicants, 100% accepted. In 2006, 64 degrees awarded. *Degree requirements:* For master's, thesis or alternative. *Entrance requirements:* For master's, GRE General Test, BSN from NLN-accredited college, Ohio RN license. Additional exam requirements/recommendations for international students: Required—TOEFL. *Application deadline:* For fall admission, 4/15 priority date for domestic students. Application fee: $25. *Financial support:* Fellowships, research assistantships, teaching assistantships, Federal Work-Study, institutionally sponsored loans, and unspecified assistantships available. Support available to part-time students. Financial award application deadline: 6/1; financial award applicants required to submit FAFSA. *Faculty research:* Clinical nursing and health, teaching, caring, pain administration, informatics and technology. *Application contact:* Theresa A. Haghnazarian, Director of Student and Alumni Affairs, 937-775-2592, Fax: 937-775-4571, E-mail: theresa.haghnazarian@wright.edu.

Xavier University, College of Social Sciences, Health and Education, Department of Nursing, Cincinnati, OH 45207. Offers clinical nurse leader (MSN); forensic nursing (MSN); healthcare law (MSN); nursing administration (MSN); school nursing (MSN); MSN/M Ed; MSN/MBA; MSN/MS. *Accreditation:* AACN. Part-time and evening/weekend programs available. *Faculty:* 12 full-time (all women), 11 part-time/adjunct (9 women). *Students:* 57 full-time (51 women), 101 part-time (97 women); includes 8 minority (5 African Americans, 3 Asian Americans or Pacific Islanders), 26 international. Average age 37. 121 applicants, 56 enrolled. In 2006, 24 degrees awarded. *Degree requirements:* For master's, thesis or alternative, scholarly project. *Entrance requirements:* For master's, portfolio (RN to MSN). Additional exam requirements/recommendations for international students: Required—TOEFL (minimum score 550 paper-based; 213 computer-based). *Application deadline:* For fall admission, 8/28 priority date for domestic students. Applications are processed on a rolling basis. Application fee: $35. Electronic applications accepted. *Expenses:* Tuition: Part-time $462 per credit hour. Part-time tuition and fees vary according to degree level, campus/location and program. *Financial support:* In 2006–07, 50 students received support. Scholarships/grants, traineeships, and unspecified assistantships available. Support available to part-time students. Financial award application deadline: 4/1; financial award applicants required to submit FAFSA. *Faculty research:* Stroke rehabilitation, informatics, gerontology, hospice, ethics, macular degeneration. *Unit head:* Dr. Susan M. Schmidt, Chair, 513-745-3815, Fax: 513-745-1087, E-mail: schmidts@xavier.edu. *Application contact:* Marilyn Gomez, Director of Nursing Student Services, 513-745-4392, Fax: 513-745-1087, E-mail: gomez@xavier.edu.

Yale University, School of Nursing, New Haven, CT 06536. Offers MSN, DN Sc, Post Master's Certificate, MSN/MBA, MSN/MPH. *Accreditation:* AACN. Part-time programs available. *Degree requirements:* For master's, thesis or alternative; for doctorate, thesis/dissertation. *Entrance requirements:* For master's, GRE General Test, undergraduate course work in statistics; for doctorate, GRE General Test, MSN; for Post Master's Certificate, MSN. Expenses: Contact institution. *Faculty research:* Family-based care, chronic illness, primary care, development, policy.

York College of Pennsylvania, Department of Nursing, York, PA 17405-7199. Offers MS. *Accreditation:* AACN; AANA/CANAEP. Part-time and evening/weekend programs available. *Entrance requirements:* For master's, GRE General Test (CRNA), minimum GPA of 3.0 with NLNAC or CCNE major. Additional exam requirements/recommendations for international students: Required—TOEFL (minimum score 530 paper-based; 200 computer-based). Electronic applications accepted. *Faculty research:* Employer and faculty beliefs about concepts in RN-BS education, evaluating effectiveness of mental health partnerships in psychiatric setting.

York University, Faculty of Graduate Studies, Faculty of Health, Program in Nursing, Toronto, ON M3J 1P3, Canada. Offers M Sc N. *Faculty:* 24 full-time (all women). *Students:* 4 full-time (all women), 18 part-time (17 women). *Unit head:* Garl Mitchell, Graduate Programme Director, 416-736-2100 Ext. 22897.

Youngstown State University, Graduate School, College of Health and Human Services, Department of Nursing, Youngstown, OH 44555-0001. Offers MSN. *Accreditation:* NLN. Part-time and evening/weekend programs available. *Degree requirements:* For master's, thesis optional. *Entrance requirements:* For master's, GRE General Test, BSN, CPR certification. Additional exam requirements/recommendations for international students: Required—TOEFL.

Acute Care/Critical Care Nursing

Allen College, Program in Nursing, Waterloo, IA 50703. Offers acute care nurse practitioner (MSN); family nurse practitioner (MSN); health education (MSN); leadership in health care delivery (MSN). *Accreditation:* AACN; NLN. Part-time and evening/weekend programs available. *Faculty:* 2 full-time (both women), 4 part-time/adjunct (all women). *Students:* 19 full-time (17 women), 42 part-time (39 women). Average age 37. 62 applicants, 94% accepted, 46 enrolled. In 2006, 3 degrees awarded. *Degree requirements:* For master's, thesis optional. *Entrance requirements:* For master's, minimum GPA of 3.0. Additional exam requirements/recommendations for international students: Required—TOEFL (minimum score 550 paper-based). *Application deadline:* For fall admission, 7/15 priority date for domestic students; for spring admission, 12/1 priority date for domestic students. Applications are processed on a rolling basis. Application fee: $50. Electronic applications accepted. *Expenses:* Tuition: Full-time $9,824; part-time $562 per credit hour. Required fees: $481. One-time fee: $220 part-time. Tuition and fees vary according to course load. *Financial support:* In 2006–07, 58 students received support, including 1 teaching assistantship (averaging $10,116 per year); institutionally sponsored loans, scholarships/grants, and traineeships also available. Support available to part-time students. Financial award application deadline: 8/15; financial award applicants required to submit FAFSA. *Faculty research:* Pain and aged, congestive heart failure. *Unit head:* Nancy Kramer, Chair, 319-226-2040, Fax: 319-226-2070, E-mail: kramerna@ihs.org.

Barry University, School of Nursing, Program in Nurse Practitioner, Miami Shores, FL 33161-6695. Offers acute care nurse practitioner (MSN); family nurse practitioner (MSN); nurse practitioner (Certificate). *Accreditation:* AACN. Part-time and evening/weekend programs available. *Students:* 10 full-time (9 women), 106 part-time (86 women); includes 69 minority (17 African Americans, 3 Asian Americans or Pacific Islanders, 49 Hispanic Americans). 43 applicants, 14% accepted, 5 enrolled. In 2006, 33 degrees awarded. *Degree requirements:* For master's, research project or thesis. *Entrance requirements:* For master's, GRE General Test or MAT, BSN, minimum GPA of 3.0, course work in statistics. *Application deadline:* For fall admission, 5/1 priority date for domestic students. Applications are processed on a rolling basis. Application fee: $30. Electronic applications accepted. *Faculty research:* Child abuse, health beliefs, teenage pregnancy, cultural and clinical studies across the lifespan. *Unit head:* Dr. Andra Hanlon, Director, 305-899-3811, Fax: 305-899-3831, E-mail: ahanlon@mail.barry.edu. *Application contact:* Dave Fletcher, Director of Graduate Admissions, 305-899-3113, Fax: 305-899-2971, E-mail: dfletcher@mail.barry.edu.

Case Western Reserve University, Frances Payne Bolton School of Nursing, Doctor of Nursing Practice Program, Cleveland, OH 44106. Offers acute care nurse practitioner (DNP); adult nurse practitioner (DNP); family nurse practitioner (DNP); gerontological nurse practitioner (DNP); graduate entry/pre-licensure option (DNP); medical-surgical nursing (DNP); midwifery/family nursing (DNP); neonatal nurse practitioner (DNP); pediatric nurse practitioner (DNP); post-licensure option (DNP); psychiatric mental health nurse practitioner (DNP); women's health nurse practitioner (DNP). Graduate entry option allows baccalaureate-prepared college graduates from non-nursing backgrounds to earn certificate and MSN in addition to ND. *Students:* 125 full-time (109 women), 308 part-time (290 women); includes 47 minority (21 African Americans, 1 American Indian/Alaska Native, 18 Asian Americans or Pacific Islanders, 7 Hispanic Americans), 7 international. 190 applicants, 70% accepted, 80 enrolled. In 2006, 35 degrees awarded. Terminal master's awarded for partial completion of doctoral program. *Degree requirements:* For doctorate, thesis/dissertation. *Entrance requirements:* For doctorate, GRE General Test or MAT. *Application deadline:* For fall admission, 6/1 priority date for domestic students. Applications are processed on a rolling basis. Application fee: $75. *Financial support:* In 2006–07, 6 students received support, including 1 teaching assistantship; research assistantships, Federal Work-Study, institutionally sponsored loans, and tuition waivers (partial) also available. Support available to part-time students. Financial award application deadline: 6/30; financial award applicants required to submit FAFSA. *Faculty research:* Clinical nursing, acute care, gerontology, mental health, critical care. *Unit head:* Dr. Georgia Narsavage, Director, 216-368-6304, Fax: 216-368-3542, E-mail: gln2@cwru.edu. *Application contact:* Peter Taylor, Recruitment and Retention Specialist, 216-368-0349, Fax: 216-368-0124, E-mail: peter.taylor@case.edu.

Case Western Reserve University, Frances Payne Bolton School of Nursing, Master's Programs in Nursing, Nurse Practitioner Program, Cleveland, OH 44106. Offers acute care cardiovascular nursing (MSN); acute care nurse practitioner (MSN); acute care/flight nurse (MSN); adult nurse practitioner (MSN); family nurse practitioner (MSN); gerontological nurse practitioner (MSN); neonatal nurse practitioner (MSN); pediatric nurse practitioner (MSN); psychiatric-mental health nurse practitioner (MSN); women's health nurse practitioner (MSN). *Accreditation:* NLN. Part-time programs available. Postbaccalaureate distance learning degree programs offered (minimal on-campus study). *Faculty:* 54 full-time (50 women), 5 part-time/adjunct (3 women). *Students:* 19 full-time (15 women), 31 part-time (29 women); includes 16 minority (9 African Americans, 5 Asian Americans or Pacific Islanders, 2 Hispanic Americans), 2 international. Average age 35. 46 applicants, 72% accepted, 18 enrolled. In 2006, 34 degrees awarded. *Degree requirements:* For master's, thesis optional. *Entrance requirements:* For master's, GRE General Test or MAT. Additional exam requirements/recommendations for international students: Required—TOEFL. *Application deadline:* For fall admission, 6/1 for domestic students. Applications are processed on a rolling basis. Application fee: $75. *Financial support:* In 2006–07, 7 teaching assistantships were awarded; research assistantships, institutionally sponsored loans and tuition waivers (partial) also available. Support available to part-time students. Financial award application deadline: 6/30. *Faculty research:* Positive and negative mood states in parents of twins, effect of a carepath on chronic obstructive pulmonary disease home care. *Application contact:* Peter Taylor, Recruitment and Retention Specialist, 216-368-0349, Fax: 216-368-0124, E-mail: peter.taylor@case.edu.

The College of New Rochelle, Graduate School, Program in Nursing, New Rochelle, NY 10805-2308. Offers acute care nurse practitioner (MS, Certificate); clinical specialist in holistic nursing (MS, Certificate); family nurse practitioner (MS, Certificate); nursing and health care management (MS); nursing education (Certificate). *Accreditation:* AACN. Part-time programs available. *Faculty:* 7 full-time (6 women), 3 part-time/adjunct (all women). *Students:* Average age 44. In 2006, 23 degrees awarded. *Degree requirements:* For master's, registration. *Entrance requirements:* For master's, GRE General Test or MAT, BSN, malpractice insurance, minimum GPA of 3.0, RN license. *Application deadline:* For fall admission, 9/1 priority date for domestic students; for spring admission, 1/15 priority date for domestic students. Applications are processed on a rolling basis. Application fee: $30. *Expenses: Contact institution. Financial support:* Traineeships available. Support available to part-time students. Financial award application deadline: 8/15. *Faculty research:* Holistic modalities, academic success variables. *Unit head:* Dr. Mary Alice Donius, Dean, 914-654-5804, Fax: 914-654-5994.

Duke University, School of Nursing, Durham, NC 27708-0586. Offers adult acute care (Certificate); adult cardiovascular (Certificate); adult oncology/HIV (Certificate); adult primary care (Certificate); clinical nurse specialist (MSN), including adult oncology/HIV, gerontology, neonatal, pediatric, pediatric/chronic acute care; clinical research management (MSN, Certificate); family (Certificate); gerontology (Certificate); health and nursing ministries (MSN, Certificate); health systems leadership and outcomes (Certificate); leadership in community based long term care (MSN, Certificate); neonatal (Certificate); neonatal/pediatric in rural health (MSN, Certificate); nurse anesthetist (MSN, Certificate); nurse practitioner (MSN), including adult acute care, adult cardiovascular, adult oncology/HIV, adult primary care, family, gerontology, neonatal, pediatric, pediatric acute care; nursing (PhD); nursing and healthcare leadership (MSN); nursing education (MSN); nursing informatics (MSN, Certificate); pediatric (Certificate); pediatric acute care (Certificate); MBA/MSN; MSN/MCM. *Accreditation:* AACN; AANA/CANAEP. Part-time programs available. Postbaccalaureate distance learning degree programs offered (minimal on-campus study). *Faculty:* 45 full-time (41 women), 169 part-time/adjunct (150 women). *Students:* 178 full-time (162 women), 140 part-time (132 women); includes 48 minority (17 African Americans, 3 American Indian/Alaska Native, 20 Asian Americans or Pacific Islanders, 8 Hispanic Americans). Average age 36. 99 applicants, 92% accepted, 91 enrolled. In 2006, 122 master's, 17 other advanced degrees awarded. *Median time to degree:* Master's–2 years full-time, 2.5 years part-time. *Degree requirements:* For master's, thesis optional. *Entrance requirements:* For master's, GRE General Test or MAT, 1 year of nursing experience, BSN, minimum GPA of 3.0, previous course work in statistics; for Certificate, MSN. Additional exam requirements/recommendations for international students: Required—TOEFL (minimum score 550 paper-based; 213 computer-based), Commission on Graduates of Foreign Nursing Schools exam. *Application deadline:* For fall admission, 7/2 priority date for domestic and international students; for spring admission, 11/15 priority date for domestic and international students. Applications are processed on a rolling basis. Application fee: $50. *Expenses: Contact institution. Financial support:* In 2006–07, 258 students received support. Career-related internships or fieldwork, institutionally sponsored loans, scholarships/grants, traineeships, and tuition waivers (partial) available. Support available to part-time students. Financial award application deadline: 4/1; financial award applicants required to submit FAFSA. *Faculty research:* Cardiovascular disease, caregiver skill training, data mining, prostate cancer, neonatal immune system. Total annual research expenditures: $3.5 million. *Unit head:* Dr. Catherine L. Gilliss, Dean/Vice Chancellor for Nursing Affairs, 919-684-9444, Fax: 919-684-9414, E-mail: gilli025@mc.duke.edu. *Application contact:* Bebe T. Mills, Director of Admissions, 919-684-9151, Fax: 919-668-4693, E-mail: mills031@mc.duke.edu.

Duquesne University, School of Nursing, Master's Program in Nursing, Pittsburgh, PA 15282-0001. Offers acute care nursing (Post-Master's Certificate); acute care nursing specialist (MSN); family nurse practitioner (MSN, Post-Master's Certificate); forensic nursing (MSN, Post-Master's Certificate); nursing administration (MSN, Post-Master's Certificate); nursing education (MSN, Post-Master's Certificate); psychiatric/mental health nursing (MSN, Post-Master's Certificate); MSN/MBA. *Accreditation:* AACN. Part-time and evening/weekend programs available. Postbaccalaureate distance learning degree programs offered (minimal on-campus study). *Faculty:* 20 full-time (19 women), 4 part-time/adjunct (all women). *Students:* 73 full-time (70 women), 83 part-time (79 women); includes 11 minority (4 African Americans, 3 American Indian/Alaska Native, 1 Asian American or Pacific Islander, 3 Hispanic Americans). 72 applicants, 75% accepted, 49 enrolled. In 2006, 20 master's, 11 other advanced degrees awarded. *Degree requirements:* For master's, culminating paper. *Entrance requirements:* For master's, MAT or GRE, 1 year of work experience, bachelor's degree in nursing, undergraduate course work in statistics, health assessment course (family nurse practitioner, nursing education, acute care clinical nurse specialist). *Application deadline:* For fall admission, 4/1 for domestic and international students; for spring admission, 11/1 for domestic and international students. Applications are processed on a rolling basis. Application fee: $50. *Expenses: Contact institution.* Tuition and fees vary according to degree level and program. *Financial support:* In 2006–07, 10 students received support, including 9 research assistantships with partial tuition reimbursements available (averaging $1,600 per year), 1 teaching assistantship with partial tuition reimbursement available (averaging $1,600 per year); fellowships with partial tuition reimbursements available, institutionally sponsored loans, scholarships/grants, traineeships, and tuition waivers (partial) also available. Financial award application deadline: 8/20. *Faculty research:* Depression, culture, vulnerable populations, ethics, health disparities, community based. Total annual research expenditures: $377,400. *Unit head:* Dr. Joan Such Lockhart, Professor and Associate Dean of Academic Affairs, 412-396-6540, Fax: 412-396-1821, E-mail: lockhart@duq.edu. *Application contact:* Susan Hardner, Nurse Recruiter, 412-396-4945, Fax: 412-396-6346, E-mail: nursing@duq.edu.

Indiana University–Purdue University Indianapolis, School of Nursing, Department of Adult Health Nursing, Indianapolis, IN 46202-2896. Offers adult clinical nurse specialist (MSN), including chronic disability, critical care, health promotion, oncology. *Accreditation:* AACN. Part-time programs available. *Students:* 4 full-time (all women), 44 part-time (41 women); includes 4 minority (2 African Americans, 2 Hispanic Americans). Average age 39. In 2006, 15 degrees awarded. *Degree requirements:* For master's, thesis. *Entrance requirements:* For master's, GRE General Test, minimum GPA of 3.0, RN license. *Application deadline:* For fall admission, 4/1 for domestic students; for spring admission, 10/1 for domestic students. Application fee: $50 ($60 for international students). *Expenses:* Tuition, state resident: full-time $5,437; part-time $227 per credit hour. Tuition, nonresident: full-time $15,694; part-time $654 per credit hour. Required fees: $620. Tuition and fees vary according to course load, campus/location and program. *Financial support:* Fellowships with full tuition reimbursements, research assistantships with full tuition reimbursements, teaching assistantships with full tuition reimbursements, Federal Work-Study, scholarships/grants, and traineeships available. Support available to part-time students. Financial award application deadline: 5/1. *Unit head:* Dr. Juanita Keck, Co-Chair, 317-274-0050.

The Johns Hopkins University, School of Nursing, Nurse Practitioner Program, Baltimore, MD 21218-2699. Offers adult acute/critical care (MSN, Certificate); adult and pediatric primary care (MSN); adult or pediatric primary care (Certificate); family primary care (MSN, Certificate). *Accreditation:* AACN; NLN (one or more programs are accredited). Part-time programs available. *Faculty:* 12 full-time (all women), 6 part-time/adjunct (5 women). *Students:* 23 full-time (22 women), 62 part-time (58 women); includes 26 minority (3 African Americans, 3 American Indian/Alaska Native, 15 Asian Americans or Pacific Islanders, 5 Hispanic Americans), 1 international. Average age 31. 157 applicants, 85% accepted, 32 enrolled. In 2006, 18 master's, 2 other advanced degrees awarded. *Degree requirements:* For master's, scholarly project or portfolio, thesis optional. *Entrance requirements:* For master's, GRE, interview, minimum GPA of 3.0, BSN, Maryland RN license. Additional exam requirements/recommendations for international students: Required—TOEFL (minimum score 550 paper-based; 230 computer-based). *Application deadline:* For fall admission, 3/1 priority date for domestic and international students; for spring admission, 7/1 priority date for domestic and international students. Application fee: $75. *Expenses: Contact institution.* Tuition and fees vary according to degree level and program. *Financial support:* In 2006–07, 16 students received support. Federal Work-Study, scholarships/grants, traineeships, and tuition waivers (partial) available. Support available to part-time students. Financial award application deadline: 3/1; financial award applicants required to submit FAFSA. *Faculty research:* Community outreach, primary care of underserved populations, substance abusing individuals, childhood violence, women's health. *Unit head:* Dr. Kathleen M. White, Director, Master's Programs, 410-614-4664, Fax: 410-955-7463, E-mail: kwhite@son.jhmi.edu. *Application contact:* Mary O'Rourke, Director of Admissions/Student Services, 410-955-7548, Fax: 410-614-7086, E-mail: orourke@son.jhmi.edu.

Loyola University Chicago, Graduate School, Marcella Niehoff School of Nursing, Acute Care Clinical Nurse Specialist Program, Chicago, IL 60611-2196. Offers MSN. *Accreditation:* AACN. Part-time and evening/weekend programs available. *Students:* Average age 29. In 2006, 2 degrees awarded. *Degree requirements:* For master's, comprehensive exam or oral thesis defense. *Entrance requirements:* For master's, BSN, Illinois license, 3 letters of recommendation, 1 year experience before starting clinical. *Application deadline:* Applications are processed on a rolling basis. Electronic applications accepted. *Financial support:* Teaching assistantships, traineeships and unspecified assistantships available. Financial award application deadline: 3/1. *Unit head:* Dr. Judith Jennrich, Associate Professor, 708-216-3813, E-mail: jjennri@luc.edu. *Application contact:* Dr. Vicki A. Keough, Associate Professor, 708-216-3582, Fax: 708-216-9555, E-mail: vkeough@luc.edu.

Loyola University Chicago, Graduate School, Marcella Niehoff School of Nursing, Acute Care Nurse Practitioner Program, Chicago, IL 60611-2196. Offers MSN. *Accreditation:* AACN. Part-time and evening/weekend programs available. *Students:* 1 (woman) full-time, 15 part-time (13 women). In 2006, 3 degrees awarded. *Degree requirements:* For master's, comprehensive exam or oral thesis defense. *Application deadline:* Applications are processed on a rolling basis. Application fee: $40. Electronic applications accepted. *Financial support:* Traineeships available. Financial award application deadline: 3/1. *Faculty research:* Critical care/trauma recidivism. *Unit head:* Dr. Judith Jennrich, Associate Professor, 708-216-3813, E-mail: jjrennri@luc.edu. *Application contact:* Dr. Vicki A. Keough, Associate Professor, 708-216-3582, Fax: 708-216-9555, E-mail: vkeough@luc.edu.

New York University, College of Dentistry, College of Nursing, Programs in Advanced Practice Nursing, New York, NY 10012-1019. Offers advanced practice nursing: adult acute care (MS, Advanced Certificate); advanced practice nursing: adult primary care (MS, Advanced Certificate); advanced practice nursing: adult primary care/geriatrics (MS); advanced practice nursing: children with special needs (Advanced Certificate); advanced practice nursing: geriatrics (MS, Advanced Certificate); advanced practice nursing: holistic nursing (MS, Advanced Certificate); advanced practice nursing: home health nursing (Advanced Certificate); advanced practice nursing: mental health (MS); advanced practice nursing: mental health nursing (Advanced Certificate); advanced practice nursing: pediatrics (MS, Advanced Certificate); advanced practice nursing: pediatrics/children with special needs (MS); midwifery (MS, Advanced Certificate); nursing administration (MS, Advanced Certificate); nursing education (MS, Advanced Certificate); nursing informatics (MS, Advanced Certificate); palliative care (MS, Advanced Certificate); MS/MS. *Accreditation:* AACN; ACNM/DOA. Part-time and evening/weekend programs available. *Faculty:* 30 full-time (all women). *Students:* 10 full-time (all women), 428 part-time (395 women); includes 166 minority (73 African Americans, 72 Asian Americans or Pacific Islanders, 21 Hispanic Americans). Average age 35. 154 applicants, 93% accepted, 118 enrolled. In 2006, 100 master's, 7 Advanced Certificates awarded. *Degree requirements:* For master's, thesis (for some programs). *Entrance requirements:* For master's, BS in nursing, AS in nursing with another BS/BA degree; for Advanced Certificate, master's degree. Additional exam requirements/recommendations for international students: Required—TOEFL. *Application deadline:* For fall admission, 7/1 priority date for domestic students, 7/1 for international students; for spring admission, 12/1 for domestic and international students. Applications are processed on a rolling basis. Application fee: $65. *Expenses:* Tuition: Part-time $1,080 per unit. Required fees: $56 per unit. $329 per term. Tuition and fees vary according to program. *Financial support:* Career-related internships or fieldwork, Federal Work-Study, institutionally sponsored loans, scholarships/grants, and tuition waivers (partial) available. Support available to part-time students. Financial award application deadline: 2/1; financial award applicants required to submit FAFSA. *Faculty research:* Elderly black diabetics, families and illness, public health nursing, parent-child nursing, health policy costs. *Unit head:* Dr. Judith Haber, Associate Dean for Graduate Programs, 212-998-5300, Fax: 212-995-3143. *Application contact:* Amy Knowles, Assistant Dean for Student Affairs and Admissions, 212-998-5333, Fax: 212-995-4302, E-mail: ak96@nyu.edu.

Northeastern University, Bouvé College of Health Sciences Graduate School, School of Nursing, Program in Critical Care-Acute Care Nurse Practitioner, Boston, MA 02115-5096. Offers MS, CAS. *Accreditation:* AACN. *Students:* 11 full-time (10 women), 10 part-time (9 women). Average age 37. In 2006, 9 degrees awarded. *Degree requirements:* For master's, thesis or alternative. *Entrance requirements:* For master's, GRE General Test, minimum GPA of 3.0, previous course work in statistics, 1-2 years of nursing experience, RN license, ICU experience; for CAS, MS in nursing. Additional exam requirements/recommendations for international students: Required—TOEFL. *Application deadline:* For fall admission, 4/1 priority date for domestic students; for spring admission, 2/1 for domestic students. Applications are processed on a rolling basis. Application fee: $50. *Financial support:* Research assistantships, teaching assistantships, tuition waivers (partial) available. Financial award application deadline: 7/1; financial award applicants required to submit FAFSA. *Unit head:* Dr. Elizabeth Howard, Director, 617-373-4590, Fax: 617-373-8672, E-mail: e.howard@neu.edu. *Application contact:* Margaret Schnabel, Director of Graduate Admissions, 617-373-2708, Fax: 617-373-4704, E-mail: bouvegrad@neu.edu.

Northeastern University, Bouvé College of Health Sciences Graduate School, School of Nursing, Program in Critical Care-Neonatal Nurse Practitioner, Boston, MA 02115-5096. Offers MS, CAS. *Accreditation:* AACN. *Students:* 11 full-time (10 women), 10 part-time (9 women). Average age 37. In 2006, 9 degrees awarded. *Degree requirements:* For master's, thesis or alternative. *Entrance requirements:* For master's, GRE General Test, minimum GPA of 3.0, previous course work in statistics, 1-2 years of nursing experience, RN license, ICU experience. Additional exam requirements/recommendations for international students: Required—TOEFL. *Application deadline:* For fall admission, 4/1 priority date for domestic students; for spring admission, 2/1 for domestic students. Applications are processed on a rolling basis. Application fee: $50. *Financial support:* Research assistantships, teaching assistantships, tuition waivers (partial) available. Financial award application deadline: 7/1; financial award applicants required to submit FAFSA. *Faculty research:* Critical thinking and diagnostic reasoning, clinical outcomes of acute and critical health problems. *Unit head:* Dr. Elizabeth Howard, Director, 617-373-4590, Fax: 617-373-8672, E-mail: e.howard@neu.edu. *Application contact:* Margaret Schnabel, Director of Graduate Admissions, 617-373-2708, Fax: 617-373-4704, E-mail: bouvegrad@neu.edu.

Rush University, College of Nursing, Department of Adult Health Nursing, Chicago, IL 60612-3832. Offers acute care nurse practitioner (MSN, Post-Master's Certificate); adult health nursing (DN Sc, DNP); adult nurse practitioner (MSN, Post-Master's Certificate); adult/gerontological nurse practitioner (MSN); anesthesia nurse practitioner (MSN, Post-Master's Certificate); critical care clinical specialist (MSN); gerontological nurse practitioner (MSN, Post-Master's Certificate); medical surgical clinical specialist (MSN). *Accreditation:* AACN; AANA/CANAEP (one or more programs are accredited). Part-time programs available. Post-baccalaureate distance learning degree programs offered (minimal on-campus study). *Faculty:* 33. *Students:* 29 full-time, 123 part-time; includes 22 minority (7 African Americans, 9 Asian Americans or Pacific Islanders, 6 Hispanic Americans). Average age 35. 101 applicants, 80% accepted, 76 enrolled. In 2006, 47 master's, 6 doctorates awarded. Terminal master's awarded for partial completion of doctoral program. *Degree requirements:* For master's, capstone project; for doctorate, thesis/dissertation, DNP leadership project. *Entrance requirements:* For master's, GRE General Test (waived if nursing GPA is above 3.0 or cumulative GPA is above 3.25), interview; for doctorate, GRE General Test, interview, course work in statistics (DN Sc). Additional exam requirements/recommendations for international students: Required—TOEFL, TWE. *Application deadline:* For fall admission, 7/1 for domestic students; for winter admission, 11/1 for domestic students; for spring admission, 1/15 for domestic students. Applications are processed on a rolling basis. Application fee: $40. Electronic applications accepted. *Financial support:* In 2006–07, 19 students received support; teaching assistantships with tuition reimbursements available, Federal Work-Study, institutionally sponsored loans, scholarships/grants, and traineeships available. Support available to part-time students. Financial award application deadline: 5/1; financial award applicants required to submit FAFSA. *Faculty research:* Complementary/alternative medicine, critical care outcomes, cardiac risk reduction, Alzheimer's Disease, telehealth monitoring. *Unit head:* Dr. Margaret Faut-Callahan, Chairperson, 312-942-7117. *Application contact:* Hicela Castruita Woods, Director, College Admissions Services, 312-942-7100, Fax: 312-942-2219, E-mail: hicela_castruita@rush.edu.

Seton Hall University, College of Nursing, Department of Graduate Nursing, Advanced Practice in Acute Care Nursing Program, South Orange, NJ 07079-2697. Offers acute care nurse practitioner (MSN). *Accreditation:* AACN. Part-time programs available. *Degree requirements:* For master's, research project. *Entrance requirements:* For master's, GRE or MAT, BSN. Additional exam requirements/recommendations for international students: Required—TOEFL. Electronic applications accepted. *Faculty research:* Pulmonary infections, stress, patient-nurse environmental interactions, open-heart surgery.

Texas Tech University Health Sciences Center, School of Nursing, Lubbock, TX 79430. Offers acute care nurse practitioner (MSN, Certificate); administration (MSN); clinical research management (MSN, Certificate); education (MSN); family nurse practitioner (MSN, Certificate); geriatric nurse practitioner (MSN, Certificate); pediatric nurse practitioner (MSN, Certificate). *Accreditation:* AACN. Part-time programs available. Postbaccalaureate distance learning degree programs offered (minimal on-campus study). *Faculty:* 17 full-time (16 women), 5 part-time/adjunct (all women). *Students:* 23 full-time (22 women), 161 part-time (137 women); includes 46 minority (8 African Americans, 2 American Indian/Alaska Native, 6 Asian Americans or Pacific Islanders, 30 Hispanic Americans). Average age 37. 97 applicants, 69% accepted, 67 enrolled. In 2006, 41 degrees awarded. *Degree requirements:* For master's, thesis optional. *Entrance requirements:* For master's, minimum GPA of 3.0, 3 letters of reference, BSN, RN license; for Certificate, minimum GPA of 3.0, 3 letters of reference, RN license. Additional exam requirements/recommendations for international students: Required—TOEFL (minimum score 550 paper-based; 213 computer-based). *Application deadline:* For fall admission, 7/15 priority date for domestic and international students; for spring admission, 11/15 priority date for domestic and international students. Applications are processed on a rolling basis. Application fee: $40. *Financial support:* In 2006–07, 184 students received support. Institutionally sponsored loans, scholarships/grants, and traineeships available. Support available to part-time students. Financial award application deadline: 12/1; financial award applicants required to submit FAFSA. *Faculty research:* Diabetes/obesity, nurse competency, disease management, intervention and measurements, health disparities. Total annual research expenditures: $2.4 million. *Unit head:* Dr. Barbara A. Johnston, Associate Dean for Administrative and Student Affairs, 806-743-3055, Fax: 806-743-1622, E-mail: barbara.johnston@ttuhsc.edu. *Application contact:* Lauren K. Sullivan, Recruiter/Transcultural Coordinator, 806-743-2730 Ext. 309, Fax: 806-743-1622, E-mail: lauren.sullivan@ttuhsc.edu.

University at Buffalo, the State University of New York, Graduate School, School of Nursing, Buffalo, NY 14260. Offers acute care nurse practitioner (MS, Certificate); adult health nursing (MS, Certificate); child health nursing (MS); family nurse practitioner (Certificate); family nursing (MS); geriatric nurse practitioner (MS, Certificate); maternal and women's health nurse practitioner (Certificate); maternal and women's health nursing (MS); nurse anesthetist (MS); nursing (PhD); nursing education (Certificate); pediatric nurse practitioner (Certificate); psychiatric/mental health nurse practitioner (Certificate); psychiatric/mental health nursing (MS). *Accreditation:* AACN; AANA/CANAEP (one or more programs are accredited). Part-time programs available. Postbaccalaureate distance learning degree programs offered. *Faculty:* 38 full-time (34 women), 15 part-time/adjunct (14 women). *Students:* 131 full-time (108 women), 64 part-time (61 women); includes 29 minority (11 African Americans, 9 Asian Americans or Pacific Islanders, 9 Hispanic Americans), 20 international. Average age 28. 346 applicants, 25% accepted, 51 enrolled. In 2006, 49 master's, 3 doctorates, 6 other advanced degrees awarded. Terminal master's awarded for partial completion of doctoral program. *Degree requirements:* For master's, comprehensive exams or project; for doctorate, thesis/dissertation, comprehensive exam. *Entrance requirements:* For master's, GRE General Test (if overall GPA is below 3.0), interview, minimum GPA of 3.0, RN license, 3 references; for doctorate, GRE General Test, minimum GPA of 3.25, RN license, BS or MS in nursing, 3 references, writing sample; for Certificate, interview, minimum GPA of 3.0 or GRE General Test, RN license, MS in nursing. Additional exam requirements/recommendations for international students: Required—TOEFL (minimum score 550 paper-based; 213 computer-based; 79 iBT), IELTS (minimum score 7). *Application deadline:* For fall admission, 6/1 priority date for domestic students, 3/1 priority date for international students; for spring admission, 11/1 for domestic students, 9/15 priority date for international students. Applications are processed on a rolling basis. Application fee: $50. Electronic applications accepted. *Financial support:* In 2006–07, 78 students received support, including 13 fellowships with full tuition reimbursements available (averaging $7,220 per year), 10 research assistantships with tuition reimbursements available (averaging $17,881 per year), 23 teaching assistantships with full tuition reimbursements available (averaging $11,245 per year); Federal Work-Study, scholarships/grants, traineeships, health care benefits, and unspecified assistantships also available. Financial award application deadline: 3/15; financial award applicants required to submit FAFSA. *Faculty research:* Oncology symptom management, end of life decision making, changing behaviors using the transtheoretical model, addictions, nursing workforce. Total annual research expenditures: $1.7 million. *Unit head:* Dr. Jean K. Brown, Dean, Interim, 716-829-2533, Fax: 716-829-2566, E-mail: jebrown@buffalo.edu. *Application contact:* Dr. Elaine R. Cusker, Assistant Dean, 716-829-2537, Fax: 716-829-2021, E-mail: ecusker@buffalo.edu.

University of Cincinnati, Graduate School, College of Nursing, Cincinnati, OH 45221-0038. Offers clinical nurse specialist (MSN), including adult health, community health, neonatal, nursing administration, occupational health, pediatric health, psychiatric nursing, women's health; nurse anesthesia (MSN); nurse midwifery (MSN); nurse practitioner (MSN), including acute care, ambulatory care, family, family/psychiatric, women's health; nursing (PhD); MBA/MSN. *Accreditation:* AACN; AANA/CANAEP (one or more programs are accredited); ACNM/DOA. Part-time programs available. Postbaccalaureate distance learning degree programs offered (no on-campus study). *Faculty:* 41 full-time (39 women), 16 part-time/adjunct (15 women). *Students:* 159 full-time (125 women), 149 part-time (145 women); includes 40 minority (22 African Americans, 1 American Indian/Alaska Native, 16 Asian Americans or Pacific Islanders, 1 Hispanic American). Average age 34. 385 applicants, 49% accepted, 132 enrolled. In 2006, 77 master's, 5 doctorates awarded. Terminal master's awarded for partial completion of doctoral program. *Median time to degree:* Of those who began their doctoral program in fall 1998, 55% received their degree in 8 years or less. *Degree requirements:* For master's, thesis or alternative, registration; for doctorate, thesis/dissertation, comprehensive exam, registration. *Entrance requirements:* For master's and doctorate, GRE General Test. Additional exam requirements/recommendations for international students: Required—TOEFL (minimum score 520 paper-based; 190 computer-based). *Application deadline:* For fall admission, 7/26 priority date for domestic and international students. Applications are processed on a rolling basis. Application fee: $40. Electronic applications accepted. *Financial support:* In 2006–07, 164 students received support, including 7 fellowships with full tuition reimbursements available (averaging $13,571 per year), research assistantships with full tuition reimbursements available (averaging $12,000 per year), 8 teaching assistantships with full tuition reimbursements available (averaging $12,000 per year); career-related internships or fieldwork, scholarships/grants, traineeships, tuition waivers (partial), and unspecified assistantships also available. Support available to part-time students. Financial award application deadline: 5/1; financial award applicants required to submit FAFSA. *Faculty research:* Substance abuse, injury and violence, symptom management. Total annual research expenditures: $1.3 million. *Unit head:* Dr. Andrea R. Lindell, Dean, 513-558-5330, Fax: 513-558-9030, E-mail: andrea.lindell@uc.edu. *Application contact:* Loren Carter, Program Coordinator, 513-558-5072, Fax: 513-558-7523, E-mail: loren.carter@uc.edu.

University of Connecticut, Graduate School, School of Nursing, Field of Nursing, Storrs, CT 06269. Offers adult acute care (Post-Master's Certificate); adult primary care (Post-Master's Certificate); community health (Post-Master's Certificate); neonatal acute care (Post-Master's Certificate); nursing (MS, PhD); patient care services and systems administration (Post-Master's Certificate); psychiatric mental health (Post-Master's Certificate). *Accreditation:* AACN. *Faculty:* 20 full-time (18 women). *Students:* 38 full-time (33 women), 70 part-time (65 women); includes 17 minority (3 African Americans, 10 Asian Americans or Pacific Islanders, 4 Hispanic Americans), 1 international. Average age 37. 64 applicants, 69% accepted, 44 enrolled. In 2006, 25 master's, 7 doctorates, 1 other advanced degree awarded. *Degree requirements:* For master's, comprehensive exam; for doctorate, thesis/dissertation. *Entrance requirements:* Additional exam requirements/recommendations for international students: Required—TOEFL (minimum score 550 paper-based; 213 computer-based). *Application deadline:* For fall admission, 2/1 priority date for domestic and international students; for spring admission, 11/1 for domestic students, 10/1 for international students. Applications are processed on a rolling basis. Application fee: $55. Electronic applications accepted. *Financial support:* In 2006–07, 4 research assistantships with full tuition reimbursements, 13 teaching assistantships with full tuition reimbursements were awarded; fellowships, Federal Work-Study, scholarships/grants, health care benefits, and unspecified assistantships also available. Financial award application deadline: 2/1; financial award applicants required to submit FAFSA. *Unit head:* E. Carol Polifroni, Chairperson, 860-486-0511, Fax: 860-486-0001, E-mail: polifron@uconn.edu. *Application contact:* Lisa Mazzola, Academic Advisor Coordinator, 860-486-1973, E-mail: lisa.mazzola@uconn.edu.

University of Guelph, Ontario Veterinary College and Graduate Program Services, Graduate Programs in Veterinary Sciences, Department of Clinical Studies, Guelph, ON N1G

Acute Care/Critical Care Nursing

University of Guelph (continued)

2W1, Canada. Offers anesthesiology (M Sc, DV Sc); cardiology (Diploma); clinical studies (Diploma); emergency/critical care (Diploma); medicine (M Sc, DV Sc); neurology (M Sc, DV Sc); ophthalmology (M Sc, DV Sc); surgery (M Sc, DV Sc). *Faculty:* 37. *Students:* 27 (19 women). *Degree requirements:* For master's, thesis/dissertation; for doctorate, thesis/dissertation, comprehensive exam. *Entrance requirements:* Additional exam requirements/recommendations for international students: Required—TOEFL (minimum score 550 paper-based; 213 computer-based), IELTS (minimum score 7). *Application deadline:* For fall admission, 12/6 for domestic students; for winter admission, 10/30 priority date for domestic students; for spring admission, 2/28 priority date for domestic students. Applications are processed on a rolling basis. Application fee: $80. Electronic applications accepted. *Financial support:* Fellowships, research assistantships, teaching assistantships, career-related internships or fieldwork and scholarships/grants available. *Faculty research:* Orthopedics, respirology, oncology, exercise physiology, cardiology. Total annual research expenditures: $1.5 million. *Unit head:* Dr. Dara Allen, Interim Chair, 519-824-4120 Ext. 54001, Fax: 519-767-0311, E-mail: dallen@ouc.uoguelph.ca. *Application contact:* Dr. J. Scott Weese, Graduate Coordinator, 519-824-4120 Ext. 54064, Fax: 519-767-0311, E-mail: jsweese@uoguelph.ca.

University of Massachusetts Worcester, Graduate School of Nursing, Worcester, MA 01655-0115. Offers adult acute/critical care nurse practitioner (MS, Certificate); adult ambulatory/community care nurse practitioner (MS, Certificate); gerontological nurse practitioner (Certificate); nurse educator (MS, Certificate); nursing (PhD). *Accreditation:* AACN. Part-time programs available. *Faculty:* 39. *Students:* 46 full-time (43 women), 6 part-time (2 women); includes 5 minority (2 African Americans, 2 Asian Americans or Pacific Islanders, 1 Hispanic American). Average age 38. 42 applicants, 71% accepted. In 2006, 26 master's, 2 doctorates, 6 other advanced degrees awarded. *Degree requirements:* For doctorate, thesis/dissertation. *Entrance requirements:* For master's, GRE General Test, BSN, previous course work in statistics; for Certificate, master's degree. *Application deadline:* For fall admission, 3/15 for domestic students. Applications are processed on a rolling basis. Application fee: $40 ($60 for international students). *Expenses:* Tuition, state resident: full-time $2,640. Tuition, nonresident: full-time $9,856. Required fees: $3,942. *Financial support:* In 2006–07, 4 students received support. Scholarships/grants and traineeships available. Support available to part-time students. Financial award application deadline: 3/22; financial award applicants required to submit FAFSA. *Faculty research:* Premature menopause with cancer treatment, quality of life and cancer, complementary therapies, psychoneuroimmunology, patient outcomes/outcomes research. *Unit head:* Dr. Janet Hale, Associate Dean, 508-856-5661, Fax: 508-856-6552. *Application contact:* Larry Shattuck, Director of Recruitment and Retention, 508-856-5801, Fax: 508-856-6552.

University of Miami, Graduate School, School of Nursing and Health Studies, Coral Gables, FL 33124. Offers acute care (MSN), including adult acute care nurse practitioner, nurse anesthesia; community health (MSN); nursing (PhD); primary care (MSN), including adult nurse practitioner, family nurse practitioner, nurse midwifery, psychiatric/mental health nursing, women's health practitioner. *Accreditation:* AACN; AANA/CANAEP; ACNM/DOA (one or more programs are accredited). Part-time programs available. *Faculty:* 10 full-time (8 women), 1 (woman) part-time/adjunct. *Students:* 33 full-time (24 women), 27 part-time (24 women); includes 28 minority (7 African Americans, 5 Asian Americans or Pacific Islanders, 16 Hispanic Americans), 2 international. Average age 34. 108 applicants, 48% accepted, 30 enrolled. In 2006, 15 master's, 1 doctorate awarded. *Degree requirements:* For master's, thesis optional; for doctorate, thesis/dissertation. *Entrance requirements:* For master's, GRE General Test, BSN, minimum GPA of 3.0, Florida RN license; for doctorate, GRE General Test, BSN or MSN, minimum GPA of 3.0. Additional exam requirements/recommendations for international students: Required—TOEFL (minimum score 550 paper-based; 213 computer-based). *Application deadline:* For fall admission, 4/30 priority date for domestic students; for spring admission, 11/1 priority date for domestic students. Applications are processed on a rolling basis. Application fee: $50. Electronic applications accepted. *Financial support:* In 2006–07, 12 students received support, including 3 research assistantships with tuition reimbursements available (averaging $9,000 per year), 5 teaching assistantships with tuition reimbursements available (averaging $9,000 per year); fellowships, Federal Work-Study, institutionally sponsored loans, scholarships/grants, and unspecified assistantships also available. Support available to part-time students. Financial award application deadline: 3/1; financial award applicants required to submit FAFSA. *Faculty research:* Transcultural nursing, exercise and depression in Alzheimer's disease, infectious diseases/HIV–AIDS, postpartum depression, outcomes assessment. Total annual research expenditures: $31.9 million. *Unit head:* Dr. Nilda Peragallo, Dean, 305-284-2107, Fax: 305-667-3787, E-mail: nperagallo@miami.edu. *Application contact:* Anne Stabb, Graduate Advisor, 305-284-2533, Fax: 305-284-4827, E-mail: astabb@miami.edu.

University of Michigan, Horace H. Rackham School of Graduate Studies, School of Nursing, Division of Acute, Critical and Long-term Care, Program in Adult Acute Care Nurse Practitioner, Ann Arbor, MI 48109. Offers MS. *Accreditation:* AACN. Part-time programs available. *Degree requirements:* For master's, thesis, registration. *Entrance requirements:* For master's, GRE General Test, licensure, minimum of B average in BSN program. Additional exam requirements/recommendations for international students: Required—TOEFL (minimum score 560 paper-based; 220 computer-based). Electronic applications accepted. *Faculty research:* The functional outcomes and quality of life in women with breast cancer, hypertension.

University of Pennsylvania, School of Nursing, Adult Acute Care Nurse Practitioner Program, Philadelphia, PA 19104. Offers acute care nurse practitioner (MSN). *Accreditation:* AACN. Part-time programs available. *Entrance requirements:* For master's, GRE General Test, BSN, minimum GPA of 3.0, previous course work in statistics. Expenses: Contact institution. *Faculty research:* Post-injury disability, bereavement and attributions in fire survivors, stress in staff nurses.

University of Pennsylvania, School of Nursing, Pediatric Critical Care Nurse Practitioner Program, Philadelphia, PA 19104. Offers MSN. *Accreditation:* AACN. *Entrance requirements:* For master's, GRE General Test, BSN, minimum GPA of 3.0, previous course work in statistics, 1 year of clinical course work. Additional exam requirements/recommendations for international students: Required—TOEFL. Expenses: Contact institution.

University of Pittsburgh, School of Nursing, Program in Nurse Practitioner Studies, Pittsburgh, PA 15260. Offers acute care nurse practitioner (MSN); adult nurse practitioner (MSN); family nurse practitioner (MSN); nursing practice (DNP); pediatric nurse practitioner (MSN); psychiatric primary care nurse practitioner (MSN). *Accreditation:* AACN. Part-time programs available. *Students:* 15 full-time (13 women), 65 part-time (57 women); includes 5 minority (3 African Americans, 2 Hispanic Americans). Average age 38. 47 applicants, 62% accepted, 27 enrolled. In 2006, 28 degrees awarded. *Degree requirements:* For master's, thesis optional. *Entrance requirements:* For master's, GRE General Test or MAT, BSN, RN license, letters of recommendation, resumé, course work in statistics, 1-3 years of nursing experience; for doctorate, GRE General Test, BSN, RN license, minimum GPA of 3.5, 3 letters of recommendation. Additional exam requirements/recommendations for international students: Required—TOEFL (minimum score 550 paper-based; 213 computer-based; 80 iBT). *Application deadline:* For fall admission, 8/1 priority date for domestic students, 8/1 for international students; for spring admission, 12/1 priority date for domestic students, 12/1 for international students. Applications are processed on a rolling basis. Application fee: $50. Electronic applications accepted.

University of South Carolina, The Graduate School, College of Nursing, Program in Advanced Practice Clinical Nursing, Columbia, SC 29208. Offers acute care nurse practitioner (Certificate); advanced practice clinical nursing (MSN). *Accreditation:* AACN. Part-time programs available. *Entrance requirements:* For master's, master's degree in nursing, RN license; for Certificate, MSN. Additional exam requirements/recommendations for international students: Required—TOEFL (minimum score 570 paper-based; 213 computer-based). Electronic applications accepted.

University of South Carolina, The Graduate School, College of Nursing, Program in Clinical Nursing, Columbia, SC 29208. Offers acute care clinical specialist (MSN); acute care nurse practitioner (MSN); women's health nurse practitioner (MSN). *Accreditation:* AACN. Part-time programs available. *Degree requirements:* For master's, thesis or alternative. *Entrance requirements:* For master's, GRE General Test or MAT, BS in nursing, RN licensure. Additional exam requirements/recommendations for international students: Required—TOEFL (minimum score 570 paper-based; 230 computer-based). Electronic applications accepted. *Faculty research:* Psychophysiological interventions, HIV/AIDS, psycho-neuroimmunology.

Vanderbilt University, School of Nursing, Nashville, TN 37235. Offers adult acute care nurse practitioner (MSN); adult health nurse practitioner/forensic (MSN); adult nurse practitioner/cardiovascular disease management and prevention (MSN); adult nurse practitioner/palliative care (MSN); clinical management (clinical nurse leader/specialist) (MSN); family nurse practitioner (MSN); gerontology nurse practitioner (MSN); health systems management (MSN); neonatal nurse practitioner (MSN); nurse midwifery (MSN); nursing informatics (MSN); nursing science (PhD); pediatric acute care nurse practitioner (MSN); pediatric primary care nurse practitioner (MSN); psychiatric-mental health nurse practitioner (MSN); women's health nurse practitioner (MSN); MBA/MSN; MSN/MTS; MSN/PhD. *Accreditation:* ACNM/DOA; NLN (one or more programs are accredited). Part-time and evening/weekend programs available. Postbaccalaureate distance learning degree programs offered (minimal on-campus study). *Faculty:* 95 full-time (83 women), 432 part-time/adjunct (314 women). *Students:* 371 full-time (325 women), 206 part-time (180 women); includes 59 minority (38 African Americans, 2 American Indian/Alaska Native, 7 Asian Americans or Pacific Islanders, 12 Hispanic Americans). Average age 27. 611 applicants, 55% accepted, 308 enrolled. In 2006, 256 master's, 2 doctorates awarded. *Degree requirements:* For doctorate, thesis/dissertation. *Entrance requirements:* For master's, GRE, interview; for doctorate, GRE, interview, 3 letters of recommendation. Additional exam requirements/recommendations for international students: Required—TOEFL. *Application deadline:* For fall admission, 12/1 priority date for domestic and international students. Applications are processed on a rolling basis. Application fee: $50. *Expenses:* Contact institution. *Financial support:* In 2006–07, 404 students received support, including 5 research assistantships (averaging $8,000 per year); Federal Work-Study, institutionally sponsored loans, and unspecified assistantships also available. Support available to part-time students. Financial award application deadline: 3/15; financial award applicants required to submit CSS PROFILE or FAFSA. *Faculty research:* Lymphedema post cancer treatment, palliative care and bereavement, patient safety and quality of care, health care workforce issues, symptom management including pain and fatigue. Total annual research expenditures: $1.1 million. *Unit head:* Dr. Colleen Conway-Welch, Dean, 615-343-8776, Fax: 615-343-7711, E-mail: colleen.conway-welch@vanderbilt.edu. *Application contact:* Cheryl Feldner, Assistant Director of Admissions, 615-322-3800, Fax: 615-343-0333, E-mail: cheryl.feldner@vanderbilt.edu.

Wayne State University, College of Nursing, Department of Adult Health, Detroit, MI 48202. Offers adult acute care nursing (MSN); adult primary care nursing (MSN). Part-time programs available. *Faculty:* 48 full-time (all women). *Students:* 14 full-time (13 women), 72 part-time (67 women); includes 22 minority (15 African Americans, 7 Asian Americans or Pacific Islanders), 9 international. Average age 36. 43 applicants, 81% accepted, 26 enrolled. In 2006, 20 degrees awarded. *Degree requirements:* For master's, thesis or alternative. *Entrance requirements:* For master's, GRE General Test, minimum GPA of 2.8. Additional exam requirements/recommendations for international students: Required—TOEFL (minimum score 550 paper-based; 213 computer-based); Recommended—TWE (minimum score 6). *Application deadline:* For fall admission, 7/1 priority date for domestic students, 6/1 for international students; for winter admission, 10/1 for international students; for spring admission, 11/1 for domestic students, 2/1 for international students. Applications are processed on a rolling basis. Application fee: $30 ($50 for international students). Electronic applications accepted. *Financial support:* In 2006–07, 1 research assistantship (averaging $17,613 per year), 1 teaching assistantship (averaging $35,350 per year) were awarded; institutionally sponsored loans, scholarships/grants, and traineeships also available. Support available to part-time students. Financial award application deadline: 7/1. Total annual research expenditures: $107,887. *Unit head:* Helene J. Krouse, Professor, 313-577-3911, E-mail: hjkrouse@wayne.edu. *Application contact:* Janet Harden, Academic Director, 313-577-4082.

Wright State University, School of Graduate Studies, College of Nursing and Health, Program in Nursing, Dayton, OH 45435. Offers acute care nurse practitioner (MS); administration of nursing and health care systems (MS); adult health (MS); child and adolescent health (MS); community health (MS); family nurse practitioner (MS); nurse practitioner (MS); school nurse (MS); MBA/MS. *Accreditation:* AACN. Part-time and evening/weekend programs available. *Students:* 46 full-time (45 women), 124 part-time (117 women); includes 16 minority (13 African Americans, 1 Asian American or Pacific Islander, 2 Hispanic Americans). Average age 39. 45 applicants, 100% accepted. In 2006, 64 degrees awarded. *Degree requirements:* For master's, thesis or alternative. *Entrance requirements:* For master's, GRE General Test, BSN from NLN-accredited college, Ohio RN license. Additional exam requirements/recommendations for international students: Required—TOEFL. *Application deadline:* For fall admission, 4/15 priority date for domestic students. Application fee: $25. *Financial support:* Fellowships, research assistantships, teaching assistantships, Federal Work-Study, institutionally sponsored loans, and unspecified assistantships also available. Support available to part-time students. Financial award application deadline: 6/1; financial award applicants required to submit FAFSA. *Faculty research:* Clinical nursing and health, teaching, caring, pain administration, informatics and technology. *Application contact:* Theresa A. Haghnazarian, Director of Student and Alumni Affairs, 937-775-2592, Fax: 937-775-4571, E-mail: theresa.haghnazarian@wright.edu.

Adult Nursing

Angelo State University, College of Graduate Studies, College of Sciences, Department of Nursing, San Angelo, TX 76909. Offers adult nurse practitioner (MSN); nurse educator (MSN). *Accreditation:* NLN. Part-time and evening/weekend programs available. *Faculty:* 10 full-time (all women). *Students:* 15 full-time (13 women), 26 part-time (23 women); includes 10 minority (1 African American, 1 Asian American or Pacific Islander, 8 Hispanic Americans). Average age 40. 25 applicants, 80% accepted, 19 enrolled. In 2006, 6 degrees awarded. *Degree requirements:* For master's, comprehensive exam. *Entrance requirements:* For master's, GRE General Test. Additional exam requirements/recommendations for international students: Required—TOEFL or IELTS. *Application deadline:* For fall admission, 7/15 priority date for domestic students, 6/15 for international students; for spring admission, 12/8 for domestic students, 11/1 for international students. Applications are processed on a rolling basis. Application fee: $40 ($50 for international students). Electronic applications accepted. *Expenses:* Tuition, state resident: full-time $2,340; part-time $130 per hour. Tuition, nonresident: full-time $7,290; part-time $405 per hour. Required fees: $906; $56 per hour. *Financial support:* In 2006–07, 24 students received support. Career-related internships or fieldwork, Federal Work-Study, and scholarships/grants available. Support available to part-time students. Financial award application deadline: 3/1. *Unit head:* Dr. Leslie M. Mayrand, Department Head, 325-942-2060 Ext. 247, E-mail: leslie.mayrand@angelo.edu. *Application contact:* Dr. Susan Wilkinson, Graduate Advisor, 325-942-2060 Ext. 290, E-mail: susan.wilkinson@angelo.edu.

Barnes-Jewish College of Nursing and Allied Health, Division of Nursing, St. Louis, MO 63110-1091. Offers adult nurse practitioner (MSN); education (MSN); gerontology nurse practitioner (MSN); holistics (MSN); management/administration (MSN); neonatal nurse practitioner (MSN); oncology (MSN). *Accreditation:* AACN; AANA/CANAEP. Part-time and evening/weekend programs available. *Degree requirements:* For master's, thesis or alternative, registration. *Entrance requirements:* For master's, minimum GPA of 3.0, 2 references, statistics course. Additional exam requirements/recommendations for international students: Required—TOEFL (minimum score 550 paper-based; 213 computer-based).

Bloomsburg University of Pennsylvania, School of Graduate Studies, College of Professional Studies, School of Health Sciences, Department of Nursing, Bloomsburg, PA 17815-1301. Offers adult and family nurse practitioner (MSN); adult health and illness (MSN); community health (MSN); nursing (MSN); nursing administration (MSN). *Accreditation:* AACN. *Faculty:* 11 full-time (all women). *Students:* 9 full-time (all women), 27 part-time (24 women). Average age 36. 10 applicants, 100% accepted, 5 enrolled. In 2006, 6 degrees awarded. *Degree requirements:* For master's, thesis. *Entrance requirements:* For master's, minimum QPA of 3.0. Additional exam requirements/recommendations for international students: Required—TOEFL. *Application deadline:* Applications are processed on a rolling basis. Application fee: $30. Electronic applications accepted. *Expenses:* Tuition, state resident: full-time $6,048; part-time $336 per credit. Tuition, nonresident: full-time $9,678; part-time $538 per credit. Required fees: $1,415. *Financial support:* Unspecified assistantships available. *Faculty research:* Cardiopulmonary nursing, cancer topics, women's health. *Application contact:* Dr. Michelle Ficca, Coordinator, 570-389-4615, Fax: 570-389-5008, E-mail: mficca@bloomu.edu.

Case Western Reserve University, Frances Payne Bolton School of Nursing, Doctor of Nursing Practice Program, Cleveland, OH 44106. Offers acute care nurse practitioner (DNP); adult nurse practitioner (DNP); family nurse practitioner (DNP); gerontological nurse practitioner (DNP); graduate entry/pre-licensure option (DNP); medical-surgical nursing (DNP); midwifery/family nursing (DNP); neonatal nurse practitioner (DNP); pediatric nurse practitioner (DNP); post-licensure option (DNP); psychiatric mental health nurse practitioner (DNP); women's health nurse practitioner (DNP). Graduate entry option allows baccalaureate-prepared college graduates from non-nursing backgrounds to earn certificate and MSN in addition to ND. *Students:* 125 full-time (109 women), 308 part-time (290 women); includes 47 minority (21 African Americans, 1 American Indian/Alaska Native, 18 Asian Americans or Pacific Islanders, 7 Hispanic Americans), 7 international. 190 applicants, 70% accepted, 80 enrolled. In 2006, 35 degrees awarded. Terminal master's awarded for partial completion of doctoral program. *Degree requirements:* For doctorate, thesis/dissertation. *Entrance requirements:* For doctorate, GRE General Test or MAT. *Application deadline:* For fall admission, 6/1 priority date for domestic students. Applications are processed on a rolling basis. Application fee: $75. *Financial support:* In 2006–07, 6 students received support, including 1 teaching assistantship; research assistantships, Federal Work-Study, institutionally sponsored loans, and tuition waivers (partial) also available. Support available to part-time students. Financial award application deadline: 6/30; financial award applicants required to submit FAFSA. *Faculty research:* Clinical nursing, acute care, gerontology, mental health, critical care. *Unit head:* Dr. Georgia Narsavage, Director, 216-368-6304, Fax: 216-368-3542, E-mail: gln2@cwru.edu. *Application contact:* Peter Taylor, Recruitment and Retention Specialist, 216-368-0349, Fax: 216-368-0124, E-mail: peter.taylor@case.edu.

Case Western Reserve University, Frances Payne Bolton School of Nursing, Master's Programs in Nursing, Nurse Practitioner Program, Cleveland, OH 44106. Offers acute care cardiovascular nursing (MSN); acute care nurse practitioner (MSN); acute care/flight nurse (MSN); adult nurse practitioner (MSN); family nurse practitioner (MSN); gerontological nurse practitioner (MSN); neonatal nurse practitioner (MSN); pediatric nurse practitioner (MSN); psychiatric-mental health nurse practitioner (MSN); women's health nurse practitioner (MSN). *Accreditation:* NLN. Part-time programs available. Postbaccalaureate distance learning degree programs offered (minimal on-campus study). *Faculty:* 54 full-time (50 women), 5 part-time/adjunct (3 women). *Students:* 19 full-time (15 women), 31 part-time (29 women); includes 16 minority (9 African Americans, 5 Asian Americans or Pacific Islanders, 2 Hispanic Americans), 2 international. Average age 35. 46 applicants, 72% accepted, 18 enrolled. In 2006, 34 degrees awarded. *Degree requirements:* For master's, thesis optional. *Entrance requirements:* For master's, GRE General Test or MAT. Additional exam requirements/recommendations for international students: Required—TOEFL. *Application deadline:* For fall admission, 6/1 for domestic students. Applications are processed on a rolling basis. Application fee: $75. *Financial support:* In 2006–07, 7 teaching assistantships were awarded; research assistantships, institutionally sponsored loans and tuition waivers (partial) also available. Support available to part-time students. Financial award application deadline: 6/30. *Faculty research:* Positive and negative mood states in parents of twins, effect of a carepath on chronic obstructive pulmonary disease home care. *Application contact:* Peter Taylor, Recruitment and Retention Specialist, 216-368-0349, Fax: 216-368-0124, E-mail: peter.taylor@case.edu.

The Catholic University of America, School of Nursing, Washington, DC 20064. Offers advanced practice nursing (MSN), including administration of nursing service, adult nurse practitioner, education, family nurse practitioner, geriatric nurse practitioner, pediatric nurse practitioner, psychiatric-mental health, school health nurse practitioner; clinical nursing (DN Sc). *Accreditation:* AACN; NLN. Part-time programs available. *Faculty:* 17 full-time (all women), 19 part-time/adjunct (18 women). *Students:* 27 full-time (25 women), 58 part-time (57 women); includes 31 minority (20 African Americans, 6 Asian Americans or Pacific Islanders, 5 Hispanic Americans), 6 international. Average age 43. 38 applicants, 76% accepted, 15 enrolled. In 2006, 15 master's, 7 doctorates awarded. *Degree requirements:* For master's, thesis optional; for doctorate, thesis/dissertation, comprehensive exam. *Entrance requirements:* For master's, GRE General Test or MAT, 3 letters of recommendation, BA in nursing, RN registration; for doctorate, GRE General Test, 3 letters of recommendation, BA in nursing, RN registration. Additional exam requirements/recommendations for international students: Required—TOEFL (minimum score 550 paper-based; 213 computer-based). *Application deadline:* For fall admission, 2/1 priority date for domestic students; for spring admission, 11/15 priority date for domestic students. Applications are processed on a rolling basis. Application fee: $55. Electronic applications accepted. *Expenses:* Tuition: Full-time $27,700; part-time $1,045 per credit hour. Required fees: $1,290. Part-time tuition and fees vary according to campus/location and program. *Financial support:* Research assistantships, teaching assistantships, career-related internships or fieldwork, Federal Work-Study, scholarships/grants, tuition waivers (full and partial), and unspecified assistantships available. Support available to part-time students. Financial award application deadline: 2/1; financial award applicants required to submit FAFSA. *Faculty research:* Outcome research–readmission of home health care patients with congestive heart failure, spirituality of chronic illness, minority multigravidos utilization of prenatal care. *Unit head:* Dr. Nalini Jairath, Dean, 202-319-5403, Fax: 202-319-6485, E-mail: jairath@cua.edu.

College of Mount Saint Vincent, School of Professional and Continuing Studies, Department of Nursing, Riverdale, NY 10471-1093. Offers adult nurse practitioner (MSN, PMC); family nurse practitioner (MSN, PMC); nurse educator (PMC); nursing administration (MSN); nursing for the adult and aged (MSN). *Accreditation:* AACN. Part-time programs available. *Faculty:* 2 full-time (1 woman), 6 part-time/adjunct (all women). *Students:* 1 (woman) full-time, 67 part-time (59 women); includes 43 minority (21 African Americans, 16 Asian Americans or Pacific Islanders, 6 Hispanic Americans). Average age 37. In 2006, 16 degrees awarded. *Degree requirements:* For master's, registration. *Entrance requirements:* For master's, BSN, interview, RN license, minimum GPA of 3.0, letters of reference. Additional exam requirements/recommendations for international students: Required—TOEFL. *Application deadline:* For fall admission, 6/1 for domestic and international students; for spring admission, 11/1 for domestic students, 10/1 for international students. Applications are processed on a rolling basis. Application fee: $50. *Expenses: Contact institution. Financial support:* Career-related internships or fieldwork available. Financial award application deadline: 6/1; financial award applicants required to submit FAFSA. *Unit head:* Carol Vicino, Director, 718-405-3354, Fax: 718-405-3286.

College of Staten Island of the City University of New York, Graduate Programs, Department of Nursing, Program in Adult Health Nursing, Staten Island, NY 10314-6600. Offers MS, 6th Year Certificate. Part-time and evening/weekend programs available. *Faculty:* 5 full-time (all women), 1 part-time/adjunct (0 women). *Students:* 1 (woman) full-time, 34 part-time (33 women); includes 10 minority (5 African Americans, 4 Asian Americans or Pacific Islanders, 1 Hispanic American), 1 international. Average age 40. 11 applicants, 82% accepted, 9 enrolled. In 2006, 5 master's, 3 other advanced degrees awarded. *Degree requirements:* For master's, 42 credits with 500 supervised hours, thesis optional; for 6th Year Certificate, 12-21 credits with 500 supervised hours. *Entrance requirements:* For master's, minimum undergraduate GPA of 3.0 in nursing courses, New York RN license, 2 professional references, specific undergraduate courses; for 6th Year Certificate, master's degree in nursing for post masters advanced certificate. Additional exam requirements/recommendations for international students: Required—TOEFL (minimum score 550 paper-based; 213 computer-based; 79 iBT). *Application deadline:* Applications are processed on a rolling basis. Application fee: $125. *Expenses:* Tuition, state resident: full-time $6,400; part-time $270 per credit. Tuition, nonresident: part-time $500 per credit. Required fees: $53 per semester. *Financial support:* Traineeships available. Financial award applicants required to submit FAFSA. *Unit head:* Dr. Margaret Lunney, Coordinator, 718-982-3823, Fax: 718-982-4124, E-mail: nursingmasters@mail.csi.cuny.edu. *Application contact:* Emmanuel Esperance, Deputy Director of Office of Recruitment and Admissions, 718-982-2190, Fax: 718-982-2500, E-mail: admissions@mail.csi.cuny.edu.

Columbia University, School of Nursing, Program in Adult Nurse Practitioner, New York, NY 10032. Offers MS, Adv C. *Accreditation:* AACN. Part-time programs available. *Faculty:* 3 full-time (all women). *Students:* 10 full-time (all women), 19 part-time (17 women); includes 6 minority (2 African Americans, 3 Asian Americans or Pacific Islanders, 1 Hispanic American), 2 international. Average age 32. In 2006, 35 degrees awarded. *Entrance requirements:* For master's, GRE General Test, BSN, 1 year of clinical experience (preferred); for Adv C, MSN. *Application deadline:* Applications are processed on a rolling basis. Application fee: $65. Electronic applications accepted. *Financial support:* Teaching assistantships available. Financial award application deadline: 2/1; financial award applicants required to submit FAFSA. *Unit head:* Prof. JoAnne Staats, Director, 212-305-7327.

Duke University, School of Nursing, Durham, NC 27708-0586. Offers adult acute care (Certificate); adult cardiovascular (Certificate); adult oncology/HIV (Certificate); adult primary care (Certificate); clinical nurse specialist (MSN), including adult oncology/HIV, gerontology, neonatal, pediatric, pediatric/chronic acute care; clinical research management (MSN, Certificate); family (Certificate); gerontology (Certificate); health and nursing ministries (MSN, Certificate); health systems leadership and outcomes (Certificate); leadership in community based long term care (MSN, Certificate); neonatal (Certificate); neonatal/pediatric in rural health (MSN, Certificate); nurse anesthetist (MSN, Certificate); nurse practitioner (MSN), including adult acute care, adult cardiovascular, adult oncology/HIV, adult primary care, family, gerontology, neonatal, pediatric, pediatric acute care; nursing (PhD); nursing and healthcare leadership (MSN); nursing education (MSN); nursing informatics (MSN, Certificate); pediatric (Certificate); pediatric acute care (Certificate); MBA/MSN; MSN/MCM. *Accreditation:* AACN; AANA/CANAEP. Part-time programs available. Postbaccalaureate distance learning degree programs offered (minimal on-campus study). *Faculty:* 45 full-time (41 women), 169 part-time/adjunct (150 women). *Students:* 178 full-time (162 women), 140 part-time (132 women); includes 48 minority (17 African Americans, 3 American Indian/Alaska Native, 20 Asian Americans or Pacific Islanders, 8 Hispanic Americans). Average age 36. 99 applicants, 92% accepted, 91 enrolled. In 2006, 122 master's, 17 other advanced degrees awarded. *Median time to degree:* Master's–2 years full-time, 2.5 years part-time. *Degree requirements:* For master's, thesis optional. *Entrance requirements:* For master's, GRE General Test or MAT, 1 year of nursing experience, BSN, minimum GPA of 3.0, previous course work in statistics; for Certificate, MSN. Additional exam requirements/recommendations for international students: Required—TOEFL (minimum score 550 paper-based; 213 computer-based), Commission on Graduates of Foreign Nursing Schools exam. *Application deadline:* For fall admission, 7/2 priority date for domestic and international students; for spring admission, 11/15 priority date for domestic and international students. Applications are processed on a rolling basis. Application fee: $50. *Expenses: Contact institution. Financial support:* In 2006–07, 258 students received support. Career-related internships or fieldwork, institutionally sponsored loans, scholarships/grants, traineeships, and tuition waivers (partial) available. Support available to part-time students. Financial award application deadline: 4/1; financial award applicants required to submit FAFSA. *Faculty research:* Cardiovascular disease, caregiver skill training, data mining, prostate cancer, neonatal immune system. Total annual research expenditures: $3.5 million. *Unit head:* Dr. Catherine L. Gilliss, Dean/Vice Chancellor for Nursing Affairs, 919-684-9444, Fax: 919-684-9414, E-mail: gilli025@mc.duke.edu. *Application contact:* Bebe T. Mills, Director of Admissions, 919-684-9151, Fax: 919-668-4693, E-mail: mills031@mc.duke.edu.

Eastern Michigan University, Graduate School, College of Health and Human Services, School of Nursing, Ypsilanti, MI 48197. Offers nursing (MSN); nursing education (Advanced Certificate). *Accreditation:* AACN. Part-time and evening/weekend programs available. Postbaccalaureate distance learning degree programs offered (minimal on-campus study). *Faculty:* 18 full-time (17 women). *Students:* 1 (woman) full-time, 25 part-time (all women); includes 9 minority (7 African Americans, 2 Asian Americans or Pacific Islanders). Average age 42. In 2006, 13 degrees awarded. *Degree requirements:* For master's, thesis optional. *Entrance requirements:* For master's, GRE General Test, Michigan RN license. Additional exam requirements/recommendations for international students: Required—TOEFL. *Application deadline:* For fall admission, 5/15 priority date for domestic students, 5/1 priority date for international students; for winter admission, 10/15 priority date for domestic students, 10/1 priority date for international students; for spring admission, 3/15 priority date for domestic students, 3/1 priority date for international students. Applications are processed on a rolling basis. Application fee: $35. *Expenses:* Tuition, state resident: part-time $341 per credit hour. Tuition, nonresident: full-time $16,104; part-time $671 per credit hour. Required fees: $816; $34 per credit hour. $40 per term. One-time fee: $82 full-time. Tuition and fees vary according to course level, course load, degree level and reciprocity agreements. *Financial support:* Fellowships, research assistantships with full tuition reimbursements, teaching assistantships with full tuition reimbursements, career-related internships or fieldwork, Federal Work-Study, institutionally sponsored loans, scholarships/grants, tuition waivers (partial), and unspecified

Adult Nursing

Eastern Michigan University (continued)
assistantships available. Support available to part-time students. Financial award applicants required to submit FAFSA. *Unit head:* Dr. Naomi Ervin, Director, 734-487-2310, Fax: 734-487-9646, E-mail: nervin@emich.edu.

Emory University, Nell Hodgson Woodruff School of Nursing, Atlanta, GA 30322-1100. Offers adult and elder health advanced practice nursing (MSN), including acute and critical care, adult nurse practitioner, gerontology, oncology; emergency nurse practitioner (MSN); family nurse practitioner (MSN); family nurse-midwife (MSN); leadership in healthcare (MSN); nurse midwifery (MSN); nursing administration (MSN); pediatric advanced nursing practice (MSN); public health nursing (MSN); women's health nurse practitioner (MSN); MSN/MPH. *Accreditation:* AACN; ACNM/DOA (one or more programs are accredited). Part-time programs available. *Entrance requirements:* For master's, GRE General Test or MAT, minimum GPA of 3.0, BS in nursing, RN license and additional course work, 3 letters of recommendation. Additional exam requirements/recommendations for international students: Required—TOEFL (minimum score 600 paper-based; 250 computer-based). Electronic applications accepted. Expenses: Contact institution. *Faculty research:* Older adult falls and injuries, minority health issues, cardiac symptoms amd quality of life, bio-ethics and decision making, menopausal issues.

See Close-Up on page 1955.

The George Washington University, School of Medicine and Health Sciences, Health Sciences Programs, Washington, DC 20052. Offers adult nurse practitioner (MSN, Post Master's Certificate); advanced family nurse practitioner (Post Master's Certificate); clinical practice management (MSHS); clinical research administration (MSHS); clinical research administration for nurses (MSN); emergency services management (MSHS); end-of-life care (MSHS, MSN); family nurse practitioner (MSN); immunohematology (MSHS); nursing leadership and management (MSN); oral biology (MSHS); physical therapy (DPT); physician assistant (MSHS); MSHS/MPH. Postbaccalaureate distance learning degree programs offered (no on-campus study). *Entrance requirements:* Additional exam requirements/recommendations for international students: Required—TOEFL (minimum score 550 paper-based; 213 computer-based). Expenses: Contact institution.

Georgia State University, College of Health and Human Sciences, School of Nursing, Atlanta, GA 30303-3083. Offers adult health (MS); child health (MS); family nurse practitioner (MS); health promotion, protection and restoration (PhD); nursing (Certificate); perinatal/women's health (MS); psychiatric/mental health (MS). *Accreditation:* AACN. Part-time and evening/weekend programs available. *Faculty:* 35 full-time (all women), 1 (woman) part-time/adjunct. *Students:* 72 full-time (66 women), 128 part-time (123 women); includes 75 minority (61 African Americans, 9 Asian Americans or Pacific Islanders, 5 Hispanic Americans), 2 international. Average age 37. 70 applicants, 54% accepted, 30 enrolled. In 2006, 39 master's, 6 doctorates awarded. *Degree requirements:* For master's, research activity; for doctorate, thesis/dissertation, comprehensive exam. *Entrance requirements:* For master's, MAT (preferred) or GRE, interview, RN license; for doctorate, GRE General Test. Additional exam requirements/recommendations for international students: Required—TOEFL (minimum score 550 paper-based; 213 computer-based). *Application deadline:* For fall admission, 3/1 priority date for domestic students; for spring admission, 10/1 priority date for domestic students. Applications are processed on a rolling basis. Application fee: $50. Electronic applications accepted. *Expenses: Contact institution. Financial support:* In 2006–07, research assistantships with full and partial tuition reimbursements (averaging $3,108 per year); fellowships with full tuition reimbursements, teaching assistantships, Federal Work-Study, institutionally sponsored loans, scholarships/grants, traineeships, and tuition waivers (partial) also available. Support available to part-time students. Financial award application deadline: 4/1; financial award applicants required to submit FAFSA. *Faculty research:* Breast cancer prevention, sexually compulsive behaviors, health risks in minority youth, asthma treatment strategies, adolescent alcohol-related issues. Total annual research expenditures: $221,691. *Unit head:* Dr. Barbara Woodring, Director, 404-651-3040. *Application contact:* Barbara Smith, Admissions Counselor II, 404-651-3834, Fax: 404-651-4871, E-mail: bbsmith@gsu.edu.

Gwynedd-Mercy College, School of Nursing, Gwynedd Valley, PA 19437-0901. Offers clinical nurse specialist (MSN), including gerontology, oncology, pediatrics; nurse practitioner (MSN), including adult health, pediatric health. *Accreditation:* NLN. *Faculty:* 5 full-time (all women), 3 part-time/adjunct (2 women). *Students:* 7 full-time (5 women), 38 part-time (35 women); includes 3 minority (1 African American, 1 Asian American or Pacific Islander, 1 Hispanic American). Average age 41. 18 applicants, 89% accepted, 11 enrolled. In 2006, 5 degrees awarded. *Degree requirements:* For master's, thesis optional. *Entrance requirements:* For master's, GRE General Test or MAT, 2 years of experience, physical assessment, course work in statistics, BSN from an NLNAC accredited program, 2 letters of recommendation, personal interview. Additional exam requirements/recommendations for international students: Required—TOEFL (minimum score 575 paper-based). *Application deadline:* For fall admission, 8/1 priority date for domestic students; for winter admission, 12/1 priority date for domestic students. Applications are processed on a rolling basis. Application fee: $25. Electronic applications accepted. *Expenses: Contact institution. Financial support:* In 2006–07, 21 students received support. Scholarships/grants, traineeships, and unspecified assistantships available. Financial award application deadline: 8/30. *Faculty research:* Critical thinking, primary care, domestic violence, multiculturalism, nursing centers. *Unit head:* Dr. Andrea D. Hollingsworth, Dean, 215-646-7300 Ext. 539, Fax: 215-641-5517, E-mail: hollingsworth.a@gmc.edu. *Application contact:* Dr. Barbara A. Jones, Director, 215-646-7300 Ext. 407, Fax: 215-641-5564, E-mail: jones.b@gmc.edu.

Hunter College of the City University of New York, Graduate School, Schools of the Health Professions, Hunter-Bellevue School of Nursing, Program in Adult Nurse Practitioner, New York, NY 10021-5085. Offers MS. *Accreditation:* AACN. *Faculty:* 24 full-time (21 women), 21 part-time/adjunct (19 women). *Students:* Average age 34. 42 applicants, 48% accepted, 15 enrolled. In 2006, 19 degrees awarded. *Degree requirements:* For master's, practicum. *Entrance requirements:* For master's, minimum GPA of 3.0, New York RN license, 2 years of professional practice experience, BSN. Additional exam requirements/recommendations for international students: Required—TOEFL. *Application deadline:* For fall admission, 4/1 for domestic students, 2/1 for international students; for spring admission, 11/1 for domestic students, 9/1 for international students. Applications are processed on a rolling basis. Application fee: $125. *Expenses:* Tuition, state resident: part-time $270 per credit. Tuition, nonresident: part-time $500 per credit. Required fees: $45 per semester. *Financial support:* Federal Work-Study, scholarships/grants, and traineeships available. Support available to part-time students. Financial award application deadline: 5/1. *Faculty research:* Adult primary care, critical care. *Unit head:* Dr. Vidette Todard-Francescli, Coordinator, 212-481-4445, Fax: 212-481-5078. *Application contact:* William Zlata, Director for Graduate Admissions, 212-772-4482, Fax: 212-650-3336, E-mail: admissions@hunter.cuny.edu.

Indiana University–Purdue University Indianapolis, School of Nursing, Department of Adult Health Nursing, Indianapolis, IN 46202-2896. Offers adult clinical nurse specialist (MSN), including chronic disability, critical care, health promotion, oncology. *Accreditation:* AACN. Part-time programs available. *Students:* 4 full-time (all women), 44 part-time (41 women); includes 4 minority (2 African Americans, 2 Hispanic Americans). Average age 39. In 2006, 15 degrees awarded. *Degree requirements:* For master's, thesis. *Entrance requirements:* For master's, GRE General Test, minimum GPA of 3.0, RN license. *Application deadline:* For fall admission, 4/1 for domestic students; for spring admission, 10/1 for domestic students. Application fee: $50 ($60 for international students). *Expenses:* Tuition, state resident: full-time $5,437; part-time $227 per credit hour. Tuition, nonresident: full-time $15,694; part-time $654 per credit hour. Required fees: $620. Tuition and fees vary according to course load, campus/location and program. *Financial support:* Fellowships with full tuition reimbursements, research assistantships with full tuition reimbursements, teaching assistantships with full tuition reimbursements, Federal Work-Study, scholarships/grants, and traineeships available. Support available to part-time students. Financial award application deadline: 5/1. *Unit head:* Dr. Juanita Keck, Co-Chair, 317-274-0050.

The Johns Hopkins University, School of Nursing, Nurse Practitioner Program, Baltimore, MD 21218-2699. Offers adult acute/critical care (MSN, Certificate); adult and pediatric primary care (MSN); adult or pediatric primary care (Certificate); family primary care (MSN, Certificate). *Accreditation:* AACN; NLN (one or more programs are accredited). Part-time programs available. *Faculty:* 12 full-time (all women), 6 part-time/adjunct (5 women). *Students:* 23 full-time (22 women), 62 part-time (58 women); includes 26 minority (3 African Americans, 3 American Indian/Alaska Native, 15 Asian Americans or Pacific Islanders, 5 Hispanic Americans), 1 international. Average age 31. 157 applicants, 85% accepted, 32 enrolled. In 2006, 18 master's, 2 other advanced degrees awarded. *Degree requirements:* For master's, scholarly project or portfolio, thesis optional. *Entrance requirements:* For master's, GRE, interview, minimum GPA of 3.0, BSN, Maryland RN license. Additional exam requirements/recommendations for international students: Required—TOEFL (minimum score 550 paper-based; 230 computer-based). *Application deadline:* For fall admission, 3/1 priority date for domestic and international students; for spring admission, 7/1 priority date for domestic and international students. Application fee: $75. *Expenses: Contact institution.* Tuition and fees vary according to degree level and program. *Financial support:* In 2006–07, 16 students received support. Federal Work-Study, scholarships/grants, traineeships, and tuition waivers (partial) available. Support available to part-time students. Financial award application deadline: 3/1; financial award applicants required to submit FAFSA. *Faculty research:* Community outreach, primary care of underserved populations, substance abusing individuals, childhood violence, women's health. *Unit head:* Dr. Kathleen M. White, Director, Master's Programs, 410-614-4664, Fax: 410-955-7463, E-mail: kwhite@son.jhmi.edu. *Application contact:* Mary O'Rourke, Director of Admissions/Student Services, 410-955-7548, Fax: 410-614-7086, E-mail: orourke@son.jhmi.edu.

La Salle University, School of Nursing and Health Sciences, Philadelphia, PA 19141-1199. Offers adult health and illness, clinical nurse specialist (MSN); gerontology (Certificate); nursing administration (MSN); nursing education (Certificate); nursing informatics (Certificate); primary care of adults-nurse practitioner (MSN); public health nursing (MSN); school nursing (Certificate); speech-language-hearing science (MS); wound, ostomy and continence nursing (Certificate); wound, ostomy, and continence nursing (MSN); MSN/MBA. *Accreditation:* AACN. Part-time programs available. Postbaccalaureate distance learning degree programs offered (minimal on-campus study). *Entrance requirements:* For master's, GRE or MAT, 1 year of professional work experience, BSN, Pennsylvania RN license. Expenses: Contact institution. *Faculty research:* Medication errors, wound care, metacognition, education of RN students.

Lehman College of the City University of New York, Division of Natural and Social Sciences, Department of Nursing, Bronx, NY 10468-1589. Offers adult health nursing (MS); nursing of older adults (MS); parent-child nursing (MS); pediatric nurse practitioner (MS). *Accreditation:* AACN. Part-time and evening/weekend programs available. *Entrance requirements:* For master's, bachelor's degree in nursing, New York RN license.

Long Island University, Brooklyn Campus, School of Nursing, Department of Adult Nurse Practitioner, Brooklyn, NY 11201-8423. Offers MS, Certificate. *Accreditation:* AACN. *Entrance requirements:* For master's, New York RN license, 2 letters of recommendation. Additional exam requirements/recommendations for international students: Required—TOEFL (minimum score 500 paper-based; 173 computer-based). Electronic applications accepted.

Louisiana State University Health Sciences Center, School of Nursing, New Orleans, LA 70112-2223. Offers adult health and illness (MN); adult health and nursing (DNS); neonatal nurse practitioner (MN); nursing (MN); nursing service administration (MN, DNS); parent-child health nursing (MN); primary care nurse practitioner (MN); psychiatric/community mental health nursing (MN, DNS); public health/community health nursing (MN, DNS). *Accreditation:* AACN; AANA/CANAEP (one or more programs are accredited). Part-time programs available. *Degree requirements:* For master's, thesis optional; for doctorate, thesis/dissertation. *Entrance requirements:* For master's, GRE General Test, MAT, minimum GPA of 3.0; for doctorate, GRE General Test, minimum GPA of 3.5. Additional exam requirements/recommendations for international students: Required—TOEFL. *Expenses:* Tuition, state resident: full-time $5,868; part-time $722 per credit. Tuition, nonresident: full-time $8,993; part-time $1,104 per credit. *Faculty research:* Advanced clinical practice, nursing education, health, social support, nursing administration.

Loyola University Chicago, Graduate School, Marcella Niehoff School of Nursing, Adult Nurse Practitioner Program, Chicago, IL 60611-2196. Offers MSN. *Accreditation:* AACN. Part-time and evening/weekend programs available. *Students:* 7 full-time (6 women), 32 part-time (30 women). Average age 29. In 2006, 5 degrees awarded. *Degree requirements:* For master's, comprehensive exam or oral thesis defense. *Entrance requirements:* For master's, BSN, minimum GPA of 3.0, professional license. *Application deadline:* Applications are processed on a rolling basis. Application fee: $40. Electronic applications accepted. *Financial support:* Traineeships available. *Faculty research:* Menopause. *Unit head:* Dr. Marijo Letizia, Associate Professor, 708-216-9325, Fax: 708-216-9555, E-mail: mletizi@luc.edu. *Application contact:* Dr. Vicki A. Keough, Associate Professor, 708-216-3582, Fax: 708-216-9555, E-mail: vkeough@luc.edu.

Loyola University Chicago, Graduate School, Marcella Niehoff School of Nursing, Program in Adult Clinical Nurse Specialist, Chicago, IL 60611-2196. Offers MSN. *Students:* 2 full-time (both women), 2 part-time (both women). In 2006, 1 degree awarded. *Entrance requirements:* For master's, Illinois license, 3 letters of recommendation. *Unit head:* Dr. Meg Gulanick, Professor, 708-216-9687, Fax: 708-216-9555, E-mail: mgulani@luc.edu. *Application contact:* Dr. Vicki A. Keough, Associate Professor, 708-216-3582, Fax: 708-216-9555, E-mail: vkeough@luc.edu.

Madonna University, Program in Nursing, Livonia, MI 48150-1173. Offers adult health: chronic health conditions (MSN); adult nurse practitioner (MSN); nursing administration (MSN); MSN/MSBA. *Accreditation:* AACN. Part-time programs available. *Faculty:* 3 full-time (all women). *Students:* 12 full-time (all women), 82 part-time (80 women); includes 9 minority (5 African Americans, 3 Asian Americans or Pacific Islanders, 1 Hispanic American), 3 international. Average age 40. 20 applicants, 50% accepted. In 2006, 10 degrees awarded. *Degree requirements:* For master's, thesis or alternative. *Entrance requirements:* For master's, GRE General Test, Michigan nursing license. *Application deadline:* For fall admission, 8/1 priority date for domestic students; for winter admission, 12/1 priority date for domestic students; for spring admission, 4/1 priority date for domestic students. Applications are processed on a rolling basis. Application fee: $25 ($200 for international students). Electronic applications accepted. *Financial support:* Career-related internships or fieldwork, Federal Work-Study, institutionally sponsored loans, and scholarships/grants available. Support available to part-time students. *Faculty research:* Coping, caring. *Unit head:* Dr. Nancy O'Connor, Chairperson, 734-432-5461, Fax: 734-432-5463, E-mail: noconnor@madonna.edu. *Application contact:* Sandra Kellums, Coordinator of Graduate Admissions and Records, 734-432-5667, Fax: 734-432-5862, E-mail: skellum@madonna.edu.

Marian College of Fond du Lac, School of Nursing, Fond du Lac, WI 54935-4699. Offers adult nurse practitioner (MSN); nurse educator (MSN). *Accreditation:* AACN. Part-time and evening/weekend programs available. *Faculty:* 4 full-time (3 women), 4 part-time/adjunct (2 women). *Students:* 13 full-time (all women), 15 part-time (all women); includes 1 minority (American Indian/Alaska Native). Average age 37. 9 applicants, 100% accepted, 9 enrolled. In 2006, 16 degrees awarded. *Degree requirements:* For master's, thesis, 675 clinical practicum hours. *Entrance requirements:* For master's, 3 letters of professional recommendation, undergraduate work in nursing research, statistics, health assessment. Additional exam requirements/recommendations for international students: Required—TOEFL (minimum score 525 paper-based). *Application deadline:* Applications are processed on a rolling basis. Application fee: $50. Electronic applications accepted. *Expenses: Contact institution. Financial support:* In 2006–07, 19 students received support. Institutionally sponsored loans and scholarships/

grants available. Support available to part-time students. Financial award application deadline: 3/1; financial award applicants required to submit FAFSA. *Unit head:* Dr. James C. McCann, Dean, School of Nursing, 920-923-8094, Fax: 920-923-8770, E-mail: jcmccann70@mariancollege.edu. *Application contact:* Dr. Lea Monahan, Director, 920-923-7608, Fax: 920-923-8770, E-mail: lmonahan@mariancollege.edu.

Marquette University, Graduate School, College of Nursing, Milwaukee, WI 53201-1881. Offers adult nurse practitioner (Certificate); advanced practice nursing (MSN), including adult, children, neonatal nurse practitioner, nurse-midwifery, older adult; gerontological nurse practitioner (Certificate); neonatal nurse practitioner (Certificate); nurse-midwifery (Certificate); nursing (PhD); pediatric nurse practitioner (Certificate). *Accreditation:* AACN. Part-time and evening/weekend programs available. *Faculty:* 29 full-time (27 women), 39 part-time/adjunct (37 women). *Students:* 104 full-time (98 women), 122 part-time (114 women); includes 18 minority (5 African Americans, 2 American Indian/Alaska Native, 4 Asian Americans or Pacific Islanders, 7 Hispanic Americans), 2 international. Average age 34. 122 applicants, 79% accepted, 73 enrolled. In 2006, 46 degrees awarded. *Degree requirements:* For master's, thesis or alternative, comprehensive exam. *Entrance requirements:* For master's, GRE General Test, BSN, Wisconsin RN license. Additional exam requirements/recommendations for international students: Required—TOEFL. Application fee: $40. *Financial support:* In 2006–07, 6 research assistantships, 1 teaching assistantship were awarded; career-related internships or fieldwork, Federal Work-Study, institutionally sponsored loans, scholarships/grants, and tuition waivers (full and partial) also available. Support available to part-time students. Financial award application deadline: 2/15. *Faculty research:* Psychosocial adjustment to chronic illness, gerontology, reminiscence, health policy: uninsured and access, hospital care delivery systems. Total annual research expenditures: $1.1 million. *Unit head:* Dr. Lea Acord, Dean, 414-288-3812, Fax: 414-288-1578. *Application contact:* Dr. Judy Miller, Director of Graduate Studies, 414-288-3810, Fax: 414-288-1578.

Medical College of Georgia, School of Graduate Studies, Programs in Nursing, Augusta, GA 30912-1500. Offers adult nursing (MSN); community health nursing (MSN); mental health nursing (MSN); nurse practitioner (MSN); nursing (DNP, PhD); nursing anesthesia (MSN); parent-child nursing (MSN). *Accreditation:* AACN; AANA/CANAEP. Part-time programs available. *Faculty:* 18 full-time (16 women), 1 part-time/adjunct (0 women). *Students:* 95 full-time (76 women), 42 part-time (37 women); includes 24 minority (20 African Americans, 4 Asian Americans or Pacific Islanders). Average age 37. 156 applicants, 35% accepted, 24 enrolled. In 2006, 28 master's, 10 doctorates awarded. *Degree requirements:* For master's, thesis (for some programs); for doctorate, thesis/dissertation. *Entrance requirements:* For master's, GRE General Test, MAT; for doctorate, GRE General Test. Additional exam requirements/recommendations for international students: Required—TOEFL (minimum score 550 paper-based; 213 computer-based). *Application deadline:* For fall admission, 7/1 for domestic students, 4/15 for international students. Applications are processed on a rolling basis. Application fee: $30. Electronic applications accepted. *Expenses:* Tuition, state resident: full-time $2,293; part-time $192 per credit hour. Tuition, nonresident: full-time $9,169; part-time $765 per credit hour. Required fees: $293 per semester. *Financial support:* In 2006–07, 78 students received support, including 9 research assistantships with partial tuition reimbursements available (averaging $23,000 per year); Federal Work-Study, institutionally sponsored loans, traineeships, tuition waivers, and unspecified assistantships also available. Support available to part-time students. Financial award application deadline: 5/31; financial award applicants required to submit FAFSA. *Unit head:* Dr. Lucy Marion, Dean, 706-721-6258, Fax: 706-721-8169, E-mail: lumarion@mail.mcg.edu.

Medical University of South Carolina, College of Nursing, Adult Nurse Practitioner Program, Charleston, SC 29425-0002. Offers MSN. Part-time programs available. Postbaccalaureate distance learning degree programs offered (minimal on-campus study). *Faculty:* 5 full-time (all women), 4 part-time/adjunct (2 women). *Students:* 5 full-time (3 women), 9 part-time (all women). Average age 36. 7 applicants, 86% accepted, 6 enrolled. In 2006, 5 degrees awarded. *Degree requirements:* For master's, thesis optional. *Entrance requirements:* For master's, GRE General Test, BSN, course work in statistics and physical assessment, nursing license, minimum GPA of 3.0. Additional exam requirements/recommendations for international students: Required—TOEFL (minimum score 600 paper-based; 250 computer-based). *Application deadline:* For fall admission, 2/1 for domestic and international students; for spring admission, 9/15 for domestic and international students. Application fee: $75. Electronic applications accepted. *Financial support:* Federal Work-Study, scholarships/grants, and traineeships available. Support available to part-time students. Financial award application deadline: 3/15; financial award applicants required to submit FAFSA. *Faculty research:* Primary and palliative care. Total annual research expenditures: $217,977. *Unit head:* Dr. Sally Stroud, Track Coordinator, 843-792-4616, Fax: 843-792-2099, E-mail: stroudsd@musc.edu. *Application contact:* Carolyn F. Page, Director, Student Services, 843-792-3844, Fax: 843-792-9258, E-mail: pagecf@musc.edu.

Mercy College, Division of Health Professions, Dobbs Ferry, NY 10522-1189. Offers adult nurse practitioner (MS, AC); communication disorders (MS); nursing (MS), including nursing administration, nursing education; occupational therapy (MS); physical therapy (MS); physician assistant (MPS, MS). *Students:* 264 full-time (200 women), 147 part-time (134 women); includes 152 minority (75 African Americans, 26 Asian Americans or Pacific Islanders, 51 Hispanic Americans), 17 international. Average age 33. In 2006, 109 degrees awarded. Application fee: $62. *Expenses:* Tuition: Part-time $595 per credit. Required fees: $9 per credit. Tuition and fees vary according to program. *Unit head:* Dr. Pat Chute, 914-674-7746, E-mail: pchute@mercy.edu. *Application contact:* Kathleen Jackson, Director of Admissions, 800-Mercy-NY, Fax: 914-674-7382, E-mail: admissions@mercy.edu.

Molloy College, Department of Nursing, Rockville Centre, NY 11571-5002. Offers adult nurse practitioner (Advanced Certificate); clinical nurse specialist: adult health (Advanced Certificate); family nurse practitioner (Advanced Certificate); nurse practitioner psychiatry (Advanced Certificate); nursing (MS); nursing administration (Advanced Certificate); nursing administration with informatics (Advanced Certificate); nursing education (Advanced Certificate); nursing informatics (Advanced Certificate); pediatric nurse practitioner (Advanced Certificate). *Accreditation:* AACN. Part-time and evening/weekend programs available. *Degree requirements:* For master's, thesis optional. *Entrance requirements:* For master's, 3 letters of reference, BS in nursing, minimum undergraduate GPA of 3.0; for Advanced Certificate, 3 letters of reference, master's degree in nursing. *Faculty research:* Hardiness and aging, alcoholism, current ethics, breast cancer, nurse role perception.

Mount Carmel College of Nursing, College of Nursing, Columbus, OH 43222. Offers adult health (MS); nursing education (MS). Part-time programs available. *Entrance requirements:* For master's, letters of recommendation, current resumé, baccalaureate degree in nursing, current Ohio RN license, cumulative GPA of 3.0. Additional exam requirements/recommendations for international students: Required—TOEFL (minimum score 550 paper-based).

See Close-Up on page 1967.

Mount Saint Mary College, Division of Nursing, Newburgh, NY 12550-3494. Offers adult nurse practitioner (MS), including nursing education, nursing management; clinical nurse specialist-adult health (MS), including nursing education, nursing management. *Accreditation:* AACN. Part-time and evening/weekend programs available. *Faculty:* 3 full-time (2 women), 1 (woman) part-time/adjunct. *Students:* 1 (woman) full-time, 28 part-time (26 women); includes 3 minority (2 African Americans, 1 Asian American or Pacific Islander). Average age 42. 12 applicants, 100% accepted, 10 enrolled. In 2006, 6 degrees awarded. *Degree requirements:* For master's, research utilization project. *Entrance requirements:* For master's, BSN, minimum GPA of 3.0, RN license. *Application deadline:* For fall admission, 6/3 priority date for domestic students; for spring admission, 10/31 priority date for domestic students. Applications are processed on a rolling basis. Application fee: $35. *Expenses:* Tuition: Full-time $11,880; part-time $660 per credit. *Financial support:* Unspecified assistantships and nursing lab assistant available. Financial award application deadline: 3/15; financial award applicants required to submit FAFSA. *Unit head:* Dr. Karen Baldwin, Coordinator, 845-569-3512, Fax: 845-562-6762, E-mail: baldwin@msmc.edu.

New Mexico State University, Graduate School, College of Health and Social Services, School of Nursing, Las Cruces, NM 88003-8001. Offers community/public health (MSN); medical-surgical (adult health) (MSN); psychiatric/mental health (MSN). *Accreditation:* AACN. Part-time programs available. Postbaccalaureate distance learning degree programs offered (minimal on-campus study). *Faculty:* 12 full-time (all women), 5 part-time/adjunct (4 women). *Students:* 27 full-time (24 women), 25 part-time (all women); includes 13 minority (1 African American, 12 Hispanic Americans), 1 international. Average age 45. 24 applicants, 83% accepted. In 2006, 14 degrees awarded. *Degree requirements:* For master's, clinical practice, RN licensure, thesis optional. *Entrance requirements:* For master's, BSN, minimum GPA of 3.0, course work in statistics, 3 letters of reference, writing sample. Additional exam requirements/recommendations for international students: Required—NCLEX. *Application deadline:* For fall admission, 3/1 priority date for domestic students; for spring admission, 10/1 priority date for domestic students. Applications are processed on a rolling basis. Application fee: $30 ($50 for international students). Electronic applications accepted. *Financial support:* In 2006–07, 2 teaching assistantships were awarded; fellowships, research assistantships, career-related internships or fieldwork, Federal Work-Study, scholarships/grants, traineeships, and health care benefits also available. Financial award application deadline: 3/1. *Faculty research:* Advanced practice nursing, evidence-based nursing practice, health policy, community outreach, clinical judgment. *Unit head:* Dr. Esperanza V. Joyce, Director, 505-646-3812, Fax: 505-646-2167, E-mail: evjoyce@nmsu.edu. *Application contact:* Dr. Mary Hoke, Associate Director for Graduate Studies, 505-646-3812, Fax: 505-646-2167, E-mail: mhoke@nmsu.edu.

New York University, College of Dentistry, College of Nursing, Programs in Advanced Practice Nursing, New York, NY 10012-1019. Offers advanced practice nursing: adult acute care (MS, Advanced Certificate); advanced practice nursing: adult primary care (MS, Advanced Certificate); advanced practice nursing: adult primary care/geriatrics (MS); advanced practice nursing: children with special needs (Advanced Certificate); advanced practice nursing: geriatrics (MS, Advanced Certificate); advanced practice nursing: holistic nursing (MS, Advanced Certificate); advanced practice nursing: home health nursing (Advanced Certificate); advanced practice nursing: mental health (MS); advanced practice nursing: mental health nursing (Advanced Certificate); advanced practice nursing: pediatrics (MS, Advanced Certificate); advanced practice nursing: pediatrics/children with special needs (MS); midwifery (MS, Advanced Certificate); nursing administration (MS, Advanced Certificate); nursing education (MS, Advanced Certificate); nursing informatics (MS, Advanced Certificate); palliative care (MS, Advanced Certificate); MS/MS. *Accreditation:* AACN; ACNM/DOA. Part-time and evening/weekend programs available. *Faculty:* 30 full-time (all women). *Students:* 10 full-time (all women), 428 part-time (395 women); includes 166 minority (73 African Americans, 72 Asian Americans or Pacific Islanders, 21 Hispanic Americans). Average age 35. 154 applicants, 93% accepted, 118 enrolled. In 2006, 100 master's, 7 Advanced Certificates awarded. *Degree requirements:* For master's, thesis (for some programs). *Entrance requirements:* For master's, BS in nursing, AS in nursing with another BS/BA degree; for Advanced Certificate, master's degree. Additional exam requirements/recommendations for international students: Required—TOEFL. *Application deadline:* For fall admission, 7/1 priority date for domestic students, 7/1 for international students; for spring admission, 12/1 for domestic and international students. Applications are processed on a rolling basis. Application fee: $65. *Expenses:* Tuition: Part-time $1,080 per unit. Required fees: $56 per unit. $329 per term. Tuition and fees vary according to program. *Financial support:* Career-related internships or fieldwork, Federal Work-Study, institutionally sponsored loans, scholarships/grants, and tuition waivers (partial) available. Support available to part-time students. Financial award application deadline: 2/1; financial award applicants required to submit FAFSA. *Faculty research:* Elderly black diabetics, families and illness, public health nursing, parent-child nursing, health policy costs. *Unit head:* Dr. Judith Haber, Associate Dean for Graduate Programs, 212-998-5300, Fax: 212-995-3143. *Application contact:* Amy Knowles, Assistant Dean for Student Affairs and Admissions, 212-998-5333, Fax: 212-995-4302, E-mail: ak96@nyu.edu.

Oakland University, Graduate Study and Lifelong Learning, School of Nursing, Program in Adult Health, Rochester, MI 48309-4401. Offers MSN. *Accreditation:* AACN. *Students:* 1 (woman) full-time, 4 part-time (3 women). Average age 40. 1 applicant, 100% accepted, 0 enrolled. *Degree requirements:* For master's, thesis (for some programs). *Entrance requirements:* For master's, GRE General Test, minimum GPA of 3.0 for unconditional admission. *Application deadline:* For fall admission, 8/1 for domestic students; for winter admission, 11/15 for domestic students. Applications are processed on a rolling basis. Application fee: $30. Electronic applications accepted. *Expenses:* Tuition, state resident: full-time $9,936; part-time $414 per credit. Tuition, nonresident: full-time $17,202; part-time $716 per credit. *Financial support:* Federal Work-Study, institutionally sponsored loans, and tuition waivers (full) available. Financial award application deadline: 3/1; financial award applicants required to submit FAFSA. *Application contact:* Mary Bray, Graduate Program Coordinator, 248-370-4482.

Oregon Health & Science University, School of Nursing, Program in Adult Health and Illness Nursing, Portland, OR 97239-3098. Offers MS, Post Master's Certificate. *Accreditation:* AACN. *Degree requirements:* For master's, thesis optional. *Entrance requirements:* For master's, GRE General Test, bachelor's degree in nursing, minimum undergraduate GPA of 3.0, previous course work in statistics; for Post Master's Certificate, master's degree in nursing.

Oregon Health & Science University, School of Nursing, Program in Primary Health Care, Portland, OR 97239-3098. Offers adult nurse practitioner (MS, Post Master's Certificate); family nurse practitioner (MS, Post Master's Certificate); geriatric nurse practitioner (Post Master's Certificate); geriatric/adult nurse practitioner (MS); pediatric nurse practitioner (MS, Post Master's Certificate). *Accreditation:* AACN. *Degree requirements:* For master's, thesis optional. *Entrance requirements:* For master's, GRE General Test, bachelor's degree in nursing, minimum undergraduate GPA of 3.0, previous course work in statistics; for Post Master's Certificate, master's degree in nursing.

Otterbein College, Department of Nursing, Westerville, OH 43081. Offers adult nurse practitioner (MSN, Certificate); clinical nurse leader (MSN); family nurse practitioner (MSN, Certificate); nurse service administration (MSN). *Accreditation:* AACN; NLN. Part-time and evening/weekend programs available. Postbaccalaureate distance learning degree programs offered (minimal on-campus study). *Students:* 7 full-time, 118 part-time; includes 5 minority (4 African Americans, 1 Hispanic American). Average age 40. 47 applicants, 94% accepted, 33 enrolled. In 2006, 37 degrees awarded. *Degree requirements:* For master's, thesis (for some programs), comprehensive exam (for some programs). *Entrance requirements:* For master's and Certificate, official transcripts, 2 reference forms, essay, resumé. Additional exam requirements/recommendations for international students: Required—TOEFL (minimum score 550 paper-based; 213 computer-based; 79 iBT). *Application deadline:* For fall admission, 8/10 priority date for domestic students, 7/10 for international students; for winter admission, 12/7 priority date for domestic students, 11/7 for international students; for spring admission, 2/28 priority date for domestic students, 1/31 for international students. Applications are processed on a rolling basis. *Expenses:* Tuition: Full-time $7,560; part-time $315 per credit. Tuition and fees vary according to program. *Financial support:* Traineeships available. Support available to part-time students. Financial award applicants required to submit FAFSA. *Faculty research:* Patient education, women's health, trauma curriculum development, administration. *Unit head:* Dr. Barbara Schaffner, Chair, 614-823-1735, Fax: 614-823-3131, E-mail: bschaffner@otterbein.edu. *Application contact:* Vicki Miller, Administrative Assistant, Office of Graduate Programs, 614-823-3210, Fax: 614-823-3208, E-mail: grad@otterbein.edu.

Quinnipiac University, School of Health Sciences, Adult Nurse Practitioner Track, Hamden, CT 06518-1940. Offers MSN, Post Master's Certificate. *Accreditation:* NLN. Part-time programs available. *Faculty:* 4 full-time (all women), 5 part-time/adjunct (4 women). *Students:* Average age 30. *Degree requirements:* For master's, clinical practicum, thesis optional. *Entrance requirements:* For master's, RN license, minimum GPA of 3.0. Additional exam requirements/

Adult Nursing

Quinnipiac University (continued)
recommendations for international students: Required—TOEFL (minimum score 575 paper-based; 233 computer-based; 90 iBT), IELTS (minimum score 7). *Application deadline:* For fall admission, 7/30 priority date for domestic students, 4/30 for international students. Applications are processed on a rolling basis. Application fee: $45. Electronic applications accepted. *Expenses:* Tuition: Part-time $675 per credit. Required fees: $30 per credit. *Financial support:* Traineeships, tuition waivers (partial), and unspecified assistantships available. Support available to part-time students. Financial award application deadline: 4/15; financial award applicants required to submit FAFSA. *Unit head:* Dr. Jeanne LeVasseur, Director of Graduate Nursing, 203-582-3484. *Application contact:* 800-462-1944, Fax: 203-582-3443, E-mail: graduate@quinnipiac.edu.

See Close-Up on page 1721.

Rutgers, The State University of New Jersey, Newark, Graduate School, Program in Nursing, Newark, NJ 07102. Offers nursing (MS), including acute care of adults and aged, advanced practice in pediatric nursing, advanced practice with childbearing families, community health nursing, family nurse practitioner, primary care of adults and aged, psychiatric/mental health nursing. *Accreditation:* AACN. Part-time programs available. *Faculty:* 33 full-time (32 women). *Students:* 11 full-time (all women), 186 part-time (175 women); includes 70 minority (28 African Americans, 30 Asian Americans or Pacific Islanders, 12 Hispanic Americans). 255 applicants, 58% accepted, 72 enrolled. In 2006, 40 master's awarded. *Degree requirements:* For master's, comprehensive exam. *Entrance requirements:* For master's, GRE General Test, RN license, minimum B average, BS in nursing. Additional exam requirements/recommendations for international students: Required—TOEFL. *Application deadline:* For fall admission, 2/15 for domestic students; for spring admission, 12/1 for domestic students. Applications are processed on a rolling basis. Application fee: $50. Electronic applications accepted. *Financial support:* In 2006–07, 3 fellowships (averaging $8,000 per year) were awarded; teaching assistantships with full tuition reimbursements, career-related internships or fieldwork, Federal Work-Study, institutionally sponsored loans, scholarships/grants, traineeships, and tuition waivers (full and partial) also available. Financial award application deadline: 4/15. *Faculty research:* HIV/AIDS, quality of life—MS and breast cancer, sleep patterns of cardiac patients. *Unit head:* Dr. Wendy Nehring, Program Director, 973-353-5293 Ext. 606, Fax: 973-353-1277, E-mail: nehring@nightingale.rutgers.edu. *Application contact:* Dr. Linda Scheetz, Associate Dean for Student Life and Services, 973-353-5060 Ext. 611, Fax: 973-353-1277, E-mail: lscheetz@andromeda.rutgers.edu.

Sage Graduate School, Graduate School, Division of Nursing, Program in Adult Health, Troy, NY 12180-4115. Offers MS. *Accreditation:* AACN. Part-time and evening/weekend programs available. *Faculty:* 8 full-time (all women), 3 part-time/adjunct (all women). *Students:* 4 full-time (all women), 14 part-time (12 women); includes 3 minority (2 African Americans, 1 Asian American or Pacific Islander). Average age 39. 11 applicants, 36% accepted, 2 enrolled. In 2006, 7 degrees awarded. *Degree requirements:* For master's, thesis or alternative. *Entrance requirements:* For master's, BS in nursing, minimum GPA of 2.75. Additional exam requirements/recommendations for international students: Required—TOEFL (minimum score 550 paper-based; 213 computer-based). *Application deadline:* Applications are processed on a rolling basis. Application fee: $40. *Expenses:* Tuition: Full-time $9,270; part-time $515 per credit hour. *Financial support:* Career-related internships or fieldwork, scholarships/grants, and unspecified assistantships available. Support available to part-time students. Financial award application deadline: 3/1; financial award applicants required to submit FAFSA. *Unit head:* Arlene Pericak, Director, 518-244-2012, E-mail: perica@sage.edu. *Application contact:* Shannon K. Easton, Director of Graduate and Adult Admission, 518-244-2443, Fax: 518-244-6880, E-mail: sgsadm@sage.edu.

Sage Graduate School, Graduate School, Division of Nursing, Program in Adult Nurse Practitioner, Troy, NY 12180-4115. Offers MS, Post Master's Certificate. *Accreditation:* AACN. Part-time and evening/weekend programs available. *Faculty:* 8 full-time (all women), 3 part-time/adjunct (all women). *Students:* 13 full-time (11 women), 20 part-time (all women); includes 1 minority (Asian American or Pacific Islander) Average age 42. 25 applicants, 76% accepted, 7 enrolled. In 2006, 9 master's, 10 other advanced degrees awarded. *Degree requirements:* For master's, thesis or alternative. *Entrance requirements:* Additional exam requirements/recommendations for international students: Required—TOEFL (minimum score 550 paper-based; 213 computer-based). *Application deadline:* Applications are processed on a rolling basis. Application fee: $40. *Expenses:* Tuition: Full-time $9,270; part-time $515 per credit hour. *Financial support:* Career-related internships or fieldwork, scholarships/grants, and unspecified assistantships available. Support available to part-time students. Financial award application deadline: 3/1; financial award applicants required to submit FAFSA. *Unit head:* Arlene Pericak, Director, 518-244-2012, E-mail: perica@sage.edu. *Application contact:* Shannon K. Easton, Director of Graduate and Adult Admission, 518-244-2443, Fax: 518-244-6880, E-mail: sgsadm@sage.edu.

Saint Xavier University, Graduate Studies, School of Nursing, Chicago, IL 60655-3105. Offers adult health clinical nurse specialist (MS); family nurse practitioner (MS, PMC); leadership in community health nursing (MS); psychiatric-mental health clinical nurse specialist (MS); psychiatric-mental health clinical specialist (PMC); MBA/MS. *Accreditation:* AACN. Part-time and evening/weekend programs available. *Faculty:* 11. *Students:* 20 full-time (14 women), 120 part-time (113 women). Average age 40. In 2006, 36 degrees awarded. *Entrance requirements:* For master's, GRE General Test or MAT, minimum GPA of 3.0, RN license. *Application deadline:* For fall admission, 2/15 for domestic students; for spring admission, 9/15 for domestic students. Applications are processed on a rolling basis. Application fee: $35. *Financial support:* Available to part-time students. Applicants required to submit FAFSA. *Unit head:* Beth Gierach, Managing Director of Admission, 773-298-3053, Fax: 773-298-3076, E-mail: gierach@sxu.edu.

Seton Hall University, College of Nursing, Department of Graduate Nursing, Advanced Practice in Primary Health Care Program, South Orange, NJ 07079-2697. Offers adult nurse practitioner (MSN); gerontological nurse practitioner (MSN); pediatric nurse practitioner (MSN); women's health nurse practitioner (MSN). *Accreditation:* AACN. Part-time programs available. *Degree requirements:* For master's, research project. *Entrance requirements:* For master's, GRE or MAT, BSN. *Faculty research:* Health promotion in well aged, practice outcomes, collaborative practice.

Southern Adventist University, School of Nursing, Collegedale, TN 37315-0370. Offers adult nurse practitioner (MSN); family nurse practitioner (MSN); nurse educator (MSN); MSN/MSBA. *Accreditation:* NLN. Part-time programs available. *Faculty:* 1 (woman) full-time, 5 part-time/adjunct (all women). *Students:* 45 full-time (41 women), 17 part-time (14 women); includes 5 minority (2 African Americans, 2 Asian Americans or Pacific Islanders, 1 Hispanic American). Average age 35. 40 applicants, 95% accepted, 31 enrolled. In 2006, 20 degrees awarded. *Degree requirements:* For master's, thesis or project. *Entrance requirements:* For master's, RN license. Additional exam requirements/recommendations for international students: Required—TOEFL (minimum score 600 paper-based). *Application deadline:* For fall admission, 7/1 for domestic and international students; for winter admission, 12/1 for domestic and international students. Applications are processed on a rolling basis. Application fee: $25. Electronic applications accepted. *Financial support:* In 2006–07, 1 teaching assistantship with partial tuition reimbursement (averaging $5,000 per year) was awarded. *Faculty research:* Pain management, ethics, corporate wellness, caring spirituality, stress. *Unit head:* Dr. Barbara James, Dean, 423-236-2940, Fax: 423-236-1940, E-mail: bjames@southern.edu. *Application contact:* Diane Proffitt, Enrollment Counselor, 423-236-2941, Fax: 423-236-1940, E-mail: dproffitt@southern.edu.

Spalding University, Graduate Studies, College of Health and Natural Sciences, School of Nursing, Louisville, KY 40203-2188. Offers adult nurse practitioner (MSN); family nurse practitioner (MSN); leadership in nursing and healthcare (MSN); pediatric nurse practitioner (MSN). *Accreditation:* AACN. Part-time and evening/weekend programs available. *Degree requirements:* For master's, thesis, comprehensive exam (for some programs). *Entrance requirements:* For master's, GRE General Test, BSN or bachelor's degree and RN licensure. *Faculty research:* Nurse educational administration, gerontology, bioterrorism, healthcare ethics, leadership.

State University of New York at New Paltz, Graduate School, Faculty of Liberal Arts and Sciences, Department of Nursing, New Paltz, NY 12561. Offers clinical nurse specialist adult health (CAS); gerontological nursing (MS). *Accreditation:* AACN. Part-time and evening/weekend programs available. *Faculty:* 6 full-time (all women), 2 part-time/adjunct (1 woman). *Students:* Average age 45. In 2006, 3 degrees awarded. *Entrance requirements:* For master's, minimum GPA of 3.0. Additional exam requirements/recommendations for international students: Required—TOEFL (minimum score 550 paper-based; 213 computer-based; 80 iBT). *Application deadline:* For fall admission, 5/15 priority date for domestic students, 5/15 for international students; for spring admission, 11/15 priority date for domestic students, 11/15 for international students. Applications are processed on a rolling basis. Application fee: $50. Electronic applications accepted. *Expenses:* Tuition, state resident: full-time $6,900; part-time $288 per credit hour. Tuition, nonresident: full-time $10,920; part-time $455 per credit hour. *Unit head:* Dr. Eleanor Richards, Chair, 845-257-2922.

State University of New York Institute of Technology, School of Nursing and Health Systems, Program in Adult Nurse Practitioner, Utica, NY 13504-3050. Offers MS, CAS. *Accreditation:* AACN. Part-time programs available. *Faculty:* 5 full-time (all women), 3 part-time/adjunct (2 women). *Degree requirements:* For master's, thesis or project. *Entrance requirements:* For master's, GRE General Test if undergraduate GPA is less than 3.3, minimum GPA of 3.0 in last 30 hours of undergraduate coursework, BS in nursing, 1 year of RN experience, RN license, interview, 2 letters of recommendation. Additional exam requirements/recommendations for international students: Required—TOEFL (minimum score 550 paper-based; 213 computer-based). *Application deadline:* For fall admission, 6/15 priority date for domestic students. Applications are processed on a rolling basis. Application fee: $50. *Expenses:* Tuition, state resident: full-time $3,452; part-time $288 per credit hour. Tuition, nonresident: full-time $10,920; part-time $455 per credit hour. Required fees: $927; $38 per credit hour. *Financial support:* Federal Work-Study, scholarships/grants, traineeships, and unspecified assistantships available. Financial award applicants required to submit FAFSA. *Faculty research:* Adult health care, critical thinking, epidemiology, ethics, moral reasoning. *Unit head:* Dr. Louise Dean-Kelly, Coordinator, 315-792-7291, Fax: 315-792-7555, E-mail: fldk@sunyit.edu. *Application contact:* Marybeth Lyons, Director of Admissions, 315-792-7500, Fax: 315-792-7837, E-mail: smbl@sunyit.edu.

Stony Brook University, State University of New York, Stony Brook University Medical Center, Health Sciences Center, School of Nursing, Program in Adult Health/Primary Care Nursing, Stony Brook, NY 11794. Offers adult health nurse practitioner (Certificate); adult health/primary care nursing (MS). *Accreditation:* AACN. *Students:* 7 full-time (5 women), 153 part-time (141 women); includes 47 minority (24 African Americans, 12 Asian Americans or Pacific Islanders, 11 Hispanic Americans). In 2006, 49 master's, 4 other advanced degrees awarded. *Degree requirements:* For master's, thesis. *Entrance requirements:* For master's, BSN, minimum GPA of 3.0, course work in statistics. *Application deadline:* For fall admission, 1/15 for domestic students. Application fee: $60. *Expenses:* Tuition, state resident: full-time $6,900; part-time $288 per credit. Tuition, nonresident: full-time $10,920; part-time $455 per credit. *Financial support:* Application deadline: 3/15. *Unit head:* Dr. Kathleen Shurpin, Chair, 631-444-3267, Fax: 631-444-3136, E-mail: kathy.shurpin@stonybrook.edu.

Texas Christian University, Harris College of Nursing and Health Sciences, Program in Nursing, Fort Worth, TX 76129-0002. Offers adult nursing (MSN). *Accreditation:* AACN; AANA/CANAEP. *Entrance requirements:* For master's, GRE General Test or MAT, 3 letters of reference, 2 years course work experience in nursing, current nursing licensure. Additional exam requirements/recommendations for international students: Required—TOEFL. Application fee: $0. *Expenses:* Tuition: Part-time $800 per credit hour. *Financial support:* Application deadline: 3/1. *Unit head:* Marinda Allender, Director of Student Affairs, 817-257-7650. *Application contact:* Dr. Kathleen Baldwin, Director of Graduate Studies, 817-257-6756, E-mail: k.baldwin@tcu.edu.

University at Buffalo, the State University of New York, Graduate School, School of Nursing, Buffalo, NY 14260. Offers acute care nurse practitioner (MS, Certificate); adult health nursing (MS, Certificate); child health nursing (MS); family nurse practitioner (Certificate); family nursing (MS); geriatric nurse practitioner (MS, Certificate); maternal and women's health nurse practitioner (Certificate); maternal and women's health nursing (MS); nurse anesthetist (MS); nursing (PhD); nursing education (Certificate); pediatric nurse practitioner (Certificate); psychiatric/mental health nurse practitioner (Certificate); psychiatric/mental health nursing (MS). *Accreditation:* AACN; AANA/CANAEP (one or more programs are accredited). Part-time programs available. Postbaccalaureate distance learning degree programs offered. *Faculty:* 38 full-time (34 women), 15 part-time/adjunct (14 women). *Students:* 131 full-time (108 women), 64 part-time (61 women); includes 29 minority (11 African Americans, 9 Asian Americans or Pacific Islanders, 9 Hispanic Americans), 20 international. Average age 28. 346 applicants, 25% accepted, 51 enrolled. In 2006, 49 master's, 3 doctorates, 6 other advanced degrees awarded. Terminal master's awarded for partial completion of doctoral program. *Degree requirements:* For master's, comprehensive exams or project; for doctorate, thesis/dissertation, comprehensive exam. *Entrance requirements:* For master's, GRE General Test (if overall GPA is below 3.0), interview, minimum GPA of 3.0, RN license, 3 references; for doctorate, GRE General Test, minimum GPA of 3.25, RN license, BS or MS in nursing, 3 references, writing sample; for Certificate, interview, minimum GPA of 3.0 or GRE General Test, RN license, MS in nursing. Additional exam requirements/recommendations for international students: Required—TOEFL (minimum score 550 paper-based; 213 computer-based; 79 iBT), IELTS (minimum score 7). *Application deadline:* For fall admission, 6/1 priority date for domestic students, 3/1 priority date for international students; for spring admission, 11/1 for domestic students, 9/15 priority date for international students. Applications are processed on a rolling basis. Application fee: $50. Electronic applications accepted. *Financial support:* In 2006–07, 78 students received support, including 13 fellowships with full tuition reimbursements available (averaging $7,220 per year), 10 research assistantships with tuition reimbursements available (averaging $17,881 per year), 23 teaching assistantships with full tuition reimbursements available (averaging $11,245 per year); Federal Work-Study, scholarships/grants, traineeships, health care benefits, and unspecified assistantships also available. Financial award application deadline: 3/15; financial award applicants required to submit FAFSA. *Faculty research:* Oncology symptom management, end of life decision making, changing behaviors using the transtheoretical model, addictions, nursing workforce. Total annual research expenditures: $1.7 million. *Unit head:* Dr. Jean K. Brown, Dean, Interim, 716-829-2533, Fax: 716-829-2566, E-mail: jebrown@buffalo.edu. *Application contact:* Dr. Elaine R. Cusker, Assistant Dean, 716-829-2537, Fax: 716-829-2021, E-mail: ecusker@buffalo.edu.

University of Central Florida, College of Health and Public Affairs, College of Nursing, Orlando, FL 32816. Offers adult practitioner (Post-Master's Certificate); family practitioner (Post-Master's Certificate); nursing (DNP, PhD); nursing education (Post-Master's Certificate); pediatric practitioner (Post-Master's Certificate). *Accreditation:* AACN. Part-time and evening/weekend programs available. *Faculty:* 35 full-time (32 women), 28 part-time/adjunct (25 women). *Students:* 84 full-time (75 women), 167 part-time (154 women); includes 41 minority (11 African Americans, 1 American Indian/Alaska Native, 8 Asian Americans or Pacific Islanders, 21 Hispanic Americans), 2 international. Average age 38. In 2006, 30 Post-Master's Certificates awarded. *Entrance requirements:* Additional exam requirements/recommendations for international students: Required—TOEFL. *Application deadline:* For fall admission, 2/15 for domestic students; for spring admission, 9/15 for domestic students. Application fee: $30. Electronic applications accepted. *Expenses:* Tuition, state resident: full-time $6,167; part-time $257 per credit hour. Tuition, nonresident: full-time $22,790; part-time $950 per credit hour. *Financial support:* In 2006–07, 35 fellowships with partial tuition reimbursements (averaging $1,550 per year), 9 research assistantships with partial tuition reimbursements (averaging

$4,500 per year), 3 teaching assistantships with partial tuition reimbursements (averaging $15,400 per year) were awarded; career-related internships or fieldwork, Federal Work-Study, institutionally sponsored loans, traineeships, and unspecified assistantships also available. Financial award application deadline: 3/1; financial award applicants required to submit FAFSA. *Unit head:* Dr. Jean D. Leuner, Dean, College of Nursing, 407-823-5496, Fax: 407-823-5675, E-mail: jleuner@mail.ucf.edu.

University of Cincinnati, Graduate School, College of Nursing, Cincinnati, OH 45221-0038. Offers clinical nurse specialist (MSN), including adult health, community health, neonatal, nursing administration, occupational health, pediatric health, psychiatric nursing, women's health; nurse anesthesia (MSN); nurse midwifery (MSN); nurse practitioner (MSN), including acute care, ambulatory care, family, family/psychiatric, women's health; nursing (PhD); MBA/MSN. *Accreditation:* AACN; AANA/CANAEP (one or more programs are accredited); ACNM/DOA. Part-time programs available. Postbaccalaureate distance learning degree programs offered (no on-campus study). *Faculty:* 41 full-time (39 women), 16 part-time/adjunct (15 women). *Students:* 159 full-time (125 women), 149 part-time (145 women); includes 40 minority (22 African Americans, 1 American Indian/Alaska Native, 16 Asian Americans or Pacific Islanders, 1 Hispanic American). Average age 34. 385 applicants, 49% accepted, 132 enrolled. In 2006, 77 master's, 5 doctorates awarded. Terminal master's awarded for partial completion of doctoral program. *Median time to degree:* Of those who began their doctoral program in fall 1998, 55% received their degree in 8 years or less. *Degree requirements:* For master's, thesis or alternative, registration; for doctorate, thesis/dissertation, comprehensive exam, registration. *Entrance requirements:* For master's and doctorate, GRE General Test. Additional exam requirements/recommendations for international students: Required—TOEFL (minimum score 520 paper-based; 190 computer-based). *Application deadline:* For fall admission, 7/26 priority date for domestic and international students. Applications are processed on a rolling basis. Application fee: $40. Electronic applications accepted. *Financial support:* In 2006–07, 164 students received support, including 7 fellowships with full tuition reimbursements available (averaging $13,571 per year), research assistantships with full tuition reimbursements available (averaging $12,000 per year), 8 teaching assistantships with full tuition reimbursements available (averaging $12,000 per year); career-related internships or fieldwork, scholarships/grants, traineeships, tuition waivers (partial), and unspecified assistantships also available. Support available to part-time students. Financial award application deadline: 5/1; financial award applicants required to submit FAFSA. *Faculty research:* Substance abuse, injury and violence, symptom management. Total annual research expenditures: $1.3 million. *Unit head:* Dr. Andrea R. Lindell, Dean, 513-558-5330, Fax: 513-558-9030, E-mail: andrea.lindell@uc.edu. *Application contact:* Loren Carter, Program Coordinator, 513-558-5072, Fax: 513-558-7523, E-mail: loren.carter@uc.edu.

University of Colorado at Colorado Springs, Graduate School, Beth-El College of Nursing, Colorado Springs, CO 80933-7150. Offers adult health nurse practitioner and clinical specialist (MSN); family practitioner (MSN), including community clinical specialist, forensic clinical specialist, holistic clinical specialist; gerontology (MSN); neonatal nurse practitioner and clinical specialist (MSN); nursing administration (MSN); women nurse practitioner (MSN). *Accreditation:* AACN. Part-time programs available. Postbaccalaureate distance learning degree programs offered (minimal on-campus study). *Faculty:* 10 full-time (7 women), 14 part-time/adjunct (7 women). *Students:* 84 full-time (77 women), 53 part-time (52 women); includes 22 minority (6 African Americans, 3 American Indian/Alaska Native, 2 Asian Americans or Pacific Islanders, 11 Hispanic Americans). Average age 37. 54 applicants, 85% accepted, 30 enrolled. In 2006, 36 degrees awarded. *Degree requirements:* For master's, thesis optional; for doctorate, capstone project. *Entrance requirements:* For master's, GRE General Test or MAT, BSN, minimum GPA of 3.0, unrestricted RN license; for doctorate, interview; active RN license; MA; minimum GPA of 3.3; National Certification as NP, CNS, or CNS; portfolio. Additional exam requirements/recommendations for international students: Required—TOEFL. *Application deadline:* For fall admission, 6/1 priority date for domestic students; for spring admission, 11/15 for domestic students. Application fee: $60 ($75 for international students). Electronic applications accepted. *Expenses: Contact institution.* Tuition and fees vary according to course load, campus/location and program. *Financial support:* Fellowships, career-related internships or fieldwork, Federal Work-Study, and institutionally sponsored loans available. Support available to part-time students. *Faculty research:* Women's health, uncertainty, empowerment, family experience in chronic illness. Total annual research expenditures: $260,389. *Unit head:* Dr. Carole Schoffstall, Dean, 719-262-4418, Fax: 719-262-4416, E-mail: cschoffs@uccs.edu.

University of Connecticut, Graduate School, School of Nursing, Field of Nursing, Storrs, CT 06269. Offers adult acute care (Post-Master's Certificate); adult primary care (Post-Master's Certificate); community health (Post-Master's Certificate); neonatal acute care (Post-Master's Certificate); nursing (MS, PhD); patient care services and systems administration (Post-Master's Certificate); psychiatric mental health (Post-Master's Certificate). *Accreditation:* AACN. *Faculty:* 20 full-time (18 women). *Students:* 38 full-time (33 women), 70 part-time (65 women); includes 17 minority (3 African Americans, 10 Asian Americans or Pacific Islanders, 4 Hispanic Americans), 1 international. Average age 37. 64 applicants, 69% accepted, 44 enrolled. In 2006, 25 master's, 7 doctorates, 1 other advanced degree awarded. *Degree requirements:* For master's, comprehensive exam; for doctorate, thesis/dissertation. *Entrance requirements:* Additional exam requirements/recommendations for international students: Required—TOEFL (minimum score 550 paper-based; 213 computer-based). *Application deadline:* For fall admission, 2/1 priority date for domestic and international students; for spring admission, 11/1 for domestic students, 10/1 for international students. Applications are processed on a rolling basis. Application fee: $55. Electronic applications accepted. *Financial support:* In 2006–07, 4 research assistantships with full tuition reimbursements, 13 teaching assistantships with full tuition reimbursements were awarded; fellowships, Federal Work-Study, scholarships/grants, health care benefits, and unspecified assistantships also available. Financial award application deadline: 2/1; financial award applicants required to submit FAFSA. *Unit head:* E. Carol Polifroni, Chairperson, 860-486-0511, Fax: 860-486-0001, E-mail: polifron@uconn.edu. *Application contact:* Lisa Mazzola, Academic Advisor Coordinator, 860-486-1973, E-mail: lisa.mazzola@uconn.edu.

University of Delaware, College of Health Sciences, School of Nursing, Newark, DE 19716. Offers adult nurse practitioner (MSN, PMC); cardiopulmonary clinical nurse specialist (MSN, PMC); cardiopulmonary clinical nurse specialist/adult nurse practitioner (MSN, PMC); family nurse practitioner (MSN, PMC); gerontology clinical nurse specialist (MSN, PMC); gerontology clinical nurse specialist geriatric nurse practitioner (PMC); gerontology clinical nurse specialist/geriatric nurse practitioner (MSN); health services administration (MSN, PMC); nursing of children clinical nurse specialist (MSN, PMC); nursing of children clinical nurse specialist/pediatric nurse practitioner (MSN, PMC); oncology/immune deficiency clinical nurse specialist (MSN, PMC); oncology/immune deficiency clinical nurse specialist/adult nurse practitioner (MSN, PMC); perinatal/women's health clinical nurse specialist (MSN, PMC); perinatal/women's health clinical nurse specialist/women's health nurse practitioner (MSN, PMC); psychiatric nursing clinical nurse specialist (MSN, PMC). *Accreditation:* AACN; NLN (one or more programs are accredited). Part-time and evening/weekend programs available. Postbaccalaureate distance learning degree programs offered (minimal on-campus study). *Degree requirements:* For master's, thesis optional. *Entrance requirements:* For master's, BSN, interview, RN license. Electronic applications accepted. *Faculty research:* Marriage and chronic illness, health promotion, congestive heart failure patient outcomes, school nursing, diabetes in children.

University of Hawaii at Manoa, Graduate Division, College of Health Sciences and Social Welfare, School of Nursing and Dental Hygiene, Honolulu, HI 96822. Offers clinical nurse specialist (MS), including adult health, community mental health; nurse practitioner (MS), including adult health, community mental health, family nurse practitioner; nursing (PhD, Graduate Certificate); nursing administration (MS). *Accreditation:* AACN; NLN (one or more programs are accredited). *Faculty:* 32 full-time (29 women), 1 (woman) part-time/adjunct. *Students:* 30 full-time (28 women), 94 part-time (83 women); includes 10 minority (3 African Americans, 1 American Indian/Alaska Native, 2 Asian Americans or Pacific Islanders, 4 Hispanic Americans), 2 international. 119 applicants, 53% accepted, 54 enrolled. In 2006, 12 master's, 4 doctorates awarded. *Median time to degree:* Of those who began their doctoral program in fall 1998, 57% received their degree in 8 years or less. *Degree requirements:* For master's, thesis optional; for doctorate, thesis/dissertation, comprehensive exam. *Entrance requirements:* For master's, Hawaii RN license. Additional exam requirements/recommendations for international students: Required—TOEFL (minimum score 580 paper-based; 237 computer-based; 92 iBT). *Application deadline:* For fall admission, 3/1 for domestic and international students. Application fee: $50. *Financial support:* In 2006–07, 1 teaching assistantship (averaging $13,296 per year) was awarded. Total annual research expenditures: $3.1 million.

University of Massachusetts Worcester, Graduate School of Nursing, Worcester, MA 01655-0115. Offers adult acute/critical care nurse practitioner (MS, Certificate); adult ambulatory/community care nurse practitioner (MS, Certificate); gerontological nurse practitioner (Certificate); nurse educator (MS, Certificate); nursing (PhD). *Accreditation:* AACN. Part-time programs available. *Faculty:* 39. *Students:* 46 full-time (43 women), 6 part-time (2 women); includes 5 minority (2 African Americans, 2 Asian Americans or Pacific Islanders, 1 Hispanic American). Average age 38. 42 applicants, 71% accepted. In 2006, 26 master's, 2 doctorates, 6 other advanced degrees awarded. *Degree requirements:* For doctorate, thesis/dissertation. *Entrance requirements:* For master's, GRE General Test, BSN, previous course work in statistics; for Certificate, master's degree. *Application deadline:* For fall admission, 3/15 for domestic students. Applications are processed on a rolling basis. Application fee: $40 ($60 for international students). *Expenses:* Tuition, state resident: full-time $2,640. Tuition, nonresident: full-time $9,856. Required fees: $3,942. *Financial support:* In 2006–07, 4 students received support. Scholarships/grants and traineeships available. Support available to part-time students. Financial award application deadline: 3/22; financial award applicants required to submit FAFSA. *Faculty research:* Premature menopause with cancer treatment, quality of life and cancer, complementary therapies, psychoneuroimmunology, patient outcomes/outcomes research. *Unit head:* Dr. Janet Hale, Associate Dean, 508-856-5661, Fax: 508-856-6552. *Application contact:* Larry Shattuck, Director of Recruitment and Retention, 508-856-5801, Fax: 508-856-6552.

University of Medicine and Dentistry of New Jersey, School of Nursing, Newark, NJ 07107-1709. Offers adult health (MSN); adult occupational health (MSN); advanced practice nursing (MSN, Post Master's Certificate); family nurse practitioner (MSN); nurse anesthesia (MSN); nursing (MSN); nursing education (MSN, Post Master's Certificate); nursing informatics (MSN); urban health (PhD); women's health practitioner (MSN). *Accreditation:* AANA/CANAEP; NLN (one or more programs are accredited). Part-time programs available. *Students:* 93 full-time (82 women), 307 part-time (274 women); includes 195 minority (92 African Americans, 1 American Indian/Alaska Native, 69 Asian Americans or Pacific Islanders, 33 Hispanic Americans), 1 international. Average age 39. 472 applicants, 63% accepted, 203 enrolled. In 2006, 57 master's, 6 other advanced degrees awarded. *Entrance requirements:* For master's, GRE, RN license; basic life support, statistics, and health assessment experience. Additional exam requirements/recommendations for international students: Required—TOEFL. *Application deadline:* Applications are processed on a rolling basis. Application fee: $50. Electronic applications accepted. *Expenses: Contact institution. Financial support:* Teaching assistantships, institutionally sponsored loans and scholarships/grants available. Support available to part-time students. Financial award application deadline: 5/1. *Faculty research:* HIV/AIDS, diabetes education, learned helplessness, nursing science, psychoeducation. *Unit head:* Dr. Susan Salmond, Interim Dean, 973-972-9239, Fax: 973-972-3225, E-mail: salmonsu@umdnj.edu.

University of Miami, Graduate School, School of Nursing and Health Studies, Coral Gables, FL 33124. Offers acute care (MSN), including acute care nurse practitioner, nurse anesthesia; community health (MSN); nursing (PhD); primary care (MSN), including adult nurse practitioner, family nurse practitioner, nurse midwifery, psychiatric/mental health nursing, women's health practitioner. *Accreditation:* AACN; AANA/CANAEP; ACNM/DOA (one or more programs are accredited). Part-time programs available. *Faculty:* 10 full-time (8 women), 1 (woman) part-time/adjunct. *Students:* 33 full-time (24 women), 27 part-time (24 women); includes 28 minority (7 African Americans, 5 Asian Americans or Pacific Islanders, 16 Hispanic Americans), 2 international. Average age 34. 108 applicants, 48% accepted, 30 enrolled. In 2006, 15 master's, 1 doctorate awarded. *Degree requirements:* For master's, thesis optional; for doctorate, thesis/dissertation. *Entrance requirements:* For master's, GRE General Test, BSN, minimum GPA of 3.0, Florida RN license; for doctorate, GRE General Test, BSN or MSN, minimum GPA of 3.0. Additional exam requirements/recommendations for international students: Required—TOEFL (minimum score 550 paper-based; 213 computer-based). *Application deadline:* For fall admission, 4/30 priority date for domestic students; for spring admission, 11/1 priority date for domestic students. Applications are processed on a rolling basis. Application fee: $50. Electronic applications accepted. *Financial support:* In 2006–07, 12 students received support, including 3 research assistantships with tuition reimbursements available (averaging $9,000 per year), 5 teaching assistantships with tuition reimbursements available (averaging $9,000 per year); fellowships, Federal Work-Study, institutionally sponsored loans, scholarships/grants, and unspecified assistantships also available. Support available to part-time students. Financial award application deadline: 3/1; financial award applicants required to submit FAFSA. *Faculty research:* Transcultural nursing, exercise and depression in Alzheimer's disease, infectious diseases/HIV–AIDS, postpartum depression, outcomes assessment. Total annual research expenditures: $31.9 million. *Unit head:* Dr. Nilda Peragallo, Dean, 305-284-2107, Fax: 305-667-3787, E-mail: nperagallo@miami.edu. *Application contact:* Anne Stabb, Graduate Advisor, 305-284-2533, Fax: 305-284-4827, E-mail: astabb@miami.edu.

University of Michigan, Horace H. Rackham School of Graduate Studies, School of Nursing, Division of Acute, Critical and Long-term Care, Program in Adult Acute Care Nurse Practitioner, Ann Arbor, MI 48109. Offers MS. *Accreditation:* AACN. Part-time programs available. *Degree requirements:* For master's, thesis, registration. *Entrance requirements:* For master's, GRE General Test, licensure, minimum of B average in BSN program. Additional exam requirements/recommendations for international students: Required—TOEFL (minimum score 560 paper-based; 220 computer-based). Electronic applications accepted. *Faculty research:* The functional outcomes and quality of life in women with breast cancer, hypertension.

University of Michigan, Horace H. Rackham School of Graduate Studies, School of Nursing, Division of Health Promotion and Risk Reduction, Program in Community Health Nursing, Ann Arbor, MI 48109. Offers adult primary care/adult nurse practitioner (MS); community care/home care (MS); family nurse practitioner (MS); occupational health nursing (MS). *Accreditation:* AACN. Part-time and evening/weekend programs available. *Degree requirements:* For master's, thesis, registration. *Entrance requirements:* For master's, GRE General Test, licensure, minimum GPA of 3.0 in BSN program. Additional exam requirements/recommendations for international students: Required—TOEFL (minimum score 560 paper-based; 220 computer-based).

University of Minnesota, Twin Cities Campus, Graduate School, School of Nursing, Program in Adult Health Clinical Nurse Specialist, Minneapolis, MN 55455-0213. Offers MS. *Accreditation:* AACN. *Students:* 8 full-time (all women), 6 part-time (all women); includes 5 minority (1 African American, 2 American Indian/Alaska Native, 2 Hispanic Americans). *Degree requirements:* For master's, final oral exam, project or thesis. *Entrance requirements:* Additional exam requirements/recommendations for international students: Required—TOEFL (minimum score 586 paper-based; 240 computer-based). *Application deadline:* For fall admission, 11/1 priority date for domestic and international students; for spring admission, 8/1 priority date for domestic and international students. Application fee: $55 ($75 for international students). *Financial support:* Fellowships, research assistantships, teaching assistantships available. *Unit head:* Dr. Cynthia Peden-McAlpine, Coordinator, 612-624-0449, E-mail: peden001@umn.edu. *Application contact:* Information Contact, 612-624-4454, Fax: 612-624-3174, E-mail: nurseoss@umn.edu.

University of Missouri–Kansas City, School of Nursing, Kansas City, MO 64110-2499. Offers adult clinical nurse specialist (MSN), including adult nurse practitioner, women's health nurse practitioner; family nurse practitioner (MSN); neonatal nurse practitioner (MSN); nurse

Adult Nursing

University of Missouri–Kansas City (continued)
educator (MSN); nurse executive (MSN); nursing (PhD); pediatric nurse practitioner (MSN). *Accreditation:* AACN. Part-time programs available. Postbaccalaureate distance learning degree programs offered (minimal on-campus study). *Faculty:* 31 full-time (26 women), 32 part-time/adjunct (31 women). *Students:* 36 full-time (all women), 213 part-time (202 women); includes 23 minority (6 African Americans, 2 American Indian/Alaska Native, 6 Asian Americans or Pacific Islanders, 9 Hispanic Americans). Average age 36. 121 applicants, 72% accepted, 71 enrolled. In 2006, 69 master's, 1 doctorate awarded. *Median time to degree:* Of those who began their doctoral program in fall 1998, 60% received their degree in 8 years or less. *Degree requirements:* For master's, thesis or alternative. *Entrance requirements:* For master's, minimum undergraduate GPA of 3.2; for doctorate, GRE, 3 letters of reference, interview and original essay by invitation. Additional exam requirements/recommendations for international students: Required—TOEFL (minimum score 550 paper-based). *Application deadline:* For fall admission, 2/1 priority date for domestic students; for spring admission, 9/15 priority date for domestic students. Application fee: $25. *Expenses:* Tuition, state resident: full-time $4,975; part-time $276 per credit. Tuition, nonresident: full-time $12,847; part-time $713 per credit. Required fees: $595; $595 per year. *Financial support:* In 2006–07, 30 students received support, including 6 research assistantships (averaging $3,450 per year), 7 teaching assistantships with partial tuition reimbursements available (averaging $12,650 per year); fellowships, career-related internships or fieldwork, Federal Work-Study, institutionally sponsored loans, and tuition waivers (full and partial) also available. Support available to part-time students. Financial award application deadline: 6/30; financial award applicants required to submit FAFSA. *Faculty research:* Geriatrics/gerontology, children's pain, neonatology, Alzheimer's care, cancer caregivers. Total annual research expenditures: $1 million. *Unit head:* Dr. Lora Lacey-Haun, Dean, 816-235-1700, Fax: 816-235-1701, E-mail: lacey-haunc@umkc.edu. *Application contact:* Leah Wilder, Coordinator for Admissions and Recruitment, 816-235-5768, Fax: 816-235-1701, E-mail: wilderl@umkc.edu.

The University of North Carolina at Charlotte, Graduate School, College of Health and Human Services, School of Nursing, Department of Adult Health Nursing, Charlotte, NC 28223-0001. Offers nursing adult health (MSN); nursing-anesthesia (MSN). *Accreditation:* AACN. *Faculty:* 9 full-time (8 women), 4 part-time/adjunct (all women). *Students:* 39 full-time (30 women), 49 part-time (40 women); includes 4 minority (1 African American, 1 Asian American or Pacific Islander, 2 Hispanic Americans). Average age 32. 62 applicants, 39% accepted, 22 enrolled. In 2006, 28 degrees awarded. *Degree requirements:* For master's, thesis or project. *Entrance requirements:* For master's, GRE General Test (nursing, anesthesia), GRE General Test or MAT (nursing, adult health), minimum undergraduate GPA of 3.0 in major. Additional exam requirements/recommendations for international students: Required—TOEFL (minimum score 557 paper-based; 220 computer-based). *Application deadline:* For fall admission, 7/1 for domestic students, 5/1 for international students; for spring admission, 11/1 for domestic students, 10/1 for international students. Applications are processed on a rolling basis. Application fee: $55. Electronic applications accepted. *Expenses:* Tuition, state resident: full-time $2,719; part-time $170 per credit. Tuition, nonresident: full-time $12,926; part-time $808 per credit. Required fees: $1,555. *Financial support:* In 2006–07, 1 research assistantship (averaging $1,204 per year), 1 teaching assistantship (averaging $4,032 per year) were awarded; fellowships, career-related internships or fieldwork, Federal Work-Study, institutionally sponsored loans, scholarships/grants, traineeships, and unspecified assistantships also available. Support available to part-time students. Financial award application deadline: 4/1; financial award applicants required to submit FAFSA. *Faculty research:* Health disparities, symptom management and chronic illness, self care chronic illness, health promotion. *Unit head:* Dr. Jacqueline A. Dienemann, Chair, 704-687-4652, Fax: 704-687-3180, E-mail: jadienem@email.uncc.edu. *Application contact:* Kathy B. Giddings, Director of Graduate Admissions, 704-687-3366, Fax: 704-687-3279, E-mail: gradadm@email.uncc.edu.

The University of North Carolina at Greensboro, Graduate School, School of Nursing, Greensboro, NC 27412-5001. Offers adult clinical nurse specialist (MSN, PMC); adult/gerontological nurse practitioner (MSN, PMC); nurse anesthesia (MSN, PMC); nursing (PhD); nursing administration (MSN); nursing education (MSN); MSN/MBA. *Accreditation:* AACN; AANA/CANAEP; NLN. *Faculty:* 24 full-time (23 women), 27 part-time/adjunct (22 women). *Students:* 231 full-time (197 women), 98 part-time (83 women); includes 56 minority (41 African Americans, 3 American Indian/Alaska Native, 9 Asian Americans or Pacific Islanders, 3 Hispanic Americans). 206 applicants, 59% accepted. *Degree requirements:* For master's, thesis or alternative. *Entrance requirements:* For master's, GRE General Test or MAT, BSN, clinical experience, liability insurance, RN license; for PMC, liability insurance, MSN, RN license. Additional exam requirements/recommendations for international students: Required—TOEFL. Application fee: $45. Electronic applications accepted. *Expenses:* Tuition, state resident: full-time $2,692. Tuition, nonresident: full-time $13,742. *Financial support:* Research assistantships with full tuition reimbursements, career-related internships or fieldwork, Federal Work-Study, scholarships/grants, and traineeships available. Support available to part-time students. *Unit head:* Dr. Lynne Pearcey, Dean, 336-334-5177, Fax: 336-334-3628, E-mail: l_pearce@uncg.edu. *Application contact:* Michelle Harkleroad, Director of Graduate Admissions, 336-334-4884, Fax: 336-334-4424, E-mail: mbharkle@uncg.edu.

University of Pennsylvania, School of Nursing, Adult Health Nurse Practitioner Program, Philadelphia, PA 19104. Offers MSN. *Accreditation:* AACN. Part-time programs available. *Entrance requirements:* For master's, GRE General Test, BSN, minimum GPA of 3.0, previous course work in basic statistics. Additional exam requirements/recommendations for international students: Required—TOEFL. Expenses: Contact institution. *Faculty research:* Restraints, incontinence, discharge planning, frail elders, quality of life across continuum of care.

University of San Diego, Hahn School of Nursing and Health Sciences, San Diego, CA 92110-2492. Offers accelerated nursing (for RNs only) (MSN); adult clinical nurse specialist (MSN, Post Master's Certificate); adult nurse practitioner (MSN, Post Master's Certificate); clinical nursing (MSN); entry-level nursing (for non-RNs) (MSN); executive nurse leader (MSN); family nurse practitioner (MSN, Post Master's Certificate); nursing science (PhD); pediatric nurse practitioner (MSN, Post Master's Certificate). *Accreditation:* AACN. Part-time and evening/weekend programs available. *Faculty:* 13 full-time (12 women), 33 part-time/adjunct (all women). *Students:* 103 full-time (85 women), 138 part-time (131 women); includes 58 minority (7 African Americans, 3 American Indian/Alaska Native, 26 Asian Americans or Pacific Islanders, 22 Hispanic Americans), 4 international. Average age 37. 261 applicants, 54% accepted, 87 enrolled. In 2006, 35 master's, 19 doctorates awarded. *Degree requirements:* For doctorate, thesis/dissertation, residency. *Entrance requirements:* For master's, GRE General Test (for entry-level nursing), BSN and current California RN licensure (for all programs except entry-level nursing); minimum GPA of 3.0; for doctorate, GRE General Test, minimum GPA of 3.5, MSN, current California RN licensure. Additional exam requirements/recommendations for international students: Required—TOEFL, TWE. *Application deadline:* Applications are processed on a rolling basis. Application fee: $45. Electronic applications accepted. *Financial support:* Scholarships/grants and traineeships available. Support available to part-time students. Financial award application deadline: 4/1; financial award applicants required to submit FAFSA. *Faculty research:* Health promotion, decision making, psychogeriatric nursing, historical nursing, leadership behavior. *Unit head:* Dr. Sally Hardin, Dean, 619-260-4550, Fax: 619-260-6814. *Application contact:* Stephen Pultz, Director of Admissions, 619-260-4524, Fax: 619-260-4158, E-mail: grads@sandiego.edu.

See Close-Up on page 1977.

University of San Francisco, School of Nursing, San Francisco, CA 94117-1080. Offers advanced practice nursing-nurse practitioner and clinical nurse specialist (MSN), including adult health nursing; nursing administration (MSN); MSN/MBA; MSN/MPA; MSN/MSIS. *Accreditation:* AACN. Part-time programs available. *Faculty:* 6 full-time (5 women), 10 part-time/adjunct (9 women). *Students:* 126 full-time (106 women), 11 part-time (10 women); includes 46 minority (3 African Americans, 36 Asian Americans or Pacific Islanders, 7 Hispanic Americans), 5 international. Average age 31. 219 applicants, 65% accepted, 47 enrolled. In 2006, 53 degrees awarded. *Entrance requirements:* For master's, minimum GPA of 3.0. *Application deadline:* Applications are processed on a rolling basis. Application fee: $40. *Expenses:* Tuition: Full-time $17,370; part-time $965 per unit. Tuition and fees vary according to degree level, campus/location and program. *Financial support:* In 2006–07, 114 students received support. Institutionally sponsored loans available. Financial award application deadline: 3/2. *Faculty research:* Direct patient/client care, providers of health care. *Unit head:* Dr. Judith Karshmer, Dean, 415-422-6681, Fax: 415-422-6877, E-mail: nursing@usfca.edu.

The University of Scranton, Graduate School, Department of Nursing, Scranton, PA 18510. Offers adult health nursing (MSN); family nurse practitioner (MSN, PMC); nurse anesthesia (MSN, PMC). Applicants accepted in odd-numbered years only. *Accreditation:* AACN; AANA/CANAEP. Part-time and evening/weekend programs available. *Faculty:* 13 full-time (all women), 2 part-time/adjunct (both women). *Students:* 44 full-time (29 women), 30 part-time (27 women); includes 5 minority (1 African American, 2 Asian Americans or Pacific Islanders, 2 Hispanic Americans). Average age 36. 63 applicants, 68% accepted. In 2006, 19 degrees awarded. *Degree requirements:* For master's, thesis (for some programs), capstone experience. *Entrance requirements:* For master's, BSN, minimum GPA of 3.0, Pennsylvania RN license. Additional exam requirements/recommendations for international students: Required—TOEFL (minimum score 500 paper-based; 173 computer-based), IELTS (minimum score 6). *Application deadline:* For fall admission, 9/1 for domestic students. Applications are processed on a rolling basis. Application fee: $50. *Expenses:* Tuition: Part-time $684 per credit. Required fees: $25 per term. *Financial support:* In 2006–07, 7 teaching assistantships with full and partial tuition reimbursements (averaging $4,085 per year) were awarded; career-related internships or fieldwork, Federal Work-Study, and unspecified assistantships also available. Support available to part-time students. Financial award application deadline: 3/1. *Faculty research:* Home care, doctoral education, health care of women and children, pain, health promotion and adolescence. *Unit head:* Dr. Patricia Harrington, Chair, 570-941-7673, Fax: 570-941-4201, E-mail: harringtonp1@scranton.edu. *Application contact:* Dr. Mary Jane Hanson, Director, 570-941-4060, Fax: 570-941-4201, E-mail: hansonm2@scranton.edu.

University of South Alabama, Graduate School, College of Nursing, Mobile, AL 36688-0002. Offers adult health nursing (MSN); community/mental health nursing (MSN); maternal/child nursing (MSN); nursing (DSN). *Accreditation:* AACN. *Faculty:* 25 full-time (23 women), 8 part-time/adjunct (all women). *Students:* 661 full-time (602 women), 127 part-time (108 women); includes 160 minority (123 African Americans, 6 American Indian/Alaska Native, 19 Asian Americans or Pacific Islanders, 12 Hispanic Americans), 1 international. In 2006, 166 degrees awarded. *Unit head:* Dr. Debra C. Davis, Dean, 251-434-3414.

University of South Carolina, The Graduate School, College of Nursing, Program in Health Nursing, Columbia, SC 29208. Offers adult nurse practitioner (MSN); community/public health clinical nurse specialist (MSN); family nurse practitioner (MSN); pediatric nurse practitioner (MSN). *Accreditation:* AACN. Part-time programs available. *Degree requirements:* For master's, thesis or alternative. *Entrance requirements:* For master's, GRE General Test or MAT, BS in nursing, nursing license. Additional exam requirements/recommendations for international students: Required—TOEFL (minimum score 570 paper-based; 230 computer-based). Electronic applications accepted. *Faculty research:* Health promotion, physical activity, adolescent health, pre-term labor, low birthrate.

University of Southern Maine, College of Nursing and Health Professions, Portland, ME 04104-9300. Offers adult health nursing (PMC); clinical nurse leader (MS); clinical nurse specialist psychiatric-mental health nursing (MS); family nursing (PMC); medical/surgical nursing (MS); nurse practitioner adult health nursing (MS); nurse practitioner family nursing (MS); nurse practitioner psychiatric/mental health nursing (MS); psychiatric-mental health nursing (PMC); MBA/MSN. *Accreditation:* AACN. Part-time programs available. *Faculty:* 13 full-time (all women), 5 part-time/adjunct (4 women). *Students:* 55 full-time (53 women), 52 part-time (50 women); includes 6 minority (all Asian Americans or Pacific Islanders) Average age 36. 88 applicants, 93% accepted, 57 enrolled. In 2006, 25 degrees awarded. *Degree requirements:* For master's, thesis optional. *Entrance requirements:* For master's, GRE General Test or MAT, minimum GPA of 3.0. Additional exam requirements/recommendations for international students: Required—TOEFL (minimum score 550 paper-based; 213 computer-based). *Application deadline:* Applications are processed on a rolling basis. Application fee: $50. Electronic applications accepted. *Expenses:* Tuition, state resident: full-time $4,860; part-time $270 per credit hour. Tuition, nonresident: full-time $13,572; part-time $754 per credit hour. Required fees: $222 per semester. Tuition and fees vary according to course load. *Financial support:* In 2006–07, 14 students received support, including 5 research assistantships with tuition reimbursements available (averaging $3,375 per year), 7 teaching assistantships with tuition reimbursements available (averaging $3,375 per year); career-related internships or fieldwork, Federal Work-Study, scholarships/grants, traineeships, tuition waivers (full and partial), and unspecified assistantships also available. Support available to part-time students. Financial award application deadline: 2/15; financial award applicants required to submit FAFSA. *Faculty research:* Women's health, nursing history, weight control, community services, substance abuse. *Unit head:* Susan Sepples, Director of Nursing Program, 207-780-4505, Fax: 207-228-8177, E-mail: sepples@usm.maine.edu. *Application contact:* Mary Sloan, Director of Graduate Admissions, 207-780-4386, Fax: 207-780-4969, E-mail: gradstudies@usm.maine.edu.

University of Southern Mississippi, Graduate School, College of Health, School of Nursing, Hattiesburg, MS 39406-0001. Offers adult health nursing (MSN); community health nursing (MSN); ethics (PhD); family nurse practitioner (MSN); leadership (PhD); nursing service administration (MSN); policy analysis (PhD); psychiatric nursing (MSN). *Accreditation:* AACN. Part-time and evening/weekend programs available. *Faculty:* 14 full-time (all women). *Students:* 39 full-time (31 women), 69 part-time (62 women); includes 18 minority (15 African Americans, 1 Asian American or Pacific Islander, 2 Hispanic Americans), 1 international. Average age 39. 46 applicants, 50% accepted, 17 enrolled. In 2006, 36 master's, 6 doctorates awarded. *Degree requirements:* For master's, thesis optional; for doctorate, thesis/dissertation, comprehensive exam, registration. *Entrance requirements:* For master's, GRE General Test, minimum GPA of 2.75, nursing license, BS in nursing; for doctorate, GRE General Test, master's degree in nursing, minimum GPA of 3.5. Additional exam requirements/recommendations for international students: Required—TOEFL. *Application deadline:* For fall admission, 3/15 priority date for domestic students, 5/1 for international students. Applications are processed on a rolling basis. Application fee: $25 ($30 for international students). Electronic applications accepted. *Financial support:* In 2006–07, 1 research assistantship with full tuition reimbursement (averaging $10,125 per year), 1 teaching assistantship (averaging $10,125 per year) were awarded; Federal Work-Study and traineeships also available. Financial award application deadline: 3/15. *Faculty research:* Gerontology, caregivers, HIV, bereavement, pain, nursing leadership. *Unit head:* Dr. Katherine Nugent, Director and Associate Dean, 601-266-5500, Fax: 601-266-5927. *Application contact:* Dr. Anne Brock, Graduate Coordinator, 601-266-5500, Fax: 601-266-5927.

The University of Tampa, Nursing Program, Tampa, FL 33606-1490. Offers adult nurse practitioner (MSN); family nurse practitioner (MSN); nursing administration (MSN); nursing education (MSN). *Accreditation:* NLN. Part-time and evening/weekend programs available. *Faculty:* 5 full-time (all women), 10 part-time/adjunct (9 women). *Students:* 3 full-time (all women), 67 part-time (63 women); includes 2 minority (both African Americans), 1 international. Average age 40. 46 applicants, 61% accepted, 18 enrolled. In 2006, 29 degrees awarded. *Degree requirements:* For master's, oral exam, practicum, thesis optional. *Entrance requirements:* For master's, GRE General Test, minimum GPA of 3.0, RN license. *Application deadline:* For fall admission, 8/20 priority date for domestic students. Applications are processed on a rolling basis. Application fee: $40. Electronic applications accepted. *Expenses:* Tuition: Part-time $426 per credit hour. Required fees: $35 per year. *Financial support:* In 2006–07, 2 students received support, including 2 research assistantships with tuition reimbursements available (averaging $1,500 per year); career-related internships or fieldwork and unspecified assistantships also available. Support available to part-time students. Financial award applicants required to submit FAFSA. *Faculty research:* Domestic violence (assessment in emergency departments, changing demographics), transcultural health assessment, priorities in maintaining autonomy of elderly. *Unit head:* Dr. Nancy Ross, Director, 813-253-6223, Fax: 813-258-7214, E-mail: nross@ut.edu. *Application contact:* Barbara P. Strickler, Vice President for Enrollment, 888-646-2738, Fax: 813-258-7398, E-mail: admissions@ut.edu.

The University of Tennessee at Chattanooga, Graduate School, College of Health, Education and Professional Studies, School of Nursing, Chattanooga, TN 37403-2598. Offers administration (MSN); adult health (MSN); education (MSN); family nurse practitioner (MSN); nurse anesthesia (MSN). *Accreditation:* AACN; AANA/CANAEP. *Faculty:* 13 full-time (all women). *Students:* 40 full-time (32 women), 47 part-time (41 women); includes 9 minority (1 African American, 2 American Indian/Alaska Native, 4 Asian Americans or Pacific Islanders, 2 Hispanic Americans). Average age 34. 14 applicants, 71% accepted, 2 enrolled. In 2006, 29 degrees awarded. *Degree requirements:* For master's, qualifying exams. *Entrance requirements:* For master's, GRE General Test, MAT, BSN, minimum GPA of 3.0, eligibility for Tennessee RN license. *Application deadline:* For fall admission, 8/1 priority date for domestic students; for spring admission, 12/1 priority date for domestic students. Applications are processed on a rolling basis. Application fee: $30. *Expenses:* Tuition, state resident: full-time $5,434; part-time $339 per hour. Tuition, nonresident: full-time $14,830; part-time $861 per hour. Required fees: $940; $178 per hour. *Financial support:* Application deadline: 4/1; *Faculty research:* Diabetes in women; health care for elderly; alternative medicine; hypertension; nurse anesthesia. Total annual research expenditures: $357,538. *Unit head:* Dr. Kay R. Lindgren, Head, 423-425-4646, Fax: 423-425-4668, E-mail: kay-lindgren@utc.edu. *Application contact:* Dr. Deborah E. Arfken, Dean of Graduate Studies, 423-425-4666, Fax: 423-425-5223, E-mail: deborah-arfken@utc.edu.

The University of Texas–Pan American, College of Health Sciences and Human Services, Department of Nursing, Edinburg, TX 78541-2999. Offers adult health nursing (MSN); family nurse practitioner (MSN); pediatric nurse practitioner (MSN). *Accreditation:* AACN. Part-time and evening/weekend programs available. *Faculty:* 8 full-time (7 women). *Students:* 19 applicants, 100% accepted, 19 enrolled. In 2006, 22 degrees awarded. *Median time to degree:* Master's–3 years part-time. *Degree requirements:* For master's, thesis optional. *Entrance requirements:* For master's, Texas RN licensure, undergraduate physical assessment courses. Additional exam requirements/recommendations for international students: Required—TOEFL (minimum score 550 paper-based). *Application deadline:* Applications are processed on a rolling basis. Application fee: $35. Electronic applications accepted. *Expenses: Contact institution. Financial support:* In 2006–07, 15 students received support. Scholarships/grants and traineeships available. *Faculty research:* Health promotion, adolescent pregnancy, herbal and nontraditional approaches, healing touch stress. Total annual research expenditures: $5,000. *Unit head:* Dr. Carolina G. Huerta, Chair, 956-381-3495, Fax: 956-381-2384, E-mail: chuerta@panam.edu. *Application contact:* Dr. Janice A. Maville, Professor and Interim Chair, 956-316-3491, Fax: 956-318-5238, E-mail: jmaville@utpa.edu.

University of Wisconsin–Oshkosh, The School of Graduate Studies, College of Nursing, Oshkosh, WI 54901. Offers adult health and illness (MSN); family nurse practitioner (MSN). *Accreditation:* AACN. Part-time programs available. *Degree requirements:* For master's, thesis or alternative, clinical paper. *Entrance requirements:* For master's, RN license, BSN, previous course work in statistics and health assessment, minimum undergraduate GPA of 3.0, letters of recommendation. Additional exam requirements/recommendations for international students: Required—TOEFL (minimum score 550 paper-based; 213 computer-based). Electronic applications accepted. *Faculty research:* Adult health and illness, nurse practitioners practice, health care service, advanced practitioner roles, natural alternative complementary healthcare.

Vanderbilt University, School of Nursing, Nashville, TN 37235. Offers adult acute care nurse practitioner (MSN); adult health nurse practitioner/forensic (MSN); adult nurse practitioner/cardiovascular disease management and prevention (MSN); adult nurse practitioner/palliative care (MSN); clinical management (clinical nurse leader/specialist) (MSN); family nurse practitioner (MSN); gerontology nurse practitioner (MSN); health systems management (MSN); neonatal nurse practitioner (MSN); nurse midwifery (MSN); nursing informatics (MSN); nursing science (PhD); pediatric acute care nurse practitioner (MSN); pediatric primary care nurse practitioner (MSN); psychiatric-mental health nurse practitioner (MSN); women's health nurse practitioner (MSN); MBA/MSN; MSN/MTS; MSN/PhD. *Accreditation:* ACNM/DOA; NLN (one or more programs are accredited). Part-time and evening/weekend programs available. Postbaccalaureate distance learning degree programs offered (minimal on-campus study). *Faculty:* 95 full-time (83 women), 432 part-time/adjunct (314 women). *Students:* 371 full-time (325 women), 206 part-time (180 women); includes 59 minority (38 African Americans, 2 American Indian/Alaska Native, 7 Asian Americans or Pacific Islanders, 12 Hispanic Americans). Average age 27. 611 applicants, 55% accepted, 308 enrolled. In 2006, 256 master's, 2 doctorates awarded. *Degree requirements:* For doctorate, thesis/dissertation. *Entrance requirements:* For master's, GRE, interview; for doctorate, GRE, interview, 3 letters of recommendation. Additional exam requirements/recommendations for international students: Required—TOEFL. *Application deadline:* For fall admission, 12/1 priority date for domestic and international students. Applications are processed on a rolling basis. Application fee: $50. *Expenses: Contact institution. Financial support:* In 2006–07, 404 students received support, including 5 research assistantships (averaging $8,000 per year); Federal Work-Study, institutionally sponsored loans, and unspecified assistantships also available. Support available to part-time students. Financial award application deadline: 3/15; financial award applicants required to submit CSS PROFILE or FAFSA. *Faculty research:* Lymphedema post cancer treatment, palliative care and bereavement, patient safety and quality of care, health care workforce issues, symptom management including pain and fatigue. Total annual research expenditures: $1.1 million. *Unit head:* Dr. Colleen Conway-Welch, Dean, 615-343-8776, Fax: 615-343-7711, E-mail: colleen.conway-welch@vanderbilt.edu. *Application contact:* Cheryl Feldner, Assistant Director of Admissions, 615-322-3800, Fax: 615-343-0333, E-mail: cheryl.feldner@vanderbilt.edu.

Villanova University, College of Nursing, Villanova, PA 19085-1690. Offers adult nurse practitioner (MSN, Post Master's Certificate); clinical case management (MSN, Post Master's Certificate); geriatric nurse practitioner (MSN, Post Master's Certificate); health care administration (MSN); nurse anesthetist (MSN, Post Master's Certificate); nursing (PhD); nursing education (MSN, Post Master's Certificate); pediatric nurse practitioner (MSN, Post Master's Certificate). *Accreditation:* AACN; AANA/CANAEP; NLN. Part-time programs available. Postbaccalaureate distance learning degree programs offered (minimal on-campus study). *Faculty:* 14 full-time (all women), 2 part-time/adjunct (both women). *Students:* 41 full-time (27 women), 164 part-time (128 women); includes 17 minority (8 African Americans, 1 American Indian/Alaska Native, 8 Asian Americans or Pacific Islanders), 6 international. Average age 31. 137 applicants, 50% accepted, 48 enrolled. In 2006, 47 degrees awarded. *Median time to degree:* Master's–2 years full-time, 5 years part-time. *Degree requirements:* For master's, independent study project; for doctorate, thesis/dissertation, comprehensive exam. *Entrance requirements:* For master's, GRE or MAT, BSN, 1 year of recent nursing experience, physical assessment, course work in statistics; for doctorate, GRE. Additional exam requirements/recommendations for international students: Required—TOEFL. *Application deadline:* For fall admission, 7/1 priority date for domestic students, 7/1 for international students; for spring admission, 12/1 priority date for domestic students, 12/1 for international students. Applications are processed on a rolling basis. Application fee: $50. *Expenses: Contact institution. Financial support:* In 2006–07, 50 students received support, including 4 teaching assistantships with full tuition reimbursements available (averaging $12,165 per year); institutionally sponsored loans, scholarships/grants, traineeships, and tuition waivers (full) also available. Financial award application deadline: 3/1; financial award applicants required to submit FAFSA. *Faculty research:* Genetics, ethics, cognitive development of students, women with disabilities, nursing leadership. *Unit head:* Dr. Marguerite K. Schlag, Assistant Dean and Director, Graduate Program, 610-519-4907, Fax: 610-519-7650, E-mail: marguerite.schlag@villanova.edu.

Virginia Commonwealth University, Graduate School, School of Nursing, Richmond, VA 23284-9005. Offers adult health nursing (MS); child health nursing (MS); family health nursing (MS); health system (PhD); immunocompetence (PhD); nurse practitioner (MS, Certificate); nursing administration (MS), including clinical nurse manager, nurse executive; psychiatric-mental health nursing (MS); risk and resilience (PhD); women's health nursing (MS). *Accreditation:* NLN (one or more programs are accredited). Part-time and evening/weekend programs available. *Faculty:* 23 full-time (21 women). *Students:* 131 full-time (125 women), 137 part-time (129 women); includes 33 minority (19 African Americans, 11 Asian Americans or Pacific Islanders, 3 Hispanic Americans), 12 international. 110 applicants, 82% accepted, 66 enrolled. In 2006, 57 master's, 1 doctorate, 3 other advanced degrees awarded. *Degree requirements:* For master's, thesis optional; for doctorate, thesis/dissertation. *Entrance requirements:* For master's, GRE General Test, BSN, minimum GPA of 2.8; for doctorate, GRE General Test. *Application deadline:* For fall admission, 2/1 priority date for domestic students. Application fee: $50. *Financial support:* Fellowships, research assistantships, teaching assistantships, career-related internships or fieldwork and institutionally sponsored loans available. *Unit head:* Dr. Nancy F. Langston, Dean, 804-828-5174, Fax: 804-828-7743, E-mail: nflangst@vcu.edu. *Application contact:* Susan Lipp, Admissions Counselor, 804-828-5171, Fax: 804-828-7743, E-mail: slipp@vcu.edu.

See Close-Up on page 1983.

Western Connecticut State University, Division of Graduate Studies, School of Professional Studies, Nursing Department, Danbury, CT 06810-6885. Offers adult nurse practitioner (MSN); clinical nurse specialist (MSN). *Accreditation:* AACN. Part-time and evening/weekend programs available. *Faculty:* 6 full-time (5 women), 1 part-time/adjunct (0 women). *Students:* Average age 42. In 2006, 11 degrees awarded. *Degree requirements:* For master's, thesis or research project. *Entrance requirements:* For master's, MAT, bachelor's degree in nursing, minimum GPA of 3.0, previous course work in statistics and nursing research, RN license. *Application deadline:* For fall admission, 8/1 priority date for domestic students. Applications are processed on a rolling basis. Application fee: $40. *Financial support:* Career-related internships or fieldwork available. Support available to part-time students. Financial award application deadline: 5/1; financial award applicants required to submit FAFSA. *Unit head:* Dr. Patricia Z. Lund, Professor, 203-837-8567. *Application contact:* Chris Shankle, Associate Director of Graduate Admissions, 203-837-8244, Fax: 203-837-8338, E-mail: shanklec@wcsu.edu.

See Close-Up on page 1985.

Winona State University, Graduate Studies, College of Nursing and Health Sciences, Winona, MN 55987-5838. Offers adult nurse practitioner (MS); clinical nurse specialist (MS); family nurse practitioner (MS); nurse administrator (MS); nurse educator (MS). *Accreditation:* AACN. Part-time programs available. *Faculty:* 10 full-time (all women). *Students:* 70 applicants, 57% accepted, 32 enrolled. In 2006, 32 master's awarded. *Degree requirements:* For master's, thesis. *Application deadline:* For fall admission, 2/1 for domestic students. Application fee: $20. *Financial support:* In 2006–07, 3 research assistantships with partial tuition reimbursements (averaging $6,000 per year) were awarded; Federal Work-Study, traineeships, and unspecified assistantships also available. Support available to part-time students. Financial award applicants required to submit FAFSA. *Unit head:* Dr. Timothy Gaspar, Graduate Director, 507-457-5122, E-mail: tgaspar@winona.msus.edu.

Wright State University, School of Graduate Studies, College of Nursing and Health, Program in Nursing, Dayton, OH 45435. Offers acute care nurse practitioner (MS); administration of nursing and health care systems (MS); adult health (MS); child and adolescent health (MS); community health (MS); family nurse practitioner (MS); nurse practitioner (MS); school nurse (MS); MBA/MS. *Accreditation:* AACN. Part-time and evening/weekend programs available. *Students:* 46 full-time (45 women), 124 part-time (117 women); includes 16 minority (13 African Americans, 1 Asian American or Pacific Islander, 2 Hispanic Americans). Average age 39. 45 applicants, 100% accepted. In 2006, 64 degrees awarded. *Degree requirements:* For master's, thesis or alternative. *Entrance requirements:* For master's, GRE General Test, BSN from NLN-accredited college, Ohio RN license. Additional exam requirements/recommendations for international students: Required—TOEFL. *Application deadline:* For fall admission, 4/15 priority date for domestic students. Application fee: $25. *Financial support:* Fellowships, research assistantships, teaching assistantships, Federal Work-Study, institutionally sponsored loans, and unspecified assistantships available. Support available to part-time students. Financial award application deadline: 6/1; financial award applicants required to submit FAFSA. *Faculty research:* Clinical nursing and health, teaching, caring, pain administration, informatics and technology. *Application contact:* Theresa A. Haghnazarian, Director of Student and Alumni Affairs, 937-775-2592, Fax: 937-775-4571, E-mail: theresa.haghnazarian@wright.edu.

Community Health Nursing

Augsburg College, Program in Transcultural Community Health Nursing, Minneapolis, MN 55454-1351. Offers MA. *Accreditation:* AACN. *Faculty:* 2 full-time (both women). *Students:* 6 full-time (all women), 43 part-time (42 women); includes 2 minority (both African Americans), 1 international. Average age 45. 120 applicants, 18% accepted, 20 enrolled. In 2006, 8 degrees awarded. *Degree requirements:* For master's, thesis or alternative. *Application deadline:* For fall admission, 8/1 for domestic students; for winter admission, 12/4 for domestic students; for spring admission, 3/9 for domestic students. Application fee: $35. *Expenses:* Tuition: Full-time $10,584; part-time $1,764 per course. Required fees: $300; $35 per course. Tuition and fees vary according to program. *Financial support:* In 2006–07, 5 students received support. Application deadline: 8/1; *Unit head:* Dr. Cheryl J. Leuning, Director, 612-330-1214, E-mail: leuning@augsburg.edu. *Application contact:* Sharon Wade, Coordinator, 612-330-1209, E-mail: wades@augsburg.edu.

Augustana College, Program in Advanced Nursing Practice in Emerging Health Systems, Sioux Falls, SD 57197. Offers community health nursing (MA). *Accreditation:* AACN. Part-time programs available. Postbaccalaureate distance learning degree programs offered (minimal on-campus study). *Degree requirements:* For master's, portfolio, oral exam, paper. *Entrance requirements:* For master's, current licensure, minimum GPA of 3.0, previous course work in statistics, bachelor's degree in nursing. Additional exam requirements/recommendations for international students: Required—TOEFL. *Faculty research:* HIV infected persons, nursing theory development, nursing workforce development.

Boston College, William F. Connell School of Nursing, Chestnut Hill, MA 02467-3800. Offers adult health nursing (MS); community health nursing (MS); family health (MS); gerontology (MS); maternal/child health nursing (MS), including pediatric and women's health; nurse anesthesia (MS); nursing (PhD); psychiatric-mental health nursing (MS); MBA/MS; MS/MA; MS/

Community Health Nursing

Boston College (continued)

PhD. *Accreditation:* AACN; AANA/CANAEP (one or more programs are accredited). Part-time programs available. *Faculty:* 46 full-time (44 women), 34 part-time/adjunct (all women). *Students:* 155 full-time (137 women), 56 part-time (54 women); includes 10 minority (4 African Americans, 5 Asian Americans or Pacific Islanders, 1 Hispanic American), 6 international. Average age 34. 276 applicants, 47% accepted, 67 enrolled. In 2006, 61 master's, 4 doctorates awarded. *Median time to degree:* Of those who began their doctoral program in fall 1998, 100% received their degree in 8 years or less. *Degree requirements:* For master's, research project; for doctorate, thesis/dissertation, computer literacy exam or foreign language, comprehensive exam. *Entrance requirements:* For master's, GRE General Test, bachelor's degree in nursing; for doctorate, GRE General Test, master's degree in nursing. Additional exam requirements/recommendations for international students: Required—TOEFL (minimum score 550 paper-based; 213 computer-based). *Application deadline:* For fall admission, 10/15 for domestic and international students; for spring admission, 3/15 for domestic and international students. Application fee: $40. Electronic applications accepted. *Financial support:* In 2006–07, 104 students received support, including 15 fellowships with partial tuition reimbursements available (averaging $10,045 per year), 3 research assistantships (averaging $10,000 per year), 4 teaching assistantships (averaging $12,548 per year); Federal Work-Study, institutionally sponsored loans, scholarships/grants, traineeships, and tuition waivers (partial) also available. Support available to part-time students. Financial award application deadline: 3/1; financial award applicants required to submit FAFSA. *Faculty research:* Ethics, reduction of risk behaviors, support during chronic illness, violence, gerontology. Total annual research expenditures: $1.1 million. *Unit head:* Dr. Barbara Hazard, Dean, 617-552-4251, Fax: 617-552-0931, E-mail: barbara.munro@bc.edu. *Application contact:* Zanifer John-Bayard, Graduate Programs Assistant, 617-552-4059, Fax: 617-552-0745, E-mail: johnza@bc.edu.

Case Western Reserve University, Frances Payne Bolton School of Nursing, Master's Programs in Nursing, Cleveland, OH 44106. Offers community health nursing (MSN); medical-surgical nursing (MSN); nurse anesthesia (MSN); nurse midwifery (MSN); nurse practitioner (MSN), including acute care cardiovascular nursing, acute care nurse practitioner, acute care/flight nurse, adult nurse practitioner, family nurse practitioner, gerontological nurse practitioner, neonatal nurse practitioner, pediatric nurse practitioner, psychiatric-mental health nurse practitioner, women's health nurse practitioner; nursing informatics (MSN). *Accreditation:* NLN. Part-time programs available. Postbaccalaureate distance learning degree programs offered (minimal on-campus study). *Faculty:* 54 full-time (50 women), 5 part-time/adjunct (3 women). *Students:* 42 full-time (30 women), 107 part-time (95 women); includes 28 minority (12 African Americans, 11 Asian Americans or Pacific Islanders, 5 Hispanic Americans), 7 international. Average age 35. 181 applicants, 43% accepted, 48 enrolled. In 2006, 75 degrees awarded. *Degree requirements:* For master's, thesis optional. *Entrance requirements:* For master's, GRE General Test or MAT. *Application deadline:* Applications are processed on a rolling basis. Application fee: $75. *Financial support:* In 2006–07, 7 teaching assistantships with tuition reimbursements were awarded; fellowships, research assistantships, institutionally sponsored loans, traineeships, and tuition waivers (partial) also available. Support available to part-time students. Financial award application deadline: 6/30. *Faculty research:* Preterm skin contact effects on electrophysiologic sleep, intergenerational caregiving to at risk youth, maintaining exercise in cardiac rehabilitation, left ventricular function and duration of mechanical ventilation. *Unit head:* Dr. Carol Savrin, Director, 216-368-6304, Fax: 215-368-3542, E-mail: cls18@case.edu. *Application contact:* Peter Taylor, Recruitment and Retention Specialist, 216-368-0349, Fax: 216-368-0124, E-mail: peter.taylor@case.edu.

Cleveland State University, College of Graduate Studies, College of Education and Human Services, School of Nursing, Cleveland, OH 44115. Offers clinical nursing leader (MSN); forensic nursing (MSN); population health nursing (MSN); MSN/MBA. *Accreditation:* AACN. Part-time programs available. *Faculty:* 8 full-time (all women). *Students:* Average age 44. In 2006, 1 degree awarded. *Degree requirements:* For master's, thesis or alternative, portfolio, population health project. *Entrance requirements:* For master's, RN license, BSN, course work in statistics. Additional exam requirements/recommendations for international students: Required—TOEFL (minimum score 525 paper-based; 197 computer-based), IELTS (minimum score 6). *Application deadline:* For fall admission, 5/1 priority date for domestic students. Applications are processed on a rolling basis. Application fee: $30. Electronic applications accepted. *Financial support:* In 2006–07, 3 students received support. Tuition waivers (full) and unspecified assistantships available. Support available to part-time students. Financial award application deadline: 3/1; financial award applicants required to submit FAFSA. *Faculty research:* Diabetes management, African-American elders medication compliance, risk in home visiting, suffering, COPD and stress. Total annual research expenditures: $204,029. *Unit head:* Dr. Noreen C. Frisch, Director, 216-523-7237, Fax: 216-687-3556, E-mail: n.frisch@csuohio.edu. *Application contact:* Dr. Sharon Radzyminski, Director, Graduate Nursing Program, 216-687-3558, Fax: 216-687-3556, E-mail: s.radzyminski@csuohio.edu.

D'Youville College, Department of Nursing, Buffalo, NY 14201-1084. Offers community health nursing/education (MSN); community health nursing/high risk parents and children (MSN); community health nursing/management (MSN); family nurse practitioner (MS); nursing and health-related professions (Certificate); nursing with clinical focus choice (MSN). *Accreditation:* AACN. Part-time and evening/weekend programs available. *Faculty:* 26 full-time (all women), 7 part-time/adjunct (6 women). *Students:* 77 full-time (72 women), 101 part-time (95 women); includes 17 minority (12 African Americans, 1 American Indian/Alaska Native, 4 Hispanic Americans), 89 international. Average age 36. 177 applicants, 58% accepted, 37 enrolled. In 2006, 41 master's, 2 other advanced degrees awarded. *Degree requirements:* For master's, membership on board of community agency, publishable paper, thesis optional. *Entrance requirements:* For master's, BS in nursing, minimum GPA of 3.0, course work in statistics and computers. Additional exam requirements/recommendations for international students: Required—TOEFL (minimum score 500 paper-based; 173 computer-based). *Application deadline:* For fall admission, 5/1 priority date for international students; for spring admission, 9/1 priority date for international students. Applications are processed on a rolling basis. Application fee: $25. Electronic applications accepted. *Financial support:* In 2006–07, 1 research assistantship with partial tuition reimbursement (averaging $3,000 per year) was awarded; Federal Work-Study and scholarships/grants also available. Support available to part-time students. Financial award application deadline: 3/1; financial award applicants required to submit FAFSA. *Faculty research:* Nursing curriculum, nursing theory-testing, wellness research, communication and socialization patterns. *Unit head:* Dr. Verna Kieffer, Chair, 716-829-7613, Fax: 716-829-8159. *Application contact:* Linda Fisher, Graduate Admissions Director, 716-829-8400, Fax: 716-829-7900, E-mail: graduateadmissions@dyc.edu.

See Close-Up on page 1953.

Georgia Southern University, Jack N. Averitt College of Graduate Studies, College of Health and Human Sciences, School of Nursing, Statesboro, GA 30460. Offers rural community health nurse practitioner (MSN); rural community health nurse specialist (Certificate); rural family nurse practitioner (MSN, Certificate); women's health nurse practitioner (MSN, Certificate). *Accreditation:* AACN. Part-time programs available. Postbaccalaureate distance learning degree programs offered. *Faculty:* 13 full-time (all women). *Students:* 6 full-time (all women), 40 part-time (38 women); includes 6 minority (all African Americans) Average age 34. 14 applicants, 100% accepted. In 2006, 15 degrees awarded. *Degree requirements:* For master's, thesis optional. *Entrance requirements:* For master's, GRE General Test or MAT, minimum GPA of 3.0, Georgia nursing license, 2 years of clinical experience, CPR certification; for Certificate, MSN. Additional exam requirements/recommendations for international students: Required—TOEFL (minimum score 550 paper-based; 213 computer-based; 80 iBT). *Application deadline:* For fall admission, 3/1 priority date for domestic students, 3/1 for international students; for spring admission, 10/1 priority date for domestic students, 10/1 for international students. Applications are processed on a rolling basis. Application fee: $50. Electronic applications accepted. *Financial support:* In 2006–07, 35 students received support, including research assistantships with partial tuition reimbursements available (averaging $5,500 per year), teaching assistantships with partial tuition reimbursements available (averaging $5,500 per year); career-related internships or fieldwork, Federal Work-Study, scholarships/grants, traineeships, tuition waivers (partial), and unspecified assistantships also available. Support available to part-time students. Financial award application deadline: 4/15; financial award applicants required to submit FAFSA. *Faculty research:* Caring, HIV disease, qualitative health research, health policy, rural nursing. Total annual research expenditures: $189,915. *Unit head:* Dr. Jean Bartels, Chair, 912-681-5479, Fax: 912-681-0536, E-mail: jbartels@georgiasouthern.edu. *Application contact:* 912-681-5384, Fax: 912-681-0740, E-mail: gradadmissions@georgiasouthern.edu.

Hawai'i Pacific University, School of Nursing, Honolulu, HI 96813. Offers community clinical nurse specialist (MSN); community clinical nurse specialist educator option (MSN); family nurse practitioner (MSN). *Accreditation:* NLN. Part-time and evening/weekend programs available. *Faculty:* 11 full-time (all women), 1 part-time/adjunct (0 women). *Students:* 26 full-time (23 women), 10 part-time (all women); includes 18 minority (2 African Americans, 1 American Indian/Alaska Native, 13 Asian Americans or Pacific Islanders, 2 Hispanic Americans). Average age 35. 22 applicants, 77% accepted, 13 enrolled. In 2006, 10 degrees awarded. *Degree requirements:* For master's, practicum, professional paper. *Entrance requirements:* For master's, bachelor's degree in nursing, minimum GPA of 3.0. Additional exam requirements/recommendations for international students: Recommended—TOEFL (minimum score 550 paper-based; 213 computer-based), TWE (minimum score 5). *Application deadline:* Applications are processed on a rolling basis. Application fee: $50. Electronic applications accepted. *Expenses:* Tuition: Full-time $10,080; part-time $560 per credit. *Financial support:* In 2006–07, 20 students received support. Career-related internships or fieldwork, Federal Work-Study, scholarships/grants, and traineeships available. Support available to part-time students. Financial award application deadline: 3/1; financial award applicants required to submit FAFSA. *Faculty research:* Hawaiian elders, traditional healing and nursing center. *Unit head:* Dr. Patricia Langotsuka, Interim Dean, 808-236-5812, Fax: 808-236-5818, E-mail: potsuka@hpu.edu. *Application contact:* Danny Lam, Assistant Director of Graduate Admissions, 808-544-1135, Fax: 808-544-0280, E-mail: graduate@hpu.edu.

See Close-Up on page 1961.

Holy Names University, Graduate Division, Department of Nursing, Oakland, CA 94619-1699. Offers community health nursing/case manager (MS); family nurse practitioner (MS). *Accreditation:* AACN. Part-time and evening/weekend programs available. *Faculty:* 1 (woman) full-time, 7 part-time/adjunct (all women). *Students:* 73 full-time (68 women), 22 part-time (20 women); includes 45 minority (22 African Americans, 1 American Indian/Alaska Native, 13 Asian Americans or Pacific Islanders, 9 Hispanic Americans). Average age 44. 52 applicants, 65% accepted, 26 enrolled. In 2006, 10 master's awarded. *Entrance requirements:* For master's, bachelor's degree in nursing or related field, California RN license or eligibility, minimum GPA of 3.0, previous course work in research or statistics. Additional exam requirements/recommendations for international students: Required—TOEFL. *Application deadline:* For fall admission, 8/1 priority date for domestic students; for spring admission, 12/1 priority date for domestic students. Applications are processed on a rolling basis. Application fee: $50. *Expenses:* Tuition: Full-time $10,800; part-time $600 per unit. Required fees: $240; $120 per term. *Financial support:* In 2006–07, 36 students received support. Scholarships/grants available. Support available to part-time students. Financial award application deadline: 3/2; financial award applicants required to submit FAFSA. *Faculty research:* Women's reproductive health, gerontology, attitudes about aging, schizophrenic families, international health issues. *Unit head:* Dr. Fay Bower, Program Director, 510-436-1127. *Application contact:* 800-430-1351, Fax: 510-436-1325, E-mail: admissions@hnu.edu.

Hunter College of the City University of New York, Graduate School, Schools of the Health Professions, Hunter-Bellevue School of Nursing, Community Health Nursing/Community Health Education Program, New York, NY 10021-5085. Offers MS/MPH. *Accreditation:* AACN. Part-time programs available. *Faculty:* 9 full-time (all women), 2 part-time/adjunct (1 woman). *Students:* Average age 32. 6 applicants, 83% accepted, 3 enrolled. *Entrance requirements:* Additional exam requirements/recommendations for international students: Required—TOEFL. *Application deadline:* For fall admission, 4/1 for domestic students, 2/1 for international students; for spring admission, 11/1 for domestic students, 9/1 for international students. Applications are processed on a rolling basis. Application fee: $125. *Expenses:* Tuition, state resident: part-time $270 per credit. Tuition, nonresident: part-time $500 per credit. Required fees: $45 per semester. *Financial support:* Federal Work-Study, scholarships/grants, traineeships, and tuition waivers (partial) available. Support available to part-time students. Financial award application deadline: 5/1; financial award applicants required to submit FAFSA. *Faculty research:* HIV/AIDS, health promotion with vulnerable populations, immigrant health. *Unit head:* Dr. Kathleen Nokes, Coordinator, 212-481-7594, Fax: 212-481-5078, E-mail: knokes@hejira.hunter.cuny.edu. *Application contact:* William Zlata, Director for Graduate Admissions, 212-772-4482, Fax: 212-650-3336, E-mail: admissions@hunter.cuny.edu.

Hunter College of the City University of New York, Graduate School, Schools of the Health Professions, Hunter-Bellevue School of Nursing, Community Health Nursing Program, New York, NY 10021-5085. Offers MS. *Accreditation:* AACN. Part-time programs available. *Faculty:* 9 full-time (all women), 2 part-time/adjunct (1 woman). *Students:* Average age 39. 3 applicants, 0% accepted. In 2006, 8 degrees awarded. *Degree requirements:* For master's, practicum. *Entrance requirements:* For master's, minimum GPA of 3.0 New York RN license, BSN. Additional exam requirements/recommendations for international students: Required—TOEFL. *Application deadline:* For fall admission, 4/1 for domestic students, 2/1 for international students; for spring admission, 11/1 for domestic students, 9/1 for international students. Applications are processed on a rolling basis. Application fee: $125. *Expenses:* Tuition, state resident: part-time $270 per credit. Tuition, nonresident: part-time $500 per credit. Required fees: $45 per semester. *Financial support:* Federal Work-Study, scholarships/grants, traineeships, and tuition waivers (partial) available. Support available to part-time students. Financial award application deadline: 5/1; financial award applicants required to submit FAFSA. *Faculty research:* HIV/AIDS, health promotion with vulnerable populations. *Unit head:* Dr. Kathleen Nokes, Coordinator, 212-481-7594, Fax: 212-481-5078, E-mail: knokes@hejira.hunter.cuny.edu. *Application contact:* William Zlata, Director for Graduate Admissions, 212-772-4482, Fax: 212-650-3336, E-mail: admissions@hunter.cuny.edu.

Indiana University–Purdue University Indianapolis, School of Nursing, Indianapolis, IN 46202-2896. Offers acute care nurse practitioner (MSN); adult health clinical nurse specialist (MSN); adult health nursing (MSN), including adult clinical nurse specialist, adult nurse practitioner (MSN); adult psychiatric/mental health nursing (MSN); child psychiatric/mental health nursing (MSN); community health nursing (MSN); family nurse practitioner (MSN); neonatal nurse practitioner (MSN); nursing science (PhD); pediatric clinical nurse specialist (MSN); women's health nurse practitioner (MSN); MSN/MPA; MSN/MPH. *Accreditation:* AACN; NLN (one or more programs are accredited). Part-time programs available. *Faculty:* 45 full-time (44 women), 1 (woman) part-time/adjunct. *Students:* 52 full-time (51 women), 415 part-time (396 women); includes 27 minority (16 African Americans, 3 Asian Americans or Pacific Islanders, 8 Hispanic Americans), 4 international. Average age 38. In 2006, 106 master's, 3 doctorates awarded. Terminal master's awarded for partial completion of doctoral program. *Degree requirements:* For master's and doctorate, thesis/dissertation. *Entrance requirements:* For master's, GRE General Test, minimum GPA of 3.0, RN license; for doctorate, GRE General Test, minimum GPA of 3.5, MSN, RN license. Additional exam requirements/recommendations for international students: Required—TOEFL. *Application deadline:* For fall admission, 2/15 for domestic students; for spring admission, 9/15 for domestic students. Application fee: $50 ($60 for international students). *Expenses:* Tuition, state resident: full-time $5,437; part-time $227 per credit hour. Tuition, nonresident: full-time $15,694; part-time $654 per credit hour. Required fees: $620. Tuition and fees vary according to course load, campus/location and program. *Financial support:* In 2006–07, 93 students received support; fellowships with full tuition reimbursements available, research assistantships with full tuition reimbursements available, teaching assistantships with full tuition reimbursements available, Federal Work-Study, institutionally sponsored loans, scholarships/grants, and tuition waivers (full) available. Support available to part-time students. Financial award application deadline: 5/1. *Faculty research:* Chronic illness, cancer, health services research, family health. Total annual research expenditures: $3 million. *Unit head:* Associate Dean for Graduate Programs, 317-274-2806, E-mail: nursing@iupui.edu. *Application contact:* Martez Plummer, Assistant Dean for Student Affairs, 317-274-2806, E-mail: mplummer@iupui.edu.

Indiana Wesleyan University, College of Graduate Studies, Division of Nursing, Marion, IN 46953-4974. Offers community health nursing (MS); nursing (Post Master's Certificate); nursing administration (MS); nursing education (MS); primary care nursing (MS). *Accreditation:* AACN. Part-time and evening/weekend programs available. *Faculty:* 2 full-time (both women), 6 part-time/adjunct (3 women). *Students:* 312 full-time (296 women), 8 part-time (4 women); includes 45 minority (41 African Americans, 2 Asian Americans or Pacific Islanders, 2 Hispanic Americans). Average age 40. In 2006, 87 degrees awarded. *Degree requirements:* For master's, thesis. *Entrance requirements:* For master's, GRE, RN license, 1 year of related experience, graduate statistics course. *Application deadline:* For fall admission, 7/31 priority date for domestic students; for winter admission, 11/15 priority date for domestic students; for spring admission, 4/15 priority date for domestic students. Electronic applications accepted. *Expenses:* Contact institution. Tuition and fees vary according to degree level, campus/ location and program. *Financial support:* In 2006–07, 15 fellowships were awarded; career-related internships or fieldwork, scholarships/grants, and traineeships also available. Support available to part-time students. Financial award application deadline: 3/15. *Faculty research:* Primary health care with international emphasis, international nursing. *Unit head:* Pam Giles, Director, 765-677-1716, E-mail: gradnurse@indwes.edu. *Application contact:* David McMillan, Assistant Director of Enrollment Management, 765-677-2688, E-mail: david.mcmillan@indwes.edu.

Inter American University of Puerto Rico, Arecibo Campus, Program in Nursing, Arecibo, PR 00614-4050. Offers community nursing (MS); primary care nursing (MS). *Entrance requirements:* For master's, EXADEP or GRE or MAT, 2 letters of recommendation, bachelor's degree in nursing, minimum GPA of 2.5 in last 60 credits, minimum 1 year nursing experience, nursing license.

The Johns Hopkins University, School of Nursing and Bloomberg School of Public Health, Joint Degree Program in Nursing and Public Health, Baltimore, MD 21218-2699. Offers MSN/ MPH. *Accreditation:* AACN; CEPH. Part-time programs available. *Faculty:* 4 full-time (all women), 2 part-time/adjunct (both women). *Students:* 27 full-time (26 women), 17 part-time (all women); includes 13 minority (3 African Americans, 9 Asian Americans or Pacific Islanders, 1 Hispanic American). Average age 31. 62 applicants, 84% accepted, 17 enrolled. *Entrance requirements:* Additional exam requirements/recommendations for international students: Required—TOEFL (minimum score 550 paper-based; 230 computer-based). *Application deadline:* For fall admission, 3/1 priority date for domestic and international students; for spring admission, 1/31 priority date for domestic and international students. Applications are processed on a rolling basis. Application fee: $75. *Expenses:* Contact institution. Tuition and fees vary according to degree level and program. *Financial support:* In 2006–07, 17 students received support. Federal Work-Study, scholarships/grants, traineeships and tuition waivers (partial) available. Support available to part-time students. Financial award application deadline: 3/1; financial award applicants required to submit FAFSA. *Faculty research:* Asthma, tuberculosis control, injury, violence, international health, women's health, substance abuse. *Unit head:* Dr. Kathleen M. White, Director, Master's Programs, 410-614-4664, Fax: 410-955-7463, E-mail: kwhite@son.jhmi.edu. *Application contact:* Mary O'Rourke, Director of Admissions/Student Services, 410-955-7548, Fax: 410-614-7086, E-mail: orourke@son.jhmi.edu.

The Johns Hopkins University, School of Nursing, Program in Public Health Nursing, Baltimore, MD 21218-2699. Offers MSN. *Accreditation:* AACN; NLN. Part-time programs available. *Faculty:* 4 full-time (all women), 2 part-time/adjunct (both women). *Students:* 1 (woman) full-time, 1 (woman) part-time; includes 1 minority (African American) Average age 31. 11 applicants, 91% accepted, 1 enrolled. In 2006, 2 degrees awarded. *Degree requirements:* For master's, scholarly project or portfolio, thesis optional. *Entrance requirements:* For master's, GRE, interview, minimum GPA of 3.0, BSN, Maryland RN license. Additional exam requirements/ recommendations for international students: Required—TOEFL (minimum score 550 paper-based; 230 computer-based). *Application deadline:* For fall admission, 3/1 priority date for domestic and international students; for spring admission, 7/1 priority date for domestic and international students. Applications are processed on a rolling basis. Application fee: $75. *Expenses:* Contact institution. Tuition and fees vary according to degree level and program. *Financial support:* Career-related internships or fieldwork, Federal Work-Study, scholarships/ grants, traineeships, and tuition waivers (partial) available. Support available to part-time students. Financial award application deadline: 3/1; financial award applicants required to submit FAFSA. *Faculty research:* Violence, community outreach, outcomes, asthma, HIV. *Unit head:* Dr. Kathleen M. White, Director, Master's Programs, 410-614-4664, Fax: 410-955-7463, E-mail: kwhite@son.jhmi.edu. *Application contact:* Mary O'Rourke, Director of Admissions/ Student Services, 410-955-7548, Fax: 410-614-7086, E-mail: orourke@son.jhmi.edu.

Kean University, College of Natural, Applied and Health Sciences, Program in Nursing, Union, NJ 07083. Offers clinical management (MSN); community health (MSN). *Accreditation:* NLN. Part-time and evening/weekend programs available. *Faculty:* 7 full-time (all women). *Students:* 5 full-time (4 women), 62 part-time (57 women); includes 42 minority (26 African Americans, 12 Asian Americans or Pacific Islanders, 4 Hispanic Americans). Average age 43. 29 applicants, 93% accepted, 19 enrolled. In 2006, 23 degrees awarded. *Degree requirements:* For master's, thesis or alternative, clinical field experience. *Entrance requirements:* For master's, BS in nursing, RN license, 2 letters of recommendation, interview. *Application deadline:* For fall admission, 5/1 for domestic students; for spring admission, 11/1 for domestic students. Application fee: $60 ($150 for international students). *Expenses:* Tuition, state resident: full-time $8,856; part-time $369 per credit. Tuition, nonresident: full-time $11,256; part-time $469 per credit. *Financial support:* Research assistantships with full tuition reimbursements available. *Unit head:* Dr. Estelle A. Pisani, Program Coordinator, 908-737-3386, E-mail: episani@kean. edu. *Application contact:* Joanne Morris, Director of Graduate Admissions, 908-737-3355, Fax: 908-737-3354, E-mail: grad-adm@kean.edu.

La Salle University, School of Nursing and Health Sciences, Philadelphia, PA 19141-1199. Offers adult health and illness, clinical nurse specialist (MSN); gerontology (Certificate); nursing administration (MSN); nursing education (Certificate); nursing informatics (Certificate); primary care of adults-nurse practitioner (MSN); public health nursing (MSN); school nursing (Certificate); speech-language-hearing science (MS); wound, ostomy and continence nursing (Certificate); wound, ostomy, and continence nursing (MSN); MSN/MBA. *Accreditation:* AACN. Part-time programs available. Postbaccalaureate distance learning degree programs offered (minimal on-campus study). *Entrance requirements:* For master's, GRE or MAT, 1 year of professional work experience, BSN, Pennsylvania RN license. *Expenses:* Contact institution. *Faculty research:* Medication errors, wound care, metacognition, education of RN students.

Louisiana State University Health Sciences Center, School of Nursing, New Orleans, LA 70112-2223. Offers adult health and illness (MN); adult health and nursing (DNS); neonatal nurse practitioner (MN); nursing (MN); nursing service administration (MN, DNS); parent-child health nursing (MN); primary care nurse practitioner (MN); psychiatric/community mental health nursing (MN, DNS); public health/community health nursing (MN, DNS). *Accreditation:* AACN; AANA/CANAEP (one or more programs are accredited). Part-time programs available. *Degree requirements:* For master's, thesis optional; for doctorate, thesis/dissertation. *Entrance requirements:* For master's, GRE General Test, MAT, minimum GPA of 3.0; for doctorate, GRE General Test, minimum GPA of 3.5. Additional exam requirements/recommendations for international students: Required—TOEFL. *Expenses:* Tuition, state resident: full-time $5,868; part-time $722 per credit. Tuition, nonresident: full-time $8,993; part-time $1,104 per credit. *Faculty research:* Advanced clinical practice, nursing education, health, social support, nursing administration.

Medical College of Georgia, School of Graduate Studies, Programs in Nursing, Augusta, GA 30912-1500. Offers adult nursing (MSN); community health nursing (MSN); mental health nursing (MSN); nurse practitioner (MSN); nursing (DNP, PhD); nursing anesthesia (MSN); parent-child nursing (MSN). *Accreditation:* AACN; AANA/CANAEP. Part-time programs available. *Faculty:* 18 full-time (16 women), 1 part-time/adjunct (0 women). *Students:* 95 full-time (76 women), 42 part-time (37 women); includes 24 minority (20 African Americans, 4 Asian Americans or Pacific Islanders). Average age 37. 156 applicants, 35% accepted, 24 enrolled. In 2006, 28 master's, 10 doctorates awarded. *Degree requirements:* For master's, thesis (for some programs); for doctorate, thesis/dissertation. *Entrance requirements:* For master's, GRE General Test, MAT; for doctorate, GRE General Test. Additional exam requirements/ recommendations for international students: Required—TOEFL (minimum score 550 paper-based; 213 computer-based). *Application deadline:* For fall admission, 7/1 for domestic students, 4/15 for international students. Applications are processed on a rolling basis. Application fee: $30. Electronic applications accepted. *Expenses:* Tuition, state resident: full-time $2,293; part-time $192 per credit hour. Tuition, nonresident: full-time $9,169; part-time $765 per credit hour. Required fees: $293 per semester. *Financial support:* In 2006–07, 78 students received support, including 9 research assistantships with partial tuition reimbursements available (averaging $23,000 per year); Federal Work-Study, institutionally sponsored loans, traineeships, tuition waivers, and unspecified assistantships also available. Support available to part-time students. Financial award application deadline: 5/31; financial award applicants required to submit FAFSA. *Unit head:* Dr. Lucy Marion, Dean, 706-721-6258, Fax: 706-721-8169, E-mail: lumarion@mail.mcg.edu.

New Mexico State University, Graduate School, College of Health and Social Services, School of Nursing, Las Cruces, NM 88003-8001. Offers community/public health (MSN); medical-surgical (adult health) (MSN); psychiatric/mental health (MSN). *Accreditation:* AACN. Part-time programs available. Postbaccalaureate distance learning degree programs offered (minimal on-campus study). *Faculty:* 12 full-time (all women), 5 part-time/adjunct (4 women). *Students:* 27 full-time (24 women), 25 part-time (all women); includes 13 minority (1 African American, 12 Hispanic Americans), 1 international. Average age 45. 24 applicants, 83% accepted. In 2006, 14 degrees awarded. *Degree requirements:* For master's, clinical practice, RN licensure, thesis optional. *Entrance requirements:* For master's, BSN, minimum GPA of 3.0, course work in statistics, 3 letters of reference, writing sample. Additional exam requirements/ recommendations for international students: Required—NCLEX. *Application deadline:* For fall admission, 3/1 priority date for domestic students; for spring admission, 10/1 priority date for domestic students. Applications are processed on a rolling basis. Application fee: $30 ($50 for international students). Electronic applications accepted. *Financial support:* In 2006–07, 2 teaching assistantships were awarded; fellowships, research assistantships, career-related internships or fieldwork, Federal Work-Study, scholarships/grants, traineeships, and health care benefits also available. Financial award application deadline: 3/1. *Faculty research:* Advanced practice nursing, evidence-based nursing practice, health policy, community outreach, clinical judgment. *Unit head:* Dr. Esperanza V. Joyce, Director, 505-646-3812, Fax: 505-646-2167, E-mail: evjoyce@nmsu.edu. *Application contact:* Dr. Mary Hoke, Associate Director for Graduate Studies, 505-646-3812, Fax: 505-646-2167, E-mail: mhoke@nmsu.edu.

Northeastern University, Bouvé College of Health Sciences Graduate School, School of Nursing, Program in Community Health Nursing, Boston, MA 02115-5096. Offers MS, CAS. *Accreditation:* AACN. *Faculty:* 23 full-time (all women), 12 part-time/adjunct (11 women). *Students:* Average age 42. 3 applicants, 100% accepted. In 2006, 1 degree awarded. *Degree requirements:* For master's, thesis optional. *Entrance requirements:* For master's, GRE General Test, minimum GPA of 3.0, previous course work in statistics, 1-2 years of nursing experience, RN license, ICU experience. Additional exam requirements/recommendations for international students: Required—TOEFL. *Application deadline:* For fall admission, 4/1 priority date for domestic students; for spring admission, 2/1 for domestic students. Applications are processed on a rolling basis. Application fee: $50. *Financial support:* Research assistantships, teaching assistantships, tuition waivers (partial) available. Financial award application deadline: 7/1; financial award applicants required to submit FAFSA. *Unit head:* Dr. Abraham N. Ndiwane, Director, 617-373-3124, Fax: 617-373-8672. *Application contact:* Margaret Schnabel, Director of Graduate Admissions, 617-373-2708, Fax: 617-373-4704, E-mail: bouvegrad@neu.edu.

Oregon Health & Science University, School of Nursing, Program in Community Health Care Systems, Portland, OR 97239-3098. Offers MS, Post Master's Certificate. *Degree requirements:* For master's, thesis optional. *Entrance requirements:* For master's, GRE General Test, bachelor's degree in nursing, minimum undergraduate GPA of 3.0, previous course work in statistics; for Post Master's Certificate, master's degree in nursing.

Oregon Health & Science University, School of Nursing, Program in Public Health Nursing, Portland, OR 97239-3098. Offers MPH. *Accreditation:* AACN. *Degree requirements:* For master's, thesis optional. *Entrance requirements:* For master's, GRE General Test, bachelor's degree in nursing, minimum undergraduate GPA of 3.0, previous course work in statistics.

Rush University, College of Nursing, Department of Community and Mental Health Nursing, Chicago, IL 60612-3832. Offers community and mental health nursing (DN Sc, DNP); family nurse practitioner (MSN, Post-Master's Certificate); psychiatric clinical specialist (MSN); psychiatric nurse practitioner—adult (MSN); psychiatric nurse practitioner—family (MSN); psychiatric-mental health clinical specialist (Post-Master's Certificate); psychiatric-mental health nurse practitioner (Post-Master's Certificate); public health nursing (MSN). *Accreditation:* AACN. Part-time programs available. Postbaccalaureate distance learning degree programs offered (minimal on-campus study). *Faculty:* 26. *Students:* 68 (65 women); includes 11 minority (6 African Americans, 4 Asian Americans or Pacific Islanders, 1 Hispanic American). Average age 35. 30 applicants, 93% accepted, 27 enrolled. In 2006, 1 master's, 13 doctorates awarded. Terminal master's awarded for partial completion of doctoral program. *Degree requirements:* For master's, capstone project; for doctorate, thesis/dissertation, DNP leadership project. *Entrance requirements:* For master's, GRE General Test (waived if nursing GPA is above 3.0 or cumulative GPA is above 3.25), interview; for doctorate, GRE General Test, interview, course work in statistics (DN Sc). *Application deadline:* For fall admission, 7/1 for domestic students; for winter admission, 11/1 for domestic students; for spring admission, 1/15 for domestic students. Applications are processed on a rolling basis. Application fee: $40. Electronic applications accepted. *Financial support:* In 2006–07, 11 students received support; teaching assistantships with tuition reimbursements available, Federal Work-Study, institutionally sponsored loans, scholarships/grants, and traineeships available. Support available to part-time students. Financial award applicants required to submit FAFSA. *Faculty research:* Immigrant mental health, de-escalation strategies, caregiver interventions, parent-teacher training, restraint use. *Unit head:* Dr. Julia Cowell, Chairperson, 312-942-7117. *Application contact:* Hicela Castruita Woods, Director, College Admissions Services, 312-942-7100, Fax: 312-942-2219, E-mail: hicela_castruita@rush.edu.

Rutgers, The State University of New Jersey, Newark, Graduate School, Program in Nursing, Newark, NJ 07102. Offers nursing (MS), including acute care of adults and aged, advanced practice in pediatric nursing, advanced practice with childbearing families, community health nursing, family nurse practitioner, primary care of adults and aged, psychiatric/ mental health nursing. *Accreditation:* AACN. Part-time programs available. *Faculty:* 33 full-time (32 women). *Students:* 11 full-time (all women), 186 part-time (175 women); includes 70 minority (28 African Americans, 30 Asian Americans or Pacific Islanders, 12 Hispanic Americans). 255 applicants, 58% accepted, 72 enrolled. In 2006, 40 master's awarded. *Degree requirements:* For master's, comprehensive exam. *Entrance requirements:* For master's, GRE General Test, RN license, minimum B average, BS in nursing. Additional exam requirements/recommendations for international students: Required—TOEFL. *Application deadline:* For fall admission, 2/15 for domestic students; for spring admission, 12/1 for domestic students. Applications are processed on a rolling basis. Application fee: $50. Electronic applications accepted. *Financial support:* In 2006–07, 3 fellowships (averaging $8,000 per year) were awarded; teaching assistantships with full tuition reimbursements, career-related internships or fieldwork, Federal Work-Study, institutionally sponsored loans, scholarships/grants, traineeships, and tuition waivers (full and

Community Health Nursing

Rutgers, The State University of New Jersey, Newark (continued)
partial) also available. Financial award application deadline: 4/15. *Faculty research:* HIV/AIDS, quality of life—MS and breast cancer, sleep patterns of cardiac patients. *Unit head:* Dr. Wendy Nehring, Program Director, 973-353-5293 Ext. 606, Fax: 973-353-1277, E-mail: nehring@nightingale.rutgers.edu. *Application contact:* Dr. Linda Scheetz, Associate Dean for Student Life and Services, 973-353-5060 Ext. 611, Fax: 973-353-1277, E-mail: lscheetz@andromeda.rutgers.edu.

Sage Graduate School, Graduate School, Division of Nursing, Program in Community Health, Troy, NY 12180-4115. Offers MS. *Accreditation:* AACN. Part-time programs available. *Faculty:* 8 full-time (all women), 3 part-time/adjunct (all women). *Students:* 3 full-time (all women), 8 part-time (all women); includes 1 minority (Hispanic American) Average age 41. 4 applicants, 100% accepted, 3 enrolled. In 2006, 5 degrees awarded. *Degree requirements:* For master's, thesis or alternative. *Entrance requirements:* For master's, BS in nursing, minimum GPA of 2.75. Additional exam requirements/recommendations for international students: Required—TOEFL (minimum score 550 paper-based; 213 computer-based). *Application deadline:* Applications are processed on a rolling basis. Application fee: $40. *Expenses:* Tuition: Full-time $9,270; part-time $515 per credit hour. *Financial support:* Career-related internships or fieldwork, scholarships/grants, and unspecified assistantships available. Support available to part-time students. Financial award application deadline: 3/1; financial award applicants required to submit FAFSA. *Unit head:* Arlene Pericak, Director, 518-244-2012, E-mail: perica@sage.edu. *Application contact:* Shannon K. Easton, Director of Graduate and Adult Admission, 518-244-2443, Fax: 518-244-6880, E-mail: sgsadm@sage.edu.

Saint Xavier University, Graduate Studies, School of Nursing, Chicago, IL 60655-3105. Offers adult health clinical nurse specialist (MS); family nurse practitioner (MS, PMC); leadership in community health nursing (MS); psychiatric-mental health clinical nurse specialist (MS); psychiatric-mental health clinical specialist (PMC); MBA/MS. *Accreditation:* AACN. Part-time and evening/weekend programs available. *Faculty:* 11. *Students:* 20 full-time (14 women), 120 part-time (113 women). Average age 40. In 2006, 36 degrees awarded. *Entrance requirements:* For master's, GRE General Test or MAT, minimum GPA of 3.0, RN license. *Application deadline:* For fall admission, 2/15 for domestic students; for spring admission, 9/15 for domestic students. Applications are processed on a rolling basis. Application fee: $35. *Financial support:* Available to part-time students. Applicants required to submit FAFSA. *Unit head:* Beth Gierach, Managing Director of Admission, 773-298-3053, Fax: 773-298-3076, E-mail: gierach@sxu.edu.

Seattle University, College of Nursing, Program in Nursing, Seattle, WA 98122-1090. Offers leadership in community nursing (MSN), including program development, spirituality and health; primary care nurse practitioner (MSN), including family nurse practitioner, psychiatric mental health nurse practitioner. *Students:* 6 full-time (all women), 8 part-time (7 women); includes 2 African Americans. Average age 40. *Application contact:* Janet Shandley, Associate Dean of Graduate Admissions, 206-296-5900, Fax: 206-298-5656, E-mail: grad_admissions@seattleu.edu.

Southern Illinois University Edwardsville, Graduate Studies and Research, School of Nursing, Program in Public Health Nursing, Edwardsville, IL 62026-0001. Offers MS, Post-Master's Certificate. *Accreditation:* AACN. *Students:* 5 full-time (all women), 4 part-time (all women); includes 1 minority (African American) Average age 33. In 2006, 2 degrees awarded. *Degree requirements:* For master's, thesis or alternative, final exam, comprehensive exam, registration. *Entrance requirements:* For master's, appropriate bachelor's degree, RN license. Additional exam requirements/recommendations for international students: Required—TOEFL. Application fee: $30. Electronic applications accepted. *Financial support:* Fellowships, career-related internships or fieldwork, Federal Work-Study, institutionally sponsored loans, scholarships/grants, and unspecified assistantships available. Support available to part-time students. Financial award application deadline: 3/1; financial award applicants required to submit FAFSA. *Unit head:* Dr. Jacquelyn Clement, Director, 618-650-3923, E-mail: jclemen@siue.edu.

University of Cincinnati, Graduate School, College of Nursing, Cincinnati, OH 45221-0038. Offers clinical nurse specialist (MSN), including adult health, community health, neonatal, nursing administration, occupational health, pediatric health, psychiatric nursing, women's health; nurse anesthesia (MSN); nurse midwifery (MSN); nurse practitioner (MSN), including acute care, ambulatory care, family, family/psychiatric, women's health; nursing (PhD); MBA/MSN. *Accreditation:* AACN; AANA/CANAEP (one or more programs are accredited); ACNM/DOA. Part-time programs available. Postbaccalaureate distance learning degree programs offered (no on-campus study). *Faculty:* 41 full-time (39 women), 16 part-time/adjunct (15 women). *Students:* 159 full-time (125 women), 149 part-time (145 women); includes 40 minority (22 African Americans, 1 American Indian/Alaska Native, 16 Asian Americans or Pacific Islanders, 1 Hispanic American). Average age 34. 385 applicants, 49% accepted, 132 enrolled. In 2006, 77 master's, 5 doctorates awarded. Terminal master's awarded for partial completion of doctoral program. *Median time to degree:* Of those who began their doctoral program in fall 1998, 55% received their degree in 8 years or less. *Degree requirements:* For master's, thesis or alternative, registration; for doctorate, thesis/dissertation, comprehensive exam, registration. *Entrance requirements:* For master's and doctorate, GRE General Test. Additional exam requirements/recommendations for international students: Required—TOEFL (minimum score 520 paper-based; 190 computer-based). *Application deadline:* For fall admission, 7/26 priority date for domestic and international students. Applications are processed on a rolling basis. Application fee: $40. Electronic applications accepted. *Financial support:* In 2006–07, 164 students received support, including 7 fellowships with full tuition reimbursements available (averaging $13,571 per year), research assistantships with full tuition reimbursements available (averaging $12,000 per year), 8 teaching assistantships with full tuition reimbursements available (averaging $12,000 per year); career-related internships or fieldwork, scholarships/grants, traineeships, tuition waivers (partial), and unspecified assistantships also available. Support available to part-time students. Financial award application deadline: 5/1; financial award applicants required to submit FAFSA. *Faculty research:* Substance abuse, injury and violence, symptom management. Total annual research expenditures: $1.3 million. *Unit head:* Dr. Andrea R. Lindell, Dean, 513-558-5330, Fax: 513-558-9030, E-mail: andrea.lindell@uc.edu. *Application contact:* Loren Carter, Program Coordinator, 513-558-5072, Fax: 513-558-7523, E-mail: loren.carter@uc.edu.

University of Colorado at Colorado Springs, Graduate School, Beth-El College of Nursing, Colorado Springs, CO 80933-7150. Offers adult health nurse practitioner and clinical specialist (MSN); family practitioner (MSN), including community clinical specialist, forensic clinical specialist, holistic clinical specialist; gerontology (MSN); neonatal nurse practitioner and clinical specialist (MSN); nursing administration (MSN); women nurse practitioner (MSN). *Accreditation:* AACN. Part-time programs available. Postbaccalaureate distance learning degree programs offered (minimal on-campus study). *Faculty:* 10 full-time (7 women), 14 part-time/adjunct (7 women). *Students:* 84 full-time (77 women), 53 part-time (52 women); includes 22 minority (6 African Americans, 3 American Indian/Alaska Native, 2 Asian Americans or Pacific Islanders, 11 Hispanic Americans). Average age 37. 54 applicants, 85% accepted, 30 enrolled. In 2006, 36 degrees awarded. *Degree requirements:* For master's, thesis optional; for doctorate, capstone project. *Entrance requirements:* For master's, GRE General Test or MAT, BSN, minimum GPA of 3.0, unrestricted RN license; for doctorate, interview; active RN license; MA; minimum GPA of 3.3; National Certification as NP, CNS, or CNS; portfolio. Additional exam requirements/recommendations for international students: Required—TOEFL. *Application deadline:* For fall admission, 6/1 priority date for domestic students; for spring admission, 11/15 for domestic students. Application fee: $60 ($75 for international students). Electronic applications accepted. *Expenses: Contact institution.* Tuition and fees vary according to course load, campus/location and program. *Financial support:* Fellowships, career-related internships or fieldwork, Federal Work-Study, and institutionally sponsored loans available. Support available to part-time students. *Faculty research:* Women's health, uncertainty, empowerment, family experience in chronic illness. Total annual research expenditures: $260,389. *Unit head:* Dr. Carole Schoffstall, Dean, 719-262-4418, Fax: 719-262-4416, E-mail: cschoffs@uccs.edu.

University of Connecticut, Graduate School, School of Nursing, Field of Nursing, Storrs, CT 06269. Offers adult acute care (Post-Master's Certificate); adult primary care (Post-Master's Certificate); community health (Post-Master's Certificate); neonatal acute care (Post-Master's Certificate); nursing (MS, PhD); patient care services and systems administration (Post-Master's Certificate); psychiatric mental health (Post-Master's Certificate). *Accreditation:* AACN. *Faculty:* 20 full-time (18 women). *Students:* 38 full-time (33 women), 70 part-time (65 women); includes 17 minority (3 African Americans, 10 Asian Americans or Pacific Islanders, 4 Hispanic Americans), 1 international. Average age 37. 64 applicants, 69% accepted, 44 enrolled. In 2006, 25 master's, 7 doctorates, 1 other advanced degree awarded. *Degree requirements:* For master's, comprehensive exam; for doctorate, thesis/dissertation. *Entrance requirements:* Additional exam requirements/recommendations for international students: Required—TOEFL (minimum score 550 paper-based; 213 computer-based). *Application deadline:* For fall admission, 2/1 priority date for domestic and international students; for spring admission, 11/1 for domestic students, 10/1 for international students. Applications are processed on a rolling basis. Application fee: $55. Electronic applications accepted. *Financial support:* In 2006–07, 4 research assistantships with full tuition reimbursements, 13 teaching assistantships with full tuition reimbursements were awarded; fellowships, Federal Work-Study, scholarships/grants, health care benefits, and unspecified assistantships also available. Financial award application deadline: 2/1; financial award applicants required to submit FAFSA. *Unit head:* E. Carol Polifroni, Chairperson, 860-486-0511, Fax: 860-486-0001, E-mail: polifron@uconn.edu. *Application contact:* Lisa Mazzola, Academic Advisor Coordinator, 860-486-1973, E-mail: lisa.mazzola@uconn.edu.

University of Hartford, College of Education, Nursing, and Health Professions, Program in Nursing, West Hartford, CT 06117-1599. Offers community/public health nursing (MSN); nursing education (MSN); nursing management (MSN). *Accreditation:* AACN. Part-time and evening/weekend programs available. *Faculty:* 6 full-time (all women), 2 part-time/adjunct (both women). *Students:* 1 (woman) full-time, 170 part-time (163 women); includes 12 minority (5 African Americans, 1 American Indian/Alaska Native, 6 Hispanic Americans). Average age 43. 60 applicants, 97% accepted, 54 enrolled. In 2006, 46 degrees awarded. *Degree requirements:* For master's, research project. *Entrance requirements:* For master's, BSN, Connecticut RN license. Additional exam requirements/recommendations for international students: Required—TOEFL (minimum score 550 paper-based; 213 computer-based). *Application deadline:* For fall admission, 4/15 priority date for domestic students; for spring admission, 12/1 for domestic students. Application fee: $40 ($55 for international students). Electronic applications accepted. *Expenses: Contact institution. Financial support:* Teaching assistantships, Federal Work-Study available. Support available to part-time students. Financial award application deadline: 6/1; financial award applicants required to submit FAFSA. *Faculty research:* Child development, women in doctoral study, applying feminist theory in teaching methods, near death experience, grandmothers as primary care providers. *Unit head:* Mary Beth Mathews, Chair, 860-768-4217, Fax: 860-768-5346, E-mail: mbmathews@hartford.edu. *Application contact:* Marlene Hall, Assistant Dean, 860-768-5116, E-mail: mhall@hartford.edu.

University of Hawaii at Manoa, Graduate Division, College of Health Sciences and Social Welfare, School of Nursing and Dental Hygiene, Honolulu, HI 96822. Offers clinical nurse specialist (MS), including adult health, community mental health; nurse practitioner (MS), including adult health, community mental health, family nurse practitioner; nursing (PhD, Graduate Certificate); nursing administration (MS). *Accreditation:* AACN; NLN (one or more programs are accredited). *Faculty:* 32 full-time (29 women), 1 (woman) part-time/adjunct. *Students:* 30 full-time (28 women), 94 part-time (83 women); includes 10 minority (3 African Americans, 1 American Indian/Alaska Native, 2 Asian Americans or Pacific Islanders, 4 Hispanic Americans), 2 international. 119 applicants, 53% accepted, 54 enrolled. In 2006, 12 master's, 4 doctorates awarded. *Median time to degree:* Of those who began their doctoral program in fall 1998, 57% received their degree in 8 years or less. *Degree requirements:* For master's, thesis optional; for doctorate, thesis/dissertation, comprehensive exam. *Entrance requirements:* For master's, Hawaii RN license. Additional exam requirements/recommendations for international students: Required—TOEFL (minimum score 580 paper-based; 237 computer-based; 92 iBT). *Application deadline:* For fall admission, 3/1 for domestic and international students. Application fee: $50. *Financial support:* In 2006–07, 1 teaching assistantship (averaging $13,296 per year) was awarded. Total annual research expenditures: $3.1 million.

University of Illinois at Chicago, Graduate College, College of Nursing, Program in Nursing Sciences (Public Health Nursing), Chicago, IL 60607-7128. Offers MS. *Accreditation:* AACN. Part-time programs available. *Degree requirements:* For master's, thesis or alternative. *Entrance requirements:* For master's, GRE General Test, minimum GPA of 2.75. Additional exam requirements/recommendations for international students: Required—TOEFL. Electronic applications accepted.

University of Maryland, Baltimore, Graduate School, School of Nursing, Master's Program in Nursing, Baltimore, MD 21201. Offers community health nursing (MS); gerontological nursing (MS); maternal-child nursing (MS); medical-surgical nursing (MS); nurse-midwifery education (MS); nursing administration (MS); nursing education (MS); nursing health policy (MS); primary care nursing (MS); psychiatric nursing (MS); MS/MBA. *Accreditation:* AANA/CANAEP; ACNM/DOA; NLN (one or more programs are accredited). Part-time programs available. *Degree requirements:* For master's, thesis or alternative, comprehensive exam (for some programs). *Entrance requirements:* For master's, GRE General Test, minimum GPA of 2.75, course work in statistics, BS in nursing. Additional exam requirements/recommendations for international students: Required—TOEFL, TOEFL or IELTS; Recommended—IELTS. Electronic applications accepted.

University of Massachusetts Dartmouth, Graduate School, College of Nursing, Department of Community Nursing, North Dartmouth, MA 02747-2300. Offers MS, PhD, Certificate, PMC. Part-time programs available. *Faculty:* 31 full-time (all women), 21 part-time/adjunct (all women). *Students:* 10 full-time (all women), 66 part-time (63 women); includes 4 minority (2 African Americans, 1 American Indian/Alaska Native, 1 Hispanic American). Average age 40. 33 applicants, 94% accepted, 26 enrolled. In 2006, 20 master's, 2 other advanced degrees awarded. *Degree requirements:* For master's, thesis. *Entrance requirements:* For master's, GRE General Test, BSN, minimum undergraduate GPA of 3.0, RN license. Additional exam requirements/recommendations for international students: Required—TOEFL (minimum score 500 paper-based). *Application deadline:* For fall admission, 4/20 for domestic students, 2/20 for international students; for spring admission, 11/15 for domestic students, 9/15 for international students. Application fee: $40 ($60 for international students). Electronic applications accepted. *Expenses:* Tuition, state resident: full-time $2,071; part-time $86 per credit. Tuition, nonresident: full-time $8,099; part-time $337 per credit. *Financial support:* In 2006–07, 10 teaching assistantships with full tuition reimbursements (averaging $4,725 per year) were awarded; research assistantships with full tuition reimbursements, Federal Work-Study and unspecified assistantships also available. Support available to part-time students. Financial award application deadline: 3/1; financial award applicants required to submit FAFSA. *Faculty research:* Maternal confidence; computerized decision support systems; pregnant and parenting teens; effect of aging, gender, and ethnicity on the absorption of medicine. Total annual research expenditures: $312,000. *Unit head:* Jeanne Leffers, Director, 508-999-8581, Fax: 508-999-9127, E-mail: jleffers@umassd.edu. *Application contact:* Carol Novo, Graduate Admissions Officer, 508-999-8604, Fax: 508-999-8183, E-mail: graduate@umassd.edu.

University of Massachusetts Lowell, Graduate School, College of Health Professions, Department of Nursing, Program in Family and Community Health Nursing, Lowell, MA 01854-2881. Offers MS. *Accreditation:* AACN. *Degree requirements:* For master's, thesis optional. *Entrance requirements:* For master's, GRE General Test.

University of Massachusetts Worcester, Graduate School of Nursing, Worcester, MA 01655-0115. Offers adult acute/critical care nurse practitioner (MS, Certificate); adult ambulatory/

community care nurse practitioner (MS, Certificate); gerontological nurse practitioner (Certificate); nurse educator (MS, Certificate); nursing (PhD). *Accreditation:* AACN. Part-time programs available. *Faculty:* 39. *Students:* 46 full-time (43 women), 6 part-time (2 women); includes 5 minority (2 African Americans, 2 Asian Americans or Pacific Islanders, 1 Hispanic American). Average age 38. 42 applicants, 71% accepted. In 2006, 26 master's, 2 doctorates, 6 other advanced degrees awarded. *Degree requirements:* For doctorate, thesis/dissertation. *Entrance requirements:* For master's, GRE General Test, BSN, previous course work in statistics; for Certificate, master's degree. *Application deadline:* For fall admission, 3/15 for domestic students. Applications are processed on a rolling basis. Application fee: $40 ($60 for international students). *Expenses:* Tuition, state resident: full-time $2,640. Tuition, nonresident: full-time $9,856. Required fees: $3,942. *Financial support:* In 2006–07, 4 students received support. Scholarships/grants and traineeships available. Support available to part-time students. Financial award application deadline: 3/22; financial award applicants required to submit FAFSA. *Faculty research:* Premature menopause with cancer treatment, quality of life and cancer, complementary therapies, psychoneuroimmunology, patient outcomes/outcomes research. *Unit head:* Dr. Janet Hale, Associate Dean, 508-856-5661, Fax: 508-856-6552. *Application contact:* Larry Shattuck, Director of Recruitment and Retention, 508-856-5801, Fax: 508-856-6552.

University of Michigan, Horace H. Rackham School of Graduate Studies, School of Nursing, Division of Health Promotion and Risk Reduction, Program in Community Health Nursing, Ann Arbor, MI 48109. Offers adult primary care/adult nurse practitioner (MS); community care/home care (MS); family nurse practitioner (MS); occupational health nursing (MS). *Accreditation:* AACN. Part-time and evening/weekend programs available. *Degree requirements:* For master's, thesis, registration. *Entrance requirements:* For master's, GRE General Test, licensure, minimum GPA of 3.0 in BSN program. Additional exam requirements/recommendations for international students: Required—TOEFL (minimum score 560 paper-based; 220 computer-based).

University of Minnesota, Twin Cities Campus, Graduate School, School of Nursing, Program in Public Health Nursing, Minneapolis, MN 55455-0213. Offers MS. *Accreditation:* AACN. Part-time programs available. Postbaccalaureate distance learning degree programs offered (minimal on-campus study). *Students:* 20 full-time (18 women), 25 part-time (24 women); includes 8 minority (1 African American, 6 American Indian/Alaska Native, 1 Asian American or Pacific Islander). *Degree requirements:* For master's, final oral exam, project or thesis. *Entrance requirements:* Additional exam requirements/recommendations for international students: Required—TOEFL (minimum score 586 paper-based; 240 computer-based). *Application deadline:* For fall admission, 11/1 priority date for domestic and international students; for spring admission, 8/1 priority date for domestic and international students. Application fee: $55 ($75 for international students). *Financial support:* Fellowships, research assistantships, teaching assistantships available. *Unit head:* Linda Olson Keller, Coordinator, 612-626-5144, E-mail: beari001@tc.umn.edu. *Application contact:* Information Contact, 612-624-4454, Fax: 612-624-3174, E-mail: nurseoss@umn.edu.

The University of North Carolina at Chapel Hill, Graduate School, School of Public Health, Public Health Leadership Program, Chapel Hill, NC 27599. Offers health care and prevention (MPH); leadership (MPH); occupational health nursing (MPH); public health nursing (MS). Part-time programs available. Postbaccalaureate distance learning degree programs offered (minimal on-campus study). *Faculty:* 6 full-time (5 women), 12 part-time/adjunct. *Students:* 168 full-time (112 women); includes 38 minority (27 African Americans, 1 American Indian/Alaska Native, 9 Asian Americans or Pacific Islanders, 1 Hispanic American), 5 international. Average age 32. 132 applicants, 73% accepted, 96 enrolled. In 2006, 87 degrees awarded. *Degree requirements:* For master's, thesis (MS), paper (MPH). *Entrance requirements:* For master's, GRE General Test, minimum GPA of 3.0, public health experience. Additional exam requirements/recommendations for international students: Required—TOEFL. *Application deadline:* For fall admission, 1/1 priority date for domestic and international students; for spring admission, 10/15 for domestic students. Applications are processed on a rolling basis. Application fee: $65. Electronic applications accepted. *Financial support:* In 2006–07, 17 fellowships with full and partial tuition reimbursements (averaging $11,608 per year) were awarded; career-related internships or fieldwork, institutionally sponsored loans, traineeships, and health care benefits also available. Financial award application deadline: 2/1; financial award applicants required to submit FAFSA. *Faculty research:* Occupational health issues, clinical outcomes, prenatal and early childcare, adolescent health, effectiveness of home visiting, issues in occupational health nursing, community-based interventions. *Unit head:* Dr. William Sollecito, Director, 919-966-5285, Fax: 919-966-0981, E-mail: bill_sollecito@unc.edu. *Application contact:* Sue Robeson, Registrar, 919-966-5305, Fax: 919-966-0981, E-mail: robeson@email.unc.edu.

The University of North Carolina at Charlotte, Graduate School, College of Health and Human Services, School of Nursing, Department of Family and Community Nursing, Charlotte, NC 28223-0001. Offers family nurse practitioner (MSN); nursing-community health (MSN). *Accreditation:* AACN. *Students:* 21 full-time (20 women), 52 part-time (all women); includes 10 minority (7 African Americans, 3 Hispanic Americans), 1 international. Average age 37. 41 applicants, 68% accepted, 22 enrolled. In 2006, 31 degrees awarded. *Degree requirements:* For master's, thesis or project. *Entrance requirements:* For master's, GRE General Test (nursing and health administration), GRE General Test or MAT (MSN), minimum GPA of 3.0 in undergraduate major. Additional exam requirements/recommendations for international students: Required—TOEFL (minimum score 557 paper-based; 220 computer-based). *Application deadline:* For fall admission, 7/1 for domestic students, 5/1 for international students; for spring admission, 11/1 for domestic students, 10/1 for international students. Applications are processed on a rolling basis. Application fee: $55. Electronic applications accepted. *Expenses:* Tuition, state resident: full-time $2,719; part-time $170 per credit. Tuition, nonresident: full-time $12,926; part-time $808 per credit. Required fees: $1,555. *Financial support:* In 2006–07, 1 research assistantship (averaging $1,024 per year), 1 teaching assistantship (averaging $4,032 per year) were awarded; fellowships, career-related internships or fieldwork, Federal Work-Study, institutionally sponsored loans, scholarships/grants, traineeships, and unspecified assistantships also available. Support available to part-time students. Financial award application deadline: 4/1; financial award applicants required to submit FAFSA. *Faculty research:* Community-based models of care, family transitions, evidence-based practice, values-based practice, living with HIV/AIDS, successful aging, bullying. *Unit head:* Dr. Lienne D. Edwards, Interim Chair, 704-687-4683, Fax: 704-687-3180. *Application contact:* Kathy B. Giddings, Director of Graduate Admissions, 704-687-3366, Fax: 704-687-3279, E-mail: gradadm@email.uncc.edu.

University of South Alabama, Graduate School, College of Nursing, Mobile, AL 36688-0002. Offers adult health nursing (MSN); community/mental health nursing (MSN); maternal/child nursing (MSN); nursing (DSN). *Accreditation:* AACN. *Faculty:* 25 full-time (23 women), 8 part-time/adjunct (all women). *Students:* 661 full-time (602 women), 127 part-time (108 women); includes 160 minority (123 African Americans, 6 American Indian/Alaska Native, 19 Asian Americans or Pacific Islanders, 12 Hispanic Americans), 1 international. In 2006, 166 degrees awarded. *Unit head:* Dr. Debra C. Davis, Dean, 251-434-3414.

University of South Carolina, The Graduate School, College of Nursing, Program in Health Nursing, Columbia, SC 29208. Offers adult nurse practitioner (MSN); community/public health

clinical nurse specialist (MSN); family nurse practitioner (MSN); pediatric nurse practitioner (MSN). *Accreditation:* AACN. Part-time programs available. *Degree requirements:* For master's, thesis or alternative. *Entrance requirements:* For master's, GRE General Test or MAT, BS in nursing, nursing license. Additional exam requirements/recommendations for international students: Required—TOEFL (minimum score 570 paper-based; 230 computer-based). Electronic applications accepted. *Faculty research:* Health promotion, physical activity, adolescent health, pre-term labor, low birthrate.

University of South Carolina, The Graduate School, College of Nursing, Program in Nursing and Public Health, Columbia, SC 29208. Offers MPH/MSN. *Accreditation:* AACN; CEPH. Part-time programs available. *Entrance requirements:* Additional exam requirements/recommendations for international students: Required—TOEFL (minimum score 570 paper-based; 230 computer-based). Electronic applications accepted. *Faculty research:* Substance abuse, violence against women, AIDS/HIV, immigrant health, organizational systems.

University of Southern Mississippi, Graduate School, College of Health, School of Nursing, Hattiesburg, MS 39406-0001. Offers adult health nursing (MSN); community health nursing (MSN); ethics (PhD); family nurse practitioner (MSN); leadership (PhD); nursing service administration (MSN); policy analysis (PhD); psychiatric nursing (MSN). *Accreditation:* AACN. Part-time and evening/weekend programs available. *Faculty:* 14 full-time (all women). *Students:* 39 full-time (31 women), 69 part-time (62 women); includes 18 minority (15 African Americans, 1 Asian American or Pacific Islander, 2 Hispanic Americans), 1 international. Average age 39. 46 applicants, 50% accepted, 17 enrolled. In 2006, 36 master's, 6 doctorates awarded. *Degree requirements:* For master's, thesis optional; for doctorate, thesis/dissertation, comprehensive exam, registration. *Entrance requirements:* For master's, GRE General Test, minimum GPA of 2.75, nursing license, BS in nursing; for doctorate, GRE General Test, master's degree in nursing, minimum GPA of 3.5. Additional exam requirements/recommendations for international students: Required—TOEFL. *Application deadline:* For fall admission, 3/15 priority date for domestic students, 5/1 for international students. Applications are processed on a rolling basis. Application fee: $25 ($30 for international students). Electronic applications accepted. *Financial support:* In 2006–07, 1 research assistantship with full tuition reimbursement (averaging $10,125 per year), 1 teaching assistantship (averaging $10,125 per year) were awarded; Federal Work-Study and traineeships also available. Financial award application deadline: 3/15. *Faculty research:* Gerontology, caregivers, HIV, bereavement, pain, nursing leadership. *Unit head:* Dr. Katherine Nugent, Director and Associate Dean, 601-266-5500, Fax: 601-266-5927. *Application contact:* Dr. Anne Brock, Graduate Coordinator, 601-266-5500, Fax: 601-266-5927.

The University of Texas at Brownsville, Graduate Studies, School of Health Sciences, Brownsville, TX 78520-4991. Offers MSN. *Accreditation:* NLN. *Degree requirements:* For master's, thesis optional.

The University of Texas at El Paso, Graduate School, College of Health Sciences, School of Nursing, El Paso, TX 79968-0001. Offers community health (MSN); community health/family nurse practitioner (MSN); nurse midwifery (MSN); nursing administration (MSN); nursing-clinical (MSN); post master's nursing (MSN); women's health care (MSN). *Accreditation:* AACN. *Degree requirements:* For master's, thesis optional. *Entrance requirements:* For master's, GRE General Test or MAT, BSN, minimum GPA of 3.0, previous course work in statistics. Additional exam requirements/recommendations for international students: Required—TOEFL. Electronic applications accepted.

Wayne State University, College of Nursing, Department of Family, Community and Mental Health, Program in Community Health Nursing, Detroit, MI 48202. Offers MSN. *Accreditation:* AACN. Part-time programs available. *Students:* Average age 40. 4 applicants, 75% accepted, 3 enrolled. In 2006, 3 degrees awarded. *Degree requirements:* For master's, thesis or alternative. *Entrance requirements:* For master's, GRE General Test, minimum GPA of 2.8. Additional exam requirements/recommendations for international students: Required—TOEFL (minimum score 550 paper-based; 213 computer-based); Recommended—TWE (minimum score 6). *Application deadline:* For fall admission, 7/1 priority date for domestic students, 6/1 for international students; for winter admission, 10/1 for international students; for spring admission, 11/1 for domestic students, 2/1 for international students. Applications are processed on a rolling basis. Application fee: $30 ($50 for international students). Electronic applications accepted. *Financial support:* In 2006–07, 2 students received support; research assistantships, institutionally sponsored loans, scholarships/grants, and traineeships available. Support available to part-time students. Financial award application deadline: 7/1; financial award applicants required to submit FAFSA. *Faculty research:* Alternative therapies, end-of-life issues, health literacy communication, physical activity and exercise, quality of nursing care. *Application contact:* Janet Harden, Academic Director, 313-577-4082.

Worcester State College, Graduate Studies, Program in Community Health Nursing, Worcester, MA 01602-2597. Offers MS. *Accreditation:* NLN. *Students:* 5 full-time (all women), 6 part-time (5 women). Average age 47. 3 applicants, 100% accepted, 1 enrolled. In 2006, 2 degrees awarded. *Degree requirements:* For master's, thesis optional. *Entrance requirements:* For master's, GRE, MAT. Additional exam requirements/recommendations for international students: Required—TOEFL (minimum score 550 paper-based; 213 computer-based). *Application deadline:* For fall admission, 1/15 for domestic and international students. Applications are processed on a rolling basis. Application fee: $30. Electronic applications accepted. *Expenses:* Contact institution. *Financial support:* Research assistantships, career-related internships or fieldwork, Federal Work-Study, scholarships/grants, and unspecified assistantships available. Support available to part-time students. *Unit head:* Ann Marie Catalano, Coordinator, 508-929-8559, Fax: 508-929-8168, E-mail: acatalano@worcester.edu. *Application contact:* Nicole Brown, Assistant Dean of Graduate and Continuing Education, 508-929-8787, Fax: 508-929-8100, E-mail: nbrown@worcester.edu.

Wright State University, School of Graduate Studies, College of Nursing and Health, Program in Nursing, Dayton, OH 45435. Offers acute care nurse practitioner (MS); administration of nursing and health care systems (MS); adult health (MS); child and adolescent health (MS); community health (MS); family nurse practitioner (MS); nurse practitioner (MS); school nurse (MS); MBA/MS. *Accreditation:* AACN. Part-time and evening/weekend programs available. *Students:* 46 full-time (45 women), 124 part-time (117 women); includes 16 minority (13 African Americans, 1 Asian American or Pacific Islander, 2 Hispanic Americans). Average age 39. 45 applicants, 100% accepted. In 2006, 64 degrees awarded. *Degree requirements:* For master's, thesis or alternative. *Entrance requirements:* For master's, GRE General Test, BSN from NLN-accredited college, Ohio RN license. Additional exam requirements/recommendations for international students: Required—TOEFL. *Application deadline:* For fall admission, 4/15 priority date for domestic students. Application fee: $25. *Financial support:* Fellowships, research assistantships, teaching assistantships, Federal Work-Study, institutionally sponsored loans, and unspecified assistantships available. Support available to part-time students. Financial award application deadline: 6/1; financial award applicants required to submit FAFSA. *Faculty research:* Clinical nursing and health, teaching, caring, pain administration, informatics and technology. *Application contact:* Theresa A. Haghnazarian, Director of Student and Alumni Affairs, 937-775-2592, Fax: 937-775-4571, E-mail: theresa.haghnazarian@wright.edu.

Family Nurse Practitioner Studies

Allen College, Program in Nursing, Waterloo, IA 50703. Offers acute care nurse practitioner (MSN); family nurse practitioner (MSN); health education (MSN); leadership in health care delivery (MSN). *Accreditation:* AACN; NLN. Part-time and evening/weekend programs available. *Faculty:* 2 full-time (both women), 4 part-time/adjunct (all women). *Students:* 19 full-time (17 women), 42 part-time (39 women). Average age 37. 62 applicants, 94% accepted, 46 enrolled. In 2006, 3 degrees awarded. *Degree requirements:* For master's, thesis optional. *Entrance requirements:* For master's, minimum GPA of 3.0. Additional exam requirements/recommendations for international students: Required—TOEFL (minimum score 550 paper-based). *Application deadline:* For fall admission, 7/15 priority date for domestic students; for spring admission, 12/1 priority date for domestic students. Applications are processed on a rolling basis. Application fee: $50. Electronic applications accepted. *Expenses:* Tuition: Full-time $9,824; part-time $562 per credit hour. Required fees: $481. One-time fee: $220 part-time. Tuition and fees vary according to course load. *Financial support:* In 2006–07, 58 students received support, including 1 teaching assistantship (averaging $10,116 per year); institutionally sponsored loans, scholarships/grants, and traineeships also available. Support available to part-time students. Financial award application deadline: 8/15; financial award applicants required to submit FAFSA. *Faculty research:* Pain and aged, congestive heart failure. *Unit head:* Nancy Kramer, Chair, 319-226-2040, Fax: 319-226-2070, E-mail: kramerna@ihs.org.

Athabasca University, Centre for Nursing and Health Studies, Athabasca, AB T9S 3A3, Canada. Offers advanced nursing practice (MN, Advanced Diploma); generalist (MN); health studies-leadership (MHS). Part-time programs available. Postbaccalaureate distance learning degree programs offered. *Faculty:* 6 full-time (all women), 40 part-time/adjunct (37 women). *Students:* Average age 40. 460 applicants, 81% accepted, 335 enrolled. In 2006, 124 degrees awarded. *Degree requirements:* For master's, comprehensive exam (for some programs), registration (for some programs). *Entrance requirements:* For master's, bachelor's degree in health-related field, 2 years professional health service experience (MHS), bachelor's degree in nursing, 2 years nursing experience (MN), minimum GPA of 3.0 in final 30 credits; for Advanced Diploma, RN license, 2 years health care experience. *Application deadline:* For fall admission, 3/1 for domestic and international students. Application fee: $60. Electronic applications accepted. *Expenses:* Contact institution. *Unit head:* Dr. Donna Romyn, Director, 780-675-6794, Fax: 780-675-6468, E-mail: dromyn@athabascau.ca. *Application contact:* Lisa Bodnarchuk, Administrative Assistant, 780-675-6381, Fax: 780-675-6468, E-mail: mhs@athabascau.ca.

Barnes-Jewish College of Nursing and Allied Health, Division of Nursing, St. Louis, MO 63110-1091. Offers adult nurse practitioner (MSN); education (MSN); gerontology nurse practitioner (MSN); holistics (MSN); management/administration (MSN); neonatal nurse practitioner (MSN); oncology (MSN). *Accreditation:* AACN; AANA/CANAEP. Part-time and evening/weekend programs available. *Degree requirements:* For master's, thesis or alternative, registration. *Entrance requirements:* For master's, minimum GPA of 3.0, 2 references, statistics course. Additional exam requirements/recommendations for international students: Required—TOEFL (minimum score 550 paper-based; 213 computer-based).

Barry University, School of Nursing, Program in Nurse Practitioner, Miami Shores, FL 33161-6695. Offers acute care nurse practitioner (MSN); family nurse practitioner (MSN); nurse practitioner (Certificate). *Accreditation:* AACN. Part-time and evening/weekend programs available. *Students:* 10 full-time (9 women), 106 part-time (86 women); includes 69 minority (17 African Americans, 3 Asian Americans or Pacific Islanders, 49 Hispanic Americans). 43 applicants, 14% accepted, 5 enrolled. In 2006, 33 degrees awarded. *Degree requirements:* For master's, research project or thesis. *Entrance requirements:* For master's, GRE General Test or MAT, BSN, minimum GPA of 3.0, course work in statistics. *Application deadline:* For fall admission, 5/1 priority date for domestic students. Applications are processed on a rolling basis. Application fee: $30. Electronic applications accepted. *Faculty research:* Child abuse, health beliefs, teenage pregnancy, cultural and clinical studies across the lifespan. *Unit head:* Dr. Andra Hanlon, Director, 305-899-3811, Fax: 305-899-3831, E-mail: ahanlon@mail.barry.edu. *Application contact:* Dave Fletcher, Director of Graduate Admissions, 305-899-3113, Fax: 305-899-2971, E-mail: dfletcher@mail.barry.edu.

Baylor University, Graduate School, Louise Herrington School of Nursing, Dallas, TX 75246. Offers family nurse practitioner (MSN); neonatal nurse practitioner (MSN); nursing administration and management (MSN). *Accreditation:* AACN. *Students:* 10 full-time (all women), 27 part-time (26 women); includes 6 minority (1 African American, 1 Asian American or Pacific Islander, 4 Hispanic Americans), 1 international. In 2006, 13 degrees awarded. *Entrance requirements:* For master's, GRE General Test. *Application deadline:* For fall admission, 8/1 for domestic students; for spring admission, 12/1 for domestic students. Applications are processed on a rolling basis. Application fee: $25. *Unit head:* Dr. Pauline Johnson, Graduate Program Director, 214-820-3361, Fax: 214-818-8692, E-mail: pauline_johnson@baylor.edu. *Application contact:* Suzanne Keener, Administrative Assistant, 254-710-3588, Fax: 254-710-3870.

Bloomsburg University of Pennsylvania, School of Graduate Studies, College of Professional Studies, School of Health Sciences, Department of Nursing, Bloomsburg, PA 17815-1301. Offers adult and family nurse practitioner (MSN); adult health and illness (MSN); community health (MSN); nursing (MSN); nursing administration (MSN). *Accreditation:* AACN. *Faculty:* 11 full-time (all women). *Students:* 9 full-time (all women), 27 part-time (24 women). Average age 36. 10 applicants, 100% accepted, 5 enrolled. In 2006, 6 degrees awarded. *Degree requirements:* For master's, thesis. *Entrance requirements:* For master's, minimum QPA of 3.0. Additional exam requirements/recommendations for international students: Required—TOEFL. *Application deadline:* Applications are processed on a rolling basis. Application fee: $30. Electronic applications accepted. *Expenses:* Tuition, state resident: full-time $6,048; part-time $336 per credit. Tuition, nonresident: full-time $9,678; part-time $538 per credit. Required fees: $1,415. *Financial support:* Unspecified assistantships available. *Faculty research:* Cardiopulmonary nursing, cancer topics, women's health. *Application contact:* Dr. Michelle Ficca, Coordinator, 570-389-4615, Fax: 570-389-5008, E-mail: mficca@bloomu.edu.

Bowie State University, Graduate Programs, Department of Nursing, Bowie, MD 20715-9465. Offers administration of nursing services (MS); family nurse practitioner (MS); nursing education (MS). *Accreditation:* NLN. Part-time programs available. *Faculty:* 7 full-time (4 women), 14 part-time/adjunct (9 women). *Students:* 9 full-time (all women), 9 part-time (8 women); includes 15 minority (all African Americans) Average age 42. 8 applicants, 88% accepted, 4 enrolled. In 2006, 7 degrees awarded. *Degree requirements:* For master's, thesis, research paper, comprehensive exam. *Entrance requirements:* For master's, minimum GPA of 2.5. *Application deadline:* For fall admission, 5/15 for domestic students. Applications are processed on a rolling basis. Application fee: $40. Electronic applications accepted. *Expenses:* Tuition, state resident: full-time $7,344; part-time $306 per credit. Tuition, nonresident: full-time $14,304; part-time $396 per credit. Required fees: $1,078; $77 per credit. $539 per term. One-time fee: $40. *Financial support:* Institutionally sponsored loans and traineeships available. Financial award application deadline: 4/1. *Faculty research:* Minority health, women's health, gerontology, leadership management. *Unit head:* Dr. Bonita Jenkins, Acting Chairperson, 301-860-3210, E-mail: mccaskill@bowiestate.edu. *Application contact:* Angela Issac, Information Contact.

Brenau University, Graduate Programs, School of Health and Science, Gainesville, GA 30501. Offers family nurse practitioner (MS); nurse educator (MS); occupational therapy (MS); psychology (MS). *Accreditation:* AOTA; NLN. Part-time and evening/weekend programs available. *Faculty:* 21 full-time (18 women), 5 part-time/adjunct (2 women). *Students:* 56 full-time (52 women), 36 part-time (35 women); includes 22 minority (18 African Americans, 1 American Indian/Alaska Native, 2 Asian Americans or Pacific Islanders, 1 Hispanic American), 1 international. Average age 31. 76 applicants, 51% accepted, 28 enrolled. In 2006, 40 degrees awarded. *Degree requirements:* For master's, clinical practicum hours. *Entrance requirements:* For master's, GRE General Test or MAT. Additional exam requirements/recommendations for international students: Required—TOEFL (minimum score 550 paper-based). *Application deadline:* Applications are processed on a rolling basis. Application fee: $30. *Expenses:* Contact institution. *Financial support:* In 2006–07, 14 students received support. Scholarships/grants available. Support available to part-time students. Financial award application deadline: 7/15; financial award applicants required to submit FAFSA. *Faculty research:* Cultural competency, family violence. *Unit head:* Dr. Gale Starich, Dean, 777-718-5305, Fax: 770-297-5929, E-mail: gstarich@brenau.edu. *Application contact:* Nathan Goss, Admissions Coordinator, 770-534-6162, Fax: 770-538-4701, E-mail: ngoss@brenau.edu.

California State University, Fresno, Division of Graduate Studies, College of Health and Human Services, Department of Nursing, Fresno, CA 93740-8027. Offers nursing (MS), including clinical specialty, primary care nurse practitioner. *Accreditation:* AACN. Part-time and evening/weekend programs available. *Degree requirements:* For master's, thesis or alternative. *Entrance requirements:* For master's, GRE General Test, 1 year of clinical practice, previous course work in statistics, BSN, minimum GPA of 3.0 in nursing. Additional exam requirements/recommendations for international students: Required—TOEFL. Electronic applications accepted. *Faculty research:* Training grant, HIV assessment.

Carlow University, School of Nursing, Pittsburgh, PA 15213-3165. Offers home health advanced practice nursing (MSN, PMC); nursing case management/leadership (MSN); nursing leadership (MSN). *Accreditation:* AACN. Part-time and evening/weekend programs available. Postbaccalaureate distance learning degree programs offered (minimal on-campus study). *Degree requirements:* For master's, thesis or alternative. *Entrance requirements:* For master's, GRE General Test, 1 year of professional experience, BSN, interview, minimum GPA of 3.0, Pennsylvania RN license, previous graduate course work in statistics, resumé, 3 letters of recommendation; for PMC, MSN. Additional exam requirements/recommendations for international students: Required—TOEFL (minimum score 550 paper-based; 213 computer-based). Electronic applications accepted. *Faculty research:* Research utilization, community and home health, medically underserved.

Carson-Newman College, Department of Nursing, Jefferson City, TN 37760. Offers family nurse practitioner (MSN). *Accreditation:* AACN. *Faculty:* 2 full-time (both women), 10 part-time/adjunct (9 women). *Students:* 21 full-time (18 women), 11 part-time (all women); includes 1 African American. Average age 32. In 2006, 6 degrees awarded. *Application deadline:* For fall admission, 7/15 priority date for domestic students. Applications are processed on a rolling basis. Application fee: $50. *Expenses:* Tuition: Part-time $270 per credit hour. *Unit head:* Dr. Patricia Kraft, Dean and Chair, 865-471-3426.

Case Western Reserve University, Frances Payne Bolton School of Nursing, Doctor of Nursing Practice Program, Cleveland, OH 44106. Offers acute care nurse practitioner (DNP); adult nurse practitioner (DNP); family nurse practitioner (DNP); gerontological nurse practitioner (DNP); graduate entry/pre-licensure option (DNP); medical-surgical nursing (DNP); midwifery/family nursing (DNP); neonatal nurse practitioner (DNP); pediatric nurse practitioner (DNP); post-licensure option (DNP); psychiatric mental health nurse practitioner (DNP); women's health nurse practitioner (DNP). Graduate entry option allows baccalaureate-prepared college graduates from non-nursing backgrounds to earn certificate and MSN in addition to ND. *Students:* 125 full-time (109 women), 308 part-time (290 women); includes 47 minority (21 African Americans, 1 American Indian/Alaska Native, 18 Asian Americans or Pacific Islanders, 7 Hispanic Americans), 7 international. 190 applicants, 70% accepted, 80 enrolled. In 2006, 35 degrees awarded. Terminal master's awarded for partial completion of doctoral program. *Degree requirements:* For doctorate, thesis/dissertation. *Entrance requirements:* For doctorate, GRE General Test or MAT. *Application deadline:* For fall admission, 6/1 priority date for domestic students. Applications are processed on a rolling basis. Application fee: $75. *Financial support:* In 2006–07, 6 students received support, including 1 teaching assistantship; research assistantships, Federal Work-Study, institutionally sponsored loans, and tuition waivers (partial) also available. Support available to part-time students. Financial award application deadline: 6/30; financial award applicants required to submit FAFSA. *Faculty research:* Clinical nursing, acute care, gerontology, mental health, critical care. *Unit head:* Dr. Georgia Narsavage, Director, 216-368-6304, Fax: 216-368-3542, E-mail: gln2@cwru.edu. *Application contact:* Peter Taylor, Recruitment and Retention Specialist, 216-368-0349, Fax: 216-368-0124, E-mail: peter.taylor@case.edu.

Case Western Reserve University, Frances Payne Bolton School of Nursing, Master's Programs in Nursing, Nurse Practitioner Program, Cleveland, OH 44106. Offers acute care cardiovascular nursing (MSN); acute care nurse practitioner (MSN); acute care/flight nurse (MSN); adult nurse practitioner (MSN); family nurse practitioner (MSN); gerontological nurse practitioner (MSN); neonatal nurse practitioner (MSN); pediatric nurse practitioner (MSN); psychiatric-mental health nurse practitioner (MSN); women's health nurse practitioner (MSN). *Accreditation:* NLN. Part-time programs available. Postbaccalaureate distance learning degree programs offered (minimal on-campus study). *Faculty:* 54 full-time (50 women), 5 part-time/adjunct (3 women). *Students:* 19 full-time (15 women), 31 part-time (29 women); includes 16 minority (9 African Americans, 5 Asian Americans or Pacific Islanders, 2 Hispanic Americans), 2 international. Average age 35. 46 applicants, 72% accepted, 18 enrolled. In 2006, 34 degrees awarded. *Degree requirements:* For master's, thesis optional. *Entrance requirements:* For master's, GRE General Test or MAT. Additional exam requirements/recommendations for international students: Required—TOEFL. *Application deadline:* For fall admission, 6/1 for domestic students. Applications are processed on a rolling basis. Application fee: $75. *Financial support:* In 2006–07, 7 teaching assistantships were awarded; research assistantships, institutionally sponsored loans and tuition waivers (partial) also available. Support available to part-time students. Financial award application deadline: 6/30. *Faculty research:* Positive and negative mood states in parents of twins, effect of a carepath on chronic obstructive pulmonary disease home care. *Application contact:* Peter Taylor, Recruitment and Retention Specialist, 216-368-0349, Fax: 216-368-0124, E-mail: peter.taylor@case.edu.

The Catholic University of America, School of Nursing, Washington, DC 20064. Offers advanced practice nursing (MSN), including administration of nursing service, adult nurse practitioner, education, family nurse practitioner, geriatric nurse practitioner, pediatric nurse practitioner, psychiatric-mental health, school health nurse practitioner; clinical nursing (DN Sc). *Accreditation:* AACN; NLN. Part-time programs available. *Faculty:* 17 full-time (all women), 19 part-time/adjunct (18 women). *Students:* 27 full-time (25 women), 58 part-time (57 women); includes 31 minority (20 African Americans, 6 Asian Americans or Pacific Islanders, 5 Hispanic Americans), 6 international. Average age 43. 38 applicants, 76% accepted, 15 enrolled. In 2006, 15 master's, 7 doctorates awarded. *Degree requirements:* For master's, thesis optional; for doctorate, thesis/dissertation, comprehensive exam. *Entrance requirements:* For master's, GRE General Test or MAT, 3 letters of recommendation, BA in nursing, RN registration; for doctorate, GRE General Test, 3 letters of recommendation, BA in nursing, RN registration. Additional exam requirements/recommendations for international students: Required—TOEFL (minimum score 550 paper-based; 213 computer-based). *Application deadline:* For fall admission, 2/1 priority date for domestic students; for spring admission, 11/15 priority date for domestic students. Applications are processed on a rolling basis. Application fee: $55. Electronic applications accepted. *Expenses:* Tuition: Full-time $27,700; part-time $1,045 per credit hour. Required fees: $1,290. Part-time tuition and fees vary according to campus/location and program. *Financial support:* Research assistantships, teaching assistantships, career-related internships or fieldwork, Federal Work-Study, scholarships/grants, tuition waivers (full and partial), and unspecified assistantships available. Support available to part-time students. Financial award application deadline: 2/1; financial award applicants required to submit FAFSA. *Faculty research:* Outcome research–readmission of home health care patients with congestive heart failure, spirituality of chronic illness, minority multigravidos utilization of prenatal care. *Unit head:* Dr. Nalini Jairath, Dean, 202-319-5403, Fax: 202-319-6485, E-mail: jairath@cua.edu.

Clarke College, Department of Nursing and Health, Dubuque, IA 52001-3198. Offers administration of nursing systems (MSN); advanced practice nursing (MSN); education (MSN); family nurse practitioner (MSN, PMC). *Accreditation:* AACN. Part-time programs available. *Entrance requirements:* For master's, GRE General Test or MAT, BSN, minimum GPA of 3.0. Electronic applications accepted. *Faculty research:* Narrative pedagogy, ethics, end-of-life care, pedagogy, family systems.

Clarkson College, Graduate Programs, Department of Nursing, Omaha, NE 68131-2739. Offers administration (MSN); education (MSN); family nurse practitioner (MSN). *Accreditation:* NLN. Part-time and evening/weekend programs available. Postbaccalaureate distance learning degree programs offered (minimal on-campus study). *Degree requirements:* For master's, on-campus skills assessment (family nurse practitioner), comprehensive exam or thesis. *Entrance requirements:* For master's, minimum GPA of 3.0, 2 references, resumé. Additional exam requirements/recommendations for international students: Required—TOEFL (minimum score 600 paper-based; 250 computer-based). Electronic applications accepted.

College of Mount Saint Vincent, School of Professional and Continuing Studies, Department of Nursing, Riverdale, NY 10471-1093. Offers adult nurse practitioner (MSN, PMC); family nurse practitioner (MSN, PMC); nurse educator (PMC); nursing administration (MSN); nursing for the adult and aged (MSN). *Accreditation:* AACN. Part-time programs available. *Faculty:* 2 full-time (1 woman), 6 part-time/adjunct (all women). *Students:* 1 (woman) full-time, 67 part-time (59 women); includes 43 minority (21 African Americans, 16 Asian Americans or Pacific Islanders, 6 Hispanic Americans). Average age 37. In 2006, 16 degrees awarded. *Degree requirements:* For master's, registration. *Entrance requirements:* For master's, BSN, interview, RN license, minimum GPA of 3.0, letters of reference. Additional exam requirements/recommendations for international students: Required—TOEFL. *Application deadline:* For fall admission, 6/1 for domestic and international students; for spring admission, 11/1 for domestic students, 10/1 for international students. Applications are processed on a rolling basis. Application fee: $50. *Expenses: Contact institution. Financial support:* Career-related internships or fieldwork available. Financial award application deadline: 6/1; financial award applicants required to submit FAFSA. *Unit head:* Carol Vicino, Director, 718-405-3354, Fax: 718-405-3286.

The College of New Jersey, Graduate Division, School of Nursing, Health and Exercise Science, Program in Nursing, Ewing, NJ 08628. Offers MSN, Certificate. *Accreditation:* AACN. *Students:* 6 applicants, 100% accepted. In 2006, 10 degrees awarded. *Degree requirements:* For master's, comprehensive exam. *Entrance requirements:* For master's, GRE, minimum GPA of 3.0 in field or 2.75 overall. Additional exam requirements/recommendations for international students: Required—TOEFL. *Application deadline:* For fall admission, 3/15 for domestic students. Application fee: $60. Electronic applications accepted. *Financial support:* Application deadline: 5/1; *Unit head:* Dr. Claire Lindberg, Chair, Advanced Nursing Education and Practice, 609-771-2510. *Application contact:* Susan L. Hydro, Office of Graduate Studies, Assistant Dean, 609-771-2300, Fax: 609-637-5105, E-mail: graduate@tcnj.edu.

Columbia University, School of Nursing, Program in Acute Care Nurse Practitioner, New York, NY 10032. Offers MS, Adv C. *Accreditation:* AACN. Part-time programs available. *Faculty:* 1 (woman) full-time, 3 part-time/adjunct (all women). *Students:* 8 full-time (6 women), 11 part-time (10 women); includes 7 minority (3 African Americans, 3 Asian Americans or Pacific Islanders, 1 Hispanic American). Average age 30. In 2006, 11 degrees awarded. *Entrance requirements:* For master's, GRE General Test, 1 year of clinical experience (preferred), BSN; for Adv C, MSN. *Application deadline:* Applications are processed on a rolling basis. Application fee: $65. Electronic applications accepted. *Financial support:* Teaching assistantships available. Financial award application deadline: 2/1; financial award applicants required to submit FAFSA. *Unit head:* Dr. Mary Donovan, Director, 212-342-4110.

Columbia University, School of Nursing, Program in Adult Nurse Practitioner, New York, NY 10032. Offers MS, Adv C. *Accreditation:* AACN. Part-time programs available. *Faculty:* 3 full-time (all women). *Students:* 10 full-time (all women), 19 part-time (17 women); includes 6 minority (2 African Americans, 3 Asian Americans or Pacific Islanders, 1 Hispanic American), 2 international. Average age 32. In 2006, 35 degrees awarded. *Entrance requirements:* For master's, GRE General Test, BSN, 1 year of clinical experience (preferred); for Adv C, MSN. *Application deadline:* Applications are processed on a rolling basis. Application fee: $65. Electronic applications accepted. *Financial support:* Teaching assistantships available. Financial award application deadline: 2/1; financial award applicants required to submit FAFSA. *Unit head:* Prof. JoAnne Staats, Director, 212-305-7327.

Columbia University, School of Nursing, Program in Family Nurse Practitioner, New York, NY 10032. Offers MS, Adv C. *Accreditation:* AACN. Part-time programs available. *Faculty:* 3 full-time (all women). *Students:* 22 full-time (all women), 74 part-time (70 women); includes 19 minority (5 African Americans, 1 American Indian/Alaska Native, 8 Asian Americans or Pacific Islanders, 5 Hispanic Americans), 3 international. Average age 32. In 2006, 15 degrees awarded. *Entrance requirements:* For master's, GRE General Test, BSN, 1 year of clinical experience (preferred); for Adv C, MSN. *Application deadline:* Applications are processed on a rolling basis. Application fee: $65. Electronic applications accepted. *Financial support:* Teaching assistantships available. Financial award application deadline: 2/1; financial award applicants required to submit FAFSA. *Unit head:* Dr. Elizabeth Hall, Director, 212-305-2806.

Columbia University, School of Nursing, Program in Geriatric Nurse Practitioner, New York, NY 10032. Offers MS, Adv C. *Accreditation:* AACN. Part-time programs available. *Faculty:* 1 (woman) full-time, 1 (woman) part-time/adjunct. *Students:* Average age 34. In 2006, 2 degrees awarded. *Entrance requirements:* For master's, GRE General Test, BSN, 1 year of clinical experience (preferred); for Adv C, MSN. *Application deadline:* Applications are processed on a rolling basis. Application fee: $65. Electronic applications accepted. *Financial support:* Teaching assistantships available. Financial award application deadline: 2/1; financial award applicants required to submit FAFSA. *Unit head:* Prof. JoAnne Staats, Director, 212-305-7327.

Columbia University, School of Nursing, Program in Neonatal Nurse Practitioner, New York, NY 10032. Offers MS, Adv C. *Accreditation:* AACN. Part-time programs available. *Students:* 1 (woman) full-time, 10 part-time (all women); includes 4 minority (3 Asian Americans or Pacific Islanders, 1 Hispanic American). Average age 33. In 2006, 6 degrees awarded. *Entrance requirements:* For master's, GRE General Test, BSN, 1 year of neonatal intensive care unit experience; for Adv C, MSN. *Application deadline:* Applications are processed on a rolling basis. Application fee: $65. Electronic applications accepted. *Financial support:* Application deadline: 2/1; *Unit head:* Dr. Ritamarie John, Head, 212-305-5542.

Columbia University, School of Nursing, Program in Pediatric Nurse Practitioner, New York, NY 10032. Offers MS, Adv C. *Accreditation:* AACN. Part-time programs available. *Faculty:* 1 (woman) full-time, 1 (woman) part-time/adjunct. *Students:* 12 full-time (all women), 38 part-time (37 women); includes 9 minority (4 African Americans, 3 Asian Americans or Pacific Islanders, 2 Hispanic Americans). Average age 30. In 2006, 18 master's, 1 other advanced degree awarded. *Entrance requirements:* For master's, GRE General Test, BSN, 1 year of clinical experience (preferred); for Adv C, MSN. *Application deadline:* Applications are processed on a rolling basis. Application fee: $65. Electronic applications accepted. *Financial support:* Teaching assistantships available. Financial award application deadline: 2/1; financial award applicants required to submit FAFSA. *Unit head:* Dr. Ritamarie John, Head, 212-305-5542.

Columbia University, School of Nursing, Program in Women's Health Nurse Practitioner, New York, NY 10032. Offers Adv C. *Accreditation:* AACN. Part-time programs available. *Faculty:* 1 (woman) full-time. *Students:* 8 full-time (all women), 10 part-time (all women); includes 5 minority (3 African Americans, 2 Hispanic Americans). Average age 31. *Entrance requirements:* For degree, MSN. *Application deadline:* Applications are processed on a rolling basis. Application fee: $65. Electronic applications accepted. *Financial support:* Teaching assistantships available. Financial award application deadline: 2/1; financial award applicants required to submit FAFSA. *Unit head:* Prof. MaryJane McEneaney, Unit Head, 212-342-5613.

Concordia University Wisconsin, Graduate Programs, School of Health and Human Services, Program in Nursing, Mequon, WI 53097-2402. Offers family nurse practitioner (MSN); geriatric nurse practitioner (MSN); nurse educator (MSN). *Accreditation:* AACN. Postbaccalaureate distance learning degree programs offered (minimal on-campus study). *Faculty:* 2 full-time (1 woman), 5 part-time/adjunct (all women). *Students:* 217 (199 women). Average age 29. In 2006, 37 degrees awarded. *Degree requirements:* For master's, thesis or alternative, comprehensive exam. *Entrance requirements:* Additional exam requirements/recommendations for international students: Required—TOEFL. *Application deadline:* For fall admission, 8/1 priority date for domestic students. Applications are processed on a rolling basis. Application fee: $35. *Expenses: Contact institution. Financial support:* Application deadline: 8/1. *Unit head:* Dr. Ruth Gresley, Director, 262-243-4452, E-mail: ruth.gresley@cuw.edu.

Coppin State University, Division of Graduate Studies, Helene Fuld School of Nursing, Baltimore, MD 21216-3698. Offers family nurse practitioner (PMC); nursing (MSN). *Accreditation:* NLN. Part-time and evening/weekend programs available. *Faculty:* 4 full-time (all women), 5 part-time/adjunct (4 women). *Students:* 25 full-time (23 women), 5 part-time (all women); includes 26 minority (all African Americans), 2 international. Average age 36. 20 applicants, 85% accepted, 13 enrolled. In 2006, 15 degrees awarded. *Degree requirements:* For master's, thesis, clinical internship, comprehensive exam, registration. *Entrance requirements:* For master's, GRE, bachelor's degree in nursing, interview, minimum GPA of 3.0, RN license. Additional exam requirements/recommendations for international students: Required—TOEFL (minimum score 550 paper-based). *Application deadline:* For fall admission, 5/30 for domestic students. Applications are processed on a rolling basis. Application fee: $45. *Financial support:* Career-related internships or fieldwork, Federal Work-Study, institutionally sponsored loans, and scholarships/grants available. Support available to part-time students. Financial award application deadline: 6/30; financial award applicants required to submit FAFSA. *Unit head:* Dr. Marcella Copes, Dean, 410-951-3991, Fax: 410-462-3032, E-mail: mcopes@coppin.edu.

Daemen College, Department of Nursing, Amherst, NY 14226-3592. Offers adult nurse practitioner (MS, Certificate); nursing executive leadership (MS); palliative care nursing (MS, Certificate). *Accreditation:* NLN. Part-time programs available. *Faculty:* 2 full-time (both women), 2 part-time/adjunct (both women). *Students:* 13 full-time (12 women), 63 part-time (59 women); includes 12 minority (10 African Americans, 1 Asian American or Pacific Islander, 1 Hispanic American), 3 international. Average age 41. 36 applicants, 58% accepted, 18 enrolled. In 2006, 9 degrees awarded. *Degree requirements:* For master's, thesis or alternative. *Entrance requirements:* For master's, 1 year medical/surgical experiences, minimum GPA of 3.25, state nursing license and registration, 1 course in statistics. Additional exam requirements/recommendations for international students: Required—TOEFL (minimum score 500 paper-based; 173 computer-based). *Application deadline:* For fall admission, 3/1 priority date for domestic and international students; for spring admission, 10/1 priority date for domestic and international students. Applications are processed on a rolling basis. Application fee: $25. Electronic applications accepted. *Expenses:* Tuition: Full-time $11,700; part-time $650 per credit hour. Required fees: $15 per credit hour. Tuition and fees vary according to course load. *Financial support:* Institutionally sponsored loans and scholarships/grants available. Financial award application deadline: 2/15; financial award applicants required to submit FAFSA. *Faculty research:* Professional stress, client behavior, drug therapy, treatment modalities and pulmonary cancers, chemical dependency. *Unit head:* Dr. Mary Lou Rusin, Chair, 716-839-8387, Fax: 716-839-8403, E-mail: mrusin@daemen.edu. *Application contact:* Karl Shallowhorn, Associate Director of Graduate Admissions, 716-839-8225, Fax: 716-839-8229, E-mail: kshallow@daemen.edu.

DePaul University, College of Liberal Arts and Sciences, Department of Nursing, Chicago, IL 60604-2287. Offers advanced practice nursing (MS); masters entry into nursing practice (MS); nurse anesthesia (MS). MS in nurse anesthesia offered jointly with Ravenswood Hospital Medical Center. *Accreditation:* AACN; AANA/CANAEP. *Faculty:* 13 full-time (10 women), 10 part-time/adjunct (all women). *Students:* 128 full-time (107 women), 36 part-time (31 women); includes 43 minority (19 African Americans, 2 American Indian/Alaska Native, 16 Asian Americans or Pacific Islanders, 6 Hispanic Americans), 2 international. Average age 39. 80 applicants, 100% accepted. In 2006, 9 master's awarded. *Degree requirements:* For master's, thesis optional. *Entrance requirements:* For master's, GRE, BSN, minimum GPA of 2.85, RN license. Application fee: $25. *Financial support:* In 2006–07, 5 fellowships (averaging $2,000 per year) were awarded; traineeships also available. *Faculty research:* Children's health, women's health, health promotion. *Unit head:* Dr. Susan Poslusny, Chair, 773-325-7280, Fax: 773-325-7282, E-mail: sposlusn@wppost.depaul.edu. *Application contact:* Christine Werdrick, Coordinator of Student Academic Services and Department Operations, 773-325-7280, Fax: 773-325-7282, E-mail: cwerdric@depaul.edu.

DeSales University, Graduate Division, Programs in Nursing, Center Valley, PA 18034-9568. Offers adult advanced practice nurse specialist (MSN); family nurse practitioner (MSN); nurse educator (MSN); MSN/MBA. *Accreditation:* NLN. Part-time and evening/weekend programs available. In 2006, 9 degrees awarded. *Degree requirements:* For master's, thesis optional. *Entrance requirements:* For master's, GRE General Test, MAT, minimum B average in undergraduate course work, health assessment course or equivalent, course work in statistics. *Application deadline:* For spring admission, 3/15 for domestic students. Applications are processed on a rolling basis. Application fee: $35. *Expenses: Contact institution. Financial support:* In 2006–07, 1 student received support. Unspecified assistantships available. Support available to part-time students. Financial award applicants required to submit FAFSA. *Faculty research:* Women's health, theory validation, needs of homeless, behavior risk evaluation, wound healing. *Unit head:* Dr. Carol Gullo Mest, Director, 610-282-1100 Ext. 1394, Fax: 610-282-2254, E-mail: carol.mest@desales.edu. *Application contact:* Megan Szivos, Secretary for MSN Program, 610-282-1100 Ext. 1664, Fax: 610-282-2254, E-mail: megan.szivos@desales.edu.

Duke University, School of Nursing, Durham, NC 27708-0586. Offers adult acute care (Certificate); adult cardiovascular (Certificate); adult oncology/HIV (Certificate); adult primary care (Certificate); clinical nurse specialist (MSN), including adult oncology/HIV, gerontology, neonatal, pediatric, pediatric/chronic acute care; clinical research management (MSN, Certificate); family (Certificate); gerontology (Certificate); health and nursing ministries (MSN, Certificate); health systems leadership and outcomes (Certificate); leadership in community based long term care (MSN, Certificate); neonatal (Certificate); neonatal/pediatric in rural health (MSN, Certificate); nurse anesthetist (MSN, Certificate); nurse practitioner (MSN), including adult acute care, adult cardiovascular, adult oncology/HIV, adult primary care, family, gerontology, neonatal, pediatric, pediatric acute care; nursing (PhD); nursing and healthcare leadership (MSN); nursing education (MSN); nursing informatics (MSN, Certificate); pediatric (Certificate); pediatric acute care (Certificate); MBA/MSN; MSN/MCM. *Accreditation:* AACN; AANA/CANAEP. Part-time programs available. Postbaccalaureate distance learning degree programs offered (minimal on-campus study). *Faculty:* 45 full-time (41 women), 169 part-time/adjunct (150 women). *Students:* 178 full-time (162 women), 140 part-time (132 women); includes 48 minority (17 African Americans, 3 American Indian/Alaska Native, 20 Asian Americans or Pacific Islanders, 8 Hispanic Americans). Average age 36. 99 applicants, 92% accepted, 91 enrolled. In 2006, 122 master's, 17 other advanced degrees awarded. *Median time to degree:* Master's–2 years full-time, 2.5 years part-time. *Degree requirements:* For master's, thesis optional. *Entrance requirements:* For master's, GRE General Test or MAT, 1 year of nursing experience, BSN, minimum GPA of 3.0, previous course work in statistics; for Certificate, MSN. Additional exam requirements/recommendations for international students: Required—TOEFL (minimum score 550 paper-based; 213 computer-based), Commission on Graduates of Foreign Nursing Schools exam. *Application deadline:* For fall admission, 7/2 priority date for domestic and international students; for spring admission, 11/15 priority date for domestic and international students. Applications are processed on a rolling basis. Application fee: $50. *Expenses: Contact institution. Financial support:* In 2006–07, 258 students received support. Career-related internships or fieldwork, institutionally sponsored loans, scholarships/grants, trainee-

Family Nurse Practitioner Studies

Duke University (continued)
ships, and tuition waivers (partial) available. Support available to part-time students. Financial award application deadline: 4/1; financial award applicants required to submit FAFSA. *Faculty research:* Cardiovascular disease, caregiver skill training, data mining, prostate cancer, neonatal immune system. Total annual research expenditures: $3.5 million. *Unit head:* Dr. Catherine L. Gilliss, Dean/Vice Chancellor for Nursing Affairs, 919-684-9444, Fax: 919-684-9414, E-mail: gilli025@mc.duke.edu. *Application contact:* Bebe T. Mills, Director of Admissions, 919-684-9151, Fax: 919-668-4693, E-mail: mills031@mc.duke.edu.

Duquesne University, School of Nursing, Master's Program in Nursing, Pittsburgh, PA 15282-0001. Offers acute care nursing (Post-Master's Certificate); acute care nursing specialist (MSN); family nurse practitioner (MSN, Post-Master's Certificate); forensic nursing (MSN, Post-Master's Certificate); nursing administration (MSN, Post-Master's Certificate); nursing education (MSN, Post-Master's Certificate); psychiatric/mental health nursing (MSN, Post-Master's Certificate); MSN/MBA. *Accreditation:* AACN. Part-time and evening/weekend programs available. Postbaccalaureate distance learning degree programs offered (minimal on-campus study). *Faculty:* 20 full-time (19 women), 4 part-time/adjunct (all women). *Students:* 73 full-time (70 women), 83 part-time (79 women); includes 11 minority (4 African Americans, 3 American Indian/Alaska Native, 1 Asian American or Pacific Islander, 3 Hispanic Americans). 72 applicants, 75% accepted, 49 enrolled. In 2006, 20 master's, 11 other advanced degrees awarded. *Degree requirements:* For master's, culminating paper. *Entrance requirements:* For master's, MAT or GRE, 1 year of work experience, bachelor's degree in nursing, undergraduate course work in statistics, health assessment course (family nurse practitioner, nursing education, acute care clinical nurse specialist). *Application deadline:* For fall admission, 4/1 for domestic and international students; for spring admission, 11/1 for domestic and international students. Applications are processed on a rolling basis. Application fee: $50. *Expenses:* Contact institution. Tuition and fees vary according to degree level and program. *Financial support:* In 2006–07, 10 students received support, including 9 research assistantships with partial tuition reimbursements available (averaging $1,600 per year), 1 teaching assistantship with partial tuition reimbursement available (averaging $1,600 per year); fellowships with partial tuition reimbursements available, institutionally sponsored loans, scholarships/grants, traineeships, and tuition waivers (partial) also available. Financial award application deadline: 8/20. *Faculty research:* Depression, culture, vulnerable populations, ethics, health disparities, community based. Total annual research expenditures: $377,400. *Unit head:* Dr. Joan Such Lockhart, Professor and Associate Dean of Academic Affairs, 412-396-6540, Fax: 412-396-1821, E-mail: lockhart@duq.edu. *Application contact:* Susan Hardner, Nurse Recruiter, 412-396-4945, Fax: 412-396-6346, E-mail: nursing@duq.edu.

D'Youville College, Department of Nursing, Buffalo, NY 14201-1084. Offers community health nursing/education (MSN); community health nursing/high risk parents and children (MSN); community health nursing/management (MSN); family nurse practitioner (MS); nursing and health-related professions (Certificate); nursing with clinical focus choice (MSN). *Accreditation:* AACN. Part-time and evening/weekend programs available. *Faculty:* 26 full-time (all women), 7 part-time/adjunct (6 women). *Students:* 77 full-time (72 women), 101 part-time (95 women); includes 17 minority (12 African Americans, 1 American Indian/Alaska Native, 4 Hispanic Americans), 89 international. Average age 36. 177 applicants, 58% accepted, 37 enrolled. In 2006, 41 master's, 2 other advanced degrees awarded. *Degree requirements:* For master's, membership on board of community agency, publishable paper, thesis optional. *Entrance requirements:* For master's, BS in nursing, minimum GPA of 3.0, course work in statistics and computers. Additional exam requirements/recommendations for international students: Required—TOEFL (minimum score 500 paper-based; 173 computer-based). *Application deadline:* For fall admission, 5/1 priority date for international students; for spring admission, 9/1 priority date for international students. Applications are processed on a rolling basis. Application fee: $25. Electronic applications accepted. *Financial support:* In 2006–07, 1 research assistantship with partial tuition reimbursement (averaging $3,000 per year) was awarded; Federal Work-Study and scholarships/grants also available. Support available to part-time students. Financial award application deadline: 3/1; financial award applicants required to submit FAFSA. *Faculty research:* Nursing curriculum, nursing theory-testing, wellness research, communication and socialization patterns. *Unit head:* Dr. Verna Kieffer, Chair, 716-829-7613, Fax: 716-829-8159. *Application contact:* Linda Fisher, Graduate Admissions Director, 716-829-8400, Fax: 716-829-7900, E-mail: graduateadmissions@dyc.edu.

See Close-Up on page 1953.

Eastern Kentucky University, The Graduate School, College of Health Sciences, Department of Nursing, Richmond, KY 40475-3102. Offers rural community health care (MSN); rural health family nurse practitioner (MSN). *Accreditation:* AACN. *Faculty:* 15 full-time (14 women), 1 part-time/adjunct (0 women). *Students:* 24 full-time (all women), 75 part-time (65 women). Average age 37. 71 applicants, 41% accepted, 27 enrolled. In 2006, 33 degrees awarded. *Entrance requirements:* For master's, GRE General Test, minimum GPA of 2.75. Application fee: $35. *Expenses:* Tuition, state resident: full-time $5,610. Tuition, nonresident: full-time $15,910. *Unit head:* Dr. Deborah Whitehouse, Chair, 859-622-1956, Fax: 859-622-1972.

East Tennessee State University, School of Graduate Studies, College of Nursing, Johnson City, TN 37614. Offers advanced nursing practice (Post Master's Certificate); health care management (Certificate); nursing (MSN, DSN). *Accreditation:* AACN. Part-time programs available. *Degree requirements:* For master's, thesis optional. *Entrance requirements:* For master's, GRE General Test, minimum GPA of 3.0, bachelor's degree in nursing, current RN license. Additional exam requirements/recommendations for international students: Required—TOEFL (minimum score 550 paper-based; 213 computer-based). *Faculty research:* Rural primary care, health care for the homeless, community health problems across the lifespan, nursing education research, school health services.

Edinboro University of Pennsylvania, Graduate Studies and Research, School of Science, Management and Technology, Department of Nursing, Edinboro, PA 16444. Offers family nurse practitioner (MSN). *Accreditation:* NLN. Part-time and evening/weekend programs available. *Faculty:* 1 (woman) full-time. *Students:* Average age 41. *Degree requirements:* For master's, thesis, competency exam. *Entrance requirements:* For master's, GRE or MAT, minimum QPA of 2.5. *Application deadline:* Applications are processed on a rolling basis. Application fee: $30. Electronic applications accepted. *Expenses:* Tuition, state resident: full-time $6,048; part-time $336 per credit. Tuition, nonresident: full-time $9,678; part-time $538 per credit. Required fees: $1,849; $42 per credit. *Financial support:* In 2006–07, 1 research assistantship with full and partial tuition reimbursement (averaging $3,850 per year) was awarded; career-related internships or fieldwork, Federal Work-Study, scholarships/grants, and unspecified assistantships also available. Support available to part-time students. Financial award application deadline: 2/15; financial award applicants required to submit FAFSA. *Unit head:* Ellen Pfadt, Acting Chairperson, 814-732-1128, Fax: 814-732-2536, E-mail: epfadt@edinboro.edu. *Application contact:* Dr. R. Scott Baldwin, Dean, 814-732-2752, Fax: 814-732-2268, E-mail: sbaldwin@edinboro.edu.

Emory University, Nell Hodgson Woodruff School of Nursing, Atlanta, GA 30322-1100. Offers adult and elder health advanced practice nursing (MSN), including acute and critical care, adult nurse practitioner, gerontology, oncology; emergency nurse practitioner (MSN); family nurse practitioner (MSN); family nurse-midwife (MSN); leadership in healthcare (MSN); nurse midwifery (MSN); nursing administration (MSN); pediatric advanced nursing practice (MSN); public health nursing (MSN); women's health nurse practitioner (MSN); MSN/MPH. *Accreditation:* AACN; ACNM/DOA (one or more programs are accredited). Part-time programs available. *Entrance requirements:* For master's, GRE General Test or MAT, minimum GPA of 3.0, BS in nursing, RN license and additional course work, 3 letters of recommendation. Additional exam requirements/recommendations for international students: Required—TOEFL (minimum score 600 paper-based; 250 computer-based). Electronic applications accepted. Expenses: Contact institution. *Faculty research:* Older adult falls and injuries, minority health issues, cardiac symptoms amd quality of life, bio-ethics and decision making, menopausal issues.

See Close-Up on page 1955.

Fairfield University, School of Nursing, Fairfield, CT 06824-5195. Offers adult nurse practitioner (MSN, PMC); family nurse practitioner (MSN, PMC); healthcare management (MSN); nurse anesthesia (MSN); psychiatric nurse practitioner (MSN, PMC). *Accreditation:* AACN; AANA/CANAEP. Part-time programs available. *Faculty:* 13 full-time (12 women), 2 part-time/adjunct (both women). *Students:* 3 full-time (all women), 39 part-time (all women); includes 5 minority (2 African Americans, 3 Asian Americans or Pacific Islanders). Average age 42. 23 applicants, 30% accepted, 3 enrolled. In 2006, 9 degrees awarded. *Degree requirements:* For master's, capstone project. *Entrance requirements:* For master's, MAT or GRE, minimum QPA of 3.0, RN license, resumé, 2 recommendations; for PMC, 1 year of work experience as a registered nurse. Additional exam requirements/recommendations for international students: Required—TOEFL (minimum score 550 paper-based; 213 computer-based; 79 iBT). *Application deadline:* For fall admission, 4/1 priority date for domestic students, 6/15 priority date for international students; for spring admission, 11/1 priority date for domestic students, 10/15 priority date for international students. Applications are processed on a rolling basis. Application fee: $55. *Expenses:* Contact institution. *Financial support:* Traineeships available. Financial award applicants required to submit FAFSA. *Faculty research:* Critical care, nursing outcomes, care of older adults, leadership, community health. *Unit head:* Dr. Jeanne M. Novotny, Dean, 203-254-4000 Ext. 2701, Fax: 203-254-4126, E-mail: jnovotny@mail.fairfield.edu. *Application contact:* Marianne Gumpper, Director of Graduate and Continuing Studies Admissions, 203-254-4184, Fax: 203-254-4073, E-mail: gradadmis@mail.fairfield.edu.

Felician College, Program in Advanced Practice Nursing, Lodi, NJ 07644-2117. Offers adult nurse practitioner (MSN, PMC); family nurse practitioner (MSN, PMC); school nurse/teacher of health education (Certificate). *Accreditation:* AACN. Part-time and evening/weekend programs available. Postbaccalaureate distance learning degree programs offered (no on-campus study). *Students:* 29 applicants, 90% accepted, 24 enrolled. *Degree requirements:* For master's, scholarly project. *Entrance requirements:* For master's, BS in nursing or equivalent, minimum GPA of 3.0, 2 letters of recommendation, RN license; for other advanced degree, RN license, minimum GPA of 2.75. Additional exam requirements/recommendations for international students: Recommended—TOEFL (minimum score 550 paper-based; 213 computer-based). *Application deadline:* Applications are processed on a rolling basis. Application fee: $40. *Expenses:* Tuition: Part-time $675 per credit. Tuition and fees vary according to program. *Financial support:* In 2006–07, 10 students received support. Traineeships available. Financial award applicants required to submit FAFSA. *Faculty research:* Anxiety and fear, curriculum innovation, health promotion. *Unit head:* Dr. Muriel Shore, Dean, Division of Health Sciences, 201-559-6030, E-mail: shorem@inet.felician.edu. *Application contact:* Wendy Lin-Cook, Director of Adult and Graduate Admission, 201-559-6077, Fax: 201-559-6138, E-mail: adultandgraduate@felician.edu.

See Close-Up on page 1957.

Florida State University, Graduate Studies, College of Nursing, Tallahassee, FL 32306. Offers family nurse practitioner (MSN, Certificate); nurse educator (MSN, Certificate); pediatric nurse practitioner (MSN, Certificate). *Accreditation:* AACN. Part-time programs available. Postbaccalaureate distance learning degree programs offered (no on-campus study). *Faculty:* 10 full-time (9 women), 1 part-time/adjunct (0 women). *Students:* 10 full-time (all women), 75 part-time (69 women); includes 16 minority (10 African Americans, 2 Asian Americans or Pacific Islanders, 4 Hispanic Americans). Average age 39. 43 applicants, 81% accepted, 32 enrolled. In 2006, 13 master's, 9 other advanced degrees awarded. *Degree requirements:* For master's, Research Project (optional), thesis optional. *Entrance requirements:* For master's, GRE General Test, minimum GPA of 3.0, BSN, Florida RN license. Additional exam requirements/recommendations for international students: Required—TOEFL (minimum score 550 paper-based). *Application deadline:* For fall admission, 7/1 for domestic students; for spring admission, 10/15 for domestic students. Applications are processed on a rolling basis. Application fee: $30. Electronic applications accepted. *Expenses:* Tuition, state resident: full-time $5,822; part-time $243 per credit hour. Tuition, nonresident: full-time $20,976; part-time $874 per credit hour. Tuition and fees vary according to program. *Financial support:* In 2006–07, 25 students received support, including 1 fellowship with partial tuition reimbursement available (averaging $6,300 per year), 3 research assistantships with partial tuition reimbursements available (averaging $3,000 per year), 13 teaching assistantships with partial tuition reimbursements available (averaging $3,000 per year); career-related internships or fieldwork, Federal Work-Study, institutionally sponsored loans, traineeships, and tuition waivers (partial) also available. Financial award application deadline: 4/15; financial award applicants required to submit FAFSA. *Faculty research:* Distance learning, gerontology, health promotion, educational strategies, rehabilitation of brain injured patients. *Unit head:* Dr. Katherine P. Mason, Dean, 850-644-5417, Fax: 850-644-7660, E-mail: kmason@mailer.fsu.edu. *Application contact:* Eddie Page, Graduate Program Coordinator, 850-644-5638, Fax: 850-645-7321, E-mail: epage@fsu.edu.

Gannon University, School of Graduate Studies, College of Sciences, Engineering, and Health Sciences, School of Health Sciences, Program in Nursing, Erie, PA 16541-0001. Offers anesthesia (MSN); business administration (MSN); case management (MSN); medical-surgical nursing (MSN); nurse anesthesia (Certificate); nursing rural practitioner (MSN). *Accreditation:* AACN; AANA/CANAEP (one or more programs are accredited). Part-time and evening/weekend programs available. *Students:* 15 full-time (5 women), 44 part-time (37 women). Average age 35. 8 applicants, 88% accepted, 5 enrolled. In 2006, 14 master's, 2 other advanced degrees awarded. *Degree requirements:* For master's, thesis. *Entrance requirements:* For master's, GRE General Test, MAT, bachelor's degree from a NLN-approved nursing program, interview, Pennsylvania RN license. Additional exam requirements/recommendations for international students: Required—TOEFL (minimum score 500 paper-based; 173 computer-based). *Application deadline:* For fall admission, 4/15 for domestic students. Application fee: $25. *Expenses:* Tuition: Full-time $12,240; part-time $680 per credit. Required fees: $496; $16 per credit. Tuition and fees vary according to course load, degree level, campus/location and program. *Financial support:* Career-related internships or fieldwork and traineeships available. Support available to part-time students. Financial award application deadline: 7/1; financial award applicants required to submit FAFSA. *Unit head:* Dr. Sharon Thompson, Interim Director, 814-871-5345, E-mail: thompson001@gannon.edu. *Application contact:* Debra Meszaros, Director of Graduate Recruitment, 814-871-5819, Fax: 814-871-5827, E-mail: cfal@gannon.edu.

George Mason University, College of Health and Human Services, Fairfax, VA 22030. Offers advanced clinical nursing (MSN); nurse practitioner (MSN); nursing (MSN, PhD); nursing administration (MSN); nursing education (Certificate); nursing educator (MSN); social work (MSW). *Accreditation:* AACN. *Faculty:* 69 full-time (55 women), 75 part-time/adjunct (66 women). *Students:* 98 full-time (81 women), 301 part-time (260 women); includes 121 minority (60 African Americans, 45 Asian Americans or Pacific Islanders, 16 Hispanic Americans), 27 international. Average age 39. 326 applicants, 61% accepted, 121 enrolled. In 2006, 89 master's, 7 doctorates, 11 other advanced degrees awarded. *Degree requirements:* For doctorate, thesis/dissertation, oral/written exams. *Entrance requirements:* For master's, RN license, minimum GPA of 3.0 in last 60 hours of course work; for doctorate, MAT, 3 years of nursing experience, master's degree, minimum GPA of 3.25, professional liability insurance. *Application deadline:* For fall admission, 5/1 for domestic students; for spring admission, 11/1 for domestic students. Application fee: $60 ($75 for international students). Electronic applications accepted. *Expenses:* Tuition, state resident: full-time $5,724; part-time $238 per credit. Tuition, nonresident: full-time $16,896; part-time $704 per credit. Required fees: $1,656; $69 per credit. *Financial support:* Fellowships, research assistantships, teaching assistantships, tuition waivers (partial) available. Support available to part-time students. Financial award application deadline: 3/1; financial award applicants required to submit FAFSA. *Unit head:* Dr. Shirley S. Travis, Dean, 703-993-1918. *Application contact:* Dr. James D. Vail, Associate Dean, Graduate Programs and Research, 703-993-1947, Fax: 703-993-1942, E-mail: nursinfo@gmu.edu.

The George Washington University, School of Medicine and Health Sciences, Health Sciences Programs, Washington, DC 20052. Offers adult nurse practitioner (MSN, Post Master's

Certificate); advanced family nurse practitioner (Post Master's Certificate); clinical practice management (MSHS); clinical research administration (MSHS); clinical research administration for nurses (MSN); emergency services management (MSHS); end-of-life care (MSHS, MSN); family nurse practitioner (MSN); immunohematology (MSHS); nursing leadership and management (MSN); oral biology (MSHS); physical therapy (DPT); physician assistant (MSHS); MSHS/MPH. Postbaccalaureate distance learning degree programs offered (no on-campus study). *Entrance requirements:* Additional exam requirements/recommendations for international students: Required—TOEFL (minimum score 550 paper-based; 213 computer-based). Expenses: Contact institution.

Georgia Southern University, Jack N. Averitt College of Graduate Studies, College of Health and Human Sciences, School of Nursing, Statesboro, GA 30460. Offers rural community health nurse practitioner (MSN); rural community health nurse specialist (Certificate); rural family nurse practitioner (MSN, Certificate); women's health nurse practitioner (MSN, Certificate). *Accreditation:* AACN. Part-time programs available. Postbaccalaureate distance learning degree programs offered. *Faculty:* 13 full-time (all women). *Students:* 6 full-time (all women), 40 part-time (38 women); includes 6 minority (all African Americans) Average age 34. 14 applicants, 100% accepted. In 2006, 15 degrees awarded. *Degree requirements:* For master's, thesis optional. *Entrance requirements:* For master's, GRE General Test or MAT, minimum GPA of 3.0, Georgia nursing license, 2 years of clinical experience, CPR certification; for Certificate, MSN. Additional exam requirements/recommendations for international students: Required—TOEFL (minimum score 550 paper-based; 213 computer-based; 80 iBT). *Application deadline:* For fall admission, 3/1 priority date for domestic students, 3/1 for international students; for spring admission, 10/1 priority date for domestic students, 10/1 for international students. Applications are processed on a rolling basis. Application fee: $50. Electronic applications accepted. *Financial support:* In 2006–07, 35 students received support, including research assistantships with partial tuition reimbursements available (averaging $5,500 per year), teaching assistantships with partial tuition reimbursements available (averaging $5,500 per year); career-related internships or fieldwork, Federal Work-Study, scholarships/grants, traineeships, tuition waivers (partial), and unspecified assistantships also available. Support available to part-time students. Financial award application deadline: 4/15; financial award applicants required to submit FAFSA. *Faculty research:* Caring, HIV disease, qualitative health research, health policy, rural nursing. Total annual research expenditures: $189,915. *Unit head:* Dr. Jean Bartels, Chair, 912-681-5479, Fax: 912-681-0536, E-mail: jbartels@georgiasouthern.edu. *Application contact:* 912-681-5384, Fax: 912-681-0740, E-mail: gradadmissionss@georgiasouthern.edu.

Georgia State University, College of Health and Human Sciences, School of Nursing, Atlanta, GA 30303-3083. Offers adult health (MS); child health (MS); family nurse practitioner (MS); health promotion, protection and restoration (PhD); nursing (Certificate); perinatal/women's health (MS); psychiatric/mental health (MS). *Accreditation:* AACN. Part-time and evening/weekend programs available. *Faculty:* 35 full-time (all women), 1 (woman) part-time/adjunct. *Students:* 72 full-time (66 women), 128 part-time (123 women); includes 75 minority (61 African Americans, 9 Asian Americans or Pacific Islanders, 5 Hispanic Americans), 2 international. Average age 37. 70 applicants, 54% accepted, 30 enrolled. In 2006, 39 master's, 6 doctorates awarded. *Degree requirements:* For master's, research activity; for doctorate, thesis/dissertation, comprehensive exam. *Entrance requirements:* For master's, MAT (preferred) or GRE, interview, RN license; for doctorate, GRE General Test. Additional exam requirements/recommendations for international students: Required—TOEFL (minimum score 550 paper-based; 213 computer-based). *Application deadline:* For fall admission, 3/1 priority date for domestic students; for spring admission, 10/1 priority date for domestic students. Applications are processed on a rolling basis. Application fee: $50. Electronic applications accepted. *Expenses: Contact institution. Financial support:* In 2006–07, research assistantships with full and partial tuition reimbursements (averaging $3,108 per year); fellowships with full tuition reimbursements, teaching assistantships, Federal Work-Study, institutionally sponsored loans, scholarships/grants, traineeships, and tuition waivers (partial) also available. Support available to part-time students. Financial award application deadline: 4/1; financial award applicants required to submit FAFSA. *Faculty research:* Breast cancer prevention, sexually compulsive behaviors, health risks in minority youth, asthma treatment strategies, adolescent alcohol-related issues. Total annual research expenditures: $221,691. *Unit head:* Dr. Barbara Woodring, Director, 404-651-3040. *Application contact:* Barbara Smith, Admissions Counselor II, 404-651-3834, Fax: 404-651-4871, E-mail: bbsmith@gsu.edu.

Graceland University, School of Nursing, Independence, MO 64050-3434. Offers family nurse practitioner (MSN, PMC); health care administration (MSN, PMC); nurse educator (MSN, PMC). Part-time programs available. Postbaccalaureate distance learning degree programs offered (minimal on-campus study). *Faculty:* 11 full-time (all women), 5 part-time/adjunct (all women). *Students:* 94 full-time (93 women), 123 part-time (102 women); includes 16 minority (10 African Americans, 4 Asian Americans or Pacific Islanders, 2 Hispanic Americans). Average age 44. 123 applicants, 90% accepted, 105 enrolled. In 2006, 42 master's, 2 other advanced degrees awarded. *Median time to degree:* Master's–2.5 years full-time, 4 years part-time. *Degree requirements:* For master's, thesis optional. *Entrance requirements:* For master's, BSN from nationally accredited program, portfolio, RN license, minimum GPA of 3.0. *Application deadline:* For fall admission, 6/1 priority date for domestic students; for winter admission, 10/1 priority date for domestic students; for spring admission, 3/1 priority date for domestic students. Applications are processed on a rolling basis. Application fee: $50. Electronic applications accepted. *Expenses: Contact institution. Financial support:* In 2006–07, 3 students received support. Institutionally sponsored loans and traineeships available. Support available to part-time students. Financial award applicants required to submit FAFSA. *Faculty research:* International nursing, family care-giving, health promotion. *Unit head:* Dr. Kathryn A Ballou, Dean, 800-833-0524 Ext. 4201, Fax: 816-833-2990, E-mail: kaballou@graceland.edu. *Application contact:* John D. Koehler, Manager of Recruiting, 816-833-0524 Ext. 4804, Fax: 816-833-2990, E-mail: jkoehler@graceland.edu.

Grambling State University, School of Graduate Studies and Research, College of Professional Studies, School of Nursing, Grambling, LA 71245. Offers family nurse practitioner (MSN, PMC); nurse educator (MSN). *Accreditation:* NLN. Part-time programs available. *Faculty:* 4 full-time (all women), 4 part-time/adjunct (2 women). *Students:* 26 full-time (21 women), 24 part-time (20 women); includes 27 minority (26 African Americans, 1 Asian American or Pacific Islander). Average age 38. In 2006, 13 degrees awarded. *Degree requirements:* For master's, thesis (for some programs), comprehensive exam (for some programs). *Entrance requirements:* For master's, GRE, minimum GPA of 3.0 on last degree, interview, 2 years experience as RN. Additional exam requirements/recommendations for international students: Required—TOEFL. *Application deadline:* For fall admission, 7/1 for domestic students; for spring admission, 12/1 for domestic students. Application fee: $20 ($30 for international students). *Expenses:* Tuition, state resident: full-time $2,232; part-time $124 per credit hour. Tuition, nonresident: full-time $7,582; part-time $124 per credit hour. Required fees: $1,127. *Financial support:* In 2006–07, 25 students received support. Application deadline: 5/31. *Unit head:* Dr. Rhonda Hensley, Director, 318-274-2897, Fax: 318-274-3491, E-mail: hensleyr@gram.edu.

Grand Valley State University, Kirkhof College of Nursing, Allendale, MI 49401-9403. Offers advanced practice (MSN); case management (MSN); nursing administration (MSN); nursing education (MSN); MSN/MBA. *Accreditation:* AACN. Part-time programs available. *Faculty:* 17 full-time (all women), 1 (woman) part-time/adjunct. *Students:* 3 full-time (all women), 46 part-time (42 women); includes 4 minority (1 African American, 1 Asian American or Pacific Islander, 2 Hispanic Americans). Average age 35. 15 applicants, 67% accepted, 8 enrolled. In 2006, 20 degrees awarded. *Degree requirements:* For master's, thesis optional. *Entrance requirements:* For master's, GRE, minimum GPA of 3.0 in upper-division course work, course work in statistics, Michigan RN license. Additional exam requirements/recommendations for international students: Required—TOEFL. *Application deadline:* For fall admission, 3/15 priority date for domestic students. Applications are processed on a rolling basis. Application fee: $30. Electronic applications accepted. *Expenses:* Tuition, state resident: full-time $5,850; part-time $325 per credit. Tuition, nonresident: full-time $10,800; part-time $600 per credit. Tuition and fees vary according to course load. *Financial support:* In 2006–07, 7 research assistantships with full and partial tuition reimbursements (averaging $8,000 per year) were awarded; career-related internships or fieldwork, Federal Work-Study, institutionally sponsored loans, and traineeships also available. Financial award application deadline: 2/15. *Faculty research:* Multigenerational health promotion, chronic disease prevention, end-of-life issues; nursing workload, family caregiver health. Total annual research expenditures: $36,000. *Unit head:* Dr. Phyllis Gendler, Dean, 616-331-7161, Fax: 616-331-7362, E-mail: gendlerp@gvsu.edu. *Application contact:* Dr. Jean Martin, Director of Graduate Programs, 616-331-7167, Fax: 616-331-7362, E-mail: martinj@gvsu.edu.

Gwynedd-Mercy College, School of Nursing, Gwynedd Valley, PA 19437-0901. Offers clinical nurse specialist (MSN), including gerontology, oncology, pediatrics; nurse practitioner (MSN), including adult health, pediatric health. *Accreditation:* NLN. *Faculty:* 5 full-time (all women), 3 part-time/adjunct (2 women). *Students:* 7 full-time (5 women), 38 part-time (35 women); includes 3 minority (1 African American, 1 Asian American or Pacific Islander, 1 Hispanic American). Average age 41. 18 applicants, 89% accepted, 11 enrolled. In 2006, 5 degrees awarded. *Degree requirements:* For master's, thesis optional. *Entrance requirements:* For master's, GRE General Test or MAT, 2 years of experience, physical assessment, course work in statistics, BSN from an NLNAC accredited program, 2 letters of recommendation, personal interview. Additional exam requirements/recommendations for international students: Required—TOEFL (minimum score 575 paper-based). *Application deadline:* For fall admission, 8/1 priority date for domestic students; for winter admission, 12/1 priority date for domestic students. Applications are processed on a rolling basis. Application fee: $25. Electronic applications accepted. *Expenses: Contact institution. Financial support:* In 2006–07, 21 students received support. Scholarships/grants, traineeships, and unspecified assistantships available. Financial award application deadline: 8/30. *Faculty research:* Critical thinking, primary care, domestic violence, multiculturalism, nursing centers. *Unit head:* Dr. Andrea D. Hollingsworth, Dean, 215-646-7300 Ext. 539, Fax: 215-641-5517, E-mail: hollingsworth.a@gmc.edu. *Application contact:* Dr. Barbara A. Jones, Director, 215-646-7300 Ext. 407, Fax: 215-641-5564, E-mail: jones.b@gmc.edu.

Hardin-Simmons University, Graduate School, School of Nursing, Abilene, TX 79698-0001. Offers advanced healthcare delivery (MSN); family nurse practitioner (MSN). *Accreditation:* AACN. Part-time programs available. *Faculty:* 5 full-time (all women). *Students:* 1 full-time (0 women), 8 part-time (6 women). Average age 39. 5 applicants, 100% accepted, 3 enrolled. In 2006, 2 degrees awarded. *Degree requirements:* For master's, thesis or alternative, comprehensive exam. *Entrance requirements:* For master's, GRE, minimum undergraduate GPA of 3.0 in major, 2.8 overall; interview; upper-level course work in statistics; CPR certification; letters of recommendation. Additional exam requirements/recommendations for international students: Required—TOEFL (minimum score 550 paper-based; 213 computer-based). *Application deadline:* For fall admission, 8/15 priority date for domestic students; for spring admission, 1/5 priority date for domestic students. Applications are processed on a rolling basis. Application fee: $50 ($100 for international students). *Expenses: Contact institution.* One-time fee: $50. Tuition and fees vary according to course load and degree level. *Financial support:* In 2006–07, 8 students received support. Career-related internships or fieldwork and scholarships/grants available. Support available to part-time students. Financial award application deadline: 6/30; financial award applicants required to submit FAFSA. *Faculty research:* Child abuse, alternative medicine, pediatric chronic disease, health promotion. *Unit head:* Dr. Janet Noles, Dean, 325-672-2441, Fax: 325-670-1564, E-mail: jnoles@hsutx.edu. *Application contact:* Dr. Gary Stanlake, Dean of Graduate Studies, 325-670-1298, Fax: 325-670-1564, E-mail: gradoff@hsutx.edu.

Hawai'i Pacific University, School of Nursing, Honolulu, HI 96813. Offers community clinical nurse specialist (MSN); community clinical nurse specialist educator option (MSN); family nurse practitioner (MSN). *Accreditation:* NLN. Part-time and evening/weekend programs available. *Faculty:* 11 full-time (all women), 1 part-time/adjunct (0 women). *Students:* 26 full-time (23 women), 10 part-time (all women); includes 18 minority (2 African Americans, 1 American Indian/Alaska Native, 13 Asian Americans or Pacific Islanders, 2 Hispanic Americans). Average age 35. 22 applicants, 77% accepted, 13 enrolled. In 2006, 10 degrees awarded. *Degree requirements:* For master's, practicum, professional paper. *Entrance requirements:* For master's, bachelor's degree in nursing, minimum GPA of 3.0. Additional exam requirements/recommendations for international students: Recommended—TOEFL (minimum score 550 paper-based; 213 computer-based), TWE (minimum score 5). *Application deadline:* Applications are processed on a rolling basis. Application fee: $50. Electronic applications accepted. *Expenses:* Tuition: Full-time $10,080; part-time $560 per credit. *Financial support:* In 2006–07, 20 students received support. Career-related internships or fieldwork, Federal Work-Study, scholarships/grants, and traineeships available. Support available to part-time students. Financial award application deadline: 3/1; financial award applicants required to submit FAFSA. *Faculty research:* Hawaiian elders, traditional healing and nursing center. *Unit head:* Dr. Patricia Langotsuka, Interim Dean, 808-236-5812, Fax: 808-236-5818, E-mail: potsuka@hpu.edu. *Application contact:* Danny Lam, Assistant Director of Graduate Admissions, 808-544-1135, Fax: 808-544-0280, E-mail: graduate@hpu.edu.

See Close-Up on page 1961.

Holy Names University, Graduate Division, Department of Nursing, Oakland, CA 94619-1699. Offers community health nursing/case manager (MS); family nurse practitioner (MS). *Accreditation:* AACN. Part-time and evening/weekend programs available. *Faculty:* 1 (woman) full-time, 7 part-time/adjunct (all women). *Students:* 73 full-time (68 women), 22 part-time (20 women); includes 45 minority (22 African Americans, 1 American Indian/Alaska Native, 13 Asian Americans or Pacific Islanders, 9 Hispanic Americans). Average age 44. 52 applicants, 65% accepted, 26 enrolled. In 2006, 10 master's awarded. *Entrance requirements:* For master's, bachelor's degree in nursing or related field, California RN license or eligibility, minimum GPA of 3.0, previous course work in research or statistics. Additional exam requirements/recommendations for international students: Required—TOEFL. *Application deadline:* For fall admission, 8/1 priority date for domestic students; for spring admission, 12/1 priority date for domestic students. Applications are processed on a rolling basis. Application fee: $50. *Expenses:* Tuition: Full-time $10,800; part-time $600 per unit. Required fees: $240; $120 per term. *Financial support:* In 2006–07, 36 students received support. Scholarships/grants available. Support available to part-time students. Financial award application deadline: 3/2; financial award applicants required to submit FAFSA. *Faculty research:* Women's reproductive health, gerontology, attitudes about aging, schizophrenic families, international health issues. *Unit head:* Dr. Fay Bower, Program Director, 510-436-1127. *Application contact:* 800-430-1351, Fax: 510-436-1325, E-mail: admissions@hnu.edu.

Howard University, College of Pharmacy, Nursing and Allied Health Sciences, Division of Nursing, Washington, DC 20059-0002. Offers nurse practitioner (Certificate); primary family health nursing (MSN). *Accreditation:* AACN. Part-time programs available. *Faculty:* 3 full-time (all women), 6 part-time/adjunct (all women). *Students:* 23 full-time (20 women), 5 part-time (all women); includes 26 minority (23 African Americans, 1 American Indian/Alaska Native, 1 Asian American or Pacific Islander, 1 Hispanic American). Average age 36. 15 applicants, 73% accepted. In 2006, 1 master's, 1 other advanced degree awarded. *Median time to degree:* Master's–4 years part-time. *Degree requirements:* For master's, thesis optional. *Entrance requirements:* For master's, RN license, minimum GPA of 3.0, BS in nursing. *Application deadline:* For fall admission, 4/1 priority date for domestic students; for spring admission, 11/1 for domestic students. Applications are processed on a rolling basis. Application fee: $45. *Financial support:* In 2006–07, teaching assistantships (averaging $16,000 per year); career-related internships or fieldwork, institutionally sponsored loans, and scholarships/grants also available. Financial award application deadline: 4/1. *Faculty research:* Urinary incontinence, breast cancer prevention, depression in the elderly, adolescent pregnancy. *Unit head:* Dr. Mamie C. Montague, Associate Dean (Interim), 202-806-7456, Fax: 202-806-5958, E-mail: mmontague@howard.edu. *Application contact:* Dr. Mamie C. Montague, Chair, Graduate Program, 202-806-7460, Fax: 202-806-5958, E-mail: mmontague@howard.edu.

Family Nurse Practitioner Studies

Hunter College of the City University of New York, Graduate School, Schools of the Health Professions, Hunter-Bellevue School of Nursing, Gerontological Nurse Practitioner Program, New York, NY 10021-5085. Offers MS. *Accreditation:* AACN. Part-time programs available. *Faculty:* 24 full-time (21 women), 21 part-time/adjunct (19 women). *Students:* 1 (woman) full-time, 40 part-time (38 women); includes 23 minority (15 African Americans, 5 Asian Americans or Pacific Islanders, 3 Hispanic Americans). Average age 39. 19 applicants, 63% accepted, 8 enrolled. In 2006, 6 degrees awarded. *Degree requirements:* For master's, practicum. *Entrance requirements:* For master's, minimum GPA of 3.0, New York RN license, 2 years of professional practice experience, BSN. Additional exam requirements/recommendations for international students: Required—TOEFL. *Application deadline:* For fall admission, 4/1 for domestic students, 2/1 for international students; for spring admission, 11/1 for domestic students, 9/1 for international students. Applications are processed on a rolling basis. Application fee: $125. *Expenses:* Tuition, state resident: part-time $270 per credit. Tuition, nonresident: part-time $500 per credit. Required fees: $45 per semester. *Financial support:* Federal Work-Study, scholarships/grants, traineeships, and tuition waivers (partial) available. Support available to part-time students. Financial award application deadline: 5/1; financial award applicants required to submit FAFSA. *Faculty research:* Primary care of older adults, lived experiences of elders. *Unit head:* Dr. Steven Baumann, Coordinator, 212-481-4457, Fax: 212-481-5078, E-mail: sbaumann@shiva.hunter.cuny.edu. *Application contact:* William Zlata, Director for Graduate Admissions, 212-772-4482, Fax: 212-650-3336, E-mail: admissions@hunter.cuny.edu.

Hunter College of the City University of New York, Graduate School, Schools of the Health Professions, Hunter-Bellevue School of Nursing, Pediatric Nurse Practitioner Program, New York, NY 10021-5085. Offers MS, AC. *Accreditation:* AACN. Part-time programs available. *Faculty:* 24 full-time (21 women), 21 part-time/adjunct (19 women). *Students:* Average age 35. 1 applicant, 100% accepted, 1 enrolled. In 2006, 5 master's, 1 AC awarded. *Degree requirements:* For master's, practicum. *Entrance requirements:* For master's, 2 years of professional practice experience, BSN, minimum GPA of 3.0, New York RN license; for AC, MSN, minimum GPA of 3.0. Additional exam requirements/recommendations for international students: Required—TOEFL. *Application deadline:* For fall admission, 4/1 for domestic students, 2/1 for international students; for spring admission, 11/1 for domestic students, 9/1 for international students. Applications are processed on a rolling basis. Application fee: $125. *Expenses:* Tuition, state resident: part-time $270 per credit. Tuition, nonresident: part-time $500 per credit. Required fees: $45 per semester. *Financial support:* Federal Work-Study, scholarships/grants, traineeships, and tuition waivers (partial) available. Support available to part-time students. Financial award application deadline: 5/1; financial award applicants required to submit FAFSA. *Faculty research:* Primary care: infants, children, and adolescents. *Unit head:* Dr. Janet N. Natapoff, Coordinator, 212-481-5070, Fax: 212-481-5078, E-mail: jnatapof@hejira.hunter.cuny.edu. *Application contact:* William Zlata, Director for Graduate Admissions, 212-772-4482, Fax: 212-650-3336, E-mail: admissions@hunter.cuny.edu.

Hunter College of the City University of New York, Graduate School, Schools of the Health Professions, Hunter-Bellevue School of Nursing, Program in Adult Nurse Practitioner, New York, NY 10021-5085. Offers MS. *Accreditation:* AACN. *Faculty:* 24 full-time (21 women), 21 part-time/adjunct (19 women). *Students:* Average age 34. 42 applicants, 48% accepted, 15 enrolled. In 2006, 19 degrees awarded. *Degree requirements:* For master's, practicum. *Entrance requirements:* For master's, minimum GPA of 3.0, New York RN license, 2 years of professional practice experience, BSN. Additional exam requirements/recommendations for international students: Required—TOEFL. *Application deadline:* For fall admission, 4/1 for domestic students, 2/1 for international students; for spring admission, 11/1 for domestic students, 9/1 for international students. Applications are processed on a rolling basis. Application fee: $125. *Expenses:* Tuition, state resident: part-time $270 per credit. Tuition, nonresident: part-time $500 per credit. Required fees: $45 per semester. *Financial support:* Federal Work-Study, scholarships/grants, and traineeships available. Support available to part-time students. Financial award application deadline: 5/1. *Faculty research:* Adult primary care, critical care. *Unit head:* Dr. Vidette Todard-Francescli, Coordinator, 212-481-4445, Fax: 212-481-5078. *Application contact:* William Zlata, Director for Graduate Admissions, 212-772-4482, Fax: 212-650-3336, E-mail: admissions@hunter.cuny.edu.

Husson College, Graduate Studies Division, Program in Nursing, Bangor, ME 04401-2999. Offers family nurse practitioner (MSN); nursing (MSN); psychiatric nursing (MSN). *Accreditation:* AACN. *Entrance requirements:* For master's, MAT, BSN. Expenses: Contact institution.

Indiana University–Purdue University Indianapolis, School of Nursing, Department of Adult Health Nursing, Indianapolis, IN 46202-2896. Offers adult clinical nurse specialist (MSN), including chronic disability, critical care, health promotion, oncology. *Accreditation:* AACN. Part-time programs available. *Students:* 4 full-time (all women), 44 part-time (41 women); includes 4 minority (2 African Americans, 2 Hispanic Americans). Average age 39. In 2006, 15 degrees awarded. *Degree requirements:* For master's, thesis. *Entrance requirements:* For master's, GRE General Test, minimum GPA of 3.0, RN license. *Application deadline:* For fall admission, 4/1 for domestic students; for spring admission, 10/1 for domestic students. Application fee: $50 ($60 for international students). *Expenses:* Tuition, state resident: full-time $5,437; part-time $227 per credit hour. Tuition, nonresident: full-time $15,694; part-time $654 per credit hour. Required fees: $620. Tuition and fees vary according to course load, campus/location and program. *Financial support:* Fellowships with full tuition reimbursements, research assistantships with full tuition reimbursements, teaching assistantships with full tuition reimbursements, Federal Work-Study, scholarships/grants, and traineeships available. Support available to part-time students. Financial award application deadline: 5/1. *Unit head:* Dr. Juanita Keck, Co-Chair, 317-274-0050.

The Johns Hopkins University, School of Nursing, Nurse Practitioner Program, Baltimore, MD 21218-2699. Offers adult acute/critical care (MSN, Certificate); adult and pediatric primary care (MSN); adult or pediatric primary care (Certificate); family primary care (MSN, Certificate). *Accreditation:* AACN; NLN (one or more programs are accredited). Part-time programs available. *Faculty:* 12 full-time (all women), 6 part-time/adjunct (5 women). *Students:* 23 full-time (22 women), 62 part-time (58 women); includes 26 minority (3 African Americans, 3 American Indian/Alaska Native, 15 Asian Americans or Pacific Islanders, 5 Hispanic Americans), 1 international. Average age 31. 157 applicants, 85% accepted, 32 enrolled. In 2006, 18 master's, 2 other advanced degrees awarded. *Degree requirements:* For master's, scholarly project or portfolio, thesis optional. *Entrance requirements:* For master's, GRE, interview, minimum GPA of 3.0, BSN, Maryland RN license. Additional exam requirements/recommendations for international students: Required—TOEFL (minimum score 550 paper-based; 230 computer-based). *Application deadline:* For fall admission, 3/1 priority date for domestic and international students; for spring admission, 7/1 priority date for domestic and international students. Application fee: $75. *Expenses: Contact institution.* Tuition and fees vary according to degree level and program. *Financial support:* In 2006–07, 16 students received support. Federal Work-Study, scholarships/grants, traineeships, and tuition waivers (partial) available. Support available to part-time students. Financial award application deadline: 3/1; financial award applicants required to submit FAFSA. *Faculty research:* Community outreach, primary care of underserved populations, substance abusing individuals, childhood violence, women's health. *Unit head:* Dr. Kathleen M. White, Director, Master's Programs, 410-614-4664, Fax: 410-955-7463, E-mail: kwhite@son.jhmi.edu. *Application contact:* Mary O'Rourke, Director of Admissions/Student Services, 410-955-7548, Fax: 410-614-7086, E-mail: orourke@son.jhmi.edu.

Kennesaw State University, College of Health and Human Services, Program in Primary Care Nurse Practitioner, Kennesaw, GA 30144-5591. Offers MSN. *Accreditation:* AACN. Part-time and evening/weekend programs available. *Faculty:* 7 full-time (6 women), 15 part-time/adjunct (10 women). *Students:* 56 full-time (53 women), 13 part-time (11 women); includes 15 minority (13 African Americans, 2 Hispanic Americans), 1 international. Average age 38. 104 applicants, 42% accepted, 40 enrolled. In 2006, 36 degrees awarded. *Entrance requirements:* For master's, GRE General Test, minimum GPA of 2.5, RN license, 3 years of professional experience. Additional exam requirements/recommendations for international students: Required—TOEFL (minimum score 550 paper-based; 213 computer-based). *Application deadline:* For fall admission, 5/31 for domestic students. Application fee: $50. Electronic applications accepted. *Expenses:* Tuition, state resident: full-time $3,044; part-time $127 per semester hour. Tuition, nonresident: full-time $12,172; part-time $508 per semester hour. Required fees: $353 per semester. Full-time tuition and fees vary according to campus/location and program. *Financial support:* In 2006–07, 2 research assistantships with full tuition reimbursements (averaging $15,000 per year) were awarded; Federal Work-Study and unspecified assistantships also available. Support available to part-time students. Financial award application deadline: 6/15; financial award applicants required to submit FAFSA. *Unit head:* Dr. B. Regina Dorman, Director, 770-423-6172, Fax: 770-423-6627, E-mail: gdorman@kennesaw.edu. *Application contact:* Vilma Marquez, Admissions Counselor, 770-420-4377, Fax: 770-423-6885, E-mail: ksugrad@kennesaw.edu.

La Roche College, School of Graduate Studies, Program in Nursing, Pittsburgh, PA 15237-5898. Offers family nurse practitioner (MSN); nursing management (MSN). *Accreditation:* AANA/CANAEP; NLN. Part-time and evening/weekend programs available. *Faculty:* 2 full-time (both women), 1 part-time/adjunct (0 women). *Students:* Average age 46. *Median time to degree:* Master's–2 years full-time, 4 years part-time. *Degree requirements:* For master's, internship, practicum, thesis optional. *Entrance requirements:* For master's, GRE General Test, BSN, nursing license, work experience. *Application deadline:* For fall admission, 8/15 priority date for domestic students; for spring admission, 12/15 priority date for domestic students. Applications are processed on a rolling basis. Application fee: $50. Electronic applications accepted. *Expenses: Contact institution. Financial support:* Application deadline: 3/31; *Faculty research:* Patient education, perception. *Unit head:* Dr. Rosemary McCarthy, Division Chair, 412-536-1173, Fax: 412-536-1175, E-mail: mccartr1@laroche.edu. *Application contact:* Hope Schiffgens, Director of Admissions for Graduate and Continuing Education, 412-536-1266, Fax: 412-536-1283, E-mail: schombh1@laroche.edu.

La Salle University, School of Nursing and Health Sciences, Philadelphia, PA 19141-1199. Offers adult health and illness, clinical nurse specialist (MSN); gerontology (Certificate); nursing administration (MSN); nursing education (Certificate); nursing informatics (Certificate); primary care of adults-nurse practitioner (MSN); public health nursing (MSN); school nursing (Certificate); speech-language-hearing science (MS); wound, ostomy and continence nursing (Certificate); wound, ostomy, and continence nursing (MSN); MSN/MBA. *Accreditation:* AACN. Part-time programs available. Postbaccalaureate distance learning degree programs offered (minimal on-campus study). *Entrance requirements:* For master's, GRE or MAT, 1 year of professional work experience, BSN, Pennsylvania RN license. Expenses: Contact institution. *Faculty research:* Medication errors, wound care, metacognition, education of RN students.

Long Island University, Brooklyn Campus, School of Nursing, Department of Adult Nurse Practitioner, Brooklyn, NY 11201-8423. Offers MS, Certificate. *Accreditation:* AACN. *Entrance requirements:* For master's, New York RN license, 2 letters of recommendation. Additional exam requirements/recommendations for international students: Required—TOEFL (minimum score 500 paper-based; 173 computer-based). Electronic applications accepted.

Long Island University, C.W. Post Campus, School of Health Professions and Nursing, Department of Nursing, Brookville, NY 11548-1300. Offers clinical nurse specialist (MS); family nurse practitioner (MS, Certificate). *Accreditation:* AACN. Part-time and evening/weekend programs available. *Degree requirements:* For master's, thesis. *Entrance requirements:* For master's, minimum GPA of 3.0 in major, bachelor's degree in nursing, NYS registered nurse, interview. Electronic applications accepted. *Faculty research:* Lactation/breast cancer, early discharge in maternity.

Louisiana State University Health Sciences Center, School of Nursing, New Orleans, LA 70112-2223. Offers adult health and illness (MN); adult health and nursing (DNS); neonatal nurse practitioner (MN); nursing (MN); nursing service administration (MN, DNS); parent-child health nursing (MN); primary care nurse practitioner (MN); psychiatric/community mental health nursing (MN, DNS); public health/community health nursing (MN, DNS). *Accreditation:* AACN; AANA/CANAEP (one or more programs are accredited). Part-time programs available. *Degree requirements:* For master's, thesis optional; for doctorate, thesis/dissertation. *Entrance requirements:* For master's, GRE General Test, MAT, minimum GPA of 3.0; for doctorate, GRE General Test, minimum GPA of 3.5. Additional exam requirements/recommendations for international students: Required—TOEFL. *Expenses:* Tuition, state resident: full-time $5,868; part-time $722 per credit. Tuition, nonresident: full-time $8,993; part-time $1,104 per credit. *Faculty research:* Advanced clinical practice, nursing education, health, social support, nursing administration.

Loyola University Chicago, Graduate School, Marcella Niehoff School of Nursing, Adult Nurse Practitioner Program, Chicago, IL 60611-2196. Offers MSN. *Accreditation:* AACN. Part-time and evening/weekend programs available. *Students:* 7 full-time (6 women), 32 part-time (30 women). Average age 29. In 2006, 5 degrees awarded. *Degree requirements:* For master's, comprehensive exam or oral thesis defense. *Entrance requirements:* For master's, BSN, minimum GPA of 3.0, professional license. *Application deadline:* Applications are processed on a rolling basis. Application fee: $40. Electronic applications accepted. *Financial support:* Traineeships available. *Faculty research:* Menopause. *Unit head:* Dr. Marijo Letizia, Associate Professor, 708-216-9325, Fax: 708-216-9555, E-mail: mletizi@luc.edu. *Application contact:* Dr. Vicki A. Keough, Associate Professor, 708-216-3582, Fax: 708-216-9555, E-mail: vkeough@luc.edu.

Loyola University Chicago, Graduate School, Marcella Niehoff School of Nursing, Cardiovascular Health and Disease Management Clinical Nurse Specialist Program, Chicago, IL 60611-2196. Offers MSN. *Accreditation:* AACN. Part-time and evening/weekend programs available. *Students:* 4 full-time (all women), 11 part-time (all women). 10 applicants, 80% accepted. In 2006, 3 degrees awarded. *Degree requirements:* For master's, comprehensive exam or oral thesis defense. *Entrance requirements:* For master's, Illinois license, 3 letters of recommendation. *Application deadline:* Applications are processed on a rolling basis. Application fee: $40. Electronic applications accepted. *Financial support:* Application deadline: 3/1. *Faculty research:* Cardiac exercise. *Unit head:* Dr. Meg Gulanick, Professor, 708-216-9687, Fax: 708-216-9555, E-mail: mgulani@luc.edu. *Application contact:* Dr. Vicki A. Keough, Associate Professor, 708-216-3582, Fax: 708-216-9555, E-mail: vkeough@luc.edu.

Loyola University Chicago, Graduate School, Marcella Niehoff School of Nursing, Family Nurse Practitioner Program, Chicago, IL 60611-2196. Offers MSN. Part-time and evening/weekend programs available. *Students:* 5 full-time (4 women), 27 part-time (23 women). In 2006, 5 degrees awarded. *Application deadline:* Applications are processed on a rolling basis. Application fee: $40. Electronic applications accepted. *Financial support:* Traineeships and employer tuition remission available. Financial award applicants required to submit FAFSA. *Unit head:* Dr. Marijo Letizia, Associate Professor, 708-216-9325, Fax: 708-216-9555, E-mail: mletizi@luc.edu. *Application contact:* Dr. Vicki A. Keough, Associate Professor, 708-216-3582, Fax: 708-216-9555, E-mail: vkeough@luc.edu.

Loyola University Chicago, Graduate School, Marcella Niehoff School of Nursing, Oncology Clinical Nurse Specialist Program, Chicago, IL 60611-2196. Offers MSN. *Accreditation:* AACN. Part-time and evening/weekend programs available. Postbaccalaureate distance learning degree programs offered (no on-campus study). *Students:* Average age 29. *Degree requirements:* For master's, comprehensive exam or oral thesis defense. *Entrance requirements:* For master's, Illinois license, 3 letters of recommendation . *Application deadline:* Applications are processed on a rolling basis. Application fee: $40. Electronic applications accepted. *Financial support:* Teaching assistantships, traineeships and unspecified assistantships available. Financial award application deadline: 3/1. *Faculty research:* Breast cancer, coping with cancer, pain. *Unit head:* Dr. Patricia Friend, Assistant Professor, 708-216-9553, Fax: 708-216-9555, E-mail: pfriend@luc.edu. *Application contact:* Dr. Vicki A. Keough, Associate Professor, 708-216-3582, Fax: 708-216-9555, E-mail: vkeough@luc.edu.

Loyola University Chicago, Graduate School, Marcella Niehoff School of Nursing, Program in Emergency Nurse Practitioner, Chicago, IL 60611-2196. Offers MSN. *Students:* 3 full-time (2 women), 10 part-time (6 women). In 2006, 2 degrees awarded. *Entrance requirements:* For master's, Illinois license, 3 letters of recommendation. Application fee: $40. *Unit head:* Dr. Vicki A. Keough, Associate Professor, 708-216-3582, Fax: 708-216-9555, E-mail: vkeough@luc.edu.

Loyola University Chicago, Graduate School, Marcella Niehoff School of Nursing, Women's Health Nurse Practitioner Program, Chicago, IL 60611-2196. Offers MSN. *Accreditation:* AACN. Part-time and evening/weekend programs available. *Students:* 2 full-time (both women), 7 part-time (all women). Average age 29. In 2006, 2 degrees awarded. *Degree requirements:* For master's, comprehensive exam or oral thesis defense. *Application deadline:* Applications are processed on a rolling basis. Application fee: $40. Electronic applications accepted. *Financial support:* Teaching assistantships, unspecified assistantships available. Financial award application deadline: 3/1. *Faculty research:* Breast feeding, postpartum depression, pre-term labor toxicity. *Unit head:* Dr. Linda Paskiewicz, Associate Professor, 708-216-9692, Fax: 708-216-9555, E-mail: lpaskie@luc.edu. *Application contact:* Dr. Vicki A. Keough, Associate Dean, 773-508-3263, Fax: 773-508-3241, E-mail: vkeough@luc.edu.

Loyola University New Orleans, City College, Program in Nursing, New Orleans, LA 70118-6195. Offers family nurse practitioner (MSN); health care systems management (MSN). *Accreditation:* NLN. Postbaccalaureate distance learning degree programs offered. *Degree requirements:* For master's, 700 hours of clinical practice. *Entrance requirements:* For master's, GRE, BSN, Louisiana nursing license, 1 year of work experience in clinical nursing, minimum undergraduate GPA of 2.8, interview. Additional exam requirements/recommendations for international students: Required—TOEFL (minimum score 550 paper-based; 213 computer-based). *Faculty research:* Increasing compliance with treatment, patient satisfaction with care provided by nurse practitioners.

Madonna University, Program in Nursing, Livonia, MI 48150-1173. Offers adult health: chronic health conditions (MSN); adult nurse practitioner (MSN); nursing administration (MSN); MSN/MSBA. *Accreditation:* AACN. Part-time programs available. *Faculty:* 3 full-time (all women). *Students:* 12 full-time (all women), 82 part-time (80 women); includes 9 minority (5 African Americans, 3 Asian Americans or Pacific Islanders, 1 Hispanic American), 3 international. Average age 40. 20 applicants, 50% accepted. In 2006, 10 degrees awarded. *Degree requirements:* For master's, thesis or alternative. *Entrance requirements:* For master's, GRE General Test, Michigan nursing license. *Application deadline:* For fall admission, 8/1 priority date for domestic students; for winter admission, 12/1 priority date for domestic students; for spring admission, 4/1 priority date for domestic students. Applications are processed on a rolling basis. Application fee: $25 ($200 for international students). Electronic applications accepted. *Financial support:* Career-related internships or fieldwork, Federal Work-Study, institutionally sponsored loans, and scholarships/grants available. Support available to part-time students. *Faculty research:* Coping, caring. *Unit head:* Dr. Nancy O'Connor, Chairperson, 734-432-5461, Fax: 734-432-5463, E-mail: noconnor@madonna.edu. *Application contact:* Sandra Kellums, Coordinator of Graduate Admissions and Records, 734-432-5667, Fax: 734-432-5862, E-mail: skellum@madonna.edu.

Malone College, School of Nursing, Graduate Program in Nursing, Canton, OH 44709-3897. Offers clinical nurse specialist (MSN); family nurse practitioner (MSN). *Accreditation:* AACN. Evening/weekend programs available. *Faculty:* 6 full-time (all women), 8 part-time/adjunct (7 women). *Students:* Average age 35. In 2006, 9 degrees awarded. *Degree requirements:* For master's, thesis. *Entrance requirements:* For master's, minimum GPA of 3.0 from BSN program, interview. *Application deadline:* For fall admission, 5/31 for international students. Applications are processed on a rolling basis. Application fee: $25. *Expenses:* Contact institution. *Financial support:* Tuition waivers (partial) available. Support available to part-time students. Financial award application deadline: 6/30. *Faculty research:* Compassion: teaching/observing/providing issues/needs of migrant populations, psychosocial care of patients close to death, the process of reconstitution, newborn health concerns in Mali, West Africa. *Unit head:* Dr. Karen R. Gehrling, Director, 330-471-8163, Fax: 330-471-8407, E-mail: kgerhling@malone.edu. *Application contact:* Dr. David Kleffman, Recruiter, 330-471-8447, Fax: 330-471-8343, E-mail: dkleffman@malone.edu.

Marquette University, Graduate School, College of Nursing, Milwaukee, WI 53201-1881. Offers adult nurse practitioner (Certificate); advanced practice nursing (MSN), including adult, children, neonatal nurse practitioner, nurse-midwifery, older adult; gerontological nurse practitioner (Certificate); neonatal nurse practitioner (Certificate); nurse-midwifery (Certificate); nursing (PhD); pediatric nurse practitioner (Certificate). *Accreditation:* AACN. Part-time and evening/weekend programs available. *Faculty:* 29 full-time (27 women), 39 part-time/adjunct (37 women). *Students:* 104 full-time (98 women), 122 part-time (114 women); includes 18 minority (5 African Americans, 2 American Indian/Alaska Native, 4 Asian Americans or Pacific Islanders, 7 Hispanic Americans), 2 international. Average age 34. 122 applicants, 79% accepted, 73 enrolled. In 2006, 46 degrees awarded. *Degree requirements:* For master's, thesis or alternative, comprehensive exam. *Entrance requirements:* For master's, GRE General Test, BSN, Wisconsin RN license. Additional exam requirements/recommendations for international students: Required—TOEFL. Application fee: $40. *Financial support:* In 2006–07, 6 research assistantships, 1 teaching assistantship were awarded; career-related internships or fieldwork, Federal Work-Study, institutionally sponsored loans, scholarships/grants, and tuition waivers (full and partial) also available. Support available to part-time students. Financial award application deadline: 2/15. *Faculty research:* Psychosocial adjustment to chronic illness, gerontology, reminiscence, health policy: uninsured and access, hospital care delivery systems. Total annual research expenditures: $1.1 million. *Unit head:* Dr. Lea Acord, Dean, 414-288-3812, Fax: 414-288-1578. *Application contact:* Dr. Judy Miller, Director of Graduate Studies, 414-288-3810, Fax: 414-288-1578.

Marymount University, School of Health Professions, Program in Nursing, Arlington, VA 22207-4299. Offers family nurse practitioner (MSN, Certificate); nursing administration (MSN, Certificate); nursing education (MSN, Certificate); RN to MSN (MSN). *Accreditation:* AACN; NLN. Part-time and evening/weekend programs available. *Faculty:* 7 full-time (all women), 1 (woman) part-time/adjunct. *Students:* 4 full-time (3 women), 36 part-time (35 women); includes 23 minority (15 African Americans, 5 Asian Americans or Pacific Islanders, 3 Hispanic Americans), 1 international. Average age 42. 17 applicants, 100% accepted, 10 enrolled. In 2006, 13 master's, 2 other advanced degrees awarded. *Degree requirements:* For master's, comprehensive exam. *Entrance requirements:* For master's, 2 letters of recommendation, interview, RN license, resumé; for Certificate, interview. *Application deadline:* Applications are processed on a rolling basis. Application fee: $40. Electronic applications accepted. *Expenses:* Tuition: Full-time $11,160; part-time $620 per credit. Required fees: $113; $630 per credit. *Financial support:* Research assistantships with partial tuition reimbursements, career-related internships or fieldwork, scholarships/grants, and unspecified assistantships available. Support available to part-time students. Financial award applicants required to submit FAFSA. *Unit head:* Dr. Susan Bidwell, Chair, 703-284-1593, Fax: 703-284-3819, E-mail: susan.bidwell@marymount.edu.

McGill University, Faculty of Graduate and Postdoctoral Studies, Faculty of Medicine, School of Nursing, Montréal, QC H3A 2T5, Canada. Offers nurse practitioner (Graduate Diploma); nursing (M Sc A, PhD). Part-time programs available. *Degree requirements:* For doctorate, thesis/dissertation. *Entrance requirements:* For master's, GRE General Test, minimum GPA of 3.0; for doctorate, GRE General Test. Additional exam requirements/recommendations for international students: Required—TOEFL. *Faculty research:* Pain, maternal-child nursing, women's health, children in hospitals, elderly.

Medical College of Georgia, School of Graduate Studies, Programs in Nursing, Augusta, GA 30912-1500. Offers adult nursing (MSN); community health nursing (MSN); mental health nursing (MSN); nurse practitioner (MSN); nursing (DNP, PhD); nursing anesthesia (MSN); parent-child nursing (MSN). *Accreditation:* AACN; AANA/CANAEP. Part-time programs available. *Faculty:* 18 full-time (16 women), 1 part-time/adjunct (0 women). *Students:* 95 full-time (76 women), 42 part-time (37 women); includes 24 minority (20 African Americans, 4 Asian Americans or Pacific Islanders). Average age 37. 156 applicants, 35% accepted, 24 enrolled. In 2006, 28 master's, 10 doctorates awarded. *Degree requirements:* For master's, thesis (for some programs); for doctorate, thesis/dissertation. *Entrance requirements:* For master's, GRE General Test, MAT; for doctorate, GRE General Test. Additional exam requirements/recommendations for international students: Required—TOEFL (minimum score 550 paper-based; 213 computer-based). *Application deadline:* For fall admission, 7/1 for domestic students, 4/15 for international students. Applications are processed on a rolling basis. Application fee: $30. Electronic applications accepted. *Expenses:* Tuition, state resident: full-time $2,293; part-time $192 per credit hour. Tuition, nonresident: full-time $9,169; part-time $765 per credit hour. Required fees: $293 per semester. *Financial support:* In 2006–07, 78 students received support, including 9 research assistantships with partial tuition reimbursements available (averaging $23,000 per year); Federal Work-Study, institutionally sponsored loans, traineeships, tuition waivers, and unspecified assistantships also available. Support available to part-time students. Financial award application deadline: 5/31; financial award applicants required to submit FAFSA. *Unit head:* Dr. Lucy Marion, Dean, 706-721-6258, Fax: 706-721-8169, E-mail: lumarion@mail.mcg.edu.

Medical University of South Carolina, College of Nursing, Family Nurse Practitioner Program, Charleston, SC 29425-0002. Offers MSN. Part-time programs available. *Faculty:* 5 full-time (all women). *Students:* 11 full-time (9 women), 15 part-time (14 women); includes 4 minority (2 African Americans, 1 American Indian/Alaska Native, 1 Hispanic American). Average age 34. 22 applicants, 55% accepted, 12 enrolled. In 2006, 11 degrees awarded. *Degree requirements:* For master's, thesis optional. *Entrance requirements:* For master's, GRE General Test, BSN, course work in statistics and physical assessment, nursing license, minimum GPA of 3.0. Additional exam requirements/recommendations for international students: Required—TOEFL (minimum score 600 paper-based; 250 computer-based). *Application deadline:* For fall admission, 2/1 for domestic and international students; for spring admission, 9/15 for domestic and international students. Application fee: $75. Electronic applications accepted. *Financial support:* Fellowships, Federal Work-Study, scholarships/grants, and traineeships available. Support available to part-time students. Financial award application deadline: 3/15; financial award applicants required to submit FAFSA. *Faculty research:* Use of PDAs in teaching, palliative care. *Unit head:* Dr. Sally Stroud, Track Coordinator, 843-792-4616, Fax: 843-792-2099, E-mail: stroudsd@musc.edu. *Application contact:* Carolyn F. Page, Director, Student Services, 843-792-3844, Fax: 843-792-9258, E-mail: pagecf@musc.edu.

Medical University of South Carolina, College of Nursing, Program in Neonatal Nurse Practitioner, Charleston, SC 29425-0002. Offers MSN. Part-time programs available. Postbaccalaureate distance learning degree programs offered. *Faculty:* 2 full-time (both women), 2 part-time/adjunct (both women). *Students:* 12 full-time (11 women), 6 part-time (all women). Average age 37. 20 applicants, 50% accepted, 10 enrolled. In 2006, 4 degrees awarded. *Degree requirements:* For master's, thesis optional. *Entrance requirements:* For master's, GRE General Test, BSN, course work in statistics and physical assessment, 1 year nursing experience, nursing license, minimum GPA of 3.0. Additional exam requirements/recommendations for international students: Required—TOEFL (minimum score 600 paper-based; 250 computer-based). *Application deadline:* For fall admission, 2/1 for domestic and international students; for spring admission, 9/15 for domestic and international students. Application fee: $75. Electronic applications accepted. *Financial support:* Federal Work-Study, scholarships/grants, and traineeships available. Support available to part-time students. Financial award application deadline: 3/15; financial award applicants required to submit FAFSA. *Faculty research:* Surfactant use in neonates. Total annual research expenditures: $147,000. *Unit head:* Robin L. Bissinger, Track Coordinator, 843-792-0531, Fax: 843-792-1741, E-mail: bissinrl@musc.edu. *Application contact:* Carolyn F. Page, Director, Student Services, 843-792-3844, Fax: 843-792-9258, E-mail: pagecf@musc.edu.

MGH Institute of Health Professions, Graduate Programs, Program in Nursing, Boston, MA 02129. Offers advanced practice nursing (MSN); gerontological nursing (MSN); pediatric nursing (MSN); psychiatric nursing (MSN); teaching and learning for health care education (Certificate); women's health nursing (MSN). *Accreditation:* NLN (one or more programs are accredited). *Faculty:* 29 full-time (28 women), 9 part-time/adjunct (7 women). *Students:* 208 full-time (188 women), 43 part-time (35 women); includes 36 minority (12 African Americans, 17 Asian Americans or Pacific Islanders, 7 Hispanic Americans), 1 international. Average age 29. 302 applicants, 62% accepted, 101 enrolled. In 2006, 77 master's, 3 other advanced degrees awarded. *Degree requirements:* For master's, thesis or alternative. *Entrance requirements:* For master's, GRE General Test, minimum GPA of 3.0. Additional exam requirements/recommendations for international students: Required—TOEFL (minimum score 550 paper-based; 213 computer-based). *Application deadline:* For fall admission, 1/10 for domestic and international students. Application fee: $50. Electronic applications accepted. *Financial support:* In 2006–07, 212 students received support, including 1 research assistantship (averaging $1,200 per year), 2 teaching assistantships (averaging $1,200 per year); career-related internships or fieldwork, scholarships/grants, traineeships, tuition waivers (full and partial), and unspecified assistantships also available. Support available to part-time students. Financial award application deadline: 3/3; financial award applicants required to submit FAFSA. *Faculty research:* Biobehavioral nursing, HIV/AIDS, gerontological nursing, women's health, vulnerable populations, health systems . *Unit head:* Margery Chisholm, Director, 617-724-0480, Fax: 617-726-8022, E-mail: mchisholm@mghihp.edu. *Application contact:* Maureen Rika Judd, Manager of Admissions, 617-726-6069, Fax: 617-726-8010, E-mail: admissions@mghihp.edu.

See Close-Up on page 1963.

Midwestern State University, Graduate Studies, College of Health Sciences and Human Services, Nursing Program, Wichita Falls, TX 76308. Offers family nurse practitioner (MSN); health services administration (MSN); nurse educator (MSN). *Accreditation:* AACN. Part-time and evening/weekend programs available. *Faculty:* 8 full-time (all women), 2 part-time/adjunct (both women). *Students:* 12 full-time (10 women), 49 part-time (40 women); includes 8 minority (1 African American, 2 American Indian/Alaska Native, 1 Asian American or Pacific Islander, 4 Hispanic Americans), 3 international. Average age 39. 19 applicants, 84% accepted, 12 enrolled. In 2006, 10 degrees awarded. *Degree requirements:* For master's, thesis optional. *Entrance requirements:* For master's, GRE General Test or MAT. Additional exam requirements/recommendations for international students: Required—TOEFL (minimum score 550 paper-based; 213 computer-based). *Application deadline:* For fall admission, 7/1 for domestic students, 4/1 for international students; for spring admission, 11/1 for domestic students, 8/1 for international students. Applications are processed on a rolling basis. Application fee: $35 ($50 for international students). Electronic applications accepted. *Financial support:* In 2006–07, 58 students received support, including 1 teaching assistantship with partial tuition reimbursement available (averaging $7,500 per year); career-related internships or fieldwork, Federal Work-Study, institutionally sponsored loans, scholarships/grants, tuition waivers (partial), and unspecified assistantships also available. Support available to part-time students. Financial award application deadline: 5/1; financial award applicants required to submit FAFSA. *Unit head:* Dr. Melissa Ford, Chair, 940-397-4601, Fax: 940-397-4513, E-mail: melissa.ford@mwsu.edu. *Application contact:* 800-842-1922, Fax: 940-397-4672, E-mail: admissions@mwsu.edu.

Minnesota State University Mankato, College of Graduate Studies, College of Allied Health and Nursing, Department of Nursing, Mankato, MN 56001. Offers family nursing (MSN), including clinical nurse specialist, educator, family nurse practitioner, manager; managed care (MSN), including clinical nurse specialist, educator, family nurse practitioner, manager. *Accreditation:* AACN; NLN. *Students:* 12 full-time (all women), 34 part-time (32 women). Average age 39. In 2006, 15 degrees awarded. *Degree requirements:* For master's, internships, research project or thesis. *Entrance requirements:* For master's, GRE General Test or on-campus essay, minimum GPA of 3.0 during previous 2 years, BSN or equivalent references. Additional exam requirements/recommendations for international students: Required—TOEFL.

Family Nurse Practitioner Studies

Minnesota State University Mankato (continued)

Application deadline: For fall admission, 1/15 priority date for domestic students; for spring admission, 11/27 for domestic students. Applications are processed on a rolling basis. Application fee: $40. Electronic applications accepted. *Financial support:* Research assistantships with full tuition reimbursements, teaching assistantships with full tuition reimbursements available. Financial award application deadline: 3/15; financial award applicants required to submit FAFSA. *Faculty research:* Psychosocial nursing, computers in nursing, family adaptation. *Unit head:* Dr. Sonja Meiers, Graduate Coordinator, 507-389-1725. *Application contact:* Collaborative MSN Program Admissions, 507-389-6022.

Molloy College, Department of Nursing, Rockville Centre, NY 11571-5002. Offers adult nurse practitioner (Advanced Certificate); clinical nurse specialist: adult health (Advanced Certificate); family nurse practitioner (Advanced Certificate); nurse practitioner psychiatry (Advanced Certificate); nursing (MS); nursing administration (Advanced Certificate); nursing administration with informatics (Advanced Certificate); nursing education (Advanced Certificate); nursing informatics (Advanced Certificate); pediatric nurse practitioner (Advanced Certificate). *Accreditation:* AACN. Part-time and evening/weekend programs available. *Degree requirements:* For master's, thesis optional. *Entrance requirements:* For master's, 3 letters of reference, BS in nursing, minimum undergraduate GPA of 3.0; for Advanced Certificate, 3 letters of reference, master's degree in nursing. *Faculty research:* Hardiness and aging, alcoholism, current ethics, breast cancer, nurse role perception.

Monmouth University, Graduate School, The Marjorie K. Unterberg School of Nursing and Health Studies, West Long Branch, NJ 07764-1898. Offers advanced practice nursing (Post-Master's Certificate); nursing (MSN); school nursing (Certificate); substance awareness coordinator (Certificate). *Accreditation:* AACN. Part-time and evening/weekend programs available. *Faculty:* 10 full-time (all women), 1 part-time/adjunct (0 women). *Students:* 5 full-time (4 women), 189 part-time (186 women); includes 26 minority (9 African Americans, 13 Asian Americans or Pacific Islanders, 4 Hispanic Americans). Average age 43. 94 applicants, 100% accepted, 44 enrolled. In 2006, 38 degrees awarded. *Entrance requirements:* For master's, GRE General Test, RN license, 1 year of work experience, minimum undergraduate GPA of 2.75. Additional exam requirements/recommendations for international students: Required—TOEFL (minimum score 550 paper-based; 213 computer-based; 79 iBT), IELTS (minimum score 5), MELAB 77, Cambridge A, B, C. *Application deadline:* For fall admission, 7/15 priority date for domestic students, 6/1 for international students; for spring admission, 11/15 priority date for domestic students, 11/1 for international students. Applications are processed on a rolling basis. Application fee: $50. Electronic applications accepted. *Expenses:* Tuition: Full-time $12,780; part-time $710 per credit. Required fees: $628; $314 per term. *Financial support:* In 2006–07, 136 fellowships (averaging $1,053 per year), 4 research assistantships (averaging $3,483 per year) were awarded; career-related internships or fieldwork, scholarships/grants, tuition waivers (partial), and unspecified assistantships also available. Support available to part-time students. Financial award application deadline: 3/1; financial award applicants required to submit FAFSA. *Faculty research:* Relationship of undergraduate GPA and GRE to succeed in a graduate nursing program. *Unit head:* Dr. Janet Mahoney, Director, 732-571-3443, Fax: 732-263-5131, E-mail: jmahoney@monmouth.edu. *Application contact:* Kevin Roane, Director, Office of Graduate Admission, 732-571-3452, Fax: 732-263-5123, E-mail: gradadm@monmouth.edu.

Montana State University, College of Graduate Studies, College of Nursing, Bozeman, MT 59717. Offers clinical nurse specialist (CNS) (MN, Post-Master's Certificate), including acute/chronic illness; family nurse practitioner (MN, Post-Master's Certificate); nursing education (Certificate). *Accreditation:* AACN. Part-time programs available. Postbaccalaureate distance learning degree programs offered (minimal on-campus study). *Faculty:* 58 full-time (53 women), 26 part-time/adjunct (25 women). *Students:* 24 full-time (20 women), 9 part-time (8 women). Average age 38. 20 applicants, 85% accepted, 12 enrolled. In 2006, 15 degrees awarded. *Degree requirements:* For master's, thesis (for some programs), comprehensive exam, registration. *Entrance requirements:* For master's, GRE General Test. Additional exam requirements/recommendations for international students: Required—TOEFL (minimum score 550 paper-based; 213 computer-based). *Application deadline:* For fall admission, 7/15 priority date for domestic students, 5/15 priority date for international students; for spring admission, 12/1 priority date for domestic students, 10/1 priority date for international students. Applications are processed on a rolling basis. Application fee: $30. Electronic applications accepted. *Expenses:* Tuition, state resident: full-time $5,113. Tuition, nonresident: full-time $12,501. *Financial support:* In 2006–07, 18 students received support, including 4 teaching assistantships with partial tuition reimbursements available (averaging $5,320 per year); institutionally sponsored loans, scholarships/grants, traineeships, tuition waivers (partial), and unspecified assistantships also available. Financial award application deadline: 3/1; financial award applicants required to submit FAFSA. *Faculty research:* Environmental health; geriatric education; enhancing rural health with clinical nurse specialists; technology and rural women with chronic illness. Total annual research expenditures: $1.4 million. *Unit head:* Dr. Elizabeth Kinion, Dean, College of Nursing, 406-994-2725, Fax: 406-994-6020, E-mail: ekinion@montana.edu.

Mountain State University, Graduate Studies, Program in Nursing, Beckley, WV 25802-9003. Offers administration/education (MSN); family nurse practitioner (MSN); nurse anesthesia (MSN); registered nurse anesthetist (Certificate). *Accreditation:* AANA/CANAEP; NLN. Part-time programs available. Postbaccalaureate distance learning degree programs offered (minimal on-campus study). *Faculty:* 6 full-time (4 women), 14 part-time/adjunct (7 women). *Students:* 80 full-time (64 women), 10 part-time (all women); includes 1 minority (African American) Average age 37. 29 applicants, 100% accepted, 17 enrolled. In 2006, 4 degrees awarded. *Median time to degree:* Master's–2 years full-time, 3 years part-time. *Degree requirements:* For master's, thesis or alternative, comprehensive exam. *Entrance requirements:* For master's, GRE. Additional exam requirements/recommendations for international students: Required—TOEFL (minimum score 550 paper-based; 213 computer-based); Recommended—IELTS (minimum score 7). *Application deadline:* For spring admission, 6/30 for domestic and international students. Applications are processed on a rolling basis. Application fee: $25 ($50 for international students). Electronic applications accepted. *Expenses: Contact institution.* Tuition and fees vary according to course load and program. *Financial support:* In 2006–07, 2 research assistantships (averaging $1,200 per year) were awarded; Federal Work-Study, scholarships/grants, and unspecified assistantships also available. Support available to part-time students. Financial award applicants required to submit FAFSA. *Unit head:* Dr. Jessica Sharp, Senior Academic Officer for Graduate Nursing, 304-929-1425, Fax: 304-929-1601, E-mail: jsharp@mountainstate.edu. *Application contact:* Melody Tilley, Program Specialist, 304-929-1576, Fax: 304-929-1601, E-mail: mtilley@mountainstate.edu.

See Close-Up on page 1965.

Mount Saint Mary College, Division of Nursing, Newburgh, NY 12550-3494. Offers adult nurse practitioner (MS), including nursing education, nursing management; clinical nurse specialist-adult health (MS), including nursing education, nursing management. *Accreditation:* AACN. Part-time and evening/weekend programs available. *Faculty:* 3 full-time (2 women), 1 (woman) part-time/adjunct. *Students:* 1 (woman) full-time, 28 part-time (26 women); includes 3 minority (2 African Americans, 1 Asian American or Pacific Islander). Average age 42. 12 applicants, 100% accepted, 10 enrolled. In 2006, 6 degrees awarded. *Degree requirements:* For master's, research utilization project. *Entrance requirements:* For master's, BSN, minimum GPA of 3.0, RN license. *Application deadline:* For fall admission, 6/3 priority date for domestic students; for spring admission, 10/31 priority date for domestic students. Applications are processed on a rolling basis. Application fee: $35. *Expenses:* Tuition: Full-time $11,880; part-time $660 per credit. *Financial support:* Unspecified assistantships and nursing lab assistant available. Financial award application deadline: 3/15; financial award applicants required to submit FAFSA. *Unit head:* Dr. Karen Baldwin, Coordinator, 845-569-3512, Fax: 845-562-6762, E-mail: baldwin@msmc.edu.

Murray State University, College of Health Sciences and Human Services, Program in Nursing, Murray, KY 42071. Offers clinical nurse specialist (MSN); family nurse practitioner (MSN); nurse anesthesia (MSN). *Accreditation:* AACN; AANA/CANAEP. *Faculty:* 8 full-time (7 women). *Students:* 37 full-time (30 women), 7 part-time (6 women); includes 2 minority (1 African American, 1 Hispanic American). 85 applicants, 35% accepted, 21 enrolled. In 2006, 22 degrees awarded. *Degree requirements:* For master's, research project. *Entrance requirements:* For master's, GRE General Test, BSN, interview, RN licensure. Additional exam requirements/recommendations for international students: Required—TOEFL (minimum score 550 paper-based). *Application deadline:* For fall admission, 3/1 for domestic students, 4/15 for international students. Application fee: $30. *Financial support:* Traineeships available. Financial award application deadline: 4/1. *Faculty research:* Fibromyalgis, primary care, rural health. *Unit head:* Dr. Nancey E. M. France, Graduate Coordinator and Professor, 270-809-6671, Fax: 270-809-6662, E-mail: nancey.france@murraystate.edu.

New York University, College of Dentistry, College of Nursing, Programs in Advanced Practice Nursing, New York, NY 10012-1019. Offers advanced practice nursing: adult acute care (MS, Advanced Certificate); advanced practice nursing: adult primary care (MS, Advanced Certificate); advanced practice nursing: adult primary care/geriatrics (MS); advanced practice nursing: children with special needs (Advanced Certificate); advanced practice nursing: geriatrics (MS, Advanced Certificate); advanced practice nursing: holistic nursing (MS, Advanced Certificate); advanced practice nursing: home health nursing (Advanced Certificate); advanced practice nursing: mental health (MS); advanced practice nursing: mental health nursing (Advanced Certificate); advanced practice nursing: pediatrics (MS, Advanced Certificate); advanced practice nursing: pediatrics/children with special needs (MS); midwifery (MS, Advanced Certificate); nursing administration (MS, Advanced Certificate); nursing education (MS, Advanced Certificate); nursing informatics (MS, Advanced Certificate); palliative care (MS, Advanced Certificate); MS/MS. *Accreditation:* AACN; ACNM/DOA. Part-time and evening/weekend programs available. *Faculty:* 30 full-time (all women). *Students:* 10 full-time (all women), 428 part-time (395 women); includes 166 minority (73 African Americans, 72 Asian Americans or Pacific Islanders, 21 Hispanic Americans). Average age 35. 154 applicants, 93% accepted, 118 enrolled. In 2006, 100 master's, 7 Advanced Certificates awarded. *Degree requirements:* For master's, thesis (for some programs). *Entrance requirements:* For master's, BS in nursing, AS in nursing with another BS/BA degree; for Advanced Certificate, master's degree. Additional exam requirements/recommendations for international students: Required—TOEFL. *Application deadline:* For fall admission, 7/1 priority date for domestic students, 7/1 for international students; for spring admission, 12/1 for domestic and international students. Applications are processed on a rolling basis. Application fee: $65. *Expenses:* Tuition: Part-time $1,080 per unit. Required fees: $56 per unit. $329 per term. Tuition and fees vary according to program. *Financial support:* Career-related internships or fieldwork, Federal Work-Study, institutionally sponsored loans, scholarships/grants, and tuition waivers (partial) available. Support available to part-time students. Financial award application deadline: 2/1; financial award applicants required to submit FAFSA. *Faculty research:* Elderly black diabetics, families and illness, public health nursing, parent-child nursing, health policy costs. *Unit head:* Dr. Judith Haber, Associate Dean for Graduate Programs, 212-998-5300, Fax: 212-995-3143. *Application contact:* Amy Knowles, Assistant Dean for Student Affairs and Admissions, 212-998-5333, Fax: 212-995-4302, E-mail: ak96@nyu.edu.

Northeastern University, Bouvé College of Health Sciences Graduate School, School of Nursing, Program in Primary Care Nursing, Boston, MA 02115-5096. Offers MS, CAS. *Accreditation:* AACN. *Students:* 31 full-time (27 women), 22 part-time (20 women). Average age 39. 17 applicants, 76% accepted. In 2006, 29 degrees awarded. *Entrance requirements:* For master's, GRE General Test, minimum GPA of 3.0, previous course work in statistics, 1-2 years of nursing experience, RN license; for CAS, MS in nursing. *Application deadline:* For fall admission, 4/1 priority date for domestic students; for spring admission, 2/1 for domestic students. Applications are processed on a rolling basis. Application fee: $50. *Financial support:* Research assistantships, teaching assistantships, tuition waivers (partial) available. Financial award application deadline: 7/1; financial award applicants required to submit FAFSA. *Faculty research:* Pediatric witness to violence. *Unit head:* Dr. Susan Jo Roberts, Director, 617-373-3130, Fax: 617-373-3050, E-mail: s.roberts@neu.edu. *Application contact:* Margaret Schnabel, Director of Graduate Admissions, 617-373-2708, Fax: 617-373-4704, E-mail: bouvegrad@neu.edu.

Northern Kentucky University, Office of Graduate Programs, School of Nursing and Health Professions, Highland Heights, KY 41099. Offers nurse practitioner advancement (Certificate); nursing (MSN, Post-Master's Certificate). Part-time and evening/weekend programs available. Postbaccalaureate distance learning degree programs offered (no on-campus study). *Students:* 25 full-time (24 women), 111 part-time (105 women); includes 6 minority (2 African Americans, 4 Asian Americans or Pacific Islanders). Average age 37. 58 applicants, 83% accepted, 42 enrolled. In 2006, 30 degrees awarded. *Entrance requirements:* For master's, GRE. Additional exam requirements/recommendations for international students: Required—TOEFL (minimum score 550 paper-based; 213 computer-based; 79 iBT), Michigan (must be taken at NKU). *Expenses:* Tuition, state resident: full-time $5,274; part-time $293 per hour. Tuition, nonresident: full-time $10,314; part-time $573 per hour. Tuition and fees vary according to course load, program and reciprocity agreements. *Financial support:* In 2006–07, 48 students received support. Unspecified assistantships available. *Unit head:* Dr. Margaret M. Anderson, Chair, Nursing and Health Professions, 859-572-5248, Fax: 859-572-1934, E-mail: andersonm@nku.edu. *Application contact:* Dr. Peg Griffin, Director of Graduate Programs, 859-572-1555, Fax: 859-572-6670, E-mail: gradprog@nku.edu.

North Georgia College & State University, Graduate Studies, Department of Nursing, Dahlonega, GA 30597. Offers family nurse practitioner (MSN); nursing education (MSN). *Accreditation:* NLN. Part-time programs available. *Faculty:* 5 full-time (all women), 1 (woman) part-time/adjunct. *Students:* 62; includes 5 minority (2 African Americans, 1 American Indian/Alaska Native, 2 Asian Americans or Pacific Islanders). Average age 32. 7 applicants, 29% accepted. In 2006, 12 degrees awarded. *Degree requirements:* For master's, one foreign language, thesis, comprehensive exam. *Entrance requirements:* For master's, GRE General Test or MAT, minimum GPA of 2.75, 3 letters of recommendation, current Georgia RN license, 1 year of post-licensure work, BSN. *Application deadline:* Applications are processed on a rolling basis. Application fee: $25. Electronic applications accepted. *Expenses:* Tuition, state resident: full-time $3,044; part-time $127 per credit hour. Tuition, nonresident: full-time $12,172; part-time $508 per credit hour. Required fees: $892; $458 per semester. *Financial support:* Career-related internships or fieldwork available. Support available to part-time students. Financial award application deadline: 5/1. *Unit head:* Dr. Toni Barnett, Department Head, 706-864-1934, Fax: 706-864-1845, E-mail: tbarnett@ngcsu.edu. *Application contact:* Dr. Donna A. Gessell, Director of Graduate Studies and External Programs, 706-864-1528, Fax: 706-867-2795, E-mail: dgessell@ngcsu.edu.

Oakland University, Graduate Study and Lifelong Learning, School of Nursing, Doctor of Nursing Practice Program, Rochester, MI 48309-4401. Offers DNP. *Students:* 4 full-time (3 women). Average age 51. 33 applicants, 36% accepted, 4 enrolled. *Expenses:* Tuition, state resident: full-time $9,936; part-time $414 per credit. Tuition, nonresident: full-time $17,202; part-time $716 per credit. *Application contact:* Mary Bray, Graduate Program Coordinator, 248-370-4482.

Oakland University, Graduate Study and Lifelong Learning, School of Nursing, Program in Family Nurse Practitioner, Rochester, MI 48309-4401. Offers MSN, Certificate. *Accreditation:* AACN. *Students:* 10 full-time (9 women), 37 part-time (36 women); includes 10 minority (7 African Americans, 2 Asian Americans or Pacific Islanders, 1 Hispanic American). Average age 36. 20 applicants, 65% accepted, 9 enrolled. In 2006, 10 master's, 1 other advanced degree awarded. *Degree requirements:* For master's, thesis. *Entrance requirements:* For master's, GRE General Test, minimum GPA of 3.0 for unconditional admission. Additional exam requirements/recommendations for international students: Required—TOEFL (minimum score 550 paper-based; 213 computer-based). *Application deadline:* For fall admission, 8/1 for domestic students, 5/1 priority date for international students; for winter admission, 11/15 for domestic students, 9/1 priority date for international students. Applications are processed on a rolling basis. Application fee: $35. Electronic applications accepted. *Expenses: Contact institution. Financial support:* Federal Work-Study, institutionally sponsored loans, and tuition waivers (full) available. Financial award application deadline: 3/1; financial award applicants required to submit FAFSA. *Unit head:* Mary Bray, Graduate Program Coordinator, 248-370-4482.

Oregon Health & Science University, School of Nursing, Program in Primary Health Care, Portland, OR 97239-3098. Offers adult nurse practitioner (MS, Post Master's Certificate); family nurse practitioner (MS, Post Master's Certificate); geriatric nurse practitioner (Post Master's Certificate); geriatric/adult nurse practitioner (MS); pediatric nurse practitioner (MS, Post Master's Certificate). *Accreditation:* AACN. *Degree requirements:* For master's, thesis optional. *Entrance requirements:* For master's, GRE General Test, bachelor's degree in nursing, minimum undergraduate GPA of 3.0, previous course work in statistics; for Post Master's Certificate, master's degree in nursing.

Oregon Health & Science University, School of Nursing, Women's Health Care Nurse Practitioner Program, Portland, OR 97239-3098. Offers MS, Post Master's Certificate. *Accreditation:* AACN. *Degree requirements:* For master's, thesis optional. *Entrance requirements:* For master's, GRE General Test, bachelor's degree in nursing, minimum undergraduate GPA of 3.0, previous course work in statistics; for Post Master's Certificate, master's degree in nursing.

Otterbein College, Department of Nursing, Westerville, OH 43081. Offers adult nurse practitioner (MSN, Certificate); clinical nurse leader (MSN); family nurse practitioner (MSN, Certificate); nurse service administration (MSN). *Accreditation:* AACN; NLN. Part-time and evening/weekend programs available. Postbaccalaureate distance learning degree programs offered (minimal on-campus study). *Students:* 7 full-time, 118 part-time; includes 5 minority (4 African Americans, 1 Hispanic American). Average age 40. 47 applicants, 94% accepted, 33 enrolled. In 2006, 37 degrees awarded. *Degree requirements:* For master's, thesis (for some programs), comprehensive exam (for some programs). *Entrance requirements:* For master's and Certificate, official transcripts, 2 reference forms, essay, resumé. Additional exam requirements/recommendations for international students: Required—TOEFL (minimum score 550 paper-based; 213 computer-based; 79 iBT). *Application deadline:* For fall admission, 8/10 priority date for domestic students, 7/10 for international students; for winter admission, 12/7 priority date for domestic students, 11/7 for international students; for spring admission, 2/28 priority date for domestic students, 1/31 for international students. Applications are processed on a rolling basis. *Expenses:* Tuition: Full-time $7,560; part-time $315 per credit. Tuition and fees vary according to program. *Financial support:* Traineeships available. Support available to part-time students. Financial award applicants required to submit FAFSA. *Faculty research:* Patient education, women's health, trauma curriculum development, administration. *Unit head:* Dr. Barbara Schaffner, Chair, 614-823-1735, Fax: 614-823-3131, E-mail: bschaffner@otterbein.edu. *Application contact:* Vicki Miller, Administrative Assistant, Office of Graduate Programs, 614-823-3210, Fax: 614-823-3208, E-mail: grad@otterbein.edu.

Pacific Lutheran University, Division of Graduate Studies, School of Nursing, Program in Family Nurse Practitioner, Tacoma, WA 98447. Offers MSN. *Accreditation:* AACN. Part-time and evening/weekend programs available. *Faculty:* 4 full-time (3 women), 3 part-time/adjunct (1 woman). *Students:* 2 full-time (both women). Average age 31. 2 applicants, 100% accepted, 2 enrolled. In 2006, 21 degrees awarded. *Degree requirements:* For master's, thesis or alternative, registration. *Entrance requirements:* For master's, GRE General Test, minimum undergraduate GPA of 3.0. Additional exam requirements/recommendations for international students: Required—TOEFL (minimum score 550 paper-based; 213 computer-based). *Application deadline:* For fall admission, 4/1 priority date for domestic students. Applications are processed on a rolling basis. Application fee: $40. *Expenses:* Tuition: Full-time $17,544. Part-time tuition and fees vary according to program. *Financial support:* Federal Work-Study, scholarships/grants, and unspecified assistantships available. Financial award application deadline: 3/1. *Unit head:* Dr. Ruth Schaffler, Unit Head, 253-535-7680. *Application contact:* Linda DuBay, Senior Office Assistant, 253-535-7151, Fax: 253-536-5136, E-mail: admissions@plu.edu.

Prairie View A&M University, Graduate School, College of Nursing, Houston, TX 77030. Offers family nurse practitioner (MSN); nursing administration (MSN); nursing education (MSN). *Accreditation:* AACN; NLN. Part-time programs available. *Faculty:* 3 full-time (all women), 4 part-time/adjunct (3 women). *Students:* 18 full-time (16 women), 59 part-time (51 women); includes 71 minority (62 African Americans, 5 Asian Americans or Pacific Islanders, 4 Hispanic Americans). Average age 38. 37 applicants, 100% accepted, 32 enrolled. In 2006, 7 degrees awarded. *Median time to degree:* Master's–1.5 years full-time, 2.5 years part-time. *Degree requirements:* For master's, thesis, comprehensive exam. *Entrance requirements:* For master's, MAT or GRE, BS in nursing; 2 years of experience as a registered nurse; 1 course each in statistics, basic health and assessment. *Application deadline:* For fall admission, 6/1 priority date for domestic students; for spring admission, 11/1 priority date for domestic students. Applications are processed on a rolling basis. Application fee: $50. *Financial support:* In 2006–07, 17 students received support. Career-related internships or fieldwork, Federal Work-Study, institutionally sponsored loans, scholarships/grants, and traineeships available. Support available to part-time students. Financial award application deadline: 4/1; financial award applicants required to submit FAFSA. *Faculty research:* Software development and violence prevention, health promotion and prevention. Total annual research expenditures: $350,000. *Unit head:* Dr. Betty N. Adams, Dean, 713-797-7009, Fax: 713-797-7013, E-mail: bnadams@pvamu.edu. *Application contact:* Dr. Pamela C. Willson, Associate Professor, 713-797-7011, Fax: 713-797-7012, E-mail: pcwillson@pvamu.edu.

Quinnipiac University, School of Health Sciences, Family Nurse Practitioner Track, Hamden, CT 06518-1940. Offers MSN; Post Master's Certificate. *Accreditation:* NLN. *Expenses:* Tuition: Part-time $675 per credit. Required fees: $30 per credit. *Unit head:* Dr. Jeanne LeVasseur, Director of Graduate Nursing, 203-582-3484.

See Close-Up on page 1721.

Regis College, Department of Nursing, Weston, MA 02493. Offers nurse educator (Certificate); nurse practitioner (Certificate); nursing (MS). *Accreditation:* NLN. Part-time and evening/weekend programs available. *Faculty:* 14 full-time (13 women), 18 part-time/adjunct (15 women). *Students:* 157 full-time (142 women), 176 part-time (166 women); includes 49 minority (35 African Americans, 1 American Indian/Alaska Native, 9 Asian Americans or Pacific Islanders, 4 Hispanic Americans). Average age 36. 167 applicants, 83% accepted, 139 enrolled. In 2006, 45 master's, 13 other advanced degrees awarded. *Degree requirements:* For master's, thesis. *Entrance requirements:* For master's, GRE General Test or MAT, minimum GPA of 3.0. *Application deadline:* Applications are processed on a rolling basis. Application fee: $50. Electronic applications accepted. *Expenses:* Tuition: Full-time $23,680; part-time $665 per credit hour. *Financial support:* In 2006–07, 31 students received support, including 8 research assistantships (averaging $35,000 per year); Federal Work-Study, scholarships/grants, traineeships, and unspecified assistantships also available. Support available to part-time students. Financial award applicants required to submit FAFSA. *Faculty research:* Health policy, education, aging, job satisfaction, psychiatric nursing, critical thinking. *Unit head:* Dr. Antoinette Hays, Dean, School of Nursing and Health Professions, 781-768-7091, Fax: 781-768-8339, E-mail: antoinette.hays@regiscollege.edu.

Research College of Nursing, Nursing Program, Kansas City, MO 64132. Offers executive nurse practitioner (MSN); family nurse practitioner (MSN); nursing education (MSN). *Accreditation:* AACN. Part-time programs available. Postbaccalaureate distance learning degree programs offered (no on-campus study). *Faculty:* 11 full-time (all women). *Students:* Average age 30. In 2006, 6 degrees awarded. *Degree requirements:* For master's, research project. *Entrance requirements:* For master's, minimum GPA of 3.0, interview, 3 letters of recommendation. Additional exam requirements/recommendations for international students: Required—TOEFL (minimum score 550 paper-based; 213 computer-based), TWE. *Application deadline:* For spring admission, 10/1 priority date for domestic students. Applications are processed on a rolling basis. Application fee: $50. *Expenses:* Tuition: Part-time $350 per credit hour. *Financial support:* Applicants required to submit FAFSA. *Unit head:* Dr. Nancy O. De Basio, President and Dean, 816-995-2815, Fax: 816-995-2817, E-mail: nancy.debasio@researchcollege.edu. *Application contact:* Leslie Ann Mendenhall, Director of Transfer and Graduate Recruitment, 816-995-2820, Fax: 816-995-2813, E-mail: leslie.mendenhall@researchcollege.edu.

Rush University, College of Nursing, Department of Adult Health Nursing, Chicago, IL 60612-3832. Offers acute care nurse practitioner (MSN, Post-Master's Certificate); adult health nursing (DN Sc, DNP); adult nurse practitioner (MSN, Post-Master's Certificate); adult/gerontological nurse practitioner (MSN); anesthesia nurse practitioner (MSN, Post-Master's Certificate); critical care clinical specialist (MSN); gerontological nurse practitioner (MSN, Post-Master's Certificate); medical surgical clinical specialist (MSN). *Accreditation:* AACN; AANA/CANAEP (one or more programs are accredited). Part-time programs available. Postbaccalaureate distance learning degree programs offered (minimal on-campus study). *Faculty:* 33. *Students:* 29 full-time, 123 part-time; includes 22 minority (7 African Americans, 9 Asian Americans or Pacific Islanders, 6 Hispanic Americans). Average age 35. 101 applicants, 80% accepted, 76 enrolled. In 2006, 47 master's, 6 doctorates awarded. Terminal master's awarded for partial completion of doctoral program. *Degree requirements:* For master's, capstone project; for doctorate, thesis/dissertation, DNP leadership project. *Entrance requirements:* For master's, GRE General Test (waived if nursing GPA is above 3.0 or cumulative GPA is above 3.25), interview; for doctorate, GRE General Test, interview, course work in statistics (DN Sc). Additional exam requirements/recommendations for international students: Required—TOEFL, TWE. *Application deadline:* For fall admission, 7/1 for domestic students; for winter admission, 11/1 for domestic students; for spring admission, 1/15 for domestic students. Applications are processed on a rolling basis. Application fee: $40. Electronic applications accepted. *Financial support:* In 2006–07, 19 students received support; teaching assistantships with tuition reimbursements available, Federal Work-Study, institutionally sponsored loans, scholarships/grants, and traineeships available. Support available to part-time students. Financial award application deadline: 5/1; financial award applicants required to submit FAFSA. *Faculty research:* Complementary/alternative medicine, critical care outcomes, cardiac risk reduction, Alzheimer's Disease, telehealth monitoring. *Unit head:* Dr. Margaret Faut-Callahan, Chairperson, 312-942-7117. *Application contact:* Hicela Castruita Woods, Director, College Admissions Services, 312-942-7100, Fax: 312-942-2219, E-mail: hicela_castruita@rush.edu.

Rush University, College of Nursing, Department of Community and Mental Health Nursing, Chicago, IL 60612-3832. Offers community and mental health nursing (DN Sc, DNP); family nurse practitioner (MSN, Post-Master's Certificate); psychiatric clinical specialist (MSN); psychiatric nurse practitioner—adult (MSN); psychiatric nurse practitioner—family (MSN); psychiatric-mental health clinical specialist (Post-Master's Certificate); psychiatric-mental health nurse practitioner (Post-Master's Certificate); public health nursing (MSN). *Accreditation:* AACN. Part-time programs available. Postbaccalaureate distance learning degree programs offered (minimal on-campus study). *Faculty:* 26. *Students:* 68 (65 women); includes 11 minority (6 African Americans, 4 Asian Americans or Pacific Islanders, 1 Hispanic American). Average age 35. 30 applicants, 93% accepted, 27 enrolled. In 2006, 1 master's, 13 doctorates awarded. Terminal master's awarded for partial completion of doctoral program. *Degree requirements:* For master's, capstone project; for doctorate, thesis/dissertation, DNP leadership project. *Entrance requirements:* For master's, GRE General Test (waived if nursing GPA is above 3.0 or cumulative GPA is above 3.25), interview; for doctorate, GRE General Test, interview, course work in statistics (DN Sc). *Application deadline:* For fall admission, 7/1 for domestic students; for winter admission, 11/1 for domestic students; for spring admission, 1/15 for domestic students. Applications are processed on a rolling basis. Application fee: $40. Electronic applications accepted. *Financial support:* In 2006–07, 11 students received support; teaching assistantships with tuition reimbursements available, Federal Work-Study, institutionally sponsored loans, scholarships/grants, and traineeships available. Support available to part-time students. Financial award applicants required to submit FAFSA. *Faculty research:* Immigrant mental health, de-escalation strategies, caregiver interventions, parent-teacher training, restraint use. *Unit head:* Dr. Julia Cowell, Chairperson, 312-942-7117. *Application contact:* Hicela Castruita Woods, Director, College Admissions Services, 312-942-7100, Fax: 312-942-2219, E-mail: hicela_castruita@rush.edu.

Rush University, College of Nursing, Department of Women's and Children's Health Nursing, Chicago, IL 60612-3832. Offers neonatal nurse practitioner (MSN, Post-Master's Certificate); pediatric acute/chronic care nurse practitioner (MSN); pediatric clinical nurse specialist (MSN); pediatric nurse practitioner (MSN, Post-Master's Certificate); women's and children's health nursing (DN Sc, DNP). *Accreditation:* AACN. Part-time programs available. Postbaccalaureate distance learning degree programs offered (minimal on-campus study). *Faculty:* 14. *Students:* 10 full-time, 75 part-time; includes 9 minority (3 African Americans, 4 Asian Americans or Pacific Islanders, 2 Hispanic Americans). Average age 35. 32 applicants, 94% accepted, 28 enrolled. In 2006, 14 master's, 5 doctorates awarded. Terminal master's awarded for partial completion of doctoral program. *Degree requirements:* For master's, capstone project; for doctorate, thesis/dissertation, DNP leadership project. *Entrance requirements:* For master's, GRE General Test (waived if nursing GPA is above 3.0 or cumulative GPA is above 3.25), interview; for doctorate, GRE General Test, interview, course work in statistics (DN Sc). Additional exam requirements/recommendations for international students: Required—TOEFL, TWE. *Application deadline:* For fall admission, 7/1 for domestic students; for winter admission, 11/1 for domestic students; for spring admission, 1/15 for domestic students. Applications are processed on a rolling basis. Application fee: $40. Electronic applications accepted. *Financial support:* In 2006–07, 16 students received support; teaching assistantships with tuition reimbursements available, Federal Work-Study, institutionally sponsored loans, scholarships/grants, and traineeships available. Support available to part-time students. Financial award applicants required to submit FAFSA. *Faculty research:* Family-centered care, women's health, health outcomes of human milk feeding for VhBW infants. *Unit head:* Dr. Deborah Gross, Chairperson, 312-942-7117. *Application contact:* Hicela Castruita Woods, Director, College Admissions Services, 312-942-7100, Fax: 312-942-2219, E-mail: hicela_castruita@rush.edu.

Rutgers, The State University of New Jersey, Newark, Graduate School, Program in Nursing, Newark, NJ 07102. Offers nursing (MS), including acute care of adults and aged, advanced practice in pediatric nursing, advanced practice with childbearing families, community health nursing, family nurse practitioner, primary care of adults and aged, psychiatric/mental health nursing. *Accreditation:* AACN. Part-time programs available. *Faculty:* 33 full-time (32 women). *Students:* 11 full-time (all women), 186 part-time (175 women); includes 70 minority (28 African Americans, 30 Asian Americans or Pacific Islanders, 12 Hispanic Americans). 255 applicants, 58% accepted, 72 enrolled. In 2006, 40 master's awarded. *Degree requirements:* For master's, comprehensive exam. *Entrance requirements:* For master's, GRE General Test, RN license, minimum B average, BS in nursing. Additional exam requirements/recommendations for international students: Required—TOEFL. *Application deadline:* For fall admission, 2/15 for domestic students; for spring admission, 12/1 for domestic students. Applications are processed on a rolling basis. Application fee: $50. Electronic applications accepted. *Financial support:* In 2006–07, 3 fellowships (averaging $8,000 per year) were awarded; teaching assistantships with full tuition reimbursements, career-related internships or fieldwork, Federal Work-Study, institutionally sponsored loans, scholarships/grants, traineeships, and tuition waivers (full and partial) also available. Financial award application deadline: 4/15. *Faculty research:* HIV/AIDS, quality of life—MS and breast cancer, sleep patterns of cardiac patients. *Unit head:* Dr. Wendy Nehring, Program Director, 973-353-5293 Ext. 606, Fax: 973-353-1277, E-mail: nehring@nightingale.rutgers.edu. *Application contact:* Dr. Linda Scheetz, Associate Dean for Student Life and Services, 973-353-5060 Ext. 611, Fax: 973-353-1277, E-mail: lscheetz@andromeda.rutgers.edu.

Sacred Heart University, Graduate Studies, College of Education and Health Professions, Faculty of Nursing, Fairfield, CT 06825-1000. Offers clinical nurse leader (MSN); family nurse practitioner (MSN); patient care services administration (MSN); MSN/MBA. *Accreditation:* AACN. Part-time and evening/weekend programs available. Postbaccalaureate distance learn-

Family Nurse Practitioner Studies

Sacred Heart University (continued)
ing degree programs offered (minimal on-campus study). *Faculty:* 12 full-time (all women). *Students:* 6 full-time (all women), 64 part-time (59 women); includes 11 minority (7 African Americans, 1 Asian American or Pacific Islander, 3 Hispanic Americans). Average age 39. 34 applicants, 94% accepted, 26 enrolled. In 2006, 10 degrees awarded. *Entrance requirements:* For master's, BSN, minimum GPA of 3.0. Additional exam requirements/recommendations for international students: Required—TOEFL (minimum score 550 paper-based; 213 computer-based). *Application deadline:* Applications are processed on a rolling basis. Application fee: $50 ($100 for international students). Electronic applications accepted. *Expenses:* Contact institution. Full-time tuition and fees vary according to degree level and program. *Financial support:* Career-related internships or fieldwork, institutionally sponsored loans, and unspecified assistantships available. Support available to part-time students. Financial award applicants required to submit FAFSA. *Unit head:* Dr. Dori Sullivan, Director, Graduate Program in Nursing, 203-371-7715. *Application contact:* Kathy Dilks, Assistant Dean of Graduate Admissions, Health Professions, 203-396-8259, Fax: 203-365-4732, E-mail: gradstudies@sacredheart.edu.

Sage Graduate School, Graduate School, Division of Nursing, Program in Adult Nurse Practitioner, Troy, NY 12180-4115. Offers MS, Post Master's Certificate. *Accreditation:* AACN. Part-time and evening/weekend programs available. *Faculty:* 8 full-time (all women), 3 part-time/adjunct (all women). *Students:* 13 full-time (11 women), 20 part-time (all women); includes 1 minority (Asian American or Pacific Islander) Average age 42. 25 applicants, 76% accepted, 7 enrolled. In 2006, 9 master's, 10 other advanced degrees awarded. *Degree requirements:* For master's, thesis or alternative. *Entrance requirements:* Additional exam requirements/recommendations for international students: Required—TOEFL (minimum score 550 paper-based; 213 computer-based). *Application deadline:* Applications are processed on a rolling basis. Application fee: $40. *Expenses:* Tuition: Full-time $9,270; part-time $515 per credit hour. *Financial support:* Career-related internships or fieldwork, scholarships/grants, and unspecified assistantships available. Support available to part-time students. Financial award application deadline: 3/1; financial award applicants required to submit FAFSA. *Unit head:* Arlene Pericak, Director, 518-244-2012, E-mail: perica@sage.edu. *Application contact:* Shannon K. Easton, Director of Graduate and Adult Admission, 518-244-2443, Fax: 518-244-6880, E-mail: sgsadm@sage.edu.

Sage Graduate School, Graduate School, Division of Nursing, Program in Family Nurse Practitioner, Troy, NY 12180-4115. Offers MS, Post Master's Certificate. *Accreditation:* AACN. Part-time and evening/weekend programs available. *Faculty:* 8 full-time (all women), 3 part-time/adjunct (all women). *Students:* 12 full-time (10 women), 14 part-time (13 women); includes 2 minority (1 African American, 1 Asian American or Pacific Islander). Average age 36. 16 applicants, 100% accepted, 12 enrolled. In 2006, 11 master's, 1 other advanced degree awarded. *Degree requirements:* For master's, thesis or alternative. *Entrance requirements:* For master's, BS in nursing, minimum GPA of 2.75. Additional exam requirements/recommendations for international students: Required—TOEFL (minimum score 550 paper-based; 213 computer-based). *Application deadline:* Applications are processed on a rolling basis. Application fee: $40. *Expenses:* Tuition: Full-time $9,270; part-time $515 per credit hour. *Financial support:* Career-related internships or fieldwork, scholarships/grants, and unspecified assistantships available. Support available to part-time students. Financial award application deadline: 3/1; financial award applicants required to submit FAFSA. *Unit head:* Arlene Pericak, Director, 518-244-2012, E-mail: perica@sage.edu. *Application contact:* Shannon K. Easton, Director of Graduate and Adult Admission, 518-244-2443, Fax: 518-244-6880, E-mail: sgsadm@sage.edu.

Sage Graduate School, Graduate School, Division of Nursing, Program in Psychiatric Mental Health Nurse Practitioner, Troy, NY 12180-4115. Offers psychiatric mental health (MS). *Accreditation:* AACN. Part-time and evening/weekend programs available. *Faculty:* 8 full-time (all women), 3 part-time/adjunct (all women). *Students:* 6 full-time (all women), 7 part-time (all women); includes 2 minority (1 African American, 1 American Indian/Alaska Native). Average age 39. 10 applicants, 90% accepted, 7 enrolled. In 2006, 7 degrees awarded. *Degree requirements:* For master's, thesis or alternative. *Entrance requirements:* For master's, BS in nursing, minimum GPA of 2.75. Additional exam requirements/recommendations for international students: Required—TOEFL (minimum score 550 paper-based; 213 computer-based). *Application deadline:* Applications are processed on a rolling basis. Application fee: $40. *Expenses:* Tuition: Full-time $9,270; part-time $515 per credit hour. *Financial support:* Career-related internships or fieldwork, scholarships/grants, and unspecified assistantships available. Support available to part-time students. Financial award application deadline: 3/1; financial award applicants required to submit FAFSA. *Unit head:* Arlene Pericak, Director, 518-244-2012, E-mail: perica@sage.edu. *Application contact:* Shannon K. Easton, Director of Graduate and Adult Admission, 518-244-2443, Fax: 518-244-6880, E-mail: sgsadm@sage.edu.

Saginaw Valley State University, Crystal M. Lange College of Nursing and Health Sciences, Program in Clinical Nurse Specialist, University Center, MI 48710. Offers MSN. *Accreditation:* AACN. Part-time and evening/weekend programs available. *Students:* 3 full-time (all women), 11 part-time (all women). Average age 38. 2 applicants, 100% accepted, 2 enrolled. *Degree requirements:* For master's, thesis optional. *Entrance requirements:* For master's, GRE. Additional exam requirements/recommendations for international students: Required—TOEFL. *Application deadline:* Applications are processed on a rolling basis. Application fee: $25. Electronic applications accepted. *Expenses:* Tuition, state resident: full-time $7,225; part-time $301 per credit hour. Tuition, nonresident: full-time $13,888; part-time $579 per credit hour. Required fees: $330; $14 per credit hour. Tuition and fees vary according to course load. *Financial support:* Fellowships with partial tuition reimbursements, research assistantships with full tuition reimbursements, Federal Work-Study available. Support available to part-time students. Financial award application deadline: 4/1; financial award applicants required to submit FAFSA. *Unit head:* Dr. Margaret Flatt, Assistant Dean, 989-964-4130, Fax: 989-964-4024, E-mail: flatt@svsu.edu.

Saginaw Valley State University, Crystal M. Lange College of Nursing and Health Sciences, Program in Nurse Practitioner, University Center, MI 48710. Offers MSN. *Accreditation:* AACN. Part-time and evening/weekend programs available. *Students:* 2 full-time (both women), 17 part-time (all women); includes 3 minority (1 African American, 1 Asian American or Pacific Islander, 1 Hispanic American). Average age 36. 5 applicants, 100% accepted, 5 enrolled. In 2006, 1 degree awarded. *Degree requirements:* For master's, thesis optional. *Entrance requirements:* For master's, GRE. Additional exam requirements/recommendations for international students: Required—TOEFL. *Application deadline:* Applications are processed on a rolling basis. Application fee: $25. Electronic applications accepted. *Expenses:* Tuition, state resident: full-time $7,225; part-time $301 per credit hour. Tuition, nonresident: full-time $13,888; part-time $579 per credit hour. Required fees: $330; $14 per credit hour. Tuition and fees vary according to course load. *Financial support:* Fellowships with partial tuition reimbursements, research assistantships with full tuition reimbursements, Federal Work-Study available. Support available to part-time students. Financial award application deadline: 4/1; financial award applicants required to submit FAFSA. *Unit head:* Dr. Margaret Flatt, Assistant Dean, 989-964-4130, Fax: 989-964-4024, E-mail: flatt@svsu.edu.

Saint Francis Medical Center College of Nursing, Graduate Program, Peoria, IL 61603-3783. Offers child and family nursing (MSN); medical-surgical nursing (MSN); nurse clinician (Post-Graduate Certificate); nurse educator (Post-Graduate Certificate). *Accreditation:* NLN. Part-time programs available. Postbaccalaureate distance learning degree programs offered (minimal on-campus study). *Faculty:* 1 (woman) full-time, 5 part-time/adjunct (all women). *Students:* 3 full-time (all women), 74 part-time (69 women); includes 5 minority (1 Asian American or Pacific Islander, 4 Hispanic Americans). Average age 28. 23 applicants, 100% accepted, 19 enrolled. In 2006, 5 degrees awarded. *Degree requirements:* For master's, research experience, portfolio, practicum. *Entrance requirements:* For master's, nursing research, health assessment, graduate course work in statistics, RN license. Additional exam requirements/recommendations for international students: Required—TOEFL. *Application deadline:* For fall admission, 6/1 priority date for domestic and international students; for spring admission, 11/15 priority date for domestic and international students. Applications are processed on a rolling basis. Application fee: $50. Electronic applications accepted. *Expenses:* Tuition: Part-time $440 per semester hour. Required fees: $130. *Financial support:* In 2006–07, 1 student received support. Application deadline: 6/15; *Faculty research:* Outcome and curriculum planning, health promotion, NCLEX-RN results, decision making program evaluation. *Unit head:* Dr. Lois J. Hamilton, Dean, 309-655-2201, Fax: 309-624-8973, E-mail: lois.j.hamilton@osfhealthcare.org. *Application contact:* Dr. Janice F. Boundy, Associate Dean Graduate Program, 309-655-2230, Fax: 309-624-8973, E-mail: jan.f.boundy@osfhealthcare.org.

St. John Fisher College, Office of the Provost, Wegmans School of Nursing, Advanced Practice Nursing Program, Rochester, NY 14618-3597. Offers advanced practice nursing (MS); clinical nurse specialist (Certificate); family nurse practitioner (Certificate); nurse educator (Certificate). *Accreditation:* AACN. Part-time and evening/weekend programs available. *Faculty:* 9 full-time (all women), 1 part-time/adjunct (0 women). *Students:* 4 full-time (all women), 72 part-time (70 women); includes 3 African Americans, 1 Asian American or Pacific Islander. Average age 40. 34 applicants, 91% accepted, 26 enrolled. In 2006, 15 degrees awarded. *Degree requirements:* For master's, clinical practice, master's project; for Certificate, clinical practice. *Entrance requirements:* For master's, BSN; minimum GPA of 3.0; undergraduate course work in statistics, health assessment, and nursing research; current New York RN license. Additional exam requirements/recommendations for international students: Required—TOEFL (minimum score 575 paper-based; 233 computer-based; 80 iBT). *Application deadline:* For fall admission, 7/1 for domestic students; for spring admission, 10/30 for domestic students. Applications are processed on a rolling basis. Application fee: $30. *Expenses:* Tuition: Part-time $615 per credit. Tuition and fees vary according to program. *Financial support:* In 2006–07, 5 students received support. Federal Work-Study, scholarships/grants, and traineeships available. Financial award application deadline: 2/15; financial award applicants required to submit FAFSA. *Faculty research:* Chronic illness, pediatric injury, women's health, public health policy, health care teams. *Unit head:* Dr. Cynthia McCloskey, Graduate Director, 585-385-8471, Fax: 585-385-8466, E-mail: cmccloskey@sjfc.edu. *Application contact:* Shannon Cleverley, Director of Graduate Admissions, 585-385-8161, Fax: 585-385-8344, E-mail: scleverley@sjfc.edu.

Saint Joseph College, Graduate Division, Department of Nursing, West Hartford, CT 06117-2700. Offers family health nurse practitioner (MS); family health nursing (MS); nursing (Post Master's Certificate); psychiatric/mental health nursing (MS). *Accreditation:* AACN. Part-time and evening/weekend programs available. *Degree requirements:* For master's and Post Master's Certificate, thesis. *Entrance requirements:* For master's, GRE General Test or MAT, 2 letters of recommendation; for Post Master's Certificate, MAT, master's degree in nursing, minimum GPA of 3.0. Additional exam requirements/recommendations for international students: Required—NCLEX. Electronic applications accepted. *Faculty research:* Reproductive health and substance abuse, problem-based learning, role of clinical faculty, students' international studies experience.

Saint Xavier University, Graduate Studies, School of Nursing, Chicago, IL 60655-3105. Offers adult health clinical nurse specialist (MS); family nurse practitioner (MS, PMC); leadership in community health nursing (MS); psychiatric-mental health clinical nurse specialist (MS); psychiatric-mental health clinical specialist (PMC); MBA/MS. *Accreditation:* AACN. Part-time and evening/weekend programs available. *Faculty:* 11. *Students:* 20 full-time (14 women), 120 part-time (113 women). Average age 40. In 2006, 36 degrees awarded. *Entrance requirements:* For master's, GRE General Test or MAT, minimum GPA of 3.0, RN license. *Application deadline:* For fall admission, 2/15 for domestic students; for spring admission, 9/15 for domestic students. Applications are processed on a rolling basis. Application fee: $35. *Financial support:* Available to part-time students. Applicants required to submit FAFSA. *Unit head:* Beth Gierach, Managing Director of Admission, 773-298-3053, Fax: 773-298-3076, E-mail: gierach@sxu.edu.

Salem State College, Graduate School, Program in Nursing, Salem, MA 01970-5353. Offers advanced practice in rehabilitation (MSN); direct entry nursing (MSN); nursing (MSN, MBA/MSN); MBA/MSN. *Accreditation:* AACN; NLN. Part-time and evening/weekend programs available. *Faculty:* 5 full-time (all women). *Students:* 19 full-time (17 women), 49 part-time (all women); includes 8 minority (6 African Americans, 1 Asian American or Pacific Islander, 1 Hispanic American), 1 international. Average age 40. In 2006, 14 degrees awarded. *Entrance requirements:* For master's, GRE General Test, MAT. *Application deadline:* Applications are processed on a rolling basis. Application fee: $35. *Unit head:* Kathleen Skrabat, Coordinator, 978-542-6646, Fax: 978-542-7215, E-mail: kskrabat@salemstate.edu.

Samuel Merritt College, School of Nursing, Oakland, CA 94609-3108. Offers case management (MSN); family nurse practitioner (MSN, Certificate); nurse anesthetist (MSN, Certificate); nursing (MSN). *Accreditation:* AACN; AANA/CANAEP (one or more programs are accredited). Part-time and evening/weekend programs available. *Degree requirements:* For master's, thesis or alternative. *Entrance requirements:* For master's, minimum GPA of 2.5 in science, 3.0 overall; previous course work in statistics; current RN license. Additional exam requirements/recommendations for international students: Required—TOEFL. *Faculty research:* Gerontology, community health, maternal-child health, sexually transmitted diseases, substance abuse, oncology.

San Francisco State University, Division of Graduate Studies, College of Health and Human Services, School of Nursing, San Francisco, CA 94132-1722. Offers case management (MS), including long-term care, primary care/family nurse practitioner; nursing administration (MS); nursing education (MS). *Accreditation:* AACN. Part-time programs available. *Faculty:* 12 full-time (10 women). *Students:* Average age 32. In 2006, 28 degrees awarded. *Degree requirements:* For master's, thesis. *Entrance requirements:* For master's, minimum GPA of 3.0. *Application deadline:* For fall admission, 11/30 priority date for domestic students; for spring admission, 5/31 for domestic students. Applications are processed on a rolling basis. Application fee: $55. *Financial support:* In 2006–07, 35 students received support, including 35 fellowships; career-related internships or fieldwork also available. Financial award application deadline: 3/1. *Faculty research:* Nursing case management and clinical outcomes, outcome of undergraduate and graduate education in nursing, patient education strategies and learning outcomes. Total annual research expenditures: $25,000. *Unit head:* Dr. Karen Johnson-Brennan, Interim Director, 415-338-1801, Fax: 415-338-0555. *Application contact:* Dr. Frank McLaughlin, Graduate Coordinator, 415-338-1802, E-mail: femc@sfsu.edu.

San Jose State University, Graduate Studies and Research, College of Applied Sciences and Arts, School of Nursing, San Jose, CA 95192-0001. Offers gerontology nurse practitioner (MS); nursing (Certificate); nursing administration (MS); nursing education (MS). *Accreditation:* AACN. Part-time and evening/weekend programs available. *Students:* 15 full-time (13 women), 70 part-time (66 women); includes 30 minority (2 African Americans, 21 Asian Americans or Pacific Islanders, 7 Hispanic Americans). Average age 41. 73 applicants, 70% accepted, 15 enrolled. In 2006, 34 degrees awarded. *Degree requirements:* For master's, thesis. *Entrance requirements:* For master's, BS in nursing, RN license. *Application deadline:* For fall admission, 6/29 for domestic students; for spring admission, 11/30 for domestic students. Applications are processed on a rolling basis. Application fee: $59. Electronic applications accepted. *Financial support:* Career-related internships or fieldwork, institutionally sponsored loans, and scholarships/grants available. Support available to part-time students. Financial award applicants required to submit FAFSA. *Faculty research:* Nurse-managed clinics, computers in nursing. *Unit head:* Jayne Cohen, Director, 408-924-3131, Fax: 408-924-3135. *Application contact:* Dr. Phyllis Connolly, Graduate Coordinator, 408-924-3144.

Seattle Pacific University, Graduate School, School of Health Sciences, Program in Nurse Practitioner, Seattle, WA 98119-1997. Offers Certificate. *Accreditation:* AACN. Part-time and evening/weekend programs available. *Students:* 4 applicants, 75% accepted, 3 enrolled.

Degree requirements: For Certificate, internships. *Entrance requirements:* For degree, MSN, minimum GPA of 3.5. *Application deadline:* For fall admission, 9/1 priority date for domestic students. Applications are processed on a rolling basis. Application fee: $50. *Expenses:* Contact institution. *Financial support:* Teaching assistantships, career-related internships or fieldwork and traineeships available. Financial award applicants required to submit FAFSA. *Faculty research:* Health promotion, intercultural/international education, empathy/spiritual care, social policy, critical care/quality of life. *Unit head:* Dr. Martha Worcester, Director, 206-281-2616, Fax: 206-281-2767.

Seattle University, College of Nursing, Program in Advanced Practice Nursing Immersion, Seattle, WA 98122-1090. Offers MSN. *Students:* 45 full-time (38 women); includes 8 minority (1 African American, 1 American Indian/Alaska Native, 6 Asian Americans or Pacific Islanders). Average age 31. *Unit head:* Katherine Camancho-Carr, Head, 206-296-5666, E-mail: kcarr@seattleu.edu.

Seattle University, College of Nursing, Program in Nursing, Seattle, WA 98122-1090. Offers leadership in community nursing (MSN), including program development, spirituality and health; primary care nurse practitioner (MSN), including family nurse practitioner, psychiatric mental health nurse practitioner. *Students:* 6 full-time (all women), 8 part-time (7 women); includes 2 African Americans. Average age 40. *Application contact:* Janet Shandley, Associate Dean of Graduate Admissions, 206-296-5900, Fax: 206-298-5656, E-mail: grad_admissions@seattleu.edu.

Seton Hall University, College of Nursing, Department of Graduate Nursing, Advanced Practice in Acute Care Nursing Program, South Orange, NJ 07079-2697. Offers acute care nurse practitioner (MSN). *Accreditation:* AACN. Part-time programs available. *Degree requirements:* For master's, research project. *Entrance requirements:* For master's, GRE or MAT, BSN. Additional exam requirements/recommendations for international students: Required—TOEFL. Electronic applications accepted. *Faculty research:* Pulmonary infections, stress, patient-nurse environmental interactions, open-heart surgery.

Seton Hall University, College of Nursing, Department of Graduate Nursing, Advanced Practice in Primary Health Care Program, South Orange, NJ 07079-2697. Offers adult nurse practitioner (MSN); gerontological nurse practitioner (MSN); pediatric nurse practitioner (MSN); women's health nurse practitioner (MSN). *Accreditation:* AACN. Part-time programs available. *Degree requirements:* For master's, research project. *Entrance requirements:* For master's, GRE or MAT, BSN. *Faculty research:* Health promotion in well aged, practice outcomes, collaborative practice.

Shenandoah University, School of Health Professions, Division of Nursing, Winchester, VA 22601-5195. Offers family nurse practitioner (Certificate); nurse-midwifery (Certificate); nursing (MSN); psychiatric mental health nurse practitioner (Certificate). *Accreditation:* AACN; ACNM/DOA. Part-time programs available. *Faculty:* 9 full-time (all women), 2 part-time/adjunct (both women). *Students:* 5 full-time (all women), 19 part-time (18 women). Average age 37. 40 applicants, 78% accepted, 19 enrolled. In 2006, 11 master's, 4 other advanced degrees awarded. *Degree requirements:* For master's, research project. *Entrance requirements:* For master's, GRE General Test, previous course work in statistics, community nursing, and physical assessment; RN license; minimum undergraduate GPA of 2.8; appropriate clinical experience; curriculum vitae; for Certificate, MSN, minimum GPA of 3.0. Additional exam requirements/recommendations for international students: Required—TOEFL (minimum score 527 paper-based; 197 computer-based; 71 iBT). *Application deadline:* For fall admission, 6/15 priority date for domestic and international students. Applications are processed on a rolling basis. Application fee: $30. Electronic applications accepted. *Expenses:* Tuition: Full-time $12,200; part-time $610 per credit. Required fees: $150. Full-time tuition and fees vary according to course load and program. *Financial support:* In 2006–07, 21 students received support, including 3 fellowships with partial tuition reimbursements available (averaging $1,500 per year), 2 teaching assistantships with partial tuition reimbursements available (averaging $3,482 per year); institutionally sponsored loans and scholarships/grants also available. Support available to part-time students. Financial award application deadline: 3/15; financial award applicants required to submit FAFSA. *Faculty research:* Nurse caring behaviors, end of life issues, women's health, gerontology, nursing diagnosis. Total annual research expenditures: $80,000. *Unit head:* Dr. Sheila Ralph, Director, 540-678-4381, Fax: 540-665-5519, E-mail: ssparks@su.edu. *Application contact:* David Anthony, Dean of Admissions, 540-665-4581, Fax: 540-665-4627, E-mail: admit@su.edu.

Simmons College, School for Health Studies, Program in Primary Health Care Nursing, Boston, MA 02115. Offers health professions education (PhD); primary health care nursing (MS, CAGS). *Accreditation:* AACN. Part-time programs available. *Faculty:* 8 full-time (7 women), 2 part-time/adjunct (both women). *Students:* 74 full-time (65 women), 84 part-time (81 women); includes 16 minority (4 African Americans, 10 Asian Americans or Pacific Islanders, 2 Hispanic Americans). Average age 30. 194 applicants, 61% accepted, 61 enrolled. In 2006, 30 master's, 1 other advanced degree awarded. *Median time to degree:* 2 years part-time. *Degree requirements:* For master's, thesis/dissertation, registration; for doctorate, thesis/dissertation, comprehensive exam, registration. *Entrance requirements:* For master's, GRE, courses in statistics and health assessment; for CAGS, previous coursework in microbiology, statistics, developmental psychology, organic and inorganic chemistry. Additional exam requirements/recommendations for international students: Required—TOEFL (minimum score 550 paper-based; 230 computer-based). *Application deadline:* For fall admission, 6/1 for domestic and international students; for winter admission, 11/1 for domestic and international students; for spring admission, 11/1 for domestic and international students. Applications are processed on a rolling basis. Application fee: $50. Electronic applications accepted. *Expenses:* Contact institution. *Financial support:* In 2006–07, 10 fellowships with partial tuition reimbursements were awarded; research assistantships, teaching assistantships, institutionally sponsored loans, scholarships/grants, and traineeships also available. Financial award application deadline: 3/1; financial award applicants required to submit FAFSA. *Faculty research:* Nursing leadership and mentoring, gerontology/home care, nurse practitioner in occupational health, adolescent pregnancy, developmental disabilities. Total annual research expenditures: $392,500. *Unit head:* Dr. Judy A. Beal, Chairperson, 617-521-2139, Fax: 617-521-3045, E-mail: judy.beal@simmons.edu. *Application contact:* Vilma Torres, Administrative Assistant, 617-521-2654, Fax: 617-521-3137, E-mail: shs@simmons.edu.

Sonoma State University, School of Science and Technology, Family Nurse Practitioner Program, Rohnert Park, CA 94928-3609. Offers MS. *Accreditation:* NLN. Part-time programs available. *Faculty:* 11 full-time (all women), 5 part-time/adjunct (all women). *Students:* 99 full-time (19 women), 7 part-time (1 woman); includes 11 minority (4 African Americans, 1 American Indian/Alaska Native, 1 Asian American or Pacific Islander, 5 Hispanic Americans). Average age 42. 62 applicants, 98% accepted, 40 enrolled. In 2006, 25 degrees awarded. *Degree requirements:* For master's, thesis or alternative, oral exams, comprehensive exam. *Entrance requirements:* For master's, GRE General Test, BSN, minimum GPA of 3.0, course work in statistics, physical assessment, RN license. *Application deadline:* For fall admission, 11/30 for domestic students. Application fee: $55. *Expenses:* Tuition, nonresident: part-time $339 per unit. Required fees: $1,464 per term. *Financial support:* Fellowships, career-related internships or fieldwork available. Financial award application deadline: 3/2. *Faculty research:* Pain management, collaborative practice. *Unit head:* Dr. Elizabeth Close, Chair, 707-664-2465, E-mail: elizabeth.close@sonoma.edu. *Application contact:* Dr. Wendy Smith, Director, 707-664-2276, E-mail: wendy.smith@sonoma.edu.

Southern Adventist University, School of Nursing, Collegedale, TN 37315-0370. Offers adult nurse practitioner (MSN); family nurse practitioner (MSN); nurse educator (MSN); MSN/MSBA. *Accreditation:* NLN. Part-time programs available. *Faculty:* 1 (woman) full-time, 5 part-time/adjunct (all women). *Students:* 45 full-time (41 women), 17 part-time (14 women); includes 5 minority (2 African Americans, 2 Asian Americans or Pacific Islanders, 1 Hispanic American). Average age 35. 40 applicants, 95% accepted, 31 enrolled. In 2006, 20 degrees awarded. *Degree requirements:* For master's, thesis or project. *Entrance requirements:* For master's, RN license. Additional exam requirements/recommendations for international students: Required—TOEFL (minimum score 600 paper-based). *Application deadline:* For fall admission, 7/1 for domestic and international students; for winter admission, 12/1 for domestic and international students. Applications are processed on a rolling basis. Application fee: $25. Electronic applications accepted. *Financial support:* In 2006–07, 1 teaching assistantship with partial tuition reimbursement (averaging $5,000 per year) was awarded. *Faculty research:* Pain management, ethics, corporate wellness, caring spirituality, stress. *Unit head:* Dr. Barbara James, Dean, 423-236-2940, Fax: 423-236-1940, E-mail: bjames@southern.edu. *Application contact:* Diane Proffitt, Enrollment Counselor, 423-236-2941, Fax: 423-236-1940, E-mail: dproffitt@southern.edu.

Southern Illinois University Edwardsville, Graduate Studies and Research, School of Nursing, Program in Family Nurse Practitioner, Edwardsville, IL 62026-0001. Offers MS, Post-Master's Certificate. *Accreditation:* AACN. *Students:* 16 full-time (15 women), 67 part-time (63 women); includes 6 minority (2 African Americans, 1 American Indian/Alaska Native, 2 Asian Americans or Pacific Islanders, 1 Hispanic American). Average age 33. 31 applicants, 39% accepted. In 2006, 9 master's, 1 other advanced degree awarded. *Degree requirements:* For master's, thesis or alternative, final exam, comprehensive exam, registration. *Entrance requirements:* For master's, appropriate bachelor's degree, RN license. Additional exam requirements/recommendations for international students: Required—TOEFL. *Application deadline:* For fall admission, 1/1 for domestic and international students. Application fee: $30. Electronic applications accepted. *Financial support:* Fellowships with full tuition reimbursements, research assistantships, career-related internships or fieldwork, Federal Work-Study, institutionally sponsored loans, scholarships/grants, and traineeships available. Support available to part-time students. Financial award application deadline: 3/1; financial award applicants required to submit FAFSA. *Unit head:* Dr. Jacquelyn Clement, Director, 618-650-3923, E-mail: jclemen@siue.edu.

Southern University and Agricultural and Mechanical College, School of Nursing, Baton Rouge, LA 70813. Offers educator/administrator (PhD); family health nursing (MSN); family nurse practitioner (Post Master's Certificate); geriatric nurse practitioner/gerontology (PhD). *Accreditation:* AACN; NLN. Part-time programs available. *Degree requirements:* For master's and doctorate, thesis/dissertation, comprehensive exam. *Entrance requirements:* For master's, GRE General Test, BSN, minimum GPA of 2.7; for doctorate, GRE General Test; for Post Master's Certificate, MSN. Additional exam requirements/recommendations for international students: Required—TOEFL (minimum score 525 paper-based; 193 computer-based). *Faculty research:* Health promotions, vulnerable populations, (community-based) cardiovascular participating research, health disparities chronic diseases, care of the elderly.

Spalding University, Graduate Studies, College of Health and Natural Sciences, School of Nursing, Louisville, KY 40203-2188. Offers adult nurse practitioner (MSN); family nurse practitioner (MSN); leadership in nursing and healthcare (MSN); pediatric nurse practitioner (MSN). *Accreditation:* AACN. Part-time and evening/weekend programs available. *Degree requirements:* For master's, thesis, comprehensive exam (for some programs). *Entrance requirements:* For master's, GRE General Test, BSN or bachelor's degree and RN licensure. *Faculty research:* Nurse educational administration, gerontology, bioterrorism, healthcare ethics, leadership.

State University of New York Downstate Medical Center, College of Nursing, Graduate Program in Nursing, Nurse Practitioner Program, Brooklyn, NY 11203-2098. Offers MS, Post Master's Certificate. *Accreditation:* AACN. Part-time programs available. *Degree requirements:* For master's, thesis optional. *Entrance requirements:* For master's, GRE, BSN; minimum GPA of 3.0; previous undergraduate course work in statistics, health assessment, and nursing research; RN license; for Post Master's Certificate, BSN; minimum GPA of 3.0; RN license; previous undergraduate course work in statistics, health assessment, and nursing research. *Expenses:* Tuition, state resident: full-time $6,900; part-time $288 per credit. Tuition, nonresident: full-time $10,920; part-time $455 per credit. Required fees: $100; $20 per credit. $50 per semester. Tuition and fees vary according to course load. *Faculty research:* Women's health.

State University of New York Institute of Technology, School of Nursing and Health Systems, Program in Family Nurse Practitioner, Utica, NY 13504-3050. Offers MS, CAS. *Accreditation:* AACN. Part-time programs available. *Faculty:* 5 full-time (all women), 3 part-time/adjunct (2 women). *Students:* 14 full-time (13 women), 16 part-time (14 women). *Degree requirements:* For master's, thesis or project. *Entrance requirements:* For master's, GRE if undergraduate GPA is under 3.3, minimum GPA of 3.0 in last 30 undergraduate hours, bachelor's degree in nursing, 1 year professional experience, RN license, interview, 2 letters of recommendation. Additional exam requirements/recommendations for international students: Required—TOEFL (minimum score 550 paper-based; 213 computer-based). *Application deadline:* For fall admission, 6/15 priority date for domestic students. Applications are processed on a rolling basis. Application fee: $50. *Expenses:* Tuition, state resident: full-time $3,452; part-time $288 per credit hour. Tuition, nonresident: full-time $10,920; part-time $455 per credit hour. Required fees: $927; $38 per credit hour. *Financial support:* In 2006–07, 2 research assistantships (averaging $2,500 per year) were awarded; Federal Work-Study, scholarships/grants, traineeships, and unspecified assistantships also available. Financial award applicants required to submit FAFSA. *Faculty research:* Adult and family healthcare, critical thinking, epidemiology, refugee and women's health, child obesity. *Unit head:* Dr. Louise Dean-Kelly, Coordinator, 315-792-7291, Fax: 315-792-7555, E-mail: fldk@sunyit.edu. *Application contact:* Marybeth Lyons, Director of Admissions, 315-792-7500, Fax: 315-792-7837, E-mail: smbl@sunyit.edu.

State University of New York Upstate Medical University, College of Nursing, Syracuse, NY 13210-2334. Offers nurse practitioner (Post Master's Certificate); nursing (MS). *Accreditation:* AACN. Part-time programs available. *Faculty:* 9 full-time (all women), 5 part-time/adjunct (4 women). *Students:* 29 full-time (all women), 62 part-time (56 women); includes 7 minority (4 African Americans, 3 Hispanic Americans). Average age 39. 41 applicants, 95% accepted, 29 enrolled. In 2006, 18 master's, 8 other advanced degrees awarded. *Degree requirements:* For master's, thesis or alternative. *Entrance requirements:* For master's, 3 years of work experience. *Application deadline:* For fall admission, 3/15 priority date for domestic and international students. Applications are processed on a rolling basis. Application fee: $40. Electronic applications accepted. *Expenses:* Tuition, state resident: full-time $6,900; part-time $288 per credit. Tuition, nonresident: full-time $10,920; part-time $455 per credit. Required fees: $496. *Financial support:* Federal Work-Study, institutionally sponsored loans, scholarships/grants, and traineeships available. Support available to part-time students. Financial award application deadline: 3/1; financial award applicants required to submit FAFSA. *Unit head:* Dr. Elvira Szigeti, Dean, 315-464-4276, Fax: 315-464-5168. *Application contact:* Donna Vavonese, Associate Director of Admissions, 315-464-4570, Fax: 315-464-8867, E-mail: vavonesd@upstate.edu.

Stony Brook University, State University of New York, Stony Brook University Medical Center, Health Sciences Center, School of Nursing, Distance Learning Program in Family Nurse Practitioner, Stony Brook, NY 11794. Offers MS, Certificate. *Accreditation:* AACN. Postbaccalaureate distance learning degree programs offered. *Students:* 5 full-time (all women), 105 part-time (98 women); includes 26 minority (14 African Americans, 8 Asian Americans or Pacific Islanders, 4 Hispanic Americans). In 2006, 31 master's, 9 other advanced degrees awarded. *Degree requirements:* For master's, thesis. *Entrance requirements:* For master's, BSN, minimum GPA of 3.0, course work in statistics. *Application deadline:* For fall admission, 1/15 for domestic students. Application fee: $60. *Expenses:* Tuition, state resident: full-time $6,900; part-time $288 per credit. Tuition, nonresident: full-time $10,920; part-time $455 per credit. *Financial support:* Application deadline: 3/15. *Application contact:* Irene Stern, Information Contact, 631-444-3286, E-mail: irene.stern@stonybrook.edu.

Stony Brook University, State University of New York, Stony Brook University Medical Center, Health Sciences Center, School of Nursing, Program in Adult Health/Primary Care Nursing, Stony Brook, NY 11794. Offers adult health nurse practitioner (Certificate); adult health/primary care nursing (MS). *Accreditation:* AACN. *Students:* 7 full-time (5 women), 153 part-time (141 women); includes 47 minority (24 African Americans, 12 Asian Americans or

Family Nurse Practitioner Studies

Stony Brook University, State University of New York (continued)
Pacific Islanders, 11 Hispanic Americans). In 2006, 49 master's, 4 other advanced degrees awarded. *Degree requirements:* For master's, thesis. *Entrance requirements:* For master's, BSN, minimum GPA of 3.0, course work in statistics. *Application deadline:* For fall admission, 1/15 for domestic students. Application fee: $60. *Expenses:* Tuition, state resident: full-time $6,900; part-time $288 per credit. Tuition, nonresident: full-time $10,920; part-time $455 per credit. *Financial support:* Application deadline: 3/15. *Unit head:* Dr. Kathleen Shurpin, Chair, 631-444-3267, Fax: 631-444-3136, E-mail: kathy.shurpin@stonybrook.edu.

Stony Brook University, State University of New York, Stony Brook University Medical Center, Health Sciences Center, School of Nursing, Program in Child Health Nursing, Stony Brook, NY 11794. Offers child health nurse practitioner (Certificate); child health nursing (MS). *Accreditation:* AACN. *Students:* 9 full-time (all women), 24 part-time (22 women); includes 1 Asian American or Pacific Islander. In 2006, 15 master's, 1 other advanced degree awarded. *Degree requirements:* For master's, thesis. *Entrance requirements:* For master's, BSN, minimum GPA of 3.0, course work in statistics. *Application deadline:* For fall admission, 1/15 for domestic students. Application fee: $60. *Expenses:* Tuition, state resident: full-time $6,900; part-time $288 per credit. Tuition, nonresident: full-time $10,920; part-time $455 per credit. *Financial support:* Application deadline: 3/15. *Unit head:* Dr. Debra Sansoucie, Chair, 631-444-3298, Fax: 631-444-3136, E-mail: debra.sansoucie@stonybrook.edu.

Stony Brook University, State University of New York, Stony Brook University Medical Center, Health Sciences Center, School of Nursing, Program in Mental Health/Psychiatric Nursing, Stony Brook, NY 11794. Offers mental health nurse practitioner (Certificate); mental health/psychiatric nursing (MS). *Accreditation:* AACN. *Students:* 19 full-time (18 women), 45 part-time (38 women); includes 4 minority (3 African Americans, 1 Hispanic American), 1 international. In 2006, 21 master's, 9 other advanced degrees awarded. *Degree requirements:* For master's, thesis. *Entrance requirements:* For master's, BSN, minimum GPA of 3.0, course work in statistics. *Application deadline:* For fall admission, 1/15 for domestic students. Application fee: $60. *Expenses:* Tuition, state resident: full-time $6,900; part-time $288 per credit. Tuition, nonresident: full-time $10,920; part-time $455 per credit. *Financial support:* Application deadline: 3/15. *Unit head:* Dr. Arlene Steckel, Chair, 631-444-3264, Fax: 631-444-3136, E-mail: arlene.steckel@stonybrook.edu.

Stony Brook University, State University of New York, Stony Brook University Medical Center, Health Sciences Center, School of Nursing, Program in Neonatal Nursing, Stony Brook, NY 11794. Offers neonatal nurse practitioner (Certificate); neonatal nursing (MS). *Accreditation:* AACN. *Students:* 11 full-time (all women), 35 part-time (33 women); includes 7 minority (4 Asian Americans or Pacific Islanders, 3 Hispanic Americans), 3 international. In 2006, 20 master's, 8 other advanced degrees awarded. *Degree requirements:* For master's, thesis. *Entrance requirements:* For master's, BSN, minimum GPA of 3.0, course work in statistics. *Application deadline:* For fall admission, 1/15 for domestic students. Application fee: $60. *Expenses:* Tuition, state resident: full-time $6,900; part-time $288 per credit. Tuition, nonresident: full-time $10,920; part-time $455 per credit. *Financial support:* Application deadline: 3/15. *Unit head:* Dr. Debra Sansoucie, Chair, 631-444-3298, Fax: 631-444-3136, E-mail: debra.sansoucie@stonybrook.edu.

Stony Brook University, State University of New York, Stony Brook University Medical Center, Health Sciences Center, School of Nursing, Program in Perinatal/Women's Health Nursing, Stony Brook, NY 11794. Offers perinatal/women's health nurse practitioner (Certificate); perinatal/women's health nursing (MS). *Accreditation:* AACN. *Students:* 2 full-time (both women), 18 part-time (all women); includes 6 minority (5 African Americans, 1 Hispanic American). In 2006, 9 master's, 2 other advanced degrees awarded. *Degree requirements:* For master's, thesis. *Entrance requirements:* For master's, BSN, minimum GPA of 3.0, course work in statistics. *Application deadline:* For fall admission, 1/15 for domestic students. Application fee: $60. *Expenses:* Tuition, state resident: full-time $6,900; part-time $288 per credit. Tuition, nonresident: full-time $10,920; part-time $455 per credit. *Financial support:* Application deadline: 3/15. *Unit head:* Dr. Debra Sansoucie, Chair, 631-444-3298, Fax: 631-444-3136, E-mail: debra.sansoucie@stonybrook.edu.

Texas A&M University–Corpus Christi, Graduate Studies and Research, College of Nursing and Health Sciences, Corpus Christi, TX 78412-5503. Offers clinical nurse specialist (MSN); family nurse practitioner (MSN); health care administration (MSN); leadership in nursing systems (MSN). *Accreditation:* AACN. Part-time and evening/weekend programs available. *Degree requirements:* For master's, thesis (for some programs), comprehensive exam, registration. *Entrance requirements:* For master's, GRE General Test. Additional exam requirements/recommendations for international students: Required—TOEFL. Electronic applications accepted.

Texas Tech University Health Sciences Center, School of Nursing, Lubbock, TX 79430. Offers acute care nurse practitioner (MSN, Certificate); administration (MSN); clinical research management (MSN, Certificate); education (MSN); family nurse practitioner (MSN, Certificate); geriatric nurse practitioner (MSN, Certificate); pediatric nurse practitioner (MSN, Certificate). *Accreditation:* AACN. Part-time programs available. Postbaccalaureate distance learning degree programs offered (minimal on-campus study). *Faculty:* 17 full-time (16 women), 5 part-time/adjunct (all women). *Students:* 23 full-time (22 women), 161 part-time (137 women); includes 46 minority (8 African Americans, 2 American Indian/Alaska Native, 6 Asian Americans or Pacific Islanders, 30 Hispanic Americans). Average age 37. 97 applicants, 69% accepted, 67 enrolled. In 2006, 41 degrees awarded. *Degree requirements:* For master's, thesis optional. *Entrance requirements:* For master's, minimum GPA of 3.0, 3 letters of reference, BSN, RN license; for Certificate, minimum GPA of 3.0, 3 letters of reference, RN license. Additional exam requirements/recommendations for international students: Required—TOEFL (minimum score 550 paper-based; 213 computer-based). *Application deadline:* For fall admission, 7/15 priority date for domestic and international students; for spring admission, 11/15 priority date for domestic and international students. Applications are processed on a rolling basis. Application fee: $40. *Financial support:* In 2006–07, 184 students received support. Institutionally sponsored loans, scholarships/grants, and traineeships available. Support available to part-time students. Financial award application deadline: 12/1; financial award applicants required to submit FAFSA. *Faculty research:* Diabetes/obesity, nurse competency, disease management, intervention and measurements, health disparities. Total annual research expenditures: $2.4 million. *Unit head:* Dr. Barbara A. Johnston, Associate Dean for Administrative and Student Affairs, 806-743-3055, Fax: 806-743-1622, E-mail: barbara.johnston@ttuhsc.edu. *Application contact:* Lauren K. Sullivan, Recruiter/Transcultural Coordinator, 806-743-2730 Ext. 309, Fax: 806-743-1622, E-mail: lauren.sullivan@ttuhsc.edu.

Texas Woman's University, Graduate School, College of Nursing, Denton, TX 76201. Offers adult health nurse practitioner (MS); health systems management (MS); nursing (MS); nursing education (MS); nursing science (PhD). *Accreditation:* AACN. Part-time programs available. Postbaccalaureate distance learning degree programs offered. *Students:* 41 full-time (38 women), 512 part-time (490 women); includes 211 minority (121 African Americans, 2 American Indian/Alaska Native, 64 Asian Americans or Pacific Islanders, 24 Hispanic Americans), 9 international. Average age 41. In 2006, 129 master's, 16 doctorates awarded. *Degree requirements:* For master's, thesis or alternative; for doctorate, thesis/dissertation, comprehensive exam. *Entrance requirements:* For master's, GRE or MAT, minimum GPA of 3.0, RN license, BS in nursing; for doctorate, GRE or MAT, MS in nursing, minimum GPA of 3.5, RN license, coursework in statistics, graduate research, 2 letters of reference. Additional exam requirements/recommendations for international students: Required—TOEFL (minimum score 550 paper-based; 213 computer-based; 79 iBT). *Application deadline:* For fall admission, 4/1 for international students; for spring admission, 8/1 for international students. Applications are processed on a rolling basis. Application fee: $30 ($50 for international students). Electronic applications accepted. *Expenses:* Tuition, area resident: Part-time $168 per unit. Tuition, state resident: full-time $4,369. Tuition, nonresident: full-time $9,373; part-time $443 per unit. Required fees: $20 per unit. $177 per term. *Financial support:* In 2006–07, 11 research assistantships (averaging $11,232 per year), 3 teaching assistantships (averaging $11,232 per year) were awarded; career-related internships or fieldwork, Federal Work-Study, institutionally sponsored loans, scholarships/grants, traineeships, health care benefits, and unspecified assistantships also available. Support available to part-time students. Financial award application deadline: 3/1; financial award applicants required to submit FAFSA. *Faculty research:* Health of women across the life span, child health issues, self-care and heart failure, smoking cessation, timing of labor and delivery. *Unit head:* Dr. Marcia Hern, Dean, 940-898-2401, Fax: 940-898-2437, E-mail: mhern@twu.edu. *Application contact:* Samuel Wheeler, Coordinator of Graduate Admissions, 940-898-3188, Fax: 940-898-3081, E-mail: wheelersr@twu.edu.

Uniformed Services University of the Health Sciences, Graduate School of Nursing, Department of Nurse Practitioner, Bethesda, MD 20814-4799. Offers MSN. Available to military officers only. *Accreditation:* AACN; NLN. *Degree requirements:* For master's, thesis or alternative. *Entrance requirements:* For master's, GRE General Test, MAT, BSN, clinical experience, minimum GPA of 3.0, previous course work in science. Electronic applications accepted. *Faculty research:* Prenatal care, distance learning, prostate cancer screening, health promotion and prevention, military health care.

Universidad de Iberoamerica, Graduate School, San Jose, Costa Rica. Offers clinical psychology (M Psych); educational psychology (M Psych); hospital and health services management (MHA); intensive care nursing (MN); medicine (MD). *Entrance requirements:* For master's, 2 letters of recommendation, interview.

University of Alaska Anchorage, College of Health and Social Welfare, School of Nursing, Anchorage, AK 99508-8060. Offers family nurse practitioner (Certificate); nursing (MS); nursing education (Certificate); psychiatric nurse practitioner (Certificate). *Accreditation:* NLN. Part-time and evening/weekend programs available. *Students:* 10 full-time (all women), 38 part-time (34 women); includes 6 minority (3 African Americans, 2 American Indian/Alaska Native, 1 Hispanic American). 15 applicants, 27% accepted. In 2006, 12 degrees awarded. *Degree requirements:* For master's, individual project. *Entrance requirements:* For master's, GRE or MAT, BS in nursing, interview, minimum GPA of 3.0, RN license, 1 year of part-time or 6 months of full-time clinical experience. Additional exam requirements/recommendations for international students: Required—TOEFL (minimum score 550 paper-based; 213 computer-based). *Application deadline:* For fall admission, 3/1 for domestic students; for spring admission, 11/1 for domestic students. Application fee: $45. *Expenses:* Tuition, state resident: part-time $268 per credit. Tuition, nonresident: part-time $547 per credit. Required fees: $124 per semester. Tuition and fees vary according to reciprocity agreements and student level. *Financial support:* Teaching assistantships, career-related internships or fieldwork, Federal Work-Study, and health care benefits available. Support available to part-time students. Financial award application deadline: 4/1; financial award applicants required to submit FAFSA. *Unit head:* Dr. Jean Ballantyne, Director, 907-786-4571, Fax: 907-786-4558. *Application contact:* Marie Samson, Coordinator of Student Affairs, 907-786-4561.

University of Central Arkansas, Graduate School, College of Health and Behavioral Sciences, Department of Nursing, Conway, AR 72035-0001. Offers clinical nurse specialist (MSN); nurse practitioner (MSN). *Accreditation:* AACN. *Faculty:* 8 full-time (all women). *Students:* 8 full-time (all women), 54 part-time (46 women); includes 8 minority (6 African Americans, 1 American Indian/Alaska Native, 1 Asian American or Pacific Islander), 1 international. 5 applicants, 100% accepted, 5 enrolled. In 2006, 8 degrees awarded. *Degree requirements:* For master's, clinicals, thesis optional. *Entrance requirements:* For master's, GRE General Test, minimum GPA of 2.7. Additional exam requirements/recommendations for international students: Required—TOEFL (minimum score 550 paper-based; 213 computer-based). *Application deadline:* For fall admission, 3/1 priority date for domestic students; for spring admission, 10/1 for domestic students. Applications are processed on a rolling basis. Application fee: $25 ($40 for international students). *Expenses: Contact institution.* One-time fee: $65 part-time. *Financial support:* Federal Work-Study, traineeships, and unspecified assistantships available. Financial award application deadline: 2/15; financial award applicants required to submit FAFSA. Total annual research expenditures: $216,643. *Unit head:* Dr. Barbara Williams, Chairperson, 501-450-3119, Fax: 501-450-5503, E-mail: barbaraw@uca.edu. *Application contact:* Nanette Fitzhugh, Administrative Assistant, 501-450-5063, Fax: 501-450-5678, E-mail: fitzhugh@uca.edu.

University of Cincinnati, Graduate School, College of Nursing, Cincinnati, OH 45221-0038. Offers clinical nurse specialist (MSN), including adult health, community health, neonatal, nursing administration, occupational health, pediatric health, psychiatric nursing, women's health; nurse anesthesia (MSN); nurse midwifery (MSN); nurse practitioner (MSN), including acute care, ambulatory care, family, family/psychiatric, women's health; nursing (PhD); MBA/MSN. *Accreditation:* AACN; AANA/CANAEP (one or more programs are accredited); ACNM/DOA. Part-time programs available. Postbaccalaureate distance learning degree programs offered (no on-campus study). *Faculty:* 41 full-time (39 women), 16 part-time/adjunct (15 women). *Students:* 159 full-time (125 women), 149 part-time (145 women); includes 40 minority (22 African Americans, 1 American Indian/Alaska Native, 16 Asian Americans or Pacific Islanders, 1 Hispanic American). Average age 34. 385 applicants, 49% accepted, 132 enrolled. In 2006, 77 master's, 5 doctorates awarded. Terminal master's awarded for partial completion of doctoral program. *Median time to degree:* Of those who began their doctoral program in fall 1998, 55% received their degree in 8 years or less. *Degree requirements:* For master's, thesis or alternative, registration; for doctorate, thesis/dissertation, comprehensive exam, registration. *Entrance requirements:* For master's and doctorate, GRE General Test. Additional exam requirements/recommendations for international students: Required—TOEFL (minimum score 520 paper-based; 190 computer-based). *Application deadline:* For fall admission, 7/26 priority date for domestic and international students. Applications are processed on a rolling basis. Application fee: $40. Electronic applications accepted. *Financial support:* In 2006–07, 164 students received support, including 7 fellowships with full tuition reimbursements available (averaging $13,571 per year), research assistantships with full tuition reimbursements available (averaging $12,000 per year), 8 teaching assistantships with full tuition reimbursements available (averaging $12,000 per year); career-related internships or fieldwork, scholarships/grants, traineeships, tuition waivers (partial), and unspecified assistantships also available. Support available to part-time students. Financial award application deadline: 5/1; financial award applicants required to submit FAFSA. *Faculty research:* Substance abuse, injury and violence, symptom management. Total annual research expenditures: $1.3 million. *Unit head:* Dr. Andrea R. Lindell, Dean, 513-558-5330, Fax: 513-558-9030, E-mail: andrea.lindell@uc.edu. *Application contact:* Loren Carter, Program Coordinator, 513-558-5072, Fax: 513-558-7523, E-mail: loren.carter@uc.edu.

University of Colorado at Colorado Springs, Graduate School, Beth-El College of Nursing, Colorado Springs, CO 80933-7150. Offers adult health nurse practitioner and clinical specialist (MSN); family practitioner (MSN), including community clinical specialist, forensic clinical specialist, holistic clinical specialist; gerontology (MSN); neonatal nurse practitioner and clinical specialist (MSN); nursing administration (MSN); women nurse practitioner (MSN). *Accreditation:* AACN. Part-time programs available. Postbaccalaureate distance learning degree programs offered (minimal on-campus study). *Faculty:* 10 full-time (7 women), 14 part-time/adjunct (7 women). *Students:* 84 full-time (77 women), 53 part-time (52 women); includes 22 minority (6 African Americans, 3 American Indian/Alaska Native, 2 Asian Americans or Pacific Islanders, 11 Hispanic Americans). Average age 37. 54 applicants, 85% accepted, 30 enrolled. In 2006, 36 degrees awarded. *Degree requirements:* For master's, thesis optional; for doctorate, capstone project. *Entrance requirements:* For master's, GRE General Test or MAT, BSN, minimum GPA of 3.0, unrestricted RN license; for doctorate, interview; active RN license; MA; minimum GPA of 3.3; National Certification as NP, CNS, or CNS; portfolio. Additional exam requirements/recommendations for international students: Required—TOEFL. *Application deadline:* For fall admission, 6/1 priority date for domestic students; for spring admission, 11/15 for domestic students. Application fee: $60 ($75 for international students). Electronic applications accepted. *Expenses: Contact institution.* Tuition and fees vary according to course load, campus/location and program. *Financial support:* Fellowships, career-related internships or fieldwork, Federal Work-Study, and institutionally sponsored loans available. Support available to part-time students. *Faculty research:* Women's health, uncertainty, empowerment, family experience in chronic illness. Total annual research expenditures: $260,389. *Unit head:* Dr. Carole Schoffstall, Dean, 719-262-4418, Fax: 719-262-4416, E-mail: cschoffs@uccs.edu.

University of Colorado at Denver and Health Sciences Center, School of Nursing, Denver, CO 80217-3364. Offers nursing (MS, PhD, Post Master's Certificate); nursing practice (DNP). *Accreditation:* AACN; ACNM/DOA (one or more programs are accredited); NLN (one or more programs are accredited). Part-time programs available. *Students:* 249 full-time (238 women), 63 part-time (47 women); includes 32 minority (6 African Americans, 4 American Indian/Alaska Native, 12 Asian Americans or Pacific Islanders, 10 Hispanic Americans), 5 international. Average age 35. 262 applicants, 73% accepted, 177 enrolled. In 2006, 69 master's, 6 doctorates awarded. *Entrance requirements:* For doctorate, minimum GPA of 2.75; resumé; courses in microbiology, anatomy, physiology, and introductory statistics; copy of RN license. Additional exam requirements/recommendations for international students: Required—TOEFL (minimum score 550 paper-based; 213 computer-based). *Application deadline:* For fall admission, 5/1 priority date for domestic students; for spring admission, 10/1 for domestic students. Application fee: $65. *Expenses:* Contact institution. *Financial support:* Fellowships, research assistantships, teaching assistantships, career-related internships or fieldwork, Federal Work-Study, and institutionally sponsored loans available. Support available to part-time students. Financial award application deadline: 3/15; financial award applicants required to submit FAFSA. *Unit head:* Patricia Moritz, Dean, 303-315-1680.

University of Delaware, College of Health Sciences, School of Nursing, Newark, DE 19716. Offers adult nurse practitioner (MSN, PMC); cardiopulmonary clinical nurse specialist (MSN, PMC); cardiopulmonary clinical nurse specialist/adult nurse practitioner (MSN, PMC); family nurse practitioner (MSN, PMC); gerontology clinical nurse specialist (MSN, PMC); gerontology clinical nurse specialist geriatric nurse practitioner (PMC); gerontology clinical nurse specialist/ geriatric nurse practitioner (MSN); health services administration (MSN, PMC); nursing of children clinical nurse specialist (MSN, PMC); nursing of children clinical nurse specialist/ pediatric nurse practitioner (MSN, PMC); oncology/immune deficiency clinical nurse specialist (MSN, PMC); oncology/immune deficiency clinical nurse specialist/adult nurse practitioner (MSN, PMC); perinatal/women's health clinical nurse specialist (MSN, PMC); perinatal/ women's health clinical nurse specialist/women's health nurse practitioner (MSN, PMC); psychiatric nursing clinical nurse specialist (MSN, PMC). *Accreditation:* AACN; NLN (one or more programs are accredited). Part-time and evening/weekend programs available. Postbaccalaureate distance learning degree programs offered (minimal on-campus study). *Degree requirements:* For master's, thesis optional. *Entrance requirements:* For master's, BSN, interview, RN license. Electronic applications accepted. *Faculty research:* Marriage and chronic illness, health promotion, congestive heart failure patient outcomes, school nursing, diabetes in children.

University of Detroit Mercy, College of Health Professions, Program in Family Nurse Practitioner, Detroit, MI 48221. Offers MSN, Certificate. *Accreditation:* AACN. *Expenses:* Tuition: Full-time $15,750; part-time $875 per credit hour. Required fees: $570.

University of Hawaii at Manoa, Graduate Division, College of Health Sciences and Social Welfare, School of Nursing and Dental Hygiene, Honolulu, HI 96822. Offers clinical nurse specialist (MS), including adult health, community mental health; nurse practitioner (MS), including adult health, community mental health, family nurse practitioner; nursing (PhD, Graduate Certificate); nursing administration (MS). *Accreditation:* AACN; NLN (one or more programs are accredited). *Faculty:* 32 full-time (29 women), 1 (woman) part-time/adjunct. *Students:* 30 full-time (28 women), 94 part-time (83 women); includes 10 minority (3 African Americans, 1 American Indian/Alaska Native, 2 Asian Americans or Pacific Islanders, 4 Hispanic Americans), 2 international. 119 applicants, 53% accepted, 54 enrolled. In 2006, 12 master's, 4 doctorates awarded. *Median time to degree:* Of those who began their doctoral program in fall 1998, 57% received their degree in 8 years or less. *Degree requirements:* For master's, thesis optional; for doctorate, thesis/dissertation, comprehensive exam. *Entrance requirements:* For master's, Hawaii RN license. Additional exam requirements/recommendations for international students: Required—TOEFL (minimum score 580 paper-based; 237 computer-based; 92 iBT). *Application deadline:* For fall admission, 3/1 for domestic and international students. Application fee: $50. *Financial support:* In 2006–07, 1 teaching assistantship (averaging $13,296 per year) was awarded. Total annual research expenditures: $3.1 million.

University of Mary, Division of Nursing, Bismarck, ND 58504-9652. Offers family nurse practitioner (MSN); nurse management (MSN); nursing educator (MSN). *Accreditation:* AACN. Part-time and evening/weekend programs available. Postbaccalaureate distance learning degree programs offered (minimal on-campus study). *Faculty:* 2 full-time (both women), 8 part-time/ adjunct (5 women). *Students:* 28 full-time (27 women), 22 part-time (all women); includes 2 minority (1 African American, 1 Hispanic American), 1 international. Average age 32. 32 applicants, 66% accepted, 19 enrolled. In 2006, 26 degrees awarded. *Degree requirements:* For master's, thesis (for some programs), internship (family nurse practitioner), practice teaching, comprehensive exam. *Entrance requirements:* For master's, minimum GPA of 3.0 in nursing, interview, letters of recommendation. *Application deadline:* For fall admission, 4/15 priority date for domestic students. Applications are processed on a rolling basis. Application fee: $40. Electronic applications accepted. *Financial support:* In 2006–07, 14 fellowships with partial tuition reimbursements, 3 teaching assistantships with partial tuition reimbursements were awarded; institutionally sponsored loans also available. Support available to part-time students. Financial award application deadline: 7/1. *Faculty research:* Gerontology issues, rural nursing, health policy, primary care, women's health. *Unit head:* Glenda Reemts, Director, 701-255-7500 Ext. 8041, Fax: 701-255-7687. *Application contact:* Traci L. Schell, Secretary, 701-355-8016, Fax: 701-255-7687, E-mail: tschell@umary.edu.

University of Massachusetts Worcester, Graduate School of Nursing, Worcester, MA 01655-0115. Offers adult acute/critical care nurse practitioner (MS, Certificate); adult ambulatory/ community care nurse practitioner (MS, Certificate); gerontological nurse practitioner (Certificate); nurse educator (MS, Certificate); nursing (PhD). *Accreditation:* AACN. Part-time programs available. *Faculty:* 39. *Students:* 46 full-time (43 women), 6 part-time (2 women); includes 5 minority (2 African Americans, 2 Asian Americans or Pacific Islanders, 1 Hispanic American). Average age 38. 42 applicants, 71% accepted. In 2006, 26 master's, 2 doctorates, 6 other advanced degrees awarded. *Degree requirements:* For doctorate, thesis/dissertation. *Entrance requirements:* For master's, GRE General Test, BSN, previous course work in statistics; for Certificate, master's degree. *Application deadline:* For fall admission, 3/15 for domestic students. Applications are processed on a rolling basis. Application fee: $40 ($60 for international students). *Expenses:* Tuition, state resident: full-time $2,640. Tuition, nonresident: full-time $9,856. Required fees: $3,942. *Financial support:* In 2006–07, 4 students received support. Scholarships/grants and traineeships available. Support available to part-time students. Financial award application deadline: 3/22; financial award applicants required to submit FAFSA. *Faculty research:* Premature menopause with cancer treatment, quality of life and cancer, complementary therapies, psychoneuroimmunology, patient outcomes/outcomes research. *Unit head:* Dr. Janet Hale, Associate Dean, 508-856-5661, Fax: 508-856-6552. *Application contact:* Larry Shattuck, Director of Recruitment and Retention, 508-856-5801, Fax: 508-856-6552.

University of Medicine and Dentistry of New Jersey, School of Nursing, Program in Advanced Practice Nursing, Newark, NJ 07107-1709. Offers MSN, Post Master's Certificate. *Entrance requirements:* Additional exam requirements/recommendations for international students: Required—TOEFL. *Application deadline:* For fall admission, 4/1 for domestic students; for spring admission, 10/1 for domestic students. Applications are processed on a rolling basis. Application fee: $50. Electronic applications accepted.

University of Miami, Graduate School, School of Nursing and Health Studies, Coral Gables, FL 33124. Offers acute care (MSN), including acute care nurse practitioner, nurse anesthesia; community health (MSN); nursing (PhD); primary care (MSN), including adult nurse practitioner, family nurse practitioner, nurse midwifery, psychiatric/mental health nursing, women's health practitioner. *Accreditation:* AACN; AANA/CANAEP; ACNM/DOA (one or more programs are accredited). Part-time programs available. *Faculty:* 10 full-time (8 women), 1 (woman) part-time/adjunct. *Students:* 33 full-time (24 women), 27 part-time (24 women); includes 28 minority (7 African Americans, 5 Asian Americans or Pacific Islanders, 16 Hispanic Americans), 2 international. Average age 34. 108 applicants, 48% accepted, 30 enrolled. In 2006, 15 master's, 1 doctorate awarded. *Degree requirements:* For master's, thesis optional; for doctorate, thesis/dissertation. *Entrance requirements:* For master's, GRE General Test, BSN, minimum GPA of 3.0, Florida RN license; for doctorate, GRE General Test, BSN or MSN, minimum GPA of 3.0. Additional exam requirements/recommendations for international students: Required—TOEFL (minimum score 550 paper-based; 213 computer-based). *Application deadline:* For fall admission, 4/30 priority date for domestic students; for spring admission, 11/1 priority date for domestic students. Applications are processed on a rolling basis. Application fee: $50. Electronic applications accepted. *Financial support:* In 2006–07, 12 students received support, including 3 research assistantships with tuition reimbursements available (averaging $9,000 per year), 5 teaching assistantships with tuition reimbursements available (averaging $9,000 per year); fellowships, Federal Work-Study, institutionally sponsored loans, scholarships/grants, and unspecified assistantships also available. Support available to part-time students. Financial award application deadline: 3/1; financial award applicants required to submit FAFSA. *Faculty research:* Transcultural nursing, exercise and depression in Alzheimer's disease, infectious diseases/HIV–AIDS, postpartum depression, outcomes assessment. Total annual research expenditures: $31.9 million. *Unit head:* Dr. Nilda Peragallo, Dean, 305-284-2107, Fax: 305-667-3787, E-mail: nperagallo@miami.edu. *Application contact:* Anne Stabb, Graduate Advisor, 305-284-2533, Fax: 305-284-4827, E-mail: astabb@miami.edu.

University of Michigan, Horace H. Rackham School of Graduate Studies, School of Nursing, Division of Acute, Critical and Long-term Care, Program in Gerontology Nursing, Ann Arbor, MI 48109. Offers gerontology nurse practitioner (MS). *Accreditation:* AACN. Part-time programs available. *Degree requirements:* For master's, thesis, registration. *Entrance requirements:* For master's, GRE General Test, licensure, minimum of B average in BSN program. Additional exam requirements/recommendations for international students: Required—TOEFL (minimum score 560 paper-based; 220 computer-based). Electronic applications accepted. *Faculty research:* Wandering in the elderly, Alzheimer's, clinical specialist and nurse practitioner roles, enhancement of cognitive function.

University of Michigan, Horace H. Rackham School of Graduate Studies, School of Nursing, Division of Acute, Critical and Long-term Care, Program in Psychiatric Mental Health Nursing, Ann Arbor, MI 48109. Offers psychiatric mental health nurse practitioner (MS); psychiatric mental health nursing (MS). *Accreditation:* AACN. Part-time programs available. *Degree requirements:* For master's, thesis, registration. *Entrance requirements:* For master's, GRE General Test, licensure, minimum of B average in BSN program. Additional exam requirements/ recommendations for international students: Required—TOEFL (minimum score 560 paper-based; 220 computer-based). Electronic applications accepted. *Faculty research:* Clinical specialist roles, depression, eating disorders, care of chronically mentally ill.

University of Michigan, Horace H. Rackham School of Graduate Studies, School of Nursing, Division of Health Promotion and Risk Reduction, Program in Community Health Nursing, Ann Arbor, MI 48109. Offers adult primary care/adult nurse practitioner (MS); community care/ home care (MS); family nurse practitioner (MS); occupational health nursing (MS). *Accreditation:* AACN. Part-time and evening/weekend programs available. *Degree requirements:* For master's, thesis, registration. *Entrance requirements:* For master's, GRE General Test, licensure, minimum GPA of 3.0 in BSN program. Additional exam requirements/recommendations for international students: Required—TOEFL (minimum score 560 paper-based; 220 computer-based).

University of Michigan, Horace H. Rackham School of Graduate Studies, School of Nursing, Division of Health Promotion and Risk Reduction, Program in Parent-Child Nursing, Ann Arbor, MI 48109. Offers infant, child, adolescent health nurse practitioner (MS); nurse midwifery (MS). *Accreditation:* AACN. Part-time programs available. Postbaccalaureate distance learning degree programs offered (minimal on-campus study). *Degree requirements:* For master's, thesis, registration. *Entrance requirements:* For master's, GRE General Test. Additional exam requirements/recommendations for international students: Required—TOEFL (minimum score 560 paper-based; 220 computer-based).

University of Minnesota, Twin Cities Campus, Graduate School, School of Nursing, Children with Special Health Care Needs Program, Minneapolis, MN 55455-0213. Offers MS. *Entrance requirements:* Additional exam requirements/recommendations for international students: Required—TOEFL (minimum score 586 paper-based; 240 computer-based). *Application deadline:* For fall admission, 11/1 priority date for domestic and international students; for spring admission, 8/1 priority date for domestic and international students. Application fee: $55 ($75 for international students). *Financial support:* Applicants required to submit FAFSA. *Unit head:* Dr. Linda Lindeke, Coordinator, 612-626-1133, Fax: 612-626-2359, E-mail: linde001@umn.edu. *Application contact:* Information Contact, 612-624-4454, Fax: 612-624-3174, E-mail: nurseoss@umn.edu.

University of Minnesota, Twin Cities Campus, Graduate School, School of Nursing, Family Nurse Practitioner Program, Minneapolis, MN 55455-0213. Offers MS. *Accreditation:* AACN. *Students:* 23 full-time (all women), 2 part-time (both women); includes 2 minority (both African Americans) *Degree requirements:* For master's, final oral exam, project or thesis. *Entrance requirements:* Additional exam requirements/recommendations for international students: Required—TOEFL (minimum score 586 paper-based; 240 computer-based). *Application deadline:* For fall admission, 11/1 priority date for domestic and international students; for spring admission, 8/1 priority date for domestic and international students. Application fee: $55 ($75 for international students). *Financial support:* Fellowships, research assistantships, teaching assistantships, career-related internships or fieldwork and traineeships available. Financial award applicants required to submit FAFSA. *Unit head:* Georgia Nygaard, Coordinator, 612-626-2881, Fax: 612-626-2359, E-mail: nygaa008@umn.edu. *Application contact:* Information Contact, 612-624-4454, Fax: 612-624-3174, E-mail: nurseoss@umn.edu.

University of Minnesota, Twin Cities Campus, Graduate School, School of Nursing, Gerontological Nurse Practitioner Program, Minneapolis, MN 55455-0213. Offers MS. *Accreditation:* AACN. *Students:* 10 full-time (8 women), 7 part-time (6 women); includes 1 minority (African American) *Degree requirements:* For master's, final oral exam, project or thesis. *Entrance requirements:* Additional exam requirements/recommendations for international students: Required—TOEFL (minimum score 586 paper-based; 240 computer-based). *Application deadline:* For fall admission, 11/1 priority date for domestic and international students; for spring admission, 8/1 priority date for domestic and international students. Application fee: $55 ($75 for international students). *Financial support:* Fellowships, research assistantships, teaching assistantships, career-related internships or fieldwork and traineeships available. *Unit head:* Dr. Christine Mueller, Coordinator, 612-626-4922. *Application contact:* Information Contact, 612-624-4454, Fax: 612-624-3174, E-mail: nurseoss@umn.edu.

University of Minnesota, Twin Cities Campus, Graduate School, School of Nursing, Pediatric Clinical Nurse Specialist Program, Minneapolis, MN 55455-0213. Offers MS. *Accreditation:* AACN. Part-time programs available. *Students:* 4 full-time (all women). *Degree requirements:* For master's, final oral exam, project or thesis. *Application deadline:* For fall admission, 11/1 priority date for domestic and international students; for spring admission, 8/1 priority date for domestic and international students. Application fee: $55 ($75 for international students). *Financial support:* Fellowships, research assistantships, teaching assistantships, career-related internships or fieldwork and traineeships available. *Unit head:* Dr. Linda Lindeke, Coordinator, 612-626-1133, Fax: 612-626-2359, E-mail: linde001@umn.edu. *Application contact:* Information Contact, 612-624-4454, Fax: 612-624-3174, E-mail: nurseoss@umn.edu.

University of Minnesota, Twin Cities Campus, Graduate School, School of Nursing, Pediatric Nurse Practitioner Program, Minneapolis, MN 55455-0213. Offers MS. *Accreditation:* AACN. *Students:* 17 full-time (all women), 2 part-time (both women); includes 1 minority (Asian

Family Nurse Practitioner Studies

University of Minnesota, Twin Cities Campus (continued)
American or Pacific Islander) *Degree requirements:* For master's, final oral exam, project or thesis. *Application deadline:* For fall admission, 11/1 priority date for domestic and international students; for spring admission, 8/1 priority date for domestic and international students. Application fee: $55 ($75 for international students). *Financial support:* Fellowships, research assistantships, teaching assistantships, career-related internships or fieldwork and traineeships available. *Unit head:* Dr. Linda Lindeke, Coordinator, 612-626-1133, Fax: 612-626-2359, E-mail: linde001@umn.edu. *Application contact:* Information Contact, 612-624-4454, Fax: 612-624-3174, E-mail: nurseoss@umn.edu.

University of Missouri–Kansas City, School of Nursing, Kansas City, MO 64110-2499. Offers adult clinical nurse specialist (MSN), including adult nurse practitioner, women's health nurse practitioner; family nurse practitioner (MSN); neonatal nurse practitioner (MSN); nurse educator (MSN); nurse executive (MSN); nursing (PhD); pediatric nurse practitioner (MSN). *Accreditation:* AACN. Part-time programs available. Postbaccalaureate distance learning degree programs offered (minimal on-campus study). *Faculty:* 31 full-time (26 women), 32 part-time/adjunct (31 women). *Students:* 36 full-time (all women), 213 part-time (202 women); includes 23 minority (6 African Americans, 2 American Indian/Alaska Native, 6 Asian Americans or Pacific Islanders, 9 Hispanic Americans). Average age 36. 121 applicants, 72% accepted, 71 enrolled. In 2006, 69 master's, 1 doctorate awarded. *Median time to degree:* Of those who began their doctoral program in fall 1998, 60% received their degree in 8 years or less. *Degree requirements:* For master's, thesis or alternative. *Entrance requirements:* For master's, minimum undergraduate GPA of 3.2; for doctorate, GRE, 3 letters of reference, interview and original essay by invitation. Additional exam requirements/recommendations for international students: Required—TOEFL (minimum score 550 paper-based). *Application deadline:* For fall admission, 2/1 priority date for domestic students; for spring admission, 9/15 priority date for domestic students. Application fee: $25. *Expenses:* Tuition, state resident: full-time $4,975; part-time $276 per credit. Tuition, nonresident: full-time $12,847; part-time $713 per credit. Required fees: $595; $595 per year. *Financial support:* In 2006–07, 30 students received support, including 6 research assistantships (averaging $3,450 per year), 7 teaching assistantships with partial tuition reimbursements available (averaging $12,650 per year); fellowships, career-related internships or fieldwork, Federal Work-Study, institutionally sponsored loans, and tuition waivers (full and partial) also available. Support available to part-time students. Financial award application deadline: 6/30; financial award applicants required to submit FAFSA. *Faculty research:* Geriatrics/gerontology, children's pain, neonatology, Alzheimer's care, cancer caregivers. Total annual research expenditures: $1 million. *Unit head:* Dr. Lora Lacey-Haun, Dean, 816-235-1700, Fax: 816-235-1701, E-mail: lacey-haunc@umkc.edu. *Application contact:* Leah Wilder, Coordinator for Admissions and Recruitment, 816-235-5768, Fax: 816-235-1701, E-mail: wilderl@umkc.edu.

University of Nevada, Las Vegas, Graduate College, Division of Health Sciences, School of Nursing, Las Vegas, NV 89154-9900. Offers family nurse practitioner (MS, Post-Master's Certificate); nursing (PhD); nursing education (MS, Post-Master's Certificate); pediatric nurse practitioner (MS). *Accreditation:* NLN. Part-time programs available. *Faculty:* 21 full-time (all women), 6 part-time/adjunct (all women). *Students:* 74 full-time (59 women), 66 part-time (61 women); includes 24 minority (2 African Americans, 15 Asian Americans or Pacific Islanders, 7 Hispanic Americans), 46 international. 190 applicants, 66% accepted, 107 enrolled. In 2006, 11 degrees awarded. *Degree requirements:* For master's, research project, thesis optional. *Entrance requirements:* For master's, GRE General Test, minimum GPA of 3.0 during previous 2 years, minimum overall GPA of 2.75. Additional exam requirements/recommendations for international students: Required—TOEFL (minimum score 550 paper-based; 213 computer-based; 80 iBT). *Application deadline:* For fall admission, 3/15 for domestic and international students. Application fee: $60 ($75 for international students). Electronic applications accepted. *Financial support:* In 2006–07, 7 research assistantships with partial tuition reimbursements (averaging $10,000 per year) were awarded; career-related internships or fieldwork, Federal Work-Study, institutionally sponsored loans, scholarships/grants, health care benefits, and unspecified assistantships also available. Support available to part-time students. Financial award application deadline: 3/1. *Unit head:* Dr. Carolyn Yucha, Dean, 702-895-3415. *Application contact:* Graduate College Admissions Evaluator, 702-895-3320, Fax: 702-895-4180, E-mail: gradcollege@unlv.edu.

University of New Brunswick Fredericton, School of Graduate Studies, Faculty of Nursing, Fredericton, NB E3B 5A3, Canada. Offers advance nurse practitioner (MN); nursing (MN). *Faculty:* 30 full-time (all women). *Students:* 6 full-time (all women), 48 part-time (all women). In 2006, 9 degrees awarded. *Entrance requirements:* For master's, undergraduate coursework in statistics and nursing research, GPA of 3.3 or better, registration as a nurse in New Brunswick (or eligible), statement of professional and research interests and career goals. Application fee: $50 Canadian dollars. *Financial support:* In 2006–07, 5 research assistantships, 4 teaching assistantships were awarded; fellowships also available. *Unit head:* Gad Storr, Director of Graduate Studies, 506-458-7643, Fax: 506-447-3057. *Application contact:* Francis Perry, Graduate Secretary, 506-451-6844, Fax: 506-447-3057, E-mail: fperry@unb.ca.

The University of North Carolina at Charlotte, Graduate School, College of Health and Human Services, School of Nursing, Department of Family and Community Nursing, Charlotte, NC 28223-0001. Offers family nurse practitioner (MSN); nursing-community health (MSN). *Accreditation:* AACN. *Students:* 21 full-time (20 women), 52 part-time (all women); includes 10 minority (7 African Americans, 3 Hispanic Americans), 1 international. Average age 37. 41 applicants, 68% accepted, 22 enrolled. In 2006, 31 degrees awarded. *Degree requirements:* For master's, thesis or project. *Entrance requirements:* For master's, GRE General Test (nursing and health administration), GRE General Test or MAT (MSN), minimum GPA of 3.0 in undergraduate major. Additional exam requirements/recommendations for international students: Required—TOEFL (minimum score 557 paper-based; 220 computer-based). *Application deadline:* For fall admission, 7/1 for domestic students, 5/1 for international students; for spring admission, 11/1 for domestic students, 10/1 for international students. Applications are processed on a rolling basis. Application fee: $55. Electronic applications accepted. *Expenses:* Tuition, state resident: full-time $2,719; part-time $170 per credit. Tuition, nonresident: full-time $12,926; part-time $808 per credit. Required fees: $1,555. *Financial support:* In 2006–07, 1 research assistantship (averaging $1,024 per year), 1 teaching assistantship (averaging $4,032 per year) were awarded; fellowships, career-related internships or fieldwork, Federal Work-Study, institutionally sponsored loans, scholarships/grants, traineeships, and unspecified assistantships also available. Support available to part-time students. Financial award application deadline: 4/1; financial award applicants required to submit FAFSA. *Faculty research:* Community-based models of care, family transitions, evidence-based practice, values-based practice, living with HIV/AIDS, successful aging, bullying. *Unit head:* Dr. Lienne D. Edwards, Interim Chair, 704-687-4683, Fax: 704-687-3180. *Application contact:* Kathy B. Giddings, Director of Graduate Admissions, 704-687-3366, Fax: 704-687-3279, E-mail: gradadm@email.uncc.edu.

The University of North Carolina at Greensboro, Graduate School, School of Nursing, Greensboro, NC 27412-5001. Offers adult clinical nurse specialist (MSN, PMC); adult/gerontological nurse practitioner (MSN, PMC); nurse anesthesia (MSN, PMC); nursing (PhD); nursing administration (MSN); nursing education (MSN); MSN/MBA. *Accreditation:* AACN; AANA/CANAEP; NLN. *Faculty:* 24 full-time (23 women), 27 part-time/adjunct (22 women). *Students:* 231 full-time (197 women), 98 part-time (83 women); includes 56 minority (41 African Americans, 3 American Indian/Alaska Native, 9 Asian Americans or Pacific Islanders, 3 Hispanic Americans). 206 applicants, 59% accepted. *Degree requirements:* For master's, thesis or alternative. *Entrance requirements:* For master's, GRE General Test or MAT, BSN, clinical experience, liability insurance, RN license; for PMC, liability insurance, MSN, RN license. Additional exam requirements/recommendations for international students: Required—TOEFL. Application fee: $45. Electronic applications accepted. *Expenses:* Tuition, state resident: full-time $2,692. Tuition, nonresident: full-time $13,742. *Financial support:* Research assistantships with full tuition reimbursements, career-related internships or fieldwork, Federal Work-Study, scholarships/grants, and traineeships available. Support available to part-time students. *Unit head:* Dr. Lynne Pearcey, Dean, 336-334-5177, Fax: 336-334-3628, E-mail: l_pearce@uncg.edu. *Application contact:* Michelle Harkleroad, Director of Graduate Admissions, 336-334-4884, Fax: 336-334-4424, E-mail: mbharkle@uncg.edu.

University of Northern Colorado, Graduate School, College of Natural and Health Sciences, School of Nursing, Greeley, CO 80639. Offers clinical nurse specialist in chronic illness (MS); family nurse practitioner (MS); nursing education (MS, PhD). *Accreditation:* AACN. Postbaccalaureate distance learning degree programs offered. *Faculty:* 12 full-time (all women). *Students:* 58 full-time (57 women), 20 part-time (19 women); includes 6 minority (2 American Indian/Alaska Native, 4 Hispanic Americans). Average age 40. 63 applicants, 68% accepted, 21 enrolled. In 2006, 21 degrees awarded. *Degree requirements:* For master's, thesis or alternative, comprehensive exam; for doctorate, thesis/dissertation, comprehensive exam. *Entrance requirements:* For master's and doctorate, GRE General Test, minimum GPA of 3.0 in last 60 hours, BS in nursing, 2 letters of recommendation. *Application deadline:* Applications are processed on a rolling basis. Application fee: $50 ($60 for international students). Electronic applications accepted. *Expenses:* Tuition, state resident: full-time $5,118; part-time $213 per credit hour. Tuition, nonresident: full-time $14,832; part-time $618 per credit hour. Required fees: $674; $34 per credit hour. *Financial support:* In 2006–07, 47 students received support, including 4 fellowships (averaging $1,006 per year), 3 research assistantships (averaging $7,108 per year), 2 teaching assistantships (averaging $4,832 per year); unspecified assistantships also available. Financial award application deadline: 3/1; financial award applicants required to submit FAFSA. *Unit head:* Dr. Diane Peters, Interim Co-Director, 970-351-2293, Fax: 970-351-1707.

University of North Florida, College of Health, School of Nursing, Jacksonville, FL 32224-2645. Offers advanced practice nursing (MSN); primary care nurse practitioner (Certificate). *Accreditation:* AACN. *Faculty:* 12 full-time (11 women). *Students:* 36 full-time (28 women), 29 part-time (25 women); includes 11 minority (3 African Americans, 1 American Indian/Alaska Native, 3 Asian Americans or Pacific Islanders, 4 Hispanic Americans), 2 international. Average age 35. 104 applicants, 45% accepted, 39 enrolled. In 2006, 11 degrees awarded. *Degree requirements:* For master's, thesis optional. *Entrance requirements:* For master's, GRE General Test, minimum GPA of 3.0 in last 60 hours of course work, BSN, clinical experience, resumé. Additional exam requirements/recommendations for international students: Required—TOEFL (minimum score 500 paper-based; 173 computer-based). *Application deadline:* For fall admission, 5/1 for domestic and international students. Applications are processed on a rolling basis. Application fee: $30. Electronic applications accepted. *Expenses:* Tuition, state resident: full-time $4,948; part-time $206 per semester hour. Tuition, nonresident: full-time $19,140; part-time $408 per semester hour. *Financial support:* In 2006–07, 33 students received support; research assistantships available. Financial award application deadline: 4/1; financial award applicants required to submit FAFSA. *Faculty research:* Teen pregnancy, diabetes, ethical decision making, family caregivers. Total annual research expenditures: $1.4 million. *Unit head:* Dr. Lilia Loriz, Director, 904-620-2684, E-mail: lloriz@unf.edu.

University of Pennsylvania, School of Nursing, Adult Acute Care Nurse Practitioner Program, Philadelphia, PA 19104. Offers acute care nurse practitioner (MSN). *Accreditation:* AACN. Part-time programs available. *Entrance requirements:* For master's, GRE General Test, BSN, minimum GPA of 3.0, previous course work in statistics. Expenses: Contact institution. *Faculty research:* Post-injury disability, bereavement and attributions in fire survivors, stress in staff nurses.

University of Pennsylvania, School of Nursing, Adult Health Nurse Practitioner Program, Philadelphia, PA 19104. Offers MSN. *Accreditation:* AACN. Part-time programs available. *Entrance requirements:* For master's, GRE General Test, BSN, minimum GPA of 3.0, previous course work in basic statistics. Additional exam requirements/recommendations for international students: Required—TOEFL. Expenses: Contact institution. *Faculty research:* Restraints, incontinence, discharge planning, frail elders, quality of life across continuum of care.

University of Pennsylvania, School of Nursing, Adult Oncology Nurse Practitioner Program, Philadelphia, PA 19104. Offers MSN. *Accreditation:* AACN. Part-time programs available. *Entrance requirements:* For master's, GRE General Test, BSN, minimum GPA of 3.0, previous course work in statistics. Additional exam requirements/recommendations for international students: Required—TOEFL. Expenses: Contact institution. *Faculty research:* Randomized clinical trials to evaluate advanced nursing practice in oncology patients and their caregivers, symptoms management.

University of Pennsylvania, School of Nursing, Family Health Nurse Practitioner Program, Philadelphia, PA 19104. Offers MSN, Certificate. *Accreditation:* AACN. Part-time programs available. *Entrance requirements:* For master's, GRE General Test, 1 year of clinical experience in area of interest, BSN, minimum GPA of 3.0, previous course work in statistics. Additional exam requirements/recommendations for international students: Required—TOEFL. Expenses: Contact institution. *Faculty research:* Evaluation of primary care practitioner practice, access to primary care.

University of Pennsylvania, School of Nursing, Neonatal Nurse Practitioner Program, Philadelphia, PA 19104. Offers MSN. *Accreditation:* AACN. Part-time programs available. *Entrance requirements:* For master's, GRE General Test, BSN, minimum GPA of 3.0, previous course work in statistics, 1 year of experience in a neonatal intensive care unit. Additional exam requirements/recommendations for international students: Required—TOEFL. Expenses: Contact institution. *Faculty research:* Neurobehavioral development, temperament, newborn sucking behaviors, parenting pre-term infants.

University of Pennsylvania, School of Nursing, Occupational Health Nurse Practitioner Program, Philadelphia, PA 19104. Offers administration/consulting (MSN); primary care (MSN). *Accreditation:* AACN. Part-time programs available. *Entrance requirements:* For master's, GRE General Test, BSN, minimum GPA of 3.0, previous course work in statistics. Additional exam requirements/recommendations for international students: Required—TOEFL. Expenses: Contact institution. *Faculty research:* Injury prevention.

University of Pennsylvania, School of Nursing, Pediatric Acute/Chronic Care Nurse Practitioner Program, Philadelphia, PA 19104. Offers MSN. *Accreditation:* AACN. Part-time programs available. Postbaccalaureate distance learning degree programs offered. *Entrance requirements:* For master's, GRE General Test, 1 year of clinical course work, BSN, minimum GPA of 3.0, previous course work in statistics. Additional exam requirements/recommendations for international students: Required—TOEFL. Expenses: Contact institution. *Faculty research:* Hispanic health, bereavement, pediatric AIDS, chronically ill children and their families.

University of Pennsylvania, School of Nursing, Pediatric Nurse Practitioner Program, Philadelphia, PA 19104. Offers MSN. *Accreditation:* AACN. Part-time programs available. *Entrance requirements:* For master's, GRE General Test, 1 year of clinical experience in area of interest, BSN, minimum GPA of 3.0, previous course work in statistics. Additional exam requirements/recommendations for international students: Required—TOEFL. Expenses: Contact institution. *Faculty research:* Adolescent behavior change, prevention of teenage pregnancy, community schools.

University of Pennsylvania, School of Nursing, Pediatric Oncology Nurse Practitioner Program, Philadelphia, PA 19104. Offers MSN. *Accreditation:* AACN. *Entrance requirements:* For master's, GRE General Test, BSN, minimum GPA of 3.0, previous course work in statistics. Additional exam requirements/recommendations for international students: Required—TOEFL. Expenses: Contact institution.

University of Pennsylvania, School of Nursing, Perinatal Advanced Practice Nurse Specialist Program, Philadelphia, PA 19104. Offers MSN. *Accreditation:* AACN. Part-time programs available. *Entrance requirements:* For master's, GRE General Test, BSN, minimum GPA of 3.0, previous course work in statistics. Additional exam requirements/recommendations for international students: Required—TOEFL. Expenses: Contact institution.

University of Pennsylvania, School of Nursing, Psychiatric Mental Health Advanced Practice Nurse Program, Philadelphia, PA 19104. Offers adult and special populations (MSN); child and family (MSN); geropsychiatrics (MSN). *Accreditation:* AACN. Part-time programs available. *Entrance requirements:* For master's, GRE General Test, BSN, minimum GPA of 3.0, previous course work in statistics. Additional exam requirements/recommendations for international students: Required—TOEFL. Expenses: Contact institution. *Faculty research:* Use of restraints in psychiatry, victims of trauma, spiritual use of prayer by cancer patients, coping strategies of African-Americans, urban health care.

University of Pennsylvania, School of Nursing, Women's Healthcare Nurse Practitioner Program, Philadelphia, PA 19104. Offers MSN. *Accreditation:* AACN. Part-time programs available. Postbaccalaureate distance learning degree programs offered (minimal on-campus study). *Entrance requirements:* For master's, GRE General Test, BSN, minimum GPA of 3.0, previous course work in statistics, physical assessment experience. Additional exam requirements/recommendations for international students: Required—TOEFL. Expenses: Contact institution. *Faculty research:* New mother and infant healthcare follow-up, adequacy of antepartum care, models of healthcare.

University of Phoenix–Bay Area Campus, The Artemis School, College of Health and Human Services, Pleasanton, CA 94588-3677. Offers administration of justice and security (MS); family nurse practitioner (MSN); health care management (MBA); marriage, family and child therapy (MSC). Evening/weekend programs available. *Faculty:* 19 full-time (8 women), 184 part-time/adjunct (85 women). *Students:* 58 full-time (51 women); includes 22 minority (6 African Americans, 12 Asian Americans or Pacific Islanders, 4 Hispanic Americans), 6 international. Average age 42. In 2006, 13 degrees awarded. *Degree requirements:* For master's, thesis (for some programs), registration. *Entrance requirements:* For master's, minimum undergraduate GPA of 2.5, 3 years of work experience, RN license. Additional exam requirements/recommendations for international students: Required—TOEFL (minimum score 550 paper-based; 213 computer-based; 79 iBT). *Application deadline:* Applications are processed on a rolling basis. Application fee: $45. Electronic applications accepted. *Expenses:* Tuition: Full-time $12,648. Required fees: $760. *Financial support:* Institutionally sponsored loans and scholarships/grants available. Financial award applicants required to submit FAFSA. *Unit head:* Dr. Gil Linne, Dean/Executive Director, 480-557-1751, E-mail: gil.linne@phoenix.edu. *Application contact:* Chair, 877-416-4100.

University of Phoenix–Detroit Campus, College of Health and Human Services, Southfield, MI 48076. Offers family nurse practitioner (MSN); health administration (MHA); health care management (MBA); nursing (MSN); MSN/MBA.

University of Phoenix–Hawaii Campus, The Artemis School, College of Health and Human Services, Honolulu, HI 96813-4317. Offers administration of justice and security (MS); community counseling (MSC); family nurse practitioner (MSN); health administration (MHA); health care management (MBA); marriage, family and child therapy (MSC); nursing (MSN); psychology (MS). Evening/weekend programs available. *Faculty:* 20 full-time (12 women), 84 part-time/adjunct (46 women). *Students:* 47 full-time (36 women); includes 20 minority (2 African Americans, 15 Asian Americans or Pacific Islanders, 3 Hispanic Americans), 9 international. Average age 41. In 2006, 13 degrees awarded. *Degree requirements:* For master's, thesis (for some programs), registration. *Entrance requirements:* For master's, minimum undergraduate GPA of 2.5, 3 years of work experience, RN license. Additional exam requirements/recommendations for international students: Required—TOEFL (minimum score 550 paper-based; 213 computer-based; 79 iBT). *Application deadline:* Applications are processed on a rolling basis. Application fee: $45. Electronic applications accepted. *Expenses:* Tuition: Full-time $11,520. Required fees: $760. *Financial support:* Institutionally sponsored loans and scholarships/grants available. Financial award applicants required to submit FAFSA. *Unit head:* Dr. Gil Linne, Dean/Executive Director, 480-557-1751, E-mail: gil.linne@phoenix.edu. *Application contact:* Chair, 808-536-2686, Fax: 808-536-3848.

University of Phoenix–Minneapolis/St. Louis Park Campus, College of Health and Human Services, St. Louis Park, MN 55426. Offers family nurse practitioner (MSN); health care management (MBA); nursing (MSN).

University of Phoenix–Phoenix Campus, The Artemis School, College of Health and Human Services, Phoenix, AZ 85040-1958. Offers community counseling (MSC); family nurse practitioner (MSN); health care management (MBA); nurse practitioner (Certificate); nursing (MSN); nursing health care education (Certificate). Evening/weekend programs available. *Faculty:* 45 full-time (20 women), 510 part-time/adjunct (308 women). *Students:* 493 full-time (420 women); includes 79 minority (17 African Americans, 4 American Indian/Alaska Native, 20 Asian Americans or Pacific Islanders, 38 Hispanic Americans), 12 international. Average age 38. In 2006, 166 degrees awarded. *Degree requirements:* For master's, thesis (for some programs), registration. *Entrance requirements:* For master's, 3 years of work experience in field, minimum undergraduate GPA of 2.5, RN license. Additional exam requirements/recommendations for international students: Required—TOEFL (minimum score 550 paper-based; 213 computer-based; 79 iBT). *Application deadline:* Applications are processed on a rolling basis. Application fee: $45. Electronic applications accepted. *Financial support:* Institutionally sponsored loans and scholarships/grants available. Financial award applicants required to submit FAFSA. *Unit head:* Dr. Gil Linne, Dean/Executive Director, 480-557-1751, E-mail: gil.linne@phoenix.edu. *Application contact:* Chair, 480-804-7400, Fax: 480-557-2320.

University of Phoenix–Sacramento Valley Campus, The Artemis School, College of Health and Human Services, Sacramento, CA 95833-3632. Offers administration of justice and security (MS); family nurse practitioner (MSN); health care management (MBA); marriage, family and child counseling (MSC); nursing (MSN); nursing education (MSN). Evening/weekend programs available. *Faculty:* 36 full-time (27 women), 270 part-time/adjunct (121 women). *Students:* 330 full-time (266 women); includes 73 minority (38 African Americans, 2 American Indian/Alaska Native, 16 Asian Americans or Pacific Islanders, 17 Hispanic Americans), 29 international. Average age 40. In 2006, 82 degrees awarded. *Degree requirements:* For master's, thesis (for some programs), registration. *Entrance requirements:* For master's, RN license, minimum undergraduate GPA of 2.5, 3 years work experience. Additional exam requirements/recommendations for international students: Required—TOEFL (minimum score 550 paper-based; 213 computer-based; 79 iBT). *Application deadline:* Applications are processed on a rolling basis. Application fee: $45. Electronic applications accepted. *Expenses:* Tuition: Full-time $12,024. Required fees: $760. *Financial support:* Institutionally sponsored loans and scholarships/grants available. Financial award applicants required to submit FAFSA. *Unit head:* Dr. Gil Linne, Dean/Executive Director, 480-557-1757, E-mail: gil.linne@phoenix.edu. *Application contact:* College Chair, 916-923-2107, Fax: 916-923-3914.

University of Phoenix–Southern Arizona Campus, The Artemis School, College of Health and Human Services, Tucson, AZ 85712-2732. Offers administration of justice and security (MS); family nurse practitioner (Certificate); health administration (MHA); marriage, family and child therapy (MSC); nursing (MSN). Evening/weekend programs available. *Faculty:* 24 full-time (17 women), 212 part-time/adjunct (127 women). *Students:* 192 full-time (158 women); includes 38 minority (16 African Americans, 3 Asian Americans or Pacific Islanders, 19 Hispanic Americans), 16 international. In 2006, 34 degrees awarded. *Degree requirements:* For master's, thesis (for some programs), registration. *Entrance requirements:* For master's, minimum undergraduate GPA of 2.5, 3 years of work experience, RN license. Additional exam requirements/recommendations for international students: Required—TOEFL (minimum score 550 paper-based; 213 computer-based; 79 iBT). *Application deadline:* Applications are processed on a rolling basis. Application fee: $45. Electronic applications accepted. *Expenses:* Tuition: Full-time $8,669. Required fees: $760. *Financial support:* Institutionally sponsored loans and scholarships/grants available. Financial award applicants required to submit FAFSA. *Unit head:* Dr. Gil Linne, Dean/Executive Director, 480-557-1757, E-mail: gil.linne@phoenix.edu. *Application contact:* Campus College Chair, 520-881-6512, Fax: 520-795-6177.

University of Phoenix–Southern California Campus, The Artemis School, College of Health and Human Services, Costa Mesa, CA 92626. Offers family nurse practitioner (MSN, Certificate); health care education (MSN); health care management (MBA); marriage, family and child therapy (MSC); nursing (MSN). Evening/weekend programs available. *Faculty:* 53 full-time (32 women), 456 part-time/adjunct (240 women). *Students:* 623 full-time (524 women); includes 237 minority (98 African Americans, 2 American Indian/Alaska Native, 62 Asian Americans or Pacific Islanders, 75 Hispanic Americans), 59 international. Average age 40. In 2006, 113 degrees awarded. *Degree requirements:* For master's, thesis (for some programs), registration. *Entrance requirements:* For master's, minimum undergraduate GPA of 2.5, 3 years work experience, RN license. Additional exam requirements/recommendations for international students: Required—TOEFL (minimum score 550 paper-based; 213 computer-based; 79 iBT). *Application deadline:* Applications are processed on a rolling basis. Application fee: $45. Electronic applications accepted. *Expenses:* Tuition: Full-time $13,512. Required fees: $760. *Financial support:* Institutionally sponsored loans and scholarships/grants available. Financial award applicants required to submit FAFSA. *Unit head:* Dr. Gil Linne, Dean/Executive Director, 480-557-1751, E-mail: gil.linne@phoenix.edu. *Application contact:* Campus College Chair, 714-398-1878, Fax: 714-378-5856.

University of Pittsburgh, School of Nursing, Advanced Specialist Role Program, Pittsburgh, PA 15260. Offers nursing administration (MSN); nursing education (MSN); nursing informatics (MSN); nursing research (MSN). *Accreditation:* AACN. Part-time programs available. *Students:* 4 full-time (2 women), 46 part-time (45 women); includes 6 minority (3 African Americans, 2 Asian Americans or Pacific Islanders, 1 Hispanic American). Average age 41. 12 applicants, 50% accepted, 5 enrolled. In 2006, 18 degrees awarded. *Degree requirements:* For master's, thesis optional. *Entrance requirements:* For master's, GRE or MAT, BSN, RN license, letters of recommendation, resumé, course work in statistics, 1-3 years of nursing experience. Additional exam requirements/recommendations for international students: Required—TOEFL (minimum score 550 paper-based; 213 computer-based; 80 iBT). *Application deadline:* For fall admission, 8/1 priority date for domestic students; for spring admission, 12/1 priority date for domestic students. Applications are processed on a rolling basis. Application fee: $50. Electronic applications accepted. *Unit head:* Dr. Helen Burns, Associate Dean for Clinical Education, 412-624-6616, Fax: 412-624-2401, E-mail: burnsh@pitt.edu. *Application contact:* Laurie Lapsley, Administrator of Graduate Student Services, 412-624-9670, Fax: 412-624-2409, E-mail: lapsleyl@pitt.edu.

University of Pittsburgh, School of Nursing, Program in Clinical Nurse Specialist, Pittsburgh, PA 15260. Offers medical/surgical clinical nurse specialist (MSN); psychiatric and mental health clinical nurse specialist (MSN). *Accreditation:* AACN. Part-time programs available. *Students:* 1 (woman) full-time, 23 part-time (21 women). Average age 37. 7 applicants, 86% accepted, 5 enrolled. In 2006, 9 degrees awarded. *Degree requirements:* For master's, thesis optional. *Entrance requirements:* For master's, GRE or MAT, BSN, RN license, letters of recommendation, resumé, course work in statistics, 1-3 years of nursing experience. Additional exam requirements/recommendations for international students: Required—TOEFL (minimum score 550 paper-based; 213 computer-based; 80 iBT). *Application deadline:* For fall admission, 8/1 priority date for domestic students; for spring admission, 12/1 priority date for domestic students. Applications are processed on a rolling basis. Application fee: $50. Electronic applications accepted. *Unit head:* Dr. Helen Burns, Associate Dean for Clinical Education, 412-624-6616, Fax: 412-624-2401, E-mail: burnsh@pitt.edu. *Application contact:* Laurie Lapsley, Administrator of Graduate Student Services, 412-624-9670, Fax: 412-624-2409, E-mail: lapsleyl@pitt.edu.

University of Pittsburgh, School of Nursing, Program in Nurse Practitioner Studies, Pittsburgh, PA 15260. Offers acute care nurse practitioner (MSN); adult nurse practitioner (MSN); family nurse practitioner (MSN); nursing practice (DNP); pediatric nurse practitioner (MSN); psychiatric primary care nurse practitioner (MSN). *Accreditation:* AACN. Part-time programs available. *Students:* 15 full-time (13 women), 65 part-time (57 women); includes 5 minority (3 African Americans, 2 Hispanic Americans). Average age 38. 47 applicants, 62% accepted, 27 enrolled. In 2006, 28 degrees awarded. *Degree requirements:* For master's, thesis optional. *Entrance requirements:* For master's, GRE General Test or MAT, BSN, RN license, letters of recommendation, resumé, course work in statistics, 1-3 years of nursing experience; for doctorate, GRE General Test, BSN, RN license, minimum GPA of 3.5, 3 letters of recommendation. Additional exam requirements/recommendations for international students: Required—TOEFL (minimum score 550 paper-based; 213 computer-based; 80 iBT). *Application deadline:* For fall admission, 8/1 priority date for domestic students, 8/1 for international students; for spring admission, 12/1 priority date for domestic students, 12/1 for international students. Applications are processed on a rolling basis. Application fee: $50. Electronic applications accepted.

University of Puerto Rico, Medical Sciences Campus, School of Nursing, San Juan, PR 00936-5067. Offers anesthesia (MSN); clinical specialist (MSN); family nurse practitioner (MSN); nurse administrator (MSN); nursing education (MSN). *Accreditation:* AACN; AANA/CANAEP. Part-time and evening/weekend programs available. *Faculty:* 12 full-time (11 women), 3 part-time/adjunct (2 women). *Students:* 115 full-time (all women), 13 part-time (9 women); includes 123 minority (all Hispanic Americans), 3 international. 70 applicants, 71% accepted. In 2006, 40 degrees awarded. *Degree requirements:* For master's, one foreign language. *Entrance requirements:* For master's, GRE or EXADEP, interview, Puerto Rico RN license or professional license for international students, general and specific point average, article analysis. *Application deadline:* For spring admission, 4/30 priority date for domestic and international students. Applications are processed on a rolling basis. Application fee: $33. Electronic applications accepted. *Financial support:* In 2006–07, research assistantships with full tuition reimbursements (averaging $28,175 per year), teaching assistantships with full tuition reimbursements (averaging $48,965 per year) were awarded; Federal Work-Study, traineeships, tuition waivers (full), and unspecified assistantships also available. Financial award application deadline: 6/30. *Faculty research:* HIV, health disparities, teen violence, women and violence, neurological disorders. *Unit head:* Dr. Suane E. Sánchez, Dean, 787-758-2525 Ext. 2100, Fax: 787-281-0721, E-mail: sesanchez@rcm.upr.edu. *Application contact:* Dr. Angelica Y. Matos, Director Graduate Department, 787-758-2525, Fax: 787-281-0721.

University of Rhode Island, Graduate School, College of Nursing, Kingston, RI 02881. Offers administration (MS); clinical specialist in gerontology (MS); clinical specialist in psychiatric/mental health (MS); family nurse practitioner (MS); nurse midwifery (MS); nursing (PhD); nursing education (MS). *Accreditation:* AACN; ACNM/DOA (one or more programs are accredited). In 2006, 34 master's, 5 doctorates awarded. *Application deadline:* For fall admission, 4/15 for domestic students. Application fee: $35. *Expenses:* Tuition, state resident: full-time $6,032; part-time $335 per credit. Tuition, nonresident: full-time $17,288; part-time $960 per credit. Required fees: $65 per credit. $30 per semester. One-time fee: $80 part-time. *Unit head:* Dayle Joseph, Dean, 401-874-2766.

University of San Diego, Hahn School of Nursing and Health Sciences, San Diego, CA 92110-2492. Offers accelerated nursing (for RNs only) (MSN); adult clinical nurse specialist (MSN, Post Master's Certificate); adult nurse practitioner (MSN, Post Master's Certificate); clinical nursing (MSN); entry-level nursing (for non-RNs) (MSN); executive nurse leader (MSN); family nurse practitioner (MSN, Post Master's Certificate); nursing science (PhD); pediatric nurse practitioner (MSN, Post Master's Certificate). *Accreditation:* AACN. Part-time and evening/weekend programs available. *Faculty:* 13 full-time (12 women), 33 part-time/adjunct (all women). *Students:* 103 full-time (85 women), 138 part-time (131 women); includes 58 minority (7 African Americans, 3 American Indian/Alaska Native, 26 Asian Americans or Pacific Islanders, 22 Hispanic Americans), 4 international. Average age 37. 261 applicants, 54% accepted, 87 enrolled. In 2006, 35 master's, 19 doctorates awarded. *Degree requirements:* For doctorate, thesis/dissertation, residency. *Entrance requirements:* For master's, GRE General Test (for

Family Nurse Practitioner Studies

University of San Diego (continued)
entry-level nursing), BSN and current California RN licensure (for all programs except entry-level nursing); minimum GPA of 3.0; for doctorate, GRE General Test, minimum GPA of 3.5, MSN, current California RN licensure. Additional exam requirements/recommendations for international students: Required—TOEFL, TWE. *Application deadline:* Applications are processed on a rolling basis. Application fee: $45. Electronic applications accepted. *Financial support:* Scholarships/grants and traineeships available. Support available to part-time students. Financial award application deadline: 4/1; financial award applicants required to submit FAFSA. *Faculty research:* Health promotion, decision making, psychogeriatric nursing, historical nursing, leadership behavior. *Unit head:* Dr. Sally Hardin, Dean, 619-260-4550, Fax: 619-260-6814. *Application contact:* Stephen Pultz, Director of Admissions, 619-260-4524, Fax: 619-260-4158, E-mail: grads@sandiego.edu.

See Close-Up on page 1977.

University of San Francisco, School of Nursing, San Francisco, CA 94117-1080. Offers advanced practice nursing-nurse practitioner and clinical nurse specialist (MSN), including adult health nursing; nursing administration (MSN); MSN/MBA; MSN/MPA; MSN/MSIS. *Accreditation:* AACN. Part-time programs available. *Faculty:* 6 full-time (5 women), 10 part-time/adjunct (9 women). *Students:* 126 full-time (106 women), 11 part-time (10 women); includes 46 minority (3 African Americans, 36 Asian Americans or Pacific Islanders, 7 Hispanic Americans), 5 international. Average age 31. 219 applicants, 65% accepted, 47 enrolled. In 2006, 53 degrees awarded. *Entrance requirements:* For master's, minimum GPA of 3.0. *Application deadline:* Applications are processed on a rolling basis. Application fee: $40. *Expenses:* Tuition: Full-time $17,370; part-time $965 per unit. Tuition and fees vary according to degree level, campus/location and program. *Financial support:* In 2006–07, 114 students received support. Institutionally sponsored loans available. Financial award application deadline: 3/2. *Faculty research:* Direct patient/client care, providers of health care. *Unit head:* Dr. Judith Karshmer, Dean, 415-422-6681, Fax: 415-422-6877, E-mail: nursing@usfca.edu.

The University of Scranton, Graduate School, Department of Nursing, Scranton, PA 18510. Offers adult health nursing (MSN); family nurse practitioner (MSN, PMC); nurse anesthesia (MSN, PMC). Applicants accepted in odd-numbered years only. *Accreditation:* AACN; AANA/CANAEP. Part-time and evening/weekend programs available. *Faculty:* 13 full-time (all women), 2 part-time/adjunct (both women). *Students:* 44 full-time (29 women), 30 part-time (27 women); includes 5 minority (1 African American, 2 Asian Americans or Pacific Islanders, 2 Hispanic Americans). Average age 36. 63 applicants, 68% accepted. In 2006, 19 degrees awarded. *Degree requirements:* For master's, thesis (for some programs), capstone experience. *Entrance requirements:* For master's, BSN, minimum GPA of 3.0, Pennsylvania RN license. Additional exam requirements/recommendations for international students: Required—TOEFL (minimum score 500 paper-based; 173 computer-based), IELTS (minimum score 6). *Application deadline:* For fall admission, 9/1 for domestic students. Applications are processed on a rolling basis. Application fee: $50. *Expenses:* Tuition: Part-time $684 per credit. Required fees: $25 per term. *Financial support:* In 2006–07, 7 teaching assistantships with full and partial tuition reimbursements (averaging $4,085 per year) were awarded; career-related internships or fieldwork, Federal Work-Study, and unspecified assistantships also available. Support available to part-time students. Financial award application deadline: 3/1. *Faculty research:* Home care, doctoral education, health care of women and children, pain, health promotion and adolescence. *Unit head:* Dr. Patricia Harrington, Chair, 570-941-7673, Fax: 570-941-4201, E-mail: harringtonp1@scranton.edu. *Application contact:* Dr. Mary Jane Hanson, Director, 570-941-4060, Fax: 570-941-4201, E-mail: hansonm2@scranton.edu.

University of South Carolina, The Graduate School, College of Nursing, Program in Advanced Practice Clinical Nursing, Columbia, SC 29208. Offers acute care nurse practitioner (Certificate); advanced practice clinical nursing (MSN). *Accreditation:* AACN. Part-time programs available. *Entrance requirements:* For master's, master's degree in nursing, RN license; for Certificate, MSN. Additional exam requirements/recommendations for international students: Required—TOEFL (minimum score 570 paper-based; 213 computer-based). Electronic applications accepted.

University of South Carolina, The Graduate School, College of Nursing, Program in Advanced Practice Nursing in Primary Care, Columbia, SC 29208. Offers MSN, Certificate. *Accreditation:* AACN. *Entrance requirements:* For master's, master's degree in nursing, RN license; for Certificate, MSN. Additional exam requirements/recommendations for international students: Required—TOEFL (minimum score 570 paper-based; 230 computer-based). Electronic applications accepted. *Faculty research:* Prenatal care, nursing ethics, Alzheimer's disease, preterm labor experience, psycho-dynamics of women's health.

University of South Carolina, The Graduate School, College of Nursing, Program in Advanced Practice Nursing in Psychiatric Mental Health, Columbia, SC 29208. Offers MSN, Certificate. Part-time programs available. *Entrance requirements:* For master's, master's degree in nursing, RN license; for Certificate, MSN. Additional exam requirements/recommendations for international students: Required—TOEFL (minimum score 570 paper-based; 213 computer-based). Electronic applications accepted.

University of South Carolina, The Graduate School, College of Nursing, Program in Health Nursing, Columbia, SC 29208. Offers adult nurse practitioner (MSN); community/public health clinical nurse specialist (MSN); family nurse practitioner (MSN); pediatric nurse practitioner (MSN). *Accreditation:* AACN. Part-time programs available. *Degree requirements:* For master's, thesis or alternative. *Entrance requirements:* For master's, GRE General Test or MAT, BS in nursing, nursing license. Additional exam requirements/recommendations for international students: Required—TOEFL (minimum score 570 paper-based; 230 computer-based). Electronic applications accepted. *Faculty research:* Health promotion, physical activity, adolescent health, pre-term labor, low birthrate.

University of Southern Maine, College of Nursing and Health Professions, Portland, ME 04104-9300. Offers adult health nursing (PMC); clinical nurse leader (MS); clinical nurse specialist psychiatric-mental health nursing (MS); family nursing (PMC); medical/surgical nursing (MS); nurse practitioner adult health nursing (MS); nurse practitioner family nursing (MS); nurse practitioner psychiatric/mental health nursing (MS); psychiatric-mental health nursing (PMC); MBA/MSN. *Accreditation:* AACN. Part-time programs available. *Faculty:* 13 full-time (all women), 5 part-time/adjunct (4 women). *Students:* 55 full-time (53 women), 52 part-time (50 women); includes 6 minority (all Asian Americans or Pacific Islanders) Average age 36. 88 applicants, 93% accepted, 57 enrolled. In 2006, 25 degrees awarded. *Degree requirements:* For master's, thesis optional. *Entrance requirements:* For master's, GRE General Test or MAT, minimum GPA of 3.0. Additional exam requirements/recommendations for international students: Required—TOEFL (minimum score 550 paper-based; 213 computer-based). *Application deadline:* Applications are processed on a rolling basis. Application fee: $50. Electronic applications accepted. *Expenses:* Tuition, state resident: full-time $4,860; part-time $270 per credit hour. Tuition, nonresident: full-time $13,572; part-time $754 per credit hour. Required fees: $222 per semester. Tuition and fees vary according to course load. *Financial support:* In 2006–07, 14 students received support, including 5 research assistantships with tuition reimbursements available (averaging $3,375 per year), 7 teaching assistantships with tuition reimbursements available (averaging $3,375 per year); career-related internships or fieldwork, Federal Work-Study, scholarships/grants, traineeships, tuition waivers (full and partial), and unspecified assistantships also available. Support available to part-time students. Financial award application deadline: 2/15; financial award applicants required to submit FAFSA. *Faculty research:* Women's health, nursing history, weight control, community services, substance abuse. *Unit head:* Susan Sepples, Director of Nursing Program, 207-780-4505, Fax: 207-228-8177, E-mail: sepples@usm.maine.edu. *Application contact:* Mary Sloan, Director of Graduate Admissions, 207-780-4386, Fax: 207-780-4969, E-mail: gradstudies@usm.maine.edu.

University of Southern Mississippi, Graduate School, College of Health, School of Nursing, Hattiesburg, MS 39406-0001. Offers adult health nursing (MSN); community health nursing (MSN); ethics (PhD); family nurse practitioner (MSN); leadership (PhD); nursing service administration (MSN); policy analysis (PhD); psychiatric nursing (MSN). *Accreditation:* AACN. Part-time and evening/weekend programs available. *Faculty:* 14 full-time (all women). *Students:* 39 full-time (31 women), 69 part-time (62 women); includes 18 minority (15 African Americans, 1 Asian American or Pacific Islander, 2 Hispanic Americans), 1 international. Average age 39. 46 applicants, 50% accepted, 17 enrolled. In 2006, 36 master's, 6 doctorates awarded. *Degree requirements:* For master's, thesis optional; for doctorate, thesis/dissertation, comprehensive exam, registration. *Entrance requirements:* For master's, GRE General Test, minimum GPA of 2.75, nursing license, BS in nursing; for doctorate, GRE General Test, master's degree in nursing, minimum GPA of 3.5. Additional exam requirements/recommendations for international students: Required—TOEFL. *Application deadline:* For fall admission, 3/15 priority date for domestic students, 5/1 for international students. Applications are processed on a rolling basis. Application fee: $25 ($30 for international students). Electronic applications accepted. *Financial support:* In 2006–07, 1 research assistantship with full tuition reimbursement (averaging $10,125 per year), 1 teaching assistantship (averaging $10,125 per year) were awarded; Federal Work-Study and traineeships also available. Financial award application deadline: 3/15. *Faculty research:* Gerontology, caregivers, HIV, bereavement, pain, nursing leadership. *Unit head:* Dr. Katherine Nugent, Director and Associate Dean, 601-266-5500, Fax: 601-266-5927. *Application contact:* Dr. Anne Brock, Graduate Coordinator, 601-266-5500, Fax: 601-266-5927.

The University of Tampa, Nursing Program, Tampa, FL 33606-1490. Offers adult nurse practitioner (MSN); family nurse practitioner (MSN); nursing administration (MSN); nursing education (MSN). *Accreditation:* NLN. Part-time and evening/weekend programs available. *Faculty:* 5 full-time (all women), 10 part-time/adjunct (9 women). *Students:* 3 full-time (all women), 67 part-time (63 women); includes 2 minority (both African Americans), 1 international. Average age 40. 46 applicants, 61% accepted, 18 enrolled. In 2006, 29 degrees awarded. *Degree requirements:* For master's, oral exam, practicum, thesis optional. *Entrance requirements:* For master's, GRE General Test, minimum GPA of 3.0, RN license. *Application deadline:* For fall admission, 8/20 priority date for domestic students. Applications are processed on a rolling basis. Application fee: $40. Electronic applications accepted. *Expenses:* Tuition: Part-time $426 per credit hour. Required fees: $35 per year. *Financial support:* In 2006–07, 2 students received support, including 2 research assistantships with tuition reimbursements available (averaging $1,500 per year); career-related internships or fieldwork and unspecified assistantships also available. Support available to part-time students. Financial award applicants required to submit FAFSA. *Faculty research:* Domestic violence (assessment in emergency departments, changing demographics), transcultural health assessment, priorities in maintaining autonomy of elderly. *Unit head:* Dr. Nancy Ross, Director, 813-253-6223, Fax: 813-258-7214, E-mail: nross@ut.edu. *Application contact:* Barbara P. Strickler, Vice President for Enrollment, 888-646-2738, Fax: 813-258-7398, E-mail: admissions@ut.edu.

The University of Tennessee at Chattanooga, Graduate School, College of Health, Education and Professional Studies, School of Nursing, Chattanooga, TN 37403-2598. Offers administration (MSN); adult health (MSN); education (MSN); family nurse practitioner (MSN); nurse anesthesia (MSN). *Accreditation:* AACN; AANA/CANAEP. *Faculty:* 13 full-time (all women). *Students:* 40 full-time (32 women), 47 part-time (41 women); includes 9 minority (1 African American, 2 American Indian/Alaska Native, 4 Asian Americans or Pacific Islanders, 2 Hispanic Americans). Average age 34. 14 applicants, 71% accepted, 2 enrolled. In 2006, 29 degrees awarded. *Degree requirements:* For master's, qualifying exams. *Entrance requirements:* For master's, GRE General Test, MAT, BSN, minimum GPA of 3.0, eligibility for Tennessee RN license. *Application deadline:* For fall admission, 8/1 priority date for domestic students; for spring admission, 12/1 priority date for domestic students. Applications are processed on a rolling basis. Application fee: $30. *Expenses:* Tuition, state resident: full-time $5,434; part-time $339 per hour. Tuition, nonresident: full-time $14,830; part-time $861 per hour. Required fees: $940; $178 per hour. *Financial support:* Application deadline: 4/1; *Faculty research:* Diabetes in women; health care for elderly; alternative medicine; hypertension; nurse anesthesia. Total annual research expenditures: $357,538. *Unit head:* Dr. Kay R. Lindgren, Head, 423-425-4646, Fax: 423-425-4668, E-mail: kay-lindgren@utc.edu. *Application contact:* Dr. Deborah E. Arfken, Dean of Graduate Studies, 423-425-4666, Fax: 423-425-5223, E-mail: deborah-arfken@utc.edu.

The University of Texas at Arlington, Graduate School, School of Nursing, Arlington, TX 76019. Offers administration/supervision of nursing (MSN); nurse practitioner (MSN); nursing science (PhD); teaching of nursing (MSN). *Accreditation:* AACN. Part-time and evening/weekend programs available. *Faculty:* 22 full-time (21 women), 11 part-time/adjunct (10 women). *Students:* 52 full-time (50 women), 334 part-time (310 women); includes 86 minority (37 African Americans, 6 American Indian/Alaska Native, 24 Asian Americans or Pacific Islanders, 19 Hispanic Americans), 18 international. Average age 37. 178 applicants, 96% accepted, 117 enrolled. In 2006, 30 degrees awarded. *Degree requirements:* For master's, comprehensive exam, thesis or master's completion project; for doctorate, thesis/dissertation, diagnostic exam after 18 hours. *Entrance requirements:* For master's, GRE General Test, minimum GPA of 3.0, Texas nursing license, minimum C in undergraduate statistics course, physical assessment course within last 3 years; for doctorate, GRE General Test, minimum undergraduate, graduate and statistics GPA of 3.0; Texas RN license; interview; 3 letters of reference. Additional exam requirements/recommendations for international students: Required—TOEFL (minimum score 550 paper-based; 213 computer-based). *Application deadline:* For fall admission, 6/16 for domestic students. Applications are processed on a rolling basis. Application fee: $35 ($50 for international students). *Expenses:* Tuition, state resident: full-time $5,528. Tuition, nonresident: full-time $10,478. International tuition: $10,608 full-time. *Financial support:* In 2006–07, 37 students received support, including 24 fellowships with partial tuition reimbursements available (averaging $3,000 per year), 6 research assistantships (averaging $7,992 per year), 7 teaching assistantships (averaging $10,080 per year); career-related internships or fieldwork and traineeships also available. Financial award application deadline: 6/1; financial award applicants required to submit FAFSA. *Unit head:* Dr. Elizabeth C. Poster, Dean, 817-272-2776, Fax: 817-272-5006, E-mail: poster@uta.edu. *Application contact:* Dr. Susan Grove, Graduate Adviser, 817-272-2776, Fax: 817-272-5006, E-mail: grove@uta.edu.

The University of Texas at El Paso, Graduate School, College of Health Sciences, School of Nursing, El Paso, TX 79968-0001. Offers community health (MSN); community health/family nurse practitioner (MSN); nurse midwifery (MSN); nursing administration (MSN); nursing-clinical (MSN); post master's nursing (MSN); women's health care (MSN). *Accreditation:* AACN. *Degree requirements:* For master's, thesis optional. *Entrance requirements:* For master's, GRE General Test or MAT, BSN, minimum GPA of 3.0, previous course work in statistics. Additional exam requirements/recommendations for international students: Required—TOEFL. Electronic applications accepted.

The University of Texas at Tyler, College of Nursing and Health Sciences, Program in Nursing, Tyler, TX 75799-0001. Offers nurse practitioner (MSN); nursing administration (MSN); nursing education (MSN); MSN/MBA. *Accreditation:* AACN. Part-time and evening/weekend programs available. Postbaccalaureate distance learning degree programs offered (no on-campus study). *Faculty:* 14 full-time (13 women), 4 part-time/adjunct (3 women). *Students:* 13 full-time (11 women), 134 part-time (122 women); includes 25 minority (16 African Americans, 2 American Indian/Alaska Native, 2 Asian Americans or Pacific Islanders, 5 Hispanic Americans). Average age 39. 37 applicants, 32 enrolled. In 2006, 15 degrees awarded. *Degree requirements:* For master's, thesis (for some programs), comprehensive exam (for some programs). *Entrance requirements:* For master's, GRE General Test or MAT, GMAT, minimum undergraduate GPA of 3.0, course work in statistics, RN license, BSN. *Application deadline:* For fall admission, 3/1 priority date for domestic students; for spring admission, 10/1 priority date for domestic students. Applications are processed on a rolling basis. Application fee: $0. Electronic applications accepted. *Expenses:* Tuition, state resident: part-time $50 per credit hour. Tuition, nonresident: part-time $328 per credit hour. Required fees: $107 per credit hour. $426 per term. *Financial support:* In 2006–07, 15 students received support, including 12 fellowships, 3 research assistantships (averaging $2,200 per year); institutionally sponsored loans and scholarships/grants also available. Financial award application deadline: 8/1; financial award applicants required to submit FAFSA. *Faculty research:* Psychosocial adjustment, aging, support/commitment of caregivers, psychological abuse and violence, hope/hopelessness, professional values, end of life cave, suicidology, clinical supervision, workforce retention and issues, global health issues. *Unit head:* Dr. Susan Yarbrough, Assistant Dean, 903-566-1220, E-mail: syarbrou@mail.uttyl.edu. *Application contact:* Bonnie Purser, Office of Graduate Studies, 903-566-7142, Fax: 903-566-7068, E-mail: bpurser@uttyler.edu.

The University of Texas–Pan American, College of Health Sciences and Human Services, Department of Nursing, Edinburg, TX 78541-2999. Offers adult health nursing (MSN); family nurse practitioner (MSN); pediatric nurse practitioner (MSN). *Accreditation:* AACN. Part-time and evening/weekend programs available. *Faculty:* 8 full-time (7 women). *Students:* 19 applicants, 100% accepted, 19 enrolled. In 2006, 22 degrees awarded. *Median time to degree:* Master's–3 years part-time. *Degree requirements:* For master's, thesis optional. *Entrance requirements:* For master's, Texas RN licensure, undergraduate physical assessment courses. Additional exam requirements/recommendations for international students: Required—TOEFL (minimum score 550 paper-based). *Application deadline:* Applications are processed on a rolling basis. Application fee: $35. Electronic applications accepted. *Expenses: Contact institution. Financial support:* In 2006–07, 15 students received support. Scholarships/grants and traineeships available. *Faculty research:* Health promotion, adolescent pregnancy, herbal and nontraditional approaches, healing touch stress. Total annual research expenditures: $5,000. *Unit head:* Dr. Carolina G. Huerta, Chair, 956-381-3495, Fax: 956-381-2384, E-mail: chuerta@panam.edu. *Application contact:* Dr. Janice A. Maville, Professor and Interim Chair, 956-316-3491, Fax: 956-318-5238, E-mail: jmaville@utpa.edu.

The University of Toledo, College of Graduate Studies, College of Nursing, Toledo, OH 43606-3390. Offers advanced practice nursing (MSN), including clinical nurse specialist, family nurse practitioner. *Accreditation:* AACN. Part-time programs available. *Faculty:* 29 full-time. *Students:* 64 full-time (58 women), 151 part-time (144 women); includes 13 minority (10 African Americans, 1 Asian American or Pacific Islander, 2 Hispanic Americans), 4 international. Average age 38. 129 applicants, 75% accepted, 87 enrolled. In 2006, 36 master's, 4 other advanced degrees awarded. *Degree requirements:* For master's, thesis or scholarly project. *Entrance requirements:* For master's, GRE General Test, BS in nursing, minimum undergraduate GPA of 3.0. *Application deadline:* For fall admission, 5/1 for domestic students; for spring admission, 9/1 for domestic students. Application fee: $45. *Expenses: Contact institution. Financial support:* Federal Work-Study, institutionally sponsored loans, and scholarships/grants available. *Faculty research:* Sexuality issues, prenatal testing, health care of homeless, nursing education, chronic/acute pain, eating disorders, low birth weight infants. Total annual research expenditures: $399,038. *Unit head:* Dr. Jeri Millstead, Dean, 419-383-5858, Fax: 419-383-6140, E-mail: mcogradschool@mco.edu. *Application contact:* Dr. Janet Robinson, Associate Dean, 419-383-5820, E-mail: jrobinson@mco.edu.

University of Victoria, Faculty of Graduate Studies, Faculty of Human and Social Development, School of Nursing, Victoria, BC V8W 2Y2, Canada. Offers advanced nursing practice; (leadership option) (MN); advanced nursing practice; (nurse practitioner option) (MN); policy and practice (MN). PhD offered by special arrangement. Part-time programs available. Postbaccalaureate distance learning degree programs offered (no on-campus study). *Entrance requirements:* Additional exam requirements/recommendations for international students: Required—TOEFL (minimum score 575 paper-based; 233 computer-based), IELTS (minimum score 7). Electronic applications accepted.

University of Wisconsin–Oshkosh, The School of Graduate Studies, College of Nursing, Oshkosh, WI 54901. Offers adult health and illness (MSN); family nurse practitioner (MSN). *Accreditation:* AACN. Part-time programs available. *Degree requirements:* For master's, thesis or alternative, clinical paper. *Entrance requirements:* For master's, RN license, BSN, previous course work in statistics and health assessment, minimum undergraduate GPA of 3.0, letters of recommendation. Additional exam requirements/recommendations for international students: Required—TOEFL (minimum score 550 paper-based; 213 computer-based). Electronic applications accepted. *Faculty research:* Adult health and illness, nurse practitioners practice, health care service, advanced practitioner roles, natural alternative complementary healthcare.

Vanderbilt University, School of Nursing, Nashville, TN 37235. Offers adult acute care nurse practitioner (MSN); adult health nurse practitioner/forensic (MSN); adult nurse practitioner/cardiovascular disease management and prevention (MSN); adult nurse practitioner/palliative care (MSN); clinical management (clinical nurse leader/specialist) (MSN); family nurse practitioner (MSN); gerontology nurse practitioner (MSN); health systems management (MSN); neonatal nurse practitioner (MSN); nurse midwifery (MSN); nursing informatics (MSN); nursing science (PhD); pediatric acute care nurse practitioner (MSN); pediatric primary care nurse practitioner (MSN); psychiatric-mental health nurse practitioner (MSN); women's health nurse practitioner (MSN); MBA/MSN; MSN/MTS; MSN/PhD. *Accreditation:* ACNM/DOA; NLN (one or more programs are accredited). Part-time and evening/weekend programs available. Postbaccalaureate distance learning degree programs offered (minimal on-campus study). *Faculty:* 95 full-time (83 women), 432 part-time/adjunct (314 women). *Students:* 371 full-time (325 women), 206 part-time (180 women); includes 59 minority (38 African Americans, 2 American Indian/Alaska Native, 7 Asian Americans or Pacific Islanders, 12 Hispanic Americans). Average age 27. 611 applicants, 55% accepted, 308 enrolled. In 2006, 256 master's, 2 doctorates awarded. *Degree requirements:* For doctorate, thesis/dissertation. *Entrance requirements:* For master's, GRE, interview; for doctorate, GRE, interview, 3 letters of recommendation. Additional exam requirements/recommendations for international students: Required—TOEFL. *Application deadline:* For fall admission, 12/1 priority date for domestic and international students. Applications are processed on a rolling basis. Application fee: $50. *Expenses: Contact institution. Financial support:* In 2006–07, 404 students received support, including 5 research assistantships (averaging $8,000 per year); Federal Work-Study, institutionally sponsored loans, and unspecified assistantships also available. Support available to part-time students. Financial award application deadline: 3/15; financial award applicants required to submit CSS PROFILE or FAFSA. *Faculty research:* Lymphedema post cancer treatment, palliative care and bereavement, patient safety and quality of care, health care workforce issues, symptom management including pain and fatigue. Total annual research expenditures: $1.1 million. *Unit head:* Dr. Colleen Conway-Welch, Dean, 615-343-8776, Fax: 615-343-7711, E-mail: colleen.conway-welch@vanderbilt.edu. *Application contact:* Cheryl Feldner, Assistant Director of Admissions, 615-322-3800, Fax: 615-343-0333, E-mail: cheryl.feldner@vanderbilt.edu.

Villanova University, College of Nursing, Villanova, PA 19085-1690. Offers adult nurse practitioner (MSN, Post Master's Certificate); clinical case management (MSN, Post Master's Certificate); geriatric nurse practitioner (MSN, Post Master's Certificate); health care administration (MSN); nurse anesthetist (MSN, Post Master's Certificate); nursing (PhD); nursing education (MSN, Post Master's Certificate); pediatric nurse practitioner (MSN, Post Master's Certificate). *Accreditation:* AACN; AANA/CANAEP; NLN. Part-time programs available. Postbaccalaureate distance learning degree programs offered (minimal on-campus study). *Faculty:* 14 full-time (all women), 2 part-time/adjunct (both women). *Students:* 41 full-time (27 women), 164 part-time (128 women); includes 17 minority (8 African Americans, 1 American Indian/Alaska Native, 8 Asian Americans or Pacific Islanders), 6 international. Average age 31. 137 applicants, 50% accepted, 48 enrolled. In 2006, 47 degrees awarded. *Median time to degree:* Master's–2 years full-time, 5 years part-time. *Degree requirements:* For master's, independent study project; for doctorate, thesis/dissertation, comprehensive exam. *Entrance requirements:* For master's, GRE or MAT, BSN, 1 year of recent nursing experience, physical assessment, course work in statistics; for doctorate, GRE. Additional exam requirements/recommendations for international students: Required—TOEFL. *Application deadline:* For fall admission, 7/1 priority date for domestic students, 7/1 for international students; for spring admission, 12/1 priority date for domestic students, 12/1 for international students. Applications are processed on a rolling basis. Application fee: $50. *Expenses: Contact institution. Financial support:* In 2006–07, 50 students received support, including 4 teaching assistantships with full tuition reimbursements available (averaging $12,165 per year); institutionally sponsored loans, scholarships/grants, traineeships, and tuition waivers (full) also available. Financial award application deadline: 3/1; financial award applicants required to submit FAFSA. *Faculty research:* Genetics, ethics, cognitive development of students, women with disabilities, nursing leadership. *Unit head:* Dr. Marguerite K. Schlag, Assistant Dean and Director, Graduate Program, 610-519-4907, Fax: 610-519-7650, E-mail: marguerite.schlag@villanova.edu.

Virginia Commonwealth University, Graduate School, School of Nursing, Nurse Practitioner Program, Richmond, VA 23284-9005. Offers MS, Certificate. *Application deadline:* For fall admission, 2/1 priority date for domestic students. Application fee: $50. *Unit head:* Susan Lipp, Admissions Counselor, 804-828-5171, Fax: 804-828-7743, E-mail: slipp@vcu.edu.

Wagner College, Division of Graduate Studies, Department of Nursing, Program in Family Nurse Practitioner, Staten Island, NY 10301-4495. Offers Certificate. Part-time and evening/weekend programs available. *Faculty:* 5 full-time (all women), 3 part-time/adjunct (all women). *Students:* Average age 28. 1 applicant, 100% accepted, 1 enrolled. *Entrance requirements:* For degree, master's degree in nursing from an NLN-accredited program, minimum GPA of 3.0. *Application deadline:* For fall admission, 8/1 priority date for domestic students; for spring admission, 12/10 for domestic students. Applications are processed on a rolling basis. Application fee: $50 ($80 for international students). *Expenses:* Tuition: Full-time $15,120; part-time $840 per credit. *Financial support:* Fellowships, unspecified assistantships available. Financial award applicants required to submit FAFSA. *Application contact:* Susan Rosenberg, Office of Graduate Studies, 718-390-3106, Fax: 718-390-3456, E-mail: graduate@wagner.edu.

Wayne State University, College of Nursing, Department of Adult Health, Program in Adult Primary Care Nursing, Detroit, MI 48202. Offers MSN. *Accreditation:* AACN. Part-time programs available. *Students:* 8 full-time (7 women), 24 part-time (all women); includes 13 minority (9 African Americans, 4 Asian Americans or Pacific Islanders), 1 international. Average age 37. 16 applicants, 81% accepted, 10 enrolled. In 2006, 13 degrees awarded. *Degree requirements:* For master's, thesis or alternative. *Entrance requirements:* For master's, GRE General Test, minimum GPA of 2.8. Additional exam requirements/recommendations for international students: Required—TOEFL (minimum score 550 paper-based; 213 computer-based); Recommended—TWE (minimum score 6). *Application deadline:* For fall admission, 7/1 priority date for domestic students, 6/1 for international students; for winter admission, 10/1 for international students; for spring admission, 11/1 for domestic students, 2/1 for international students. Applications are processed on a rolling basis. Application fee: $30 ($50 for international students). Electronic applications accepted. *Financial support:* In 2006–07, 3 students received support; research assistantships, traineeships available. Support available to part-time students. Financial award application deadline: 7/1; financial award applicants required to submit FAFSA. *Faculty research:* Smoking risk behaviors in adolescents, sleep disturbances in postmenopausal women, health disparities in urban environments, nurse practitioner interventions, caregiving and pain management. *Application contact:* Janet Harden, Academic Director, 313-577-4082.

Western Connecticut State University, Division of Graduate Studies, School of Professional Studies, Nursing Department, Danbury, CT 06810-6885. Offers adult nurse practitioner (MSN); clinical nurse specialist (MSN). *Accreditation:* AACN. Part-time and evening/weekend programs available. *Faculty:* 6 full-time (5 women), 1 part-time/adjunct (0 women). *Students:* Average age 42. In 2006, 11 degrees awarded. *Degree requirements:* For master's, thesis or research project. *Entrance requirements:* For master's, MAT, bachelor's degree in nursing, minimum GPA of 3.0, previous course work in statistics and nursing research, RN license. *Application deadline:* For fall admission, 8/1 priority date for domestic students. Applications are processed on a rolling basis. Application fee: $40. *Financial support:* Career-related internships or fieldwork available. Support available to part-time students. Financial award application deadline: 5/1; financial award applicants required to submit FAFSA. *Unit head:* Dr. Patricia Z. Lund, Professor, 203-837-8567. *Application contact:* Chris Shankle, Associate Director of Graduate Admissions, 203-837-8244, Fax: 203-837-8338, E-mail: shanklec@wcsu.edu.

See Close-Up on page 1985.

Western University of Health Sciences, College of Graduate Nursing, Pomona, CA 91766-1854. Offers family nurse practitioner (MSN). *Accreditation:* AACN. Part-time and evening/weekend programs available. Postbaccalaureate distance learning degree programs offered. *Faculty:* 8 full-time (all women), 9 part-time/adjunct (7 women). *Students:* 149 full-time (129 women), 7 part-time (all women); includes 83 minority (7 African Americans, 56 Asian Americans or Pacific Islanders, 20 Hispanic Americans), 1 international. Average age 33. 163 applicants, 48% accepted, 67 enrolled. In 2006, 13 degrees awarded. *Degree requirements:* For master's, culminating project. *Entrance requirements:* For master's, GRE General Test, BSN or bachelor's degree in related field, certificate nurse practitioner, minimum GPA of 3.0, interview, letters of recommendation. Additional exam requirements/recommendations for international students: Required—TOEFL. *Application deadline:* For fall admission, 3/1 priority date for domestic students. Applications are processed on a rolling basis. Application fee: $60. *Expenses: Contact institution. Financial support:* Institutionally sponsored loans, scholarships/grants, and Veterans Educational Benefits available. Financial award application deadline: 3/2; financial award applicants required to submit FAFSA. *Unit head:* Karen J. Hanford, Dean, 909-469-5243, Fax: 909-469-5521, E-mail: khanford@westernu.edu. *Application contact:* Audrey Navarro, Information Contact, 909-469-5335, Fax: 909-469-5570, E-mail: admissions@westernu.edu.

Westminster College, School of Nursing and Health Sciences, Salt Lake City, UT 84105-3697. Offers family nurse practitioner (MSN); nurse anesthesia (MSNA); nursing (MSN); nursing education (MSN). *Accreditation:* AACN; AANA/CANAEP. Part-time and evening/weekend programs available. *Faculty:* 9 full-time (8 women). *Students:* 44 full-time (31 women), 13 part-time (9 women); includes 4 minority (1 African American, 2 Asian Americans or Pacific Islanders, 1 Hispanic American), 1 international. Average age 39. 57 applicants, 65% accepted, 32 enrolled. In 2006, 5 degrees awarded. *Degree requirements:* For master's, project or thesis. *Entrance requirements:* For master's, resumé, Utah RN license in good standing, minimum GPA of 3.0, 3 letters of recommendation, proof of completed BSN from accredited nursing school, proof of clear state and federal background check, drug test results, personal interview. Additional exam requirements/recommendations for international students: Required—TOEFL (minimum score 550 paper-based; 213 computer-based). *Application deadline:* For fall admission, 8/1 priority date for domestic students. Applications are processed on a rolling basis. Application fee: $40. Electronic applications accepted. *Financial support:* In 2006–07, 39 students received support. Career-related internships or fieldwork and tuition remissions available. Support available to part-time students. Financial award applicants required to submit FAFSA. *Faculty research:* Learning styles assessment, curriculum simulation, self-esteem and learning success. *Unit head:* Dr. Jean Dyer, Dean, 801-832-2168, Fax: 801-832-3110, E-mail: jdyer@westminstercollege.edu. *Application contact:* Joel Bauman, Vice President of Enrollment Services, 801-832-2200, Fax: 801-832-3101, E-mail: admission@westminstercollege.edu.

Wichita State University, Graduate School, College of Health Professions, School of Nursing, Wichita, KS 67260. Offers clinical nurse specialist (MSN); nurse midwifery (MSN); nurse practitioner (MSN); nursing and health care systems administration (MSN); MSN/MBA. *Accreditation:* AACN. Part-time programs available. *Degree requirements:* For master's,

Family Nurse Practitioner Studies

Wichita State University (continued)
thesis optional. *Entrance requirements:* For master's, GRE, BSN, minimum undergraduate GPA of 2.75. Additional exam requirements/recommendations for international students: Required—TOEFL. Electronic applications accepted. *Faculty research:* Adolescent pregnancy, alcoholism, arthritis and chronic disease, health practices of elderly, diabetes.

Wilmington College, Division of Nursing, New Castle, DE 19720-6491. Offers adult nurse practitioner (MSN); family nurse practitioner (MSN); gerontology (MSN); leadership (MSN); nursing (MSN); women's nurse practitioner (MSN). *Accreditation:* AACN; NLN. Part-time programs available. *Students:* 30 full-time (28 women), 195 part-time (176 women); includes 24 minority (19 African Americans, 3 Asian Americans or Pacific Islanders, 2 Hispanic Americans). Average age 39. 54 applicants, 100% accepted, 48 enrolled. In 2006, 58 degrees awarded. *Degree requirements:* For master's, thesis. *Entrance requirements:* For master's, BSN, RN license, interview, 3 letters of recommendation. Additional exam requirements/recommendations for international students: Required—TOEFL (minimum score 500 paper-based; 173 computer-based). *Application deadline:* For fall admission, 3/31 priority date for domestic students. Applications are processed on a rolling basis. Application fee: $25. *Financial support:* In 2006–07, 28 fellowships with tuition reimbursements (averaging $2,200 per year) were awarded; traineeships also available. Financial award applicants required to submit FAFSA. *Faculty research:* Outcomes assessment, student writing ability. *Unit head:* Dr. Mary Letitia Gallagher, Chair, 302-328-9401 Ext. 161, Fax: 302-328-7081, E-mail: tgall@wilmcoll.edu. *Application contact:* Chris Ferguson, Director of Admissions and Financial Aid, 302-328-9407 Ext. 256, Fax: 302-328-5164, E-mail: inquire@wilmcoll.edu.

Winona State University, Graduate Studies, College of Nursing and Health Sciences, Winona, MN 55987-5838. Offers adult nurse practitioner (MS); clinical nurse specialist (MS); family nurse practitioner (MS); nurse administrator (MS); nurse educator (MS). *Accreditation:* AACN. Part-time programs available. *Faculty:* 10 full-time (all women). *Students:* 70 applicants, 57% accepted, 32 enrolled. In 2006, 32 master's awarded. *Degree requirements:* For master's, thesis. *Application deadline:* For fall admission, 2/1 for domestic students. Application fee: $20. *Financial support:* In 2006–07, 3 research assistantships with partial tuition reimbursements (averaging $6,000 per year) were awarded; Federal Work-Study, traineeships, and unspecified assistantships also available. Support available to part-time students. Financial award applicants required to submit FAFSA. *Unit head:* Dr. Timothy Gaspar, Graduate Director, 507-457-5122, E-mail: tgaspar@winona.msus.edu.

Wright State University, School of Graduate Studies, College of Nursing and Health, Program in Nursing, Dayton, OH 45435. Offers acute care nurse practitioner (MS); administration of nursing and health care systems (MS); adult health (MS); child and adolescent health (MS); community health (MS); family nurse practitioner (MS); nurse practitioner (MS); school nurse (MS); MBA/MS. *Accreditation:* AACN. Part-time and evening/weekend programs available. *Students:* 46 full-time (45 women), 124 part-time (117 women); includes 16 minority (13 African Americans, 1 Asian American or Pacific Islander, 2 Hispanic Americans). Average age 39. 45 applicants, 100% accepted. In 2006, 64 degrees awarded. *Degree requirements:* For master's, thesis or alternative. *Entrance requirements:* For master's, GRE General Test, BSN from NLN-accredited college, Ohio RN license. Additional exam requirements/recommendations for international students: Required—TOEFL. *Application deadline:* For fall admission, 4/15 priority date for domestic students. Application fee: $25. *Financial support:* Fellowships, research assistantships, teaching assistantships, Federal Work-Study, institutionally sponsored loans, and unspecified assistantships available. Support available to part-time students. Financial award application deadline: 6/1; financial award applicants required to submit FAFSA. *Faculty research:* Clinical nursing and health, teaching, caring, pain administration, informatics and technology. *Application contact:* Theresa A. Haghnazarian, Director of Student and Alumni Affairs, 937-775-2592, Fax: 937-775-4571, E-mail: theresa.haghnazarian@wright.edu.

Xavier University, College of Social Sciences, Health and Education, Department of Nursing, Cincinnati, OH 45207. Offers clinical nurse leader (MSN); forensic nursing (MSN); healthcare law (MSN); nursing administration (MSN); school nursing (MSN); MSN/M Ed; MSN/MBA; MSN/MS. *Accreditation:* AACN. Part-time and evening/weekend programs available. *Faculty:* 12 full-time (all women), 11 part-time/adjunct (9 women). *Students:* 57 full-time (51 women), 101 part-time (97 women); includes 8 minority (5 African Americans, 3 Asian Americans or Pacific Islanders), 26 international. Average age 37. 121 applicants, 56 enrolled. In 2006, 24 degrees awarded. *Degree requirements:* For master's, thesis or alternative, scholarly project. *Entrance requirements:* For master's, portfolio (RN to MSN). Additional exam requirements/recommendations for international students: Required—TOEFL (minimum score 550 paper-based; 213 computer-based). *Application deadline:* For fall admission, 8/28 priority date for domestic students. Applications are processed on a rolling basis. Application fee: $35. Electronic applications accepted. *Expenses:* Tuition: Part-time $462 per credit hour. Part-time tuition and fees vary according to degree level, campus/location and program. *Financial support:* In 2006–07, 50 students received support. Scholarships/grants, traineeships, and unspecified assistantships available. Support available to part-time students. Financial award application deadline: 4/1; financial award applicants required to submit FAFSA. *Faculty research:* Stroke rehabilitation, informatics, gerontology, hospice, ethics, macular degeneration. *Unit head:* Dr. Susan M. Schmidt, Chair, 513-745-3815, Fax: 513-745-1087, E-mail: schmidts@xavier.edu. *Application contact:* Marilyn Gomez, Director of Nursing Student Services, 513-745-4392, Fax: 513-745-1087, E-mail: gomez@xavier.edu.

Forensic Nursing

Cleveland State University, College of Graduate Studies, College of Education and Human Services, School of Nursing, Cleveland, OH 44115. Offers clinical nursing leader (MSN); forensic nursing (MSN); population health nursing (MSN); MSN/MBA. *Accreditation:* AACN. Part-time programs available. *Faculty:* 8 full-time (all women). *Students:* Average age 44. In 2006, 1 degree awarded. *Degree requirements:* For master's, thesis or alternative, portfolio, population health project. *Entrance requirements:* For master's, RN license, BSN, course work in statistics. Additional exam requirements/recommendations for international students: Required—TOEFL (minimum score 525 paper-based; 197 computer-based), IELTS (minimum score 6). *Application deadline:* For fall admission, 5/1 priority date for domestic students. Applications are processed on a rolling basis. Application fee: $30. Electronic applications accepted. *Financial support:* In 2006–07, 3 students received support. Tuition waivers (full) and unspecified assistantships available. Support available to part-time students. Financial award application deadline: 3/1; financial award applicants required to submit FAFSA. *Faculty research:* Diabetes management, African-American elders medication compliance, risk in home visiting, suffering, COPD and stress. Total annual research expenditures: $204,029. *Unit head:* Dr. Noreen C. Frisch, Director, 216-523-7237, Fax: 216-687-3556, E-mail: n.frisch@csuohio.edu. *Application contact:* Dr. Sharon Radzyminski, Director, Graduate Nursing Program, 216-687-3558, Fax: 216-687-3556, E-mail: s.radzyminski@csuohio.edu.

Duquesne University, School of Nursing, Master's Program in Nursing, Pittsburgh, PA 15282-0001. Offers acute care nursing (Post-Master's Certificate); acute care nursing specialist (MSN); family nurse practitioner (MSN, Post-Master's Certificate); forensic nursing (MSN, Post-Master's Certificate); nursing administration (MSN, Post-Master's Certificate); nursing education (MSN, Post-Master's Certificate); psychiatric/mental health nursing (MSN, Post-Master's Certificate); MSN/MBA. *Accreditation:* AACN. Part-time and evening/weekend programs available. Postbaccalaureate distance learning degree programs offered (minimal on-campus study). *Faculty:* 20 full-time (19 women), 4 part-time/adjunct (all women). *Students:* 73 full-time (70 women), 83 part-time (79 women); includes 11 minority (4 African Americans, 3 American Indian/Alaska Native, 1 Asian American or Pacific Islander, 3 Hispanic Americans). 72 applicants, 75% accepted, 49 enrolled. In 2006, 20 master's, 11 other advanced degrees awarded. *Degree requirements:* For master's, culminating paper. *Entrance requirements:* For master's, MAT or GRE, 1 year of work experience, bachelor's degree in nursing, undergraduate course work in statistics, health assessment course (family nurse practitioner, nursing education, acute care clinical nurse specialist). *Application deadline:* For fall admission, 4/1 for domestic and international students; for spring admission, 11/1 for domestic and international students. Applications are processed on a rolling basis. Application fee: $50. *Expenses: Contact institution.* Tuition and fees vary according to degree level and program. *Financial support:* In 2006–07, 10 students received support, including 9 research assistantships with partial tuition reimbursements available (averaging $1,600 per year), 1 teaching assistantship with partial tuition reimbursement available (averaging $1,600 per year); fellowships with partial tuition reimbursements available, institutionally sponsored loans, scholarships/grants, traineeships, and tuition waivers (partial) also available. Financial award application deadline: 8/20. *Faculty research:* Depression, culture, vulnerable populations, ethics, health disparities, community based. Total annual research expenditures: $377,400. *Unit head:* Dr. Joan Such Lockhart, Professor and Associate Dean of Academic Affairs, 412-396-6540, Fax: 412-396-1821, E-mail: lockhart@duq.edu. *Application contact:* Susan Hardner, Nurse Recruiter, 412-396-4945, Fax: 412-396-6346, E-mail: nursing@duq.edu.

Fitchburg State College, Division of Graduate and Continuing Education, Program in Forensic Nursing, Fitchburg, MA 01420-2697. Offers MS, Certificate. *Accreditation:* AACN. Part-time and evening/weekend programs available. *Students:* Average age 38. 5 applicants, 100% accepted, 4 enrolled. In 2006, 8 degrees awarded. *Entrance requirements:* For master's, GRE General Test or MAT, bachelor's degree in nursing from accredited program, 1 year of clinical practice, nursing license, letters of recommendation, resumé. Additional exam requirements/recommendations for international students: Required—TOEFL (minimum score 550 paper-based; 213 computer-based; 79 iBT). *Application deadline:* Applications are processed on a rolling basis. Application fee: $25 ($50 for international students). *Expenses:* Tuition, state resident: part-time $150 per credit. Tuition, nonresident: part-time $150 per credit. Required fees: $90 per credit. *Financial support:* In 2006–07, research assistantships with partial tuition reimbursements (averaging $5,500 per year); Federal Work-Study, scholarships/grants, and unspecified assistantships also available. Support available to part-time students. Financial award application deadline: 3/1; financial award applicants required to submit FAFSA. *Unit head:* Dr. Rachel Boersma, Chair, 978-665-3036, Fax: 978-665-3658, E-mail: gce@fsc.edu. *Application contact:* Director of Admissions, 978-665-3144, Fax: 978-665-4540, E-mail: admissions@fsc.edu.

Quinnipiac University, School of Health Sciences, Forensic Nurse Clinical Specialist Track, Hamden, CT 06518-1940. Offers MSN, Post Master's Certificate. *Accreditation:* NLN. Part-time programs available. *Faculty:* 2 full-time (both women), 3 part-time/adjunct (2 women). *Students:* 5 full-time (all women), 29 part-time (all women). 16 applicants, 94% accepted, 15 enrolled. *Degree requirements:* For master's, thesis or alternative, clinical practicum. *Entrance requirements:* For master's, MAT or GRE, RN license, minimum GPA of 3.0. *Application deadline:* For fall admission, 7/30 priority date for domestic students. Applications are processed on a rolling basis. Application fee: $45. Electronic applications accepted. *Expenses:* Tuition: Part-time $675 per credit. Required fees: $30 per credit. *Financial support:* Tuition waivers (partial) and unspecified assistantships available. Support available to part-time students. Financial award application deadline: 4/15; financial award applicants required to submit FAFSA. *Unit head:* Dr. Jeanne LeVasseur, Director of Graduate Nursing, 203-582-3484. *Application contact:* Louise M. Howe, Director of Marketing Communications for Admissions, 203-582-5221, Fax: 203-582-3443, E-mail: louise.howe@quinnipiac.edu.

See Close-Up on page 1721.

University of Colorado at Colorado Springs, Graduate School, Beth-El College of Nursing, Colorado Springs, CO 80933-7150. Offers adult health nurse practitioner and clinical specialist (MSN); family practitioner (MSN), including community clinical specialist, forensic clinical specialist, holistic clinical specialist; gerontology (MSN); neonatal nurse practitioner and clinical specialist (MSN); nursing administration (MSN); women nurse practitioner (MSN). *Accreditation:* AACN. Part-time programs available. Postbaccalaureate distance learning degree programs offered (minimal on-campus study). *Faculty:* 10 full-time (7 women), 14 part-time/adjunct (7 women). *Students:* 84 full-time (77 women), 53 part-time (52 women); includes 22 minority (6 African Americans, 3 American Indian/Alaska Native, 2 Asian Americans or Pacific Islanders, 11 Hispanic Americans). Average age 37. 54 applicants, 85% accepted, 30 enrolled. In 2006, 36 degrees awarded. *Degree requirements:* For master's, thesis optional; for doctorate, capstone project. *Entrance requirements:* For master's, GRE General Test or MAT, BSN, minimum GPA of 3.0, unrestricted RN license; for doctorate, interview; active RN license; MA; minimum GPA of 3.3; National Certification as NP, CNS, or CNS; portfolio. Additional exam requirements/recommendations for international students: Required—TOEFL. *Application deadline:* For fall admission, 6/1 priority date for domestic students; for spring admission, 11/15 for domestic students. Application fee: $60 ($75 for international students). Electronic applications accepted. *Expenses: Contact institution.* Tuition and fees vary according to course load, campus/location and program. *Financial support:* Fellowships, career-related internships or fieldwork, Federal Work-Study, and institutionally sponsored loans available. Support available to part-time students. *Faculty research:* Women's health, uncertainty, empowerment, family experience in chronic illness. Total annual research expenditures: $260,389. *Unit head:* Dr. Carole Schoffstall, Dean, 719-262-4418, Fax: 719-262-4416, E-mail: cschoffs@uccs.edu.

Vanderbilt University, School of Nursing, Nashville, TN 37235. Offers adult acute care nurse practitioner (MSN); adult health nurse practitioner/forensic (MSN); adult nurse practitioner/cardiovascular disease management and prevention (MSN); adult nurse practitioner/palliative care (MSN); clinical management (clinical nurse leader/specialist) (MSN); family nurse practitioner (MSN); gerontology nurse practitioner (MSN); health systems management (MSN); neonatal nurse practitioner (MSN); nurse midwifery (MSN); nursing informatics (MSN); nursing science (PhD); pediatric acute care nurse practitioner (MSN); pediatric primary care nurse practitioner (MSN); psychiatric-mental health nurse practitioner (MSN); women's health nurse practitioner (MSN); MBA/MSN; MSN/MTS; MSN/PhD. *Accreditation:* ACNM/DOA; NLN (one or more programs are accredited). Part-time and evening/weekend programs available. Postbaccalaureate distance learning degree programs offered (minimal on-campus study). *Faculty:* 95 full-time (83 women), 432 part-time/adjunct (314 women). *Students:* 371 full-time (325 women), 206 part-time (180 women); includes 59 minority (38 African Americans, 2 American

Indian/Alaska Native, 7 Asian Americans or Pacific Islanders, 12 Hispanic Americans). Average age 27. 611 applicants, 55% accepted, 308 enrolled. In 2006, 256 master's, 2 doctorates awarded. *Degree requirements:* For doctorate, thesis/dissertation. *Entrance requirements:* For master's, GRE, interview; for doctorate, GRE, interview, 3 letters of recommendation. Additional exam requirements/recommendations for international students: Required—TOEFL. *Application deadline:* For fall admission, 12/1 priority date for domestic and international students. Applications are processed on a rolling basis. Application fee: $50. *Expenses:* Contact institution. *Financial support:* In 2006–07, 404 students received support, including 5 research assistantships (averaging $8,000 per year); Federal Work-Study, institutionally sponsored loans, and unspecified assistantships also available. Support available to part-time students. Financial award application deadline: 3/15; financial award applicants required to submit CSS PROFILE or FAFSA. *Faculty research:* Lymphedema post cancer treatment, palliative care and bereavement, patient safety and quality of care, health care workforce issues, symptom management including pain and fatigue. Total annual research expenditures: $1.1 million. *Unit head:* Dr. Colleen Conway-Welch, Dean, 615-343-8776, Fax: 615-343-7711, E-mail: colleen.conway-welch@vanderbilt.edu. *Application contact:* Cheryl Feldner, Assistant Director of Admissions, 615-322-3800, Fax: 615-343-0333, E-mail: cheryl.feldner@vanderbilt.edu.

Gerontological Nursing

Abilene Christian University, Graduate School, College of Arts and Sciences, Department of Sociology and Family Studies, Program in Gerontology, Certificate in Gerontology, Abilene, TX 79699-9100. Offers Certificate. *Faculty:* 4 part-time/adjunct (0 women). Application fee: $25 ($45 for international students). Electronic applications accepted. *Expenses:* Tuition: Full-time $12,504; part-time $521 per hour. Required fees: $700; $34 per hour. *Unit head:* Dr. Charlie D. Pruett, Director of the Center for Aging, 325-674-2350, Fax: 325-674-6804, E-mail: pruettc@acu.edu. *Application contact:* William Horn, Graduate Admissions Counselor, 325-674-2656, Fax: 325-674-6717, E-mail: gradinfo@acu.edu.

Arkansas State University, Graduate School, College of Nursing and Health Professions, Department of Nursing, Jonesboro, State University, AR 72467. Offers aging studies (Certificate); nurse anesthesia (MSN); nursing (MSN). *Accreditation:* AANA/CANAEP (one or more programs are accredited); NLN. Part-time programs available. *Faculty:* 8 full-time (7 women), 3 part-time/adjunct (all women). *Students:* 63 full-time (28 women), 110 part-time (73 women); includes 27 minority (22 African Americans, 1 Asian American or Pacific Islander, 4 Hispanic Americans). Average age 33. 89 applicants, 72% accepted, 64 enrolled. In 2006, 55 degrees awarded. *Degree requirements:* For master's, thesis or alternative, comprehensive exam. *Entrance requirements:* For master's, GRE General Test or MAT, appropriate bachelor's degree, current Arkansas nursing license, CPR certification, acceptable immunization status, physical examination, professional liability insurance, official transcript. Additional exam requirements/recommendations for international students: Required—TOEFL (minimum score 213 computer-based). *Application deadline:* Applications are processed on a rolling basis. Application fee: $30 ($40 for international students). Electronic applications accepted. *Expenses:* Contact institution. *Financial support:* Career-related internships or fieldwork, scholarships/grants, and unspecified assistantships available. Financial award application deadline: 7/1; financial award applicants required to submit FAFSA.

Barnes-Jewish College of Nursing and Allied Health, Division of Nursing, St. Louis, MO 63110-1091. Offers adult nurse practitioner (MSN); education (MSN); gerontology nurse practitioner (MSN); holistics (MSN); management/administration (MSN); neonatal nurse practitioner (MSN); oncology (MSN). *Accreditation:* AACN; AANA/CANAEP. Part-time and evening/weekend programs available. *Degree requirements:* For master's, thesis or alternative, registration. *Entrance requirements:* For master's, minimum GPA of 3.0, 2 references, statistics course. Additional exam requirements/recommendations for international students: Required—TOEFL (minimum score 550 paper-based; 213 computer-based).

Boston College, William F. Connell School of Nursing, Chestnut Hill, MA 02467-3800. Offers adult health nursing (MS); community health nursing (MS); family health (MS); gerontology (MS); maternal/child health nursing (MS), including pediatric and women's health; nurse anesthesia (MS); nursing (PhD); psychiatric-mental health nursing (MS); MBA/MS; MS/MA; MS/PhD. *Accreditation:* AACN; AANA/CANAEP (one or more programs are accredited). Part-time programs available. *Faculty:* 46 full-time (44 women), 34 part-time/adjunct (all women). *Students:* 155 full-time (137 women), 56 part-time (54 women); includes 10 minority (4 African Americans, 5 Asian Americans or Pacific Islanders, 1 Hispanic American), 6 international. Average age 34. 276 applicants, 47% accepted, 67 enrolled. In 2006, 61 master's, 4 doctorates awarded. *Median time to degree:* Of those who began their doctoral program in fall 1998, 100% received their degree in 8 years or less. *Degree requirements:* For master's, research project; for doctorate, thesis/dissertation, computer literacy exam or foreign language, comprehensive exam. *Entrance requirements:* For master's, GRE General Test, bachelor's degree in nursing; for doctorate, GRE General Test, master's degree in nursing. Additional exam requirements/recommendations for international students: Required—TOEFL (minimum score 550 paper-based; 213 computer-based). *Application deadline:* For fall admission, 10/15 for domestic and international students; for spring admission, 3/15 for domestic and international students. Application fee: $40. Electronic applications accepted. *Financial support:* In 2006–07, 104 students received support, including 15 fellowships with partial tuition reimbursements available (averaging $10,045 per year), 3 research assistantships (averaging $10,000 per year), 4 teaching assistantships (averaging $12,548 per year); Federal Work-Study, institutionally sponsored loans, scholarships/grants, traineeships, and tuition waivers (partial) also available. Support available to part-time students. Financial award application deadline: 3/1; financial award applicants required to submit FAFSA. *Faculty research:* Ethics, reduction of risk behaviors, support during chronic illness, violence, gerontology. Total annual research expenditures: $1.1 million. *Unit head:* Dr. Barbara Hazard, Dean, 617-552-4251, Fax: 617-552-0931, E-mail: barbara.munro@bc.edu. *Application contact:* Zanifer John-Bayard, Graduate Programs Assistant, 617-552-4059, Fax: 617-552-0745, E-mail: johnza@bc.edu.

Caribbean University, Graduate School, Bayamón, PR 00960-0493. Offers accounting (MBA); administration and supervision (MA Ed); criminal justice (MA); curriculum and instruction (MA Ed); education (PhD); gerontology (MSN); human resources (MBA); museology, archiving and art history (MA Ed); neonatal pediatrics (MSN); physical education (MA Ed); special education (MA Ed). *Entrance requirements:* For master's, interview, minimum GPA of 2.5.

Case Western Reserve University, Frances Payne Bolton School of Nursing, Doctor of Nursing Practice Program, Cleveland, OH 44106. Offers acute care nurse practitioner (DNP); adult nurse practitioner (DNP); family nurse practitioner (DNP); gerontological nurse practitioner (DNP); graduate entry/pre-licensure option (DNP); medical-surgical nursing (DNP); midwifery/family nursing (DNP); neonatal nurse practitioner (DNP); pediatric nurse practitioner (DNP); post-licensure option (DNP); psychiatric mental health nurse practitioner (DNP); women's health nurse practitioner (DNP). Graduate entry option allows baccalaureate-prepared college graduates from non-nursing backgrounds to earn certificate and MSN in addition to ND. *Students:* 125 full-time (109 women), 308 part-time (290 women); includes 47 minority (21 African Americans, 1 American Indian/Alaska Native, 18 Asian Americans or Pacific Islanders, 7 Hispanic Americans), 7 international. 190 applicants, 70% accepted, 80 enrolled. In 2006, 35 degrees awarded. Terminal master's awarded for partial completion of doctoral program. *Degree requirements:* For doctorate, thesis/dissertation. *Entrance requirements:* For doctorate, GRE General Test or MAT. *Application deadline:* For fall admission, 6/1 priority date for domestic students. Applications are processed on a rolling basis. Application fee: $75. *Financial support:* In 2006–07, 6 students received support, including 1 teaching assistantship; research assistantships, Federal Work-Study, institutionally sponsored loans, and tuition waivers (partial) also available. Support available to part-time students. Financial award application deadline: 6/30; financial award applicants required to submit FAFSA. *Faculty research:* Clinical nursing, acute care, gerontology, mental health, critical care. *Unit head:* Dr. Georgia Narsavage, Director, 216-368-6304, Fax: 216-368-3542, E-mail: gln2@cwru.edu. *Application contact:* Peter Taylor, Recruitment and Retention Specialist, 216-368-0349, Fax: 216-368-0124, E-mail: peter.taylor@case.edu.

Case Western Reserve University, Frances Payne Bolton School of Nursing, Master's Programs in Nursing, Nurse Practitioner Program, Cleveland, OH 44106. Offers acute care cardiovascular nursing (MSN); acute care nurse practitioner (MSN); acute care/flight nurse (MSN); adult nurse practitioner (MSN); family nurse practitioner (MSN); gerontological nurse practitioner (MSN); neonatal nurse practitioner (MSN); pediatric nurse practitioner (MSN); psychiatric-mental health nurse practitioner (MSN); women's health nurse practitioner (MSN). *Accreditation:* NLN. Part-time programs available. Postbaccalaureate distance learning degree programs offered (minimal on-campus study). *Faculty:* 54 full-time (50 women), 5 part-time/adjunct (3 women). *Students:* 19 full-time (15 women), 31 part-time (29 women); includes 16 minority (9 African Americans, 5 Asian Americans or Pacific Islanders, 2 Hispanic Americans), 2 international. Average age 35. 46 applicants, 72% accepted, 18 enrolled. In 2006, 34 degrees awarded. *Degree requirements:* For master's, thesis optional. *Entrance requirements:* For master's, GRE General Test or MAT. Additional exam requirements/recommendations for international students: Required—TOEFL. *Application deadline:* For fall admission, 6/1 for domestic students. Applications are processed on a rolling basis. Application fee: $75. *Financial support:* In 2006–07, 7 teaching assistantships were awarded; research assistantships, institutionally sponsored loans and tuition waivers (partial) also available. Support available to part-time students. Financial award application deadline: 6/30. *Faculty research:* Positive and negative mood states in parents of twins, effect of a carepath on chronic obstructive pulmonary disease home care. *Application contact:* Peter Taylor, Recruitment and Retention Specialist, 216-368-0349, Fax: 216-368-0124, E-mail: peter.taylor@case.edu.

The Catholic University of America, School of Nursing, Washington, DC 20064. Offers advanced practice nursing (MSN), including administration of nursing service, adult nurse practitioner, education, family nurse practitioner, geriatric nurse practitioner, pediatric nurse practitioner, psychiatric-mental health, school health nurse practitioner; clinical nursing (DN Sc). *Accreditation:* AACN; NLN. Part-time programs available. *Faculty:* 17 full-time (all women), 19 part-time/adjunct (18 women). *Students:* 27 full-time (25 women), 58 part-time (57 women); includes 31 minority (20 African Americans, 6 Asian Americans or Pacific Islanders, 5 Hispanic Americans), 6 international. Average age 43. 38 applicants, 76% accepted, 15 enrolled. In 2006, 15 master's, 7 doctorates awarded. *Degree requirements:* For master's, thesis optional; for doctorate, thesis/dissertation, comprehensive exam. *Entrance requirements:* For master's, GRE General Test or MAT, 3 letters of recommendation, BA in nursing, RN registration; for doctorate, GRE General Test, 3 letters of recommendation, BA in nursing, RN registration. Additional exam requirements/recommendations for international students: Required—TOEFL (minimum score 550 paper-based; 213 computer-based). *Application deadline:* For fall admission, 2/1 priority date for domestic students; for spring admission, 11/15 priority date for domestic students. Applications are processed on a rolling basis. Application fee: $55. Electronic applications accepted. *Expenses:* Tuition: Full-time $27,700; part-time $1,045 per credit hour. Required fees: $1,290. Part-time tuition and fees vary according to campus/location and program. *Financial support:* Research assistantships, teaching assistantships, career-related internships or fieldwork, Federal Work-Study, scholarships/grants, tuition waivers (full and partial), and unspecified assistantships available. Support available to part-time students. Financial award application deadline: 2/1; financial award applicants required to submit FAFSA. *Faculty research:* Outcome research–readmission of home health care patients with congestive heart failure, spirituality of chronic illness, minority multigravidos utilization of prenatal care. *Unit head:* Dr. Nalini Jairath, Dean, 202-319-5403, Fax: 202-319-6485, E-mail: jairath@cua.edu.

College of Mount Saint Vincent, School of Professional and Continuing Studies, Department of Nursing, Riverdale, NY 10471-1093. Offers adult nurse practitioner (MSN, PMC); family nurse practitioner (MSN, PMC); nurse educator (PMC); nursing administration (MSN); nursing for the adult and aged (MSN). *Accreditation:* AACN. Part-time programs available. *Faculty:* 2 full-time (1 woman), 6 part-time/adjunct (all women). *Students:* 1 (woman) full-time, 67 part-time (59 women); includes 43 minority (21 African Americans, 16 Asian Americans or Pacific Islanders, 6 Hispanic Americans). Average age 37. In 2006, 16 degrees awarded. *Degree requirements:* For master's, registration. *Entrance requirements:* For master's, BSN, interview, RN license, minimum GPA of 3.0, letters of reference. Additional exam requirements/recommendations for international students: Required—TOEFL. *Application deadline:* For fall admission, 6/1 for domestic and international students; for spring admission, 11/1 for domestic students, 10/1 for international students. Applications are processed on a rolling basis. Application fee: $50. *Expenses:* Contact institution. *Financial support:* Career-related internships or fieldwork available. Financial award application deadline: 6/1; financial award applicants required to submit FAFSA. *Unit head:* Carol Vicino, Director, 718-405-3354, Fax: 718-405-3286.

College of Staten Island of the City University of New York, Graduate Programs, Department of Nursing, Program in Gerontological Nursing, Staten Island, NY 10314-6600. Offers MS, 6th Year Certificate. Part-time and evening/weekend programs available. *Faculty:* 1 (woman) part-time/adjunct. *Students:* Average age 38. *Degree requirements:* For master's, 42 credits with 500 supervised hours, thesis optional; for 6th Year Certificate, 12-21 credits with 500 supervised hours. *Entrance requirements:* For master's, minimum undergraduate GPA of 3.0 in nursing courses, New York RN license, 2 professional references, specific undergraduate courses; for 6th Year Certificate, master's degree in nursing for post masters advanced certificates. Additional exam requirements/recommendations for international students: Required—TOEFL (minimum score 550 paper-based; 213 computer-based; 79 iBT). *Application deadline:* Applications are processed on a rolling basis. Application fee: $125. *Expenses:* Tuition, state resident: full-time $6,400; part-time $270 per credit. Tuition, nonresident: part-time $500 per credit. Required fees: $53 per semester. *Financial support:* Traineeships available. Financial award applicants required to submit FAFSA. *Unit head:* Dr. Margaret Lunney, Coordinator, 718-982-3823, Fax: 718-982-4124, E-mail: nursingmasters@mail.csi.cuny.edu. *Application contact:* Emmanuel Esperance, Deputy Director of Office of Recruitment and Admissions, 718-982-2190, Fax: 718-982-2500, E-mail: admissions@mail.csi.cuny.edu.

Columbia University, School of Nursing, Program in Geriatric Nurse Practitioner, New York, NY 10032. Offers MS, Adv C. *Accreditation:* AACN. Part-time programs available. *Faculty:* 1 (woman) full-time, 1 (woman) part-time/adjunct. *Students:* Average age 34. In 2006, 2 degrees awarded. *Entrance requirements:* For master's, GRE General Test, BSN, 1 year of clinical experience (preferred); for Adv C, MSN. *Application deadline:* Applications are processed on a rolling basis. Application fee: $65. Electronic applications accepted. *Financial support:* Teaching assistantships available. Financial award application deadline: 2/1; financial award applicants required to submit FAFSA. *Unit head:* Prof. JoAnne Staats, Director, 212-305-7327.

Gerontological Nursing

Concordia University Wisconsin, Graduate Programs, School of Health and Human Services, Program in Nursing, Mequon, WI 53097-2402. Offers family nurse practitioner (MSN); geriatric nurse practitioner (MSN); nurse educator (MSN). *Accreditation:* AACN. Postbaccalaureate distance learning degree programs offered (minimal on-campus study). *Faculty:* 2 full-time (1 woman), 5 part-time/adjunct (all women). *Students:* 217 (199 women). Average age 29. In 2006, 37 degrees awarded. *Degree requirements:* For master's, thesis or alternative, comprehensive exam. *Entrance requirements:* Additional exam requirements/recommendations for international students: Required—TOEFL. *Application deadline:* For fall admission, 8/1 priority date for domestic students. Applications are processed on a rolling basis. Application fee: $35. *Expenses:* Contact institution. *Financial support:* Application deadline: 8/1. *Unit head:* Dr. Ruth Gresley, Director, 262-243-4452, E-mail: ruth.gresley@cuw.edu.

Duke University, School of Nursing, Durham, NC 27708-0586. Offers adult acute care (Certificate); adult cardiovascular (Certificate); adult oncology/HIV (Certificate); adult primary care (Certificate); clinical nurse specialist (MSN), including adult oncology/HIV, gerontology, neonatal, pediatric, pediatric/chronic acute care; clinical research management (MSN, Certificate); family (Certificate); gerontology (Certificate); health and nursing ministries (MSN, Certificate); health systems leadership and outcomes (Certificate); leadership in community based long term care (MSN, Certificate); neonatal (Certificate); neonatal/pediatric in rural health (MSN, Certificate); nurse anesthetist (MSN, Certificate); nurse practitioner (MSN), including adult acute care, adult cardiovascular, adult oncology/HIV, adult primary care, family, gerontology, neonatal, pediatric, pediatric acute care; nursing (PhD); nursing and healthcare leadership (MSN); nursing education (MSN); nursing informatics (MSN, Certificate); pediatric (Certificate); pediatric acute care (Certificate); MBA/MSN; MSN/MCM. *Accreditation:* AACN; AANA/CANAEP. Part-time programs available. Postbaccalaureate distance learning degree programs offered (minimal on-campus study). *Faculty:* 45 full-time (41 women), 169 part-time/adjunct (150 women). *Students:* 178 full-time (162 women), 140 part-time (132 women); includes 48 minority (17 African Americans, 3 American Indian/Alaska Native, 20 Asian Americans or Pacific Islanders, 8 Hispanic Americans). Average age 36. 99 applicants, 92% accepted, 91 enrolled. In 2006, 122 master's, 17 other advanced degrees awarded. *Median time to degree:* Master's–2 years full-time, 2.5 years part-time. *Degree requirements:* For master's, thesis optional. *Entrance requirements:* For master's, GRE General Test or MAT, 1 year of nursing experience, BSN, minimum GPA of 3.0, previous course work in statistics; for Certificate, MSN. Additional exam requirements/recommendations for international students: Required—TOEFL (minimum score 550 paper-based; 213 computer-based), Commission on Graduates of Foreign Nursing Schools exam. *Application deadline:* For fall admission, 7/2 priority date for domestic and international students; for spring admission, 11/15 priority date for domestic and international students. Applications are processed on a rolling basis. Application fee: $50. *Expenses:* Contact institution. *Financial support:* In 2006–07, 258 students received support. Career-related internships or fieldwork, institutionally sponsored loans, scholarships/grants, traineeships, and tuition waivers (partial) available. Support available to part-time students. Financial award application deadline: 4/1; financial award applicants required to submit FAFSA. *Faculty research:* Cardiovascular disease, caregiver skill training, data mining, prostate cancer, neonatal immune system. Total annual research expenditures: $3.5 million. *Unit head:* Dr. Catherine L. Gilliss, Dean/Vice Chancellor for Nursing Affairs, 919-684-9444, Fax: 919-684-9414, E-mail: gilli025@mc.duke.edu. *Application contact:* Bebe T. Mills, Director of Admissions, 919-684-9151, Fax: 919-668-4693, E-mail: mills031@mc.duke.edu.

Gwynedd-Mercy College, School of Nursing, Gwynedd Valley, PA 19437-0901. Offers clinical nurse specialist (MSN), including gerontology, oncology, pediatrics; nurse practitioner (MSN), including adult health, pediatric health. *Accreditation:* NLN. *Faculty:* 5 full-time (all women), 3 part-time/adjunct (2 women). *Students:* 7 full-time (5 women), 38 part-time (35 women); includes 3 minority (1 African American, 1 Asian American or Pacific Islander, 1 Hispanic American). Average age 41. 18 applicants, 89% accepted, 11 enrolled. In 2006, 5 degrees awarded. *Degree requirements:* For master's, thesis optional. *Entrance requirements:* For master's, GRE General Test or MAT, 2 years of experience, physical assessment, course work in statistics, BSN from an NLNAC accredited program, 2 letters of recommendation, personal interview. Additional exam requirements/recommendations for international students: Required—TOEFL (minimum score 575 paper-based). *Application deadline:* For fall admission, 8/1 priority date for domestic students; for winter admission, 12/1 priority date for domestic students. Applications are processed on a rolling basis. Application fee: $25. Electronic applications accepted. *Expenses:* Contact institution. *Financial support:* In 2006–07, 21 students received support. Scholarships/grants, traineeships, and unspecified assistantships available. Financial award application deadline: 8/30. *Faculty research:* Critical thinking, primary care, domestic violence, multiculturalism, nursing centers. *Unit head:* Dr. Andrea D. Hollingsworth, Dean, 215-646-7300 Ext. 539, Fax: 215-641-5517, E-mail: hollingsworth.a@gmc.edu. *Application contact:* Dr. Barbara A. Jones, Director, 215-646-7300 Ext. 407, Fax: 215-641-5564, E-mail: jones.b@gmc.edu.

Hunter College of the City University of New York, Graduate School, Schools of the Health Professions, Hunter-Bellevue School of Nursing, Gerontological Nurse Practitioner Program, New York, NY 10021-5085. Offers MS. *Accreditation:* AACN. Part-time programs available. *Faculty:* 24 full-time (21 women), 21 part-time/adjunct (19 women). *Students:* 1 (woman) full-time, 40 part-time (38 women); includes 23 minority (15 African Americans, 5 Asian Americans or Pacific Islanders, 3 Hispanic Americans). Average age 39. 19 applicants, 63% accepted, 8 enrolled. In 2006, 6 degrees awarded. *Degree requirements:* For master's, practicum. *Entrance requirements:* For master's, minimum GPA of 3.0, New York RN license, 2 years of professional practice experience, BSN. Additional exam requirements/recommendations for international students: Required—TOEFL. *Application deadline:* For fall admission, 4/1 for domestic students, 2/1 for international students; for spring admission, 11/1 for domestic students, 9/1 for international students. Applications are processed on a rolling basis. Application fee: $125. *Expenses:* Tuition, state resident: part-time $270 per credit. Tuition, nonresident: part-time $500 per credit. Required fees: $45 per semester. *Financial support:* Federal Work-Study, scholarships/grants, traineeships, and tuition waivers (partial) available. Support available to part-time students. Financial award application deadline: 5/1; financial award applicants required to submit FAFSA. *Faculty research:* Primary care of older adults, lived experiences of elders. *Unit head:* Dr. Steven Baumann, Coordinator, 212-481-4457, Fax: 212-481-5078, E-mail: sbaumann@shiva.hunter.cuny.edu. *Application contact:* William Zlata, Director for Graduate Admissions, 212-772-4482, Fax: 212-650-3336, E-mail: admissions@hunter.cuny.edu.

Lehman College of the City University of New York, Division of Natural and Social Sciences, Department of Nursing, Bronx, NY 10468-1589. Offers adult health nursing (MS); nursing of older adults (MS); parent-child nursing (MS); pediatric nurse practitioner (MS). *Accreditation:* AACN. Part-time and evening/weekend programs available. *Entrance requirements:* For master's, bachelor's degree in nursing, New York RN license.

Loma Linda University, Department of Graduate Nursing, Program in Adult and Aging Family Nursing, Loma Linda, CA 92350. Offers MS. *Accreditation:* AACN. Part-time programs available. *Degree requirements:* For master's, thesis or alternative. *Entrance requirements:* For master's, GRE General Test. *Faculty research:* Coping, integration of research.

Marquette University, Graduate School, College of Nursing, Milwaukee, WI 53201-1881. Offers adult nurse practitioner (Certificate); advanced practice nursing (MSN), including adult, children, neonatal nurse practitioner, nurse-midwifery, older adult; gerontological nurse practitioner (Certificate); neonatal nurse practitioner (Certificate); nurse-midwifery (Certificate); nursing (PhD); pediatric nurse practitioner (Certificate). *Accreditation:* AACN. Part-time and evening/weekend programs available. *Faculty:* 29 full-time (27 women), 39 part-time/adjunct (37 women). *Students:* 104 full-time (98 women), 122 part-time (114 women); includes 18 minority (5 African Americans, 2 American Indian/Alaska Native, 4 Asian Americans or Pacific Islanders, 7 Hispanic Americans), 2 international. Average age 34. 122 applicants, 79% accepted, 73 enrolled. In 2006, 46 degrees awarded. *Degree requirements:* For master's, thesis or alternative, comprehensive exam. *Entrance requirements:* For master's, GRE General Test, BSN, Wisconsin RN license. Additional exam requirements/recommendations for international students: Required—TOEFL. Application fee: $40. *Financial support:* In 2006–07, 6 research assistantships, 1 teaching assistantship were awarded; career-related internships or fieldwork, Federal Work-Study, institutionally sponsored loans, scholarships/grants, and tuition waivers (full and partial) also available. Support available to part-time students. Financial award application deadline: 2/15. *Faculty research:* Psychosocial adjustment to chronic illness, gerontology, reminiscence, health policy: uninsured and access, hospital care delivery systems. Total annual research expenditures: $1.1 million. *Unit head:* Dr. Lea Acord, Dean, 414-288-3812, Fax: 414-288-1578. *Application contact:* Dr. Judy Miller, Director of Graduate Studies, 414-288-3810, Fax: 414-288-1578.

Medical University of South Carolina, College of Nursing, Program in Gerontological Nurse Practitioner, Charleston, SC 29425-0002. Offers MSN. *Accreditation:* AACN. Part-time programs available. *Faculty:* 4 full-time (all women). *Students:* 4 full-time (3 women), 1 (woman) part-time. *Degree requirements:* For master's, thesis optional. *Entrance requirements:* For master's, GRE General Test, BSN, course work in statistics and physical assessment, nursing license, minimum GPA of 3.0. Additional exam requirements/recommendations for international students: Required—TOEFL (minimum score 600 paper-based; 250 computer-based). *Application deadline:* For fall admission, 2/1 for domestic and international students; for spring admission, 9/15 for domestic and international students. Application fee: $75. Electronic applications accepted. *Financial support:* Federal Work-Study, scholarships/grants, and traineeships available. Support available to part-time students. Financial award application deadline: 3/15; financial award applicants required to submit FAFSA. *Faculty research:* Meals at end of life, primary and palliative care. Total annual research expenditures: $146,000. *Unit head:* Dr. Barbara J. Edlund, Track Coordinator, 843-792-4653, Fax: 843-792-1741, E-mail: edlundb@musc.edu. *Application contact:* Carolyn F. Page, Director, Student Services, 843-792-3844, Fax: 843-792-9258, E-mail: pagecf@musc.edu.

MGH Institute of Health Professions, Graduate Programs, Program in Nursing, Boston, MA 02129. Offers advanced practice nursing (MSN); gerontological nursing (MSN); pediatric nursing (MSN); psychiatric nursing (MSN); teaching and learning for health care education (Certificate); women's health nursing (MSN). *Accreditation:* NLN (one or more programs are accredited). *Faculty:* 29 full-time (28 women), 9 part-time/adjunct (7 women). *Students:* 208 full-time (188 women), 43 part-time (35 women); includes 36 minority (12 African Americans, 17 Asian Americans or Pacific Islanders, 7 Hispanic Americans), 1 international. Average age 29. 302 applicants, 62% accepted, 101 enrolled. In 2006, 77 master's, 3 other advanced degrees awarded. *Degree requirements:* For master's, thesis or alternative. *Entrance requirements:* For master's, GRE General Test, minimum GPA of 3.0. Additional exam requirements/recommendations for international students: Required—TOEFL (minimum score 550 paper-based; 213 computer-based). *Application deadline:* For fall admission, 1/10 for domestic and international students. Application fee: $50. Electronic applications accepted. *Financial support:* In 2006–07, 212 students received support, including 1 research assistantship (averaging $1,200 per year), 2 teaching assistantships (averaging $1,200 per year); career-related internships or fieldwork, scholarships/grants, traineeships, tuition waivers (full and partial), and unspecified assistantships also available. Support available to part-time students. Financial award application deadline: 3/3; financial award applicants required to submit FAFSA. *Faculty research:* Biobehavioral nursing, HIV/AIDS, gerontological nursing, women's health, vulnerable populations, health systems . *Unit head:* Margery Chisholm, Director, 617-724-0480, Fax: 617-726-8022, E-mail: mchisholm@mghihp.edu. *Application contact:* Maureen Rika Judd, Manager of Admissions, 617-726-6069, Fax: 617-726-8010, E-mail: admissions@mghihp.edu.

See Close-Up on page 1963.

Nazareth College of Rochester, Graduate Studies, Department of Nursing, Gerontological Nurse Practitioner Program, Rochester, NY 14618-3790. Offers MS. *Accreditation:* AACN. Part-time programs available. *Faculty:* 3 full-time (all women), 1 (woman) part-time/adjunct. *Students:* 1 (woman) full-time, 19 part-time (18 women); includes 5 minority (3 African Americans, 1 American Indian/Alaska Native, 1 Asian American or Pacific Islander). Average age 33. 2 applicants, 100% accepted, 2 enrolled. *Entrance requirements:* For master's, minimum GPA of 3.0. *Application deadline:* For fall admission, 8/1 priority date for domestic students; for spring admission, 11/1 for domestic students. Applications are processed on a rolling basis. Application fee: $40. *Financial support:* Research assistantships with partial tuition reimbursements, career-related internships or fieldwork available. Support available to part-time students. Financial award application deadline: 3/1; financial award applicants required to submit FAFSA. *Unit head:* Dr. Linda Janelli, Director, 585-389-2713, Fax: 585-389-2452, E-mail: ljanell6@naz.edu. *Application contact:* Judith G. Baker, Director, Graduate Admissions, 585-389-2050, Fax: 585-389-2817, E-mail: gradstudies@naz.edu.

New York University, College of Dentistry, College of Nursing, Programs in Advanced Practice Nursing, New York, NY 10012-1019. Offers advanced practice nursing: adult acute care (MS, Advanced Certificate); advanced practice nursing: adult primary care (MS, Advanced Certificate); advanced practice nursing: adult primary care/geriatrics (MS); advanced practice nursing: children with special needs (Advanced Certificate); advanced practice nursing: geriatrics (MS, Advanced Certificate); advanced practice nursing: holistic nursing (MS, Advanced Certificate); advanced practice nursing: home health nursing (Advanced Certificate); advanced practice nursing: mental health (MS); advanced practice nursing: mental health nursing (Advanced Certificate); advanced practice nursing: pediatrics (MS, Advanced Certificate); advanced practice nursing: pediatrics/children with special needs (MS); midwifery (MS, Advanced Certificate); nursing administration (MS, Advanced Certificate); nursing education (MS, Advanced Certificate); nursing informatics (MS, Advanced Certificate); palliative care (MS, Advanced Certificate); MS/MS. *Accreditation:* AACN; ACNM/DOA. Part-time and evening/weekend programs available. *Faculty:* 30 full-time (all women). *Students:* 10 full-time (all women), 428 part-time (395 women); includes 166 minority (73 African Americans, 72 Asian Americans or Pacific Islanders, 21 Hispanic Americans). Average age 35. 154 applicants, 93% accepted, 118 enrolled. In 2006, 100 master's, 7 Advanced Certificates awarded. *Degree requirements:* For master's, thesis (for some programs). *Entrance requirements:* For master's, BS in nursing, AS in nursing with another BS/BA degree; for Advanced Certificate, master's degree. Additional exam requirements/recommendations for international students: Required—TOEFL. *Application deadline:* For fall admission, 7/1 priority date for domestic students, 7/1 for international students; for spring admission, 12/1 for domestic and international students. Applications are processed on a rolling basis. Application fee: $65. *Expenses:* Tuition: Part-time $1,080 per unit. Required fees: $56 per unit. $329 per term. Tuition and fees vary according to program. *Financial support:* Career-related internships or fieldwork, Federal Work-Study, institutionally sponsored loans, scholarships/grants, and tuition waivers (partial) available. Support available to part-time students. Financial award application deadline: 2/1; financial award applicants required to submit FAFSA. *Faculty research:* Elderly black diabetics, families and illness, public health nursing, parent-child nursing, health policy costs. *Unit head:* Dr. Judith Haber, Associate Dean for Graduate Programs, 212-998-5300, Fax: 212-995-3143. *Application contact:* Amy Knowles, Assistant Dean for Student Affairs and Admissions, 212-998-5333, Fax: 212-995-4302, E-mail: ak96@nyu.edu.

Oakland University, Graduate Study and Lifelong Learning, School of Nursing, Adult Gerontological Nurse Practitioner Program, Rochester, MI 48309-4401. Offers MSN, Certificate. *Students:* 7 full-time (all women), 14 part-time (all women); includes 4 minority (2 African Americans, 1 Asian American or Pacific Islander, 1 Hispanic American), 1 international. Average age 41. 7 applicants, 71% accepted, 3 enrolled.Application fee: $35. *Expenses:* Tuition, state resident: full-time $9,936; part-time $414 per credit. Tuition, nonresident: full-time $17,202; part-time $716 per credit. *Application contact:* Mary Bray, Graduate Program Coordinator, 248-370-4482.

Oregon Health & Science University, School of Nursing, PhD Nursing Program, Portland, OR 97239-3098. Offers families in health, illness, and transition (PhD); gerontological nursing (PhD). Part-time programs available. *Degree requirements:* For doctorate, thesis/dissertation.

Entrance requirements: For doctorate, GRE General Test, master's degree in nursing; minimum undergraduate GPA of 3.0, 3.5 graduate.

Oregon Health & Science University, School of Nursing, Program in Gerontological Nursing, Portland, OR 97239-3098. Offers MS, Post Master's Certificate. *Accreditation:* AACN. *Degree requirements:* For master's, thesis optional. *Entrance requirements:* For master's, GRE General Test, bachelor's degree in nursing, minimum undergraduate GPA of 3.0, previous course work in statistics; for Post Master's Certificate, master's or associate's degree in nursing.

Oregon Health & Science University, School of Nursing, Program in Primary Health Care, Portland, OR 97239-3098. Offers adult nurse practitioner (MS, Post Master's Certificate); family nurse practitioner (MS, Post Master's Certificate); geriatric nurse practitioner (Post Master's Certificate); geriatric/adult nurse practitioner (MS); pediatric nurse practitioner (MS, Post Master's Certificate). *Accreditation:* AACN. *Degree requirements:* For master's, thesis optional. *Entrance requirements:* For master's, GRE General Test, bachelor's degree in nursing, minimum undergraduate GPA of 3.0, previous course work in statistics; for Post Master's Certificate, master's degree in nursing.

Rush University, College of Nursing, Department of Adult Health Nursing, Chicago, IL 60612-3832. Offers acute care nurse practitioner (MSN, Post-Master's Certificate); adult health nursing (DN Sc, DNP); adult nurse practitioner (MSN, Post-Master's Certificate); adult/gerontological nurse practitioner (MSN); anesthesia nurse practitioner (MSN, Post-Master's Certificate); critical care clinical specialist (MSN); gerontological nurse practitioner (MSN, Post-Master's Certificate); medical surgical clinical specialist (MSN). *Accreditation:* AACN; AANA/CANAEP (one or more programs are accredited). Part-time programs available. Postbaccalaureate distance learning degree programs offered (minimal on-campus study). *Faculty:* 33. *Students:* 29 full-time, 123 part-time; includes 22 minority (7 African Americans, 9 Asian Americans or Pacific Islanders, 6 Hispanic Americans). Average age 35. 101 applicants, 80% accepted, 76 enrolled. In 2006, 47 master's, 6 doctorates awarded. Terminal master's awarded for partial completion of doctoral program. *Degree requirements:* For master's, capstone project; for doctorate, thesis/dissertation, DNP leadership project. *Entrance requirements:* For master's, GRE General Test (waived if nursing GPA is above 3.0 or cumulative GPA is above 3.25), interview; for doctorate, GRE General Test, interview, course work in statistics (DN Sc). Additional exam requirements/recommendations for international students: Required—TOEFL, TWE. *Application deadline:* For fall admission, 7/1 for domestic students; for winter admission, 11/1 for domestic students; for spring admission, 1/15 for domestic students. Applications are processed on a rolling basis. Application fee: $40. Electronic applications accepted. *Financial support:* In 2006–07, 19 students received support; teaching assistantships with tuition reimbursements available, Federal Work-Study, institutionally sponsored loans, scholarships/grants, and traineeships available. Support available to part-time students. Financial award application deadline: 5/1; financial award applicants required to submit FAFSA. *Faculty research:* Complementary/alternative medicine, critical care outcomes, cardiac risk reduction, Alzheimer's Disease, telehealth monitoring. *Unit head:* Dr. Margaret Faut-Callahan, Chairperson, 312-942-7117. *Application contact:* Hicela Castruita Woods, Director, College Admissions Services, 312-942-7100, Fax: 312-942-2219, E-mail: hicela_castruita@rush.edu.

Rutgers, The State University of New Jersey, Newark, Graduate School, Program in Nursing, Newark, NJ 07102. Offers nursing (MS), including acute care of adults and aged, advanced practice in pediatric nursing, advanced practice with childbearing families, community health nursing, family nurse practitioner, primary care of adults and aged, psychiatric/mental health nursing. *Accreditation:* AACN. Part-time programs available. *Faculty:* 33 full-time (32 women). *Students:* 11 full-time (all women), 186 part-time (175 women); includes 70 minority (28 African Americans, 30 Asian Americans or Pacific Islanders, 12 Hispanic Americans). 255 applicants, 58% accepted, 72 enrolled. In 2006, 40 master's awarded. *Degree requirements:* For master's, comprehensive exam. *Entrance requirements:* For master's, GRE General Test, RN license, minimum B average, BS in nursing. Additional exam requirements/recommendations for international students: Required—TOEFL. *Application deadline:* For fall admission, 2/15 for domestic students; for spring admission, 12/1 for domestic students. Applications are processed on a rolling basis. Application fee: $50. Electronic applications accepted. *Financial support:* In 2006–07, 3 fellowships (averaging $8,000 per year) were awarded; teaching assistantships with full tuition reimbursements, career-related internships or fieldwork, Federal Work-Study, institutionally sponsored loans, scholarships/grants, traineeships, and tuition waivers (full and partial) also available. Financial award application deadline: 4/15. *Faculty research:* HIV/AIDS, quality of life—MS and breast cancer, sleep patterns of cardiac patients. *Unit head:* Dr. Wendy Nehring, Program Director, 973-353-5293 Ext. 606, Fax: 973-353-1277, E-mail: nehring@nightingale.rutgers.edu. *Application contact:* Dr. Linda Scheetz, Associate Dean for Student Life and Services, 973-353-5060 Ext. 611, Fax: 973-353-1277, E-mail: lscheetz@andromeda.rutgers.edu.

San Jose State University, Graduate Studies and Research, College of Applied Sciences and Arts, School of Nursing, San Jose, CA 95192-0001. Offers gerontology nurse practitioner (MS); nursing (Certificate); nursing administration (MS); nursing education (MS). *Accreditation:* AACN. Part-time and evening/weekend programs available. *Students:* 15 full-time (13 women), 70 part-time (66 women); includes 30 minority (2 African Americans, 21 Asian Americans or Pacific Islanders, 7 Hispanic Americans). Average age 41. 73 applicants, 70% accepted, 15 enrolled. In 2006, 34 degrees awarded. *Degree requirements:* For master's, thesis. *Entrance requirements:* For master's, BS in nursing, RN license. *Application deadline:* For fall admission, 6/29 for domestic students; for spring admission, 11/30 for domestic students. Applications are processed on a rolling basis. Application fee: $59. Electronic applications accepted. *Financial support:* Career-related internships or fieldwork, institutionally sponsored loans, and scholarships/grants available. Support available to part-time students. Financial award applicants required to submit FAFSA. *Faculty research:* Nurse-managed clinics, computers in nursing. *Unit head:* Jayne Cohen, Director, 408-924-3131, Fax: 408-924-3135. *Application contact:* Dr. Phyllis Connolly, Graduate Coordinator, 408-924-3144.

Seton Hall University, College of Nursing, Department of Graduate Nursing, Advanced Practice in Primary Health Care Program, South Orange, NJ 07079-2697. Offers adult nurse practitioner (MSN); gerontological nurse practitioner (MSN); pediatric nurse practitioner (MSN); women's health nurse practitioner (MSN). *Accreditation:* AACN. Part-time programs available. *Degree requirements:* For master's, research project. *Entrance requirements:* For master's, GRE or MAT, BSN. *Faculty research:* Health promotion in well aged, practice outcomes, collaborative practice.

Southern University and Agricultural and Mechanical College, School of Nursing, Baton Rouge, LA 70813. Offers educator/administrator (PhD); family health nursing (MSN); family nurse practitioner (Post Master's Certificate); geriatric nurse practitioner/gerontology (PhD). *Accreditation:* AACN; NLN. Part-time programs available. *Degree requirements:* For master's and doctorate, thesis/dissertation, comprehensive exam. *Entrance requirements:* For master's, GRE General Test, BSN, minimum GPA of 2.7; for doctorate, GRE General Test; for Post Master's Certificate, MSN. Additional exam requirements/recommendations for international students: Required—TOEFL (minimum score 525 paper-based; 193 computer-based). *Faculty research:* Health promotions, vulnerable populations, (community-based) cardiovascular participating research, health disparities chronic diseases, care of the elderly.

State University of New York at New Paltz, Graduate School, Faculty of Liberal Arts and Sciences, Department of Nursing, New Paltz, NY 12561. Offers clinical nurse specialist adult health (CAS); gerontological nursing (MS). *Accreditation:* AACN. Part-time and evening/weekend programs available. *Faculty:* 6 full-time (all women), 2 part-time/adjunct (1 woman). *Students:* Average age 45. In 2006, 3 degrees awarded. *Entrance requirements:* For master's, minimum GPA of 3.0. Additional exam requirements/recommendations for international students: Required—TOEFL (minimum score 550 paper-based; 213 computer-based; 80 iBT). *Application deadline:* For fall admission, 5/15 priority date for domestic students, 5/15 for international students; for spring admission, 11/15 priority date for domestic students, 11/15 for international students. Applications are processed on a rolling basis. Application fee: $50. Electronic applications accepted. *Expenses:* Tuition, state resident: full-time $6,900; part-time $288 per credit hour. Tuition, nonresident: full-time $10,920; part-time $455 per credit hour. *Unit head:* Dr. Eleanor Richards, Chair, 845-257-2922.

State University of New York Institute of Technology, School of Nursing and Health Systems, Program in Gerontological Nurse Practitioner, Utica, NY 13504-3050. Offers MS, CAS. *Faculty:* 5 full-time (all women), 3 part-time/adjunct (2 women). *Entrance requirements:* For master's, GRE General Test if undergraduate GPA is less than 3.3 , minimum GPA of 3.0 in last 30 hours of undergraduate work, bachelor's degree in nursing, 1 year professional experience, RN license, interview, 2 letters of recommendation . Additional exam requirements/recommendations for international students: Required—TOEFL (minimum score 550 paper-based; 213 computer-based). *Application deadline:* For fall admission, 6/15 for domestic students. Applications are processed on a rolling basis. Application fee: $50. *Expenses:* Tuition, state resident: full-time $3,452; part-time $288 per credit hour. Tuition, nonresident: full-time $10,920; part-time $455 per credit hour. Required fees: $927; $38 per credit hour. *Financial support:* Traineeships available. *Faculty research:* Gerontological health issues, assessment of eldercare, nursing shortages, nursing faculty shortages. *Unit head:* Dr. Louisde Kelly, Coordinator, Fax: 315-792-7555, E-mail: fldk@sunyit.edu. *Application contact:* Marybeth Lyons, Director of Admissions, 315-792-7500, Fax: 315-792-7837, E-mail: smbl@sunyit.edu.

Stony Brook University, State University of New York, Stony Brook University Medical Center, Health Sciences Center, School of Nursing, Program in Gerontological Nursing, Stony Brook, NY 11794. Offers MS. *Accreditation:* AACN. *Degree requirements:* For master's, thesis. *Entrance requirements:* For master's, BSN, minimum GPA of 3.0, course work in statistics. *Application deadline:* For fall admission, 1/15 for domestic students. Application fee: $50. *Expenses:* Tuition, state resident: full-time $6,900; part-time $288 per credit. Tuition, nonresident: full-time $10,920; part-time $455 per credit. *Financial support:* Application deadline: 3/15. *Unit head:* Dr. Carole L. Blair, Coordinator, 631-444-3258, Fax: 631-444-3136.

Texas Tech University Health Sciences Center, School of Nursing, Lubbock, TX 79430. Offers acute care nurse practitioner (MSN, Certificate); administration (MSN); clinical research management (MSN, Certificate); education (MSN); family nurse practitioner (MSN, Certificate); geriatric nurse practitioner (MSN, Certificate); pediatric nurse practitioner (MSN, Certificate). *Accreditation:* AACN. Part-time programs available. Postbaccalaureate distance learning degree programs offered (minimal on-campus study). *Faculty:* 17 full-time (16 women), 5 part-time/adjunct (all women). *Students:* 23 full-time (22 women), 161 part-time (137 women); includes 46 minority (8 African Americans, 2 American Indian/Alaska Native, 6 Asian Americans or Pacific Islanders, 30 Hispanic Americans). Average age 37. 97 applicants, 69% accepted, 67 enrolled. In 2006, 41 degrees awarded. *Degree requirements:* For master's, thesis optional. *Entrance requirements:* For master's, minimum GPA of 3.0, 3 letters of reference, BSN, RN license; for Certificate, minimum GPA of 3.0, 3 letters of reference, RN license. Additional exam requirements/recommendations for international students: Required—TOEFL (minimum score 550 paper-based; 213 computer-based). *Application deadline:* For fall admission, 7/15 priority date for domestic and international students; for spring admission, 11/15 priority date for domestic and international students. Applications are processed on a rolling basis. Application fee: $40. *Financial support:* In 2006–07, 184 students received support. Institutionally sponsored loans, scholarships/grants, and traineeships available. Support available to part-time students. Financial award application deadline: 12/1; financial award applicants required to submit FAFSA. *Faculty research:* Diabetes/obesity, nurse competency, disease management, intervention and measurements, health disparities. Total annual research expenditures: $2.4 million. *Unit head:* Dr. Barbara A. Johnston, Associate Dean for Administrative and Student Affairs, 806-743-3055, Fax: 806-743-1622, E-mail: barbara.johnston@ttuhsc.edu. *Application contact:* Lauren K. Sullivan, Recruiter/Transcultural Coordinator, 806-743-2730 Ext. 309, Fax: 806-743-1622, E-mail: lauren.sullivan@ttuhsc.edu.

Texas Wesleyan University, Graduate Programs, Programs in Business Administration, Fort Worth, TX 76105-1536. Offers business administration (MBA); geriatrics (MSHA); health administration (MSHA); public health (MSHA). *Accreditation:* ACBSP. Part-time and evening/weekend programs available. *Faculty:* 13 full-time (3 women), 4 part-time/adjunct (1 woman). *Students:* 15 full-time (7 women), 42 part-time (30 women); includes 27 minority (14 African Americans, 1 American Indian/Alaska Native, 4 Asian Americans or Pacific Islanders, 8 Hispanic Americans). Average age 31. In 2006, 18 degrees awarded. *Degree requirements:* For master's, capstone course. *Entrance requirements:* For master's, GMAT, minimum GPA of 3.0 in final 60 hours of undergraduate course work, 2.75 overall. *Application deadline:* Applications are processed on a rolling basis. Application fee: $30 ($50 for international students). Electronic applications accepted. *Expenses: Contact institution.* Tuition and fees vary according to program. *Financial support:* Federal Work-Study, scholarships/grants, and tuition waivers (full and partial) available. Support available to part-time students. Financial award application deadline: 3/15; financial award applicants required to submit FAFSA. *Unit head:* Dr. Charles Little, Director, 817-531-6500, Fax: 817-531-6585.

University at Buffalo, the State University of New York, Graduate School, School of Nursing, Buffalo, NY 14260. Offers acute care nurse practitioner (MS, Certificate); adult health nursing (MS, Certificate); child health nursing (MS); family nurse practitioner (Certificate); family nursing (MS); geriatric nurse practitioner (MS, Certificate); maternal and women's health nurse practitioner (Certificate); maternal and women's health nursing (MS); nurse anesthetist (MS); nursing (PhD); nursing education (Certificate); pediatric nurse practitioner (Certificate); psychiatric/mental health nurse practitioner (Certificate); psychiatric/mental health nursing (MS). *Accreditation:* AACN; AANA/CANAEP (one or more programs are accredited). Part-time programs available. Postbaccalaureate distance learning degree programs offered. *Faculty:* 38 full-time (34 women), 15 part-time/adjunct (14 women). *Students:* 131 full-time (108 women), 64 part-time (61 women); includes 29 minority (11 African Americans, 9 Asian Americans or Pacific Islanders, 9 Hispanic Americans), 20 international. Average age 28. 346 applicants, 25% accepted, 51 enrolled. In 2006, 49 master's, 3 doctorates, 6 other advanced degrees awarded. Terminal master's awarded for partial completion of doctoral program. *Degree requirements:* For master's, comprehensive exams or project; for doctorate, thesis/dissertation, comprehensive exam. *Entrance requirements:* For master's, GRE General Test (if overall GPA is below 3.0), interview, minimum GPA of 3.0, RN license, 3 references; for doctorate, GRE General Test, minimum GPA of 3.25, RN license, BS or MS in nursing, 3 references, writing sample; for Certificate, interview, minimum GPA of 3.0 or GRE General Test, RN license, MS in nursing. Additional exam requirements/recommendations for international students: Required—TOEFL (minimum score 550 paper-based; 213 computer-based; 79 iBT), IELTS (minimum score 7). *Application deadline:* For fall admission, 6/1 priority date for domestic students, 3/1 priority date for international students; for spring admission, 11/1 for domestic students, 9/15 priority date for international students. Applications are processed on a rolling basis. Application fee: $50. Electronic applications accepted. *Financial support:* In 2006–07, 78 students received support, including 13 fellowships with full tuition reimbursements available (averaging $7,220 per year), 10 research assistantships with tuition reimbursements available (averaging $17,881 per year), 23 teaching assistantships with full tuition reimbursements available (averaging $11,245 per year); Federal Work-Study, scholarships/grants, traineeships, health care benefits, and unspecified assistantships also available. Financial award application deadline: 3/15; financial award applicants required to submit FAFSA. *Faculty research:* Oncology symptom management, end of life decision making, changing behaviors using the transtheoretical model, addictions, nursing workforce. Total annual research expenditures: $1.7 million. *Unit head:* Dr. Jean K. Brown, Dean, Interim, 716-829-2533, Fax: 716-829-2566, E-mail: jebrown@buffalo.edu. *Application contact:* Dr. Elaine R. Cusker, Assistant Dean, 716-829-2537, Fax: 716-829-2021, E-mail: ecusker@buffalo.edu.

University of Colorado at Colorado Springs, Graduate School, Beth-El College of Nursing, Colorado Springs, CO 80933-7150. Offers adult health nurse practitioner and clinical specialist (MSN); family practitioner (MSN), including community clinical specialist, forensic clinical specialist, holistic clinical specialist; gerontology (MSN); neonatal nurse practitioner and clinical specialist (MSN); nursing administration (MSN); women nurse practitioner (MSN).

Gerontological Nursing

University of Colorado at Colorado Springs (continued)
Accreditation: AACN. Part-time programs available. Postbaccalaureate distance learning degree programs offered (minimal on-campus study). *Faculty:* 10 full-time (7 women), 14 part-time/adjunct (7 women). *Students:* 84 full-time (77 women), 53 part-time (52 women); includes 22 minority (6 African Americans, 3 American Indian/Alaska Native, 2 Asian Americans or Pacific Islanders, 11 Hispanic Americans). Average age 37. 54 applicants, 85% accepted, 30 enrolled. In 2006, 36 degrees awarded. *Degree requirements:* For master's, thesis optional; for doctorate, capstone project. *Entrance requirements:* For master's, GRE General Test or MAT, BSN, minimum GPA of 3.0, unrestricted RN license; for doctorate, interview; active RN license; MA; minimum GPA of 3.3; National Certification as NP, CNS, or CNS; portfolio. Additional exam requirements/recommendations for international students: Required—TOEFL. *Application deadline:* For fall admission, 6/1 priority date for domestic students; for spring admission, 11/15 for domestic students. Application fee: $60 ($75 for international students). Electronic applications accepted. *Expenses: Contact institution.* Tuition and fees vary according to course load, campus/location and program. *Financial support:* Fellowships, career-related internships or fieldwork, Federal Work-Study, and institutionally sponsored loans available. Support available to part-time students. *Faculty research:* Women's health, uncertainty, empowerment, family experience in chronic illness. Total annual research expenditures: $260,389. *Unit head:* Dr. Carole Schoffstall, Dean, 719-262-4418, Fax: 719-262-4416, E-mail: cschoffs@uccs.edu.

University of Delaware, College of Health Sciences, School of Nursing, Newark, DE 19716. Offers adult nurse practitioner (MSN, PMC); cardiopulmonary clinical nurse specialist (MSN, PMC); cardiopulmonary clinical nurse specialist/adult nurse practitioner (MSN, PMC); family nurse practitioner (MSN, PMC); gerontology clinical nurse specialist (MSN, PMC); gerontology clinical nurse specialist geriatric nurse practitioner (PMC); gerontology clinical nurse specialist/geriatric nurse practitioner (MSN); health services administration (MSN, PMC); nursing of children clinical nurse specialist (MSN, PMC); nursing of children clinical nurse specialist/pediatric nurse practitioner (MSN, PMC); oncology/immune deficiency clinical nurse specialist (MSN, PMC); oncology/immune deficiency clinical nurse specialist/adult nurse practitioner (MSN, PMC); perinatal/women's health clinical nurse specialist (MSN, PMC); perinatal/women's health clinical nurse specialist/women's health nurse practitioner (MSN, PMC); psychiatric nursing clinical nurse specialist (MSN, PMC). *Accreditation:* AACN; NLN (one or more programs are accredited). Part-time and evening/weekend programs available. Postbaccalaureate distance learning degree programs offered (minimal on-campus study). *Degree requirements:* For master's, thesis optional. *Entrance requirements:* For master's, BSN, interview, RN license. Electronic applications accepted. *Faculty research:* Marriage and chronic illness, health promotion, congestive heart failure patient outcomes, school nursing, diabetes in children.

University of Maryland, Baltimore, Graduate School, School of Nursing, Master's Program in Nursing, Baltimore, MD 21201. Offers community health nursing (MS); gerontological nursing (MS); maternal-child nursing (MS); medical-surgical nursing (MS); nurse-midwifery education (MS); nursing administration (MS); nursing education (MS); nursing health policy (MS); primary care nursing (MS); psychiatric nursing (MS); MS/MBA. *Accreditation:* AANA/CANAEP; ACNM/DOA; NLN (one or more programs are accredited). Part-time programs available. *Degree requirements:* For master's, thesis or alternative, comprehensive exam (for some programs). *Entrance requirements:* For master's, GRE General Test, minimum GPA of 2.75, course work in statistics, BS in nursing. Additional exam requirements/recommendations for international students: Required—TOEFL, TOEFL or IELTS; Recommended—IELTS. Electronic applications accepted.

University of Massachusetts Lowell, Graduate School, College of Health Professions, Department of Nursing, Program in Gerontological Nursing, Lowell, MA 01854-2881. Offers MS. *Accreditation:* AACN. *Degree requirements:* For master's, thesis optional. *Entrance requirements:* For master's, GRE General Test.

University of Massachusetts Worcester, Graduate School of Nursing, Worcester, MA 01655-0115. Offers adult acute/critical care nurse practitioner (MS, Certificate); adult ambulatory/community care nurse practitioner (MS, Certificate); gerontological nurse practitioner (Certificate); nurse educator (MS, Certificate); nursing (PhD). *Accreditation:* AACN. Part-time programs available. *Faculty:* 39. *Students:* 46 full-time (43 women), 6 part-time (2 women); includes 5 minority (2 African Americans, 2 Asian Americans or Pacific Islanders, 1 Hispanic American). Average age 38. 42 applicants, 71% accepted. In 2006, 26 master's, 2 doctorates, 6 other advanced degrees awarded. *Degree requirements:* For doctorate, thesis/dissertation. *Entrance requirements:* For master's, GRE General Test, BSN, previous course work in statistics; for Certificate, master's degree. *Application deadline:* For fall admission, 3/15 for domestic students. Applications are processed on a rolling basis. Application fee: $40 ($60 for international students). *Expenses:* Tuition, state resident: full-time $2,640. Tuition, nonresident: full-time $9,856. Required fees: $3,942. *Financial support:* In 2006–07, 4 students received support. Scholarships/grants and traineeships available. Support available to part-time students. Financial award application deadline: 3/22; financial award applicants required to submit FAFSA. *Faculty research:* Premature menopause with cancer treatment, quality of life and cancer, complementary therapies, psychoneuroimmunology, patient outcomes/outcomes research. *Unit head:* Dr. Janet Hale, Associate Dean, 508-856-5661, Fax: 508-856-6552. *Application contact:* Larry Shattuck, Director of Recruitment and Retention, 508-856-5801, Fax: 508-856-6552.

University of Michigan, Horace H. Rackham School of Graduate Studies, School of Nursing, Division of Acute, Critical and Long-term Care, Program in Gerontology Nursing, Ann Arbor, MI 48109. Offers gerontology nurse practitioner (MS). *Accreditation:* AACN. Part-time programs available. *Degree requirements:* For master's, thesis, registration. *Entrance requirements:* For master's, GRE General Test, licensure, minimum of B average in BSN program. Additional exam requirements/recommendations for international students: Required—TOEFL (minimum score 560 paper-based; 220 computer-based). Electronic applications accepted. *Faculty research:* Wandering in the elderly, Alzheimer's, clinical specialist and nurse practitioner roles, enhancement of cognitive function.

University of Minnesota, Twin Cities Campus, Graduate School, School of Nursing, Gerontological Nurse Practitioner Program, Minneapolis, MN 55455-0213. Offers MS. *Accreditation:* AACN. *Students:* 10 full-time (8 women), 7 part-time (6 women); includes 1 minority (African American) *Degree requirements:* For master's, final oral exam, project or thesis. *Entrance requirements:* Additional exam requirements/recommendations for international students: Required—TOEFL (minimum score 586 paper-based; 240 computer-based). *Application deadline:* For fall admission, 11/1 priority date for domestic and international students; for spring admission, 8/1 priority date for domestic and international students. Application fee: $55 ($75 for international students). *Financial support:* Fellowships, research assistantships, teaching assistantships, career-related internships or fieldwork and traineeships available. *Unit head:* Dr. Christine Mueller, Coordinator, 612-626-4922. *Application contact:* Information Contact, 612-624-4454, Fax: 612-624-3174, E-mail: nurseoss@umn.edu.

University of Minnesota, Twin Cities Campus, Graduate School, School of Nursing, Program in Gerontological Clinical Nurse Specialist, Minneapolis, MN 55455-0213. Offers advanced clinical specialist in gerontology (MS). *Accreditation:* AACN. Part-time programs available. *Students:* 2 full-time (1 woman), 2 part-time (both women). *Degree requirements:* For master's, final oral exam, project or thesis. *Entrance requirements:* Additional exam requirements/recommendations for international students: Required—TOEFL (minimum score 586 paper-based; 240 computer-based). *Application deadline:* For fall admission, 11/1 priority date for domestic and international students; for spring admission, 8/1 priority date for domestic and international students. Application fee: $55 ($75 for international students). *Financial support:* Fellowships, research assistantships, teaching assistantships, career-related internships or fieldwork available. *Unit head:* Dr. Christine Mueller, Coordinator, 612-626-4922. *Application contact:* Information Contact, 612-624-4454, Fax: 612-624-3174, E-mail: nurseoss@umn.edu.

The University of North Carolina at Greensboro, Graduate School, School of Nursing, Greensboro, NC 27412-5001. Offers adult clinical nurse specialist (MSN, PMC); adult/gerontological nurse practitioner (MSN, PMC); nurse anesthesia (MSN, PMC); nursing (PhD); nursing administration (MSN); nursing education (MSN); MSN/MBA. *Accreditation:* AACN; AANA/CANAEP; NLN. *Faculty:* 24 full-time (23 women), 27 part-time/adjunct (22 women). *Students:* 231 full-time (197 women), 98 part-time (83 women); includes 56 minority (41 African Americans, 3 American Indian/Alaska Native, 9 Asian Americans or Pacific Islanders, 3 Hispanic Americans). 206 applicants, 59% accepted. *Degree requirements:* For master's, thesis or alternative. *Entrance requirements:* For master's, GRE General Test or MAT, BSN, clinical experience, liability insurance, RN license; for PMC, liability insurance, MSN, RN license. Additional exam requirements/recommendations for international students: Required—TOEFL. Application fee: $45. Electronic applications accepted. *Expenses:* Tuition, state resident: full-time $2,692. Tuition, nonresident: full-time $13,742. *Financial support:* Research assistantships with full tuition reimbursements, career-related internships or fieldwork, Federal Work-Study, scholarships/grants, and traineeships available. Support available to part-time students. *Unit head:* Dr. Lynne Pearcey, Dean, 336-334-5177, Fax: 336-334-3628, E-mail: l_pearce@uncg.edu. *Application contact:* Michelle Harkleroad, Director of Graduate Admissions, 336-334-4884, Fax: 336-334-4424, E-mail: mbharkle@uncg.edu.

University of Utah, The Graduate School, College of Nursing, Center on Aging, Salt Lake City, UT 84112-1107. Offers MS, Certificate. *Accreditation:* AACN. Part-time programs available. *Students:* 2 full-time (both women), 3 part-time (2 women). Average age 42. 5 applicants, 60% accepted, 0 enrolled. In 2006, 3 degrees awarded. *Degree requirements:* For master's, thesis optional. *Entrance requirements:* For master's, GRE General Test, minimum undergraduate GPA of 3.0. Additional exam requirements/recommendations for international students: Required—TOEFL (minimum score 500 paper-based; 173 computer-based). *Application deadline:* For fall admission, 3/1 for domestic students. Applications are processed on a rolling basis. Application fee: $20 ($65 for international students). *Expenses: Contact institution.* Tuition and fees vary according to class time and program. *Financial support:* In 2006–07, 2 research assistantships were awarded; fellowships, teaching assistantships, scholarships/grants also available. Financial award application deadline: 9/15. *Faculty research:* Spousal bereavement, family caregiving, healthy promotion and self-care, environmental issues, geriatric care management. *Unit head:* Dr. Sue E. Huether, Interim Director, 801-581-8198, Fax: 801-581-4642, E-mail: sue.huether@nurs.utah.edu. *Application contact:* Ribana Milas, Secretary, 801-581-8198, Fax: 801-581-4642, E-mail: ribana.dragicevic@nurs.utah.edu.

Vanderbilt University, School of Nursing, Nashville, TN 37235. Offers adult acute care nurse practitioner (MSN); adult health nurse practitioner/forensic (MSN); adult nurse practitioner/cardiovascular disease management and prevention (MSN); adult nurse practitioner/palliative care (MSN); clinical management (clinical nurse leader/specialist) (MSN); family nurse practitioner (MSN); gerontology nurse practitioner (MSN); health systems management (MSN); neonatal nurse practitioner (MSN); nurse midwifery (MSN); nursing informatics (MSN); nursing science (PhD); pediatric acute care nurse practitioner (MSN); pediatric primary care nurse practitioner (MSN); psychiatric-mental health nurse practitioner (MSN); women's health nurse practitioner (MSN); MBA/MSN; MSN/MTS; MSN/PhD. *Accreditation:* ACNM/DOA; NLN (one or more programs are accredited). Part-time and evening/weekend programs available. Postbaccalaureate distance learning degree programs offered (minimal on-campus study). *Faculty:* 95 full-time (83 women), 432 part-time/adjunct (314 women). *Students:* 371 full-time (325 women), 206 part-time (180 women); includes 59 minority (38 African Americans, 2 American Indian/Alaska Native, 7 Asian Americans or Pacific Islanders, 12 Hispanic Americans). Average age 27. 611 applicants, 55% accepted, 308 enrolled. In 2006, 256 master's, 2 doctorates awarded. *Degree requirements:* For doctorate, thesis/dissertation. *Entrance requirements:* For master's, GRE, interview; for doctorate, GRE, interview, 3 letters of recommendation. Additional exam requirements/recommendations for international students: Required—TOEFL. *Application deadline:* For fall admission, 12/1 priority date for domestic and international students. Applications are processed on a rolling basis. Application fee: $50. *Expenses: Contact institution.* *Financial support:* In 2006–07, 404 students received support, including 5 research assistantships (averaging $8,000 per year); Federal Work-Study, institutionally sponsored loans, and unspecified assistantships also available. Support available to part-time students. Financial award application deadline: 3/15; financial award applicants required to submit CSS PROFILE or FAFSA. *Faculty research:* Lymphedema post cancer treatment, palliative care and bereavement, patient safety and quality of care, health care workforce issues, symptom management including pain and fatigue. Total annual research expenditures: $1.1 million. *Unit head:* Dr. Colleen Conway-Welch, Dean, 615-343-8776, Fax: 615-343-7711, E-mail: colleen.conway-welch@vanderbilt.edu. *Application contact:* Cheryl Feldner, Assistant Director of Admissions, 615-322-3800, Fax: 615-343-0333, E-mail: cheryl.feldner@vanderbilt.edu.

Villanova University, College of Nursing, Villanova, PA 19085-1690. Offers adult nurse practitioner (MSN, Post Master's Certificate); clinical case management (MSN, Post Master's Certificate); geriatric nurse practitioner (MSN, Post Master's Certificate); health care administration (MSN); nurse anesthetist (MSN, Post Master's Certificate); nursing (PhD); nursing education (MSN, Post Master's Certificate); pediatric nurse practitioner (MSN, Post Master's Certificate). *Accreditation:* AACN; AANA/CANAEP; NLN. Part-time programs available. Postbaccalaureate distance learning degree programs offered (minimal on-campus study). *Faculty:* 14 full-time (all women), 2 part-time/adjunct (both women). *Students:* 41 full-time (27 women), 164 part-time (128 women); includes 17 minority (8 African Americans, 1 American Indian/Alaska Native, 8 Asian Americans or Pacific Islanders), 6 international. Average age 31. 137 applicants, 50% accepted, 48 enrolled. In 2006, 47 degrees awarded. *Median time to degree:* Master's–2 years full-time, 5 years part-time. *Degree requirements:* For master's, independent study project; for doctorate, thesis/dissertation, comprehensive exam. *Entrance requirements:* For master's, GRE or MAT, BSN, 1 year of recent nursing experience, physical assessment, course work in statistics; for doctorate, GRE. Additional exam requirements/recommendations for international students: Required—TOEFL. *Application deadline:* For fall admission, 7/1 priority date for domestic students, 7/1 for international students; for spring admission, 12/1 priority date for domestic students, 12/1 for international students. Applications are processed on a rolling basis. Application fee: $50. *Expenses: Contact institution.* *Financial support:* In 2006–07, 50 students received support, including 4 teaching assistantships with full tuition reimbursements available (averaging $12,165 per year); institutionally sponsored loans, scholarships/grants, traineeships, and tuition waivers (full) also available. Financial award application deadline: 3/1; financial award applicants required to submit FAFSA. *Faculty research:* Genetics, ethics, cognitive development of students, women with disabilities, nursing leadership. *Unit head:* Dr. Marguerite K. Schlag, Assistant Dean and Director, Graduate Program, 610-519-4907, Fax: 610-519-7650, E-mail: marguerite.schlag@villanova.edu.

HIV/AIDS Nursing

Duke University, School of Nursing, Durham, NC 27708-0586. Offers adult acute care (Certificate); adult cardiovascular (Certificate); adult oncology/HIV (Certificate); adult primary care (Certificate); clinical nurse specialist (MSN), including adult oncology/HIV, gerontology, neonatal, pediatric, pediatric/chronic acute care; clinical research management (MSN, Certificate); family (Certificate); gerontology (Certificate); health and nursing ministries (MSN, Certificate); health systems leadership and outcomes (Certificate); leadership in community based long term care (MSN, Certificate); neonatal (Certificate); neonatal/pediatric in rural health (MSN, Certificate); nurse anesthetist (MSN, Certificate); nurse practitioner (MSN), including adult acute care, adult cardiovascular, adult oncology/HIV, adult primary care, family, gerontology, neonatal, pediatric, pediatric acute care; nursing (PhD); nursing and healthcare leadership (MSN); nursing education (MSN); nursing informatics (MSN, Certificate); pediatric (Certificate); pediatric acute care (Certificate); MBA/MSN; MSN/MCM. *Accreditation:* AACN; AANA/CANAEP. Part-time programs available. Postbaccalaureate distance learning degree programs offered (minimal on-campus study). *Faculty:* 45 full-time (41 women), 169 part-time/adjunct (150 women). *Students:* 178 full-time (162 women), 140 part-time (132 women); includes 48 minority (17 African Americans, 3 American Indian/Alaska Native, 20 Asian Americans or Pacific Islanders, 8 Hispanic Americans). Average age 36. 99 applicants, 92% accepted, 91 enrolled. In 2006, 122 master's, 17 other advanced degrees awarded. *Median time to degree:* Master's–2 years full-time, 2.5 years part-time. *Degree requirements:* For master's, thesis optional. *Entrance requirements:* For master's, GRE General Test or MAT, 1 year of nursing experience, BSN, minimum GPA of 3.0, previous course work in statistics; for Certificate, MSN. Additional exam requirements/recommendations for international students: Required—TOEFL (minimum score 550 paper-based; 213 computer-based), Commission on Graduates of Foreign Nursing Schools exam. *Application deadline:* For fall admission, 7/2 priority date for domestic and international students; for spring admission, 11/15 priority date for domestic and international students. Applications are processed on a rolling basis. Application fee: $50. *Expenses:* Contact institution. *Financial support:* In 2006–07, 258 students received support. Career-related internships or fieldwork, institutionally sponsored loans, scholarships/grants, traineeships, and tuition waivers (partial) available. Support available to part-time students. Financial award application deadline: 4/1; financial award applicants required to submit FAFSA. *Faculty research:* Cardiovascular disease, caregiver skill training, data mining, prostate cancer, neonatal immune system. Total annual research expenditures: $3.5 million. *Unit head:* Dr. Catherine L. Gilliss, Dean/Vice Chancellor for Nursing Affairs, 919-684-9444, Fax: 919-684-9414, E-mail: gilli025@mc.duke.edu. *Application contact:* Bebe T. Mills, Director of Admissions, 919-684-9151, Fax: 919-668-4693, E-mail: mills031@mc.duke.edu.

University of Delaware, College of Health Sciences, School of Nursing, Newark, DE 19716. Offers adult nurse practitioner (MSN, PMC); cardiopulmonary clinical nurse specialist (MSN, PMC); cardiopulmonary clinical nurse specialist/adult nurse practitioner (MSN, PMC); family nurse practitioner (MSN, PMC); gerontology clinical nurse specialist (MSN, PMC); gerontology clinical nurse specialist geriatric nurse practitioner (PMC); gerontology clinical nurse specialist/geriatric nurse practitioner (MSN); health services administration (MSN, PMC); nursing of children clinical nurse specialist (MSN, PMC); nursing of children clinical nurse specialist/pediatric nurse practitioner (MSN, PMC); oncology/immune deficiency clinical nurse specialist (MSN, PMC); oncology/immune deficiency clinical nurse specialist/adult nurse practitioner (MSN, PMC); perinatal/women's health clinical nurse specialist (MSN, PMC); perinatal/women's health clinical nurse specialist/women's health nurse practitioner (MSN, PMC); psychiatric nursing clinical nurse specialist (MSN, PMC). *Accreditation:* AACN; NLN (one or more programs are accredited). Part-time and evening/weekend programs available. Postbaccalaureate distance learning degree programs offered (minimal on-campus study). *Degree requirements:* For master's, thesis optional. *Entrance requirements:* For master's, BSN, interview, RN license. Electronic applications accepted. *Faculty research:* Marriage and chronic illness, health promotion, congestive heart failure patient outcomes, school nursing, diabetes in children.

Hospice Nursing

Madonna University, Program in Hospice, Livonia, MI 48150-1173. Offers MSH. Part-time and evening/weekend programs available. *Degree requirements:* For master's, thesis or alternative. *Entrance requirements:* For master's, GRE General Test. Electronic applications accepted.

Maternal and Child/Neonatal Nursing

Barnes-Jewish College of Nursing and Allied Health, Division of Nursing, St. Louis, MO 63110-1091. Offers adult nurse practitioner (MSN); education (MSN); gerontology nurse practitioner (MSN); holistics (MSN); management/administration (MSN); neonatal nurse practitioner (MSN); oncology (MSN). *Accreditation:* AACN; AANA/CANAEP. Part-time and evening/weekend programs available. *Degree requirements:* For master's, thesis or alternative, registration. *Entrance requirements:* For master's, minimum GPA of 3.0, 2 references, statistics course. Additional exam requirements/recommendations for international students: Required—TOEFL (minimum score 550 paper-based; 213 computer-based).

Baylor University, Graduate School, Louise Herrington School of Nursing, Dallas, TX 75246. Offers family nurse practitioner (MSN); neonatal nurse practitioner (MSN); nursing administration and management (MSN). *Accreditation:* AACN. *Students:* 10 full-time (all women), 27 part-time (26 women); includes 6 minority (1 African American, 1 Asian American or Pacific Islander, 4 Hispanic Americans), 1 international. In 2006, 13 degrees awarded. *Entrance requirements:* For master's, GRE General Test. *Application deadline:* For fall admission, 8/1 for domestic students; for spring admission, 12/1 for domestic students. Applications are processed on a rolling basis. Application fee: $25. *Unit head:* Dr. Pauline Johnson, Graduate Program Director, 214-820-3361, Fax: 214-818-8692, E-mail: pauline_johnson@baylor.edu. *Application contact:* Suzanne Keener, Administrative Assistant, 254-710-3588, Fax: 254-710-3870.

Boston College, William F. Connell School of Nursing, Chestnut Hill, MA 02467-3800. Offers adult health nursing (MS); community health nursing (MS); family health (MS); gerontology (MS); maternal/child health nursing (MS), including pediatric and women's health; nurse anesthesia (MS); nursing (PhD); psychiatric-mental health nursing (MS); MBA/MS; MS/MA; MS/PhD. *Accreditation:* AACN; AANA/CANAEP (one or more programs are accredited). Part-time programs available. *Faculty:* 46 full-time (44 women), 34 part-time/adjunct (all women). *Students:* 155 full-time (137 women), 56 part-time (54 women); includes 10 minority (4 African Americans, 5 Asian Americans or Pacific Islanders, 1 Hispanic American), 6 international. Average age 34. 276 applicants, 47% accepted, 67 enrolled. In 2006, 61 master's, 4 doctorates awarded. *Median time to degree:* Of those who began their doctoral program in fall 1998, 100% received their degree in 8 years or less. *Degree requirements:* For master's, research project; for doctorate, thesis/dissertation, computer literacy exam or foreign language, comprehensive exam. *Entrance requirements:* For master's, GRE General Test, bachelor's degree in nursing; for doctorate, GRE General Test, master's degree in nursing. Additional exam requirements/recommendations for international students: Required—TOEFL (minimum score 550 paper-based; 213 computer-based). *Application deadline:* For fall admission, 10/15 for domestic and international students; for spring admission, 3/15 for domestic and international students. Application fee: $40. Electronic applications accepted. *Financial support:* In 2006–07, 104 students received support, including 15 fellowships with partial tuition reimbursements available (averaging $10,045 per year), 3 research assistantships (averaging $10,000 per year), 4 teaching assistantships (averaging $12,548 per year); Federal Work-Study, institutionally sponsored loans, scholarships/grants, traineeships, and tuition waivers (partial) also available. Support available to part-time students. Financial award application deadline: 3/1; financial award applicants required to submit FAFSA. *Faculty research:* Ethics, reduction of risk behaviors, support during chronic illness, violence, gerontology. Total annual research expenditures: $1.1 million. *Unit head:* Dr. Barbara Hazard, Dean, 617-552-4251, Fax: 617-552-0931, E-mail: barbara.munro@bc.edu. *Application contact:* Zanifer John-Bayard, Graduate Programs Assistant, 617-552-4059, Fax: 617-552-0745, E-mail: johnza@bc.edu.

Columbia University, School of Nursing, Program in Neonatal Nurse Practitioner, New York, NY 10032. Offers MS, Adv C. *Accreditation:* AACN. Part-time programs available. *Students:* 1 (woman) full-time, 10 part-time (all women); includes 4 minority (3 Asian Americans or Pacific Islanders, 1 Hispanic American). Average age 33. In 2006, 6 degrees awarded. *Entrance requirements:* For master's, GRE General Test, BSN, 1 year of neonatal intensive care unit experience; for Adv C, MSN. *Application deadline:* Applications are processed on a rolling basis. Application fee: $65. Electronic applications accepted. *Financial support:* Application deadline: 2/1; *Unit head:* Dr. Ritamarie John, Head, 212-305-5542.

Duke University, School of Nursing, Durham, NC 27708-0586. Offers adult acute care (Certificate); adult cardiovascular (Certificate); adult oncology/HIV (Certificate); adult primary care (Certificate); clinical nurse specialist (MSN), including adult oncology/HIV, gerontology, neonatal, pediatric, pediatric/chronic acute care; clinical research management (MSN, Certificate); family (Certificate); gerontology (Certificate); health and nursing ministries (MSN, Certificate); health systems leadership and outcomes (Certificate); leadership in community based long term care (MSN, Certificate); neonatal (Certificate); neonatal/pediatric in rural health (MSN, Certificate); nurse anesthetist (MSN, Certificate); nurse practitioner (MSN), including adult acute care, adult cardiovascular, adult oncology/HIV, adult primary care, family, gerontology, neonatal, pediatric, pediatric acute care; nursing (PhD); nursing and healthcare leadership (MSN); nursing education (MSN); nursing informatics (MSN, Certificate); pediatric (Certificate); pediatric acute care (Certificate); MBA/MSN; MSN/MCM. *Accreditation:* AACN; AANA/CANAEP. Part-time programs available. Postbaccalaureate distance learning degree programs offered (minimal on-campus study). *Faculty:* 45 full-time (41 women), 169 part-time/adjunct (150 women). *Students:* 178 full-time (162 women), 140 part-time (132 women); includes 48 minority (17 African Americans, 3 American Indian/Alaska Native, 20 Asian Americans or Pacific Islanders, 8 Hispanic Americans). Average age 36. 99 applicants, 92% accepted, 91 enrolled. In 2006, 122 master's, 17 other advanced degrees awarded. *Median time to degree:* Master's–2 years full-time, 2.5 years part-time. *Degree requirements:* For master's, thesis optional. *Entrance requirements:* For master's, GRE General Test or MAT, 1 year of nursing experience, BSN, minimum GPA of 3.0, previous course work in statistics; for Certificate, MSN. Additional exam requirements/recommendations for international students: Required—TOEFL (minimum score 550 paper-based; 213 computer-based), Commission on Graduates of Foreign Nursing Schools exam. *Application deadline:* For fall admission, 7/2 priority date for domestic and international students; for spring admission, 11/15 priority date for domestic and international students. Applications are processed on a rolling basis. Application fee: $50. *Expenses:* Contact institution. *Financial support:* In 2006–07, 258 students received support. Career-related internships or fieldwork, institutionally sponsored loans, scholarships/grants, traineeships, and tuition waivers (partial) available. Support available to part-time students. Financial award application deadline: 4/1; financial award applicants required to submit FAFSA. *Faculty research:* Cardiovascular disease, caregiver skill training, data mining, prostate cancer, neonatal immune system. Total annual research expenditures: $3.5 million. *Unit head:* Dr. Catherine L. Gilliss, Dean/Vice Chancellor for Nursing Affairs, 919-684-9444, Fax: 919-684-9414, E-mail: gilli025@mc.duke.edu. *Application contact:* Bebe T. Mills, Director of Admissions, 919-684-9151, Fax: 919-668-4693, E-mail: mills031@mc.duke.edu.

Hardin-Simmons University, Graduate School, School of Nursing, Abilene, TX 79698-0001. Offers advanced healthcare delivery (MSN); family nurse practitioner (MSN). *Accreditation:* AACN. Part-time programs available. *Faculty:* 5 full-time (all women). *Students:* 1 full-time (0 women), 8 part-time (6 women). Average age 39. 5 applicants, 100% accepted, 3 enrolled. In 2006, 2 degrees awarded. *Degree requirements:* For master's, thesis or alternative, comprehensive exam. *Entrance requirements:* For master's, GRE, minimum undergraduate GPA of 3.0 in major, 2.8 overall; interview; upper-level course work in statistics; CPR certification; letters of recommendation. Additional exam requirements/recommendations for international students: Required—TOEFL (minimum score 550 paper-based; 213 computer-based). *Application deadline:* For fall admission, 8/15 priority date for domestic students; for spring admission, 1/5 priority date for domestic students. Applications are processed on a rolling basis. Application fee: $50 ($100 for international students). *Expenses:* Contact institution. One-time fee: $50. Tuition and fees vary according to course load and degree level. *Financial support:* In 2006–07, 8 students received support. Career-related internships or fieldwork and scholarships/grants available. Support available to part-time students. Financial award application deadline: 6/30; financial award applicants required to submit FAFSA. *Faculty research:* Child abuse, alternative medicine, pediatric chronic disease, health promotion. *Unit head:* Dr. Janet Noles, Dean, 325-672-2441, Fax: 325-670-1564, E-mail: jnoles@hsutx.edu. *Application contact:* Dr. Gary Stanlake, Dean of Graduate Studies, 325-670-1298, Fax: 325-670-1564, E-mail: gradoff@hsutx.edu.

Maternal and Child/Neonatal Nursing

Hunter College of the City University of New York, Graduate School, Schools of the Health Professions, Hunter-Bellevue School of Nursing, Program in Maternal Child-Health Nursing, New York, NY 10021-5085. Offers MS. *Accreditation:* AACN. Part-time programs available. *Faculty:* 24 full-time (21 women), 21 part-time/adjunct (19 women). *Students:* Average age 36. 3 applicants, 100% accepted, 3 enrolled. In 2006, 2 degrees awarded. *Degree requirements:* For master's, practicum. *Entrance requirements:* For master's, minimum GPA of 3.0, New York RN license, BSN. Additional exam requirements/recommendations for international students: Required—TOEFL. *Application deadline:* For fall admission, 4/1 for domestic students, 2/1 for international students; for spring admission, 11/1 for domestic students, 9/1 for international students. Applications are processed on a rolling basis. Application fee: $50. *Expenses:* Tuition, state resident: part-time $270 per credit. Tuition, nonresident: part-time $500 per credit. Required fees: $45 per semester. *Financial support:* Federal Work-Study, scholarships/grants, traineeships, and tuition waivers (partial) available. Support available to part-time students. Financial award application deadline: 5/1; financial award applicants required to submit FAFSA. *Faculty research:* Material-infant attachment, children's perception of health. *Unit head:* Dr. Janet N. Natapoff, Coordinator, 212-481-5070, Fax: 212-481-5078, E-mail: jnatapof@hejira.hunter.cuny.edu. *Application contact:* William Zlata, Director for Graduate Admissions, 212-772-4482, Fax: 212-650-3336, E-mail: admissions@hunter.cuny.edu.

Indiana University–Purdue University Indianapolis, School of Nursing, Indianapolis, IN 46202-2896. Offers acute care nurse practitioner (MSN); adult health clinical nurse specialist (MSN); adult health nursing (MSN), including adult clinical nurse specialist, adult nurse practitioner (MSN); adult psychiatric/mental health nursing (MSN); child psychiatric/mental health nursing (MSN); community health nursing (MSN); family nurse practitioner (MSN); neonatal nurse practitioner (MSN); nursing science (PhD); pediatric clinical nurse specialist (MSN); women's health nurse practitioner (MSN); MSN/MPA; MSN/MPH. *Accreditation:* AACN; NLN (one or more programs are accredited). Part-time programs available. *Faculty:* 45 full-time (44 women), 1 (woman) part-time/adjunct. *Students:* 52 full-time (51 women), 415 part-time (396 women); includes 27 minority (16 African Americans, 3 Asian Americans or Pacific Islanders, 8 Hispanic Americans), 4 international. Average age 38. In 2006, 106 master's, 3 doctorates awarded. Terminal master's awarded for partial completion of doctoral program. *Degree requirements:* For master's and doctorate, thesis/dissertation. *Entrance requirements:* For master's, GRE General Test, minimum GPA of 3.0, RN license; for doctorate, GRE General Test, minimum GPA of 3.5, MSN, RN license. Additional exam requirements/recommendations for international students: Required—TOEFL. *Application deadline:* For fall admission, 2/15 for domestic students; for spring admission, 9/15 for domestic students. Application fee: $50 ($60 for international students). *Expenses:* Tuition, state resident: full-time $5,437; part-time $227 per credit hour. Tuition, nonresident: full-time $15,694; part-time $654 per credit hour. Required fees: $620. Tuition and fees vary according to course load, campus/location and program. *Financial support:* In 2006–07, 93 students received support; fellowships with full tuition reimbursements available, research assistantships with full tuition reimbursements available, teaching assistantships with full tuition reimbursements available, Federal Work-Study, institutionally sponsored loans, scholarships/grants, and tuition waivers (full) available. Support available to part-time students. Financial award application deadline: 5/1. *Faculty research:* Chronic illness, cancer, health services research, family health. Total annual research expenditures: $3 million. *Unit head:* Associate Dean for Graduate Programs, 317-274-2806, E-mail: nursing@iupui.edu. *Application contact:* Martez Plummer, Assistant Dean for Student Affairs, 317-274-2806, E-mail: mplummer@iupui.edu.

Lehman College of the City University of New York, Division of Natural and Social Sciences, Department of Nursing, Bronx, NY 10468-1589. Offers adult health nursing (MS); nursing of older adults (MS); parent-child nursing (MS); pediatric nurse practitioner (MS). *Accreditation:* AACN. Part-time and evening/weekend programs available. *Entrance requirements:* For master's, bachelor's degree in nursing, New York RN license.

Marquette University, Graduate School, College of Nursing, Milwaukee, WI 53201-1881. Offers adult nurse practitioner (Certificate); advanced practice nursing (MSN), including adult, children, neonatal nurse practitioner, nurse-midwifery, older adult; gerontological nurse practitioner (Certificate); neonatal nurse practitioner (Certificate); nurse-midwifery (Certificate); nursing (PhD); pediatric nurse practitioner (Certificate). *Accreditation:* AACN. Part-time and evening/weekend programs available. *Faculty:* 29 full-time (27 women), 39 part-time/adjunct (37 women). *Students:* 104 full-time (98 women), 122 part-time (114 women); includes 18 minority (5 African Americans, 2 American Indian/Alaska Native, 4 Asian Americans or Pacific Islanders, 7 Hispanic Americans), 2 international. Average age 34. 122 applicants, 79% accepted, 73 enrolled. In 2006, 46 degrees awarded. *Degree requirements:* For master's, thesis or alternative, comprehensive exam. *Entrance requirements:* For master's, GRE General Test, BSN, Wisconsin RN license. Additional exam requirements/recommendations for international students: Required—TOEFL. Application fee: $40. *Financial support:* In 2006–07, 6 research assistantships, 1 teaching assistantship were awarded; career-related internships or fieldwork, Federal Work-Study, institutionally sponsored loans, scholarships/grants, and tuition waivers (full and partial) also available. Support available to part-time students. Financial award application deadline: 2/15. *Faculty research:* Psychosocial adjustment to chronic illness, gerontology, reminiscence, health policy: uninsured and access, hospital care delivery systems. Total annual research expenditures: $1.1 million. *Unit head:* Dr. Lea Acord, Dean, 414-288-3812, Fax: 414-288-1578. *Application contact:* Dr. Judy Miller, Director of Graduate Studies, 414-288-3810, Fax: 414-288-1578.

Medical College of Georgia, School of Graduate Studies, Programs in Nursing, Augusta, GA 30912-1500. Offers adult nursing (MSN); community health nursing (MSN); mental health nursing (MSN); nurse practitioner (MSN); nursing (DNP, PhD); nursing anesthesia (MSN); parent-child nursing (MSN). *Accreditation:* AACN; AANA/CANAEP. Part-time programs available. *Faculty:* 18 full-time (16 women), 1 part-time/adjunct (0 women). *Students:* 95 full-time (76 women), 42 part-time (37 women); includes 24 minority (20 African Americans, 4 Asian Americans or Pacific Islanders). Average age 37. 156 applicants, 35% accepted, 24 enrolled. In 2006, 28 master's, 10 doctorates awarded. *Degree requirements:* For master's, thesis (for some programs); for doctorate, thesis/dissertation. *Entrance requirements:* For master's, GRE General Test, MAT; for doctorate, GRE General Test. Additional exam requirements/recommendations for international students: Required—TOEFL (minimum score 550 paper-based; 213 computer-based). *Application deadline:* For fall admission, 7/1 for domestic students, 4/15 for international students. Applications are processed on a rolling basis. Application fee: $30. Electronic applications accepted. *Expenses:* Tuition, state resident: full-time $2,293; part-time $192 per credit hour. Tuition, nonresident: full-time $9,169; part-time $765 per credit hour. Required fees: $293 per semester. *Financial support:* In 2006–07, 78 students received support, including 9 research assistantships with partial tuition reimbursements available (averaging $23,000 per year); Federal Work-Study, institutionally sponsored loans, traineeships, tuition waivers, and unspecified assistantships also available. Support available to part-time students. Financial award application deadline: 5/31; financial award applicants required to submit FAFSA. *Unit head:* Dr. Lucy Marion, Dean, 706-721-6258, Fax: 706-721-8169, E-mail: lumarion@mail.mcg.edu.

Medical University of South Carolina, College of Nursing, Program in Neonatal Nurse Practitioner, Charleston, SC 29425-0002. Offers MSN. Part-time programs available. Postbaccalaureate distance learning degree programs offered. *Faculty:* 2 full-time (both women), 2 part-time/adjunct (both women). *Students:* 12 full-time (11 women), 6 part-time (all women). Average age 37. 20 applicants, 50% accepted, 10 enrolled. In 2006, 4 degrees awarded. *Degree requirements:* For master's, thesis optional. *Entrance requirements:* For master's, GRE General Test, BSN, course work in statistics and physical assessment, 1 year nursing experience, nursing license, minimum GPA of 3.0. Additional exam requirements/recommendations for international students: Required—TOEFL (minimum score 600 paper-based; 250 computer-based). *Application deadline:* For fall admission, 2/1 for domestic and international students; for spring admission, 9/15 for domestic and international students. Application fee: $75. Electronic applications accepted. *Financial support:* Federal Work-Study, scholarships/grants, and traineeships available. Support available to part-time students. Financial award application deadline: 3/15; financial award applicants required to submit FAFSA. *Faculty research:* Surfactant use in neonates. Total annual research expenditures: $147,000. *Unit head:* Robin L. Bissinger, Track Coordinator, 843-792-0531, Fax: 843-792-1741, E-mail: bissinrl@musc.edu. *Application contact:* Carolyn F. Page, Director, Student Services, 843-792-3844, Fax: 843-792-9258, E-mail: pagecf@musc.edu.

Medical University of South Carolina, College of Nursing, Program in Pediatric Nursing, Charleston, SC 29425-0002. Offers MSN. *Accreditation:* AACN. Part-time programs available. *Faculty:* 4 full-time (all women). *Students:* 5 full-time (all women), 7 part-time (all women). 11 applicants, 91% accepted, 8 enrolled. In 2006, 7 degrees awarded. *Degree requirements:* For master's, thesis optional. *Entrance requirements:* For master's, GRE General Test, BSN, course work in statistics and physical assessment, nursing license, minimum GPA of 3.0. Additional exam requirements/recommendations for international students: Required—TOEFL (minimum score 600 paper-based; 250 computer-based). *Application deadline:* For fall admission, 2/1 for domestic and international students; for spring admission, 9/15 for domestic and international students. Application fee: $75. Electronic applications accepted. *Financial support:* Federal Work-Study, scholarships/grants, and traineeships available. Support available to part-time students. Financial award application deadline: 3/15; financial award applicants required to submit FAFSA. *Faculty research:* Epilepsy management, ADHD/ADD management, school-based clinics. Total annual research expenditures: $340,405. *Unit head:* Dianna Inman, Track Coordinator, 843-792-7201, Fax: 843-792-1741, E-mail: inmandd@musc.edu. *Application contact:* Carolyn F. Page, Director, Student Services, 843-792-3844, Fax: 843-792-9258, E-mail: pagecf@musc.edu.

Rush University, College of Nursing, Department of Women's and Children's Health Nursing, Chicago, IL 60612-3832. Offers neonatal nurse practitioner (MSN, Post-Master's Certificate); pediatric acute/chronic care nurse practitioner (MSN); pediatric clinical nurse specialist (MSN); pediatric nurse practitioner (MSN, Post-Master's Certificate); women's and children's health nursing (DN Sc, DNP). *Accreditation:* AACN. Part-time programs available. Postbaccalaureate distance learning degree programs offered (minimal on-campus study). *Faculty:* 14. *Students:* 10 full-time, 75 part-time; includes 9 minority (3 African Americans, 4 Asian Americans or Pacific Islanders, 2 Hispanic Americans). Average age 35. 32 applicants, 94% accepted, 28 enrolled. In 2006, 14 master's, 5 doctorates awarded. Terminal master's awarded for partial completion of doctoral program. *Degree requirements:* For master's, capstone project; for doctorate, thesis/dissertation, DNP leadership project. *Entrance requirements:* For master's, GRE General Test (waived if nursing GPA is above 3.0 or cumulative GPA is above 3.25), interview; for doctorate, GRE General Test, interview, course work in statistics (DN Sc). Additional exam requirements/recommendations for international students: Required—TOEFL, TWE. *Application deadline:* For fall admission, 7/1 for domestic students; for winter admission, 11/1 for domestic students; for spring admission, 1/15 for domestic students. Applications are processed on a rolling basis. Application fee: $40. Electronic applications accepted. *Financial support:* In 2006–07, 16 students received support; teaching assistantships with tuition reimbursements available, Federal Work-Study, institutionally sponsored loans, scholarships/grants, and traineeships available. Support available to part-time students. Financial award applicants required to submit FAFSA. *Faculty research:* Family-centered care, women's health, health outcomes of human milk feeding for VhBW infants. *Unit head:* Dr. Deborah Gross, Chairperson, 312-942-7117. *Application contact:* Hicela Castruita Woods, Director, College Admissions Services, 312-942-7100, Fax: 312-942-2219, E-mail: hicela_castruita@rush.edu.

Rutgers, The State University of New Jersey, Newark, Graduate School, Program in Nursing, Newark, NJ 07102. Offers nursing (MS), including acute care of adults and aged, advanced practice in pediatric nursing, advanced practice with childbearing families, community health nursing, family nurse practitioner, primary care of adults and aged, psychiatric/mental health nursing. *Accreditation:* AACN. Part-time programs available. *Faculty:* 33 full-time (32 women). *Students:* 11 full-time (all women), 186 part-time (175 women); includes 70 minority (28 African Americans, 30 Asian Americans or Pacific Islanders, 12 Hispanic Americans). 255 applicants, 58% accepted, 72 enrolled. In 2006, 40 master's awarded. *Degree requirements:* For master's, comprehensive exam. *Entrance requirements:* For master's, GRE General Test, RN license, minimum B average, BS in nursing. Additional exam requirements/recommendations for international students: Required—TOEFL. *Application deadline:* For fall admission, 2/15 for domestic students; for spring admission, 12/1 for domestic students. Applications are processed on a rolling basis. Application fee: $50. Electronic applications accepted. *Financial support:* In 2006–07, 3 fellowships (averaging $8,000 per year) were awarded; teaching assistantships with full tuition reimbursements, career-related internships or fieldwork, Federal Work-Study, institutionally sponsored loans, scholarships/grants, traineeships, and tuition waivers (full and partial) also available. Financial award application deadline: 4/15. *Faculty research:* HIV/AIDS, quality of life—MS and breast cancer, sleep patterns of cardiac patients. *Unit head:* Dr. Wendy Nehring, Program Director, 973-353-5293 Ext. 606, Fax: 973-353-1277, E-mail: nehring@nightingale.rutgers.edu. *Application contact:* Dr. Linda Scheetz, Associate Dean for Student Life and Services, 973-353-5060 Ext. 611, Fax: 973-353-1277, E-mail: lscheetz@andromeda.rutgers.edu.

Saint Joseph College, Graduate Division, Department of Nursing, West Hartford, CT 06117-2700. Offers family health nurse practitioner (MS); family health nursing (MS); nursing (Post Master's Certificate); psychiatric/mental health nursing (MS). *Accreditation:* AACN. Part-time and evening/weekend programs available. *Degree requirements:* For master's and Post Master's Certificate, thesis. *Entrance requirements:* For master's, GRE General Test or MAT, 2 letters of recommendation; for Post Master's Certificate, MAT, master's degree in nursing, minimum GPA of 3.0. Additional exam requirements/recommendations for international students: Required—NCLEX. Electronic applications accepted. *Faculty research:* Reproductive health and substance abuse, problem-based learning, role of clinical faculty, students' international studies experience.

Stony Brook University, State University of New York, Stony Brook University Medical Center, Health Sciences Center, School of Nursing, Program in Neonatal Nursing, Stony Brook, NY 11794. Offers neonatal nurse practitioner (Certificate); neonatal nursing (MS). *Accreditation:* AACN. *Students:* 11 full-time (all women), 35 part-time (33 women); includes 7 minority (4 Asian Americans or Pacific Islanders, 3 Hispanic Americans), 3 international. In 2006, 20 master's, 8 other advanced degrees awarded. *Degree requirements:* For master's, thesis. *Entrance requirements:* For master's, BSN, minimum GPA of 3.0, course work in statistics. *Application deadline:* For fall admission, 1/15 for domestic students. Application fee: $60. *Expenses:* Tuition, state resident: full-time $6,900; part-time $288 per credit. Tuition, nonresident: full-time $10,920; part-time $455 per credit. *Financial support:* Application deadline: 3/15. *Unit head:* Dr. Debra Sansoucie, Chair, 631-444-3298, Fax: 631-444-3136, E-mail: debra.sansoucie@stonybrook.edu.

Stony Brook University, State University of New York, Stony Brook University Medical Center, Health Sciences Center, School of Nursing, Program in Perinatal/Women's Health Nursing, Stony Brook, NY 11794. Offers perinatal/women's health nurse practitioner (Certificate); perinatal/women's health nursing (MS). *Accreditation:* AACN. *Students:* 2 full-time (both women), 18 part-time (all women); includes 6 minority (5 African Americans, 1 Hispanic American). In 2006, 9 master's, 2 other advanced degrees awarded. *Degree requirements:* For master's, thesis. *Entrance requirements:* For master's, BSN, minimum GPA of 3.0, course work in statistics. *Application deadline:* For fall admission, 1/15 for domestic students. Application fee: $60. *Expenses:* Tuition, state resident: full-time $6,900; part-time $288 per credit. Tuition, nonresident: full-time $10,920; part-time $455 per credit. *Financial support:* Application deadline: 3/15. *Unit head:* Dr. Debra Sansoucie, Chair, 631-444-3298, Fax: 631-444-3136, E-mail: debra.sansoucie@stonybrook.edu.

Université de Montréal, Faculty of Medicine and Faculty of Graduate Studies, Graduate Programs in Medicine, Program in Specialized Studies, Montréal, QC H3C 3J7, Canada. Offers anesthesia (DESS); diagnostic radiology (DESS); family medicine (DESS); medical biochemistry (DESS); medical genetics (DESS); medicine (DESS); microbiology and infectious diseases (DESS); nuclear medicine (DESS); obstetrics and gynecology (DESS); ophthalmology (DESS); pediatrics (DESS); psychiatry (DESS); radiology-oncology (DESS); surgery (DESS). *Faculty:* 159 full-time (37 women), 345 part-time/adjunct (102 women). *Entrance requirements:* For degree, proficiency in French. *Application deadline:* For fall admission, 2/1 priority date for domestic students; for winter admission, 11/1 priority date for domestic students; for spring admission, 2/1 priority date for domestic students. Application fee: $30. Electronic applications accepted. *Unit head:* Dr. Pierre Boyle, Vice Dean of Studies, 514-343-6300, Fax: 514-343-5751, E-mail: pierre.boyle@umontreal.ca.

University at Buffalo, the State University of New York, Graduate School, School of Nursing, Buffalo, NY 14260. Offers acute care nurse practitioner (MS, Certificate); adult health nursing (MS, Certificate); child health nursing (MS); family nurse practitioner (Certificate); family nursing (MS); geriatric nurse practitioner (MS, Certificate); maternal and women's health nurse practitioner (Certificate); maternal and women's health nursing (MS); nurse anesthetist (MS); nursing (PhD); nursing education (Certificate); pediatric nurse practitioner (Certificate); psychiatric/mental health nurse practitioner (Certificate); psychiatric/mental health nursing (MS). *Accreditation:* AACN; AANA/CANAEP (one or more programs are accredited). Part-time programs available. Postbaccalaureate distance learning degree programs offered. *Faculty:* 38 full-time (34 women), 15 part-time/adjunct (14 women). *Students:* 131 full-time (108 women), 64 part-time (61 women); includes 29 minority (11 African Americans, 9 Asian Americans or Pacific Islanders, 9 Hispanic Americans), 20 international. Average age 28. 346 applicants, 25% accepted, 51 enrolled. In 2006, 49 master's, 3 doctorates, 6 other advanced degrees awarded. Terminal master's awarded for partial completion of doctoral program. *Degree requirements:* For master's, comprehensive exams or project; for doctorate, thesis/dissertation, comprehensive exam. *Entrance requirements:* For master's, GRE General Test (if overall GPA is below 3.0), interview, minimum GPA of 3.0, RN license, 3 references; for doctorate, GRE General Test, minimum GPA of 3.25, RN license, BS or MS in nursing, 3 references, writing sample; for Certificate, interview, minimum GPA of 3.0 or GRE General Test, RN license, MS in nursing. Additional exam requirements/recommendations for international students: Required—TOEFL (minimum score 550 paper-based; 213 computer-based; 79 iBT), IELTS (minimum score 7). *Application deadline:* For fall admission, 6/1 priority date for domestic students, 3/1 priority date for international students; for spring admission, 11/1 for domestic students, 9/15 priority date for international students. Applications are processed on a rolling basis. Application fee: $50. Electronic applications accepted. *Financial support:* In 2006–07, 78 students received support, including 13 fellowships with full tuition reimbursements available (averaging $7,220 per year), 10 research assistantships with tuition reimbursements available (averaging $17,881 per year), 23 teaching assistantships with full tuition reimbursements available (averaging $11,245 per year); Federal Work-Study, scholarships/grants, traineeships, health care benefits, and unspecified assistantships also available. Financial award application deadline: 3/15; financial award applicants required to submit FAFSA. *Faculty research:* Oncology symptom management, end of life decision making, changing behaviors using the transtheoretical model, addictions, nursing workforce. Total annual research expenditures: $1.7 million. *Unit head:* Dr. Jean K. Brown, Dean, Interim, 716-829-2533, Fax: 716-829-2566, E-mail: jebrown@buffalo.edu. *Application contact:* Dr. Elaine R. Cusker, Assistant Dean, 716-829-2537, Fax: 716-829-2021, E-mail: ecusker@buffalo.edu.

The University of Alabama in Huntsville, School of Graduate Studies, College of Nursing, Huntsville, AL 35899. Offers family nurse practitioner (Certificate); nursing (MSN). *Accreditation:* AACN. Part-time and evening/weekend programs available. Postbaccalaureate distance learning degree programs offered. *Faculty:* 11 full-time (10 women), 8 part-time/adjunct (5 women). *Students:* 54 full-time (53 women), 79 part-time (72 women); includes 22 minority (13 African Americans, 5 American Indian/Alaska Native, 4 Hispanic Americans). Average age 36. 94 applicants, 93% accepted, 70 enrolled. In 2006, 44 master's, 12 other advanced degrees awarded. *Degree requirements:* For master's, thesis or alternative, oral and written exams, comprehensive exam, registration. *Entrance requirements:* For master's, MAT or GRE, Alabama RN license, BSN, minimum GPA of 3.0. Additional exam requirements/recommendations for international students: Required—TOEFL (minimum score 500 paper-based; 173 computer-based). *Application deadline:* For fall admission, 5/30 priority date for domestic students, 2/28 priority date for international students; for spring admission, 10/10 priority date for domestic students, 7/10 priority date for international students. Applications are processed on a rolling basis. Application fee: $40. *Expenses:* Tuition, state resident: full-time $6,072; part-time $253 per credit hour. Tuition, nonresident: full-time $12,476; part-time $519 per credit hour. *Financial support:* In 2006–07, 61 students received support, including 54 fellowships with full and partial tuition reimbursements available (averaging $1,937 per year), 7 teaching assistantships with full and partial tuition reimbursements available (averaging $6,540 per year); research assistantships, career-related internships or fieldwork, Federal Work-Study, institutionally sponsored loans, scholarships/grants, traineeships, health care benefits, and unspecified assistantships also available. Support available to part-time students. Financial award application deadline: 4/1; financial award applicants required to submit FAFSA. *Faculty research:* Home health care, gerontology, pediatric nursing, family nurse practitioner, adult acute care administration. Total annual research expenditures: $19,540. *Unit head:* Dr. Fay Raines, Dean, 256-824-6345, Fax: 256-824-6026, E-mail: rainesc@email.uah.edu. *Application contact:* Lavan Wilson, Director of Student Affairs, 256-824-6742, Fax: 256-824-6026, E-mail: wilsonol@email.uah.edu.

University of Alberta, Faculty of Medicine and Dentistry and Faculty of Graduate Studies and Research, Graduate Programs in Medicine, Department of Obstetrics and Gynecology, Edmonton, AB T6G 2E1, Canada. Offers MD. *Faculty:* 3 full-time (1 woman). *Students:* 3 full-time (2 women), 1 international. Average age 26. 1 applicant. *Entrance requirements:* Additional exam requirements/recommendations for international students: Required—TOEFL. *Application deadline:* Applications are processed on a rolling basis. Application fee: $60. *Financial support:* Fellowships, scholarships/grants, traineeships, tuition waivers (partial), and unspecified assistantships available. *Faculty research:* Parturition, fetal/neonatal lung development, nitric oxide, vascular reactivity, pre-eclampsia gestational diabetes. Total annual research expenditures: $650,000. *Unit head:* Dr. J. Wylam Faught, Chair, 780-735-4927, Fax: 780-477-4981.

University of Cincinnati, Graduate School, College of Nursing, Cincinnati, OH 45221-0038. Offers clinical nurse specialist (MSN), including adult health, community health, neonatal, nursing administration, occupational health, pediatric health, psychiatric nursing, women's health; nurse anesthesia (MSN); nurse midwifery (MSN); nurse practitioner (MSN), including acute care, ambulatory care, family, family/psychiatric, women's health; nursing (PhD); MBA/MSN. *Accreditation:* AACN; AANA/CANAEP (one or more programs are accredited); ACNM/DOA. Part-time programs available. Postbaccalaureate distance learning degree programs offered (no on-campus study). *Faculty:* 41 full-time (39 women), 16 part-time/adjunct (15 women). *Students:* 159 full-time (125 women), 149 part-time (145 women); includes 40 minority (22 African Americans, 1 American Indian/Alaska Native, 16 Asian Americans or Pacific Islanders, 1 Hispanic American). Average age 34. 385 applicants, 49% accepted, 132 enrolled. In 2006, 77 master's, 5 doctorates awarded. Terminal master's awarded for partial completion of doctoral program. *Median time to degree:* Of those who began their doctoral program in fall 1998, 55% received their degree in 8 years or less. *Degree requirements:* For master's, thesis or alternative, registration; for doctorate, thesis/dissertation, comprehensive exam, registration. *Entrance requirements:* For master's and doctorate, GRE General Test. Additional exam requirements/recommendations for international students: Required—TOEFL (minimum score 520 paper-based; 190 computer-based). *Application deadline:* For fall admission, 7/26 priority date for domestic and international students. Applications are processed on a rolling basis. Application fee: $40. Electronic applications accepted. *Financial support:* In 2006–07, 164 students received support, including 7 fellowships with full tuition reimbursements available (averaging $13,571 per year), research assistantships with full tuition reimbursements available (averaging $12,000 per year), 8 teaching assistantships with full tuition reimbursements available (averaging $12,000 per year); career-related internships or fieldwork, scholarships/grants, traineeships, tuition waivers (partial), and unspecified assistantships also available. Support available to part-time students. Financial award application deadline: 5/1; financial award applicants required to submit FAFSA. *Faculty research:* Substance abuse, injury and violence, symptom management. Total annual research expenditures: $1.3 million. *Unit head:* Dr. Andrea R. Lindell, Dean, 513-558-5330, Fax: 513-558-9030, E-mail: andrea.lindell@uc.edu. *Application contact:* Loren Carter, Program Coordinator, 513-558-5072, Fax: 513-558-7523, E-mail: loren.carter@uc.edu.

University of Colorado at Colorado Springs, Graduate School, Beth-El College of Nursing, Colorado Springs, CO 80933-7150. Offers adult health nurse practitioner and clinical specialist (MSN); family practitioner (MSN), including community clinical specialist, forensic clinical specialist, holistic clinical specialist; gerontology (MSN); neonatal nurse practitioner and clinical specialist (MSN); nursing administration (MSN); women nurse practitioner (MSN). *Accreditation:* AACN. Part-time programs available. Postbaccalaureate distance learning degree programs offered (minimal on-campus study). *Faculty:* 10 full-time (7 women), 14 part-time/adjunct (7 women). *Students:* 84 full-time (77 women), 53 part-time (52 women); includes 22 minority (6 African Americans, 3 American Indian/Alaska Native, 2 Asian Americans or Pacific Islanders, 11 Hispanic Americans). Average age 37. 54 applicants, 85% accepted, 30 enrolled. In 2006, 36 degrees awarded. *Degree requirements:* For master's, thesis optional; for doctorate, capstone project. *Entrance requirements:* For master's, GRE General Test or MAT, BSN, minimum GPA of 3.0, unrestricted RN license; for doctorate, interview; active RN license; MA; minimum GPA of 3.3; National Certification as NP, CNS, or CNS; portfolio. Additional exam requirements/recommendations for international students: Required—TOEFL. *Application deadline:* For fall admission, 6/1 priority date for domestic students; for spring admission, 11/15 for domestic students. Application fee: $60 ($75 for international students). Electronic applications accepted. *Expenses: Contact institution.* Tuition and fees vary according to course load, campus/location and program. *Financial support:* Fellowships, career-related internships or fieldwork, Federal Work-Study, and institutionally sponsored loans available. Support available to part-time students. *Faculty research:* Women's health, uncertainty, empowerment, family experience in chronic illness. Total annual research expenditures: $260,389. *Unit head:* Dr. Carole Schoffstall, Dean, 719-262-4418, Fax: 719-262-4416, E-mail: cschoffs@uccs.edu.

University of Connecticut, Graduate School, School of Nursing, Field of Nursing, Storrs, CT 06269. Offers adult acute care (Post-Master's Certificate); adult primary care (Post-Master's Certificate); community health (Post-Master's Certificate); neonatal acute care (Post-Master's Certificate); nursing (MS, PhD); patient care services and systems administration (Post-Master's Certificate); psychiatric mental health (Post-Master's Certificate). *Accreditation:* AACN. *Faculty:* 20 full-time (18 women). *Students:* 38 full-time (33 women), 70 part-time (65 women); includes 17 minority (3 African Americans, 10 Asian Americans or Pacific Islanders, 4 Hispanic Americans), 1 international. Average age 37. 64 applicants, 69% accepted, 44 enrolled. In 2006, 25 master's, 7 doctorates, 1 other advanced degree awarded. *Degree requirements:* For master's, comprehensive exam; for doctorate, thesis/dissertation. *Entrance requirements:* Additional exam requirements/recommendations for international students: Required—TOEFL (minimum score 550 paper-based; 213 computer-based). *Application deadline:* For fall admission, 2/1 priority date for domestic and international students; for spring admission, 11/1 for domestic students, 10/1 for international students. Applications are processed on a rolling basis. Application fee: $55. Electronic applications accepted. *Financial support:* In 2006–07, 4 research assistantships with full tuition reimbursements, 13 teaching assistantships with full tuition reimbursements were awarded; fellowships, Federal Work-Study, scholarships/grants, health care benefits, and unspecified assistantships also available. Financial award application deadline: 2/1; financial award applicants required to submit FAFSA. *Unit head:* E. Carol Polifroni, Chairperson, 860-486-0511, Fax: 860-486-0001, E-mail: polifron@uconn.edu. *Application contact:* Lisa Mazzola, Academic Advisor Coordinator, 860-486-1973, E-mail: lisa.mazzola@uconn.edu.

University of Delaware, College of Health Sciences, School of Nursing, Newark, DE 19716. Offers adult nurse practitioner (MSN, PMC); cardiopulmonary clinical nurse specialist (MSN, PMC); cardiopulmonary clinical nurse specialist/adult nurse practitioner (MSN, PMC); family nurse practitioner (MSN, PMC); gerontology clinical nurse specialist (MSN, PMC); gerontology clinical nurse specialist geriatric nurse practitioner (PMC); gerontology clinical nurse specialist/geriatric nurse practitioner (MSN); health services administration (MSN, PMC); nursing of children clinical nurse specialist (MSN, PMC); nursing of children clinical nurse specialist/pediatric nurse practitioner (MSN, PMC); oncology/immune deficiency clinical nurse specialist (MSN, PMC); oncology/immune deficiency clinical nurse specialist/adult nurse practitioner (MSN, PMC); perinatal/women's health clinical nurse specialist (MSN, PMC); perinatal/women's health clinical nurse specialist/women's health nurse practitioner (MSN, PMC); psychiatric nursing clinical nurse specialist (MSN, PMC). *Accreditation:* AACN; NLN (one or more programs are accredited). Part-time and evening/weekend programs available. Postbaccalaureate distance learning degree programs offered (minimal on-campus study). *Degree requirements:* For master's, thesis optional. *Entrance requirements:* For master's, BSN, interview, RN license. Electronic applications accepted. *Faculty research:* Marriage and chronic illness, health promotion, congestive heart failure patient outcomes, school nursing, diabetes in children.

University of Illinois at Chicago, Graduate College, College of Nursing, Program in Nursing Sciences (Maternal Child), Chicago, IL 60607-7128. Offers maternity nursing/nurse midwifery (MS); pediatric nursing (MS); perinatal nursing (MS). *Accreditation:* AACN; ACNM/DOA. Part-time programs available. *Degree requirements:* For master's, thesis or alternative. *Entrance requirements:* For master's, GRE General Test, minimum GPA of 2.75. Additional exam requirements/recommendations for international students: Required—TOEFL. Electronic applications accepted.

University of Maryland, Baltimore, Graduate School, School of Nursing, Master's Program in Nursing, Baltimore, MD 21201. Offers community health nursing (MS); gerontological nursing (MS); maternal-child nursing (MS); medical-surgical nursing (MS); nurse-midwifery education (MS); nursing administration (MS); nursing education (MS); nursing health policy (MS); primary care nursing (MS); psychiatric nursing (MS); MS/MBA. *Accreditation:* AANA/CANAEP; ACNM/DOA; NLN (one or more programs are accredited). Part-time programs available. *Degree requirements:* For master's, thesis or alternative, comprehensive exam (for some programs). *Entrance requirements:* For master's, GRE General Test, minimum GPA of 2.75, course work in statistics, BS in nursing. Additional exam requirements/recommendations for international students: Required—TOEFL, TOEFL or IELTS; Recommended—IELTS. Electronic applications accepted.

University of Missouri–Kansas City, School of Nursing, Kansas City, MO 64110-2499. Offers adult clinical nurse specialist (MSN), including adult nurse practitioner, women's health nurse practitioner; family nurse practitioner (MSN); neonatal nurse practitioner (MSN); nurse educator (MSN); nurse executive (MSN); nursing (PhD); pediatric nurse practitioner (MSN). *Accreditation:* AACN. Part-time programs available. Postbaccalaureate distance learning degree programs offered (minimal on-campus study). *Faculty:* 31 full-time (26 women), 32 part-time/adjunct (31 women). *Students:* 36 full-time (all women), 213 part-time (202 women); includes 23 minority (6 African Americans, 2 American Indian/Alaska Native, 6 Asian Americans or Pacific Islanders, 9 Hispanic Americans). Average age 36. 121 applicants, 72% accepted, 71 enrolled. In 2006, 69 master's, 1 doctorate awarded. *Median time to degree:* Of those who began their doctoral program in fall 1998, 60% received their degree in 8 years or less. *Degree requirements:* For master's, thesis or alternative. *Entrance requirements:* For master's, minimum undergraduate GPA of 3.2; for doctorate, GRE, 3 letters of reference, interview and original essay by invitation. Additional exam requirements/recommendations for international students: Required—TOEFL (minimum score 550 paper-based). *Application deadline:* For fall admission, 2/1 priority date for domestic students; for spring admission, 9/15 priority date for domestic students. Application fee: $25. *Expenses:* Tuition, state resident: full-time $4,975; part-time $276 per credit. Tuition, nonresident: full-time $12,847; part-time $713 per credit. Required fees: $595; $595 per year. *Financial support:* In 2006–07, 30 students received support, including 6 research assistantships (averaging $3,450 per year), 7 teaching assistant-

Maternal and Child/Neonatal Nursing

University of Missouri–Kansas City (continued)
ships with partial tuition reimbursements available (averaging $12,650 per year); fellowships, career-related internships or fieldwork, Federal Work-Study, institutionally sponsored loans, and tuition waivers (full and partial) also available. Support available to part-time students. Financial award application deadline: 6/30; financial award applicants required to submit FAFSA. *Faculty research:* Geriatrics/gerontology, children's pain, neonatology, Alzheimer's care, cancer caregivers. Total annual research expenditures: $1 million. *Unit head:* Dr. Lora Lacey-Haun, Dean, 816-235-1700, Fax: 816-235-1701, E-mail: lacey-haunc@umkc.edu. *Application contact:* Leah Wilder, Coordinator for Admissions and Recruitment, 816-235-5768, Fax: 816-235-1701, E-mail: wilderl@umkc.edu.

University of Pennsylvania, School of Nursing, Family Health Nurse Practitioner Program, Philadelphia, PA 19104. Offers MSN, Certificate. *Accreditation:* AACN. Part-time programs available. *Entrance requirements:* For master's, GRE General Test, 1 year of clinical experience in area of interest, BSN, minimum GPA of 3.0, previous course work in statistics. Additional exam requirements/recommendations for international students: Required—TOEFL. Expenses: Contact institution. *Faculty research:* Evaluation of primary care practitioner practice, access to primary care.

University of Pennsylvania, School of Nursing, Neonatal Nurse Practitioner Program, Philadelphia, PA 19104. Offers MSN. *Accreditation:* AACN. Part-time programs available. *Entrance requirements:* For master's, GRE General Test, BSN, minimum GPA of 3.0, previous course work in statistics, 1 year of experience in a neonatal intensive care unit. Additional exam requirements/recommendations for international students: Required—TOEFL. Expenses: Contact institution. *Faculty research:* Neurobehavioral development, temperament, newborn sucking behaviors, parenting pre-term infants.

University of Pennsylvania, School of Nursing, Perinatal Advanced Practice Nurse Specialist Program, Philadelphia, PA 19104. Offers MSN. *Accreditation:* AACN. Part-time programs available. *Entrance requirements:* For master's, GRE General Test, BSN, minimum GPA of 3.0, previous course work in statistics. Additional exam requirements/recommendations for international students: Required—TOEFL. Expenses: Contact institution.

University of South Alabama, Graduate School, College of Nursing, Mobile, AL 36688-0002. Offers adult health nursing (MSN); community/mental health nursing (MSN); maternal/child nursing (MSN); nursing (DSN). *Accreditation:* AACN. *Faculty:* 25 full-time (23 women), 8 part-time/adjunct (all women). *Students:* 661 full-time (602 women), 127 part-time (108 women); includes 160 minority (123 African Americans, 6 American Indian/Alaska Native, 19 Asian Americans or Pacific Islanders, 12 Hispanic Americans), 1 international. In 2006, 166 degrees awarded. *Unit head:* Dr. Debra C. Davis, Dean, 251-434-3414.

University of Southern Mississippi, Graduate School, College of Health, School of Nursing, Hattiesburg, MS 39406-0001. Offers adult health nursing (MSN); community health nursing (MSN); ethics (PhD); family nurse practitioner (MSN); leadership (PhD); nursing service administration (MSN); policy analysis (PhD); psychiatric nursing (MSN). *Accreditation:* AACN. Part-time and evening/weekend programs available. *Faculty:* 14 full-time (all women). *Students:* 39 full-time (31 women), 69 part-time (62 women); includes 18 minority (15 African Americans, 1 Asian American or Pacific Islander, 2 Hispanic Americans), 1 international. Average age 39. 46 applicants, 50% accepted, 17 enrolled. In 2006, 36 master's, 6 doctorates awarded. *Degree requirements:* For master's, thesis optional; for doctorate, thesis/dissertation, comprehensive exam, registration. *Entrance requirements:* For master's, GRE General Test, minimum GPA of 2.75, nursing license, BS in nursing; for doctorate, GRE General Test, master's degree in nursing, minimum GPA of 3.5. Additional exam requirements/recommendations for international students: Required—TOEFL. *Application deadline:* For fall admission, 3/15 priority date for domestic students, 5/1 for international students. Applications are processed on a rolling basis. Application fee: $25 ($30 for international students). Electronic applications accepted. *Financial support:* In 2006–07, 1 research assistantship with full tuition reimbursement (averaging $10,125 per year), 1 teaching assistantship (averaging $10,125 per year) were awarded; Federal Work-Study and traineeships also available. Financial award application deadline: 3/15. *Faculty research:* Gerontology, caregivers, HIV, bereavement, pain, nursing leadership. *Unit head:* Dr. Katherine Nugent, Director and Associate Dean, 601-266-5500, Fax: 601-266-5927. *Application contact:* Dr. Anne Brock, Graduate Coordinator, 601-266-5500, Fax: 601-266-5927.

Vanderbilt University, School of Nursing, Nashville, TN 37235. Offers adult acute care nurse practitioner (MSN); adult health nurse practitioner/forensic (MSN); adult nurse practitioner/cardiovascular disease management and prevention (MSN); adult nurse practitioner/palliative care (MSN); clinical management (clinical nurse leader/specialist) (MSN); family nurse practitioner (MSN); gerontology nurse practitioner (MSN); health systems management (MSN); neonatal nurse practitioner (MSN); nurse midwifery (MSN); nursing informatics (MSN); nursing science (PhD); pediatric acute care nurse practitioner (MSN); pediatric primary care nurse practitioner (MSN); psychiatric-mental health nurse practitioner (MSN); women's health nurse practitioner (MSN); MBA/MSN; MSN/MTS; MSN/PhD. *Accreditation:* ACNM/DOA; NLN (one or more programs are accredited). Part-time and evening/weekend programs available. Postbaccalaureate distance learning degree programs offered (minimal on-campus study). *Faculty:* 95 full-time (83 women), 432 part-time/adjunct (314 women). *Students:* 371 full-time (325 women), 206 part-time (180 women); includes 59 minority (38 African Americans, 2 American Indian/Alaska Native, 7 Asian Americans or Pacific Islanders, 12 Hispanic Americans). Average age 27. 611 applicants, 55% accepted, 308 enrolled. In 2006, 256 master's, 2 doctorates awarded. *Degree requirements:* For doctorate, thesis/dissertation. *Entrance requirements:* For master's, GRE, interview; for doctorate, GRE, interview, 3 letters of recommendation. Additional exam requirements/recommendations for international students: Required—TOEFL. *Application deadline:* For fall admission, 12/1 priority date for domestic and international students. Applications are processed on a rolling basis. Application fee: $50. *Expenses:* Contact institution. *Financial support:* In 2006–07, 404 students received support, including 5 research assistantships (averaging $8,000 per year); Federal Work-Study, institutionally sponsored loans, and unspecified assistantships also available. Support available to part-time students. Financial award application deadline: 3/15; financial award applicants required to submit CSS PROFILE or FAFSA. *Faculty research:* Lymphedema post cancer treatment, palliative care and bereavement, patient safety and quality of care, health care workforce issues, symptom management including pain and fatigue. Total annual research expenditures: $1.1 million. *Unit head:* Dr. Colleen Conway-Welch, Dean, 615-343-8776, Fax: 615-343-7711, E-mail: colleen.conway-welch@vanderbilt.edu. *Application contact:* Cheryl Feldner, Assistant Director of Admissions, 615-322-3800, Fax: 615-343-0333, E-mail: cheryl.feldner@vanderbilt.edu.

Wayne State University, College of Nursing, Department of Family, Community and Mental Health, Program in Advanced Practice Nursing with Women, Neonates and Children, Detroit, MI 48202. Offers advanced practice nursing with women, neonates and children (MSN); neonatal nurse practitioner (Certificate). *Accreditation:* AACN. Part-time programs available. *Students:* 13 full-time (12 women), 47 part-time (all women); includes 10 minority (7 African Americans, 2 Asian Americans or Pacific Islanders, 1 Hispanic American). Average age 35. 13 applicants, 85% accepted, 11 enrolled. In 2006, 1 degree awarded. *Degree requirements:* For master's, thesis or alternative. *Entrance requirements:* For master's, GRE General Test, minimum GPA of 2.8. Additional exam requirements/recommendations for international students: Required—TOEFL (minimum score 550 paper-based; 213 computer-based); Recommended—TWE (minimum score 6). *Application deadline:* For fall admission, 7/1 priority date for domestic students, 6/1 for international students; for winter admission, 10/1 for international students; for spring admission, 11/1 for domestic students, 2/1 for international students. Applications are processed on a rolling basis. Application fee: $30 ($50 for international students). Electronic applications accepted. *Financial support:* In 2006–07, 17 students received support, including 2 research assistantships; institutionally sponsored loans, scholarships/grants, and traineeships also available. Financial award application deadline: 7/1; financial award applicants required to submit FAFSA. *Faculty research:* Acculturation and parenting, domestic violence, evidence-based midwifery practice, pain in children, trauma and community violence. *Application contact:* Janet Harden, Academic Director, 313-577-4082.

Medical/Surgical Nursing

Angelo State University, College of Graduate Studies, College of Sciences, Department of Nursing, San Angelo, TX 76909. Offers adult nurse practitioner (MSN); nurse educator (MSN). *Accreditation:* NLN. Part-time and evening/weekend programs available. *Faculty:* 10 full-time (all women). *Students:* 15 full-time (13 women), 26 part-time (23 women); includes 10 minority (1 African American, 1 Asian American or Pacific Islander, 8 Hispanic Americans). Average age 40. 25 applicants, 80% accepted, 19 enrolled. In 2006, 6 degrees awarded. *Degree requirements:* For master's, comprehensive exam. *Entrance requirements:* For master's, GRE General Test. Additional exam requirements/recommendations for international students: Required—TOEFL or IELTS. *Application deadline:* For fall admission, 7/15 priority date for domestic students, 6/15 for international students; for spring admission, 12/8 for domestic students, 11/1 for international students. Applications are processed on a rolling basis. Application fee: $40 ($50 for international students). Electronic applications accepted. *Expenses:* Tuition, state resident: full-time $2,340; part-time $130 per hour. Tuition, nonresident: full-time $7,290; part-time $405 per hour. Required fees: $906; $56 per hour. *Financial support:* In 2006–07, 24 students received support. Career-related internships or fieldwork, Federal Work-Study, and scholarships/grants available. Support available to part-time students. Financial award application deadline: 3/1. *Unit head:* Dr. Leslie M. Mayrand, Department Head, 325-942-2060 Ext. 247, E-mail: leslie.mayrand@angelo.edu. *Application contact:* Dr. Susan Wilkinson, Graduate Advisor, 325-942-2060 Ext. 290, E-mail: susan.wilkinson@angelo.edu.

Case Western Reserve University, Frances Payne Bolton School of Nursing, Doctor of Nursing Practice Program, Cleveland, OH 44106. Offers acute care nurse practitioner (DNP); adult nurse practitioner (DNP); family nurse practitioner (DNP); gerontological nurse practitioner (DNP); graduate entry/pre-licensure option (DNP); medical-surgical nursing (DNP); midwifery/family nursing (DNP); neonatal nurse practitioner (DNP); pediatric nurse practitioner (DNP); post-licensure option (DNP); psychiatric mental health nurse practitioner (DNP); women's health nurse practitioner (DNP). Graduate entry option allows baccalaureate-prepared college graduates from non-nursing backgrounds to earn certificate and MSN in addition to ND. *Students:* 125 full-time (109 women), 308 part-time (290 women); includes 47 minority (21 African Americans, 1 American Indian/Alaska Native, 18 Asian Americans or Pacific Islanders, 7 Hispanic Americans), 7 international. 190 applicants, 70% accepted, 80 enrolled. In 2006, 35 degrees awarded. Terminal master's awarded for partial completion of doctoral program. *Degree requirements:* For doctorate, thesis/dissertation. *Entrance requirements:* For doctorate, GRE General Test or MAT. *Application deadline:* For fall admission, 6/1 priority date for domestic students. Applications are processed on a rolling basis. Application fee: $75. *Financial support:* In 2006–07, 6 students received support, including 1 teaching assistantship; research assistantships, Federal Work-Study, institutionally sponsored loans, and tuition waivers (partial) also available. Support available to part-time students. Financial award application deadline: 6/30; financial award applicants required to submit FAFSA. *Faculty research:* Clinical nursing, acute care, gerontology, mental health, critical care. *Unit head:* Dr. Georgia Narsavage, Director, 216-368-6304, Fax: 216-368-3542, E-mail: gln2@cwru.edu. *Application contact:* Peter Taylor, Recruitment and Retention Specialist, 216-368-0349, Fax: 216-368-0124, E-mail: peter.taylor@case.edu.

Case Western Reserve University, Frances Payne Bolton School of Nursing, Master's Programs in Nursing, Program in Medical-Surgical Nursing, Cleveland, OH 44106. Offers MSN. *Accreditation:* NLN. Part-time programs available. *Students:* Average age 35. 1 applicant, 100% accepted, 1 enrolled. In 2006, 5 degrees awarded. *Degree requirements:* For master's, thesis optional. *Entrance requirements:* For master's, GRE General Test or MAT. *Application deadline:* For fall admission, 6/1 priority date for domestic students. Applications are processed on a rolling basis. Application fee: $75. *Financial support:* In 2006–07, 7 teaching assistantships were awarded; fellowships, research assistantships, institutionally sponsored loans and tuition waivers (partial) also available. Support available to part-time students. Financial award application deadline: 6/30. *Faculty research:* Clinical nursing, oncology, acute care, critical care, mobilization in the Intensive Care Unit. *Unit head:* C. Winkleman, Head, 216-368-0700. *Application contact:* Peter Taylor, Recruitment and Retention Specialist, 216-368-0349, Fax: 216-368-0124, E-mail: peter.taylor@case.edu.

Columbia University, School of Nursing, Program in Acute Care Nurse Practitioner, New York, NY 10032. Offers MS, Adv C. *Accreditation:* AACN. Part-time programs available. *Faculty:* 1 (woman) full-time, 3 part-time/adjunct (all women). *Students:* 8 full-time (6 women), 11 part-time (10 women); includes 7 minority (3 African Americans, 3 Asian Americans or Pacific Islanders, 1 Hispanic American). Average age 30. In 2006, 11 degrees awarded. *Entrance requirements:* For master's, GRE General Test, 1 year of clinical experience (preferred), BSN; for Adv C, MSN. *Application deadline:* Applications are processed on a rolling basis. Application fee: $65. Electronic applications accepted. *Financial support:* Teaching assistantships available. Financial award application deadline: 2/1; financial award applicants required to submit FAFSA. *Unit head:* Dr. Mary Donovan, Director, 212-342-4110.

Daemen College, Department of Nursing, Amherst, NY 14226-3592. Offers adult nurse practitioner (MS, Certificate); nursing executive leadership (MS); palliative care nursing (MS, Certificate). *Accreditation:* NLN. Part-time programs available. *Faculty:* 2 full-time (both women), 2 part-time/adjunct (both women). *Students:* 13 full-time (12 women), 63 part-time (59 women); includes 12 minority (10 African Americans, 1 Asian American or Pacific Islander, 1 Hispanic American), 3 international. Average age 41. 36 applicants, 58% accepted, 18 enrolled. In 2006, 9 degrees awarded. *Degree requirements:* For master's, thesis or alternative. *Entrance requirements:* For master's, 1 year medical/surgical experiences, minimum GPA of 3.25, state nursing license and registration, 1 course in statistics. Additional exam requirements/recommendations for international students: Required—TOEFL (minimum score 500 paper-based; 173 computer-based). *Application deadline:* For fall admission, 3/1 priority date for domestic and international students; for spring admission, 10/1 priority date for domestic and international students. Applications are processed on a rolling basis. Application fee: $25. Electronic applications accepted. *Expenses:* Tuition: Full-time $11,700; part-time $650 per credit hour. Required fees: $15 per credit hour. Tuition and fees vary according to course load. *Financial support:* Institutionally sponsored loans and scholarships/grants available. Financial award application deadline: 2/15; financial award applicants required to submit FAFSA. *Faculty research:* Professional stress, client behavior, drug therapy, treatment modalities and pulmonary cancers, chemical dependency. *Unit head:* Dr. Mary Lou Rusin, Chair, 716-839-8387, Fax:

716-839-8403, E-mail: mrusin@daemen.edu. *Application contact:* Karl Shallowhorn, Associate Director of Graduate Admissions, 716-839-8225, Fax: 716-839-8229, E-mail: kshallow@daemen.edu.

Eastern Virginia Medical School, Surgical Assistant Program, Norfolk, VA 23501-1980. Offers Certificate, Graduate Certificate. *Faculty:* 8. *Students:* 24 full-time (18 women); includes 6 minority (4 African Americans, 1 Asian American or Pacific Islander, 1 Hispanic American). 23 applicants, 57% accepted, 12 enrolled. *Application deadline:* For winter admission, 3/20 for domestic students. Applications are processed on a rolling basis. Application fee: $50. *Expenses:* Contact institution. *Financial support:* In 2006–07, 18 students received support. *Unit head:* R. Clinton Crews, Program Director, 757-446-8961, Fax: 757-446-6179, E-mail: crewsrc@evms.edu. *Application contact:* Nancy Stromann, Program Coordinator, 757-446-6100, Fax: 757-446-6179, E-mail: stromand@evms.edu.

Emory University, Nell Hodgson Woodruff School of Nursing, Atlanta, GA 30322-1100. Offers adult and elder health advanced practice nursing (MSN), including acute and critical care, adult nurse practitioner, gerontology, oncology; emergency nurse practitioner (MSN); family nurse practitioner (MSN); family nurse-midwife (MSN); leadership in healthcare (MSN); nurse midwifery (MSN); nursing administration (MSN); pediatric advanced nursing practice (MSN); public health nursing (MSN); women's health nurse practitioner (MSN); MSN/MPH. *Accreditation:* AACN; ACNM/DOA (one or more programs are accredited). Part-time programs available. *Entrance requirements:* For master's, GRE General Test or MAT, minimum GPA of 3.0, BS in nursing, RN license and additional course work, 3 letters of recommendation. Additional exam requirements/recommendations for international students: Required—TOEFL (minimum score 600 paper-based; 250 computer-based). Electronic applications accepted. Expenses: Contact institution. *Faculty research:* Older adult falls and injuries, minority health issues, cardiac symptoms amd quality of life, bio-ethics and decision making, menopausal issues.

See Close-Up on page 1955.

Gannon University, School of Graduate Studies, College of Sciences, Engineering, and Health Sciences, School of Health Sciences, Program in Nursing, Erie, PA 16541-0001. Offers anesthesia (MSN); business administration (MSN); case management (MSN); medical-surgical nursing (MSN); nurse anesthesia (Certificate); nursing rural practitioner (MSN). *Accreditation:* AACN; AANA/CANAEP (one or more programs are accredited). Part-time and evening/weekend programs available. *Students:* 15 full-time (5 women), 44 part-time (37 women). Average age 35. 8 applicants, 88% accepted, 5 enrolled. In 2006, 14 master's, 2 other advanced degrees awarded. *Degree requirements:* For master's, thesis. *Entrance requirements:* For master's, GRE General Test, MAT, bachelor's degree from a NLN-approved nursing program, interview, Pennsylvania RN license. Additional exam requirements/recommendations for international students: Required—TOEFL (minimum score 500 paper-based; 173 computer-based). *Application deadline:* For fall admission, 4/15 for domestic students. Application fee: $25. *Expenses:* Tuition: Full-time $12,240; part-time $680 per credit. Required fees: $496; $16 per credit. Tuition and fees vary according to course load, degree level, campus/location and program. *Financial support:* Career-related internships or fieldwork and traineeships available. Support available to part-time students. Financial award application deadline: 7/1; financial award applicants required to submit FAFSA. *Unit head:* Dr. Sharon Thompson, Interim Director, 814-871-5345, E-mail: thompson001@gannon.edu. *Application contact:* Debra Meszaros, Director of Graduate Recruitment, 814-871-5819, Fax: 814-871-5827, E-mail: cfal@gannon.edu.

George Mason University, College of Health and Human Services, Fairfax, VA 22030. Offers advanced clinical nursing (MSN); nurse practitioner (MSN); nursing (MSN, PhD); nursing administration (MSN); nursing education (Certificate); nursing educator (MSN); social work (MSW). *Accreditation:* AACN. *Faculty:* 69 full-time (55 women), 75 part-time/adjunct (66 women). *Students:* 98 full-time (81 women), 301 part-time (260 women); includes 121 minority (60 African Americans, 45 Asian Americans or Pacific Islanders, 16 Hispanic Americans), 27 international. Average age 39. 326 applicants, 61% accepted, 121 enrolled. In 2006, 89 master's, 7 doctorates, 11 other advanced degrees awarded. *Degree requirements:* For doctorate, thesis/dissertation, oral/written exams. *Entrance requirements:* For master's, RN license, minimum GPA of 3.0 in last 60 hours of course work; for doctorate, MAT, 3 years of nursing experience, master's degree, minimum GPA of 3.25, professional liability insurance. *Application deadline:* For fall admission, 5/1 for domestic students; for spring admission, 11/1 for domestic students. Application fee: $60 ($75 for international students). Electronic applications accepted. *Expenses:* Tuition, state resident: full-time $5,724; part-time $238 per credit. Tuition, nonresident: full-time $16,896; part-time $704 per credit. Required fees: $1,656; $69 per credit. *Financial support:* Fellowships, research assistantships, teaching assistantships, tuition waivers (partial) available. Support available to part-time students. Financial award application deadline: 3/1; financial award applicants required to submit FAFSA. *Unit head:* Dr. Shirley S. Travis, Dean, 703-993-1918. *Application contact:* Dr. James D. Vail, Associate Dean, Graduate Programs and Research, 703-993-1947, Fax: 703-993-1942, E-mail: nursinfo@gmu.edu.

Hunter College of the City University of New York, Graduate School, Schools of the Health Professions, Hunter-Bellevue School of Nursing, Program in Medical/Surgical Nursing, New York, NY 10021-5085. Offers MS. *Accreditation:* AACN. Part-time programs available. *Faculty:* 24 full-time (21 women), 21 part-time/adjunct (19 women). In 2006, 1 degree awarded. *Degree requirements:* For master's, practicum. *Entrance requirements:* For master's, minimum GPA of 3.0, New York RN license, BSN. Additional exam requirements/recommendations for international students: Required—TOEFL. *Application deadline:* For fall admission, 4/1 for domestic students, 2/1 for international students; for spring admission, 11/1 for domestic students, 9/1 for international students. Applications are processed on a rolling basis. *Expenses:* Tuition, state resident: part-time $270 per credit. Tuition, nonresident: part-time $500 per credit. Required fees: $45 per semester. *Financial support:* Federal Work-Study, scholarships/grants, traineeships, and tuition waivers (partial) available. Support available to part-time students. Financial award application deadline: 5/1; financial award applicants required to submit FAFSA. *Faculty research:* Adult health, critical care. *Unit head:* Dr. Joan Sayre, Coordinator, 212-481-4343, Fax: 212-481-5078, E-mail: jsayre@shiva.hunter.cuny.edu. *Application contact:* William Zlata, Director for Graduate Admissions, 212-772-4482, Fax: 212-650-3336, E-mail: admissions@hunter.cuny.edu.

Kent State University, College of Nursing, Kent, OH 44242-0001. Offers clinical nursing (MSN), including nursing of the adult (medical/surgical nursing), psychiatric mental health nursing; nursing (PhD); nursing administration (MSN); nursing education (MSN); parent-child nursing (MSN). *Accreditation:* AACN. Part-time programs available. *Degree requirements:* For master's, thesis optional; for doctorate, thesis/dissertation, comprehensive exam, registration. *Entrance requirements:* For master's, GRE if undergraduate GPA is less than 3.0, minimum GPA of 2.75; for doctorate, GRE, MSN. Additional exam requirements/recommendations for international students: Required—TOEFL. Electronic applications accepted. Expenses: Contact institution. *Faculty research:* Women and violence, methodological specialties, osteoporosis in women, new caregivers and the elderly.

La Salle University, School of Nursing and Health Sciences, Philadelphia, PA 19141-1199. Offers adult health and illness, clinical nurse specialist (MSN); gerontology (Certificate); nursing administration (MSN); nursing education (Certificate); nursing informatics (Certificate); primary care of adults-nurse practitioner (MSN); public health nursing (MSN); school nursing (Certificate); speech-language-hearing science (MS); wound, ostomy and continence nursing (Certificate); wound, ostomy, and continence nursing (MSN); MSN/MBA. *Accreditation:* AACN. Part-time programs available. Postbaccalaureate distance learning degree programs offered (minimal on-campus study). *Entrance requirements:* For master's, GRE or MAT, 1 year of professional work experience, BSN, Pennsylvania RN license. Expenses: Contact institution. *Faculty research:* Medication errors, wound care, metacognition, education of RN students.

New Mexico State University, Graduate School, College of Health and Social Services, School of Nursing, Las Cruces, NM 88003-8001. Offers community/public health (MSN); medical-surgical (adult health) (MSN); psychiatric/mental health (MSN). *Accreditation:* AACN. Part-time programs available. Postbaccalaureate distance learning degree programs offered (minimal on-campus study). *Faculty:* 12 full-time (all women), 5 part-time/adjunct (4 women). *Students:* 27 full-time (24 women), 25 part-time (all women); includes 13 minority (1 African American, 12 Hispanic Americans), 1 international. Average age 45. 24 applicants, 83% accepted. In 2006, 14 degrees awarded. *Degree requirements:* For master's, clinical practice, RN licensure, thesis optional. *Entrance requirements:* For master's, BSN, minimum GPA of 3.0, course work in statistics, 3 letters of reference, writing sample. Additional exam requirements/recommendations for international students: Required—NCLEX. *Application deadline:* For fall admission, 3/1 priority date for domestic students; for spring admission, 10/1 priority date for domestic students. Applications are processed on a rolling basis. Application fee: $30 ($50 for international students). Electronic applications accepted. *Financial support:* In 2006–07, 2 teaching assistantships were awarded; fellowships, research assistantships, career-related internships or fieldwork, Federal Work-Study, scholarships/grants, traineeships, and health care benefits also available. Financial award application deadline: 3/1. *Faculty research:* Advanced practice nursing, evidence-based nursing practice, health policy, community outreach, clinical judgment. *Unit head:* Dr. Esperanza V. Joyce, Director, 505-646-3812, Fax: 505-646-2167, E-mail: evjoyce@nmsu.edu. *Application contact:* Dr. Mary Hoke, Associate Director for Graduate Studies, 505-646-3812, Fax: 505-646-2167, E-mail: mhoke@nmsu.edu.

Pontifical Catholic University of Puerto Rico, College of Sciences, Department of Nursing, Ponce, PR 00717-0777. Offers medical-surgical nursing (MS); mental health and psychiatric nursing (MS). *Accreditation:* NLN. Part-time and evening/weekend programs available. *Degree requirements:* For master's, thesis, clinical research paper, comprehensive exam (for some programs), registration. *Entrance requirements:* For master's, GRE General Test, 2 letters of recommendation, interview, minimum GPA of 2.5. Electronic applications accepted.

Rush University, College of Nursing, Department of Adult Health Nursing, Chicago, IL 60612-3832. Offers acute care nurse practitioner (MSN, Post-Master's Certificate); adult health nursing (DN Sc, DNP); adult nurse practitioner (MSN, Post-Master's Certificate); adult/gerontological nurse practitioner (MSN); anesthesia nurse practitioner (MSN, Post-Master's Certificate); critical care clinical specialist (MSN); gerontological nurse practitioner (MSN, Post-Master's Certificate); medical surgical clinical specialist (MSN). *Accreditation:* AACN; AANA/CANAEP (one or more programs are accredited). Part-time programs available. Postbaccalaureate distance learning degree programs offered (minimal on-campus study). *Faculty:* 33. *Students:* 29 full-time, 123 part-time; includes 22 minority (7 African Americans, 9 Asian Americans or Pacific Islanders, 6 Hispanic Americans). Average age 35. 101 applicants, 80% accepted, 76 enrolled. In 2006, 47 master's, 6 doctorates awarded. Terminal master's awarded for partial completion of doctoral program. *Degree requirements:* For master's, capstone project; for doctorate, thesis/dissertation, DNP leadership project. *Entrance requirements:* For master's, GRE General Test (waived if nursing GPA is above 3.0 or cumulative GPA is above 3.25), interview; for doctorate, GRE General Test, interview, course work in statistics (DN Sc). Additional exam requirements/recommendations for international students: Required—TOEFL, TWE. *Application deadline:* For fall admission, 7/1 for domestic students; for winter admission, 11/1 for domestic students; for spring admission, 1/15 for domestic students. Applications are processed on a rolling basis. Application fee: $40. Electronic applications accepted. *Financial support:* In 2006–07, 19 students received support; teaching assistantships with tuition reimbursements available, Federal Work-Study, institutionally sponsored loans, scholarships/grants, and traineeships available. Support available to part-time students. Financial award application deadline: 5/1; financial award applicants required to submit FAFSA. *Faculty research:* Complementary/alternative medicine, critical care outcomes, cardiac risk reduction, Alzheimer's Disease, telehealth monitoring. *Unit head:* Dr. Margaret Faut-Callahan, Chairperson, 312-942-7117. *Application contact:* Hicela Castruita Woods, Director, College Admissions Services, 312-942-7100, Fax: 312-942-2219, E-mail: hicela_castruita@rush.edu.

Sage Graduate School, Graduate School, Division of Nursing, Program in Nursing-Medical Surgical, Troy, NY 12180-4115. Offers MS. *Accreditation:* AACN. In 2006, 1 degree awarded. *Entrance requirements:* Additional exam requirements/recommendations for international students: Required—TOEFL (minimum score 550 paper-based; 213 computer-based). Application fee: $40. *Expenses:* Tuition: Full-time $9,270; part-time $515 per credit hour. *Unit head:* Arlene Pericak, Director, 518-244-2012, E-mail: perica@sage.edu. *Application contact:* Shannon K. Easton, Director of Graduate and Adult Admission, 518-244-2443, Fax: 518-244-6880, E-mail: sgsadm@sage.edu.

Saint Francis Medical Center College of Nursing, Graduate Program, Peoria, IL 61603-3783. Offers child and family nursing (MSN); medical-surgical nursing (MSN); nurse clinician (Post-Graduate Certificate); nurse educator (Post-Graduate Certificate). *Accreditation:* NLN. Part-time programs available. Postbaccalaureate distance learning degree programs offered (minimal on-campus study). *Faculty:* 1 (woman) full-time, 5 part-time/adjunct (all women). *Students:* 3 full-time (all women), 74 part-time (69 women); includes 5 minority (1 Asian American or Pacific Islander, 4 Hispanic Americans). Average age 28. 23 applicants, 100% accepted, 19 enrolled. In 2006, 5 degrees awarded. *Degree requirements:* For master's, research experience, portfolio, practicum. *Entrance requirements:* For master's, nursing research, health assessment, graduate course work in statistics, RN license. Additional exam requirements/recommendations for international students: Required—TOEFL. *Application deadline:* For fall admission, 6/1 priority date for domestic and international students; for spring admission, 11/15 priority date for domestic and international students. Applications are processed on a rolling basis. Application fee: $50. Electronic applications accepted. *Expenses:* Tuition: Part-time $440 per semester hour. Required fees: $130. *Financial support:* In 2006–07, 1 student received support. Application deadline: 6/15; *Faculty research:* Outcome and curriculum planning, health promotion, NCLEX-RN results, decision making program evaluation. *Unit head:* Dr. Lois J. Hamilton, Dean, 309-655-2201, Fax: 309-624-8973, E-mail: lois.j.hamilton@osfhealthcare.org. *Application contact:* Dr. Janice F. Boundy, Associate Dean Graduate Program, 309-655-2230, Fax: 309-624-8973, E-mail: jan.f.boundy@osfhealthcare.org.

University of Illinois at Chicago, Graduate College, College of Nursing, Program in Nursing Sciences (Medical/Surgical), Chicago, IL 60607-7128. Offers MS. *Accreditation:* AACN. Part-time programs available. *Degree requirements:* For master's, thesis or alternative. *Entrance requirements:* For master's, GRE General Test, minimum GPA of 2.75. Additional exam requirements/recommendations for international students: Required—TOEFL. Electronic applications accepted.

University of Maryland, Baltimore, Graduate School, School of Nursing, Master's Program in Nursing, Baltimore, MD 21201. Offers community health nursing (MS); gerontological nursing (MS); maternal-child nursing (MS); medical-surgical nursing (MS); nurse-midwifery education (MS); nursing administration (MS); nursing education (MS); nursing health policy (MS); primary care nursing (MS); psychiatric nursing (MS); MS/MBA. *Accreditation:* AANA/CANAEP; ACNM/DOA; NLN (one or more programs are accredited). Part-time programs available. *Degree requirements:* For master's, thesis or alternative, comprehensive exam (for some programs). *Entrance requirements:* For master's, GRE General Test, minimum GPA of 2.75, course work in statistics, BS in nursing. Additional exam requirements/recommendations for international students: Required—TOEFL, TOEFL or IELTS; Recommended—IELTS. Electronic applications accepted.

University of Michigan, Horace H. Rackham School of Graduate Studies, School of Nursing, Division of Acute, Critical and Long-term Care, Program in Medical-Surgical Clinical Nurse Specialist, Ann Arbor, MI 48109. Offers MS. *Accreditation:* AACN. Part-time programs available. *Degree requirements:* For master's, thesis, registration. *Entrance requirements:* For master's, GRE General Test, licensure, B average in BSN. Additional exam requirements/recommendations for international students: Required—TOEFL (minimum score 560 paper-

Medical/Surgical Nursing

University of Michigan (continued)
based; 220 computer-based). Electronic applications accepted. *Faculty research:* Clinical specialist and nurse practitioner roles, obesity, breast cancer, Alzheimer's, neurological disorders.

University of South Carolina, The Graduate School, College of Nursing, Program in Clinical Nursing, Columbia, SC 29208. Offers acute care clinical specialist (MSN); acute care nurse practitioner (MSN); women's health nurse practitioner (MSN). *Accreditation:* AACN. Part-time programs available. *Degree requirements:* For master's, thesis or alternative. *Entrance requirements:* For master's, GRE General Test or MAT, BS in nursing, RN licensure. Additional exam requirements/recommendations for international students: Required—TOEFL (minimum score 570 paper-based; 230 computer-based). Electronic applications accepted. *Faculty research:* Psychophysiological interventions, HIV/AIDS, psycho-neuroimmunology.

University of Southern Maine, College of Nursing and Health Professions, Portland, ME 04104-9300. Offers adult health nursing (PMC); clinical nurse leader (MS); clinical nurse specialist psychiatric-mental health nursing (MS); family nursing (PMC); medical/surgical nursing (MS); nurse practitioner adult health nursing (MS); nurse practitioner family nursing (MS); nurse practitioner psychiatric/mental health nursing (MS); psychiatric-mental health nursing (PMC); MBA/MSN. *Accreditation:* AACN. Part-time programs available. *Faculty:* 13 full-time (all women), 5 part-time/adjunct (4 women). *Students:* 55 full-time (53 women), 52 part-time (50 women); includes 6 minority (all Asian Americans or Pacific Islanders) Average age 36. 88 applicants, 93% accepted, 57 enrolled. In 2006, 25 degrees awarded. *Degree requirements:* For master's, thesis optional. *Entrance requirements:* For master's, GRE General Test or MAT, minimum GPA of 3.0. Additional exam requirements/recommendations for international students: Required—TOEFL (minimum score 550 paper-based; 213 computer-based). *Application deadline:* Applications are processed on a rolling basis. Application fee: $50. Electronic applications accepted. *Expenses:* Tuition, state resident: full-time $4,860; part-time $270 per credit hour. Tuition, nonresident: full-time $13,572; part-time $754 per credit hour. Required fees: $222 per semester. Tuition and fees vary according to course load. *Financial support:* In 2006–07, 14 students received support, including 5 research assistantships with tuition reimbursements available (averaging $3,375 per year), 7 teaching assistantships with tuition reimbursements available (averaging $3,375 per year); career-related internships or fieldwork, Federal Work-Study, scholarships/grants, traineeships, tuition waivers (full and partial), and unspecified assistantships also available. Support available to part-time students. Financial award application deadline: 2/15; financial award applicants required to submit FAFSA. *Faculty research:* Women's health, nursing history, weight control, community services, substance abuse. *Unit head:* Susan Sepples, Director of Nursing Program, 207-780-4505, Fax: 207-228-8177, E-mail: sepples@usm.maine.edu. *Application contact:* Mary Sloan, Director of Graduate Admissions, 207-780-4386, Fax: 207-780-4969, E-mail: gradstudies@usm.maine.edu.

Vanderbilt University, School of Nursing, Nashville, TN 37235. Offers adult acute care nurse practitioner (MSN); adult health nurse practitioner/forensic (MSN); adult nurse practitioner/cardiovascular disease management and prevention (MSN); adult nurse practitioner/palliative care (MSN); clinical management (clinical nurse leader/specialist) (MSN); family nurse practitioner (MSN); gerontology nurse practitioner (MSN); health systems management (MSN); neonatal nurse practitioner (MSN); nurse midwifery (MSN); nursing informatics (MSN); nursing science (PhD); pediatric acute care nurse practitioner (MSN); pediatric primary care nurse practitioner (MSN); psychiatric-mental health nurse practitioner (MSN); women's health nurse practitioner (MSN); MBA/MSN; MSN/MTS; MSN/PhD. *Accreditation:* ACNM/DOA; NLN (one or more programs are accredited). Part-time and evening/weekend programs available. Post-baccalaureate distance learning degree programs offered (minimal on-campus study). *Faculty:* 95 full-time (83 women), 432 part-time/adjunct (314 women). *Students:* 371 full-time (325 women), 206 part-time (180 women); includes 59 minority (38 African Americans, 2 American Indian/Alaska Native, 7 Asian Americans or Pacific Islanders, 12 Hispanic Americans). Average age 27. 611 applicants, 55% accepted, 308 enrolled. In 2006, 256 master's, 2 doctorates awarded. *Degree requirements:* For doctorate, thesis/dissertation. *Entrance requirements:* For master's, GRE, interview; for doctorate, GRE, interview, 3 letters of recommendation. Additional exam requirements/recommendations for international students: Required—TOEFL. *Application deadline:* For fall admission, 12/1 priority date for domestic and international students. Applications are processed on a rolling basis. Application fee: $50. *Expenses:* Contact institution. *Financial support:* In 2006–07, 404 students received support, including 5 research assistantships (averaging $8,000 per year); Federal Work-Study, institutionally sponsored loans, and unspecified assistantships also available. Support available to part-time students. Financial award application deadline: 3/15; financial award applicants required to submit CSS PROFILE or FAFSA. *Faculty research:* Lymphedema post cancer treatment, palliative care and bereavement, patient safety and quality of care, health care workforce issues, symptom management including pain and fatigue. Total annual research expenditures: $1.1 million. *Unit head:* Dr. Colleen Conway-Welch, Dean, 615-343-8776, Fax: 615-343-7711, E-mail: colleen.conway-welch@vanderbilt.edu. *Application contact:* Cheryl Feldner, Assistant Director of Admissions, 615-322-3800, Fax: 615-343-0333, E-mail: cheryl.feldner@vanderbilt.edu.

Wayne State University, College of Nursing, Department of Adult Health, Program in Adult Acute Care Nursing, Detroit, MI 48202. Offers MSN. *Accreditation:* AACN. Part-time programs available. *Students:* 6 full-time (all women), 48 part-time (43 women); includes 9 minority (6 African Americans, 3 Asian Americans or Pacific Islanders), 8 international. Average age 35. 27 applicants, 81% accepted, 16 enrolled. In 2006, 7 degrees awarded. *Degree requirements:* For master's, thesis or alternative. *Entrance requirements:* For master's, GRE General Test, minimum GPA of 2.8. Additional exam requirements/recommendations for international students: Required—TOEFL (minimum score 550 paper-based; 213 computer-based); Recommended—TWE (minimum score 6). *Application deadline:* For fall admission, 7/1 priority date for domestic students, 6/1 for international students; for winter admission, 10/1 for international students; for spring admission, 11/1 for domestic students, 2/1 for international students. Applications are processed on a rolling basis. Application fee: $30 ($50 for international students). Electronic applications accepted. *Financial support:* In 2006–07, 5 students received support; research assistantships, institutionally sponsored loans, scholarships/grants, and traineeships available. Financial award application deadline: 7/1; financial award applicants required to submit FAFSA. *Faculty research:* Cardiovascular nursing with vulnerable populations, wound healing, symptom management.

Nurse Anesthesia

Albany Medical College, Center for Nurse Anesthesiology, Albany, NY 12208-3479. Offers MS. *Accreditation:* AANA/CANAEP. Postbaccalaureate distance learning degree programs offered (minimal on-campus study). *Faculty:* 4 full-time (all women). *Students:* 45 full-time (26 women), 3 part-time (all women); includes 4 minority (1 African American, 2 Asian Americans or Pacific Islanders, 1 Hispanic American). Average age 33. 52 applicants, 38% accepted, 17 enrolled. In 2006, 16 master's awarded. *Degree requirements:* For master's, thesis, thesis proposal/clinical research. *Entrance requirements:* For master's, GRE General Test, BSN or appropriate bachelor's degree, current RN license, critical care experience, organic chemistry, reasonable math. Additional exam requirements/recommendations for international students: Required—TOEFL. *Application deadline:* For fall admission, 3/15 priority date for domestic students. Applications are processed on a rolling basis. Application fee: $60. *Expenses:* Contact institution. *Financial support:* Scholarships/grants and traineeships available. Financial award applicants required to submit FAFSA. *Unit head:* Dr. Denise Martin-Sheridan, Graduate Director, 518-262-4303, Fax: 518-262-5170, E-mail: amcnap@mail.amc.edu. *Application contact:* Helene M. Gregory, Coordinator, 518-262-4303, Fax: 518-262-5170, E-mail: amcnap@mail.amc.edu.

Arkansas State University, Graduate School, College of Nursing and Health Professions, Department of Nursing, Jonesboro, State University, AR 72467. Offers aging studies (Certificate); nurse anesthesia (MSN); nursing (MSN). *Accreditation:* AANA/CANAEP (one or more programs are accredited); NLN. Part-time programs available. *Faculty:* 8 full-time (7 women), 3 part-time/adjunct (all women). *Students:* 63 full-time (28 women), 110 part-time (73 women); includes 27 minority (22 African Americans, 1 Asian American or Pacific Islander, 4 Hispanic Americans). Average age 33. 89 applicants, 72% accepted, 64 enrolled. In 2006, 55 degrees awarded. *Degree requirements:* For master's, thesis or alternative, comprehensive exam. *Entrance requirements:* For master's, GRE General Test or MAT, appropriate bachelor's degree, current Arkansas nursing license, CPR certification, acceptable immunization status, physical examination, professional liability insurance, official transcript. Additional exam requirements/recommendations for international students: Required—TOEFL (minimum score 213 computer-based). *Application deadline:* Applications are processed on a rolling basis. Application fee: $30 ($40 for international students). Electronic applications accepted. *Expenses:* Contact institution. *Financial support:* Career-related internships or fieldwork, scholarships/grants, and unspecified assistantships available. Financial award application deadline: 7/1; financial award applicants required to submit FAFSA.

Barry University, School of Natural and Health Sciences, Program in Anesthesiology, Miami Shores, FL 33161-6695. Offers MS. *Accreditation:* AANA/CANAEP. *Students:* 147 full-time (111 women); includes 47 minority (15 African Americans, 11 Asian Americans or Pacific Islanders, 21 Hispanic Americans). 199 applicants, 39% accepted, 71 enrolled. In 2006, 55 degrees awarded. *Degree requirements:* For master's, comprehensive exam. *Entrance requirements:* For master's, GRE General Test, minimum GPA of 3.0; 2 courses in chemistry (1 with lab); minimum 1 year critical care experience; BSN or RN; 4-year bachelor's degree in health sciences, nursing, biology, or chemistry. *Application deadline:* For spring admission, 9/1 for domestic students. Applications are processed on a rolling basis. Application fee: $30. Electronic applications accepted. *Financial support:* Application deadline: 5/1; *Faculty research:* Use of computers in education, psychological well-bring of health care providers. *Unit head:* John McFadden, Program Director, 305-899-3287, Fax: 305-899-3366, E-mail: jmcfadden@mail.barry.edu. *Application contact:* Jocelyn Goulet, Director, Health Services Admissions Operation, 305-899-3541, Fax: 305-899-3232, E-mail: jgoulet@mail.barry.edu.

Baylor College of Medicine, School of Allied Health Sciences, Program in Nurse Anesthesia, Houston, TX 77030-3498. Offers MS. *Accreditation:* AANA/CANAEP. *Faculty:* 9 full-time (6 women). *Students:* 34 full-time (24 women); includes 8 minority (2 African Americans, 4 Asian Americans or Pacific Islanders, 2 Hispanic Americans). Average age 32. 108 applicants, 12% accepted, 10 enrolled. In 2006, 12 degrees awarded. *Entrance requirements:* For master's, GRE General Test, Texas nursing license, 1 year of work experience in acute care nursing, minimum GPA of 3.0. *Application deadline:* For fall admission, 12/1 for domestic students. Application fee: $70. Electronic applications accepted. *Expenses:* Contact institution. *Financial support:* In 2006–07, 34 students received support. Career-related internships or fieldwork, Federal Work-Study, institutionally sponsored loans, scholarships/grants, and traineeships available. Financial award application deadline: 5/11; financial award applicants required to submit FAFSA. *Unit head:* James R. Walker, Director, 713-793-2860, Fax: 713-793-2867, E-mail: jrwalker@bcm.edu.

Boston College, William F. Connell School of Nursing, Chestnut Hill, MA 02467-3800. Offers adult health nursing (MS); community health nursing (MS); family health (MS); gerontology (MS); maternal/child health nursing (MS), including pediatric and women's health; nurse anesthesia (MS); nursing (PhD); psychiatric-mental health nursing (MS); MBA/MS; MS/MA; MS/PhD. *Accreditation:* AACN; AANA/CANAEP (one or more programs are accredited). Part-time programs available. *Faculty:* 46 full-time (44 women), 34 part-time/adjunct (all women). *Students:* 155 full-time (137 women), 56 part-time (54 women); includes 10 minority (4 African Americans, 5 Asian Americans or Pacific Islanders, 1 Hispanic American), 6 international. Average age 34. 276 applicants, 47% accepted, 67 enrolled. In 2006, 61 master's, 4 doctorates awarded. *Median time to degree:* Of those who began their doctoral program in fall 1998, 100% received their degree in 8 years or less. *Degree requirements:* For master's, research project; for doctorate, thesis/dissertation, computer literacy exam or foreign language, comprehensive exam. *Entrance requirements:* For master's, GRE General Test, bachelor's degree in nursing; for doctorate, GRE General Test, master's degree in nursing. Additional exam requirements/recommendations for international students: Required—TOEFL (minimum score 550 paper-based; 213 computer-based). *Application deadline:* For fall admission, 10/15 for domestic and international students; for spring admission, 3/15 for domestic and international students. Application fee: $40. Electronic applications accepted. *Financial support:* In 2006–07, 104 students received support, including 15 fellowships with partial tuition reimbursements available (averaging $10,045 per year), 3 research assistantships (averaging $10,000 per year), 4 teaching assistantships (averaging $12,548 per year); Federal Work-Study, institutionally sponsored loans, scholarships/grants, traineeships, and tuition waivers (partial) also available. Support available to part-time students. Financial award application deadline: 3/1; financial award applicants required to submit FAFSA. *Faculty research:* Ethics, reduction of risk behaviors, support during chronic illness, violence, gerontology. Total annual research expenditures: $1.1 million. *Unit head:* Dr. Barbara Hazard, Dean, 617-552-4251, Fax: 617-552-0931, E-mail: barbara.munro@bc.edu. *Application contact:* Zanifer John-Bayard, Graduate Programs Assistant, 617-552-4059, Fax: 617-552-0745, E-mail: johnza@bc.edu.

Bradley University, Graduate School, College of Education and Health Sciences, Department of Nursing, Peoria, IL 61625-0002. Offers nurse administered anesthesia (MSN); nursing administration (MSN). *Accreditation:* AANA/CANAEP; NLN. Part-time and evening/weekend programs available. *Students:* 3 full-time (0 women), 47 part-time (29 women); includes 6 minority (1 African American, 1 American Indian/Alaska Native, 4 Asian Americans or Pacific Islanders). 16 applicants, 19% accepted, 3 enrolled. In 2006, 24 degrees awarded. *Degree requirements:* For master's, thesis optional. *Entrance requirements:* For master's, GRE General Test or MAT, interview, Illinois RN license, advanced cardiac life support certification, pediatric advanced life support certification, 3 letters of recommendation. Additional exam requirements/recommendations for international students: Required—TOEFL (minimum score 550 paper-based; 213 computer-based; 79 iBT). *Application deadline:* For fall admission, 5/15 priority date for domestic and international students; for spring admission, 10/15 priority date for domestic and international students. Applications are processed on a rolling basis. Application fee: $40 ($50 for international students). *Financial support:* Research assistantships, scholarships/grants, tuition waivers (partial), and unspecified assistantships available. Financial award application deadline: 4/1. *Unit head:* Dr. Francesca Armmer, Chairperson, 309-677-2528, E-mail: faa@bradley.edu.

Case Western Reserve University, Frances Payne Bolton School of Nursing, Master's Programs in Nursing, Program in Nurse Anesthesia, Cleveland, OH 44106. Offers MSN. *Accreditation:* AANA/CANAEP. *Students:* 32 full-time (23 women), 36 part-time (29 women); includes 10 minority (2 African Americans, 5 Asian Americans or Pacific Islanders, 3

Hispanic Americans). 113 applicants, 28% accepted, 24 enrolled. In 2006, 23 degrees awarded. *Degree requirements:* For master's, thesis optional. *Entrance requirements:* For master's, GRE General Test or MAT. *Application deadline:* For fall admission, 1/15 for domestic students. Application fee: $75. *Financial support:* Research assistantships, teaching assistantships, institutionally sponsored loans and tuition waivers (partial) available. Support available to part-time students. Financial award application deadline: 6/30. *Faculty research:* Mechanical ventilation antioxidant trial; intravenous function and mechanical ventilation; impact of taxane on peripheral nerve function. *Unit head:* Jack Kless, Head. *Application contact:* Peter Taylor, Recruitment and Retention Specialist, 216-368-0349, Fax: 216-368-0124, E-mail: peter.taylor@case.edu.

Central Connecticut State University, School of Graduate Studies, School of Arts and Sciences, Department of Biology, New Britain, CT 06050-4010. Offers anesthesia (MS); biological sciences (MA, MS), including ecology and environmental sciences (MA), general biology (MA); biology (Certificate); general health (MS). Part-time and evening/weekend programs available. *Faculty:* 12 full-time (4 women), 7 part-time/adjunct (4 women). *Students:* 105 full-time (69 women), 29 part-time (17 women); includes 16 minority (5 African Americans, 1 American Indian/Alaska Native, 8 Asian Americans or Pacific Islanders, 2 Hispanic Americans), 2 international. Average age 33. 38 applicants, 79% accepted, 20 enrolled. In 2006, 34 master's, 1 other advanced degree awarded. *Degree requirements:* For master's, thesis or alternative, comprehensive exam; for Certificate, qualifying exam. *Entrance requirements:* For master's, minimum GPA of 2.7. Additional exam requirements/recommendations for international students: Required—TOEFL. *Application deadline:* For fall admission, 7/1 for domestic students; for spring admission, 12/1 for domestic students. Applications are processed on a rolling basis. Application fee: $50. Electronic applications accepted. *Expenses:* Tuition, area resident: Full-time $3,970; part-time $380 per credit. Tuition, state resident: full-time $5,955; part-time $380 per credit. Tuition, nonresident: full-time $11,061; part-time $380 per credit. Required fees: $3,189. One-time fee: $62 part-time. Tuition and fees vary according to degree level and program. *Financial support:* In 2006–07, 27 students received support, including 2 research assistantships; career-related internships or fieldwork, Federal Work-Study, scholarships/grants, and unspecified assistantships also available. Support available to part-time students. Financial award application deadline: 3/1; financial award applicants required to submit FAFSA. *Faculty research:* Environmental science, anesthesia, health sciences, zoology, animal behavior. *Unit head:* Dr. Jeremiah Jarrett, Chair, 860-832-2645.

Columbia University, School of Nursing, Program in Nurse Anesthesia, New York, NY 10032. Offers MS, Adv C. *Accreditation:* AACN; AANA/CANAEP. *Faculty:* 1 (woman) full-time, 3 part-time/adjunct (2 women). *Students:* 48 full-time (41 women), 9 part-time (8 women); includes 18 minority (3 African Americans, 9 Asian Americans or Pacific Islanders, 6 Hispanic Americans). Average age 32. In 2006, 25 master's, 3 other advanced degrees awarded. *Entrance requirements:* For master's, GRE General Test, BSN, 1 year of intensive care unit experience; for Adv C, MSN, 1 year of intensive care unit experience. *Application deadline:* For fall admission, 11/1 for domestic and international students. Application fee: $65. Electronic applications accepted. *Financial support:* Application deadline: 2/1; *Unit head:* Dr. Eileen Evanina, Director, 212-305-4196. *Application contact:* Dr. Eileen Evanina, Director, 212-305-4196.

DePaul University, College of Liberal Arts and Sciences, Department of Nursing, Chicago, IL 60604-2287. Offers advanced practice nursing (MS); masters entry into nursing practice (MS); nurse anesthesia (MS). MS in nurse anesthesia offered jointly with Ravenswood Hospital Medical Center. *Accreditation:* AACN; AANA/CANAEP. *Faculty:* 13 full-time (10 women), 10 part-time/adjunct (all women). *Students:* 128 full-time (107 women), 36 part-time (31 women); includes 43 minority (19 African Americans, 2 American Indian/Alaska Native, 16 Asian Americans or Pacific Islanders, 6 Hispanic Americans), 2 international. Average age 39. 80 applicants, 100% accepted. In 2006, 9 master's awarded. *Degree requirements:* For master's, thesis optional. *Entrance requirements:* For master's, GRE, BSN, minimum GPA of 2.85, RN license. Application fee: $25. *Financial support:* In 2006–07, 5 fellowships (averaging $2,000 per year) were awarded; traineeships also available. *Faculty research:* Children's health, women's health, health promotion. *Unit head:* Dr. Susan Poslusny, Chair, 773-325-7280, Fax: 773-325-7282, E-mail: sposlusn@wppost.depaul.edu. *Application contact:* Christine Werdrick, Coordinator of Student Academic Services and Department Operations, 773-325-7280, Fax: 773-325-7282, E-mail: cwerdric@depaul.edu.

Drexel University, College of Nursing and Health Professions, Program in Nurse Anesthesia, Philadelphia, PA 19104-2875. Offers MSN. *Accreditation:* AACN; AANA/CANAEP. Electronic applications accepted.

Duke University, School of Nursing, Durham, NC 27708-0586. Offers adult acute care (Certificate); adult cardiovascular (Certificate); adult oncology/HIV (Certificate); adult primary care (Certificate); clinical nurse specialist (MSN), including adult oncology/HIV, gerontology, neonatal, pediatric, pediatric/chronic acute care; clinical research management (MSN, Certificate); family (Certificate); gerontology (Certificate); health and nursing ministries (MSN, Certificate); health systems leadership and outcomes (Certificate); leadership in community based long term care (MSN, Certificate); neonatal (Certificate); neonatal/pediatric in rural health (MSN, Certificate); nurse anesthetist (MSN, Certificate); nurse practitioner (MSN), including adult acute care, adult cardiovascular, adult oncology/HIV, adult primary care, family, gerontology, neonatal, pediatric, pediatric acute care; nursing (PhD); nursing and healthcare leadership (MSN); nursing education (MSN); nursing informatics (MSN, Certificate); pediatric (Certificate); pediatric acute care (Certificate); MBA/MSN; MSN/MCM. *Accreditation:* AACN; AANA/CANAEP. Part-time programs available. Postbaccalaureate distance learning degree programs offered (minimal on-campus study). *Faculty:* 45 full-time (41 women), 169 part-time/adjunct (150 women). *Students:* 178 full-time (162 women), 140 part-time (132 women); includes 48 minority (17 African Americans, 3 American Indian/Alaska Native, 20 Asian Americans or Pacific Islanders, 8 Hispanic Americans). Average age 36. 99 applicants, 92% accepted, 91 enrolled. In 2006, 122 master's, 17 other advanced degrees awarded. *Median time to degree:* Master's–2 years full-time, 2.5 years part-time. *Degree requirements:* For master's, thesis optional. *Entrance requirements:* For master's, GRE General Test or MAT, 1 year of nursing experience, BSN, minimum GPA of 3.0, previous course work in statistics; for Certificate, MSN. Additional exam requirements/recommendations for international students: Required—TOEFL (minimum score 550 paper-based; 213 computer-based), Commission on Graduates of Foreign Nursing Schools exam. *Application deadline:* For fall admission, 7/2 priority date for domestic and international students; for spring admission, 11/15 priority date for domestic and international students. Applications are processed on a rolling basis. Application fee: $50. *Expenses:* Contact institution. *Financial support:* In 2006–07, 258 students received support. Career-related internships or fieldwork, institutionally sponsored loans, scholarships/grants, traineeships, and tuition waivers (partial) available. Support available to part-time students. Financial award application deadline: 4/1; financial award applicants required to submit FAFSA. *Faculty research:* Cardiovascular disease, caregiver skill training, data mining, prostate cancer, neonatal immune system. Total annual research expenditures: $3.5 million. *Unit head:* Dr. Catherine L. Gilliss, Dean/Vice Chancellor for Nursing Affairs, 919-684-9444, Fax: 919-684-9414, E-mail: gilli025@mc.duke.edu. *Application contact:* Bebe T. Mills, Director of Admissions, 919-684-9151, Fax: 919-668-4693, E-mail: mills031@mc.duke.edu.

Emory University, School of Medicine, Programs in Allied Health Professions, Atlanta, GA 30322-1100. Offers anesthesiology (MM Sc); anesthesiology/patient monitoring systems (MM Sc); ophthalmic technology (MM Sc); physical therapy (DPT); physician assistant (MM Sc). Postbaccalaureate distance learning degree programs offered. *Faculty:* 27 full-time (16 women), 57 part-time/adjunct (32 women). *Students:* 322 full-time (227 women), 6 part-time (5 women); includes 69 minority (33 African Americans, 4 American Indian/Alaska Native, 28 Asian Americans or Pacific Islanders, 4 Hispanic Americans). Average age 28. 1,149 applicants, 16% accepted, 132 enrolled. In 2006, 80 master's, 21 doctorates awarded. *Entrance requirements:* For master's and doctorate, GRE. *Expenses:* Contact institution. *Financial support:* In 2006–07, 289 students received support. Federal Work-Study, institutionally sponsored loans, and scholarships/grants available. Support available to part-time students. Financial award application deadline: 2/15; financial award applicants required to submit CSS PROFILE or FAFSA. *Unit head:* Dr. J. Alan Otsuki, Assistant Dean, Office of Medical Education and Student Affairs, 404-727-5655, Fax: 404-727-0045, E-mail: jotsuki@emory.edu. *Application contact:* Roselyn Branch, Associate Director of Registration and Student Affairs, 404-727-5682, Fax: 404-727-0045, E-mail: roselyn.branch@emory.edu.

Fairfield University, School of Nursing, Fairfield, CT 06824-5195. Offers adult nurse practitioner (MSN, PMC); family nurse practitioner (MSN, PMC); healthcare management (MSN); nurse anesthesia (MSN); psychiatric nurse practitioner (MSN, PMC). *Accreditation:* AACN; AANA/CANAEP. Part-time programs available. *Faculty:* 13 full-time (12 women), 2 part-time/adjunct (both women). *Students:* 3 full-time (all women), 39 part-time (all women); includes 5 minority (2 African Americans, 3 Asian Americans or Pacific Islanders). Average age 42. 23 applicants, 30% accepted, 3 enrolled. In 2006, 9 degrees awarded. *Degree requirements:* For master's, capstone project. *Entrance requirements:* For master's, MAT or GRE, minimum QPA of 3.0, RN license, resumé, 2 recommendations; for PMC, 1 year of work experience as a registered nurse. Additional exam requirements/recommendations for international students: Required—TOEFL (minimum score 550 paper-based; 213 computer-based; 79 iBT). *Application deadline:* For fall admission, 4/1 priority date for domestic students, 6/15 priority date for international students; for spring admission, 11/1 priority date for domestic students, 10/15 priority date for international students. Applications are processed on a rolling basis. Application fee: $55. *Expenses:* Contact institution. *Financial support:* Traineeships available. Financial award applicants required to submit FAFSA. *Faculty research:* Critical care, nursing outcomes, care of older adults, leadership, community health. *Unit head:* Dr. Jeanne M. Novotny, Dean, 203-254-4000 Ext. 2701, Fax: 203-254-4126, E-mail: jnovotny@mail.fairfield.edu. *Application contact:* Marianne Gumpper, Director of Graduate and Continuing Studies Admissions, 203-254-4184, Fax: 203-254-4073, E-mail: gradadmis@mail.fairfield.edu.

Gannon University, School of Graduate Studies, College of Sciences, Engineering, and Health Sciences, School of Health Sciences, Program in Nursing, Erie, PA 16541-0001. Offers anesthesia (MSN); business administration (MSN); case management (MSN); medical-surgical nursing (MSN); nurse anesthesia (Certificate); nursing rural practitioner (MSN). *Accreditation:* AACN; AANA/CANAEP (one or more programs are accredited). Part-time and evening/weekend programs available. *Students:* 15 full-time (5 women), 44 part-time (37 women). Average age 35. 8 applicants, 88% accepted, 5 enrolled. In 2006, 14 master's, 2 other advanced degrees awarded. *Degree requirements:* For master's, thesis. *Entrance requirements:* For master's, GRE General Test, MAT, bachelor's degree from a NLN-approved nursing program, interview, Pennsylvania RN license. Additional exam requirements/recommendations for international students: Required—TOEFL (minimum score 500 paper-based; 173 computer-based). *Application deadline:* For fall admission, 4/15 for domestic students. Application fee: $25. *Expenses:* Tuition: Full-time $12,240; part-time $680 per credit. Required fees: $496; $16 per credit. Tuition and fees vary according to course load, degree level, campus/location and program. *Financial support:* Career-related internships or fieldwork and traineeships available. Support available to part-time students. Financial award application deadline: 7/1; financial award applicants required to submit FAFSA. *Unit head:* Dr. Sharon Thompson, Interim Director, 814-871-5345, E-mail: thompson001@gannon.edu. *Application contact:* Debra Meszaros, Director of Graduate Recruitment, 814-871-5819, Fax: 814-871-5827, E-mail: cfal@gannon.edu.

Gonzaga University, School of Education, Program in Anesthesiology Education, Spokane, WA 99258. Offers M Anesth Ed. *Accreditation:* AANA/CANAEP. *Faculty:* 3 full-time (2 women), 5 part-time/adjunct (2 women). *Students:* 8 full-time (6 women), 8 part-time (3 women). Average age 34. In 2006, 7 degrees awarded. *Degree requirements:* For master's, comprehensive exam. *Entrance requirements:* For master's, GRE General Test or MAT. Additional exam requirements/recommendations for international students: Required—TOEFL. *Application deadline:* For fall admission, 12/1 for domestic students. Application fee: $40. *Expenses:* Tuition: Full-time $10,620; part-time $590 per credit. *Financial support:* Application deadline: 3/1. *Unit head:* Dr. Janet Brougher, Academic Director, 509-328-4220 Ext. 3502.

Gooding Institute of Nurse Anesthesia, Program in Nurse Anesthesia, Panama City, FL 32401. Offers MS. *Accreditation:* AANA/CANAEP. *Degree requirements:* For master's, thesis, comprehensive exam. *Entrance requirements:* For master's, GRE General Test, BSN or BA, RN license.

Inter American University of Puerto Rico, Arecibo Campus, Program in Anesthesia, Arecibo, PR 00614-4050. Offers MS. *Accreditation:* AANA/CANAEP. *Degree requirements:* For master's, thesis optional. *Entrance requirements:* For master's, GRE, EXADEP, 2 letters of recommendation, bachelor's degree in nursing, interview, minimum GPA of 3.0 in last 60 credits, minimum 1 year experience.

La Roche College, School of Graduate Studies, Program in Health Sciences, Pittsburgh, PA 15237-5898. Offers nurse anesthesia (MS). *Accreditation:* AANA/CANAEP. *Faculty:* 2 full-time (0 women), 1 part-time/adjunct (0 women). *Students:* 60 full-time (35 women), 32 part-time (22 women); includes 1 minority (Asian American or Pacific Islander) Average age 35. 18 applicants, 100% accepted, 18 enrolled. In 2006, 47 degrees awarded. *Median time to degree:* Master's–2 years full-time. *Degree requirements:* For master's, thesis optional. *Entrance requirements:* For master's, GRE General Test, prior acceptance to the Allegheny Valley School of Anesthesia. *Application deadline:* For fall admission, 12/31 for domestic students. Application fee: $50. Electronic applications accepted. *Expenses:* Tuition: Full-time $9,900; part-time $550 per credit. Required fees: $14 per credit. *Financial support:* Application deadline: 3/31; *Unit head:* Dr. Don Fujito, Coordinator, 412-536-1157, Fax: 412-536-1175, E-mail: fujitod1@laroche.edu. *Application contact:* Hope Schiffgens, Director of Admissions for Graduate and Continuing Education, 412-536-1266, Fax: 412-536-1283, E-mail: schombh1@laroche.edu.

Mayo School of Health Sciences, Program in Nurse Anesthesia, Rochester, MN 55905. Offers MNA. *Accreditation:* AANA/CANAEP. *Faculty:* 1 (woman) full-time, 2 part-time/adjunct (1 woman). *Students:* 117 full-time (65 women); includes 10 minority (5 African Americans, 4 Asian Americans or Pacific Islanders, 1 Hispanic American). Average age 30. 83 applicants, 30 enrolled. In 2006, 30 degrees awarded. *Degree requirements:* For master's, research project. *Entrance requirements:* For master's, GRE General Test, minimum GPA of 3.0, minimum 1 year of critical care experience. Additional exam requirements/recommendations for international students: Required—TOEFL. *Application deadline:* For fall admission, 10/15 for domestic students. Applications are processed on a rolling basis. Application fee: $50. Electronic applications accepted. *Expenses:* Contact institution. *Financial support:* Scholarships/grants, health care benefits, and stipends available. Financial award applicants required to submit FAFSA. *Unit head:* Mary E. Marienau, Director, 507-284-3293, Fax: 507-284-0656, E-mail: marienau.mary@mayo.edu. *Application contact:* Val Martin, Administrative Assistant, 507-284-3678, Fax: 507-284-0656.

Medical College of Georgia, School of Graduate Studies, Programs in Nursing, Augusta, GA 30912-1500. Offers adult nursing (MSN); community health nursing (MSN); mental health nursing (MSN); nurse practitioner (MSN); nursing (DNP, PhD); nursing anesthesia (MSN); parent-child nursing (MSN). *Accreditation:* AACN; AANA/CANAEP. Part-time programs available. *Faculty:* 18 full-time (16 women), 1 part-time/adjunct (0 women). *Students:* 95 full-time (76 women), 42 part-time (37 women); includes 24 minority (20 African Americans, 4 Asian Americans or Pacific Islanders). Average age 37. 156 applicants, 35% accepted, 24 enrolled. In 2006, 28 master's, 10 doctorates awarded. *Degree requirements:* For master's, thesis (for some programs); for doctorate, thesis/dissertation. *Entrance requirements:* For master's, GRE General Test, MAT; for doctorate, GRE General Test. Additional exam requirements/recommendations for international students: Required—TOEFL (minimum score 550 paper-based; 213 computer-based). *Application deadline:* For fall admission, 7/1 for domestic students, 4/15 for international students. Applications are processed on a rolling basis. Application fee: $30. Electronic applications accepted. *Expenses:* Tuition, state resident: full-time $2,293; part-time $192 per credit hour. Tuition, nonresident: full-time $9,169; part-time $765 per

Nurse Anesthesia

Medical College of Georgia (continued)

credit hour. Required fees: $293 per semester. *Financial support:* In 2006–07, 78 students received support, including 9 research assistantships with partial tuition reimbursements available (averaging $23,000 per year); Federal Work-Study, institutionally sponsored loans, traineeships, tuition waivers, and unspecified assistantships also available. Support available to part-time students. Financial award application deadline: 5/31; financial award applicants required to submit FAFSA. *Unit head:* Dr. Lucy Marion, Dean, 706-721-6258, Fax: 706-721-8169, E-mail: lumarion@mail.mcg.edu.

Medical University of South Carolina, College of Health Professions, Department of Clinical Services, Anesthesia for Nurses Program, Charleston, SC 29425-0002. Offers MS. *Accreditation:* AANA/CANAEP. *Faculty:* 2 full-time (0 women). *Students:* 65 full-time (40 women); includes 8 minority (2 African Americans, 2 American Indian/Alaska Native, 3 Asian Americans or Pacific Islanders, 1 Hispanic American). Average age 32. 81 applicants, 37% accepted, 28 enrolled. In 2006, 20 degrees awarded. *Degree requirements:* For master's, research proposal, clinical practica. *Entrance requirements:* For master's, GRE General Test, interview, minimum GPA of 3.0, 2 years of RN (ICU) experience, RN license. Additional exam requirements/recommendations for international students: Required—TOEFL (minimum score 600 paper-based; 250 computer-based). *Application deadline:* For fall admission, 11/30 priority date for domestic and international students. Application fee: $75. Electronic applications accepted. *Financial support:* Federal Work-Study, scholarships/grants, and tuition waivers (partial) available. Support available to part-time students. Financial award application deadline: 3/15; financial award applicants required to submit FAFSA. *Unit head:* Dr. Anthony Chipas, Director, 843-792-3785, Fax: 843-792-1984, E-mail: chipas@musc.edu. *Application contact:* Jerri Snider, Administrative Specialist, 843-792-3785, Fax: 843-792-1984, E-mail: sniderj@musc.edu.

Middle Tennessee School of Anesthesia, Program in Nurse Anesthesia, Madison, TN 37116. Offers MS. *Accreditation:* AANA/CANAEP. *Degree requirements:* For master's, project. *Entrance requirements:* For master's, GRE General Test, RN license, 1 year of critical-care nursing experience, BSN, general chemistry (3 semester hours minimum).

Midwestern University, Glendale Campus, College of Health Sciences, Arizona Campus, Program in Nurse Anesthesia, Glendale, AZ 85308. Offers MS. *Accreditation:* AANA/CANAEP. *Faculty:* 5 full-time (3 women), 5 part-time/adjunct (3 women). *Students:* 28 full-time (19 women); includes 5 minority (2 African Americans, 3 Hispanic Americans). Average age 34. 131 applicants, 16% accepted, 16 enrolled.Application fee: $50. *Expenses: Contact institution. Unit head:* Sandra L. Lovell, Head, 623-572-3227, E-mail: slovel@midwestern.edu. *Application contact:* James Walter, Director of Admissions, 888-247-9277, Fax: 623-572-3229, E-mail: admissaz@midwestern.edu.

Missouri State University, Graduate College, College of Health and Human Services, Department of Biomedical Sciences, Program in Nurse Anesthesia, Springfield, MO 65804-0094. Offers MS. *Accreditation:* AANA/CANAEP. *Students:* 30 full-time (19 women), 3 part-time (all women); includes 1 minority (American Indian/Alaska Native). Average age 33. 19 applicants, 26% accepted, 5 enrolled. In 2006, 13 degrees awarded. *Degree requirements:* For master's, thesis or alternative, oral exams, comprehensive exam. *Entrance requirements:* For master's, GRE General Test, 1 year of experience in acute care nursing, current RN license, interview, minimum GPA of 3.0 during final 60 hours of course work. Additional exam requirements/recommendations for international students: Required—TOEFL (minimum score 550 paper-based; 213 computer-based; 79 iBT). *Application deadline:* For fall admission, 1/1 priority date for domestic students; for spring admission, 8/1 priority date for domestic students. Applications are processed on a rolling basis. Application fee: $35. *Expenses:* Tuition, state resident: full-time $3,582; part-time $199 per credit hour. Tuition, nonresident: full-time $6,984; part-time $199 per credit hour. Required fees: $548. Full-time tuition and fees vary according to course level, course load, program and reciprocity agreements. *Financial support:* Career-related internships or fieldwork, scholarships/grants, and unspecified assistantships available. Support available to part-time students. Financial award application deadline: 3/31; financial award applicants required to submit FAFSA.

Mountain State University, Graduate Studies, Program in Nursing, Beckley, WV 25802-9003. Offers administration/education (MSN); family nurse practitioner (MSN); nurse anesthesia (MSN); registered nurse anesthetist (Certificate). *Accreditation:* AANA/CANAEP; NLN. Part-time programs available. Postbaccalaureate distance learning degree programs offered (minimal on-campus study). *Faculty:* 6 full-time (4 women), 14 part-time/adjunct (7 women). *Students:* 80 full-time (64 women), 10 part-time (all women); includes 1 minority (African American) Average age 37. 29 applicants, 100% accepted, 17 enrolled. In 2006, 4 degrees awarded. *Median time to degree:* Master's–2 years full-time, 3 years part-time. *Degree requirements:* For master's, thesis or alternative, comprehensive exam. *Entrance requirements:* For master's, GRE. Additional exam requirements/recommendations for international students: Required—TOEFL (minimum score 550 paper-based; 213 computer-based); Recommended—IELTS (minimum score 7). *Application deadline:* For spring admission, 6/30 for domestic and international students. Applications are processed on a rolling basis. Application fee: $25 ($50 for international students). Electronic applications accepted. *Expenses: Contact institution.* Tuition and fees vary according to course load and program. *Financial support:* In 2006–07, 2 research assistantships (averaging $1,200 per year) were awarded; Federal Work-Study, scholarships/grants, and unspecified assistantships also available. Support available to part-time students. Financial award applicants required to submit FAFSA. *Unit head:* Dr. Jessica Sharp, Senior Academic Officer for Graduate Nursing, 304-929-1425, Fax: 304-929-1601, E-mail: jsharp@mountainstate.edu. *Application contact:* Melody Tilley, Program Specialist, 304-929-1576, Fax: 304-929-1601, E-mail: mtilley@mountainstate.edu.

See Close-Up on page 1965.

Mount Marty College, Graduate Studies Division, Yankton, SD 57078-3724. Offers business administration (MBA); nurse anesthesia (MS); pastoral ministries (MPM). *Accreditation:* AANA/CANAEP (one or more programs are accredited). *Faculty:* 4 full-time (3 women), 1 part-time/adjunct (0 women). *Students:* 70 full-time (42 women); includes 4 minority (2 African Americans, 1 Asian American or Pacific Islander, 1 Hispanic American). 140 applicants, 28% accepted, 39 enrolled. In 2006, 37 degrees awarded. *Degree requirements:* For master's, thesis or alternative. *Entrance requirements:* For master's, GRE General Test, minimum GPA of 3.0. *Application deadline:* For fall admission, 12/1 priority date for domestic students. Applications are processed on a rolling basis. Application fee: $35. Electronic applications accepted. *Financial support:* In 2006–07, 70 students received support. Scholarships/grants available. Financial award application deadline: 8/1; financial award applicants required to submit FAFSA. *Faculty research:* Clinical anesthesia, professional characteristics, motivations of applicants. *Unit head:* Brandi Tschumper, Vice President of Enrollment, 800-658-4552, Fax: 605-688-1508, E-mail: mmcadmit@mtmc.edu.

Murray State University, College of Health Sciences and Human Services, Program in Nursing, Murray, KY 42071. Offers clinical nurse specialist (MSN); family nurse practitioner (MSN); nurse anesthesia (MSN). *Accreditation:* AACN; AANA/CANAEP. *Faculty:* 8 full-time (7 women). *Students:* 37 full-time (30 women), 7 part-time (6 women); includes 2 minority (1 African American, 1 Hispanic American). 85 applicants, 35% accepted, 21 enrolled. In 2006, 22 degrees awarded. *Degree requirements:* For master's, research project. *Entrance requirements:* For master's, GRE General Test, BSN, interview, RN licensure. Additional exam requirements/recommendations for international students: Required—TOEFL (minimum score 550 paper-based). *Application deadline:* For fall admission, 3/1 for domestic students, 4/15 for international students. Application fee: $30. *Financial support:* Traineeships available. Financial award application deadline: 4/1. *Faculty research:* Fibromyalgis, primary care, rural health. *Unit head:* Dr. Nancey E. M. France, Graduate Coordinator and Professor, 270-809-6671, Fax: 270-809-6662, E-mail: nancey.france@murraystate.edu.

Newman University, School of Nursing and Allied Health, Wichita, KS 67213-2097. Offers nurse anesthesia (MS). *Accreditation:* AANA/CANAEP. *Faculty:* 4 full-time (3 women), 1 part-time/adjunct (0 women). *Students:* 24 full-time (13 women), 2 part-time; includes 4 minority (1 African American, 1 Asian American or Pacific Islander, 2 Hispanic Americans). Average age 34. 94 applicants, 15% accepted, 12 enrolled. In 2006, 12 degrees awarded. *Degree requirements:* For master's, thesis optional. *Entrance requirements:* For master's, GRE General Test, interview, minimum GPA of 3.0. Additional exam requirements/recommendations for international students: Required—TOEFL (minimum score 600 paper-based; 250 computer-based). *Application deadline:* For fall admission, 12/1 for domestic and international students. Applications are processed on a rolling basis. Application fee: $25 ($40 for international students). Electronic applications accepted. *Expenses: Contact institution. Financial support:* Federal Work-Study and tuition waivers (full) available. Financial award application deadline: 8/15; financial award applicants required to submit FAFSA. *Unit head:* Sharon Niemann, Director, 316-942-4291 Ext. 2272, Fax: 316-942-4483, E-mail: niemanns@newmanu.edu. *Application contact:* Linda Kay Sabala, Director of Graduate Admissions, 316-942-4291 Ext. 2230, Fax: 316-942-4483, E-mail: sabalal@newmanu.edu.

Northeastern University, Bouvé College of Health Sciences Graduate School, School of Nursing, Program in Nurse Anesthesia, Boston, MA 02115-5096. Offers MS. *Accreditation:* AACN; AANA/CANAEP. *Students:* 46 full-time (32 women). 56 applicants, 46% accepted. In 2006, 12 degrees awarded. *Degree requirements:* For master's, thesis or alternative. *Entrance requirements:* For master's, GRE General Test, minimum GPA of 3.0, previous course work in statistics, 1-2 years of nursing experience, RN license, ICU experience. Additional exam requirements/recommendations for international students: Required—TOEFL. *Application deadline:* For fall admission, 10/1 for domestic students. Application fee: $50. *Financial support:* Research assistantships, teaching assistantships, tuition waivers (partial) available. Financial award application deadline: 7/1; financial award applicants required to submit FAFSA. *Unit head:* Dr. Steve Alves, Director, 617-373-7962. *Application contact:* Margaret Schnabel, Director of Graduate Admissions, 617-373-2708, Fax: 617-373-4704, E-mail: bouvegrad@neu.edu.

Oakland University, Graduate Study and Lifelong Learning, School of Nursing, Program in Nurse Anesthetist, Rochester, MI 48309-4401. Offers MSN, Certificate. Programs offered jointly with Beaumont Hospital Corporation. *Accreditation:* AACN; AANA/CANAEP. *Students:* 47 full-time (37 women), 28 part-time (17 women); includes 9 minority (3 African Americans, 4 Asian Americans or Pacific Islanders, 2 Hispanic Americans), 1 international. Average age 33. 108 applicants, 33% accepted, 24 enrolled. In 2006, 19 degrees awarded. *Degree requirements:* For master's, thesis (for some programs). *Entrance requirements:* For master's, GRE General Test. Additional exam requirements/recommendations for international students: Required—TOEFL (minimum score 550 paper-based; 213 computer-based). *Application deadline:* For fall admission, 10/15 for domestic and international students. Application fee: $35. Electronic applications accepted. *Expenses: Contact institution. Financial support:* Federal Work-Study, institutionally sponsored loans, and tuition waivers (full) available. Financial award application deadline: 3/1; financial award applicants required to submit FAFSA. *Unit head:* Mary Bray, Graduate Program Coordinator, 248-370-4482.

Rush University, College of Nursing, Department of Adult Health Nursing, Chicago, IL 60612-3832. Offers acute care nurse practitioner (MSN, Post-Master's Certificate); adult health nursing (DN Sc, DNP); adult nurse practitioner (MSN, Post-Master's Certificate); adult/gerontological nurse practitioner (MSN); anesthesia nurse practitioner (MSN, Post-Master's Certificate); critical care clinical specialist (MSN); gerontological nurse practitioner (MSN, Post-Master's Certificate); medical surgical clinical specialist (MSN). *Accreditation:* AACN; AANA/CANAEP (one or more programs are accredited). Part-time programs available. Postbaccalaureate distance learning degree programs offered (minimal on-campus study). *Faculty:* 33. *Students:* 29 full-time, 123 part-time; includes 22 minority (7 African Americans, 9 Asian Americans or Pacific Islanders, 6 Hispanic Americans). Average age 35. 101 applicants, 80% accepted, 76 enrolled. In 2006, 47 master's, 6 doctorates awarded. Terminal master's awarded for partial completion of doctoral program. *Degree requirements:* For master's, capstone project; for doctorate, thesis/dissertation, DNP leadership project. *Entrance requirements:* For master's, GRE General Test (waived if nursing GPA is above 3.0 or cumulative GPA is above 3.25), interview; for doctorate, GRE General Test, interview, course work in statistics (DN Sc). Additional exam requirements/recommendations for international students: Required—TOEFL, TWE. *Application deadline:* For fall admission, 7/1 for domestic students; for winter admission, 11/1 for domestic students; for spring admission, 1/15 for domestic students. Applications are processed on a rolling basis. Application fee: $40. Electronic applications accepted. *Financial support:* In 2006–07, 19 students received support; teaching assistantships with tuition reimbursements available, Federal Work-Study, institutionally sponsored loans, scholarships/grants, and traineeships available. Support available to part-time students. Financial award application deadline: 5/1; financial award applicants required to submit FAFSA. *Faculty research:* Complementary/alternative medicine, critical care outcomes, cardiac risk reduction, Alzheimer's Disease, telehealth monitoring. *Unit head:* Dr. Margaret Faut-Callahan, Chairperson, 312-942-7117. *Application contact:* Hicela Castruita Woods, Director, College Admissions Services, 312-942-7100, Fax: 312-942-2219, E-mail: hicela_castruita@rush.edu.

Saint Joseph's University, College of Arts and Sciences, Department of Health Services, Philadelphia, PA 19131-1395. Offers health administration (MS); health education (MS); nurse anesthesia (MS). Evening/weekend programs available. *Faculty:* 5 full-time (2 women), 12 part-time/adjunct (6 women). *Students:* 45 full-time (27 women), 147 part-time (107 women); includes 51 minority (45 African Americans, 3 Asian Americans or Pacific Islanders, 3 Hispanic Americans), 9 international. Average age 34. In 2006, 62 degrees awarded. *Entrance requirements:* For master's, 2 letters of recommendation. Additional exam requirements/recommendations for international students: Required—TOEFL. *Application deadline:* For fall admission, 7/15 for domestic students. Application fee: $35. *Financial support:* Fellowships, career-related internships or fieldwork available. *Unit head:* Dr. John Newhouse, Chair, 610-660-1578.

Saint Mary's University of Minnesota, School of Graduate and Professional Programs, Nurse Anesthesia Program, Minneapolis, MN 55404. Offers MS. Offered jointly with the Minneapolis School of Anesthesia. *Accreditation:* AANA/CANAEP. *Unit head:* Merri Moody, Director, 612-728-5133, Fax: 612-728-5121, E-mail: mmoody@smumn.edu.

Samuel Merritt College, School of Nursing, Oakland, CA 94609-3108. Offers case management (MSN); family nurse practitioner (MSN, Certificate); nurse anesthetist (MSN, Certificate); nursing (MSN). *Accreditation:* AACN; AANA/CANAEP (one or more programs are accredited). Part-time and evening/weekend programs available. *Degree requirements:* For master's, thesis or alternative. *Entrance requirements:* For master's, minimum GPA of 2.5 in science, 3.0 overall; previous course work in statistics; current RN license. Additional exam requirements/recommendations for international students: Required—TOEFL. *Faculty research:* Gerontology, community health, maternal-child health, sexually transmitted diseases, substance abuse, oncology.

Southern Illinois University Edwardsville, Graduate Studies and Research, School of Nursing, Program in Nurse Anesthesia, Edwardsville, IL 62026-0001. Offers MS, Post-Master's Certificate. *Accreditation:* AANA/CANAEP. *Students:* 48 full-time (30 women), 11 part-time (9 women); includes 7 minority (3 African Americans, 3 Asian Americans or Pacific Islanders, 1 Hispanic American). Average age 33. 43 applicants, 19% accepted. In 2006, 13 master's, 2 other advanced degrees awarded. *Degree requirements:* For master's, thesis or alternative, final exam, comprehensive exam, registration. *Entrance requirements:* For master's, appropriate bachelor's degree, RN license. Additional exam requirements/recommendations for international students: Required—TOEFL. *Application deadline:* For fall admission, 8/1 for domestic and international students. Application fee: $30. Electronic applications accepted. *Financial support:* Fellowships with full tuition reimbursements, research assistantships, teaching assistantships, career-related internships or fieldwork, Federal Work-Study, scholarships/grants, and unspecified assistantships available. Support available to part-time students. Financial award application deadline: 3/1; financial award applicants required to submit FAFSA. *Unit head:* Dr. Jacquelyn Clement, Director, 618-650-3923, E-mail: jclemen@siue.edu.

State University of New York Downstate Medical Center, College of Nursing, Graduate Program in Nursing, Program in Nurse Anesthesia, Brooklyn, NY 11203-2098. Offers MS. *Accreditation:* AACN; AANA/CANAEP. *Degree requirements:* For master's, thesis optional. *Entrance requirements:* For master's, GRE, BSN; minimum GPA of 3.0; previous undergraduate course work in statistics, health assessment, and nursing research; RN license. *Expenses:* Tuition, state resident: full-time $6,900; part-time $288 per credit. Tuition, nonresident: full-time $10,920; part-time $455 per credit. Required fees: $100; $20 per credit. $50 per semester. Tuition and fees vary according to course load.

Texas Christian University, Harris College of Nursing and Health Sciences, School of Nurse Anesthesia, Fort Worth, TX 76129-0002. Offers MSNA. *Expenses:* Tuition: Part-time $800 per credit hour. *Unit head:* Dr. Kay K. Sanders, Director, 817-257-7887.

Texas Wesleyan University, Graduate Programs, Programs in Nurse Anesthesia, Fort Worth, TX 76105-1536. Offers MHS, MSNA. *Accreditation:* AANA/CANAEP (one or more programs are accredited). *Faculty:* 4 full-time (1 woman), 7 part-time/adjunct (2 women). *Students:* 377 full-time (191 women); includes 55 minority (15 African Americans, 2 American Indian/Alaska Native, 21 Asian Americans or Pacific Islanders, 17 Hispanic Americans). Average age 33. *Entrance requirements:* For master's, GRE General Test, minimum GPA of 3.0 in final 60 hours of undergraduate course work, Texas RN license with acute care experience, current cardiac life support certification. *Application deadline:* For fall admission, 2/1 for domestic students. Applications are processed on a rolling basis. Application fee: $30 ($50 for international students). *Expenses: Contact institution.* Tuition and fees vary according to program. *Financial support:* Federal Work-Study, institutionally sponsored loans, scholarships/grants, and tuition waivers (full and partial) available. Support available to part-time students. Financial award application deadline: 3/15; financial award applicants required to submit FAFSA. *Unit head:* John Martin, Director, 817-531-4406, Fax: 817-531-6508.

Uniformed Services University of the Health Sciences, Graduate School of Nursing, Department of Nurse Anesthesia, Bethesda, MD 20814-4799. Offers MSN. Available to military officers only. *Accreditation:* AACN; AANA/CANAEP. Postbaccalaureate distance learning degree programs offered (no on-campus study). *Degree requirements:* For master's, thesis or alternative. *Entrance requirements:* For master's, GRE General Test, MAT, BSN, clinical experience, minimum GPA of 3.0, previous course work in science. Electronic applications accepted. *Faculty research:* International nurse anesthesia practice, pharmacology, neuroscience, malignant hyperthermia, pain management.

Union University, School of Nursing, Jackson, TN 38305-3697. Offers nurse anesthetist (PMC); nursing education (MSN, PMC). *Accreditation:* AACN; AANA/CANAEP. *Faculty:* 15 full-time (14 women), 3 part-time/adjunct (2 women). *Students:* 47 full-time (36 women); includes 12 minority (10 African Americans, 1 American Indian/Alaska Native, 1 Asian American or Pacific Islander). Average age 38. 12 applicants, 100% accepted, 12 enrolled. In 2006, 9 degrees awarded. *Degree requirements:* For master's, thesis or alternative, registration. *Entrance requirements:* For master's, GRE, 3 letters of reference, bachelor's degree in nursing, minimum GPA of 3.0. Additional exam requirements/recommendations for international students: Required—TOEFL (minimum score 560 paper-based; 220 computer-based). *Application deadline:* For fall admission, 8/1 priority date for domestic students, 8/1 for international students. Application fee: $25. Electronic applications accepted. *Financial support:* Traineeships available. Financial award applicants required to submit FAFSA. *Faculty research:* Children's health, occupational rehabilitation, informatics, health promotion. *Unit head:* Dr. Tim Smith, Dean, 731-661-5200, Fax: 731-661-5504. *Application contact:* Elsie Cressman, Coordinator of MSN Programs, 731-661-5120, Fax: 731-661-5504, E-mail: ecressman@uu.edu.

Université de Montréal, Faculty of Medicine and Faculty of Graduate Studies, Graduate Programs in Medicine, Program in Specialized Studies, Montréal, QC H3C 3J7, Canada. Offers anesthesia (DESS); diagnostic radiology (DESS); family medicine (DESS); medical biochemistry (DESS); medical genetics (DESS); medicine (DESS); microbiology and infectious diseases (DESS); nuclear medicine (DESS); obstetrics and gynecology (DESS); ophthalmology (DESS); pediatrics (DESS); psychiatry (DESS); radiology-oncology (DESS); surgery (DESS). *Faculty:* 159 full-time (37 women), 345 part-time/adjunct (102 women). *Entrance requirements:* For degree, proficiency in French. *Application deadline:* For fall admission, 2/1 priority date for domestic students; for winter admission, 11/1 priority date for domestic students; for spring admission, 2/1 priority date for domestic students. Application fee: $30. Electronic applications accepted. *Unit head:* Dr. Pierre Boyle, Vice Dean of Studies, 514-343-6300, Fax: 514-343-5751, E-mail: pierre.boyle@umontreal.ca.

University at Buffalo, the State University of New York, Graduate School, School of Nursing, Buffalo, NY 14260. Offers acute care nurse practitioner (MS, Certificate); adult health nursing (MS, Certificate); child health nursing (MS); family nurse practitioner (Certificate); family nursing (MS); geriatric nurse practitioner (MS, Certificate); maternal and women's health nurse practitioner (Certificate); maternal and women's health nursing (MS); nurse anesthetist (MS); nursing (PhD); nursing education (Certificate); pediatric nurse practitioner (Certificate); psychiatric/mental health nurse practitioner (Certificate); psychiatric/mental health nursing (MS). *Accreditation:* AACN; AANA/CANAEP (one or more programs are accredited). Part-time programs available. Postbaccalaureate distance learning degree programs offered. *Faculty:* 38 full-time (34 women), 15 part-time/adjunct (14 women). *Students:* 131 full-time (108 women), 64 part-time (61 women); includes 29 minority (11 African Americans, 9 Asian Americans or Pacific Islanders, 9 Hispanic Americans), 20 international. Average age 28. 346 applicants, 25% accepted, 51 enrolled. In 2006, 49 master's, 3 doctorates, 6 other advanced degrees awarded. Terminal master's awarded for partial completion of doctoral program. *Degree requirements:* For master's, comprehensive exams or project; for doctorate, thesis/dissertation, comprehensive exam. *Entrance requirements:* For master's, GRE General Test (if overall GPA is below 3.0), interview, minimum GPA of 3.0, RN license, 3 references; for doctorate, GRE General Test, minimum GPA of 3.25, RN license, BS or MS in nursing, 3 references, writing sample; for Certificate, interview, minimum GPA of 3.0 or GRE General Test, RN license, MS in nursing. Additional exam requirements/recommendations for international students: Required—TOEFL (minimum score 550 paper-based; 213 computer-based; 79 iBT), IELTS (minimum score 7). *Application deadline:* For fall admission, 6/1 priority date for domestic students, 3/1 priority date for international students; for spring admission, 11/1 for domestic students, 9/15 priority date for international students. Applications are processed on a rolling basis. Application fee: $50. Electronic applications accepted. *Financial support:* In 2006–07, 78 students received support, including 13 fellowships with full tuition reimbursements available (averaging $7,220 per year), 10 research assistantships with tuition reimbursements available (averaging $17,881 per year), 23 teaching assistantships with full tuition reimbursements available (averaging $11,245 per year); Federal Work-Study, scholarships/grants, traineeships, health care benefits, and unspecified assistantships also available. Financial award application deadline: 3/15; financial award applicants required to submit FAFSA. *Faculty research:* Oncology symptom management, end of life decision making, changing behaviors using the transtheoretical model, addictions, nursing workforce. Total annual research expenditures: $1.7 million. *Unit head:* Dr. Jean K. Brown, Dean, Interim, 716-829-2533, Fax: 716-829-2566, E-mail: jebrown@buffalo.edu. *Application contact:* Dr. Elaine R. Cusker, Assistant Dean, 716-829-2537, Fax: 716-829-2021, E-mail: ecusker@buffalo.edu.

The University of Alabama at Birmingham, School of Health Professions, Department of Critical Care, Program in Nurse Anesthesia, Birmingham, AL 35294. Offers MNA. *Accreditation:* AACN; AANA/CANAEP. *Students:* 206 full-time (140 women); includes 23 minority (16 African Americans, 7 Asian Americans or Pacific Islanders). 59 applicants, 59% accepted. In 2006, 67 degrees awarded. *Entrance requirements:* For master's, GRE, MAT, minimum GPA of 3.0, RN license, 1 year of critical care experience. *Application deadline:* For fall admission, 11/20 priority date for domestic students. Application fee: $35 ($60 for international students). Electronic applications accepted. *Expenses:* Tuition, state resident: part-time $170 per credit hour. Tuition, nonresident: part-time $425 per credit hour. Required fees: $15 per credit hour. $122 per term. Tuition and fees vary according to program. *Financial support:* In 2006–07, 66 students received support. *Faculty research:* Technology in health care, perioperative temperature control, outcome research. *Unit head:* Joe Rue Williams, Director, 205-934-3209, Fax: 205-934-3212, E-mail: williams@uab.edu.

University of Cincinnati, Graduate School, College of Nursing, Cincinnati, OH 45221-0038. Offers clinical nurse specialist (MSN), including adult health, community health, neonatal, nursing administration, occupational health, pediatric health, psychiatric nursing, women's health; nurse anesthesia (MSN); nurse midwifery (MSN); nurse practitioner (MSN), including acute care, ambulatory care, family, family/psychiatric, women's health; nursing (PhD); MBA/MSN. *Accreditation:* AACN; AANA/CANAEP (one or more programs are accredited); ACNM/DOA. Part-time programs available. Postbaccalaureate distance learning degree programs offered (no on-campus study). *Faculty:* 41 full-time (39 women), 16 part-time/adjunct (15 women). *Students:* 159 full-time (125 women), 149 part-time (145 women); includes 40 minority (22 African Americans, 1 American Indian/Alaska Native, 16 Asian Americans or Pacific Islanders, 1 Hispanic American). Average age 34. 385 applicants, 49% accepted, 132 enrolled. In 2006, 77 master's, 5 doctorates awarded. Terminal master's awarded for partial completion of doctoral program. *Median time to degree:* Of those who began their doctoral program in fall 1998, 55% received their degree in 8 years or less. *Degree requirements:* For master's, thesis or alternative, registration; for doctorate, thesis/dissertation, comprehensive exam, registration. *Entrance requirements:* For master's and doctorate, GRE General Test. Additional exam requirements/recommendations for international students: Required—TOEFL (minimum score 520 paper-based; 190 computer-based). *Application deadline:* For fall admission, 7/26 priority date for domestic and international students. Applications are processed on a rolling basis. Application fee: $40. Electronic applications accepted. *Financial support:* In 2006–07, 164 students received support, including 7 fellowships with full tuition reimbursements available (averaging $13,571 per year), research assistantships with full tuition reimbursements available (averaging $12,000 per year), 8 teaching assistantships with full tuition reimbursements available (averaging $12,000 per year); career-related internships or fieldwork, scholarships/grants, traineeships, tuition waivers (partial), and unspecified assistantships also available. Support available to part-time students. Financial award application deadline: 5/1; financial award applicants required to submit FAFSA. *Faculty research:* Substance abuse, injury and violence, symptom management. Total annual research expenditures: $1.3 million. *Unit head:* Dr. Andrea R. Lindell, Dean, 513-558-5330, Fax: 513-558-9030, E-mail: andrea.lindell@uc.edu. *Application contact:* Loren Carter, Program Coordinator, 513-558-5072, Fax: 513-558-7523, E-mail: loren.carter@uc.edu.

University of Detroit Mercy, College of Health Professions, Program in Nurse Anesthesiology, Detroit, MI 48221. Offers MS. *Accreditation:* AANA/CANAEP. *Entrance requirements:* For master's, GRE General Test, minimum GPA of 3.0. Expenses: Contact institution.

University of Kansas, Graduate Studies Medical Center, School of Allied Health, Department of Nurse Anesthesia Education, Lawrence, KS 66045. Offers nurse anesthesia (MS). *Accreditation:* AANA/CANAEP. *Faculty:* 29 full-time (12 women). *Students:* 72 full-time (38 women), 1 (woman) part-time; includes 6 minority (2 African Americans, 3 Asian Americans or Pacific Islanders, 1 Hispanic American). Average age 31. 98 applicants, 30% accepted, 22 enrolled. In 2006, 27 degrees awarded. *Median time to degree:* Master's–2.56 years full-time. *Degree requirements:* For master's, thesis or alternative, comprehensive exam. *Entrance requirements:* For master's, bachelor's degree in related field, RN license, 2 years of experience as an RN including 1 year of experience in ICU. Additional exam requirements/recommendations for international students: Required—TOEFL. *Application deadline:* For fall admission, 7/1 for domestic students, 9/15 for international students. Application fee: $60. *Expenses:* Tuition, area resident: Part-time $227 per credit. Tuition, state resident: part-time $543 per credit. Tuition and fees vary according to course load, campus/location, program and reciprocity agreements. *Financial support:* Traineeships available. *Faculty research:* Use of technology in education, stimulation training, diaphragm fatigue, delirium and pain assessment in ICU patients, RN satisfaction. *Unit head:* Dr. Carol Elliott, Chair, 913-588-6612, Fax: 913-588-3334, E-mail: celliott@kumc.edu.

University of Medicine and Dentistry of New Jersey, School of Nursing, Newark, NJ 07107-1709. Offers adult health (MSN); adult occupational health (MSN); advanced practice nursing (MSN, Post Master's Certificate); family nurse practitioner (MSN); nurse anesthesia (MSN); nursing (MSN); nursing education (MSN, Post Master's Certificate); nursing informatics (MSN); urban health (PhD); women's health practitioner (MSN). *Accreditation:* AANA/CANAEP; NLN (one or more programs are accredited). Part-time programs available. *Students:* 93 full-time (82 women), 307 part-time (274 women); includes 195 minority (92 African Americans, 1 American Indian/Alaska Native, 69 Asian Americans or Pacific Islanders, 33 Hispanic Americans), 1 international. Average age 39. 472 applicants, 63% accepted, 203 enrolled. In 2006, 57 master's, 6 other advanced degrees awarded. *Entrance requirements:* For master's, GRE, RN license; basic life support, statistics, and health assessment experience. Additional exam requirements/recommendations for international students: Required—TOEFL. *Application deadline:* Applications are processed on a rolling basis. Application fee: $50. Electronic applications accepted. *Expenses: Contact institution. Financial support:* Teaching assistantships, institutionally sponsored loans and scholarships/grants available. Support available to part-time students. Financial award application deadline: 5/1. *Faculty research:* HIV/AIDS, diabetes education, learned helplessness, nursing science, psychoeducation. *Unit head:* Dr. Susan Salmond, Interim Dean, 973-972-9239, Fax: 973-972-3225, E-mail: salmonsu@umdnj.edu.

University of Miami, Graduate School, School of Nursing and Health Studies, Coral Gables, FL 33124. Offers acute care (MSN), including acute care nurse practitioner, nurse anesthesia; community health (MSN); nursing (PhD); primary care (MSN), including adult nurse practitioner, family nurse practitioner, nurse midwifery, psychiatric/mental health nursing, women's health practitioner. *Accreditation:* AACN; AANA/CANAEP; ACNM/DOA (one or more programs are accredited). Part-time programs available. *Faculty:* 10 full-time (8 women), 1 (woman) part-time/adjunct. *Students:* 33 full-time (24 women), 27 part-time (24 women); includes 28 minority (7 African Americans, 5 Asian Americans or Pacific Islanders, 16 Hispanic Americans), 2 international. Average age 34. 108 applicants, 48% accepted, 30 enrolled. In 2006, 15 master's, 1 doctorate awarded. *Degree requirements:* For master's, thesis optional; for doctorate, thesis/dissertation. *Entrance requirements:* For master's, GRE General Test, BSN, minimum GPA of 3.0, Florida RN license; for doctorate, GRE General Test, BSN or MSN, minimum GPA of 3.0. Additional exam requirements/recommendations for international students: Required—TOEFL (minimum score 550 paper-based; 213 computer-based). *Application deadline:* For fall admission, 4/30 priority date for domestic students; for spring admission, 11/1 priority date for domestic students. Applications are processed on a rolling basis. Application fee: $50. Electronic applications accepted. *Financial support:* In 2006–07, 12 students received support, including 3 research assistantships with tuition reimbursements available (averaging $9,000 per year), 5 teaching assistantships with tuition reimbursements available (averaging $9,000 per year); fellowships, Federal Work-Study, institutionally sponsored loans, scholarships/grants, and unspecified assistantships also available. Support available to part-time students. Financial award application deadline: 3/1; financial award applicants required to submit FAFSA. *Faculty research:* Transcultural nursing, exercise and depression in Alzheimer's disease, infectious diseases/HIV–AIDS, postpartum depression, outcomes assessment. Total annual research expenditures: $31.9 million. *Unit head:* Dr. Nilda Peragallo, Dean, 305-284-2107, Fax: 305-667-3787, E-mail: nperagallo@miami.edu. *Application contact:* Anne Stabb, Graduate Advisor, 305-284-2533, Fax: 305-284-4827, E-mail: astabb@miami.edu.

University of Michigan–Flint, School of Health Professions and Studies, Program in Anesthesia, Flint, MI 48502-1950. Offers MS. *Accreditation:* AACN; AANA/CANAEP. Part-time programs available. *Faculty:* 4 full-time (1 woman), 2 part-time/adjunct (0 women). *Students:* 34 full-time (28 women), 2 part-time (both women); includes 1 minority (Asian American or Pacific Islander) Average age 31. 76 applicants, 24% accepted, 18 enrolled. In 2006, 21 degrees awarded. *Degree requirements:* For master's, thesis. *Entrance requirements:* For master's, GRE, BSN or BS in science, critical care experience, RN license. Additional exam requirements/

Nurse Anesthesia

University of Michigan–Flint (continued)
recommendations for international students: Required—TOEFL (minimum score 550 paper-based; 220 computer-based), IELTS (minimum score 7). *Application deadline:* For fall admission, 8/1 priority date for domestic students, 3/1 priority date for international students; for winter admission, 11/15 priority date for domestic students, 7/1 priority date for international students; for spring admission, 3/15 priority date for domestic students, 11/1 priority date for international students. Application fee: $55. *Expenses: Contact institution.* Full-time tuition and fees vary according to degree level and program. Part-time tuition and fees vary according to course load and degree level. *Financial support:* Career-related internships or fieldwork, scholarships/grants, and traineeships available. Support available to part-time students. Financial award applicants required to submit FAFSA. *Faculty research:* CRNA expected retirement patterns, factors of importance in CENA selection of first job, lidocaine 4% in ETT cuff and reducing in coughing on emergence, orientation of spinal needle benel, length of time to discharge outpatients. *Unit head:* Dr. Lynn Lebeck, Director, 810-257-9264, Fax: 810-760-0839, E-mail: lynnlebeck@hurleymc.com. *Application contact:* Bradley T. Maki, Director of Graduate Admissions, 810-762-3171, Fax: 810-766-6789, E-mail: bmaki@umflint.edu.

University of Minnesota, Twin Cities Campus, Graduate School, School of Nursing, Program in Nurse Anesthetist, Minneapolis, MN 55455-0213. Offers MS. *Accreditation:* AANA/CANAEP. *Students:* 10 full-time (6 women). *Entrance requirements:* Additional exam requirements/recommendations for international students: Required—TOEFL (minimum score 586 paper-based; 240 computer-based). *Application deadline:* For fall admission, 8/1 for domestic and international students; for spring admission, 8/15 priority date for domestic students. Application fee: $55 ($75 for international students). *Unit head:* Dr. Kathleen Fagerlund, Coordinator, 612-624-1115, Fax: 612-624-3174, E-mail: fager003@umn.edu. *Application contact:* Information Contact, 612-624-4454, Fax: 612-624-3174, E-mail: nurseoss@umn.edu.

University of New England, College of Health Professions, Program in Nurse Anesthesia, Biddeford, ME 04005-9526. Offers MS. Offered in association with Eastern Maine Medical Center, St. Joseph Hospital, and Harlem Hospital. *Accreditation:* AANA/CANAEP. *Faculty:* 4 full-time (3 women), 8 part-time/adjunct (5 women). *Students:* 84 full-time (56 women); includes 10 minority (5 African Americans, 3 Asian Americans or Pacific Islanders, 2 Hispanic Americans). Average age 36. 59 applicants, 51% accepted, 26 enrolled. In 2006, 31 degrees awarded. *Degree requirements:* For master's, thesis or alternative, practicum. *Entrance requirements:* For master's, GRE, RN license, 1 year of acute care experience, 3 letters of reference, recent completion of organic or biochemistry course. *Application deadline:* For fall admission, 2/1 for domestic and international students. Applications are processed on a rolling basis. Application fee: $40. Electronic applications accepted. *Expenses: Contact institution. Financial support:* Application deadline: 5/1; *Faculty research:* Evaluation, faculty perceptions of student characteristics and success during clinical practicum. *Unit head:* Nina Turcato, Director, 207-283-0171 Ext. 4517, Fax: 207-282-6379, E-mail: nturcato@une.edu. *Application contact:* Peggy Warden, Assistant Dean of Graduate Admissions, 207-221-4225, Fax: 207-221-4898, E-mail: admissions@une.edu.

The University of North Carolina at Charlotte, Graduate School, College of Health and Human Services, School of Nursing, Department of Adult Health Nursing, Charlotte, NC 28223-0001. Offers nursing adult health (MSN); nursing-anesthesia (MSN). *Accreditation:* AACN. *Faculty:* 9 full-time (8 women), 4 part-time/adjunct (all women). *Students:* 39 full-time (30 women), 49 part-time (40 women); includes 4 minority (1 African American, 1 Asian American or Pacific Islander, 2 Hispanic Americans). Average age 32. 62 applicants, 39% accepted, 22 enrolled. In 2006, 28 degrees awarded. *Degree requirements:* For master's, thesis or project. *Entrance requirements:* For master's, GRE General Test (nursing, anesthesia), GRE General Test or MAT (nursing, adult health), minimum undergraduate GPA of 3.0 in major. Additional exam requirements/recommendations for international students: Required—TOEFL (minimum score 557 paper-based; 220 computer-based). *Application deadline:* For fall admission, 7/1 for domestic students, 5/1 for international students; for spring admission, 11/1 for domestic students, 10/1 for international students. Applications are processed on a rolling basis. Application fee: $55. Electronic applications accepted. *Expenses:* Tuition, state resident: full-time $2,719; part-time $170 per credit. Tuition, nonresident: full-time $12,926; part-time $808 per credit. Required fees: $1,555. *Financial support:* In 2006–07, 1 research assistantship (averaging $1,204 per year), 1 teaching assistantship (averaging $4,032 per year) were awarded; fellowships, career-related internships or fieldwork, Federal Work-Study, institutionally sponsored loans, scholarships/grants, traineeships, and unspecified assistantships also available. Support available to part-time students. Financial award application deadline: 4/1; financial award applicants required to submit FAFSA. *Faculty research:* Health disparities, symptom management and chronic illness, self care chronic illness, health promotion. *Unit head:* Dr. Jacqueline A. Dienemann, Chair, 704-687-4652, Fax: 704-687-3180, E-mail: jadienem@email.uncc.edu. *Application contact:* Kathy B. Giddings, Director of Graduate Admissions, 704-687-3366, Fax: 704-687-3279, E-mail: gradadm@email.uncc.edu.

The University of North Carolina at Greensboro, Graduate School, School of Nursing, Greensboro, NC 27412-5001. Offers adult clinical nurse specialist (MSN, PMC); adult/gerontological nurse practitioner (MSN, PMC); nurse anesthesia (MSN, PMC); nursing (PhD); nursing administration (MSN); nursing education (MSN); MSN/MBA. *Accreditation:* AACN; AANA/CANAEP; NLN. *Faculty:* 24 full-time (23 women), 27 part-time/adjunct (22 women). *Students:* 231 full-time (197 women), 98 part-time (83 women); includes 56 minority (41 African Americans, 3 American Indian/Alaska Native, 9 Asian Americans or Pacific Islanders, 3 Hispanic Americans). 206 applicants, 59% accepted. *Degree requirements:* For master's, thesis or alternative. *Entrance requirements:* For master's, GRE General Test or MAT, BSN, clinical experience, liability insurance, RN license; for PMC, liability insurance, MSN, RN license. Additional exam requirements/recommendations for international students: Required—TOEFL. Application fee: $45. Electronic applications accepted. *Expenses:* Tuition, state resident: full-time $2,692. Tuition, nonresident: full-time $13,742. *Financial support:* Research assistantships with full tuition reimbursements, career-related internships or fieldwork, Federal Work-Study, scholarships/grants, and traineeships available. Support available to part-time students. *Unit head:* Dr. Lynne Pearcey, Dean, 336-334-5177, Fax: 336-334-3628, E-mail: l_pearce@uncg.edu. *Application contact:* Michelle Harkleroad, Director of Graduate Admissions, 336-334-4884, Fax: 336-334-4424, E-mail: mbharkle@uncg.edu.

University of Pennsylvania, School of Nursing, Nurse Anesthetist Program, Philadelphia, PA 19104. Offers MSN.

University of Pittsburgh, School of Nursing, Program in Anesthesia Nursing, Pittsburgh, PA 15260. Offers MSN. *Accreditation:* AACN; AANA/CANAEP. *Students:* 123 full-time (88 women), 17 part-time (15 women); includes 10 minority (5 African Americans, 5 Asian Americans or Pacific Islanders). Average age 32. 124 applicants, 24% accepted, 30 enrolled. In 2006, 44 degrees awarded. *Degree requirements:* For master's, thesis optional. *Entrance requirements:* For master's, GRE General Test, BSN, RN license, 1-3 years nursing experience, letters of recommendation, resumé, course work in statistics. Additional exam requirements/recommendations for international students: Required—TOEFL (minimum score 550 paper-based; 213 computer-based; 80 iBT). *Application deadline:* For fall admission, 1/2 for domestic students. Application fee: $50. Electronic applications accepted. *Unit head:* John O'Donnell, Director, 412-624-4860, Fax: 412-624-2401. *Application contact:* Laurie Lapsley, Administrator of Graduate Student Services, 412-624-9670, Fax: 412-624-2409, E-mail: lapsleyl@pitt.edu.

University of Puerto Rico, Medical Sciences Campus, School of Nursing, San Juan, PR 00936-5067. Offers anesthesia (MSN); clinical specialist (MSN); family nurse practitioner (MSN); nurse administrator (MSN); nursing education (MSN). *Accreditation:* AACN; AANA/CANAEP. Part-time and evening/weekend programs available. *Faculty:* 12 full-time (11 women), 3 part-time/adjunct (2 women). *Students:* 115 full-time (all women), 13 part-time (9 women); includes 123 minority (all Hispanic Americans), 3 international. 70 applicants, 71% accepted. In 2006, 40 degrees awarded. *Degree requirements:* For master's, one foreign language. *Entrance requirements:* For master's, GRE or EXADEP, interview, Puerto Rico RN license or professional license for international students, general and specific point average, article analysis. *Application deadline:* For spring admission, 4/30 priority date for domestic and international students. Applications are processed on a rolling basis. Application fee: $33. Electronic applications accepted. *Financial support:* In 2006–07, research assistantships with full tuition reimbursements (averaging $28,175 per year), teaching assistantships with full tuition reimbursements (averaging $48,965 per year) were awarded; Federal Work-Study, traineeships, tuition waivers (full), and unspecified assistantships also available. Financial award application deadline: 6/30. *Faculty research:* HIV, health disparities, teen violence, women and violence, neurological disorders. *Unit head:* Dr. Suane E. Sánchez, Dean, 787-758-2525 Ext. 2100, Fax: 787-281-0721, E-mail: sesanchez@rcm.upr.edu. *Application contact:* Dr. Angelica Y. Matos, Director Graduate Department, 787-758-2525, Fax: 787-281-0721.

The University of Scranton, Graduate School, Department of Nursing, Scranton, PA 18510. Offers adult health nursing (MSN); family nurse practitioner (MSN, PMC); nurse anesthesia (MSN, PMC). Applicants accepted in odd-numbered years only. *Accreditation:* AACN; AANA/CANAEP. Part-time and evening/weekend programs available. *Faculty:* 13 full-time (all women), 2 part-time/adjunct (both women). *Students:* 44 full-time (29 women), 30 part-time (27 women); includes 5 minority (1 African American, 2 Asian Americans or Pacific Islanders, 2 Hispanic Americans). Average age 36. 63 applicants, 68% accepted. In 2006, 19 degrees awarded. *Degree requirements:* For master's, thesis (for some programs), capstone experience. *Entrance requirements:* For master's, BSN, minimum GPA of 3.0, Pennsylvania RN license. Additional exam requirements/recommendations for international students: Required—TOEFL (minimum score 500 paper-based; 173 computer-based), IELTS (minimum score 6). *Application deadline:* For fall admission, 9/1 for domestic students. Applications are processed on a rolling basis. Application fee: $50. *Expenses:* Tuition: Part-time $684 per credit. Required fees: $25 per term. *Financial support:* In 2006–07, 7 teaching assistantships with full and partial tuition reimbursements (averaging $4,085 per year) were awarded; career-related internships or fieldwork, Federal Work-Study, and unspecified assistantships also available. Support available to part-time students. Financial award application deadline: 3/1. *Faculty research:* Home care, doctoral education, health care of women and children, pain, health promotion and adolescence. *Unit head:* Dr. Patricia Harrington, Chair, 570-941-7673, Fax: 570-941-4201, E-mail: harringtonp1@scranton.edu. *Application contact:* Dr. Mary Jane Hanson, Director, 570-941-4060, Fax: 570-941-4201, E-mail: hansonm2@scranton.edu.

University of South Carolina, School of Medicine and The Graduate School, Graduate Programs in Medicine, Program in Nurse Anesthesia, Columbia, SC 29208. Offers MNA. *Accreditation:* AACN; AANA/CANAEP. *Degree requirements:* For master's, practicum. *Entrance requirements:* For master's, GRE, 1 year of critical care experience, RN license. Electronic applications accepted. Expenses: Contact institution. *Faculty research:* Neuroscience, cardiovascular, hormones.

The University of Tennessee at Chattanooga, Graduate School, College of Health, Education and Professional Studies, School of Nursing, Chattanooga, TN 37403-2598. Offers administration (MSN); adult health (MSN); education (MSN); family nurse practitioner (MSN); nurse anesthesia (MSN). *Accreditation:* AACN; AANA/CANAEP. *Faculty:* 13 full-time (all women). *Students:* 40 full-time (32 women), 47 part-time (41 women); includes 9 minority (1 African American, 2 American Indian/Alaska Native, 4 Asian Americans or Pacific Islanders, 2 Hispanic Americans). Average age 34. 14 applicants, 71% accepted, 2 enrolled. In 2006, 29 degrees awarded. *Degree requirements:* For master's, qualifying exams. *Entrance requirements:* For master's, GRE General Test, MAT, BSN, minimum GPA of 3.0, eligibility for Tennessee RN license. *Application deadline:* For fall admission, 8/1 priority date for domestic students; for spring admission, 12/1 priority date for domestic students. Applications are processed on a rolling basis. Application fee: $30. *Expenses:* Tuition, state resident: full-time $5,434; part-time $339 per hour. Tuition, nonresident: full-time $14,830; part-time $861 per hour. Required fees: $940; $178 per hour. *Financial support:* Application deadline: 4/1; *Faculty research:* Diabetes in women; health care for elderly; alternative medicine; hypertension; nurse anesthesia. Total annual research expenditures: $357,538. *Unit head:* Dr. Kay R. Lindgren, Head, 423-425-4646, Fax: 423-425-4668, E-mail: kay-lindgren@utc.edu. *Application contact:* Dr. Deborah E. Arfken, Dean of Graduate Studies, 423-425-4666, Fax: 423-425-5223, E-mail: deborah-arfken@utc.edu.

University of Wisconsin–La Crosse, Office of University Graduate Studies, College of Science and Health, Department of Biology, La Crosse, WI 54601-3742. Offers aquatic sciences (MS); biology (MS); cellular and molecular biology (MS); clinical microbiology (MS); microbiology (MS); nurse anesthesia (MS); physiology (MS). *Accreditation:* AANA/CANAEP. Part-time programs available. *Faculty:* 17 full-time (5 women), 1 part-time/adjunct (0 women). *Students:* 18 full-time (11 women), 52 part-time (23 women); includes 4 minority (2 American Indian/Alaska Native, 2 Asian Americans or Pacific Islanders), 3 international. Average age 27. 60 applicants, 40% accepted, 16 enrolled. In 2006, 13 degrees awarded. *Degree requirements:* For master's, thesis, comprehensive exam, registration. *Entrance requirements:* For master's, GRE General Test, minimum GPA of 2.85. Additional exam requirements/recommendations for international students: Required—TOEFL (minimum score 550 paper-based; 213 computer-based). *Application deadline:* For fall admission, 3/1 priority date for domestic students. Applications are processed on a rolling basis. Application fee: $45. Electronic applications accepted. *Financial support:* In 2006–07, 22 research assistantships with partial tuition reimbursements (averaging $49,881 per year) were awarded; career-related internships or fieldwork, Federal Work-Study, health care benefits, unspecified assistantships, and grant-funded positions also available. Support available to part-time students. Financial award application deadline: 3/15; financial award applicants required to submit FAFSA. *Faculty research:* Cell and molecular biology, physiology, environmental sciences, mycology, biomedical general. Total annual research expenditures: $700,000. *Unit head:* Dr. Tom Volk, Program Director, 608-785-6972, Fax: 608-785-6959, E-mail: volk.thom@uwlax.edu. *Application contact:* Kathryn Kiefer, Associate Director of Admissions, 608-785-8939, E-mail: admissions@uwlax.edu.

Villanova University, College of Nursing, Villanova, PA 19085-1690. Offers adult nurse practitioner (MSN, Post Master's Certificate); clinical case management (MSN, Post Master's Certificate); geriatric nurse practitioner (MSN, Post Master's Certificate); health care administration (MSN); nurse anesthetist (MSN, Post Master's Certificate); nursing (PhD); nursing education (MSN, Post Master's Certificate); pediatric nurse practitioner (MSN, Post Master's Certificate). *Accreditation:* AACN; AANA/CANAEP; NLN. Part-time programs available. Postbaccalaureate distance learning degree programs offered (minimal on-campus study). *Faculty:* 14 full-time (all women), 2 part-time/adjunct (both women). *Students:* 41 full-time (27 women), 164 part-time (128 women); includes 17 minority (8 African Americans, 1 American Indian/Alaska Native, 8 Asian Americans or Pacific Islanders), 6 international. Average age 31. 137 applicants, 50% accepted, 48 enrolled. In 2006, 47 degrees awarded. *Median time to degree:* Master's–2 years full-time, 5 years part-time. *Degree requirements:* For master's, independent study project; for doctorate, thesis/dissertation, comprehensive exam. *Entrance requirements:* For master's, GRE or MAT, BSN, 1 year of recent nursing experience, physical assessment, course work in statistics; for doctorate, GRE. Additional exam requirements/recommendations for international students: Required—TOEFL. *Application deadline:* For fall admission, 7/1 priority date for domestic students, 7/1 for international students; for spring admission, 12/1 priority date for domestic students, 12/1 for international students. Applications are processed on a rolling basis. Application fee: $50. *Expenses: Contact institution. Financial support:* In 2006–07, 50 students received support, including 4 teaching assistantships with full tuition reimbursements available (averaging $12,165 per year); institutionally sponsored loans, scholarships/grants, traineeships, and tuition waivers (full) also available. Financial award application deadline: 3/1; financial award applicants required to submit FAFSA. *Faculty research:* Genetics, ethics, cognitive development of students, women with disabilities, nursing leadership. *Unit head:* Dr. Marguerite K. Schlag, Assistant Dean and Director, Graduate Program, 610-519-4907, Fax: 610-519-7650, E-mail: marguerite.schlag@villanova.edu.

Virginia Commonwealth University, Graduate School, School of Allied Health Professions, Department of Health Administration, Doctoral Program in Health Related Sciences, Richmond,

VA 23284-9005. Offers clinical laboratory sciences (PhD); gerontology (PhD); health administration (PhD); nurse anesthesia (PhD); occupational therapy (PhD); physical therapy (PhD); radiation sciences (PhD); rehabilitation leadership (PhD). *Faculty:* 2 full-time (1 woman). *Students:* 4 full-time (all women), 13 part-time (7 women); includes 7 minority (1 African American, 6 Asian Americans or Pacific Islanders), 3 international. In 2006, 2 degrees awarded. *Unit head:* Monica L. White, Director of Student Services, 804-828-3273, Fax: 804-828-8656, E-mail: mlwhite1@vcu.edu.

See Close-Up on page 1745.

Virginia Commonwealth University, Graduate School, School of Allied Health Professions, Department of Nurse Anesthesia, Richmond, VA 23284-9005. Offers MSNA. *Accreditation:* AANA/CANAEP. *Faculty:* 7 full-time (3 women). *Students:* 86 full-time (60 women); includes 9 minority (3 African Americans, 5 Asian Americans or Pacific Islanders, 1 Hispanic American). 106 applicants, 39% accepted, 35 enrolled. In 2006, 23 degrees awarded. *Degree requirements:* For master's, thesis. *Entrance requirements:* For master's, GRE General Test, 1 year experience in acute critical care nursing, BSN, current state RPN license. *Application deadline:* For fall admission, 2/1 priority date for domestic students. Application fee: $50. *Faculty research:* Obstetrical anesthesia, ambulatory anesthesia, regional anesthesia, practice profiles, clinical practice. *Unit head:* Dr. Michael D. Fallacaro, Chair, 804-828-6735, Fax: 804-828-0581, E-mail: mdfallac@hsc.vcu.edu.

See Close-Up on page 1981.

Wayne State University, Eugene Applebaum College of Pharmacy and Health Sciences, Department of Health Care Sciences, Program in Nursing Anesthesia, Detroit, MI 48202. Offers nurse anesthesia (MS); pediatric nurse anesthesia (Certificate). *Accreditation:* AACN; AANA/CANAEP. *Faculty:* 1 (woman) full-time, 6 part-time/adjunct (3 women). *Students:* 10 full-time (8 women), 1 (woman) part-time; includes 3 minority (2 African Americans, 1 Asian American or Pacific Islander), 1 international. Average age 34. 26 applicants, 92% accepted. In 2006, 17 degrees awarded. *Degree requirements:* For master's, thesis optional. *Entrance requirements:* For master's, GRE General Test, BSN, 1 year of ICU experience. Additional exam requirements/recommendations for international students: Required—TOEFL (minimum score 550 paper-based; 213 computer-based); Recommended—TWE (minimum score 6). *Application deadline:* For fall admission, 6/1 for international students; for winter admission, 10/1 for international students; for spring admission, 2/1 for international students. Applications are processed on a rolling basis. Application fee: $30 ($50 for international students). Electronic applications accepted. *Financial support:* Career-related internships or fieldwork and scholarships/grants available. Support available to part-time students. *Faculty research:* Maternal oxygen administration, re-activated epidural anesthesia, temperate monitoring modalities, sedation, anesthesia outcomes. *Unit head:* Prudentia A. Worth, Academic Director, 313-745-3610, Fax: 313-993-7729, E-mail: aa1635@wayne.edu.

Webster University, College of Arts and Sciences, Department of Biological Sciences, Program in Nurse Anesthesia, St. Louis, MO 63119-3194. Offers MS. *Accreditation:* AANA/CANAEP. Postbaccalaureate distance learning degree programs offered. *Students:* 40 full-time (27 women), 17 part-time (12 women); includes 5 minority (3 African Americans, 2 Hispanic Americans). Average age 31. In 2006, 18 degrees awarded. *Degree requirements:* For master's, thesis. *Entrance requirements:* For master's, 1 year of work-related experience, 75 hours of graduate course work, BSN, interview, minimum GPA of 3.0. *Application deadline:* For spring admission, 5/1 for domestic students. Applications are processed on a rolling basis. Application fee: $40 ($50 for international students). *Expenses:* Tuition: Full-time $8,820; part-time $490 per credit. Tuition and fees vary according to degree level, campus/location and program. *Financial support:* Applicants required to submit FAFSA. *Faculty research:* Clinical anesthesia, substance abuse education in the health professions, technology and education, clinical pharmacology. *Unit head:* Dr. Gary Clark, Director, 314-968-5916, Fax: 314-968-7194, E-mail: clarkga@webster.edu. *Application contact:* Director of Graduate and Evening Student Admissions, Fax: 314-968-7116, E-mail: gadmit@webster.edu.

Westminster College, School of Nursing and Health Sciences, Salt Lake City, UT 84105-3697. Offers family nurse practitioner (MSN); nurse anesthesia (MSNA); nursing (MSN); nursing education (MSN). *Accreditation:* AACN; AANA/CANAEP. Part-time and evening/weekend programs available. *Faculty:* 9 full-time (8 women). *Students:* 44 full-time (31 women), 13 part-time (9 women); includes 4 minority (1 African American, 2 Asian Americans or Pacific Islanders, 1 Hispanic American), 1 international. Average age 39. 57 applicants, 65% accepted, 32 enrolled. In 2006, 5 degrees awarded. *Degree requirements:* For master's, project or thesis. *Entrance requirements:* For master's, resumé, Utah RN license in good standing, minimum GPA of 3.0, 3 letters of recommendation, proof of completed BSN from accredited nursing school, proof of clear state and federal background check, drug test results, personal interview. Additional exam requirements/recommendations for international students: Required—TOEFL (minimum score 550 paper-based; 213 computer-based). *Application deadline:* For fall admission, 8/1 priority date for domestic students. Applications are processed on a rolling basis. Application fee: $40. Electronic applications accepted. *Financial support:* In 2006–07, 39 students received support. Career-related internships or fieldwork and tuition remissions available. Support available to part-time students. Financial award applicants required to submit FAFSA. *Faculty research:* Learning styles assessment, curriculum simulation, self-esteem and learning success. *Unit head:* Dr. Jean Dyer, Dean, 801-832-2168, Fax: 801-832-3110, E-mail: jdyer@westminstercollege.edu. *Application contact:* Joel Bauman, Vice President of Enrollment Services, 801-832-2200, Fax: 801-832-3101, E-mail: admission@westminstercollege.edu.

Nurse Midwifery

Bastyr University, Graduate and Professional Programs, School of Naturopathic Medicine, Kenmore, WA 98028-4966. Offers midwifery (Certificate); naturopathic medicine (ND). *Accreditation:* CNME; MEAC. *Students:* 488 full-time (400 women), 2 part-time (1 woman); includes 64 minority (15 African Americans, 32 Asian Americans or Pacific Islanders, 17 Hispanic Americans), 13 international. Average age 29. 271 applicants, 73% accepted, 120 enrolled. In 2006, 83 doctorates, 1 other advanced degree awarded. *Degree requirements:* For doctorate, comprehensive exam. *Entrance requirements:* For doctorate and Certificate, BS or BA with 1 year of course work in biology, chemistry, organic chemistry and physics. Additional exam requirements/recommendations for international students: Required—TOEFL (minimum score 550 paper-based; 213 computer-based). *Application deadline:* For fall admission, 2/1 priority date for domestic and international students. Applications are processed on a rolling basis. Application fee: $75. *Expenses:* Tuition: Full-time $18,845; part-time $325 per credit hour. Required fees: $1,365. Tuition and fees vary according to course load and degree level. *Financial support:* Career-related internships or fieldwork, Federal Work-Study, and scholarships/grants available. Support available to part-time students. Financial award application deadline: 4/15; financial award applicants required to submit FAFSA. *Unit head:* Dr. Gannady Raskin, Dean, 425-823-1300, Fax: 425-823-6222. *Application contact:* Admissions Office, 425-602-3330, Fax: 425-602-3090, E-mail: admiss@bastyr.edu.

See Close-Up on page 2201.

Boston University, School of Public Health, Maternal and Child Health Department, Boston, MA 02215. Offers maternal and child health (MPH); nurse midwifery education (Certificate). *Students:* 33 full-time (31 women), 20 part-time (19 women); includes 11 minority (3 African Americans, 6 Asian Americans or Pacific Islanders, 2 Hispanic Americans), 7 international. Average age 27. *Entrance requirements:* For master's, GRE General Test. Additional exam requirements/recommendations for international students: Required—TOEFL or IELTS. *Application deadline:* For fall admission, 2/1 for domestic students; for spring admission, 10/15 for domestic students. Applications are processed on a rolling basis. Application fee: $60. Electronic applications accepted. *Expenses:* Tuition: Full-time $33,330; part-time $1,042 per credit. Required fees: $462; $40. *Financial support:* Scholarships/grants and tuition waivers (partial) available. *Unit head:* Dr. Milton Kotelchuck, Head, 617-638-5375, E-mail: askmch@bu.edu. *Application contact:* LePhan Quan, Assistant Director of Admissions, 617-638-4640, Fax: 617-638-5299, E-mail: asksph@bu.edu.

Case Western Reserve University, Frances Payne Bolton School of Nursing, Doctor of Nursing Practice Program, Cleveland, OH 44106. Offers acute care nurse practitioner (DNP); adult nurse practitioner (DNP); family nurse practitioner (DNP); gerontological nurse practitioner (DNP); graduate entry/pre-licensure option (DNP); medical-surgical nursing (DNP); midwifery/family nursing (DNP); neonatal nurse practitioner (DNP); pediatric nurse practitioner (DNP); post-licensure option (DNP); psychiatric mental health nurse practitioner (DNP); women's health nurse practitioner (DNP). Graduate entry option allows baccalaureate-prepared college graduates from non-nursing backgrounds to earn certificate and MSN in addition to ND. *Students:* 125 full-time (109 women), 308 part-time (290 women); includes 47 minority (21 African Americans, 1 American Indian/Alaska Native, 18 Asian Americans or Pacific Islanders, 7 Hispanic Americans), 7 international. 190 applicants, 70% accepted, 80 enrolled. In 2006, 35 degrees awarded. Terminal master's awarded for partial completion of doctoral program. *Degree requirements:* For doctorate, thesis/dissertation. *Entrance requirements:* For doctorate, GRE General Test or MAT. *Application deadline:* For fall admission, 6/1 priority date for domestic students. Applications are processed on a rolling basis. Application fee: $75. *Financial support:* In 2006–07, 6 students received support, including 1 teaching assistantship; research assistantships, Federal Work-Study, institutionally sponsored loans, and tuition waivers (partial) also available. Support available to part-time students. Financial award application deadline: 6/30; financial award applicants required to submit FAFSA. *Faculty research:* Clinical nursing, acute care, gerontology, mental health, critical care. *Unit head:* Dr. Georgia Narsavage, Director, 216-368-6304, Fax: 216-368-3542, E-mail: gln2@cwru.edu. *Application contact:* Peter Taylor, Recruitment and Retention Specialist, 216-368-0349, Fax: 216-368-0124, E-mail: peter.taylor@case.edu.

Case Western Reserve University, Frances Payne Bolton School of Nursing, Master's Programs in Nursing, Program in Nurse Midwifery, Cleveland, OH 44106. Offers MSN. *Accreditation:* ACNM/DOA. *Students:* 3 full-time (all women), 9 part-time (all women). 6 applicants, 67% accepted, 1 enrolled. In 2006, 4 degrees awarded. *Degree requirements:* For master's, thesis optional. *Entrance requirements:* For master's, GRE General Test or MAT. *Application deadline:* Applications are processed on a rolling basis. Application fee: $75. *Financial support:* Fellowships, research assistantships, teaching assistantships, institutionally sponsored loans and tuition waivers (partial) available. Support available to part-time students. Financial award application deadline: 6/30. *Faculty research:* Clinical nursing, normal childbearing, descriptive studies of care, high risk pregnancy side effects of bedrest, strengthening and expanding nursing services. *Unit head:* Gretchen Mettler, Head, 216-368-0671, E-mail: ggm@case.edu. *Application contact:* Peter Taylor, Recruitment and Retention Specialist, 216-368-0349, Fax: 216-368-0124, E-mail: peter.taylor@case.edu.

Columbia University, School of Nursing, Program in Nurse Midwifery, New York, NY 10032. Offers MS. *Accreditation:* AACN; ACNM/DOA. Part-time programs available. *Faculty:* 5 full-time (3 women), 2 part-time/adjunct (both women). *Students:* 7 full-time (all women), 11 part-time (all women); includes 1 minority (African American) Average age 29. In 2006, 8 degrees awarded. *Entrance requirements:* For master's, GRE General Test, BSN, 1 year of clinical experience (preferred). *Application deadline:* For fall admission, 11/15 priority date for domestic and international students. Application fee: $65. Electronic applications accepted. *Financial support:* Teaching assistantships available. Financial award application deadline: 2/1; financial award applicants required to submit FAFSA. *Unit head:* Dr. Laura Zeidenstein, Director, 212-305-5887.

Emory University, Nell Hodgson Woodruff School of Nursing, Atlanta, GA 30322-1100. Offers adult and elder health advanced practice nursing (MSN), including acute and critical care, adult nurse practitioner, gerontology, oncology; emergency nurse practitioner (MSN); family nurse practitioner (MSN); family nurse-midwife (MSN); leadership in healthcare (MSN); nurse midwifery (MSN); nursing administration (MSN); pediatric advanced nursing practice (MSN); public health nursing (MSN); women's health nurse practitioner (MSN); MSN/MPH. *Accreditation:* AACN; ACNM/DOA (one or more programs are accredited). Part-time programs available. *Entrance requirements:* For master's, GRE General Test or MAT, minimum GPA of 3.0, BS in nursing, RN license and additional course work, 3 letters of recommendation. Additional exam requirements/recommendations for international students: Required—TOEFL (minimum score 600 paper-based; 250 computer-based). Electronic applications accepted. Expenses: Contact institution. *Faculty research:* Older adult falls and injuries, minority health issues, cardiac symptoms amd quality of life, bio-ethics and decision making, menopausal issues.

See Close-Up on page 1955.

Frontier School of Midwifery and Family Nursing, Graduate Programs, Hyden, KY 41749. Offers community-based family nurse practitioner (MSN, Post Master's Certificate); community-based nurse-midwifery education (MSN, Post Master's Certificate); community-based women[0092]s health care nurse practitioner (MSN, Post Master's Certificate). *Accreditation:* ACNM; NLN.

Illinois State University, Graduate School, Mennonite College of Nursing, Normal, IL 61790. Offers family nurse practitioner (PMC); nursing (MSN). *Accreditation:* AACN. *Faculty:* 7 full-time (all women). *Students:* 17 full-time (16 women), 21 part-time (18 women); includes 3 minority (1 African American, 2 Asian Americans or Pacific Islanders), 1 international. 11 applicants, 100% accepted. In 2006, 13 master's, 1 other advanced degree awarded. Application fee: $40. *Expenses:* Tuition, state resident: full-time $3,330; part-time $185 per credit hour. Tuition, nonresident: full-time $6,948; part-time $438 per credit hour. Required fees: $1,259; $52 per credit hour. *Financial support:* In 2006–07, 4 research assistantships (averaging $6,694 per year) were awarded. *Faculty research:* Expanding the teaching-nursing home culture in the state of Illinois, advanced education nursing traineeship program, collaborative doctoral program-caring for older adults. Total annual research expenditures: $757,962. *Unit head:* Nancy Ridenour, Dean, 309-438-7400, Fax: 309-438-2620.

Marquette University, Graduate School, College of Nursing, Milwaukee, WI 53201-1881. Offers adult nurse practitioner (Certificate); advanced practice nursing (MSN), including adult children, neonatal nurse practitioner, nurse-midwifery, older adult; gerontological nurse practitioner (Certificate); neonatal nurse practitioner (Certificate); nurse-midwifery (Certificate); nursing (PhD); pediatric nurse practitioner (Certificate). *Accreditation:* AACN. Part-time and evening/weekend programs available. *Faculty:* 29 full-time (27 women), 39 part-time/adjunct (37

Nurse Midwifery

Marquette University (continued)
women). *Students:* 104 full-time (98 women), 122 part-time (114 women); includes 18 minority (5 African Americans, 2 American Indian/Alaska Native, 4 Asian Americans or Pacific Islanders, 7 Hispanic Americans), 2 international. Average age 34. 122 applicants, 79% accepted, 73 enrolled. In 2006, 46 degrees awarded. *Degree requirements:* For master's, thesis or alternative, comprehensive exam. *Entrance requirements:* For master's, GRE General Test, BSN, Wisconsin RN license. Additional exam requirements/recommendations for international students: Required—TOEFL. Application fee: $40. *Financial support:* In 2006–07, 6 research assistantships, 1 teaching assistantship were awarded; career-related internships or fieldwork, Federal Work-Study, institutionally sponsored loans, scholarships/grants, and tuition waivers (full and partial) also available. Support available to part-time students. Financial award application deadline: 2/15. *Faculty research:* Psychosocial adjustment to chronic illness, gerontology, reminiscence, health policy: uninsured and access, hospital care delivery systems. Total annual research expenditures: $1.1 million. *Unit head:* Dr. Lea Acord, Dean, 414-288-3812, Fax: 414-288-1578. *Application contact:* Dr. Judy Miller, Director of Graduate Studies, 414-288-3810, Fax: 414-288-1578.

Medical University of South Carolina, College of Nursing, Program in Nurse Midwifery, Charleston, SC 29425-0002. Offers MSN. *Accreditation:* ACNM/DOA. Postbaccalaureate distance learning degree programs offered. *Faculty:* 4 full-time (all women). *Students:* 6 full-time (all women), 5 part-time (all women); includes 1 minority (African American) Average age 29. 5 applicants, 100% accepted, 4 enrolled. In 2006, 3 degrees awarded. *Degree requirements:* For master's, thesis optional. *Entrance requirements:* For master's, GRE General Test, BSN, course work in statistics and physical assessment, 1 year of nursing experience, nursing license, minimum GPA of 3.0. Additional exam requirements/recommendations for international students: Required—TOEFL (minimum score 600 paper-based; 250 computer-based). *Application deadline:* For fall admission, 2/1 for domestic and international students; for spring admission, 9/15 for domestic and international students. Application fee: $75. *Financial support:* Federal Work-Study, scholarships/grants, and traineeships available. Support available to part-time students. Financial award application deadline: 3/15; financial award applicants required to submit FAFSA. *Faculty research:* Breast-feeding teens, cervical cancer, prevention and follow-up. *Unit head:* Lee S. Horton, Track Coordinator, 843-792-5857, Fax: 843-792-1741, E-mail: hortonl@musc.edu. *Application contact:* Carolyn F. Page, Director, Student Services, 843-792-3844, Fax: 843-792-9258, E-mail: pagecf@musc.edu.

National College of Midwifery, Graduate Programs, Taos, NM 87571. Offers MS, PhD. *Accreditation:* MEAC. Part-time and evening/weekend programs available. Postbaccalaureate distance learning degree programs offered (no on-campus study). *Degree requirements:* For master's, thesis, publication; for doctorate, thesis/dissertation, presentation, publication. *Entrance requirements:* For master's and doctorate, midwifery license or certification. Electronic applications accepted.

New York University, College of Dentistry, College of Nursing, Programs in Advanced Practice Nursing, New York, NY 10012-1019. Offers advanced practice nursing: adult acute care (MS, Advanced Certificate); advanced practice nursing: adult primary care (MS, Advanced Certificate); advanced practice nursing: adult primary care/geriatrics (MS); advanced practice nursing: children with special needs (Advanced Certificate); advanced practice nursing: geriatrics (MS, Advanced Certificate); advanced practice nursing: holistic nursing (MS, Advanced Certificate); advanced practice nursing: home health nursing (Advanced Certificate); advanced practice nursing: mental health (MS); advanced practice nursing: mental health nursing (Advanced Certificate); advanced practice nursing: pediatrics (MS, Advanced Certificate); advanced practice nursing: pediatrics/children with special needs (MS); midwifery (MS, Advanced Certificate); nursing administration (MS, Advanced Certificate); nursing education (MS, Advanced Certificate); nursing informatics (MS, Advanced Certificate); palliative care (MS, Advanced Certificate); MS/MS. *Accreditation:* AACN; ACNM/DOA. Part-time and evening/weekend programs available. *Faculty:* 30 full-time (all women). *Students:* 10 full-time (all women), 428 part-time (395 women); includes 166 minority (73 African Americans, 72 Asian Americans or Pacific Islanders, 21 Hispanic Americans). Average age 35. 154 applicants, 93% accepted, 118 enrolled. In 2006, 100 master's, 7 Advanced Certificates awarded. *Degree requirements:* For master's, thesis (for some programs). *Entrance requirements:* For master's, BS in nursing, AS in nursing with another BS/BA degree; for Advanced Certificate, master's degree. Additional exam requirements/recommendations for international students: Required—TOEFL. *Application deadline:* For fall admission, 7/1 priority date for domestic students, 7/1 for international students; for spring admission, 12/1 for domestic and international students. Applications are processed on a rolling basis. Application fee: $65. *Expenses:* Tuition: Part-time $1,080 per unit. Required fees: $56 per unit. $329 per term. Tuition and fees vary according to program. *Financial support:* Career-related internships or fieldwork, Federal Work-Study, institutionally sponsored loans, scholarships/grants, and tuition waivers (partial) available. Support available to part-time students. Financial award application deadline: 2/1; financial award applicants required to submit FAFSA. *Faculty research:* Elderly black diabetics, families and illness, public health nursing, parent-child nursing, health policy costs. *Unit head:* Dr. Judith Haber, Associate Dean for Graduate Programs, 212-998-5300, Fax: 212-995-3143. *Application contact:* Amy Knowles, Assistant Dean for Student Affairs and Admissions, 212-998-5333, Fax: 212-995-4302, E-mail: ak96@nyu.edu.

Oregon Health & Science University, School of Nursing, Program in Nurse Midwifery, Portland, OR 97239-3098. Offers MS, Post Master's Certificate. *Accreditation:* AACN; ACNM/DOA (one or more programs are accredited). *Degree requirements:* For master's, thesis optional. *Entrance requirements:* For master's, GRE General Test, bachelor's degree in nursing, minimum undergraduate GPA of 3.0, previous course work in statistics; for Post Master's Certificate, master's degree in nursing.

Philadelphia University, School of Science and Health, Program in Midwifery, Philadelphia, PA 19144-5497. Offers midwifery (MS); nurse midwifery (Postbaccalaureate Certificate). *Accreditation:* ACNM/DOA. Part-time and evening/weekend programs available. Postbaccalaureate distance learning degree programs offered (minimal on-campus study). *Faculty:* 5 part-time/adjunct (3 women). *Students:* 22 full-time (all women), 22 part-time (all women). 36 applicants, 53% accepted, 19 enrolled. In 2006, 31 degrees awarded. *Entrance requirements:* For master's, GRE or MAT. Additional exam requirements/recommendations for international students: Required—TOEFL (minimum score 550 paper-based; 213 computer-based; 79 iBT). *Application deadline:* Applications are processed on a rolling basis. Application fee: $35. Electronic applications accepted. *Financial support:* Career-related internships or fieldwork and Federal Work-Study available. Support available to part-time students. Financial award applicants required to submit FAFSA. *Application contact:* Jack A. Klett, Director of Graduate Admissions, 215-951-2943, Fax: 215-951-2907, E-mail: gradadm@philau.edu.

Shenandoah University, School of Health Professions, Division of Nursing, Winchester, VA 22601-5195. Offers family nurse practitioner (Certificate); nurse-midwifery (Certificate); nursing (MSN); psychiatric mental health nurse practitioner (Certificate). *Accreditation:* AACN; ACNM/DOA. Part-time programs available. *Faculty:* 9 full-time (all women), 2 part-time/adjunct (both women). *Students:* 5 full-time (all women), 19 part-time (18 women). Average age 37. 40 applicants, 78% accepted, 19 enrolled. In 2006, 11 master's, 4 other advanced degrees awarded. *Degree requirements:* For master's, research project. *Entrance requirements:* For master's, GRE General Test, previous course work in statistics, community nursing, and physical assessment; RN license; minimum undergraduate GPA of 2.8; appropriate clinical experience; curriculum vitae; for Certificate, MSN, minimum GPA of 3.0. Additional exam requirements/recommendations for international students: Required—TOEFL (minimum score 527 paper-based; 197 computer-based; 71 iBT). *Application deadline:* For fall admission, 6/15 priority date for domestic and international students. Applications are processed on a rolling basis. Application fee: $30. Electronic applications accepted. *Expenses:* Tuition: Full-time $12,200; part-time $610 per credit. Required fees: $150. Full-time tuition and fees vary according to course load and program. *Financial support:* In 2006–07, 21 students received support, including 3 fellowships with partial tuition reimbursements available (averaging $1,500 per year), 2 teaching assistantships with partial tuition reimbursements available (averaging $3,482 per year); institutionally sponsored loans and scholarships/grants also available. Support available to part-time students. Financial award application deadline: 3/15; financial award applicants required to submit FAFSA. *Faculty research:* Nurse caring behaviors, end of life issues, women's health, gerontology, nursing diagnosis. Total annual research expenditures: $80,000. *Unit head:* Dr. Sheila Ralph, Director, 540-678-4381, Fax: 540-665-5519, E-mail: ssparks@su.edu. *Application contact:* David Anthony, Dean of Admissions, 540-665-4581, Fax: 540-665-4627, E-mail: admit@su.edu.

Stony Brook University, State University of New York, Stony Brook University Medical Center, Health Sciences Center, School of Nursing, Program in Nurse-Midwifery, Stony Brook, NY 11794. Offers MS, Certificate. *Accreditation:* AACN; ACNM/DOA. *Students:* 7 full-time (all women), 17 part-time (all women); includes 5 minority (2 African Americans, 1 American Indian/Alaska Native, 2 Hispanic Americans). In 2006, 24 master's, 7 other advanced degrees awarded. *Degree requirements:* For master's, thesis. *Entrance requirements:* For master's, BSN, minimum GPA of 3.0, course work in statistics. *Application deadline:* For fall admission, 1/15 for domestic students. Application fee: $60. *Expenses:* Tuition, state resident: full-time $6,900; part-time $288 per credit. Tuition, nonresident: full-time $10,920; part-time $455 per credit. *Financial support:* Fellowships, research assistantships, teaching assistantships available. Financial award application deadline: 3/15. *Unit head:* Dr. Debra Sansoucie, Chair, 631-444-3298, Fax: 631-444-3136, E-mail: debra.sansoucie@stonybrook.edu.

University of Cincinnati, Graduate School, College of Nursing, Cincinnati, OH 45221-0038. Offers clinical nurse specialist (MSN), including adult health, community health, neonatal, nursing administration, occupational health, pediatric health, psychiatric nursing, women's health; nurse anesthesia (MSN); nurse midwifery (MSN); nurse practitioner (MSN), including acute care, ambulatory care, family, family/psychiatric, women's health; nursing (PhD); MBA/MSN. *Accreditation:* AACN; AANA/CANAEP (one or more programs are accredited); ACNM/DOA. Part-time programs available. Postbaccalaureate distance learning degree programs offered (no on-campus study). *Faculty:* 41 full-time (39 women), 16 part-time/adjunct (15 women). *Students:* 159 full-time (125 women), 149 part-time (145 women); includes 40 minority (22 African Americans, 1 American Indian/Alaska Native, 16 Asian Americans or Pacific Islanders, 1 Hispanic American). Average age 34. 385 applicants, 49% accepted, 132 enrolled. In 2006, 77 master's, 5 doctorates awarded. Terminal master's awarded for partial completion of doctoral program. *Median time to degree:* Of those who began their doctoral program in fall 1998, 55% received their degree in 8 years or less. *Degree requirements:* For master's, thesis or alternative, registration; for doctorate, thesis/dissertation, comprehensive exam, registration. *Entrance requirements:* For master's and doctorate, GRE General Test. Additional exam requirements/recommendations for international students: Required—TOEFL (minimum score 520 paper-based; 190 computer-based). *Application deadline:* For fall admission, 7/26 priority date for domestic and international students. Applications are processed on a rolling basis. Application fee: $40. Electronic applications accepted. *Financial support:* In 2006–07, 164 students received support, including 7 fellowships with full tuition reimbursements available (averaging $13,571 per year), research assistantships with full tuition reimbursements available (averaging $12,000 per year), 8 teaching assistantships with full tuition reimbursements available (averaging $12,000 per year); career-related internships or fieldwork, scholarships/grants, traineeships, tuition waivers (partial), and unspecified assistantships also available. Support available to part-time students. Financial award application deadline: 5/1; financial award applicants required to submit FAFSA. *Faculty research:* Substance abuse, injury and violence, symptom management. Total annual research expenditures: $1.3 million. *Unit head:* Dr. Andrea R. Lindell, Dean, 513-558-5330, Fax: 513-558-9030, E-mail: andrea.lindell@uc.edu. *Application contact:* Loren Carter, Program Coordinator, 513-558-5072, Fax: 513-558-7523, E-mail: loren.carter@uc.edu.

University of Illinois at Chicago, Graduate College, College of Nursing, Program in Nursing Sciences (Maternal Child), Chicago, IL 60607-7128. Offers maternity nursing/nurse midwifery (MS); pediatric nursing (MS); perinatal nursing (MS). *Accreditation:* AACN; ACNM/DOA. Part-time programs available. *Degree requirements:* For master's, thesis or alternative. *Entrance requirements:* For master's, GRE General Test, minimum GPA of 2.75. Additional exam requirements/recommendations for international students: Required—TOEFL. Electronic applications accepted.

University of Indianapolis, Graduate Programs, School of Nursing, Indianapolis, IN 46227-3697. Offers family practice (post-RN) (MSN); gerontological nurse practitioner (MSN); nurse-midwifery (MSN); nursing (MSN); nursing administration (MSN); nursing education (MSN); MBA/MSN. *Accreditation:* AACN; ACNM. *Faculty:* 7 full-time (all women), 3 part-time/adjunct (all women). *Students:* 9 full-time (all women), 121 part-time (115 women); includes 17 minority (16 African Americans, 1 Asian American or Pacific Islander). Average age 41. In 2006, 7 degrees awarded. *Entrance requirements:* For master's, minimum GPA of 3.0, interview, letters of recommendation, resumé, IN nursing license, 1 year professional practice. Additional exam requirements/recommendations for international students: Required—TOEFL (minimum score 550 paper-based; 213 computer-based). *Application deadline:* For fall admission, 8/1 for domestic students; for winter admission, 12/15 for domestic students; for spring admission, 4/15 for domestic students. Applications are processed on a rolling basis. Application fee: $50. *Financial support:* Federal Work-Study available. *Unit head:* Dr. Sharon Isaac, Dean, 317-788-3207, E-mail: isaac@uindy.edu. *Application contact:* T.C. Crum, 317-788-2128, Fax: 317-788-3542, E-mail: tcrum@uindy.edu.

University of Kansas, Graduate Studies Medical Center, School of Nursing, Kansas City, KS 66160. Offers nurse educator (PMC); nurse midwife (PMC); nursing (MS, PhD); psychiatric/mental health nurse practitioner (PMC). *Accreditation:* AACN; ACNM/DOA. Part-time programs available. Postbaccalaureate distance learning degree programs offered (minimal on-campus study). *Faculty:* 53 full-time (50 women), 3 part-time/adjunct (all women). *Students:* 63 full-time (59 women), 200 part-time (190 women); includes 37 minority (16 African Americans, 3 American Indian/Alaska Native, 12 Asian Americans or Pacific Islanders, 6 Hispanic Americans), 4 international. Average age 38. 88 applicants, 82% accepted, 62 enrolled. In 2006, 39 master's, 5 doctorates awarded. Terminal master's awarded for partial completion of doctoral program. *Median time to degree:* Master's–2.05 years full-time, 2.95 years part-time; doctorate–3.26 years part-time. Of those who began their doctoral program in fall 1998, 66% received their degree in 8 years or less. *Degree requirements:* For master's, general oral exam, thesis optional; for doctorate, one foreign language, thesis/dissertation, comprehensive oral and written exam. *Entrance requirements:* For master's, GRE General Test, bachelor's degree in nursing, minimum GPA of 3.0, RN license, 1 year of clinical experience; for doctorate, GRE General Test, master's degree in nursing, minimum GPA of 3.5. Additional exam requirements/recommendations for international students: Required—TOEFL. *Application deadline:* For fall admission, 4/1 for domestic students; for winter admission, 7/1 for domestic students; for spring admission, 9/1 for domestic students. Application fee: $50. *Expenses:* Tuition, area resident: Part-time $227 per credit. Tuition, state resident: part-time $543 per credit. Tuition and fees vary according to course load, campus/location, program and reciprocity agreements. *Financial support:* In 2006–07, 106 students received support, including 7 research assistantships (averaging $19,000 per year), 23 teaching assistantships with full and partial tuition reimbursements available (averaging $19,000 per year); traineeships also available. Financial award application deadline: 7/7. *Faculty research:* Breastfeeding practices of teen mothers, prevention of pressure ulcers, caregiving of families of patients using technology in the home, self care talk intervention partnership between caregivers of stroke survivors and nurses, smoking cessation. *Unit head:* Dr. Karen L. Miller, Dean, 913-588-1604, Fax: 913-588-1660, E-mail: kmiller@kumc.edu. *Application contact:* Dr. Rita K. Clifford, Associate Dean, Student Affairs, 913-588-1619, Fax: 913-588-1615, E-mail: rcliffor@kumc.edu.

University of Maryland, Baltimore, Graduate School, School of Nursing, Master's Program in Nursing, Baltimore, MD 21201. Offers community health nursing (MS); gerontological nursing (MS); maternal-child nursing (MS); medical-surgical nursing (MS); nurse-midwifery education (MS); nursing administration (MS); nursing education (MS); nursing health policy (MS); primary care nursing (MS); psychiatric nursing (MS); MS/MBA. *Accreditation:* AANA/CANAEP; ACNM/DOA; NLN (one or more programs are accredited). Part-time programs available. *Degree requirements:* For master's, thesis or alternative, comprehensive exam (for some programs). *Entrance requirements:* For master's, GRE General Test, minimum GPA of 2.75, course work in statistics, BS in nursing. Additional exam requirements/recommendations for international students: Required—TOEFL, TOEFL or IELTS; Recommended—IELTS. Electronic applications accepted.

University of Medicine and Dentistry of New Jersey, School of Health Related Professions, Department of Primary Care, Program in Nurse Midwifery, Newark, NJ 07107-1709. Offers Certificate. *Accreditation:* ACNM/DOA. *Entrance requirements:* For degree, 2 years professional experience in maternal/neonatal health care, bachelor's degree in related area, current RN license, minimum GPA of 2.5, physical assessment course within last 5 years. Additional exam requirements/recommendations for international students: Required—TOEFL. *Application deadline:* For fall admission, 2/15 for domestic students. Applications are processed on a rolling basis. Application fee: $50. Electronic applications accepted. *Unit head:* Dr. Elaine K. Diegmann, Director, 973-972-4249, E-mail: diegmaek@umdnj.edu.

University of Miami, Graduate School, School of Nursing and Health Studies, Coral Gables, FL 33124. Offers acute care (MSN), including acute care nurse practitioner, nurse anesthesia; community health (MSN); nursing (PhD); primary care (MSN), including adult nurse practitioner, family nurse practitioner, nurse midwifery, psychiatric/mental health nursing, women's health practitioner. *Accreditation:* AACN; AANA/CANAEP; ACNM/DOA (one or more programs are accredited). Part-time programs available. *Faculty:* 10 full-time (8 women), 1 (woman) part-time/adjunct. *Students:* 33 full-time (24 women), 27 part-time (24 women); includes 28 minority (7 African Americans, 5 Asian Americans or Pacific Islanders, 16 Hispanic Americans), 2 international. Average age 34. 108 applicants, 48% accepted, 30 enrolled. In 2006, 15 master's, 1 doctorate awarded. *Degree requirements:* For master's, thesis optional; for doctorate, thesis/dissertation. *Entrance requirements:* For master's, GRE General Test, BSN, minimum GPA of 3.0, Florida RN license; for doctorate, GRE General Test, BSN or MSN, minimum GPA of 3.0. Additional exam requirements/recommendations for international students: Required—TOEFL (minimum score 550 paper-based; 213 computer-based). *Application deadline:* For fall admission, 4/30 priority date for domestic students; for spring admission, 11/1 priority date for domestic students. Applications are processed on a rolling basis. Application fee: $50. Electronic applications accepted. *Financial support:* In 2006–07, 12 students received support, including 3 research assistantships with tuition reimbursements available (averaging $9,000 per year), 5 teaching assistantships with tuition reimbursements available (averaging $9,000 per year); fellowships, Federal Work-Study, institutionally sponsored loans, scholarships/grants, and unspecified assistantships also available. Support available to part-time students. Financial award application deadline: 3/1; financial award applicants required to submit FAFSA. *Faculty research:* Transcultural nursing, exercise and depression in Alzheimer's disease, infectious diseases/HIV–AIDS, postpartum depression, outcomes assessment. Total annual research expenditures: $31.9 million. *Unit head:* Dr. Nilda Peragallo, Dean, 305-284-2107, Fax: 305-667-3787, E-mail: nperagallo@miami.edu. *Application contact:* Anne Stabb, Graduate Advisor, 305-284-2533, Fax: 305-284-4827, E-mail: astabb@miami.edu.

University of Michigan, Horace H. Rackham School of Graduate Studies, School of Nursing, Division of Health Promotion and Risk Reduction, Program in Parent-Child Nursing, Ann Arbor, MI 48109. Offers infant, child, adolescent health nurse practitioner (MS); nurse midwifery (MS). *Accreditation:* AACN. Part-time programs available. Postbaccalaureate distance learning degree programs offered (minimal on-campus study). *Degree requirements:* For master's, thesis, registration. *Entrance requirements:* For master's, GRE General Test. Additional exam requirements/recommendations for international students: Required—TOEFL (minimum score 560 paper-based; 220 computer-based).

University of Minnesota, Twin Cities Campus, Graduate School, School of Nursing, Nurse Midwifery Program, Minneapolis, MN 55455-0213. Offers MS. *Accreditation:* ACNM/DOA. Postbaccalaureate distance learning degree programs offered (minimal on-campus study). *Students:* 17 full-time (all women), 3 part-time (all women); includes 2 minority (1 African American, 1 American Indian/Alaska Native). *Degree requirements:* For master's, final oral exam, project or thesis. *Entrance requirements:* Additional exam requirements/recommendations for international students: Required—TOEFL (minimum score 586 paper-based; 240 computer-based). *Application deadline:* For fall admission, 11/1 priority date for domestic and international students; for spring admission, 8/1 priority date for domestic and international students. Application fee: $55 ($75 for international students). *Financial support:* Fellowships, research assistantships, teaching assistantships, career-related internships or fieldwork and traineeships available. *Unit head:* Dr. Melissa Avery, Coordinator, 612-624-5933, Fax: 612-626-2359, E-mail: avery003@umn.edu. *Application contact:* Information Contact, 612-624-4454, Fax: 612-624-3174, E-mail: nurseoss@umn.edu.

University of Pennsylvania, School of Nursing, Program in Nurse Midwifery, Philadelphia, PA 19104. Offers MSN. *Accreditation:* AACN; ACNM/DOA. Part-time programs available. *Entrance requirements:* For master's, GRE General Test, BSN, minimum GPA of 3.0, previous course work in statistics, physical assessment. Additional exam requirements/recommendations for international students: Required—TOEFL. Expenses: Contact institution. *Faculty research:* Breast-feeding protocols, history of midwifery, hydrotherapy in labor, cocaine abuse during pregnancy, stress in pregnancy.

University of Puerto Rico, Medical Sciences Campus, Graduate School of Public Health, Department of Human Development, Program in Nurse Midwifery, San Juan, PR 00936-5067. Offers MPH, Certificate. *Accreditation:* ACNM/DOA. Part-time programs available. *Entrance requirements:* For master's, GRE, previous course work in algebra. *Application deadline:* For fall admission, 3/15 for domestic students. Application fee: $20. *Financial support:* Application deadline: 4/30. *Unit head:* Prof. Irene De la Torre, Coordinator, 787-758-2525 Ext. 2401, Fax: 787-756-6719, E-mail: idelatorre@rcm.upr.edu. *Application contact:* Prof. Mayra E. Santiago-Vargas, Counselor, 787-756-5244, Fax: 787-759-6719, E-mail: msantiago@rcm.upr.edu.

University of Rhode Island, Graduate School, College of Nursing, Kingston, RI 02881. Offers administration (MS); clinical specialist in gerontology (MS); clinical specialist in psychiatric/mental health (MS); family nurse practitioner (MS); nurse midwifery (MS); nursing (PhD); nursing education (MS). *Accreditation:* AACN; ACNM/DOA (one or more programs are accredited). In 2006, 34 master's, 5 doctorates awarded. *Application deadline:* For fall admission, 4/15 for domestic students. Application fee: $35. *Expenses:* Tuition, state resident: full-time $6,032; part-time $335 per credit. Tuition, nonresident: full-time $17,288; part-time $960 per credit. Required fees: $65 per credit. $30 per semester. One-time fee: $80 part-time. *Unit head:* Dayle Joseph, Dean, 401-874-2766.

The University of Texas at El Paso, Graduate School, College of Health Sciences, School of Nursing, El Paso, TX 79968-0001. Offers community health (MSN); community health/family nurse practitioner (MSN); nurse midwifery (MSN); nursing administration (MSN); nursing-clinical (MSN); post master's nursing (MSN); women's health care (MSN). *Accreditation:* AACN. *Degree requirements:* For master's, thesis optional. *Entrance requirements:* For master's, GRE General Test or MAT, BSN, minimum GPA of 3.0, previous course work in statistics. Additional exam requirements/recommendations for international students: Required—TOEFL. Electronic applications accepted.

Vanderbilt University, School of Nursing, Nashville, TN 37235. Offers adult acute care nurse practitioner (MSN); adult health nurse practitioner/forensic (MSN); adult nurse practitioner/cardiovascular disease management and prevention (MSN); adult nurse practitioner/palliative care (MSN); clinical management (clinical nurse leader/specialist) (MSN); family nurse practitioner (MSN); gerontology nurse practitioner (MSN); health systems management (MSN); neonatal nurse practitioner (MSN); nurse midwifery (MSN); nursing informatics (MSN); nursing science (PhD); pediatric acute care nurse practitioner (MSN); pediatric primary care nurse practitioner (MSN); psychiatric-mental health nurse practitioner (MSN); women's health nurse practitioner (MSN); MBA/MSN; MSN/MTS; MSN/PhD. *Accreditation:* ACNM/DOA; NLN (one or more programs are accredited). Part-time and evening/weekend programs available. Postbaccalaureate distance learning degree programs offered (minimal on-campus study). *Faculty:* 95 full-time (83 women), 432 part-time/adjunct (314 women). *Students:* 371 full-time (325 women), 206 part-time (180 women); includes 59 minority (38 African Americans, 2 American Indian/Alaska Native, 7 Asian Americans or Pacific Islanders, 12 Hispanic Americans). Average age 27. 611 applicants, 55% accepted, 308 enrolled. In 2006, 256 master's, 2 doctorates awarded. *Degree requirements:* For doctorate, thesis/dissertation. *Entrance requirements:* For master's, GRE, interview; for doctorate, GRE, interview, 3 letters of recommendation. Additional exam requirements/recommendations for international students: Required—TOEFL. *Application deadline:* For fall admission, 12/1 priority date for domestic and international students. Applications are processed on a rolling basis. Application fee: $50. *Expenses:* Contact institution. *Financial support:* In 2006–07, 404 students received support, including 5 research assistantships (averaging $8,000 per year); Federal Work-Study, institutionally sponsored loans, and unspecified assistantships also available. Support available to part-time students. Financial award application deadline: 3/15; financial award applicants required to submit CSS PROFILE or FAFSA. *Faculty research:* Lymphedema post cancer treatment, palliative care and bereavement, patient safety and quality of care, health care workforce issues, symptom management including pain and fatigue. Total annual research expenditures: $1.1 million. *Unit head:* Dr. Colleen Conway-Welch, Dean, 615-343-8776, Fax: 615-343-7711, E-mail: colleen.conway-welch@vanderbilt.edu. *Application contact:* Cheryl Feldner, Assistant Director of Admissions, 615-322-3800, Fax: 615-343-0333, E-mail: cheryl.feldner@vanderbilt.edu.

Wichita State University, Graduate School, College of Health Professions, School of Nursing, Wichita, KS 67260. Offers clinical nurse specialist (MSN); nurse midwifery (MSN); nurse practitioner (MSN); nursing and health care systems administration (MSN); MSN/MBA. *Accreditation:* AACN. Part-time programs available. *Degree requirements:* For master's, thesis optional. *Entrance requirements:* For master's, GRE, BSN, minimum undergraduate GPA of 2.75. Additional exam requirements/recommendations for international students Required—TOEFL. Electronic applications accepted. *Faculty research:* Adolescent pregnancy alcoholism, arthritis and chronic disease, health practices of elderly, diabetes.

Nursing and Healthcare Administration

Allen College, Program in Nursing, Waterloo, IA 50703. Offers acute care nurse practitioner (MSN); family nurse practitioner (MSN); health education (MSN); leadership in health care delivery (MSN). *Accreditation:* AACN; NLN. Part-time and evening/weekend programs available. *Faculty:* 2 full-time (both women), 4 part-time/adjunct (all women). *Students:* 19 full-time (17 women), 42 part-time (39 women). Average age 37. 62 applicants, 94% accepted, 46 enrolled. In 2006, 3 degrees awarded. *Degree requirements:* For master's, thesis optional. *Entrance requirements:* For master's, minimum GPA of 3.0. Additional exam requirements/recommendations for international students: Required—TOEFL (minimum score 550 paper-based). *Application deadline:* For fall admission, 7/15 priority date for domestic students; for spring admission, 12/1 priority date for domestic students. Applications are processed on a rolling basis. Application fee: $50. Electronic applications accepted. *Expenses:* Tuition: Full-time $9,824; part-time $562 per credit hour. Required fees: $481. One-time fee: $220 part-time. Tuition and fees vary according to course load. *Financial support:* In 2006–07, 58 students received support, including 1 teaching assistantship (averaging $10,116 per year); institutionally sponsored loans, scholarships/grants, and traineeships also available. Support available to part-time students. Financial award application deadline: 8/15; financial award applicants required to submit FAFSA. *Faculty research:* Pain and aged, congestive heart failure. *Unit head:* Nancy Kramer, Chair, 319-226-2040, Fax: 319-226-2070, E-mail: kramerna@ihs.org.

Athabasca University, Centre for Nursing and Health Studies, Athabasca, AB T9S 3A3, Canada. Offers advanced nursing practice (MN, Advanced Diploma); generalist (MN); health studies-leadership (MHS). Part-time programs available. Postbaccalaureate distance learning degree programs offered. *Faculty:* 6 full-time (all women), 40 part-time/adjunct (37 women). *Students:* Average age 40. 460 applicants, 81% accepted, 335 enrolled. In 2006, 126 degrees awarded. *Degree requirements:* For master's, comprehensive exam (for some programs), registration (for some programs). *Entrance requirements:* For master's, bachelor's degree in health-related field, 2 years professional health service experience (MHS), bachelor's degree in nursing, 2 years nursing experience (MN), minimum GPA of 3.0 in final 30 credits; for Advanced Diploma, RN license, 2 years health care experience. *Application deadline:* For fall admission, 3/1 for domestic and international students. Application fee: $60. Electronic applications accepted. *Expenses:* Contact institution. *Unit head:* Dr. Donna Romyn, Director, 780-675-6794, Fax: 780-675-6468, E-mail: dromyn@athabascau.ca. *Application contact:* Lisa Bodnarchuk, Administrative Assistant, 780-675-6381, Fax: 780-675-6468, E-mail: mhs@athabascau.ca.

Barry University, School of Nursing, Program in Nursing Administration, Miami Shores, FL 33161-6695. Offers MSN, PhD, Certificate. *Accreditation:* AACN. Part-time and evening/weekend programs available. *Students:* 12 full-time (10 women), 18 part-time (17 women); includes 21 minority (8 African Americans, 1 Asian American or Pacific Islander, 12 Hispanic Americans). 15 applicants, 67% accepted, 10 enrolled. In 2006, 17 degrees awarded. *Degree requirements:* For master's, research project or thesis. *Entrance requirements:* For master's, GRE General Test or MAT, BSN, minimum GPA of 3.0, course work in statistics. *Application deadline:* For fall admission, 5/1 priority date for domestic students. Applications are processed on a rolling basis. Application fee: $30. Electronic applications accepted. *Faculty research:* Power/empowerment, health delivery systems, managed care, employee health and well being. Total annual research expenditures: $2,000. *Unit head:* Dr. Claudette Spalding, Associate Dean for Graduate Programs, 305-899-3838, Fax: 305-899-3831, E-mail: cspalding@mail.barry.edu. *Application contact:* Dave Fletcher, Director of Graduate Admissions, 305-899-3113, Fax: 305-899-2971, E-mail: dfletcher@mail.barry.edu.

Barry University, School of Nursing and Andreas School of Business, Program in Nursing Administration and Business Administration, Miami Shores, FL 33161-6695. Offers MSN/MBA. *Accreditation:* AACN. Part-time and evening/weekend programs available. *Students:* 3 applicants, 0% accepted. *Application deadline:* For fall admission, 5/1 priority date for domestic students. Applications are processed on a rolling basis. Application fee: $30. Electronic applications accepted. *Faculty research:* Power/empowerment, health delivery systems, managed care, employee health well-being. *Unit head:* Dr. Claudette Spalding, Associate Dean for Graduate Programs, 305-899-3838, Fax: 305-899-3831, E-mail: cspalding@mail.barry.edu.

Nursing and Healthcare Administration

Barry University (continued)
Application contact: Dave Fletcher, Director of Graduate Admissions, 305-899-3113, Fax: 305-899-2971, E-mail: dfletcher@mail.barry.edu.

Baylor University, Graduate School, Louise Herrington School of Nursing, Dallas, TX 75246. Offers family nurse practitioner (MSN); neonatal nurse practitioner (MSN); nursing administration and management (MSN). *Accreditation:* AACN. *Students:* 10 full-time (all women), 27 part-time (26 women); includes 6 minority (1 African American, 1 Asian American or Pacific Islander, 4 Hispanic Americans), 1 international. In 2006, 13 degrees awarded. *Entrance requirements:* For master's, GRE General Test. *Application deadline:* For fall admission, 8/1 for domestic students; for spring admission, 12/1 for domestic students. Applications are processed on a rolling basis. Application fee: $25. *Unit head:* Dr. Pauline Johnson, Graduate Program Director, 214-820-3361, Fax: 214-818-8692, E-mail: pauline_johnson@baylor.edu. *Application contact:* Suzanne Keener, Administrative Assistant, 254-710-3588, Fax: 254-710-3870.

Bellarmine University, Donna and Allan Lansing School of Nursing and Health Sciences, Louisville, KY 40205-0671. Offers nursing administration (MSN); nursing education (MSN); physical therapy (DPT). *Accreditation:* AACN; APTA. *Faculty:* 15 full-time (11 women), 8 part-time/adjunct (7 women). *Students:* 112 full-time (87 women), 70 part-time (66 women); includes 12 minority (7 African Americans, 4 Asian Americans or Pacific Islanders, 1 Hispanic American), 1 international. Average age 31. In 2006, 44 degrees awarded. *Degree requirements:* For doctorate, comprehensive exam. *Entrance requirements:* For master's, GRE General Test, minimum undergraduate GPA of 2.75, RN license; for doctorate, minimum prerequisites coursework GPA of 2.75, 2.5 overall; 25 hours of documented service in physical therapy; physical ability to perform tasks of a physical therapist. Additional exam requirements/recommendations for international students: Required—TOEFL (minimum score 550 paper-based; 213 computer-based; 80 iBT). *Application deadline:* For fall admission, 10/15 priority date for domestic students. Applications are processed on a rolling basis. Application fee: $25. Electronic applications accepted. *Expenses:* Contact institution. Tuition and fees vary according to program. *Financial support:* Career-related internships or fieldwork and scholarships/grants available. *Faculty research:* Pain, empathy, leadership styles, control. *Unit head:* Dr. Susan H. Davis, Dean, 800-274-4723 Ext. 8217, E-mail: sdavis@bellarmine.edu. *Application contact:* Julie Armstrong-Binnix, Health Science Recruiter, 800-274-4723 Ext. 8364, E-mail: julieab@bellarmine.edu.

Bloomsburg University of Pennsylvania, School of Graduate Studies, College of Professional Studies, School of Health Sciences, Department of Nursing, Bloomsburg, PA 17815-1301. Offers adult and family nurse practitioner (MSN); adult health and illness (MSN); community health (MSN); nursing (MSN); nursing administration (MSN). *Accreditation:* AACN. *Faculty:* 11 full-time (all women). *Students:* 9 full-time (all women), 27 part-time (24 women). Average age 36. 10 applicants, 100% accepted, 5 enrolled. In 2006, 6 degrees awarded. *Degree requirements:* For master's, thesis. *Entrance requirements:* For master's, minimum QPA of 3.0. Additional exam requirements/recommendations for international students: Required—TOEFL. *Application deadline:* Applications are processed on a rolling basis. Application fee: $30. Electronic applications accepted. *Expenses:* Tuition, state resident: full-time $6,048; part-time $336 per credit. Tuition, nonresident: full-time $9,678; part-time $538 per credit. Required fees: $1,415. *Financial support:* Unspecified assistantships available. *Faculty research:* Cardiopulmonary nursing, cancer topics, women's health. *Application contact:* Dr. Michelle Ficca, Coordinator, 570-389-4615, Fax: 570-389-5008, E-mail: mficca@bloomu.edu.

Bowie State University, Graduate Programs, Department of Nursing, Bowie, MD 20715-9465. Offers administration of nursing services (MS); family nurse practitioner (MS); nursing education (MS). *Accreditation:* NLN. Part-time programs available. *Faculty:* 7 full-time (4 women), 14 part-time/adjunct (9 women). *Students:* 9 full-time (all women), 9 part-time (8 women); includes 15 minority (all African Americans) Average age 42. 8 applicants, 88% accepted, 4 enrolled. In 2006, 7 degrees awarded. *Degree requirements:* For master's, thesis, research paper, comprehensive exam. *Entrance requirements:* For master's, minimum GPA of 2.5. *Application deadline:* For fall admission, 5/15 for domestic students. Applications are processed on a rolling basis. Application fee: $40. Electronic applications accepted. *Expenses:* Tuition, state resident: full-time $7,344; part-time $306 per credit. Tuition, nonresident: full-time $14,304; part-time $396 per credit. Required fees: $1,078; $77 per credit. $539 per term. One-time fee: $40. *Financial support:* Institutionally sponsored loans and traineeships available. Financial award application deadline: 4/1. *Faculty research:* Minority health, women's health, gerontology, leadership management. *Unit head:* Dr. Bonita Jenkins, Acting Chairperson, 301-860-3210, E-mail: mccaskill@bowiestate.edu. *Application contact:* Angela Issac, Information Contact.

Bradley University, Graduate School, College of Education and Health Sciences, Department of Nursing, Peoria, IL 61625-0002. Offers nurse administered anesthesia (MSN); nursing administration (MSN). *Accreditation:* AANA/CANAEP; NLN. Part-time and evening/weekend programs available. *Students:* 3 full-time (0 women), 47 part-time (29 women); includes 6 minority (1 African American, 1 American Indian/Alaska Native, 4 Asian Americans or Pacific Islanders). 16 applicants, 19% accepted, 3 enrolled. In 2006, 24 degrees awarded. *Degree requirements:* For master's, thesis optional. *Entrance requirements:* For master's, GRE General Test or MAT, interview, Illinois RN license, advanced cardiac life support certification, pediatric advanced life support certification, 3 letters of recommendation. Additional exam requirements/recommendations for international students: Required—TOEFL (minimum score 550 paper-based; 213 computer-based; 79 iBT). *Application deadline:* For fall admission, 5/15 priority date for domestic and international students; for spring admission, 10/15 priority date for domestic and international students. Applications are processed on a rolling basis. Application fee: $40 ($50 for international students). *Financial support:* Research assistantships, scholarships/grants, tuition waivers (partial), and unspecified assistantships available. Financial award application deadline: 4/1. *Unit head:* Dr. Francesca Armmer, Chairperson, 309-677-2528, E-mail: faa@bradley.edu.

Capital University, School of Nursing, Columbus, OH 43209-2394. Offers administration (MSN); legal studies (MSN); theological studies (MSN); JD/MSN; MBA/MSN; MSN/MTS. *Accreditation:* AACN. Part-time and evening/weekend programs available. *Faculty:* 11 full-time (all women), 2 part-time/adjunct (both women). *Students:* 16 full-time (15 women), 72 part-time (67 women); includes 5 minority (4 African Americans, 1 Asian American or Pacific Islander), 8 international. Average age 41. 20 applicants, 90% accepted, 18 enrolled. In 2006, 14 degrees awarded. *Degree requirements:* For master's, thesis or alternative, registration. *Entrance requirements:* For master's, BSN, current RN license, minimum GPA of 3.0, undergraduate courses in statistics and research. Additional exam requirements/recommendations for international students: Required—TOEFL (minimum score 550 paper-based). *Application deadline:* For fall admission, 3/30 priority date for domestic and international students; for spring admission, 9/30 priority date for domestic and international students. Applications are processed on a rolling basis. Application fee: $25. *Expenses:* Contact institution. Part-time tuition and fees vary according to program. *Financial support:* In 2006–07, 2 students received support. Career-related internships or fieldwork and traineeships available. Financial award applicants required to submit FAFSA. *Faculty research:* Bereavement, wellness/health promotion, emergency cardiac care, critical thinking, complementary and alternative healthcare. *Unit head:* Dr. Elaine F. Haynes, Dean and Professor, 614-236-6703, Fax: 614-236-6157, E-mail: ehaynes@capital.edu. *Application contact:* Dr. Jill D Steuer, Professor and Director of the MSN Program, 614-236-6393, Fax: 614-236-6157, E-mail: jsteuer@capital.edu.

Carlow University, School of Nursing, Pittsburgh, PA 15213-3165. Offers home health advanced practice nursing (MSN, PMC); nursing case management/leadership (MSN); nursing leadership (MSN). *Accreditation:* AACN. Part-time and evening/weekend programs available. Postbaccalaureate distance learning degree programs offered (minimal on-campus study). *Degree requirements:* For master's, thesis or alternative. *Entrance requirements:* For master's, GRE General Test, 1 year of professional experience, BSN, interview, minimum GPA of 3.0, Pennsylvania RN license, previous graduate course work in statistics, resumé, 3 letters of recommendation; for PMC, MSN. Additional exam requirements/recommendations for international students: Required—TOEFL (minimum score 550 paper-based; 213 computer-based). Electronic applications accepted. *Faculty research:* Research utilization, community and home health, medically underserved.

The Catholic University of America, School of Nursing, Washington, DC 20064. Offers advanced practice nursing (MSN), including administration of nursing service, adult nurse practitioner, education, family nurse practitioner, geriatric nurse practitioner, pediatric nurse practitioner, psychiatric-mental health, school health nurse practitioner; clinical nursing (DN Sc). *Accreditation:* AACN; NLN. Part-time programs available. *Faculty:* 17 full-time (all women), 19 part-time/adjunct (18 women). *Students:* 27 full-time (25 women), 58 part-time (57 women); includes 31 minority (20 African Americans, 6 Asian Americans or Pacific Islanders, 5 Hispanic Americans), 6 international. Average age 43. 38 applicants, 76% accepted, 15 enrolled. In 2006, 15 master's, 7 doctorates awarded. *Degree requirements:* For master's, thesis optional; for doctorate, thesis/dissertation, comprehensive exam. *Entrance requirements:* For master's, GRE General Test or MAT, 3 letters of recommendation, BA in nursing, RN registration; for doctorate, GRE General Test, 3 letters of recommendation, BA in nursing, RN registration. Additional exam requirements/recommendations for international students: Required—TOEFL (minimum score 550 paper-based; 213 computer-based). *Application deadline:* For fall admission, 2/1 priority date for domestic students; for spring admission, 11/15 priority date for domestic students. Applications are processed on a rolling basis. Application fee: $55. Electronic applications accepted. *Expenses:* Tuition: Full-time $27,700; part-time $1,045 per credit hour. Required fees: $1,290. Part-time tuition and fees vary according to campus/location and program. *Financial support:* Research assistantships, teaching assistantships, career-related internships or fieldwork, Federal Work-Study, scholarships/grants, tuition waivers (full and partial), and unspecified assistantships available. Support available to part-time students. Financial award application deadline: 2/1; financial award applicants required to submit FAFSA. *Faculty research:* Outcome research–readmission of home health care patients with congestive heart failure, spirituality of chronic illness, minority multigravidos utilization of prenatal care. *Unit head:* Dr. Nalini Jairath, Dean, 202-319-5403, Fax: 202-319-6485, E-mail: jairath@cua.edu.

Clarke College, Department of Nursing and Health, Dubuque, IA 52001-3198. Offers administration of nursing systems (MSN); advanced practice nursing (MSN); education (MSN); family nurse practitioner (MSN, PMC). *Accreditation:* AACN. Part-time programs available. *Entrance requirements:* For master's, GRE General Test or MAT, BSN, minimum GPA of 3.0. Electronic applications accepted. *Faculty research:* Narrative pedagogy, ethics, end-of-life care, pedagogy, family systems.

Clarkson College, Graduate Programs, Department of Nursing, Omaha, NE 68131-2739. Offers administration (MSN); education (MSN); family nurse practitioner (MSN). *Accreditation:* NLN. Part-time and evening/weekend programs available. Postbaccalaureate distance learning degree programs offered (minimal on-campus study). *Degree requirements:* For master's, on-campus skills assessment (family nurse practitioner), comprehensive exam or thesis. *Entrance requirements:* For master's, minimum GPA of 3.0, 2 references, resumé. Additional exam requirements/recommendations for international students: Required—TOEFL (minimum score 600 paper-based; 250 computer-based). Electronic applications accepted.

College of Mount Saint Vincent, School of Professional and Continuing Studies, Department of Nursing, Riverdale, NY 10471-1093. Offers adult nurse practitioner (MSN, PMC); family nurse practitioner (MSN, PMC); nurse educator (PMC); nursing administration (MSN); nursing for the adult and aged (MSN). *Accreditation:* AACN. Part-time programs available. *Faculty:* 2 full-time (1 woman), 6 part-time/adjunct (all women). *Students:* 1 (woman) full-time, 67 part-time (59 women); includes 43 minority (21 African Americans, 16 Asian Americans or Pacific Islanders, 6 Hispanic Americans). Average age 37. In 2006, 16 degrees awarded. *Degree requirements:* For master's, registration. *Entrance requirements:* For master's, BSN, interview, RN license, minimum GPA of 3.0, letters of reference. Additional exam requirements/recommendations for international students: Required—TOEFL. *Application deadline:* For fall admission, 6/1 for domestic and international students; for spring admission, 11/1 for domestic students, 10/1 for international students. Applications are processed on a rolling basis. Application fee: $50. *Expenses:* Contact institution. *Financial support:* Career-related internships or fieldwork available. Financial award application deadline: 6/1; financial award applicants required to submit FAFSA. *Unit head:* Carol Vicino, Director, 718-405-3354, Fax: 718-405-3286.

The College of New Rochelle, Graduate School, Program in Nursing, New Rochelle, NY 10805-2308. Offers acute care nurse practitioner (MS, Certificate); clinical specialist in holistic nursing (MS, Certificate); family nurse practitioner (MS, Certificate); nursing and health care management (MS); nursing education (Certificate). *Accreditation:* AACN. Part-time programs available. *Faculty:* 7 full-time (6 women), 3 part-time/adjunct (all women). *Students:* Average age 44. In 2006, 23 degrees awarded. *Degree requirements:* For master's, registration. *Entrance requirements:* For master's, GRE General Test or MAT, BSN, malpractice insurance, minimum GPA of 3.0, RN license. *Application deadline:* For fall admission, 9/1 priority date for domestic students; for spring admission, 1/15 priority date for domestic students. Applications are processed on a rolling basis. Application fee: $30. *Expenses:* Contact institution. *Financial support:* Traineeships available. Support available to part-time students. Financial award application deadline: 8/15. *Faculty research:* Holistic modalities, academic success variables. *Unit head:* Dr. Mary Alice Donius, Dean, 914-654-5804, Fax: 914-654-5994.

Daemen College, Department of Nursing, Amherst, NY 14226-3592. Offers adult nurse practitioner (MS, Certificate); nursing executive leadership (MS); palliative care nursing (MS, Certificate). *Accreditation:* NLN. Part-time programs available. *Faculty:* 2 full-time (both women), 2 part-time/adjunct (both women). *Students:* 13 full-time (12 women), 63 part-time (59 women); includes 12 minority (10 African Americans, 1 Asian American or Pacific Islander, 1 Hispanic American), 3 international. Average age 41. 36 applicants, 58% accepted, 18 enrolled. In 2006, 9 degrees awarded. *Degree requirements:* For master's, thesis or alternative. *Entrance requirements:* For master's, 1 year medical/surgical experiences, minimum GPA of 3.25, state nursing license and registration, 1 course in statistics. Additional exam requirements/recommendations for international students: Required—TOEFL (minimum score 500 paper-based; 173 computer-based). *Application deadline:* For fall admission, 3/1 priority date for domestic and international students; for spring admission, 10/1 priority date for domestic and international students. Applications are processed on a rolling basis. Application fee: $25. Electronic applications accepted. *Expenses:* Tuition: Full-time $11,700; part-time $650 per credit hour. Required fees: $15 per credit hour. Tuition and fees vary according to course load. *Financial support:* Institutionally sponsored loans and scholarships/grants available. Financial award application deadline: 2/15; financial award applicants required to submit FAFSA. *Faculty research:* Professional stress, client behavior, drug therapy, treatment modalities and pulmonary cancers, chemical dependency. *Unit head:* Dr. Mary Lou Rusin, Chair, 716-839-8387, Fax: 716-839-8403, E-mail: mrusin@daemen.edu. *Application contact:* Karl Shallowhorn, Associate Director of Graduate Admissions, 716-839-8225, Fax: 716-839-8229, E-mail: kshallow@daemen.edu.

Duke University, School of Nursing, Durham, NC 27708-0586. Offers adult acute care (Certificate); adult cardiovascular (Certificate); adult oncology/HIV (Certificate); adult primary care (Certificate); clinical nurse specialist (MSN), including adult oncology/HIV, gerontology, neonatal, pediatric, pediatric/chronic acute care; clinical research management (MSN, Certificate); family (Certificate); gerontology (Certificate); health and nursing ministries (MSN, Certificate); health systems leadership and outcomes (Certificate); leadership in community based long term care (MSN, Certificate); neonatal (Certificate); neonatal/pediatric in rural health (MSN, Certificate); nurse anesthetist (MSN, Certificate); nurse practitioner (MSN), including adult acute care, adult cardiovascular, adult oncology/HIV, adult primary care, family, gerontology, neonatal, pediatric, pediatric acute care; nursing (PhD); nursing and healthcare leadership (MSN); nursing education (MSN); nursing informatics (MSN, Certificate); pediatric (Certificate); pediatric acute care (Certificate); MBA/MSN; MSN/MCM. *Accreditation:* AACN;

AANA/CANAEP. Part-time programs available. Postbaccalaureate distance learning degree programs offered (minimal on-campus study). *Faculty:* 45 full-time (41 women), 169 part-time/adjunct (150 women). *Students:* 178 full-time (162 women), 140 part-time (132 women); includes 48 minority (17 African Americans, 3 American Indian/Alaska Native, 20 Asian Americans or Pacific Islanders, 8 Hispanic Americans). Average age 36. 99 applicants, 92% accepted, 91 enrolled. In 2006, 122 master's, 17 other advanced degrees awarded. *Median time to degree:* Master's–2 years full-time, 2.5 years part-time. *Degree requirements:* For master's, thesis optional. *Entrance requirements:* For master's, GRE General Test or MAT, 1 year of nursing experience, BSN, minimum GPA of 3.0, previous course work in statistics; for Certificate, MSN. Additional exam requirements/recommendations for international students: Required—TOEFL (minimum score 550 paper-based; 213 computer-based), Commission on Graduates of Foreign Nursing Schools exam. *Application deadline:* For fall admission, 7/2 priority date for domestic and international students; for spring admission, 11/15 priority date for domestic and international students. Applications are processed on a rolling basis. Application fee: $50. *Expenses:* Contact institution. *Financial support:* In 2006–07, 258 students received support. Career-related internships or fieldwork, institutionally sponsored loans, scholarships/grants, traineeships, and tuition waivers (partial) available. Support available to part-time students. Financial award application deadline: 4/1; financial award applicants required to submit FAFSA. *Faculty research:* Cardiovascular disease, caregiver skill training, data mining, prostate cancer, neonatal immune system. Total annual research expenditures: $3.5 million. *Unit head:* Dr. Catherine L. Gilliss, Dean/Vice Chancellor for Nursing Affairs, 919-684-9444, Fax: 919-684-9414, E-mail: gilli025@mc.duke.edu. *Application contact:* Bebe T. Mills, Director of Admissions, 919-684-9151, Fax: 919-668-4693, E-mail: mills031@mc.duke.edu.

Duquesne University, School of Nursing, Master's Program in Nursing, Pittsburgh, PA 15282-0001. Offers acute care nursing (Post-Master's Certificate); acute care nursing specialist (MSN); family nurse practitioner (MSN, Post-Master's Certificate); forensic nursing (MSN, Post-Master's Certificate); nursing administration (MSN, Post-Master's Certificate); nursing education (MSN, Post-Master's Certificate); psychiatric/mental health nursing (MSN, Post-Master's Certificate); MSN/MBA. *Accreditation:* AACN. Part-time and evening/weekend programs available. Postbaccalaureate distance learning degree programs offered (minimal on-campus study). *Faculty:* 20 full-time (19 women), 4 part-time/adjunct (all women). *Students:* 73 full-time (70 women), 83 part-time (79 women); includes 11 minority (4 African Americans, 3 American Indian/Alaska Native, 1 Asian American or Pacific Islander, 3 Hispanic Americans). 72 applicants, 75% accepted, 49 enrolled. In 2006, 20 master's, 11 other advanced degrees awarded. *Degree requirements:* For master's, culminating paper. *Entrance requirements:* For master's, MAT or GRE, 1 year of work experience, bachelor's degree in nursing, undergraduate course work in statistics, health assessment course (family nurse practitioner, nursing education, acute care clinical nurse specialist). *Application deadline:* For fall admission, 4/1 for domestic and international students; for spring admission, 11/1 for domestic and international students. Applications are processed on a rolling basis. Application fee: $50. *Expenses:* Contact institution. Tuition and fees vary according to degree level and program. *Financial support:* In 2006–07, 10 students received support, including 9 research assistantships with partial tuition reimbursements available (averaging $1,600 per year), 1 teaching assistantship with partial tuition reimbursement available (averaging $1,600 per year); fellowships with partial tuition reimbursements available, institutionally sponsored loans, scholarships/grants, traineeships, and tuition waivers (partial) also available. Financial award application deadline: 8/20. *Faculty research:* Depression, culture, vulnerable populations, ethics, health disparities, community based. Total annual research expenditures: $377,400. *Unit head:* Dr. Joan Such Lockhart, Professor and Associate Dean of Academic Affairs, 412-396-6540, Fax: 412-396-1821, E-mail: lockhart@duq.edu. *Application contact:* Susan Hardner, Nurse Recruiter, 412-396-4945, Fax: 412-396-6346, E-mail: nursing@duq.edu.

D'Youville College, Department of Nursing, Buffalo, NY 14201-1084. Offers community health nursing/education (MSN); community health nursing/high risk parents and children (MSN); community health nursing/management (MSN); family nurse practitioner (MS); nursing and health-related professions (Certificate); nursing with clinical focus choice (MSN). *Accreditation:* AACN. Part-time and evening/weekend programs available. *Faculty:* 26 full-time (all women), 7 part-time/adjunct (6 women). *Students:* 77 full-time (72 women), 101 part-time (95 women); includes 17 minority (12 African Americans, 1 American Indian/Alaska Native, 4 Hispanic Americans), 89 international. Average age 36. 177 applicants, 58% accepted, 37 enrolled. In 2006, 41 master's, 2 other advanced degrees awarded. *Degree requirements:* For master's, membership on board of community agency, publishable paper, thesis optional. *Entrance requirements:* For master's, BS in nursing, minimum GPA of 3.0, course work in statistics and computers. Additional exam requirements/recommendations for international students: Required—TOEFL (minimum score 500 paper-based; 173 computer-based). *Application deadline:* For fall admission, 5/1 priority date for international students; for spring admission, 9/1 priority date for international students. Applications are processed on a rolling basis. Application fee: $25. Electronic applications accepted. *Financial support:* In 2006–07, 1 research assistantship with partial tuition reimbursement (averaging $3,000 per year) was awarded; Federal Work-Study and scholarships/grants also available. Support available to part-time students. Financial award application deadline: 3/1; financial award applicants required to submit FAFSA. *Faculty research:* Nursing curriculum, nursing theory-testing, wellness research, communication and socialization patterns. *Unit head:* Dr. Verna Kieffer, Chair, 716-829-7613, Fax: 716-829-8159. *Application contact:* Linda Fisher, Graduate Admissions Director, 716-829-8400, Fax: 716-829-7900, E-mail: graduateadmissions@dyc.edu.

See Close-Up on page 1953.

Eastern Michigan University, Graduate School, College of Health and Human Services, School of Health Sciences, Program in Clinical Research Administration, Ypsilanti, MI 48197. Offers MS. Part-time and evening/weekend programs available. Postbaccalaureate distance learning degree programs offered (minimal on-campus study). *Students:* 1 (woman) full-time, 21 part-time (20 women); includes 8 minority (1 African American, 7 Asian Americans or Pacific Islanders), 1 international. Average age 35. In 2006, 3 degrees awarded. *Entrance requirements:* Additional exam requirements/recommendations for international students: Required—TOEFL. *Application deadline:* For fall admission, 5/15 priority date for domestic students, 5/1 priority date for international students; for winter admission, 10/15 priority date for domestic students, 10/1 priority date for international students; for spring admission, 3/15 priority date for domestic students, 3/1 priority date for international students. Applications are processed on a rolling basis. Application fee: $35. *Expenses:* Tuition, state resident: part-time $341 per credit hour. Tuition, nonresident: full-time $16,104; part-time $671 per credit hour. Required fees: $816; $34 per credit hour. $40 per term. One-time fee: $82 full-time. Tuition and fees vary according to course level, course load, degree level and reciprocity agreements. *Financial support:* Fellowships, research assistantships with full tuition reimbursements, teaching assistantships with full tuition reimbursements, career-related internships or fieldwork, Federal Work-Study, institutionally sponsored loans, scholarships/grants, tuition waivers (partial), and unspecified assistantships available. Support available to part-time students. Financial award applicants required to submit FAFSA. *Unit head:* Dr. Elizabeth Francis Connolly, Director, School of Health Sciences, 734-487-4094, Fax: 734-487-4095, E-mail: elizabeth.francis-connolly@emich.edu.

Emory University, Nell Hodgson Woodruff School of Nursing, Atlanta, GA 30322-1100. Offers adult and elder health advanced practice nursing (MSN), including acute and critical care, adult nurse practitioner, gerontology, oncology; emergency nurse practitioner (MSN); family nurse practitioner (MSN); family nurse-midwife (MSN); leadership in healthcare (MSN); nurse midwifery (MSN); nursing administration (MSN); pediatric advanced nursing practice (MSN); public health nursing (MSN); women's health nurse practitioner (MSN); MSN/MPH. *Accreditation:* AACN; ACNM/DOA (one or more programs are accredited). Part-time programs available. *Entrance requirements:* For master's, GRE General Test or MAT, minimum GPA of 3.0, BS in nursing, RN license and additional course work, 3 letters of recommendation. Additional exam requirements/recommendations for international students: Required—TOEFL (minimum score 600 paper-based; 250 computer-based). Electronic applications accepted. Expenses: Contact

institution. *Faculty research:* Older adult falls and injuries, minority health issues, cardiac symptoms amd quality of life, bio-ethics and decision making, menopausal issues.

See Close-Up on page 1955.

Excelsior College, School of Health Sciences, Albany, NY 12203-5159. Offers healthcare informatics (Certificate); hospice and palliative care (Certificate); nursing management (Certificate). Part-time and evening/weekend programs available. Postbaccalaureate distance learning degree programs offered (no on-campus study). *Faculty:* 1 (woman) full-time, 28 part-time/adjunct (24 women). *Students:* Average age 47. *Entrance requirements:* For degree, bachelor's degree in applicable field. *Application deadline:* Applications are processed on a rolling basis. Application fee: $100. Electronic applications accepted. *Expenses:* Tuition: Part-time $365 per credit hour. *Financial support:* In 2006–07, 1 student received support. Scholarships/grants available. Support available to part-time students. *Faculty research:* Use of technology in online learning. *Unit head:* Deborah Sopczyk, Director, 518-464-8500, Fax: 518-464-8777, E-mail: informatics@excelsior.edu. *Application contact:* Laura Goff, Student Service Coordinator, 518-464-8500, Fax: 518-464-8777, E-mail: lgoff@excelsior.edu.

Ferris State University, College of Allied Health Sciences, School of Nursing, Big Rapids, MI 49307. Offers nursing (MS); nursing administration (MS); nursing education (MS); nursing informatics (MS). Part-time and evening/weekend programs available. Postbaccalaureate distance learning degree programs offered (minimal on-campus study). *Faculty:* 2 full-time (1 woman). *Students:* Average age 39. 22 applicants, 100% accepted, 22 enrolled. In 2006, 2 degrees awarded. *Median time to degree:* Master's–3 years part-time. *Degree requirements:* For master's, thesis, practicum, comprehensive exam. *Entrance requirements:* For master's, BS in nursing, writing sample, letters of reference, 2 years clinical experience. Additional exam requirements/recommendations for international students: Required—TOEFL (minimum score 550 paper-based). *Application deadline:* For fall admission, 8/26 for domestic students; for winter admission, 12/16 for domestic students. Applications are processed on a rolling basis. Application fee: $30. Electronic applications accepted. *Expenses:* Tuition, state resident: part-time $355 per credit hour. Tuition, nonresident: part-time $687 per credit hour. *Financial support:* In 2006–07, 3 students received support. Scholarships/grants available. *Faculty research:* Nursing education-minority student focus student attitudes toward aging. *Unit head:* Dr. Julie A. Coon, Director, 231-591-2267, Fax: 231-591-2325, E-mail: coonj@ferris.edu.

Florida Agricultural and Mechanical University, Division of Graduate Studies, Research, and Continuing Education, School of Allied Health Sciences, Tallahassee, FL 32307-3200. Offers health administration (MS); physical therapy (MPT). *Degree requirements:* For master's, thesis (for some programs). *Entrance requirements:* For master's, GRE General Test or GMAT, minimum GPA of 3.0. Additional exam requirements/recommendations for international students: Required—TOEFL (minimum score 550 paper-based).

Florida Atlantic University, College of Business, Department of Management, International Business and Entrepreneurship, Boca Raton, FL 33431-0991. Offers business administration (Exec MBA, MBA), including accounting (MBA), electronic commerce (MBA), finance (MBA), financial planning (MBA), global entrepreneurship (MBA), health administration (MBA), international business (MBA), marketing (MBA), operations management (MBA), real estate (MBA), sport management (MBA). *Faculty:* 64 full-time (17 women), 15 part-time/adjunct (3 women). *Students:* 215 full-time (89 women), 365 part-time (189 women); includes 150 minority (49 African Americans, 2 American Indian/Alaska Native, 36 Asian Americans or Pacific Islanders, 63 Hispanic Americans), 54 international. Average age 32. 414 applicants, 55% accepted, 167 enrolled. In 2006, 196 master's awarded. *Degree requirements:* For master's, thesis optional. *Entrance requirements:* For master's, GMAT, minimum GPA of 3.0. Additional exam requirements/recommendations for international students: Required—TOEFL (minimum score 600 paper-based; 250 computer-based). *Application deadline:* For fall admission, 7/1 priority date for domestic students, 2/15 priority date for international students; for winter admission, 11/1 priority date for domestic students, 8/15 priority date for international students; for spring admission, 4/1 priority date for domestic students, 1/15 priority date for international students. Applications are processed on a rolling basis. Application fee: $30. Electronic applications accepted. *Expenses:* Tuition, area resident: Full-time $4,394. Tuition, nonresident: full-time $16,441. *Financial support:* Research assistantships, teaching assistantships, career-related internships or fieldwork, Federal Work-Study, institutionally sponsored loans, tuition waivers (partial), and unspecified assistantships available. Support available to part-time students. Financial award application deadline: 3/1; financial award applicants required to submit FAFSA. *Unit head:* Dr. Brenda Richey, Head, 561-297-3194, E-mail: brichey@fau.edu. *Application contact:* Fredrick G. Taylor, Graduate Adviser, 561-297-2768, Fax: 561-297-1315, E-mail: mba@fau.edu.

Gannon University, School of Graduate Studies, College of Sciences, Engineering, and Health Sciences, School of Health Sciences, Program in Nursing, Erie, PA 16541-0001. Offers anesthesia (MSN); business administration (MSN); case management (MSN); medical-surgical nursing (MSN); nurse anesthesia (Certificate); nursing rural practitioner (MSN). *Accreditation:* AACN; AANA/CANAEP (one or more programs are accredited). Part-time and evening/weekend programs available. *Students:* 15 full-time (5 women), 44 part-time (37 women). Average age 35. 8 applicants, 88% accepted, 5 enrolled. In 2006, 14 master's, 2 other advanced degrees awarded. *Degree requirements:* For master's, thesis. *Entrance requirements:* For master's, GRE General Test, MAT, bachelor's degree from a NLN-approved nursing program, interview, Pennsylvania RN license. Additional exam requirements/recommendations for international students: Required—TOEFL (minimum score 500 paper-based; 173 computer-based). *Application deadline:* For fall admission, 4/15 for domestic students. Application fee: $25. *Expenses:* Tuition: Full-time $12,240; part-time $680 per credit. Required fees: $496; $16 per credit. Tuition and fees vary according to course load, degree level, campus/location and program. *Financial support:* Career-related internships or fieldwork and traineeships available. Support available to part-time students. Financial award application deadline: 7/1; financial award applicants required to submit FAFSA. *Unit head:* Dr. Sharon Thompson, Interim Director, 814-871-5345, E-mail: thompson001@gannon.edu. *Application contact:* Debra Meszaros, Director of Graduate Recruitment, 814-871-5819, Fax: 814-871-5827, E-mail: cfal@gannon.edu.

George Mason University, College of Health and Human Services, Fairfax, VA 22030. Offers advanced clinical nursing (MSN); nurse practitioner (MSN); nursing (MSN, PhD); nursing administration (MSN); nursing education (Certificate); nursing educator (MSN); social work (MSW). *Accreditation:* AACN. *Faculty:* 69 full-time (55 women), 75 part-time/adjunct (66 women). *Students:* 98 full-time (81 women), 301 part-time (260 women); includes 121 minority (60 African Americans, 45 Asian Americans or Pacific Islanders, 16 Hispanic Americans), 27 international. Average age 39. 326 applicants, 61% accepted, 121 enrolled. In 2006, 89 master's, 7 doctorates, 11 other advanced degrees awarded. *Degree requirements:* For doctorate, thesis/dissertation, oral/written exams. *Entrance requirements:* For master's, RN license, minimum GPA of 3.0 in last 60 hours of course work; for doctorate, MAT, 3 years of nursing experience, master's degree, minimum GPA of 3.25, professional liability insurance. *Application deadline:* For fall admission, 5/1 for domestic students; for spring admission, 11/1 for domestic students. Application fee: $60 ($75 for international students). Electronic applications accepted. *Expenses:* Tuition, state resident: full-time $5,724; part-time $238 per credit. Tuition, nonresident: full-time $16,896; part-time $704 per credit. Required fees: $1,656; $69 per credit. *Financial support:* Fellowships, research assistantships, teaching assistantships, tuition waivers (partial) available. Support available to part-time students. Financial award application deadline: 3/1; financial award applicants required to submit FAFSA. *Unit head:* Dr. Shirley S. Travis, Dean, 703-993-1918. *Application contact:* Dr. James D. Vail, Associate Dean, Graduate Programs and Research, 703-993-1947, Fax: 703-993-1942, E-mail: nursinfo@gmu.edu.

The George Washington University, School of Medicine and Health Sciences, Health Sciences Programs, Washington, DC 20052. Offers adult nurse practitioner (MSN, Post Master's Certificate); advanced family nurse practitioner (Post Master's Certificate); clinical practice

Nursing and Healthcare Administration

The George Washington University (continued)

management (MSHS); clinical research administration (MSHS); clinical research administration for nurses (MSN); emergency services management (MSHS); end-of-life care (MSHS, MSN); family nurse practitioner (MSN); immunohematology (MSHS); nursing leadership and management (MSN); oral biology (MSHS); physical therapy (DPT); physician assistant (MSHS); MSHS/MPH. Postbaccalaureate distance learning degree programs offered (no on-campus study). *Entrance requirements:* Additional exam requirements/recommendations for international students: Required—TOEFL (minimum score 550 paper-based; 213 computer-based). Expenses: Contact institution.

Graceland University, School of Nursing, Independence, MO 64050-3434. Offers family nurse practitioner (MSN, PMC); health care administration (MSN, PMC); nurse educator (MSN, PMC). Part-time programs available. Postbaccalaureate distance learning degree programs offered (minimal on-campus study). *Faculty:* 11 full-time (all women), 5 part-time/adjunct (all women). *Students:* 94 full-time (93 women), 123 part-time (102 women); includes 16 minority (10 African Americans, 4 Asian Americans or Pacific Islanders, 2 Hispanic Americans). Average age 44. 123 applicants, 90% accepted, 105 enrolled. In 2006, 42 master's, 2 other advanced degrees awarded. *Median time to degree:* Master's–2.5 years full-time, 4 years part-time. *Degree requirements:* For master's, thesis optional. *Entrance requirements:* For master's, BSN from nationally accredited program, portfolio, RN license, minimum GPA of 3.0. *Application deadline:* For fall admission, 6/1 priority date for domestic students; for winter admission, 10/1 priority date for domestic students; for spring admission, 3/1 priority date for domestic students. Applications are processed on a rolling basis. Application fee: $50. Electronic applications accepted. *Expenses:* Contact institution. *Financial support:* In 2006–07, 3 students received support. Institutionally sponsored loans and traineeships available. Support available to part-time students. Financial award applicants required to submit FAFSA. *Faculty research:* International nursing, family care-giving, health promotion. *Unit head:* Dr. Kathryn A Ballou, Dean, 800-833-0524 Ext. 4201, Fax: 816-833-2990, E-mail: kaballou@graceland.edu. *Application contact:* John D. Koehler, Manager of Recruiting, 816-833-0524 Ext. 4804, Fax: 816-833-2990, E-mail: jkoehler@graceland.edu.

Grand Valley State University, Kirkhof College of Nursing, Allendale, MI 49401-9403. Offers advanced practice (MSN); case management (MSN); nursing administration (MSN); nursing education (MSN); MSN/MBA. *Accreditation:* AACN. Part-time programs available. *Faculty:* 17 full-time (all women), 1 (woman) part-time/adjunct. *Students:* 3 full-time (all women), 46 part-time (42 women); includes 4 minority (1 African American, 1 Asian American or Pacific Islander, 2 Hispanic Americans). Average age 35. 15 applicants, 67% accepted, 8 enrolled. In 2006, 20 degrees awarded. *Degree requirements:* For master's, thesis optional. *Entrance requirements:* For master's, GRE, minimum GPA of 3.0 in upper-division course work, course work in statistics, Michigan RN license. Additional exam requirements/recommendations for international students: Required—TOEFL. *Application deadline:* For fall admission, 3/15 priority date for domestic students. Applications are processed on a rolling basis. Application fee: $30. Electronic applications accepted. *Expenses:* Tuition, state resident: full-time $5,850; part-time $325 per credit. Tuition, nonresident: full-time $10,800; part-time $600 per credit. Tuition and fees vary according to course load. *Financial support:* In 2006–07, 7 research assistantships with full and partial tuition reimbursements (averaging $8,000 per year) were awarded; career-related internships or fieldwork, Federal Work-Study, institutionally sponsored loans, and traineeships also available. Financial award application deadline: 2/15. *Faculty research:* Multigenerational health promotion, chronic disease prevention, end-of-life issues; nursing workload, family caregiver health. Total annual research expenditures: $36,000. *Unit head:* Dr. Phyllis Gendler, Dean, 616-331-7161, Fax: 616-331-7362, E-mail: gendlerp@gvsu.edu. *Application contact:* Dr. Jean Martin, Director of Graduate Programs, 616-331-7167, Fax: 616-331-7362, E-mail: martinj@gvsu.edu.

Indiana University–Purdue University Fort Wayne, School of Health Sciences, Department of Nursing, Fort Wayne, IN 46805-1499. Offers nursing administration (MS, Certificate). Part-time programs available. *Faculty:* 9 full-time (all women). *Students:* Average age 47. 9 applicants, 100% accepted, 5 enrolled. In 2006, 2 degrees awarded. *Entrance requirements:* For master's, GRE Writing Test, BS in nursing, eligibility for Indiana RN license, minimum GPA of 3.0. Additional exam requirements/recommendations for international students: Required—TOEFL (minimum score 600 paper-based; 260 computer-based). *Application deadline:* For fall admission, 8/1 priority date for domestic students; for spring admission, 12/1 for domestic students. Application fee: $55. Electronic applications accepted. *Expenses:* Tuition, state resident: full-time $4,039; part-time $224 per credit. Tuition, nonresident: full-time $9,220; part-time $512 per credit. Required fees: $429; $24 per credit. Tuition and fees vary according to course load. *Financial support:* Scholarships/grants available. Support available to part-time students. Financial award application deadline: 3/1; financial award applicants required to submit FAFSA. Total annual research expenditures: $333,000. *Unit head:* Dr. Carol Sternberger, Chair, 260-481-6816, Fax: 260-481-5707, E-mail: sternber@ipfw.edu.

Indiana Wesleyan University, College of Graduate Studies, Division of Nursing, Marion, IN 46953-4974. Offers community health nursing (MS); nursing (Post Master's Certificate); nursing administration (MS); nursing education (MS); primary care nursing (MS). *Accreditation:* AACN. Part-time and evening/weekend programs available. *Faculty:* 2 full-time (both women), 6 part-time/adjunct (3 women). *Students:* 312 full-time (296 women), 8 part-time (4 women); includes 45 minority (41 African Americans, 2 Asian Americans or Pacific Islanders, 2 Hispanic Americans). Average age 40. In 2006, 87 degrees awarded. *Degree requirements:* For master's, thesis. *Entrance requirements:* For master's, GRE, RN license, 1 year of related experience, graduate statistics course. *Application deadline:* For fall admission, 7/31 priority date for domestic students; for winter admission, 11/15 priority date for domestic students; for spring admission, 4/15 priority date for domestic students. Electronic applications accepted. *Expenses:* Contact institution. Tuition and fees vary according to degree level, campus/location and program. *Financial support:* In 2006–07, 15 fellowships were awarded; career-related internships or fieldwork, scholarships/grants, and traineeships also available. Support available to part-time students. Financial award application deadline: 3/15. *Faculty research:* Primary health care with international emphasis, international nursing. *Unit head:* Pam Giles, Director, 765-677-1716, E-mail: gradnurse@indwes.edu. *Application contact:* David McMillan, Assistant Director of Enrollment Management, 765-677-2688, E-mail: david.mcmillan@indwes.edu.

Jefferson College of Health Sciences, Program in Nursing, Roanoke, VA 24031-3186. Offers nursing education (MSN); nursing management (MSN). *Accreditation:* AACN.

The Johns Hopkins University, School of Nursing, Dual Major in Clinical Nurse Specialist and Health Systems Management, Baltimore, MD 21218-2699. Offers MSN. *Accreditation:* AACN. Part-time programs available. *Faculty:* 3 full-time (2 women). *Students:* 1 (woman) full-time, 6 part-time (all women); includes 3 minority (all Asian Americans or Pacific Islanders) Average age 31. 7 applicants, 86% accepted, 3 enrolled. In 2006, 2 degrees awarded. *Degree requirements:* For master's, scholarly project or portfolio, thesis optional. *Entrance requirements:* For master's, GRE, interview, minimum GPA of 3.0, BSN, Maryland RN license. Additional exam requirements/recommendations for international students: Required—TOEFL (minimum score 550 paper-based; 230 computer-based). *Application deadline:* For fall admission, 3/1 priority date for domestic and international students; for spring admission, 7/1 priority date for domestic and international students. Applications are processed on a rolling basis. Application fee: $75. *Expenses:* Tuition: Full-time $32,976. Tuition and fees vary according to degree level and program. *Financial support:* In 2006–07, 1 student received support. Federal Work-Study, scholarships/grants, traineeships, and tuition waivers (partial) available. Support available to part-time students. Financial award application deadline: 3/15; financial award applicants required to submit FAFSA. *Faculty research:* Maternal/child health, outcomes measurement, symptom management, oncology, HIV/AIDS. *Unit head:* Dr. Kathleen M. White, Director, Master's Programs, 410-614-4664, Fax: 410-955-7463, E-mail: kwhite@son.jhmi.edu. *Application contact:* Mary O'Rourke, Director of Admissions/Student Services, 410-955-7548, Fax: 410-614-7086, E-mail: orourke@son.jhmi.edu.

The Johns Hopkins University, School of Nursing, Program in Clinical Nurse Specialist, Baltimore, MD 21218-2699. Offers MSN. *Accreditation:* AACN. Part-time programs available. *Faculty:* 2 full-time (1 woman). *Students:* 4 full-time (all women), 16 part-time (all women); includes 1 minority (African American) Average age 31. 23 applicants, 74% accepted, 6 enrolled. In 2006, 5 degrees awarded. *Degree requirements:* For master's, scholarly project or portfolio, thesis optional. *Entrance requirements:* For master's, GRE, interview, minimum GPA of 3.0, BSN, Maryland RN license. Additional exam requirements/recommendations for international students: Required—TOEFL (minimum score 550 paper-based; 230 computer-based). *Application deadline:* For fall admission, 3/1 priority date for domestic and international students; for spring admission, 7/1 priority date for domestic and international students. Applications are processed on a rolling basis. Application fee: $75. *Expenses:* Contact institution. Tuition and fees vary according to degree level and program. *Financial support:* In 2006–07, 1 student received support. Federal Work-Study, scholarships/grants, traineeships, and tuition waivers (partial) available. Support available to part-time students. Financial award application deadline: 3/1; financial award applicants required to submit FAFSA. *Faculty research:* Maternal child health, symptom management, cardiovascular risk reduction, asthma, hypertension. *Unit head:* Dr. Kathleen M. White, Director, Master's Programs, 410-614-4664, Fax: 410-955-7463, E-mail: kwhite@son.jhmi.edu. *Application contact:* Mary O'Rourke, Director of Admissions/Student Services, 410-955-7548, Fax: 410-614-7086, E-mail: orourke@son.jhmi.edu.

The Johns Hopkins University, School of Nursing, Program in Health Systems Management, Baltimore, MD 21218-2699. Offers MSN. *Accreditation:* AACN. Part-time programs available. *Faculty:* 2 full-time (both women), 2 part-time/adjunct (1 woman). *Students:* Average age 30. 19 applicants, 95% accepted, 15 enrolled. In 2006, 4 degrees awarded. *Degree requirements:* For master's, scholarly project or portfolio, thesis optional. *Entrance requirements:* For master's, GRE, interview, minimum GPA of 3.0, BSN, Maryland RN license. Additional exam requirements/recommendations for international students: Required—TOEFL (minimum score 550 paper-based; 230 computer-based). *Application deadline:* For fall admission, 3/1 priority date for domestic and international students; for spring admission, 7/1 priority date for domestic and international students. Applications are processed on a rolling basis. Application fee: $75. *Expenses:* Contact institution. Tuition and fees vary according to degree level and program. *Financial support:* Federal Work-Study, scholarships/grants, traineeships, and tuition waivers (partial) available. Support available to part-time students. Financial award application deadline: 3/1; financial award applicants required to submit FAFSA. *Faculty research:* Program evaluation, program development, staff satisfaction, quality and safety. *Unit head:* Dr. Kathleen M. White, Director, Master's Programs, 410-614-4664, Fax: 410-955-7463, E-mail: kwhite@son.jhmi.edu. *Application contact:* Mary O'Rourke, Director of Admissions/Student Services, 410-955-7548, Fax: 410-614-7086, E-mail: orourke@son.jhmi.edu.

Kean University, College of Natural, Applied and Health Sciences, Program in Nursing, Union, NJ 07083. Offers clinical management (MSN); community health (MSN). *Accreditation:* NLN. Part-time and evening/weekend programs available. *Faculty:* 7 full-time (all women). *Students:* 5 full-time (4 women), 62 part-time (57 women); includes 42 minority (26 African Americans, 12 Asian Americans or Pacific Islanders, 4 Hispanic Americans). Average age 43. 29 applicants, 93% accepted, 19 enrolled. In 2006, 23 degrees awarded. *Degree requirements:* For master's, thesis or alternative, clinical field experience. *Entrance requirements:* For master's, BS in nursing, RN license, 2 letters of recommendation, interview. *Application deadline:* For fall admission, 5/1 for domestic students; for spring admission, 11/1 for domestic students. Application fee: $60 ($150 for international students). *Expenses:* Tuition, state resident: full-time $8,856; part-time $369 per credit. Tuition, nonresident: full-time $11,256; part-time $469 per credit. *Financial support:* Research assistantships with full tuition reimbursements available. *Unit head:* Dr. Estelle A. Pisani, Program Coordinator, 908-737-3386, E-mail: episani@kean.edu. *Application contact:* Joanne Morris, Director of Graduate Admissions, 908-737-3355, Fax: 908-737-3354, E-mail: grad-adm@kean.edu.

Kent State University, College of Nursing, Kent, OH 44242-0001. Offers clinical nursing (MSN), including nursing of the adult (medical/surgical nursing), psychiatric mental health nursing; nursing (PhD); nursing administration (MSN); nursing education (MSN); parent-child nursing (MSN). *Accreditation:* AACN. Part-time programs available. *Degree requirements:* For master's, thesis optional; for doctorate, thesis/dissertation, comprehensive exam, registration. *Entrance requirements:* For master's, GRE if undergraduate GPA is less than 3.0, minimum GPA of 2.75; for doctorate, GRE, MSN. Additional exam requirements/recommendations for international students: Required—TOEFL. Electronic applications accepted. Expenses: Contact institution. *Faculty research:* Women and violence, methodological specialties, osteoporosis in women, new caregivers and the elderly.

Lamar University, College of Graduate Studies, College of Arts and Sciences, Department of Nursing, Beaumont, TX 77710. Offers nursing administration online (MSN); nursing education online (MSN); MSN/MBA. *Accreditation:* NLN. Part-time and evening/weekend programs available. *Faculty:* 10 full-time (all women). *Students:* 2 full-time (0 women), 7 part-time (4 women). Average age 42. 10 applicants, 40% accepted, 2 enrolled. In 2006, 2 master's awarded. *Median time to degree:* Of those who began their doctoral program in fall 1998, 100% received their degree in 8 years or less. *Degree requirements:* For master's, practicum project presentation, evidence-based project. *Entrance requirements:* For master's, GRE General Test, MAT, criminal background check, RN license, NLN-accredited BSN, college course work in graduate statistics in past 5 years, letters of recommendation, minimum undergraduate GPA of 3.0. Additional exam requirements/recommendations for international students: Required—TOEFL, MAT. *Application deadline:* For fall admission, 8/1 priority date for domestic students; for spring admission, 12/1 priority date for domestic students. Applications are processed on a rolling basis. Application fee: $25 ($50 for international students). *Expenses:* Tuition, nonresident: part-time $33 per hour. Required fees: $43 per hour. $110 per semester. *Financial support:* In 2006–07, 3 students received support, including 2 teaching assistantships (averaging $24,000 per year); scholarships/grants and traineeships also available. Financial award application deadline: 4/1. *Faculty research:* Student retention, theory, caregiving, on-line course and research. Total annual research expenditures: $6,000. *Unit head:* Dr. Nancy Blume, Director of Graduate Nursing Studies, 409-880-8820, Fax: 409-880-8698, E-mail: nancy.blume@lamar.edu. *Application contact:* Shelly R. Belk, Administrative Associate, 409-880-7720.

La Roche College, School of Graduate Studies, Program in Nursing, Pittsburgh, PA 15237-5898. Offers family nurse practitioner (MSN); nursing management (MSN). *Accreditation:* AANA/CANAEP; NLN. Part-time and evening/weekend programs available. *Faculty:* 2 full-time (both women), 1 part-time/adjunct (0 women). *Students:* Average age 46. *Median time to degree:* Master's–2 years full-time, 4 years part-time. *Degree requirements:* For master's, internship, practicum, thesis optional. *Entrance requirements:* For master's, GRE General Test, BSN, nursing license, work experience. *Application deadline:* For fall admission, 8/15 priority date for domestic students; for spring admission, 12/15 priority date for domestic students. Applications are processed on a rolling basis. Application fee: $50. Electronic applications accepted. *Expenses:* Contact institution. *Financial support:* Application deadline: 3/31; *Faculty research:* Patient education, perception. *Unit head:* Dr. Rosemary McCarthy, Division Chair, 412-536-1173, Fax: 412-536-1175, E-mail: mccartr1@laroche.edu. *Application contact:* Hope Schiffgens, Director of Admissions for Graduate and Continuing Education, 412-536-1266, Fax: 412-536-1283, E-mail: schombh1@laroche.edu.

La Salle University, School of Nursing and Health Sciences, Philadelphia, PA 19141-1199. Offers adult health and illness, clinical nurse specialist (MSN); gerontology (Certificate); nursing administration (MSN); nursing education (Certificate); nursing informatics (Certificate); primary care of adults-nurse practitioner (MSN); public health nursing (MSN); school nursing (Certificate); speech-language-hearing science (MS); wound, ostomy and continence nursing (Certificate); wound, ostomy, and continence nursing (MSN); MSN/MBA. *Accreditation:* AACN. Part-time programs available. Postbaccalaureate distance learning degree programs offered (minimal on-campus study). *Entrance requirements:* For master's, GRE or MAT, 1 year of professional work experience, BSN, Pennsylvania RN license. Expenses: Contact institution. *Faculty research:* Medication errors, wound care, metacognition, education of RN students.

Lewis University, College of Nursing and Health Professions, Program in Nursing, Romeoville, IL 60446. Offers case management (MSN); nursing administration (MSN); nursing education (MSN); MSN/MBA. *Accreditation:* AACN. Part-time and evening/weekend programs available. *Degree requirements:* For master's, clinical practicum. *Entrance requirements:* For master's, GRE General Test, GRE Subject Test, minimum undergraduate GPA of 2.75, degree in nursing, RN license, letter of recommendation, interview, resumé or curriculum vitae. Additional exam requirements/recommendations for international students: Required—TOEFL (minimum score 550 paper-based; 213 computer-based). Electronic applications accepted. *Faculty research:* Cancer prevention, phenomenological methods, public policy analysis.

Loma Linda University, Department of Graduate Nursing, Program in Nursing Administration, Loma Linda, CA 92350. Offers MS, Certificate. *Accreditation:* AACN. Part-time programs available. *Degree requirements:* For master's, thesis or alternative. *Entrance requirements:* For master's, GRE General Test. *Faculty research:* Job aspects contributing to satisfaction among leaders in health care institutions, leadership content significant to RN graduates.

Long Island University, Brooklyn Campus, School of Nursing, Department of Nurse Executive, Brooklyn, NY 11201-8423. Offers MS. *Accreditation:* AACN. *Entrance requirements:* For master's, New York RN license, 2 letters of recommendation. Additional exam requirements/recommendations for international students: Required—TOEFL (minimum score 500 paper-based; 173 computer-based).

Louisiana State University Health Sciences Center, School of Nursing, New Orleans, LA 70112-2223. Offers adult health and illness (MN); adult health and nursing (DNS); neonatal nurse practitioner (MN); nursing (MN); nursing service administration (MN, DNS); parent-child health nursing (MN); primary care nurse practitioner (MN); psychiatric/community mental health nursing (MN, DNS); public health/community health nursing (MN, DNS). *Accreditation:* AACN; AANA/CANAEP (one or more programs are accredited). Part-time programs available. *Degree requirements:* For master's, thesis optional; for doctorate, thesis/dissertation. *Entrance requirements:* For master's, GRE General Test, MAT, minimum GPA of 3.0; for doctorate, GRE General Test, minimum GPA of 3.5. Additional exam requirements/recommendations for international students: Required—TOEFL. *Expenses:* Tuition, state resident: full-time $5,868; part-time $722 per credit. Tuition, nonresident: full-time $8,993; part-time $1,104 per credit. *Faculty research:* Advanced clinical practice, nursing education, health, social support, nursing administration.

Loyola University Chicago, Graduate School, Marcella Niehoff School of Nursing, Health Systems Management Program, Chicago, IL 60611-2196. Offers MSN, MSN/MBA. Part-time and evening/weekend programs available. *Students:* 3 full-time (all women), 20 part-time (all women). Average age 36. 20 applicants, 90% accepted. In 2006, 10 degrees awarded. *Degree requirements:* For master's, comprehensive exam or oral thesis defense. *Application deadline:* Applications are processed on a rolling basis. Application fee: $40. Electronic applications accepted. *Financial support:* Teaching assistantships, traineeships and unspecified assistantships available. Financial award application deadline: 3/1. *Faculty research:* Patient classification systems, career/job mobility. *Unit head:* Dr. Ida Androwich, Dean, 773-508-3255, E-mail: iandrow@luc.edu. *Application contact:* Dr. Vicki A. Keough, Associate Professor, 708-216-3582, Fax: 708-216-9555, E-mail: vkeough@luc.edu.

Madonna University, Program in Nursing, Livonia, MI 48150-1173. Offers adult health: chronic health conditions (MSN); adult nurse practitioner (MSN); nursing administration (MSN); MSN/MSBA. *Accreditation:* AACN. Part-time programs available. *Faculty:* 3 full-time (all women). *Students:* 12 full-time (all women), 82 part-time (80 women); includes 9 minority (5 African Americans, 3 Asian Americans or Pacific Islanders, 1 Hispanic American), 3 international. Average age 40. 20 applicants, 50% accepted. In 2006, 10 degrees awarded. *Degree requirements:* For master's, thesis or alternative. *Entrance requirements:* For master's, GRE General Test, Michigan nursing license. *Application deadline:* For fall admission, 8/1 priority date for domestic students; for winter admission, 12/1 priority date for domestic students; for spring admission, 4/1 priority date for domestic students. Applications are processed on a rolling basis. Application fee: $25 ($200 for international students). Electronic applications accepted. *Financial support:* Career-related internships or fieldwork, Federal Work-Study, institutionally sponsored loans, and scholarships/grants available. Support available to part-time students. *Faculty research:* Coping, caring. *Unit head:* Dr. Nancy O'Connor, Chairperson, 734-432-5461, Fax: 734-432-5463, E-mail: noconnor@madonna.edu. *Application contact:* Sandra Kellums, Coordinator of Graduate Admissions and Records, 734-432-5667, Fax: 734-432-5862, E-mail: skellum@madonna.edu.

Marymount University, School of Health Professions, Program in Nursing, Arlington, VA 22207-4299. Offers family nurse practitioner (MSN, Certificate); nursing administration (MSN, Certificate); nursing education (MSN, Certificate); RN to MSN (MSN). *Accreditation:* AACN; NLN. Part-time and evening/weekend programs available. *Faculty:* 7 full-time (all women), 1 (woman) part-time/adjunct. *Students:* 4 full-time (3 women), 36 part-time (35 women); includes 23 minority (15 African Americans, 5 Asian Americans or Pacific Islanders, 3 Hispanic Americans), 1 international. Average age 42. 17 applicants, 100% accepted, 10 enrolled. In 2006, 13 master's, 2 other advanced degrees awarded. *Degree requirements:* For master's, comprehensive exam. *Entrance requirements:* For master's, 2 letters of recommendation, interview, RN license, resumé; for Certificate, interview. *Application deadline:* Applications are processed on a rolling basis. Application fee: $40. Electronic applications accepted. *Expenses:* Tuition: Full-time $11,160; part-time $620 per credit. Required fees: $113; $630 per credit. *Financial support:* Research assistantships with partial tuition reimbursements, career-related internships or fieldwork, scholarships/grants, and unspecified assistantships available. Support available to part-time students. Financial award applicants required to submit FAFSA. *Unit head:* Dr. Susan Bidwell, Chair, 703-284-1593, Fax: 703-284-3819, E-mail: susan.bidwell@marymount.edu.

Marywood University, Academic Affairs, College of Health and Human Services, Department of Nursing and Public Administration, Program in Nursing Administration, Scranton, PA 18509-1598. Offers MS. *Accreditation:* NLN. *Students:* 1 (woman) full-time, 13 part-time (all women). Average age 42. In 2006, 2 degrees awarded. *Degree requirements:* For master's, thesis or alternative, internship/practicum. Application fee: $30. *Expenses:* Tuition: Part-time $672 per credit. Tuition and fees vary according to degree level, campus/location and program.

Medical University of South Carolina, College of Nursing, Program in Nursing Administration, Charleston, SC 29425-0002. Offers MSN. *Accreditation:* AACN. Part-time programs available. Postbaccalaureate distance learning degree programs offered. *Faculty:* 9 full-time (8 women). *Students:* 4 full-time (3 women), 15 part-time (13 women); includes 4 minority (all African Americans) 14 applicants, 71% accepted, 10 enrolled. In 2006, 7 degrees awarded. *Degree requirements:* For master's, thesis optional. *Entrance requirements:* For master's, GRE General Test, BSN, nursing license, minimum GPA of 3.0. Additional exam requirements/recommendations for international students: Required—TOEFL (minimum score 600 paper-based; 250 computer-based). *Application deadline:* For fall admission, 2/1 for domestic and international students; for spring admission, 9/15 for domestic and international students. Application fee: $75. Electronic applications accepted. *Financial support:* Federal Work-Study, scholarships/grants, and traineeships available. Support available to part-time students. Financial award application deadline: 3/15; financial award applicants required to submit FAFSA. *Unit head:* Dr. Mary M. Martin, Track Coordinator, 843-792-3084, Fax: 843-792-1741, E-mail: martinmm@musc.edu. *Application contact:* Carolyn F. Page, Director, Student Services, 843-792-3844, Fax: 843-792-9258, E-mail: pagecf@musc.edu.

Mercy College, Division of Health Professions, Program in Nursing, Dobbs Ferry, NY 10522-1189. Offers nursing administration (MS); nursing education (MS). *Accreditation:* AACN. Part-time programs available. *Students:* 18 full-time (8 women), 65 part-time (62 women); includes 36 minority (28 African Americans, 6 Asian Americans or Pacific Islanders, 2 Hispanic Americans), 14 international. Average age 41. In 2006, 15 degrees awarded. *Degree requirements:* For master's, comprehensive project. *Entrance requirements:* For master's, GRE General Test or MAT, BSN, minimum GPA of 3.0, 2 letters of reference, interview, US RN registration. *Application deadline:* For fall admission, 8/15 priority date for domestic students; for spring admission, 2/15 for domestic students. Applications are processed on a rolling basis. Application fee: $62. *Expenses:* Tuition: Part-time $595 per credit. Required fees: $9 per credit. Tuition and fees vary according to program. *Financial support:* Career-related internships or fieldwork, Federal Work-Study, and institutionally sponsored loans available. Support available to part-time students. *Faculty research:* Program evaluation, cost and home care, children of alcoholic parents, clinical decision making. *Unit head:* Dr. Mary McGuiness, Director, Nursing Programs, 914-674-7863 Ext. 551, E-mail: mmcguiness@mercy.edu. *Application contact:* Kathleen Jackson, Director of Admissions, 800-Mercy-NY, Fax: 914-674-7382, E-mail: admissions@mercy.edu.

Minnesota State University Mankato, College of Graduate Studies, College of Allied Health and Nursing, Department of Nursing, Mankato, MN 56001. Offers family nursing (MSN), including clinical nurse specialist, educator, family nurse practitioner, manager; managed care (MSN), including clinical nurse specialist, educator, family nurse practitioner, manager. *Accreditation:* AACN; NLN. *Students:* 12 full-time (all women), 34 part-time (32 women). Average age 39. In 2006, 15 degrees awarded. *Degree requirements:* For master's, internships, research project or thesis. *Entrance requirements:* For master's, GRE General Test or on-campus essay, minimum GPA of 3.0 during previous 2 years, BSN or equivalent references. Additional exam requirements/recommendations for international students: Required—TOEFL. *Application deadline:* For fall admission, 1/15 priority date for domestic students; for spring admission, 11/27 for domestic students. Applications are processed on a rolling basis. Application fee: $40. Electronic applications accepted. *Financial support:* Research assistantships with full tuition reimbursements, teaching assistantships with full tuition reimbursements available. Financial award application deadline: 3/15; financial award applicants required to submit FAFSA. *Faculty research:* Psychosocial nursing, computers in nursing, family adaptation. *Unit head:* Dr. Sonja Meiers, Graduate Coordinator, 507-389-1725. *Application contact:* Collaborative MSN Program Admissions, 507-389-6022.

Molloy College, Department of Nursing, Rockville Centre, NY 11571-5002. Offers adult nurse practitioner (Advanced Certificate); clinical nurse specialist: adult health (Advanced Certificate); family nurse practitioner (Advanced Certificate); nurse practitioner psychiatry (Advanced Certificate); nursing (MS); nursing administration (Advanced Certificate); nursing administration with informatics (Advanced Certificate); nursing education (Advanced Certificate); nursing informatics (Advanced Certificate); pediatric nurse practitioner (Advanced Certificate). *Accreditation:* AACN. Part-time and evening/weekend programs available. *Degree requirements:* For master's, thesis optional. *Entrance requirements:* For master's, 3 letters of reference BS in nursing, minimum undergraduate GPA of 3.0; for Advanced Certificate, 3 letters of reference, master's degree in nursing. *Faculty research:* Hardiness and aging, alcoholism, current ethics, breast cancer, nurse role perception.

Mountain State University, Graduate Studies, Program in Nursing, Beckley, WV 25802-9003. Offers administration/education (MSN); family nurse practitioner (MSN); nurse anesthesia (MSN); registered nurse anesthetist (Certificate). *Accreditation:* AANA/CANAEP; NLN. Part-time programs available. Postbaccalaureate distance learning degree programs offered (minimal on-campus study). *Faculty:* 6 full-time (4 women), 14 part-time/adjunct (7 women). *Students:* 80 full-time (64 women), 10 part-time (all women); includes 1 minority (African American) Average age 37. 29 applicants, 100% accepted, 17 enrolled. In 2006, 4 degrees awarded. *Median time to degree:* Master's–2 years full-time, 3 years part-time. *Degree requirements:* For master's, thesis or alternative, comprehensive exam. *Entrance requirements:* For master's, GRE. Additional exam requirements/recommendations for international students: Required—TOEFL (minimum score 550 paper-based; 213 computer-based); Recommended—IELTS (minimum score 7). *Application deadline:* For spring admission, 6/30 for domestic and international students. Applications are processed on a rolling basis. Application fee: $25 ($50 for international students). Electronic applications accepted. *Expenses:* Contact institution. Tuition and fees vary according to course load and program. *Financial support:* In 2006–07, 2 research assistantships (averaging $1,200 per year) were awarded; Federal Work-Study, scholarships/grants, and unspecified assistantships also available. Support available to part-time students. Financial award applicants required to submit FAFSA. *Unit head:* Dr. Jessica Sharp, Senior Academic Officer for Graduate Nursing, 304-929-1425, Fax: 304-929-1601, E-mail: jsharp@mountainstate.edu. *Application contact:* Melody Tilley, Program Specialist, 304-929-1576, Fax: 304-929-1601, E-mail: mtilley@mountainstate.edu.

See Close-Up on page 1965.

Mount Saint Mary College, Division of Nursing, Newburgh, NY 12550-3494. Offers adult nurse practitioner (MS), including nursing education, nursing management; clinical nurse specialist-adult health (MS), including nursing education, nursing management. *Accreditation:* AACN. Part-time and evening/weekend programs available. *Faculty:* 3 full-time (2 women), 1 (woman) part-time/adjunct. *Students:* 1 (woman) full-time, 28 part-time (26 women); includes 3 minority (2 African Americans, 1 Asian American or Pacific Islander). Average age 42. 12 applicants, 100% accepted, 10 enrolled. In 2006, 6 degrees awarded. *Degree requirements:* For master's, research utilization project. *Entrance requirements:* For master's, BSN, minimum GPA of 3.0, RN license. *Application deadline:* For fall admission, 6/3 priority date for domestic students; for spring admission, 10/31 priority date for domestic students. Applications are processed on a rolling basis. Application fee: $35. *Expenses:* Tuition: Full-time $11,880; part-time $660 per credit. *Financial support:* Unspecified assistantships and nursing lab assistant available. Financial award application deadline: 3/15; financial award applicants required to submit FAFSA. *Unit head:* Dr. Karen Baldwin, Coordinator, 845-569-3512, Fax: 845-562-6762, E-mail: baldwin@msmc.edu.

Northeastern University, Bouvé College of Health Sciences Graduate School, School of Nursing, Program in Nursing Administration, Boston, MA 02115-5096. Offers MS, MS/MBA. *Accreditation:* AACN. *Students:* 6 full-time (5 women), 15 part-time (12 women). Average age 42. 6 applicants, 50% accepted. In 2006, 6 degrees awarded. *Degree requirements:* For master's, thesis or alternative. *Entrance requirements:* For master's, GRE General Test, minimum GPA of 3.0, previous course work in statistics, 1-2 years of nursing experience, RN license, ICU experience. Additional exam requirements/recommendations for international students: Required—TOEFL. *Application deadline:* For fall admission, 4/1 priority date for domestic students; for spring admission, 2/1 for domestic students. Applications are processed on a rolling basis. Application fee: $50. *Financial support:* Research assistantships, teaching assistantships, tuition waivers (partial) available. Financial award application deadline: 7/1; financial award applicants required to submit FAFSA. *Faculty research:* Nursing informatics. *Unit head:* Dr. Jane Aroian, Director, 617-373-3128, E-mail: j.aroian@neu.edu. *Application contact:* Margaret Schnabel, Director of Graduate Admissions, 617-373-2708, Fax: 617-373-4704, E-mail: bouvegrad@neu.edu.

Norwich University, School of Graduate Studies, Program in Nursing Administration, Northfield, VT 05663. Offers MSN. Postbaccalaureate distance learning degree programs offered. *Students:* 26 full-time (20 women). *Entrance requirements:* For master's, minimum undergraduate degree GPA of 2.75. Additional exam requirements/recommendations for international students: Required—TOEFL (minimum score 550 paper-based). *Application deadline:* For fall admission, 7/1 for domestic and international students; for winter admission, 11/1 for domestic and international students; for spring admission, 3/1 for domestic and international students. Application fee: $50. Electronic applications accepted. *Financial support:* Scholarships/grants available. *Unit head:* Dr. Cynthia Scalzi, Unit Head, 802-485-2730.

Otterbein College, Department of Nursing, Westerville, OH 43081. Offers adult nurse practitioner (MSN, Certificate); clinical nurse leader (MSN); family nurse practitioner (MSN, Certificate); nurse service administration (MSN). *Accreditation:* AACN; NLN. Part-time and

Nursing and Healthcare Administration

Otterbein College (continued)
evening/weekend programs available. Postbaccalaureate distance learning degree programs offered (minimal on-campus study). *Students:* 7 full-time, 118 part-time; includes 5 minority (4 African Americans, 1 Hispanic American). Average age 40. 47 applicants, 94% accepted, 33 enrolled. In 2006, 37 degrees awarded. *Degree requirements:* For master's, thesis (for some programs), comprehensive exam (for some programs). *Entrance requirements:* For master's and Certificate, official transcripts, 2 reference forms, essay, resumé. Additional exam requirements/recommendations for international students: Required—TOEFL (minimum score 550 paper-based; 213 computer-based; 79 iBT). *Application deadline:* For fall admission, 8/10 priority date for domestic students, 7/10 for international students; for winter admission, 12/7 priority date for domestic students, 11/7 for international students; for spring admission, 2/28 priority date for domestic students, 1/31 for international students. Applications are processed on a rolling basis. *Expenses:* Tuition: Full-time $7,560; part-time $315 per credit. Tuition and fees vary according to program. *Financial support:* Traineeships available. Support available to part-time students. Financial award applicants required to submit FAFSA. *Faculty research:* Patient education, women's health, trauma curriculum development, administration. *Unit head:* Dr. Barbara Schaffner, Chair, 614-823-1735, Fax: 614-823-3131, E-mail: bschaffner@otterbein.edu. *Application contact:* Vicki Miller, Administrative Assistant, Office of Graduate Programs, 614-823-3210, Fax: 614-823-3208, E-mail: grad@otterbein.edu.

Pacific Lutheran University, Division of Graduate Studies, School of Nursing, Program in Care and Outcomes Manager, Tacoma, WA 98447. Offers client systems management (MSN); health care systems management (MSN). *Accreditation:* AACN. Part-time and evening/weekend programs available. *Faculty:* 4 full-time (3 women), 3 part-time/adjunct (1 woman). *Students:* 7 full-time (all women), 1 (woman) part-time; includes 1 minority (African American) Average age 44. 1 applicant, 100% accepted, 1 enrolled. In 2006, 9 degrees awarded. *Degree requirements:* For master's, thesis or alternative, registration. *Entrance requirements:* For master's, GRE General Test, minimum undergraduate GPA of 3.0. Additional exam requirements/recommendations for international students: Required—TOEFL (minimum score 550 paper-based; 213 computer-based). *Application deadline:* For fall admission, 4/1 priority date for domestic students. Applications are processed on a rolling basis. Application fee: $40. *Expenses:* Tuition: Full-time $17,544. Part-time tuition and fees vary according to program. *Financial support:* Federal Work-Study, scholarships/grants, and unspecified assistantships available. Financial award application deadline: 3/1. *Unit head:* Dr. Patsy Maloney, Unit Head, 253-535-7685. *Application contact:* Linda DuBay, Senior Office Assistant, 253-535-7151, Fax: 253-536-5136, E-mail: admissions@plu.edu.

Prairie View A&M University, Graduate School, College of Nursing, Houston, TX 77030. Offers family nurse practitioner (MSN); nursing administration (MSN); nursing education (MSN). *Accreditation:* AACN; NLN. Part-time programs available. *Faculty:* 3 full-time (all women), 4 part-time/adjunct (3 women). *Students:* 18 full-time (16 women), 59 part-time (51 women); includes 71 minority (62 African Americans, 5 Asian Americans or Pacific Islanders, 4 Hispanic Americans). Average age 38. 37 applicants, 100% accepted, 32 enrolled. In 2006, 7 degrees awarded. *Median time to degree:* Master's–1.5 years full-time, 2.5 years part-time. *Degree requirements:* For master's, thesis, comprehensive exam. *Entrance requirements:* For master's, MAT or GRE, BS in nursing; 2 years of experience as a registered nurse; 1 course each in statistics, basic health and assessment. *Application deadline:* For fall admission, 6/1 priority date for domestic students; for spring admission, 11/1 priority date for domestic students. Applications are processed on a rolling basis. Application fee: $50. *Financial support:* In 2006–07, 17 students received support. Career-related internships or fieldwork, Federal Work-Study, institutionally sponsored loans, scholarships/grants, and traineeships available. Support available to part-time students. Financial award application deadline: 4/1; financial award applicants required to submit FAFSA. *Faculty research:* Software development and violence prevention, health promotion and prevention. Total annual research expenditures: $350,000. *Unit head:* Dr. Betty N. Adams, Dean, 713-797-7009, Fax: 713-797-7013, E-mail: bnadams@pvamu.edu. *Application contact:* Dr. Pamela C. Willson, Associate Professor, 713-797-7011, Fax: 713-797-7012, E-mail: pcwillson@pvamu.edu.

Queens University of Charlotte, Hayworth College, Division of Nursing, Charlotte, NC 28274-0002. Offers nursing management (MSN). *Accreditation:* AACN. *Faculty:* 2 full-time (both women), 3 part-time/adjunct (all women). *Students:* 2 full-time (both women), 17 part-time (13 women); includes 6 minority (all African Americans) Average age 27. 11 applicants, 82% accepted, 9 enrolled. In 2006, 10 degrees awarded. *Degree requirements:* For master's, research project. *Entrance requirements:* For master's, minimum GPA of 3.0. Additional exam requirements/recommendations for international students: Required—TOEFL. *Application deadline:* Applications are processed on a rolling basis. Application fee: $40. Electronic applications accepted. *Expenses:* Contact institution. *Unit head:* Dr. William K. Cody, Chair, 704-337-2542. *Application contact:* Holly Boyd, Director of Admissions, 704-337-2574, Fax: 704-337-2415.

Rivier College, School of Graduate Studies, Department of Business Administration, Nashua, NH 03060-5086. Offers business administration (MBA); health care administration (MBA); human resources management (MS); organizational leadership (EMBA). Part-time and evening/weekend programs available. *Faculty:* 4 full-time (2 women), 21 part-time/adjunct (6 women). *Students:* 12 full-time (10 women), 60 part-time (35 women); includes 7 minority (2 African Americans, 2 Asian Americans or Pacific Islanders, 3 Hispanic Americans), 6 international. Average age 36. In 2006, 37 degrees awarded. *Degree requirements:* For master's, registration. *Application deadline:* Applications are processed on a rolling basis. Application fee: $25. *Financial support:* Available to part-time students. Application deadline: 2/1; *Unit head:* Maria Matarazzo, Division Chair, 603-897-8532, Fax: 603-897-8885, E-mail: mmatarazzo@rivier.edu. *Application contact:* Diane Monahan, Director of Graduate Admissions, 603-897-8129, Fax: 603-897-8810, E-mail: gradadm@rivier.edu.

Roberts Wesleyan College, Division of Nursing, Rochester, NY 14624-1997. Offers nursing administration (MSN); nursing education (MSN). *Faculty:* 13 full-time (all women), 6 part-time/adjunct (4 women). *Entrance requirements:* For master's, minimum GPA of 3.0; BS in nursing; interview; RN license; resumé; course work in statistics and health assessment. Additional exam requirements/recommendations for international students: Required—TOEFL. *Unit head:* Dr. Susanne M. Mohnkern, Chair, 585-594-6000, E-mail: mohnkerns@roberts.edu. *Application contact:* Yvonne Strong, Admissions Coordinator, 585-594-6388, E-mail: strong_yvonne@roberts.edu.

Sacred Heart University, Graduate Studies, College of Education and Health Professions, Faculty of Nursing, Fairfield, CT 06825-1000. Offers clinical nurse leader (MSN); family nurse practitioner (MSN); patient care services administration (MSN); MSN/MBA. *Accreditation:* AACN. Part-time and evening/weekend programs available. Postbaccalaureate distance learning degree programs offered (minimal on-campus study). *Faculty:* 12 full-time (all women). *Students:* 6 full-time (all women), 64 part-time (59 women); includes 11 minority (7 African Americans, 1 Asian American or Pacific Islander, 3 Hispanic Americans). Average age 39. 34 applicants, 94% accepted, 26 enrolled. In 2006, 10 degrees awarded. *Entrance requirements:* For master's, BSN, minimum GPA of 3.0. Additional exam requirements/recommendations for international students: Required—TOEFL (minimum score 550 paper-based; 213 computer-based). *Application deadline:* Applications are processed on a rolling basis. Application fee: $50 ($100 for international students). Electronic applications accepted. *Expenses:* Contact institution. Full-time tuition and fees vary according to degree level and program. *Financial support:* Career-related internships or fieldwork, institutionally sponsored loans, and unspecified assistantships available. Support available to part-time students. Financial award applicants required to submit FAFSA. *Unit head:* Dr. Dori Sullivan, Director, Graduate Program in Nursing, 203-371-7715. *Application contact:* Kathy Dilks, Assistant Dean of Graduate Admissions, Health Professions, 203-396-8259, Fax: 203-365-4732, E-mail: gradstudies@sacredheart.edu.

Saginaw Valley State University, Crystal M. Lange College of Nursing and Health Sciences, Program in Health System Nurse Specialist, University Center, MI 48710. Offers MSN. *Accreditation:* AACN. Part-time and evening/weekend programs available. *Students:* Average age 40. 12 applicants, 100% accepted, 9 enrolled. In 2006, 3 degrees awarded. *Degree requirements:* For master's, thesis optional. *Entrance requirements:* For master's, GRE. Additional exam requirements/recommendations for international students: Required—TOEFL. *Application deadline:* Applications are processed on a rolling basis. Application fee: $25. Electronic applications accepted. *Expenses:* Tuition, state resident: full-time $7,225; part-time $301 per credit hour. Tuition, nonresident: full-time $13,888; part-time $579 per credit hour. Required fees: $330; $14 per credit hour. Tuition and fees vary according to course load. *Financial support:* Fellowships with partial tuition reimbursements, research assistantships with full tuition reimbursements, Federal Work-Study available. Support available to part-time students. Financial award application deadline: 4/1; financial award applicants required to submit FAFSA. *Unit head:* Dr. Margaret Flatt, Assistant Dean, 989-964-4130, Fax: 989-964-4024, E-mail: flatt@svsu.edu.

Saint Joseph's College of Maine, Department of Nursing, Standish, ME 04084-5263. Offers nursing (MS); nursing administration and leadership (Certificate); nursing and health care education (Certificate). MS degree offered only through faculty-directed independent study. *Accreditation:* AACN. Part-time programs available. Postbaccalaureate distance learning degree programs offered (minimal on-campus study). *Faculty:* 2 full-time (both women), 8 part-time/adjunct (all women). *Students:* Average age 43. 65 applicants, 91% accepted, 54 enrolled. In 2006, 26 degrees awarded. *Degree requirements:* For master's, summer residency. *Entrance requirements:* For master's, MAT. *Application deadline:* Applications are processed on a rolling basis. Application fee: $50. Electronic applications accepted. *Expenses:* Tuition: Part-time $350 per credit. *Financial support:* Institutionally sponsored loans available. Support available to part-time students. *Unit head:* Dr. Margaret Hourigan, Chair, 207-893-7970, Fax: 207-892-7423, E-mail: mhourigan@sjcme.edu. *Application contact:* 800-752-4723, Fax: 207-892-7480, E-mail: info@sjcme.edu.

Saint Xavier University, Graduate Studies, School of Nursing, Chicago, IL 60655-3105. Offers adult health clinical nurse specialist (MS); family nurse practitioner (MS, PMC); leadership in community health nursing (MS); psychiatric-mental health clinical nurse specialist (MS); psychiatric-mental health clinical specialist (PMC); MBA/MS. *Accreditation:* AACN. Part-time and evening/weekend programs available. *Faculty:* 11. *Students:* 20 full-time (14 women), 120 part-time (113 women). Average age 40. In 2006, 36 degrees awarded. *Entrance requirements:* For master's, GRE General Test or MAT, minimum GPA of 3.0, RN license. *Application deadline:* For fall admission, 2/15 for domestic students; for spring admission, 9/15 for domestic students. Applications are processed on a rolling basis. Application fee: $35. *Financial support:* Available to part-time students. Applicants required to submit FAFSA. *Unit head:* Beth Gierach, Managing Director of Admission, 773-298-3053, Fax: 773-298-3076, E-mail: gierach@sxu.edu.

Samuel Merritt College, School of Nursing, Oakland, CA 94609-3108. Offers case management (MSN); family nurse practitioner (MSN, Certificate); nurse anesthetist (MSN, Certificate); nursing (MSN). *Accreditation:* AACN; AANA/CANAEP (one or more programs are accredited). Part-time and evening/weekend programs available. *Degree requirements:* For master's, thesis or alternative. *Entrance requirements:* For master's, minimum GPA of 2.5 in science, 3.0 overall; previous course work in statistics; current RN license. Additional exam requirements/recommendations for international students: Required—TOEFL. *Faculty research:* Gerontology, community health, maternal-child health, sexually transmitted diseases, substance abuse, oncology.

San Francisco State University, Division of Graduate Studies, College of Health and Human Services, School of Nursing, San Francisco, CA 94132-1722. Offers case management (MS), including long-term care, primary care/family nurse practitioner; nursing administration (MS); nursing education (MS). *Accreditation:* AACN. Part-time programs available. *Faculty:* 12 full-time (10 women). *Students:* Average age 32. In 2006, 28 degrees awarded. *Degree requirements:* For master's, thesis. *Entrance requirements:* For master's, minimum GPA of 3.0. *Application deadline:* For fall admission, 11/30 priority date for domestic students; for spring admission, 5/31 for domestic students. Applications are processed on a rolling basis. Application fee: $55. *Financial support:* In 2006–07, 35 students received support, including 35 fellowships; career-related internships or fieldwork also available. Financial award application deadline: 3/1. *Faculty research:* Nursing case management and clinical outcomes, outcome of undergraduate and graduate education in nursing, patient education strategies and learning outcomes. Total annual research expenditures: $25,000. *Unit head:* Dr. Karen Johnson-Brennan, Interim Director, 415-338-1801, Fax: 415-338-0555. *Application contact:* Dr. Frank McLaughlin, Graduate Coordinator, 415-338-1802, E-mail: femc@sfsu.edu.

San Jose State University, Graduate Studies and Research, College of Applied Sciences and Arts, School of Nursing, San Jose, CA 95192-0001. Offers gerontology nurse practitioner (MS); nursing (Certificate); nursing administration (MS); nursing education (MS). *Accreditation:* AACN. Part-time and evening/weekend programs available. *Students:* 15 full-time (13 women), 70 part-time (66 women); includes 30 minority (2 African Americans, 21 Asian Americans or Pacific Islanders, 7 Hispanic Americans). Average age 41. 73 applicants, 70% accepted, 15 enrolled. In 2006, 34 degrees awarded. *Degree requirements:* For master's, thesis. *Entrance requirements:* For master's, BS in nursing, RN license. *Application deadline:* For fall admission, 6/29 for domestic students; for spring admission, 11/30 for domestic students. Applications are processed on a rolling basis. Application fee: $59. Electronic applications accepted. *Financial support:* Career-related internships or fieldwork, institutionally sponsored loans, and scholarships/grants available. Support available to part-time students. Financial award applicants required to submit FAFSA. *Faculty research:* Nurse-managed clinics, computers in nursing. *Unit head:* Jayne Cohen, Director, 408-924-3131, Fax: 408-924-3135. *Application contact:* Dr. Phyllis Connolly, Graduate Coordinator, 408-924-3144.

Seattle Pacific University, Graduate School, School of Health Sciences, Program in Nursing Leadership, Seattle, WA 98119-1997. Offers MSN. *Accreditation:* AACN. *Students:* 13 applicants, 69% accepted, 5 enrolled. In 2006, 15 degrees awarded. *Degree requirements:* For master's, thesis. *Application deadline:* For fall admission, 9/1 priority date for domestic students. Applications are processed on a rolling basis. Application fee: $50. *Expenses:* Contact institution. *Unit head:* Dr. Emily Hitchens, Graduate Program Director, 206-281-2616, Fax: 206-281-2767.

Seattle University, College of Nursing, Program in Nursing, Seattle, WA 98122-1090. Offers leadership in community nursing (MSN), including program development, spirituality and health; primary care nurse practitioner (MSN), including family nurse practitioner, psychiatric mental health nurse practitioner. *Students:* 6 full-time (all women), 8 part-time (7 women); includes 2 African Americans. Average age 40.*Application contact:* Janet Shandley, Associate Dean of Graduate Admissions, 206-296-5900, Fax: 206-298-5656, E-mail: grad_admissions@seattleu.edu.

Seton Hall University, College of Nursing, Department of Graduate Nursing, Nursing Case Management Program, South Orange, NJ 07079-2697. Offers MSN. *Accreditation:* AACN. *Degree requirements:* For master's, research project. *Entrance requirements:* For master's, GRE or MAT.

Southern Adventist University, School of Nursing, Collegedale, TN 37315-0370. Offers adult nurse practitioner (MSN); family nurse practitioner (MSN); nurse educator (MSN); MSN/MSBA. *Accreditation:* NLN. Part-time programs available. *Faculty:* 1 (woman) full-time, 5 part-time/adjunct (all women). *Students:* 45 full-time (41 women), 17 part-time (14 women); includes 5 minority (2 African Americans, 2 Asian Americans or Pacific Islanders, 1 Hispanic American). Average age 35. 40 applicants, 95% accepted, 31 enrolled. In 2006, 20 degrees awarded. *Degree requirements:* For master's, thesis or project. *Entrance requirements:* For master's, RN license. Additional exam requirements/recommendations for international students: Required—TOEFL (minimum score 600 paper-based). *Application deadline:* For fall admission, 7/1 for domestic and international students; for winter admission, 12/1 for domestic and international students. Applications are processed on a rolling basis. Application fee: $25. Electronic applications accepted. *Financial support:* In 2006–07, 1 teaching assistantship with partial tuition reimbursement (averaging $5,000 per year) was awarded. *Faculty research:* Pain management, ethics, corporate wellness, caring spirituality, stress. *Unit head:* Dr. Barbara James, Dean, 423-236-2940, Fax: 423-236-1940, E-mail: bjames@southern.edu. *Application contact:* Diane Proffitt, Enrollment Counselor, 423-236-2941, Fax: 423-236-1940, E-mail: dproffitt@southern.edu.

Southern Connecticut State University, School of Graduate Studies, School of Health and Human Services, Department of Nursing, New Haven, CT 06515-1355. Offers nursing administration (MSN); nursing education (MSN). *Accreditation:* AACN; AANA/CANAEP. Part-time and evening/weekend programs available. *Faculty:* 6 full-time, 1 part-time/adjunct. *Students:* 2 full-time (both women), 29 part-time (27 women); includes 4 minority (3 African Americans, 1 Hispanic American). 15 applicants, 93% accepted, 10 enrolled. In 2006, 14 degrees awarded. *Degree requirements:* For master's, thesis. *Entrance requirements:* For master's, GRE, MAT, interview, minimum QPA of 2.8, RN license, minimum 1 year of professional nursing experience. *Application deadline:* For fall admission, 7/15 priority date for domestic students. Applications are processed on a rolling basis. Application fee: $50. Electronic applications accepted. *Financial support:* Application deadline: 4/15; *Unit head:* Dr. Cesarina Thompson, Chairperson, 203-392-6487, Fax: 203-392-6493, E-mail: thompson_c@southernct.edu. *Application contact:* Dr. Eileen Crutchlow, Graduate Coordinator, 203-392-6489, Fax: 203-392-6493, E-mail: crutchlow1@southernct.edu.

Southern Illinois University Edwardsville, Graduate Studies and Research, School of Nursing, Program in Health Care and Nursing Administration, Edwardsville, IL 62026-0001. Offers MS, Post-Master's Certificate. *Students:* 15 applicants, 47% accepted. In 2006, 2 degrees awarded. *Degree requirements:* For master's, thesis or alternative, final exam. *Entrance requirements:* Additional exam requirements/recommendations for international students: Required—TOEFL. *Application deadline:* For fall admission, 1/1 for domestic and international students. Application fee: $30. Electronic applications accepted. *Unit head:* Dr. Jacquelyn Clement, Director, 618-650-3923, E-mail: jclemen@siue.edu.

Southern Nazarene University, Graduate College, School of Nursing, Bethany, OK 73008. Offers nursing education (MS); nursing leadership (MS). *Accreditation:* AACN. Part-time and evening/weekend programs available. *Students:* 30. In 2006, 14 degrees awarded. *Expenses:* Tuition: Part-time $507 per credit. *Unit head:* Dr. Carol Dorough, Dean, 405-491-6365, E-mail: cdorough@snu.edu.

Southern University and Agricultural and Mechanical College, School of Nursing, Baton Rouge, LA 70813. Offers educator/administrator (PhD); family health nursing (MSN); family nurse practitioner (Post Master's Certificate); geriatric nurse practitioner/gerontology (PhD). *Accreditation:* AACN; NLN. Part-time programs available. *Degree requirements:* For master's and doctorate, thesis/dissertation, comprehensive exam. *Entrance requirements:* For master's, GRE General Test, BSN, minimum GPA of 2.7; for doctorate, GRE General Test; for Post Master's Certificate, MSN. Additional exam requirements/recommendations for international students: Required—TOEFL (minimum score 525 paper-based; 193 computer-based). *Faculty research:* Health promotions, vulnerable populations, (community-based) cardiovascular participating research, health disparities chronic diseases, care of the elderly.

Spalding University, Graduate Studies, College of Health and Natural Sciences, School of Nursing, Louisville, KY 40203-2188. Offers adult nurse practitioner (MSN); family nurse practitioner (MSN); leadership in nursing and healthcare (MSN); pediatric nurse practitioner (MSN). *Accreditation:* AACN. Part-time and evening/weekend programs available. *Degree requirements:* For master's, thesis, comprehensive exam (for some programs). *Entrance requirements:* For master's, GRE General Test, BSN or bachelor's degree and RN licensure. *Faculty research:* Nurse educational administration, gerontology, bioterrorism, healthcare ethics, leadership.

State University of New York Institute of Technology, School of Nursing and Health Systems, Program in Nursing Administration, Utica, NY 13504-3050. Offers MS, CAS. *Accreditation:* AACN. Part-time programs available. *Faculty:* 4 full-time (all women), 2 part-time/adjunct (both women). *Students:* 1 (woman) full-time, 14 part-time (all women), 1 international. *Degree requirements:* For master's, thesis or project. *Entrance requirements:* For master's, GRE General Test if undergraduate GPA is less than 3.3, minimum GPA of 3.0, 2 letters of recommendation. Additional exam requirements/recommendations for international students: Required—TOEFL (minimum score 550 paper-based; 213 computer-based). *Application deadline:* For fall admission, 6/15 priority date for domestic students. Applications are processed on a rolling basis. Application fee: $50. *Expenses:* Tuition, state resident: full-time $3,452; part-time $288 per credit hour. Tuition, nonresident: full-time $10,920; part-time $455 per credit hour. Required fees: $927; $38 per credit hour. *Financial support:* Federal Work-Study, scholarships/grants, traineeships, and unspecified assistantships available. Financial award applicants required to submit FAFSA. *Faculty research:* Community health, critical thinking, leadership, nursing informatics, child obesity, evidence-based practice. *Unit head:* Dr. Kathleen Sellers, Coordinator, 315-792-7815, Fax: 315-792-7555, E-mail: kathleen.sellers@sunyit.edu. *Application contact:* Marybeth Lyons, Director of Admissions, 315-792-7500, Fax: 315-792-7837, E-mail: smbl@sunyit.edu.

Teachers College Columbia University, Graduate Faculty of Education, Department of Organization and Leadership, Program in Nurse Executive, New York, NY 10027-6696. Offers Ed M, MA, Ed D. *Faculty:* 1 (woman) full-time. *Students:* 42 full-time (38 women), 9 part-time (all women); includes 24 minority (11 African Americans, 10 Asian Americans or Pacific Islanders, 3 Hispanic Americans). Average age 41. 60 applicants, 78% accepted, 38 enrolled. In 2006, 19 master's, 2 doctorates awarded. *Degree requirements:* For master's, capstone project; for doctorate, thesis/dissertation. *Entrance requirements:* For master's, BSN; for doctorate, GRE General Test or MAT, BSN, nursing license. *Application deadline:* For fall admission, 5/15 for domestic students; for spring admission, 12/1 for domestic students. Application fee: $65. *Expenses:* Tuition: Full-time $23,400; part-time $975 per credit. Required fees: $320 per term. *Financial support:* Career-related internships or fieldwork, Federal Work-Study, institutionally sponsored loans, traineeships, and tuition waivers (full and partial) available. Support available to part-time students. Financial award application deadline: 2/1. *Faculty research:* Health care administration, health care law, nursing administration and education, consumer satisfaction with health care. *Application contact:* Debbie Lesperance, Assistant Director of Admission, 212-678-3710, Fax: 212-678-4171.

See Close-Up on page 1131.

Texas A&M University–Corpus Christi, Graduate Studies and Research, College of Nursing and Health Sciences, Corpus Christi, TX 78412-5503. Offers clinical nurse specialist (MSN); family nurse practitioner (MSN); health care administration (MSN); leadership in nursing systems (MSN). *Accreditation:* AACN. Part-time and evening/weekend programs available. *Degree requirements:* For master's, thesis (for some programs), comprehensive exam, registration. *Entrance requirements:* For master's, GRE General Test. Additional exam requirements/recommendations for international students: Required—TOEFL. Electronic applications accepted.

Texas Tech University Health Sciences Center, School of Nursing, Lubbock, TX 79430. Offers acute care nurse practitioner (MSN, Certificate); administration (MSN); clinical research management (MSN, Certificate); education (MSN); family nurse practitioner (MSN, Certificate); geriatric nurse practitioner (MSN, Certificate); pediatric nurse practitioner (MSN, Certificate). *Accreditation:* AACN. Part-time programs available. Postbaccalaureate distance learning degree programs offered (minimal on-campus study). *Faculty:* 17 full-time (16 women), 5 part-time/adjunct (all women). *Students:* 23 full-time (22 women), 161 part-time (137 women); includes 46 minority (8 African Americans, 2 American Indian/Alaska Native, 6 Asian Americans or Pacific Islanders, 30 Hispanic Americans). Average age 37. 97 applicants, 69% accepted, 67 enrolled. In 2006, 41 degrees awarded. *Degree requirements:* For master's, thesis optional. *Entrance requirements:* For master's, minimum GPA of 3.0, 3 letters of reference, BSN, RN license; for Certificate, minimum GPA of 3.0, 3 letters of reference, RN license. Additional exam requirements/recommendations for international students: Required—TOEFL (minimum score 550 paper-based; 213 computer-based). *Application deadline:* For fall admission, 7/15 priority date for domestic and international students; for spring admission, 11/15 priority date for domestic and international students. Applications are processed on a rolling basis. Application fee: $40. *Financial support:* In 2006–07, 184 students received support. Institutionally sponsored loans, scholarships/grants, and traineeships available. Support available to part-time students. Financial award application deadline: 12/1; financial award applicants required to submit FAFSA. *Faculty research:* Diabetes/obesity, nurse competency, disease management, intervention and measurements, health disparities. Total annual research expenditures: $2.4 million. *Unit head:* Dr. Barbara A. Johnston, Associate Dean for Administrative and Student Affairs, 806-743-3055, Fax: 806-743-1622, E-mail: barbara.johnston@ttuhsc.edu. *Application contact:* Lauren K. Sullivan, Recruiter/Transcultural Coordinator, 806-743-2730 Ext. 309, Fax: 806-743-1622, E-mail: lauren.sullivan@ttuhsc.edu.

Touro University International, College of Health Sciences, Program in Health Sciences, Cypress, CA 90630. Offers clinical research administration (MS, Certificate); emergency and disaster management (MS, Certificate); environmental health science (Certificate); health care administration (PhD); health care management (MS), including health informatics; health education (MS, Certificate); health informatics (Certificate); health sciences (PhD); international health (MS); international health: educator or researcher option (PhD); international health: practitioner option (PhD); law and expert witness studies (MS, Certificate); public health (MS); quality assurance (Certificate). Part-time and evening/weekend programs available. Postbaccalaureate distance learning degree programs offered (no on-campus study). In 2006, 322 master's, 21 doctorates awarded. *Degree requirements:* For doctorate, thesis/dissertation, defense of dissertation, comprehensive exam. *Entrance requirements:* For master's, minimum GPA of 3.0; for doctorate, minimum GPA of 3.4, curriculum vitae, course work in research methods or statistics. Additional exam requirements/recommendations for international students: Required—TOEFL (minimum score 550 paper-based). Application fee: $75. *Expenses:* Tuition: Part-time $300 per credit hour. Tuition and fees vary according to course level and program. *Unit head:* Dr. Edith Neumann, Vice President for Academic Affairs, College of Health Sciences, 714-816-0366 Ext. 2030, Fax: 714-226-9844, E-mail: eneumann@tourou.edu.

University of Cincinnati, Graduate School, College of Nursing, Cincinnati, OH 45221-0038. Offers clinical nurse specialist (MSN), including adult health, community health, neonatal, nursing administration, occupational health, pediatric health, psychiatric nursing, women's health; nurse anesthesia (MSN); nurse midwifery (MSN); nurse practitioner (MSN), including acute care, ambulatory care, family, family/psychiatric, women's health; nursing (PhD); MBA/MSN. *Accreditation:* AACN; AANA/CANAEP (one or more programs are accredited); ACNM/DOA. Part-time programs available. Postbaccalaureate distance learning degree programs offered (no on-campus study). *Faculty:* 41 full-time (39 women), 16 part-time/adjunct (15 women). *Students:* 159 full-time (125 women), 149 part-time (145 women); includes 40 minority (22 African Americans, 1 American Indian/Alaska Native, 16 Asian Americans or Pacific Islanders, 1 Hispanic American). Average age 34. 385 applicants, 49% accepted, 132 enrolled. In 2006, 77 master's, 5 doctorates awarded. Terminal master's awarded for partial completion of doctoral program. *Median time to degree:* Of those who began their doctoral program in fall 1998, 55% received their degree in 8 years or less. *Degree requirements:* For master's, thesis or alternative, registration; for doctorate, thesis/dissertation, comprehensive exam, registration. *Entrance requirements:* For master's and doctorate, GRE General Test. Additional exam requirements/recommendations for international students: Required—TOEFL (minimum score 520 paper-based; 190 computer-based). *Application deadline:* For fall admission, 7/26 priority date for domestic and international students. Applications are processed on a rolling basis. Application fee: $40. Electronic applications accepted. *Financial support:* In 2006–07, 164 students received support, including 7 fellowships with full tuition reimbursements available (averaging $13,571 per year), research assistantships with full tuition reimbursements available (averaging $12,000 per year), 8 teaching assistantships with full tuition reimbursements available (averaging $12,000 per year); career-related internships or fieldwork, scholarships/grants, traineeships, tuition waivers (partial), and unspecified assistantships also available. Support available to part-time students. Financial award application deadline: 5/1; financial award applicants required to submit FAFSA. *Faculty research:* Substance abuse, injury and violence, symptom management. Total annual research expenditures: $1.3 million. *Unit head:* Dr. Andrea R. Lindell, Dean, 513-558-5330, Fax: 513-558-9030, E-mail: andrea.lindell@uc.edu. *Application contact:* Loren Carter, Program Coordinator, 513-558-5072, Fax: 513-558-7523, E-mail: loren.carter@uc.edu.

University of Colorado at Colorado Springs, Graduate School, Beth-El College of Nursing, Colorado Springs, CO 80933-7150. Offers adult health nurse practitioner and clinical specialist (MSN); family practitioner (MSN), including community clinical specialist, forensic clinical specialist, holistic clinical specialist; gerontology (MSN); neonatal nurse practitioner and clinical specialist (MSN); nursing administration (MSN); women nurse practitioner (MSN). *Accreditation:* AACN. Part-time programs available. Postbaccalaureate distance learning degree programs offered (minimal on-campus study). *Faculty:* 10 full-time (7 women), 14 part-time/adjunct (7 women). *Students:* 84 full-time (77 women), 53 part-time (52 women); includes 22 minority (6 African Americans, 3 American Indian/Alaska Native, 2 Asian Americans or Pacific Islanders, 11 Hispanic Americans). Average age 37. 54 applicants, 85% accepted, 30 enrolled. In 2006, 36 degrees awarded. *Degree requirements:* For master's, thesis optional; for doctorate, capstone project. *Entrance requirements:* For master's, GRE General Test or MAT, BSN, minimum GPA of 3.0, unrestricted RN license; for doctorate, interview; active RN license; MA; minimum GPA of 3.3; National Certification as NP, CNS, or CNS; portfolio. Additional exam requirements/recommendations for international students: Required—TOEFL. *Application deadline:* For fall admission, 6/1 priority date for domestic students; for spring admission, 11/15 for domestic students. Application fee: $60 ($75 for international students). Electronic applications accepted. *Expenses: Contact institution.* Tuition and fees vary according to course load, campus/location and program. *Financial support:* Fellowships, career-related internships or fieldwork, Federal Work-Study, and institutionally sponsored loans available. Support available to part-time students. *Faculty research:* Women's health, uncertainty, empowerment family experience in chronic illness. Total annual research expenditures: $260,389. *Unit head:* Dr. Carole Schoffstall, Dean, 719-262-4418, Fax: 719-262-4416, E-mail: cschoffs@uccs.edu.

University of Connecticut, Graduate School, School of Nursing, Field of Nursing, Storrs, CT 06269. Offers adult acute care (Post-Master's Certificate); adult primary care (Post-Master's Certificate); community health (Post-Master's Certificate); neonatal acute care (Post-Master's Certificate); nursing (MS, PhD); patient care services and systems administration (Post-Master's Certificate); psychiatric mental health (Post-Master's Certificate). *Accreditation:* AACN. *Faculty:* 20 full-time (18 women). *Students:* 38 full-time (33 women), 70 part-time (65 women); includes 17 minority (3 African Americans, 10 Asian Americans or Pacific Islanders, 4 Hispanic Americans), 1 international. Average age 37. 64 applicants, 69% accepted, 44 enrolled. In 2006, 25 master's, 7 doctorates, 1 other advanced degree awarded. *Degree requirements:* For master's, comprehensive exam; for doctorate, thesis/dissertation. *Entrance requirements:* Additional exam requirements/recommendations for international students: Required—TOEFL (minimum score 550 paper-based; 213 computer-based). *Application deadline:* For fall admission, 2/1 priority date for domestic and international students; for spring admission, 11/1 for domestic students, 10/1 for international students. Applications are processed on a rolling basis. Application fee: $55. Electronic applications accepted. *Financial support:* In 2006–07, 4 research assistantships with full tuition reimbursements, 13 teaching assistantships with full tuition reimbursements were awarded; fellowships, Federal Work-Study, scholarships/grants, health care benefits, and unspecified assistantships also available. Financial award application deadline: 2/1; financial award applicants required to submit FAFSA. *Unit head:* E. Carol Polifroni, Chairperson, 860-486-0511, Fax: 860-486-0001, E-mail: polifron@uconn.edu. *Applica-*

Nursing and Healthcare Administration

University of Connecticut (continued)
tion contact: Lisa Mazzola, Academic Advisor Coordinator, 860-486-1973, E-mail: lisa.mazzola@uconn.edu.

University of Delaware, College of Health Sciences, School of Nursing, Newark, DE 19716. Offers adult nurse practitioner (MSN, PMC); cardiopulmonary clinical nurse specialist (MSN, PMC); cardiopulmonary clinical nurse specialist/adult nurse practitioner (MSN, PMC); family nurse practitioner (MSN, PMC); gerontology clinical nurse specialist (MSN, PMC); gerontology clinical nurse specialist geriatric nurse practitioner (PMC); gerontology clinical nurse specialist/geriatric nurse practitioner (MSN); health services administration (MSN, PMC); nursing of children clinical nurse specialist (MSN, PMC); nursing of children clinical nurse specialist/pediatric nurse practitioner (MSN, PMC); oncology/immune deficiency clinical nurse specialist (MSN, PMC); oncology/immune deficiency clinical nurse specialist/adult nurse practitioner (MSN, PMC); perinatal/women's health clinical nurse specialist (MSN, PMC); perinatal/women's health clinical nurse specialist/women's health nurse practitioner (MSN, PMC); psychiatric nursing clinical nurse specialist (MSN, PMC). *Accreditation:* AACN; NLN (one or more programs are accredited). Part-time and evening/weekend programs available. Postbaccalaureate distance learning degree programs offered (minimal on-campus study). *Degree requirements:* For master's, thesis optional. *Entrance requirements:* For master's, BSN, interview, RN license. Electronic applications accepted. *Faculty research:* Marriage and chronic illness, health promotion, congestive heart failure patient outcomes, school nursing, diabetes in children.

University of Hawaii at Manoa, Graduate Division, College of Health Sciences and Social Welfare, School of Nursing and Dental Hygiene, Honolulu, HI 96822. Offers clinical nurse specialist (MS), including adult health, community mental health; nurse practitioner (MS), including adult health, community mental health, family nurse practitioner; nursing (PhD, Graduate Certificate); nursing administration (MS). *Accreditation:* AACN; NLN (one or more programs are accredited). *Faculty:* 32 full-time (29 women), 1 (woman) part-time/adjunct. *Students:* 30 full-time (28 women), 94 part-time (83 women); includes 10 minority (3 African Americans, 1 American Indian/Alaska Native, 2 Asian Americans or Pacific Islanders, 4 Hispanic Americans), 2 international. 119 applicants, 53% accepted, 54 enrolled. In 2006, 12 master's, 4 doctorates awarded. *Median time to degree:* Of those who began their doctoral program in fall 1998, 57% received their degree in 8 years or less. *Degree requirements:* For master's, thesis optional; for doctorate, thesis/dissertation, comprehensive exam. *Entrance requirements:* For master's, Hawaii RN license. Additional exam requirements/recommendations for international students: Required—TOEFL (minimum score 580 paper-based; 237 computer-based; 92 iBT). *Application deadline:* For fall admission, 3/1 for domestic and international students. Application fee: $50. *Financial support:* In 2006–07, 1 teaching assistantship (averaging $13,296 per year) was awarded. Total annual research expenditures: $3.1 million.

University of Illinois at Chicago, Graduate College, College of Nursing, Program in Nursing Sciences (Nursing Administration), Chicago, IL 60607-7128. Offers MS. *Accreditation:* AACN. Part-time programs available. *Degree requirements:* For master's, thesis or alternative. *Entrance requirements:* For master's, GRE General Test, minimum GPA of 2.75. Additional exam requirements/recommendations for international students: Required—TOEFL. Electronic applications accepted.

University of Indianapolis, Graduate Programs, School of Nursing, Indianapolis, IN 46227-3697. Offers family practice (post-RN) (MSN); gerontological nurse practitioner (MSN); nurse-midwifery (MSN); nursing (MSN); nursing administration (MSN); nursing education (MSN); MBA/MSN. *Accreditation:* AACN; ACNM. *Faculty:* 7 full-time (all women), 3 part-time/adjunct (all women). *Students:* 9 full-time (all women), 121 part-time (115 women); includes 17 minority (16 African Americans, 1 Asian American or Pacific Islander). Average age 41. In 2006, 7 degrees awarded. *Entrance requirements:* For master's, minimum GPA of 3.0, interview, letters of recommendation, resumé, IN nursing license, 1 year professional practice. Additional exam requirements/recommendations for international students: Required—TOEFL (minimum score 550 paper-based; 213 computer-based). *Application deadline:* For fall admission, 8/1 for domestic students; for winter admission, 12/15 for domestic students; for spring admission, 4/15 for domestic students. Applications are processed on a rolling basis. Application fee: $50. *Financial support:* Federal Work-Study available. *Unit head:* Dr. Sharon Isaac, Dean, 317-788-3207, E-mail: isaac@uindy.edu. *Application contact:* T.C. Crum, 317-788-2128, Fax: 317-788-3542, E-mail: tcrum@uindy.edu.

University of Mary, Division of Nursing, Bismarck, ND 58504-9652. Offers family nurse practitioner (MSN); nurse management (MSN); nursing educator (MSN). *Accreditation:* AACN. Part-time and evening/weekend programs available. Postbaccalaureate distance learning degree programs offered (minimal on-campus study). *Faculty:* 2 full-time (both women), 8 part-time/adjunct (5 women). *Students:* 28 full-time (27 women), 22 part-time (all women); includes 2 minority (1 African American, 1 Hispanic American), 1 international. Average age 32. 32 applicants, 66% accepted, 19 enrolled. In 2006, 26 degrees awarded. *Degree requirements:* For master's, thesis (for some programs), internship (family nurse practitioner), practice teaching, comprehensive exam. *Entrance requirements:* For master's, minimum GPA of 3.0 in nursing, interview, letters of recommendation. *Application deadline:* For fall admission, 4/15 priority date for domestic students. Applications are processed on a rolling basis. Application fee: $40. Electronic applications accepted. *Financial support:* In 2006–07, 14 fellowships with partial tuition reimbursements, 3 teaching assistantships with partial tuition reimbursements were awarded; institutionally sponsored loans also available. Support available to part-time students. Financial award application deadline: 7/1. *Faculty research:* Gerontology issues, rural nursing, health policy, primary care, women's health. *Unit head:* Glenda Reemts, Director, 701-255-7500 Ext. 8041, Fax: 701-255-7687. *Application contact:* Traci L. Schell, Secretary, 701-355-8016, Fax: 701-255-7687, E-mail: tschell@umary.edu.

University of Maryland, Baltimore, Graduate School, School of Nursing, Master's Program in Nursing, Baltimore, MD 21201. Offers community health nursing (MS); gerontological nursing (MS); maternal-child nursing (MS); medical-surgical nursing (MS); nurse-midwifery education (MS); nursing administration (MS); nursing education (MS); nursing health policy (MS); primary care nursing (MS); psychiatric nursing (MS); MS/MBA. *Accreditation:* AANA/CANAEP; ACNM/DOA; NLN (one or more programs are accredited). Part-time programs available. *Degree requirements:* For master's, thesis or alternative, comprehensive exam (for some programs). *Entrance requirements:* For master's, GRE General Test, minimum GPA of 2.75, course work in statistics, BS in nursing. Additional exam requirements/recommendations for international students: Required—TOEFL, TOEFL or IELTS; Recommended—IELTS. Electronic applications accepted.

University of Massachusetts Lowell, Graduate School, College of Health Professions, Department of Nursing, Program in Administration of Nursing Services, Lowell, MA 01854-2881. Offers health promotion (PhD). *Accreditation:* AACN. *Degree requirements:* For doctorate, thesis/dissertation. *Entrance requirements:* For doctorate, GRE General Test.

University of Michigan, Horace H. Rackham School of Graduate Studies, School of Nursing, Division of Nursing and Health Care Systems Administration, Ann Arbor, MI 48109. Offers nursing business and health systems (MS); MBA/MS; MHSA/MS; MS/MS. MS/MS offered with School of Information. *Accreditation:* AACN. Part-time and evening/weekend programs available. Postbaccalaureate distance learning degree programs offered (minimal on-campus study). *Degree requirements:* For master's, thesis. *Entrance requirements:* For master's, GRE General Test, minimum GPA of 3.0. Electronic applications accepted. *Faculty research:* Outcomes research, nursing language, change management and innovation, nurse staffing, and informatics.

University of Minnesota, Twin Cities Campus, Graduate School, School of Nursing, Program in Nursing and Health Care Systems Administration, Minneapolis, MN 55455-0213. Offers MS. *Accreditation:* AACN. Part-time programs available. *Students:* 5 full-time (all women), 8 part-time (all women); includes 3 minority (1 African American, 1 Asian American or Pacific Islander, 1 Hispanic American), 9 international. *Degree requirements:* For master's, final oral exam, project or thesis. *Entrance requirements:* Additional exam requirements/recommendations for international students: Required—TOEFL (minimum score 586 paper-based; 240 computer-based). *Application deadline:* For fall admission, 1/2 priority date for domestic and international students; for spring admission, 8/1 priority date for domestic and international students. Application fee: $55 ($75 for international students). *Financial support:* Fellowships, research assistantships, teaching assistantships available. *Unit head:* Dr. Helen Hansen, Coordinator, 612-624-3102. *Application contact:* Information Contact, 612-624-4454, Fax: 612-624-3174, E-mail: nurseoss@umn.edu.

University of Missouri–Kansas City, School of Nursing, Kansas City, MO 64110-2499. Offers adult clinical nurse specialist (MSN), including adult nurse practitioner, women's health nurse practitioner; family nurse practitioner (MSN); neonatal nurse practitioner (MSN); nurse educator (MSN); nurse executive (MSN); nursing (PhD); pediatric nurse practitioner (MSN). *Accreditation:* AACN. Part-time programs available. Postbaccalaureate distance learning degree programs offered (minimal on-campus study). *Faculty:* 31 full-time (26 women), 32 part-time/adjunct (31 women). *Students:* 36 full-time (all women), 213 part-time (202 women); includes 23 minority (6 African Americans, 2 American Indian/Alaska Native, 6 Asian Americans or Pacific Islanders, 9 Hispanic Americans). Average age 36. 121 applicants, 72% accepted, 71 enrolled. In 2006, 69 master's, 1 doctorate awarded. *Median time to degree:* Of those who began their doctoral program in fall 1998, 60% received their degree in 8 years or less. *Degree requirements:* For master's, thesis or alternative. *Entrance requirements:* For master's, minimum undergraduate GPA of 3.2; for doctorate, GRE, 3 letters of reference, interview and original essay by invitation. Additional exam requirements/recommendations for international students: Required—TOEFL (minimum score 550 paper-based). *Application deadline:* For fall admission, 2/1 priority date for domestic students; for spring admission, 9/15 priority date for domestic students. Application fee: $25. *Expenses:* Tuition, state resident: full-time $4,975; part-time $276 per credit. Tuition, nonresident: full-time $12,847; part-time $713 per credit. Required fees: $595; $595 per year. *Financial support:* In 2006–07, 30 students received support, including 6 research assistantships (averaging $3,450 per year), 7 teaching assistantships with partial tuition reimbursements available (averaging $12,650 per year); fellowships, career-related internships or fieldwork, Federal Work-Study, institutionally sponsored loans, and tuition waivers (full and partial) also available. Support available to part-time students. Financial award application deadline: 6/30; financial award applicants required to submit FAFSA. *Faculty research:* Geriatrics/gerontology, children's pain, neonatology, Alzheimer's care, cancer caregivers. Total annual research expenditures: $1 million. *Unit head:* Dr. Lora Lacey-Haun, Dean, 816-235-1700, Fax: 816-235-1701, E-mail: lacey-haunc@umkc.edu. *Application contact:* Leah Wilder, Coordinator for Admissions and Recruitment, 816-235-5768, Fax: 816-235-1701, E-mail: wilderl@umkc.edu.

The University of North Carolina at Greensboro, Graduate School, School of Nursing, Greensboro, NC 27412-5001. Offers adult clinical nurse specialist (MSN, PMC); adult/gerontological nurse practitioner (MSN, PMC); nurse anesthesia (MSN, PMC); nursing (PhD); nursing administration (MSN); nursing education (MSN); MSN/MBA. *Accreditation:* AACN; AANA/CANAEP; NLN. *Faculty:* 24 full-time (23 women), 27 part-time/adjunct (22 women). *Students:* 231 full-time (197 women), 98 part-time (83 women); includes 56 minority (41 African Americans, 3 American Indian/Alaska Native, 9 Asian Americans or Pacific Islanders, 3 Hispanic Americans). 206 applicants, 59% accepted. *Degree requirements:* For master's, thesis or alternative. *Entrance requirements:* For master's, GRE General Test or MAT, BSN, clinical experience, liability insurance, RN license; for PMC, liability insurance, MSN, RN license. Additional exam requirements/recommendations for international students: Required—TOEFL. Application fee: $45. Electronic applications accepted. *Expenses:* Tuition, state resident: full-time $2,692. Tuition, nonresident: full-time $13,742. *Financial support:* Research assistantships with full tuition reimbursements, career-related internships or fieldwork, Federal Work-Study, scholarships/grants, and traineeships available. Support available to part-time students. *Unit head:* Dr. Lynne Pearcey, Dean, 336-334-5177, Fax: 336-334-3628, E-mail: l_pearce@uncg.edu. *Application contact:* Michelle Harkleroad, Director of Graduate Admissions, 336-334-4884, Fax: 336-334-4424, E-mail: mbharkle@uncg.edu.

University of Pennsylvania, School of Nursing, Health Leadership Program, Philadelphia, PA 19104. Offers MSN. *Accreditation:* AACN. Part-time programs available. *Entrance requirements:* For master's, GRE General Test, BSN, minimum GPA of 3.0, previous course work in statistics, 1 year of clinical experience in area of interest. Additional exam requirements/recommendations for international students: Required—TOEFL. Expenses: Contact institution. *Faculty research:* Payment structures for nurse practitioners, delirium in older adults.

University of Pennsylvania, School of Nursing, Program in Nursing and Health Care Administration, Philadelphia, PA 19104. Offers MSN, PhD, MBA/MSN. *Accreditation:* AACN. Part-time programs available. Terminal master's awarded for partial completion of doctoral program. *Degree requirements:* For doctorate, thesis/dissertation. *Entrance requirements:* For master's, GMAT (MBA/MSN), GRE General Test, BSN, minimum GPA of 3.0, previous course work in statistics; for doctorate, GMAT (MBA/PhD), GRE General Test, BSN or MSN, minimum GPA of 3.0. Additional exam requirements/recommendations for international students: Required—TOEFL. Expenses: Contact institution. *Faculty research:* Nursing services and policy, home health services utilization.

University of Phoenix–Springfield Campus, College of Health and Human Services, Springfield, MO 65804-7211. Offers administration/health care management (MSN); health administration (MHA); health care management (MBA); nursing (MSN); MSN/MBA; MSN/MHA.

University of Pittsburgh, School of Nursing, Advanced Specialist Role Program, Pittsburgh, PA 15260. Offers nursing administration (MSN); nursing education (MSN); nursing informatics (MSN); nursing research (MSN). *Accreditation:* AACN. Part-time programs available. *Students:* 4 full-time (2 women), 46 part-time (45 women); includes 6 minority (3 African Americans, 2 Asian Americans or Pacific Islanders, 1 Hispanic American). Average age 41. 12 applicants, 50% accepted, 5 enrolled. In 2006, 18 degrees awarded. *Degree requirements:* For master's, thesis optional. *Entrance requirements:* For master's, GRE or MAT, BSN, RN license, letters of recommendation, resumé, course work in statistics, 1-3 years of nursing experience. Additional exam requirements/recommendations for international students: Required—TOEFL (minimum score 550 paper-based; 213 computer-based; 80 iBT). *Application deadline:* For fall admission, 8/1 priority date for domestic students; for spring admission, 12/1 priority date for domestic students. Applications are processed on a rolling basis. Application fee: $50. Electronic applications accepted. *Unit head:* Dr. Helen Burns, Associate Dean for Clinical Education, 412-624-6616, Fax: 412-624-2401, E-mail: burnsh@pitt.edu. *Application contact:* Laurie Lapsley, Administrator of Graduate Student Services, 412-624-9670, Fax: 412-624-2409, E-mail: lapsleyl@pitt.edu.

University of Puerto Rico, Medical Sciences Campus, School of Nursing, San Juan, PR 00936-5067. Offers anesthesia (MSN); clinical specialist (MSN); family nurse practitioner (MSN); nurse administrator (MSN); nursing education (MSN). *Accreditation:* AACN; AANA/CANAEP. Part-time and evening/weekend programs available. *Faculty:* 12 full-time (11 women), 3 part-time/adjunct (2 women). *Students:* 115 full-time (all women), 13 part-time (9 women); includes 123 minority (all Hispanic Americans), 3 international. 70 applicants, 71% accepted. In 2006, 40 degrees awarded. *Degree requirements:* For master's, one foreign language. *Entrance requirements:* For master's, GRE or EXADEP, interview, Puerto Rico RN license or professional license for international students, general and specific point average, article analysis. *Application deadline:* For spring admission, 4/30 priority date for domestic and international students. Applications are processed on a rolling basis. Application fee: $33. Electronic applications accepted. *Financial support:* In 2006–07, research assistantships with full tuition reimbursements (averaging $28,175 per year), teaching assistantships with full tuition reimbursements (averaging $48,965 per year) were awarded; Federal Work-Study, traineeships, tuition waivers (full), and unspecified assistantships also available. Financial award application deadline: 6/

30. *Faculty research:* HIV, health disparities, teen violence, women and violence, neurological disorders. *Unit head:* Dr. Suane E. Sánchez, Dean, 787-758-2525 Ext. 2100, Fax: 787-281-0721, E-mail: sesanchez@rcm.upr.edu. *Application contact:* Dr. Angelica Y. Matos, Director Graduate Department, 787-758-2525, Fax: 787-281-0721.

University of Rhode Island, Graduate School, College of Nursing, Kingston, RI 02881. Offers administration (MS); clinical specialist in gerontology (MS); clinical specialist in psychiatric/mental health (MS); family nurse practitioner (MS); nurse midwifery (MS); nursing (PhD); nursing education (MS). *Accreditation:* AACN; ACNM/DOA (one or more programs are accredited). In 2006, 34 master's, 5 doctorates awarded. *Application deadline:* For fall admission, 4/15 for domestic students. Application fee: $35. *Expenses:* Tuition, state resident: full-time $6,032; part-time $335 per credit. Tuition, nonresident: full-time $17,288; part-time $960 per credit. Required fees: $65 per credit. $30 per semester. One-time fee: $80 part-time. *Unit head:* Dayle Joseph, Dean, 401-874-2766.

University of San Diego, Hahn School of Nursing and Health Sciences, San Diego, CA 92110-2492. Offers accelerated nursing (for RNs only) (MSN); adult clinical nurse specialist (MSN, Post Master's Certificate); adult nurse practitioner (MSN, Post Master's Certificate); clinical nursing (MSN); entry-level nursing (for non-RNs) (MSN); executive nurse leader (MSN); family nurse practitioner (MSN, Post Master's Certificate); nursing science (PhD); pediatric nurse practitioner (MSN, Post Master's Certificate). *Accreditation:* AACN. Part-time and evening/weekend programs available. *Faculty:* 13 full-time (12 women), 33 part-time/adjunct (all women). *Students:* 103 full-time (85 women), 138 part-time (131 women); includes 58 minority (7 African Americans, 3 American Indian/Alaska Native, 26 Asian Americans or Pacific Islanders, 22 Hispanic Americans), 4 international. Average age 37. 261 applicants, 54% accepted, 87 enrolled. In 2006, 35 master's, 19 doctorates awarded. *Degree requirements:* For doctorate, thesis/dissertation, residency. *Entrance requirements:* For master's, GRE General Test (for entry-level nursing), BSN and current California RN licensure (for all programs except entry-level nursing); minimum GPA of 3.0; for doctorate, GRE General Test, minimum GPA of 3.5, MSN, current California RN licensure. Additional exam requirements/recommendations for international students: Required—TOEFL, TWE. *Application deadline:* Applications are processed on a rolling basis. Application fee: $45. Electronic applications accepted. *Financial support:* Scholarships/grants and traineeships available. Support available to part-time students. Financial award application deadline: 4/1; financial award applicants required to submit FAFSA. *Faculty research:* Health promotion, decision making, psychogeriatric nursing, historical nursing, leadership behavior. *Unit head:* Dr. Sally Hardin, Dean, 619-260-4550, Fax: 619-260-6814. *Application contact:* Stephen Pultz, Director of Admissions, 619-260-4524, Fax: 619-260-4158, E-mail: grads@sandiego.edu.

See Close-Up on page 1977.

University of San Francisco, School of Nursing, San Francisco, CA 94117-1080. Offers advanced practice nursing-nurse practitioner and clinical nurse specialist (MSN), including adult health nursing; nursing administration (MSN); MSN/MBA; MSN/MPA; MSN/MSIS. *Accreditation:* AACN. Part-time programs available. *Faculty:* 6 full-time (5 women), 10 part-time/adjunct (9 women). *Students:* 126 full-time (106 women), 11 part-time (10 women); includes 46 minority (3 African Americans, 36 Asian Americans or Pacific Islanders, 7 Hispanic Americans), 5 international. Average age 31. 219 applicants, 65% accepted, 47 enrolled. In 2006, 53 degrees awarded. *Entrance requirements:* For master's, minimum GPA of 3.0. *Application deadline:* Applications are processed on a rolling basis. Application fee: $40. *Expenses:* Tuition: Full-time $17,370; part-time $965 per unit. Tuition and fees vary according to degree level, campus/location and program. *Financial support:* In 2006–07, 114 students received support. Institutionally sponsored loans available. Financial award application deadline: 3/2. *Faculty research:* Direct patient/client care, providers of health care. *Unit head:* Dr. Judith Karshmer, Dean, 415-422-6681, Fax: 415-422-6877, E-mail: nursing@usfca.edu.

University of South Carolina, The Graduate School, College of Nursing, Program in Nursing Administration, Columbia, SC 29208. Offers MSN. *Accreditation:* AACN. Part-time programs available. *Degree requirements:* For master's, thesis or alternative. *Entrance requirements:* For master's, GRE General Test or MAT, BS in nursing, nursing license. Additional exam requirements/recommendations for international students: Required—TOEFL (minimum score 570 paper-based; 230 computer-based). Electronic applications accepted. *Faculty research:* Case management, head nurse-staff, measurement of teaching effectiveness.

University of Southern Mississippi, Graduate School, College of Health, School of Nursing, Hattiesburg, MS 39406-0001. Offers adult health nursing (MSN); community health nursing (MSN); ethics (PhD); family nurse practitioner (MSN); leadership (PhD); nursing service administration (MSN); policy analysis (PhD); psychiatric nursing (MSN). *Accreditation:* AACN. Part-time and evening/weekend programs available. *Faculty:* 14 full-time (all women). *Students:* 39 full-time (31 women), 69 part-time (62 women); includes 18 minority (15 African Americans, 1 Asian American or Pacific Islander, 2 Hispanic Americans), 1 international. Average age 39. 46 applicants, 50% accepted, 17 enrolled. In 2006, 36 master's, 6 doctorates awarded. *Degree requirements:* For master's, thesis optional; for doctorate, thesis/dissertation, comprehensive exam, registration. *Entrance requirements:* For master's, GRE General Test, minimum GPA of 2.75, nursing license, BS in nursing; for doctorate, GRE General Test, master's degree in nursing, minimum GPA of 3.5. Additional exam requirements/recommendations for international students: Required—TOEFL. *Application deadline:* For fall admission, 3/15 priority date for domestic students, 5/1 for international students. Applications are processed on a rolling basis. Application fee: $25 ($30 for international students). Electronic applications accepted. *Financial support:* In 2006–07, 1 research assistantship with full tuition reimbursement (averaging $10,125 per year), 1 teaching assistantship (averaging $10,125 per year) were awarded; Federal Work-Study and traineeships also available. Financial award application deadline: 3/15. *Faculty research:* Gerontology, caregivers, HIV, bereavement, pain, nursing leadership. *Unit head:* Dr. Katherine Nugent, Director and Associate Dean, 601-266-5500, Fax: 601-266-5927. *Application contact:* Dr. Anne Brock, Graduate Coordinator, 601-266-5500, Fax: 601-266-5927.

The University of Tampa, Nursing Program, Tampa, FL 33606-1490. Offers adult nurse practitioner (MSN); family nurse practitioner (MSN); nursing administration (MSN); nursing education (MSN). *Accreditation:* NLN. Part-time and evening/weekend programs available. *Faculty:* 5 full-time (all women), 10 part-time/adjunct (9 women). *Students:* 3 full-time (all women), 67 part-time (63 women); includes 2 minority (both African Americans), 1 international. Average age 40. 46 applicants, 61% accepted, 18 enrolled. In 2006, 29 degrees awarded. *Degree requirements:* For master's, oral exam, practicum, thesis optional. *Entrance requirements:* For master's, GRE General Test, minimum GPA of 3.0, RN license. *Application deadline:* For fall admission, 8/20 priority date for domestic students. Applications are processed on a rolling basis. Application fee: $40. Electronic applications accepted. *Expenses:* Tuition: Part-time $426 per credit hour. Required fees: $35 per year. *Financial support:* In 2006–07, 2 students received support, including 2 research assistantships with tuition reimbursements available (averaging $1,500 per year); career-related internships or fieldwork and unspecified assistantships also available. Support available to part-time students. Financial award applicants required to submit FAFSA. *Faculty research:* Domestic violence (assessment in emergency departments, changing demographics), transcultural health assessment, priorities in maintaining autonomy of elderly. *Unit head:* Dr. Nancy Ross, Director, 813-253-6223, Fax: 813-258-7214, E-mail: nross@ut.edu. *Application contact:* Barbara P. Strickler, Vice President for Enrollment, 888-646-2738, Fax: 813-258-7398, E-mail: admissions@ut.edu.

The University of Tennessee at Chattanooga, Graduate School, College of Health, Education and Professional Studies, School of Nursing, Chattanooga, TN 37403-2598. Offers administration (MSN); adult health (MSN); education (MSN); family nurse practitioner (MSN); nurse anesthesia (MSN). *Accreditation:* AACN; AANA/CANAEP. *Faculty:* 13 full-time (all women). *Students:* 40 full-time (32 women), 47 part-time (41 women); includes 9 minority (1 African American, 2 American Indian/Alaska Native, 4 Asian Americans or Pacific Islanders, 2 Hispanic Americans). Average age 34. 14 applicants, 71% accepted, 2 enrolled. In 2006, 29 degrees awarded. *Degree requirements:* For master's, qualifying exams. *Entrance requirements:* For master's, GRE General Test, MAT, BSN, minimum GPA of 3.0, eligibility for Tennessee RN license. *Application deadline:* For fall admission, 8/1 priority date for domestic students; for spring admission, 12/1 priority date for domestic students. Applications are processed on a rolling basis. Application fee: $30. *Expenses:* Tuition, state resident: full-time $5,434; part-time $339 per hour. Tuition, nonresident: full-time $14,830; part-time $861 per hour. Required fees: $940; $178 per hour. *Financial support:* Application deadline: 4/1; *Faculty research:* Diabetes in women; health care for elderly; alternative medicine; hypertension; nurse anesthesia. Total annual research expenditures: $357,538. *Unit head:* Dr. Kay R. Lindgren, Head, 423-425-4646, Fax: 423-425-4668, E-mail: kay-lindgren@utc.edu. *Application contact:* Dr. Deborah E. Arfken, Dean of Graduate Studies, 423-425-4666, Fax: 423-425-5223, E-mail: deborah-arken@utc.edu.

The University of Texas at Arlington, Graduate School, School of Nursing, Arlington, TX 76019. Offers administration/supervision of nursing (MSN); nurse practitioner (MSN); nursing science (PhD); teaching of nursing (MSN). *Accreditation:* AACN. Part-time and evening/weekend programs available. *Faculty:* 22 full-time (21 women), 11 part-time/adjunct (10 women). *Students:* 52 full-time (50 women), 334 part-time (310 women); includes 86 minority (37 African Americans, 6 American Indian/Alaska Native, 24 Asian Americans or Pacific Islanders, 19 Hispanic Americans), 18 international. Average age 37. 178 applicants, 96% accepted, 117 enrolled. In 2006, 30 degrees awarded. *Degree requirements:* For master's, comprehensive exam, thesis or master's completion project; for doctorate, thesis/dissertation, diagnostic exam after 18 hours. *Entrance requirements:* For master's, GRE General Test, minimum GPA of 3.0, Texas nursing license, minimum C in undergraduate statistics course, physical assessment course within last 3 years; for doctorate, GRE General Test, minimum undergraduate, graduate and statistics GPA of 3.0; Texas RN license; interview; 3 letters of reference. Additional exam requirements/recommendations for international students: Required—TOEFL (minimum score 550 paper-based; 213 computer-based). *Application deadline:* For fall admission, 6/16 for domestic students. Applications are processed on a rolling basis. Application fee: $35 ($50 for international students). *Expenses:* Tuition, state resident: full-time $5,528. Tuition, nonresident: full-time $10,478. International tuition: $10,608 full-time. *Financial support:* In 2006–07, 37 students received support, including 24 fellowships with partial tuition reimbursements available (averaging $3,000 per year), 6 research assistantships (averaging $7,992 per year), 7 teaching assistantships (averaging $10,080 per year); career-related internships or fieldwork and traineeships also available. Financial award application deadline: 6/1; financial award applicants required to submit FAFSA. *Unit head:* Dr. Elizabeth C. Poster, Dean, 817-272-2776, Fax: 817-272-5006, E-mail: poster@uta.edu. *Application contact:* Dr. Susan Grove, Graduate Adviser, 817-272-2776, Fax: 817-272-5006, E-mail: grove@uta.edu.

The University of Texas at El Paso, Graduate School, College of Health Sciences, School of Nursing, El Paso, TX 79968-0001. Offers community health (MSN); community health/family nurse practitioner (MSN); nurse midwifery (MSN); nursing administration (MSN); nursing-clinical (MSN); post master's nursing (MSN); women's health care (MSN). *Accreditation:* AACN. *Degree requirements:* For master's, thesis optional. *Entrance requirements:* For master's, GRE General Test or MAT, BSN, minimum GPA of 3.0, previous course work in statistics. Additional exam requirements/recommendations for international students: Required—TOEFL. Electronic applications accepted.

The University of Texas at Tyler, College of Nursing and Health Sciences, Program in Nursing, Tyler, TX 75799-0001. Offers nurse practitioner (MSN); nursing administration (MSN); nursing education (MSN); MSN/MBA. *Accreditation:* AACN. Part-time and evening/weekend programs available. Postbaccalaureate distance learning degree programs offered (no on-campus study). *Faculty:* 14 full-time (13 women), 4 part-time/adjunct (3 women). *Students:* 13 full-time (11 women), 134 part-time (122 women); includes 25 minority (16 African Americans, 2 American Indian/Alaska Native, 2 Asian Americans or Pacific Islanders, 5 Hispanic Americans). Average age 39. 37 applicants, 32 enrolled. In 2006, 15 degrees awarded. *Degree requirements:* For master's, thesis (for some programs), comprehensive exam (for some programs). *Entrance requirements:* For master's, GRE General Test or MAT, GMAT, minimum undergraduate GPA of 3.0, course work in statistics, RN license, BSN. *Application deadline:* For fall admission, 3/1 priority date for domestic students; for spring admission, 10/1 priority date for domestic students. Applications are processed on a rolling basis. Application fee: $0. Electronic applications accepted. *Expenses:* Tuition, state resident: part-time $50 per credit hour. Tuition, nonresident: part-time $328 per credit hour. Required fees: $107 per credit hour. $426 per term. *Financial support:* In 2006–07, 15 students received support, including 12 fellowships, 3 research assistantships (averaging $2,200 per year); institutionally sponsored loans and scholarships/grants also available. Financial award application deadline: 8/1; financial award applicants required to submit FAFSA. *Faculty research:* Psychosocial adjustment, aging, support/commitment of caregivers, psychological abuse and violence, hope/hopelessness, professional values, end of life cave, suicidology, clinical supervision, workforce retention and issues, global health issues. *Unit head:* Dr. Susan Yarbrough, Assistant Dean, 903-566-1220, E-mail: syarbrou@mail.uttyl.edu. *Application contact:* Bonnie Purser, Office of Graduate Studies, 903-566-7142, Fax: 903-566-7068, E-mail: bpurser@uttyler.edu.

Vanderbilt University, School of Nursing, Nashville, TN 37235. Offers adult acute care nurse practitioner (MSN); adult health nurse practitioner/forensic (MSN); adult nurse practitioner/cardiovascular disease management and prevention (MSN); adult nurse practitioner/palliative care (MSN); clinical management (clinical nurse leader/specialist) (MSN); family nurse practitioner (MSN); gerontology nurse practitioner (MSN); health systems management (MSN); neonatal nurse practitioner (MSN); nurse midwifery (MSN); nursing informatics (MSN); nursing science (PhD); pediatric acute care nurse practitioner (MSN); pediatric primary care nurse practitioner (MSN); psychiatric-mental health nurse practitioner (MSN); women's health nurse practitioner (MSN); MBA/MSN; MSN/MTS; MSN/PhD. *Accreditation:* ACNM/DOA; NLN (one or more programs are accredited). Part-time and evening/weekend programs available. Postbaccalaureate distance learning degree programs offered (minimal on-campus study). *Faculty:* 95 full-time (83 women), 432 part-time/adjunct (314 women). *Students:* 371 full-time (325 women), 206 part-time (180 women); includes 59 minority (38 African Americans, 2 American Indian/Alaska Native, 7 Asian Americans or Pacific Islanders, 12 Hispanic Americans). Average age 27. 611 applicants, 55% accepted, 308 enrolled. In 2006, 256 master's, 2 doctorates awarded. *Degree requirements:* For doctorate, thesis/dissertation. *Entrance requirements:* For master's, GRE, interview; for doctorate, GRE, interview, 3 letters of recommendation. Additional exam requirements/recommendations for international students: Required—TOEFL. *Application deadline:* For fall admission, 12/1 priority date for domestic and international students. Applications are processed on a rolling basis. Application fee: $50. *Expenses:* Contact institution. *Financial support:* In 2006–07, 404 students received support, including 5 research assistantships (averaging $8,000 per year); Federal Work-Study, institutionally sponsored loans, and unspecified assistantships also available. Support available to part-time students. Financial award application deadline: 3/15; financial award applicants required to submit CSS PROFILE or FAFSA. *Faculty research:* Lymphedema post cancer treatment, palliative care and bereavement, patient safety and quality of care, health care workforce issues, symptom management including pain and fatigue. Total annual research expenditures: $1.1 million. *Unit head:* Dr. Colleen Conway-Welch, Dean, 615-343-8776, Fax: 615-343-7711, E-mail: colleen.conway-welch@vanderbilt.edu. *Application contact:* Cheryl Feldner, Assistant Director of Admissions, 615-322-3800, Fax: 615-343-0333, E-mail: cheryl.feldner@vanderbilt.edu.

Villanova University, College of Nursing, Villanova, PA 19085-1690. Offers adult nurse practitioner (MSN, Post Master's Certificate); clinical case management (MSN, Post Master's Certificate); geriatric nurse practitioner (MSN, Post Master's Certificate); health care administration (MSN); nurse anesthetist (MSN, Post Master's Certificate); nursing (PhD); nursing education (MSN, Post Master's Certificate); pediatric nurse practitioner (MSN, Post Master's Certificate). *Accreditation:* AACN; AANA/CANAEP; NLN. Part-time programs available. Postbaccalaureate distance learning degree programs offered (minimal on-campus study). *Faculty:* 14 full-time (all women), 2 part-time/adjunct (both women). *Students:* 41 full-time (27 women),

Nursing and Healthcare Administration

Villanova University (continued)
164 part-time (128 women); includes 17 minority (8 African Americans, 1 American Indian/Alaska Native, 8 Asian Americans or Pacific Islanders), 6 international. Average age 31. 137 applicants, 50% accepted, 48 enrolled. In 2006, 47 degrees awarded. *Median time to degree:* Master's–2 years full-time, 5 years part-time. *Degree requirements:* For master's, independent study project; for doctorate, thesis/dissertation, comprehensive exam. *Entrance requirements:* For master's, GRE or MAT, BSN, 1 year of recent nursing experience, physical assessment, course work in statistics; for doctorate, GRE. Additional exam requirements/recommendations for international students: Required—TOEFL. *Application deadline:* For fall admission, 7/1 priority date for domestic students, 7/1 for international students; for spring admission, 12/1 priority date for domestic students, 12/1 for international students. Applications are processed on a rolling basis. Application fee: $50. *Expenses:* Contact institution. *Financial support:* In 2006–07, 50 students received support, including 4 teaching assistantships with full tuition reimbursements available (averaging $12,165 per year); institutionally sponsored loans, scholarships/grants, traineeships, and tuition waivers (full) also available. Financial award application deadline: 3/1; financial award applicants required to submit FAFSA. *Faculty research:* Genetics, ethics, cognitive development of students, women with disabilities, nursing leadership. *Unit head:* Dr. Marguerite K. Schlag, Assistant Dean and Director, Graduate Program, 610-519-4907, Fax: 610-519-7650, E-mail: marguerite.schlag@villanova.edu.

Virginia Commonwealth University, Graduate School, School of Nursing, Richmond, VA 23284-9005. Offers adult health nursing (MS); child health nursing (MS); family health nursing (MS); health system (PhD); immunocompetence (PhD); nurse practitioner (MS, Certificate); nursing administration (MS), including clinical nurse manager, nurse executive; psychiatric-mental health nursing (MS); risk and resilience (PhD); women's health nursing (MS). *Accreditation:* NLN (one or more programs are accredited). Part-time and evening/weekend programs available. *Faculty:* 23 full-time (21 women). *Students:* 131 full-time (125 women), 137 part-time (129 women); includes 33 minority (19 African Americans, 11 Asian Americans or Pacific Islanders, 3 Hispanic Americans), 12 international. 110 applicants, 82% accepted, 66 enrolled. In 2006, 57 master's, 1 doctorate, 3 other advanced degrees awarded. *Degree requirements:* For master's, thesis optional; for doctorate, thesis/dissertation. *Entrance requirements:* For master's, GRE General Test, BSN, minimum GPA of 2.8; for doctorate, GRE General Test. *Application deadline:* For fall admission, 2/1 priority date for domestic students. Application fee: $50. *Financial support:* Fellowships, research assistantships, teaching assistantships, career-related internships or fieldwork and institutionally sponsored loans available. *Unit head:* Dr. Nancy F. Langston, Dean, 804-828-5174, Fax: 804-828-7743, E-mail: nflangst@vcu.edu. *Application contact:* Susan Lipp, Admissions Counselor, 804-828-5171, Fax: 804-828-7743, E-mail: slipp@vcu.edu.

See Close-Up on page 1983.

Wichita State University, Graduate School, College of Health Professions, School of Nursing, Wichita, KS 67260. Offers clinical nurse specialist (MSN); nurse midwifery (MSN); nurse practitioner (MSN); nursing and health care systems administration (MSN); MSN/MBA. *Accreditation:* AACN. Part-time programs available. *Degree requirements:* For master's, thesis optional. *Entrance requirements:* For master's, GRE, BSN, minimum undergraduate GPA of 2.75. Additional exam requirements/recommendations for international students: Required—TOEFL. Electronic applications accepted. *Faculty research:* Adolescent pregnancy, alcoholism, arthritis and chronic disease, health practices of elderly, diabetes.

Winona State University, Graduate Studies, College of Nursing and Health Sciences, Winona, MN 55987-5838. Offers adult nurse practitioner (MS); clinical nurse specialist (MS); family nurse practitioner (MS); nurse administrator (MS); nurse educator (MS). *Accreditation:* AACN. Part-time programs available. *Faculty:* 10 full-time (all women). *Students:* 70 applicants, 57% accepted, 32 enrolled. In 2006, 32 master's awarded. *Degree requirements:* For master's, thesis. *Application deadline:* For fall admission, 2/1 for domestic students. Application fee: $20. *Financial support:* In 2006–07, 3 research assistantships with partial tuition reimbursements (averaging $6,000 per year) were awarded; Federal Work-Study, traineeships, and unspecified assistantships also available. Support available to part-time students. Financial award applicants required to submit FAFSA. *Unit head:* Dr. Timothy Gaspar, Graduate Director, 507-457-5122, E-mail: tgaspar@winona.msus.edu.

Wright State University, School of Graduate Studies, College of Nursing and Health, Program in Nursing, Dayton, OH 45435. Offers acute care nurse practitioner (MS); administration of nursing and health care systems (MS); adult health (MS); child and adolescent health (MS); community health (MS); family nurse practitioner (MS); nurse practitioner (MS); school nurse (MS); MBA/MS. *Accreditation:* AACN. Part-time and evening/weekend programs available. *Students:* 46 full-time (45 women), 124 part-time (117 women); includes 16 minority (13 African Americans, 1 Asian American or Pacific Islander, 2 Hispanic Americans). Average age 39. 45 applicants, 100% accepted. In 2006, 64 degrees awarded. *Degree requirements:* For master's, thesis or alternative. *Entrance requirements:* For master's, GRE General Test, BSN from NLN-accredited college, Ohio RN license. Additional exam requirements/recommendations for international students: Required—TOEFL. *Application deadline:* For fall admission, 4/15 priority date for domestic students. Application fee: $25. *Financial support:* Fellowships, research assistantships, teaching assistantships, Federal Work-Study, institutionally sponsored loans, and unspecified assistantships available. Support available to part-time students. Financial award application deadline: 6/1; financial award applicants required to submit FAFSA. *Faculty research:* Clinical nursing and health, teaching, caring, pain administration, informatics and technology. *Application contact:* Theresa A. Haghnazarian, Director of Student and Alumni Affairs, 937-775-2592, Fax: 937-775-4571, E-mail: theresa.haghnazarian@wright.edu.

Xavier University, College of Social Sciences, Health and Education, Department of Nursing, Cincinnati, OH 45207. Offers clinical nurse leader (MSN); forensic nursing (MSN); healthcare law (MSN); nursing administration (MSN); school nursing (MSN); MSN/M Ed; MSN/MBA; MSN/MS. *Accreditation:* AACN. Part-time and evening/weekend programs available. *Faculty:* 12 full-time (all women), 11 part-time/adjunct (9 women). *Students:* 57 full-time (51 women), 101 part-time (97 women); includes 8 minority (5 African Americans, 3 Asian Americans or Pacific Islanders), 26 international. Average age 37. 121 applicants, 56 enrolled. In 2006, 24 degrees awarded. *Degree requirements:* For master's, thesis or alternative, scholarly project. *Entrance requirements:* For master's, portfolio (RN to MSN). Additional exam requirements/recommendations for international students: Required—TOEFL (minimum score 550 paper-based; 213 computer-based). *Application deadline:* For fall admission, 8/28 priority date for domestic students. Applications are processed on a rolling basis. Application fee: $35. Electronic applications accepted. *Expenses:* Tuition: Part-time $462 per credit hour. Part-time tuition and fees vary according to degree level, campus/location and program. *Financial support:* In 2006–07, 50 students received support. Scholarships/grants, traineeships, and unspecified assistantships available. Support available to part-time students. Financial award application deadline: 4/1; financial award applicants required to submit FAFSA. *Faculty research:* Stroke rehabilitation, informatics, gerontology, hospice, ethics, macular degeneration. *Unit head:* Dr. Susan M. Schmidt, Chair, 513-745-3815, Fax: 513-745-1087, E-mail: schmidts@xavier.edu. *Application contact:* Marilyn Gomez, Director of Nursing Student Services, 513-745-4392, Fax: 513-745-1087, E-mail: gomez@xavier.edu.

Nursing Education

Angelo State University, College of Graduate Studies, College of Sciences, Department of Nursing, San Angelo, TX 76909. Offers adult nurse practitioner (MSN); nurse educator (MSN). *Accreditation:* NLN. Part-time and evening/weekend programs available. *Faculty:* 10 full-time (all women). *Students:* 15 full-time (13 women), 26 part-time (23 women); includes 10 minority (1 African American, 1 Asian American or Pacific Islander, 8 Hispanic Americans). Average age 40. 25 applicants, 80% accepted, 19 enrolled. In 2006, 6 degrees awarded. *Degree requirements:* For master's, comprehensive exam. *Entrance requirements:* For master's, GRE General Test. Additional exam requirements/recommendations for international students: Required—TOEFL or IELTS. *Application deadline:* For fall admission, 7/15 priority date for domestic students, 6/15 for international students; for spring admission, 12/8 for domestic students, 11/1 for international students. Applications are processed on a rolling basis. Application fee: $40 ($50 for international students). Electronic applications accepted. *Expenses:* Tuition, state resident: full-time $2,340; part-time $130 per hour. Tuition, nonresident: full-time $7,290; part-time $405 per hour. Required fees: $906; $56 per hour. *Financial support:* In 2006–07, 24 students received support. Career-related internships or fieldwork, Federal Work-Study, and scholarships/grants available. Support available to part-time students. Financial award application deadline: 3/1. *Unit head:* Dr. Leslie M. Mayrand, Department Head, 325-942-2060 Ext. 247, E-mail: leslie.mayrand@angelo.edu. *Application contact:* Dr. Susan Wilkinson, Graduate Advisor, 325-942-2060 Ext. 290, E-mail: susan.wilkinson@angelo.edu.

Azusa Pacific University, School of Nursing, Azusa, CA 91702-7000. Offers nursing (MSN); nursing education (PhD). *Accreditation:* AACN. Part-time and evening/weekend programs available. *Faculty:* 12 full-time (11 women). *Students:* 56 full-time (49 women), 100 part-time (96 women); includes 73 minority (12 African Americans, 1 American Indian/Alaska Native, 33 Asian Americans or Pacific Islanders, 27 Hispanic Americans), 5 international. In 2006, 16 degrees awarded. *Degree requirements:* For master's, thesis optional. *Entrance requirements:* For master's, BSN. *Application deadline:* Applications are processed on a rolling basis. Application fee: $45 ($65 for international students). *Expenses:* Tuition: Part-time $475 per credit. *Financial support:* Teaching assistantships, scholarships/grants, traineeships, and unspecified assistantships available. Support available to part-time students. Financial award application deadline: 10/15. *Faculty research:* Family adaptation to illness and crisis, bioethical issues in nursing, self-care activities, quality of life issues, home health. Total annual research expenditures: $177,950. *Unit head:* Dr. Aja Lesh, Interim Dean/Professor, 626-815-5386, E-mail: alesh@apu.edu. *Application contact:* Barb Barthelmess, Graduate Program Secretary, 626-815-5391, Fax: 626-815-5414.

Barnes-Jewish College of Nursing and Allied Health, Division of Nursing, St. Louis, MO 63110-1091. Offers adult nurse practitioner (MSN); education (MSN); gerontology nurse practitioner (MSN); holistics (MSN); management/administration (MSN); neonatal nurse practitioner (MSN); oncology (MSN). *Accreditation:* AACN; AANA/CANAEP. Part-time and evening/weekend programs available. *Degree requirements:* For master's, thesis or alternative, registration. *Entrance requirements:* For master's, minimum GPA of 3.0, 2 references, statistics course. Additional exam requirements/recommendations for international students: Required—TOEFL (minimum score 550 paper-based; 213 computer-based).

Barry University, School of Nursing, Program in Nursing Education, Miami Shores, FL 33161-6695. Offers MSN, Certificate. *Accreditation:* AACN. Part-time and evening/weekend programs available. *Students:* 12 full-time (all women), 14 part-time (all women); includes 14 minority (5 African Americans, 9 Hispanic Americans). 9 applicants, 44% accepted, 3 enrolled. In 2006, 13 degrees awarded. *Degree requirements:* For master's, research project or thesis. *Entrance requirements:* For master's, GRE General Test or MAT, BSN, minimum GPA of 3.0, course work in statistics. *Application deadline:* For fall admission, 5/1 priority date for domestic students. Applications are processed on a rolling basis. Application fee: $30. Electronic applications accepted. *Faculty research:* HIV/AIDS, gerontology. *Unit head:* Dr. Claudette Spalding, Associate Dean for Graduate Programs, 305-899-3838, Fax: 305-899-3831, E-mail: cspalding@mail.barry.edu. *Application contact:* Dave Fletcher, Director of Graduate Admissions, 305-899-3113, Fax: 305-899-2971, E-mail: dfletcher@mail.barry.edu.

Bellarmine University, Donna and Allan Lansing School of Nursing and Health Sciences, Louisville, KY 40205-0671. Offers nursing administration (MSN); nursing education (MSN); physical therapy (DPT). *Accreditation:* AACN; APTA. *Faculty:* 15 full-time (11 women), 8 part-time/adjunct (7 women). *Students:* 112 full-time (87 women), 70 part-time (66 women); includes 12 minority (7 African Americans, 4 Asian Americans or Pacific Islanders, 1 Hispanic American), 1 international. Average age 31. In 2006, 44 degrees awarded. *Degree requirements:* For doctorate, comprehensive exam. *Entrance requirements:* For master's, GRE General Test, minimum undergraduate GPA of 2.75, RN license; for doctorate, minimum prerequisites course-work GPA of 2.75, 2.5 overall; 25 hours of documented service in physical therapy; physical ability to perform tasks of a physical therapist. Additional exam requirements/recommendations for international students: Required—TOEFL (minimum score 550 paper-based; 213 computer-based; 80 iBT). *Application deadline:* For fall admission, 10/15 priority date for domestic students. Applications are processed on a rolling basis. Application fee: $25. Electronic applications accepted. *Expenses:* Contact institution. Tuition and fees vary according to program. *Financial support:* Career-related internships or fieldwork and scholarships/grants available. *Faculty research:* Pain, empathy, leadership styles, control. *Unit head:* Dr. Susan H. Davis, Dean, 800-274-4723 Ext. 8217, E-mail: sdavis@bellarmine.edu. *Application contact:* Julie Armstrong-Binnix, Health Science Recruiter, 800-274-4723 Ext. 8364, E-mail: julieab@bellarmine.edu.

Bethel University, Graduate School, Department of Nursing, St. Paul, MN 55112-6999. Offers Christian health ministry (MA); healthcare leadership (MA); nursing education (MA, Certificate). *Accreditation:* AACN. *Faculty:* 12 full-time (10 women). *Students:* 44 full-time (all women), 10 part-time (8 women); includes 2 minority (1 African American, 1 Hispanic American). Average age 41. In 2006, 7 master's, 2 other advanced degrees awarded. *Degree requirements:* For master's, thesis, internship, comprehensive exam. *Entrance requirements:* For master's, MAT, interview, minimum GPA of 3.0, RN experience, BSN, letters of reference, course work in statistics. Additional exam requirements/recommendations for international students: Required—TOEFL (minimum score 550 paper-based; 213 computer-based). *Application deadline:* For fall admission, 3/20 priority date for domestic students. Application fee: $25. Electronic applications accepted. *Expenses:* Tuition: Part-time $395 per credit. Tuition and fees vary according to program. *Financial support:* Institutionally sponsored loans and scholarships/grants available. *Unit head:* Dr. Mary P. Reuland, Director, 651-638-6189, Fax: 651-635-8604, E-mail: reumar@bethel.edu. *Application contact:* Karen Akslen, Graduate Admissions Adviser, 651-635-8011, Fax: 651-635-1464, E-mail: k-akslen@bethel.edu.

Bowie State University, Graduate Programs, Department of Nursing, Bowie, MD 20715-9465. Offers administration of nursing services (MS); family nurse practitioner (MS); nursing education (MS). *Accreditation:* NLN. Part-time programs available. *Faculty:* 7 full-time (4 women), 14 part-time/adjunct (9 women). *Students:* 9 full-time (all women), 9 part-time (8 women); includes 15 minority (all African Americans) Average age 42. 8 applicants, 88% accepted, 4 enrolled. In 2006, 7 degrees awarded. *Degree requirements:* For master's, thesis, research paper, comprehensive exam. *Entrance requirements:* For master's, minimum GPA of 2.5. *Application deadline:* For fall admission, 5/15 for domestic students. Applications are processed on a rolling basis. Application fee: $40. Electronic applications accepted. *Expenses:* Tuition, state resident: full-time $7,344; part-time $306 per credit. Tuition, nonresident: full-time $14,304; part-time $396 per credit. Required fees: $1,078; $77 per credit. $539 per term. One-time fee: $40. *Financial support:* Institutionally sponsored loans and traineeships available. Financial award application deadline: 4/1. *Faculty research:* Minority health, women's health, gerontology, leadership management. *Unit head:* Dr. Bonita Jenkins, Acting Chairperson, 301-860-3210, E-mail: mccaskill@bowiestate.edu. *Application contact:* Angela Issac, Information Contact.

Brenau University, Graduate Programs, School of Health and Science, Gainesville, GA 30501. Offers family nurse practitioner (MS); nurse educator (MS); occupational therapy (MS); psychology (MS). *Accreditation:* AOTA; NLN. Part-time and evening/weekend programs available. *Faculty:* 21 full-time (18 women), 5 part-time/adjunct (2 women). *Students:* 56 full-time (52 women), 36 part-time (35 women); includes 22 minority (18 African Americans, 1 American Indian/Alaska Native, 2 Asian Americans or Pacific Islanders, 1 Hispanic American), 1 international. Average age 31. 76 applicants, 51% accepted, 28 enrolled. In 2006, 40 degrees awarded. *Degree requirements:* For master's, clinical practicum hours. *Entrance requirements:* For master's, GRE General Test or MAT. Additional exam requirements/recommendations for international students: Required—TOEFL (minimum score 550 paper-based). *Application deadline:* Applications are processed on a rolling basis. Application fee: $30. *Expenses:* Contact institution. *Financial support:* In 2006–07, 14 students received support. Scholarships/grants available. Support available to part-time students. Financial award application deadline: 7/15; financial award applicants required to submit FAFSA. *Faculty research:* Cultural competency, family violence. *Unit head:* Dr. Gale Starich, Dean, 777-718-5305, Fax: 770-297-5929, E-mail: gstarich@brenau.edu. *Application contact:* Nathan Goss, Admissions Coordinator, 770-534-6162, Fax: 770-538-4701, E-mail: ngoss@brenau.edu.

The Catholic University of America, School of Nursing, Washington, DC 20064. Offers advanced practice nursing (MSN), including administration of nursing service, adult nurse practitioner, education, family nurse practitioner, geriatric nurse practitioner, pediatric nurse practitioner, psychiatric-mental health, school health nurse practitioner; clinical nursing (DN Sc). *Accreditation:* AACN; NLN. Part-time programs available. *Faculty:* 17 full-time (all women), 19 part-time/adjunct (18 women). *Students:* 27 full-time (25 women), 58 part-time (57 women); includes 31 minority (20 African Americans, 6 Asian Americans or Pacific Islanders, 5 Hispanic Americans), 6 international. Average age 43. 38 applicants, 76% accepted, 15 enrolled. In 2006, 15 master's, 7 doctorates awarded. *Degree requirements:* For master's, thesis optional; for doctorate, thesis/dissertation, comprehensive exam. *Entrance requirements:* For master's, GRE General Test or MAT, 3 letters of recommendation, BA in nursing, RN registration; for doctorate, GRE General Test, 3 letters of recommendation, BA in nursing, RN registration. Additional exam requirements/recommendations for international students: Required—TOEFL (minimum score 550 paper-based; 213 computer-based). *Application deadline:* For fall admission, 2/1 priority date for domestic students; for spring admission, 11/15 priority date for domestic students. Applications are processed on a rolling basis. Application fee: $55. Electronic applications accepted. *Expenses:* Tuition: Full-time $27,700; part-time $1,045 per credit hour. Required fees: $1,290. Part-time tuition and fees vary according to campus/location and program. *Financial support:* Research assistantships, teaching assistantships, career-related internships or fieldwork, Federal Work-Study, scholarships/grants, tuition waivers (full and partial), and unspecified assistantships available. Support available to part-time students. Financial award application deadline: 2/1; financial award applicants required to submit FAFSA. *Faculty research:* Outcome research–readmission of home health care patients with congestive heart failure, spirituality of chronic illness, minority multigravidos utilization of prenatal care. *Unit head:* Dr. Nalini Jairath, Dean, 202-319-5403, Fax: 202-319-6485, E-mail: jairath@cua.edu.

Clarke College, Department of Nursing and Health, Dubuque, IA 52001-3198. Offers administration of nursing systems (MSN); advanced practice nursing (MSN); education (MSN); family nurse practitioner (MSN, PMC). *Accreditation:* AACN. Part-time programs available. *Entrance requirements:* For master's, GRE General Test or MAT, BSN, minimum GPA of 3.0. Electronic applications accepted. *Faculty research:* Narrative pedagogy, ethics, end-of-life care, pedagogy, family systems.

Clarkson College, Graduate Programs, Department of Nursing, Omaha, NE 68131-2739. Offers administration (MSN); education (MSN); family nurse practitioner (MSN). *Accreditation:* NLN. Part-time and evening/weekend programs available. Postbaccalaureate distance learning degree programs offered (minimal on-campus study). *Degree requirements:* For master's, on-campus skills assessment (family nurse practitioner), comprehensive exam or thesis. *Entrance requirements:* For master's, minimum GPA of 3.0, 2 references, resumé. Additional exam requirements/recommendations for international students: Required—TOEFL (minimum score 600 paper-based; 250 computer-based). Electronic applications accepted.

College of Mount Saint Vincent, School of Professional and Continuing Studies, Department of Nursing, Riverdale, NY 10471-1093. Offers adult nurse practitioner (MSN, PMC); family nurse practitioner (MSN, PMC); nurse educator (PMC); nursing administration (MSN); nursing for the adult and aged (MSN). *Accreditation:* AACN. Part-time programs available. *Faculty:* 2 full-time (1 woman), 6 part-time/adjunct (all women). *Students:* 1 (woman) full-time, 67 part-time (59 women); includes 43 minority (21 African Americans, 16 Asian Americans or Pacific Islanders, 6 Hispanic Americans). Average age 37. In 2006, 16 degrees awarded. *Degree requirements:* For master's, registration. *Entrance requirements:* For master's, BSN, interview, RN license, minimum GPA of 3.0, letters of reference. Additional exam requirements/recommendations for international students: Required—TOEFL. *Application deadline:* For fall admission, 6/1 for domestic and international students; for spring admission, 11/1 for domestic students, 10/1 for international students. Applications are processed on a rolling basis. Application fee: $50. *Expenses:* Contact institution. *Financial support:* Career-related internships or fieldwork available. Financial award application deadline: 6/1; financial award applicants required to submit FAFSA. *Unit head:* Carol Vicino, Director, 718-405-3354, Fax: 718-405-3286.

The College of New Rochelle, Graduate School, Program in Nursing, New Rochelle, NY 10805-2308. Offers acute care nurse practitioner (MS, Certificate); clinical specialist in holistic nursing (MS, Certificate); family nurse practitioner (MS, Certificate); nursing and health care management (MS); nursing education (Certificate). *Accreditation:* AACN. Part-time programs available. *Faculty:* 7 full-time (6 women), 3 part-time/adjunct (all women). *Students:* Average age 44. In 2006, 23 degrees awarded. *Degree requirements:* For master's, registration. *Entrance requirements:* For master's, GRE General Test or MAT, BSN, malpractice insurance, minimum GPA of 3.0, RN license. *Application deadline:* For fall admission, 9/1 priority date for domestic students; for spring admission, 1/15 priority date for domestic students. Applications are processed on a rolling basis. Application fee: $30. *Expenses:* Contact institution. *Financial support:* Traineeships available. Support available to part-time students. Financial award application deadline: 8/15. *Faculty research:* Holistic modalities, academic success variables. *Unit head:* Dr. Mary Alice Donius, Dean, 914-654-5804, Fax: 914-654-5994.

Concordia University Wisconsin, Graduate Programs, School of Health and Human Services, Program in Nursing, Mequon, WI 53097-2402. Offers family nurse practitioner (MSN); geriatric nurse practitioner (MSN); nurse educator (MSN). *Accreditation:* AACN. Postbaccalaureate distance learning degree programs offered (minimal on-campus study). *Faculty:* 2 full-time (1 woman), 5 part-time/adjunct (all women). *Students:* 217 (199 women). Average age 29. In 2006, 37 degrees awarded. *Degree requirements:* For master's, thesis or alternative, comprehensive exam. *Entrance requirements:* Additional exam requirements/recommendations for international students: Required—TOEFL. *Application deadline:* For fall admission, 8/1 priority date for domestic students. Applications are processed on a rolling basis. Application fee: $35. *Expenses:* Contact institution. *Financial support:* Application deadline: 8/1. *Unit head:* Dr. Ruth Gresley, Director, 262-243-4452, E-mail: ruth.gresley@cuw.edu.

DeSales University, Graduate Division, Programs in Nursing, Center Valley, PA 18034-9568. Offers adult advanced practice nurse specialist (MSN); family nurse practitioner (MSN); nurse educator (MSN); MSN/MBA. *Accreditation:* NLN. Part-time and evening/weekend programs available. In 2006, 9 degrees awarded. *Degree requirements:* For master's, thesis optional. *Entrance requirements:* For master's, GRE General Test, MAT, minimum B average in undergraduate course work, health assessment course or equivalent, course work in statistics. *Application deadline:* For spring admission, 3/15 for domestic students. Applications are processed on a rolling basis. Application fee: $35. *Expenses:* Contact institution. *Financial support:* In 2006–07, 1 student received support. Unspecified assistantships available. Support available to part-time students. Financial award applicants required to submit FAFSA. *Faculty research:* Women's health, theory validation, needs of homeless, behavior risk evaluation, wound healing. *Unit head:* Dr. Carol Gullo Mest, Director, 610-282-1100 Ext. 1394, Fax: 610-282-2254, E-mail: carol.mest@desales.edu. *Application contact:* Megan Szivos, Secretary for MSN Program, 610-282-1100 Ext. 1664, Fax: 610-282-2254, E-mail: megan.szivos@desales.edu.

Dominican University of California, Graduate Programs, School of Arts and Sciences, Program in Nursing, San Rafael, CA 94901-2298. Offers geriatric and nurse educator (MS); integrated health practices (MS). *Accreditation:* AACN. Part-time and evening/weekend programs available. *Degree requirements:* For master's, thesis, registration. *Entrance requirements:* For master's, minimum GPA of 3.0, clinical experience, course work in nursing research and statistics, CPR certification, professional liability and malpractice insurance, interview. Additional exam requirements/recommendations for international students: Required—TOEFL (minimum score 550 paper-based; 213 computer-based). Electronic applications accepted.

Duke University, School of Nursing, Durham, NC 27708-0586. Offers adult acute care (Certificate); adult cardiovascular (Certificate); adult oncology/HIV (Certificate); adult primary care (Certificate); clinical nurse specialist (MSN), including adult oncology/HIV, gerontology, neonatal, pediatric, pediatric/chronic acute care; clinical research management (MSN, Certificate); family (Certificate); gerontology (Certificate); health and nursing ministries (MSN, Certificate); health systems leadership and outcomes (Certificate); leadership in community based long term care (MSN, Certificate); neonatal (Certificate); neonatal/pediatric in rural health (MSN, Certificate); nurse anesthetist (MSN, Certificate); nurse practitioner (MSN), including adult acute care, adult cardiovascular, adult oncology/HIV, adult primary care, family, gerontology, neonatal, pediatric, pediatric acute care; nursing (PhD); nursing and healthcare leadership (MSN); nursing education (MSN); nursing informatics (MSN, Certificate); pediatric (Certificate); pediatric acute care (Certificate); MBA/MSN; MSN/MCM. *Accreditation:* AACN; AANA/CANAEP. Part-time programs available. Postbaccalaureate distance learning degree programs offered (minimal on-campus study). *Faculty:* 45 full-time (41 women), 169 part-time/adjunct (150 women). *Students:* 178 full-time (162 women), 140 part-time (132 women); includes 48 minority (17 African Americans, 3 American Indian/Alaska Native, 20 Asian Americans or Pacific Islanders, 8 Hispanic Americans). Average age 36. 99 applicants, 92% accepted, 91 enrolled. In 2006, 122 master's, 17 other advanced degrees awarded. *Median time to degree:* Master's–2 years full-time, 2.5 years part-time. *Degree requirements:* For master's, thesis optional. *Entrance requirements:* For master's, GRE General Test or MAT, 1 year of nursing experience, BSN, minimum GPA of 3.0, previous course work in statistics; for Certificate, MSN. Additional exam requirements/recommendations for international students: Required—TOEFL (minimum score 550 paper-based; 213 computer-based), Commission on Graduates of Foreign Nursing Schools exam. *Application deadline:* For fall admission, 7/2 priority date for domestic and international students; for spring admission, 11/15 priority date for domestic and international students. Applications are processed on a rolling basis. Application fee: $50. *Expenses:* Contact institution. *Financial support:* In 2006–07, 258 students received support. Career-related internships or fieldwork, institutionally sponsored loans, scholarships/grants, traineeships, and tuition waivers (partial) available. Support available to part-time students. Financial award application deadline: 4/1; financial award applicants required to submit FAFSA. *Faculty research:* Cardiovascular disease, caregiver skill training, data mining, prostate cancer, neonatal immune system. Total annual research expenditures: $3.5 million. *Unit head:* Dr. Catherine L. Gilliss, Dean/Vice Chancellor for Nursing Affairs, 919-684-9444, Fax: 919-684-9414, E-mail: gilli025@mc.duke.edu. *Application contact:* Bebe T. Mills, Director of Admissions, 919-684-9151, Fax: 919-668-4693, E-mail: mills031@mc.duke.edu.

Duquesne University, School of Nursing, Master's Program in Nursing, Pittsburgh, PA 15282-0001. Offers acute care nursing (Post-Master's Certificate); acute care nursing specialist (MSN); family nurse practitioner (MSN, Post-Master's Certificate); forensic nursing (MSN, Post-Master's Certificate); nursing administration (MSN, Post-Master's Certificate); nursing education (MSN, Post-Master's Certificate); psychiatric/mental health nursing (MSN, Post-Master's Certificate); MSN/MBA. *Accreditation:* AACN. Part-time and evening/weekend programs available. Postbaccalaureate distance learning degree programs offered (minimal on-campus study). *Faculty:* 20 full-time (19 women), 4 part-time/adjunct (all women). *Students:* 73 full-time (70 women), 83 part-time (79 women); includes 11 minority (4 African Americans, 3 American Indian/Alaska Native, 1 Asian American or Pacific Islander, 3 Hispanic Americans). 72 applicants, 75% accepted, 49 enrolled. In 2006, 20 master's, 11 other advanced degrees awarded. *Degree requirements:* For master's, culminating paper. *Entrance requirements:* For master's, MAT or GRE, 1 year of work experience, bachelor's degree in nursing, undergraduate course work in statistics, health assessment course (family nurse practitioner, nursing education, acute care clinical nurse specialist). *Application deadline:* For fall admission, 4/1 for domestic and international students; for spring admission, 11/1 for domestic and international students. Applications are processed on a rolling basis. Application fee: $50. *Expenses:* Contact institution. Tuition and fees vary according to degree level and program. *Financial support:* In 2006–07, 10 students received support, including 9 research assistantships with partial tuition reimbursements available (averaging $1,600 per year), 1 teaching assistantship with partial tuition reimbursement available (averaging $1,600 per year); fellowships with partial tuition reimbursements available, institutionally sponsored loans, scholarships/grants, traineeships, and tuition waivers (partial) also available. Financial award application deadline: 8/20. *Faculty research:* Depression, culture, vulnerable populations, ethics, health disparities, community based. Total annual research expenditures: $377,400. *Unit head:* Dr. Joan Such Lockhart, Professor and Associate Dean of Academic Affairs, 412-396-6540, Fax: 412-396-1821, E-mail: lockhart@duq.edu. *Application contact:* Susan Hardner, Nurse Recruiter, 412-396-4945, Fax: 412-396-6346, E-mail: nursing@duq.edu.

D'Youville College, Department of Nursing, Buffalo, NY 14201-1084. Offers community health nursing/education (MSN); community health nursing/high risk parents and children (MSN); community health nursing/management (MSN); family nurse practitioner (MS); nursing and health-related professions (Certificate); nursing with clinical focus choice (MSN). *Accreditation:* AACN. Part-time and evening/weekend programs available. *Faculty:* 26 full-time (all women), 7 part-time/adjunct (6 women). *Students:* 77 full-time (72 women), 101 part-time (95 women); includes 17 minority (12 African Americans, 1 American Indian/Alaska Native, 4 Hispanic Americans), 89 international. Average age 36. 177 applicants, 58% accepted, 37 enrolled. In 2006, 41 master's, 2 other advanced degrees awarded. *Degree requirements:* For master's, membership on board of community agency, publishable paper, thesis optional. *Entrance requirements:* For master's, BS in nursing, minimum GPA of 3.0, course work in statistics and computers. Additional exam requirements/recommendations for international students: Required—TOEFL (minimum score 500 paper-based; 173 computer-based). *Application deadline:* For fall admission, 5/1 priority date for international students; for spring admission, 9/1 priority date for international students. Applications are processed on a rolling basis. Application fee: $25. Electronic applications accepted. *Financial support:* In 2006–07, 1 research assistantship with partial tuition reimbursement (averaging $3,000 per year) was awarded; Federal Work-Study and scholarships/grants also available. Support available to part-time students. Financial award application deadline: 3/1; financial award applicants required to submit FAFSA. *Faculty research:* Nursing curriculum, nursing theory-testing, wellness research, communication and socialization patterns. *Unit head:* Dr. Verna Kieffer, Chair, 716-829-7613, Fax: 716-829-8159. *Application contact:* Linda Fisher, Graduate Admissions Director, 716-829-8400, Fax: 716-829-7900, E-mail: graduateadmissions@dyc.edu.

See Close-Up on page 1953.

Nursing Education

Eastern Michigan University, Graduate School, College of Health and Human Services, School of Nursing, Ypsilanti, MI 48197. Offers nursing (MSN); nursing education (Advanced Certificate). *Accreditation:* AACN. Part-time and evening/weekend programs available. Postbaccalaureate distance learning degree programs offered (minimal on-campus study). *Faculty:* 18 full-time (17 women). *Students:* 1 (woman) full-time, 25 part-time (all women); includes 9 minority (7 African Americans, 2 Asian Americans or Pacific Islanders). Average age 42. In 2006, 13 degrees awarded. *Degree requirements:* For master's, thesis optional. *Entrance requirements:* For master's, GRE General Test, Michigan RN license. Additional exam requirements/recommendations for international students: Required—TOEFL. *Application deadline:* For fall admission, 5/15 priority date for domestic students, 5/1 priority date for international students; for winter admission, 10/15 priority date for domestic students, 10/1 priority date for international students; for spring admission, 3/15 priority date for domestic students, 3/1 priority date for international students. Applications are processed on a rolling basis. Application fee: $35. *Expenses:* Tuition, state resident: part-time $341 per credit hour. Tuition, nonresident: full-time $16,104; part-time $671 per credit hour. Required fees: $816; $34 per credit hour. $40 per term. One-time fee: $82 full-time. Tuition and fees vary according to course level, course load, degree level and reciprocity agreements. *Financial support:* Fellowships, research assistantships with full tuition reimbursements, teaching assistantships with full tuition reimbursements, career-related internships or fieldwork, Federal Work-Study, institutionally sponsored loans, scholarships/grants, tuition waivers (partial), and unspecified assistantships available. Support available to part-time students. Financial award applicants required to submit FAFSA. *Unit head:* Dr. Naomi Ervin, Director, 734-487-2310, Fax: 734-487-9646, E-mail: nervin@emich.edu.

Eastern Washington University, Graduate Studies, Intercollegiate College of Nursing, Cheney, WA 99004-2431. Offers MN. *Degree requirements:* For master's, thesis, comprehensive exam. *Entrance requirements:* For master's, GRE General Test, minimum GPA of 3.0.

Ferris State University, College of Allied Health Sciences, School of Nursing, Big Rapids, MI 49307. Offers nursing (MS); nursing administration (MS); nursing education (MS); nursing informatics (MS). Part-time and evening/weekend programs available. Postbaccalaureate distance learning degree programs offered (minimal on-campus study). *Faculty:* 2 full-time (1 woman). *Students:* Average age 39. 22 applicants, 100% accepted, 22 enrolled. In 2006, 2 degrees awarded. *Median time to degree:* Master's–3 years part-time. *Degree requirements:* For master's, thesis, practicum, comprehensive exam. *Entrance requirements:* For master's, BS in nursing, writing sample, letters of reference, 2 years clinical experience. Additional exam requirements/recommendations for international students: Required—TOEFL (minimum score 550 paper-based). *Application deadline:* For fall admission, 8/26 for domestic students; for winter admission, 12/16 for domestic students. Applications are processed on a rolling basis. Application fee: $30. Electronic applications accepted. *Expenses:* Tuition, state resident: part-time $355 per credit hour. Tuition, nonresident: part-time $687 per credit hour. *Financial support:* In 2006–07, 3 students received support. Scholarships/grants available. *Faculty research:* Nursing education-minority student focus student attitudes toward aging. *Unit head:* Dr. Julie A. Coon, Director, 231-591-2267, Fax: 231-591-2325, E-mail: coonj@ferris.edu.

Florida State University, Graduate Studies, College of Nursing, Tallahassee, FL 32306. Offers family nurse practitioner (MSN, Certificate); nurse educator (MSN, Certificate); pediatric nurse practitioner (MSN, Certificate). *Accreditation:* AACN. Part-time programs available. Postbaccalaureate distance learning degree programs offered (no on-campus study). *Faculty:* 10 full-time (9 women), 1 part-time/adjunct (0 women). *Students:* 10 full-time (all women), 75 part-time (69 women); includes 16 minority (10 African Americans, 2 Asian Americans or Pacific Islanders, 4 Hispanic Americans). Average age 39. 43 applicants, 81% accepted, 32 enrolled. In 2006, 13 master's, 9 other advanced degrees awarded. *Degree requirements:* For master's, Research Project (optional), thesis optional. *Entrance requirements:* For master's, GRE General Test, minimum GPA of 3.0, BSN, Florida RN license. Additional exam requirements/recommendations for international students: Required—TOEFL (minimum score 550 paper-based). *Application deadline:* For fall admission, 7/1 for domestic students; for spring admission, 10/15 for domestic students. Applications are processed on a rolling basis. Application fee: $30. Electronic applications accepted. *Expenses:* Tuition, state resident: full-time $5,822; part-time $243 per credit hour. Tuition, nonresident: full-time $20,976; part-time $874 per credit hour. Tuition and fees vary according to program. *Financial support:* In 2006–07, 25 students received support, including 1 fellowship with partial tuition reimbursement available (averaging $6,300 per year), 3 research assistantships with partial tuition reimbursements available (averaging $3,000 per year), 13 teaching assistantships with partial tuition reimbursements available (averaging $3,000 per year); career-related internships or fieldwork, Federal Work-Study, institutionally sponsored loans, traineeships, and tuition waivers (partial) also available. Financial award application deadline: 4/15; financial award applicants required to submit FAFSA. *Faculty research:* Distance learning, gerontology, health promotion, educational strategies, rehabilitation of brain injured patients. *Unit head:* Dr. Katherine P. Mason, Dean, 850-644-5417, Fax: 850-644-7660, E-mail: kmason@mailer.fsu.edu. *Application contact:* Eddie Page, Graduate Program Coordinator, 850-644-5638, Fax: 850-645-7321, E-mail: epage@fsu.edu.

George Mason University, College of Health and Human Services, Fairfax, VA 22030. Offers advanced clinical nursing (MSN); nurse practitioner (MSN); nursing (MSN, PhD); nursing administration (MSN); nursing education (Certificate); nursing educator (MSN); social work (MSW). *Accreditation:* AACN. *Faculty:* 69 full-time (55 women), 75 part-time/adjunct (66 women). *Students:* 98 full-time (81 women), 301 part-time (260 women); includes 121 minority (60 African Americans, 45 Asian Americans or Pacific Islanders, 16 Hispanic Americans), 27 international. Average age 39. 326 applicants, 61% accepted, 121 enrolled. In 2006, 89 master's, 7 doctorates, 11 other advanced degrees awarded. *Degree requirements:* For doctorate, thesis/dissertation, oral/written exams. *Entrance requirements:* For master's, RN license, minimum GPA of 3.0 in last 60 hours of course work; for doctorate, MAT, 3 years of nursing experience, master's degree, minimum GPA of 3.25, professional liability insurance. *Application deadline:* For fall admission, 5/1 for domestic students; for spring admission, 11/1 for domestic students. Application fee: $60 ($75 for international students). Electronic applications accepted. *Expenses:* Tuition, state resident: full-time $5,724; part-time $238 per credit. Tuition, nonresident: full-time $16,896; part-time $704 per credit. Required fees: $1,656; $69 per credit. *Financial support:* Fellowships, research assistantships, teaching assistantships, tuition waivers (partial) available. Support available to part-time students. Financial award application deadline: 3/1; financial award applicants required to submit FAFSA. *Unit head:* Dr. Shirley S. Travis, Dean, 703-993-1918. *Application contact:* Dr. James D. Vail, Associate Dean, Graduate Programs and Research, 703-993-1947, Fax: 703-993-1942, E-mail: nursinfo@gmu.edu.

Graceland University, School of Nursing, Independence, MO 64050-3434. Offers family nurse practitioner (MSN, PMC); health care administration (MSN, PMC); nurse educator (MSN, PMC). Part-time programs available. Postbaccalaureate distance learning degree programs offered (minimal on-campus study). *Faculty:* 11 full-time (all women), 5 part-time/adjunct (all women). *Students:* 94 full-time (93 women), 123 part-time (102 women); includes 16 minority (10 African Americans, 4 Asian Americans or Pacific Islanders, 2 Hispanic Americans). Average age 44. 123 applicants, 90% accepted, 105 enrolled. In 2006, 42 master's, 2 other advanced degrees awarded. *Median time to degree:* Master's–2.5 years full-time, 4 years part-time. *Degree requirements:* For master's, thesis optional. *Entrance requirements:* For master's, BSN from nationally accredited program, portfolio, RN license, minimum GPA of 3.0. *Application deadline:* For fall admission, 6/1 priority date for domestic students; for winter admission, 10/1 priority date for domestic students; for spring admission, 3/1 priority date for domestic students. Applications are processed on a rolling basis. Application fee: $50. Electronic applications accepted. *Expenses: Contact institution. Financial support:* In 2006–07, 3 students received support. Institutionally sponsored loans and traineeships available. Support available to part-time students. Financial award applicants required to submit FAFSA. *Faculty research:* International nursing, family care-giving, health promotion. *Unit head:* Dr. Kathryn A. Ballou, Dean, 800-833-0524 Ext. 4201, Fax: 816-833-2990, E-mail: kaballou@graceland.edu. *Application contact:* John D. Koehler, Manager of Recruiting, 816-833-0524 Ext. 4804, Fax: 816-833-2990, E-mail: jkoehler@graceland.edu.

Grambling State University, School of Graduate Studies and Research, College of Professional Studies, School of Nursing, Grambling, LA 71245. Offers family nurse practitioner (MSN, PMC); nurse educator (MSN). *Accreditation:* NLN. Part-time programs available. *Faculty:* 4 full-time (all women), 4 part-time/adjunct (2 women). *Students:* 26 full-time (21 women), 24 part-time (20 women); includes 27 minority (26 African Americans, 1 Asian American or Pacific Islander). Average age 38. In 2006, 13 degrees awarded. *Degree requirements:* For master's, thesis (for some programs), comprehensive exam (for some programs). *Entrance requirements:* For master's, GRE, minimum GPA of 3.0 on last degree, interview, 2 years experience as RN. Additional exam requirements/recommendations for international students: Required—TOEFL. *Application deadline:* For fall admission, 7/1 for domestic students; for spring admission, 12/1 for domestic students. Application fee: $20 ($30 for international students). *Expenses:* Tuition, state resident: full-time $2,232; part-time $124 per credit hour. Tuition, nonresident: full-time $7,582; part-time $124 per credit hour. Required fees: $1,127. *Financial support:* In 2006–07, 25 students received support. Application deadline: 5/31. *Unit head:* Dr. Rhonda Hensley, Director, 318-274-2897, Fax: 318-274-3491, E-mail: hensleyr@gram.edu.

Grand Valley State University, Kirkhof College of Nursing, Allendale, MI 49401-9403. Offers advanced practice (MSN); case management (MSN); nursing administration (MSN); nursing education (MSN); MSN/MBA. *Accreditation:* AACN. Part-time programs available. *Faculty:* 17 full-time (all women), 1 (woman) part-time/adjunct. *Students:* 3 full-time (all women), 46 part-time (42 women); includes 4 minority (1 African American, 1 Asian American or Pacific Islander, 2 Hispanic Americans). Average age 35. 15 applicants, 67% accepted, 8 enrolled. In 2006, 20 degrees awarded. *Degree requirements:* For master's, thesis optional. *Entrance requirements:* For master's, minimum GPA of 3.0 in upper-division course work, course work in statistics, Michigan RN license. Additional exam requirements/recommendations for international students: Required—TOEFL. *Application deadline:* For fall admission, 3/15 priority date for domestic students. Applications are processed on a rolling basis. Application fee: $30. Electronic applications accepted. *Expenses:* Tuition, state resident: full-time $5,850; part-time $325 per credit. Tuition, nonresident: full-time $10,800; part-time $600 per credit. Tuition and fees vary according to course load. *Financial support:* In 2006–07, 7 research assistantships with full and partial tuition reimbursements (averaging $8,000 per year) were awarded; career-related internships or fieldwork, Federal Work-Study, institutionally sponsored loans, and traineeships also available. Financial award application deadline: 2/15. *Faculty research:* Multigenerational health promotion, chronic disease prevention, end-of-life issues; nursing workload, family caregiver health. Total annual research expenditures: $36,000. *Unit head:* Dr. Phyllis Gendler, Dean, 616-331-7161, Fax: 616-331-7362, E-mail: gendlerp@gvsu.edu. *Application contact:* Dr. Jean Martin, Director of Graduate Programs, 616-331-7167, Fax: 616-331-7362, E-mail: martinj@gvsu.edu.

Indiana Wesleyan University, College of Graduate Studies, Division of Nursing, Marion, IN 46953-4974. Offers community health nursing (MS); nursing (Post Master's Certificate); nursing administration (MS); nursing education (MS); primary care nursing (MS). *Accreditation:* AACN. Part-time and evening/weekend programs available. *Faculty:* 2 full-time (both women), 6 part-time/adjunct (3 women). *Students:* 312 full-time (296 women), 8 part-time (4 women); includes 45 minority (41 African Americans, 2 Asian Americans or Pacific Islanders, 2 Hispanic Americans). Average age 40. In 2006, 87 degrees awarded. *Degree requirements:* For master's, thesis. *Entrance requirements:* For master's, GRE, RN license, 1 year of related experience, graduate statistics course. *Application deadline:* For fall admission, 7/31 priority date for domestic students; for winter admission, 11/15 priority date for domestic students; for spring admission, 4/15 priority date for domestic students. Electronic applications accepted. *Expenses: Contact institution.* Tuition and fees vary according to degree level, campus/location and program. *Financial support:* In 2006–07, 15 fellowships were awarded; career-related internships or fieldwork, scholarships/grants, and traineeships also available. Support available to part-time students. Financial award application deadline: 3/15. *Faculty research:* Primary health care with international emphasis, international nursing. *Unit head:* Pam Giles, Director, 765-677-1716, E-mail: gradnurse@indwes.edu. *Application contact:* David McMillan, Assistant Director of Enrollment Management, 765-677-2688, E-mail: david.mcmillan@indwes.edu.

Jefferson College of Health Sciences, Program in Nursing, Roanoke, VA 24031-3186. Offers nursing education (MSN); nursing management (MSN). *Accreditation:* AACN.

Kent State University, College of Nursing, Kent, OH 44242-0001. Offers clinical nursing (MSN), including nursing of the adult (medical/surgical nursing), psychiatric mental health nursing; nursing (PhD); nursing administration (MSN); nursing education (MSN); parent-child nursing (MSN). *Accreditation:* AACN. Part-time programs available. *Degree requirements:* For master's, thesis optional; for doctorate, thesis/dissertation, comprehensive exam, registration. *Entrance requirements:* For master's, GRE if undergraduate GPA is less than 3.0, minimum GPA of 2.75; for doctorate, GRE, MSN. Additional exam requirements/recommendations for international students: Required—TOEFL. Electronic applications accepted. Expenses: Contact institution. *Faculty research:* Women and violence, methodological specialties, osteoporosis in women, new caregivers and the elderly.

Lamar University, College of Graduate Studies, College of Arts and Sciences, Department of Nursing, Beaumont, TX 77710. Offers nursing administration online (MSN); nursing education online (MSN); MSN/MBA. *Accreditation:* NLN. Part-time and evening/weekend programs available. *Faculty:* 10 full-time (all women). *Students:* 2 full-time (0 women), 7 part-time (4 women). Average age 42. 10 applicants, 40% accepted, 2 enrolled. In 2006, 2 master's awarded. *Median time to degree:* Of those who began their doctoral program in fall 1998, 100% received their degree in 8 years or less. *Degree requirements:* For master's, practicum project presentation, evidence-based project. *Entrance requirements:* For master's, GRE General Test, MAT, criminal background check, RN license, NLN-accredited BSN, college course work in graduate statistics in past 5 years, letters of recommendation, minimum undergraduate GPA of 3.0. Additional exam requirements/recommendations for international students: Required—TOEFL, MAT. *Application deadline:* For fall admission, 8/1 priority date for domestic students; for spring admission, 12/1 priority date for domestic students. Applications are processed on a rolling basis. Application fee: $25 ($50 for international students). *Expenses:* Tuition, nonresident: part-time $33 per hour. Required fees: $43 per hour. $110 per semester. *Financial support:* In 2006–07, 3 students received support, including 2 teaching assistantships (averaging $24,000 per year); scholarships/grants and traineeships also available. Financial award application deadline: 4/1. *Faculty research:* Student retention, theory, caregiving, on-line course and research. Total annual research expenditures: $6,000. *Unit head:* Dr. Nancy Blume, Director of Graduate Nursing Studies, 409-880-8820, Fax: 409-880-8698, E-mail: nancy.blume@lamar.edu. *Application contact:* Shelly R. Belk, Administrative Associate, 409-880-7720.

La Salle University, School of Nursing and Health Sciences, Philadelphia, PA 19141-1199. Offers adult health and illness, clinical nurse specialist (MSN); gerontology (Certificate); nursing administration (MSN); nursing education (Certificate); nursing informatics (Certificate); primary care of adults-nurse practitioner (MSN); public health nursing (MSN); school nursing (Certificate); speech-language-hearing science (MS); wound, ostomy and continence nursing (Certificate); wound, ostomy, and continence nursing (MSN); MSN/MBA. *Accreditation:* AACN. Part-time programs available. Postbaccalaureate distance learning degree programs offered (minimal on-campus study). *Entrance requirements:* For master's, GRE or MAT, 1 year of professional work experience, BSN, Pennsylvania RN license. Expenses: Contact institution. *Faculty research:* Medication errors, wound care, metacognition, education of RN students.

Lewis University, College of Nursing and Health Professions, Program in Nursing, Romeoville, IL 60446. Offers case management (MSN); nursing administration (MSN); nursing education (MSN); MSN/MBA. *Accreditation:* AACN. Part-time and evening/weekend programs available. *Degree requirements:* For master's, clinical practicum. *Entrance requirements:* For master's, GRE General Test, GRE Subject Test, minimum undergraduate GPA of 2.75, degree in nursing, RN license, letter of recommendation, interview, resumé or curriculum vitae. Additional exam requirements/recommendations for international students: Required—TOEFL (minimum score 550 paper-based; 213 computer-based). Electronic applications accepted. *Faculty research:* Cancer prevention, phenomenological methods, public policy analysis.

Marian College of Fond du Lac, School of Nursing, Fond du Lac, WI 54935-4699. Offers adult nurse practitioner (MSN); nurse educator (MSN). *Accreditation:* AACN. Part-time and evening/weekend programs available. *Faculty:* 4 full-time (3 women), 4 part-time/adjunct (2 women). *Students:* 13 full-time (all women), 15 part-time (all women); includes 1 minority (American Indian/Alaska Native). Average age 37. 9 applicants, 100% accepted, 9 enrolled. In 2006, 16 degrees awarded. *Degree requirements:* For master's, thesis, 675 clinical practicum hours. *Entrance requirements:* For master's, 3 letters of professional recommendation, undergraduate work in nursing research, statistics, health assessment. Additional exam requirements/recommendations for international students: Required—TOEFL (minimum score 525 paper-based). *Application deadline:* Applications are processed on a rolling basis. Application fee: $50. Electronic applications accepted. *Expenses: Contact institution. Financial support:* In 2006–07, 19 students received support. Institutionally sponsored loans and scholarships/grants available. Support available to part-time students. Financial award application deadline: 3/1; financial award applicants required to submit FAFSA. *Unit head:* Dr. James C. McCann, Dean, School of Nursing, 920-923-8094, Fax: 920-923-8770, E-mail: jcmccann70@mariancollege.edu. *Application contact:* Dr. Lea Monahan, Director, 920-923-7608, Fax: 920-923-8770, E-mail: lmonahan@mariancollege.edu.

Marymount University, School of Health Professions, Program in Nursing, Arlington, VA 22207-4299. Offers family nurse practitioner (MSN, Certificate); nursing administration (MSN, Certificate); nursing education (MSN, Certificate); RN to MSN (MSN). *Accreditation:* AACN; NLN. Part-time and evening/weekend programs available. *Faculty:* 7 full-time (all women), 1 (woman) part-time/adjunct. *Students:* 4 full-time (3 women), 36 part-time (35 women); includes 23 minority (15 African Americans, 5 Asian Americans or Pacific Islanders, 3 Hispanic Americans), 1 international. Average age 42. 17 applicants, 100% accepted, 10 enrolled. In 2006, 13 master's, 2 other advanced degrees awarded. *Degree requirements:* For master's, comprehensive exam. *Entrance requirements:* For master's, 2 letters of recommendation, interview, RN license, resumé; for Certificate, interview. *Application deadline:* Applications are processed on a rolling basis. Application fee: $40. Electronic applications accepted. *Expenses:* Tuition: Full-time $11,160; part-time $620 per credit. Required fees: $113; $630 per credit. *Financial support:* Research assistantships with partial tuition reimbursements, career-related internships or fieldwork, scholarships/grants, and unspecified assistantships available. Support available to part-time students. Financial award applicants required to submit FAFSA. *Unit head:* Dr. Susan Bidwell, Chair, 703-284-1593, Fax: 703-284-3819, E-mail: susan.bidwell@marymount.edu.

Medical University of South Carolina, College of Nursing, Program in Nurse Educator, Charleston, SC 29425-0002. Offers MSN. Part-time and evening/weekend programs available. Postbaccalaureate distance learning degree programs offered. *Faculty:* 11 full-time (10 women). *Students:* 6 full-time (5 women), 10 part-time (all women); includes 1 minority (Asian American or Pacific Islander) Average age 35. 10 applicants, 60% accepted, 6 enrolled. In 2006, 1 degree awarded. *Degree requirements:* For master's, thesis optional. *Entrance requirements:* For master's, GRE General Test, BSN, course work in statistics and physical assessment, nursing license, minimum GPA of 3.0. Additional exam requirements/recommendations for international students: Required—TOEFL (minimum score 600 paper-based; 250 computer-based). *Application deadline:* For fall admission, 2/1 for domestic and international students; for spring admission, 9/15 for domestic and international students. Application fee: $75. Electronic applications accepted. *Financial support:* Federal Work-Study, scholarships/grants, and traineeships available. Support available to part-time students. Financial award application deadline: 3/15; financial award applicants required to submit FAFSA. *Faculty research:* Prenatal care outcomes, perinatal wellness in Hispanic women, community-based breast cancer screening. Total annual research expenditures: $26,866. *Unit head:* Dr. Kathleen A. Simon, Track Coordinator, 843-792-3389, Fax: 843-792-1741, E-mail: simonk@musc.edu. *Application contact:* Carolyn F. Page, Director, Student Services, 843-792-3844, Fax: 843-792-9258, E-mail: pagecf@musc.edu.

Mercy College, Division of Health Professions, Program in Nursing, Dobbs Ferry, NY 10522-1189. Offers nursing administration (MS); nursing education (MS). *Accreditation:* AACN. Part-time programs available. *Students:* 18 full-time (8 women), 65 part-time (62 women); includes 36 minority (28 African Americans, 6 Asian Americans or Pacific Islanders, 2 Hispanic Americans), 14 international. Average age 41. In 2006, 15 degrees awarded. *Degree requirements:* For master's, comprehensive project. *Entrance requirements:* For master's, GRE General Test or MAT, BSN, minimum GPA of 3.0, 2 letters of reference, interview, US RN registration. *Application deadline:* For fall admission, 8/15 priority date for domestic students; for spring admission, 2/15 for domestic students. Applications are processed on a rolling basis. Application fee: $62. *Expenses:* Tuition: Part-time $595 per credit. Required fees: $9 per credit. Tuition and fees vary according to program. *Financial support:* Career-related internships or fieldwork, Federal Work-Study, and institutionally sponsored loans available. Support available to part-time students. *Faculty research:* Program evaluation, cost and home care, children of alcoholic parents, clinical decision making. *Unit head:* Dr. Mary McGuiness, Director, Nursing Programs, 914-674-7863 Ext. 551, E-mail: mmcguiness@mercy.edu. *Application contact:* Kathleen Jackson, Director of Admissions, 800-Mercy-NY, Fax: 914-674-7382, E-mail: admissions@mercy.edu.

MGH Institute of Health Professions, Graduate Programs, Program in Nursing, Boston, MA 02129. Offers advanced practice nursing (MSN); gerontological nursing (MSN); pediatric nursing (MSN); psychiatric nursing (MSN); teaching and learning for health care education (Certificate); women's health nursing (MSN). *Accreditation:* NLN (one or more programs are accredited). *Faculty:* 29 full-time (28 women), 9 part-time/adjunct (7 women). *Students:* 208 full-time (188 women), 43 part-time (35 women); includes 36 minority (12 African Americans, 17 Asian Americans or Pacific Islanders, 7 Hispanic Americans), 1 international. Average age 29. 302 applicants, 62% accepted, 101 enrolled. In 2006, 77 master's, 3 other advanced degrees awarded. *Degree requirements:* For master's, thesis or alternative. *Entrance requirements:* For master's, GRE General Test, minimum GPA of 3.0. Additional exam requirements/recommendations for international students: Required—TOEFL (minimum score 550 paper-based; 213 computer-based). *Application deadline:* For fall admission, 1/10 for domestic and international students. Application fee: $50. Electronic applications accepted. *Financial support:* In 2006–07, 212 students received support, including 1 research assistantship (averaging $1,200 per year), 2 teaching assistantships (averaging $1,200 per year); career-related internships or fieldwork, scholarships/grants, traineeships, tuition waivers (full and partial), and unspecified assistantships also available. Support available to part-time students. Financial award application deadline: 3/3; financial award applicants required to submit FAFSA. *Faculty research:* Biobehavioral nursing, HIV/AIDS, gerontological nursing, women's health, vulnerable populations, health systems . *Unit head:* Margery Chisholm, Director, 617-724-0480, Fax: 617-726-8022, E-mail: mchisholm@mghihp.edu. *Application contact:* Maureen Rika Judd, Manager of Admissions, 617-726-6069, Fax: 617-726-8010, E-mail: admissions@mghihp.edu.

See Close-Up on page 1963.

Midwestern State University, Graduate Studies, College of Health Sciences and Human Services, Nursing Program, Wichita Falls, TX 76308. Offers family nurse practitioner (MSN); health services administration (MSN); nurse educator (MSN). *Accreditation:* AACN. Part-time and evening/weekend programs available. *Faculty:* 8 full-time (all women), 2 part-time/adjunct (both women). *Students:* 12 full-time (10 women), 49 part-time (40 women); includes 8 minority (1 African American, 2 American Indian/Alaska Native, 1 Asian American or Pacific Islander, 4 Hispanic Americans), 3 international. Average age 39. 19 applicants, 84% accepted, 12 enrolled. In 2006, 10 degrees awarded. *Degree requirements:* For master's, thesis optional. *Entrance requirements:* For master's, GRE General Test or MAT. Additional exam requirements/recommendations for international students: Required—TOEFL (minimum score 550 paper-based; 213 computer-based). *Application deadline:* For fall admission, 7/1 for domestic students, 4/1 for international students; for spring admission, 11/1 for domestic students, 8/1 for international students. Applications are processed on a rolling basis. Application fee: $35 ($50 for international students). Electronic applications accepted. *Financial support:* In 2006–07, 58 students received support, including 1 teaching assistantship with partial tuition reimbursement available (averaging $7,500 per year); career-related internships or fieldwork, Federal Work-Study, institutionally sponsored loans, scholarships/grants, tuition waivers (partial), and unspecified assistantships also available. Support available to part-time students. Financial award application deadline: 5/1; financial award applicants required to submit FAFSA. *Unit head:* Dr. Melissa Ford, Chair, 940-397-4601, Fax: 940-397-4513, E-mail: melissa.ford@mwsu.edu. *Application contact:* 800-842-1922, Fax: 940-397-4672, E-mail: admissions@mwsu.edu.

Minnesota State University Mankato, College of Graduate Studies, College of Allied Health and Nursing, Department of Nursing, Mankato, MN 56001. Offers family nursing (MSN), including clinical nurse specialist, educator, family nurse practitioner, manager; managed care (MSN), including clinical nurse specialist, educator, family nurse practitioner, manager. *Accreditation:* AACN; NLN. *Students:* 12 full-time (all women), 34 part-time (32 women). Average age 39. In 2006, 15 degrees awarded. *Degree requirements:* For master's, internships, research project or thesis. *Entrance requirements:* For master's, GRE General Test or on-campus essay, minimum GPA of 3.0 during previous 2 years, BSN or equivalent references. Additional exam requirements/recommendations for international students: Required—TOEFL. *Application deadline:* For fall admission, 1/15 priority date for domestic students; for spring admission, 11/27 for domestic students. Applications are processed on a rolling basis. Application fee: $40. Electronic applications accepted. *Financial support:* Research assistantships with full tuition reimbursements, teaching assistantships with full tuition reimbursements available. Financial award application deadline: 3/15; financial award applicants required to submit FAFSA. *Faculty research:* Psychosocial nursing, computers in nursing, family adaptation. *Unit head:* Dr. Sonja Meiers, Graduate Coordinator, 507-389-1725. *Application contact:* Collaborative MSN Program Admissions, 507-389-6022.

Minnesota State University Moorhead, Graduate Studies, College of Education and Human Services, Tri-College University Nursing Consortium, Moorhead, MN 56563-0002. Offers MS. Program offered jointly with North Dakota State University and Concordia College. *Accreditation:* AACN. *Faculty:* 4 full-time (all women), 1 (woman) part-time/adjunct. *Students:* 7 full-time (all women), 19 part-time (18 women), 1 international. 10 applicants, 100% accepted. In 2006, 3 degrees awarded. *Degree requirements:* For master's, thesis or alternative, final oral exam. *Entrance requirements:* For master's, 3 letters of recommendation, minimum GPA of 3.0, RN licensure, bachelor's degree with nursing major. Additional exam requirements/recommendations for international students: Required—TOEFL (minimum score 550 paper-based; 213 computer-based). *Application deadline:* For fall admission, 2/15 priority date for domestic students, 1/15 for international students. Applications are processed on a rolling basis. Application fee: $20. Electronic applications accepted. *Expenses: Contact institution. Financial support:* In 2006–07, 1 research assistantship (averaging $1,000 per year) was awarded; traineeships also available. *Unit head:* Dr. Jane Giedt, Coordinator, 218-477-4699, E-mail: giedt@mnstate.edu.

Molloy College, Department of Nursing, Rockville Centre, NY 11571-5002. Offers adult nurse practitioner (Advanced Certificate); clinical nurse specialist: adult health (Advanced Certificate); family nurse practitioner (Advanced Certificate); nurse practitioner psychiatry (Advanced Certificate); nursing (MS); nursing administration (Advanced Certificate); nursing administration with informatics (Advanced Certificate); nursing education (Advanced Certificate); nursing informatics (Advanced Certificate); pediatric nurse practitioner (Advanced Certificate). *Accreditation:* AACN. Part-time and evening/weekend programs available. *Degree requirements:* For master's, thesis optional. *Entrance requirements:* For master's, 3 letters of reference, BS in nursing, minimum undergraduate GPA of 3.0; for Advanced Certificate, 3 letters of reference, master's degree in nursing. *Faculty research:* Hardiness and aging, alcoholism, current ethics, breast cancer, nurse role perception.

Montana State University, College of Graduate Studies, College of Nursing, Bozeman, MT 59717. Offers clinical nurse specialist (CNS) (MN, Post-Master's Certificate), including acute/chronic illness; family nurse practitioner (MN, Post-Master's Certificate); nursing education (Certificate). *Accreditation:* AACN. Part-time programs available. Postbaccalaureate distance learning degree programs offered (minimal on-campus study). *Faculty:* 58 full-time (53 women), 26 part-time/adjunct (25 women). *Students:* 24 full-time (20 women), 9 part-time (8 women). Average age 38. 20 applicants, 85% accepted, 12 enrolled. In 2006, 15 degrees awarded. *Degree requirements:* For master's, thesis (for some programs), comprehensive exam, registration. *Entrance requirements:* For master's, GRE General Test. Additional exam requirements/recommendations for international students: Required—TOEFL (minimum score 550 paper-based; 213 computer-based). *Application deadline:* For fall admission, 7/15 priority date for domestic students, 5/15 priority date for international students; for spring admission, 12/1 priority date for domestic students, 10/1 priority date for international students. Applications are processed on a rolling basis. Application fee: $30. Electronic applications accepted. *Expenses:* Tuition, state resident: full-time $5,113. Tuition, nonresident: full-time $12,501. *Financial support:* In 2006–07, 18 students received support, including 4 teaching assistantships with partial tuition reimbursements available (averaging $5,320 per year); institutionally sponsored loans, scholarships/grants, traineeships, tuition waivers (partial), and unspecified assistantships also available. Financial award application deadline: 3/1; financial award applicants required to submit FAFSA. *Faculty research:* Environmental health; geriatric education; enhancing rural health with clinical nurse specialists; technology and rural women with chronic illness. Total annual research expenditures: $1.4 million. *Unit head:* Dr. Elizabeth Kinion, Dean, College of Nursing, 406-994-2725, Fax: 406-994-6020, E-mail: ekinion@montana.edu.

Mountain State University, Graduate Studies, Program in Nursing, Beckley, WV 25802-9003. Offers administration/education (MSN); family nurse practitioner (MSN); nurse anesthesia (MSN); registered nurse anesthetist (Certificate). *Accreditation:* AANA/CANAEP; NLN. Part-time programs available. Postbaccalaureate distance learning degree programs offered (minimal on-campus study). *Faculty:* 6 full-time (4 women), 14 part-time/adjunct (7 women). *Students:* 80 full-time (64 women), 10 part-time (all women); includes 1 minority (African American) Average age 37. 29 applicants, 100% accepted, 17 enrolled. In 2006, 4 degrees awarded. *Median time to degree:* Master's–2 years full-time, 3 years part-time. *Degree requirements:* For master's, thesis or alternative, comprehensive exam. *Entrance requirements:* For master's, GRE. Additional exam requirements/recommendations for international students: Required—TOEFL (minimum score 550 paper-based; 213 computer-based); Recommended—IELTS (minimum score 7). *Application deadline:* For spring admission, 6/30 for domestic and international students. Applications are processed on a rolling basis. Application fee: $25 ($50 for international students). Electronic applications accepted. *Expenses: Contact institution.* Tuition and fees vary according to course load and program. *Financial support:* In 2006–07, 2 research assistantships (averaging $1,200 per year) were awarded; Federal Work-Study scholarships/grants, and unspecified assistantships also available. Support available to part-time students. Financial award applicants required to submit FAFSA. *Unit head:* Dr. Jessica Sharp, Senior Academic Officer for Graduate Nursing, 304-929-1425, Fax: 304-929-1601, E-mail: jsharp@mountainstate.edu. *Application contact:* Melody Tilley, Program Specialist, 304-929-1576, Fax: 304-929-1601, E-mail: mtilley@mountainstate.edu.

See Close-Up on page 1965.

Mount Carmel College of Nursing, College of Nursing, Columbus, OH 43222. Offers adult health (MS); nursing education (MS). Part-time programs available. *Entrance requirements:* For master's, letters of recommendation, current resumé, baccalaureate degree in nursing, current Ohio RN license, cumulative GPA of 3.0. Additional exam requirements/recommendations for international students: Required—TOEFL (minimum score 550 paper-based).

See Close-Up on page 1967.

Nursing Education

Mount Saint Mary College, Division of Nursing, Newburgh, NY 12550-3494. Offers adult nurse practitioner (MS), including nursing education, nursing management; clinical nurse specialist-adult health (MS), including nursing education, nursing management. *Accreditation:* AACN. Part-time and evening/weekend programs available. *Faculty:* 3 full-time (2 women), 1 (woman) part-time/adjunct. *Students:* 1 (woman) full-time, 28 part-time (26 women); includes 3 minority (2 African Americans, 1 Asian American or Pacific Islander). Average age 42. 12 applicants, 100% accepted, 10 enrolled. In 2006, 6 degrees awarded. *Degree requirements:* For master's, research utilization project. *Entrance requirements:* For master's, BSN, minimum GPA of 3.0, RN license. *Application deadline:* For fall admission, 6/3 priority date for domestic students; for spring admission, 10/31 priority date for domestic students. Applications are processed on a rolling basis. Application fee: $35. *Expenses:* Tuition: Full-time $11,880; part-time $660 per credit. *Financial support:* Unspecified assistantships and nursing lab assistant available. Financial award application deadline: 3/15; financial award applicants required to submit FAFSA. *Unit head:* Dr. Karen Baldwin, Coordinator, 845-569-3512, Fax: 845-562-6762, E-mail: baldwin@msmc.edu.

New York University, College of Dentistry, College of Nursing, Programs in Advanced Practice Nursing, New York, NY 10012-1019. Offers advanced practice nursing: adult acute care (MS, Advanced Certificate); advanced practice nursing: adult primary care (MS, Advanced Certificate); advanced practice nursing: adult primary care/geriatrics (MS); advanced practice nursing: children with special needs (Advanced Certificate); advanced practice nursing: geriatrics (MS, Advanced Certificate); advanced practice nursing: holistic nursing (MS, Advanced Certificate); advanced practice nursing: home health nursing (Advanced Certificate); advanced practice nursing: mental health (MS); advanced practice nursing: mental health nursing (Advanced Certificate); advanced practice nursing: pediatrics (MS, Advanced Certificate); advanced practice nursing: pediatrics/children with special needs (MS); midwifery (MS, Advanced Certificate); nursing administration (MS, Advanced Certificate); nursing education (MS, Advanced Certificate); nursing informatics (MS, Advanced Certificate); palliative care (MS, Advanced Certificate); MS/MS. *Accreditation:* AACN; ACNM/DOA. Part-time and evening/weekend programs available. *Faculty:* 30 full-time (all women). *Students:* 10 full-time (all women), 428 part-time (395 women); includes 166 minority (73 African Americans, 72 Asian Americans or Pacific Islanders, 21 Hispanic Americans). Average age 35. 154 applicants, 93% accepted, 118 enrolled. In 2006, 100 master's, 7 Advanced Certificates awarded. *Degree requirements:* For master's, thesis (for some programs). *Entrance requirements:* For master's, BS in nursing, AS in nursing with another BS/BA degree; for Advanced Certificate, master's degree. Additional exam requirements/recommendations for international students: Required—TOEFL. *Application deadline:* For fall admission, 7/1 priority date for domestic students, 7/1 for international students; for spring admission, 12/1 for domestic and international students. Applications are processed on a rolling basis. Application fee: $65. *Expenses:* Tuition: Part-time $1,080 per unit. Required fees: $56 per unit. $329 per term. Tuition and fees vary according to program. *Financial support:* Career-related internships or fieldwork, Federal Work-Study, institutionally sponsored loans, scholarships/grants, and tuition waivers (partial) available. Support available to part-time students. Financial award application deadline: 2/1; financial award applicants required to submit FAFSA. *Faculty research:* Elderly black diabetics, families and illness, public health nursing, parent-child nursing, health policy costs. *Unit head:* Dr. Judith Haber, Associate Dean for Graduate Programs, 212-998-5300, Fax: 212-995-3143. *Application contact:* Amy Knowles, Assistant Dean for Student Affairs and Admissions, 212-998-5333, Fax: 212-995-4302, E-mail: ak96@nyu.edu.

North Georgia College & State University, Graduate Studies, Department of Nursing, Dahlonega, GA 30597. Offers family nurse practitioner (MSN); nursing education (MSN). *Accreditation:* NLN. Part-time programs available. *Faculty:* 5 full-time (all women), 1 (woman) part-time/adjunct. *Students:* 62; includes 5 minority (2 African Americans, 1 American Indian/Alaska Native, 2 Asian Americans or Pacific Islanders). Average age 32. 7 applicants, 29% accepted. In 2006, 12 degrees awarded. *Degree requirements:* For master's, one foreign language, thesis, comprehensive exam. *Entrance requirements:* For master's, GRE General Test or MAT, minimum GPA of 2.75, 3 letters of recommendation, current Georgia RN license, 1 year of post-licensure work, BSN. *Application deadline:* Applications are processed on a rolling basis. Application fee: $25. Electronic applications accepted. *Expenses:* Tuition: State resident: full-time $3,044; part-time $127 per credit hour. Tuition, nonresident: full-time $12,172; part-time $508 per credit hour. Required fees: $892; $458 per semester. *Financial support:* Career-related internships or fieldwork available. Support available to part-time students. Financial award application deadline: 5/1. *Unit head:* Dr. Toni Barnett, Department Head, 706-864-1934, Fax: 706-864-1845, E-mail: tbarnett@ngcsu.edu. *Application contact:* Dr. Donna A. Gessell, Director of Graduate Studies and External Programs, 706-864-1528, Fax: 706-867-2795, E-mail: dgessell@ngcsu.edu.

Oakland University, Graduate Study and Lifelong Learning, School of Nursing, Program in Nursing Education, Rochester, MI 48309-4401. Offers MSN, Certificate. *Students:* 3 full-time (all women), 37 part-time (all women); includes 5 minority (4 African Americans, 1 American Indian/Alaska Native). Average age 43. 16 applicants, 81% accepted, 12 enrolled. In 2006, 10 degrees awarded. Application fee: $35. *Expenses:* Tuition, state resident: full-time $9,936; part-time $414 per credit. Tuition, nonresident: full-time $17,202; part-time $716 per credit. *Application contact:* Mary Bray, Graduate Program Coordinator, 248-370-4482.

Prairie View A&M University, Graduate School, College of Nursing, Houston, TX 77030. Offers family nurse practitioner (MSN); nursing administration (MSN); nursing education (MSN). *Accreditation:* AACN; NLN. Part-time programs available. *Faculty:* 3 full-time (all women), 4 part-time/adjunct (3 women). *Students:* 18 full-time (16 women), 59 part-time (51 women); includes 71 minority (62 African Americans, 5 Asian Americans or Pacific Islanders, 4 Hispanic Americans). Average age 38. 37 applicants, 100% accepted, 32 enrolled. In 2006, 7 degrees awarded. *Median time to degree:* Master's–1.5 years full-time, 2.5 years part-time. *Degree requirements:* For master's, thesis, comprehensive exam. *Entrance requirements:* For master's, MAT or GRE, BS in nursing; 2 years of experience as a registered nurse; 1 course each in statistics, basic health and assessment. *Application deadline:* For fall admission, 6/1 priority date for domestic students; for spring admission, 11/1 priority date for domestic students. Applications are processed on a rolling basis. Application fee: $50. *Financial support:* In 2006–07, 17 students received support. Career-related internships or fieldwork, Federal Work-Study, institutionally sponsored loans, scholarships/grants, and traineeships available. Support available to part-time students. Financial award application deadline: 4/1; financial award applicants required to submit FAFSA. *Faculty research:* Software development and violence prevention, health promotion and prevention. Total annual research expenditures: $350,000. *Unit head:* Dr. Betty N. Adams, Dean, 713-797-7009, Fax: 713-797-7013, E-mail: bnadams@pvamu.edu. *Application contact:* Dr. Pamela C. Willson, Associate Professor, 713-797-7011, Fax: 713-797-7012, E-mail: pcwillson@pvamu.edu.

Regis College, Department of Nursing, Weston, MA 02493. Offers nurse educator (Certificate); nurse practitioner (Certificate); nursing (MS). *Accreditation:* NLN. Part-time and evening/weekend programs available. *Faculty:* 14 full-time (13 women), 18 part-time/adjunct (15 women). *Students:* 157 full-time (142 women), 176 part-time (166 women); includes 49 minority (35 African Americans, 1 American Indian/Alaska Native, 9 Asian Americans or Pacific Islanders, 4 Hispanic Americans). Average age 36. 167 applicants, 83% accepted, 139 enrolled. In 2006, 45 master's, 13 other advanced degrees awarded. *Degree requirements:* For master's, thesis. *Entrance requirements:* For master's, GRE General Test or MAT, minimum GPA of 3.0. *Application deadline:* Applications are processed on a rolling basis. Application fee: $50. Electronic applications accepted. *Expenses:* Tuition: Full-time $23,680; part-time $665 per credit hour. *Financial support:* In 2006–07, 31 students received support, including 8 research assistantships (averaging $35,000 per year); Federal Work-Study, scholarships/grants, traineeships, and unspecified assistantships also available. Support available to part-time students. Financial award applicants required to submit FAFSA. *Faculty research:* Health policy, education, aging, job satisfaction, psychiatric nursing, critical thinking. *Unit head:* Dr. Antoinette Hays, Dean, School of Nursing and Health Professions, 781-768-7091, Fax: 781-768-8339, E-mail: antoinette.hays@regiscollege.edu.

Research College of Nursing, Nursing Program, Kansas City, MO 64132. Offers executive nurse practitioner (MSN); family nurse practitioner (MSN); nursing education (MSN). *Accreditation:* AACN. Part-time programs available. Postbaccalaureate distance learning degree programs offered (no on-campus study). *Faculty:* 11 full-time (all women). *Students:* Average age 30. In 2006, 6 degrees awarded. *Degree requirements:* For master's, research project. *Entrance requirements:* For master's, minimum GPA of 3.0, interview, 3 letters of recommendation. Additional exam requirements/recommendations for international students: Required—TOEFL (minimum score 550 paper-based; 213 computer-based), TWE. *Application deadline:* For spring admission, 10/1 priority date for domestic students. Applications are processed on a rolling basis. Application fee: $50. *Expenses:* Tuition: Part-time $350 per credit hour. *Financial support:* Applicants required to submit FAFSA. *Unit head:* Dr. Nancy O. De Basio, President and Dean, 816-995-2815, Fax: 816-995-2817, E-mail: nancy.debasio@researchcollege.edu. *Application contact:* Leslie Ann Mendenhall, Director of Transfer and Graduate Recruitment, 816-995-2820, Fax: 816-995-2813, E-mail: leslie.mendenhall@researchcollege.edu.

Rivier College, School of Graduate Studies, Department of Nursing and Health Sciences, Nashua, NH 03060-5086. Offers family nurse practitioner (MS); nursing education (MS). *Accreditation:* NLN. Part-time and evening/weekend programs available. *Faculty:* 5 full-time (4 women), 2 part-time/adjunct (0 women). *Students:* 6 full-time (all women), 28 part-time (27 women); includes 1 minority (Asian American or Pacific Islander) Average age 41. In 2006, 18 degrees awarded. *Degree requirements:* For master's, registration. *Entrance requirements:* For master's, GRE, MAT. *Application deadline:* Applications are processed on a rolling basis. Application fee: $25. Electronic applications accepted. *Financial support:* Available to part-time students. Application deadline: 2/1. *Unit head:* Dr. Paula Williams, Head, 603-897-8529. *Application contact:* Diane Monahan, Director of Graduate Admissions, 603-897-8129, Fax: 603-897-8810, E-mail: gradadm@rivier.edu.

Roberts Wesleyan College, Division of Nursing, Rochester, NY 14624-1997. Offers nursing administration (MSN); nursing education (MSN). *Faculty:* 13 full-time (all women), 6 part-time/adjunct (4 women). *Entrance requirements:* For master's, minimum GPA of 3.0; BS in nursing; interview; RN license; resumé; course work in statistics and health assessment. Additional exam requirements/recommendations for international students: Required—TOEFL. *Unit head:* Dr. Susanne M. Mohnkern, Chair, 585-594-6000, E-mail: mohnkerns@roberts.edu. *Application contact:* Yvonne Strong, Admissions Coordinator, 585-594-6388, E-mail: strong_yvonne@roberts.edu.

Saint Francis Medical Center College of Nursing, Graduate Program, Peoria, IL 61603-3783. Offers child and family nursing (MSN); medical-surgical nursing (MSN); nurse clinician (Post-Graduate Certificate); nurse educator (Post-Graduate Certificate). *Accreditation:* NLN. Part-time programs available. Postbaccalaureate distance learning degree programs offered (minimal on-campus study). *Faculty:* 1 (woman) full-time, 5 part-time/adjunct (all women). *Students:* 3 full-time (all women), 74 part-time (69 women); includes 5 minority (1 Asian American or Pacific Islander, 4 Hispanic Americans). Average age 28. 23 applicants, 100% accepted, 19 enrolled. In 2006, 5 degrees awarded. *Degree requirements:* For master's, research experience, portfolio, practicum. *Entrance requirements:* For master's, nursing research, health assessment, graduate course work in statistics, RN license. Additional exam requirements/recommendations for international students: Required—TOEFL. *Application deadline:* For fall admission, 6/1 priority date for domestic and international students; for spring admission, 11/15 priority date for domestic and international students. Applications are processed on a rolling basis. Application fee: $50. Electronic applications accepted. *Expenses:* Tuition: Part-time $440 per semester hour. Required fees: $130. *Financial support:* In 2006–07, 1 student received support. Application deadline: 6/15. *Faculty research:* Outcome and curriculum planning, health promotion, NCLEX-RN results, decision making program evaluation. *Unit head:* Dr. Lois J. Hamilton, Dean, 309-655-2201, Fax: 309-624-8973, E-mail: lois.j.hamilton@osfhealthcare.org. *Application contact:* Dr. Janice F. Boundy, Associate Dean Graduate Program, 309-655-2230, Fax: 309-624-8973, E-mail: jan.f.boundy@osfhealthcare.org.

St. John Fisher College, Office of the Provost, Wegmans School of Nursing, Advanced Practice Nursing Program, Rochester, NY 14618-3597. Offers advanced practice nursing (MS); clinical nurse specialist (Certificate); family nurse practitioner (Certificate); nurse educator (Certificate). *Accreditation:* AACN. Part-time and evening/weekend programs available. *Faculty:* 9 full-time (all women), 1 part-time/adjunct (0 women). *Students:* 4 full-time (all women), 72 part-time (70 women); includes 3 African Americans, 1 Asian American or Pacific Islander. Average age 40. 34 applicants, 91% accepted, 26 enrolled. In 2006, 15 degrees awarded. *Degree requirements:* For master's, clinical practice, master's project; for Certificate, clinical practice. *Entrance requirements:* For master's, BSN, minimum GPA of 3.0; undergraduate course work in statistics, health assessment, and nursing research; current New York RN license. Additional exam requirements/recommendations for international students: Required—TOEFL (minimum score 575 paper-based; 233 computer-based; 80 iBT). *Application deadline:* For fall admission, 7/1 for domestic students; for spring admission, 10/30 for domestic students. Applications are processed on a rolling basis. Application fee: $30. *Expenses:* Tuition: Part-time $615 per credit. Tuition and fees vary according to program. *Financial support:* In 2006–07, 5 students received support. Federal Work-Study, scholarships/grants, and traineeships available. Financial award application deadline: 2/15; financial award applicants required to submit FAFSA. *Faculty research:* Chronic illness, pediatric injury, women's health, public health policy, health care teams. *Unit head:* Dr. Cynthia McCloskey, Graduate Director, 585-385-8471, Fax: 585-385-8466, E-mail: cmccloskey@sjfc.edu. *Application contact:* Shannon Cleverley, Director of Graduate Admissions, 585-385-8161, Fax: 585-385-8344, E-mail: scleverley@sjfc.edu.

Saint Joseph's College of Maine, Department of Nursing, Standish, ME 04084-5263. Offers nursing (MS); nursing administration and leadership (Certificate); nursing and health care education (Certificate). MS degree offered only through faculty-directed independent study. *Accreditation:* AACN. Part-time programs available. Postbaccalaureate distance learning degree programs offered (minimal on-campus study). *Faculty:* 2 full-time (both women), 8 part-time/adjunct (all women). *Students:* Average age 43. 65 applicants, 91% accepted, 54 enrolled. In 2006, 26 degrees awarded. *Degree requirements:* For master's, summer residency. *Entrance requirements:* For master's, MAT. *Application deadline:* Applications are processed on a rolling basis. Application fee: $50. Electronic applications accepted. *Expenses:* Tuition: Part-time $350 per credit. *Financial support:* Institutionally sponsored loans available. Support available to part-time students. *Unit head:* Dr. Margaret Hourigan, Chair, 207-893-7970, Fax: 207-892-7423, E-mail: mhourigan@sjcme.edu. *Application contact:* 800-752-4723, Fax: 207-892-7480, E-mail: info@sjcme.edu.

San Francisco State University, Division of Graduate Studies, College of Health and Human Services, School of Nursing, San Francisco, CA 94132-1722. Offers case management (MS); including long-term care, primary care/family nurse practitioner; nursing administration (MS); nursing education (MS). *Accreditation:* AACN. Part-time programs available. *Faculty:* 12 full-time (10 women). *Students:* Average age 32. In 2006, 28 degrees awarded. *Degree requirements:* For master's, thesis. *Entrance requirements:* For master's, minimum GPA of 3.0. *Application deadline:* For fall admission, 11/30 priority date for domestic students; for spring admission, 5/31 for domestic students. Applications are processed on a rolling basis. Application fee: $55. *Financial support:* In 2006–07, 35 students received support, including 35 fellowships; career-related internships or fieldwork also available. Financial award application deadline: 3/1. *Faculty research:* Nursing case management and clinical outcomes, outcome of undergraduate and graduate education in nursing, patient education strategies and learning outcomes. Total annual research expenditures: $25,000. *Unit head:* Dr. Karen Johnson-Brennan, Interim Director, 415-338-1801, Fax: 415-338-0555. *Application contact:* Dr. Frank McLaughlin, Graduate Coordinator, 415-338-1802, E-mail: femc@sfsu.edu.

San Jose State University, Graduate Studies and Research, College of Applied Sciences and Arts, School of Nursing, San Jose, CA 95192-0001. Offers gerontology nurse practitioner (MS); nursing (Certificate); nursing administration (MS); nursing education (MS). *Accreditation:*

AACN. Part-time and evening/weekend programs available. *Students:* 15 full-time (13 women), 70 part-time (66 women); includes 30 minority (2 African Americans, 21 Asian Americans or Pacific Islanders, 7 Hispanic Americans). Average age 41. 73 applicants, 70% accepted, 15 enrolled. In 2006, 34 degrees awarded. *Degree requirements:* For master's, thesis. *Entrance requirements:* For master's, BS in nursing, RN license. *Application deadline:* For fall admission, 6/29 for domestic students; for spring admission, 11/30 for domestic students. Applications are processed on a rolling basis. Application fee: $59. Electronic applications accepted. *Financial support:* Career-related internships or fieldwork, institutionally sponsored loans, and scholarships/grants available. Support available to part-time students. Financial award applicants required to submit FAFSA. *Faculty research:* Nurse-managed clinics, computers in nursing. *Unit head:* Jayne Cohen, Director, 408-924-3131, Fax: 408-924-3135. *Application contact:* Dr. Phyllis Connolly, Graduate Coordinator, 408-924-3144.

Seton Hall University, College of Nursing, Department of Graduate Nursing, Nursing Education Program, South Orange, NJ 07079-2697. Offers MA, MSN/MA. *Accreditation:* AACN. Part-time programs available. *Degree requirements:* For master's, research project. *Entrance requirements:* For master's, GRE or MAT, BSN. *Faculty research:* Teaching methods for adult learners.

Southern Connecticut State University, School of Graduate Studies, School of Health and Human Services, Department of Nursing, New Haven, CT 06515-1355. Offers nursing administration (MSN); nursing education (MSN). *Accreditation:* AACN; AANA/CANAEP. Part-time and evening/weekend programs available. *Faculty:* 6 full-time, 1 part-time/adjunct. *Students:* 2 full-time (both women), 29 part-time (27 women); includes 4 minority (3 African Americans, 1 Hispanic American). 15 applicants, 93% accepted, 10 enrolled. In 2006, 14 degrees awarded. *Degree requirements:* For master's, thesis. *Entrance requirements:* For master's, GRE, MAT, interview, minimum QPA of 2.8, RN license, minimum 1 year of professional nursing experience. *Application deadline:* For fall admission, 7/15 priority date for domestic students. Applications are processed on a rolling basis. Application fee: $50. Electronic applications accepted. *Financial support:* Application deadline: 4/15; *Unit head:* Dr. Cesarina Thompson, Chairperson, 203-392-6487, Fax: 203-392-6493, E-mail: thompson_c@southernct.edu. *Application contact:* Dr. Eileen Crutchlow, Graduate Coordinator, 203-392-6489, Fax: 203-392-6493, E-mail: crutchlow1@southernct.edu.

Southern Illinois University Edwardsville, Graduate Studies and Research, School of Nursing, Program in Nurse Educator, Edwardsville, IL 62026-0001. Offers MS, Post-Master's Certificate. *Students:* 3 full-time (all women), 29 part-time (28 women); includes 2 minority (both African Americans) 5 applicants, 60% accepted. In 2006, 7 degrees awarded. *Degree requirements:* For master's, thesis or alternative, final exam. *Entrance requirements:* Additional exam requirements/recommendations for international students: Required—TOEFL. *Application deadline:* For fall admission, 1/1 for domestic and international students. Application fee: $30. Electronic applications accepted. *Unit head:* Dr. Jacquelyn Clement, Director, 618-650-3923, E-mail: jclemen@siue.edu.

Southern Nazarene University, Graduate College, School of Nursing, Bethany, OK 73008. Offers nursing education (MS); nursing leadership (MS). *Accreditation:* AACN. Part-time and evening/weekend programs available. *Students:* 30. In 2006, 14 degrees awarded. *Expenses:* Tuition: Part-time $507 per credit. *Unit head:* Dr. Carol Dorough, Dean, 405-491-6365, E-mail: cdorough@snu.edu.

Southern University and Agricultural and Mechanical College, School of Nursing, Baton Rouge, LA 70813. Offers educator/administrator (PhD); family health nursing (MSN); family nurse practitioner (Post Master's Certificate); geriatric nurse practitioner/gerontology (PhD). *Accreditation:* AACN; NLN. Part-time programs available. *Degree requirements:* For master's and doctorate, thesis/dissertation, comprehensive exam. *Entrance requirements:* For master's, GRE General Test, BSN, minimum GPA of 2.7; for doctorate, GRE General Test; for Post Master's Certificate, MSN. Additional exam requirements/recommendations for international students: Required—TOEFL (minimum score 525 paper-based; 193 computer-based). *Faculty research:* Health promotions, vulnerable populations, (community-based) cardiovascular participating research, health disparities chronic diseases, care of the elderly.

State University of New York Institute of Technology, School of Nursing and Health Systems, Program in Nursing Education, Utica, NY 13504-3050. Offers MS, CAS. *Faculty:* 5 full-time (all women), 1 (woman) part-time/adjunct. *Students:* 6 full-time (all women), 6 part-time (all women). *Entrance requirements:* For master's, GRE General Test if undergraduate GPA is less than 3.3, minimum GPA of 3.0 in last 30 hours of undergraduate work, bachelor's in nursing, 1 year RN experience, RN license, 2 letters of recommendation, interview. Additional exam requirements/recommendations for international students: Required—TOEFL (minimum score 550 paper-based; 213 computer-based). *Application deadline:* For fall admission, 6/15 for domestic students. Applications are processed on a rolling basis. Application fee: $50. *Expenses:* Tuition, state resident: full-time $3,452; part-time $288 per credit hour. Tuition, nonresident: full-time $10,920; part-time $455 per credit hour. Required fees: $927; $38 per credit hour. *Financial support:* In 2006–07, 2 research assistantships (averaging $2,500 per year) were awarded; Federal Work-Study, scholarships/grants, traineeships, and unspecified assistantships also available. Financial award applicants required to submit FAFSA. *Faculty research:* Nursing faculty shortages, curriculum enhancements, measurement and assessment, evidence-based practice. *Unit head:* Marybeth Lyons, Director of Admissions, 315-792-7500, Fax: 315-792-7837, E-mail: smbl@sunyit.edu.

Teachers College Columbia University, Graduate Faculty of Education, Department of Health and Behavioral Studies, Program in Nursing, Professional Role, New York, NY 10027-6696. Offers Ed M, MA, Ed D. *Faculty:* 1 (woman) full-time. *Students:* 2 full-time (1 woman), 14 part-time (13 women); includes 4 minority (3 African Americans, 1 Asian American or Pacific Islander), 1 international. Average age 47. 5 applicants, 20% accepted, 0 enrolled. In 2006, 3 degrees awarded. *Degree requirements:* For master's, capstone project; for doctorate, thesis/dissertation. *Entrance requirements:* For master's, BSN, nursing license; for doctorate, GRE General Test or MAT, BSN, nursing license. *Application deadline:* For fall admission, 5/15 for domestic students; for spring admission, 12/1 for domestic students. Application fee: $50. *Expenses:* Tuition: Full-time $23,400; part-time $975 per credit. Required fees: $320 per term. *Financial support:* Career-related internships or fieldwork, Federal Work-Study, institutionally sponsored loans, traineeships, and tuition waivers (full and partial) available. Support available to part-time students. Financial award application deadline: 2/1. *Faculty research:* Empathy in nurses, clinical teaching for basic nursing students, interdisciplinary health care team. *Application contact:* Peter Shon, Assistant Director of Admission, 212-678-3305, Fax: 212-678-4171, E-mail: shon@exchange.tc.columbia.edu.

See Close-Up on page 1129.

Teachers College Columbia University, Graduate Faculty of Education, Department of Organization and Leadership, New York, NY 10027-6696. Offers adult education (MA, Ed D); education leadership (Ed M, MA, Ed D, PhD), including education leadership (PhD), education leadership studies (Ed M, MA, Ed D), leadership, policy and politics, private school leadership (Ed M, MA, Ed D), public school and school district leadership (Ed M, MA, Ed D); educational administration (Ed M, MA, Ed D, PhD); higher education (Ed M, MA, Ed D, PhD); inquiry in education leadership (Ed D); nurse executive (Ed M, MA, Ed D); politics and education (Ed M, MA, Ed D, PhD); social and organizational psychology (MA, Ed D, PhD), including organizational psychology, social psychology (Ed D, PhD); student personnel administration (Ed M, MA, Ed D); MBA/Ed D. Part-time and evening/weekend programs available. *Faculty:* 23 full-time (12 women). *Students:* 349 full-time (203 women), 503 part-time (265 women); includes 249 minority (109 African Americans, 2 American Indian/Alaska Native, 83 Asian Americans or Pacific Islanders, 55 Hispanic Americans), 53 international. Average age 35. 839 applicants, 61% accepted, 261 enrolled. In 2006, 210 master's, 97 doctorates awarded. *Degree requirements:* For doctorate, thesis/dissertation. *Application deadline:* For fall admission, 5/15 for domestic students. Application fee: $65. *Expenses:* Tuition: Full-time $23,400; part-time $975 per credit. Required fees: $320 per term. *Financial support:* Fellowships, research assistantships, career-related internships or fieldwork, Federal Work-Study, institutionally sponsored loans, and tuition waivers (full and partial) available. Support available to part-time students. Financial award application deadline: 2/1. *Unit head:* Warner Burke, Chair, 212-678-3258. *Application contact:* Debbie Lesperance, Assistant Director of Admission, 212-678-3710, Fax: 212-678-4171.

See Close-Up on page 1131.

Texas Tech University Health Sciences Center, School of Nursing, Lubbock, TX 79430. Offers acute care nurse practitioner (MSN, Certificate); administration (MSN); clinical research management (MSN, Certificate); education (MSN); family nurse practitioner (MSN, Certificate); geriatric nurse practitioner (MSN, Certificate); pediatric nurse practitioner (MSN, Certificate). *Accreditation:* AACN. Part-time programs available. Postbaccalaureate distance learning degree programs offered (minimal on-campus study). *Faculty:* 17 full-time (16 women), 5 part-time/adjunct (all women). *Students:* 23 full-time (22 women), 161 part-time (137 women); includes 46 minority (8 African Americans, 2 American Indian/Alaska Native, 6 Asian Americans or Pacific Islanders, 30 Hispanic Americans). Average age 37. 97 applicants, 69% accepted, 67 enrolled. In 2006, 41 degrees awarded. *Degree requirements:* For master's, thesis optional. *Entrance requirements:* For master's, minimum GPA of 3.0, 3 letters of reference, BSN, RN license; for Certificate, minimum GPA of 3.0, 3 letters of reference, RN license. Additional exam requirements/recommendations for international students: Required—TOEFL (minimum score 550 paper-based; 213 computer-based). *Application deadline:* For fall admission, 7/15 priority date for domestic and international students; for spring admission, 11/15 priority date for domestic and international students. Applications are processed on a rolling basis. Application fee: $40. *Financial support:* In 2006–07, 184 students received support. Institutionally sponsored loans, scholarships/grants, and traineeships available. Support available to part-time students. Financial award application deadline: 12/1; financial award applicants required to submit FAFSA. *Faculty research:* Diabetes/obesity, nurse competency, disease management, intervention and measurements, health disparities. Total annual research expenditures: $2.4 million. *Unit head:* Dr. Barbara A. Johnston, Associate Dean for Administrative and Student Affairs, 806-743-3055, Fax: 806-743-1622, E-mail: barbara.johnston@ttuhsc.edu. *Application contact:* Lauren K. Sullivan, Recruiter/Transcultural Coordinator, 806-743-2730 Ext. 309, Fax: 806-743-1622, E-mail: lauren.sullivan@ttuhsc.edu.

Texas Woman's University, Graduate School, College of Nursing, Denton, TX 76201. Offers adult health nurse practitioner (MS); health systems management (MS); nursing (MS); nursing education (MS); nursing science (PhD). *Accreditation:* AACN. Part-time programs available. Postbaccalaureate distance learning degree programs offered. *Students:* 41 full-time (38 women), 512 part-time (490 women); includes 211 minority (121 African Americans, 2 American Indian/Alaska Native, 64 Asian Americans or Pacific Islanders, 24 Hispanic Americans), 9 international. Average age 41. In 2006, 129 master's, 16 doctorates awarded. *Degree requirements:* For master's, thesis or alternative; for doctorate, thesis/dissertation, comprehensive exam. *Entrance requirements:* For master's, GRE or MAT, minimum GPA of 3.0, RN license, BS in nursing; for doctorate, GRE or MAT, MS in nursing, minimum GPA of 3.5, RN license, coursework in statistics, graduate research, 2 letters of reference. Additional exam requirements/recommendations for international students: Required—TOEFL (minimum score 550 paper-based; 213 computer-based; 79 iBT). *Application deadline:* For fall admission, 4/1 for international students; for spring admission, 8/1 for international students. Applications are processed on a rolling basis. Application fee: $30 ($50 for international students). Electronic applications accepted. *Expenses:* Tuition, area resident: Part-time $168 per unit. Tuition, state resident: full-time $4,369. Tuition, nonresident: full-time $9,373; part-time $443 per unit. Required fees: $20 per unit. $177 per term. *Financial support:* In 2006–07, 11 research assistantships (averaging $11,232 per year), 3 teaching assistantships (averaging $11,232 per year) were awarded; career-related internships or fieldwork, Federal Work-Study, institutionally sponsored loans, scholarships/grants, traineeships, health care benefits, and unspecified assistantships also available. Support available to part-time students. Financial award application deadline: 3/1; financial award applicants required to submit FAFSA. *Faculty research:* Health of women across the life span, child health issues, self-care and heart failure, smoking cessation, timing of labor and delivery. *Unit head:* Dr. Marcia Hern, Dean, 940-898-2401, Fax: 940-898-2437, E-mail: mhern@twu.edu. *Application contact:* Samuel Wheeler, Coordinator of Graduate Admissions, 940-898-3188, Fax: 940-898-3081, E-mail: wheelersr@twu.edu.

Union University, School of Nursing, Jackson, TN 38305-3697. Offers nurse anesthetist (PMC); nursing education (MSN, PMC). *Accreditation:* AACN; AANA/CANAEP. *Faculty:* 15 full-time (14 women), 3 part-time/adjunct (2 women). *Students:* 47 full-time (36 women); includes 12 minority (10 African Americans, 1 American Indian/Alaska Native, 1 Asian American or Pacific Islander). Average age 38. 12 applicants, 100% accepted, 12 enrolled. In 2006, 9 degrees awarded. *Degree requirements:* For master's, thesis or alternative, registration. *Entrance requirements:* For master's, GRE, 3 letters of reference, bachelor's degree in nursing, minimum GPA of 3.0. Additional exam requirements/recommendations for international students: Required—TOEFL (minimum score 560 paper-based; 220 computer-based). *Application deadline:* For fall admission, 8/1 priority date for domestic students, 8/1 for international students. Application fee: $25. Electronic applications accepted. *Financial support:* Traineeships available. Financial award applicants required to submit FAFSA. *Faculty research:* Children's health, occupational rehabilitation, informatics, health promotion. *Unit head:* Dr. Tim Smith, Dean, 731-661-5200, Fax: 731-661-5504. *Application contact:* Elsie Cressman, Coordinator of MSN Programs, 731-661-5120, Fax: 731-661-5504, E-mail: ecressman@uu.edu.

University of Alaska Anchorage, College of Health and Social Welfare, School of Nursing, Anchorage, AK 99508-8060. Offers family nurse practitioner (Certificate); nursing (MS); nursing education (Certificate); psychiatric nurse practitioner (Certificate). *Accreditation:* NLN. Part-time and evening/weekend programs available. *Students:* 10 full-time (all women), 38 part-time (34 women); includes 6 minority (3 African Americans, 2 American Indian/Alaska Native, 1 Hispanic American). 15 applicants, 27% accepted. In 2006, 12 degrees awarded. *Degree requirements:* For master's, individual project. *Entrance requirements:* For master's, GRE or MAT, BS in nursing, interview, minimum GPA of 3.0, RN license, 1 year of part-time or 6 months of full-time clinical experience. Additional exam requirements/recommendations for international students: Required—TOEFL (minimum score 550 paper-based; 213 computer-based). *Application deadline:* For fall admission, 3/1 for domestic students; for spring admission, 11/1 for domestic students. Application fee: $45. *Expenses:* Tuition, state resident: part-time $268 per credit. Tuition, nonresident: part-time $547 per credit. Required fees: $124 per semester. Tuition and fees vary according to reciprocity agreements and student level. *Financial support:* Teaching assistantships, career-related internships or fieldwork, Federal Work-Study, and health care benefits available. Support available to part-time students. Financial award application deadline: 4/1; financial award applicants required to submit FAFSA. *Unit head:* Dr. Jean Ballantyne, Director, 907-786-4571, Fax: 907-786-4558. *Application contact:* Marie Samson, Coordinator of Student Affairs, 907-786-4561.

University of Central Florida, College of Health and Public Affairs, College of Nursing, Orlando, FL 32816. Offers adult practitioner (Post-Master's Certificate); family practitioner (Post-Master's Certificate); nursing (DNP, PhD); nursing education (Post-Master's Certificate); pediatric practitioner (Post-Master's Certificate). *Accreditation:* AACN. Part-time and evening/weekend programs available. *Faculty:* 35 full-time (32 women), 28 part-time/adjunct (25 women). *Students:* 84 full-time (75 women), 167 part-time (154 women); includes 41 minority (11 African Americans, 1 American Indian/Alaska Native, 8 Asian Americans or Pacific Islanders, 21 Hispanic Americans), 2 international. Average age 38. In 2006, 30 Post-Master's Certificates awarded. *Entrance requirements:* Additional exam requirements/recommendations for international students: Required—TOEFL. *Application deadline:* For fall admission, 2/15 for domestic students; for spring admission, 9/15 for domestic students. Application fee: $30. Electronic applications accepted. *Expenses:* Tuition, state resident: full-time $6,167; part-time $257 per credit hour. Tuition, nonresident: full-time $22,790; part-time $950 per credit hour. *Financial support:* In 2006–07, 35 fellowships with partial tuition reimbursements (averaging

Nursing Education

University of Central Florida (continued)
$1,550 per year), 9 research assistantships with partial tuition reimbursements (averaging $4,500 per year), 3 teaching assistantships with partial tuition reimbursements (averaging $15,400 per year) were awarded; career-related internships or fieldwork, Federal Work-Study, institutionally sponsored loans, traineeships, and unspecified assistantships also available. Financial award application deadline: 3/1; financial award applicants required to submit FAFSA. *Unit head:* Dr. Jean D. Leuner, Dean, College of Nursing, 407-823-5496, Fax: 407-823-5675, E-mail: jleuner@mail.ucf.edu.

University of Hartford, College of Education, Nursing, and Health Professions, Program in Nursing, West Hartford, CT 06117-1599. Offers community/public health nursing (MSN); nursing education (MSN); nursing management (MSN). *Accreditation:* AACN. Part-time and evening/weekend programs available. *Faculty:* 6 full-time (all women), 2 part-time/adjunct (both women). *Students:* 1 (woman) full-time, 170 part-time (163 women); includes 12 minority (5 African Americans, 1 American Indian/Alaska Native, 6 Hispanic Americans). Average age 43. 60 applicants, 97% accepted, 54 enrolled. In 2006, 46 degrees awarded. *Degree requirements:* For master's, research project. *Entrance requirements:* For master's, BSN, Connecticut RN license. Additional exam requirements/recommendations for international students: Required—TOEFL (minimum score 550 paper-based; 213 computer-based). *Application deadline:* For fall admission, 4/15 priority date for domestic students; for spring admission, 12/1 for domestic students. Application fee: $40 ($55 for international students). Electronic applications accepted. *Expenses:* Contact institution. *Financial support:* Teaching assistantships, Federal Work-Study available. Support available to part-time students. Financial award application deadline: 6/1; financial award applicants required to submit FAFSA. *Faculty research:* Child development, women in doctoral study, applying feminist theory in teaching methods, near death experience, grandmothers as primary care providers. *Unit head:* Mary Beth Mathews, Chair, 860-768-4217, Fax: 860-768-5346, E-mail: mbmathews@hartford.edu. *Application contact:* Marlene Hall, Assistant Dean, 860-768-5116, E-mail: mhall@hartford.edu.

University of Indianapolis, Graduate Programs, School of Nursing, Indianapolis, IN 46227-3697. Offers family practice (post-RN) (MSN); gerontological nurse practitioner (MSN); nurse-midwifery (MSN); nursing (MSN); nursing administration (MSN); nursing education (MSN); MBA/MSN. *Accreditation:* AACN; ACNM. *Faculty:* 7 full-time (all women), 3 part-time/adjunct (all women). *Students:* 9 full-time (all women), 121 part-time (115 women); includes 17 minority (16 African Americans, 1 Asian American or Pacific Islander). Average age 41. In 2006, 7 degrees awarded. *Entrance requirements:* For master's, minimum GPA of 3.0, interview, letters of recommendation, resumé, IN nursing license, 1 year professional practice. Additional exam requirements/recommendations for international students: Required—TOEFL (minimum score 550 paper-based; 213 computer-based). *Application deadline:* For fall admission, 8/1 for domestic students; for winter admission, 12/15 for domestic students; for spring admission, 4/15 for domestic students. Applications are processed on a rolling basis. Application fee: $50. *Financial support:* Federal Work-Study available. *Unit head:* Dr. Sharon Isaac, Dean, 317-788-3207, E-mail: isaac@uindy.edu. *Application contact:* T.C. Crum, 317-788-2128, Fax: 317-788-3542, E-mail: tcrum@uindy.edu.

University of Kansas, Graduate Studies Medical Center, School of Nursing, Kansas City, KS 66160. Offers nurse educator (PMC); nurse midwife (PMC); nursing (MS, PhD); psychiatric/mental health nurse practitioner (PMC). *Accreditation:* AACN; ACNM/DOA. Part-time programs available. Postbaccalaureate distance learning degree programs offered (minimal on-campus study). *Faculty:* 53 full-time (50 women), 3 part-time/adjunct (all women). *Students:* 63 full-time (59 women), 200 part-time (190 women); includes 37 minority (16 African Americans, 3 American Indian/Alaska Native, 12 Asian Americans or Pacific Islanders, 6 Hispanic Americans), 4 international. Average age 38. 88 applicants, 82% accepted, 62 enrolled. In 2006, 39 master's, 5 doctorates awarded. Terminal master's awarded for partial completion of doctoral program. *Median time to degree:* Master's–2.05 years full-time, 2.95 years part-time; doctorate–3.26 years part-time. Of those who began their doctoral program in fall 1998, 66% received their degree in 8 years or less. *Degree requirements:* For master's, general oral exam, thesis optional; for doctorate, one foreign language, thesis/dissertation, comprehensive oral and written exam. *Entrance requirements:* For master's, GRE General Test, bachelor's degree in nursing, minimum GPA of 3.0, RN license, 1 year of clinical experience; for doctorate, GRE General Test, master's degree in nursing, minimum GPA of 3.5. Additional exam requirements/recommendations for international students: Required—TOEFL. *Application deadline:* For fall admission, 4/1 for domestic students; for winter admission, 7/1 for domestic students; for spring admission, 9/1 for domestic students. Application fee: $50. *Expenses:* Tuition, area resident: Part-time $227 per credit. Tuition, state resident: part-time $543 per credit. Tuition and fees vary according to course load, campus/location, program and reciprocity agreements. *Financial support:* In 2006–07, 106 students received support, including 7 research assistantships (averaging $19,000 per year), 23 teaching assistantships with full and partial tuition reimbursements available (averaging $19,000 per year); traineeships also available. Financial award application deadline: 7/7. *Faculty research:* Breastfeeding practices of teen mothers, prevention of pressure ulcers, caregiving of families of patients using technology in the home, self care talk intervention partnership between caregivers of stroke survivors and nurses, smoking cessation. *Unit head:* Dr. Karen L. Miller, Dean, 913-588-1604, Fax: 913-588-1660, E-mail: kmiller@kumc.edu. *Application contact:* Dr. Rita K. Clifford, Associate Dean, Student Affairs, 913-588-1619, Fax: 913-588-1615, E-mail: rcliffor@kumc.edu.

University of Mary, Division of Nursing, Bismarck, ND 58504-9652. Offers family nurse practitioner (MSN); nurse management (MSN); nursing educator (MSN). *Accreditation:* AACN. Part-time and evening/weekend programs available. Postbaccalaureate distance learning degree programs offered (minimal on-campus study). *Faculty:* 2 full-time (both women), 8 part-time/adjunct (5 women). *Students:* 28 full-time (27 women), 22 part-time (all women); includes 2 minority (1 African American, 1 Hispanic American), 1 international. Average age 32. 32 applicants, 66% accepted, 19 enrolled. In 2006, 26 degrees awarded. *Degree requirements:* For master's, thesis (for some programs), internship (family nurse practitioner), practice teaching, comprehensive exam. *Entrance requirements:* For master's, minimum GPA of 3.0 in nursing, interview, letters of recommendation. *Application deadline:* For fall admission, 4/15 priority date for domestic students. Applications are processed on a rolling basis. Application fee: $40. Electronic applications accepted. *Financial support:* In 2006–07, 14 fellowships with partial tuition reimbursements, 3 teaching assistantships with partial tuition reimbursements were awarded; institutionally sponsored loans also available. Support available to part-time students. Financial award application deadline: 7/1. *Faculty research:* Gerontology issues, rural nursing, health policy, primary care, women's health. *Unit head:* Glenda Reemts, Director, 701-255-7500 Ext. 8041, Fax: 701-255-7687. *Application contact:* Traci L. Schell, Secretary, 701-355-8016, Fax: 701-255-7687, E-mail: tschell@umary.edu.

University of Maryland, Baltimore, Graduate School, School of Nursing, Master's Program in Nursing, Baltimore, MD 21201. Offers community health nursing (MS); gerontological nursing (MS); maternal-child nursing (MS); medical-surgical nursing (MS); nurse-midwifery education (MS); nursing administration (MS); nursing education (MS); nursing health policy (MS); primary care nursing (MS); psychiatric nursing (MS); MS/MBA. *Accreditation:* AANA/CANAEP; ACNM/DOA; NLN (one or more programs are accredited). Part-time programs available. *Degree requirements:* For master's, thesis or alternative, comprehensive exam (for some programs). *Entrance requirements:* For master's, GRE General Test, minimum GPA of 2.75, course work in statistics, BS in nursing. Additional exam requirements/recommendations for international students: Required—TOEFL, TOEFL or IELTS; Recommended—IELTS. Electronic applications accepted.

University of Massachusetts Worcester, Graduate School of Nursing, Worcester, MA 01655-0115. Offers adult acute/critical care nurse practitioner (MS, Certificate); adult ambulatory/community care nurse practitioner (MS, Certificate); gerontological nurse practitioner (Certificate); nurse educator (MS, Certificate); nursing (PhD). *Accreditation:* AACN. Part-time programs available. *Faculty:* 39. *Students:* 46 full-time (43 women), 6 part-time (2 women); includes 5 minority (2 African Americans, 2 Asian Americans or Pacific Islanders, 1 Hispanic American). Average age 38. 42 applicants, 71% accepted. In 2006, 26 master's, 2 doctorates, 6 other advanced degrees awarded. *Degree requirements:* For doctorate, thesis/dissertation. *Entrance requirements:* For master's, GRE General Test, BSN, previous course work in statistics; for Certificate, master's degree. *Application deadline:* For fall admission, 3/15 for domestic students. Applications are processed on a rolling basis. Application fee: $40 ($60 for international students). *Expenses:* Tuition, state resident: full-time $2,640. Tuition, nonresident: full-time $9,856. Required fees: $3,942. *Financial support:* In 2006–07, 4 students received support. Scholarships/grants and traineeships available. Support available to part-time students. Financial award application deadline: 3/22; financial award applicants required to submit FAFSA. *Faculty research:* Premature menopause with cancer treatment, quality of life and cancer, complementary therapies, psychoneuroimmunology, patient outcomes/outcomes research. *Unit head:* Dr. Janet Hale, Associate Dean, 508-856-5661, Fax: 508-856-6552. *Application contact:* Larry Shattuck, Director of Recruitment and Retention, 508-856-5801, Fax: 508-856-6552.

University of Medicine and Dentistry of New Jersey, School of Nursing, Program in Nursing Education, Newark, NJ 07107-1709. Offers MSN, Post Master's Certificate. Part-time programs available. *Degree requirements:* For master's, registration. *Entrance requirements:* Additional exam requirements/recommendations for international students: Required—TOEFL. *Application deadline:* For spring admission, 4/15 priority date for domestic students, 4/15 for international students. Applications are processed on a rolling basis. Application fee: $50. Electronic applications accepted. *Financial support:* Institutionally sponsored loans, scholarships/grants, and traineeships available. *Faculty research:* Computer anxiety, adolescent pregnancy prevention. *Unit head:* Dr. Kathleen M. Burke, Assistant Dean, 201-684-7737, Fax: 201-684-7954, E-mail: kmburke@umdnj.edu.

University of Missouri–Kansas City, School of Nursing, Kansas City, MO 64110-2499. Offers adult clinical nurse specialist (MSN), including adult nurse practitioner, women's health nurse practitioner; family nurse practitioner (MSN); neonatal nurse practitioner (MSN); nurse educator (MSN); nurse executive (MSN); nursing (PhD); pediatric nurse practitioner (MSN). *Accreditation:* AACN. Part-time programs available. Postbaccalaureate distance learning degree programs offered (minimal on-campus study). *Faculty:* 31 full-time (26 women), 32 part-time/adjunct (31 women). *Students:* 36 full-time (all women), 213 part-time (202 women); includes 23 minority (6 African Americans, 2 American Indian/Alaska Native, 6 Asian Americans or Pacific Islanders, 9 Hispanic Americans). Average age 36. 121 applicants, 72% accepted, 71 enrolled. In 2006, 69 master's, 1 doctorate awarded. *Median time to degree:* Of those who began their doctoral program in fall 1998, 60% received their degree in 8 years or less. *Degree requirements:* For master's, thesis or alternative. *Entrance requirements:* For master's, minimum undergraduate GPA of 3.2; for doctorate, GRE, 3 letters of reference, interview and original essay by invitation. Additional exam requirements/recommendations for international students: Required—TOEFL (minimum score 550 paper-based). *Application deadline:* For fall admission, 2/1 priority date for domestic students; for spring admission, 9/15 priority date for domestic students. Application fee: $25. *Expenses:* Tuition, state resident: full-time $4,975; part-time $276 per credit. Tuition, nonresident: full-time $12,847; part-time $713 per credit. Required fees: $595; $595 per year. *Financial support:* In 2006–07, 30 students received support, including 6 research assistantships (averaging $3,450 per year), 7 teaching assistantships with partial tuition reimbursements available (averaging $12,650 per year); fellowships, career-related internships or fieldwork, Federal Work-Study, institutionally sponsored loans, and tuition waivers (full and partial) also available. Support available to part-time students. Financial award application deadline: 6/30; financial award applicants required to submit FAFSA. *Faculty research:* Geriatrics/gerontology, children's pain, neonatology, Alzheimer's care, cancer caregivers. Total annual research expenditures: $1 million. *Unit head:* Dr. Lora Lacey-Haun, Dean, 816-235-1700, Fax: 816-235-1701, E-mail: lacey-haunc@umkc.edu. *Application contact:* Leah Wilder, Coordinator for Admissions and Recruitment, 816-235-5768, Fax: 816-235-1701, E-mail: wilderl@umkc.edu.

University of Nevada, Las Vegas, Graduate College, Division of Health Sciences, School of Nursing, Las Vegas, NV 89154-9900. Offers family nurse practitioner (MS, Post-Master's Certificate); nursing (PhD); nursing education (MS, Post-Master's Certificate); pediatric nurse practitioner (MS). *Accreditation:* NLN. Part-time programs available. *Faculty:* 21 full-time (all women), 6 part-time/adjunct (all women). *Students:* 74 full-time (59 women), 66 part-time (61 women); includes 24 minority (2 African Americans, 15 Asian Americans or Pacific Islanders, 7 Hispanic Americans), 46 international. 190 applicants, 66% accepted, 107 enrolled. In 2006, 11 degrees awarded. *Degree requirements:* For master's, research project, thesis optional. *Entrance requirements:* For master's, GRE General Test, minimum GPA of 3.0 during previous 2 years, minimum overall GPA of 2.75. Additional exam requirements/recommendations for international students: Required—TOEFL (minimum score 550 paper-based; 213 computer-based; 80 iBT). *Application deadline:* For fall admission, 3/15 for domestic and international students. Application fee: $60 ($75 for international students). Electronic applications accepted. *Financial support:* In 2006–07, 7 research assistantships with partial tuition reimbursements (averaging $10,000 per year) were awarded; career-related internships or fieldwork, Federal Work-Study, institutionally sponsored loans, scholarships/grants, health care benefits, and unspecified assistantships also available. Support available to part-time students. Financial award application deadline: 3/1. *Unit head:* Dr. Carolyn Yucha, Dean, 702-895-3415. *Application contact:* Graduate College Admissions Evaluator, 702-895-3320, Fax: 702-895-4180, E-mail: gradcollege@unlv.edu.

The University of North Carolina at Greensboro, Graduate School, School of Nursing, Greensboro, NC 27412-5001. Offers adult clinical nurse specialist (MSN, PMC); adult/gerontological nurse practitioner (MSN, PMC); nurse anesthesia (MSN, PMC); nursing (PhD); nursing administration (MSN); nursing education (MSN); MSN/MBA. *Accreditation:* AACN; AANA/CANAEP; NLN. *Faculty:* 24 full-time (23 women), 27 part-time/adjunct (22 women). *Students:* 231 full-time (197 women), 98 part-time (83 women); includes 56 minority (41 African Americans, 3 American Indian/Alaska Native, 9 Asian Americans or Pacific Islanders, 3 Hispanic Americans). 206 applicants, 59% accepted. *Degree requirements:* For master's, thesis or alternative. *Entrance requirements:* For master's, GRE General Test or MAT, BSN, clinical experience, liability insurance, RN license; for PMC, liability insurance, MSN, RN license. Additional exam requirements/recommendations for international students: Required—TOEFL. Application fee: $45. Electronic applications accepted. *Expenses:* Tuition, state resident: full-time $2,692. Tuition, nonresident: full-time $13,742. *Financial support:* Research assistantships with full tuition reimbursements, career-related internships or fieldwork, Federal Work-Study, scholarships/grants, and traineeships available. Support available to part-time students. *Unit head:* Dr. Lynne Pearcey, Dean, 336-334-5177, Fax: 336-334-3628, E-mail: l_pearce@uncg.edu. *Application contact:* Michelle Harkleroad, Director of Graduate Admissions, 336-334-4884, Fax: 336-334-4424, E-mail: mbharkle@uncg.edu.

University of Northern Colorado, Graduate School, College of Natural and Health Sciences, School of Nursing, Greeley, CO 80639. Offers clinical nurse specialist in chronic illness (MS); family nurse practitioner (MS); nursing education (MS, PhD). *Accreditation:* AACN. Postbaccalaureate distance learning degree programs offered. *Faculty:* 12 full-time (all women). *Students:* 58 full-time (57 women), 20 part-time (19 women); includes 6 minority (2 American Indian/Alaska Native, 4 Hispanic Americans). Average age 40. 63 applicants, 68% accepted, 21 enrolled. In 2006, 21 degrees awarded. *Degree requirements:* For master's, thesis or alternative, comprehensive exam; for doctorate, thesis/dissertation, comprehensive exam. *Entrance requirements:* For master's and doctorate, GRE General Test, minimum GPA of 3.0 in last 60 hours, BS in nursing, 2 letters of recommendation. *Application deadline:* Applications are processed on a rolling basis. Application fee: $50 ($60 for international students). Electronic applications accepted. *Expenses:* Tuition, state resident: full-time $5,118; part-time $213 per credit hour. Tuition, nonresident: full-time $14,832; part-time $618 per credit hour. Required fees: $674; $34 per credit hour. *Financial support:* In 2006–07, 47 students received support, including 4 fellowships (averaging $1,006 per year), 3 research assistantships (averaging $7,108 per year), 2 teaching assistantships (averaging $4,832 per year); unspecified assistantships also available. Financial award application deadline: 3/1; financial award applicants required to submit FAFSA. *Unit head:* Dr. Diane Peters, Interim Co-Director, 970-351-2293, Fax: 970-351-1707.

University of Phoenix–Cheyenne Campus, College of Health and Human Services, Cheyenne, WY 82009. Offers health administration (MHA); health care education (MSN); health care management (MBA); nursing (MSN); MSN/MBA; MSN/MHA.

University of Phoenix–Fort Lauderdale Campus, The Artemis School, College of Health and Human Services, Fort Lauderdale, FL 33309. Offers health administration (MHA); health care education (MSN); health care management (MBA); nursing (MSN); MSN/MBA. Evening/weekend programs available. *Faculty:* 22 full-time (10 women), 56 part-time/adjunct (28 women). *Students:* 197 full-time (173 women); includes 73 minority (60 African Americans, 2 Asian Americans or Pacific Islanders, 11 Hispanic Americans), 33 international. Average age 43. In 2006, 52 degrees awarded. *Degree requirements:* For master's, thesis (for some programs), registration. *Entrance requirements:* For master's, minimum undergraduate GPA of 2.5, 3 years work experience, RN license. Additional exam requirements/recommendations for international students: Required—TOEFL (minimum score 550 paper-based; 213 computer-based; 79 iBT). *Application deadline:* Applications are processed on a rolling basis. Application fee: $45. Electronic applications accepted. *Expenses:* Tuition: Full-time $9,450. Required fees: $760. *Financial support:* Institutionally sponsored loans and scholarships/grants available. Financial award applicants required to submit FAFSA. *Unit head:* Dr. Gil Linne, Dean/Executive Director, 480-557-1751, E-mail: gil.linne@phoenix.edu. *Application contact:* 954-382-5303, Fax: 954-382-5303.

University of Phoenix–Harrisburg Campus, College of Health and Human Services, Harrisburg, PA 17112. Offers health administration (MHA); health care management (MBA); nursing (MSN); nursing/health care education (MSN); MSN/MBA; MSN/MHA.

University of Phoenix–Maryland Campus, The Artemis School, College of Health and Human Services, Columbia, MD 21045-5424. Offers administration of justice and security (MS); nursing (MSN); nursing education (MSN); psychology (MS); MSN/MBA; MSN/MHA. Evening/weekend programs available. *Faculty:* 8 part-time/adjunct (7 women). *Students:* 1 (woman) full-time; minority (African American) Average age 27. *Degree requirements:* For master's, thesis (for some programs), registration. *Entrance requirements:* For master's, minimum undergraduate GPA of 2.5, 3 years work experience. Additional exam requirements/recommendations for international students: Required—TOEFL (minimum score 550 paper-based; 213 computer-based; 79 iBT). *Application deadline:* Applications are processed on a rolling basis. Application fee: $45. Electronic applications accepted. *Expenses:* Tuition: Full-time $13,200. Required fees: $760. *Financial support:* Institutionally sponsored loans and scholarships/grants available. Financial award applicants required to submit FAFSA. *Unit head:* Dr. Gil Linne, Dean/Executive Director, 480-557-1751, E-mail: gil.line@phoenix.com. *Application contact:* Campus Chair, 410-872-9001.

University of Phoenix—Northern Nevada Campus, College of Health and Human Services, Reno, NV 89511. Offers health administration (MHA); health care management (MBA); nursing (MSN); nursing/health care education (MSN); MSN/MBA; MSN/MHA.

University of Phoenix–North Florida Campus, The Artemis School, College of Health and Human Services, Jacksonville, FL 32216-0959. Offers health administration (MHA); health care education (MSN); health care management (MBA); nursing (MSN); MSN/MBA. Evening/weekend programs available. *Faculty:* 13 full-time (10 women), 58 part-time/adjunct (42 women). *Students:* 69 full-time (52 women); includes 33 minority (26 African Americans, 5 Asian Americans or Pacific Islanders, 2 Hispanic Americans), 7 international. Average age 41. In 2006, 15 master's awarded. *Degree requirements:* For master's, thesis (for some programs), registration. *Entrance requirements:* For master's, minimum undergraduate GPA of 2.5, 3 years work experience, RN license. Additional exam requirements/recommendations for international students: Required—TOEFL (minimum score 550 paper-based; 213 computer-based; 79 iBT). *Application deadline:* Applications are processed on a rolling basis. Application fee: $45. Electronic applications accepted. *Financial support:* Institutionally sponsored loans and scholarships/grants available. Financial award applicants required to submit FAFSA. *Unit head:* Dr. Gil Linne, Dean, 480-557-1751, E-mail: gil.linne@phoenix.edu. *Application contact:* Chair, 904-636-6645, Fax: 904-636-0998.

University of Phoenix–Northwest Arkansas Campus, College of Health and Human Services, Rogers, AR 72756-9615. Offers health administration (MHA); health care education (MSN); health care management (MBA); nursing (MSN); MSN/MBA.

University of Phoenix–Northwest Indiana, College of Health and Human Services, Merrillville, IN 46410. Offers health administration (MHA); nursing (MSN); nursing/health care education (MSN); MSN/MBA; MSN/MHA.

University of Phoenix Online Campus, The Artemis School, College of Health and Human Services, Phoenix, AZ 85034-7209. Offers administration of justice and security (MS); health care administration (MHA); health care management (MBA, MSN); nurse practitioner (MSN); nursing (MSN); nursing education (MSN); psychology (MS); MSN/MBA-HCM; MSN/MHA. *Accreditation:* AACN. Evening/weekend programs available. *Faculty:* 10 full-time (9 women), 1,743 part-time/adjunct (1,042 women). *Students:* 8,196 full-time (6,937 women); includes 1,916 minority (1,301 African Americans, 56 American Indian/Alaska Native, 268 Asian Americans or Pacific Islanders, 291 Hispanic Americans), 849 international. Average age 40. In 2006, 6,951 master's awarded. *Degree requirements:* For master's, thesis (for some programs), registration. *Entrance requirements:* For master's, 3 years of work experience, minimum undergraduate GPA of 2.5, RN license. Additional exam requirements/recommendations for international students: Required—TOEFL (minimum score 550 paper-based; 213 computer-based; 79 iBT). *Application deadline:* Applications are processed on a rolling basis. Application fee: $45. Electronic applications accepted. *Expenses:* Tuition: Full-time $12,664. Required fees: $760. *Financial support:* Institutionally sponsored loans and scholarships/grants available. Financial award applicants required to submit FAFSA. *Unit head:* Dr. Gil Linne, Dean/Executive Director, 480-552-1751, E-mail: gil.linne@phoenix.edu. *Application contact:* Dr. Gil Linne, Dean/Executive Director, 480-552-1751, E-mail: gil.linne@phoenix.edu.

University of Phoenix–Pittsburgh Campus, The Artemis School, College of Health and Human Services, Pittsburgh, PA 15276. Offers administration of justice and security (MS); health administration (MHA); health care management (MBA); nursing (MSN); nursing education (MSN); psychology (MS); MSN/MBA; MSN/MHA. Evening/weekend programs available. *Faculty:* 2 full-time (0 women), 10 part-time/adjunct (1 woman). *Students:* 11 full-time (8 women); includes 3 minority (all African Americans) Average age 36. In 2006, 1 degree awarded. *Degree requirements:* For master's, thesis (for some programs), registration. *Entrance requirements:* For master's, minimum undergraduate GPA of 2.5, 3 years work experience, current RN license (nursing). Additional exam requirements/recommendations for international students: Required—TOEFL (minimum score 550 paper-based; 213 computer-based; 79 iBT). *Application deadline:* Applications are processed on a rolling basis. Application fee: $45. Electronic applications accepted. *Expenses:* Tuition: Full-time $13,560. Required fees: $760. *Financial support:* Institutionally sponsored loans and scholarships/grants available. *Unit head:* Dr. Gil Linne, Dean/Executive Director, 480-557-1751, E-mail: gil.linne@phoenix.edu.

University of Phoenix–Renton Learning Center, College of Health and Human Services, Renton, WA 98005. Offers health administration (MHA); health care education (MSN); health care management (MBA); nursing (MSN); MSN/MBA; MSN/MHA.

University of Phoenix–Sacramento Valley Campus, The Artemis School, College of Health and Human Services, Sacramento, CA 95833-3632. Offers administration of justice and security (MS); family nurse practitioner (MSN); health care management (MBA); marriage, family and child counseling (MSC); nursing (MSN); nursing education (MSN). Evening/weekend programs available. *Faculty:* 36 full-time (27 women), 270 part-time/adjunct (121 women). *Students:* 330 full-time (266 women); includes 73 minority (38 African Americans, 2 American Indian/Alaska Native, 16 Asian Americans or Pacific Islanders, 17 Hispanic Americans), 29 international. Average age 40. In 2006, 82 degrees awarded. *Degree requirements:* For master's, thesis (for some programs), registration. *Entrance requirements:* For master's, RN license, minimum undergraduate GPA of 2.5, 3 years work experience. Additional exam requirements/recommendations for international students: Required—TOEFL (minimum score 550 paper-based; 213 computer-based; 79 iBT). *Application deadline:* Applications are processed on a rolling basis. Application fee: $45. Electronic applications accepted. *Expenses:* Tuition: Full-time $12,024. Required fees: $760. *Financial support:* Institutionally sponsored loans and scholarships/grants available. Financial award applicants required to submit FAFSA. *Unit head:* Dr. Gil Linne, Dean/Executive Director, 480-557-1757, E-mail: gil.linne@phoenix.edu. *Application contact:* College Chair, 916-923-2107, Fax: 916-923-3914.

University of Phoenix–Savannah Campus, College of Health and Human Services, Savannah, GA 31405-7400. Offers health administration (MHA); health care management (MBA); nursing (MSN); nursing/health care education (MSN); MSN/MBA; MSN/MHA.

University of Phoenix–Southern California Campus, The Artemis School, College of Health and Human Services, Costa Mesa, CA 92626. Offers family nurse practitioner (MSN, Certificate); health care education (MSN); health care management (MBA); marriage, family and child therapy (MSC); nursing (MSN). Evening/weekend programs available. *Faculty:* 53 full-time (32 women), 456 part-time/adjunct (240 women). *Students:* 623 full-time (524 women); includes 237 minority (98 African Americans, 2 American Indian/Alaska Native, 62 Asian Americans or Pacific Islanders, 75 Hispanic Americans), 59 international. Average age 40. In 2006, 113 degrees awarded. *Degree requirements:* For master's, thesis (for some programs), registration. *Entrance requirements:* For master's, minimum undergraduate GPA of 2.5, 3 years work experience, RN license. Additional exam requirements/recommendations for international students: Required—TOEFL (minimum score 550 paper-based; 213 computer-based; 79 iBT). *Application deadline:* Applications are processed on a rolling basis. Application fee: $45. Electronic applications accepted. *Expenses:* Tuition: Full-time $13,512. Required fees: $760. *Financial support:* Institutionally sponsored loans and scholarships/grants available. Financial award applicants required to submit FAFSA. *Unit head:* Dr. Gil Linne, Dean/Executive Director, 480-557-1751, E-mail: gil.linne@phoenix.edu. *Application contact:* Campus College Chair, 714-398-1878, Fax: 714-378-5856.

University of Phoenix–West Florida Campus, The Artemis School, College of Health and Human Services, Temple Terrace, FL 33637. Offers health administration (MHA); health care education (MSN); health care management (MBA); MSN/MBA. Evening/weekend programs available. Postbaccalaureate distance learning degree programs offered. *Faculty:* 19 full-time (12 women), 56 part-time/adjunct (31 women). *Students:* 87 full-time (79 women); includes 21 minority (12 African Americans, 1 Asian American or Pacific Islander, 8 Hispanic Americans), 10 international. Average age 45. In 2006, 18 degrees awarded. *Degree requirements:* For master's, thesis (for some programs), registration. *Entrance requirements:* For master's, minimum undergraduate GPA of 2.5, RN license, 3 years work experience. Additional exam requirements/recommendations for international students: Required—TOEFL (minimum score 550 paper-based; 213 computer-based; 79 iBT). *Application deadline:* Applications are processed on a rolling basis. Application fee: $45. Electronic applications accepted. *Expenses:* Tuition: Full-time $9,450. Required fees: $760. *Financial support:* Institutionally sponsored loans and scholarships/grants available. Financial award applicants required to submit FAFSA. *Unit head:* Dr. Gil Linne, Dean, 480-557-1751, E-mail: gil.linne@phoenix.edu. *Application contact:* Chair, 813-626-7911, Fax: 813-977-1449.

University of Pittsburgh, School of Nursing, Advanced Specialist Role Program, Pittsburgh, PA 15260. Offers nursing administration (MSN); nursing education (MSN); nursing informatics (MSN); nursing research (MSN). *Accreditation:* AACN. Part-time programs available. *Students:* 4 full-time (2 women), 46 part-time (45 women); includes 6 minority (3 African Americans, 2 Asian Americans or Pacific Islanders, 1 Hispanic American). Average age 41. 12 applicants, 50% accepted, 5 enrolled. In 2006, 18 degrees awarded. *Degree requirements:* For master's, thesis optional. *Entrance requirements:* For master's, GRE or MAT, BSN, RN license, letters of recommendation, resumé, course work in statistics, 1-3 years of nursing experience. Additional exam requirements/recommendations for international students: Required—TOEFL (minimum score 550 paper-based; 213 computer-based; 80 iBT). *Application deadline:* For fall admission, 8/1 priority date for domestic students; for spring admission, 12/1 priority date for domestic students. Applications are processed on a rolling basis. Application fee: $50. Electronic applications accepted. *Unit head:* Dr. Helen Burns, Associate Dean for Clinical Education, 412-624-6616, Fax: 412-624-2401, E-mail: burnsh@pitt.edu. *Application contact:* Laurie Lapsley, Administrator of Graduate Student Services, 412-624-9670, Fax: 412-624-2409, E-mail: lapsleyl@pitt.edu.

University of Puerto Rico, Medical Sciences Campus, School of Nursing, San Juan, PR 00936-5067. Offers anesthesia (MSN); clinical specialist (MSN); family nurse practitioner (MSN); nurse administrator (MSN); nursing education (MSN). *Accreditation:* AACN; AANA/CANAEP. Part-time and evening/weekend programs available. *Faculty:* 12 full-time (11 women), 3 part-time/adjunct (2 women). *Students:* 115 full-time (all women), 13 part-time (9 women); includes 123 minority (all Hispanic Americans), 3 international. 70 applicants, 71% accepted. In 2006, 40 degrees awarded. *Degree requirements:* For master's, one foreign language. *Entrance requirements:* For master's, GRE or EXADEP, interview, Puerto Rico RN license or professional license for international students, general and specific point average, article analysis. *Application deadline:* For spring admission, 4/30 priority date for domestic and international students. Applications are processed on a rolling basis. Application fee: $33. Electronic applications accepted. *Financial support:* In 2006–07, research assistantships with full tuition reimbursements (averaging $28,175 per year), teaching assistantships with full tuition reimbursements (averaging $48,965 per year) were awarded; Federal Work-Study, traineeships, tuition waivers (full), and unspecified assistantships also available. Financial award application deadline: 6/30. *Faculty research:* HIV, health disparities, teen violence, women and violence, neurological disorders. *Unit head:* Dr. Suane E. Sánchez, Dean, 787-758-2525 Ext. 2100, Fax: 787-281-0721, E-mail: sesanchez@rcm.upr.edu. *Application contact:* Dr. Angelica Y. Matos, Director Graduate Department, 787-758-2525, Fax: 787-281-0721.

University of Rhode Island, Graduate School, College of Nursing, Kingston, RI 02881. Offers administration (MS); clinical specialist in gerontology (MS); clinical specialist in psychiatric/mental health (MS); family nurse practitioner (MS); nurse midwifery (MS); nursing (PhD); nursing education (MS). *Accreditation:* AACN; ACNM/DOA (one or more programs are accredited). In 2006, 34 master's, 5 doctorates awarded. *Application deadline:* For fall admission, 4/15 for domestic students. Application fee: $35. *Expenses:* Tuition, state resident: full-time $6,032; part-time $335 per credit. Tuition, nonresident: full-time $17,288; part-time $960 per credit. Required fees: $65 per credit. $30 per semester. One-time fee: $80 part-time. *Unit head:* Dayle Joseph, Dean, 401-874-2766.

The University of Tampa, Nursing Program, Tampa, FL 33606-1490. Offers adult nurse practitioner (MSN); family nurse practitioner (MSN); nursing administration (MSN); nursing education (MSN). *Accreditation:* NLN. Part-time and evening/weekend programs available. *Faculty:* 5 full-time (all women), 10 part-time/adjunct (9 women). *Students:* 3 full-time (all women), 67 part-time (63 women); includes 2 minority (both African Americans), 1 international. Average age 40. 46 applicants, 61% accepted, 18 enrolled. In 2006, 29 degrees awarded. *Degree requirements:* For master's, oral exam, practicum, thesis optional. *Entrance requirements:* For master's, GRE General Test, minimum GPA of 3.0, RN license. *Application deadline:* For fall admission, 8/20 priority date for domestic students. Applications are processed on a rolling basis. Application fee: $40. Electronic applications accepted. *Expenses:* Tuition: Part-time $426 per credit hour. Required fees: $35 per year. *Financial support:* In 2006–07, 2 students received support, including 2 research assistantships with tuition reimbursements available (averaging $1,500 per year); career-related internships or fieldwork and unspecified assistantships also available. Support available to part-time students. Financial award applicants required to submit FAFSA. *Faculty research:* Domestic violence (assessment in emergency

Nursing Education

The University of Tampa (continued)
departments, changing demographics), transcultural health assessment, priorities in maintaining autonomy of elderly. *Unit head:* Dr. Nancy Ross, Director, 813-253-6223, Fax: 813-258-7214, E-mail: nross@ut.edu. *Application contact:* Barbara P. Strickler, Vice President for Enrollment, 888-646-2738, Fax: 813-258-7398, E-mail: admissions@ut.edu.

The University of Tennessee at Chattanooga, Graduate School, College of Health, Education and Professional Studies, School of Nursing, Chattanooga, TN 37403-2598. Offers administration (MSN); adult health (MSN); education (MSN); family nurse practitioner (MSN); nurse anesthesia (MSN). *Accreditation:* AACN; AANA/CANAEP. *Faculty:* 13 full-time (all women). *Students:* 40 full-time (32 women), 47 part-time (41 women); includes 9 minority (1 African American, 2 American Indian/Alaska Native, 4 Asian Americans or Pacific Islanders, 2 Hispanic Americans). Average age 34. 14 applicants, 71% accepted, 2 enrolled. In 2006, 29 degrees awarded. *Degree requirements:* For master's, qualifying exams. *Entrance requirements:* For master's, GRE General Test, MAT, BSN, minimum GPA of 3.0, eligibility for Tennessee RN license. *Application deadline:* For fall admission, 8/1 priority date for domestic students; for spring admission, 12/1 priority date for domestic students. Applications are processed on a rolling basis. Application fee: $30. *Expenses:* Tuition, state resident: full-time $5,434; part-time $339 per hour. Tuition, nonresident: full-time $14,830; part-time $861 per hour. Required fees: $940; $178 per hour. *Financial support:* Application deadline: 4/1; *Faculty research:* Diabetes in women; health care for elderly; alternative medicine; hypertension; nurse anesthesia. Total annual research expenditures: $357,538. *Unit head:* Dr. Kay R. Lindgren, Head, 423-425-4646, Fax: 423-425-4668, E-mail: kay-lindgren@utc.edu. *Application contact:* Dr. Deborah E. Arfken, Dean of Graduate Studies, 423-425-4666, Fax: 423-425-5223, E-mail: deborah-arfken@utc.edu.

The University of Texas at Arlington, Graduate School, School of Nursing, Arlington, TX 76019. Offers administration/supervision of nursing (MSN); nurse practitioner (MSN); nursing science (PhD); teaching of nursing (MSN). *Accreditation:* AACN. Part-time and evening/weekend programs available. *Faculty:* 22 full-time (21 women), 11 part-time/adjunct (10 women). *Students:* 52 full-time (50 women), 334 part-time (310 women); includes 86 minority (37 African Americans, 6 American Indian/Alaska Native, 24 Asian Americans or Pacific Islanders, 19 Hispanic Americans), 18 international. Average age 37. 178 applicants, 96% accepted, 117 enrolled. In 2006, 30 degrees awarded. *Degree requirements:* For master's, comprehensive exam, thesis or master's completion project; for doctorate, thesis/dissertation, diagnostic exam after 18 hours. *Entrance requirements:* For master's, GRE General Test, minimum GPA of 3.0, Texas nursing license, minimum C in undergraduate statistics course, physical assessment course within last 3 years; for doctorate, GRE General Test, minimum undergraduate, graduate and statistics GPA of 3.0; Texas RN license; interview; 3 letters of reference. Additional exam requirements/recommendations for international students: Required—TOEFL (minimum score 550 paper-based; 213 computer-based). *Application deadline:* For fall admission, 6/16 for domestic students. Applications are processed on a rolling basis. Application fee: $35 ($50 for international students). *Expenses:* Tuition, state resident: full-time $5,528. Tuition, nonresident: full-time $10,478. International tuition: $10,608 full-time. *Financial support:* In 2006–07, 37 students received support, including 24 fellowships with partial tuition reimbursements available (averaging $3,000 per year), 6 research assistantships (averaging $7,992 per year), 7 teaching assistantships (averaging $10,080 per year); career-related internships or fieldwork and traineeships also available. Financial award application deadline: 6/1; financial award applicants required to submit FAFSA. *Unit head:* Dr. Elizabeth C. Poster, Dean, 817-272-2776, Fax: 817-272-5006, E-mail: poster@uta.edu. *Application contact:* Dr. Susan Grove, Graduate Adviser, 817-272-2776, Fax: 817-272-5006, E-mail: grove@uta.edu.

The University of Texas at Tyler, College of Nursing and Health Sciences, Program in Nursing, Tyler, TX 75799-0001. Offers nurse practitioner (MSN); nursing administration (MSN); nursing education (MSN); MSN/MBA. *Accreditation:* AACN. Part-time and evening/weekend programs available. Postbaccalaureate distance learning degree programs offered (no on-campus study). *Faculty:* 14 full-time (13 women), 4 part-time/adjunct (3 women). *Students:* 13 full-time (11 women), 134 part-time (122 women); includes 25 minority (16 African Americans, 2 American Indian/Alaska Native, 2 Asian Americans or Pacific Islanders, 5 Hispanic Americans). Average age 39. 37 applicants, 32 enrolled. In 2006, 15 degrees awarded. *Degree requirements:* For master's, thesis (for some programs), comprehensive exam (for some programs). *Entrance requirements:* For master's, GRE General Test or MAT, GMAT, minimum undergraduate GPA of 3.0, course work in statistics, RN license, BSN. *Application deadline:* For fall admission, 3/1 priority date for domestic students; for spring admission, 10/1 priority date for domestic students. Applications are processed on a rolling basis. Application fee: $0. Electronic applications accepted. *Expenses:* Tuition, state resident: part-time $50 per credit hour. Tuition, nonresident: part-time $328 per credit hour. Required fees: $107 per credit hour. $426 per term. *Financial support:* In 2006–07, 15 students received support, including 12 fellowships, 3 research assistantships (averaging $2,200 per year); institutionally sponsored loans and scholarships/grants also available. Financial award application deadline: 8/1; financial award applicants required to submit FAFSA. *Faculty research:* Psychosocial adjustment, aging, support/commitment of caregivers, psychological abuse and violence, hope/hopelessness, professional values, end of life cave, suicidology, clinical supervision, workforce retention and issues, global health issues. *Unit head:* Dr. Susan Yarbrough, Assistant Dean, 903-566-1220, E-mail: syarbrou@mail.uttyl.edu. *Application contact:* Bonnie Purser, Office of Graduate Studies, 903-566-7142, Fax: 903-566-7068, E-mail: bpurser@uttyler.edu.

Villanova University, College of Nursing, Villanova, PA 19085-1690. Offers adult nurse practitioner (MSN, Post Master's Certificate); clinical case management (MSN, Post Master's Certificate); geriatric nurse practitioner (MSN, Post Master's Certificate); health care administration (MSN); nurse anesthetist (MSN, Post Master's Certificate); nursing (PhD); nursing education (MSN, Post Master's Certificate); pediatric nurse practitioner (MSN, Post Master's Certificate). *Accreditation:* AACN; AANA/CANAEP; NLN. Part-time programs available. Postbaccalaureate distance learning degree programs offered (minimal on-campus study). *Faculty:* 14 full-time (all women), 2 part-time/adjunct (both women). *Students:* 41 full-time (27 women), 164 part-time (128 women); includes 17 minority (8 African Americans, 1 American Indian/Alaska Native, 8 Asian Americans or Pacific Islanders), 6 international. Average age 31. 137 applicants, 50% accepted, 48 enrolled. In 2006, 47 degrees awarded. *Median time to degree:* Master's–2 years full-time, 5 years part-time. *Degree requirements:* For master's, independent study project; for doctorate, thesis/dissertation, comprehensive exam. *Entrance requirements:* For master's, GRE or MAT, BSN, 1 year of recent nursing experience, physical assessment, course work in statistics; for doctorate, GRE. Additional exam requirements/recommendations for international students: Required—TOEFL. *Application deadline:* For fall admission, 7/1 priority date for domestic students, 7/1 for international students; for spring admission, 12/1 priority date for domestic students, 12/1 for international students. Applications are processed on a rolling basis. Application fee: $50. *Expenses:* Contact institution. *Financial support:* In 2006–07, 50 students received support, including 4 teaching assistantships with full tuition reimbursements available (averaging $12,165 per year); institutionally sponsored loans, scholarships/grants, traineeships, and tuition waivers (full) also available. Financial award application deadline: 3/1; financial award applicants required to submit FAFSA. *Faculty research:* Genetics, ethics, cognitive development of students, women with disabilities, nursing leadership. *Unit head:* Dr. Marguerite K. Schlag, Assistant Dean and Director, Graduate Program, 610-519-4907, Fax: 610-519-7650, E-mail: marguerite.schlag@villanova.edu.

Wayne State University, College of Nursing, Program in Nursing Education, Detroit, MI 48202. Offers nursing education (Certificate); transcultural nursing (MSN, Certificate). *Students:* Average age 40. 1 applicant, 100% accepted, 1 enrolled. In 2006, 7 degrees awarded. *Entrance requirements:* For degree, GRE General Test, minimum GPA of 2.8. Additional exam requirements/recommendations for international students: Required—TOEFL (minimum score 550 paper-based; 213 computer-based); Recommended—TWE (minimum score 6). *Application deadline:* For fall admission, 7/1 priority date for domestic students, 6/1 for international students; for winter admission, 10/1 for international students; for spring admission, 11/1 for domestic students, 2/1 for international students. Applications are processed on a rolling basis. Application fee: $30 ($50 for international students). Electronic applications accepted. *Financial support:* Institutionally sponsored loans, scholarships/grants, and traineeships available. Financial award application deadline: 7/1. *Faculty research:* Clinical teaching, curriculum development and evaluation, teaching methodology. *Application contact:* Nancy Artinian, Professor, 313-577-4143, E-mail: n.artinian@wayne.edu.

West Chester University of Pennsylvania, Graduate Studies, School of Health Sciences, Department of Nursing, West Chester, PA 19383. Offers nursing (MSN); nursing education (MSN). *Accreditation:* AACN. Part-time and evening/weekend programs available. *Students:* 10 full-time (9 women), 40 part-time (all women); includes 2 African Americans. Average age 42. 19 applicants, 100% accepted, 15 enrolled. In 2006, 12 degrees awarded. *Degree requirements:* For master's, thesis optional. *Entrance requirements:* For master's, GRE General Test or MAT, RN license. *Application deadline:* For fall admission, 4/15 priority date for domestic students; for spring admission, 10/15 for domestic students. Applications are processed on a rolling basis. Application fee: $35. *Financial support:* In 2006–07, research assistantships with full tuition reimbursements (averaging $5,000 per year); unspecified assistantships also available. Support available to part-time students. Financial award application deadline: 2/15; financial award applicants required to submit FAFSA. *Faculty research:* Violence against women. *Unit head:* Dr. Ann Coghlan Stowe, Chair, 610-436-2331, E-mail: astowe@wcupa.edu.

Westminster College, School of Nursing and Health Sciences, Salt Lake City, UT 84105-3697. Offers family nurse practitioner (MSN); nurse anesthesia (MSNA); nursing (MSN); nursing education (MSN). *Accreditation:* AACN; AANA/CANAEP. Part-time and evening/weekend programs available. *Faculty:* 9 full-time (8 women). *Students:* 44 full-time (31 women), 13 part-time (9 women); includes 4 minority (1 African American, 2 Asian Americans or Pacific Islanders, 1 Hispanic American), 1 international. Average age 39. 57 applicants, 65% accepted, 32 enrolled. In 2006, 5 degrees awarded. *Degree requirements:* For master's, project or thesis. *Entrance requirements:* For master's, resumé, Utah RN license in good standing, minimum GPA of 3.0, 3 letters of recommendation, proof of completed BSN from accredited nursing school, proof of clear state and federal background check, drug test results, personal interview. Additional exam requirements/recommendations for international students: Required—TOEFL (minimum score 550 paper-based; 213 computer-based). *Application deadline:* For fall admission, 8/1 priority date for domestic students. Applications are processed on a rolling basis. Application fee: $40. Electronic applications accepted. *Financial support:* In 2006–07, 39 students received support. Career-related internships or fieldwork and tuition remissions available. Support available to part-time students. Financial award applicants required to submit FAFSA. *Faculty research:* Learning styles assessment, curriculum simulation, self-esteem and learning success. *Unit head:* Dr. Jean Dyer, Dean, 801-832-2168, Fax: 801-832-3110, E-mail: jdyer@westminstercollege.edu. *Application contact:* Joel Bauman, Vice President of Enrollment Services, 801-832-2200, Fax: 801-832-3101, E-mail: admission@westminstercollege.edu.

Winona State University, Graduate Studies, College of Nursing and Health Sciences, Winona, MN 55987-5838. Offers adult nurse practitioner (MS); clinical nurse specialist (MS); family nurse practitioner (MS); nurse administrator (MS); nurse educator (MS). *Accreditation:* AACN. Part-time programs available. *Faculty:* 10 full-time (all women). *Students:* 70 applicants, 57% accepted, 32 enrolled. In 2006, 32 master's awarded. *Degree requirements:* For master's, thesis. *Application deadline:* For fall admission, 2/1 for domestic students. Application fee: $20. *Financial support:* In 2006–07, 3 research assistantships with partial tuition reimbursements (averaging $6,000 per year) were awarded; Federal Work-Study, traineeships, and unspecified assistantships also available. Support available to part-time students. Financial award applicants required to submit FAFSA. *Unit head:* Dr. Timothy Gaspar, Graduate Director, 507-457-5122, E-mail: tgaspar@winona.msus.edu.

Nursing Informatics

Case Western Reserve University, Frances Payne Bolton School of Nursing, Master's Programs in Nursing, Program in Nursing Informatics, Cleveland, OH 44106. Offers MSN. Part-time programs available. *Students:* 1 (woman) full-time, 2 part-time (both women), 2 international. 2 applicants, 0% accepted. In 2006, 3 degrees awarded. *Entrance requirements:* For master's, GRE General Test or MAT. Additional exam requirements/recommendations for international students: Required—TOEFL. Application fee: $75. *Unit head:* Chris Hudak, Head, 216-368-6315. *Application contact:* Peter Taylor, Recruitment and Retention Specialist, 216-368-0349, Fax: 216-368-0124, E-mail: peter.taylor@case.edu.

Duke University, School of Nursing, Durham, NC 27708-0586. Offers adult acute care (Certificate); adult cardiovascular (Certificate); adult oncology/HIV (Certificate); adult primary care (Certificate); clinical nurse specialist (MSN), including adult oncology/HIV, gerontology, neonatal, pediatric, pediatric/chronic acute care; clinical research management (MSN, Certificate); family (Certificate); gerontology (Certificate); health and nursing ministries (MSN, Certificate); health systems leadership and outcomes (Certificate); leadership in community based long term care (MSN, Certificate); neonatal (Certificate); neonatal/pediatric in rural health (MSN, Certificate); nurse anesthetist (MSN, Certificate); nurse practitioner (MSN), including adult acute care, adult cardiovascular, adult oncology/HIV, adult primary care, family, gerontology, neonatal, pediatric, pediatric acute care; nursing (PhD); nursing and healthcare leadership (MSN); nursing education (MSN); nursing informatics (MSN, Certificate); pediatric (Certificate); pediatric acute care (Certificate); MBA/MSN; MSN/MCM. *Accreditation:* AACN; AANA/CANAEP. Part-time programs available. Postbaccalaureate distance learning degree programs offered (minimal on-campus study). *Faculty:* 45 full-time (41 women), 169 part-time/adjunct (150 women). *Students:* 178 full-time (162 women), 140 part-time (132 women); includes 48 minority (17 African Americans, 3 American Indian/Alaska Native, 20 Asian Americans or Pacific Islanders, 8 Hispanic Americans). Average age 36. 99 applicants, 92% accepted, 91 enrolled. In 2006, 122 master's, 17 other advanced degrees awarded. *Median time to degree:* Master's–2 years full-time, 2.5 years part-time. *Degree requirements:* For master's, thesis optional. *Entrance requirements:* For master's, GRE General Test or MAT, 1 year of nursing experience, BSN, minimum GPA of 3.0, previous course work in statistics; for Certificate, MSN. Additional exam requirements/recommendations for international students: Required—TOEFL (minimum score 550 paper-based; 213 computer-based), Commission on Graduates of Foreign Nursing Schools exam. *Application deadline:* For fall admission, 7/2 priority date for domestic and international students; for spring admission, 11/15 priority date for domestic and international students. Applications are processed on a rolling basis. Application fee: $50. *Expenses:* Contact institution. *Financial support:* In 2006–07, 258 students received support. Career-related internships or fieldwork, institutionally sponsored loans, scholarships/grants, traineeships, and tuition waivers (partial) available. Support available to part-time students. Financial award application deadline: 4/1; financial award applicants required to submit FAFSA. *Faculty research:* Cardiovascular disease, caregiver skill training, data mining, prostate cancer, neonatal immune system. Total annual research expenditures: $3.5 million. *Unit head:* Dr. Catherine L. Gilliss, Dean/Vice Chancellor for Nursing Affairs, 919-684-9444, Fax: 919-684-9414, E-mail: gilli025@mc.duke.edu. *Application contact:* Bebe T. Mills, Director of Admissions, 919-684-9151, Fax: 919-668-4693, E-mail: mills031@mc.duke.edu.

Ferris State University, College of Allied Health Sciences, School of Nursing, Big Rapids, MI 49307. Offers nursing (MS); nursing administration (MS); nursing education (MS); nursing informatics (MS). Part-time and evening/weekend programs available. Postbaccalaureate distance learning degree programs offered (minimal on-campus study). *Faculty:* 2 full-time (1 woman). *Students:* Average age 39. 22 applicants, 100% accepted, 22 enrolled. In 2006, 2 degrees awarded. *Median time to degree:* Master's–3 years part-time. *Degree requirements:* For master's, thesis, practicum, comprehensive exam. *Entrance requirements:* For master's, BS in nursing, writing sample, letters of reference, 2 years clinical experience. Additional exam requirements/recommendations for international students: Required—TOEFL (minimum score 550 paper-based). *Application deadline:* For fall admission, 8/26 for domestic students; for winter admission, 12/16 for domestic students. Applications are processed on a rolling basis. Application fee: $30. Electronic applications accepted. *Expenses:* Tuition, state resident: part-time $355 per credit hour. Tuition, nonresident: part-time $687 per credit hour. *Financial support:* In 2006–07, 3 students received support. Scholarships/grants available. *Faculty research:* Nursing education-minority student focus student attitudes toward aging. *Unit head:* Dr. Julie A. Coon, Director, 231-591-2267, Fax: 231-591-2325, E-mail: coonj@ferris.edu.

La Salle University, School of Nursing and Health Sciences, Philadelphia, PA 19141-1199. Offers adult health and illness, clinical nurse specialist (MSN); gerontology (Certificate); nursing administration (MSN); nursing education (Certificate); nursing informatics (Certificate); primary care of adults-nurse practitioner (MSN); public health nursing (MSN); schoo nursing (Certificate); speech-language-hearing science (MS); wound, ostomy and continence nursing (Certificate); wound, ostomy, and continence nursing (MSN); MSN/MBA. *Accreditation:* AACN. Part-time programs available. Postbaccalaureate distance learning degree programs offered (minimal on-campus study). *Entrance requirements:* For master's, GRE or MAT, 1 year of professional work experience, BSN, Pennsylvania RN license. Expenses: Contact institution. *Faculty research:* Medication errors, wound care, metacognition, education of RN students.

Molloy College, Department of Nursing, Rockville Centre, NY 11571-5002. Offers adult nurse practitioner (Advanced Certificate); clinical nurse specialist: adult health (Advanced Certificate); family nurse practitioner (Advanced Certificate); nurse practitioner psychiatry (Advanced Certificate); nursing (MS); nursing administration (Advanced Certificate); nursing administration with informatics (Advanced Certificate); nursing education (Advanced Certificate); nursing informatics (Advanced Certificate); pediatric nurse practitioner (Advanced Certificate). *Accreditation:* AACN. Part-time and evening/weekend programs available. *Degree requirements:* For master's, thesis optional. *Entrance requirements:* For master's, 3 letters of reference, BS in nursing, minimum undergraduate GPA of 3.0; for Advanced Certificate, 3 letters of reference, master's degree in nursing. *Faculty research:* Hardiness and aging, alcoholism, current ethics, breast cancer, nurse role perception.

New York University, College of Dentistry, College of Nursing, Programs in Advanced Practice Nursing, New York, NY 10012-1019. Offers advanced practice nursing: adult acute care (MS, Advanced Certificate); advanced practice nursing: adult primary care (MS, Advanced Certificate); advanced practice nursing: adult primary care/geriatrics (MS); advanced practice nursing: children with special needs (Advanced Certificate); advanced practice nursing: geriatrics (MS, Advanced Certificate); advanced practice nursing: holistic nursing (MS, Advanced Certificate); advanced practice nursing: home health nursing (Advanced Certificate); advanced practice nursing: mental health (MS); advanced practice nursing: mental health nursing (Advanced Certificate); advanced practice nursing: pediatrics (MS, Advanced Certificate); advanced practice nursing: pediatrics/children with special needs (MS); midwifery (MS, Advanced Certificate); nursing administration (MS, Advanced Certificate); nursing education (MS, Advanced Certificate); nursing informatics (MS, Advanced Certificate); palliative care (MS, Advanced Certificate); MS/MS. *Accreditation:* AACN; ACNM/DOA. Part-time and evening/weekend programs available. *Faculty:* 30 full-time (all women). *Students:* 10 full-time (all women), 428 part-time (395 women); includes 166 minority (73 African Americans, 72 Asian Americans or Pacific Islanders, 21 Hispanic Americans). Average age 35. 154 applicants, 93% accepted, 118 enrolled. In 2006, 100 master's, 7 Advanced Certificates awarded. *Degree requirements:* For master's, thesis (for some programs). *Entrance requirements:* For master's, BS in nursing, AS in nursing with another BS/BA degree; for Advanced Certificate, master's degree. Additional exam requirements/recommendations for international students: Required—TOEFL. *Application deadline:* For fall admission, 7/1 priority date for domestic students, 7/1 for international students; for spring admission, 12/1 for domestic and international students. Applications are processed on a rolling basis. Application fee: $65. *Expenses:* Tuition: Part-time $1,080 per unit. Required fees: $56 per unit. $329 per term. Tuition and fees vary according to program. *Financial support:* Career-related internships or fieldwork, Federal Work-Study, institutionally sponsored loans, scholarships/grants, and tuition waivers (partial) available. Support available to part-time students. Financial award application deadline: 2/1; financial award applicants required to submit FAFSA. *Faculty research:* Elderly black diabetics, families and illness, public health nursing, parent-child nursing, health policy costs. *Unit head:* Dr. Judith Haber, Associate Dean for Graduate Programs, 212-998-5300, Fax: 212-995-3143. *Application contact:* Amy Knowles, Assistant Dean for Student Affairs and Admissions, 212-998-5333, Fax: 212-995-4302, E-mail: ak96@nyu.edu.

University of Medicine and Dentistry of New Jersey, School of Nursing, Program in Nursing Informatics—Newark, Newark, NJ 07107-1709. Offers MSN. *Entrance requirements:* Additional exam requirements/recommendations for international students: Required—TOEFL. *Application deadline:* For fall admission, 4/1 for domestic students; for spring admission, 10/1 for domestic students. Applications are processed on a rolling basis. Application fee: $50. Electronic applications accepted. *Financial support:* Application deadline: 5/1. *Unit head:* Dr. Rosario P. Estrada, Track Coordinator, 973-972-8551, Fax: 973-972-7453, E-mail: estradrp@umdnj.edu.

University of Medicine and Dentistry of New Jersey, School of Nursing, Program in Nursing Informatics—Stratford, Newark, NJ 07107-1709. Offers MSN. *Entrance requirements:* Additional exam requirements/recommendations for international students: Required—TOEFL. *Application deadline:* For fall admission, 4/1 for domestic students; for spring admission, 10/1 for domestic students. Applications are processed on a rolling basis. Application fee: $50. Electronic applications accepted. *Financial support:* Application deadline: 5/1. *Unit head:* Dr. Rosario P. Estrada, Track Coordinator, 973-972-8551, Fax: 973-972-7453, E-mail: estradrp@umdnj.edu.

Vanderbilt University, School of Nursing, Nashville, TN 37235. Offers adult acute care nurse practitioner (MSN); adult health nurse practitioner/forensic (MSN); adult nurse practitioner/cardiovascular disease management and prevention (MSN); adult nurse practitioner/palliative care (MSN); clinical management (clinical nurse leader/specialist) (MSN); family nurse practitioner (MSN); gerontology nurse practitioner (MSN); health systems management (MSN); neonatal nurse practitioner (MSN); nurse midwifery (MSN); nursing informatics (MSN); nursing science (PhD); pediatric acute care nurse practitioner (MSN); pediatric primary care nurse practitioner (MSN); psychiatric-mental health nurse practitioner (MSN); women's health nurse practitioner (MSN); MBA/MSN; MSN/MTS; MSN/PhD. *Accreditation:* ACNM/DOA; NLN (one or more programs are accredited). Part-time and evening/weekend programs available. Postbaccalaureate distance learning degree programs offered (minimal on-campus study). *Faculty:* 95 full-time (83 women), 432 part-time/adjunct (314 women). *Students:* 371 full-time (325 women), 206 part-time (180 women); includes 59 minority (38 African Americans, 2 American Indian/Alaska Native, 7 Asian Americans or Pacific Islanders, 12 Hispanic Americans). Average age 27. 611 applicants, 55% accepted, 308 enrolled. In 2006, 256 master's, 2 doctorates awarded. *Degree requirements:* For doctorate, thesis/dissertation. *Entrance requirements:* For master's, GRE, interview; for doctorate, GRE, interview, 3 letters of recommendation. Additional exam requirements/recommendations for international students: Required—TOEFL. *Application deadline:* For fall admission, 12/1 priority date for domestic and international students. Applications are processed on a rolling basis. Application fee: $50. *Expenses:* Contact institution. *Financial support:* In 2006–07, 404 students received support, including 5 research assistantships (averaging $8,000 per year); Federal Work-Study, institutionally sponsored loans, and unspecified assistantships also available. Support available to part-time students. Financial award application deadline: 3/15; financial award applicants required to submit CSS PROFILE or FAFSA. *Faculty research:* Lymphedema post cancer treatment, palliative care and bereavement, patient safety and quality of care, health care workforce issues, symptom management including pain and fatigue. Total annual research expenditures: $1.1 million. *Unit head:* Dr. Colleen Conway-Welch, Dean, 615-343-8776, Fax: 615-343-7711, E-mail: colleen.conway-welch@vanderbilt.edu. *Application contact:* Cheryl Feldner, Assistant Director of Admissions, 615-322-3800, Fax: 615-343-0333, E-mail: cheryl.feldner@vanderbilt.edu.

Occupational Health Nursing

University of Cincinnati, Graduate School, College of Nursing, Cincinnati, OH 45221-0038. Offers clinical nurse specialist (MSN), including adult health, community health, neonatal, nursing administration, occupational health, pediatric health, psychiatric nursing, women's health; nurse anesthesia (MSN); nurse midwifery (MSN); nurse practitioner (MSN), including acute care, ambulatory care, family, family/psychiatric, women's health; nursing (PhD); MBA/MSN. *Accreditation:* AACN; AANA/CANAEP (one or more programs are accredited); ACNM/DOA. Part-time programs available. Postbaccalaureate distance learning degree programs offered (no on-campus study). *Faculty:* 41 full-time (39 women), 16 part-time/adjunct (15 women). *Students:* 159 full-time (125 women), 149 part-time (145 women); includes 40 minority (22 African Americans, 1 American Indian/Alaska Native, 16 Asian Americans or Pacific Islanders, 1 Hispanic American). Average age 34. 385 applicants, 49% accepted, 132 enrolled. In 2006, 77 master's, 5 doctorates awarded. Terminal master's awarded for partial completion of doctoral program. *Median time to degree:* Of those who began their doctoral program in fall 1998, 55% received their degree in 8 years or less. *Degree requirements:* For master's, thesis or alternative, registration; for doctorate, thesis/dissertation, comprehensive exam, registration. *Entrance requirements:* For master's and doctorate, GRE General Test. Additional exam requirements/recommendations for international students: Required—TOEFL (minimum score 520 paper-based; 190 computer-based). *Application deadline:* For fall admission, 7/26 priority date for domestic and international students. Applications are processed on a rolling basis. Application fee: $40. Electronic applications accepted. *Financial support:* In 2006–07, 164 students received support, including 7 fellowships with full tuition reimbursements available (averaging $13,571 per year), research assistantships with full tuition reimbursements available (averaging $12,000 per year), 8 teaching assistantships with full tuition reimbursements available (averaging $12,000 per year); career-related internships or fieldwork, scholarships/grants, traineeships, tuition waivers (partial), and unspecified assistantships also available. Support available to part-time students. Financial award application deadline: 5/1; financial award applicants required to submit FAFSA. *Faculty research:* Substance abuse, injury and violence, symptom management. Total annual research expenditures: $1.3 million. *Unit head:* Dr. Andrea R. Lindell, Dean, 513-558-5330, Fax: 513-558-9030, E-mail: andrea.lindell@uc.edu. *Application contact:* Loren Carter, Program Coordinator, 513-558-5072, Fax: 513-558-7523, E-mail: loren.carter@uc.edu.

University of Massachusetts Lowell, Graduate School, College of Health Professions, Department of Nursing, Program in Occupational Health Nursing, Lowell, MA 01854-2881. Offers adult psychiatric nursing (MS); occupational health nursing (MS). *Accreditation:* AACN. *Degree requirements:* For master's, thesis optional. *Entrance requirements:* For master's, GRE General Test.

University of Medicine and Dentistry of New Jersey, School of Nursing, Newark, NJ 07107-1709. Offers adult health (MSN); adult occupational health (MSN); advanced practice nursing (MSN, Post Master's Certificate); family nurse practitioner (MSN); nurse anesthesia (MSN); nursing (MSN); nursing education (MSN, Post Master's Certificate); nursing informatics (MSN); urban health (PhD); women's health practitioner (MSN). *Accreditation:* AANA/CANAEP; NLN (one or more programs are accredited). Part-time programs available. *Students:* 93 full-time (82 women), 307 part-time (274 women); includes 195 minority (92 African Americans, 1 American Indian/Alaska Native, 69 Asian Americans or Pacific Islanders, 33 Hispanic Americans), 1 international. Average age 39. 472 applicants, 63% accepted, 203 enrolled. In 2006, 57 master's, 6 other advanced degrees awarded. *Entrance requirements:* For master's, GRE, RN license; basic life support, statistics, and health assessment experience. Additional exam requirements/recommendations for international students: Required—TOEFL. *Application deadline:* Applications are processed on a rolling basis. Application fee: $50. Electronic applications accepted. *Expenses:* Contact institution. *Financial support:* Teaching assistantships, institutionally sponsored loans and scholarships/grants available. Support available to part-time students. Financial award application deadline: 5/1. *Faculty research:* HIV/AIDS, diabetes education, learned helplessness, nursing science, psychoeducation. *Unit head:* Dr. Susan Salmond, Interim Dean, 973-972-9239, Fax: 973-972-3225, E-mail: salmonsu@umdnj.edu.

University of Michigan, Horace H. Rackham School of Graduate Studies, School of Nursing, Division of Health Promotion and Risk Reduction, Program in Community Health Nursing, Ann Arbor, MI 48109. Offers adult primary care/adult nurse practitioner (MS); community care/home care (MS); family nurse practitioner (MS); occupational health nursing (MS). *Accreditation:* AACN. Part-time and evening/weekend programs available. *Degree requirements:* For master's, thesis, registration. *Entrance requirements:* For master's, GRE General Test, licensure, minimum GPA of 3.0 in BSN program. Additional exam requirements/recommendations for international students: Required—TOEFL (minimum score 560 paper-based; 220 computer-based).

University of Minnesota, Twin Cities Campus, School of Public Health, Division of Environmental Health Sciences, Area in Occupational Health Nursing, Minneapolis, MN 55455-0213. Offers MPH, MS, PhD, MPH/MS. *Accreditation:* AACN. *Degree requirements:* For doctorate, thesis/dissertation. *Entrance requirements:* For master's and doctorate, GRE General Test.

Occupational Health Nursing

University of Minnesota, Twin Cities Campus (continued)
Expenses: Tuition, state resident: full-time $9,302; part-time $775 per credit. Tuition, nonresident: full-time $16,400; part-time $1,367 per credit. Full-time tuition and fees vary according to class time, course load, program, reciprocity agreements and student level.

The University of North Carolina at Chapel Hill, Graduate School, School of Public Health, Public Health Leadership Program, Chapel Hill, NC 27599. Offers health care and prevention (MPH); leadership (MPH); occupational health nursing (MPH); public health nursing (MS). Part-time programs available. Postbaccalaureate distance learning degree programs offered (minimal on-campus study). *Faculty:* 6 full-time (5 women), 12 part-time/adjunct. *Students:* 168 full-time (112 women); includes 38 minority (27 African Americans, 1 American Indian/Alaska Native, 9 Asian Americans or Pacific Islanders, 1 Hispanic American), 5 international. Average age 32. 132 applicants, 73% accepted, 96 enrolled. In 2006, 87 degrees awarded. *Degree requirements:* For master's, thesis (MS), paper (MPH). *Entrance requirements:* For master's, GRE General Test, minimum GPA of 3.0, public health experience. Additional exam requirements/recommendations for international students: Required—TOEFL. *Application deadline:* For fall admission, 1/1 priority date for domestic and international students; for spring admission, 10/15 for domestic students. Applications are processed on a rolling basis. Application fee: $65. Electronic applications accepted. *Financial support:* In 2006–07, 17 fellowships with full and partial tuition reimbursements (averaging $11,608 per year) were awarded; career-related internships or fieldwork, institutionally sponsored loans, traineeships, and health care benefits also available. Financial award application deadline: 2/1; financial award applicants required to submit FAFSA. *Faculty research:* Occupational health issues, clinical outcomes, prenatal and early childcare, adolescent health, effectiveness of home visiting, issues in occupational health nursing, community-based interventions. *Unit head:* Dr. William Sollecito, Director, 919-966-5285, Fax: 919-966-0981, E-mail: bill_sollecito@unc.edu. *Application contact:* Sue Robeson, Registrar, 919-966-5305, Fax: 919-966-0981, E-mail: robeson@email.unc.edu.

University of Pennsylvania, School of Nursing, Occupational Health Nurse Practitioner Program, Philadelphia, PA 19104. Offers administration/consulting (MSN); primary care (MSN). *Accreditation:* AACN. Part-time programs available. *Entrance requirements:* For master's, GRE General Test, BSN, minimum GPA of 3.0, previous course work in statistics. Additional exam requirements/recommendations for international students: Required—TOEFL. Expenses: Contact institution. *Faculty research:* Injury prevention.

Oncology Nursing

Barnes-Jewish College of Nursing and Allied Health, Division of Nursing, St. Louis, MO 63110-1091. Offers adult nurse practitioner (MSN); education (MSN); gerontology nurse practitioner (MSN); holistics (MSN); management/administration (MSN); neonatal nurse practitioner (MSN); oncology (MSN). *Accreditation:* AACN; AANA/CANAEP. Part-time and evening/weekend programs available. *Degree requirements:* For master's, thesis or alternative, registration. *Entrance requirements:* For master's, minimum GPA of 3.0, 2 references, statistics course. Additional exam requirements/recommendations for international students: Required—TOEFL (minimum score 550 paper-based; 213 computer-based).

Columbia University, School of Nursing, Program in Oncology Nursing, New York, NY 10032. Offers MS, Adv C. *Accreditation:* AACN. Part-time programs available. *Students:* 3 full-time (all women), 4 part-time (all women); includes 2 minority (1 African American, 1 Asian American or Pacific Islander). Average age 32. In 2006, 9 degrees awarded. *Entrance requirements:* For master's, GRE General Test, BSN, 1 year of clinical experience (preferred); for Adv C, MSN. *Application deadline:* Applications are processed on a rolling basis. Application fee: $65. Electronic applications accepted. *Financial support:* Teaching assistantships available. Financial award application deadline: 2/1; financial award applicants required to submit FAFSA. *Unit head:* Prof. Anita Nirenberg, Director, 212-305-1110.

Duke University, School of Nursing, Durham, NC 27708-0586. Offers adult acute care (Certificate); adult cardiovascular (Certificate); adult oncology/HIV (Certificate); adult primary care (Certificate); clinical nurse specialist (MSN), including adult oncology/HIV, gerontology, neonatal, pediatric, pediatric/chronic acute care; clinical research management (MSN, Certificate); family (Certificate); gerontology (Certificate); health and nursing ministries (MSN, Certificate); health systems leadership and outcomes (Certificate); leadership in community based long term care (MSN, Certificate); neonatal (Certificate); neonatal/pediatric in rural health (MSN, Certificate); nurse anesthetist (MSN, Certificate); nurse practitioner (MSN), including adult acute care, adult cardiovascular, adult oncology/HIV, adult primary care, family, gerontology, neonatal, pediatric, pediatric acute care; nursing (PhD); nursing and healthcare leadership (MSN); nursing education (MSN); nursing informatics (MSN, Certificate); pediatric (Certificate); pediatric acute care (Certificate); MBA/MSN; MSN/MCM. *Accreditation:* AACN; AANA/CANAEP. Part-time programs available. Postbaccalaureate distance learning degree programs offered (minimal on-campus study). *Faculty:* 45 full-time (41 women), 169 part-time/adjunct (150 women). *Students:* 178 full-time (162 women), 140 part-time (132 women); includes 48 minority (17 African Americans, 3 American Indian/Alaska Native, 20 Asian Americans or Pacific Islanders, 8 Hispanic Americans). Average age 36. 99 applicants, 92% accepted, 91 enrolled. In 2006, 122 master's, 17 other advanced degrees awarded. *Median time to degree:* Master's–2 years full-time, 2.5 years part-time. *Degree requirements:* For master's, thesis optional. *Entrance requirements:* For master's, GRE General Test or MAT, 1 year of nursing experience, BSN, minimum GPA of 3.0, previous course work in statistics; for Certificate, MSN. Additional exam requirements/recommendations for international students: Required—TOEFL (minimum score 550 paper-based; 213 computer-based), Commission on Graduates of Foreign Nursing Schools exam. *Application deadline:* For fall admission, 7/2 priority date for domestic and international students; for spring admission, 11/15 priority date for domestic and international students. Applications are processed on a rolling basis. Application fee: $50. *Expenses: Contact institution. Financial support:* In 2006–07, 258 students received support. Career-related internships or fieldwork, institutionally sponsored loans, scholarships/grants, traineeships, and tuition waivers (partial) available. Support available to part-time students. Financial award application deadline: 4/1; financial award applicants required to submit FAFSA. *Faculty research:* Cardiovascular disease, caregiver skill training, data mining, prostate cancer, neonatal immune system. Total annual research expenditures: $3.5 million. *Unit head:* Dr. Catherine L. Gilliss, Dean/Vice Chancellor for Nursing Affairs, 919-684-9444, Fax: 919-684-9414, E-mail: gilli025@mc.duke.edu. *Application contact:* Bebe T. Mills, Director of Admissions, 919-684-9151, Fax: 919-668-4693, E-mail: mills031@mc.duke.edu.

Emory University, Nell Hodgson Woodruff School of Nursing, Atlanta, GA 30322-1100. Offers adult and elder health advanced practice nursing (MSN), including acute and critical care, adult nurse practitioner, gerontology, oncology; emergency nurse practitioner (MSN); family nurse practitioner (MSN); family nurse-midwife (MSN); leadership in healthcare (MSN); nurse midwifery (MSN); nursing administration (MSN); pediatric advanced nursing practice (MSN); public health nursing (MSN); women's health nurse practitioner (MSN); MSN/MPH. *Accreditation:* AACN; ACNM/DOA (one or more programs are accredited). Part-time programs available. *Entrance requirements:* For master's, GRE General Test or MAT, minimum GPA of 3.0, BS in nursing, RN license and additional course work, 3 letters of recommendation. Additional exam requirements/recommendations for international students: Required—TOEFL (minimum score 600 paper-based; 250 computer-based). Electronic applications accepted. Expenses: Contact institution. *Faculty research:* Older adult falls and injuries, minority health issues, cardiac symptoms amd quality of life, bio-ethics and decision making, menopausal issues.

See Close-Up on page 1955.

Gwynedd-Mercy College, School of Nursing, Gwynedd Valley, PA 19437-0901. Offers clinical nurse specialist (MSN), including gerontology, oncology, pediatrics; nurse practitioner (MSN), including adult health, pediatric health. *Accreditation:* NLN. *Faculty:* 5 full-time (all women), 3 part-time/adjunct (2 women). *Students:* 7 full-time (5 women), 38 part-time (35 women); includes 3 minority (1 African American, 1 Asian American or Pacific Islander, 1 Hispanic American). Average age 41. 18 applicants, 89% accepted, 11 enrolled. In 2006, 5 degrees awarded. *Degree requirements:* For master's, thesis optional. *Entrance requirements:* For master's, GRE General Test or MAT, 2 years of experience, physical assessment, course work in statistics, BSN from an NLNAC accredited program, 2 letters of recommendation, personal interview. Additional exam requirements/recommendations for international students: Required—TOEFL (minimum score 575 paper-based). *Application deadline:* For fall admission, 8/1 priority date for domestic students; for winter admission, 12/1 priority date for domestic students. Applications are processed on a rolling basis. Application fee: $25. Electronic applications accepted. *Expenses: Contact institution. Financial support:* In 2006–07, 21 students received support. Scholarships/grants, traineeships, and unspecified assistantships available. Financial award application deadline: 8/30. *Faculty research:* Critical thinking, primary care, domestic violence, multiculturalism, nursing centers. *Unit head:* Dr. Andrea D. Hollingsworth, Dean, 215-646-7300 Ext. 539, Fax: 215-641-5517, E-mail: hollingsworth.a@gmc.edu. *Application contact:* Dr. Barbara A. Jones, Director, 215-646-7300 Ext. 407, Fax: 215-641-5564, E-mail: jones.b@gmc.edu.

Loyola University Chicago, Graduate School, Marcella Niehoff School of Nursing, Oncology Clinical Nurse Specialist Program, Chicago, IL 60611-2196. Offers MSN. *Accreditation:* AACN. Part-time and evening/weekend programs available. Postbaccalaureate distance learning degree programs offered (no on-campus study). *Students:* Average age 29. *Degree requirements:* For master's, comprehensive exam or oral thesis defense. *Entrance requirements:* For master's, Illinois license, 3 letters of recommendation . *Application deadline:* Applications are processed on a rolling basis. Application fee: $40. Electronic applications accepted. *Financial support:* Teaching assistantships, traineeships and unspecified assistantships available. Financial award application deadline: 3/1. *Faculty research:* Breast cancer, coping with cancer, pain. *Unit head:* Dr. Patricia Friend, Assistant Professor, 708-216-9553, Fax: 708-216-9555, E-mail: pfriend@luc.edu. *Application contact:* Dr. Vicki A. Keough, Associate Professor, 708-216-3582, Fax: 708-216-9555, E-mail: vkeough@luc.edu.

University of Delaware, College of Health Sciences, School of Nursing, Newark, DE 19716. Offers adult nurse practitioner (MSN, PMC); cardiopulmonary clinical nurse specialist (MSN, PMC); cardiopulmonary clinical nurse specialist/adult nurse practitioner (MSN, PMC); family nurse practitioner (MSN, PMC); gerontology clinical nurse specialist (MSN, PMC); gerontology clinical nurse specialist geriatric nurse practitioner (PMC); gerontology clinical nurse specialist/geriatric nurse practitioner (MSN); health services administration (MSN, PMC); nursing of children clinical nurse specialist (MSN, PMC); nursing of children clinical nurse specialist/pediatric nurse practitioner (MSN, PMC); oncology/immune deficiency clinical nurse specialist (MSN, PMC); oncology/immune deficiency clinical nurse specialist/adult nurse practitioner (MSN, PMC); perinatal/women's health clinical nurse specialist (MSN, PMC); perinatal/women's health clinical nurse specialist/women's health nurse practitioner (MSN, PMC); psychiatric nursing clinical nurse specialist (MSN, PMC). *Accreditation:* AACN; NLN (one or more programs are accredited). Part-time and evening/weekend programs available. Postbaccalaureate distance learning degree programs offered (minimal on-campus study). *Degree requirements:* For master's, thesis optional. *Entrance requirements:* For master's, BSN, interview, RN license. Electronic applications accepted. *Faculty research:* Marriage and chronic illness, health promotion, congestive heart failure patient outcomes, school nursing, diabetes in children.

University of Pennsylvania, School of Nursing, Adult Oncology Nurse Practitioner Program, Philadelphia, PA 19104. Offers MSN. *Accreditation:* AACN. Part-time programs available. *Entrance requirements:* For master's, GRE General Test, BSN, minimum GPA of 3.0, previous course work in statistics. Additional exam requirements/recommendations for international students: Required—TOEFL. Expenses: Contact institution. *Faculty research:* Randomized clinical trials to evaluate advanced nursing practice in oncology patients and their caregivers, symptoms management.

University of Pennsylvania, School of Nursing, Pediatric Oncology Nurse Practitioner Program, Philadelphia, PA 19104. Offers MSN. *Accreditation:* AACN. *Entrance requirements:* For master's, GRE General Test, BSN, minimum GPA of 3.0, previous course work in statistics. Additional exam requirements/recommendations for international students: Required—TOEFL. Expenses: Contact institution.

Pediatric Nursing

Baylor University, Graduate School, Louise Herrington School of Nursing, Dallas, TX 75246. Offers family nurse practitioner (MSN); neonatal nurse practitioner (MSN); nursing administration and management (MSN). *Accreditation:* AACN. *Students:* 10 full-time (all women), 27 part-time (26 women); includes 6 minority (1 African American, 1 Asian American or Pacific Islander, 4 Hispanic Americans), 1 international. In 2006, 13 degrees awarded. *Entrance requirements:* For master's, GRE General Test. *Application deadline:* For fall admission, 8/1 for domestic students; for spring admission, 12/1 for domestic students. Applications are processed on a rolling basis. Application fee: $25. *Unit head:* Dr. Pauline Johnson, Graduate Program Director, 214-820-3361, Fax: 214-818-8692, E-mail: pauline_johnson@baylor.edu. *Application contact:* Suzanne Keener, Administrative Assistant, 254-710-3588, Fax: 254-710-3870.

Caribbean University, Graduate School, Bayamón, PR 00960-0493. Offers accounting (MBA); administration and supervision (MA Ed); criminal justice (MA); curriculum and instruction (MA Ed); education (PhD); gerontology (MSN); human resources (MBA); museology, archiving and art history (MA Ed); neonatal pediatrics (MSN); physical education (MA Ed); special education (MA Ed). *Entrance requirements:* For master's, interview, minimum GPA of 2.5.

Case Western Reserve University, Frances Payne Bolton School of Nursing, Doctor of Nursing Practice Program, Cleveland, OH 44106. Offers acute care nurse practitioner (DNP); adult nurse practitioner (DNP); family nurse practitioner (DNP); gerontological nurse practitioner (DNP); graduate entry/pre-licensure option (DNP); medical-surgical nursing (DNP); midwifery/family nursing (DNP); neonatal nurse practitioner (DNP); pediatric nurse practitioner (DNP); post-licensure option (DNP); psychiatric mental health nurse practitioner (DNP); women's health nurse practitioner (DNP). Graduate entry option allows baccalaureate-prepared college graduates from non-nursing backgrounds to earn certificate and MSN in addition to ND. *Students:* 125 full-time (109 women), 308 part-time (290 women); includes 47 minority (21 African Americans, 1 American Indian/Alaska Native, 18 Asian Americans or Pacific Islanders, 7 Hispanic Americans), 7 international. 190 applicants, 70% accepted, 80 enrolled. In 2006, 35 degrees awarded. Terminal master's awarded for partial completion of doctoral program. *Degree requirements:* For doctorate, thesis/dissertation. *Entrance requirements:* For doctorate, GRE General Test or MAT. *Application deadline:* For fall admission, 6/1 priority date for domestic students. Applications are processed on a rolling basis. Application fee: $75. *Financial support:* In 2006–07, 6 students received support, including 1 teaching assistantship; research assistantships, Federal Work-Study, institutionally sponsored loans, and tuition waivers (partial) also available. Support available to part-time students. Financial award application deadline: 6/30; financial award applicants required to submit FAFSA. *Faculty research:* Clinical nursing, acute care, gerontology, mental health, critical care. *Unit head:* Dr. Georgia Narsavage, Director, 216-368-6304, Fax: 216-368-3542, E-mail: gln2@cwru.edu. *Application contact:* Peter Taylor, Recruitment and Retention Specialist, 216-368-0349, Fax: 216-368-0124, E-mail: peter.taylor@case.edu.

Case Western Reserve University, Frances Payne Bolton School of Nursing, Master's Programs in Nursing, Nurse Practitioner Program, Cleveland, OH 44106. Offers acute care cardiovascular nursing (MSN); acute care nurse practitioner (MSN); acute care/flight nurse (MSN); adult nurse practitioner (MSN); family nurse practitioner (MSN); gerontological nurse practitioner (MSN); neonatal nurse practitioner (MSN); pediatric nurse practitioner (MSN); psychiatric-mental health nurse practitioner (MSN); women's health nurse practitioner (MSN). *Accreditation:* NLN. Part-time programs available. Postbaccalaureate distance learning degree programs offered (minimal on-campus study). *Faculty:* 54 full-time (50 women), 5 part-time/adjunct (3 women). *Students:* 19 full-time (15 women), 31 part-time (29 women); includes 16 minority (9 African Americans, 5 Asian Americans or Pacific Islanders, 2 Hispanic Americans), 2 international. Average age 35. 46 applicants, 72% accepted, 18 enrolled. In 2006, 34 degrees awarded. *Degree requirements:* For master's, thesis optional. *Entrance requirements:* For master's, GRE General Test or MAT. Additional exam requirements/recommendations for international students: Required—TOEFL. *Application deadline:* For fall admission, 6/1 for domestic students. Applications are processed on a rolling basis. Application fee: $75. *Financial support:* In 2006–07, 7 teaching assistantships were awarded; research assistantships, institutionally sponsored loans and tuition waivers (partial) also available. Support available to part-time students. Financial award application deadline: 6/30. *Faculty research:* Positive and negative mood states in parents of twins, effect of a carepath on chronic obstructive pulmonary disease home care. *Application contact:* Peter Taylor, Recruitment and Retention Specialist, 216-368-0349, Fax: 216-368-0124, E-mail: peter.taylor@case.edu.

The Catholic University of America, School of Nursing, Washington, DC 20064. Offers advanced practice nursing (MSN), including administration of nursing service, adult nurse practitioner, education, family nurse practitioner, geriatric nurse practitioner, pediatric nurse practitioner, psychiatric-mental health, school health nurse practitioner; clinical nursing (DN Sc). *Accreditation:* AACN; NLN. Part-time programs available. *Faculty:* 17 full-time (all women), 19 part-time/adjunct (18 women). *Students:* 27 full-time (25 women), 58 part-time (57 women); includes 31 minority (20 African Americans, 6 Asian Americans or Pacific Islanders, 5 Hispanic Americans), 6 international. Average age 43. 38 applicants, 76% accepted, 15 enrolled. In 2006, 15 master's, 7 doctorates awarded. *Degree requirements:* For master's, thesis optional; for doctorate, thesis/dissertation, comprehensive exam. *Entrance requirements:* For master's, GRE General Test or MAT, 3 letters of recommendation, BA in nursing, RN registration; for doctorate, GRE General Test, 3 letters of recommendation, BA in nursing, RN registration. Additional exam requirements/recommendations for international students: Required—TOEFL (minimum score 550 paper-based; 213 computer-based). *Application deadline:* For fall admission, 2/1 priority date for domestic students; for spring admission, 11/15 priority date for domestic students. Applications are processed on a rolling basis. Application fee: $55. Electronic applications accepted. *Expenses:* Tuition: Full-time $27,700; part-time $1,045 per credit hour. Required fees: $1,290. Part-time tuition and fees vary according to campus/location and program. *Financial support:* Research assistantships, teaching assistantships, career-related internships or fieldwork, Federal Work-Study, scholarships/grants, tuition waivers (full and partial), and unspecified assistantships available. Support available to part-time students. Financial award application deadline: 2/1; financial award applicants required to submit FAFSA. *Faculty research:* Outcome research–readmission of home health care patients with congestive heart failure, spirituality of chronic illness, minority multigravidos utilization of prenatal care. *Unit head:* Dr. Nalini Jairath, Dean, 202-319-5403, Fax: 202-319-6485, E-mail: jairath@cua.edu.

Columbia University, School of Nursing, Program in Pediatric Nurse Practitioner, New York, NY 10032. Offers MS, Adv C. *Accreditation:* AACN. Part-time programs available. *Faculty:* 1 (woman) full-time, 1 (woman) part-time/adjunct. *Students:* 12 full-time (all women), 38 part-time (37 women); includes 9 minority (4 African Americans, 3 Asian Americans or Pacific Islanders, 2 Hispanic Americans). Average age 30. In 2006, 18 master's, 1 other advanced degree awarded. *Entrance requirements:* For master's, GRE General Test, BSN, 1 year of clinical experience (preferred); for Adv C, MSN. *Application deadline:* Applications are processed on a rolling basis. Application fee: $65. Electronic applications accepted. *Financial support:* Teaching assistantships available. Financial award application deadline: 2/1; financial award applicants required to submit FAFSA. *Unit head:* Dr. Ritamarie John, Head, 212-305-5542.

Duke University, School of Nursing, Durham, NC 27708-0586. Offers adult acute care (Certificate); adult cardiovascular (Certificate); adult oncology/HIV (Certificate); adult primary care (Certificate); clinical nurse specialist (MSN), including adult oncology/HIV, gerontology, neonatal, pediatric, pediatric/chronic acute care; clinical research management (MSN, Certificate); family (Certificate); gerontology (Certificate); health and nursing ministries (MSN, Certificate); health systems leadership and outcomes (Certificate); leadership in community based long term care (MSN, Certificate); neonatal (Certificate); neonatal/pediatric in rural health (MSN, Certificate); nurse anesthetist (MSN, Certificate); nurse practitioner (MSN), including adult acute care, adult cardiovascular, adult oncology/HIV, adult primary care, family, gerontology, neonatal, pediatric, pediatric acute care; nursing (PhD); nursing and healthcare leadership (MSN); nursing education (MSN); nursing informatics (MSN, Certificate); pediatric (Certificate); pediatric acute care (Certificate); MBA/MSN; MSN/MCM. *Accreditation:* AACN; AANA/CANAEP. Part-time programs available. Postbaccalaureate distance learning degree programs offered (minimal on-campus study). *Faculty:* 45 full-time (41 women), 169 part-time/adjunct (150 women). *Students:* 178 full-time (162 women), 140 part-time (132 women); includes 48 minority (17 African Americans, 3 American Indian/Alaska Native, 20 Asian Americans or Pacific Islanders, 8 Hispanic Americans). Average age 36. 99 applicants, 92% accepted, 91 enrolled. In 2006, 122 master's, 17 other advanced degrees awarded. *Median time to degree:* Master's–2 years full-time, 2.5 years part-time. *Degree requirements:* For master's, thesis optional. *Entrance requirements:* For master's, GRE General Test or MAT, 1 year of nursing experience, BSN, minimum GPA of 3.0, previous course work in statistics; for Certificate, MSN. Additional exam requirements/recommendations for international students: Required—TOEFL (minimum score 550 paper-based; 213 computer-based), Commission on Graduates of Foreign Nursing Schools exam. *Application deadline:* For fall admission, 7/2 priority date for domestic and international students; for spring admission, 11/15 priority date for domestic and international students. Applications are processed on a rolling basis. Application fee: $50. *Expenses:* Contact institution. *Financial support:* In 2006–07, 258 students received support. Career-related internships or fieldwork, institutionally sponsored loans, scholarships/grants, traineeships, and tuition waivers (partial) available. Support available to part-time students. Financial award application deadline: 4/1; financial award applicants required to submit FAFSA. *Faculty research:* Cardiovascular disease, caregiver skill training, data mining, prostate cancer, neonatal immune system. Total annual research expenditures: $3.5 million. *Unit head:* Dr. Catherine L. Gilliss, Dean/Vice Chancellor for Nursing Affairs, 919-684-9444, Fax: 919-684-9414, E-mail: gilli025@mc.duke.edu. *Application contact:* Bebe T. Mills, Director of Admissions, 919-684-9151, Fax: 919-668-4693, E-mail: mills031@mc.duke.edu.

Emory University, Nell Hodgson Woodruff School of Nursing, Atlanta, GA 30322-1100. Offers adult and elder health advanced practice nursing (MSN), including acute and critical care, adult nurse practitioner, gerontology, oncology; emergency nurse practitioner (MSN); family nurse practitioner (MSN); family nurse-midwife (MSN); leadership in healthcare (MSN); nurse midwifery (MSN); nursing administration (MSN); pediatric advanced nursing practice (MSN); public health nursing (MSN); women's health nurse practitioner (MSN); MSN/MPH. *Accreditation:* AACN; ACNM/DOA (one or more programs are accredited). Part-time programs available. *Entrance requirements:* For master's, GRE General Test or MAT, minimum GPA of 3.0, BS in nursing, RN license and additional course work, 3 letters of recommendation. Additional exam requirements/recommendations for international students: Required—TOEFL (minimum score 600 paper-based; 250 computer-based). Electronic applications accepted. Expenses: Contact institution. *Faculty research:* Older adult falls and injuries, minority health issues, cardiac symptoms amd quality of life, bio-ethics and decision making, menopausal issues.

See Close-Up on page 1955.

Florida State University, Graduate Studies, College of Nursing, Tallahassee, FL 32306. Offers family nurse practitioner (MSN, Certificate); nurse educator (MSN, Certificate); pediatric nurse practitioner (MSN, Certificate). *Accreditation:* AACN. Part-time programs available. Postbaccalaureate distance learning degree programs offered (no on-campus study). *Faculty:* 10 full-time (9 women), 1 part-time/adjunct (0 women). *Students:* 10 full-time (all women), 75 part-time (69 women); includes 16 minority (10 African Americans, 2 Asian Americans or Pacific Islanders, 4 Hispanic Americans). Average age 39. 43 applicants, 81% accepted, 32 enrolled. In 2006, 13 master's, 9 other advanced degrees awarded. *Degree requirements:* For master's, Research Project (optional), thesis optional. *Entrance requirements:* For master's, GRE General Test, minimum GPA of 3.0, BSN, Florida RN license. Additional exam requirements/recommendations for international students: Required—TOEFL (minimum score 550 paper-based). *Application deadline:* For fall admission, 7/1 for domestic students; for spring admission, 10/15 for domestic students. Applications are processed on a rolling basis. Application fee: $30. Electronic applications accepted. *Expenses:* Tuition, state resident: full-time $5,822; part-time $243 per credit hour. Tuition, nonresident: full-time $20,976; part-time $874 per credit hour. Tuition and fees vary according to program. *Financial support:* In 2006–07, 25 students received support, including 1 fellowship with partial tuition reimbursement available (averaging $6,300 per year), 3 research assistantships with partial tuition reimbursements available (averaging $3,000 per year), 13 teaching assistantships with partial tuition reimbursements available (averaging $3,000 per year); career-related internships or fieldwork, Federal Work-Study, institutionally sponsored loans, traineeships, and tuition waivers (partial) also available. Financial award application deadline: 4/15; financial award applicants required to submit FAFSA. *Faculty research:* Distance learning, gerontology, health promotion, educational strategies, rehabilitation of brain injured patients. *Unit head:* Dr. Katherine P. Mason, Dean, 850-644-5417, Fax: 850-644-7660, E-mail: kmason@mailer.fsu.edu. *Application contact:* Eddie Page, Graduate Program Coordinator, 850-644-5638, Fax: 850-645-7321, E-mail: epage@fsu.edu.

Georgia State University, College of Health and Human Sciences, School of Nursing, Atlanta, GA 30303-3083. Offers adult health (MS); child health (MS); family nurse practitioner (MS); health promotion, protection and restoration (PhD); nursing (Certificate); perinatal/women's health (MS); psychiatric/mental health (MS). *Accreditation:* AACN. Part-time and evening/weekend programs available. *Faculty:* 35 full-time (all women), 1 (woman) part-time/adjunct. *Students:* 72 full-time (66 women), 128 part-time (123 women); includes 75 minority (61 African Americans, 9 Asian Americans or Pacific Islanders, 5 Hispanic Americans), 2 international. Average age 37. 70 applicants, 54% accepted, 30 enrolled. In 2006, 39 master's, 6 doctorates awarded. *Degree requirements:* For master's, research activity; for doctorate, thesis/dissertation, comprehensive exam. *Entrance requirements:* For master's, MAT (preferred) or GRE, interview, RN license; for doctorate, GRE General Test. Additional exam requirements/recommendations for international students: Required—TOEFL (minimum score 550 paper-based; 213 computer-based). *Application deadline:* For fall admission, 3/1 priority date for domestic students; for spring admission, 10/1 priority date for domestic students. Applications are processed on a rolling basis. Application fee: $50. Electronic applications accepted. *Expenses:* Contact institution. *Financial support:* In 2006–07, research assistantships with full and partial tuition reimbursements (averaging $3,108 per year); fellowships with full tuition reimbursements, teaching assistantships, Federal Work-Study, institutionally sponsored loans, scholarships/grants, traineeships, and tuition waivers (partial) also available. Support available to part-time students. Financial award application deadline: 4/1; financial award applicants required to submit FAFSA. *Faculty research:* Breast cancer prevention, sexually compulsive behaviors, health risks in minority youth, asthma treatment strategies, adolescent alcohol-related issues. Total annual research expenditures: $221,691. *Unit head:* Dr. Barbara Woodring, Director, 404-651-3040. *Application contact:* Barbara Smith, Admissions Counselor II, 404-651-3834, Fax: 404-651-4871, E-mail: bbsmith@gsu.edu.

Gwynedd-Mercy College, School of Nursing, Gwynedd Valley, PA 19437-0901. Offers clinical nurse specialist (MSN), including gerontology, oncology, pediatrics; nurse practitioner (MSN), including adult health, pediatric health. *Accreditation:* NLN. *Faculty:* 5 full-time (all women), 3 part-time/adjunct (2 women). *Students:* 7 full-time (5 women), 38 part-time (35 women); includes 3 minority (1 African American, 1 Asian American or Pacific Islander, 1 Hispanic American). Average age 41. 18 applicants, 89% accepted, 11 enrolled. In 2006, 5 degrees awarded. *Degree requirements:* For master's, thesis optional. *Entrance requirements:* For master's, GRE General Test or MAT, 2 years of experience, physical assessment, course work in statistics, BSN from an NLNAC accredited program, 2 letters of recommendation, personal interview. Additional exam requirements/recommendations for international students: Required—TOEFL (minimum score 575 paper-based). *Application deadline:* For fall admission, 8/1 priority date for domestic students; for winter admission, 12/1 priority date for domestic students. Applications are processed on a rolling basis. Application fee: $25. Electronic applica-

Pediatric Nursing

Gwynedd-Mercy College (continued)
tions accepted. *Expenses:* Contact institution. *Financial support:* In 2006–07, 21 students received support. Scholarships/grants, traineeships, and unspecified assistantships available. Financial award application deadline: 8/30. *Faculty research:* Critical thinking, primary care, domestic violence, multiculturalism, nursing centers. *Unit head:* Dr. Andrea D. Hollingsworth, Dean, 215-646-7300 Ext. 539, Fax: 215-641-5517, E-mail: hollingsworth.a@gmc.edu. *Application contact:* Dr. Barbara A. Jones, Director, 215-646-7300 Ext. 407, Fax: 215-641-5564, E-mail: jones.b@gmc.edu.

Hunter College of the City University of New York, Graduate School, Schools of the Health Professions, Hunter-Bellevue School of Nursing, Pediatric Nurse Practitioner Program, New York, NY 10021-5085. Offers MS, AC. *Accreditation:* AACN. Part-time programs available. *Faculty:* 24 full-time (21 women), 21 part-time/adjunct (19 women). *Students:* Average age 35. 1 applicant, 100% accepted, 1 enrolled. In 2006, 5 master's, 1 AC awarded. *Degree requirements:* For master's, practicum. *Entrance requirements:* For master's, 2 years of professional practice experience, BSN, minimum GPA of 3.0, New York RN license; for AC, MSN, minimum GPA of 3.0. Additional exam requirements/recommendations for international students: Required—TOEFL. *Application deadline:* For fall admission, 4/1 for domestic students, 2/1 for international students; for spring admission, 11/1 for domestic students, 9/1 for international students. Applications are processed on a rolling basis. Application fee: $125. *Expenses:* Tuition, state resident: part-time $270 per credit. Tuition, nonresident: part-time $500 per credit. Required fees: $45 per semester. *Financial support:* Federal Work-Study, scholarships/grants, traineeships, and tuition waivers (partial) available. Support available to part-time students. Financial award application deadline: 5/1; financial award applicants required to submit FAFSA. *Faculty research:* Primary care: infants, children, and adolescents. *Unit head:* Dr. Janet N. Natapoff, Coordinator, 212-481-5070, Fax: 212-481-5078, E-mail: jnatapof@hejira.hunter.cuny.edu. *Application contact:* William Zlata, Director for Graduate Admissions, 212-772-4482, Fax: 212-650-3336, E-mail: admissions@hunter.cuny.edu.

Indiana University–Purdue University Indianapolis, School of Nursing, Indianapolis, IN 46202-2896. Offers acute care nurse practitioner (MSN); adult health clinical nurse specialist (MSN); adult health nursing (MSN), including adult clinical nurse specialist; adult nurse practitioner (MSN); adult psychiatric/mental health nursing (MSN); child psychiatric/mental health nursing (MSN); community health nursing (MSN); family nurse practitioner (MSN); neonatal nurse practitioner (MSN); nursing science (PhD); pediatric clinical nurse specialist (MSN); women's health nurse practitioner (MSN); MSN/MPA; MSN/MPH. *Accreditation:* AACN; NLN (one or more programs are accredited). Part-time programs available. *Faculty:* 45 full-time (44 women), 1 (woman) part-time/adjunct. *Students:* 52 full-time (51 women), 415 part-time (396 women); includes 27 minority (16 African Americans, 3 Asian Americans or Pacific Islanders, 8 Hispanic Americans), 4 international. Average age 38. In 2006, 106 master's, 3 doctorates awarded. Terminal master's awarded for partial completion of doctoral program. *Degree requirements:* For master's and doctorate, thesis/dissertation. *Entrance requirements:* For master's, GRE General Test, minimum GPA of 3.0, RN license; for doctorate, GRE General Test, minimum GPA of 3.5, MSN, RN license. Additional exam requirements/recommendations for international students: Required—TOEFL. *Application deadline:* For fall admission, 2/15 for domestic students; for spring admission, 9/15 for domestic students. Application fee: $50 ($60 for international students). *Expenses:* Tuition, state resident: full-time $5,437; part-time $227 per credit hour. Tuition, nonresident: full-time $15,694; part-time $654 per credit hour. Required fees: $620. Tuition and fees vary according to course load, campus/location and program. *Financial support:* In 2006–07, 93 students received support; fellowships with full tuition reimbursements available, research assistantships with full tuition reimbursements available, teaching assistantships with full tuition reimbursements available, Federal Work-Study, institutionally sponsored loans, scholarships/grants, and tuition waivers (full) available. Support available to part-time students. Financial award application deadline: 5/1. *Faculty research:* Chronic illness, cancer, health services research, family health. Total annual research expenditures: $3 million. *Unit head:* Associate Dean for Graduate Programs, 317-274-2806, E-mail: nursing@iupui.edu. *Application contact:* Martez Plummer, Assistant Dean for Student Affairs, 317-274-2806, E-mail: mplummer@iupui.edu.

The Johns Hopkins University, School of Nursing, Nurse Practitioner Program, Baltimore, MD 21218-2699. Offers adult acute/critical care (MSN, Certificate); adult and pediatric primary care (MSN); adult or pediatric primary care (Certificate); family primary care (MSN, Certificate). *Accreditation:* AACN; NLN (one or more programs are accredited). Part-time programs available. *Faculty:* 12 full-time (all women), 6 part-time/adjunct (5 women). *Students:* 23 full-time (22 women), 62 part-time (58 women); includes 26 minority (3 African Americans, 3 American Indian/Alaska Native, 15 Asian Americans or Pacific Islanders, 5 Hispanic Americans), 1 international. Average age 31. 157 applicants, 85% accepted, 32 enrolled. In 2006, 18 master's, 2 other advanced degrees awarded. *Degree requirements:* For master's, scholarly project or portfolio, thesis optional. *Entrance requirements:* For master's, GRE, interview, minimum GPA of 3.0, BSN, Maryland RN license. Additional exam requirements/recommendations for international students: Required—TOEFL (minimum score 550 paper-based; 230 computer-based). *Application deadline:* For fall admission, 3/1 priority date for domestic and international students; for spring admission, 7/1 priority date for domestic and international students. Application fee: $75. *Expenses:* Contact institution. Tuition and fees vary according to degree level and program. *Financial support:* In 2006–07, 16 students received support. Federal Work-Study, scholarships/grants, traineeships, and tuition waivers (partial) available. Support available to part-time students. Financial award application deadline: 3/1; financial award applicants required to submit FAFSA. *Faculty research:* Community outreach, primary care of underserved populations, substance abusing individuals, childhood violence, women's health. *Unit head:* Dr. Kathleen M. White, Director, Master's Programs, 410-614-4664, Fax: 410-955-7463, E-mail: kwhite@son.jhmi.edu. *Application contact:* Mary O'Rourke, Director of Admissions/Student Services, 410-955-7548, Fax: 410-614-7086, E-mail: orourke@son.jhmi.edu.

Kent State University, College of Nursing, Kent, OH 44242-0001. Offers clinical nursing (MSN), including nursing of the adult (medical/surgical nursing), psychiatric mental health nursing; nursing (PhD); nursing administration (MSN); nursing education (MSN); parent-child nursing (MSN). *Accreditation:* AACN. Part-time programs available. *Degree requirements:* For master's, thesis optional; for doctorate, thesis/dissertation, comprehensive exam, registration. *Entrance requirements:* For master's, GRE if undergraduate GPA is less than 3.0, minimum GPA of 2.75; for doctorate, GRE, MSN. Additional exam requirements/recommendations for international students: Required—TOEFL. Electronic applications accepted. Expenses: Contact institution. *Faculty research:* Women and violence, methodological specialties, osteoporosis in women, new caregivers and the elderly.

Lehman College of the City University of New York, Division of Natural and Social Sciences, Department of Nursing, Bronx, NY 10468-1589. Offers adult health nursing (MS); nursing of older adults (MS); parent-child nursing (MS); pediatric nurse practitioner (MS). *Accreditation:* AACN. Part-time and evening/weekend programs available. *Entrance requirements:* For master's, bachelor's degree in nursing, New York RN license.

Loma Linda University, Department of Graduate Nursing, Program in Growing Family Nursing, Loma Linda, CA 92350. Offers MS. *Accreditation:* AACN. Part-time programs available. *Degree requirements:* For master's, thesis or alternative. *Entrance requirements:* For master's, GRE General Test. *Faculty research:* Family coping in chronic illness; women, identity, and career/family issues.

Louisiana State University Health Sciences Center, School of Nursing, New Orleans, LA 70112-2223. Offers adult health and illness (MN); adult health and nursing (DNS); neonatal nurse practitioner (MN); nursing (MN); nursing service administration (MN, DNS); parent-child health nursing (MN); primary care nurse practitioner (MN); psychiatric/community mental health nursing (MN, DNS); public health/community health nursing (MN, DNS). *Accreditation:* AACN; AANA/CANAEP (one or more programs are accredited). Part-time programs available. *Degree requirements:* For master's, thesis optional; for doctorate, thesis/dissertation. *Entrance requirements:* For master's, GRE General Test, MAT, minimum GPA of 3.0; for doctorate, GRE General Test, minimum GPA of 3.5. Additional exam requirements/recommendations for international students: Required—TOEFL. *Expenses:* Tuition, state resident: full-time $5,868; part-time $722 per credit. Tuition, nonresident: full-time $8,993; part-time $1,104 per credit. *Faculty research:* Advanced clinical practice, nursing education, health, social support, nursing administration.

Marquette University, Graduate School, College of Nursing, Milwaukee, WI 53201-1881. Offers adult nurse practitioner (Certificate); advanced practice nursing (MSN), including adult, children, neonatal nurse practitioner, nurse-midwifery, older adult; gerontological nurse practitioner (Certificate); neonatal nurse practitioner (Certificate); nurse-midwifery (Certificate); nursing (PhD); pediatric nurse practitioner (Certificate). *Accreditation:* AACN. Part-time and evening/weekend programs available. *Faculty:* 29 full-time (27 women), 39 part-time/adjunct (37 women). *Students:* 104 full-time (98 women), 122 part-time (114 women); includes 18 minority (5 African Americans, 2 American Indian/Alaska Native, 4 Asian Americans or Pacific Islanders, 7 Hispanic Americans), 2 international. Average age 34. 122 applicants, 79% accepted, 73 enrolled. In 2006, 46 degrees awarded. *Degree requirements:* For master's, thesis or alternative, comprehensive exam. *Entrance requirements:* For master's, GRE General Test, BSN, Wisconsin RN license. Additional exam requirements/recommendations for international students: Required—TOEFL. Application fee: $40. *Financial support:* In 2006–07, 6 research assistantships, 1 teaching assistantship were awarded; career-related internships or fieldwork, Federal Work-Study, institutionally sponsored loans, scholarships/grants, and tuition waivers (full and partial) also available. Support available to part-time students. Financial award application deadline: 2/15. *Faculty research:* Psychosocial adjustment to chronic illness, gerontology, reminiscence, health policy: uninsured and access, hospital care delivery systems. Total annual research expenditures: $1.1 million. *Unit head:* Dr. Lea Acord, Dean, 414-288-3812, Fax: 414-288-1578. *Application contact:* Dr. Judy Miller, Director of Graduate Studies, 414-288-3810, Fax: 414-288-1578.

MGH Institute of Health Professions, Graduate Programs, Program in Nursing, Boston, MA 02129. Offers advanced practice nursing (MSN); gerontological nursing (MSN); pediatric nursing (MSN); psychiatric nursing (MSN); teaching and learning for health care education (Certificate); women's health nursing (MSN). *Accreditation:* NLN (one or more programs are accredited). *Faculty:* 29 full-time (28 women), 9 part-time/adjunct (7 women). *Students:* 208 full-time (188 women), 43 part-time (35 women); includes 36 minority (12 African Americans, 17 Asian Americans or Pacific Islanders, 7 Hispanic Americans), 1 international. Average age 29. 302 applicants, 62% accepted, 101 enrolled. In 2006, 77 master's, 3 other advanced degrees awarded. *Degree requirements:* For master's, thesis or alternative. *Entrance requirements:* For master's, GRE General Test, minimum GPA of 3.0. Additional exam requirements/recommendations for international students: Required—TOEFL (minimum score 550 paper-based; 213 computer-based). *Application deadline:* For fall admission, 1/10 for domestic and international students. Application fee: $50. Electronic applications accepted. *Financial support:* In 2006–07, 212 students received support, including 1 research assistantship (averaging $1,200 per year), 2 teaching assistantships (averaging $1,200 per year); career-related internships or fieldwork, scholarships/grants, traineeships, tuition waivers (full and partial), and unspecified assistantships also available. Support available to part-time students. Financial award application deadline: 3/3; financial award applicants required to submit FAFSA. *Faculty research:* Biobehavioral nursing, HIV/AIDS, gerontological nursing, women's health, vulnerable populations, health systems . *Unit head:* Margery Chisholm, Director, 617-724-0480, Fax: 617-726-8022, E-mail: mchisholm@mghihp.edu. *Application contact:* Maureen Rika Judd, Manager of Admissions, 617-726-6069, Fax: 617-726-8010, E-mail: admissions@mghihp.edu.

See Close-Up on page 1963.

Molloy College, Department of Nursing, Rockville Centre, NY 11571-5002. Offers adult nurse practitioner (Advanced Certificate); clinical nurse specialist: adult health (Advanced Certificate); family nurse practitioner (Advanced Certificate); nurse practitioner psychiatry (Advanced Certificate); nursing (MS); nursing administration (Advanced Certificate); nursing administration with informatics (Advanced Certificate); nursing education (Advanced Certificate); nursing informatics (Advanced Certificate); pediatric nurse practitioner (Advanced Certificate). *Accreditation:* AACN. Part-time and evening/weekend programs available. *Degree requirements:* For master's, thesis optional. *Entrance requirements:* For master's, 3 letters of reference, BS in nursing, minimum undergraduate GPA of 3.0; for Advanced Certificate, 3 letters of reference, master's degree in nursing. *Faculty research:* Hardiness and aging, alcoholism, current ethics, breast cancer, nurse role perception.

New York University, College of Dentistry, College of Nursing, Programs in Advanced Practice Nursing, New York, NY 10012-1019. Offers advanced practice nursing: adult acute care (MS, Advanced Certificate); advanced practice nursing: adult primary care (MS, Advanced Certificate); advanced practice nursing: adult primary care/geriatrics (MS); advanced practice nursing: children with special needs (Advanced Certificate); advanced practice nursing: geriatrics (MS, Advanced Certificate); advanced practice nursing: holistic nursing (MS, Advanced Certificate); advanced practice nursing: home health nursing (Advanced Certificate); advanced practice nursing: mental health (MS); advanced practice nursing: mental health nursing (Advanced Certificate); advanced practice nursing: pediatrics (MS, Advanced Certificate); advanced practice nursing: pediatrics/children with special needs (MS); midwifery (MS, Advanced Certificate); nursing administration (MS, Advanced Certificate); nursing education (MS, Advanced Certificate); nursing informatics (MS, Advanced Certificate); palliative care (MS, Advanced Certificate); MS/MS. *Accreditation:* AACN; ACNM/DOA. Part-time and evening/weekend programs available. *Faculty:* 30 full-time (all women). *Students:* 10 full-time (all women), 428 part-time (395 women); includes 166 minority (73 African Americans, 72 Asian Americans or Pacific Islanders, 21 Hispanic Americans). Average age 35. 154 applicants, 93% accepted, 118 enrolled. In 2006, 100 master's, 7 Advanced Certificates awarded. *Degree requirements:* For master's, thesis (for some programs). *Entrance requirements:* For master's, BS in nursing, AS in nursing with another BS/BA degree; for Advanced Certificate, master's degree. Additional exam requirements/recommendations for international students: Required—TOEFL. *Application deadline:* For fall admission, 7/1 priority date for domestic students, 7/1 for international students; for spring admission, 12/1 for domestic and international students. Applications are processed on a rolling basis. Application fee: $65. *Expenses:* Tuition: Part-time $1,080 per unit. Required fees: $56 per unit. $329 per term. Tuition and fees vary according to program. *Financial support:* Career-related internships or fieldwork, Federal Work-Study, institutionally sponsored loans, scholarships/grants, and tuition waivers (partial) available. Support available to part-time students. Financial award application deadline: 2/1; financial award applicants required to submit FAFSA. *Faculty research:* Elderly black diabetics, families and illness, public health nursing, parent-child nursing, health policy issues. *Unit head:* Dr. Judith Haber, Associate Dean for Graduate Programs, 212-998-5300, Fax: 212-995-3143. *Application contact:* Amy Knowles, Assistant Dean for Student Affairs and Admissions, 212-998-5333, Fax: 212-995-4302, E-mail: ak96@nyu.edu.

Northeastern University, Bouvé College of Health Sciences Graduate School, School of Nursing, Program in Critical Care-Neonatal Nurse Practitioner, Boston, MA 02115-5096. Offers MS, CAS. *Accreditation:* AACN. *Students:* 11 full-time (10 women), 10 part-time (9 women). Average age 37. In 2006, 9 degrees awarded. *Degree requirements:* For master's, thesis or alternative. *Entrance requirements:* For master's, GRE General Test, minimum GPA of 3.0, previous course work in statistics, 1-2 years of nursing experience, RN license, ICU experience. Additional exam requirements/recommendations for international students: Required—TOEFL. *Application deadline:* For fall admission, 4/1 priority date for domestic students; for spring admission, 2/1 for domestic students. Applications are processed on a rolling basis. Application fee: $50. *Financial support:* Research assistantships, teaching assistantships, tuition waivers (partial) available. Financial award application deadline: 7/1; financial award applicants required to submit FAFSA. *Faculty research:* Critical thinking and diagnostic reasoning, clinical outcomes of acute and critical health problems. *Unit head:* Dr. Elizabeth

Howard, Director, 617-373-4590, Fax: 617-373-8672, E-mail: e.howard@neu.edu. *Application contact:* Margaret Schnabel, Director of Graduate Admissions, 617-373-2708, Fax: 617-373-4704, E-mail: bouvegrad@neu.edu.

Oregon Health & Science University, School of Nursing, Program in Primary Health Care, Portland, OR 97239-3098. Offers adult nurse practitioner (MS, Post Master's Certificate); family nurse practitioner (MS, Post Master's Certificate); geriatric nurse practitioner (Post Master's Certificate); geriatric/adult nurse practitioner (MS); pediatric nurse practitioner (MS, Post Master's Certificate). *Accreditation:* AACN. *Degree requirements:* For master's, thesis optional. *Entrance requirements:* For master's, GRE General Test, bachelor's degree in nursing, minimum undergraduate GPA of 3.0, previous course work in statistics; for Post Master's Certificate, master's degree in nursing.

Rush University, College of Nursing, Department of Women's and Children's Health Nursing, Chicago, IL 60612-3832. Offers neonatal nurse practitioner (MSN, Post-Master's Certificate); pediatric acute/chronic care nurse practitioner (MSN); pediatric clinical nurse specialist (MSN); pediatric nurse practitioner (MSN, Post-Master's Certificate); women's and children's health nursing (DN Sc, DNP). *Accreditation:* AACN. Part-time programs available. Postbaccalaureate distance learning degree programs offered (minimal on-campus study). *Faculty:* 14. *Students:* 10 full-time, 75 part-time; includes 9 minority (3 African Americans, 4 Asian Americans or Pacific Islanders, 2 Hispanic Americans). Average age 35. 32 applicants, 94% accepted, 28 enrolled. In 2006, 14 master's, 5 doctorates awarded. Terminal master's awarded for partial completion of doctoral program. *Degree requirements:* For master's, capstone project; for doctorate, thesis/dissertation, DNP leadership project. *Entrance requirements:* For master's, GRE General Test (waived if nursing GPA is above 3.0 or cumulative GPA is above 3.25), interview; for doctorate, GRE General Test, interview, course work in statistics (DN Sc). Additional exam requirements/recommendations for international students: Required—TOEFL, TWE. *Application deadline:* For fall admission, 7/1 for domestic students; for winter admission, 11/1 for domestic students; for spring admission, 1/15 for domestic students. Applications are processed on a rolling basis. Application fee: $40. Electronic applications accepted. *Financial support:* In 2006–07, 16 students received support; teaching assistantships with tuition reimbursements available, Federal Work-Study, institutionally sponsored loans, scholarships/grants, and traineeships available. Support available to part-time students. Financial award applicants required to submit FAFSA. *Faculty research:* Family-centered care, women's health, health outcomes of human milk feeding for VhBW infants. *Unit head:* Dr. Deborah Gross, Chairperson, 312-942-7117. *Application contact:* Hicela Castruita Woods, Director, College Admissions Services, 312-942-7100, Fax: 312-942-2219, E-mail: hicela_castruita@rush.edu.

Seton Hall University, College of Nursing, Department of Graduate Nursing, Advanced Practice in Primary Health Care Program, South Orange, NJ 07079-2697. Offers adult nurse practitioner (MSN); gerontological nurse practitioner (MSN); pediatric nurse practitioner (MSN); women's health nurse practitioner (MSN). *Accreditation:* AACN. Part-time programs available. *Degree requirements:* For master's, research project. *Entrance requirements:* For master's, GRE or MAT, BSN. *Faculty research:* Health promotion in well aged, practice outcomes, collaborative practice.

Spalding University, Graduate Studies, College of Health and Natural Sciences, School of Nursing, Louisville, KY 40203-2188. Offers adult nurse practitioner (MSN); family nurse practitioner (MSN); leadership in nursing and healthcare (MSN); pediatric nurse practitioner (MSN). *Accreditation:* AACN. Part-time and evening/weekend programs available. *Degree requirements:* For master's, thesis, comprehensive exam (for some programs). *Entrance requirements:* For master's, GRE General Test, BSN or bachelor's degree and RN licensure. *Faculty research:* Nurse educational administration, gerontology, bioterrorism, healthcare ethics, leadership.

Stony Brook University, State University of New York, Stony Brook University Medical Center, Health Sciences Center, School of Nursing, Program in Child Health Nursing, Stony Brook, NY 11794. Offers child health nurse practitioner (Certificate); child health nursing (MS). *Accreditation:* AACN. *Students:* 9 full-time (all women), 24 part-time (22 women); includes 1 Asian American or Pacific Islander. In 2006, 15 master's, 1 other advanced degree awarded. *Degree requirements:* For master's, thesis. *Entrance requirements:* For master's, BSN, minimum GPA of 3.0, course work in statistics. *Application deadline:* For fall admission, 1/15 for domestic students. Application fee: $60. *Expenses:* Tuition, state resident: full-time $6,900; part-time $288 per credit. Tuition, nonresident: full-time $10,920; part-time $455 per credit. *Financial support:* Application deadline: 3/15. *Unit head:* Dr. Debra Sansoucie, Chair, 631-444-3298, Fax: 631-444-3136, E-mail: debra.sansoucie@stonybrook.edu.

Texas Tech University Health Sciences Center, School of Nursing, Lubbock, TX 79430. Offers acute care nurse practitioner (MSN, Certificate); administration (MSN); clinical research management (MSN, Certificate); education (MSN); family nurse practitioner (MSN, Certificate); geriatric nurse practitioner (MSN, Certificate); pediatric nurse practitioner (MSN, Certificate). *Accreditation:* AACN. Part-time programs available. Postbaccalaureate distance learning degree programs offered (minimal on-campus study). *Faculty:* 17 full-time (16 women), 5 part-time/adjunct (all women). *Students:* 23 full-time (22 women), 161 part-time (137 women); includes 46 minority (8 African Americans, 2 American Indian/Alaska Native, 6 Asian Americans or Pacific Islanders, 30 Hispanic Americans). Average age 37. 97 applicants, 69% accepted, 67 enrolled. In 2006, 41 degrees awarded. *Degree requirements:* For master's, thesis optional. *Entrance requirements:* For master's, minimum GPA of 3.0, 3 letters of reference, BSN, RN license; for Certificate, minimum GPA of 3.0, 3 letters of reference, RN license. Additional exam requirements/recommendations for international students: Required—TOEFL (minimum score 550 paper-based; 213 computer-based). *Application deadline:* For fall admission, 7/15 priority date for domestic and international students; for spring admission, 11/15 priority date for domestic and international students. Applications are processed on a rolling basis. Application fee: $40. *Financial support:* In 2006–07, 184 students received support. Institutionally sponsored loans, scholarships/grants, and traineeships available. Support available to part-time students. Financial award application deadline: 12/1; financial award applicants required to submit FAFSA. *Faculty research:* Diabetes/obesity, nurse competency, disease management, intervention and measurements, health disparities. Total annual research expenditures: $2.4 million. *Unit head:* Dr. Barbara A. Johnston, Associate Dean for Administrative and Student Affairs, 806-743-3055, Fax: 806-743-1622, E-mail: barbara.johnston@ttuhsc.edu. *Application contact:* Lauren K. Sullivan, Recruiter/Transcultural Coordinator, 806-743-2730 Ext. 309, Fax: 806-743-1622, E-mail: lauren.sullivan@ttuhsc.edu.

University at Buffalo, the State University of New York, Graduate School, School of Nursing, Buffalo, NY 14260. Offers acute care nurse practitioner (MS, Certificate); adult health nursing (MS, Certificate); child health nursing (MS); family nurse practitioner (Certificate); family nursing (MS); geriatric nurse practitioner (MS, Certificate); maternal and women's health nurse practitioner (Certificate); maternal and women's health nursing (MS); nurse anesthetist (MS); nursing (PhD); nursing education (Certificate); pediatric nurse practitioner (Certificate); psychiatric/mental health nurse practitioner (Certificate); psychiatric/mental health nursing (MS). *Accreditation:* AACN; AANA/CANAEP (one or more programs are accredited). Part-time programs available. Postbaccalaureate distance learning degree programs offered. *Faculty:* 38 full-time (34 women), 15 part-time/adjunct (14 women). *Students:* 131 full-time (108 women), 64 part-time (61 women); includes 29 minority (11 African Americans, 9 Asian Americans or Pacific Islanders, 9 Hispanic Americans), 20 international. Average age 28. 346 applicants, 25% accepted, 51 enrolled. In 2006, 49 master's, 3 doctorates, 6 other advanced degrees awarded. Terminal master's awarded for partial completion of doctoral program. *Degree requirements:* For master's, comprehensive exams or project; for doctorate, thesis/dissertation, comprehensive exam. *Entrance requirements:* For master's, GRE General Test (if overall GPA is below 3.0), interview, minimum GPA of 3.0, RN license, 3 references; for doctorate, GRE General Test, minimum GPA of 3.25, RN license, BS or MS in nursing, 3 references, writing sample; for Certificate, interview, minimum GPA of 3.0 or GRE General Test, RN license, MS in nursing. Additional exam requirements/recommendations for international students: Required—TOEFL (minimum score 550 paper-based; 213 computer-based; 79 iBT), IELTS (minimum score 7). *Application deadline:* For fall admission, 6/1 priority date for domestic students, 3/1 priority date for international students; for spring admission, 11/1 for domestic students, 9/15 priority date for international students. Applications are processed on a rolling basis. Application fee: $50. Electronic applications accepted. *Financial support:* In 2006–07, 78 students received support, including 13 fellowships with full tuition reimbursements available (averaging $7,220 per year), 10 research assistantships with tuition reimbursements available (averaging $17,881 per year), 23 teaching assistantships with full tuition reimbursements available (averaging $11,245 per year); Federal Work-Study, scholarships/grants, traineeships, health care benefits, and unspecified assistantships also available. Financial award application deadline: 3/15; financial award applicants required to submit FAFSA. *Faculty research:* Oncology symptom management, end of life decision making, changing behaviors using the transtheoretical model, addictions, nursing workforce. Total annual research expenditures: $1.7 million. *Unit head:* Dr. Jean K. Brown, Dean, Interim, 716-829-2533, Fax: 716-829-2566, E-mail: jebrown@buffalo.edu. *Application contact:* Dr. Elaine R. Cusker, Assistant Dean, 716-829-2537, Fax: 716-829-2021, E-mail: ecusker@buffalo.edu.

University of Central Florida, College of Health and Public Affairs, College of Nursing, Orlando, FL 32816. Offers adult practitioner (Post-Master's Certificate); family practitioner (Post-Master's Certificate); nursing (DNP, PhD); nursing education (Post-Master's Certificate); pediatric practitioner (Post-Master's Certificate). *Accreditation:* AACN. Part-time and evening/weekend programs available. *Faculty:* 35 full-time (32 women), 28 part-time/adjunct (25 women). *Students:* 84 full-time (75 women), 167 part-time (154 women); includes 41 minority (11 African Americans, 1 American Indian/Alaska Native, 8 Asian Americans or Pacific Islanders, 21 Hispanic Americans), 2 international. Average age 38. In 2006, 30 Post-Master's Certificates awarded. *Entrance requirements:* Additional exam requirements/recommendations for international students: Required—TOEFL. *Application deadline:* For fall admission, 2/15 for domestic students; for spring admission, 9/15 for domestic students. Application fee: $30. Electronic applications accepted. *Expenses:* Tuition, state resident: full-time $6,167; part-time $257 per credit hour. Tuition, nonresident: full-time $22,790; part-time $950 per credit hour. *Financial support:* In 2006–07, 35 fellowships with partial tuition reimbursements (averaging $1,550 per year), 9 research assistantships with partial tuition reimbursements (averaging $4,500 per year), 3 teaching assistantships with partial tuition reimbursements (averaging $15,400 per year) were awarded; career-related internships or fieldwork, Federal Work-Study, institutionally sponsored loans, traineeships, and unspecified assistantships also available. Financial award application deadline: 3/1; financial award applicants required to submit FAFSA. *Unit head:* Dr. Jean D. Leuner, Dean, College of Nursing, 407-823-5496, Fax: 407-823-5675, E-mail: jleuner@mail.ucf.edu.

University of Cincinnati, Graduate School, College of Nursing, Cincinnati, OH 45221-0038. Offers clinical nurse specialist (MSN), including adult health, community health, neonatal, nursing administration, occupational health, pediatric health, psychiatric nursing, women's health; nurse anesthesia (MSN); nurse midwifery (MSN); nurse practitioner (MSN), including acute care, ambulatory care, family, family/psychiatric, women's health; nursing (PhD); MBA/MSN. *Accreditation:* AACN; AANA/CANAEP (one or more programs are accredited); ACNM/DOA. Part-time programs available. Postbaccalaureate distance learning degree programs offered (no on-campus study). *Faculty:* 41 full-time (39 women), 16 part-time/adjunct (15 women). *Students:* 159 full-time (125 women), 149 part-time (145 women); includes 40 minority (22 African Americans, 1 American Indian/Alaska Native, 16 Asian Americans or Pacific Islanders, 1 Hispanic American). Average age 34. 385 applicants, 49% accepted, 132 enrolled. In 2006, 77 master's, 5 doctorates awarded. Terminal master's awarded for partial completion of doctoral program. *Median time to degree:* Of those who began their doctoral program in fall 1998, 55% received their degree in 8 years or less. *Degree requirements:* For master's, thesis or alternative, registration; for doctorate, thesis/dissertation, comprehensive exam, registration. *Entrance requirements:* For master's and doctorate, GRE General Test. Additional exam requirements/recommendations for international students: Required—TOEFL (minimum score 520 paper-based; 190 computer-based). *Application deadline:* For fall admission, 7/26 priority date for domestic and international students. Applications are processed on a rolling basis. Application fee: $40. Electronic applications accepted. *Financial support:* In 2006–07, 164 students received support, including 7 fellowships with full tuition reimbursements available (averaging $13,571 per year), research assistantships with full tuition reimbursements available (averaging $12,000 per year), 8 teaching assistantships with full tuition reimbursements available (averaging $12,000 per year); career-related internships or fieldwork, scholarships/grants, traineeships, tuition waivers (partial), and unspecified assistantships also available. Support available to part-time students. Financial award application deadline: 5/1; financial award applicants required to submit FAFSA. *Faculty research:* Substance abuse, injury and violence, symptom management. Total annual research expenditures: $1.3 million. *Unit head:* Dr. Andrea R. Lindell, Dean, 513-558-5330, Fax: 513-558-9030, E-mail: andrea.lindell@uc.edu. *Application contact:* Loren Carter, Program Coordinator, 513-558-5072, Fax: 513-558-7523, E-mail: loren.carter@uc.edu.

University of Delaware, College of Health Sciences, School of Nursing, Newark, DE 19716. Offers adult nurse practitioner (MSN, PMC); cardiopulmonary clinical nurse specialist (MSN, PMC); cardiopulmonary clinical nurse specialist/adult nurse practitioner (MSN, PMC); family nurse practitioner (MSN, PMC); gerontology clinical nurse specialist (MSN, PMC); gerontology clinical nurse specialist geriatric nurse practitioner (PMC); gerontology clinical nurse specialist/geriatric nurse practitioner (MSN); health services administration (MSN, PMC); nursing of children clinical nurse specialist (MSN, PMC); nursing of children clinical nurse specialist/pediatric nurse practitioner (MSN, PMC); oncology/immune deficiency clinical nurse specialist (MSN, PMC); oncology/immune deficiency clinical nurse specialist/adult nurse practitioner (MSN, PMC); perinatal/women's health clinical nurse specialist (MSN, PMC); perinatal/women's health clinical nurse specialist/women's health nurse practitioner (MSN, PMC); psychiatric nursing clinical nurse specialist (MSN, PMC). *Accreditation:* AACN; NLN (one or more programs are accredited). Part-time and evening/weekend programs available. Postbaccalaureate distance learning degree programs offered (minimal on-campus study). *Degree requirements:* For master's, thesis optional. *Entrance requirements:* For master's, BSN, interview, RN license. Electronic applications accepted. *Faculty research:* Marriage and chronic illness, health promotion, congestive heart failure patient outcomes, school nursing, diabetes in children.

University of Illinois at Chicago, Graduate College, College of Nursing, Program in Nursing Sciences (Maternal Child), Chicago, IL 60607-7128. Offers maternity nursing/nurse midwifery (MS); pediatric nursing (MS); perinatal nursing (MS). *Accreditation:* AACN; ACNM/DOA. Part-time programs available. *Degree requirements:* For master's, thesis or alternative. *Entrance requirements:* For master's, GRE General Test, minimum GPA of 2.75. Additional exam requirements/recommendations for international students: Required—TOEFL. Electronic applications accepted.

University of Maryland, Baltimore, Graduate School, School of Nursing, Master's Program in Nursing, Baltimore, MD 21201. Offers community health nursing (MS); gerontological nursing (MS); maternal-child nursing (MS); medical-surgical nursing (MS); nurse-midwifery education (MS); nursing administration (MS); nursing education (MS); nursing health policy (MS); primary care nursing (MS); psychiatric nursing (MS); MS/MBA. *Accreditation:* AANA/CANAEP; ACNM/DOA; NLN (one or more programs are accredited). Part-time programs available. *Degree requirements:* For master's, thesis or alternative, comprehensive exam (for some programs). *Entrance requirements:* For master's, GRE General Test, minimum GPA of 2.75, course work in statistics, BS in nursing. Additional exam requirements/recommendations for international students: Required—TOEFL, TOEFL or IELTS; Recommended—IELTS. Electronic applications accepted.

University of Michigan, Horace H. Rackham School of Graduate Studies, School of Nursing, Division of Health Promotion and Risk Reduction, Program in Parent-Child Nursing, Ann Arbor, MI 48109. Offers infant, child, adolescent health nurse practitioner (MS); nurse

Pediatric Nursing

University of Michigan (continued)
midwifery (MS). *Accreditation:* AACN. Part-time programs available. Postbaccalaureate distance learning degree programs offered (minimal on-campus study). *Degree requirements:* For master's, thesis, registration. *Entrance requirements:* For master's, GRE General Test. Additional exam requirements/recommendations for international students: Required—TOEFL (minimum score 560 paper-based; 220 computer-based).

University of Minnesota, Twin Cities Campus, Graduate School, School of Nursing, Children with Special Health Care Needs Program, Minneapolis, MN 55455-0213. Offers MS. *Entrance requirements:* Additional exam requirements/recommendations for international students: Required—TOEFL (minimum score 586 paper-based; 240 computer-based). *Application deadline:* For fall admission, 11/1 priority date for domestic and international students; for spring admission, 8/1 priority date for domestic and international students. Application fee: $55 ($75 for international students). *Financial support:* Applicants required to submit FAFSA. *Unit head:* Dr. Linda Lindeke, Coordinator, 612-626-1133, Fax: 612-626-2359, E-mail: linde001@umn.edu. *Application contact:* Information Contact, 612-624-4454, Fax: 612-624-3174, E-mail: nurseoss@umn.edu.

University of Minnesota, Twin Cities Campus, Graduate School, School of Nursing, Pediatric Clinical Nurse Specialist Program, Minneapolis, MN 55455-0213. Offers MS. *Accreditation:* AACN. Part-time programs available. *Students:* 4 full-time (all women). *Degree requirements:* For master's, final oral exam, project or thesis. *Application deadline:* For fall admission, 11/1 priority date for domestic and international students; for spring admission, 8/1 priority date for domestic and international students. Application fee: $55 ($75 for international students). *Financial support:* Fellowships, research assistantships, teaching assistantships, career-related internships or fieldwork and traineeships available. *Unit head:* Dr. Linda Lindeke, Coordinator, 612-626-1133, Fax: 612-626-2359, E-mail: linde001@umn.edu. *Application contact:* Information Contact, 612-624-4454, Fax: 612-624-3174, E-mail: nurseoss@umn.edu.

University of Minnesota, Twin Cities Campus, Graduate School, School of Nursing, Pediatric Nurse Practitioner Program, Minneapolis, MN 55455-0213. Offers MS. *Accreditation:* AACN. *Students:* 17 full-time (all women), 2 part-time (both women); includes 1 minority (Asian American or Pacific Islander) *Degree requirements:* For master's, final oral exam, project or thesis. *Application deadline:* For fall admission, 11/1 priority date for domestic and international students; for spring admission, 8/1 priority date for domestic and international students. Application fee: $55 ($75 for international students). *Financial support:* Fellowships, research assistantships, teaching assistantships, career-related internships or fieldwork and traineeships available. *Unit head:* Dr. Linda Lindeke, Coordinator, 612-626-1133, Fax: 612-626-2359, E-mail: linde001@umn.edu. *Application contact:* Information Contact, 612-624-4454, Fax: 612-624-3174, E-mail: nurseoss@umn.edu.

University of Minnesota, Twin Cities Campus, Graduate School, School of Nursing, Program in Adolescent Nursing, Minneapolis, MN 55455-0213. Offers MS. *Accreditation:* AACN. Part-time programs available. *Students:* 2 full-time (both women), 1 (woman) part-time. *Degree requirements:* For master's, final oral exam, project or thesis. *Entrance requirements:* Additional exam requirements/recommendations for international students: Required—TOEFL (minimum score 586 paper-based; 240 computer-based). *Application deadline:* For fall admission, 11/1 priority date for domestic and international students; for spring admission, 8/1 priority date for domestic and international students. Application fee: $55 ($75 for international students). *Unit head:* Dr. Linda Bearinger, Coordinator, 612-624-5157, E-mail: beari001@tc.umn.edu. *Application contact:* Information Contact, 612-624-4454, Fax: 612-624-3174, E-mail: nurseoss@umn.edu.

University of Missouri–Kansas City, School of Nursing, Kansas City, MO 64110-2499. Offers adult clinical nurse specialist (MSN), including adult nurse practitioner, women's health nurse practitioner; family nurse practitioner (MSN); neonatal nurse practitioner (MSN); nurse educator (MSN); nurse executive (MSN); nursing (PhD); pediatric nurse practitioner (MSN). *Accreditation:* AACN. Part-time programs available. Postbaccalaureate distance learning degree programs offered (minimal on-campus study). *Faculty:* 31 full-time (26 women), 32 part-time/adjunct (31 women). *Students:* 36 full-time (all women), 213 part-time (202 women); includes 23 minority (6 African Americans, 2 American Indian/Alaska Native, 6 Asian Americans or Pacific Islanders, 9 Hispanic Americans). Average age 36. 121 applicants, 72% accepted, 71 enrolled. In 2006, 69 master's, 1 doctorate awarded. *Median time to degree:* Of those who began their doctoral program in fall 1998, 60% received their degree in 8 years or less. *Degree requirements:* For master's, thesis or alternative. *Entrance requirements:* For master's, minimum undergraduate GPA of 3.2; for doctorate, GRE, 3 letters of reference, interview and original essay by invitation. Additional exam requirements/recommendations for international students: Required—TOEFL (minimum score 550 paper-based). *Application deadline:* For fall admission, 2/1 priority date for domestic students; for spring admission, 9/15 priority date for domestic students. Application fee: $25. *Expenses:* Tuition, state resident: full-time $4,975; part-time $276 per credit. Tuition, nonresident: full-time $12,847; part-time $713 per credit. Required fees: $595; $595 per year. *Financial support:* In 2006–07, 30 students received support, including 6 research assistantships (averaging $3,450 per year), 7 teaching assistantships with partial tuition reimbursements available (averaging $12,650 per year); fellowships, career-related internships or fieldwork, Federal Work-Study, institutionally sponsored loans, and tuition waivers (full and partial) also available. Support available to part-time students. Financial award application deadline: 6/30; financial award applicants required to submit FAFSA. *Faculty research:* Geriatrics/gerontology, children's pain, neonatology, Alzheimer's care, cancer caregivers. Total annual research expenditures: $1 million. *Unit head:* Dr. Lora Lacey-Haun, Dean, 816-235-1700, Fax: 816-235-1701, E-mail: lacey-haunc@umkc.edu. *Application contact:* Leah Wilder, Coordinator for Admissions and Recruitment, 816-235-5768, Fax: 816-235-1701, E-mail: wilderl@umkc.edu.

University of Nevada, Las Vegas, Graduate College, Division of Health Sciences, School of Nursing, Las Vegas, NV 89154-9900. Offers family nurse practitioner (MS, Post-Master's Certificate); nursing (PhD); nursing education (MS, Post-Master's Certificate); pediatric nurse practitioner (MS). *Accreditation:* NLN. Part-time programs available. *Faculty:* 21 full-time (all women), 6 part-time/adjunct (all women). *Students:* 74 full-time (59 women), 66 part-time (61 women); includes 24 minority (2 African Americans, 15 Asian Americans or Pacific Islanders, 7 Hispanic Americans), 46 international. 190 applicants, 66% accepted, 107 enrolled. In 2006, 11 degrees awarded. *Degree requirements:* For master's, research project, thesis optional. *Entrance requirements:* For master's, GRE General Test, minimum GPA of 3.0 during previous 2 years, minimum overall GPA of 2.75. Additional exam requirements/recommendations for international students: Required—TOEFL (minimum score 550 paper-based; 213 computer-based; 80 iBT). *Application deadline:* For fall admission, 3/15 for domestic and international students. Application fee: $60 ($75 for international students). Electronic applications accepted. *Financial support:* In 2006–07, 7 research assistantships with partial tuition reimbursements (averaging $10,000 per year) were awarded; career-related internships or fieldwork, Federal Work-Study, institutionally sponsored loans, scholarships/grants, health care benefits, and unspecified assistantships also available. Support available to part-time students. Financial award application deadline: 3/1. *Unit head:* Dr. Carolyn Yucha, Dean, 702-895-3415. *Application contact:* Graduate College Admissions Evaluator, 702-895-3320, Fax: 702-895-4180, E-mail: gradcollege@unlv.edu.

University of Pennsylvania, School of Nursing, Pediatric Acute/Chronic Care Nurse Practitioner Program, Philadelphia, PA 19104. Offers MSN. *Accreditation:* AACN. Part-time programs available. Postbaccalaureate distance learning degree programs offered. *Entrance requirements:* For master's, GRE General Test, 1 year of clinical course work, BSN, minimum GPA of 3.0, previous course work in statistics. Additional exam requirements/recommendations for international students: Required—TOEFL. Expenses: Contact institution. *Faculty research:* Hispanic health, bereavement, pediatric AIDS, chronically ill children and their families.

University of Pennsylvania, School of Nursing, Pediatric Critical Care Nurse Practitioner Program, Philadelphia, PA 19104. Offers MSN. *Accreditation:* AACN. *Entrance requirements:* For master's, GRE General Test, BSN, minimum GPA of 3.0, previous course work in statistics, 1 year of clinical course work. Additional exam requirements/recommendations for international students: Required—TOEFL. Expenses: Contact institution.

University of Pennsylvania, School of Nursing, Pediatric Nurse Practitioner Program, Philadelphia, PA 19104. Offers MSN. *Accreditation:* AACN. Part-time programs available. *Entrance requirements:* For master's, GRE General Test, 1 year of clinical experience in area of interest, BSN, minimum GPA of 3.0, previous course work in statistics. Additional exam requirements/recommendations for international students: Required—TOEFL. Expenses: Contact institution. *Faculty research:* Adolescent behavior change, prevention of teenage pregnancy, community schools.

University of Pittsburgh, School of Nursing, Program in Nurse Practitioner Studies, Pittsburgh, PA 15260. Offers acute care nurse practitioner (MSN); adult nurse practitioner (MSN); family nurse practitioner (MSN); nursing practice (DNP); pediatric nurse practitioner (MSN); psychiatric primary care nurse practitioner (MSN). *Accreditation:* AACN. Part-time programs available. *Students:* 15 full-time (13 women), 65 part-time (57 women); includes 5 minority (3 African Americans, 2 Hispanic Americans). Average age 38. 47 applicants, 62% accepted, 27 enrolled. In 2006, 28 degrees awarded. *Degree requirements:* For master's, thesis optional. *Entrance requirements:* For master's, GRE General Test or MAT, BSN, RN license, letters of recommendation, resumé, course work in statistics, 1-3 years of nursing experience; for doctorate, GRE General Test, BSN, RN license, minimum GPA of 3.5, 3 letters of recommendation. Additional exam requirements/recommendations for international students: Required—TOEFL (minimum score 550 paper-based; 213 computer-based; 80 iBT). *Application deadline:* For fall admission, 8/1 priority date for domestic students, 8/1 for international students; for spring admission, 12/1 priority date for domestic students, 12/1 for international students. Applications are processed on a rolling basis. Application fee: $50. Electronic applications accepted.

University of San Diego, Hahn School of Nursing and Health Sciences, San Diego, CA 92110-2492. Offers accelerated nursing (for RNs only) (MSN); adult clinical nurse specialist (MSN, Post Master's Certificate); adult nurse practitioner (MSN, Post Master's Certificate); clinical nursing (MSN); entry-level nursing (for non-RNs) (MSN); executive nurse leader (MSN); family nurse practitioner (MSN, Post Master's Certificate); nursing science (PhD); pediatric nurse practitioner (MSN, Post Master's Certificate). *Accreditation:* AACN. Part-time and evening/weekend programs available. *Faculty:* 13 full-time (12 women), 33 part-time/adjunct (all women). *Students:* 103 full-time (85 women), 138 part-time (131 women); includes 58 minority (7 African Americans, 3 American Indian/Alaska Native, 26 Asian Americans or Pacific Islanders, 22 Hispanic Americans), 4 international. Average age 37. 261 applicants, 54% accepted, 87 enrolled. In 2006, 35 master's, 19 doctorates awarded. *Degree requirements:* For doctorate, thesis/dissertation, residency. *Entrance requirements:* For master's, GRE General Test (for entry-level nursing), BSN and current California RN licensure (for all programs except entry-level nursing); minimum GPA of 3.0; for doctorate, GRE General Test, minimum GPA of 3.5, MSN, current California RN licensure. Additional exam requirements/recommendations for international students: Required—TOEFL, TWE. *Application deadline:* Applications are processed on a rolling basis. Application fee: $45. Electronic applications accepted. *Financial support:* Scholarships/grants and traineeships available. Support available to part-time students. Financial award application deadline: 4/1; financial award applicants required to submit FAFSA. *Faculty research:* Health promotion, decision making, psychogeriatric nursing, historical nursing, leadership behavior. *Unit head:* Dr. Sally Hardin, Dean, 619-260-4550, Fax: 619-260-6814. *Application contact:* Stephen Pultz, Director of Admissions, 619-260-4524, Fax: 619-260-4158, E-mail: grads@sandiego.edu.

See Close-Up on page 1977.

University of South Carolina, The Graduate School, College of Nursing, Program in Health Nursing, Columbia, SC 29208. Offers adult nurse practitioner (MSN); community/public health clinical nurse specialist (MSN); family nurse practitioner (MSN); pediatric nurse practitioner (MSN). *Accreditation:* AACN. Part-time programs available. *Degree requirements:* For master's, thesis or alternative. *Entrance requirements:* For master's, GRE General Test or MAT, BS in nursing, nursing license. Additional exam requirements/recommendations for international students: Required—TOEFL (minimum score 570 paper-based; 230 computer-based). Electronic applications accepted. *Faculty research:* Health promotion, physical activity, adolescent health, pre-term labor, low birthrate.

The University of Texas–Pan American, College of Health Sciences and Human Services, Department of Nursing, Edinburg, TX 78541-2999. Offers adult health nursing (MSN); family nurse practitioner (MSN); pediatric nurse practitioner (MSN). *Accreditation:* AACN. Part-time and evening/weekend programs available. *Faculty:* 8 full-time (7 women). *Students:* 19 applicants, 100% accepted, 19 enrolled. In 2006, 22 degrees awarded. *Median time to degree:* Master's–3 years part-time. *Degree requirements:* For master's, thesis optional. *Entrance requirements:* For master's, Texas RN licensure, undergraduate physical assessment courses. Additional exam requirements/recommendations for international students: Required—TOEFL (minimum score 550 paper-based). *Application deadline:* Applications are processed on a rolling basis. Application fee: $35. Electronic applications accepted. *Expenses: Contact institution. Financial support:* In 2006–07, 15 students received support. Scholarships/grants and traineeships available. *Faculty research:* Health promotion, adolescent pregnancy, herbal and nontraditional approaches, healing touch stress. Total annual research expenditures: $5,000. *Unit head:* Dr. Carolina G. Huerta, Chair, 956-381-3495, Fax: 956-381-2384, E-mail: chuerta@panam.edu. *Application contact:* Dr. Janice A. Maville, Professor and Interim Chair, 956-316-3491, Fax: 956-318-5238, E-mail: jmaville@utpa.edu.

Vanderbilt University, School of Nursing, Nashville, TN 37235. Offers adult acute care nurse practitioner (MSN); adult health nurse practitioner/forensic (MSN); adult nurse practitioner/cardiovascular disease management and prevention (MSN); adult nurse practitioner/palliative care (MSN); clinical management (clinical nurse leader/specialist) (MSN); family nurse practitioner (MSN); gerontology nurse practitioner (MSN); health systems management (MSN); neonatal nurse practitioner (MSN); nurse midwifery (MSN); nursing informatics (MSN); nursing science (PhD); pediatric acute care nurse practitioner (MSN); pediatric primary care nurse practitioner (MSN); psychiatric-mental health nurse practitioner (MSN); women's health nurse practitioner (MSN); MBA/MSN; MSN/MTS; MSN/PhD. *Accreditation:* ACNM/DOA; NLN (one or more programs are accredited). Part-time and evening/weekend programs available. Postbaccalaureate distance learning degree programs offered (minimal on-campus study). *Faculty:* 95 full-time (83 women), 432 part-time/adjunct (314 women). *Students:* 371 full-time (325 women), 206 part-time (180 women); includes 59 minority (38 African Americans, 2 American Indian/Alaska Native, 7 Asian Americans or Pacific Islanders, 12 Hispanic Americans). Average age 27. 611 applicants, 55% accepted, 308 enrolled. In 2006, 256 master's, 2 doctorates awarded. *Degree requirements:* For doctorate, thesis/dissertation. *Entrance requirements:* For master's, GRE, interview; for doctorate, GRE, interview, 3 letters of recommendation. Additional exam requirements/recommendations for international students: Required—TOEFL. *Application deadline:* For fall admission, 12/1 priority date for domestic and international students. Applications are processed on a rolling basis. Application fee: $50. *Expenses:* Contact institution. *Financial support:* In 2006–07, 404 students received support, including 5 research assistantships (averaging $8,000 per year); Federal Work-Study, institutionally sponsored loans, and unspecified assistantships also available. Support available to part-time students. Financial award application deadline: 3/15; financial award applicants required to submit CSS PROFILE or FAFSA. *Faculty research:* Lymphedema post cancer treatment, palliative care and bereavement, patient safety and quality of care, health care workforce issues, symptom management including pain and fatigue. Total annual research expenditures: $1.1 million. *Unit head:* Dr. Colleen Conway-Welch, Dean, 615-343-8776, Fax: 615-343-7711,

E-mail: colleen.conway-welch@vanderbilt.edu. *Application contact:* Cheryl Feldner, Assistant Director of Admissions, 615-322-3800, Fax: 615-343-0333, E-mail: cheryl.feldner@vanderbilt.edu.

Villanova University, College of Nursing, Villanova, PA 19085-1690. Offers adult nurse practitioner (MSN, Post Master's Certificate); clinical case management (MSN, Post Master's Certificate); geriatric nurse practitioner (MSN, Post Master's Certificate); health care administration (MSN); nurse anesthetist (MSN, Post Master's Certificate); nursing (PhD); nursing education (MSN, Post Master's Certificate); pediatric nurse practitioner (MSN, Post Master's Certificate). *Accreditation:* AACN; AANA/CANAEP; NLN. Part-time programs available. Postbaccalaureate distance learning degree programs offered (minimal on-campus study). *Faculty:* 14 full-time (all women), 2 part-time/adjunct (both women). *Students:* 41 full-time (27 women), 164 part-time (128 women); includes 17 minority (8 African Americans, 1 American Indian/Alaska Native, 8 Asian Americans or Pacific Islanders), 6 international. Average age 31. 137 applicants, 50% accepted, 48 enrolled. In 2006, 47 degrees awarded. *Median time to degree:* Master's–2 years full-time, 5 years part-time. *Degree requirements:* For master's, independent study project; for doctorate, thesis/dissertation, comprehensive exam. *Entrance requirements:* For master's, GRE or MAT, BSN, 1 year of recent nursing experience, physical assessment, course work in statistics; for doctorate, GRE. Additional exam requirements/recommendations for international students: Required—TOEFL. *Application deadline:* For fall admission, 7/1 priority date for domestic students, 7/1 for international students; for spring admission, 12/1 priority date for domestic students, 12/1 for international students. Applications are processed on a rolling basis. Application fee: $50. *Expenses:* Contact institution. *Financial support:* In 2006–07, 50 students received support, including 4 teaching assistantships with full tuition reimbursements available (averaging $12,165 per year); institutionally sponsored loans, scholarships/grants, traineeships, and tuition waivers (full) also available. Financial award application deadline: 3/1; financial award applicants required to submit FAFSA. *Faculty research:* Genetics, ethics, cognitive development of students, women with disabilities, nursing leadership. *Unit head:* Dr. Marguerite K. Schlag, Assistant Dean and Director, Graduate Program, 610-519-4907, Fax: 610-519-7650, E-mail: marguerite.schlag@villanova.edu.

Virginia Commonwealth University, Graduate School, School of Nursing, Richmond, VA 23284-9005. Offers adult health nursing (MS); child health nursing (MS); family health nursing (MS); health system (PhD); immunocompetence (PhD); nurse practitioner (MS, Certificate); nursing administration (MS), including clinical nurse manager, nurse executive; psychiatric-mental health nursing (MS); risk and resilience (PhD); women's health nursing (MS). *Accreditation:* NLN (one or more programs are accredited). Part-time and evening/weekend programs available. *Faculty:* 23 full-time (21 women). *Students:* 131 full-time (125 women), 137 part-time (129 women); includes 33 minority (19 African Americans, 11 Asian Americans or Pacific Islanders, 3 Hispanic Americans), 12 international. 110 applicants, 82% accepted, 66 enrolled. In 2006, 57 master's, 1 doctorate, 3 other advanced degrees awarded. *Degree requirements:* For master's, thesis optional; for doctorate, thesis/dissertation. *Entrance requirements:* For master's, GRE General Test, BSN, minimum GPA of 2.8; for doctorate, GRE General Test. *Application deadline:* For fall admission, 2/1 priority date for domestic students. Application fee: $50. *Financial support:* Fellowships, research assistantships, teaching assistantships, career-related internships or fieldwork and institutionally sponsored loans available. *Unit head:* Dr. Nancy F. Langston, Dean, 804-828-5174, Fax: 804-828-7743, E-mail: nflangst@vcu.edu. *Application contact:* Susan Lipp, Admissions Counselor, 804-828-5171, Fax: 804-828-7743, E-mail: slipp@vcu.edu.

See Close-Up on page 1983.

Wayne State University, College of Nursing, Department of Family, Community and Mental Health, Program in Advanced Practice Nursing with Women, Neonates and Children, Detroit, MI 48202. Offers advanced practice nursing with women, neonates and children (MSN); neonatal nurse practitioner (Certificate). *Accreditation:* AACN. Part-time programs available. *Students:* 13 full-time (12 women), 47 part-time (all women); includes 10 minority (7 African Americans, 2 Asian Americans or Pacific Islanders, 1 Hispanic American). Average age 35. 13 applicants, 85% accepted, 11 enrolled. In 2006, 1 degree awarded. *Degree requirements:* For master's, thesis or alternative. *Entrance requirements:* For master's, GRE General Test, minimum GPA of 2.8. Additional exam requirements/recommendations for international students: Required—TOEFL (minimum score 550 paper-based; 213 computer-based); Recommended—TWE (minimum score 6). *Application deadline:* For fall admission, 7/1 priority date for domestic students, 6/1 for international students; for winter admission, 10/1 for international students; for spring admission, 11/1 for domestic students, 2/1 for international students. Applications are processed on a rolling basis. Application fee: $30 ($50 for international students). Electronic applications accepted. *Financial support:* In 2006–07, 17 students received support, including 2 research assistantships; institutionally sponsored loans, scholarships/grants, and traineeships also available. Financial award application deadline: 7/1; financial award applicants required to submit FAFSA. *Faculty research:* Acculturation and parenting, domestic violence, evidence-based midwifery practice, pain in children, trauma and community violence. *Application contact:* Janet Harden, Academic Director, 313-577-4082.

Wright State University, School of Graduate Studies, College of Nursing and Health, Program in Nursing, Dayton, OH 45435. Offers acute care nurse practitioner (MS); administration of nursing and health care systems (MS); adult health (MS); child and adolescent health (MS); community health (MS); family nurse practitioner (MS); nurse practitioner (MS); school nurse (MS); MBA/MS. *Accreditation:* AACN. Part-time and evening/weekend programs available. *Students:* 46 full-time (45 women), 124 part-time (117 women); includes 16 minority (13 African Americans, 1 Asian American or Pacific Islander, 2 Hispanic Americans). Average age 39. 45 applicants, 100% accepted. In 2006, 64 degrees awarded. *Degree requirements:* For master's, thesis or alternative. *Entrance requirements:* For master's, GRE General Test, BSN from NLN-accredited college, Ohio RN license. Additional exam requirements/recommendations for international students: Required—TOEFL. *Application deadline:* For fall admission, 4/15 priority date for domestic students. Application fee: $25. *Financial support:* Fellowships, research assistantships, teaching assistantships, Federal Work-Study, institutionally sponsored loans, and unspecified assistantships available. Support available to part-time students. Financial award application deadline: 6/1; financial award applicants required to submit FAFSA. *Faculty research:* Clinical nursing and health, teaching, caring, pain administration, informatics and technology. *Application contact:* Theresa A. Haghnazarian, Director of Student and Alumni Affairs, 937-775-2592, Fax: 937-775-4571, E-mail: theresa.haghnazarian@wright.edu.

Psychiatric Nursing

Boston College, William F. Connell School of Nursing, Chestnut Hill, MA 02467-3800. Offers adult health nursing (MS); community health nursing (MS); family health (MS); gerontology (MS); maternal/child health nursing (MS), including pediatric and women's health; nurse anesthesia (MS); nursing (PhD); psychiatric-mental health nursing (MS); MBA/MS; MS/MA; MS/PhD. *Accreditation:* AACN; AANA/CANAEP (one or more programs are accredited). Part-time programs available. *Faculty:* 46 full-time (44 women), 34 part-time/adjunct (all women). *Students:* 155 full-time (137 women), 56 part-time (54 women); includes 10 minority (4 African Americans, 5 Asian Americans or Pacific Islanders, 1 Hispanic American), 6 international. Average age 34. 276 applicants, 47% accepted, 67 enrolled. In 2006, 61 master's, 4 doctorates awarded. *Median time to degree:* Of those who began their doctoral program in fall 1998, 100% received their degree in 8 years or less. *Degree requirements:* For master's, research project; for doctorate, thesis/dissertation, computer literacy exam or foreign language, comprehensive exam. *Entrance requirements:* For master's, GRE General Test, bachelor's degree in nursing; for doctorate, GRE General Test, master's degree in nursing. Additional exam requirements/recommendations for international students: Required—TOEFL (minimum score 550 paper-based; 213 computer-based). *Application deadline:* For fall admission, 10/15 for domestic and international students; for spring admission, 3/15 for domestic and international students. Application fee: $40. Electronic applications accepted. *Financial support:* In 2006–07, 104 students received support, including 15 fellowships with partial tuition reimbursements available (averaging $10,045 per year), 3 research assistantships (averaging $10,000 per year), 4 teaching assistantships (averaging $12,548 per year); Federal Work-Study, institutionally sponsored loans, scholarships/grants, traineeships, and tuition waivers (partial) also available. Support available to part-time students. Financial award application deadline: 3/1; financial award applicants required to submit FAFSA. *Faculty research:* Ethics, reduction of risk behaviors, support during chronic illness, violence, gerontology. Total annual research expenditures: $1.1 million. *Unit head:* Dr. Barbara Hazard, Dean, 617-552-4251, Fax: 617-552-0931, E-mail: barbara.munro@bc.edu. *Application contact:* Zanifer John-Bayard, Graduate Programs Assistant, 617-552-4059, Fax: 617-552-0745, E-mail: johnza@bc.edu.

Case Western Reserve University, Frances Payne Bolton School of Nursing, Doctor of Nursing Practice Program, Cleveland, OH 44106. Offers acute care nurse practitioner (DNP); adult nurse practitioner (DNP); family nurse practitioner (DNP); gerontological nurse practitioner (DNP); graduate entry/pre-licensure option (DNP); medical-surgical nursing (DNP); midwifery/family nursing (DNP); neonatal nurse practitioner (DNP); pediatric nurse practitioner (DNP); post-licensure option (DNP); psychiatric mental health nurse practitioner (DNP); women's health nurse practitioner (DNP). Graduate entry option allows baccalaureate-prepared college graduates from non-nursing backgrounds to earn certificate and MSN in addition to ND. *Students:* 125 full-time (109 women), 308 part-time (290 women); includes 47 minority (21 African Americans, 1 American Indian/Alaska Native, 18 Asian Americans or Pacific Islanders, 7 Hispanic Americans), 7 international. 190 applicants, 70% accepted, 80 enrolled. In 2006, 35 degrees awarded. Terminal master's awarded for partial completion of doctoral program. *Degree requirements:* For doctorate, thesis/dissertation. *Entrance requirements:* For doctorate, GRE General Test or MAT. *Application deadline:* For fall admission, 6/1 priority date for domestic students. Applications are processed on a rolling basis. Application fee: $75. *Financial support:* In 2006–07, 6 students received support, including 1 teaching assistantship; research assistantships, Federal Work-Study, institutionally sponsored loans, and tuition waivers (partial) also available. Support available to part-time students. Financial award application deadline: 6/30; financial award applicants required to submit FAFSA. *Faculty research:* Clinical nursing, acute care, gerontology, mental health, critical care. *Unit head:* Dr. Georgia Narsavage, Director, 216-368-6304, Fax: 216-368-3542, E-mail: gln2@cwru.edu. *Application contact:* Peter Taylor, Recruitment and Retention Specialist, 216-368-0349, Fax: 216-368-0124, E-mail: peter.taylor@case.edu.

Case Western Reserve University, Frances Payne Bolton School of Nursing, Master's Programs in Nursing, Nurse Practitioner Program, Cleveland, OH 44106. Offers acute care cardiovascular nursing (MSN); acute care nurse practitioner (MSN); acute care/flight nurse (MSN); adult nurse practitioner (MSN); family nurse practitioner (MSN); gerontological nurse practitioner (MSN); neonatal nurse practitioner (MSN); pediatric nurse practitioner (MSN); psychiatric-mental health nurse practitioner (MSN); women's health nurse practitioner (MSN). *Accreditation:* NLN. Part-time programs available. Postbaccalaureate distance learning degree programs offered (minimal on-campus study). *Faculty:* 54 full-time (50 women), 5 part-time/adjunct (3 women). *Students:* 19 full-time (15 women), 31 part-time (29 women); includes 16 minority (9 African Americans, 5 Asian Americans or Pacific Islanders, 2 Hispanic Americans), 2 international. Average age 35. 46 applicants, 72% accepted, 18 enrolled. In 2006, 34 degrees awarded. *Degree requirements:* For master's, thesis optional. *Entrance requirements:* For master's, GRE General Test or MAT. Additional exam requirements/recommendations for international students: Required—TOEFL. *Application deadline:* For fall admission, 6/1 for domestic students. Applications are processed on a rolling basis. Application fee: $75. *Financial support:* In 2006–07, 7 teaching assistantships were awarded; research assistantships, institutionally sponsored loans and tuition waivers (partial) also available. Support available to part-time students. Financial award application deadline: 6/30. *Faculty research:* Positive and negative mood states in parents of twins, effect of a carepath on chronic obstructive pulmonary disease home care. *Application contact:* Peter Taylor, Recruitment and Retention Specialist, 216-368-0349, Fax: 216-368-0124, E-mail: peter.taylor@case.edu.

The Catholic University of America, School of Nursing, Washington, DC 20064. Offers advanced practice nursing (MSN), including administration of nursing service, adult nurse practitioner, education, family nurse practitioner, geriatric nurse practitioner, pediatric nurse practitioner, psychiatric-mental health, school health nurse practitioner; clinical nursing (DN Sc). *Accreditation:* AACN; NLN. Part-time programs available. *Faculty:* 17 full-time (all women), 19 part-time/adjunct (18 women). *Students:* 27 full-time (25 women), 58 part-time (57 women); includes 31 minority (20 African Americans, 6 Asian Americans or Pacific Islanders, 5 Hispanic Americans), 6 international. Average age 43. 38 applicants, 76% accepted, 15 enrolled. In 2006, 15 master's, 7 doctorates awarded. *Degree requirements:* For master's, thesis optional; for doctorate, thesis/dissertation, comprehensive exam. *Entrance requirements:* For master's, GRE General Test or MAT, 3 letters of recommendation, BA in nursing, RN registration; for doctorate, GRE General Test, 3 letters of recommendation, BA in nursing, RN registration. Additional exam requirements/recommendations for international students: Required—TOEFL (minimum score 550 paper-based; 213 computer-based). *Application deadline:* For fall admission, 2/1 priority date for domestic students; for spring admission, 11/15 priority date for domestic students. Applications are processed on a rolling basis. Application fee: $55. Electronic applications accepted. *Expenses:* Tuition: Full-time $27,700; part-time $1,045 per credit hour. Required fees: $1,290. Part-time tuition and fees vary according to campus/location and program. *Financial support:* Research assistantships, teaching assistantships, career-related internships or fieldwork, Federal Work-Study, scholarships/grants, tuition waivers (full and partial), and unspecified assistantships available. Support available to part-time students. Financial award application deadline: 2/1; financial award applicants required to submit FAFSA. *Faculty research:* Outcome research–readmission of home health care patients with congestive heart failure, spirituality of chronic illness, minority multigravidos utilization of prenatal care. *Unit head:* Dr. Nalini Jairath, Dean, 202-319-5403, Fax: 202-319-6485, E-mail: jairath@cua.edu.

Columbia University, School of Nursing, Program in Psychiatric Mental Health Nursing, New York, NY 10032. Offers MS, Adv C. *Accreditation:* AACN. Part-time programs available. *Faculty:* 3 full-time (all women), 2 part-time/adjunct (both women). *Students:* 6 full-time (5 women), 28 part-time (26 women); includes 2 minority (1 African American, 1 Asian American or Pacific Islander). Average age 32. In 2006, 10 master's, 1 other advanced degree awarded. *Entrance requirements:* For master's, GRE General Test, BSN, 1 year of clinical experience (preferred); for Adv C, MSN. *Application deadline:* Applications are processed on a rolling basis. Application fee: $65. Electronic applications accepted. *Financial support:* Teaching assistantships available. Financial award application deadline: 2/1; financial award applicants required to submit FAFSA. *Unit head:* Prof. Penelope Buschman, Head, 212-305-3199. *Application contact:* Prof. Penelope Buschman, Head, 212-305-3199.

Psychiatric Nursing

Duquesne University, School of Nursing, Master's Program in Nursing, Pittsburgh, PA 15282-0001. Offers acute care nursing (Post-Master's Certificate); acute care nursing specialist (MSN); family nurse practitioner (MSN, Post-Master's Certificate); forensic nursing (MSN, Post-Master's Certificate); nursing administration (MSN, Post-Master's Certificate); nursing education (MSN, Post-Master's Certificate); psychiatric/mental health nursing (MSN, Post-Master's Certificate); MSN/MBA. *Accreditation:* AACN. Part-time and evening/weekend programs available. Postbaccalaureate distance learning degree programs offered (minimal on-campus study). *Faculty:* 20 full-time (19 women), 4 part-time/adjunct (all women). *Students:* 73 full-time (70 women), 83 part-time (79 women); includes 11 minority (4 African Americans, 3 American Indian/Alaska Native, 1 Asian American or Pacific Islander, 3 Hispanic Americans). 72 applicants, 75% accepted, 49 enrolled. In 2006, 20 master's, 11 other advanced degrees awarded. *Degree requirements:* For master's, culminating paper. *Entrance requirements:* For master's, MAT or GRE, 1 year of work experience, bachelor's degree in nursing, undergraduate course work in statistics, health assessment course (family nurse practitioner, nursing education, acute care clinical nurse specialist). *Application deadline:* For fall admission, 4/1 for domestic and international students; for spring admission, 11/1 for domestic and international students. Applications are processed on a rolling basis. Application fee: $50. *Expenses: Contact institution.* Tuition and fees vary according to degree level and program. *Financial support:* In 2006–07, 10 students received support, including 9 research assistantships with partial tuition reimbursements available (averaging $1,600 per year), 1 teaching assistantship with partial tuition reimbursement available (averaging $1,600 per year); fellowships with partial tuition reimbursements available, institutionally sponsored loans, scholarships/grants, traineeships, and tuition waivers (partial) also available. Financial award application deadline: 8/20. *Faculty research:* Depression, culture, vulnerable populations, ethics, health disparities, community based. Total annual research expenditures: $377,400. *Unit head:* Dr. Joan Such Lockhart, Professor and Associate Dean of Academic Affairs, 412-396-6540, Fax: 412-396-1821, E-mail: lockhart@duq.edu. *Application contact:* Susan Hardner, Nurse Recruiter, 412-396-4945, Fax: 412-396-6346, E-mail: nursing@duq.edu.

Fairfield University, School of Nursing, Fairfield, CT 06824-5195. Offers adult nurse practitioner (MSN, PMC); family nurse practitioner (MSN, PMC); healthcare management (MSN); nurse anesthesia (MSN); psychiatric nurse practitioner (MSN, PMC). *Accreditation:* AACN; AANA/CANAEP. Part-time programs available. *Faculty:* 13 full-time (12 women), 2 part-time/adjunct (both women). *Students:* 3 full-time (all women), 39 part-time (all women); includes 5 minority (2 African Americans, 3 Asian Americans or Pacific Islanders). Average age 42. 23 applicants, 30% accepted, 3 enrolled. In 2006, 9 degrees awarded. *Degree requirements:* For master's, capstone project. *Entrance requirements:* For master's, MAT or GRE, minimum QPA of 3.0, RN license, resumé, 2 recommendations; for PMC, 1 year of work experience as a registered nurse. Additional exam requirements/recommendations for international students: Required—TOEFL (minimum score 550 paper-based; 213 computer-based; 79 iBT). *Application deadline:* For fall admission, 4/1 priority date for domestic students, 6/15 priority date for international students; for spring admission, 11/1 priority date for domestic students, 10/15 priority date for international students. Applications are processed on a rolling basis. Application fee: $55. *Expenses: Contact institution. Financial support:* Traineeships available. Financial award applicants required to submit FAFSA. *Faculty research:* Critical care, nursing outcomes, care of older adults, leadership, community health. *Unit head:* Dr. Jeanne M. Novotny, Dean, 203-254-4000 Ext. 2701, Fax: 203-254-4126, E-mail: jnovotny@mail.fairfield.edu. *Application contact:* Marianne Gumpper, Director of Graduate and Continuing Studies Admissions, 203-254-4184, Fax: 203-254-4073, E-mail: gradadmis@mail.fairfield.edu.

Georgia State University, College of Health and Human Sciences, School of Nursing, Atlanta, GA 30303-3083. Offers adult health (MS); child health (MS); family nurse practitioner (MS); health promotion, protection and restoration (PhD); nursing (Certificate); perinatal/women's health (MS); psychiatric/mental health (MS). *Accreditation:* AACN. Part-time and evening/weekend programs available. *Faculty:* 35 full-time (all women), 1 (woman) part-time/adjunct. *Students:* 72 full-time (66 women), 128 part-time (123 women); includes 75 minority (61 African Americans, 9 Asian Americans or Pacific Islanders, 5 Hispanic Americans), 2 international. Average age 37. 70 applicants, 54% accepted, 30 enrolled. In 2006, 39 master's, 6 doctorates awarded. *Degree requirements:* For master's, research activity; for doctorate, thesis/dissertation, comprehensive exam. *Entrance requirements:* For master's, MAT (preferred) or GRE, interview, RN license; for doctorate, GRE General Test. Additional exam requirements/recommendations for international students: Required—TOEFL (minimum score 550 paper-based; 213 computer-based). *Application deadline:* For fall admission, 3/1 priority date for domestic students; for spring admission, 10/1 priority date for domestic students. Applications are processed on a rolling basis. Application fee: $50. Electronic applications accepted. *Expenses: Contact institution. Financial support:* In 2006–07, research assistantships with full and partial tuition reimbursements (averaging $3,108 per year); fellowships with full tuition reimbursements, teaching assistantships, Federal Work-Study, institutionally sponsored loans, scholarships/grants, traineeships, and tuition waivers (partial) also available. Support available to part-time students. Financial award application deadline: 4/1; financial award applicants required to submit FAFSA. *Faculty research:* Breast cancer prevention, sexually compulsive behaviors, health risks in minority youth, asthma treatment strategies, adolescent alcohol-related issues. Total annual research expenditures: $221,691. *Unit head:* Dr. Barbara Woodring, Director, 404-651-3040. *Application contact:* Barbara Smith, Admissions Counselor II, 404-651-3834, Fax: 404-651-4871, E-mail: bbsmith@gsu.edu.

Hunter College of the City University of New York, Graduate School, Schools of the Health Professions, Hunter-Bellevue School of Nursing, Program in Psychiatric Nursing, New York, NY 10021-5085. Offers MS. *Accreditation:* AACN. Part-time programs available. *Faculty:* 24 full-time (21 women), 21 part-time/adjunct (19 women). *Students:* Average age 48. 11 applicants, 73% accepted, 7 enrolled. In 2006, 2 degrees awarded. *Degree requirements:* For master's, practicum. *Entrance requirements:* For master's, minimum GPA of 3.0, New York RN license, BSN. Additional exam requirements/recommendations for international students: Required—TOEFL. *Application deadline:* For fall admission, 4/1 for domestic students, 2/1 for international students; for spring admission, 11/1 for domestic students, 9/1 for international students. Applications are processed on a rolling basis. Application fee: $125. *Expenses:* Tuition, state resident: part-time $270 per credit. Tuition, nonresident: part-time $500 per credit. Required fees: $45 per semester. *Financial support:* Federal Work-Study, scholarships/grants, traineeships, and tuition waivers (partial) available. Support available to part-time students. Financial award application deadline: 5/1; financial award applicants required to submit FAFSA. *Faculty research:* Nursing approaches with the homeless, chronic mentally ill, and depressed; power and empathy. *Unit head:* Dr. Vidette Todard-Francescli, Coordinator, 212-481-4449, Fax: 212-481-5078. *Application contact:* William Zlata, Director for Graduate Admissions, 212-772-4482, Fax: 212-650-3336, E-mail: admissions@hunter.cuny.edu.

Husson College, Graduate Studies Division, Program in Nursing, Bangor, ME 04401-2999. Offers family nurse practitioner (MSN); nursing (MSN); psychiatric nursing (MSN). *Accreditation:* AACN. *Entrance requirements:* For master's, MAT, BSN. Expenses: Contact institution.

Indiana University–Purdue University Indianapolis, School of Nursing, Indianapolis, IN 46202-2896. Offers acute care nurse practitioner (MSN); adult health clinical nurse specialist (MSN); adult health nursing (MSN), including adult clinical nurse specialist; adult nurse practitioner (MSN); adult psychiatric/mental health nursing (MSN); child psychiatric/mental health nursing (MSN); community health nursing (MSN); family nurse practitioner (MSN); neonatal nurse practitioner (MSN); nursing science (PhD); pediatric clinical nurse specialist (MSN); women's health nurse practitioner (MSN); MSN/MPA; MSN/MPH. *Accreditation:* AACN; NLN (one or more programs are accredited). Part-time programs available. *Faculty:* 45 full-time (44 women), 1 (woman) part-time/adjunct. *Students:* 52 full-time (51 women), 415 part-time (396 women); includes 27 minority (16 African Americans, 3 Asian Americans or Pacific Islanders, 8 Hispanic Americans), 4 international. Average age 38. In 2006, 106 master's, 3 doctorates awarded. Terminal master's awarded for partial completion of doctoral program. *Degree requirements:* For master's and doctorate, thesis/dissertation. *Entrance requirements:* For master's, GRE General Test, minimum GPA of 3.0, RN license; for doctorate, GRE General Test, minimum GPA of 3.5, MSN, RN license. Additional exam requirements/recommendations for international students: Required—TOEFL. *Application deadline:* For fall admission, 2/15 for domestic students; for spring admission, 9/15 for domestic students. Application fee: $50 ($60 for international students). *Expenses:* Tuition, state resident: full-time $5,437; part-time $227 per credit hour. Tuition, nonresident: full-time $15,694; part-time $654 per credit hour. Required fees: $620. Tuition and fees vary according to course load, campus/location and program. *Financial support:* In 2006–07, 93 students received support; fellowships with full tuition reimbursements available, research assistantships with full tuition reimbursements available, teaching assistantships with full tuition reimbursements available, Federal Work-Study, institutionally sponsored loans, scholarships/grants, and tuition waivers (full) available. Support available to part-time students. Financial award application deadline: 5/1. *Faculty research:* Chronic illness, cancer, health services research, family health. Total annual research expenditures: $3 million. *Unit head:* Associate Dean for Graduate Programs, 317-274-2806, E-mail: nursing@iupui.edu. *Application contact:* Martez Plummer, Assistant Dean for Student Affairs, 317-274-2806, E-mail: mplummer@iupui.edu.

Kent State University, College of Nursing, Kent, OH 44242-0001. Offers clinical nursing (MSN), including nursing of the adult (medical/surgical nursing), psychiatric mental health nursing; nursing (PhD); nursing administration (MSN); nursing education (MSN); parent-child nursing (MSN). *Accreditation:* AACN. Part-time programs available. *Degree requirements:* For master's, thesis optional; for doctorate, thesis/dissertation, comprehensive exam, registration. *Entrance requirements:* For master's, GRE if undergraduate GPA is less than 3.0, minimum GPA of 2.75; for doctorate, GRE, MSN. Additional exam requirements/recommendations for international students: Required—TOEFL. Electronic applications accepted. Expenses: Contact institution. *Faculty research:* Women and violence, methodological specialties, osteoporosis in women, new caregivers and the elderly.

Louisiana State University Health Sciences Center, School of Nursing, New Orleans, LA 70112-2223. Offers adult health and illness (MN); adult health and nursing (DNS); neonatal nurse practitioner (MN); nursing (MN); nursing service administration (MN, DNS); parent-child health nursing (MN); primary care nurse practitioner (MN); psychiatric/community mental health nursing (MN, DNS); public health/community health nursing (MN, DNS). *Accreditation:* AACN; AANA/CANAEP (one or more programs are accredited). Part-time programs available. *Degree requirements:* For master's, thesis optional; for doctorate, thesis/dissertation. *Entrance requirements:* For master's, GRE General Test, MAT, minimum GPA of 3.0; for doctorate, GRE General Test, minimum GPA of 3.5. Additional exam requirements/recommendations for international students: Required—TOEFL. *Expenses:* Tuition, state resident: full-time $5,868; part-time $722 per credit. Tuition, nonresident: full-time $8,993; part-time $1,104 per credit. *Faculty research:* Advanced clinical practice, nursing education, health, social support, nursing administration.

Medical College of Georgia, School of Graduate Studies, Programs in Nursing, Augusta, GA 30912-1500. Offers adult nursing (MSN); community health nursing (MSN); mental health nursing (MSN); nurse practitioner (MSN); nursing (DNP, PhD); nursing anesthesia (MSN); parent-child nursing (MSN). *Accreditation:* AACN; AANA/CANAEP. Part-time programs available. *Faculty:* 18 full-time (16 women), 1 part-time/adjunct (0 women). *Students:* 95 full-time (76 women), 42 part-time (37 women); includes 24 minority (20 African Americans, 4 Asian Americans or Pacific Islanders). Average age 37. 156 applicants, 35% accepted, 24 enrolled. In 2006, 28 master's, 10 doctorates awarded. *Degree requirements:* For master's, thesis (for some programs); for doctorate, thesis/dissertation. *Entrance requirements:* For master's, GRE General Test, MAT; for doctorate, GRE General Test. Additional exam requirements/recommendations for international students: Required—TOEFL (minimum score 550 paper-based; 213 computer-based). *Application deadline:* For fall admission, 7/1 for domestic students, 4/15 for international students. Applications are processed on a rolling basis. Application fee: $30. Electronic applications accepted. *Expenses:* Tuition, state resident: full-time $2,293; part-time $192 per credit hour. Tuition, nonresident: full-time $9,169; part-time $765 per credit hour. Required fees: $293 per semester. *Financial support:* In 2006–07, 78 students received support, including 9 research assistantships with partial tuition reimbursements available (averaging $23,000 per year); Federal Work-Study, institutionally sponsored loans, traineeships, tuition waivers, and unspecified assistantships also available. Support available to part-time students. Financial award application deadline: 5/31; financial award applicants required to submit FAFSA. *Unit head:* Dr. Lucy Marion, Dean, 706-721-6258, Fax: 706-721-8169, E-mail: lumarion@mail.mcg.edu.

Medical University of South Carolina, College of Nursing, Program in Psychiatric Mental Health Nurse Practitioner, Charleston, SC 29425-0002. Offers MSN. Part-time programs available. *Faculty:* 10 full-time (9 women). *Students:* 7 full-time (6 women), 1 (woman) part-time; includes 2 minority (both African Americans) Average age 35. 7 applicants, 86% accepted, 3 enrolled. In 2006, 2 degrees awarded. *Degree requirements:* For master's, thesis optional. *Entrance requirements:* For master's, GRE General Test, BSN, course work in statistics and physical assessment, nursing license, minimum GPA of 3.0. Additional exam requirements/recommendations for international students: Required—TOEFL (minimum score 600 paper-based; 250 computer-based). *Application deadline:* For fall admission, 2/1 for domestic and international students; for spring admission, 9/15 for domestic and international students. Application fee: $75. Electronic applications accepted. *Financial support:* Federal Work-Study, scholarships/grants, and traineeships available. Support available to part-time students. Financial award application deadline: 3/15; financial award applicants required to submit FAFSA. *Faculty research:* Adolescent suicide, family drug court. Total annual research expenditures: $9,955. *Unit head:* Dr. Janet A. Grossman, Track Coordinator, 843-792-5645, Fax: 843-792-1741, E-mail: grossmja@musc.edu. *Application contact:* Carolyn F. Page, Director, Student Services, 843-792-3844, Fax: 843-792-9258, E-mail: pagecf@musc.edu.

MGH Institute of Health Professions, Graduate Programs, Program in Nursing, Boston, MA 02129. Offers advanced practice nursing (MSN); gerontological nursing (MSN); pediatric nursing (MSN); psychiatric nursing (MSN); teaching and learning for health care education (Certificate); women's health nursing (MSN). *Accreditation:* NLN (one or more programs are accredited). *Faculty:* 29 full-time (28 women), 9 part-time/adjunct (7 women). *Students:* 208 full-time (188 women), 43 part-time (35 women); includes 36 minority (12 African Americans, 17 Asian Americans or Pacific Islanders, 7 Hispanic Americans), 1 international. Average age 29. 302 applicants, 62% accepted, 101 enrolled. In 2006, 77 master's, 3 other advanced degrees awarded. *Degree requirements:* For master's, thesis or alternative. *Entrance requirements:* For master's, GRE General Test, minimum GPA of 3.0. Additional exam requirements/recommendations for international students: Required—TOEFL (minimum score 550 paper-based; 213 computer-based). *Application deadline:* For fall admission, 1/10 for domestic and international students. Application fee: $50. Electronic applications accepted. *Financial support:* In 2006–07, 212 students received support, including 1 research assistantship (averaging $1,200 per year), 2 teaching assistantships (averaging $1,200 per year); career-related internships or fieldwork, scholarships/grants, traineeships, tuition waivers (full and partial), and unspecified assistantships also available. Support available to part-time students. Financial award application deadline: 3/3; financial award applicants required to submit FAFSA. *Faculty research:* Biobehavioral nursing, HIV/AIDS, gerontological nursing, women's health, vulnerable populations, health systems . *Unit head:* Margery Chisholm, Director, 617-724-0480, Fax: 617-726-8022, E-mail: mchisholm@mghihp.edu. *Application contact:* Maureen Rika Judd, Manager of Admissions, 617-726-6069, Fax: 617-726-8010, E-mail: admissions@mghihp.edu.

See Close-Up on page 1963.

Molloy College, Department of Nursing, Rockville Centre, NY 11571-5002. Offers adult nurse practitioner (Advanced Certificate); clinical nurse specialist: adult health (Advanced Certificate); family nurse practitioner (Advanced Certificate); nurse practitioner psychiatry (Advanced Certificate); nursing (MS); nursing administration (Advanced Certificate); nursing administration with informatics (Advanced Certificate); nursing education (Advanced Certificate); nursing informatics (Advanced Certificate); pediatric nurse practitioner (Advanced Certificate). *Accreditation:* AACN. Part-time and evening/weekend programs available. *Degree requirements:* For master's, thesis optional. *Entrance requirements:* For master's, 3 letters of reference, BS in nursing, minimum undergraduate GPA of 3.0; for Advanced Certificate, 3 letters of reference, master's degree in nursing. *Faculty research:* Hardiness and aging, alcoholism, current ethics, breast cancer, nurse role perception.

New Mexico State University, Graduate School, College of Health and Social Services, School of Nursing, Las Cruces, NM 88003-8001. Offers community/public health (MSN); medical-surgical (adult health) (MSN); psychiatric/mental health (MSN). *Accreditation:* AACN. Part-time programs available. Postbaccalaureate distance learning degree programs offered (minimal on-campus study). *Faculty:* 12 full-time (all women), 5 part-time/adjunct (4 women). *Students:* 27 full-time (24 women), 25 part-time (all women); includes 13 minority (1 African American, 12 Hispanic Americans), 1 international. Average age 45. 24 applicants, 83% accepted. In 2006, 14 degrees awarded. *Degree requirements:* For master's, clinical practice, RN licensure, thesis optional. *Entrance requirements:* For master's, BSN, minimum GPA of 3.0, course work in statistics, 3 letters of reference, writing sample. Additional exam requirements/recommendations for international students: Required—NCLEX. *Application deadline:* For fall admission, 3/1 priority date for domestic students; for spring admission, 10/1 priority date for domestic students. Applications are processed on a rolling basis. Application fee: $30 ($50 for international students). Electronic applications accepted. *Financial support:* In 2006–07, 2 teaching assistantships were awarded; fellowships, research assistantships, career-related internships or fieldwork, Federal Work-Study, scholarships/grants, traineeships, and health care benefits also available. Financial award application deadline: 3/1. *Faculty research:* Advanced practice nursing, evidence-based nursing practice, health policy, community outreach, clinical judgment. *Unit head:* Dr. Esperanza V. Joyce, Director, 505-646-3812, Fax: 505-646-2167, E-mail: evjoyce@nmsu.edu. *Application contact:* Dr. Mary Hoke, Associate Director for Graduate Studies, 505-646-3812, Fax: 505-646-2167, E-mail: mhoke@nmsu.edu.

New York University, College of Dentistry, College of Nursing, Programs in Advanced Practice Nursing, New York, NY 10012-1019. Offers advanced practice nursing: adult acute care (MS, Advanced Certificate); advanced practice nursing: adult primary care (MS, Advanced Certificate); advanced practice nursing: adult primary care/geriatrics (MS); advanced practice nursing: children with special needs (Advanced Certificate); advanced practice nursing: geriatrics (MS, Advanced Certificate); advanced practice nursing: holistic nursing (MS, Advanced Certificate); advanced practice nursing: home health nursing (Advanced Certificate); advanced practice nursing: mental health (MS); advanced practice nursing: mental health nursing (Advanced Certificate); advanced practice nursing: pediatrics (MS, Advanced Certificate); advanced practice nursing: pediatrics/children with special needs (MS); midwifery (MS, Advanced Certificate); nursing administration (MS, Advanced Certificate); nursing education (MS, Advanced Certificate); nursing informatics (MS, Advanced Certificate); palliative care (MS, Advanced Certificate); MS/MS. *Accreditation:* AACN; ACNM/DOA. Part-time and evening/weekend programs available. *Faculty:* 30 full-time (all women). *Students:* 10 full-time (all women), 428 part-time (395 women); includes 166 minority (73 African Americans, 72 Asian Americans or Pacific Islanders, 21 Hispanic Americans). Average age 35. 154 applicants, 93% accepted, 118 enrolled. In 2006, 100 master's, 7 Advanced Certificates awarded. *Degree requirements:* For master's, thesis (for some programs). *Entrance requirements:* For master's, BS in nursing, AS in nursing with another BS/BA degree; for Advanced Certificate, master's degree. Additional exam requirements/recommendations for international students: Required—TOEFL. *Application deadline:* For fall admission, 7/1 priority date for domestic students, 7/1 for international students; for spring admission, 12/1 for domestic and international students. Applications are processed on a rolling basis. Application fee: $65. *Expenses:* Tuition: Part-time $1,080 per unit. Required fees: $56 per unit. $329 per term. Tuition and fees vary according to program. *Financial support:* Career-related internships or fieldwork, Federal Work-Study, institutionally sponsored loans, scholarships/grants, and tuition waivers (partial) available. Support available to part-time students. Financial award application deadline: 2/1; financial award applicants required to submit FAFSA. *Faculty research:* Elderly black diabetics, families and illness, public health nursing, parent-child nursing, health policy costs. *Unit head:* Dr. Judith Haber, Associate Dean for Graduate Programs, 212-998-5300, Fax: 212-995-3143. *Application contact:* Amy Knowles, Assistant Dean for Student Affairs and Admissions, 212-998-5333, Fax: 212-995-4302, E-mail: ak96@nyu.edu.

Northeastern University, Bouvé College of Health Sciences Graduate School, School of Nursing, Program in Psychiatric-Mental Health Nursing, Boston, MA 02115-5096. Offers MS, CAS. *Accreditation:* AACN. *Students:* 7 full-time (6 women), 15 part-time (14 women). Average age 45. 8 applicants, 63% accepted. In 2006, 2 degrees awarded. *Degree requirements:* For master's, thesis or alternative. *Entrance requirements:* For master's, GRE General Test, minimum GPA of 3.0, previous course work in statistics, 1-2 years of nursing experience, RN license, ICU experience; for CAS, MS in nursing. Additional exam requirements/recommendations for international students: Required—TOEFL. *Application deadline:* For fall admission, 4/1 priority date for domestic students; for spring admission, 2/1 for domestic students. Applications are processed on a rolling basis. Application fee: $50. *Financial support:* Research assistantships, teaching assistantships, tuition waivers (partial) available. Financial award application deadline: 7/1; financial award applicants required to submit FAFSA. *Faculty research:* Clinical psychopharmacology, access to mental health care, child abuse, seasonal affective disorder (SAD), chronic and persistent mental illness. *Application contact:* Margaret Schnabel, Director of Graduate Admissions, 617-373-2708, Fax: 617-373-4704, E-mail: bouvegrad@neu.edu.

Oregon Health & Science University, School of Nursing, Program in Mental Health Nursing, Portland, OR 97239-3098. Offers MS, Post Master's Certificate. *Accreditation:* AACN. *Degree requirements:* For master's, thesis optional. *Entrance requirements:* For master's, GRE General Test, bachelor's degree in nursing, minimum undergraduate GPA of 3.0, previous course work in statistics; for Post Master's Certificate, master's degree in nursing.

Pontifical Catholic University of Puerto Rico, College of Sciences, Department of Nursing, Ponce, PR 00717-0777. Offers medical-surgical nursing (MS); mental health and psychiatric nursing (MS). *Accreditation:* NLN. Part-time and evening/weekend programs available. *Degree requirements:* For master's, thesis, clinical research paper, comprehensive exam (for some programs), registration. *Entrance requirements:* For master's, GRE General Test, 2 letters of recommendation, interview, minimum GPA of 2.5. Electronic applications accepted.

Rush University, College of Nursing, Department of Community and Mental Health Nursing, Chicago, IL 60612-3832. Offers community and mental health nursing (DN Sc, DNP); family nurse practitioner (MSN, Post-Master's Certificate); psychiatric clinical specialist (MSN); psychiatric nurse practitioner—adult (MSN); psychiatric nurse practitioner—family (MSN); psychiatric-mental health clinical specialist (Post-Master's Certificate); psychiatric-mental health nurse practitioner (Post-Master's Certificate); public health nursing (MSN). *Accreditation:* AACN. Part-time programs available. Postbaccalaureate distance learning degree programs offered (minimal on-campus study). *Faculty:* 26. *Students:* 68 (65 women); includes 11 minority (6 African Americans, 4 Asian Americans or Pacific Islanders, 1 Hispanic American). Average age 35. 30 applicants, 93% accepted, 27 enrolled. In 2006, 1 master's, 13 doctorates awarded. Terminal master's awarded for partial completion of doctoral program. *Degree requirements:* For master's, capstone project; for doctorate, thesis/dissertation, DNP leadership project. *Entrance requirements:* For master's, GRE General Test (waived if nursing GPA is above 3.0 or cumulative GPA is above 3.25), interview; for doctorate, GRE General Test, interview, course work in statistics (DN Sc). *Application deadline:* For fall admission, 7/1 for domestic students; for winter admission, 11/1 for domestic students; for spring admission, 1/15 for domestic students. Applications are processed on a rolling basis. Application fee: $40. Electronic applications accepted. *Financial support:* In 2006–07, 11 students received support; teaching assistantships with tuition reimbursements available, Federal Work-Study, institutionally sponsored loans, scholarships/grants, and traineeships available. Support available to part-time students. Financial award applicants required to submit FAFSA. *Faculty research:* Immigrant mental health, de-escalation strategies, caregiver interventions, parent-teacher training, restraint use. *Unit head:* Dr. Julia Cowell, Chairperson, 312-942-7117. *Application contact:* Hicela Castruita Woods, Director, College Admissions Services, 312-942-7100, Fax: 312-942-2219, E-mail: hicela_castruita@rush.edu.

Rutgers, The State University of New Jersey, Newark, Graduate School, Program in Nursing, Newark, NJ 07102. Offers nursing (MS), including acute care of adults and aged, advanced practice in pediatric nursing, advanced practice with childbearing families, community health nursing, family nurse practitioner, primary care of adults and aged, psychiatric/mental health nursing. *Accreditation:* AACN. Part-time programs available. *Faculty:* 33 full-time (32 women). *Students:* 11 full-time (all women), 186 part-time (175 women); includes 70 minority (28 African Americans, 30 Asian Americans or Pacific Islanders, 12 Hispanic Americans). 255 applicants, 58% accepted, 72 enrolled. In 2006, 40 master's awarded. *Degree requirements:* For master's, comprehensive exam. *Entrance requirements:* For master's, GRE General Test, RN license, minimum B average, BS in nursing. Additional exam requirements/recommendations for international students: Required—TOEFL. *Application deadline:* For fall admission, 2/15 for domestic students; for spring admission, 12/1 for domestic students. Applications are processed on a rolling basis. Application fee: $50. Electronic applications accepted. *Financial support:* In 2006–07, 3 fellowships (averaging $8,000 per year) were awarded; teaching assistantships with full tuition reimbursements, career-related internships or fieldwork, Federal Work-Study, institutionally sponsored loans, scholarships/grants, traineeships, and tuition waivers (full and partial) also available. Financial award application deadline: 4/15. *Faculty research:* HIV/AIDS, quality of life—MS and breast cancer, sleep patterns of cardiac patients. *Unit head:* Dr. Wendy Nehring, Program Director, 973-353-5293 Ext. 606, Fax: 973-353-1277, E-mail: nehring@nightingale.rutgers.edu. *Application contact:* Dr. Linda Scheetz, Associate Dean for Student Life and Services, 973-353-5060 Ext. 611, Fax: 973-353-1277, E-mail: lscheetz@andromeda.rutgers.edu.

Sage Graduate School, Graduate School, Division of Nursing, Program in Psychiatric Mental Health Nurse Practitioner, Troy, NY 12180-4115. Offers psychiatric mental health (MS). *Accreditation:* AACN. Part-time and evening/weekend programs available. *Faculty:* 8 full-time (all women), 3 part-time/adjunct (all women). *Students:* 6 full-time (all women), 7 part-time (all women); includes 2 minority (1 African American, 1 American Indian/Alaska Native). Average age 39. 10 applicants, 90% accepted, 7 enrolled. In 2006, 7 degrees awarded. *Degree requirements:* For master's, thesis or alternative. *Entrance requirements:* For master's, BS in nursing, minimum GPA of 2.75. Additional exam requirements/recommendations for international students: Required—TOEFL (minimum score 550 paper-based; 213 computer-based). *Application deadline:* Applications are processed on a rolling basis. Application fee: $40. *Expenses:* Tuition: Full-time $9,270; part-time $515 per credit hour. *Financial support:* Career-related internships or fieldwork, scholarships/grants, and unspecified assistantships available. Support available to part-time students. Financial award application deadline: 3/1; financial award applicants required to submit FAFSA. *Unit head:* Arlene Pericak, Director, 518-244-2012, E-mail: perica@sage.edu. *Application contact:* Shannon K. Easton, Director of Graduate and Adult Admission, 518-244-2443, Fax: 518-244-6880, E-mail: sgsadm@sage.edu.

Saint Joseph College, Graduate Division, Department of Nursing, West Hartford, CT 06117-2700. Offers family health nurse practitioner (MS); family health nursing (MS); nursing (Post Master's Certificate); psychiatric/mental health nursing (MS). *Accreditation:* AACN. Part-time and evening/weekend programs available. *Degree requirements:* For master's and Post Master's Certificate, thesis. *Entrance requirements:* For master's, GRE General Test or MAT, 2 letters of recommendation; for Post Master's Certificate, MAT, master's degree in nursing, minimum GPA of 3.0. Additional exam requirements/recommendations for international students: Required—NCLEX. Electronic applications accepted. *Faculty research:* Reproductive health and substance abuse, problem-based learning, role of clinical faculty, students' international studies experience.

Saint Xavier University, Graduate Studies, School of Nursing, Chicago, IL 60655-3105. Offers adult health clinical nurse specialist (MS); family nurse practitioner (MS, PMC); leadership in community health nursing (MS); psychiatric-mental health clinical nurse specialist (MS); psychiatric-mental health clinical specialist (PMC); MBA/MS. *Accreditation:* AACN. Part-time and evening/weekend programs available. *Faculty:* 11. *Students:* 20 full-time (14 women), 120 part-time (113 women). Average age 40. In 2006, 36 degrees awarded. *Entrance requirements:* For master's, GRE General Test or MAT, minimum GPA of 3.0, RN license. *Application deadline:* For fall admission, 2/15 for domestic students; for spring admission, 9/15 for domestic students. Applications are processed on a rolling basis. Application fee: $35. *Financial support:* Available to part-time students. Applicants required to submit FAFSA. *Unit head:* Beth Gierach, Managing Director of Admission, 773-298-3053, Fax: 773-298-3076, E-mail: gierach@sxu.edu.

Seattle University, College of Nursing, Program in Nursing, Seattle, WA 98122-1090. Offers leadership in community nursing (MSN), including program development, spirituality and health; primary care nurse practitioner (MSN), including family nurse practitioner, psychiatric mental health nurse practitioner. *Students:* 6 full-time (all women), 8 part-time (7 women); includes 2 African Americans. Average age 40.*Application contact:* Janet Shandley, Associate Dean of Graduate Admissions, 206-296-5900, Fax: 206-298-5656, E-mail: grad_admissions@seattleu.edu.

Stony Brook University, State University of New York, Stony Brook University Medical Center, Health Sciences Center, School of Nursing, Program in Mental Health/Psychiatric Nursing, Stony Brook, NY 11794. Offers mental health nurse practitioner (Certificate); mental health/psychiatric nursing (MS). *Accreditation:* AACN. *Students:* 19 full-time (18 women), 45 part-time (38 women); includes 4 minority (3 African Americans, 1 Hispanic American), 1 international. In 2006, 21 master's, 9 other advanced degrees awarded. *Degree requirements:* For master's, thesis. *Entrance requirements:* For master's, BSN, minimum GPA of 3.0, course work in statistics. *Application deadline:* For fall admission, 1/15 for domestic students. Application fee: $60. *Expenses:* Tuition, state resident: full-time $6,900; part-time $288 per credit. Tuition, nonresident: full-time $10,920; part-time $455 per credit. *Financial support:* Application deadline: 3/15. *Unit head:* Dr. Arlene Steckel, Chair, 631-444-3264, Fax: 631-444-3136, E-mail: arlene.steckel@stonybrook.edu.

University at Buffalo, the State University of New York, Graduate School, School of Nursing, Buffalo, NY 14260. Offers acute care nurse practitioner (MS, Certificate); adult health nursing (MS, Certificate); child health nursing (MS); family nurse practitioner (Certificate); family nursing (MS); geriatric nurse practitioner (MS, Certificate); maternal and women's health nurse practitioner (Certificate); maternal and women's health nursing (MS); nurse anesthetist (MS); nursing (PhD); nursing education (Certificate); pediatric nurse practitioner (Certificate); psychiatric/mental health nurse practitioner (Certificate); psychiatric/mental health nursing (MS). *Accreditation:* AACN; AANA/CANAEP (one or more programs are accredited). Part-time programs available. Postbaccalaureate distance learning degree programs offered. *Faculty:* 38 full-time (34 women), 15 part-time/adjunct (14 women). *Students:* 131 full-time (108 women), 64 part-time (61 women); includes 29 minority (11 African Americans, 9 Asian Americans or Pacific Islanders, 9 Hispanic Americans), 20 international. Average age 28. 346 applicants, 25% accepted, 51 enrolled. In 2006, 49 master's, 3 doctorates, 6 other advanced degrees awarded. Terminal master's awarded for partial completion of doctoral program. *Degree requirements:* For master's, comprehensive exams or project; for doctorate, thesis/dissertation, comprehensive exam. *Entrance requirements:* For master's, GRE General Test (if overall GPA is below 3.0), interview, minimum GPA of 3.0, RN license, 3 references; for doctorate, GRE General Test, minimum GPA of 3.25, RN license, BS or MS in nursing, 3 references, writing sample; for Certificate, interview, minimum GPA of 3.0 or GRE General Test, RN license, MS in nursing. Additional exam requirements/recommendations for international students: Required—TOEFL (minimum score 550 paper-based; 213 computer-based; 79 iBT), IELTS (minimum score 7). *Application deadline:* For fall admission, 6/1 priority date for

Psychiatric Nursing

University at Buffalo, the State University of New York (continued)

domestic students, 3/1 priority date for international students; for spring admission, 11/1 for domestic students, 9/15 priority date for international students. Applications are processed on a rolling basis. Application fee: $50. Electronic applications accepted. *Financial support:* In 2006–07, 78 students received support, including 13 fellowships with full tuition reimbursements available (averaging $7,220 per year), 10 research assistantships with tuition reimbursements available (averaging $17,881 per year), 23 teaching assistantships with full tuition reimbursements available (averaging $11,245 per year); Federal Work-Study, scholarships/grants, traineeships, health care benefits, and unspecified assistantships also available. Financial award application deadline: 3/15; financial award applicants required to submit FAFSA. *Faculty research:* Oncology symptom management, end of life decision making, changing behaviors using the transtheoretical model, addictions, nursing workforce. Total annual research expenditures: $1.7 million. *Unit head:* Dr. Jean K. Brown, Dean, Interim, 716-829-2533, Fax: 716-829-2566, E-mail: jebrown@buffalo.edu. *Application contact:* Dr. Elaine R. Cusker, Assistant Dean, 716-829-2537, Fax: 716-829-2021, E-mail: ecusker@buffalo.edu.

University of Alaska Anchorage, College of Health and Social Welfare, School of Nursing, Anchorage, AK 99508-8060. Offers family nurse practitioner (Certificate); nursing (MS); nursing education (Certificate); psychiatric nurse practitioner (Certificate). *Accreditation:* NLN. Part-time and evening/weekend programs available. *Students:* 10 full-time (all women), 38 part-time (34 women); includes 6 minority (3 African Americans, 2 American Indian/Alaska Native, 1 Hispanic American). 15 applicants, 27% accepted. In 2006, 12 degrees awarded. *Degree requirements:* For master's, individual project. *Entrance requirements:* For master's, GRE or MAT, BS in nursing, interview, minimum GPA of 3.0, RN license, 1 year of part-time or 6 months of full-time clinical experience. Additional exam requirements/recommendations for international students: Required—TOEFL (minimum score 550 paper-based; 213 computer-based). *Application deadline:* For fall admission, 3/1 for domestic students; for spring admission, 11/1 for domestic students. Application fee: $45. *Expenses:* Tuition, state resident: part-time $268 per credit. Tuition, nonresident: part-time $547 per credit. Required fees: $124 per semester. Tuition and fees vary according to reciprocity agreements and student level. *Financial support:* Teaching assistantships, career-related internships or fieldwork, Federal Work-Study, and health care benefits available. Support available to part-time students. Financial award application deadline: 4/1; financial award applicants required to submit FAFSA. *Unit head:* Dr. Jean Ballantyne, Director, 907-786-4571, Fax: 907-786-4558. *Application contact:* Marie Samson, Coordinator of Student Affairs, 907-786-4561.

University of Cincinnati, Graduate School, College of Nursing, Cincinnati, OH 45221-0038. Offers clinical nurse specialist (MSN), including adult health, community health, neonatal, nursing administration, occupational health, pediatric health, psychiatric nursing, women's health; nurse anesthesia (MSN); nurse midwifery (MSN); nurse practitioner (MSN), including acute care, ambulatory care, family, family/psychiatric, women's health; nursing (PhD); MBA/MSN. *Accreditation:* AACN; AANA/CANAEP (one or more programs are accredited); ACNM/DOA. Part-time programs available. Postbaccalaureate distance learning degree programs offered (no on-campus study). *Faculty:* 41 full-time (39 women), 16 part-time/adjunct (15 women). *Students:* 159 full-time (125 women), 149 part-time (145 women); includes 40 minority (22 African Americans, 1 American Indian/Alaska Native, 16 Asian Americans or Pacific Islanders, 1 Hispanic American). Average age 34. 385 applicants, 49% accepted, 132 enrolled. In 2006, 77 master's, 5 doctorates awarded. Terminal master's awarded for partial completion of doctoral program. *Median time to degree:* Of those who began their doctoral program in fall 1998, 55% received their degree in 8 years or less. *Degree requirements:* For master's, thesis or alternative, registration; for doctorate, thesis/dissertation, comprehensive exam, registration. *Entrance requirements:* For master's and doctorate, GRE General Test. Additional exam requirements/recommendations for international students: Required—TOEFL (minimum score 520 paper-based; 190 computer-based). *Application deadline:* For fall admission, 7/26 priority date for domestic and international students. Applications are processed on a rolling basis. Application fee: $40. Electronic applications accepted. *Financial support:* In 2006–07, 164 students received support, including 7 fellowships with full tuition reimbursements available (averaging $13,571 per year), research assistantships with full tuition reimbursements available (averaging $12,000 per year), 8 teaching assistantships with full tuition reimbursements available (averaging $12,000 per year); career-related internships or fieldwork, scholarships/grants, traineeships, tuition waivers (partial), and unspecified assistantships also available. Support available to part-time students. Financial award application deadline: 5/1; financial award applicants required to submit FAFSA. *Faculty research:* Substance abuse, injury and violence, symptom management. Total annual research expenditures: $1.3 million. *Unit head:* Dr. Andrea R. Lindell, Dean, 513-558-5330, Fax: 513-558-9030, E-mail: andrea.lindell@uc.edu. *Application contact:* Loren Carter, Program Coordinator, 513-558-5072, Fax: 513-558-7523, E-mail: loren.carter@uc.edu.

University of Connecticut, Graduate School, School of Nursing, Field of Nursing, Storrs, CT 06269. Offers adult acute care (Post-Master's Certificate); adult primary care (Post-Master's Certificate); community health (Post-Master's Certificate); neonatal acute care (Post-Master's Certificate); nursing (MS, PhD); patient care services and systems administration (Post-Master's Certificate); psychiatric mental health (Post-Master's Certificate). *Accreditation:* AACN. *Faculty:* 20 full-time (18 women). *Students:* 38 full-time (33 women), 70 part-time (65 women); includes 17 minority (3 African Americans, 10 Asian Americans or Pacific Islanders, 4 Hispanic Americans), 1 international. Average age 37. 64 applicants, 69% accepted, 44 enrolled. In 2006, 25 master's, 7 doctorates, 1 other advanced degree awarded. *Degree requirements:* For master's, comprehensive exam; for doctorate, thesis/dissertation. *Entrance requirements:* Additional exam requirements/recommendations for international students: Required—TOEFL (minimum score 550 paper-based; 213 computer-based). *Application deadline:* For fall admission, 2/1 priority date for domestic and international students; for spring admission, 11/1 for domestic students, 10/1 for international students. Applications are processed on a rolling basis. Application fee: $55. Electronic applications accepted. *Financial support:* In 2006–07, 4 research assistantships with full tuition reimbursements, 13 teaching assistantships with full tuition reimbursements were awarded; fellowships, Federal Work-Study, scholarships/grants, health care benefits, and unspecified assistantships also available. Financial award application deadline: 2/1; financial award applicants required to submit FAFSA. *Unit head:* E. Carol Polifroni, Chairperson, 860-486-0511, Fax: 860-486-0001, E-mail: polifron@uconn.edu. *Application contact:* Lisa Mazzola, Academic Advisor Coordinator, 860-486-1973, E-mail: lisa.mazzola@uconn.edu.

University of Delaware, College of Health Sciences, School of Nursing, Newark, DE 19716. Offers adult nurse practitioner (MSN, PMC); cardiopulmonary clinical nurse specialist (MSN, PMC); cardiopulmonary clinical nurse specialist/adult nurse practitioner (MSN, PMC); family nurse practitioner (MSN, PMC); gerontology clinical nurse specialist (MSN, PMC); gerontology clinical nurse specialist geriatric nurse practitioner (PMC); gerontology clinical nurse specialist/geriatric nurse practitioner (MSN); health services administration (MSN, PMC); nursing of children clinical nurse specialist (MSN, PMC); nursing of children clinical nurse specialist/pediatric nurse practitioner (MSN, PMC); oncology/immune deficiency clinical nurse specialist (MSN, PMC); oncology/immune deficiency clinical nurse specialist/adult nurse practitioner (MSN, PMC); perinatal/women's health clinical nurse specialist (MSN, PMC); perinatal/women's health clinical nurse specialist/women's health nurse practitioner (MSN, PMC); psychiatric nursing clinical nurse specialist (MSN, PMC). *Accreditation:* AACN; NLN (one or more programs are accredited). Part-time and evening/weekend programs available. Postbaccalaureate distance learning degree programs offered (minimal on-campus study). *Degree requirements:* For master's, thesis optional. *Entrance requirements:* For master's, BSN, interview, RN license. Electronic applications accepted. *Faculty research:* Marriage and chronic illness, health promotion, congestive heart failure patient outcomes, school nursing, diabetes in children.

University of Illinois at Chicago, Graduate College, College of Nursing, Program in Nursing Sciences (Psychiatric Nursing), Chicago, IL 60607-7128. Offers MS. *Accreditation:* AACN. Part-time programs available. *Degree requirements:* For master's, thesis or alternative. *Entrance requirements:* For master's, GRE General Test, minimum GPA of 2.75. Additional exam requirements/recommendations for international students: Required—TOEFL. Electronic applications accepted.

University of Kansas, Graduate Studies Medical Center, School of Nursing, Kansas City, KS 66160. Offers nurse educator (PMC); nurse midwife (PMC); nursing (MS, PhD); psychiatric/mental health nurse practitioner (PMC). *Accreditation:* AACN; ACNM/DOA. Part-time programs available. Postbaccalaureate distance learning degree programs offered (minimal on-campus study). *Faculty:* 53 full-time (50 women), 3 part-time/adjunct (all women). *Students:* 63 full-time (59 women), 200 part-time (190 women); includes 37 minority (16 African Americans, 3 American Indian/Alaska Native, 12 Asian Americans or Pacific Islanders, 6 Hispanic Americans), 4 international. Average age 38. 88 applicants, 82% accepted, 62 enrolled. In 2006, 39 master's, 5 doctorates awarded. Terminal master's awarded for partial completion of doctoral program. *Median time to degree:* Master's–2.05 years full-time, 2.95 years part-time; doctorate–3.26 years part-time. Of those who began their doctoral program in fall 1998, 66% received their degree in 8 years or less. *Degree requirements:* For master's, general oral exam, thesis optional; for doctorate, one foreign language, thesis/dissertation, comprehensive oral and written exam. *Entrance requirements:* For master's, GRE General Test, bachelor's degree in nursing, minimum GPA of 3.0, RN license, 1 year of clinical experience; for doctorate, GRE General Test, master's degree in nursing, minimum GPA of 3.5. Additional exam requirements/recommendations for international students: Required—TOEFL. *Application deadline:* For fall admission, 4/1 for domestic students; for winter admission, 7/1 for domestic students; for spring admission, 9/1 for domestic students. Application fee: $50. *Expenses:* Tuition, area resident: Part-time $227 per credit. Tuition, state resident: part-time $543 per credit. Tuition and fees vary according to course load, campus/location, program and reciprocity agreements. *Financial support:* In 2006–07, 106 students received support, including 7 research assistantships (averaging $19,000 per year), 23 teaching assistantships with full and partial tuition reimbursements available (averaging $19,000 per year); traineeships also available. Financial award application deadline: 7/7. *Faculty research:* Breastfeeding practices of teen mothers, prevention of pressure ulcers, caregiving of families of patients using technology in the home, self care talk intervention partnership between caregivers of stroke survivors and nurses, smoking cessation. *Unit head:* Dr. Karen L. Miller, Dean, 913-588-1604, Fax: 913-588-1660, E-mail: kmiller@kumc.edu. *Application contact:* Dr. Rita K. Clifford, Associate Dean, Student Affairs, 913-588-1619, Fax: 913-588-1615, E-mail: rcliffor@kumc.edu.

University of Maryland, Baltimore, Graduate School, School of Nursing, Master's Program in Nursing, Baltimore, MD 21201. Offers community health nursing (MS); gerontological nursing (MS); maternal-child nursing (MS); medical-surgical nursing (MS); nurse-midwifery education (MS); nursing administration (MS); nursing education (MS); nursing health policy (MS); primary care nursing (MS); psychiatric nursing (MS); MS/MBA. *Accreditation:* AANA/CANAEP; ACNM/DOA; NLN (one or more programs are accredited). Part-time programs available. *Degree requirements:* For master's, thesis or alternative, comprehensive exam (for some programs). *Entrance requirements:* For master's, GRE General Test, minimum GPA of 2.75, course work in statistics, BS in nursing. Additional exam requirements/recommendations for international students: Required—TOEFL, TOEFL or IELTS; Recommended—IELTS. Electronic applications accepted.

University of Massachusetts Lowell, Graduate School, College of Health Professions, Department of Nursing, Program in Occupational Health Nursing, Lowell, MA 01854-2881. Offers adult psychiatric nursing (MS); occupational health nursing (MS). *Accreditation:* AACN. *Degree requirements:* For master's, thesis optional. *Entrance requirements:* For master's, GRE General Test.

University of Miami, Graduate School, School of Nursing and Health Studies, Coral Gables, FL 33124. Offers acute care (MSN), including acute care nurse practitioner, nurse anesthesia; community health (MSN); nursing (PhD); primary care (MSN), including adult nurse practitioner, family nurse practitioner, nurse midwifery, psychiatric/mental health nursing, women's health practitioner. *Accreditation:* AACN; AANA/CANAEP; ACNM/DOA (one or more programs are accredited). Part-time programs available. *Faculty:* 10 full-time (8 women), 1 (woman) part-time/adjunct. *Students:* 33 full-time (24 women), 27 part-time (24 women); includes 28 minority (7 African Americans, 5 Asian Americans or Pacific Islanders, 16 Hispanic Americans), 2 international. Average age 34. 108 applicants, 48% accepted, 30 enrolled. In 2006, 15 master's, 1 doctorate awarded. *Degree requirements:* For master's, thesis optional; for doctorate, thesis/dissertation. *Entrance requirements:* For master's, GRE General Test, BSN, minimum GPA of 3.0, Florida RN license; for doctorate, GRE General Test, BSN or MSN, minimum GPA of 3.0. Additional exam requirements/recommendations for international students: Required—TOEFL (minimum score 550 paper-based; 213 computer-based). *Application deadline:* For fall admission, 4/30 priority date for domestic students; for spring admission, 11/1 priority date for domestic students. Applications are processed on a rolling basis. Application fee: $50. Electronic applications accepted. *Financial support:* In 2006–07, 12 students received support, including 3 research assistantships with tuition reimbursements available (averaging $9,000 per year), 5 teaching assistantships with tuition reimbursements available (averaging $9,000 per year); fellowships, Federal Work-Study, institutionally sponsored loans, scholarships/grants, and unspecified assistantships also available. Support available to part-time students. Financial award application deadline: 3/1; financial award applicants required to submit FAFSA. *Faculty research:* Transcultural nursing, exercise and depression in Alzheimer's disease, infectious diseases/HIV–AIDS, postpartum depression, outcomes assessment. Total annual research expenditures: $31.9 million. *Unit head:* Dr. Nilda Peragallo, Dean, 305-284-2107, Fax: 305-667-3787, E-mail: nperagallo@miami.edu. *Application contact:* Anne Stabb, Graduate Advisor, 305-284-2533, Fax: 305-284-4827, E-mail: astabb@miami.edu.

University of Michigan, Horace H. Rackham School of Graduate Studies, School of Nursing, Division of Acute, Critical and Long-term Care, Program in Psychiatric Mental Health Nursing, Ann Arbor, MI 48109. Offers psychiatric mental health nurse practitioner (MS); psychiatric mental health nursing (MS). *Accreditation:* AACN. Part-time programs available. *Degree requirements:* For master's, thesis, registration. *Entrance requirements:* For master's, GRE General Test, licensure, minimum of B average in BSN program. Additional exam requirements/recommendations for international students: Required—TOEFL (minimum score 560 paper-based; 220 computer-based). Electronic applications accepted. *Faculty research:* Clinical specialist roles, depression, eating disorders, care of chronically mentally ill.

University of Minnesota, Twin Cities Campus, Graduate School, School of Nursing, Program in Psychiatric Mental Health Clinical Nurse Specialist, Minneapolis, MN 55455-0213. Offers MS. *Accreditation:* AACN. Part-time programs available. *Students:* 6 full-time (5 women), 7 part-time (all women), 12 international. *Entrance requirements:* Additional exam requirements/recommendations for international students: Required—TOEFL (minimum score 586 paper-based; 240 computer-based). *Application deadline:* For fall admission, 11/1 priority date for domestic and international students; for spring admission, 8/1 priority date for domestic and international students. Application fee: $55 ($75 for international students). *Unit head:* Dr. Merrie Kaas, Coordinator, 612-626-3781, Fax: 612-624-3174. *Application contact:* Information Contact, 612-624-4454, Fax: 612-624-3174, E-mail: nurseoss@umn.edu.

University of Pennsylvania, School of Nursing, Psychiatric Mental Health Advanced Practice Nurse Program, Philadelphia, PA 19104. Offers adult and special populations (MSN); child and family (MSN); geropsychiatrics (MSN). *Accreditation:* AACN. Part-time programs available. *Entrance requirements:* For master's, GRE General Test, BSN, minimum GPA of 3.0, previous course work in statistics. Additional exam requirements/recommendations for international students: Required—TOEFL. Expenses: Contact institution. *Faculty research:* Use of restraints in psychiatry, victims of trauma, spiritual use of prayer by cancer patients, coping strategies of African-Americans, urban health care.

University of Pittsburgh, School of Nursing, Program in Clinical Nurse Specialist, Pittsburgh, PA 15260. Offers medical/surgical clinical nurse specialist (MSN); psychiatric and mental health clinical nurse specialist (MSN). *Accreditation:* AACN. Part-time programs available. *Students:* 1 (woman) full-time, 23 part-time (21 women). Average age 37. 7 applicants, 86% accepted, 5 enrolled. In 2006, 9 degrees awarded. *Degree requirements:* For master's, thesis optional. *Entrance requirements:* For master's, GRE or MAT, BSN, RN license, letters of recommendation, resumé, course work in statistics, 1-3 years of nursing experience. Additional exam requirements/recommendations for international students: Required—TOEFL (minimum score 550 paper-based; 213 computer-based; 80 iBT). *Application deadline:* For fall admission, 8/1 priority date for domestic students; for spring admission, 12/1 priority date for domestic students. Applications are processed on a rolling basis. Application fee: $50. Electronic applications accepted. *Unit head:* Dr. Helen Burns, Associate Dean for Clinical Education, 412-624-6616, Fax: 412-624-2401, E-mail: burnsh@pitt.edu. *Application contact:* Laurie Lapsley, Administrator of Graduate Student Services, 412-624-9670, Fax: 412-624-2409, E-mail: lapsleyl@pitt.edu.

University of Pittsburgh, School of Nursing, Program in Nurse Practitioner Studies, Pittsburgh, PA 15260. Offers acute care nurse practitioner (MSN); adult nurse practitioner (MSN); family nurse practitioner (MSN); nursing practice (DNP); pediatric nurse practitioner (MSN); psychiatric primary care nurse practitioner (MSN). *Accreditation:* AACN. Part-time programs available. *Students:* 15 full-time (13 women), 65 part-time (57 women); includes 5 minority (3 African Americans, 2 Hispanic Americans). Average age 38. 47 applicants, 62% accepted, 27 enrolled. In 2006, 28 degrees awarded. *Degree requirements:* For master's, thesis optional. *Entrance requirements:* For master's, GRE General Test or MAT, BSN, RN license, letters of recommendation, resumé, course work in statistics, 1-3 years of nursing experience; for doctorate, GRE General Test, BSN, RN license, minimum GPA of 3.5, 3 letters of recommendation. Additional exam requirements/recommendations for international students: Required—TOEFL (minimum score 550 paper-based; 213 computer-based; 80 iBT). *Application deadline:* For fall admission, 8/1 priority date for domestic students, 8/1 for international students; for spring admission, 12/1 priority date for domestic students, 12/1 for international students. Applications are processed on a rolling basis. Application fee: $50. Electronic applications accepted.

University of Rhode Island, Graduate School, College of Nursing, Kingston, RI 02881. Offers administration (MS); clinical specialist in gerontology (MS); clinical specialist in psychiatric/mental health (MS); family nurse practitioner (MS); nurse midwifery (MS); nursing (PhD); nursing education (MS). *Accreditation:* AACN; ACNM/DOA (one or more programs are accredited). In 2006, 34 master's, 5 doctorates awarded. *Application deadline:* For fall admission, 4/15 for domestic students. Application fee: $35. *Expenses:* Tuition, state resident: full-time $6,032; part-time $335 per credit. Tuition, nonresident: full-time $17,288; part-time $960 per credit. Required fees: $65 per credit. $30 per semester. One-time fee: $80 part-time. *Unit head:* Dayle Joseph, Dean, 401-874-2766.

University of South Carolina, The Graduate School, College of Nursing, Program in Advanced Practice Nursing in Psychiatric Mental Health, Columbia, SC 29208. Offers MSN, Certificate. Part-time programs available. *Entrance requirements:* For master's, master's degree in nursing, RN license; for Certificate, MSN. Additional exam requirements/recommendations for international students: Required—TOEFL (minimum score 570 paper-based; 213 computer-based). Electronic applications accepted.

University of South Carolina, The Graduate School, College of Nursing, Program in Community Mental Health and Psychiatric Health Nursing, Columbia, SC 29208. Offers psychiatric/mental health nurse practitioner (MSN); psychiatric/mental health specialist (MSN). *Accreditation:* AACN. Part-time programs available. *Degree requirements:* For master's, thesis or alternative. *Entrance requirements:* For master's, GRE General Test, MAT, BS in nursing, nursing license. Additional exam requirements/recommendations for international students: Required—TOEFL (minimum score 570 paper-based; 230 computer-based). Electronic applications accepted. *Faculty research:* Substance abuse, violence against women, AIDS/HIV.

University of Southern Maine, College of Nursing and Health Professions, Portland, ME 04104-9300. Offers adult health nursing (PMC); clinical nurse leader (MS); clinical nurse specialist psychiatric-mental health nursing (MS); family nursing (PMC); medical/surgical nursing (MS); nurse practitioner adult health nursing (MS); nurse practitioner family nursing (MS); nurse practitioner psychiatric/mental health nursing (MS); psychiatric-mental health nursing (PMC); MBA/MSN. *Accreditation:* AACN. Part-time programs available. *Faculty:* 13 full-time (all women), 5 part-time/adjunct (4 women). *Students:* 55 full-time (53 women), 52 part-time (50 women); includes 6 minority (all Asian Americans or Pacific Islanders) Average age 36. 88 applicants, 93% accepted, 57 enrolled. In 2006, 25 degrees awarded. *Degree requirements:* For master's, thesis optional. *Entrance requirements:* For master's, GRE General Test or MAT, minimum GPA of 3.0. Additional exam requirements/recommendations for international students: Required—TOEFL (minimum score 550 paper-based; 213 computer-based). *Application deadline:* Applications are processed on a rolling basis. Application fee: $50. Electronic applications accepted. *Expenses:* Tuition, state resident: full-time $4,860; part-time $270 per credit hour. Tuition, nonresident: full-time $13,572; part-time $754 per credit hour. Required fees: $222 per semester. Tuition and fees vary according to course load. *Financial support:* In 2006–07, 14 students received support, including 5 research assistantships with tuition reimbursements available (averaging $3,375 per year), 7 teaching assistantships with tuition reimbursements available (averaging $3,375 per year); career-related internships or fieldwork, Federal Work-Study, scholarships/grants, traineeships, tuition waivers (full and partial), and unspecified assistantships also available. Support available to part-time students. Financial award application deadline: 2/15; financial award applicants required to submit FAFSA. *Faculty research:* Women's health, nursing history, weight control, community services, substance abuse. *Unit head:* Susan Sepples, Director of Nursing Program, 207-780-4505, Fax: 207-228-8177, E-mail: sepples@usm.maine.edu. *Application contact:* Mary Sloan, Director of Graduate Admissions, 207-780-4386, Fax: 207-780-4969, E-mail: gradstudies@usm.maine.edu.

University of Southern Mississippi, Graduate School, College of Health, School of Nursing, Hattiesburg, MS 39406-0001. Offers adult health nursing (MSN); community health nursing (MSN); ethics (PhD); family nurse practitioner (MSN); leadership (PhD); nursing service administration (MSN); policy analysis (PhD); psychiatric nursing (MSN). *Accreditation:* AACN. Part-time and evening/weekend programs available. *Faculty:* 14 full-time (all women). *Students:* 39 full-time (31 women), 69 part-time (62 women); includes 18 minority (15 African Americans, 1 Asian American or Pacific Islander, 2 Hispanic Americans), 1 international. Average age 39. 46 applicants, 50% accepted, 17 enrolled. In 2006, 36 master's, 6 doctorates awarded. *Degree requirements:* For master's, thesis optional; for doctorate, thesis/dissertation, comprehensive exam, registration. *Entrance requirements:* For master's, GRE General Test, minimum GPA of 2.75, nursing license, BS in nursing; for doctorate, GRE General Test, master's degree in nursing, minimum GPA of 3.5. Additional exam requirements/recommendations for international students: Required—TOEFL. *Application deadline:* For fall admission, 3/15 priority date for domestic students, 5/1 for international students. Applications are processed on a rolling basis. Application fee: $25 ($30 for international students). Electronic applications accepted. *Financial support:* In 2006–07, 1 research assistantship with full tuition reimbursement (averaging $10,125 per year), 1 teaching assistantship (averaging $10,125 per year) were awarded; Federal Work-Study and traineeships also available. Financial award application deadline: 3/15. *Faculty research:* Gerontology, caregivers, HIV, bereavement, pain, nursing leadership. *Unit head:* Dr. Katherine Nugent, Director and Associate Dean, 601-266-5500, Fax: 601-266-5927. *Application contact:* Dr. Anne Brock, Graduate Coordinator, 601-266-5500, Fax: 601-266-5927.

Vanderbilt University, School of Nursing, Nashville, TN 37235. Offers adult acute care nurse practitioner (MSN); adult health nurse practitioner/forensic (MSN); adult nurse practitioner/cardiovascular disease management and prevention (MSN); adult nurse practitioner/palliative care (MSN); clinical management (clinical nurse leader/specialist) (MSN); family nurse practitioner (MSN); gerontology nurse practitioner (MSN); health systems management (MSN); neonatal nurse practitioner (MSN); nurse midwifery (MSN); nursing informatics (MSN); nursing science (PhD); pediatric acute care nurse practitioner (MSN); pediatric primary care nurse practitioner (MSN); psychiatric-mental health nurse practitioner (MSN); women's health nurse practitioner (MSN); MBA/MSN; MSN/MTS; MSN/PhD. *Accreditation:* ACNM/DOA; NLN (one or more programs are accredited). Part-time and evening/weekend programs available. Postbaccalaureate distance learning degree programs offered (minimal on-campus study). *Faculty:* 95 full-time (83 women), 432 part-time/adjunct (314 women). *Students:* 371 full-time (325 women), 206 part-time (180 women); includes 59 minority (38 African Americans, 2 American Indian/Alaska Native, 7 Asian Americans or Pacific Islanders, 12 Hispanic Americans). Average age 27. 611 applicants, 55% accepted, 308 enrolled. In 2006, 256 master's, 2 doctorates awarded. *Degree requirements:* For doctorate, thesis/dissertation. *Entrance requirements:* For master's, GRE, interview; for doctorate, GRE, interview, 3 letters of recommendation. Additional exam requirements/recommendations for international students: Required—TOEFL. *Application deadline:* For fall admission, 12/1 priority date for domestic and international students. Applications are processed on a rolling basis. Application fee: $50. *Expenses:* Contact institution. *Financial support:* In 2006–07, 404 students received support, including 5 research assistantships (averaging $8,000 per year); Federal Work-Study, institutionally sponsored loans, and unspecified assistantships also available. Support available to part-time students. Financial award application deadline: 3/15; financial award applicants required to submit CSS PROFILE or FAFSA. *Faculty research:* Lymphedema post cancer treatment, palliative care and bereavement, patient safety and quality of care, health care workforce issues, symptom management including pain and fatigue. Total annual research expenditures: $1.1 million. *Unit head:* Dr. Colleen Conway-Welch, Dean, 615-343-8776, Fax: 615-343-7711, E-mail: colleen.conway-welch@vanderbilt.edu. *Application contact:* Cheryl Feldner, Assistant Director of Admissions, 615-322-3800, Fax: 615-343-0333, E-mail: cheryl.feldner@vanderbilt.edu.

Virginia Commonwealth University, Graduate School, School of Nursing, Richmond, VA 23284-9005. Offers adult health nursing (MS); child health nursing (MS); family health nursing (MS); health system (PhD); immunocompetence (PhD); nurse practitioner (MS, Certificate); nursing administration (MS), including clinical nurse manager, nurse executive; psychiatric-mental health nursing (MS); risk and resilience (PhD); women's health nursing (MS). *Accreditation:* NLN (one or more programs are accredited). Part-time and evening/weekend programs available. *Faculty:* 23 full-time (21 women). *Students:* 131 full-time (125 women), 137 part-time (129 women); includes 33 minority (19 African Americans, 11 Asian Americans or Pacific Islanders, 3 Hispanic Americans), 12 international. 110 applicants, 82% accepted, 66 enrolled. In 2006, 57 master's, 1 doctorate, 3 other advanced degrees awarded. *Degree requirements:* For master's, thesis optional; for doctorate, thesis/dissertation. *Entrance requirements:* For master's, GRE General Test, BSN, minimum GPA of 2.8; for doctorate, GRE General Test. *Application deadline:* For fall admission, 2/1 priority date for domestic students. Application fee: $50. *Financial support:* Fellowships, research assistantships, teaching assistantships, career-related internships or fieldwork and institutionally sponsored loans available. *Unit head:* Dr. Nancy F. Langston, Dean, 804-828-5174, Fax: 804-828-7743, E-mail: nflangst@vcu.edu. *Application contact:* Susan Lipp, Admissions Counselor, 804-828-5171, Fax: 804-828-7743, E-mail: slipp@vcu.edu.

See Close-Up on page 1983.

Wayne State University, College of Nursing, Department of Family, Community and Mental Health, Program in Psychiatric Mental Health Nurse Practitioner, Detroit, MI 48202. Offers MSN, Certificate. *Accreditation:* AACN. Part-time programs available. *Students:* 1 (woman) full-time, 7 part-time (6 women); includes 2 minority (1 African American, 1 Hispanic American). Average age 43. 4 applicants, 100% accepted, 3 enrolled. In 2006, 2 degrees awarded. *Degree requirements:* For master's, thesis or alternative. *Entrance requirements:* For master's, GRE General Test, minimum GPA of 2.8. Additional exam requirements/recommendations for international students: Required—TOEFL (minimum score 550 paper-based; 213 computer-based); Recommended—TWE (minimum score 6). *Application deadline:* For fall admission, 7/1 priority date for domestic students, 6/1 for international students; for winter admission, 10/1 for international students; for spring admission, 11/1 for domestic students, 2/1 for international students. Applications are processed on a rolling basis. Application fee: $30 ($50 for international students). Electronic applications accepted. *Financial support:* In 2006–07, 1 student received support; research assistantships, institutionally sponsored loans and scholarships/grants available. Support available to part-time students. Financial award application deadline: 7/1; financial award applicants required to submit FAFSA. *Faculty research:* Immigrant and minority health, homelessness, HIV/AIDS, promotion of sleep, substance abuse. *Application contact:* Janet Harden, Academic Director, 313-577-4082.

School Nursing

Kutztown University of Pennsylvania, College of Graduate Studies and Extended Learning, College of Liberal Arts and Sciences, Program in School Nursing, Kutztown, PA 19530-0730. Offers Certificate. Part-time and evening/weekend programs available. *Students:* Average age 34. 7 applicants, 100% accepted, 5 enrolled. *Entrance requirements:* Additional exam requirements/recommendations for international students: Required—TOEFL. *Application deadline:* Applications are processed on a rolling basis. Application fee: $35. Electronic applications accepted. *Expenses:* Tuition, state resident: full-time $6,048; part-time $336 per credit. Tuition, nonresident: full-time $9,678; part-time $538 per credit. *Unit head:* Dr. Kim Johnston, Graduate Coordinator, 610-683-4328, Fax: 610-683-4708, E-mail: johnston@kutztown.edu.

La Salle University, School of Nursing and Health Sciences, Philadelphia, PA 19141-1199. Offers adult health and illness, clinical nurse specialist (MSN); gerontology (Certificate); nursing administration (MSN); nursing education (Certificate); nursing informatics (Certificate); primary care of adults-nurse practitioner (MSN); public health nursing (MSN); school nursing (Certificate); speech-language-hearing science (MS); wound, ostomy and continence nursing (Certificate); wound, ostomy, and continence nursing (MSN); MSN/MBA. *Accreditation:* AACN. Part-time programs available. Postbaccalaureate distance learning degree programs offered (minimal on-campus study). *Entrance requirements:* For master's, GRE or MAT, 1 year of professional work experience, BSN, Pennsylvania RN license. Expenses: Contact institution. *Faculty research:* Medication errors, wound care, metacognition, education of RN students.

Monmouth University, Graduate School, The Marjorie K. Unterberg School of Nursing and Health Studies, West Long Branch, NJ 07764-1898. Offers advanced practice nursing (Post-Master's Certificate); nursing (MSN); school nursing (Certificate); substance awareness coordinator (Certificate). *Accreditation:* AACN. Part-time and evening/weekend programs available.

School Nursing

Monmouth University (continued)
Faculty: 10 full-time (all women), 1 part-time/adjunct (0 women). *Students:* 5 full-time (4 women), 189 part-time (186 women); includes 26 minority (9 African Americans, 13 Asian Americans or Pacific Islanders, 4 Hispanic Americans). Average age 43. 94 applicants, 100% accepted, 44 enrolled. In 2006, 38 degrees awarded. *Entrance requirements:* For master's, GRE General Test, RN license, 1 year of work experience, minimum undergraduate GPA of 2.75. Additional exam requirements/recommendations for international students: Required—TOEFL (minimum score 550 paper-based; 213 computer-based; 79 iBT), IELTS (minimum score 5), MELAB 77, Cambridge A, B, C. *Application deadline:* For fall admission, 7/15 priority date for domestic students, 6/1 for international students; for spring admission, 11/15 priority date for domestic students, 11/1 for international students. Applications are processed on a rolling basis. Application fee: $50. Electronic applications accepted. *Expenses:* Tuition: Full-time $12,780; part-time $710 per credit. Required fees: $628; $314 per term. *Financial support:* In 2006–07, 136 fellowships (averaging $1,053 per year), 4 research assistantships (averaging $3,483 per year) were awarded; career-related internships or fieldwork, scholarships/grants, tuition waivers (partial), and unspecified assistantships also available. Support available to part-time students. Financial award application deadline: 3/1; financial award applicants required to submit FAFSA. *Faculty research:* Relationship of undergraduate GPA and GRE to succeed in a graduate nursing program. *Unit head:* Dr. Janet Mahoney, Director, 732-571-3443, Fax: 732-263-5131, E-mail: jmahoney@monmouth.edu. *Application contact:* Kevin Roane, Director, Office of Graduate Admission, 732-571-3452, Fax: 732-263-5123, E-mail: gradadm@monmouth.edu.

Seton Hall University, College of Nursing, Department of Graduate Nursing, School Nurse Program, South Orange, NJ 07079-2697. Offers MSN.

Wright State University, School of Graduate Studies, College of Nursing and Health, Program in Nursing, Dayton, OH 45435. Offers acute care nurse practitioner (MS); administration of nursing and health care systems (MS); adult health (MS); child and adolescent health (MS); community health (MS); family nurse practitioner (MS); nurse practitioner (MS); school nurse (MS); MBA/MS. *Accreditation:* AACN. Part-time and evening/weekend programs available. *Students:* 46 full-time (45 women), 124 part-time (117 women); includes 16 minority (13 African Americans, 1 Asian American or Pacific Islander, 2 Hispanic Americans). Average age 39. 45 applicants, 100% accepted. In 2006, 64 degrees awarded. *Degree requirements:* For master's, thesis or alternative. *Entrance requirements:* For master's, GRE General Test, BSN from NLN-accredited college, Ohio RN license. Additional exam requirements/recommendations for international students: Required—TOEFL. *Application deadline:* For fall admission, 4/15 priority date for domestic students. Application fee: $25. *Financial support:* Fellowships, research assistantships, teaching assistantships, Federal Work-Study, institutionally sponsored loans, and unspecified assistantships available. Support available to part-time students. Financial award application deadline: 6/1; financial award applicants required to submit FAFSA. *Faculty research:* Clinical nursing and health, teaching, caring, pain administration, informatics and technology. *Application contact:* Theresa A. Haghnazarian, Director of Student and Alumni Affairs, 937-775-2592, Fax: 937-775-4571, E-mail: theresa.haghnazarian@wright.edu.

Transcultural Nursing

Augsburg College, Program in Transcultural Community Health Nursing, Minneapolis, MN 55454-1351. Offers MA. *Accreditation:* AACN. *Faculty:* 2 full-time (both women). *Students:* 6 full-time (all women), 43 part-time (42 women); includes 2 minority (both African Americans), 1 international. Average age 45. 120 applicants, 18% accepted, 20 enrolled. In 2006, 8 degrees awarded. *Degree requirements:* For master's, thesis or alternative. *Application deadline:* For fall admission, 8/1 for domestic students; for winter admission, 12/4 for domestic students; for spring admission, 3/9 for domestic students. Application fee: $35. *Expenses:* Tuition: Full-time $10,584; part-time $1,764 per course. Required fees: $300; $35 per course. Tuition and fees vary according to program. *Financial support:* In 2006–07, 5 students received support. Application deadline: 8/1; *Unit head:* Dr. Cheryl J. Leuning, Director, 612-330-1214, E-mail: leuning@augsburg.edu. *Application contact:* Sharon Wade, Coordinator, 612-330-1209, E-mail: wades@augsburg.edu.

New Jersey City University, Graduate and Continuing Education, College of Professional Studies, Department of Nursing, Jersey City, NJ 07305-1597. Offers holistic nursing (MSN); urban health (MSN). Part-time and evening/weekend programs available. *Faculty:* 1. *Students:* Average age 57. In 2006, 1 degree awarded. *Application deadline:* For fall admission, 8/1 priority date for domestic students; for spring admission, 12/1 for domestic students. Applications are processed on a rolling basis. Application fee: $0. *Expenses:* Tuition, state resident: full-time $7,038; part-time $391 per credit. Tuition, nonresident: full-time $12,510; part-time $695 per credit. Required fees: $65 per credit. *Unit head:* Dr. Gloria Boseman, Chair, 201-200-3157, E-mail: gboseman@njcu.edu.

University of Medicine and Dentistry of New Jersey, School of Nursing, Program in Urban Health, Newark, NJ 07107-1709. Offers PhD. Part-time and evening/weekend programs available. *Entrance requirements:* Additional exam requirements/recommendations for international students: Required—TOEFL. *Application deadline:* For fall admission, 4/1 for domestic students; for spring admission, 10/1 for domestic students. Applications are processed on a rolling basis. Application fee: $50. Electronic applications accepted. *Financial support:* Institutionally sponsored loans, scholarships/grants, and traineeships available. Support available to part-time students. *Unit head:* Dr. Jeffrey Backstand, Director, 973-972-9731, Fax: 973-972-7453, E-mail: backstjr@umdnj.edu.

Women's Health Nursing

Case Western Reserve University, Frances Payne Bolton School of Nursing, Doctor of Nursing Practice Program, Cleveland, OH 44106. Offers acute care nurse practitioner (DNP); adult nurse practitioner (DNP); family nurse practitioner (DNP); gerontological nurse practitioner (DNP); graduate entry/pre-licensure option (DNP); medical-surgical nursing (DNP); midwifery/family nursing (DNP); neonatal nurse practitioner (DNP); pediatric nurse practitioner (DNP); post-licensure option (DNP); psychiatric mental health nurse practitioner (DNP); women's health nurse practitioner (DNP). Graduate entry option allows baccalaureate-prepared college graduates from non-nursing backgrounds to earn certificate and MSN in addition to ND. *Students:* 125 full-time (109 women), 308 part-time (290 women); includes 47 minority (21 African Americans, 1 American Indian/Alaska Native, 18 Asian Americans or Pacific Islanders, 7 Hispanic Americans), 7 international. 190 applicants, 70% accepted, 80 enrolled. In 2006, 35 degrees awarded. Terminal master's awarded for partial completion of doctoral program. *Degree requirements:* For doctorate, thesis/dissertation. *Entrance requirements:* For doctorate, GRE General Test or MAT. *Application deadline:* For fall admission, 6/1 priority date for domestic students. Applications are processed on a rolling basis. Application fee: $75. *Financial support:* In 2006–07, 6 students received support, including 1 teaching assistantship; research assistantships, Federal Work-Study, institutionally sponsored loans, and tuition waivers (partial) also available. Support available to part-time students. Financial award application deadline: 6/30; financial award applicants required to submit FAFSA. *Faculty research:* Clinical nursing, acute care, gerontology, mental health, critical care. *Unit head:* Dr. Georgia Narsavage, Director, 216-368-6304, Fax: 216-368-3542, E-mail: gln2@cwru.edu. *Application contact:* Peter Taylor, Recruitment and Retention Specialist, 216-368-0349, Fax: 216-368-0124, E-mail: peter.taylor@case.edu.

Case Western Reserve University, Frances Payne Bolton School of Nursing, Master's Programs in Nursing, Nurse Practitioner Program, Cleveland, OH 44106. Offers acute care cardiovascular nursing (MSN); acute care nurse practitioner (MSN); acute care/flight nurse (MSN); adult nurse practitioner (MSN); family nurse practitioner (MSN); gerontological nurse practitioner (MSN); neonatal nurse practitioner (MSN); pediatric nurse practitioner (MSN); psychiatric-mental health nurse practitioner (MSN); women's health nurse practitioner (MSN). *Accreditation:* NLN. Part-time programs available. Postbaccalaureate distance learning degree programs offered (minimal on-campus study). *Faculty:* 54 full-time (50 women), 5 part-time/adjunct (3 women). *Students:* 19 full-time (15 women), 31 part-time (29 women); includes 16 minority (9 African Americans, 5 Asian Americans or Pacific Islanders, 2 Hispanic Americans), 2 international. Average age 35. 46 applicants, 72% accepted, 18 enrolled. In 2006, 34 degrees awarded. *Degree requirements:* For master's, thesis optional. *Entrance requirements:* For master's, GRE General Test or MAT. Additional exam requirements/recommendations for international students: Required—TOEFL. *Application deadline:* For fall admission, 6/1 for domestic students. Applications are processed on a rolling basis. Application fee: $75. *Financial support:* In 2006–07, 7 teaching assistantships were awarded; research assistantships, institutionally sponsored loans and tuition waivers (partial) also available. Support available to part-time students. Financial award application deadline: 6/30. *Faculty research:* Positive and negative mood states in parents of twins, effect of a carepath on chronic obstructive pulmonary disease home care. *Application contact:* Peter Taylor, Recruitment and Retention Specialist, 216-368-0349, Fax: 216-368-0124, E-mail: peter.taylor@case.edu.

Columbia University, School of Nursing, Program in Women's Health Nurse Practitioner, New York, NY 10032. Offers Adv C. *Accreditation:* AACN. Part-time programs available. *Faculty:* 1 (woman) full-time. *Students:* 8 full-time (all women), 10 part-time (all women); includes 5 minority (3 African Americans, 2 Hispanic Americans). Average age 31. *Entrance requirements:* For degree, MSN. *Application deadline:* Applications are processed on a rolling basis. Application fee: $65. Electronic applications accepted. *Financial support:* Teaching assistantships available. Financial award application deadline: 2/1; financial award applicants required to submit FAFSA. *Unit head:* Prof. MaryJane McEneaney, Unit Head, 212-342-5613.

Emory University, Nell Hodgson Woodruff School of Nursing, Atlanta, GA 30322-1100. Offers adult and elder health advanced practice nursing (MSN), including acute and critical care, adult nurse practitioner, gerontology, oncology; emergency nurse practitioner (MSN); family nurse practitioner (MSN); family nurse-midwife (MSN); leadership in healthcare (MSN); nurse midwifery (MSN); nursing administration (MSN); pediatric advanced nursing practice (MSN); public health nursing (MSN); women's health nurse practitioner (MSN); MSN/MPH. *Accreditation:* AACN; ACNM/DOA (one or more programs are accredited). Part-time programs available. *Entrance requirements:* For master's, GRE General Test or MAT, minimum GPA of 3.0, BS in nursing, RN license and additional course work, 3 letters of recommendation. Additional exam requirements/recommendations for international students: Required—TOEFL (minimum score 600 paper-based; 250 computer-based). Electronic applications accepted. Expenses: Contact institution. *Faculty research:* Older adult falls and injuries, minority health issues, cardiac symptoms and quality of life, bio-ethics and decision making, menopausal issues.

See Close-Up on page 1955.

Frontier School of Midwifery and Family Nursing, Graduate Programs, Hyden, KY 41749. Offers community-based family nurse practitioner (MSN, Post Master's Certificate); community-based nurse-midwifery education (MSN, Post Master's Certificate); community-based women[0092]s health care nurse practitioner (MSN, Post Master's Certificate). *Accreditation:* ACNM; NLN.

Georgia Southern University, Jack N. Averitt College of Graduate Studies, College of Health and Human Sciences, School of Nursing, Statesboro, GA 30460. Offers rural community health nurse practitioner (MSN); rural community health nurse specialist (Certificate); rural family nurse practitioner (MSN, Certificate); women's health nurse practitioner (MSN, Certificate). *Accreditation:* AACN. Part-time programs available. Postbaccalaureate distance learning degree programs offered. *Faculty:* 13 full-time (all women). *Students:* 6 full-time (all women), 40 part-time (38 women); includes 6 minority (all African Americans) Average age 34. 14 applicants, 100% accepted. In 2006, 15 degrees awarded. *Degree requirements:* For master's, thesis optional. *Entrance requirements:* For master's, GRE General Test or MAT, minimum GPA of 3.0, Georgia nursing license, 2 years of clinical experience, CPR certification; for Certificate, MSN. Additional exam requirements/recommendations for international students: Required—TOEFL (minimum score 550 paper-based; 213 computer-based; 80 iBT). *Application deadline:* For fall admission, 3/1 priority date for domestic students, 3/1 for international students; for spring admission, 10/1 priority date for domestic students, 10/1 for international students. Applications are processed on a rolling basis. Application fee: $50. Electronic applications accepted. *Financial support:* In 2006–07, 35 students received support, including research assistantships with partial tuition reimbursements available (averaging $5,500 per year), teaching assistantships with partial tuition reimbursements available (averaging $5,500 per year); career-related internships or fieldwork, Federal Work-Study, scholarships/grants, traineeships, tuition waivers (partial), and unspecified assistantships also available. Support available to part-time students. Financial award application deadline: 4/15; financial award applicants required to submit FAFSA. *Faculty research:* Caring, HIV disease, qualitative health research, health policy, rural nursing. Total annual research expenditures: $189,915. *Unit head:* Dr. Jean Bartels, Chair, 912-681-5479, Fax: 912-681-0536, E-mail: jbartels@georgiasouthern.edu. *Application contact:* 912-681-5384, Fax: 912-681-0740, E-mail: gradadmissionss@georgiasouthern.edu.

Georgia State University, College of Health and Human Sciences, School of Nursing, Atlanta, GA 30303-3083. Offers adult health (MS); child health (MS); family nurse practitioner

(MS); health promotion, protection and restoration (PhD); nursing (Certificate); perinatal/women's health (MS); psychiatric/mental health (MS). *Accreditation:* AACN. Part-time and evening/weekend programs available. *Faculty:* 35 full-time (all women), 1 (woman) part-time/adjunct. *Students:* 72 full-time (66 women), 128 part-time (123 women); includes 75 minority (61 African Americans, 9 Asian Americans or Pacific Islanders, 5 Hispanic Americans), 2 international. Average age 37. 70 applicants, 54% accepted, 30 enrolled. In 2006, 39 master's, 6 doctorates awarded. *Degree requirements:* For master's, research activity; for doctorate, thesis/dissertation, comprehensive exam. *Entrance requirements:* For master's, MAT (preferred) or GRE, interview, RN license; for doctorate, GRE General Test. Additional exam requirements/recommendations for international students: Required—TOEFL (minimum score 550 paper-based; 213 computer-based). *Application deadline:* For fall admission, 3/1 priority date for domestic students; for spring admission, 10/1 priority date for domestic students. Applications are processed on a rolling basis. Application fee: $50. Electronic applications accepted. *Expenses: Contact institution. Financial support:* In 2006–07, research assistantships with full and partial tuition reimbursements (averaging $3,108 per year); fellowships with full tuition reimbursements, teaching assistantships, Federal Work-Study, institutionally sponsored loans, scholarships/grants, traineeships, and tuition waivers (partial) also available. Support available to part-time students. Financial award application deadline: 4/1; financial award applicants required to submit FAFSA. *Faculty research:* Breast cancer prevention, sexually compulsive behaviors, health risks in minority youth, asthma treatment strategies, adolescent alcohol-related issues. Total annual research expenditures: $221,691. *Unit head:* Dr. Barbara Woodring, Director, 404-651-3040. *Application contact:* Barbara Smith, Admissions Counselor II, 404-651-3834, Fax: 404-651-4871, E-mail: bbsmith@gsu.edu.

Indiana University–Purdue University Indianapolis, School of Nursing, Indianapolis, IN 46202-2896. Offers acute care nurse practitioner (MSN); adult health clinical nurse specialist (MSN); adult health nursing (MSN), including adult clinical nurse specialist; adult nurse practitioner (MSN); adult psychiatric/mental health nursing (MSN); child psychiatric/mental health nursing (MSN); community health nursing (MSN); family nurse practitioner (MSN); neonatal nurse practitioner (MSN); nursing science (PhD); pediatric clinical nurse specialist (MSN); women's health nurse practitioner (MSN); MSN/MPA; MSN/MPH. *Accreditation:* AACN; NLN (one or more programs are accredited). Part-time programs available. *Faculty:* 45 full-time (44 women), 1 (woman) part-time/adjunct. *Students:* 52 full-time (51 women), 415 part-time (396 women); includes 27 minority (16 African Americans, 3 Asian Americans or Pacific Islanders, 8 Hispanic Americans), 4 international. Average age 38. In 2006, 106 master's, 3 doctorates awarded. Terminal master's awarded for partial completion of doctoral program. *Degree requirements:* For master's and doctorate, thesis/dissertation. *Entrance requirements:* For master's, GRE General Test, minimum GPA of 3.0, RN license; for doctorate, GRE General Test, minimum GPA of 3.5, MSN, RN license. Additional exam requirements/recommendations for international students: Required—TOEFL. *Application deadline:* For fall admission, 2/15 for domestic students; for spring admission, 9/15 for domestic students. Application fee: $50 ($60 for international students). *Expenses:* Tuition, state resident: full-time $5,437; part-time $227 per credit hour. Tuition, nonresident: full-time $15,694; part-time $654 per credit hour. Required fees: $620. Tuition and fees vary according to course load, campus/location and program. *Financial support:* In 2006–07, 93 students received support; fellowships with full tuition reimbursements available, research assistantships with full tuition reimbursements available, teaching assistantships with full tuition reimbursements available, Federal Work-Study, institutionally sponsored loans, scholarships/grants, and tuition waivers (full) available. Support available to part-time students. Financial award application deadline: 5/1. *Faculty research:* Chronic illness, cancer, health services research, family health. Total annual research expenditures: $3 million. *Unit head:* Associate Dean for Graduate Programs, 317-274-2806, E-mail: nursing@iupui.edu. *Application contact:* Martez Plummer, Assistant Dean for Student Affairs, 317-274-2806, E-mail: mplummer@iupui.edu.

Loyola University Chicago, Graduate School, Marcella Niehoff School of Nursing, Women's Health Nurse Practitioner Program, Chicago, IL 60611-2196. Offers MSN. *Accreditation:* AACN. Part-time and evening/weekend programs available. *Students:* 2 full-time (both women), 7 part-time (all women). Average age 29. In 2006, 2 degrees awarded. *Degree requirements:* For master's, comprehensive exam or oral thesis defense. *Application deadline:* Applications are processed on a rolling basis. Application fee: $40. Electronic applications accepted. *Financial support:* Teaching assistantships, unspecified assistantships available. Financial award application deadline: 3/1. *Faculty research:* Breast feeding, postpartum depression, pre-term labor toxicity. *Unit head:* Dr. Linda Paskiewicz, Associate Professor, 708-216-9692, Fax: 708-216-9555, E-mail: lpaskie@luc.edu. *Application contact:* Dr. Vicki A. Keough, Associate Dean, 773-508-3263, Fax: 773-508-3241, E-mail: vkeough@luc.edu.

MGH Institute of Health Professions, Graduate Programs, Program in Nursing, Boston, MA 02129. Offers advanced practice nursing (MSN); gerontological nursing (MSN); pediatric nursing (MSN); psychiatric nursing (MSN); teaching and learning for health care education (Certificate); women's health nursing (MSN). *Accreditation:* NLN (one or more programs are accredited). *Faculty:* 29 full-time (28 women), 9 part-time/adjunct (7 women). *Students:* 208 full-time (188 women), 43 part-time (35 women); includes 36 minority (12 African Americans, 17 Asian Americans or Pacific Islanders, 7 Hispanic Americans), 1 international. Average age 29. 302 applicants, 62% accepted, 101 enrolled. In 2006, 77 master's, 3 other advanced degrees awarded. *Degree requirements:* For master's, thesis or alternative. *Entrance requirements:* For master's, GRE General Test, minimum GPA of 3.0. Additional exam requirements/recommendations for international students: Required—TOEFL (minimum score 550 paper-based; 213 computer-based). *Application deadline:* For fall admission, 1/10 for domestic and international students. Application fee: $50. Electronic applications accepted. *Financial support:* In 2006–07, 212 students received support, including 1 research assistantship (averaging $1,200 per year), 2 teaching assistantships (averaging $1,200 per year); career-related internships or fieldwork, scholarships/grants, traineeships, tuition waivers (full and partial), and unspecified assistantships also available. Support available to part-time students. Financial award application deadline: 3/3; financial award applicants required to submit FAFSA. *Faculty research:* Biobehavioral nursing, HIV/AIDS, gerontological nursing, women's health, vulnerable populations, health systems . *Unit head:* Margery Chisholm, Director, 617-724-0480, Fax: 617-726-8022, E-mail: mchisholm@mghihp.edu. *Application contact:* Maureen Rika Judd, Manager of Admissions, 617-726-6069, Fax: 617-726-8010, E-mail: admissions@mghihp.edu.

See Close-Up on page 1963.

Oregon Health & Science University, School of Nursing, Women's Health Care Nurse Practitioner Program, Portland, OR 97239-3098. Offers MS, Post Master's Certificate. *Accreditation:* AACN. *Degree requirements:* For master's, thesis optional. *Entrance requirements:* For master's, GRE General Test, bachelor's degree in nursing, minimum undergraduate GPA of 3.0, previous course work in statistics; for Post Master's Certificate, master's degree in nursing.

Seton Hall University, College of Nursing, Department of Graduate Nursing, Advanced Practice in Primary Health Care Program, South Orange, NJ 07079-2697. Offers adult nurse practitioner (MSN); gerontological nurse practitioner (MSN); pediatric nurse practitioner (MSN); women's health nurse practitioner (MSN). *Accreditation:* AACN. Part-time programs available. *Degree requirements:* For master's, research project. *Entrance requirements:* For master's, GRE or MAT, BSN. *Faculty research:* Health promotion in well aged, practice outcomes, collaborative practice.

Stony Brook University, State University of New York, Stony Brook University Medical Center, Health Sciences Center, School of Nursing, Program in Perinatal/Women's Health Nursing, Stony Brook, NY 11794. Offers perinatal/women's health nurse practitioner (Certificate); perinatal/women's health nursing (MS). *Accreditation:* AACN. *Students:* 2 full-time (both women), 18 part-time (all women): includes 6 minority (5 African Americans, 1 Hispanic American). In 2006, 9 master's, 2 other advanced degrees awarded. *Degree requirements:* For master's, thesis. *Entrance requirements:* For master's, BSN, minimum GPA of 3.0, course work in statistics. *Application deadline:* For fall admission, 1/15 for domestic students. Application fee: $60. *Expenses:* Tuition, state resident: full-time $6,900; part-time $288 per credit. Tuition, nonresident: full-time $10,920; part-time $455 per credit. *Financial support:* Application deadline: 3/15. *Unit head:* Dr. Debra Sansoucie, Chair, 631-444-3298, Fax: 631-444-3136, E-mail: debra.sansoucie@stonybrook.edu.

University at Buffalo, the State University of New York, Graduate School, School of Nursing, Buffalo, NY 14260. Offers acute care nurse practitioner (MS, Certificate); adult health nursing (MS, Certificate); child health nursing (MS); family nurse practitioner (Certificate); family nursing (MS); geriatric nurse practitioner (MS, Certificate); maternal and women's health nurse practitioner (Certificate); maternal and women's health nursing (MS); nurse anesthetist (MS); nursing (PhD); nursing education (Certificate); pediatric nurse practitioner (Certificate); psychiatric/mental health nurse practitioner (Certificate); psychiatric/mental health nursing (MS). *Accreditation:* AACN; AANA/CANAEP (one or more programs are accredited). Part-time programs available. Postbaccalaureate distance learning degree programs offered. *Faculty:* 38 full-time (34 women), 15 part-time/adjunct (14 women). *Students:* 131 full-time (108 women), 64 part-time (61 women); includes 29 minority (11 African Americans, 9 Asian Americans or Pacific Islanders, 9 Hispanic Americans), 20 international. Average age 28. 346 applicants, 25% accepted, 51 enrolled. In 2006, 49 master's, 3 doctorates, 6 other advanced degrees awarded. Terminal master's awarded for partial completion of doctoral program. *Degree requirements:* For master's, comprehensive exams or project; for doctorate, thesis/dissertation, comprehensive exam. *Entrance requirements:* For master's, GRE General Test (if overall GPA is below 3.0), interview, minimum GPA of 3.0, RN license, 3 references; for doctorate, GRE General Test, minimum GPA of 3.25, RN license, BS or MS in nursing, 3 references, writing sample; for Certificate, interview, minimum GPA of 3.0 or GRE General Test, RN license, MS in nursing. Additional exam requirements/recommendations for international students: Required—TOEFL (minimum score 550 paper-based; 213 computer-based; 79 iBT), IELTS (minimum score 7). *Application deadline:* For fall admission, 6/1 priority date for domestic students, 3/1 priority date for international students; for spring admission, 11/1 for domestic students, 9/15 priority date for international students. Applications are processed on a rolling basis. Application fee: $50. Electronic applications accepted. *Financial support:* In 2006–07, 78 students received support, including 13 fellowships with full tuition reimbursements available (averaging $7,220 per year), 10 research assistantships with tuition reimbursements available (averaging $17,881 per year), 23 teaching assistantships with full tuition reimbursements available (averaging $11,245 per year); Federal Work-Study, scholarships/grants, traineeships, health care benefits, and unspecified assistantships also available. Financial award application deadline: 3/15; financial award applicants required to submit FAFSA. *Faculty research:* Oncology symptom management, end of life decision making, changing behaviors using the transtheoretical model, addictions, nursing workforce. Total annual research expenditures: $1.7 million. *Unit head:* Dr. Jean K. Brown, Dean, Interim, 716-829-2533, Fax: 716-829-2566, E-mail: jebrown@buffalo.edu. *Application contact:* Dr. Elaine R. Cusker, Assistant Dean, 716-829-2537, Fax: 716-829-2021, E-mail: ecusker@buffalo.edu.

University of Cincinnati, Graduate School, College of Nursing, Cincinnati, OH 45221-0038. Offers clinical nurse specialist (MSN), including adult health, community health, neonatal, nursing administration, occupational health, pediatric health, psychiatric nursing, women's health; nurse anesthesia (MSN); nurse midwifery (MSN); nurse practitioner (MSN), including acute care, ambulatory care, family, family/psychiatric, women's health; nursing (PhD); MBA/MSN. *Accreditation:* AACN; AANA/CANAEP (one or more programs are accredited); ACNM/DOA. Part-time programs available. Postbaccalaureate distance learning degree programs offered (no on-campus study). *Faculty:* 41 full-time (39 women), 16 part-time/adjunct (15 women). *Students:* 159 full-time (125 women), 149 part-time (145 women); includes 40 minority (22 African Americans, 1 American Indian/Alaska Native, 16 Asian Americans or Pacific Islanders, 1 Hispanic American). Average age 34. 385 applicants, 49% accepted, 132 enrolled. In 2006, 77 master's, 5 doctorates awarded. Terminal master's awarded for partial completion of doctoral program. *Median time to degree:* Of those who began their doctoral program in fall 1998, 55% received their degree in 8 years or less. *Degree requirements:* For master's, thesis or alternative, registration; for doctorate, thesis/dissertation, comprehensive exam, registration. *Entrance requirements:* For master's and doctorate, GRE General Test. Additional exam requirements/recommendations for international students: Required—TOEFL (minimum score 520 paper-based; 190 computer-based). *Application deadline:* For fall admission, 7/26 priority date for domestic and international students. Applications are processed on a rolling basis. Application fee: $40. Electronic applications accepted. *Financial support:* In 2006–07, 164 students received support, including 7 fellowships with full tuition reimbursements available (averaging $13,571 per year), research assistantships with full tuition reimbursements available (averaging $12,000 per year), 8 teaching assistantships with full tuition reimbursements available (averaging $12,000 per year); career-related internships or fieldwork, scholarships/grants, traineeships, tuition waivers (partial), and unspecified assistantships also available. Support available to part-time students. Financial award application deadline: 5/1; financial award applicants required to submit FAFSA. *Faculty research:* Substance abuse, injury and violence, symptom management. Total annual research expenditures: $1.3 million. *Unit head:* Dr. Andrea R. Lindell, Dean, 513-558-5330, Fax: 513-558-9030, E-mail: andrea.lindell@uc.edu. *Application contact:* Loren Carter, Program Coordinator, 513-558-5072, Fax: 513-558-7523, E-mail: loren.carter@uc.edu.

University of Colorado at Colorado Springs, Graduate School, Beth-El College of Nursing, Colorado Springs, CO 80933-7150. Offers adult health nurse practitioner and clinical specialist (MSN); family practitioner (MSN), including community clinical specialist, forensic clinical specialist, holistic clinical specialist; gerontology (MSN); neonatal nurse practitioner and clinical specialist (MSN); nursing administration (MSN); women nurse practitioner (MSN). *Accreditation:* AACN. Part-time programs available. Postbaccalaureate distance learning degree programs offered (minimal on-campus study). *Faculty:* 10 full-time (7 women), 14 part-time/adjunct (7 women). *Students:* 84 full-time (77 women), 53 part-time (52 women); includes 22 minority (6 African Americans, 3 American Indian/Alaska Native, 2 Asian Americans or Pacific Islanders, 11 Hispanic Americans). Average age 37. 54 applicants, 85% accepted, 30 enrolled. In 2006, 36 degrees awarded. *Degree requirements:* For master's, thesis optional; for doctorate, capstone project. *Entrance requirements:* For master's, GRE General Test or MAT, BSN, minimum GPA of 3.0, unrestricted RN license; for doctorate, interview; active RN license; MA; minimum GPA of 3.3; National Certification as NP, CNS, or CNS; portfolio. Additional exam requirements/recommendations for international students: Required—TOEFL. *Application deadline:* For fall admission, 6/1 priority date for domestic students; for spring admission, 11/15 for domestic students. Application fee: $60 ($75 for international students). Electronic applications accepted. *Expenses: Contact institution.* Tuition and fees vary according to course load, campus/location and program. *Financial support:* Fellowships, career-related internships or fieldwork, Federal Work-Study, and institutionally sponsored loans available. Support available to part-time students. *Faculty research:* Women's health, uncertainty, empowerment, family experience in chronic illness. Total annual research expenditures: $260,389. *Unit head:* Dr. Carole Schoffstall, Dean, 719-262-4418, Fax: 719-262-4416, E-mail: cschoffs@uccs.edu.

University of Delaware, College of Health Sciences, School of Nursing, Newark, DE 19716. Offers adult nurse practitioner (MSN, PMC); cardiopulmonary clinical nurse specialist (MSN, PMC); cardiopulmonary clinical nurse specialist/adult nurse practitioner (MSN, PMC); family nurse practitioner (MSN, PMC); gerontology clinical nurse specialist (MSN, PMC); gerontology clinical nurse specialist geriatric nurse practitioner (PMC); gerontology clinical nurse specialist/geriatric nurse practitioner (MSN); health services administration (MSN, PMC); nursing of children clinical nurse specialist (MSN, PMC); nursing of children clinical nurse specialist/pediatric nurse practitioner (MSN, PMC); oncology/immune deficiency clinical nurse specialist (MSN, PMC); oncology/immune deficiency clinical nurse specialist/adult nurse practitioner (MSN, PMC); perinatal/women's health clinical nurse specialist (MSN, PMC); perinatal/women's health clinical nurse specialist/women's health nurse practitioner (MSN, PMC); psychiatric nursing clinical nurse specialist (MSN, PMC). *Accreditation:* AACN; NLN (one or

Women's Health Nursing

University of Delaware (continued)
more programs are accredited). Part-time and evening/weekend programs available. Post-baccalaureate distance learning degree programs offered (minimal on-campus study). *Degree requirements:* For master's, thesis optional. *Entrance requirements:* For master's, BSN, interview, RN license. Electronic applications accepted. *Faculty research:* Marriage and chronic illness, health promotion, congestive heart failure patient outcomes, school nursing, diabetes in children.

University of Medicine and Dentistry of New Jersey, School of Nursing, Newark, NJ 07107-1709. Offers adult health (MSN); adult occupational health (MSN); advanced practice nursing (MSN, Post Master's Certificate); family nurse practitioner (MSN); nurse anesthesia (MSN); nursing (MSN); nursing education (MSN, Post Master's Certificate); nursing informatics (MSN); urban health (PhD); women's health practitioner (MSN). *Accreditation:* AANA/CANAEP; NLN (one or more programs are accredited). Part-time programs available. *Students:* 93 full-time (82 women), 307 part-time (274 women); includes 195 minority (92 African Americans, 1 American Indian/Alaska Native, 69 Asian Americans or Pacific Islanders, 33 Hispanic Americans), 1 international. Average age 39. 472 applicants, 63% accepted, 203 enrolled. In 2006, 57 master's, 6 other advanced degrees awarded. *Entrance requirements:* For master's, GRE, RN license; basic life support, statistics, and health assessment experience. Additional exam requirements/recommendations for international students: Required—TOEFL. *Application deadline:* Applications are processed on a rolling basis. Application fee: $50. Electronic applications accepted. *Expenses:* Contact institution. *Financial support:* Teaching assistantships, institutionally sponsored loans and scholarships/grants available. Support available to part-time students. Financial award application deadline: 5/1. *Faculty research:* HIV/AIDS, diabetes education, learned helplessness, nursing science, psychoeducation. *Unit head:* Dr. Susan Salmond, Interim Dean, 973-972-9239, Fax: 973-972-3225, E-mail: salmonsu@umdnj.edu.

University of Michigan, Horace H. Rackham School of Graduate Studies, School of Nursing, Division of Health Promotion and Risk Reduction, Ann Arbor, MI 48109. Offers community health nursing (MS), including adult primary care/adult nurse practitioner, community care/home care, family nurse practitioner, occupational health nursing; parent-child nursing (MS), including infant, child, adolescent health nurse practitioner, nurse midwifery; women's health (Post Master's Certificate). Part-time programs available. *Degree requirements:* For master's, thesis, registration. *Entrance requirements:* For master's, GRE General Test, licensure, minimum GPA of 3.0 in BSN program. Electronic applications accepted. *Faculty research:* Child and adolescent health and risk behavior, women's health, substance abuse prevention and intervention, primary care outcomes.

University of Minnesota, Twin Cities Campus, Graduate School, School of Nursing, Program in Women's Health Nurse Practitioner, Minneapolis, MN 55455-0213. Offers MS. *Accreditation:* AACN. Postbaccalaureate distance learning degree programs offered (minimal on-campus study). *Students:* 11 full-time (all women), 4 part-time (all women). *Entrance requirements:* Additional exam requirements/recommendations for international students: Required—TOEFL (minimum score 586 paper-based; 240 computer-based). *Application deadline:* For fall admission, 11/1 priority date for domestic and international students; for spring admission, 8/1 priority date for domestic and international students. Application fee: $55 ($75 for international students). *Unit head:* Dr. Cathy Juve, Coordinator, 612-624-9605, E-mail: cjuve@umn.edu. *Application contact:* Information Contact, 612-625-5965, Fax: 612-624-3174, E-mail: nurseoss@umn.edu.

University of Missouri–Kansas City, School of Nursing, Kansas City, MO 64110-2499. Offers adult clinical nurse specialist (MSN), including adult nurse practitioner, women's health nurse practitioner; family nurse practitioner (MSN); neonatal nurse practitioner (MSN); nurse educator (MSN); nurse executive (MSN); nursing (PhD); pediatric nurse practitioner (MSN). *Accreditation:* AACN. Part-time programs available. Postbaccalaureate distance learning degree programs offered (minimal on-campus study). *Faculty:* 31 full-time (26 women), 32 part-time/adjunct (31 women). *Students:* 36 full-time (all women), 213 part-time (202 women); includes 23 minority (6 African Americans, 2 American Indian/Alaska Native, 6 Asian Americans or Pacific Islanders, 9 Hispanic Americans). Average age 36. 121 applicants, 72% accepted, 71 enrolled. In 2006, 69 master's, 1 doctorate awarded. *Median time to degree:* Of those who began their doctoral program in fall 1998, 60% received their degree in 8 years or less. *Degree requirements:* For master's, thesis or alternative. *Entrance requirements:* For master's, minimum undergraduate GPA of 3.2; for doctorate, GRE, 3 letters of reference, interview and original essay by invitation. Additional exam requirements/recommendations for international students: Required—TOEFL (minimum score 550 paper-based). *Application deadline:* For fall admission, 2/1 priority date for domestic students; for spring admission, 9/15 priority date for domestic students. Application fee: $25. *Expenses:* Tuition, state resident: full-time $4,975; part-time $276 per credit. Tuition, nonresident: full-time $12,847; part-time $713 per credit. Required fees: $595; $595 per year. *Financial support:* In 2006–07, 30 students received support, including 6 research assistantships (averaging $3,450 per year), 7 teaching assistantships with partial tuition reimbursements available (averaging $12,650 per year); fellowships, career-related internships or fieldwork, Federal Work-Study, institutionally sponsored loans, and tuition waivers (full and partial) also available. Support available to part-time students. Financial award application deadline: 6/30; financial award applicants required to submit FAFSA. *Faculty research:* Geriatrics/gerontology, children's pain, neonatology, Alzheimer's care, cancer caregivers. Total annual research expenditures: $1 million. *Unit head:* Dr. Lora Lacey-Haun, Dean, 816-235-1700, Fax: 816-235-1701, E-mail: lacey-haunc@umkc.edu. *Application contact:* Leah Wilder, Coordinator for Admissions and Recruitment, 816-235-5768, Fax: 816-235-1701, E-mail: wilderl@umkc.edu.

University of Pennsylvania, School of Nursing, Women's Healthcare Nurse Practitioner Program, Philadelphia, PA 19104. Offers MSN. *Accreditation:* AACN. Part-time programs available. Postbaccalaureate distance learning degree programs offered (minimal on-campus study). *Entrance requirements:* For master's, GRE General Test, BSN, minimum GPA of 3.0, previous course work in statistics, physical assessment experience. Additional exam requirements/recommendations for international students: Required—TOEFL. Expenses: Contact institution. *Faculty research:* New mother and infant healthcare follow-up, adequacy of antepartum care, models of healthcare.

University of South Carolina, The Graduate School, College of Nursing, Program in Clinical Nursing, Columbia, SC 29208. Offers acute care clinical specialist (MSN); acute care nurse practitioner (MSN); women's health nurse practitioner (MSN). *Accreditation:* AACN. Part-time programs available. *Degree requirements:* For master's, thesis or alternative. *Entrance requirements:* For master's, GRE General Test or MAT, BS in nursing, RN licensure. Additional exam requirements/recommendations for international students: Required—TOEFL (minimum score 570 paper-based; 230 computer-based). Electronic applications accepted. *Faculty research:* Psychophysiological interventions, HIV/AIDS, psycho-neuroimmunology.

The University of Texas at El Paso, Graduate School, College of Health Sciences, School of Nursing, El Paso, TX 79968-0001. Offers community health (MSN); community health/family nurse practitioner (MSN); nurse midwifery (MSN); nursing administration (MSN); nursing-clinical (MSN); post master's nursing (MSN); women's health care (MSN). *Accreditation:* AACN. *Degree requirements:* For master's, thesis optional. *Entrance requirements:* For master's, GRE General Test or MAT, BSN, minimum GPA of 3.0, previous course work in statistics. Additional exam requirements/recommendations for international students: Required—TOEFL. Electronic applications accepted.

Vanderbilt University, School of Nursing, Nashville, TN 37235. Offers adult acute care nurse practitioner (MSN); adult health nurse practitioner/forensic (MSN); adult nurse practitioner/cardiovascular disease management and prevention (MSN); adult nurse practitioner/palliative care (MSN); clinical management (clinical nurse leader/specialist) (MSN); family nurse practitioner (MSN); gerontology nurse practitioner (MSN); health systems management (MSN); neonatal nurse practitioner (MSN); nurse midwifery (MSN); nursing informatics (MSN); nursing science (PhD); pediatric acute care nurse practitioner (MSN); pediatric primary care nurse practitioner (MSN); psychiatric-mental health nurse practitioner (MSN); women's health nurse practitioner (MSN); MBA/MSN; MSN/MTS; MSN/PhD. *Accreditation:* ACNM/DOA; NLN (one or more programs are accredited). Part-time and evening/weekend programs available. Postbaccalaureate distance learning degree programs offered (minimal on-campus study). *Faculty:* 95 full-time (83 women), 432 part-time/adjunct (314 women). *Students:* 371 full-time (325 women), 206 part-time (180 women); includes 59 minority (38 African Americans, 2 American Indian/Alaska Native, 7 Asian Americans or Pacific Islanders, 12 Hispanic Americans). Average age 27. 611 applicants, 55% accepted, 308 enrolled. In 2006, 256 master's, 2 doctorates awarded. *Degree requirements:* For doctorate, thesis/dissertation. *Entrance requirements:* For master's, GRE, interview; for doctorate, GRE, interview, 3 letters of recommendation. Additional exam requirements/recommendations for international students: Required—TOEFL. *Application deadline:* For fall admission, 12/1 priority date for domestic and international students. Applications are processed on a rolling basis. Application fee: $50. *Expenses:* Contact institution. *Financial support:* In 2006–07, 404 students received support, including 5 research assistantships (averaging $8,000 per year); Federal Work-Study, institutionally sponsored loans, and unspecified assistantships also available. Support available to part-time students. Financial award application deadline: 3/15; financial award applicants required to submit CSS PROFILE or FAFSA. *Faculty research:* Lymphedema post cancer treatment, palliative care and bereavement, patient safety and quality of care, health care workforce issues, symptom management including pain and fatigue. Total annual research expenditures: $1.1 million. *Unit head:* Dr. Colleen Conway-Welch, Dean, 615-343-8776, Fax: 615-343-7711, E-mail: colleen.conway-welch@vanderbilt.edu. *Application contact:* Cheryl Feldner, Assistant Director of Admissions, 615-322-3800, Fax: 615-343-0333, E-mail: cheryl.feldner@vanderbilt.edu.

Virginia Commonwealth University, Graduate School, School of Nursing, Richmond, VA 23284-9005. Offers adult health nursing (MS); child health nursing (MS); family health nursing (MS); health system (PhD); immunocompetence (PhD); nurse practitioner (MS, Certificate); nursing administration (MS), including clinical nurse manager, nurse executive; psychiatric-mental health nursing (MS); risk and resilience (PhD); women's health nursing (MS). *Accreditation:* NLN (one or more programs are accredited). Part-time and evening/weekend programs available. *Faculty:* 23 full-time (21 women). *Students:* 131 full-time (125 women), 137 part-time (129 women); includes 33 minority (19 African Americans, 11 Asian Americans or Pacific Islanders, 3 Hispanic Americans), 12 international. 110 applicants, 82% accepted, 66 enrolled. In 2006, 57 master's, 1 doctorate, 3 other advanced degrees awarded. *Degree requirements:* For master's, thesis optional; for doctorate, thesis/dissertation. *Entrance requirements:* For master's, GRE General Test, BSN, minimum GPA of 2.8; for doctorate, GRE General Test. *Application deadline:* For fall admission, 2/1 priority date for domestic students. Application fee: $50. *Financial support:* Fellowships, research assistantships, teaching assistantships, career-related internships or fieldwork and institutionally sponsored loans available. *Unit head:* Dr. Nancy F. Langston, Dean, 804-828-5174, Fax: 804-828-7743, E-mail: nflangst@vcu.edu. *Application contact:* Susan Lipp, Admissions Counselor, 804-828-5171, Fax: 804-828-7743, E-mail: slipp@vcu.edu.

See Close-Up on page 1983.

Wilmington College, Division of Nursing, New Castle, DE 19720-6491. Offers adult nurse practitioner (MSN); family nurse practitioner (MSN); gerontology (MSN); leadership (MSN); nursing (MSN); women's nurse practitioner (MSN). *Accreditation:* AACN; NLN. Part-time programs available. *Students:* 30 full-time (28 women), 195 part-time (176 women); includes 24 minority (19 African Americans, 3 Asian Americans or Pacific Islanders, 2 Hispanic Americans). Average age 39. 54 applicants, 100% accepted, 48 enrolled. In 2006, 58 degrees awarded. *Degree requirements:* For master's, thesis. *Entrance requirements:* For master's, BSN, RN license, interview, 3 letters of recommendation. Additional exam requirements/recommendations for international students: Required—TOEFL (minimum score 500 paper-based; 173 computer-based). *Application deadline:* For fall admission, 3/31 priority date for domestic students. Applications are processed on a rolling basis. Application fee: $25. *Financial support:* In 2006–07, 28 fellowships with tuition reimbursements (averaging $2,200 per year) were awarded; traineeships also available. Financial award applicants required to submit FAFSA. *Faculty research:* Outcomes assessment, student writing ability. *Unit head:* Dr. Mary Letitia Gallagher, Chair, 302-328-9401 Ext. 161, Fax: 302-328-7081, E-mail: tgall@wilmcoll.edu. *Application contact:* Chris Ferguson, Director of Admissions and Financial Aid, 302-328-9407 Ext. 256, Fax: 302-328-5164, E-mail: inquire@wilmcoll.edu.

ADELPHI UNIVERSITY

School of Nursing

Programs of Study

The School of Nursing at Adelphi University offers the Master of Science (M.S.) in adult health nurse practitioner, the M.S. in nursing administration, the M.S. in nursing education, the M.S. in emergency nursing and disaster management, a joint Master of Science/Master of Business Administration (M.S./M.B.A.) program, a new Ph.D. in nursing program, and post-master's certificate programs in adult health nurse practitioner, nursing administration, emergency nursing and disaster management, and nursing education.

The M.S. in adult health nurse practitioner program (42 credits) entails in-depth study of adult-health nursing. The curriculum integrates theoretical knowledge and practical skills while exploring the issues and forces within the health-care delivery system that affect the roles of the advanced practice nurse. The program emphasizes scientific inquiry as a tool for building clinical knowledge and testing the validity of the theoretical assumptions underlying nursing practice. Students have opportunities to work with advanced practice nurses and other health professionals in a variety of clinical settings.

The M.S. in nursing administration program (39 credits) prepares nurse managers who can function in a variety of health-care settings. Topics include nursing theories, group dynamics, communication, and professional issues and trends. To prepare to serve as leaders in improving health-care services, students study leadership roles in the health-care field. Through the program's research component, students gain practice in analyzing and implementing research findings.

The new emergency nursing/emergency management program (M.S. and post-master's certificate) was created in response to the increasing number of emergency room visits in the United States and the growing number and magnitude of natural, technological, and manmade disaster situations that are occurring throughout the world. Graduates acquire skills in planning, response, and recovery efforts at organizational and community-wide levels, which prepare them to assume leadership positions in emergency nursing and disaster management. Adelphi is currently the only university in the New York metropolitan region—and one of the few in the country—to offer this specialization in nursing. The 39-credit master's degree program utilizes courses from both the School of Nursing (24 credits) and the College of Arts and Sciences emergency management program (15 credits). The post-master's certificate program consists of 18 credits that are earned from a selection of courses offered for the master's degree.

The 75-credit M.S./M.B.A. program is offered with the School of Business. The program, which is designed for registered nurses with a bachelor's degree, incorporates contemporary management theory, business fundamentals and essential core competencies, and the knowledge, skills, and values of advanced professional nursing practice. The objective of this joint-degree program is to prepare leaders who facilitate and embody the competencies required to help transform health-service organizations and health systems as a whole.

The new Ph.D. in nursing program is the only one of its kind on Long Island. This innovative 54-credit program is designed to advance health-care teaching, research, and leadership by educating nurses with a master's degree to become nursing scholars and educators. The plan of study offers strong core courses in both nursing science and research. The program may be taken on a full-time (9 to 12 credits) or part-time basis following a progressive program plan. Most of the courses are offered one day a week and are held on Fridays. Students are admitted only in the fall semester and proceed through the program in cohorts, taking classes together.

The post-master's certificate program in nursing administration or adult health nurse practitioner is designed for students who already hold a master's degree in nursing and want to specialize in another discipline. The program aims to strengthen the administrative or clinical capability of master's-prepared nurses who are planning or are already involved in a role expansion or role change. The program is a part-time course of study that includes 28 to 30 credits of master's courses, at least 12 of which must be taken at Adelphi University.

Research Facilities

The Nursing Resource Center features learning laboratories that simulate hospital and clinical settings. A clinical coordinator provides supervision as students gain invaluable practice. One laboratory is set up with all appropriate hospital supplies and equipment, including advanced patient-care mannequins and simulators. The second laboratory is equipped with state-of-the-art nursing tools for complete assessment practice. The computer laboratory offers online learning and practice programs.

The University's primary research holdings are at Swirbul Library and include 657,000 volumes (including bound periodicals and government publications), 805,000 microformats, 27,000 audiovisual items, 33,000 electronic journal titles, more than 135 electronic databases, and general and special-accessibility computer facilities.

Financial Aid

Adelphi University offers a wide variety of federal aid programs, state grants, scholarship and fellowship programs, on- and off-campus employment, and teaching and research assistantships. For the Ph.D., program, the Federal Faculty Loan Program enables qualified students to borrow up to two years of the cost of their education. Ph.D. students who agree to work on a nursing faculty for four years following graduation may have 85 percent of their federal loans forgiven. More information is available at the Office of Student Financial Services Web site at http://ecampus.adelphi.edu/sfs/.

Cost of Study

For the 2006–07 academic year, the tuition rate is $690 per credit. University fees range from $175 to $275 per semester.

Living and Housing Costs

The University assists single and married students in finding suitable accommodations whenever possible. The cost of living depends on the location and number of rooms rented.

Student Group

Of the 170 students, 98 percent are women and 44 percent are members of minority groups. The average age is 43.5; more than half of the students major in nursing administration.

Location

Located in historic Garden City, New York, 45 minutes from Manhattan and 20 minutes from Queens, Adelphi's 75-acre suburban campus is known for the beauty of its landscape and architecture. The campus is a short walk from the Long Island Railroad and is convenient to New York's major airports and several major highways. Off-campus centers are located in Manhattan, Hauppauge, and Poughkeepsie.

The University and The School

Founded in 1896, Adelphi is a fully accredited, private university with 8,110 undergraduate, graduate, and returning-adult students in the arts and sciences, business, clinical psychology, education, nursing, and social work. Students come from forty-three states and from thirty-seven countries. *The Princeton Review* named Adelphi University a 2005 Best College in the Northeastern Region, and the *Fiske Guide to Colleges 2007* recognized Adelphi as a "Best Buy" in higher education. The University is the only private institution on Long Island and one of only twenty-six in the nation to earn this recognition.

The School of Nursing is dedicated to providing students with the skills, knowledge, and specialized training to succeed as qualified caregivers and leaders in the nursing profession. The course of study combines theory, research, clinical practice, and community service. Adelphi's extensive school and community partnerships provide wide-ranging opportunities to gain fieldwork experience. The curricula of the School of Nursing are registered by the New York State Education Department, Division of Professional Education, and are accredited by the Commission on Collegiate Nursing Education (CCNE).

Applying

Each master's degree applicant should have a bachelor's degree in nursing, with a course in basic statistics, and be licensed as a professional registered nurse. Students must submit the completed application form, the $50 application fee, official college transcripts, and two letters of recommendation. In addition, applicants to the M.S./M.B.A. program must send in a personal statement and GMAT scores. Applications are processed on a rolling basis.

Applicants for the Ph.D. program must have an M.S. or M.S.N. degree from an accredited nursing program (CCNE or NLNAC approved) and submit the completed application form, three professional letters of reference (from a supervisor, committee chair, former professor, etc.), satisfactory GRE scores (taken within the last five years); licensure as an RN in New York; and a professional writing sample. All application materials must be received by March 15 to be considered for the following fall semester for the Ph.D. program.

Correspondence and Information

School of Nursing
Alumnae Hall, Room 220
Adelphi University
1 South Avenue
Garden City, New York 11530
Phone: 516-877-4510
Fax: 516-877-4558
E-mail: coonan@adelphi.edu
Web site: http://nursing.adelphi.edu/

Adelphi University

THE FACULTY AND THEIR RESEARCH

Veronica Arikian, Associate Professor. Alterations in holistic integrity managed in the community.

Deborah A. Ambrosio-Mawhirter, Clinical Assistant Professor; M.S., Adelphi; RN. Human assessment: a holistic approach.

Stefni R. Bogard, Clinical Assistant Professor and Clinical Administrator, Nurse Practitioner Program; M.S.N., Pennsylvania, 1986.

Jacqueline Brandwein, Clinical Assistant Professor; Ph.D., CUNY, 1997. Alterations in the holistic integrity of the childbearing family, alterations of holistic integrity of children.

Elizabeth Cohn, Assistant Professor; D.N.Sc., Columbia, 2004. Bridging the gap between academic nursing education and nursing practice.

Xiaomei Cong, Assistant Professor; Ph.D., Case Western Reserve. Pain assessment and management in preterm infants, using kangaroo care as an intervention for preterm infants' pain.

Christine Coughlin, Associate Professor; Ed.D., Columbia Teachers College. Patient/family perception of care, leadership qualities of front-line nursing leaders.

Diane Dembicki, Assistant Professor; Ph.D., Colorado State, 1995. Public health/community nutrition, international health and nutrition, cultural diversity, developmental education.

Bonnie Marie Ewing, Assistant Professor; Ph.D., Adelphi, 1996.

Maryann Forbes, Associate Professor; Ph.D., Adelphi, 1999. Effects of long-term mechanical ventilation on patients and families, nursing care of the COPD patient, simulation in nursing education, gerontology.

Yvonne D. Gray, Visiting Assistant Professor. Independent study technology information literacy, professionalism in the provision of holistic care.

Linda Sue Greenfield, Assistant Professor; Ph.D., Adelphi, 1998. Medical surgical nursing, pharmacology, nurse anesthesia, alternative medicine.

Mary T. Hickey, Assistant Professor; M.S., Adelphi.

Erica Kathryn, Associate Professor; Ph.D., Case Western Reserve, 1996. Family nurse practice; nurse-midwifery; applied bioethics, epistemology and philosophy in nursing; professional development of nursing; theory development, analysis, and application; community/institutional/academic partnerships on health initiatives; research methods.

David Keepnews, Associate Professor; Ph.D., J.D., RN.

Robert Kerner, Clinical Assistant Professor; J.D., New York Law, 1997.

Marilyn B. Klainberg, Associate Professor; Ed.D., Columbia Teachers College, 1994. Use of computers to enhance nursing practice and nursing education.

Teresa Mascitti, Clinical Assistant Professor; M.S.N., Molloy, 1997; CANP.

Roberta Marpet, Visiting Associate Professor; Ph.D., NYU; RN. Alterations in mental health: a holistic approach, research in nursing.

Elaine A. Pasquali, Professor; Ph.D., SUNY at Stony Brook.

M. Denise Pollard, Associate Professor; M.P.H., CUNY, Hunter; M.S., D.N.Sc., Columbia, 2006.

Kristine Lori Qureshi, Assistant Professor; D.N.Sc., Columbia, 2003.

Kenneth Rondello, Assistant Professor of Management, Marketing, and Decision Sciences; M.D., St. George's (West Indies); M.P.H., Yale. Health management in times of disaster, hospital and health-care policy and management.

Marybeth Ryan, Associate Professor; Ph.D., Hofstra, 1985; RN, ANP. Evidence-based practice.

Lorraine Sanders, Assistant Professor; M.S., SUNY at Stony Brook, 1989. HIV-positive women and childbearing, mental illness and women's health, ethics in clinical practice, emergency preparedness/vulnerable populations.

Arlene Trolman, Associate Professor; Ed.D., Columbia, 1984. Alterations holistic integrity managed in the community.

Joan Valas, Associate Professor; Ph.D., Columbia/Columbia Teachers College; RN. Technology and information.

Shiow-ying Yang, Assistant Professor; D.N.Sc., RN.

BRIGHAM YOUNG UNIVERSITY

College of Nursing

Programs of Study

The Brigham Young University (BYU) College of Nursing offers a Master of Science (M.S.) degree that prepares students as family nurse practitioners (FNP). A post-master's family nurse practitioner degree is available for those who have already received a master's degree in nursing. Graduates are eligible to apply for certification examinations. The program can be completed in six semesters of full-time study.

Research Facilities

The research center offers work space for faculty members and students, research resources, research journals, and eight computer work stations. Current software includes several programs for quantitative and qualitative data analysis, media presentation preparation, scanning, and word processing. Statistical consultation services are available to students with data analysis during the thesis/project process.

Financial Aid

Tuition scholarships are available, along with research and teaching assistantships. State and federal monies specific to nurses are available. University loans and Federal Stafford Student Loans are also available.

Cost of Study

Tuition at BYU is charged on the basis of the student's membership or nonmembership in the Church of Jesus Christ of Latter-Day Saints (LDS). Full-time graduate nursing students enrolled in the fall or winter semester pay $2430 if they are LDS members or $4860 if they are nonmembers. Those enrolled in the spring or summer term pay $1215 if they are LDS members or $2430 if they are nonmembers. Part-time tuition per credit hour is $270 for LDS students and $540 for non-LDS students. During fall and winter semesters, full-time study consists of 8.5 or more hours, and for spring and summer terms it consists of at least 4.5 credit hours.

Living and Housing Costs

A variety of on-campus and off-campus housing is available. A large number of off-campus apartments are also available.

Student Groups

There are approximately 32 students in the graduate program. Students gain knowledge and are provided opportunities to develop the commitment to service and lifelong learning. Students are highly recruited.

Location

The University is nestled at the foot of the beautifully rugged Wasatch Range of the Rocky Mountains. The campus is the focal point of the Provo/Orem community of 163,000 people. The valley lies 45 miles south of Salt Lake City; it is bounded on the west by Utah Lake and on the east by the Wasatch Mountains. The setting offers a variety of recreational opportunities, including numerous ski resorts, mountain climbing, and spectacular national parks.

The University and The College

Brigham Young University is sponsored and operated by the Church of Jesus Christ of Latter-Day Saints. Founded in 1875, BYU is the largest privately owned, church-sponsored university in the United States, with approximately 1,500 faculty members and 30,000 students. Students represent all fifty states and more than ninety other countries. In keeping with an inscription at the entrance of the campus, The World is Our Campus, the University offers students many local and international learning experiences. Facilities and programs include a 793-acre research farm, a PBS television station, a 3-million-volume library, and study centers in Washington, D.C.; London; Vienna; and Jerusalem. Programs also extend into South America, the Middle East, Africa, Eastern Europe, and other parts of the world.

The College of Nursing was established in 1952. Following in the footsteps of pioneer nurses and midwives, College alumni have established a legacy of service as clinicians, nurse practitioners, administrators, educators, health and welfare missionaries, and scholars. The University and the College of Nursing endeavor to provide students with the broad-based education and skills necessary for becoming professionals and informed citizens.

Applying

Applicants can obtain application forms from the University Web site listed in this In-Depth Description, or the Office of Graduate Studies, B-356 ASB, Provo, Utah 84602-1339 (telephone: 801-422-4091). Application packages should include a statement of intent for graduate education, official transcripts of previous academic work, standardized test scores, and three letters of recommendation from former instructors or employers. Application may be made online or by regular mail. The deadline for submission of the form and supporting documents is December 1. Entry to both M.S. programs is restricted to spring semester. A personal interview with faculty members and completion of a short writing exercise are necessary. The application fee is $50.

Correspondence and Information

Denise Gibbons Davis
Graduate Program
400 Spencer W. Kimball Tower (SWKT)
Brigham Young University
Provo, Utah 84602
Phone: 801-422-4142
Fax: 801-422-0536
E-mail: denise_gibbons@byu.edu
Web site: http://nursing.byu.edu

Brigham Young University

THE FACULTY AND THEIR RESEARCH

Renea Beckstrand, Associate Professor; Ph.D., Utah, 2001. Comprehensive care of the adult client with acute health problems.
Judith Berry, Assistant Professor; M.S.N., Catholic University, 1984; Ph.D., Rush, 2006. Rural primary health care.
Kent Blad, Associate Teaching Professor; M.S., Brigham Young, 2000. Acute care.
Lynn Callister, Professor; Ph.D., Utah, 1993. Cultural meanings of childbirth, women's health.
Catherine R. Coverston, Associate Professor; Ph.D., Utah, 2001. Maternal and child care.
Amy Cox, Assistant Teaching Professor; M.S., Brigham Young, 2000. Pediatric topics.
Karen Dearing, Assistant Professor; Ph.D., Utah, 2003. Schizophrenia recovery, nurse-patient relations.
Donna Freeborn, Instructor; M.S., UCLA, 1994. Women's issues.
Barbara Heise, Assistant Professor; Ph.D., Virginia, 2006. Adult and gerontological mental health, alcohol and drug abuse.
Barbara L. Mandleco, Professor; Ph.D., Brigham Young, 1991. Growth and development, resilience in children.
Erin Maughan, Assistant Professor; Ph.D., Utah, 2006. Community nursing, specializing in school nursing.
Elaine Sorensen Marshall, Professor; Ph.D., Utah, 1987. Children and stress, family adaptation, descriptive methods.
Patty Ravert, Assistant Professor and Director, Nursing Learning Center; Ph.D., Utah, 2004. Outcomes of simulated learning experiences.
Mary Williams, Associate Professor; Ph.D., Arizona, 1991. Transplant anxiety, management, qualitative methodology.

CLEMSON UNIVERSITY

Master of Science in Nursing

Program of Study	The School of Nursing at Clemson University offers the Master of Science (M.S.) with a major in nursing and a strong emphasis on the family. The curriculum is designed to build on prior course work and experiences of each student. Theory, research, and role development are emphasized, enabling the graduate to participate in the development of nursing knowledge and to contribute to the advancement of the nursing profession.
	Students may select one of the four study options: clinical nurse specialist (CNS) in either material/child/adolescent nursing or adult/gerontological nursing, nurse practitioner (NP) in either family nurse practitioner (FNP) studies or adult/gerontological nurse practitioner (A/GNP) studies, nursing administration, or nursing education. The program is two years (four semesters) of full-time study, with a maximum of six years. Part-time study is also available. Clemson has a strong placement rate within two months of graduation. Graduates practice in a variety of settings, provide leadership in their specialty area, and initiate collaborative and consultative relationships with others to improve health and influence health policy.
Research Facilities	Clemson's Smart Classrooms represent the cutting edge in interactive education. The rooms are designed as the ultimate in connectivity and adaptability. Clinical facilities include Community Health Agencies, the Joseph F. Sullivan Center for Nursing and Wellness, and a variety of inpatient and outpatient settings throughout the region.
Financial Aid	Graduate assistantships provide an hourly stipend (for 10 hours per week for fifteen weeks a semester), tuition, and a reduction in University charges and fees. Federal traineeship funds, scholarships, and fellowships are also available. Most full-time graduate students at Clemson University receive some form of financial assistance, primarily through graduate assistantships, fellowships, traineeships, hourly employment, and loans.
Cost of Study	Tuition for the 2007–08 academic year is $3960 per semester for in-state students and $7923 per semester for nonresidents. Off-campus rates are $330 per hour for in-state students and $660 per hour for nonresidents. Graduate assistants pay a flat fee of $750 per semester and $348 per summer session. Graduate fellows pay South Carolina resident fees.
Living and Housing Costs	On-campus housing is available; for information, prospective students should visit http://www.housing.clemson.edu. The cost of living in Clemson is quite low compared to the national average; students who choose to live off campus typically spend $300–$400 per month for rent, depending on location, amenities, roommates, and other factors.
Student Group	There are approximately 100 students enrolled in the graduate program.
Location	Clemson is a small, beautiful college town near the Blue Ridge Mountains and Lake Hartwell in upstate South Carolina. The Upstate is one of the country's fastest-growing areas and is an important part of the I-85 corridor, a multistate area along Interstate 85 that runs from metro Atlanta to Richmond, Virginia, and encompasses Charlotte, North Carolina, and North Carolina's Research Triangle. Atlanta and Charlotte are each a 2-hour drive away. Many financial institutions and other industries have their national headquarters in the Upstate, including Wachovia, Bank of America, BMW, Bon Secours St. Francis Health System, Bosch North America, Bowater, Charter Communications, Ernst and Young, Fluor Corporation, IBM, Microsoft, Michelin of North America, and many others.
The University and The School	Clemson is classified by the Carnegie Foundation as a Research University (high research activity), a category comprising just 10 percent of all graduate degree-granting universities in America. The University's mission is to fulfill the covenant between its founder and the people of South Carolina to establish a "high seminary of learning" through its responsibilities of teaching, research, and extended public service. The University has identified eight areas of academic emphasis that create collaborations that, in turn, help fulfill the University's mission.
	The School of Nursing is committed to teaching, research, and service to the public of South Carolina, the nation, and the world. The School strives to prepare nurses for professional practice and leadership in health care and to advance nursing knowledge.
Applying	In addition to meeting University admission requirements, applicants should be graduates of a nationally accredited baccalaureate nursing program, should have completed an undergraduate statistics course, should demonstrate evidence of current basic client assessment skills, and should have documented recent clinical experience (at least 600 hours during the twelve months prior to acceptance into the program).
	Applicants may apply on the Web at http://www.grad.clemson.edu/p_apply.html. The completed application for admission, the $50 application fee, official transcripts, and a satisfactory score on the General Test of the Graduate Record Examinations (GRE) must be submitted. The application deadline is April 1 for the fall semester and October 1 for the spring.
Correspondence and Information	Ms. Lynne G. McGuirt, M.Ed. Student Services Coordinator Clemson University School of Nursing Clemson University 225 South Pleasantburg Drive, Suite B-5 Greenville, South Carolina 29606 Phone: 864-250-8881 Fax: 864-250-6711 E-mail: lgm@clemson.edu Web site: http://www.hehd.clemson.edu/nursing/

Clemson University

THE FACULTY AND THEIR RESEARCH

Full-Time Faculty

Janet B. Craig, Assistant Professor; D.H.A., Medical University of South Carolina. Health systems, management.
Stephanie Davis, Assistant Professor; Ph.D., South Carolina. Women's health.
Cathy Dyches, Assistant Professor; Ph.D., Georgia; RN, MSN. Nursing administration.
Julia A. Eggert, Assistant Professor and Coordinator of the RN-B.S. Program; Ph.D., Clemson. Breast cancer (early detection and prevention).
Carol Elliott, Assistant Professor; Ph.D., Boston College. Psychiatric and mental health nursing.
Corky Harmon, Assistant Professor; Ed.D., Georgia; RN. Critical care.
Bonnie Holaday, D.S.N., California, San Francisco; RN. Chronic illness in children.
Linda A. Howe, Assistant Professor; Ph.D., South Carolina. CHF, historical nursing, educational research.
Arlene Johnson, Assistant Professor; Ph.D., Capella; RN, CNP. Pediatrics and distance learning.
Connie W. Lee, Associate Professor; Ed.D., Georgia. Evidence-based outcomes and case management.
Nancy K. Meehan, Associate Professor; Ph.D., Texas at Austin. Health communication and information.
Kristen Montgomery, Assistant Professor; Ph.D., Case Western University; Maternal and child nursing.
Veronica G. Parker, Associate Professor; Ph.D., Medical University of South Carolina. Health risk behavior in college students and young adults.
Rosanne H. Pruitt, Professor and Director; Ph.D., Maryland; RN, FNP. Autonomy legislation, advanced practice.
Patricia T. Smart, Professor; Ph.D., Georgia. Health policy, women's health.
Janet L. Timms, Associate Professor; Ed.D., Georgia. End-of-life care.
Margaret Ann Wetsel, Associate Professor; Ph.D., Texas at Austin. Limited nutrition, poverty, ADD.
Deborah F. Willoughby, Associate Professor; Ph.D., Georgia State. Type 2 diabetes.

Part-Time Faculty

Pat Maybee, Lecturer; Ed.D., Georgia.
Kelly Smith, Instructor; M.S., Clemson; RN, FNP.
Mary Beth Steck, Instructor; M.S.N., Clemson.
Mary Strossner, Instructor; M.N., South Carolina.

COLUMBIA UNIVERSITY

School of Nursing

Programs of Study

Columbia University School of Nursing is distinguished by the clinical excellence of its programs and graduates. The School strives to accommodate the widely varying pool of applicants with multiple pathways to reach the master's degree, including the Combined B.S./M.S. (ETP) program for college graduates with non-nursing degrees. The School offers specialization in eleven different graduate majors, including adult, geriatric, pediatric, family, and neonatal primary care; acute care; psychiatric–mental health; oncology; nurse anesthesia; nurse midwifery; and women's health. In addition, subspecialization is available in HIV/AIDS, addictive behaviors, integrative therapies, clinical genetics, emergency preparedness response, and palliative/end-of-life care. The Doctor of Nursing Science (D.N.Sc.) program is a research-intensive curriculum preparing nurse scholars who are ready to conduct research in outcomes and health policy independently and as part of interdisciplinary teams. The Doctor of Nursing Practice (Dr.N.P.), prepares nurse clinicians with the knowledge and skills necessary for fully accountable practice with patients across sites and over time. More than 90 percent of master's graduates are working as advanced practice nurses.

Research Facilities

The School of Nursing is part of the Columbia University Medical Center, along with the School of Public Health, the School of Dental Medicine, and the College of Physicians and Surgeons, which, together with New York-Presbyterian Hospital, create one of the world's greatest academic health centers. Other facilities include the Neurological Institute, the Eye Institute, Babies and Children's Hospital, Sloane Hospital for Women, the Center for Geriatrics and Gerontology, the Organ Transplant Center, and the Center for Health Promotion and Disease Prevention. In addition, approximately 200 other sites in the tristate area are available for clinical education. The Augustus C. Long Library is the fourth-largest academic medical library in the country and is part of the Columbia University Library system, which encompasses approximately forty libraries and more than 4 million volumes. The Long Library houses more than 400,000 volumes and receives more than 4,500 journals, most of which can be accessed through online computer search programs. The Media and Computer Center contains more than 3,000 audiovisual and computer-assisted instruction programs, including slides, videodiscs, tapes, and a wide variety of personal computer applications. The Special Collections section houses several thousand rare and unique works, including the Florence Nightingale Collection, which is featured at exhibitions along with rare holdings of Freud and Webster. The School of Nursing's Technology Learning Center contains two patient units, which provide a hands-on environment for developing psychomotor skills, as well as state-of-the-art, computer-assisted monitoring equipment that simulates a real clinical environment.

Financial Aid

The goal of the School of Nursing financial aid program is to provide as many students as possible with sufficient resources to meet their needs, distributing funds to eligible students in a fair and equitable manner. Financial aid is met through a combination of scholarships, grants, work, and loans. Students should be able to meet all expenses for the academic year through a combination of these resources.

Cost of Study

During the 2007–08 academic year, graduate tuition ranged from $1042 to $1322 per credit.

Living and Housing Costs

Housing costs on the Health Sciences Campus range from $4000 to $6000 per term. Other expenses, including health fees, books, personal expenses, transportation, and uniforms, are estimated at $5000.

Student Group

The nearly 600 students enrolled in the School of Nursing represent a diverse group of nursing professionals. They come from all over the country, but most are from the tristate area.

Student Outcomes

Columbia University School of Nursing's faculty members are outstanding educators who are committed to providing the best educational experience possible. They are responsive to student needs and to changes in the health-care market. As a result, Columbia graduates are sought after by employers, and more than 90 percent of recent graduates have secured employment in positions that are consistent with their education.

Location

The School of Nursing is part of the Columbia University Medical Center, a 20-acre campus overlooking the Hudson River on Manhattan's Upper West Side. Students can take advantage of the world-renowned recreational, cultural, educational, and entertainment events and sites that have made New York City famous.

The University and The School

By royal charter of King George II of England, Columbia University was founded in 1754 as King's College. It is the oldest institution of higher learning in New York State and the fifth oldest in the nation. A private, nonsectarian institution, Columbia University is organized into fifteen schools and is associated with more than seventy research and public service institutions and twenty-two scholarly journals. Founded in 1892 as the Presbyterian Hospital School of Nursing, the School began offering baccalaureate degrees when it joined Columbia University's Faculty of Medicine in 1937. In 1956, it became the first nursing program in the country to award a master's degree in a clinical nursing specialty.

Applying

Columbia University School of Nursing has two semesters: one begins in September (fall semester) and the other in May (summer semester). The School has rolling admission for most master's specialties. All clinical sequences begin in the fall semester.

The Nurse Anesthesia program enrolls once per year in May. Applications are due by November 1. The Post-Master's Certificate in Anesthesia program enrolls in September.

The Combined B.S./M.S. Program (ETP) enrolls just once per year at the end of May. Applications are due by November 15.

The Doctor of Nursing Science Program (D.N.Sc.) enrolls once per year in September. Applications are due by February 1.

The Doctor of Nursing Practice Program (Dr.N.P.) enrolls once per year in September. Applications are due by February 1.

The University Statutory Certificate program enrolls once per year in September. Applications can be submitted throughout the year and no later than July 1.

Admission is based on past academic and professional performance. Admission requirements include an online application form with a fee; a typed, double-spaced, twelve-point font, one-page personal statement describing professional goals and aspirations; three competed recommendation forms; official transcripts from all postsecondary schools; official GRE scores; resume or CV; a copy of an RN license and current registration (if applicable); and an undergraduate course in statistics and in physical assessment. Students should consult the School of Nursing Web site for specific admission criteria.

Correspondence and Information

Office of Admissions
Columbia University School of Nursing
630 West 168th Street, Box 6
New York, New York 10032
Phone: 212-305-5756
        800-899-8895 (toll-free)
E-mail: nursing@columbia.edu
Web site: http://www.nursing.columbia.edu

Columbia University

THE FACULTY

The faculty at Columbia University School of Nursing is composed of a multitalented group of researchers, practitioners, and educators.

Research faculty members are all doctorally prepared and engaged in a variety of funded research projects, such as symptom management of HIV/AIDS using alternative and complementary medicine, evaluation of advanced practice nursing, domestic violence, health-care needs of perimenopausal women, health policy, and infection control. They have received national and international recognition for their work.

Practice faculty members are all nationally certified in their clinical specialties and maintain a faculty practice that is consistent with their certification. The practice faculty members are on the leading edge of advanced practice nursing and have received national and international recognition for innovative practice endeavors.

Dean and Centennial Professor of Health Policy: Mary O'Neil Mundinger, Dr.P.H.

D'YOUVILLE COLLEGE

Department of Nursing

Programs of Study	At the graduate level, nursing programs include Master of Science (M.S.) in community health nursing with concentrations in advanced clinical nursing, high-risk parents and children, nursing management, and nursing education; Master of Science in nursing with choice of clinical focus; and Master of Science in family nurse practitioner studies as well as a post-master's certificate in family nurse practitioner studies. A five-year Bachelor of Science in Nursing/Master of Science in nursing (B.S.N./M.S.) degree program, degree-completion programs for nurses who have already received their associate degrees, RN to B.S.N./M.S. program, and an RN to B.S.N./M.S. in community health nursing program are also available.
	Innovative class scheduling provides working nursing professionals the opportunity to study full-time by attending only one day per week. This alternative scheduling allows students to continue working in their professions while earning their degrees.
Research Facilities	D'Youville's modern Library Resource Center, which was completed in fall 1999, contains 154,000 volumes, including microtext and software, and subscriptions to 870 periodicals and newspapers. The multimillion-dollar Health Science Building houses laboratories, including those for anatomy, organic chemistry, quantitative analysis, and computer science. It also houses classrooms, faculty member offices, and development centers, including one for career development. This is augmented by a modern academic center that opened in fall 2001.
Financial Aid	D'Youville attempts to provide financial aid for students who would not otherwise be able to attend. Determination of aid is based on the Free Application for Federal Student Aid. Aid is available in the form of grants, loans, and employment on campus. In addition, D'Youville offers scholarships for academic achievement to incoming students.
	Graduate students must be matriculated for 6 or more credits in a degree program. Nurse traineeship assistance is available to students enrolled for a minimum of 9 credit hours per semester in the graduate nursing program. Canadian students (citizens and landed immigrants), except those enrolled in the RN degree-completion program, are offered a 20 percent tuition reduction and may also apply for the Ontario Student Assistance Program (OSAP). All students enrolled in the RN degree-completion program are offered a 50 percent tuition reduction.
Cost of Study	Graduate tuition for 2007–08 is $635 per credit hour for master's and advanced certificate programs and $680 per credit hour for doctoral programs. A general College fee of between $30 and $60 is required, based on credit hours taken.
Living and Housing Costs	Marguerite Hall, the residence facility, houses men and women on separate floors and includes a coed floor for graduate and adult students. For 2007–08, room and board cost $4375 per semester. Overnight accommodations are available at a rate of $23 per night (space permitting). A new residence-apartment complex opened in January 2005 and houses 175 junior, senior, and graduate students in one- and four-bedroom apartments. In 2007–08, the new resident apartment complex rates are around $3575 per semester, based on the type of apartment reserved.
Student Group	Graduate degree programs are enhanced by a 13:1 student-faculty ratio. The current enrollment is 1,113 full-time and 443 part-time graduate students. Seventy-four percent of the students are women, 5 percent are members of minority groups, and 62 percent are internationals students. D'Youville's proximity to the Canadian border accounts for the majority of the international student population.
Location	D'Youville is situated on Buffalo's residential west side. The College is within minutes of many social attractions, including the downtown shopping center, the Kleinhans Music hall, the Albright-Knox Art Gallery, two museums, and several theaters that offer stage productions. Seasonal changes in the area offer a variety of recreational opportunities. Buffalo is only 90 miles from Toronto and 25 minutes from Niagara Falls, making it a gateway to recreation areas in western New York and Ontario. Holiday Valley, a skier's paradise, is an hour's drive away. The city is serviced by the New York State Thruway, Amtrak, Greyhound and Trailways bus lines, and most major airlines.
	D'Youville enjoys a diversified interchange with the community due to its affiliations with schools, hospitals, and social agencies in the area. College students in the Buffalo area number more than 60,000.
The College	Commencing in 1942, D'Youville College was the first private college in New York State to offer a four-year Bachelor of Science in Nursing degree program. The College offers four doctoral, eight master's-level, and five postbaccalaureate programs as well as baccalaureate and advanced certificate programs. Graduate programs in addition to nursing include childhood, adolescence, and special education; health services administration; international business; and occupational therapy. Doctoral programs include chiropractic, educational leadership, health policy and health education, and physical therapy. D'Youville offers the undergraduate degrees of Bachelor of Arts (B.A.), Bachelor of Science (B.S.), and Bachelor of Science in Nursing (B.S.N.). Majors include accounting, biology, business management, chiropractic (seven-year B.S./D.C.), dietetics, education (early childhood, childhood, adolescence, and special), English, exercise and sports studies, global studies, health services, history, information technology, nursing, occupational therapy, philosophy, physical therapy, physician assistant, preprofessional studies (dental, law, medicine, and veterinary studies), psychology, and sociology. Five-year combined bachelor's/master's (B.S./M.S.) programs are offered in dietetics, education, information technology (B.S.)/international business (M.S.), nursing, and occupational therapy. A six-year B.S./D.P.T. program is offered in physical therapy.
Applying	A baccalaureate degree in nursing from an approved or accredited college or university and RN licensure are required for admission to the graduate nursing programs. Licensure as a registered nurse in New York State and a minimum of one year of experience as a registered nurse are required of candidates applying to the nurse practitioner programs. Admissions to graduate programs is based on an overall evaluation of credentials, including the applicant's undergraduate record, with a minimum 3.0 GPA average in the major field. Applicants who do not fulfill admission requirements may be admitted provisionally. Applicants whose native language is not English must submit a minimum TOEFL score of 500. Graduate application files are reviewed on a rolling basis.
Correspondence and Information	Linda E. Fisher Director of Graduate Admission D'Youville College One D'Youville Square 320 Porter Avenue Buffalo, New York 14201 Phone: 716-829-8400 800-777-3921 (toll-free) E-mail: graduateadmissions@dyc.edu Web site: http://www.dyc.edu

D'Youville College

THE FACULTY AND THEIR RESEARCH

Patricia Bahn, Associate Professor; M.S; RN. Adult health/nursing administration, holistic health/oncology.

Denise Dunford, Assistant Professor and Director of Family Nurse Practitioner Program; D.N.S., SUNY at Buffalo. Family/ambulatory/emergency nursing.

Carol A. Gutt, Associate Professor; Ed.D., SUNY at Buffalo. Wellness, child health, curriculum, women's health, women's issues, stress management, leadership roles.

Verna Kieffer, Assistant Professor and Department Chair; D.N.S., SUNY at Buffalo. Adult health, critical care, qualitative research, quality of life issues, professional practice issues.

Edith Malizia, Assistant Professor and Assistant to the Chair; Ed.D., SUNY at Buffalo. Adult health, professional issues, professional socialization, leadership and management.

Pamela Miller, Clinical Coordinator; M.S., SUNY at Buffalo; RN. Women's health nurse practitioner.

Judith Stanley, Assistant Professor; D.H.Sc., Nova Southeastern.

EMORY

NELL HODGSON
WOODRUFF
SCHOOL OF
NURSING

EMORY UNIVERSITY

Nell Hodgson Woodruff School of Nursing

Programs of Study

Emory University School of Nursing graduate programs prepare students with advanced nursing knowledge, produce nurse leaders in practice and research, and create forerunners in the design of new models of care. The graduate curriculum combines comprehensive nursing theory and research with a rich clinical core and extensive specialty courses. A wealth of clinical venues are available in the Atlanta metropolitan area, and clinical experiences are precisely geared to students' career focus.

Programs of study leading to the Master of Science in Nursing (M.S.N.) include the following specialties: acute care nurse practitioner, adult nurse practitioner, adult oncology nurse practitioner, emergency nurse practitioner, family nurse midwife, family nurse practitioner, gerontological nurse practitioner, international health (M.S.N./M.P.H. only), leadership and administration in health care, nurse midwifery, pediatric nurse practitioner-acute care, pediatric nurse practitioner-primary care, public health nursing leadership, women's health (Title X), women's health nurse practitioner, and women's health/adult health nurse practitioner. Areas of concentration include faith-based health care, management, and teaching. The length of the specialty programs ranges from three (one calendar year) to five consecutive semesters of full-time study; part-time study is available. Upon completion of the M.S.N. degree students are eligible to sit for certification as a certified nurse midwife or nurse practitioner. An RN-M.S.N. bridge program is available for associate degree or diploma prepared nurses. Students in the RN-M.S.N. program complete 24 semester hours of bridge course work prior to beginning the specialty curriculum of choice. A dual Master of Science in Nursing/Master of Public Health (M.S.N./M.P.H.) is available in conjunction with Emory's Rollins School of Public Health. Post-master's options are available in all graduate specialty areas, except the emergency nurse practitioner.

The Ph.D. in nursing offers flexible specialization options and is a four-year, full-time program.

Research Facilities

In 2001, the School of Nursing opened a state-of-the-art facility for nursing study and research. The building unites scholarship and teaching under one roof and enhances the School's mission of social responsibility and service. Designed with tomorrow's technology in mind, the building offers ample space for research and clinical training. In 2000, the School of Nursing opened the Lillian Carter Center for International Nursing. The center focuses on improving the health of vulnerable people worldwide through nursing practice, education, and research. The School of Nursing is part of the Robert W. Woodruff Health Sciences Center, a major provider of patient care and a national leader in clinical and research programs. The other components are Emory University School of Medicine, Rollins School of Public Health, Yerkes Regional Primate Research Center, Emory HealthCare, the Emory Clinic, and the Wesley Woods Center of Emory University, Inc. Emory University is a close collaborator with the Carter Center, a nonprofit, nonpartisan public policy institute founded by former President Jimmy Carter and his wife Rosalynn. The center is dedicated to fighting disease, hunger, poverty, conflict, and oppression on a worldwide basis. Holdings of the five Emory libraries total approximately 2.5 million volumes. The libraries also offer access to thousands of electronic information resources. The primary research resources for nursing students are the Asa Griggs Candler Library, the Health Sciences Library, and the Robert W. Woodruff Library for Advanced Studies. EUCLID, the library's integrated library computer system, can be searched at all Emory libraries and through the campus network.

Financial Aid

Ninety-five percent of currently enrolled School of Nursing graduate students receive some form of financial assistance. A variety of need-based and merit-based awards are available. Dean's Scholarships are awarded to students based on academic achievement. Five full-tuition Woodruff Fellowships are awarded to incoming graduate students each year based on academic achievement, leadership, and service. Students may be eligible to receive Advanced Education Nursing Traineeships based on financial need, academic achievement, and future work plans. Need-based grants and loans are also available.

Ph.D. students receive a full-tuition fellowship and a stipend.

Cost of Study

Tuition for full-time study was $14,400 per semester and $1200 per credit hour for the 2006–07 academic year. Activity and athletic fees were $173 per semester.

Living and Housing Costs

On-campus housing is available to full-time graduate students. Emory's location in the middle of a residential area offers ample opportunities for off-campus housing. More information may be obtained by contacting the Office of Residence Life of Emory University.

Student Group

During the 2006–07 academic year, the School of Nursing enrolled 213 undergraduate and 177 graduate students. Eighty-four percent of graduate students were women, 7 percent were men, and 54 percent pursued the graduate degree full-time. The students represented seventeen states and three countries. Faculty members look for high academic achievement, solid verbal and written communication skills, and a strong commitment to advanced practice nursing.

Location

The School of Nursing is located on the 631-acre Emory campus in Atlanta, Georgia. It is situated 15 minutes from downtown Atlanta and is positioned along the Clifton Corridor, which also includes the U.S. Centers for Disease Control and Prevention and the American Cancer Society. Atlanta is the fastest-growing city in the South, with premier athletic teams, museums, and theaters.

The University and The Department

Emory University has approximately 12,000 students and 2,500 faculty members who represent all regions of the U.S. and ninety countries. Emory has nine major academic divisions, numerous centers for advanced study, and a host of prestigious affiliated institutions. The academic units include an undergraduate college; a graduate school of arts and sciences; professional schools of medicine, theology, law, nursing, public health, and business; and a two-year undergraduate division. Emory was founded by the Methodist Church in 1836.

Applying

Admission requirements include graduation from a National League for Nursing–accredited or Commission on Collegiate Nursing Education–accredited Bachelor of Science program in nursing with a minimum grade point average of 3.0, a current license to practice nursing, a recommended minimum of one year of work experience, an application, statement of purpose, satisfactory scores on the Graduate Record Examinations (GRE) or Miller Analogies Test (MAT), three recommendations, transcripts from all institutions attended, and a faculty interview. Admission decisions are on a rolling basis. The priority deadline for admission and scholarships for fall and summer term is January 15; however, applications will continue to be reviewed on a space available basis.

Correspondence and Information

Office of Admission
School of Nursing
Emory University
1520 Clifton Road
Atlanta, Georgia 30322
Phone: 404-727-7980
          800-222-3879 (toll-free)
Fax: 404-727-8509
E-mail: admit@nursing.emory.edu
Web site: http://www.nursing.emory.edu

Emory University

THE FACULTY

Corrine Abraham, Associate; M.N., Emory, 1985. Adult and elder health.

Kelly Brewer, Associate; M.S.N., Arkansas, 1992. Adult and elder health.

Holly L. Brown, Associate; M.S.N., Pennsylvania, 1989. Adult and elder health.

Ann Connor, Clinical Assistant Professor; M.S.N., Alabama, 1980. Family and community nursing.

Jo Ann Dalton, Professor and Chair, Adult and Elder Health; Ed.D., North Carolina State, 1984.

Madge M. Donnellan, Clinical Associate Professor; Ph.D., Tennessee, 1988. Family and community nursing.

Elizabeth Downes, Clinical Assistant Professor; M.S.N., Tennessee, 1986. Family and community nursing.

Sandra B. Dunbar, Professor and Coordinator of the Doctoral Program; D.S.N., Alabama at Birmingham, 1982. Adaptation to the stresses of acute and chronic cardiovascular illness.

Sara Edwards, Instructor; M.S.N./M.P.H., Emory, 1994. Family and community nursing.

Sarah B. Freeman, Clinical Professor; Ph.D., Georgia State, 1989. Family and community nursing.

Mary L. Garvin-Surpris, Instructor; M.S., New Rochelle, 1993. Adult and elder health.

Maggie P. Gilead, Associate Professor; Ph.D., Emory, 1981. Adult and elder health.

Judy Gretz, Instructor; M.S., Texas Woman's, 1977. Family and community nursing.

Jill Hamilton, Assistant Professor; Ph.D., North Carolina at Chapel Hill, 2001. Adult and elder health.

Kenneth Hepburn, Associate Dean for Research; Ph.D., Washington, 1968.

Leslie Holmes, Instructor; M.S.N., Medical University of South Carolina, 1993. Family and community nursing.

Barbara Kaplan, Instructor; M.S.N., Emory, 1992. Family and community nursing.

Maureen A. Kelley, Clinical Associate Professor and Chair, Family and Community Nursing; Ph.D., Medical College of Georgia, 1993. Midwifery.

Joyce L. King, Clinical Assistant Professor; Ph.D., Emory, 1995. Family and community nursing.

Sally T. Lehr, Clinical Assistant Professor; Ph.D., Georgia State, 2001. Adult and elder health.

Marsha Lewis, Associate Dean for Education; Ph.D., Minnesota, 1992.

Maureen O. Lobb, Clinical Assistant Professor; Ph.D., Georgia State, 1992. Family and community nursing.

Kathy Markowski, Associate; M.S.N., DePaul, 1980. Adult and elder health.

Jane L. Mashburn, Clinical Associate Professor and Director, M.S.N. Program; M.N., Emory, 1978. Midwifery, family and community nursing.

Kathryn Matthews, Instructor; M.S.N., Pennsylvania, 1976. Family and community nursing.

Joyce P. Murray, Professor; Ed.D., Georgia, 1989. Adult and elder health.

Lynda P. Nauright, Professor; Ed.D., Georgia, 1975. Adult and elder health.

Michael W. Neville, Clinical Associate Professor; Pharm.D., Georgia, 1992. Adult and elder health.

Helen S. O'Shea, Professor Emerita; Ph.D., Georgia State, 1980. Adult health.

Kathy Parker, Professor; Ph.D., Georgia State, 1990. Family and community nursing.

Quyen Phan, Instructor; M.S.N., Emory, 2004. Adult and elder health.

Marcene L. Powell, Professor; D.S.W., Utah, 1981. Family and community nursing.

Barbara D. Reeves, Clinical Assistant Professor; M.S.N., Vanderbilt, 1979. Family and community nursing.

Bethany D. Robertson, Instructor; M.S.N., Emory, 1992. Family and community nursing.

Martha F. Rogers, Clinical Professor; M.D., Medical College of Georgia, 1976. Family and community nursing.

Deborah A. Ryan, Clinical Associate Professor and Director, B.S.N. Program; M.S.N., Marquette, 1981. Family and community nursing.

Marla E. Salmon, Professor, Dean, and Director of LCCIN; Sc.D., Johns Hopkins, 1977. Health workforce and health services.

Lynn Sibley, Associate Professor; Ph.D., Colorado, 1993. Family and community nursing.

Linda Smith, Instructor; M.N., South Carolina, 1980; M.Div., Emory, 2004. Adult and elder health.

Linda Spencer, Clinical Associate Professor; Ph.D., Georgia State, 1988. Family and community nursing.

Ora Strickland, Professor; Ph.D., North Carolina at Greensboro, 1977. Family and community nursing.

Darla R. Ura, Clinical Associate Professor; M.A., Ball State, 1974. Adult and elder health.

Jeannie Weston, Instructor; M.S., Maryland, 1982. Family and community nursing.

Lynette Wright, Clinical Associate Professor; M.N., Emory, 1974. Distance learning strategies.

Erin M. York, Associate; M.S., Georgia State, 1995. Family and community nursing.

Weihua Zhang, Clinical Assistant Professor; Ph.D., Georgia State, 2004. Adult and elder health.

FELICIAN COLLEGE

Advanced Practice Nursing

Programs of Study

The Online Master of Science in Nursing (M.S.N.) Program at Felician College is designed to prepare the registered nurse with a B.S.N. degree for advanced practice in primary-care settings. The program, also available entirely online, emphasizes nursing care of families or adults, with a specific focus on vulnerable and underserved populations.

Felician College offers two advanced practitioner tracks: adult nurse practitioner and family nurse practitioner. The adult nurse practitioner track requires 43 credits and 600 clinical hours, while the family nurse practitioner track requires 46 credits and 780 clinical hours. Courses are taught on a trimester schedule, and terms start in September, January, and April. Students generally take at least two courses per term and can complete the degree in as little as two years. All students are required to take 28 credits of professional core courses before they complete the course work required for their track of choice. Graduates are eligible to take the advanced practice national certification examination in family or adult health.

The Post-Master's Certificate Program prepares a nurse with a master's degree in nursing for primary-care practice in family or adult advanced practice. The credits required for the certificate range from 12 to 31, based on the student's educational background and prerequisite course work. The program consists of four foundation courses, with more courses in the chosen area of specialization, as well as clinical experience.

The School Nurse/Health Education Post-Baccalaureate Certificate Program prepares registered nurses to provide health care and health education for K–12 in the school setting.

Research Facilities

The Nursing Resource Center, a multifaceted center of learning for all nursing students, is located on the Lodi campus. The center has a state-of-the-art computer room, where CD-ROM and interactive video programs are used to intensify the learning experience. The Nursing Resource Center staff members assist students with clinical competencies through the use of mannequins and other equipment that simulates clinical procedures. Individual tutoring and workshops are offered to enhance theory comprehension.

A center for child care and simulated nursing practice is also available on the Lodi campus. The first floor is devoted to a well-equipped Child Care Center for the convenience of students and faculty members. The upper floor houses the Nursing Skills Laboratory, which provides a simulated hospital setting for the clinical training of students in the nursing programs.

The College Library is a two-story building that serves the needs of students, faculty and staff members, and alumni with more than 110,000 books and over 800 periodical subscriptions. This collection is enhanced by large holdings of materials in microform, which can be used on the library's reader/printer equipment. With its computers linked to information services such as DIALOG and OCLC, and as a member of the New Jersey Library Network and VALE, the library locates and obtains information, journal articles, and books not available in its collection from sources all over the country. Computerized databases can also be accessed directly by users through the online First Search workstation, where up-to-date information on 40 million books and an index of 15,000 periodicals is available. The library is also connected to the Internet and has several CD-ROM workstations. Through EBSCOhost, Bell & Howell's Proquest, CINAHL, and other services, students and faculty and staff members have access to numerous online journal indexes—as well as articles from thousands of periodicals—from anywhere on the campus computer network or from their home computers. An experienced staff of professional librarians is available to assist users.

The College's computer facilities include an academic and administrative network, four computerized labs, a computerized learning center, and two computer centers that are available for students, with a total of about 200 computers available for student/faculty member use. All classrooms, offices, and facilities are wired for Internet and e-mail.

Financial Aid

Fellowships and loans are available. To qualify for financial aid, a student must complete the Free Application for Federal Student Aid (FAFSA).

Cost of Study

In 2006–07, graduate tuition was $675 per credit. Fees are additional.

Living and Housing Costs

Students are housed in two dormitories on the Rutherford campus, Milton and Elliott Halls. Both buildings have housing organized around student suites containing semiprivate baths. On-campus room and board ranges between $3200 and $5500 per semester. On-campus housing is not available to married students.

Student Group

In total, there are about 1,800 students. In fall 2005, there were 34 students (2 percent) enrolled in the graduate nursing programs.

Location

Felician College's Lodi campus is located on the banks of the Saddle River on a beautifully landscaped campus of 27 acres and offers a collegiate setting in suburban Bergen County, within easy driving distance of New York City. The Felician College Rutherford Campus is set on 10.5 beautifully landscaped acres in the heart of the historic community of Rutherford, New Jersey. Only 15 minutes from the Lodi campus, the Rutherford complex contains student residences, classroom buildings, a student center, and a gymnasium. The campus is a short distance from downtown Rutherford, where there are many shops and businesses of interest to students.

The College

Felician College, a coeducational liberal arts college, is a Catholic, private, independent institution for students representing diverse religious, racial, and ethnic backgrounds. The College operates on two campuses in Lodi and Rutherford, New Jersey. The College is one of the institutions of higher learning conducted by the Felician Sisters in the United States. Its mission is to provide a values-oriented education based in the liberal arts while it prepares students for meaningful lives and careers in contemporary society. To meet the needs of students and to provide personal enrichment courses to matriculated and nonmatriculated students, Felician College offers day, evening, and weekend programs. The College is accredited by the Middle States Association of Colleges and Schools and carries program accreditation from the National League for Nursing Accrediting Commission, the National Accrediting Agency for Clinical Laboratory Sciences, and the International Assembly for Collegiate Business Education.

Applying

In addition to being licensed as a registered nurse, applicants must have an accredited bachelor's degree from a nursing program, with a minimum cumulative GPA of 3.0. Undergraduate courses in nursing research, statistics, pathophysiology, and health assessment should have been completed. Applicants must submit the completed application, the $30 nonrefundable application fee, official transcripts, a copy of the student's nursing license, and two letters of recommendation. An interview with the chair of graduate nursing may be required. International credential requirements are reviewed on an individual basis. Applications are processed on a rolling basis.

Correspondence and Information

Programs in Advanced Practice Nursing
Felician College
262 South Main Street
Lodi, New Jersey 07644-2117
Phone: 201-559-6077
Fax: 201-559-6138
E-mail: adultandgraduate@felician.edu
Web site: http://www.felician.edu/academics/mahp/

Felician College

THE FACULTY

Nancy Brey, Assistant Professor of Nursing; M.S.N., CUNY, Hunter; RN.
Dorothy Carolina, Assistant Professor of Nursing; M.S.N., Columbia; RN.
Janet Daly, Instructor of Nursing; M.A., NYU; RN.
John Fajvan, Nursing Resource Coordinator.
Diane Holbrow, Associate Nursing Resource Coordinator.
Catherine Jennings, Instructor; M.S.N., SUNY at Stony Brook; RN, APNC.
Sr. Patricia Kennedy, Assistant Nursing Resource Coordinator.
Christine Mihal, Assistant Professor and Chair, RN-B.S.N. Programs; M.S.N., Seton Hall; RN, ANCC.
Maureen Murphy-Ruocco, Professor and Chair, School Nurse/Health Education Program; Ed.D., Columbia Teachers College; RN, APNC.
Mary Norton, Professor and Associate Dean of Graduate Nursing; Ed.D., Columbia; RN, APNC.
Patricia O'Brien-Barry, Associate Professor; Ph.D., NYU.
Susan Schwade, Assistant Professor; M.S.N., Wayne State.
Muriel M. Shore, Professor and Dean; Ed.D., Seton Hall; RN.
Salimah Walani, Assistant Professor; M.S.N., Simmons; M.P.H., Harvard; RN.
Elizabeth Zweighaft, Assistant Professor and Associate Dean of Undergraduate Nursing; Ed.M., Columbia Teachers College.

FLORIDA INTERNATIONAL UNIVERSITY

Ph.D. in Nursing Program

Programs of Study
The College of Nursing and Health Sciences at Florida International University (FIU) offers a doctoral program that is grounded in a research-focused curriculum and designed to prepare students for leadership roles in nursing education, research, and service in a variety of health-care organizations. The Ph.D. in Nursing Program trains individuals to generate and apply the science needed to guide nursing practice and provides the knowledge and skills to direct and guide applications that improve the health of people from diverse cultures. An important goal of the program is to increase the number of Ph.D. nurses from minority groups and to produce clinically relevant research on health issues concerning minority and underserved populations.

The degree requires the completion of 36 credit hours of course work and 24 credit hours of dissertation. Course work includes foundations of scientific inquiry and nursing science, research methods and data analysis, foundations for conducting research with multicultural groups, cognates to provide in-depth study in focused areas, and courses in analyzing and understanding requirements for successful functioning within academic and health-care systems and the accessing, managing, and packaging of information. Elective cognates provide a broadened substantive base for the student's specialized content area. A wide range of courses are available in the areas of aging, anthropology and sociology, economics and financing, education, health-care administration, and psychology. Once admitted into the program, a student is assigned a faculty mentor whose program of research matches the student's interest. Students pursue individualized areas of study under the mentorship of research-active faculty members.

The Ph.D. in Nursing Program can be completed in four years of full-time study; an overall GPA of 3.0 or higher is required to complete the program. Students are expected to complete the dissertation five years from the date of advancement to candidacy, which includes successful completion of written and oral examinations, favorable recommendation of the supervisory/guidance committee, and an approved dissertation proposal.

The College is accredited by the National League for Nursing Accrediting Commission, the Council on Accreditation of Nurse Anesthesia Educational Programs, and the Florida State Board of Nursing.

Research Facilities
The University Park Library and Biscayne Bay Campus Libraries have a combined collection of more than 1.5 million volumes, in addition to substantial holdings of federal, state, local, and international documents, periodicals, maps, microfilms, institutional archives, and curriculum materials. The library subscribes to approximately 9,700 journals and serials and offers a wide variety of online resources. Its online computer catalog provides information on the collections of all libraries of the State University System of Florida.

The Center of Health Research and Policy provides competency-based education and training in public health, communication, preparedness, and response; contributes to the study of public health policy in order to effectively influence future policy; fosters academic and community-based research on public health; and meets the public health needs of diverse populations in south Florida.

Financial Aid
Graduate assistantships in teaching or research range from $1700 to $6000 per semester depending on the nature of the job and the number of hours worked. A limited amount of scholarship funds is available through the Dean's office. Traineeship funds are also available through the HRSA Advanced Nurse Education Traineeship program. Full-time enrollment is a requirement. More generous scholarships for qualified students are available from the Financial Aid Office at http://www.fiu.edu/orgs/finaid.

Cost of Study
In 2006–07, tuition was $259.73 per credit hour for Florida residents and $763.80 per credit hour for out-of-state students. Additional per-semester fees, such as intercollegiate athletics, health services, and transportational access, are not included.

Living and Housing Costs
Housing is limited and should be petitioned for with ample time. Campus housing includes apartment-style accommodations ranging from studio apartments to shared units. Costs vary within the choice of housing and residential life. Off-campus housing near the University is also available. Information is available from the University Housing Office at http://www.fiu.edu/~housing.

Student Group
Students in the program hold master's degrees in nursing, with an average GPA of 3.3, and have a GRE score of 1120 or higher. In addition, they hold current Registered Nurse (RN) licensure or RN licensure with Advanced Registered Nurse Practitioner (ARNP) certification in the state of Florida and maintain professional liability insurance.

Student Outcomes
The program prepares graduates for leadership roles and research careers in academia, health care, and government and private organizations that are focused on health care. Individuals become leaders in generating and applying the science needed to guide nursing practice, and they gain the knowledge and skills to improve the health of people from diverse cultures.

Location
The University is located in Miami, Florida's largest urban center and a major transportation and business hub of the southeastern United States. Miami is an exciting, dynamic global marketplace. Miami Beach is known for its historic art deco district and the numerous hotels that line its beaches. Miami has been reinvented into a hemispheric crossroads for trade, travel, culture, and communications.

The University
Established in 1972, Florida International University offers more than 190 baccalaureate, master's, and doctoral degree programs in nineteen colleges and schools. *U.S. News & World Report* has ranked FIU among the top 100 public national universities, and FIU has been recognized as one of the top ten public commuter universities in the nation by *Money*. FIU has 35,000 students, 1,100 full-time faculty members, and 110,000 alumni—making it the largest university in south Florida and among the nation's thirty largest colleges and universities.

Applying
Prospective students must meet all admission requirements stipulated in the FIU Graduate Policies and Procedures. In addition, candidates for the Ph.D. in Nursing Program must have a master's degree in nursing with a clinical specialty from an accredited institution, a master's program GPA of at least 3.3 on a 4.0 scale, and a combined score of 1120 or higher on the verbal and quantitative sections of the Graduate Record Examinations (GRE), taken within five years of the date of application. Applicants whose native language is not English must take the Test of English as a Foreign Language (TOEFL) and score at least 550 on the paper test or 213 on the computer version. A satisfactory interview by members of the College of Nursing and Health Sciences Doctoral Program Admissions Committee (DPAC) is required.

A completed application form must be sent with official transcripts of prior undergraduate and graduate work, GRE or TOEFL scores, three letters of recommendation from academic and professional references, a statement of no more than 500 words addressing the goals for pursuing a Ph.D., proof of nursing licensure or certification and professional liability insurance, and a $30 application fee. The deadline to apply is June 1 for the fall semester, October 1 for the spring semester, and March 1 for the summer semester.

Correspondence and Information
Dr. Luz S. Porter, Ph.D. Program Coordinator
College of Nursing and Health Sciences
Room HLS 378
University Park Campus
Florida International University
11200 Southwest 8th Street
Miami, Florida 33199
Phone: 305-348-7744
E-mail: porterl@fiu.edu
Web site: http://nursing.fiu.edu/

Florida International University

THE FACULTY AND THEIR RESEARCH

Kathryn Anderson, Associate Professor; Ph.D., Minnesota; RN, LMFT. Impact of cancer on couple interaction, psychosocial impact of illness on the family, family dynamics in health and illness, nursing interventions with families in health and illness.

Kathleen Blais, Associate Professor; Ed.D., Florida Atlantic; RN. Gerontology, medication errors, medicinal substance abuse in special populations.

Dorothy Brooten, Professor; Ph.D., Pennsylvania; RN, FAAN. High-risk pregnancy, health services, intervention, outcomes, advanced practice.

Daisy Ciocon, Associate Professor; Ph.D., Miami (Florida); RN, CCRN, ARNP. Geriatric clinical research, geriatric syndromes, enteral nutrition, fall prevention.

Marie-Luise Friedemann, Professor; Ph.D., Michigan; RN. Family functioning, family measurement, family theory, dynamics of care-giving, families with elderly, family and substance abuse, family treatment modalities, family and juvenile delinquency in girls.

Jeffrey Groom, Professor and Director, Anesthesiology Nursing Program; Ph.D., Nova Southeastern, 2006; CRNA. Patient stimulation–based instruction.

Sandra Jones, Assistant Professor; Ph.D., Barry; RN-BC, ACRN, ARNP. Symptom management in HIV/AIDS, medication adherence/side-effect management of HIV/AIDS medications, HIV prevention.

Sandra Lobar, Associate Professor; Ph.D., Miami (Florida); RN, ARNP. Life management for chronically ill children, parenting, infant adoption, behavioral pediatrics, Attention Deficit Hyperactivity Disorder.

Suzanne Phillips, Associate Professor; Ed.D., Florida International; RN, ARNP. Evaluation of nursing programs, critical-thinking skills, Attention Deficit Hyperactivity Disorder, parenting and nursing management, adoptive parenting.

Luz Porter, Professor and Coordinator, Ph.D. in Nursing Program; Ph.D., NYU; RN, ARNP, FNP, FAAN. Parenting enhancement, infant massage, growth and development, substance-abusing women, teenage pregnancy, demographics, role orientations, obesity, cross-cultural interventions, outcomes.

JoAnne Youngblut, Professor; Ph.D., Michigan; RN, FAAN. Critically ill children and their families, maternal employment, functioning of child-rearing families.

HAWAI'I PACIFIC UNIVERSITY

School of Nursing

Programs of Study

Hawai'i Pacific University's Master of Science in Nursing (M.S.N.) degree program is designed to prepare students to assume enhanced roles in community-based care as advanced practice nurses. With three concentrations, community clinical nurse specialist (CNS) studies, community clinical nurse specialist educator option, or family nurse practitioner (FNP) studies, students learn contemporary approaches for delivering cost-effective, qualitative health care, especially to chronically underserved populations such as the poor, elderly, and those in multiethnic communities. The program focuses on those skills needed by nurses to succeed in the changing health-care environment: enhanced critical-thinking, assessment, problem-solving, the education of future nurses, and communication skills.

The RN-M.S.N. pathway allows registered nurses without baccalaureate degrees in nursing to transition into the M.S.N. program. Students entering the RN-M.S.N. pathway are granted provisional admission status until all prerequisites have been completed. Students who successfully complete the program receive an M.S.N. degree.

Hawai'i Pacific University offers the joint Master of Science in Nursing and Master of Business Administration program to complement a nurse's clinical skills with a solid business foundation. The joint program focuses on skills needed by both health-care and business leaders: analytical reasoning, leadership, and effective communication.

Research Facilities

To support graduate studies, University libraries, with a collection exceeding 153,000 volumes, add an average of 2,500 volumes annually. Periodical titles number more than 1,700, and 205,000 pieces of microfiche and 5,300 rolls of microfilm are maintained. Dial-up and online access to local area databases of public and state university catalogs are also available.

Financial Aid

The University participates in all federal financial aid programs designated for graduate students. These programs provide aid in the form of subsidized (need-based) and unsubsidized (non-need-based) Federal Stafford Student Loans. Through these loans, funds may be available to cover the student's entire cost of education. To apply for aid, students must submit the Free Application for Federal Student Aid (FAFSA) after January 1. Mailing of student award letters usually begins by the end of March. The University also offers several institutional scholarships and assistantships.

Cost of Study

For the 2007–08 academic year, graduate tuition is $560 per credit hour, and books cost approximately $1500 for the entire program. The RN-M.S.N. pathway tuition is $398 per credit hour.

Living and Housing Costs

The University has both residence halls and an apartment referral service. Including tuition, books, housing, food, health insurance, and miscellaneous expenses, the cost of living for a typical single student for two semesters (nine months) is approximately $25,840.

Student Group

University enrollment currently stands at nearly 9,000, including more than 1,200 graduate students. All fifty states and more than 100 countries are represented.

Student Outcomes

M.S.N. program graduates are eligible to sit for certification as family nurse practitioners or advanced practice nurse educators when they complete their degree. Course work and practicum time in the Clinical Nurse Specialist track can also focus on the nurse educator role.

Location

The University has three campuses linked by shuttle. Hawai'i Pacific combines the excitement of an urban, downtown campus with the serenity of the windward side of the island. The main campus is located in downtown Honolulu, the business and financial center of the Pacific. The Hawai'i Loa campus is 8 miles away situated on 135 acres in Kaneohe at the base of the Ko'olau Mountains; it is the site of the School of Nursing, the marine science program, and a variety of other course offerings. The third campus, Oceanic Institute, is an applied aquaculture research facility located on a 56-acre site at Makapu'u Point on the windward coast.

The University

Hawai'i Pacific University is the largest private postsecondary institution in the state of Hawai'i. The University is coeducational, with a faculty of more than 300 members, a student-faculty ratio of 18:1, and an average class size of 20. A wide range of counseling and student support services are available. There are more than ninety student organizations, including the Graduate Student Organization.

Applying

Hawai'i Pacific University seeks students with academic promise, outstanding career potential, and high motivation. Applicants should complete and forward a graduate admissions application form, have official transcripts sent from all colleges or universities attended, and submit two original and current letters of recommendation (one from a professional associate, preferably with a graduate degree, and one from an immediate supervisor detailing the applicant's clinical performance). Applicants should also submit two essays, a resume, and a current license as a registered nurse in the state of Hawai'i. Admissions decisions are made on a rolling basis, and applicants are notified one to two weeks after all documents have been submitted. Applicants to Hawai'i Pacific University's graduate program are encouraged to submit applications online at http://www.hpu.edu/msn.

Correspondence and Information

Graduate Admissions
Hawai'i Pacific University
1164 Bishop Street, #911
Honolulu, Hawai'i 96813
Phone: 808-544-1135
          866-GRAD-HPU (toll-free)
Fax: 808-544-0280
E-mail: graduate@hpu.edu
Web site: http://www.hpu.edu/grad

Hawai'i Pacific University

THE FACULTY AND THEIR RESEARCH

Dale Allison, Ph.D.; RNC, APRN-Rx, FAAN. Underserved populations, multiethnic communities, APRN delivery models for care, outreach programs, service learning.

Margaret Anderson, Ed.D., M.S.N.; RN, APRN. Education, anxiety disorders, mental health.

Patricia Burrell, Ph.D.; RN, APRN, BC. Women's health issues, noncancerous hysterectomy outcomes, transcultural nursing, HIV-AIDS and its effect on women's lives, depth psychology.

ReNel Davis, Ph.D.; RN. Elder health, community health, transcultural health, service learning.

Hobie Feagai, Ed.D., M.S.N.; RN, APRN, FNP, BC. Transcultural practice.

Janice Haley, Ph.D.; APRN, BC, CPNP, FNP. Medically fragile children, strengths of parent caregivers.

Judith Holland, Ph.D., M.S.N. Post-traumatic stress disorder (PTSD), guilt and health psychology.

Patricia Lange-Otsuka, Ed.D., M.S.N.; APRN, BC, CNE. HIV-AIDS issues, educational assessment, NCLEX predictors, chronic illness management, genetics.

Michelle Marineau, Ph.D., M.S.N.; RN, APRN, FNP. Infectious disease management, clinical drug studies, telehealth, SARS.

Catherine Ryan, D.N.P., M.S.N.; RN, APRN, CNM. Women's health, nurse midwifery, NCLEX success, leadership and management.

MGH INSTITUTE
OF HEALTH PROFESSIONS
an academic affiliate of Massachusetts General Hospital

MGH INSTITUTE OF HEALTH PROFESSIONS

Graduate Programs in Nursing, Physical Therapy,
Communication Sciences and Disorders,
Clinical Investigation, and Medical Imaging

Programs of Study

The graduate programs offered at the Institute combine a rigorous academic curriculum with clinical practicums in multiple settings, designed to prepare graduates for leadership positions in their respective professions. Founded by, and affiliated with, Massachusetts General Hospital (MGH) in Boston, the Institute offers an interdisciplinary curriculum as well as different tracks and specialties within a field. Opportunities for postprofessional certification (Certificates of Advanced Study) exist in several of the programs.

The Master of Science in Nursing degree program accepts both college graduates without a nursing background and nurses with bachelor's degrees in nursing or other fields. For students without a nursing background, the program requires three years of full-time study and consists of generalist and advanced practice nursing courses. There is also an admission pathway for associate degree and diploma RNs who have completed selected additional general education requirements prior to matriculating into the program. Both the entry-level and the RN programs offer opportunities to develop specializations in a variety of areas: women's health, gerontology, and psychiatric–mental health. Acute-care, pediatric, adult, and family nurse practitioner tracks allow all students to prepare for certification; an acute-care track is offered to RN students. RN students may complete the program on a full- or part-time basis, with courses offered in the daytime and evening and during the summer.

Graduate programs in physical therapy offer both entry-level and postprofessional (advanced) curricula. The Doctor of Physical Therapy (D.P.T.) program, which prepares students who hold a bachelor's degree in another field to become physical therapists, is a full-time, two-year program, followed by a one-year clinical internship. The Post-Professional Master of Science in Physical Therapy program, offered on a full- or part-time basis, admits U.S.-licensed physical therapists who have had at least one year of clinical experience. Specialty areas include cardiopulmonary, neurologic, and orthopedic physical therapy, or a student may design an individualized program of study. A clinical preceptorship and thesis are required. Other postprofessional study options are a Certificate of Advanced Study, an International Scholars program designed for practicing physical therapists from other countries with at least eighteen months of clinical experience, and a transitional D.P.T. program for U.S. licensed therapists who want to obtain the D.P.T. credential.

The Master of Science degree program in speech-language pathology offers a curriculum based on a solid foundation in the normal processes and disorders of human communication across the life span. The Graduate Program in Communication Sciences and Disorders prepares students to provide speech-language pathology services in multiple settings, including acute care, rehabilitation, long-term care, community clinics, and both special and regular public schools. Unique features of the program include the opportunity to pursue additional certification in written language (reading) and cross-registration with the Harvard Graduate School of Education.

The Master of Science degree program in clinical investigation is a three-semester program (based on full-time study; part-time study takes longer) that prepares health-care professionals and other qualified students to be team members and leaders in clinical research through participation in the development of new and improved therapies and interventions, implementation of clinical trials, data management, regulatory affairs, medical writing, outcomes research, and study oversight. Features of this program include all didactic work in a distance learning format and the Certificate of Advanced Study option.

The postbaccalaureate certificate in medical imaging is designed to meet the needs of career changers as well as recent graduates and provides an alternative route to licensure as a radiologic technologist. The instructional format is competency based and uses an alternating structure of online academic instruction, laboratory, and hands-on clinical experience. This seventeen-month fast-track program is intended to help students reach their educational goals in a timely manner, while fulfilling the requirements to sit for the certification/licensure examination in radiography.

Research Facilities

Clinical and research opportunities are provided at MGH and in more than 500 other major health-care centers and community settings in the greater Boston area. Through MGH's Treadwell Library, with major basic science, medical, and nursing collections, students may access online computer databases and an extensive reference and periodical collection. Students working on research projects may also access the Countway Library of Medicine at Harvard Medical School. In addition, the Institute houses the Ruth Sleeper Learning Center, which provides computers and modern technology for interactive learning.

Financial Aid

Financial assistance is supplemental to the student's financial resources. Whenever possible, financial need is met through a combination of sources that may include federal loans, partial scholarships, graduate assistantships, and federal traineeships.

Cost of Study

Tuition for the 2007–08 academic year is approximately $855 per credit hour, with the number of credits dependent on individual program requirements. Fees include a general student fee and an anatomy fee for the entry-level program in physical therapy. Books and supplies are estimated to cost about $1500.

Living and Housing Costs

The Institute does not provide housing for students; however, the Office of Students Affairs does provide limited assistance to students who are relocating. Rents in the area vary. It is estimated that annual expenses for a single student living alone in Boston run about $15,000 per year.

Student Group

Total enrollment for fall 2006 was approximately 800. With many of these students making career changes, the student body is composed of highly talented individuals from diverse backgrounds who wish to become leaders in the health professions.

Student Outcomes

Graduates of the Institute are equipped to meet the challenges of managed care in a variety of settings: major teaching hospitals, ambulatory health-care environments, educational institutions, hospital-based systems, and private practice. Many continue their education at the doctoral level.

Location

Located along the waterfront of the historic Charleston Navy Yard, which is conveniently near the edge of Boston Harbor and Massachusetts General Hospital, the Institute offers students a stimulating environment. There are numerous opportunities for extracurricular activities—theaters, museums, concerts, and professional sports events. Boston has an excellent public transportation system and is located in proximity to rivers, lakes, mountains, and parks.

The Institute

The Institute was founded in 1977 by the Massachusetts General Hospital and maintains a close affiliation with the hospital while being separately incorporated. The Institute's faculty members are engaged in teaching, clinical practice, and research. As model practitioners, faculty members integrate theory with the care of patients, evaluation of that care, and the design and implementation of student research to improve health care. Students test theories through clinical application with faculty assistance. Interdisciplinary study is an integral part of the Institute's educational philosophy.

Applying

All applicants must submit a completed online application along with a $65 fee, official transcripts from all colleges and universities attended, GRE General Test scores (taken within the last five years if required for the program), three letters of recommendation, and an essay. International applicants and applicants who did not receive their undergraduate degree from an English-speaking institution must have their degree transcript evaluated by an American credentialing agency. They are also required to submit Test of English as a Foreign Language (TOEFL) scores.

Correspondence and Information

Office of Student Affairs
MGH Institute of Health Professions
P.O. Box 6357
Boston, Massachusetts 02114-0016

Phone: 617-726-3140
Fax: 617-726-8010
E-mail: admissions@mghihp.edu
Web site: http://www.mghihp.edu

MGH Institute of Health Professions

FACULTY AND RESEARCH AREAS

Nursing

Linda Andrist, Associate Professor; Ph.D., RNC, WHNP.
Debra A. Bradford, Clinical Instructor; M.S.N, RNCS, ANP-BC.
Elaine L. Bridge, Clinical Instructor; M.B.A.
Cheryl A. Cahill, Amelia Peabody Professor in Nursing Research; Ph.D., RN.
Jeanne M. Cartier, Assistant Professor; Ph.D., APRN, BC.
Denise M. Celli, Clinical Instructor; M.S.N.
Margery Chisholm, Professor and Director; Ed.D., RN, CS, ABPP.
Stephen E. Coffey, Clinical Instructor; M.S.N., RN-C, ARNP.
Inge B. Corless, Professor; Ph.D., RN, FAAN.
Deborah D'Avolio, Assistant Professor; Ph.D., RN, CS.
Jeanette Ives Erickson, Clinical Assistant Professor; M.S., RN, CAN.
Joan B. Fitzmaurice, Associate Professor; Ph.D., RN, FAAN.
Elizabeth B. Friedlander, Clinical Assistant Professor; M.S.N., M.Ed., RN.
M. Patricia Gibbons, Assistant Professor; D.N.Sc., RN.
Janice H. Goodman, Assistant Professor; Ph.D., RN, CS, IBCLC.
J. Alexander Hoyt, Instructor; M.S.N., RN.
Veronica R. Kane, Clinical Assistant Professor; M.S.N., RN, CPNP.
Ursula Kelly, Assistant Professor; Ph.D., APRN-BC.
Elissa C. Ladd, Clinical Assistant Professor; Ph.D., APRN, ANP/FNP.
Ellen Long-Middleton, Assistant Professor; Ph.D., RN.
Ruth Palan Lopez, Assistant Professor; Ph.D., APRN, BC.
Patricia Lussier-Duynstee, Assistant Professor; Ph.D., RN.
Diane Feeney Mahoney, Jacques Mohr Professor in Geriatric Nursing; Ph.D., ARNP, BC.
Maureen J. Marre, Clinical Instructor; M.S.N., RN, FNP.
Talli Craig McCormick, Clinical Assistant Professor; M.S.N., RNC, GNP.
Janice Bell Meisenhelder, Associate Professor; D.N.Sc., RN.
Jacqueline S. (Sue) Myers, Assistant Professor; Ph.D., RN.
Patrice Kenneally Nicholas, Professor; D.N.Sc., M.P.H., APRN, BC.
Joanne O'Sullivan, Assistant Professor; Ph.D., RN, FNP.
Alexandra Paul-Simon, Assistant Professor; Ph.D., RN.
Patricia A. Reidy, Clinical Instructor; M.S., APRN, BC-FNP.
Marcia P. Reissig, Clinical Instructor; M.S., RN, CHCE.
Deborah A. Rosenbloom, Clinical Instructor; M.S., RN, NP.
Pamela M. Senesac, Assistant Professor and Associate Director; Ph.D., SM, RN.
Katherine F. Simmonds, Clinical Assistant Professor; M.S.N., RNC.
Kathleen H. Solomon, Clinical Assistant Professor; M.S., RN, NP.
Sharon P. Sullivan, Clinical Instructor; M.S., RN.
Nancy M. Terres, Assistant Professor; Ph.D., RNC.
Carmela A. Townsend, Clinical Instructor and Academic Coordinator of Clinical Education; M.S./M.B.A., RN.
John G. Twomey Jr., Associate Professor; Ph.D., RN, CS.
Karen Anne Wolf, Clinical Associate Professor; Ph.D., RN, CS.

Physical Therapy

Donna Applebaum, Clinical Assistant Professor and Associate Director of Clinical Education; D.P.T.
Marianne Beninato, Assistant Professor; D.P.T., Ph.D.
Joann M. Brooks, Clinical Assistant Professor; D.P.T., M.P.H., OCS.
Kathleen Grimes, Clinical Assistant Professor; D.P.T., CCS.
Bette Ann Harris, Clinical Professor; D.P.T.
Maura D. Iversen, Professor and Associate Director; D.Sc., M.P.H., PT.
Anne McCarthy Jacobson, Clinical Assistant Professor; D.P.T.; NCS.
Colleen Mary Kigin, Assistant Professor; D.P.T.; M.P.A.
Aimee B. Klein, Clinical Assistant Professor; D.P.T., OCS.

Mary S. Knab, Assistant Professor and Director of Clinical Education; D.P.T.
David E. Krebs, Professor; D.P.T., Ph.D.
Claire F. McCarthy, Associate Professor; M.S., PT.
Theresa Hoskins Michel, Clinical Associate Professor; D.P.T., D.Sc., CCS.
Leslie G. Portney, Professor and Director; D.P.T., Ph.D., FAPTA.
Michael S. Puniello, Clinical Assistant Professor and Coordinator, Orthopaedic Residency Program; D.P.T., OCS, FAAOMPT.
Linda A. Steiner, Clinical Assistant Professor; D.P.T., OCS.
Michael G. Sullivan, Clinical Assistant Professor; D.P.T., M.B.A.
Patricia E. Sullivan, Associate Professor; D.P.T., Ph.D.
Elise Townsend, Assistant Professor; Ph.D., PT.
Mary P. Watkins, Clinical Associate Professor; D.P.T.
Cynthia Coffin Zadai, Assistant Professor and Coordinator, Transitional D.P.T. Program; D.P.T., CCS, FAPTA.

Communication Sciences and Disorders

Denise M. Ambrosi, Clinical Instructor; M.S., CCC-SLP.
Julie Atwood, Professor; M.Ed., CCC-SLP.
Lynne A. Davis, Assistant Professor; Ph.D., CCC-AUD.
Christine R. Doyle, Clinical Instructor; M.S., CCC-SLP.
Charles W. Haynes, Associate Professor; Ed.D., CCC-SLP.
Robert E. Hillman, Professor; Ph.D., CCC-SLP.
Pamela E. Hook, Associate Professor; Ph.D.
Charles Jeans, Clinical Instructor; M.S., CCC-SLP.
Sandra Jones, Associate Professor; Ph.D.
Kevin P. Kearns, Professor and Director; Ph.D., CCC-SLP.
Gregory L. Lof, Associate Professor and Associate Director; Ph.D., CCC-SLP.
Jennifer E. Mackey, Clinical Assistant Professor and Coordinator of Clinical Education; M.A., CCC-SLP.
Lesley A. Maxwell, Assistant Clinical Professor and Director of the Language Laboratory; M.S., CCC-SLP.
Marjorie L. Nicholas, Associate Professor; Ph.D., CCC-SLP.
Isabel B. Phillips, Clinical Associate Professor; Ed.D.
Mary K. Riotte, Clinical Instructor; M.S., CCC-SLP.
Howard C. Shane, Professor; Ph.D., CCC-SLP.
Sharyn L. Tucceri, Clinical Instructor; M.S., CCC-SLP.
Carmen Vega-Barachowitz, Clinical Instructor; M.S., CCC-SLP.
Anne M. Waters, Clinical Instructor; M.S., CCC-SLP.
Sharon Weiss-Kapp, Clinical Assistant Professor; M.Ed., CCC-SLP.

Clinical Investigation

Paul A. Boepple, Professor and Director; M.D.
Cheryl A. Cahill, Amelia Peabody Professor in Nursing Research; Ph.D., RN.
Mary Carey, Professor and Academic Dean; Ph.D.
James L. Parmentier, Associate Professor; Ph.D.

Medical Imaging

Sandra Creaser, Clinical Associate Professor and Clinical Coordinator; M.M., RT(R), (N), (M), CNMT.
Kimberly L. Metcalf, Assistant Professor; Ed.D., M.B.A., AART.
Richard Terrass, Clinical Assistant Professor and Director; M.Ed., RT(R).

Interdisciplinary

Ellen A. Moloney, Clinical Instructor; M.B.A.
Denis G. Stratford, Associate Professor; M.S.
Ruth Purtilo, Professor and Chair, Ethics Initiative; Ph.D.

MOUNTAIN STATE UNIVERSITY

Master of Science in Nursing Programs

■ Mountain State University™

Programs of Study

Mountain State University (MSU) offers the Master of Science in Nursing (M.S.N.) with concentrations in family nurse practitioner (FNP) studies, nursing administration and education, and nurse anesthesia, as well as family nurse practitioner and nurse anesthesia graduate certificate programs. The FNP and nursing administration and education programs are offered on both the Beckley and Martinsburg campuses and can be completed full-time (two years) or part-time (three to four years). Both of these programs offer great flexibility in helping nurses meet their goals. The didactic portion of the programs requires a full day of classes one day each week. Because most students in the programs continue to work full- or part-time during their graduate studies, services such as registration, advising, and library research assistance are available in the evening as well as during the day, and whenever possible, the clinical portion of the program is scheduled in the student's local city or town. The nurse anesthesia concentration, based on the Beckley campus and offered through a combination of on-site and distance learning, is designed as a thirty-month full-time program of study.

The family nurse practitioner concentration prepares nurses to become primary-care providers for individuals, groups, and communities. With a focus on health across the entire life span, FNPs may provide prenatal care, family planning services, and well child care; they encourage healthy aging and recommend elder care. Family nurse practitioners obtain medical histories and perform physical examinations, diagnose and treat acute health problems or chronic diseases, and prescribe medications and other treatments. This practice is grounded within informatics and research as well as the ability to provide leadership.

The nursing administration and education concentration prepares nurse managers and nurse administrators for first- or middle-level leadership positions in a variety of health-care organizations, and it also prepares nurse educators for teaching in any educational area. Becoming an educator is a great option for those who love to teach and are looking for a flexible schedule without a full-time clinical commitment. Other students already working in health-care administration look to the M.S.N. program to boost them to levels of higher management responsibility. The MSU program of study incorporates an interdisciplinary perspective by combining the two areas of administration and education. Both course work and clinical practice emphasize the development of leadership skills and the application of theories of leadership, education, informatics, and research.

Mountain State University's nurse anesthesia program prepares RNs who have completed a minimum of a bachelor's degree in nursing for entry into advanced practice nursing within the anesthesia specialization. Students receive clinical and didactic experiences that meet or exceed the requirements to take the certification exam of the Council on Accreditation of Nurse Anesthesia Educational Programs and Council on Certification of Nurse Anesthetists.

There is a serious shortage of certified registered nurse anesthetists (CRNAs) in West Virginia as well as the entire United States. It is estimated that certified registered nurse anesthetists administer approximately 65 percent of the 26 million anesthetics given to patients in the U.S. each year. CRNAs are needed in a variety of settings in the public, private, and military sectors, including hospital operating rooms, ambulatory surgery centers, pain clinics, and physicians' offices. Nurse anesthetists are the sole anesthesia providers for many rural hospitals, enabling these health-care facilities to offer obstetrical, surgical, and trauma stabilization services. CRNAs are in-demand, highly compensated professionals.

The 79-credit-hour MSU CRNA program, offered through a combination of on-site and distance learning, is a full-time master's-level program that can be completed in thirty months. The MSU program is the first in the country to offer distance learning combined with practical clinical experience. Students attend on-site labs, discussion groups, workshops, and simulation experiences in three- to four-day blocks every three to four weeks. Most lectures are delivered on CDs, and most other interactions with the faculty members are assigned, delivered, and graded via the Internet.

Both the clinical and didactic phases are intense. Participants average 15 credit hours of graduate work per semester for the first four semesters and then have clinicals for the next four semesters. Each phase requires a commitment of 65 to 70 hours per week without a break, from the first day until graduation. With principal educational settings in West Virginia (Huntington, Charleston, and Beckley), eastern Kentucky, and western Virginia, the CRNA program is designed to keep students as close to home as possible for clinical practicums. However, some relocation may be needed to accommodate the requirements of the Council on Accreditation of Nurse Anesthesia Educational Programs and Council on Certification of Nurse Anesthetists.

Research Facilities

Learning resources include multimedia classrooms, computer laboratories, computer-assisted instruction, nursing and health assessment labs, and laboratories for the basic sciences. For CRNA education, SimMan and SimBaby have full-body physiologic parameters programmed to respond to student input. The Robert C. Byrd Learning Resource Center includes a student-centered library and media center. The collection comprises more than 95,000 titles, supplemented both by interlibrary loan and by extensive electronic resources, including ProQuest, Cumulative Index to Nursing and Allied Health Literature (CINAL), Social Issues Resources Index (SIRS), EBSCOhost, Westlaw, Wilson Web, Newsbank, and Medline. The newly created Technology Zone includes state-of-the-art telecommunication links, technology equipment, high-speed access and software, and a 3-D immersion module.

Financial Aid

Eligible graduate students may qualify for Federal Stafford Student Loans. Prospective students must submit the Free Application for Federal Student Aid (FAFSA) for determination of eligibility. Most graduate students receive some sort of financial assistance.

Cost of Study

Tuition in 2006–07 for the FNP and nursing administration and education concentrations was $335 per credit hour. Payment plans are available. Additional fees are charged for graduation, thesis review, and thesis binding.

Tuition for the CNRA program was $465 per credit hour. During each clinical semester, the student pays an additional $3500 fee ($14,000 for four semesters). At the beginning of the program, students must purchase a computer and all required textbooks from the Mountain State University Bookstore. The computer is designed to interface with the MSU computer system, maintain compatibility with the software used, and cut down on computer-related problems. The estimated cost of the computer and books is $6000.

Living and Housing Costs

Most students in the graduate nursing programs are commuters; however, many affordable housing opportunities are available in the neighborhoods surrounding the campus and in other nearby areas, which range from suburban to rural. Monthly rents average $300 to $600. Graduate students may also live in the residence hall on campus. Residence hall fees for 2006–07 were $1405 per semester for double occupancy and $2100 per semester for a private room. Students living on campus are required to purchase one of the University's meal plans.

Student Group

Mountain State University serves more than 6,000 students a year. Graduate enrollment and programming have grown steadily since the University's first graduate program was launched in 1998.

Location

Mountain State University's main campus is located near downtown Beckley, West Virginia, a small city in the heart of the southern West Virginia mountains that serves as a regional center for business, health care, education, and tourism. The Beckley area offers the excitement of city life, the quiet of a small town, and a wealth of recreational and cultural opportunities. Nearby recreational opportunities include white-water rafting on the famed New and Gauley Rivers, skiing, hiking, biking, climbing and rappelling, and other outdoor pursuits. Beckley is an hour's drive from the state capital of Charleston and just a few hours from Pittsburgh; Washington, D.C.; and other eastern metropolitan areas.

The University

For more than seventy years, Mountain State University has been a leader in overcoming barriers to higher education and in offering academic programs that combine a liberal arts foundation with career-oriented studies. The University features innovative programming, flexible learning arrangements, well-qualified and deeply committed faculty members, and outstanding student services, all in a relaxed atmosphere. Graduate degree programs are offered through the University's School of Graduate Studies, some in conjunction with the Center for Distance Education.

Applying

Students should consult the nursing programs Web site for specific application requirements.

Correspondence and Information

Information Center
Mountain State University
P.O. Box 9003
Beckley, West Virginia 25802-9003
Phone: 304-929-INFO (4636)
       866-FOR-MSU1 (367-6781; toll-free)
Web site: http://www.mountainstate.edu

Mountain State University

THE FULL-TIME GRADUATE FACULTY

Wayne Ellis, Professor and Director, CRNA Program; Ph.D., Texas A&M; RN, CRNA, ARNP.
Patsy Haslam, Professor and Senior Academic Officer, Health Sciences; Ed.D., West Virginia; RN.
Jessica Sharp, Professor and Senior Academic Officer, Graduate Nursing; Ph.D., George Mason; RN, FNP-C, BC-APN.

MOUNT CARMEL
College of Nursing

MOUNT CARMEL COLLEGE OF NURSING

Master of Science Program

Programs of Study	Mount Carmel College of Nursing (MCCN) offers a Master of Science (M.S.) program in adult health and nursing education. The program of study is designed for baccalaureate-prepared nurses who wish to pursue careers at a higher level. This dynamic master's program focuses on adult health and nursing education and includes the clinical practice hours needed to take the Clinical Nurse Specialist (CNS) exam in medical-surgical nursing. With a master's degree from Mount Carmel, students can increase professional responsibility, teach patients, and educate future nurses and health-care workers.
	Offered on both a full- and part-time basis, the master's program offers flexibility for the nurse seeking his or her level of expertise. Class sizes are small and designed to meet the individual needs of the student.
	Other advantages to Mount Carmel's program are that students attend classes only one day a week, there are no GRE requirements for admission, undergraduate work and nursing licensure count toward requirements, and there is flexible scheduling of classes.
	The College also offers a Post-Master's Certificate in Nursing Education, a Dietetic Internship Program, and programs through its Division of Continuing Education. Offered online or on-site, the Post-Master's Certificate in Nursing Education program prepares licensed registered nurses who already have a master's degree in nursing for another level of practice—the role of qualified educator in an academic or a health-care setting.
Research Facilities	Various clinical learning experiences are offered at several locations throughout central Ohio. Among them are long-term care facilities, academic institutions, and hospitals, including those within the Mount Carmel network. The clinical areas of study provide students with an excellent and well-rounded opportunity to experience all elements of nursing care in a variety of environments.
	As part of a large health-care delivery system, students at MCCN have access to a full professional library. The library provides a full range of reference, bibliographic, and interlibrary loan services.
	Students also have access to the new Center for Learning and Education (CLE), which is located on campus and is designed specifically to support studies. The center includes a fully equipped computer lab, and a multimedia area, which houses state-of-the-art instructional technology. Completed in early 2004, the state-of-the-art CLE includes new research labs, an auditorium, classrooms, and a library.
Financial Aid	Numerous financial aid options are available to students. Financial aid is awarded based on demonstrated financial need, scholastic achievement, and other considerations in the form of loans, employment opportunities, scholarships, and grants. Students may find assistance through the College's own financial aid programs and through federal programs. Representatives from the MCCN financial aid department can assist students in exploring various options.
Cost of Study	Tuition and fees were $14,574 for the 42-credit-hour program in 2006–07. Admission, processing, and graduation fees were $250.
Living and Housing Costs	For students wishing to live on campus, MCCN maintains a full-service dormitory within the College for easy access to classes and the faculty. Housing costs associated with living in the dormitory are $964 per semester for double occupancy. Also, students, both commuter and resident, have access to three on-campus dining options, the hospital cafeteria, Wendy's, and Tim Hortons.
Student Group	The master's program is composed of baccalaureate-prepared professional registered nurses at varying stages of their careers and personal interests. More than 550 students are enrolled in the College's undergraduate Bachelor of Science in Nursing (B.S.N.) degree and certification programs. Faculty and staff members are committed to fostering personal and academic growth, an approach that transcends into such areas as student recruitment and retention rates.
Location	Mount Carmel College of Nursing is located on the near west side of Columbus, Ohio, on the hospital campus of Mount Carmel West. With more than 1 million residents in its metropolitan area, Columbus is a diverse city. Mount Carmel is located just minutes from the exciting downtown area, which is conveniently located to shopping theaters, sporting events, and parks.
	Columbus has all the benefits of a large city without losing the feeling of small-town warmth and spontaneity.
The College	MCCN is a private, specialized institution of higher education offering the B.S.N. degree, a Master of Science program in adult health and nursing education, the RN-B.S.N. Completion Program, a dietetic internship program, a Post-Master's Certificate in Nursing Education, and programs through its Division of Continuing Education. The College's baccalaureate degree in nursing includes both the prelicensure program as well as a curriculum option called the RN-B.S.N. Completion Program for registered nurses seeking a baccalaureate degree.
	The College is accredited by the Higher Learning Commission and the nursing program is accredited by the National League for Nursing Accrediting Commission. The master's program, offered for the first time in 2003, is authorized by the Ohio Board of Regents, and is under review by the Higher Learning Commission and accreditation is being sought.
	Mount Carmel College of Nursing is a subsidiary of Trinity Health and has one of the largest undergraduate nursing programs among all Ohio private colleges with nursing programs. The learning is enhanced by experiences and opportunities made possible by the College's inclusion in Mount Carmel Health System, an integrated delivery system. Mount Carmel includes three acute-care hospitals, community outreach programs, hospice, home health, and ambulatory care centers.
	Founded in 1903 by the Congregation of the Sisters of the Holy Cross, Mount Carmel offered a diploma program until 1993. In 1993, Mount Carmel College of Nursing was established. MCCN offers small classes and one-on-one instruction. MCCN is committed to respect for all persons, holistic development of individuals, and encouragement of social responsibility.
Applying	Admission to the program is determined on the following criteria: a baccalaureate degree in nursing from an accredited program/accreditation by either NLNAC or CCNE, a current unrestricted Ohio RN license, a minimum cumulative GPA of 3.0 (on a 4.0 scale) in a baccalaureate nursing program, and a minimum score of 550 on the TOEFL for international students whose native language is not English.
	Admission materials to be submitted include official transcripts from all previous academic work; a current resume; a statement of career goals, objectives, and plans for graduate study; and letters of recommendation from professional associates. Additional materials to be submitted prior to course enrollment include current CPR certification, current professional liability insurance, a completed health form, and a criminal background check. To schedule a visit and tour, students should call the College.
Correspondence and Information	Office of Admission Mount Carmel College of Nursing 127 South Davis Avenue Columbus, Ohio 43222 Phone: 614-234-4CON 800-556-6942 (toll-free) Web site: http://www.mccn.edu

Mount Carmel College of Nursing

THE FACULTY AND THEIR RESEARCH

The program was approved by the Ohio Board of Regents in June 2003. While the graduate program is new, Mount Carmel has been providing nursing education for more than 100 years, with 2003 marking the institution's centennial celebration.

The Graduate Council is the faculty planning group for the graduate program. All 8 faculty members are doctorally prepared and seasoned educators. With the development of the adult health and nursing education specialty, faculty members are aggressively pursuing additional development opportunities that enhance their teaching and their scholarship.

Individualized attention, small classes, and highly experienced and caring faculty members foster excellence in education at Mount Carmel College of Nursing.

OAKLAND UNIVERSITY

Master of Science in Nursing

Program of Study

The School of Nursing graduate degree program at Oakland University (OU) prepares professional nurses for advanced nursing practice, leadership in the nursing profession, and future doctoral study. Five tracks are offered: Adult Acute Care Clinical Nurse Specialist, Adult/Gerontological Nurse Practitioner, Family Nurse Practitioner, Nurse Anesthesia, and Nursing Education. The master's program is accredited by the Commission on Collegiate Nursing Education. In addition, the Nurse Anesthesia program is accredited by the Council on Accreditation of Nurse Anesthesia Educational Programs.

In keeping with the philosophy of the School of Nursing, master's degree graduates achieve the following outcome competencies: 1) Incorporate concepts and theories from nursing and related disciplines into advanced nursing practice, 2) Provide advanced nursing care in a variety of settings in accordance with the American Nurses Association (ANA) Scope and Standards of Advanced Practice Registered Nursing and appropriate subspecialty standards, and 3) Exemplify in practice the American Nurses Association Standards of Professional Performance as detailed in the Scope and Standards of Advanced Practice Registered Nursing as well as other appropriate advanced standards of care.

Oakland also offers a Doctor of Nursing practice degree.

Research Facilities

The Office of Grants, Contracts and Sponsored Research supports research and scholarship at Oakland University. In particular, the office acts as the coordinating office between Oakland University and the federal and state agencies, foundations, and public and private corporations that provide funds for research, education, training, and service programs.

Located in the center of campus, the Kresge Library houses collections of books, journals, reference works, government documents, musical scores, and recordings as well as a wireless network and computer workstations to access an array of digital resources. The Kresge Library's collections include over 727,000 books, approximately 1,400 print journal subscriptions, and electronic access to more than 15,000 titles, over 240,000 federal and state documents, and more than 1.1 million microforms. The Library's Homepage and online catalog serve as gateways to dozens of specialized and general research databases and hundreds of full-text electronic journals and e-books covering a wide range of disciplines and research areas.

Financial Aid

In order to assist eligible graduate students in financing their education, Oakland University participates in the Federal College Work-Study Program and the William Ford Federal Direct Loan Program.

Cost of Study

Graduate tuition in the 2007–08 academic year is $472.50 per credit hour for Michigan residents and $814.50 per credit hour for nonresidents. For current tuition rates, students should visit http://www.oakland.edu/tuitionandfees.

Living and Housing Costs

The 2006–07 rate for room and board was $6385 for the academic year. Facilities with a selected number of single rooms are available to graduate students. For students with families, a limited number of two-bedroom town houses and two- to four-bedroom student apartments are available.

Student Group

Total enrollment at OU for fall 2006 was 17,737. Graduate students make up 23 percent of the total enrollment. Within the graduate enrollment, 66 percent are women and 11.4 percent are members of ethnic minority groups. The diverse student body includes international students representing many different countries.

Location

Oakland University is located in Oakland County, the third-most-affluent county in the United States and the fastest growing county in Michigan. Rochester, Michigan, is OU's hometown. Rochester was named thirty-ninth in a list of top 100 cities to live—and the highest-ranking Michigan city in the survey—by *Money* magazine and *CNN Money* in 2005. The ranking was based on population, number of educational facilities, safety, environment, housing affordability, taxes, weather, commute times, and job market.

In addition, the area's rolling hills, wetlands, and woodlands provide beautiful neighborhoods and plenty of year-round recreation. The surrounding community also offers an abundance of entertainment, cultural, and social opportunities. Together, all this makes Oakland County and Rochester a great place to live, work, and go to school.

The University

Oakland University, founded in 1957, is a comprehensive state-supported institution of higher education. The University is organized into the College of Arts and Sciences and the Schools of Business Administration, Education and Human Services, Engineering and Computer Science, Health Sciences, and Nursing.

Applying

Students applying to the M.S.N. program need to submit the Application for Admission to Graduate Study, application processing fee, and supporting documents to Graduate Admissions. Both a paper and online application process are available. Information about application requirements and deadlines is available online at http://www.oakland.edu/grad/apply.

Correspondence and Information

Graduate Admissions
160 North Foundation Hall
Oakland University
Rochester, Minnesota 48309
Phone: 248-370-3167
E-mail: gradmail@oakland.edu
Web site: http://www.oakland.edu/gograd

Oakland University

THE FACULTY AND THEIR RESEARCH

Linda S. Thompson Adams, Dr.P.H., Johns Hopkins; RN, FAAN. Childhood obesity and prevention, health of vulnerable children, juvenile justice and systems reform.

Karen Dunn, Ph.D., Wayne State; RN. Aging and spirituality, chronic pain, stress and coping, end-of-life care.

Wanda Gibson-Scipio, M.S.N., Michigan State; RNC, FNP. Social support, self-regulation, asthma self-management, health-related quality of life.

Barbara Harrison, Ph.D., Michigan; RN. Dementia behaviors, memory and cognitive skills assessment, oral health of older adults.

Frances C. Jackson, Ph.D., Wayne State; RN. HIV/AIDS and older African Americans, influence of culture/ethnicity on end-of-life decisions.

Suha Kridli, Ph.D., Missouri, Columbia; RN. Family planning, health promotion, Middle Eastern health beliefs and practices, diabetes.

Anahid Kulwicki, D.N.S., Indiana; RN. Tobacco use in Arab Americans, Arab American health, domestic violence, parent-child relationship.

Morris A. Magnan, Ph.D., Wayne State; RN.

Anne M. Mitchell, Ph.D., Wayne State; RN.

Mary E. Mittelstaedt, Ph.D., Michigan State; RN. Psychosocial issues of at-risk childbearing and early childrearing families, including postpartum depression, parent-infant relationships, eating disorders, and infertility.

Gary Moore, Ph.D., Wayne State; RN. Nursing education outcomes, music therapy, animal-assisted therapy.

Sarah E. Newton, Ph.D., Michigan; RN. Return-to-work post–liver transplantation, writing abilities of nursing students, graduate study in nursing.

Diane M. Norris, Ph.D., Michigan; RN. Ethical nursing practice, nurses' job satisfaction, student group testing.

Barbara B. Penprase, Ph.D., Wayne State; RN. Complexity theory, management/leadership, gerontology nursing, student group testing, qualitative research methodology.

Cheryl K. Riley-Doucet, Ph.D., Wayne State; RN. Pain control in older adults, activities to promote successful aging, nursing interventions with families of older adults who suffer from chronic illness.

F. Darlene Schott-Baer, Ph.D., Wayne State; RN. Women's self-care, evidence-based practice, self-care of caregivers.

PACE UNIVERSITY

Lienhard School of Nursing

Programs of Study	The Lienhard School of Nursing offers the Master of Science (M.S.) in family nurse practitioner studies and the Master of Arts (M.A.) in nursing education. Certificates of Advanced Graduate Study (CAGS) are offered in family nurse practitioner studies and nursing education. All programs are offered for both full- and part-time study and require a clinical curriculum component. The M.S. program in family nurse practitioner studies is 42 credits and focuses on health promotion, illness prevention, health maintenance, detection of alterations in health status, and restoration of health care. Additional foci are advanced nursing practice strategies, research, and leadership. Graduates are eligible for New York State (NYS) certification as family nurse practitioners with full prescriptive privileges.
	The newly approved Master of Arts (M.A.) in nursing education prepares students to assume the role of educator in a variety of educational and practice settings. The specialty in education provides students with the concepts, theories, and ideas that support teaching and learning in the academic setting at the level of clinical instructor or in associate degree programs as well as educational roles in health care organizations. The specialty in administration gives students a background in management and leadership principles and practices in order for them to successfully assume leadership roles in health care organizations. The program is 39 credits for the M.A. degree and 18 credits for the CAGS.
	The Combined Degree Program (CDP) is a specially designed, accelerated curriculum for non-nurse college graduates who wish to study nursing in a first professional degree program (B.S.N.), combined with the option of an advanced professional degree program (M.S.). The Lienhard School of Nursing has long been a leader in second-degree education for non-nursing college graduates and has offered the CDP in Pleasantville since 1984. Acceleration is possible for the B.S.N. portion by giving recognit on to previous baccalaureate education and by recognizing that the college graduate is an able learner by virtue of previous educational and life experiences. The CDP (B.S.N. and M.S. portions) is now available at both the Pleasantville and New York City campuses. The B.S.N. can be completed in one calendar year of full-time study, consisting of 50 credits in the nursing major, including 6 graduate credits that can be counted toward the M.S. degree. The optional M.S. portion of the CDP can be started the semester immediately following B.S.N. graduation and, depending on the major chosen, can be completed in a full-time sequence of four semesters.
Research Facilities	The Pace University Library is a comprehensive teaching library and student-learning center, a virtual library that combines strong core collections with ubiquitous access to global Internet resources to support broad and diversified curricula. Reciprocal borrowing and access accords, traditional interlibrary loan services, and commercial document delivery options supplement the aggregate library. Pace offers Instructional Services Librarians, a state-of-the-art electronic classroom, digital reference services, and multimedia applications. Pace's computer resource centers are linked to high-speed data networks and feature sophisticated hardware and software to facilitate active learning. Recognized as one of America's most wired universities, Pace supports high-speed Internet and Internet2 access on every campus; residential facilities are wired, and most public areas are enabled for wireless connectivity. Full-motion videoconference facilities enable remote delivery of instruction between campus sites for synchronous learning applications. Many courses are Web-assisted with state-of-the-art software, and some courses and programs are completely Web-based.
Financial Aid	Pace's comprehensive student financial aid assistance program includes scholarships, graduate assistantships, student loans, and tuition payment plans. Scholarships are awarded to students in recognition of academic achievement and are available for full- and part-time study. Highly qualified students may be eligible for assistantships awarded by departments, which paid stipends of up to $5100 and tuition remission of up to 24 credits during the 2006–07 academic year. Pace participates in all major federal and state financial aid programs, such as direct loans, New York State Tuition Assistance Program (TAP), Perkins Loans, and Federal Work-Study. All students are encouraged to apply for these programs by filing the Free Application for Federal Student Aid (FAFSA).
Cost of Study	Tuition for graduate courses is $734 per credit in 2007–08.
Living and Housing Costs	Residence facilities are available on campus in both New York City and Westchester. Double occupancy rooms range from approximately $8500 to $12,000 for 2007–08. University-operated, off-campus housing is available within proximity of the New York City campus.
Student Group	Pace students represent diversified personal, cultural, and educational backgrounds. Many students are employed and pursue graduate study for personal growth and career advancement opportunities; 86 percent are enrolled part-time in evening classes. Current enrollment in the graduate nursing program is approximately 190 students.
Location	Pace University is a multicampus institution with campuses in both New York City and Westchester County, New York. All locations are within reach of cultural, business, and social resources and opportunities. The downtown Manhattan campus is adjacent to Wall Street and City Hall. Pace's Midtown Center is a short distance from Times Square, theaters, and Grand Central Station. In Westchester County, the Pleasantville/Briarcliff campus is a suburban setting, surrounded by towns offering various forms of recreation. The Graduate Center and the School of Law are located in White Plains among major retail districts and many corporate headquarters. All locations are accessible by public transportation. Graduate nursing programs, as well as the CDP program, are available at both the New York City and Pleasantville campuses.
The University	Founded in 1906, Pace University is a private, nonsectarian coeducational institution. Originally founded as a school of accounting, Pace Institution was designated Pace College in 1948. Through growth and various successes, it was renamed Pace University in 1973, as approved by the New York State Board of Regents. Today, Pace offers comprehensive undergraduate, graduate, doctoral, and professional programs at several campus locations through six schools and colleges.
Applying	Admission to Pace University's graduate programs requires successful completion of a U.S. baccalaureate degree or its equivalent from an accredited institution. Students must submit a completed application, application fee, official transcripts from all post-secondary institutions, a personal statement, a resume, and two letters of recommendation. International students must submit official TOEFL scores and official transcripts in their native language with a professional English translation. Applicants for the master's programs must have RN licensure. Completion of one year of nursing is recommended. The CDP is highly competitive, and applicants must demonstrate satisfactory performance on the GRE General Test or the Miller Analogies Test (MAT). Applications for M.S. programs should be submitted by August 1 for the fall semester, December 1 for the spring semester, and May 1 for the summer sessions. Applications for the CDP should be submitted by June 1 for fall admission and October 15 for spring admission. International applications should be submitted one month prior to these dates.
Correspondence and Information	Office of Graduate Admission Pace University 1 Pace Plaza New York, New York 10038 Phone: 212-346-1531 Fax: 212-346-1585 E-mail: gradnyc@pace.edu Web site: http://www.pace.edu	Office of Graduate Admission Pace University 1 Martine Avenue White Plains, New York 10606 Phone: 914-422-4283 Fax: 914-422-4287 E-mail: gradwp@pace.edu Web site: http://www.pace.edu

Pace University

THE FACULTY AND THEIR RESEARCH

Ann Marie Bova, Clinical Instructor; M.S., Pace, 1997; RN.

Susan Del Bene, Associate Professor; Ph.D., CUNY Graduate Center, 1985; RN. Women's health.

Lin J. Drury, Associate Professor; D.N.Sc., Rush, 1995; RN. Community health, primary care, and the underserved.

David Ekstrom, Assistant Professor; Ph.D., NYU, 1995; RN. Gender and nurse caring, nursing via the Internet, international exchanges in nursing education, baccalaureate completion for RNs.

Harriet R. Feldman, Professor and Dean; Ph.D., NYU, 1984; RN, FAAN. Pain perception and management, legislative influence of nursing leaders, smoking cessation and gender.

Louise Gallagher, Associate Professor; Ed.D., Columbia Teachers College, 1985; RN. Adverse drug reactions in the elderly, nurses' knowledge of medications, the elderly and social support.

Susan Gordon, Professor; Ed.D., Columbia Teachers College, 1972; RN. Medical-surgical nursing, psychiatric nursing, stress and aging, baccalaureate education for registered nurses.

Martha Greenberg, Associate Professor; Ph.D., NYU, 1995; RN. Humor and other integrative modalities for pain management in adults.

Karen (Toby) Haghenbeck, Assistant Professor; Ph.D., Adelphi, 2001; RN. Critical-care nurses' use of technology, technological education in critical care, critical care nursing staff development, cardiac disease/heart disease.

Donna Hallas, Associate Professor and Chairperson, Department of Undergraduate Studies; Ph.D., Adelphi, 1999; RN. Managing pediatric emergencies in the pediatric office setting, assessing critical thinking in nursing students through the use of computer-assisted instruction, attitudes and beliefs of pediatric nurse practitioners and pediatricians in collaborative practice, increasing influenza immunization rates, evidence-based research supports putting recommendations into practice.

Martha Kelly, Assistant Professor and Chairperson, Department of Undergraduate Studies; Ed.D., Florida Atlantic, 1991; RN. Nursing education and distance learning.

Sandra Lewenson, Professor and Associate Dean for Academic Affairs; Ed.D., Columbia Teachers College, 1989; RN, FAAN. Historical research, nursing's role in the women's movement, community health, accreditation, legislative influence of nursing leaders.

Margaret M. McCarthy, Clinical Instructor; M.S., Pace, 1994; RN, FNP.

Jean Mary O'Connor-Kenny, Lecturer; M.S., M.P.H., New York Medical College, 1995; RN, FNP. Health promotion, infectious disease, psychiatric nursing.

Ida Rosario-Heber, Lecturer; Ed.D. candidate, Nova Southeastern; RN.

Paula Scharf, Associate Professor; Ph.D., NYU, 1986; RN. Burnout, predictors of success for baccalaureate students.

JoAnn Sciacca, Clinical Instructor; M.A., NYU; RN.

Lillie Shortridge-Baggett, Professor and Executive Director of the Center for Nursing Research, Clinical Practice, and International Affairs; Ed.D., Columbia Teachers College, 1977; RN, FAAN. Family stress and coping, self-efficacy and health behaviors, international collaborative research.

Joanne K. Singleton, Professor; Ph.D., Adelphi, 1993; RN. Family primary care, self-care, healthy aging, smoking cessation, evidence-based practice.

Shirlee A. Stokes, Professor; Ed.D., Columbia Teachers College, 1972; RN, FAAN. Stress and aging, health promotion for the aged.

Marie Truglio-Londrigan, Associate Professor and Chairperson, Department of Graduate Studies; Ph.D., Adelphi, 1997; RN. Experience of wisdom in nursing practice, reminiscing and depression in the elderly, older adults and community support, smoking cessation and gender.

ST. JOSEPH'S COLLEGE, NEW YORK

Department of Nursing
Master of Science with a Major in Nursing

Programs of Study

St. Joseph's College (SJC) offers the Master of Science degree with a major in nursing. The program, registered with the New York State Education Department, enrolled its first class in 2005. Students pick one of two concentrations—clinical nurse specialist (CNS) studies in adult health or nursing education.

The graduate curriculum, consisting of a core and specialty concentrations, builds on the knowledge base and practice competencies of the baccalaureate-prepared nurse and prepares the graduate for advanced professional practice. Graduates of the clinical nurse specialist studies in adult health concentration (38 credits) are prepared to actualize the multifaceted role of the CNS in a variety of health-care settings, reflecting three spheres of relationships—patient and client, nurses and nursing practice, and organizations and systems. Graduates of the nursing education concentration (37 credits) are ready to assume nurse educator positions in either academic or service settings or in patient education.

The program meets the needs of the working professional. Designed for part-time study, the program can be completed in seven semesters. Each class enters as a cohort group, attending classes one day per week during the fall and spring semesters and one summer. Additional hours are required for clinical/practicum courses.

Research Facilities

The Callahan Library at the Suffolk Campus is a modern, 25,000-square-foot freestanding facility with seating for more than 300 readers. A curriculum library, seminar rooms, administrative offices, and two classrooms are housed in this building. Holdings include more than 105,000 volumes and 307 periodical titles, and they are supplemented by videos and other instructional aids. Patrons have access to the Internet and to several online academic databases. A fully automated library system, Endeavor, ensures the efficient retrieval and management of all library resources. Other resources include the library at St. Joseph's Brooklyn Campus, with more than 109,000 volumes and membership in the Long Island Library Resources Council. This facilitates cooperative associations with the academic and special libraries on Long Island. Internet access, subscriptions to several online full-text databases, and membership in the international bibliographic utility OCLC allow almost limitless access to available information.

McEntegart Hall is a fully air-conditioned five-level structure. Three spacious reading areas with a capacity for 300 readers, including individual study carrels and shelf space for 200,000 volumes, provide an excellent environment for research. In addition, McEntegart Hall houses the College archives, a curriculum library, three computer laboratories, a nursing education laboratory, and a videoconference room. There are eight classrooms, a chapel, a cafeteria, and faculty and student lounges.

A high-speed fiber-optic intracampus network connects all offices, instructional facilities, computer laboratories, and libraries on both the Brooklyn and Patchogue Campuses. The network provides Internet access to all students and faculty and staff members. An integrated online library system enables students to search for and check out books at either campus. Online databases and other electronic resources are available to students from either campus or from their home computers. Two wireless laptop classrooms with smart-classroom features provide flexible instruction spaces with the latest technologies. Videoconferencing facilities connect the two campuses, allowing for real-time distance learning in a small-group setting.

Financial Aid

Financial aid is available in the form of federal and private loans, scholarships, and work-study programs. Students should contact the Financial Aid Office for more information (Brooklyn Campus, telephone: 718-636-6808; Suffolk Campus, telephone: 631-447-3214).

Cost of Study

In 2006–07, tuition was $530 per credit. The College and technology fees per semester for 12 or more credits totaled $200, and the nursing lab fee was $100.

Living and Housing Costs

On-campus housing is not available. The St. George Hotel, New York's number one resource for student housing, and St. Joseph's College have partnered to offer off-campus housing. In 2006–07, the cost was $5450 per semester, or $10,900 for the year. Accommodations include a double room, cable TV, high-speed Internet access, a completely furnished bedroom, a full bath, a closet, a kitchen on each floor, and 24-hour security. Housing applications are available online.

Student Group

The total enrollment for all graduate programs on both campuses is 508.

Location

St. Joseph's College has two campuses—the main campus in the residential Clinton Hill section of Brooklyn and the Suffolk branch campus in Patchogue, Long Island. The main campus offers easy access to all transit lines; to the Long Island Expressway; to all bridges in Brooklyn, Manhattan, and Queens; and to the Verrazano-Narrows Bridge to Staten Island. Within 30 minutes, students leaving St. Joseph's College can find themselves at the Metropolitan Museum of Art, the 42nd Street Library, Carnegie Hall and Lincoln Center, the Broadway theater district, Madison Square Garden, or Shea Stadium. The College itself stands in the center of one of the nation's most diversified academic communities, consisting of six colleges and universities within a 2-mile radius of each other. The 27-acre Suffolk Campus, adjacent to Great Patchogue Lake, is an ideal setting for studying, socializing, and partaking in extracurricular activities. Located just off Sunrise Highway, the Suffolk Campus is easily accessible from all parts of Long Island.

The University and The Department

St. Joseph's College is a fully accredited institution that has been dedicated to providing a diverse population of students in the New York metropolitan area with an affordable education rooted in the liberal arts tradition since 1916. Independent and coeducational, the College provides a strong academic and value-oriented education at the undergraduate and graduate levels. For the fifth year in a row, the 2007 ranking of "America's Best Colleges" by *U.S. News & World Report* named St. Joseph's College to the top tier of the Northern Comprehensive Colleges–Bachelor's category.

The mission of the Department of Nursing is to provide professional nursing education that prepares the student to think critically and to utilize nursing theory, related sciences, and humanities to improve their practice; assists the student to internalize professional values and standards of practice; provides learning experiences that acknowledge the needs of a diversified student population with varied nursing practice experience; encourages students to actively participate in all aspects of their educational experiences; and facilitates student development of a spirit of inquiry and an appreciation of learning as a lifelong process.

Applying

Students must possess a B.S. degree with a major in nursing from a nationally accredited nursing program (NLNAC or CCNE). Prerequisite courses include an undergraduate health assessment course and an undergraduate statistics course. Students should have a minimum GPA of 3.0; preference is given to applicants with a GPA of 3.3 or above. One year of professional clinical practice should be completed prior to admission. Applicants must submit the completed application, the application fee, official transcripts, a current curriculum vitae, a personal statement, and two letters of recommendation. In addition, applicants must provide proof of New York State RN licensure, current professional registration, and professional malpractice insurance. An interview is required.

Correspondence and Information

Brooklyn Campus
St. Joseph's College
245 Clinton Avenue
Brooklyn, New York 11205
Phone: 718-399-0068
E-mail: msmbab@sjcny.edu
Web site: http://www.sjcny.edu/page.php/prmID/1244

Suffolk Campus
St. Joseph's College
155 West Roe Boulevard
Patchogue, New York 11772
Phone: 631-447-3250
E-mail: msmbab@sjcny.edu

St. Joseph's College, New York

THE FACULTY

Lorraine Brown, Assistant Professor; M.S.N., Boston University; RN.
Barbara Carlstrom, Assistant Professor; M.S.N., Stony Brook, SUNY; RN.
Maria Fletcher, Associate Professor; Ph.D., Adelphi; RN.
Laurel Janssen-Breen, Assistant Professor; M.A., NYU; RN.
Florence Jerdan, Associate Professor; Ph.D., Adelphi; RN.
Tae Sook Kim, Associate Professor; Ph.D., NYU; RN.
Linda Morgante, Assistant Professor; M.S.N., CUNY, Hunter; RN.
Catherine Pearsall, Assistant Professor; Ph.D., Duquesne; CNE, FNP, ANPC, RN.
Barbara Sands, Professor and Director; Ph.D., Adelphi; RN.
Boas Yu, Assistant Professor; Ed.D., Columbia Teachers College; RN.

THOMAS JEFFERSON UNIVERSITY

School of Nursing

Programs of Study

The graduate program in the Jefferson College of Health Professions School of Nursing at Thomas Jefferson University (TJU) awards the Master of Science in Nursing (M.S.N.) degree and the Doctor of Nursing Practice (D.N.P.) degree. The purpose of the graduate program is to prepare advanced practice practitioners to anticipate and respond to changing societal, health-care, and professional needs; develop practitioners who use advanced skills and knowledge in implementing their professional roles; and foster continuing development of nursing science, professional foundations, and nursing roles. The Master of Science in Nursing program prepares nurses for advanced and sophisticated clinical practice in roles such as clinical nurse specialist, case manager, nurse practitioner, and nurse administrator. The Doctor of Nursing Practice program provides academic preparation for professional nurses who will practice at the most advanced level of nursing.

The School of Nursing offers nurse practitioner, clinical nurse specialist, and post-master's certificate programs in acute care, adult health, community systems administration, nursing informatics, oncology, and pediatrics as well as family nurse practitioner, nurse anesthesia (CRNA), and neonatal nurse practitioner options. In addition, a family nurse practitioner/community systems administration integrated program is available. A 12-credit minor in nursing education is available, and a post-master's certificate in nursing education is available to students with an M.S.N. degree.

The School also offers accelerated options to the M.S.N. program for highly motivated, academically talented registered nurses and students who hold a bachelor's degree in a field other than nursing. The RN to B.S.N./M.S.N. option is designed for registered nurse students who have obtained their basic nursing education through either a diploma or associate degree program. The option enables RN students to qualify for admission to graduate nursing education through a combined B.S.N./M.S.N. program. The goal of the option is to provide a mechanism for RN students to earn both degrees in a seamless, integrated curriculum.

The curriculum is predicated on the School of Nursing's belief that professional nursing is both an art and a science and incorporates theory, research, and clinical practice. The curriculum is organized using a core curriculum concept. All students enrolled in the M.S.N. program share a core curriculum. All specialty areas require 36 credits, except for the nurse anesthesia program, which requires 74 credits (2.5 years). All students enrolled in the D.N.P. program share a core curriculum. The D.N.P. program requires 36 credits. Full-time students can complete the M.S.N. course of study in fifteen months, beginning in the summer semester. Full-time students can complete the D.N.P. course of study in twelve months, beginning in the fall semester. Part-time options, designed for the working professional nurse, enable students to take up to five years to complete the program. Courses are available via the Internet.

Research Facilities

The University shares its campus with Thomas Jefferson University Hospital (TJUH), one of the nation's premier health-care facilities. The multi-institutional Jefferson Health System (JHS) and other leading hospitals and agencies throughout the region offer outstanding learning opportunities in a broad array of health-care settings. The specialty options offered by the School of Nursing were selected to complement the areas of clinical and research excellence at TJUH and JHS, such as the Kimmel Cancer Center and the Pain Management Center. The Scott Library provides resources and facilities for study and research by students and faculty and staff members. In addition to extensive holdings of books and periodicals, direct online access to full-text periodicals is available. The computing services available to the University community are extensive. Jeffline provides access to the Internet. In addition to the computing stations located throughout Scott Library, the College of Health Professions' Learning Resource Center houses computers and computer classrooms and contains a wide variety of audiovisual materials, training models, computer software programs, simulations, and a clinical learning laboratory.

Financial Aid

Jefferson is committed to meeting the financial needs of its students. More than 82 percent of the current students receive financial assistance. Aid can include Pell Grants, National Direct Student Loans, nursing scholarships, nursing loans, state grants, work scholarships, state-guaranteed loans, and academic scholarships. Completed applications must be received by the financial aid office no later than May 1 to ensure the maximum award. The School of Nursing offers scholarships, stipends, and traineeships. Applications are available through the department.

Cost of Study

Tuition for full-time M.S.N. students for the 2007–08 academic year is $26,203. Part-time tuition is $800 per credit.

Living and Housing Costs

On-campus housing is available for rental by matriculated students and their immediate families. The Department of Housing and Residence Life administers three on-campus facilities and maintains a listing of available off-campus housing in the area.

Student Group

The School currently enrolls approximately 300 graduate students, who represent a diverse population. The majority of students are practicing professionals with a wide range of clinical backgrounds, who attend class on a part-time basis.

Location

Thomas Jefferson University is located in historic Center City Philadelphia, the fourth-largest city in the United States. It is within walking distance of theaters, museums, art galleries, and many places of historical interest. Convenient bus, rail, and subway lines offer transportation to Jefferson as well as to a variety of interesting attractions.

The University and The School

Thomas Jefferson University is a private, nonsectarian academic health center and is one of the oldest and largest academic health centers in the United States. It was founded as Jefferson Medical College in 1824. In 1969, the College of Graduate Studies and the College of Health Professions joined Jefferson Medical College to form the Thomas Jefferson University. The goals of TJU are to educate qualified students as physicians, nurses, biomedical scientists, and health professionals; to expand the understanding of human beings and their environment—especially their health and diseases—through research; and to provide and promote health services as a basis for clinical education. The University fosters a community of biologically, medically, and health-oriented scholars, teachers, and clinicians who are dedicated to these goals. Presently, the total student body exceeds 2,400 students.

Nursing education has been an integral part of TJU since its inception in 1891 as the Jefferson Medical College Hospital School of Nursing. The School of Nursing was established in 1970 in the College of Health Professions and awards the B.S.N., M.S.N., and D.N.P. degrees. Both the undergraduate and graduate programs are accredited by the Commission on Collegiate Nursing Education.

Applying

Applications to the M.S.N. program are accepted and evaluated on an ongoing basis; full-time students begin the program in the summer. Applications to the D.N.P. program are accepted annually on April 15; full-time students begin the program in the fall. Part-time students may begin in the fall, spring, or summer. Admission requirements include competitive scores on the GRE or MAT, which may be waived if undergraduate B.S.N. GPA is at least 3.2; RN licensure; undergraduate statistics, nursing research, and physical assessment; computer literacy; three letters of reference; a resume; and a personal statement addressing professional goals. Applicants to the accelerated options for the M.S.N. program and the RN to B.S.N./M.S.N. program must submit a completed application, transcripts of all college work, and a personal statement of academic and professional intent, as well as an essay, three letters of recommendation, professional license as indicated, and GRE or MAT scores as indicated.

Correspondence and Information

For an application, contact:
Donald Sharples
Office of Admissions and Enrollment Management
Edison Building Lobby
Thomas Jefferson University
130 South 9th Street
Philadelphia, Pennsylvania 19107
Phone: 215-503-1044
          877-JEFFCHP (533-3247; toll-free)
Fax: 215-503-7241
Web site: http://www.jefferson.edu/jchp

For information, contact:
Beth Ann Swan, Ph.D., CRNP, FAAN
Associate Dean, Graduate Programs
Thomas Jefferson University
130 South 9th Street, 1230A
Philadelphia, Pennsylvania 19107
Phone: 215-503-8057
Fax: 215-923-1468
E-mail: beth.swan@jefferson.edu

Thomas Jefferson University

THE FACULTY AND THEIR RESEARCH

Dr. Jennifer Bellot, Assistant Professor. Leadership change.

Dr. Cecilia Borden, Assistant Professor. Gerontology nursing.

Elizabeth Elkind, Instructor. Informatics.

Julia Feliciano, Instructor. Nurse anesthesia.

Dr. Holly Harner, Assistant Professor. Teen pregnancy, violence, women's health.

Kathleen Higgins, Instructor. Acute care.

Norma Mann, Instructor. Family health.

Dr. Mary Lou Manning, Associate Professor. Leadership, quality and safety.

Dr. Mary Powell, Assistant Professor. Adult health, health literacy.

Candace Pratt, Instructor. Nurse anesthesia.

Dr. Molly A. Rose, Professor. Women and HIV/AIDS, AIDS and the elderly, caregivers of children with HIV/AIDS, health promotion, disease prevention, community health.

Mary G. Schaal, Professor and Dean. Curriculum design and development, distance learning, community/public health.

Dr. Beth Ann Swan, Associate Professor. Technology applications for evidence-based care, delirium.

Dr. Ksenia Zukowsky, Assistant Professor. Neonatal care.

Dr. Theresa Yeo, Assistant Professor. Oncology and acute care.

UNIVERSITY OF SAN DIEGO

Hahn School of Nursing and Health Science

Programs of Study

The School of Nursing at the University of San Diego (USD) offers the Ph.D., master's, and baccalaureate degrees to registered nurses and a Master's Entry Program in Nursing (MEPN) for those with a baccalaureate or higher degree in a field other than nursing. Programs have full accreditation from the Commission on Collegiate Nursing Education (CCNE) and the California Board of Registered Nursing. The School specializes in personalized attention and small classes, labs, and clinical practicums that are taught by doctorally prepared and/or clinically certified faculty members. Classes in the nursing programs are offered in traditional fifteen-week semesters in the spring and fall and also in concentrated intersession and summer semesters, allowing students to take courses throughout the year.

The master's degree program includes advanced practice nursing programs (nurse practitioner studies, clinical nurse specialist studies, and executive nurse leader studies, with an option for a joint M.S.N./M.B.A. program) and the clinical nursing program. The nurse practitioner studies master's and post-master's certificate programs offer family, adult, and pediatric nurse practitioner studies specialties. Gerontological, Latino health-care, and mind-body integrative health-care options are available to nurse practitioner studies students as subspecialties.

The Ph.D. program prepares beginning-level nurse scientists, nursing faculty members, and executive nurse leaders. Successful graduates think critically, conduct research to improve the health status of consumers, lead the profession and public to policies that promote health, serve as successful collaborators and principal investigators on interdisciplinary research teams, lead health-care agencies, and prepare the next generation of nurse scientists and faculty members. To achieve this, students are educated and socialized for their roles both didactically and experientially. The program of study includes a minimum of 48 units of post-master's course work and a dissertation. These 48 units comprise 9 units of core course work, 18 units of research course work, 9 units in the student's research emphasis area, and a minimum of 12 dissertation units.

The Master of Science in Nursing curriculum consists of two core courses and additional courses designed to prepare graduates for advanced practice or specialist nursing at the bedside. The specialty tracks range in length from 30 to 42 semester units. Graduates of the family, adult (including gerontological subspecialty), pediatric, and clinical nurse specialist studies programs are eligible for certification by the American Nurses Credentialing Center (ANCC). In addition, pediatric nurse practitioner studies graduates are eligible for certification by the National Certification Board of Pediatric Nurse Practitioners. Graduates of the executive nurse leader studies program are eligible for certification by the ANCC.

The Master's Entry Program in Nursing is designed for students with bachelor's or higher degrees in non-nursing disciplines who are seeking a new career in nursing and have completed prerequisite courses in the physical and behavioral sciences. Following successful completion of five consecutive semesters of course and clinical work, students are eligible to take the National Council Licensure Examination (NCLEX) for registered nurse licensure and receive the master's degree as a bedside clinical nurse. Students are eligible to continue on toward the Ph.D. or one of the advanced practice nursing programs. The Accelerated RN to Master of Science in Nursing program leads to both the B.S.N. and M.S.N. degrees and eligibility for certification as a public health nurse in the state of California. Students take graduate courses in nursing research, health-care issues and policy, and health-care systems analysis as part of the B.S.N. degree requirements. The master's degree portion of the program offers students any of the track and specialization options available in the M.S.N. program.

Research Facilities

The University provides students access to state-of-the-art computer laboratories and the Helen K. and James C. Copley Library, which houses 500,000 volumes, 351,000 titles, and 2,200 print periodical subscriptions and provides access to about 18,000 current periodicals in electronic form, including a well-serviced health sciences collection. Students and faculty members have access to the School of Law Legal Research Center as well as additional resources in area medical and health sciences libraries. The San Diego Library Circuit, a collaborative effort among San Diego State University; the University of California, San Diego; California State University, San Marcos; and the University of San Diego, allows access to an additional 2 million titles.

The Hahn School of Nursing and Health Science occupies a well-appointed, recently renovated two-story building with 18,000 square feet of space and the newly renovated and equipped 3,000-square-foot Barcelona Advanced Nursing Skills Laboratory. The main building houses administrative office suites, office space for 62 faculty members and administrative personnel, a large auditorium-style classroom, two midsized classrooms, four seminar rooms, a primary computer lab, conference rooms, and a library with videoconferencing capabilities. Each classroom is a smart classroom. Other equipment includes interactive conferencing, software (Access, Excel, PowerPoint, Word, Netscape, Office 97, SPSS, N-Query, QSD, NUD*IST, NVIVO, SPSS, ADAM, Atlas of Clinical Anatomy, 64 Diagnostic Reasoning Cases, Doctor's Dilemma, Human Physiology, Interactive Electrocardiography, Immunology, and FLIPS), Scantron with a Scanbook computer, copiers, color printers, fax machines, and a Wi-Fi system for the building.

The Barcelona Nursing Skills Laboratory contains a hospital area with six fully equipped patient units; four fully equipped exam rooms, including a pediatric examination room; a fifteen-station computer laboratory; and three faculty offices. A ceiling-mounted data projector and screen also enable this laboratory to be used for computer training sessions.

Financial Aid

Many financial resources, including merit scholarships, traineeships, federal and state forgivable loans, and other types of loans, are available to help students.

Cost of Study

Tuition costs for the 2006–07 academic year were $1050 per unit for the M.S.N. and $1065 per unit for the doctoral program. Other educational expenses, including books, immunizations, instruments, insurance, travel to clinical sites, and student fees, total approximately $5000.

Living and Housing Costs

Since most students are registered nurses, they seldom live in campus housing. However, living expenses, including room and board, transportation, and personal expenses, are estimated at approximately $12,000.

Student Group

During the last three decades, the University's enrollment has tripled to 7,500 students. Current enrollment in the School consists of 250 registered nurse (B.S.N./M.S.N.), MEPN, advanced practice master's, and Ph.D. students.

Location

San Diego offers a wide variety of clinical and biomedical resources and recreational, business, science, art, and cultural activities. With an average temperature of 64°F in February and 76°F in August, the area is perfect for biking, jogging, tennis, softball, and all aquatic sports. San Diego is also noted for a world-famous zoo, museums, Spanish missions, Sea World, and major sports programs. USD and its beautiful 182-acre campus reflecting Spanish Renaissance architecture, which has attained landmark status, rests on a prominent hilltop in proximity to the scientific, health-care, and business resources of California's birthplace and second-largest city. The campus has commanding views of the Pacific Ocean, Mission Bay, San Diego Bay, and the surrounding mountains.

The University and The School

Chartered in 1949, the University of San Diego is an independent, private Catholic institution of higher education that is known for its commitment to teaching, research, the formation of values, and community involvement. As an independent Catholic school, USD is a nonprofit corporation governed by a Board of Trustees. *U.S. News & World Report* ranks USD in the top 100 universities in the United States. The University has active chapters of Phi Beta Kappa and Mortar Board and has obtained Carnegie Research II status. USD comprises a community of scholars who are committed to teaching and research, both in and out of the classroom. Of the full-time faculty members, 97 percent hold the Ph.D. or other terminal degree. Professors, rather than teaching assistants, teach all classes and supervise laboratories.

Since its inception in 1974, the Hahn School of Nursing and Health Science has provided high-quality education to more than 1,400 alumni and 150 doctorally prepared nurse scientists. The School has consistently placed in the top tier of graduate nursing programs nationally. The School seeks to deepen its commitment to social justice and health care as a human right by influencing health policy and promoting an ethical approach to nursing, characterized by compassion and respect for the dignity of the individual.

In addition, the School provides volunteer international clinical, research, and cultural immersion experiences in Mexico, the Dominican Republic, Northern Ireland, and England and African and Pacific Rim countries. Students who elect to participate in these opportunities are accompanied by faculty members who are experts in international health.

The School is affiliated with a wide variety of clinical resources, including UCSD Medical Center, Sharp Health Care (hospitals and clinics), Scripps Health (hospitals and clinics), Children's Hospital, Veterans Administration Hospital, Kaiser Permanente, and Balboa Naval Hospital.

Applying

Applicants to all nursing degree programs, except the Master's Entry Program, must have California RN licensure and professional liability and malpractice insurance. The Accelerated RN to M.S.N. and MEPN programs require completion of all nursing program prerequisites prior to admission and a GPA of at least 3.0 on a 4.0 scale. The master's and post-master's programs further require a bachelor's or a master's degree in nursing, respectively, from an approved, accredited institution; a minimum GPA of 3.0 on a 4.0 scale; letters of reference; and a 3-unit course in statistics. GRE scores are encouraged. Additional requirements for the Ph.D. program include a minimum GPA of 3.5 on a 4.0 scale, GRE scores (taken in the past five years), two letters of reference from doctorally prepared faculty members, and a sample of scholarly writing. Applicants with non-nursing baccalaureate or master's degrees may be considered for admission to the M.S.N. and Ph.D. programs, respectively. All applicants must show proof of required immunizations and screening tests, including a recent physical examination. Students should contact the appropriate office at the University for complete information about admission requirements and application deadlines.

Correspondence and Information

Office of Graduate Admissions
University of San Diego
5998 Alcala Park
San Diego, California 92110-2492
Phone: 619-260-4524
Fax: 619-260-4158
Web site: http://www.sandiego.edu/academics/nursing

University of San Diego

THE FACULTY

Cheryl K. Ahern-Lehmann, Clinical Associate Professor; Ph.D., RN-C, ANP.
Susan Bonnell, Clinical Instructor; M.S.N., RN, CPNP.
Mary Jo Clark, Professor; Ph.D., RN.
Cynthia D. Connelly, Professor; Ph.D., RN, FAAN.
Connie Curran, Clinical Instructor; M.S.N., RN, CNS.
Carol Enright, Adjunct Clinical Instructor; M.S.N., RN.
Anastasia Fisher, Associate Professor; D.N.Sc., RN.
Nancy Gaffrey, Clinical Placement Coordinator; M.S.N., RN, CNS.
Michael Gates, Assistant Professor; Ph.D., RN.
Jane Georges, Associate Professor; Ph.D., RN.
Dale Glazer, Adjunct Assistant Professor; Ph.D.
Sally Brosz Hardin, Professor and Dean; Ph.D., RN, FAAN.
Diane Hatton, Professor; D.N.Sc., CS.
Anita Hunter, Associate Professor and Director, Master's Entry Program in Nursing and RN-to-B.S.N. Programs; Ph.D., RN, CPNP.
Susan Instone, Associate Professor and Director, Advanced Practice Nursing Programs; D.N.Sc., RN, CPNP.
Kathy Shadle James, Associate Professor; D.N.Sc., RN, CNP.
Sheryl E. Leary, Clinical Instructor; M.S.N., RN.
Sharon Ann McGuire, Assistant Professor; Ph.D., RN, CNP.
Mary-Rose Mueller, Associate Professor; Ph.D., RN.
Patricia Quinn, Clinical Associate Professor; Ph.D. candidate, ANP.
Linda A. Robinson, Associate Professor; Ph.D., RN, CS.
Patricia Roth, Professor and Director, Ph.D. Program; Ed.D., RN.
Nancy Jex Sabin, Clinical Instructor; M.S., RN, FNP.
Linda D. Urden, Clinical Professor; D.N.Sc., CNA-BC; FAAN.

UNIVERSITY OF SOUTH FLORIDA

College of Nursing

Programs of Study

The University of South Florida (USF) College of Nursing is committed to providing excellent nursing education and advancing the nursing profession through research, practice, and community service. The College is accredited by the National League for Nursing Accrediting Commission (NLNAC) and the Commission on Collegiate Nursing Education (CCNE). The College of Nursing offers the Master of Science (M.S.) degree with a major in nursing, a post-master's certificate program, a Doctor of Philosophy (Ph.D.) in nursing, a Doctor of Nursing Practice (D.N.P.), and a B.S. to Ph.D. in nursing program. The master's program emphasizes the preparation of expert clinicians who are able to manage complex nursing situations. Advanced practice specialty programs are acute care; clinical nurse leader; gerontology; geropsychiatry; nurse anesthesia; oncology; primary care of the adult, child, and family; and psychiatric nursing. An occupational health nursing dual-degree program with the College of Public Health (M.S./M.P.H.) is also offered. The College also offers a Graduate Certificate in hospice and palliative care, nurse practitioner, nursing education, and nursing informatics.

Research Facilities

The College has access to a variety of excellent clinical teaching, research, and administration experiences for student learning, including the University Medical Clinics, H. Lee Moffitt Cancer Center, Shriner's Hospital for Children, Florida Mental Health Institute, James A. Haley Veterans Administrative Hospital, Tampa General Hospital, University Community Hospital, All Children's Hospital, and the Bay Care Network. In addition, the College of Nursing has affiliations with more than 120 health-care facilities that participate in the educational experiences of the master's students.

Financial Aid

Financial aid at USF is awarded on the basis of financial need and/or merit. State, federal, institutional, and other funds are available. Full-time and part-time students are eligible to apply for assistance. In addition, the federal Advanced Education Nursing Traineeships, the Nurse Faculty Loan, and the Scholarships for Disadvantaged Students programs and a substantial number of College-based scholarships are available to qualified applicants. In 2005–06, the College awarded more than $600,000 in financial aid and scholarships.

Cost of Study

Tuition fees for the 2006–07 year were $251.98 per credit hour for in-state students and $897.05 per credit hour for out-of-state students. Fees vary slightly at regional campuses. Master's degree programs range from 44 to 50 credit hours.

Living and Housing Costs

Students at the University of South Florida have numerous choices for living on campus. New graduate dorm apartments opened in fall 2002. Double rooms range from $1652 to $2736 per semester. Campus housing information can be viewed on the University Web site at http://www.housing.usf.edu/. In addition, the surrounding community offers many choices for economical apartment living.

Student Group

African-American, Asian, Hispanic, and Native American students make up 26 percent of the College of Nursing's population. Students are active in their professional organizations as officers in the Florida Nursing Association and have been recognized through national and state awards for their contributions. Currently, the total student enrollment is 821, which includes 352 master's students and 40 doctoral students.

Student Outcomes

Nurses are in high demand in the Tampa Bay area and surrounding counties. Students at the USF College of Nursing assume a wide variety of professional positions that include clinical practice, education, research, and hospital administration.

Location

Tampa is located on the Gulf Coast of central Florida, one of the most rapidly growing areas in the country. Metropolitan Tampa is home to approximately 1.5 million people, or 16 percent of Florida's population. Many cultural and entertainment activities are available, including performances by the Gulf Coast Symphony, art exhibits, and professional football, hockey, and baseball. The climate is conducive to many forms of outdoor recreational activities. Well-known attractions, such as Busch Gardens, Walt Disney World, Epcot Center, and Universal Studios, are within easy reach of the University.

The University

Established in 1956, the University of South Florida, a Research I university, is the thirteenth-largest university in the nation, with more than 39,170 students at four campuses (Tampa, St. Petersburg, Sarasota, and Lakeland). The University is the home of the largest distance learning program in Florida and houses a virtual library that brings educational resources to students in their homes.

Applying

Application to the College of Nursing may be submitted online at http://hsccf.hsc.usf.edu/con_online_app/index.cfm. All documentation materials should be sent together in a packet to the College of Nursing Office of Student Affairs. Admissions criteria vary from program to program but may include a personal goal statement, a resume, three letters of reference, transcripts from previous institutions, an individual interview, and GRE General Test scores. Applicants whose native language is not English are required to submit TOEFL scores.

Correspondence and Information

Office of Student Affairs
College of Nursing
University of South Florida
12901 Bruce B. Downs Boulevard, MDC Box 22
Tampa, Florida 33612
Phone: 813-974-9305
      888-974-9488 (toll-free)
Web site: http://www.hsc.usf.edu/nursing/

University of South Florida

THE FACULTY AND THEIR RESEARCH

USF's College of Nursing enjoys its highly regarded reputation in undergraduate and graduate nursing education in part because of the faculty's commitment to outstanding teaching, scholarly research, and service to the profession and community. This distinctive group of highly motivated members is leading USF in its mission to become the premier institution for those striving to achieve leadership in nursing.

Pat Albright, M.P.H.; RN. Public health.

Barbara Battin, B.S.N., M.P.H. Maternal-child health, public health.

Theresa M. Beckie, Ph.D.; RN. Quality of life and cardiovascular disease, critical-thinking implementation and evaluation, measurement and LISREL modeling, end-of-life issues.

Jason W. Beckstead, Ph.D. Health services delivery and patient perception, social network analysis of health-care systems, functionally impaired health-care professionals.

Adrienne Berarducci, Ph.D.; ARNP, CS. Health promotion, women's health, osteoporosis.

Dorit Breiter, M.S.N.; ARNP. Psychiatry.

Candace M. Burns, Ph.D.; RN. Health promotion/modification of risk factors, impaired professionals (nurses), occupational stress and strain.

Patricia A. Burns, Ph.D.; RN, FAAN. Female urinary incontinence.

Cas Cahill, M.S. Pain management.

Deborah J. Cantero, M.S.; ARNP. Hypertension and wellness health-care practices in the elderly.

Teresa Dowdell, R.Ph. Pharmacology

Janet Dubois, M.S.; ARNP. Primary care women/child.

Allison Edmonds, M.S.; ARNP. Adult health.

Sharon Edwards, Ph.D.; RN. Adult health, pulmonary critical care.

Mary E. Evans, Ph.D.; RN, FAAN. Implementation of systems of care legislation.

Laura Gonzalez, M.S.; RN, ARNP. Adult health, occupational/emergency.

Lois O. Gonzalez, Ph.D.; ARNP. Interpersonal factors and depression at end of life, alternative therapies.

S. Joan Gregory, Ph.D.; ARNP. Quality-of-life issues and learning-style profiles (Native Americans).

Clyde Gwinn, M.D. Pathophysiology, infectious disease.

Tomka Harris, M.S.N.; ARNP.

Katie Jerla, M.S.N.; ARNP. Adolescents/women's health.

Cecilia Jevitt, Ph.D.; RN, CNM, ARNP. Prenatal care, obesity prevention, oral health in pregnancy.

Afriyie Johnson, M.S.; RN, FCNS, CFNP. Differences in reported symptoms and/or risk factors and clinical breast exam findings in low-income white and black women.

Lilyan Kay, B.S.N., M.S., M.P.H.; FNP, CNM. Midwifery, women's health, jail health.

Nagi Kumar, Ph.D.; RN. Nutrition.

Cecile A. Lengacher, Ph.D.; RN. Women's health, psychoneuroimmunology and breast cancer, role strain, health promotion, cancer and complementary therapies, organizational redesign, measurement (instrument development and testing).

Susan C. McMillan, Ph.D.; RN, FAAN. Symptom management in persons with cancer, quality of life at end of life, cancer prevention and early detection, program evaluation, instrument development and testing.

Linda E. Moody, Ph.D.; RN, FAAN. End-of-life issues (symptom management and quality of life), aging and chronic illness (COPD), measurement (instrument development and testing) and meta-analysis.

Audrey Nelson, Ph.D., M.S.N. Patient safety, safe patient handling, movement.

Janine Overcash, Ph.D.; ARNP. Geriatrics/oncology.

Barbara A. Redding, Ed.D.; RN. Perinatal substance abuse education.

Elaine Slocumb, Ph.D.; RN. Information systems management, strengthening hospital nursing.

Mary S. Webb, Ph.D.; RN. Hypertension in African American women, dyspnea in end-stage pulmonary patients.

VIRGINIA COMMONWEALTH UNIVERSITY

Department of Nurse Anesthesia

Programs of Study

First organized in 1969, the Department of Nurse Anesthesia has a long and proud heritage of educating high-quality professional nurse anesthetists. In fact, the Department was first in the nation to offer a master's degree in nurse anesthesia over 23 years ago. Nine academic nurse anesthesia faculty members work in concert with more than 50 adjunct faculty members, 2 staff members, and fifteen clinical affiliated training sites to offer exceptional training to graduate students. The Department offers a Master of Science in Nurse Anesthesia (M.S.N.A.), a post-master's Doctor of Nurse Anesthesia Practice (D.N.A.P.), and a combined degree program (M.S.N.A.-D.N.A.P.). The Department's programs are offered on the Medical College of Virginia Campus in Richmond and at the Southwest Virginia Higher Education Center in Abingdon, Virginia, using state-of-the-art telecommunications technology.

The M.S.N.A. is a 72-credit, seven-semester program that prepares the registered nurse with a baccalaureate degree for entry into practice as a nurse anesthetist. Graduates are eligible to take the national certification examination given by the Council on Certification of Nurse Anesthetists. The M.S.N.A. is a full-time program.

The D.N.A.P. is a clinical doctorate for certified registered nurse anesthetists with a previous master's degree who wish to expand their knowledge in the areas of patient safety, evidence-based practice, education, and leadership. The program is designed to prepare CRNAs to assume leadership roles in education, management, and patient care. The program is 33 credits and can be completed in three semesters of full-time study or longer on a part-time basis.

The combined degree M.S.N.A.-D.N.A.P. is an optional program for students enrolled in the entry-level master's program. The combined-degree option is 96 credits and includes 9 credit hours of shared course work between the two programs. The M.S.N.A.-D.N.A.P. can be completed in eight semesters of full-time study.

Students can earn a Ph.D. in health-related sciences with a concentration in nurse anesthesia through the School of Allied Health Professions. Structured as a four-year course of study, the program is intended to meet the critical national need for allied health professionals who are prepared at the doctoral level in the areas of teaching, research, and administration. The program curriculum consists of a total of 51 credit hours (18 credits of common interdisciplinary core courses, 12 credits of research methods core courses, 9 hours of specialty track courses, and 12 hours of dissertation research).

Research Facilities

The Center for Research in Human Simulation is dedicated to integrating simulation into the graduate curriculum to advance the art and science of anesthesiology and to improve patient safety. The center was established in 1998 and supports research in the areas of human simulation, education, human error, and patient safety. The facility occupies more than 1,500 square feet and features two full-body Laerdal patient simulators (SimMan and SimBaby), which can be used in operating-room, critical-care, or emergency medical settings. The recent addition of the Medical Education Technologies Inc. (METI) Pedia-Sim ECS patient simulator provides the unique opportunity for clinical interventions and medication administration relevant to pediatric anesthesia practice. The Pedia-Sim ECS generates realistic and automatic responses to learner interventions. State-of-the-art audiovisual equipment enables instructors to record training activities and provide detailed and subsequent debriefings for simulation participants. The center houses an adjoining classroom and on-site conference room with closed-circuit television and a projection screen that offers live viewing from the simulation lab. An intercom system enables observing participants to communicate directly with the simulation lab, allowing for immediate interaction during live sessions. A study area is located within the facility for participants to work on computer-based educational programs. The Center for Research in Human Simulation provides realistic, procedure-based training of fiber-optic intubation and bronchoscopy cognitive and dexterity skills via the Immersion Medical Pre-Op Endoscopy Simulator.

Financial Aid

Students may apply for need-based assistance with the University's Financial Aid Office. Current information on financial aid programs, policies, and procedures is available at http://www.vcu.edu/enroll/finaid.

Cost of Study

In 2007–08, Virginia residents enrolled full-time (9–15 credits) in the M.S.N.A. and D.N.A.P. programs pay tuition and fees of $4452 per semester; nonresidents, $8876 per semester. For part-time study, Virginia residents pay tuition and fees of $465 per hour; nonresidents, $954 per hour. All students enrolled in the D.N.A.P. program pay an additional $200 per credit hour doctoral program fee. Additional fees may apply as tuition, fees, and other expenses vary in the medicine, pharmacy, nurse anesthesia, dentistry, and School of Allied Health programs.

Living and Housing Costs

Graduate student housing is available on both the MCV campus and the academic campus of Virginia Commonwealth University. Many graduate students live in off-campus housing, which is reasonably priced and readily available in a variety of styles and settings in nearby residential areas or within easy commuting distance. On- and off-campus housing information is available on the Web at http://www.housing.vcu.edu/.

Student Group

VCU enrolls 30,452 students, 7,611 of whom are graduate students. More than 200 clubs and organizations reflect the diverse social, recreational, educational, political, and religious interests of the student body.

Location

Richmond is Virginia's capital and a major East Coast financial and manufacturing center that offers students a wide range of cultural, educational, and recreational activities. Richmond is located in central Virginia at the intersection of Interstates 95 and 64, 2 hours south of Washington, D.C., and nestled between the Blue Ridge Mountains and the Atlantic coast. The Richmond region is easily accessible by plane, car, and train. With nearly 1 million residents, the historic city of Richmond combines big-city offerings with small-town hospitality. Applicants are encouraged to explore http://www.visit.richmond.com/ for more information on the city.

The University

VCU is a state-supported coeducational university with a graduate school, a major teaching hospital, and twelve academic and professional units that offer fifty-two undergraduate, twenty-two postbaccalaureate certificate, sixty-five master's, six post-master's certificate, and twenty-nine Ph.D. programs. VCU also offers M.D., D.D.S., D.P.T., and Pharm.D. programs as well as cooperative degree programs with other major Virginia colleges and universities. VCU has one of the largest evening colleges in the United States. The academic campus is located in Richmond's historic Fan District. The health sciences campus and hospital are located 2 miles east in the downtown business district. A University bus service provides free intercampus transportation for faculty members and students.

With more than $211 million in annual research funding, Virginia Commonwealth University is classified as one of the nation's top research universities by the Carnegie Foundation for the Advancement of Teaching. More than 29,000 undergraduate, certificate, graduate, post-master's, professional, and doctoral students are enrolled in 162 academic programs, forty of which are unique in the commonwealth of Virginia. The faculty members represent the finest American and international graduate institutions and enhance the University's position among the important institutions of higher learning in the United States and the world via their work in the classroom, laboratory, studio, and clinic and in their scholarly publications.

Applying

Admission procedures and program requirements are detailed in the *Graduate Bulletin*. Application deadlines and materials, including the application and the *Graduate Bulletin*, are available online at the Graduate School Web site at http://www.graduate.vcu.edu. Virginia Commonwealth University is an equal opportunity/affirmative action institution providing access to education and employment without regard to age, race, color, national origin, gender, religion, sexual orientation, veteran's status, political affiliation, or disability.

Correspondence and Information

Michael D. Fallacaro, D.N.S., CRNA, Chair
Department of Nurse Anesthesia
School of Allied Health Professions
Virginia Commonwealth University
P.O. Box 980226
Richmond, Virginia 23298-0226
Phone: 804-828-9808
Fax: 804-828-0581
E-mail: nuapply@mail2.vcu.edu
Web site: http://www.sahp.vcu.edu/nrsa/index.htm

Virginia Commonwealth University

THE FACULTY AND THEIR RESEARCH

Chuck Biddle, Professor and Director of Research; Ph.D., Missouri; CRNA. Patient safety.

Thomas Corey Davis, Assistant Professor and Director of Clinical Education; M.S.N.A., Virginia Commonwealth; CRNA. Education and training of health-care professionals, especially through advanced human simulation.

Cecil Drain, Dean of the School of Allied Health Professions; Ph.D., Texas A&M; CRNA, FAAN. Post-anesthesia nursing.

Michael D. Fallacaro, Professor and Chair; D.N.S., SUNY at Buffalo; CRNA. Anesthesia delivery in medically underserved and nurse-shortage areas across the United States.

Beverly George-Gay, Assistant Professor and Coordinator of Distance Education; M.S.N., Florida; CCRN. Cardiovascular nursing, human simulation, quality outcomes with distance education.

William Hartland, Associate Professor and Director of Education; Ph.D., Virginia Commonwealth; CRNA. Classroom/clinical teaching effectiveness with the use of "Trigger Films" and patient safety.

Donna Johnson, Assistant Professor and Assistant Director of Education; M.S.N.A., Virginia Commonwealth; CRNA. Patient safety, regional anesthesia, malignant hyperthermia, pediatrics.

Elizabeth Monti-Seibert, Director of Doctoral Education; Ph.D., South Carolina; CRNA. Patient safety, safety culture, rural nurse anesthesia practice.

Suzanne Wright, Assistant Professor and Director of the Center for Research in Human Simulation; M.S.N.A., Virginia Commonwealth; CRNA. Simulation in education, clinical decision-making, patient safety.

VIRGINIA COMMONWEALTH UNIVERSITY

School of Nursing

Programs of Study

The School of Nursing at Virginia Commonwealth University (VCU) offers a program of study in advanced practice nursing—that is, the specialized and expanded practice of nursing—that leads to a Master of Science degree. Individuals can choose from several tracks, including the traditional M.S., the M.S. for registered nurses who do not have a B.S.N., the RN-M.S., and the accelerated master's program. Along with a general core, students take courses in a specialty concentration, such as adult health–acute care nursing (CNS or ACNP), adult health–primary care nursing (ANP), child health nursing (PNP preparation), community health nursing (for individuals with a M.P.H.), community health nursing and public health (dual-degree program), family health nursing (FNP preparation), integrative psychiatric–mental health nursing (CNS and/or PANP), nursing administration and leadership, or women's health nursing (WHNP preparation).

For those seeking additional certification or specialization in nursing, the School also offers a post-master's certificate in several concentration areas—adult health–acute care nurse practitioner, adult health–primary care nurse practitioner, child health nurse practitioner, family nurse practitioner, integrative psychiatric–mental health (for ANCC-certified PMH CNS or for the non-PMH M.S. applicant), nursing administration and leadership, nursing in faith communities, and women's health nurse practitioner.

In addition, a Ph.D. in nursing is offered. The purpose of the doctoral program is to prepare scholars and researchers in nursing to engage in knowledge development and transmission in areas critical to the advancement of clinical nursing practice. The program prepares nursing scholars for a lifetime of intellectual inquiry and cutting-edge research as well as for academic or research positions. Students may enroll in the post-B.S. to Ph.D. track or the traditional Ph.D. track. The doctoral program consists of three focus areas of inquiry—healing, risk and resilience, and biobehavioral clinical.

Research Facilities

The VCU School of Nursing has a Clinical Learning Center (CLC) that transforms the clinical education of its students. This specialized, state-of-the-art facility provides an interactive environment that simulates a variety of clinical settings. Clinical simulations are based on clinical situations with identified learning objectives. They provide students structured experimental learning opportunities, especially for patient conditions that occur infrequently in actual supervised clinical situations. Simulation allows for practicing clinical skills, decision making, developing clinical judgment, and priority setting. There are twenty-six patient areas in the CLC, with new physical exam tables and new hospital beds. Specialty equipment areas include an area for pulmonary and respiratory care, intravenous insertion arms for IV starts and blood drawing, and two Virtual IV tm computer stations. There is also a 40-student audiovisual classroom.

Computerized lifelike Human Patient Simulators (HPS) are sometimes referred to as high-fidelity simulators. These manikins simulate patient responses such as heart sounds, lung sounds, and verbal responses. Some HPS manikins breathe, have audible heart sounds, and can be programmed to have specific responses after desired interactions are implemented. Not all scenarios are high tech. Some scenarios deal with sample patient-nurse communication or high-risk or difficult communication situations. The CLC is able to simulate an actual inpatient hospital setting. Using actual patient (without identifying data) situations, multidisciplinary teams can interact by making patient rounds, practice patient-to-health-care-provider communication, and develop priorities in care. Students or manikins can be "patients" in these situations.

Financial Aid

For Ph.D. students, faculty support for predoctoral fellowship grant submissions, research and teaching assistantships for two years of study, scholarships, and internal dissertation support are available. All students may apply for need-based assistance with the University's Financial Aid Office. Current information on financial aid programs, policies, and procedures is available at http://www.vcu.edu/enroll/finaid.

Cost of Study

For full-time study (9–15 credits) in 2007–08, Virginia residents pay tuition and fees of $4452 per semester; nonresidents, $8876 per semester. For part-time study, Virginia residents pay tuition and fees of $465 per hour; nonresidents, $954 per hour. Some programs require additional fees. On the Medical College of Virginia (MCV) campus, tuition, fees, and other expenses vary in the medicine, pharmacy, nursing, nurse anesthesia, dentistry, and School of Allied Health programs.

Living and Housing Costs

Graduate student housing is available on both the MCV campus and the academic campus of Virginia Commonwealth University. Many graduate students live in off-campus housing, which is reasonably priced and readily available in a variety of styles and settings in nearby residential areas or within easy commuting distance. On- and off-campus housing information is available on the Web at http://www.housing.vcu.edu/.

Student Group

VCU enrolls 30,452 students, 7,611 of whom are graduate students. More than 200 clubs and organizations reflect the diverse social, recreational, educational, political, and religious interests of the student body.

Location

Richmond is Virginia's capital and a major East Coast financial and manufacturing center that offers students a wide range of cultural, educational, and recreational activities. Richmond is located in central Virginia at the intersection of Interstates 95 and 64, 2 hours south of Washington, D.C., and nestled between the Blue Ridge Mountains and the Atlantic coast. The Richmond region is easily accessible by plane, car, and train. With nearly 1 million residents, the historic city of Richmond combines big-city offerings with small-town hospitality. Applicants are encouraged to explore http://www.visit.richmond.com/ for more information on the city.

The University

VCU is a state-supported coeducational university with a graduate school, a major teaching hospital, and twelve academic and professional units that offer fifty-two undergraduate, twenty-two postbaccalaureate certificate, sixty-five master's, six post-master's certificate, and twenty-nine Ph.D. programs. VCU also offers M.D., D.D.S., D.P.T., and Pharm.D. programs as well as cooperative degree programs with other major Virginia colleges and universities. VCU has one of the largest evening colleges in the United States. The academic campus is located in Richmond's historic Fan District. The health sciences campus and hospital are located 2 miles east in the downtown business district. A University bus service provides free intercampus transportation for faculty members and students. With more than $211 million in annual research funding, Virginia Commonwealth University is classified as one of the nation's top research universities by the Carnegie Foundation for the Advancement of Teaching. More than 29,000 undergraduate, certificate, graduate, post-master's, professional, and doctoral students are enrolled in 162 academic programs, forty of which are unique in the commonwealth of Virginia. The faculty members represent the finest American and international graduate institutions and enhance the University's position among the important institutions of higher learning in the United States and the world via their work in the classroom, laboratory, studio, and clinic and in their scholarly publications.

Applying

Admission procedures and program requirements are detailed in the *Graduate Bulletin*. Application deadlines and materials, including the application and the *Graduate Bulletin,* are available online at the Graduate School Web site at http://www.graduate.vcu.edu. Virginia Commonwealth University is an equal opportunity/affirmative action institution providing access to education and employment without regard to age, race, color, national origin, gender, religion, sexual orientation, veteran's status, political affiliation, or disability.

Correspondence and Information

Susan L. Lipp, Director
Office of Enrollment and Student Services
School of Nursing
Virginia Commonwealth University
1100 East Leigh Street
P.O. Box 980567
Richmond, Virginia 23219

Phone: 804-828-5171
Fax: 804-828-1839
E-mail: slipp@vcu.edu
Web site: http://www.nursing.vcu.edu

Virginia Commonwealth University

THE FACULTY AND THEIR RESEARCH

DEPARTMENT OF ADULT HEALTH

Sadeeka Al-Majid, Assistant Professor; Ph.D., Wisconsin–Madison; RN. Biobehavioral clinical, immunocompetence.

Anne Boyle, Clinical Assistant Professor; Ph.D., Virginia; RN. Respiratory nursing.

Elizabeth Crooks, Clinical Assistant Professor; M.S.N., Case Western Reserve; RN. Multidisciplinary management of the patient with dementia, Alzheimer's disease management.

Mary Grap, Professor; Ph.D., Georgia State; RN, FAAN, ACNP. Biobehavioral clinical.

Dorothy Gray, Associate Professor and Chair; Ph.D., Utah; RN. Healing, immunocompetence.

Tanya Huff, Clinical Assistant Professor; M.S.N., Virginia; RN, CCRN. Trauma.

Lisa N. Lee, Instructor and Graduate Clinical Coordinator; M.S.N., George Mason; RN, ANP, ACNP, APRN, BC. Acute and primary-care nursing.

Nancy McCain, Professor; D.S.N., Alabama; RN, FAAN. PNI-based stress management in early breast cancer.

Cindy Munro, Professor; Ph.D., Virginia Commonwealth; RN, FAAN. Oral-care intervention in mechanically ventilated adults, sedation effects in mechanically ventilated patients.

Jeanne Salyer, Associate Professor; Ph.D., Virginia Commonwealth; RN. Immunocompetence, risk and resilience.

DEPARTMENT OF INTEGRATIVE SYSTEMS

Jennifer Field Brown, Assistant Professor; Ph.D., Virginia Commonwealth; APRN-PMH. Psychiatric–mental health nursing.

Carol Cutler, Clinical Assistant Professor; D.N.Sc., Catholic University; RN. Psychiatric–mental health nursing.

Anthony J. DeLellis, Associate Professor and Assistant Dean of Administration; Ed.D., Virginia.

Melissa A. Forsythe, Assistant Professor; Ph.D., Virginia Commonwealth; RN. Nursing administration and leadership.

Lauren Goodloe, Clinical Associate Professor; Ph.D., Virginia Commonwealth; RN. Nursing administration and leadership.

Martha Moon, Associate Professor; Ph.D., California, San Francisco; RN. Community health nursing, risk and resilience.

C. Fay Parpart, Assistant Professor; M.S., Virginia Commonwealth; RN, AACRN. Immune conditions.

Inez Tuck, Professor and Chair; Ph.D., North Carolina at Greensboro; RN. Psychiatric–mental health nursing.

DEPARTMENT OF MATERNAL CHILD HEALTH

Jennifer Black, Clinical Assistant Professor; M.S., Virginia Commonwealth; RN, WHNP.

Lisa Brown, Assistant Professor; Ph.D., Wisconsin–Madison; RN. Early development of the attachment system of premature infants to their mothers.

Marie Chapin, Clinical Instructor; M.S., Virginia Commonwealth; RN, CPNP. Children's health.

Ching-Yu Cheng, Assistant Professor; Ph.D., Texas at Austin; RN. Health of pregnant women and postpartum mothers, with focuses on various aspects of health and factors that influence health, particularly cultural issues, with a specialty in Asian cultures.

Martha Hart, Clinical Instructor; M.S., Virginia Commonwealth; RNC, PNP, NNP. Pediatric nursing.

Debra K. Hearington, Assistant Professor; M.S., Virginia Commonwealth; RN, PNP, CS.

Robin Hills, Clinical Assistant Professor; M.S., Virginia Commonwealth; RNC, WHNP. Women's health.

Susan L. Lindner, Clinical Instructor; M.S.N., Old Dominion; RNC. Women's health.

Debra Lyon, Associate Professor; Ph.D., Virginia Commonwealth; RN. Nursing theory and research; family, children's, and women's health.

Jacqueline M. McGrath, Associate Professor; Ph.D., Pennsylvania; RN, NNP, FNAP. Integration of developmental interventions with infants and families.

Rita Pickler, Professor and Chair; Ph.D., Virginia; RN, PNP. Feeding readiness in preterm infants.

Sandra Voll, Director of Clinical Learning Center; M.S.N., Virginia Commonwealth; RN, CNM, WHNP, FNP.

Janet Younger, Associate Professor and Associate Dean; Ph.D., Virginia; RN, CPNP.

WESTERN CONNECTICUT STATE UNIVERSITY

Program in Nursing

WESTERN CONNECTICUT STATE UNIVERSITY

Program of Study

The Master of Science (M.S.) in Nursing program at Western Connecticut State University (WCSU) prepares nurses for leadership positions in nursing practice as Advanced Practice Registered Nurses. Two tracks are offered: Adult Nurse Practitioner and Adult Clinical Nurse Specialist. The program is designed for part-time study, with courses offered in the evening. Part-time study requires approximately four years for completion of the degree, although students are granted up to six years to complete the requirements. The program is accredited by the Collegiate Commission of Nursing Education.

In order to earn the degree, students must complete 36 credits of specialized professional course work. The first 11 credits come from foundational courses, which address the theoretical bases of nursing practice as well as contemporary issues and research relevant to the nursing profession. The next 13 credits come from advanced practice courses, in which students become familiar with pathophysiology, clinical pharmacology, and management of the chronically ill—either as a direct care provider or as a mediator of services. Students can then choose between the Adult Nurse Practitioner track or the Clinical Nurse Specialist track, in which they complete another 8 credits and a clinical practicum that encompasses all aspects of their selected roles. The program is completed with a 4-credit capstone thesis or research project. Upon completion of the program, students are eligible to sit for the national certification examination for their chosen role.

The Department of Nursing also offers post-master's course work that prepares adult nurse practitioners to be eligible to take the adult nurse practitioner certificate exam. Students are required to earn at least 19 credits in health assessment and nursing management.

Research Facilities

The collections of the WCSU Libraries include more than 175,000 volumes, with approximately 6,500 volumes added annually, as well as current subscriptions to over 900 periodicals. The Haas Library also owns more than 8,700 media titles, including over 80 percent of the titles on the National Film Registry, a small but growing collection of archival materials, and a well-established curriculum collection that supports the education students. The WCSU Libraries share an online catalog with the Connecticut State Library and the three other Connecticut State University libraries, which also provides access to a variety of online databases and indexes, including EBSCO and OCLC FirstSearch.

Financial Aid

Prospective students should contact the Financial Aid Office at 203-837-5880 for information regarding financial aid opportunities.

Cost of Study

In 2006–07, full-time tuition is $1985 for residents and $5530.50 for nonresidents. All full-time students are also required to pay a general fee of $868, a University fee of $410, an information technology fee of $111.50, a SAF fee of $67.50, and a health insurance fee of $625. Part-time tuition is $346 per credit plus a $60 registration fee.

Living and Housing Costs

Students living on-campus typically pay $2797 to $3484 for a single room, $2258 to $2900 for a double room in a two-bedroom apartment, or $2500 to $2750 for a double room in a four-bedroom apartment. Meal plans range from $100 for a flexible meal plan to $1616.50 for a full meal plan. Other fees include an $80 telecommunication fee and a $17.50 social fee. Affordable off-campus housing is also available.

Student Group

The program is designed for registered nurses who are currently working in a hospital or other health-care facility.

Student Outcomes

Graduates of the program are prepared to generate research for the purpose of expanding nursing science, provide care to individuals and groups from diverse backgrounds across the health spectrum, collaborate with professionals in other disciplines to improve patient care and outcomes, and understand how policy formulation impacts nursing practice and health-care delivery.

Location

Danbury, the seventh-largest city in Connecticut, continues to revitalize itself in order to better serve residents and tourists alike. It features numerous museums, including the birthplace of classical music composer Charles Ives, as well as excellent theater, shopping, and dining. The Old Quarry Nature Center features 80 acres of nature trails, and the Still River is a perfect place to go hiking and fishing.

The University

Western Connecticut State University was founded in 1903 to meet the educational needs of a diversified student body through instruction, scholarship, and public service. By combining a strong liberal arts foundation with opportunities for experiential learning, the University equips its students with the necessary background to be successful in their chosen careers and to be productive members of society.

Applying

Applications for admission to the master's program are made through the Division of Graduate Studies. Applicants must submit official transcripts of all undergraduate and graduate work with the completed application form (available to download at http://wcsu.edu/graduate/application.asp) and the $50 graduate application fee. Admission to the program is selective. Candidates must have earned a Bachelor of Science in nursing degree from a recognized accrediting agency (or equivalent undergraduate preparation), have achieved a satisfactory score on the Miller Analogies Test (required for those applicants with an undergraduate QPA of less than 3.3), and hold a current RN license. At the time of application, candidates must provide a resume and one letter of recommendation from an employer. As part of the admission process, the applicant must meet with the M.S. program coordinator to develop a plan of study.

Correspondence and Information

For program information or to send applications:
Division of Graduate Studies
Western Connecticut State University
181 White Street
Danbury, Connecticut 06810
Phone: 203-837-8243

Graduate Program Coordinator:
Dr. Patricia Lund, RN.
Program in Nursing
Western Connecticut State University
181 White Street
Danbury, Connecticut 06810
Phone: 203-837-8567
E-mail: Lundp@wcsu.edu
Web site: http://www.wcsu.edu/nursing/

Western Connecticut State University

THE FACULTY AND THEIR RESEARCH

Joseph Oyeniyi Aina, Associate Professor; Ph.D., NYU. Mental health and homelessness.

Carol Avery, Professor; Ed.D., Columbia Teachers College. Student nurse clinical practice, graduate nurse competency.

Jeanette H. Bjurback-Lupinacci, Assistant Professor; M.S., Western Connecticut State. Rehabilitation nursing.

Daryle L. Brown, Associate Professor; Ed.D., Columbia. Mathematic competencies of beginning baccalaureate-degree nursing students, faculty-student interactions that promote diversity.

Karen Crouse, Assistant Professor; Ed.D., Hartford. Critical and emergency nursing care, professional development and vitality of nursing faculty, nursing and nursing education in China.

Karen Daley, Assistant Professor; Ph.D. candidate, Rutgers. Medical surgical nursing, decision making in asthma, assessment of outcomes in nursing programs through standardized testing.

Colleen Delaney, Associate Professor and Coordinator, RN-B.S.N. Program; M.S., Connecticut. Women and heart disease, health informatics, spirituality.

Eileen "Pat" Geraci, Associate Professor and Coordinator, B.S.N. Program; Ph.D. candidate, Connecticut; APN. Effects of computerization on nurses and nursing practice.

Laurel Halloran, Professor, Department Co-Chair, and Coordinator, M.S.N. Program; Ph.D., Connecticut; FNP. Women's presenting symptoms of myocardial infarction.

Laura Hunnibell, Assistant Professor; M.S., Southern Connecticut State; FNP. Pain and symptom management in oncology and hospice patients.

Debra Lajoie, Assistant Professor; Ph.D. candidate, Wisconsin–Milwaukee. Health-care policy and law, evidence-based practice and translating research into policy, health-care access and health-care disparities, the economics of health care.

Patricia Z. Lund, Professor and Graduate Coordinator; Ed.D., Columbia; RN. Parent-child nursing, nursing education, direct entry to specialty practice.

Patricia Moreland, Assistant Professor; D.N.Sc. candidate, Columbia. Pediatrics and emergency medicine; family-centered care in the emergency department, focusing on the needs of family members of acute and critically ill patients.

Joan Palladino, Assistant Professor; Ed.D. candidate, Hartford; CCRN. Mentoring programs for both student nurses and new graduate nurses.

Barbara Piscopo, Professor and Chairperson of Department of Nursing; Ed.D., Columbia Teachers College; RN. Training new nurse educators.

Catherine Rice, Associate Professor; Ed.D., Bridgeport. International education, ethics in education, educational law, leadership principles in higher education, advanced nursing practice.

Maryann Riley, Professor; M.A., M.Ed., Columbia. Practice of geriatrics as it relates to medical/surgical nursing.

Section 31
Public Health

This section contains a directory of institutions offering graduate work in public health, followed by in-depth entries submitted by institutions that chose to prepare detailed program descriptions. Additional information about programs listed in the directory but not augmented by an in-depth entry may be obtained by writing directly to the dean of a graduate school or chair of a department at the address given in the directory.

For programs offering related work, see also in this book Allied Health, Education, Health Services, and Nursing; in Book 2, Family and Consumer Sciences (Gerontology) and Sociology, Anthropology, and Archaeology (Demography and Population Studies); in Book 3, Biological and Biomedical Sciences; Ecology, Environmental Biology, and Evolutionary Biology; Microbiological Sciences; and Nutrition; in Book 4, Mathematical Sciences and Environmental Sciences and Management; and in Book 5, Biomedical Engineering and Biotechnology, Civil and Environmental Engineering, Industrial Engineering, Energy and Power Engineering (Nuclear Engineering), and Management of Engineering and Technology.

CONTENTS

Program Directories

Announcements

Close-Ups

See also:

Public Health—General

Adelphi University, Graduate School of Arts and Sciences, Department of Emergency Management, Garden City, NY 11530-0701. Offers Certificate. Part-time and evening/weekend programs available. *Students:* Average age 47. In 2006, 4 degrees awarded. *Application deadline:* For fall admission, 5/1 for international students; for spring admission, 12/1 for international students. Applications are processed on a rolling basis. Application fee: $50. Electronic applications accepted. *Financial support:* Research assistantships with partial tuition reimbursements, Federal Work-Study and institutionally sponsored loans available. *Faculty research:* Emergency nursing, disaster management, disaster preparedness. *Unit head:* Dr. John Vetter, Chairperson, 516-877-4110, E-mail: vetter@adelphi.edu. *Application contact:* Christine Murphy, Director of Admissions, 516-877-3050, Fax: 516-877-3039, E-mail: graduateadmissions@adelphi.edu.

American Public University System, AMU/APU Graduate Programs, Charles Town, WV 25414. Offers business administration (MBA); criminal justice (MA); emergency and disaster management (MA); environmental policy and management (MS); history (MA); homeland security (MA); humanities (MA); intelligence (MA Strategic Intelligence); international relations and conflict resolution (MA); management (MA); military history (MA); national security studies (MA); political science (MA); public administration (MA); public health (MS); security management (MA); space studies (MS); sports management (MA); transportation and logistics management (MA). Programs offered via distance learning only. Part-time and evening/weekend programs available. Postbaccalaureate distance learning degree programs offered (no on-campus study). *Faculty:* 10 full-time (3 women), 183 part-time/adjunct (57 women). *Students:* 498 full-time (104 women), 5,272 part-time (1,209 women). Average age 34. 6,574 applicants, 100% accepted, 3508 enrolled. In 2006, 358 degrees awarded. *Degree requirements:* For master's, comprehensive exam, registration. *Entrance requirements:* For master's, bachelor's degree or equivalent, minimum GPA of 2.7 in last 60 hours of course work. *Application deadline:* For fall admission, 9/1 priority date for domestic students; for winter admission, 1/1 priority date for domestic students; for spring admission, 5/1 priority date for domestic students. Applications are processed on a rolling basis. Application fee: $0. Electronic applications accepted. *Expenses:* Tuition: Full-time $4,950; part-time $275 per credit. One-time fee: $200 full-time. *Financial support:* Applicants required to submit FAFSA. *Faculty research:* Military history, criminal justice, management performance, national security. *Unit head:* Dr. Frank McCluskey, Provost, 877-468-6268, Fax: 304-724-3780. *Application contact:* Terry Grant, Director of Enrollment Management, 877-468-6268, Fax: 304-724-3780, E-mail: info@apus.edu.

American University of Beirut, Graduate Programs, Faculty of Health Sciences, Beirut, Lebanon. Offers environmental health (MSES); epidemiology (MS); population health (MS); population science (MS); public health (MPH). Part-time programs available. *Faculty:* 21 full-time (16 women), 4 part-time/adjunct (0 women). *Students:* 42 full-time (34 women), 63 part-time (54 women). Average age 27. 158 applicants, 74% accepted, 47 enrolled. In 2006, 47 degrees awarded. *Degree requirements:* For master's, one foreign language, thesis (for some programs), comprehensive exam, registration. *Entrance requirements:* For master's, letter of recommendation. Additional exam requirements/recommendations for international students: Required—TOEFL (minimum score 600 paper-based; 250 computer-based; 100 iBT), IELTS (minimum score 8). *Application deadline:* For fall admission, 4/30 for domestic and international students; for spring admission, 11/1 for domestic and international students. Application fee: $50. *Financial support:* In 2006–07, 6 students received support. Career-related internships or fieldwork, institutionally sponsored loans, scholarships/grants, health care benefits, and unspecified assistantships available. Financial award application deadline: 2/2. *Faculty research:* Urban health, challenging childbirth in the Arab region, tobacco control, HIV/AIDS surveillance, water quality and management. Total annual research expenditures: $632,411. *Unit head:* Huda Zurayk, Dean, 961-1340119 Ext. 4600, Fax: 961-1744470, E-mail: hzurayk@aub.edu.lb. *Application contact:* Dr. Salim Kanaan, Director of Admissions Office, 961-1-374374 Ext. 2592, Fax: 961-1-750775, E-mail: admissions@aub.edu.lb.

Armstrong Atlantic State University, School of Graduate Studies, Program in Health Science, Savannah, GA 31419-1997. Offers health services administration (MHSA); public health (MPH). *Accreditation:* CAHME; CEPH. Part-time and evening/weekend programs available. Postbaccalaureate distance learning degree programs offered (no on-campus study). *Faculty:* 4 full-time (0 women), 3 part-time/adjunct (0 women). *Students:* 30 full-time (22 women), 72 part-time (51 women); includes 37 minority (33 African Americans, 1 American Indian/Alaska Native, 1 Asian American or Pacific Islander, 2 Hispanic Americans), 6 international. Average age 34. In 2006, 23 degrees awarded. *Degree requirements:* For master's, internship, thesis optional. *Entrance requirements:* For master's, GMAT or GRE General Test, MAT, minimum GPA of 2.6. Additional exam requirements/recommendations for international students: Required—TOEFL (minimum score 523 paper-based; 193 computer-based). *Application deadline:* For fall admission, 7/1 priority date for domestic and international students; for spring admission, 11/15 priority date for domestic and international students. Applications are processed on a rolling basis. Application fee: $25. Electronic applications accepted. *Expenses:* Tuition, state resident: full-time $2,286; part-time $127 per credit. Tuition, nonresident: full-time $9,144; part-time $508 per credit. One-time fee: $257. *Financial support:* In 2006–07, research assistantships with partial tuition reimbursements (averaging $2,500 per year); career-related internships or fieldwork, Federal Work-Study, scholarships/grants, tuition waivers (full), and unspecified assistantships also available. Support available to part-time students. Financial award applicants required to submit FAFSA. *Faculty research:* Health administration, community health, health education. *Unit head:* Dr. James Streater, Department Head, 912-921-7346, Fax: 912-921-7350, E-mail: mssm@mail.armstrong.edu.

A.T. Still University of Health Sciences, School of Health Management, Kirksville, MO 63501. Offers geriatric healthcare (MGH); health administration (MHA); health education (DH Ed, MH Ed); public health (MPH). Part-time and evening/weekend programs available. Postbaccalaureate distance learning degree programs offered (no on-campus study). *Faculty:* 1 full-time (0 women), 45 part-time/adjunct (17 women). *Students:* 18 full-time (14 women), 194 part-time (130 women); includes 39 minority (20 African Americans, 8 American Indian/Alaska Native, 9 Asian Americans or Pacific Islanders, 2 Hispanic Americans). Average age 34. In 2006, 75 degrees awarded. *Degree requirements:* For master's, thesis (for some programs), capstone project. *Entrance requirements:* For master's, minimum GPA of 2.5, bachelor's degree or equivalent from U.S. institution. Additional exam requirements/recommendations for international students: Required—TOEFL (minimum score 500 paper-based; 222 computer-based). *Application deadline:* For fall admission, 8/27 for domestic students, 8/4 for international students; for winter admission, 10/25 for domestic students, 11/26 for international students; for spring admission, 2/10 for domestic students, 3/17 for international students. Applications are processed on a rolling basis. Electronic applications accepted. *Expenses:* Contact institution. *Financial support:* Application deadline: 5/1; *Unit head:* Dr. Jon Persavich, Dean, 660-626-2820, Fax: 660-626-2826, E-mail: jpersavich@atsu.edu. *Application contact:* Donna Sparks, Associate Director for Admissions, 660-626-2237, Fax: 660-626-2969, E-mail: admissions@atsu.edu.

Barry University, School of Graduate Medical Sciences and School of Natural and Health Sciences, Program in Public Health, Miami Shores, FL 33161-6695. Offers MPH. *Students:* 12 full-time (9 women), 19 part-time (15 women); includes 24 minority (12 African Americans, 5 Asian Americans or Pacific Islanders, 7 Hispanic Americans), 2 international. 47 applicants, 38% accepted, 15 enrolled. In 2006, 13 degrees awarded. *Entrance requirements:* For master's, GRE. *Unit head:* Dr. Richard Patton, Director, 305-899-3257, Fax: 305-899-3253, E-mail: rpatton@mail.barry.edu. *Application contact:* Marc A. Weiner, Director of Graduate and Medical Sciences Admissions and Marketing, 305-899-3130, Fax: 305-899-3253, E-mail: mweiner@mail.barry.edu.

Benedictine University, Graduate Programs, Program in Public Health, Lisle, IL 60532-0900. Offers MPH, MBA/MPH, MPH/MS. Part-time and evening/weekend programs available. *Faculty:* 2 full-time (0 women), 8 part-time/adjunct (3 women). *Students:* 98 (78 women); includes 41 minority (17 African Americans, 18 Asian Americans or Pacific Islanders, 6 Hispanic Americans) 4 international. Average age 33. 36 applicants, 86% accepted, 19 enrolled. In 2006, 42 degrees awarded. *Entrance requirements:* For master's, MAT, GRE, or GMAT. Additional exam requirements/recommendations for international students: Required—TOEFL (minimum score 550 paper-based; 213 computer-based). *Application deadline:* For fall admission, 9/1 for domestic students; for winter admission, 12/1 for domestic students; for spring admission, 2/15 for domestic students. Application fee: $40. *Expenses:* Tuition: Full-time $12,150; part-time $450 per credit hour. *Financial support:* Career-related internships or fieldwork and health care benefits available. Support available to part-time students. *Unit head:* Dr. Alan Gorr, Director, 630-829-6566, Fax: 630-960-1126, E-mail: agorr@ben.edu. *Application contact:* Kari Gibbons, Director, Admissions, 630-829-6200, Fax: 630-829-6584, E-mail: kgibbons@ben.edu.

Boise State University, Graduate College, College of Health Science, Boise, ID 83725-0399. Offers MHS. Part-time programs available. *Faculty:* 11 full-time (5 women), 41 part-time/adjunct (24 women). *Students:* 6 full-time (5 women), 60 part-time (38 women); includes 5 minority (1 African American, 1 American Indian/Alaska Native, 2 Asian Americans or Pacific Islanders, 1 Hispanic American), 1 international. Average age 38. 30 applicants, 100% accepted, 16 enrolled. In 2006, 11 degrees awarded. *Degree requirements:* For master's, thesis. *Entrance requirements:* For master's, GRE General Test, GMAT or MAT, minimum GPA of 3.0. *Application deadline:* For fall admission, 3/1 priority date for domestic students; for spring admission, 10/1 priority date for domestic students. Applications are processed on a rolling basis. Application fee: $0. Electronic applications accepted. *Financial support:* In 2006–07, 2 research assistantships with partial tuition reimbursements (averaging $4,080 per year) were awarded; career-related internships or fieldwork, Federal Work-Study, institutionally sponsored loans, and unspecified assistantships also available. Support available to part-time students. Financial award application deadline: 3/1. *Unit head:* Dr. James T. Girvan, Dean, 208-426-4116, Fax: 208-426-3469. *Application contact:* Dr. Tedd McDonald, Program Director, 208-426-2425, E-mail: tmcdonal@boisestate.edu.

Boston University, Goldman School of Dental Medicine, Graduate Programs in Dentistry, Boston, MA 02215. Offers advanced general dentistry (CAGS); dental public health (MS, MSD, D Sc D, CAGS); dentistry (DMD); endodontics (MSD, D Sc D, CAGS); implantology (CAGS); operative dentistry (MSD, D Sc D, CAGS); oral and maxillofacial surgery (MSD, D Sc D, CAGS); oral biology (MSD, D Sc, D Sc D, PhD); orthodontics (MSD, D Sc D, CAGS); pediatric dentistry (MSD, D Sc D, CAGS); periodontology (MSD, D Sc D, CAGS); prosthodontics (MSD, D Sc D, CAGS). *Students:* 152 full-time (62 women); includes 13 minority (1 African American, 11 Asian Americans or Pacific Islanders, 1 Hispanic American), 75 international. Average age 29. In 2006, 224 first professional degrees, 22 master's, 10 doctorates, 63 other advanced degrees awarded. *Degree requirements:* For master's and doctorate, thesis/dissertation; for CAGS, thesis (for some programs). *Entrance requirements:* For DMD, DAT, minimum GPA of 3.0; for CAGS, dental degree. *Application deadline:* For fall admission, 5/1 for domestic students. Applications are processed on a rolling basis. Application fee: $60. *Expenses: Contact institution. Financial support:* Career-related internships or fieldwork and institutionally sponsored loans available. Financial award application deadline: 4/15; financial award applicants required to submit CSS PROFILE or FAFSA. *Faculty research:* Defensive mechanisms, bone-cell regulation, protein biochemistry, molecular biology, biomaterials. *Application contact:* 617-638-4787, Fax: 617-638-4798.

See Close-Up on page 2179.

Boston University, School of Public Health, Boston, MA 02215. Offers M Sc, MA, MPH, D Sc, Dr PH, PhD, Certificate, JD/MPH, MBA/MPH, MD/MPH, MPH/MA, MSW/MPH. *Accreditation:* CEPH. Part-time and evening/weekend programs available. *Faculty:* 90 full-time (45 women), 223 part-time/adjunct (98 women). *Students:* 304 full-time (238 women), 404 part-time (323 women); includes 136 minority (40 African Americans, 77 Asian Americans or Pacific Islanders, 19 Hispanic Americans), 75 international. Average age 28. In 2006, 246 master's, 9 doctorates awarded. *Degree requirements:* For doctorate, one foreign language, thesis/dissertation, comprehensive written and oral exams. *Entrance requirements:* For master's, GRE General Test; for doctorate, GRE General Test, MPH or equivalent. Additional exam requirements/recommendations for international students: Required—TOEFL (550 paper-based, 213 computer-based) or IELTS. *Application deadline:* For fall admission, 2/1 for domestic students; for spring admission, 10/15 for domestic students. Applications are processed on a rolling basis. Application fee: $95. Electronic applications accepted. *Expenses: Contact institution. Financial support:* Career-related internships or fieldwork, Federal Work-Study, institutionally sponsored loans, and scholarships/grants available. Support available to part-time students. *Faculty research:* Chemical carcinogenesis, patients' rights, health services, elderly medical care, HIV and other sexually transmitted diseases. *Unit head:* Dr. Robert F. Meenan, Dean, 617-638-4640, Fax: 617-638-5299. *Application contact:* LePhan Quan, Assistant Director of Admissions, 617-638-4640, Fax: 617-638-5299, E-mail: asksph@bu.edu.

Bowling Green State University, Graduate College, College of Health and Human Services, Program in Public Health, Bowling Green, OH 43403. Offers MPH. *Accreditation:* CEPH. Part-time programs available. *Faculty:* 5 full-time (2 women). *Students:* 11 full-time (10 women), 58 part-time (43 women); includes 16 minority (12 African Americans, 2 Asian Americans or Pacific Islanders, 2 Hispanic Americans), 7 international. Average age 31. 38 applicants, 100% accepted, 30 enrolled. *Degree requirements:* For master's, thesis or alternative. *Entrance requirements:* For master's, GRE General Test, minimum GPA of 3.0. Additional exam requirements/recommendations for international students: Required—TOEFL. *Application deadline:* For fall admission, 6/15 for domestic students, 2/15 for international students; for spring admission, 10/15 for domestic students. Application fee: $30. Electronic applications accepted. *Expenses:* Tuition, state resident: part-time $535 per hour. Tuition, nonresident: part-time $884 per hour. *Financial support:* In 2006–07, 4 research assistantships (averaging $7,105 per year), 1 teaching assistantship (averaging $8,120 per year) were awarded. Financial award applicants required to submit FAFSA. *Unit head:* Dr. L. Fleming Fallon, Chair, 419-372-8316.

Brooklyn College of the City University of New York, Division of Graduate Studies, Department of Health and Nutrition Science, Program in Public Health, Brooklyn, NY 11210-2889. Offers community health (MPH); health care management (MPH); health care policy and administration (MPH). *Accreditation:* CEPH. *Students:* 3 full-time (2 women), 49 part-time (35 women); includes 27 minority (18 African Americans, 5 Asian Americans or Pacific Islanders, 4 Hispanic Americans), 7 international. 45 applicants, 71% accepted, 11 enrolled. In 2006, 5 degrees awarded. *Entrance requirements:* For master's, GRE, 2 letters of recommendation, essay. *Application deadline:* For fall admission, 3/1 priority date for domestic students, 2/1 priority date for international students; for spring admission, 11/1 priority date for domestic students, 10/1 priority date for international students. Applications are processed on a rolling basis. Application fee: $125. Electronic applications accepted. *Expenses:* Tuition, state resident: full-time $6,400; part-time $270 per credit. Tuition, nonresident: full-time $12,000; part-time $500 per credit. Required fees: $118 per semester. *Financial support:* Application deadline: 5/1. *Unit head:* Dr. Jean Grassman, Graduate Deputy Chairperson, 718-951-5026, Fax: 718-951-4670, E-mail: grassman@brooklyn.cuny.edu. *Application contact:* Karen Alleyne-Pierre, Director of Admissions Services and Enrollment Communications, 718-951-5902, Fax: 718-951-4506, E-mail: grads@brooklyn.cuny.edu.

Brown University, Graduate School, Division of Biology and Medicine, Department of Community Health, Program in Public Health, Providence, RI 02912. Offers MPH. *Accreditation:* CEPH. *Entrance requirements:* For master's, GRE General Test or MCAT. Additional exam requirements/recommendations for international students: Required—TOEFL.

California College for Health Sciences, Program in Public Health, Salt Lake City, UT 84107. Offers MPH. Part-time and evening/weekend programs available. Postbaccalaureate distance learning degree programs offered (no on-campus study). *Degree requirements:* For master's, final project or thesis.

California State University, Fresno, Division of Graduate Studies, College of Health and Human Services, Department of Public Health, Fresno, CA 93740-8027. Offers environmental/occupational health (MPH); health administration (MPH); health promotion (MPH). *Accreditation:* CEPH. Part-time and evening/weekend programs available. *Degree requirements:* For master's, thesis or alternative. *Entrance requirements:* For master's, GRE General Test, minimum GPA of 2.5. Additional exam requirements/recommendations for international students: Required—TOEFL. Electronic applications accepted. *Faculty research:* Foster parent training, geriatrics, tobacco control.

California State University, Fullerton, Graduate Studies, College of Health and Human Development, Department of Health Science, Fullerton, CA 92834-9480. Offers public health (MPH). *Students:* 30 full-time (22 women), 31 part-time (27 women); includes 34 minority (5 African Americans, 18 Asian Americans or Pacific Islanders, 11 Hispanic Americans), 3 international. 83 applicants, 49% accepted, 26 enrolled. In 2006, 5 degrees awarded. *Expenses:* Tuition, nonresident: part-time $339 per unit. Required fees: $1,155 per semester. *Unit head:* Dr. Shari McMahan, Department Head, 714-278-7000.

Case Western Reserve University, Frances Payne Bolton School of Nursing, Nursing/Public Health Program, Cleveland, OH 44106. Offers MSN/MPH. Application fee: $75. *Unit head:* Dr. Deborah Lindell, Head, 216-368-3740, E-mail: dxl41@case.edu. *Application contact:* Peter Taylor, Recruitment and Retention Specialist, 216-368-0349, Fax: 216-368-0124, E-mail: peter.taylor@case.edu.

Case Western Reserve University, School of Medicine and School of Graduate Studies, Graduate Programs in Medicine, Department of Epidemiology and Biostatistics, Program in Public Health Program, Cleveland, OH 44106. Offers MPH. *Accreditation:* CEPH. Part-time programs available. *Faculty:* 22 full-time (11 women), 15 part-time/adjunct (7 women). *Students:* 28 full-time (25 women), 68 part-time (43 women); includes 27 minority (10 African Americans, 1 American Indian/Alaska Native, 11 Asian Americans or Pacific Islanders, 5 Hispanic Americans), 11 international. Average age 29. 82 applicants, 78% accepted, 40 enrolled. In 2006, 11 degrees awarded. *Degree requirements:* For master's, essay, field experience, presentation. *Entrance requirements:* For master's, GRE General Test (MCAT may be substituted), 3 letters of recommendation. Additional exam requirements/recommendations for international students: Required—TOEFL. *Application deadline:* For fall admission, 5/1 priority date for domestic and international students; for winter admission, 10/1 priority date for domestic students. Applications are processed on a rolling basis. Application fee: $50. Electronic applications accepted. *Financial support:* In 2006–07, 16 students received support. Career-related internships or fieldwork and scholarships/grants available. *Faculty research:* Public policy and aging, statistical modeling, behavioral medicine and evaluation, continuous quality improvement; tobacco cessation and prevention. *Unit head:* Dr. Scott H. Frank, Director, 216-368-3725, Fax: 216-368-3970, E-mail: shf2@case.edu. *Application contact:* Virginia C. Morrison, Administrative Director, 216-368-3128, Fax: 216-368-3970, E-mail: vxg6@cwru.edu.

College of St. Catherine, Graduate Programs, Program in Holistic Health Studies, St. Paul, MN 55105-1789. Offers MA. Part-time programs available. *Degree requirements:* For master's, thesis optional. *Entrance requirements:* For master's, 1 course in anatomy, physiology and psychology. Expenses: Contact institution.

Columbia University, Mailman School of Public Health, New York, NY 10032. Offers Exec MPH, MPH, MS, Dr PH, PhD, DDS/MPH, MBA/MPH, MD/MPH, MPA/MPH, MPH/MIA, MPH/MOT, MPH/MS, MPH/MSN, MPH/MSSW. PhD offered in cooperation with the Graduate School of Arts and Sciences. *Accreditation:* CEPH (one or more programs are accredited). Part-time and evening/weekend programs available. *Faculty:* 165 full-time (83 women), 230 part-time/adjunct. *Students:* 635 full-time (431 women), 317 part-time (271 women); includes 311 minority (105 African Americans, 2 American Indian/Alaska Native, 139 Asian Americans or Pacific Islanders, 65 Hispanic Americans), 108 international. Average age 28. 1,718 applicants, 60% accepted, 414 enrolled. In 2006, 321 master's, 16 doctorates awarded. *Degree requirements:* For master's, thesis (for some programs), registration; for doctorate, thesis/dissertation, comprehensive exam, registration. *Entrance requirements:* For master's, GRE General Test; for doctorate, GRE General Test, MPH or equivalent (Dr PH). Additional exam requirements/recommendations for international students: Required—TOEFL (minimum score 600 paper-based; 250 computer-based; 100 iBT). *Application deadline:* For fall admission, 2/1 for domestic and international students; for spring admission, 10/1 for domestic and international students. Applications are processed on a rolling basis. Application fee: $60. Electronic applications accepted. *Expenses: Contact institution. Financial support:* In 2006–07, 512 students received support; fellowships, research assistantships, teaching assistantships, career-related internships or fieldwork, Federal Work-Study, and traineeships available. Support available to part-time students. Financial award application deadline: 2/1; financial award applicants required to submit FAFSA. *Unit head:* Dr. Allan Rosenfield, Dean, 212-305-3927. *Application contact:* June Saunders, Associate Director of Admissions, 212-305-3927, Fax: 212-342-4861, E-mail: ph-admit@columbia.edu.

See Close-Up on page 2031.

Columbia University, Mailman School of Public Health, Division of Environmental Health Sciences, Program in Medical Physics/Health Physics, New York, NY 10027. Offers public health (MPH, Dr PH), including health, medical physics. Part-time programs available. *Degree requirements:* For doctorate, thesis/dissertation. *Entrance requirements:* For master's, GRE General Test, bachelor's degree in physics, engineering, or mathematics; for doctorate, GRE General Test, bachelor's degree in physics, engineering, or mathematics; MPH or equivalent (Dr PH). *Application deadline:* For spring admission, 10/1 for domestic students. Applications are processed on a rolling basis. Application fee: $60. *Financial support:* Career-related internships or fieldwork and Federal Work-Study available. Support available to part-time students. Financial award application deadline: 3/15; financial award applicants required to submit FAFSA. *Faculty research:* Health effects of radiation and other physical agents. *Unit head:* Dr. Cheng Shie Wuu, Professor of Clinical Radiation Oncology and Public Health, 212-305-3464, Fax: 212-305-4012.

Dartmouth College, School of Arts and Sciences, Center for the Evaluative Clinical Sciences, Program in Public Health, Hanover, NH 03755. Offers MPH. Degree awarded through Medical School. *Accreditation:* CEPH. Part-time programs available. *Faculty:* 26 full-time (12 women), 10 part-time/adjunct (9 women). *Students:* 49 full-time (32 women), 13 part-time (4 women); includes 17 minority (3 African Americans, 1 American Indian/Alaska Native, 13 Asian Americans or Pacific Islanders), 2 international. Average age 30. 118 applicants, 69% accepted, 44 enrolled. In 2006, 49 degrees awarded. *Degree requirements:* For master's, research project or practicum. *Entrance requirements:* For master's, GRE or MCAT, 3 letters of recommendation. Additional exam requirements/recommendations for international students: Required—TOEFL. *Application deadline:* For fall admission, 1/15 for domestic students. Applications are processed on a rolling basis. Application fee: $50. *Expenses:* Tuition: Full-time $33,297. *Application contact:* Susan M. Benson, Academic Programs Director, 603-650-1782, Fax: 603-650-1900, E-mail: susan.benson@dartmouth.edu.

Des Moines University, College of Health Sciences, Program in Public Health, Des Moines, IA 50312-4104. Offers MPH. *Accreditation:* CEPH. Part-time and evening/weekend programs available. *Faculty:* 1 (woman) full-time, 1 (woman) part-time/adjunct. *Students:* 60 full-time (40 women), 12 part-time (7 women); includes 12 minority (5 African Americans, 3 Asian Americans or Pacific Islanders, 4 Hispanic Americans), 2 international. 42 applicants, 60% accepted, 25 enrolled. In 2006, 31 degrees awarded. *Entrance requirements:* For master's, minimum GPA of 3.0. Additional exam requirements/recommendations for international students: Required—TOEFL (minimum score 600 paper-based). *Application deadline:* For fall admission, 8/25 priority date for domestic and international students; for winter admission, 1/5 priority date for domestic and international students; for spring admission, 5/1 priority date for domestic and international students. Applications are processed on a rolling basis. Application fee: $35. Electronic applications accepted. *Expenses: Contact institution. Financial support:* In 2006–07, 1 student received support. Career-related internships or fieldwork, institutionally sponsored loans, scholarships/grants, and university employment available. Financial award applicants required to submit FAFSA. *Faculty research:* Quality improvement, women's health, health promotion, patient education. *Unit head:* Dr. Wendy Ringgenberg, Director, 515-271-1367, E-mail: wendy.ringgenberg@dmu.edu. *Application contact:* Lisa Vroegh, Admissions Coordinator, 515-271-1364, Fax: 515-271-7162, E-mail: hmadmit@dmu.edu.

Dominican University of California, Graduate Programs, School of Arts and Sciences, Program in Nursing, San Rafael, CA 94901-2298. Offers geriatric and nurse educator (MS); integrated health practices (MS). *Accreditation:* AACN. Part-time and evening/weekend programs available. *Degree requirements:* For master's, thesis, registration. *Entrance requirements:* For master's, minimum GPA of 3.0, clinical experience, course work in nursing research and statistics, CPR certification, professional liability and malpractice insurance, interview. Additional exam requirements/recommendations for international students: Required—TOEFL (minimum score 550 paper-based; 213 computer-based). Electronic applications accepted.

Drexel University, School of Public Health, Philadelphia, PA 19104-2875. Offers MPH. *Entrance requirements:* For master's, GMAT, GRE, LSAT, or MCAT, previous course work in statistics and word processing. Additional exam requirements/recommendations for international students: Required—TOEFL. Electronic applications accepted. Expenses: Contact institution. *Faculty research:* Epidemiology, behavioral and social sciences, problem-based learning.

East Carolina University, Brody School of Medicine, Program in Public Health, Greenville, NC 27858-4353. Offers MPH. *Accreditation:* CEPH. Part-time programs available. *Faculty:* 4 full-time (2 women). *Students:* 33 full-time (22 women), 23 part-time (19 women); includes 16 minority (12 African Americans, 3 Asian Americans or Pacific Islanders, 1 Hispanic American), 1 international. Average age 28. 31 applicants, 74% accepted. In 2006, 16 degrees awarded. *Degree requirements:* For master's, field placement professional paper. *Entrance requirements:* For master's, GRE or MCAT. Additional exam requirements/recommendations for international students: Required—TOEFL (minimum score 550 paper-based; 213 computer-based). *Application deadline:* For fall admission, 4/15 for domestic and international students; for spring admission, 10/15 for domestic and international students. Application fee: $50. Electronic applications accepted. *Financial support:* In 2006–07, 4 research assistantships with full tuition reimbursements (averaging $3,750 per year) were awarded; unspecified assistantships also available. Financial award applicants required to submit FAFSA. *Faculty research:* Public health, disparities in public health. *Unit head:* Dr. Lloyd F. Novick, Chairman (Family Medicine), 252-744-4079, Fax: 252-744-2987, E-mail: novickl@ecu.edu. *Application contact:* Dean of Graduate School, 252-328-6012, Fax: 252-328-6071, E-mail: gradschool@ecu.edu.

East Carolina University, Graduate School, College of Fine Arts and Communication, School of Communication, Greenville, NC 27858-4353. Offers health communication (MA). *Students:* 17 full-time (15 women), 2 part-time (both women); includes 5 minority (3 African Americans, 2 Asian Americans or Pacific Islanders). Average age 24. *Entrance requirements:* For master's, GRE. *Financial support:* Teaching assistantships available. *Unit head:* Dr. Tim Hudson, Head, 252-328-2814, E-mail: hudsont@ecu.edu.

Eastern Virginia Medical School, Master of Public Health Program, Norfolk, VA 23501-1980. Offers MPH. *Accreditation:* CEPH. Evening/weekend programs available. Postbaccalaureate distance learning degree programs offered (minimal on-campus study). *Faculty:* 5 full-time (3 women), 6 part-time/adjunct (3 women). *Students:* 51. 71 applicants, 70% accepted, 30 enrolled. In 2006, 19 degrees awarded. *Degree requirements:* For master's, field practicum, integrative seminar. *Entrance requirements:* For master's, GRE General Test, MCAT. Additional exam requirements/recommendations for international students: Required—TOEFL (minimum score 650 paper-based; 278 computer-based). *Application deadline:* For fall admission, 5/3 priority date for domestic students, 4/30 for international students. Application fee: $50 ($100 for international students). *Expenses: Contact institution. Financial support:* In 2006–07, 33 students received support. Career-related internships or fieldwork and institutionally sponsored loans available. Financial award application deadline: 5/1; financial award applicants required to submit FAFSA. *Faculty research:* Community-based health research. *Unit head:* Dr. David O. Matson, Director, 757-466-6120, Fax: 757-446-6121, E-mail: matsondo@evms.edu. *Application contact:* Paula M. Swartz, Administrative Support Coordinator, 757-446-6120, Fax: 757-446-6121, E-mail: swartzpm@evms.edu.

East Stroudsburg University of Pennsylvania, Graduate School, School of Health Sciences and Human Performance, Program in Public Health, East Stroudsburg, PA 18301-2999. Offers community health education (MPH). Part-time and evening/weekend programs available. Postbaccalaureate distance learning degree programs offered (minimal on-campus study). *Faculty:* 3 full-time (2 women), 1 (woman) part-time/adjunct. *Students:* 14 full-time (9 women), 5 part-time (all women); includes 4 minority (1 African American, 2 Asian Americans or Pacific Islanders, 1 Hispanic American), 5 international. Average age 33. In 2006, 9 degrees awarded. *Degree requirements:* For master's, publishable paper. *Entrance requirements:* For master's, GRE, 3 letters of recommendation. Additional exam requirements/recommendations for international students: Required—TOEFL (minimum score 560 paper-based; 220 computer-based; 83 iBT). *Application deadline:* For fall admission, 7/31 priority date for domestic students, 5/1 priority date for international students; for spring admission, 11/30 for domestic students, 10/1 for international students. Applications are processed on a rolling basis. Application fee: $50. Electronic applications accepted. *Expenses:* Tuition, state resident: full-time $6,048; part-time $336 per credit. Tuition, nonresident: full-time $9,678; part-time $538 per credit. Required fees: $1,353; $67 per credit. One-time fee: $37 part-time. *Financial support:* In 2006–07, 9 research assistantships with partial tuition reimbursements were awarded; career-related internships or fieldwork and unspecified assistantships also available. *Faculty research:* Public health infrastructure. Total annual research expenditures: $500,000. *Unit head:* Dr. Carolyn Woodhouse, MPH Program Director, 570-422-3702, E-mail: cwoodhouse@po-box.esu.edu.

East Tennessee State University, School of Graduate Studies, College of Public and Allied Health, Department of Public Health, Johnson City, TN 37614. Offers community health (MPH); epidemiology (Certificate); gerontology (Certificate); health care management (Certificate); public health (MPH); public health administration (MPH). *Accreditation:* CEPH. Part-time programs available. *Degree requirements:* For master's, thesis optional. *Entrance requirements:* For master's, GRE General Test, 2 years of community health experience. Additional exam requirements/recommendations for international students: Required—TOEFL (minimum score 550 paper-based; 213 computer-based). *Faculty research:* Rural health issues, youth and adolescent health, health of the elderly, environmental epidemiology, spatial analysis of data.

Emerson College, Graduate Studies, School of Communication, Department of Marketing Communication, Boston, MA 02116-4624. Offers global marketing communication and advertising (MA); health communication (MA); integrated marketing communication (MA). *Entrance requirements:* For master's, GRE General Test. Additional exam requirements/recommendations for international students: Required—TOEFL. Electronic applications accepted.

See Close-Up on page 2033.

Emory University, Rollins School of Public Health, Atlanta, GA 30322-1100. Offers MPH, MSPH, PhD, JD/MPH, MBA/MPH, MD/MPH, MSN/MPH. *Accreditation:* CEPH (one or more programs are accredited). Part-time and evening/weekend programs available. Postbaccalaureate distance learning degree programs offered (minimal on-campus study). *Faculty:* 160 full-time (75 women), 200 part-time/adjunct (66 women). *Students:* 557 full-time (461 women), 148 part-time (102 women); includes 251 minority (156 African Americans, 3 American

Public Health—General

Emory University (continued)
Indian/Alaska Native, 63 Asian Americans or Pacific Islanders, 29 Hispanic Americans), 68 international. Average age 27. 1,000 applicants, 71% accepted, 324 enrolled. In 2006, 300 degrees awarded. *Degree requirements:* For master's, thesis (for some programs), practicum. *Entrance requirements:* For master's, GRE General Test. Additional exam requirements/recommendations for international students: Required—TOEFL (minimum score 550 paper-based; 213 computer-based). *Application deadline:* For fall admission, 1/5 priority date for domestic and international students. Application fee: $75. Electronic applications accepted. *Expenses: Contact institution. Financial support:* In 2006–07, 350 students received support; fellowships with full and partial tuition reimbursements available, research assistantships, teaching assistantships, career-related internships or fieldwork, Federal Work-Study, institutionally sponsored loans, scholarships/grants, traineeships, and health care benefits available. Support available to part-time students. Financial award application deadline: 1/5; financial award applicants required to submit FAFSA. *Faculty research:* Cancer risk and occurrence, AIDS prevention, infectious disease models, violence prevention, minority health. Total annual research expenditures: $24.3 million. *Unit head:* Dr. Richard Levinson, Executive Associate Dean for Academic Affairs, 404-727-3956, Fax: 404-712-9853, E-mail: admit@sph.emory.edu. *Application contact:* Kara Brown Robinson, Director of Admissions and Recruitment, 404-727-3317, Fax: 404-727-3996, E-mail: admit@sph.emory.edu.

See Close-Up on page 2035.

Florida Agricultural and Mechanical University, Division of Graduate Studies, Research, and Continuing Education, College of Pharmacy and Pharmaceutical Sciences, Institute of Public Health, Tallahassee, FL 32307-3200. Offers MPH. *Accreditation:* CEPH. *Entrance requirements:* Additional exam requirements/recommendations for international students: Required—TOEFL.

Florida International University, School of Public Health, Department of Public Health, Miami, FL 33199. Offers MPH. *Accreditation:* CEPH. Part-time programs available. *Faculty:* 5 full-time (1 woman). *Students:* 120 full-time (86 women), 135 part-time (103 women); includes 175 minority (73 African Americans, 22 Asian Americans or Pacific Islanders, 80 Hispanic Americans), 26 international. Average age 32. 161 applicants, 60% accepted, 47 enrolled. In 2006, 45 degrees awarded. *Degree requirements:* For master's, thesis optional. *Entrance requirements:* For master's, GRE General Test, minimum GPA of 3.0. Additional exam requirements/recommendations for international students: Required—TOEFL. *Application deadline:* For fall admission, 4/1 priority date for domestic students; for spring admission, 10/1 for domestic students. Applications are processed on a rolling basis. Application fee: $25. *Expenses:* Tuition, state resident: part-time $249 per credit hour. Tuition, nonresident: part-time $753 per credit hour. Tuition and fees vary according to program. *Faculty research:* Drugs/AIDS intervention among migrant workers, provision of services for active/recovering drug users with HIV. *Unit head:* Nasar Ahmed, Director, 305-348-1093, Fax: 305-348-4901, E-mail: nasar.ahmed@fiu.edu.

See Close-Up on page 2037.

Fort Valley State University, College of Graduate Studies and Extended Education, Program in Public Health, Fort Valley, GA 31030-4313. Offers environmental health (MPH). *Degree requirements:* For master's, thesis. *Entrance requirements:* For master's, GRE General Test.

Georgetown University, Graduate School of Arts and Sciences, Programs in Biomedical Sciences, Department of Microbiology and Immunology, Washington, DC 20057. Offers biohazardous threat agents and emerging infectious diseases (MS); general microbiology and immunology (MS); global infectious diseases (PhD); microbiology and immunology research (PhD); science policy and advocacy (MS). Part-time programs available. *Faculty:* 20 full-time (4 women), 16 part-time/adjunct (3 women). *Students:* 42 full-time (32 women), 13 part-time (8 women); includes 15 minority (2 African Americans, 11 Asian Americans or Pacific Islanders, 2 Hispanic Americans), 6 international. Average age 24. 94 applicants, 55% accepted, 41 enrolled. In 2006, 37 master's, 5 doctorates awarded. *Median time to degree:* Master's–1 year full-time, 2 years part-time; doctorate–5 years full-time. *Degree requirements:* For master's, 30 credit hours of coursework; for doctorate, thesis/dissertation, comprehensive exam. *Entrance requirements:* For master's, GRE General Test, 3 letters of reference, bachelor's degree in related field; for doctorate, GRE General Test, 3 letters of reference, graduate degree in related field. Additional exam requirements/recommendations for international students: Required—TOEFL (minimum score 505 paper-based; 213 computer-based). *Application deadline:* For fall admission, 7/1 for domestic students, 6/1 priority date for international students; for winter admission, 2/2 priority date for domestic students, 1/2 priority date for international students; for spring admission, 11/1 for domestic students, 10/1 priority date for international students. Applications are processed on a rolling basis. Application fee: $70. Electronic applications accepted. *Financial support:* In 2006–07, 17 students received support, including 2 fellowships with full tuition reimbursements available (averaging $23,772 per year). *Faculty research:* Pathogenesis and basic biology of the fungus Candida albicans, molecular biology of viral hepatitis, molecular and cellular biology of the Hepatitis B and Delta viruses, dengue virus, immunopathological mechanisms in Multiple Sclerosis. *Unit head:* Dr. Adam Myers, Associate Dean, E-mail: myersa@georgetown.edu. *Application contact:* Eugenia Pyntikova, Coordinator, Graduate Programs, 202-687-3422, Fax: 202-687-1800, E-mail: ep72@georgetown.edu.

The George Washington University, School of Public Health and Health Services, Department of Global Health, Washington, DC 20052. Offers international health policy and programs (MPH); international health promotion (MPH); JD/MPH; LL M/MPH; MD/MPH. *Accreditation:* CEPH. *Degree requirements:* For master's, case study or special project. *Entrance requirements:* For master's, GMAT, GRE General Test, or MCAT. Additional exam requirements/recommendations for international students: Required—TOEFL.

The George Washington University, School of Public Health and Health Services, Department of Health Services Management and Leadership, Washington, DC 20052. Offers health management and leadership (MHSA); health policy (MHSA); health services administration (Specialist); public health management (MPH). *Accreditation:* CAHME (one or more programs are accredited). *Degree requirements:* For master's, internship or residency. *Entrance requirements:* For master's, GMAT or GRE; for Specialist, GMAT or GRE, master's degree in related field. Additional exam requirements/recommendations for international students: Required—TOEFL. *Faculty research:* Hospital administration, ambulatory health care, social gerontology, health care financing, health care ethics.

The George Washington University, School of Public Health and Health Services, Department of Prevention and Community Health, Washington, DC 20052. Offers community-oriented primary care (MPH); health promotion (MPH); maternal and child health (MPH); public health and emergency management (Certificate). *Accreditation:* CEPH. *Entrance requirements:* For master's, GRE or GMAT, 2 letters of recommendation, resumé. Additional exam requirements/recommendations for international students: Required—TOEFL.

The George Washington University, School of Public Health and Health Services, Doctoral Program in Public Health, Washington, DC 20052. Offers environmental and occupational health (Dr PH); health behavior (Dr PH); health policy (Dr PH). *Accreditation:* CEPH. *Faculty research:* Community organization, tele-medicine, long-term care, financing for vulnerable populations, quantitative analysis in public health policy.

Georgia Southern University, Jack N. Averitt College of Graduate Studies, Jiann-Ping Hsu College of Public Health, Program in Public Health, Statesboro, GA 30460. Offers MPH. Part-time and evening/weekend programs available. *Students:* 21 full-time (13 women), 6 part-time (4 women); includes 7 minority (6 African Americans, 1 Asian American or Pacific Islander), 9 international. Average age 28. 21 applicants, 62% accepted, 8 enrolled. In 2006, 9 degrees awarded. *Degree requirements:* For master's, thesis optional. *Entrance requirements:* For master's, GRE General Test, minimum GPA of 2.75, resumé. Additional exam requirements/recommendations for international students: Required—TOEFL (minimum score 550 paper-based; 213 computer-based; 80 iBT). *Application deadline:* For fall admission, 3/1 priority date for domestic students, 3/1 for international students; for spring admission, 10/1 priority date for domestic students, 10/1 for international students. Applications are processed on a rolling basis. Application fee: $50. Electronic applications accepted. *Financial support:* In 2006–07, 23 students received support, including research assistantships with partial tuition reimbursements available (averaging $5,500 per year), teaching assistantships with partial tuition reimbursements available (averaging $5,500 per year); career-related internships or fieldwork, Federal Work-Study, scholarships/grants, tuition waivers (partial), and unspecified assistantships also available. Support available to part-time students. Financial award applicants required to submit FAFSA. *Application contact:* 912-681-5384, Fax: 912-681-0740, E-mail: gradadmissions@georgiasouthern.edu.

Georgia State University, College of Health and Human Sciences, Institute of Public Health, Atlanta, GA 30303-3083. Offers MPH, Certificate. *Accreditation:* CEPH. Part-time and evening/weekend programs available. *Faculty:* 7 full-time (2 women), 1 part-time/adjunct (0 women). *Students:* 45 full-time (29 women), 39 part-time (34 women). 146 applicants, 37% accepted, 21 enrolled. In 2006, 13 master's, 1 other advanced degree awarded. *Degree requirements:* For master's, thesis, practicum. *Entrance requirements:* For master's, GRE. Additional exam requirements/recommendations for international students: Required—TOEFL (minimum score 550 paper-based; 213 computer-based). *Application deadline:* For fall admission, 3/1 for domestic students; for spring admission, 10/1 for domestic students. Application fee: $50. *Financial support:* In 2006–07, research assistantships with partial tuition reimbursements (averaging $3,108 per year); Federal Work-Study, scholarships/grants, tuition waivers (partial), and unspecified assistantships also available. Support available to part-time students. Total annual research expenditures: $1.1 million. *Unit head:* Michael P Eriksen, Director, 404-651-4133, E-mail: meriksen@gsu.edu. *Application contact:* Denise Gouveia, Application Contact, 404-651-3064, Fax: 404-651-4571, E-mail: dgouveia@gsu.edu.

Harvard University, Graduate School of Arts and Sciences, Program in Biological Sciences in Public Health (BPH), Boston, MA 02115. Offers PhD. *Degree requirements:* For doctorate, thesis/dissertation, qualifying exam. *Entrance requirements:* For doctorate, GRE General Test, GRE Subject Test. Additional exam requirements/recommendations for international students: Required—TOEFL. *Application deadline:* For fall admission, 12/15 for domestic students. Application fee: $60. *Expenses:* Tuition: Full-time $30,275. Full-time tuition and fees vary according to program and student level. *Financial support:* Fellowships, research assistantships, teaching assistantships, institutionally sponsored loans and tuition waivers (full) available. Financial award application deadline: 1/1. *Faculty research:* Nutrition biochemistry, molecular and cellular toxicology, cardiovascular disease, cancer biology, tropical public health, environmental health physiology. *Unit head:* Ruth Kenworthy, Administrator, 617-432-2932, Fax: 617-432-0433, E-mail: kenworthy@cvlab.harvard.edu. *Application contact:* Leah W. Simons.

Harvard University, School of Public Health, Boston, MA 02115-6096. Offers MOH, MPH, SM, DPH, PhD, SD, JD/MPH, MD/MPH. *Accreditation:* CEPH (one or more programs are accredited). Part-time programs available. *Degree requirements:* For doctorate, thesis/dissertation, qualifying exam. *Entrance requirements:* For master's and doctorate, GRE. Additional exam requirements/recommendations for international students: Required—TOEFL (minimum score 560 paper-based; 220 computer-based); Recommended—IELTS (minimum score 7). Electronic applications accepted. Expenses: Contact institution. Full-time tuition and fees vary according to program and student level.

See Close-Up on page 2039.

Hunter College of the City University of New York, Graduate School, Schools of the Health Professions, Programs in Urban Public Health, New York, NY 10021-5085. Offers environmental and occupational health sciences (MS); public health (MPH); MS/MPH. *Accreditation:* CEPH. Part-time programs available. *Faculty:* 2 full-time (0 women), 2 part-time/adjunct (1 woman). *Students:* 12 full-time (8 women), 119 part-time (96 women); includes 40 minority (13 African Americans, 9 Asian Americans or Pacific Islanders, 18 Hispanic Americans). Average age 33. In 2006, 57 degrees awarded. *Degree requirements:* For master's, comprehensive exam. *Entrance requirements:* For master's, GRE General Test, undergraduate major in natural or social sciences, health studies, nutrition or related field; 1 year of work or volunteer experience related to public health, nutrition, environmental health, social services, or community organization. Additional exam requirements/recommendations for international students: Required—TOEFL. *Application deadline:* For fall admission, 4/1 for domestic students, 2/1 for international students; for spring admission, 11/1 for domestic students, 9/1 for international students. Application fee: $125. *Expenses:* Tuition, state resident: part-time $270 per credit. Tuition, nonresident: part-time $500 per credit. Required fees: $45 per semester. *Financial support:* Application deadline: 3/1. *Unit head:* Dr. Nicholas Freudenberg, Director, 212-481-4363, Fax: 212-481-5260, E-mail: nfreuden@hunter.cuny.edu.

Idaho State University, Office of Graduate Studies, College of Education, Department of Educational Foundations, Pocatello, ID 83209. Offers child and family studies (M Ed); curriculum leadership (M Ed); education (M Ed); educational administration (M Ed); educational foundations (5th Year Certificate); elementary education (M Ed), including K-12 education, literacy, secondary education. Part-time and evening/weekend programs available. Post-baccalaureate distance learning degree programs offered (no on-campus study). *Faculty:* 12 full-time (8 women). *Students:* 16 full-time (11 women), 161 part-time (102 women); includes 2 minority (1 Asian American or Pacific Islander, 1 Hispanic American), 2 international. Average age 40. In 2006, 15 degrees awarded. *Degree requirements:* For master's, oral exam, written exam, thesis optional; for 5th Year Certificate, thesis (for some programs), oral exam, written exam, comprehensive exam, registration (for some programs). *Entrance requirements:* For master's, GRE General Test or MAT, minimum undergraduate GPA of 3.0; for 5th Year Certificate, GRE General Test, minimum undergraduate GPA of 3.0, master's degree. Additional exam requirements/recommendations for international students: Required—TOEFL (minimum score 550 paper-based; 213 computer-based; 80 iBT). *Application deadline:* For fall admission, 7/1 for domestic students, 6/1 for international students; for spring admission, 12/1 for domestic students, 11/1 for international students. Applications are processed on a rolling basis. Application fee: $55. *Expenses:* Tuition, state resident: part-time $251 per credit. Tuition, nonresident: part-time $366 per credit. Tuition and fees vary according to degree level, program and reciprocity agreements. *Financial support:* Career-related internships or fieldwork, Federal Work-Study, institutionally sponsored loans, scholarships/grants, tuition waivers, and unspecified assistantships available. Support available to part-time students. Financial award application deadline: 1/1. *Faculty research:* Child and families studies; business education; special education; math, science, and technology education. *Unit head:* Dr. Jack Newsome, Chair, 208-282-4838, E-mail: newsjack@isu.edu. *Application contact:* Dr. Peter Denner, Assistant Dean, 208-282-3807, Fax: 208-282-4697, E-mail: dennpete@isu.edu.

Idaho State University, Office of Graduate Studies, Kasiska College of Health Professions, Department of Health and Nutrition Sciences, Program in Public Health, Pocatello, ID 83209. Offers MPH. *Accreditation:* CEPH. *Students:* 12 full-time (3 women), 23 part-time (14 women), 9 international. Average age 35. In 2006, 4 degrees awarded. *Degree requirements:* For master's, internship, thesis optional. *Entrance requirements:* For master's, GRE General Test, minimum GPA of 3.0 for upper division classes, 2 letters of recommendation. Additional exam requirements/recommendations for international students: Required—TOEFL (minimum score 600 paper-based; 213 computer-based). *Application deadline:* For fall admission, 7/1 for domestic students, 6/1 for international students; for spring admission, 12/1 for domestic students, 11/1 for international students. Applications are processed on a rolling basis. Application fee: $55. *Financial support:* In 2006–07, teaching assistantships with full and partial tuition reimbursements (averaging $8,694 per year); career-related internships or fieldwork, Federal Work-Study, scholarships/grants, and unspecified assistantships also available. Financial award application deadline: 1/1. *Application contact:* Ellen Combs, Graduate School Technical Records Specialist, 208-282-2150, Fax: 208-282-4847.

Indiana University Bloomington, School of Health, Physical Education and Recreation, Department of Applied Health Science, Bloomington, IN 47405-7000. Offers health behavior (PhD); health promotion (MS); human development/family studies (MS); nutrition science (MS); public health (MPH); safety management (MS); school and college health education (MS). PhD offered through the University Graduate School. *Accreditation:* CEPH (one or more programs are accredited). *Faculty:* 21 full-time (11 women), 1 (woman) part-time/adjunct. *Students:* 72 full-time (54 women), 44 part-time (30 women); includes 18 minority (15 African Americans, 2 Asian Americans or Pacific Islanders, 1 Hispanic American), 17 international. Average age 30. 94 applicants, 88% accepted, 54 enrolled. In 2006, 50 master's, 7 doctorates awarded. *Degree requirements:* For master's, thesis optional; for doctorate, thesis/dissertation, registration. *Entrance requirements:* For master's, GRE (MS in nutrition science), 3 recommendations; for doctorate, GRE, 3 recommendations. Additional exam requirements/recommendations for international students: Required—TOEFL (minimum score 550 paper-based; 213 computer-based; 79 iBT). *Application deadline:* For fall admission, 4/30 priority date for domestic students, 12/1 priority date for international students; for spring admission, 11/15 priority date for domestic students, 9/1 priority date for international students. Application fee: $50 ($60 for international students). *Expenses:* Tuition, state resident: full-time $5,791; part-time $241 per credit hour. Tuition, nonresident: full-time $16,866; part-time $703 per credit hour. *Financial support:* In 2006–07, teaching assistantships with full and partial tuition reimbursements (averaging $11,666 per year); fellowships, career-related internships or fieldwork, Federal Work-Study, institutionally sponsored loans, scholarships/grants, tuition waivers (partial), and fee remissions also available. Financial award application deadline: 3/1. *Faculty research:* Cancer education, HIV/AIDS and drug education, public health, parent-child interactions, safety education. *Unit head:* Dr. Mohammad R. Torabi, Chair, 812-855-4808, Fax: 812-855-3936, E-mail: torabi@indiana.edu.

Indiana University–Purdue University Indianapolis, Indiana University School of Medicine, Department of Public Health, Indianapolis, IN 46202-2896. Offers MPH. *Accreditation:* CEPH. *Students:* 1 (woman) full-time, 4 part-time (all women); includes 2 minority (both African Americans) *Expenses:* Tuition, state resident: full-time $5,437; part-time $227 per credit hour. Tuition, nonresident: full-time $15,694; part-time $654 per credit hour. Required fees: $620. Tuition and fees vary according to course load, campus/location and program. *Unit head:* Greg Wilson, Director, 317-274-0388.

The Johns Hopkins University, Bloomberg School of Public Health, Baltimore, MD 21205. Offers MHS, MPH, Sc M, Dr PH, PhD, Sc D, JD/MPH, MBA/MPH, MHS/MA, MSN/MPH, MSW/MPH. *Accreditation:* CEPH (one or more programs are accredited). Part-time and evening/weekend programs available. Postbaccalaureate distance learning degree programs offered (minimal on-campus study). *Faculty:* 517 full-time (253 women), 572 part-time/adjunct (222 women). *Students:* 1,197 full-time (872 women), 454 part-time (279 women); includes 388 minority (107 African Americans, 5 American Indian/Alaska Native, 218 Asian Americans or Pacific Islanders, 58 Hispanic Americans), 388 international. Average age 29. 3,047 applicants, 52% accepted, 755 enrolled. In 2006, 507 master's, 123 doctorates awarded. *Median time to degree:* Of those who began their doctoral program in fall 1998, 70% received their degree in 8 years or less. *Degree requirements:* For master's, thesis (for some programs), comprehensive exam (for some programs), registration; for doctorate, thesis/dissertation, comprehensive exam, registration. *Entrance requirements:* For master's and doctorate, GRE General Test, 3 letters of recommendation, resumé. Additional exam requirements/recommendations for international students: Required—TOEFL (minimum score 600 paper-based; 250 computer-based). *Application deadline:* Applications are processed on a rolling basis. Application fee: $45. Electronic applications accepted. *Expenses:* Tuition: Full-time $32,976. Tuition and fees vary according to degree level and program. *Financial support:* In 2006–07, 1,650 students received support, including 38 fellowships (averaging $34,333 per year), 59 research assistantships (averaging $23,525 per year), 11 teaching assistantships (averaging $3,126 per year); career-related internships or fieldwork, Federal Work-Study, institutionally sponsored loans, scholarships/grants, traineeships, health care benefits, and stipends also available. Support available to part-time students. Financial award application deadline: 3/15; financial award applicants required to submit FAFSA. *Faculty research:* Biodefense studies, infectious/chronic disease, human nutrition, environmental hazards, genetics. Total annual research expenditures: $290 million. *Unit head:* Dr. Michael J. Klag, Dean, 410-955-3540, Fax: 410-955-0121, E-mail: mklag@jhsph.edu. *Application contact:* Jennifer L. Kerilla, Associate Director of Admissions: Communications, Recruitment and Special Projects, 410-955-3543, Fax: 410-955-0464, E-mail: jkerilla@jhsph.edu.

See Close-Up on page 2041.

Kansas State University, Graduate School, College of Human Ecology, Department of Human Nutrition, Program in Public Health, Manhattan, KS 66506. Offers MS. *Students:* 8 full-time (3 women), 6 part-time (5 women); includes 2 minority (1 African American, 1 Hispanic American), 2 international. 5 applicants, 100% accepted, 2 enrolled. In 2006, 4 degrees awarded. *Entrance requirements:* For master's, GRE, minimum undergraduate GPA of 3.0. Additional exam requirements/recommendations for international students: Required—TOEFL (minimum score 550 paper-based; 213 computer-based). *Application deadline:* For fall admission, 8/1 priority date for domestic students; for spring admission, 11/1 priority date for domestic students. Application fee: $30 ($55 for international students). *Expenses:* Tuition, state resident: full-time $6,352; part-time $240 per credit hour. Tuition, nonresident: full-time $14,296; part-time $571 per credit hour. Required fees: $585. *Financial support:* Research assistantships available. *Faculty research:* Food safety and biosecurity; public health physical activity; breast-feeding and childhood obesity; zoonotic and emerging infections; health literacy. *Unit head:* Carol Ann Holcomb, Interim Head, 785-532-1318, Fax: 785-532-3796, E-mail: carolann@ksu.edu.

Kent State University, Graduate School of Education, Health, and Human Services, Northeastern Ohio Universities Public Health Program, Kent, OH 44242-0001. Offers MPH. *Accreditation:* CEPH. Part-time programs available. *Students:* 1 full-time (0 women), 17 part-time (13 women); includes 1 minority (Asian American or Pacific Islander) 9 applicants, 100% accepted. In 2006, 1 degree awarded. *Entrance requirements:* For master's, GRE General Test, minimum undergraduate GPA of 2.75, graduate 3.0. Additional exam requirements/recommendations for international students: Required—TOEFL (minimum score 550 paper-based; 213 computer-based). *Application deadline:* For fall admission, 3/1 for domestic and international students. Application fee: $30. *Expenses: Contact institution. Faculty research:* Health education, collaborative community practice, physical education, nursing. *Unit head:* Dr. Davina Gosnell, Coordinator, 330-672-2228, E-mail: dgosnell@kent.edu. *Application contact:* Amy Lee, Administrative Director Community Health Services, 330-325-6179, E-mail: afl@neoucom.edu.

Loma Linda University, School of Public Health, Loma Linda, CA 92350. Offers MHA, MPH, MSPH, Dr PH. *Accreditation:* CEPH (one or more programs are accredited). Part-time programs available. *Degree requirements:* For doctorate, thesis/dissertation. *Entrance requirements:* For doctorate, GRE General Test. Additional exam requirements/recommendations for international students: Required—Michigan English Language Assessment Battery or TOEFL. *Faculty research:* Lifestyle and health, nutrition and cancer, nutrition and cardiovascular disease, smoking and health, aging and longevity.

Louisiana State University Health Sciences Center, School of Graduate Studies in New Orleans, Department of Public Health and Preventive Medicine, New Orleans, LA 70112-2223. Offers MPH. Open only to currently enrolled medical students. Part-time and evening/weekend programs available. *Faculty:* 2 full-time (0 women), 10 part-time/adjunct (2 women). *Students:* Average age 24. In 2006, 2 degrees awarded. *Degree requirements:* For master's, thesis. *Entrance requirements:* For master's, GRE General Test, interview. Additional exam requirements/recommendations for international students: Required—TOEFL. *Application deadline:* For winter admission, 6/15 priority date for domestic students; for spring admission, 10/15 priority date for domestic students. Applications are processed on a rolling basis. Application fee: $30. *Expenses:* Tuition, state resident: full-time $5,868; part-time $722 per credit. Tuition, nonresident: full-time $8,993; part-time $1,104 per credit. *Faculty research:* Health care outcomes, occupational medicine, health status measurement, Rasch measurement, civil rights litigation. *Unit head:* Dr. Elizabeth Fontham, Head, E-mail: efonth@lsuhsc.edu. *Application contact:* Alice Isabelle LeBlanc, Program Administrator, 504-599-1299, E-mail: alebla@lsuhsc.edu.

Medical College of Wisconsin, Medical School, Department of Preventive Medicine, Milwaukee, WI 53226-0509. Offers general preventive medicine and public health (MPH); occupational medicine (MPH). *Accreditation:* CEPH. Part-time programs available. Postbaccalaureate distance learning degree programs offered (no on-campus study). *Degree requirements:* For master's, project. *Entrance requirements:* For master's, MD/DO license to practice medicine in U.S. or Canada. Additional exam requirements/recommendations for international students: Required—TOEFL. *Faculty research:* Environmental medicine, ergonomics, epidemiology, surveillance, distance education.

Missouri State University, Graduate College, College of Health and Human Services, Department of Health, Physical Education, and Recreation, Springfield, MO 65804-0094. Offers health promotion and wellness management (MS); public health (MPH); secondary education (MS Ed), including physical education. Part-time programs available. *Faculty:* 12 full-time (4 women). *Students:* 43 full-time (11 women), 36 part-time (18 women); includes 1 minority (Hispanic American), 45 international. Average age 27. 126 applicants, 73% accepted, 37 enrolled. In 2006, 15 degrees awarded. *Degree requirements:* For master's, thesis or alternative, comprehensive exam. *Entrance requirements:* For master's, GRE (MS, MPH), minimum GPA of 2.8 (MS), minimum GPA of 3.0 (MPH), 9-12 teaching certification (MS Ed). Additional exam requirements/recommendations for international students: Required—TOEFL (minimum score 550 paper-based; 213 computer-based; 79 iBT). *Application deadline:* For fall admission, 7/20 priority date for domestic students; for spring admission, 12/20 priority date for domestic students. Applications are processed on a rolling basis. Application fee: $35. Electronic applications accepted. *Expenses:* Tuition, state resident: full-time $3,582; part-time $199 per credit hour. Tuition, nonresident: full-time $6,984; part-time $199 per credit hour. Required fees: $548. Full-time tuition and fees vary according to course level, course load, program and reciprocity agreements. *Financial support:* In 2006–07, 6 teaching assistantships with full tuition reimbursements (averaging $6,780 per year) were awarded; research assistantships with full tuition reimbursements, Federal Work-Study, scholarships/grants, and unspecified assistantships also available. Financial award application deadline: 3/31; financial award applicants required to submit FAFSA. *Unit head:* Dr. Sarah McCallister, Acting Head, 417-836-6582, Fax: 417-836-5371, E-mail: sarahmccallister@missouristate.edu. *Application contact:* Dr. Sarah McCallister, Acting Head, 417-836-6582, Fax: 417-836-5371, E-mail: sarahmccallister@missouristate.edu.

Morehouse School of Medicine, Master of Public Health Program, Atlanta, GA 30310-1495. Offers MPH. *Accreditation:* CEPH. Part-time programs available. *Degree requirements:* For master's, thesis, practicum. *Entrance requirements:* For master's, GRE General Test, public health or human service experience. Additional exam requirements/recommendations for international students: Required—TOEFL (minimum score 550 paper-based; 200 computer-based). Electronic applications accepted. Expenses: Contact institution. *Faculty research:* Women's and adolescent health, violence prevention, cancer epidemiology/disparities, substance abuse prevention.

Morgan State University, School of Graduate Studies, School of Public Health and Policy, Baltimore, MD 21251. Offers MPH, Dr PH. *Accreditation:* CEPH. *Faculty:* 17. *Students:* 76; includes 1 Asian American or Pacific Islander. In 2006, 2 master's, 5 doctorates awarded. *Degree requirements:* For doctorate, thesis/dissertation. *Entrance requirements:* For doctorate, GRE, minimum GPA of 3.0. Additional exam requirements/recommendations for international students: Required—TOEFL (minimum score 550 paper-based; 213 computer-based). *Application deadline:* For fall admission, 2/1 priority date for domestic students; for spring admission, 10/1 priority date for domestic students. Applications are processed on a rolling basis. Application fee: $0. *Expenses:* Tuition, state resident: part-time $272 per credit. Tuition, nonresident: part-time $478 per credit. Required fees: $38 per credit. *Financial support:* Fellowships, research assistantships, career-related internships or fieldwork, Federal Work-Study, institutionally sponsored loans, scholarships/grants, health care benefits, tuition waivers (full and partial), and unspecified assistantships available. Support available to part-time students. Financial award application deadline: 2/1. *Unit head:* Dr. Allan Noonan, Dean, 443-885-3238. *Application contact:* Dr. Maurice C. Taylor, Dean, 443-885-3185, Fax: 443-885-8226, E-mail: mctaylor@moac.morgan.edu.

New Jersey Institute of Technology, Office of Graduate Studies, College of Science and Liberal Arts, Department of Humanities and Social Sciences, Program in Public Health, Newark, NJ 07102. Offers MS. *Accreditation:* CEPH. Part-time and evening/weekend programs available. *Students:* Average age 28. *Entrance requirements:* For master's, GRE General Test. Additional exam requirements/recommendations for international students: Required—TOEFL (minimum score 550 paper-based; 213 computer-based). *Application deadline:* For fall admission, 6/5 priority date for domestic students; for spring admission, 10/15 for domestic students. Applications are processed on a rolling basis. Application fee: $60. Electronic applications accepted. *Expenses:* Tuition, state resident: full-time $11,896; part-time $648 per credit. Tuition, nonresident: full-time $16,900; part-time $892 per credit. Required fees: $336; $66 per credit. $168 per term. Tuition and fees vary according to course load. *Financial support:* Fellowships with full and partial tuition reimbursements, research assistantships with full and partial tuition reimbursements, teaching assistantships with full and partial tuition reimbursements, career-related internships or fieldwork, Federal Work-Study, institutionally sponsored loans, and unspecified assistantships available. Financial award application deadline: 3/15. *Application contact:* Kathryn Kelly, Director of Admissions, 973-596-3300, Fax: 973-596-3461, E-mail: admissions@njit.edu.

New Mexico State University, Graduate School, College of Health and Social Services, Department of Health Science, Las Cruces, NM 88003-8001. Offers MPH. *Accreditation:* CEPH. Part-time and evening/weekend programs available. *Faculty:* 5 full-time (2 women), 3 part-time/adjunct (0 women). *Students:* 25 full-time (17 women), 18 part-time (15 women); includes 17 minority (1 African American, 4 American Indian/Alaska Native, 1 Asian American or Pacific Islander, 11 Hispanic Americans), 6 international. Average age 32. 31 applicants, 68% accepted. In 2006, 19 degrees awarded. *Degree requirements:* For master's, thesis optional. *Entrance requirements:* For master's, GRE or MAT, 6 hours in psychosocial course work, 4 hours in biology, 3 hours in statistics. *Application deadline:* For fall admission, 7/1 for domestic students; for spring admission, 11/1 for domestic students. Applications are processed on a rolling basis. Application fee: $30 ($50 for international students). Electronic applications accepted. *Financial support:* In 2006–07, 5 teaching assistantships were awarded; research assistantships, career-related internships or fieldwork and health care benefits also available. Financial award application deadline: 3/1. *Faculty research:* Community health education, health issues of U.S.-Mexico border, health policy and management, victims of violence (spatial abuse), environmental and occupational health issues. *Unit head:* Dr. Stephen Anderson, Interim Head, 505-646-4300, Fax: 505-646-4343, E-mail: stephen@nmsu.edu.

New York Medical College, School of Public Health, Valhalla, NY 10595-1691. Offers MPH, MS, DPT, Dr PH, Graduate Certificate. Part-time and evening/weekend programs available. *Faculty:* 42 full-time (22 women), 182 part-time/adjunct (99 women). *Students:* 143 full-time (114 women), 314 part-time (212 women). Average age 31. 154 applicants, 71% accepted, 37 enrolled. In 2006, 76 master's, 13 doctorates awarded. *Degree requirements:* For master's, thesis, registration; for doctorate, thesis/dissertation, project, comprehensive exam, registration. *Entrance requirements:* For master's and doctorate, GRE General Test, minimum undergraduate GPA of 3.0. Additional exam requirements/recommendations for international students:

Public Health—General

New York Medical College (continued)
Required—TOEFL (minimum score 600 paper-based; 250 computer-based; 100 iBT), IELTS (minimum score 7). *Application deadline:* For fall admission, 8/1 priority date for domestic students, 5/15 for international students; for spring admission, 12/1 priority date for domestic students, 10/15 for international students. Applications are processed on a rolling basis. Application fee: $50 ($100 for international students). Electronic applications accepted. *Expenses:* Contact institution. *Financial support:* In 2006–07, 139 students received support; research assistantships with full and partial tuition reimbursements available, teaching assistantships with full and partial tuition reimbursements available, career-related internships or fieldwork, Federal Work-Study, institutionally sponsored loans, health care benefits, tuition waivers (partial), and tuition reimbursements available. Support available to part-time students. Financial award applicants required to submit FAFSA. *Faculty research:* Disaster preparedness, autism, health literacy, adolescent HIV, health disparities. Total annual research expenditures: $500,000. *Unit head:* Dr. Robert W. Amler, Dean, 914-594-4531, Fax: 914-594-4292, E-mail: robert_amler@nymc.edu. *Application contact:* Marian F. McGowan, Information Contact, 914-594-4510, Fax: 914-594-4292, E-mail: sph_admissions@nymc.edu.

See Close-Up on page 2043.

Northern Arizona University, Consortium of Professional Schools and Colleges, College of Health Professions, Program in Public Health, Flagstaff, AZ 86011. Offers health education and health promotion (MPH). *Degree requirements:* For master's, internship. *Entrance requirements:* For master's, GRE General Test or MCAT, minimum GPA of 3.0.

Northern Illinois University, Graduate School, College of Health and Human Sciences, School of Allied Health Professions, De Kalb, IL 60115-2854. Offers physical therapy (MPT); public health (MPH). Admission to MPT program as undergraduate only. *Accreditation:* APTA; CEPH. Part-time programs available. *Faculty:* 9 full-time (6 women). *Students:* 72 full-time (53 women), 31 part-time (26 women); includes 17 minority (8 African Americans, 7 Asian Americans or Pacific Islanders, 2 Hispanic Americans), 30 international. Average age 27. 186 applicants, 55% accepted, 17 enrolled. In 2006, 56 degrees awarded. *Degree requirements:* For master's, internship, research paper in public health, thesis optional. *Entrance requirements:* For master's, GRE General Test, minimum GPA of 2.75. Additional exam requirements/recommendations for international students: Required—TOEFL (minimum score 550 paper-based; 213 computer-based). *Application deadline:* For fall admission, 6/1 for domestic students, 5/1 for international students; for spring admission, 11/1 for domestic students, 10/1 for international students. Applications are processed on a rolling basis. Application fee: $30. Electronic applications accepted. *Financial support:* In 2006–07, 18 research assistantships with full tuition reimbursements were awarded; fellowships with full tuition reimbursements, teaching assistantships with full tuition reimbursements, career-related internships or fieldwork, Federal Work-Study, scholarships/grants, tuition waivers (full), and unspecified assistantships also available. Support available to part-time students. Financial award applicants required to submit FAFSA. *Faculty research:* Stroke rehabilitation, radon exposure prevention, environmental causes of cancer, body image in young girls. *Unit head:* Interim Chair, 815-753-6329, Fax: 815-753-0720.

Northwestern University, The Graduate School, Program in Public Health, Evanston, IL 60208. Offers MPH. *Accreditation:* CEPH. Part-time and evening/weekend programs available. *Entrance requirements:* For master's, GRE General Test. Additional exam requirements/recommendations for international students: Required—TOEFL. *Faculty research:* Cardiovascular epidemiology, cancer epidemiology, nutritional interventions for the prevention of cardiovascular disease and cancer, women's health, outcomes research.

Nova Southeastern University, Health Professions Division, College of Osteopathic Medicine, Program in Public Health, Fort Lauderdale, FL 33314-7796. Offers MPH. *Accreditation:* CEPH. Part-time programs available. *Faculty:* 8 full-time (4 women). *Students:* 16 full-time (8 women), 21 part-time (15 women); includes 18 minority (6 African Americans, 4 Asian Americans or Pacific Islanders, 8 Hispanic Americans), 3 international. Average age 30. 20 applicants, 95% accepted, 17 enrolled. In 2006, 24 degrees awarded. *Degree requirements:* For master's, field experience. *Entrance requirements:* For master's, GRE, MCAT, DAT. Additional exam requirements/recommendations for international students: Required—TOEFL. *Application deadline:* Applications are processed on a rolling basis. Application fee: $50. Electronic applications accepted. *Expenses:* Contact institution. *Financial support:* Teaching assistantships, Federal Work-Study, institutionally sponsored loans, scholarships/grants, and unspecified assistantships available. Financial award applicants required to submit FAFSA. *Unit head:* Dr. Cyril Blaro, Director, E-mail: cblaro@nsu.nova.edu. *Application contact:* James Lawrence, Admissions Counselor, 954-262-1114.

The Ohio State University, College of Public Health, School of Public Health, Columbus, OH 43210. Offers MHA, MPH, MS, PhD, MHA/MBA, MHA/MPA, MHA/MS. *Accreditation:* CAHME; CEPH. Part-time and evening/weekend programs available. *Faculty:* 28 full-time (13 women), 9 part-time/adjunct (2 women). *Students:* 128 full-time (89 women), 95 part-time (65 women); includes 42 minority (19 African Americans, 19 Asian Americans or Pacific Islanders, 4 Hispanic Americans), 14 international. 242 applicants, 71% accepted, 33 enrolled. In 2006, 65 master's, 5 doctorates awarded. Terminal master's awarded for partial completion of doctoral program. *Degree requirements:* For master's, thesis (for some programs), project paper, comprehensive exam; for doctorate, thesis/dissertation. *Entrance requirements:* For master's, GRE or GMAT or MCAT (with permission of program). Additional exam requirements/recommendations for international students: Required—TOEFL (minimum score 600 paper-based; 250 computer-based). *Application deadline:* For fall admission, 8/15 priority date for domestic students, 7/1 priority date for international students; for winter admission, 12/1 priority date for domestic students, 11/1 priority date for international students; for spring admission, 3/1 priority date for domestic students, 2/1 priority date for international students. Applications are processed on a rolling basis. Application fee: $40 ($50 for international students). Electronic applications accepted. *Expenses:* Tuition, state resident: full-time $9,438. Tuition, nonresident: full-time $22,791. Tuition and fees vary according to course load, campus/location and program. *Financial support:* In 2006–07, 12 fellowships with full tuition reimbursements (averaging $14,400 per year), 21 research assistantships with full tuition reimbursements (averaging $12,000 per year) were awarded; Federal Work-Study, institutionally sponsored loans, traineeships, and unspecified assistantships also available. Support available to part-time students. Financial award application deadline: 7/1. *Faculty research:* Occupational epidemiology, carcinogenesis and chemoprevention, cancer epidemiology and control, environmental exposure and the health of rural populations, substance abuse prevention. Total annual research expenditures: $2.6 million. *Unit head:* Robert J. Caswell, Graduate Studies Committee Chair, 614-293-4014, Fax: 614-293-3937, E-mail: caswell.1@osu.edu. *Application contact:* 614-292-9444, Fax: 614-292-3895, E-mail: domestic.grad@osu.edu.

Old Dominion University, College of Health Sciences, Program in Community Health and Environmental Health, Norfolk, VA 23529. Offers community health professions (MS); environmental health (MS); health care administration (MS); long-term care administration (MS); wellness and promotion (MS). Part-time and evening/weekend programs available. Post-baccalaureate distance learning degree programs offered (no on-campus study). *Faculty:* 5 full-time (4 women), 5 part-time/adjunct (1 woman). *Students:* 10 full-time (7 women), 33 part-time (24 women); includes 6 minority (5 African Americans, 1 Asian American or Pacific Islander), 8 international. Average age 33. 32 applicants, 88% accepted, 15 enrolled. In 2006, 19 degrees awarded. *Degree requirements:* For master's, oral exam, written exam, thesis optional. *Entrance requirements:* For master's, GRE General Test, minimum GPA of 2.75. Additional exam requirements/recommendations for international students: Required—TOEFL. *Application deadline:* For fall admission, 8/1 priority date for domestic students, 7/1 priority date for international students; for winter admission, 11/1 priority date for domestic students, 10/1 priority date for international students; for spring admission, 4/1 priority date for domestic students, 3/1 priority date for international students. Applications are processed on a rolling basis. Application fee: $40. Electronic applications accepted. *Expenses:* Tuition, area resident: Part-time $285 per credit hour. Tuition, nonresident: part-time $715 per credit hour. Required fees: $94 per semester. *Financial support:* In 2006–07, 5 research assistantships with tuition reimbursements (averaging $14,000 per year) were awarded; career-related internships or fieldwork, institutionally sponsored loans, scholarships/grants, and tuition waivers (partial) also available. Support available to part-time students. Financial award applicants required to submit FAFSA. *Faculty research:* Toxicology, domestic violence, health policy and planning, environmental hazards, obesity, substance abuse, minority health spirituality, women's health. Total annual research expenditures: $150,133. *Unit head:* Dr. Clare Houseman, Chair, 757-683-4259, Fax: 757-683-4410, E-mail: chpgdd@odu.edu.

Old Dominion University, College of Health Sciences, Program in Public Health, Norfolk, VA 23529. Offers MPH. *Faculty:* 4 full-time (2 women), 6 part-time/adjunct (3 women). *Students:* 2 full-time (1 woman), 52 part-time (23 women); includes 10 African Americans, 3 Asian Americans or Pacific Islanders. Average age 30. 67 applicants, 60% accepted, 28 enrolled. In 2006, 7 degrees awarded. *Degree requirements:* For master's, field practicum, integrative seminar. *Entrance requirements:* For master's, GRE, MCAT. Additional exam requirements/recommendations for international students: Required—TOEFL (minimum score 650 paper-based; 278 computer-based). *Application deadline:* For fall admission, 5/31 priority date for domestic students, 4/30 for international students. Application fee: $50 ($100 for international students). Electronic applications accepted. *Expenses:* Tuition, area resident: Part-time $285 per credit hour. Tuition, nonresident: part-time $715 per credit hour. Required fees: $94 per semester. *Financial support:* Application deadline: 5/1; *Faculty research:* Community-based health research. *Unit head:* Dr. David Matson, Graduate Program Director, 757-446-6120, Fax: 757-446-6121, E-mail: mphinfo@evms.edu.

Oregon State University, Graduate School, College of Health and Human Sciences, Department of Public Health, Corvallis, OR 97331. Offers environmental health and occupational safety management (MAIS, MS); health management and policy (MS); health promotion and health behavior (MAIS, MAT, MS); public health (MPH, PhD). *Accreditation:* CEPH. *Faculty:* 11 full-time (7 women), 5 part-time/adjunct (3 women). *Students:* 67 full-time (54 women), 31 part-time (21 women); includes 16 minority (4 African Americans, 1 American Indian/Alaska Native, 7 Asian Americans or Pacific Islanders, 4 Hispanic Americans), 7 international. Average age 33. In 2006, 20 master's, 5 doctorates awarded. Terminal master's awarded for partial completion of doctoral program. *Degree requirements:* For doctorate, one foreign language, thesis/dissertation. *Entrance requirements:* For master's and doctorate, minimum GPA of 3.0 in last 90 hours. Additional exam requirements/recommendations for international students: Required—TOEFL. *Application deadline:* For fall admission, 3/1 for domestic students. Applications are processed on a rolling basis. Application fee: $50. *Financial support:* Fellowships, research assistantships, teaching assistantships, career-related internships or fieldwork, Federal Work-Study, and institutionally sponsored loans available. Support available to part-time students. Financial award application deadline: 2/1. *Faculty research:* Traffic safety, health safety, injury control, health promotion. *Unit head:* Dr. S. Marie Harvey, Chair, 541-737-2686, Fax: 541-737-4001.

Ponce School of Medicine, Program in Public Health, Ponce, PR 00732-7004. Offers MPH. *Degree requirements:* For master's, one foreign language, comprehensive exam, registration. *Entrance requirements:* For master's, GRE General Test or EXADEP, proficiency in Spanish and English, minimum GPA of 2.7, 3 letters of recommendation.

Portland State University, Graduate Studies, College of Urban and Public Affairs, School of Community Health, Portland, OR 97207-0751. Offers gerontology (Certificate); health education (MA, MS); health education and health promotion (MPH); health studies (MPA, MPH), including health administration and policy. *Accreditation:* CEPH. Part-time programs available. *Faculty:* 13 full-time (9 women), 8 part-time/adjunct (6 women). *Students:* 36 full-time (30 women), 34 part-time (27 women); includes 9 minority (1 African American, 1 Asian American or Pacific Islander, 7 Hispanic Americans), 5 international. Average age 32. 73 applicants, 84% accepted, 34 enrolled. In 2006, 20 degrees awarded. *Degree requirements:* For master's, oral and written exams. *Entrance requirements:* For master's, GRE General Test, 3 letters of recommendation. Additional exam requirements/recommendations for international students: Required—TOEFL (minimum score 550 paper-based; 213 computer-based). *Application deadline:* For fall admission, 2/1 for domestic and international students. Application fee: $50. *Expenses:* Tuition, state resident: full-time $6,426; part-time $238 per credit. Tuition, nonresident: full-time $11,016; part-time $408 per credit. Tuition and fees vary according to course load. *Financial support:* In 2006–07, 4 research assistantships with full tuition reimbursements (averaging $7,286 per year) were awarded; fellowships, teaching assistantships, career-related internships or fieldwork, Federal Work-Study, scholarships/grants, and unspecified assistantships also available. Support available to part-time students. Financial award application deadline: 3/1; financial award applicants required to submit FAFSA. Total annual research expenditures: $766,046. *Unit head:* Carlos J. Crespo, Interim Director, 503-725-5102, Fax: 503-725-5100. *Application contact:* Elizabeth Bull, Assistant to the Director, 503-725-4592, Fax: 503-725-5100, E-mail: bulle@pdx.edu.

Purdue University, School of Veterinary Medicine and Graduate School, Graduate Programs in Veterinary Medicine, Department of Comparative Pathobiology, West Lafayette, IN 47907. Offers biochemistry and molecular biology (MS, PhD); comparative epidemiology (MS, PhD); epidemiology (MS, PhD); immunology (MS, PhD); infectious diseases (MS, PhD); interdisciplinary genetics (PhD); laboratory animal medicine (MS, PhD); microbiology (MS, PhD); molecular virology (MS, PhD); parasitology (MS, PhD); pathobiology (MS, PhD); public health epidemiology (MS, PhD); toxicology (MS, PhD); veterinary anatomic pathology (MS, PhD); veterinary clinical pathology (MS, PhD); virology (MS, PhD). *Faculty:* 34 full-time (8 women). *Students:* 45 full-time (19 women), 3 part-time (1 woman); includes 1 minority (African American), 29 international. Average age 35. In 2006, 3 master's, 2 doctorates awarded. Terminal master's awarded for partial completion of doctoral program. *Degree requirements:* For master's, thesis (for some programs); for doctorate, thesis/dissertation. *Entrance requirements:* For master's and doctorate, GRE General Test. Additional exam requirements/recommendations for international students: Required—TOEFL (minimum score 575 paper-based; 232 computer-based), IELTS (minimum score 7), TWE (minimum score 4). *Application deadline:* For fall admission, 8/12 for domestic students, 6/15 for international students; for spring admission, 1/12 for domestic students, 10/15 for international students. Application fee: $55. Electronic applications accepted. *Financial support:* Fellowships, research assistantships, teaching assistantships available. Financial award application deadline: 3/1; financial award applicants required to submit FAFSA. *Unit head:* Dr. H. Hogen Esch, Head, 765-494-7543.

Regis College, Department of Health Product Regulation and Health Policy, Weston, MA 02493. Offers MS. Part-time and evening/weekend programs available. *Faculty:* 2 part-time/adjunct (1 woman). *Students:* 2 full-time (1 woman), 25 part-time (20 women); includes 2 minority (1 African American, 1 Asian American or Pacific Islander). Average age 35. 11 applicants, 100% accepted, 9 enrolled. In 2006, 6 degrees awarded. *Degree requirements:* For master's, internship, thesis optional. *Entrance requirements:* For master's, GRE or MAT. Application fee: $50. *Expenses:* Tuition: Full-time $23,680; part-time $665 per credit hour. *Financial support:* Career-related internships or fieldwork available. Financial award applicants required to submit FAFSA. *Faculty research:* FDA regulatory affairs medical device. *Unit head:* Charles Burr, Director, 781-768-7008, E-mail: charles.burr@regiscollege.edu.

Rutgers, The State University of New Jersey, New Brunswick, Edward J. Bloustein School of Planning and Public Policy, Program in Public Health, New Brunswick, NJ 08901-1281. Offers MPH, Dr PH, PhD, MBA/MPH, MD/MPH. *Accreditation:* CEPH. Part-time and evening/weekend programs available. *Degree requirements:* For master's, internship; for doctorate, thesis/dissertation. *Entrance requirements:* For master's, GMAT, GRE General Test; for doctorate, GRE General Test, MPH (Dr PH). Additional exam requirements/recommendations for international students: Required—TOEFL. *Faculty research:* Epidemiology, risk perception, statistical research design, health care utilization, health promotion.

Saint Louis University, Graduate School, School of Public Health and Graduate School, Department of Health Management and Policy, St. Louis, MO 63103-2097. Offers health administration (MHA); public health studies (PhD). *Accreditation:* CAHME. Part-time programs available. *Faculty:* 11 full-time (4 women), 15 part-time/adjunct (0 women). *Students:* 33 full-time (17 women), 8 part-time (6 women); includes 11 minority (8 African Americans, 3 Asian Americans or Pacific Islanders), 2 international. Average age 29. 79 applicants, 68% accepted, 17 enrolled. In 2006, 28 master's, 3 doctorates awarded. *Degree requirements:* For master's, internship. *Entrance requirements:* For master's, GMAT or GRE General Test, LSAT, MCAT, letters of recommendation, resumé. Additional exam requirements/recommendations for international students: Required—TOEFL (minimum score 525 paper-based; 194 computer-based). *Application deadline:* For fall admission, 7/1 for domestic students, 5/1 for international students; for spring admission, 11/1 for domestic students. Applications are processed on a rolling basis. Application fee: $40. *Expenses:* Tuition: Part-time $800 per credit hour. Required fees: $105 per semester. *Financial support:* In 2006–07, 17 students received support. Federal Work-Study, scholarships/grants, traineeships, health care benefits, and unspecified assistantships available. Support available to part-time students. Financial award application deadline: 6/1; financial award applicants required to submit FAFSA. *Faculty research:* Management of HIV/AIDS, rural health services, prevention of asthma, genetics and health services use, health insurance and access to care. *Unit head:* Dr. Richard S. Kurz, Chairperson, 314-977-8111, Fax: 314-977-8150, E-mail: kurzrs@slu.edu. *Application contact:* Gary Behrman, Associate Dean of the Graduate School, 314-977-3827, E-mail: behrmang@slu.edu.

Saint Xavier University, Graduate Studies, Graham School of Management, Chicago, IL 60655-3105. Offers e-commerce (MBA); employee health benefits (Certificate); finance (MBA, MS); financial analysis and investments (MBA); financial planning (MBA, Certificate); financial trading and practice (MBA, Certificate); generalist/administration (MBA); health administration (MBA, MS); managed care (Certificate); management (MBA, MS); marketing (MBA); public and non-profit management (MBA); public health (MPH); service management (MBA); training and performance management (MBA); MBA/MS. *Accreditation:* ACBSP. Part-time and evening/weekend programs available. *Faculty:* 27. *Students:* 67 full-time (32 women), 291 part-time (152 women). Average age 35. In 2006, 61 degrees awarded. *Entrance requirements:* For master's, GMAT, minimum GPA of 3.0, 2 years of work experience. *Application deadline:* For fall admission, 8/15 for domestic students. Applications are processed on a rolling basis. Application fee: $35. Electronic applications accepted. *Expenses:* Contact institution. *Financial support:* Career-related internships or fieldwork available. Support available to part-time students. Financial award applicants required to submit FAFSA. *Unit head:* Dr. John Eber, Dean, 773-298-3601, Fax: 773-298-3601, E-mail: eber@sxu.edu. *Application contact:* Beth Gierach, Managing Director of Admission, 773-298-3053, Fax: 773-298-3076, E-mail: gierach@sxu.edu.

San Diego State University, Graduate and Research Affairs, College of Health and Human Services, Graduate School of Public Health, San Diego, CA 92182. Offers environmental health (MPH); epidemiology (MPH, PhD), including biostatistics (MPH); global emergency preparedness and response (MS); health behavior (PhD); health promotion (MPH); health services administration (MPH); toxicology (MS); MSW/MPH. *Accreditation:* ABET (one or more programs are accredited); CAHME (one or more programs are accredited); CEPH (one or more programs are accredited). Part-time programs available. *Degree requirements:* For master's, thesis (for some programs), comprehensive exam (for some programs); for doctorate, thesis/dissertation. *Entrance requirements:* For master's, GMAT (health services administration MPH), GRE General Test; for doctorate, GRE General Test. Additional exam requirements/recommendations for international students: Required—TOEFL. *Faculty research:* Evaluation of tobacco, AIDS prevalence and prevention, mammography, infant death project, Alzheimer's in elderly Chinese.

San Francisco State University, Division of Graduate Studies, College of Health and Human Services, Department of Health Education, San Francisco, CA 94132-1722. Offers MPH. *Accreditation:* CEPH. Part-time programs available. *Faculty:* 4 full-time (all women), 1 (woman) part-time/adjunct. *Students:* Average age 36. In 2006, 20 degrees awarded. *Degree requirements:* For master's, culminating project. *Entrance requirements:* For master's, minimum GPA of 2.5 in last 60 units. *Application deadline:* For fall admission, 11/30 priority date for domestic students. Applications are processed on a rolling basis. Application fee: $55. *Financial support:* Application deadline: 3/1. *Faculty research:* Health behavior, gerontology, homelessness, community health. *Unit head:* Dr. Mary Beth Love, Chair, 415-338-1413, E-mail: love@sfsu.edu.

San Jose State University, Graduate Studies and Research, College of Applied Sciences and Arts, Department of Health Science, San Jose, CA 95192-0001. Offers applied social gerontology (Certificate); community health education (MPH). *Accreditation:* CEPH (one or more programs are accredited). *Students:* 26 full-time (22 women), 45 part-time (37 women); includes 30 minority (3 African Americans, 12 Asian Americans or Pacific Islanders, 15 Hispanic Americans), 4 international. Average age 35. 112 applicants, 33% accepted, 20 enrolled. In 2006, 30 degrees awarded. *Entrance requirements:* For master's, GRE General Test. *Application deadline:* For fall admission, 6/29 for domestic students; for spring admission, 11/30 for domestic students. Applications are processed on a rolling basis. Application fee: $59. Electronic applications accepted. *Financial support:* Career-related internships or fieldwork, Federal Work-Study, and institutionally sponsored loans available. Support available to part-time students. Financial award applicants required to submit FAFSA. *Faculty research:* Behavioral science in occupational and health care settings, epidemiology in health care settings. *Unit head:* Kathleen Roe, Chair, 408-924-2970, Fax: 408-924-2979.

Sarah Lawrence College, Graduate Studies, Program in Health Advocacy, Bronxville, NY 10708-5999. Offers MA. Part-time programs available. *Faculty:* 11 part-time/adjunct (8 women). *Students:* 12 full-time (all women), 16 part-time (all women); includes 2 minority (1 African American, 1 Hispanic American). Average age 45. 13 applicants, 92% accepted, 7 enrolled. In 2006, 9 degrees awarded. *Degree requirements:* For master's, fieldwork. *Entrance requirements:* For master's, previous course work in biology and microeconomics, minimum B average in undergraduate course work. Additional exam requirements/recommendations for international students: Required—TOEFL (minimum score 600 paper-based). *Application deadline:* For fall admission, 3/31 priority date for domestic students. Applications are processed on a rolling basis. Application fee: $60. *Expenses:* Contact institution. Tuition and fees vary according to program and student level. *Financial support:* In 2006–07, 8 fellowships (averaging $2,922 per year) were awarded; career-related internships or fieldwork and scholarships/grants also available. Support available to part-time students. Financial award application deadline: 3/1. *Unit head:* Marsha H. Huist, Director, 914-395-2371, E-mail: mhuist@mail.slc.edu. *Application contact:* Susan Guma, Dean of Graduate Studies, 914-395-2373, E-mail: sguma@mail.slc.edu.

See Close-Up on page 2049.

Southern Connecticut State University, School of Graduate Studies, School of Health and Human Services, Department of Public Health, New Haven, CT 06515-1355. Offers MPH. *Accreditation:* CEPH. Part-time and evening/weekend programs available. *Faculty:* 9 full-time. *Students:* 34 full-time (29 women), 51 part-time (39 women); includes 19 minority (13 African Americans, 6 Asian Americans or Pacific Islanders), 2 international. 56 applicants, 63% accepted, 29 enrolled. In 2006, 25 degrees awarded. *Degree requirements:* For master's, thesis or alternative. *Entrance requirements:* For master's, minimum undergraduate QPA of 3.0 in graduate major field or 2.5 overall, interview. *Application deadline:* For fall admission, 3/15 for domestic students. Application fee: $50. Electronic applications accepted. *Financial support:* In 2006–07, 1 teaching assistantship was awarded; career-related internships or fieldwork also available. Financial award application deadline: 4/15; financial award applicants required to submit FAFSA. *Unit head:* Dr. William Faraclas, Chairperson, 203-392-6950, Fax: 203-392-6965, E-mail: faraclas@southernct.edu. *Application contact:* Dr. Michael Perlin, Graduate Coordinator, 203-392-6950, Fax: 203-392-6965, E-mail: perlin@southernct.edu.

State University of New York Downstate Medical Center, College of Medicine, Program in Public Health, Brooklyn, NY 11203-2098. Offers urban and immigrant health (MPH); MD/MPH. *Accreditation:* CEPH. Part-time programs available. *Degree requirements:* For master's, practicum. *Entrance requirements:* For master's, GRE, MCAT or OAT, 2 letters of recommendation, minimum undergraduate GPA of 3.0. Additional exam requirements/recommendations for international students: Required—TOEFL (minimum score 550 paper-based). *Expenses:* Tuition, state resident: full-time $6,900; part-time $288 per credit. Tuition, nonresident: full-time $10,920; part-time $455 per credit. Required fees: $100; $20 per credit. $50 per semester. Tuition and fees vary according to course load.

See Close-Up on page 2051.

Stony Brook University, State University of New York, Stony Brook University Medical Center, School of Medicine, Program in Public Health, Stony Brook, NY 11794. Offers community health (MPH); evaluation sciences (MPH); family violence (MPH); health economics (MPH); population health (MPH); substance abuse (MPH). *Faculty:* 7 full-time (3 women), 1 part-time/adjunct (0 women). *Students:* 10 full-time (9 women), 28 part-time (23 women); includes 6 minority (4 African Americans, 2 Asian Americans or Pacific Islanders), 3 international. Average age 39. 83 applicants, 57% accepted. In 2006, 3 degrees awarded. *Entrance requirements:* For master's, GRE, 3 references. Additional exam requirements/recommendations for international students: Required—TOEFL. *Application deadline:* For fall admission, 1/15 for domestic and international students. Application fee: $60. Electronic applications accepted. *Expenses:* Tuition, state resident: full-time $6,900; part-time $288 per credit. Tuition, nonresident: full-time $10,920; part-time $455 per credit. *Faculty research:* Population health, health service research, health economics. *Unit head:* Dr. Raymond L. Goldsteen, Director, 631-444-2074, Fax: 631-444-3480, E-mail: raymond.goldsteen@stonybrook.edu. *Application contact:* Patricia M. Villa, Assistant, 631-444-2074, Fax: 631-444-3480, E-mail: patricia.villa@stonybrook.edu.

Announcement: The Graduate Program in Public Health is a small, selective program in the School of Medicine that awards a Master of Public Health (MPH) degree. The mission of the program is to train individuals with strong analytical skills for public health practice. The program emphasizes population health and clinical outcomes research.

See Close-Up on page 2053.

Temple University, Health Sciences Center and Graduate School, College of Health Professions, Department of Public Health, Philadelphia, PA 19122-6096. Offers Ed M, MPH, MS, PhD. *Accreditation:* CEPH (one or more programs are accredited). Part-time and evening/weekend programs available. *Faculty:* 8 full-time (5 women). *Students:* 22 full-time (16 women), 75 part-time (51 women); includes 32 minority (24 African Americans, 3 Asian Americans or Pacific Islanders, 5 Hispanic Americans), 4 international. 92 applicants, 47% accepted, 26 enrolled. In 2006, 21 master's, 7 doctorates awarded. Terminal master's awarded for partial completion of doctoral program. *Degree requirements:* For doctorate, thesis/dissertation. *Entrance requirements:* For master's and doctorate, minimum undergraduate GPA of 3.0. Additional exam requirements/recommendations for international students: Required—TOEFL (minimum score 550 paper-based; 213 computer-based; 79 iBT). Application fee: $50. Electronic applications accepted. *Expenses:* Tuition, state resident: full-time $12,264; part-time $511 per credit. Tuition, nonresident: full-time $17,904; part-time $746 per credit. Required fees: $84 per course. Tuition and fees vary according to program. *Financial support:* Fellowships with tuition reimbursements, research assistantships with tuition reimbursements, teaching assistantships with tuition reimbursements, career-related internships or fieldwork, Federal Work-Study, institutionally sponsored loans, scholarships/grants, and tuition waivers (partial) available. Financial award application deadline: 1/15; financial award applicants required to submit FAFSA. *Faculty research:* Program development and evaluation in HIV prevention, violence prevention, women's health policy, psychosocial aspects of disability. *Unit head:* Dr. Alice Hausman, Chair, 215-204-8726, Fax: 215-204-1854, E-mail: alice.hausman@temple.edu.

Texas A&M Health Science Center, School of Rural Public Health, College Station, TX 77843-1266. Offers environmental/occupational health (MPH); epidemiology/biostatistics (MPH); health policy/management (MPH); social and behavioral health (MPH). *Accreditation:* CEPH. Part-time programs available. Postbaccalaureate distance learning degree programs offered (no on-campus study). *Faculty:* 16 full-time (7 women), 4 part-time/adjunct (1 woman). *Students:* 43 full-time (27 women), 118 part-time (76 women); includes 63 minority (13 African Americans, 13 Asian Americans or Pacific Islanders, 37 Hispanic Americans), 1 international. Average age 32. 162 applicants, 83% accepted, 118 enrolled. In 2006, 10 degrees awarded. *Degree requirements:* For master's, thesis optional. *Entrance requirements:* For master's, GRE General Test, minimum undergraduate GPA of 3.0. *Application deadline:* For fall admission, 8/27 for domestic students; for spring admission, 1/14 for domestic students. Applications are processed on a rolling basis. Application fee: $35 ($75 for international students). Electronic applications accepted. *Financial support:* In 2006–07, research assistantships (averaging $10,800 per year). *Faculty research:* Tobacco cessation, youth health risk. Total annual research expenditures: $1.7 million. *Unit head:* Dr. Ciro V. Sumaya, Dean. *Application contact:* Dr. James Robinson, Professor/Special Advisor to the Dean, 409-845-2387, Fax: 409-862-8371, E-mail: jrobinson@medicine.tamu.edu.

Texas A&M University, College of Veterinary Medicine, Graduate Programs in Veterinary Medicine, Department of Veterinary Integrative Biosciences, College Station, TX 77843. Offers epidemiology (MS); food safety/toxicology (MS); veterinary anatomy (MS, PhD); veterinary public health (MS). *Faculty:* 22 full-time (8 women), 6 part-time/adjunct (2 women). *Students:* 30 full-time (22 women), 11 part-time (8 women); includes 4 minority (1 American Indian/Alaska Native, 3 Asian Americans or Pacific Islanders), 9 international. Average age 30. 14 applicants, 93% accepted, 11 enrolled. In 2006, 4 master's, 1 doctorate awarded. Terminal master's awarded for partial completion of doctoral program. *Degree requirements:* For master's and doctorate, thesis/dissertation, comprehensive exam, registration. *Entrance requirements:* For master's and doctorate, GRE General Test, minimum undergraduate GPA of 3.0. Additional exam requirements/recommendations for international students: Required—TOEFL. *Application deadline:* For fall admission, 7/15 priority date for domestic students, 4/1 priority date for international students; for spring admission, 10/1 priority date for domestic students, 9/15 priority date for international students. Applications are processed on a rolling basis. Application fee: $50 ($75 for international students). Electronic applications accepted. *Expenses:* Tuition, state resident: full-time $4,697. Tuition, nonresident: full-time $11,297. Required fees: $2,272. *Financial support:* In 2006–07, fellowships (averaging $18,000 per year), research assistantships (averaging $15,600 per year), teaching assistantships (averaging $15,600 per year) were awarded; institutionally sponsored loans, unspecified assistantships, and clinical associateships also available. Financial award application deadline: 7/15; financial award applicants required to submit FAFSA. *Faculty research:* Metal toxicology, reproductive biology, genetics of neural development, developmental biology, environmental toxicology. *Unit head:* Dr. Evelyn Tiffany-Castiglioni, Head, 979-845-2828, Fax: 979-847-8981, E-mail: ecastiglioni@cvm.tamu.edu. *Application contact:* Dr. Jane Welsh, Chair, Fax: 979-847-8981, E-mail: jwelsh@cum.tamu.edu.

Texas Wesleyan University, Graduate Programs, Programs in Business Administration, Fort Worth, TX 76105-1536. Offers business administration (MBA); geriatrics (MSHA); health administration (MSHA); public health (MSHA). *Accreditation:* ACBSP. Part-time and evening/weekend programs available. *Faculty:* 13 full-time (3 women), 4 part-time/adjunct (1 woman). *Students:* 15 full-time (7 women), 42 part-time (30 women); includes 27 minority (14 African Americans, 1 American Indian/Alaska Native, 4 Asian Americans or Pacific Islanders, 8 Hispanic Americans). Average age 31. In 2006, 18 degrees awarded. *Degree requirements:* For master's, capstone course. *Entrance requirements:* For master's, GMAT, minimum GPA of 3.0 in final 60 hours of undergraduate course work, 2.75 overall. *Application deadline:* Applications are processed on a rolling basis. Application fee: $30 ($50 for international students). Electronic applications accepted. *Expenses:* Contact institution. Tuition and fees vary according to program. *Financial support:* Federal Work-Study, scholarships/grants, and tuition waivers (full and partial) available. Support available to part-time students. Financial award application

Public Health—General

Texas Wesleyan University (continued)
deadline: 3/15; financial award applicants required to submit FAFSA. *Unit head:* Dr. Charles Little, Director, 817-531-6500, Fax: 817-531-6585.

Thomas Jefferson University, Jefferson College of Graduate Studies, Program in Public Health, Philadelphia, PA 19107. Offers MS. Part-time and evening/weekend programs available. *Students:* 34 applicants, 65% accepted, 17 enrolled. In 2006, 15 degrees awarded. *Entrance requirements:* For master's, GRE General Test or MCAT, minimum GPA of 3.0. Additional exam requirements/recommendations for international students: Required—TOEFL (minimum score 213 computer-based). *Application deadline:* For fall admission, 3/1 priority date for domestic and international students; for winter admission, 12/1 priority date for domestic students, 6/1 priority date for international students; for spring admission, 4/1 priority date for domestic students. Application fee: $50. *Expenses:* Tuition: Full-time $15,340; part-time $790 per credit. Required fees: $300. *Financial support:* In 2006–07, 7 students received support. *Unit head:* Dr. Dennis M. Gross, Associate Dean, 215-503-0156, Fax: 215-503-3433, E-mail: dennis.gross@jefferson.edu. *Application contact:* Eleanor M. Gorman, Assistant Coordinator, Graduate Center Programs, 215-503-5799, Fax: 215-503-3433, E-mail: eleanor.gorman@jefferson.edu.

Touro University College of Osteopathic Medicine, Professional Program, Vallejo, CA 94592. Offers education (MA); osteopathic medicine (DO); pharmacy (Pharm D); physician assistant studies (MS); public health (MPH). *Accreditation:* AOsA; ARC-PA. *Faculty:* 61 full-time (26 women), 30 part-time/adjunct (16 women). *Students:* 950 full-time (579 women); includes 354 minority (39 African Americans, 5 American Indian/Alaska Native, 258 Asian Americans or Pacific Islanders, 52 Hispanic Americans). Average age 26. 2,113 applicants, 13% accepted, 269 enrolled. In 2006, 109 first professional degrees, 43 master's awarded. *Median time to degree:* Of those who began their doctoral program in fall 1998, 98% received their degree in 8 years or less. *Entrance requirements:* For first professional degree and master's, BS/BA. *Application deadline:* For fall admission, 6/1 for domestic students. Applications are processed on a rolling basis. Application fee: $100. Electronic applications accepted. *Financial support:* In 2006–07, 3 fellowships (averaging $3,000 per year) were awarded. *Faculty research:* Diabetes, heart disease. *Application contact:* Steve Davis, Admissions Counselor, 707-638-5527, Fax: 707-638-5270, E-mail: sdavis@touro.edu.

Touro University International, College of Health Sciences, Cypress, CA 90630. Offers MS, PhD, Certificate. Part-time and evening/weekend programs available. Postbaccalaureate distance learning degree programs offered (no on-campus study). In 2006, 322 master's, 21 doctorates awarded. *Entrance requirements:* For master's, minimum GPA of 3.0; for doctorate, minimum GPA of 3.4. Additional exam requirements/recommendations for international students: Required—TOEFL (minimum score 550 paper-based). Application fee: $75. *Expenses:* Tuition: Part-time $300 per credit hour. Tuition and fees vary according to course level and program. *Unit head:* Dr. Edith Neumann, Vice President for Academic Affairs, 714-816-0366 Ext. 2030, Fax: 714-226-9844, E-mail: eneumann@tourou.edu.

Trinity (Washington) University, School of Professional Studies, Washington, DC 20017-1094. Offers business administration (MBA); communication (MA); information security management (MS); organizational management (MSA), including federal program management, human resource management, nonprofit management, organizational development, public and community health. Part-time and evening/weekend programs available. *Degree requirements:* For master's, thesis (for some programs), capstone project (MSA). *Entrance requirements:* For master's, minimum GPA of 2.5. Additional exam requirements/recommendations for international students: Required—TOEFL (minimum score 550 paper-based; 213 computer-based).

Tufts University, School of Medicine, Public Health and Professional Degree Programs, Medford, MA 02155. Offers biomedical sciences (MS); health communication (MS); pain research, education and policy (MS); public health (MPH). *Accreditation:* CEPH (one or more programs are accredited). Part-time and evening/weekend programs available. *Students:* 92 full-time (64 women), 40 part-time (30 women); includes 22 minority (5 African Americans, 12 Asian Americans or Pacific Islanders, 5 Hispanic Americans), 7 international. 220 applicants, 77% accepted, 69 enrolled. In 2006, 62 degrees awarded. *Degree requirements:* For master's, thesis (for some programs). *Entrance requirements:* For master's, GRE General Test. Additional exam requirements/recommendations for international students: Required—TOEFL. *Application deadline:* For fall admission, 4/15 priority date for domestic students, 4/15 for international students; for spring admission, 10/25 priority date for domestic students, 10/1 for international students. Applications are processed on a rolling basis. Application fee: $65. Electronic applications accepted. *Expenses:* Contact institution. Tuition and fees vary according to degree level and program. *Financial support:* Federal Work-Study and scholarships/grants available. Support available to part-time students. Financial award application deadline: 4/13; financial award applicants required to submit FAFSA. *Faculty research:* Environmental and occupational health, nutrition, epidemiology, health communication, health services management and policy. *Unit head:* Dr. Harris Berman, Dean, Public Health and Professional Degree Programs, 617-636-0935. *Application contact:* Peg Martin, Assistant Director of Admissions and Student Services, 617-636-0935, Fax: 617-636-3949, E-mail: med-phpd@tufts.edu.

Tulane University, School of Public Health and Tropical Medicine, New Orleans, LA 70118-5669. Offers MHA, MMM, MPH, MPHTM, MS, MSPH, Dr PH, PhD, Sc D, Diploma, JD/MHA, JD/MSPH, MD/MPH, MD/MPHTM, MD/MSPH, MD/PhD, MSW/MPH. MS, PhD offered through the Graduate School. *Accreditation:* CAHME (one or more programs are accredited); CEPH (one or more programs are accredited). Part-time and evening/weekend programs available. Postbaccalaureate distance learning degree programs offered (no on-campus study). *Faculty:* 118 full-time, 42 part-time/adjunct. *Students:* 791 full-time, 412 part-time; includes 135 minority (39 African Americans, 2 American Indian/Alaska Native, 17 Asian Americans or Pacific Islanders, 77 Hispanic Americans), 234 international. 855 applicants, 82% accepted, 380 enrolled. In 2006, 420 master's, 9 doctorates awarded. Terminal master's awarded for partial completion of doctoral program. *Degree requirements:* For master's, comprehensive exam (for some programs); for doctorate, thesis/dissertation, comprehensive exam. *Entrance requirements:* For master's and doctorate, GRE General Test. Additional exam requirements/recommendations for international students: Required—TOEFL. *Application deadline:* For fall admission, 4/15 priority date for domestic and international students; for winter admission, 10/15 priority date for domestic and international students. Applications are processed on a rolling basis. Application fee: $40. Electronic applications accepted. *Expenses:* Contact institution. *Financial support:* Fellowships, research assistantships, teaching assistantships, Federal Work-Study, scholarships/grants, and traineeships available. Support available to part-time students. Financial award application deadline: 4/15; financial award applicants required to submit FAFSA. Total annual research expenditures: $12.9 million. *Unit head:* Dr. Pierre Beukens, Dean, 504-588-5397, Fax: 504-588-5718. *Application contact:* Jeffrey T. Johnson, Associate Dean for Admissions and Student Affairs, 504-588-5387, Fax: 504-584-1667, E-mail: jeff@tulane.edu.

Uniformed Services University of the Health Sciences, School of Medicine, Programs in Biomedical Sciences, Bethesda, MD 20814-4799. Offers emerging infectious diseases (PhD); medical and clinical psychology (PhD), including clinical psychology, medical psychology; medical history (MMH); microbiology and immunology (PhD); molecular and cell biology (PhD); neuroscience (PhD); pathology (PhD), including comparative pathology, molecular pathobiology; preventive medicine and biometrics (MPH, MSPH, MTMH, Dr PH, PhD), including environmental health science (PhD), medical zoology (PhD), public health (MPH, MSPH, Dr PH), tropical medicine and hygiene (MTMH). Terminal master's awarded for partial completion of doctoral program. *Degree requirements:* For master's, thesis or alternative, comprehensive exam; for doctorate, thesis/dissertation, qualifying exam, comprehensive exam. *Entrance requirements:* For master's, GRE General Test; for doctorate, GRE General Test, minimum GPA of 3.0. Additional exam requirements/recommendations for international students: Required—TOEFL.

Uniformed Services University of the Health Sciences, School of Medicine, Programs in Biomedical Sciences, Department of Preventive Medicine and Biometrics, Program in Public Health, Bethesda, MD 20814-4799. Offers MPH, MSPH, Dr PH. *Accreditation:* CEPH (one or more programs are accredited). *Degree requirements:* For master's, comprehensive exam; for doctorate, thesis/dissertation, qualifying exam. *Entrance requirements:* For master's, GRE General Test; for doctorate, GRE General Test, minimum GPA of 3.0. Additional exam requirements/recommendations for international students: Required—TOEFL. *Faculty research:* Epidemiology, biostatistics, health services administration, environmental and occupational health, tropical public health.

Universidad Central del Este, Graduate School, San Pedro de Macoris, Dominican Republic. Offers accounting (M Ad); administration (M Ad); architecture (M Arch); civil engineering (ME); electromechanical engineering (ME); human resources (M Ad); industrial engineering (ME); public health (MPH). *Entrance requirements:* For master's, letters of recommendation.

Université de Montréal, Faculty of Medicine and Faculty of Graduate Studies, Graduate Programs in Medicine, Program in Communal and Public Health, Montréal, QC H3C 3J7, Canada. Offers community health (M Sc, DESS); public health (PhD). *Accreditation:* CEPH. Part-time programs available. *Students:* 101 full-time (64 women), 3 part-time (1 woman). 67 applicants, 16% accepted, 10 enrolled. In 2006, 22 master's, 12 doctorates, 3 other advanced degrees awarded. Terminal master's awarded for partial completion of doctoral program. *Degree requirements:* For master's, thesis; for doctorate, thesis/dissertation, general exam. *Entrance requirements:* For master's and doctorate, proficiency in French, knowledge of English; for DESS, proficiency in French. *Application deadline:* For fall admission, 2/1 priority date for domestic students; for winter admission, 11/1 priority date for domestic students; for spring admission, 2/1 priority date for domestic students. Application fee: $30. Electronic applications accepted. *Financial support:* Fellowships with partial tuition reimbursements, scholarships/grants and tuition waivers (partial) available. *Faculty research:* Epidemiology, health services utilization, health promotion and education, health behaviors, poverty and child health. *Unit head:* Marie-France Raynault, Director, 514-343-6140, Fax: 514-343-5645. *Application contact:* Francine Gazaille, Information Contact, 514-343-6111 Ext. 2755, Fax: 514-343-5645, E-mail: francine.gazaille@umontreal.ca.

University at Albany, State University of New York, School of Public Health, Program in Public Health, Rensselaer, NY 12144. Offers MPH, Dr PH. *Students:* 124 full-time (96 women), 69 part-time (50 women). Average age 32. In 2006, 45 master's, 2 doctorates awarded. *Degree requirements:* For master's and doctorate, thesis/dissertation. *Entrance requirements:* For master's and doctorate, GRE General Test. Additional exam requirements/recommendations for international students: Required—TOEFL (minimum score 550 paper-based; 213 computer-based). *Application deadline:* For fall admission, 4/1 for domestic students, 5/1 for international students; for spring admission, 10/31 for domestic students, 11/1 for international students. Applications are processed on a rolling basis. Application fee: $75. Electronic applications accepted. *Expenses:* Tuition, state resident: full-time $6,900; part-time $288 per credit. Tuition, nonresident: full-time $10,920; part-time $455 per credit. Required fees: $1,139. *Financial support:* Application deadline: 5/30. *Unit head:* Dr. Mary Jane Schneider, Director, 518-402-0404.

University at Buffalo, the State University of New York, Graduate School, School of Public Health and Health Professions, Department of Social and Preventive Medicine, Buffalo, NY 14260. Offers community health (PhD); epidemiology (MS, PhD); public health (MPH). Part-time programs available. *Faculty:* 11 full-time (7 women), 11 part-time/adjunct (5 women). *Students:* 20 full-time (7 women), 20 part-time (13 women); includes 5 minority (2 African Americans, 3 Asian Americans or Pacific Islanders), 8 international. Average age 27. 136 applicants, 41% accepted, 25 enrolled. In 2006, 2 master's, 6 doctorates awarded. Terminal master's awarded for partial completion of doctoral program. *Median time to degree:* Of those who began their doctoral program in fall 1998, 86% received their degree in 8 years or less. *Degree requirements:* For master's and doctorate, thesis/dissertation, comprehensive exam. *Entrance requirements:* For master's and doctorate, GRE General Test. Additional exam requirements/recommendations for international students: Required—TOEFL (minimum score 600 paper-based; 250 computer-based; 100 iBT). *Application deadline:* For fall admission, 2/1 priority date for domestic and international students. Applications are processed on a rolling basis. Application fee: $50. Electronic applications accepted. *Financial support:* In 2006–07, 13 students received support, including 2 fellowships with full tuition reimbursements available (averaging $15,000 per year), 11 research assistantships with full tuition reimbursements available (averaging $15,000 per year); teaching assistantships with full tuition reimbursements available, career-related internships or fieldwork, Federal Work-Study, institutionally sponsored loans, health care benefits, and unspecified assistantships also available. Financial award application deadline: 2/1; financial award applicants required to submit FAFSA. *Faculty research:* Epidemiology of community health services including cancer and nutrition, cardiovascular disease, epidemiology of cancer, cardiovascular diseases; health services research. Total annual research expenditures: $6 million. *Unit head:* Dr. Jo Freudenheim, Chair, 716-829-2975 Ext. 612, Fax: 716-829-2979, E-mail: jfreuden@buffalo.edu. *Application contact:* Dr. Carl Li, Director of Graduate Studies, 716-829-2975 Ext. 618, Fax: 716-829-2979, E-mail: carlli@buffalo.edu.

The University of Akron, Graduate School, College of Nursing, Akron, OH 44325. Offers nursing (MSN, PhD); public health (MPH). *Accreditation:* AACN; AANA/CANAEP (one or more programs are accredited). Part-time programs available. *Faculty:* 22 full-time (all women), 17 part-time/adjunct (15 women). *Students:* 67 full-time (53 women), 167 part-time (139 women); includes 24 minority (16 African Americans, 8 Asian Americans or Pacific Islanders), 1 international. Average age 36. 67 applicants, 81% accepted, 40 enrolled. In 2006, 60 master's, 1 doctorate awarded. *Degree requirements:* For master's, thesis optional (MSN), capstone project (MPH); for doctorate, one foreign language, thesis/dissertation, qualifying exam. *Entrance requirements:* For master's, GRE or MAT, minimum GPA of 3.0, interview, license (MSN), minimum GPA of 2.75 (MPH), letters of recommendation; for doctorate, GRE, minimum GPA of 3.0, MSN, licensure or eligibility for licensure, writing sample, letters of recommendation, interview. Additional exam requirements/recommendations for international students: Required—TOEFL (minimum score 550 paper-based; 213 computer-based; 79 iBT). *Application deadline:* For fall admission, 8/15 for domestic students. Applications are processed on a rolling basis. Application fee: $30 ($40 for international students). Electronic applications accepted. *Expenses:* Tuition, state resident: full-time $6,164; part-time $342 per credit. Tuition, nonresident: full-time $10,575; part-time $588 per credit. Required fees: $806; $43 per credit. $12 per term. Tuition and fees vary according to course load, degree level and program. *Financial support:* In 2006–07, 15 fellowships with full tuition reimbursements, 14 research assistantships with full tuition reimbursements, 12 teaching assistantships with full tuition reimbursements were awarded; career-related internships or fieldwork, Federal Work-Study, and tuition waivers (full) also available. *Faculty research:* Health promotion and chronic disease prevention; mental health and psychosocial resilience; gerontological health, trauma and violence; gut oxygenation during shock and trauma. Total annual research expenditures: $295,321. *Unit head:* Dr. Margaret Wineman, Interim Dean, 330-972-7551, E-mail: wineman@uakron.edu.

The University of Alabama at Birmingham, School of Public Health, Program in Public Health, Birmingham, AL 35294. Offers MPH, MSPH, DPH. *Accreditation:* CEPH. *Students:* 245 full-time (141 women), 87 part-time (51 women); includes 72 minority (44 African Americans, 23 Asian Americans or Pacific Islanders, 5 Hispanic Americans), 111 international. 390 applicants, 81% accepted. In 2006, 127 master's, 9 doctorates awarded. *Expenses:* Tuition, state resident: part-time $170 per credit hour. Tuition, nonresident: part-time $425 per credit hour. Required fees: $15 per credit hour. $122 per term. Tuition and fees vary according to program. *Application contact:* Nancy O. Pinson, Coordinator of Student Admissions, 205-934-4993, Fax: 205-975-5484.

University of Alaska Anchorage, College of Health and Social Welfare, Division of Health Sciences, Anchorage, AK 99508-8060. Offers public health practice (MPH). Part-time programs available. *Faculty:* 2 full-time (both women). *Students:* 2 full-time (1 woman), 46 part-time (39 women); includes 10 minority (4 American Indian/Alaska Native, 3 Asian Americans or Pacific Islanders, 3 Hispanic Americans). 23 applicants, 48% accepted. In 2006, 4 degrees awarded. *Degree requirements:* For master's, thesis, comprehensive exam, registration. *Entrance requirements:* For master's, writing sample. Additional exam requirements/recommendations for international students: Required—TOEFL (minimum score 550 paper-based; 213 computer-based). *Application deadline:* For fall admission, 3/1 for domestic and international students; for spring admission, 10/1 for domestic and international students. Application fee: $45. *Expenses:* Tuition, state resident: part-time $268 per credit. Tuition, nonresident: part-time $547 per credit. Required fees: $124 per semester. Tuition and fees vary according to reciprocity agreements and student level. *Unit head:* Dr. Rhonda Johnson, Chair, 907-786-6565.

University of Alberta, School of Public Health, Department of Public Health Sciences, Edmonton, AB T6G 2E1, Canada. Offers clinical epidemiology (M Sc, MPH); environmental and occupational health (MPH); environmental health sciences (M Sc); epidemiology (M Sc); global health (M Sc, MPH); health policy and management (MPH); health policy research (M Sc); health technology assessment (MPH); occupational health (M Sc); population health (M Sc); public health leadership (MPH); public health sciences (PhD); quantitative methods (MPH). *Accreditation:* CEPH (one or more programs are accredited). *Faculty:* 24 full-time (5 women), 59 part-time/adjunct (13 women). *Students:* 49 full-time, 49 part-time. 81 applicants, 31% accepted. In 2006, 28 degrees awarded. Terminal master's awarded for partial completion of doctoral program. *Degree requirements:* For master's, thesis (for some programs); for doctorate, thesis/dissertation. *Entrance requirements:* For master's, GMAT or GRE General Test. Additional exam requirements/recommendations for international students: Required—TOEFL (paper-based 550; computer-based 213) or IELTS (paper-based 6). *Application deadline:* For fall admission, 3/15 for domestic students, 7/1 for international students; for winter admission, 11/1 for international students; for spring admission, 3/1 for international students. Applications are processed on a rolling basis. Application fee: $0. Electronic applications accepted. *Financial support:* In 2006–07, 11 students received support, including 6 research assistantships with tuition reimbursements available (averaging $2,200 per year); fellowships, teaching assistantships, career-related internships or fieldwork and tuition waivers (partial) also available. Financial award application deadline: 2/1. *Faculty research:* Biostatistics, health promotion and socio-behavioral health science. Total annual research expenditures: $5.7 million. *Unit head:* L. Duncan Saunders, Acting Chair, 780-492-6814, Fax: 780-492-0364. *Application contact:* Felicity R. Hey, Graduate Programs Administrator, 780-492-6407, Fax: 780-492-0364, E-mail: felicity.hey@ualberta.ca.

The University of Arizona, College of Medicine, Graduate Programs in Medicine, Program in Public Health, Tucson, AZ 85721. Offers MPH. *Accreditation:* CEPH. Part-time programs available. *Entrance requirements:* For master's, GRE General Test. *Faculty research:* Prevention, health preparation, epidemiology, nutritional sciences.

The University of Arizona, Graduate College, Arizona Graduate Program in Public Health, Tucson, AZ 85721. Offers MPH. *Accreditation:* CEPH. *Entrance requirements:* Additional exam requirements/recommendations for international students: Required—TOEFL.

University of California, Berkeley, Graduate Division, Haas School of Business and School of Public Health, Concurrent MBA/MPH Program, Berkeley, CA 94720-1500. Offers MBA/MPH. *Accreditation:* AACSB; CAHME; CEPH. *Students:* 34 full-time (22 women); includes 12 minority (1 African American, 10 Asian Americans or Pacific Islanders, 1 Hispanic American), 5 international. Average age 28. *Entrance requirements:* Additional exam requirements/recommendations for international students: Required—TOEFL. *Application deadline:* For fall admission, 3/10 for domestic and international students. Application fee: $175. Electronic applications accepted. *Financial support:* Fellowships with tuition reimbursements, teaching assistantships with tuition reimbursements, career-related internships or fieldwork, scholarships/grants, and unspecified assistantships available. Financial award application deadline: 3/2; financial award applicants required to submit FAFSA. *Unit head:* Prof. Kristi Raube, Director, Health Services Management Program, 510-642-5023, Fax: 510-643-6659, E-mail: raube@haas.berkeley.edu. *Application contact:* Lee Forgue, Student Affairs Officer, 510-642-5023, Fax: 510-643-6659, E-mail: eilis@haas.berkeley.edu.

University of California, Berkeley, Graduate Division, School of Public Health, Division of Environmental Health Sciences, Berkeley, CA 94720-1500. Offers MPH, MS, Dr PH, PhD. *Degree requirements:* For master's, comprehensive exam (MPH), project or thesis (MS); for doctorate, thesis/dissertation, departmental and qualifying exams. *Entrance requirements:* For master's, GRE General Test, minimum GPA of 3.0; previous course work in biology, calculus, and chemistry; for doctorate, GRE General Test, master's degree in relevant scientific discipline or engineering; minimum GPA of 3.0; previous course work in biology, calculus, and chemistry. Additional exam requirements/recommendations for international students: Required—TOEFL. *Application deadline:* For fall admission, 12/1 for domestic students. Applications are processed on a rolling basis. Application fee: $60 ($80 for international students). *Financial support:* Fellowships, research assistantships, teaching assistantships, unspecified assistantships available. *Faculty research:* Toxicology, industrial hygiene, exposure assessment, risk assessment, ergonomics. *Unit head:* Katharine Hammond, Chair, 510-643-0289, E-mail: hammondk@berkeley.edu. *Application contact:* Norma Firestone, Graduate Assistant for Admission, 510-643-5160, Fax: 510-642-5815, E-mail: sphinfo@berkeley.edu.

University of California, Berkeley, Graduate Division, School of Public Health, Division of Health Policy and Management, Berkeley, CA 94720-1500. Offers MPH, MBA/MPH, MCP/MPH, MPP/MPH. *Accreditation:* CAHME; CEPH. *Degree requirements:* For master's, comprehensive exam. *Entrance requirements:* For master's, GRE General Test, minimum GPA of 3.0. *Application deadline:* Applications are processed on a rolling basis. Application fee: $60 ($80 for international students). *Financial support:* Fellowships, research assistantships, teaching assistantships, Federal Work-Study and unspecified assistantships available. *Unit head:* James C. Robinson, Professor, 510-642-0564. *Application contact:* Greta Gebhardt, Administrative Assistant, 510-642-4578, Fax: 510-643-6981, E-mail: gretag@uclink.berkeley.edu.

University of California, Berkeley, Graduate Division, School of Public Health, Division of Public Health Biology and Epidemiology, Berkeley, CA 94720-1500. Offers epidemiology (MS, PhD); infectious diseases (MPH, PhD). *Accreditation:* CEPH (one or more programs are accredited). *Degree requirements:* For master's, comprehensive exam; for doctorate, thesis/dissertation, oral and written exam. *Entrance requirements:* For master's, GRE General Test, minimum GPA of 3.0; MD, DDS, DVM, or PhD in biomedical science (MPH); for doctorate, GRE General Test, minimum GPA of 3.0. *Application deadline:* For fall admission, 12/1 for domestic students. Applications are processed on a rolling basis. Application fee: $60 ($80 for international students). *Financial support:* Fellowships, research assistantships, teaching assistantships, Federal Work-Study and unspecified assistantships available. *Unit head:* Dr. Arthur L. Reingold, Head, 510-642-0327. *Application contact:* Ron Jeremicz, Graduate Assistant, 510-643-0881, Fax: 510-643-5163, E-mail: sphinfo@berkeley.edu.

University of California, Berkeley, Graduate Division, School of Public Health, Master's Internationalist Program, Berkeley, CA 94720-1500. Offers community health education (MPH); epidemiology (MPH); interdisciplinary (MPH); maternal and child health (MPH); public health nutrition (MPH). *Accreditation:* CEPH. *Entrance requirements:* For master's, GRE General Test, minimum GPA of 3.0. *Application deadline:* For fall admission, 12/1 for domestic students. Applications are processed on a rolling basis. Application fee: $60 ($80 for international students). *Financial support:* Fellowships, research assistantships, teaching assistantships, Federal Work-Study and unspecified assistantships available. *Application contact:* Information Contact, 510-643-0881, E-mail: sphinfo@berkeley.edu.

University of California, Berkeley, Graduate Division, School of Public Health, Program in Health and Social Behavior, Berkeley, CA 94720-1500. Offers MPH. *Accreditation:* CEPH. *Entrance requirements:* For master's, GRE General Test, minimum GPA of 3.0. *Application deadline:* For fall admission, 12/1 for domestic students. Applications are processed on a rolling basis. Application fee: $60 ($80 for international students). *Financial support:* Unspecified assistantships available. *Unit head:* William Satariano, Director, 510-642-3997. *Application contact:* Greta Gebhardt, Administrative Assistant, 510-642-4578, Fax: 510-643-6981, E-mail: gretag@uclink.berkeley.edu.

University of California, Berkeley, Graduate Division, School of Public Health, Program in Maternal and Child Health, Berkeley, CA 94720-1500. Offers MPH. *Entrance requirements:* For master's, GRE General Test, minimum GPA of 3.0. *Application deadline:* For fall admission, 12/1 for domestic students. Applications are processed on a rolling basis. Application fee: $60 ($80 for international students). *Financial support:* Fellowships, research assistantships, unspecified assistantships available. *Unit head:* Sylvia Guendelman, Chair, 510-642-1512. *Application contact:* Steve Purser, Assistant Director, 510-643-4991, Fax: 510-643-8236, E-mail: spurser@uclink.berkeley.edu.

University of California, Berkeley, Graduate Division, School of Public Health, Programs in Public Health, Berkeley, CA 94720-1500. Offers MPH, Dr PH. *Accreditation:* CEPH. *Degree requirements:* For doctorate, thesis/dissertation, exam. *Entrance requirements:* For doctorate, GRE General Test, minimum GPA of 3.0. *Application deadline:* For fall admission, 12/1 for domestic students. Applications are processed on a rolling basis. Application fee: $60 ($80 for international students). *Financial support:* Unspecified assistantships available. *Unit head:* Richard S. Stephens, Head, 510-643-9400, E-mail: rss@berkeley.edu. *Application contact:* Rick Love, Student Affairs Officer, 510-643-8452, E-mail: sphdocs@uclink.berkeley.edu.

University of California, Los Angeles, Graduate Division, School of Public Health, Los Angeles, CA 90095. Offers MPH, MS, D Env, Dr PH, PhD, MBA/MPH, MD/PhD, MPH/MA. *Accreditation:* CAHME (one or more programs are accredited); CEPH (one or more programs are accredited). *Degree requirements:* For doctorate, thesis/dissertation, oral and written qualifying exams. *Entrance requirements:* For master's, GRE General Test, minimum GPA of 3.0; for doctorate, GRE General Test, minimum undergraduate GPA of 3.0. Electronic applications accepted.

University of California, San Diego, Office of Graduate Studies, Program in Public Health and Epidemiology, La Jolla, CA 92093. Offers PhD. Electronic applications accepted.

University of Colorado at Denver and Health Sciences Center, Graduate School, Department of Preventive Medicine and Biometrics, Program in Public Health, Denver, CO 80217-3364. Offers MSPH. *Accreditation:* CEPH. *Students:* 91 full-time (71 women), 6 part-time (1 woman); includes 13 minority (2 African Americans, 1 American Indian/Alaska Native, 4 Asian Americans or Pacific Islanders, 6 Hispanic Americans), 3 international. 69 applicants, 49% accepted, 34 enrolled. In 2006, 19 degrees awarded. *Degree requirements:* For master's, thesis or alternative. *Entrance requirements:* For master's, GRE General Test, minimum GPA of 3.0, 4 letters of recommendation. Additional exam requirements/recommendations for international students: Required—TOEFL (minimum score 550 paper-based; 213 computer-based). *Application deadline:* For fall admission, 2/1 for domestic students. Application fee: $50. *Financial support:* Fellowships, research assistantships, teaching assistantships, Federal Work-Study and institutionally sponsored loans available. Financial award application deadline: 3/1; financial award applicants required to submit FAFSA. *Faculty research:* Perinatal epidemiology, chronic disease epidemiology, injury epidemiology, statistical methodology. *Unit head:* Dr. Phoebe Lindsey Barton, Director, 303-315-8357, E-mail: phoebe.barton@uchsc.edu. *Application contact:* Robin Ripley, Coordinator, 303-315-8357, E-mail: robin.ripley@uchsc.edu.

See Close-Up on page 2055.

University of Connecticut, Graduate School, University of Connecticut Health Center, Field of Public Health, Storrs, CT 06269. Offers MPH, JD/MPH. *Faculty:* 49 full-time (19 women). *Students:* 20 full-time (15 women), 115 part-time (84 women); includes 33 minority (14 African Americans, 10 Asian Americans or Pacific Islanders, 9 Hispanic Americans), 1 international. Average age 36. 118 applicants, 40% accepted, 47 enrolled. In 2006, 44 degrees awarded. *Degree requirements:* For master's, comprehensive exam. *Entrance requirements:* Additional exam requirements/recommendations for international students: Required—TOEFL (minimum score 550 paper-based; 213 computer-based). *Application deadline:* For fall admission, 2/1 priority date for domestic and international students; for spring admission, 11/1 for domestic students, 10/1 for international students. Applications are processed on a rolling basis. Application fee: $55. Electronic applications accepted. *Financial support:* In 2006–07, 4 research assistantships with full tuition reimbursements were awarded; teaching assistantships with full tuition reimbursements, Federal Work-Study, scholarships/grants, health care benefits, and unspecified assistantships also available. Financial award application deadline: 2/1; financial award applicants required to submit FAFSA. *Unit head:* Holger Hansen, Director, 860-674-3402. *Application contact:* Joan Siegel, Administrative Assistant, 860-679-1509, E-mail: mpa@nso.uchc.edu.

University of Connecticut Health Center, Graduate School, Program in Public Health, Farmington, CT 06030. Offers MPH, DMD/MPH, MD/MPH. *Accreditation:* CEPH. Part-time and evening/weekend programs available. *Degree requirements:* For master's, thesis optional. *Entrance requirements:* Additional exam requirements/recommendations for international students: Required—TOEFL (minimum score 550 paper-based; 213 computer-based). Electronic applications accepted. *Faculty research:* Cancer epidemiology, birth defects, gerontology, health manpower, health services.

University of Florida, College of Medicine, Program in Clinical Investigation, Gainesville, FL 32611. Offers clinical investigation (MS); epidemiology (MS); public health (MPH). Part-time programs available. *Faculty:* 40. In 2006, 2 degrees awarded. *Entrance requirements:* For master's, GRE, MD, PhD, DMD/DDS or Pharm D. *Application deadline:* For fall admission, 2/15 priority date for domestic students. Applications are processed on a rolling basis. Application fee: $30. *Expenses:* Tuition, state resident: full-time $6,827. Tuition, nonresident: full-time $21,951. Required fees: $999. *Unit head:* Dr. Marian Limacher, Director, 352-846-1228, E-mail: limacmc@medicine.ufl.edu. *Application contact:* Eve Johnson, Program Assistant, 352-846-1228, Fax: 352-846-1217, E-mail: eve11@ufl.edu.

University of Florida, Graduate School, College of Public Health and Health Professions and College of Medicine, Programs in Public Health, Gainesville, FL 32611. Offers biostatistics (MPH); environmental health (MPH); epidemiology (MPH); public health management and policy (MPH); public health practice (MPH); social and behavioral sciences (MPH). *Faculty:* 10. *Entrance requirements:* For master's, GRE General Test, minimum GPA of 3.0. Additional exam requirements/recommendations for international students: Required—TOEFL (minimum score 550 paper-based; 213 computer-based). Application fee: $30. *Expenses:* Tuition, state resident: full-time $6,827. Tuition, nonresident: full-time $21,951. Required fees: $999. *Unit head:* Dr. Mary Peoples-Sheps, Associate Dean for Academic Affairs, 352-273-6084, Fax: 352-273-6448, E-mail: mpeoplessheps@phhp.ufl.edu. *Application contact:* Brigette Hart, Program Assistant, 352-273-6443, E-mail: bhart@phhp.ufl.edu.

University of Hawaii at Manoa, John A. Burns School of Medicine, Department of Public Health Sciences and Epidemiology, Program in Public Health, Honolulu, HI 96822. Offers MPH, MS. *Faculty:* 32 full-time (12 women). *Students:* 27 full-time (23 women), 10 part-time (9 women); includes 4 minority (1 African American, 1 American Indian/Alaska Native, 2 Asian Americans or Pacific Islanders), 2 international. 59 applicants, 59% accepted, 18 enrolled. In 2006, 24 degrees awarded. *Degree requirements:* For master's, thesis optional. *Entrance requirements:* For master's, GRE General Test. Additional exam requirements/recommendations for international students: Required—TOEFL (minimum score 550 paper-based; 213 computer-based; 79 iBT). *Application deadline:* For fall admission, 1/15 for domestic and international students. Application fee: $50. *Financial support:* In 2006–07, 6 research assistantships (averaging $16,513 per year) were awarded. Total annual research expenditures: $2.5 million. *Application contact:* Jason Maddock, 808-956-8267, Fax: 808-956-6041.

Public Health—General

University of Illinois at Chicago, Graduate College, School of Public Health, Chicago, IL 60607-7128. Offers biostatistics (MS, PhD); community health sciences (MPH, MS, Dr PH, PhD); environmental and occupational health sciences (MPH, MS, Dr PH, PhD); epidemiology (MPH, MS, Dr PH, PhD); health policy administration (MPH, MS, Dr PH, PhD); DDS/MPH; MBA/MPH; MD/PhD; MPH/MS. *Accreditation:* CEPH (one or more programs are accredited). Part-time programs available. Terminal master's awarded for partial completion of doctoral program. *Degree requirements:* For master's, thesis, field practicum; for doctorate, thesis/dissertation, independent research, internship. *Entrance requirements:* For master's and doctorate, GRE General Test, minimum GPA of 2.75. Additional exam requirements/recommendations for international students: Required—TOEFL. Electronic applications accepted.

University of Illinois at Springfield, Graduate Programs, College of Public Affairs and Administration, Program in Public Health, Springfield, IL 62703-5407. Offers MPH. Part-time and evening/weekend programs available. *Faculty:* 3 full-time (2 women), 2 part-time/adjunct (0 women). *Students:* 19 full-time (6 women), 22 part-time (10 women); includes 5 minority (3 African Americans, 2 Asian Americans or Pacific Islanders), 21 international. Average age 30. 129 applicants, 60% accepted, 6 enrolled. In 2006, 17 degrees awarded. *Degree requirements:* For master's, internship. *Entrance requirements:* For master's, GRE, 3 letters of reference, minimum undergraduate GPA of 3.0, 3 semester hours of course work in biology. Additional exam requirements/recommendations for international students: Required—TOEFL (minimum score 580 paper-based). *Application deadline:* Applications are processed on a rolling basis. Application fee: $50 ($60 for international students). Electronic applications accepted. *Expenses:* Tuition, state resident: full-time $4,722; part-time $197 per credit hour. Tuition, nonresident: full-time $12,558; part-time $523 per credit hour. Required fees: $1,614; $8 per credit hour. $597 per term. *Financial support:* In 2006–07, research assistantships with full tuition reimbursements (averaging $7,425 per year), teaching assistantships with full tuition reimbursements (averaging $7,425 per year) were awarded; career-related internships or fieldwork, Federal Work-Study, scholarships/grants, health care benefits, and unspecified assistantships also available. Support available to part-time students. Financial award application deadline: 11/15; financial award applicants required to submit FAFSA. *Faculty research:* Epidemiology of breast cancer. *Unit head:* Dr. Remi Imeokparia, Program Administrator, 217-206-7576, Fax: 217-206-7279, E-mail: imeokparia.remi@uis.edu.

The University of Iowa, College of Dentistry and Graduate College, Graduate Programs in Dentistry, Department of Preventive and Community Dentistry, Iowa City, IA 52242-1316. Offers dental public health (MS). *Degree requirements:* For master's, thesis. *Entrance requirements:* For master's, GRE, DDS. Additional exam requirements/recommendations for international students: Required—TOEFL.

The University of Iowa, Graduate College, College of Public Health, Iowa City, IA 52242-1316. Offers MHA, MPH, MS, PhD, Certificate, DVM/MPH, JD/MHA, JD/MPH, MBA/MHA, MD/MPH, MHA/MA, MHA/MS, MS/MA, MS/MS, MSN/MPH, Pharm D/MPH. *Accreditation:* CEPH. *Faculty:* 60 full-time, 45 part-time/adjunct. *Students:* 161 full-time (94 women), 100 part-time (62 women); includes 30 minority (6 African Americans, 2 American Indian/Alaska Native, 17 Asian Americans or Pacific Islanders, 5 Hispanic Americans), 64 international. 346 applicants, 37% accepted, 55 enrolled. In 2006, 111 master's, 6 doctorates awarded. *Degree requirements:* For master's, exam; for doctorate, thesis/dissertation, comprehensive exam, registration. *Entrance requirements:* For master's and doctorate, GRE General Test, minimum GPA of 3.0. Additional exam requirements/recommendations for international students: Required—TOEFL. *Application deadline:* Applications are processed on a rolling basis. Application fee: $60 ($85 for international students). Electronic applications accepted. *Expenses: Contact institution. Financial support:* In 2006–07, 3 fellowships, 121 research assistantships with partial tuition reimbursements, 22 teaching assistantships with partial tuition reimbursements were awarded. Financial award applicants required to submit FAFSA. *Unit head:* Dr. James A. Merchant, Dean, 319-384-5452, Fax: 319-384-5462, E-mail: james-merchant@uiowa.edu.

University of Kansas, Graduate Studies Medical Center, Interdisciplinary Graduate Program in Biomedical Sciences, Department of Preventive Medicine, Lawrence, KS 66045. Offers MPH, MS, MD/MPH. *Accreditation:* CEPH. Part-time programs available. *Faculty:* 26 full-time (14 women), 5 part-time/adjunct (all women). *Students:* 29 full-time (18 women), 64 part-time (43 women); includes 20 minority (6 African Americans, 2 American Indian/Alaska Native, 12 Asian Americans or Pacific Islanders), 5 international. Average age 33. 41 applicants, 51% accepted, 10 enrolled. In 2006, 23 degrees awarded. *Median time to degree:* Master's–1.47 years full-time, 2.37 years part-time. *Degree requirements:* For master's, thesis, comprehensive exam. *Entrance requirements:* For master's, GRE General Test, minimum GPA of 3.0. Additional exam requirements/recommendations for international students: Required—TOEFL. *Application deadline:* For fall admission, 3/31 priority date for domestic students; for spring admission, 11/1 for domestic students. Applications are processed on a rolling basis. Application fee: $35. *Expenses:* Tuition, area resident: Part-time $227 per credit. Tuition, state resident: part-time $543 per credit. Tuition and fees vary according to course load, campus/location, program and reciprocity agreements. *Financial support:* In 2006–07, 24 research assistantships (averaging $6,400 per year) were awarded; career-related internships or fieldwork, Federal Work-Study, scholarships/grants, and unspecified assistantships also available. Financial award application deadline: 3/30; financial award applicants required to submit FAFSA. *Faculty research:* Cancer screening and prevention, smoking cessation, obesity and physical activity, health services/outcomes research. *Unit head:* Dr. Edward F. Ellerbeale, Chairman, 913-588-2774, Fax: 913-588-2780, E-mail: eellerbe@kumc.edu. *Application contact:* Mary Ann Woirhaye, Assistant Director, KU-MPH, 913-588-2720, Fax: 913-588-8505, E-mail: mwoirhaye@kumc.edu.

University of Kentucky, Graduate School, College of Public Health, Program in Public Health, Lexington, KY 40506-0032. Offers MPH. *Accreditation:* CEPH. *Faculty:* 36 full-time (12 women), 3 part-time/adjunct (1 woman). *Students:* 73 full-time (52 women), 55 part-time (37 women); includes 24 minority (20 African Americans, 1 American Indian/Alaska Native, 2 Asian Americans or Pacific Islanders, 1 Hispanic American), 16 international. Average age 32. 158 applicants, 69% accepted, 54 enrolled. In 2006, 30 degrees awarded. *Entrance requirements:* For master's, GRE General Test, minimum undergraduate GPA of 2.75. Additional exam requirements/recommendations for international students: Required—TOEFL (minimum score 550 paper-based; 213 computer-based). *Application deadline:* For fall admission, 7/17 priority date for domestic students, 2/1 priority date for international students; for spring admission, 12/13 priority date for domestic students, 6/15 priority date for international students. Application fee: $40 ($55 for international students). Electronic applications accepted. *Expenses:* Tuition, state resident: full-time $7,670; part-time $401 per credit hour. Tuition, nonresident: full-time $16,158; part-time $873 per credit hour. *Financial support:* In 2006–07, 24 students received support, including 15 fellowships with full tuition reimbursements available (averaging $4,708 per year), 9 research assistantships with full tuition reimbursements available (averaging $8,252 per year); teaching assistantships with full tuition reimbursements available, Federal Work-Study, scholarships/grants, traineeships, health care benefits, tuition waivers (partial), and unspecified assistantships also available. Support available to part-time students. Financial award application deadline: 3/15. *Unit head:* Dr. Timothy Scott Prince, Director of Graduate Studies, 859-257-5678, Fax: 859-257-9862, E-mail: tprince@uky.edu. *Application contact:* Dr. Brian Jackson, Senior Associate Dean, 859-257-4667, Fax: 859-257-4676, E-mail: brian.jackson@uky.edu.

University of Louisville, Graduate School, School of Public Health, Program in Public Health, Louisville, KY 40292-0001. Offers clinical investigation (Certificate); public health (MPH). *Students:* 44 full-time (33 women), 14 part-time (9 women); includes 14 minority (9 African Americans, 3 Asian Americans or Pacific Islanders, 2 Hispanic Americans), 2 international. Average age 29. In 2006, 23 master's, 3 other advanced degrees awarded. *Unit head:* Dr. Robert Jacobs, Head, 502-852-0196, Fax: 502-852-3294, E-mail: rrjaco01@louisville.edu.

University of Maryland, College Park, Graduate Studies, College of Health and Human Performance, Department of Public and Community Health, College Park, MD 20742. Offers community health education (MPH); public/community health (PhD). *Accreditation:* CEPH. Part-time and evening/weekend programs available. *Faculty:* 35 full-time (17 women), 6 part-time/adjunct (all women). *Students:* 48 full-time (44 women), 32 part-time (30 women); includes 29 minority (17 African Americans, 5 Asian Americans or Pacific Islanders, 7 Hispanic Americans), 7 international. 48 applicants, 27% accepted, 7 enrolled. In 2006, 19 master's, 3 doctorates awarded. *Median time to degree:* Of those who began their doctoral program in fall 1998, 33% received their degree in 8 years or less. *Degree requirements:* For master's, thesis optional; for doctorate, thesis/dissertation, comprehensive exam. *Entrance requirements:* For master's, GRE General Test, minimum GPA of 3.0, 3 letters of recommendation; for doctorate, GRE General Test, minimum GPA of 3.5, 3 letters of recommendation. Additional exam requirements/recommendations for international students: Required—TOEFL. *Application deadline:* For fall admission, 1/15 for domestic students, 2/1 for international students. Applications are processed on a rolling basis. Application fee: $60. Electronic applications accepted. *Financial support:* In 2006–07, 3 fellowships with full tuition reimbursements (averaging $15,139 per year), 6 research assistantships with tuition reimbursements (averaging $14,562 per year), 2 teaching assistantships with tuition reimbursements (averaging $14,467 per year) were awarded; career-related internships or fieldwork, Federal Work-Study, and scholarships/grants also available. Support available to part-time students. Financial award applicants required to submit FAFSA. *Faculty research:* Controlling stress and tension, women's health, aging and public policy, adolescent health, long term care. Total annual research expenditures: $2 million. *Unit head:* Dr. Elbert Glover, Chair, 301-405-2467, Fax: 301-314-9167, E-mail: eglover1@umd.edu. *Application contact:* Dean of Graduate School, 301-405-0358, Fax: 301-314-9305.

University of Massachusetts Amherst, Graduate School, School of Public Health and Health Sciences, Department of Nutrition, Amherst, MA 01003. Offers nutrition (MPH, MS); public health (PhD). *Faculty:* 8 full-time (4 women). *Students:* 11 full-time (all women), 3 part-time (all women), 9 international. Average age 28. 22 applicants, 68% accepted, 3 enrolled. In 2006, 2 degrees awarded. *Degree requirements:* For master's, thesis or alternative. *Entrance requirements:* For master's, GRE General Test. Additional exam requirements/recommendations for international students: Required—TOEFL (minimum score 530 paper-based; 197 computer-based). *Application deadline:* For fall admission, 2/1 priority date for domestic and international students; for spring admission, 10/1 for domestic and international students. Applications are processed on a rolling basis. Application fee: $40 ($65 for international students). Electronic applications accepted. *Expenses:* Tuition, state resident: full-time $2,640; part-time $110 per credit. Tuition, nonresident: full-time $9,936; part-time $414 per credit. Required fees: $8,969; $3,129 per term. One-time fee: $257 full-time. Tuition and fees vary according to class time, course load, campus/location and reciprocity agreements. *Financial support:* In 2006–07, 8 research assistantships with full tuition reimbursements (averaging $4,525 per year), 10 teaching assistantships with full tuition reimbursements (averaging $7,162 per year) were awarded; fellowships with full tuition reimbursements, career-related internships or fieldwork, Federal Work-Study, scholarships/grants, traineeships, and unspecified assistantships also available. Support available to part-time students. Financial award application deadline: 2/1. *Unit head:* Dr. Nancy Cohen, Acting Head, 413-545-0470, Fax: 413-545-1074, E-mail: cohen@nutrition.umass.edu.

University of Massachusetts Amherst, Graduate School, School of Public Health and Health Sciences, Department of Public Health, Amherst, MA 01003. Offers MPH, MS, PhD. *Accreditation:* CEPH (one or more programs are accredited). Part-time programs available. *Faculty:* 22 full-time (10 women). *Students:* 92 full-time (54 women), 211 part-time (132 women); includes 39 minority (20 African Americans, 16 Asian Americans or Pacific Islanders, 3 Hispanic Americans), 58 international. Average age 36. 264 applicants, 62% accepted, 43 enrolled. In 2006, 96 master's, 1 doctorate awarded. *Degree requirements:* For master's, thesis (for some programs); for doctorate, thesis/dissertation. *Entrance requirements:* For master's and doctorate, GRE General Test. Additional exam requirements/recommendations for international students: Required—TOEFL (minimum score 530 paper-based; 197 computer-based). *Application deadline:* For fall admission, 2/1 priority date for domestic and international students; for spring admission, 10/1 for domestic and international students. Applications are processed on a rolling basis. Application fee: $40 ($65 for international students). Electronic applications accepted. *Expenses:* Tuition, state resident: full-time $2,640; part-time $110 per credit. Tuition, nonresident: full-time $9,936; part-time $414 per credit. Required fees: $8,969; $3,129 per term. One-time fee: $257 full-time. Tuition and fees vary according to class time, course load, campus/location and reciprocity agreements. *Financial support:* In 2006–07, 3 fellowships with full tuition reimbursements (averaging $5,862 per year), 32 research assistantships with full tuition reimbursements (averaging $5,174 per year), 27 teaching assistantships with full tuition reimbursements (averaging $4,626 per year) were awarded; career-related internships or fieldwork, Federal Work-Study, scholarships/grants, traineeships, tuition waivers (full), and unspecified assistantships also available. Support available to part-time students. Financial award application deadline: 2/1. *Unit head:* Susan Sturgeon, Chairman, 413-545-2288.

University of Medicine and Dentistry of New Jersey, UMDNJ–School of Public Health (UMDNJ, Rutgers, NJIT) Newark Campus, Newark, NJ 07107-1709. Offers MPH, Dr PH, PhD, Certificate, DMD/MPH, MD/MPH, MS/MPH. *Degree requirements:* For master's, internship. *Entrance requirements:* For master's, GRE General Test. Additional exam requirements/recommendations for international students: Required—TOEFL. *Application deadline:* For fall admission, 4/1 for domestic students; for spring admission, 10/1 for domestic students. Application fee: $95. Electronic applications accepted. *Unit head:* Rhonda Barnes, 973-972-7212, Fax: 973-972-8032, E-mail: barnesb@umdnj.edu. *Application contact:* Yvette J. Holding-Ford, Information Contact, 973-972-7212, Fax: 973-972-8032, E-mail: holdinys@umdnj.edu.

See Close-Up on page 2057.

University of Medicine and Dentistry of New Jersey, UMDNJ–School of Public Health (UMDNJ, Rutgers, NJIT) Piscataway/New Brunswick Campus, Piscataway, NJ 08854. Offers biostatistics (MS); epidemiology (Certificate); general public health (Certificate); public health (MPH, Dr PH, PhD); DO/MPH; MD/MPH; MPH/MBA; MPH/MSPA; Psy D/MPH. *Degree requirements:* For master's, internship; for doctorate, thesis/dissertation. *Entrance requirements:* For master's, GRE General Test; for doctorate, GRE General Test, MPH (Dr PH); MA, MPH, or MS (PhD). Additional exam requirements/recommendations for international students: Required—TOEFL. *Application deadline:* For fall admission, 4/1 for domestic students; for spring admission, 10/1 for domestic students. Application fee: $95. Electronic applications accepted. *Unit head:* Janet Zamorski, 732-235-4646, Fax: 732-235-5476, E-mail: zamorsja@umdnj.edu. *Application contact:* Dr. Mark G. Robson, Assistant Dean, 732-235-4646, Fax: 732-235-5476, E-mail: robson@eohsi.rutgers.edu.

See Close-Up on page 2057.

University of Medicine and Dentistry of New Jersey, UMDNJ–School of Public Health (UMDNJ, Rutgers, NJIT) Stratford/Camden Campus, Stratford, NJ 08084. Offers general public health (Certificate); public health (MPH); DO/MPH. *Degree requirements:* For master's, internship. *Entrance requirements:* For master's, GRE General Test. Additional exam requirements/recommendations for international students: Required—TOEFL. *Application deadline:* For fall admission, 4/1 for domestic students; for spring admission, 10/1 for domestic students. Application fee: $95. Electronic applications accepted. *Unit head:* Vanessa Jago, 856-566-2790, Fax: 856-566-2882, E-mail: jagovi@umdnj.edu. *Application contact:* 732-235-4317, Fax: 856-566-2882.

See Close-Up on page 2057.

University of Miami, Graduate School, Miller School of Medicine, Graduate Programs in Medicine, Department of Epidemiology and Public Health, Teaching Programs in Public Health, Coral Gables, FL 33124. Offers MPH, MSPH, JD/MPH, MD/MPH, MPA/MPH, MPH/MAIA. *Accreditation:* CEPH. Part-time programs available. *Faculty:* 18 full-time (8 women), 8 part-time/adjunct (5 women). *Students:* 7 full-time (6 women), 23 part-time (14 women); includes 12 minority (3 African Americans, 2 Asian Americans or Pacific Islanders, 7 Hispanic Americans), 4 international. Average age 28. 70 applicants, 21% accepted, 5 enrolled. In 2006, 11 degrees awarded. *Degree requirements:* For master's, thesis (for some programs), project, practicum. *Entrance requirements:* For master's, GRE General Test, minimum GPA of 3.0, 3 letters of recommendation. Additional exam requirements/recommendations for international students: Required—TOEFL (minimum score 550 paper-based; 213 computer-based). *Application deadline:* For fall admission, 4/1 for domestic students, 3/1 priority date for international students; for spring admission, 11/15 for domestic students, 10/15 priority date for international students. Applications are processed on a rolling basis. Application fee: $50. Electronic applications accepted. *Financial support:* In 2006–07, 22 students received support, including 4 teaching assistantships; career-related internships or fieldwork, Federal Work-Study, institutionally sponsored loans, tuition waivers (partial), and graduate administrative assistantships also available. Support available to part-time students. Financial award application deadline: 2/1; financial award applicants required to submit FAFSA. *Faculty research:* Behavioral epidemiology, AIDS, cardiovascular diseases, cancer prevention, substance abuse epidemiology, women's health. *Unit head:* Dr. James D. Wilkinson, Director, Teaching Programs, 305-243-3022, Fax: 305-243-3384, E-mail: jwilkins@med.miami.edu. *Application contact:* Heather Mc Anany, Administrator, 305-243-2209, Fax: 305-243-3384, E-mail: hmcanany@med.miami.edu.

See Close-Up on page 2059.

University of Michigan, School of Public Health, Ann Arbor, MI 48109. Offers MHSA, MPH, MS, Dr PH, PhD, JD/MHSA, MD/MPH, MHSA/MBA, MHSA/MNA, MHSA/MPP, MHSA/MSIOE, MPH/AM, MPH/JD, MPH/MPP, MSW/MPH. MS and PhD offered through the Horace H. Rackham School of Graduate Studies. *Accreditation:* CAHME (one or more programs are accredited); CEPH (one or more programs are accredited). Part-time and evening/weekend programs available. Terminal master's awarded for partial completion of doctoral program. *Degree requirements:* For doctorate, oral defense of dissertation, preliminary exam. *Entrance requirements:* For master's and doctorate, GRE General Test. Additional exam requirements/recommendations for international students: Required—TOEFL (minimum score 560 paper-based; 220 computer-based). Electronic applications accepted.

University of Minnesota, Twin Cities Campus, School of Public Health, Minneapolis, MN 55455. Offers MHA, MPH, MS, PhD, Certificate, DVM/MPH, JD/MS, JD/PhD, MD/MPH, MD/PhD, MPH/JD, MPH/MSN, MPP/MS. *Accreditation:* CEPH (one or more programs are accredited). Part-time programs available. Postbaccalaureate distance learning degree programs offered (minimal on-campus study). Terminal master's awarded for partial completion of doctoral program. *Degree requirements:* For doctorate, thesis/dissertation. *Entrance requirements:* For master's and doctorate, GRE General Test. Additional exam requirements/recommendations for international students: Required—TOEFL. Electronic applications accepted. Expenses: Contact institution. Full-time tuition and fees vary according to class time, course load, program, reciprocity agreements and student level.

University of Missouri–Columbia, School of Medicine and Graduate School, Graduate Programs in Medicine, Program in Public Health, Columbia, MO 65211. Offers MPH. *Students:* 2 full-time (0 women). In 2006, 4 degrees awarded. Application fee: $45 ($60 for international students). *Unit head:* Dr. Kristofer Hagglund, Associate Dean, 573-884-7050, E-mail: hagglundk@missouri.edu.

The University of Montana, Programs in Public Health, Missoula, MT 59812-0002. Offers MPH, CPH.

University of Nebraska at Omaha, Graduate Studies and Research, Program in Public Health, Omaha, NE 68182. Offers MPH. Program is interdisciplinary. *Accreditation:* CEPH. Part-time and evening/weekend programs available. *Students:* Average age 32. 19 applicants, 37% accepted, 4 enrolled. In 2006, 3 degrees awarded. *Degree requirements:* For master's, thesis (for some programs), comprehensive exam. *Entrance requirements:* For master's, minimum GPA of 3.0, resumé, personal statement. Additional exam requirements/recommendations for international students: Required—TOEFL (minimum score 550 paper-based; 213 computer-based; 80 iBT). *Application deadline:* For fall admission, 4/15 for domestic students; for spring admission, 9/1 for domestic students. Applications are processed on a rolling basis. Application fee: $45. Electronic applications accepted. *Financial support:* In 2006–07, 9 students received support. Application deadline: 3/1; *Application contact:* Jessica Tschirren, Coordinator, 402-561-7566, Fax: 402-561-7599.

University of Nebraska Medical Center, Graduate Studies, Graduate Program in Public Health, Omaha, NE 68198. Offers MPH. *Accreditation:* CEPH. Part-time programs available. Postbaccalaureate distance learning degree programs offered (minimal on-campus study). *Faculty:* 19 part-time/adjunct (11 women). *Students:* 5 full-time (4 women), 21 part-time (14 women); includes 2 minority (both African Americans), 4 international. Average age 36. 12 applicants, 50% accepted, 5 enrolled. In 2006, 10 degrees awarded. *Degree requirements:* For master's, service-learning capstone course. *Entrance requirements:* Additional exam requirements/recommendations for international students: Required—TOEFL (minimum score 550 paper-based; 213 computer-based), GRE. *Application deadline:* For fall admission, 4/15 for domestic students, 4/15 priority date for international students; for spring admission, 9/1 for domestic students, 9/1 priority date for international students. Application fee: $45. Electronic applications accepted. *Financial support:* In 2006–07, 1 research assistantship with full tuition reimbursement (averaging $13,000 per year) was awarded. *Faculty research:* Ethics, environmental health, cultural influence on health, rural health policy, cancer prevention. *Unit head:* Dr. Alice Schumaker, Program Director, 402-554-2589, Fax: 402-554-2682, E-mail: aschumaker@mail.unomaha.edu. *Application contact:* Jessica Tschirren, Coordinator, 402-561-7586, Fax: 402-561-7599, E-mail: jtschirren@unmc.edu.

University of Nevada, Las Vegas, Graduate College, Division of Health Sciences, School of Public Health, Las Vegas, NV 89154-9900. Offers health promotion (M Ed); public health (MPH). *Faculty:* 4 full-time (0 women), 13 part-time/adjunct (3 women). *Students:* 29 full-time (20 women), 27 part-time (16 women); includes 19 minority (7 African Americans, 1 American Indian/Alaska Native, 7 Asian Americans or Pacific Islanders, 4 Hispanic Americans), 4 international. 41 applicants, 66% accepted, 18 enrolled. In 2006, 12 degrees awarded. *Entrance requirements:* For master's, GRE General Test or GMAT, minimum GPA of 3.0 in last 2 years of course work. Additional exam requirements/recommendations for international students: Required—TOEFL (minimum score 550 paper-based; 213 computer-based; 80 iBT). *Application deadline:* For fall admission, 6/1 for domestic students, 5/1 for international students; for spring admission, 11/1 for domestic students, 10/1 for international students. Application fee: $60 ($75 for international students). Electronic applications accepted. *Financial support:* In 2006–07, 4 research assistantships with partial tuition reimbursements (averaging $10,000 per year) were awarded; career-related internships or fieldwork, Federal Work-Study, institutionally sponsored loans, scholarships/grants, health care benefits, and unspecified assistantships also available. Support available to part-time students. *Unit head:* Dr. Mary Guinan, Interim Dean, 702-895-5090. *Application contact:* Graduate College Admissions Evaluator, 702-895-3320, Fax: 702-895-4180, E-mail: gradcollege@unlv.edu.

University of Nevada, Reno, Graduate School, College of Health and Human Sciences, Department of Public Health, Reno, NV 89557. Offers MPH. *Faculty:* 16. *Students:* 12 full-time (8 women), 15 part-time (13 women); includes 3 minority (1 African American, 1 American Indian/Alaska Native, 1 Asian American or Pacific Islander), 3 international. Average age 38. 13 applicants, 77% accepted, 6 enrolled. In 2006, 15 degrees awarded. *Degree requirements:* For master's, culminating experience, thesis optional. *Entrance requirements:* For master's, GRE General Test, minimum GPA of 2.75. Additional exam requirements/recommendations for international students: Required—TOEFL. *Application deadline:* For fall admission, 3/1 priority date for domestic students; for spring admission, 11/1 for domestic students. Applications are processed on a rolling basis. Application fee: $60 ($95 for international students). *Financial support:* Research assistantships, teaching assistantships, Federal Work-Study, institutionally sponsored loans, and tuition waivers (full) available. Financial award application deadline: 3/1.

Faculty research: Biomechanics and basic fundamentals of skiing, social psychology in sports and recreation, fitness and aging, elementary physical education, body fat evaluation. *Unit head:* Dr. Paul Devereau, Graduate Program Director, 775-682-7090.

University of New England, College of Osteopathic Medicine, Program in Public Health, Biddeford, ME 04005-9526. Offers MPH, Certificate. Part-time programs available. Postbaccalaureate distance learning degree programs offered. *Faculty:* 2 full-time (both women), 11 part-time/adjunct (9 women). *Students:* 3 full-time (1 woman), 32 part-time (24 women). Average age 37. 25 applicants, 96% accepted, 16 enrolled. In 2006, 1 degree awarded. *Degree requirements:* For Certificate, practicum. *Entrance requirements:* For degree, undergraduate course work in math and science. Additional exam requirements/recommendations for international students: Required—TOEFL (minimum score 550 paper-based; 213 computer-based). *Application deadline:* Applications are processed on a rolling basis. Electronic applications accepted. *Expenses:* Contact institution. *Financial support:* Available to part-time students. Application deadline: 5/1; *Unit head:* Becky Wittemore, Director, 207-283-0170 Ext. 2886, E-mail: bwittemore@une.edu. *Application contact:* Diane Labbe, Staff Assistant, 207-283-0170 Ext. 2886, Fax: 207-602-5916, E-mail: dlabbe@une.edu.

University of New Hampshire, Graduate School, School of Health and Human Services, Department of Health Management and Policy, Durham, NH 03824. Offers public health: ecology (MPH); public health: nursing (MPH); public health: policy and management (MPH). *Accreditation:* CEPH. Part-time and evening/weekend programs available. *Faculty:* 9 full-time. *Students:* 16 full-time (14 women), 34 part-time (25 women); includes 3 minority (1 African American, 1 Asian American or Pacific Islander, 1 Hispanic American). Average age 29. 29 applicants, 90% accepted, 14 enrolled. In 2006, 15 degrees awarded. *Entrance requirements:* For master's, GMAT or GRE General Test. Additional exam requirements/recommendations for international students: Required—TOEFL (minimum score 550 paper-based; 213 computer-based). *Application deadline:* For fall admission, 4/1 priority date for domestic students, 4/1 for international students. Applications are processed on a rolling basis. Application fee: $60. Electronic applications accepted. *Expenses:* Contact institution. Tuition and fees vary according to course load, program and reciprocity agreements. *Financial support:* In 2006–07, 1 fellowship was awarded; research assistantships, teaching assistantships, scholarships/grants also available. Financial award application deadline: 2/15. *Unit head:* Dr. John Seavey, Chairperson, 603-862-3414. *Application contact:* Chris Hamann, Administrative Assistant, 603-862-2733, E-mail: masterof.publichealth@unh.edu.

University of New Hampshire at Manchester, Center for Graduate and Professional Studies, Manchester, NH 03101-1113. Offers business administration (MBA); counseling (M Ed); education (M Ed, MAT); educational administration and supervision (M Ed, CAGS); industrial statistics (Certificate); public administration (MPA); public health (MPH, Certificate); social work (MSW).

University of New Mexico, School of Medicine, Program in Public Health, Albuquerque, NM 87131-5196. Offers MPH. *Accreditation:* CEPH. Part-time programs available. Postbaccalaureate distance learning degree programs offered. *Degree requirements:* For master's, thesis. *Entrance requirements:* For master's, GRE, MCAT, 2 years of experience in health field. Additional exam requirements/recommendations for international students: Required—TOEFL. *Faculty research:* Epidemiology, rural health, environmental health, Native American health issues.

The University of North Carolina at Chapel Hill, Graduate School, School of Public Health, Chapel Hill, NC 27599. Offers MHA, MPH, MS, MSEE, MSPH, Dr PH, PhD, DDS/MPH, JD/MPH, MBA/MHA, MD/MPH, MHA/MBA, MHA/MSIS, MHA/MSLS, MPH/MRP, MPH/MSW, MSPH/MSW. *Accreditation:* CAHME (one or more programs are accredited); CEPH (one or more programs are accredited). Part-time programs available. Postbaccalaureate distance learning degree programs offered (minimal on-campus study). *Faculty:* 212 full-time (99 women), 328 part-time/adjunct. *Students:* 1,204 full-time (839 women); includes 246 minority (120 African Americans, 9 American Indian/Alaska Native, 88 Asian Americans or Pacific Islanders, 29 Hispanic Americans), 142 international. Average age 27. 1,792 applicants, 43% accepted, 489 enrolled. In 2006, 372 master's, 72 doctorates awarded. Terminal master's awarded for partial completion of doctoral program. *Median time to degree:* Of those who began their doctoral program in fall 1998, 100% received their degree in 8 years or less. *Degree requirements:* For master's, thesis, master's paper, capstone, comprehensive exam, registration; for doctorate, thesis/dissertation, comprehensive exam, registration. *Entrance requirements:* For master's and doctorate, GRE General Test, minimum GPA of 3.0. Additional exam requirements/recommendations for international students: Required—TOEFL. *Application deadline:* For fall admission, 1/1 priority date for domestic and international students. Applications are processed on a rolling basis. Application fee: $70. Electronic applications accepted. *Financial support:* In 2006–07, 148 fellowships with full and partial tuition reimbursements (averaging $20,000 per year), 298 research assistantships with partial tuition reimbursements (averaging $12,023 per year), 79 teaching assistantships with partial tuition reimbursements (averaging $8,375 per year) were awarded; career-related internships or fieldwork, Federal Work-Study, institutionally sponsored loans, scholarships/grants, traineeships, and unspecified assistantships also available. Support available to part-time students. Financial award application deadline: 1/1; financial award applicants required to submit FAFSA. *Faculty research:* Health promotion and disease prevention, injury prevention, international health, environmental studies, occupational health studies. *Unit head:* Dr. Barbara K. Rimer, Dean, 919-966-3245, Fax: 919-966-7678. *Application contact:* Sherry Rhodes, Director of Student Services, 919-966-2499, Fax: 919-966-6352, E-mail: srhodes@email.unc.edu.

The University of North Carolina at Charlotte, Graduate School, College of Health and Human Services, Department of Health Behavior and Administration, Charlotte, NC 28223-0001. Offers health behavior and administration (MHA); public health (MSPH). *Faculty:* 10 full-time (5 women), 5 part-time/adjunct (2 women). *Students:* 40 full-time (26 women), 14 part-time (10 women); includes 14 minority (9 African Americans, 5 Asian Americans or Pacific Islanders), 12 international. Average age 30. 44 applicants, 93% accepted, 15 enrolled. In 2006, 16 degrees awarded. *Degree requirements:* For master's, thesis or comprehensive exam. *Entrance requirements:* For master's, GRE or MAT (public health), GRE or GMAT (health administration), minimum GPA of 3.0 during previous 2 years, 2.75 overall. Additional exam requirements/recommendations for international students: Required—TOEFL (minimum score 557 paper-based; 220 computer-based). *Application deadline:* For fall admission, 7/1 for domestic students, 5/1 for international students; for spring admission, 11/1 for domestic students, 10/1 for international students. Applications are processed on a rolling basis. Application fee: $55. Electronic applications accepted. *Expenses:* Tuition, state resident: full-time $2,719; part-time $170 per credit. Tuition, nonresident: full-time $12,926; part-time $808 per credit. Required fees: $1,555. *Financial support:* In 2006–07, 3 research assistantships (averaging $7,940 per year) were awarded; fellowships, teaching assistantships, career-related internships or fieldwork, Federal Work-Study, institutionally sponsored loans, scholarships/grants, and unspecified assistantships also available. Support available to part-time students. Financial award application deadline: 4/1; financial award applicants required to submit FAFSA. *Faculty research:* Pediatric asthma self-management, reproductive epidemiology, social aspects of injury prevention, chronic illness self-care, competency-based professional education. Total annual research expenditures: $561,332. *Unit head:* Dr. Andrew R. Harver, Chair, 704-687-2957, Fax: 704-687-6122, E-mail: arharver@email.uncc.edu. *Application contact:* Kathy B. Giddings, Director of Graduate Admissions, 704-687-3366, Fax: 704-687-3279, E-mail: gradadm@email.uncc.edu.

University of Northern Colorado, Graduate School, College of Natural and Health Sciences, School of Human Sciences, Program in Public Health and Nutrition, Greeley, CO 80639. Offers public health education (MPH). *Accreditation:* CEPH. *Faculty:* 3 full-time (2 women). *Students:* 42 full-time (34 women), 7 part-time (5 women); includes 7 minority (2 African Americans, 1 Asian American or Pacific Islander, 4 Hispanic Americans), 1 international. Average age 31. 28 applicants, 100% accepted, 14 enrolled. In 2006, 16 degrees awarded.

Public Health—General

University of Northern Colorado (continued)
Degree requirements: For master's, thesis or alternative, comprehensive exam. *Entrance requirements:* For master's, GRE General test, 2 letters of recommendation. *Application deadline:* Applications are processed on a rolling basis. Application fee: $50 ($60 for international students). Electronic applications accepted. *Expenses:* Tuition, state resident: full-time $5,118; part-time $213 per credit hour. Tuition, nonresident: full-time $14,832; part-time $618 per credit hour. Required fees: $674; $34 per credit hour. *Financial support:* In 2006–07, 27 students received support, including 5 fellowships (averaging $1,025 per year), 4 research assistantships (averaging $10,914 per year); teaching assistantships, unspecified assistantships also available. Financial award application deadline: 3/1; financial award applicants required to submit FAFSA. *Unit head:* Dr. Kathy Zavela, Program Coordinator, 970-351-2403.

University of North Florida, College of Health, Department of Public Health, Jacksonville, FL 32224-2645. Offers community health (MPH); geriatric management (MSH); health administration (MHA); health behavior research and evaluation (Certificate); nutrition (MSH); rehabilitation counseling (MS). *Accreditation:* CORE. Part-time and evening/weekend programs available. *Faculty:* 21 full-time (16 women). *Students:* 78 full-time (60 women), 54 part-time (40 women); includes 31 minority (16 African Americans, 7 Asian Americans or Pacific Islanders, 8 Hispanic Americans), 10 international. Average age 32. 136 applicants, 47% accepted, 38 enrolled. In 2006, 50 degrees awarded. *Degree requirements:* For master's, thesis optional. *Entrance requirements:* For master's, GRE General Test (MSH, MS, MPH), GMAT or GRE General Test (MHA), minimum GPA of 3.0 in last 60 hours. Additional exam requirements/recommendations for international students: Required—TOEFL (minimum score 500 paper-based; 173 computer-based). *Application deadline:* For fall admission, 7/1 priority date for domestic students, 5/1 for international students; for spring admission, 11/10 priority date for domestic students, 10/1 for international students. Applications are processed on a rolling basis. Application fee: $30. Electronic applications accepted. *Expenses:* Tuition, state resident: full-time $4,948; part-time $206 per semester hour. Tuition, nonresident: full-time $19,140; part-time $408 per semester hour. *Financial support:* In 2006–07, 64 students received support, including 11 teaching assistantships (averaging $2,942 per year); research assistantships, career-related internships or fieldwork, Federal Work-Study, scholarships/grants, and tuition waivers (partial) also available. Support available to part-time students. Financial award application deadline: 4/1; financial award applicants required to submit FAFSA. *Faculty research:* Dietary supplements; alcohol, tobacco, and other drug use prevention; turnover among health professionals; aging; psychosocial aspects of disabilities. Total annual research expenditures: $438,597. *Unit head:* Dr. Judith Perkin, Chair, 904-620-2840, Fax: 904-620-2848, E-mail: jperkin@unf.edu. *Application contact:* Rachel Broderick, Director of Advising, 904-620-2817, Fax: 904-620-1770, E-mail: rbroderi@unf.edu.

University of North Texas Health Science Center at Fort Worth, School of Public Health, Fort Worth, TX 76107-2699. Offers biostatistics (MPH); community health (MPH); disease control and prevention (Dr PH); environmental health (MPH); epidemiology (MPH); health behavior (MPH); health policy and management (MPH, Dr PH); DO/MPH; MA/MPH; MS/MPH; PhD/MPH. *Accreditation:* CEPH. Part-time and evening/weekend programs available. *Degree requirements:* For master's, thesis or alternative, supervised internship; for doctorate, thesis/dissertation, supervised internship. *Entrance requirements:* For master's, GRE General Test. Additional exam requirements/recommendations for international students: Required—TOEFL. Electronic applications accepted.

University of Oklahoma Health Sciences Center, Graduate College, College of Public Health, Program in General Public Health, Oklahoma City, OK 73190. Offers MPH, Dr PH.

University of Oklahoma Health Sciences Center, Graduate College, College of Public Health, Program in Preparedness and Terrorism, Oklahoma City, OK 73190. Offers MPH.

University of Ottawa, Faculty of Graduate and Postdoctoral Studies, Interdisciplinary Programs, Program in Population Health, Ottawa, ON K1N 6N5, Canada. Offers PhD. *Degree requirements:* For doctorate, thesis/dissertation, comprehensive exam. Electronic applications accepted. *Faculty research:* Population health.

University of Pittsburgh, Graduate School of Public Health, Pittsburgh, PA 15260. Offers MHA, MPH, MS, Dr PH, PhD, Certificate, JD/MPH, MD/MPH, MD/PhD, MID/MPH, MPH/MPA, MPH/MSW, MPH/PhD. *Accreditation:* CEPH (one or more programs are accredited). Part-time programs available. *Faculty:* 162 full-time (71 women), 110 part-time/adjunct (36 women). *Students:* 349 full-time (243 women), 179 part-time (121 women); includes 93 minority (47 African Americans, 1 American Indian/Alaska Native, 35 Asian Americans or Pacific Islanders, 10 Hispanic Americans), 138 international. Average age 31. 885 applicants, 60% accepted, 185 enrolled. In 2006, 97 master's, 25 doctorates, 6 other advanced degrees awarded. Terminal master's awarded for partial completion of doctoral program. *Degree requirements:* For master's, thesis/dissertation, comprehensive exam (for some programs), registration; for doctorate, thesis/dissertation, comprehensive exam, registration. *Entrance requirements:* For master's, doctorate, and Certificate, GRE, bachelor's degree, recommendations, prerequisite courses, professional student. Additional exam requirements/recommendations for international students: Required—TOEFL (minimum score 550 paper-based; 213 computer-based; 80 iBT). *Application deadline:* For fall admission, 4/1 for international students; for winter admission, 9/1 for international students; for spring admission, 2/1 for international students. Applications are processed on a rolling basis. Application fee: $50 ($60 for international students). Electronic applications accepted. *Expenses:* Contact institution. *Financial support:* In 2006–07, 4 fellowships with full tuition reimbursements, 149 research assistantships with full tuition reimbursements (averaging $20,575 per year), 13 teaching assistantships with full tuition reimbursements (averaging $13,996 per year) were awarded; career-related internships or fieldwork, scholarships/grants, traineeships, health care benefits, tuition waivers (partial), and unspecified assistantships also available. Support available to part-time students. Financial award applicants required to submit FAFSA. *Faculty research:* Clampsia and fetal, maternal factors, cardiovascular disease and sexual identity, health disparities, protein families and genomes, J cell immunity to human immunodeficiency virus. Total annual research expenditures: $73.5 million. *Unit head:* Dr. Donald S. Burke, Dean, 412-624-3001, Fax: 412-624-3309, E-mail: donburke@pitt.edu. *Application contact:* 412-624-5200, Fax: 412-624-3755, E-mail: stuaff@pitt.edu.

Announcement: The Graduate School of Public Health offers master's and doctoral degrees in many areas, including biostatistics, public health statistics, human genetics, public health genetics, genetic counseling, epidemiology, infectious diseases and microbiology, behavioral and community health sciences, health administration, health promotion and education, risk assessment, and environmental and occupational health. Certificate programs include public health preparedness and disaster response, global health, environmental health risk assessment, minority health research, LGBTQ health, public health genetics, evaluation of health education programs, and recruitment of research subjects. A multidisciplinary MPH is offered for doctoral-level health professionals, some experienced professionals, and advanced health profession students. Also available are joint-degree programs (JD/MPH, MPH/MPA, MPH/MID, MPH/PhD-anthropology, MPH/PhD-social work, MD/PhD, MPH (EOH)/MD, MPH/MSW, and MPH-Public Health Genetics/MS-Genetic Counseling).

See Close-Up on page 2061.

University of Puerto Rico, Medical Sciences Campus, Graduate School of Public Health, Department of Health Services Administration, Program in Public Health, San Juan, PR 00936-5067. Offers MPH. *Accreditation:* CEPH. Part-time programs available. *Students:* 78 (50 women) 3 international. 56 applicants, 73% accepted. In 2006, 23 degrees awarded. *Entrance requirements:* For master's, GRE, previous course work in algebra. *Application deadline:* For fall admission, 3/15 for domestic students. Application fee: $20. *Financial support:* Research assistantships, teaching assistantships, Federal Work-Study and institutionally sponsored loans available. Financial award application deadline: 4/30. *Unit head:* Dr. José M. Cobos, Coordinator, 787-758-2525 Ext. 1442, Fax: 787-759-6719. *Application contact:* Prof. Mayra E. Santiago-Vargas, Counselor, 787-756-5244, Fax: 787-759-6719, E-mail: msantiago@rcm.upr.edu.

University of Rochester, School of Medicine and Dentistry, Graduate Programs in Medicine and Dentistry, Department of Community and Preventive Medicine, Program in Public Health, Rochester, NY 14627-0250. Offers MPH, MBA/MPH, MD/MPH, MPH/MS, MPH/PhD. *Accreditation:* CEPH. *Entrance requirements:* For master's, GRE General Test.

University of South Carolina, The Graduate School, Arnold School of Public Health, Program in General Public Health, Columbia, SC 29208. Offers MPH. *Accreditation:* CEPH. Part-time programs available. *Degree requirements:* For master's, practicum. *Entrance requirements:* For master's, DAT or MCAT, GRE General Test, previously earned MD or doctoral degree. Additional exam requirements/recommendations for international students: Required—TOEFL (minimum score 570 paper-based; 230 computer-based). Electronic applications accepted.

University of South Carolina, The Graduate School, Arnold School of Public Health, Program in Physical Activity and Public Health, Columbia, SC 29208. Offers MPH. *Accreditation:* CEPH. *Degree requirements:* For master's, practicum. *Entrance requirements:* For master's, GRE.

University of South Carolina, The Graduate School, College of Nursing, Program in Nursing and Public Health, Columbia, SC 29208. Offers MPH/MSN. *Accreditation:* AACN; CEPH. Part-time programs available. *Entrance requirements:* Additional exam requirements/recommendations for international students: Required—TOEFL (minimum score 570 paper-based; 230 computer-based). Electronic applications accepted. *Faculty research:* Substance abuse, violence against women, AIDS/HIV, immigrant health, organizational systems.

University of Southern California, Keck School of Medicine and Graduate School, Graduate Programs in Medicine, Department of Preventive Medicine, Master of Public Health Program, Los Angeles, CA 90089. Offers biometry/epidemiology (MPH); health communication (MPH); health promotion (MPH); preventive nutrition (MPH). *Accreditation:* CEPH. Part-time programs available. *Faculty:* 22 full-time (12 women), 3 part-time/adjunct (0 women). *Students:* 148 full-time (118 women), 7 part-time (6 women); includes 77 minority (17 African Americans, 45 Asian Americans or Pacific Islanders, 15 Hispanic Americans), 24 international. Average age 26. 310 applicants, 66% accepted, 85 enrolled. In 2006, 53 degrees awarded. *Degree requirements:* For master's, practicum, final report, oral presentation. *Entrance requirements:* For master's, GRE General Test, MCAT, GMAT, DAT, minimum GPA of 3.0. Additional exam requirements/recommendations for international students: Required—TOEFL (minimum score 600 paper-based; 250 computer-based; 100 iBT). *Application deadline:* For fall admission, 6/1 priority date for domestic and international students; for spring admission, 11/15 priority date for domestic students, 10/1 priority date for international students. Applications are processed on a rolling basis. Application fee: $85. Electronic applications accepted. *Expenses:* Tuition: Full-time $33,314; part-time $1,121 per credit. Required fees: $522. Full-time tuition and fees vary according to program. *Financial support:* In 2006–07, 131 students received support, including 11 research assistantships with full tuition reimbursements available (averaging $11,109 per year), 18 teaching assistantships with partial tuition reimbursements available (averaging $11,109 per year); career-related internships or fieldwork, Federal Work-Study, institutionally sponsored loans, scholarships/grants, health care benefits, unspecified assistantships, and staff tuition remission also available. Support available to part-time students. Financial award application deadline: 5/1; financial award applicants required to submit CSS PROFILE or FAFSA. *Faculty research:* Substance abuse prevention, cancer and heart disease prevention, mass media and health communication research, health promotion, treatment compliance. Total annual research expenditures: $93.8 million. *Unit head:* Dr. Thomas W. Valente, Director, 626-457-6678, Fax: 626-457-6699, E-mail: tvalente@usc.edu. *Application contact:* Nemesia P. Kelly, Program Specialist, 626-457-6603, Fax: 626-457-6699, E-mail: nkelly@usc.edu.

See Close-Up on page 2065.

University of Southern Mississippi, Graduate School, College of Health, Department of Community Health Sciences, Hattiesburg, MS 39406-0001. Offers epidemiology and biostatistics (MPH); health education (MPH); health policy/administration (MPH); occupational/environmental health (MPH); public health nutrition (MPH). *Accreditation:* CEPH. Part-time and evening/weekend programs available. *Faculty:* 10 full-time (3 women). *Students:* 53 full-time (32 women), 13 part-time (10 women); includes 25 minority (24 African Americans, 1 Asian American or Pacific Islander), 15 international. Average age 30. 114 applicants, 84% accepted, 35 enrolled. In 2006, 27 degrees awarded. *Degree requirements:* For master's, thesis (for some programs), comprehensive exam, registration. *Entrance requirements:* For master's, GRE General Test, minimum GPA of 2.75 in last 60 hours. Additional exam requirements/recommendations for international students: Required—TOEFL. *Application deadline:* For fall admission, 3/1 for domestic and international students. Applications are processed on a rolling basis. Application fee: $25 ($30 for international students). *Financial support:* In 2006–07, 9 research assistantships with full tuition reimbursements (averaging $5,906 per year) were awarded; teaching assistantships with full tuition reimbursements, career-related internships or fieldwork and Federal Work-Study also available. Financial award application deadline: 3/15. *Faculty research:* Rural health care delivery, school health, nutrition of pregnant teens, risk factor reduction, sexually transmitted diseases. *Unit head:* Dr. James McGuire, Chair, 601-266-5437, Fax: 601-266-5043.

University of South Florida, Graduate School, College of Public Health, Tampa, FL 33620-9951. Offers MHA, MPH, MSPH, PhD. *Accreditation:* CEPH (one or more programs are accredited). Part-time and evening/weekend programs available. Postbaccalaureate distance learning degree programs offered (minimal on-campus study). *Faculty:* 63 full-time (31 women), 22 part-time/adjunct (7 women). *Students:* 292 full-time (196 women), 312 part-time (204 women); includes 161 minority (68 African Americans, 2 American Indian/Alaska Native, 39 Asian Americans or Pacific Islanders, 52 Hispanic Americans), 92 international. Average age 33. 319 applicants, 68% accepted, 105 enrolled. In 2006, 132 master's, 17 doctorates awarded. *Median time to degree:* Master's–1.58 years full-time, 3.17 years part-time. Of those who began their doctoral program in fall 1998, 100% received their degree in 8 years or less. *Degree requirements:* For master's, thesis (for some programs), comprehensive exam; for doctorate, thesis/dissertation, comprehensive exam. *Entrance requirements:* For master's and doctorate, GRE General Test, minimum GPA of 3.0 in upper-level course work. Additional exam requirements/recommendations for international students: Required—TOEFL (minimum score 550 paper-based; 213 computer-based; 79 iBT). *Application deadline:* For fall admission, 6/1 for domestic students, 1/2 for international students; for spring admission, 10/15 for domestic students, 7/1 for international students. Applications are processed on a rolling basis. Application fee: $30. Electronic applications accepted. *Financial support:* In 2006–07, 16 fellowships with full tuition reimbursements (averaging $10,006 per year), 88 research assistantships with full and partial tuition reimbursements (averaging $4,532 per year), 83 teaching assistantships (averaging $3,140 per year) were awarded; career-related internships or fieldwork, Federal Work-Study, institutionally sponsored loans, scholarships/grants, traineeships, and unspecified assistantships also available. Support available to part-time students. Financial award applicants required to submit FAFSA. Total annual research expenditures: $16.5 million. *Unit head:* Dr. Donna J. Petersen, Dean, 813-974-3623, Fax: 813-974-7390. *Application contact:* Michelle Robinson, Academic Advisor, 813-974-6665, Fax: 813-974-8121, E-mail: mrobinso@health.usf.edu.

The University of Tennessee, Graduate School, College of Education, Health and Human Sciences, Program in Public Health, Knoxville, TN 37996. Offers community health education (MPH); gerontology (MPH); health planning/administration (MPH); MS/MPH. *Accreditation:* CEPH. *Students:* 42 (36 women); includes 3 minority (2 African Americans, 1 Hispanic American) 3 international. 48 applicants, 54% accepted. In 2006, 34 degrees awarded. *Degree requirements:* For master's, thesis optional. *Entrance requirements:* For master's, minimum GPA of 2.7. Additional exam requirements/recommendations for international students:

Required—TOEFL. *Application deadline:* For fall admission, 2/1 priority date for domestic students. Applications are processed on a rolling basis. Application fee: $35. Electronic applications accepted. *Expenses:* Tuition, state resident: full-time $5,574. Tuition, nonresident: full-time $16,840. Required fees: $792. *Financial support:* Application deadline: 2/1; *Unit head:* Dr. Charles B. Hamilton, Graduate Representative, 865-974-6674, E-mail: cbhamilton@utk.edu.

The University of Texas Health Science Center at Houston, School of Public Health, Houston, TX 77225-0036. Offers MPH, MS, Dr PH, PhD, Certificate, JD/MPH, MD/MPH, MS/MPH, MSN/MPH, MSW/MPH, PhD/MPH. Part-time programs available. *Faculty:* 139 full-time (64 women), 12 part-time/adjunct (4 women). *Students:* 347 full-time (219 women), 436 part-time (329 women); includes 287 minority (78 African Americans, 6 American Indian/Alaska Native, 91 Asian Americans or Pacific Islanders, 112 Hispanic Americans), 179 international. Average age 34. 713 applicants, 65% accepted, 261 enrolled. In 2006, 175 master's, 32 doctorates awarded. *Median time to degree:* Of those who began their doctoral program in fall 1998, 63% received their degree in 8 years or less. *Degree requirements:* For master's, thesis/dissertation; for doctorate, thesis/dissertation, comprehensive exam. *Entrance requirements:* For master's and doctorate, GRE General Test. Additional exam requirements/recommendations for international students: Required—TOEFL (minimum score 565 paper-based; 225 computer-based). *Application deadline:* For fall admission, 2/1 for domestic and international students; for spring admission, 8/1 for domestic and international students. Applications are processed on a rolling basis. Application fee: $30. Electronic applications accepted. *Financial support:* In 2006–07, 25 fellowships (averaging $31,994 per year), 105 research assistantships (averaging $17,054 per year), 76 teaching assistantships (averaging $17,434 per year) were awarded; career-related internships or fieldwork, institutionally sponsored loans, scholarships/grants, traineeships, health care benefits, and unspecified assistantships also available. Support available to part-time students. Financial award application deadline: 5/5; financial award applicants required to submit FAFSA. *Faculty research:* Big-security and public health preparedness, health promotion and prevention research, health services research, infectious diseases, environmental and occupational health. Total annual research expenditures: $42.3 million. *Unit head:* Dr. Guy S. Parcel, Dean, 713-500-9050, Fax: 713-500-9068, E-mail: guy.s.parcel@uth.tmc.edu. *Application contact:* Marius P. Reyes, Pre-Enrollment Services Coordinator, 713-500-9035, Fax: 713-500-9068, E-mail: marius.p.reyes@uth.tmc.edu.

The University of Texas Medical Branch, Graduate School of Biomedical Sciences, Program in Preventive Medicine and Community Health, Program in Public Health, Galveston, TX 77555. Offers MPH. *Accreditation:* CEPH. *Faculty:* 14 full-time (4 women), 11 part-time/adjunct (4 women). *Students:* 21 full-time (4 women); includes 7 minority (3 African Americans, 1 Asian American or Pacific Islander, 3 Hispanic Americans), 1 international. Average age 42. In 2006, 5 degrees awarded. *Degree requirements:* For master's, thesis, registration. *Entrance requirements:* For master's, GRE, USMLE or NBE, preventive medicine resident. Additional exam requirements/recommendations for international students: Required—TOEFL (minimum score 550 paper-based; 213 computer-based). *Application deadline:* For fall admission, 7/1 priority date for domestic and international students; for winter admission, 11/1 priority date for domestic and international students; for spring admission, 3/1 priority date for domestic and international students. Applications are processed on a rolling basis. Application fee: $30 ($75 for international students). Electronic applications accepted. *Financial support:* Applicants required to submit FAFSA. *Unit head:* Dr. Billy U. Philips, Director, 409-772-2551, Fax: 409-772-2573, E-mail: bphilips@utmb.edu. *Application contact:* Tonya R. Groh, Coordinator II Special programs, 409-772-1123, Fax: 409-772-5272, E-mail: trgroh@utmb.edu.

University of the Sciences in Philadelphia, College of Graduate Studies, Program in Public Health, Philadelphia, PA 19104-4495. Offers MPH. *Faculty:* 5 full-time (2 women), 9 part-time/adjunct (3 women). *Students:* 2 full-time (both women). Average age 32. *Expenses:* Tuition: Part-time $1,058 per credit. Tuition and fees vary according to program. *Financial support:* In 2006–07, 2 students received support; fellowships, research assistantships, teaching assistantships available. *Unit head:* Dr. Richard Stefanacci, Program Director, 215-596-7466. *Application contact:* Joyce D'Angelo.

The University of Toledo, College of Graduate Studies, College of Health Science and Human Service, Division of Human Services, Toledo, OH 43606-3390. Offers counselor education and school psychology (MA, PhD, Ed S), including counselor education, guidance/counselor education (PhD), school psychology (MA, Ed S); criminal justice (MA, Certificate), including criminal justice (MA), juvenile justice (Certificate), severe behavioral spectrum (Certificate); health education (PhD); kinesiology (MSX, PhD), including exercise science; public health and rehabilitative services (MA, MPH), including public health (MPH), speech language pathology (MA); recreation and leisure (MA); social work (MS); speech-language pathology (MA). *Students:* 398 full-time (319 women), 270 part-time (194 women); includes 78 minority (60 African Americans, 8 Asian Americans or Pacific Islanders, 10 Hispanic Americans), 23 international. 641 applicants, 51% accepted, 246 enrolled.Application fee: $45. *Unit head:* Dr. Jerome M. Sulivan, Dean, College of Health Science and Human Service, 419-530-4180.

The University of Toledo, College of Graduate Studies, College of Health Science and Human Service, Division of Human Services, Department of Public Health and Rehabilitative Services, Program in Public Health, Toledo, OH 43606-3390. Offers MPH. *Students:* 35 full-time (27 women), 61 part-time (43 women); includes 17 minority (11 African Americans, 4 Asian Americans or Pacific Islanders, 2 Hispanic Americans), 11 international. 56 applicants, 82% accepted, 33 enrolled.Application fee: $45. *Unit head:* Dr. Michael Bisesi, Head, 419-383-4235, E-mail: mbisesi@utoledo.edu. *Application contact:* Mary Alderman, Student Contact, 419-383-5356, E-mail: malderman@meduohio.edu.

University of Toronto, School of Graduate Studies, Life Sciences Division, Department of Public Health Sciences, Toronto, ON M5S 1A1, Canada. Offers M Sc, MH Sc, PhD, Diploma. *Accreditation:* CAHME (one or more programs are accredited); CEPH (one or more programs are accredited). Part-time programs available. *Degree requirements:* For master's, thesis (for some programs), practicum; for doctorate, thesis/dissertation, oral thesis defense, comprehensive exam. *Entrance requirements:* For master's, 2 letters of reference, relevant professional/research experience, minimum B average in final year; for doctorate, 2 letters of reference, relevant professional/research experience, minimum B+ average. Additional exam requirements/recommendations for international students: Required—TOEFL (minimum score 580 paper-based; 237 computer-based), TWE (minimum score 5). Expenses: Contact institution.

University of Utah, School of Medicine and The Graduate School, Graduate Programs in Medicine, Programs in Public Health, Salt Lake City, UT 84112-1107. Offers biostatistics (M Stat); public health (MPH, MSPH, PhD). *Accreditation:* CEPH (one or more programs are accredited). Part-time programs available. *Faculty:* 8 full-time (2 women), 49 part-time/adjunct (9 women). *Students:* 56 full-time (33 women), 47 part-time (32 women); includes 15 minority (2 African Americans, 2 American Indian/Alaska Native, 6 Asian Americans or Pacific Islanders, 5 Hispanic Americans), 2 international. Average age 35. 89 applicants, 56% accepted, 39 enrolled. In 2006, 48 degrees awarded. *Degree requirements:* For master's, thesis (for some programs), thesis or project (MSPH), comprehensive exam, registration; for doctorate, thesis/dissertation, comprehensive exam, registration. *Entrance requirements:* For master's and doctorate, GRE General Test, 3 letters of reference, in-person interviews, minimum GPA of 3.0, personal statement. Additional exam requirements/recommendations for international students: Required—TOEFL (minimum score 550 paper-based; 175 computer-based). *Application deadline:* For fall admission, 2/15 for domestic students, 1/15 for international students. Application fee: $45 ($65 for international students). Electronic applications accepted. *Expenses:* Tuition, state resident: full-time $3,208. Tuition, nonresident: full-time $11,326. Required fees: $608. Tuition and fees vary according to class time and program. *Financial support:* In 2006–07, 2 fellowships (averaging $5,200 per year), 3 research assistantships with full tuition reimbursements (averaging $10,500 per year), 2 teaching assistantships with full tuition reimbursements (averaging $10,500 per year) were awarded. *Faculty research:* Health services, health policy, epidemiology of chronic disease, infectious disease epidemiology, cancer

epidemiology. *Unit head:* Dr. George L. White, Director, 801-587-3315, Fax: 801-587-3353, E-mail: george.white@utah.edu. *Application contact:* Peggy Christensen, Administrative Program Coordinator, 801-587-3315, Fax: 801-587-3353, E-mail: peggy.christensen@utah.edu.

University of Virginia, School of Medicine, Department of Public Health Sciences, Program in Public Health, Charlottesville, VA 22903. Offers MPH. *Accreditation:* CEPH. *Students:* 17 full-time (11 women), 4 part-time (2 women); includes 8 minority (5 African Americans, 3 Asian Americans or Pacific Islanders). Average age 33. 53 applicants, 47% accepted, 13 enrolled. *Entrance requirements:* For master's, GRE or MCAT. Additional exam requirements/recommendations for international students: Required—TOEFL. *Application deadline:* Applications are processed on a rolling basis. Application fee: $60. Electronic applications accepted. *Financial support:* Applicants required to submit FAFSA. *Application contact:* Robyn Kells, Coordinator, 434-924-8646, Fax: 434-924-8437, E-mail: ms-hes@virginia.edu.

University of Washington, Graduate School, School of Public Health and Community Medicine, Seattle, WA 98195-7230. Offers EMHA, MHA, MPH, MS, PhD, DDS/PhD, MD/MPH, MD/PhD, MHA/MBA, MHA/MD, MHA/MPA, MN/MPH, MPH/MAIS, MPH/MHA, MPH/MN, MPH/MPA, MPH/MS, MPH/MSW, MS/MPA. *Accreditation:* CAHME (one or more programs are accredited); CEPH (one or more programs are accredited). Part-time and evening/weekend programs available. Postbaccalaureate distance learning degree programs offered (minimal on-campus study). Terminal master's awarded for partial completion of doctoral program. *Degree requirements:* For master's, thesis (for some programs), practicum (MPH), capstone project (MHA); for doctorate, thesis/dissertation, comprehensive exam, registration. *Entrance requirements:* For master's and doctorate, GRE General Test, minimum GPA of 3.0. Additional exam requirements/recommendations for international students: Required—TOEFL (minimum score 580 paper-based; 237 computer-based). *Faculty research:* Health services (health care delivery/health policy), epidemiology, biostatistics, environmental and occupational sciences, pathobiology (infectious disease).

University of West Florida, College of Arts and Sciences: Sciences, Division of Life and Health Sciences, Program in Public Health, Pensacola, FL 32514-5750. Offers MPH. Part-time and evening/weekend programs available. *Students:* 1 (woman) full-time, 2 part-time (1 woman), 1 international. Average age 38. 7 applicants, 29% accepted, 0 enrolled. *Entrance requirements:* Additional exam requirements/recommendations for international students: Required—TOEFL (minimum score 550 paper-based; 213 computer-based). *Application deadline:* For fall admission, 6/1 for domestic students, 5/15 for international students; for spring admission, 11/1 for domestic students, 10/1 for international students. Applications are processed on a rolling basis. Application fee: $30. *Expenses:* Tuition, state resident: full-time $5,871; part-time $245 per credit hour. Tuition, nonresident: full-time $21,241; part-time $885 per credit hour. *Financial support:* Application deadline: 4/15; *Unit head:* Dr. George L. Stewart, Chairperson, Division of Life and Health Sciences, 850-474-2748.

University of Wisconsin–Eau Claire, College of Nursing and Health Sciences, Department of Public Health Professions, Eau Claire, WI 54702-4004. Offers environmental and public health (MS). *Faculty:* 4 full-time (2 women), 1 (woman) part-time/adjunct. *Students:* 5 full-time (3 women), 1 part-time; includes 2 minority (both African Americans), 1 international. Average age 37. 8 applicants, 50% accepted, 3 enrolled. In 2006, 3 degrees awarded. *Degree requirements:* For master's, thesis, oral and written exams. *Entrance requirements:* For master's, bachelor's degree in environmental health or related sciences. *Application deadline:* For fall admission, 3/1 for domestic students. Applications are processed on a rolling basis. Application fee: $45. *Expenses:* Tuition, state resident: full-time $6,533; part-time $363 per credit. Tuition, nonresident: full-time $17,143; part-time $952 per credit. Tuition and fees vary according to program and reciprocity agreements. *Financial support:* In 2006–07, 4 students received support, including 4 teaching assistantships (averaging $5,800 per year); Federal Work-Study also available. Financial award application deadline: 3/1; financial award applicants required to submit FAFSA. *Unit head:* Dr. Douglas Olson, Chair, 715-836-2628, Fax: 715-836-3379, E-mail: olsondou@uwec.edu.

University of Wisconsin–La Crosse, Office of University Graduate Studies, College of Science and Health, Department of Health Education and Health Promotion, La Crosse, WI 54601-3742. Offers community health education (MPH, MS); school health education (MS). *Accreditation:* CEPH (one or more programs are accredited). Part-time and evening/weekend programs available. *Faculty:* 6 full-time (4 women). *Students:* 14 full-time (all women), 21 part-time (17 women); includes 2 minority (both African Americans), 3 international. Average age 30. 9 applicants, 78% accepted, 3 enrolled. In 2006, 10 degrees awarded. *Degree requirements:* For master's, thesis (for some programs), community health education preceptorship. *Entrance requirements:* For master's, GRE General Test, GRE Subject Test (MPH), minimum GPA of 3.0 (MPH), minimum GPA of 2.85 (MS). Additional exam requirements/recommendations for international students: Required—TOEFL (minimum score 550 paper-based; 213 computer-based). *Application deadline:* For spring admission, 2/15 for domestic students. Applications are processed on a rolling basis. Application fee: $45. Electronic applications accepted. *Financial support:* Research assistantships with partial tuition reimbursements, career-related internships or fieldwork, traineeships, health care benefits, unspecified assistantships, and grant-funded positions available. Support available to part-time students. Financial award application deadline: 2/15; financial award applicants required to submit FAFSA. *Faculty research:* Stress management, wellness inventories, needs assessment, health promotion, drug and alcohol use, education, school curriculum. *Unit head:* Dr. Dan Duquette, Chair, 608-785-8161, Fax: 608-785-6742, E-mail: duquette.rode@uwlax.edu. *Application contact:* Kathryn Kiefer, Associate Director of Admissions, 608-785-8939, E-mail: admissions@uwlax.edu.

Vanderbilt University, School of Medicine, Program in Public Health, Nashville, TN 37240-1001. Offers MPH. *Degree requirements:* For master's, thesis, project. *Entrance requirements:* For master's, curriculum vitae. *Application deadline:* For fall admission, 2/28 for domestic students. *Expenses:* Tuition: full-time $24,462. Required fees: $2,515. One-time fee: $30 full-time. Full-time tuition and fees vary according to course load, degree level and program. *Unit head:* Cindty Naron, Coordinator, 615-343-6338, Fax: 615-343-8722, E-mail: cindy.naron@vanderbilt.edu.

Virginia Commonwealth University, Medical College of Virginia-Professional Programs, School of Medicine and Graduate Programs, School of Medicine Graduate Programs, Department of Epidemiology and Community Health, Richmond, VA 23284-9005. Offers epidemiology and community health (PhD); public health (MPH); MD/MPH. *Faculty:* 13 full-time (5 women). *Students:* 1 full-time (0 women), 1 international. In 2006, 8 degrees awarded. *Degree requirements:* For master's, research project. *Entrance requirements:* For master's, GMAT or MCAT, DAT or GRE General Test. *Application deadline:* For fall admission, 4/1 for domestic students. Application fee: $50. *Unit head:* Dr. Tilahun Adera, Chair, 804-828-9785, Fax: 804-828-9773, E-mail: tadera@vcu.edu.

See Close-Up on page 2071.

Walden University, Graduate Programs, School of Health and Human Services, Minneapolis, MN 55401. Offers health services (PhD); human services (PhD); nursing (MS); public health (MPH, PhD). Part-time and evening/weekend programs available. Postbaccalaureate distance learning degree programs offered (minimal on-campus study). *Faculty:* 100. *Students:* 2,383 full-time (2,074 women), 1,082 part-time (876 women); includes 840 minority (662 African Americans, 18 American Indian/Alaska Native, 83 Asian Americans or Pacific Islanders, 77 Hispanic Americans), 24 international. Average age 42. 1,164 applicants, 85% accepted, 813 enrolled. In 2006, 212 master's, 30 doctorates awarded. *Degree requirements:* For master's, thesis (for some programs); for doctorate, thesis/dissertation. *Entrance requirements:* For master's, minimum GPA of 3.0; for doctorate, 3 years of professional experience, master's degree. Additional exam requirements/recommendations for international students: Required—TOEFL (minimum score 550 paper-based; 213 computer-based), IELTS (minimum score 7). *Application deadline:* For fall admission, 8/15 priority date

Public Health—General

Walden University (continued)

for domestic and international students; for winter admission, 11/15 priority date for domestic and international students; for spring admission, 12/15 priority date for domestic and international students. Applications are processed on a rolling basis. Application fee: $50. Electronic applications accepted. *Financial support:* Fellowships with partial tuition reimbursements, tuition waivers (partial) available. Support available to part-time students. Financial award applicants required to submit FAFSA. *Unit head:* Dr. Gary J. Burkholder, Dean, 800-925-3368, Fax: 612-338-5092. *Application contact:* 866-4-WALDEN, Fax: 410-843-8780, E-mail: request@waldenu.edu.

Wayne State University, School of Medicine, Graduate Programs in Medicine, Department of Community Medicine, Detroit, MI 48202. Offers community health (MS); community health services (Certificate); public health (MPH); public health practice (Certificate). *Faculty:* 3 full-time (1 woman). *Students:* 5 full-time (4 women), 23 part-time (17 women); includes 11 minority (8 African Americans, 3 Asian Americans or Pacific Islanders), 7 international. Average age 35. 28 applicants, 32% accepted, 0 enrolled. *Degree requirements:* For master's, thesis (for some programs). *Entrance requirements:* For master's, GRE, minimum GPA of 2.6. Additional exam requirements/recommendations for international students: Required—TOEFL (minimum score 550 paper-based; 213 computer-based); Recommended—TWE (minimum score 6). *Application deadline:* For fall admission, 8/1 for domestic students, 6/1 for international students; for winter admission, 10/1 for international students; for spring admission, 2/1 for international students. Applications are processed on a rolling basis. Application fee: $30 ($50 for international students). Electronic applications accepted. *Financial support:* Research assistantships with tuition reimbursements, career-related internships or fieldwork, Federal Work-Study, and scholarships/grants available. Support available to part-time students. Financial award application deadline: 6/1. *Faculty research:* Urban health disparities, community health promotion, substance abuse etiology and prevention, HIV/AIDS, interpersonal violence. Total annual research expenditures: $54,800. *Unit head:* Dr. Antonia Abbey, Chair, 313-577-6686, Fax: 313-577-0316, E-mail: ab8222@wayne.edu. *Application contact:* James Moseley, Director, 313-577-7948, Fax: 313-577-0316, E-mail: jmosele@med.wayne.edu.

West Chester University of Pennsylvania, Graduate Studies, School of Health Sciences, Department of Health, West Chester, PA 19383. Offers emergency preparedness (Certificate); environmental health (MS); gerontology (MS); health care administration (Certificate); health services (MSA); integrative health (Certificate); public health (MPH, MS); school health (M Ed). Part-time and evening/weekend programs available. *Students:* 35 full-time (27 women), 65 part-time (50 women); includes 19 African Americans, 1 Asian American or Pacific Islander, 9 international. Average age 34. 58 applicants, 98% accepted, 30 enrolled. In 2006, 36 degrees awarded. *Degree requirements:* For master's, thesis (for some programs), comprehensive exam. *Entrance requirements:* For master's, GRE. *Application deadline:* For fall admission, 4/15 priority date for domestic students; for spring admission, 10/15 for domestic students. Applications are processed on a rolling basis. Application fee: $35. *Financial support:* In 2006–07, 9 research assistantships with full tuition reimbursements (averaging $5,000 per year) were awarded; unspecified assistantships also available. Support available to part-time students. Financial award application deadline: 2/15; financial award applicants required to submit FAFSA. *Faculty research:* HIV/AIDS education, teacher preparation, water quality. *Unit head:* Dr. Roger Mustalish, Chair, 610-436-2931, E-mail: rmustalish@wcupa.edu. *Application contact:* Dr. Bethann Cinelli, Graduate Coordinator, 610-436-2267, E-mail: bcinelli@wcupa.edu.

Western Kentucky University, Graduate Studies, College of Health and Human Services, Department of Public Health, Bowling Green, KY 42101. Offers healthcare administration (MHA); public health (MPH). *Accreditation:* CEPH. Part-time and evening/weekend programs available. *Faculty:* 13 full-time (4 women), 4 part-time/adjunct (2 women). *Students:* 89 full-time (33 women), 45 part-time (23 women); includes 14 minority (10 African Americans, 2 Asian Americans or Pacific Islanders, 2 Hispanic Americans), 88 international. Average age 28. 170 applicants, 38% accepted, 32 enrolled. In 2006, 32 degrees awarded. *Degree requirements:* For master's, thesis or alternative, comprehensive exam. *Entrance requirements:* For master's, GRE General Test, minimum GPA of 2.75. Additional exam requirements/recommendations for international students: Required—TOEFL (minimum score 555 paper-based; 213 computer-based; 79 iBT). *Application deadline:* For fall admission, 7/1 priority date for domestic students, 4/1 for international students; for spring admission, 11/1 for domestic students, 9/1 for international students. Applications are processed on a rolling basis. Application fee: $35. *Expenses:* Tuition, state resident: full-time $6,520; part-time $226 per hour. Tuition, nonresident: full-time $7,140; part-time $357 per hour. International tuition: $15,820 full-time. *Financial support:* In

2006–07, 10 research assistantships with partial tuition reimbursements (averaging $9,500 per year) were awarded; career-related internships or fieldwork, Federal Work-Study, institutionally sponsored loans, tuition waivers (partial), unspecified assistantships, and service awards also available. Support available to part-time students. Financial award application deadline: 4/1; financial award applicants required to submit FAFSA. *Faculty research:* Health education training, driver traffic safety, community readiness, occupational injuries, local health departments. Total annual research expenditures: $88,907. *Unit head:* Dr. David Dunn, Interim Head, 270-745-6395, Fax: 270-745-4437, E-mail: david.dunn@wku.edu.

West Virginia University, School of Medicine, Department of Community Medicine, Program in Public Health, Morgantown, WV 26506. Offers community health/preventative medicine (MPH). *Accreditation:* CEPH. Part-time programs available. Postbaccalaureate distance learning degree programs offered (minimal on-campus study). *Students:* Average age 31. In 2006, 10 degrees awarded. *Degree requirements:* For master's, practicum, project. *Entrance requirements:* For master's, GRE General Test, MCAT, medical degree; medical internship. *Application deadline:* For fall admission, 4/15 priority date for domestic students; for spring admission, 12/1 for domestic students. Applications are processed on a rolling basis. *Expenses:* Contact institution. Tuition and fees vary according to program. *Financial support:* In 2006–07, 15 research assistantships, 3 teaching assistantships were awarded. Financial award application deadline: 2/1; financial award applicants required to submit FAFSA. *Faculty research:* Occupational health, environmental health, clinical epidemiology, health care management, prevention. Total annual research expenditures: $500,000. *Unit head:* Dr. Ian Rockett, Director of Educational Programs, 304-293-5325, Fax: 304-293-3755, E-mail: irockett@hsc.wvu.edu. *Application contact:* Leah A. Adkins, Senior Program Coordinator, 304-293-1098, Fax: 304-293-3755, E-mail: ladkins@hsc.wvu.edu.

Wichita State University, Graduate School, College of Health Professions, Department of Public Health, Wichita, KS 67260. Offers MPH. *Entrance requirements:* For master's, GRE, bachelor's degree in health, minimum GPA of 3.0, 1 year of work experience. Additional exam requirements/recommendations for international students: Required—TOEFL. Electronic applications accepted.

Wright State University, School of Medicine, Program in Public Health, Dayton, OH 45435. Offers health promotion and education (MPH); public health management (MPH); public health nursing (MPH). *Accreditation:* CEPH. *Unit head:* Dr. Richard J. Schuster, Director, 937-258-5555, Fax: 937-258-5544, E-mail: richard.schuster@wright.edu.

Yale University, School of Medicine, School of Public Health, New Haven, CT 06520. Offers biostatistics (MPH, MS, PhD); chronic disease epidemiology (MPH, PhD); environmental health sciences (MPH, PhD); epidemiology of microbial diseases (MPH, PhD); global health (MPH); health management (MPH); health policy and administration (MPH, PhD); parasitology (PhD); social and behavioral sciences (MPH); MBA/MPH; MD/MPH; MPH/MA; MSN/MPH. MS and PhD offered through the Graduate School. Part-time programs available. *Faculty:* 67 full-time (37 women), 53 part-time/adjunct (18 women). *Students:* 209 full-time (169 women), 8 part-time (4 women); includes 77 minority (24 African Americans, 44 Asian Americans or Pacific Islanders, 9 Hispanic Americans), 21 international. Average age 26. 413 applicants, 71% accepted. In 2006, 124 master's, 8 doctorates awarded. Terminal master's awarded for partial completion of doctoral program. *Degree requirements:* For master's, thesis, internship; for doctorate, thesis/dissertation, residency, comprehensive exam. *Entrance requirements:* For master's, GMAT, GRE, or MCAT, previous undergraduate course work in mathematics and science; for doctorate, GRE General Test. Additional exam requirements/recommendations for international students: Required—TOEFL. *Application deadline:* For fall admission, 1/15 for domestic and international students. Application fee: $60. Electronic applications accepted. *Expenses:* Contact institution. *Financial support:* In 2006–07, 21 fellowships with full tuition reimbursements (averaging $12,560 per year), 4 research assistantships with full tuition reimbursements (averaging $24,910 per year) were awarded; teaching assistantships with full tuition reimbursements, career-related internships or fieldwork, Federal Work-Study, institutionally sponsored loans, scholarships/grants, and tuition waivers (full and partial) also available. Support available to part-time students. Financial award application deadline: 3/1; financial award applicants required to submit FAFSA. *Faculty research:* Genetic and emerging infections epidemiology, virology, cost/quality, vector biology, quantitative methods. *Unit head:* Dr. Paul D. Cleary, Dean and Chairman, 203-785-2867, Fax: 203-785-6103, E-mail: paul.cleary@yale.edu. *Application contact:* Jacqui Comshaw, Director of Admissions, 203-785-2844, Fax: 203-785-4845, E-mail: eph.admissions@yale.edu.

See Close-Up on page 2073.

Community Health

Adelphi University, School of Education, Program in Health Studies, Garden City, NY 11530-0701. Offers community health education (MA, Certificate); school health education (MA). Part-time and evening/weekend programs available. *Students:* 10 full-time (9 women), 95 part-time (51 women); includes 6 minority (3 African Americans, 3 Hispanic Americans), 1 international. Average age 29. In 2006, 30 degrees awarded. *Degree requirements:* For master's, internship. *Entrance requirements:* For master's, 3 letters of recommendation, resumé, minimum cumulative GPA of 2.75. Additional exam requirements/recommendations for international students: Required—TOEFL (minimum score 550 paper-based; 213 computer-based). *Application deadline:* Applications are processed on a rolling basis. Application fee: $50. Electronic applications accepted. *Financial support:* Fellowships, research assistantships with partial tuition reimbursements, teaching assistantships, career-related internships or fieldwork, Federal Work-Study, institutionally sponsored loans, and tuition waivers (full) available. Support available to part-time students. Financial award application deadline: 2/15; financial award applicants required to submit FAFSA. *Faculty research:* Alcohol abuse, tobacco cessation, drug abuse, healthy family lives, healthy personal living. *Unit head:* Dr. Stanley Snegroff, Director, 516-877-4283, E-mail: snegroff@adelphi.edu. *Application contact:* Christine Murphy, Director of Admissions, 516-877-3050, Fax: 516-877-3039, E-mail: graduateadmissions@adelphi.edu.

Arcadia University, Graduate Studies, Department of Medical Science and Community Health, Glenside, PA 19038-3295. Offers MM Sc, MSHE, MSPH, MM Sc/MAHE, MM Sc/MSPH. *Students:* 124 full-time (99 women); includes 7 minority (2 African Americans, 4 Asian Americans or Pacific Islanders, 1 Hispanic American), 1 international. In 2006, 56 degrees awarded. *Entrance requirements:* For master's, GRE General Test or MCAT. Additional exam requirements/recommendations for international students: Required—TOEFL. *Application deadline:* For fall admission, 1/5 priority date for domestic students. Application fee: $50. *Expenses:* Contact institution. *Financial support:* Tuition waivers (partial) available. *Unit head:* Michael Dryer, Chair, 215-572-2083. *Application contact:* 215-572-2910, Fax: 215-572-4041, E-mail: admiss@arcadia.edu.

Bloomsburg University of Pennsylvania, School of Graduate Studies, College of Professional Studies, School of Health Sciences, Department of Nursing, Bloomsburg, PA 17815-1301. Offers adult and family nurse practitioner (MSN); adult health and illness (MSN); community health (MSN); nursing (MSN); nursing administration (MSN). *Accreditation:* AACN. *Faculty:* 11 full-time (all women). *Students:* 9 full-time (all women), 27 part-time (24 women). Average age 36. 10 applicants, 100% accepted, 5 enrolled. In 2006, 6 degrees awarded.

Degree requirements: For master's, thesis. *Entrance requirements:* For master's, minimum QPA of 3.0. Additional exam requirements/recommendations for international students: Required—TOEFL. *Application deadline:* Applications are processed on a rolling basis. Application fee: $30. Electronic applications accepted. *Expenses:* Tuition, state resident: full-time $6,048; part-time $336 per credit. Tuition, nonresident: full-time $9,678; part-time $538 per credit. Required fees: $1,415. *Financial support:* Unspecified assistantships available. *Faculty research:* Cardiopulmonary nursing, cancer topics, women's health. *Application contact:* Dr. Michelle Ficca, Coordinator, 570-389-4615, Fax: 570-389-5008, E-mail: mficca@bloomu.edu.

Brooklyn College of the City University of New York, Division of Graduate Studies, Department of Health and Nutrition Science, Program in Community Health, Brooklyn, NY 11210-2889. Offers community health education (MA); computer science and health science (MS); thanatology (MA). *Accreditation:* CEPH. *Students:* 23 applicants, 70% accepted, 4 enrolled. In 2006, 11 degrees awarded. *Degree requirements:* For master's, thesis or alternative. *Entrance requirements:* For master's, 18 credits in health-related areas, 2 letters of recommendation, essay. Additional exam requirements/recommendations for international students: Required—TOEFL. *Application deadline:* For fall admission, 3/1 priority date for domestic students, 2/1 priority date for international students; for spring admission, 11/1 priority date for domestic students, 10/1 priority date for international students. Applications are processed on a rolling basis. Application fee: $125. Electronic applications accepted. *Expenses:* Tuition, state resident: full-time $6,400; part-time $270 per credit. Tuition, nonresident: full-time $12,000; part-time $500 per credit. Required fees: $118 per semester. *Financial support:* Federal Work-Study, institutionally sponsored loans, and scholarships/grants available. Support available to part-time students. Financial award application deadline: 5/1; financial award applicants required to submit FAFSA. *Faculty research:* Diet restriction, religious practices in bereavement, diabetes, stress management, palliative care. *Unit head:* Dr. Jean Grassman, Graduate Deputy Chairperson, 718-951-5026, Fax: 718-951-4670, E-mail: grassman@brooklyn.cuny.edu. *Application contact:* Karen Alleyne-Pierre, Director of Admissions Services and Enrollment Communications, 718-951-5902, Fax: 718-951-4506, E-mail: grads@brooklyn.cuny.edu.

Brooklyn College of the City University of New York, Division of Graduate Studies, Department of Health and Nutrition Science, Program in Public Health, Brooklyn, NY 11210-2889. Offers community health (MPH); health care management (MPH); health care policy and administration (MPH). *Accreditation:* CEPH. *Students:* 3 full-time (2 women), 49 part-time (35 women); includes 27 minority (18 African Americans, 5 Asian Americans or Pacific Islanders, 4 Hispanic Americans), 7 international. 45 applicants, 71% accepted, 11 enrolled. In 2006, 5 degrees awarded. *Entrance requirements:* For master's, GRE, 2 letters of recommendation, essay. *Application deadline:* For fall admission, 3/1 priority date for domestic students, 2/1 priority date for international students; for spring admission, 11/1 priority date for domestic students, 10/1 priority date for international students. Applications are processed on a rolling basis. Application fee: $125. Electronic applications accepted. *Expenses:* Tuition, state resident: full-time $6,400; part-time $270 per credit. Tuition, nonresident: full-time $12,000; part-time $500 per credit. Required fees: $118 per semester. *Financial support:* Application deadline: 5/1. *Unit head:* Dr. Jean Grassman, Graduate Deputy Chairperson, 718-951-5026, Fax: 718-951-4670, E-mail: grassman@brooklyn.cuny.edu. *Application contact:* Karen Alleyne-Pierre, Director of Admissions Services and Enrollment Communications, 718-951-5902, Fax: 718-951-4506, E-mail: grads@brooklyn.cuny.edu.

Brown University, Graduate School, Division of Biology and Medicine, Department of Community Health, Providence, RI 02912. Offers health services research (MS, PhD); public health (MPH); statistical science (MS, PhD), including biostatistics, epidemiology; MD/PhD. *Accreditation:* CEPH. *Degree requirements:* For doctorate, thesis/dissertation, preliminary exam. *Entrance requirements:* For master's and doctorate, GRE General Test. Additional exam requirements/recommendations for international students: Required—TOEFL.

California College for Health Sciences, Program in Health Services, Salt Lake City, UT 84107. Offers community health (MSHS); wellness promotion (MSHS). Part-time and evening/weekend programs available. Postbaccalaureate distance learning degree programs offered (no on-campus study). *Degree requirements:* For master's, fieldwork, internship, final project (wellness promotion). *Entrance requirements:* For master's, previous course work in psychology.

Columbia University, Mailman School of Public Health, Division of Sociomedical Sciences, New York, NY 10032. Offers MPH, Dr PH, PhD. PhD offered in cooperation with the Graduate School of Arts and Sciences. *Accreditation:* CEPH (one or more programs are accredited). Part-time programs available. *Students:* 246. In 2006, 35 master's, 1 doctorate awarded. *Degree requirements:* For master's and doctorate, thesis/dissertation. *Entrance requirements:* For master's, GRE General Test; for doctorate, GRE General Test, MPH or equivalent (Dr PH). *Application deadline:* For fall admission, 2/1 for domestic students; for spring admission, 10/1 for domestic students. Application fee: $60. Electronic applications accepted. *Financial support:* Research assistantships, teaching assistantships, career-related internships or fieldwork and Federal Work-Study available. Support available to part-time students. Financial award application deadline: 2/1; financial award applicants required to submit FAFSA. *Faculty research:* Social and cultural factors in health and health care, health services delivery and utilization, health promotion and disease prevention, AIDS. *Unit head:* Dr. Richard Parker, Chair, 212-305-5656. *Application contact:* June Saunders, Associate Director of Admissions, 212-305-3927, Fax: 212-342-4861, E-mail: ph-admit@columbia.edu.

Dalhousie University, Faculty of Graduate Studies, Department of Community Health and Epidemiology, Halifax, NS B3H 4R2, Canada. Offers M Sc. Part-time programs available. *Degree requirements:* For master's, thesis. *Entrance requirements:* Additional exam requirements/recommendations for international students: Required—TOEFL. Expenses: Contact institution. *Faculty research:* Population health, health promotion and disease prevention, health services utilization, chronic disease epidemiology.

Eastern Kentucky University, The Graduate School, College of Health Sciences, Department of Health Promotion and Administration, Richmond, KY 40475-3102. Offers chemical abuse and dependency (MPH); community health (MPH). *Faculty:* 7 full-time (5 women). *Students:* 23 full-time (13 women), 10 part-time (7 women); includes 3 minority (all African Americans), 17 international. Average age 28. 139 applicants, 22% accepted. In 2006, 8 degrees awarded. Application fee: $35. *Expenses:* Tuition, state resident: full-time $5,610. Tuition, nonresident: full-time $15,910. *Unit head:* Dr. Michael Ballard, Chair, 859-622-1142, Fax: 859-622-2916.

East Stroudsburg University of Pennsylvania, Graduate School, School of Health Sciences and Human Performance, Program in Public Health, East Stroudsburg, PA 18301-2999. Offers community health education (MPH). Part-time and evening/weekend programs available. Postbaccalaureate distance learning degree programs offered (minimal on-campus study). *Faculty:* 3 full-time (2 women), 1 (woman) part-time/adjunct. *Students:* 14 full-time (9 women), 5 part-time (all women); includes 4 minority (1 African American, 2 Asian Americans or Pacific Islanders, 1 Hispanic American), 5 international. Average age 33. In 2006, 9 degrees awarded. *Degree requirements:* For master's, publishable paper. *Entrance requirements:* For master's, GRE, 3 letters of recommendation. Additional exam requirements/recommendations for international students: Required—TOEFL (minimum score 560 paper-based; 220 computer-based; 83 iBT). *Application deadline:* For fall admission, 7/31 priority date for domestic students, 5/1 priority date for international students; for spring admission, 11/30 for domestic students, 10/1 for international students. Applications are processed on a rolling basis. Application fee: $50. Electronic applications accepted. *Expenses:* Tuition, state resident: full-time $6,048; part-time $336 per credit. Tuition, nonresident: full-time $9,678; part-time $538 per credit. Required fees: $1,353; $67 per credit. One-time fee: $37 part-time. *Financial support:* In 2006–07, 9 research assistantships with partial tuition reimbursements were awarded; career-related internships or fieldwork and unspecified assistantships also available. *Faculty research:* Public health infrastructure. Total annual research expenditures: $500,000. *Unit head:* Dr. Carolyn Woodhouse, MPH Program Director, 570-422-3702, E-mail: cwoodhouse@po-box.esu.edu.

East Tennessee State University, School of Graduate Studies, College of Public and Allied Health, Department of Public Health, Johnson City, TN 37614. Offers community health (MPH); epidemiology (Certificate); gerontology (Certificate); health care management (Certificate); public health (MPH); public health administration (MPH). *Accreditation:* CEPH. Part-time programs available. *Degree requirements:* For master's, thesis optional. *Entrance requirements:* For master's, GRE General Test, 2 years of community health experience. Additional exam requirements/recommendations for international students: Required—TOEFL (minimum score 550 paper-based; 213 computer-based). *Faculty research:* Rural health issues, youth and adolescent health, health of the elderly, environmental epidemiology, spatial analysis of data.

Emory University, Rollins School of Public Health, Department of Behavioral Sciences and Health Education, Atlanta, GA 30322-1100. Offers MPH, PhD. *Accreditation:* CEPH. Part-time programs available. *Students:* 145 full-time (138 women), 18 part-time (16 women). Average age 27. 215 applicants, 72% accepted, 80 enrolled. In 2006, 49 degrees awarded. *Degree requirements:* For master's, thesis, practicum, comprehensive exam. *Entrance requirements:* For master's, GRE General Test. Additional exam requirements/recommendations for international students: Required—TOEFL (minimum score 550 paper-based; 220 computer-based). *Application deadline:* For fall admission, 1/5 priority date for domestic and international students. Application fee: $75. Electronic applications accepted. *Expenses:* Tuition: Full-time $30,246. *Financial support:* Fellowships with full and partial tuition reimbursements, career-related internships or fieldwork, Federal Work-Study, institutionally sponsored loans, and scholarships/grants available. Support available to part-time students. Financial award application deadline: 1/5. *Unit head:* Dr. Michael Windle, Professor, 404-727-9868, Fax: 404-712-4299. *Application contact:* Melissa Krancer, Assistant Director, Academic Programs, 404-727-3899, E-mail: mkrancer@sph.emory.edu.

See Close-Up on page 2035.

The George Washington University, School of Public Health and Health Services, Department of Prevention and Community Health, Washington, DC 20052. Offers community-oriented primary care (MPH); health promotion (MPH); maternal and child health (MPH); public health and emergency management (Certificate). *Accreditation:* CEPH. *Entrance requirements:* For master's, GRE or GMAT, 2 letters of recommendation, resumé. Additional exam requirements/recommendations for international students: Required—TOEFL.

Idaho State University, Office of Graduate Studies, Kasiska College of Health Professions, Department of Family Medicine, Pocatello, ID 83209. Offers Post-Master's Certificate. *Faculty:* 1 full-time (0 women). *Degree requirements:* For Post-Master's Certificate, 3 year residency program, thesis optional. *Entrance requirements:* For degree, GRE General Test, MD or DO. Additional exam requirements/recommendations for international students: Required—TOEFL (minimum score 600 paper-based; 213 computer-based). *Application deadline:* For fall admission, 7/1 for domestic students, 6/1 for international students; for spring admission, 12/1 for domestic students, 11/1 for international students. Applications are processed on a rolling basis. Application fee: $55. *Financial support:* Application deadline: 1/1. *Faculty research:* Rural medicine, rural health data bases. Total annual research expenditures: $448,581. *Unit head:* Dr. Jonathan Cree, Director, 208-282-4704, Fax: 208-282-4818, E-mail: joncree@otc.isu.edu. *Application contact:* Ellen Combs, Graduate School Technical Records Specialist, 208-282-2150, Fax: 208-282-4847.

Indiana State University, School of Graduate Studies, College of Health and Human Performance, Department of Health, Safety, and Environmental Health Sciences, Terre Haute, IN 47809-1401. Offers community health promotion (MA, MS); occupational safety management (MA, MS); school health and safety (MA, MS). *Accreditation:* NCATE (one or more programs are accredited). *Faculty:* 9 full-time (1 woman), 2 part-time/adjunct (1 woman). *Students:* 3 full-time (2 women), 19 part-time (5 women); includes 4 minority (3 African Americans, 1 Hispanic American), 1 international. Average age 37. 8 applicants, 63% accepted, 2 enrolled. In 2006, 3 degrees awarded. *Degree requirements:* For master's, thesis or alternative. *Entrance requirements:* For master's, GRE General Test. *Application deadline:* For fall admission, 7/1 priority date for domestic students; for spring admission, 11/1 priority date for domestic students. Applications are processed on a rolling basis. Application fee: $35. Electronic applications accepted. *Expenses:* Tuition, state resident: part-time $278 per credit. Tuition, nonresident: part-time $552 per credit. *Financial support:* In 2006–07, 1 research assistantship (averaging $3,150 per year) was awarded; teaching assistantships, tuition waivers (full) and unspecified assistantships also available. Financial award application deadline: 3/1; financial award applicants required to submit FAFSA. *Unit head:* Dr. Ernest Sheldon, Interim Chairperson, 812-237-3071.

The Johns Hopkins University, Bloomberg School of Public Health, Department of Health, Behavior and Society, Baltimore, MD 21218-2699. Offers behavioral sciences and health education (MHS); genetic counseling (Sc M); social and behavioral sciences (PhD, Sc D). *Faculty:* 36 full-time (28 women), 27 part-time/adjunct (15 women). *Students:* 62 full-time (59 women), 3 part-time (all women); includes 16 minority (6 African Americans, 6 Asian Americans or Pacific Islanders, 4 Hispanic Americans), 6 international. Average age 27. 179 applicants, 31% accepted, 26 enrolled. In 2006, 10 master's, 6 doctorates awarded. *Degree requirements:* For master's, thesis (for some programs), comprehensive exam (for some programs), registration (for some programs); for doctorate, thesis/dissertation, comprehensive exam, registration. *Entrance requirements:* For master's and doctorate, GRE, transcripts, curriculum vitae, statement, 3 recommendation letters. *Application deadline:* For fall admission, 12/1 for domestic and international students. Electronic applications accepted. *Expenses:* Tuition: Full-time $32,976. Tuition and fees vary according to degree level and program. *Financial support:* In 2006–07, 2 fellowships with tuition reimbursements (averaging $24,000 per year), 7 teaching assistantships (averaging $4,770 per year) were awarded; career-related internships or fieldwork, Federal Work-Study, scholarships/grants, traineeships, health care benefits, and unspecified assistantships also available. Financial award application deadline: 3/15. *Faculty research:* Structural and community-level inventions to improve health communication and health education behavioral and social aspects of genetic counseling. Total annual research expenditures: $4.6 million. *Unit head:* Georgean Smith, Administrator, 410-502-3715, Fax: 410-502-4333, E-mail: gesmith@jhsph.edu. *Application contact:* Barbara W. Diehl, Senior Academic Program Coordinator, 410-502-4415, Fax: 410-502-4333, E-mail: bdiehl@jhsph.edu.

Long Island University, Brooklyn Campus, School of Health Professions, Department of Community Health, Brooklyn, NY 11201-8423. Offers community mental health (MS); family health (MS); health management (MS). Part-time and evening/weekend programs available. *Entrance requirements:* For master's, 2 letters of recommendation. Additional exam requirements/recommendations for international students: Required—TOEFL (minimum score 500 paper-based; 173 computer-based). Electronic applications accepted.

McGill University, Faculty of Graduate and Postdoctoral Studies, Faculty of Medicine, Departments of Epidemiology and Biostatistics, and Occupational Health, Montréal, QC H3A 2T5, Canada. Offers community health (M Sc); environmental health (M Sc); epidemiology and biostatistics (M Sc, PhD, Diploma); health care evaluation (M Sc); medical statistics (M Sc); occupational health (M Sc). *Accreditation:* CEPH (one or more programs are accredited). *Degree requirements:* For master's, thesis optional; for doctorate, thesis/dissertation. *Entrance requirements:* For master's, GRE, minimum GPA of 3.0; for doctorate, GRE. *Faculty research:* Chronic and infectious disease epidemiology, health services research, pharmacoepidemiology.

Meharry Medical College, School of Graduate Studies, Division of Community Health Sciences, Nashville, TN 37208-9989. Offers general preventive medicine (MSPH); health services administration (MSPH); occupational medicine (MSPH); public health administration (MSPH). Part-time and evening/weekend programs available. *Degree requirements:* For master's, thesis, externship. *Entrance requirements:* For master's, GRE General Test, GMAT. Expenses: Contact institution. *Faculty research:* Policy and management, health care financing, health education and promotion.

Memorial University of Newfoundland, Faculty of Medicine and School of Graduate Studies, Graduate Programs in Medicine, Division of Community Health, St. John's, NL A1C 5S7, Canada. Offers clinical epidemiology (M Sc, PhD, Diploma); community health (M Sc, PhD, Diploma). Part-time programs available. *Degree requirements:* For master's, thesis; for doctorate, thesis/dissertation, oral defense of thesis, comprehensive exam. *Entrance requirements:* For master's, MD or B Sc; for doctorate, MD or M Sc; for Diploma, bachelor's degree in health-related field. Additional exam requirements/recommendations for international students: Required—TOEFL. *Faculty research:* Epidemiology of chronic diseases, health care delivery and administration, health services, psychosocial, aging.

Minnesota State University Mankato, College of Graduate Studies, College of Allied Health and Nursing, Department of Health Science, Mankato, MN 56001. Offers chemical dependency studies (MS); community health (MS); health science (MS, MT); school health (MS). Part-time programs available. *Students:* 14 full-time (11 women), 35 part-time (28 women). Average age 32. In 2006, 10 degrees awarded. *Degree requirements:* For master's, thesis or alternative, comprehensive exam. *Entrance requirements:* For master's, minimum GPA of 3.0 during previous 2 years. *Application deadline:* For fall admission, 7/1 for domestic students, 5/1 for international students; for spring admission, 11/1 for domestic students, 10/1 for international students. Applications are processed on a rolling basis. Application fee: $40. Electronic applications accepted. *Financial support:* Research assistantships with full tuition reimbursements, teaching assistantships with full tuition reimbursements, career-related internships or fieldwork and Federal Work-Study available. Support available to part-time students. Financial award application deadline: 3/15; financial award applicants required to submit FAFSA. *Faculty research:* Teaching methods, stress prophylaxis and management, effects of alcohol. *Unit head:* Dr. Dawn Larsen, Graduate Coordinator, 507-389-2113. *Application contact:* 507-389-2321, E-mail: grad@mnsu.edu.

Mount Sinai School of Medicine of New York University, Graduate School of Biological Sciences, New York, NY 10029-6504. Offers bioethics (MS); biophysics, structural biology and biomathematics (PhD); community medicine (MPH); genetic counseling (MS); genetics and genomic sciences (PhD); mechanisms of disease and therapy (PhD); microbiology (PhD);

Community Health

Mount Sinai School of Medicine of New York University (continued)
molecular, cellular, biochemical and developmental sciences (PhD); neurosciences (PhD); MD/PhD. Terminal master's awarded for partial completion of doctoral program. *Degree requirements:* For master's, registration; for doctorate, thesis/dissertation, registration. *Entrance requirements:* For doctorate, GRE General Test, GRE Subject Test, 3 years of college pre-med course work. Additional exam requirements/recommendations for international students: Required—TOEFL. Electronic applications accepted. *Faculty research:* Cancer, gene therapy, minimally invasive surgery, cardiac translational research.

New Jersey City University, Graduate and Continuing Education, College of Professional Studies, Department of Health Sciences, Jersey City, NJ 07305-1597. Offers community health education (MS); health administration (MS); school health education (MS). Part-time and evening/weekend programs available. *Faculty:* 5. *Students:* Average age 42. In 2006, 25 degrees awarded. *Degree requirements:* For master's, thesis or alternative, internship. *Entrance requirements:* For master's, GRE General Test or MAT. Additional exam requirements/recommendations for international students: Required—TOEFL. *Application deadline:* For fall admission, 8/1 priority date for domestic students; for spring admission, 12/1 for domestic students. Applications are processed on a rolling basis. Application fee: $0. *Expenses:* Tuition, state resident: full-time $7,038; part-time $391 per credit. Tuition, nonresident: full-time $12,510; part-time $695 per credit. Required fees: $65 per credit. *Financial support:* Career-related internships or fieldwork and unspecified assistantships available. *Unit head:* Dr. Lilliam Rosado, Chairperson, 201-200-3461.

New York Medical College, School of Public Health, Department of Behavioral Sciences and Community Health, Program in General Public Health, Valhalla, NY 10595-1691. Offers MPH. Part-time and evening/weekend programs available. *Degree requirements:* For master's, thesis, registration. *Entrance requirements:* For master's, minimum undergraduate GPA of 3.0. *Application deadline:* For fall admission, 8/1 priority date for domestic students, 5/15 for international students; for spring admission, 12/1 priority date for domestic students, 10/15 for international students. Applications are processed on a rolling basis. Application fee: $35 ($60 for international students). Electronic applications accepted. *Financial support:* Career-related internships or fieldwork, Federal Work-Study, and institutionally sponsored loans available. Financial award application deadline: 6/15; financial award applicants required to submit FAFSA. *Unit head:* Dr. Cathey Falvo, Director, 914-594-4250, E-mail: falvo@nymc.edu. *Application contact:* Marian F. McGowan, Information Contact, 914-594-4510, Fax: 914-594-4292, E-mail: sph_admissions@nymc.edu.

See Close-Up on page 2043.

Old Dominion University, College of Health Sciences, Program in Community Health and Environmental Health, Norfolk, VA 23529. Offers community health professions (MS); environmental health (MS); health care administration (MS); long-term care administration (MS); wellness and promotion (MS). Part-time and evening/weekend programs available. Postbaccalaureate distance learning degree programs offered (no on-campus study). *Faculty:* 5 full-time (4 women), 5 part-time/adjunct (1 woman). *Students:* 10 full-time (7 women), 33 part-time (24 women); includes 6 minority (5 African Americans, 1 Asian American or Pacific Islander), 8 international. Average age 33. 32 applicants, 88% accepted, 15 enrolled. In 2006, 19 degrees awarded. *Degree requirements:* For master's, oral exam, written exam, thesis optional. *Entrance requirements:* For master's, GRE General Test, minimum GPA of 2.75. Additional exam requirements/recommendations for international students: Required—TOEFL. *Application deadline:* For fall admission, 8/1 priority date for domestic students, 7/1 priority date for international students; for winter admission, 11/1 priority date for domestic students, 10/1 priority date for international students; for spring admission, 4/1 priority date for domestic students, 3/1 priority date for international students. Applications are processed on a rolling basis. Application fee: $40. Electronic applications accepted. *Expenses:* Tuition, area resident: Part-time $285 per credit hour. Tuition, nonresident: part-time $715 per credit hour. Required fees: $94 per semester. *Financial support:* In 2006–07, 5 research assistantships with tuition reimbursements (averaging $14,000 per year) were awarded; career-related internships or fieldwork, institutionally sponsored loans, scholarships/grants, and tuition waivers (partial) also available. Support available to part-time students. Financial award applicants required to submit FAFSA. *Faculty research:* Toxicology, domestic violence, health policy and planning, environmental hazards, obesity, substance abuse, minority health spirituality, women's health. Total annual research expenditures: $150,133. *Unit head:* Dr. Clare Houseman, Chair, 757-683-4259, Fax: 757-683-4410, E-mail: chpgdd@odu.edu.

Sage Graduate School, Graduate School, Division of Psychology, Program in Community Psychology, Troy, NY 12180-4115. Offers child care and children's services (MA); community counseling (MA); community health education (MA); general psychology (MA). Part-time and evening/weekend programs available. *Faculty:* 4 full-time (all women), 6 part-time/adjunct (5 women). *Students:* 51 full-time (42 women), 70 part-time (65 women); includes 16 minority (7 African Americans, 2 American Indian/Alaska Native, 2 Asian Americans or Pacific Islanders, 5 Hispanic Americans), 1 international. Average age 30. 77 applicants, 66% accepted, 26 enrolled. In 2006, 22 degrees awarded. *Degree requirements:* For master's, thesis or alternative. *Entrance requirements:* For master's, minimum GPA of 2.75. Additional exam requirements/recommendations for international students: Required—TOEFL (minimum score 550 paper-based; 213 computer-based). *Application deadline:* Applications are processed on a rolling basis. Application fee: $40. *Expenses:* Tuition: Full-time $9,270; part-time $515 per credit hour. *Financial support:* Career-related internships or fieldwork, scholarships/grants, and unspecified assistantships available. Support available to part-time students. Financial award application deadline: 3/1; financial award applicants required to submit FAFSA. *Unit head:* Dr. Bronna Romanoff, Director, 518-244-2260, E-mail: romanb@sage.edu. *Application contact:* Shannon K. Easton, Director of Graduate and Adult Admission, 518-244-2443, Fax: 518-244-6880, E-mail: sgsadm@sage.edu.

Saint Louis University, Graduate School, School of Public Health and Graduate School, Department of Community Health, St. Louis, MO 63103-2097. Offers MPH. *Accreditation:* CEPH. Part-time programs available. *Faculty:* 32 full-time (16 women), 21 part-time/adjunct (7 women). *Students:* 137 full-time (110 women), 103 part-time (62 women); includes 47 minority (24 African Americans, 18 Asian Americans or Pacific Islanders, 5 Hispanic Americans), 26 international. Average age 31. 230 applicants, 66% accepted, 81 enrolled. In 2006, 66 degrees awarded. *Degree requirements:* For master's, comprehensive exam. *Entrance requirements:* For master's, GRE General Test, LSAT, GMAT, MCAT, letters of recommendation, resumé. Additional exam requirements/recommendations for international students: Required—TOEFL (minimum score 525 paper-based; 194 computer-based). *Application deadline:* For fall admission, 7/1 for domestic students, 5/1 for international students; for spring admission, 11/1 for domestic students. Applications are processed on a rolling basis. Application fee: $40. *Expenses:* Tuition: Part-time $800 per credit hour. Required fees: $105 per semester. *Financial support:* In 2006–07, 70 students received support, including 6 research assistantships with full tuition reimbursements available (averaging $10,750 per year); Federal Work-Study, scholarships/grants, traineeships, health care benefits, and unspecified assistantships also available. Support available to part-time students. Financial award application deadline: 6/1; financial award applicants required to submit FAFSA. *Unit head:* Dr. Terry L. Leet, Chairperson, 314-977-8126, E-mail: lettl@slu.edu. *Application contact:* Gary Behrman, Associate Dean of the Graduate School, 314-977-3827, E-mail: behrmang@slu.edu.

Southern Illinois University Carbondale, Graduate School, College of Education, Department of Health Education and Recreation, Program in Community Health Education, Carbondale, IL 62901-4701. Offers MPH. *Students:* 12 full-time (9 women), 12 part-time (10 women); includes 6 minority (5 African Americans, 1 American Indian/Alaska Native), 3 international. 21 applicants, 14% accepted, 2 enrolled. In 2006, 3 degrees awarded. *Application contact:* Carol Reynolds, Administrative Assistant, 618-453-2415, Fax: 618-453-1829, E-mail: creynolds@siu.edu.

Southern New Hampshire University, School of Liberal Arts, Manchester, NH 03106-1045. Offers clinical services for adults psychiatric disabilities (Certificate); clinical services for children and adolescents with psychiatric disabilities (Certificate); clinical services for persons with co-occurring substance abuse and psychiatric disabilities (Certificate); community mental health (MS); fiction writing (MFA); non-fiction writing (MFA); teaching English as a foreign language (MS). Part-time and evening/weekend programs available. *Faculty:* 18 full-time. *Students:* 187 full-time, 12 part-time. Average age 35. In 2006, 35 degrees awarded. *Degree requirements:* For master's, one foreign language, thesis, registration (for some programs). *Entrance requirements:* For master's, minimum GPA of 2.75: MS-TEFL, 3.0: MFA. Additional exam requirements/recommendations for international students: Required—TOEFL (minimum score 550 paper-based; 213 computer-based; 79 iBT), IELTS (minimum score 7), TWE (minimum score 5). *Application deadline:* For fall admission, 7/1 priority date for domestic students; for winter admission, 11/1 priority date for domestic students; for spring admission, 6/1 priority date for domestic students. Applications are processed on a rolling basis. Application fee: $40. Electronic applications accepted. *Expenses:* Contact institution. *Financial support:* In 2006–07, 4 research assistantships were awarded; career-related internships or fieldwork and scholarships/grants also available. Financial award applicants required to submit FAFSA. *Faculty research:* Action research, state of the art practice in behavioral health services, wraparound approaches to working with youth, learning styles. *Unit head:* Dr. Karen Erickson, Dean, 603-668-2211, E-mail: k.erickson@shnu.edu. *Application contact:* Scott Durand, Director of Graduate Enrollment Services, 603-644-3102 Ext. 3338, Fax: 603-644-3144, E-mail: s.durand@snhu.edu.

State University of New York Downstate Medical Center, College of Medicine, Program in Public Health, Brooklyn, NY 11203-2098. Offers urban and immigrant health (MPH); MD/MPH. *Accreditation:* CEPH. Part-time programs available. *Degree requirements:* For master's, practicum. *Entrance requirements:* For master's, GRE, MCAT or OAT, 2 letters of recommendation, minimum undergraduate GPA of 3.0. Additional exam requirements/recommendations for international students: Required—TOEFL (minimum score 550 paper-based). *Expenses:* Tuition, state resident: full-time $6,900; part-time $288 per credit. Tuition, nonresident: full-time $10,920; part-time $455 per credit. Required fees: $100; $20 per credit. $50 per semester. Tuition and fees vary according to course load.

See Close-Up on page 2051.

Stony Brook University, State University of New York, Stony Brook University Medical Center, Health Sciences Center, School of Health Technology and Management, Stony Brook, NY 11794. Offers community health (Advanced Certificate); health care management (Advanced Certificate); health care policy and management (MS); occupational therapy (MS); physical therapy (MS, DPT). *Accreditation:* APTA. Part-time programs available. *Faculty:* 26 full-time (15 women), 21 part-time/adjunct (12 women). *Students:* 198 full-time (147 women), 130 part-time (89 women); includes 87 minority (29 African Americans, 1 American Indian/Alaska Native, 37 Asian Americans or Pacific Islanders, 20 Hispanic Americans), 4 international. 907 applicants, 25% accepted. In 2006, 33 master's, 106 doctorates, 15 other advanced degrees awarded. *Degree requirements:* For master's, thesis. *Entrance requirements:* For master's, GRE General Test, minimum GPA of 3.0, work experience in field. *Application deadline:* For fall admission, 1/15 for domestic students. Application fee: $60. *Expenses:* Tuition, state resident: full-time $6,900; part-time $288 per credit. Tuition, nonresident: full-time $10,920; part-time $455 per credit. *Financial support:* In 2006–07, 1 fellowship was awarded; career-related internships or fieldwork, Federal Work-Study, and institutionally sponsored loans also available. Financial award application deadline: 3/15. *Faculty research:* Health promotion and disease prevention. Total annual research expenditures: $527,101. *Unit head:* Dr. Craig A. Lehmann, Dean, 631-444-2251, Fax: 631-444-7621. *Application contact:* Alan Leiken, Associate Dean for Graduate Studies, 631-444-3240, Fax: 631-444-7621.

Stony Brook University, State University of New York, Stony Brook University Medical Center, School of Medicine, Program in Public Health, Stony Brook, NY 11794. Offers community health (MPH); evaluation sciences (MPH); family violence (MPH); health economics (MPH); population health (MPH); substance abuse (MPH). *Faculty:* 7 full-time (3 women), 1 part-time/adjunct (0 women). *Students:* 10 full-time (9 women), 28 part-time (23 women); includes 6 minority (4 African Americans, 2 Asian Americans or Pacific Islanders), 3 international. Average age 39. 83 applicants, 57% accepted. In 2006, 3 degrees awarded. *Entrance requirements:* For master's, GRE, 3 references. Additional exam requirements/recommendations for international students: Required—TOEFL. *Application deadline:* For fall admission, 1/15 for domestic and international students. Application fee: $60. Electronic applications accepted. *Expenses:* Tuition, state resident: full-time $6,900; part-time $288 per credit. Tuition, nonresident: full-time $10,920; part-time $455 per credit. *Faculty research:* Population health, health service research, health economics. *Unit head:* Dr. Raymond L. Goldsteen, Director, 631-444-2074, Fax: 631-444-3480, E-mail: raymond.goldsteen@stonybrook.edu. *Application contact:* Patricia M. Villa, Assistant, 631-444-2074, Fax: 631-444-3480, E-mail: patricia.villa@stonybrook.edu.

See Close-Up on page 2053.

Temple University, Health Sciences Center and Graduate School, College of Health Professions, Department of Public Health, Program in Community Health Education, Philadelphia, PA 19122-6096. Offers MPH. *Accreditation:* CEPH. Part-time programs available. *Entrance requirements:* For master's, GRE General Test. Additional exam requirements/recommendations for international students: Required—TOEFL (minimum score 550 paper-based; 213 computer-based; 79 iBT). *Application deadline:* For fall admission, 2/15 for domestic students, 12/15 for international students; for spring admission, 10/15 for domestic students, 8/1 for international students. Application fee: $50. Electronic applications accepted. *Expenses:* Tuition, state resident: full-time $12,264; part-time $511 per credit. Tuition, nonresident: full-time $17,904; part-time $746 per credit. Required fees: $84 per course. Tuition and fees vary according to program. *Financial support:* Application deadline: 1/15; *Unit head:* Dr. Brenda Seals, Director, 215-204-6780, Fax: 215-204-1854, E-mail: bseals4@temple.edu.

Université de Montréal, Faculty of Medicine and Faculty of Graduate Studies, Graduate Programs in Medicine, Program in Communal and Public Health, Montréal, QC H3C 3J7, Canada. Offers community health (M Sc, DESS); public health (PhD). *Accreditation:* CEPH. Part-time programs available. *Students:* 101 full-time (64 women), 3 part-time (1 woman). 67 applicants, 16% accepted, 10 enrolled. In 2006, 22 master's, 12 doctorates, 3 other advanced degrees awarded. Terminal master's awarded for partial completion of doctoral program. *Degree requirements:* For master's, thesis; for doctorate, thesis/dissertation, general exam. *Entrance requirements:* For master's and doctorate, proficiency in French, knowledge of English; for DESS, proficiency in French. *Application deadline:* For fall admission, 2/1 priority date for domestic students; for winter admission, 11/1 priority date for domestic students; for spring admission, 2/1 priority date for domestic students. Application fee: $30. Electronic applications accepted. *Financial support:* Fellowships with partial tuition reimbursements, scholarships/grants and tuition waivers (partial) available. *Faculty research:* Epidemiology, health services utilization, health promotion and education, health behaviors, poverty and child health. *Unit head:* Marie-France Raynault, Director, 514-343-6140, Fax: 514-343-5645. *Application contact:* Francine Gazaille, Information Contact, 514-343-6111 Ext. 2755, Fax: 514-343-5645, E-mail: francine.gazaille@umontreal.ca.

Université Laval, Faculty of Medicine, Graduate Programs in Medicine, Department of Social and Preventive Medicine, Program in Community Health, Québec, QC G1K 7P4, Canada. Offers M Sc, PhD. Part-time programs available. Terminal master's awarded for partial completion of doctoral program. *Degree requirements:* For master's, thesis (for some programs); for doctorate, thesis/dissertation, comprehensive exam. *Entrance requirements:* For master's, knowledge of French, comprehension of written English; for doctorate, French exam, comprehension of French, written comprehension of English. Electronic applications accepted.

Université Laval, Faculty of Medicine, Post-Professional Programs in Medical Studies, Québec, QC G1K 7P4, Canada. Offers anatomy–pathology (DESS); anesthesiology (DESS); cardiology (DESS); care of older people (Diploma); clinical research (DESS); community health (DESS); dermatology (DESS); diagnostic radiology (DESS); emergency medicine (Diploma); family medicine (DESS); general surgery (DESS); geriatrics (DESS); hematology (DESS); internal medicine (DESS); maternal and fetal medicine (Diploma); medical biochemistry (DESS); medical microbiology and infectious diseases (DESS); medical oncology (DESS); nephrology (DESS); neurology (DESS); neurosurgery (DESS); obstetrics and gynecology (DESS); ophthalmology (DESS); orthopedic surgery (DESS); oto-rhino-laryngology (DESS); palliative medicine (Diploma); pediatrics (DESS); plastic surgery (DESS); psychiatry (DESS); pulmonary medicine (DESS); radiology–oncology (DESS); thoracic surgery (DESS); urology (DESS). *Degree requirements:* For other advanced degree, comprehensive exam. *Entrance requirements:* For degree, knowledge of French. Electronic applications accepted.

University at Buffalo, the State University of New York, Graduate School, School of Public Health and Health Professions, Department of Social and Preventive Medicine, Buffalo, NY 14260. Offers community health (PhD); epidemiology (MS, PhD); public health (MPH). Part-time programs available. *Faculty:* 11 full-time (7 women), 11 part-time/adjunct (5 women). *Students:* 20 full-time (7 women), 20 part-time (13 women); includes 5 minority (2 African Americans, 3 Asian Americans or Pacific Islanders), 8 international. Average age 27. 136 applicants, 41% accepted, 25 enrolled. In 2006, 2 master's, 6 doctorates awarded. Terminal master's awarded for partial completion of doctoral program. *Median time to degree:* Of those who began their doctoral program in fall 1998, 86% received their degree in 8 years or less. *Degree requirements:* For master's and doctorate, thesis/dissertation, comprehensive exam. *Entrance requirements:* For master's and doctorate, GRE General Test. Additional exam requirements/recommendations for international students: Required—TOEFL (minimum score 600 paper-based; 250 computer-based; 100 iBT). *Application deadline:* For fall admission, 2/1 priority date for domestic and international students. Applications are processed on a rolling basis. Application fee: $50. Electronic applications accepted. *Financial support:* In 2006–07, 13 students received support, including 2 fellowships with full tuition reimbursements available (averaging $15,000 per year), 11 research assistantships with full tuition reimbursements available (averaging $15,000 per year); teaching assistantships with full tuition reimbursements available, career-related internships or fieldwork, Federal Work-Study, institutionally sponsored loans, health care benefits, and unspecified assistantships also available. Financial award application deadline: 2/1; financial award applicants required to submit FAFSA. *Faculty research:* Epidemiology of community health services including cancer and nutrition, cardiovascular disease, epidemiology of cancer, cardiovascular diseases; health services research. Total annual research expenditures: $6 million. *Unit head:* Dr. Jo Freudenheim, Chair, 716-829-2975 Ext. 612, Fax: 716-829-2979, E-mail: jfreuden@buffalo.edu. *Application contact:* Dr. Carl Li, Director of Graduate Studies, 716-829-2975 Ext. 618, Fax: 716-829-2979, E-mail: carlli@buffalo.edu.

University of Alberta, School of Public Health, Department of Public Health Sciences, Edmonton, AB T6G 2E1, Canada. Offers clinical epidemiology (M Sc, MPH); environmental and occupational health (MPH); environmental health sciences (M Sc); epidemiology (M Sc); global health (M Sc, MPH); health policy and management (MPH); health policy research (M Sc); health technology assessment (MPH); occupational health (M Sc); population health (M Sc); public health leadership (MPH); public health sciences (PhD); quantitative methods (MPH). *Accreditation:* CEPH (one or more programs are accredited). *Faculty:* 24 full-time (5 women), 59 part-time/adjunct (13 women). *Students:* 49 full-time, 49 part-time. 81 applicants, 31% accepted. In 2006, 28 degrees awarded. Terminal master's awarded for partial completion of doctoral program. *Degree requirements:* For master's, thesis (for some programs); for doctorate, thesis/dissertation. *Entrance requirements:* For master's, GMAT or GRE General Test. Additional exam requirements/recommendations for international students: Required—TOEFL (paper-based 550; computer-based 213) or IELTS (paper-based 6). *Application deadline:* For fall admission, 3/15 for domestic students, 7/1 for international students; for winter admission, 11/1 for international students; for spring admission, 3/1 for international students. Applications are processed on a rolling basis. Application fee: $50. Electronic applications accepted. *Financial support:* In 2006–07, 11 students received support, including 6 research assistantships with tuition reimbursements available (averaging $2,200 per year); fellowships, teaching assistantships, career-related internships or fieldwork and tuition waivers (partial) also available. Financial award application deadline: 2/1. *Faculty research:* Biostatistics, health promotion and sociobehavioral health science. Total annual research expenditures: $5.7 million. *Unit head:* L. Duncan Saunders, Acting Chair, 780-492-6814, Fax: 780-492-0364. *Application contact:* Felicity R. Hey, Graduate Programs Administrator, 780-492-6407, Fax: 780-492-0364, E-mail: felicity.hey@ualberta.ca.

The University of British Columbia, Faculty of Medicine, Department of Health Care and Epidemiology, Vancouver, BC V6T 1W5, Canada. Offers clinical epidemiology (MH Sc); community health (MH Sc); epidemiology/clinical epidemiology (M Sc, PhD); health administration (MHA); health services research (M Sc, PhD); occupational and environmental health (M Sc, PhD); occupational health (MH Sc). *Accreditation:* CEPH (one or more programs are accredited). Part-time programs available. *Faculty:* 27 full-time (7 women). *Students:* 27 full-time (4 women), 10 part-time (2 women). Average age 31. 91 applicants, 30% accepted. In 2006, 14 master's, 1 doctorate awarded. *Degree requirements:* For master's and doctorate, thesis/dissertation. *Entrance requirements:* For master's, GRE General Test, MD or equivalent (MH Sc); for doctorate, work experience. *Application deadline:* For fall admission, 3/31 for domestic students. Applications are processed on a rolling basis. Application fee: $65. Electronic applications accepted. *Financial support:* In 2006–07, 7 students received support, including 1 fellowship; career-related internships or fieldwork also available. *Faculty research:* AIDS, public health, environmental toxicology, infectious diseases, health evaluation, epidemiology. Total annual research expenditures: $4.8 million. *Unit head:* M. T. Schechter, Head, 604-822-3910, Fax: 604-822-4994, E-mail: martin.schechter@ubc.ca. *Application contact:* Laurel Slaney, Program Assistant, 604-822-5405, Fax: 604-822-4994, E-mail: laurel.slaney@ubc.ca.

University of Calgary, Faculty of Graduate Studies, Faculty of Education, Graduate Division of Educational Research, Calgary, AB T2N 1N4, Canada. Offers community rehabilitation and disability studies (M Ed, M Sc, Ed D, PhD, Graduate Certificate, Graduate Diploma); curriculum, teaching and learning (M Ed, M Sc, MA, Ed D, PhD, Graduate Certificate, Graduate Diploma); educational contexts (M Ed, MA, Ed D, PhD, Graduate Certificate, Graduate Diploma); educational leadership (M Ed, MA, Ed D, PhD, Graduate Certificate, Graduate Diploma); educational technology (M Ed, M Sc, MA, Ed D, PhD, Graduate Certificate, Graduate Diploma); gifted education (M Sc, MA, Ed D, PhD, Graduate Certificate, Graduate Diploma); higher education administration (Ed D); interpretive studies in education (M Ed, M Sc, MA, Ed D, PhD, Graduate Certificate, Graduate Diploma); second language teaching (M Ed, Ed D, PhD, Graduate Certificate, Graduate Diploma); teaching English as a second language (M Ed, M Sc, MA, Ed D, PhD, Graduate Certificate, Graduate Diploma); workplace and adult learning (M Ed, MA, Ed D, PhD, Graduate Certificate, Graduate Diploma). Ed D in both higher education administration and educational leadership offered via distance delivery. Part-time and evening/weekend programs available. Postbaccalaureate distance learning degree programs offered (minimal on-campus study). *Faculty:* 44 full-time, 52 part-time/adjunct. *Students:* 488 full-time, 550 part-time. 400 applicants, 50% accepted. In 2006, 102 master's, 18 doctorates awarded. *Degree requirements:* For master's, thesis (for some programs); for doctorate, thesis/dissertation, candidacy exam. *Entrance requirements:* For master's, minimum GPA of 3.0, 3 letters of reference; for doctorate, minimum GPA of 3.5, 3 letters of reference; for other advanced degree, minimum GPA of 3.0. Additional exam requirements/recommendations for international students: Required—TOEFL, IELTS. *Application deadline:* For fall admission, 2/15 for domestic students, 2/5 for international students; for winter admission, 6/15 for domestic and international students. Application fee: $100. Electronic applications accepted. *Financial support:* In 2006–07, research assistantships (averaging $3,920 per year); teaching assistantships, career-related internships or fieldwork, scholarships/grants, and unspecified assistantships also available. Financial award application deadline: 2/1. *Faculty research:* Curriculum, leadership, technology, contexts, gifted, second language teaching, work place and adult learning. *Unit head:* Dr. Charles F. Webber, Associate Dean, 403-220-5675, Fax: 403-282-3005, E-mail: cwebber@ucalgary.ca. *Application contact:* Patricia A. Brown, Program Officer, Graduate Division of Educational Research, 403-220-3178, Fax: 403-282-3005, E-mail: brownp@ucalgary.ca.

University of Calgary, Faculty of Medicine and Faculty of Graduate Studies, Department of Community Health Sciences, Calgary, AB T2N 1N4, Canada. Offers M Sc, MCM, PhD. *Faculty:* 68 full-time (28 women), 24 part-time/adjunct (13 women). *Students:* 85 full-time (60 women), 5 part-time (2 women). Average age 34. 78 applicants, 45% accepted, 25 enrolled. In 2006, 18 master's, 4 doctorates awarded. *Degree requirements:* For master's, thesis; for doctorate, thesis/dissertation, candidacy exam. *Entrance requirements:* For master's and doctorate, minimum GPA of 3.2. Additional exam requirements/recommendations for international students: Required—TOEFL (minimum score 600 paper-based; 250 computer-based). *Application deadline:* For fall admission, 2/15 for domestic and international students. Application fee: $100 ($130 for international students). Electronic applications accepted. *Financial support:* In 2006–07, 34 students received support, including 6 fellowships (averaging $12,000 per year), 14 research assistantships (averaging $4,100 per year), 7 teaching assistantships (averaging $6,915 per year); scholarships/grants and tuition waivers (partial) also available. Financial award application deadline: 1/15. *Faculty research:* Epidemiology, health research, biostatistics, health economics, health policy. Total annual research expenditures: $47.2 million. *Unit head:* Dr. Marilynne A. Hebert, Graduate Coordinator, 403-220-7452, Fax: 403-270-7307, E-mail: hebert@ucalgary.ca. *Application contact:* Crystal Elliott, Graduate Program Administrator, 403-220-4288, Fax: 403-270-7307, E-mail: chsgrad@ucalgary.ca.

University of California, Los Angeles, Graduate Division, School of Public Health, Department of Community Health Sciences, Los Angeles, CA 90095. Offers public health (MS, PhD). *Degree requirements:* For master's, comprehensive exam or thesis; for doctorate, thesis/dissertation, oral and written qualifying exams. *Entrance requirements:* For master's, GRE General Test, minimum GPA of 3.0; for doctorate, GRE General Test, minimum undergraduate GPA of 3.0. Electronic applications accepted.

University of Illinois at Chicago, Graduate College, School of Public Health, Program in Community Health Sciences, Chicago, IL 60607-7128. Offers MPH, MS, Dr PH, PhD. *Accreditation:* CEPH (one or more programs are accredited). Part-time programs available. Terminal master's awarded for partial completion of doctoral program. *Degree requirements:* For master's, thesis, field practicum; for doctorate, thesis/dissertation, independent research, internship. *Entrance requirements:* For master's and doctorate, GRE General Test, minimum GPA of 2.75. Additional exam requirements/recommendations for international students: Required—TOEFL. Electronic applications accepted.

University of Illinois at Urbana–Champaign, Graduate College, College of Applied Health Studies, Department of Kinesiology and Community Health, Champaign, IL 61820. Offers community health (MS, MSPH, PhD); kinesiology (MS, PhD). *Faculty:* 26 full-time (12 women), 1 part-time/adjunct (0 women). *Students:* 87 full-time (55 women), 4 part-time (2 women); includes 17 minority (11 African Americans, 5 Asian Americans or Pacific Islanders, 1 Hispanic American), 13 international. 95 applicants, 52% accepted, 29 enrolled. In 2006, 15 master's, 6 doctorates awarded. *Degree requirements:* For doctorate, thesis/dissertation. *Entrance requirements:* For master's, GRE General Test, minimum GPA of 3.0; for doctorate, GRE, minimum graduate GPA of 3.5. Additional exam requirements/recommendations for international students: Required—TOEFL. *Application deadline:* For fall admission, 1/15 priority date for domestic students. Applications are processed on a rolling basis. Application fee: $50 ($60 for international students). Electronic applications accepted. *Financial support:* In 2006–07, 13 fellowships, 43 research assistantships, 76 teaching assistantships were awarded; tuition waivers (full and partial) also available. Financial award application deadline: 2/15. *Unit head:* Wojtek Chodzko-Zajko, Head, 217-244-0823, Fax: 217-244-7322, E-mail: wojtek@uiuc.edu. *Application contact:* Deb Shilts, Administrative Aide, 217-333-1083, Fax: 217-244-7322, E-mail: dshilts@uiuc.edu.

The University of Iowa, Graduate College, College of Public Health, Department of Community and Behavioral Health, Iowa City, IA 52242-1316. Offers MS, PhD. *Faculty:* 8 full-time, 2 part-time/adjunct. *Students:* 3 full-time (all women), 8 part-time (all women); includes 2 minority (1 African American, 1 Asian American or Pacific Islander). 22 applicants, 9% accepted, 0 enrolled. In 2006, 3 degrees awarded. *Degree requirements:* For master's, thesis/dissertation, registration; for doctorate, thesis/dissertation, comprehensive exam, registration. *Entrance requirements:* For master's and doctorate, GRE General Test, minimum GPA of 3.0. Additional exam requirements/recommendations for international students: Required—TOEFL (minimum score 600 paper-based; 250 computer-based; 100 iBT). *Application deadline:* For fall admission, 4/1 priority date for domestic and international students; for spring admission, 10/1 priority date for domestic students. Applications are processed on a rolling basis. Application fee: $60 ($85 for international students). Electronic applications accepted. *Financial support:* In 2006–07, 7 research assistantships with partial tuition reimbursements, 1 teaching assistantship with partial tuition reimbursement were awarded. Financial award applicants required to submit FAFSA. *Unit head:* John Lowe, Head, 319-384-5383, Fax: 319-335-5385.

University of Manitoba, Faculty of Medicine and Faculty of Graduate Studies, Graduate Programs in Medicine, Department of Community Health Sciences, Winnipeg, MB R3T 2N2, Canada. Offers M Sc, PhD. Part-time programs available. *Degree requirements:* For master's and doctorate, thesis/dissertation. *Entrance requirements:* For master's and doctorate, minimum GPA of 3.0. *Faculty research:* Health services, aboriginal health, health policy, epidemiology, environmental and occupational health.

University of Miami, Graduate School, School of Nursing and Health Studies, Coral Gables, FL 33124. Offers acute care (MSN), including acute care nurse practitioner, nurse anesthesia; community health (MSN); nursing (PhD); primary care (MSN), including adult nurse practitioner, family nurse practitioner, nurse midwifery, psychiatric/mental health nursing, women's health practitioner. *Accreditation:* AACN; AANA/CANAEP; ACNM/DOA (one or more programs are accredited). Part-time programs available. *Faculty:* 10 full-time (8 women), 1 (woman) part-time/adjunct. *Students:* 33 full-time (24 women), 27 part-time (24 women); includes 28 minority (7 African Americans, 5 Asian Americans or Pacific Islanders, 16 Hispanic Americans), 2 international. Average age 34. 108 applicants, 48% accepted, 30 enrolled. In 2006, 15 master's, 1 doctorate awarded. *Degree requirements:* For master's, thesis optional; for doctorate, thesis/dissertation. *Entrance requirements:* For master's, GRE General Test, BSN, minimum GPA of 3.0, Florida RN license; for doctorate, GRE General Test, BSN or MSN, minimum GPA of 3.0. Additional exam requirements/recommendations for international students: Required—TOEFL (minimum score 550 paper-based; 213 computer-based). *Application deadline:* For fall admission, 4/30 priority date for domestic students; for spring admission, 11/1 priority date for domestic students. Applications are processed on a rolling basis. Application fee: $50. Electronic applications accepted. *Financial support:* In 2006–07, 12 students received support, including 3 research assistantships with tuition reimbursements available (averaging $9,000 per year), 5 teaching assistantships with tuition reimbursements available (averaging $9,000 per year); fellowships, Federal Work-Study, institutionally sponsored loans, scholarships/grants, and unspecified assistantships also available. Support available to part-time students. Financial award application deadline: 3/1; financial award applicants required to submit FAFSA. *Faculty research:* Transcultural nursing, exercise and depression in Alzheimer's disease, infectious diseases/HIV–AIDS, postpartum depression, outcomes assessment. Total annual research expenditures: $31.9 million. *Unit head:* Dr. Nilda Peragallo, Dean, 305-284-2107, Fax: 305-667-3787, E-mail: nperagallo@miami.edu. *Application contact:* Anne Stabb, Graduate Advisor, 305-284-2533, Fax: 305-284-4827, E-mail: astabb@miami.edu.

University of Minnesota, Twin Cities Campus, School of Public Health, Major in Community Health Education, Minneapolis, MN 55455-0213. Offers MPH. *Accreditation:* CEPH. Part-time programs available. *Degree requirements:* For master's, fieldwork, master's project. *Entrance requirements:* For master's, GRE General Test. Additional exam requirements/recommendations for international students: Required—TOEFL. Electronic applications accepted. *Expenses:* Tuition, state resident: full-time $9,302; part-time $775 per credit. Tuition, nonresident: full-time

Community Health

University of Minnesota, Twin Cities Campus (continued)
$16,400; part-time $1,367 per credit. Full-time tuition and fees vary according to class time, course load, program, reciprocity agreements and student level. *Faculty research:* Assessing population behavior, designing community-wide prevention and treatment, preventing alcohol and drug abuse, influencing health policies.

The University of North Carolina at Greensboro, Graduate School, School of Health and Human Performance, Department of Public Health Education, Greensboro, NC 27412-5001. Offers community health education (MPH, Dr PH). *Accreditation:* CEPH; NCATE. *Faculty:* 16 full-time (7 women), 7 part-time/adjunct (3 women). *Students:* 63 full-time (53 women), 5 part-time (3 women); includes 26 minority (20 African Americans, 5 Asian Americans or Pacific Islanders, 1 Hispanic American). 92 applicants, 36% accepted. *Degree requirements:* For master's, thesis or alternative, comprehensive exam. *Entrance requirements:* For master's, GRE General Test or MAT. Additional exam requirements/recommendations for international students: Required—TOEFL. *Application deadline:* For fall admission, 3/15 priority date for domestic students; for spring admission, 11/1 for domestic students. Applications are processed on a rolling basis. Application fee: $45. Electronic applications accepted. *Expenses:* Tuition, state resident: full-time $2,692. Tuition, nonresident: full-time $13,742. *Financial support:* Fellowships, research assistantships, teaching assistantships, career-related internships or fieldwork, Federal Work-Study, institutionally sponsored loans, scholarships/grants, and traineeships available. Support available to part-time students. *Faculty research:* Peer facilitator training, innovative health education approaches. *Unit head:* Dr. Dan Bibeau, Head, 336-334-5532, Fax: 336-334-3238, E-mail: bibeau@uncg.edu. *Application contact:* Michelle Harkleroad, Director of Graduate Admissions, 336-334-4884, Fax: 336-334-4424, E-mail: mbharkle@uncg.edu.

University of Northern British Columbia, Office of Graduate Studies, Prince George, BC V2N 4Z9, Canada. Offers business administration (Diploma); community health science (M Sc); disability management (MA); education (M Ed); first nations studies (MA); gender studies (MA); history (MA); interdisciplinary studies (MA); international studies (MA); mathematical, computer and physical sciences (M Sc); natural resources and environmental studies (M Sc, MA, MNRES, PhD); political science (MA); psychology (M Sc, PhD); social work (MSW). Part-time and evening/weekend programs available. Postbaccalaureate distance learning degree programs offered (no on-campus study). *Degree requirements:* For master's and doctorate, thesis/dissertation. *Entrance requirements:* For master's, GRE, minimum B average in undergraduate course work; for doctorate, candidacy exam, minimum A average in graduate course work.

University of Northern Colorado, Graduate School, College of Natural and Health Sciences, School of Human Sciences, Program in Public Health and Nutrition, Greeley, CO 80639. Offers public health education (MPH). *Accreditation:* CEPH. *Faculty:* 3 full-time (2 women). *Students:* 42 full-time (34 women), 7 part-time (5 women); includes 7 minority (2 African Americans, 1 Asian American or Pacific Islander, 4 Hispanic Americans), 1 international. Average age 31. 28 applicants, 100% accepted, 14 enrolled. In 2006, 16 degrees awarded. *Degree requirements:* For master's, thesis or alternative, comprehensive exam. *Entrance requirements:* For master's, GRE General test, 2 letters of recommendation. *Application deadline:* Applications are processed on a rolling basis. Application fee: $50 ($60 for international students). Electronic applications accepted. *Expenses:* Tuition, state resident: full-time $5,118; part-time $213 per credit hour. Tuition, nonresident: full-time $14,832; part-time $618 per credit hour. Required fees: $674; $34 per credit hour. *Financial support:* In 2006–07, 27 students received support, including 5 fellowships (averaging $1,025 per year), 4 research assistantships (averaging $10,914 per year); teaching assistantships, unspecified assistantships also available. Financial award application deadline: 3/1; financial award applicants required to submit FAFSA. *Unit head:* Dr. Kathy Zavela, Program Coordinator, 970-351-2403.

University of Northern Iowa, Graduate College, College of Education, School of Health, Physical Education, and Leisure Services, Cedar Falls, IA 50614. Offers community health education (Ed D); health education (MA, Ed D); leisure services (MA, Ed D), including leisure services (Ed D), program administration (MA), youth/human services administration (MA); physical education (MA), including physical education, scientific basis of physical education, teaching/coaching; rehabilitation studies (Ed D). Part-time and evening/weekend programs available. *Faculty:* 34 full-time (17 women). *Students:* 98 full-time (49 women), 31 part-time (17 women); includes 21 minority (18 African Americans, 3 Hispanic Americans), 23 international. 94 applicants, 74% accepted, 59 enrolled. In 2006, 35 degrees awarded. *Degree requirements:* For master's, thesis or alternative, comprehensive exam; for doctorate, thesis/dissertation. *Entrance requirements:* For master's, minimum GPA of 3.5, 3 years of educational experience; for doctorate, GRE. Additional exam requirements/recommendations for international students: Required—TOEFL (minimum score 500 paper-based; 180 computer-based; 61 iBT). *Application deadline:* Applications are processed on a rolling basis. Application fee: $30 ($50 for international students). *Expenses:* Tuition, state resident: full-time $5,936. Tuition, nonresident: full-time $14,074. *Financial support:* Career-related internships or fieldwork, Federal Work-Study, institutionally sponsored loans, scholarships/grants, tuition waivers (full and partial), and unspecified assistantships available. Support available to part-time students. Financial award application deadline: 2/1. *Unit head:* Dr. Christopher R. Edginton, Director, 319-273-2840, Fax: 319-273-5958, E-mail: christopher.edginton@uni.edu.

University of North Florida, College of Health, Department of Public Health, Jacksonville, FL 32224-2645. Offers community health (MPH); geriatric management (MSH); health administration (MHA); health behavior research and evaluation (Certificate); nutrition (MSH); rehabilitation counseling (MS). *Accreditation:* CORE. Part-time and evening/weekend programs available. *Faculty:* 21 full-time (16 women). *Students:* 78 full-time (60 women), 54 part-time (40 women); includes 31 minority (16 African Americans, 7 Asian Americans or Pacific Islanders, 8 Hispanic Americans), 10 international. Average age 32. 136 applicants, 47% accepted, 38 enrolled. In 2006, 50 degrees awarded. *Degree requirements:* For master's, thesis optional. *Entrance requirements:* For master's, GRE General Test (MSH, MS, MPH), GMAT or GRE General Test (MHA), minimum GPA of 3.0 in last 60 hours. Additional exam requirements/recommendations for international students: Required—TOEFL (minimum score 500 paper-based; 173 computer-based). *Application deadline:* For fall admission, 7/1 priority date for domestic students, 5/1 for international students; for spring admission, 11/10 priority date for domestic students, 10/1 for international students. Applications are processed on a rolling basis. Application fee: $30. Electronic applications accepted. *Expenses:* Tuition, state resident: full-time $4,948; part-time $206 per semester hour. Tuition, nonresident: full-time $19,140; part-time $408 per semester hour. *Financial support:* In 2006–07, 64 students received support, including 11 teaching assistantships (averaging $2,942 per year); research assistantships, career-related internships or fieldwork, Federal Work-Study, scholarships/grants, and tuition waivers (partial) also available. Support available to part-time students. Financial award application deadline: 4/1; financial award applicants required to submit FAFSA. *Faculty research:* Dietary supplements; alcohol, tobacco, and other drug use prevention; turnover among health professionals; aging; psychosocial aspects of disabilities. Total annual research expenditures: $438,597. *Unit head:* Dr. Judith Perkin, Chair, 904-620-2840, Fax: 904-620-2848, E-mail: jperkin@unf.edu. *Application contact:* Rachel Broderick, Director of Advising, 904-620-2817, Fax: 904-620-1770, E-mail: rbroderi@unf.edu.

University of North Texas, Robert B. Toulouse School of Graduate Studies, College of Education, Department of Kinesiology, Health Promotion, and Recreation, Program in Health Promotion, Denton, TX 76203. Offers community health (MS); school health (MS). Part-time programs available. *Faculty:* 16 full-time (6 women). *Students:* 1 (woman) full-time. Average age 27. 2 applicants, 100% accepted, 0 enrolled. In 2006, 2 degrees awarded. *Degree requirements:* For master's, thesis (for some programs). *Entrance requirements:* For master's, GRE General Test. Additional exam requirements/recommendations for international students: Recommended—TOEFL (minimum score 550 paper-based; 213 computer-based). *Application deadline:* For fall admission, 7/15 for domestic students. Application fee: $50 ($75 for international students). *Expenses:* Tuition, state resident: full-time $3,573; part-time $198 per credit. Tuition, nonresident: full-time $8,577; part-time $476 per credit. Required fees: $1,258; $126 per credit. One-time fee: $150 full-time. Tuition and fees vary according to course load. *Financial support:* Teaching assistantships, career-related internships or fieldwork, Federal Work-Study, and institutionally sponsored loans available. Financial award application deadline: 4/1. *Application contact:* Dr. John Collins, Adviser, 940-565-3422, Fax: 940-565-4904, E-mail: collins@unt.edu.

University of North Texas Health Science Center at Fort Worth, School of Public Health, Fort Worth, TX 76107-2699. Offers biostatistics (MPH); community health (MPH); disease control and prevention (Dr PH); environmental health (MPH); epidemiology (MPH); health behavior (MPH); health policy and management (MPH, Dr PH); DO/MPH; MA/MPH; MS/MPH; PhD/MPH. *Accreditation:* CEPH. Part-time and evening/weekend programs available. *Degree requirements:* For master's, thesis or alternative, supervised internship; for doctorate, thesis/dissertation, supervised internship. *Entrance requirements:* For master's, GRE General Test. Additional exam requirements/recommendations for international students: Required—TOEFL. Electronic applications accepted.

University of Ottawa, Faculty of Graduate and Postdoctoral Studies, Faculty of Medicine, Department of Epidemiology and Community Medicine, Ottawa, ON K1N 6N5, Canada. Offers epidemiology (M Sc), including health technology assessment. *Degree requirements:* For master's, thesis. *Entrance requirements:* For master's, honors degree or equivalent, minimum B average. Electronic applications accepted. *Faculty research:* Epidemiologic concepts and methods, health technology assessment.

University of Ottawa, Faculty of Graduate and Postdoctoral Studies, Interdisciplinary Programs, Ottawa, ON K1N 6N5, Canada. Offers e-business (Certificate); e-commerce (Certificate); finance (Certificate); health services and policies research (Diploma); population health (PhD); population health risk assessment and management (Certificate); public management and governance (Certificate); systems science (Certificate).

University of Pittsburgh, Graduate School of Public Health, Department of Behavioral and Community Health Sciences, Pittsburgh, PA 15260. Offers behavioral and community health sciences (MPH, Dr PH); lesbian, gay, bisexual and transgender health and wellness (Certificate); minority health and health disparities (Certificate); program evaluation (Certificate); public health and aging (Certificate); public health preparedness (Certificate); MID/MPH; MPH/MPA; MPH/MSW; MPH/PhD. *Accreditation:* CAHME (one or more programs are accredited). Part-time programs available. *Faculty:* 20 full-time (9 women), 17 part-time/adjunct (8 women). *Students:* 48 full-time (39 women), 33 part-time (27 women); includes 21 minority (14 African Americans, 1 American Indian/Alaska Native, 5 Asian Americans or Pacific Islanders, 1 Hispanic American), 3 international. Average age 31. 125 applicants, 62% accepted, 28 enrolled. In 2006, 24 master's, 2 doctorates awarded. *Median time to degree:* Of those who began their doctoral program in fall 1998, 100% received their degree in 8 years or less. *Degree requirements:* For master's, thesis; for doctorate, thesis/dissertation, preliminary exams, comprehensive exam. *Entrance requirements:* For master's and Certificate, GRE; for doctorate, GRE, master's degree in public health or related field. Additional exam requirements/recommendations for international students: Required—TOEFL (minimum score 550 paper-based; 213 computer-based). *Application deadline:* For fall admission, 5/1 priority date for domestic students, 4/1 for international students; for winter admission, 9/1 for international students; for spring admission, 10/1 priority date for domestic students, 2/1 for international students. Applications are processed on a rolling basis. Application fee: $50 ($60 for international students). Electronic applications accepted. *Financial support:* In 2006–07, 20 students received support, including 14 research assistantships with tuition reimbursements available, 6 teaching assistantships with tuition reimbursements available; career-related internships or fieldwork, scholarships/grants, and unspecified assistantships also available. Support available to part-time students. *Faculty research:* Maternal and child health, program evaluation, community-based participatory research, minority health and health disparities, aging. Total annual research expenditures: $1.3 million. *Unit head:* Dr. Robert M. Goodman, Chairman, 412-624-3100, Fax: 412-624-5510, E-mail: rmg16@pitt.edu. *Application contact:* Natalie C Arnold, Recruitment and Academic Affairs Administrator, 412-624-3107, Fax: 412-624-5510, E-mail: narnold@pi.edu.

University of Saskatchewan, College of Medicine, Department of Community Health and Epidemiology, Saskatoon, SK S7N 5A2, Canada. Offers M Sc, PhD. *Faculty:* 14. *Students:* 41; includes 3 minority (all American Indian/Alaska Native). *Degree requirements:* For master's, thesis/dissertation, registration; for doctorate, thesis/dissertation. *Entrance requirements:* Additional exam requirements/recommendations for international students: Required—TOEFL. *Application deadline:* For fall admission, 7/1 priority date for domestic students. Applications are processed on a rolling basis. Application fee: $50. *Financial support:* Fellowships, research assistantships, teaching assistantships available. Financial award application deadline: 3/31. *Unit head:* Dr. Nazeem Muhajarine, Graduate Chair, 306-966-7945, Fax: 306-966-7920, E-mail: nazeem.muhajarine@usask.ca. *Application contact:* Dr. S. Abonyi, Graduate Chair, 306-966-2194, Fax: 306-966-7920, E-mail: sylvia.abonyi@usask.ca.

University of South Florida, Graduate School, College of Public Health, Department of Community and Family Health, Tampa, FL 33620-9951. Offers MPH, MSPH, PhD. *Accreditation:* CEPH (one or more programs are accredited). Part-time and evening/weekend programs available. *Faculty:* 16 full-time (12 women), 5 part-time/adjunct (2 women). *Students:* 71 full-time (59 women), 61 part-time (50 women); includes 42 minority (20 African Americans, 1 American Indian/Alaska Native, 8 Asian Americans or Pacific Islanders, 13 Hispanic Americans), 18 international. Average age 32. 73 applicants, 55% accepted, 22 enrolled. In 2006, 19 master's, 9 doctorates awarded. *Median time to degree:* Master's–1.67 years full-time, 3.33 years part-time; doctorate–6.63 years part-time. Of those who began their doctoral program in fall 1998, 100% received their degree in 8 years or less. *Degree requirements:* For master's, thesis (for some programs), comprehensive exam; for doctorate, thesis/dissertation, comprehensive exam. *Entrance requirements:* For master's and doctorate, GRE General Test, minimum GPA of 3.0 in upper-level course work. Additional exam requirements/recommendations for international students: Required—TOEFL (minimum score 550 paper-based; 213 computer-based; 79 iBT). *Application deadline:* For fall admission, 6/1 for domestic students, 1/2 for international students; for spring admission, 10/15 for domestic students, 7/1 for international students. Applications are processed on a rolling basis. Application fee: $30. Electronic applications accepted. *Financial support:* In 2006–07, 6 fellowships with full tuition reimbursements (averaging $10,100 per year), 53 research assistantships with full and partial tuition reimbursements (averaging $4,296 per year), 15 teaching assistantships (averaging $3,060 per year) were awarded; career-related internships or fieldwork, Federal Work-Study, institutionally sponsored loans, scholarships/grants, traineeships, and unspecified assistantships also available. Support available to part-time students. Financial award applicants required to submit FAFSA. *Faculty research:* Family violence, high-risk infant, medical material and child health, healthy start, social marketing, adolescent health, high-risk behaviors. Total annual research expenditures: $4.9 million. *Unit head:* Dr. Jeannine Coreil, Chairperson, 813-974-4867, Fax: 813-974-5172, E-mail: jcoreil@hsc.usf.edu. *Application contact:* Michelle Robinson, Academic Advisor, 813-974-6665, Fax: 813-974-8121, E-mail: mrobinso@health.usf.edu.

The University of Tennessee, Graduate School, College of Education, Health and Human Sciences, Program in Human Ecology, Knoxville, TN 37996. Offers child and family studies (PhD); community health (PhD); nutrition science (PhD); retailing and consumer sciences (PhD); textile science (PhD). *Students:* 45 (37 women); includes 3 minority (all African Americans) 12 international. 39 applicants, 44% accepted. In 2006, 12 degrees awarded. *Degree requirements:* For doctorate, thesis/dissertation. *Entrance requirements:* For doctorate, GRE General Test, minimum GPA of 2.7. Additional exam requirements/recommendations for international students: Required—TOEFL. *Application deadline:* For fall admission, 2/1 priority date for domestic students. Applications are processed on a rolling basis. Application fee: $35. Electronic applications accepted. *Expenses:* Tuition, state resident: full-time $5,574. Tuition, nonresident: full-time $16,840. Required fees: $792. *Financial support:* Fellowships, research assistantships, teaching assistantships, Federal Work-Study, institutionally sponsored loans, and unspecified assistantships available. Financial award application deadline: 2/1; financial award applicants required to submit FAFSA. *Unit head:* Dr. Billie J. Collier, Interim Head, 865-974-5224, E-mail: bcollier@utk.edu.

The University of Tennessee, Graduate School, College of Education, Health and Human Sciences, Program in Public Health, Knoxville, TN 37996. Offers community health education (MPH); gerontology (MPH); health planning/administration (MPH); MS/MPH. *Accreditation:* CEPH. *Students:* 42 (36 women); includes 3 minority (2 African Americans, 1 Hispanic American) 3 international. 48 applicants, 54% accepted. In 2006, 34 degrees awarded. *Degree requirements:* For master's, thesis optional. *Entrance requirements:* For master's, minimum GPA of 2.7. Additional exam requirements/recommendations for international students: Required—TOEFL. *Application deadline:* For fall admission, 2/1 priority date for domestic students. Applications are processed on a rolling basis. Application fee: $35. Electronic applications accepted. *Expenses:* Tuition, state resident: full-time $5,574. Tuition, nonresident: full-time $16,840. Required fees: $792. *Financial support:* Application deadline: 2/1; *Unit head:* Dr. Charles B. Hamilton, Graduate Representative, 865-974-6674, E-mail: cbhamilton@utk.edu.

The University of Texas Medical Branch, Graduate School of Biomedical Sciences, Program in Preventive Medicine and Community Health, Galveston, TX 77555. Offers MPH, MS, PhD. *Accreditation:* CEPH. *Faculty:* 28 full-time (8 women), 36 part-time/adjunct (13 women). *Students:* 34 full-time (20 women), 5 part-time (3 women); includes 9 minority (4 Asian Americans or Pacific Islanders, 5 Hispanic Americans), 8 international. Average age 35. In 2006, 5 master's, 7 doctorates awarded. *Degree requirements:* For master's and doctorate, thesis/dissertation. *Entrance requirements:* For master's, GRE General Test or MAT; for doctorate, GRE General Test. Additional exam requirements/recommendations for international students: Required—TOEFL (minimum score 550 paper-based; 213 computer-based). *Application deadline:* Applications are processed on a rolling basis. Application fee: $30 ($75 for international students). Electronic applications accepted. *Financial support:* In 2006–07, fellowships (averaging $25,000 per year), research assistantships with full tuition reimbursements (averaging $25,000 per year) were awarded. Financial award applicants required to submit FAFSA. *Unit head:* Dr. Billy U. Philips, Director, 409-772-2551, Fax: 409-772-2573, E-mail: bphilips@utmb.edu. *Application contact:* Tonya R. Groh, Coordinator II Special Programs, 409-772-1123, Fax: 409-772-5272, E-mail: trgroh@utmb.edu.

University of Wisconsin–La Crosse, Office of University Graduate Studies, College of Science and Health, Department of Health Education and Health Promotion, Program in Community Health Education, La Crosse, WI 54601-3742. Offers MPH, MS. *Accreditation:* CEPH. *Students:* 11 full-time (all women), 19 part-time (16 women); includes 2 minority (both African Americans), 3 international. Average age 33. 8 applicants, 75% accepted, 3 enrolled. In 2006, 6 degrees awarded. *Degree requirements:* For master's, thesis. *Entrance requirements:* For master's, GRE General Test, GRE Subject Test (MPH), 3 letters of recommendation. Additional exam requirements/recommendations for international students: Required—TOEFL (minimum score 550 paper-based; 213 computer-based). Application fee: $45. *Financial support:* In 2006–07, 3 students received support, including 3 research assistantships (averaging $6,479 per year). *Faculty research:* School-based and community-based wellness strategies, violence prevention, alcohol and drug abuse prevention, competencies update project for health education, exercise and healthful pregnancy. *Unit head:* Dr. Gary Gilmore, Director, 608-785-8163, E-mail: gilmore.gary@uwlax.edu. *Application contact:* Kathryn Kiefer, Associate Director of Admissions, 608-785-8939, E-mail: admissions@uwlax.edu.

University of Wisconsin–Madison, School of Medicine and Public Health and Graduate School, Graduate Programs in Medicine, Population Health Graduate Program, Madison, WI 53706-1380. Offers MPH, MS, PhD. Part-time programs available. *Faculty:* 82 full-time (36 women), 2 part-time/adjunct (0 women). *Students:* 54 full-time (31 women), 42 part-time (31 women); includes 14 minority (5 African Americans, 7 Asian Americans or Pacific Islanders, 2 Hispanic Americans), 10 international. Average age 31. 114 applicants, 56% accepted, 43 enrolled. In 2006, 12 master's, 3 doctorates awarded. Terminal master's awarded for partial completion of doctoral program. Median time to degree: Of those who began their doctoral program in fall 1998, 100% received their degree in 8 years or less. *Degree requirements:* For master's, thesis, master's defense; for doctorate, thesis/dissertation, qualifying exam, preliminary exam, dissertation defense; for degree. *Entrance requirements:* For master's and doctorate, GRE, minimum GPA of 3.0, quantitative preparation (calculus, statistics, or other) with a grade of B or better. Additional exam requirements/recommendations for international students: Required—TOEFL (minimum score 580 paper-based; 237 computer-based; 92 iBT). *Application deadline:* For fall admission, 1/15 for domestic and international students; for spring admission, 8/15 for domestic and international students. Application fee: $45. Electronic applications accepted. *Financial support:* In 2006–07, 39 students received support, including

6 fellowships with full tuition reimbursements available (averaging $20,722 per year), 18 research assistantships with full tuition reimbursements available (averaging $16,088 per year), 3 teaching assistantships with full tuition reimbursements available (averaging $12,600 per year); traineeships, health care benefits, and unspecified assistantships also available. Support available to part-time students. *Faculty research:* Chronic and environmental epidemiology, health economics, health policy, determinants of population health, medical outcomes. Total annual research expenditures: $8.2 million. *Unit head:* Dr. F. Javier Nieto, Chair, 608-265-5242, Fax: 608-263-2820, E-mail: fjnieto@facstaff.wisc.edu. *Application contact:* Kelly Haslam, Graduate Program Coordinator, 608-265-8108, Fax: 608-263-2820, E-mail: haslam@wisc.edu.

Virginia Commonwealth University, Medical College of Virginia-Professional Programs, School of Medicine and Graduate Programs, School of Medicine Graduate Programs, Department of Epidemiology and Community Health, Program in Epidemiology and Community Health, Richmond, VA 23284-9005. Offers PhD. *Accreditation:* CEPH. Part-time programs available. *Faculty:* 13 full-time (4 women). *Students:* 42 full-time (36 women), 23 part-time (16 women); includes 17 minority (10 African Americans, 6 Asian Americans or Pacific Islanders, 1 Hispanic American), 4 international. 10 applicants, 20% accepted, 2 enrolled. *Degree requirements:* For doctorate, thesis/dissertation, comprehensive exam. *Entrance requirements:* For doctorate, GRE General Test, interview, 3 letters of recommendation, minimum graduate GPA of 3.0, master's degree in public health or related field including epidemiology and biostatistics. Additional exam requirements/recommendations for international students: Required—TOEFL (minimum score 600 paper-based). *Application deadline:* For spring admission, 4/1 priority date for domestic students, 1/1 priority date for international students. Applications are processed on a rolling basis. Application fee: $50. Electronic applications accepted. *Financial support:* Fellowships with full tuition reimbursements, tuition waivers (partial) available. *Faculty research:* Sickle cell anemia, breast cancer, HIV/AIDS, hospital epidemiology, infectious diseases. *Unit head:* Elizabeth Eustice-Turf, Director, 804-828-9705, Fax: 804-828-9773, E-mail: eturf@mail1.vcu.edu.

See Close-Up on page 2069.

Wayne State University, School of Medicine, Graduate Programs in Medicine, Department of Community Medicine, Detroit, MI 48202. Offers community health (MS); community health services (Certificate); public health (MPH); public health practice (Certificate). *Faculty:* 3 full-time (1 woman). *Students:* 5 full-time (4 women), 23 part-time (17 women); includes 11 minority (8 African Americans, 3 Asian Americans or Pacific Islanders), 7 international. Average age 35. 28 applicants, 32% accepted, 0 enrolled. *Degree requirements:* For master's, thesis (for some programs). *Entrance requirements:* For master's, GRE, minimum GPA of 2.6. Additional exam requirements/recommendations for international students: Required—TOEFL (minimum score 550 paper-based; 213 computer-based); Recommended—TWE (minimum score 6). *Application deadline:* For fall admission, 8/1 for domestic students, 6/1 for international students; for winter admission, 10/1 for international students; for spring admission, 2/1 for international students. Applications are processed on a rolling basis. Application fee: $30 ($50 for international students). Electronic applications accepted. *Financial support:* Research assistantships with tuition reimbursements, career-related internships or fieldwork, Federal Work-Study, and scholarships/grants available. Support available to part-time students. Financial award application deadline: 6/1. *Faculty research:* Urban health disparities, community health promotion, substance abuse etiology and prevention, HIV/AIDS, interpersonal violence. Total annual research expenditures: $54,800. *Unit head:* Dr. Antonia Abbey, Chair, 313-577-6686, Fax: 313-577-0316, E-mail: ab8222@wayne.edu. *Application contact:* James Moseley, Director, 313-577-7948, Fax: 313-577-0316, E-mail: jmosele@med.wayne.edu.

West Virginia University, School of Medicine, Department of Community Medicine, Program in Public Health, Morgantown, WV 26506. Offers community health/preventative medicine (MPH). *Accreditation:* CEPH. Part-time programs available. Postbaccalaureate distance learning degree programs offered (minimal on-campus study). *Students:* Average age 31. In 2006, 10 degrees awarded. *Degree requirements:* For master's, practicum, project. *Entrance requirements:* For master's, GRE General Test, MCAT, medical degree, medical internship. *Application deadline:* For fall admission, 4/15 priority date for domestic students; for spring admission, 12/1 for domestic students. Applications are processed on a rolling basis. *Expenses:* Contact institution. Tuition and fees vary according to program. *Financial support:* In 2006–07, 15 research assistantships, 3 teaching assistantships were awarded. Financial award application deadline: 2/1; financial award applicants required to submit FAFSA. *Faculty research:* Occupational health, environmental health, clinical epidemiology, health care management, prevention. Total annual research expenditures: $500,000. *Unit head:* Dr. Ian Rockett, Director of Educational Programs, 304-293-5325, Fax: 304-293-3755, E-mail: irockett@hsc.wvu.edu. *Application contact:* Leah A. Adkins, Senior Program Coordinator, 304-293-1098, Fax: 304-293-3755, E-mail: ladkins@hsc.wvu.edu.

Environmental and Occupational Health

American University of Beirut, Graduate Programs, Faculty of Health Sciences, Beirut, Lebanon. Offers environmental health (MSES); epidemiology (MS); population health (MS); population science (MS); public health (MPH). Part-time programs available. *Faculty:* 21 full-time (16 women), 4 part-time/adjunct (0 women). *Students:* 42 full-time (34 women), 63 part-time (54 women). Average age 27. 158 applicants, 74% accepted, 47 enrolled. In 2006, 47 degrees awarded. *Degree requirements:* For master's, one foreign language, thesis (for some programs), comprehensive exam, registration. *Entrance requirements:* For master's, letter of recommendation. Additional exam requirements/recommendations for international students: Required—TOEFL (minimum score 600 paper-based; 250 computer-based; 100 iBT), IELTS (minimum score 8). *Application deadline:* For fall admission, 4/30 for domestic and international students; for spring admission, 11/1 for domestic and international students. Application fee: $50. *Financial support:* In 2006–07, 6 students received support. Career-related internships or fieldwork, institutionally sponsored loans, scholarships/grants, health care benefits, and unspecified assistantships available. Financial award application deadline: 2/2. *Faculty research:* Urban health, challenging childbirth in the Arab region, tobacco control, HIV/AIDS surveillance, water quality and management. Total annual research expenditures: $632,411. *Unit head:* Huda Zurayls, Dean, 961-1340119 Ext. 4600, Fax: 961-1744470, E-mail: hzurayk@aub.edu.lb. *Application contact:* Dr. Salim Kanaan, Director of Admissions Office, 961-1-374374 Ext. 2592, Fax: 961-1-750775, E-mail: admissions@aub.edu.lb.

Anna Maria College, Graduate Division, Program in Occupational and Environmental Health and Safety, Paxton, MA 01612. Offers MS. Part-time and evening/weekend programs available. *Faculty:* 2 full-time (1 woman), 4 part-time/adjunct (1 woman). *Students:* Average age 40. In 2006, 2 degrees awarded. *Degree requirements:* For master's, thesis. *Entrance requirements:* For master's, minimum GPA of 2.7. *Application deadline:* For fall admission, 3/1 priority date for domestic and international students; for spring admission, 11/1 priority date for domestic and international students. Applications are processed on a rolling basis. Application fee: $40. Electronic applications accepted. *Financial support:* Applicants required to submit FAFSA. *Unit head:* Dr. Susan Swedis, Director, 508-849-3382, E-mail: sswedis@annamaria.edu. *Application contact:* Janet LaPointe, Admissions Coordinator, Graduate and Continuing Education, 508-849-3234, Fax: 508-819-3362, E-mail: jlapointe@annamaria.edu.

Boston University, School of Public Health, Environmental Health Department, Boston, MA 02215. Offers MPH, D Sc. *Accreditation:* CEPH (one or more programs are accredited).

Students: 13 full-time (11 women), 29 part-time (23 women); includes 6 minority (2 African Americans, 4 Asian Americans or Pacific Islanders), 3 international. Average age 29. *Degree requirements:* For doctorate, one foreign language, thesis/dissertation, comprehensive written and oral exams. *Entrance requirements:* For master's, GRE General Test; for doctorate, GRE General Test, MPH or equivalent. Additional exam requirements/recommendations for international students: Required—TOEFL or IELTS. *Application deadline:* For fall admission, 2/1 for domestic students; for spring admission, 10/15 for domestic students. Applications are processed on a rolling basis. Application fee: $95. Electronic applications accepted. *Expenses:* Tuition: Full-time $33,330; part-time $1,042 per credit. Required fees: $462; $40. *Financial support:* Career-related internships or fieldwork, Federal Work-Study, institutionally sponsored loans, scholarships/grants, and tuition waivers (partial) available. Support available to part-time students. *Unit head:* Dr. Roberta White, Chair, 617-638-4620, E-mail: envhlth@bu.edu. *Application contact:* LePhan Quan, Assistant Director of Admissions, 617-638-4640, Fax: 617-638-5299, E-mail: asksph@bu.edu.

California State University, Fresno, Division of Graduate Studies, College of Health and Human Services, Department of Public Health, Fresno, CA 93740-8027. Offers environmental/occupational health (MPH); health administration (MPH); health promotion (MPH). *Accreditation:* CEPH. Part-time and evening/weekend programs available. *Degree requirements:* For master's, thesis or alternative. *Entrance requirements:* For master's, GRE General Test, minimum GPA of 2.5. Additional exam requirements/recommendations for international students: Required—TOEFL. Electronic applications accepted. *Faculty research:* Foster parent training, geriatrics, tobacco control.

California State University, Northridge, Graduate Studies, College of Health and Human Development, Department of Environmental and Occupational Health, Northridge, CA 91330. Offers industrial hygiene (MS). *Faculty:* 5 full-time (0 women), 11 part-time/adjunct (3 women). *Students:* 14 full-time (3 women), 21 part-time (11 women); includes 16 minority (2 African Americans, 9 Asian Americans or Pacific Islanders, 5 Hispanic Americans), 2 international. Average age 31. 24 applicants, 75% accepted, 14 enrolled. In 2006, 18 degrees awarded. *Entrance requirements:* For master's, GRE General Test or minimum GPA of 3.0. Additional exam requirements/recommendations for international students: Required—TOEFL. *Application deadline:* For fall admission, 11/30 for domestic students. Application fee: $55. *Expenses:*

Environmental and Occupational Health

California State University, Northridge (continued)
Tuition, nonresident: full-time $8,136; part-time $4,068 per year. Required fees: $3,624; $1,161 per term. *Financial support:* Application deadline: 3/1. *Unit head:* Dr. Thomas Hatfield, Chair, 818-677-7476.

Colorado State University, College of Veterinary Medicine and Biomedical Sciences, Department of Environmental and Radiological Health Sciences, Fort Collins, CO 80523-0015. Offers environmental health (MS, PhD); radiological health sciences (MS, PhD). *Faculty:* 22 full-time (3 women), 2 part-time/adjunct (0 women). *Students:* 36 full-time (16 women), 38 part-time (17 women); includes 2 American Indian/Alaska Native, 5 Asian Americans or Pacific Islanders, 2 Hispanic Americans, 8 international. Average age 32. 38 applicants, 66% accepted, 13 enrolled. In 2006, 13 master's, 6 doctorates awarded. Terminal master's awarded for partial completion of doctoral program. *Median time to degree:* Of those who began their doctoral program in fall 1998, 100% received their degree in 8 years or less. *Degree requirements:* For master's, thesis (for some programs), publishable paper; for doctorate, thesis/dissertation, publishable paper, comprehensive exam, registration. *Entrance requirements:* For master's and doctorate, GRE General Test, 1 year of course work in biology lab and chemistry lab, 1 semester of course work in organic chemistry, course work in calculus; recommend 1 year of physics with lab; anatomy/physiology. Additional exam requirements/recommendations for international students: Required—TOEFL (minimum score 550 paper-based; 213 computer-based). *Application deadline:* For fall admission, 3/1 for domestic students, 2/1 priority date for international students; for spring admission, 10/1 for domestic students. Application fee: $50. Electronic applications accepted. *Expenses:* Tuition, state resident: full-time $4,248; part-time $236 per credit. Tuition, nonresident: full-time $15,642; part-time $869 per credit. Required fees: $66 per credit. Tuition and fees vary according to program. *Financial support:* In 2006–07, 5 fellowships with partial tuition reimbursements (averaging $6,840 per year), 3 teaching assistantships with full tuition reimbursements (averaging $11,441 per year) were awarded; career-related internships or fieldwork, Federal Work-Study, institutionally sponsored loans, traineeships, and unspecified assistantships also available. Support available to part-time students. Financial award application deadline: 2/1. *Faculty research:* Epidemiology, toxicology, industrial hygiene, occupational health, radiation therapy. Total annual research expenditures: $9.9 million. *Unit head:* Dr. John D. Zimbrick, Head, 970-491-7038, Fax: 970-491-6023, E-mail: zimbrick@colostate.edu. *Application contact:* Norma Jean Bulera, Administrative Assistant, 970-491-0241, Fax: 970-491-0623, E-mail: cmb@colostate.edu.

Columbia Southern University, Program in Occupational Safety and Health, Orange Beach, AL 36561. Offers environmental management (MS). Part-time and evening/weekend programs available. Postbaccalaureate distance learning degree programs offered (no on-campus study). *Entrance requirements:* Additional exam requirements/recommendations for international students: Required—TOEFL. Electronic applications accepted.

Columbia University, Mailman School of Public Health, Division of Environmental Health Sciences, New York, NY 10032. Offers MPH, Dr PH, PhD. PhD offered in cooperation with the Graduate School of Arts and Sciences. *Accreditation:* CEPH (one or more programs are accredited). Part-time programs available. *Students:* 68. In 2006, 30 master's, 2 doctorates awarded. *Degree requirements:* For master's, thesis optional; for doctorate, thesis/dissertation. *Entrance requirements:* For master's, GRE General Test, 1 year of course work in biology, general chemistry, organic chemistry, and mathematics; for doctorate, GRE General Test, MPH or equivalent (Dr PH). *Application deadline:* For fall admission, 2/1 for domestic students; for spring admission, 10/1 for domestic students. Applications are processed on a rolling basis. Application fee: $60. Electronic applications accepted. *Financial support:* Research assistantships, teaching assistantships, career-related internships or fieldwork and Federal Work-Study available. Support available to part-time students. Financial award application deadline: 2/1; financial award applicants required to submit FAFSA. *Faculty research:* Health effects of environmental and occupational exposure to chemicals and radiation, molecular epidemiology, risk assessment. *Unit head:* Dr. Paul Brandt-Rauf, Department Chair, 212-305-3464, Fax: 212-305-4012, E-mail: prvb1@columbia.edu. *Application contact:* June Saunders, Associate Director of Admissions, 212-305-3927, Fax: 212-342-4861, E-mail: ph-admit@columbia.edu.

Duke University, Graduate School, Integrated Toxicology and Environmental Health Program, Durham, NC 27708. Offers PhD, Certificate. *Faculty:* 33 full-time. *Students:* 7 full-time (2 women); includes 2 minority (1 African American, 1 Asian American or Pacific Islander). 19 applicants, 11% accepted, 2 enrolled. *Entrance requirements:* For doctorate, GRE General Test, GRE Subject Test (recommended). Additional exam requirements/recommendations for international students: Required—TOEFL (minimum score 550 paper-based; 213 computer-based; 83 iBT), IELTS (minimum score 7). *Application deadline:* For fall admission, 12/15 priority date for domestic and international students. Application fee: $75. Electronic applications accepted. *Financial support:* Fellowships available. Financial award application deadline: 12/31. *Unit head:* Theodore Slotkin, Director, 919-613-8078.

Duke University, Nicholas School of the Environment and Earth Sciences, Durham, NC 27708-0328. Offers coastal environmental management (MEM); DEL-environmental leadership (MEM); energy and environment (MEM); environmental economics and policy (MEM); environmental health and security (MEM); forest resource management (MF); global environmental change (MEM); resource ecology (MEM); water and air resources (MEM); JD/AM; JD/MEM; JD/MF; MAT/MEM; MBA/MEM; MBA/MF; MEM/MPP; MF/MPP. *Accreditation:* SAF (one or more programs are accredited). Part-time programs available. *Faculty:* 58 full-time (14 women), 61 part-time/adjunct (21 women). *Students:* 257 full-time (162 women). Average age 26. In 2006, 115 degrees awarded. *Median time to degree:* Master's–2 years full-time. *Degree requirements:* For master's, thesis, registration. *Entrance requirements:* For master's, GRE General Test, previous course work in biology or ecology, calculus, statistics, and microeconomics; computer familiarity with word processing and data analysis. Additional exam requirements/recommendations for international students: Required—TOEFL (minimum score 550 paper-based; 213 computer-based). *Application deadline:* For fall admission, 2/1 for domestic and international students; for spring admission, 10/15 for domestic and international students. Applications are processed on a rolling basis. Application fee: $75. Electronic applications accepted. *Expenses: Contact institution. Financial support:* In 2006–07, 143 fellowships (averaging $10,000 per year), 48 research assistantships (averaging $2,800 per year) were awarded; career-related internships or fieldwork, Federal Work-Study, institutionally sponsored loans, scholarships/grants, and unspecified assistantships also available. Financial award application deadline: 2/1; financial award applicants required to submit FAFSA. *Faculty research:* Ecosystem management, conservation ecology, earth systems, risk assessment. *Unit head:* Dr. William Schlesinger, Dean, 919-613-8004, Fax: 919-613-8719. *Application contact:* Cynthia Peters, Assistant Dean for Enrollment Services, 919-613-8070, Fax: 919-613-8719, E-mail: admissions@nicholas.duke.edu.

East Carolina University, Graduate School, College of Health and Human Performance, Department of Health Education and Promotion, Greenville, NC 27858-4353. Offers environmental health (MS); health education (MA, MA Ed). *Accreditation:* NCATE. *Students:* 36 full-time (23 women), 82 part-time (54 women); includes 32 minority (29 African Americans, 2 American Indian/Alaska Native, 1 Hispanic American), 1 international. Average age 29. 14 applicants, 29% accepted, 3 enrolled. In 2006, 29 degrees awarded. *Degree requirements:* For master's, thesis optional. *Entrance requirements:* For master's, GRE General Test or MAT. Additional exam requirements/recommendations for international students: Required—TOEFL. *Application deadline:* For fall admission, 6/1 priority date for domestic students. Applications are processed on a rolling basis. Application fee: $50. *Financial support:* In 2006–07, 4 fellowships (averaging $4,000 per year), 4 research assistantships (averaging $7,500 per year), 15 teaching assistantships (averaging $7,500 per year) were awarded; career-related internships or fieldwork also available. Support available to part-time students. Financial award application deadline: 6/1. *Faculty research:* Community health education, worksite health promotion, school health education, environmental health. Total annual research expenditures: $300,000. *Unit head:* Dr. David M. White, Chair, 252-328-6000, Fax: 252-328-1285, E-mail: whited@ecu.edu.

Eastern Kentucky University, The Graduate School, College of Health Sciences, Department of Clinical Laboratory Science/Environmental Health Science, Richmond, KY 40475-3102. Offers environmental health science (MPH). *Faculty:* 2 full-time (1 woman). *Students:* 9 full-time (6 women), 9 part-time (3 women); includes 5 minority (2 African Americans, 1 Asian American or Pacific Islander, 2 Hispanic Americans), 2 international. Average age 32. 29 applicants, 72% accepted, 11 enrolled.Application fee: $30. *Expenses:* Tuition, state resident: full-time $5,610. Tuition, nonresident: full-time $15,910. *Unit head:* Darryl Barnett, Chair, 859-622-3078, Fax: 859-622-1939.

East Tennessee State University, School of Graduate Studies, College of Public and Allied Health, Department of Environmental Health, Johnson City, TN 37614. Offers environmental health (MSEH), including administrative option, specialist option. Part-time programs available. *Degree requirements:* For master's, thesis optional. *Entrance requirements:* For master's, GRE, 30 hours of course work in natural and physical sciences, minimum GPA of 2.5. Additional exam requirements/recommendations for international students: Required—TOEFL (minimum score 550 paper-based; 213 computer-based). *Faculty research:* Water quality, ecotoxicology, occupational health.

Emory University, Rollins School of Public Health, Department of Environmental and Occupational Health, Atlanta, GA 30322-1100. Offers MPH, MSPH. *Accreditation:* CEPH. Part-time programs available. *Students:* 36 full-time (25 women), 4 part-time (3 women). Average age 27. 33 applicants, 76% accepted, 10 enrolled. In 2006, 21 degrees awarded. *Degree requirements:* For master's, thesis (for some programs), practicum. *Entrance requirements:* For master's, GRE General Test. Additional exam requirements/recommendations for international students: Required—TOEFL. *Application deadline:* For fall admission, 1/5 priority date for domestic and international students. Application fee: $75. Electronic applications accepted. *Expenses:* Tuition: Full-time $30,246. *Financial support:* Fellowships with full and partial tuition reimbursements, career-related internships or fieldwork, Federal Work-Study, institutionally sponsored loans, and scholarships/grants available. Support available to part-time students. Financial award application deadline: 1/5. *Unit head:* Dr. Paige Tolbert, Interim Chair, 404-727-0196, Fax: 404-727-8744, E-mail: ptolber@sph.emory.edu. *Application contact:* Ariadne Switchenberg, Assistant Director of Academic Programs, 404-727-7905, Fax: 404-727-8744, E-mail: ariadne.switchenberg@sph.emory.edu.

See Close-Up on page 2035.

Fort Valley State University, College of Graduate Studies and Extended Education, Program in Public Health, Fort Valley, GA 31030-4313. Offers environmental health (MPH). *Degree requirements:* For master's, thesis. *Entrance requirements:* For master's, GRE General Test.

Gannon University, School of Graduate Studies, College of Sciences, Engineering, and Health Sciences, School of Sciences, Program in Environmental and Occupational Science and Health, Erie, PA 16541-0001. Offers Certificate. *Students:* Average age 52. 1 applicant, 100% accepted, 1 enrolled. *Entrance requirements:* Additional exam requirements/recommendations for international students: Required—TOEFL (minimum score 500 paper-based; 173 computer-based). *Application deadline:* Applications are processed on a rolling basis. Application fee: $25. *Expenses:* Tuition: Full-time $12,240; part-time $680 per credit. Required fees: $496; $16 per credit. Tuition and fees vary according to course load, degree level, campus/location and program. *Financial support:* Application deadline: 7/1; *Unit head:* Dr. Harry Diz, Chair, 814-871-7633, E-mail: diz001@gannon.edu. *Application contact:* Debra Meszaros, Director of Graduate Recruitment, 814-871-5819, Fax: 814-871-5827, E-mail: cfal@gannon.edu.

Gannon University, School of Graduate Studies, College of Sciences, Engineering, and Health Sciences, School of Sciences, Program in Environmental Health and Engineering, Erie, PA 16541-0001. Offers MS. Part-time and evening/weekend programs available. *Students:* 5 full-time (3 women), 11 part-time (4 women); includes 1 minority (African American), 2 international. Average age 29. 15 applicants, 73% accepted, 2 enrolled. In 2006, 4 degrees awarded. *Entrance requirements:* Additional exam requirements/recommendations for international students: Required—TOEFL (minimum score 500 paper-based; 173 computer-based). *Application deadline:* Applications are processed on a rolling basis. Application fee: $25. *Expenses:* Tuition: Full-time $12,240; part-time $680 per credit. Required fees: $496; $16 per credit. Tuition and fees vary according to course load, degree level, campus/location and program. *Financial support:* Application deadline: 7/1; *Unit head:* Dr. Harry Diz, Chair, 814-871-7633, E-mail: diz001@gannon.edu. *Application contact:* Debra Meszaros, Director of Graduate Recruitment, 814-871-5819, Fax: 814-871-5827, E-mail: cfal@gannon.edu.

The George Washington University, School of Public Health and Health Services, Department of Environmental and Occupational Health, Washington, DC 20052. Offers MPH. *Accreditation:* CEPH. *Degree requirements:* For master's, case study or special project. *Entrance requirements:* For master's, GMAT, GRE General Test, or MCAT. Additional exam requirements/recommendations for international students: Required—TOEFL.

The George Washington University, School of Public Health and Health Services, Doctoral Program in Public Health, Washington, DC 20052. Offers environmental and occupational health (Dr PH); health behavior (Dr PH); health policy (Dr PH). *Accreditation:* CEPH. *Faculty research:* Community organization, tele-medicine, long-term care, financing for vulnerable populations, quantitative analysis in public health policy.

Harvard University, School of Public Health, Department of Environmental Health, Boston, MA 02115-6096. Offers environmental health (MOH, SM, DPH, PhD, SD); occupational health (MOH, SM, DPH, SD); physiology (PhD, SD). Part-time programs available. *Degree requirements:* For doctorate, thesis/dissertation, qualifying exam. *Entrance requirements:* For master's and doctorate, GRE. Additional exam requirements/recommendations for international students: Required—TOEFL (minimum score 560 paper-based; 220 computer-based); Recommended—IELTS (minimum score 7). Electronic applications accepted. *Expenses:* Tuition: Full-time $30,275. Full-time tuition and fees vary according to program and student level. *Faculty research:* Industrial hygiene and occupational safety, population genetics, indoor and outdoor air pollution, cell and molecular biology of the lungs, infectious diseases.

See Close-Up on page 2039.

Hunter College of the City University of New York, Graduate School, Schools of the Health Professions, Programs in Urban Public Health, Program in Environmental and Occupational Health Sciences, New York, NY 10021-5085. Offers MS. *Accreditation:* ABET. Part-time and evening/weekend programs available. *Faculty:* 2 full-time (0 women), 2 part-time/adjunct (1 woman). *Students:* 4 full-time (2 women), 21 part-time (7 women); includes 7 minority (1 African American, 4 Asian Americans or Pacific Islanders, 2 Hispanic Americans). Average age 34. 9 applicants, 44% accepted, 4 enrolled. In 2006, 15 degrees awarded. *Degree requirements:* For master's, internship, thesis optional. *Entrance requirements:* For master's, GRE General Test, previous course work in calculus and statistics. Additional exam requirements/recommendations for international students: Required—TOEFL. *Application deadline:* For fall admission, 4/1 for domestic students, 2/1 for international students; for spring admission, 11/1 for domestic students, 9/1 for international students. Application fee: $125. *Expenses:* Tuition, state resident: part-time $270 per credit. Tuition, nonresident: part-time $500 per credit. Required fees: $45 per semester. *Financial support:* In 2006–07, 6 fellowships were awarded; career-related internships or fieldwork, Federal Work-Study, institutionally sponsored loans, and tuition waivers (partial) also available. Support available to part-time students. Financial award application deadline: 3/1. *Faculty research:* Hazardous waste, asbestos, lead exposures, worker training, public employees. *Unit head:* Jack Caravanos, Director, 212-481-7569. *Applica-*

tion contact: William Zlata, Director for Graduate Admissions, 212-772-4482, Fax: 212-650-3336, E-mail: admissions@hunter.cuny.edu.

Illinois Institute of Technology, Graduate College, College of Science and Letters, Department of Social Sciences, Chicago, IL 60616-3793. Offers nonprofit management (MPA); public administration (MPA); public safety and crisis management (MPA); JD/MPA; MBA/MPA. Part-time and evening/weekend programs available. *Faculty:* 10 full-time (3 women), 10 part-time/adjunct (3 women). *Students:* 29 full-time (18 women), 40 part-time (23 women); includes 23 minority (17 African Americans, 1 American Indian/Alaska Native, 1 Asian American or Pacific Islander, 4 Hispanic Americans), 24 international. Average age 35. 116 applicants, 91% accepted, 45 enrolled. In 2006, 65 degrees awarded. *Degree requirements:* For master's, capstone course (practicum). *Entrance requirements:* For master's, minimum undergraduate GPA of 3.0, 2 letters of recommendation. Additional exam requirements/recommendations for international students: Required—TOEFL (minimum score 550 paper-based; 213 computer-based). *Application deadline:* For fall admission, 5/1 for domestic and international students; for spring admission, 10/15 for domestic and international students. Applications are processed on a rolling basis. Application fee: $40. Electronic applications accepted. *Expenses:* Tuition: Full-time $13,086; part-time $727 per credit. Required fees: $7 per credit. $235 per term. Tuition and fees vary according to class time, course level, course load, program and student level. *Financial support:* Federal Work-Study, institutionally sponsored loans, scholarships/grants, and health care benefits available. Support available to part-time students. Financial award applicants required to submit FAFSA. *Faculty research:* Science policy, city management, urban politics, urban ethnography, social impact of science and technology. *Unit head:* Dr. Ullica C. Segerstrale, Chair, 312-567-5134, Fax: 312-567-6821, E-mail: segerstrale@iit.edu. *Application contact:* Lawerence Ruffolo, Assistant Director, Graduate Program in Public Administration, 312-906-5197, Fax: 312-906-5199, E-mail: ruffolo@iit.edu.

Indiana State University, School of Graduate Studies, College of Health and Human Performance, Department of Health, Safety, and Environmental Health Sciences, Terre Haute, IN 47809-1401. Offers community health promotion (MA, MS); occupational safety management (MA, MS); school health and safety (MA, MS). *Accreditation:* NCATE (one or more programs are accredited). *Faculty:* 9 full-time (1 woman), 2 part-time/adjunct (1 woman). *Students:* 3 full-time (2 women), 19 part-time (5 women); includes 4 minority (3 African Americans, 1 Hispanic American), 1 international. Average age 37. 8 applicants, 63% accepted, 2 enrolled. In 2006, 3 degrees awarded. *Degree requirements:* For master's, thesis or alternative. *Entrance requirements:* For master's, GRE General Test. *Application deadline:* For fall admission, 7/1 priority date for domestic students; for spring admission, 11/1 priority date for domestic students. Applications are processed on a rolling basis. Application fee: $35. Electronic applications accepted. *Expenses:* Tuition, state resident: part-time $278 per credit. Tuition, nonresident: part-time $552 per credit. *Financial support:* In 2006–07, 1 research assistantship (averaging $3,150 per year) was awarded; teaching assistantships, tuition waivers (full) and unspecified assistantships also available. Financial award application deadline: 3/1; financial award applicants required to submit FAFSA. *Unit head:* Dr. Ernest Sheldon, Interim Chairperson, 812-237-3071.

Indiana University of Pennsylvania, School of Graduate Studies and Research, College of Health and Human Services, Department of Safety Sciences, Program in Safety Sciences, Indiana, PA 15705-1087. Offers MS. Part-time programs available. *Faculty:* 2 full-time (1 woman). *Students:* 5 full-time (2 women), 33 part-time (8 women); includes 2 minority (both African Americans), 2 international. Average age 36. 63 applicants, 54% accepted. In 2006, 19 degrees awarded. *Degree requirements:* For master's, thesis optional. *Entrance requirements:* For master's, 2 letters of recommendation. Additional exam requirements/recommendations for international students: Required—TOEFL. *Application deadline:* For fall admission, 7/1 priority date for domestic students; for spring admission, 11/1 for domestic students. Applications are processed on a rolling basis. Application fee: $30. *Expenses:* Tuition, state resident: full-time $6,048; part-time $336 per credit. Tuition, nonresident: full-time $9,678; part-time $538 per credit. Required fees: $1,069; $148 per year. *Financial support:* In 2006–07, 5 research assistantships with full and partial tuition reimbursements (averaging $2,955 per year) were awarded. Financial award application deadline: 3/15; financial award applicants required to submit FAFSA. *Unit head:* Dr. Chris Janicak, Graduate Coordinator, 724-357-3270.

The Johns Hopkins University, Bloomberg School of Public Health, Department of Environmental Health Sciences, Baltimore, MD 21218-2699. Offers environmental health engineering (PhD); environmental health sciences (MHS, Dr PH); molecular imaging (PhD); occupational and environmental health (PhD); occupational and environmental hygiene (MHS); physiology (PhD); toxicology (PhD). *Faculty:* 67 full-time (23 women), 44 part-time/adjunct (18 women). *Students:* 77 full-time (51 women), 14 part-time (11 women); includes 23 minority (5 African Americans, 13 Asian Americans or Pacific Islanders, 5 Hispanic Americans), 17 international. Average age 30. 106 applicants, 59% accepted, 26 enrolled. In 2006, 10 master's, 11 doctorates awarded. *Median time to degree:* Master's–1 year full-time; doctorate–6 years full-time, 11 years part-time. Of those who began their doctoral program in fall 1998, 57% received their degree in 8 years or less. *Degree requirements:* For master's, essay and presentation; for doctorate, thesis/dissertation, 1 year full-time residency, oral and written exams, comprehensive exam, registration. *Entrance requirements:* For master's and doctorate, GRE General Test or MCAT, 3 letters of recommendation, transcripts. Additional exam requirements/recommendations for international students: Required—TOEFL (minimum score 250 computer-based). *Application deadline:* For fall admission, 12/15 priority date for domestic and international students. Applications are processed on a rolling basis. Application fee: $45. Electronic applications accepted. *Expenses:* Tuition: Full-time $32,976. Tuition and fees vary according to degree level and program. *Financial support:* In 2006–07, 1 fellowship (averaging $23,500 per year) was awarded; Federal Work-Study, institutionally sponsored loans, scholarships/grants, traineeships, health care benefits, and stipends also available. Support available to part-time students. Financial award application deadline: 3/15; financial award applicants required to submit FAFSA. *Faculty research:* Respiratory and cardiovascular physiology, chemical carcinogenesis, antioxidants and drug metabolism, nuclear medicine, nuclear imaging. Total annual research expenditures: $20.5 million. *Unit head:* Dr. John Davis Groopman, Chair, 410-955-3720, Fax: 410-955-0617, E-mail: jgroopma@jhsph.edu. *Application contact:* Nina Kulacki, Senior Academic Coordinator, 410-955-2212, Fax: 410-955-0617, E-mail: nkulacki@jhsph.edu.

Loma Linda University, School of Public Health, Programs in Environmental and Occupational Health, Loma Linda, CA 92350. Offers MPH, MSPH. *Accreditation:* CEPH. *Entrance requirements:* Additional exam requirements/recommendations for international students: Required—Michigan English Language Assessment Battery or TOEFL. *Faculty research:* Human exposure to toxins, smog.

Loyola University Chicago, Graduate School, Marcella Niehoff School of Nursing, Population-Based Infection Control and Environmental Safety Program, Chicago, IL 60611-2196. Offers MSN. Part-time and evening/weekend programs available. *Entrance requirements:* For master's, Illinois license, 3 letters of recommendation. *Unit head:* Dr. Ida Androwich, Dean, 773-508-3255, E-mail: iandrow@luc.edu. *Application contact:* Dr. Vicki A. Keough, Associate Dean, 773-508-3263, Fax: 773-508-3241, E-mail: vkeough@luc.edu.

McGill University, Faculty of Graduate and Postdoctoral Studies, Faculty of Medicine, Departments of Epidemiology and Biostatistics, and Occupational Health, Montréal, QC H3A 2T5, Canada. Offers community health (M Sc); environmental health (M Sc); epidemiology and biostatistics (M Sc, PhD, Diploma); health care evaluation (M Sc); medical statistics (M Sc); occupational health (M Sc). *Accreditation:* CEPH (one or more programs are accredited). *Degree requirements:* For master's, thesis optional; for doctorate, thesis/dissertation. *Entrance requirements:* For master's, GRE, minimum GPA of 3.0; for doctorate, GRE. *Faculty research:* Chronic and infectious disease epidemiology, health services research, pharmacoepidemiology.

Medical College of Wisconsin, Medical School, Department of Preventive Medicine, Milwaukee, WI 53226-0509. Offers general preventive medicine and public health (MPH); occupational medicine (MPH). *Accreditation:* CEPH. Part-time programs available. Postbaccalaureate distance learning degree programs offered (no on-campus study). *Degree requirements:* For master's, project. *Entrance requirements:* For master's, MD/DO license to practice medicine in U.S. or Canada. Additional exam requirements/recommendations for international students: Required—TOEFL. *Faculty research:* Environmental medicine, ergonomics, epidemiology, surveillance, distance education.

Meharry Medical College, School of Graduate Studies, Division of Community Health Sciences, Nashville, TN 37208-9989. Offers general preventive medicine (MSPH); health services administration (MSPH); occupational medicine (MSPH); public health administration (MSPH). Part-time and evening/weekend programs available. *Degree requirements:* For master's, thesis, externship. *Entrance requirements:* For master's, GRE General Test, GMAT. Expenses: Contact institution. *Faculty research:* Policy and management, health care financing, health education and promotion.

Mississippi Valley State University, Department of Natural Science and Environmental Health, Program in Environmental Health, Itta Bena, MS 38941-1400. Offers MS. Evening/weekend programs available.

Montclair State University, The Graduate School, College of Science and Mathematics, Department of Earth and Environmental Studies, Montclair, NJ 07043-1624. Offers environmental management (MA, D Env M); environmental studies (MS), including environmental education, environmental health, environmental management, environmental science; geoscience (MS, Certificate), including geoscience (MS), water resource management (Certificate). Part-time and evening/weekend programs available. *Faculty:* 17 full-time (3 women), 9 part-time/adjunct (3 women). *Students:* 24 full-time (11 women), 45 part-time (20 women); includes 6 minority (3 African Americans, 1 Asian American or Pacific Islander, 2 Hispanic Americans), 8 international. 33 applicants, 39% accepted, 7 enrolled. In 2006, 18 master's, 3 other advanced degrees awarded. *Degree requirements:* For master's, thesis or alternative, comprehensive exam; for doctorate, thesis/dissertation. *Entrance requirements:* For master's, GRE General Test, 2 letters of recommendation. Additional exam requirements/recommendations for international students: Required—TOEFL (minimum score 83 computer-based). *Application deadline:* For fall admission, 6/1 for international students; for spring admission, 10/1 for international students. Applications are processed on a rolling basis. Application fee: $60. Electronic applications accepted. *Expenses:* Tuition, state resident: part-time $450 per credit. Tuition, nonresident: part-time $682 per credit. Tuition and fees vary according to degree level and program. *Financial support:* In 2006–07, 14 research assistantships with full tuition reimbursements were awarded; Federal Work-Study, scholarships/grants, and unspecified assistantships also available. Support available to part-time students. Financial award application deadline: 3/1; financial award applicants required to submit FAFSA. *Faculty research:* Antarctica, carbon pools, contaminated sediments, wetlands. Total annual research expenditures: $127,880. *Unit head:* Dr. Gregory Pope, Chairperson, 973-655-7385. *Application contact:* Dr. Harbans Singh, Adviser, 973-655-7383.

Murray State University, College of Health Sciences and Human Services, Program in Occupational Safety and Health, Murray, KY 42071. Offers environmental science (MS); industrial hygiene (MS); safety management (MS). *Accreditation:* ABET. Part-time programs available. *Faculty:* 9 full-time (3 women), 2 part-time/adjunct (0 women). *Students:* Average age 25. 15 applicants, 100% accepted, 12 enrolled. In 2006, 15 degrees awarded. *Degree requirements:* For master's, professional internship, thesis optional. *Application deadline:* Applications are processed on a rolling basis. Application fee: $25. Electronic applications accepted. *Financial support:* In 2006–07, 16 students received support. Career-related internships or fieldwork, Federal Work-Study, institutionally sponsored loans, scholarships/grants, tuition waivers (full), and unspecified assistantships available. Support available to part-time students. *Faculty research:* Light effects on plant growth, ergonomics, toxic effects of pets' pesticides, traffic safety. *Unit head:* Dr. David G. Kraemer, Chairman, 270-809-6654, Fax: 270-809-3630, E-mail: david.kraemer@murraystate.edu. *Application contact:* Dr. Bassam H. Atieh, Professor, 270-809-6652, Fax: 270-809-3630, E-mail: bassam.atieh@murraystate.edu.

New Jersey Institute of Technology, Office of Graduate Studies, College of Science and Liberal Arts, Department of Chemistry and Environmental Science, Program in Occupational Safety and Industrial Hygiene, Newark, NJ 07102. Offers MS. Part-time and evening/weekend programs available. *Entrance requirements:* For master's, GRE General Test. Additional exam requirements/recommendations for international students: Required—TOEFL (minimum score 550 paper-based; 213 computer-based). *Application deadline:* For fall admission, 6/5 priority date for domestic students; for spring admission, 10/15 for domestic students. Applications are processed on a rolling basis. Application fee: $60. Electronic applications accepted. *Expenses:* Tuition, state resident: full-time $11,896; part-time $648 per credit. Tuition, nonresident: full-time $16,900; part-time $892 per credit. Required fees: $336; $66 per credit. $168 per term. Tuition and fees vary according to course load. *Financial support:* Fellowships with full and partial tuition reimbursements, research assistantships with full and partial tuition reimbursements, teaching assistantships with full and partial tuition reimbursements, career-related internships or fieldwork, Federal Work-Study, institutionally sponsored loans, and unspecified assistantships available. Financial award application deadline: 3/15. *Application contact:* Kathryn Kelly, Director of Admissions, 973-596-3300, Fax: 973-596-3461, E-mail: admissions@njit.edu.

New York Medical College, School of Public Health, Department of Environmental Health Science, Valhalla, NY 10595-1691. Offers MPH. Part-time and evening/weekend programs available. In 2006, 4 degrees awarded. *Degree requirements:* For master's, thesis, registration. *Entrance requirements:* For master's, minimum undergraduate GPA of 3.0. Additional exam requirements/recommendations for international students: Required—TOEFL (minimum score 600 paper-based; 250 computer-based). *Application deadline:* For fall admission, 8/1 priority date for domestic students, 5/15 for international students; for spring admission, 12/1 priority date for domestic students, 10/15 for international students. Applications are processed on a rolling basis. Application fee: $35 ($60 for international students). Electronic applications accepted. *Financial support:* Career-related internships or fieldwork, Federal Work-Study, and institutionally sponsored loans available. Financial award application deadline: 6/15; financial award applicants required to submit FAFSA. *Unit head:* Dr. Robert W. Amler, Acting Chair, 914-594-4804, Fax: 914-594-4292, E-mail: robert_amler@nymc.edu. *Application contact:* Marian F. McGowan, Information Contact, 914-594-4510, Fax: 914-594-4292, E-mail: sph_admissions@nymc.edu.

See Close-Up on page 2043.

New York University, Graduate School of Arts and Science, Department of Environmental Medicine, New York, NY 10012-1019. Offers environmental health sciences (MS, PhD), including biostatistics (PhD), environmental hygiene (MS), epidemiology (PhD), ergonomics and biomechanics (PhD), exposure assessment and health effects (PhD), molecular toxicology/carcinogenesis (PhD), toxicology. Part-time programs available. *Faculty:* 26 full-time (7 women). *Students:* 49 full-time (40 women), 17 part-time (8 women); includes 12 minority (3 African Americans, 6 Asian Americans or Pacific Islanders, 3 Hispanic Americans), 25 international. Average age 31. 65 applicants, 45% accepted, 16 enrolled. In 2006, 10 master's, 4 doctorates awarded. Terminal master's awarded for partial completion of doctoral program. *Degree requirements:* For master's, thesis or alternative; for doctorate, one foreign language, thesis/dissertation, oral and written exams. *Entrance requirements:* For master's and doctorate, GRE General Test, GRE Subject Test, minimum GPA of 3.0; bachelor's degree in biological, physical, or engineering science. Additional exam requirements/recommendations for international students: Required—TOEFL. *Application deadline:* For fall admission, 12/15 for domestic students. Application fee: $80. *Expenses:* Tuition: Part-time $1,080 per unit. Required fees: $56 per unit. $329 per term. Tuition and fees vary according to program. *Financial support:* Fellowships with tuition reimbursements, teaching assistantships with tuition reimbursements, career-related internships or fieldwork, Federal Work-Study, institutionally sponsored loans, and health care benefits available. Financial award application deadline: 12/15; financial

Environmental and Occupational Health

New York University (continued)
award applicants required to submit FAFSA. *Unit head:* Dr. Max Costa, Chair, 845-731-3661, Fax: 845-351-3317, E-mail: ehs@env.med.nyu.edu. *Application contact:* Dr. Jerome J. Solomon, Director of Graduate Studies, 845-731-3661, Fax: 845-351-3317, E-mail: ehs@env.med.nyu.edu.

Oakland University, Graduate Study and Lifelong Learning, School of Health Sciences, Program in Safety Management, Rochester, MI 48309-4401. Offers MS. *Students:* Average age 35. 7 applicants, 100% accepted, 5 enrolled. *Application deadline:* For fall admission, 8/1 for domestic students; for winter admission, 12/1 for domestic students; for spring admission, 4/1 for domestic students. Application fee: $35. *Expenses:* Tuition, state resident: full-time $9,936; part-time $414 per credit. Tuition, nonresident: full-time $17,202; part-time $716 per credit. *Unit head:* Dr. Charles McGlothlin, Director, 248-370-2664, E-mail: mcglothl@oakland.edu.

See Close-Up on page 2047.

OGI School of Science & Engineering at Oregon Health & Science University, Graduate Studies, Department of Environmental and Biomolecular Systems, Beaverton, OR 97006-8921. Offers biochemistry and molecular biology (MS, PhD); environmental health systems (MS); environmental information technology (MS, PhD); environmental science and engineering (MS, PhD). Part-time programs available. *Faculty:* 15 full-time (5 women), 3 part-time/adjunct (0 women). *Students:* 29 full-time (11 women), 22 part-time (11 women); includes 23 minority (2 American Indian/Alaska Native, 21 Asian Americans or Pacific Islanders), 5 international. Average age 28. 40 applicants, 63% accepted, 12 enrolled. In 2006, 14 master's, 6 doctorates awarded. Terminal master's awarded for partial completion of doctoral program. *Median time to degree:* Of those who began their doctoral program in fall 1998, 100% received their degree in 8 years or less. *Degree requirements:* For master's, thesis optional; for doctorate, oral defense of dissertation. *Entrance requirements:* For master's and doctorate, GRE General Test. Additional exam requirements/recommendations for international students: Required—TOEFL. Application fee: $65. Electronic applications accepted. *Expenses:* Tuition, nonresident: full-time $22,760; part-time $625 per credit. Required fees: $65 per term. *Financial support:* In 2006–07, 4 fellowships with full and partial tuition reimbursements (averaging $18,500 per year), 22 research assistantships with full and partial tuition reimbursements (averaging $18,500 per year) were awarded; teaching assistantships with full and partial tuition reimbursements, Federal Work-Study, scholarships/grants, and tuition waivers (full and partial) also available. Financial award application deadline: 2/15. *Faculty research:* Air and water science, hydrogeology, estuarine and coastal modeling, environmental microbiology, contaminant transport, biochemistry, biomolecular systems. Total annual research expenditures: $4.9 million. *Unit head:* Dr. Brad Tebo, Head, 503-748-1992, Fax: 503-748-1273, E-mail: tebob@ebs.ogi.edu. *Application contact:* Nancy Christie, Information Contact, 800-748-1070, Fax: 503-748-1464, E-mail: christin@ohsu.edu.

Old Dominion University, College of Health Sciences, Program in Community Health and Environmental Health, Norfolk, VA 23529. Offers community health professions (MS); environmental health (MS); health care administration (MS); long-term care administration (MS); wellness and promotion (MS). Part-time and evening/weekend programs available. Postbaccalaureate distance learning degree programs offered (no on-campus study). *Faculty:* 5 full-time (4 women), 5 part-time/adjunct (1 woman). *Students:* 10 full-time (7 women), 33 part-time (24 women); includes 6 minority (5 African Americans, 1 Asian American or Pacific Islander), 8 international. Average age 33. 32 applicants, 88% accepted, 15 enrolled. In 2006, 19 degrees awarded. *Degree requirements:* For master's, oral exam, written exam, thesis optional. *Entrance requirements:* For master's, GRE General Test, minimum GPA of 2.75. Additional exam requirements/recommendations for international students: Required—TOEFL. *Application deadline:* For fall admission, 8/1 priority date for domestic students, 7/1 priority date for international students; for winter admission, 11/1 priority date for domestic students, 10/1 priority date for international students; for spring admission, 4/1 priority date for domestic students, 3/1 priority date for international students. Applications are processed on a rolling basis. Application fee: $40. Electronic applications accepted. *Expenses:* Tuition, area resident: Part-time $285 per credit hour. Tuition, nonresident: part-time $715 per credit hour. Required fees: $94 per semester. *Financial support:* In 2006–07, 5 research assistantships with tuition reimbursements (averaging $14,000 per year) were awarded; career-related internships or fieldwork, institutionally sponsored loans, scholarships/grants, and tuition waivers (partial) also available. Support available to part-time students. Financial award applicants required to submit FAFSA. *Faculty research:* Toxicology, domestic violence, health policy and planning, environmental hazards, obesity, substance abuse, minority health spirituality, women's health. Total annual research expenditures: $150,133. *Unit head:* Dr. Clare Houseman, Chair, 757-683-4259, Fax: 757-683-4410, E-mail: chpgdd@odu.edu.

Oregon State University, Graduate School, College of Health and Human Sciences, Department of Public Health, Program in Environmental Health and Occupational Safety Management, Corvallis, OR 97331. Offers MAIS, MS. *Students:* 1 (woman) full-time. Average age 32. *Degree requirements:* For master's, thesis. *Entrance requirements:* For master's, GRE General Test, minimum GPA of 3.0 in last 90 hours. Additional exam requirements/recommendations for international students: Required—TOEFL. *Application deadline:* For fall admission, 3/1 for domestic students. Applications are processed on a rolling basis. Application fee: $50. *Financial support:* Research assistantships, teaching assistantships, career-related internships or fieldwork, Federal Work-Study, and institutionally sponsored loans available. Support available to part-time students. Financial award application deadline: 2/1. *Unit head:* Dr. Cathy Neumann, Coordinator, 541-737-3833, Fax: 541-737-4001, E-mail: cathy.neumann@orst.edu. *Application contact:* Annette M. Rossignal, Professor, 541-737-3840, Fax: 541-737-3643, E-mail: anne.rossignal@orst.edu.

Penn State University Park, Graduate School, College of Earth and Mineral Sciences, Department of Energy and Geo-Environmental Engineering, State College, University Park, PA 16802-1503. Offers energy and geo-environmental engineering (MS, PhD); industrial health and safety (MS); mineral processing (MS, PhD); mining engineering (MS, PhD); petroleum and mining engineering (MS, PhD). *Unit head:* Dr. Yaw D. Yeboah, Head, 814-865-3437, E-mail: ydy1@psu.edu. *Application contact:* Information Contact, E-mail: egee@ems.psu.edu.

Saint Joseph's University, College of Arts and Sciences, Public Safety and Environmental Protection Institute, Philadelphia, PA 19131-1395. Offers environmental protection and safety management (MS, Post-Master's Certificate); public safety (MS, Post-Master's Certificate). *Students:* 10 full-time (4 women), 72 part-time (13 women); includes 10 minority (all African Americans) Average age 36. In 2006, 28 degrees awarded. *Entrance requirements:* For master's, GRE (may be required), 2 letters of recommendation, resum[00e9]. *Application deadline:* For fall admission, 7/15 for domestic students. Application fee: $35. *Unit head:* Dr. Vincent P. McNally, Director, 610-660-1641, Fax: 610-660-2903, E-mail: vmcnally@sju.edu.

Saint Mary's University of Minnesota, School of Graduate and Professional Programs, Program in Public Safety Administration, Winona, MN 55987-1399. Offers MA. *Unit head:* Donald S. Winger, Director, 612-728-5195, Fax: 612-728-5121, E-mail: dwinger@smumn.edu.

San Diego State University, Graduate and Research Affairs, College of Health and Human Services, Graduate School of Public Health, San Diego, CA 92182. Offers environmental health (MPH); epidemiology (MPH, PhD), including biostatistics (MPH); global emergency preparedness and response (MS); health behavior (PhD); health promotion (MPH); health services administration (MPH); toxicology (MS); MSW/MPH. *Accreditation:* ABET (one or more programs are accredited); CAHME (one or more programs are accredited); CEPH (one or more programs are accredited). Part-time programs available. *Degree requirements:* For master's, thesis (for some programs), comprehensive exam (for some programs); for doctorate, thesis/dissertation. *Entrance requirements:* For master's, GMAT (health services administration MPH), GRE General Test; for doctorate, GRE General Test. Additional exam requirements/recommendations for international students: Required—TOEFL. *Faculty research:* Evaluation of tobacco, AIDS prevalence and prevention, mammography, infant death project, Alzheimer's in elderly Chinese.

Stony Brook University, State University of New York, School of Professional Development, Stony Brook, NY 11794. Offers adolescence education: mathematics (Certificate); biology 7-12 (MAT); chemistry-grade 7-12 (MAT); coaching (Certificate); computer integrated engineering (Certificate); cultural studies (Certificate); earth science-grade 7-12 (MAT); educational computing (Advanced Certificate, Certificate); English-grade 7-12 (MAT); environmental and waste management (MS, Advanced Certificate); environmental systems management (Certificate); environmental/occupational health and safety (Certificate); French-grade 7-12 (MAT); German-grade 7-12 (MAT); human resource management (Certificate); industrial management (Certificate); information systems management (Certificate); Italian-grade 7-12 (MAT); liberal studies (MA); liberal studies online (MA); Long Island regional studies (Certificate); operation research (Certificate); physics-grade 7-12 (MAT); Russian-grade 7-12 (MAT); school administration and supervision (Certificate); school district administration (Certificate); social science and the professions (MPS), including human resources management, labor management, public affairs, waste management; social studies 7-12 (MAT); waste management (Certificate); women's studies (Certificate). Part-time and evening/weekend programs available. Postbaccalaureate distance learning degree programs offered. *Faculty:* 1 full-time (0 women), 118 part-time/adjunct (45 women). *Students:* 322 full-time (202 women), 1,188 part-time (728 women); includes 164 minority (69 African Americans, 2 American Indian/Alaska Native, 29 Asian Americans or Pacific Islanders, 64 Hispanic Americans), 11 international. Average age 28. In 2006, 738 master's, 405 other advanced degrees awarded. *Degree requirements:* For master's, one foreign language, thesis or alternative. *Application deadline:* Applications are processed on a rolling basis. Application fee: $62. *Expenses:* Tuition, state resident: full-time $6,900; part-time $288 per credit. Tuition, nonresident: full-time $10,920; part-time $455 per credit. *Financial support:* In 2006–07, 5 teaching assistantships were awarded; fellowships, research assistantships, career-related internships or fieldwork also available. Support available to part-time students. *Unit head:* Dr. Paul J. Edelson, Dean, 631-632-7052, Fax: 631-632-9046, E-mail: paul.edelson@sunysb.edu. *Application contact:* Sandra Romansky, Director of Admissions and Advisement, 631-632-7050, Fax: 631-632-9046, E-mail: sandra.romansky@sunysb.edu.

Temple University, Health Sciences Center and Graduate School, College of Health Professions, Department of Public Health, Program in Environmental Health, Philadelphia, PA 19122-6096. Offers MS. Part-time and evening/weekend programs available. *Students:* 1 full-time (0 women), 14 part-time (8 women). 13 applicants, 54% accepted. In 2006, 6 degrees awarded. *Entrance requirements:* For master's, GRE General Test. Additional exam requirements/recommendations for international students: Required—TOEFL (minimum score 550 paper-based; 213 computer-based; 79 iBT). *Application deadline:* For fall admission, 2/15 for domestic students, 12/15 for international students; for spring admission, 10/15 for domestic students, 8/1 for international students. Applications are processed on a rolling basis. Application fee: $50. Electronic applications accepted. *Expenses:* Tuition, state resident: full-time $12,264; part-time $511 per credit. Tuition, nonresident: full-time $17,904; part-time $746 per credit. Required fees: $84 per course. Tuition and fees vary according to program. *Financial support:* Fellowships, teaching assistantships with full tuition reimbursements, career-related internships or fieldwork, Federal Work-Study, and institutionally sponsored loans available. Financial award application deadline: 1/15; financial award applicants required to submit FAFSA. *Faculty research:* Air pollution, industrial hygiene, exposure assessment, nonionizing radiation. *Unit head:* Dr. Robert M. Patterson, Director, 215-204-1665, Fax: 215-204-1854, E-mail: rpatters@temple.edu.

Texas A&M Health Science Center, School of Rural Public Health, College Station, TX 77843-1266. Offers environmental/occupational health (MPH); epidemiology/biostatistics (MPH); health policy/management (MPH); social and behavioral health (MPH). *Accreditation:* CEPH. Part-time programs available. Postbaccalaureate distance learning degree programs offered (no on-campus study). *Faculty:* 16 full-time (7 women), 4 part-time/adjunct (1 woman). *Students:* 43 full-time (27 women), 118 part-time (76 women); includes 63 minority (13 African Americans, 13 Asian Americans or Pacific Islanders, 37 Hispanic Americans), 1 international. Average age 32. 162 applicants, 83% accepted, 118 enrolled. In 2006, 10 degrees awarded. *Degree requirements:* For master's, thesis optional. *Entrance requirements:* For master's, GRE General Test, minimum undergraduate GPA of 3.0. *Application deadline:* For fall admission, 8/27 for domestic students; for spring admission, 1/14 for domestic students. Applications are processed on a rolling basis. Application fee: $35 ($75 for international students). Electronic applications accepted. *Financial support:* In 2006–07, research assistantships (averaging $10,800 per year). *Faculty research:* Tobacco cessation, youth health risk. Total annual research expenditures: $1.7 million. *Unit head:* Dr. Ciro V. Sumaya, Dean. *Application contact:* Dr. James Robinson, Professor/Special Advisor to the Dean, 409-845-2387, Fax: 409-862-8371, E-mail: jrobinson@medicine.tamu.edu.

Touro University International, College of Health Sciences, Program in Health Sciences, Cypress, CA 90630. Offers clinical research administration (MS, Certificate); emergency and disaster management (MS, Certificate); environmental health science (Certificate); health care administration (PhD); health care management (MS), including health informatics; health education (MS, Certificate); health informatics (Certificate); health sciences (PhD); international health (MS); international health: educator or researcher option (PhD); international health: practitioner option (PhD); law and expert witness studies (MS, Certificate); public health (MS); quality assurance (Certificate). Part-time and evening/weekend programs available. Postbaccalaureate distance learning degree programs offered (no on-campus study). In 2006, 322 master's, 21 doctorates awarded. *Degree requirements:* For doctorate, thesis/dissertation, defense of dissertation, comprehensive exam. *Entrance requirements:* For master's, minimum GPA of 3.0; for doctorate, minimum GPA of 3.4, curriculum vitae, course work in research methods or statistics. Additional exam requirements/recommendations for international students: Required—TOEFL (minimum score 550 paper-based). Application fee: $75. *Expenses:* Tuition: Part-time $300 per credit hour. Tuition and fees vary according to course level and program. *Unit head:* Dr. Edith Neumann, Vice President for Academic Affairs, College of Health Sciences, 714-816-0366 Ext. 2030, Fax: 714-226-9844, E-mail: eneumann@tourou.edu.

Towson University, Graduate School, Program in Occupational Science, Towson, MD 21252-0001. Offers Sc D. Part-time and evening/weekend programs available. *Faculty:* 5 full-time (all women), 1 (woman) part-time/adjunct. *Students:* 5 applicants, 60% accepted, 2 enrolled. *Degree requirements:* For doctorate, thesis/dissertation, comprehensive assessment. *Entrance requirements:* For doctorate, GRE or MAT, NBCOT certification, minimum GPA of 3.25. Additional exam requirements/recommendations for international students: Required—TOEFL (minimum score 600 paper-based; 250 computer-based). *Application deadline:* For fall admission, 8/15 priority date for domestic and international students; for winter admission, 11/15 priority date for domestic and international students; for spring admission, 1/15 priority date for domestic and international students. Applications are processed on a rolling basis. Application fee: $50. Electronic applications accepted. *Expenses:* Tuition, state resident: part-time $275 per unit. Tuition, nonresident: part-time $577 per unit. Required fees: $72 per unit. *Financial support:* In 2006–07, 2 fellowships with full tuition reimbursements (averaging $7,500 per year), teaching assistantships with partial tuition reimbursements (averaging $3,000 per year) were awarded; research assistantships with partial tuition reimbursements, career-related internships or fieldwork and unspecified assistantships also available. Financial award application deadline: 4/1; financial award applicants required to submit FAFSA. *Faculty research:* Successful aging, family quality of life, community living and individuals with mental illness. *Unit head:* Dr. Janet Delany, Graduate Program Director, 410-704-2371, Fax: 410-704-2322, E-mail: jdelany@towson.edu. *Application contact:* 410-704-2501, Fax: 410-704-4675, E-mail: grads@towson.edu.

Tufts University, School of Engineering, Department of Civil and Environmental Engineering, Medford, MA 02155. Offers civil engineering (ME, MS, PhD), including geotechnical engineering, structural engineering; environmental engineering (ME, MS, PhD), including environmental engineering and environmental sciences, environmental geotechnology, environmental health, environmental science and management, hazardous materials management, water resources engineering. Part-time programs available. *Faculty:* 16 full-time, 7 part-time/adjunct. *Students:* 68 (39 women); includes 3 minority (1 African American, 2 Asian Americans or Pacific Islanders) 9 international. 88 applicants, 68% accepted, 20 enrolled. In 2006, 24 degrees awarded. Terminal master's awarded for partial completion of doctoral program. *Degree requirements:* For master's, thesis or alternative; for doctorate, thesis/dissertation. *Entrance requirements:* Additional exam requirements/recommendations for international students: Required—TOEFL (minimum score 550 paper-based; 213 computer-based; 80 iBT). *Application deadline:* For fall admission, 1/15 priority date for domestic students, 12/30 for international students; for spring admission, 10/15 for domestic students, 9/15 for international students. Applications are processed on a rolling basis. Application fee: $70. Electronic applications accepted. *Expenses:* Tuition: Full-time $33,672. Tuition and fees vary according to degree level and program. *Financial support:* Fellowships with full tuition reimbursements, research assistantships with full and partial tuition reimbursements, teaching assistantships with full and partial tuition reimbursements, Federal Work-Study, scholarships/grants, and tuition waivers (partial) available. Support available to part-time students. Financial award application deadline: 1/15; financial award applicants required to submit FAFSA. *Unit head:* Dr. Christopher Swan, Chair, 617-627-3211, Fax: 617-627-3994.

Tulane University, School of Public Health and Tropical Medicine, Department of Environmental Health Sciences, New Orleans, LA 70118-5669. Offers MPH, MSPH, Dr PH, PhD, JD/MSPH. *Accreditation:* ABET (one or more programs are accredited); CEPH (one or more programs are accredited). *Faculty:* 13 full-time (6 women), 8 part-time/adjunct (3 women). *Students:* 182 full-time (83 women), 16 part-time (8 women). *Degree requirements:* For doctorate, thesis/dissertation, comprehensive exam. *Entrance requirements:* For master's and doctorate, GRE General Test. Additional exam requirements/recommendations for international students: Required—TOEFL. *Application deadline:* For fall admission, 4/15 priority date for domestic and international students; for spring admission, 10/15 priority date for domestic and international students. Applications are processed on a rolling basis. Application fee: $40. Electronic applications accepted. *Financial support:* Federal Work-Study, scholarships/grants, and traineeships available. Support available to part-time students. Financial award application deadline: 4/15. *Unit head:* Dr. Assaf Abdelghani, Chair, 504-588-5374. *Application contact:* Erica Geary, Program Coordinator, 504-588-5374, E-mail: egeary@tulane.edu.

Uniformed Services University of the Health Sciences, School of Medicine, Programs in Biomedical Sciences, Bethesda, MD 20814-4799. Offers emerging infectious diseases (PhD); medical and clinical psychology (PhD), including clinical psychology, medical psychology; medical history (MMH); microbiology and immunology (PhD); molecular and cell biology (PhD); neuroscience (PhD); pathology (PhD), including comparative pathology, molecular pathobiology; preventive medicine and biometrics (MPH, MSPH, MTMH, Dr PH, PhD), including environmental health science (PhD), medical zoology (PhD), public health (MPH, MSPH, Dr PH), tropical medicine and hygiene (MTMH). Terminal master's awarded for partial completion of doctoral program. *Degree requirements:* For master's, thesis or alternative, comprehensive exam; for doctorate, thesis/dissertation, qualifying exam, comprehensive exam. *Entrance requirements:* For master's, GRE General Test; for doctorate, GRE General Test, minimum GPA of 3.0. Additional exam requirements/recommendations for international students: Required—TOEFL.

Uniformed Services University of the Health Sciences, School of Medicine, Programs in Biomedical Sciences, Department of Preventive Medicine and Biometrics, Program in Environmental Health Science, Bethesda, MD 20814-4799. Offers PhD. *Accreditation:* CEPH. *Degree requirements:* For doctorate, thesis/dissertation, qualifying exam, comprehensive exam. *Entrance requirements:* For doctorate, GRE, minimum GPA of 3.0. Additional exam requirements/recommendations for international students: Required—TOEFL.

Université de Montréal, Faculty of Medicine and Faculty of Graduate Studies, Graduate Programs in Medicine, Department of Environmental and Occupational Health, Montréal, QC H3C 3J7, Canada. Offers M Sc, DESS. *Accreditation:* CEPH. *Faculty:* 10 full-time (1 woman), 8 part-time/adjunct (3 women). *Students:* 42 full-time (30 women), 6 part-time (5 women). 35 applicants, 43% accepted, 14 enrolled. In 2006, 20 degrees awarded. *Degree requirements:* For master's, thesis. *Entrance requirements:* For master's, proficiency in French, knowledge of English; for DESS, proficiency in French. *Application deadline:* For fall admission, 2/1 priority date for domestic students; for winter admission, 11/1 priority date for domestic students; for spring admission, 2/1 priority date for domestic students. Applications are processed on a rolling basis. Application fee: $30. Electronic applications accepted. *Faculty research:* Metabolism of chemical substances, toxicity, biological surveillance, risk analysis. Total annual research expenditures: $590,120. *Unit head:* Joseph Zayed, Director, 514-343-5912, Fax: 514-343-6668, E-mail: joseph.zayed@umontreal.ca. *Application contact:* Adolf Vyskocil, Program Director, 514-343-6146, Fax: 514-343-2200.

Université du Québec à Montréal, Graduate Programs, Program in Ergonomics in Occupational Health and Safety, Montréal, QC H3C 3P8, Canada. Offers Diploma. Part-time programs available. *Entrance requirements:* For degree, appropriate bachelor's degree or equivalent, proficiency in French.

Université Laval, Faculty of Medicine, Graduate Programs in Medicine, Department of Social and Preventive Medicine, Program in Accident Prevention and Occupational Health and Safety Management, Québec, QC G1K 7P4, Canada. Offers Diploma. Part-time programs available. *Entrance requirements:* For degree, knowledge of French. Electronic applications accepted.

University at Albany, State University of New York, School of Public Health, Department of Environmental Health Sciences, Albany, NY 12222-0001. Offers environmental and analytical chemistry (MS, PhD); environmental and occupational health (MS, PhD); toxicology (MS, PhD). *Students:* 24 full-time (15 women), 17 part-time (9 women). Average age 31. In 2006, 1 master's, 2 doctorates awarded. *Degree requirements:* For master's and doctorate, thesis/dissertation. *Entrance requirements:* For master's and doctorate, GRE General Test, GRE Subject Test, 3 letters of reference. Additional exam requirements/recommendations for international students: Required—TOEFL (minimum score 600 paper-based; 213 computer-based). *Application deadline:* For fall admission, 1/15 for domestic students. Applications are processed on a rolling basis. Application fee: $75. Electronic applications accepted. *Expenses:* Tuition, state resident: full-time $6,900; part-time $288 per credit. Tuition, nonresident: full-time $10,920; part-time $455 per credit. Required fees: $1,139. *Financial support:* Fellowships, research assistantships, scholarships/grants and unspecified assistantships available. Financial award application deadline: 2/1. *Unit head:* Dr. Laurence Kaminsky, Chair, 518-473-7553. *Application contact:* Caitlin Reid, Assistant to the Chair, E-mail: reid@wadsworth.org.

The University of Alabama at Birmingham, School of Public Health, Department of Environmental Health Sciences, Birmingham, AL 35294. Offers environmental health (PhD); environmental toxicology (PhD); industrial hygiene (PhD). *Faculty:* 9. *Students:* 6 full-time (4 women); includes 3 minority (all African Americans) 4 applicants, 0% accepted. In 2006, 2 degrees awarded. *Degree requirements:* For doctorate, thesis/dissertation. *Entrance requirements:* For doctorate, GRE General Test. Additional exam requirements/recommendations for international students: Required—TOEFL. *Application deadline:* For fall admission, 4/1 for domestic students. Application fee: $35 ($60 for international students). Electronic applications accepted. *Expenses:* Tuition, state resident: part-time $170 per credit hour. Tuition, nonresident: part-time $425 per credit hour. Required fees: $15 per credit hour. $122 per term. Tuition and fees vary according to program. *Financial support:* Fellowships, career-related internships or fieldwork, scholarships/grants, and unspecified assistantships available. *Faculty research:* Aquatic toxicology, virology. *Unit head:* Dr. Edward M. Postlethwait, Chair, 205-934-7032, Fax: 205-975-6341. *Application contact:* Nancy O. Pinson, Coordinator of Student Admissions, 205-934-4993, Fax: 205-975-5484.

University of Alberta, School of Public Health, Department of Public Health Sciences, Edmonton, AB T6G 2E1, Canada. Offers clinical epidemiology (M Sc, MPH); environmental and occupational health (MPH); environmental health sciences (M Sc); epidemiology (M Sc); global health (M Sc, MPH); health policy and management (MPH); health policy research (M Sc); health technology assessment (MPH); occupational health (M Sc); population health (M Sc); public health leadership (MPH); public health sciences (PhD); quantitative methods (MPH). *Accreditation:* CEPH (one or more programs are accredited). *Faculty:* 24 full-time (5 women), 59 part-time/adjunct (13 women). *Students:* 49 full-time, 49 part-time. 81 applicants, 31% accepted. In 2006, 28 degrees awarded. Terminal master's awarded for partial completion of doctoral program. *Degree requirements:* For master's, thesis (for some programs); for doctorate, thesis/dissertation. *Entrance requirements:* For master's, GMAT or GRE General Test. Additional exam requirements/recommendations for international students: Required—TOEFL (paper-based 550; computer-based 213) or IELTS (paper-based 6). *Application deadline:* For fall admission, 3/15 for domestic students, 7/1 for international students; for winter admission, 11/1 for international students; for spring admission, 3/1 for international students. Applications are processed on a rolling basis. Application fee: $0. Electronic applications accepted. *Financial support:* In 2006–07, 11 students received support, including 6 research assistantships with tuition reimbursements available (averaging $2,200 per year); fellowships, teaching assistantships, career-related internships or fieldwork and tuition waivers (partial) also available. Financial award application deadline: 2/1. *Faculty research:* Biostatistics, health promotion and sociobehavioral health science. Total annual research expenditures: $5.7 million. *Unit head:* L. Duncan Saunders, Acting Chair, 780-492-6814, Fax: 780-492-0364. *Application contact:* Felicity R. Hey, Graduate Programs Administrator, 780-492-6407, Fax: 780-492-0364, E-mail: felicity.hey@ualberta.ca.

University of Arkansas for Medical Sciences, Graduate School, Graduate Programs in Biomedical Sciences, Occupational and Environmental Health Program, Little Rock, AR 72205-7199. Offers MS. Offered jointly with the University of Arkansas at Little Rock and the National Center for Toxicological Research. *Accreditation:* CEPH. *Faculty:* 10 full-time (1 woman), 7 part-time/adjunct (0 women). *Students:* 1 full-time, 2 part-time. *Degree requirements:* For master's, thesis or alternative. *Entrance requirements:* For master's, GRE General Test. Application fee: $0. *Financial support:* Fellowships available. Support available to part-time students. *Unit head:* Dr. Jay Gandy, Director, 501-686-5239, E-mail: jgandy@uams.edu. *Application contact:* Dr. Jay Gandy, Information Contact, 501-686-5289.

The University of British Columbia, Faculty of Graduate Studies, School of Occupational and Environmental Hygiene, Vancouver, BC V6T 1Z1, Canada. Offers M Sc, PhD. Part-time programs available. *Faculty:* 4 full-time (1 woman), 22 part-time/adjunct (9 women). *Students:* 15 full-time (13 women), 5 part-time (1 woman). Average age 25. 26 applicants, 46% accepted, 7 enrolled. In 2006, 8 degrees awarded. *Degree requirements:* For master's, thesis optional; for doctorate, thesis/dissertation, comprehensive exam. *Entrance requirements:* For master's and doctorate, GRE. Additional exam requirements/recommendations for international students: Required—TOEFL (minimum score 600 paper-based; 250 computer-based); Recommended—TWE. *Application deadline:* For fall admission, 1/31 for domestic and international students. Application fee: $90 Canadian dollars ($150 Canadian dollars for international students). Electronic applications accepted. *Financial support:* In 2006–07, 1 fellowship (averaging $8,000 per year), 4 research assistantships (averaging $16,000 per year), 6 teaching assistantships (averaging $2,300 per year) were awarded; career-related internships or fieldwork and institutionally sponsored loans also available. *Faculty research:* Acoustics, exposure assessment and epidemiology, occupational and environmental respiratory disease, occupational and environmental policy. *Unit head:* Dr. Michael Brauer, Director, 604-822-9595, Fax: 604-822-9588, E-mail: brauer@interchange.ubc.ca. *Application contact:* Dr. Paul Demers, Graduate Advisor, 604-822-0585, Fax: 604-822-9588, E-mail: pdemers@interchange.ubc.ca.

The University of British Columbia, Faculty of Medicine, Department of Health Care and Epidemiology, Vancouver, BC V6T 1W5, Canada. Offers clinical epidemiology (MH Sc); community health (MH Sc); epidemiology/clinical epidemiology (M Sc, PhD); health administration (MHA); health services research (M Sc, PhD); occupational and environmental health (M Sc, PhD); occupational health (MH Sc). *Accreditation:* CEPH (one or more programs are accredited). Part-time programs available. *Faculty:* 27 full-time (7 women). *Students:* 27 full-time (4 women), 10 part-time (2 women). Average age 31. 91 applicants, 30% accepted. In 2006, 14 master's, 1 doctorate awarded. *Degree requirements:* For master's and doctorate, thesis/dissertation. *Entrance requirements:* For master's, GRE General Test, MD or equivalent (MH Sc); for doctorate, work experience. *Application deadline:* For fall admission, 3/31 for domestic students. Applications are processed on a rolling basis. Application fee: $65. Electronic applications accepted. *Financial support:* In 2006–07, 7 students received support, including 1 fellowship; career-related internships or fieldwork also available. *Faculty research:* AIDS, public health, environmental toxicology, infectious diseases, health evaluation, epidemiology. Total annual research expenditures: $4.8 million. *Unit head:* M. T. Schechter, Head, 604-822-3910, Fax: 604-822-4994, E-mail: martin.schechter@ubc.ca. *Application contact:* Laurel Slaney, Program Assistant, 604-822-5405, Fax: 604-822-4994, E-mail: laurel.slaney@ubc.ca.

University of California, Berkeley, Graduate Division, School of Public Health, Division of Environmental Health Sciences, Berkeley, CA 94720-1500. Offers MPH, MS, Dr PH, PhD. *Degree requirements:* For master's, comprehensive exam (MPH), project or thesis (MS); for doctorate, thesis/dissertation, departmental and qualifying exams. *Entrance requirements:* For master's, GRE General Test, minimum GPA of 3.0; previous course work in biology, calculus, and chemistry; for doctorate, GRE General Test, master's degree in relevant scientific discipline or engineering; minimum GPA of 3.0; previous course work in biology, calculus, and chemistry. Additional exam requirements/recommendations for international students: Required—TOEFL. *Application deadline:* For fall admission, 12/1 for domestic students. Applications are processed on a rolling basis. Application fee: $60 ($80 for international students). *Financial support:* Fellowships, research assistantships, teaching assistantships, unspecified assistantships available. *Faculty research:* Toxicology, industrial hygiene, exposure assessment, risk assessment, ergonomics. *Unit head:* Katharine Hammond, Chair, 510-643-0289, E-mail: hammondk@berkeley.edu. *Application contact:* Norma Firestone, Graduate Assistant for Admission, 510-643-5160, Fax: 510-642-5815, E-mail: sphinfo@berkeley.edu.

University of California, Los Angeles, Graduate Division, School of Public Health, Department of Environmental Health Sciences, Los Angeles, CA 90095. Offers environmental health sciences (MS, PhD); molecular toxicology (PhD). *Accreditation:* ABET (one or more programs are accredited). *Degree requirements:* For master's, comprehensive exam or thesis; for doctorate, thesis/dissertation, oral and written qualifying exams. *Entrance requirements:* For master's, GRE General Test, minimum GPA of 3.0; for doctorate, GRE General Test, minimum undergraduate GPA of 3.0. Electronic applications accepted.

University of Central Missouri, The Graduate School, College of Health and Human Services, Department of Safety Sciences, Warrensburg, MO 64093. Offers fire science (MS); human services/public services (Ed S); industrial hygiene (MS); industrial safety management (MS); loss control (MS); occupational safety management (MS); public safety (MS); security (MS); transportation safety (MS). *Accreditation:* ABET (one or more programs are accredited). Part-time programs available. *Faculty:* 18 full-time (3 women). *Students:* 14 full-time (4 women), 18 part-time (6 women); includes 6 minority (2 African Americans, 1 American Indian/Alaska Native, 3 Hispanic Americans), 1 international. Average age 36. 9 applicants, 78% accepted, 6 enrolled. In 2006, 6 degrees awarded. *Degree requirements:* For master's, comprehensive exam. *Entrance requirements:* For master's, GRE General Test, minimum GPA of 2.5, 15 hours of course work in related area; for Ed S, master's degree in related field. Additional exam requirements/recommendations for international students: Required—TOEFL (minimum score 500 paper-based; 173 computer-based). *Application deadline:* For fall admission, 6/1 priority date for domestic students, 5/1 priority date for international students; for spring admission, 10/1 priority date for domestic students, 10/1 for international students. Applications are processed on a rolling basis. Application fee: $30 ($50 for international students). *Expenses:* Tuition, state resident: full-time $5,448; part-time $227 per credit hour. Tuition, nonresident:

Environmental and Occupational Health

University of Central Missouri (continued)
full-time $10,896; part-time $454 per credit hour. Required fees: $336; $14 per credit hour. *Financial support:* In 2006–07, 5 students received support. Federal Work-Study, scholarships/grants, unspecified assistantships, and administrative and laboratory assistantships available. Support available to part-time students. Financial award application deadline: 3/1; financial award applicants required to submit FAFSA. *Faculty research:* Workplace and school safety, industrial hygiene assessment methods, lead and take-home toxins, rural emergency management, cultural aspects of safety, health, and the environment. Total annual research expenditures: $60,999. *Unit head:* Dr. Dennis Laster, Interim Chair, 660-543-4017, E-mail: laster@cmsu1.cmsu.edu.

University of Cincinnati, Division of Research and Advanced Studies, College of Medicine, Graduate Programs in Biomedical Sciences, Department of Environmental Health, Cincinnati, OH 45267. Offers environmental and industrial hygiene (MS, PhD); environmental and occupational medicine (MS); environmental genetics and molecular toxicology (MS, PhD); epidemiology and biostatistics (MS, PhD); occupational safety and ergonomics (MS, PhD). *Accreditation:* ABET (one or more programs are accredited). *Faculty:* 26 full-time (10 women). *Students:* 75 full-time (32 women), 59 part-time (33 women); includes 7 minority (5 African Americans, 1 American Indian/Alaska Native, 1 Asian American or Pacific Islander), 55 international. 136 applicants, 28% accepted. In 2006, 13 master's, 7 doctorates awarded. Terminal master's awarded for partial completion of doctoral program. *Median time to degree:* Master's–2.3 years full-time, 3.5 years part-time; doctorate–5.3 years full-time, 7.3 years part-time. Of those who began their doctoral program in fall 1998, 100% received their degree in 8 years or less. *Degree requirements:* For master's, thesis; for doctorate, thesis/dissertation, qualifying exam. *Entrance requirements:* For master's, GRE General Test, bachelor's degree in science; for doctorate, GRE General Test. Additional exam requirements/recommendations for international students: Required—TOEFL (minimum score 600 paper-based; 250 computer-based; 100 iBT). *Application deadline:* For fall admission, 3/1 priority date for domestic and international students. Applications are processed on a rolling basis. Application fee: $40. Electronic applications accepted. *Financial support:* In 2006–07, 69 students received support, including research assistantships with full tuition reimbursements available (averaging $17,850 per year); career-related internships or fieldwork, scholarships/grants, traineeships, tuition waivers (partial), and unspecified assistantships also available. Financial award application deadline: 5/1. *Faculty research:* Carcinogens and mutagenesis, pulmonary studies, reproduction and development. Total annual research expenditures: $16.9 million. *Unit head:* Dr. Shuk-Mei Ho, Chairman, 513-558-5701, Fax: 513-558-4397, E-mail: hosm@ucmail.uc.edu. *Application contact:* Stephanie W. Starkey, Graduate Program Coordinator, 513-558-5704, Fax: 513-558-5457, E-mail: stephanie.starkey@uc.edu.

University of Connecticut, Graduate School, Center for Continuing Studies, Program in Occupational Safety and Health Management, Storrs, CT 06269. Offers MPS. *Faculty:* 3 full-time (0 women). *Students:* 1 (woman) full-time, 9 part-time (5 women); includes 3 minority (2 African Americans, 1 American Indian/Alaska Native). Average age 35. 14 applicants, 50% accepted, 7 enrolled.

University of Florida, Graduate School, College of Public Health and Health Professions and College of Medicine, Programs in Public Health, Gainesville, FL 32611. Offers biostatistics (MPH); environmental health (MPH); epidemiology (MPH); public health management and policy (MPH); public health practice (MPH); social and behavioral sciences (MPH). *Faculty:* 10. *Entrance requirements:* For master's, GRE General Test, minimum GPA of 3.0. Additional exam requirements/recommendations for international students: Required—TOEFL (minimum score 550 paper-based; 213 computer-based). Application fee: $30. *Expenses:* Tuition, state resident: full-time $6,827. Tuition, nonresident: full-time $21,951. Required fees: $999. *Unit head:* Dr. Mary Peoples-Sheps, Associate Dean for Academic Affairs, 352-273-6084, Fax: 352-273-6448, E-mail: mpeoplessheps@phhp.ufl.edu. *Application contact:* Brigette Hart, Program Assistant, 352-273-6443, E-mail: bhart@phhp.ufl.edu.

University of Georgia, College of Public Health, Department of Environmental Health Science, Athens, GA 30602. Offers MS, PhD. *Faculty:* 6 full-time (4 women), 1 (woman) part-time/adjunct. *Students:* 19 full-time (9 women), 3 part-time (1 woman); includes 4 minority (2 African Americans, 1 Asian American or Pacific Islander, 1 Hispanic American), 3 international. Average age 25. 16 applicants, 50% accepted, 7 enrolled. In 2006, 3 master's, 2 doctorates awarded. Terminal master's awarded for partial completion of doctoral program. *Degree requirements:* For master's, thesis/dissertation; for doctorate, thesis/dissertation, comprehensive exam. *Entrance requirements:* For master's and doctorate, GRE General Test. Additional exam requirements/recommendations for international students: Required—TOEFL. *Application deadline:* For fall admission, 3/1 priority date for domestic students; for spring admission, 11/15 for domestic students. Application fee: $50. Electronic applications accepted. *Financial support:* Research assistantships with full tuition reimbursements available. *Faculty research:* Risk assessment, environmental toxicology, water quality, air quality. *Unit head:* Dr. Marsha C. Black, Interim Head, 706-542-0998, Fax: 706-542-7472, E-mail: mblack@uga.edu. *Application contact:* Dr. Mary Alice Smith, Graduate Coordinator, 706-542-2454, Fax: 706-542-7472, E-mail: masmith@uga.edu.

University of Illinois at Chicago, Graduate College, School of Public Health, Program in Environmental and Occupational Health Sciences, Chicago, IL 60607-7128. Offers MPH, MS, Dr PH, PhD. *Accreditation:* ABET (one or more programs are accredited); CEPH (one or more programs are accredited). Part-time programs available. Terminal master's awarded for partial completion of doctoral program. *Degree requirements:* For master's, thesis, field practicum; for doctorate, thesis/dissertation, independent research, internship. *Entrance requirements:* For master's and doctorate, GRE General Test, minimum GPA of 2.75. Additional exam requirements/recommendations for international students: Required—TOEFL. Electronic applications accepted.

The University of Iowa, Graduate College, College of Public Health, Department of Occupational and Environmental Health, Iowa City, IA 52242-1316. Offers MS, PhD, Certificate, MS/MA, MS/MS. *Accreditation:* ABET (one or more programs are accredited). *Faculty:* 17 full-time, 16 part-time/adjunct. *Students:* 20 full-time (11 women), 10 part-time (3 women); includes 4 minority (1 African American, 2 Asian Americans or Pacific Islanders, 1 Hispanic American), 11 international. 25 applicants, 56% accepted, 7 enrolled. In 2006, 5 master's, 1 doctorate awarded. *Degree requirements:* For master's, exam, thesis optional; for doctorate, thesis/dissertation, comprehensive exam, registration. *Entrance requirements:* For master's and doctorate, GRE General Test, minimum GPA of 3.0. Additional exam requirements/recommendations for international students: Required—TOEFL (minimum score 600 paper-based; 250 computer-based; 100 iBT). *Application deadline:* For fall admission, 7/1 priority date for domestic students. Applications are processed on a rolling basis. Application fee: $60 ($85 for international students). Electronic applications accepted. *Financial support:* In 2006–07, 1 fellowship, 12 research assistantships with partial tuition reimbursements, 1 teaching assistantship with partial tuition reimbursement were awarded. Financial award applicants required to submit FAFSA. *Unit head:* Dr. Craig Zwerling, Head, 319-335-4428, Fax: 319-335-4225.

University of Miami, Graduate School, College of Engineering, Department of Industrial Engineering, Program in Environmental Health and Safety, Coral Gables, FL 33124. Offers environmental health and safety (MS, MSEVH); occupational ergonomics and safety (MSOES). Part-time programs available. *Faculty:* 4 full-time (0 women). *Students:* 4 full-time (2 women), 1 international. Average age 34. 2 applicants, 100% accepted, 2 enrolled. *Degree requirements:* For master's, thesis optional. *Entrance requirements:* For master's, GRE General Test, minimum GPA of 3.0. Additional exam requirements/recommendations for international students: Required—TOEFL (minimum score 550 paper-based; 213 computer-based). *Application deadline:* For fall admission, 12/1 priority date for domestic and international students; for spring admission, 11/1 priority date for domestic and international students. Applications are processed on a rolling basis. Application fee: $50. Electronic applications accepted. *Financial support:* In 2006–07, 2 students received support, including 2 research assistantships with full tuition reimbursements available (averaging $14,400 per year); fellowships, teaching assistantships with full tuition reimbursements available, career-related internships or fieldwork, institutionally sponsored loans, and unspecified assistantships also available. Support available to part-time students. Financial award application deadline: 12/1; financial award applicants required to submit FAFSA. *Faculty research:* Noise, heat stress, water pollution, survey pain. *Application contact:* Dr. Eleftherios Iakovou, Graduate Advisor, 305-284-2344, Fax: 305-284-4040, E-mail: eiakovou@miami.edu.

University of Michigan, School of Public Health, Department of Environmental Health Sciences, Program in Environmental Health, Ann Arbor, MI 48109. Offers MPH, MS, Dr PH, PhD. MS and PhD offered through the Horace H. Rackham School of Graduate Studies. *Accreditation:* CEPH (one or more programs are accredited). *Entrance requirements:* For master's and doctorate, GRE General Test.

University of Michigan, School of Public Health, Department of Environmental Health Sciences, Program in Occupational Health, Ann Arbor, MI 48109. Offers industrial hygiene (MS, PhD); occupational and environmental epidemiology (MPH). MS and PhD offered through the Horace H. Rackham School of Graduate Studies. *Entrance requirements:* For master's and doctorate, GRE General Test. Electronic applications accepted.

University of Minnesota, Twin Cities Campus, School of Public Health, Division of Environmental Health Sciences, Area in Environmental Health Policy, Minneapolis, MN 55455-0213. Offers MPH, MS, PhD. *Accreditation:* CEPH (one or more programs are accredited). *Degree requirements:* For doctorate, thesis/dissertation. *Entrance requirements:* For master's and doctorate, GRE General Test. *Expenses:* Tuition, state resident: full-time $9,302; part-time $775 per credit. Tuition, nonresident: full-time $16,400; part-time $1,367 per credit. Full-time tuition and fees vary according to class time, course load, program, reciprocity agreements and student level.

University of Minnesota, Twin Cities Campus, School of Public Health, Division of Environmental Health Sciences, Area in Occupational Medicine, Minneapolis, MN 55455-0213. Offers MPH. *Accreditation:* CEPH. *Entrance requirements:* For master's, GRE General Test. *Expenses:* Tuition, state resident: full-time $9,302; part-time $775 per credit. Tuition, nonresident: full-time $16,400; part-time $1,367 per credit. Full-time tuition and fees vary according to class time, course load, program, reciprocity agreements and student level.

University of Minnesota, Twin Cities Campus, School of Public Health, Major in Public Health Practice, Minneapolis, MN 55455-0213. Offers core concepts (Certificate); food safety and biosecurity (Certificate); occupational health and safety (Certificate); preparedness, response and recovery (Certificate); public health practice (MPH); DVM/MPH; MD/MPH. Part-time programs available. Postbaccalaureate distance learning degree programs offered (no on-campus study). *Degree requirements:* For master's, thesis, registration. *Entrance requirements:* For master's, GRE, MCAT, United States Medical Licensing Exam. Additional exam requirements/recommendations for international students: Required—TOEFL (minimum score 600 paper-based; 250 computer-based). Electronic applications accepted. *Expenses:* Tuition, state resident: full-time $9,302; part-time $775 per credit. Tuition, nonresident: full-time $16,400; part-time $1,367 per credit. Full-time tuition and fees vary according to class time, course load, program, reciprocity agreements and student level.

University of Nevada, Reno, Graduate School, Interdisciplinary Program in Environmental Sciences and Health, Reno, NV 89557. Offers MS, PhD. *Faculty:* 4. *Students:* 6 full-time (2 women), 16 part-time (10 women); includes 1 minority (Hispanic American), 5 international. Average age 32. 3 applicants, 100% accepted, 3 enrolled. In 2006, 4 master's, 2 doctorates awarded. *Degree requirements:* For master's and doctorate, thesis/dissertation. *Entrance requirements:* For master's, GRE General Test, minimum GPA of 2.75; for doctorate, GRE General Test, minimum GPA of 3.0. Additional exam requirements/recommendations for international students: Required—TOEFL. *Application deadline:* For fall admission, 3/1 for domestic students; for spring admission, 11/1 for domestic students. Applications are processed on a rolling basis. Application fee: $60 ($95 for international students). *Financial support:* In 2006–07, 1 research assistantship was awarded; fellowships, teaching assistantships also available. Financial award application deadline: 3/1. *Unit head:* Dr. Mark Walker, Graduate Program Director, 775-784-1938, Fax: 775-784-1142.

University of New Haven, Graduate School, Henry C. Lee College of Criminal Justice and Forensic Sciences, Program in Occupational Safety and Health Management, West Haven, CT 06516-1916. Offers MS. *Degree requirements:* For master's, thesis or alternative.

The University of North Carolina at Chapel Hill, Graduate School, School of Public Health, Department of Environmental Sciences and Engineering, Chapel Hill, NC 27599. Offers air, radiation and industrial hygiene (MPH, MS, MSEE, MSPH, PhD); aquatic and atmospheric sciences (MPH, MS, MSPH, PhD); environmental engineering (MPH, MS, MSEE, MSPH, PhD); environmental health sciences (MPH, MS, MSPH, PhD); environmental management and policy (MPH, MS, MSPH, PhD). *Faculty:* 29 full-time (2 women), 14 part-time/adjunct. *Students:* 139 full-time (70 women); includes 21 minority (9 African Americans, 1 American Indian/Alaska Native, 8 Asian Americans or Pacific Islanders, 3 Hispanic Americans), 17 international. Average age 27. 191 applicants, 48% accepted, 41 enrolled. In 2006, 26 master's, 17 doctorates awarded. Terminal master's awarded for partial completion of doctoral program. *Median time to degree:* Of those who began their doctoral program in fall 1998, 100% received their degree in 8 years or less. *Degree requirements:* For master's, thesis (for some programs), research paper, comprehensive exam, registration; for doctorate, thesis/dissertation, comprehensive exam, registration. *Entrance requirements:* For master's and doctorate, GRE General Test, minimum GPA of 3.0. Additional exam requirements/recommendations for international students: Required—TOEFL. *Application deadline:* For fall admission, 1/1 priority date for domestic and international students; for spring admission, 9/15 for domestic students. Applications are processed on a rolling basis. Application fee: $70. Electronic applications accepted. *Financial support:* In 2006–07, 29 fellowships with tuition reimbursements (averaging $12,903 per year), 61 research assistantships with tuition reimbursements (averaging $13,114 per year), 13 teaching assistantships with tuition reimbursements (averaging $11,846 per year) were awarded; career-related internships or fieldwork, Federal Work-Study, traineeships, health care benefits, and unspecified assistantships also available. Support available to part-time students. Financial award application deadline: 1/1; financial award applicants required to submit FAFSA. *Faculty research:* Air, radiation and industrial hygiene, aquatic and atmospheric sciences, environmental health sciences, environmental management and policy, water resources engineering. *Unit head:* Dr. Michael Aitken, Chair, 919-966-1024, Fax: 919-966-7911, E-mail: mike_aitken@unc.edu. *Application contact:* Jack Whaley, Registrar, 919-966-3844, Fax: 919-966-7911, E-mail: jack_whaley@unc.edu.

University of North Texas Health Science Center at Fort Worth, School of Public Health, Fort Worth, TX 76107-2699. Offers biostatistics (MPH); community health (MPH); disease control and prevention (Dr PH); environmental health (MPH); epidemiology (MPH); health behavior (MPH); health policy and management (MPH, Dr PH); DO/MPH; MA/MPH; MS/MPH; PhD/MPH. *Accreditation:* CEPH. Part-time and evening/weekend programs available. *Degree requirements:* For master's, thesis or alternative, supervised internship; for doctorate, thesis/dissertation, supervised internship. *Entrance requirements:* For master's, GRE General Test. Additional exam requirements/recommendations for international students: Required—TOEFL. Electronic applications accepted.

University of Oklahoma, Graduate College, College of Engineering, School of Civil Engineering and Environmental Science, Program in Environmental Science, Norman, OK 73019-0390. Offers air (M Env Sc); environmental science (PhD); groundwater management (M Env Sc); hazardous solid waste (M Env Sc); occupational safety and health (M Env Sc); process design (M Env Sc); water quality resources (M Env Sc). *Students:* 12 full-time (8 women), 5 part-time (3 women); includes 2 minority (1 African American, 1 American Indian/Alaska Native), 5 international. 19 applicants, 63% accepted, 5 enrolled. In 2006, 3 degrees awarded. Terminal master's awarded for partial completion of doctoral program. *Degree requirements:* For master's, oral exams; for doctorate, thesis/dissertation, oral and qualifying exams, comprehensive exam. *Entrance requirements:* For master's, minimum GPA of 3.0; for doctorate, minimum graduate GPA of 3.5. Additional exam requirements/recommendations for international students: Required—TOEFL (minimum score 600 paper-based; 250 computer-based). *Application deadline:* For fall admission, 4/1 priority date for domestic students, 4/1 for international students; for spring admission, 11/1 for domestic students, 9/1 for international students. Applications are processed on a rolling basis. Application fee: $40 ($90 for international students). *Expenses:* Tuition, state resident: full-time $3,180; part-time $133 per credit hour. Tuition, nonresident: full-time $11,347; part-time $473 per credit hour. Required fees: $1,729; $62 per credit hour. $117 per semester. Tuition and fees vary according to course load and program. *Financial support:* Fellowships, research assistantships with partial tuition reimbursements, teaching assistantships with partial tuition reimbursements, scholarships/grants available. Financial award application deadline: 3/1; financial award applicants required to submit FAFSA. *Faculty research:* Treatment wetlands, soil remediation, biomediation.

University of Oklahoma Health Sciences Center, Graduate College, College of Public Health, Department of Occupational and Environmental Health, Oklahoma City, OK 73190. Offers MPH, MS, Dr PH, PhD, JD/MPH, JD/MS. *Accreditation:* ABET (one or more programs are accredited); CEPH (one or more programs are accredited). Part-time programs available. *Degree requirements:* For master's, thesis (for some programs), comprehensive exam; for doctorate, thesis/dissertation, comprehensive exam. *Entrance requirements:* For master's, GRE General Test (all except occupational medicine), 3 letters of recommendation, resumé; for doctorate, GRE (all except occupational medicine), 3 letters of recommendation, resumé. Additional exam requirements/recommendations for international students: Required—TOEFL (minimum score 570 paper-based; 230 computer-based). *Faculty research:* Environmental safety, accident prevention and injury control.

University of Pittsburgh, Graduate School of Public Health, Department of Environmental and Occupational Health, Program in Occupational Medicine, Pittsburgh, PA 15260. Offers MPH. Program restricted to licensed physicians. *Accreditation:* CEPH. Part-time programs available. *Faculty:* 2 full-time (0 women). *Students:* 3 full-time (2 women), 2 part-time (1 woman); includes 1 minority (Asian American or Pacific Islander) Average age 36. 5 applicants, 60% accepted, 2 enrolled. In 2006, 3 degrees awarded. *Degree requirements:* For master's, thesis, registration. *Entrance requirements:* For master's, MD. *Application deadline:* For fall admission, 6/1 for domestic students; for winter admission, 3/1 for domestic students; for spring admission, 10/1 for domestic students. Applications are processed on a rolling basis. Application fee: $50 ($60 for international students). *Financial support:* Scholarships/grants, traineeships, and unspecified assistantships available. Support available to part-time students. Financial award application deadline: 4/30; financial award applicants required to submit FAFSA. *Faculty research:* Mesenchymal stem cell interstitial lung disease, medical surveillance, occupational diseases, occupational exposure, occupational health. *Application contact:* Donna L Murr, Program Administrator, 412-624-3155, Fax: 412-624-3040, E-mail: dmurr@eoh.pitt.edu.

University of Puerto Rico, Medical Sciences Campus, Graduate School of Public Health, Department of Environmental Health, Doctoral Program in Environmental Health, San Juan, PR 00936-5067. Offers Dr PH. Part-time programs available. *Students:* 136 (83 women). 85 applicants, 65% accepted. *Application deadline:* For fall admission, 3/15 for domestic students. Application fee: $20. *Expenses: Contact institution. Financial support:* Research assistantships, teaching assistantships, Federal Work-Study and institutionally sponsored loans available. Financial award application deadline: 4/30. *Unit head:* Dr. Imar Mansilla-Rivera, Coordinator, 787-758-2525 Ext. 1425, Fax: 757-759-6719, E-mail: imansilla@rcm.upr.edu. *Application contact:* Prof. Mayra E. Santiago-Vargas, Counselor, 787-756-5244, Fax: 787-759-6719, E-mail: msantiago@rcm.upr.edu.

University of Puerto Rico, Medical Sciences Campus, Graduate School of Public Health, Department of Environmental Health, Master's Program in Environmental Health, San Juan, PR 00936-5067. Offers MS. *Degree requirements:* For master's, thesis. *Entrance requirements:* For master's, GRE, course work in biology, chemistry, mathematics, and physics. Application fee: $20. *Expenses: Contact institution. Application contact:* Prof. Mayra E. Santiago-Vargas, Counselor, 787-756-5244, Fax: 787-759-6719, E-mail: msantiago@rcm.upr.edu.

University of South Alabama, Graduate School, Program in Environmental Toxicology, Mobile, AL 36688-0002. Offers MS. *Students:* 6 full-time (1 woman), 5 international. In 2006, 1 degree awarded. *Unit head:* Dr. Julio F. Turrens, Director, 251-380-2785.

University of South Carolina, The Graduate School, Arnold School of Public Health, Department of Environmental Health Sciences, Program in Environmental Quality, Columbia, SC 29208. Offers MPH, MSPH, PhD. *Accreditation:* CEPH (one or more programs are accredited). Part-time programs available. *Degree requirements:* For master's, thesis (for some programs), practicum (MPH), comprehensive exam; for doctorate, one foreign language, thesis/dissertation, comprehensive exam. *Entrance requirements:* For master's and doctorate, GRE General Test. Additional exam requirements/recommendations for international students: Required—TOEFL (minimum score 570 paper-based; 230 computer-based). Electronic applications accepted. *Faculty research:* Environmental assessment and planning; environmental toxicology; ecosystems analysis; air quality monitoring and modeling.

See Close-Up on page 2063.

University of Southern Mississippi, Graduate School, College of Health, Department of Community Health Sciences, Hattiesburg, MS 39406-0001. Offers epidemiology and biostatistics (MPH); health education (MPH); health policy/administration (MPH); occupational/environmental health (MPH); public health nutrition (MPH). *Accreditation:* CEPH. Part-time and evening/weekend programs available. *Faculty:* 10 full-time (3 women). *Students:* 53 full-time (32 women), 13 part-time (10 women); includes 25 minority (24 African Americans, 1 Asian American or Pacific Islander), 15 international. Average age 30. 114 applicants, 84% accepted, 35 enrolled. In 2006, 27 degrees awarded. *Degree requirements:* For master's, thesis (for some programs), comprehensive exam, registration. *Entrance requirements:* For master's, GRE General Test, minimum GPA of 2.75 in last 60 hours. Additional exam requirements/recommendations for international students: Required—TOEFL. *Application deadline:* For fall admission, 3/1 for domestic and international students. Applications are processed on a rolling basis. Application fee: $25 ($30 for international students). *Financial support:* In 2006–07, 9 research assistantships with full tuition reimbursements (averaging $5,906 per year) were awarded; teaching assistantships with full tuition reimbursements, career-related internships or fieldwork and Federal Work-Study also available. Financial award application deadline: 3/15. *Faculty research:* Rural health care delivery, school health, nutrition of pregnant teens, risk factor reduction, sexually transmitted diseases. *Unit head:* Dr. James McGuire, Chair, 601-266-5437, Fax: 601-266-5043.

University of South Florida, Graduate School, College of Public Health, Department of Environmental and Occupational Health, Tampa, FL 33620-9951. Offers MPH, MSPH, PhD. *Accreditation:* ABET (one or more programs are accredited); CEPH (one or more programs are accredited). Part-time and evening/weekend programs available. *Faculty:* 8 full-time (1 woman), 7 part-time/adjunct (2 women). *Students:* 22 full-time (8 women), 45 part-time (21 women); includes 7 minority (1 African American, 3 Asian Americans or Pacific Islanders, 3 Hispanic Americans), 6 international. Average age 38. 32 applicants, 81% accepted, 10 enrolled. In 2006, 14 master's, 5 doctorates awarded. *Median time to degree:* Master's–1.33 years full-time, 3.17 years part-time; doctorate–5.6 years part-time. Of those who began their doctoral program in fall 1998, 100% received their degree in 8 years or less. *Degree requirements:* For master's, thesis (for some programs), comprehensive exam; for doctorate, thesis/dissertation, comprehensive exam. *Entrance requirements:* For master's and doctorate, GRE General Test, minimum GPA of 3.0 in upper-level course work. Additional exam requirements/recommendations for international students: Required—TOEFL (minimum score 550 paper-based; 213 computer-based; 79 iBT). *Application deadline:* For fall admission, 6/1 for domestic students, 1/2 for international students; for spring admission, 10/15 for domestic students, 7/1 for international students. Applications are processed on a rolling basis. Application fee: $30. Electronic applications accepted. *Financial support:* In 2006–07, 2 fellowships with full tuition reimbursements (averaging $13,500 per year), 5 research assistantships with full and partial tuition reimbursements (averaging $2,935 per year), 4 teaching assistantships with tuition reimbursements (averaging $4,269 per year) were awarded; Federal Work-Study, institutionally sponsored loans, scholarships/grants, traineeships, and unspecified assistantships also available. Support available to part-time students. Financial award applicants required to submit FAFSA. *Faculty research:* Biomedical assessment/stress test, risk impact, nitrobenzes on mammalism glutathion transferases, lysimeter research management, independent hygiene development. Total annual research expenditures: $6.5 million. *Unit head:* Dr. Thomas Bernard, Chairperson, 813-974-3144, Fax: 813-974-4986. *Application contact:* Michelle Robinson, Academic Advisor, 813-974-6665, Fax: 813-974-8121, E-mail: mrobinso@health.usf.edu.

University of the Sacred Heart, Graduate Programs, Department of Natural Sciences, Program in Occupational Health, San Juan, PR 00914-0383. Offers MS.

The University of Toledo, College of Graduate Studies, College of Health Science and Human Service, Division of Health, Program in Occupational Health, Toledo, OH 43606-3390. Offers MS. *Students:* 3 applicants, 100% accepted, 3 enrolled.Application fee: $45. *Unit head:* Dr. Michael Bisesi, Head, 419-530-4636. *Application contact:* Mary Alderman, Student Contact, 419-530-4636.

University of Washington, Graduate School, School of Public Health and Community Medicine, Department of Environmental and Occupational Health Sciences, Seattle, WA 98195. Offers environmental and occupational health (MPH); environmental and occupational hygiene (PhD); environmental health (MS); industrial hygiene and safety (MS); occupational medicine (MPH); safety and ergonomics (MS); toxicology (MS, PhD). Part-time programs available. Terminal master's awarded for partial completion of doctoral program. *Degree requirements:* For master's, thesis (for some programs), practicum (MPH); for doctorate, thesis/dissertation, comprehensive exam, registration. *Entrance requirements:* For master's and doctorate, GRE General Test, minimum GPA of 3.0, prerequisite course work in biology, chemistry, physics, calculus. Additional exam requirements/recommendations for international students: Required—TOEFL (minimum score 580 paper-based; 237 computer-based). Electronic applications accepted. *Faculty research:* Developmental toxicology, biochemical toxicology, exposure assessment, hazardous waste, industrial chemistry.

See Close-Up on page 2067.

University of Wisconsin–Eau Claire, College of Nursing and Health Sciences, Department of Public Health Professions, Program in Environmental and Public Health, Eau Claire, WI 54702-4004. Offers MS. *Faculty:* 4 full-time (2 women), 1 (woman) part-time/adjunct. *Students:* 5 full-time (3 women), 1 part-time; includes 2 minority (both African Americans), 1 international. Average age 37. 8 applicants, 50% accepted, 3 enrolled. In 2006, 3 degrees awarded. *Degree requirements:* For master's, thesis, oral and written exams. *Entrance requirements:* For master's, bachelor's degree in environmental health or related sciences. *Application deadline:* For fall admission, 3/1 for domestic students. Applications are processed on a rolling basis. Application fee: $45. *Expenses:* Tuition, state resident: full-time $6,533; part-time $363 per credit. Tuition, nonresident: full-time $17,143; part-time $952 per credit. Tuition and fees vary according to program and reciprocity agreements. *Financial support:* In 2006–07, 4 students received support, including 4 teaching assistantships (averaging $5,800 per year); Federal Work-Study also available. Financial award application deadline: 3/1; financial award applicants required to submit FAFSA. *Unit head:* Dr. Crispin Pierce, Program Coordinator, 715-836-5589, Fax: 715-836-3379, E-mail: piercech@uwec.edu.

University of Wisconsin–Whitewater, School of Graduate Studies, College of Education, Department of Occupational and Environmental Safety, Whitewater, WI 53190-1790. Offers safety (MS). Part-time and evening/weekend programs available. Postbaccalaureate distance learning degree programs offered (no on-campus study). *Students:* 5 full-time (0 women), 15 part-time (5 women); includes 3 minority (2 Asian Americans or Pacific Islanders, 1 Hispanic American). Average age 42. 6 applicants, 67% accepted, 3 enrolled. In 2006, 15 degrees awarded. *Degree requirements:* For master's, thesis or alternative. *Entrance requirements:* For master's, 3 letters of recommendation, interview. Additional exam requirements/recommendations for international students: Required—TOEFL (minimum score 550 paper-based; 213 computer-based). *Application deadline:* For fall admission, 7/15 priority date for domestic and international students; for spring admission, 12/1 priority date for domestic and international students. Applications are processed on a rolling basis. Application fee: $45. Electronic applications accepted. *Expenses:* Tuition, state resident: full-time $3,311. Tuition, nonresident: full-time $8,616. Required fees: $368 per credit. *Financial support:* Research assistantships, Federal Work-Study, unspecified assistantships, and out of state fee waiver available. Support available to part-time students. Financial award application deadline: 3/15; financial award applicants required to submit FAFSA. *Faculty research:* Industrial ergonomics; work, measurement, and design; product design/evaluation. *Unit head:* Dr. Alvaro Taveira, Coordinator, 262-472-5427, Fax: 262-472-1091, E-mail: taveiraa@uww.edu. *Application contact:* Sally A. Lange, School of Graduate Studies, 262-472-1006, Fax: 262-472-5027, E-mail: gradschl@uww.edu.

Virginia Commonwealth University, Graduate School, College of Humanities and Sciences, Center for Environmental Studies, Richmond, VA 23284-9005. Offers environmental communication (MIS); environmental health (MIS); environmental policy (MIS); environmental sciences (MIS). *Faculty:* 1 full-time (0 women). *Students:* 15 full-time (10 women), 21 part-time (14 women); includes 2 minority (both African Americans), 1 international. Average age 33. 22 applicants, 68% accepted, 7 enrolled. In 2006, 13 degrees awarded. *Degree requirements:* For master's, thesis. *Entrance requirements:* For master's, GRE General Test. Application fee: $50. *Unit head:* Dr. Gregory C. Garman, Director, 804-828-1574, Fax: 804-828-0503, E-mail: gcgarman@vcu.edu.

Washington State University Tri-Cities, Graduate Programs, Program in Environmental Science, Richland, WA 99352-1671. Offers applied environmental science (MS); atmospheric science (MS); earth science (MS); environmental and occupational health science (MS); environmental regulatory compliance (MS); environmental science (PhD); environmental toxicology and risk assessment (MS); water resource science (MS). Part-time programs available. *Faculty:* 1 full-time, 53 part-time/adjunct. *Students:* 1 full-time (0 women), 35 part-time (17 women); includes 1 minority (Hispanic American), 1 international. Average age 41. 62 applicants, 10% accepted, 6 enrolled. *Degree requirements:* For master's, thesis (for some programs), oral exam, comprehensive exam, registration; for doctorate, thesis/dissertation, comprehensive exam. *Entrance requirements:* For master's, GRE General Test, minimum GPA of 3.0, 3 letters of recommendation. Additional exam requirements/recommendations for international students: Required—TOEFL (minimum score 550 paper-based; 213 computer-based). *Application deadline:* For fall admission, 2/1 priority date for domestic students, 3/1 for international students; for spring admission, 9/1 priority date for domestic students, 7/1 for international students. Application fee: $50. *Expenses:* Tuition, state resident: full-time $7,066. Tuition, nonresident: full-time $17,204. *Financial support:* In 2006–07, 8 students received support, including 1 fellowship (averaging $2,200 per year), research assistantships with full and partial tuition reimbursements available (averaging $13,917 per year), teaching assistantships with full and partial tuition reimbursements available (averaging $13,056 per year); Federal Work-Study, scholarships/grants, health care benefits, and unspecified assistantships also available. *Faculty research:* Radiation ecology, cytogenetics. *Unit head:* Dr. Gene Schreckhise, Associate Dean/Coordinator, 509-372-7323, E-mail: gschreck@wsu.edu. *Application contact:* Graduate School Admissions, 800-GRADWSU, Fax: 509-335-1949, E-mail: gradsch@wsu.edu.

Environmental and Occupational Health

Wayne State University, Eugene Applebaum College of Pharmacy and Health Sciences, Department of Fundamental and Applied Sciences, Program in Occupational and Environmental Health Sciences, Detroit, MI 48202. Offers MPH, MS, Certificate, Post-Master's Certificate. *Faculty:* 19 full-time (11 women), 12 part-time/adjunct (0 women). *Students:* Average age 39. In 2006, 4 degrees awarded. *Financial support:* In 2006–07, 1 research assistantship (averaging $13,500 per year) was awarded. *Application contact:* Peter Warner, Graduate Director, 313-577-1551, E-mail: aa4631@wayne.edu.

West Chester University of Pennsylvania, Graduate Studies, School of Health Sciences, Department of Health, West Chester, PA 19383. Offers emergency preparedness (Certificate); environmental health (MS); gerontology (MS); health care administration (Certificate); health services (MSA); integrative health (Certificate); public health (MPH, MS); school health (M Ed). Part-time and evening/weekend programs available. *Students:* 35 full-time (27 women), 65 part-time (50 women); includes 19 African Americans, 1 Asian American or Pacific Islander, 9 international. Average age 34. 58 applicants, 98% accepted, 30 enrolled. In 2006, 36 degrees awarded. *Degree requirements:* For master's, thesis (for some programs), comprehensive exam. *Entrance requirements:* For master's, GRE. *Application deadline:* For fall admission, 4/15 priority date for domestic students; for spring admission, 10/15 for domestic students. Applications are processed on a rolling basis. Application fee: $35. *Financial support:* In 2006–07, 9 research assistantships with full tuition reimbursements (averaging $5,000 per year) were awarded; unspecified assistantships also available. Support available to part-time students. Financial award application deadline: 2/15; financial award applicants required to submit FAFSA. *Faculty research:* HIV/AIDS education, teacher preparation, water quality. *Unit head:* Dr. Roger Mustalish, Chair, 610-436-2931, E-mail: rmustalish@wcupa.edu. *Application contact:* Dr. Bethann Cinelli, Graduate Coordinator, 610-436-2267, E-mail: bcinelli@wcupa.edu.

West Virginia University, College of Engineering and Mineral Resources, Department of Industrial and Management Systems Engineering, Program in Occupational Safety and Health, Morgantown, WV 26506. Offers PhD. Part-time programs available. Postbaccalaureate distance learning degree programs offered (minimal on-campus study). *Students:* 2 full-time (0 women), 3 part-time (1 woman), 2 international. Average age 34. 4 applicants, 25% accepted. *Degree requirements:* For doctorate, thesis/dissertation, comprehensive exam, registration. *Entrance requirements:* For doctorate, GRE General Test, Minimum GPA of 3.5. Additional exam requirements/recommendations for international students: Required—TOEFL. *Application deadline:* For fall admission, 6/15 priority date for domestic and international students; for spring admission, 11/1 for domestic and international students. Applications are processed on a rolling basis. Application fee: $50. *Expenses:* Tuition, state resident: full-time $4,926; part-time $276 per credit hour. Tuition, nonresident: full-time $14,278; part-time $796 per credit hour. Tuition and fees vary according to program. *Financial support:* In 2006–07, 2 research assistantships with full tuition reimbursements (averaging $13,850 per year) were awarded; fellowships, teaching assistantships, career-related internships or fieldwork, Federal Work-Study, institutionally sponsored loans, traineeships, health care benefits, tuition waivers (full and partial), and unspecified assistantships also available. Financial award application deadline: 4/1; financial award applicants required to submit FAFSA. *Faculty research:* Safety management, ergonomics and workplace design, safety and health training, construction safety. *Unit head:* Gary Winn, Coordinator, 304-293-4821 Ext. 3744, Fax: 304-293-4970, E-mail: gary.winn@mail.wvu.edu.

Yale University, School of Medicine, School of Public Health, Division of Environmental Health Sciences, New Haven, CT 06520. Offers MPH, PhD. PhD offered through the Graduate School. *Accreditation:* CEPH (one or more programs are accredited). Part-time programs available. *Faculty:* 3 full-time (0 women), 11 part-time/adjunct (4 women). *Students:* Average age 26. In 2006, 10 master's, 1 doctorate awarded. Terminal master's awarded for partial completion of doctoral program. *Degree requirements:* For master's, thesis, internship. *Entrance requirements:* For master's, GMAT, GRE, or MCAT, previous undergraduate course work in mathematics and science. Additional exam requirements/recommendations for international students: Required—TOEFL. *Application deadline:* For fall admission, 1/15 for domestic and international students. Electronic applications accepted. *Expenses:* Contact institution. *Financial support:* Career-related internships or fieldwork, Federal Work-Study, institutionally sponsored loans, and scholarships/grants available. Support available to part-time students. Financial award application deadline: 3/1; financial award applicants required to submit FAFSA. *Faculty research:* Asthma and environmental agents, environmental epidemiology, sensory perceptions, indoor/outdoor air quality, exercise physiology. *Unit head:* Dr. Tongzhang Zheng, Division Head, 203-785-2880, Fax: 203-737-6023, E-mail: tongzhang.zheng@yale.edu. *Application contact:* Jacqui Comshaw, Director of Admissions, 203-785-2844, Fax: 203-785-4845, E-mail: eph.admissions@yale.edu.

See Close-Up on page 2073.

Epidemiology

American University of Beirut, Graduate Programs, Faculty of Health Sciences, Beirut, Lebanon. Offers environmental health (MSES); epidemiology (MS); population health (MS); population science (MS); public health (MPH). Part-time programs available. *Faculty:* 21 full-time (16 women), 4 part-time/adjunct (0 women). *Students:* 42 full-time (34 women), 63 part-time (54 women). Average age 27. 158 applicants, 74% accepted, 47 enrolled. In 2006, 47 degrees awarded. *Degree requirements:* For master's, one foreign language, thesis (for some programs), comprehensive exam, registration. *Entrance requirements:* For master's, letter of recommendation. Additional exam requirements/recommendations for international students: Required—TOEFL (minimum score 600 paper-based; 250 computer-based; 100 iBT), IELTS (minimum score 8). *Application deadline:* For fall admission, 4/30 for domestic and international students; for spring admission, 11/1 for domestic and international students. Application fee: $50. *Financial support:* In 2006–07, 6 students received support. Career-related internships or fieldwork, institutionally sponsored loans, scholarships/grants, health care benefits, and unspecified assistantships available. Financial award application deadline: 2/2. *Faculty research:* Urban health, challenging childbirth in the Arab region, tobacco control, HIV/AIDS surveillance, water quality and management. Total annual research expenditures: $632,411. *Unit head:* Huda Zurayls, Dean, 961-1340119 Ext. 4600, Fax: 961-1744470, E-mail: hzurayk@aub.edu.lb. *Application contact:* Dr. Salim Kanaan, Director of Admissions Office, 961-1-374374 Ext. 2592, Fax: 961-1-750775, E-mail: admissions@aub.edu.lb.

Boston University, School of Public Health, Epidemiology Department, Boston, MA 02215. Offers M Sc, MPH, D Sc. *Accreditation:* CEPH (one or more programs are accredited). *Students:* 73 full-time (58 women), 90 part-time (60 women); includes 33 minority (7 African Americans, 23 Asian Americans or Pacific Islanders, 3 Hispanic Americans), 17 international. Average age 28. *Entrance requirements:* For master's, GRE General Test; for doctorate, GRE General Test, MPH or equivalent. Additional exam requirements/recommendations for international students: Required—TOEFL or IELTS. *Application deadline:* For fall admission, 2/1 for domestic students; for spring admission, 10/15 for domestic students. Application fee: $95. Electronic applications accepted. *Expenses:* Tuition: Full-time $33,330; part-time $1,042 per credit. Required fees: $462; $40. *Financial support:* Career-related internships or fieldwork, Federal Work-Study, institutionally sponsored loans, and scholarships/grants available. Support available to part-time students. *Unit head:* Dr. C. Robert Horsburgh, Chair, 617-638-7775, E-mail: epi@bu.edu. *Application contact:* LePhan Quan, Assistant Director of Admissions, 617-638-4640, Fax: 617-638-5299, E-mail: asksph@bu.edu.

Brown University, Graduate School, Division of Biology and Medicine, Department of Community Health, Providence, RI 02912. Offers health services research (MS, PhD); public health (MPH); statistical science (MS, PhD), including biostatistics, epidemiology; MD/PhD. *Accreditation:* CEPH. *Degree requirements:* For doctorate, thesis/dissertation, preliminary exam. *Entrance requirements:* For master's and doctorate, GRE General Test. Additional exam requirements/recommendations for international students: Required—TOEFL.

Brown University, Graduate School, Division of Biology and Medicine, Department of Community Health, Center for Statistical Science, Program in Epidemiology, Providence, RI 02912. Offers MS, PhD, MD/PhD. *Degree requirements:* For doctorate, thesis/dissertation, preliminary exam. *Entrance requirements:* For master's and doctorate, GRE General Test.

Case Western Reserve University, School of Medicine and School of Graduate Studies, Graduate Programs in Medicine, Department of Epidemiology and Biostatistics, Program in Epidemiology, Cleveland, OH 44106. Offers MS, PhD. *Accreditation:* CEPH. Part-time programs available. *Faculty:* 10 full-time (6 women), 15 part-time/adjunct (4 women). *Students:* 30 full-time (16 women); includes 16 minority (9 African Americans, 6 Asian Americans or Pacific Islanders, 1 Hispanic American). Average age 38. 25 applicants, 68% accepted, 3 enrolled. In 2006, 4 master's, 2 doctorates awarded. Terminal master's awarded for partial completion of doctoral program. *Degree requirements:* For master's and doctorate, thesis/dissertation, comprehensive exam. *Entrance requirements:* For master's, GRE General Test (MCAT may be substituted), 3 recommendations; for doctorate, GRE General Test, 3 recommendations. Additional exam requirements/recommendations for international students: Required—TOEFL (minimum score 550 paper-based; 213 computer-based). *Application deadline:* For fall admission, 2/1 priority date for domestic and international students. Applications are processed on a rolling basis. Application fee: $50. Electronic applications accepted. *Financial support:* In 2006–07, 17 students received support, including 4 fellowships with full and partial tuition reimbursements available (averaging $20,772 per year), 5 research assistantships with full and partial tuition reimbursements available (averaging $20,772 per year); career-related internships or fieldwork, scholarships/grants, traineeships, tuition waivers (partial), and unspecified assistantships also available. Support available to part-time students. Financial award application deadline: 2/1. *Faculty research:* Cardiovascular epidemiology, cancer risk factors, HIV in underserved populations, effectiveness studies in Medicare patients. Total annual research expenditures: $5.5 million. *Unit head:* Dr. Christopher C Whalen, Acting Director of the Division of Epidemiology, 216-368-4192, Fax: 216-368-3970, E-mail: ccw@case.edu. *Application contact:* Alicia M Boscarello, Graduate Student Coordinator, 216-368-5957, Fax: 216-368-3970, E-mail: amb62@case.edu.

Columbia University, Mailman School of Public Health, Division of Epidemiology, New York, NY 10027. Offers MPH, MS, Dr PH, PhD. PhD offered in cooperation with the Graduate School of Arts and Sciences. *Accreditation:* CEPH (one or more programs are accredited). Part-time programs available. *Students:* 167. In 2006, 19 degrees awarded. *Degree requirements:* For master's and doctorate, thesis/dissertation. *Entrance requirements:* For master's, GRE General Test; for doctorate, GRE General Test, MPH or equivalent (Dr PH). *Application deadline:* For fall admission, 2/1 for domestic students; for spring admission, 10/1 for domestic students. Application fee: $60. Electronic applications accepted. *Financial support:* Research assistantships, teaching assistantships, career-related internships or fieldwork and Federal Work-Study available. Support available to part-time students. Financial award application deadline: 2/1; financial award applicants required to submit FAFSA. *Faculty research:* Psychiatric epidemiology; epidemiology of neurological disorders, cancer, and cardiovascular disease. *Unit head:* Ezra Susser, Chair, 212-305-9412, Fax: 212-305-9413. *Application contact:* June Saunders, Associate Director of Admissions, 212-305-3927, Fax: 212-342-4861, E-mail: ph-admit@columbia.edu.

Cornell University, Graduate School, Graduate Fields of Comparative Biomedical Sciences, Field of Comparative Biomedical Sciences, Ithaca, NY 14853-0001. Offers cellular and molecular medicine (MS, PhD); developmental and reproductive biology (MS, PhD); infectious diseases (MS, PhD); population medicine and epidemiology (MS); population medicine and epidemiology sciences (PhD); structural and functional biology (MS, PhD). *Faculty:* 107 full-time (30 women). *Students:* 50 full-time (29 women); includes 4 minority (1 African American, 3 Asian Americans or Pacific Islanders), 25 international. Average age 31. 58 applicants, 60% accepted, 33 enrolled. In 2006, 6 degrees awarded. *Degree requirements:* For master's, thesis/dissertation; for doctorate, thesis/dissertation, comprehensive exam. *Entrance requirements:* For master's and doctorate, GRE General Test, 2 letters of recommendation. Additional exam requirements/recommendations for international students: Required—TOEFL (minimum score 550 paper-based; 213 computer-based). *Application deadline:* For fall admission, 12/15 for domestic students. Application fee: $60. Electronic applications accepted. *Expenses:* Tuition: Full-time $32,800. Full-time tuition and fees vary according to program. *Financial support:* In 2006–07, 47 students received support, including 14 fellowships with full tuition reimbursements available, 33 research assistantships with full tuition reimbursements available; teaching assistantships with full tuition reimbursements available, institutionally sponsored loans, scholarships/grants, health care benefits, tuition waivers (full and partial), and unspecified assistantships also available. Financial award applicants required to submit FAFSA. *Faculty research:* Receptors and signal transduction, viral and bacterial infectious diseases, tumor metastasis, clinical sciences/nutritional disease, developmental/neurological disorders. *Unit head:* Director of Graduate Studies, 607-253-3276, Fax: 607-253-3756. *Application contact:* Graduate Field Assistant, 607-253-3276, Fax: 607-253-3756, E-mail: graduate_edcvm@cornell.edu.

Cornell University, Joan and Sanford I. Weill Medical College and Graduate School of Medical Sciences, Weill Graduate School of Medical Sciences, Program in Clinical Epidemiology and Health Services Research, New York, NY 10021. Offers MS. *Faculty:* 17 full-time (6 women), 3 part-time/adjunct (0 women). *Students:* 14 full-time (9 women); includes 6 minority (2 African Americans, 2 Asian Americans or Pacific Islanders, 2 Hispanic Americans), 1 international. 2 applicants, 100% accepted, 2 enrolled. In 2006, 6 degrees awarded. *Degree requirements:* For master's, thesis. *Entrance requirements:* For master's, 3 years of work experience, MD or RN certificate. *Application deadline:* For fall admission, 12/15 for domestic students. Application fee: $60. *Financial support:* Scholarships/grants available. *Unit head:* Dr. Carol Mancuso, Director. *Application contact:* Susan Toro, Administrator, 212-746-1607.

Dalhousie University, Faculty of Graduate Studies, Department of Community Health and Epidemiology, Halifax, NS B3H 4R2, Canada. Offers M Sc. Part-time programs available. *Degree requirements:* For master's, thesis. *Entrance requirements:* Additional exam requirements/recommendations for international students: Required—TOEFL. Expenses: Contact institution. *Faculty research:* Population health, health promotion and disease prevention, health services utilization, chronic disease epidemiology.

East Tennessee State University, School of Graduate Studies, College of Public and Allied Health, Department of Public Health, Johnson City, TN 37614. Offers community health (MPH); epidemiology (Certificate); gerontology (Certificate); health care management

(Certificate); public health (MPH); public health administration (MPH). *Accreditation:* CEPH. Part-time programs available. *Degree requirements:* For master's, thesis optional. *Entrance requirements:* For master's, GRE General Test, 2 years of community health experience. Additional exam requirements/recommendations for international students: Required—TOEFL (minimum score 550 paper-based; 213 computer-based). *Faculty research:* Rural health issues, youth and adolescent health, health of the elderly, environmental epidemiology, spatial analysis of data.

Emory University, Rollins School of Public Health, Department of Epidemiology, Atlanta, GA 30322-1100. Offers MPH, MSPH, PhD. *Accreditation:* CEPH. Part-time programs available. *Students:* 170 full-time (127 women), 10 part-time (4 women). Average age 27. 305 applicants, 44% accepted, 51 enrolled. In 2006, 60 master's awarded. *Degree requirements:* For master's, thesis, practicum; for doctorate, written qualifying exam. *Entrance requirements:* For master's, GRE General Test. Additional exam requirements/recommendations for international students: Required—TOEFL (minimum score 550 paper-based; 213 computer-based). *Application deadline:* For fall admission, 1/5 priority date for domestic and international students. Application fee: $75. Electronic applications accepted. *Expenses: Contact institution. Financial support:* Fellowships with full and partial tuition reimbursements, career-related internships or fieldwork, Federal Work-Study, institutionally sponsored loans, and scholarships/grants available. Support available to part-time students. Financial award application deadline: 1/5. *Faculty research:* Cancer, infectious diseases, epidemiological methods, environmental/occupational health, women's and children's health. *Unit head:* Dr. Jack S. Mandel, Professor and Chair, 404-712-2679, Fax: 404-727-8737, E-mail: jsmande@sph.emory.edu. *Application contact:* Missy McCall, Assistant Director of Academic Programs, 404-727-8729, Fax: 404-727-8737, E-mail: missy.mccall@emory.edu.

See Close-Up on page 2035.

Emory University, Rollins School of Public Health, Program in Career Public Health, Atlanta, GA 30322-1100. Offers applied epidemiology (MPH); outcomes option (MPH); prevention (MPH). Part-time and evening/weekend programs available. Postbaccalaureate distance learning degree programs offered (minimal on-campus study). *Students:* 11 full-time (10 women), 101 part-time (69 women). Average age 40. 69 applicants, 68% accepted, 37 enrolled. In 2006, 18 degrees awarded. *Degree requirements:* For master's, thesis, practicum. *Entrance requirements:* Additional exam requirements/recommendations for international students: Required—TOEFL (minimum score 550 paper-based; 213 computer-based). *Application deadline:* For fall admission, 1/5 priority date for domestic students, 1/5 for international students. Applications are processed on a rolling basis. Application fee: $75. Electronic applications accepted. *Expenses:* Tuition: Full-time $30,246. *Financial support:* Fellowships with full and partial tuition reimbursements, career-related internships or fieldwork, institutionally sponsored loans, and scholarships/grants available. Support available to part-time students. Financial award application deadline: 1/5. *Unit head:* Dr. Iris Smith, Director, 404-727-2925, Fax: 404-727-3996, E-mail: ismith@sph.emory.edu. *Application contact:* Robie Freeman Burks, Assistant Director of Academic Programs, 404-727-8739, Fax: 404-727-8768, E-mail: rfreem2@sph.emory.edu.

Georgetown University, Graduate School of Arts and Sciences, Programs in Biomedical Sciences, Division of Biostatistics and Epidemiology, Washington, DC 20057. Offers MS. *Entrance requirements:* For master's, GRE General Test. Additional exam requirements/recommendations for international students: Required—TOEFL. *Faculty research:* Occupation epidemiology, cancer.

The George Washington University, Columbian College of Arts and Sciences, Program in Epidemiology, Washington, DC 20052. Offers MS, PhD. Part-time and evening/weekend programs available. *Degree requirements:* For master's, comprehensive exam; for doctorate, thesis/dissertation, general exam. *Entrance requirements:* For master's and doctorate, GRE General Test, minimum GPA of 3.0. Additional exam requirements/recommendations for international students: Required—TOEFL (minimum score 550 paper-based; 213 computer-based). Electronic applications accepted.

The George Washington University, School of Public Health and Health Services, Department of Epidemiology and Biostatistics, Washington, DC 20052. Offers biostatistics (MPH); epidemiology (MPH); health information systems (MPH); microbiology and emerging infectious diseases (MSPH). *Degree requirements:* For master's, case study or special project. *Entrance requirements:* For master's, GMAT, GRE General Test, or MCAT. Additional exam requirements/recommendations for international students: Required—TOEFL.

Harvard University, School of Public Health, Department of Epidemiology, Boston, MA 02115-6096. Offers epidemiology (SM, DPH, SD); exposure, epidemiology and risk (SM, SD). Part-time programs available. *Degree requirements:* For doctorate, thesis/dissertation, qualifying exam. *Entrance requirements:* For master's and doctorate, GRE. Additional exam requirements/recommendations for international students: Required—TOEFL (minimum score 560 paper-based; 220 computer-based); Recommended—IELTS (minimum score 7). Electronic applications accepted. *Expenses:* Tuition: Full-time $30,275. Full-time tuition and fees vary according to program and student level. *Faculty research:* Cancer prevention and epidemiology, cardiovascular epidemiology, environmental and occupational epidemiology, pharmacoepidemiology, psychiatric epidemiology.

Harvard University, School of Public Health, Department of Nutrition, Boston, MA 02115-6096. Offers nutrition (DPH, PhD, SD); nutritional epidemiology (DPH, SD); public health nutrition (DPH, SD). *Degree requirements:* For doctorate, thesis/dissertation, qualifying exam. *Entrance requirements:* For doctorate, GRE. Additional exam requirements/recommendations for international students: Required—TOEFL (minimum score 560 paper-based; 220 computer-based); Recommended—IELTS (minimum score 7). Electronic applications accepted. *Expenses:* Tuition: Full-time $30,275. Full-time tuition and fees vary according to program and student level.

The Johns Hopkins University, Bloomberg School of Public Health, Department of Epidemiology, Baltimore, MD 21205. Offers cancer epidemiology (MHS, Sc M, PhD, Sc D); cardiovascular disease epidemiology (MHS, Sc M, PhD, Sc D); clinical epidemiology (MHS, Sc M, PhD, Sc D); clinical trials (PhD, Sc D); epidemiology (Dr PH); epidemiology (general) (MHS, Sc M, PhD, Sc D); epidemiology of aging (MHS, Sc M, PhD, Sc D); human genetics/genetic epidemiology (MHS, Sc M, PhD, Sc D); infectious disease epidemiology (MHS, Sc M, PhD, Sc D); occupational/environmental epidemiology (MHS, Sc M, PhD, Sc D). *Faculty:* 81 full-time (43 women), 98 part-time/adjunct (44 women). *Students:* 153 full-time (109 women), 42 part-time (32 women); includes 52 minority (12 African Americans, 36 Asian Americans or Pacific Islanders, 4 Hispanic Americans), 41 international. Average age 30. 274 applicants, 46% accepted, 55 enrolled. In 2006, 20 master's, 22 doctorates awarded. *Median time to degree:* Of those who began their doctoral program in fall 1998, 72% received their degree in 8 years or less. *Degree requirements:* For master's, thesis, 1 year full-time residency, comprehensive exam, registration; for doctorate, thesis/dissertation, 2 years full-time residency, oral and written exams, teaching requirement, comprehensive exam, registration. *Entrance requirements:* For master's, GRE General Test, 3 letters of recommendation, curriculum vitae, statement of objectives, academic records from all schools; for doctorate, GRE General Test or MCAT, minimum 1 year work experience, 3 letters of recommendation, curriculum vitae, statement, transcripts. Additional exam requirements/recommendations for international students: Required—TOEFL (minimum score 600 paper-based; 250 computer-based). *Application deadline:* For fall admission, 12/1 priority date for domestic students. Applications are processed on a rolling basis. Application fee: $45. Electronic applications accepted. *Expenses:* Tuition: Full-time $32,976. Tuition and fees vary according to degree level and program. *Financial support:* In 2006–07, 2 fellowships (averaging $28,859 per year) were awarded; Federal Work-Study, institutionally sponsored loans, scholarships/grants, traineeships, tuition waivers (partial), and stipends also available. Support available to part-time students. Financial award application deadline: 3/15; financial award applicants required to submit FAFSA. *Faculty research:* Cancer and congenital malformations, nutritional epidemiology, AIDS, tuberculosis, cardiovascular disease, risk assessment. Total annual research expenditures: $47.8 million. *Unit head:* Dr. Jonathan M. Samet, Chairman, 410-955-3286, Fax: 410-955-0863, E-mail: jsamet@jhsph.edu. *Application contact:* Frances S. Burman, Senior Academic Coordinator, 410-955-3926, Fax: 410-955-0863, E-mail: fburman@jhsph.edu.

The Johns Hopkins University, Bloomberg School of Public Health, Department of International Health, Baltimore, MD 21218-2699. Offers disease prevention and control (MHS, PhD); health systems (MHS, PhD); human nutrition (MHS, PhD); international health (Dr PH); social and behavioral interventions (MHS, PhD). *Faculty:* 119 full-time (63 women), 170 part-time/adjunct (55 women). *Students:* 197 full-time (159 women), 7 part-time (4 women); includes 36 minority (4 African Americans, 1 American Indian/Alaska Native, 25 Asian Americans or Pacific Islanders, 6 Hispanic Americans), 58 international. Average age 27. 376 applicants, 46% accepted, 68 enrolled. In 2006, 39 master's, 19 doctorates awarded. *Median time to degree:* Of those who began their doctoral program in fall 1998, 63% received their degree in 8 years or less. *Degree requirements:* For master's, thesis (for some programs), internship, comprehensive exam, registration; for doctorate, thesis/dissertation, 1 year full-time residency, oral and written exams, comprehensive exam, registration. *Entrance requirements:* For master's, GRE General Test or MCAT, 3 letters of recommendation, resumé; for doctorate, GRE General Test, 3 letters of recommendation, resumé. Additional exam requirements/recommendations for international students: Required—TOEFL (minimum score 600 paper-based; 280 computer-based). *Application deadline:* For fall admission, 1/2 priority date for domestic and international students. Applications are processed on a rolling basis. Application fee: $45. Electronic applications accepted. *Expenses:* Tuition: Full-time $32,976. Tuition and fees vary according to degree level and program. *Financial support:* In 2006–07, 203 students received support, including 9 fellowships (averaging $32,000 per year); Federal Work-Study, institutionally sponsored loans, scholarships/grants, traineeships, and stipends also available. Support available to part-time students. Financial award application deadline: 3/15; financial award applicants required to submit FAFSA. *Faculty research:* Nutrition, infectious diseases, health systems, economics, humanitarian emergencies. Total annual research expenditures: $62 million. *Unit head:* Dr. Robert E. Black, Chairman, 410-955-3934, Fax: 410-955-7159, E-mail: rblack@jhsph.edu. *Application contact:* Jennifer Shaffer, Academic Program Administrator, 410-955-3734, Fax: 410-955-7159, E-mail: jshaffer@jhsph.edu.

Loma Linda University, School of Public Health, Programs in Epidemiology and Biostatistics, Loma Linda, CA 92350. Offers MPH, MSPH. *Entrance requirements:* Additional exam requirements/recommendations for international students: Required—Michigan English Language Assessment Battery or TOEFL.

McGill University, Faculty of Graduate and Postdoctoral Studies, Faculty of Medicine, Departments of Epidemiology and Biostatistics, and Occupational Health, Montréal, QC H3A 2T5, Canada. Offers community health (M Sc); environmental health (M Sc); epidemiology and biostatistics (M Sc, PhD, Diploma); health care evaluation (M Sc); medical statistics (M Sc); occupational health (M Sc). *Accreditation:* CEPH (one or more programs are accredited). *Degree requirements:* For master's, thesis optional; for doctorate, thesis/dissertation. *Entrance requirements:* For master's, GRE, minimum GPA of 3.0; for doctorate, GRE. *Faculty research:* Chronic and infectious disease epidemiology, health services research, pharmacoepidemiology.

Medical College of Wisconsin, Graduate School of Biomedical Sciences, Program in Epidemiology, Milwaukee, WI 53226-0509. Offers MS. Part-time programs available. *Degree requirements:* For master's, thesis, registration. *Entrance requirements:* For master's, GRE General Test, interview. Additional exam requirements/recommendations for international students: Required—TOEFL. *Faculty research:* Descriptive epidemiology of health care delivery using large databases.

Medical University of South Carolina, College of Graduate Studies, Department of Biostatistics, Bioinformatics, and Epidemiology, Charleston, SC 29425-0002. Offers bioinformatics (MS, PhD); biostatistics (MS, PhD); clinical research (MS); epidemiology (MS, PhD); DMD/PhD; MD/PhD. *Faculty:* 26 full-time (9 women). *Students:* 40 full-time (26 women); includes 3 minority (1 African American, 2 Asian Americans or Pacific Islanders), 6 international. Average age 28. 181 applicants, 34% accepted. In 2006, 7 master's, 4 doctorates awarded. Terminal master's awarded for partial completion of doctoral program. *Degree requirements:* For master's, thesis, research seminar; for doctorate, thesis/dissertation, teaching and research seminar, oral and written exams. *Entrance requirements:* For master's, GRE General Test; for doctorate, GRE General Test, interview. Additional exam requirements/recommendations for international students: Required—TOEFL (minimum score 600 paper-based; 250 computer-based). *Application deadline:* For fall admission, 1/15 priority date for domestic and international students. Applications are processed on a rolling basis. Application fee: $0 ($75 for international students). Electronic applications accepted. *Financial support:* In 2006–07, 8 students received support, including fellowships with partial tuition reimbursements available (averaging $21,000 per year); Federal Work-Study and scholarships/grants also available. Support available to part-time students. Financial award application deadline: 3/15; financial award applicants required to submit FAFSA. *Faculty research:* Health disparities, central nervous system injuries, radiation exposure, analysis of clinical trial data, biomedical information. *Unit head:* Dr. Barbara Tilley, Chair, 873-876-1327, Fax: 873-792-6950, E-mail: tilleybc@musc.edu.

Memorial University of Newfoundland, Faculty of Medicine and School of Graduate Studies, Graduate Programs in Medicine, Division of Community Health, St. John's, NL A1C 5S7, Canada. Offers clinical epidemiology (M Sc, PhD, Diploma); community health (M Sc, PhD, Diploma). Part-time programs available. *Degree requirements:* For master's, thesis; for doctorate, thesis/dissertation, oral defense of thesis, comprehensive exam. *Entrance requirements:* For master's, MD or B Sc; for doctorate, MD or M Sc; for Diploma, bachelor's degree in health-related field. Additional exam requirements/recommendations for international students: Required—TOEFL. *Faculty research:* Epidemiology of chronic diseases, health care delivery and administration, health services, psychosocial, aging.

Michigan State University, College of Human Medicine and The Graduate School, Graduate Programs in Human Medicine, Department of Epidemiology, East Lansing, MI 48824. Offers MS, PhD. *Faculty:* 11 full-time (3 women). *Students:* 28 full-time (18 women), 16 part-time (11 women); includes 6 minority (3 African Americans, 3 Asian Americans or Pacific Islanders), 12 international. Average age 32. 36 applicants, 31% accepted. In 2006, 4 degrees awarded. *Degree requirements:* For master's, oral thesis defense. *Entrance requirements:* Additional exam requirements/recommendations for international students: Required—TOEFL. *Application deadline:* Applications are processed on a rolling basis. Electronic applications accepted. *Expenses:* Tuition, state resident: part-time $346 per credit hour. Tuition, nonresident: part-time $730 per credit hour. Tuition and fees vary according to program. *Financial support:* In 2006–07, 10 fellowships with tuition reimbursements, 11 research assistantships with tuition reimbursements (averaging $13,276 per year) were awarded. Total annual research expenditures: $4.4 million. *Unit head:* Dr. James C. Anthony, Chairperson, 517-353-8623, Fax: 517-432-1130, E-mail: janthony@epi.msu.edu. *Application contact:* Jayne Goeddeke, Graduate Secretary, 517-432-3921, Fax: 517-432-2229, E-mail: epigrad@epi.msu.edu.

New York Medical College, School of Public Health, Department of Epidemiology and Biostatistics, Valhalla, NY 10595-1691. Offers biostatistics (MPH, MS); epidemiology (MPH, Dr PH); public health informatics (Graduate Certificate). Part-time and evening/weekend programs available. In 2006, 4 degrees awarded. *Degree requirements:* For master's and doctorate, thesis/dissertation, registration. *Entrance requirements:* For master's, minimum undergraduate GPA of 3.0; for doctorate, GRE General Test, minimum undergraduate GPA of 3.5. Additional exam requirements/recommendations for international students: Required—TOEFL (minimum score 600 paper-based; 250 computer-based). *Application deadline:* For fall admission, 8/1 priority date for domestic students, 5/15 for international students; for spring admission, 12/1 priority date for domestic students, 12/1 for international students. Applications are processed on a rolling basis. Application fee: $35 ($60 for international students). Electronic applications accepted. *Financial support:* Career-related internships or fieldwork, Federal Work-Study, and institutionally sponsored loans available. Financial award application deadline: 6/15;

Epidemiology

New York Medical College (continued)
financial award applicants required to submit FAFSA. *Unit head:* Dr. Paul Visintainer, Chair, 914-594-4817, Fax: 914-594-4292, E-mail: visint@nymc.edu. *Application contact:* Marian F. McGowan, Information Contact, 914-594-4510, Fax: 914-594-4292, E-mail: sph_admissions@nymc.edu.

See Close-Ups on pages 2045 and 2043.

New York University, Graduate School of Arts and Science, Department of Environmental Medicine, New York, NY 10012-1019. Offers environmental health sciences (MS, PhD), including biostatistics (PhD), environmental hygiene (MS), epidemiology (PhD), ergonomics and biomechanics (PhD), exposure assessment and health effects (PhD), molecular toxicology/carcinogenesis (PhD), toxicology. Part-time programs available. *Faculty:* 26 full-time (7 women). *Students:* 49 full-time (40 women), 17 part-time (8 women); includes 12 minority (3 African Americans, 6 Asian Americans or Pacific Islanders, 3 Hispanic Americans), 25 international. Average age 31. 65 applicants, 45% accepted, 16 enrolled. In 2006, 10 master's, 4 doctorates awarded. Terminal master's awarded for partial completion of doctoral program. *Degree requirements:* For master's, thesis or alternative; for doctorate, one foreign language, thesis/dissertation, oral and written exams. *Entrance requirements:* For master's and doctorate, GRE General Test, GRE Subject Test, minimum GPA of 3.0; bachelor's degree in biological, physical, or engineering science. Additional exam requirements/recommendations for international students: Required—TOEFL. *Application deadline:* For fall admission, 12/15 for domestic students. Application fee: $80. *Expenses:* Tuition: Part-time $1,080 per unit. Required fees: $56 per unit. $329 per term. Tuition and fees vary according to program. *Financial support:* Fellowships with tuition reimbursements, teaching assistantships with tuition reimbursements, career-related internships or fieldwork, Federal Work-Study, institutionally sponsored loans, and health care benefits available. Financial award application deadline: 12/15; financial award applicants required to submit FAFSA. *Unit head:* Dr. Max Costa, Chair, 845-731-3661, Fax: 845-351-3317, E-mail: ehs@env.med.nyu.edu. *Application contact:* Dr. Jerome J. Solomon, Director of Graduate Studies, 845-731-3661, Fax: 845-351-3317, E-mail: ehs@env.med.nyu.edu.

North Carolina State University, College of Veterinary Medicine, Program in Comparative Biomedical Sciences, Raleigh, NC 27695. Offers cell biology and morphology (MS, PhD); epidemiology and population medicine (MS, PhD); immunology (MS, PhD); microbiology and immunology (MS, PhD); pathology (MS, PhD); pharmacology (MS, PhD); specialized veterinary medicine (MS). Part-time programs available. *Degree requirements:* For master's and doctorate, thesis/dissertation. *Entrance requirements:* For master's and doctorate, GRE General Test. Additional exam requirements/recommendations for international students: Required—TOEFL (minimum score 550 paper-based; 213 computer-based). Electronic applications accepted. Expenses: Contact institution. *Faculty research:* Infectious diseases, cell biology, pharmacology and toxicology, genomics, pathology and population medicine.

Oregon Health & Science University, School of Medicine, Department of Public Health and Preventive Medicine, Portland, OR 97239-3098. Offers epidemiology and biostatistics (MPH); MD/MPH. *Accreditation:* CEPH. Part-time programs available. *Degree requirements:* For master's, thesis, fieldwork/internship. *Entrance requirements:* For master's, GRE General Test, previous undergraduate course work in statistics. Additional exam requirements/recommendations for international students: Required—TOEFL. *Faculty research:* Health services, health care access, health policy, environmental and occupational health.

Purdue University, School of Veterinary Medicine and Graduate School, Graduate Programs in Veterinary Medicine, Department of Comparative Pathobiology, West Lafayette, IN 47907. Offers biochemistry and molecular biology (MS, PhD); comparative epidemiology (MS, PhD); epidemiology (MS, PhD); immunology (MS, PhD); infectious diseases (MS, PhD); interdisciplinary genetics (PhD); laboratory animal medicine (MS, PhD); microbiology (MS, PhD); molecular virology (MS, PhD); parasitology (MS, PhD); pathobiology (MS, PhD); public health epidemiology (MS, PhD); toxicology (MS, PhD); veterinary anatomic pathology (MS, PhD); veterinary clinical pathology (MS, PhD); virology (MS, PhD). *Faculty:* 34 full-time (8 women). *Students:* 45 full-time (19 women), 3 part-time (1 woman); includes 1 minority (African American), 29 international. Average age 35. In 2006, 3 master's, 2 doctorates awarded. Terminal master's awarded for partial completion of doctoral program. *Degree requirements:* For master's, thesis (for some programs); for doctorate, thesis/dissertation. *Entrance requirements:* For master's and doctorate, GRE General Test. Additional exam requirements/recommendations for international students: Required—TOEFL (minimum score 575 paper-based; 232 computer-based), IELTS (minimum score 7), TWE (minimum score 4). *Application deadline:* For fall admission, 8/12 for domestic students, 6/15 for international students; for spring admission, 1/12 for domestic students, 10/15 for international students. Application fee: $55. Electronic applications accepted. *Financial support:* Fellowships, research assistantships, teaching assistantships available. Financial award application deadline: 3/1; financial award applicants required to submit FAFSA. *Unit head:* Dr. H. Hogen Esch, Head, 765-494-7543.

Queen's University at Kingston, School of Graduate Studies and Research, Faculty of Health Sciences, Department of Community Health and Epidemiology, Kingston, ON K7L 3N6, Canada. Offers epidemiology (M Sc). Part-time programs available. *Degree requirements:* For master's, thesis. *Entrance requirements:* For master's, GRE General Test (strongly recommended). Additional exam requirements/recommendations for international students: Required—TOEFL (minimum score 600 paper-based; 250 computer-based). *Faculty research:* Cancer epidemiology, clinical trials, biostatistics health services research, health policy.

San Diego State University, Graduate and Research Affairs, College of Health and Human Services, Graduate School of Public Health, San Diego, CA 92182. Offers environmental health (MPH); epidemiology (MPH, PhD), including biostatistics (MPH); global emergency preparedness and response (MS); health behavior (PhD); health promotion (MPH); health services administration (MPH); toxicology (MS); MSW/MPH. *Accreditation:* ABET (one or more programs are accredited); CAHME (one or more programs are accredited); CEPH (one or more programs are accredited). Part-time programs available. *Degree requirements:* For master's, thesis (for some programs), comprehensive exam (for some programs); for doctorate, thesis/dissertation. *Entrance requirements:* For master's, GMAT (health services administration MPH), GRE General Test; for doctorate, GRE General Test. Additional exam requirements/recommendations for international students: Required—TOEFL. *Faculty research:* Evaluation of tobacco, AIDS prevalence and prevention, mammography, infant death project, Alzheimer's in elderly Chinese.

Stanford University, School of Medicine, Graduate Programs in Medicine, Department of Epidemiology, Stanford, CA 94305-9991. Offers MS, PhD. *Degree requirements:* For master's, thesis; for doctorate, thesis/dissertation, qualifying examinations. *Entrance requirements:* For doctorate, GRE General Test or MCAT. Additional exam requirements/recommendations for international students: Required—TOEFL. Electronic applications accepted.

Temple University, Health Sciences Center and Graduate School, College of Health Professions, Department of Public Health, Program in Epidemiology, Philadelphia, PA 19122-6096. Offers MS. Part-time and evening/weekend programs available. *Entrance requirements:* For master's, GRE or MCAT. Additional exam requirements/recommendations for international students: Required—TOEFL (minimum score 550 paper-based; 213 computer-based; 79 iBT). *Application deadline:* For fall admission, 2/15 for domestic students, 12/15 for international students. Applications are processed on a rolling basis. Application fee: $50. Electronic applications accepted. *Expenses:* Tuition, state resident: full-time $12,264; part-time $511 per credit. Tuition, nonresident: full-time $17,904; part-time $746 per credit. Required fees: $84 per course. Tuition and fees vary according to program. *Financial support:* Application deadline: 1/15; *Unit head:* Dr. Deborah Nelson, Director, 215-204-9659, Fax: 215-204-1854, E-mail: dnelson@temple.edu.

Texas A&M Health Science Center, School of Rural Public Health, College Station, TX 77843-1266. Offers environmental/occupational health (MPH); epidemiology/biostatistics (MPH); health policy/management (MPH); social and behavioral health (MPH). *Accreditation:* CEPH. Part-time programs available. Postbaccalaureate distance learning degree programs offered (no on-campus study). *Faculty:* 16 full-time (7 women), 4 part-time/adjunct (1 woman). *Students:* 43 full-time (27 women), 118 part-time (76 women); includes 63 minority (13 African Americans, 13 Asian Americans or Pacific Islanders, 37 Hispanic Americans), 1 international. Average age 32. 162 applicants, 83% accepted, 118 enrolled. In 2006, 10 degrees awarded. *Degree requirements:* For master's, thesis optional. *Entrance requirements:* For master's, GRE General Test, minimum undergraduate GPA of 3.0. *Application deadline:* For fall admission, 8/27 for domestic students; for spring admission, 1/14 for domestic students. Applications are processed on a rolling basis. Application fee: $35 ($75 for international students). Electronic applications accepted. *Financial support:* In 2006–07, research assistantships (averaging $10,800 per year). *Faculty research:* Tobacco cessation, youth health risk. Total annual research expenditures: $1.7 million. *Unit head:* Dr. Ciro V. Sumaya, Dean. *Application contact:* Dr. James Robinson, Professor/Special Advisor to the Dean, 409-845-2387, Fax: 409-862-8371, E-mail: jrobinson@medicine.tamu.edu.

Texas A&M University, College of Veterinary Medicine, Graduate Programs in Veterinary Medicine, Department of Veterinary Integrative Biosciences, College Station, TX 77843. Offers epidemiology (MS); food safety/toxicology (MS); veterinary anatomy (MS, PhD); veterinary public health (MS). *Faculty:* 22 full-time (8 women), 6 part-time/adjunct (2 women). *Students:* 30 full-time (22 women), 11 part-time (8 women); includes 4 minority (1 American Indian/Alaska Native, 3 Asian Americans or Pacific Islanders), 9 international. Average age 30. 14 applicants, 93% accepted, 11 enrolled. In 2006, 4 master's, 1 doctorate awarded. Terminal master's awarded for partial completion of doctoral program. *Degree requirements:* For master's and doctorate, thesis/dissertation, comprehensive exam, registration. *Entrance requirements:* For master's and doctorate, GRE General Test, minimum undergraduate GPA of 3.0. Additional exam requirements/recommendations for international students: Required—TOEFL. *Application deadline:* For fall admission, 7/15 priority date for domestic students, 4/1 priority date for international students; for spring admission, 10/1 priority date for domestic students, 9/15 priority date for international students. Applications are processed on a rolling basis. Application fee: $50 ($75 for international students). Electronic applications accepted. *Expenses:* Tuition, state resident: full-time $4,697. Tuition, nonresident: full-time $11,297. Required fees: $2,272. *Financial support:* In 2006–07, fellowships (averaging $18,000 per year), research assistantships (averaging $15,600 per year), teaching assistantships (averaging $15,600 per year) were awarded; institutionally sponsored loans, unspecified assistantships, and clinical associateships also available. Financial award application deadline: 7/15; financial award applicants required to submit FAFSA. *Faculty research:* Metal toxicology, reproductive biology, genetics of neural development, developmental biology, environmental toxicology. *Unit head:* Dr. Evelyn Tiffany-Castiglioni, Head, 979-845-2828, Fax: 979-847-8981, E-mail: ecastiglioni@cvm.tamu.edu. *Application contact:* Dr. Jane Welsh, Chair, Fax: 979-847-8981, E-mail: jwelsh@cum.tamu.edu.

Tufts University, Graduate School of Arts and Sciences, Graduate Certificate Programs, Program in Epidemiology, Medford, MA 02155. Offers Certificate. *Students:* Average age 31. 6 applicants, 100% accepted, 6 enrolled. *Application deadline:* For fall admission, 8/15 priority date for domestic students; for spring admission, 12/12 priority date for domestic students. Applications are processed on a rolling basis. Application fee: $65. Electronic applications accepted. *Expenses:* Tuition: Full-time $33,672. Tuition and fees vary according to degree level and program. *Financial support:* Available to part-time students. Application deadline: 5/1. *Application contact:* Angela Foss, Program Administrator, 617-627-3395, Fax: 617-627-3016, E-mail: gradschool@ase.tufts.edu.

Tufts University, Sackler School of Graduate Biomedical Sciences, Division of Clinical Care Research, Medford, MA 02155. Offers MS, PhD. Part-time programs available. *Faculty:* 33 full-time (10 women). *Students:* 19 full-time (10 women), 1 part-time; includes 3 minority (all Asian Americans or Pacific Islanders), 3 international. Average age 34. 19 applicants, 47% accepted, 8 enrolled. In 2006, 13 master's, 1 doctorate awarded. Terminal master's awarded for partial completion of doctoral program. *Degree requirements:* For master's and doctorate, thesis/dissertation. *Entrance requirements:* For master's and doctorate, MD or PhD, strong clinical research background. Additional exam requirements/recommendations for international students: Required—TOEFL. *Application deadline:* For fall admission, 1/15 priority date for domestic and international students. Applications are processed on a rolling basis. Application fee: $65. Electronic applications accepted. *Expenses:* Tuition: Full-time $33,672. Tuition and fees vary according to degree level and program. *Financial support:* In 2006–07, 20 fellowships with full tuition reimbursements (averaging $44,000 per year) were awarded. Financial award application deadline: 1/15. *Faculty research:* Clinical study design, mathematical modeling, meta analysis, epidemiologic research, coronary heart disease. *Unit head:* Dr. Harry P. Selker, Program Director, 617-636-5009, Fax: 617-636-8023, E-mail: hselker@lifespan.org. *Application contact:* 617-636-6767, Fax: 617-636-0375, E-mail: sackler-school@tufts.edu.

Tulane University, School of Public Health and Tropical Medicine, Department of Epidemiology, New Orleans, LA 70118-5669. Offers MPH, MS, Dr PH, PhD. MS and PhD offered through the Graduate School. *Accreditation:* CEPH (one or more programs are accredited). Part-time programs available. *Faculty:* 20 full-time (10 women), 6 part-time/adjunct (4 women). *Students:* 99 full-time (48 women), 32 part-time (14 women). *Degree requirements:* For doctorate, thesis/dissertation, comprehensive exam. *Entrance requirements:* For master's and doctorate, GRE General Test. Additional exam requirements/recommendations for international students: Required—TOEFL. *Application deadline:* For fall admission, 4/15 priority date for domestic and international students; for spring admission, 10/15 priority date for domestic and international students. Applications are processed on a rolling basis. Application fee: $40. Electronic applications accepted. *Financial support:* In 2006–07, 2 research assistantships were awarded; teaching assistantships, Federal Work-Study, scholarships/grants, and traineeships also available. Support available to part-time students. Financial award application deadline: 4/15. *Faculty research:* Environment, cancer, cardiovascular epidemiology, women's health. *Unit head:* Dr. Jiang He, Chairman, 504-988-5164, Fax: 504-988-1568, E-mail: jhe@tulane.edu. *Application contact:* Therese Carter, Program Coordinator, 504-988-6809, Fax: 504-988-1568, E-mail: tcarter1@tulane.edu.

Université Laval, Faculty of Medicine, Graduate Programs in Medicine, Department of Medicine, Programs in Epidemiology, Québec, QC G1K 7P4, Canada. Offers M Sc, PhD. Terminal master's awarded for partial completion of doctoral program. *Degree requirements:* For master's, thesis/dissertation; for doctorate, thesis/dissertation, comprehensive exam. *Entrance requirements:* For master's and doctorate, knowledge of French, comprehension of written English. Electronic applications accepted.

University at Albany, State University of New York, School of Public Health, Department of Epidemiology and Biostatistics, Albany, NY 12222-0001. Offers MS, PhD. *Students:* 27 full-time (18 women), 15 part-time (11 women). Average age 32. In 2006, 5 master's, 2 doctorates awarded. *Degree requirements:* For master's and doctorate, thesis/dissertation. *Entrance requirements:* For master's and doctorate, GRE General Test. Additional exam requirements/recommendations for international students: Required—TOEFL (minimum score 550 paper-based; 213 computer-based). *Application deadline:* For fall admission, 6/30 for domestic students, 5/1 for international students; for spring admission, 11/30 for domestic students, 11/1 for international students. Applications are processed on a rolling basis. Application fee: $75. Electronic applications accepted. *Expenses:* Tuition, state resident: full-time $6,900; part-time $288 per credit. Tuition, nonresident: full-time $10,920; part-time $455 per credit. Required fees: $1,139. *Financial support:* Application deadline: 4/1. *Unit head:* Dr. David Strogatz, Chair, 518-402-0400. *Application contact:* Nikki Malachowski, Assistant to the Chair, 518-402-0372.

University at Buffalo, the State University of New York, Graduate School, School of Public Health and Health Professions, Department of Social and Preventive Medicine, Buffalo, NY

14260. Offers community health (PhD); epidemiology (MS, PhD); public health (MPH). Part-time programs available. *Faculty:* 11 full-time (7 women), 11 part-time/adjunct (5 women). *Students:* 20 full-time (7 women), 20 part-time (13 women); includes 5 minority (2 African Americans, 3 Asian Americans or Pacific Islanders), 8 international. Average age 27. 136 applicants, 41% accepted, 25 enrolled. In 2006, 2 master's, 6 doctorates awarded. Terminal master's awarded for partial completion of doctoral program. *Median time to degree:* Of those who began their doctoral program in fall 1998, 86% received their degree in 8 years or less. *Degree requirements:* For master's and doctorate, thesis/dissertation, comprehensive exam. *Entrance requirements:* For master's and doctorate, GRE General Test. Additional exam requirements/recommendations for international students: Required—TOEFL (minimum score 600 paper-based; 250 computer-based; 100 iBT). *Application deadline:* For fall admission, 2/1 priority date for domestic and international students. Applications are processed on a rolling basis. Application fee: $50. Electronic applications accepted. *Financial support:* In 2006–07, 13 students received support, including 2 fellowships with full tuition reimbursements available (averaging $15,000 per year), 11 research assistantships with full tuition reimbursements available (averaging $15,000 per year); teaching assistantships with full tuition reimbursements available, career-related internships or fieldwork, Federal Work-Study, institutionally sponsored loans, health care benefits, and unspecified assistantships also available. Financial award application deadline: 2/1; financial award applicants required to submit FAFSA. *Faculty research:* Epidemiology of community health services including cancer and nutrition, cardiovascular disease, epidemiology of cancer, cardiovascular diseases; health services research. Total annual research expenditures: $6 million. *Unit head:* Dr. Jo Freudenheim, Chair, 716-829-2975 Ext. 612, Fax: 716-829-2979, E-mail: jfreuden@buffalo.edu. *Application contact:* Dr. Carl Li, Director of Graduate Studies, 716-829-2975 Ext. 618, Fax: 716-829-2979, E-mail: carlli@buffalo.edu.

The University of Alabama at Birmingham, School of Public Health, Department of Epidemiology, Birmingham, AL 35294. Offers PhD. *Students:* 6 full-time (3 women), 7 part-time (3 women); includes 3 minority (1 African American, 2 Asian Americans or Pacific Islanders), 2 international. 27 applicants, 19% accepted. In 2006, 1 degree awarded. *Degree requirements:* For doctorate, thesis/dissertation. *Entrance requirements:* For doctorate, GRE General Test or MAT, MPH or MSPH. *Application deadline:* Applications are processed on a rolling basis. Application fee: $35 ($60 for international students). Electronic applications accepted. *Expenses:* Tuition, state resident: part-time $170 per credit hour. Tuition, nonresident: part-time $425 per credit hour. Required fees: $15 per credit hour. $122 per term. Tuition and fees vary according to program. *Financial support:* Career-related internships or fieldwork available. *Faculty research:* Biometry. *Unit head:* Dr. Donna K. Arnett, Chair, 205-934-7066, Fax: 205-934-8665, E-mail: arnett@uab.edu. *Application contact:* Nancy O. Pinson, Coordinator of Student Admissions, 205-934-4993, Fax: 205-975-5484.

University of Alberta, School of Public Health, Department of Public Health Sciences, Edmonton, AB T6G 2E1, Canada. Offers clinical epidemiology (M Sc, MPH); environmental and occupational health (MPH); environmental health sciences (M Sc); epidemiology (M Sc); global health (M Sc, MPH); health policy and management (MPH); health policy research (M Sc); health technology assessment (MPH); occupational health (M Sc); population health (M Sc); public health leadership (MPH); public health sciences (PhD); quantitative methods (MPH). *Accreditation:* CEPH (one or more programs are accredited). *Faculty:* 24 full-time (5 women), 59 part-time/adjunct (13 women). *Students:* 49 full-time, 49 part-time. 81 applicants, 31% accepted. In 2006, 28 degrees awarded. Terminal master's awarded for partial completion of doctoral program. *Degree requirements:* For master's, thesis (for some programs); for doctorate, thesis/dissertation. *Entrance requirements:* For master's, GMAT or GRE General Test. Additional exam requirements/recommendations for international students: Required—TOEFL (paper-based 550; computer-based 213) or IELTS (paper-based 6). *Application deadline:* For fall admission, 3/15 for domestic students, 7/1 for international students; for winter admission, 11/1 for international students; for spring admission, 3/1 for international students. Applications are processed on a rolling basis. Application fee: $0. Electronic applications accepted. *Financial support:* In 2006–07, 11 students received support, including 6 research assistantships with tuition reimbursements available (averaging $2,200 per year); fellowships, teaching assistantships, career-related internships or fieldwork and tuition waivers (partial) also available. Financial award application deadline: 2/1. *Faculty research:* Biostatistics, health promotion and socio-behavioral health science. Total annual research expenditures: $5.7 million. *Unit head:* L. Duncan Saunders, Acting Chair, 780-492-6814, Fax: 780-492-0364. *Application contact:* Felicity R. Hey, Graduate Programs Administrator, 780-492-6407, Fax: 780-492-0364, E-mail: felicity.hey@ualberta.ca.

The University of British Columbia, Faculty of Medicine, Department of Health Care and Epidemiology, Vancouver, BC V6T 1W5, Canada. Offers clinical epidemiology (MH Sc); community health (MH Sc); epidemiology/clinical epidemiology (M Sc, PhD); health administration (MHA); health services research (M Sc, PhD); occupational and environmental health (M Sc, PhD); occupational health (MH Sc). *Accreditation:* CEPH (one or more programs are accredited). Part-time programs available. *Faculty:* 27 full-time (7 women). *Students:* 27 full-time (4 women), 10 part-time (2 women). Average age 31. 91 applicants, 30% accepted. In 2006, 14 master's, 1 doctorate awarded. *Degree requirements:* For master's and doctorate, thesis/dissertation. *Entrance requirements:* For master's, GRE General Test, MD or equivalent (MH Sc); for doctorate, work experience. *Application deadline:* For fall admission, 3/31 for domestic students. Applications are processed on a rolling basis. Application fee: $65. Electronic applications accepted. *Financial support:* In 2006–07, 7 students received support, including 1 fellowship; career-related internships or fieldwork also available. *Faculty research:* AIDS, public health, environmental toxicology, infectious diseases, health evaluation, epidemiology. Total annual research expenditures: $4.8 million. *Unit head:* M. T. Schechter, Head, 604-822-3910, Fax: 604-822-4994, E-mail: martin.schechter@ubc.ca. *Application contact:* Laurel Slaney, Program Assistant, 604-822-5405, Fax: 604-822-4994, E-mail: laurel.slaney@ubc.ca.

University of Calgary, Faculty of Medicine and Faculty of Graduate Studies, Department of Microbiology and Infectious Diseases, Calgary, AB T2N 1N4, Canada. Offers M Sc, PhD. *Faculty:* 21. *Students:* 21 full-time (12 women), 1 (woman) part-time. Average age 29. 25 applicants, 36% accepted. In 2006, 2 master's, 6 doctorates awarded. *Degree requirements:* For master's, thesis, oral thesis exam; for doctorate, thesis/dissertation, candidacy exam, oral thesis exam. *Entrance requirements:* For master's and doctorate, minimum GPA of 3.2. Additional exam requirements/recommendations for international students: Required—TOEFL (minimum score 580 paper-based; 237 computer-based). *Application deadline:* For fall admission, 5/15 for domestic students, 4/15 for international students; for winter admission, 9/15 for domestic students, 8/15 for international students; for spring admission, 4/15 for domestic students, 2/15 for international students. Applications are processed on a rolling basis. Application fee: $100 ($130 for international students). Electronic applications accepted. *Financial support:* In 2006–07, 7 fellowships (averaging $13,370 per year), 24 research assistantships (averaging $51,600 per year) were awarded. Financial award application deadline: 2/1. *Faculty research:* Bacteriology, virology, parasitology, immunology. Total annual research expenditures: $5.6 million. *Unit head:* Dr. Donald E. Woods, Graduate Coordinator, E-mail: midgrad@ucalgary.ca. *Application contact:* Julie Boyd, Graduate Program Administrator, 403-220-2558, Fax: 403-210-8109, E-mail: boydj@ucalgary.ca.

University of California, Berkeley, Graduate Division, School of Public Health, Division of Public Health Biology and Epidemiology, Group in Epidemiology, Berkeley, CA 94720-1500. Offers MS, PhD. *Accreditation:* CEPH. *Degree requirements:* For master's, comprehensive exam; for doctorate, thesis/dissertation, oral and written qualifying exams. *Entrance requirements:* For master's, GRE General Test, minimum GPA of 3.0; MD, DDS, DVM, or PhD in biomedical science (MPH); for doctorate, GRE General Test, minimum GPA of 3.0. *Application deadline:* For fall admission, 12/1 for domestic students. Applications are processed on a rolling basis. Application fee: $60 ($80 for international students). *Financial support:* Fellowships, research assistantships, unspecified assistantships available. *Application contact:* Ron Jeremicz, Graduate Assistant, 510-643-0881, Fax: 510-643-5163, E-mail: sphinfo@berkeley.edu.

University of California, Davis, Graduate Studies, Graduate Group in Epidemiology, Davis, CA 95616. Offers MS, PhD. Terminal master's awarded for partial completion of doctoral program. *Degree requirements:* For master's, thesis (for some programs), comprehensive exam (for some programs); for doctorate, thesis/dissertation. *Entrance requirements:* For master's and doctorate, GRE General Test, GRE Subject Test (biology), minimum GPA of 3.25. Additional exam requirements/recommendations for international students: Required—TOEFL (minimum score 550 paper-based; 213 computer-based). Electronic applications accepted. *Faculty research:* Environmental/occupational wildlife, reproductive and veterinary epidemiology, infectious/chronic disease epidemiology, public health.

University of California, Los Angeles, Graduate Division, School of Public Health, Department of Epidemiology, Los Angeles, CA 90095. Offers MS, PhD. *Degree requirements:* For master's, comprehensive exam or thesis; for doctorate, thesis/dissertation, oral and written qualifying exams. *Entrance requirements:* For master's, GRE General Test, minimum GPA of 3.0; for doctorate, GRE General Test, minimum undergraduate GPA of 3.0. Electronic applications accepted.

University of California, San Diego, Office of Graduate Studies, Program in Public Health and Epidemiology, La Jolla, CA 92093. Offers PhD. Electronic applications accepted.

University of Cincinnati, Division of Research and Advanced Studies, College of Medicine, Graduate Programs in Biomedical Sciences, Department of Environmental Health, Cincinnati, OH 45267. Offers environmental and industrial hygiene (MS, PhD); environmental and occupational medicine (MS); environmental genetics and molecular toxicology (MS, PhD); epidemiology and biostatistics (MS, PhD); occupational safety and ergonomics (MS, PhD). *Accreditation:* ABET (one or more programs are accredited). *Faculty:* 26 full-time (10 women). *Students:* 75 full-time (32 women), 59 part-time (33 women); includes 7 minority (5 African Americans, 1 American Indian/Alaska Native, 1 Asian American or Pacific Islander), 55 international. 136 applicants, 28% accepted. In 2006, 13 master's, 7 doctorates awarded. Terminal master's awarded for partial completion of doctoral program. *Median time to degree:* Master's–2.3 years full-time, 3.5 years part-time; doctorate–5.3 years full-time, 7.3 years part-time. Of those who began their doctoral program in fall 1998, 100% received their degree in 8 years or less. *Degree requirements:* For master's, thesis; for doctorate, thesis/dissertation, qualifying exam. *Entrance requirements:* For master's, GRE General Test, bachelor's degree in science; for doctorate, GRE General Test. Additional exam requirements/recommendations for international students: Required—TOEFL (minimum score 600 paper-based; 250 computer-based; 100 iBT). *Application deadline:* For fall admission, 3/1 priority date for domestic and international students. Applications are processed on a rolling basis. Application fee: $40. Electronic applications accepted. *Financial support:* In 2006–07, 69 students received support, including research assistantships with full tuition reimbursements available (averaging $17,850 per year); career-related internships or fieldwork, scholarships/grants, traineeships, tuition waivers (partial), and unspecified assistantships also available. Financial award application deadline: 5/1. *Faculty research:* Carcinogens and mutagenesis, pulmonary studies, reproduction and development. Total annual research expenditures: $16.9 million. *Unit head:* Dr. Shuk-Mei Ho, Chairman, 513-558-5701, Fax: 513-558-4397, E-mail: hosm@ucmail.uc.edu. *Application contact:* Stephanie W. Starkey, Graduate Program Coordinator, 513-558-5704, Fax: 513-558-5457, E-mail: stephanie.starkey@uc.edu.

University of Colorado at Denver and Health Sciences Center, Graduate School, Department of Preventive Medicine and Biometrics, Program in Epidemiology, Denver, CO 80217-3364. Offers analytic health sciences (PhD). *Degree requirements:* For doctorate, thesis/dissertation, comprehensive exam. *Entrance requirements:* For doctorate, GRE, minimum GPA of 3.0, 2 semesters of course work in calculus, 1 semester of organic chemistry, 4 letters of reference. Additional exam requirements/recommendations for international students: Required—TOEFL (minimum score 550 paper-based; 213 computer-based). *Application deadline:* For fall admission, 2/1 for domestic students. Application fee: $50. *Financial support:* Application deadline: 3/15; *Faculty research:* Cancer prevention by nutrition, cancer survivorship outcomes, social and cultural factors related to health. *Unit head:* Dr. John Hokansan, Director, 303-315-0862, E-mail: john.hokansan@uchsc.edu. *Application contact:* Fayette Augillard, Program Coordinator, 303-315-7605, Fax: 303-315-1010, E-mail: fayette.augillard@uchsc.edu.

University of Florida, College of Medicine, Program in Clinical Investigation, Gainesville, FL 32611. Offers clinical investigation (MS); epidemiology (MS); public health (MPH). Part-time programs available. *Faculty:* 40. In 2006, 2 degrees awarded. *Entrance requirements:* For master's, GRE, MD, PhD, DMD/DDS or Pharm D. *Application deadline:* For fall admission, 2/15 priority date for domestic students. Applications are processed on a rolling basis. Application fee: $30. *Expenses:* Tuition, state resident: full-time $6,827. Tuition, nonresident: full-time $21,951. Required fees: $999. *Unit head:* Dr. Marian Limacher, Director, 352-846-1228, E-mail: limacmc@medicine.ufl.edu. *Application contact:* Eve Johnson, Program Assistant, 352-846-1228, Fax: 352-846-1217, E-mail: eve11@ufl.edu.

University of Florida, Graduate School, College of Public Health and Health Professions and College of Medicine, Programs in Public Health, Gainesville, FL 32611. Offers biostatistics (MPH); environmental health (MPH); epidemiology (MPH); public health management and policy (MPH); public health practice (MPH); social and behavioral sciences (MPH). *Faculty:* 10. *Entrance requirements:* For master's, GRE General Test, minimum GPA of 3.0. Additional exam requirements/recommendations for international students: Required—TOEFL (minimum score 550 paper-based; 213 computer-based). Application fee: $30. *Expenses:* Tuition, state resident: full-time $6,827. Tuition, nonresident: full-time $21,951. Required fees: $999. *Unit head:* Dr. Mary Peoples-Sheps, Associate Dean for Academic Affairs, 352-273-6084, Fax: 352-273-6448, E-mail: mpeoplessheps@phhp.ufl.edu. *Application contact:* Brigette Hart, Program Assistant, 352-273-6443, E-mail: bhart@phhp.ufl.edu.

University of Guelph, Ontario Veterinary College and Graduate Program Services, Graduate Programs in Veterinary Sciences, Department of Population Medicine, Guelph, ON N1G 2W1, Canada. Offers epidemiology (M Sc, DV Sc, PhD); health management (M Sc, DV Sc); population medicine (Diploma); theriogenology (M Sc, DV Sc). *Degree requirements:* For master's, thesis/dissertation; for doctorate, thesis/dissertation, comprehensive exam. *Entrance requirements:* Additional exam requirements/recommendations for international students: Required—TOEFL.

University of Hawaii at Manoa, John A. Burns School of Medicine, Department of Public Health Sciences and Epidemiology, Program in Epidemiology, Honolulu, HI 96822. Offers PhD. *Faculty:* 22 full-time (8 women), 1 part-time/adjunct (0 women). *Students:* 4 full-time (3 women), 1 (woman) part-time; includes 1 minority (Asian American or Pacific Islander), 2 international. 6 applicants, 33% accepted, 1 enrolled. *Degree requirements:* For doctorate, thesis/dissertation, comprehensive exam. *Entrance requirements:* For doctorate, GRE General Test. Additional exam requirements/recommendations for international students: Required—TOEFL (minimum score 600 paper-based; 250 computer-based; 100 iBT). *Application deadline:* For fall admission, 3/1 for domestic and international students; for spring admission, 9/1 for domestic and international students. Application fee: $50. *Financial support:* In 2006–07, 2 research assistantships (averaging $17,160 per year) were awarded. *Application contact:* F. DeWolfe Miller, Information Contact, 808-692-1605, Fax: 808-692-1979.

University of Illinois at Chicago, Graduate College, School of Public Health, Program in Epidemiology, Chicago, IL 60607-7128. Offers MPH, MS, Dr PH, PhD. *Accreditation:* CEPH (one or more programs are accredited). Part-time programs available. Terminal master's awarded for partial completion of doctoral program. *Degree requirements:* For master's, thesis, field practicum; for doctorate, thesis/dissertation, independent research, internship. *Entrance requirements:* For master's and doctorate, GRE General Test, minimum GPA of 2.75. Additional exam requirements/recommendations for international students: Required—TOEFL. Electronic applications accepted.

Epidemiology

The University of Iowa, Graduate College, College of Public Health, Department of Epidemiology, Iowa City, IA 52242-1316. Offers clinical investigation (MS); epidemiology (MS, PhD). *Faculty:* 12 full-time, 16 part-time/adjunct. *Students:* 18 full-time (13 women), 33 part-time (19 women); includes 7 minority (1 African American, 5 Asian Americans or Pacific Islanders, 1 Hispanic American), 8 international. 32 applicants, 38% accepted, 5 enrolled. In 2006, 17 master's, 2 doctorates awarded. *Degree requirements:* For master's, exam, thesis optional; for doctorate, thesis/dissertation, comprehensive exam, registration. *Entrance requirements:* For master's and doctorate, GRE General Test, minimum GPA of 3.0. Additional exam requirements/recommendations for international students: Required—TOEFL (minimum score 550 paper-based; 213 computer-based; 81 iBT). *Application deadline:* Applications are processed on a rolling basis. Application fee: $60 ($85 for international students). Electronic applications accepted. *Financial support:* In 2006–07, 19 research assistantships with partial tuition reimbursements, 4 teaching assistantships with partial tuition reimbursements were awarded; fellowships also available. Financial award applicants required to submit FAFSA. *Unit head:* Dr. James C. Torner, Head, 319-384-5001, Fax: 319-384-5004.

University of Maryland, Baltimore, Graduate School, Graduate Programs in Pharmacy, Department of Pharmaceutical Health Service Research, Baltimore, MD 21201. Offers epidemiology (MS); pharmacy administration (PhD); Pharm D/PhD. Part-time programs available. *Faculty:* 14 full-time (8 women). *Students:* 21 full-time (10 women), 5 part-time (1 woman); includes 3 minority (2 African Americans, 1 Hispanic American), 20 international. Average age 26. 39 applicants, 15% accepted, 5 enrolled. In 2006, 2 degrees awarded. *Degree requirements:* For doctorate, thesis/dissertation, comprehensive exam. *Entrance requirements:* For doctorate, GRE General Test. Additional exam requirements/recommendations for international students: Required—TOEFL (minimum score 550 paper-based; 215 computer-based), IELTS. *Application deadline:* For fall admission, 7/1 for domestic students, 1/15 for international students; for winter admission, 12/1 for domestic students, 5/1 for international students. Applications are processed on a rolling basis. Application fee: $125. *Financial support:* In 2006–07, 1 fellowship with tuition reimbursement (averaging $20,000 per year), 4 research assistantships with full tuition reimbursements (averaging $21,772 per year), 4 teaching assistantships with full tuition reimbursements (averaging $21,772 per year) were awarded; career-related internships or fieldwork, scholarships/grants, traineeships, and unspecified assistantships also available. Financial award application deadline: 2/15; financial award applicants required to submit FAFSA. *Faculty research:* Pharmacoeconomics, outcomes research, public health policy, drug therapy and aging. Total annual research expenditures: $1.5 million. *Unit head:* Diane Kaufman, Administrative Director, 410-706-3555, E-mail: dkaufman@rx.umaryland.edu. *Application contact:* Tracie Jones, Graduate Coordinator, 410-706-7613, Fax: 410-706-5394, E-mail: tjones@umaryland.edu.

University of Maryland, Baltimore, School of Medicine, Department of Epidemiology and Preventive Medicine, Baltimore, MD 21201. Offers biostatistics (MS); clinical research (MS); epidemiology (MS, PhD); gerontology (PhD); molecular epidemiology (PhD); toxicology (MS, PhD); MD/MS; MD/PhD. Part-time programs available. *Degree requirements:* For doctorate, one foreign language, thesis/dissertation, qualifying exam. *Entrance requirements:* For master's and doctorate, GRE General Test, minimum GPA of 3.0. Additional exam requirements/recommendations for international students: Required—TOEFL; Recommended—IELTS. Electronic applications accepted. *Faculty research:* Chronic and infectious disease epidemiology, environmental and occupational health, biostatistics, gerontology.

University of Maryland, Baltimore County, Graduate School, College of Arts, Humanities and Social Sciences, Department of Emergency Health Services, Baltimore, MD 21250. Offers administration, planning, and policy (MS); education (MS); emergency health services (MS); preventive medicine and epidemiology (MS). Part-time and evening/weekend programs available. Postbaccalaureate distance learning degree programs offered (no on-campus study). *Faculty:* 4 full-time (0 women), 7 part-time/adjunct (1 woman). *Students:* 3 full-time (2 women), 32 part-time (12 women); includes 3 African Americans, 1 American Indian/Alaska Native, 3 Hispanic Americans. Average age 33. 22 applicants, 59% accepted, 11 enrolled. In 2006, 9 degrees awarded. *Median time to degree:* Master's–2.3 years full-time, 5 years part-time. *Degree requirements:* For master's, thesis (for some programs), comprehensive exam. *Entrance requirements:* For master's, GRE General Test, minimum GPA of 3.0. Additional exam requirements/recommendations for international students: Required—TOEFL (minimum score 550 paper-based; 213 computer-based; 80 iBT). *Application deadline:* For fall admission, 7/1 for domestic students. Applications are processed on a rolling basis. Application fee: $45. *Expenses:* Tuition, state resident: part-time $412 per credit hour. Tuition, nonresident: part-time $681 per credit hour. Required fees: $91 per credit hour. One-time fee: $75 part-time. *Financial support:* In 2006–07, fellowships with tuition reimbursements (averaging $55,000 per year), research assistantships with tuition reimbursements (averaging $21,000 per year) were awarded; teaching assistantships, career-related internships or fieldwork, Federal Work-Study, health care benefits, and unspecified assistantships also available. Financial award application deadline: 5/30; financial award applicants required to submit FAFSA. *Faculty research:* EMS management, disaster health services, emergency management. Total annual research expenditures: $500,000. *Unit head:* Dr. Bruce Walz, Chairman, 410-455-3223. *Application contact:* Dr. Rick Bissell, Program Director, 410-455-3776, Fax: 410-455-3045, E-mail: bissell@umbc.edu.

University of Massachusetts Lowell, Graduate School, James B. Francis College of Engineering, Department of Work Environment, Lowell, MA 01854-2881. Offers cleaner production and pollution prevention (MS, Sc D); environmental risk assessment (Certificate); identification and control of ergonomic hazards (Certificate); industrial hygiene (MS, Sc D); job stress and healthy job redesign (Certificate); occupational epidemiology (MS, Sc D); occupational ergonomics (MS, Sc D); radiological health physics and general work environment protection (Certificate); work environmental policy (MS, Sc D). *Accreditation:* ABET (one or more programs are accredited). Part-time programs available. Terminal master's awarded for partial completion of doctoral program. *Degree requirements:* For master's, thesis optional; for doctorate, thesis/dissertation. *Entrance requirements:* For master's and doctorate, GRE General Test. Additional exam requirements/recommendations for international students: Required—TOEFL. *Faculty research:* Ergonomics, industrial hygiene, epidemiology, work environment policy, pollution prevention.

University of Massachusetts Worcester, Graduate School of Biomedical Sciences, Program in Clinical and Population Health Research, Worcester, MA 01655-0115. Offers PhD. *Faculty:* 46 full-time (18 women). *Entrance requirements:* For doctorate, GRE General Test, master's degree in public health, clinical research, or in one of the social, psychological, physical, or biological sciences, with adequate introductory course work in biostatistics and epidemiology; 3 letters of recommendation. *Application deadline:* For fall admission, 1/15 for domestic students. Application fee: $25 ($50 for international students). *Expenses:* Tuition, state resident: full-time $2,640. Tuition, nonresident: full-time $9,856. Required fees: $3,942. *Financial support:* All full-time graduate students received annual stipend support ($25,740) for the duration of their study available. *Unit head:* Dr. Carole Upshur, Associate Dean, 508-334-7267. *Application contact:* Colleen Corey, Program Coordinator, 508-334-2112.

See Close-Up on page 1821.

University of Medicine and Dentistry of New Jersey, UMDNJ–School of Public Health (UMDNJ, Rutgers, NJIT) Piscataway/New Brunswick Campus, Piscataway, NJ 08854. Offers biostatistics (MS); epidemiology (Certificate); general public health (Certificate); public health (MPH, Dr PH, PhD); DO/MPH; MD/MPH; MPH/MBA; MPH/MSPA; Psy D/MPH. *Degree requirements:* For master's, internship; for doctorate, thesis/dissertation. *Entrance requirements:* For master's, GRE General Test; for doctorate, GRE General Test, MPH (Dr PH); MA, MPH, or MS (PhD). Additional exam requirements/recommendations for international students: Required—TOEFL. *Application deadline:* For fall admission, 4/1 for domestic students; for spring admission, 10/1 for domestic students. Application fee: $95. Electronic applications accepted. *Unit head:* Janet Zamorski, 732-235-4646, Fax: 732-235-5476, E-mail: zamorsja@umdnj.edu. *Application contact:* Dr. Mark G. Robson, Assistant Dean, 732-235-4646, Fax: 732-235-5476, E-mail: robson@eohsi.rutgers.edu.

See Close-Up on page 2057.

University of Miami, Graduate School, Miller School of Medicine, Graduate Programs in Medicine, Department of Epidemiology and Public Health, Teaching Programs in Epidemiology, Coral Gables, FL 33124. Offers PhD, MD/PhD. *Faculty:* 18 full-time (8 women), 8 part-time/adjunct (5 women). *Students:* 10 full-time (6 women), 2 part-time (1 woman); includes 3 minority (2 African Americans, 1 Hispanic American), 2 international. Average age 31. 31 applicants, 13% accepted, 4 enrolled. In 2006, 3 degrees awarded. *Median time to degree:* Of those who began their doctoral program in fall 1998, 100% received their degree in 8 years or less. *Degree requirements:* For doctorate, thesis/dissertation, comprehensive exam, registration. *Entrance requirements:* For doctorate, GRE General Test, minimum GPA of 3.0, course work in epidemiology and statistics, 3 letters of recommendation. Additional exam requirements/recommendations for international students: Required—TOEFL (minimum score 550 paper-based; 213 computer-based). *Application deadline:* For fall admission, 1/31 for domestic students, 12/31 priority date for international students. Applications are processed on a rolling basis. Application fee: $50. Electronic applications accepted. *Financial support:* Teaching assistantships, career-related internships or fieldwork, Federal Work-Study, institutionally sponsored loans, and tuition waivers (full) available. Financial award application deadline: 2/1. *Faculty research:* Behavioral epidemiology, substance abuse, AIDS, cardiovascular diseases, cancer epidemiology. *Unit head:* Dr. James D. Wilkinson, Director, Teaching Programs, 305-243-3022, Fax: 305-243-3384, E-mail: jwilkins@med.miami.edu. *Application contact:* Heather Mc Anany, Administrator, 305-243-2209, Fax: 305-243-3384, E-mail: hmcanany@med.miami.edu.

See Close-Up on page 2059.

University of Michigan, School of Public Health, Department of Epidemiology, Ann Arbor, MI 48109. Offers dental public health (MPH); epidemiological science (PhD); epidemiology (MPH, Dr PH); hospital and molecular epidemiology (MPH); international health (MPH). PhD offered through the Horace H. Rackham School of Graduate Studies. *Accreditation:* CEPH (one or more programs are accredited). Terminal master's awarded for partial completion of doctoral program. *Entrance requirements:* For master's and doctorate, GRE General Test, MCAT. Additional exam requirements/recommendations for international students: Required—TOEFL (minimum score 560 paper-based; 220 computer-based). Electronic applications accepted. *Faculty research:* Molecular virology, infectious diseases, women's health, genetics, social epidemiology.

University of Minnesota, Twin Cities Campus, School of Public Health, Division of Environmental Health Sciences, Area in Environmental and Occupational Epidemiology, Minneapolis, MN 55455-0213. Offers MPH, MS, PhD. *Accreditation:* CEPH (one or more programs are accredited). *Degree requirements:* For doctorate, thesis/dissertation. *Entrance requirements:* For master's and doctorate, GRE General Test. *Expenses:* Tuition, state resident: full-time $9,302; part-time $775 per credit. Tuition, nonresident: full-time $16,400; part-time $1,367 per credit. Full-time tuition and fees vary according to class time, course load, program, reciprocity agreements and student level.

University of Minnesota, Twin Cities Campus, School of Public Health, Major in Epidemiology, Minneapolis, MN 55455-0213. Offers MPH, PhD. *Accreditation:* CEPH (one or more programs are accredited). Part-time programs available. Terminal master's awarded for partial completion of doctoral program. *Degree requirements:* For master's, fieldwork, master's project; for doctorate, thesis/dissertation, comprehensive exam. *Entrance requirements:* For master's, GRE General Test; for doctorate, GRE General Test, master's degree in related field. Additional exam requirements/recommendations for international students: Required—TOEFL. Electronic applications accepted. Expenses: Contact institution. Full-time tuition and fees vary according to class time, course load, program, reciprocity agreements and student level. *Faculty research:* Prevention of cardiovascular disease, nutrition, genetic epidemiology, behavioral interventions, research methods.

The University of North Carolina at Chapel Hill, Graduate School, School of Public Health, Department of Epidemiology, Chapel Hill, NC 27599. Offers MPH, MSPH, PhD. *Accreditation:* CEPH (one or more programs are accredited). *Faculty:* 46 full-time (27 women), 94 part-time/adjunct. *Students:* 162 full-time (124 women); includes 35 minority (13 African Americans, 1 American Indian/Alaska Native, 18 Asian Americans or Pacific Islanders, 3 Hispanic Americans), 20 international. Average age 28. 259 applicants, 32% accepted, 42 enrolled. In 2006, 23 master's, 25 doctorates awarded. Terminal master's awarded for partial completion of doctoral program. *Median time to degree:* Of those who began their doctoral program in fall 1998, 100% received their degree in 8 years or less. *Degree requirements:* For master's, major paper; for doctorate, thesis/dissertation, comprehensive exam, registration. *Entrance requirements:* For master's and doctorate, GRE General Test, minimum GPA of 3.0. Additional exam requirements/recommendations for international students: Required—TOEFL. *Application deadline:* For fall admission, 1/1 priority date for domestic and international students. Applications are processed on a rolling basis. Application fee: $70. Electronic applications accepted. *Financial support:* In 2006–07, 4 fellowships with partial tuition reimbursements, 44 research assistantships with partial tuition reimbursements (averaging $11,103 per year), 13 teaching assistantships with partial tuition reimbursements (averaging $8,364 per year) were awarded; career-related internships or fieldwork, Federal Work-Study, institutionally sponsored loans, scholarships/grants, traineeships, and health care benefits also available. Support available to part-time students. Financial award application deadline: 1/1; financial award applicants required to submit FAFSA. *Faculty research:* Chronic disease: cancer, cardiovascular, nutritional; environmental/occupational injury; infectious diseases; reproductive diseases; healthcare. *Unit head:* Dr. Andrew Olshan, Interim Chair, 919-966-7458, Fax: 919-966-2089, E-mail: andy_olshan@unc.edu. *Application contact:* Carmen Woody, Registrar, 919-966-7458, Fax: 919-966-2089, E-mail: carmen_woody@unc.edu.

University of North Texas Health Science Center at Fort Worth, School of Public Health, Fort Worth, TX 76107-2699. Offers biostatistics (MPH); community health (MPH); disease control and prevention (Dr PH); environmental health (MPH); epidemiology (MPH); health behavior (MPH); health policy and management (MPH, Dr PH); DO/MPH; MA/MPH; MS/MPH; PhD/MPH. *Accreditation:* CEPH. Part-time and evening/weekend programs available. *Degree requirements:* For master's, thesis or alternative, supervised internship; for doctorate, thesis/dissertation, supervised internship. *Entrance requirements:* For master's, GRE General Test. Additional exam requirements/recommendations for international students: Required—TOEFL. Electronic applications accepted.

University of Oklahoma Health Sciences Center, Graduate College, College of Public Health, Program in Biostatistics and Epidemiology, Oklahoma City, OK 73190. Offers biostatistics (MPH, MS, Dr PH, PhD); epidemiology (MPH, MS, Dr PH, PhD). *Accreditation:* CEPH (one or more programs are accredited). Part-time programs available. *Degree requirements:* For master's, thesis (for some programs), comprehensive exam; for doctorate, thesis/dissertation, comprehensive exam. *Entrance requirements:* For master's, 3 letters of recommendation, resumé; for doctorate, GRE General Test, letters of recommendation. Additional exam requirements/recommendations for international students: Required—TOEFL (minimum score 570 paper-based; 230 computer-based), TWE. *Faculty research:* Statistical methodology, applied statistics, acute and chronic disease epidemiology.

University of Ottawa, Faculty of Graduate and Postdoctoral Studies, Faculty of Medicine, Department of Epidemiology and Community Medicine, Ottawa, ON K1N 6N5, Canada. Offers epidemiology (M Sc), including health technology assessment. *Degree requirements:* For master's, thesis. *Entrance requirements:* For master's, honors degree or equivalent, minimum B average. Electronic applications accepted. *Faculty research:* Epidemiologic concepts and methods, health technology assessment.

University of Pennsylvania, School of Medicine, Center for Clinical Epidemiology and Bio-statistics, Philadelphia, PA 19104. Offers clinical epidemiology (MSCE); epidemiology (PhD). PhD offered through the School of Arts and Sciences. *Accreditation:* CEPH. Part-time programs available. *Faculty:* 64 full-time (27 women), 117 part-time/adjunct (39 women). *Students:* 70 full-time (40 women), 42 part-time (22 women); includes 31 minority (6 African Americans, 22 Asian Americans or Pacific Islanders, 3 Hispanic Americans). Average age 30. 56 applicants, 88% accepted, 41 enrolled. In 2006, 27 degrees awarded. *Median time to degree:* Master's–3 years full-time, 4 years part-time. *Degree requirements:* For master's, thesis, comprehensive exam; for doctorate, thesis/dissertation, qualifying exam, preliminary exam. *Entrance requirements:* For master's and doctorate, GRE General Test or MCAT, advanced degree, clinical experience. Additional exam requirements/recommendations for international students: Required—TOEFL. *Application deadline:* For fall admission, 1/15 priority date for domestic and international students. Applications are processed on a rolling basis. *Expenses: Contact institution. Financial support:* In 2006–07, 65 students received support, including 60 fellowships with full and partial tuition reimbursements available (averaging $40,000 per year); career-related internships or fieldwork, scholarships/grants, health care benefits, unspecified assistantships, and faculty/staff benefits for partial tuition coverage also available. Financial award application deadline: 1/15. *Faculty research:* Health services research, pharmacoepidemiology, women's health, cancer epidemiology, genetic epidemiology. Total annual research expenditures: $22.3 million. *Unit head:* Dr. Harold I. Feldman, Director, 215-573-2382, Fax: 215-573-2265, E-mail: hfeldman@mail.med.upenn.edu. *Application contact:* Shanta C. Layton, Associate Director for Graduate Training in Epidemiology, 215-573-2382, Fax: 215-573-5315, E-mail: shanta2@mail.med.upenn.edu.

University of Pittsburgh, Graduate School of Public Health, Department of Epidemiology, Pittsburgh, PA 15260. Offers MPH, MS, Dr PH, PhD, MD/PhD. *Accreditation:* CEPH (one or more programs are accredited). Part-time programs available. *Faculty:* 42 full-time (24 women), 42 part-time/adjunct (16 women). *Students:* 106 full-time (78 women), 36 part-time (31 women); includes 31 minority (19 African Americans, 8 Asian Americans or Pacific Islanders, 4 Hispanic Americans), 29 international. Average age 30. 230 applicants, 63% accepted, 43 enrolled. In 2006, 18 master's, 12 doctorates awarded. Terminal master's awarded for partial completion of doctoral program. *Degree requirements:* For master's, thesis, comprehensive exam (for some programs); registration; for doctorate, one foreign language, thesis/dissertation, teaching practicum, comprehensive exam, registration. *Entrance requirements:* For master's, DCAT, GRE General Test, MCAT, 3 credits of course work in biology and mathematics, 6 credits of course work in behavioral science, minimum QPA of 3.0; for doctorate, DCAT, GRE General Test, MCAT, 3 credits of course work in biology and math, 6 credits of course work in behavioral science, minimum QPA of 3.0. Additional exam requirements/recommendations for international students: Required—TOEFL (minimum score 550 paper-based; 213 computer-based; 80 iBT). *Application deadline:* For fall admission, 2/1 priority date for domestic and international students; for winter admission, 2/1 priority date for domestic students, 9/1 priority date for international students; for spring admission, 1/1 priority date for international students. Applications are processed on a rolling basis. Application fee: $50 ($60 for international students). Electronic applications accepted. *Financial support:* In 2006–07, 9 fellowships with full tuition reimbursements (averaging $21,840 per year), 38 research assistantships with full tuition reimbursements were awarded; career-related internships or fieldwork, scholarships/grants, and traineeships also available. Support available to part-time students. Financial award applicants required to submit FAFSA. *Faculty research:* Aging, cardiovascular, clinical trials, psychiatric, women's health, molecular. Total annual research expenditures: $36.9 million. *Unit head:* Dr. Roberta B. Ness, Chairman, 412-624-3056, Fax: 412-624-3737, E-mail: repro@pitt.edu. *Application contact:* Lori S. Smith, Student Services Coordinator, 412-383-5269, E-mail: smithl@edc.pitt.edu.

See Close-Up on page 2061.

University of Prince Edward Island, Atlantic Veterinary College, Graduate Program in Veterinary Medicine, Charlottetown, PE C1A 4P3, Canada. Offers anatomy (M Sc, PhD); bacteriology (M Sc, PhD); clinical pharmacology (M Sc, PhD); clinical sciences (M Sc, PhD); epidemiology (M Sc, PhD), including reproduction; fish health (M Sc, PhD); food animal nutrition (M Sc, PhD); immunology (M Sc, PhD); microanatomy (M Sc, PhD); parasitology (M Sc, PhD); pathology (M Sc, PhD); pharmacology (M Sc, PhD); physiology (M Sc, PhD); toxicology (M Sc, PhD); veterinary science (M Vet Sc); virology (M Sc, PhD). Part-time programs available. *Faculty:* 76 full-time (25 women), 49 part-time/adjunct (8 women). *Students:* 55 full-time (28 women), 5 part-time (all women). Average age 30. 37 applicants, 51% accepted, 18 enrolled. In 2006, 5 master's, 7 doctorates awarded. *Degree requirements:* For master's and doctorate, thesis/dissertation. *Entrance requirements:* For master's, DVM, B Sc honors degree, or equivalent; for doctorate, M Sc. Additional exam requirements/recommendations for international students: Required—TOEFL (minimum score 550 paper-based; 213 computer-based; 80 iBT). *Application deadline:* Applications are processed on a rolling basis. Application fee: $75 ($100 for international students). *Expenses: Contact institution. Financial support:* In 2006–07, 4 fellowships (averaging $25,000 Canadian dollars per year), 4 research assistantships (averaging $16,500 Canadian dollars per year) were awarded; career-related internships or fieldwork also available. *Faculty research:* Animal health management, infectious diseases, fin fish and shellfish health, basic biomedical sciences, ecosystem health. Total annual research expenditures: $1.2 million Canadian dollars. *Unit head:* Dr. James Bellamy, Associate Dean of Graduate Studies and Research, 902-566-0856, E-mail: bellamy@upei.ca. *Application contact:* Jack MacDougall, Registrar's Office, 902-566-0781, Fax: 902-566-0795, E-mail: registrar@upei.ca.

University of Puerto Rico, Medical Sciences Campus, Graduate School of Public Health, Department of Biostatistics and Epidemiology, Program in Epidemiology, San Juan, PR 00936-5067. Offers MPH, MS. *Accreditation:* CEPH (one or more programs are accredited). Part-time programs available. *Students:* 38 (31 women). 40 applicants, 68% accepted. In 2006, 16 degrees awarded. *Entrance requirements:* For master's, GRE, previous course work in biology, chemistry, physics, mathematics, and social sciences. *Application deadline:* For fall admission, 3/15 for domestic students. Application fee: $20. *Expenses: Contact institution. Financial support:* Research assistantships, teaching assistantships, Federal Work-Study and institutionally sponsored loans available. Financial award application deadline: 4/30. *Unit head:* Dr. Cynthia Perez-Cardona, Coordinator, 787-758-2525 Ext. 1400, E-mail: cperez@rcm.upr.edu. *Application contact:* Prof. Mayra E. Santiago-Vargas, Counselor, 787-756-5244, Fax: 787-759-6719, E-mail: msantiago@rcm.upr.edu.

University of Rochester, School of Medicine and Dentistry, Graduate Programs in Medicine and Dentistry, Department of Community and Preventive Medicine, Program in Epidemiology, Rochester, NY 14627-0250. Offers MS, PhD. *Degree requirements:* For doctorate, thesis/dissertation, qualifying exam. *Entrance requirements:* For doctorate, GRE General Test.

University of Saskatchewan, College of Medicine, Department of Community Health and Epidemiology, Saskatoon, SK S7N 5A2, Canada. Offers M Sc, PhD. *Faculty:* 14. *Students:* 41; includes 3 minority (all American Indian/Alaska Native). *Degree requirements:* For master's, thesis/dissertation, registration; for doctorate, thesis/dissertation. *Entrance requirements:* Additional exam requirements/recommendations for international students: Required—TOEFL. *Application deadline:* For fall admission, 7/1 priority date for domestic students. Applications are processed on a rolling basis. Application fee: $50. *Financial support:* Fellowships, research assistantships, teaching assistantships available. Financial award application deadline: 3/31. *Unit head:* Dr. Nazeem Muhajarine, Graduate Chair, 306-966-7945, Fax: 306-966-7920, E-mail: nazeem.muhajarine@usask.ca. *Application contact:* Dr. S. Abonyi, Graduate Chair, 306-966-2194, Fax: 306-966-7920, E-mail: sylvia.abonyi@usask.ca.

University of South Carolina, The Graduate School, Arnold School of Public Health, Department of Epidemiology/Biostatistics, Program in Epidemiology, Columbia, SC 29208. Offers MPH, MSPH, Dr PH, PhD. *Accreditation:* CEPH (one or more programs are accredited). Part-time programs available. *Degree requirements:* For master's, thesis (for some programs),

practicum (MPH), comprehensive exam; for doctorate, thesis/dissertation, comprehensive exam. *Entrance requirements:* For master's and doctorate, GRE General Test. Additional exam requirements/recommendations for international students: Required—TOEFL (minimum score 570 paper-based; 230 computer-based). Electronic applications accepted. *Faculty research:* Cancer epidemiology, infectious disease epidemiology, mental health epidemiology, health effects of physical activity.

University of Southern California, Keck School of Medicine and Graduate School, Graduate Programs in Medicine, Department of Preventive Medicine, Division of Biostatistics, Los Angeles, CA 90089. Offers applied biostatistics/epidemiology (MS); biostatistics (MS, PhD); epidemiology (PhD); genetic epidemiology and statistical genetics (PhD); molecular epidemiology (MS, PhD). *Faculty:* 74 full-time (33 women). *Students:* 102 full-time (65 women); includes 32 minority (24 Asian Americans or Pacific Islanders, 8 Hispanic Americans), 47 international. Average age 30. 85 applicants, 68% accepted, 31 enrolled. In 2006, 14 master's, 4 doctorates awarded. Terminal master's awarded for partial completion of doctoral program. *Median time to degree:* Of those who began their doctoral program in fall 1998, 100% received their degree in 8 years or less. *Degree requirements:* For master's and doctorate, thesis/dissertation. *Entrance requirements:* For master's, GRE General Test, GRE Subject Test, minimum GPA of 3.0; for doctorate, GRE General Test, GRE Subject Test, minimum GPA of 3.5. Additional exam requirements/recommendations for international students: Required—TOEFL (minimum score 580 paper-based; 243 computer-based; 93 iBT). *Application deadline:* For fall admission, 1/15 priority date for domestic students. Applications are processed on a rolling basis. Application fee: $65 ($75 for international students). Electronic applications accepted. *Expenses:* Tuition: Full-time $33,314; part-time $1,121 per credit. Required fees: $522. Full-time tuition and fees vary according to program. *Financial support:* In 2006–07, 3 fellowships with tuition reimbursements (averaging $27,530 per year), 47 research assistantships with tuition reimbursements (averaging $27,530 per year), 16 teaching assistantships with tuition reimbursements (averaging $27,530 per year) were awarded; career-related internships or fieldwork, Federal Work-Study, institutionally sponsored loans, scholarships/grants, and tuition waivers (partial) also available. Financial award application deadline: 4/1. *Faculty research:* Clinical trials in ophthalmology and cancer research, methods of analysis for epidemiological studies, genetic epidemiology. Total annual research expenditures: $1.3 million. *Unit head:* Dr. Stanley P. Azen, Co-Director, 323-442-1810, Fax: 323-442-2993, E-mail: mtrujill@usc.edu. *Application contact:* Mary L. Trujillo, Student Adviser, 323-442-1810, Fax: 323-442-2993, E-mail: mtrujill@usc.edu.

University of Southern California, Keck School of Medicine and Graduate School, Graduate Programs in Medicine, Department of Preventive Medicine, Master of Public Health Program, Los Angeles, CA 90089. Offers biometry/epidemiology (MPH); health communication (MPH); health promotion (MPH); preventive nutrition (MPH). *Accreditation:* CEPH. Part-time programs available. *Faculty:* 22 full-time (12 women), 3 part-time/adjunct (0 women). *Students:* 148 full-time (118 women), 7 part-time (6 women); includes 77 minority (17 African Americans, 45 Asian Americans or Pacific Islanders, 15 Hispanic Americans), 24 international. Average age 26. 310 applicants, 66% accepted, 85 enrolled. In 2006, 53 degrees awarded. *Degree requirements:* For master's, practicum, final report, oral presentation. *Entrance requirements:* For master's, GRE General Test, MCAT, GMAT, DAT, minimum GPA of 3.0. Additional exam requirements/recommendations for international students: Required—TOEFL (minimum score 600 paper-based; 250 computer-based; 100 iBT). *Application deadline:* For fall admission, 6/1 priority date for domestic and international students; for spring admission, 11/15 priority date for domestic students, 10/1 priority date for international students. Applications are processed on a rolling basis. Application fee: $85. Electronic applications accepted. *Expenses:* Tuition: Full-time $33,314; part-time $1,121 per credit. Required fees: $522. Full-time tuition and fees vary according to program. *Financial support:* In 2006–07, 131 students received support, including 11 research assistantships with full tuition reimbursements available (averaging $11,109 per year), 18 teaching assistantships with partial tuition reimbursements available (averaging $11,109 per year); career-related internships or fieldwork, Federal Work-Study, institutionally sponsored loans, scholarships/grants, health care benefits, unspecified assistantships, and staff tuition remission also available. Support available to part-time students. Financial award application deadline: 5/1; financial award applicants required to submit CSS PROFILE or FAFSA. *Faculty research:* Substance abuse prevention, cancer and heart disease prevention, mass media and health communication research, health promotion, treatment compliance. Total annual research expenditures: $93.8 million. *Unit head:* Dr. Thomas W. Valente, Director, 626-457-6678, Fax: 626-457-6699, E-mail: tvalente@usc.edu. *Application contact:* Nemesia P. Kelly, Program Specialist, 626-457-6603, Fax: 626-457-6699, E-mail: nkelly@usc.edu.

See Close-Up on page 2065.

University of Southern Mississippi, Graduate School, College of Health, Department of Community Health Sciences, Hattiesburg, MS 39406-0001. Offers epidemiology and biostatistics (MPH); health education (MPH); health policy/administration (MPH); occupational/environmental health (MPH); public health nutrition (MPH). *Accreditation:* CEPH. Part-time and evening/weekend programs available. *Faculty:* 10 full-time (3 women). *Students:* 53 full-time (32 women), 13 part-time (10 women); includes 25 minority (24 African Americans, 1 Asian American or Pacific Islander), 15 international. Average age 30. 114 applicants, 84% accepted, 35 enrolled. In 2006, 27 degrees awarded. *Degree requirements:* For master's, thesis (for some programs), comprehensive exam, registration. *Entrance requirements:* For master's, GRE General Test, minimum GPA of 2.75 in last 60 hours. Additional exam requirements/recommendations for international students: Required—TOEFL. *Application deadline:* For fall admission, 3/1 for domestic and international students. Applications are processed on a rolling basis. Application fee: $25 ($30 for international students). *Financial support:* In 2006–07, 9 research assistantships with full tuition reimbursements (averaging $5,906 per year) were awarded; teaching assistantships with full tuition reimbursements, career-related internships or fieldwork and Federal Work-Study also available. Financial award application deadline: 3/15. *Faculty research:* Rural health care delivery, school health, nutrition of pregnant teens, risk factor reduction, sexually transmitted diseases. *Unit head:* Dr. James McGuire, Chair, 601-266-5437, Fax: 601-266-5043.

University of South Florida, Graduate School, College of Public Health, Department of Epidemiology and Biostatistics, Tampa, FL 33620-9951. Offers MPH, MSPH, PhD. *Accreditation:* CEPH (one or more programs are accredited). Part-time and evening/weekend programs available. *Faculty:* 17 full-time (7 women), 3 part-time/adjunct (1 woman). *Students:* 59 full-time (39 women), 51 part-time (31 women); includes 27 minority (11 African Americans, 6 Asian Americans or Pacific Islanders, 10 Hispanic Americans), 29 international. Average age 31. 65 applicants, 62% accepted, 15 enrolled. In 2006, 18 master's, 1 doctorate awarded. *Median time to degree:* Master's–1.7 years full-time, 3.15 years part-time; doctorate–3.67 years part-time. Of those who began their doctoral program in fall 1998, 100% received their degree in 8 years or less. *Degree requirements:* For master's and doctorate, thesis/dissertation, comprehensive exam. *Entrance requirements:* For master's and doctorate, GRE General Test, minimum GPA of 3.0 in upper-level course work. Additional exam requirements/recommendations for international students: Required—TOEFL (minimum score 550 paper-based; 213 computer-based; 79 iBT). *Application deadline:* For fall admission, 6/1 for domestic students, 1/2 for international students; for spring admission, 10/15 for domestic students, 7/1 for international students. Applications are processed on a rolling basis. Application fee: $30. Electronic applications accepted. *Financial support:* In 2006–07, 3 fellowships with full tuition reimbursements (averaging $10,333 per year), 13 research assistantships with full and partial tuition reimbursements (averaging $5,777 per year), 13 teaching assistantships (averaging $3,295 per year) were awarded; career-related internships or fieldwork, Federal Work-Study, institutionally sponsored loans, scholarships/grants, traineeships, and unspecified assistantships also available. Support available to part-time students. Financial award applicants required to submit FAFSA. *Faculty research:* Dementia, mental illness, mental health preventative trails, rural health outreach, clinical and administrative studies. Total annual research expenditures: $2.2 million. *Unit head:* Dr. Heather Stockwell, Chairperson, 813-974-4860, Fax: 813-974-4719, E-mail:

Epidemiology

University of South Florida (continued)

stockwell@hsc.usf.edu. *Application contact:* Michelle Robinson, Academic Advisor, 813-974-6665, Fax: 813-974-8121, E-mail: mrobinso@health.usf.edu.

University of Washington, Graduate School, School of Public Health and Community Medicine, Department of Epidemiology, Seattle, WA 98195. Offers epidemiology (MPH, MS, PhD); international health (MPH); maternal/child health (MPH); nutritional sciences (MPH, MS, PhD); public health genetics (MPH, MS, PhD), including genetic epidemiology (MS), public health genetics (MPH, PhD). *Accreditation:* CEPH (one or more programs are accredited). Part-time programs available. Terminal master's awarded for partial completion of doctoral program. *Degree requirements:* For master's, thesis, practicum (MPH); for doctorate, thesis/dissertation, preliminary exam, general exam, final exam, comprehensive exam, registration. *Entrance requirements:* For master's, GRE General Test, research experience in health sciences (preferred), minimum GPA of 3.0; for doctorate, GRE General Test, master's degree in health sciences or related field from US institution, experience in health science (preferred), minimum GPA of 3.0. Additional exam requirements/recommendations for international students: Required—TOEFL (minimum score 580 paper-based; 237 computer-based). Electronic applications accepted. Expenses: Contact institution. *Faculty research:* Chronic diseases, sexually transmitted diseases, injury epidemiology, materials and child health, molecular and genetic epidemiology.

The University of Western Ontario, Faculty of Graduate Studies, Biosciences Division, Department of Epidemiology and Biostatistics, London, ON N6A 5B8, Canada. Offers M Sc, PhD. *Accreditation:* CEPH (one or more programs are accredited). Part-time programs available. *Students:* 28. In 2006, 3 master's, 1 doctorate awarded. *Degree requirements:* For master's, thesis; for doctorate, thesis proposal defense. *Entrance requirements:* For master's, BA or B Sc honors degree, minimum B+ average in last 10 courses; for doctorate, M Sc or equivalent, minimum B+ average in last 10 courses. *Application deadline:* For fall admission, 2/1 for domestic students. Application fee: $20. *Financial support:* Research assistantships, teaching assistantships, career-related internships or fieldwork available. Financial award application deadline: 4/1. *Faculty research:* Chronic disease epidemiology, clinical epidemiology. *Unit head:* Dr. Karen Campbell, Chair, 519-661-2111 Ext. 86267, E-mail: karen.campbell@schulich.uwo.ca. *Application contact:* Pam Eaton, Graduate Assistant, E-mail: peaton@uwo.ca.

Virginia Commonwealth University, Medical College of Virginia-Professional Programs, School of Medicine and Graduate Programs, School of Medicine Graduate Programs, Department of Epidemiology and Community Health, Program in Epidemiology and Community Health, Richmond, VA 23284-9005. Offers PhD. *Accreditation:* CEPH. Part-time programs available. *Faculty:* 13 full-time (4 women). *Students:* 42 full-time (36 women), 23 part-time (16 women); includes 17 minority (10 African Americans, 6 Asian Americans or Pacific Islanders, 1 Hispanic American), 4 international. 10 applicants, 20% accepted, 2 enrolled. *Degree requirements:* For doctorate, thesis/dissertation, comprehensive exam. *Entrance requirements:* For doctorate, GRE General Test, interview, 3 letters of recommendation, minimum graduate GPA of 3.0, master's degree in public health or related field including epidemiology and biostatistics. Additional exam requirements/recommendations for international students: Required—TOEFL (minimum score 600 paper-based). *Application deadline:* For spring admission, 4/1 priority date for domestic students, 1/1 priority date for international students. Applications are processed on a rolling basis. Application fee: $50. Electronic applications accepted. *Financial support:* Fellowships with full tuition reimbursements, tuition waivers (partial) available. *Faculty research:* Sickle cell anemia, breast cancer, HIV/AIDS, hospital epidemiology, infectious diseases. *Unit head:* Elizabeth Eustice-Turf, Director, 804-828-9705, Fax: 804-828-9773, E-mail: eturf@mail1.vcu.edu.

See Close-Up on page 2069.

Yale University, School of Medicine, School of Public Health, Division of Chronic Disease Epidemiology, New Haven, CT 06520. Offers MPH, PhD. PhD offered through the Graduate School. *Accreditation:* CEPH (one or more programs are accredited). Part-time programs available. *Faculty:* 18 full-time (12 women), 12 part-time/adjunct (5 women). *Students:* 61; includes 20 minority (7 African Americans, 11 Asian Americans or Pacific Islanders, 2 Hispanic Americans), 3 international. Average age 26. In 2006, 27 master's, 27 doctorates awarded. Terminal master's awarded for partial completion of doctoral program. *Degree requirements:* For master's, thesis, internship. *Entrance requirements:* For master's, GMAT, GRE, LSAT, or MCAT, previous undergraduate course work in mathematics and science. Additional exam requirements/recommendations for international students: Required—TOEFL. *Application deadline:* For fall admission, 1/15 for domestic and international students. Electronic applications accepted. *Expenses: Contact institution. Financial support:* Fellowships, research assistantships, teaching assistantships, career-related internships or fieldwork, Federal Work-Study, institutionally sponsored loans, scholarships/grants, and tuition waivers (full and partial) available. Support available to part-time students. Financial award application deadline: 3/1; financial award applicants required to submit FAFSA. *Faculty research:* Perinatal epidemiology, epidemiology of aging, psychiatric and social epidemiology, cancer and cardiovascular epidemiology, pharmacoepidemiology. *Unit head:* Dr. Stanislav V. Kasl, Division Head, 203-785-2886, Fax: 203-785-6980, E-mail: stanislav.kasl@yale.edu. *Application contact:* Jacqui Comshaw, Director of Admissions, 203-785-2844, Fax: 203-785-4845, E-mail: eph.admissions@yale.edu.

See Close-Up on page 2073.

Yale University, School of Medicine, School of Public Health, Division of Epidemiology of Microbial Diseases, New Haven, CT 06520. Offers MPH, PhD. PhD offered through the Graduate School. *Accreditation:* CEPH (one or more programs are accredited). Part-time programs available. *Faculty:* 21 full-time (14 women), 12 part-time/adjunct (1 woman). *Students:* 39; includes 13 minority (2 African Americans, 9 Asian Americans or Pacific Islanders, 2 Hispanic Americans), 6 international. Average age 26. In 2006, 21 master's, 1 doctorate awarded. Terminal master's awarded for partial completion of doctoral program. *Degree requirements:* For master's, thesis, internship. *Entrance requirements:* For master's, GMAT, GRE, or MCAT, previous undergraduate course work in mathematics and science. Additional exam requirements/recommendations for international students: Required—TOEFL. *Application deadline:* For fall admission, 1/15 for domestic and international students. Electronic applications accepted. *Expenses: Contact institution. Financial support:* Career-related internships or fieldwork, Federal Work-Study, institutionally sponsored loans, and scholarships/grants available. Support available to part-time students. Financial award application deadline: 3/1; financial award applicants required to submit FAFSA. *Faculty research:* Insect vector competence, vector biology, emerging infections, parasitology, microbial diseases and defense. *Unit head:* Dr. Serap Aksoy, Division Head, 203-737-2180, Fax: 203-785-4782, E-mail: serap.aksoy@yale.edu. *Application contact:* Jacqui Comshaw, Director of Admissions, 203-785-2844, Fax: 203-785-4845, E-mail: eph.admissions@yale.edu.

See Close-Up on page 2073.

Health Promotion

Auburn University, Graduate School, College of Education, Department of Health and Human Performance, Auburn University, AL 36849. Offers exercise science (M Ed, MS, PhD); health promotion (M Ed, MS); physical education/teacher education (M Ed, MS, Ed D, Ed S). *Accreditation:* NCATE. Part-time programs available. *Faculty:* 13 full-time (5 women). *Students:* 40 full-time (18 women), 27 part-time (6 women); includes 7 minority (5 African Americans, 2 Hispanic Americans), 6 international. Average age 28. 67 applicants, 79% accepted, 24 enrolled. In 2006, 17 master's, 2 doctorates awarded. *Degree requirements:* For master's, thesis (for some programs); for doctorate, thesis/dissertation; for Ed S, exam, field project. *Entrance requirements:* For master's, GRE General Test; for doctorate and Ed S, GRE General Test, interview, master's degree. *Application deadline:* For fall admission, 7/7 for domestic students; for spring admission, 11/24 for domestic students. Applications are processed on a rolling basis. Application fee: $25 ($50 for international students). Electronic applications accepted. *Expenses:* Tuition, state resident: full-time $5,000. Tuition, nonresident: full-time $15,000. Required fees: $416. Tuition and fees vary according to program. *Financial support:* Research assistantships, teaching assistantships, Federal Work-Study available. Support available to part-time students. Financial award application deadline: 3/15. *Faculty research:* Biomechanics, exercise physiology, motor skill learning, school health, curriculum development. *Unit head:* Dr. Mary E Rudisill, Acting Head, 334-844-4483. *Application contact:* Dr. Joe Pittman, Interim Dean of the Graduate School, 334-844-4700.

Ball State University, Graduate School, College of Applied Science and Technology, Fisher Institute for Wellness, Interdepartmental Program in Wellness Management, Muncie, IN 47306-1099. Offers MA, MS. *Faculty:* 3. *Students:* 14 full-time (10 women), 9 part-time (7 women); includes 2 minority (1 African American, 1 Asian American or Pacific Islander), 2 international. Average age 25. 11 applicants, 82% accepted, 8 enrolled. In 2006, 8 degrees awarded. *Entrance requirements:* For master's, GRE General Test, interview. Application fee: $25 ($35 for international students). *Financial support:* In 2006–07, 10 teaching assistantships (averaging $7,921 per year) were awarded; research assistantships with full tuition reimbursements, career-related internships or fieldwork also available. Financial award application deadline:3/1. *Unit head:* Dr. Jane Ellery, Head, 765-285-8259.

Barnes-Jewish College of Nursing and Allied Health, Division of Allied Health, St. Louis, MO 63110-1091. Offers dietetic internship (Certificate); education (MSAH); management (MSAH); nutrition (MSAH). Part-time and evening/weekend programs available. *Degree requirements:* For master's, thesis or alternative, registration. *Entrance requirements:* For master's, minimum GPA of 3.0, 2 references, statistics course. Additional exam requirements/recommendations for international students: Required—TOEFL (minimum score 550 paper-based; 213 computer-based).

Benedictine University, Graduate Programs, Program in Nutrition and Wellness, Lisle, IL 60532-0900. Offers MS. *Students:* 14 full-time (all women), 6 part-time (all women); includes 1 minority (Asian American or Pacific Islander) 24 applicants, 46% accepted, 10 enrolled. *Entrance requirements:* Additional exam requirements/recommendations for international students: Required—TOEFL (minimum score 550 paper-based; 213 computer-based). *Application deadline:* For fall admission, 9/1 for domestic students; for winter admission, 12/1 for domestic students; for spring admission, 2/15 for domestic students. Applications are processed on a rolling basis. Application fee: $40. Electronic applications accepted. *Expenses:* Tuition: Full-time $12,150; part-time $450 per credit hour. *Financial support:* Career-related internships or fieldwork and health care benefits available. Support available to part-time students. *Faculty research:* Community and corporate wellness risk assessment, health behavior change, self-efficacy, evaluation of health program impact and effectiveness. Total annual research expenditures: $8,335. *Unit head:* Catherine Arnold, Director, 630-829-6534, E-mail: carnold@ben.edu. *Application contact:* Kari Gibbons, Director, Admissions, 630-829-6200, Fax: 630-829-6584, E-mail: kgibbons@ben.edu.

Boston University, School of Public Health, Social and Behavioral Sciences Department, Boston, MA 02215. Offers health behavior, health promotion, and disease prevention (MPH); social behavioral sciences (Dr PH). *Accreditation:* CEPH. *Students:* 24 full-time (23 women), 81 part-time (73 women); includes 19 minority (11 African Americans, 5 Asian Americans or Pacific Islanders, 3 Hispanic Americans), 5 international. Average age 27. *Entrance requirements:* For master's, GRE General Test. Additional exam requirements/recommendations for international students: Required—TOEFL or IELTS. *Application deadline:* For fall admission, 2/1 for domestic students; for spring admission, 10/15 for domestic students. Applications are processed on a rolling basis. Application fee: $60. Electronic applications accepted. *Expenses:* Tuition: Full-time $33,330; part-time $1,042 per credit. Required fees: $462; $40. *Financial support:* Career-related internships or fieldwork, Federal Work-Study, institutionally sponsored loans, scholarships/grants, and tuition waivers (partial) available. Support available to part-time students. *Unit head:* Dr. Deborah Bowen, Chair, 617-638-5160, E-mail: socbeh@bu.edu. *Application contact:* LePhan Quan, Assistant Director of Admissions, 617-638-4640, Fax: 617-638-5299, E-mail: asksph@bu.edu.

Bridgewater State College, School of Graduate Studies, School of Education and Allied Science, Department of Movement Arts, Health Promotion, and Leisure Studies, Program in Health Promotion, Bridgewater, MA 02325-0001. Offers M Ed. Part-time and evening/weekend programs available. *Entrance requirements:* For master's, GRE General Test. *Application deadline:* For fall admission, 3/1 priority date for domestic students; for spring admission, 10/1 priority date for domestic students. Application fee: $50. *Financial support:* Career-related internships or fieldwork, health care benefits, and unspecified assistantships available. Support available to part-time students.

Brigham Young University, Graduate Studies, College of Health and Human Performance, Department of Exercise Sciences, Provo, UT 84602-1001. Offers athletic training (MS); exercise physiology (MS, PhD); health promotion (MS, PhD); physical medicine and rehabilitation (PhD); sports pedagogy (MS). *Faculty:* 19 full-time (3 women), 1 (woman) part-time/adjunct. *Students:* 23 full-time (10 women), 48 part-time (21 women); includes 7 minority (3 American Indian/Alaska Native, 1 Asian American or Pacific Islander, 3 Hispanic Americans). Average age 28. 30 applicants, 70% accepted, 14 enrolled. In 2006, 9 master's, 4 doctorates awarded. *Median time to degree:* Of those who began their doctoral program in fall 1998, 100% received their degree in 8 years or less. *Degree requirements:* For master's, thesis, oral defense; for doctorate, thesis/dissertation, oral defense, oral and written exams, comprehensive exam. *Entrance requirements:* For master's, GRE General Test, minimum GPA of 3.0 in last 60 hours of course work; for doctorate, GRE General Test, minimum GPA of 3.5 in last 60 hours of course work. Additional exam requirements/recommendations for international students: Required—TOEFL (minimum score 580 paper-based; 237 computer-based; 85 iBT), IELTS (minimum score 7). *Application deadline:* For fall admission, 2/1 for domestic and international students. Application fee: $50. Electronic applications accepted. *Financial support:* In 2006–07, 18 research assistantships with full and partial tuition reimbursements (averaging $3,324 per year), 45 teaching assistantships with full and partial tuition reimbursements (averaging $11,080 per year) were awarded; fellowships, career-related internships or fieldwork, institutionally sponsored loans, tuition waivers (full and partial), and unspecified assistantships also available. Financial award application deadline: 3/1. *Faculty research:* Injury prevention and rehabilitation, human skeletal muscle adaptation, cardiovascular health and fitness, lifestyle modification and health promotion. Total annual research expenditures: $250,125. *Unit head:* Dr. Larry Hall, Chair, 801-422-7303, Fax: 801-422-0543, E-mail: larry_hall@byu.edu. *Applica-*

tion contact: Dr. J. William Myrer, Graduate Coordinator, 801-422-2690, Fax: 801-422-0557, E-mail: bill_myrer@byu.edu.

California College for Health Sciences, Program in Health Services, Salt Lake City, UT 84107. Offers community health (MSHS); wellness promotion (MSHS). Part-time and evening/weekend programs available. Postbaccalaureate distance learning degree programs offered (no on-campus study). *Degree requirements:* For master's, fieldwork, internship, final project (wellness promotion). *Entrance requirements:* For master's, previous course work in psychology.

California State University, Fresno, Division of Graduate Studies, College of Health and Human Services, Department of Public Health, Fresno, CA 93740-8027. Offers environmental/occupational health (MPH); health administration (MPH); health promotion (MPH). *Accreditation:* CEPH. Part-time and evening/weekend programs available. *Degree requirements:* For master's, thesis or alternative. *Entrance requirements:* For master's, GRE General Test, minimum GPA of 2.5. Additional exam requirements/recommendations for international students: Required—TOEFL. Electronic applications accepted. *Faculty research:* Foster parent training, geriatrics, tobacco control.

Canisius College, Graduate Division, School of Education and Human Services, Department of Health and Human Performance, Buffalo, NY 14208-1098. Offers MS. Part-time and evening/weekend programs available. *Faculty:* 4 full-time (0 women), 3 part-time/adjunct (1 woman). *Students:* 9 full-time (6 women), 7 part-time (all women). Average age 24. 12 applicants, 75% accepted, 6 enrolled. In 2006, 5 degrees awarded. *Degree requirements:* For master's, thesis, project internship. Application fee: $25. *Expenses:* Tuition: Part-time $645 per credit hour. Required fees: $19 per credit hour. Tuition and fees vary according to program. *Financial support:* In 2006–07, 9 students received support, including 1 teaching assistantship with tuition reimbursement available (averaging $6,000 per year); career-related internships or fieldwork, institutionally sponsored loans, health care benefits, and unspecified assistantships also available. *Faculty research:* Delayed onset of muscle soreness, exercising muscle blood flow, aging. Total annual research expenditures: $13,000. *Unit head:* Dr. Peter M. Koehneke, Chair, 716-888-2954, E-mail: koehneke@canisius.edu.

Central Michigan University, College of Graduate Studies, The Herbert H. and Grace A. Dow College of Health Professions, School of Health Sciences, Mount Pleasant, MI 48859. Offers health promotion and program management (MA). *Degree requirements:* For master's, thesis or alternative, registration. *Faculty research:* Children's fitness and active video games, obesity and weight control, international health education, school health education.

Eastern Michigan University, Graduate School, College of Health and Human Services, School of Health Promotion and Human Performance, Ypsilanti, MI 48197. Offers health and physical education (MS); orthotics and prosthetics (MS); sports management (MS); sports medicine (MS). Part-time and evening/weekend programs available. Postbaccalaureate distance learning degree programs offered (minimal on-campus study). *Faculty:* 19 full-time (10 women). *Students:* 9 full-time (6 women), 67 part-time (31 women); includes 10 minority (9 African Americans, 1 Hispanic American), 4 international. Average age 29. In 2006, 22 degrees awarded. *Entrance requirements:* Additional exam requirements/recommendations for international students: Required—TOEFL. *Application deadline:* For fall admission, 5/15 priority date for domestic students, 5/1 priority date for international students; for winter admission, 10/15 priority date for domestic students, 10/1 priority date for international students; for spring admission, 3/15 priority date for domestic students, 3/1 priority date for international students. Applications are processed on a rolling basis. Application fee: $35. *Expenses:* Tuition, state resident: part-time $341 per credit hour. Tuition, nonresident: full-time $16,104; part-time $671 per credit hour. Required fees: $816; $34 per credit hour. $40 per term. One-time fee: $82 full-time. Tuition and fees vary according to course level, course load, degree level and reciprocity agreements. *Financial support:* Fellowships, research assistantships with full tuition reimbursements, teaching assistantships with full tuition reimbursements, career-related internships or fieldwork, Federal Work-Study, institutionally sponsored loans, scholarships/grants, tuition waivers (partial), and unspecified assistantships available. Support available to part-time students. Financial award applicants required to submit FAFSA. *Unit head:* Dr. Murali Nair, Director, 734-487-0090, Fax: 734-487-2024, E-mail: murali.nair@emich.edu.

Emerson College, Graduate Studies, School of Communication, Department of Marketing Communication, Boston, MA 02116-4624. Offers global marketing communication and advertising (MA); health communication (MA); integrated marketing communication (MA). *Entrance requirements:* For master's, GRE General Test. Additional exam requirements/recommendations for international students: Required—TOEFL. Electronic applications accepted.

Emory University, Rollins School of Public Health, Program in Career Public Health, Atlanta, GA 30322-1100. Offers applied epidemiology (MPH); outcomes option (MPH); prevention (MPH). Part-time and evening/weekend programs available. Postbaccalaureate distance learning degree programs offered (minimal on-campus study). *Students:* 11 full-time (10 women), 101 part-time (69 women). Average age 40. 69 applicants, 68% accepted, 37 enrolled. In 2006, 18 degrees awarded. *Degree requirements:* For master's, thesis, practicum. *Entrance requirements:* Additional exam requirements/recommendations for international students: Required—TOEFL (minimum score 550 paper-based; 213 computer-based). *Application deadline:* For fall admission, 1/5 priority date for domestic students, 1/5 for international students. Applications are processed on a rolling basis. Application fee: $75. Electronic applications accepted. *Expenses:* Tuition: Full-time $30,246. *Financial support:* Fellowships with full and partial tuition reimbursements, career-related internships or fieldwork, institutionally sponsored loans, and scholarships/grants available. Support available to part-time students. Financial award application deadline: 1/5. *Unit head:* Dr. Iris Smith, Director, 404-727-2925, Fax: 404-727-3996, E-mail: ismith@sph.emory.edu. *Application contact:* Robie Freeman Burks, Assistant Director of Academic Programs, 404-727-8739, Fax: 404-727-8768, E-mail: rfreem2@sph.emory.edu.

Florida Atlantic University, College of Education, Department of Exercise Science and Health Promotion, Boca Raton, FL 33431-0991. Offers M Ed, MS. Part-time and evening/weekend programs available. *Faculty:* 8 full-time (2 women), 4 part-time/adjunct (2 women). *Students:* 19 full-time (11 women), 7 part-time (6 women); includes 7 minority (1 African American, 2 Asian Americans or Pacific Islanders, 4 Hispanic Americans), 3 international. Average age 28. 22 applicants, 64% accepted, 7 enrolled. In 2006, 10 degrees awarded. *Degree requirements:* For master's, thesis optional. *Entrance requirements:* For master's, GRE General Test, minimum GPA of 3.0 during last 60 hours of course work. Additional exam requirements/recommendations for international students: Required—TOEFL (minimum score 500 paper-based). *Application deadline:* For fall admission, 7/1 priority date for domestic students; for spring admission, 4/1 priority date for domestic students. Applications are processed on a rolling basis. Application fee: $30. *Expenses:* Tuition, area resident: Full-time $4,394. Tuition, nonresident: full-time $16,441. *Financial support:* In 2006–07, 4 research assistantships with partial tuition reimbursements (averaging $12,000 per year), 11 teaching assistantships with partial tuition reimbursements (averaging $12,000 per year) were awarded; career-related internships or fieldwork also available. *Faculty research:* Pulmonary limitations during exercise, metabolism regulation, determinants of performance, age related change in functional mobility and geriatric exercise, behavioral change aimed at promoting active lifestyles. Total annual research expenditures: $280,000. *Unit head:* Dr. Sue Graves, Chair, 954-236-1261, Fax: 954-236-1259. *Application contact:* Dr. Joseph A. O'Kroy, Graduate Coordinator, 954-236-1266, Fax: 954-236-1259, E-mail: okroy@fau.edu.

Georgetown University, Graduate School of Arts and Sciences, Programs in Biomedical Sciences, Department of Microbiology and Immunology, Washington, DC 20057. Offers biohazardous threat agents and emerging infectious diseases (MS); general microbiology and immunology (MS); global infectious diseases (PhD); microbiology and immunology research (PhD); science policy and advocacy (MS). Part-time programs available. *Faculty:* 20 full-time (4 women), 16 part-time/adjunct (3 women). *Students:* 42 full-time (32 women), 13 part-time (8

women); includes 15 minority (2 African Americans, 11 Asian Americans or Pacific Islanders, 2 Hispanic Americans), 6 international. Average age 24. 94 applicants, 55% accepted, 41 enrolled. In 2006, 37 master's, 5 doctorates awarded. *Median time to degree:* Master's–1 year full-time, 2 years part-time; doctorate–5 years full-time. *Degree requirements:* For master's, 30 credit hours of coursework; for doctorate, thesis/dissertation, comprehensive exam. *Entrance requirements:* For master's, GRE General Test, 3 letters of reference, bachelor's degree in related field; for doctorate, GRE General Test, 3 letters of reference, graduate degree in related field. Additional exam requirements/recommendations for international students: Required—TOEFL (minimum score 505 paper-based; 213 computer-based). *Application deadline:* For fall admission, 7/1 for domestic students, 6/1 priority date for international students; for winter admission, 2/2 priority date for domestic students, 1/2 priority date for international students; for spring admission, 11/1 for domestic students, 10/1 priority date for international students. Applications are processed on a rolling basis. Application fee: $70. Electronic applications accepted. *Financial support:* In 2006–07, 17 students received support, including 2 fellowships with full tuition reimbursements available (averaging $23,772 per year). *Faculty research:* Pathogenesis and basic biology of the fungus Candida albicans, molecular biology of viral hepatitis, molecular and cellular biology of the Hepatitis B and Delta viruses, dengue virus, immunopathological mechanisms in Multiple Sclerosis. *Unit head:* Dr. Adam Myers, Associate Dean, E-mail: myersa@georgetown.edu. *Application contact:* Eugenia Pyntikova, Coordinator, Graduate Programs, 202-687-3422, Fax: 202-687-1800, E-mail: ep72@georgetown.edu.

The George Washington University, School of Public Health and Health Services, Department of Global Health, Washington, DC 20052. Offers international health policy and programs (MPH); international health promotion (MPH); JD/MPH; LL M/MPH; MD/MPH. *Accreditation:* CEPH. *Degree requirements:* For master's, case study or special project. *Entrance requirements:* For master's, GMAT, GRE General Test, or MCAT. Additional exam requirements/recommendations for international students: Required—TOEFL.

The George Washington University, School of Public Health and Health Services, Department of Prevention and Community Health, Washington, DC 20052. Offers community-oriented primary care (MPH); health promotion (MPH); maternal and child health (MPH); public health and emergency management (Certificate). *Accreditation:* CEPH. *Entrance requirements:* For master's, GRE or GMAT, 2 letters of recommendation, resumé. Additional exam requirements/recommendations for international students: Required—TOEFL.

Georgia State University, College of Health and Human Sciences, School of Nursing, Atlanta, GA 30303-3083. Offers adult health (MS); child health (MS); family nurse practitioner (MS); health promotion, protection and restoration (PhD); nursing (Certificate); perinatal/women's health (MS); psychiatric/mental health (MS). *Accreditation:* AACN. Part-time and evening/weekend programs available. *Faculty:* 35 full-time (all women), 1 (woman) part-time/adjunct. *Students:* 72 full-time (66 women), 128 part-time (123 women); includes 75 minority (61 African Americans, 9 Asian Americans or Pacific Islanders, 5 Hispanic Americans), 2 international. Average age 37. 70 applicants, 54% accepted, 30 enrolled. In 2006, 39 master's, 6 doctorates awarded. *Degree requirements:* For master's, research activity; for doctorate, thesis/dissertation, comprehensive exam. *Entrance requirements:* For master's, MAT (preferred) or GRE, interview, RN license; for doctorate, GRE General Test. Additional exam requirements/recommendations for international students: Required—TOEFL (minimum score 550 paper-based; 213 computer-based). *Application deadline:* For fall admission, 3/1 priority date for domestic students; for spring admission, 10/1 priority date for domestic students. Applications are processed on a rolling basis. Application fee: $50. Electronic applications accepted. *Expenses:* Contact institution. *Financial support:* In 2006–07, research assistantships with full and partial tuition reimbursements (averaging $3,108 per year); fellowships with full tuition reimbursements, teaching assistantships, Federal Work-Study, institutionally sponsored loans, scholarships/grants, traineeships, and tuition waivers (partial) also available. Support available to part-time students. Financial award application deadline: 4/1; financial award applicants required to submit FAFSA. *Faculty research:* Breast cancer prevention, sexually compulsive behaviors, health risks in minority youth, asthma treatment strategies, adolescent alcohol-related issues. Total annual research expenditures: $221,691. *Unit head:* Dr. Barbara Woodring, Director, 404-651-3040. *Application contact:* Barbara Smith, Admissions Counselor II, 404-651-3834, Fax: 404-651-4871, E-mail: bbsmith@gsu.edu.

Goddard College, Graduate Program, Program in Health Arts and Sciences, Plainfield, VT 05667-9432. Offers MA. *Faculty:* 6 part-time/adjunct (5 women). *Students:* 15 full-time. Average age 43. 8 applicants, 88% accepted, 5 enrolled. *Degree requirements:* For master's, thesis, registration. *Entrance requirements:* For master's, 3 letters of recommendation, study plan, bibliography. *Application deadline:* Applications are processed on a rolling basis. Application fee: $40. Electronic applications accepted. *Expenses:* Tuition: Full-time $12,506; part-time $10,392 per year. Required fees: $998; $499 per term. *Financial support:* In 2006–07, 14 students received support. Applicants required to submit FAFSA. *Unit head:* Suzanne Richman, Director, 802-454-8311 Ext. 211, Fax: 802-454-1029, E-mail: richmans@goddard.edu. *Application contact:* 800-906-8312, Fax: 802-454-1029, E-mail: admissions@goddard.edu.

Harvard University, School of Public Health, Department of Society, Human Development and Health, Boston, MA 02115-6096. Offers SM, DPH, SD. Part-time programs available. *Degree requirements:* For doctorate, thesis/dissertation, qualifying exam. *Entrance requirements:* For master's and doctorate, GRE. Additional exam requirements/recommendations for international students: Required—TOEFL (minimum score 560 paper-based; 220 computer-based); Recommended—IELTS (minimum score 7). Electronic applications accepted. *Expenses:* Tuition: Full-time $30,275. Full-time tuition and fees vary according to program and student level. *Faculty research:* Social determinants of health, program design and planned social change, health and social policy.

Indiana State University, School of Graduate Studies, College of Health and Human Performance, Department of Health, Safety, and Environmental Health Sciences, Terre Haute, IN 47809-1401. Offers community health promotion (MA, MS); occupational safety management (MA, MS); school health and safety (MA, MS). *Accreditation:* NCATE (one or more programs are accredited). *Faculty:* 9 full-time (1 woman), 2 part-time/adjunct (1 woman). *Students:* 3 full-time (2 women), 19 part-time (5 women); includes 4 minority (3 African Americans, 1 Hispanic American), 1 international. Average age 37. 8 applicants, 63% accepted, 2 enrolled. In 2006, 3 degrees awarded. *Degree requirements:* For master's, thesis or alternative. *Entrance requirements:* For master's, GRE General Test. *Application deadline:* For fall admission, 7/1 priority date for domestic students; for spring admission, 11/1 priority date for domestic students. Applications are processed on a rolling basis. Application fee: $35. Electronic applications accepted. *Expenses:* Tuition, state resident: part-time $278 per credit. Tuition, nonresident: part-time $552 per credit. *Financial support:* In 2006–07, 1 research assistantship (averaging $3,150 per year) was awarded; teaching assistantships, tuition waivers (full) and unspecified assistantships also available. Financial award application deadline: 3/1; financial award applicants required to submit FAFSA. *Unit head:* Dr. Ernest Sheldon, Interim Chairperson, 812-237-3071.

Indiana University Bloomington, School of Health, Physical Education and Recreation, Department of Applied Health Science, Bloomington, IN 47405-7000. Offers health behavior (PhD); health promotion (MS); human development/family studies (MS); nutrition science (MS); public health (MPH); safety management (MS); school and college health education (MS). PhD offered through the University Graduate School. *Accreditation:* CEPH (one or more programs are accredited). *Faculty:* 21 full-time (11 women), 1 (woman) part-time/adjunct. *Students:* 72 full-time (54 women), 44 part-time (30 women); includes 18 minority (15 African Americans, 2 Asian Americans or Pacific Islanders, 1 Hispanic American), 17 international. Average age 30. 94 applicants, 88% accepted, 54 enrolled. In 2006, 50 master's, 7 doctorates awarded. *Degree requirements:* For master's, thesis optional; for doctorate, thesis/dissertation, registration. *Entrance requirements:* For master's, GRE (MS in nutrition science), 3 recommendations; for doctorate, GRE, 3 recommendations. Additional exam requirements/

Health Promotion

Indiana University Bloomington (continued)
recommendations for international students: Required—TOEFL (minimum score 550 paper-based; 213 computer-based; 79 iBT). *Application deadline:* For fall admission, 4/30 priority date for domestic students, 12/1 priority date for international students; for spring admission, 11/15 priority date for domestic students, 9/1 priority date for international students. Application fee: $50 ($60 for international students). *Expenses:* Tuition, state resident: full-time $5,791; part-time $241 per credit hour. Tuition, nonresident: full-time $16,866; part-time $703 per credit hour. *Financial support:* In 2006–07, teaching assistantships with full and partial tuition reimbursements (averaging $11,666 per year); fellowships, career-related internships or fieldwork, Federal Work-Study, institutionally sponsored loans, scholarships/grants, tuition waivers (partial), and fee remissions also available. Financial award application deadline: 3/1. *Faculty research:* Cancer education, HIV/AIDS and drug education, public health, parent-child interactions, safety education. *Unit head:* Dr. Mohammad R. Torabi, Chair, 812-855-4808, Fax: 812-855-3936, E-mail: torabi@indiana.edu.

Lehman College of the City University of New York, Division of Natural and Social Sciences, Department of Health Sciences, Program in Health Education and Promotion, Bronx, NY 10468-1589. Offers MA. *Accreditation:* NCATE. Part-time and evening/weekend programs available. *Degree requirements:* For master's, thesis or alternative. *Entrance requirements:* For master's, minimum GPA of 2.7.

Loma Linda University, School of Public Health, Programs in Health Promotion and Education, Loma Linda, CA 92350. Offers MPH, Dr PH. *Accreditation:* CEPH (one or more programs are accredited). *Degree requirements:* For doctorate, thesis/dissertation. *Entrance requirements:* For doctorate, GRE General Test. Additional exam requirements/recommendations for international students: Required—Michigan English Language Assessment Battery or TOEFL.

Marymount University, School of Health Professions, Program in Health Promotion Management, Arlington, VA 22207-4299. Offers MS. Part-time and evening/weekend programs available. *Students:* 7 full-time (5 women), 20 part-time (19 women); includes 6 minority (5 African Americans, 1 Asian American or Pacific Islander), 1 international. Average age 32. 15 applicants, 100% accepted, 10 enrolled. In 2006, 8 degrees awarded. *Degree requirements:* For master's, thesis or alternative. *Entrance requirements:* For master's, GRE General Test or MAT, interview, 2 letters of recommendation. Additional exam requirements/recommendations for international students: Required—TOEFL (minimum score 600 paper-based; 250 computer-based). *Application deadline:* Applications are processed on a rolling basis. Application fee: $40. Electronic applications accepted. *Expenses:* Tuition: Full-time $11,160; part-time $620 per credit. Required fees: $113; $630 per credit. *Financial support:* Research assistantships with full tuition reimbursements, career-related internships or fieldwork, scholarships/grants, and unspecified assistantships available. Support available to part-time students. Financial award applicants required to submit FAFSA. *Unit head:* Dr. Michael Nordvall, Chair, 703-526-6876, Fax: 703-284-3819, E-mail: michael.nordvall@marymount.edu.

McNeese State University, Graduate School, College of Education, Department of Health and Human Performance, Lake Charles, LA 70609. Offers exercise physiology (MS); health promotion (MS). *Accreditation:* NCATE. Evening/weekend programs available. *Faculty:* 5 full-time (2 women). *Students:* 18 full-time (11 women), 8 part-time (5 women); includes 4 minority (3 African Americans, 1 Asian American or Pacific Islander), 3 international. In 2006, 13 degrees awarded. *Entrance requirements:* For master's, GRE, UG major or minor in health and human performance or related field of study. *Application deadline:* For fall admission, 5/15 priority date for domestic students. Applications are processed on a rolling basis. Application fee: $20 ($30 for international students). *Expenses:* Tuition, area resident: Full-time $2,226; part-time $193 per hour. Required fees: $919; $106 per hour. *Financial support:* Application deadline: 5/1. *Unit head:* Dr. Michael Soileau, Head, 337-475-5374, Fax: 337-475-5947, E-mail: msoileau@mcneese.edu.

Missouri State University, Graduate College, College of Health and Human Services, Department of Health, Physical Education, and Recreation, Springfield, MO 65804-0094. Offers health promotion and wellness management (MS); public health (MPH); secondary education (MS Ed), including physical education. Part-time programs available. *Faculty:* 12 full-time (4 women). *Students:* 43 full-time (11 women), 36 part-time (18 women); includes 1 minority (Hispanic American), 45 international. Average age 27. 126 applicants, 73% accepted, 37 enrolled. In 2006, 15 degrees awarded. *Degree requirements:* For master's, thesis or alternative, comprehensive exam. *Entrance requirements:* For master's, GRE (MS, MPH), minimum GPA of 2.8 (MS), minimum GPA of 3.0 (MPH), 9-12 teaching certification (MS Ed). Additional exam requirements/recommendations for international students: Required—TOEFL (minimum score 550 paper-based; 213 computer-based; 79 iBT). *Application deadline:* For fall admission, 7/20 priority date for domestic students; for spring admission, 12/20 priority date for domestic students. Applications are processed on a rolling basis. Application fee: $35. Electronic applications accepted. *Expenses:* Tuition, state resident: full-time $3,582; part-time $199 per credit hour. Tuition, nonresident: full-time $6,984; part-time $199 per credit hour. Required fees: $548. Full-time tuition and fees vary according to course level, course load, program and reciprocity agreements. *Financial support:* In 2006–07, 6 teaching assistantships with full tuition reimbursements (averaging $6,780 per year) were awarded; research assistantships with full tuition reimbursements, Federal Work-Study, scholarships/grants, and unspecified assistantships also available. Financial award application deadline: 3/31; financial award applicants required to submit FAFSA. *Unit head:* Dr. Sarah McCallister, Acting Head, 417-836-6582, Fax: 417-836-5371, E-mail: sarahmccallister@missouristate.edu. *Application contact:* Dr. Sarah McCallister, Acting Head, 417-836-6582, Fax: 417-836-5371, E-mail: sarahmccallister@missouristate.edu.

Nebraska Methodist College, Program in Health Promotion Management, Omaha, NE 68114. Offers MS. Evening/weekend programs available. Postbaccalaureate distance learning degree programs offered (minimal on-campus study). *Faculty:* 9 part-time/adjunct (5 women). *Students:* 20 full-time (all women); includes 1 minority (Hispanic American) Average age 34. 19 applicants, 84% accepted, 13 enrolled. In 2006, 10 degrees awarded. *Degree requirements:* For master's, thesis. *Entrance requirements:* For master's, interview. Additional exam requirements/recommendations for international students: Required—TOEFL (minimum score 550 paper-based; 213 computer-based; 80 iBT). *Application deadline:* Applications are processed on a rolling basis. Application fee: $25. *Expenses:* Tuition: Part-time $486 per credit hour. Required fees: $25 per credit hour. Full-time tuition and fees vary according to program. *Financial support:* In 2006–07, 13 students received support; research assistantships with full and partial tuition reimbursements available, scholarships/grants available. Support available to part-time students. Financial award applicants required to submit FAFSA. *Faculty research:* Congregational health promotion, fitness testing with elderly, educational assessment, statistics instruction. *Unit head:* Sarah Bonney, Program Director, 402-354-7200, Fax: 402-354-7020. *Application contact:* Deann Sterner, Director of Admissions, 402-354-7200, Fax: 402-354-7020, E-mail: admissions@methodistcollege.edu.

New York Medical College, School of Public Health, Department of Behavioral Sciences and Community Health, Valhalla, NY 10595-1691. Offers behavioral sciences and health promotion (MPH); general public health (MPH); international health (MPH); maternal and child health (MPH). Part-time and evening/weekend programs available. In 2006, 3 degrees awarded. *Degree requirements:* For master's, thesis, registration. *Entrance requirements:* For master's, minimum undergraduate GPA of 3.0. Additional exam requirements/recommendations for international students: Required—TOEFL (minimum score 600 paper-based; 250 computer-based). *Application deadline:* For fall admission, 8/1 priority date for domestic students, 5/15 for international students; for spring admission, 12/1 priority date for domestic students, 10/15 for international students. Applications are processed on a rolling basis. Application fee: $35 ($60 for international students). Electronic applications accepted. *Financial support:* Career-related internships or fieldwork, Federal Work-Study, and institutionally sponsored loans available. Financial award application deadline: 6/15; financial award applicants required to submit FAFSA. *Unit head:* Dr. Frank Baker, Chair, 914-594-3480. *Application contact:* Marian F. McGowan, Information Contact, 914-594-4510, Fax: 914-594-4292, E-mail: sph_admissions@nymc.edu.

See Close-Up on page 2043.

New York University, Steinhardt School of Culture, Education and Human Development, Department of Applied Psychology, Program in Counselor Education, New York, NY 10012-1019. Offers counseling and guidance (MA, Advanced Certificate), including bilingual school counseling (MA), school counseling (MA); counseling for mental health and wellness (MA); counseling psychology (PhD). *Accreditation:* APA (one or more programs are accredited). Part-time and evening/weekend programs available. *Faculty:* 9 full-time (5 women). *Students:* 137 full-time (107 women), 81 part-time (67 women); includes 78 minority (34 African Americans, 19 Asian Americans or Pacific Islanders, 25 Hispanic Americans), 18 international. 463 applicants, 41% accepted, 90 enrolled. In 2006, 79 master's, 8 doctorates awarded. Terminal master's awarded for partial completion of doctoral program. *Degree requirements:* For master's, thesis (for some programs); for doctorate, thesis/dissertation. *Entrance requirements:* For doctorate, GRE General Test, interview. Additional exam requirements/recommendations for international students: Required—TOEFL. *Application deadline:* For fall admission, 1/15 priority date for domestic and international students; for spring admission, 11/1 for domestic and international students. Applications are processed on a rolling basis. Application fee: $50. *Expenses:* Tuition: Part-time $1,080 per unit. Required fees: $56 per unit. $329 per term. Tuition and fees vary according to program. *Financial support:* Fellowships with full and partial tuition reimbursements, teaching assistantships with partial tuition reimbursements, career-related internships or fieldwork, Federal Work-Study, institutionally sponsored loans, scholarships/grants, tuition waivers (partial), and unspecified assistantships available. Support available to part-time students. Financial award application deadline: 2/1; financial award applicants required to submit FAFSA. *Faculty research:* Cross-cultural counseling; group dynamics; culture, race and ethnicity; religiosity and psychological development; well-being and mental health. *Unit head:* Dr. Mary Sue Richardson, Director, 212-998-5559, Fax: 212-995-4358. *Application contact:* 212-998-5030, Fax: 212-995-4328, E-mail: steinhardt.gradadmissions@nyu.edu.

Northern Arizona University, Consortium of Professional Schools and Colleges, College of Health Professions, Program in Public Health, Flagstaff, AZ 86011. Offers health education and health promotion (MPH). *Degree requirements:* For master's, internship. *Entrance requirements:* For master's, GRE General Test or MCAT, minimum GPA of 3.0.

Oakland University, Graduate Study and Lifelong Learning, School of Health Sciences, Program in Complimentary Medicine and Wellness, Rochester, MI 48309-4401. Offers Certificate. *Students:* 1 (woman) full-time, 9 part-time (all women). Average age 43. 6 applicants, 100% accepted, 4 enrolled.Application fee: $35. *Expenses:* Tuition, state resident: full-time $9,936; part-time $414 per credit. Tuition, nonresident: full-time $17,202; part-time $716 per credit. *Unit head:* Dr. Robert Janski, Director, 248-370-4191.

Old Dominion University, College of Health Sciences, Program in Community Health and Environmental Health, Norfolk, VA 23529. Offers community health professions (MS); environmental health (MS); health care administration (MS); long-term care administration (MS); wellness and promotion (MS). Part-time and evening/weekend programs available. Postbaccalaureate distance learning degree programs offered (no on-campus study). *Faculty:* 5 full-time (4 women), 5 part-time/adjunct (1 woman). *Students:* 10 full-time (7 women), 33 part-time (24 women); includes 6 minority (5 African Americans, 1 Asian American or Pacific Islander), 8 international. Average age 33. 32 applicants, 88% accepted, 15 enrolled. In 2006, 19 degrees awarded. *Degree requirements:* For master's, oral exam, written exam, thesis optional. *Entrance requirements:* For master's, GRE General Test, minimum GPA of 2.75. Additional exam requirements/recommendations for international students: Required—TOEFL. *Application deadline:* For fall admission, 8/1 priority date for domestic students, 7/1 priority date for international students; for winter admission, 11/1 priority date for domestic students, 10/1 priority date for international students; for spring admission, 4/1 priority date for domestic students, 3/1 priority date for international students. Applications are processed on a rolling basis. Application fee: $40. Electronic applications accepted. *Expenses:* Tuition, area resident: Part-time $285 per credit hour. Tuition, nonresident: part-time $715 per credit hour. Required fees: $94 per semester. *Financial support:* In 2006–07, 5 research assistantships with tuition reimbursements (averaging $14,000 per year) were awarded; career-related internships or fieldwork, institutionally sponsored loans, scholarships/grants, and tuition waivers (partial) also available. Support available to part-time students. Financial award applicants required to submit FAFSA. *Faculty research:* Toxicology, domestic violence, health policy and planning, environmental hazards, obesity, substance abuse, minority health spirituality, women's health. Total annual research expenditures: $150,133. *Unit head:* Dr. Clare Houseman, Chair, 757-683-4259, Fax: 757-683-4410, E-mail: chpgdd@odu.edu.

Old Dominion University, Darden College of Education, Program in Physical Education, Exercise and Wellness Emphasis, Norfolk, VA 23529. Offers MS Ed. Part-time and evening/weekend programs available. *Faculty:* 7 full-time (4 women). *Students:* 20 full-time (13 women), 2 part-time (1 woman); includes 3 minority (all African Americans), 4 international. Average age 26. 12 applicants, 92% accepted, 8 enrolled. In 2006, 3 degrees awarded. *Degree requirements:* For master's, thesis or alternative, internship, research project, comprehensive exam. *Entrance requirements:* For master's, GRE, minimum GPA of 2.8 overall, minimum of 3.0 in major. Additional exam requirements/recommendations for international students: Required—TOEFL (minimum score 500 paper-based; 200 computer-based). *Application deadline:* For fall admission, 7/1 for domestic students; for spring admission, 11/1 for domestic students. Applications are processed on a rolling basis. Application fee: $40. *Expenses:* Tuition, area resident: Part-time $285 per credit hour. Tuition, nonresident: part-time $715 per credit hour. Required fees: $94 per semester. *Financial support:* In 2006–07, fellowships (averaging $1,500 per year), 2 research assistantships with partial tuition reimbursements (averaging $9,000 per year), 1 teaching assistantship with partial tuition reimbursement (averaging $9,000 per year) were awarded; career-related internships or fieldwork and scholarships/grants also available. Financial award application deadline: 4/15. *Faculty research:* Diabetes, exercise, prescription, gait and balance. Total annual research expenditures: $105,000. *Unit head:* Liz Dowling, Graduate Program Director, 757-683-4514, E-mail: ldowling@odu.edu. *Application contact:* Robert Spina, Graduate Program Director, 757-683-6029, E-mail: rspina@odu.edu.

Oregon State University, Graduate School, College of Health and Human Sciences, Department of Public Health, Program in Health Promotion and Health Behavior, Corvallis, OR 97331. Offers MAIS, MAT, MS. *Entrance requirements:* For master's, California Basic Educational Skills Test, NTE, minimum GPA of 3.0 in last 90 hours. Additional exam requirements/recommendations for international students: Required—TOEFL. *Application deadline:* For fall admission, 3/1 for domestic students. Applications are processed on a rolling basis. Application fee: $50. *Financial support:* Fellowships, career-related internships or fieldwork, Federal Work-Study, and institutionally sponsored loans available. Support available to part-time students. Financial award application deadline: 2/1. *Unit head:* Dr. Sheryl Thorburn, Coordinator, 541-737-9493, Fax: 541-737-4001.

Portland State University, Graduate Studies, College of Urban and Public Affairs, School of Community Health, Portland, OR 97207-0751. Offers gerontology (Certificate); health education (MA, MS); health education and health promotion (MPH); health studies (MPA, MPH), including health administration and policy. *Accreditation:* CEPH. Part-time programs available. *Faculty:* 13 full-time (9 women), 8 part-time/adjunct (6 women). *Students:* 36 full-time (30 women), 34 part-time (27 women); includes 9 minority (1 African American, 1 Asian American or Pacific Islander, 7 Hispanic Americans), 5 international. Average age 32. 73 applicants, 84% accepted, 34 enrolled. In 2006, 20 degrees awarded. *Degree requirements:* For master's, oral and written exams. *Entrance requirements:* For master's, GRE General Test, 3 letters of recommendation. Additional exam requirements/recommendations for international students: Required—TOEFL (minimum score 550 paper-based; 213 computer-based). *Application deadline:* For fall admission, 2/1 for domestic and international students. Application fee: $50. *Expenses:* Tuition, state resident: full-time $6,426; part-time $238 per credit. Tuition, nonresident:

full-time $11,016; part-time $408 per credit. Tuition and fees vary according to course load. *Financial support:* In 2006–07, 4 research assistantships with full tuition reimbursements (averaging $7,286 per year) were awarded; fellowships, teaching assistantships, career-related internships or fieldwork, Federal Work-Study, scholarships/grants, and unspecified assistantships also available. Support available to part-time students. Financial award application deadline: 3/1; financial award applicants required to submit FAFSA. Total annual research expenditures: $766,046. *Unit head:* Carlos J. Crespo, Interim Director, 503-725-5102, Fax: 503-725-5100. *Application contact:* Elizabeth Bull, Assistant to the Director, 503-725-4592, Fax: 503-725-5100, E-mail: bulle@pdx.edu.

Purdue University, Graduate School, College of Liberal Arts, Department of Health and Kinesiology, West Lafayette, IN 47907. Offers exercise, human physiology of movement and sport (PhD); health and fitness (MS); health promotion (MS); health promotion and disease prevention (PhD); movement and sport science (MS); pedagogy and administration (MS); pedagogy of physical activity and health (PhD); psychology of sport and exercise, and motor behavior (PhD). Part-time programs available. *Faculty:* 16 full-time (5 women), 6 part-time/adjunct (0 women). *Students:* 60 full-time (37 women), 25 part-time (12 women); includes 8 minority (3 African Americans, 1 American Indian/Alaska Native, 1 Asian American or Pacific Islander, 3 Hispanic Americans), 15 international. Average age 28. 92 applicants, 63% accepted, 33 enrolled. In 2006, 13 master's, 3 doctorates awarded. *Degree requirements:* For master's, thesis (for some programs); for doctorate, thesis/dissertation. *Entrance requirements:* For master's and doctorate, GRE General Test. Additional exam requirements/recommendations for international students: Required—TOEFL. *Application deadline:* For fall admission, 2/1 for domestic and international students. Applications are processed on a rolling basis. Application fee: $55. Electronic applications accepted. *Financial support:* In 2006–07, 4 fellowships with partial tuition reimbursements (averaging $12,000 per year), 2 research assistantships with partial tuition reimbursements (averaging $10,000 per year), 22 teaching assistantships with partial tuition reimbursements (averaging $10,000 per year) were awarded; Federal Work-Study also available. Support available to part-time students. Financial award applicants required to submit FAFSA. *Faculty research:* Wellness, motivation, teaching effectiveness, learning and development. *Unit head:* Dr. William Harper, Head, 765-494-3178, Fax: 765-494-496-1239. *Application contact:* Graduate Studies Office, 765-494-3162, Fax: 765-496-1239, E-mail: hkgrad@purdue.edu.

San Diego State University, Graduate and Research Affairs, College of Health and Human Services, Graduate School of Public Health, San Diego, CA 92182. Offers environmental health (MPH); epidemiology (MPH, PhD), including biostatistics (MPH); global emergency preparedness and response (MS); health behavior (PhD); health promotion (MPH); health services administration (MPH); toxicology (MS); MSW/MPH. *Accreditation:* ABET (one or more programs are accredited); CAHME (one or more programs are accredited); CEPH (one or more programs are accredited). Part-time programs available. *Degree requirements:* For master's, thesis (for some programs), comprehensive exam (for some programs); for doctorate, thesis/dissertation. *Entrance requirements:* For master's, GMAT (health services administration MPH), GRE General Test; for doctorate, GRE General Test. Additional exam requirements/recommendations for international students: Required—TOEFL. *Faculty research:* Evaluation of tobacco, AIDS prevalence and prevention, mammography, infant death project, Alzheimer's in elderly Chinese.

Simmons College, School for Health Studies, Program in Nutrition and Health Promotion, Boston, MA 02115. Offers didactic program in dietetics (Certificate); nutrition (dietetic internship) (Certificate); nutrition and health promotion (MS); sports nutrition (Certificate). Certificate program offered entirely online. Part-time and evening/weekend programs available. Postbaccalaureate distance learning degree programs offered (no on-campus study). *Faculty:* 5 full-time (all women), 4 part-time/adjunct (all women). *Students:* 7 full-time (all women), 19 part-time (all women); includes 4 minority (2 Asian Americans or Pacific Islanders, 2 Hispanic Americans). 53 applicants, 42% accepted, 16 enrolled. In 2006, 6 master's, 8 other advanced degrees awarded. *Degree requirements:* For master's, research project. *Entrance requirements:* For master's, GRE, courses in community nutrition, nutritional metabolism, introduction to nutrition, organic and inorganic chemistry, statistics, anatomy and physiology. Additional exam requirements/recommendations for international students: Required—TOEFL (minimum score 550 paper-based; 230 computer-based; 88 iBT). *Application deadline:* For fall admission, 6/1 for domestic students; for spring admission, 11/1 for domestic students. Application fee: $50. Electronic applications accepted. *Expenses: Contact institution. Financial support:* In 2006–07, research assistantships (averaging $6,000 per year), teaching assistantships (averaging $6,000 per year) were awarded; fellowships, unspecified assistantships also available. Financial award application deadline: 3/1. *Faculty research:* Nutrition supplements of athletes' nutrition, cancer and vitamin A, dietary patterns and chronic disease development, obesity bias among health professions, poly oils in baked goods, food security and obesity, childhood overweight. Total annual research expenditures: $60,000. *Unit head:* Dr. Nancie Herbold, Director, 617-521-2711, Fax: 617-521-3137, E-mail: herbold@simmons.edu. *Application contact:* Staff Assistant, 617-521-2718, Fax: 617-521-3137, E-mail: gshsadm@simmons.edu.

Université de Montréal, Faculty of Graduate Studies, Department of Kinesiology, Montréal, QC H3C 3J7, Canada. Offers kinesiology (M Sc, DESS); physical activity (M Sc, PhD); physical activity and health promotion (DESS). *Faculty:* 14 full-time (5 women), 8 part-time/adjunct (2 women). *Students:* 50 full-time (14 women), 14 part-time (10 women). Average age 26. 49 applicants, 45% accepted, 19 enrolled. In 2006, 11 master's, 7 doctorates awarded. *Degree requirements:* For master's, one foreign language, thesis (for some programs); for doctorate, one foreign language, thesis/dissertation, general exam. *Application deadline:* For fall admission, 2/1 priority date for domestic students; for winter admission, 11/1 priority date for domestic students; for spring admission, 2/1 priority date for domestic students. Application fee: $30. Electronic applications accepted. *Financial support:* In 2006–07, 3 fellowships (averaging $20,000 per year), 10 research assistantships (averaging $5,000 per year), 6 teaching assistantships (averaging $7,000 per year) were awarded. Financial award application deadline: 2/1. *Faculty research:* Physiology of exercise, psychology of sports, biomechanics, dance, sociology of sports. Total annual research expenditures: $600,000. *Unit head:* Director, 514-343-6166, Fax: 514-343-2181. *Application contact:* Francine Normandeau, Information Contact, 514-343-6152, E-mail: francine.normandeau@umontreal.ca.

The University of Alabama, Graduate School, College of Human Environmental Sciences, Department of Health Science, Tuscaloosa, AL 35487. Offers health education and promotion (PhD); health studies (MA). Part-time and evening/weekend programs available. Postbaccalaureate distance learning degree programs offered (no on-campus study). *Faculty:* 3 full-time (1 woman), 3 part-time/adjunct (1 woman). *Students:* 39 full-time (25 women), 77 part-time (52 women); includes 27 minority (21 African Americans, 2 American Indian/Alaska Native, 3 Asian Americans or Pacific Islanders, 1 Hispanic American), 2 international. Average age 34. 52 applicants, 75% accepted, 33 enrolled. In 2006, 51 master's, 2 doctorates awarded. *Median time to degree:* Master's–1.3 years full-time, 2 years part-time. Of those who began their doctoral program in fall 1998, 100% received their degree in 8 years or less. *Degree requirements:* For doctorate, one foreign language, thesis/dissertation. *Entrance requirements:* For master's and doctorate, GRE General Test or MAT, minimum GPA of 3.0. Additional exam requirements/recommendations for international students: Required—TOEFL. *Application deadline:* For fall admission, 7/6 for domestic students. Applications are processed on a rolling basis. Application fee: $25. *Financial support:* In 2006–07, 8 research assistantships with full tuition reimbursements (averaging $8,100 per year), teaching assistantships with full tuition reimbursements (averaging $8,100 per year) were awarded; career-related internships or fieldwork, Federal Work-Study, and institutionally sponsored loans also available. Financial award application deadline: 7/14. *Faculty research:* Program planning, adolescent health, worksite health, data management, health behavior. Total annual research expenditures:$43,097. *Unit head:* Dr. Michael A. Perko, Department Head and Associate Professor, 205-348-2956, Fax: 205-348-7568.

The University of Alabama at Birmingham, School of Education, Department of Human Studies, Program in Health Education/Health Promotion, Birmingham, AL 35294. Offers PhD. *Accreditation:* NCATE. *Students:* 6 full-time (5 women), 26 part-time (20 women); includes 14 minority (13 African Americans, 1 Hispanic American). 11 applicants, 82% accepted. In 2006, 4 degrees awarded. *Degree requirements:* For doctorate, thesis/dissertation. *Entrance requirements:* For doctorate, GRE General Test, MAT, minimum GPA of 3.25. Application fee: $35 ($60 for international students). Electronic applications accepted. *Expenses:* Tuition, state resident: part-time $170 per credit hour. Tuition, nonresident: part-time $425 per credit hour. Required fees: $15 per credit hour. $122 per term. Tuition and fees vary according to program. *Unit head:* Dr. David M. Macrina, Chair, Department of Human Studies, 205-934-2446, Fax: 205-975-8040, E-mail: dmacrina@uab.edu.

University of Alberta, Faculty of Graduate Studies and Research, Centre for Health Promotion Studies, Edmonton, AB T6G 2E1, Canada. Offers M Sc, Postgraduate Diploma. Part-time programs available. Postbaccalaureate distance learning degree programs offered (minimal on-campus study). *Faculty:* 1 (woman) full-time, 23 part-time/adjunct (18 women). *Students:* 19 full-time (18 women), 69 part-time (64 women). 100 applicants, 32% accepted, 28 enrolled. In 2006, 21 master's, 1 Postgraduate Diploma awarded. *Degree requirements:* For master's, thesis (for some programs). *Entrance requirements:* For master's and Postgraduate Diploma, minimum GPA of 3.0. Additional exam requirements/recommendations for international students: Required—TOEFL (minimum score 580 paper-based; 237 computer-based). *Application deadline:* For fall admission, 3/31 for domestic students. Application fee: $0. Electronic applications accepted. *Financial support:* In 2006–07, 10 fellowships with partial tuition reimbursements, 15 research assistantships were awarded; career-related internships or fieldwork and scholarships/grants also available. *Faculty research:* Addictions, heart health, diabetics, social, physical activity behavior. *Unit head:* Dr. Helen M. Madill, Graduate Coordinator, 780-492-8661, Fax: 780-492-9347, E-mail: helen.madill@ualberta.ca. *Application contact:* Sue Muhlfeld, Graduate Programs Assistant, 780-492-9347, Fax: 780-492-9579, E-mail: health.promotion@ualberta.ca.

University of Alberta, School of Public Health, Centre for Health Promotion Studies, Edmonton, AB T6G 2E1, Canada. Offers health promotion (M Sc, Postgraduate Diploma). Part-time programs available. Postbaccalaureate distance learning degree programs offered. *Unit head:* Kim Raine, Director, 780-492-9415, E-mail: kim.raine@ualberta.ca. *Application contact:* Dr. Helen M. Madill, Graduate Coordinator, 780-492-8661, Fax: 780-492-9347, E-mail: helen.madill@ualberta.ca.

University of Central Florida, College of Education, Department of Teaching and Learning Principles, Orlando, FL 32816. Offers art education (M Ed, MA); coaching (Certificate); educational media (M Ed); elementary education (M Ed, MA); English language arts education (M Ed, MA); foreign language education (Certificate); health and wellness (Certificate); K-8 mathematics and science education (M Ed, Certificate); mathematics education (M Ed, MA); music education (M Ed, MA); online educational media (Certificate); reading education (M Ed, MA, Certificate); science education (M Ed, MA); social science education (M Ed, MA); sports leadership (Certificate); vocational education (M Ed, MA); world studies education (Certificate); writing education (Certificate). Part-time and evening/weekend programs available. *Faculty:* 57 full-time (44 women), 62 part-time/adjunct (42 women). *Students:* 101 full-time (77 women), 323 part-time (269 women); includes 60 minority (24 African Americans, 13 Asian Americans or Pacific Islanders, 23 Hispanic Americans), 5 international. 221 applicants, 76% accepted, 115 enrolled. In 2006, 158 master's, 40 other advanced degrees awarded. *Degree requirements:* For Certificate, thesis or alternative. *Entrance requirements:* For degree, GRE General Test, minimum GPA of 3.0. Additional exam requirements/recommendations for international students: Required—TOEFL. *Application deadline:* For fall admission, 7/15 for domestic students; for spring admission, 12/15 for domestic students. Application fee: $30. Electronic applications accepted. *Expenses:* Tuition, state resident: full-time $6,167; part-time $257 per credit hour. Tuition, nonresident: full-time $22,790; part-time $950 per credit hour. *Financial support:* Fellowships with partial tuition reimbursements, research assistantships with partial tuition reimbursements, teaching assistantships with partial tuition reimbursements, career-related internships or fieldwork, Federal Work-Study, institutionally sponsored loans, tuition waivers (partial), and unspecified assistantships available. Financial award application deadline: 3/1; financial award applicants required to submit FAFSA. *Unit head:* Dr. Robert Williams, Chair, 407-823-1768, E-mail: rdwilliams@mail.ucf.edu. *Application contact:* Information Contact, 407-823-2053.

University of Chicago, Division of the Biological Sciences, Program in Health Studies, Chicago, IL 60637-1513. Offers MS. *Faculty:* 14 full-time (4 women), 4 part-time/adjunct (3 women). *Students:* Average age 35. 10 applicants, 60% accepted, 5 enrolled. *Application deadline:* For fall admission, 12/28 priority date for domestic and international students. Application fee: $55. Electronic applications accepted. *Expenses:* Tuition: Full-time $34,920. Required fees: $612. One-time fee: $35 full-time. Full-time tuition and fees vary according to course load, degree level and program. *Unit head:* Dr. Ronald Thisted, Chair, 773-834-1242, Fax: 773-702-1979, E-mail: thisted@health.bsd.uchicago.edu. *Application contact:* Michele Thompson, Education Program Manager, 773-834-1836, E-mail: mthompso@health.bsd.uchicago.edu.

University of Delaware, College of Health Sciences, Department of Health, Nutrition, and Exercise Sciences, Newark, DE 19716. Offers exercise science (MS), including biomechanics, exercise physiology, motor control; health promotion (MS); human nutrition (MS). Part-time programs available. *Degree requirements:* For master's, thesis, registration. *Entrance requirements:* For master's, GRE General Test, interview, minimum GPA of 3.0. Additional exam requirements/recommendations for international students: Required—TOEFL (minimum score 550 paper-based; 213 computer-based). Electronic applications accepted. *Faculty research:* Sport biomechanics, rehabilitation biomechanics, vascular dynamics.

University of Georgia, College of Public Health, Department of Health Promotion and Behavior, Athens, GA 30602. Offers M Ed, MA, MPH, PhD, Ed S. *Accreditation:* NCATE (one or more programs are accredited). *Faculty:* 7 full-time (5 women). *Students:* 12 full-time (10 women), 4 part-time (all women); includes 6 minority (5 African Americans, 1 Hispanic American). 52 applicants, 77% accepted. In 2006, 4 master's, 4 doctorates awarded. *Degree requirements:* For master's, thesis (MA); for doctorate, thesis/dissertation. *Entrance requirements:* For master's, GRE General Test or MAT; for doctorate, GRE General Test. *Application deadline:* For fall admission, 7/1 priority date for domestic students; for spring admission, 11/15 for domestic students. Application fee: $50. Electronic applications accepted. *Financial support:* Fellowships, research assistantships, teaching assistantships, unspecified assistantships available. *Unit head:* Dr. Mark G. Wilson, Head, 706-542-4364, Fax: 706-542-4956, E-mail: mwilson@coe.uga.edu. *Application contact:* Pamela Orpinas, Graduate Coordinator, 706-542-4372, Fax: 706-542-4956, E-mail: porpinas@uga.edu.

University of Kentucky, Graduate School, College of Education, Program in Kinesiology and Health Promotion, Lexington, KY 40506-0032. Offers exercise science (PhD); kinesiology (MS, Ed D). *Faculty:* 13 full-time (4 women). *Students:* 82 full-time (46 women), 31 part-time (12 women); includes 15 minority (10 African Americans, 3 Asian Americans or Pacific Islanders, 2 Hispanic Americans), 2 international. Average age 29. 127 applicants, 55% accepted, 46 enrolled. In 2006, 37 master's, 3 doctorates awarded. Terminal master's awarded for partial completion of doctoral program. *Median time to degree:* Of those who began their doctoral program in fall 1998, 75% received their degree in 8 years or less. *Degree requirements:* For master's, thesis optional; for doctorate, thesis/dissertation, comprehensive exam. *Entrance requirements:* For master's, GRE General Test, minimum undergraduate GPA of 2.75; for doctorate, GRE General Test, minimum graduate GPA of 3.0. Additional exam requirements/recommendations for international students: Required—TOEFL (minimum score 550 paper-based; 213 computer-based). *Application deadline:* For fall admission, 7/17 priority date for domestic students, 2/1 priority date for international students; for spring admission, 12/13 priority date for domestic students, 6/15 priority date for international students. Application fee: $40 ($55 for international students). Electronic applications accepted. *Expenses:* Tuition, state resident: full-time $7,670; part-time $401 per credit hour. Tuition, nonresident: full-time $16,158;

Health Promotion

University of Kentucky (continued)

part-time $873 per credit hour. *Financial support:* In 2006–07, 2 fellowships with full tuition reimbursements (averaging $4,500 per year), 17 research assistantships with full tuition reimbursements (averaging $9,500 per year), 19 teaching assistantships with full tuition reimbursements (averaging $7,446 per year) were awarded; career-related internships or fieldwork, Federal Work-Study, institutionally sponsored loans, scholarships/grants, traineeships, health care benefits, tuition waivers (partial), and unspecified assistantships also available. Support available to part-time students. Financial award application deadline: 3/15. *Unit head:* Dr. Richard Riggs, Director of Graduate Studies, 859-257-3645, Fax: 859-323-1090. *Application contact:* Dr. Brian Jackson, Senior Associate Dean, 859-257-4667, Fax: 859-257-4676, E-mail: brian.jackson@uky.edu.

University of Massachusetts Lowell, Graduate School, College of Health Professions, Department of Nursing, Program in Administration of Nursing Services, Lowell, MA 01854-2881. Offers health promotion (PhD). *Accreditation:* AACN. *Degree requirements:* For doctorate, thesis/dissertation. *Entrance requirements:* For doctorate, GRE General Test.

University of Memphis, Graduate School, College of Education, Department of Health and Sport Sciences, Memphis, TN 38152. Offers clinical nutrition (MS); exercise and sport science (MS); health promotion (MS); physical education teacher education (MS), including teacher education; sport and leisure commerce (MS). Part-time and evening/weekend programs available. *Faculty:* 26 full-time (10 women), 8 part-time/adjunct (5 women). *Students:* Average age 28. 50 applicants, 62% accepted. In 2006, 14 degrees awarded. *Degree requirements:* For master's, thesis, comprehensive exam. *Entrance requirements:* For master's, GRE General Test or GMAT (sport and leisure commerce). *Application deadline:* For fall admission, 5/1 priority date for domestic students; for spring admission, 11/1 for domestic students. Applications are processed on a rolling basis. Application fee: $25 ($50 for international students). *Financial support:* In 2006–07, 13 research assistantships with full tuition reimbursements (averaging $6,000 per year), 4 teaching assistantships with full tuition reimbursements (averaging $6,000 per year) were awarded; career-related internships or fieldwork, tuition waivers (partial), and community assistantships also available. *Faculty research:* Sport marketing and consumer analysis, health psychology, smoking cessation, psychosocial aspects of cardiovascular disease, global health promotion. Total annual research expenditures: $1.3 million. *Unit head:* Dr. Michael H. Hamrick, Chairman, 901-678-4165, Fax: 901-678-3591, E-mail: mhamrick@memphis.edu. *Application contact:* Christina Little, Academic Services Coordinator, 901-678-4316, Fax: 901-678-3591, E-mail: aclittle@memphis.edu.

University of Michigan, School of Public Health, Department of Health Behavior and Health Education, Ann Arbor, MI 48109. Offers MPH, PhD, MSW/MPH. PhD offered through the Horace H. Rackham School of Graduate Studies. *Accreditation:* CEPH (one or more programs are accredited). Terminal master's awarded for partial completion of doctoral program. *Entrance requirements:* For master's and doctorate, GRE General Test. Additional exam requirements/recommendations for international students: Required—TOEFL (minimum score 560 paper-based; 220 computer-based). Electronic applications accepted. *Faculty research:* Asthma management, women and heart disease, cancer prevention and control.

The University of Montana, Graduate School, School of Education, Department of Health and Human Performance, Missoula, MT 59812-0002. Offers exercise science (MS); health and human performance (MS); health promotion (MS). *Accreditation:* NCATE. Part-time programs available. *Entrance requirements:* For master's, GRE General Test. Additional exam requirements/recommendations for international students: Required—TOEFL. *Faculty research:* Exercise physiology, performance psychology, nutrition, pre-employment physical screening, program evaluation.

University of Nevada, Las Vegas, Graduate College, Division of Health Sciences, School of Public Health, Department of Health Promotion, Las Vegas, NV 89154-9900. Offers M Ed. Part-time and evening/weekend programs available. *Faculty:* 8 full-time (3 women), 6 part-time/adjunct (4 women). *Students:* 21 full-time (18 women), 43 part-time (38 women); includes 23 minority (8 African Americans, 10 Asian Americans or Pacific Islanders, 5 Hispanic Americans). 29 applicants, 83% accepted, 19 enrolled. In 2006, 13 degrees awarded. *Degree requirements:* For master's, project. *Entrance requirements:* For master's, minimum GPA of 3.0. Additional exam requirements/recommendations for international students: Required—TOEFL (minimum score 550 paper-based; 213 computer-based; 80 iBT). *Application deadline:* For fall admission, 6/15 for domestic students, 5/1 for international students; for spring admission, 11/15 for domestic students, 10/1 for international students. Application fee: $60 ($75 for international students). Electronic applications accepted. *Financial support:* In 2006–07, 3 research assistantships with partial tuition reimbursements (averaging $10,000 per year), 1 teaching assistantship with partial tuition reimbursement (averaging $10,000 per year) were awarded; career-related internships or fieldwork, Federal Work-Study, institutionally sponsored loans, scholarships/grants, health care benefits, and unspecified assistantships also available. Support available to part-time students. *Unit head:* Dr. Chuck Regin, Chair, 702-895-4030, Fax: 702-895-3979. *Application contact:* Graduate College Admissions Evaluator, 702-895-3320, Fax: 702-895-4180, E-mail: gradcollege@unlv.edu.

The University of North Carolina at Chapel Hill, Graduate School, School of Public Health, Public Health Leadership Program, Chapel Hill, NC 27599. Offers health care and prevention (MPH); leadership (MPH); occupational health nursing (MPH); public health nursing (MS). Part-time programs available. Postbaccalaureate distance learning degree programs offered (minimal on-campus study). *Faculty:* 6 full-time (5 women), 12 part-time/adjunct. *Students:* 168 full-time (112 women); includes 38 minority (27 African Americans, 1 American Indian/Alaska Native, 9 Asian Americans or Pacific Islanders, 1 Hispanic American), 5 international. Average age 32. 132 applicants, 73% accepted, 96 enrolled. In 2006, 87 degrees awarded. *Degree requirements:* For master's, thesis (MS), paper (MPH). *Entrance requirements:* For master's, GRE General Test, minimum GPA of 3.0, public health experience. Additional exam requirements/recommendations for international students: Required—TOEFL. *Application deadline:* For fall admission, 1/1 priority date for domestic and international students; for spring admission, 10/15 for domestic students. Applications are processed on a rolling basis. Application fee: $65. Electronic applications accepted. *Financial support:* In 2006–07, 17 fellowships with full and partial tuition reimbursements (averaging $11,608 per year) were awarded; career-related internships or fieldwork, institutionally sponsored loans, traineeships, and health care benefits also available. Financial award application deadline: 2/1; financial award applicants required to submit FAFSA. *Faculty research:* Occupational health issues, clinical outcomes, prenatal and early childcare, adolescent health, effectiveness of home visiting, issues in occupational health nursing, community-based interventions. *Unit head:* Dr. William Sollecito, Director, 919-966-5285, Fax: 919-966-0981, E-mail: bill_sollecito@unc.edu. *Application contact:* Sue Robeson, Registrar, 919-966-5305, Fax: 919-966-0981, E-mail: robeson@email.unc.edu.

University of North Texas, Robert B. Toulouse School of Graduate Studies, College of Education, Department of Kinesiology, Health Promotion, and Recreation, Program in Health Promotion, Denton, TX 76203. Offers community health (MS); school health (MS). Part-time programs available. *Faculty:* 16 full-time (6 women). *Students:* 1 (woman) full-time. Average age 27. 2 applicants, 100% accepted, 0 enrolled. In 2006, 2 degrees awarded. *Degree requirements:* For master's, thesis (for some programs). *Entrance requirements:* For master's, GRE General Test. Additional exam requirements/recommendations for international students: Recommended—TOEFL (minimum score 550 paper-based; 213 computer-based). *Application deadline:* For fall admission, 7/15 for domestic students. Application fee: $50 ($75 for international students). *Expenses:* Tuition, state resident: full-time $3,573; part-time $198 per credit. Tuition, nonresident: full-time $8,577; part-time $476 per credit. Required fees: $1,258; $126 per credit. One-time fee: $150 full-time. Tuition and fees vary according to course load. *Financial support:* Teaching assistantships, career-related internships or fieldwork, Federal Work-Study, and institutionally sponsored loans available. Financial award application deadline: 4/1. *Application contact:* Dr. John Collins, Adviser, 940-565-3422, Fax: 940-565-4904, E-mail: collins@unt.edu.

University of Oklahoma Health Sciences Center, Graduate College, College of Public Health, Department of Health Promotion Sciences, Oklahoma City, OK 73190. Offers MPH, MS, Dr PH, PhD. *Accreditation:* CEPH (one or more programs are accredited). Part-time programs available. *Degree requirements:* For master's, thesis (for some programs), comprehensive exam; for doctorate, 2 foreign languages, thesis/dissertation, comprehensive exam. *Entrance requirements:* For master's, letters of recommendation, resumé; for doctorate, GRE, letters of recommendation. Additional exam requirements/recommendations for international students: Required—TOEFL (minimum score 570 paper-based; 230 computer-based). *Faculty research:* Health education, school health, health behavior, American Indian health.

University of Puerto Rico, Medical Sciences Campus, Graduate School of Public Health, Department of Social Sciences, Program in School Health Promotion, San Juan, PR 00936-5067. Offers Certificate. *Application contact:* Prof. Mayra E. Santiago-Vargas, Counselor, 787-756-5244, Fax: 787-759-6719, E-mail: msantiago@rcm.upr.edu.

University of South Carolina, The Graduate School, Arnold School of Public Health, Department of Health Promotion, Education and Behavior, Columbia, SC 29208. Offers alcohol and drug studies (Certificate); health education administration (Ed D); health promotion and education (MAT, MPH, MS, MSPH, Dr PH, PhD); school health education (Certificate). MAT and Ed D offered in cooperation with the College of Education. *Accreditation:* CEPH (one or more programs are accredited); NCATE (one or more programs are accredited). *Degree requirements:* For master's, thesis or alternative, practicum (MPH), project (MS), comprehensive exam; for doctorate, thesis/dissertation, comprehensive exam. *Entrance requirements:* For master's and doctorate, GRE General Test. Additional exam requirements/recommendations for international students: Required—TOEFL (minimum score 570 paper-based; 230 computer-based). Electronic applications accepted. *Faculty research:* Implementation and evaluation of health behavior change programs, nutrition behavior, work site health promotion, AIDS education.

University of South Carolina, The Graduate School, Arnold School of Public Health, Program in Physical Activity and Public Health, Columbia, SC 29208. Offers MPH. *Accreditation:* CEPH. *Degree requirements:* For master's, practicum. *Entrance requirements:* For master's, GRE.

University of Southern California, Keck School of Medicine and Graduate School, Graduate Programs in Medicine, Department of Preventive Medicine, Master of Public Health Program, Los Angeles, CA 90089. Offers biometry/epidemiology (MPH); health communication (MPH); health promotion (MPH); preventive nutrition (MPH). *Accreditation:* CEPH. Part-time programs available. *Faculty:* 22 full-time (12 women), 3 part-time/adjunct (0 women). *Students:* 148 full-time (118 women), 7 part-time (6 women); includes 77 minority (17 African Americans, 45 Asian Americans or Pacific Islanders, 15 Hispanic Americans), 24 international. Average age 26. 310 applicants, 66% accepted, 85 enrolled. In 2006, 53 degrees awarded. *Degree requirements:* For master's, practicum, final report, oral presentation. *Entrance requirements:* For master's, GRE General Test, MCAT, GMAT, DAT, minimum GPA of 3.0. Additional exam requirements/recommendations for international students: Required—TOEFL (minimum score 600 paper-based; 250 computer-based; 100 iBT). *Application deadline:* For fall admission, 6/1 priority date for domestic and international students; for spring admission, 11/15 priority date for domestic students, 10/1 priority date for international students. Applications are processed on a rolling basis. Application fee: $85. Electronic applications accepted. *Expenses:* Tuition: Full-time $33,314; part-time $1,121 per credit. Required fees: $522. Full-time tuition and fees vary according to program. *Financial support:* In 2006–07, 131 students received support, including 11 research assistantships with full tuition reimbursements available (averaging $11,109 per year), 18 teaching assistantships with partial tuition reimbursements available (averaging $11,109 per year); career-related internships or fieldwork, Federal Work-Study, institutionally sponsored loans, scholarships/grants, health care benefits, unspecified assistantships, and staff tuition remission also available. Support available to part-time students. Financial award application deadline: 5/1; financial award applicants required to submit CSS PROFILE or FAFSA. *Faculty research:* Substance abuse prevention, cancer and heart disease prevention, mass media and health communication research, health promotion, treatment compliance. Total annual research expenditures: $93.8 million. *Unit head:* Dr. Thomas W. Valente, Director, 626-457-6678, Fax: 626-457-6699, E-mail: tvalente@usc.edu. *Application contact:* Nemesia P. Kelly, Program Specialist, 626-457-6603, Fax: 626-457-6699, E-mail: nkelly@usc.edu.

See Close-Up on page 2065.

The University of Tennessee, Graduate School, College of Education, Health and Human Sciences, Program in Health Promotion and Health Education, Knoxville, TN 37996. Offers MS. *Accreditation:* CEPH. Part-time programs available. *Students:* 4 full-time (3 women), 11 part-time (all women). 4 applicants, 50% accepted. In 2006, 1 degree awarded. *Degree requirements:* For master's, thesis optional. *Entrance requirements:* For master's, minimum GPA of 2.7. Additional exam requirements/recommendations for international students: Required—TOEFL. *Application deadline:* For fall admission, 2/1 priority date for domestic students. Applications are processed on a rolling basis. Application fee: $35. Electronic applications accepted. *Expenses:* Tuition, state resident: full-time $5,574. Tuition, nonresident: full-time $16,840. Required fees: $792. *Financial support:* Application deadline: 2/1; *Unit head:* Dr. Paula Zemel, Graduate Representative, 865-974-5041, E-mail: pzemel@utk.edu.

University of Utah, The Graduate School, College of Health, Department of Health Promotion and Education, Salt Lake City, UT 84112-1107. Offers M Phil, MS, Ed D, PhD. Part-time and evening/weekend programs available. *Faculty:* 7 full-time (3 women). *Students:* 26 full-time (20 women), 26 part-time (19 women); includes 1 minority (Hispanic American), 1 international. Average age 37. 24 applicants, 100% accepted, 19 enrolled. In 2006, 5 master's, 4 doctorates awarded. Terminal master's awarded for partial completion of doctoral program. *Median time to degree:* Of those who began their doctoral program in fall 1998, 100% received their degree in 8 years or less. *Degree requirements:* For master's and doctorate, thesis/dissertation or alternative, field experience, comprehensive exam. *Entrance requirements:* For master's, GRE General Test, minimum GPA of 3.0; for doctorate, GRE General Test, minimum GPA of 3.2. Additional exam requirements/recommendations for international students: Required—TOEFL (minimum score 500 paper-based; 173 computer-based). *Application deadline:* For winter admission, 2/15 for domestic students. Application fee: $45 ($65 for international students). *Expenses:* Tuition, state resident: full-time $3,208. Tuition, nonresident: full-time $11,326. Required fees: $608. Tuition and fees vary according to class time and program. *Financial support:* In 2006–07, 7 students received support, including 2 research assistantships with full tuition reimbursements available (averaging $10,650 per year), 3 teaching assistantships with full tuition reimbursements available (averaging $10,650 per year); career-related internships or fieldwork, Federal Work-Study, and institutionally sponsored loans also available. Financial award application deadline: 2/15; financial award applicants required to submit FAFSA. *Faculty research:* Health behavior and counseling, health service administration, evaluation of health programs. Total annual research expenditures: $151,482. *Unit head:* Les Chatelain, Interim Chair, 801-581-4512, Fax: 801-585-3646, E-mail: les.chatelain@health.utah.edu. *Application contact:* Tim Behrens, Graduate Director, 801-581-8114, E-mail: tim.behrens@hsc.utah.edu.

University of Wisconsin–Madison, School of Medicine and Public Health and Graduate School, Graduate Programs in Medicine, Madison, WI 53706-1380. Offers biomolecular chemistry (MS, PhD); cancer biology (PhD); genetics and medical genetics (MS, PhD), including genetics (PhD), medical genetics (MS); medical physics (MS, PhD), including health physics (MS), medical physics; microbiology (PhD); molecular and cellular pharmacology (PhD); pathology and laboratory medicine (PhD); physiology (PhD); population health (MPH, MS, PhD); MD/PhD. Part-time programs available. Postbaccalaureate distance learning degree programs offered (minimal on-campus study). Terminal master's awarded for partial completion of doctoral program. Application fee: $45. Electronic applications accepted. *Expenses:* Contact institution. *Financial support:* Fellowships with full tuition reimbursements, research assistantships with full tuition reimbursements, teaching assistantships with full tuition reimbursements, scholarships/grants, traineeships, and tuition waivers (full) available. *Unit head:* Dr. Paul M. DeLuca, Associate Dean of Research and Graduate Studies, 608-265-0524, Fax: 608-265-0522, E-mail: pmdeluca@facstaff.wisc.edu.

University of Wisconsin–Stevens Point, College of Professional Studies, School of Health Promotion and Human Development, Stevens Point, WI 54481-3897. Offers human and community resources (MS); nutritional sciences (MS). Part-time programs available. *Faculty:* 10 full-time (5 women), 1 (woman) part-time/adjunct. *Students:* 6 full-time (4 women), 13 part-time (all women); includes 1 minority (Asian American or Pacific Islander) In 2006, 15 degrees awarded. *Degree requirements:* For master's, thesis or alternative. *Entrance requirements:* For master's, minimum GPA of 2.75. *Application deadline:* For fall admission, 5/1 priority date for domestic students. Applications are processed on a rolling basis. Application fee: $45. *Expenses:* Tuition, state resident: full-time $5,910; part-time $328 per credit. Tuition, nonresident: full-time $16,520; part-time $918 per credit. Required fees: $756; $73 per credit. *Financial support:* Research assistantships, teaching assistantships, career-related internships or fieldwork, Federal Work-Study, and unspecified assistantships available. Support available to part-time students. Financial award application deadline: 5/1; financial award applicants required to submit FAFSA. *Unit head:* Marty Loy, Head, 715-346-2830, Fax: 715-346-2720. *Application contact:* Jasia Steinmetz, Information Contact, 715-346-2830, Fax: 715-346-2720, E-mail: jsteinme@uwsp.edu.

West Virginia University, School of Medicine, Department of Community Medicine, Morgantown, WV 26506. Offers public health (MPH), including community health/preventative medicine; public health sciences (PhD). *Accreditation:* CEPH. Part-time and evening/weekend programs available. Postbaccalaureate distance learning degree programs offered (minimal on-campus study). *Faculty:* 18 full-time (10 women), 4 part-time/adjunct (2 women). *Students:* 63 full-time (28 women), 17 part-time (9 women); includes 4 minority (2 African Americans, 2 Hispanic Americans), 33 international. Average age 36. 84 applicants, 51% accepted, 19 enrolled. In 2006, 41 degrees awarded. *Degree requirements:* For master's, thesis (for some programs). *Entrance requirements:* For master's, minimum GPA of 3.0. Additional exam requirements/recommendations for international students: Required—TOEFL. *Application deadline:* For fall admission, 3/1 priority date for domestic students. Applications are processed on a rolling basis. Application fee: $50. *Expenses:* Tuition, state resident: full-time $4,926; part-time $276 per credit hour. Tuition, nonresident: full-time $14,278; part-time $796 per credit hour. Tuition and fees vary according to program. *Financial support:* In 2006–07, 17 research assistantships with full tuition reimbursements (averaging $9,228 per year), 3 teaching assistantships with full tuition reimbursements (averaging $9,228 per year) were awarded; career-related internships or fieldwork, Federal Work-Study, institutionally sponsored loans, tuition waivers (partial), and unspecified assistantships also available. Financial award application deadline: 2/1; financial award applicants required to submit FAFSA. *Faculty research:* Adolescent smoking cessation, cardiovascular disease, women's health, worker's health. Total annual research expenditures: $3.5 million. *Unit head:* Dr. Alan Ducatman, Professor/Chair, 304-293-2502, Fax: 304-293-2629, E-mail: han.ducatman@hsc.wvu.edu. *Application contact:* Leah A. Adkins, Senior Program Coordinator, 304-293-1098, Fax: 304-293-3755, E-mail: ladkins@hsc.wvu.edu.

Wright State University, School of Medicine, Program in Public Health, Dayton, OH 45435. Offers health promotion and education (MPH); public health management (MPH); public health nursing (MPH). *Accreditation:* CEPH. *Unit head:* Dr. Richard J. Schuster, Director, 937-258-5555, Fax: 937-258-5544, E-mail: richard.schuster@wright.edu.

Industrial Hygiene

California State University, Northridge, Graduate Studies, College of Health and Human Development, Department of Environmental and Occupational Health, Northridge, CA 91330. Offers industrial hygiene (MS). *Faculty:* 5 full-time (0 women), 11 part-time/adjunct (3 women). *Students:* 14 full-time (3 women), 21 part-time (11 women); includes 16 minority (2 African Americans, 9 Asian Americans or Pacific Islanders, 5 Hispanic Americans), 2 international. Average age 31. 24 applicants, 75% accepted, 14 enrolled. In 2006, 18 degrees awarded. *Entrance requirements:* For master's, GRE General Test or minimum GPA of 3.0. Additional exam requirements/recommendations for international students: Required—TOEFL. *Application deadline:* For fall admission, 11/30 for domestic students. Application fee: $55. *Expenses:* Tuition, nonresident: full-time $8,136; part-time $4,068 per year. Required fees: $3,624; $1,161 per term. *Financial support:* Application deadline: 3/1. *Unit head:* Dr. Thomas Hatfield, Chair, 818-677-7476.

Montana Tech of The University of Montana, Graduate School, Industrial Hygiene Program, Butte, MT 59701-8997. Offers MS. *Accreditation:* ABET. Part-time programs available. *Faculty:* 5 full-time (2 women). *Students:* 6 full-time (all women), 15 part-time (5 women); includes 2 minority (1 American Indian/Alaska Native, 1 Hispanic American). 17 applicants, 82% accepted, 12 enrolled. In 2006, 3 degrees awarded. *Degree requirements:* For master's, thesis, registration. *Entrance requirements:* For master's, GRE General Test, minimum GPA of 3.0. Additional exam requirements/recommendations for international students: Required—TOEFL (minimum score 525 paper-based; 195 computer-based; 71 iBT). *Application deadline:* For fall admission, 4/1 priority date for domestic students; for spring admission, 10/1 priority date for domestic students. Applications are processed on a rolling basis. Application fee: $30. Electronic applications accepted. *Expenses:* Tuition, state resident: part-time $219 per credit. Tuition, nonresident: part-time $480 per credit. Required fees: $305 per credit. *Financial support:* In 2006–07, 8 students received support, including 1 research assistantship with partial tuition reimbursement available (averaging $1,200 per year), 6 teaching assistantships with partial tuition reimbursements available (averaging $1,542 per year); career-related internships or fieldwork, institutionally sponsored loans, and tuition waivers (full and partial) also available. Financial award application deadline: 4/1; financial award applicants required to submit FAFSA. *Faculty research:* Ergonomics, metal bioavailability, aerosols, particulate sizing, respiration protection. Total annual research expenditures: $101,546. *Unit head:* Dr. Terry Spear, Department Head, 406-496-4445, Fax: 406-496-4650, E-mail: tspear@mtech.edu. *Application contact:* Cindy Dunstan, Administrator, Graduate School, 406-496-4304, Fax: 406-496-4710, E-mail: cdunstan@mtech.edu.

Murray State University, College of Health Sciences and Human Services, Program in Occupational Safety and Health, Murray, KY 42071. Offers environmental science (MS); industrial hygiene (MS); safety management (MS). *Accreditation:* ABET. Part-time programs available. *Faculty:* 9 full-time (3 women), 2 part-time/adjunct (0 women). *Students:* Average age 25. 15 applicants, 100% accepted, 12 enrolled. In 2006, 15 degrees awarded. *Degree requirements:* For master's, professional internship, thesis optional. *Application deadline:* Applications are processed on a rolling basis. Application fee: $25. Electronic applications accepted. *Financial support:* In 2006–07, 16 students received support. Career-related internships or fieldwork, Federal Work-Study, institutionally sponsored loans, scholarships/grants, tuition waivers (full), and unspecified assistantships available. Support available to part-time students. *Faculty research:* Light effects on plant growth, ergonomics, toxic effects of pets' pesticides, traffic safety. *Unit head:* Dr. David G. Kraemer, Chairman, 270-809-6654, Fax: 270-809-3630, E-mail: david.kraemer@murraystate.edu. *Application contact:* Dr. Bassam H. Atieh, Professor, 270-809-6652, Fax: 270-809-3630, E-mail: bassam.atieh@murraystate.edu.

New Jersey Institute of Technology, Office of Graduate Studies, College of Science and Liberal Arts, Department of Chemistry and Environmental Science, Program in Occupational Safety and Industrial Hygiene, Newark, NJ 07102. Offers MS. Part-time and evening/weekend programs available. *Entrance requirements:* For master's, GRE General Test. Additional exam requirements/recommendations for international students: Required—TOEFL (minimum score 550 paper-based; 213 computer-based). *Application deadline:* For fall admission, 6/5 priority date for domestic students; for spring admission, 10/15 for domestic students. Applications are processed on a rolling basis. Application fee: $60. Electronic applications accepted. *Expenses:* Tuition, state resident: full-time $11,896; part-time $648 per credit. Tuition, nonresident: full-time $16,900; part-time $892 per credit. Required fees: $336; $66 per credit. $168 per term. Tuition and fees vary according to course load. *Financial support:* Fellowships with full and partial tuition reimbursements, research assistantships with full and partial tuition reimbursements, teaching assistantships with full and partial tuition reimbursements, career-related internships or fieldwork, Federal Work-Study, institutionally sponsored loans, and unspecified assistantships available. Financial award application deadline: 3/15. *Application contact:* Kathryn Kelly, Director of Admissions, 973-596-3300, Fax: 973-596-3461, E-mail: admissions@njit.edu.

The University of Alabama at Birmingham, School of Public Health, Department of Environmental Health Sciences, Birmingham, AL 35294. Offers environmental health (PhD); environmental toxicology (PhD); industrial hygiene (PhD). *Faculty:* 9. *Students:* 6 full-time (4 women); includes 3 minority (all African Americans) 4 applicants, 0% accepted. In 2006, 2 degrees awarded. *Degree requirements:* For doctorate, thesis/dissertation. *Entrance requirements:* For doctorate, GRE General Test. Additional exam requirements/recommendations for international students: Required—TOEFL. *Application deadline:* For fall admission, 4/1 for domestic students. Application fee: $35 ($60 for international students). Electronic applications accepted. *Expenses:* Tuition, state resident: part-time $170 per credit hour. Tuition, nonresident: part-time $425 per credit hour. Required fees: $15 per credit hour. $122 per term. Tuition and fees vary according to program. *Financial support:* Fellowships, career-related internships or fieldwork, scholarships/grants, and unspecified assistantships available. *Faculty research:* Aquatic toxicology, virology. *Unit head:* Dr. Edward M. Postlethwait, Chair, 205-934-7032, Fax: 205-975-6341. *Application contact:* Nancy O. Pinson, Coordinator of Student Admissions, 205-934-4993, Fax: 205-975-5484.

University of Central Missouri, The Graduate School, College of Health and Human Services, Department of Safety Sciences, Warrensburg, MO 64093. Offers fire science (MS); human services/public services (Ed S); industrial hygiene (MS); industrial safety management (MS); loss control (MS); occupational safety management (MS); public safety (MS); security (MS); transportation safety (MS). *Accreditation:* ABET (one or more programs are accredited). Part-time programs available. *Faculty:* 18 full-time (3 women). *Students:* 14 full-time (4 women), 18 part-time (6 women); includes 6 minority (2 African Americans, 1 American Indian/Alaska Native, 3 Hispanic Americans), 1 international. Average age 36. 9 applicants, 78% accepted, 6 enrolled. In 2006, 6 degrees awarded. *Degree requirements:* For master's, comprehensive exam. *Entrance requirements:* For master's, GRE General Test, minimum GPA of 2.5, 15 hours of course work in related area; for Ed S, master's degree in related field. Additional exam requirements/recommendations for international students: Required—TOEFL (minimum score 500 paper-based; 173 computer-based). *Application deadline:* For fall admission, 6/1 priority date for domestic students, 5/1 priority date for international students; for spring admission, 10/1 priority date for domestic students, 10/1 for international students. Applications are processed on a rolling basis. Application fee: $30 ($50 for international students). *Expenses:* Tuition, state resident: full-time $5,448; part-time $227 per credit hour. Tuition, nonresident: full-time $10,896; part-time $454 per credit hour. Required fees: $336; $14 per credit hour. *Financial support:* In 2006–07, 5 students received support. Federal Work-Study, scholarships/grants, unspecified assistantships, and administrative and laboratory assistantships available. Support available to part-time students. Financial award application deadline: 3/1; financial award applicants required to submit FAFSA. *Faculty research:* Workplace and school safety, industrial hygiene assessment methods, lead and take-home toxins, rural emergency management, cultural aspects of safety, health, and the environment. Total annual research expenditures: $60,999. *Unit head:* Dr. Dennis Laster, Interim Chair, 660-543-4017, E-mail: laster@cmsu1.cmsu.edu.

University of Cincinnati, Division of Research and Advanced Studies, College of Medicine, Graduate Programs in Biomedical Sciences, Department of Environmental Health, Cincinnati, OH 45267. Offers environmental and industrial hygiene (MS, PhD); environmental and occupational medicine (MS); environmental genetics and molecular toxicology (MS, PhD); epidemiology and biostatistics (MS, PhD); occupational safety and ergonomics (MS, PhD). *Accreditation:* ABET (one or more programs are accredited). *Faculty:* 26 full-time (10 women). *Students:* 75 full-time (32 women), 59 part-time (33 women); includes 7 minority (5 African Americans, 1 American Indian/Alaska Native, 1 Asian American or Pacific Islander), 55 international. 136 applicants, 28% accepted. In 2006, 13 master's, 7 doctorates awarded. Terminal master's awarded for partial completion of doctoral program. *Median time to degree:* Master's–2.3 years full-time, 3.5 years part-time; doctorate–5.3 years full-time, 7.3 years part-time. Of those who began their doctoral program in fall 1998, 100% received their degree in 8 years or less. *Degree requirements:* For master's, thesis; for doctorate, thesis/dissertation, qualifying exam. *Entrance requirements:* For master's, GRE General Test, bachelor's degree in science; for doctorate, GRE General Test. Additional exam requirements/recommendations for international students: Required—TOEFL (minimum score 600 paper-based; 250 computer-based; 100 iBT). *Application deadline:* For fall admission, 3/1 priority date for domestic and international students. Applications are processed on a rolling basis. Application fee: $40. Electronic applications accepted. *Financial support:* In 2006–07, 69 students received support, including research assistantships with full tuition reimbursements available (averaging $17,850 per year); career-related internships or fieldwork, scholarships/grants, traineeships, tuition waivers (partial), and unspecified assistantships also available. Financial award application deadline: 5/1. *Faculty research:* Carcinogens and mutagenesis, pulmonary studies, reproduction and development. Total annual research expenditures: $16.9 million. *Unit head:* Dr. Shuk-Mei Ho, Chairman, 513-558-5701, Fax: 513-558-4397, E-mail: hosm@ucmail.uc.edu. *Application contact:* Stephanie W. Starkey, Graduate Program Coordinator, 513-558-5704, Fax: 513-558-5457, E-mail: stephanie.starkey@uc.edu.

University of Massachusetts Lowell, Graduate School, James B. Francis College of Engineering, Department of Work Environment, Lowell, MA 01854-2881. Offers cleaner production and pollution prevention (MS, Sc D); environmental risk assessment (Certificate); identification and control of ergonomic hazards (Certificate); industrial hygiene (MS, Sc D); job stress and healthy job redesign (Certificate); occupational epidemiology (MS, Sc D); occupational ergonomics (MS, Sc D); radiological health physics and general work environment protection (Certificate); work environmental policy (MS, Sc D). *Accreditation:* ABET (one or more programs are accredited). Part-time programs available. Terminal master's awarded for partial completion of doctoral program. *Degree requirements:* For master's, thesis optional; for doctorate, thesis/dissertation. *Entrance requirements:* For master's and doctorate, GRE General Test. Additional exam requirements/recommendations for international students: Required—TOEFL. *Faculty research:* Ergonomics, industrial hygiene, epidemiology, work environment policy, pollution prevention.

Industrial Hygiene

University of Michigan, School of Public Health, Department of Environmental Health Sciences, Program in Occupational Health, Ann Arbor, MI 48109. Offers industrial hygiene (MS, PhD); occupational and environmental epidemiology (MPH). MS and PhD offered through the Horace H. Rackham School of Graduate Studies. *Entrance requirements:* For master's and doctorate, GRE General Test. Electronic applications accepted.

University of Minnesota, Twin Cities Campus, School of Public Health, Division of Environmental Health Sciences, Area in Industrial Hygiene, Minneapolis, MN 55455-0213. Offers MPH, MS, PhD. *Accreditation:* ABET (one or more programs are accredited); CEPH (one or more programs are accredited). *Degree requirements:* For doctorate, thesis/dissertation. *Entrance requirements:* For master's and doctorate, GRE General Test. *Expenses:* Tuition, state resident: full-time $9,302; part-time $775 per credit. Tuition, nonresident: full-time $16,400; part-time $1,367 per credit. Full-time tuition and fees vary according to class time, course load, program, reciprocity agreements and student level.

University of New Haven, Graduate School, Henry C. Lee College of Criminal Justice and Forensic Sciences, Program in Industrial Hygiene, West Haven, CT 06516-1916. Offers MS. *Degree requirements:* For master's, thesis or alternative.

The University of North Carolina at Chapel Hill, Graduate School, School of Public Health, Department of Environmental Sciences and Engineering, Chapel Hill, NC 27599. Offers air, radiation and industrial hygiene (MPH, MS, MSEE, MSPH, PhD); aquatic and atmospheric sciences (MPH, MS, MSPH, PhD); environmental engineering (MPH, MS, MSEE, MSPH, PhD); environmental health sciences (MPH, MS, MSPH, PhD); environmental management and policy (MPH, MS, MSPH, PhD). *Faculty:* 29 full-time (2 women), 14 part-time/adjunct. *Students:* 139 full-time (70 women); includes 21 minority (9 African Americans, 1 American Indian/Alaska Native, 8 Asian Americans or Pacific Islanders, 3 Hispanic Americans), 17 international. Average age 27. 191 applicants, 48% accepted, 41 enrolled. In 2006, 26 master's, 17 doctorates awarded. Terminal master's awarded for partial completion of doctoral program. *Median time to degree:* Of those who began their doctoral program in fall 1998, 100% received their degree in 8 years or less. *Degree requirements:* For master's, thesis (for some programs), research paper, comprehensive exam, registration; for doctorate, thesis/dissertation, comprehensive exam, registration. *Entrance requirements:* For master's and doctorate, GRE General Test, minimum GPA of 3.0. Additional exam requirements/recommendations for international students: Required—TOEFL. *Application deadline:* For fall admission, 1/1 priority date for domestic and international students; for spring admission, 9/15 for domestic students. Applications are processed on a rolling basis. Application fee: $70. Electronic applications accepted. *Financial support:* In 2006–07, 29 fellowships with tuition reimbursements (averaging $12,903 per year), 61 research assistantships with tuition reimbursements (averaging $13,114 per year), 13 teaching assistantships with tuition reimbursements (averaging $11,846 per year) were awarded; career-related internships or fieldwork, Federal Work-Study, traineeships, health care benefits, and unspecified assistantships also available. Support available to part-time students. Financial award application deadline: 1/1; financial award applicants required to submit FAFSA. *Faculty research:* Air, radiation and industrial hygiene, aquatic and atmospheric sciences, environmental health sciences, environmental management and policy, water resources engineering. *Unit head:* Dr. Michael Aitken, Chair, 919-966-1024, Fax: 919-966-7911, E-mail: mike_aitken@unc.edu. *Application contact:* Jack Whaley, Registrar, 919-966-3844, Fax: 919-966-7911, E-mail: jack_whaley@unc.edu.

University of Puerto Rico, Medical Sciences Campus, Graduate School of Public Health, Department of Environmental Health, Program in Industrial Hygiene, San Juan, PR 00936-5067. Offers MS. Part-time programs available. *Students:* 44 (30 women). 33 applicants, 33% accepted. In 2006, 4 degrees awarded. *Degree requirements:* For master's, thesis. *Entrance requirements:* For master's, GRE, previous course work in biology, chemistry, mathematics, and physics. *Application deadline:* For fall admission, 3/15 for domestic students. Application fee: $20. *Expenses:* Contact institution. *Financial support:* Research assistantships, teaching assistantships, Federal Work-Study and institutionally sponsored loans available. Financial award application deadline: 4/30. *Unit head:* Dr. Jesús Gonzalez, Coordinator, 787-758-2525 Ext. 1437, Fax: 787-759-6719, E-mail: jgonzalez@rcm.upr.edu. *Application contact:* Prof. Mayra E. Santiago-Vargas, Counselor, 787-756-5244, Fax: 787-759-6719, E-mail: msantiago@rcm.upr.edu.

University of South Carolina, The Graduate School, Arnold School of Public Health, Department of Environmental Health Sciences, Program in Industrial Hygiene, Columbia, SC 29208. Offers MPH, MSPH, PhD. *Accreditation:* ABET (one or more programs are accredited); CEPH (one or more programs are accredited). *Degree requirements:* For master's, thesis (for some programs), practicum (MPH), comprehensive exam; for doctorate, one foreign language, thesis/dissertation, comprehensive exam. *Entrance requirements:* For master's and doctorate, GRE General Test. Additional exam requirements/recommendations for international students: Required—TOEFL (minimum score 570 paper-based; 230 computer-based). Electronic applications accepted. *Faculty research:* Sampling and calibration method development, exposure and risk assessment, respirator and dermal protective equipment, ergonomics, air cleaning methods and devices.

See Close-Up on page 2063.

University of Washington, Graduate School, School of Public Health and Community Medicine, Department of Environmental and Occupational Health Sciences, Seattle, WA 98195. Offers environmental and occupational health (MPH); environmental and occupational hygiene (PhD); environmental health (MS); industrial hygiene and safety (MS); occupational medicine (MPH); safety and ergonomics (MS); toxicology (MS, PhD). Part-time programs available. Terminal master's awarded for partial completion of doctoral program. *Degree requirements:* For master's, thesis (for some programs), practicum (MPH); for doctorate, thesis/dissertation, comprehensive exam, registration. *Entrance requirements:* For master's and doctorate, GRE General Test, minimum GPA of 3.0, prerequisite course work in biology, chemistry, physics, calculus. Additional exam requirements/recommendations for international students: Required—TOEFL (minimum score 580 paper-based; 237 computer-based). Electronic applications accepted. *Faculty research:* Developmental toxicology, biochemical toxicology, exposure assessment, hazardous waste, industrial chemistry.

See Close-Up on page 2067.

University of Wisconsin–Stout, Graduate School, College of Technology, Engineering, and Management, Program in Risk Control, Menomonie, WI 54751. Offers MS. Part-time programs available. *Faculty:* 8 full-time (0 women). *Students:* 13 full-time (3 women), 11 part-time (3 women); includes 1 minority (African American), 1 international. Average age 33. 10 applicants, 90% accepted, 5 enrolled. In 2006, 8 degrees awarded. *Degree requirements:* For master's, thesis. *Entrance requirements:* For master's, minimum GPA of 3.0. Additional exam requirements/recommendations for international students: Required—TOEFL (minimum score 500 paper-based; 173 computer-based; 61 iBT). *Application deadline:* For fall admission, 6/1 priority date for domestic and international students; for spring admission, 12/1 priority date for domestic and international students. Applications are processed on a rolling basis. Application fee: $45. Electronic applications accepted. *Expenses:* Tuition, state resident: part-time $317 per credit. Tuition, nonresident: part-time $543 per credit. Tuition and fees vary according to reciprocity agreements. *Financial support:* In 2006–07, 2 research assistantships with partial tuition reimbursements (averaging $6,518 per year) were awarded; Federal Work-Study, scholarships/grants, health care benefits, tuition waivers (full and partial), and unspecified assistantships also available. Support available to part-time students. Financial award application deadline: 4/1; financial award applicants required to submit FAFSA. *Faculty research:* Environmental microbiology, water supply safety, facilities planning, industrial ventilation, bioterrorism. *Unit head:* Dr. Brian Finder, Director, 715-232-1422, E-mail: finderb@uwstout.edu. *Application contact:* Anne E. Johnson, Graduate Student Evaluator, 715-232-1322, Fax: 715-232-2413, E-mail: johnsona@uwstout.edu.

West Virginia University, College of Engineering and Mineral Resources, Department of Industrial and Management Systems Engineering, Program in Industrial Hygiene, Morgantown, WV 26506. Offers MS. *Accreditation:* ABET. Part-time programs available. *Students:* 17 full-time (6 women), 2 part-time (1 woman); includes 2 minority (1 Asian American or Pacific Islander, 1 Hispanic American). Average age 28. 16 applicants, 88% accepted, 9 enrolled. In 2006, 5 degrees awarded. *Degree requirements:* For master's, thesis or alternative, registration. *Entrance requirements:* For master's, GRE General Test, minimum GPA of 3.0. Additional exam requirements/recommendations for international students: Required—TOEFL. *Application deadline:* For fall admission, 6/15 priority date for domestic and international students; for spring admission, 11/1 for domestic and international students. Applications are processed on a rolling basis. Application fee: $50. *Expenses:* Tuition, state resident: full-time $4,926; part-time $276 per credit hour. Tuition, nonresident: full-time $14,278; part-time $796 per credit hour. Tuition and fees vary according to program. *Financial support:* In 2006–07, 4 fellowships with full tuition reimbursements (averaging $10,000 per year), 3 research assistantships with full tuition reimbursements (averaging $12,600 per year) were awarded; career-related internships or fieldwork, institutionally sponsored loans, scholarships/grants, traineeships, health care benefits, tuition waivers (full and partial), and unspecified assistantships also available. Financial award application deadline: 4/1; financial award applicants required to submit FAFSA. *Faculty research:* Safety management, ergonomics and workplace design, safety and health training, construction safety. *Unit head:* Steven Guffey, Coordinator, 304-293-4607 Ext. 3707, Fax: 304-293-4970, E-mail: steve.guffey@mail.wvu.edu.

International Health

Boston University, School of Public Health, International Health Department, Boston, MA 02215. Offers MPH, Dr PH, Certificate. *Accreditation:* CEPH (one or more programs are accredited). *Students:* 101 full-time (68 women), 79 part-time (70 women); includes 28 minority (8 African Americans, 15 Asian Americans or Pacific Islanders, 5 Hispanic Americans), 27 international. Average age 27. *Degree requirements:* For master's, thesis. *Entrance requirements:* For master's, GRE General Test. Additional exam requirements/recommendations for international students: Required—TOEFL or IELTS. *Application deadline:* For fall admission, 2/1 for domestic students; for spring admission, 10/15 for domestic students. Applications are processed on a rolling basis. Application fee: $60. Electronic applications accepted. *Expenses:* Tuition: Full-time $33,330; part-time $1,042 per credit. Required fees: $462; $40. *Financial support:* Career-related internships or fieldwork, Federal Work-Study, institutionally sponsored loans, scholarships/grants, and tuition waivers (partial) available. *Unit head:* Dr. Jonathon Simon, Chair, 617-638-5234, E-mail: ih@bu.edu. *Application contact:* LePhan Quan, Assistant Director of Admissions, 617-638-4640, Fax: 617-638-5299, E-mail: asksph@bu.edu.

Brandeis University, The Heller School for Social Policy and Management, Program in International Health Policy and Management, Waltham, MA 02454-9110. Offers MS. *Entrance requirements:* For master's, GMAT or GRE recommended, 3 letters of recommendation, curriculum vitae or resumé. Additional exam requirements/recommendations for international students: Required—TOEFL.

See Close-Up on page 2029.

Emory University, Rollins School of Public Health, Department of Global Health, Atlanta, GA 30322-1100. Offers global health (MPH); public nutrition (MSPH, PhD). *Accreditation:* CEPH. Part-time programs available. *Students:* 133 full-time (112 women), 8 part-time (6 women). Average age 27. 264 applicants, 65% accepted, 69 enrolled. In 2006, 77 degrees awarded. *Degree requirements:* For master's, thesis, practicum. *Entrance requirements:* For master's, GRE General Test. Additional exam requirements/recommendations for international students: Required—TOEFL (minimum score 550 paper-based; 213 computer-based). *Application deadline:* For fall admission, 1/5 priority date for domestic and international students. Application fee: $75. Electronic applications accepted. *Expenses:* Tuition: Full-time $30,246. *Financial support:* Fellowships with full and partial tuition reimbursements, career-related internships or fieldwork, Federal Work-Study, institutionally sponsored loans, and scholarships/grants available. Support available to part-time students. Financial award application deadline: 1/5. *Unit head:* Dr. Reynaldo Martorell, Chair, 404-727-9888, Fax: 404-727-1278, E-mail: rmart77@sph.emory.edu. *Application contact:* Theresa Nash, Assistant Director of Academic Programs, 404-727-5724, Fax: 404-727-4590, E-mail: tnash@sph.emory.edu.

See Close-Up on page 2035.

The George Washington University, School of Public Health and Health Services, Department of Global Health, Washington, DC 20052. Offers international health policy and programs (MPH); international health promotion (MPH); JD/MPH; LL M/MPH; MD/MPH. *Accreditation:* CEPH. *Degree requirements:* For master's, case study or special project. *Entrance requirements:* For master's, GMAT, GRE General Test, or MCAT. Additional exam requirements/recommendations for international students: Required—TOEFL.

Harvard University, School of Public Health, Department of Population and International Health, Boston, MA 02115-6096. Offers SM, DPH, SD. Part-time programs available. *Degree requirements:* For master's, thesis; for doctorate, thesis/dissertation, qualifying exam. *Entrance requirements:* For master's and doctorate, GRE. Additional exam requirements/recommendations for international students: Required—TOEFL (minimum score 560 paper-based; 220 computer-based); Recommended—IELTS (minimum score 7). Electronic applications accepted. *Expenses:* Tuition: Full-time $30,275. Full-time tuition and fees vary according to program and student level. *Faculty research:* International health policy, economics, reproductive health, ecology.

The Johns Hopkins University, Bloomberg School of Public Health, Department of International Health, Baltimore, MD 21218-2699. Offers disease prevention and control (MHS, PhD); health systems (MHS, PhD); human nutrition (MHS, PhD); international health (Dr PH); social and behavioral interventions (MHS, PhD). *Faculty:* 119 full-time (63 women), 170 part-time/adjunct (55 women). *Students:* 197 full-time (159 women), 7 part-time (4 women); includes 36 minority (4 African Americans, 1 American Indian/Alaska Native, 25 Asian Americans or Pacific Islanders, 6 Hispanic Americans), 58 international. Average age 27. 376 applicants, 46% accepted, 68 enrolled. In 2006, 39 master's, 19 doctorates awarded. *Median time to degree:* Of those who began their doctoral program in fall 1998, 63% received their degree in 8 years or less. *Degree requirements:* For master's, thesis (for some programs), internship, comprehensive exam, registration; for doctorate, thesis/dissertation, 1 year full-time residency, oral and written exams, comprehensive exam, registration. *Entrance requirements:* For master's, GRE General Test or MCAT, 3 letters of recommendation, resumé; for doctorate, GRE General Test, 3 letters of recommendation, resumé. Additional exam requirements/recommendations for international students: Required—TOEFL (minimum score 600 paper-based; 280 computer-based). *Application deadline:* For fall admission, 1/2 priority date for domestic and international students. Applications are processed on a rolling basis. Application fee: $45. Electronic applications accepted. *Expenses:* Tuition: Full-time $32,976. Tuition and fees vary according to degree level and program. *Financial support:* In 2006–07, 203 students received support, including 9 fellowships (averaging $32,000 per year); Federal Work-Study, institutionally sponsored loans, scholarships/grants, traineeships, and stipends also available. Support available to part-time students. Financial award application deadline: 3/15; financial award applicants required to submit FAFSA. *Faculty research:* Nutrition, infectious diseases, health systems, economics, humanitarian emergencies. Total annual research expenditures: $62 million. *Unit head:* Dr. Robert E. Black, Chairman, 410-955-3934, Fax: 410-955-7159, E-mail: rblack@jhsph.edu. *Application contact:* Jennifer Shaffer, Academic Program Administrator, 410-955-3734, Fax: 410-955-7159, E-mail: jshaffer@jhsph.edu.

Loma Linda University, School of Public Health, Programs in Global Health, Loma Linda, CA 92350. Offers MPH. *Accreditation:* CEPH. *Entrance requirements:* Additional exam requirements/recommendations for international students: Required—Michigan English Language Assessment Battery or TOEFL.

New York Medical College, School of Public Health, Department of Behavioral Sciences and Community Health, Program in International Health, Valhalla, NY 10595-1691. Offers MPH. Part-time and evening/weekend programs available. *Degree requirements:* For master's, thesis, registration. *Entrance requirements:* For master's, 2-3 years of health-related experience (recommended), minimum GPA of 3.0. Additional exam requirements/recommendations for international students: Required—TOEFL (minimum score 600 paper-based; 250 computer-based). *Application deadline:* For fall admission, 8/1 priority date for domestic students, 5/15 for international students; for spring admission, 12/1 priority date for domestic students, 10/15 for international students. Applications are processed on a rolling basis. Application fee: $35 ($60 for international students). Electronic applications accepted. *Financial support:* Career-related internships or fieldwork, Federal Work-Study, and institutionally sponsored loans available. Financial award application deadline: 6/15; financial award applicants required to submit FAFSA. *Unit head:* Dr. Cathey Falvo, Director, 914-594-4250, E-mail: falvo@nymc.edu. *Application contact:* Marian F. McGowan, Information Contact, 914-594-4510, Fax: 914-594-4292, E-mail: sph_admissions@nymc.edu.

See Close-Up on page 2043.

New York University, Steinhardt School of Culture, Education and Human Development, Department of Nutrition, Food Studies, and Public Health, Program in Community Public Health, New York, NY 10012-1019. Offers community health (MPH); international community health (MPH); public health (PhD); public health nutrition (MPH). *Accreditation:* CEPH. Part-time and evening/weekend programs available. *Faculty:* 5 full-time (4 women). *Students:* 64 full-time (54 women), 43 part-time (39 women); includes 38 minority (12 African Americans, 1 American Indian/Alaska Native, 20 Asian Americans or Pacific Islanders, 5 Hispanic Americans), 4 international. 188 applicants, 76% accepted, 42 enrolled. In 2006, 21 master's, 1 doctorate awarded. *Degree requirements:* For master's, thesis (for some programs). *Entrance requirements:* For master's, GRE General Test; for doctorate, GRE General Test, interview. Additional exam requirements/recommendations for international students: Required—TOEFL. *Application deadline:* For fall admission, 12/15 priority date for domestic and international students; for spring admission, 11/1 for domestic and international students. Applications are processed on a rolling basis. Application fee: $50. *Expenses:* Tuition: Part-time $1,080 per unit. Required fees: $56 per unit. $329 per term. Tuition and fees vary according to program. *Financial support:* Career-related internships or fieldwork, Federal Work-Study, scholarships/grants, and tuition waivers (partial) available. Support available to part-time students. Financial award application deadline: 2/1; financial award applicants required to submit FAFSA. *Faculty research:* Social epidemiology, primary health care, global health, immigrants and health, infectious disease prevention. *Unit head:* Sally Guttmacher, Director, 212-998-5580, Fax: 212-995-4192. *Application contact:* 212-998-5030, Fax: 212-995-4328, E-mail: steinhardt.gradadmissions@nyu.edu.

Touro University International, College of Health Sciences, Program in Health Sciences, Cypress, CA 90630. Offers clinical research administration (MS, Certificate); emergency and disaster management (MS, Certificate); environmental health science (Certificate); health care administration (PhD); health care management (MS), including health informatics; health education (MS, Certificate); health informatics (Certificate); health sciences (PhD); international health (MS); international health: educator or researcher option (PhD); international health: practitioner option (PhD); law and expert witness studies (MS, Certificate); public health (MS); quality assurance (Certificate). Part-time and evening/weekend programs available. Postbaccalaureate distance learning degree programs offered (no on-campus study). In 2006, 322 master's, 21 doctorates awarded. *Degree requirements:* For doctorate, thesis/dissertation, defense of dissertation, comprehensive exam. *Entrance requirements:* For master's, minimum GPA of 3.0; for doctorate, minimum GPA of 3.4, curriculum vitae, course work in research methods or statistics. Additional exam requirements/recommendations for international students: Required—TOEFL (minimum score 550 paper-based). Application fee: $75. *Expenses:* Tuition: Part-time $300 per credit hour. Tuition and fees vary according to course level and program. *Unit head:* Dr. Edith Neumann, Vice President for Academic Affairs, College of Health Sciences, 714-816-0366 Ext. 2030, Fax: 714-226-9844, E-mail: eneumann@tourou.edu.

Tufts University, Fletcher School of Law and Diplomacy, Medford, MA 02155. Offers MA, MAHA, MALD, PhD, DVM/MA, JD/MALD, MALD/MA, MALD/MBA, MALD/MS, MD/MA. Postbaccalaureate distance learning degree programs offered (minimal on-campus study). *Faculty:* 34 full-time (7 women), 31 part-time/adjunct (8 women). *Students:* 527 full-time (268 women), 9 part-time (4 women); includes 61 minority (12 African Americans, 1 American Indian/Alaska Native, 32 Asian Americans or Pacific Islanders, 16 Hispanic Americans), 212 international. Average age 31. 1,605 applicants, 40% accepted, 234 enrolled. In 2006, 203 master's, 10 doctorates awarded. *Median time to degree:* Of those who began their doctoral program in fall 1998, 75% received their degree in 8 years or less. *Degree requirements:* For master's, one foreign language, thesis, registration; for doctorate, one foreign language, thesis/dissertation, dissertation defense, comprehensive exam, registration. *Entrance requirements:* For master's and doctorate, GMAT or GRE General Test. Additional exam requirements/recommendations for international students: Required—TOEFL (minimum score 600 paper-based; 250 computer-based; 100 iBT), IELTS (minimum score 7). *Application deadline:* For fall admission, 1/15 for domestic and international students; for spring admission, 10/15 for domestic and international students. Application fee: $65. Electronic applications accepted. *Expenses: Contact institution.* Tuition and fees vary according to degree level and program. *Financial support:* Federal Work-Study, institutionally sponsored loans, scholarships/grants, and tuition waivers (partial) available. Financial award application deadline: 1/15; financial award applicants required to submit FAFSA. *Faculty research:* Negotiation and conflict resolution, international organizations, international business and economic law, security studies, development economics. *Unit head:* Stephen W. Bosworth, Dean, 617-627-3050, Fax: 617-627-3712. *Application contact:* Laurie A. Hurley, Director of Admissions and Financial Aid, 617-627-2410, Fax: 617-627-3712, E-mail: fletcheradmissions@tufts.edu.

Tulane University, School of Public Health and Tropical Medicine, Department of International Health and Development, New Orleans, LA 70118-5669. Offers MPH, Dr PH, PhD, MSW/MPH. *Accreditation:* CEPH (one or more programs are accredited). Part-time programs available. *Faculty:* 28 full-time (14 women), 4 part-time/adjunct (3 women). *Students:* 300 full-time (255 women), 74 part-time (54 women). Terminal master's awarded for partial completion of doctoral program. *Degree requirements:* For master's, one foreign language; for doctorate, one foreign language, thesis/dissertation, comprehensive exam. *Entrance requirements:* For master's and doctorate, GRE General Test. Additional exam requirements/recommendations for international students: Required—TOEFL. *Application deadline:* For fall admission, 4/15 priority date for domestic and international students; for spring admission, 10/15 priority date for domestic and international students. Applications are processed on a rolling basis. Application fee: $40. Electronic applications accepted. *Financial support:* Federal Work-Study, scholarships/grants, and traineeships available. Support available to part-time students. Financial award application deadline: 4/15. *Faculty research:* Reproductive health, HIV/AIDS, nutrition and food security, health financing, program evaluation. Total annual research expenditures: $4.1 million. *Unit head:* Dr. Carl Kendall, Chair, 504-988-3655, Fax: 504-584-3653, E-mail: ckendall@tulane.edu. *Application contact:* Penny Jessop, Coordinator, 504-588-5399, Fax: 504-584-3653, E-mail: pjessop@tulane.edu.

Uniformed Services University of the Health Sciences, School of Medicine, Programs in Biomedical Sciences, Bethesda, MD 20814-4799. Offers emerging infectious diseases (PhD); medical and clinical psychology (PhD), including clinical psychology, medical psychology; medical history (MMH); microbiology and immunology (PhD); molecular and cell biology (PhD); neuroscience (PhD); pathology (PhD), including comparative pathology, molecular pathobiology; preventive medicine and biometrics (MPH, MSPH, MTMH, Dr PH, PhD), including environmental health science (PhD), medical zoology (PhD), public health (MPH, MSPH, Dr PH), tropical medicine and hygiene (MTMH). Terminal master's awarded for partial completion of doctoral program. *Degree requirements:* For master's, thesis or alternative, comprehensive exam; for doctorate, thesis/dissertation, qualifying exam, comprehensive exam. *Entrance requirements:* For master's, GRE General Test; for doctorate, GRE General Test, minimum GPA of 3.0. Additional exam requirements/recommendations for international students: Required—TOEFL.

Uniformed Services University of the Health Sciences, School of Medicine, Programs in Biomedical Sciences, Department of Preventive Medicine and Biometrics, Program in Tropical Medicine and Hygiene, Bethesda, MD 20814-4799. Offers MTMH. *Accreditation:* CEPH. *Degree requirements:* For master's, comprehensive exam. *Entrance requirements:* For master's, GRE General Test, MD, US citizenship. *Faculty research:* Epidemiology, biostatistics, tropical public health.

University of Alberta, School of Public Health, Department of Public Health Sciences, Edmonton, AB T6G 2E1, Canada. Offers clinical epidemiology (M Sc, MPH); environmental and occupational health (MPH); environmental health sciences (M Sc); epidemiology (M Sc); global health (M Sc, MPH); health policy and management (MPH); health policy research (M Sc); health technology assessment (MPH); occupational health (M Sc); population health (M Sc); public health leadership (MPH); public health sciences (PhD); quantitative methods (MPH). *Accreditation:* CEPH (one or more programs are accredited). *Faculty:* 24 full-time (5 women), 59 part-time/adjunct (13 women). *Students:* 49 full-time, 49 part-time. 81 applicants, 31% accepted. In 2006, 28 degrees awarded. Terminal master's awarded for partial completion of doctoral program. *Degree requirements:* For master's, thesis (for some programs); for doctorate, thesis/dissertation. *Entrance requirements:* For master's, GMAT or GRE General Test. Additional exam requirements/recommendations for international students: Required—TOEFL (paper-based 550; computer-based 213) or IELTS (paper-based 6). *Application deadline:* For fall admission, 3/15 for domestic students, 7/1 for international students; for winter admission, 11/1 for international students; for spring admission, 3/1 for international students. Applications are processed on a rolling basis. Application fee: $0. Electronic applications accepted. *Financial support:* In 2006–07, 11 students received support, including 6 research assistantships with tuition reimbursements available (averaging $2,200 per year); fellowships, teaching assistantships, career-related internships or fieldwork and tuition waivers (partial) also available. Financial award application deadline: 2/1. *Faculty research:* Biostatistics, health promotion and socio-behavioral health science. Total annual research expenditures: $5.7 million. *Unit head:* L. Duncan Saunders, Acting Chair, 780-492-6814, Fax: 780-492-0364. *Application contact:* Felicity R. Hey, Graduate Programs Administrator, 780-492-6407, Fax: 780-492-0364, E-mail: felicity.hey@ualberta.ca.

University of Michigan, School of Public Health, Department of Epidemiology, Ann Arbor, MI 48109. Offers dental public health (MPH); epidemiological science (PhD); epidemiology (MPH, Dr PH); hospital and molecular epidemiology (MPH); international health (MPH). PhD offered through the Horace H. Rackham School of Graduate Studies. *Accreditation:* CEPH (one or more programs are accredited). Terminal master's awarded for partial completion of doctoral program. *Entrance requirements:* For master's and doctorate, GRE General Test, MCAT. Additional exam requirements/recommendations for international students: Required—TOEFL (minimum score 560 paper-based; 220 computer-based). Electronic applications accepted. *Faculty research:* Molecular virology, infectious diseases, women's health, genetics, social epidemiology.

University of South Florida, Graduate School, College of Public Health, Department of Global Health, Tampa, FL 33620-9951. Offers MPH, MSPH, PhD. Part-time and evening/weekend programs available. *Faculty:* 9 full-time (3 women), 9 part-time/adjunct (7 women). *Students:* 80 full-time (58 women), 32 part-time (24 women); includes 31 minority (13 African Americans, 1 American Indian/Alaska Native, 7 Asian Americans or Pacific Islanders, 10 Hispanic Americans), 18 international. Average age 29. 69 applicants, 83% accepted, 31 enrolled. In 2006, 38 master's, 2 doctorates awarded. *Median time to degree:* Master's–1.67 years full-time, 2.54 years part-time; doctorate–3.67 years part-time. *Degree requirements:* For master's, thesis (for some programs), comprehensive exam; for doctorate, thesis/dissertation, comprehensive exam. *Entrance requirements:* For master's and doctorate, GRE General Test, minimum GPA of 3.0 in upper-level course work. Additional exam requirements/recommendations for international students: Required—TOEFL (minimum score 550 paper-based; 213 computer-based; 79 iBT). *Application deadline:* For fall admission, 6/1 for domestic students, 1/2 for international students; for spring admission, 10/15 for domestic students, 7/1 for international students. Applications are processed on a rolling basis. Application fee: $30. Electronic applications accepted. *Financial support:* In 2006–07, 4 fellowships (averaging $8,500 per year), 8 research assistantships with partial tuition reimbursements (averaging $6,961 per year), 36 teaching assistantships with full and partial tuition reimbursements (averaging $3,038 per year) were awarded; career-related internships or fieldwork, Federal Work-Study, institutionally sponsored loans, scholarships/grants, traineeships, and unspecified assistantships also available. Support available to part-time students. Total annual research expenditures: $2.1 million. *Unit head:* Boo Kwa, Chairperson, 813-974-1122, Fax: 813-974-8506. *Application contact:* Michelle Robinson, Academic Advisor, 813-974-6665, Fax: 813-974-8121, E-mail: mrobinso@health.usf.edu.

University of Washington, Graduate School, School of Public Health and Community Medicine, Department of Epidemiology, Seattle, WA 98195. Offers epidemiology (MPH, MS, PhD); international health (MPH); maternal/child health (MPH); nutritional sciences (MPH, MS, PhD); public health genetics (MPH, MS, PhD), including genetic epidemiology (MS), public health genetics (MPH, PhD). *Accreditation:* CEPH (one or more programs are accredited). Part-time programs available. Terminal master's awarded for partial completion of doctoral program. *Degree requirements:* For master's, thesis, practicum (MPH); for doctorate, thesis/dissertation, preliminary exam, general exam, final exam, comprehensive exam, registration. *Entrance requirements:* For master's, GRE General Test, research experience in health sciences (preferred), minimum GPA of 3.0; for doctorate, GRE General Test, master's degree in health sciences or related field from US institution, experience in health science (preferred), minimum GPA of 3.0. Additional exam requirements/recommendations for international students: Required—TOEFL (minimum score 580 paper-based; 237 computer-based). Electronic applications accepted. Expenses: Contact institution. *Faculty research:* Chronic diseases, sexually transmitted diseases, injury epidemiology, materials and child health, molecular and genetic epidemiology.

Yale University, School of Medicine, School of Public Health, Division of Global Health, New Haven, CT 06520. Offers MPH. *Accreditation:* CEPH. Part-time programs available. *Faculty:* 3 full-time (2 women), 1 (woman) part-time/adjunct. *Students:* 25; includes 10 minority (3 African Americans, 4 Asian Americans or Pacific Islanders, 3 Hispanic Americans), 4 international.

International Health

Yale University (continued)
Average age 26. In 2006, 15 degrees awarded. *Degree requirements:* For master's, one foreign language, thesis, internship. *Entrance requirements:* For master's, GMAT, GRE, or MCAT, previous undergraduate course work in mathematics and science. Additional exam requirements/recommendations for international students: Required—TOEFL. *Application deadline:* For fall admission, 1/15 for domestic and international students. Electronic applications accepted. *Expenses:* Contact institution. *Financial support:* Career-related internships or fieldwork, Federal Work-Study, institutionally sponsored loans, and scholarships/grants available. Support available to part-time students. Financial award application deadline: 3/1; financial award applicants required to submit FAFSA. *Faculty research:* International health promotion and healthy public policy, community health planning, health of elderly and disabled persons. *Unit head:* Dr. Brian P. Leaderer, Acting Division Head, 203-785-6269, Fax: 203-785-6103, E-mail: brian.leaderer@yale.edu. *Application contact:* Jacqui Comshaw, Director of Admissions, 203-785-2844, Fax: 203-785-4845, E-mail: eph.admissions@yale.edu.

See Close-Up on page 2073.

Maternal and Child Health

Bank Street College of Education, Graduate School, Department of Curriculum and Instruction, Program in Infant and Parent Development and Early Intervention, New York, NY 10025. Offers infant and parent development and early intervention (MS Ed); infant and parent development and early intervention/early childhood special and general education (MS Ed); infant and parent development and early intervention/early childhood special education (Ed M). *Accreditation:* NCATE. *Students:* 14 full-time (all women), 29 part-time (27 women); includes 10 minority (3 African Americans, 7 Hispanic Americans). Average age 31. 27 applicants, 63% accepted, 12 enrolled. In 2006, 7 degrees awarded. *Degree requirements:* For master's, thesis, registration. *Entrance requirements:* For master's, interview. Additional exam requirements/recommendations for international students: Required—TOEFL (minimum score 600 paper-based; 250 computer-based). *Application deadline:* For fall admission, 3/1 priority date for domestic students; for spring admission, 11/1 priority date for domestic students. Applications are processed on a rolling basis. Application fee: $50. *Expenses:* Tuition: Part-time $940 per credit. Required fees: $100 per term. *Financial support:* Career-related internships or fieldwork, Federal Work-Study, scholarships/grants, and unspecified assistantships available. Support available to part-time students. Financial award application deadline: 4/15; financial award applicants required to submit FAFSA. *Faculty research:* Early intervention, early attachment practice in infant and toddler childcare, parenting skills in adolescents. *Unit head:* Carla Poole, Director, 212-875-4523, Fax: 212-875-4753, E-mail: @bankstreet.edu. *Application contact:* Ann Morgan, Director of Graduate Admissions, 212-875-4403, Fax: 212-875-4678, E-mail: amorgan@bankstreet.edu.

Bank Street College of Education, Graduate School, Program in Child Life, New York, NY 10025. Offers MS. *Students:* 20 full-time (all women), 5 part-time (all women); includes 5 minority (2 African Americans, 2 Asian Americans or Pacific Islanders, 1 Hispanic American). Average age 27. 19 applicants, 74% accepted, 13 enrolled. In 2006, 5 degrees awarded. *Degree requirements:* For master's, thesis. *Entrance requirements:* For master's, interview. Additional exam requirements/recommendations for international students: Required—TOEFL (minimum score 600 paper-based; 250 computer-based). *Application deadline:* For fall admission, 3/1 priority date for domestic students; for spring admission, 11/1 priority date for domestic students. Applications are processed on a rolling basis. Application fee: $50. *Expenses:* Tuition: Part-time $940 per credit. Required fees: $100 per term. *Financial support:* Career-related internships or fieldwork, Federal Work-Study, scholarships/grants, and unspecified assistantships available. Support available to part-time students. Financial award application deadline: 4/15; financial award applicants required to submit FAFSA. *Faculty research:* Therapeutic play in child life setting, child advocacy, psychosocial and educational intervention with care of sick children. *Unit head:* Troy Pinkney-Ragsdale, Director, 212-875-4473, Fax: 212-875-4753, E-mail: tpinkneyragsdale@bankstreet.edu. *Application contact:* Ann Morgan, Director of Graduate Admissions, 212-875-4403, Fax: 212-875-4678, E-mail: amorgan@bankstreet.edu.

Boston University, School of Public Health, Maternal and Child Health Department, Boston, MA 02215. Offers maternal and child health (MPH); nurse midwifery education (Certificate). *Students:* 33 full-time (31 women), 20 part-time (19 women); includes 11 minority (3 African Americans, 6 Asian Americans or Pacific Islanders, 2 Hispanic Americans), 7 international. Average age 27. *Entrance requirements:* For master's, GRE General Test. Additional exam requirements/recommendations for international students: Required—TOEFL or IELTS. *Application deadline:* For fall admission, 2/1 for domestic students; for spring admission, 10/15 for domestic students. Applications are processed on a rolling basis. Application fee: $60. Electronic applications accepted. *Expenses:* Tuition: Full-time $33,330; part-time $1,042 per credit. Required fees: $462; $40. *Financial support:* Scholarships/grants and tuition waivers (partial) available. *Unit head:* Dr. Milton Kotelchuck, Head, 617-638-5375, E-mail: askmch@bu.edu. *Application contact:* LePhan Quan, Assistant Director of Admissions, 617-638-4640, Fax: 617-638-5299, E-mail: asksph@bu.edu.

Columbia University, Mailman School of Public Health, Division of Population and Family Health, New York, NY 10032. Offers MPH. *Accreditation:* CEPH. Part-time programs available. *Students:* 95. In 2006, 25 degrees awarded. *Entrance requirements:* For master's, GRE General Test. *Application deadline:* For fall admission, 2/1 for domestic students; for spring admission, 10/1 for domestic students. Application fee: $60. *Financial support:* Research assistantships, career-related internships or fieldwork and Federal Work-Study available. Financial award application deadline: 2/1; financial award applicants required to submit FAFSA. *Faculty research:* Women's sexual and reproductive health, adolescent sexual and reproductive behavior, infant and child health, maternal mortality, reproductive rights. *Unit head:* Dr. John Santelli, Head, 212-304-5200. *Application contact:* June Saunders, Associate Director of Admissions, 212-305-3927, Fax: 212-342-4861, E-mail: ph-admit@columbia.edu.

The George Washington University, School of Public Health and Health Services, Department of Prevention and Community Health, Washington, DC 20052. Offers community-oriented primary care (MPH); health promotion (MPH); maternal and child health (MPH); public health and emergency management (Certificate). *Accreditation:* CEPH. *Entrance requirements:* For master's, GRE or GMAT, 2 letters of recommendation, resumé. Additional exam requirements/recommendations for international students: Required—TOEFL.

New York Medical College, School of Public Health, Department of Behavioral Sciences and Community Health, Program in Maternal and Child Health, Valhalla, NY 10595-1691. Offers MPH. Part-time and evening/weekend programs available. *Degree requirements:* For master's, thesis, registration. *Entrance requirements:* For master's, minimum undergraduate GPA of 3.0, work experience. Additional exam requirements/recommendations for international students: Required—TOEFL (minimum score 600 paper-based; 250 computer-based). *Application deadline:* For fall admission, 8/1 priority date for domestic students, 5/15 for international students; for spring admission, 12/1 priority date for domestic students, 10/15 for international students. Applications are processed on a rolling basis. Application fee: $35 ($60 for international students). Electronic applications accepted. *Financial support:* Career-related internships or fieldwork, Federal Work-Study, and institutionally sponsored loans available. Financial award application deadline: 6/15; financial award applicants required to submit FAFSA. *Unit head:* Director, 914-594-3480. *Application contact:* Marian F. McGowan, Information Contact, 914-594-4510, Fax: 914-594-4292, E-mail: sph_admissions@nymc.edu.

See Close-Up on page 2043.

Oakland University, Graduate Study and Lifelong Learning, School of Health Sciences, Program in Physical Therapy, Rochester, MI 48309-4401. Offers neurological rehabilitation (Certificate); orthopedic manual physical therapy (Certificate); orthopedic physical therapy (Certificate); pediatric rehabilitation (Certificate); physical therapy (MSPT, DPT, Dr Sc PT); teaching and learning for rehabilitation professionals (Certificate). *Accreditation:* APTA. *Faculty:* 10 full-time (8 women), 1 (woman) part-time/adjunct. *Students:* 117 full-time (98 women), 77 part-time (59 women); includes 23 minority (9 African Americans, 12 Asian Americans or Pacific Islanders, 2 Hispanic Americans), 20 international. Average age 27. 205 applicants, 39% accepted, 56 enrolled. In 2006, 4 master's, 27 doctorates, 13 Certificates awarded. *Degree requirements:* For master's, thesis (for some programs). *Entrance requirements:* For master's, acceptance in the 2-year preparatory post-baccalaureate program, minimum GPA of 3.0; for doctorate, GRE General Test. Additional exam requirements/recommendations for international students: Required—TOEFL (minimum score 550 paper-based; 213 computer-based). *Application deadline:* For fall admission, 10/15 for domestic and international students. Application fee: $35. *Expenses:* Contact institution. *Financial support:* Federal Work-Study, institutionally sponsored loans, and tuition waivers (full) available. Financial award application deadline: 3/1; financial award applicants required to submit FAFSA. *Unit head:* Dr. Kristine A. Thompson, Program Director, 248-370-4041, E-mail: marcoux@oakland.edu.

Tulane University, School of Public Health and Tropical Medicine, Department of Community Health Sciences, Program in Maternal and Child Health, New Orleans, LA 70118-5669. Offers MPH, Dr PH, MSW/MPH. *Accreditation:* CEPH (one or more programs are accredited). *Faculty:* 3 full-time (2 women), 3 part-time/adjunct (2 women). *Students:* 37 full-time (31 women), 25 part-time (13 women); includes 22 minority (20 African Americans, 2 Asian Americans or Pacific Islanders), 1 international. *Degree requirements:* For doctorate, thesis/dissertation, comprehensive exam. *Entrance requirements:* For master's and doctorate, GRE General Test. Additional exam requirements/recommendations for international students: Required—TOEFL. *Application deadline:* For fall admission, 4/15 priority date for domestic and international students; for spring admission, 10/15 for domestic students, 10/15 priority date for international students. Applications are processed on a rolling basis. Application fee: $40. *Financial support:* Application deadline: 4/15. *Unit head:* Dr. Jeanette Magnus, Section Head.

The University of Alabama at Birmingham, School of Public Health, Department of Maternal and Child Health, Birmingham, AL 35294. Offers MSPH. *Degree requirements:* For master's, research project. *Application deadline:* Applications are processed on a rolling basis. Application fee: $35 ($60 for international students). Electronic applications accepted. *Expenses:* Tuition, state resident: part-time $170 per credit hour. Tuition, nonresident: part-time $425 per credit hour. Required fees: $15 per credit hour. $122 per term. Tuition and fees vary according to program. *Unit head:* Dr. Greg R. Alexander, Chair, 205-934-7161, Fax: 205-934-8248, E-mail: alexandg@uab.edu. *Application contact:* Nancy O. Pinson, Coordinator of Student Admissions, 205-934-4993, Fax: 205-975-5484.

University of California, Berkeley, Graduate Division, School of Public Health, Master's Internationalist Program, Berkeley, CA 94720-1500. Offers community health education (MPH); epidemiology (MPH); interdisciplinary (MPH); maternal and child health (MPH); public health nutrition (MPH). *Accreditation:* CEPH. *Entrance requirements:* For master's, GRE General Test, minimum GPA of 3.0. *Application deadline:* For fall admission, 12/1 for domestic students. Applications are processed on a rolling basis. Application fee: $60 ($80 for international students). *Financial support:* Fellowships, research assistantships, teaching assistantships, Federal Work-Study and unspecified assistantships available. *Application contact:* Information Contact, 510-643-0881, E-mail: sphinfo@berkeley.edu.

University of California, Berkeley, Graduate Division, School of Public Health, Program in Maternal and Child Health, Berkeley, CA 94720-1500. Offers MPH. *Entrance requirements:* For master's, GRE General Test, minimum GPA of 3.0. *Application deadline:* For fall admission, 12/1 for domestic students. Applications are processed on a rolling basis. Application fee: $60 ($80 for international students). *Financial support:* Fellowships, research assistantships, unspecified assistantships available. *Unit head:* Sylvia Guendelman, Chair, 510-642-1512. *Application contact:* Steve Purser, Assistant Director, 510-643-4991, Fax: 510-643-8236, E-mail: spurser@uclink.berkeley.edu.

University of California, Davis, Graduate Studies, Program in Maternal and Child Nutrition, Davis, CA 95616. Offers MAS. *Degree requirements:* For master's, comprehensive exam. *Entrance requirements:* Additional exam requirements/recommendations for international students: Required—TOEFL (minimum score 550 paper-based; 213 computer-based).

University of Minnesota, Twin Cities Campus, School of Public Health, Major in Maternal and Child Health, Minneapolis, MN 55455-0213. Offers MPH. *Accreditation:* CEPH. Part-time programs available. *Degree requirements:* For master's, fieldwork, master's project. *Entrance requirements:* For master's, GRE General Test, 1 year of relevant experience. Additional exam requirements/recommendations for international students: Required—TOEFL. Electronic applications accepted. Expenses: Contact institution. Full-time tuition and fees vary according to class time, course load, program, reciprocity agreements and student level. *Faculty research:* Reproductive and perinatal health, family planning, child adolescent and family health, risk reduction and resiliency, child and family adaptation to chronic health conditions.

University of Mississippi Medical Center, School of Graduate Studies in the Health Sciences, Department of Maternal-Fetal Medicine, Jackson, MS 39216-4505. Offers MS. *Faculty:* 6 full-time (0 women). *Students:* 3 full-time (0 women). Average age 36. *Degree requirements:* For master's, thesis. *Entrance requirements:* For master's, status as obstetrician-gynecologist in the Department of Obstetrics and Gynecology's Maternal-Fetal Medicine Fellowship Program. Application fee: $10. *Expenses:* Tuition, state resident: full-time $4,523. Tuition, nonresident: full-time $10,566. *Unit head:* Dr. Bryan D. Cowan, Chairman, 601-984-5342, Fax: 601-984-6904, E-mail: bcowan@ob-gyn.umsmed.edu. *Application contact:* Dr. James A. Bofill, Program Director and Chief, 601-984-6719, Fax: 601-984-6773, E-mail: jbofill@ob-gyn.umsmed.edu.

The University of North Carolina at Chapel Hill, Graduate School, School of Public Health, Department of Maternal and Child Health, Chapel Hill, NC 27599. Offers MPH, MSPH, Dr PH, PhD, MPH/MSW, MSPH/MSW. *Accreditation:* CEPH (one or more programs are accredited). *Faculty:* 20 full-time (13 women), 60 part-time/adjunct. *Students:* 80 full-time (77 women); includes 18 minority (8 African Americans, 3 American Indian/Alaska Native, 5 Asian Americans or Pacific Islanders, 2 Hispanic Americans), 8 international. Average age 27. 131 applicants, 34% accepted, 36 enrolled. In 2006, 42 master's, 6 doctorates awarded. *Median time to degree:* Of those who began their doctoral program in fall 1998, 100% received their degree in 8 years or less. *Degree requirements:* For master's, major paper; for doctorate, thesis/dissertation, comprehensive exam, registration. *Entrance requirements:* For master's, GRE

General Test or MCAT, minimum GPA of 3.0, paid MHCH-related work experience (preferred); for doctorate, GRE General Test, minimum GPA of 3.0, paid MHCH-related work experience (preferred). Additional exam requirements/recommendations for international students: Required—TOEFL. *Application deadline:* For fall admission, 1/1 priority date for domestic and international students. Applications are processed on a rolling basis. Application fee: $70. Electronic applications accepted. *Financial support:* In 2006–07, 50 students received support, including 14 fellowships with full tuition reimbursements available (averaging $6,869 per year), 26 research assistantships with full tuition reimbursements available (averaging $9,809 per year), 3 teaching assistantships with full and partial tuition reimbursements available (averaging $7,252 per year); career-related internships or fieldwork, institutionally sponsored loans, traineeships, health care benefits, and unspecified assistantships also available. Financial award application deadline: 1/1; financial award applicants required to submit FAFSA. *Faculty research:* Women's health, prenatal health, family planning, program evaluation, child health policy and priorities. *Unit head:* Dr. Herbert B. Peterson, Chair, 919-966-5981, Fax: 919-966-0458, E-mail: herbert_peterson@unc.edu. *Application contact:* Linda Southern, Registrar, 919-966-2018, Fax: 919-966-0458, E-mail: southern@email.unc.edu.

University of Puerto Rico, Medical Sciences Campus, Graduate School of Public Health, Department of Human Development, Program in Mother and Child Health, San Juan, PR 00936-5067. Offers MPH. Part-time and evening/weekend programs available. *Students:* 7 (6 women). 9 applicants, 67% accepted. In 2006, 9 degrees awarded. *Entrance requirements:* For master's, GRE, previous course work in algebra. *Application deadline:* For fall admission, 3/15 for domestic students. Application fee: $20. *Financial support:* Research assistantships, teaching assistantships, Federal Work-Study and institutionally sponsored loans available. Financial award application deadline: 4/30. *Application contact:* Prof. Mayra E. Santiago-Vargas, Counselor, 787-756-5244, Fax: 787-759-6719, E-mail: msantiago@rcm.upr.edu.

University of Washington, Graduate School, School of Public Health and Community Medicine, Department of Epidemiology, Seattle, WA 98195. Offers epidemiology (MPH, MS, PhD); international health (MPH); maternal/child health (MPH); nutritional sciences (MPH, MS, PhD); public health genetics (MPH, MS, PhD), including genetic epidemiology (MS), public health genetics (MPH, PhD). *Accreditation:* CEPH (one or more programs are accredited). Part-time programs available. Terminal master's awarded for partial completion of doctoral program. *Degree requirements:* For master's, thesis, practicum (MPH); for doctorate, thesis/dissertation, preliminary exam, general exam, final exam, comprehensive exam, registration. *Entrance requirements:* For master's, GRE General Test, research experience in health sciences (preferred), minimum GPA of 3.0; for doctorate, GRE General Test, master's degree in health sciences or related field from US institution, experience in health science (preferred), minimum GPA of 3.0. Additional exam requirements/recommendations for international students: Required—TOEFL (minimum score 580 paper-based; 237 computer-based). Electronic applications accepted. Expenses: Contact institution. *Faculty research:* Chronic diseases, sexually transmitted diseases, injury epidemiology, materials and child health, molecular and genetic epidemiology.

BRANDEIS UNIVERSITY

The Heller School for Social Policy and Management
International Health Policy and Management Program

Programs of Study

The Master of Science (M.S.) in international health policy and management at Brandeis University prepares students to address the challenges of creating equitable, cost-effective, and efficient policies and health-care programs that improve the well-being of people in developing countries as well as that of vulnerable and disadvantaged populations in developed countries.

Bringing together experts in international development, health financing, and health systems, the International Health Policy and Management Program teaches students how to make the best use of policy analysis to determine which plans work and which are the most cost-effective. The program also provides students with a conceptual framework and the tools and techniques to engage in policy development and evaluation as well as the skills to manage implementation. By bridging these gaps, students are better equipped to meet the challenges of helping governments manage health-care markets, dealing with the relationship between chronic illness—including HIV/AIDS—and macroeconomic growth, and managing the transition from diseases of poverty to those of higher-income populations.

During this one-year program, students are required to take 20 credits each semester as well as workshops during the winter break that cover management style, interpersonal communications, task delegation, and conflict mediation. The program culminates in a Capstone Seminar, in which students apply their analytical and managerial skills to a specific problem. The program offers tracks in policy and management, for which specific courses are required, and students may take approved electives from other schools within the University.

Research Facilities

The Schneider Institutes for Health Policy at the Heller School work on a variety of substantive issues that bridge the domains of health services and health policy research. The staff includes researchers, administrators, and technical assistance experts with backgrounds in economics, mental health, public policy, public health, sociology, political science, psychology, health administration, finance and operations, and business management. The Family and Child Policy Center (FCPC) brings together faculty members, research staff members, and students in activities that foster the well-being of children and their families. The center conducts policy research, promotes active public engagement, and contributes to the teaching activities of the School. The Center for International Development engages in research that furthers knowledge about sustainable development and helps build local capacity to solve problems and plan sound development strategies. The center works in partnership with development organizations and universities abroad and in the United States.

Financial Aid

The program provides a full scholarship, covering tuition and fees, to 1 student each year with a demonstrated commitment to effective health policy and management. World Bank Scholarships offer tuition and fees to graduate students from World Bank member countries, including airfare to and from the student's home country. Royal Ambassadorial Scholarships award one year of tuition to students from other countries. Students in the program are also eligible for Fulbright Scholarships and Ford Foundation International Fellowships or Federal Perkins Loans, or they may qualify for Federal Direct Stafford Student Loans of up to $20,500 per year. Detailed information about financial aid opportunities is available from the Admissions Office.

Cost of Study

In the 2006–07 academic year, full-time tuition was $32,951. Students must also pay mandatory fees of $100 and mandatory medical insurance of $1475 (unless they are otherwise insured by an acceptable policy).

Living and Housing Costs

Students can expect to pay approximately $12,000, or $1333 per month, in living expenses and $500 for books and other course materials each semester.

Student Group

Students in the program are early-career to midcareer professionals from throughout the world who have at least two years of relevant experience working on problems of underdevelopment, marginalization, and project implementation in low- and middle-income countries or with the marginalized communities in high-income countries.

Student Outcomes

Students are trained to take on increasingly responsible roles in health policy planning and in the management of policy and program implementation in health ministries and planning agencies, multilateral and bilateral development organizations, and nongovernmental organizations (NGOs). Students learn how to make the best use of policy analysis to determine which plans work, which are the most cost-effective, and which are sensitive to a country's values and culture.

Location

Located in Waltham, Massachusetts, 16 miles west of Boston, Brandeis University is part of a metropolitan area that includes educational institutions, museums and galleries, theaters, cultural events, and other attractions of the city. Students are able to travel easily into Cambridge or Boston via either the commuter train or public bus, both of which stop within steps of the campus.

The University and The School

Brandeis University is ranked in the top tier of the nation's universities. It is the youngest private research university in the country. The Heller School is committed to developing new knowledge and insights in the field of social policy and in health and human services management. As a research institution, Heller has pioneered in a variety of policy areas, including mental health, substance abuse, international and community development, developmental disabilities, and poverty and hunger.

Applying

Application for admission requires an application form, a curriculum vitae/resume, a statement of purpose, three letters of recommendation (one professional, one academic, and the third professional or academic), official transcripts of undergraduate and any graduate work, proof of English proficiency if English is not the native language, and a $55 application fee. Official scores from either the GRE or GMAT tests are preferred but are not required.

Correspondence and Information

Admissions Office
The Heller School for Social Policy and Management
MS 035
Brandeis University
P.O. Box 549110
Waltham, Massachusetts 02454-9110
Phone: 781-736-3820
Fax: 781-736-2774
E-mail: helleradmissions@brandeis.edu
Web site: http://heller.brandeis.edu/sid/

Brandeis University

THE FACULTY AND THEIR RESEARCH

Sarita Bhalotra, Assistant Professor and Co-Chair, Concentration in Health Policy and Health Services; M.D., Delhi (India). Financing and delivery of health care; utilization, cost, and outcomes evaluation of patients with chronic disease in different delivery systems; impact on cardiovascular disease of a lifestyle-modification program.

Jon A. Chilingerian, Associate Professor of Management and Director, Management and Organizational Sciences Research; Ph.D. (management), MIT (Sloan), 1987. Productive efficiency of health-care organizations and providers, study of executive leadership.

Barry L. Friedman, Professor of Economics; Ph.D., MIT. Social security and income maintenance, studies relating welfare and work.

Andrew B. Hahn, Professor and Director, Institute for Sustainable Development; Ph.D., Brandeis, 1978. Effective strategies for assisting America's most vulnerable youth.

Susan Holcombe, Associate Professor and Associate Director (Academics), Sustainable International Development (SID) program; Ph.D. (public administration), New York for Women. Development management, demographics of development, monitoring and evaluation.

Constance M. Horgan, Professor; Director, Center on Behavioral Health in the Schneider Institutes for Health Policy; and Co-Chair, Concentration in Health Policy and Health Services; Sc.D. (health policy and management), Johns Hopkins, 1984. How substance-abuse and mental health services are financed, organized, and delivered in the public and private sectors.

A. K. Nandakumar, Associate Professor; Ph.D. (economics), Boston University. International health policy issues, including financing, national health accounts, household demand and expenditures on health, and aging populations and their economic impact on health systems; strengthening health systems in developing countries, including Egypt, Gaza, Jordan, Kenya, Lebanon, Rwanda, Western Samoa, and Yemen.

Donald S. Shepard, Professor and Director, Schneider Institutes for Health Policy's Cost-effectiveness Group; Ph.D. (public policy), Harvard (JFK). Cost and cost-effectiveness analysis in health, health financing.

Laurence R. Simon, Professor of International Development; Director, Master of Arts Program in Sustainable International Development; and Director, Center for International Development; Ph.D. (geography), Clark. Poverty and vulnerability in developing nations, development program management.

Stanley S. Wallack, Professor, Executive Director, and Co-Founder, Schneider Institutes for Health Policy; Ph.D. (economics), Washington (St. Louis), 1969. Developing effective reimbursement systems and organizational arrangements for acute and chronic health care; cost, use, and value of prescription drugs.

COLUMBIA UNIVERSITY

Mailman School of Public Health

Programs of Study	The Mailman School of Public Health, located within the Columbia University Medical Center, offers programs leading to the Master of Public Health (M.P.H.), Master of Science (M.S.), and Doctor of Public Health (Dr.P.H.). The Doctor of Philosophy (Ph.D.) degree is also offered in collaboration with the Graduate School of Arts and Sciences. Concentrations are available in biostatistics, environmental health sciences, epidemiology, health policy and management, population and family health, and sociomedical sciences. The M.P.H. program requires 45 course credits, practical training (practicum) equivalent to one term, and a culminating experience. A two-year Weekend Executive M.P.H. program in health services management and an evening program in health promotion are also available for working professionals. The course requirements for the M.S. and doctoral programs vary, depending on each candidate's program. Part-time study is an option in many of the School's programs. Formal dual-degree programs exist with the Schools of Business (M.B.A./M.P.H.), Architecture and Urban Planning (M.S.U.P./M.P.H.), Dentistry (D.D.S./M.P.H.), Law (J.D./M.P.H.), Medicine (M.D./M.P.H.), Nursing (M.S.N./M.P.H.), International Affairs (M.I.A./M.P.H., M.P.A./M.P.H.), Social Work (M.S.S.W./M.P.H.), and Occupational Therapy (M.S.O.T./M.P.H.).
Research Facilities	Faculty members in all departments of the School of Public Health are involved in research programs, most of which afford opportunities for student participation. Faculty involvement in research projects enriches classroom and tutorial experiences for students and contributes to the body of knowledge on health issues and the application of that knowledge to health care and health-care delivery. The facilities of the Health Sciences Center are available through faculty members with appointments in the various schools, institutes, centers, and hospitals of the Columbia-Presbyterian Center. The Health Sciences Library is one of the largest medical center libraries in the United States, with more than 500,000 volumes, 4,400 periodicals, and computerized literature-searching on several databases, including MEDLARS.
Financial Aid	A limited number of assistantships, scholarships, traineeships, and student loans are available. Applicants requesting financial aid are encouraged to contact the School's Financial Aid Office (212-305-4113) early in the application process.
Cost of Study	The tuition was $1100 per credit in 2006–07. Health services and hospital insurance plans are available for individual students and members of their family and are required for full-time students. Health coverage for individual students was $3020 in 2006–07.
Living and Housing Costs	There is some housing available for single students and for couples at or near the Columbia University Medical Center. Accommodations are limited in number and may not be available to all students accepted into the School. Estimated personal and living expenses for students maintaining their own residence were approximately $18,835 for the nine-month academic year in 2006–07. New York offers a wide variety of living options, and actual expenses may vary. Applicants are encouraged to explore off-campus housing options if possible.
Student Group	In fall 2006, the School enrolled approximately 860 graduate students. While the majority are pursuing the M.P.H. degree, approximately 25 percent are engaged in doctoral studies. Entering students averaged 27 years of age. Their backgrounds reflect the broad range of public health issues. Approximately 15 percent of the students are from underrepresented minority groups; 11 percent are international students. More than 30 percent of the students are engaged in part-time study. Many of these students are midcareer professionals broadening their knowledge base and acquiring new skills. Students at the Mailman School of Public Health are part of the Health Sciences Division of Columbia University. Approximately 2,500 students in medicine, dentistry, nursing, public health, and occupational and physical therapy study at this site.
Location	New York City offers the world's most comprehensive networks of private and public health-care and social services. Students have the opportunity to study and observe the latest in their area of interest and to work with the leaders in the field, both in the classroom and through the practicum. The campus, located in upper Manhattan a few blocks south of the George Washington Bridge, offers outstanding resources: the College of Physicians and Surgeons, the School of Dental and Oral Surgery, the School of Nursing, the Center for Geriatrics and Gerontology, the Institute of Human Nutrition, the Center for Population and Family Health, the Columbia-Presbyterian Cancer Center, the Sergievsky Center for epidemiological research, the Upper West Side Health Center, and the clinical programs of the New York Presbyterian Hospital and the New York State Psychiatric Institute. The School has close ties to the New York City Department of Health (NYCDOH), providing excellent opportunities for student field experience. It also participates with Harlem Hospital in a major Prevention Center activity.
The University and The School	Columbia's role is that of education for excellence—a term that embraces high quality in teaching and the furtherance of knowledge through research, preeminence in the professions, and leadership in community and national affairs. Columbia's status as a private institution, its location, its faculty, and its international reputation provide the basis for this diversified educational purpose. The Mailman School of Public Health is one of the first three schools of public health in the country. It was founded originally as an institute of the medical school, reflecting an early concern in the Faculty of Medicine with the principles of the health of populations and the administrative sciences of health care. It became the School of Public Health in 1945 and today encompasses global as well as national and community health perspectives. Although the School's offerings are diverse and the breadth of preparation provided is wide, the School of Public Health remains small. A dedicated faculty upholds a basic tenet of the School—the importance of the individual student—and shares a major commitment to flexibility in the learning process.
Applying	The application deadline for regular fall admission to the M.P.H. or M.S. program is February 1 and for the Executive M.P.H. program and the Columbia on the Job (COTJ) program, June 15. All applicants must have a bachelor's degree from a recognized university or college, show evidence of satisfactory preparation in quantitative subject areas, and have an acceptable academic record. The program is designed for applicants with appropriate professional or other work experience. Some programs have specific preadmission requirements. The GRE General Test or another appropriate test (MCAT, GMAT, LSAT, DAT) is required for admission. The TOEFL is required of all applicants whose native language is not English. The application deadline for the Dr.P.H. program is January 3.
Correspondence and Information	Office of Admission Mailman School of Public Health Columbia University 722 West 168th Street, Suite 1030 New York, New York 10032 Phone: 212-342-5127 Fax: 212-342-1830 E-mail: ph-admit@columbia.edu Web site: http://www.mailman.hs.columbia.edu

Columbia University

DEPARTMENTS AND PROGRAMS

Biostatistics. (M.P.H., M.S., Dr.P.H., Ph.D.) Department Chair: Bruce Levin, Ph.D. The collection, analysis, and presentation of data have wide applicability to every area of public health. The Biostatistics Department programs provide a strong base of statistical techniques used to measure and evaluate health status, health hazards, and health measures in the public and private sectors. This diversity is reflected in the backgrounds of those entering the program. Some are mathematicians, others are from the natural or social sciences, and still others are professionals in such areas as medicine or dentistry. The common thread is an affinity for quantitative methods and pleasure in the utilization of mathematics to solve practical problems. Knowledge of calculus is strongly recommended. Courses in statistical methodology cover such areas as applied probability theory, vital statistics, analysis of categorical data, regression analysis, multivariate analysis, and sampling. The department has tracks in clinical research methods, patient-oriented research, and theory and methods and an accelerated track for predoctoral training leading to an M.S. degree. An M.P.H. in general biostatistics is also available. These are of special interest to clinicians pursuing careers in academic medicine who need formal, rigorous training in skills essential for the design, conduct, and analysis of clinical research studies and for those interested in research careers or in earning a Ph.D. degree. (Contact: Dr. Melissa Begg, telephone: 212-305-9398; e-mail: clinical_ms@biostat.columbia.edu.)

Environmental Health Sciences. (M.P.H., Dr.P.H., Ph.D.) Department Chair: Paul Brandt-Rauf, M.D., Dr.P.H. This rapidly expanding field requires a broad range of basic and applied scientific skills. The program is primarily oriented at understanding and predicting the health effects of environmental and occupational exposure to chemicals and radiation. Research activities of the faculty strive to generate scientific data that ultimately serve as the underpinnings of environmental policy decisions. Because the field is so broad, students are encouraged to focus on particular areas, including medical/health physics, environment and molecular epidemiology, environment and molecular toxicology, and environmental health policy. Each of these is taught with some consideration of national, international, and global policy issues. The program typically attracts students with a wide variety of backgrounds and interests. Several academic prerequisites are required for admission, such as one year each of undergraduate biology and mathematics (which must be calculus for the medical/health physics track) and one year each of general and organic chemistry. Admission may be contingent upon completing any of the missing prerequisites during the first year. A global health track has been added to this department to meet the needs of students who are interested in becoming global health practitioners within this area of public health interest.

Epidemiology. (Dr.P.H., M.P.H., M.S., Ph.D.) Department Chair: Ezra Susser, M.D., Dr.P.H. Epidemiology is an integral part of human ecology. Its area of concern includes the distribution, determinants, and dynamics of health and disease in populations—from communicable and chronic diseases, child health and development, and mental retardation to stress in health disorders, psychiatric problems, and evaluation of programs and services. The areas of interest to faculty members include cancer, schizophrenia, coronary heart disease, immunology, and neurological disorders. Epidemiologic methodology is also applied to social problems such as homelessness. Special resources available to the student of epidemiology include the Gertrude H. Sergievsky Center for epidemiologic research. The center focuses on the study of epilepsy, cerebral palsy, and the development of brain disorders and provides a rich resource in epidemiologic research and training in neuroepidemiology. An academic background in health, the biological or social sciences, or mathematics and statistics is desirable for candidates wishing to enter this field. A global health track has been added to this department to meet the needs of students who are interested in becoming global health practitioners within this area of public health interest.

Health Policy and Management. (M.P.H., Executive M.P.H.) Department Chair: Sherry Glied, Ph.D. This program encompasses studies in the formulation and implementation of health-care policy and the planning and management of the increasingly diverse range of institutions that provide health care. The growth of the health services sector demands a better understanding of the production and distribution of care and how to gauge its effectiveness in relation to costs. Just as policymakers should be trained to examine the feasibility of their goals in light of managers' capacities and constraints, so too managers should be equipped to understand the policy projects that increasingly define the environment in which they work. The department's full-time, part-time, and weekend programs provide students with analytical skills and methodological tools useful to policymakers and managers in the public, voluntary, and private sectors. Students focusing on management take courses in accounting and budgeting, financial management, health economics, and organizational theory. Students focusing on policy substitute advanced health economics and applied regression for the finance sequence. For students interested in specializing in a particular area of health policy and management, the department offers the opportunity for specific concentrations, such as the economics of health care and a track in effectiveness and outcomes research leading to an M.P.H. (Contact: Dr. Joshua Zivin, telephone: 212-305-3524; e-mail: jz126@columbia.edu). Students interested in the Columbia on the Job part-time program should contact Susan Cohen (telephone: 212-305-5152; e-mail: sc33@columbia.edu). An Executive M.P.H. program in health services management, a two-year course of study, is available for employed health professionals seeking to advance in management positions (Program Director: Michael Sparer, J.D., Ph.D., telephone: 212-305-5611; e-mail: mss16@columbia.edu). A global health track has been added to this department to meet the needs of students who are interested in becoming global health practitioners within this area of public health interest.

Population and Family Health. (M.P.H.) Department Chair: John Santelli, M.D. This program aims to provide leadership in the search for solutions to the critical public health problems in population and family health, including reproductive, adolescent, and child health in developed and developing countries, and forced migration and health. The curriculum, which combines theory and practice, provides the necessary base of knowledge and skills to develop and implement policies, programs, and research that address the important issues within these areas. The program is designed for professionals representing the disciplines of pediatrics, obstetrics, nursing, social work, health-care delivery, management, law, and social sciences as well as for those with other relevant professional background or field experience. Prior to admission, students must have work experience in the field. The community- and school-based programs developed and run by the Heilbrunn Center for Population and Family Health provide rich and varied training opportunities where students can apply their knowledge and skills. A global health track has been added to this department to meet the needs of students who are interested in becoming global health practitioners within this area of public health interest.

Sociomedical Sciences. (M.P.H., Ph.D., Dr.P.H.) Department Chair: Richard Parker, Ph.D. The department brings together a multidisciplinary faculty of social scientists and health professionals who study the influence of social and cultural factors on health and health-care delivery. Major areas of interest include preventive health behavior, social and economic determinants of health and disease, sexuality and policy, the role of social supports, ethical issues in health, research methods, health and human rights, evaluation of health-care programs, organization and delivery of health care, HIV/AIDS, adolescent health, and disability. The department has six M.P.H. tracks. The first focuses on public health research with a strong social science orientation. The second concentrates on health promotion and disease prevention, including program planning, implementation, and evaluation. This track offers a day and evening program. Applicants to this program should have prior work experience in public health or a related field. An evening M.P.H. program in health promotion and disease prevention is open to working professionals. The third M.P.H. program, the history of public health and medicine, focuses on historical approaches and responses to public health and the insights that history can offer to those concerned with contemporary policy. The fourth track, aging and public health, offers a public health perspective on aging that encompasses both applied and policy dimensions. The fifth track is in sexuality and health, and the sixth one is in urbanism and community health. In addition, the department offers the Ph.D. degree, with study divided between the School of Public Health and one social science department in Columbia University's Graduate School of Arts and Sciences (Anthropology, Economics, History, Philosophy, Political Science, or Sociology). Students may also obtain the Dr.P.H., focusing on research issues in public health. A global health track has been added to this department to meet the needs of students who are interested in becoming global health practitioners within this area of public health interest.

General Public Health. (M.P.H.) Program Director: Jeanne Stellman, Ph.D. This program is intended for candidates who already have professional health training and/or considerable public health experience and are generally seeking formal training in methods and issues addressed by several public health disciplines that would allow them broader participation in the field. Since their career needs often require an interdisciplinary approach going beyond the scope of any single department, applicants to this program need to identify their substantive area(s) of interest and the technical skills (administration, research, program development, etc.) they want to acquire from two or more of the School's departments. This program is also available to students in the dual-degree programs offered by the School and to students with other professional degrees (e.g., law, journalism) where an individualized, interdisciplinary curriculum is deemed particularly suitable.

EMERSON COLLEGE

School of Communication
Master of Arts in Health Communication Program

Programs of Study	Health communicators enhance countless lives by planning awareness campaigns, developing patient materials, and advocating health initiatives. The Emerson College Master of Arts (M.A.) in Health Communication program, unlike those in public health, affords students the opportunity to focus on communication issues in a variety of health-related contexts.
	In collaboration with Tufts University School of Medicine, Emerson M.A. candidates ground their studies in both communication and health sciences. Emerson graduates thrive in careers as health communication directors, advocates, and communication experts in hospitals, research facilities, HMOs and insurers, media outlets, volunteer and government agencies, public relations firms, pharmaceutical companies, and more.
	For more information about Emerson's M.A. in Health Communication Program, students should visit http://admission.emerson.edu/admission/graduate/academics/hc.cfm.
Research Facilities	The Emerson College library has more than 200,000 volumes, 20,000 journals (paper and electronic), 8,000 e-books, 10,000 nonprint materials, and 10,000 microforms in its collection that focuses on communication studies and the performing arts. Through membership in the Fenway Consortium, graduate students have access to more than 2 million volumes. Computer-assisted reference services provide bibliographic databases through Dialog, BRS, and other online services. The Online Computer Library Center is used for student research support.
	M.A. candidates gain valuable hands-on experience in the Media Services Center, which provides students with access to approximately 2,400 films, videos, laser discs, and DVDs. The center is home to audio, video, and multimedia production facilities; a video studio; and several nonlinear editing suites comparable to those of any television studio in a major U.S. city. In addition, a marketing suite that opened in fall 2003 features a focus group room with an observation booth. There are also fully-mediated classrooms.
Financial Aid	Emerson College offers several financial assistance programs that make an Emerson education possible: merit-based awards (domestic and international applicants), low-interest federal loans (domestic applicants only), Federal Work-Study (domestic applicants only), private loans (domestic and international applicants), Student Employment (domestic and international applicants), and alternative payment plans (domestic and international applicants). For detailed information, prospective students should visit the Office of Student Financial Services Web site at http://www.emerson.edu/financial_services/info-grad.cfm. The deadline for merit aid consideration is March 1 for the fall semester and November 1 for the spring semester.
Cost of Study	Tuition for the 2007–08 academic year is $840 per credit hour. Other fees vary and may apply.
Living and Housing Costs	Though on-campus housing is not available for its graduate students, the Emerson College Office of Off-Campus Student Services (http://www.emerson.edu/offcampus_housing/) offers assistance in finding housing, including local apartment listings, realtor lists, temporary accommodations, search tips, pertinent neighborhood information, a roommate networking service, and more. Costs for housing are comparable to those of rental properties available in larger East Coast cities.
Student Group	More than 950 graduate students representing forty-five states and sixty countries are enrolled in Emerson programs.
Student Outcomes	As health communication directors, marketing specialists, campaign strategists, and health advocates, graduates bring scientific and communication skills to their work in hospitals, research facilities, HMOs and insurers, schools, media outlets, volunteer and government agencies, consulting and public relations firms, and pharmaceutical and biotech companies. Many graduates have experienced a smooth transition between for-profit and nonprofit organizations and quickly advance to senior positions.
Location	Situated in the heart of downtown Boston, Emerson offers access to the vast resources of a city that is home to the nation's finest educational institutions and an international hub of culture, media production, writing, publishing, communication, commerce, and medical innovation. Boston is a career launching pad for Emerson's students, many of whom intern or work at world-renowned organizations throughout the city. Emerson students from around the country and the world absorb the city's unique blend of local and global culture, and many find that Boston is an education in itself.
The College	Emerson College, founded in 1880 by Charles Wesley Emerson, has expanded upon its original mission of promoting the study of oratory and the performing arts by offering some of the nation's most distinctive graduate programs in communication.
Applying	Emerson's graduate programs welcome applicants from across the United States and around the world. Admission is competitive and selective. The College is looking for students whose academic and professional backgrounds, communication skills, and passion for the field meet the demands of their chosen program and promise a successful career.
	The final application deadline is June 1 for domestic applicants and May 1 for international applicants for fall enrollment, and November 1 for spring enrollment. Applications that are not complete by the final deadline are not reviewed by the admission committee. Applicants are responsible for ensuring the completion of their application. Application fees are nonrefundable; application forms and supporting materials become the property of the Office of Graduate Admission once they are sent to the office and are not returned.
	All application materials, with the exception of GRE/GMAT test scores, must be submitted together in one package to ensure timely review. A complete application includes the application form (students may apply online or download the PDF version), the application fee ($60 for domestic applicants; $75 for international applicants), official transcripts from all colleges/universities previously attended, three letters of recommendation (by persons best able to assess academic and professional qualifications, including motivation and goals), GRE/GMAT test scores, an essay, and a professional resume.
	Applicants whose native language is not English must provide evidence of English proficiency by submitting official TOEFL or IELTS test results. (Students from India and the Philippines are considered nonnative English speakers and are required to take the TOEFL.) Emerson College's school code for the TOEFL is 3367; no department code is needed. The minimum TOEFL score is 550 on the paper-based test (213 on the computer-based test or 80 on the Internet-based test). The minimum IELTS score is 6.5. Applicants who do not meet this requirement will not be reviewed for admission. For more information about these tests, students should visit http://www.toefl.org or http://www.ielts.org.
	Decisions are made on complete applications within six to eight weeks. Deadlines for merit-based and federal aid applications for fall are March 1 and April 1, respectively. Students seeking additional information about financing their graduate education should visit http://www.emerson.edu/financial_services/info-grad.cfm/.
Correspondence and Information	For more information, students may contact:
	Office of Graduate Admission Emerson College 120 Boylston Street Boston, Massachusetts 02116
	Phone: 617-824-8610 Fax: 617-824-8614 E-mail: gradapp@emerson.edu Web site: http://admission.emerson.edu/admission/graduate

Emerson College

THE FACULTY AND THEIR RESEARCH

Emerson College faculty members are specialists in public and interpersonal health communication areas that include mental health, adolescent health, immunization, HIV/AIDS, and diabetes. They continue to remain active in the field and bring their diverse experiences to the classroom. Tufts faculty members are epidemiologists and physicians who also continue their work in their fields. All faculty members actively seek to mentor students, working closely with them to help them achieve professional goals.

Joann M. Montepare, Chair of Marketing Communication and Associate Professor of Psychology; Ph.D., Brandeis. Dr. Montepare is a social-developmental psychologist who teaches courses in social psychology, developmental psychology, nonverbal communication, and face perception. Her research in person perception, emotion communication, and age-identity across the life span has been widely published in prominent journals such as the *Journal of Personality and Social Psychology*, *Developmental Psychology*, *Psychology and Aging*, *Advances in Experimental Social Psychology*, *Science*, and *Communication Research*. Dr. Montepare has also contributed to edited books such as *First Impressions*, *Ageism: Stereotyping and Prejudice Against Older Persons*, *The Social Psychology of Stigma*, and *Evolution and Social Psychology*. She is the Associate Editor for Special Issues for the *Journal of Nonverbal Behavior* and serves on the editorial board for the *Journal of Adult Development*.

Timothy Edgar, Graduate Program Director, Health Communication Program, and Associate Professor of Marketing Communication; Ph.D., Purdue. Dr. Edgar's professional career has been devoted to conducting quantitative and qualitative health-communication research on topics as diverse as HIV/AIDS, physical activity for adolescents, childhood and adult immunization, diabetes, epilepsy, and peptic ulcers. Prior to working at Emerson, Dr. Edgar was a Senior Study Director with Westat, a social science research firm in Rockville, Maryland. Dr. Edgar has also taught health communication and research methods at the University of Maryland, University of Wisconsin, and The George Washington University. Dr. Edgar has published widely in professional journals such as the *Journal of Health Communication*, *Health Education Research*, and *Health Communication*, and he has contributed to edited volumes such as *The Handbook of Health Communication*. He also co-edited the book, *AIDS: A Communication Perspective*. Dr. Edgar currently serves on the editorial board of *Health Communication*, and the *Journal of Health Communication*.

Thomas Vogel, Graduate Program Director, Global Marketing Communication and Advertising Program and Associate Professor of Marketing Communication; M.F.A., Academy of Fine Arts (Stuttgart). Mr. Vogel is a specialist in strategic communication on the Internet, online usability, and branding on the Internet. At the University of Applied Sciences in Wiesbaden, Germany, he was a Professor of Media Design in the Department of Media Management and also served as the Founding Dean from 1993 to 1999. Professor Vogel is an active public speaker, panelist, and consultant and is involved in special projects for the Internet, advertising, and multimedia. His current research focuses on the strategic design and usability aspects of interactive media, developing efficient experience design and online communication. He is also a founding partner of Mediaman, a German-based communications agency that specializes in integrated communication and advertising with a special focus on interactive communication. Formerly, he has worked as art director and creative director in New York City at Grey Advertising, Lois GGK, J. Walter Thompson, and Communication House.

Cathy Waters, Graduate Program Director, Integrated Marketing Communication Program and Executive-in-Residence; M.B.A., Boston College. Ms. Waters is a specialist in market analysis, forecasting, technical sales and sales management, personnel recruitment/development, and customer relations. Her career has spanned both the academic and professional worlds. Before coming to Emerson, she served on the faculty of Boston College's Carroll School of Management where she taught undergraduate and graduate courses in marketing, applied marketing management, product planning, and strategy as well as professional selling and sales management. Complementing her academic work is twelve years of experience in the corporate world with IMB where she held positions in sales and marketing management. Her combined expertise comes together in cases published in *Strategic Marketing Management Cases* and the *Journal of Business Research*.

William G. Anderson, Executive-in-Residence; M.B.A., Pennsylvania (Wharton). Mr. Anderson brings extensive, high-level experience to his teaching having worked for such corporations as Welch, Currier, Curry, Anderson, and Hill, Holliday, Connors, Cosmopulos. He has worked on major advertising assignments for brands, including Ameritech and Ocean Spray. At Emerson, Anderson collaborated to develop Marketing Finance for the IMC program and Financial and Strategic Context of Global Market Planning. His reputation for exceptional teaching has made his "Brands" classes very popular.

Karl Baehr, Executive-in-Residence; Ph.D., Regent University (Virginia). Dr. Baehr is a communication professional, scholar, and corporate leader whose career of more than twenty-five years is highlighted by a series of successes in the new media and technology venture evolution, communication curriculum development, and pedagogy. He has extensive knowledge of mass media and Internet new media industries, marketing strategies and tactics, communication technologies and trends, broadcasting operations and management, audience research methods, distance education, and computer-mediated communication.

Silvia Hodges, Executive-in-Residence; Ph.D. candidate, Nottingham Trent (England). Ms. Hodges is a pioneer in legal marketing with expertise in continental European jurisdictions. Over the course of ten years as a communications and business development consultant, she as written several books and articles on law firm marketing. She is the founder of the Legal Marketing Italia network, writes a regular column on legal marketing for *Italia Ogg*, and has conducted professional seminars and workshops on legal marketing in Italy, Germany, England, and the United States. As a recipient of a scholarship from the German Department of Education and Research, she is completing her doctoral studies in law firm marketing with a special focus on marketing legal services to medium-size companies.

Abbott Ikeler, Executive-in-Residence; Ph.D., London. Dr. Ikeler taught literature and writing at Bowdoin College, University of Muenster, and Rhode Island College before entering the corporate world. His academic achievements include a Senior Fulbright Fellowship, a book on nineteenth-century aesthetics, and numerous articles on Victorian fiction. From the mid-1980s to 2001, he held public relations and advertising positions with three multinational organizations and a full-service agency. Immediately before coming to Emerson, Dr. Ikeler was Director of Communications and Public Affairs for the Internet and Networking Division of Motorola, a post he held for three years. The focus of his current research is global public relations, especially the impact of such nonmedia influencers as industry and financial analysts.

Julie C. Lellis, Instructor of Marketing Communication; Ph.D. candidate, North Carolina at Chapel Hill. Ms. Lellis brings experience teaching public relations issues and public relations writing, enhanced by service-learning practices in the classroom. Her award-winning research writing is influenced by her training in rehabilitation psychology and counseling coupled with mass communication and focuses on nonprofit communication about disability and chronic illness. She has worked in program development and clinical settings to aid adolescents. Her work has been presented at national and international conferences in public relations, mass media, and health communication.

Kristin Lieb, Instructor of Marketing Communication; Ph.D. candidate, Syracuse. Ms. Lieb's expertise combines executive experience in marketing and business development with scholarship in public communications. Her career has brought her from the interactive side of Newbury Comics to writing case studies for the Harvard Business School. She has served as the vice president for business development for Digital Media on Demand, Swap It, and Atomic Pop as well as consultant for America Online and UPS. She has been a freelance writer for *Billboard*, *Rolling Stone*, the *Boston Phoenix*, and the *Boston Globe*. Her research explores the branding of popular female celebrities and informs issues related to body image, gender, and aging.

Douglas Quintal, Lecturer; M.A., Emerson College. A lecturer in the Department of Communication, Mr. Quintal teaches courses in integrated marketing communication, writing for marketing communication, advertising, public relations, and entertainment marketing. His professional experience includes work with Virgin Records, Hard Rock Café, Rogers and Cowen, Braithewaite and Katz, and the Charles Playhouse. He is on the Board of Directors for the Jennifer Stowers Quintal Education Foundation and is a member of the academic committee for the American Advertising Federation. He is an avid musician and has opened for NoFX, Bad Religion, Rancid, and Blink 182.

James Rowean, Executive-in-Residence; M.A., Michigan State. Mr. Rowean brings twenty-five years of professional experience in advertising and marketing to his teaching of integrated marketing communication. A former account executive for Cronin/Wallwork Curry, Arnold Worldwide, and Campbell Ewald (Detroit), he also directed marketing for Dunkin' Donuts and Bread & Circus/Whole Foods Supermarkets. He has brand experience with Ocean Spray, Kimberly-Clark, Reebok, Timex, and Steinway Pianos. Rowean has been a guest lecturer at Boston University, New York University, and Boston College.

Tracy Worrell, Assistant Professor of Marketing Communication; Ph.D., Michigan State. Dr. Worrell is a rising scholar in the area of advertising, media, and health. Her timely work on television portrayals of weight, consumption, physical disability, and media impact has gained attention at national conferences and has been published in *Health Communication* and the *Journal of Creative Communications*. In addition to teaching core courses in human communication, she has taught courses in mass media, public relations, and public speaking. Her applied work in the television industry as a traffic manager, continuity director, and disc jockey complements her scholarly expertise.

Seounmi Han Youn, Assistant Professor of Marketing Communication; Ph.D., Minnesota. Dr. Youn has established a productive line of research focusing on the antecedents, correlates, and consequences of online consumer socialization among the young. In addition to presenting her work at national and international conferences, it has been featured in professional journals such as the *Journal of Advertising Research*, *Psychology and Marketing*, the *Journal of Interactive Advertising*, and the *Journal of Broadcasting and Electronic Media*. Dr. Youn's instruction in courses that deal with global applications and research methodology is enhanced by her industry experience with DongSeo Marketing Research in Seoul, Korea.

EMORY UNIVERSITY

Rollins School of Public Health

Programs of Study

The Rollins School of Public Health (RSPH) of Emory University offers programs leading to the Master of Public Health (M.P.H.) degree, with concentrations in behavioral sciences and health education, biostatistics, environmental and occupational health, epidemiology, global environmental health, global epidemiology, global health, and health policy and management. The M.S.P.H. is also available in some departments. Several dual-degree programs are available with the Schools of Nursing (M.S.N./M.P.H.), Business (M.B.A./M.P.H.), Law (J.D./M.P.H.), and Medicine (M.D./M.P.H. and M.M.Sc./M.P.H.). Ph.D. programs in behavioral sciences and health education, biostatistics, epidemiology, health services research and health policy, and nutrition and health sciences and a Master of Science program in clinical research are administered through the Graduate School of Arts and Sciences. A residency program in occupational and environmental medicine is offered by the Rollins School of Public Health.

The M.P.H. program meets the needs of both full-time and part-time students and is intended for recent baccalaureate degree graduates who have a strong interest in a health career, physicians and other health professionals who wish to link advanced study in public health with another academic or professional field, international health professionals seeking career development, and currently employed health professionals desiring advanced studies. Each student's program is determined individually. An interdisciplinary approach is emphasized, along with practical public health experiences.

The School also offers midcareer professionals the option of distance learning with the Career M.P.H. degree, including a track in health-care outcomes, prevention, and applied epidemiology (new track for 2007). The Career M.P.H. degree is a mixed format of both Web-based learning environments and traditional face-to-face seminars.

Research Facilities

The ten-story Grace Crum Rollins Public Health Building offers 137,000 square feet of state-of-the-art public health research and training facilities, including advanced computer technology with laboratories for programs in toxicology, biochemistry, molecular biology, and infectious diseases.

Financial Aid

Information about federal loans is available through the Office of Financial Aid (phone: 404-727-6039). Non-U.S. citizens are ineligible for federal loans. The Rollins School of Public Health also offers several financial assistance programs. All applicants with complete admission materials received by the financial assistance deadline are considered for these awards. Eligible applicants are reviewed for need-based grants. The Graduate School of Arts and Sciences Fellowship provides full tuition coverage and stipends for eligible Ph.D. students.

Cost of Study

The 2006–07 tuition for M.P.H. and M.S.P.H. students was $10,000 per semester.

Living and Housing Costs

Living expenses for a single person attending Emory University are estimated to be approximately $17,000 per year. Information regarding University and off-campus housing in the surrounding area may be obtained from the Housing Office at 404-727-7631 or via the Web at http://www.emory.edu/HOUSING.

Student Group

Approximately 760 M.P.H./M.S.P.H. and special-standing students and 40 Ph.D. students are enrolled in the School. Approximately 14 percent are international students, representing forty-eight different countries.

Student Outcomes

The RSPH houses a Career Services Center to assist recent graduates in finding employment as researchers, policy analysts, consultants, health educators, administrators, and clinicians in local, state, and federal health agencies; universities; business enterprises; state and federal government offices; private health organizations; managed-care corporations; professional associations; nongovernmental international health organizations; and health ministries around the world. The RSPH is also home to the Public Health Employment Connection, which can be accessed via the Web at http://cfusion.sph.emory.edu/PHEC/phec.cfm. It is the first Web site dedicated to a database of jobs, internships, and fellowships aimed at public health students and professionals.

Location

Often described as the "public health capital of the world," Atlanta is home to the Centers for Disease Control and Prevention (CDC), CARE, the national home office of the American Cancer Society, the Carter Center, the Arthritis Foundation, Global Health Action, numerous state and regional health agencies, and the patient-care, teaching, and health-related research programs of Emory University's Robert W. Woodruff Health Sciences Center. With a metropolitan population of 3.8 million, a strong corporate base, and a wide array of cultural, sports, and entertainment activities, Atlanta is one of the leading cities of the Southeast.

The University and The School

Emory University's student body of 11,700 includes 6,316 undergraduates and 5,384 graduate and professional school students. The Robert W. Woodruff Health Sciences Center of Emory University includes the Schools of Medicine, Nursing, and Public Health. A main corridor through the campus incorporates the expanding medical complex with the headquarters of the CDC and the American Cancer Society. Affiliated resources, such as the Georgia Department of Human Resources, the Carter Center, and Grady Memorial Hospital, are nearby. The Rollins School of Public Health, established in 1990, is located in suburban Atlanta on the main University campus. The M.P.H. and M.S.P.H. degree programs and the School are accredited by the Council on Education for Public Health.

Applying

Requirements for admission include satisfactory completion of a four-year baccalaureate degree program and a strong interest in a public-health career. Applicants are admitted for studies beginning in the fall semester. A complete application consists of the application form, college transcripts, appropriate test scores, and reference letters. All applicants not holding a doctoral-level degree are required to submit GRE scores. In some cases, applicants may submit MCAT scores. Applicants who have completed doctoral-level degrees are not required to submit test scores unless otherwise specified by the department. Applicants to the M.S., M.S.P.H., and Ph.D. programs should have a strong undergraduate background in the mathematical and biological sciences. For all programs, international students whose native language is not English must submit TOEFL scores.

Correspondence and Information

For additional information and to apply online for M.P.H. and M.S.P.H. programs:

The Rollins School of Public Health
1518 Clifton Road, NE
Atlanta, Georgia 30322
Phone: 404-727-3956
Web site: http://www.sph.emory.edu/APPLY

For additional information on M.S. and Ph.D. programs:
Web site:
   http://www.emory.edu/GSOAS/prospective/admissions_info

Emory University

THE FACULTY AND THEIR RESEARCH

Behavioral Sciences and Health Education. Melissa Alperin, M.P.H., Emory, 1991: applied evaluation of community-based programs. Kimberly Jacob Arriola, Ph.D., Northeastern, 1998: HIV/AIDS among African Americans, violence and abuse toward women, organ and tissue donation in the black community. Susan Butler, Ed.D., Tennessee, 1992: tobacco use prevention and control, physical activity, women's health, public health advocacy. Ralph DiClemente, Ph.D., Berkeley, 1984: design and evaluation of STD and HIV prevention interventions tailored for adolescents and women. Colleen DiIorion, Ph.D., NYU, 1981: HIV medication adherence, HIV prevention with families, epilepsy for adults. Kristin L. Dunkle, Ph.D., Michigan, 2003: HIV/AIDS, gender and violence, sexual and reproductive health, health and South Africa. Cam Escoffery, Ph.D., Georgia, 2002: training public health professionals, curriculum development and instructional design. Karen Glanz, Ph.D., Michigan, 1979: theories of health behavior, cancer prevention and control, ethnic differences in health behavior, nutrition education, program evaluation and research. Kimberly Sessions Hagen, Ph.D., Georgia, 1998: HIV/AIDS, program planning, curriculum development, instructional design, program evaluation. Michelle Kegler, Dr.P.H., North Carolina at Chapel Hill, 1995: evaluating community interventions, environmental justice, tobacco use prevention. Howard Kushner, Ph.D., Cornell, 1970: Historical and clinical aspects of addiction, history and etiology of Kawasaki's disease. Delia L. Lang, Ph.D., Loma Linda, 2001: HIV/AIDS, adolescent health, sexual behavior. Richard Levinson, Ph.D., Wisconsin, 1975: social determinants of health-risk behavior, access to health care. Francis A. McCarty, Ph.D., Georgia State, 2001: quantitative methods, development and evaluation of psychosocial measures, use of advanced statistical methods in public health research. Kathleen Miner, Ph.D., Georgia State, 1984: design and evaluation of domestic and international community-based interventions primarily focused on public health workforce development, with emphasis on distance education; tobacco prevention and control; cancer education; bioterrorism. Laura F. Salazar, Ph.D., Georgia State, 2001: STD/HIV prevention and control, adolescent health, violence against women, program evaluation. Iris Smith, Ph.D., Georgia State, 2000: substance abuse, program evaluation; cancer-related psychosocial research. Claire Sterk, Ph.D., Utrecht, 1983; Ph.D., Rotterdam/CUNY, 1990: women's and adolescent health, HIV/AIDS, addiction, mental health. Jo Ellen Stryker, Ph.D., Pennsylvania, 2000: health campaigns, mass media and public health, communication and health behavior. Colin L. Talley, Ph.D., California, San Francisco, 1998: history of smoking and health; phenomenology of persistent smoking; history of multiple sclerosis; history of public health, medicine, and disease in the United States. Nancy Thompson, Ph.D., Georgia State, 1988: behavioral and psychiatric epidemiology, injury and violence prevention and control, applications of psychological theory to public health, mental health. Winifred W. Thompson, Ph.D., South Carolina, 2006: psychosocial variables that affect women in using holistic (mind, body, and spirit) approaches to potentially eliminate health disparities in cardiovascular disease, cancer prevention and control, birth outcomes among African American women. Michael Windle, Ph.D., Penn State, 1984: developmental psychopathology, with a focus on substance use and mental health among children and families; development and application of longitudinal quantitative models. Gina Wingood, Sc.D., Harvard, 1995: social factors (partner violence and media) that influence women's risk of STDs and HIV.

Biostatistics. Students should visit the department's Web site at http://www.sph.emory.edu/bios/facultylist.html for faculty and research information.

Distance Learning (Career M.P.H.). Students should visit the program's Web site at http://www.sph.emory.edu/CMPH/Temp/index.html for faculty and research information.

Environmental and Occupational Health. Howard Frumkin, M.D., Pennsylvania, 1982; Dr.P.H., Harvard, 1993: clinical occupational medicine, occupational and environmental epidemiology, urban sprawl and public health, global environmental health (currently on leave of absence). Debra Houry, M.D., M.P.H., Tulane, 1998: violence prevention, domestic violence, emergency medicine. Barry Johnson, Ph.D., Iowa State, 1967: environmental and occupational health policy. Mitchel Klein, Ph.D., Emory, 1998: epidemiologic methods. Chensheng (Alex) Lu, Ph.D., Washington (Seattle), 1996: environmental and occupational exposure and risk assessment. Gary W. Miller, Ph.D., Georgia, 1995: neurotoxicology. Christine Moe, Ph.D., North Carolina at Chapel Hill, 1989: environmental transmission of infectious agents; epidemiology of foodborne and waterborne diseases; environmental microbiology; water, sanitation, and health. Joel F. Moorhead, M.D., Cincinnati, 1978; M.P.H., Arizona, 1995: clinical, occupational, and environmental medicine and rehabilitative medicine. Karen Mumford, Ph.D., Minnesota, 2002: physical activity and the built environment, parks and urban health. Melvin Myers, M.P.A., Indiana, 1977: environmental and occupational health policy. Rick Rheingans, Ph.D., Yale, 1996: environmental health economics, economics of infectious diseases in developing countries, household decision making, risk assessment and modeling. Anne Riederer, Sc.D., Harvard, 2004: biomarker validation, exposure assessment, global environmental health. P. Barry Ryan, Ph.D., Wesleyan, 1979: environmental exposure assessment, environmental epidemiology, environmental chemistry. Jeremy Sarnat, Sc.D., Harvard, 2001: exposure assessment, environmental and occupational epidemiology. Stefanie Sarnat, Sc.D., Harvard, 2004: air pollution epidemiology. N. Kyle Steenland, Ph.D., SUNY at Buffalo, 1974; Ph.D., Pennsylvania, 1985: environmental and occupational epidemiology. Paige Tolbert, Ph.D., North Carolina, 1989: environmental and occupational epidemiology, cancer epidemiology. Mary White, Sc.D., Harvard, 1986: environmental epidemiology.

Epidemiology. Students should visit the department's Web site at http://www.sph.emory.edu/epi/epifaculty.html for faculty and research information.

Global Health. Susan Allen, M.D., Duke, 1986: HIV risk, transmission, and prevention. C. Rafael Flores Ayala, Dr.P.H., UCLA, 1989: design, implementation, monitoring, and evaluation of public health and public health nutrition policies and programs; consequences of early malnutrition. Peter Bell, M.P.A., Princeton, 1964: health, development, and disasters. Philip S. Brachman, M.D., Wisconsin, 1953: preventive medicine, epidemiology of infectious diseases, hospital infections, bioterrorism. Peter Brown, Ph.D., Emory, 1979: Department of Anthropology. Ann M. DiGirolamo, Ph.D., Indiana, 1994: child development, effects of caregiving on child health and nutrition, mental health. Dabney Evans, M.P.H., Arizona, 1996: health and human rights. William H. Foege, M.D., Washington (Seattle), 1961: disease eradication and agricultural projects of Global 2000 of the Carter Center, child survival and development, global tobacco plague, medical ethics, preventive medicine, injury control. Stanley O. Foster, M.D., Rochester, 1960: international health policy; primary health-care planning and management; working with NGOs to strengthen community and health system capacity in promotion, prevention, and case management; child survival and immunization. Eugene J. Gangarosa, M.D., Rochester, 1954: control of foodborne and waterborne diseases, child survival issues, primary health care. Gary R. Gunderson, D.Min., Interdenominational Theological Center, 1999: exploring strengths of religious congregations as agents in building healthy communities. Monique Hennink, Ph.D., Southampton, 1997: demography, family planning and sexual behavior, reproductive health service provision, men's reproductive health, HIV/AIDS prevention, sex education, evaluation of health programs. Miriam Kiser, M.P.H., Emory, 1993; RN: interfaith health program. Keith P. Klugman, Ph.D., Witwatersrand (Johannesburg), 1981: global spread of antimicrobial resistance, acute respiratory infections, bacterial vaccines, typhoid fever. Glen F. Maberly, M.D., New South Wales (Sydney), 1983: micronutrient malnutrition, endocrinology. Reynaldo Martorell, Ph.D., Washington (Seattle), 1973: protein-energy malnutrition, maternal and child nutrition, child growth, nutrition and infection, functional consequences of malnutrition, design and evaluation of nutrition interventions, food and nutrition policy. Deborah A. McFarland, Ph.D., Tennessee, 1987: health policy, health financing in developing countries, comparative health policy, health systems reform, equity and the poor, economic burden of disease. Leslie McGee, Ph.D., Witwatersrand (Johannesburg), 2001: molecular epidemiology and molecular basis of antibiotic-resistant *Streptococcus pneumoniae*. Christine L. Moe, Ph.D., North Carolina at Chapel Hill, 1989: environmental transmission of infectious agents; epidemiology of foodborne and waterborne diseases; environmental microbiology; water, sanitation, and health. K. M. Venkat Narayan, M.Sc., Edinburgh, 1987; M.F.P.H.M., Royal College of Physicians, 1988; M.B.A., Heriot-Watt, 1995: diabetes, obesity and nutrition. Eric A. Ottesen, M.D., Harvard, 1970: epidemiology and immunology of parasitic diseases. Usha Ramakrishnan, Ph.D., Cornell, 1993: childhood malnutrition, maternal and child nutrition, micronutrient malnutrition. Richard Rheingans, Ph.D., Yale, 1996: environmental health economics, economics of infectious diseases in developing countries, household decision making, risk assessment and modeling. Roger W. Rochat, M.D., Washington (Seattle), 1966: maternal, infant, and child health epidemiology; maternal and child health epidemiology capacity building in state health departments; maternal death and abortion surveillance; unintended-pregnancy outcomes. James Setzer, M.P.H., Tulane, 1983: program planning and management, health finance. Aryeh D. Stein, Ph.D., Columbia, 1992: nutritional epidemiology, diet and chronic disease, intergenerational effects on health. Rob Stephenson, Ph.D., Southampton, 1999: reproductive health. Sandra L. Thurman, B.S., Mercer: President and CEO, International AIDS Trust. Frits van der Haar, Ph.D., Agricultural University (Netherlands), 1977: food and nutrition policy, global elimination of micronutrient malnutrition, public-private-civic partnerships. Kate Winskell, Ph.D., Courtauld Institute (London), 1995: HIV/AIDS communication. Kathryn M. Yount, Ph.D., Johns Hopkins, 1999: social demography, reproductive health, and gender studies in the Middle East and less developed countries.

Health Policy and Management. Students should visit the department's Web site at http://www.sph.emory.edu/hpm/index.php for faculty and research information.

FLORIDA INTERNATIONAL UNIVERSITY

Robert Stempel School of Public Health

Programs of Study	The Robert Stempel School of Public Health at Florida International University (FIU) seeks to serve as a model for stimulating educational programs and community-based research in the advancement of public health. Its mission is to educate and train future leaders, researchers, and health professionals from diverse backgrounds; to conduct innovative research and to translate that research into practice; and to promote healthy lives for the diverse communities of southern Florida. Graduates are prepared to work in the areas of community nutrition, health promotion and disease prevention, health policy and management, epidemiology and biostatistics, and environmental and occupational health.
	One of the strengths of the School is its location. Students benefit from the cultural and ethnic diversity of the community and have a unique opportunity to study the impact of the blending of natural and man-made environments and population growth on population health. Practitioners, academic researchers, and the community are brought together to study the impact of environmental, social, and behavioral factors on public health.
	The School offers master's programs in biostatistics, community nutrition, dietetics and nutrition, environmental and occupational health, epidemiology, health policy and management, health promotion and disease prevention, and health services administration. Degree requirements vary, but each program comprises a mix of required courses, elective courses, and a cumulative project in the form of field experience or a capstone, research, or thesis project.
	Doctoral degrees are available in community nutrition, dietetics and nutrition, environmental and occupational health, epidemiology, and health promotion and disease prevention. The Ph.D. program requires 75 credit hours, including 12 credits in shared courses and 24 dissertation credits.
Research Facilities	FIU has state-of-the-art library and research facilities. The library houses more than 1.5 million volumes and 9,000 journal subscriptions and hosts a wireless network for computerized searches. The Center for Health Research and Policy aims to increase the number of members of underrepresented minority groups entering health professions programs and to increase the number of public health agencies building personnel and training systems around competencies in essential public health services. The Institute for Public Management and Community Service is involved in governance reform projects that focus on legislative development, civil service reform, and the promotion of governmental and political accountability. The National Resource Center on Nutrition, Physical Activity, and Aging provides technical assistance and disseminates information to help older adults and their caregivers improve their quality of life by reducing their risk for malnutrition and functional disabilities. The Center on Aging seeks to design and implement comprehensive gerontological education and training programs and to demonstrate new concepts to serve older persons. The Institute for Children and Families at Risk conducts research on the issues confronting high-risk families, engages in service and outreach activities, and provides technical assistance and opportunities for education and training.
Financial Aid	Graduate fee grants of up to $2500 per semester are awarded to full-time students who demonstrate financial need. Graduate teaching and research assistantships are available to qualified students. The stipend typically ranges from $1700 to $6000 per semester and carries a partial or full tuition waiver. Matriculation fee waivers cover the in-state portion of tuition for students working at least 10 hours per week in a graduate assistantship; nonresident fee waivers cover the out-of-state portion. A limited number of scholarships are available through the Dean's office, and other scholarships may be available from private sources. Award amounts and eligibility criteria may vary.
Cost of Study	In 2006–07, tuition was $249.15 per credit hour for Florida residents and $753.22 per credit hour for nonresidents. Additional costs included a photo ID fee of $10 per year, an athletic fee of $10 per semester, and a health services fee of $67.20 per semester.
Living and Housing Costs	Housing is limited and should be petitioned for within ample time. Campus housing includes apartment-style accommodations, which are available in the form of everything from studio apartments through shared units. Costs vary depending on the choice of housing and residential life. Off-campus housing near the University is also available. Additional information can be obtained from the University Housing Office at http://www.fiu.edu/~housing.
Student Group	Approximately 125 students enroll in the School's programs each year, with women outnumbering men 2:1. The demographic makeup is very diverse—20 percent are African American, 20 percent are Hispanic, and 25 percent are from countries other than the U.S. Approximately 78 percent of students have a GPA greater than 3.5.
Student Outcomes	Alumni have established careers in governmental and voluntary settings within the community; in regional, state, and national systems; and in academia, research, and industry.
Location	The University is located in Miami, Florida's largest urban center and a major transportation and business hub of the southeastern U.S. Miami is an exciting, dynamic global marketplace. Miami Beach is known for its historic art deco district and the numerous hotels that line its beaches. Miami has been reinvented into a hemispheric crossroads for trade, travel, culture, and communications.
The University	Florida International University opened in 1972 with 5,667 students, the largest opening-day enrollment in U.S. collegiate history. Today, it has more than 38,000 students enrolled in over 200 degree programs, making it the largest university in southern Florida. FIU is the youngest university to have been awarded a chapter of Phi Beta Kappa, and *Kiplinger's Personal Finance* magazine ranked it among the best values in public higher education in the country.
Applying	Prospective students are required to submit an application; official transcripts of previous college course work; official GRE or GMAT scores showing a combined minimum of 1120 or 570, respectively; and a $30 application fee. The deadline to apply is June 1 for fall admission, October 1 for spring admission, and March 1 for summer admission. Applications may be submitted online or mailed to the Graduate Admissions Office, Florida International University, P.O. Box 659004, Miami, Florida 33265-9004.
Correspondence and Information	Robert Stempel School of Public Health University Park, HLS 595 Florida International University 11200 Southwest 8th Street Miami, Florida 33199 Phone: 305-348-4903 Fax: 305-348-4901 E-mail: ph@fiu.edu Web site: http://ssph.fiu.edu

Florida International University

THE FACULTY AND STAFF

Office of the Dean
Michelle Ciccazzo, Interim Dean.
Zaida Agramonte, Accountant.
Mary Ann Camps-Gato, Director of Budget and Operations.
Chris Townsend, Program Assistant.
Gianni Bajarano, Student Assistant, Budget and Operations.
Maggie Pagan, Office Manager.

Student and Alumni Affairs
Saul Sztam, Assistant Dean and Director.
Carrie Sanchez, Assistant Director.
Julia D. C. Gonzalez Pampin, Coordinator, Student Services.
Christina Rajkumar, Coordinator, Student Services.
Cheryl Gomez, Program Assistant.

Dietetics and Nutrition
Fatma Huffman, Chairperson.
Victoria Castellanos, Ph.D. Program Director.
Evelyn Enrione, M.S. Program Director.
Donna Greenwood, B.S. Program Director.
Olga Perez, Program Assistant.
Karen Harvey, Senior Secretary.
Marianna Baum, Professor.
Adriana Campa, Professor.
Zisca Dixon, Professor.
Valerie George, Professor.
Susan Himburg, Professor.
Marcia Magnus, Professor.
Terese Maitland, Professor.
Tania Rivera, Professor.
Dian Weddle, Professor.
Nancy Wellman, Professor.

Health and Policy Management
Gloria Deckard, Chairperson.
Charlene Brown, Secretary.

Gullicin Gumus, Professor.
Fred Newman, Professor.
Won Suh, Professor.
Mustafa Younis, Professor.

Epidemiology and Biostatistics
Nasar Ahmed, Chairperson.
Ethel Davis, Senior Secretary.
Caridad Galvez, Senior Secretary.
Daniel Feaster, Professor.
WayWay Hlaing, Professor.
Sunny Kim, Professor.
Theophile Niyonsenga, Professor.
Vukosava Pekovic, Professor.
Guillermo Prado, Professor.
Mary Jo Trepka, Professor.

Environmental and Occupational Health
Deodutta Roy, Chairperson.
Quentin Felty, Professor.
Janvier Gasana, Professor.
Jai Parkash, Professor.
Berrin Serdar, Professor.

Health Promotion and Disease Prevention
Virginia McCoy, Chairperson.
Monica Cabrera, Senior Secretary.
Luther Brewster, Professor.
William Darrow, Professor.
Richard Palmer, Professor.
Jesus Sanchez, Professor.

HARVARD UNIVERSITY

School of Public Health

Programs of Study

The School of Public Health offers programs leading to the graduate degrees of Master of Public Health (M.P.H.), Doctor of Public Health (D.P.H.), Master of Occupational Health (M.O.H.), Master of Science in a specified field (S.M. in that field), and Doctor of Science in a specified field (S.D. in that field). Doctor of Philosophy (Ph.D.) degrees are offered in specific fields of study through the Graduate School of Arts and Sciences. Programs are offered in biostatistics, environmental health, epidemiology, genetics and complex diseases, health policy and management, immunology and infectious diseases, nutrition, occupational health, population and international health, and society, human development, and health. Some programs are designed for physicians, lawyers, managers, and other health-care professionals; some for college graduates who wish to train for health careers; and others for individuals who hold graduate degrees in medicine, law, business, government, education, and other fields who wish to apply their special skills to public health problems. Special programs include the Master of Science in occupational health or maternal and child health nursing, administered jointly by HSPH and Simmons College; the doctoral program in oral epidemiology, administered jointly by HSPH and the Harvard School of Dental Medicine; the combined M.D./M.P.H. program offered in conjunction with medical schools; and the J.D./M.P.H joint-degree program offered by HSPH and Harvard Law School. The School offers residency training leading to certification by the American Board of Preventive Medicine in occupational medicine.

Research Facilities

The main buildings of the School are the Sebastian S. Kresge Educational Facilities Building at 677 Huntington Avenue, the François-Xavier Bagnoud Building at 651 Huntington Avenue, and the Health Sciences Laboratories at 665 Huntington Avenue. The School maintains well-equipped research laboratories containing sophisticated instrumentation and supporting animal facilities. Computing and data processing resources are also available to students through the Instructional Computing Facility. The Francis A. Countway Library serves the library needs of the School. It holds more than 630,000 volumes, subscribes to 3,500 current journal titles, and houses over 10,000 noncurrent biomedical journal titles in addition to its extensive collection of historical materials, making it the largest library in the country serving a medical and health-related school.

Financial Aid

Financial aid at the School of Public Health can come from a variety of sources. Some departments have training grants offering students full tuition plus a stipend. Through need- and merit-based programs, other students are offered grants that range from half to full tuition. To supplement other aid, many students borrow through one or more of the federal educational loan programs and work at part-time jobs at Harvard and in the community.

Cost of Study

Full-time tuition for 2006–07 is $31,800 per year. Health insurance, health services, and registration fees are required, and total costs are $2856. Books and supplies cost approximately $1315 in 2006–07.

Living and Housing Costs

For the academic year 2006–07, it is estimated that a single student needs a minimum of $15,900: $8985 for rent and utilities and $6915 for other expenses. Limited housing is available in the Shattuck International House, with preference given to international students. Most students arrange for housing in the adjacent communities.

Student Group

There were 1,055 graduate students (624 women and 431 men) enrolled in 2005–06. Sixty-three nations are represented.

Student Outcomes

Graduates from the Harvard School of Public Health find employment in a variety of settings, depending in part upon their previous experience and in part upon department and degree programs from which they graduate. Recent graduates have found positions in research institutes, with pharmaceutical companies and governmental and nongovernmental agencies, within the health-care industry, and as faculty members of universities.

Location

Boston is a heterogeneous metropolis rich in history and charm. Athletic, cultural, and recreational activities are abundant. The School is within walking distance of museums, colleges and universities, waterways, and parks.

The University and The School

Harvard College was founded in 1636, and, until the establishment of professorships in medicine in 1782, it composed the whole of the institution now called Harvard University. In addition to the college, ten graduate schools are now part of the University.

Activity in professional education in the field of public health had been steadily increasing at Harvard University for more than two decades before the actual founding of the School in 1922. The primary mission of the School is to carry out teaching and research aimed at improving the health of population groups throughout the world. The School emphasizes not only the development and implementation of disease prevention and treatment programs but also the planning and management of systems involved in the delivery of health services in this country and abroad. The School cooperates with the Medical School in teaching and research and has close ties with other Harvard faculties. The School has more than 374 full-time and part-time faculty members and eleven academic departments representing major biomedical and social disciplines.

Applying

HSPH participates in the Schools of Public Health Application Service (SOPHAS), which is an online, common application service designed to provide a more efficient application process. Students should visit the SOPHAS Web site at http://www.sophas.org for more specific information and for access to the application for admission. All applicants to the School are required to submit scores from the GRE; applicants are urged to take the test no later than November, since applications are not considered without the scores. Applicants may submit the DAT, GMAT, or MCAT, as appropriate to the applicant's background, in lieu of the GRE. Lawyers applying to the M.P.H. program may submit LSAT scores. Applicants with prior test scores may submit them with their application materials. In addition, applicants must persuade the Committee on Admissions and Degrees of their ability to meet academic standards and of their overall qualifications to undertake advanced study at a graduate level. Students should visit the School's Web site (http://www.hsph.harvard.edu/) for information concerning the deadline to apply for admission and to apply online.

As a matter of policy, law, and commitment, Harvard University does not discriminate against applicants or students in admission, educational policies, or scholarship and loan programs on the basis of race, religion, sex, sexual orientation, marital or parental status, veteran status, national origin, color, creed, handicap, or age. Members of minority groups are strongly encouraged to apply.

Correspondence and Information

Catalogs and applications:
Admissions Office
Harvard School of Public Health
677 Huntington Avenue, Room G4
Boston, Massachusetts 02115-6096

Phone: 617-432-1031
Fax: 617-432-2009
E-mail: admisofc@hsph.harvard.edu
Web site: http://www.hsph.harvard.edu/

Counseling and program information:
Vincent W. James, Director
Kerri Noonan, Assistant Director
Admissions Office
Harvard School of Public Health
677 Huntington Avenue, Room G4
Boston, Massachusetts 02115-6096

Phone: 617-432-1031
E-mail: admisofc@hsph.harvard.edu

Harvard University

FACULTY CHAIRS AND DEPARTMENTAL ACTIVITIES

Biostatistics (617-432-1056)
Chair: Louise Ryan, Ph.D. The program combines both theory and application of statistical science to analyze public health problems and further biomedical research. Students are prepared for academic and private-sector research careers. Faculty research spans both methodological developments on new statistical techniques and important subject-matter applications that lead to significant advances in the health sciences. Current departmental research on statistical and computing methods for observational studies and clinical trials includes survival analysis, missing-data problems, and causal inference. Other areas of investigation include environmental research; statistical aspects of the study of AIDS and cancer; quantitative problems in health-risk analysis, technology assessment, and clinical decision making; statistical methodology in psychiatric research and in genetic studies; and statistical genetics and computational biology.

Environmental Health (617-432-1270)
Chair: Douglas Dockery, S.D. The mission of the Department of Environmental Health is to advance the health of all people in the United States and around the world through research and training in environmental health. The department emphasizes the role of air, water, the built environment, and the workplace as critical determinants of health. Faculty members in the department study the pathogenesis and prevention of environmentally produced illnesses and act as catalysts for scientifically based public health advances. Research approaches range from the molecular to the epidemiologic. Teaching and research activities of the department are carried out through three concentrations: exposure, epidemiology, and risk; occupational health; and physiology.

Epidemiology (617-432-1050)
Chair: Meir Stampfer, M.D., Dr.P.H. Epidemiology, the study of the frequency, distribution, and determinants of disease in humans, is a fundamental science of public health. Epidemiologists use many approaches, but the ultimate aim of epidemiologic research is the prevention or effective control of human disease. Current research involves the role of viruses in the etiology of cancer; the connection between diet and risk of cancer, cardiovascular disease, and other major chronic diseases; the relationship between exposure to chemicals in the workplace and the development of cancer; the epidemiology of infectious disease; factors in early life predisposing individuals to chronic diseases; and causes of human infertility.

Genetics and Complex Diseases (617-432-0054)
Chair: Gökhan Hotamisligil, M.D., Ph.D. The complex interplay of biological processes with environmental factors as they apply to chronic, multigenic, and multifactorial diseases is the emphasis of the Department of Genetics and Complex Diseases. Research programs in the department focus on molecular mechanisms of adaptive responses to environmental signals to elucidate the mechanisms underlying the intricate interaction between genetic determinants and their divergent responses to stress signals. Alterations in these integrated adaptive mechanisms have a major impact on the health of human populations. The diseases under study include nutritional and metabolic diseases (obesity, diabetes, and cardiovascular diseases), cancer, and aging, both at the mechanistic level and in the context of population studies.

Health Policy and Management (617-432-1090)
Chair: Arnold Epstein, M.D. The department is mission-oriented in its concern with improving the health-care delivery system and mitigating public health risks in the United States and abroad. It is dedicated to resolving major management and health policy problems through original research, advanced training, and dispute resolution. Research priorities are organized into nine broad areas, including health financing and insurance, management of health hazards, study of the causes and etiology of injury, management of health-care organizations, evaluation and management of medical technology, business and labor in health, international health, quality of health-care, and health-care reform.

Immunology and Infectious Diseases (617-432-2334)
Chair: Dyann Wirth, Ph.D. The department focuses on the biological, immunological, epidemiological, and ecological aspects of viral, bacterial, protozoan, and helminthic diseases of animals and humans and the vectors that transmit some of these infectious agents. Emphasis is on research identifying basic pathogenic mechanisms that may lead to better diagnostic tools and the development of vaccines and other interventions for prevention and control of infections and disease, as well as the identification of new targets for antiviral and antiparasitic drugs.

Nutrition (617-432-1333)
Chair: Walter C. Willett, M.D., Dr.P.H. The department's mission is to improve human health through enhanced nutrition. It strives to accomplish this goal through research aimed at improved understanding of how diet influences health, the dissemination of new knowledge about nutrition to health professionals and the public, the development of nutritional strategies, and the education of researchers and practitioners. Department research ranges from molecular biology to human studies of cancer and heart disease, including the conduct of population-based intervention trials. Current research covers a wide range of topics, including large prospective studies of dietary factors in relation to heart disease, cancer, diabetes, and ophthalmologic disease; development of methods to assess nutritional status by analysis of body tissue; the interaction of nutritional factors with genetic determinants of disease; and the interaction of nutritional factors and infectious agents.

Population and International Health (617-432-1232)
Chair: David Bloom, Ph.D. The department seeks to improve global health through education, research, and service from a population based perspective. Research interests span a wide spectrum of topics, including social and economic development, health policy, and demography; design and financing of health-care systems; women's health and children's health; and prevention and control of infectious and chronic diseases. The department has a special concern with questions of health equity and human rights, particularly in relation to health and population issues in developing countries.

Society, Human Development, and Health (617-432-1135)
Chair: Lisa Berkman, Ph.D. The mission of the Department of Society, Human Development, and Health is to improve health throughout the lifespan, including a special emphasis on children and adolescents. This mission is achieved through research to identify the social and behavioral determinants of health, development and evaluation of interventions and policies leading to the improvement of population health, and the preparation of professionals and researchers who fill leadership positions in advocacy and public service. The department's educational mission is to train both scholars and practitioners: scholars whose research illuminates basic social determinants of health and who identify and test innovative social policy and service interventions, and practitioners who are skilled in designing, implementing, and evaluating health-enhancing interventions in action settings.

Division of Biological Sciences (617-432-4470)
Director: Laurie Glimcher, M.D. The Division of Biological Sciences is an umbrella organization encompassing the HSPH Departments of Environmental Health, Genetics and Complex Diseases, Immunology and Infectious Diseases, and Nutrition. In most of these departments, two doctoral degrees are offered: the Doctor of Philosophy (Ph.D.) and the Doctor of Science (S.D.). The Ph.D. programs generally center on laboratory-based investigation in the biological sciences, whereas the S.D. programs emphasize epidemiological analysis. The Ph.D. programs are administered by the Division of Biological Sciences.

Master of Public Health Program (617-432-0090)
Director: Richard R. Monson, M.D., Associate Dean for Professional Education. The program is designed to provide both a general background and flexibility of specialization in public health. The seven areas of concentration are clinical effectiveness, family and community health, health care management and policy, international health, law and public health, occupational and environmental health, and quantitative methods.

THE JOHNS HOPKINS UNIVERSITY

Bloomberg School of Public Health

Programs of Study
The Johns Hopkins Bloomberg School of Public Health offers programs leading to the graduate degrees of Master of Public Health (M.P.H.), Master of Health Science (M.H.S.), Master of Science (Sc.M.), Doctor of Public Health (Dr.P.H.), Doctor of Science (Sc.D.), and Doctor of Philosophy (Ph.D.) degrees. Depending on the department and specific area of study, the M.H.S. and Sc.M. provide students with opportunities for advanced study and research or prepare students to begin or advance their careers as public health professionals in their chosen area of study. The Ph.D. is primarily a degree for those individuals with research or teaching or both as their goal. The Sc.D. provides training emphasizing the mastery of principles and methodology in fields covered by the interests of the departments of the school. The Dr.P.H. furthers M.P.H. training to provide graduates with a career in high-level administration, teaching, or practice. Combined programs include M.P.H./M.B.A., M.P.H./M.S.W., M.P.H./M.S.N., M.P.H./J.D., M.A./M.H.S., B.A./M.H.S., M.D./Ph.D., M.H.S./Doctoral, and Sc.M./Ph.D. Postdoctoral training and residency programs in general preventive medicine or occupational medicine are available. Some programs offer a part-time option, including the M.P.H. program, which is also offered through the Internet-based distance education option.

Research Facilities
Well-equipped research laboratories are available for use by graduate students in the various departments of the School. There also are opportunities for field training in many local, state, national, and international health- and medical-care organizations. Students have access to all the University library facilities, which provide more than 2.5 million volumes selected to support the studies of all departments and divisions of the University. The William H. Welch Medical Library coordinates access to biomedical literature and online databases for the Johns Hopkins Medical Institutions. The Abraham M. Lilienfeld Library is the primary information resource within the School of Public Health. Wireless access to networked resources is available in labs, classrooms, and common areas throughout the School.

Financial Aid
Financial assistance includes scholarships, traineeships, student loans, and the Federal Work-Study Program. Eligibility for financial aid is based on a combination of factors, such as financial need, merit, and the availability of funds. Prospective students should note that the decision to offer or deny financial aid is totally separate from the decision to offer or deny admission. The Office of Student Financial Services administers all student educational loan programs and the Federal Work-Study Program. In addition to determining a student's eligibility for loan assistance and work-study, the Office of Student Financial Services provides personal and confidential financial counseling to all aid applicants.

Cost of Study
Tuition was $32,976 for the nine-month 2006–07 academic year; tuition for the eleven-month M.P.H. program was $41,220. All new full-time students are assessed a one-time matriculation fee of $500. Books and instructional supplies average $2000 per year.

Living and Housing Costs
Yearly living expenses were estimated at $18,007 to $23,876 for 2006–07. The cost of living in Baltimore is comparable to that in most urban centers in the United States, and students may choose from a wide variety of affordable housing. Information on apartments and houses as well as University accommodations may be obtained from the Office of Housing, Reed Hall, 1620 McElderry Street, Baltimore, Maryland 21205, or by visiting http://www.hopkinsmedicine.org/housing.

Student Group
The Bloomberg School of Public Health has 2,005 graduate students from more than eighty nations. Over half of the students are women; 23 percent of Americans are members of minority groups.

Student Outcomes
Graduates are readily absorbed into the job market and find employment at all levels of the U.S. or international governments, academic institutions, hospitals, and other health-care facilities; profit, nonprofit, and nongovernmental organizations; managed-care organizations; and consulting firms. Selected job titles include primary health-care project evaluator, public health specialist, health educator, epidemiologist, technical support manager, community education facilitator, public health officer, director of maternal and child health program, and public health associate.

Location
Baltimore is among the largest of U.S. industrial and seaport cities, offering a mix of tradition and progress, with an easy, pleasant, and affordable style. The city is conveniently situated on the mid-Atlantic corridor, 45 minutes away from Washington, D.C., and 4 hours' driving time from New York. Because Baltimore is close to both the Chesapeake Bay and mountainous areas, year-round recreational opportunities abound. In 2005, *Frommer's* named Baltimore one of the Top 10 Up and Coming Travel Destinations in the World. The School is on the subway route, providing students with access to the Inner Harbor area where the National Aquarium, as well as the Ravens and Orioles stadiums, are located.

The University and The School
Recognized as the first true university in America, Johns Hopkins University was incorporated in 1867 by Johns Hopkins, a Quaker merchant of Baltimore. The medical campus in East Baltimore is composed of the Bloomberg School of Public Health, the School of Medicine, the School of Nursing, the Welch Medical Library, and the Johns Hopkins Hospital. The Bloomberg School of Public Health is the oldest school of public health in the world. It was established in 1916 by persons of vision who planned a school of the biological, physical, social, and behavioral sciences. Its goal, now as then, is to preserve and improve the health of the public through the advancement of knowledge and the preparation of students for a variety of careers in public health. A 485-member full-time faculty represents major biomedical and social disciplines; ten academic departments offer graduate training. The campus includes a residence hall and the Denton A. Cooley Center, which has an indoor jogging track; a sauna; racquetball, squash, and tennis courts; and an outdoor swimming pool. Excellent athletics and cultural facilities also are available at the nearby Homewood campus.

Applying
The online application is available at http://www.jhsph.edu/admissions. Schoolwide application requirements include standardized test scores, such as GRE (varies per department); TOEFL scores for applicants whose native language is not English; statement of purpose; official transcripts from all universities attended; letters of recommendation; and a resume or curriculum vitae. There is a $45 nonrefundable application fee. Application deadlines and specific requirements vary per department; students should visit http://www.jhsph.edu/admissions for complete details.

Correspondence and Information
Director of Admissions
The Johns Hopkins Bloomberg School of Public Health
615 North Wolfe Street, Suite E-1002
Baltimore, Maryland 21205
Phone: 410-955-3543
Fax: 410-955-0464
E-mail: admiss@jhsph.edu
Web site: http://www.jhsph.edu

The Johns Hopkins University

DEPARTMENTS AND PROGRAMS

Biochemistry and Molecular Biology. Chair: Roger McMacken, Ph.D. The goal of the department is to increase current knowledge of the biochemical and molecular bases of normal and abnormal cellular processes and train highly qualified scientists who, through research, teaching, and service, will continue to provide new insights into the biochemical, biophysical, and molecular aspects of biomedical issues that have an impact on public health. Critical biomedical issues in reproductive health are addressed in the Division of Reproductive Biology. Programs lead to the Ph.D., Sc.M., and M.H.S. degrees.

Biostatistics. Chair: Scott L. Zeger, Ph.D. Programs cover the creation and application of methods for quantitative research in the health sciences. Research addresses the spectrum of statistical science from foundations of inference to the discovery of new methodology to health applications. The designs and analytic methods enable health scientists and professionals in academia, government, pharmaceutical companies, medical research organizations, and elsewhere to efficiently acquire knowledge and draw valid conclusions from their ever-expanding sources of information. Programs lead to the Ph.D. and Sc.M. degrees as well as an M.H.S. in biostatistics for students earning a Ph.D. in another department of the School. Related careers are research biostatisticians in academia, government, and industry.

Environmental Health Sciences. Chair: John D. Groopman, Ph.D. Students in this interdisciplinary field examine how biological, chemical, and physical environmental agents affect human health. Faculty members undertake mechanistic studies of the body's response to the environment as well as risk assessment and epidemiology to develop techniques to control the effects of air and water pollution and quality, occupational health and safety, toxic substances and hazardous wastes, and radiation. The department has four divisions: environmental health engineering, occupational and environmental health, physiology, and toxicological sciences. Programs leading to M.H.S., Sc.D., Sc.M., Dr.P.H., and Ph.D. degrees are offered. Related careers are research and professional practice in chemistry, toxicology, occupational health, environmental epidemiology, and environmental engineering.

Epidemiology. Chair: Jonathan Samet, M.D. Students study the distribution of diseases and the determinants of health and disease risk in human populations. Epidemiology, one of the quantitative foundations of public health and clinical research, provides a basis for the preventive approaches in medicine and public health. Faculty members investigate the genetics of disease, cancer, infectious diseases, and cardiovascular and renal diseases; vision research; aging; clinical trials; international AIDS research; occupational and environmental research; tuberculosis; and clinical research. Programs lead to the M.H.S., Sc.D., Sc.M., Dr.P.H., and Ph.D. degrees. Related careers are research epidemiologists and practitioners in academic institutions, public health agencies, international organizations, and biotechnological and pharmaceutical firms.

Health, Behavior, and Society. Chair: David Holtgrave, Ph.D. This department uses a multidisciplinary, multilevel approach to study the determinants of disease and injury and develop, test, and disseminate effective public health interventions. Theoretical, methodological, and applied studies are conducted in three signature areas: social determinants of health and structural- and community-level interventions to improve health, health communication and health education, and behavioral and social aspects of genetics and genetic counseling. Programs lead to an M.H.S. in behavioral sciences and health education, an Sc.M. in genetic counseling, and Ph.D. and Sc.D. degrees. Related careers are researchers, teachers, and practitioners in academic institutions, government agencies, and private industry.

Health Policy and Management. Chair: Ellen MacKenzie, Ph.D. This multidisciplinary field seeks to improve health and prevent disease and disability through the education of future public health leaders and research on the causes and remedies of significant public health problems facing the United States and other industrialized countries. Faculty and student research seeks to identify policy options and behavioral interventions that promote and protect the health status of populations; design strategies that improve access to health and preventive services, particularly among the most vulnerable; develop methods that enhance the effectiveness and efficiency of health care for medical and mental illness; and create models for improving the financing, organization, and delivery of preventive and curative health services. Programs lead to an M.H.S. in health finance and management; an M.H.S. in health policy; a Ph.D. in health and public policy; and a Dr.P.H. in health care management and leadership. Related careers are health-care administration, research and teaching, public health agencies, and private industry.

International Health. Chair: Robert E. Black, M.D., M.P.H. This department draws on all public health disciplines and applies them to international settings. There are four programs: disease prevention and control, health systems, human nutrition, and social and behavioral interventions. Faculty members work to implement cost-effective strategies for health-care delivery; to design health promotion interventions to disadvantaged communities; develop vaccines; conduct clinical trials, prevention trials, and behavioral studies; develop policy for disease control; and develop methods to assess nutritional status and propose effective strategies for nutritional problems. Programs lead to an M.H.S.; Ph.D.; and Sc.D. training for research in defined fields of specialization in international health; and a Dr.P.H. Related careers are international health agencies, national assistance organizations such as the Agency for International Development, private foundations, and voluntary organizations or firms.

Internet-Based Education. Director: Sukon Kanchanaraksa, Ph.D. The School offers two programs to help professionals continue their education on a part-time basis online. The Internet-based M.P.H. allows students from around the globe to interact with faculty members at one of the leading schools of public health in the United States—without having to relocate to Baltimore. Students can matriculate into the program by participating in two weeks of orientation and course work in Baltimore in January or June. Required and elective courses can be chosen from more than fifty full online courses and from Summer and Winter Institutes. The Graduate Certificate in Public Health is intended for members of the public health workforce who seek formal education and training in public health principles, problem-solving skills, quantitative methods, social and behavioral determinants of disease, organization and management of health programs, and preparation for new and emerging threats to the health of the public. The certificate program begins with two weeks of course work in Baltimore then continues via the Internet, where students take required courses in different discipline areas.

Mental Health. Chair: William W. Eaton, Ph.D. Students study the prevention and control of mental disorders, including alcohol and drug dependence syndromes and neuropsychiatric conditions such as Alzheimer's disease. Research aims to discover the causes of these disorders; identify the factors that promote or attenuate their occurrence, persistence, or severity; devise methods of intervention to prevent the disorders or limit their consequences; and disseminate the insights and accrued knowledge of others through an active program of teaching and community education and service. Programs lead to M.H.S., Sc.D., and Ph.D. degrees. Related careers are in the government and private industry.

Molecular Microbiology and Immunology. Chair: Diane E. Griffin, M.D., Ph.D. This department integrates many disciplines (vector biology, ecology, virology, bacteriology, parasitology, immunology) concerned with the study of the transmission, molecular biology, and pathogenesis of bacterial, parasitic, viral, and immunological diseases. Research is carried out at the population, organismal, cellular, and molecular levels. This broad approach reflects the belief that public health problems can best be addressed by understanding basic biological mechanisms. In the laboratory, clinic, and field, faculty members study diseases such as malaria, sexually transmitted infections, mosquito-borne encephalitis, tuberculosis, measles, AIDS, and autoimmunity. Programs lead to M.H.S., Sc.M., and Ph.D. degrees and careers as faculty members and research scientists in universities, research institutes, and government agencies as well as in the biotechnology and pharmaceutical industries.

M.P.H. Degree Program. Chair: Ron Brookmeyer, Ph.D. A Schoolwide program designed to provide health professionals with a population perspective on health. The program prepares students to become leading public health professionals capable of addressing current global public health problems through multidisciplinary approaches that apply the latest scientific knowledge. M.P.H. students obtain a common grounding in public health theory and practice, with opportunities to specialize in one of ten multidisciplinary concentration areas.

Population, Family, and Reproductive Health. Chair: Robert Blum, M.D., Ph.D. This interdisciplinary department uses the sciences of demography, developmental psychology, epidemiology, sociology, health services research, medicine, nursing, nutrition, economics, communication sciences, and policy analysis. To address the changing patterns of population growth and reproduction globally and ensure the health and development of human populations across their life span, the department focuses on vulnerable populations throughout the world—mothers and infants, families, adolescents, children with special health-care needs, women, and the elderly. Research and practice prepare future researchers and administrators for such organizations as the U.S. Census Bureau, managed-care organizations, government ministries, universities, research institutes, and advocacy groups.

NEW YORK MEDICAL COLLEGE

School of Public Health

Programs of Study

The School of Public Health at New York Medical College is a member of the Association of Schools of Public Health (ASPH). The School of Public Health offers the Master of Public Health (M.P.H.) degree in behavioral sciences and health promotion, biostatistics, disability and human development, environmental health science, epidemiology, health policy and management, and international health. Candidates for the M.P.H. degree must complete a minimum of 46 credits, which includes a 1-credit practicum. The Master of Science (M.S.) degree is offered in biostatistics and in speech-language pathology. Candidates for the M.S. degree in biostatistics must complete a minimum of 36 credits, and candidates for the M.S. in speech-language pathology, 72 credits. The Speech-Language Pathology Program is a two-year, full-time day program. A Doctor of Public Health (Dr.P.H.) degree in epidemiology is also offered. The total number of credits required for the Dr.P.H. degree depends upon the individual's educational profile at the time of application. The Doctor of Physical Therapy (D.P.T.) degree program is a three-year, full-time day program requiring 120 credits.

With the exception of the two full-time day programs, classes are offered in the early evening, Monday through Thursday, and students may be full- or part-time. An individual may apply for a degree program as a matriculated student or take courses on a nonmatriculated basis for up to 9 credits. Similarly, a student enrolled in a graduate degree program at another institution may enroll as a nonmatriculated visiting student.

The Department of Health Policy and Management and the Center for Disaster Medicine within the School of Public Health offer a concentration in emergency preparedness and a 15-credit graduate certificate. Through several other departments of the school, certificates are offered in health promotion, environmental health sciences, public health, public health informatics, international health, maternal and child health, children with special health-care needs, managed care, and management of long-term-care facilities.

Research Facilities

Research facilities include the Alumni Computer Learning Laboratory and the Health Sciences Library, which maintain a collection of approximately 200,000 volumes and 10,454 journals. A dynamic list of online and Web-based resources, including Scopus, PsycINFO, CINAHL, and Science Citation Index, are available. The program in disability and human development draws upon the professional resources of the Westchester Institute for Human Development. In addition, the School of Public Health benefits from the presence of the basic science laboratories that serve the School of Medicine and the Graduate School of Basic Medical Sciences and from eight research centers and institutes that focus on such issues as AIDS, Lyme disease, and adolescent health.

Financial Aid

Financial aid is available for matriculated students. Students are encouraged to talk to the financial aid staff members, who are available to assist them in planning financial aid packages.

Cost of Study

For 2006–07, tuition was $645 per credit hour. The entrance fee is $100, and the student activity and network fees total $10. Tuition for the Physical Therapy Program was $23,500 per year; tuition for the Speech-Language Pathology Program was also $23,500. Annual fees for both programs totaled $270. Health insurance through New York Medical College is separate.

Living and Housing Costs

Students must be matriculating full-time to be eligible for housing on the Valhalla campus. Assistance in obtaining off-campus housing is available from the Office of Student Housing. Housing costs are approximately $505 to $675 per month for a single student.

Student Group

Approximately 500 students are enrolled in the School of Public Health. The majority of these students attend part-time and many work full-time in the health-care system as administrators, physicians, nurses, corporate benefits administrators, nutritionists, technologists, engineers, and researchers.

Graduates work in a variety of settings, including government, private practice, nursing homes, home health agencies, public health agencies, corporations, environmental and pharmaceutical laboratories, and community service organizations.

Location

New York Medical College is located on a 565-acre campus shared with Westchester Medical Center in Valhalla, New York. Its suburban site in the center of Westchester County is approximately 20 miles north of New York City. There are ample educational, recreational, and cultural opportunities available locally and in the New York metropolitan area.

The University and The School

Founded in 1860, New York Medical College has a strong history of involvement in medical and health education and in training, research, and professional and community service. It is chartered by the Regents of the State of New York and is a member of the Middle States Association of Colleges and Secondary Schools. The School of Public Health is pre-accredited by the Council on Education for Public Health (CEPH).

The scope of the College's earliest mission—to prepare physicians to be outstanding clinicians—has been broadened to include the educational preparation of scientists and public health professionals. Today it is chartered as a health sciences university, and its mission is carried out through three schools: the School of Medicine, the Graduate School of Basic Medical Sciences, and the School of Public Health. The School of Public Health seeks to respond to the growing need for well-educated health professionals on the local, national, and international levels.

Applying

Applicants must hold a baccalaureate degree from an accredited college or university. Applicants for the Dr.P.H. program must also hold an M.P.H. or M.S. in epidemiology or an M.P.H. in a health-related field from a school or program accredited in public health. Prerequisite requirements vary by program. Two to three years of relevant work experience is desirable, although not required. The admission decision is based on the information provided in the applicant's completed application. This includes past academic performance (undergraduate and graduate, if any), a personal statement, recommendations, work experience, community involvement, and school extracurricular activities. The application fee for the general programs is $50 ($100 for international students). The application fee for the Physical Therapy Program is $75. The Speech-Language Pathology Program also requires a $75 application fee.

Applicants whose native language is not English are required to obtain a minimum TOEFL score of 600 on the paper-based exam, 250 on the computer-based exam, or 100 on the Internet-based exam (the Speech-Language Pathology Program and Dr.P.H. program have higher score requirements). In addition, international applicants should be prepared to furnish proof of health insurance, statement of planned residence, affidavit of support, and accompanying U.S. bank statements to cover all school and living expenses. The application fee for international students is $100.

Students are admitted for the fall, spring, and summer terms, except for the following programs: the Physical Therapy Program admits new students by April for the academic year that begins in June, the Speech-Language Pathology Program admits new students by May for the academic year that begins in September, and the Dr.P.H. program admits students in April for the fall semester, which begins in September.

Correspondence and Information

Marian McGowan, Assistant Dean for Admissions
School of Public Health
New York Medical College
Valhalla, New York 10595
Phone: 914-594-4510
      888-336-NYMC (toll-free)
Fax: 914-594-4292
E-mail: sph_admissions@nymc.edu
Web site: http://www.nymc.edu/sph/index.htm

New York Medical College

DEPARTMENT CHAIRS AND PROGRAM DIRECTORS

Robert W. Amler, M.D., Interim Chair, Environmental Health Sciences.
Amy Ansehl, M.S.N., RN, FNPC, Executive Director, Partnership for a Healthy Population, and Practicum Coordinator.
Ansley Bacon, Ph.D., Chair, Disability and Human Development, and Director, Center on Disability and Health.
Frank Baker, Ph.D., Chair, Behavioral Sciences and Community Health.
Annette Choolfaian, M.P.A., RN, Chair, Health Policy and Management.
Michael J. Majsak, Ed.D., PT, Chair, Physical Therapy.
David Markenson, M.D., Director, Center for Disaster Medicine.
Paul F. Visintainer, Ph.D., Chair, Epidemiology and Biostatistics.
Ben C. Watson, Ph.D., Chair, Speech-Language Pathology.

Research Activities

Standardization of the CAT/CLAMS instrument for developmental milestones.
Low-weight births in minority populations.
Birth outcomes of Medicaid mothers in a nurse-midwife program.
Patient satisfaction with dental care.
Neuron-specific enolase as a predictor of brain injury in low-birth-weight preterm neonates.
Integrating the Palm Pilot into the clinical medical.
The effects of cognitive retraining on patients who have undergone coronary artery bypass graft surgery.
The effects of exercise training on heart variability and the correlation with changes in right heart echocardiography in patients with chronic obstructive pulmonary disease.
Transfer of training among exercise types.
A multicenter trial for stage 1b cardiac rehabilitation.
Community-based strategies of physical therapy education.
Motor control and motor learning in patients with Parkinson's disease.
Falls risk assessments for the elderly.
Efficacy of an apparatus to promote functional use of the upper limb following stroke.
Relationship between the Visual Analog Rating Scale and verbal comments on the American Physical Therapy Association Clinical Performance Instrument.
A structure for teaching statistics, research design, and critical analysis in health sciences.
Fecal incontinence in the elderly.
Formal evaluation of change in curriculum to improve analysis skills in PT students.
Clinical issues in geriatrics.
Diadochokinetics in normal aged speakers.
Cortical correlates of fluent and dysfluent speech production in adult, developmental stutterers.
Cortical electrophysiological activity (resting EEG and EP) in children with developmental stuttering.
Survey of speech-language pathologists who work within hospice organizations.
Development of literacy skills in individuals with severe disabilities who use augmentative and alternative communication services.
The effects of voice output communication aids (VOCAs) on the interaction patterns of individuals with autism.
Assessment of residents of a local agency for appropriate AAC interventions and training of staff on the use of the AAC interventions.
The development of protocols or guidelines for developing protocols for the efficient and functionally effective use of biofeedback in the context of motor learning theory.
Community physicians' treatment of Lyme disease.
Resistant *Candida albicans*.
Physician practice patterns.
Biofeedback in speech and swallowing rehabilitation.
Phonological deficits in Landon-Kleffner syndrome.
Strong phoneme knowledge in the presence of problems segmenting connected speech.
Speech, language, and brain function in child stutterers.
Augmentative/alternative communication in an acute-care setting.
Effects of voice output communication on language skills.
Analysis of motor variability in individuals with Huntington's disease.
Effectiveness of a home exercise program to improve gait and balance in individuals with Huntington's disease.
The implementation of functionally relevant goal writing in New York City public schools.
Predictors of falls and functional decline in individuals residing in nursing homes.
Response of oral musculature to hypoxia and hypercapnia.
The effect of sleep on learning and behavior in the adolescent.
A survey of knowledge, attitudes, and beliefs regarding breast cancer.

NEW YORK MEDICAL COLLEGE

School of Public Health
Program in Epidemiology

Programs of Study
The School of Public Health at New York Medical College (NYMC) offers the Master of Public Health (M.P.H.) and Doctor of Public Health (Dr.P.H.) degrees in epidemiology. The Master of Public Health degree provides students with the knowledge and quantitative skills necessary to participate in medical, clinical, and public health research. The M.P.H. program is designed for those with undergraduate degrees in biology, mathematics, psychology, or other health sciences–related areas and for those with a keen interest in medical, clinical, and public health research. Students must complete a master's thesis involving an analysis of new or existing data on a subject relevant to the field of epidemiology or public health. Students must also complete a practicum, which assures that they have practical experience to support academic skills and information acquired before they enter the world of public health practice. To fulfill this requirement, students must register for a 1-credit pass/fail course beyond the 45 credits required for the degree. Those who can demonstrate appropriate practice experience prior to beginning their M.P.H. studies may apply for a waiver. All M.P.H. students are required to show evidence of computer literacy through the successful completion of the Computer Literacy Competency Project.

The Doctor of Public Health (Dr.P.H.) in epidemiology addresses the need for health-care professionals who are prepared to examine, at the highest level of scholarly achievement, the conditions and determinants of health and disease in the population. The program has three components—18-credit course work, a 12-credit internship, and 15-credit dissertation research. All students are required to take a minimum of 18 credits of didactic course work, including the 3-credit doctoral-level course on research ethics. There is a two-year minimum residency requirement. Students have opportunities to interact with other health-care professionals in a variety of settings and to apply their skills to real-world problems, under the guidance of a mentor. These internships make use of the rich academic and practice environment offered by New York Medical College, its hospitals, the county health department affiliates, and other health-related organizations. At enrollment, students are accepted as provisional candidates for the doctoral degree. Upon passing the qualifying exam (usually taken after one year of course work), students are admitted to full candidacy. Students must pass the qualifying exam in order to begin work on their doctoral dissertation and complete the doctoral degree. The dissertation serves as the culmination of the research competency of the doctoral program and must address an original research question. Doctoral candidates must orally defend their research proposal and completed research study. Students' progress through the doctoral program is assessed through grades in course work and through mentor and adviser evaluations during internships. In addition, students must exhibit satisfactory performance on three milestone evaluations. The School of Public Health is a member of the Association of Schools of Public Health (ASPH).

Research Facilities
As one of the nation's largest private health sciences universities and the only academic biomedical research center between New York City and Albany, New York Medical College offers campuswide research facilities to support the biomedical community. More than $40 million in research and programs sponsored by the National Institutes of Health and other sources are ongoing at the university. Two hundred scientists located on campus and at twenty-two affiliated hospitals advance research in heart disease, cancer, kidney disease, AIDS, Lyme disease, and the neurosciences. Researchers also collaborate with biopharmaceutical companies that are looking for ways to supplement existing resources with new platform technology or product ideas. The College provides access on a fee-for-service basis to centralized research facilities commonly used in drug discovery and development. These facilities serve as a conduit for biomedical industries to interact with the campus research community and afford access to sophisticated research equipment, without the costs associated with purchase and maintenance. The Technology Development Division, created in 1994, expands basic and clinical research through collaborations with the biomedical community.

Financial Aid
Advisement concerning how to pay the cost of education is available to admitted students through the Student Financial Planning Office. Generally, most students are eligible for loan programs sufficient to cover the cost of tuition, fees, books, and, if needed, living expenses.

Cost of Study
Tuition for the 2006–07 academic year was $645 per credit. In addition, there are student activity and network access fees. Full-time students may elect to purchase health insurance through the College and to secure use of the College Health Services for a separate fee.

Living and Housing Costs
Limited on-campus housing is available for single and married students. The Student Housing Office works with students to obtain housing either on-campus or at nearby off-campus locations.

Student Group
There are 1,660 students enrolled—760 in the School of Medicine (M.D. degree), 500 in the School of Public Health (doctoral, Master of Public Health, and Master of Science degrees), and 250 in the Graduate School of Basic Medical Sciences (doctoral and Master of Science degrees). Students come from across the United States and from many other countries.

Location
The School of Public Health at New York Medical College is located on a beautiful 565-acre campus shared with Westchester Medical Center and the Westchester Institute for Human Development (WIHD). The campus is centrally located in Westchester, close to several major roadways, including the Cross Westchester Expressway (I-287), the Sprain Brook Parkway, the Taconic State Parkway, and the Saw Mill River Parkway. It is a 45-minute drive from midtown Manhattan.

The College
New York Medical College is chartered as a health sciences university, and its mission is carried out through three schools: the School of Medicine, the School of Public Health, and the Graduate School of Basic Medical Sciences. New York Medical College has geographic and administrative ties to a number of organizations that offer opportunities for students to obtain exceptional experience during their internships.

Applying
Admissions requirements for the M.P.H. program include a bachelor's degree from an accredited institution and a GPA of at least 3.0. Undergraduate courses in calculus, statistics, or research methods are desirable. Scores from the Graduate Record Examinations (GRE) are not required. Scores from the TOEFL exam may be required. Applicants must submit a nonrefundable $50 application fee ($100 for international students), along with the application, two recommendations, a resume, and official transcripts from all postsecondary institutions attended. Application deadline dates are August 1 for fall, December 1 for spring, and May 1 for summer. Deadline dates for international students are May 15, October 15, and March 15, respectively.

Admissions requirements for the Dr.P.H. program include an M.P.H. or M.S. degree in epidemiology or an M.P.H. in a health-related field from an ASPH accredited program or institution and a GPA of at least 3.5. GRE scores are required. Scores from the TOEFL exam may be required. Applicants must submit a nonrefundable $75 application fee ($100 for international students), along with the application, three recommendations, a resume, and official transcripts from all postsecondary institutions attended. Students may begin in the fall semester only. The deadline date is March 15. The deadline date for international students is January 15. Qualified applicants are invited for an interview, and acceptance is contingent upon the number of spaces available in the program. Accepted students may be waitlisted. A nonrefundable deposit of $500 to be applied towards tuition is required from accepted students.

Correspondence and Information
Paul Visintainer, Professor and Department Chair
Department of Epidemiology and Biostatistics
School of Public Health
New York Medical College
Valhalla, New York 10595
Phone: 914-594-4804
E-mail: visint@nymc.edu
Web site: http://www.nymc.edu/sph/programs/epidemiology.asp

Marian F. McGowan, Assistant Dean for Admissions
School of Public Health
New York Medical College
Valhalla, New York 10595
Phone: 914-594-4510
888-336-NYMC (toll-free)
E-mail: sph_admissions@nymc.edu

New York Medical College

THE FACULTY

Oscar Alleyne, Lecturer; M.P.H., SUNY, Albany.
Harry C. Barrett, Distinguished Lecturer; M.P.H., Columbia; M.Ed., St. John's; D.Min., New York Theological Seminary.
Denton C. Brosius, Assistant Professor of Biostatistics; Ph.D., Clark.
Heather L. Brumberg, Assistant Professor of Clinical Public Health; M.D., Tufts; M.P.H., Yale; FAAP.
Peter Paul Cervoni, Distinguished Lecturer; Ph.D., Washington (Seattle).
Paul Christos, Lecturer; M.S., M.P.H., New York Medical College.
Stephen Dusza, Lecturer; M.P.H., New York Medical College.
Dorothy L. Faulkner, Associate Professor of Epidemiology; M.P.H., Alabama at Birmingham; Ph.D., Michigan.
Martin J. Glassman, Assistant Professor of Clinical Public Health; D.M.D., Pennsylvania.
Susan Hailpern, Lecturer; B.S.N., Colorado; M.P.H., M.S., New York Medical College; RN.
John Hammond, Senior Lecturer; M.B.A., SUNY at Buffalo.
Clayton J. Heydorn, Lecturer; B.A., Borromeo Seminary of Ohio; CIP.
Wei-Nchih Lee, Assistant Professor of Clinical Public Health; M.D., CUNY, Mount Sinai; M.P.H., Columbia.
Elayne Livote, Lecturer; M.A., SUNY, Albany; M.S., M.P.H., New York Medical College.
Maureen Miller, Associate Professor; Ph.D., Columbia.
Erin Ray Pascaretti, Lecturer; M.P.H., New York Medical College; RD.
Patricia A. Patrick, Lecturer; M.P.H., New York Medical College.
Joann Petrini, Lecturer; M.P.H., Yale; M.P.A., Ph.D., NYU.
Qiuhu Shi, Associate Professor of Biostatistics; M.S., Shanghai Teacher's; M.S., Ph.D., Columbia.
Nancy Stambler, Lecturer; M.S., SUNY at Stony Brook, M.S., Uniformed Services of the Health Sciences.
Renee Stolove, Lecturer; M.A., Columbia Teachers College; M.P.H., New York Medical College; PT.
Julia Y. Tai, Lecturer; M.A., CUNY, Hunter.
Elizabeth Vazquez, Lecturer; M.P.H., Columbia.
Anita Verga, Lecturer; M.P.H., Columbia.
Paul Visintainer, Professor of Epidemiology and Chair; Ph.D., Pittsburgh.
Marsha Zion, Lecturer; M.S., M.P.H., New York Medical College.

OAKLAND UNIVERSITY

Program in Safety Management

Program of Study

The Master of Science in Safety Management (MSSM) Program was developed through a cooperative effort between the School of Health Sciences and the School of Business Administration at Oakland University (OU). This master's degree program focuses on the business aspects of safety management in the workplace and combines an effective balance of core M.B.A. course work with application of those business skills to safety-related case studies in risk assessment, loss control, risk management, and safety program planning, administration, and management.

This Master of Science degree is intended to benefit college graduates and in-service safety professionals with a safety-related bachelor's degree or other bachelor's degree coupled with safety-related work experience or required prerequisite safety courses. The goal of the MSSM Program is to provide the analytical tools and skills necessary for making sound management decisions in business and industry as they relate to occupational safety, health, and environmental issues in the workplace.

Upon completion of this Master of Science in Safety Management Program, the graduate is able to communicate effectively with top management and cost-justify interventions necessary to protect employees, property, and the environment; enhance management commitment to workplace improvements in safety and health through development of better management understanding of the safety and health impact on bottom line performance; encourage increased employee involvement in the development of safety and health interventions through better understanding of the business ramifications and needs for safety and health improvements in the workplace; implement safety and health programs/interventions that optimize business and safety performance in unison; develop return of investment evaluations that demonstrate understanding of the financial and operational impacts of safety interventions in the workplace; effectively integrate occupational safety and health programs that play a significant role in business total quality management efforts and that enhance operational efficiency and productivity; translate moral, ethical, legal, and operational needs for safety and health programs/interventions into terms that a business CEO or other corporate manager can recognize as a valid business need; identify strategies that align safety and health improvements with organizational priorities; demonstrate that safety in the workplace makes good business sense; and contribute as a key member of an organizational management team.

Research Facilities

The Office of Grants, Contracts, and Sponsored Research supports research and scholarship at Oakland University. In particular, the office acts as the coordinating office between Oakland University and the federal and state agencies, foundations, and public and private corporations that provide funds for research, education, training, and service programs.

Located in the center of campus, the Kresge Library houses collections of books, journals, reference works, government documents, musical scores, and recordings as well as a wireless network and computer workstations to access an array of digital resources. The Kresge Library's collections include over 727,000 books, approximately 1,400 print journal subscriptions and electronic access to more than 15,000 titles, over 240,000 federal and state documents, and more than 1.1 million microforms. The Library's homepage and online catalog serve as gateways to dozens of specialized and general research databases and hundreds of full-text electronic journals and e-books covering a wide range of disciplines and research areas.

Financial Aid

In order to assist eligible graduate students in financing their education, Oakland University participates in the Federal College Work-Study Program and the William Ford Federal Direct Loan Program.

Cost of Study

Graduate tuition in the 2007–08 academic year is $472.50 per credit hour for Michigan residents and $814.50 per credit hour for non-residents. For current tuition rates, interested students should visit http://www.oakland.edu/tuitionandfees.

Living and Housing Costs

The 2006–07 rate for room and board was $6385 for the academic year. Facilities with a limited number of single rooms are available to graduate students. For students with families, a limited number of two-bedroom town houses and two- to four-bedroom student apartments are available.

Student Group

Total enrollment at OU for fall 2006 was 17,737. Twenty-three percent of the total enrollment are graduate students. Within the graduate enrollment, 66 percent are women and 11.4 percent are members of ethnic minority groups. The diverse student body includes international students representing many different countries.

Location

Oakland University is located in Oakland County, the third-most-affluent county in the United States and the fastest growing county in Michigan. Rochester, Michigan, is OU's hometown. Rochester was named thirty-ninth in a list of top 100 cities in which to live, and the highest-ranking Michigan city in the survey, by *Money* magazine and *CNN Money* in 2005. Rochester and the surrounding area was ranked based on population, number of educational facilities, safety, environment, housing affordability, taxes, weather, commute times, and job market.

In addition, the area's rolling hills, wetlands, and woodlands provide beautiful neighborhoods and plenty of year-round recreation. The surrounding community also offers an abundance of entertainment, cultural, and social opportunities. Together, all this makes Oakland County and Rochester great places to live, work, and go to school.

The University

Oakland University, founded in 1957, is a comprehensive state-supported institution of higher education. The University is organized into the College of Arts and Sciences and the Schools of Business Administration, Education and Human Services, Engineering and Computer Science, Health Sciences, and Nursing.

Applying

Students applying to the MSSM Program need to submit the Application for Admission to Graduate Study, the application processing fee, and supporting documents to Graduate Admissions. Both a paper and online application process are available. Information about application requirements and deadlines is available online at http://www.oakland.edu/grad/apply.

Correspondence and Information

Graduate Admissions
160 North Foundation Hall
Oakland University
Rochester, Michigan 48309
Phone: 248-370-3167
E-mail: gradmail@oakland.edu
Web site: http://www.oakland.edu/gograd

Oakland University

THE FACULTY

Charles McGlothlin Jr., Program Director; Ph.D., Colorado State.
Richard Rozek, Associate Professor; Ph.D., Wayne State.
Thomas Schenk, Adjunct Professor; Ph.D., SUNY.

SARAH LAWRENCE COLLEGE

Human Genetics and Health Advocacy Graduate Programs

Programs of Study	Sarah Lawrence College offers two unique master's programs in health. The College's Health Advocacy Program and its Joan H. Marks Graduate Program in Human Genetics, each leading to a master's degree (M.A. and M.S., respectively), train health professionals devoted to the health concerns of patients. The interdisciplinary curriculum in each program consists of 40 academic course credits and at least 600 hours of clinical work or other fieldwork. The location of Sarah Lawrence College in the metropolitan New York area offers a rich network of settings—hospitals, clinics, and community agencies—for students to do fieldwork that integrates theoretical knowledge learned in the classroom with practice. The faculty includes professionals and academicians drawn from health and medical disciplines. Small classes and close faculty-student interaction offer a productive and stimulating environment for professional growth. Both programs make use of invited speakers, professional workshops, and community involvement to enrich the learning experience and expose students to new developments in the field. A joint degree in human genetics and health advocacy (M.S./M.A.) is also offered.
	In 1980, Sarah Lawrence established the nation's first master's degree program in health advocacy. The program, usually completed over four semesters and one summer (or longer on a part-time basis), leads to a Master of Arts degree and meets the educational requirements for challenging and rewarding careers in this multifaceted field. The course of study prepares graduates to work in direct care as patient representatives, ombudsmen, educators, and health advisers; to help patients and families navigate the health-care system and ensure that their medical and health needs are met; to work collaboratively with other health-care providers to mediate conflict and facilitate positive change; and to work as educators and health-information specialists empowering others. Graduates also work in government and voluntary associations as policy advocates, in research settings protecting human subjects, and in community-based programs. Course work includes a core sequence on the theory and practice of health advocacy, and other courses address legal, ethical, policy, economic, historical, and other disciplinary aspects of health advocacy. Course work is conducted in seminars and tutorials, with an emphasis on student participation.
	In 1969, Sarah Lawrence College established the human genetics program, the first master's-level program in genetic counseling, which has set the standard for the field. The program fulfills all the requirements for certification of genetic counselors, available through the American Board of Medical Genetics. The genetic counselor, as a member of a medical genetics team, provides individuals and families with genetic information, emotional support, and help with crucial decisions at times of emotional distress. The required curriculum can be completed on a full-time basis in two years or part-time in three years. The program leads to the Master of Science degree. From courses, seminars, and fieldwork experiences, the students acquire competence in both medical genetics and genetic counseling. There is a strong emphasis on psychological counseling.
	In the summer of 2006, Sarah Lawrence College began offering new certificate programs for health-care professionals who seek career change and advancement in public health genetics/genomics and applied research ethics. These programs are designed on a "low-residency" model with the working professional in mind. The courses are offered on weekends and in short, intensive sessions that require minimal time off from work, and the program accommodates multiple points of entry. To earn the certificate, participants must complete all modules associated with the program. Alternatively, modules may also be taken for continuing education units.
Research Facilities	Sarah Lawrence College has established affiliations with more than thirty medical and research centers in the metropolitan New York area. Placement with leading researchers at area institutions is readily available for students with research interests. A well-equipped human genetics lab serves the human genetics program. The College maintains a library of books, periodicals, and reference materials of interest to students in the genetics and health advocacy programs. In addition, students in both programs have access to the rich resources of libraries, hospitals, and community agencies throughout metropolitan New York. Both programs emphasize professional roles in research and human subject protection.
Financial Aid	All graduate grants and loans are awarded based on financial need as determined by information provided on the PROFILE and the FAFSA. Applicants with financial need are considered for Sarah Lawrence College gift aid, Federal Perkins Loans, and Federal Stafford Student Loans. Sarah Lawrence College is unable to offer federal financial aid to students who are not citizens or permanent residents of the United States. However, international students may apply for Sarah Lawrence gift aid by filling out the PROFILE. International students are also advised to investigate other financing opportunities offered by their governments or through private institutions.
Cost of Study	Tuition for the human genetics program in 2007–08 is $931 per academic credit. Tuition for the health advocacy program is $908 per academic credit and $200 per field placement.
Living and Housing Costs	Although housing is not available on campus, off-campus single rooms and shared apartments are available for $400 to $800 per month. The minimum cost for an apartment in the area is $500 per month. Housing information is available from the Office of Graduate Studies. Meals at reasonable rates are available at the College's dining halls.
Student Group	The student body of the entire Sarah Lawrence graduate studies program is diverse, with more than 300 students, including both recent college graduates and adults changing careers. Students in the Human Genetics and Health Advocacy Graduate Programs come from across the country and often have extensive work experience.
Student Outcomes	Health advocates work as patient representatives in hospital settings and in community health, government agencies, or advocacy organizations. Examples of positions held by graduates include policy analyst, program health service administrator, and community health organizer.
	The majority of graduates from the human genetics program enter the field as genetic counselors in a range of settings; average time to find and fill such positions is less than two months. As the field of human genetics grows and diversifies, alumni increasingly fill other roles in research, public health, policy, and other settings. Recent graduates of the program at Sarah Lawrence are employed at Memorial Sloan-Kettering Cancer Center, Massachusetts General Hospital, and Columbia Presbyterian Medical Center, among other institutions.
Location	The College is located in the Bronxville/Yonkers suburban community in southern Westchester County, New York, 15 miles from midtown Manhattan, thus offering students the comforts of suburban living within a 30-minute commute of the city. Regular vans to New York City, notices of special events, and general information about New York are all provided by the Office of Student Affairs. The commuter train station is a short walk from campus.
The College	Founded in 1926, Sarah Lawrence College is a liberal arts and sciences college for men and women. It is a lively community of students, scholars, and artists and is nationally renowned for its unique academic structure, which combines small classes with individual student-faculty conferences.
Applying	The human genetics program seeks qualified applicants who can demonstrate a well-developed interest in medical genetic services. Prerequisites for admission are general biology, developmental biology (vertebrate embryology), genetics (Mendelian and molecular), basic chemistry, and probability and statistics. Other recommended courses include organic chemistry, psychology of personality, and Spanish. A personal interview is required. The deadline for applications and all supporting documents is January 15. The health advocacy program invites health professionals, consumers active in health or social welfare networks, adults changing careers, and recent college graduates with a commitment to improving people's access to health services, to apply. The admissions committee looks for writing and analytical skills, demonstrated interest in public service, a personal sense of the importance of advocacy, and clear motivation to enter new and challenging areas of health care. Prerequisites for admission are completion of a bachelor's degree, with a strong undergraduate record, and work in the social sciences, and facility in a second language, especially Spanish, is considered advantageous. Writing skills and critical analytic abilities are important for admission. A personal interview is required. GRE scores are not required. The preferred application deadline is March 31.
Correspondence and Information	Susan Guma, Dean of Graduate Studies Sarah Lawrence College Bronxville, New York 10708 Phone: 914-395-2371 Fax: 914-395-2664 E-mail: grad@slc.edu Web site: http://www.sarahlawrence.edu/health-programs

Sarah Lawrence College

THE FACULTY

Health Advocacy Program
Laura Weil, Interim Director; M.A. (health advocacy), Sarah Lawrence.
Peter Arno, Ph.D., New School.
Patricia Banta, B.S.N., Mount Saint Vincent; M.A. (health advocacy), Sarah Lawrence.
Bruce Berg, Associate Professor and Chair, Department of Political Science at Fordham University; Ph.D., American.
Sayantani DasGupta, M.D., M.P.H., Johns Hopkins.
Rachel Grob, Ph.D. (sociology), CUNY Graduate Center.
Catherine M. Handy, Ph.D., NYU.
Alice Herb, J.D., LL.M., NYU.
Margaret Keller, J.D., M.S. (administrative medicine), Columbia.
Laura Long, M.S. (human genetics), Sarah Lawrence.
Terry Mizrahi, Ph.D. (sociology), Virginia.
Constance Peterson, M.A. (health advocacy), Sarah Lawrence.

Human Genetics Program
Caroline Lieber, Director; M.S., Sarah Lawrence.
James W. Speer, Associate Director; M.S., Sarah Lawrence.
Jessica Davis, Director, Clinical Training; M.D., Columbia.
Judith Durcan, M.S., Sarah Lawrence.

Susanne Carter, M.S., Sarah Lawrence.
Sayantani DasGupta, M.D., M.P.H., Johns Hopkins.
Peggy Cottrell, M.S., Sarah Lawrence
Siobhan Dolan, M.D., Harvard.
Marvin Frankel, Ph.D., Chicago.
Eva Bostein Griepp, M.D., NYU.
Susan Gross, M.D., Toronto.
Alice Herb, J.D., LL.M., NYU.
Laura Hercher, M.S., Sarah Lawrence; M.S., Columbia.
Judith Hull, M.S., Sarah Lawrence.
David Kronn, M.D., Trinity College (Dublin).
Sharon LaVigne, M.S., Sarah Lawrence.
Laura Long, M.S., Sarah Lawrence.
Robert Marion, M.D., Yeshiva (Einstein).
Diana Punales Morejon, M.S., Sarah Lawrence.
Sally Nolin, Ph.D., SUNY Health Science Center at Brooklyn.
Elsa Reich, M.S., Sarah Lawrence.
Michael J. Smith, D.S.W., Columbia.
Jennifer Scalia Wilbur, M.S., Sarah Lawrence.

Sarah Lawrence is in suburban Westchester, 15 miles from New York City.

STATE UNIVERSITY OF NEW YORK DOWNSTATE MEDICAL CENTER
Department of Preventive Medicine and Community Health
Master of Public Health Program

Program of Study

The Master of Public Health (M.P.H.) Program at the State University of New York (SUNY) Downstate Medical Center (also known as the SUNY Health Science Center at Brooklyn) offers an M.P.H. degree to students on a part-time basis. With an initial concentration in urban and immigrant health, the program has recently expanded to include a new track in social and behavioral sciences. The M.P.H. Program is intended for students who have completed at least a baccalaureate degree program at an accredited institution and have a strong interest in careers related to public health research and practice. Concurrent degrees with the College of Medicine, College of Nursing, and College of Health Related Professions are also available to interested M.P.H. students. Students who attend the program on a part-time basis and take approximately 6 credit hours per semester can expect to complete the program within two years. In addition to the academic requirements of the program, students must complete a 250-hour Culminating Experience.

Research Facilities

The Health Science Education Building is the central location for one of the largest medical libraries in the United States. The Medical Research Library of Brooklyn offers the resources of more than 200 databases, 600 electronic full-text journals, more than seventy-five electronic books, and a constantly expanding collection of resources as well as the assistance of a professional reference staff. In addition, a Learning Resource Center provides networked workstations with a variety of software programs that access library resources, statistical programs, curriculum materials, e-mail, and the Internet. This building also houses some classrooms, laboratories, and an auditorium.

Clinical facilities include the University Hospital of Brooklyn and Kings County Hospital Center as well as other affiliated institutions throughout the New York metro area and several community clinics operated by SUNY Downstate staff members. University Hospital is a major referral center for tertiary care and has one of the largest kidney transplantation programs in the Eastern United States.

Financial Aid

Information about financial aid, including federal loans, can be obtained by calling the Office of Financial Aid at 718-270-2488 or by visiting the Web site at http://sls.downstate.edu/financialaid/index.html.

Cost of Study

Current tuition for in-state residents of New York is $288 per credit hour; $455 per credit hour for out-of-state residents. Students taking less than a full-time schedule (less than 12 credit hours) are eligible for part-time financial assistance. For the purposes of financial aid, a student must have a minimum of 9 credit hours to be eligible for full-time grants and/or loans. Part-time students are ineligible for the Tuition Assistance Program (TAP) but may be eligible for other forms of aid, depending on the credit load.

Living and Housing Costs

Living expenses for students attending the Downstate M.P.H. Program are estimated to be approximately $13,000 per year. Students who choose to live on campus in the dormitories are charged between $2300 and $6000 per semester, depending on the size of accommodations. Additional fees are approximately $500 per year.

Student Group

Students range from faculty physicians, physician's assistants, nurses, occupational therapists, and other health professionals to recent undergraduates. Students are racially and ethnically diverse and reflect Brooklyn's many multiethnic communities.

Location

Located in the heart of Brooklyn, SUNY Downstate Medical Center was founded in 1860 to help people making their way in the New World by treating health problems carried from the Old. At SUNY Downstate, students live, work, and study in one of the most diverse, dynamic, and vibrant urban environments in the world. Representatives from local, state, and national organizations share their experience and knowledge in lectures, seminars, and the other special events that an international city such as New York provides.

The Medical Center

As one of only 125 academic medical centers across the country, SUNY Downstate has four colleges: Medicine, Nursing, Health Related Professions, and Graduate Studies. The M.P.H. Program joins these noted schools to graduate highly trained and community-minded health professionals engaged in public health. The SUNY Downstate M.P.H. Program is housed in the medical center's Department of Preventive Medicine and Community Health of the College of Medicine. The program's faculty includes nationally respected leaders in public health who have distinguished themselves through teaching, research, and service. Located in the heart of Brooklyn, SUNY Downstate offers students the opportunity to live, study, and work in one of the most diverse, dynamic, and vibrant urban environments in the world. Students graduating from this program can expect to understand and deal with many issues facing public health professionals in diverse communities throughout the world.

Applying

Requirements for admission include satisfactory completion of a baccalaureate degree from an accredited institution, an undergraduate GPA of 3.0 or better in the major course of study, letters of recommendation, and appropriate test scores. Applicants for concurrent degrees with other programs in the medical center must apply to and be accepted by each program. The admissions requirements for each degree apply. Students applying for concurrent degrees should indicate their intent on each application.

The SUNY Downstate M.P.H. Program application can be downloaded from the M.P.H. Web site, listed below, or interested applicants can call the M.P.H. Program at the phone number listed below. Complete applications should be sent to the Office of Admissions at SUNY Downstate Office of Admissions (450 Clarkson Avenue, Box 60, Brooklyn, New York, 11203-2098; telephone: 718-270-2446).

The M.P.H. Program offers rolling admission for other than M.D./M.P.H. applicants. Applications are accepted in the spring, summer, and fall semesters of each calendar year. M.D./M.P.H. applicants must submit M.P.H. applications directly to the SUNY Downstate Office of Admissions. American Medical College Application Service (AMCAS) applications must be submitted according to the instructions for that application. Deadlines for applications are as follows: February 15 for the summer semester, April 15 for the fall semester, and October 15 for the spring semester.

Correspondence and Information

Master of Public Health Program
State University of New York Downstate Medical Center
450 Clarkson Avenue, Box 60
Brooklyn, New York 11203-2098

Phone: 718-270-1065
Fax: 718-270-2533
E-mail: mphprogram@downstate.edu
Web site: http://www.downstate.edu/mphprogram

State University of New York Downstate Medical Center

THE FACULTY AND THEIR RESEARCH

Pascal James Imperato, M.D., M.P.H.T.M., Distinguished Service Professor; Chair, Department of Preventive Medicine and Community Health; and Director, Master of Public Health Program. Served for six years as a medical epidemiologist for the Centers for Disease Control and Prevention in West Africa, directing mass immunization campaigns against smallpox, measles, yellow fever, cholera, and meningococcal meningitis; awarded the Meritorious Honor Award and Medal by the U.S. Department of State for his work in Africa; served as Commissioner of Health of New York City and Chair of the Board, New York City Health and Hospitals Corporation.

Abraham Aragones, M.D., M.S.C.I., Assistant Professor of Preventive Medicine and Community Health. Immigrant populations and cancer health disparities and chronic care in these populations, colorectal cancer screening among Latinos, cancer-screening referrals among immigrants, impact of the Chronic Care Model in the Latino immigrant population.

Karen Benker, M.D., M.P.H., Assistant Professor of Preventive Medicine and Community Health, Voluntary Attending Physician in Family Practice, and Founder and Director, Downstate's Freedom from Tobacco Project. Delivering primary care to innercity and immigrant populations, research and intervention on HIV-related issues and smoking cessation.

Denise Bruno, M.D., M.P.H., Assistant Professor of Preventive Medicine and Community Health and Co-Director of the fourth-year medical student elective, Health Care in Developing Countries. General pediatric public health issues such as immunization, asthma, perinatal hepatitis B, lead poisoning prevention, and newborn screening.

Laura Geer, Ph.D., Assistant Professor of Preventive Medicine and Community Health and has been consultant for U.S. Environmental Protection Agency and Exposure Measurements and Analysis Branch (EMAB) at the National Exposure Research Laboratory (NERL). Worker dermal exposure to chemicals, environmental perinatal exposures and infant morbidity and mortality outcomes.

Michael A. Joseph, Ph.D., M.P.H., Assistant Professor of Preventive Medicine and Community Health. Chronic disease epidemiology; epidemiology of benign prostatic hyperplasia (BPH) and lower urinary tract symptoms (LUTS); morbidity in African American men; social epidemiology, particularly issues of behavioral and cultural determinants of cancer screening practices among communities of color.

Judith H. LaRosa, Ph.D., Professor of Preventive Medicine and Community Health and Deputy Director, Master of Public Health Program; RN. Was first Deputy Director of the National Institutes of Health's Office of Research on Women's Health; Professor and Chair, Department of Community Health Sciences, Tulane University School of Public Health and Tropical Medicine; and Director, Tulane Xavier National Center of Excellence in Women's Health. Women's health, public health, cardiovascular disease.

Edmond S. Malka, M.P.H., Assistant Professor of Preventive Medicine and Community Health. Life Fellow of the American Institute of Chemists, member of the Royal Society of Chemistry (UK), Certified Professional Chemist (National Certification Commission in Chemistry and Chemical Engineering, USA), and Chartered Chemist (The Royal Society of Chemistry, UK).

Theresa Montini, M.S.W., Ph.D., Assistant Professor of Preventive Medicine and Community Health. Health policy, substance abuse, adoption of evidence-based medicine, tobacco control, adoption of evidenced-based practice, women's health.

Timothy Prinz, Ph.D., Assistant Professor of Preventive Medicine and Community Health. Was Director of the Community Health Institute at Affinity Health Plan and Senior Policy Analyst at the United Hospital Fund, awarded an APSA Congressional Fellowship in 1995, served as legislative assistant to Senator Tom Daschle, and named Robert Wood Johnson Scholar in Health Policy at the University of California, Berkeley, from 1996 to 1998.

Rebecca Schwartz, Ph.D., Assistant Professor of Preventive Medicine and Community Health. Role of psychosocial and behavioral factors in health promotion and risk prevention among low-income urban populations; clinical work with children, adolescents, and families; therapeutic interventions for youth who are HIV positive.

Jeanne Mager Stellman, Ph.D., Professor of Preventive Medicine and Community Health, Head of the Division of Environmental Health Sciences, and Associate Director for Research. Occupational and environmental health, directed major research study on Agent Orange exposure for National Academy of Sciences, Editor-in-Chief 4th edition *ILO Encyclopaedia Occupational Safety & Health*, Editor, *Women and Health*, 1986–2004.

Scyatta A. Wallace, Ph.D., Assistant Professor of Preventive Medicine and Community Health. Cultural and contextual considerations in behavioral health interventions with youth populations, health education and health-care utilization among black populations, ethical issues in health care and health-related research with vulnerable populations.

Tracey E. Wilson, Ph.D., Assistant Professor of Preventive Medicine and Community Health. Prevention of unintended pregnancy, STDs, HIV, and other health-related issues among women living in innercity areas of New York City; sexual and contraceptive behaviors of HIV infected and uninfected women; issues associated with medication adherence.

Part-Time Faculty

Alvin M. Berk, Ph.D., Assistant Professor of Preventive Medicine and Community Health and Assistant Vice President, Downstate's Management Systems. Role of grass-roots organizations in formulating public policy; regular contributions to *Newsday*, the *New York Post*, and the *New York Times*, and television; since 1989, chairman of Brooklyn Community Board 14; since 1993, chair of the Coalition of Brooklyn Community Boards.

George Braman, M.D., Assistant Professor of Preventive Medicine and Community Health and has been Director, Quality Management, and assistant attending physician, Elmhurst Hospital Center in Queens; seven years as public health physician, New York State Department of Health; clinical and teaching positions in geriatric medicine.

Ruth C. Browne, M.P.P., M.P.H., Sc.D., Assistant Professor in the College of Health Related Professions and in Preventive Medicine and Community Health at the SUNY Downstate Medical Center. Founding Executive Director of the Arthur Ashe Institute for Urban Health (AAIUH).

Gerald W. Deas, M.D., M.P.H., Clinical Assistant Professor of Preventive Medicine and Community Health and Director, Health Education Communication. Primary-care practice in innercity area of Queens, health education, medical reporter on *McCreary Report* on Fox Television (Channel 5), discussion of issues of health promotion and disease prevention on WLIB radio, shows on Time-Warner cable TV as well as Brooklyn Cable Access TV (BCAT) and Brooklyn/Queens Cable TV, articles in the *Amsterdam News, Caribe News,* and *New York Voice*.

Barbara G. Delano, M.D., M.P.H., Professor of Medicine and of Preventive Medicine and Community Health; Director, Home Dialysis Program, Kings County Hospital/Downstate Medical Center; and Associate Director, Renal Disease Division of State University Hospital. Hemodialysis, numerous publications in the field.

Imogene A. Drakes, M.S., M.B.A., Assistant Professor of Preventive Medicine and Community Health. Health-care from forensic science (in particular, forensic toxicology) to clinical laboratory science, currently a third-year toxicology student in the Doctor of Public Health program at Columbia University.

Francesca Gany, M.D., Assistant Professor of Preventive Medicine and Community Health at the Downstate Medical Center, Executive Director of the New York Task Force on Immigrant Health, and Director of the Center for Immigrant Health. Attending physician at New York University Medical Center.

Judith Hey-Hadavi, M.D., D.D.S., Assistant Professor of Clinical Medicine and Assistant Professor of Clinical Dentistry at Columbia University and Medical Director of Medical Regulatory Affairs for the Metabolic and Cardiovascular Group at Pfizer, Inc. Research design.

Larry I. Lutwick, M.D., Professor of Medicine and Director of the Division of Infectious Diseases at the Veterans Administration New York Harbor Health Care System, Brooklyn Campus. Was Director of the Division of Infectious Diseases at Maimonides Medical Center.

Suzanne M. Lutwick, M.P.H., RN, Project Epidemiologist with the New York Anti-microbial Project at the Public Health Research Institute of New York. Was Director of Infection Control at Maimonides Medical Center.

Karen A. M. Myrie, M.D., M.P.H., Assistant Professor of Preventive Medicine and Community Health. Attending pediatrician at Lutheran Medical Center in Brooklyn, on the board of the Edwin Gould Services for Children and Families, active in the New York Coalition of 100 Black Women.

Pamela Sass, M.D., Assistant Professor of the Department of Family Practice, Director of Community Medicine Activities, and Course Director of Community Oriented Primary Care for Family Practice Residents. Curriculum reform for the College of Medicine, was physician and Medical Director, Montefiore Medical Center's Valentine Lane Family Practice Center.

Mahfouz H. Zaki, M.D., Dr.P.H., Clinical Professor of Preventive Medicine and Community Health. Preceptor for Department's first- and second-year small-group teaching programs for more than twenty-five years, former Director of Public Health for Suffolk County, scientific research on public-health issues widely cited in literature, innovative public-health interventions regularly duplicated throughout U.S., former Peace Corps physician, adviser in public health for Afghanistan.

STATE UNIVERSITY OF NEW YORK
STONY BROOK
THE GRADUATE SCHOOL

STONY BROOK UNIVERSITY, STATE UNIVERSITY OF NEW YORK
Medical Center
Graduate Program in Public Health

Program of Study

The Graduate Program in Public Health is a small, selective program that awards a Master of Public Health (M.P.H.) degree. The mission of the program is to train individuals who wish to integrate public health knowledge, skills, and values into their careers and provide leadership in the field.

The program emphasizes the population-health approach to public health. The hallmarks of population health are an ecological understanding of the determinants of health and a systems approach to solving health problems, an emphasis on proactively stabilizing and improving health among all populations, and insistence on accountability, evidence-based practice, and continuous performance improvement. The population-health approach requires multidisciplinary collaboration among scholars in the social, behavioral, clinical, and basic sciences and the humanities; development of comprehensive, sophisticated health-information systems; and use of advanced analytical tools to examine health problems and evaluate responses to them.

The program is designed for students with an advanced clinical or related degree or who are currently studying for such a degree, as well as for students who have only a bachelor's degree. The curriculum is 45 credits and consists of a public health core (24 credits), a practicum, a capstone seminar, and a concentration in evaluative sciences, community health, or the public health generalist. The core consists of ten required courses, including biostatistics, epidemiology, environmental and occupational health, data management and informatics, public health law, health systems performance, cost-benefit analysis, and the social and behavioral determinants of health. The practicum is a field-based experience that introduces students to the real world of public health practice. Most courses are offered in the late afternoon and evening, and there are course offerings throughout the year.

The Master of Public Health (M.P.H.) degree can be obtained concurrently with the M.D. degree. Medical students are advised to begin their course work for the M.P.H. degree early in their medical school training in order to complete the program within four years. During the academic year, tuition for the M.P.H. program is waived for full-time medical students. During the summer, medical students must pay tuition for M.P.H. courses. There may be scholarships and loans available for summer study.

Research Facilities

The Graduate Program in Public Health has established the Center for Health Services and Outcomes Research (CHSOR). The Center is a multidisciplinary research unit that combines expertise in economics, statistics, epidemiology, and medicine to address substantive issues in health-care delivery. As part of its research mission, the Center seeks to develop joint projects with researchers at Stony Brook University and health organizations throughout Long Island.

The Health Sciences Library serves the educational, clinical, and research needs of the faculty, staff, and students in the program; the Medical Center; and the University. It also functions as a regional resource, assisting health-care professionals throughout Nassau and Suffolk counties. It contains a large, well-equipped computer laboratory for students.

Financial Aid

Financial aid for graduate students is divided into three categories: grants, loans, and employment opportunities. Some financial aid programs are administered by the University, others by federal and state agencies to which the student applies directly. Special-purpose scholarships are also available to health professionals through private foundations and government agencies to which the student must apply directly. For more information, students should contact the Office of Student Services at the Health Sciences Center.

Cost of Study

In 2006–07, full-time tuition at 12 credits for entering in-state residents was $3450 per semester, while out-of-state residents and international students paid $5460. Additional fees for each semester, including (but not limited to) the infirmary, activity, technology, and transportation fee, amount to about $430. International students also pay a service fee of $35 per semester and an orientation fee of $50. Fees for the mandatory Student Health Insurance Plan vary depending on citizenship and employment status.

Living and Housing Costs

For 2006–07, Stony Brook calculated the cost of education excluding tuition, fees, and insurance at $13,520 per year. On-campus apartments range in cost from approximately $316 per month to approximately $1456 per month, depending on the size of the unit and the number of students sharing the space. Off-campus housing options include rooms, houses, and apartments that can be rented from $350 to $2500 per month. Costs including books, food, and transportation may vary depending on academic program and/or personal circumstances.

Student Group

In fall 2005, 43 percent of graduate students at Stony Brook University were men, 55 percent were white, 6 percent were of African origin, 7 percent were Asian American, 4 percent were Hispanic American, and 19 percent were international students.

Location

Close to the historic village of Stony Brook at the geographic midpoint of Long Island, the University lies about 50 miles east of Manhattan and 60 miles west of Montauk Point. It is only a short distance to the beaches of Fire Island, the elegant resorts of the Hamptons, and the vineyards of the East End. The internationally recognized research facilities of Brookhaven National Laboratory are nearby.

The University

In the forty years since its founding, the University has grown tremendously and is now recognized as one of the nation's important centers of learning and scholarship. Stony Brook recently joined the prestigious Association of American Universities, which is the invitation-only organization of the best research universities in the country. Stony Brook has been listed as one of the "100 Best Values in Higher Education" among public universities by *Kiplinger's Personal Finance* magazine.

Applying

Although admissions requirements are rigorous, the Graduate Program in Public Health aims to develop camaraderie, cooperation, and cohesiveness among students in each cohort. For this reason, admission to the program is during the fall semester only.

The admissions requirements for the program include a bachelor's degree from an accredited college or university, with a 3.0 GPA or better. The major must have an equivalent at the State University of New York (SUNY). Also required are official transcripts from all postsecondary schools. Transcripts for all degrees earned in schools outside the U.S. or Canada must be evaluated by an agency accredited by the National Association of Credential Evaluation Services, but the requirement for evaluation of transcripts is waived for graduates of foreign medical schools with a current license to practice in the U.S. Proof of licensure and good standing must be submitted for licensed health professionals. Applicants must submit official GRE (verbal, quantitative, and analytical), MCAT, DAT, or GMAT scores. This requirement is waived for applicants who have been awarded a doctoral degree from an accredited U.S. or Canadian college or university. Applicants currently employed for more than three years in the public health field may request a waiver of this requirement.

Three references must be provided from people who can address the applicant's capacity to provide leadership in public health and complete a course of graduate study. If the applicant is a student or has graduated within the last two years, at least one letter must be from a college or university faculty member with whom the applicant has studied. If the applicant is a member of the public health workforce, at least one letter must be from a senior administrator in the organization who is familiar with the applicant's work. Two essays of no more than 500 words each (applicants should visit the Web site for details) are required, as well as a personal interview, if requested by the Admissions Committee and any other requirements of the Graduate School.

The Admissions Committee considers all factors, including grades, GRE scores, recommendation letters, essays, prior training, and professional experience. It is a goal of the Admissions Committee to select applicants who have the academic capability, aptitude, character, personal qualities, and commitment to provide future value to society through leadership and creative contributions to the field of public health. In addition, the program requires that each entering student take a mathematics placement examination prior to enrollment. Also, students without a clinical background must provide certificates of completion for the following two online courses: Anatomy and Physiology 101 and Medical Terminology 101, available at http://www.universalclass.com. Students are admitted to the program on the condition that these courses will be completed by the end of the first semester.

There are special admission requirements for international students.

Correspondence and Information

Judy Greene, Practicum Coordinator
Graduate Program in Public Health
HSC Level 3, Room 071
Stony Brook University, State University of New York
Stony Brook, New York 11794-8338
Phone: 631-444-2074
E-mail: hsc_mph_stonybrook@notes.cc.sunysb.edu
Web site: http://www.hsc.stonybrook.edu/public_health_program/index.cfm

Stony Brook University, State University of New York

THE FACULTY AND THEIR RESEARCH

Core Faculty

Raymond L. Goldsteen, Professor and Director, Graduate Program; Dr.P.H., Columbia. Fairness and effectiveness of allocation policies for health-care resources.

Norman H. Edelman, Professor; M.D., NYU. Pulmonary medicine, health policy.

Karen Goldsteen, Research Associate Professor; Ph.D., Illinois at Urbana-Champaign. Social determinants of child health and well-being.

Melody Goodman, Assistant Professor; Ph.D., Harvard. Biostatistics, health disparities.

Lauren E. Hale, Assistant Professor; Ph.D., Princeton. Social determinants of health, demography.

Evonne Kaplan-Liss, Research Assistant Professor; M.P.H., Columbia; M.D., CUNY, Mount Sinai. Pediatrics, medical journalism, environmental health.

Hongdao Meng, Assistant Professor; Ph.D., Rochester. Health-services research.

John A. Rizzo, Professor; Ph.D., Brown. Health economics, clinical outcomes research.

Mohammed Saad, Professor; M.D., Egypt. Epidemiology of diabetes and cardiovascular diseases.

Affiliated Faculty

Lisa A. Benz Scott, Clinical Associate Professor of Health-Care Policy and Management; Ph.D., Johns Hopkins. Cardiovascular outcomes research.

Candyce Berger, Associate Professor of Social Welfare; Ph.D., UCLA. Child and maternal health.

David L. Ferguson, Professor of Technology and Society; Ph.D., Berkeley. Quantitative reasoning, problem solving, educational technologies, decision making.

Pierce Gardner, Professor of Medicine; M.D., Harvard. International health.

David G. Graham, Adjunct Professor; Chief Deputy Commissioner, Suffolk County Department of Health Services; M.D., M.P.H.

Steven Jonas, Professor of Preventive Medicine; M.D., Harvard. Health policy.

Thomas O'Riordan, Associate Professor of Medicine; M.D., University College (Dublin). Asthma, COPD, other respiratory diseases.

Nanci Rice, Clinical Associate Professor of Health-Care Policy and Management; Ph.D., NYU. Women's health.

Charles L. Robbins, Professor of Social Welfare; D.S.W., Yeshiva. Health, violence, and ethics; social justice; gender issues.

Warren C. Sanderson, Professor of Economics; Ph.D., Stanford. Economic history, demography.

Nancy J. Tomes, Professor of History; Ph.D., Pennsylvania. History of medicine and public health.

S. Van McCrary, Associate Professor of Preventive Medicine; M.P.H., Johns Hopkins; J.D., Tennessee; Ph.D., Texas Medical Branch. Bioethics, health law.

Mahfouz Zaki, Adjunct Professor; Suffolk County Department of Health Services; M.D.

UNIVERSITY OF COLORADO AT DENVER AND HEALTH SCIENCES CENTER
Department of Preventive Medicine and Biometrics
Master of Science in Public Health Program

Program of Study

The degree program leading to the Master of Science in Public Health (M.S.P.H.) is intended to provide graduate-level training that introduces students to the core content areas of public health. Specific program emphases include epidemiological research, community needs assessment, public health practice and ethics, environmental and occupational health, and health policy. The program's goals are to provide education for students in the core content and methodological areas of public health (epidemiology, biostatistics, health-care systems, occupational and environmental health, and social and community factors in health); to prepare students for practical application of acquired skills and knowledge to public and community health research, community needs assessment, and program planning and evaluation; to direct students to relevant elective course work and help them to apply all areas of program learning experiences to their individual interests and activities in the health field; to give students an opportunity to demonstrate an integration of acquired skills and knowledge, as well as an ability to organize, synthesize, and communicate these skills orally and in writing, through preparation and defense of a publishable research paper or a thesis; and to enrich graduate medical education programs and continuing education for public health professionals. The program would be of interest to those working or expecting to work in academic or clinical settings, industry, or government health agencies. It is accredited by the Council on Education for Public Health.

The program includes a core of required courses and a choice of electives that enable the student, in consultation with a faculty adviser, to plan an individual course of study that is responsive to the student's needs and interests. Electives may include Departmental offerings as well as a broad range of course offerings in other programs of the University of Colorado at Denver and Health Sciences Center and on the Boulder and Denver campuses of the University. Independent study may be organized with Departmental faculty members and through a variety of health agencies with which the Department enjoys excellent working relationships. Completion of the degree program requires 40 semester hours, including 4 hours toward a research project resulting in either a thesis or publishable research paper. Both full- and part-time study is encouraged. Full-time students normally graduate in about two years. Part-time students are allowed up to four years to complete the program. The program is committed to maintaining the high quality of faculty-student interactions and thus will remain relatively small, admitting approximately 35 new students each year.

Research Facilities

The Department houses a computer-user room, with personal computers and appropriate analytical software, which is available to students and faculty members in the Department. The Dennison Memorial Library serves the Health Sciences Center campus and contains more than 240,000 volumes and 1,900 periodicals. Research opportunities are available both through research projects directed by faculty members and through arrangements with the Colorado Department of Health, county health departments, and community health agencies.

Financial Aid

The Department grants a limited number of assistantships through funds available from the Graduate School. Other aid is available through the Office of Financial Aid, to which application can be made only after a student has been admitted to the program. Funds can include Federal Perkins Loans and Colorado Graduate Loans. Inquiries regarding financial aid should be addressed to the Office of Financial Aid, UCHSC, 4200 East Ninth Avenue, Box A-088 (telephone: 303-315-8364).

Cost of Study

The tuition for the 2005–06 academic year was $391 per credit hour for Colorado residents and $752 per credit hour for nonresidents. In addition, approximately $1500 is needed annually for the activity fees and medical insurance.

Living and Housing Costs

There is no on-campus housing, but there is an ample supply of apartments, duplexes, and houses in the Denver metropolitan area. Many of these accommodations are within walking distance of the University of Colorado at Denver and Health Sciences Center and are usually available for immediate occupancy. Average monthly rents for unfurnished housing near campus are $700 for one-bedroom apartments and $1000 for two-bedroom apartments. Houses rent for $1000 and up per month. Total monthly expenses, including costs of food and moderate entertainment, are estimated at $1000 for a single student and $1500 for a couple.

Student Group

Approximately 95 students are currently enrolled in the Master of Science in Public Health Program. They have a very broad range of experiences and career goals. Eighty percent are women, and about 30 percent are physicians.

Student Outcomes

A survey conducted in 2005 indicated that 85 percent of the respondents are currently working in the public health field. The majority of respondents indicated that they are currently working in a government or academic setting. The largest number of respondents described their current position as epidemiological research.

Location

The University of Colorado Health Sciences Center campus is located in a medical/public health complex approximately 3 miles from downtown Denver and the Colorado state capitol. The Denver metropolitan area is located at the foot of the Rocky Mountains. It offers all the cultural, recreational, athletic, and economic opportunities to be found in a major city.

The Center and The Department

The University of Colorado at Denver and Health Sciences Center is one of the two Denver campuses of the University of Colorado; the University also has a campus in Boulder and one in Colorado Springs. It includes the dental, medical, pharmacy, and nursing schools, University Hospital, and the graduate programs of the departments in the various schools.

The Department of Preventive Medicine and Biometrics has a multidisciplinary faculty actively involved in medical and graduate education, residency training, research, and service to the public health community and to the medical community at large. Faculty research interests include chronic disease epidemiology, perinatal epidemiology, injury epidemiology, medical care evaluation, health policy, medical ethics, preventive health care, environmental epidemiology, and biostatistics.

Applying

Application materials, which describe the admission requirements in detail, are available from the program office. A baccalaureate degree is required as a minimum. GRE General Test scores are required of all applicants. A brief statement describing the applicant's career goals and reasons for applying to the program is also expected. Interviews with faculty members may also be required. All application materials must be received by February 1 for entry in either the summer or fall semester.

Correspondence and Information

Director
Master of Science in Public Health Program
University of Colorado at Denver and Health Sciences Center
4200 East Ninth Avenue, Box B-119
Denver, Colorado 80262

Phone: 303-315-8359
E-mail: annette.hays@uchsc.edu
Web site: http://pmb.uchsc.edu/MSPH/index.html

University of Colorado at Denver and Health Sciences Center

THE FACULTY AND THEIR RESEARCH

Anna E. Barón, Professor; Ph.D., Texas, 1984. Biostatistics, epidemiology, discriminate analysis, survival analysis.

Phoebe Lindsey Barton, Professor and Director, M.S.P.H. Program; Ph.D., UCLA, 1987. Health policy, health financing, Medicaid, AIDS.

Judith Baxter, Assistant Professor; M.A., Denver, 1981. Demography, diabetes epidemiology.

Tim Byers, Professor; M.D./M.P.H., Indiana, 1973. Cancer epidemiology.

Lori Crane, Associate Professor; Ph.D., UCLA, 1991. Behavioral science and cancer.

Dana Dabelea, Associate Professor; M.D./Ph.D., Romania, 1990. Diabetes epidemiology, chronic disease epidemiology, life course epidemiology.

Carolyn DiGuiseppi, Associate Professor; M.D./M.P.H., Virginia, 1983. Pediatrics, preventive medicine, maternal and child health.

Judith Glazner, Assistant Professor; M.S.B.A., Denver, 1968. Indigent health care, health-care policy.

Richard F. Hamman, Professor and Chairman; M.D., Case Western Reserve, 1972; Dr.P.H., Johns Hopkins, 1978. Chronic disease epidemiology, environmental radiation, epidemiologic methods, clinical trials.

John Hokanson, Associate Professor; Ph.D., Washington (Seattle), 1998. Cardiovascular epidemiology, genetic epidemiology.

John Kittelson, Associate Professor; Ph.D., Arizona, 1996. Statistics.

Jenn Leiferman, Assistant Professor; Ph.D., Texas, 2000. Maternal and child health.

Dennis C. Lezotte, Professor; Ph.D., SUNY at Buffalo, 1975; Multivariate statistical techniques for clinical laboratory data, decision support systems.

Jill Litt, Assistant Professor; Ph.D., Johns Hopkins, 2000. Environmental health.

Julie A. Marshall, Professor; Ph.D., Washington (Seattle), 1987. Epidemiologic methods, diabetes epidemiology, disease etiology, nutrition.

Lee Newman, Professor; M.D., Vanderbilt, 1980. Occupational lung and allergic disorders, pulmonary immunology, toxicology, granulomatous diseases.

Jill Norris, Professor; Ph.D., Pennsylvania, 1990. Diabetes epidemiology, nutrition.

A. James Ruttenber, Associate Professor; M.D./Ph.D., Emory, 1981. Occupational and environmental health, risk assessment, environmental epidemiology, drug abuse epidemiology.

Mark Yarborough, Associate Professor Adjoint; Ph.D., Tennessee, 1984. Biomedical ethics.

Gary O. Zerbe, Professor; Ph.D., Ohio State, 1973. Growth curve analysis, applied multivariate analysis.

Selected Affiliated and Clinical Faculty

Ned Calonge, Assistant Professor; M.D., Colorado Health Sciences Center, 1981; M.P.H., Washington (Seattle), 1986. Family medicine.

Arthur J. Davidson, Assistant Professor; M.D., Einstein (Yeshiva), 1979; M.S.P.H., Colorado Health Sciences Center, 1988. Communicable disease epidemiology, community health.

Jackie Glover, Associate Professor; Ph.D., Georgetown, 1988. Bioethics.

Richard Hoffman, Assistant Clinical Professor; M.D., Texas, 1975; M.P.H., Johns Hopkins, 1983.

Steve Lowenstein, Professor; M.D./M.P.H., CUNY, Mount Sinai, 1974. Injury epidemiology and preventive medicine.

Dann Milne, Assistant Clinical Professor; Ph.D., Texas, 1975. Health economics.

Ann Christine Nyquist, Associate Professor; M.D./M.P.H., Michigan, 1987. Infectious diseases, pediatrics.

John Steiner, Assistant Professor; M.D., Pennsylvania, 1982; M.P.H., Washington (Seattle), 1987. Internal medicine, preventive medicine.

UNIVERSITY OF MEDICINE AND DENTISTRY OF NEW JERSEY

School of Public Health

Programs of Study	The University of Medicine and Dentistry of New Jersey (UMDNJ) School of Public Health is built on the expertise and strong partnership of the University of Medicine and Dentistry of New Jersey; Rutgers, The State University of New Jersey (RU); and New Jersey Institute of Technology (NJIT). Founded on a long history of public-health education between UMDNJ and RU that began in 1983 in New Jersey, the UMDNJ–School of Public Health was established in 1998 and is a statewide, multi-institutional, multicampus scholarly community dedicated to improving the health of diverse populations in New Jersey and elsewhere through collaborative teaching, research, and service. The School was fully accredited in 2001 as the first collaborative school of public health by the Council on Education for Public Health.
	The UMDNJ–School of Public Health confers the M.S. degree in biostatistics, the M.P.H. degree (jointly with RU and NJIT), and the Dr.P.H. and Ph.D. degrees (jointly with RU).
	Three campuses are strategically located within New Jersey and offer a variety of M.P.H. degree concentrations. Concentrations at the Newark Campus include dental public health, quantitative methods (biostatistics and epidemiology), and urban health administration; at the Piscataway/New Brunswick Campus, concentrations include biostatistics, environmental and occupational health, epidemiology, health education and behavioral science, and health systems and policy; and at the Stratford/Camden Campus, concentrations include health systems and policy.
	Several dual-degree programs are also offered with the seven other UMDNJ schools in partnership with RU and NJIT: New Jersey Medical School, Robert Wood Johnson Medical School, New Jersey Dental School, the School of Nursing, the School of Osteopathic Medicine, the School of Health Related Professions, and the Graduate School of Biomedical Sciences. The dual-degree programs are M.D./M.P.H., D.O./M.P.H., D.M.D./M.P.H., Psy.D./M.P.H., M.S. (in biomedical sciences)/M.P.H., M.S. (in community health nursing)/M.P.H., M.S.N./M.P.H., M.P.H./M.B.A., and M.P.H./M.S.P.A.
	Articulated B.S./M.P.H. programs with RU and William Paterson University of New Jersey and a B.A./M.P.H. program with RU offer highly qualified undergraduate students early coordinated pathways into M.P.H. degree programs.
	Certificate programs are also offered in clinical epidemiology (Newark; Piscataway/New Brunswick); environmental and occupational health (Piscataway/New Brunswick); General Public Health (all campuses); and public policy and oral health services administration (Newark).
	The master's degree program requires 45 credit hours. Full-time students may complete the program within two years; part-time students up to five years. The curriculum requirements include core courses (15–18 credits), courses required by the department (12–24 credits), elective courses (5–15 credits), and a final integrating experience that includes both a fieldwork project and a written report (6–9 credits). The Ph.D. degree program in public health is offered by the biostatistics, environmental and occupational health, epidemiology, health education and behavioral science, and health systems and policy departments. The Dr.P.H. degree program is offered by the biostatistics, environmental and occupational health, epidemiology, health education and behavioral science, and health systems and policy departments.
Research Facilities	A number of campus research facilities are available to provide integral resources in support of students and faculty members in public health degree programs at UMDNJ, Rutgers, and NJIT. Research is frequently conducted with a number of institutes and centers located throughout New Jersey, such as the Environmental and Occupational Health Sciences Institute; The Cancer Institute of New Jersey; the Ozone Research Center; the Rutgers University Institute for Health, Health Care Policy and Aging Research; the Violence Institute of New Jersey at UMDNJ; the UMDNJ–School of Public Health's Institute for the Elimination of Health Disparities; the UMDNJ–School of Public Health's Tobacco Dependence Program; the UMDNJ–School of Public Health's New Jersey Center for Public Health Preparedness at UMDNJ; and the National Tuberculosis Center. The sociodemographic and environmental factors that combine to make graduate public health training in New Jersey timely and useful also form the mandate for the School's research agenda.
Financial Aid	Financial aid includes the Federal Perkins Loan program, Federal Stafford Student Loan (subsidized and unsubsidized), New Jersey Class Loan, and other alternative loan programs. Grants include the Educational Opportunity Fund (EOF) and Disadvantaged Student Fund (DSF). There are also teaching assistantships that provide annual stipends plus remission of tuition.
Cost of Study	Tuition for the academic year 2006–07 for New Jersey residents was $431 per credit hour. Tuition for out-of-state residents was $633 per credit hour. The average increase in tuition over the past three years has been 9 percent.
Living and Housing Costs	The national cost-of-living index places the area at about the median. Attractive and comfortable residence facilities for graduate students are available.
Student Group	As of fall 2006, there were nearly 411 students enrolled in the School of Public Health. This number includes both full- and part-time students currently employed in the health field (i.e., dentists, nurses, physicians, and environmental scientists) as well as students who recently received their bachelor's degree and those pursuing a dual degree in conjunction with other programs offered at the schools.
Location	The UMDNJ–School of Public Health has three locations. The Newark Campus is located in northern New Jersey and the Piscataway/New Brunswick Campus is located in central New Jersey; both campuses are within a 1-hour commute of New York City by car, train, or bus. The Stratford/Camden Campus is located in southern New Jersey and is within a 30-minute commute by car or train of Philadelphia.
The School	The UMDNJ–School of Public Health is a statewide institution. It is a multicampus scholarly community dedicated to improving the health of diverse populations in New Jersey and elsewhere through its collaborative teaching, research, and service.
Applying	For the M.P.H., M.S., Ph.D., and Dr.P.H. degree programs, the application process is online through the Schools of Public Health Application Service Web sit located at http://www.sophas.org.
	The UMDNJ–School of Public Health recognizes the need for a separate application for applicants who are part of a residency/fellowship program, have a UMDNJ faculty appointment, or are interested in applying for certificates, dual degrees, or nonmatriculation status. Applicants who fall into any of these categories should contact one of the three Campus Administrative Offices to request an application.
	Applicants interested in taking two courses only and/or enrolling for a single semester should complete the "nonmatriculating short form" that can be found on the School's Web site (http://sph.umdnj.edu) under Admissions, How to Apply.
	A bachelor's degree with at least a B average in academic work is required for admission to the M.P.H. degree program. An applicant's qualifications are substantiated by academic transcripts, GRE General Test scores, and references. As part of the application, an essay is required. A master's degree in a relevant field is required to enter either the Dr.P.H. or the Ph.D. program, as are GRE scores and three letters of recommendation, of which at least two must be from people who have known the candidate in an academic setting. With regard to all the programs of study, TOEFL scores are required of students from countries in which English is not the native language. All M.P.H. and M.S. degree and certificate program applicants for the semester must submit materials by May 1 or by February 15 for early decision. The application deadline for spring semester is October 1. All doctoral program applicants must apply by April 1 or by January 1 for early decision.

Correspondence and Information		

Newark Campus:
Rhonda Barnes
Stanley S. Bergen Jr. Building, SSB701
UMDNJ–School of Public Health
65 Bergen Street
P.O. Box 1709
Newark, New Jersey 07107-1709
Phone: 973-972-7212
Fax: 973-972-8032
E-mail: barnesrb@umdnj.edu

Piscataway/New Brunswick Campus:
Janet Zamorski
First Floor, Room 135
UMDNJ–School of Public Health
683 Hoes Lane, West
P.O. Box 9
Piscataway, New Jersey 08854
Phone: 732-235-4646
Fax: 732-235-5476
E-mail: zamorsja@umdnj.edu

Stratford/Camden Campus:
Vanessa Jago
Primary Care Center, Suite 243
UMDNJ–School of Public Health
40 East Laurel Road
Stratford, New Jersey 08084
Phone: 856-566-2790
Fax: 856-566-2882
E-mail: jagovj@umdnj.edu

University of Medicine and Dentistry of New Jersey

THE FACULTY

Biostatistics

Weichung Shih, Ph.D., Professor and Department Chair.
Irving Hwang, Ph.D., Adjunct Professor.
Leo Korn, Ph.D., Adjunct Assistant Professor.
K. Gordon Lan, Ph.D., Adjunct Professor.
Michael Lee, Ph.D., Adjunct Assistant Professor.
Yong Lin, Ph.D., Associate Professor.
Kaifeng Lu, Ph.D., Adjunct Assistant Professor
Shou-En Lu, Ph.D., Assistant Professor.
Dirk Moore, Ph.D., Associate Professor.
Hui Quan, Ph.D., Adjunct Associate Professor.
Pamela Ohman Strickland, Ph.D., Associate Professor.
Yujun Wu, Ph.D., Assistant Professor.

Dental Public Health

Rufus Caine Jr., D.D.S., M.P.H., Associate Professor and Department Chair; primary at UMDNJ–New Jersey Dental School.
Michael Conte, D.D.S., D.M.D., M.P.H., Assistant Professor; primary at UMDNJ–New Jersey Dental School.
Joseph Holtzman, Ph.D., Professor; primary at UMDNJ–New Jersey Dental School.
Richard Montgomery, D.D.S., M.P.H., Associate Professor; primary at UMDNJ–New Jersey Dental School.
Samuel Quek, D.M.D., M.P.H., Adjunct Assistant Professor; primary at UMDNJ–New Jersey Dental School.

Environmental and Occupational Health

Junfeng Zhang, Ph.D., Professor and Department Chair.
Brian Buckley, Ph.D., Adjunct Associate Professor; primary at Rutgers University.
Joanna Burger, Ph.D., Professor; primary at the Department of Cell Biology and Neuroscience, Rutgers University.
Gary J. Centifonti, M.S., Adjunct Instructor.
Robert Chapman, M.D., M.P.H., Adjunct Professor.
John Dobi, Ph.D., Adjunct Associate Professor; primary at New Jersey Institute of Technology.
Fred Ellerbusch, Ph.D., M.P.H., Adjunct Assistant Professor.
Linda Erdreich, Ph.D., Adjunct Associate Professor.
Mitchell Erickson, Ph.D., Adjunct Professor.
Nancy Fiedler, Ph.D., Associate Professor; primary at UMDNJ–Robert Wood Johnson Medical School.
Adam Finkel, Sc.D., M.P.P., CIH, Professor.
Michael Gallo, Ph.D., Professor; primary at UMDNJ–Robert Wood Johnson Medical School.
Gary Garetano, Ph.D., Adjunct Instructor.
Seymour Garte, Ph.D., Adjunct Professor; primary at Graduate School of Public Health, University of Pittsburgh.
Michael Gochfeld, M.D., Ph.D., Professor; primary at UMDNJ–Robert Wood Johnson Medical School.
Jay Goldring, Ph.D., M.S.P.H., Adjunct Assistant Professor.
Robert M. Goodman, Ph.D., Professor, primary at Cook College, Rutgers University.
George Hamilton, Ph.D., Professor; primary at Cook College, Rutgers University.
Drew Harris, D.P.M., M.P.H., Assistant Professor.
Jun-Yan Hong, Ph.D., Professor.
Paromita Hore, Ph.D., M.P.H., Adjunct Assistant Professor.
Howard Kipen, M.D., M.P.H., Professor; primary at UMDNJ–Robert Wood Johnson Medical School.
Robert Laumbach, M.P.H., M.D., CIH, Assistant Professor; primary at UMDNJ–Robert Wood Johnson Medical School.
Paul Lioy, Ph.D., Professor; primary at UMDNJ–Robert Wood Johnson Medical School.
Jill Lipoti, Ph.D., Adjunct Assistant Professor.
Florence J. Lotrowski, J.D., Adjunct Assistant Professor.
Gediminas Mainelis, Ph.D., Assistant Professor; primary at Cook College, Rutgers University.
Leroy Meyer, M.S., Adjunct Instructor.
Sandra N. Mohr, M.D., M.P.H., Adjunct Associate Professor.
Omowunmi Osinubi, M.D., Assistant Professor.
Douglas Pastore, M.S., Adjunct Instructor.
Glenn Paulson, Ph.D., Professor and Associate Dean for Research.
Joseph Ponessa, Ph.D., Professor; primary at Cook College, Rutgers University.
Mark G. Robson, Ph.D., M.P.H., Associate Professor; primary at Cook College, Rutgers University.
Edward V. Sargent, Ph.D., M.P.H., Adjunct Professor.
Robert Snyder, Ph.D., Professor; primary at the Ernest Mario School of Pharmacy, Rutgers University.
Alan Stern, Dr.P.H., M.P.H., Adjunct Associate Professor.
Robert Tate, Ph.D., Professor; primary at Cook College, Rutgers University.
Rodney Turpin, M.S., Adjunct Assistant Professor.
Iris Udasin, M.D., Associate Professor; primary at UMDNJ–Robert Wood Johnson Medical School.
Eric Vowinkel, Ph.D., Adjunct Associate Professor.
Clifford Weisel, Ph.D., Professor; primary at UMDNJ–Robert Wood Johnson Medical School.

Epidemiology

George Rhoads, M.D., M.P.H., Professor, Acting Department Chair, and Associate Dean.
Cande Ananth, Ph.D., M.P.H., Associate Professor; primary at UMDNJ–Robert Wood Johnson Medical School.
Roger Anderson, Dr.P.H., Adjunct Professor.
Elisa Bandera, M.D., Ph.D., Assistant Professor; primary at UMDNJ–Robert Wood Johnson Medical School.
Eddy Bresnitz, M.D., Adjunct Professor.
Randall S. Burd, M.D., Ph.D., Associate Professor; primary at UMDNJ-Robert Wood Johnson Medical School.
Ronald Cody, Ed.D., Adjunct Professor.
Benjamin Crabtree, Ph.D., Professor; primary at UMDNJ–Robert Wood Johnson Medical School.
Kitaw Demissie, M.D., Ph.D., Associate Professor.
George DiFerdinando, M.D., M.P.H., Adjunct Professor.
Robert Epstein, M.D., Adjunct Professor.
Joanne K. Fagan, Ph.D., M.P.H., Assistant Professor.
Kristina Feja, M.D., M.P.H., Adjunct Assistant Professor.
Mark Fulcomer, Ph.D., Adjunct Associate Professor.
Michael Greenberg, Ph.D., Professor; primary at the Edward J. Bloustein School of Planning and Public Policy, Rutgers University.
Steven Kairys, M.D., M.P.H., Adjunct Professor.
Judith Klotz, Dr.P.H., Adjunct Associate Professor.
Stephen Marcella, M.D., M.P.H., Assistant Professor.
Elizabeth Marshall, Ph.D., Adjunct Associate Professor.
Jane Miller, Ph.D., Associate Professor; primary at the Edward J. Bloustein School of Planning and Public Policy, Rutgers University.
Barbara E. Montana, M.D., M.P.H., Adjunct Assistant Professor.
Robert Morgan, M.D., M.P.H., Assistant Professor.
Sindy Paul, M.D., M.P.H., Adjunct Associate Professor.
Sherry Pomerantz, Ph.D., Adjunct Assistant Professor; primary at UMDNJ–School of Osteopathic Medicine.
David Rich, Sc.D., M.P.H., Assistant Professor.
Dona Schneider, M.P.H., Ph.D., Professor; primary at the Edward J. Bloustein School of Planning and Public Policy, Rutgers University.
John Smulian, M.D., M.P.H., Professor; primary at UMDNJ–Robert Wood Johnson Medical School.
Elizabeth Sosnowska, M.S.L.I.S., Adjunct Instructor.
Patty Vitale, M.D., M.P.H., Adjunct Assistant Professor.
Daniel Wartenberg, Ph.D., Professor; primary at UMDNJ–Robert Wood Johnson Medical School.

Health Education and Behavioral Science

Lynn Waishwell, M.H.E., Ph.D., CHES, Assistant Professor and Department Chair.
Diane Abatemarco, M.S.W., Ph.D., Adjunct Assistant Professor.
Neal Boyd, M.S.P.H., Ed.D., Professor, Associate Dean for Education and Assessment, and Associate Dean, Newark Campus.
Diane Brown, Ph.D., Professor and Executive Director, Institute for the Elimination of Health Disparities, UMDNJ–School of Public Health.
Patrick Clifford, Ph.D., Professor.
H. Liesel Copeland, Ph.D., Adjunct Assistant Professor.
Cristine Delnevo, M.P.H., Ph.D., Associate Professor.
Jonathan Foulds, Ph.D., Associate Professor and Director, Tobacco Dependence Program, UMDNJ–School of Public Health.
Denise C. Fyffe, Ph.D., Assistant Professor.
Fern Goodhart, M.S., Adjunct Instructor.
Audrey Gotsch, Dr.P.H., CHES, Professor and Dean.
Mary Hrywna, M.P.H., Instructor.
Rickie Kashdan, M.P.H., Adjunct Instructor.
Susan Lachenmayr, M.P.H., CHES, Adjunct Instructor.
Jane Lewis, Dr.P.H., Associate Professor.
Andrew F. Pleasant, Ph.D., Assistant Professor; primary at Cook College, Rutgers University.
Linda S. Potter, Dr.P.H., Adjunct Assistant Professor.
Donna Richardson, M.S.W., Instructor.
Gloria Rodriguez, D.S.W., Adjunct Assistant Professor.
Mitchel Rosen, M.S.P.H., Instructor and Director, Office of Public Health Practice, UMDNJ–School of Public Health.
Susan Santos, Ph.D., Assistant Professor.
Barry Schlegel, Ed.D., CIH, Assistant Professor.
Louise Weidner, M.S.P.H., Ph.D., Adjunct Assistant Professor.
Jill Williams, M.D., Associate Professor; primary at UMDNJ–Robert Wood Johnson Medical School.
Tsering Yangdon, M.Sc.P.H., CHES, Adjunct Instructor.

Health Systems and Policy

Lois Grau, Ph.D., Associate Professor and Department Chair.
Peter V. Abatemarco, J.D., Adjunct Assistant Professor.
John Beckley, M.P.H., Adjunct Instructor.
Joel Cantor, Sc.D., Professor; primary at the Edward J. Bloustein School of Planning and Public Policy, Rutgers University.
Stephen Crystal, Ph.D., Professor; primary at the Graduate School of Social Work, Rutgers University.
Ethan Ellis, M.A., Adjunct Associate Professor.
Vicki Freedman, Ph.D., Professor.
James Garnett, Ph.D., Professor; primary at the Graduate School, Rutgers University, Camden.
Irina Grafova, Ph.D., Assistant Professor.
Andrew Greene, M.H.C.A., Adjunct Associate Professor.
Susan Hammerman, Ph.D., Assistant Professor.
George Hampton, B.A., Assistant Professor.
Stephen K. Jones, M.A. Adjunct Instructor.
Frank Lautenberg, B.S., Distinguished Visiting Professor.
Donald Light, Ph.D., Professor; primary at UMDNJ–School of Osteopathic Medicine.
Micki McIntyre, M.S., Adjunct Instructor.
Russell McIntyre, Th.D., Professor; primary at UMDNJ–Robert Wood Johnson Medical School.
Andrew Miller, M.P.H., M.D., Adjunct Associate Professor.
Alan Monheit, Ph.D., Professor.
Sanjay Pandey, Ph.D., Assistant Professor; primary at the Graduate School, Rutgers University, Camden.
Jeannette Rogowski, Ph.D., University Professor and Director, Center for Health Economics and Health Policy, UMDNJ–School of Public Health.
Usha Sambamoorthi, Ph.D., Adjunct Associate Professor.
Marcia Sass, Sc.D., Assistant Professor.
Shirley Smoyak, Ph.D., Professor; primary at the Edward J. Bloustein School of Planning and Public Policy, Rutgers University.
Michael Steinberg, M.P.H., M.D., Assistant Professor; primary at UMDNJ–Robert Wood Johnson Medical School.
Dong-Churl Suh, Ph.D., Associate Professor; primary at the Ernest Mario School of Pharmacy, Rutgers University.
Bernadette West, Ph.D., Assistant Professor and Assistant Dean, Stratford/Camden Campus and Community Health.
Nancy Wolff, Ph.D., Associate Professor; primary at the Edward J. Bloustein School of Planning and Public Policy, Rutgers University.
Douglas Ziedonis, M.P.H., M.D., Professor; primary at UMDNJ–Robert Wood Johnson Medical School.
Leah Ziskin, M.D., Adjunct Associate Professor.

Quantitative Methods: Biostatistics and Epidemiology

William Halperin, M.D., Dr.P.H., Professor and Department Chair; primary at UMDNJ–New Jersey Medical School.
Stephen Baker, M.P.H., M.D., Professor; primary at UMDNJ–New Jersey Medical School.
John Bogden, Ph.D., Professor; primary at UMDNJ–New Jersey Medical School.
Michael Brimacombe, Ph.D., Associate Professor; primary at UMDNJ–New Jersey Medical School.
Amy Davidow, Ph.D., Associate Professor; primary at UMDNJ–New Jersey Medical School.
Andrew Dean, M.P.H., M.D., Adjunct Professor; primary at UMDNJ–New Jersey Medical School.
Patricia Fleming, Ph.D., Professor; primary at UMDNJ–New Jersey Medical School.
Katherine Hempstead, Ph.D., Adjunct Assistant Professor.
Bart Holland, M.P.H., Ph.D., Associate Professor; primary at UMDNJ–New Jersey Medical School.
David Hom, M.S., Assistant Professor; primary at UMDNJ–New Jersey Medical School.
Wansoo Im, Ph.D., Adjunct Instructor.
Debra Kantor, Ph.D., Assistant Professor; primary at UMDNJ–New Jersey Medical School.
Cheryl Kennedy, M.D., Associate Professor; primary at UMDNJ–New Jersey Medical School.
Soyeon Kim, Sc.D., Assistant Professor; primary at UMDNJ–New Jersey Medical School.
Patricia Kloser, M.P.H., M.D., Professor; primary at UMDNJ–New Jersey Medical School.
Marvin Lavenhar, Ph.D., M.P.H., Adjunct Professor; primary at UMDNJ–New Jersey Medical School.
Robert Lavery, M.A., Adjunct Instructor.
Bonita Mangura, M.D., Professor; primary at UMDNJ–New Jersey Medical School.
G. Reza Najem, M.P.H., M.D., Ph.D., Professor; primary at UMDNJ–New Jersey Medical School.
Cheongeun Oh, Ph.D., Assistant Professor; primary at UMDNJ–New Jersey Medical School.
James Oleske, M.P.H., M.D., Professor; primary at UMDNJ–New Jersey Medical School.
Marian Passannante, Ph.D., Associate Professor; primary at UMDNJ–New Jersey Medical School.
Lee Reichman, M.P.H., M.D., Professor; primary at UMDNJ–New Jersey Medical School.
Mitchell Singal, M.D., M.P.H., Adjunct Instructor.
Anushua Sinha, M.D., M.P.H., Assistant Professor; primary at UMDNJ–New Jersey Medical School.
Joan Skurnick, Ph.D., Associate Professor; primary at UMDNJ–New Jersey Medical School.
Zdravko Vassilev, M.D., M.P.H., Assistant Professor; primary at UMDNJ–New Jersey Medical School.
Stanley Weiss, M.D., Professor; primary at UMDNJ–New Jersey Medical School.
Peter Wenger, M.D., Associate Professor; primary at UMDNJ–New Jersey Medical School.

Urban Health Administration

Evan Stark, Ph.D., Associate Professor and Department Chair; primary at the College of Arts and Sciences, Rutgers University, Newark.
W. Patrick Beaton, Ph.D., Professor; primary at New Jersey Institute of Technology.
Kathleen Callahan, Ph.D., Assistant Professor; primary at the College of Arts and Sciences, Rutgers University, Newark.
John Douard, J.D., Ph.D., Adjunct Assistant Professor.
Lucille Eller, Ph.D., Assistant Professor; primary at the College of Nursing, Rutgers University.
Norbert Elliot, Ph.D., Professor; primary at New Jersey Institute of Technology.
Terry Konn, Ph.D., Adjunct Instructor.
Cynthia Lischick, Ph.D., Adjunct Instructor.
Gerald Miller, Ph.D., Professor, primary at the College of Arts and Sciences, Rutgers University, Newark.
Dorothy Olshfski, Ph.D., Associate Professor; primary at the College of Arts and Sciences, Rutgers University, Newark.
Chimezie Ozurumba, M.A., Adjunct Instructor; primary at Graduate School, Rutgers University, Camden.
Suzanne Piotrowski, Ph.D., Assistant Professor; primary at the College of Arts and Sciences, Rutgers University, Newark.
Byron Price, Ph.D., Assistant Professor; primary at the College of Arts and Sciences, Rutgers University, Newark.
Norma Riccucci, Ph.D., Professor; primary at the College of Arts and Sciences, Rutgers University, Newark.

UNIVERSITY OF MIAMI

Miller School of Medicine
Department of Epidemiology and Public Health
Teaching Programs

Programs of Study

The Department of Epidemiology and Public Health (DEPH) offers the Master of Public Health (M.P.H.) degree, the Master of Science in Public Health (M.S.P.H.) degree, and a Ph.D. degree in epidemiology. The mission of the Department is to provide up-to-date educational programs to practicing health professionals and to students newly entering the field; to conduct, stimulate, and guide research activities relevant to health needs; and to provide assistance to health agencies for disease prevention, health promotion and education, environmental health, and the planning, analysis, and management of health services. The M.P.H. program is accredited by the Council on Education for Public Health. It is a 45-credit-hour program requiring 27 credit hours of core courses, 6 credit hours for supervised field placement (capstone experience), and 12 credit hours of electives. Full-time students can be expected to complete the program in two years. A joint degree in public health and public health administration (M.P.A./M.P.H.) is offered through the School of Business and the DEPH. The School of Law and the DEPH collaborate to offer a J.D./M.P.H. degree. Students can also pursue the M.P.H. degree jointly with the Master of Arts in International Administration (M.A.I.A.) degree. For students who are enrolled in the University of Miami's Medical School, the Department offers a combined M.D./M.P.H. degree. In addition, the DEPH program is affiliated with the M.P.H. program at Florida International University and the Palm Beach County Health Department's Preventive Medicine Residency Program. The M.S.P.H. program is an academic research degree designed for students who wish to prepare for further study at the doctoral level or to prepare for research or technical positions in government, industry, academia, or private institutions. Studies include many of the core disciplines included in the M.P.H. degree, with an additional emphasis on advanced research methods and quantitative analysis skills. The M.S.P.H. program is a 45-credit-hour program requiring 24 credit hours of core courses, 6 credit hours for the capstone experience, and 15 credit hours of electives in area(s) of interest. The Doctor of Philosophy (Ph.D.) program in epidemiology is an intensive research training program for students with prior training in epidemiology or related disciplines. It provides advanced education and training for students seeking a professional career in medical- and health-related research, as well as physicians and other persons who have attained professional degrees who seek to integrate epidemiologic research and methods into their ongoing careers. The program is primarily designed for persons who have an M.P.H. degree, as well as physicians and others who have a master's or doctoral degree in a related discipline and who have completed prerequisite courses in epidemiology and biostatistics. The Ph.D. curriculum is planned on an individual basis and is based on a core of 27 credit hours, 9 credit hours in elective courses, and a minimum of 24 credit hours in a doctoral dissertation. Students should expect to complete formal course work within two years of admission to the program.

Research Facilities

Facilities of the Department of Epidemiology and Public Health and affiliated research centers include a student computer laboratory, the HIV/AIDS Surveillance Program, the Alpha 1 Foundation Registry, the Florida Cancer Data System, the Firefighter's Fitness Assessment Center, the Drug Abuse and AIDS Research Center (DAARC), the Center for Treatment Research on Adolescent Drug Abuse (CTRADA), and an Assessment Center that provides facilities and trained personnel for clinical assessments, phlebotomy, focus groups, and personal and computer-assisted interviews. Library facilities include the Calder Medical Library, the Richter Library on the Coral Gables campus, and various other libraries located within specific schools.

Financial Aid

A variety of financial assistance programs are available through the Office of Financial Assistance Services, including grants, educational loans, student employment, and tuition payment plans. The Department has research and teaching assistantships that are available based on faculty grants and Departmental funding.

Cost of Study

Graduate tuition was $1280 per credit hour for the 2006–07 school year. Funds may be available to subsidize the tuition costs of master's students. Subsidized credits and tuition are subject to change each academic year. For Ph.D. students, tuition may be covered internally.

Living and Housing Costs

There is no on-campus housing available for graduate students. However, off-campus housing is available in the vicinity. The cost of living in Miami, including housing, food, entertainment, and transportation, is equivalent to that of other metropolitan areas.

Student Group

In 2005–06, there were 94 students enrolled in the DEPH teaching programs: 54 M.P.H. students, 17 Ph.D. students, 19 students from other departments or the postbaccalaureate program, and 4 students from the affiliated program at Florida International University. Sixteen percent are physicians, and 42 percent are employed in the public health sector. Sixty-six percent of the students are women, and more than 40 percent are members of minority groups.

Student Outcomes

Career planning and placement is available from the DEPH Teaching Programs Office, the Teaching Programs director and academic advisers, the Toppel Career Planning and Placement Center, the Ziff Graduate Placement Center for M.P.A./M.P.H. students, and the Law School Placement Center for J.D./M.PH. students. All graduates who have sought employment have obtained positions as research assistants or project directors, administrators, and public health providers for the University, various hospitals, nonprofit organizations, and federal, state, or local public health programs.

Location

Miami is a cosmopolitan, multilingual community. It offers a variety of sporting events, concerts, plays, festivals, and operas. Nearby parks, ocean beaches, tropical gardens, and wildlife sanctuaries offer abundant opportunities for outdoor recreation.

The University

The University, founded in 1925, is an independent, private institution that consists of fourteen colleges and schools. The Department of Epidemiology and Public Health is located in the School of Medicine, near downtown Miami, adjacent to several hospitals. The Coral Gables campus of the University is about 15 minutes away and is easily accessible by Metrorail.

Applying

Admission into the master's programs (M.P.H. and M.S.P.H.) is offered in the fall and spring terms. Application deadlines are April 1 and November 15, respectively. The criteria for admission include a 400-word letter of intent and a minimum guideline combined verbal and quantitative score of 1100 on the Graduate Record Examinations (GRE) taken within the last five years. Ph.D. applications are accepted for the fall semester only, with a submission deadline of January 31. The criteria for admission into the Ph.D. program include a 1,000-word letter of intent and a minimum guideline combined verbal and quantitative score of 1100 on the GRE taken within the last five years, with a suggested minimum score of 550 on each section. The Ph.D. program requires previous course work in epidemiology and biostatistics. Highly qualified Ph.D. candidates are also contacted to schedule an interview with faculty members as part of the admissions process. All applicants for the master's or Ph.D. programs are required to submit a completed application, official transcripts from all previous colleges or universities that show courses and a minimum grade point average of 3.0, a written letter of intent, supporting evidence of computer literacy and competency, three letters of recommendation, and an updated resume or curriculum vitae. International applicants are also required to pass the TOEFL with a guideline minimum score of 213 (computer-based) or 550 (paper-based).

Correspondence and Information

James Wilkinson, M.D., M.P.H.
Director, Teaching Programs
Department of Epidemiology and Public Health (R-669)
Miller School of Medicine
University of Miami
P.O. Box 016069
Miami, Florida 33101
Phone: 305-243-6759
Fax: 305-243-3384
E-mail: gpph@med.miami.edu
Web site: http://www.biomed.miami.edu/epi/

University of Miami

THE FACULTY AND THEIR RESEARCH

Kristopher Arheart, Research Associate Professor; Ed.D., Memphis, 1993. Research methods, design and analysis of experiments, hierarchical models.

John C. Beier, Professor; Sc.D., Johns Hopkins, 1980. Tropical medicine, infectious diseases, insect physiology, malaria.

Margaret Byrne, Research Assistant Professor; Ph.D., Florida, 1996. Cancer screening and prevention, financial incentives, human subjects research, medical ethics.

Lee Crandall, Professor; Ph.D., Purdue, 1976. Rural health care, substance abuse, HIV/AIDS, bioethics.

Gayle A. Dakof, Research Assistant Professor; Ph.D., Berkeley, 1986. Adolescent drug abuse, family therapy, drug abuse prevention.

Robert C. Duncan, Professor; Ph.D., Oklahoma, 1966. Clinical trials, mathematical modeling.

Lora E. Fleming, Associate Professor; M.D./M.P.H., Harvard, 1984; Ph.D., Yale, 1997. Occupational and environmental health, epidemiology, medicine.

Orlando Gomez-Marin, Associate Professor; Ph.D., Minnesota, 1981. Biostatistics, clinical trials, cardiovascular disease, epidemiology and prevention, women's health.

Kenneth Goodman, Research Assistant Professor; Ph.D., Miami (Florida), 1991. Philosophy of science, bioethics, medical informatics.

Dolores Katz, Voluntary Assistant Professor; Ph.D., Michigan, 1995. Infectious diseases, cardiovascular diseases, study design, epidemiologic methods.

David J. Lee, Associate Professor; Ph.D., Texas Medical Branch, 1989. Cardiovascular disease epidemiology and prevention, psychosocial factors and health.

Howard A. Liddle, Professor; Ed.D., Northern Illinois, 1974. Adolescent drug abuse, family therapy, drug abuse prevention.

Kathryn E. McCollister, Research Assistant Professor; Ph.D., Florida International, 1999. Health economics, health policy.

Clyde B. McCoy, Professor and Chair; Ph.D., Cincinnati, 1970. Substance abuse, cancer, HIV/AIDS, demography, community health.

Shari Messinger, Assistant Professor; Ph.D., Michigan, 2002. Biostatistics, outcomes research.

Lisa Metsch, Associate Professor; Ph.D., Florida, 1994. Health services research, substance abuse policy, women's health.

Margaret Pereyra, Research Assistant Professor; Dr.P.H., UCLA, 2003. Health services research, maternal and child health, international health, applied biostatistics.

Joshua A. Perper, Voluntary Clinical Professor and Broward County Medical Examiner; M.D., 1962, LL.B., 1966, Hebrew (Jerusalem). Sudden unexpected natural deaths, alcoholism and drug related deaths, environmental diseases, suicide and violent deaths.

Tatiana Perrino, Assistant Professor; Psy.D., Rutgers, 1998. HIV and drug abuse prevention, health promotion in minority populations, risk reduction interventions for adolescents.

Sherri Porcelain, Voluntary Instructor; M.P.H., Miami (Florida), 1985. International health planning and policy implementation, community-based health programs, women and international health concerns, overexposure to sun and skin cancer.

Isildinha M. Reis, Research Assistant Professor; Dr.P.H., UCLA, 1996. Statistical methods, design and analysis of clinical trials.

Cynthia Rowe, Assistant Professor; Ph.D., Temple, 1998. Adolescent substance abuse, adolescent drug treatment, intervention design.

Eleni Sfakianki, Voluntary Associate Professor and Medical Executive Director, Dade County Health Department; M.D., Thessaloniki, 1964; M.S.P.H., Miami (Florida), 1983. Maternal and child health, development of systems for provision of health care to indigent populations.

Donna E. Shalala, Professor; Ph.D., Syracuse, 1970. Public policy, state/urban government and finance, political economy of education.

Edward J. Trapido, Professor; Vice Chair; Director, Ph.D. Program in Epidemiology; and Director, Teaching Programs in Epidemiology and Public Health; Sc.D., Harvard, 1981. Cancer epidemiology, breast cancer, disease surveillance, cancer prevention and control.

James D. Wilkinson, Research Assistant Professor and Director, Master's Programs in Public Health; M.D., South Florida, 1978; M.P.H., Miami (Florida), 1999. Cancer epidemiology, cancer prevention and control, disease surveillance, AIDS epidemiology.

UNIVERSITY OF PITTSBURGH

Graduate School of Public Health

Programs of Study

The Graduate School of Public Health (GSPH) offers courses of study and research in many areas, including biostatistics, chronic disease epidemiology, community health sciences, health administration, health policy analysis, human genetics, genetic counseling, environmental and occupational health, environmental and occupational medicine, health promotion and education, infectious disease epidemiology, infectious diseases and microbiology, psychiatric epidemiology, public health social work, public health statistics, and telecommunications and health. Involvement in such specific research units as the Center for Public Health Practice, Center for Minority Health, Health Policy Institute, Pittsburgh Genetics Institute, Center for Public Health Preparedness, and others is possible.

The degrees offered are the Master of Health Administration, Master of Public Health, Master of Science, Doctor of Philosophy, and Doctor of Public Health. The following joint degrees are available: J.D./M.P.H., M.P.H./M.I.D., M.P.H./M.P.A., M.P.H./Ph.D. in anthropology, M.P.H./Ph.D. in social work, M.P.H./M.S.W, and M.S. in genetic counseling/M.P.H. in public health genetics. A multidisciplinary M.P.H. is offered for experienced health professionals and advanced students. Certificates in the evaluation of health education programs; global health; lesbian, gay, bisexual, and transgender (LGBT) health; minority health research; public health genetics; public health preparedness and disaster response; recruitment of research subjects; and risk assessment are offered.

Research Facilities

GSPH is a major research institution, with research activities ranging from the basic laboratory sciences to applied public health evaluations. The School currently ranks third among public health schools in total NIH funding. It has made direct contributions to public health through its research programs, which are characterized by substantial interaction across departments and schools and with local industries, health departments, agencies, and hospitals. Student involvement in research is extensive, and the majority of the School's full-time doctoral students are provided tuition and stipends for work on research projects. The School is equipped with modern laboratories, very large population datasets, a whole-body counter, a telephone survey research center for conducting social and behavioral research, a mass spectrometer, and computer teaching laboratories. The Falk Library of the Health Sciences contains more than 50,000 volumes and 150 journals of interest to GSPH, and the library is supplemented by other University libraries. The School houses a number of centers, including the Centers for Public Health Practice, the Center for Public Health Preparedness, the Center for Minority Health, the Center for Environmental and Occupational Health, the Center for Research on Health and Sexual Orientation, the Center for Research on Health Care, the Health Policy Institute, a nutrition counseling center, and a WHO collaborating center.

Financial Aid

Every eligible student is considered for some aid to the extent of funds available. Certain programs have fellowships or traineeships for qualified students enrolled in those programs. They include predoctoral and postdoctoral fellowships in aging, alcohol, cardiovascular, and psychiatric epidemiology and traineeships for social workers holding the M.S.W. degree who are concentrating in public health social work. Eligibility for the preceding aid requires U.S. citizenship or, in the case of international students, permanent residence or immigrant status. In addition, many programs offer graduate student assistantships that provide students with a stipend and a tuition scholarship in exchange for approximately 20 hours of work per week. Approximately one third of all students received assistantships in 2006–07.

Cost of Study

For full-time students, the tuition charge per term for 2006–07 was $8192 for state residents and $15,115 for out-of-state students. This did not include such costs as student health service fees and student activity fees. For part-time students, the cost per credit hour was $671 for state residents and $1243 for nonresidents.

Living and Housing Costs

The University has no housing for graduate students, but the Off-Campus Housing Office assists students in obtaining housing. A conservative estimate of monthly living expenses would include approximately $400–$500 for rent, $250 for food, and $100 for miscellaneous expenses.

Student Group

There were approximately 570 students registered in the School in 2006–07, of whom about 25 percent are from other countries. Approximately 40 percent of the students are pursuing doctoral studies. Graduates of the School of Public Health have come from all fifty states and nearly seventy countries.

Location

Pittsburgh, known as the Renaissance City of America, is renowned throughout the world as a center of steel and coal production, which is constantly applying and developing new technologies. Prominent features of the city include the headquarters of major industrial concerns; excellent cultural opportunities that include the symphony, ballet, opera, theater productions, concerts, fairs, and art museums (including the Andy Warhol Museum); and many parks and recreational facilities. Recreational opportunities include golf, hunting, and fishing in nearby mountain areas; skiing within a few hours' drive of the city; hiking, camping, and stream and lake sports; and professional baseball, football, and hockey.

The School is located in the Oakland area of Pittsburgh, which also includes the Carnegie Library and Museum, Scaife Galleries, the educational television station, four of the city's colleges and universities, and the University of Pittsburgh Medical Center complex.

The School

The Graduate School of Public Health was established in 1948 by the trustees of the University of Pittsburgh as a result of a gift of $13.6 million from the A. W. Mellon Educational and Charitable Trust. In 1957, the School moved into an eight-story building with a capacity of more than 2 million cubic feet, which it soon outgrew. An extension with 48,000 square feet of floor space has since been added. A building designed specifically for toxicological research houses the Department of Environmental and Occupational Health.

Applying

To be considered for fall admission, students are encouraged to submit applications by February 1, but earlier deadlines apply to some programs. Admission to the spring and summer terms is possible under certain circumstances. An undergraduate average of at least 3.0 (on a 4.0 scale) is usually required, and applicants who do not have a postbaccalaureate degree must send scores from the General Test of the Graduate Record Examinations (GRE). Some programs require the GRE scores of all applicants. In some cases, LSAT, MCAT, or DAT scores may be used. International students must furnish certification of English proficiency and financial responsibility. All applicants must have successfully completed 3 college credits of algebra or more advanced mathematics. In addition, M.P.H., M.H.A., and certificate applicants must have 6 credits in the social sciences. Specific departments may have additional requirements. Both paper and online applications are accepted. For more information, students should contact the School.

Correspondence and Information

Office of Student Affairs
Graduate School of Public Health
114 Parran Hall
University of Pittsburgh
Pittsburgh, Pennsylvania 15261
Phone: 412-624-3002
Fax: 412-624-3755
E-mail: stuaff@pitt.edu
Web site: http://www.publichealth.pitt.edu/

University of Pittsburgh

DEPARTMENT CHAIRS AND RESEARCH ACTIVITIES

Donald S. Burke, M.D., Dean, UPMC–Jonas Salk Chair in Global Health.
Phalguni Gupta, Ph.D., Associate Dean for Academic Affairs.
Margaret A. Potter, J.D., Associate Dean for Public Health Practice.
Sandra Crouse Quinn, Ph.D., Associate Dean for Student Affairs and Education.
Stephen R. Wisniewski, Ph.D., Associate Dean for Research.
Mary M. Derkach, J.D., M.S.I.S., Assistant Dean for Student Affairs.

Behavioral and Community Health Sciences. Robert Goodman, Ph.D., Chair. Research and training activities focus on social and behavioral factors that influence the health and welfare of populations, including social justice issues and the elimination of health disparities as top priorities. Degrees offered are the M.P.H. degree and the Dr.P.H. degree. Students in the M.P.H. program are prepared as practitioners who can apply social/behavioral theory, concepts, and methods to design, implement, and evaluate public health interventions. At the master's level, joint degrees (M.P.H./M.I.D. or M.P.A., M.P.H./M.S.W., M.P.H./Ph.D.) are offered in conjunction with the University of Pittsburgh Graduate School of Public and International Affairs, the School of Social Work, and the Department of Anthropology, School of Arts and Sciences. The Dr.P.H. program prepares students for the consideration and examination of complex problems in public and community-care systems, allowing them to pursue research, teaching, and leadership positions in health-promotion organizations in both academic and practice settings. Strands of academic concentration for both degree programs include community health assessment, applied research, community development, health communication, program planning, and theories of health behavior and education. Certificate programs in evaluation of public health promotion and health education, health disparities and minority health, public health preparedness, women's studies, global health, and Latin American studies, as well as a certification in public health and aging, are also available through the department or through other University departments.

Biostatistics. Howard E. Rockette, Ph.D., Chair. Research is focused in biostatistical theory, methods, and applications. Areas of particular emphasis include the development and application of quantitative methods to evaluate health effects associated with urban and industrial environments; the methodology, design, conduct, and analysis of large-scale collaborative clinical trials; and statistical computing applications in public health and medicine. In addition, faculty members provide expertise in quantitative methods and their applications in public health problems through multidisciplinary projects in collaboration with other departments within the School, the University, local and state health departments, and other agencies charged with the promotion of health. Research, teaching assistantship, and training grants are available. GRE scores are required of all applicants.

Environmental and Occupational Health. Bruce R. Pitt, Ph.D., Chair. Research and training opportunities are provided in basic science (molecular biology, physiology, biochemistry, toxicology, and occupational medicine) of environmental and occupational health. Emphasis is placed on molecular basis of toxicological sciences aimed at identifying genetic contributions that underlie sensitivity and susceptibility of mammals to environmental toxins. Current laboratory-based initiatives include pulmonary toxicology, including sensitivity of vascular endothelium to metals and nitrosative stress, repair, and remodeling of airway epithelium in response to inhaled toxicants and chemical-induced airway hyperreactivity; the role of oxidative and nitrosative stress in cardiovascular, respiratory, and CNS pathophysiology; regulation of voltage-gated potassium channels in excitable tissue; DNA damage, mutagenesis, cytogenetics, biomarkers, risk assessment, and their contributions in carcinogenesis; and computational toxicology. Training opportunities exist for Ph.D. and M.S. students in molecular toxicology. Molecular toxicology is also a specialized track within the University's Interdisciplinary Biomedical Graduate Program that includes additional fundamental approaches in biomedical science. Training opportunities for master's students include a residency/M.P.H. program in occupational medicine, an M.P.H. program in EOH/risk assessment, and a certificate in risk assessment. Extensive collaboration exists with basic science and clinical departments in the University of Pittsburgh School of Medicine as well as other departments in the Graduate School of Public Health, Carnegie Mellon University, and NIOSH in Morgantown, West Virginia.

Epidemiology. Roberta Ness, M.D., M.P.H., Chair. The department offers doctoral programs (Ph.D., Dr.P.H.), 45-credit M.P.H. and M.S. degrees, and a 30-credit M.P.H. degree. Educational and research areas include the epidemiology of aging, alcohol, cancer, cardiovascular disease, clinical trials, diabetes, environmental health, infectious disease, injuries, physical activity, and reproductive health. Research is oriented toward the prevention and control of major public health disease problems in the urban community. A number of studies address women's health issues, health in minority populations, telecommunications in public health, the role of physical activity in the development of chronic diseases, and molecular epidemiology. The Department of Epidemiology has collaborative arrangements with all departments in the Graduate School of Public Health, the University of Pittsburgh Health Center, other schools of the health professions, and both state and local health departments. In addition, the department houses one of the CDC's network of prevention research centers focusing on "healthy aging" as a theme and a public health goal. Currently, the department also is maintaining a number of registries for diseases such as Alzheimer's disease, cardiovascular disease, breast cancer, and diabetes mellitus. A WHO-collaborating diabetes research center is responsible for the maintenance of diabetes registries, for training in the epidemiology of diabetes, and for research studies in the prevention of diabetes complications and of diabetes itself. The Epidemiology Data Center coordinates multicenter clinical trials and registries and tests treatment strategies for chronic diseases. The department is also the home of the Global Health Network Supercourse, a resource of more than 10,000 lectures on public health issues.

Health Policy and Management. Judith R. Lave, Ph.D., Chair. The department offers multiple master's programs, including a Master of Health Administration (M.H.A.), Master of Public Health (M.P.H.) degree with a choice of three distinct areas of concentration (health policy, health management, and public health administration), and a joint J.D./M.P.H. degree. The M.H.A. program focuses on early career students with targeted interactions with the world of practice. All programs feature nationally known faculty members and a high faculty-student ratio. The department's faculty members maintain a broad base of multidisciplinary research and scholarship, which serves as the intellectual foundation for the department's educational programs. The multidisciplinary nature of health policy and health management presents many opportunities for collaborative study with researchers and clinicians in a variety of disciplines across the schools of the health sciences and professional schools within the University. The department's core faculty members represent the disciplines of business administration, health economics, health policy, health services research, organization studies, and accounting and finance. Many high-level executives from the area serve on the adjunct faculty. The Health Policy and Management (HPM) faculty members are engaged in interdisciplinary research, addressing a range of problems relevant to public policy and organization and management within health-care organizations and systems as well as disease outcome research. The specific research and scholarly interests of the HPM faculty members include health-care financing and insurance issues, including the costs of graduate medical education, funding health care for children, the economics of mental health, and the economic burden of disease; strategic management and governance in health-care organizations and the role of health-care organizations as corporate citizens; organization studies, including administrative ethics and leadership in health care; evaluation (outcomes and process) research in community health; management development for integrated health-care systems and networks; health law and public health law; barriers to access for uninsured/underinsured populations; health policy, including the context and processes of policymaking and such issue areas as pharmaceutical policy and health disparities among rural, minority, and other populations; and applications of health economic analysis, including the effects of managed care, employment and health-care financing, financing of behavioral health services, worker's compensation and health, and patient preferences and shared decision making.

Human Genetics. M. Ilyas Kamboh, Ph.D., Acting Chair. Ph.D. and M.S. training and research are oriented toward identifying genes that contribute to common diseases and understanding the mechanisms by which these genes contribute to disease susceptibility. The faculty includes clinical geneticists who identify and recruit patients and families for genetic studies; molecular and biochemical geneticists and cytogeneticists who characterize individuals at the chromosomal, cellular, and molecular levels; and mathematical geneticists who develop and apply the theories of population genetics and statistical methods to clinical and laboratory data in order to localize genes, to identify specific disease genes, and to quantify their contribution to disease risk. The M.S. program in genetic counseling trains students to apply this knowledge to the identification of individuals and families who are at increased risk of disease and to counsel those individuals regarding their risk and their options with respect to genetic testing and medical interventions. The M.P.H. in public health genetics trains students to integrate genetics into the broader field of public health. Research and training in the department is multidisciplinary and collaborative, involving investigators from the School of Public Health, the School of Medicine, other schools of the health sciences, and the Faculty of Arts and Sciences. The genetic counseling program is accredited by the American Board of Genetic Counselors. Specialty training in biochemical and molecular genetics and cytogenetics is accredited by the American Board of Medical Genetics, and the M.D. in clinical genetics program is accredited by the Council for Graduate Medical Education.

Infectious Diseases and Microbiology. Charles R. Rinaldo Jr., Ph.D., Chair. The disciplines of microbiology, molecular biology, immunology, and epidemiology are merged with infectious disease education and prevention to provide a unique research environment in which basic scientists, clinicians, and public health educators work together to study infectious diseases at the cellular and molecular levels, as well as prevention of the spread of infectious agents through education and vaccine development. This multidisciplinary approach provides the graduate student with an opportunity to focus on a specific infectious agent and to study the host-pathogen interaction at the cellular and molecular level or at the population level. Close associations are maintained with the University of Pittsburgh, School of Medicine and Cancer Institute, which lend additional flexibility to the design and implementation of graduate research projects. Areas of research include molecular and immunological studies of the pathogenesis of HIV; molecular mechanisms of HIV drug resistance; molecular mechanism of sexual transmission of HIV; molecular and immunological studies of Epstein-Barr virus, Kaposi's sarcoma herpes virus, and malaria infections and the regulation of viral gene expression; host and microbial genetics of malaria, HIV, and other infectious diseases, such as tuberculosis; basic research in the development of vaccines for HIV, SIV, influenza virus, and West Nile virus; and early intervention and prevention of HIV infection and other sexually transmitted diseases.

Multidisciplinary M.P.H. Program. Director: Ronald D. Stall, Ph.D. This M.P.H. degree program provides clinically trained, doctoral-level health professionals with the opportunity to attain expertise in preventive medicine, environmental health, and health policy in preparation for assuming public health leadership positions. The program meets the needs of health science professionals who wish to practice in academic, public health, or community-based settings where data-based concepts, health management, and public health practice are of benefit. The program is open primarily to holders of a doctoral degree in the clinical health sciences and medical and dental students.

UNIVERSITY OF SOUTH CAROLINA

Department of Environmental Health Sciences

Programs of Study

Exploration of the complex interaction between humans and the environment involves numerous disciplines, including biology, chemistry, engineering, public health, and medicine. The Department of Environmental Health Sciences was created to promote a clearer understanding of this interaction; develop methods for preventing environmental degradation; and provide information for policymakers to encourage societal action toward sustaining a healthy environment. The Department offers four degrees, the M.S., M.P.H., M.S.P.H., and the Ph.D. Graduates of the program are prepared for varied careers in public and environmental health, including environmental management, occupational health, public policy creation, and cutting-edge environmental research.

The Master of Public Health (M.P.H.) degree helps students develop a broad background in public health. The degree requires 42 credits, including 16 credits in core courses, 20 credits in major and cognate courses, and 6 credits in a thesis project. The Master of Science in Public Health (M.S.P.H.) emphasizes the scientific basis of public health and problem-solving research in the environmental health sciences. This degree requires 42 credits, including 9 credits in core courses, 27 credits in major and cognate courses, and 6 thesis credits. Students in these two programs may follow a program track in environmental quality, industrial hygiene, or hazardous materials management.

The Master of Science (M.S.) degree, which may be tailored to individual interests, combines real-world problem solving and research skills with other technical, health, and related skills. The degree requires 36 credits, including 18 credits in Departmental courses, 12 credits in quantitative and technical skills, and 6 thesis credits. Doctor of Philosophy students must complete 45 hours of course work beyond the master's degree, including 12 credit hours of dissertation preparation. Students must pass a qualifying examination after the first year of study, pass an oral and/or written comprehensive examination upon completion of all course work, and then prepare and defend a dissertation that represents significant research in their area of advanced study.

Research Facilities

The University's Thomas Cooper Library provides access to more than 7.5 million volumes, periodicals, microfilm entries, and manuscripts in the University system through the USCAN integrated information system. Computer facilities include an Intel Paragon high-performance parallel computer system and an IBM 3090-400E mainframe computer. An extensive fiber-optic network connects local area networks to the Internet's global resources.

The Geographic Information Processing (GIP) Laboratory, directed by Dr. Dwayne Porter and located within the Belle W. Baruch Institute for Marine and Coastal Sciences, is responsible for research, development, and application of spatial analytical tools and models to address estuarine and marine environmental issues. The GIP Lab is an integration of the technologies of digital image processing, geographic information systems (GIS), global positioning systems (GPS), remote sensing, and geostatistics. The GIP Lab provides powerful state-of-the-art tools for examining, evaluating, and modeling a multitude of coastal, marine, and other environmental research issues.

The USC Environmental Genomics Laboratory is scheduled to open in the Public Health Research Center in summer 2007. It will provide cutting-edge genomic sequencing and gene expression analyses to researchers interested in gene-level response of organisms to environmental agents or change. A Roche Scientific 454 GS-20 sequencer, an Affymetrix gene expression array system, ABI 7900 quantitative RT-PCR equipment, Eppendorf microinjectors and liquid-handling systems, microplate washers/readers, Leica FLIM and Raman quantitative confocal microscopes, and various capillary sequencing instruments will reside in the facility.

The USC Mass Spectrometry Facility is available to all environmental health researchers at low cost for state-of-the-art detection and quantification of chemical agents in soil, sediments, air, and water. It holds GC-MS/MS, LC-MS/MS, high-resolution ICP-MS, time-of-flight MS, and negative CI-MS instrumentation.

Financial Aid

A variety of graduate assistantships, NIOSH traineeships, and Graduate School fellowships are available for students in the Department. Most assistantships are linked to faculty research grants and provide tuition relief with stipends of $12,000 to $25,000 per year. The Graduate School Centennial Fellowship awards twenty scholarships of $1000 each to graduate students across campus. A number of scholarships are also available from the Graduate School; award amounts and eligibility requirements vary.

Cost of Study

In the 2006–07 academic year, graduate tuition was $411 per credit hour for South Carolina residents and $874 for nonresidents. Students also paid a matriculation fee of $50, a technology fee of $17 per credit hour, a health fee of $146, and a lab fee of $40.

Living and Housing Costs

Housing is available on campus for $580 to $775 per month for a one-bedroom apartment, $655 to $905 for two bedrooms, and $690 for three bedrooms. Meal plans range from $512 per semester for five meals per week to $1242 for twenty-one meals per week. Block meal plans are also available. Campus parking fees are $30 to $60 per semester. Off-campus housing is also available. (Costs are subject to change.)

Student Group

Students in the program come from a wide variety of academic and professional backgrounds, but most have undergraduate degrees in the physical or life sciences or have completed sufficient course work in these areas.

Location

Columbia, the capital of the state, has a population of approximately 500,000 residents within the metropolitan area. The University is located near the main downtown areas and the state government complex of buildings. Greater Columbia offers a wide range of cultural attractions and entertainment, including the Koger Center for the Arts, the Colonial Center, the South Carolina Orchestra Association, the Columbia City Ballet, the Columbia Art Museum, the South Carolina State Museum, several excellent community and children's theaters, and the nationally known Riverbanks Zoo. The city is located in the center of the state, and an excellent network of roads makes it easy to drive to the ocean and the mountains. Lake Murray, one of the largest lakes in the state and the setting for a wide range of aquatic activities, is only 15 miles from Columbia. Golf and tennis may be enjoyed year-round.

The University and The Department

The University was founded in 1801, the first state college to be supported by annual public appropriations. Having expanded through the years around the original horseshoe-shaped campus, the University today is the state's largest public institution of higher learning. Expansion in the last twenty years has been particularly rapid, and some of the most striking architecture of the region can be found on the campus. The University has launched the first phase of its research campus, "INNOVISTA," in downtown Columbia.

The Department of Environmental Health Sciences is located in the Arnold School of Public Health's new state-of-the-art research center, which opened in fall 2006. This building is the first in INNOVISTA and has a new environmental genomics laboratory with the latest whole-genome sequencing and analytical gene expression technologies. The Department's faculty members have expertise in a broad range of disciplines necessary for the solution of problems in the environmental health sciences. Many have extensive practical experience, and most serve as consultants in environmental or occupational health. The faculty's high level of professional activity is evidenced by numerous technical publications in professional journals, by presentations at technical meetings, and by service on local and national boards and committees.

Applying

Prospective students must submit an application for admission; official college transcripts showing a minimum 3.0 GPA and course work in science, engineering, or technology; official GRE scores; three letters of recommendation; a personal essay describing academic and professional objectives; a current resume; and an application fee. The application deadline is July 15 for spring admission and January 15 for fall admission. To obtain additional information and to apply, prospective students should visit http://www.sph.sc.edu/futurestudents/index.htm.

Correspondence and Information

Dr. Dwayne Porter, Graduate Director
Department of Environmental Health Sciences
921 Assembly Street, Room 401
University of South Carolina
Columbia, South Carolina 29208
Phone: 803-777-4615
Fax: 803-777-3391
E-mail: porter@sc.edu
Web site: http://www.sph.sc.edu/enhs/default.htm

University of South Carolina

THE FACULTY AND THEIR RESEARCH

C. Marjorie Aelion, Professor and Associate Dean for Research; Ph.D., North Carolina at Chapel Hill, 1988. Environmental contamination and fate, transport, and biodegradation of organic and inorganic contaminants in aquatic sediments and groundwater.

G. Thomas Chandler, Professor and Department Chair; Ph.D., LSU, 1986. Aquatic/marine ecotoxicology in sediments and water, organismal to population effects of endocrine-disrupting chemicals, use of stable isotopic and trace-metal compositions of microcosm cultured deep-sea benthic foraminifera as indicators of environmental change.

Alan W. Decho, Professor; Ph.D., LSU, 1987. Aquatic systems and microbial biofilms, extracellular (EPS) matrix, chemical and spectroscopic characterization of EPS, bioavailability of pesticides and metals, marine stromatolite genesis and microbial mats, pathogen survival in biofilms, bacterial quorum sensing, animal-microbe interactions.

Charles E. Feigley, Professor; Ph.D., North Carolina at Chapel Hill, 1978. Environmental exposure assessment; air sampling, especially diffusive sampling; applications of computational fluid dynamics.

Christopher J. Hintz, Research Faculty; Ph.D., South Carolina, 2005. Trace-element distribution coefficient determinations in benthic foraminiferal calcite, benthic foraminiferal culturing for environmentally controlled studies of growth and metal incorporation, trace-metal analytical technique development.

Lee A. Newman, Assistant Professor; Ph.D., Rutgers, 1993. Environmental remediation, fate of contaminants in plant systems, genetic and molecular properties of plants for metabolism of contaminants, genetic engineering of plants for enhanced remediation of contaminants, ecological restoration.

R. Sean Norman, Research Assistant Professor; Ph.D., Medical University of South Carolina, 2003. Microbial environmental genomics, bacterial degradation of environmental contaminants, pathogen identification and environmental fate, microbial community metagenomics.

Dwayne E. Porter, Associate Professor and Graduate Director; Ph.D., South Carolina, 1995. Resource management and environmental decision making, coastal zone environmental management, spatial modeling, human health–environmental landscape interactions.

Tara Sabo-Attwood, Assistant Professor. Ph.D., Florida, 2003. Cell signaling pathways impacted by airborne pollutants relevant to environmental lung disease, role of estrogen in lung cancer, molecular mechanisms of xenoestrogens in aquatic models.

Geoffrey I. Scott, Research Professor; Ph.D., South Carolina. 1979. Estuarine ecotoxicology, marine pathogen dynamics and source tracking, marine environmental policy and management.

Dwight W. Underhill, Professor; Sc.D., Harvard, 1967. Industrial hygiene, exposure assessment in indoor environments, passive sampling of radon and other radioactive agents in air, adsorption of toxicants onto activated carbon.

UNIVERSITY OF SOUTHERN CALIFORNIA

Institute for Health Promotion and Disease Prevention Research
Master of Public Health Program

Program of Study

The Keck School of Medicine at the University of Southern California (USC) offers the Master of Public Health (M.P.H.) degree. The mission of the M.P.H. Program is to assist in creating healthy communities by preparing graduates to lead and collaborate with others in organized community efforts across a variety of settings, focusing on disease prevention and health promotion among diverse populations. The program addresses behavioral theory, intervention strategies, and evaluation procedures for community health promotion and primary and secondary prevention. The program is built upon the strength of its faculty members, who are world leaders in the implementation and evaluation of school- and community-based health promotion programs. Faculty members command expertise in substance use prevention, unhealthful patterns of diet and physical activity, HIV/AIDS, cancer, and cardiovascular disease. Faculty members also specialize in developing culturally tailored public health interventions.

The M.P.H. is a 43- to 47-unit program designed to give students a solid foundation in the core areas of public health theory, research, and practice. Students begin with five core courses and then pursue an area of concentrated study from one of six tracks: health promotion, biostatistics/epidemiology, nutrition, health communication, child and family health, and global health leadership. To integrate concepts and skills gained in the academic program, students complete a supervised field training experience in an area of public health practice within a county, state, federal, community-based agency, or University-sponsored research project. Students also have the opportunity to serve as research or teaching assistants and are encouraged to engage in service work with community groups and agencies. The M.P.H. Program accommodates the needs of both full-time and part-time students. Program requirements may be completed in one year full-time or within two to four years part-time. Four dual-degree programs are available with the Schools of Psychology (Ph.D./M.P.H.), Medicine (M.D./M.P.H.), Pharmacy (Pharm.D./M.P.H.), and Physical Therapy (D.P.T./M.P.H.). The program also offers an M.P.H. Progressive degree, in which a maximum of one third of the course units for the M.P.H. degree may overlap with course units for a bachelor's degree at USC.

Research Facilities

Founded in 1880, USC is the oldest and largest private research university in the American West, ranking among the top ten research universities in the nation, based on federal research and development support. M.P.H. students have access to USC's numerous libraries, including the comprehensive Norris Medical Library and the Institute's own dedicated library. The Institute offers extensive research opportunities in tobacco use prevention and cessation, alcohol and drug abuse prevention, physical activity and nutrition, obesity, cancer and diabetes control and prevention, gender and cultural issues in health promotion, cardiovascular disease epidemiology and prevention, health communication, prevention of HIV/STDs, dissemination of prevention technologies, and prevention policy.

Financial Aid

The M.P.H. Program has a limited number of training opportunities in research and teaching available for fall, spring, and summer semesters. Interested students are encouraged to submit an online application for consideration. Applicants pursing federal and private financial aid, grants, scholarships, and fellowships are strongly encouraged to contact the USC Keck School of Medicine Financial Aid Office.

Cost of Study

Based on the 2007–08 academic year, the following are estimated two-semester costs at USC for a full-time master's student (8–14 units) living in University or non-University housing (not with parents or relatives, other than a spouse): $23,700 for tuition and fees, $13,146 for room and board, $1008 for books and supplies, $1828 for personal and miscellaneous expenses, and $2028 for transportation, for a total estimated cost of $41,710. Students should also add $29 for the orientation fee in their first semester at USC. Tuition costs vary by course load.

Living and Housing Costs

Off-campus apartment and housing rental rates vary widely by community, ranging from $600 to $2000 per month for a one-bedroom unit.

Student Group

The M.P.H. Program maintains an enrollment of more than 120 students annually. The student population is ethnically diverse and international and includes the following: African American (11 percent), Hispanic/Latino (9 percent), Asian/Pacific Islander (44 percent), Native American (1 percent), and non-Hispanic white (36 percent). Women make up 76 percent of the student body, while the international student population accounts for 20 percent.

Student Outcomes

Program graduates are trained to assess health needs of individuals and communities; design, implement, and evaluate effective health promotion interventions; coordinate and manage collaborative programs in health service provision; and communicate with leaders in government and industry about public health policy.

Location

Program offices, classrooms, and the Institute for Prevention Research (IPR) library are located at the USC Health Sciences Campus, Alhambra, a business park–like complex in the San Gabriel Valley. The city of Alhambra is a multicultural community, just minutes from USC's University Park and Health Sciences–Los Angeles Campuses. M.P.H. classes are also held at the Health Sciences and University Park Campuses. Shuttle buses connect the Alhambra Campus with neighboring campuses.

The University and The Program

The program is currently ranked twelfth among all U.S. public health programs, according to *U.S. News & World Report*. The M.P.H. Program is proud to exemplify the excellence in academics, research, and community involvement that earned USC its recognition as "College of the Year" in 2000.

Applying

The M.P.H. Program accepts applicants for both fall and spring semesters. The fall application deadline is June 1 (final). Extended application deadlines for fall may be possible. Spring application deadlines are November 15 for domestic applicants and October 1 for international applicants. The new summer application deadline is March 1. Admissions requirements include the University graduate application; the M.P.H. supplemental application; a bachelor's degree from an accredited university, with a minimum cumulative GPA of 3.0; official transcripts from each college or university attended; Graduate Record Examinations (GRE) scores of at least 1000 (verbal/quantitative combined); a personal statement; three letters of recommendation (must include one academic reference); and a curriculum vitae or resume. The Test of English as a Foreign Language (TOEFL), with a minimum Internet-based score of 100 (equivalent to a computer score of 250 and paper score of 600), is required of international students.

Correspondence and Information

M.P.H. Program
Keck School of Medicine
University of Southern California/IPR
1000 South Fremont Avenue
Building A-5, Suite 5128
Alhambra, California 91803
Phone: 626-457-6676
E-mail: mphusc@usc.edu
Web site: http://www.usc.edu/medicine/mph

Financial Aid Office
Keck School of Medicine
Health Science Campus
University of Southern California
1975 Zonal Avenue, KAM B-22
Los Angeles, California 90089-9033
Phone: 323-442-1016
Fax: 323-442-2943
Web site: http://www.usc.edu/dept/fao

University of Southern California

THE FACULTY AND THEIR RESEARCH

All faculty members are in the Preventive Medicine Department unless otherwise noted.

Teaching Faculty

Stanley P. Azen, Ph.D., Professor and Co-Director, Biometry/Biostatistics Division. Biostatistical methodology with applications in the areas of atherosclerosis and cardiovascular disease, ophthalmology, diabetes, and gerontology. (sazen@usc.edu)

Lourdes Baezconde-Garbanati, Ph.D., M.P.H., Assistant Professor, Preventive Medicine and Sociology. Cancer control research with special emphasis on minority populations. (baezcond@usc.edu)

Ricardo Calderon, M.D., M.P.H., Adjunct Associate Professor, Preventive Medicine. Applied public health practice through strategic leadership, planning and management of programs. (mrcalderon@dhs.co.la.ca.us)

Alex Y. Chen, M.D., Assistant Professor, Pediatrics and Preventive Medicine. Access and utilization of health-care services, inequalities in medical expenditures by socioeconomic factors, as well as other issues related to health and health-care disparities. (achen@chla.usc.edu)

Myles Cockburn, Ph.D., Assistant Professor, Preventive Medicine. (cockburn@usc.edu)

Michael Cousineau, Dr.P.H., Associate Professor, Family Medicine. Issues that impact public health, in particular, access to primary care for the low income uninsured; impact of privatization on safety-net providers, including public hospitals and community-based clinics and health centers; vulnerable populations. (cousinea@usc.edu)

Wendy Cozen, D.O., Assistant Professor of Clinical. Epidemiology of hematologic neoplasms, particularly Hodgkin's disease, non-Hodgkin's lymphoma, and multiple myeloma; analysis of cancer clusters. (wcozen@usc.edu)

N. Tess Boley Cruz, Ph.D., M.P.H., Assistant Professor of Research. Public health communications research, antitobacco media and pro-tobacco marketing effects. (tesscruz@usc.edu)

William J. Gauderman, Ph.D., Assistant Professor. Biostatistical methodology, statistical methods for genetic-epidemiological analysis of pedigree data, design and analysis of studies relating health outcomes to environmental exposures. (jimg@usc.edu)

Anne Bradford Harris, Ph.D., M.P.H., Assistant Professor, Pediatrics and Preventive Medicine; RD. Public health nutrition; child development and developmental disabilities; nutrition and feeding for children with, or at risk for, special health-care needs; interdisciplinary leadership training. (abradfor@usc.edu)

C. Anderson Johnson, Ph.D., Sidney Garfield Professor of Health Sciences; Professor of Preventive Medicine and Psychology; Director, Institute for Health Promotion and Disease Prevention Research and Transdisciplinary Tobacco Use Research Center (TTURC); and Director, Postdoctoral Training Programs in Health Behavior Research. Determinants of health-related lifestyles and approaches to prevention of behavioral, social, environmental, and genetic risks for disease. (carljohn@usc.edu)

Carol Koprowski, Ph.D., Assistant Professor; RD. Diet and nutrition, relationship between diet and physical activity among adolescent girls, nutrition for dialysis patients and those with diabetes. (koprowsk@usc.edu)

Mary Ann P. Limbos, M.D., M.P.H. Assistant Professor, Pediatrics. (mlimbos@chla.usc.edu)

Rob McConnell, M.D., Associate Professor. Epidemiology of respiratory disease in children, studies examining causes of asthma and its relationship with indoor and outdoor air pollution. (rmcconne@usc.edu)

Roberta McKean-Cowdin, Ph.D., Visiting Assistant Professor of Research. Epidemiology of breast cancer, including the role of endogenous sex hormones and hormone replacement therapy; epidemiology of childhood brain tumors, including developmental genetics. (mckeanco@usc.edu)

Paula H. Palmer, Ph.D., Assistant Professor of Clinical. Social and cultural determinants of health in ethnically diverse populations; school- and community-based research. (ppalmer@usc.edu)

Louise Ann Rohrbach, Ph.D., M.P.H., Associate Professor of Research. Community-based interventions for disease prevention and health promotion, with emphasis on interventions for prevention of tobacco, alcohol, and other drug abuse. (rohrbac@usc.edu)

Darleen V. Schuster, Ph.D., M.P.H., Instructor of Preventive Medicine and Assistant Director, Master of Public Health Program; CHES. Public health communications research, antitobacco media and pro-tobacco marketing effects. (dschuste@usc.edu)

Thomas W. Valente, Ph.D., Associate Professor. Evaluation of health promotion and substance abuse prevention programs, application of social network analysis and mathematical models to health-related behavior. (tvalente@usc.edu)

Participating Faculty

Chih-Ping Chou, Ph.D., Associate Professor. Evaluation of approaches to substance abuse prevention among adolescents, evaluation of substance abuse treatment, statistical methods in prevention research. (cchou@usc.edu)

Clyde W. Dent, Ph.D., Associate Professor. Evaluation of research that examines the onset, prevention, and cessation of tobacco, alcohol, and other drugs in large-scale contexts, such as schools, medical clinics, and worksites. (cdent@usc.edu)

Michael Goran, Ph.D., Professor of Preventive Medicine, Physiology, and Biophysics. Etiology and prevention of obesity and type 2 diabetes in children. (goran@usc.edu)

Elahe Nezami, Ph.D., Assistant Professor. Determinants of behavior risk factors for chronic diseases, in particular, cancer and cardiovascular disease. (nezami@usc.edu)

Mary Ann Pentz, Ph.D., Professor. Community-level tobacco, alcohol, and drug abuse prevention, prevention policy, and large-scale dissemination. (pentz@usc.edu)

Kim Reynolds, Ph.D., Associate Professor and Director, Ph.D. Program in Health Behavior Research. Diet and physical activity involving the prevention of cancer, heart disease, diabetes, and other chronic diseases through the modification of diet, physical activity, sun-safety behavior, and substance use. (kdreynol@usc.edu)

Jean Richardson, Dr.P.H., Professor. Cancer control research that interfaces closely with clinical and epidemiological research and draws upon behavioral research and epidemiological research methods. (jeanr@usc.edu)

Kimberly D. Siegmund, Ph.D., Assistant Professor. Statistical methods for genetic-epidemiology studies. (kims@usc.edu)

Donna Spruijt-Metz, Ph.D., Assistant Professor. Adolescent health, particularly in the areas of physical activity and obesity. (dmetz@usc.edu)

Alan Stacy, Ph.D., Associate Professor. Memory models of addiction and prevention; projects include studying alternative models of alcohol and drug abuse etiology, prevention of drug abuse, and effects of alcohol labeling legislation on adolescents. (astacy@usc.edu)

Ping Sun, Ph.D., Assistant Professor. Technology-facilitated interventions to prevent behavioral risk factors of cardiovascular disease and cancer (e.g., cigarette smoking and obesity). (sping@usc.edu)

Steven Y. Sussman, Ph.D., Professor, Preventive Medicine and Psychology. Drug abuse prevention and cessation; school-based adolescent alcohol, tobacco, and other drug abuse prevention and cessation research. (ssussma@usc.edu)

Jennifer B. Unger, Ph.D., Assistant Professor. Role of psychosocial and cultural factors in adolescent health risk behaviors. (unger@usc.edu)

The USC Institute for Health Promotion and Disease Prevention Research.

UNIVERSITY OF WASHINGTON

School of Public Health and Community Medicine
Department of Environmental and Occupational Health Sciences

Programs of Study	The Department of Environmental and Occupational Health Sciences at the University of Washington (UW) offers three graduate degrees: the M.S., the M.P.H., and the Ph.D. The areas of emphasis are environmental and occupational health (M.P.H.), environmental and occupational hygiene (Ph.D.), environmental health (M.S.), occupational and environmental exposure sciences (M.S.), occupational and environmental medicine (M.P.H.), and toxicology (M.S., Ph.D.).

The M.P.H. in environmental and occupational health provides an opportunity for students to focus on the recognition, assessment, and control of environmental and occupational hazards; the impact of these hazards on health and society; and approaches to regulation, enforcement, and policy development. The Ph.D. in environmental and occupational hygiene focuses on the assessment of exposures, health effects, and control strategies in community and work environments. The M.S. in environmental health focuses on community exposures to biological and chemical agents in commonly encountered environmental media including air, water, food, and soil. The M.S. in occupational and environmental exposure science focuses on the recognition, evaluation, and control of workplace hazards that cause occupational illness and injury. For individuals with an earned M.D. or D.O. degree, the M.P.H. in occupational and environmental medicine and concurrent residency program provide training in the public health sciences with a focus on occupational and environmental health. The M.S. and Ph.D. in toxicology focus on research and application of basic scientific principles toward a better understanding of the health effects of toxic substances in the workplace and general environment.

The Department also offers concurrent M.P.H./M.P.A. or M.S./M.P.A. programs with the Daniel J. Evans School of Public Affairs. These programs seek to educate students so that they can bring substantive public health knowledge and a strong policy and management orientation to their professional careers.

Research Facilities
Home to thirteen national and regional research and education centers, the Department has more than $18 million in funded research grants. Well-equipped laboratories contain facilities for environmental chemistry, in vivo and in vitro toxicology, industrial hygiene, and human exposure studies. School relationships include those with the University of Washington Medical Center and affiliated hospitals, the Fred Hutchinson Cancer Research Center, the Group Health Cooperative, and state and local health agencies. The Health Sciences Library provides access to more than 136,000 bound volumes, 1,500 current print journal subscriptions, 1,865 electronic journals, and access to 100 research databases. Department computing resources include two student computer labs, equipment available for student checkout, and additional computers available to students in many faculty labs.

Financial Aid
Ninety percent of full-time graduate students in the Department receive financial assistance as research assistants, teaching assistants, or trainees. Support includes a stipend or salary, a tuition waiver, and health and dental coverage.

Cost of Study
Tuition for 2006–07 ranged from $2940 to $3023 per quarter for state residents and from $6881 to $6964 per quarter for nonresident students. Tuition rates for 2007–08 are expected to be $3139 to $3306 per quarter for state residents and from $7155 to $7322 per quarter for nonresident students.

Living and Housing Costs
A wide selection of privately owned rental units in various price ranges is available in the area. General information about off-campus housing is available from the Student Housing Office. The University's Housing and Food Services Office offers assistance to students wishing to use campus facilities.

Student Group
In 2005–06, the total enrollment in the Department of Environmental and Occupational Health was 72 graduate students, including 28 M.S. students, 19 M.P.H. students, and 25 Ph.D. students.

Location
Seattle is the cultural center of the Pacific Northwest, with a professional symphony orchestra, a major art museum, and ballet and opera companies. It is a center for the arts, with more than a dozen thriving theater companies and two major music festivals a year. A science center, a bustling farmers' market, and a restored "Pioneer Square" are popular attractions for visitors and natives, as are the city's professional football, basketball, and baseball teams. Seattle's temperate climate and its location on Puget Sound, between the Cascade and Olympic mountain ranges, provide superb opportunities for year-round sailing, kayaking, hiking, and mountaineering. Cross-country and downhill ski areas are within an hour's drive.

The University
The University of Washington's Seattle campus occupies 693 acres on the shores of Lake Washington. Established in 1861, it was the first state university on the West Coast. Today it is recognized for the high quality of its research and graduate programs. For several years, UW has ranked among the top five institutions in the country in the amount of competitive grant and contract support received from federal sources. The 39,000 students of the University represent all ethnic groups, most geographic areas in the nation, and most of the countries of the world; 30 percent are graduate students. There is a Graduate and Professional Student Senate as well as more than 350 student organizations and an intramural sports program.

Applying
Acceptance by the UW Graduate School and adequate preparation for the applicant's field of interest are required for admission to the Department. Information on the programs, prerequisites, application procedures, and application forms are available on the Department's Web site. International applications must be completed by January 15. The priority application deadline for domestic applicants is January 15. Domestic applications completed after January 15 are considered on a space-available basis.

Correspondence and Information
Graduate Program Office
Department of Environmental and Occupational Health Sciences
University of Washington
Box 357234
Seattle, Washington 98195-7234
Phone: 206-543-3199
Fax: 206-543-9616
E-mail: ehgrad@u.washington.edu
Web site: http://depts.washington.edu/envhlth

University of Washington

THE FACULTY AND THEIR RESEARCH

Scott Barnhart, M.D., M.P.H. Occupational, environmental, and pulmonary medicine; bronchial hyperreactivity; attribution of impairment and disability in occupational respiratory diseases; musculoskeletal disorders from repetitive motion.

Thomas Burbacher, Ph.D. Behavioral toxicology, developmental effects of prenatal and postnatal exposure to environmental contaminants.

Janice Camp, M.S. Field industrial hygiene and safety, ergonomics, program evaluation, exposure assessment.

Harvey Checkoway, Ph.D. Occupational and environmental epidemiology, chemical and physical hazards, epidemiologic methods, Parkinson's disease.

Lucio G. Costa. Dr. Pharm. Neurotoxicology, signal-transduction systems in developmental neurotoxicity, molecular mechanisms and biochemical markers of neurotoxicity.

William Daniell, M.D., M.P.H. Occupational medicine and epidemiology, noise-induced hearing loss, use of workers' compensation data for guiding interventions, neuropsychological sequelae of solvent/pesticide exposure.

David L. Eaton. Ph.D. Biochemical toxicology, aflatoxin carcinogenesis, glutathione-mediated biotransformations of toxic chemicals, genetic susceptibility to environmental carcinogens, "gene-environment" interactions.

Elaine Faustman, Ph.D. Developmental toxicology, risk assessment methodologies, toxicology of N-nitroso compounds.

Richard Fenske, Ph.D. Exposure assessment, occupational health and safety, pesticide exposure, children's health, environmental risk and policy, agricultural health and safety, sustainable agriculture.

Jordan Firestone, M.D., Ph.D., M.P.H. Neurology, clinical toxicology, epidemiology, worker safety, environmental health.

Gary Franklin, M.D., M.P.H. Occupational injury, neurological epidemiology, outcomes research.

Evan Gallagher, Ph.D. Human and aquatic toxicology: mechanisms of aldehyde-induced oxidative liver damage, protective glutathione S-transferase enzymes, and chemical injury in salmonids.

Peter Johnson, Ph.D. Ergonomics, bioengineering, computer-related disorders, developing hardware and software technologies for assessing exposures to physical risk factors.

David Kalman, Ph.D. Environmental chemistry, detection and fate of chemical hazards in natural and man-made environments.

Joel Kaufman, M.D., M.P.H. Environmental and occupational epidemiology, health effects of diesel exhaust exposures, environmental factors in cardiovascular and respiratory disease, occupational asthma.

Terrance J. Kavanagh, Ph.D. Glutathione metabolism, analytical cytology, in vitro toxicology, toxicology of oxygen-free radicals, toxicogenomics, transgenic models, liver toxicology, cardiorespiratory toxicology, immunotoxicology, development and aging.

Matthew C. Keifer, M.D., M.P.H. Agricultural health and safety, international occupational health, community-based participatory action research. environmental justice.

John C. Kissel, Ph.D. Human exposure assessment, environmental risk assessment, hazardous waste management, soil cleanup, water quality.

Jane Q. Koenig, Ph.D. Respiratory physiology, pulmonary effects of inhalation of airborne pollutants on susceptible populations.

Joellen Lewtas, Ph.D. Air pollution; human exposure, source apportionment and health effects of particulate matter and organic species.

Daniel L. Luchtel, Ph.D. Respiratory toxicology, lung histopathology and pathophysiology, optical and electron microscopic techniques.

John Scott Meschke, Ph.D. Pathogen survival, mobility, and detection in the environment; microbial risk assessment; water and wastewater treatment; public health and environmental microbiology.

Lee Monteith, M.S. Absorption process in passive dosimeter badges, methods for the measurements of glove permeation, methods for the detection and measurement of trace compounds in the environment.

Michael S. Morgan, Sc.D. Applied respiratory physiology, inhalation toxicology.

Marilyn Roberts, Ph.D. Joint with Pathobiology. Bacteria antibiotic resistance genes and gene exchange in the environment, molecular epidemiology, bacterial mercury resistance.

Michael Rosenfeld, Ph.D. Joint with Pathobiology. Effects of environmental factors on the turnover of arterial macrophages and on the stability of advanced atherosclerotic lesions in transgenic hyperlipidemic mouse models.

Noah Seixas, Ph.D. Exposure assessment methods for occupational and epidemiologic studies, modeling exposure-response relationships.

Lianne Sheppard, Ph.D. Air pollution health effect and occupational epidemiology studies, estimation of health effects from environmental and occupational exposures, incorporating group information in epidemiologic studies.

Gwy-am Shin, Ph.D. Aquatic microbiology; physicochemical and disinfection processes; molecular biological methods.

Dennis Shusterman, M.D., M.P.H. Latex allergy; vocal cord dysfunction; workplace hazards, such as solvents and chlorine, and effects of irritants on the upper airway.

Christopher Simpson, Ph.D. Application of analytical chemistry to the development of techniques for assessment of exposure to toxic chemicals.

Charles D. (Chuck) Treser, M.P.H. Environmental health practice, law regulation, policy analysis, decision making, program planning and evaluation, education of environmental health workforce, housing, vector control.

Sverre Vedal, M.D. Pulmonology, effects of air pollution on patients with asthma and with COPD.

James S. Woods, Ph.D. Biochemical toxicology of heavy metals, metal effects on signal transduction and cell death processes, biological markers of metal exposure.

Zhengui Xia, Ph.D. Mechanisms for regulation of apoptosis in animal cells, mechanisms of neurogenesis.

Michael Yost, Ph.D. Optical remote sensing of chemicals in the environment, physical agents in the workplace: noise, vibration, nonionizing radiation.

VIRGINIA COMMONWEALTH UNIVERSITY

Program in Epidemiology

Program of Study

The Department of Epidemiology and Community Health at Virginia Commonwealth University (VCU) provides a course of study leading to the Ph.D. in epidemiology, the only program of its kind in Virginia. Students are prepared for research-oriented careers in clinical and population-based research. The program includes a foundation of 41 credits of epidemiology and biostatistics course work in which students learn methods for studying disease etiology and prevention in populations. Other requirements include six core courses and two semesters of the journal club as a special topic, five electives, and two courses offered by other departments. Once the majority of the course work has been completed, students take a written comprehensive exam, followed by an oral comprehensive exam. Students then implement an original, hypothesis-based analytical epidemiology research project under the supervision of an experienced faculty adviser. The doctoral degree must be obtained within seven years of matriculation. Most full-time students satisfy all requirements within four to five years.

The mission of the Ph.D. program in epidemiology is to serve the citizens of Virginia by educating and training students to become independent, competent, and self-directed research scientists so they can conduct outstanding clinical and population-based research. Students learn methods for studying disease etiology and prevention in populations and evaluating interventions, diagnostic tests, and treatment efficacy; they implement such methods in an independent research study under the mentorship of an experienced epidemiology researcher.

Upon graduation, students are able to define specific research questions or hypotheses; work either independently or in collaboration with other departments, programs, or organizations; design and conduct the appropriate research studies to address the questions/hypotheses; clearly communicate the findings to appropriate audiences; and guide the use of such findings in clinical practice and public health policy.

The University has numerous research faculty members who are interested in working with epidemiology doctoral students. Within the Department of Preventive Medicine and Community Health, research interests include youth violence prevention, women's health and domestic violence, cancer prevention, substance abuse, hearing loss, and nutrition. Additional research topics that have faculty interest and support include sickle cell anemia, breast cancer, HIV/AIDS, hospital epidemiology, and infectious diseases. Students with a specific interest should contact the program director to learn more about the possibility of working with a researcher in that area.

Research Facilities

VCU libraries provide a combined capacity of more than 1.7 million volumes and 10,200 periodical titles and an online bibliographic search service accessing hundreds of databases. In addition, the Virginia state and Richmond public libraries are within walking distance of both VCU campuses. Academic Computing provides a variety of microcomputer, minicomputer, and mainframe computing services to support the research and instructional endeavors of its faculty members and students, including consultation, instruction, and computer acquisition. Other research facilities operated by VCU include the Anderson Art Gallery Conservation Laboratory, the Burn Trauma Clinic, the Virginia Institute for Developmental Disabilities, the Massey Cancer Center, the Pharmacokinetics Laboratory, the School of the Arts Library and Slide Collections, the Sickle Cell Anemia Clinic, the Survey Research Laboratory, the Virginia Center on Aging, the Virginia Biotechnology Research Park, and the Virginia Real Estate Research Center.

Financial Aid

A limited number of assistantships are available each year for doctoral students matriculating in the fall. The assistantships cover tuition and provide a stipend for living expenses. Recipients are expected to work in the department part-time as research or teaching assistants or in similar roles. Students may apply for need-based assistance with the University's Financial Aid Office. Current information on financial aid programs, policies, and procedures is available at http://www.vcu.edu/enroll/finaid.

Cost of Study

For full-time study (9–15 credits) in 2007–08, Virginia residents pay tuition and fees of $4452 per semester; nonresidents, $8876 per semester. For part-time study, Virginia residents pay tuition and fees of $465 per credit hour; nonresidents, $954 per credit hour. Some programs require additional fees. On the Medical College of Virginia (MCV) campus, tuition, fees, and other expenses vary in the medicine, pharmacy, nurse anesthesia, dentistry, and School of Allied Health programs.

Living and Housing Costs

Graduate student housing is available on both the MCV campus and the academic campus of Virginia Commonwealth University. Many graduate students live in off-campus housing, which is reasonably priced and readily available in a variety of styles and settings in nearby residential areas or within easy commuting distance. On- and off-campus housing information is available on the Web at http://www.students.vcu.edu/housing.

Student Group

VCU enrolls 30,452 students, 7,611 of whom are graduate students. More than 200 clubs and organizations reflect the diverse social, recreational, educational, political, and religious interests of the student body.

Location

Richmond is Virginia's capital and a major East Coast financial and manufacturing center that offers students a wide range of cultural, educational, and recreational activities. Richmond is located in central Virginia at the intersection of Interstates 95 and 64, 2 hours south of Washington, D.C., and nestled between the Blue Ridge Mountains and the Atlantic Coast. The Richmond region is easily accessible by plane, car, and train. With nearly 1 million residents, the historic city of Richmond combines big-city offerings with small-town hospitality. Applicants are encouraged to explore http://www.visit.richmond.com/ for more information on the city.

The University

VCU is a state-supported coeducational university with a graduate school, a major teaching hospital, and twelve academic and professional units that offer fifty-two undergraduate, twenty-two postbaccalaureate certificate, sixty-five master's, six post-master's certificate, and twenty-nine Ph.D. programs. VCU also offers M.D., D.D.S., D.P.T., and Pharm.D. programs as well as cooperative degree programs with other major Virginia colleges and universities. VCU has one of the largest evening colleges in the United States. The academic campus is located in Richmond's historic Fan District. The health sciences campus and hospital are located 2 miles east in the downtown business district. A University bus service provides free intercampus transportation for faculty members and students. With more than $211 million in annual research funding, the Carnegie Foundation for the Advancement of Teaching ranks Virginia Commonwealth University as one of the nation's top research universities. More than 29,000 undergraduate, certificate, graduate, post-master's, professional, and doctoral students are enrolled in 162 academic programs, forty of which are unique in the commonwealth of Virginia. The faculty members at Virginia Commonwealth University represent the finest American and international graduate institutions and enhance the University's position among the important institutions of higher learning in the United States and the world via their work in the classroom, laboratory, studio, and clinic and in their scholarly publications.

Applying

Admission procedures and program requirements are detailed in the *Graduate Bulletin*. Application deadlines and materials, including the application and the *Graduate Bulletin*, are available online at the Graduate School Web site at http://www.graduate.vcu.edu. Virginia Commonwealth University is an equal opportunity/affirmative action institution providing access to education and employment without regard to age, race, color, national origin, gender, religion, sexual orientation, veteran's status, political affiliation, or disability.

Correspondence and Information

Elizabeth Eustis Turf, Director
Department of Epidemiology and Community Health
School of Medicine
Virginia Commonwealth University
1000 East Clay Street
P.O. Box 980212
Richmond, Virginia 23298-0212
Phone: 804-828-9785
Fax: 804-828-9773
E-mail: eturf@vcu.edu
Web site: http://www.epidemiology.vcu.edu/PhD/phd-index.htm

Virginia Commonwealth University

THE FACULTY AND THEIR RESEARCH

Core Faculty

Tilahun Adera, Professor and Chairman; Ph.D., Oregon State, 1987. Effect of minimal hearing and vision loss on academic performance in underserved schoolchildren, effect of chemicals and noise on occupational hearing loss, developing methods for evaluating hearing-loss prevention programs, effect of statin drugs on bone mineral density, risk factors for osteoporosis, hypercholesterolemia and coronary heart disease in the elderly, oral contraceptive use and abortion as risk factors for breast cancer, risk factors for low back pain, premenstrual syndrome.

Obesity as a risk factor for premenstrual syndrome. *J. Psychosom. Obstet. Gynaecol.* 26(1):33–9, 2005 (with Masho and South-Paul).

Gonzalo Bearman, Assistant Professor; M.D., SUNY at Buffalo, 1997. Epidemiology of hospital-acquired infections.

Hospital-acquired *Clostridium difficile*–associated disease in the intensive care unit setting: Epidemiology, clinical course and outcome. *BMC Infect. Dis.* 7:42, 2007 (with Marra, Edmond, and Wenzel).

C. M. G. Buttery, Adjunct Clinical Professor; M.P.H., Johns Hopkins, 1968. Primary care, health systems, translational technology, public health GIS.

I. Marilyn Buzzard, Associate Professor Emeritus; Ph.D., Syracuse, 1979. Methods for measuring food and nutrient intakes for epidemiological studies, dietary data collection and nutrient calculation, nutrition education and intervention, maintenance of food composition database.

Derek A. Chapman, Assistant Professor; Ph.D., Miami, 1999. Prevention of developmental disabilities, impact of sociodemographic factors on children's health and development, data linkage methodology.

Cumulative risk and low income children's language and behavioral development. *Top. Early Child. Special Educ.* 24:227–37, 2004 (with Stanton-Chapman and Kaiser).

Michael Edmond, Professor; M.D., West Virginia, 1986. Epidemiology of nosocomial infections.

A statewide survey of nosocomial infection surveillance in acute care hospitals. *Am. J. Infect. Control* 33:480–2, 2005 (with White-Russell, Woolard, Ober, and Bearman).

Resa M. Jones, Assistant Professor; Ph.D., Minnesota, 2004. Cancer screening and the predictors and barriers of cancer-screening behavior, predominantly, colorectal cancer screening; developing and implementing community interventions to increase healthy behaviors, such as increasing cancer screening rates in the general population and preventing and decreasing tobacco use among adolescents.

Colorectal cancer screening adherence in a general population. *Cancer Epidemiol. Biomarkers Prev.* 13(4):654–7, 2004 (with Yeazel et al.).

May G. Kennedy, Associate Professor; Ph.D., Georgia State, 1982. Social marketing, health-risk communication strategies, social and health policy applications of social science, prevention technology transfer, domestic and international HIV/AIDS prevention, adolescent health, program evaluation.

Increases in calls to the CDC national STD and AIDS hotline following AIDS-related episodes in a soap opera. *J. Commun.* 54:287–301, 2004 (with O'Leary, Beck, Pollard, and Simpson).

Jack O. Lanier, Professor; Dr.P.H., Texas, 1975. Health policy, community health.

Correlation between high-risk obesity groups and low socioeconomic status in school children. *South. Med. J.* 100(1):8, 2007.

Saba Woldemichael Masho, Assistant Professor; M.D., Addis Ababa, 1987; Dr.P.H., Berkeley, 1997. Women's health, sexual assault, maternal and child health, teen pregnancy, perinatal health, violence and injury prevention.

Youth violence prevention for public health students. *Am. J. Prevent. Med.* 29(5S2):240–6, 2005 (with Meyer).

Charles O'Keeffe, Professor; M.B.A., Loyola, 1978; FCPDD. Domestic and international drug abuse policy, with particular emphasis on addiction treatment policy and the effect of overall national and international policy on addiction treatment outcomes.

From morphine clinics to buprenorphine: Regulating opioid agonist treatment of addiction in the United States. *Drug Alcohol Depend.* 70(S1):3–11, 2003 (with Jaffe).

Jodi L. Teitelman, Associate Professor; Ph.D., Virginia Commonwealth, 1983. Persons with Alzheimer's disease and their family caregivers.

Elizabeth Eustis Turf, Director, Graduate Programs; Ph.D., Wayne State, 1985. Addiction research and education, infectious disease, needs assessments, cohort methodologies.

Comparative utility of Barona formulae, WTAR demographic algorithms, and WRAT-3 reading for estimating premorbid ability in a diverse research sample. *Clin. Neuropsychol.* 21(3):422–33, 2007 (with Ball, Hart, Stutts, and Barth).

Robert Leonard Vance, Associate Professor; Ph.D., Virginia, 1969; J.D., Richmond, 1975. Occupational and environmental health, environmental law.

Affiliate Faculty

Emmanuel Anum, M.P.H.
Al Best, Ph.D.
Judith B. Bradford, Ph.D.
Teqwyn Brickhouse, D.D.S., Ph.D.
Rene Cabral-Daniels, J.D.
James Cisek, M.D.
Homer M. Cole, M.S.P.H.
David Compton, M.D.
Thomas Franck, M.D.
Norma Geddes, Ph.D., RN.
Constance Hanna, M.D.
Spencer E. Harpe, Pharm.D., Ph.D.
Paula Inserra, Ph.D., RD.
Suzanne Jenkins, V.M.D.
M. A. Karim, Ph.D., PE.
John Keene, Dr.P.H.
Kathleen Kreutzer, M.Ed.
John Marr, M.D., FACP.
James May, Ph.D.

John McGurl, M.D.
Margaret McLellan, M.S., RDCDE.
Aleta L. Meyer, Ph.D.
Edward Murrelle, Ph.D., M.S.P.H.
William Nelson, M.D., M.P.H.
Napoleon Peoples, Ph.D.
James Person, Dr.P.H.
Valentina Petkov, M.D.
Melvin Pinn Jr., M.D.
River Pugsley, M.P.H.
Kerry Redican, Ph.D.
Dianne Reynolds-Cane, M.D.
James W. Ross, M.D.
Wally R. Smith, M.D.
Robert Stroube, M.D.
Curtis Thorpe, M.D.
Theodore Tweel, M.D.
James Wesdock, M.D.

VIRGINIA COMMONWEALTH UNIVERSITY

Department of Epidemiology and Community Health
Programs in Public Health

Programs of Study

Virginia Commonwealth University (VCU) offers the Master of Public Health (M.P.H.), a four-semester course of study and the first M.P.H. program in Virginia. It is fully accredited by the Council for Education in Public Health. The program is closely linked with local, state, and national public health agencies, organizations, and professionals in order to enhance the student's appreciation and understanding of the application of public health principles to practice. Under the guidance of a faculty adviser, each student must conduct a scientific investigation on a topic relevant to public health and prepare and report the results of this research. The program provides students with the skills for employment in a broad range of positions in local, state, and national public health agencies.

Students choose from four tracks—addiction studies, environmental health, epidemiology, and generalist. The addiction studies track is designed for persons interested in learning more about the impact of addiction on the health of populations. Study in this track focuses on addiction issues and how data are used to develop policy and plan preventions. The environmental health track provides expertise in the impact of the environment on the health of populations and training in methods designed to evaluate health risks presented by the environment. The epidemiology track is designed to train students who want to specialize in research methods and analysis and interpretation of public health data. The generalist track gives students a broad overview of public health issues and training in epidemiologic and biostatistical methods commonly used by public health professionals. This track can be used by students to design a curriculum in a focused area of interest for which there is no track currently available. A minimum of 45 credits is necessary to complete the degree requirements.

Four dual-degree programs are also available. The M.D./M.P.H. provides an opportunity for medical students who wish to pursue a public health or research career to graduate from medical school trained in both clinical and preventive population-oriented medicine. The five-year program consists of four years of medical school and one year of study in the M.P.H. program. Graduates are prepared for positions in preventive medicine, primary care, research, community-based health centers, and local health departments.

The M.P.H./M.S. in nursing—public health and community health nursing is a five-semester program that prepares students with the skills, knowledge, and competencies necessary to conduct needs assessments of populations, perform program planning and evaluation, understand the effects of contemporary issues and health policies on the public's health, and provide care and services to prevent disease and promote and preserve the health of populations.

The M.P.H./Pharm.D. offers students the opportunity to achieve a doctorate in pharmacy, with a focus on research and community pharmacy practice. This is a five-year program in which students spend the fourth year pursuing the M.P.H. then transition back to pharmacy for advance-practice experiences.

The M.S.W./M.P.H. prepares graduates to work with individuals, families, groups, communities, and/or organizations; advocate for social, health-care, and economic justice in a diverse and multicultural society; and promote physical and mental health across the lifespan. Students are required to complete a minimum of 45 M.S.W. credits and a minimum of 33 M.P.H. credits, for a total of 78 semester credit hours.

Research Facilities

VCU libraries provide a combined capacity of more than 1.7 million volumes and 10,200 periodical titles and an online bibliographic search service accessing hundreds of databases. In addition, the Virginia State and Richmond Public Libraries are within walking distance of both VCU campuses. Academic Computing provides a variety of microcomputer, minicomputer, and mainframe computing services to support the research and instructional endeavors of the faculty and students, including consultation, instruction, and computer acquisition.

Financial Aid

Graduate assistantships may be available intermittently for master's students. Students may apply for need-based assistance with the University's Financial Aid Office. Current information on financial aid programs, policies, and procedures is available at http://www.vcu.edu/enroll/finaid.

Cost of Study

For full-time study (9–15 credits) in 2007–08, Virginia residents pay tuition and fees of $4452 per semester; nonresidents, $8876 per semester. For part-time study, Virginia residents pay tuition and fees of $465 per hour; nonresidents, $954 per hour. Some programs require additional fees. On the Medical College of Virginia (MCV) campus, tuition, fees, and other expenses vary in the medicine, pharmacy, nurse anesthesia, dentistry, and School of Allied Health programs.

Living and Housing Costs

Graduate student housing is available on both the MCV campus and the academic campus of Virginia Commonwealth University. Many graduate students live in off-campus housing, which is reasonably priced and readily available in a variety of styles and settings in nearby residential areas or within easy commuting distance. On- and off-campus housing information is available on the Web at http://www.housing.vcu.edu/.

Student Group

VCU enrolls 30,452 students, 7,611 of whom are graduate students. More than 200 clubs and organizations reflect the diverse social, recreational, educational, political, and religious interests of the student body.

Location

Richmond is Virginia's capital and a major East Coast financial and manufacturing center that offers students a wide range of cultural, educational, and recreational activities. Richmond is located in central Virginia at the intersection of Interstates 95 and 64, 2 hours south of Washington, D.C., and nestled between the Blue Ridge Mountains and the Atlantic coast. The Richmond region is easily accessible by plane, car, and train. With nearly 1 million residents, the historic city of Richmond combines big-city offerings with small-town hospitality. Applicants are encouraged to explore http://www.visit.richmond.com/ for more information on the city.

The University

VCU is a state-supported coeducational university with a graduate school, a major teaching hospital, and twelve academic and professional units that offer fifty-two undergraduate, twenty-two postbaccalaureate certificate, sixty-five master's, six post-master's certificate, and twenty-nine Ph.D. programs. VCU also offers M.D., D.D.S., D.P.T., and Pharm.D. programs as well as cooperative degree programs with other major Virginia colleges and universities. VCU has one of the largest evening colleges in the United States. The academic campus is located in Richmond's historic Fan District. The health sciences campus and hospital are located 2 miles east in the downtown business district. A University bus service provides free intercampus transportation for faculty members and students.

With more than $211 million in annual research funding, Virginia Commonwealth University is classified as one of the nation's top research universities by the Carnegie Foundation for the Advancement of Teaching. More than 29,000 undergraduate, certificate, graduate, post-master's, professional, and doctoral students are enrolled in 162 academic programs, forty of which are unique in the commonwealth of Virginia. The faculty members represent the finest American and international graduate institutions and enhance the University's position among the important institutions of higher learning in the United States and the world via their work in the classroom, laboratory, studio, and clinic and in their scholarly publications.

Applying

Admission procedures and program requirements are detailed in the *Graduate Bulletin*. Application deadlines and materials, including the application and the *Graduate Bulletin*, are available online at the Graduate School Web site at http://www.graduate.vcu.edu. Virginia Commonwealth University is an equal opportunity/affirmative action institution providing access to education and employment without regard to age, race, color, national origin, gender, religion, sexual orientation, veteran's status, political affiliation, or disability.

Correspondence and Information

Karen Bryant, Graduate Recruitment Contact
Department of Epidemiology and Community Health
School of Medicine
Virginia Commonwealth University
1000 East Clay Street
P.O. Box 980212
Richmond, Virginia 23298-0212
Phone: 804-828-9786
Fax: 804-828-9773
E-mail: kpbryant@vcu.edu
Web site: http://www.epidemiology.vcu.edu/academics.htm

Virginia Commonwealth University

THE CORE FACULTY AND THEIR RESEARCH

Tilahun Adera, Professor and Chairman; Ph.D., Oregon State. Effect of minimal hearing and vision loss on academic performance in underserved schoolchildren, effect of chemicals and noise on occupational hearing loss, developing methods for evaluating hearing-loss-prevention programs, effect of statin drugs on bone mineral density, risk factors for osteoporosis, hypercholesterolemia and coronary heart disease in the elderly, oral contraceptive use and abortion as risk factors for breast cancer, risk factors for low back pain, premenstrual syndrome.

Obesity as a risk factor for premenstrual syndrome. *J. Psychosom. Obstet. Gynaecol.* 26(1):33–9, 2005. With Masho and South-Paul.

Elizabeth Eustis Turf, Director of the Graduate Programs; Ph.D., Wayne State. Addiction research and education, infectious disease, needs assessments, cohort methodologies.

Comparative utility of Barona formulae, WTAR demographic algorithms, and WRAT-3 reading for estimating premorbid ability in a diverse research sample. *Clin. Neuropsychol.* 21(3):422–33, 2007. With Ball, Hart, Stutts, and Barth.

Gonzalo Bearman, Assistant Professor of Internal Medicine; M.D., SUNY at Buffalo. Epidemiology of hospital-acquired infections.

Hospital-acquired Clostridium difficile–associated disease in the intensive care unit setting: Epidemiology, clinical course and outcome. *BMC Infect. Dis.* 7:42, 2007. With Marra, Edmond, and Wenzel.

C. M. G. Buttery, Adjunct Clinical Professor of Public Health; M.P.H., Johns Hopkins. Primary care, health systems, translational technology, public health GIS.

I. Marilyn Buzzard, Associate Professor Emeritus; Ph.D., Syracuse. Methods for measuring food and nutrient intakes for epidemiological studies, dietary data collection and nutrient calculation, nutrition education and intervention, maintenance of food composition database.

Derek A. Chapman, Assistant Professor; Ph.D., Miami. Prevention of developmental disabilities, the impact of socio-demographic factors on children's health and development, and data linkage methodology.

Cumulative risk and low income children's language and behavioral development. *Topics Early Childhood Special Educ.* 24:227–37, 2004. With Stanton-Chapman and Kaiser.

Michael Edmond, Professor of Internal Medicine, Epidemiology, and Community Health; M.D., West Virginia. Epidemiology of nosocomial infections.

A statewide survey of nosocomial infection surveillance in acute care hospitals. *Am. J. Infection Control* 33:480–2, 2005. With White-Russell, Woolard, Ober, and Bearman.

Resa M. Jones, Assistant Professor; Ph.D., Minnesota. Cancer screening and the predictors and barriers of cancer-screening behavior, predominantly colorectal cancer screening; developing and implementing community interventions to increase healthy behaviors, such as increasing cancer screening rates in the general population and preventing and decreasing tobacco use among adolescents.

Colorectal cancer screening adherence in a general population. *Cancer Epidemiol. Biomarkers Prevention* 13(4):654–7, 2004. With Yeazel et al.

May G. Kennedy, Associate Professor; Ph.D., Georgia State, 1982. Social marketing, health risk communication strategies, social and health policy applications of social science, prevention technology transfer, domestic and international HIV/AIDS prevention, adolescent health, program evaluation.

Increases in calls to the CDC national STD and AIDS hotline following AIDS-related episodes in a soap opera. *J. Communication* 54:287–301, 2004. With O' Leary, Beck, Pollard, and Simpson.

Jack O. Lanier, Professor; Dr.P.H., Texas, 1975. Health policy, community health.

Correlation between high-risk obesity groups and low socioeconomic status in school children. *Southern Med. J.* 100(1), January 2007.

Saba Woldemichael Masho, Assistant Professor; M.D., Addis Ababa; Dr.P.H., Berkeley. Women's health, sexual assault, maternal and child health, teen pregnancy, perinatal health, violence and injury prevention.

Youth violence prevention for public health students. *Am. J. Preventive Med.* 29(5S2):240–6, 2005. With Meyer.

Charles O'Keeffe, Professor; M.B.A., Loyola; FCPDD, Domestic and international drug abuse policy, with particular emphasis on addiction treatment policy and the effect of overall national and international policy on addiction treatment outcomes.

From morphine clinics to buprenorphine: Regulating opioid agonist treatment of addiction in the United States. *Drug Alcohol Dependence* 70(S1):3–11, 2003. With Jaffe.

Robert Leonard Vance, Associate Professor; Ph.D., Virginia; J.D., Richmond. Occupational and environmental health, environmental law.

YALE UNIVERSITY

School of Public Health

Programs of Study

Yale's School of Public Health is a department within the Yale School of Medicine but is also an independently accredited school of public health. It offers the Master of Public Health (M.P.H.) degree through the School of Medicine, as well as the Master of Science (M.S.) in biostatistics and chronic disease epidemiology and the Doctor of Philosophy (Ph.D.) through the Graduate School of Arts and Sciences.

The School is one of the few accredited schools of public health with direct access to clinical and basic science departments, because of its medical school base, as well as direct access to private and public institutions and community health agencies. These multiple resources allow the School to implement its mission of improving the status of community and individual health.

Many specialties are available through the following academic areas of concentration: biostatistics, chronic disease epidemiology, environmental health sciences, epidemiology of microbial diseases, health management, health policy, social and behavioral sciences, and a One-Year M.P.H. Program. Some of these specialties are cardiovascular, psychosocial, aging, and cancer epidemiology; tropical diseases; epidemic investigation; AIDS epidemiology; parasitology; environmental risk assessment, management, and policy; and health practice and administration and policy analysis.

The School of Public Health also offers formal joint-degree programs with the Schools of Medicine, Nursing, Management, Law, Divinity, and Forestry and Environmental Studies and with the Center for International and Area Studies and the International and Development Economics Program in the Graduate School of Arts and Sciences.

Most M.P.H. students spend two years in residence, although those with earned health doctorates may be eligible for the One-Year M.P.H. Program. Doctoral candidates usually receive their degrees within five years. Postdoctoral fellows are appointed subject to the availability of funds.

The One-Year M.P.H. Program is a generalist track designed for mature individuals with clear career goals in public health. The program provides a general grounding in the core areas of public health (epidemiology, biostatistics, environmental health sciences, health services administration, and social and behavioral sciences). Students have the opportunity to focus on a specific area of interest. This intensive program is only open to individuals with a doctoral-level degree in a field related to public health.

Yale is a research-oriented institution. Research is emphasized in the teaching program and culminates in the master's thesis, capstone course, or doctoral dissertation. Faculty advisers help students with all aspects of their programs. A schoolwide M.P.H. core curriculum, combined with divisional requirements, electives, and field experiences, promotes employment flexibility. M.P.H. graduates, aided by Career Services, secure a wide array of positions in the health field. Doctoral students usually choose academic careers, though a number are employed in research settings.

Research Facilities

The School's facilities include basic science and computer laboratories. Libraries include two within the School, as well as the exceptionally well stocked School of Medicine and University libraries. Several major research centers are also located in the School, for example, the Center for Perinatal, Pediatric, and Environmental Epidemiology, the first of its kind in the U.S.; the Cancer Prevention and Control Research Program; the Emerging Infections Program; and the Center for Interdisciplinary Research on AIDS.

Financial Aid

Financial aid consists primarily of student loans, supplemented by scholarships, grants, and work-study funds. Most aid is offered on the basis of financial need, but, in addition, the Admission Committee awards some merit-based scholarships. Ph.D. candidates are supported by training grants, research grants, and teaching fellowships. Fellowship and trainee support from federal funds is limited to citizens and permanent residents of the United States.

Cost of Study

Tuition for the 2007–08 academic year is $28,850. Additional fees for those students in residence include a hospitalization premium of $1615 per year, $1725 for books and supplies, and a $125 student activity fee.

Living and Housing Costs

For 2007–08, the standard nine-month budget for a single student at Yale University is estimated to be a total of $46,635.

Student Group

The School of Public Health admits from 100 to 110 students each year to its M.P.H. program. About 50 students are enrolled in the doctoral programs. Students vary in age, experience, and interest and come from many different states and countries. The majority of students attend full-time. Students from minority groups accounted for 15 percent of the 2006 entering class. The student diversity stimulates faculty members to share ideas and experiences in seminars and in research and community projects.

Location

New Haven is known for its theater, art museums, and medical resources. The School, located on the medical school campus, is within easy walking distance of the University campus, where lectures, concerts, art exhibits, and sports events attract both University staff and local residents. Being midway between New York City and Boston places Yale in one of the Northeast's most dynamic corridors.

The University and The School

Yale encourages interdisciplinary study with the ten professional schools, the Graduate School, and the College. All offer disciplinary depth as well as a remarkable range of course offerings. A notable strength of the University is the attention it pays to the individual student. The Schools of Medicine and Public Health carry out research, service, and teaching missions involving the full spectrum of health and disease. Other professional schools—chiefly Law, Management, Forestry and Environmental Studies, and Nursing—broaden the range of courses and research opportunities available to M.P.H. and doctoral students.

Applying

Prospective M.P.H. candidates must apply online through the Schools of Public Health Application Service at http://www.sophas.org. The application deadline is January 15 for the M.P.H. program and December 15 for the Ph.D. program. The School requires GRE scores for M.P.H. and doctoral applicants. GMAT or MCAT scores may be substituted for the GRE. The TOEFL is also required of all international applicants. The field of public health can accommodate many interests, and each application is carefully reviewed by a faculty committee. Students from minority groups are encouraged to apply. The need for financial aid is not considered in the admission process.

Correspondence and Information

For M.P.H.:
Admissions Office
Yale School of Public Health
47 College Street, Suite 108
New Haven, Connecticut 06510
Phone: 203-785-2844
E-mail: eph.admissions@yale.edu
Web site: http://publichealth.yale.edu

For Ph.D.:
Admissions Office
Yale Graduate School of Arts and Sciences
Yale Station, P.O. Box 208323
New Haven, Connecticut 06520-8323
Phone: 203-432-2771
E-mail: eph.doctoral@yale.edu
Web site: http://www.yale.edu/graduateschool

Yale University

THE FACULTY AND THEIR RESEARCH

Biostatistics
The research interests of this division are concerned with developing a statistical basis for medical and health policy decisions that may advance public health around the world. Areas include methodological issues in clinical trials, modeling of biomedical time series data, regulatory affairs, statistical methods in epidemiology, analysis of time trends in cancer incidence, categorical data analysis, goodness of fit tests, statistical genetics, genetic epidemiology, cancer genetics, applications of probability and statistics to molecular biology and genetics, regression methods, and issues in multivariable analysis.

Faculty: L. Calvocoressi, Ph.D.; E. B. Claus, Ph.D., M.D.; Y. Guan, Ph.D.; R. Gueorguieva, Ph.D.; P. Hartigan, M.P.H., Ph.D.; T. R. Holford, Ph.D.; H. Lin, M.D., Ph.D.; S. Ma, Ph.D.; R. W. Makuch, Ph.D.; A. M. Molinaro, Ph.D.; P. M. Nadkarni, M.D.; P. N. Peduzzi, Ph.D.; N. Sun, Ph.D.; C. White, M.B.B.S.; D. Zelterman, Ph.D.; H. Zhang, Ph.D.; H. Zhao, Ph.D.

Chronic Disease Epidemiology/Social and Behavioral Sciences
The five principal areas of faculty research and teaching are cancer epidemiology, with an emphasis on cancer control and on etiologic studies in association with the Yale Cancer Center; cardiovascular epidemiology, focused on coronary heart disease and hypertension and work with the cardiology division of the Department of Internal Medicine; the epidemiology of aging, centered on predictors of disability, hospitalization, nursing home admission, and mortality in association with the Program on Aging; a perinatal epidemiology unit, where research includes effects of tobacco smoke, acid aerosols, and electromagnetic fields on infants and mothers, in collaboration with the Departments of Obstetrics and Gynecology and of Pediatrics; and psychosocial epidemiology, focusing on bereavement, social support, depression, and other predictors of morbidity and mortality in association with the Department of Psychiatry. Cancer research includes lung cancer in nonsmokers, invasive cervical cancer, multiple primary breast cancer, malignant melanoma, gastrointestinal cancer, male breast cancer, childhood cancers, risk of cancer after exposure to radiation and to herbicides, and changes in cancer trends over time.

Faculty: S. G. Austin, Ph.D.; L. Barry, Ph.D., M.P.H.; K. D. Belanger, Ph.D.; K. M. Blankenship, Ph.D.; E. A. Bortnichak, Ph.D.; M. B. Bracken, M.P.H., Ph.D.; K. D. Brownell, Ph.D.; B. Cartmel, Ph.D.; P. A. Charpentier, M.P.H.; M. G. McCrea Curnen, M.D., Dr.T.M., Dr. P.H.; A. S. Darefsky, M.P.H., Ph.D.; M. Desai, M.P.H., Ph.D.; V. T. DeVita Jr., M.D.; R. D. Dubrow, M.D., Ph.D.; T. Gill, M.D.; E. Grigorenkp, Ph.D.; L. M. Grosso, Ph.D.; J. Hoh, Ph.D.; J. R. Ickovics, Ph.D.; M. L. Irwin, Ph.D.; S. Jacobs, M.P.H., M.D.; G. Jacobsen, M.D., Dr. P.H.; B. A. Jones, M.P.H., Ph.D.; S. V. Kasl, Ph.D.; T. S. Kershaw, M.P.H., M.D.; B. R. Levy, Ph.D.; T. Lewis, Ph.D.; D. Li, Ph.D.; J. H. Lichtman, M.P.H., Ph.D.; X. Ma, Ph.D.; L. Mayes, M.D.; S. T. Mayne, Ph.D.; R. McCorkle, Ph.D.; L. M. Mueller, Ph.D.; J. M. Mullen, M.D., M.P.H.; A. M. Ostfeld, M.D.; J. Rawlings, M.P.H., R.P.H.; H. A. Risch, M.D., Ph.D.; P. Salovey, Ph.D.; B. P. Schachtel, M.D.; D. Shenson, M.D., M.P.H.; D. L. Snow, Ph.D.; D. E. Stevens, Ph.D.; J. K. Tebes, Ph.D.; M. E. Tinetti, M.D.; E. W. Triche, Ph.D.; P. H. Van Ness, M.P.H., Ph.D.; K. Yonkers, M.D.; M. U. Yood, Ph.D., M.D.

Environmental Health Sciences
Research involves environmental factors affecting respiration and circulation, various aspects of thermoregulatory physiology, exercise physiology, sensory processes, aging, human exposures to environmental contaminants, perceptions of risks, and risk management.

Faculty: D. D. Aye, Ph.D.; M. Bell, Ph.D.; A. L. Boissevain, M.P.H.; J. B. Borak, M.D.; A. Caccone, Ph.D.; P. F. Canny, Ph.D.; D. C. Cone, M.D.; M. R. Cullen, M.D.; L. C. Degutis, Dr. P.H.; L. DiPietro, M.P.H., Ph.D.; A. B. DuBois, M.D.; J. D. Dunn, Ph.D.; C. Fields, M.P.H.; J. F. Gent, Ph.D.; G. L. Ginsberg, Ph.D.; C. H. Grantham-Millman, M.P.H.; B. P. Leaderer, Ph.D.; L. E. Marks, Ph.D.; K. McCarty, M.P.H., S.D.; M. V. Roberto, Dr. P.H.; M. Russi, M.D., M.P.H.; J. A. Sparer, M.Sc.E.; N. S. Stachenfeld, Ph.D.; J. T. Stitt, Ph.D.; J. A. J. Stolwijk, Ph.D.; M. H. Stowe, Ph.D.; C. Yeckel, Ph.D.; Y. Zhang, M.D., Ph.D.; T. Zheng, B.Med., Sc.D., Sc.M.; Y. Zhu, Ph.D.

Epidemiology of Microbial Diseases
Research focuses on understanding the epidemiology and biology of parasitic, bacterial, and viral diseases. Emphasis is placed on understanding the interactions of pathogens with their vertebrate hosts and vectors in order to better understand the transmission, maintenance, and pathogenesis of disease. These studies are conducted at both the molecular and organismal level.

Faculty: N. Abdala, Ph.D., D.V.M.; S. Aksoy, Ph.D.; L. Alexander, Ph.D.; J. F. Anderson, Ph.D.; W. A. Andiman, M.D.; T. G. Andreadis, Ph.D.; M. Y. K. Armstrong, M.D.; R. S. Baltimore, M.D.; R. Bucala, M.D., Ph.D.; M. Cappello, M.D.; M. L. Cartter, M.D.; J. E. Childs, Ph.D.; L. M. Dembry, M.D.; M. A. Diuk-Wasser, Ph.D.; E. Fikrig, M.D.; D. Fish, Ph.D.; B. A. Fontes, M.P.H.; G. H. Friedland, M.D.; A. P. Galvani, Ph.D.; L. E. Grau, Ph.D.; J. L. Hadler, M.D., M.P.H.; R. Heimer, Ph.D.; V. H. Hodgkinson, Ph.D.; H. Kampen, Ph.D.; K. Khoshnood, M.P.H., Ph.D.; L. A. Magnarelli, Ph.D.; R. Marcus, M.P.H.; D. McMahon-Pratt, Ph.D.; I. G. Miller, M.D.; L. E. Munstermann, Ph.D.; L. M. Niccolai, Ph.D.; C. Ocampo-Duran, Ph.D.; C. L. Patton, Ph.D.; M. M. Pettigrew, Ph.D.; D. J. Richardson, Ph.D.; N. H. Ruddle, Ph.D.; N. G. Saravia, Ph.D.; E. D. Shapiro, M.D.; A. N. Sofair, M.D.; G. H. Tignor, D.Sc.; C. Tschudi, Ph.D.

Global Health
Faculty: M. Barry, M.D.; A. Durante, Ph.D.; J. Fernando, Ph.D.; A. M. Foltz, M.P.H., Ph.D.; N. E. Groce, Ph.D.; B. M. Halpaap, Pharm.D.; K. Hartwig, Dr. P.H.; N. Hirschhorn, M.D.; D. L. Humphries, Ph.D., M.P.H.; J. F. Jekel, M.D., M.P.H.; L. S. Levin, Ed.D., M.P.H.; C. K. Pope, Ph.D.; J. P. Ruger, Ph.D.; J. Wack, Ph.D.; H. Wang, M.D., Ph.D.; F. Zhao, M.P.H., M.D., Ph.D.; E. Ziglio, Ph.D.

Health Policy and Administration/Health Management
Research focuses on the joint application of the methods and theory of epidemiology, economics, and political science to public policy analysis, quality of care issues, and management in health-care systems. Areas of emphasis are the organization and financing of health services, mental health (depression and the elderly), the politics of health-care reform, maternal and child health (teenage pregnancy; access, quality, and effectiveness of prenatal care; disabilities; foster care), cost-effectiveness analysis of medical care and health-related programs (e.g., as applied to substance abuse), and the application of the social and behavioral sciences to health-care issues.

Faculty: H. M. Allen, Ph.D.; T. Balcezak, M.D., M.P.H.; C. L. Barry, Ph.D.; M. P. Borgstrom, M.P.H.; E. H. Bradley, Ph.D.; J. C. Bradley, M.B.A.; S. H. Busch, Ph.D.; M. M. Callaway, M.B.A.; G. L. Capozzalo, M.S.P.H; K. H. Clark, M.P.H.; J. G. Culhane, J.D.; L. Curry, M.P.H., Ph.D.; M. Dale, M.P.H.; R. A. Desai, Ph.D., M.P.H.; H. G. Dove, Ph.D.; A. J. Epstein, Ph.D.; J. Fletcher, Ph.D.; H. Forman, M.B.A., Ph.D.; W. T. Gallo, Ph.D.; S. G. Geballe, J.D., M.P.H.; W. Gillespie, M.D.; S. M. Horwitz, Ph.D., M.P.H.; B. Jennings, M.A.; A. C. Justice, M.D., Ph.D.; E. H. Kaplan, Ph.D.; P. S. Keenan, Ph.D., M.H.S.; B. D. Kerker, Ph.D.; H. M. Krumholz, M.D.; M. A. Lee, M.S.N., Ph.D.; D. L. Leslie, Ph.D.; J. Mattera, M.P.H.; S. M. Merz, M.H.S.A.; I. M. Nembhard, Ph.D.; A. D. Paltiel, Ph.D.; W. P. Quinn, M.P.H.; R. A. Rosenheck, M.D.; T. W. Ruger, J.D.; M. J. Schlesinger, Ph.D.; J. L. Sindelar, Ph.D.; S. Spangler, M.D.; D. M. G. Wild, M.D., M.P.H.; J. A. Zaccagnino, M.P.H.

ACADEMIC AND PROFESSIONAL PROGRAMS IN LAW

Section 32
Law

This section contains a directory of institutions offering graduate work in law, followed by in-depth entries submitted by institutions that chose to prepare detailed program descriptions. Additional information about programs listed in the directory but not augmented by an in-depth entry may be obtained by writing directly to the dean of a graduate school or chair of a department at the address given in the directory.

For programs offering related work, see also in this book Business Administration and Management and Social Work; in Book 2, Criminology and Forensics; Public, Regional, and Industrial Affairs; Economics; and Political Science and International Affairs; in Book 4, Environmental Sciences and Management; and in Book 5, Management of Engineering and Technology.

CONTENTS

Program Directories

Law

Albany Law School of Union University, Professional Program, Albany, NY 12208-3494. Offers JD, LL M, MSLS, JD/MBA, JD/MPA, JD/MRP, JD/MSW. *Accreditation:* ABA. Part-time programs available. *Entrance requirements:* For JD, LSAT; for master's, GRE or LSAT. Additional exam requirements/recommendations for international students: Recommended—TOEFL (minimum score 600 paper-based; 250 computer-based). Expenses: Contact institution. *Faculty research:* Federal tax, constitutional law, secured transactions, international law, American politics.

American University, Washington College of Law, Program in International Legal Studies, Washington, DC 20016-8001. Offers LL M, Certificate. Part-time and evening/weekend programs available. *Students:* 29 full-time (11 women), 104 part-time (63 women); includes 6 minority (1 African American, 2 Asian Americans or Pacific Islanders, 3 Hispanic Americans), 93 international. Average age 30. In 2006, 110 degrees awarded. *Entrance requirements:* For master's, JD. Additional exam requirements/recommendations for international students: Required—TOEFL. *Application deadline:* For fall admission, 6/1 for domestic students; for spring admission, 11/1 for domestic students. Applications are processed on a rolling basis. Application fee: $55. *Expenses:* Tuition: Full-time $18,864; part-time $1,048 per credit. Required fees: $380. Tuition and fees vary according to program. *Financial support:* Fellowships, research assistantships, teaching assistantships, career-related internships or fieldwork and tuition waivers (partial) available. Financial award application deadline: 2/15; financial award applicants required to submit FAFSA. *Unit head:* Daniel D. Bradlow, Director, 202-274-4205.

American University, Washington College of Law, Program in Law, Washington, DC 20016-8001. Offers JD, JD/MA, JD/MBA, JD/MS. *Accreditation:* ABA. Part-time and evening/weekend programs available. *Students:* 1,216 full-time (683 women), 267 part-time (135 women); includes 441 minority (108 African Americans, 15 American Indian/Alaska Native, 142 Asian Americans or Pacific Islanders, 176 Hispanic Americans), 32 international. Average age 26. In 2006, 407 degrees awarded. *Entrance requirements:* LSAT. *Application deadline:* For fall admission, 3/1 for domestic students. Applications are processed on a rolling basis. Application fee: $55. *Expenses:* Tuition: Full-time $18,864; part-time $1,048 per credit. Required fees: $380. Tuition and fees vary according to program. *Financial support:* Fellowships, career-related internships or fieldwork, Federal Work-Study, institutionally sponsored loans, and tuition waivers (partial) available. Support available to part-time students. Financial award application deadline: 2/15. *Application contact:* Brooke Sandoval, Information Contact, 202-274-4101, Fax: 202-274-4107, E-mail: wcladmit@american.edu.

American University, Washington College of Law, Program in Law and Government, Washington, DC 20016-8001. Offers LL M. *Students:* 7 full-time (3 women), 26 part-time (12 women); includes 11 minority (9 African Americans, 1 Asian American or Pacific Islander, 1 Hispanic American), 6 international. Average age 35. In 2006, 33 degrees awarded. *Degree requirements:* For master's, thesis optional. *Entrance requirements:* For master's, JD. Additional exam requirements/recommendations for international students: Required—TOEFL. *Application deadline:* For fall admission, 6/1 priority date for domestic students; for spring admission, 11/1 priority date for domestic students. Applications are processed on a rolling basis. Application fee: $55. *Expenses:* Tuition: Full-time $18,864; part-time $1,048 per credit. Required fees: $380. Tuition and fees vary according to program. *Financial support:* Fellowships with partial tuition reimbursements, career-related internships or fieldwork and institutionally sponsored loans available. Support available to part-time students. Financial award application deadline: 2/15. *Unit head:* Jamin Raskin, Director, 202-885-4011.

Appalachian School of Law, Professional Program in Law, Grundy, VA 24614. Offers JD. *Accreditation:* ABA. Part-time programs available. *Faculty:* 20 full-time, 4 part-time/adjunct. *Students:* 369 full-time (114 women); includes 21 minority (5 African Americans, 1 American Indian/Alaska Native, 4 Asian Americans or Pacific Islanders, 11 Hispanic Americans). Average age 27. 1,714 applicants, 42% accepted, 163 enrolled. In 2006, 108 degrees awarded. *Median time to degree:* 3 years full-time. *Entrance requirements:* LSAT. *Application deadline:* For spring admission, 4/15 priority date for domestic students. Applications are processed on a rolling basis. Application fee: $60. Electronic applications accepted. *Expenses:* Tuition: Full-time $22,500. Required fees: $275. *Financial support:* In 2006–07, 205 students received support, including 12 research assistantships (averaging $1,000 per year); career-related internships or fieldwork, Federal Work-Study, institutionally sponsored loans, scholarships/grants, and tuition waivers (full and partial) also available. Financial award application deadline: 7/1; financial award applicants required to submit FAFSA. *Faculty research:* Appalachian legal issues, dispute resolution, constitutional law, professional ethics, intellectual property. *Unit head:* Clinton W. Shinn, Dean, 276-935-4349, Fax: 276-935-8261, E-mail: wshinn@asl.edu. *Application contact:* Nancy M. Pruitt, Director of Student Services and Registrar, 276-935-4349 Ext. 1229, Fax: 276-935-8261, E-mail: npruitt@asl.edu.

Arizona State University, College of Law, Tempe, AZ 85287-7906. Offers JD, JD/MBA, JD/PhD. *Accreditation:* ABA. *Degree requirements:* For first-professional, paper. *Entrance requirements:* LSAT. Additional exam requirements/recommendations for international students: Required—TOEFL (minimum score 550 paper-based; 213 computer-based). Expenses: Contact institution. *Faculty research:* Genetics and law, forensics and the law, science and law, Indian law, jurisprudence.

Ave Maria School of Law, School of Law, Ann Arbor, MI 48105-2550. Offers JD. *Accreditation:* ABA. *Faculty:* 29 full-time (13 women), 8 part-time/adjunct (2 women). *Students:* 380 full-time (126 women), 1 (woman) part-time; includes 62 minority (6 African Americans, 4 American Indian/Alaska Native, 28 Asian Americans or Pacific Islanders, 24 Hispanic Americans), 8 international. Average age 26. 941 applicants, 53% accepted, 131 enrolled. In 2006, 88 degrees awarded. *Entrance requirements:* LSAT, 2 letters of recommendation. Additional exam requirements/recommendations for international students: Required—TOEFL (minimum score 600 paper-based; 250 computer-based). *Application deadline:* For fall admission, 6/10 priority date for domestic and international students. Applications are processed on a rolling basis. Application fee: $50. Electronic applications accepted. *Expenses:* Tuition: Full-time $30,345. Tuition and fees vary according to student level. *Financial support:* In 2006–07, 220 students received support. Career-related internships or fieldwork, Federal Work-Study, and scholarships/grants available. Financial award application deadline: 6/1; financial award applicants required to submit FAFSA. *Application contact:* Rachele Conner, Assistant Director of Admissions, 734-827-8063, Fax: 734-622-0123, E-mail: rconner@avemarialaw.edu.

Barry University, School of Law, Orlando, FL 32807. Offers JD, JD/MS. *Accreditation:* ABA. *Students:* 556 full-time (267 women), 19 part-time (9 women); includes 108 minority (26 African Americans, 4 American Indian/Alaska Native, 25 Asian Americans or Pacific Islanders, 53 Hispanic Americans), 3 international. Average age 29. 2,122 applicants, 46% accepted, 207 enrolled. In 2006, 102 degrees awarded. *Application deadline:* For fall admission, 4/1 priority date for domestic students. *Unit head:* Leticia Diaz, Dean, 321-206-5602, E-mail: ldiaz@mail.barry.edu. *Application contact:* Sheri Lagomarsino, Director of Admissions, 321-206-5654, Fax: 321-206-5620, E-mail: slagomarsino@mail.barry.edu.

Baylor University, School of Law, Waco, TX 76798-7288. Offers JD, JD/MBA, JD/MPPA, JD/MT. *Accreditation:* ABA. *Faculty:* 24 full-time (4 women), 36 part-time/adjunct (2 women). *Students:* 391 full-time (168 women), 7 part-time (4 women); includes 42 minority (5 African Americans, 1 American Indian/Alaska Native, 22 Asian Americans or Pacific Islanders, 14 Hispanic Americans), 3 international. Average age 24. 2,082 applicants, 21% accepted, 94 enrolled. In 2006, 151 degrees awarded. *Entrance requirements:* LSAT. *Application deadline:* For fall admission, 3/1 for domestic students; for spring admission, 11/1 for domestic students. Applications are processed on a rolling basis. Application fee: $40. Electronic applications accepted. *Expenses:* Contact institution. *Financial support:* In 2006–07, 394 students received support. Career-related internships or fieldwork, Federal Work-Study, institutionally sponsored loans, and scholarships/grants available. Financial award applicants required to submit FAFSA. *Unit head:* Dr. Bradley J. B. Toben, Dean, 254-710-1911, Fax: 254-710-2316. *Application contact:* Heather Creed, Director of Student Relations, 254-710-1911, Fax: 254-710-2316, E-mail: heather_creed@baylor.edu.

Boston College, Law School, Newton, MA 02459. Offers JD, JD/MA, JD/MBA, JD/MSW. *Accreditation:* ABA. *Faculty:* 52 full-time (22 women), 35 part-time/adjunct (10 women). *Students:* 781 full-time (353 women); includes 187 minority (40 African Americans, 1 American Indian/Alaska Native, 94 Asian Americans or Pacific Islanders, 52 Hispanic Americans), 22 international. Average age 25. 6,321 applicants, 19% accepted, 254 enrolled. In 2006, 288 degrees awarded. *Entrance requirements:* LSAT. Additional exam requirements/recommendations for international students: Required—TOEFL. *Application deadline:* For fall admission, 3/1 for domestic and international students. Applications are processed on a rolling basis. Application fee: $75. Electronic applications accepted. *Expenses:* Contact institution. *Financial support:* In 2006–07, 448 students received support. Career-related internships or fieldwork, Federal Work-Study, institutionally sponsored loans, scholarships/grants, and tuition waivers (partial) available. Financial award application deadline: 3/15; financial award applicants required to submit FAFSA. *Faculty research:* Commercial law, labor law, legal history, comparative law, international law. *Unit head:* John H. Garvey, Dean, 617-552-4340. *Application contact:* Rita C. Jones, Assistant Dean for Admissions and Financial Aid, 617-522-4351, Fax: 617-522-2917, E-mail: rita.jones@bc.edu.

Boston University, School of Law, Boston, MA 02215. Offers American law (LL M); banking law (LL M); intellectual property law (LL M); law (JD); taxation (LL M); JD/LL M; JD/MA; JD/MBA; JD/MPH; JD/MS; JD/MSW. *Accreditation:* ABA. Part-time and evening/weekend programs available. *Faculty:* 69 full-time (21 women), 72 part-time/adjunct (20 women). *Students:* 987 full-time (495 women), 103 part-time (52 women); includes 195 minority (38 African Americans, 2 American Indian/Alaska Native, 125 Asian Americans or Pacific Islanders, 30 Hispanic Americans), 132 international. Average age 27. 7,265 applicants, 19% accepted, 285 enrolled. In 2006, 262 JDs, 162 master's awarded. *Degree requirements:* For JD, thesis, research project resulting in a paper; for master's, thesis (for some programs). *Entrance requirements:* For JD, LSAT; for master's, JD. Additional exam requirements/recommendations for international students: Required—TOEFL (minimum score 600 paper-based; 250 computer-based). *Application deadline:* For fall admission, 3/1 for domestic and international students. Applications are processed on a rolling basis. Application fee: $60. Electronic applications accepted. *Expenses:* Tuition: Full-time $33,330; part-time $1,042 per credit. Required fees: $462; $40. *Financial support:* In 2006–07, 681 students received support. Career-related internships or fieldwork, Federal Work-Study, institutionally sponsored loans, and scholarships/grants available. Financial award application deadline: 3/1; financial award applicants required to submit CSS PROFILE or FAFSA. *Faculty research:* Litigation and dispute resolution, intellectual property law, business organizations and finance law, international law, health law. *Unit head:* Maureen O'Rourke, Interim Dean, 617-353-3112, Fax: 617-353-7400. *Application contact:* Joan Horgan, Director of Admissions and Financial Aid, 617-353-3100, Fax: 617-353-0578, E-mail: bulawadm@bu.edu.

Brigham Young University, Graduate Studies, J. Reuben Clark Law School, Provo, UT 84602-8000. Offers JD, LL M, JD/Ed D, JD/M Acc, JD/M Ed, JD/MBA, JD/MPA, JD/PhD. *Accreditation:* ABA. *Faculty:* 37 full-time (7 women), 33 part-time/adjunct (14 women). *Students:* 472 full-time (179 women); includes 82 minority (6 African Americans, 5 American Indian/Alaska Native, 38 Asian Americans or Pacific Islanders, 33 Hispanic Americans), 6 international. Average age 26. 940 applicants, 27% accepted, 153 enrolled. In 2006, 164 degrees awarded. *Entrance requirements:* LSAT. Additional exam requirements/recommendations for international students: Required—TOEFL (minimum score 590 paper-based; 243 computer-based). *Application deadline:* For fall admission, 3/1 for domestic students. Applications are processed on a rolling basis. Application fee: $50. *Expenses:* Contact institution. *Financial support:* In 2006–07, 252 students received support, including 243 fellowships (averaging $1,500 per year); research assistantships, teaching assistantships, career-related internships or fieldwork, institutionally sponsored loans, scholarships/grants, and health care benefits also available. Financial award application deadline: 6/1; financial award applicants required to submit FAFSA. *Faculty research:* International law, federal taxation, real property law, constitutional law, business organization law. Total annual research expenditures: $10,363. *Unit head:* Kevin J Worthen, Dean, 801-422-6383, Fax: 801-422-0389, E-mail: worthenk@lawgate.byu.edu. *Application contact:* GaeLynn Kuchar, Admissions Director, 801-422-4277, Fax: 801-422-0389, E-mail: kucharg@lawgate.byu.edu.

Brooklyn Law School, Professional Program, Brooklyn, NY 11201-3798. Offers JD, JD/MA, JD/MBA, JD/MS, JD/MUP. *Accreditation:* ABA. Part-time and evening/weekend programs available. *Faculty:* 66 full-time (30 women), 70 part-time/adjunct (19 women). *Students:* 1,156 full-time (571 women), 345 part-time (164 women); includes 394 minority (88 African Americans, 2 American Indian/Alaska Native, 221 Asian Americans or Pacific Islanders, 83 Hispanic Americans), 8 international. Average age 26. 5,003 applicants, 29% accepted, 493 enrolled. In 2006, 494 degrees awarded. *Entrance requirements:* LSAT, dean's certification, 2 faculty letters of evaluation. Additional exam requirements/recommendations for international students: Recommended—TOEFL (minimum score 600 paper-based; 250 computer-based), TWE. *Application deadline:* For fall admission, 2/1 priority date for domestic and international students. Applications are processed on a rolling basis. Application fee: $65. Electronic applications accepted. *Financial support:* In 2006–07, 1,280 students received support, including 48 fellowships with partial tuition reimbursements available (averaging $5,000 per year), 91 research assistantships with partial tuition reimbursements available (averaging $2,680 per year); career-related internships or fieldwork, Federal Work-Study, scholarships/grants, and tuition waivers (partial) also available. Support available to part-time students. Financial award application deadline: 4/28; financial award applicants required to submit FAFSA. *Faculty research:* Civil procedure, securities regulation, family law, corporate finance, international business and law, health law. *Unit head:* Joan G. Wexler, Dean, 718-780-7900, Fax: 718-780-0393. *Application contact:* Henry W. Haverstick, Dean of Admissions and Financial Aid, 718-780-7906, Fax: 718-780-0395, E-mail: admitq@brooklaw.edu.

California Western School of Law, Graduate and Professional Programs, San Diego, CA 92101-3090. Offers law (JD, LL M); JD/MBA; JD/MSW; JD/PhD; MCL/LL M. *Accreditation:* ABA. Part-time programs available. *Entrance requirements:* LSAT. Additional exam requirements/recommendations for international students: Required—TOEFL. Electronic applications accepted. *Faculty research:* Biotechnology, child and family law, international law, labor and employment law, sports law.

Campbell University, Graduate and Professional Programs, Norman Adrian Wiggins School of Law, Buies Creek, NC 27506. Offers JD. *Accreditation:* ABA. *Faculty:* 23 full-time (5 women), 23 part-time/adjunct (4 women). *Students:* 343 full-time (165 women); includes 12 minority (7 African Americans, 3 American Indian/Alaska Native, 2 Hispanic Americans), 5 international. Average age 26. 1,032 applicants, 26% accepted, 122 enrolled. In 2006, 99 degrees awarded. *Entrance requirements:* LSAT, interview. *Application deadline:* For fall admission, 3/31 priority date for domestic students. Applications are processed on a rolling basis. Application fee: $50. Electronic applications accepted. *Expenses:* Contact institution. *Financial support:* In 2006–07, 326 students received support, including 15 research assistantships (averaging $960 per year), 15 teaching assistantships (averaging $4,000 per year); career-related internships or fieldwork, Federal Work-Study, institutionally sponsored loans, and scholarships/grants also available. Financial award application deadline: 4/15; financial award applicants required to submit FAFSA. *Faculty research:* Interdisciplinary approaches to legal problems, management and planning for lawyers, church/state constitutional problems, basic research in substantive legal areas. *Unit head:* Melissa A. Essary, Dean, 910-893-1750, Fax: 910-893-1780, E-mail: essary@law.campbell.edu. *Application contact:* Lewis Hutchison, Assistant Dean for Admissions, 910-893-1754, Fax: 910-893-1780, E-mail: hutchison@law.campbell.edu.

Capital University, Law School, Columbus, OH 43215-3200. Offers JD, LL M, MT, JD/LL M, JD/MBA, JD/MSA, JD/MSN, JD/MTS. *Accreditation:* ABA. Part-time and evening/weekend programs available. *Degree requirements:* For master's, thesis or alternative. *Entrance requirements:* For JD, LSAT, LSDAS; for master's, previous course work in accounting, business law, and taxation. Additional exam requirements/recommendations for international students: Required—TOEFL. Electronic applications accepted. Expenses: Contact institution. Part-time tuition and fees vary according to program. *Faculty research:* Dispute resolution, remedies, taxation, commercial law, election law.

Case Western Reserve University, School of Law, Cleveland, OH 44106. Offers law (JD); U.S. legal studies (LL M); JD/CNM; JD/MA; JD/MBA; JD/MD; JD/MNO; JD/MPH; JD/MS; JD/MSSA. *Accreditation:* ABA. Part-time programs available. *Faculty:* 52 full-time (16 women), 130 part-time/adjunct (43 women). *Students:* 670 full-time (273 women), 3 part-time (all women); includes 113 minority (29 African Americans, 2 American Indian/Alaska Native, 73 Asian Americans or Pacific Islanders, 9 Hispanic Americans), 7 international. Average age 25. 2,653 applicants, 28% accepted, 228 enrolled. In 2006, 241 JDs, 34 master's awarded. *Entrance requirements:* LSAT, LSDAS. *Application deadline:* For fall admission, 2/1 priority date for domestic students, 4/1 priority date for international students. Applications are processed on a rolling basis. Application fee: $40. Electronic applications accepted. *Expenses: Contact institution. Financial support:* In 2006–07, 560 students received support. Career-related internships or fieldwork, Federal Work-Study, and scholarships/grants available. Support available to part-time students. Financial award application deadline: 3/15; financial award applicants required to submit FAFSA. *Unit head:* Gary J. Simson, Dean, 216-368-3283. *Application contact:* Alyson Alber, Interim Assistant Dean for Admissions, 216-368-3600, Fax: 216-368-1042, E-mail: lawadmissions@case.edu.

The Catholic University of America, Columbus School of Law, Washington, DC 20064. Offers JD, JD/JCL, JD/MA, JD/MLS, JD/MSW. *Accreditation:* ABA. Part-time and evening/weekend programs available. *Entrance requirements:* LSAT. Additional exam requirements/recommendations for international students: Required—TOEFL. Electronic applications accepted. Expenses: Contact institution. Part-time tuition and fees vary according to campus/location and program.

The Catholic University of America, School of Arts and Sciences, Department of Psychology, Program in Psychology/Law, Washington, DC 20064. Offers JD/MA. Part-time programs available. *Entrance requirements:* Additional exam requirements/recommendations for international students: Required—TOEFL (minimum score 580 paper-based; 237 computer-based). *Application deadline:* For fall admission, 2/1 priority date for domestic students; for spring admission, 11/15 priority date for domestic students. Applications are processed on a rolling basis. Application fee: $55. Electronic applications accepted. *Expenses:* Tuition: Full-time $27,700; part-time $1,045 per credit hour. Required fees: $1,290. Part-time tuition and fees vary according to campus/location and program. *Financial support:* Career-related internships or fieldwork, Federal Work-Study, scholarships/grants, tuition waivers (full and partial), and unspecified assistantships available. Support available to part-time students. Financial award application deadline: 2/1; financial award applicants required to submit FAFSA. *Faculty research:* Psychological methodology, human memory, social and moral development.

Central European University, Graduate Studies, Department of Legal Studies, Budapest, Hungary. Offers comparative constitutional law (LL M); economic and legal studies (LL M, MA); human rights (LL M, MA); international business law (LL M); legal studies (SJD). *Faculty:* 7 full-time (2 women), 3 part-time/adjunct (1 woman). *Students:* 115 full-time (58 women). Average age 26. 579 applicants, 21% accepted, 88 enrolled. In 2006, 40 master's, 4 doctorates awarded. Terminal master's awarded for partial completion of doctoral program. *Median time to degree:* Of those who began their doctoral program in fall 1998, 75% received their degree in 8 years or less. *Degree requirements:* For master's, one foreign language, thesis/dissertation, registration; for doctorate, one foreign language, thesis/dissertation, comprehensive exam, registration. *Entrance requirements:* For master's and doctorate, LSAT, CEU admissions exams. Additional exam requirements/recommendations for international students: Required—TOEFL (minimum score 570 paper-based; 230 computer-based). *Application deadline:* For fall admission, 1/5 for domestic and international students. Application fee: $0. Electronic applications accepted. *Expenses: Contact institution. Financial support:* In 2006–07, 84 students received support, including 65 fellowships with full and partial tuition reimbursements available (averaging $5,000 per year); career-related internships or fieldwork, institutionally sponsored loans, scholarships/grants, and tuition waivers (full and partial) also available. Financial award application deadline: 1/5. *Faculty research:* Institutional, constitutional and human rights in European Union law, biomedical law and reproductive rights, data protection law, Islamic banking and finance. *Unit head:* Dr. Stefan Messmann, Head, 361-327-3274, Fax: 361-327-3198, E-mail: legalst@ceu.hu. *Application contact:* Maria Balla, Coordinator, 361-327-3204, Fax: 361-327-3198, E-mail: ballam@ceu.hu.

Chapman University, Graduate Studies, School of Law, Orange, CA 92866. Offers law (JD); taxation (LL M); JD/MBA. *Accreditation:* ABA. Part-time and evening/weekend programs available. *Faculty:* 36 full-time (15 women), 30 part-time/adjunct (5 women). *Students:* 509 full-time (235 women), 75 part-time (36 women); includes 134 minority (5 African Americans, 3 American Indian/Alaska Native, 90 Asian Americans or Pacific Islanders, 36 Hispanic Americans), 7 international. Average age 26. 2,385 applicants, 33% accepted, 197 enrolled. In 2006, 181 JDs, 15 master's awarded. *Degree requirements:* For master's, registration. *Entrance requirements:* LSAT, minimum undergraduate GPA of 2.75. Additional exam requirements/recommendations for international students: Required—TOEFL (minimum score 600 paper-based). *Application deadline:* Applications are processed on a rolling basis. Application fee: $60. Electronic applications accepted. *Expenses: Contact institution. Financial support:* In 2006–07, 492 students received support; fellowships, Federal Work-Study available. Financial award application deadline: 6/30; financial award applicants required to submit FAFSA. *Unit head:* Dr. Parham Williams, Dean, 714-628-2500. *Application contact:* Demetrius L. Greer, Office of Admissions, 888-242-1913, E-mail: greer@chapman.edu.

City University of New York School of Law at Queens College, Professional Program, Flushing, NY 11367-1358. Offers JD. *Accreditation:* ABA. *Faculty:* 27 full-time (14 women), 16 part-time/adjunct (10 women). *Students:* 417 full-time (274 women), 4 part-time (3 women); includes 131 minority (30 African Americans, 1 American Indian/Alaska Native, 66 Asian Americans or Pacific Islanders, 34 Hispanic Americans), 17 international. Average age 27. 2,457 applicants, 23% accepted, 144 enrolled. In 2006, 128 degrees awarded. *Entrance requirements:* LSAT, LSDAS. *Application deadline:* For fall admission, 3/15 priority date for domestic students. Applications are processed on a rolling basis. Application fee: $50. Electronic applications accepted. *Expenses:* Tuition, state resident: full-time $8,900. Tuition, nonresident: full-time $14,800. Required fees: $1,662. *Financial support:* In 2006–07, 124 students received support, including 20 fellowships (averaging $8,900 per year), 35 research assistantships (averaging $3,000 per year), 3 teaching assistantships (averaging $1,920 per year); career-related internships or fieldwork, Federal Work-Study, scholarships/grants, and tuition waivers (partial) also available. Financial award application deadline: 5/1; financial award applicants required to submit FAFSA. *Unit head:* Michelle J. Anderson, Professor of Law, 718-340-4201, Fax: 718-340-4482. *Application contact:* Yvonne Cherena-Pacheco, Assistant Dean for Enrollment Management and Director of Admissions, 718-340-4210, Fax: 718-340-4435, E-mail: admissions@mail.law.cuny.edu.

Cleveland State University, Cleveland-Marshall College of Law, Cleveland, OH 44115. Offers JD, LL M, JD/MAES, JD/MBA, JD/MPA, JD/MSES, JD/MUPDD. *Accreditation:* ABA. Part-time and evening/weekend programs available. *Faculty:* 42 full-time (17 women), 25 part-time/adjunct (7 women). *Students:* 436 full-time (214 women), 312 part-time (150 women); includes 92 minority (45 African Americans, 4 American Indian/Alaska Native, 25 Asian Americans or Pacific Islanders, 18 Hispanic Americans), 12 international. Average age 28. 1,814 applicants, 31% accepted, 247 enrolled. In 2006, 197 degrees awarded. *Degree requirements:* For master's, thesis (for some programs). *Entrance requirements:* For JD, LSAT; for master's, JD or LL B. Additional exam requirements/recommendations for international students: Required—TOEFL, TWE. *Application deadline:* For fall admission, 5/1 for domestic and international students. Applications are processed on a rolling basis. Application fee: $35. Electronic applications accepted. *Expenses: Contact institution. Financial support:* In 2006–07, 205 students received support, including 4 teaching assistantships with partial tuition reimbursements available (averaging $2,400 per year); career-related internships or fieldwork, Federal Work-Study, institutionally sponsored loans, scholarships/grants, tuition waivers (full and partial), and unspecified assistantships also available. Support available to part-time students. Financial award application deadline: 5/1; financial award applicants required to submit FAFSA. *Faculty research:* Criminal law, law and medicine, intellectual property, commercial law, business organizations. *Unit head:* Geoffrey S. Mearns, Dean, 216-687-2300, Fax: 216-687-6881, E-mail: geoffrey.mearns@law.csuohio.edu. *Application contact:* Christopher Lucak, Assistant Dean for Admissions, 216-687-4692, Fax: 216-687-6881, E-mail: christopher.lucak@law.csuohio.edu.

The College of William and Mary, William & Mary Law School, Williamsburg, VA 23187-8795. Offers JD, LL M, JD/MA, JD/MBA, JD/MPP. *Accreditation:* ABA. *Faculty:* 32 full-time (10 women), 30 part-time/adjunct (11 women). *Students:* 620 full-time (281 women), 3 part-time (all women); includes 87 minority (49 African Americans, 1 American Indian/Alaska Native, 29 Asian Americans or Pacific Islanders, 8 Hispanic Americans), 4 international. Average age 26. 4,209 applicants, 24% accepted, 204 enrolled. In 2006, 206 JDs, 11 master's awarded. *Degree requirements:* For JD and master's, major paper. *Entrance requirements:* For JD, LSAT; for master's, law degree. Additional exam requirements/recommendations for international students: Required—TOEFL (minimum score 600 paper-based; 250 computer-based). *Application deadline:* For fall admission, 3/1 priority date for domestic and international students. Application fee: $50. Electronic applications accepted. *Expenses: Contact institution.* Tuition and fees vary according to program. *Financial support:* In 2006–07, 338 students received support, including 222 research assistantships with partial tuition reimbursements available (averaging $4,000 per year), 26 teaching assistantships (averaging $4,300 per year); career-related internships or fieldwork, Federal Work-Study, institutionally sponsored loans, and scholarships/grants also available. Financial award application deadline: 2/15; financial award applicants required to submit FAFSA. *Faculty research:* Intellectual property law, corporate law, environmental law, international law, constitutional law. Total annual research expenditures: $43,859. *Unit head:* W. Taylor Reveley, Dean, 757-221-3800, Fax: 757-221-3261, E-mail: taylor@wm.edu. *Application contact:* Faye F. Shealy, Associate Dean for Admission, 757-221-3785, Fax: 757-221-3261, E-mail: ffshea@wm.edu.

Columbia University, School of Law, New York, NY 10027. Offers JD, LL M, JSD, JD/M Phil, JD/MA, JD/MBA, JD/MFA, JD/MIA, JD/MPA, JD/MPH, JD/MSW. *Accreditation:* ABA. *Entrance requirements:* LSAT. Electronic applications accepted. Expenses: Contact institution. *Faculty research:* Human rights, law and philosophy, corporate governance, regulation of the workplace, death penalty.

Concord Law School, Program in Law, Los Angeles, CA 90024. Offers EJD, JD. Part-time and evening/weekend programs available. Postbaccalaureate distance learning degree programs offered (no on-campus study). *Degree requirements:* For first-professional, comprehensive exam. *Entrance requirements:* Online admissions test. Additional exam requirements/recommendations for international students: Required—TOEFL (minimum score 520 paper-based). Electronic applications accepted.

Cornell University, Cornell Law School, Ithaca, NY 14853-4901. Offers JD, LL M, JD/DESS, JD/LL M, JD/MA, JD/MBA, JD/MILR, JD/MLLP, JD/MLP, JD/MPA, JD/MRP, JD/Maitrise en Droit, JD/PhD. JD/MLLP offered jointly with Humboldt University, Berlin; JD/DESS offered jointly with Institut d[0092][00c9]tudes Politiques de Paris ('Sciences Po") and Paris I. *Accreditation:* ABA. *Faculty:* 57 full-time (16 women), 51 part-time/adjunct (12 women). *Students:* 632 full-time (307 women). Average age 25. 5,131 applicants. In 2006, 192 JDs, 56 master's awarded. *Entrance requirements:* LSAT. *Application deadline:* For fall admission, 2/1 for domestic students. Applications are processed on a rolling basis. Application fee: $70. Electronic applications accepted. *Expenses: Contact institution.* Full-time tuition and fees vary according to program. *Financial support:* In 2006–07, 250 students received support. Career-related internships or fieldwork, Federal Work-Study, and scholarships/grants available. Financial award application deadline: 3/15; financial award applicants required to submit FAFSA. *Faculty research:* International law, constitutional law, corporate laws, public interest law, feminist legal theory. *Unit head:* Stewart J. Schawb, Dean, 607-255-3527. *Application contact:* Richard D. Geiger, Associate Dean, 607-255-5141, Fax: 607-255-7193, E-mail: rdg9@cornell.edu.

Cornell University, Graduate School, Graduate Field in the Law School, Ithaca, NY 14853-0001. Offers LL M, JSD. *Faculty:* 37 full-time (9 women). *Students:* 73 full-time (38 women); includes 7 minority (4 Asian Americans or Pacific Islanders, 3 Hispanic Americans), 41 international. Average age 29. 856 applicants, 32% accepted, 61 enrolled. In 2006, 64 master's, 5 doctorates awarded. *Entrance requirements:* For doctorate, JD, LL M, or equivalent; 2 letters of recommendation. Additional exam requirements/recommendations for international students: Required—TOEFL (minimum score 550 paper-based; 213 computer-based). *Application deadline:* For fall admission, 5/1 for domestic students. Application fee: $60. Electronic applications accepted. *Expenses: Contact institution.* Full-time tuition and fees vary according to program. *Financial support:* In 2006–07, 8 students received support, including 8 fellowships with full tuition reimbursements available; research assistantships with full tuition reimbursements available, teaching assistantships with full tuition reimbursements available, institutionally sponsored loans, scholarships/grants, health care benefits, tuition waivers (full and partial), and unspecified assistantships also available. Financial award applicants required to submit FAFSA. *Faculty research:* International economic integration (WTO and EU), international commercial arbitration, feminist jurisprudence, human rights. *Unit head:* Director of Graduate Studies, 607-255-5141. *Application contact:* Graduate Field Assistant, 607-255-5141, E-mail: gradlaw@law.mail.cornell.edu.

Creighton University, School of Law, Omaha, NE 68178. Offers JD, MS, JD/MA, JD/MBA, JD/MS. *Accreditation:* ABA. Part-time programs available. *Faculty:* 26 full-time (6 women), 32 part-time/adjunct (8 women). *Students:* 452 full-time (195 women), 16 part-time (7 women); includes 46 minority (10 African Americans, 3 American Indian/Alaska Native, 15 Asian Americans or Pacific Islanders, 18 Hispanic Americans), 1 international. Average age 24. 1,334 applicants, 40% accepted, 161 enrolled. In 2006, 148 degrees awarded. *Entrance requirements:* LSAT. *Application deadline:* For fall admission, 5/1 priority date for domestic students. Applications are processed on a rolling basis. Application fee: $45. Electronic applications accepted. *Expenses: Contact institution. Financial support:* In 2006–07, 419 students received support. Career-related internships or fieldwork, institutionally sponsored loans, scholarships/grants, and unspecified assistantships available. Support available to part-time students. Financial award application deadline: 7/1; financial award applicants required to submit FAFSA. *Faculty research:* Bankruptcy, conflict of laws, international human rights, casino gaming, alternative dispute resolution. *Unit head:* Patrick J. Borchers, Dean, 402-280-2874, Fax: 402-280-3161. *Application contact:* Andrea D. Bashara, Assistant Dean, 402-280-2872, Fax: 402-280-3161, E-mail: bashara@creighton.edu.

Dalhousie University, Faculty of Graduate Studies, Faculty of Law, Halifax, NS B3H 4R2, Canada. Offers LL M, JSD, LL B/MBA, LL B/MHSA, LL B/MLIS, LL B/MPA. Part-time programs available. *Degree requirements:* For master's, thesis or alternative; for doctorate, thesis/dissertation. *Entrance requirements:* Additional exam requirements/recommendations for international students: Required—TOEFL. Expenses: Contact institution. *Faculty research:* Marine and environmental law, international comparative law, health law, general public and private law fields.

DePaul University, College of Law, Chicago, IL 60604-2287. Offers JD, LL M, JD/MA, JD/MAIS, JD/MBA, JD/MPS, JD/MS. *Accreditation:* ABA. Part-time programs available. *Faculty:* 45 full-time (18 women), 54 part-time/adjunct (16 women). *Students:* 943 full-time (468 women), 236 part-time (119 women); includes 222 minority (72 African Americans, 3 American Indian/Alaska Native, 72 Asian Americans or Pacific Islanders, 75 Hispanic Americans), 16 international.

Law

DePaul University (continued)
Average age 27. 5,028 applicants, 28% accepted, 330 enrolled. In 2006, 311 degrees awarded. *Entrance requirements:* LSAT, LSDAS. Additional exam requirements/recommendations for international students: Required—TOEFL (minimum score 600 paper-based; 250 computer-based). *Application deadline:* For fall admission, 3/1 for domestic students. Applications are processed on a rolling basis. Application fee: $60. Electronic applications accepted. *Expenses:* Contact institution. *Financial support:* In 2006–07, 527 students received support, including 38 fellowships with tuition reimbursements available, 98 research assistantships (averaging $1,200 per year), 16 teaching assistantships (averaging $2,000 per year); career-related internships or fieldwork, Federal Work-Study, scholarships/grants, and tuition waivers (full and partial) also available. Support available to part-time students. Financial award application deadline: 3/1; financial award applicants required to submit FAFSA. *Faculty research:* Health law, international law, constitutional law, human rights law, church-state studies. Total annual research expenditures: $750,000. *Unit head:* Glen Weissenberger, Dean, 312-362-8088, E-mail: gweissen@depaul.edu. *Application contact:* Michael S Burns, Director of Law Admission and Assistant Dean, 312-362-6831, Fax: 312-362-5280, E-mail: lawinfo@depaul.edu.

Drake University, Law School, Des Moines, IA 50311-4505. Offers JD, JD/MA, JD/MBA, JD/MPA, JD/MS, JD/MSW, JD/Pharm D. *Accreditation:* ABA. *Faculty:* 17 part-time/adjunct (5 women). *Students:* 432 full-time (203 women), 6 part-time (5 women); includes 43 minority (21 African Americans, 7 American Indian/Alaska Native, 3 Asian Americans or Pacific Islanders, 12 Hispanic Americans), 7 international. Average age 25. 1,106 applicants, 46% accepted. In 2006, 158 degrees awarded. *Degree requirements:* For first-professional, internships (2). *Entrance requirements:* LSAT, LSDAS Report. Additional exam requirements/recommendations for international students: Required—TOEFL (minimum score 560 paper-based; 220 computer-based), TWE. *Application deadline:* For fall admission, 4/1 priority date for domestic and international students. Applications are processed on a rolling basis. Application fee: $40. Electronic applications accepted. *Expenses:* Contact institution. *Financial support:* In 2006–07, 20 research assistantships (averaging $757 per year), 6 teaching assistantships (averaging $2,142 per year) were awarded; career-related internships or fieldwork, Federal Work-Study, institutionally sponsored loans, scholarships/grants, and tuition waivers (full and partial) also available. Support available to part-time students. Financial award application deadline: 3/1; financial award applicants required to submit FAFSA. *Faculty research:* Agricultural law. Total annual research expenditures: $167,106. *Unit head:* David Walker, Dean, 515-271-1805, Fax: 515-271-4118, E-mail: david.walker@drake.edu. *Application contact:* J. Kara Blanchard, Director of Admission and Financial Aid, 515-271-2953, Fax: 515-271-2530, E-mail: kara.blanchard@drake.edu.

See Close-Up on page 2099.

Duke University, School of Law, Durham, NC 27708. Offers JD, LL M, MLS, SJD, JD/AM, JD/LL M, JD/MA, JD/MBA, JD/MEM, JD/MPP, JD/MS, JD/MTS, JD/PhD, MD/JD. LL M and SJD offered only to international students. *Accreditation:* ABA. *Faculty:* 50 full-time (14 women), 43 part-time/adjunct (18 women). *Students:* 630 full-time (273 women); includes 149 minority (64 African Americans, 2 American Indian/Alaska Native, 60 Asian Americans or Pacific Islanders, 23 Hispanic Americans), 6 international. Average age 26. 4,341 applicants, 23% accepted, 205 enrolled. In 2006, 220 JDs, 96 master's awarded. *Degree requirements:* For doctorate, thesis/dissertation. *Entrance requirements:* LSAT. Additional exam requirements/recommendations for international students: Required—TOEFL (minimum score 600 paper-based). *Application deadline:* For fall admission, 2/15 for domestic students. Applications are processed on a rolling basis. Application fee: $70. Electronic applications accepted. *Expenses:* Contact institution. *Financial support:* In 2006–07, 370 students received support. Federal Work-Study, institutionally sponsored loans, and scholarships/grants available. Financial award application deadline: 4/15; financial award applicants required to submit FAFSA. *Faculty research:* International and comparative law; constitutional and public law; intellectual property, science and technology; business, finance, and corporate law; environmental law and policy. *Unit head:* William J. Hoye, Associate Dean, Admissions and Financial Aid, 919-613-7020, Fax: 919-613-7257, E-mail: hoye@law.duke.edu.

Duquesne University, Bayer School of Natural and Environmental Sciences, Program in Forensic Science and the Law, Pittsburgh, PA 15282-0001. Offers MS. *Faculty:* 1 full-time (0 women), 8 part-time/adjunct (1 woman). *Students:* 42 full-time (30 women); includes 4 minority (all African Americans) In 2006, 9 degrees awarded. *Expenses:* Tuition: Part-time $723 per credit. Required fees: $71 per credit. Tuition and fees vary according to degree level and program. *Financial support:* Fellowships, research assistantships, teaching assistantships available. *Faculty research:* Extraction protocols, mass spectrometry, synthetic fiber analysis, synthetic polymer characterization, trace analysis. *Unit head:* Dr. Federick W. Fochtman, Director, 412-396-6373, E-mail: fochtman@duq.edu.

Duquesne University, School of Law, Pittsburgh, PA 15282-0700. Offers JD, LL M, JD/M Div, JD/MBA, JD/MS, JD/MSEM. *Accreditation:* ABA. Part-time and evening/weekend programs available. *Faculty:* 24 full-time (5 women), 44 part-time/adjunct (13 women). *Students:* 462 full-time (205 women), 186 part-time (92 women). Average age 23. In 2006, 168 degrees awarded. *Entrance requirements:* LSAT, minimum GPA of 3.25. Additional exam requirements/recommendations for international students: Required—TOEFL (minimum score 600 paper-based). *Application deadline:* For fall admission, 4/1 for domestic students. Applications are processed on a rolling basis. Application fee: $50. *Expenses:* Contact institution. Tuition and fees vary according to degree level and program. *Financial support:* In 2006–07, 267 students received support; research assistantships, teaching assistantships, career-related internships or fieldwork, Federal Work-Study, scholarships/grants, tuition waivers (partial), and grant-in-aid awards available. Support available to part-time students. Financial award application deadline: 5/31. *Faculty research:* Clinical legal education, litigation/trial advocacy. Total annual research expenditures: $100,000. *Unit head:* Donald J. Guter, Dean, 412-396-6280, Fax: 412-396-1073, E-mail: guterd@duq.edu. *Application contact:* Joseph P. Campion, Director, Admissions/Law School, 412-396-6296, Fax: 412-396-1073, E-mail: campion@duq.edu.

Elon University, Program in Law, Elon, NC 27244-2010. Offers JD. *Faculty:* 7 full-time (3 women). *Students:* 115 full-time (53 women); includes 9 minority (7 African Americans, 2 Asian Americans or Pacific Islanders). Average age 25. 534 applicants, 36% accepted, 115 enrolled. *Entrance requirements:* LSAT, LSDAS. Additional exam requirements/recommendations for international students: Required—TOEFL (minimum score 550 paper-based; 213 computer-based; 79 iBT). *Application deadline:* For spring admission, 4/1 priority date for domestic students. Applications are processed on a rolling basis. Application fee: $50. Electronic applications accepted. *Expenses:* Contact institution. *Financial support:* In 2006–07, 54 students received support. Federal Work-Study and scholarships/grants available. Financial award applicants required to submit FAFSA. *Faculty research:* Quality of life and job satisfaction; civil procedure; damages; assessment for development for instruments; psychological types. *Unit head:* Leary Davis, Dean, 336-279-9201, E-mail: davislaw@elon.edu. *Application contact:* Alan Woodlief, Associate Dean for Admissions and Administration, 336-279-9203, E-mail: awoodlief@elon.edu.

Emory University, School of Law, Atlanta, GA 30322-2770. Offers JD, LL M, Certificate, JD/Certificate, JD/LL M, JD/M Div, JD/MA, JD/MBA, JD/MPH, JD/MTS, JD/PhD. *Accreditation:* ABA. *Faculty:* 57 full-time (22 women), 26 part-time/adjunct (4 women). *Students:* 674 full-time (323 women); includes 177 minority (62 African Americans, 72 Asian Americans or Pacific Islanders, 43 Hispanic Americans), 16 international. Average age 24. 3,591 applicants, 29% accepted, 207 enrolled. In 2006, 221 JDs, 12 other advanced degrees awarded. *Median time to degree:* JD–3 years full-time; Certificate–1 year full-time. *Entrance requirements:* LSAT, 2 letters of recommendation. Additional exam requirements/recommendations for international students: Required—TOEFL (minimum score 600 paper-based; 250 computer-based). *Application deadline:* For fall admission, 3/1 for domestic and international students. Applications are processed on a rolling basis. Application fee: $70. Electronic applications accepted. *Expenses:* Contact institution. *Financial support:* In 2006–07, 604 students received support, including 15 fellowships with full tuition reimbursements available (averaging $3,000 per year), 48 research assistantships (averaging $8,580 per year); career-related internships or fieldwork, Federal Work-Study, institutionally sponsored loans, scholarships/grants, and tuition waivers (full and partial) also available. Financial award application deadline: 3/1; financial award applicants required to submit FAFSA. *Faculty research:* Law and economics, law and religion, international law, human rights, feminism and legal theory. Total annual research expenditures: $1.9 million. *Unit head:* David F. Partlett, Dean, 404-712-8815, Fax: 404-727-0866, E-mail: david.partlett@emory.edu. *Application contact:* Lynell A. Cadray, Assistant Dean for Admissions, 404-727-6802, Fax: 404-727-2477, E-mail: lcadray@law.emory.edu.

Facultad de derecho Eugenio María de Hostos, School of Law, Mayagüez, PR 00681. Offers JD. *Entrance requirements:* EXADEP, LSAT, 2 letters of recommendation.

Faulkner University, Thomas Goode Jones School of Law, Montgomery, AL 36109-3398. Offers JD. Part-time and evening/weekend programs available. *Faculty:* 25 full-time (9 women), 4 part-time/adjunct (3 women). *Students:* 182 full-time (69 women), 92 part-time (42 women); includes 28 minority (20 African Americans, 3 American Indian/Alaska Native, 3 Asian Americans or Pacific Islanders, 2 Hispanic Americans). Average age 28. 316 applicants, 58% accepted, 106 enrolled. In 2006, 54 degrees awarded. *Entrance requirements:* LSAT. *Application deadline:* For fall admission, 5/1 for domestic students. Applications are processed on a rolling basis. Application fee: $25. Electronic applications accepted. *Financial support:* In 2006–07, 78 students received support. Career-related internships or fieldwork, scholarships/grants, and tuition waivers (full and partial) available. Support available to part-time students. Financial award application deadline: 5/1; financial award applicants required to submit FAFSA. *Unit head:* Charles I. Nelson, Dean, 334-386-7220, Fax: 334-386-7545, E-mail: cnelson@faulkner.edu. *Application contact:* Andrew R Matthews, Assistant Dean for Student Services, 334-386-7910, Fax: 334-386-7908, E-mail: amatthews@faulkner.edu.

Florida Agricultural and Mechanical University, College of Law, Tallahassee, FL 32307-3200. Offers JD. *Entrance requirements:* LSAT, LSDAS, 2 letters of recommendation. Additional exam requirements/recommendations for international students: Required—TOEFL. Expenses: Contact institution.

Florida Coastal School of Law, Professional Program, Jacksonville, FL 32256. Offers JD. *Accreditation:* ABA. Part-time programs available. *Faculty:* 58 full-time (36 women), 34 part-time/adjunct (8 women). *Students:* 824 full-time (379 women), 216 part-time (108 women); includes 233 minority (95 African Americans, 15 American Indian/Alaska Native, 53 Asian Americans or Pacific Islanders, 70 Hispanic Americans), 7 international. Average age 26. 4,940 applicants, 48% accepted, 553 enrolled. In 2006, 219 degrees awarded. *Entrance requirements:* LSAT. Additional exam requirements/recommendations for international students: Recommended—TOEFL (minimum score 600 paper-based; 250 computer-based). *Application deadline:* Applications are processed on a rolling basis. Application fee: $50. Electronic applications accepted. *Expenses:* Contact institution. *Financial support:* In 2006–07, 513 students received support, including 14 research assistantships (averaging $2,000 per year), 12 teaching assistantships (averaging $2,000 per year); scholarships/grants and tuition waivers (full and partial) also available. Support available to part-time students. Financial award applicants required to submit FAFSA. *Faculty research:* Law and business, law technology and intellectual property, juvenile justice and family law, constitutional law, labor law. Total annual research expenditures: $50,000. *Unit head:* Peter Goplerud, Dean, E-mail: pgoplerud@fcsl.edu. *Application contact:* 904-680-7710, Fax: 904-680-7776, E-mail: admissions@fcsl.edu.

Florida International University, College of Law, Miami, FL 33199. Offers JD. *Accreditation:* ABA. *Faculty:* 23 full-time (9 women), 1 part-time/adjunct (0 women). *Students:* 370 full-time (172 women), 13 part-time (4 women); includes 217 minority (38 African Americans, 2 American Indian/Alaska Native, 8 Asian Americans or Pacific Islanders, 169 Hispanic Americans), 1 international. 1,323 applicants, 19% accepted, 155 enrolled. In 2006, 82 degrees awarded. *Entrance requirements:* LSAT, 3 letters of recommendation. Application fee: $25. *Expenses:* Tuition, state resident: part-time $249 per credit hour. Tuition, nonresident: part-time $753 per credit hour. Tuition and fees vary according to program. *Unit head:* Dr. Leonard Strickman, Dean, 305-348-1118, Fax: 305-348-1159, E-mail: leonard.strickman@fiu.edu.

Florida State University, College of Law, Tallahassee, FL 32306-1601. Offers JD, JD/MBA, JD/MPA, JD/MS, JD/MSP, JD/MSW. *Accreditation:* ABA. *Faculty:* 46 full-time (18 women), 14 part-time/adjunct (4 women). *Students:* 765 full-time (305 women); includes 143 minority (43 African Americans, 6 American Indian/Alaska Native, 33 Asian Americans or Pacific Islanders, 61 Hispanic Americans), 12 international. Average age 23. 3,313 applicants, 24% accepted, 196 enrolled. In 2006, 244 degrees awarded. *Entrance requirements:* LSAT. Additional exam requirements/recommendations for international students: Required—TOEFL. *Application deadline:* For fall admission, 3/15 priority date for domestic students. Applications are processed on a rolling basis. Application fee: $30. Electronic applications accepted. *Expenses:* Contact institution. Tuition and fees vary according to program. *Financial support:* In 2006–07, 260 fellowships (averaging $1,500 per year), 58 research assistantships (averaging $3,300 per year), 6 teaching assistantships (averaging $2,069 per year) were awarded; scholarships/grants also available. Financial award application deadline: 4/1; financial award applicants required to submit FAFSA. *Faculty research:* Administrative law, business law, international law, environmental law and land use law. *Unit head:* Donald J. Weidner, Dean, 850-644-3400, Fax: 850-644-5487, E-mail: dweidner@law.fsu.edu. *Application contact:* Sharon J. Booker, Director of Admissions and Records, 850-644-3787, Fax: 850-644-7284, E-mail: admissions@law.fsu.edu.

Fordham University, School of Law, New York, NY 10023. Offers banking, corporate and finance law (LL M); intellectual property and information law (LL M); international business and trade law (LL M); law (JD); JD/MA; JD/MBA; JD/MSW. *Accreditation:* ABA. Part-time and evening/weekend programs available. *Faculty:* 78 full-time (30 women), 128 part-time/adjunct (44 women). *Students:* 1,259 full-time (592 women), 373 part-time (165 women). 7,080 applicants, 26% accepted, 564 enrolled. In 2006, 477 JDs, 65 master's awarded. *Entrance requirements:* LSAT, personal statement. Additional exam requirements/recommendations for international students: Required—TOEFL. *Application deadline:* For fall admission, 3/1 for domestic students. Applications are processed on a rolling basis. Application fee: $65. Electronic applications accepted. *Expenses:* Contact institution. *Financial support:* In 2006–07, 1,143 students received support. Career-related internships or fieldwork, institutionally sponsored loans, and scholarships/grants available. Support available to part-time students. Financial award application deadline: 4/1; financial award applicants required to submit CSS PROFILE or FAFSA. *Unit head:* William Michael Treanor, Dean, 212-636-6875, Fax: 212-636-6921, E-mail: wtreanor@law.fordham.edu. *Application contact:* Stephen G. Brown, Assistant Dean for Admissions and Financial Aid, 212-636-6810, E-mail: lawadmissins@law.fordham.edu.

Franklin Pierce Law Center, Professional Program, Concord, NH 03301-4197. Offers intellectual property (Diploma); intellectual property, commerce and technology (LL M, MIP); law (JD); JD/MIP. Diploma awarded as part of Intellectual Property Summer Institute. *Accreditation:* ABA. *Entrance requirements:* LSAT. Additional exam requirements/recommendations for international students: Required—TOEFL (minimum score 600 paper-based; 250 computer-based); Recommended—TWE. Electronic applications accepted. Expenses: Contact institution. *Faculty research:* Legal applications of artificial intelligence, intellectual property.

Friends University, Graduate School, Division of Business, Technology, and Leadership, Program of Studies in Business Law, Wichita, KS 67213. Offers MBL. Evening/weekend programs available. *Faculty:* 1 (woman) full-time, 3 part-time/adjunct (1 woman). *Students:* 33 full-time. In 2006, 19 degrees awarded. *Entrance requirements:* Additional exam requirements/recommendations for international students: Required—TOEFL (minimum score 560 paper-based; 220 computer-based). *Application deadline:* For fall admission, 6/1 priority date for domestic and international students. Applications are processed on a rolling basis. Application fee: $45 ($65 for international students). Electronic applications accepted. *Unit head:* Dr. Dixie

Madden, Director, 800-794-6945 Ext. 5906. *Application contact:* Craig Davis, Director of Graduate Admissions, 800-794-6945 Ext. 5573, Fax: 316-295-5050, E-mail: cdavis@friends.edu.

George Mason University, School of Law, Arlington, VA 22201. Offers intellectual property (LL M); law (JD); law and economics (LL M); JD/MA; JD/MPP; JD/PhD. *Accreditation:* ABA. Part-time and evening/weekend programs available. *Entrance requirements:* LSAT. Electronic applications accepted. Expenses: Contact institution.

Georgetown University, Law Center, Washington, DC 20001. Offers advocacy (LL M); common law studies (LL M); general (LL M); international and comparative law (LL M); labor and employment law (LL M); law (JD, SJD); securities regulation (LL M); taxation (LL M); JD/MA; JD/MBA; JD/MPH; JD/MS; JD/PhD. *Accreditation:* ABA. Part-time and evening/weekend programs available. *Degree requirements:* For master's and doctorate, thesis/dissertation. *Entrance requirements:* For JD, LSAT; for master's and doctorate, JD, LL B, or first law degree earned in country of origin. Additional exam requirements/recommendations for international students: Required—TOEFL. Expenses: Contact institution. *Faculty research:* Constitutional law, legal history, jurisprudence.

The George Washington University, Law School, Washington, DC 20052. Offers JD, LL M, SJD, JD/MA, JD/MBA, JD/MPA, JD/MPH, LL M/MA, LL M/MPH. *Accreditation:* ABA. Part-time and evening/weekend programs available. *Degree requirements:* For doctorate, thesis/dissertation. *Entrance requirements:* For JD, LSAT; for master's, JD or equivalent; for doctorate, LL M or equivalent. Expenses: Contact institution.

Georgia State University, College of Law, Atlanta, GA 30302-4037. Offers JD, JD/MA, JD/MBA, JD/MCRP, JD/MHA, JD/MPA, JD/MSHA. *Accreditation:* ABA. Part-time and evening/weekend programs available. *Faculty:* 46 full-time (21 women), 49 part-time/adjunct (17 women). *Students:* 453 full-time (226 women), 210 part-time (89 women); includes 128 minority (73 African Americans, 3 American Indian/Alaska Native, 33 Asian Americans or Pacific Islanders, 19 Hispanic Americans). Average age 28. 2,910 applicants, 21% accepted, 213 enrolled. In 2006, 181 degrees awarded. *Entrance requirements:* LSAT, LSDAS, 2 letters of recommendation. Additional exam requirements/recommendations for international students: Recommended—TOEFL (minimum score 630 paper-based). *Application deadline:* For fall admission, 3/15 for domestic students, 3/15 priority date for international students. Applications are processed on a rolling basis. Application fee: $50. Electronic applications accepted. *Expenses: Contact institution. Financial support:* In 2006–07, 127 research assistantships with full and partial tuition reimbursements (averaging $1,000 per year) were awarded; career-related internships or fieldwork, Federal Work-Study, institutionally sponsored loans, scholarships/grants, tuition waivers (partial), and unspecified assistantships also available. Support available to part-time students. Financial award application deadline: 4/1; financial award applicants required to submit FAFSA. *Faculty research:* Corporate/commercial law, tax law, labor law, criminal law, constitutional law. Total annual research expenditures: $196,654. *Unit head:* Dr. Steven J. Kaminshine, Dean, 404-651-2035, Fax: 404-651-2570, E-mail: skaminshine@gsu.edu. *Application contact:* Dr. Cheryl Jester Jackson, Director of Admissions, 404-651-2048, Fax: 404-651-1244, E-mail: cjgeorge@gsulaw.gsu.edu.

Golden Gate University, School of Law, San Francisco, CA 94105-2968. Offers environmental law (LL M); intellectual property law (LL M); international legal studies (LL M, SJD); law (JD); taxation (LL M); U.S. legal studies (LL M); JD/MBA; JD/PhD. *Accreditation:* ABA. Part-time and evening/weekend programs available. *Faculty:* 49 full-time (22 women), 68 part-time/adjunct (31 women). *Students:* 733 full-time (415 women), 345 part-time (196 women); includes 276 minority (47 African Americans, 4 American Indian/Alaska Native, 168 Asian Americans or Pacific Islanders, 57 Hispanic Americans), 74 international. Average age 28. 2,761 applicants, 49% accepted, 222 enrolled. In 2006, 168 JDs, 113 master's, 3 doctorates awarded. *Entrance requirements:* LSAT. Additional exam requirements/recommendations for international students: Required—TOEFL (minimum score 600 paper-based; 250 computer-based). *Application deadline:* For fall admission, 4/1 for domestic students, 4/15 for international students; for spring admission, 11/15 for international students. Applications are processed on a rolling basis. Application fee: $60. Electronic applications accepted. *Expenses: Contact institution. Financial support:* In 2006–07, 331 students received support, including 3 fellowships (averaging $36,000 per year), 60 research assistantships (averaging $2,400 per year), 30 teaching assistantships (averaging $2,400 per year); career-related internships or fieldwork, Federal Work-Study, institutionally sponsored loans, scholarships/grants, tuition waivers (full and partial), and unspecified assistantships also available. Support available to part-time students. Financial award application deadline: 3/1; financial award applicants required to submit FAFSA. *Faculty research:* International law, intellectual property law, environmental law, real estate, civil rights. *Unit head:* Frederic White, Dean, 415-442-6600, Fax: 415-442-6609. *Application contact:* Sherolyn Hurst, Director of Admissions, 415-442-6630, Fax: 415-442-6631, E-mail: lawadmit@ggu.edu.

Gonzaga University, School of Law, Spokane, WA 99220-3528. Offers JD, JD/M Acc, JD/MBA. *Accreditation:* ABA. Part-time programs available. *Faculty:* 30 full-time (12 women), 35 part-time/adjunct (7 women). *Students:* 544 full-time (240 women), 11 part-time (8 women); includes 46 minority (1 African American, 11 American Indian/Alaska Native, 25 Asian Americans or Pacific Islanders, 9 Hispanic Americans), 3 international. Average age 27. In 2006, 187 degrees awarded. *Entrance requirements:* LSAT. *Application deadline:* For fall admission, 4/1 priority date for domestic students. Applications are processed on a rolling basis. Application fee: $40. *Expenses: Contact institution. Financial support:* In 2006–07, 425 students received support. Career-related internships or fieldwork, Federal Work-Study, institutionally sponsored loans, and scholarships/grants available. Support available to part-time students. Financial award application deadline: 3/15; financial award applicants required to submit FAFSA. *Faculty research:* Environmental law, business law, public interest law, tax law. Total annual research expenditures: $28,500. *Unit head:* Earl Martin, Dean, 509-328-4220 Ext. 3700. *Application contact:* Susan Lee, Director of Admissions, 509-323-5532, Fax: 509-323-3857, E-mail: admissions@lawschool.gonzaga.edu.

Hamline University, School of Law, St. Paul, MN 55104. Offers JD, LL M, JD/MAM, JD/MANM, JD/MAOL, JD/MAPA, JD/MLIS. *Accreditation:* ABA. Part-time and evening/weekend programs available. *Faculty:* 44 full-time (20 women), 55 part-time/adjunct (21 women). *Students:* 498 full-time (257 women), 218 part-time (112 women); includes 91 minority (22 African Americans, 4 American Indian/Alaska Native, 36 Asian Americans or Pacific Islanders, 29 Hispanic Americans), 7 international. Average age 28. 1,510 applicants, 47% accepted, 250 enrolled. In 2006, 184 first professional degrees, 9 master's awarded. *Entrance requirements:* LSAT, 2 letters of recommendation. Additional exam requirements/recommendations for international students: Required—TOEFL (minimum score 600 paper-based; 250 computer-based). *Application deadline:* For fall admission, 5/1 priority date for domestic students. Applications are processed on a rolling basis. Application fee: $40. Electronic applications accepted. *Expenses: Contact institution.* One-time fee: $175. Tuition and fees vary according to course load, degree level and program. *Financial support:* In 2006–07, 669 students received support, including 20 fellowships with full and partial tuition reimbursements available (averaging $3,000 per year); career-related internships or fieldwork, Federal Work-Study, and scholarships/grants also available. Support available to part-time students. Financial award applicants required to submit FAFSA. *Faculty research:* Alternative dispute resolution, international trade, uniform commercial code, health law. *Unit head:* Jon M. Garon, Dean, 651-523-2968, Fax: 651-523-2435, E-mail: jgaron@hamline.edu. *Application contact:* Robin C. Ingli, Director of Admissions, 800-388-3688, Fax: 651-523-3064, E-mail: ringli@hamline.edu.

Harvard University, Law School, Graduate Programs in Law, Cambridge, MA 02138. Offers LL M, SJD. *Degree requirements:* For master's, thesis optional; for doctorate, thesis/dissertation. *Entrance requirements:* Additional exam requirements/recommendations for international students: Required—TOEFL. *Expenses:* Tuition: Full-time $30,275. Full-time tuition and fees vary according to program and student level. *Faculty research:* Corporation finance, national and international law, legal ethics, family law, criminal law, administrative law, constitutional law.

Harvard University, Law School, Professional Programs in Law, Cambridge, MA 02138. Offers JD, JD/MALD, JD/MBA, JD/MPP, JD/PhD. *Accreditation:* ABA. *Degree requirements:* For first-professional, 3rd-year paper. *Entrance requirements:* LSAT. *Expenses:* Tuition: Full-time $30,275. Full-time tuition and fees vary according to program and student level. *Faculty research:* Constitutional law, voting rights law, cyber law.

Hodges University, Graduate Programs, Naples, FL 34119. Offers business administration (MBA); computer information technology (MS); criminal justice (MCJ); education (MPS); information systems management (MIS); interdisciplinary (MPS); law (MPS); management (MSM); professional studies (MPS); psychology (MPS); public administration (MPA) Part-time and evening/weekend programs available. Postbaccalaureate distance learning degree programs offered (no on-campus study). *Faculty:* 17 full-time (4 women). *Students:* 35 full-time (22 women), 156 part-time (100 women); includes 52 minority (24 African Americans, 1 American Indian/Alaska Native, 4 Asian Americans or Pacific Islanders, 23 Hispanic Americans). Average age 32. In 2006, 101 degrees awarded. *Median time to degree:* Master's–1.5 years full-time, 2.5 years part-time. *Degree requirements:* For master's, comprehensive exam (for some programs), registration. *Entrance requirements:* For master's, in-house entrance exam. Application fee: $50. Electronic applications accepted. *Financial support:* Federal Work-Study and scholarships/grants available. Financial award applicants required to submit FAFSA. *Unit head:* Terry McMahan, President, 239-513-1122, Fax: 239-598-6253, E-mail: tmcmahan@internationalcollege.edu. *Application contact:* Rita Lampus, Vice President of Student Enrollment Management, 239-513-1122, Fax: 239-598-6253, E-mail: rlampus@internationalcollege.edu.

Hofstra University, School of Law, Hempstead, NY 11549. Offers American legal studies (LL M); family law (LL M); international law (LL M); law (JD); JD/MBA. *Accreditation:* ABA. Part-time and evening/weekend programs available. *Faculty:* 58 full-time (21 women), 37 part-time/adjunct (7 women). *Students:* 891 full-time (416 women), 257 part-time (127 women); includes 245 minority (87 African Americans, 2 American Indian/Alaska Native, 92 Asian Americans or Pacific Islanders, 64 Hispanic Americans), 22 international. Average age 26. 4,810 applicants, 43% accepted, 461 enrolled. In 2006, 300 JDs, 10 master's awarded. *Degree requirements:* For JD, set of required courses, number of credits; for master's, thesis, number of credits, select courses required. *Entrance requirements:* LSAT, 1 letter of recommendation, application form, personal statement, undergraduate transcripts. Additional exam requirements/recommendations for international students: Required—TOEFL (minimum score 580 paper-based; 237 computer-based). *Application deadline:* For fall admission, 4/15 priority date for domestic and international students. Applications are processed on a rolling basis. Application fee: $60. Electronic applications accepted. *Expenses: Contact institution. Financial support:* In 2006–07, 591 students received support, including 483 fellowships with tuition reimbursements available (averaging $14,864 per year), 1 research assistantship with full and partial tuition reimbursement available (averaging $3,825 per year); Federal Work-Study, scholarships/grants, health care benefits, and unspecified assistantships also available. Financial award applicants required to submit FAFSA. *Faculty research:* International and comparative law, family law, gender and LGBT issues, legal history, commercial and corporate law. *Unit head:* Nora V. Demleitner, Interim Dean, 516-463-6190, Fax: 516-463-6091, E-mail: lawnvd@hofstra.edu. *Application contact:* Noreen A. O'Brien, Director of Law School Enrollment- Operations, 516-463-5243, Fax: 516-463-6264, E-mail: lawadmissions@hofstra.edu.

Howard University, School of Law, Washington, DC 20008. Offers JD, LL M, JD/MBA. *Accreditation:* ABA. *Degree requirements:* For JD, thesis (for some programs), registration; for master's, one foreign language, thesis, registration. *Entrance requirements:* LSAT. Additional exam requirements/recommendations for international students: Required—TOEFL. Electronic applications accepted. Expenses: Contact institution. *Faculty research:* Criminal law, family law, telecommunications, religion, antitrust.

Humphreys College, Laurence Drivon School of Law, Stockton, CA 95207-3896. Offers JD. *Faculty:* 2 full-time (1 woman), 23 part-time/adjunct (5 women). *Students:* Average age 36. 101 applicants, 41% accepted, 32 enrolled. In 2006, 7 degrees awarded. *Entrance requirements:* LSAT, minimum GPA of 2.5. *Application deadline:* For fall admission, 7/1 priority date for domestic students. Applications are processed on a rolling basis. Application fee: $35. Electronic applications accepted. *Expenses:* Tuition: Part-time $315 per unit. *Financial support:* In 2006–07, 62 students received support. Federal Work-Study available. Support available to part-time students. Financial award application deadline: 7/1; financial award applicants required to submit FAFSA. *Unit head:* Leo Patrick Piggott, Dean, 209-478-0800 Ext. 243, Fax: 209-235-2889. *Application contact:* Santa Lopez-Minatre, Admission Counselor, 209-478-0800 Ext. 202, Fax: 209-478-8721, E-mail: slopez@humphreys.edu.

Illinois Institute of Technology, Chicago-Kent College of Law, Chicago, IL 60661-3691. Offers family law (LL M); financial services (LL M); international intellectual property (LL M); international law (LL M); law (JD); taxation (LL M); JD/LL M; JD/MBA; JD/MPA; JD/MPH; JD/MS. *Accreditation:* ABA. Part-time and evening/weekend programs available. *Faculty:* 61 full-time (20 women), 132 part-time/adjunct (34 women). *Students:* 827 full-time (395 women), 302 part-time (130 women); includes 221 minority (61 African Americans, 4 American Indian/Alaska Native, 95 Asian Americans or Pacific Islanders, 61 Hispanic Americans), 70 international. Average age 27. 3,510 applicants, 31% accepted, 307 enrolled. In 2006, 283 JDs, 28 master's awarded. *Entrance requirements:* LSAT, LSDAS. *Application deadline:* For fall admission, 3/1 priority date for domestic and international students. Applications are processed on a rolling basis. Application fee: $60. Electronic applications accepted. *Expenses: Contact institution.* Tuition and fees vary according to class time, course level, course load, program and student level. *Financial support:* In 2006–07, 573 students received support. Career-related internships or fieldwork, institutionally sponsored loans, scholarships/grants, and tuition waivers (full) available. Support available to part-time students. Financial award application deadline: 3/15; financial award applicants required to submit FAFSA. *Faculty research:* Constitutional law, bioethics, environmental law. Total annual research expenditures: $1.2 million. *Unit head:* Harold J. Krent, Dean, 312-906-5010, Fax: 312-906-5335, E-mail: hkrent@kentlaw.edu. *Application contact:* Nicole Vilches, Assistant Dean, 312-906-5020, Fax: 312-906-5274, E-mail: admit@kentlaw.edu.

Indiana University Bloomington, School of Law, Bloomington, IN 47405-7000. Offers comparative law (MCL); juridical science (SJD); law (JD, LL M); law and social sciences (PhD); legal studies (Certificate); JD/MA; JD/MBA; JD/MLS; JD/MPA; JD/MS; JD/MSES. *Faculty:* 59 full-time (19 women), 15 part-time/adjunct (4 women). *Students:* 654 full-time (274 women), 74 part-time (29 women); includes 95 minority (39 African Americans, 35 Asian Americans or Pacific Islanders, 21 Hispanic Americans), 101 international. Average age 26. 2,718 applicants, 39% accepted, 211 enrolled. In 2006, 211 first professional degrees, 62 master's, 3 doctorates awarded. *Median time to degree:* Of those who began their doctoral program in fall 1998, 100% received their degree in 8 years or less. *Degree requirements:* For JD, research seminar; for master's, thesis or practicum; for doctorate, thesis/dissertation (for some programs). *Entrance requirements:* For JD, LSAT; for master's, LSAT, 3 letters of recommendation, law degree or license to practice, 3-5 years of experience; for doctorate, LSAT, 3 letters of recommendation, LL M or JD. Additional exam requirements/recommendations for international students: Required—TOEFL (minimum score 560 paper-based; 213 computer-based; 80 iBT). *Application deadline:* For fall admission, 3/1 priority date for domestic and international students. Applications are processed on a rolling basis. Application fee: $35 ($60 for international students). Electronic applications accepted. *Expenses:* Tuition, state resident: full-time $5,791; part-time $241 per credit hour. Tuition, nonresident: full-time $16,866; part-time $703 per credit hour. *Financial support:* In 2006–07, 581 students received support, including 477 fellowships (averaging $7,982 per year), 99 research assistantships (averaging $811 per year), 5 teaching assistantships (averaging $3,000 per year); career-related intern-

Law

Indiana University Bloomington (continued)

ships or fieldwork, Federal Work-Study, institutionally sponsored loans, scholarships/grants, health care benefits, and unspecified assistantships also available. Financial award application deadline: 3/1; financial award applicants required to submit FAFSA. *Faculty research:* Environmental risk assessment and policy analysis, information privacy and security, judicial independence, accountability, ethics. Total annual research expenditures: $1.4 million. *Unit head:* Lauren K. Robel, Dean, 812-855-8885, Fax: 812-855-7057, E-mail: lrobel@indiana.edu. *Application contact:* Patricia S. Clark, Director of Admissions, 812-855-2704, Fax: 812-855-0555, E-mail: psclark@indiana.edu.

Indiana University–Purdue University Indianapolis, School of Law, Indianapolis, IN 46202-2896. Offers JD, LL M, SJD, JD/MBA, JD/MLS, JD/MPA, JD/MPH. *Faculty:* 1 (woman) full-time. *Students:* 728 full-time (365 women), 290 part-time (130 women); includes 633 minority (60 African Americans, 1 American Indian/Alaska Native, 23 Asian Americans or Pacific Islanders, 549 Hispanic Americans), 73 international. Average age 28. In 2006, 250 JDs, 36 master's awarded. *Entrance requirements:* Additional exam requirements/recommendations for international students: Required—TOEFL. *Application deadline:* For fall admission, 11/30 priority date for domestic students. Application fee: $50 ($60 for international students). *Expenses:* Tuition, state resident: full-time $5,437; part-time $227 per credit hour. Tuition, nonresident: full-time $15,694; part-time $654 per credit hour. Required fees: $620. Tuition and fees vary according to course load, campus/location and program. *Financial support:* Research assistantships with full and partial tuition reimbursements, Federal Work-Study, institutionally sponsored loans, and scholarships/grants available. Support available to part-time students. Financial award applicants required to submit FAFSA. *Unit head:* Susanah M. Mead, Interim Dean, 317-274-8523. *Application contact:* Patricia Kinney, Director of Admissions, 317-274-2459, Fax: 317-278-4780, E-mail: pkkinney@iupui.edu.

Indiana University School of Law-Bloomington, School of Law, Bloomington, IN 47405. Offers comparative law (MCL); law (JD, LL M, SJD); legal studies (Certificate); JD/MA; JD/MBA; JD/MLS; JD/MPA; JD/MPAF; JD/MS; JD/MSES. *Accreditation:* ABA. *Degree requirements:* For JD, research seminar; for master's, thesis (for some programs), practicum; for doctorate, thesis/dissertation. *Entrance requirements:* For JD, master's, and doctorate, LSAT, LSDAS. Additional exam requirements/recommendations for international students: Required—TOEFL (minimum score 560 paper-based; 213 computer-based). *Faculty research:* International law, constitutional law, litigation and dispute resolution, commercial law, communications law.

Indiana University School of Law-Indianapolis, School of Law, Indianapolis, IN 46202-3225. Offers American law for foreign lawyers (LL M); health law, policy and bioethics (LL M); intellectual property law (LL M); international and comparative law (LL M); international human rights law (LL M); law (JD); JD/MBA; JD/MHA; JD/MPA; JD/MPH. *Accreditation:* ABA. Part-time and evening/weekend programs available. *Faculty:* 52 full-time (21 women), 54 part-time/adjunct (16 women). *Students:* 728 full-time (365 women), 290 part-time (130 women); includes 113 minority (60 African Americans, 1 American Indian/Alaska Native, 23 Asian Americans or Pacific Islanders, 29 Hispanic Americans), 73 international. Average age 28. 1,820 applicants, 26% accepted, 286 enrolled. In 2006, 250 first professional degrees, 36 master's awarded. *Degree requirements:* For master's, thesis (for some programs). *Entrance requirements:* LSAT, LSDAS. Additional exam requirements/recommendations for international students: Required—TOEFL. *Application deadline:* For fall admission, 3/1 priority date for domestic and international students. Applications are processed on a rolling basis. Application fee: $50 ($60 for international students). Electronic applications accepted. *Expenses: Contact institution.* Tuition and fees vary according to course load and program. *Financial support:* In 2006–07, 682 students received support, including 149 fellowships with partial tuition reimbursements available (averaging $4,520 per year); career-related internships or fieldwork, Federal Work-Study, and scholarships/grants also available. Support available to part-time students. Financial award application deadline: 6/30; financial award applicants required to submit FAFSA. *Faculty research:* Constitutional law, environmental law, health care, international law. Total annual research expenditures: $300,000. *Unit head:* Susanah M. Mead, Dean, School of Law, 317-274-2581, Fax: 317-274-3955. *Application contact:* Patricia K. Kinney, Director of Admissions, 317-274-2459, Fax: 317-278-4780, E-mail: pkkinney@iupui.edu.

Instituto Tecnológico y de Estudios Superiores de Monterrey, Campus Ciudad de México, Division of Humanities and Social Sciences, Ciudad de Mexico, Mexico. Offers LL B. Part-time and evening/weekend programs available. *Entrance requirements:* Instituto entrance exam. Additional exam requirements/recommendations for international students: Required—TOEFL. *Faculty research:* Law; politics; international relations.

Inter American University of Puerto Rico School of Law, Professional Program, San Juan, PR 00936-8351. Offers JD. *Accreditation:* ABA. Part-time and evening/weekend programs available. *Entrance requirements:* LSAT, PAEG, minimum GPA of 2.5. Expenses: Contact institution.

John F. Kennedy University, School of Law, Pleasant Hill, CA 94523-4817. Offers JD. Part-time and evening/weekend programs available. *Entrance requirements:* LSAT, interview. Additional exam requirements/recommendations for international students: Required—TOEFL. Expenses: Contact institution.

John Marshall Law School, Graduate and Professional Programs, Chicago, IL 60604-3968. Offers comparative legal studies (LL M); employee benefits (LL M, MS); information technology (LL M, MS); intellectual property (LL M); international business and trade (LL M); law (JD); real estate (LL M, MS); taxation (LL M, MS); JD/LL M; JD/MA; JD/MBA; JD/MPA. *Accreditation:* ABA. Part-time and evening/weekend programs available. *Faculty:* 64 full-time (23 women), 113 part-time/adjunct (29 women). *Students:* 1,157 full-time (479 women), 421 part-time (187 women); includes 253 minority (76 African Americans, 10 American Indian/Alaska Native, 101 Asian Americans or Pacific Islanders, 66 Hispanic Americans), 48 international. Average age 27. 3,169 applicants, 37% accepted, 333 enrolled. In 2006, 347 JDs, 69 master's awarded. *Entrance requirements:* For JD, LSAT; for master's, JD. Additional exam requirements/recommendations for international students: Required—TOEFL. *Application deadline:* For fall admission, 3/1 priority date for domestic and international students; for spring admission, 10/15 priority date for domestic and international students. Applications are processed on a rolling basis. Application fee: $60. Electronic applications accepted. *Expenses: Contact institution. Financial support:* In 2006–07, 1,339 students received support. Scholarships/grants and tuition waivers (full and partial) available. Support available to part-time students. Financial award application deadline: 6/1; financial award applicants required to submit FAFSA. *Unit head:* John Corkery, Dean, 312-427-2737. *Application contact:* William B. Powers, Associate Dean of Admission and Student Affairs, 800-537-4280, Fax: 312-427-5136, E-mail: admission@jmls.edu.

The Johns Hopkins University, Paul H. Nitze School of Advanced International Studies, Washington, DC 20036. Offers emerging markets (Certificate); interdisciplinary studies (MA, PhD), including African studies (MA), American foreign policy (MA), Asian studies (MA), Canadian studies (MA), conflict management (MA), energy, environment, science and technology (MA), European studies (MA), global theory and history (MA), international development (MA), international law, and organization (MA), international relations (MA), Latin American studies (MA), Middle East studies (MA), Russian and Eurasian studies (MA), strategic studies (MA); international public policy (MIPP); international studies (Certificate); JD/MA; MBA/MA; MHS/MA. Terminal master's awarded for partial completion of doctoral program. *Degree requirements:* For master's, one foreign language, comprehensive exam; for doctorate, 2 foreign languages, thesis/dissertation. *Entrance requirements:* For master's, GMAT or GRE General Test, previous course work in economics, foreign language; for doctorate, GRE General Test. Additional exam requirements/recommendations for international students: Required—TOEFL (minimum score 600 paper-based; 250 computer-based). Electronic applications accepted. Expenses: Contact institution. Tuition and fees vary according to degree level and program. *Faculty research:* Comparative politics, regional studies, foreign language.

The Judge Advocate General's School, U.S. Army, Graduate Programs, Charlottesville, VA 22903-1781. Offers military law (LL M). Only active duty military lawyers attend this school. *Accreditation:* ABA. *Degree requirements:* For master's, thesis optional. *Entrance requirements:* For master's, active duty military lawyer, international military officer, or DOD civilian attorney, JD or LL B. *Faculty research:* Criminal law, administrative and civil law, contract law, international law, legal research and writing.

Lewis & Clark College, Lewis & Clark School of Law, Portland, OR 97203. Offers environmental and natural resources law (LL M); law (JD). *Accreditation:* ABA. Part-time and evening/weekend programs available. *Faculty:* 46 full-time (20 women), 27 part-time/adjunct (13 women). *Students:* 543 full-time (256 women), 185 part-time (84 women); includes 134 minority (16 African Americans, 10 American Indian/Alaska Native, 70 Asian Americans or Pacific Islanders, 38 Hispanic Americans), 13 international. Average age 28. 2,273 applicants, 40% accepted, 225 enrolled. In 2006, 232 JDs, 8 master's awarded. *Entrance requirements:* LSAT. *Application deadline:* For fall admission, 3/1 priority date for domestic students, 1/15 priority date for international students. Applications are processed on a rolling basis. Application fee: $50. Electronic applications accepted. *Expenses: Contact institution. Financial support:* In 2006–07, 674 students received support, including 44 research assistantships (averaging $1,250 per year), 26 teaching assistantships (averaging $1,788 per year); fellowships, career-related internships or fieldwork, Federal Work-Study, scholarships/grants, and tuition waivers (partial) also available. Support available to part-time students. Financial award application deadline: 3/1; financial award applicants required to submit FAFSA. Total annual research expenditures: $222,175. *Unit head:* Robert H. Klonoff, Dean, School of Law, 503-768-6602, Fax: 503-768-6671. *Application contact:* 503-768-6613, Fax: 503-768-6793, E-mail: lawadmss@lclark.edu.

Liberty University, School of Law, Lynchburg, VA 24502. Offers JD. *Faculty:* 14 full-time (4 women), 4 part-time/adjunct (1 woman). *Students:* 157 full-time (59 women), 2 part-time (1 woman); includes 15 minority (9 African Americans, 1 American Indian/Alaska Native, 3 Asian Americans or Pacific Islanders, 2 Hispanic Americans), 3 international. Average age 28. 226 applicants, 47% accepted, 73 enrolled. *Entrance requirements:* LSAT, 2 letters of recommendation, interview, subscription to LSDAS. Additional exam requirements/recommendations for international students: Required—TOEFL (minimum score 600 paper-based; 250 computer-based). *Application deadline:* For fall admission, 6/1 for domestic students. Application fee: $50. Electronic applications accepted. *Financial support:* In 2006–07, 157 students received support. *Unit head:* Mathew D. Staver, Dean, 434-592-5300, Fax: 434-522-0404, E-mail: law@liberty.edu. *Application contact:* Michelle Crawford Rickert, Assistant Dean, Admissions for the School of Law, 434-592-5471, Fax: 434-522-0404, E-mail: mcrawfordrickert@liberty.edu.

Louisiana State University and Agricultural and Mechanical College, Paul M. Hebert Law Center, Baton Rouge, LA 70803. Offers JD, LL M, MCL, JD/MBA, JD/MPA. *Accreditation:* ABA. *Faculty:* 45 full-time (13 women), 51 part-time/adjunct (6 women). *Students:* 578 full-time (286 women); includes 57 minority (42 African Americans, 2 American Indian/Alaska Native, 7 Asian Americans or Pacific Islanders, 6 Hispanic Americans), 1 international. Average age 26. 1,353 applicants, 35% accepted, 204 enrolled. *Degree requirements:* For master's, thesis. *Entrance requirements:* LSAT, 2 letters of recommendation. Additional exam requirements/recommendations for international students: Required—TOEFL (minimum score 600 paper-based; 250 computer-based). *Application deadline:* For fall admission, 3/1 priority date for domestic students, 2/1 priority date for international students. Applications are processed on a rolling basis. Application fee: $25. Electronic applications accepted. *Expenses: Contact institution. Financial support:* In 2006–07, 5 fellowships with tuition reimbursements were awarded; scholarships/grants and tuition waivers (full and partial) also available. Financial award applicants required to submit FAFSA. *Unit head:* John J. Costonis, Chancellor, 225-578-8491, Fax: 225-578-8202, E-mail: john.costonis@law.lsu.edu. *Application contact:* Michele Forbes, Director of Student Affairs and Registrar, 225-578-8646, Fax: 225-578-8647, E-mail: michele.forbes@law.lsu.edu.

Loyola Marymount University, Loyola Law School, Los Angeles, CA 90015. Offers American law and international practice (LL M); law (JD); taxation (LL M); JD/MBA. *Accreditation:* ABA. Part-time and evening/weekend programs available. *Faculty:* 65 full-time (26 women), 61 part-time/adjunct (27 women). *Students:* 1,022 full-time, 343 part-time; includes 233 minority (55 African Americans, 8 American Indian/Alaska Native, 42 Asian Americans or Pacific Islanders, 128 Hispanic Americans), 20 international. Average age 23. 4,537 applicants, 30% accepted, 423 enrolled. In 2006, 419 JDs, 15 master's awarded. *Entrance requirements:* For JD, LSAT; for master's, JD (LLM). Additional exam requirements/recommendations for international students: Required—TOEFL. *Application deadline:* For fall admission, 2/1 priority date for domestic and international students. Applications are processed on a rolling basis. Application fee: $65. Electronic applications accepted. *Financial support:* In 2006–07, 246 students received support; research assistantships, Federal Work-Study and scholarships/grants available. Financial award application deadline: 3/15; financial award applicants required to submit FAFSA. *Unit head:* David W. Burcham, Dean, 213-736-1028, Fax: 213-487-6736, E-mail: david.burcham@lls.edu. *Application contact:* Janell Lundy Roberts, Assistant Dean, Admissions, 213-736-1074, Fax: 213-736-6523, E-mail: admissions@lls.edu.

Loyola University Chicago, School of Law, Chicago, IL 60611. Offers business law (LL M, MJ); child and family law (LL M, MJ); health law (LL M, MJ, D Law, SJD); law (JD); JD/MA; JD/MBA; JD/MSW; MJ/MSW. *Accreditation:* ABA. Part-time programs available. *Faculty:* 41 full-time (15 women), 97 part-time/adjunct (53 women). *Students:* 607 full-time (318 women), 252 part-time (123 women); includes 137 minority (39 African Americans, 2 American Indian/Alaska Native, 62 Asian Americans or Pacific Islanders, 34 Hispanic Americans), 12 international. Average age 26. 4,469 applicants, 22% accepted, 295 enrolled. In 2006, 264 JDs, 37 master's awarded. *Entrance requirements:* LSAT. Additional exam requirements/recommendations for international students: Required—TOEFL (minimum score 650 paper-based; 280 computer-based). *Application deadline:* For fall admission, 4/1 for domestic and international students. Applications are processed on a rolling basis. Application fee: $50. Electronic applications accepted. *Expenses: Contact institution. Financial support:* In 2006–07, 494 students received support; fellowships, research assistantships, Federal Work-Study, institutionally sponsored loans, scholarships/grants, tuition waivers (partial), and unspecified assistantships available. Support available to part-time students. Financial award application deadline: 3/1; financial award applicants required to submit FAFSA. *Unit head:* David N. Yellen, Dean, 312-815-7120. *Application contact:* Pamela A. Bloomquist, Assistant Dean, Law Admission and Financial Assistance, 312-915-7170, Fax: 312-915-7906, E-mail: law-admissions@luc.edu.

Loyola University New Orleans, School of Law, New Orleans, LA 70118. Offers JD, JD/MA, JD/MBA, JD/MPA, JD/MURP. *Accreditation:* ABA. Part-time and evening/weekend programs available. *Entrance requirements:* LSAT, LSDAS. Electronic applications accepted. Expenses: Contact institution. *Faculty research:* Louisiana civil code, international law, commercial law, comparative law.

Marquette University, Law School, Milwaukee, WI 53201-1881. Offers JD, JD/Certificate, JD/MA, JD/MBA. *Accreditation:* ABA. Part-time and evening/weekend programs available. *Faculty:* 42 full-time (19 women), 71 part-time/adjunct (23 women). *Students:* 499 full-time (200 women), 190 part-time (94 women); includes 63 minority (15 African Americans, 5 American Indian/Alaska Native, 19 Asian Americans or Pacific Islanders, 24 Hispanic Americans), 5 international. Average age 25. 1,908 applicants, 40% accepted, 222 enrolled. In 2006, 201 degrees awarded. *Median time to degree:* 3 years full-time, 4.5 years part-time. *Entrance requirements:* LSAT. Additional exam requirements/recommendations for international students: Required—TOEFL. *Application deadline:* For fall admission, 4/1 for domestic students. Applications are processed on a rolling basis. Application fee: $50. Electronic applications accepted. *Expenses: Contact institution. Financial support:* In 2006–07, 302 students received support. Career-related internships or fieldwork, Federal Work-Study, and scholarships/grants available. Support available to part-time students. Financial award application deadline: 3/1; financial award applicants required to submit FAFSA. *Faculty research:* Constitutional law, sports law, dispute resolution, intellectual property, legal ethics. *Unit head:* Joseph D. Kearney, Dean, 414-288-7090, Fax: 414-288-6403, E-mail: joseph.kearney@marquette.edu. *Application contact:* Sean Reilly, Assistant Dean for Admissions, 414-288-6767, Fax: 414-288-0676, E-mail: sean.reilly@marquette.edu.

Massachusetts School of Law at Andover, Professional Program, Andover, MA 01810. Offers JD. Part-time and evening/weekend programs available. *Faculty:* 20 full-time (10 women), 65 part-time/adjunct (25 women). *Students:* 260 full-time (130 women), 390 part-time (195 women). 320 applicants, 63% accepted, 166 enrolled. In 2006, 120 degrees awarded. *Median time to degree:* 3 years full-time, 4 years part-time. *Entrance requirements:* Massachusetts School of Law Aptitude Test (MSLAT), interview. *Application deadline:* Applications are processed on a rolling basis. Application fee: $40. Electronic applications accepted. *Expenses:* Tuition: Full-time $13,320. One-time fee: $750 full-time. *Unit head:* Paula Colby-Clements, Director of Admissions, 978-681-0800, Fax: 978-684-7517, E-mail: pcolby@mslaw.edu. *Application contact:* Paula Colby-Clements, Director of Admissions, 978-681-0800, Fax: 978-684-7517, E-mail: pcolby@mslaw.edu.

See Close-Up on page 2101.

McGill University, Faculty of Graduate and Postdoctoral Studies, Faculty of Law, Montréal, QC H3A 2T5, Canada. Offers air and space law (LL M, DCL, Certificate); bioethics (LL M); comparative law (LL M, DCL, Certificate); law (LL M, DCL). Applications for LL M with specialization in bioethics are made initially through the Biomedical Ethics Unit in the Faculty of Medicine. *Degree requirements:* For master's, thesis (for some programs), registration; for doctorate, thesis/dissertation, comprehensive exam, registration. *Entrance requirements:* For master's, law degree, minimum GPA of 3.0, knowledge of French preferred or required depending on subject; for doctorate, LL M. Additional exam requirements/recommendations for international students: Required—TOEFL (minimum score 600 paper-based; 250 computer-based), IELTS (minimum score 8), For air and space law degrees: TOEFL 575 paper-based, 233 computer-based; IELTS 7.0. Electronic applications accepted. *Faculty research:* International law, international business law, human rights, legal theory and traditions, regulation and technology.

Mercer University, Walter F. George School of Law, Macon, GA 31207. Offers JD, JD/MBA. *Accreditation:* ABA. Part-time programs available. *Faculty:* 31 full-time (10 women), 34 part-time/adjunct (9 women). *Students:* 451 full-time (194 women); includes 74 minority (50 African Americans, 2 American Indian/Alaska Native, 12 Asian Americans or Pacific Islanders, 10 Hispanic Americans), 3 international. Average age 24. 1,290 applicants, 35% accepted, 176 enrolled. In 2006, 127 degrees awarded. *Entrance requirements:* LSAT. *Application deadline:* For fall admission, 3/15 priority date for domestic students. Applications are processed on a rolling basis. Application fee: $50. Electronic applications accepted. *Expenses: Contact institution. Financial support:* In 2006–07, 383 students received support, including 15 fellowships (averaging $3,800 per year), 13 research assistantships (averaging $476 per year); career-related internships or fieldwork, Federal Work-Study, institutionally sponsored loans, scholarships/grants, tuition waivers (partial), and institutional work-study also available. Support available to part-time students. Financial award application deadline: 4/1; financial award applicants required to submit FAFSA. *Faculty research:* Legal ethics, environmental law, employment discrimination, intellectual property, legal writing. *Unit head:* Daisy H. Floyd, Dean, 478-301-2602, Fax: 478-301-2101, E-mail: floyd_dh@mercer.edu. *Application contact:* Susan Martin, Admissions Assistant, 478-301-2605, Fax: 478-301-2989, E-mail: martin_sv@mercer.edu.

Michigan State University College of Law, Professional Program, East Lansing, MI 48824-1300. Offers American legal system (LL M); intellectual property (LL M); law (JD). *Accreditation:* ABA. Part-time and evening/weekend programs available. *Entrance requirements:* LSAT. Additional exam requirements/recommendations for international students: Required—TOEFL (minimum score 600 paper-based; 250 computer-based). Electronic applications accepted. Expenses: Contact institution. *Faculty research:* International, constitutional, health, tax and environmental law; intellectual property, health law, trial practice, corporate law.

Mississippi College, School of Law, Jackson, MS 39201. Offers civil law studies (Certificate); law (JD); JD/MBA. *Accreditation:* ABA. *Faculty:* 19 full-time (7 women), 33 part-time/adjunct (12 women). *Students:* 522 full-time (210 women), 6 part-time (4 women); includes 40 minority (34 African Americans, 1 American Indian/Alaska Native, 2 Asian Americans or Pacific Islanders, 3 Hispanic Americans). 1,171 applicants, 41% accepted, 195 enrolled. In 2006, 129 degrees awarded. *Degree requirements:* For first-professional, thesis. *Entrance requirements:* LSAT, LDAS report. Additional exam requirements/recommendations for international students: Recommended—IELTS. *Application deadline:* For fall admission, 6/1 priority date for domestic students. Applications are processed on a rolling basis. Application fee: $50. Electronic applications accepted. *Expenses: Contact institution.* Tuition and fees vary according to campus/location and program. *Financial support:* In 2006–07, 490 students received support. Federal Work-Study and scholarships/grants available. Financial award applicants required to submit FAFSA. *Unit head:* James H. Rosenblatt, Dean, 601-925-7101, Fax: 601-925-7115, E-mail: rosenblatt@mc.edu. *Application contact:* Patricia H. Evans, Assistant Dean for Admissions, 601-925-7151, Fax: 601-925-7166, E-mail: pevans@mc.edu.

New College of California, School of Law, San Francisco, CA 94102-5206. Offers JD. Part-time programs available. *Faculty:* 6 full-time (4 women), 18 part-time/adjunct (6 women). *Students:* 70 full-time (45 women), 50 part-time (28 women). Average age 30. 100 applicants, 50% accepted. In 2006, 22 degrees awarded. *Entrance requirements:* LSAT. *Application deadline:* For fall admission, 12/1 priority date for domestic students; for spring admission, 3/1 priority date for domestic students. Applications are processed on a rolling basis. Application fee: $55. Electronic applications accepted. *Expenses: Contact institution. Financial support:* Career-related internships or fieldwork, Federal Work-Study, and scholarships/grants available. Support available to part-time students. Financial award application deadline: 3/1; financial award applicants required to submit FAFSA. *Faculty research:* Public interest, practical skills development. *Unit head:* Debrenia Madison, Dean, 415-241-1325, Fax: 415-241-1353, E-mail: madison@newcollege.edu. *Application contact:* Sharon Pittman, Associate Dean for Admissions, 415-241-1374, Fax: 415-241-9525, E-mail: lawadmissions@newcollege.edu.

See Close-Up on page 2103.

New England School of Law, Professional Program, Boston, MA 02116-5687. Offers JD. *Accreditation:* ABA. Part-time and evening/weekend programs available. *Faculty:* 33 full-time (12 women), 83 part-time/adjunct (29 women). *Students:* 719 full-time (398 women), 381 part-time (190 women); includes 127 minority (20 African Americans, 2 American Indian/Alaska Native, 71 Asian Americans or Pacific Islanders, 34 Hispanic Americans). Average age 27. 3,362 applicants, 50% accepted, 393 enrolled. In 2006, 315 degrees awarded. *Entrance requirements:* LSAT, LSDAS. Additional exam requirements/recommendations for international students: Required—TOEFL (minimum score 600 paper-based; 250 computer-based; 100 iBT). *Application deadline:* For fall admission, 3/15 for domestic students. Applications are processed on a rolling basis. Application fee: $65. Electronic applications accepted. *Expenses:* Tuition: Full-time $25,800; part-time $19,350 per year. One-time fee: $65 full-time. *Financial support:* In 2006–07, 454 students received support. Federal Work-Study, institutionally sponsored loans, scholarships/grants, and tuition waivers (full and partial) available. Support available to part-time students. Financial award application deadline: 4/20; financial award applicants required to submit FAFSA. *Unit head:* John F. O'Brien, Dean, 617-422-7221, Fax: 617-422-7333, E-mail: jobrien@admin.nesl.edu. *Application contact:* Michelle L'Etoile, Director of Admissions, 617-422-7210, Fax: 617-422-7201, E-mail: admit@admin.nesl.edu.

New York Law School, Professional Program, New York, NY 10013. Offers law (JD); tax (LL M); JD/MBA. *Accreditation:* ABA. Part-time and evening/weekend programs available. *Faculty:* 76 full-time (28 women), 94 part-time/adjunct (36 women). *Students:* 1,168 full-time (629 women), 394 part-time (203 women); includes 355 minority (93 African Americans, 3 American Indian/Alaska Native, 142 Asian Americans or Pacific Islanders, 117 Hispanic Americans), 9 international. Average age 28. 5,557 applicants, 44% accepted, 549 enrolled. In 2006, 521 degrees awarded. *Entrance requirements:* LSAT, letters of recommendation, resumé. Additional exam requirements/recommendations for international students: Recommended—TOEFL (minimum score 600 paper-based; 250 computer-based). *Application deadline:* For fall admission, 4/1 priority date for domestic and international students. Applications are processed on a rolling basis. Application fee: $60. Electronic applications accepted. *Expenses:* Tuition: Full-time $38,535. Required fees: $809. Tuition and fees vary according to degree level and student level. *Financial support:* In 2006–07, 679 students received support, including 202 research assistantships (averaging $3,920 per year), 5 teaching assistantships (averaging $1,000 per year); career-related internships or fieldwork, Federal Work-Study, institutionally sponsored loans, and scholarships/grants also available. Support available to part-time students. Financial award application deadline: 4/2; financial award applicants required to submit FAFSA. *Unit head:* Richard A. Matasar, President and Dean, 212-431-2840, Fax: 212-219-3752, E-mail: rmatasar@nyls.edu. *Application contact:* William D. Perez, Assistant Dean for Admissions and Financial Aid, 212-431-2888, Fax: 212-966-1522, E-mail: wperez@nyls.edu.

New York University, School of Law, New York, NY 10012-1019. Offers law (JD, LL M, JSD); law and business (Advanced Certificate); tax (Advanced Certificate); JD/LL M; JD/MA; JD/MBA; JD/MPA; JD/MSW; JD/PhD. *Accreditation:* ABA. Part-time programs available. *Faculty:* 117 full-time (35 women), 64 part-time/adjunct (18 women). *Students:* 1,442 full-time (667 women); includes 345 minority (124 African Americans, 153 Asian Americans or Pacific Islanders, 68 Hispanic Americans), 53 international. 7,571 applicants, 448 enrolled. In 2006, 465 JDs, 472 master's, 6 doctorates awarded. *Entrance requirements:* LSAT. *Application deadline:* For fall admission, 2/1 for domestic students. Application fee: $85. Electronic applications accepted. *Expenses: Contact institution.* Tuition and fees vary according to program. *Financial support:* Fellowships, research assistantships, teaching assistantships, career-related internships or fieldwork, Federal Work-Study, institutionally sponsored loans, scholarships/grants, tuition waivers (partial), and loan repayment assistance available. Financial award application deadline: 4/15; financial award applicants required to submit FAFSA. *Faculty research:* Constitutional law, environmental law, corporate law, globalization of law, philosophy of law. *Unit head:* Richard L. Revesz, Dean, 212-998-6000, Fax: 212-995-3150. *Application contact:* Kenneth J. Kleinrock, Assistant Dean for Admissions, 212-998-6060, Fax: 212-995-4527.

North Carolina Central University, Division of Academic Affairs, School of Law, Durham, NC 27707. Offers JD, LL B, JD/MLS. *Accreditation:* ABA. Part-time and evening/weekend programs available. *Entrance requirements:* LSAT, LSDAS. Additional exam requirements/recommendations for international students: Required—TOEFL. Expenses: Contact institution.

Northeastern University, School of Law, Boston, MA 02115-5005. Offers JD, JD/MBA, JD/MPH, JD/MS/MBA, JD/PhD. *Accreditation:* ABA. *Faculty:* 34 full-time (18 women), 15 part-time/adjunct. *Students:* Average age 26. 3,354 applicants, 213 enrolled. In 2006, 192 degrees awarded. *Entrance requirements:* LSAT. *Application deadline:* For fall admission, 3/1 for domestic students. Applications are processed on a rolling basis. Application fee: $75. Electronic applications accepted. *Expenses: Contact institution. Financial support:* In 2006–07, 405 students received support, including 39 teaching assistantships (averaging $3,500 per year); fellowships, research assistantships, career-related internships or fieldwork, Federal Work-Study, institutionally sponsored loans, scholarships/grants, and tuition waivers (full and partial) also available. Financial award application deadline: 2/15; financial award applicants required to submit CSS PROFILE or FAFSA. *Faculty research:* Domestic violence, certiorari/criminal appeals, prisoners' rights, tobacco control, poverty law and practice. *Unit head:* Emily A. Spieler, Dean, 617-373-3307, Fax: 617-373-8793, E-mail: e.spieler@neu.edu. *Application contact:* Judy Cote, Information Contact, 617-373-2395, Fax: 617-373-8865, E-mail: lawadmissions@neu.edu.

Northern Illinois University, College of Law, DeKalb, IL 60115. Offers JD. *Accreditation:* ABA. Part-time programs available. *Faculty:* 22 full-time (11 women). *Students:* 314 full-time (163 women), 1 part-time; includes 62 minority (27 African Americans, 1 American Indian/Alaska Native, 13 Asian Americans or Pacific Islanders, 21 Hispanic Americans). Average age 25. 1,514 applicants, 26% accepted, 105 enrolled. In 2006, 109 degrees awarded. *Entrance requirements:* LSAT. Additional exam requirements/recommendations for international students: Required—TOEFL. *Application deadline:* For fall admission, 5/15 priority date for domestic and international students. Applications are processed on a rolling basis. Application fee: $35 ($50 for international students). Electronic applications accepted. *Expenses: Contact institution. Financial support:* In 2006–07, 10 teaching assistantships were awarded; research assistantships, career-related internships or fieldwork, Federal Work-Study, tuition waivers (full and partial), and unspecified assistantships also available. Support available to part-time students. Financial award application deadline: 3/1; financial award applicants required to submit FAFSA. *Faculty research:* Feminist legal theory, environment law, agricultural law, administrative law, constitutional law. *Unit head:* LeRoy Pernell, Dean, 815-753-1067, Fax: 815-753-1310, E-mail: lpernell@niu.edu. *Application contact:* Judith L. Malen, Director of Admissions and Financial Aid, 815-753-1420, E-mail: jmalen@niu.edu.

Northern Kentucky University, Salmon P. Chase College of Law, Highland Heights, KY 41099. Offers JD, JD/MBA. *Accreditation:* ABA. Part-time and evening/weekend programs available. *Faculty:* 36 full-time (13 women), 24 part-time/adjunct (11 women). *Students:* 283 full-time (126 women), 241 part-time (109 women); includes 40 minority (19 African Americans, 3 American Indian/Alaska Native, 5 Asian Americans or Pacific Islanders, 13 Hispanic Americans). Average age 27. 1,117 applicants, 31% accepted, 150 enrolled. In 2006, 142 degrees awarded. *Entrance requirements:* LSAT. Additional exam requirements/recommendations for international students: Required—TOEFL. *Application deadline:* For fall admission, 4/1 for domestic and international students. Applications are processed on a rolling basis. Application fee: $40. Electronic applications accepted. *Expenses: Contact institution. Financial support:* In 2006–07, 8 fellowships (averaging $6,000 per year), 20 research assistantships (averaging $1,200 per year) were awarded; career-related internships or fieldwork, Federal Work-Study, scholarships/grants, and unspecified assistantships also available. Support available to part-time students. Financial award application deadline: 3/1; financial award applicants required to submit FAFSA. *Faculty research:* ADR, torts, evidence, criminal procedure, disability. *Unit head:* Dennis R. Honabach, Dean, 859-572-6406, Fax: 859-572-6183, E-mail: honabachd1@nku.edu. *Application contact:* Ashley Folger Gray, Director of Admissions, 859-572-5841, Fax: 859-572-6081, E-mail: folger@nku.edu.

Northwestern University, The Graduate School, Program in Law and Social Science, Evanston, IL 60208. Offers Certificate. *Degree requirements:* For Certificate, research project. *Faculty research:* Law and social science.

Northwestern University, Law School, Chicago, IL 60611-3069. Offers executive law (LL M); international law (JD); law (JD, LL M); JD/LL M; JD/MBA; JD/PhD; LL M/Certificate; MSJ/MSL. *Accreditation:* ABA. *Faculty:* 100 full-time (53 women), 71 part-time/adjunct (17 women). *Students:* 768 full-time (354 women); includes 266 minority (64 African Americans, 5 American Indian/Alaska Native, 133 Asian Americans or Pacific Islanders, 64 Hispanic Americans), 32 international. Average age 26. 5,015 applicants, 17% accepted, 233 enrolled. In 2006, 265 degrees awarded. *Median time to degree:* 3 years full-time. *Entrance requirements:* For JD, LSAT, 1 letter of recommendation, resumé; for master's, law degree or equivalent, letter of recommendation, resumé. Additional exam requirements/recommendations for international students: Required—TOEFL. *Application deadline:* For fall admission, 2/15 for domestic students, 2/1 for international students. Applications are processed on a rolling basis. Application fee: $80 ($85 for international students). Electronic applications accepted. *Expenses: Contact institution. Financial support:* In 2006–07, 254 fellowships (averaging $20,000 per year) were awarded; career-related internships or fieldwork, Federal Work-Study, institutionally sponsored loans, and scholarships/grants also available. Financial award application deadline: 2/15; financial award applicants required to submit FAFSA. *Faculty research:* Constitutional law, corporate law, international law, law and social policy, negotiation and dispute resolution. *Unit head:* David Van Zandt, Chair, 847-491-8024, Fax: 847-467-1035. *Application contact:* Johann

Law

Northwestern University (continued)

H. Lee, Assistant Dean of Admissions and Financial Aid, 312-503-8465, Fax: 312-503-0178, E-mail: johann@law.northwestern.edu.

Nova Southeastern University, Shepard Broad Law Center, Ft. Lauderdale, FL 33314. Offers education law (MS); employment law (MS); health law (MS); law (JD); JD/MBA; JD/MS; JD/MURP. *Accreditation:* ABA. Part-time and evening/weekend programs available. Postbaccalaureate distance learning degree programs offered (minimal on-campus study). *Faculty:* 66 full-time (37 women), 53 part-time/adjunct (17 women). *Students:* 966 full-time (506 women), 29 part-time (18 women); includes 265 minority (63 African Americans, 3 American Indian/Alaska Native, 27 Asian Americans or Pacific Islanders, 172 Hispanic Americans), 11 international. Average age 27. 2,821 applicants, 34% accepted, 315 enrolled. In 2006, 261 JDs, 24 master's awarded. *Degree requirements:* For first-professional, thesis. *Entrance requirements:* LSAT. *Application deadline:* For fall admission, 3/1 priority date for domestic students. Applications are processed on a rolling basis. Application fee: $50. Electronic applications accepted. *Expenses: Contact institution. Financial support:* In 2006–07, 58 fellowships were awarded; research assistantships, teaching assistantships, Federal Work-Study, scholarships/grants, tuition waivers (full and partial), unspecified assistantships, and mediation programs also available. Support available to part-time students. Financial award application deadline: 4/15; financial award applicants required to submit FAFSA. *Faculty research:* Legal issues in family law, civil rights, business associations, criminal law, law and popular culture. *Unit head:* Joseph D. Harbaugh, Dean, 954-262-6105, Fax: 954-262-3834, E-mail: harbaughj@nsu.law.nova.edu. *Application contact:* Beth Hall, Assistant Dean of Admissions, 954-262-6121, Fax: 954-262-3844, E-mail: hallb@nsu.law.nova.edu.

Ohio Northern University, Claude W. Pettit College of Law, Ada, OH 45810-1599. Offers JD. *Accreditation:* ABA. *Entrance requirements:* LSAT. Additional exam requirements/recommendations for international students: Required—TOEFL. Electronic applications accepted. Expenses: Contact institution. *Faculty research:* Constitutional law, environmental law, business law and taxation, criminal law, public interest law, death penalty for women and juveniles, international human rights, sports violence.

The Ohio State University, Moritz College of Law, Columbus, OH 43210. Offers JD, LL M, MSL, JD/MBA, JD/MD, JD/MHA, JD/MPA, JD/PhD. *Accreditation:* ABA. *Faculty:* 43 full-time (12 women). *Students:* 672 full-time (282 women), 6 part-time (3 women); includes 133 minority (56 African Americans, 2 American Indian/Alaska Native, 58 Asian Americans or Pacific Islanders, 17 Hispanic Americans), 11 international. Average age 25. In 2006, 258 degrees awarded. *Entrance requirements:* For JD, LSAT; for master's, GRE or GMAT or MCAT. *Application deadline:* For fall admission, 3/1 priority date for domestic students. Applications are processed on a rolling basis. Electronic applications accepted. *Expenses: Contact institution.* Tuition and fees vary according to course load, campus/location and program. *Financial support:* In 2006–07, 550 students received support. Career-related internships or fieldwork, Federal Work-Study, institutionally sponsored loans, and scholarships/grants available. Financial award application deadline: 3/1; financial award applicants required to submit FAFSA. *Faculty research:* Alternative dispute resolution, law and policy, clinical programs, criminal law, intellectual property, cyberlaw. *Unit head:* Nancy H. Rogers, Dean, 614-292-5992, Fax: 614-292-1492, E-mail: rogers.23@osu.edu. *Application contact:* Graduate Studies Committee Chair, 614-292-9444, Fax: 614-292-3895, E-mail: domestic.grad@osu.edu.

See Close-Up on page 2105.

Oklahoma City University, School of Law, Oklahoma City, OK 73106-1402. Offers JD, JD/MBA. *Accreditation:* ABA. Part-time and evening/weekend programs available. *Faculty:* 30 full-time (10 women), 41 part-time/adjunct (12 women). *Students:* 472 full-time (192 women), 133 part-time (56 women); includes 107 minority (17 African Americans, 41 American Indian/Alaska Native, 21 Asian Americans or Pacific Islanders, 28 Hispanic Americans), 6 international. In 2006, 215 degrees awarded. *Entrance requirements:* LSAT. *Application deadline:* For fall admission, 6/1 for domestic students. Application fee: $50 ($70 for international students). Electronic applications accepted. *Expenses: Contact institution. Financial support:* Career-related internships or fieldwork, Federal Work-Study, institutionally sponsored loans, and tuition waivers (partial) available. Support available to part-time students. Financial award application deadline: 8/1; financial award applicants required to submit FAFSA. *Faculty research:* Family law, environmental law, consumer law, alternative dispute resolution, criminal law and procedure. *Unit head:* Dr. Larry Hellman, Dean, 405-208-5337, Fax: 405-208-6041, E-mail: lhellman@okcu.edu. *Application contact:* Tamara Martinez-Anderson, Assistant Dean, Law School Admissions, 800-633-7242 Ext. 2, Fax: 405-208-5354, E-mail: tmartinezanderson@okcu.edu.

Pace University, School of Law, White Plains, NY 10603. Offers comparative legal studies (LL M); environmental law (LL M, SJD); law (JD); JD/MA; JD/MBA; JD/MEM; JD/MPA; JD/MS. *Accreditation:* ABA. Part-time and evening/weekend programs available. *Faculty:* 44 full-time, 56 part-time/adjunct. *Students:* 511 full-time (305 women), 279 part-time (149 women); includes 138 minority (24 African Americans, 1 American Indian/Alaska Native, 73 Asian Americans or Pacific Islanders, 40 Hispanic Americans), 15 international. Average age 26. 2,935 applicants, 31% accepted, 273 enrolled. In 2006, 224 JDs, 20 master's awarded. *Entrance requirements:* For JD, LSAT; for doctorate, LL M in comparative or environmental law. Additional exam requirements/recommendations for international students: Required—TOEFL (minimum score 600 paper-based; 250 computer-based); Recommended—TWE. *Application deadline:* For fall admission, 3/1 priority date for domestic students. Applications are processed on a rolling basis. Application fee: $65. Electronic applications accepted. *Expenses: Contact institution. Financial support:* Career-related internships or fieldwork, Federal Work-Study, institutionally sponsored loans, and scholarships/grants available. Support available to part-time students. Financial award application deadline: 2/1; financial award applicants required to submit FAFSA. *Faculty research:* Torts products liability, international environmental law, land use law, prosecutorial misconduct, nonprofit corporation law, voting rights issues. *Unit head:* Stephen J. Friedman, Dean, 914-422-4407, E-mail: sfriedman@law.pace.edu. *Application contact:* Cathy Alexander, Director of Law Admissions, 914-422-4210, Fax: 914-989-8714, E-mail: calexander@law.pace.edu.

See Close-Up on page 2107.

Park University, College of Graduate and Professional Studies, Kansas City, MO 54105. Offers adult education (M Ed); at-risk students (M Ed); disaster and emergency management (MPA); educational administration (M Ed); entrepreneurship (MBA); general business (MBA); general education (M Ed); government/business relations (MPA); healthcare/services management (MBA, MPA); international business (MBA); K-12 certification (MAT); management information systems (MBA); management of information systems (MPA); middle school certification (MAT); multi-cultural education (M Ed); nonprofit management (MPA); public management (MPA); school law (M Ed); secondary school certification (MAT); special education (M Ed). Part-time and evening/weekend programs available. Postbaccalaureate distance learning degree programs offered (no on-campus study). *Degree requirements:* For master's, thesis (for some programs), comprehensive exam, registration. *Entrance requirements:* For master's, GRE, GMAT, teacher certification (M Ed). Additional exam requirements/recommendations for international students: Required—TOEFL (minimum score 550 paper-based). Electronic applications accepted. *Faculty research:* Literacy, leadership, brain based research, multicultural education, diversity.

Penn State Dickinson School of Law, Graduate and Professional Programs, Carlisle, PA 17013-2899. Offers comparative law (LL M); law (JD). *Accreditation:* ABA. Part-time programs available. *Faculty:* 56 full-time (23 women), 39 part-time/adjunct (9 women). *Students:* 552 full-time (249 women), 68 part-time (36 women); includes 108 minority (59 African Americans, 1 American Indian/Alaska Native, 42 Asian Americans or Pacific Islanders, 6 Hispanic Americans), 24 international. Average age 25. 3,350 applicants, 31% accepted, 237 enrolled. In 2006, 200 JDs, 9 master's awarded. *Entrance requirements:* For JD, LSAT, employment record, 2 letters of recommendation; for master's, application appraisals. Additional exam requirements/recommendations for international students: Required—TOEFL (JD). *Application deadline:* For fall admission, 3/1 priority date for domestic students. Applications are processed on a rolling basis. Application fee: $60. Electronic applications accepted. *Financial support:* In 2006–07, 519 students received support; research assistantships, Federal Work-Study, institutionally sponsored loans, and scholarships/grants available. Support available to part-time students. Financial award application deadline: 3/1; financial award applicants required to submit FAFSA. *Faculty research:* Arbitration, sports law, international human rights law, alternate dispute resolution. *Unit head:* Philip J. McConnaughay, Dean, 717-240-5000, Fax: 717-240-5213, E-mail: pjm30@psu.edu. *Application contact:* Barbara W. Guillaume, Director, Law Admissions, 717-240-5207, Fax: 717-241-3503, E-mail: dsladmit@psu.edu.

Pepperdine University, School of Law, Professional Program, Malibu, CA 90263. Offers JD, JD/MBA. *Accreditation:* ABA. *Students:* 638 full-time (322 women), 1 (woman) part-time; includes 110 minority (24 African Americans, 3 American Indian/Alaska Native, 51 Asian Americans or Pacific Islanders, 32 Hispanic Americans), 5 international. 3,440 applicants, 26% accepted, 276 enrolled. In 2006, 204 degrees awarded. *Entrance requirements:* LSAT, 2 letters of recommendation. *Application deadline:* For fall admission, 3/1 for domestic and international students. Applications are processed on a rolling basis. Application fee: $50. *Expenses: Contact institution.* Full-time tuition and fees vary according to program. *Financial support:* Federal Work-Study, institutionally sponsored loans, and scholarships/grants available. Financial award application deadline: 4/1; financial award applicants required to submit FAFSA. *Unit head:* Dr. Richard L. Cupp, Associate Dean, Academics, 310-506-4623, E-mail: richard.cupp@pepperdine.edu. *Application contact:* Shannon Phillips, Director of Admissions/Records, 310-506-4631, Fax: 310-506-4266, E-mail: shannon.phillips@pepperdine.edu.

Pontifical Catholic University of Puerto Rico, School of Law, Ponce, PR 00717-0777. Offers JD. *Accreditation:* ABA. Part-time and evening/weekend programs available. *Entrance requirements:* LSAT, PAEG, 3 letters of recommendation.

Queen's University at Kingston, Faculty of Law, Kingston, ON K7L 3N6, Canada. Offers LL B, LL M, LL B/MIR. Part-time programs available. *Degree requirements:* For master's, thesis. *Entrance requirements:* LSAT, minimum 2 years of college. Additional exam requirements/recommendations for international students: Required—TOEFL, TWE. *Faculty research:* Labor relations law, tax law and policy, criminal law and policy, critical legal theories, international legal relations.

Quinnipiac University, School of Law, Hamden, CT 06518. Offers health law (LL M); law (JD); JD/MBA. *Accreditation:* ABA. Part-time and evening/weekend programs available. *Faculty:* 33 full-time (15 women), 36 part-time/adjunct (10 women). *Students:* 393 full-time (202 women), 153 part-time (79 women); includes 52 minority (10 African Americans, 2 American Indian/Alaska Native, 28 Asian Americans or Pacific Islanders, 12 Hispanic Americans). Average age 28. 2,550 applicants, 24% accepted, 132 enrolled. In 2006, 205 degrees awarded. *Entrance requirements:* LSAT. *Application deadline:* For fall admission, 3/1 priority date for domestic students. Applications are processed on a rolling basis. Application fee: $40. Electronic applications accepted. *Expenses: Contact institution. Financial support:* In 2006–07, 516 students received support, including 23 fellowships (averaging $1,330 per year), 47 research assistantships (averaging $620 per year); career-related internships or fieldwork, Federal Work-Study, and scholarships/grants also available. Support available to part-time students. Financial award application deadline: 4/15; financial award applicants required to submit FAFSA. *Faculty research:* Tax, health, public interest, corporate law, dispute resolution; intellectual property. *Unit head:* Brad Saxton, Dean, 203-582-3200, Fax: 203-582-3209, E-mail: ladm@quinnipiac.edu. *Application contact:* Edwin Wilkes, Executive Dean of Law School Admissions, 203-582-3400, Fax: 203-582-3339, E-mail: ladm@quinnipiac.edu.

Regent University, Graduate School, Robertson School of Government, Virginia Beach, VA 23464-9800. Offers health care policy and administration (MA); international politics (MA); law and public policy (MA); political leadership and management (MA); political management (MA); public administration (MA); public policy (MA); terrorism and homeland defense (MA); world economies and political development (MA); JD/MA; M Div/MA; M Ed/MA; MBA/MA. Part-time programs available. *Faculty:* 7 full-time (2 women), 7 part-time/adjunct (0 women). *Students:* 73 full-time (48 women), 78 part-time (40 women); includes 42 minority (28 African Americans, 5 Asian Americans or Pacific Islanders, 9 Hispanic Americans), 3 international. Average age 31. 189 applicants, 51% accepted, 63 enrolled. In 2006, 31 degrees awarded. *Degree requirements:* For master's, internship, thesis optional. *Entrance requirements:* For master's, GRE General Test or LSAT, minimum undergraduate GPA of 2.75, writing sample, resumé, interview, references. Additional exam requirements/recommendations for international students: Required—TOEFL (minimum score 577 paper-based; 233 computer-based). *Application deadline:* For fall admission, 5/1 priority date for domestic students; for spring admission, 11/1 priority date for domestic students. Applications are processed on a rolling basis. Application fee: $50. Electronic applications accepted. *Expenses: Contact institution. Financial support:* In 2006–07, 151 students received support. Scholarships/grants and unspecified assistantships available. Support available to part-time students. Financial award application deadline: 9/1; financial award applicants required to submit FAFSA. *Faculty research:* Education reform, political character issues, social capital concerns, administrative ethics, biblical law and public policy. *Unit head:* Dr. Charles W. Dunn, Dean, 757-226-4322, Fax: 757-226-4643, E-mail: cwdunn@regent.edu. *Application contact:* Althea Bishard, Registrar and Executive Director of Enrollment and Academic Services, 800-373-5504, Fax: 757-226-4381, E-mail: admissions@regent.edu.

Regent University, Graduate School, School of Law, Virginia Beach, VA 23464. Offers JD, JD/MA, JD/MBA. *Accreditation:* ABA. Part-time and evening/weekend programs available. Postbaccalaureate distance learning degree programs offered (minimal on-campus study). *Faculty:* 26 full-time (5 women), 59 part-time/adjunct (12 women). *Students:* 475 full-time (237 women), 8 part-time (5 women); includes 55 minority (26 African Americans, 4 American Indian/Alaska Native, 16 Asian Americans or Pacific Islanders, 9 Hispanic Americans), 3 international. Average age 27. 698 applicants, 44% accepted, 167 enrolled. In 2006, 142 degrees awarded. *Entrance requirements:* LSAT, minimum undergraduate GPA of 2.75, 3 letters of recommendation, resumé. Additional exam requirements/recommendations for international students: Required—TOEFL (minimum score 600 paper-based; 250 computer-based). *Application deadline:* For fall admission, 3/1 for domestic students. Applications are processed on a rolling basis. Application fee: $50. Electronic applications accepted. *Expenses: Contact institution. Financial support:* Scholarships/grants and tuition waivers (full and partial) available. Support available to part-time students. Financial award application deadline: 2/1. *Faculty research:* Family law, constitutional law, law and culture, evidence and practice, intellectual property. *Unit head:* Jeffrey Brauch, Dean, 757-226-4040, Fax: 757-226-4595, E-mail: jeffbra@regent.edu. *Application contact:* Althea Bishard, Registrar and Executive Director of Enrollment and Academic Services, 800-373-5504, Fax: 757-226-4381, E-mail: admissions@regent.edu.

Roger Williams University, Ralph R. Papitto School of Law, Bristol, RI 02809-5171. Offers JD, JD/MLRHR, JD/MMA, JD/MSCJ. *Accreditation:* ABA. *Faculty:* 32 full-time (13 women), 31 part-time/adjunct (11 women). *Students:* 533 full-time (262 women), 60 part-time (24 women); includes 69 minority (19 African Americans, 2 American Indian/Alaska Native, 27 Asian Americans or Pacific Islanders, 21 Hispanic Americans), 5 international. Average age 27. 1,677 applicants, 51% accepted, 204 enrolled. In 2006, 177 degrees awarded. *Entrance requirements:* LSAT. Additional exam requirements/recommendations for international students: Required—TOEFL (minimum score 600 paper-based; 250 computer-based). *Application deadline:* For fall admission, 3/15 priority date for domestic and international students. Applications are processed on a rolling basis. Application fee: $60. Electronic applications accepted. *Expenses:* Tuition: Part-time $362 per credit. Tuition and fees vary according to program. *Financial support:* In 2006–07, 245 students received support, including 6 fellowships, 40 research assistantships; career-related internships or fieldwork, Federal Work-Study, scholarships/grants, and tuition waivers (full and partial) also available. Financial award application deadline: 3/15; financial award applicants required to submit FAFSA. *Faculty research:* Civil rights, admiralty, labor, intellectual property, international and comparative law. Total annual research expenditures: $81,100. *Unit head:* David A. Logan, Dean, 401-254-4500, Fax: 401-254-3525, E-mail: dlogan@rwu.edu. *Application contact:* Michael W. Boylen, Assistant Dean of Admissions, 401-254-4555, Fax: 401-254-4516, E-mail: mboylen@rwu.edu.

Rutgers, The State University of New Jersey, Camden, School of Law, Camden, NJ 08102. Offers JD, JD/DO, JD/MA, JD/MBA, JD/MCRP, JD/MD, JD/MPA, JD/MS, JD/MSW. *Accreditation:* ABA. Part-time and evening/weekend programs available. *Entrance requirements:* LSAT. Electronic applications accepted. Expenses: Contact institution. *Faculty research:* International law, commercial law, public law, health law, constitutional law, jurisprudence.

Rutgers, The State University of New Jersey, Newark, School of Law, Newark, NJ 07102-3094. Offers JD, JD/MA, JD/MCRP, JD/PhD. *Accreditation:* ABA. Part-time and evening/weekend programs available. *Entrance requirements:* LSAT. Expenses: Contact institution. *Faculty research:* Civil rights and liberties, women and the law, international human rights and world order, corporate law, employment law.

St. John's University, School of Law, Program in Law, Queens, NY 11439. Offers JD. *Faculty:* 55 full-time (23 women), 43 part-time/adjunct (11 women). *Students:* 726 full-time (350 women), 196 part-time (97 women); includes 222 minority (55 African Americans, 2 American Indian/Alaska Native, 94 Asian Americans or Pacific Islanders, 71 Hispanic Americans), 10 international. Average age 26. In 2006, 319 degrees awarded. *Expenses:* Tuition: Full-time $18,480; part-time $770 per credit. Required fees: $125 per semester. Tuition and fees vary according to program. *Application contact:* Robert Harrison, Assistant Dean and Director of Admissions, 718-990-2310, Fax: 718-990-6699, E-mail: lawinfo@stjohns.edu.

Saint Joseph's University, College of Arts and Sciences, Department of Criminal Justice/Sociology, Philadelphia, PA 19131-1395. Offers administration/police executive (MS); behavior analysis (MS); behavior management and justice (MS); criminal justice (MS, Post-Master's Certificate); criminology (MS); federal law (MS); intelligence and crime (MS); probation, parole, and corrections (MS). Evening/weekend programs available. *Faculty:* 3 full-time (all women), 14 part-time/adjunct (5 women). *Students:* 46 full-time (25 women), 146 part-time (91 women); includes 71 minority (62 African Americans, 2 Asian Americans or Pacific Islanders, 7 Hispanic Americans), 2 international. Average age 29. In 2006, 110 degrees awarded. *Degree requirements:* For master's, thesis. *Entrance requirements:* For master's, GRE General Test or minimum GPA of 3.0, 2 letters of recommendation, personal statement. Additional exam requirements/recommendations for international students: Required—TOEFL. *Application deadline:* For fall admission, 7/15 for domestic students; for spring admission, 11/15 for domestic students. Application fee: $35. *Financial support:* Fellowships, research assistantships, career-related internships or fieldwork available. *Unit head:* Patricia Griffin, Director, 610-660-1294.

Saint Louis University, School of Law, St. Louis, MO 63108. Offers JD, LL M. *Accreditation:* ABA. Part-time and evening/weekend programs available. *Faculty:* 43 full-time (18 women), 27 part-time/adjunct (10 women). *Students:* 716 full-time (357 women), 234 part-time (108 women); includes 103 minority (48 African Americans, 5 American Indian/Alaska Native, 32 Asian Americans or Pacific Islanders, 18 Hispanic Americans), 12 international. Average age 26. 2,278 applicants, 47% accepted, 346 enrolled. In 2006, 247 JDs, 6 master's awarded. *Degree requirements:* For master's, thesis (for some programs). *Entrance requirements:* For JD, LSAT, letters of recommendation; for master's, JD or equivalent. Additional exam requirements/recommendations for international students: Required—TOEFL (minimum score 525 paper-based; 194 computer-based). *Application deadline:* For fall admission, 3/1 for domestic and international students. Applications are processed on a rolling basis. Application fee: $55. Electronic applications accepted. *Expenses: Contact institution. Financial support:* In 2006–07, 372 students received support. Federal Work-Study, scholarships/grants, traineeships, health care benefits, tuition waivers, and unspecified assistantships available. Support available to part-time students. Financial award application deadline: 6/1; financial award applicants required to submit FAFSA. *Faculty research:* Health law, employment law, international comparative law, lawyering skills (clinical). *Unit head:* Dr. Jeffrey E. Lewis, Dean, 314-977-2766, Fax: 314-977-3333, E-mail: lewisje@slu.edu. *Application contact:* Michael J. Kolnik, Director of Admissions, 314-977-2800, E-mail: kolnikmj@slu.edu.

St. Mary's University of San Antonio, School of Law, San Antonio, TX 78228-8602. Offers JD, JD/M Acc, JD/MA, JD/MBA, JD/MPA, JD/MS. *Accreditation:* ABA. *Faculty:* 36 full-time (11 women), 14 part-time/adjunct (5 women). *Students:* 734 full-time, 15 part-time; includes 205 minority (15 African Americans, 8 American Indian/Alaska Native, 26 Asian Americans or Pacific Islanders, 156 Hispanic Americans), 6 international. Average age 27. 2,170 applicants, 32% accepted, 295 enrolled. In 2006, 242 degrees awarded. *Entrance requirements:* LSAT. Additional exam requirements/recommendations for international students: Required—TOEFL (minimum score 600 paper-based; 213 computer-based). *Application deadline:* For fall admission, 3/1 for domestic students. Application fee: $55. Electronic applications accepted. *Expenses: Contact institution.* Tuition and fees vary according to degree level. *Financial support:* In 2006–07, 59 research assistantships (averaging $1,000 per year), 35 teaching assistantships (averaging $1,250 per year) were awarded; career-related internships or fieldwork, Federal Work-Study, institutionally sponsored loans, scholarships/grants, and health care benefits also available. Financial award application deadline: 2/15; financial award applicants required to submit FAFSA. *Faculty research:* Ethics, church and state, exclusionary rule, civil rights, tort law. *Unit head:* Robert William Piatt, Dean, 210-436-3424, Fax: 210-436-3515. *Application contact:* Dr. William Charles Wilson, Assistant Dean and Director of Admissions, 210-436-3523, Fax: 210-431-4202.

St. Thomas University, School of Law, Miami, FL 33054-6459. Offers international human rights (LL M); international taxation (LL M); law (JD); JD/MBA; JD/MS. *Accreditation:* ABA. Postbaccalaureate distance learning degree programs offered (no on-campus study). *Degree requirements:* For master's, thesis (international taxation). *Entrance requirements:* LSAT. Electronic applications accepted. Expenses: Contact institution.

Samford University, Cumberland School of Law, Birmingham, AL 35229. Offers JD, MCL, JD/M Acc, JD/M Div, JD/MBA, JD/MPA, JD/MPH, JD/MSEM, JD/MTS. *Accreditation:* ABA. *Faculty:* 26 full-time (6 women), 14 part-time/adjunct (5 women). *Students:* 492 full-time (210 women), 7 part-time (4 women); includes 60 minority (43 African Americans, 4 American Indian/Alaska Native, 7 Asian Americans or Pacific Islanders, 6 Hispanic Americans). Average age 25. 1,425 applicants, 15% accepted, 199 enrolled. In 2006, 193 JDs, 3 master's awarded. *Entrance requirements:* LSAT. Additional exam requirements/recommendations for international students: Required—TOEFL (minimum score 550 paper-based; 213 computer-based). *Application deadline:* For fall admission, 2/28 priority date for domestic students. Applications are processed on a rolling basis. Application fee: $50. *Expenses: Contact institution.* One-time fee: $25 part-time. Full-time tuition and fees vary according to program and student level. *Financial support:* In 2006–07, 196 students received support. Career-related internships or fieldwork, Federal Work-Study, institutionally sponsored loans, and scholarships/grants available. Financial award application deadline: 3/1; financial award applicants required to submit FAFSA. *Faculty research:* Constitutional law (commerce clause), law and literature, legal history, law and ethics, evidence. *Unit head:* John L. Carroll, Dean, 205-726-2704, Fax: 205-726-4107, E-mail: jlcarrol@samford.edu. *Application contact:* M. Giselle Gauthier, Director of Admissions, 205-726-2702, Fax: 205-726-2057, E-mail: law.admissions@samford.edu.

San Joaquin College of Law, Law Program, Clovis, CA 93612-1312. Offers JD. Part-time and evening/weekend programs available. *Entrance requirements:* LSAT.

Santa Clara University, School of Law, Santa Clara, CA 95053. Offers high technology law (Certificate); intellectual property law (LL M); international and comparative law (LL M); international law (Certificate); law (JD); public interest and social justice law (Certificate); U.S. law for foreign lawyers (LL M); JD/MBA. *Accreditation:* ABA. Part-time and evening/weekend programs available. *Faculty:* 58 full-time (29 women), 34 part-time/adjunct (15 women). *Students:* 881 full-time (439 women), 53 part-time (29 women); includes 362 minority (45 African Americans, 4 American Indian/Alaska Native, 229 Asian Americans or Pacific Islanders, 84 Hispanic Americans), 16 international. Average age 28. 3,782 applicants, 41% accepted, 329 enrolled. In 2006, 286 JDs, 17 master's awarded. *Entrance requirements:* LSAT, LSDAS. *Application deadline:* For fall admission, 2/1 for domestic students. Application fee: $75. *Expenses: Contact institution.* Tuition and fees vary according to program. *Financial support:* Fellowships, research assistantships, career-related internships or fieldwork, Federal Work-Study, institutionally sponsored loans, and scholarships/grants available. Support available to part-time students. Financial award application deadline: 2/1; financial award applicants required to submit FAFSA. *Unit head:* Donald Polden, Dean, 408-554-4361. *Application contact:* Julia Yaffee, Director of Admissions, 408-554-4800, Fax: 408-554-7897.

Seattle University, School of Law, Seattle, WA 98122-4340. Offers JD, JD/MBA, JD/MIB, JD/MPA, JD/MSF, JD/MSL. *Accreditation:* ABA. Part-time programs available. *Faculty:* 67 full-time (33 women), 40 part-time/adjunct (9 women). *Students:* 861 full-time (470 women), 229 part-time (107 women); includes 265 minority (47 African Americans, 16 American Indian/Alaska Native, 142 Asian Americans or Pacific Islanders, 60 Hispanic Americans), 9 international. Average age 28. 3,151 applicants, 29% accepted, 352 enrolled. In 2006, 343 degrees awarded. *Entrance requirements:* LSAT. Additional exam requirements/recommendations for international students: Required—TOEFL (minimum score 600 paper-based; 250 computer-based; 92 iBT). *Application deadline:* For fall admission, 4/1 priority date for domestic and international students. Applications are processed on a rolling basis. Application fee: $50. Electronic applications accepted. *Expenses: Contact institution. Financial support:* Career-related internships or fieldwork, Federal Work-Study, institutionally sponsored loans, and scholarships/grants available. Support available to part-time students. Financial award application deadline: 4/1; financial award applicants required to submit FAFSA. *Faculty research:* Brain finger printing and the 4th Amendment/globe bioethics/intellectual property in developing countries, role of debtor health in the discharge of educational debt. Total annual research expenditures: $283,000. *Unit head:* Kellye Y. Testy, Dean, 206-398-4309, Fax: 206-398-4310, E-mail: ktesty@seattleu.edu. *Application contact:* Carol T. Cochran, Assistant Dean for Admission, 206-398-4200, Fax: 206-398-4058, E-mail: lawadmis@seattleu.edu.

Seton Hall University, School of Law, Newark, NJ 07102-5210. Offers JD, LL M, MSJ, JD/MADIR, JD/MBA, MD/JD, MD/MSJ. *Accreditation:* ABA. Part-time and evening/weekend programs available. *Faculty:* 61 full-time (24 women), 81 part-time/adjunct (24 women). *Students:* 729 full-time (313 women), 435 part-time (224 women); includes 219 minority (52 African Americans, 3 American Indian/Alaska Native, 107 Asian Americans or Pacific Islanders, 57 Hispanic Americans). Average age 27. 3,005 applicants, 36% accepted, 359 enrolled. In 2006, 370 JDs, 17 master's awarded. *Entrance requirements:* For JD, LSAT, active LSDAS registration, letters of recommendation, JD; for master's, professional experience, letters of recommendation. *Application deadline:* For fall admission, 4/1 for domestic and international students. Applications are processed on a rolling basis. Application fee: $65. Electronic applications accepted. *Expenses: Contact institution. Financial support:* In 2006–07, 979 students received support, including 26 fellowships (averaging $3,000 per year), 95 research assistantships (averaging $3,731 per year), 2 teaching assistantships (averaging $3,000 per year); career-related internships or fieldwork, Federal Work-Study, institutionally sponsored loans, scholarships/grants, and unspecified assistantships also available. Support available to part-time students. Financial award application deadline: 4/1; financial award applicants required to submit FAFSA. *Faculty research:* Employment law, constitutional law, health law, intellectual property. Total annual research expenditures: $958,000. *Unit head:* Patrick E. Hobbs, Dean and Professor of Law, 973-642-8750, Fax: 973-642-8031, E-mail: hobbspat@shu.edu. *Application contact:* Gisele Joachim, Assistant Dean for Admissions and Financial Resource Management, 973-642-8747, Fax: 973-642-8876, E-mail: admitme@shu.edu.

Southern Illinois University Carbondale, School of Law, Carbondale, IL 62901-6804. Offers general law (LL M); health law and policy (LL M); law (JD); legal studies (MLS), including general law, health law and policy; JD/M Acc; JD/MBA; JD/MD; JD/MPA; JD/MSW; JD/PhD. *Accreditation:* ABA. Part-time programs available. *Faculty:* 23 full-time (11 women), 12 part-time/adjunct (6 women). *Students:* 380 full-time (143 women), 3 part-time (1 women); includes 29 minority (9 African Americans, 1 American Indian/Alaska Native, 12 Asian Americans or Pacific Islanders, 7 Hispanic Americans), 2 international. Average age 27. 802 applicants, 50% accepted, 158 enrolled. In 2006, 107 degrees awarded. *Entrance requirements:* LSAT. Additional exam requirements/recommendations for international students: Required—TOEFL (minimum score 600 paper-based). *Application deadline:* For fall admission, 3/1 for domestic and international students. Applications are processed on a rolling basis. Application fee: $50. Electronic applications accepted. *Expenses: Contact institution. Financial support:* In 2006–07, 326 students received support. Career-related internships or fieldwork, Federal Work-Study, institutionally sponsored loans, scholarships/grants, and health care benefits available. Support available to part-time students. Financial award application deadline: 4/1; financial award applicants required to submit FAFSA. *Faculty research:* Health care law, criminal law, environmental law, international law, tort reform. *Unit head:* Peter C. Alexander, Dean, 618-453-8761, Fax: 618-453-8769. *Application contact:* Michael P. Ruiz, Assistant Dean for Admissions, 618-453-8858, Fax: 618-453-8769, E-mail: lawadmit@siu.edu.

Southern Methodist University, Dedman School of Law, Dallas, TX 75275-0110. Offers comparative and international law (LL M); law (JD, SJD); law-general (LL M); taxation (LL M); JD/MA; JD/MBA. *Accreditation:* ABA. Part-time and evening/weekend programs available. *Faculty:* 37 full-time (15 women), 27 part-time/adjunct (6 women). *Students:* 922 full-time (424 women), 76 part-time (34 women); includes 193 minority (44 African Americans, 3 American Indian/Alaska Native, 75 Asian Americans or Pacific Islanders, 66 Hispanic Americans), 46 international. Average age 27. 2,640 applicants, 23% accepted, 275 enrolled. In 2006, 261 JDs, 45 master's awarded. *Median time to degree:* 3 years full-time, 4 years part-time. *Degree requirements:* For JD, 30 hours of public service; for master's, thesis optional; for doctorate, thesis/dissertation. *Entrance requirements:* For JD, LSAT, 2 letters of recommendation, resumé, personal statement; for master's, JD (LL M in law, taxation), foreign law degree (LL M in comparative and international law); for doctorate, LL M. Additional exam requirements/recommendations for international students: Required—TOEFL (minimum score 575 paper-based; 233 computer-based). *Application deadline:* For fall admission, 2/15 priority date for domestic students. Applications are processed on a rolling basis. Application fee: $75. Electronic applications accepted. *Expenses: Contact institution. Financial support:* Career-related internships or fieldwork, Federal Work-Study, and scholarships/grants available. Financial award application deadline: 2/15; financial award applicants required to submit FAFSA. *Faculty research:* Corporate law, intellectual property, international law, commercial law, dispute resolution. *Unit head:* John B. Attanasio, Dean, 214-768-8999, Fax: 214-768-2182, E-mail: jba@mail.smu.edu. *Application contact:* Virginia Keehan, Assistant Dean for Admissions, 214-768-2550, Fax: 214-768-2549, E-mail: lawadmit@smu.edu.

Southern New England School of Law, Professional Program, North Dartmouth, MA 02747-1252. Offers JD. Part-time and evening/weekend programs available. *Faculty:* 11 full-time (5 women), 19 part-time/adjunct (5 women). *Students:* 156 full-time (86 women), 110 part-time (69 women); includes 68 minority (41 African Americans, 15 Asian Americans or Pacific Islanders, 12 Hispanic Americans), 7 international. Average age 32. 256 applicants, 82% accepted, 105 enrolled. In 2006, 68 degrees awarded. *Entrance requirements:* LSAT. *Application deadline:* For fall admission, 6/30 for domestic students. Applications are processed on a rolling basis. Application fee: $50. *Expenses:* Tuition: Full-time $19,486; part-time $685 per credit. Required fees: $375. *Financial support:* In 2006–07, 242 students received support, including 3 research assistantships (averaging $2,400 per year); scholarships/grants, tuition waivers (full and partial), and SNESL summer stipends also available. Support available to part-time students. Financial award application deadline: 6/30; financial award applicants required to submit FAFSA. *Unit head:* Robert V. Ward, Dean, 508-998-9600 Ext. 170, Fax:

Law

Southern New England School of Law (continued)
508-998-9561, E-mail: rward@snesl.edu. *Application contact:* Nancy Fitzsimmons Hebert, Director of Admissions, 508-998-9400 Ext. 113, Fax: 508-998-9561, E-mail: nhebert@snesl.edu.

Southern University and Agricultural and Mechanical College, Southern University Law Center, Baton Rouge, LA 70813. Offers JD. *Accreditation:* ABA. Part-time and evening/weekend programs available. *Entrance requirements:* LSAT. Electronic applications accepted. Expenses: Contact institution. *Faculty research:* Civil law, comparative law, constitutional law, civil rights law.

See Close-Up on page 2109.

South Texas College of Law, Professional Program, Houston, TX 77002-7000. Offers JD. *Accreditation:* ABA. Part-time and evening/weekend programs available. *Faculty:* 58 full-time (21 women), 69 part-time/adjunct (18 women). *Students:* 913 full-time (412 women), 324 part-time (136 women); includes 279 minority (44 African Americans, 10 American Indian/Alaska Native, 122 Asian Americans or Pacific Islanders, 103 Hispanic Americans), 3 international. Average age 28. 2,185 applicants, 43% accepted, 339 enrolled. In 2006, 374 degrees awarded. *Degree requirements:* For first-professional, registration. *Entrance requirements:* LSAT (within 4 years of application date). *Application deadline:* For fall admission, 2/15 for domestic and international students; for spring admission, 10/1 for domestic and international students. Application fee: $50. Electronic applications accepted. *Expenses:* Tuition: Full-time $21,840; part-time $14,560 per year. Required fees: $600. *Financial support:* In 2006–07, 1,175 students received support. Federal Work-Study, scholarships/grants, and tuition waivers (full and partial) available. Support available to part-time students. Financial award application deadline: 5/1; financial award applicants required to submit FAFSA. *Unit head:* James J. Alfini, President and Dean, 713-646-1819, Fax: 713-646-2909, E-mail: jalfini@stcl.edu. *Application contact:* Alicia K. Cramer, Assistant Dean of Admissions, 713-646-1810, Fax: 713-646-2906, E-mail: admissions@stcl.edu.

Southwestern Law School, Graduate Program, Los Angeles, CA 90010. Offers entertainment and media law (LL M); law (JD). *Accreditation:* ABA. Part-time and evening/weekend programs available. *Faculty:* 57 full-time (22 women), 24 part-time/adjunct (7 women). *Students:* 676 full-time (353 women), 288 part-time (150 women); includes 343 minority (50 African Americans, 7 American Indian/Alaska Native, 175 Asian Americans or Pacific Islanders, 111 Hispanic Americans), 12 international. Average age 27. 3,555 applicants, 31% accepted, 348 enrolled. In 2006, 269 JDs, 7 master's awarded. *Entrance requirements:* For JD, LSAT, LSDAS; for master's, JD. Additional exam requirements/recommendations for international students: Required—TOEFL. *Application deadline:* For fall admission, 4/1 for domestic and international students. Applications are processed on a rolling basis. Application fee: $50. Electronic applications accepted. *Expenses:* Tuition: Full-time $31,700; part-time $19,100 per year. Required fees: $200. Tuition and fees vary according to class time, course load, program and student level. *Financial support:* Research assistantships, career-related internships or fieldwork, Federal Work-Study, institutionally sponsored loans, scholarships/grants, and tuition waivers (full and partial) available. Support available to part-time students. Financial award application deadline: 6/1; financial award applicants required to submit FAFSA. *Faculty research:* International trade and law, mediation/arbitration, land use and urban planning, antitrust law. *Unit head:* Bryant Garth, Dean, 213-738-6710, Fax: 213-383-1688. *Application contact:* Lisa Gear, Interim Director of Admissions, 213-738-6717, Fax: 213-383-1688, E-mail: admissions@swlaw.edu.

Stanford University, Law School, Stanford, CA 94305-8610. Offers JD, JSM, MLS, JSD, JD/MBA, JD/PhD. *Accreditation:* ABA. *Degree requirements:* For doctorate, thesis/dissertation. *Entrance requirements:* LSAT. Electronic applications accepted. Expenses: Contact institution.

Stetson University, College of Law, Gulfport, FL 33707-3299. Offers JD, LL M, JD/MBA. *Accreditation:* ABA. *Students:* 853 full-time (450 women), 204 part-time (112 women); includes 204 minority (61 African Americans, 6 American Indian/Alaska Native, 27 Asian Americans or Pacific Islanders, 110 Hispanic Americans), 22 international. Average age 27. In 2006, 294 degrees awarded. *Entrance requirements:* LSAT, LSDAS. *Application deadline:* For fall admission, 3/1 priority date for domestic students; for spring admission, 9/1 for domestic students. Application fee: $50. *Expenses: Contact institution. Financial support:* Research assistantships, teaching assistantships, career-related internships or fieldwork, institutionally sponsored loans, and scholarships/grants available. Financial award application deadline: 4/1; financial award applicants required to submit FAFSA. *Unit head:* Dr. Darby Dickerson, Dean, 727-562-7810. *Application contact:* Pamela Coleman, Assistant Dean and Director of Admissions, 727-562-7802, E-mail: lawadmit@law.stetson.edu.

Suffolk University, Law School, Boston, MA 02108. Offers civil litigation (JD); financial services (JD); global law and technology (LL M); health care/biotechnology law (JD); intellectual property law (JD); international law (JD); U.S. law for international business lawyers (LL M); JD/MBA; JD/MPA; JD/MSCJ; JD/MSF; JD/MSIE. *Accreditation:* ABA. Part-time and evening/weekend programs available. *Faculty:* 79 full-time (25 women), 124 part-time/adjunct (30 women). *Students:* 1,032 full-time (504 women), 612 part-time (301 women); includes 211 minority (47 African Americans, 8 American Indian/Alaska Native, 105 Asian Americans or Pacific Islanders, 51 Hispanic Americans), 23 international. Average age 26. 3,069 applicants, 49% accepted, 550 enrolled. In 2006, 498 JDs, 18 master's awarded. *Degree requirements:* For master's, legal writing. *Entrance requirements:* For JD, LSAT, LSDAS, dean's certification, recommendation; for master's, 2 letters of recommendation, resumé. Additional exam requirements/recommendations for international students: Required—TOEFL (minimum score 600 paper-based; 250 computer-based; 100 iBT). *Application deadline:* For fall admission, 3/1 priority date for domestic and international students. Applications are processed on a rolling basis. Application fee: $60. Electronic applications accepted. *Expenses: Contact institution. Financial support:* In 2006–07, 627 students received support. Career-related internships or fieldwork, Federal Work-Study, institutionally sponsored loans, and scholarships/grants available. Support available to part-time students. Financial award application deadline: 3/1; financial award applicants required to submit FAFSA. *Faculty research:* Civil law, international law, health/biomedical law, business and finance, intellectual property. *Unit head:* Gail N. Ellis, Dean of Admissions, 617-573-8144, Fax: 617-523-1367, E-mail: gellis@suffolk.edu. *Application contact:* Ian A. Menchini, Associate Director, Law Admissions, 617-573-8144, Fax: 617-523-1367, E-mail: imenchin@suffolk.edu.

Syracuse University, College of Law, Syracuse, NY 13244-1030. Offers JD, JD/MA, JD/MBA, JD/MLS, JD/MPA, JD/MPS, JD/MS, JD/MS Acct, JD/MSW, JD/PhD. *Accreditation:* ABA. Part-time programs available. *Entrance requirements:* LSAT. Additional exam requirements/recommendations for international students: Required—TOEFL (minimum score 600 paper-based; 250 computer-based), TWE. Expenses: Contact institution. *Faculty research:* Interdisciplinary legal studies, law and technology, international law, advocacy training, family law.

Temple University, James E. Beasley School of Law, Philadelphia, PA 19122. Offers law (JD); taxation (LL M); transnational law (LL M); trial advocacy (LL M); JD/LL M; JD/MBA. *Accreditation:* ABA. Part-time and evening/weekend programs available. *Degree requirements:* For first-professional, 87 credits, completion of professional responsibility course and two writing courses. *Entrance requirements:* LSAT. Electronic applications accepted. Expenses: Contact institution. Tuition and fees vary according to program. *Faculty research:* Public health law/AIDS, religious rights, sexual harassment, children's rights, products liability.

Texas Southern University, Thurgood Marshall School of Law, Houston, TX 77004-4584. Offers JD, JD/MA, JD/MCP, JD/MPA. *Accreditation:* ABA. *Faculty:* 35 full-time (17 women), 18 part-time/adjunct (7 women). *Students:* 663 full-time (351 women), 2 part-time; includes 530 minority (328 African Americans, 6 American Indian/Alaska Native, 47 Asian Americans or Pacific Islanders, 149 Hispanic Americans), 22 international. Average age 28. 308 applicants, 100% accepted, 253 enrolled. In 2006, 195 degrees awarded. *Entrance requirements:* LSAT. *Application deadline:* For fall admission, 4/1 priority date for domestic students. Applications are processed on a rolling basis. Application fee: $55. Electronic applications accepted. *Expenses: Contact institution. Financial support:* In 2006–07, 75 students received support, including 24 research assistantships (averaging $1,050 per year), 19 teaching assistantships (averaging $1,000 per year); fellowships, career-related internships or fieldwork, Federal Work-Study, institutionally sponsored loans, scholarships/grants, and tuition waivers (partial) also available. Financial award application deadline: 4/1; financial award applicants required to submit FAFSA. *Faculty research:* Sports law, civil rights and minors, international economics regulation, contracts principle, standards of judicial review. *Unit head:* McKen V. Carrington, Dean, 713-313-1076, Fax: 713-313-1049, E-mail: carrington_mv@tsulaw.edu. *Application contact:* Edward Rene, Director of Admissions, 713-313-7115 Ext. 1004, Fax: 713-313-1049, E-mail: erene@tsulaw.edu.

Texas Tech University, School of Law, Lubbock, TX 79409-0004. Offers JD, JD/MBA, JD/MPA, JD/MS. *Accreditation:* ABA. *Faculty:* 11 full-time (4 women), 6 part-time/adjunct (1 woman). *Students:* 695 full-time (310 women), 7 part-time (4 women); includes 137 minority (28 African Americans, 5 American Indian/Alaska Native, 30 Asian Americans or Pacific Islanders, 74 Hispanic Americans), 2 international. Average age 26. 1,790 applicants, 26% accepted, 225 enrolled. In 2006, 200 degrees awarded. *Entrance requirements:* LSAT. *Application deadline:* For fall admission, 2/1 priority date for domestic and international students. Applications are processed on a rolling basis. Application fee: $50 ($60 for international students). *Expenses: Contact institution. Financial support:* In 2006–07, 646 students received support, including 16 teaching assistantships with partial tuition reimbursements available (averaging $6,979 per year); research assistantships with partial tuition reimbursements available, career-related internships or fieldwork, Federal Work-Study, and institutionally sponsored loans also available. Financial award application deadline: 4/15; financial award applicants required to submit FAFSA. *Faculty research:* Bioterrorism, water law, forensic mental health law, oil and gas law, international art law. Total annual research expenditures: $10,046. *Unit head:* Walter Burl Huffman, Dean, 806-742-3990, Fax: 806-742-4014, E-mail: walter.huffman@ttu.edu. *Application contact:* Terence Cook, Assistant Dean of Admissions and Recruitment, 806-742-3990, Fax: 806-742-4617, E-mail: terence.cook@ttu.edu.

Texas Wesleyan University, School of Law, Fort Worth, TX 76102. Offers JD. *Accreditation:* ABA. Part-time and evening/weekend programs available. *Faculty:* 25 full-time (8 women), 28 part-time/adjunct (11 women). *Students:* 444 full-time (208 women), 307 part-time (145 women); includes 149 minority (40 African Americans, 12 American Indian/Alaska Native, 36 Asian Americans or Pacific Islanders, 61 Hispanic Americans). Average age 29. In 2006, 151 degrees awarded. *Entrance requirements:* LSAT. Additional exam requirements/recommendations for international students: Required—TOEFL. *Application deadline:* For fall admission, 5/1 priority date for domestic students. Applications are processed on a rolling basis. Application fee: $50. Electronic applications accepted. *Expenses: Contact institution.* Tuition and fees vary according to program. *Financial support:* Career-related internships or fieldwork, scholarships/grants, and tuition waivers (full and partial) available. Support available to part-time students. Financial award application deadline: 3/15; financial award applicants required to submit FAFSA. *Unit head:* Cynthia Fountaine, Interim Dean, 817-212-4000, Fax: 817-212-4199. *Application contact:* Lynda Culver, Assistant Dean/Director of Admissions, 817-212-4045, Fax: 817-212-4002, E-mail: law_admissions@law.txwes.edu.

Thomas Jefferson School of Law, Professional Program, San Diego, CA 92110-2905. Offers JD. *Accreditation:* ABA. Part-time and evening/weekend programs available. *Faculty:* 37 full-time (19 women), 34 part-time/adjunct (11 women). *Students:* 580 full-time (255 women), 190 part-time (85 women); includes 150 minority (36 African Americans, 4 American Indian/Alaska Native, 56 Asian Americans or Pacific Islanders, 54 Hispanic Americans). Average age 26. 3,285 applicants, 47% accepted, 294 enrolled. In 2006, 279 degrees awarded. *Entrance requirements:* LSAT. Additional exam requirements/recommendations for international students: Required—TOEFL. *Application deadline:* For fall admission, 8/20 priority date for domestic students; for spring admission, 1/7 priority date for domestic students. Applications are processed on a rolling basis. Application fee: $35. Electronic applications accepted. *Expenses:* Tuition: Full-time $30,100; part-time $9,450 per semester. Tuition and fees vary according to course load. *Financial support:* In 2006–07, 346 fellowships with full and partial tuition reimbursements (averaging $11,622 per year) were awarded; career-related internships or fieldwork, Federal Work-Study, scholarships/grants, and tuition waivers also available. Support available to part-time students. Financial award application deadline: 4/30; financial award applicants required to submit FAFSA. *Faculty research:* Tenant's rights, fetal rights/medical ethics, bilateral treaties/international law, sexual harassment and gender treatment. *Unit head:* Rudolph C. Hasl, Dean and President, 619-297-9700 Ext. 1404, E-mail: hasl@tjsl.edu. *Application contact:* M. Elizabeth Kransberger, Assistant Dean for Admissions, Financial Aid, and Student Counseling Services, 619-297-9700 Ext. 1616, Fax: 619-294-4713, E-mail: bkransberger@tjsl.edu.

Thomas M. Cooley Law School, Professional Program, Lansing, MI 48901-3038. Offers JD, LL M. *Accreditation:* ABA. Part-time and evening/weekend programs available. *Faculty:* 87 full-time (35 women), 154 part-time/adjunct (53 women). *Students:* 566 full-time (253 women), 3,066 part-time (1,468 women); includes 810 minority (394 African Americans, 14 American Indian/Alaska Native, 219 Asian Americans or Pacific Islanders, 183 Hispanic Americans), 137 international. Average age 26. 5,718 applicants, 66% accepted, 1691 enrolled. In 2006, 665 JDs awarded. *Median time to degree:* 3 years full-time, 4 years part-time. *Degree requirements:* For first-professional, clinical experience. *Entrance requirements:* LSAT, LSDAS. *Application deadline:* For fall admission, 9/1 for domestic students; for winter admission, 1/1 for domestic students; for spring admission, 5/1 for domestic students. Applications are processed on a rolling basis. Application fee: $0. Electronic applications accepted. *Expenses:* Tuition: Full-time $24,220. Tuition and fees vary according to course load. *Financial support:* In 2006–07, 3,304 students received support, including 11 research assistantships with tuition reimbursements available (averaging $5,092 per year), 60 teaching assistantships with tuition reimbursements available; career-related internships or fieldwork, Federal Work-Study, scholarships/grants, and unspecified assistantships also available. Support available to part-time students. Financial award applicants required to submit FAFSA. *Faculty research:* Wrongful convictions, civil rights, environmental law, litigation techniques, death penalty. *Application contact:* Stephanie Gregg, Dean of Admissions, 517-371-5140, Fax: 517-334-5718, E-mail: greggs@cooley.edu.

Touro College, Jacob D. Fuchsberg Law Center, Huntington, NY 11743. Offers law (JD); U.S. law for foreign lawyers (LL M). *Accreditation:* ABA. Part-time and evening/weekend programs available. *Entrance requirements:* LSAT. Expenses: Contact institution. *Faculty research:* Business law, civil rights, international law, criminal justice.

Trinity International University, Trinity Law School, Santa Ana, CA 92705. Offers JD. Part-time and evening/weekend programs available. *Faculty:* 3 full-time (0 women), 21 part-time/adjunct (5 women). *Students:* 107 full-time (54 women), 65 part-time (32 women). In 2006, 37 degrees awarded. *Entrance requirements:* LSAT. Additional exam requirements/recommendations for international students: Required—TOEFL (minimum score 580 paper-based). *Application deadline:* For fall admission, 5/1 priority date for domestic and international students; for spring admission, 12/1 priority date for domestic and international students. Applications are processed on a rolling basis. Application fee: $30. *Expenses: Contact institution. Financial support:* Scholarships/grants available. Financial award application deadline: 8/15; financial award applicants required to submit FAFSA. *Unit head:* Kevin P. Holsclaw, Academic Dean, 714-836-7160, Fax: 714-796-7190, E-mail: kholscla@tiu.edu. *Application contact:* Joseph Wyse, Director of Admissions and Records, 714-796-7141, Fax: 714-796-7190, E-mail: jwyse@tiu.edu.

Tulane University, School of Law, New Orleans, LA 70118. Offers admiralty (LL M); American business law (LL M); energy and environment (LL M); international and comparative law (LL M); law (JD, LL M, SJD); JD/M Acct; JD/MA; JD/MBA; JD/MHA; JD/MPH; JD/MS; JD/MSW. *Accreditation:* ABA. *Faculty:* 54 full-time (15 women), 103 part-time/adjunct (18 women).

Students: 1,023 full-time (513 women), 8 part-time (6 women); includes 182 minority (80 African Americans, 7 American Indian/Alaska Native, 51 Asian Americans or Pacific Islanders, 44 Hispanic Americans), 50 international. Average age 24. 4,100 applicants, 26% accepted, 300 enrolled. In 2006, 336 JDs, 51 master's, 1 doctorate awarded. Terminal master's awarded for partial completion of doctoral program. *Degree requirements:* For doctorate, thesis/dissertation. *Entrance requirements:* LSAT. Additional exam requirements/recommendations for international students: Required—TOEFL (minimum score 575 paper-based; 233 computer-based). *Application deadline:* For fall admission, 3/15 priority date for domestic and international students. Applications are processed on a rolling basis. Application fee: $60. Electronic applications accepted. *Expenses: Contact institution. Financial support:* In 2006–07, 625 students received support, including 3 fellowships with full and partial tuition reimbursements available; career-related internships or fieldwork, Federal Work-Study, institutionally sponsored loans, scholarships/grants, and tuition waivers (full and partial) also available. Financial award application deadline: 2/15; financial award applicants required to submit FAFSA. *Faculty research:* Civil law. *Unit head:* Lawrence Ponoroff, Dean, 504-865-5937, Fax: 504-862-8746, E-mail: lponoroff@law.tulane.edu. *Application contact:* Susan Krinsky, Associate Dean, 504-865-5930, Fax: 504-865-6710, E-mail: skrinsky@law.tulane.edu.

Universidad Central del Este, Law School, San Pedro de Macoris, Dominican Republic. Offers JD.

Université de Moncton, Faculty of Law, Moncton, NB E1A 3E9, Canada. Offers LL B, LL M, Diploma, LL B/MBA, LL B/MEE, LL B/MPA. Programs offered exclusively in French. *Degree requirements:* For LL B, one foreign language; for master's, 2 foreign languages. *Entrance requirements:* For LL B and master's, proficiency in French. *Faculty research:* Minority language rights, legal translation, rights of the elderly, student rights, constitutional rights.

Université de Montréal, Faculty of Graduate Studies, Faculty of Law, Montréal, QC H3C 3J7, Canada. Offers LL B, LL M, LL D, DDN, DESS. Part-time programs available. *Faculty:* 57 full-time (19 women), 5 part-time/adjunct (2 women). *Students:* 375 full-time (208 women), 89 part-time (53 women). 698 applicants, 40% accepted, 216 enrolled. In 2006, 53 master's, 4 doctorates, 78 other advanced degrees awarded. *Degree requirements:* For master's, thesis; for doctorate, thesis/dissertation, project; for other advanced degree, thesis (for some programs). *Application deadline:* For fall admission, 2/1 priority date for domestic students; for winter admission, 11/1 priority date for domestic students; for spring admission, 2/1 priority date for domestic students. Application fee: $30. Electronic applications accepted. *Financial support:* Fellowships, research assistantships, teaching assistantships available. *Faculty research:* Legal theory; constitutional, private, and public law. *Unit head:* Anne-Marie Boisvert, Dean, 514-343-2356, Fax: 514-343-2199, E-mail: anne-marie.boisvert@umontreal.ca. *Application contact:* Michel Morin, Vice Dean, 514-343-2409, E-mail: michel.morin.3@umontreal.ca.

Université de Sherbrooke, Faculty of Law, Sherbrooke, QC J1K 2R1, Canada. Offers alternative dispute resolution (LL M, Diploma); biotechnology (LL B); business administration (LL B); business law (Diploma); health law (LL M, Diploma); law (LL B, LL D); legal management (Diploma); notarial law (DDN); transnational law (Diploma). Part-time and evening/weekend programs available. *Degree requirements:* For master's, thesis; for other advanced degree, one foreign language. *Entrance requirements:* For master's and other advanced degree, LL B. Electronic applications accepted.

Université du Québec à Montréal, Graduate Programs, Program in Social and Labor Law, Montréal, QC H3C 3P8, Canada. Offers LL M. *Entrance requirements:* For master's, appropriate bachelor's degree or equivalent and proficiency in French.

Université Laval, Faculty of Law, Programs in Law, Québec, QC G1K 7P4, Canada. Offers international and transnational law (Diploma); law (LL M, LL D); law of business (Diploma). Part-time programs available. Terminal master's awarded for partial completion of doctoral program. *Degree requirements:* For master's, thesis (for some programs); for doctorate, thesis/dissertation. *Entrance requirements:* For master's, doctorate, and Diploma, knowledge of French and English. Electronic applications accepted.

University at Buffalo, the State University of New York, Graduate School, Law School, Buffalo, NY 14260. Offers criminal law (LL M); general law for international students (LL M); law (JD); JD/MA; JD/MBA; JD/MLS; JD/MPH; JD/MSW; JD/MUP; JD/PhD; JD/Pharm D. *Accreditation:* ABA. *Faculty:* 54 full-time (24 women), 51 part-time/adjunct (19 women). *Students:* 764 full-time (372 women), 5 part-time (3 women); includes 126 minority (42 African Americans, 4 American Indian/Alaska Native, 48 Asian Americans or Pacific Islanders, 32 Hispanic Americans), 29 international. Average age 25. 1,544 applicants, 36% accepted, 247 enrolled. In 2006, 248 degrees awarded. *Entrance requirements:* For JD, LSAT, minimum undergraduate GPA of 2.0; for master's, JD. Additional exam requirements/recommendations for international students: Required—TOEFL (minimum score 650 paper-based; 280 computer-based). *Application deadline:* For fall admission, 3/15 priority date for domestic students. Applications are processed on a rolling basis. Application fee: $50. Electronic applications accepted. *Expenses: Contact institution. Financial support:* In 2006–07, 660 students received support, including 25 fellowships with full and partial tuition reimbursements available (averaging $10,000 per year), 34 research assistantships (averaging $1,135 per year); career-related internships or fieldwork, Federal Work-Study, institutionally sponsored loans, scholarships/grants, tuition waivers (full and partial), and unspecified assistantships also available. Financial award application deadline: 3/1; financial award applicants required to submit FAFSA. *Faculty research:* Criminal law, environmental law, international law, human rights, labor and employment law. Total annual research expenditures: $121,000. *Unit head:* R. Nils Olsen, Dean, 716-645-2052, Fax: 716-645-5968, E-mail: law-deans@buffalo.edu. *Application contact:* Lillie V. Wiley-Upshaw, Associate Dean and Director of Admissions and Financial Aid, 716-645-2907, Fax: 716-645-6676, E-mail: law-admissions@buffalo.edu.

The University of Akron, School of Law, Akron, OH 44325-2901. Offers JD, JD/MAP, JD/M Tax, JD/MBA, JD/MPA, JD/MSM, JD/MSMHR. *Accreditation:* ABA. Part-time and evening/weekend programs available. *Faculty:* 31 full-time (11 women), 24 part-time/adjunct (6 women). *Students:* 314 full-time (136 women), 225 part-time (95 women); includes 71 minority (38 African Americans, 22 Asian Americans or Pacific Islanders, 11 Hispanic Americans), 1 international. Average age 28. 2,230 applicants, 28% accepted, 186 enrolled. In 2006, 138 JDs awarded. *Entrance requirements:* LSAT, LSDAS. Additional exam requirements/recommendations for international students: Required—TOEFL (minimum score 650 paper-based; 230 computer-based; 115 iBT). *Application deadline:* For fall admission, 3/1 priority date for domestic and international students. Applications are processed on a rolling basis. Application fee: $35. Electronic applications accepted. *Expenses: Contact institution.* Tuition and fees vary according to course load, degree level and program. *Financial support:* In 2006–07, 197 students received support. Career-related internships or fieldwork, scholarships/grants, and tuition waivers (full and partial) available. Support available to part-time students. Financial award applicants required to submit FAFSA. *Faculty research:* Intellectual property; law and science; trust and elder law, including taxation and retirement benefits; professional responsibility and judicial ethics; constitutional law, theory, and process. Total annual research expenditures: $35,751. *Unit head:* Richard L. Aynes, Dean, 330-972-7331, Fax: 330-258-2343, E-mail: raynes@uakron.edu. *Application contact:* Lauri S. File, Assistant Dean of Admission and Financial Aid, 330-972-7331, Fax: 330-258-2343, E-mail: lfile@uakron.edu.

The University of Alabama, School of Law, Tuscaloosa, AL 35487. Offers JD, LL M, LL M in Tax, JD/MBA. *Accreditation:* ABA. Postbaccalaureate distance learning degree programs offered (no on-campus study). *Faculty:* 35 full-time (11 women), 31 part-time/adjunct (5 women). *Students:* 497 full-time (188 women), 2 part-time; includes 53 minority (40 African Americans, 4 American Indian/Alaska Native, 4 Asian Americans or Pacific Islanders, 5 Hispanic Americans), 1 international. Average age 25. 1,071 applicants, 26% accepted, 157 enrolled. In 2006, 176 JDs, 28 master's awarded. *Median time to degree:* Master's–2 years part-time. *Degree requirements:* For first-professional, seminar. *Entrance requirements:* LSAT, LSDAS registration. Additional exam requirements/recommendations for international students: Required—TOEFL. *Application deadline:* For fall admission, 3/1 for domestic and international students. Applications are processed on a rolling basis. Application fee: $35. Electronic applications accepted. *Expenses: Contact institution. Financial support:* In 2006–07, 383 students received support, including 54 research assistantships; career-related internships or fieldwork, Federal Work-Study, institutionally sponsored loans, and tuition waivers (full and partial) also available. Financial award application deadline: 5/15. *Faculty research:* Environmental law, legal history, white-collar crime, pensions, comparative law. *Unit head:* Kenneth C. Randall, Dean, 205-348-5117, Fax: 205-348-3917, E-mail: krandall@law.ua.edu. *Application contact:* Marquita Henderson, Admissions Coordinator, 205-348-5440, Fax: 205-348-3917, E-mail: admissions@law.ua.edu.

University of Alberta, Faculty of Law, Edmonton, AB T6G 2H5, Canada. Offers LL B, LL M, MBA/LL B. Part-time programs available. *Degree requirements:* For master's, thesis, registration. *Entrance requirements:* For LL B, LSAT; for master's, minimum GPA of 3.0. Additional exam requirements/recommendations for international students: Required—TOEFL (minimum score 600 paper-based; 250 computer-based). Electronic applications accepted. *Faculty research:* Health law, environmental law, native law issues, constitutional law, human rights.

The University of Arizona, James E. Rogers College of Law, Tucson, AZ 85721-0176. Offers international indigenous peoples' rights and policy (LL M); international trade law (LL M); law (JD); JD/MA; JD/MBA; JD/MPA; JD/PhD. *Accreditation:* ABA. *Degree requirements:* For first-professional, publishable paper. *Entrance requirements:* LSAT, LSDAS, resumé, 2 letters of recommendation. Additional exam requirements/recommendations for international students: Required—TOEFL. Electronic applications accepted. Expenses: Contact institution. *Faculty research:* Tax law, employment law, corporate law, torts, trial practice and skills, constitutional law, Indian law, family law, estates and trusts.

University of Arkansas, School of Law, Fayetteville, AR 72701. Offers agricultural law (LL M); law (JD). *Accreditation:* ABA. *Students:* 440 full-time (245 women); includes 110 minority (79 African Americans, 8 American Indian/Alaska Native, 14 Asian Americans or Pacific Islanders, 9 Hispanic Americans), 2 international. In 2006, 146 JDs awarded. *Entrance requirements:* LSAT. *Application deadline:* For fall admission, 4/1 for domestic students. Applications are processed on a rolling basis. Application fee: $0. *Expenses: Contact institution. Financial support:* In 2006–07, 131 students received support, including fellowships with full tuition reimbursements available (averaging $6,000 per year), 10 research assistantships (averaging $2,500 per year), 1 teaching assistantship; career-related internships or fieldwork, Federal Work-Study, and scholarships/grants also available. Support available to part-time students. Financial award application deadline: 4/1; financial award applicants required to submit FAFSA. *Unit head:* Cynthia Nance, Dean, 479-575-5601, Fax: 479-575-3320, E-mail: cnance@uark.edu. *Application contact:* James K. Miller, Associate Dean for Students, 479-575-3102, E-mail: jkmiller@uark.edu.

University of Arkansas at Little Rock, William H. Bowen School of Law, Little Rock, AR 72202-5142. Offers JD, JD/MBA, JD/MD, JD/MPA, JD/MPH. *Accreditation:* ABA. Part-time and evening/weekend programs available. *Entrance requirements:* LSAT. Electronic applications accepted. Expenses: Contact institution. *Faculty research:* Employment discrimination, uniform commercial code, Arkansas legal history, scientific evidence, mediation.

University of Baltimore, School of Law, Baltimore, MD 21201. Offers law (JD); taxation (LL M); JD/LL M; JD/MBA; JD/MPA; JD/MS; JD/PhD. *Accreditation:* ABA. Part-time and evening/weekend programs available. *Faculty:* 60 full-time (23 women), 92 part-time/adjunct (24 women). *Students:* 726 full-time, 306 part-time; includes 181 minority (106 African Americans, 5 American Indian/Alaska Native, 50 Asian Americans or Pacific Islanders, 20 Hispanic Americans), 7 international. Average age 27. 2,896 applicants, 41% accepted, 382 enrolled. In 2006, 276 degrees awarded. *Entrance requirements:* LSAT. *Application deadline:* For fall admission, 3/1 priority date for domestic students. Applications are processed on a rolling basis. Application fee: $60. Electronic applications accepted. *Expenses: Contact institution. Financial support:* In 2006–07, 650 students received support, including 27 teaching assistantships; research assistantships, career-related internships or fieldwork, Federal Work-Study, institutionally sponsored loans, and scholarships/grants also available. Support available to part-time students. Financial award application deadline: 4/1; financial award applicants required to submit FAFSA. *Faculty research:* Plain view doctrine, statute of limitations, bankruptcy, family law, international and comparative law. *Unit head:* Phillip J. Closius, Dean, 410-837-4458. *Application contact:* Mark Bell, Assistant Director of Law Admissions, 410-837-4464, Fax: 410-837-4450, E-mail: kbell@ubalt.edu.

The University of British Columbia, Faculty of Graduate Studies, Faculty of Law, Vancouver, BC V6T 1Z1, Canada. Offers LL M, PhD. Part-time programs available. *Faculty:* 44 full-time (11 women), 89 part-time/adjunct. *Students:* 75 full-time (45 women); includes 24 minority (4 African Americans, 4 American Indian/Alaska Native, 13 Asian Americans or Pacific Islanders, 3 Hispanic Americans), 25 international. Average age 30. 130 applicants, 42% accepted, 33 enrolled. *Median time to degree:* Master's–2 years full-time. *Entrance requirements:* For master's, LL B, thesis proposal, 3 letters of reference; for doctorate, LL B, LL M, thesis proposal, 3 letters of reference. Additional exam requirements/recommendations for international students: Required—TOEFL (minimum score 600 paper-based; 250 computer-based; 100 iBT), IELTS. *Application deadline:* For fall admission, 2/1 for domestic and international students. Applications are processed on a rolling basis. Application fee: $90 ($150 for international students). Electronic applications accepted. *Financial support:* In 2006–07, 10 fellowships (averaging $7,000 per year), 5 research assistantships, 8 teaching assistantships (averaging $9,933 per year) were awarded; Federal Work-Study, scholarships/grants, and unspecified assistantships also available. Financial award application deadline: 9/30. *Faculty research:* Aboriginal rights/native law, Asian legal studies, criminal law, environmental law, international law, corporate, human rights, intellectual property, dispute resolution, entertainment. *Unit head:* Prof. Catherine Dauvergne, Associate Dean, Graduate Studies and Research, 604-822-6506, Fax: 604-822-4781. *Application contact:* Joanne Y. Chung, Graduate Administrator, 604-822-6449, Fax: 604-822-4781, E-mail: graduates@law.ubc.ca.

University of Calgary, Faculty of Law, Calgary, AB T2N 1N4, Canada. Offers LL B, LL M, Graduate Certificate. *Faculty:* 18 full-time (8 women), 23 part-time/adjunct (8 women). *Students:* 241 full-time (138 women). Average age 26. 915 applicants, 9% accepted, 85 enrolled. In 2006, 69 LL Bs, 2 master's awarded. *Degree requirements:* For master's, thesis. *Entrance requirements:* For LL B, LSAT; for master's, minimum GPA of 3.0. Additional exam requirements/recommendations for international students: Required—TOEFL (minimum score 600 paper-based; 250 computer-based; 100 iBT). Application fee: $100. *Expenses: Contact institution. Financial support:* In 2006–07, 2 research assistantships (averaging $4,100 per year) were awarded; scholarships/grants and study awards also available. Financial award application deadline: 2/1. *Faculty research:* Resources law, family law, legal history, taxation law, human rights. *Unit head:* Alastair Lucas, Acting Dean, 403-220-7116, Fax: 403-282-8325, E-mail: lawdean@ucalgary.ca. *Application contact:* Karen Argento, Admissions and Student Affairs Officer, 403-220-8154, Fax: 403-210-9662, E-mail: kargento@ucalgary.ca.

University of California, Berkeley, Graduate Division, Haas School of Business and School of Law, Concurrent JD/MBA Program, Berkeley, CA 94720-1500. Offers JD/MBA. *Accreditation:* AACSB; ABA. *Students:* 2 full-time (both women); includes 1 minority (Asian American or Pacific Islander) Average age 28. *Entrance requirements:* Additional exam requirements/recommendations for international students: Required—TOEFL. *Application deadline:* For fall admission, 3/10 for domestic and international students. Application fee: $175. Electronic applications accepted. *Financial support:* Fellowships, career-related internships or fieldwork, scholarships/grants, and unspecified assistantships available. Financial award application deadline: 3/2; financial award applicants required to submit FAFSA. *Unit head:* Julia Hwang, Director, MBA Program, 510-642-1405, Fax: 510-643-6659, E-mail: julia_hwang@haas.berkeley.edu. *Application contact:* Office of Admissions, 510-642-1405, Fax: 510-643-6659, E-mail: admissions@boalt.berkeley.edu.

Law

University of California, Berkeley, School of Law, Berkeley, CA 94720-7200. Offers jurisprudence and social policy (PhD); law (JD, LL M, JSD); JD/MA; JD/MBA; JD/MCP; JD/MJ; JD/MPP; JD/MSW. *Accreditation:* ABA. Terminal master's awarded for partial completion of doctoral program. *Degree requirements:* For JD, writing requirement, professional responsibility; for master's, thesis; for doctorate, one foreign language, thesis/dissertation, oral qualifying exam. *Entrance requirements:* For JD, LSAT, LSDAS, letters of recommendation, writing sample; for master's, letters of recommendation; for doctorate, GRE General Test, letters of recommendation. Additional exam requirements/recommendations for international students: Required—TOEFL. Expenses: Contact institution. *Faculty research:* Law and technology; social justice; environmental law; business, law and economics; international/comparative law.

University of California, Davis, School of Law, Davis, CA 95616-5201. Offers JD, LL M, JD/MA, JD/MBA. *Accreditation:* ABA. *Faculty:* 36 full-time (16 women), 16 part-time/adjunct (5 women). *Students:* 582 full-time (321 women); includes 192 minority (9 African Americans, 2 American Indian/Alaska Native, 133 Asian Americans or Pacific Islanders, 48 Hispanic Americans), 6 international. Average age 24. 3,493 applicants, 28% accepted, 188 enrolled. In 2006, 189 JDs, 10 master's awarded. *Entrance requirements:* LSAT. *Application deadline:* For fall admission, 2/1 for domestic and international students. Applications are processed on a rolling basis. Application fee: $75. Electronic applications accepted. *Expenses: Contact institution. Financial support:* In 2006–07, 523 students received support, including 9 research assistantships with partial tuition reimbursements available, 78 teaching assistantships with partial tuition reimbursements available; Federal Work-Study, institutionally sponsored loans, scholarships/grants, and health care benefits also available. Financial award application deadline: 3/2; financial award applicants required to submit FAFSA. *Faculty research:* International law, international trade, immigration, environmental law, public interest law. *Unit head:* Rex R. Perschbacher, Dean, 530-752-0243, Fax: 530-752-7279, E-mail: rrperschbacher@ucdavis.edu. *Application contact:* Sharon Pinkney, Director, Admissions, 530-752-6477, Fax: 530-754-8371, E-mail: lawadmissions@ucdavis.edu.

University of California, Hastings College of the Law, Graduate Program, San Francisco, CA 94102-4978. Offers JD, LL M. *Accreditation:* ABA. *Degree requirements:* For JD and master's, registration. *Entrance requirements:* LSAT, LSDAS, 2 letters of recommendation. Electronic applications accepted. *Faculty research:* Immigration and refugee law, civil procedure and evidence, taxation law, environmental law and policy, constitutional law and civil rights.

University of California, Los Angeles, School of Law, Los Angeles, CA 90024. Offers JD, LL M, JD/MA, JD/MBA, JD/MSW, JD/PhD. *Accreditation:* ABA. *Entrance requirements:* LSAT. Expenses: Contact institution.

University of Chicago, The Law School, Chicago, IL 60637. Offers JD, LL M, MCL, DCL, JSD, JD/AM, JD/MBA, JD/MPP. *Accreditation:* ABA. *Faculty:* 69 full-time (10 women), 58 part-time/adjunct (11 women). *Students:* 658 full-time (293 women); includes 179 minority (43 African Americans, 4 American Indian/Alaska Native, 77 Asian Americans or Pacific Islanders, 55 Hispanic Americans), 63 international. Average age 24. 4,818 applicants. In 2006, 192 JDs, 51 master's, 1 doctorate awarded. *Entrance requirements:* LSAT, 2 letters of recommendation, resumé, personal statement. Additional exam requirements/recommendations for international students: Required—TOEFL. *Application deadline:* For fall admission, 2/1 priority date for domestic students. Applications are processed on a rolling basis. Application fee: $75. Electronic applications accepted. *Expenses: Contact institution.* One-time fee: $35 full-time. Full-time tuition and fees vary according to course load, degree level and program. *Financial support:* In 2006–07, 307 students received support, including 7 fellowships (averaging $3,000 per year); research assistantships, teaching assistantships, career-related internships or fieldwork, institutionally sponsored loans, and scholarships/grants also available. Financial award application deadline: 3/1; financial award applicants required to submit FAFSA. *Unit head:* Saul Levmore, Dean, 773-702-9494, Fax: 773-834-4409. *Application contact:* Ann K. Perry, Dean of Admissions, 773-834-4425, Fax: 773-834-0942, E-mail: admissions@law.uchicago.edu.

University of Cincinnati, College of Law, Cincinnati, OH 45221-0040. Offers JD, JD/MA, JD/MBA, JD/MCP, JD/MS, JD/PhD. *Accreditation:* ABA. *Faculty:* 32 full-time (16 women), 23 part-time/adjunct (3 women). *Students:* 376 full-time (184 women); includes 66 minority (26 African Americans, 3 American Indian/Alaska Native, 23 Asian Americans or Pacific Islanders, 14 Hispanic Americans). Average age 24. 1,183 applicants, 34% accepted, 113 enrolled. In 2006, 123 degrees awarded. *Entrance requirements:* LSAT. *Application deadline:* For fall admission, 4/1 priority date for domestic students. Applications are processed on a rolling basis. Application fee: $35. Electronic applications accepted. *Expenses: Contact institution. Financial support:* In 2006–07, 240 students received support, including 240 fellowships (averaging $8,000 per year); research assistantships, career-related internships or fieldwork, Federal Work-Study, scholarships/grants, tuition waivers (full and partial), and unspecified assistantships also available. Financial award application deadline: 4/1; financial award applicants required to submit FAFSA. *Faculty research:* International human rights, corporate law, intellectual property law, criminal law. *Unit head:* Louis D. Bilionois, Dean, 513-556-0121, Fax: 513-556-2391, E-mail: louis.bilionis@uc.edu. *Application contact:* Al Watson, Assistant Dean and Director of Admissions, 513-556-0077, Fax: 513-556-2391, E-mail: al.watson@uc.edu.

University of Colorado at Boulder, School of Law, Boulder, CO 80309-0401. Offers JD, JD/MBA, JD/MPA, JD/MS, JD/PhD. *Accreditation:* ABA. *Faculty:* 32 full-time (11 women). *Students:* 509 full-time (256 women), 1 part-time; includes 116 minority (19 African Americans, 17 American Indian/Alaska Native, 44 Asian Americans or Pacific Islanders, 36 Hispanic Americans), 5 international. Average age 27. 677 applicants, 100% accepted. In 2006, 169 JDs awarded. *Entrance requirements:* LSAT, minimum undergraduate GPA of 2.75. *Application deadline:* For fall admission, 2/15 for domestic students. Applications are processed on a rolling basis. Application fee: $50 ($60 for international students). *Expenses: Contact institution. Financial support:* In 2006–07, 118 fellowships (averaging $1,613 per year), 11 teaching assistantships (averaging $1,639 per year) were awarded; research assistantships, Federal Work-Study and institutionally sponsored loans also available. Financial award application deadline: 3/1; financial award applicants required to submit FAFSA. Total annual research expenditures: $60,476. *Unit head:* Harold H. Bruff, Dean, 303-492-8047, Fax: 303-492-1757, E-mail: harold.bruff@colorado.edu. *Application contact:* Graduate Program Assistant, 303-492-7203, Fax: 303-492-2542, E-mail: lawadmin@colorado.edu.

University of Connecticut, School of Law, Hartford, CT 06105. Offers JD, JD/LL M, JD/MBA, JD/MLS, JD/MPA, JD/MPH, JD/MSW. *Accreditation:* ABA. Part-time and evening/weekend programs available. *Faculty:* 44 full-time (13 women), 21 part-time/adjunct (5 women). *Students:* 480 full-time (230 women), 224 part-time (99 women); includes 117 minority (39 African Americans, 4 American Indian/Alaska Native, 26 Asian Americans or Pacific Islanders, 48 Hispanic Americans), 35 international. Average age 25. 2,017 applicants, 18% accepted, 212 enrolled. In 2006, 216 JDs awarded. *Median time to degree:* JD–3 years full-time, 4 years part-time. *Degree requirements:* For first-professional, extensive research paper. *Entrance requirements:* LSAT. Additional exam requirements/recommendations for international students: Required—TOEFL. *Application deadline:* For fall admission, 3/1 for domestic and international students. Applications are processed on a rolling basis. Application fee: $30. Electronic applications accepted. *Expenses: Contact institution. Financial support:* In 2006–07, 364 students received support; research assistantships, teaching assistantships, career-related internships or fieldwork, Federal Work-Study, scholarships/grants, and tuition waivers (full and partial) available. Support available to part-time students. Financial award application deadline: 3/1; financial award applicants required to submit FAFSA. *Faculty research:* International law, constitutional law, tax law, intellectual property, human rights law. *Unit head:* Ellen Keane Rutt, Associate Dean of Admissions, Career Services, and Student Finance, 860-570-5100, Fax: 860-570-5153, E-mail: admit@law.uconn.edu. *Application contact:* Karen L. DeMeola, Assistant Dean for Admissions and Student Finance, 860-570-5162, Fax: 860-570-5153, E-mail: karen.demeola@law.uconn.edu.

University of Dayton, School of Law, Dayton, OH 45469-2772. Offers JD, LL M, MSL, JD/M Ed, JD/MBA. *Accreditation:* ABA. *Faculty:* 28 full-time, 23 part-time/adjunct. *Students:* 458 full-time (197 women); includes 55 minority (22 African Americans, 4 American Indian/Alaska Native, 12 Asian Americans or Pacific Islanders, 17 Hispanic Americans), 2 international. Average age 25. 2,400 applicants, 39% accepted, 181 enrolled. In 2006, 164 degrees awarded. *Entrance requirements:* LSAT, accredited bachelor's degree or foreign equivalent. *Application deadline:* For fall admission, 5/1 priority date for domestic students, 3/1 priority date for international students; for spring admission, 2/1 priority date for international students. Applications are processed on a rolling basis. Application fee: $0. Electronic applications accepted. *Expenses: Contact institution.* Tuition and fees vary according to degree level and program. *Financial support:* In 2006–07, 245 students received support. Career-related internships or fieldwork, scholarships/grants, and tuition waivers (full and partial) available. Financial award application deadline: 3/1; financial award applicants required to submit FAFSA. *Faculty research:* Bankruptcy, criminal procedure, corporate practice, torts, computer law. *Unit head:* Lisa A. Kloppenberg, Dean, 937-229-3795, Fax: 937-229-2469. *Application contact:* Janet L. Hein, Assistant Dean, Director of Admissions and Financial Aid, 937-229-3555, Fax: 937-229-4194, E-mail: lawinfo@notes.udayton.edu.

University of Denver, College of Law, Professional Program, Denver, CO 80208. Offers JD. *Accreditation:* ABA. Part-time and evening/weekend programs available. *Students:* 1,087 full-time (515 women), 45 part-time (16 women); includes 209 minority (54 African Americans, 38 American Indian/Alaska Native, 54 Asian Americans or Pacific Islanders, 63 Hispanic Americans), 11 international. Average age 29. 3,676 applicants, 28% accepted. In 2006, 366 degrees awarded. *Entrance requirements:* LSAT. *Application deadline:* For fall admission, 3/1 priority date for domestic students. Applications are processed on a rolling basis. Application fee: $60. *Expenses:* Tuition: Full-time $29,628; part-time $823 per credit. *Financial support:* Career-related internships or fieldwork, Federal Work-Study, institutionally sponsored loans, and tutorships available. Support available to part-time students. Financial award application deadline: 2/15; financial award applicants required to submit FAFSA. *Faculty research:* Lawyering skills, international and legal studies, natural resources law (domestic and international), transportation law, public interest law, business and commercial law. *Application contact:* Admissions, 303-871-6135, Fax: 303-871-6992, E-mail: admissions@law.du.edu.

University of Denver, College of Law, Programs in American and Comparative Law and International Natural Resources Law, Denver, CO 80208. Offers American and comparative law (LL M); international natural resources law (LL M, MRLS). *Students:* 29 full-time (17 women), 11 part-time (7 women); includes 4 minority (1 American Indian/Alaska Native, 2 Asian Americans or Pacific Islanders, 1 Hispanic American), 6 international. Average age 31. 79 applicants, 92% accepted. In 2006, 48 degrees awarded. *Degree requirements:* For master's, internship. *Entrance requirements:* For master's, JD from US institution. Additional exam requirements/recommendations for international students: Required—TOEFL, TWE. *Application deadline:* Applications are processed on a rolling basis. Application fee: $45. Electronic applications accepted. *Expenses:* Tuition: Full-time $29,628; part-time $823 per credit. *Financial support:* Federal Work-Study and institutionally sponsored loans available. Support available to part-time students. Financial award application deadline: 2/15; financial award applicants required to submit FAFSA. *Unit head:* James Otto, Director, 303-871-6052. *Application contact:* Lucy Daberkow, Admissions, 303-871-6324, Fax: 303-871-6378, E-mail: llm@law.du.edu.

University of Detroit Mercy, School of Law, Detroit, MI 48226. Offers JD, JD/LL B, JD/MBA. *Accreditation:* ABA. Part-time programs available. *Entrance requirements:* LSAT. Expenses: Contact institution.

University of Florida, Levin College of Law, Gainesville, FL 32611. Offers comparative law (LL M); international taxation (LL M); law (JD); taxation (LL M, SJD). *Accreditation:* ABA. *Faculty:* 61 full-time (31 women), 46 part-time/adjunct (11 women). *Students:* 1,364 full-time (636 women); includes 281 minority (82 African Americans, 3 American Indian/Alaska Native, 68 Asian Americans or Pacific Islanders, 128 Hispanic Americans), 51 international. Average age 25. 2,535 applicants, 41% accepted, 447 enrolled. In 2006, 310 first professional degrees awarded. *Median time to degree:* 3 years full-time. *Degree requirements:* For first-professional, thesis or alternative. *Entrance requirements:* LSAT. Additional exam requirements/recommendations for international students: Required—TOEFL. *Application deadline:* For fall admission, 1/15 for domestic and international students. Applications are processed on a rolling basis. Application fee: $30. Electronic applications accepted. *Expenses: Contact institution. Financial support:* In 2006–07, 241 students received support, including 4 fellowships (averaging $3,655 per year); Federal Work-Study, institutionally sponsored loans, and scholarships/grants also available. Financial award application deadline: 4/1; financial award applicants required to submit FAFSA. *Faculty research:* Environmental and land use law, taxation, family law, international law, constitutional law. *Unit head:* Robert Jerry, Dean, 352-273-0600, Fax: 352-392-8727, E-mail: jerryr@law.ufl.edu. *Application contact:* J. Michael Patrick, Assistant Dean for Admissions, 352-273-0890, Fax: 352-392-4087, E-mail: patrick@law.ufl.edu.

University of Georgia, School of Law and Graduate School, Graduate Program in Law, Athens, GA 30602. Offers LL M. *Students:* 15 full-time (9 women), 2 part-time; includes 2 minority (1 African American, 1 Hispanic American), 13 international. 55 applicants, 36% accepted, 15 enrolled. In 2006, 9 degrees awarded. *Degree requirements:* For master's, thesis. *Entrance requirements:* Additional exam requirements/recommendations for international students: Required—TOEFL (minimum score 600 paper-based; 250 computer-based). *Application deadline:* For fall admission, 4/15 for domestic and international students. Application fee: $50. *Expenses: Contact institution. Financial support:* Fellowships, research assistantships, teaching assistantships, Federal Work-Study, institutionally sponsored loans, and unspecified assistantships available. Financial award application deadline: 4/15. *Unit head:* Prof. Gabriel M. Wilner, Graduate Coordinator, 706-542-5238, Fax: 706-542-4145, E-mail: wilner@uga.edu. *Application contact:* Information Contact, E-mail: intlgrad@uga.edu.

University of Georgia, School of Law, Professional Program in Law, Athens, GA 30602. Offers JD. *Accreditation:* ABA. *Students:* 665 full-time (329 women), 2 part-time (both women); includes 130 minority (89 African Americans, 2 American Indian/Alaska Native, 25 Asian Americans or Pacific Islanders, 14 Hispanic Americans), 2 international. In 2006, 251 degrees awarded. *Entrance requirements:* LSAT. *Application contact:* Giles Kennedy, Director of Law Admissions, 706-542-7060.

University of Hawaii at Manoa, William S. Richardson School of Law, Honolulu, HI 96822. Offers JD, Graduate Certificate, JD/Certificate, JD/MA, JD/MBA, JD/MLI Sc, JD/MS, JD/MURP, JD/PhD. *Accreditation:* ABA. *Degree requirements:* For first-professional, 6 semesters of full-time residency. *Entrance requirements:* LSAT. Additional exam requirements/recommendations for international students: Required—TOEFL. *Expenses: Contact institution. Financial support:* Fellowships, research assistantships, career-related internships or fieldwork, Federal Work-Study, institutionally sponsored loans, and tuition waivers (full and partial) available. Financial award application deadline: 3/1; financial award applicants required to submit FAFSA. *Faculty research:* Law of the sea, Asian and Pacific comparative law, native Hawaiian rights, environmental law. *Application contact:* Laurie A. Tochiki, Assistant Dean, 808-956-7966, Fax: 808-956-3813, E-mail: lawadm@hawaii.edu.

University of Houston, Law Center, Houston, TX 77204-6060. Offers JD, LL M, JD/MA, JD/MBA, JD/MPH, JD/PhD. *Accreditation:* ABA. Part-time and evening/weekend programs available. *Faculty:* 40 full-time (8 women), 51 part-time/adjunct (14 women). *Students:* 849 full-time (371 women), 247 part-time (107 women); includes 267 minority (45 African Americans, 11 American Indian/Alaska Native, 115 Asian Americans or Pacific Islanders, 96 Hispanic Americans), 26 international. Average age 28. 991 applicants, 98% accepted, 313 enrolled. In 2006, 312 JDs, 49 master's awarded. *Degree requirements:* For JD, research paper; for master's, thesis. *Entrance requirements:* For JD, LSAT; for master's, LSAT, JD. Additional exam requirements/recommendations for international students: Required—TOEFL. *Application deadline:* For fall admission, 2/15 priority date for domestic students. Applications are processed on a rolling basis. Application fee: $50 ($75 for international students). Electronic applications accepted. *Expenses: Contact institution. Financial support:* In 2006–07, 691 students received support; fellowships with full tuition reimbursements available, research assistantships with full tuition reimbursements available, teaching assistantships with full tuition reimbursements available, career-related internships or fieldwork, Federal Work-Study, institutionally sponsored loans, scholarships/grants, health care benefits, and unspecified assistantships available. Support available to part-time students. Financial award application deadline: 3/10; financial award applicants required to submit FAFSA. *Faculty research:* Health law, international, tax, environmental/energy, information law/intellectual property. Total annual research expenditures: $77,127. *Unit head:* Raymond Nimmer, Interim Dean, 713-743-2100, Fax: 713-743-2122, E-mail: rnimmer@uh.edu. *Application contact:* Sondra B. Tennessee, Assistant Dean for Admissions, 713-743-2181.

University of Idaho, College of Law, Moscow, ID 83844-2321. Offers JD. *Accreditation:* ABA. *Students:* 313 (130 women). Average age 29. In 2006, 84 degrees awarded. *Entrance requirements:* LSAT. *Application deadline:* For fall admission, 2/1 for domestic students. Application fee: $55 ($60 for international students). *Expenses:* Tuition, nonresident: full-time $9,600; part-time $140 per credit. Required fees: $4,740; $227 per credit. *Financial support:* Career-related internships or fieldwork, Federal Work-Study, and institutionally sponsored loans available. Financial award application deadline: 2/15. *Unit head:* Donald L. Burnett, Dean, 208-885-4977.

University of Illinois at Urbana–Champaign, College of Law, Champaign, IL 61820. Offers JD, JD/DVM, JD/MCS, JD/MHRIR, LL M, MCL, JSD, JD/MBA, JD/MUP, MD/JD. *Accreditation:* ABA. *Faculty:* 36 full-time (9 women), 22 part-time/adjunct (11 women). *Students:* 665 full-time (254 women), 6 part-time (1 woman); includes 188 minority (36 African Americans, 3 American Indian/Alaska Native, 100 Asian Americans or Pacific Islanders, 49 Hispanic Americans), 56 international. 958 applicants, 42% accepted, 259 enrolled. In 2006, 214 JDs, 36 master's, 1 doctorate awarded. *Degree requirements:* For master's, thesis. *Entrance requirements:* LSAT, minimum GPA of 2.5. *Application deadline:* Applications are processed on a rolling basis. Application fee: $50 ($60 for international students). Electronic applications accepted. *Expenses: Contact institution. Financial support:* In 2006–07, 1 fellowship, 3 research assistantships, 24 teaching assistantships were awarded; tuition waivers (full and partial) also available. *Unit head:* Heidi M. Hurd, Dean, 217-333-9857, Fax: 217-244-1478, E-mail: hhurd@law.uiuc.edu. *Application contact:* Patricia Camp, Admissions Coordinator, 217-244-6415, Fax: 217-244-1478, E-mail: pcamp@law.uiuc.edu.

The University of Iowa, College of Law, Iowa City, IA 52242. Offers JD, LL M, JD/MA, JD/MBA, JD/MD, JD/MHA, JD/MPH, JD/MS, JD/PhD. *Accreditation:* ABA. *Faculty:* 43 full-time (14 women), 16 part-time/adjunct (6 women). *Students:* 655 full-time (311 women); includes 111 minority (28 African Americans, 6 American Indian/Alaska Native, 45 Asian Americans or Pacific Islanders, 32 Hispanic Americans), 8 international. 1,809 applicants, 33% accepted, 210 enrolled. In 2006, 261 JDs, 8 master's awarded. *Entrance requirements:* LSAT. Additional exam requirements/recommendations for international students: Required—TOEFL or IELTS. *Application deadline:* For fall admission, 3/1 for domestic and international students. Applications are processed on a rolling basis. Application fee: $60 ($85 for international students). Electronic applications accepted. *Expenses: Contact institution. Financial support:* In 2006–07, 594 students received support, including 25 fellowships with partial tuition reimbursements available, 236 research assistantships with partial tuition reimbursements available (averaging $1,803 per year); career-related internships or fieldwork, Federal Work-Study, institutionally sponsored loans, scholarships/grants, health care benefits, and unspecified assistantships also available. Financial award application deadline: 1/1; financial award applicants required to submit FAFSA. *Faculty research:* International and comparative law, health law, business law, intellectual property law, antitrust law. Total annual research expenditures: $2 million. *Unit head:* Carolyn Jones, Dean, 319-335-9034, E-mail: carolyn-jones@uiowa.edu. *Application contact:* Collins Byrd, Associate Dean of Admissions, 319-335-9095, Fax: 319-335-9646, E-mail: law-admissions@uiowa.edu.

University of Kansas, School of Law, Lawrence, KS 66045. Offers JD, JD/MA, JD/MBA, JD/MHSA, JD/MPA, JD/MSW, JD/MUP. *Accreditation:* ABA. *Faculty:* 39 full-time (16 women), 20 part-time/adjunct (5 women). *Students:* 482 full-time (190 women); includes 73 minority (9 African Americans, 13 American Indian/Alaska Native, 27 Asian Americans or Pacific Islanders, 24 Hispanic Americans), 18 international. Average age 26. 1,121 applicants, 31% accepted, 160 enrolled. In 2006, 173 degrees awarded. *Entrance requirements:* LSAT, letter of recommendation, personal statement. Additional exam requirements/recommendations for international students: Required—TOEFL. *Application deadline:* For fall admission, 3/15 for domestic students. Applications are processed on a rolling basis. Application fee: $50. Electronic applications accepted. *Expenses: Contact institution.* Tuition and fees vary according to course load, campus/location, program and reciprocity agreements. *Financial support:* In 2006–07, 350 students received support, including 38 research assistantships (averaging $1,263 per year), 11 teaching assistantships (averaging $1,700 per year); career-related internships or fieldwork, Federal Work-Study, institutionally sponsored loans, and scholarships/grants also available. Financial award application deadline: 3/1; financial award applicants required to submit FAFSA. *Faculty research:* International law, business law, criminal law, environmental law, elder law, law and public policy. *Unit head:* Gail B Agrawal, Dean, 785-864-4550, Fax: 785-864-5054. *Application contact:* Jacqlene Nance, Director of Admissions, 866-220-3654, E-mail: admitlaw@ku.edu.

University of Kentucky, College of Law, Lexington, KY 40506-0048. Offers JD, JD/MA, JD/MBA, JD/MPA. *Accreditation:* ABA. *Entrance requirements:* LSAT, LSDAS. Additional exam requirements/recommendations for international students: Required—TOEFL. Electronic applications accepted. Expenses: Contact institution. *Faculty research:* ADR, white collar crime, international trade law, corporate mergers, taxation of Internet transactions.

University of La Verne, College of Law, La Verne, CA 91750-4443. Offers JD. Also available at San Fernando Valley Campus. Part-time and evening/weekend programs available. *Faculty:* 18 full-time (7 women), 14 part-time/adjunct (2 women). *Students:* 174 full-time (68 women), 87 part-time (45 women); includes 80 minority (14 African Americans, 1 American Indian/Alaska Native, 30 Asian Americans or Pacific Islanders, 35 Hispanic Americans), 5 international. Average age 27. 641 applicants, 42% accepted, 89 enrolled. In 2006, 67 degrees awarded. *Median time to degree:* 3 years full-time, 4 years part-time. *Entrance requirements:* LSAT. Additional exam requirements/recommendations for international students: Required—TOEFL (minimum score 550 paper-based; 213 computer-based). *Application deadline:* For fall admission, 7/1 priority date for domestic students; for spring admission, 11/1 priority date for domestic students. Applications are processed on a rolling basis. Application fee: $60. Electronic applications accepted. *Expenses: Contact institution. Financial support:* Federal Work-Study and scholarships/grants available. Support available to part-time students. Financial award application deadline: 3/2; financial award applicants required to submit FAFSA. *Unit head:* Donald J. Dunn, Dean, 909-460-2000, Fax: 909-460-2081, E-mail: lawadm@ulv.edu. *Application contact:* Alexis E. Thompson, Assistant Dean of Admissions, 909-460-2001, Fax: 909-460-2082, E-mail: lawadm@ulv.edu.

University of Louisville, Louis D. Brandeis School of Law, Louisville, KY 40292. Offers JD, JD/M Div, JD/MA, JD/MBA, JD/MSW, JD/MUP. *Accreditation:* ABA. Part-time and evening/weekend programs available. *Faculty:* 29 full-time (11 women), 6 part-time/adjunct (1 woman). *Students:* 319 full-time (134 women), 98 part-time (47 women); includes 17 minority (10 African Americans, 2 American Indian/Alaska Native, 1 Asian American or Pacific Islander, 4 Hispanic Americans), 1 international. Average age 24. 1,244 applicants, 32% accepted, 142 enrolled. In 2006, 104 degrees awarded. *Degree requirements:* For first-professional, 30 work hours of pro-bono service. *Entrance requirements:* LSAT. *Application deadline:* For fall admission, 3/1 priority date for domestic students, 3/1 for international students. Applications are processed on a rolling basis. Application fee: $50. Electronic applications accepted. *Financial support:* Fellowships, research assistantships, teaching assistantships, career-related internships or fieldwork, Federal Work-Study, scholarships/grants, and tuition waivers (partial) available. Support available to part-time students. Financial award application deadline: 6/1; financial award applicants required to submit FAFSA. *Unit head:* James Chen, Dean, 502-852-6879, E-mail: jim.chen@louisville.edu. *Application contact:* Jack D Cox, Assistant Dean for Admission and Financial Aid, 502-852-6391, Fax: 502-852-8971, E-mail: lawadmissions@louisville.edu.

University of Manitoba, Faculty of Law, Winnipeg, MB R3T 2N2, Canada. Offers interdisciplinary studies (MA); law (LL M). *Degree requirements:* For master's, thesis, registration. *Entrance requirements:* For master's, thesis proposal. Additional exam requirements/recommendations for international students: Required—TOEFL (minimum score 600 paper-based; 240 computer-based). Electronic applications accepted. *Faculty research:* Constitutional law, legal history, human rights laws, international trade law, medicine and law.

University of Maryland, Baltimore, School of Law, Baltimore, MD 21201. Offers JD, JD/MA, JD/MBA, JD/MCP, JD/MPH, JD/MPM, JD/MPP, JD/MS, JD/MSN, JD/MSW, JD/PhD, JD/Pharm D. *Accreditation:* ABA. Part-time and evening/weekend programs available. *Faculty:* 57 full-time (29 women), 64 part-time/adjunct (19 women). *Students:* 673 full-time (402 women), 153 part-time (79 women); includes 262 minority (123 African Americans, 4 American Indian/Alaska Native, 81 Asian Americans or Pacific Islanders, 54 Hispanic Americans), 10 international. Average age 26. 4,331 applicants, 16% accepted, 263 enrolled. In 2006, 253 degrees awarded. *Degree requirements:* For first-professional, writing certification. *Entrance requirements:* LSAT, LSDAS. Additional exam requirements/recommendations for international students: Recommended—TOEFL (minimum score 600 paper-based; 250 computer-based). *Application deadline:* For fall admission, 3/1 priority date for domestic and international students. Applications are processed on a rolling basis. Application fee: $65. Electronic applications accepted. *Expenses: Contact institution. Financial support:* In 2006–07, 639 students received support. Federal Work-Study, institutionally sponsored loans, and scholarships/grants available. Support available to part-time students. Financial award application deadline: 3/1; financial award applicants required to submit FAFSA. *Faculty research:* Environmental regulation, health care policy, intellectual property, civil rights and race history and policy, international and comparative law. Total annual research expenditures: $1.9 million. *Unit head:* Karen H. Rothenberg, Dean and Marjorie Cook Professor of Law, 410-706-7214, Fax: 410-706-4045. *Application contact:* Connie Beals, Executive Director of Admissions, 410-706-3492, Fax: 410-706-1793, E-mail: admissions@law.umaryland.edu.

University of Maryland, College Park, Graduate Studies, Robert H. Smith School of Business, Program in Business Management/Law, College Park, MD 20742. Offers JD/MBA. *Accreditation:* AACSB. *Students:* 5 full-time (0 women); includes 3 minority (1 African American, 1 Asian American or Pacific Islander, 1 Hispanic American). 11 applicants, 55% accepted, 4 enrolled. *Entrance requirements:* Additional exam requirements/recommendations for international students: Required—TOEFL. *Application deadline:* For fall admission, 2/1 for domestic and international students. Applications are processed on a rolling basis. Application fee: $60. *Financial support:* In 2006–07, 1 fellowship (averaging $23,814 per year), 1 teaching assistantship (averaging $13,224 per year) were awarded. Financial award applicants required to submit FAFSA. *Application contact:* Dean of Graduate School, 301-405-0358, Fax: 301-314-9305.

University of Maryland, College Park, Graduate Studies, School of Public Policy, Joint Program in Public Policy/Law, College Park, MD 20742. Offers JD/MPM. *Students:* 3 full-time (0 women), 2 part-time; includes 1 minority (Hispanic American) 12 applicants, 83% accepted, 2 enrolled. *Application deadline:* For fall admission, 12/15 for domestic students, 2/1 for international students; for spring admission, 10/1 for domestic students, 6/1 for international students. Applications are processed on a rolling basis. Application fee: $60. Electronic applications accepted. *Financial support:* In 2006–07, 2 teaching assistantships (averaging $12,528 per year) were awarded; fellowships also available. Financial award applicants required to submit FAFSA. *Application contact:* Dean of Graduate School, 301-405-0358, Fax: 301-314-9305.

University of Memphis, Cecil C. Humphreys School of Law, Memphis, TN 38152-3140. Offers JD, JD/MBA. *Accreditation:* ABA. Part-time programs available. *Faculty:* 20 full-time (8 women), 24 part-time/adjunct (11 women). *Students:* 379 full-time (160 women), 29 part-time (20 women); includes 74 minority (63 African Americans, 2 American Indian/Alaska Native, 6 Asian Americans or Pacific Islanders, 3 Hispanic Americans). Average age 25. 1,113 applicants, 26% accepted, 144 enrolled. In 2006, 125 JDs awarded. *Entrance requirements:* LSAT, LSDAS, letters of recommendation, non-resident must submit 'Why Memphis" statement. Additional exam requirements/recommendations for international students: Required—TOEFL. *Application deadline:* For fall admission, 3/1 priority date for domestic and international students. Applications are processed on a rolling basis. Application fee: $25 ($40 for international students). Electronic applications accepted. *Expenses: Contact institution. Financial support:* In 2006–07, 326 students received support, including 22 research assistantships with full and partial tuition reimbursements available (averaging $3,136 per year), 2 teaching assistantships (averaging $3,000 per year); fellowships, career-related internships or fieldwork, scholarships/grants, tuition waivers (full), and unspecified assistantships also available. Financial award application deadline: 4/1; financial award applicants required to submit FAFSA. *Faculty research:* Constitutional and civil rights law, inheritance and family law, intellectual property, environmental law, employment law. Total annual research expenditures: $69,000. *Unit head:* James R. Smoot, Dean, 901-678-2421, Fax: 901-678-5210, E-mail: jrsmoot@memphis.edu. *Application contact:* Dr. Sue Ann McClellan, Assistant Dean for Law Admissions, 901-678-5403, Fax: 901-678-5210, E-mail: smcclell@memphis.edu.

University of Miami, Graduate School, School of Law, Coral Gables, FL 33124-8087. Offers comparative law (LL M); estate planning (LL M); inter-American law (LL M); international law (LL M); law (JD); ocean and coastal law (LL M); real property development (LL M); taxation (LL M); JD/LL M; JD/MA; JD/MBA; JD/MPH. *Accreditation:* ABA. *Faculty:* 55 full-time (17 women), 42 part-time/adjunct (15 women). *Students:* 1,163 full-time (518 women), 45 part-time (8 women); includes 280 minority (84 African Americans, 3 American Indian/Alaska Native, 51 Asian Americans or Pacific Islanders, 142 Hispanic Americans), 51 international. Average age 24. 4,923 applicants, 48% accepted, 420 enrolled. In 2006, 331 JDs awarded. *Entrance requirements:* LSAT, 2 letters of recommendation, personal statement. Additional exam requirements/recommendations for international students: Required—TOEFL (minimum score 600 paper-based; 250 computer-based; 75 iBT). *Application deadline:* For fall admission, 2/5 priority date for domestic and international students. Applications are processed on a rolling basis. Application fee: $60. Electronic applications accepted. *Expenses: Contact institution. Financial support:* In 2006–07, 991 students received support, including 77 fellowships (averaging $2,200 per year), 80 research assistantships (averaging $1,800 per year); career-related internships or fieldwork, Federal Work-Study, institutionally sponsored loans, scholarships/grants, and unspecified assistantships also available. Financial award application deadline: 3/1; financial award applicants required to submit FAFSA. *Faculty research:* National security law, international finance, Internet law/law of electronic commerce, law of the seas, art law/cultural heritage law. Total annual research expenditures: $21,000. *Unit head:* Michael Goodnight, Assistant Dean of Admissions, 305-284-2527, Fax: 305-284-3084, E-mail: mgoodnig@law.miami.edu. *Application contact:* Therese Lambert, Director of Student Recruiting, 305-284-6746, Fax: 305-284-3084, E-mail: tlambert@law.miami.edu.

University of Michigan, Law School, Ann Arbor, MI 48109-1215. Offers comparative law (MCL); law (JD, LL M, SJD); JD/AM; JD/MA; JD/MBA; JD/MHSA; JD/MPH; JD/MPP; JD/MS; JD/MSI; JD/MSW; JD/MUP; JD/PhD. *Accreditation:* ABA. *Entrance requirements:* For JD, master's, and doctorate, LSAT. Expenses: Contact institution.

University of Minnesota, Twin Cities Campus, Law School, Minneapolis, MN 55455. Offers JD, LL M, JD/MA, JD/MBA, JD/MBT, JD/MD, JD/MP, JD/MPA, JD/MPH, JD/MPP, JD/MS, JD/MURP, JD/PhD. *Accreditation:* ABA. *Entrance requirements:* LSAT. Additional exam requirements/recommendations for international students: Required—TOEFL. Electronic applications accepted. Expenses: Contact institution. Full-time tuition and fees vary according to class

Law

University of Minnesota, Twin Cities Campus (continued)
time, course load, program, reciprocity agreements and student level. *Faculty research:* International law, constitutional law, corporate law, criminal law, public law.

University of Mississippi, School of Law, Oxford, University, MS 38677. Offers JD, JD/MBA. *Accreditation:* ABA. *Faculty:* 26 full-time (9 women), 10 part-time/adjunct (3 women). *Students:* 505 full-time (228 women), 1 (woman) part-time; includes 62 minority (50 African Americans, 2 American Indian/Alaska Native, 7 Asian Americans or Pacific Islanders, 3 Hispanic Americans), 2 international. Average age 24. 1,069 applicants, 42% accepted, 160 enrolled. In 2006, 208 degrees awarded. *Entrance requirements:* LSAT, LSDAS. Additional exam requirements/recommendations for international students: Required—TOEFL. *Application deadline:* For fall admission, 4/1 for domestic students. Application fee: $40. *Expenses: Contact institution. Financial support:* Fellowships, research assistantships, teaching assistantships, career-related internships or fieldwork, Federal Work-Study, institutionally sponsored loans, and scholarships/grants available. Support available to part-time students. Financial award application deadline: 3/1; financial award applicants required to submit FAFSA. *Unit head:* Dr. Samuel Davis, Dean, 662-915-7361, Fax: 662-915-5313, E-mail: smdavis@olemiss.edu. *Application contact:* Barbara Vinson, Coordinator of Admissions, 662-915-7361, E-mail: bvinson@olemiss.edu.

University of Missouri–Columbia, School of Law, Columbia, MO 65211. Offers JD, LL M, JD/MA, JD/MBA, JD/MPA. *Accreditation:* ABA. *Faculty:* 32 full-time (10 women). *Students:* 455 full-time (176 women), 12 part-time (6 women); includes 54 minority (23 African Americans, 5 American Indian/Alaska Native, 16 Asian Americans or Pacific Islanders, 10 Hispanic Americans), 11 international. Average age 25. In 2006, 143 JDs, 11 master's awarded. *Entrance requirements:* LSAT. Additional exam requirements/recommendations for international students: Required—TOEFL. *Application deadline:* For fall admission, 3/1 priority date for domestic students. Applications are processed on a rolling basis. *Expenses: Contact institution. Financial support:* Fellowships, Federal Work-Study and institutionally sponsored loans available. Financial award application deadline: 3/1; financial award applicants required to submit FAFSA. *Unit head:* Dr. R. Lawrence Dessem, Dean, 573-882-3246, E-mail: dessemrl@law.missouri.edu.

University of Missouri–Kansas City, School of Law, Kansas City, MO 64110-2499. Offers law (JD, LL M), including general (LL M), taxation (LL M); JD/LL M; JD/MBA; LL M/MPA. *Accreditation:* ABA. Part-time programs available. *Faculty:* 34 full-time (13 women). *Students:* 496 full-time (214 women), 41 part-time (20 women); includes 45 minority (15 African Americans, 3 American Indian/Alaska Native, 17 Asian Americans or Pacific Islanders, 10 Hispanic Americans), 6 international. Average age 27. 1,327 applicants, 40% accepted, 216 enrolled. In 2006, 156 JDs, 22 master's awarded. *Degree requirements:* For master's, thesis (general). *Entrance requirements:* For JD, LSAT; for master's, LSAT, minimum GPA of 3.0 (general), 2.7 (taxation). Additional exam requirements/recommendations for international students: Required—TOEFL. *Application deadline:* For fall admission, 4/1 priority date for domestic students. Applications are processed on a rolling basis. Application fee: $50. Electronic applications accepted. *Expenses: Contact institution. Financial support:* In 2006–07, 162 students received support, including 1 research assistantship (averaging $54,667 per year), 38 teaching assistantships with partial tuition reimbursements available (averaging $2,587 per year); fellowships with partial tuition reimbursements available, career-related internships or fieldwork, Federal Work-Study, institutionally sponsored loans, scholarships/grants, and tuition waivers (full and partial) also available. Support available to part-time students. *Faculty research:* Family and children's issues, litigation, estate planning, urban law, business, tax entrepreneurial law. *Unit head:* Ellen Y. Suni, Dean, 816-235-1677, Fax: 816-235-5276, E-mail: sunie@umkc.edu. *Application contact:* Debbie Brooks, Director of Admissions, 816-325-1644, Fax: 816-235-5276, E-mail: brooksdv@umkc.edu.

The University of Montana, School of Law, Missoula, MT 59812. Offers JD, JD/MBA, JD/MPA. *Accreditation:* ABA. *Degree requirements:* For first-professional, oral presentation, paper. *Entrance requirements:* LSAT. Expenses: Contact institution. *Faculty research:* Legal education curriculum, business and probate law reform, rules of civil procedure reform, tribal courts, women's issues.

University of Nebraska–Lincoln, College of Law, Lincoln, NE 68583-0902. Offers JD, MLS, JD/MA, JD/MBA, JD/MCRP, JD/MPA, JD/PhD. *Accreditation:* ABA. *Entrance requirements:* LSAT. Electronic applications accepted. Expenses: Contact institution. *Faculty research:* Law and medicine, constitutional law, criminal procedure, international trade.

University of Nevada, Las Vegas, William S. Boyd School of Law, Las Vegas, NV 89154-1003. Offers JD, JD/MBA, JD/MSW. *Accreditation:* ABA. Part-time and evening/weekend programs available. *Faculty:* 42 full-time (21 women), 23 part-time/adjunct (5 women). *Students:* 338 full-time (168 women), 133 part-time (60 women); includes 127 minority (22 African Americans, 6 American Indian/Alaska Native, 57 Asian Americans or Pacific Islanders, 42 Hispanic Americans). 2,206 applicants, 16% accepted, 156 enrolled. In 2006, 124 degrees awarded. *Entrance requirements:* LSAT. *Application deadline:* For fall admission, 3/15 priority date for domestic and international students. Applications are processed on a rolling basis. Application fee: $50. Electronic applications accepted. *Expenses: Contact institution. Financial support:* In 2006–07, 343 students received support. Career-related internships or fieldwork and scholarships/grants available. Support available to part-time students. Financial award application deadline: 2/1; financial award applicants required to submit FAFSA. *Faculty research:* Civil procedure, constitutional law, federal courts, professional responsibility, juvenile justice. Total annual research expenditures: $250,000. *Unit head:* Richard J. Morgan, Dean, 702-895-3671, Fax: 702-895-1095, E-mail: morgan@ccmail.nevada.edu. *Application contact:* Gerald Sequiera, Director of Admissions, E-mail: gerald.sequeira@unlv.edu.

University of New Brunswick Fredericton, Faculty of Law, Fredericton, NB E3B 5A3, Canada. Offers LL B, LL B/MBA. *Faculty:* 20 full-time (6 women), 12 part-time/adjunct (6 women). *Students:* 245 full-time (126 women). Average age 24. 831 applicants, 24% accepted, 89 enrolled. In 2006, 64 degrees awarded. *Entrance requirements:* LSAT. *Application deadline:* For fall admission, 3/1 for domestic students. Applications are processed on a rolling basis. Application fee: $50. Electronic applications accepted. *Financial support:* Scholarships/grants available. *Faculty research:* Property studies, legal history, family violence, law and technology, international law. *Unit head:* Philip Bryden, Dean, 506-453-4627, Fax: 506-453-4604, E-mail: bryden@unb.ca. *Application contact:* Robin Dickson, Director of Admissions, 506-453-4693, Fax: 506-458-7722, E-mail: rjd@unb.ca.

University of New Mexico, School of Law, Albuquerque, NM 87131-0001. Offers JD, JD/MA, JD/MBA, JD/MPA, JD/MS, JD/PhD. *Accreditation:* ABA. *Faculty:* 34 full-time (18 women), 27 part-time/adjunct (12 women). *Students:* 343 full-time; includes 155 minority (12 African Americans, 40 American Indian/Alaska Native, 9 Asian Americans or Pacific Islanders, 94 Hispanic Americans). 1,405 applicants, 18% accepted, 115 enrolled. In 2006, 119 degrees awarded. *Degree requirements:* For first-professional, advanced writing piece, clinic. *Entrance requirements:* LSAT, Bachelor's degree. Additional exam requirements/recommendations for international students: Required—TOEFL (minimum score 600 paper-based; 250 computer-based; 100 iBT). *Application deadline:* For fall admission, 2/15 priority date for domestic students, 2/15 for international students. Applications are processed on a rolling basis. Application fee: $50. Electronic applications accepted. *Expenses: Contact institution. Financial support:* Career-related internships or fieldwork, Federal Work-Study, and scholarships/grants available. Financial award application deadline: 3/1; financial award applicants required to submit FAFSA. *Unit head:* Suellyn Scarnecchia, Dean, 505-277-4700, Fax: 505-277-1597, E-mail: scarnecchia@law.unm.edu. *Application contact:* Susan L. Mitchell, Assistant Dean for Admissions and Financial Aid, 505-277-0959, Fax: 505-277-9958, E-mail: mitchell@law.unm.edu.

The University of North Carolina at Chapel Hill, School of Law, Chapel Hill, NC 27599-3380. Offers JD, JD/MBA, JD/MPA, JD/MPH, JD/MRP, JD/MSW, JD/MAPPS. *Accreditation:* ABA. *Entrance requirements:* LSAT. Additional exam requirements/recommendations for international students: Required—TOEFL (minimum score 650 paper-based). Electronic applications accepted. Expenses: Contact institution. *Faculty research:* Death penalty, feminist legal theory, urban reform risk-based environmental policy, state and U.S. constitutional law, health law policy.

University of North Dakota, School of Law, Grand Forks, ND 58202. Offers JD. *Accreditation:* ABA. *Faculty:* 15 full-time (8 women). *Students:* 238 full-time (110 women); includes 20 minority (1 African American, 5 American Indian/Alaska Native, 9 Asian Americans or Pacific Islanders, 5 Hispanic Americans), 7 international. Average age 27. 650 applicants, 13% accepted, 76 enrolled. In 2006, 60 degrees awarded. *Entrance requirements:* LSAT. *Application deadline:* For fall admission, 4/1 priority date for domestic students. Applications are processed on a rolling basis. Application fee: $35. *Expenses: Contact institution.* Tuition and fees vary according to reciprocity agreements. *Financial support:* In 2006–07, 4 teaching assistantships with full tuition reimbursements were awarded; career-related internships or fieldwork, Federal Work-Study, scholarships/grants, and tuition waivers (full and partial) also available. Financial award application deadline: 4/15; financial award applicants required to submit FAFSA. Total annual research expenditures: $323,012. *Unit head:* Paul LeBel, Dean, 701-777-2104. *Application contact:* Ben Hoffman, Admissions and Records Officer, 701-777-2260, Fax: 701-777-2217, E-mail: benjam.n.hoffman@thor.law.und.nodak.edu.

University of Notre Dame, Law School, Notre Dame, IN 46556-0780. Offers human rights (LL M, JSD); international and comparative law (LL M); law (JD). *Accreditation:* ABA. *Faculty:* 47 full-time (14 women), 41 part-time/adjunct (18 women). *Students:* 570 full-time (210 women), 1 (woman) part-time; includes 128 minority (28 African Americans, 9 American Indian/Alaska Native, 42 Asian Americans or Pacific Islanders, 49 Hispanic Americans), 6 international. 3,502 applicants, 24% accepted, 199 enrolled. In 2006, 173 JDs, 20 master's, 2 doctorates awarded. *Degree requirements:* For master's and doctorate, thesis/dissertation, 1 year residency. *Entrance requirements:* For JD, LSAT; for doctorate, LL M. Additional exam requirements/recommendations for international students: Required—TOEFL. *Application deadline:* For fall admission, 11/1 priority date for domestic students; for winter admission, 3/1 for domestic students. Applications are processed on a rolling basis. Application fee: $55. Electronic applications accepted. *Expenses: Contact institution. Financial support:* In 2006–07, 376 fellowships (averaging $13,446 per year), 29 research assistantships (averaging $3,000 per year), 7 teaching assistantships were awarded; career-related internships or fieldwork, Federal Work-Study, institutionally sponsored loans, scholarships/grants, and university dormitory rector assistants also available. Financial award application deadline: 3/1; financial award applicants required to submit FAFSA. *Unit head:* Patricia A. O'Hara, Dean, 574-631-6789, Fax: 574-631-8400, E-mail: o'hara.3@nd.edu. *Application contact:* Marie E. Bensman, Director of Admissions and Financial Aid, 574-631-6626, Fax: 574-631-5474, E-mail: lawadmit@nd.edu.

University of Oklahoma, College of Law, Norman, OK 73019. Offers JD, JD/MBA, JD/MPH, JD/MSEM, JD/MSHA, JD/MSOH. *Accreditation:* ABA. *Faculty:* 37 full-time (15 women), 17 part-time/adjunct (6 women). *Students:* 501 full-time (224 women); includes 122 minority (28 African Americans, 52 American Indian/Alaska Native, 22 Asian Americans or Pacific Islanders, 20 Hispanic Americans). Average age 23. 1,055 applicants, 32% accepted, 164 enrolled. In 2006, 169 degrees awarded. *Entrance requirements:* LSAT. *Application deadline:* For fall admission, 3/15 for domestic students. Applications are processed on a rolling basis. Application fee: $50. Electronic applications accepted. *Expenses: Contact institution.* Tuition and fees vary according to course load and program. *Financial support:* In 2006–07, 414 students received support. Career-related internships or fieldwork, Federal Work-Study, institutionally sponsored loans, scholarships/grants, and tuition waivers (full and partial) available. Support available to part-time students. Financial award application deadline: 3/1; financial award applicants required to submit FAFSA. Total annual research expenditures: $94,969. *Unit head:* Dr. Andrew M. Coats, Dean, 405-325-4699, Fax: 405-325-7712, E-mail: acoats@ou.edu. *Application contact:* Kathie Madden, Admissions Coordinator, 405-325-4728, Fax: 405-325-0502, E-mail: kmadden@ou.edu.

University of Oregon, School of Law, Eugene, OR 97403. Offers JD, MA, MS, JD/MBA, JD/MS. *Accreditation:* ABA. *Faculty:* 27 full-time (10 women), 4 part-time/adjunct (1 woman). *Students:* 558 full-time (243 women), 36 part-time (15 women); includes 99 minority (19 African Americans, 10 American Indian/Alaska Native, 40 Asian Americans or Pacific Islanders, 30 Hispanic Americans), 8 international. 1,174 applicants, 53% accepted. In 2006, 149 degrees awarded. *Entrance requirements:* LSAT. *Application deadline:* For fall admission, 2/15 priority date for domestic students. Application fee: $50. *Expenses: Contact institution. Financial support:* In 2006–07, 27 teaching assistantships were awarded; career-related internships or fieldwork, Federal Work-Study, institutionally sponsored loans, and tuition waivers (partial) also available. Financial award application deadline: 2/1; financial award applicants required to submit FAFSA. *Unit head:* Margaret Paris, Interim Dean, 541-346-3852, Fax: 541-346-1564. *Application contact:* Jee Muntz, Information Contact, Office of Admissions, 541-346-1810, Fax: 541-346-1564.

University of Ottawa, Faculty of Graduate and Postdoctoral Studies, Faculty of Law, Ottawa, ON K1N 6N5, Canada. Offers LL M, LL D. Part-time and evening/weekend programs available. *Degree requirements:* For master's, thesis or alternative; for doctorate, thesis/dissertation. *Entrance requirements:* For master's, minimum B average, LL B; for doctorate, LL M, minimum B+ average. Electronic applications accepted. *Faculty research:* International law, human rights law, family law.

University of Pennsylvania, Law School, Philadelphia, PA 19104. Offers JD, LL CM, LL M, SJD, JD/DESS, JD/M Bioethics, JD/MA, JD/MBA, JD/MCP, JD/MD, JD/MES, JD/MGA, JD/MPH, JD/MS, JD/MS Ed, JD/MSW, JD/PhD. *Accreditation:* ABA. *Faculty:* 53 full-time (13 women), 41 part-time/adjunct (11 women). *Students:* 762 full-time (355 women); includes 231 minority (61 African Americans, 5 American Indian/Alaska Native, 110 Asian Americans or Pacific Islanders, 55 Hispanic Americans), 35 international. Average age 24. 5,649 applicants, 16% accepted, 249 enrolled. In 2006, 274 JDs, 93 master's, 2 doctorates awarded. *Degree requirements:* For master's, thesis optional; for doctorate, thesis/dissertation. *Entrance requirements:* For JD, LSAT; for doctorate, LL M. Additional exam requirements/recommendations for international students: Required—TOEFL. *Application deadline:* For fall admission, 2/15 for domestic students. Applications are processed on a rolling basis. Application fee: $75. Electronic applications accepted. *Expenses: Contact institution. Financial support:* In 2006–07, 644 students received support, including 2 research assistantships with tuition reimbursements available (averaging $16,500 per year), 21 teaching assistantships (averaging $1,750 per year); fellowships, career-related internships or fieldwork, Federal Work-Study, institutionally sponsored loans, and scholarships/grants also available. Financial award application deadline: 3/1; financial award applicants required to submit FAFSA. *Faculty research:* Law and business, public law and the Constitution, international and comparative law, law and health sciences, intellectual property. Total annual research expenditures: $188,827. *Unit head:* Michael A. Fitts, Dean, 215-898-7400, Fax: 215-573-2025. *Application contact:* Renee Post, Associate Dean of Admissions and Financial Aid, 215-898-7400, Fax: 215-898-9606, E-mail: admissions@law.upenn.edu.

University of Pittsburgh, School of Law, John P. Gismondi Civil Litigation Certificate Program, Pittsburgh, PA 15260. Offers Certificate. *Faculty:* 4 full-time (3 women), 18 part-time/adjunct (3 women). *Students:* 46 full-time (14 women). *Unit head:* Marvin Fein, Associate Professor of Legal Writing and Director, 412-648-9815, Fax: 412-648-1352, E-mail: fein@law.pitt.edu.

University of Pittsburgh, School of Law, Professional Programs in Law, Pittsburgh, PA 15260. Offers JD, JD/MA, JD/MBA, JD/MID, JD/MPA, JD/MPH, JD/MPIA, JD/MS. *Accreditation:* ABA. *Faculty:* 46 full-time (16 women), 85 part-time/adjunct (23 women). *Students:* 731 full-time (306 women); includes 95 minority (43 African Americans, 1 American Indian/Alaska Native, 40 Asian Americans or Pacific Islanders, 11 Hispanic Americans). 2,369 applicants, 31% accepted, 243 enrolled. In 2006, 212 degrees awarded. *Entrance requirements:* LSAT. Additional exam requirements/recommendations for international students: Required—TOEFL.

Application deadline: For fall admission, 3/1 for domestic students. Applications are processed on a rolling basis. Application fee: $55. Electronic applications accepted. *Expenses: Contact institution. Financial support:* In 2006–07, 387 students received support, including 36 research assistantships (averaging $5,440 per year), 13 teaching assistantships (averaging $1,200 per year); career-related internships or fieldwork, Federal Work-Study, scholarships/grants, and unspecified assistantships also available. Financial award application deadline: 3/1; financial award applicants required to submit FAFSA. *Faculty research:* Civil and criminal justice, constitutional law, health law, international law, law and society. Total annual research expenditures: $320,000. *Application contact:* Charmaine McCall, Assistant Dean of Admissions and Financial Aid, 412-648-1413, Fax: 412-648-1318, E-mail: mccall@law.pitt.edu.

University of Pittsburgh, School of Law, Program in Environmental Law, Science and Policy, Pittsburgh, PA 15260. Offers Certificate. *Faculty:* 46 full-time (16 women), 85 part-time/adjunct (23 women). *Students:* 17 full-time (7 women). *Unit head:* Jennifer L. Poller, Director, Environmental Law Science and Policy Certificate Program, 412-648-1408, Fax: 412-624-4843, E-mail: poller@law.pitt.edu.

University of Pittsburgh, School of Law, Program in Intellectual Property and Technology Law, Pittsburgh, PA 15260. Offers Certificate. *Faculty:* 4 full-time (1 woman), 7 part-time/adjunct (1 woman). *Students:* 42 full-time (14 women). *Faculty research:* Patent, copyright, trademark, cyberspace, biotechnology. *Unit head:* Prof. Janice M Mueller, Professor and Director, 412-648-5300, Fax: 412-648-2648, E-mail: mueller@law.pitt.edu.

University of Pittsburgh, School of Law, Program in International and Comparative Law, Pittsburgh, PA 15260. Offers international and comparative law (LL M). Offered to international students only. *Faculty:* 22 full-time (7 women), 17 part-time/adjunct (4 women). *Students:* 14 full-time (7 women); includes 1 minority (African American), 11 international. Average age 25. 61 applicants, 82% accepted, 14 enrolled. In 2006, 13 degrees awarded. *Degree requirements:* For master's, seminar paper. *Entrance requirements:* For master's, law degree from foreign university. Additional exam requirements/recommendations for international students: Required—TOEFL (minimum score 600 paper-based; 250 computer-based; 100 iBT); Recommended—IELTS (minimum score 7). *Application deadline:* For fall admission, 3/30 priority date for international students. Applications are processed on a rolling basis. Application fee: $40. *Expenses: Contact institution. Financial support:* In 2006–07, 6 students received support, including 4 fellowships with partial tuition reimbursements available (averaging $10,000 per year); career-related internships or fieldwork and scholarships/grants also available. *Faculty research:* International business transactions, transnational litigation, international trade, international transactions. *Unit head:* Ronald A. Brand, Director CILE, 412-648-7023, Fax: 412-648-2648, E-mail: brand@law.pitt.edu. *Application contact:* Gina Clark, Program Administrator, 412-648-2023, Fax: 412-648-2648, E-mail: cile@law.pitt.edu.

University of Pittsburgh, School of Law, Program in International Law, Pittsburgh, PA 15260. Offers Certificate. *Faculty:* 48 full-time (19 women), 91 part-time/adjunct (24 women). *Students:* 98 full-time (53 women); includes 9 minority (4 African Americans, 3 Asian Americans or Pacific Islanders, 2 Hispanic Americans), 1 international. Average age 24. *Unit head:* Ronald A. Brand, Director CILE, 412-648-7023, Fax: 412-648-2648, E-mail: brand@law.pitt.edu. *Application contact:* Gina Clark, Program Administrator, 412-648-2023, Fax: 412-648-2648, E-mail: cile@law.pitt.edu.

University of Puerto Rico, Río Piedras, School of Law, San Juan, PR 00931-3349. Offers JD, LL M. *Accreditation:* ABA. Part-time and evening/weekend programs available. *Students:* 678 full-time (403 women), 41 part-time (27 women); includes 718 minority (all Hispanic Americans) Average age 22. In 2006, 170 degrees awarded. *Entrance requirements:* For JD, GMAT, GRE, LSAT, EXADEP, minimum GPA of 3.0; for master's, LSAT, minimum GPA of 3.0, letter of recommendation. Additional exam requirements/recommendations for international students: Required—TOEFL. *Application deadline:* For fall admission, 2/1 for domestic students. Application fee: $17. *Expenses:* Tuition, commonwealth resident: part-time $100 per credit. Tuition, nonresident: part-time $291 per credit. Required fees: $72 per semester. *Financial support:* Fellowships, research assistantships, teaching assistantships, career-related internships or fieldwork, Federal Work-Study, institutionally sponsored loans, and tuition waivers (partial) available. Financial award application deadline: 5/31. *Faculty research:* Civil code; Puerto Rico constitutional law; professional behavior, rules and regulations; international law; expert testimony. *Unit head:* Dr. Efrén Rivera-Ramos, Dean, 787-999-9527, Fax: 787-764-2765. *Application contact:* Information Contact, 787-764-2675 Ext. 3843, Fax: 787-764-2675.

University of Richmond, School of Law, Richmond, University of Richmond, VA 23173. Offers JD, JD/MA, JD/MBA, JD/MHA, JD/MPA, JD/MS, JD/MSW, JD/MURP. *Accreditation:* ABA. *Entrance requirements:* LSAT. Electronic applications accepted. Expenses: Contact institution.

University of St. Thomas, Graduate Studies, School of Law, Minneapolis, MN 55105-1096. Offers JD, JD/MA, JD/MBA, JD/MSW. *Accreditation:* ABA. *Faculty:* 29 full-time (12 women), 40 part-time/adjunct (15 women). *Students:* 443 full-time (214 women); includes 64 minority (19 African Americans, 4 American Indian/Alaska Native, 24 Asian Americans or Pacific Islanders, 17 Hispanic Americans). Average age 27. 1,135 applicants, 46% accepted, 155 enrolled. In 2006, 119 degrees awarded. *Median time to degree:* 3 years full-time. *Degree requirements:* For first-professional, mentor externship, public service. *Entrance requirements:* LSAT, 2 letters of recommendation. Additional exam requirements/recommendations for international students: Required—TOEFL (minimum score 550 paper-based; 213 computer-based), IELTS (minimum score 7), Michigan English Language Assessment Battery (score of 80). *Application deadline:* For fall admission, 7/1 priority date for domestic and international students. Applications are processed on a rolling basis. Application fee: $50. Electronic applications accepted. *Financial support:* In 2006–07, 317 students received support. Scholarships/grants available. Financial award application deadline: 7/1; financial award applicants required to submit FAFSA. *Faculty research:* Civil litigation with federal government; ethics of the profession; federal rules of appellate procedure; integration of faith and professional life; law and religion. *Unit head:* Thomas M. Mengler, Dean, 651-962-4880, Fax: 651-962-4881, E-mail: tmmengler@stthomas.edu. *Application contact:* Cari Haaland, Director of Admissions, 651-962-4895, Fax: 651-962-4876, E-mail: lawschool@stthomas.edu.

University of San Diego, School of Law, San Diego, CA 92110. Offers business and corporate law (LL M); comparative law (LL M); general studies (LL M); international law (LL M); law (JD); taxation (LL M, Diploma); JD/IMBA; JD/MA; JD/MBA. *Accreditation:* ABA. Part-time and evening/weekend programs available. *Faculty:* 53 full-time (20 women), 44 part-time/adjunct (9 women). *Students:* 796 full-time (363 women), 333 part-time (151 women); includes 324 minority (34 African Americans, 11 American Indian/Alaska Native, 165 Asian Americans or Pacific Islanders, 114 Hispanic Americans), 21 international. Average age 27. 4,818 applicants, 31% accepted, 342 enrolled. In 2006, 313 JDs, 59 master's awarded. *Entrance requirements:* For JD, LSAT; for master's, JD, LLB or equivalent from an ABA-accredited law school. Additional exam requirements/recommendations for international students: Required—TOEFL. *Application deadline:* For fall admission, 2/1 priority date for domestic students. Applications are processed on a rolling basis. Application fee: $50. Electronic applications accepted. *Expenses: Contact institution. Financial support:* In 2006–07, 60 research assistantships were awarded; career-related internships or fieldwork, Federal Work-Study, institutionally sponsored loans, and scholarships/grants also available. Support available to part-time students. Financial award application deadline: 3/1; financial award applicants required to submit FAFSA. *Unit head:* Kevin Cole, Dean, 619-260-2330, Fax: 619-260-2218. *Application contact:* Carl J. Eging, Director of Admissions and Financial Aid, 619-260-4528, Fax: 619-260-2218, E-mail: eging@sandiego.edu.

University of San Francisco, School of Law, San Francisco, CA 94117-1080. Offers law (JD, LL M), including intellectual property and technology law (LL M), international transactions and comparative law (LL M); JD/MBA. *Accreditation:* ABA. Part-time and evening/weekend programs available. *Faculty:* 16 full-time (6 women), 78 part-time/adjunct (32 women). *Students:* 567 full-time (292 women), 141 part-time (69 women); includes 216 minority (34 African Americans, 3 American Indian/Alaska Native, 119 Asian Americans or Pacific Islanders, 60 Hispanic Americans), 7 international. Average age 27. 3,512 applicants, 33% accepted, 246 enrolled. In 2006, 242 JDs, 6 master's awarded. *Entrance requirements:* LSAT, minimum undergraduate GPA of 3.2. *Application deadline:* For fall admission, 4/1 for domestic students. Applications are processed on a rolling basis. *Expenses: Contact institution.* Tuition and fees vary according to degree level, campus/location and program. *Financial support:* In 2006–07, 629 students received support. Career-related internships or fieldwork, Federal Work-Study, and institutionally sponsored loans available. Support available to part-time students. Financial award application deadline: 3/2; financial award applicants required to submit FAFSA. *Unit head:* Jeffrey Brand, Dean, 415-422-6304. *Application contact:* Alan P. Guerrero, Director of Admissions, 415-422-6586, E-mail: lawadmissions@usfca.edu.

University of Saskatchewan, College of Graduate Studies and Research, College of Law, Saskatoon, SK S7N 5A2, Canada. Offers LL B, LL M. Part-time programs available. *Degree requirements:* For master's, thesis, registration. *Entrance requirements:* For LL B, LSAT; for master's, LL B. Additional exam requirements/recommendations for international students: Required—TOEFL. *Faculty research:* Cooperative, native/aboriginal, constitutional, commercial, consumer, and natural resource law; criminal justice; human rights.

University of South Carolina, School of Law, Columbia, SC 29208. Offers JD, JD/IMBA, JD/M Acc, JD/MCJ, JD/MEERM, JD/MHA, JD/MHR, JD/MIBS, JD/MPA, JD/MSEL, JD/MSW. *Accreditation:* ABA. *Degree requirements:* For first-professional, thesis. *Entrance requirements:* LSAT. Expenses: Contact institution.

The University of South Dakota, School of Law, Vermillion, SD 57069-2390. Offers JD, JD/MA, JD/MBA, JD/MP Acc, JD/MPA, JD/MS. *Accreditation:* ABA. Part-time programs available. *Faculty:* 16 full-time (4 women), 3 part-time/adjunct (0 women). *Students:* 231 full-time (96 women), 4 part-time (3 women); includes 10 minority (1 African American, 4 American Indian/Alaska Native, 1 Asian American or Pacific Islander, 4 Hispanic Americans). Average age 27. 448 applicants, 37% accepted, 72 enrolled. In 2006, 90 degrees awarded. *Entrance requirements:* LSAT. Additional exam requirements/recommendations for international students: Required—TOEFL (minimum score 600 paper-based; 250 computer-based). *Application deadline:* For fall admission, 3/1 priority date for domestic students. Applications are processed on a rolling basis. Application fee: $35. Electronic applications accepted. *Expenses: Contact institution. Financial support:* In 2006–07, 212 students received support, including 15 research assistantships with partial tuition reimbursements available (averaging $4,812 per year); career-related internships or fieldwork, Federal Work-Study, scholarships/grants, and unspecified assistantships also available. Financial award application deadline: 4/1; financial award applicants required to submit FAFSA. *Faculty research:* Indian law, skills training, international law, family law, evidence. Total annual research expenditures: $67,000. *Unit head:* Barry R. Vickrey, Dean, 605-677-5443. *Application contact:* Jean Henriques, Admissions Officer/Registrar, 605-677-5443, Fax: 605-677-5417, E-mail: law.school@usd.edu.

University of Southern California, Graduate School, Gould School of Law, Los Angeles, CA 90089-0071. Offers JD, LL M, JD/MA, JD/MBA, JD/MBT, JD/MPA, JD/MRED, JD/MS, JD/MSW. *Accreditation:* ABA. *Students:* 609 full-time (290 women); includes 225 minority (53 African Americans, 1 American Indian/Alaska Native, 104 Asian Americans or Pacific Islanders, 67 Hispanic Americans), 12 international. In 2006, 206 JDs, 64 master's awarded. *Entrance requirements:* LSAT. *Application deadline:* Applications are processed on a rolling basis. *Expenses:* Tuition: Full-time $33,314; part-time $1,121 per credit. Required fees: $522. Full-time tuition and fees vary according to program. *Financial support:* Fellowships, research assistantships, teaching assistantships, Federal Work-Study, institutionally sponsored loans, and scholarships/grants available. Support available to part-time students. Financial award application deadline: 2/15; financial award applicants required to submit FAFSA. *Unit head:* Edward McCaffy, Dean, 213-740-6473, E-mail: dean@law.usc.edu.

University of Southern Maine, University of Maine School of Law, Portland, ME 04102. Offers JD, JD/MBA, JD/MPPM. Part-time programs available. *Faculty:* 18 full-time (11 women), 13 part-time/adjunct (1 woman). *Students:* 258 full-time (137 women), 3 part-time (2 women); includes 11 minority (3 African Americans, 7 Asian Americans or Pacific Islanders, 1 Hispanic American). Average age 28. 760 applicants, 43% accepted, 101 enrolled. In 2006, 82 degrees awarded. *Entrance requirements:* LSAT. Additional exam requirements/recommendations for international students: Required—TOEFL. *Application deadline:* For fall admission, 3/1 for domestic and international students. Applications are processed on a rolling basis. Application fee: $50. Electronic applications accepted. *Expenses: Contact institution.* Tuition and fees vary according to course load. *Financial support:* In 2006–07, 242 students received support. Career-related internships or fieldwork, Federal Work-Study, scholarships/grants, and tuition waivers (full and partial) available. Support available to part-time students. Financial award application deadline: 2/1; financial award applicants required to submit FAFSA. *Faculty research:* Securitization transactions and bankruptcy dynamic; law/science/ecosystem approach to marine fisheries; European integration: past, present, future; commercial law aspects of intellectual property. *Unit head:* Peter R. Pitegoff, Dean, 207-780-4344, Fax: 207-780-4239. *Application contact:* David Pallozzi, Assistant Dean for Admissions, 207-780-4341, Fax: 207-780-4239, E-mail: mainelaw@usm.maine.edu.

The University of Tennessee, College of Law, Knoxville, TN 37996-1810. Offers JD, JD/MBA, JD/MPA. *Accreditation:* ABA. *Faculty:* 51 full-time (24 women), 66 part-time/adjunct (23 women). *Students:* 449 full-time (226 women); includes 71 minority (61 African Americans, 2 American Indian/Alaska Native, 3 Asian Americans or Pacific Islanders, 5 Hispanic Americans). Average age 24. 1,390 applicants, 28% accepted, 151 enrolled. In 2006, 136 degrees awarded. *Entrance requirements:* LSAT. Additional exam requirements/recommendations for international students: Required—TOEFL. *Application deadline:* For fall admission, 3/1 priority date for domestic and international students. Applications are processed on a rolling basis. Application fee: $15. Electronic applications accepted. *Expenses: Contact institution. Financial support:* In 2006–07, 397 students received support, including 7 research assistantships with full tuition reimbursements available (averaging $4,400 per year); career-related internships or fieldwork, Federal Work-Study, institutionally sponsored loans, scholarships/grants, and unspecified assistantships also available. Support available to part-time students. Financial award application deadline: 3/1; financial award applicants required to submit FAFSA. *Faculty research:* Legal expert systems, medical malpractice remedies, professional ethics, insanity defense. *Unit head:* Dr. Karen R. Britton, Director of Admissions, Financial Aid and Career Services, 865-974-4131, Fax: 865-974-1572, E-mail: lawadmit@utk.edu. *Application contact:* Janet S. Hatcher, Admissions and Financial Aid Advisor, 865-974-4131, Fax: 865-974-1572, E-mail: hatcher@utk.edu.

The University of Texas at Austin, School of Law, Austin, TX 78705. Offers JD, LL M, JD/MA, JD/MBA, JD/MP Aff, JD/MSCRP. *Accreditation:* ABA. *Faculty:* 124 full-time (39 women), 41 part-time/adjunct (16 women). *Students:* 1,365 full-time (556 women); includes 416 minority (77 African Americans, 8 American Indian/Alaska Native, 73 Asian Americans or Pacific Islanders, 258 Hispanic Americans). Average age 24. 4,999 applicants, 22% accepted, 433 enrolled. In 2006, 542 JDs, 24 master's awarded. *Entrance requirements:* LSAT, minimum GPA of 2.2. *Application deadline:* For fall admission, 2/1 for domestic students. Application fee: $70. Electronic applications accepted. *Expenses: Contact institution. Financial support:* In 2006–07, 1,167 students received support, including 100 research assistantships, 32 teaching assistantships (averaging $3,900 per year); career-related internships or fieldwork, scholarships/grants, and tuition waivers (full) also available. Financial award application deadline: 3/31; financial award applicants required to submit FAFSA. *Faculty research:* Constitutional law, corporate law, environmental law, employment and labor law, intellectual property law. *Unit head:* Lawrence Sager, Interim Dean, 512-232-1120, Fax: 512-471-6987, E-mail: lsager@law.utexas.edu. *Application contact:* 512-232-1200, Fax: 512-471-2765, E-mail: admissions@law.texas.edu.

Law

University of the District of Columbia, David A. Clarke School of Law, Washington, DC 20008. Offers JD. *Accreditation:* ABA. *Entrance requirements:* LSAT. Electronic applications accepted. Expenses: Contact institution. *Faculty research:* HIV law, juvenile law, legislative law, community development, small business.

University of the Pacific, McGeorge School of Law, Sacramento, CA 95817. Offers government and public policy (LL M); international law (LL M); international waters resources law (LL M); law (JD); transnational business practice (LL M); JD/MBA; JD/MPPA. *Accreditation:* ABA. Part-time and evening/weekend programs available. *Faculty:* 39 full-time (12 women), 31 part-time/adjunct (7 women). *Students:* 686 full-time, 321 part-time. Average age 24. 3,621 applicants, 31% accepted. In 2006, 261 JDs, 19 master's awarded. *Degree requirements:* For master's, thesis (for some programs); for doctorate, thesis/dissertation. *Entrance requirements:* For JD, LSAT; for master's, JD; for doctorate, LL M. Additional exam requirements/recommendations for international students: Required—TOEFL (minimum score 600 paper-based). *Application deadline:* For fall admission, 5/1 priority date for domestic students. Applications are processed on a rolling basis. Application fee: $50. Electronic applications accepted. *Expenses: Contact institution.* Tuition and fees vary according to course load. *Financial support:* In 2006–07, 528 students received support, including 9 fellowships, 20 research assistantships (averaging $6,485 per year); career-related internships or fieldwork, Federal Work-Study, institutionally sponsored loans, and scholarships/grants also available. Support available to part-time students. Financial award applicants required to submit FAFSA. *Faculty research:* Taxation and business, family and juvenile law, governmental affairs, environmental law, intellectual property law. *Unit head:* Elizabeth Rindskopf Parker, Dean, 916-739-7151, E-mail: elizabeth@uop.edu. *Application contact:* 916-739-7105, Fax: 916-739-7134, E-mail: admissionsmcgeorge@uop.edu.

The University of Toledo, College of Law, Toledo, OH 43606. Offers JD, MLW, JD/MACJ, JD/MBA, JD/MPA, JD/MSE. *Accreditation:* ABA. Part-time and evening/weekend programs available. *Faculty:* 31 full-time (13 women), 14 part-time/adjunct (5 women). *Students:* 345 full-time (140 women), 186 part-time (74 women); includes 41 minority (16 African Americans, 2 American Indian/Alaska Native, 10 Asian Americans or Pacific Islanders, 13 Hispanic Americans). Average age 27. 1,216 applicants, 28% accepted, 190 enrolled. In 2006, 140 degrees awarded. *Entrance requirements:* LSAT. *Application deadline:* For fall admission, 7/31 priority date for domestic students, 7/31 for international students. Applications are processed on a rolling basis. Application fee: $45. Electronic applications accepted. *Expenses: Contact institution. Financial support:* In 2006–07, 455 students received support, including 15 research assistantships (averaging $689 per year), 47 teaching assistantships; career-related internships or fieldwork, Federal Work-Study, and scholarships/grants also available. Support available to part-time students. Financial award application deadline: 8/1; financial award applicants required to submit FAFSA. *Faculty research:* Federal courts/political ends; federal Superfund statute; just-cause termination rules; recklessness in tort & criminal law; detainee treatment; domestic violence-related deaths. Total annual research expenditures: $60,000. *Unit head:* Douglas E. Ray, Dean, 419-530-2379, Fax: 419-530-4526, E-mail: douglas.ray@utoledo.edu. *Application contact:* Carol E. Frendt, Assistant Dean of Law Admissions, 419-530-4131, Fax: 419-530-4345, E-mail: law.admissions@utoledo.edu.

University of Toronto, Faculty of Law and School of Graduate Studies, Graduate Programs in Law, Toronto, ON M5S 1A1, Canada. Offers LL M, MSL, SJD. *Degree requirements:* For master's, thesis (for some programs); for doctorate, thesis/dissertation.

University of Toronto, Faculty of Law, Professional Program in Law, Toronto, ON M5S 1A1, Canada. Offers JD, JD/Certificate, JD/M I St, JD/MA, JD/MBA, JD/MSW, JD/PhD. *Entrance requirements:* LSAT. Expenses: Contact institution.

University of Tulsa, College of Law, Tulsa, OK 74104. Offers alternative methods of dispute resolution (Certificate); American Indian and indigenous law (LL M); American law for foreign lawyers (LL M); comparative and international law (Certificate); entrepreneurial law (Certificate); health law (Certificate); law (JD); lawyering skills (Certificate); Native American law (Certificate); public policy and regulation (Certificate); resources, energy, and environmental law (Certificate); JD/M Acct; JD/M Tax; JD/MA; JD/MBA; JD/MS; MCS/JD. *Accreditation:* ABA. Part-time programs available. *Faculty:* 37 full-time (19 women), 31 part-time/adjunct (9 women). *Students:* 464 full-time (153 women), 81 part-time (35 women); includes 57 minority (17 African Americans, 24 American Indian/Alaska Native, 6 Asian Americans or Pacific Islanders, 10 Hispanic Americans), 5 international. Average age 28. 1,436 applicants, 41% accepted, 183 enrolled. In 2006, 199 JDs, 8 other advanced degrees awarded. *Entrance requirements:* For JD, LSAT; for master's, JD or equivalent from non-US university. Additional exam requirements/recommendations for international students: Required—TOEFL (minimum score 570 paper-based; 230 computer-based). *Application deadline:* For fall admission, 2/1 priority date for domestic and international students. Applications are processed on a rolling basis. Application fee: $30. Electronic applications accepted. *Expenses: Contact institution. Financial support:* In 2006–07, 181 students received support, including fellowships (averaging $25,000 per year); Federal Work-Study and scholarships/grants also available. Support available to part-time students. Financial award applicants required to submit FAFSA. *Unit head:* Robert Butkin, Dean, 918-631-2400, Fax: 918-631-3126, E-mail: robert-butkin@utulsa.edu. *Application contact:* Martha T. Cordell, Assistant Dean of Admissions and Financial Aid, 918-631-2406, Fax: 918-631-3630, E-mail: martha-cordell@utulsa.edu.

University of Utah, S.J. Quinney College of Law, Salt Lake City, UT 84112-0730. Offers JD, LL M, JD/MBA, JD/MPA. *Accreditation:* ABA. *Faculty:* 39 full-time (13 women), 28 part-time/adjunct (6 women). *Students:* 391 full-time (148 women); includes 40 minority (2 African Americans, 2 American Indian/Alaska Native, 21 Asian Americans or Pacific Islanders, 15 Hispanic Americans), 1 international. Average age 28. 1,130 applicants, 32% accepted, 122 enrolled. In 2006, 129 JDs, 2 master's awarded. *Entrance requirements:* LSAT, LSDAS. Additional exam requirements/recommendations for international students: Required—TOEFL (minimum score 600 paper-based; 250 computer-based). *Application deadline:* For fall admission, 2/1 for domestic and international students. Applications are processed on a rolling basis. Application fee: $60. *Expenses: Contact institution.* Tuition and fees vary according to class time and program. *Financial support:* In 2006–07, 167 students received support, including 45 fellowships with full and partial tuition reimbursements available (averaging $1,332 per year), 2 research assistantships with partial tuition reimbursements available (averaging $5,000 per year); career-related internships or fieldwork, Federal Work-Study, institutionally sponsored loans, and scholarships/grants also available. Financial award application deadline: 3/15; financial award applicants required to submit FAFSA. *Faculty research:* Environmental law, natural resources law, international law, criminal law, corporate law. *Unit head:* Hiram E. Chodosh, Dean, 801-581-6833, Fax: 801-581-6897. *Application contact:* Reyes Aguilar, Associate Dean for Admission and Financial Aid, 801-581-7479, Fax: 801-581-6897, E-mail: aguilarr@law.utah.edu.

University of Victoria, Faculty of Law, Victoria, BC V8W 2Y2, Canada. Offers LL B, LL M, PhD, LL B/MAIG, MBA/LL B, MPA/LL B. Part-time programs available. *Faculty:* 33 full-time (14 women), 33 part-time/adjunct (6 women). *Students:* 393 full-time (217 women), 10 part-time (6 women). Average age 26. 1,038 applicants, 27% accepted, 108 enrolled. In 2006, 122 LL Bs, 10 master's awarded. *Median time to degree:* LL B–3 years full-time, 4.5 years part-time; master's–1 year full-time, 2 years part-time. *Degree requirements:* For LL B, major research paper; for master's and doctorate, thesis/dissertation, registration. *Entrance requirements:* For LL B, LSAT, minimum 3 years of full-time study or part-time equivalent leading toward a bachelor's degree; for master's and doctorate, LL B. Additional exam requirements/recommendations for international students: Required—TOEFL (minimum score 600 paper-based; 250 computer-based; 100 iBT). *Application deadline:* For fall admission, 2/1 for domestic and international students. Applications are processed on a rolling basis. Application fee: $75 Canadian dollars. Electronic applications accepted. *Expenses: Contact institution. Financial support:* In 2006–07, 250 students received support, including 11 fellowships (averaging $8,000 Canadian dollars per year), 20 research assistantships (averaging $8,000 Canadian dollars per year); career-related internships or fieldwork, Federal Work-Study, institutionally sponsored loans, scholarships/grants, health care benefits, unspecified assistantships, and course prizes, merit-based awards also available. Support available to part-time students. Financial award application deadline: 6/1. *Faculty research:* Environmental law and policy, Asian-Pacific law, alternative dispute resolution, intellectual property law, Aboriginal law. *Unit head:* Andrew J. Petter, Dean, 250-721-8147, Fax: 250-472-7299, E-mail: dean@law.uvic.ca. *Application contact:* Neela Paige, Admissions Assistant, 250-721-8151, Fax: 250-721-6390, E-mail: lawadmss@uvic.ca.

University of Virginia, School of Law, Charlottesville, VA 22903-1789. Offers JD, LL M, SJD, JD/MA, JD/MBA, JD/MP, JD/MPH, JD/MS. *Accreditation:* ABA. *Faculty:* 73 full-time (17 women), 2 part-time/adjunct (1 woman). *Students:* 1,174 full-time (461 women), 1 part-time; includes 199 minority (98 African Americans, 8 American Indian/Alaska Native, 72 Asian Americans or Pacific Islanders, 21 Hispanic Americans), 41 international. Average age 25. 5,286 applicants, 27% accepted, 441 enrolled. In 2006, 369 JDs, 30 master's, 1 doctorate awarded. *Degree requirements:* For doctorate, thesis/dissertation, oral exam. *Entrance requirements:* LSAT. Additional exam requirements/recommendations for international students: Required—TOEFL. *Application deadline:* For fall admission, 1/16 priority date for domestic students. Applications are processed on a rolling basis. Application fee: $70. *Expenses: Contact institution. Financial support:* Fellowships, Federal Work-Study available. Financial award application deadline: 1/15; financial award applicants required to submit FAFSA. *Unit head:* John C. Jeffries, Dean, 434-924-7354. *Application contact:* Susan Palmer, Associate Dean of Admissions, 434-924-7351, Fax: 434-982-2128, E-mail: lawadmit@virginia.edu.

University of Washington, School of Law, Seattle, WA 98195-3020. Offers Asian law (LL M, PhD); intellectual property law and policy (LL M); law (JD); law of sustainable international development (LL M); taxation (LL M); JD/LL M; JD/MA; JD/MAIS; JD/MBA; JD/MPA; JD/MS; JD/PhD. *Accreditation:* ABA. *Degree requirements:* For master's and doctorate, thesis/dissertation. *Entrance requirements:* For JD, LSAT; for master's, language proficiency (LL M in Asian law). Additional exam requirements/recommendations for international students: Required—TOEFL. Expenses: Contact institution. *Faculty research:* Asian, international and comparative law, intellectual property law, health law, environmental law, taxation.

The University of Western Ontario, Faculty of Law, London, ON N6A 5B8, Canada. Offers LL B, LL M, Diploma, LL B/MBA. *Entrance requirements:* LSAT, minimum B+ average. *Application deadline:* For fall admission, 11/1 for domestic students. Applications are processed on a rolling basis. Application fee: $50. *Expenses: Contact institution. Faculty research:* Taxation, administrative law, torts, drug and alcohol law and policy, property. *Unit head:* Dr. Craig Brown, Acting Dean, 519-661-2111 Ext. 88442, E-mail: cbrown3@uwo.ca. *Application contact:* D. Sandler, Director, Graduate Program, 519-661-3356, E-mail: dsandler@uwo.ca.

University of Wisconsin–Madison, Law School, Graduate Programs in Law, Madison, WI 53706-1380. Offers LL M, SJD. *Students:* 37 full-time (15 women); includes 4 minority (1 African American, 1 Asian American or Pacific Islander, 2 Hispanic Americans), 33 international. Average age 33. 57 applicants, 37% accepted, 20 enrolled. In 2006, 5 master's, 8 doctorates awarded. *Entrance requirements:* Additional exam requirements/recommendations for international students: Required—TOEFL (minimum score 625 paper-based; 263 computer-based). *Application deadline:* For fall admission, 3/1 for domestic and international students; for spring admission, 10/1 for domestic and international students. Applications are processed on a rolling basis. Application fee: $45. *Financial support:* In 2006–07, 7 fellowships with tuition reimbursements (averaging $10,000 per year) were awarded; career-related internships or fieldwork, Federal Work-Study, and institutionally sponsored loans also available. Financial award application deadline: 3/1. *Unit head:* Gerald Thain, Chairperson, 608-262-9120.

University of Wyoming, College of Law, Laramie, WY 82071. Offers JD, JD/MPA. *Accreditation:* ABA. *Faculty:* 16 full-time (8 women), 14 part-time/adjunct (8 women). *Students:* 233 full-time (107 women), 3 part-time (1 woman); includes 16 minority (1 African American, 2 American Indian/Alaska Native, 6 Asian Americans or Pacific Islanders, 7 Hispanic Americans), 5 international. Average age 29. 780 applicants, 24% accepted, 82 enrolled. In 2006, 69 degrees awarded. *Entrance requirements:* LSAT. Additional exam requirements/recommendations for international students: Required—TOEFL. *Application deadline:* For fall admission, 3/15 for domestic students. Applications are processed on a rolling basis. Application fee: $35. *Expenses: Contact institution. Financial support:* In 2006–07, 161 students received support, including 18 research assistantships (averaging $1,610 per year), 7 teaching assistantships with full and partial tuition reimbursements available (averaging $2,337 per year); fellowships, career-related internships or fieldwork, Federal Work-Study, institutionally sponsored loans, and scholarships/grants also available. Financial award application deadline: 5/1; financial award applicants required to submit FAFSA. *Faculty research:* Environmental, public land, constitutional, securities law, criminal law. *Unit head:* Jerry Parkinson, Dean, 307-766-6416, E-mail: jparkins@wyo.edu. *Application contact:* Sheryl Sullivan, Assistant Dean, 307-766-6416, E-mail: lawadmis@wyo.edu.

Valparaiso University, School of Law, Valparaiso, IN 46383. Offers JD, LL M, JD/MA, JD/MALS, JD/MBA, JD/MS, JD/MSSA. *Accreditation:* ABA. Part-time programs available. *Faculty:* 36 full-time (16 women), 25 part-time/adjunct (11 women). *Students:* 466 full-time (208 women), 54 part-time (24 women); includes 60 minority (24 African Americans, 1 American Indian/Alaska Native, 11 Asian Americans or Pacific Islanders, 24 Hispanic Americans), 12 international. Average age 24. 2,736 applicants, 30% accepted, 200 enrolled. In 2006, 160 JDs, 5 master's awarded. *Entrance requirements:* LSAT. Additional exam requirements/recommendations for international students: Required—TOEFL. *Application deadline:* For fall admission, 4/15 priority date for domestic students. Applications are processed on a rolling basis. Application fee: $50. Electronic applications accepted. *Expenses: Contact institution.* Tuition and fees vary according to program. *Financial support:* In 2006–07, 470 students received support, including 23 research assistantships (averaging $500 per year), 10 teaching assistantships (averaging $2,000 per year); career-related internships or fieldwork, Federal Work-Study, institutionally sponsored loans, scholarships/grants, and tuition waivers (partial) also available. Support available to part-time students. Financial award application deadline: 3/1; financial award applicants required to submit FAFSA. *Faculty research:* Jurisprudence, international law, Constitutional law, civil procedure, law and religion. *Unit head:* Jay Conison, Dean, 219-465-7834, Fax: 219-465-7872, E-mail: jay.conison@valpo.edu. *Application contact:* Tony O. Credit, Executive Director of Admissions, 219-465-7829, Fax: 219-465-7808, E-mail: tony.credit@valpo.edu.

Vanderbilt University, Law School, Nashville, TN 37203. Offers law (JD, LL M); law and economics (PhD); JD/M Div; JD/MA; JD/MBA; JD/MD; JD/MPP; JD/MTS; JD/PhD; LL M/MA. *Accreditation:* ABA. *Faculty:* 50 full-time (15 women), 70 part-time/adjunct (26 women). *Students:* 653 full-time (299 women); includes 116 minority (51 African Americans, 5 American Indian/Alaska Native, 41 Asian Americans or Pacific Islanders, 19 Hispanic Americans), 35 international. Average age 25. 3,640 applicants, 25% accepted, 190 enrolled. In 2006, 203 first professional degrees, 10 master's awarded. *Entrance requirements:* LSAT. *Application deadline:* For fall admission, 3/15 for domestic students. Applications are processed on a rolling basis. Application fee: $50. Electronic applications accepted. *Expenses: Contact institution.* One-time fee: $30 full-time. Full-time tuition and fees vary according to course load, degree level and program. *Financial support:* In 2006–07, 90 students received support. Career-related internships or fieldwork, Federal Work-Study, institutionally sponsored loans, and scholarships/grants available. Financial award application deadline: 2/15; financial award applicants required to submit FAFSA. *Unit head:* Edward L Rubin, Dean, 615-322-2615. *Application contact:* G. Todd Morton, Assistant Dean for Admissions, 615-322-6452, Fax: 615-322-1531.

Vermont Law School, Law School, Professional Program, South Royalton, VT 05068-0096. Offers JD, JD/MSEL. *Accreditation:* ABA. *Faculty:* 48 full-time (23 women), 28 part-time/adjunct (12 women). *Students:* Average age 27. 1,119 applicants, 56% accepted, 202 enrolled. In 2006, 168 degrees awarded. *Entrance requirements:* LSAT, LSDAS/registration, resumé. Additional exam requirements/recommendations for international students: Required—TOEFL (minimum score 600 paper-based). *Application deadline:* For fall admission, 3/15 priority date for domestic students; for spring admission, 11/15 priority date for domestic students. Applications are processed on a rolling basis. Application fee: $60. Electronic applications accepted. *Financial support:* Career-related internships or fieldwork, Federal Work-Study, institutionally sponsored loans, scholarships/grants, and tuition waivers (partial) available. Financial award application deadline: 2/15; financial award applicants required to submit FAFSA. *Faculty research:* Environmental law, national security, law and medicine. *Application contact:* Kathy Hartman, Associate Dean for Enrollment Management, 802-831-1239, Fax: 802-763-7071, E-mail: admiss@vermontlaw.edu.

Villanova University, School of Law, Program in Law, Villanova, PA 19085-1699. Offers JD, JD/LL M, JD/MBA, JD/PhD. *Faculty:* 42 full-time (20 women), 96 part-time/adjunct (29 women). *Students:* 720 full-time (344 women), 9 part-time (8 women); includes 126 minority (39 African Americans, 3 American Indian/Alaska Native, 55 Asian Americans or Pacific Islanders, 29 Hispanic Americans), 5 international. Average age 25. 2,834 applicants, 36% accepted, 250 enrolled. In 2006, 259 degrees awarded. *Entrance requirements:* LSAT. *Application deadline:* For fall admission, 3/1 for domestic and international students. Applications are processed on a rolling basis. Application fee: $75. Electronic applications accepted. *Expenses: Contact institution. Financial support:* In 2006–07, 273 students received support, including 91 research assistantships, 13 teaching assistantships; career-related internships or fieldwork, Federal Work-Study, institutionally sponsored loans, and scholarships/grants also available. Financial award application deadline: 3/15; financial award applicants required to submit FAFSA. *Faculty research:* International law, evidence, criminal procedure, torts/products liability, sex crimes/feminist jurisprudence. *Application contact:* Noe Bernal, Assistant Dean for Admissions, 610-519-7010, Fax: 610-519-6291, E-mail: admissions@law.villanova.edu.

Wake Forest University, School of Law, Winston-Salem, NC 27109. Offers JD, LL M, JD/MBA. LL M for foreign law graduates in American law. *Accreditation:* ABA. *Faculty:* 45 full-time, 26 part-time/adjunct. *Students:* 471 full-time (221 women), 20 part-time (13 women); includes 51 minority (27 African Americans, 18 Asian Americans or Pacific Islanders, 6 Hispanic Americans), 5 international. Average age 25. 2,142 applicants, 30% accepted. In 2006, 171 degrees awarded. *Entrance requirements:* LSAT. Additional exam requirements/recommendations for international students: Required—TOEFL. *Application deadline:* For fall admission, 3/1 for domestic students. Applications are processed on a rolling basis. Application fee: $60. Electronic applications accepted. *Expenses: Contact institution. Financial support:* In 2006–07, 183 students received support. Career-related internships or fieldwork, Federal Work-Study, institutionally sponsored loans, and scholarships/grants available. Financial award application deadline: 4/30; financial award applicants required to submit FAFSA. *Faculty research:* Constitutional law, family law, land use planning, torts, taxation. *Unit head:* Robert K. Walsh, Dean, 336-758-5435, Fax: 336-758-4632. *Application contact:* Melanie E. Nutt, Director of Admissions and Financial Aid, 336-758-5437, Fax: 336-758-3930, E-mail: admissions@law.wfu.edu.

Washburn University, School of Law, Topeka, KS 66621. Offers JD. *Accreditation:* ABA. *Entrance requirements:* LSAT. Electronic applications accepted. Expenses: Contact institution. *Faculty research:* Constitutional law, family law, energy law, banking and securities law, agricultural law.

Washington and Lee University, School of Law, Lexington, VA 24450. Offers law (JD); U.S. law (LL M). *Accreditation:* ABA. *Faculty:* 36 full-time (11 women), 6 part-time/adjunct (2 women). *Students:* 403 full-time (165 women); includes 62 minority (18 African Americans, 7 American Indian/Alaska Native, 31 Asian Americans or Pacific Islanders, 6 Hispanic Americans), 13 international. Average age 25. 2,764 applicants, 31% accepted, 126 enrolled. In 2006, 129 JDs awarded. *Entrance requirements:* LSAT. Additional exam requirements/recommendations for international students: Required—TOEFL (minimum score 560 paper-based; 220 computer-based; 83 iBT). *Application deadline:* For fall admission, 1/15 priority date for domestic students. Applications are processed on a rolling basis. Application fee: $50. Electronic applications accepted. *Expenses:* Tuition: Full-time $30,500. Required fees: $800. *Financial support:* In 2006–07, 329 students received support, including 6 teaching assistantships (averaging $4,200 per year); fellowships, career-related internships or fieldwork, Federal Work-Study, institutionally sponsored loans, and scholarships/grants also available. Financial award application deadline: 2/15; financial award applicants required to submit FAFSA. *Unit head:* Rodney A. Smolla, Dean, 540-458-8502, Fax: 540-458-8488, E-mail: smollar@wlu.edu. *Application contact:* Andrea Hilton Howe, Director of Admissions, 540-458-8503, Fax: 540-458-8586, E-mail: hiltonhowea@wlu.edu.

Washington University in St. Louis, School of Law, St. Louis, MO 63130-4899. Offers JD, LL M, MJS, JSD, JD/MA, JD/MBA, JD/MHA, JD/MS, JD/MSW, JD/PhD. *Accreditation:* ABA. *Faculty:* 59 full-time (28 women), 118 part-time/adjunct (24 women). *Students:* 861 full-time (366 women), 29 part-time (8 women). Average age 27. 3,325 applicants, 27% accepted, 241 enrolled. In 2006, 251 degrees awarded. *Entrance requirements:* LSAT. *Application deadline:* For fall admission, 3/1 priority date for domestic students. Application fee: $70. Electronic applications accepted. *Expenses: Contact institution. Financial support:* Career-related internships or fieldwork, Federal Work-Study, institutionally sponsored loans, scholarships/grants, and health care benefits available. Support available to part-time students. Financial award application deadline: 3/1; financial award applicants required to submit FAFSA. *Faculty research:* International law, environmental law, employment discrimination, reproductive rights, bankruptcy and white-collar crime. *Unit head:* Kent D Syvervd, Dean, 314-935-6400. *Application contact:* Mary Ann Clifford, Assistant Dean for Admissions, 314-935-4525, Fax: 314-935-8778, E-mail: admiss@wulaw.wustl.edu.

Wayne State University, Law School, Detroit, MI 48202. Offers JD, LL M, PhD, JD/MA, JD/MADR, JD/MBA. *Accreditation:* ABA. Part-time and evening/weekend programs available. *Faculty:* 56 full-time (21 women), 23 part-time/adjunct (3 women). *Students:* 576 full-time (278 women), 177 part-time (81 women); includes 144 minority (78 African Americans, 3 American Indian/Alaska Native, 35 Asian Americans or Pacific Islanders, 28 Hispanic Americans), 13 international. Average age 27. 1,582 applicants, 42% accepted, 238 enrolled. In 2006, 225 JDs, 25 master's awarded. *Degree requirements:* For master's, thesis. *Entrance requirements:* For JD, LSAT; for master's, JD. Additional exam requirements/recommendations for international students: Required—TOEFL (minimum score 550 paper-based; 213 computer-based); Recommended—TWE (minimum score 6). *Application deadline:* For fall admission, 4/15 for domestic students, 6/1 for international students; for winter admission, 10/1 for international students; for spring admission, 2/1 for international students. Application fee: $30 ($50 for international students). Electronic applications accepted. *Expenses: Contact institution. Financial support:* In 2006–07, 460 students received support. Federal Work-Study available. Support available to part-time students. Financial award application deadline: 4/30; financial award applicants required to submit FAFSA. *Faculty research:* Constitutional law, intellectual property, comparative law, commercial law, health law. *Unit head:* Frank Wu, Dean, 313-577-3933, Fax: 313-577-2620, E-mail: aw7545@wayne.edu. *Application contact:* Linda Fowler Sims, Assistant Dean for Recruitment and Admissions, 313-577-3937, Fax: 313-577-9049, E-mail: ab2594@wayne.edu.

Western New England College, School of Law, Springfield, MA 01119. Offers estate planning/elder law (LL M); law (JD). *Accreditation:* ABA. Part-time and evening/weekend programs available. *Entrance requirements:* LSAT.. Electronic applications accepted. Expenses: Contact institution.

Western State University College of Law, Professional Program, Fullerton, CA 92831-3000. Offers JD. Part-time and evening/weekend programs available. *Faculty:* 22 full-time (9 women), 26 part-time/adjunct (9 women). *Students:* 310 full-time (162 women), 141 part-time (73 women); includes 156 minority (18 African Americans, 5 American Indian/Alaska Native, 83 Asian Americans or Pacific Islanders, 50 Hispanic Americans). Average age 30. 1,637 applicants, 40% accepted, 155 enrolled. In 2006, 148 degrees awarded. *Entrance requirements:* LSAT, 2 letters of recommendation. Additional exam requirements/recommendations for international students: Required—TOEFL (minimum score 550 paper-based; 213 computer-based). *Application deadline:* For fall admission, 5/1 priority date for domestic students; for spring admission, 10/1 priority date for domestic students. Applications are processed on a rolling basis. Application fee: $50. Electronic applications accepted. *Expenses:* Tuition: Full-time $27,220; part-time $9,160 per term. Required fees: $283; $130 per term. One-time fee: $23 part-time. *Financial support:* In 2006–07, 434 students received support. Federal Work-Study and scholarships/grants available. Support available to part-time students. Financial award application deadline: 9/15; financial award applicants required to submit FAFSA. *Faculty research:* Criminal law and practice, entrepreneurship, teaching effectiveness and student success, learning theory and legal education. *Application contact:* Gloria Switzer, Assistant Dean of Admission, 714-459-1101, Fax: 714-441-1748, E-mail: adm@wsulaw.edu.

West Virginia University, College of Law, Morgantown, WV 26506-6130. Offers JD, JD/MBA, JD/MPA. *Accreditation:* ABA. Part-time programs available. *Faculty:* 25 full-time (8 women), 24 part-time/adjunct (10 women). *Students:* 475 full-time (214 women), 6 part-time (4 women); includes 48 minority (31 African Americans, 2 American Indian/Alaska Native, 10 Asian Americans or Pacific Islanders, 5 Hispanic Americans), 4 international. Average age 26. 903 applicants, 30% accepted, 176 enrolled. In 2006, 139 degrees awarded. *Entrance requirements:* LSAT. Additional exam requirements/recommendations for international students: Required—TOEFL. *Application deadline:* For fall admission, 2/1 for domestic and international students. Applications are processed on a rolling basis. Application fee: $50. Electronic applications accepted. *Expenses: Contact institution.* Tuition and fees vary according to program. *Financial support:* In 2006–07, 405 students received support, including 5 research assistantships, 3 teaching assistantships; fellowships, career-related internships or fieldwork, Federal Work-Study, institutionally sponsored loans, scholarships/grants, tuition waivers (full), unspecified assistantships, and graduate administrative assistantships, graduate resident assistantships also available. Support available to part-time students. Financial award application deadline: 3/1. *Faculty research:* Constitutional law, public interest law, corporate law, environment and natural resources innocence project. Total annual research expenditures: $76,695. *Unit head:* John W. Fisher, Dean, 304-293-3199, Fax: 304-293-6891, E-mail: john.fisher@mail.wvu.edu. *Application contact:* Janet Long Armistead, Assistant Dean for Admissions and Student Affairs, 304-293-7320, Fax: 304-293-6891, E-mail: janet.armistead@mail.wvu.edu.

Whittier College, Whittier Law School, Costa Mesa, CA 92626. Offers foreign legal studies (LL M); law (JD). *Accreditation:* ABA. Part-time and evening/weekend programs available. *Entrance requirements:* For JD, LSAT; for master's, first degree in law. Additional exam requirements/recommendations for international students: Required—TOEFL (minimum score 600 paper-based; 250 computer-based). Electronic applications accepted. Expenses: Contact institution. *Faculty research:* Intellectual property, international law, health law, children's rights.

Widener University, School of Human Service Professions, Institute for Graduate Clinical Psychology, Law-Psychology Program, Chester, PA 19013-5792. Offers JD/Psy D. Electronic applications accepted.

Widener University, School of Law, Harrisburg, PA 17106-9381. Offers JD. *Accreditation:* ABA. Part-time programs available. *Entrance requirements:* LSAT. Electronic applications accepted. Expenses: Contact institution. *Faculty research:* Health law, toxic torts, constitutional law, intellectual property, corporate law.

See Close-Up on page 2111.

Widener University, School of Law at Wilmington, Wilmington, DE 19803-0474. Offers corporate law and finance (LL M); health law (LL M, MJ, D Law); juridical science (SJD); law (JD). *Accreditation:* ABA. Part-time programs available. *Degree requirements:* For doctorate, thesis/dissertation. *Entrance requirements:* For JD, LSAT; for master's, GMAT; for doctorate, GRE.

Willamette University, College of Law, Salem, OR 97301-3922. Offers JD, LL M, JD/MBA. *Accreditation:* ABA. *Faculty:* 25 full-time (8 women), 20 part-time/adjunct (6 women). *Students:* 424 full-time (179 women); includes 36 minority (3 African Americans, 7 American Indian/Alaska Native, 18 Asian Americans or Pacific Islanders, 8 Hispanic Americans), 3 international. Average age 27. 1,329 applicants, 38% accepted, 159 enrolled. In 2006, 137 JDs, 2 master's awarded. *Degree requirements:* For JD and master's, thesis. *Entrance requirements:* LSAT. Additional exam requirements/recommendations for international students: Required—TOEFL (minimum score 600 paper-based; 250 computer-based). *Application deadline:* For fall admission, 4/1 priority date for domestic students, 4/1 for international students. Applications are processed on a rolling basis. Application fee: $50. Electronic applications accepted. *Expenses: Contact institution. Financial support:* In 2006–07, 390 students received support; fellowships with partial tuition reimbursements available, research assistantships with partial tuition reimbursements available, Federal Work-Study, scholarships/grants, and tuition waivers (full and partial) available. Financial award application deadline: 3/1; financial award applicants required to submit FAFSA. *Faculty research:* Dispute resolution, international law, business law, law and government. Total annual research expenditures: $120,000. *Unit head:* Symeon C. Symeonides, Dean, 503-370-6402, Fax: 503-370-6828, E-mail: symeon@willamette.edu. *Application contact:* Carolyn Dennis, Director of Admission, 503-370-6282, Fax: 503-370-6087, E-mail: law-admission@willamette.edu.

William Howard Taft University, Graduate Programs, Bernard E. Witkin School of Law, Santa Ana, CA 92704. Offers American jurisprudence (LL M); law (JD); taxation (LL M).

William Mitchell College of Law, Professional Program, St. Paul, MN 55105-3076. Offers JD. *Accreditation:* ABA. Part-time and evening/weekend programs available. *Faculty:* 35 full-time (13 women), 212 part-time/adjunct (87 women). *Students:* 738 full-time (403 women), 365 part-time (184 women); includes 121 minority (33 African Americans, 5 American Indian/Alaska Native, 57 Asian Americans or Pacific Islanders, 26 Hispanic Americans), 7 international. Average age 29. 1,487 applicants, 55% accepted, 352 enrolled. In 2006, 322 degrees awarded. *Entrance requirements:* LSAT. Additional exam requirements/recommendations for international students: Required—TOEFL (minimum score 600 paper-based; 250 computer-based; 100 iBT). *Application deadline:* For fall admission, 5/1 for domestic and international students. Applications are processed on a rolling basis. Application fee: $50. Electronic applications accepted. *Expenses:* Tuition: Full-time $27,480; part-time $19,888 per year. Required fees: $50. *Financial support:* In 2006–07, 621 students received support, including 62 research assistantships (averaging $1,487 per year); Federal Work-Study and scholarships/grants also available. Support available to part-time students. Financial award application deadline: 3/15; financial award applicants required to submit FAFSA. *Faculty research:* Comparative law: Japan and India, copyright law, lawyers and pro bono work, choice of entity law, administrative law. Total annual research expenditures: $15,000. *Unit head:* Allen K. Easley, President/Dean, 651-290-6310, Fax: 651-290-6426, E-mail: allen.easley@wmitchell.edu. *Application contact:* Kendra Dane, Assistant Dean and Director of Admissions, 651-290-6343, Fax: 651-290-6414, E-mail: admissions@wmitchell.edu.

Yale University, Yale Law School, New Haven, CT 06520-8215. Offers JD, LL M, MSL, JSD, JD/MA, JD/MAR, JD/MBA, JD/MD, JD/MES, JD/PhD. *Accreditation:* ABA. *Faculty:* 71 full-time, 45 part-time/adjunct. *Students:* 586 full-time (260 women). Average age 24. 3,677 applicants, 7% accepted, 189 enrolled. In 2006, 203 JDs, 29 master's, 10 doctorates awarded. *Entrance requirements:* LSAT. Additional exam requirements/recommendations for international students: Required—TOEFL (minimum score 600 paper-based; 250 computer-based). *Application deadline:* For fall admission, 2/1 for domestic students. Applications are processed on a rolling basis. Application fee: $70. Electronic applications accepted. *Expenses: Contact institution. Financial support:* Application deadline: 3/15; *Unit head:* Harold Hongju Koh, Dean, 203-432-1660. *Application contact:* Asha Rangappa, Assistant Dean, 203-432-4995, E-mail: admissions.law@yale.edu.

Yeshiva University, Benjamin N. Cardozo School of Law, New York, NY 10003-4301. Offers comparative legal thought (LL M); general studies (LL M); intellectual property law (LL M); law (JD). *Accreditation:* ABA. Part-time programs available. *Faculty:* 50 full-time (20 women), 64

Yeshiva University (continued)
part-time/adjunct (15 women). *Students:* 1,007 full-time (492 women), 101 part-time (62 women); includes 228 minority (42 African Americans, 3 American Indian/Alaska Native, 115 Asian Americans or Pacific Islanders, 68 Hispanic Americans), 60 international. Average age 25. 4,785 applicants, 29% accepted, 351 enrolled. In 2006, 362 JDs, 65 master's awarded. *Entrance requirements:* LSAT, 2 letters of recommendation. *Application deadline:* For fall admission, 4/1 for domestic students; for spring admission, 12/1 for domestic students. Applications are processed on a rolling basis. Application fee: $65. Electronic applications accepted. *Expenses: Contact institution. Financial support:* In 2006–07, 944 students received support, including 65 research assistantships; career-related internships or fieldwork, Federal Work-Study, institutionally sponsored loans, scholarships/grants, health care benefits, and tuition waivers (full and partial) also available. Support available to part-time students. Financial award application deadline: 4/15; financial award applicants required to submit FAFSA. *Faculty research:* Corporate and commercial law, intellectual property law, criminal law and litigation, tax, constitutional law and legal history. *Unit head:* David G. Martinidez, Dean of Admissions, 212-790-0274, Fax: 212-790-0482, E-mail: lawinfo@yu.edu.

York University, Faculty of Graduate Studies, Atkinson Faculty of Liberal and Professional Studies, Program in Public Policy, Administration and Law, Toronto, ON M3J 1P3, Canada. Offers MPPAL. *Unit head:* Ian Greene, Head, 416-736-2100 Ext. 77083, E-mail: igreene@yorku.ca.

York University, Faculty of Graduate Studies, Program in Law, Toronto, ON M3J 1P3, Canada. Offers LL B, LL M, PhD, MBA/LL B, MES/LL B, MPA/LL B. Part-time and evening/weekend programs available. *Faculty:* 52 full-time (21 women), 4 part-time/adjunct (0 women). *Students:* 90 full-time (41 women), 312 part-time (145 women). 162 applicants, 59% accepted. In 2006, 7 master's, 8 doctorates awarded. *Degree requirements:* For master's, thesis/dissertation, registration; for doctorate, thesis/dissertation, comprehensive exam, registration. *Entrance requirements:* LSAT. *Application deadline:* For fall admission, 1/31 for domestic students. Application fee: $80. Electronic applications accepted. *Financial support:* In 2006–07, 26 fellowships (averaging $15,533 per year), 32 research assistantships (averaging $4,306 per year), 36 teaching assistantships (averaging $12,096 per year) were awarded; fee bursaries also available. *Unit head:* Liora Salter, Director, 416-736-5046.

Legal and Justice Studies

American University, Washington College of Law, Humphrey Fellows Program in Human Rights and the Law, Washington, DC 20016-8001. Offers Certificate. *Students:* 4 full-time (2 women), 8 part-time (4 women), (all international). Average age 34. *Expenses:* Tuition: Full-time $18,864; part-time $1,048 per credit. Required fees: $380. Tuition and fees vary according to program. *Unit head:* Daniel D. Bradlow, Director, 202-274-4205.

American University, Washington College of Law, Program in International Legal Studies, Washington, DC 20016-8001. Offers LL M, Certificate. Part-time and evening/weekend programs available. *Students:* 29 full-time (11 women), 104 part-time (63 women); includes 6 minority (1 African American, 2 Asian Americans or Pacific Islanders, 3 Hispanic Americans), 93 international. Average age 30. In 2006, 110 degrees awarded. *Entrance requirements:* For master's, JD. Additional exam requirements/recommendations for international students: Required—TOEFL. *Application deadline:* For fall admission, 6/1 for domestic students; for spring admission, 11/1 for domestic students. Applications are processed on a rolling basis. Application fee: $55. *Expenses:* Tuition: Full-time $18,864; part-time $1,048 per credit. Required fees: $380. Tuition and fees vary according to program. *Financial support:* Fellowships, research assistantships, teaching assistantships, career-related internships or fieldwork and tuition waivers (partial) available. Financial award application deadline: 2/15; financial award applicants required to submit FAFSA. *Unit head:* Daniel D. Bradlow, Director, 202-274-4205.

American University, Washington College of Law, Program in Judicial Sciences, Washington, DC 20016-8001. Offers SJD. *Students:* 1 full-time (0 women), 14 part-time (4 women), 12 international. Average age 38. In 2006, 2 degrees awarded. *Entrance requirements:* For doctorate, JD, LL M or LL B. *Application deadline:* Applications are processed on a rolling basis. Application fee: $55. *Expenses:* Tuition: Full-time $18,864; part-time $1,048 per credit. Required fees: $380. Tuition and fees vary according to program. *Unit head:* Daniel D. Bradlow, Director, 202-274-4205.

American University, Washington College of Law, Program in Law and Government, Washington, DC 20016-8001. Offers LL M. *Students:* 7 full-time (3 women), 26 part-time (12 women); includes 11 minority (9 African Americans, 1 Asian American or Pacific Islander, 1 Hispanic American), 6 international. Average age 35. In 2006, 33 degrees awarded. *Degree requirements:* For master's, thesis optional. *Entrance requirements:* For master's, JD. Additional exam requirements/recommendations for international students: Required—TOEFL. *Application deadline:* For fall admission, 6/1 priority date for domestic students; for spring admission, 11/1 priority date for domestic students. Applications are processed on a rolling basis. Application fee: $55. *Expenses:* Tuition: Full-time $18,864; part-time $1,048 per credit. Required fees: $380. Tuition and fees vary according to program. *Financial support:* Fellowships with partial tuition reimbursements, career-related internships or fieldwork and institutionally sponsored loans available. Support available to part-time students. Financial award application deadline: 2/15. *Unit head:* Jamin Raskin, Director, 202-885-4011.

Arizona State University, Division of Graduate Studies, College of Liberal Arts and Sciences, Division of Social Sciences, School of Justice and Social Inquiry, Tempe, AZ 85287. Offers MS, PhD, MA/MS. *Degree requirements:* For master's, thesis optional. *Entrance requirements:* For master's, GRE. Additional exam requirements/recommendations for international students: Required—TOEFL.

Boston University, School of Public Health, Health Law, Bioethics and Human Rights Department, Boston, MA 02215. Offers MPH. *Students:* 16 full-time (13 women), 18 part-time (13 women); includes 4 minority (3 Asian Americans or Pacific Islanders, 1 Hispanic American), 3 international. Average age 25. *Entrance requirements:* For master's, GRE General Test. Additional exam requirements/recommendations for international students: Required—TOEFL or IELTS. *Application deadline:* For fall admission, 2/1 for domestic students; for spring admission, 10/15 for domestic students. Applications are processed on a rolling basis. Application fee: $95. Electronic applications accepted. *Expenses:* Tuition: Full-time $33,330; part-time $1,042 per credit. Required fees: $462; $40. *Financial support:* Career-related internships or fieldwork, Federal Work-Study, institutionally sponsored loans, scholarships/grants, and tuition waivers (partial) available. Support available to part-time students. *Unit head:* Prof. George Annas, Chair, 617-638-4626. *Application contact:* LePhan Quan, Assistant Director of Admissions, 617-638-4640, Fax: 617-638-5299, E-mail: asksph@bu.edu.

Brock University, Faculty of Graduate Studies, Faculty of Social Sciences, Program in Social Justice and Equity Studies, St. Catharines, ON L2S 3A1, Canada. Offers MA. Part-time programs available. *Faculty:* 27 full-time (16 women). *Students:* 16 full-time (11 women), 4 part-time (3 women). 45 applicants, 31% accepted, 9 enrolled. In 2006, 7 degrees awarded. *Degree requirements:* For master's, thesis optional. *Entrance requirements:* For master's, honors degree. Additional exam requirements/recommendations for international students: Required—TOEFL (minimum score 550 paper-based; 213 computer-based; 80 iBT), IELTS (minimum score 7), TWE (minimum score 4). *Application deadline:* For fall admission, 2/1 for domestic students. Application fee: $75. Electronic applications accepted. *Financial support:* Fellowships, research assistantships, teaching assistantships, scholarships/grants, unspecified assistantships, and bursaries available. *Faculty research:* Social inequality, social movements, gender, racism, environmental justice. *Unit head:* Dr. Jane Helleiner, Graduate Program Director, 905-688-5550 Ext. 3711, E-mail: jhellein@brocku.ca.

California University of Pennsylvania, School of Graduate Studies and Research, Department of Professional Studies, California, PA 15419-1394. Offers legal studies (MS), including homeland security, law and public policy. Part-time and evening/weekend programs available. Postbaccalaureate distance learning degree programs offered (no on-campus study). *Faculty:* 3 full-time (0 women), 12 part-time/adjunct (2 women). *Students:* 57 full-time (29 women), 57 part-time (30 women); includes 18 minority (15 African Americans, 3 Hispanic Americans). Average age 35. 74 applicants, 93% accepted, 38 enrolled. In 2006, 31 degrees awarded. *Median time to degree:* Master's–2 years full-time, 2.25 years part-time. *Degree requirements:* For master's, thesis optional. *Entrance requirements:* For master's, interview, minimum QPA of 3.0. Additional exam requirements/recommendations for international students: Required—TOEFL (minimum score 550 paper-based; 213 computer-based; 80 iBT). *Application deadline:* For fall admission, 8/1 priority date for domestic and international students; for winter admission, 12/1 priority date for domestic and international students; for spring admission, 5/1 priority date for domestic and international students. Applications are processed on a rolling basis. Application fee: $25. Electronic applications accepted. *Expenses:* Tuition, state resident: full-time $6,048; part-time $336 per credit. Tuition, nonresident: full-time $9,678; part-time $538 per credit. Required fees: $1,854; $263 per credit. Full-time tuition and fees vary according to course load, campus/location and program. *Financial support:* Career-related internships or fieldwork, scholarships/grants, traineeships, and unspecified assistantships available. Financial award applicants required to submit FAFSA. *Faculty research:* Ethics in political practice, ethics and law, law and morality, St. Thomas Aquinas and crime, police policy. Total annual research expenditures: $10,000. *Unit head:* Dr. Charles Nemeth, Director and Chairperson, 412-565-2328, Fax: 412-565-5082, E-mail: nemeth@cup.edu.

Capital University, School of Nursing, Columbus, OH 43209-2394. Offers administration (MSN); legal studies (MSN); theological studies (MSN); JD/MSN; MBA/MSN; MSN/MTS. *Accreditation:* AACN. Part-time and evening/weekend programs available. *Faculty:* 11 full-time (all women), 2 part-time/adjunct (both women). *Students:* 16 full-time (15 women), 72 part-time (67 women); includes 5 minority (4 African Americans, 1 Asian American or Pacific Islander), 8 international. Average age 41. 20 applicants, 90% accepted, 18 enrolled. In 2006, 14 degrees awarded. *Degree requirements:* For master's, thesis or alternative, registration. *Entrance requirements:* For master's, BSN, current RN license, minimum GPA of 3.0, undergraduate courses in statistics and research. Additional exam requirements/recommendations for international students: Required—TOEFL (minimum score 550 paper-based). *Application deadline:* For fall admission, 3/30 priority date for domestic and international students; for spring admission, 9/30 priority date for domestic and international students. Applications are processed on a rolling basis. Application fee: $25. *Expenses: Contact institution.* Part-time tuition and fees vary according to program. *Financial support:* In 2006–07, 2 students received support. Career-related internships or fieldwork and traineeships available. Financial award applicants required to submit FAFSA. *Faculty research:* Bereavement, wellness/health promotion, emergency cardiac care, critical thinking, complementary and alternative healthcare. *Unit head:* Dr. Elaine F. Haynes, Dean and Professor, 614-236-6703, Fax: 614-236-6157, E-mail: ehaynes@capital.edu. *Application contact:* Dr. Jill D Steuer, Professor and Director of the MSN Program, 614-236-6393, Fax: 614-236-6157, E-mail: jsteuer@capital.edu.

Carleton University, Faculty of Graduate Studies, Faculty of Public Affairs and Management, Department of Law, Ottawa, ON K1S 5B6, Canada. Offers conflict resolution (Certificate); legal studies (MA). *Degree requirements:* For master's, thesis. *Entrance requirements:* For master's, honors degree. Additional exam requirements/recommendations for international students: Required—TOEFL. *Application deadline:* Applications are processed on a rolling basis. Application fee: $75 Canadian dollars. *Financial support:* Fellowships, teaching assistantships, institutionally sponsored loans, scholarships/grants, and unspecified assistantships available. *Faculty research:* Legal and social theory; women, law, and gender relations; law, crime, and social order; political economy of law; international law. *Unit head:* Peter Swan, Chair, 613-520-2600 Ext. 3690, Fax: 613-520-4467, E-mail: law@ccs.carleton.ca. *Application contact:* Ron Saunders, Graduate Supervisor, 613-520-2600 Ext. 3690, Fax: 613-520-4467, E-mail: law@cs.carleton.ca.

Case Western Reserve University, School of Law, Cleveland, OH 44106. Offers law (JD); U.S. legal studies (LL M); JD/CNM; JD/MA; JD/MBA; JD/MD; JD/MNO; JD/MPH; JD/MS; JD/MSSA. *Accreditation:* ABA. Part-time programs available. *Faculty:* 52 full-time (16 women), 130 part-time/adjunct (43 women). *Students:* 670 full-time (273 women), 3 part-time (all women); includes 113 minority (29 African Americans, 2 American Indian/Alaska Native, 73 Asian Americans or Pacific Islanders, 9 Hispanic Americans), 7 international. Average age 25. 2,653 applicants, 28% accepted, 228 enrolled. In 2006, 241 JDs, 34 master's awarded. *Entrance requirements:* LSAT, LSDAS. *Application deadline:* For fall admission, 2/1 priority date for domestic students, 4/1 priority date for international students. Applications are processed on a rolling basis. Application fee: $40. Electronic applications accepted. *Expenses: Contact institution. Financial support:* In 2006–07, 560 students received support. Career-related internships or fieldwork, Federal Work-Study, and scholarships/grants available. Support available to part-time students. Financial award application deadline: 3/15; financial award applicants required to submit FAFSA. *Unit head:* Gary J. Simson, Dean, 216-368-3283. *Application contact:* Alyson Alber, Interim Assistant Dean for Admissions, 216-368-3600, Fax: 216-368-1042, E-mail: lawadmissions@case.edu.

The Catholic University of America, School of Canon Law, Washington, DC 20064. Offers JCD, JCL, JD/JCL. *Faculty:* 6 full-time (1 woman). *Students:* 30 full-time (3 women), 27 part-time (7 women); includes 6 minority (2 African Americans, 1 Asian American or Pacific Islander, 3 Hispanic Americans), 9 international. Average age 42. 42 applicants, 81% accepted, 22 enrolled. *Degree requirements:* For doctorate, 2 foreign languages, thesis/dissertation. *Entrance requirements:* For doctorate, GRE General Test, 2 letters of recommendation. Additional exam requirements/recommendations for international students: Required—TOEFL (minimum score 580 paper-based; 237 computer-based). *Application deadline:* For fall admission, 2/1 priority date for domestic students; for spring admission, 11/15 priority date for domestic students. Applications are processed on a rolling basis. Application fee: $55. Electronic applications accepted. *Expenses:* Tuition: Full-time $27,700; part-time $1,045 per credit hour. Required fees: $1,290. Part-time tuition and fees vary according to campus/location and program. *Financial support:* Fellowships, research assistantships, teaching assistantships, career-related internships or fieldwork, Federal Work-Study, scholarships/grants, tuition waivers (full and partial), and unspecified assistantships available. Support available to part-time students. Financial award application deadline: 2/1; financial award applicants required to submit FAFSA. *Unit head:* Rev. Msgr. Brian Ferme, Dean, 202-319-5492, Fax: 202-319-4187, E-mail: ferme@cua.edu.

Central European University, Graduate Studies, Department of Legal Studies, Budapest, Hungary. Offers comparative constitutional law (LL M); economic and legal studies (LL M, MA); human rights (LL M, MA); international business law (LL M); legal studies (SJD). *Faculty:* 7 full-time (2 women), 3 part-time/adjunct (1 woman). *Students:* 115 full-time (58 women). Average age 26. 579 applicants, 21% accepted, 88 enrolled. In 2006, 40 master's, 4 doctorates awarded. Terminal master's awarded for partial completion of doctoral program. *Median time to degree:* Of those who began their doctoral program in fall 1998, 75% received their degree in 8 years or less. *Degree requirements:* For master's, one foreign language, thesis/dissertation, registration; for doctorate, one foreign language, thesis/dissertation, comprehensive exam, registration. *Entrance requirements:* For master's and doctorate, LSAT, CEU admissions exams. Additional exam requirements/recommendations for international students: Required—TOEFL (minimum score 570 paper-based; 230 computer-based). *Application deadline:* For fall admission, 1/5 for domestic and international students. Application fee: $0. Electronic applications accepted. *Expenses: Contact institution. Financial support:* In 2006–07, 84 students received support, including 65 fellowships with full and partial tuition reimbursements available (averaging $5,000 per year); career-related internships or fieldwork, institutionally sponsored loans, scholarships/grants, and tuition waivers (full and partial) also available. Financial award application deadline: 1/5. *Faculty research:* Institutional, constitutional and human rights in European Union law, biomedical law and reproductive rights, data protection law, Islamic banking and finance. *Unit head:* Dr. Stefan Messmann, Head, 361-327-3274, Fax: 361-327-3198, E-mail: legalst@ceu.hu. *Application contact:* Maria Balla, Coordinator, 361-327-3204, Fax: 361-327-3198, E-mail: ballam@ceu.hu.

College of Charleston, Graduate School, School of Humanities and Social Sciences, Program in Bilingual Legal Interpreting, Charleston, SC 29424-0001. Offers MA, Certificate. *Entrance requirements:* For master's, GRE General Test, Interpreting Aptitude Exam. Electronic applications accepted. Expenses: Contact institution.

College of the Humanities and Sciences, Harrison Middleton University, Graduate Program, Tempe, AZ 85282. Offers education (MA, Ed D); humanities (MA); imaginative literature (MA); jurisprudence (MA); natural science (MA); philosophy and religion (MA); social science (MA). Part-time and evening/weekend programs available. Postbaccalaureate distance learning degree programs offered (no on-campus study). *Faculty:* 17 full-time (7 women), 5 part-time/adjunct (2 women). *Students:* 38 full-time (9 women). In 2006, 10 degrees awarded. Application fee: $50. *Expenses:* Tuition: Part-time $275 per credit hour. *Application contact:* Kathleen Mirabile, Vice-President, Provost, 877-248-6724, Fax: 800-762-1622, E-mail: kmirabile@chumsci.edu.

DePaul University, School of Public Service, Chicago, IL 60604-2287. Offers financial administration management (Certificate); health administration (Certificate); health law and policy (MS); international public services (MS); metropolitan planning (Certificate); public administration (MS); public service management (MS), including association management, fundraising and philanthropy, healthcare administration, higher education administration, metropolitan planning, non-profit administration, public administration, public policy; public services (Certificate); JD/MS; MA/MS. Part-time and evening/weekend programs available. Postbaccalaureate distance learning degree programs offered (minimal on-campus study). *Faculty:* 11 full-time (2 women), 19 part-time/adjunct (16 women). *Students:* 195 full-time (146 women), 132 part-time (89 women); includes 114 minority (58 African Americans, 1 American Indian/Alaska Native, 27 Asian Americans or Pacific Islanders, 28 Hispanic Americans). 140 applicants, 96% accepted, 96 enrolled. In 2006, 89 degrees awarded. *Degree requirements:* For master's, thesis or integrative seminar. *Entrance requirements:* For master's, minimum GPA of 2.7. Additional exam requirements/recommendations for international students: Required—TOEFL (minimum score 550 paper-based; 213 computer-based; 80 iBT), IELTS (minimum score 7). *Application deadline:* Applications are processed on a rolling basis. Application fee: $25. Electronic applications accepted. *Financial support:* In 2006–07, 28 students received support, including 3 research assistantships with full tuition reimbursements available (averaging $7,000 per year); career-related internships or fieldwork, Federal Work-Study, institutionally sponsored loans, scholarships/grants, and tuition waivers (partial) also available. Support available to part-time students. Financial award application deadline: 7/1; financial award applicants required to submit FAFSA. *Faculty research:* Government financing, transportation, leadership, health care, volunteerism and organizational behavior, non-profit organizations. Total annual research expenditures: $20,000. *Unit head:* Dr. J. Patrick Murphy, Director, 312-362-5608, Fax: 312-362-5506, E-mail: jpmurphy@depaul.edu. *Application contact:* Megan B. Balderston, Director of Admissions and Marketing, 312-362-5565, Fax: 312-362-5506, E-mail: pubserv@depaul.edu.

Golden Gate University, School of Law, San Francisco, CA 94105-2968. Offers environmental law (LL M); intellectual property law (LL M); international legal studies (LL M, SJD); law (JD); taxation (LL M); U.S. legal studies (LL M); JD/MBA; JD/PhD. *Accreditation:* ABA. Part-time and evening/weekend programs available. *Faculty:* 49 full-time (22 women), 68 part-time/adjunct (31 women). *Students:* 733 full-time (415 women), 345 part-time (196 women); includes 276 minority (47 African Americans, 4 American Indian/Alaska Native, 168 Asian Americans or Pacific Islanders, 57 Hispanic Americans), 74 international. Average age 28. 2,761 applicants, 49% accepted, 222 enrolled. In 2006, 168 JDs, 113 master's, 3 doctorates awarded. *Entrance requirements:* LSAT. Additional exam requirements/recommendations for international students: Required—TOEFL (minimum score 600 paper-based; 250 computer-based). *Application deadline:* For fall admission, 4/1 for domestic students, 4/15 for international students; for spring admission, 11/15 for international students. Applications are processed on a rolling basis. Application fee: $60. Electronic applications accepted. *Expenses: Contact institution. Financial support:* In 2006–07, 331 students received support, including 3 fellowships (averaging $36,000 per year), 60 research assistantships (averaging $2,400 per year), 30 teaching assistantships (averaging $2,400 per year); career-related internships or fieldwork, Federal Work-Study, institutionally sponsored loans, scholarships/grants, tuition waivers (full and partial), and unspecified assistantships also available. Support available to part-time students. Financial award application deadline: 3/1; financial award applicants required to submit FAFSA. *Faculty research:* International law, intellectual property law, environmental law, real estate, civil rights. *Unit head:* Frederic White, Dean, 415-442-6600, Fax: 415-442-6609. *Application contact:* Sherolyn Hurst, Director of Admissions, 415-442-6630, Fax: 415-442-6631, E-mail: lawadmit@ggu.edu.

Governors State University, College of Arts and Sciences, Program in Political and Justice Studies, University Park, IL 60466-0975. Offers MA. Part-time and evening/weekend programs available. *Students:* 11 full-time, 43 part-time. Average age 35. *Degree requirements:* For master's, thesis or alternative. *Entrance requirements:* For master's, bachelor's degree in related field. *Application deadline:* For fall admission, 7/15 priority date for domestic students; for spring admission, 11/10 for domestic students. Applications are processed on a rolling basis. Application fee: $25. *Expenses:* Tuition, state resident: full-time $4,104; part-time $171 per hour. Tuition, nonresident: part-time $513 per hour. *Financial support:* Research assistantships, Federal Work-Study, institutionally sponsored loans, and scholarships/grants available. Support available to part-time students. Financial award application deadline: 5/1. *Unit head:* Dr. Eric V. Martin, Interim Dean, College of Arts and Sciences, 708-534-4101.

Hofstra University, School of Law, Hempstead, NY 11549. Offers American legal studies (LL M); family law (LL M); international law (LL M); law (JD); JD/MBA. *Accreditation:* ABA. Part-time and evening/weekend programs available. *Faculty:* 58 full-time (21 women), 37 part-time/adjunct (7 women). *Students:* 891 full-time (416 women), 257 part-time (127 women); includes 245 minority (87 African Americans, 2 American Indian/Alaska Native, 92 Asian Americans or Pacific Islanders, 64 Hispanic Americans), 22 international. Average age 26. 4,810 applicants, 43% accepted, 461 enrolled. In 2006, 300 JDs, 10 master's awarded. *Degree requirements:* For JD, set of required courses, number of credits; for master's, thesis, number of credits, select courses required. *Entrance requirements:* LSAT, 1 letter of recommendation, application form, personal statement, undergraduate transcripts. Additional exam requirements/recommendations for international students: Required—TOEFL (minimum score 580 paper-based; 237 computer-based). *Application deadline:* For fall admission, 4/15 priority date for domestic and international students. Applications are processed on a rolling basis. Application fee: $60. Electronic applications accepted. *Expenses: Contact institution. Financial support:* In 2006–07, 591 students received support, including 483 fellowships with tuition reimbursements available (averaging $14,864 per year), 1 research assistantship with full and partial tuition reimbursement available (averaging $3,825 per year); Federal Work-Study, scholarships/grants, health care benefits, and unspecified assistantships also available. Financial award applicants required to submit FAFSA. *Faculty research:* International and comparative law, family law, gender and LGBT issues, legal history, commercial and corporate law. *Unit head:* Nora V. Demleitner, Interim Dean, 516-463-6190, Fax: 516-463-6091, E-mail: lawnvd@hofstra.edu. *Application contact:* Noreen A. O'Brien, Director of Law School Enrollment- Operations, 516-463-5243, Fax: 516-463-6264, E-mail: lawadmissions@hofstra.edu.

Indiana University School of Law-Bloomington, School of Law, Bloomington, IN 47405. Offers comparative law (MCL); law (JD, LL M, SJD); legal studies (Certificate); JD/MA; JD/MBA; JD/MLS; JD/MPA; JD/MPAF; JD/MS; JD/MSES. *Accreditation:* ABA. *Degree requirements:* For JD, research seminar; for master's, thesis (for some programs), practicum; for doctorate, thesis/dissertation. *Entrance requirements:* For JD, master's, and doctorate, LSAT, LSDAS. Additional exam requirements/recommendations for international students: Required—TOEFL (minimum score 560 paper-based; 213 computer-based). *Faculty research:* International law, constitutional law, litigation and dispute resolution, commercial law, communications law.

John Jay College of Criminal Justice of the City University of New York, Graduate Studies, Programs in Criminal Justice, New York, NY 10019-1093. Offers criminal justice (MA, PhD); criminology and deviance (PhD); forensic psychology (PhD); forensic science (PhD); law and philosophy (PhD); organizational behavior (PhD); public policy (PhD). Part-time and evening/weekend programs available. Terminal master's awarded for partial completion of doctoral program. *Degree requirements:* For master's, thesis or alternative; for doctorate, one foreign language, thesis/dissertation. *Entrance requirements:* For master's, GRE General Test, minimum B average; for doctorate, GRE General Test. Additional exam requirements/recommendations for international students: Required—TOEFL (minimum score 500 paper-based; 173 computer-based).

John Marshall Law School, Graduate and Professional Programs, Chicago, IL 60604-3968. Offers comparative legal studies (LL M); employee benefits (LL M, MS); information technology (LL M, MS); intellectual property (LL M); international business and trade (LL M); law (JD); real estate (LL M, MS); taxation (LL M, MS); JD/LL M; JD/MA; JD/MBA; JD/MPA. *Accreditation:* ABA. Part-time and evening/weekend programs available. *Faculty:* 64 full-time (23 women), 113 part-time/adjunct (29 women). *Students:* 1,157 full-time (479 women), 421 part-time (187 women); includes 253 minority (76 African Americans, 10 American Indian/Alaska Native, 101 Asian Americans or Pacific Islanders, 66 Hispanic Americans), 48 international. Average age 27. 3,169 applicants, 37% accepted, 333 enrolled. In 2006, 347 JDs, 69 master's awarded. *Entrance requirements:* For JD, LSAT; for master's, JD. Additional exam requirements/recommendations for international students: Required—TOEFL. *Application deadline:* For fall admission, 3/1 priority date for domestic and international students; for spring admission, 10/15 priority date for domestic and international students. Applications are processed on a rolling basis. Application fee: $60. Electronic applications accepted. *Expenses: Contact institution. Financial support:* In 2006–07, 1,339 students received support. Scholarships/grants and tuition waivers (full and partial) available. Support available to part-time students. Financial award application deadline: 6/1; financial award applicants required to submit FAFSA. *Unit head:* John Corkery, Dean, 312-427-2737. *Application contact:* William B. Powers, Associate Dean of Admission and Student Affairs, 800-537-4280, Fax: 312-427-5136, E-mail: admission@jmls.edu.

Marygrove College, Graduate Division, Program in Social Justice, Detroit, MI 48221-2599. Offers MA.

Marymount University, School of Business Administration, Program in Legal Administration, Arlington, VA 22207-4299. Offers legal administration (MA); paralegal studies (Certificate). Part-time and evening/weekend programs available. *Students:* 3 full-time (all women), 24 part-time (19 women); includes 14 minority (13 African Americans, 1 Hispanic American). Average age 33. 19 applicants, 100% accepted, 13 enrolled. In 2006, 14 master's, 8 other advanced degrees awarded. *Entrance requirements:* For master's, GMAT or GRE General Test, resumé; for Certificate, resumé. Additional exam requirements/recommendations for international students: Required—TOEFL (minimum score 600 paper-based; 250 computer-based). *Application deadline:* Applications are processed on a rolling basis. Application fee: $40. Electronic applications accepted. *Expenses:* Tuition: Full-time $11,160; part-time $620 per credit. Required fees: $113; $630 per credit. *Financial support:* Research assistantships with full tuition reimbursements, career-related internships or fieldwork, scholarships/grants, and unspecified assistantships available. Support available to part-time students. Financial award applicants required to submit FAFSA. *Unit head:* Susan Ninassi, Director, 703-284-5917, Fax: 703-527-3830.

Michigan State University College of Law, Professional Program, East Lansing, MI 48824-1300. Offers American legal system (LL M); intellectual property (LL M); law (JD). *Accreditation:* ABA. Part-time and evening/weekend programs available. *Entrance requirements:* LSAT. Additional exam requirements/recommendations for international students: Required—TOEFL (minimum score 600 paper-based; 250 computer-based). Electronic applications accepted. Expenses: Contact institution. *Faculty research:* International, constitutional, health, tax and environmental law; intellectual property, health law, trial practice, corporate law.

Mississippi College, Graduate School, College of Arts and Sciences, School of Humanities and Social Sciences, Department of History and Political Science, Clinton, MS 39058. Offers administration of justice (MSS); history (M Ed, MA, MSS); paralegal studies (Certificate); political science (MSS); social sciences (M Ed, MSS). Part-time programs available. *Faculty:* 6 full-time (1 woman), 2 part-time/adjunct (0 women). *Students:* 12 full-time (6 women), 24 part-time (19 women); includes 18 minority (17 African Americans, 1 American Indian/Alaska Native), 1 international. Average age 30. In 2006, 13 master's, 1 other advanced degree awarded. *Degree requirements:* For master's, one foreign language, thesis (for some programs), comprehensive exam, registration. *Entrance requirements:* For master's, GRE or NTE, minimum GPA of 2.5. Additional exam requirements/recommendations for international students: Recommended—IELTS. *Application deadline:* For fall admission, 8/15 priority date for domestic students. Applications are processed on a rolling basis. Application fee: $25. Electronic applications accepted. *Expenses:* Tuition: Full-time $7,290; part-time $405 per hour. Required fees: $150 per term. Tuition and fees vary according to campus/location and program. *Financial support:* Teaching assistantships, Federal Work-Study, scholarships/grants, and unspecified assistantships available. Support available to part-time students. Financial award application deadline: 4/1; financial award applicants required to submit FAFSA. *Unit head:* Dr. Kirk Ford, Chair, 601-925-3326, E-mail: ford@mc.edu.

Montclair State University, The Graduate School, College of Humanities and Social Sciences, Department of Justice Studies, Montclair, NJ 07043-1624. Offers dispute resolution (MA); governance, compliance and regulation (MA); law office management and technology (MA); paralegal (Certificate). Part-time and evening/weekend programs available. *Faculty:* 8 full-time (6 women), 14 part-time/adjunct (5 women). *Students:* 19 full-time (16 women), 54 part-time (47 women); includes 30 minority (14 African Americans, 5 Asian Americans or Pacific Islanders, 11 Hispanic Americans), 3 international. 36 applicants, 53% accepted, 14 enrolled. In 2006, 12 master's, 14 other advanced degrees awarded. *Degree requirements:* For master's, thesis or alternative, comprehensive exam. *Entrance requirements:* For master's, GRE General Test, minimum undergraduate GPA of 2.75, 2 letters of recommendation; for Certificate, 2 letters of recommendation. Additional exam requirements/recommendations for international students: Required—TOEFL (minimum score 83 computer-based). *Application deadline:* For fall admission, 6/1 for international students; for spring admission, 10/1 for international students. Applications are processed on a rolling basis. Application fee: $60.

Legal and Justice Studies

Montclair State University (continued)
Electronic applications accepted. *Expenses:* Tuition, state resident: part-time $450 per credit. Tuition, nonresident: part-time $682 per credit. Tuition and fees vary according to degree level and program. *Financial support:* Research assistantships with full tuition reimbursements, Federal Work-Study, scholarships/grants, and unspecified assistantships available. Support available to part-time students. Financial award application deadline: 3/1. *Unit head:* Dr. Norma Connolly, Chairperson, 973-655-4152, E-mail: connolyn@mail.montclair.edu. *Application contact:* Prof. Jack Baldwin-LeClair, Adviser, E-mail: leclairj@mail.montclair.edu.

New York University, Graduate School of Arts and Science and School of Law, Institute for Law and Society, New York, NY 10012-1019. Offers MA, PhD, JD/MA, JD/PhD. *Faculty:* 3 full-time (1 woman). *Students:* 19 full-time (15 women), 1 part-time; includes 2 minority (both Asian Americans or Pacific Islanders), 5 international. Average age 32. 52 applicants, 10% accepted, 3 enrolled. In 2006, 2 master's, 2 doctorates awarded. *Degree requirements:* For doctorate, one foreign language, thesis/dissertation. *Entrance requirements:* For doctorate, GRE. Additional exam requirements/recommendations for international students: Required—TOEFL. *Application deadline:* For fall admission, 12/15 for domestic students. Application fee: $80. *Expenses:* Tuition: Part-time $1,080 per unit. Required fees: $56 per unit. $329 per term. Tuition and fees vary according to program. *Financial support:* Fellowships with tuition reimbursements, teaching assistantships with tuition reimbursements, career-related internships or fieldwork, Federal Work-Study, institutionally sponsored loans, scholarships/grants, health care benefits, and unspecified assistantships available. Financial award application deadline: 12/15; financial award applicants required to submit FAFSA. *Faculty research:* Politics of law, law and social policy, law in comparative global perspective, rights and social movements. *Unit head:* Lewis Kornhauser, Director, 212-998-8536, Fax: 212-995-4034, E-mail: law.society@nyu.edu. *Application contact:* Jo Dixon, Director of Graduate Studies, 212-998-8536, Fax: 212-995-4034, E-mail: law.society@nyu.edu.

Northeastern University, College of Arts and Sciences, Program in Law, Policy, and Society, Boston, MA 02115-5096. Offers MS, PhD, JD/PhD. Part-time and evening/weekend programs available. *Faculty:* 24 full-time (9 women). *Students:* 43 full-time (31 women), 45 part-time (23 women). Average age 40. 72 applicants, 25% accepted. In 2006, 3 master's, 6 doctorates awarded. *Degree requirements:* For master's, comprehensive exam; for doctorate, thesis/dissertation, comprehensive exam. *Entrance requirements:* For master's, GRE General Test; for doctorate, GRE General Test or LSAT. *Application deadline:* For fall admission, 2/1 for domestic students. Application fee: $50. *Financial support:* In 2006–07, 15 fellowships with tuition reimbursements, 4 teaching assistantships with tuition reimbursements (averaging $13,624 per year) were awarded; research assistantships with tuition reimbursements, tuition waivers (full and partial) and unspecified assistantships also available. Financial award application deadline: 2/1; financial award applicants required to submit FAFSA. *Faculty research:* Policy issues in health, crime, and labor; urban studies; education; law and environmental issues; economic development, international trade and law. *Unit head:* Dr. Joan Fitzgerald, Director, 617-373-3644, Fax: 617-373-4691, E-mail: jo.fitzgerald@neu.edu.

Nova Southeastern University, Shepard Broad Law Center, Program in Health Law, Fort Lauderdale, FL 33314-7796. Offers MS. Part-time and evening/weekend programs available. Postbaccalaureate distance learning degree programs offered (minimal on-campus study). *Faculty:* 12 full-time (5 women), 11 part-time/adjunct (5 women). *Students:* 66 full-time (52 women); includes 30 minority (19 African Americans, 2 Asian Americans or Pacific Islanders, 9 Hispanic Americans). Average age 43. 66 applicants, 59% accepted, 35 enrolled. In 2006, 24 degrees awarded. *Entrance requirements:* Additional exam requirements/recommendations for international students: Required—TOEFL (minimum score 600 paper-based; 250 computer-based). *Application deadline:* For fall admission, 5/31 priority date for domestic and international students. Applications are processed on a rolling basis. Application fee: $50. Electronic applications accepted. *Financial support:* In 2006–07, 44 students received support. Tuition waivers (full and partial) available. Financial award application deadline: 7/4; financial award applicants required to submit FAFSA. *Unit head:* William Adams, Associate Dean, 954-262-6331, Fax: 954-262-6301, E-mail: adamsb@nsu.law.nova.edu. *Application contact:* Jennifer McIntyre, Assistant Dean for Online Programs, 954-262-6079, Fax: 954-262-6301, E-mail: mcintyrej@nsu.law.nova.edu.

Pace University, School of Law, White Plains, NY 10603. Offers comparative legal studies (LL M); environmental law (LL M, SJD); law (JD); JD/MA; JD/MBA; JD/MEM; JD/MPA; JD/MS. *Accreditation:* ABA. Part-time and evening/weekend programs available. *Faculty:* 44 full-time, 56 part-time/adjunct. *Students:* 511 full-time (305 women), 279 part-time (149 women); includes 138 minority (24 African Americans, 1 American Indian/Alaska Native, 73 Asian Americans or Pacific Islanders, 40 Hispanic Americans), 15 international. Average age 26. 2,935 applicants, 31% accepted, 273 enrolled. In 2006, 224 JDs, 20 master's awarded. *Entrance requirements:* For JD, LSAT; for doctorate, LL M in comparative or environmental law. Additional exam requirements/recommendations for international students: Required—TOEFL (minimum score 600 paper-based; 250 computer-based); Recommended—TWE. *Application deadline:* For fall admission, 3/1 priority date for domestic students. Applications are processed on a rolling basis. Application fee: $65. Electronic applications accepted. *Expenses: Contact institution. Financial support:* Career-related internships or fieldwork, Federal Work-Study, institutionally sponsored loans, and scholarships/grants available. Support available to part-time students. Financial award application deadline: 2/1; financial award applicants required to submit FAFSA. *Faculty research:* Torts products liability, international environmental law, land use law, prosecutorial misconduct, nonprofit corporation law, voting rights issues. *Unit head:* Stephen J. Friedman, Dean, 914-422-4407, E-mail: sfriedman@law.pace.edu. *Application contact:* Cathy Alexander, Director of Law Admissions, 914-422-4210, Fax: 914-989-8714, E-mail: calexander@law.pace.edu.

See Close-Up on page 2107.

Prairie View A&M University, Graduate School, College of Juvenile Justice and Psychology, Prairie View, TX 77446-0519. Offers clinical adolescent psychology (PhD); juvenile forensic psychology (MSJFP); juvenile justice (MSJJ, PhD). Part-time and evening/weekend programs available. *Faculty:* 11 full-time (4 women), 6 part-time/adjunct (2 women). *Students:* 45 full-time (33 women), 29 part-time (19 women); includes 54 minority (48 African Americans, 1 American Indian/Alaska Native, 1 Asian American or Pacific Islander, 4 Hispanic Americans). Average age 26. In 2006, 4 master's, 1 doctorate awarded. *Degree requirements:* For master's, thesis (for some programs), comprehensive exam (for some programs); for doctorate, thesis/dissertation, comprehensive exam. *Entrance requirements:* For master's, GRE, minimum GPA of 2.75; for doctorate, GRE, previous course work in clinical adolescent psychology, minimum GPA of 3.5. Additional exam requirements/recommendations for international students: Required—TOEFL. *Application deadline:* For fall admission, 3/1 for domestic students; for spring admission, 10/1 for domestic students. Applications are processed on a rolling basis. Application fee: $50. *Financial support:* In 2006–07, 18 students received support, including teaching assistantships (averaging $18,000 per year); research assistantships, career-related internships or fieldwork, Federal Work-Study, institutionally sponsored loans, tuition waivers (full and partial), and unspecified assistantships also available. Support available to part-time students. Financial award application deadline: 3/1; financial award applicants required to submit FAFSA. *Faculty research:* Juvenile justice, juvenile forensic psychology, teen court, graduate education, capital punishment. *Unit head:* Dr. Elaine Rodney, Dean, 936-261-520, Fax: 936-261-5252. *Application contact:* Sandy Siegmund, Executive Secretary, Graduate Program, 936-857-3831, Fax: 936-857-3846, E-mail: sandy_siegmund@pvamu.edu.

Quinnipiac University, School of Law, Health Law Program, Hamden, CT 06518-1940. Offers LL M. *Faculty:* 32 full-time (12 women), 33 part-time/adjunct (8 women). *Students:* 318 full-time (166 women), 146 part-time (68 women); includes 51 minority (11 African Americans, 3 American Indian/Alaska Native, 24 Asian Americans or Pacific Islanders, 13 Hispanic Americans), 2 international. 2,865 applicants, 28% accepted, 127 enrolled. *Expenses:* Tuition: Part-time $675 per credit. Required fees: $30 per credit. *Application contact:* Edwin Wilkes, Executive Dean of Law School Admissions, 203-582-3400, Fax: 203-582-3339, E-mail: ladm@quinnipiac.edu.

Regis University, School for Professional Studies, MA Program, Denver, CO 80221-1099. Offers fine arts administration (Certificate); language and communication (MA); mediation (Certificate); psychology (MA); social justice, peace, and reconciliation (Certificate); social science (MA); technical communication (Certificate). Program also offered in Henderson and Las Vegas (Summerlin), NV. Part-time and evening/weekend programs available. Postbaccalaureate distance learning degree programs offered (minimal on-campus study). *Faculty:* 93. *Students:* Average age 35. In 2006, 38 degrees awarded. *Degree requirements:* For master's, thesis, research project. *Entrance requirements:* For master's, resumé, recommendations. Additional exam requirements/recommendations for international students: Required—TOEFL, TWE (minimum score 5). *Application deadline:* For fall admission, 8/13 priority date for domestic students, 7/13 priority date for international students; for winter admission, 10/8 priority date for domestic students, 9/8 priority date for international students; for spring admission, 12/17 priority date for domestic students, 11/17 for international students. Applications are processed on a rolling basis. Application fee: $75. Electronic applications accepted. *Expenses: Contact institution. Financial support:* Federal Work-Study available. Support available to part-time students. Financial award application deadline: 3/15; financial award applicants required to submit FAFSA. *Faculty research:* Independent/nonresidential graduate study: new methods and models, adult learning and the capstone experience. *Unit head:* Dr. Robert Collins, Chair, 303-458-4302, Fax: 303-964-5538. *Application contact:* Graduate Admissions, 800-677-9270 Ext. 4080, Fax: 303-964-5538, E-mail: masters@regis.edu.

The Richard Stockton College of New Jersey, Graduate Programs, Paralegal Certificate Program, Pomona, NJ 08240-0195. Offers Certificate. *Faculty:* 9 part-time/adjunct (5 women). *Students:* Average age 30.Application fee: $50. *Expenses:* Tuition, state resident: full-time $9,746. Tuition, nonresident: full-time $14,462. Required fees: $2,340. *Unit head:* Melanie Contreras, Coordinator, 609-652-4298, E-mail: paralegal.studies@stockton.edu. *Application contact:* Alison Henry, Associate Director of Admissions, 609-652-4261, Fax: 609-626-5541, E-mail: admissions@stockton.edu.

Rutgers, The State University of New Jersey, New Brunswick, Graduate School, Program in Political Science, New Brunswick, NJ 08901-1281. Offers American political institutions (PhD); comparative politics (PhD); international relations (PhD); political economy (PhD); political theory (PhD); public law (PhD); women and politics (PhD). *Degree requirements:* For doctorate, one foreign language, thesis/dissertation, comprehensive exam. *Entrance requirements:* For doctorate, GRE General Test. Additional exam requirements/recommendations for international students: Required—TOEFL.

St. John's University, College of Professional Studies, Department of Criminal Justice and Legal Studies, Queens, NY 11439. Offers MPS. *Faculty:* 17 full-time (6 women), 43 part-time/adjunct (10 women). *Students:* 10 full-time (7 women), 58 part-time (29 women); includes 25 minority (11 African Americans, 1 American Indian/Alaska Native, 3 Asian Americans or Pacific Islanders, 10 Hispanic Americans), 1 international. Average age 30. 39 applicants, 69% accepted, 15 enrolled. In 2006, 50 degrees awarded. *Degree requirements:* For master's, comprehensive exam. *Entrance requirements:* Additional exam requirements/recommendations for international students: Required—TOEFL (minimum score 500 paper-based; 173 computer-based). *Application deadline:* For fall admission, 5/1 priority date for domestic and international students; for spring admission, 11/1 priority date for domestic and international students. Applications are processed on a rolling basis. Application fee: $40. Electronic applications accepted. *Expenses:* Tuition: Full-time $18,480; part-time $770 per credit. Required fees: $125 per semester. Tuition and fees vary according to program. *Financial support:* Research assistantships available. *Faculty research:* Fire litigation, forensic psychology, organized crime, probation and parole, leadership studies, criminal justice ethics and integration control. *Unit head:* Dr. Angelo L. Pisani, Chair, 718-390-4317, E-mail: pisania@stjohns.edu. *Application contact:* Br. Shamus McGrenra, Senior Associate Director, Office of Admission, 718-990-1601, Fax: 718-990-2346, E-mail: gradhelp@stjohns.edu.

Salve Regina University, Graduate Studies, Programs in Administration of Justice, Newport, RI 02840-4192. Offers justice and homeland security (MS); law enforcement leadership (MS, MSM). *Unit head:* Dr. Daniel Knight, Director, 401-341-3255, E-mail: knightd@salve.edu. *Application contact:* Karen E. Johnson, Graduate Admissions Counselor, 401-341-2153, Fax: 401-341-2973, E-mail: johnsoke@salve.edu.

San Francisco State University, Division of Graduate Studies, College of Education, Department of Administration and Interdisciplinary Studies, San Francisco, CA 94132-1722. Offers adult education (MA Ed, AC); educational administration (MA, AC); equity and social justice (AC); equity and social justice in education (MA Ed); special interest (MA Ed). Part-time programs available. *Students:* 93 (72 women). *Entrance requirements:* For master's, minimum GPA of 2.5 in last 60 units. *Application deadline:* For fall admission, 11/30 priority date for domestic students. Applications are processed on a rolling basis. Application fee: $55. *Financial support:* Application deadline: 3/1. *Unit head:* Dr. Marilyn Stepney, Chair, 415-338-2369, E-mail: mstepney@sfsu.edu. *Application contact:* Anarose Schelstrate, Administrative Office Coordinator, 415-338-1479, E-mail: aschels@sfsu.edu.

Southern Illinois University Carbondale, Graduate School, Program in Legal Studies, Carbondale, IL 62901-4701. Offers general law (MLS); health law and policy (MLS). *Students:* 16 applicants, 38% accepted, 3 enrolled. In 2006, 1 degree awarded. *Unit head:* Thomas Britton, Director, 618-453-8980, E-mail: llmadmit@siu.edu. *Application contact:* Barb Smith, Office Specialist, 618-453-8858, E-mail: mlsadmit@siu.edu.

Southern Illinois University Carbondale, School of Law, Carbondale, IL 62901-6804. Offers general law (LL M); health law and policy (LL M); law (JD); legal studies (MLS), including general law, health law and policy; JD/M Acc; JD/MBA; JD/MD; JD/MPA; JD/MSW; JD/PhD. *Accreditation:* ABA. Part-time programs available. *Faculty:* 23 full-time (11 women), 12 part-time/adjunct (6 women). *Students:* 380 full-time (143 women), 3 part-time (1 woman); includes 29 minority (9 African Americans, 1 American Indian/Alaska Native, 12 Asian Americans or Pacific Islanders, 7 Hispanic Americans), 2 international. Average age 27. 802 applicants, 50% accepted, 158 enrolled. In 2006, 107 degrees awarded. *Entrance requirements:* LSAT. Additional exam requirements/recommendations for international students: Required—TOEFL (minimum score 600 paper-based). *Application deadline:* For fall admission, 3/1 for domestic and international students. Applications are processed on a rolling basis. Application fee: $50. Electronic applications accepted. *Expenses: Contact institution. Financial support:* In 2006–07, 326 students received support. Career-related internships or fieldwork, Federal Work-Study, institutionally sponsored loans, scholarships/grants, and health care benefits available. Support available to part-time students. Financial award application deadline: 4/1; financial award applicants required to submit FAFSA. *Faculty research:* Health care law, criminal law, environmental law, international law, tort reform. *Unit head:* Peter C. Alexander, Dean, 618-453-8761, Fax: 618-453-8769. *Application contact:* Michael P. Ruiz, Assistant Dean for Admissions, 618-453-8858, Fax: 618-453-8769, E-mail: lawadmit@siu.edu.

State University of New York at Binghamton, Graduate School, School of Arts and Sciences, Social, Legal and Legal Philosophy Program, Binghamton, NY 13902-6000. Offers MA, PhD. Application fee: $60. *Unit head:* Dr. Bat-Ami Bar-On, Chairperson, 607-777-6198, E-mail: ami@binghamton.edu.

Texas State University-San Marcos, Graduate School, College of Liberal Arts, Department of Political Science, Program in Legal Studies, San Marcos, TX 78666. Offers MA. *Students:* 34 full-time (25 women), 50 part-time (39 women); includes 35 minority (11 African Americans, 2 Asian Americans or Pacific Islanders, 22 Hispanic Americans), 1 international. Average age 32. 23 applicants, 100% accepted, 17 enrolled. In 2006, 21 degrees awarded. *Application deadline:* For fall admission, 6/15 priority date for domestic students, 6/1 priority date for international students; for spring admission, 10/15 priority date for domestic students, 10/1 priority date for international students. Applications are processed on a rolling basis. Application fee: $40 ($90 for international students). *Financial support:* In 2006–07, 59 students received support. *Unit head:* Dr. Terry L. Hull, Graduate Advisor, 512-245-3286, Fax: 512-245-7815, E-mail: th10@swt.edu.

Université Laval, Faculty of Law, Program in Notarial Law, Québec, QC G1K 7P4, Canada. Offers Diploma. Part-time programs available. *Entrance requirements:* For degree, knowledge of French. Electronic applications accepted.

University of Baltimore, Graduate School, The Yale Gordon College of Liberal Arts, Division of Legal, Ethical and Historical Studies, Program in Legal and Ethical Studies, Baltimore, MD 21201-5779. Offers MA. Part-time and evening/weekend programs available. *Faculty:* 14 full-time (7 women), 12 part-time/adjunct (4 women). *Students:* 12 full-time (7 women), 57 part-time (41 women); includes 47 minority (43 African Americans, 1 Asian American or Pacific Islander, 3 Hispanic Americans). Average age 35. 30 applicants, 83% accepted, 19 enrolled. In 2006, 22 degrees awarded. *Degree requirements:* For master's, thesis optional. *Entrance requirements:* For master's, minimum GPA of 3.0. Additional exam requirements/recommendations for international students: Required—TOEFL (minimum score 550 paper-based; 213 computer-based). *Application deadline:* For fall admission, 8/1 for domestic students, 6/1 for international students; for spring admission, 12/1 for domestic students, 11/1 for international students. Applications are processed on a rolling basis. Application fee: $45. Electronic applications accepted. *Expenses:* Tuition, state resident: full-time $5,322; part-time $591 per credit. Tuition, nonresident: full-time $7,527; part-time $830 per credit. *Financial support:* In 2006–07, 3 research assistantships were awarded; fellowships, career-related internships or fieldwork and Federal Work-Study also available. Support available to part-time students. Financial award application deadline: 4/1; financial award applicants required to submit FAFSA. *Faculty research:* Morality in law and economics, religion in lawmaking, comparative legal history, law and social change, critical issues in constitutional law, theories of justice. Total annual research expenditures: $24,077. *Unit head:* Dr. Jeffrey Sawyer, Director, Program in Legal Studies, 410-837-5320, E-mail: jsawyer@ubalt.edu. *Application contact:* Dean Dreibelbis, Assistant Director, Office of Graduate Admissions, 410-837-6565, Fax: 410-837-4793, E-mail: gradadmissions@ubalt.edu.

University of Calgary, Faculty of Law, Programs in Natural Resources, Energy and Environmental Law, Calgary, AB T2N 1N4, Canada. Offers LL M, Graduate Certificate. *Entrance requirements:* Additional exam requirements/recommendations for international students: Required—TOEFL. *Application deadline:* For fall admission, 2/1 for domestic and international students. Applications are processed on a rolling basis. *Application contact:* Karen Argento, Admissions and Student Affairs Officer, 403-220-8154, Fax: 403-210-9662, E-mail: kargento@ucalgary.ca.

University of California, Berkeley, School of Law, Program in Jurisprudence and Social Policy, Berkeley, CA 94720-1500. Offers PhD. *Degree requirements:* For doctorate, one foreign language, thesis/dissertation, oral qualifying exam. *Entrance requirements:* For doctorate, GRE General Test, sample of written work, letters of recommendation. Electronic applications accepted. Expenses: Contact institution. *Faculty research:* Law and philosophy, legal history, law and economics, law and political science, law and sociology.

University of Denver, College of Law, Program in Legal Administration, Denver, CO 80204. Offers MSLA, Certificate. Part-time and evening/weekend programs available. *Students:* 21 full-time (13 women), 22 part-time (14 women); includes 8 minority (2 African Americans, 3 Asian Americans or Pacific Islanders, 3 Hispanic Americans), 2 international. Average age 30. 37 applicants, 100% accepted. In 2006, 23 degrees awarded. *Degree requirements:* For master's, internship. *Entrance requirements:* For master's, GMAT, GRE, or LSAT. *Application deadline:* Applications are processed on a rolling basis. Application fee: $25. Electronic applications accepted. *Expenses:* Tuition: Full-time $29,628; part-time $823 per credit. *Financial support:* Career-related internships or fieldwork and Federal Work-Study available. Support available to part-time students. Financial award application deadline: 2/15; financial award applicants required to submit FAFSA. *Unit head:* Hope Kentnor, Interim Director, 305-871-6308. *Application contact:* Lucy Daberkow, Admissions, 303-871-6324, Fax: 303-871-6378, E-mail: msln@law.du.edu.

University of Illinois at Springfield, Graduate Programs, College of Public Affairs and Administration, Program in Legal Studies, Springfield, IL 62703-5407. Offers MA. Part-time and evening/weekend programs available. Postbaccalaureate distance learning degree programs offered. *Faculty:* 5 full-time (3 women). *Students:* 12 full-time (9 women), 15 part-time (12 women); includes 3 minority (2 African Americans, 1 Hispanic American), 2 international. Average age 30. 12 applicants, 75% accepted, 9 enrolled. In 2006, 6 degrees awarded. *Degree requirements:* For master's, thesis or seminar, thesis optional. *Entrance requirements:* For master's, writing sample, minimum undergraduate GPA of 3.0, at least 1 undergraduate course in American government. Additional exam requirements/recommendations for international students: Required—TOEFL (minimum score 550 paper-based; 213 computer-based). *Application deadline:* Applications are processed on a rolling basis. Application fee: $50 ($60 for international students). Electronic applications accepted. *Expenses:* Tuition, state resident: full-time $4,722; part-time $197 per credit hour. Tuition, nonresident: full-time $12,558; part-time $523 per credit hour. Required fees: $1,614; $8 per credit hour. $597 per term. *Financial support:* In 2006–07, research assistantships with full tuition reimbursements (averaging $7,425 per year), teaching assistantships with full tuition reimbursements (averaging $7,425 per year) were awarded; career-related internships or fieldwork, Federal Work-Study, scholarships/grants, health care benefits, and unspecified assistantships also available. Support available to part-time students. Financial award application deadline: 11/15; financial award applicants required to submit FAFSA. *Faculty research:* Labor law, First Amendment issues, civil practice, constitutional law, civil rights law. *Unit head:* Kathryn E. Eisenhart, Program Administrator, 217-206-7882, Fax: 217-206-7807, E-mail: eisenhart.kathryn@uis.edu.

University of Manitoba, Faculty of Law, Winnipeg, MB R3T 2N2, Canada. Offers interdisciplinary studies (MA); law (LL M). *Degree requirements:* For master's, thesis, registration. *Entrance requirements:* For master's, thesis proposal. Additional exam requirements/recommendations for international students: Required—TOEFL (minimum score 600 paper-based; 240 computer-based). Electronic applications accepted. *Faculty research:* Constitutional law, legal history, human rights laws, international trade law, medicine and law.

University of Nebraska–Lincoln, College of Law, Program in Legal Studies, Lincoln, NE 68588. Offers MLS. *Entrance requirements:* For master's, GRE or LSAT. Additional exam requirements/recommendations for international students: Required—TOEFL (minimum score 600 paper-based; 250 computer-based). Electronic applications accepted.

University of Nevada, Reno, Graduate School, Interdisciplinary Program in Judicial Studies, Reno, NV 89557. Offers MJS. Offered jointly with the National Judicial College and the National Council of Juvenile and Family Court Judges. Part-time programs available. *Faculty:* 11 part-time/adjunct (2 women). *Students:* 26 applicants, 77% accepted. In 2006, 3 master's awarded. *Degree requirements:* For master's, thesis. *Entrance requirements:* For master's, sitting judge, law degree from an accredited school. Additional exam requirements/recommendations for international students: Required—TOEFL. *Application deadline:* For fall admission, 3/1 for domestic students; for spring admission, 11/1 for domestic students. Applications are processed on a rolling basis. Application fee: $40. *Expenses: Contact institution. Financial support:* Fellowships available. Support available to part-time students. *Faculty research:* Jury research, capital punishment, expert testimony, environmental law, medical issues. *Unit head:* Dr. James T. Richardson, Graduate Program Director, 775-784-6270, Fax: 775-784-1300.

University of New Hampshire, Graduate School, College of Liberal Arts, Department of Justice Studies, Durham, NH 03824. Offers MA. Part-time programs available. *Faculty:* 29 full-time. *Students:* 17 full-time (8 women), 14 part-time (9 women); includes 1 minority (Hispanic American) Average age 26. 21 applicants, 100% accepted, 11 enrolled. In 2006, 12 degrees awarded. *Degree requirements:* For master's, thesis optional. *Entrance requirements:* For master's, GRE. Additional exam requirements/recommendations for international students: Required—TOEFL (minimum score 550 paper-based; 213 computer-based); Recommended—TWE. *Application deadline:* For fall admission, 4/1 for domestic students, 2/15 priority date for international students; for winter admission, 12/1 for domestic students; for spring admission, 4/1 for domestic students. Applications are processed on a rolling basis. Application fee: $60. Electronic applications accepted. *Expenses:* Tuition, state resident: full-time $8,540; part-time $474 per credit hour. Tuition, nonresident: full-time $20,990; part-time $862 per credit hour. Required fees: $1,343; $356 per term. Tuition and fees vary according to course load, program and reciprocity agreements. *Financial support:* Fellowships, research assistantships, teaching assistantships, career-related internships or fieldwork, Federal Work-Study, scholarships/grants, and tuition waivers (full and partial) available. Support available to part-time students. Financial award application deadline: 2/15. *Unit head:* Dr. Ellen Cohn, Chairperson, 603-862-3197, E-mail: ellen.cohn@unh.edu. *Application contact:* Deborah Briand, Administrative Assistant, 603-862-1716, E-mail: justice.studies@unh.edu.

University of Pittsburgh, School of Law, Master of Studies in Law Program, Pittsburgh, PA 15260. Offers business law (MSL), including commercial law, corporate law, general business law, international business, tax law; constitutional law (MSL); criminal justice (MSL); disabilities law (MSL); dispute resolution (MSL); education law (MSL); elder and estate planning law (MSL); employment and labor law (MSL); environment and real estate law (MSL); family law (MSL); general law and jurisprudence (MSL); health law (MSL); intellectual property and technology (MSL); international and comparative law (MSL); personal injury and civil litigation (MSL); regulatory law (MSL); self-designed (MSL). Part-time programs available. *Faculty:* 45 full-time (15 women), 77 part-time/adjunct (20 women). *Students:* 7 full-time (2 women), 17 part-time (12 women); includes 3 minority (1 African American, 2 Asian Americans or Pacific Islanders). Average age 31. In 2006, 7 degrees awarded. *Entrance requirements:* Additional exam requirements/recommendations for international students: Required—TOEFL (minimum score 600 paper-based; 250 computer-based; 100 iBT). *Application deadline:* For fall admission, 6/30 for domestic students, 5/31 for international students. Applications are processed on a rolling basis. Application fee: $0. *Faculty research:* Law, health law, business law, contracts. *Unit head:* Prof. Alan Meisel, Director, 412-648-1384, Fax: 412-648-2649, E-mail: meisel@pitt.edu. *Application contact:* Bethann Pischke, Administrative Coordinator, 412-648-7120, Fax: 412-648-2649, E-mail: pischke@pitt.edu.

University of Pittsburgh, School of Law, Program in Health Law, Pittsburgh, PA 15260. Offers MA, Certificate. *Faculty:* 46 full-time (16 women), 85 part-time/adjunct (23 women). *Students:* 29 full-time (16 women). *Application deadline:* For spring admission, 7/31 for domestic students. Applications are processed on a rolling basis. *Unit head:* Prof. Alan Meisel, Professor and Director, Health Law Certificate Program, 412-648-1384, Fax: 412-648-2649, E-mail: meisel@pitt.edu. *Application contact:* Bethann Pischke, Program Administrator, 412-648-7120, Fax: 412-648-2649, E-mail: pischke@pitt.edu.

University of San Diego, School of Law, San Diego, CA 92110. Offers business and corporate law (LL M); comparative law (LL M); general studies (LL M); international law (LL M); law (JD); taxation (LL M, Diploma); JD/IMBA; JD/MA; JD/MBA. *Accreditation:* ABA. Part-time and evening/weekend programs available. *Faculty:* 53 full-time (20 women), 44 part-time/adjunct (9 women). *Students:* 796 full-time (363 women), 333 part-time (151 women); includes 324 minority (34 African Americans, 11 American Indian/Alaska Native, 165 Asian Americans or Pacific Islanders, 114 Hispanic Americans), 21 international. Average age 27. 4,818 applicants, 31% accepted, 342 enrolled. In 2006, 313 JDs, 59 master's awarded. *Entrance requirements:* For JD, LSAT; for master's, JD, LLB or equivalent from an ABA-accredited law school. Additional exam requirements/recommendations for international students: Required—TOEFL. *Application deadline:* For fall admission, 2/1 priority date for domestic students. Applications are processed on a rolling basis. Application fee: $50. Electronic applications accepted. *Expenses: Contact institution. Financial support:* In 2006–07, 60 research assistantships were awarded; career-related internships or fieldwork, Federal Work-Study, institutionally sponsored loans, and scholarships/grants also available. Support available to part-time students. Financial award application deadline: 3/1; financial award applicants required to submit FAFSA. *Unit head:* Kevin Cole, Dean, 619-260-2330, Fax: 619-260-2218. *Application contact:* Carl J. Eging, Director of Admissions and Financial Aid, 619-260-4528, Fax: 619-260-2218, E-mail: eging@sandiego.edu.

University of the Pacific, McGeorge School of Law, Sacramento, CA 95817. Offers government and public policy (LL M); international law (LL M); international waters resources law (LL M); law (JD); transnational business practice (LL M); JD/MBA; JD/MPPA. *Accreditation:* ABA. Part-time and evening/weekend programs available. *Faculty:* 39 full-time (12 women), 31 part-time/adjunct (7 women). *Students:* 686 full-time, 321 part-time. Average age 24. 3,621 applicants, 31% accepted. In 2006, 261 JDs, 19 master's awarded. *Degree requirements:* For master's, thesis (for some programs); for doctorate, thesis/dissertation. *Entrance requirements:* For JD, LSAT; for master's, JD; for doctorate, LL M. Additional exam requirements/recommendations for international students: Required—TOEFL (minimum score 600 paper-based). *Application deadline:* For fall admission, 5/1 priority date for domestic students. Applications are processed on a rolling basis. Application fee: $50. Electronic applications accepted. *Expenses: Contact institution.* Tuition and fees vary according to course load. *Financial support:* In 2006–07, 528 students received support, including 9 fellowships, 20 research assistantships (averaging $6,485 per year); career-related internships or fieldwork, Federal Work-Study, institutionally sponsored loans, and scholarships/grants also available. Support available to part-time students. Financial award applicants required to submit FAFSA. *Faculty research:* Taxation and business, family and juvenile law, governmental affairs, environmental law, intellectual property law. *Unit head:* Elizabeth Rindskopf Parker, Dean, 916-739-7151, E-mail: elizabeth@uop.edu. *Application contact:* 916-739-7105, Fax: 916-739-7134, E-mail: admissionsmcgeorge@uop.edu.

University of the Sacred Heart, Graduate Programs, Program in Systems of Justice, San Juan, PR 00914-0383. Offers human rights and anti-discriminatory processes (MASJ); mediation and transformation of conflicts (MASJ).

University of Washington, School of Law, Seattle, WA 98195-3020. Offers Asian law (LL M, PhD); intellectual property law and policy (LL M); law (JD); law of sustainable international development (LL M); taxation (LL M); JD/LL M; JD/MA; JD/MAIS; JD/MBA; JD/MPA; JD/MS; JD/PhD. *Accreditation:* ABA. *Degree requirements:* For master's and doctorate, thesis/dissertation. *Entrance requirements:* For JD, LSAT; for master's, language proficiency (LL M in Asian law). Additional exam requirements/recommendations for international students: Required—TOEFL. Expenses: Contact institution. *Faculty research:* Asian, international and comparative law, intellectual property law, health law, environmental law, taxation.

University of Windsor, Faculty of Graduate Studies and Research, Faculty of Arts and Social Sciences, Department of Communication Studies, Windsor, ON N9B 3P4, Canada. Offers communication and social justice (MA). *Degree requirements:* For master's, thesis. *Entrance requirements:* For master's, writing sample/media production or multimedia portfolio, minimum B average. Additional exam requirements/recommendations for international students: Required—TOEFL (minimum score 600 paper-based; 250 computer-based). Electronic applications accepted. *Faculty research:* Sociology of news, media ownership and control, communication networks and social movements, issues of media representation.

University of Wisconsin–Madison, Law School and Graduate School, Department of Legal Institutions, Madison, WI 53706-1380. Offers MLI. *Students:* 37 full-time (24 women), 1 (woman) part-time, 36 international. Average age 28. 96 applicants, 67% accepted, 35 enrolled. In 2006, 29 degrees awarded. *Entrance requirements:* Additional exam requirements/

Legal and Justice Studies

University of Wisconsin–Madison *(continued)*
recommendations for international students: Required—TOEFL (minimum score 580 paper-based; 237 computer-based). *Application deadline:* For fall admission, 2/1 for domestic and international students. Applications are processed on a rolling basis. Application fee: $45. Electronic applications accepted. *Financial support:* Career-related internships or fieldwork and institutionally sponsored loans available. Support available to part-time students. Financial award application deadline: 2/1. *Unit head:* Gerald Thain, Chairperson, 608-262-9120.

Vermont Law School, Law School, Environmental Law Center, South Royalton, VT 05068-0096. Offers LL M, MSEL, JD/MSEL. Part-time programs available. *Faculty:* 12 full-time (6 women), 8 part-time/adjunct (4 women). *Students:* 43 full-time (28 women), 5 part-time (4 women); includes 3 minority (2 Asian Americans or Pacific Islanders, 1 Hispanic American), 1 international. Average age 30. 74 applicants, 78% accepted, 30 enrolled. In 2006, 82 degrees awarded. *Entrance requirements:* For master's, GRE General Test or LSAT. Additional exam requirements/recommendations for international students: Required—TOEFL. *Application deadline:* For fall admission, 3/15 priority date for domestic students. Applications are processed on a rolling basis. Application fee: $60. *Financial support:* In 2006–07, 2 fellowships with full tuition reimbursements (averaging $5,000 per year) were awarded; career-related internships or fieldwork, Federal Work-Study, institutionally sponsored loans, scholarships/grants, and tuition waivers (partial) also available. Support available to part-time students. Financial award application deadline: 2/15; financial award applicants required to submit FAFSA. *Faculty research:* Environment and technology; takings; international environmental law; interaction among science, law, and environmental policy; air pollution. Total annual research expenditures: $52,000. *Unit head:* Karin Sheldon, Associate Dean, 802-831-1342, Fax: 802-763-2490, E-mail: admiss@vermontlaw.edu. *Application contact:* Anne Mansfield, Associate Director, 802-831-1338, Fax: 802-763-2940, E-mail: admiss@vermontlaw.edu.

Weber State University, College of Social and Behavioral Sciences, Program in Criminal Justice, Ogden, UT 84408-1001. Offers MCJ. Part-time and evening/weekend programs available. *Faculty:* 4 full-time (0 women), 2 part-time/adjunct (1 woman). *Students:* 8 full-time (2 women), 22 part-time (7 women). Average age 32. 16 applicants, 94% accepted, 13 enrolled. In 2006, 20 degrees awarded. *Entrance requirements:* For master's, GRE General Test, resume. *Application deadline:* Applications are processed on a rolling basis. Application fee: $0. *Expenses:* Tuition, state resident: full-time $3,950; part-time $203 per semester. Tuition, nonresident: full-time $10,371; part-time $518 per semester. Required fees: $544; $24 per semester. Tuition and fees vary according to course load and program. *Financial support:* In 2006–07, 1 student received support. *Unit head:* Dr. L. Kay Gillespie, Chair, 801-626-6245, Fax: 801-626-6145, E-mail: lgillespie@weber.edu. *Application contact:* Dr. Robert C. Wadman, Associate Professor, 801-626-6149, Fax: 801-626-6145, E-mail: rwadman1@weber.edu.

Webster University, College of Arts and Sciences, Department of Behavioral and Social Sciences, Program in Legal Analysis, St. Louis, MO 63119-3194. Offers MA. *Students:* 4 full-time (3 women), 41 part-time (32 women); includes 23 minority (22 African Americans, 1 Hispanic American). Average age 40. In 2006, 11 degrees awarded. Application fee: $25 ($50 for international students). *Expenses:* Tuition: Full-time $8,820; part-time $490 per credit. Tuition and fees vary according to degree level, campus/location and program. *Unit head:* Robin Jefferson Higgins, Director, 314-961-2660 Ext. 8724, Fax: 314-968-7403.

Webster University, College of Arts and Sciences, Department of Behavioral and Social Sciences, Program in Legal Studies, St. Louis, MO 63119-3194. Offers MA. Part-time and evening/weekend programs available. *Students:* 8 full-time (7 women), 27 part-time (22 women); includes 13 minority (11 African Americans, 2 Asian Americans or Pacific Islanders). Average age 33. In 2006, 17 degrees awarded. *Degree requirements:* For master's, thesis optional. *Application deadline:* Applications are processed on a rolling basis. Application fee: $25 ($50 for international students). *Expenses:* Tuition: Full-time $8,820; part-time $490 per credit. Tuition and fees vary according to degree level, campus/location and program. *Financial support:* Career-related internships or fieldwork and Federal Work-Study available. Support available to part-time students. Financial award application deadline: 4/1; financial award applicants required to submit FAFSA. *Faculty research:* Intellectual property rights, emerging torts, death penalty, juvenile justice, confidentiality issues in banking. *Unit head:* Robin Jefferson Higgins, Director, 314-961-2660 Ext. 8724, Fax: 314-968-7403. *Application contact:* Director of Graduate and Evening Student Admissions, Fax: 314-968-7116, E-mail: gadmit@webster.edu.

Webster University, College of Arts and Sciences, Department of Behavioral and Social Sciences, Program in Patent Agency, St. Louis, MO 63119-3194. Offers MA. Part-time and evening/weekend programs available. *Students:* Average age 36. *Application deadline:* Applications are processed on a rolling basis. Application fee: $25 ($50 for international students). *Expenses:* Tuition: Full-time $8,820; part-time $490 per credit. Tuition and fees vary according to degree level, campus/location and program. *Financial support:* Application deadline: 4/1; *Faculty research:* Intellectual property rights, emerging torts, death penalty, juvenile justice, confidentiality issues in banking. *Unit head:* Robin Jefferson Higgins, Director, 314-961-2660 Ext. 8724, Fax: 314-968-7403. *Application contact:* Director of Graduate and Evening Student Admissions, Fax: 314-968-7116, E-mail: gadmit@webster.edu.

West Virginia University, Eberly College of Arts and Sciences, Program in Legal Studies, Morgantown, WV 26506. Offers MLS. Part-time and evening/weekend programs available. *Students:* Average age 44. 10 applicants, 0% accepted. In 2006, 4 degrees awarded. *Degree requirements:* For master's, capstone research. *Entrance requirements:* For master's, GRE or LSAT, minimum GPA of 2.75. *Expenses:* Tuition, state resident: full-time $4,926; part-time $276 per credit hour. Tuition, nonresident: full-time $14,278; part-time $796 per credit hour. Tuition and fees vary according to program. *Financial support:* In 2006–07, 2 students received support. *Application contact:* Dr. Joan Gorham, Associate Dean, 304-293-4611, Fax: 304-293-6858, E-mail: joan.gorham@mail.wvu.edu.

Whittier College, Whittier Law School, Costa Mesa, CA 92626. Offers foreign legal studies (LL M); law (JD). *Accreditation:* ABA. Part-time and evening/weekend programs available. *Entrance requirements:* For JD, LSAT; for master's, first degree in law. Additional exam requirements/recommendations for international students: Required—TOEFL (minimum score 600 paper-based; 250 computer-based). Electronic applications accepted. Expenses: Contact institution. *Faculty research:* Intellectual property, international law, health law, children's rights.

William Howard Taft University, Graduate Programs, Bernard E. Witkin School of Law, Santa Ana, CA 92704. Offers American jurisprudence (LL M); law (JD); taxation (LL M).

DRAKE UNIVERSITY

Drake Law School

Programs of Study	Drake Law School at Drake University offers top-quality programs leading to the Juris Doctor (J.D.) degree. One of the oldest law schools in the country, Drake combines strong theoretical underpinnings with practical experience and professional skills development. The result is well-prepared students who, upon graduation, are ready to practice law in a variety of settings.
	A Drake legal education is not limited to the classroom. Drake's location in Des Moines, Iowa's capital, provides numerous opportunities for internships and clerkships with private firms, government agencies, and federal and state judges at both the trial and appellate levels. Extensive clinical programs, housed in a state-of-the-art clinical facility, allow students to gain practical experience. Prominent lawyers, jurists, and legal scholars visit regularly. Since 1988, 9 Supreme Court justices have delivered major lectures at Drake; in 1999, 2002, and 2006, justices returned for one-week residencies with the students.
	Drake offers certification programs in food and agricultural law, legislative practice, constitutional law and civil rights, and litigation and dispute resolution. The Legal Clinic offers a number of public service and practice opportunities. Through joint-degree programs, students may obtain advanced degrees in agricultural economics, business, political science, public administration, social work, and pharmacy.
Research Facilities	Drake Law School's facilities are among the best in the country. Opperman Hall and Law Library has won several architectural and design awards and has received international recognition. The entire law school is covered by a wireless network and the library includes two computer labs, Westlaw and LEXIS legal research training centers, and easy access to the Internet and electronic resources. In addition, there are two main reading areas conducive to individual study, nineteen small-group study rooms, and several conference and seminar rooms. The library has a collection of approximately 320,000 volumes and adjoins Cartwright Hall, the main classroom building. The Neal and Bea Smith Law Center also has its own library as well as a fully computerized courtroom with laptop power connections at each seat.
Financial Aid	Drake Law School awards more than $3 million annually in scholarship assistance, and more than 90 percent of students receive financial aid of some type. Scholarships are available based on both need and academic performance, and awards range from partial to full tuition. Five full-tuition merit scholarships plus $10,000 living stipends are awarded annually to entering students. General scholarship assistance is available to entering students as well as to second- and third-year students who did not previously receive awards. Loan programs also are available.
Cost of Study	Tuition for the 2006–07 academic year was $25,800 per year for students taking 10 or more hours per semester. For those students who carried fewer than 10 hours, the tuition rate was $900 per hour.
Living and Housing Costs	The cost of living in Des Moines is low compared to that of many metropolitan areas, particularly in housing expenses. There are numerous apartments within walking distance of the campus. Rent for one-bedroom apartments typically ranges from $400 to $600 per month, and two-bedroom apartments range from $550 to $750 per month.
Student Group	The enrollment in the Law School is approximately 430 students, 46 percent of whom are women. The median GPA for the fall 2006 entering class was 3.4, and the median LSAT score was 155. Law School students are a diverse group, representing twenty-five states and sixty-three undergraduate institutions; approximately 45 percent of the students come from outside of Iowa.
Student Outcomes	Drake Law School has alumni in all fifty states and several other countries in positions ranging from state Supreme Court justices to practicing attorneys to corporate CEOs. Historically, more than 90 percent of graduates secure employment within six months of graduation, which is above the national average.
Location	The Law School is located on the Drake University campus, a 150-acre community within 10 minutes of downtown Des Moines. With a metropolitan population of approximately 450,000, Des Moines is the hub of the state's legal community as well as the state capital, resulting in opportunities for students in government, insurance, and banking as well as clerking opportunities.
The University and The Law School	Founded in 1881, Drake University is a private, independent university that offers a strong liberal arts foundation complemented by excellent career-oriented programs. Located on the Drake campus, the Law School is one of the twenty-five oldest law schools in the country and is accredited by the American Bar Association and the Association of American Law Schools.
Applying	Applications may be obtained from the Law School Admission Office. The application form should be returned with a personal statement and a nonrefundable application fee of $50. Although letters of recommendation from academic sources are not required, applicants are strongly encouraged to submit them.
Correspondence and Information	Kara Blanchard, Director of Admission and Financial Aid Drake Law School Drake University 2507 University Avenue Des Moines, Iowa 50311 Phone: 515-271-2782 800-44-DRAKE Ext. 2782 (toll-free) Fax: 515-271-1990 E-mail: lawadmit@drake.edu Web site: http://www.law.drake.edu/

Drake University

THE FACULTY

David S. Walker, The Dwight D. Opperman Distinguished Professor of Law and Dean; LL.B., Virginia, 1969.
Russell E. Lovell II, Professor and Associate Dean; LL.M., Missouri–Kansas City, 1971.

James A. Adams, The Ellis and Nelle Levitt Distinguished Professor of Law; J.D., Duke, 1967.
James A. Albert, Professor; J.D., Notre Dame, 1976.
Jerry L. Anderson, The Richard M. and Anita Calkins Distinguished Professor of Law; J.D., Stanford, 1984.
Martin D. Begleiter, The Ellis and Nelle Levitt Distinguished Professor of Law; J.D., Cornell, 1970.
Kristi Bowman, Assistant Professor; J.D., Duke, 2001.
Andrea S. Charlow, Professor; LL.M., Columbia, 1982.
Hunter R. Clark, Professor; J.D., Harvard, 1979.
Laurie Kratky Doré, The Ellis and Nelle Levitt Distinguished Professor of Law; J.D., SMU, 1984.
Matthew G. Doré, The Richard M. and Anita Calkins Distinguished Professor of Law; J.D., Texas at Austin, 1984.
John D. Edwards, Professor, Director of the Law Library, and Associate Dean for Information Resources and Technology; J.D., Missouri–Kansas City, 1977; M.A.L.S., Missouri–Columbia, 1979.
Jerry Foxhoven, Associate Professor and Director, Middleton Center for Children's Rights; J.D., Drake, 1977.
Sally Frank, Professor; J.D., NYU, 1983; M.A.T., Antioch, 1998.
Neil D. Hamilton, The Dwight D. Opperman Chair and Director, Agricultural Law Center; J.D., Iowa, 1979.
Robert C. Hunter, Professor; J.D., Duke, 1967.
Mark S. Kende, The James Madison Chair in Constitutional Law and Director, Constitutional Law Center; J.D., Chicago, 1986.
Suzanne Levitt, Professor and Executive Director of Legal Clinic; LL.M., Yale, 1989.
Cathy Lesser Mansfield, Professor; J.D., Virginia, 1987.
J. Karnale Manuel, Visiting Associate Professor; J.D., Drake, 1978.
David E. McCord, Professor; J.D., Harvard, 1978.
Keith C. Miller, The Ellis and Nelle Levitt Distinguished Professor of Law; LL.M., Michigan, 1979.
James R. Monroe, Professor; M.B.A., Denver, 1967; LL.M., NYU, 1977.
Lisa Penland, Assistant Professor; J.D., Drake, 1985.
Lawrence E. Pope, Professor and Director, Legislative Practice Center; LL.M., NYU, 1969.
Robert Rigg, Visiting Associate Professor and Criminal Defense Program Director; J.D., Drake, 1977.
Danielle Shelton, Assistant Professor; J.D., Harvard, 1995.
Maura I. Strassberg, Professor; J.D., Columbia, 1984.
Melissa Weresh, Professor and Assistant Director of Legal Writing; J.D., Iowa, 1992.
Ellen Yee, Assistant Professor; J.D., Minnesota, 1997.

MASSACHUSETTS SCHOOL OF LAW AT ANDOVER

Professional Program

Programs of Study

Massachusetts School of Law offers day and evening programs for full-time and part-time students, as well as two summer sessions that allow students to accelerate their program. The full-time program requires that students take 15 credits per semester, while part-time students take 11–12 credits per semester. During the first year, students take courses in civil procedure and conflict resolution, contracts, property, torts, and research and writing. In subsequent years, course work focuses on criminal procedure, legal ethics, litigation, and other topics. Specializations are also available in litigation, criminal law, family law, real estate, labor law, and business and corporate law.

The Clinical Law Program affords students the opportunity to begin the transition from law school to law practice. In the classroom component, students learn the substantive and procedural law they must know to practice in their area of concentration. They also practice law under the supervision of a member of the American Bar Association, working as counselors, negotiators, advocates, and problem solvers for their clients.

Research Facilities

The School's Information Resource Center is well equipped to meet the research, practice, and study needs of students, faculty members, and alumni, as well as local attorneys and law firms. Its goal is to provide the legal materials and services to support both the academic programs of the School and research interests of all members of the law school community. The library contains more than 60,000 hardbound and microfiche volumes. The collection is national in scope and covers most major subjects of American law. Most of the material is on open shelves for easy access, while course materials, study aids, current periodicals, reference books, and other frequently used materials are kept on reserve to ensure availability. The Information Resource Center also has access to millions of volumes and megabytes of information through computer databases, interlibrary loans, and information ordered from other document delivery services. In addition, a number of CD-ROM titles are available.

Financial Aid

The Thomas McGovern Educational Scholarship is awarded to graduates of educational institutions located in Bristol County, Massachusetts. United Cerebral Palsy of Metro Boston offers the John J. Ingalls Memorial Scholarship to students who have been diagnosed with a physical disability; this award gives up to 3 applicants per year an unrestricted amount of $5000 to be used toward tuition. The financial aid office offers an additional $3000 in Graduate PLUS Loans.

Cost of Study

In the 2006–07 academic year, tuition was $444 per credit hour, for a total of $6660 per semester for full-time students and $4884 for part-time students. When registering for the first semester, students are assessed a one-time nonrefundable building fund charge of $750.

Living and Housing Costs

The School does not provide housing. However, apartments are available in the area. A two-bedroom apartment typically costs $850 to $1500 per month, depending on size and location.

Student Group

In keeping with the School's mission, many of the students are from working-class and middle-class backgrounds, members of minority groups, midlife individuals who are looking to change careers, and immigrants.

Student Outcomes

Graduates of the School are eligible to take the bar examination immediately upon graduation in Massachusetts and Connecticut. After passing the examination in Massachusetts, they are immediately eligible to take the bar exam in a number of jurisdictions. Graduates are practicing at law firms throughout Massachusetts and across the country, and several are working as district attorneys in their respective jurisdictions.

Location

Andover is located approximately 25 miles north of Boston. Best known as the home of Phillips Academy, Andover offers other attractions, including a variety of performing arts venues, museums, and historical sites, as well as golf, cross-country skiing, and canoeing along the Shawsheen River. Companies operating in Andover include Raytheon, Philips Electronics, Verizon, Compaq, and Gillette.

The School

Massachusetts School of Law is committed to providing a practical yet technologically sophisticated approach to legal education to college students and working professionals. As the most affordable law school in all of New England, its mission is to make practical, affordable, high-quality legal education, and resulting social and economic mobility, available to capable but less privileged persons who have been traditionally excluded from the legal profession. Through a rigorous, useful, affordable legal education, students improve their lives and better serve their communities. The School is accredited by the New England Association of Schools and Colleges.

Applying

To be considered for admission, prospective students must submit the following to the Admission Department: an application, official college transcripts, a personal statement of no more than 550 words, three letters of recommendation, and a $40 application fee. Each applicant must complete a personal interview, at which time he or she takes the Massachusetts School of Law Aptitude Test, which replaces the traditional LSAT. There is no formal deadline, but applications should be submitted as soon as possible.

Correspondence and Information

Paula Colby-Clements, Director of Admissions
Massachusetts School of Law
500 Federal Street
Andover, Massachusetts 01810
Phone: 978-681-0800 Ext. 38
E-mail: pcolby@mslaw.edu
Web site: http://www.mslaw.edu/

Massachusetts School of Law at Andover

THE FACULTY AND THEIR RESEARCH

Timothy R. Cagle, Assistant Professor; J.D., Suffolk. Medical malpractice, torts, evidence, negotiation in the legal context.

Anthony A. Copani, Associate Professor; J.D., Suffolk. Family law, case preparation and strategy, evidence.

Philip Coppola, Assistant Professor; J.D., Suffolk. Consumer law, criminal law, criminal procedure, oral advocacy, prosecution and adjudication.

Michael L. Coyne, Professor and Associate Dean; J.D., Suffolk. Civil procedure and conflict resolution, evidence, case preparation and strategy, remedies.

Joseph Devlin, Professor and Assistant Dean; J.D., Boston University. Wills and trusts; contracts; accounting for lawyers; creating and representing new businesses; drafting wills and trusts; drafting contracts and business agreements; business associations; logic, analysis, and the law.

Paula Kaldis, Professor; J.D., New England Law. Legal research and writing, juvenile law.

Mary Kilpatrick, Assistant Professor; J.D., NYU. Research and writing, film and the legal process, race in American law.

Peter M. Malaguti, Professor; J.D., Suffolk. Property, conveyancing, land-use regulation, local government law, landlord-tenant law.

Thomas H. Martin, Assistant Professor; J.D., Harvard. Civil procedure and conflict resolution, environmental law, torts, restitution.

Kurt Olson, Assistant Professor; J.D., Massachusetts School of Law. Research and writing, legal ethics, introduction to the Internet, law office technology, cyberspace and the law.

Constance Rudnick, Professor; J.D., Case Western Reserve. Legal ethics, constitutional law, advanced litigation skills.

Andrej Starkis, Assistant Professor; J.D., Boston College. Business associations, motions and litigation practice.

Diane Sullivan, Professor; J.D., Massachusetts School of Law. Uniform Commercial Code, contracts, issues impacting women, animal law.

Holly Vietzke, Assistant Professor; J.D., Massachusetts School of Law. Writing and legal reasoning.

Judith Wolfe, Assistant Professor; J.D., Missouri–Columbia. Advanced research skills, motions and litigation practice, asset protection and planning.

NEW COLLEGE OF CALIFORNIA

School of Law

Program of Study

New College of California School of Law is the oldest public interest law school in the nation. Since 1973, New College has offered an innovative program of legal education, combining practical skills training, rigorous classroom work, and supportive services, all in the pursuit of training talented, creative, and compassionate lawyers who will work in the public interest in new and dynamic ways. There are now hundreds of New College attorneys practicing law in neighborhood offices, government agencies, and community organizations, all sharing a special bond based on their experience at this unique school.

The curriculum centers on courses in fundamental doctrine, trial practice and skills courses, and clinical programs—both on and off campus. The Apprenticeship Program places advanced students in law offices and agencies to earn academic credit while learning about the practice of law. The on-campus Criminal Defense Program gives third-year students the opportunity to provide direct legal representation for clients. The Housing Advocacy Clinic trains second- and third-year law students to provide legal assistance to low-income tenants facing wrongful evictions. The fundamental doctrine courses, covering those topics tested on the California bar exam, emphasize the intricacies of existing rules and doctrines while offering a critical perspective on the role of law in promoting or hindering social change.

Academic support services are available to all students, regardless of academic standing, in the form of counseling, tutorials, and workshops. The J.D. degree can be earned through either a full-time (three-year) or part-time (four-year) program of study.

Research Facilities

The Law Library plays a central role in the legal education provided at New College. In addition to its collection of more than 10,000 volumes, the library provides students with unlimited access to computer-assisted legal research through WESTLAW and other databases. The collection meets the requirements of the State Bar of California and includes an extensive array of practice-oriented materials. In addition, New College participates in the interlibrary loan network, making more than 20 million titles available on request. The Law Library also maintains program and word processing stations.

Financial Aid

New College School of Law assists many of its students in obtaining the necessary funding to meet the costs of a legal education. The Financial Aid Office administers various state and federal financial aid programs, including grants, loans, and work-study awards. New College also administers several private financial aid programs, such as the Third World Scholarship Fund for students from minority groups with unmet financial need (made possible with funds from the Leon and Esther Blum Foundation) and the M. Jay Kramer Foundation Awards for students pursuing careers in public interest law.

Cost of Study

For 2006–07, tuition was $15,214 per year for full-time students and $11,390 per year for part-time students. A $45 application fee and a student services fee of $50 per semester are also required.

Living and Housing Costs

San Francisco provides several residential neighborhoods with affordable housing within short distances of the campus. The cost of living varies from student to student, depending on living arrangements and other factors.

Student Group

New College School of Law maintains a small, supportive environment with an overall enrollment of 140 students, with an entering first-year class of about 47 students. The student population is highly diverse, with 55 percent women and more than 40 percent of the students from minority groups. In addition, there is a significant presence of lesbian and gay students. There are more than 900 alumni, the majority practicing law in California in public-sector jobs such as in public defender or legal aid offices or in private practice. Alumni obtained many of these positions through contacts made while they were law students participating in the clinical programs.

Location

New College is housed in a four-story landmark building in the heart of San Francisco's Civic Center, within walking distance of numerous government agencies, state and federal trial courts, appellate courts, and law offices where students apprentice as part of their legal education. The Civic Center is also the site of the San Francisco Opera, Symphony, Ballet, Public Libraries, and Asian Arts Museum. All public transportation, including BART and MUNI, serves the area.

The College

New College is fully accredited by the Committee of Bar Examiners of the State Bar of California and by the Western Association of Schools and Colleges. Graduates are qualified to sit for the bar examination in California. New College law graduates may petition to sit for the bar exam in some other states after having practiced in California for a certain number of years. The School of Law is an integral part of New College of California, which was founded in 1971 and which offers a wide range of undergraduate and graduate programs, annually serving more than 850 students as an alternative to mainstream education.

Applying

New College School of Law seeks to attract socially concerned students from diverse backgrounds who intend to pursue careers in public interest law. The Admissions Office considers factors such as motivation, work and community experience, maturity, and public interest awareness along with standard academic criteria such as LSAT scores and academic histories. First consideration is given to applicants who apply by March 1 of each year. Applicants are expected to take the LSAT no later than February of the year for which they are applying. Most applicants hold a bachelor's degree, but those with less than four years of college and significant life experience may be eligible for admission. Full details are available from the Admissions Office.

Correspondence and Information

Admissions Office
New College of California School of Law
50 Fell Street
San Francisco, California 94102
Phone: 415-241-1300
E-mail: lawinfo@ncgate.newcollege.edu
Web site: http://www.newcollege.edu/law/

New College of California

THE FACULTY

New College law faculty members are dedicated legal practitioners and educators who teach because of their desire to participate in the education of competent public interest lawyers and because of their commitment to social and political change. The faculty has an outstanding reputation in the San Francisco Bay Area legal community for its involvement in public service activities and progressive causes and for its scholarship in the field of critical legal theory.

The faculty at New College is one of the most diverse law faculties in the nation. Women make up more than 40 percent of the faculty, and one third of the faculty are members of minority groups. In addition, more than 15 percent of the faculty members are gay or lesbian. This multicultural faculty adds an important component to the legal education of socially responsible lawyers.

Fania Davis, J.D., Berkeley, 1978. Indigenous mediation theory.
Peter Gabel, Professor of Law and President of New College of California; J.D., Harvard; Ph.D., Wright Institute.
Paul Harris, Professor of Law; J.D., Berkeley.
Chris Gus Kanios, Professor of Law; J.D., New College of California.
Debrenia Madison, Professor of Law and Dean; J.D., Georgetown.
John Timothy Philipsborn, Professor of Law; J.D., California, Davis.
Ora Prochovnick, Professor of Law; J.D., New College of California.
Edward R. Roybal, Professor of Law; J.D., Berkeley.
Steven Royston, Professor-in-Residence; J.D., Western State, Fullerton, 1980. Civil procedure and civil trial skills.
Rebecca Young, J.D., Golden Gate, 1985. Criminal pretrial skills.
In addition to the senior core and associate faculty, New College has a talented group of adjunct faculty members teaching on a regular, part-time basis.
Stephanie Adraktas, J.D., NYU. Criminal law.
Charles Carbone, J.D., SUNY at Buffalo. Ethics.
Thomas Flemming, J.D., Yale, 1988. Criminal trial skills.
Lindsey Elizabeth Harris, J.D., Stanford, 1989. Critical legal theories seminar.
Ian Kelly, J.D., New College of California, 2001.
Mathew Kumin, J.D., California, Hastings Law. Evidence.
Reichi Lee, J.D., California, Hastings Law. Legal analysis.
Sharon Pittman, J.D., New College of California, 1997. Small claims clinic.
Sondra Roberto, J.D., Brooklyn Law. Legal writing and research.
Lois Schwartz, J.D., Berkeley, 1989. Legal writing/research.
Robert Shepard, J.D., New College of California, 1997. Small claims clinic.
Belinda Sifford, J.D., CUNY, City College, 1986. Contracts.
Sondra Solovag, J.D., Berkeley. Torts.
Victoria Stafford, J.D., Berkeley, 1990. Legal writing and research.

Oklahoma Professor Anita Hill delivered New College School of Law's commencement address in 1992. Hill was awarded an honorary doctorate by the School.

College of Law

THE OHIO STATE UNIVERSITY

Michael E. Moritz College of Law
Master of Laws Program for Foreign Lawyers

Program of Study

The Ohio State University Moritz College of Law is a diverse and dynamic community of students and scholars, with faculty members known nationally for their scholarship and teaching. The Moritz College faculty is equally dedicated to preparing students for the legal profession and to exploring the cutting edge of their disciplines. The Moritz College of Law offers a nationally ranked program and certificate in the emerging area of alternative dispute resolution as well as an exceptionally broad array of clinical programs, including clinics in civil and criminal practice, mediation, legislation, and juvenile law. The curriculum provides excellent preparation in criminal law, intellectual property law, employment and labor law, commercial law, international law, and many other fields.

The Moritz College of Law is offering a new Master of Laws (LL.M.) Program for Foreign Lawyers. The College plans to welcome its first class in August 2007. The one-year Moritz LL.M. program is designed for lawyers from other countries who wish to advance their legal education in a stimulating academic environment and provides them with a basic understanding of the United States' legal system through a rigorous program of legal training. Two of the program's primary goals are to immerse such lawyers in a year of U.S. legal education and to foster interaction between United States J.D. students and the LL.M. students. In large part, this is accomplished by integrating the LL.M. students into the J.D. curriculum, ensuring that both groups will benefit from the interaction and graduate from their respective programs well prepared to participate in an increasingly globalized world.

Students are required to successfully complete 24 semester credits to earn the LL.M. degree. LL.M. studies can be structured three different ways. Students can choose from more than 145 classes and seminars to craft the LL.M. program that best suits their interests and career goals. In the first option, LL.M. students may choose to pursue a general degree program that provides a broad understanding of the fundamentals of U.S. law, with courses in such subjects as torts, contracts, and constitutional law. In the second option, LL.M. students may focus on areas of particular interest or relevance to their career by tailoring an individual selection of courses. Finally, students may choose to fulfill the requirements for one of the six designated LL.M. concentrations: business law; criminal law and procedure; dispute resolution; intellectual property and information law; international law; or labor and employment law. Regardless of the path chosen, LL.M. students will graduate from this program with new skills to further their career in their home country as well as with the tools needed to function effectively in an increasingly global economy.

Research Facilities

With a collection of more than 770,000 volumes and access to a myriad of online resources, the Moritz Law Library is the fourteenth-largest among law school libraries in the nation. The library's collection is particularly strong in the areas of dispute resolution, health-care law, international law, and socio-legal studies. The Moritz Law Library participates in OhioLINK, which links Ohio's major institutions of higher education—including eight law school libraries. A large and talented research staff is always available to assist students with difficult research assignments.

Financial Aid

Financial aid is only available to citizens or permanent residents of the United States. A very limited number of scholarships are available. Interested students should contact the LL.M. Program Office at 001-614-688-5328 for additional information.

Cost of Study

The cost of study for the LL.M. Program for Foreign Lawyers is consistent with the cost of study for the J.D. program, with a differential between resident and nonresident fees. Students who have resided in Ohio for at least one year pay $17,538 in tuition; nonresident students pay $34,232. There is an estimated annual cost of $2950 for books and supplies. International students must provide an affidavit of proof of availability of funds before they are granted their visa and admission to the LL.M. program.

Living and Housing Costs

Living and housing costs are approximately $10,000 per year. Columbus, Ohio, has one of the lowest costs of living of large Midwestern cities along with a very manageable lifestyle. Information about off-campus housing can be obtained by visiting the Web site at http://offcampus. osu.edu/ or calling 001-614-292-0100.

Student Group

Students are encouraged to take part in one or more of the College's fifty-five student organizations or committees. Through involvement, students develop both personally and professionally and become acquainted with students in other sections and in other classes at the Moritz College of Law, as well as with students and faculty members who have common interests and backgrounds. Student organizations range from those that emphasize public-interest advocacy and professional development to those that serve the particular interests of the members.

Location

With a metropolitan population of more than 1.5 million residents, 20 percent of whom represent various ethnic minorities, Columbus is a stimulating, urban environment. Centrally located in the state of Ohio, the Columbus metropolitan area is headquarters for five Fortune 500 companies and more than 700 law firms. The economy thrives with a strong mix of government, service, retail, and manufacturing, yet Columbus has a cost of living that is significantly lower than other major cities. Columbus celebrates its diverse heritage with more than a dozen ethnic/cultural festivals each year.

The University

Moritz LL.M. students become part of The Ohio State University and all that it has to offer. Ranked by *U.S. News & World Report* as one of the top twenty public universities, The University is a leading comprehensive teaching and research university and, with nearly 50,000 students, it is one of the largest in the country. The University combines a responsibility for the advancement and dissemination of knowledge with a land-grant heritage of public service, offering an extensive range of academic programs in the liberal arts, the sciences, and the professions. Few universities can match Ohio State's breadth of academic offerings and related interdisciplinary opportunities that include 176 undergraduate majors, 220 graduate fields of study, and numerous professional programs. Ohio State has long attracted a wide range of international students. Currently there are nearly 4,000 international scholars on campus and 1,500 visiting international students. The University has more than 300 formal partnerships with universities in fifty-two countries and has an infrastructure of support and resources in place to serve its international student population.

Applying

LL.M. program applicants are limited to students who have obtained an LL.B. from an institution in another country, have completed (in another country) the university-based legal education required to take the equivalent of the bar examination in that country, are qualified to practice law in another country, or have the equivalent qualifications thereof as determined by the LL.M. Admissions Committee.

When making the admission decision, the LL.M. Admissions Committee also considers factors such as outstanding academic performance, professional experience, and the quality of the undergraduate institution. An applicant for whom English is a second language must present evidence of a Test of English as a Foreign Language (TOEFL) score of at least 600 on the paper-based test, 250 on the computer-based test, or 100 on the Internet-based test or a minimum score of 8.0 on the IETLS. The admission process is ongoing, with a final application deadline of May 30, but prospective students should apply early to increase their chances of admission. Applicants for admission may apply by the preferred method of using an electronic application through the Web site for the Law School Admission Council's LL.M. Credential Assembly Services at http://llm.lsac.org/ or by using a paper application, which can be downloaded at http://moritzlaw.osu.edu/programs/ llm/application.pdf.

Correspondence and Information

LL.M. Program Office
Moritz College of Law
The Ohio State University
55 West 12th Avenue
Columbus, Ohio 43210-1391
Phone: 614-688-5328
Fax: 614-292-2035
E-mail: MoritzLLM@osu.edu
Web site: http://moritzlaw.osu.edu/programs/llm

The Ohio State University

THE FACULTY

Nancy Hardin Rogers, Dean and Michael E. Moritz Chair in Dispute Resolution; J.D., Yale, 1972. Professor Rogers became Dean in August 2001, after serving for two years as Vice Provost for Academic Administration for The Ohio State University. She is the President of the Association of American Law Schools. Dean Rogers has taught and written primarily in the area of dispute resolution.

Ellen E. Deason, Professor of Law and Director, Master of Laws (LL.M.) Program for Foreign Lawyers; J.D., Michigan, 1985. Background: Associate Professor, University of Illinois College of Law; Litigation Associate with Morrison & Foerster, Washington, D.C., Law Clerk for Judge Harry T. Edwards, U.S. Court of Appeals, District of Columbia Circuit; Law Clerk for Justice Harry A. Blackmun, U.S. Supreme Court. Legal Assistant to Arbitrator Howard M. Holtzman, Iran–United States Claims Tribunal, The Hague, The Netherlands. Professor Deason teaches Mediation, Lawyering in Dispute Resolution Processes, Comparative Dispute Resolution, and Law and Genetics.

Daniel Chow, Robert J. Nordstrom Designated Professor of Law; J.D., Yale. Background: Law Clerk to the Honorable Constance Baker Motley, Chief Judge, Southern District of New York; Associate with Debevoise & Plimpton, LLP, New York. Professor Chow teaches International Law, International Transactions, Jurisprudence, Asian Law, and Property.

John B. Quigley, President's Club Professor of Law and Adjunct Professor of Political Science; LL.B., Harvard. Background: Research Scholar, Moscow State University; Research Associate in Comparative Law, Harvard Law School; Visiting Professor at University of Dar es Salaam, Tanzania (1982–83). Professor Quigley is active in international human rights work. His numerous publications include books and articles on human rights, the United Nations, war and peace, law of Eastern Europe, African law, and the Arab-Israeli conflict. In 1995, he was the recipient of The Ohio State University Distinguished Scholar Award. Professor Quigley teaches International Law and Comparative Law.

Mary E. Ming, Assistant Dean for Graduate and International Programs; J.D., Dayton. Assistant Dean Ming is primarily responsible for recruiting and administration of the Master of Laws (LL.M.) Program for Foreign Lawyers. (MoritzLLM@osu.edu; 614-688-5328).

Campus life at The Ohio State University.

The Ohio State University Moritz College of Law.

PACE UNIVERSITY

School of Law

Program of Study

The curriculum at the School of Law at Pace University is devoted to preparing graduates to become able and ethical lawyers who can make a difference in improving society. Pace is dedicated to excellence in teaching and training in the specialized areas where the need for skilled lawyers is greatest. The majority of classes have fewer than 35 students, which enables close faculty-student relationships. Deans, administrators, and faculty members maintain an open-door policy for students. Students participate actively in formulating law school policy through the Student Bar Association and by serving on most faculty committees.

Pace University's legal program attracts highly qualified students from across the country and around the world. The School of Law offers programs of study leading to the Juris Doctor (J.D.), Master of Laws (LL.M.), and Doctor of Juridical Science (S.J.D.) degrees. There are also joint degree and certificate program options. Students who wish to obtain the J.D. degree may choose to receive a certificate of specialization in one of two areas: environmental law or international law. Concentrations include business law, constitutional law, criminal law, family law, health law, intellectual property law, public interest and advocacy law, and real estate and land-use law. The joint program options allow students to work toward a degree in law while earning an M.P.A. degree from Dyson College of Arts and Sciences, an M.B.A. degree from Pace's Lubin School of Business, a joint J.D./M.E.M. degree with the Yale University School of Forestry and Environmental Studies, a J.D./M.A. degree with Sarah Lawrence College in women's studies, or a J.D./M.S. degree with Bard College Center for Environmental Policy.

The Environmental Law Program was one of the first in the country and consistently ranks as one of the best in the country in terms of academic and clinical opportunities available. Students may obtain the Master of Laws (LL.M.) in environmental law or the Doctor of Juridical Science (S.J.D.) in environmental law. The LL.M. in comparative legal studies is available for graduates of law schools outside the U.S. and is designed to meet the specific needs of students who want to obtain a degree in law within the U.S. that they can apply wherever they might practice.

School of Law students who wish to gain some international experience may also participate in the London Law Program or the Human Rights in Action Program and live, study, and work abroad as part of their degree requirements.

A mandatory first-year moot court competition is part of the Criminal Law and Legal Writing curriculum. The School of Law also competes in interscholastic moot court competitions, including the Willem C. Vis International Commercial Arbitration Moot in Vienna, and hosts the National Environmental Moot Court Competition, the largest of its kind in the country. Team members are selected by professors and chosen based on writing ability and oral presentation skills. The School of Law also sponsors an intraschool moot, which culminates in the Grand Moot Competition each spring.

Pace School of Law publishes three law reviews, the *Pace Law Review*, the *Pace Environmental Law Review*, and the *Pace International Law Review*. Admission to the reviews is based upon academic standing and a writing competition.

Research Facilities

First-year students receive formal instruction in LexisNexis and WESTLAW. Additional instruction on advanced research techniques and on research in specialized areas of law is always available. The Law Library's many computer terminals provide access to word processing and e-mail and give students free access to all the information in the LexisNexis, WESTLAW, and Dialog databases; CD-ROMs; and other Internet-based databases to which the library subscribes. In addition, the entire library facility provides wireless access to the Law Library computer network.

Financial Aid

The School of Law awards scholarships to qualified students on the basis of academic merit, leadership and work experience, community service, and financial need. A variety of scholarships are available to first-year law students, ranging from partial to full tuition. A comprehensive aid program has been developed that includes grants, employment, scholarships, and loans. Pace School of Law dedicated $2.5 million in scholarships and grants to law students during the 2006–07 academic year.

Living and Housing Costs

Pace University offers on-campus housing for single law students in Dannat Hall, located on the White Plains campus near the Law Library and an on-campus dining facility. Dannat Hall is a five-story building equipped with a kitchen, laundry room, recreation room, and weight room. Furnished single rooms were available at the rate of $5240 per semester or $10,480 for the 2006–07 academic year. A variety of off-campus housing is available in White Plains and the surrounding area. The Student Life Office maintains a list of off-campus housing to assist Pace students, as well as a list of students interested in sharing apartments.

Student Group

In 2006, there were 198 full-time day students, 9 part-time day students, and 69 part-time evening students; 57 percent of the students are women and 16 percent are members of minority groups. The average age of full-time students was 25, and the average age of part-time students was 31. The average LSAT and GPA for students offered admission was 156 and 3.4, respectively.

Student Outcomes

The first-time bar passage rate for the 2006 graduates was 83 percent. In a survey of the class of 2006, 93 percent of the respondents reported employment within nine months of graduation. The Center for Career Development actively solicits law job listings for part-time and summer positions for students, including full-time jobs for evening students, while they are in school, and permanent positions for graduates. The center works closely with alumni to expand career opportunities for students and assist alumni in their own midcareer, lateral job searches. All job listings for students and alumni, as well as important career information, are maintained on the center's dedicated Web site. The Center for Career Development conducts a fall on-campus interview program for large-firm and government employers and a spring on-campus interview program for smaller to medium-sized law firms and public interest organizations. The center also administers more than forty career panels and programs each academic year, including a videotaped mock interview program, an intensive interview preparation workshop, an alumni mentorship program, and practice area presentations by faculty, alumni, and prominent practitioners.

In a recent survey of Pace School of Law graduates, students had chosen the following areas of practice: academic, 1.1 percent; business/industry, 24.9 percent; government, 15.9 percent; judicial clerkships, 2.6 percent; law firm private practice, 51.3 percent; and public interest, 2.1 percent.

Location

The School of Law is located at Pace University's White Plains campus in Westchester County, New York, just 25 miles from New York City. The spacious 12-acre campus offers a combination of historic and modern buildings as well as the Judicial Institute of the State of New York. White Plains is home to a number of national corporations, law firms, government agencies, and county, state, and federal courts. Pace's location creates the ideal setting for clinical, externship, and career opportunities for students.

The University and The School

Pace University is a comprehensive, independent, urban, and suburban New York institution that offers a wide range of academic and professional programs at the graduate and undergraduate levels. Pace considers teaching and learning to be its highest goals. In recognizing that educational leadership implies broadening obligations, the University has become increasingly attentive to integrating scholarship and service with excellent teaching. Pace's commitment to the individual needs of its students is at the heart of its teaching mission. By offering access and opportunity to qualified men and women, Pace embraces persons of diverse talents, interests, experiences, and origins who have the will to learn and the desire to participate in university life.

The School of Law features wireless networked classrooms, a law library, a cafeteria, an activities center, student housing, and on-site parking. It offers more than thirty-three organizations in which students can participate. Available activities include professional organizations, minority student groups, issue-centered organizations, political groups, social action groups, religious groups, a student bar association, and a student newspaper.

Applying

To apply for admission to Pace School of Law, students should complete the online application. Students may submit the application for admission through the Law School Admission Council (http://www.lsac.org) or print a PDF of the application by going to http://www.law.pace.edu.

Correspondence and Information

Office of Admissions
School of Law
Pace University
78 North Broadway
White Plains, New York 10603
Phone: 914-422-4210
Fax: 914-989-8714
E-mail: admissions@law.pace.edu
Web site: http://www.law.pace.edu

Pace University

THE FACULTY

The primary goal of the faculty at Pace School of Law is to produce a quality educational experience for the students. The emphasis on teaching is reflected in the time devoted to class preparation and is notable in the faculty's commitment to being accessible to students outside of class. Professors make a point of being on campus at least four days a week, and an open door policy prevails.

The majority of faculty members have had significant careers in legal practice prior to becoming legal educators. Their experience in law firms, as corporate counsel, and as federal and state regulators adds important perspectives to the theoretical principles of law.

Horace Anderson, J.D., Pennsylvania.
Barbara Atwell, J.D., Columbia.
Adele Bernhard, J.D., NYU.
Jay Carlisle, J.D., California, Davis.
David Cassuto, J.D., Berkeley.
Karl Coplan, J.D., Columbia.
Bridget Crawford, J.D., Pennsylvania.
Don Doernberg, J.D., Columbia.
David Dorfman, J.D., Chicago.
Linda Fentiman, J.D., SUNY at Buffalo; LL.M., Harvard.
James Fishman, J.D., NYU.
Leslie Garfield, J.D., Florida.
Bennett Gershman, J.D., NYU.
Steven Goldberg, J.D., Minnesota.
Shelby Green, J.D., Georgetown.
Alexander Greenwalt, J.D., Columbia.
Lissa Griffin, B.A., Michigan.
Jill Gross, J.D., Harvard.
Jo Ann Harris, J.D., NYU.
John Humbach, J.D., Ohio State.
Ronald Jensen, LL.B., Harvard.
Irene Johnson, J.D., Columbia.
Janet Johnson, J.D., Drake; LL.M., Virginia.
R. F. Kennedy Jr., J.D., Virginia; LL.M., Pace.
Norman Lichtenstein, LL.B., Yale.
Thomas McDonnell, J.D., Fordham.
Randolph McLaughlin, J.D., Harvard.
Vanessa Merton, J.D., NYU.
Jeffrey Miller, LL.B., Harvard.
Gary Munneke, J.D., Texas.
Michael Mushlin, J.D., Northwestern.
Marie Newman, J.D., Rutgers.
John Nolon, J.D., Michigan.
Richard Ottinger, LL.B., Harvard.
Ann Powers, J.D., Georgetown.
Nicholas Robinson, J.D., Columbia.
Audrey Rogers, J.D., St. John's (New York).
Darren Rosenblum, J.D., Pennsylvania.
Michelle Simon, J.D., Syracuse.
Merril Sobie, J.D., NYU.
Ralph Stein, J.D., Hofstra.
Emily Waldman, J.D., Harvard.
Gayl Westerman, J.D., Pace; LL.M., Yale; J.S.D., Yale.

SOUTHERN UNIVERSITY
AND AGRICULTURAL AND MECHANICAL COLLEGE
Southern University Law Center

Program of Study

Southern University Law Center offers a three-year full-time and a four-year part-time curriculum leading to the Juris Doctor degree. The curriculum is based upon the standard professional courses usually given in member schools accredited by the American Bar Association. It requires a full six semesters of residence for full-time students and eight semesters of residency for part-time students. Any study undertaken in a summer semester does not count toward residence requirements. Electives are integrated as part of the curriculum, and students must take courses specified for the respective years.

The program of study is designed to give students a comprehensive knowledge of both the civil law and common law. While emphasis is given to the substantive and procedural law of Louisiana, with its French and Spanish origins, Anglo-American law is strongly integrated into the curriculum. Fundamental differences in method and approach and the results reached in the two systems are analyzed. Students are trained in the art of advocacy, legal research, and the sources and social purposes of legal principles. The teaching of techniques to discipline students' minds in legal reasoning is an important part of the educational objectives of the Center. Students are instructed in the ethics of the legal profession and the professional responsibility of the lawyer to society.

Research Facilities

The Law Library contains 475,081 volumes and offers research assistance and reference service to students, faculty members, and the public. The collection of the library is adequate to support the curriculum and conforms to the standards of the American Bar Association. Both the federal and the Louisiana state governments have designated the Southern University Law Library an official depository for government documents. A complete collection of Louisiana legal materials, including Continuing Legal Education materials of the Louisiana Bar Association, is provided in the library. Although library acquisitions reflect the civil law tradition of Louisiana, sufficient materials for research in the common law and a substantial number of basic legal reference works are available. The legal periodical collection contains 801 titles, and several new titles are added every year. In addition to print materials, the library has collections of microforms and tapes dealing with a wide range of legal subjects. Media equipment in the library includes copying machines for print materials and microforms and a multimedia workstation.

Arrangements have been made with the Louisiana State University Law Center Library, which has one of the largest Anglo-American and civil law collections in the South, to make its resources available for research purposes to the Southern University Law Library.

Financial Aid

A limited number of direct Law Center assistance awards are available, based upon students' academic averages and demonstrated financial need. Applications for these scholarships should be directed to the Scholarship Committee at the Southern University Law Center. Applicants seeking Federal Stafford Student Loans must apply to the Financial Aid Office at Southern University Law Center.

Cost of Study

Tuition per semester was $3305.95 for Louisiana residents and $5605.95 for nonresident students in 2006–07.

Living and Housing Costs

Room and board on campus cost approximately $2000 per semester in 2006–07. It costs approximately $2000 per month for a married student living off campus for housing, food, and moderate entertainment in order to live at local standards. It costs a single student about $1500 per month for similar expenses.

Student Group

The current enrollment at the Law Center is approximately 490 men and women who have come from colleges and universities across the nation and from international institutions. Students participate in the Student Bar Association; the *Law Review;* the Moot Court Program; the Law Student Division, American Bar Association; the Black Law Students Association; Phi Alpha Delta and Delta Theta Phi law fraternities; *The Public Defender,* the law student newspaper; and other on-campus activities. An active intramural athletic program is well established at Southern.

Location

Baton Rouge, the capital of Louisiana, is a large industrial center and is the fifth-largest port in the United States, with a population of 500,000. The Law Center is located less than 5 miles from the state capitol, and it is situated in the midst of local law firms, a short drive from state and federal court buildings, government law offices, and regulatory agencies, in downtown Baton Rouge. Aside from the cultural, social, and athletic activities on and off campus in Baton Rouge, the fabled city of New Orleans, 85 miles away, offers many attractions. Other tourist attractions and historic sites in southern Louisiana are within easy reach of Baton Rouge.

The University and The Center

Southern University Law Center, established in 1947 as Southern University School of Law, is a progressive, innovative law school. It is located on the eastern bank of the historic Mississippi River in Baton Rouge, Louisiana. The Center is fully approved by the American Bar Association and the Supreme Court of Louisiana and accredited by the Southern Association of Colleges and Schools. It is also fully approved by the Veterans Administration for the training of eligible veterans. The Law Center maintains a high standard of professional education and adheres to the principle of equal opportunity. The University is proud of its rich academic program and culturally diverse student body, and it continues to be receptive to the introduction of new courses in response to a changing society.

Applying

Admission at Southern University Law Center is competitive and is based on a number of factors, including the undergraduate grade point average and scores on the Law School Admission Test (LSAT). All applications for admission are reviewed by a special committee. Among the factors considered by the committee, in addition to those stated above, are work experience, past pursuits, and recommendations.

Students beginning the study of law are admitted only in the fall semester. Applications for admission should be filed at the end of the fall semester of the year prior to the desired date of admission. Applications received later than February 28 for full-time and May 1 for part-time evening students may not be processed for admission in August.

Correspondence and Information

Office of Admission
Southern University Law Center
P.O. Box 9294
Baton Rouge, Louisiana 70813
Phone: 225-771-4976
Web site: http://www.sulc.edu/

Southern University and Agricultural and Mechanical College

THE FACULTY

Ruby Andrew, Assistant Professor; J.D., Boston.
Steve Barbre, Associate Professor; J.D., Chicago.
Cleveland Coon, Associate Professor; J.D., Southern Law.
Alfreda S. Diamond, Professor; LL.M., Columbia.
Ernest Easterly III, Professor; J.D., LSU.
Christian Fasullo, Assistant Clinical Professor; LL.M., SMU.
Linda Fowler, Visiting Instructor; J.D., LSU.
Maurice Franks, Professor; J.D., Memphis State.
Michelle R. Ghetti, Professor; J.D., LSU.
Shenequa L. Grey, Assistant Professor; J.D., Southern Law.
Stanley A. Halpin Jr., Professor; J.D., Tulane.
Dorothy F. Jackson, Assistant Clinical Professor; J.D., Southern Law.
Russell L. Jones, Professor and Vice Chancellor; LL.M., Georgetown.
Virginia Listach, Assistant Clinical Professor; J.D., Southern Law.
Ollivette Mencer, Associate Professor; J.D., Southern Law.
Jacqueline Nash, Assistant Clinical Professor; J.D., Southern Law.
Nadia Nedzel, Assistant Professor; LL.M., Northwestern.
Donald North, Associate Professor and Director of Clinical Education; J.D., Southern Law.
Okechukwu Oko, Professor; J.S.D., Yale.
Judith Perhay, Associate Professor; LL.M., Tulane.
Cynthia Picou, Professor; J.D., LSU.
John K. Pierre, Professor and Vice Chancellor for Special Projects; J.D., SMU.
Freddie Pitcher Jr., Professor and Chancellor; J.D., Southern Law.
Paul Race, Visiting Professor; J.D., Duke.
Thomas Richard, Professor; J.D., LSU.
Winston Riddick, Professor; J.D., LSU.
Arthur E. Stallworth, Professor; J.D., Southern Law.
Gail Stephenson, Assistant Professor and Director of Legal Writing; J.D., LSU.
Donald Tibbs, Assistant Professor and Director of Civil Rights and Justice Institute; J.D., Pittsburgh.
Shawn Vance, Instructor; LL.M., Georgetown.
Prentice White, Instructor; J.D., Southern Law.
Roederick White, Professor and Associate Vice Chancellor for Student Affairs; J.D., Southern Law.
Evelyn Wilson, Professor; J.D., LSU.

WIDENER UNIVERSITY

School of Law

Programs of Study

The School of Law confers the Juris Doctor (J.D.) degree, Master of Laws (LL.M.) degrees in corporate law and finance and in health law, the Master of Jurisprudence (M.J.) degree in health law for nonlawyers, a Doctor of Juridical Science (S.J.D.) degree in health law, and a Doctor of Laws (D.L.) degree in health law for nonlawyers. Joint degrees are offered with Widener's Institute for Clinical Psychology (J.D./Psy.D.) and School of Business Administration (J.D./M.B.A.). The School also offers a J.D./Master of Science in Library Science (M.S.L.S.) in cooperation with Clarion University of Pennsylvania. All candidates for the J.D. must complete a required minimum of 87 semester hours of study. After the first year, this averages a minimum of 14 hours per semester in the Regular Division (three-year program, full-time) and 11 hours per semester in the Extended Division (four-year program, day or evening). The M.J. degree requires 30 semester hours of study and the LL.M. degree requires 24 semester hours of course work. The S.J.D. and D.L. in health law are individually tailored to each candidate.

The School of Law also offers certificate programs through the Health Law Institute, the Law and Government Institute, the Institute of Delaware Corporate Law, and the Trial Advocacy Institute. In addition, the School offers clinics in civil law, consumer credit, criminal defense, environmental and natural resources law, and veterans' assistance as well as international programs in Geneva, Nairobi, Sydney, and Venice.

The School has been certified as an accredited sponsor for continuing legal education in Delaware and by the Pennsylvania Supreme Court as an official provider for continuing legal education in Pennsylvania. The Widener University School of Law is accredited by the ABA and is a member of AALS.

Research Facilities

The School of Law's library, the Legal Information Center, houses one of the most significant legal collections in the region, exceeding 600,000 volumes. The Legal Information Center consists of two branches—one on the Delaware Campus and one on the Harrisburg Campus. The Delaware Campus branch has outstanding collections in corporate law and health law to support the School's LL.M. programs. The Harrisburg Campus collection reflects its proximity to the state capital, with an emphasis on administrative, legislative, and public interest law. High-speed computers are available for legal research, searching the Internet, and word processing. All students are instructed in LexisNexis and Westlaw. Numerous other databases provide access to legal as well as interdisciplinary resources both on and off campus. A high-speed wireless network is available throughout the library and on each campus. An interactive video library simulates actual trial practice, aiding students in the development of courtroom skills. Advanced telecommunications permit total linkage between the Delaware and Harrisburg Campuses. Each branch has access to resources on the other campus.

Financial Aid

Students at Widener may receive financial assistance from federal programs, institutional grants, and endowed and other School scholarship funds. All aid programs are administered by the School's Office of Financial Aid (phone: 302-477-2272 for the Delaware Campus; 717-541-3961 for the Harrisburg Campus). Financial aid is awarded on a rolling basis. Students are encouraged to pursue the following: Federal Work-Study Program awards, Federal Perkins Loans, Federal Stafford Student Loans, unsubsidized Federal Stafford Student Loans, and Delaware State Grants. Financial assistance is also offered directly to students by various organizations or individuals, such as state bar associations, veterans' organizations, ethnic and church groups, and alumni associations. Major scholarships are awarded to students with outstanding credentials as well as returning students who have demonstrated high achievement in their law studies.

Cost of Study

Tuition for 2006–07 was $29,330 for incoming Regular Division students for full-time study in the J.D. program. For incoming Extended Division students, the cost was $21,950 per year. LL.M. and S.J.D. students paid $855 per credit, and M.J. students paid $725 per credit. For the combined programs, the cost of Psy.D. courses in the J.D./Psy.D. program was $740 per credit; the cost of business courses in the J.D./M.B.A. program was $680 per credit. In these combined programs, the J.D. courses cost $870 per credit.

Living and Housing Costs

The Delaware Campus maintains two student housing facilities available to law students only, which include 152 single-occupancy, fully furnished and air-conditioned rooms. Twenty-four one- and two-bedroom apartments are also available. Although the Harrisburg Campus does not maintain on-campus housing, a considerable number of apartment complexes offering a wide range of choices are located within a short distance of campus. Detailed information on available housing near the Harrisburg Campus is available by contacting the Office of Admissions at 717-541-3903.

Student Group

Total enrollment is approximately 1,500 students, with an alumni body of close to 11,000 practicing throughout the United States and a variety of other countries. Students can take advantage of a variety of cocurricular and extracurricular programs. Cocurricular activities include three law reviews, Moot Court Honor Society, Moe Levine Trial Advocacy Honor Society, and Order of Barristers. Extracurricular activities include Student Bar Association; American Trial Lawyers Association; Black Law Student Association, Inc.; national legal fraternities; Sports and Entertainment Law Society; state bar association affiliations; and Women's Law Caucus. Other organizations include American Civil Liberties Union, Asian Pacific American Law Students Association, Association of Latin and Hispanic Students, Brehon Society, Christian Legal Society, Club Rugby and Soccer, Environmental Law Society, International Law Society, Jewish Law Students Association, and Justinian Society.

Location

Widener University School of Law occupies two campuses—one in Wilmington, Delaware, and the other in Harrisburg, Pennsylvania. The Delaware Campus is in the heart of the Brandywine Valley and just minutes from downtown Wilmington, one of the corporate capitals of the United States. The Harrisburg Campus is nestled in the rolling foothills of the Appalachian mountains, 7 miles from the downtown area and a few minutes from the state capitol. Most of the major urban legal centers of the eastern United States are within 2 hours of both campuses.

The School

Founded in 1971 as the Delaware Law School, the School affiliated with Widener University in 1975 and graduated its first class of 267 that same year. At both campus locations, the emphasis is on teaching, and the primary mission is to provide the highest quality legal education to all students.

Applying

The application deadline is May 15. Admission is on a rolling basis with first acceptances offered in December. Candidates must have a bachelor's degree from an accredited college or university and must submit LSAT scores (LSATs given in June, October, December, and February). A graduate degree, work experience, extracurricular activities, and life experiences are also considered.

Correspondence and Information

Office of Admissions
Widener University School of Law
4601 Concord Pike
P.O. Box 7474
Wilmington, Delaware 19803-0474

Phone: 302-477-2162
E-mail: law.admissions@law.widener.edu
Web site: http://www.law.widener.edu

Office of Admissions
Widener University School of Law
3800 Vartan Way
P.O. Box 69381
Wilmington, Delaware 19803-0474

Phone: 717-541-3903
E-mail: law.admissions@law.widener.edu
Web site: http://www.law.widener.edu

Widener University

THE ADMINISTRATION

Linda Ammons, J.D., Dean of the School of Law.
Barbara L. Ayars, J.D., Assistant Dean for Admissions, Delaware and Harrisburg Campuses.
Susan L. Goldberg, LL.M., Associate Dean for Student Affairs, Delaware Campus.
Russell A. Hakes, J.D., Professor of Law and Vice Dean, Delaware Campus.
Edmund Luce, Legal Writing Professor, Delaware Campus; Assistant Dean of Student Affairs; and Administrative Director of Graduate Programs.
Lorén D. Prescott Jr., LL.M., Professor of Law and Vice Dean, Harrisburg Campus.
Elizabeth G. Simcox, J.D., Dean of Students, Harrisburg Campus.
Serena M. Williams, Professor of Law, Delaware Campus, and Assistant Dean of Student Affairs.

The Widener University School of Law students in the Ruby R. Vale Moot Courtroom.

The administration building on the Widener University School of Law Harrisburg Campus.

The Widener University School of Law building houses faculty offices, classrooms, Delaware Volunteer Legal Services offices, and the Ruby R. Vale Moot Courtroom.

ACADEMIC AND PROFESSIONAL PROGRAMS IN LIBRARY AND INFORMATION STUDIES

Section 33
Library and Information Studies

This section contains a directory of institutions offering graduate work in library and information studies, followed by in-depth entries submitted by institutions that chose to prepare detailed program descriptions. Additional information about programs listed in the directory but not augmented by an in-depth entry may be obtained by writing directly to the dean of a graduate school or chair of a department at the address given in the directory.

For programs offering related work, see also in this book Education. In Book 5, see Computer Science and Information Technology.

CONTENTS

Program Directories

Information Studies

The Catholic University of America, School of Library and Information Science, Washington, DC 20064. Offers MSLS, JD/MSLS, MSLS/MA, MSLS/MS. *Accreditation:* ALA (one or more programs are accredited). Part-time and evening/weekend programs available. Post-baccalaureate distance learning degree programs offered (minimal on-campus study). *Faculty:* 7 full-time (5 women), 19 part-time/adjunct (9 women). *Students:* 36 full-time (33 women), 207 part-time (166 women); includes 26 minority (17 African Americans, 2 Asian Americans or Pacific Islanders, 7 Hispanic Americans), 3 international. Average age 35. 155 applicants, 86% accepted, 64 enrolled. In 2006, 80 degrees awarded. *Degree requirements:* For master's, comprehensive exam. *Entrance requirements:* For master's, GRE General Test, 3 letters of recommendation. Additional exam requirements/recommendations for international students: Required—TOEFL (minimum score 550 paper-based; 213 computer-based). *Application deadline:* For fall admission, 2/1 priority date for domestic students; for spring admission, 11/15 priority date for domestic students. Applications are processed on a rolling basis. Application fee: $55. Electronic applications accepted. *Expenses: Contact institution.* Part-time tuition and fees vary according to campus/location and program. *Financial support:* Fellowships, research assistantships, career-related internships or fieldwork, Federal Work-Study, scholarships/grants, tuition waivers (full and partial), and unspecified assistantships available. Support available to part-time students. Financial award application deadline: 2/1; financial award applicants required to submit FAFSA. *Faculty research:* Information transfer, archives and manuscripts, legal libraries, information seeking, information storage and retrieval, special collections, information systems. *Unit head:* Dr. Martha L. Hale, Dean, 202-319-5085, Fax: 202-319-5574, E-mail: halem@cua.edu.

Central Connecticut State University, School of Graduate Studies, School of Arts and Sciences, Department of Information Design, New Britain, CT 06050-4010. Offers graphic information design (MA). *Faculty:* 4 full-time (2 women), 2 part-time/adjunct (both women). *Students:* 1 (woman) full-time, 2 part-time (both women), 1 international. Average age 30. 7 applicants, 57% accepted, 2 enrolled. In 2006, 3 degrees awarded. *Entrance requirements:* For master's, minimum GPA of 3.0. *Application deadline:* For fall admission, 7/1 for domestic students; for spring admission, 12/1 for domestic students. Applications are processed on a rolling basis. Application fee: $50. Electronic applications accepted. *Expenses:* Tuition, area resident: Full-time $3,970; part-time $380 per credit. Tuition, state resident: full-time $5,955; part-time $380 per credit. Tuition, nonresident: full-time $11,061; part-time $380 per credit. Required fees: $3,189. One-time fee: $62 part-time. Tuition and fees vary according to degree level and program. *Financial support:* Research assistantships, career-related internships or fieldwork, Federal Work-Study, scholarships/grants, and unspecified assistantships available. Support available to part-time students. Financial award application deadline: 3/1; financial award applicants required to submit FAFSA. *Unit head:* Susan Vial, Chair, 860-832-2557.

Claremont Graduate University, Graduate Programs, School of Arts and Humanities, Department of History, Claremont, CA 91711-6160. Offers Africana history (Certificate); American studies (MA, PhD); archival studies (MA); early modern studies (MA, PhD); European studies (MA, PhD); oral history (MA, PhD); MBA/MA; MBA/PhD. *Faculty:* 3 full-time (2 women), 2 part-time/adjunct (1 woman). *Students:* 81 full-time (40 women), 7 part-time (4 women); includes 17 minority (2 African Americans, 2 Asian Americans or Pacific Islanders, 13 Hispanic Americans), 3 international. Average age 37. In 2006, 6 master's, 3 doctorates awarded. *Degree requirements:* For master's, 2 foreign languages, thesis/dissertation; for doctorate, 2 foreign languages, thesis/dissertation, comprehensive exam. *Entrance requirements:* For master's and doctorate, GRE General Test. *Application deadline:* For fall admission, 2/15 priority date for domestic students. Applications are processed on a rolling basis. Electronic applications accepted. *Financial support:* Fellowships, research assistantships, Federal Work-Study and institutionally sponsored loans available. Support available to part-time students. Financial award application deadline: 2/15; financial award applicants required to submit FAFSA. *Faculty research:* Intellectual and social history, cultural studies, gender studies, Western history, Chicano history. *Unit head:* Janet Farrell Brodie, Chair, 909-621-8880, Fax: 909-621-8609, E-mail: janet.bradie@cgu.edu.

College of St. Catherine, Graduate Programs, Program in Library and Information Science, St. Paul, MN 55105-1789. Offers MA. Part-time and evening/weekend programs available. *Degree requirements:* For master's, microcomputer competency. *Entrance requirements:* For master's, minimum GPA of 3.2 or GRE. Additional exam requirements/recommendations for international students: Required—Michigan English Language Assessment Battery or TOEFL.

Cornell University, Graduate School, Graduate Fields of Arts and Sciences, Field of Information Science, Ithaca, NY 14853-0001. Offers cognition (PhD); human computer interaction (PhD); information systems (PhD); social aspects of information (PhD). *Faculty:* 28 full-time (8 women). *Students:* 6 full-time (2 women), 4 international. Average age 30. 78 applicants, 6% accepted, 2 enrolled. In 2006, 1 degree awarded. *Degree requirements:* For doctorate, thesis/dissertation, comprehensive exam. *Entrance requirements:* For doctorate, GRE General Test, 3 letters of recommendation. Additional exam requirements/recommendations for international students: Required—TOEFL (minimum score 550 paper-based; 213 computer-based). *Application deadline:* For fall admission, 1/1 for domestic students. Application fee: $60. Electronic applications accepted. *Expenses:* Tuition: Full-time $32,800. Full-time tuition and fees vary according to program. *Financial support:* In 2006–07, 6 students received support, including 1 fellowship with full tuition reimbursement available, 5 teaching assistantships with full tuition reimbursements available; research assistantships with full tuition reimbursements available, institutionally sponsored loans, scholarships/grants, tuition waivers (full and partial), and unspecified assistantships also available. Financial award applicants required to submit FAFSA. *Faculty research:* Digital libraries, game theory, data mining, human-computer interaction, computational linguistics. *Unit head:* Director of Graduate Studies, 607-255-5925. *Application contact:* Graduate Field Assistant, 607-255-5925, E-mail: info@infosci.cornell.edu.

Dalhousie University, Faculty of Graduate Studies, Faculty of Management, School of Library and Information Studies, Halifax, NS B3H 4R2, Canada. Offers MLIS, LL B/MLIS. *Accreditation:* ALA (one or more programs are accredited). Part-time programs available. *Degree requirements:* For master's, one foreign language, thesis optional. *Entrance requirements:* Additional exam requirements/recommendations for international students: Required—TOEFL. *Faculty research:* Information-seeking behavior, electronic text design, browsing in digital environments, information diffusion among scientists.

Dominican University, Graduate School of Library and Information Science, River Forest, IL 60305-1099. Offers MLIS, CSS, MBA/MLIS, MLIS/M Div, MLIS/MA, MLIS/MM. *Accreditation:* ALA (one or more programs are accredited). Part-time and evening/weekend programs available. Postbaccalaureate distance learning degree programs offered (minimal on-campus study). *Faculty:* 15 full-time (10 women), 28 part-time/adjunct (19 women). *Students:* 137 full-time (101 women), 588 part-time (484 women); includes 43 minority (11 African Americans, 1 American Indian/Alaska Native, 12 Asian Americans or Pacific Islanders, 19 Hispanic Americans), 5 international. Average age 36. 179 applicants, 99% accepted, 127 enrolled. In 2006, 269 degrees awarded. *Entrance requirements:* For master's, minimum GPA of 3.0 or GRE General Test or MAT. Additional exam requirements/recommendations for international students: Required—TOEFL. *Application deadline:* For fall admission, 6/1 priority date for domestic students; for winter admission, 3/1 priority date for domestic students; for spring admission, 10/1 priority date for domestic students. Applications are processed on a rolling basis. Application fee: $25. *Expenses: Contact institution.* Tuition and fees vary according to campus/location and program. *Financial support:* Fellowships, research assistantships, career-related internships or fieldwork, Federal Work-Study, scholarships/grants, and tuition waivers (partial) available. Support available to part-time students. Financial award application deadline: 4/15; financial award applicants required to submit FAFSA. *Faculty research:* Productivity and the information environment, bibliometrics, library history, subject access, library materials and services for children. *Unit head:* Susan Roman, Dean, 708-524-6986, Fax: 708-524-6657,

E-mail: sroman@dom.edu. *Application contact:* Tracie Hall, Assistant Dean, 708-524-6848, Fax: 708-524-6657, E-mail: thall@dom.edu.

Drexel University, College of Information Science and Technology, Philadelphia, PA 19104-2875. Offers information science and technology (PhD); information studies (PhD, CAS); information systems (MSIS); library and information science (MS). *Accreditation:* ALA (one or more programs are accredited). Part-time and evening/weekend programs available. Postbaccalaureate distance learning degree programs offered (no on-campus study). *Degree requirements:* For doctorate, thesis/dissertation. *Entrance requirements:* For master's and doctorate, GRE General Test. Additional exam requirements/recommendations for international students: Required—TOEFL. Electronic applications accepted. Expenses: Contact institution. *Faculty research:* Human-computer interaction, computer-supported cooperative work, digital libraries, software engineering, information retrieval/information visualization/bibliometrics.

See Close-Up on page 2129.

Emporia State University, School of Graduate Studies, School of Library and Information Management, Program in Legal Information Management, Emporia, KS 66801-5087. Offers MLM, Certificate. Part-time and evening/weekend programs available. Postbaccalaureate distance learning degree programs offered (minimal on-campus study). *Entrance requirements:* For master's, GRE. Additional exam requirements/recommendations for international students: Required—TOEFL (minimum score 450 paper-based; 133 computer-based). *Application deadline:* For fall admission, 8/15 priority date for domestic students. Applications are processed on a rolling basis. Application fee: $30 ($75 for international students). Electronic applications accepted. *Expenses:* Tuition, state resident: full-time $3,438; part-time $143 per credit hour. Tuition, nonresident: full-time $10,398; part-time $433 per credit hour. Required fees: $724; $44 per credit hour. *Financial support:* Application deadline: 3/15;

Emporia State University, School of Graduate Studies, School of Library and Information Management, Program in Library and Information Management, Emporia, KS 66801-5087. Offers MLS, PhD, Certificate. Part-time and evening/weekend programs available. Postbaccalaureate distance learning degree programs offered (minimal on-campus study). *Faculty:* 10 full-time (8 women). *Students:* 9 full-time (4 women), 302 part-time (244 women); includes 11 minority (3 African Americans, 3 Asian Americans or Pacific Islanders, 5 Hispanic Americans), 5 international. 46 applicants, 74% accepted, 26 enrolled. In 2006, 123 master's, 1 doctorate, 4 other advanced degrees awarded. *Entrance requirements:* For master's, GRE. Additional exam requirements/recommendations for international students: Required—TOEFL. *Application deadline:* For fall admission, 8/15 priority date for domestic students. Applications are processed on a rolling basis. Application fee: $30 ($75 for international students). Electronic applications accepted. *Expenses:* Tuition, state resident: full-time $3,438; part-time $143 per credit hour. Tuition, nonresident: full-time $10,398; part-time $433 per credit hour. Required fees: $724; $44 per credit hour. *Financial support:* In 2006–07, 2 research assistantships (averaging $6,752 per year), 10 teaching assistantships (averaging $6,752 per year) were awarded; Federal Work-Study, institutionally sponsored loans, and unspecified assistantships also available. Financial award application deadline: 3/15; financial award applicants required to submit FAFSA. *Application contact:* Daniel Roland, Assistant to the Dean, 620-341-5064, Fax: 620-341-5233, E-mail: droland@emporia.edu.

Florida State University, Graduate Studies, College of Information, Tallahassee, FL 32306. Offers library and information studies (MS, PhD, Specialist). *Accreditation:* ALA (one or more programs are accredited). Part-time and evening/weekend programs available. Postbaccalaureate distance learning degree programs offered (no on-campus study). *Faculty:* 29 full-time (14 women), 8 part-time/adjunct (4 women). *Students:* 47 full-time (31 women), 746 part-time (541 women); includes 151 minority (76 African Americans, 4 American Indian/Alaska Native, 23 Asian Americans or Pacific Islanders, 48 Hispanic Americans), 47 international. Average age 35. 502 applicants, 75% accepted, 263 enrolled. In 2006, 202 master's, 5 doctorates, 4 other advanced degrees awarded. *Median time to degree:* Master's—2.6 years full-time; doctorate—6.6 years full-time; Specialist—2.8 years full-time. *Degree requirements:* For master's, thesis optional; for doctorate, thesis/dissertation, comprehensive exam, registration; for Specialist, thesis or alternative, registration. *Entrance requirements:* For master's, GRE or minimum GPA of 3.0 on last 2 years of baccalaureate degree; for doctorate, GRE, minimum GPA of 3.0 on last degree program; research paper; resumé; 3 letters of recommendation; for Specialist, GRE, minimum graduate GPA of 3.2, resumé, 3 letters of recommendation. Additional exam requirements/recommendations for international students: Required—TOEFL (minimum score 550 paper-based; 80 iBT). *Application deadline:* For fall admission, 6/1 priority date for domestic students, 6/1 for international students. Applications are processed on a rolling basis. Application fee: $30. Electronic applications accepted. *Expenses:* Tuition, state resident: full-time $5,822; part-time $243 per credit hour. Tuition, nonresident: full-time $20,976; part-time $874 per credit hour. Tuition and fees vary according to program. *Financial support:* In 2006–07, 209 students received support, including 13 fellowships with full tuition reimbursements available, 102 research assistantships with full tuition reimbursements available, 94 teaching assistantships with full tuition reimbursements available; career-related internships or fieldwork, Federal Work-Study, scholarships/grants, and unspecified assistantships also available. Financial award application deadline: 3/1; financial award applicants required to submit FAFSA. *Faculty research:* Needs assessment, information policy, usability analysis, human information behavior, youth services. Total annual research expenditures: $654,946. *Unit head:* Dr. Lawrence Dennis, Dean, 850-644-2216, Fax: 850-644-9763, E-mail: ldennis@ci.fsu.edu. *Application contact:* Delores Bryant, Graduate Program Assistant, 850-644-5775, Fax: 850-644-9763, E-mail: grad@ci.fsu.edu.

Indiana University Bloomington, School of Library and Information Science, Bloomington, IN 47405-7000. Offers MIS, MLS, PhD, Sp LIS, JD/MLS, MIS/MA, MLS/MA, MPA/MIS, MPA/MLS. PhD offered through the University Graduate School. *Accreditation:* ALA (one or more programs are accredited). Part-time programs available. *Faculty:* 12 full-time (7 women). *Students:* 211 full-time (152 women), 120 part-time (81 women); includes 28 minority (9 African Americans, 1 American Indian/Alaska Native, 7 Asian Americans or Pacific Islanders, 11 Hispanic Americans), 31 international. Average age 30. In 2006, 165 master's, 1 doctorate awarded. *Degree requirements:* For doctorate, thesis/dissertation. *Entrance requirements:* For master's and doctorate, GRE General Test, 3 letters of reference. Additional exam requirements/recommendations for international students: Required—TOEFL (minimum score 600 paper-based; 250 computer-based). *Application deadline:* For fall admission, 5/15 priority date for domestic students, 12/1 priority date for international students; for spring admission, 3/15 priority date for domestic students, 9/1 priority date for international students. Applications are processed on a rolling basis. Application fee: $50 ($60 for international students). Electronic applications accepted. *Expenses: Contact institution. Financial support:* Fellowships with full and partial tuition reimbursements, Federal Work-Study, institutionally sponsored loans, and scholarships/grants available. Support available to part-time students. *Faculty research:* Scholarly communication, interface design, public library policy, computer-mediated communication, information retrieval. Total annual research expenditures: $179,634. *Unit head:* Debora Shaw, Dean, 812-855-2018, Fax: 812-855-6166. *Application contact:* Rhonda Spencer, Information Contact, 812-855-2018, Fax: 812-855-6166.

See Close-Up on page 2131.

Long Island University, C.W. Post Campus, College of Information and Computer Science, Palmer School of Library and Information Science, Brookville, NY 11548-1300. Offers archives and records management (Certificate); information studies (PhD); library and information science (MS); library media specialist (MS); public library management (Certificate). *Accreditation:* ALA (one or more programs are accredited). Part-time and evening/weekend programs available. Postbaccalaureate distance learning degree programs offered (minimal on-campus study).

Degree requirements: For master's, internship, thesis optional; for doctorate, thesis/dissertation, qualifying exam. *Entrance requirements:* For master's, GRE or MAT, minimum undergraduate GPA of 3.0, resumé. Electronic applications accepted. *Faculty research:* Information retrieval, digital libraries, scientometric and infometric studies, preservation/archiving and electronic records.

Long Island University, Westchester Graduate Campus, Program in Library and Information Science, Purchase, NY 10577. Offers MS. Part-time and evening/weekend programs available. *Faculty:* 1 (woman) full-time, 19 part-time/adjunct (11 women). *Students:* 110 (88 women). 22 applicants, 91% accepted, 18 enrolled. In 2006, 35 degrees awarded. *Application deadline:* Applications are processed on a rolling basis. Application fee: $30. *Expenses:* Tuition: Part-time $790 per credit. *Financial support:* In 2006–07, 24 students received support. Scholarships/grants, tuition waivers, and unspecified assistantships available. *Unit head:* Trudy Katz, Coordinator, 914-831-2712, E-mail: trudy.katz@liu.edu. *Application contact:* Ellen Brief, Coordinator of Admissions, Marketing, Student Services and Public Relations, 914-831-2701, Fax: 914-251-5959, E-mail: ellen.brief@liu.edu.

Louisiana State University and Agricultural and Mechanical College, Graduate School, School of Library and Information Science, Baton Rouge, LA 70803. Offers MLIS, CAS. *Accreditation:* ALA (one or more programs are accredited). Evening/weekend programs available. *Faculty:* 11 full-time (9 women). *Students:* 63 full-time (47 women), 101 part-time (90 women); includes 19 minority (13 African Americans, 5 American Indian/Alaska Native, 1 Asian American or Pacific Islander), 6 international. Average age 36. 48 applicants, 73% accepted, 17 enrolled. In 2006, 63 master's awarded. *Degree requirements:* For master's, thesis optional. *Entrance requirements:* For master's, GRE General Test, minimum GPA of 3.0. Additional exam requirements/recommendations for international students: Required—TOEFL (minimum score 550 paper-based; 213 computer-based; 79 iBT). *Application deadline:* For fall admission, 1/25 priority date for domestic students, 5/15 for international students; for spring admission, 10/15 for international students. Applications are processed on a rolling basis. Application fee: $25. Electronic applications accepted. *Financial support:* In 2006–07, 33 students received support, including 10 research assistantships with partial tuition reimbursements available (averaging $8,878 per year), 14 teaching assistantships with partial tuition reimbursements available (averaging $10,730 per year); fellowships, career-related internships or fieldwork, Federal Work-Study, institutionally sponsored loans, scholarships/grants, and unspecified assistantships also available. Support available to part-time students. Financial award applicants required to submit FAFSA. *Faculty research:* Information retrieval, management, collection development, public libraries. Total annual research expenditures: $16,801. *Unit head:* Dr. Beth M. Paskoff, Dean, 225-578-3158, Fax: 225-578-4581, E-mail: lspask@lsu.edu.

Mansfield University of Pennsylvania, Graduate Studies, Program in School Library and Information Technologies, Mansfield, PA 16933. Offers library science (M Ed). Part-time and evening/weekend programs available. Postbaccalaureate distance learning degree programs offered. *Faculty:* 1 (woman) full-time, 13 part-time/adjunct (all women). *Students:* 7 full-time (all women), 202 part-time (182 women); includes 26 minority (18 African Americans, 3 American Indian/Alaska Native, 2 Asian Americans or Pacific Islanders, 3 Hispanic Americans). Average age 39. 374 applicants, 48% accepted, 68 enrolled. In 2006, 34 degrees awarded. *Degree requirements:* For master's, thesis optional. *Entrance requirements:* For master's, minimum GPA of 3.0. Additional exam requirements/recommendations for international students: Required—TOEFL (minimum score 550 paper-based; 220 computer-based). *Application deadline:* Applications are processed on a rolling basis. Application fee: $25. Electronic applications accepted. *Expenses:* Contact institution. Tuition and fees vary according to course load and reciprocity agreements. *Financial support:* In 2006–07, 41 students received support. Unspecified assistantships available. Financial award application deadline: 5/1; financial award applicants required to submit FAFSA. *Unit head:* Cindy Keller, Chair, E-mail: ckeller@mansfield.edu. *Application contact:* Judi Brayer, Assistant Director of Enrollment Management/Graduate Admissions, 570-662-4818, Fax: 570-662-4121, E-mail: jbrayer@mansfield.edu.

McGill University, Faculty of Graduate and Postdoctoral Studies, Faculty of Education, Graduate School of Library and Information Studies, Montréal, QC H3A 2T5, Canada. Offers MLIS, PhD, Certificate, Diploma. *Accreditation:* ALA (one or more programs are accredited). Part-time programs available. *Degree requirements:* For master's, registration; for doctorate, thesis/dissertation, registration. *Entrance requirements:* For master's, minimum GPA of 3.0; for doctorate, MLIS or equivalent. Additional exam requirements/recommendations for international students: Required—TOEFL (minimum score 600 paper-based; 250 computer-based), IELTS (minimum score 8). Electronic applications accepted. *Faculty research:* Information seeking behavior, information resources in context, knowledge management and representation, human computer interaction.

Metropolitan State University, College of Management, St. Paul, MN 55106-5000. Offers finance (MBA); human resource management (MBA); information management (MMIS); international business (MBA); law enforcement (MPNA); management information systems (MBA); marketing (MBA); nonprofit management (MPNA); organizational studies (MBA); public administration (MPNA); purchasing management (MBA); systems management (MMIS). Part-time and evening/weekend programs available. *Degree requirements:* For master's, computer language (MMIS), thesis optional. *Entrance requirements:* For master's, GMAT (MBA), resumé. Additional exam requirements/recommendations for international students: Required—TOEFL (minimum score 550 paper-based; 213 computer-based). *Faculty research:* Yugoslav economic system, workers' cooperatives, participative management and job enrichment, global business systems.

North Carolina Central University, Division of Academic Affairs, School of Library and Information Sciences, Durham, NC 27707-3129. Offers MIS, MLS. *Accreditation:* ALA (one or more programs are accredited). Part-time and evening/weekend programs available. *Degree requirements:* For master's, one foreign language. *Entrance requirements:* For master's, GRE, 90 hours in liberal arts, minimum B average. Additional exam requirements/recommendations for international students: Required—TOEFL. *Faculty research:* African-American resources, planning and evaluation, analysis of economic and physical resources, geography of information, artificial intelligence.

Pratt Institute, School of Information and Library Science, Brooklyn, NY 11205-3899. Offers MS, Adv C, JD/MS, MS/MS. *Accreditation:* ALA. Part-time and evening/weekend programs available. *Faculty:* 9 full-time (6 women), 27 part-time/adjunct (15 women). *Students:* 121 full-time (93 women), 224 part-time (165 women); includes 78 minority (33 African Americans, 1 American Indian/Alaska Native, 21 Asian Americans or Pacific Islanders, 23 Hispanic Americans), 9 international. Average age 33. 254 applicants, 81% accepted, 110 enrolled. In 2006, 100 degrees awarded. *Degree requirements:* For master's, thesis. *Entrance requirements:* Additional exam requirements/recommendations for international students: Required—TOEFL (minimum score 550 paper-based; 213 computer-based). *Application deadline:* For fall admission, 2/1 for domestic students; for spring admission, 10/1 for domestic students. Application fee: $40 ($90 for international students). Electronic applications accepted. *Expenses:* Contact institution. Tuition and fees vary according to course load and program. *Financial support:* In 2006–07, 10 fellowships (averaging $2,000 per year), 10 research assistantships (averaging $2,500 per year) were awarded; career-related internships or fieldwork, Federal Work-Study, institutionally sponsored loans, scholarships/grants, and unspecified assistantships also available. Support available to part-time students. Financial award application deadline: 2/1; financial award applicants required to submit FAFSA. *Faculty research:* Development of urban libraries and information centers, medical and law librarianship, information management. *Unit head:* Tula Gianinni, Dean, 212-647-7682. *Application contact:* Young Hah, Director of Graduate Admissions, 718-636-3683, Fax: 718-399-4242, E-mail: yhah@pratt.edu.

See Close-Up on page 2133.

Queens College of the City University of New York, Division of Graduate Studies, Social Science Division, Graduate School of Library and Information Studies, Flushing, NY 11367-1597. Offers MLS, AC. *Accreditation:* ALA (one or more programs are accredited). Part-time and evening/weekend programs available. *Faculty:* 17 full-time (11 women). *Students:* 29 full-time (25 women), 348 part-time (249 women). 259 applicants, 92% accepted, 184 enrolled. In 2006, 188 degrees awarded. *Degree requirements:* For master's, thesis; for AC, thesis optional. *Entrance requirements:* For master's, minimum GPA of 3.0; for AC, master's degree or equivalent. Additional exam requirements/recommendations for international students: Required—TOEFL. *Application deadline:* For fall admission, 4/1 for domestic students; for spring admission, 11/1 for domestic students. Applications are processed on a rolling basis. Application fee: $125. *Financial support:* Career-related internships or fieldwork, Federal Work-Study, institutionally sponsored loans, and tuition waivers (partial) available. Support available to part-time students. Financial award application deadline: 4/1; financial award applicants required to submit FAFSA. *Faculty research:* Multimedia and video studies, ethnicity and librarianship, information science and computer applications. *Unit head:* Dr. Virgil Blake, Director/Chair, 718-997-3790. *Application contact:* Dr. Karen Smith, Graduate Adviser, 718-997-3790, E-mail: karen_smith@qc.edu.

Rutgers, The State University of New Jersey, New Brunswick, Graduate School, Program in Communication, Information and Library Studies, New Brunswick, NJ 08901-1281. Offers PhD. Part-time programs available. *Degree requirements:* For doctorate, thesis/dissertation, qualifying exams, comprehensive exam. *Entrance requirements:* For doctorate, GRE General Test, proficiency in statistics. Additional exam requirements/recommendations for international students: Required—TOEFL (minimum score 600 paper-based; 250 computer-based). Electronic applications accepted. *Faculty research:* Information science, communication, media studies, library studies.

Rutgers, The State University of New Jersey, New Brunswick, School of Communication, Information and Library Studies, Program in Communication and Information Studies, New Brunswick, NJ 08901-1281. Offers MCIS. Part-time programs available. *Faculty:* 20 full-time (10 women). *Students:* 27 full-time (23 women), 25 part-time (19 women); includes 17 minority (5 African Americans, 9 Asian Americans or Pacific Islanders, 3 Hispanic Americans), 4 international. Average age 31. 79 applicants, 28% accepted, 19 enrolled. In 2006, 20 degrees awarded. *Entrance requirements:* For master's, GRE General Test. Additional exam requirements/recommendations for international students: Required—TOEFL. *Application deadline:* For fall admission, 2/1 priority date for domestic students, 2/1 for international students; for spring admission, 9/15 for domestic and international students. Applications are processed on a rolling basis. Application fee: $50. Electronic applications accepted. *Financial support:* In 2006–07, 7 fellowships with full tuition reimbursements (averaging $18,348 per year) were awarded; career-related internships or fieldwork, Federal Work-Study, and institutionally sponsored loans also available. Support available to part-time students. Financial award application deadline: 2/1; financial award applicants required to submit FAFSA. *Faculty research:* Communication processes and systems, information process and systems, human information and communication behavior. *Unit head:* Dr. Laurie Lewis, Director, 732-932-7500 Ext. 8141, Fax: 732-932-6916, E-mail: mcis@scils.rutgers.edu.

St. John's University, St. John's College of Liberal Arts and Sciences, Division of Library and Information Science, Queens, NY 11439. Offers MLS, Adv C, MA/MLS, MS/MLS. *Accreditation:* ALA (one or more programs are accredited). Part-time and evening/weekend programs available. *Faculty:* 5 full-time (3 women), 3 part-time/adjunct (1 woman). *Students:* 7 full-time (all women), 85 part-time (69 women); includes 14 minority (4 African Americans, 4 Asian Americans or Pacific Islanders, 6 Hispanic Americans), 3 international. Average age 34. 45 applicants, 84% accepted, 18 enrolled. In 2006, 35 degrees awarded. *Degree requirements:* For master's, residence. *Entrance requirements:* For master's, interview, minimum GPA of 3.0. Additional exam requirements/recommendations for international students: Required—TOEFL (minimum score 500 paper-based; 173 computer-based). *Application deadline:* For fall admission, 5/1 priority date for domestic and international students; for spring admission, 11/1 priority date for domestic and international students. Applications are processed on a rolling basis. Application fee: $40. Electronic applications accepted. *Expenses:* Contact institution. Tuition and fees vary according to program. *Financial support:* Research assistantships, career-related internships or fieldwork and scholarships/grants available. Support available to part-time students. Financial award application deadline: 3/1; financial award applicants required to submit FAFSA. *Faculty research:* On-line database management, public library patronage, medieval monastic libraries and archives, children's literature, indexing. *Unit head:* Dr. Jeffrey Olson, Director, 718-990-5705, E-mail: olsonj@stjohns.edu. *Application contact:* Matthew Whelan, Director, Office of Admissions, 718-990-2000, Fax: 718-990-2096, E-mail: admissions@stjohns.edu.

San Jose State University, Graduate Studies and Research, College of Applied Sciences and Arts, School of Library and Information Science, San Jose, CA 95192-0001. Offers MLIS. *Accreditation:* ALA. Part-time and evening/weekend programs available. *Students:* 238 full-time (177 women), 577 part-time (458 women); includes 169 minority (19 African Americans, 8 American Indian/Alaska Native, 84 Asian Americans or Pacific Islanders, 58 Hispanic Americans), 1 international. Average age 37. 672 applicants, 80% accepted, 211 enrolled. In 2006, 338 degrees awarded. *Degree requirements:* For master's, comprehensive exam. *Entrance requirements:* Additional exam requirements/recommendations for international students: Required—TOEFL (minimum score 600 paper-based). *Application deadline:* For fall admission, 6/29 for domestic students; for spring admission, 11/30 for domestic students. Applications are processed on a rolling basis. Application fee: $59. Electronic applications accepted. *Financial support:* Career-related internships or fieldwork, Federal Work-Study, and institutionally sponsored loans available. Support available to part-time students. Financial award application deadline: 8/20; financial award applicants required to submit FAFSA. *Faculty research:* Evaluation of information services online, search strategy, organizational behavior. *Unit head:* Ken Haycock, Director, 408-924-2490, Fax: 408-924-2476.

Simmons College, Graduate School of Library and Information Science, Boston, MA 02115. Offers library and information science (PhD); school library teacher (MS, Certificate); MS/MA. MS/DA and MS/MA offered jointly with Department of History. *Accreditation:* ALA (one or more programs are accredited). Part-time and evening/weekend programs available. *Faculty:* 17 full-time (11 women), 30 part-time/adjunct (21 women). *Students:* 26 full-time (20 women), 528 part-time (412 women); includes 41 minority (13 African Americans, 2 American Indian/Alaska Native, 16 Asian Americans or Pacific Islanders, 10 Hispanic Americans), 7 international. Average age 35. 342 applicants, 86% accepted, 159 enrolled. In 2006, 314 master's, 1 doctorate awarded. *Degree requirements:* For master's, technology competency. *Entrance requirements:* For master's, GRE General Test or minimum GPA of 3.0; interview; for doctorate, GRE General Test or MAT, interview. Additional exam requirements/recommendations for international students: Required—TOEFL (minimum score 550 paper-based; 213 computer-based; 79 iBT). *Application deadline:* For fall admission, 3/1 priority date for domestic students, 3/1 for international students; for spring admission, 7/1 priority date for domestic students. Applications are processed on a rolling basis. Application fee: $35. Electronic applications accepted. *Expenses:* Contact institution. *Financial support:* In 2006–07, 4 research assistantships with full tuition reimbursements were awarded; career-related internships or fieldwork, Federal Work-Study, institutionally sponsored loans, scholarships/grants, and tuition waivers (full and partial) also available. Support available to part-time students. Financial award application deadline: 3/1; financial award applicants required to submit FAFSA. *Faculty research:* Visual communications, database management, information policy, digitization of libraries, international librarianship. Total annual research expenditures: $475,862. *Unit head:* Dr. Michele V. Cloonan, Dean, 617-521-2806, Fax: 617-521-3192, E-mail: cloonan@simmons.edu. *Application contact:* Denise Davis, Assistant Dean for Admission and Recruitment, 617-521-2801, Fax: 617-521-3192, E-mail: denise.davis@simmons.edu.

Southern Connecticut State University, School of Graduate Studies, School of Communication, Information and Library Science, Department of Library Science and Instructional Technology, New Haven, CT 06515-1355. Offers instructional technology (MS); library science (MLS); library/information studies (Diploma); JD/MLS; MLS/MA; MLS/MS. Part-time and evening/

Information Studies

Southern Connecticut State University (continued)
weekend programs available. Postbaccalaureate distance learning degree programs offered (no on-campus study). *Faculty:* 12 full-time, 5 part-time/adjunct. *Students:* 50 full-time (38 women), 255 part-time (223 women); includes 18 minority (5 African Americans, 10 Asian Americans or Pacific Islanders, 3 Hispanic Americans). 139 applicants, 86% accepted, 104 enrolled. In 2006, 127 master's, 12 other advanced degrees awarded. *Degree requirements:* For master's and Diploma, thesis or alternative. *Entrance requirements:* For master's, GRE General Test, interview, minimum QPA of 2.7, introductory computer science course; for Diploma, master's degree in library science or information science. *Application deadline:* For fall admission, 7/15 priority date for domestic students. Applications are processed on a rolling basis. Application fee: $50. Electronic applications accepted. *Financial support:* Research assistantships available. Financial award application deadline: 4/15; financial award applicants required to submit FAFSA. *Unit head:* Dr. Josephine Sche, Chairperson, 203-392-5710, Fax: 203-392-5780, E-mail: schej1@southernct.edu.

Syracuse University, Graduate School, School of Information Studies, Information Management Program, Syracuse, NY 13244. Offers MS, MS/CAS. Part-time and evening/weekend programs available. Postbaccalaureate distance learning degree programs offered (minimal on-campus study). *Students:* 124 full-time (43 women), 76 part-time (28 women); includes 33 minority (17 African Americans, 1 American Indian/Alaska Native, 10 Asian Americans or Pacific Islanders, 5 Hispanic Americans), 102 international. 211 applicants, 81% accepted, 63 enrolled. *Entrance requirements:* For master's, GRE General Test. *Application deadline:* For fall admission, 2/14 priority date for domestic students; for spring admission, 11/1 priority date for domestic students. Application fee: $65. Electronic applications accepted. *Expenses:* Tuition: Full-time $16,920; part-time $940 per credit hour. Required fees: $930; $930 per year. *Unit head:* Dr. Robert Heckman, Director, 315-443-4479, Fax: 315-443-6886, E-mail: rheckman@syr.edu. *Application contact:* Susan Corieri, Director of Enrollment Management, 315-443-6885, E-mail: ist@syr.edu.

See Close-Up on page 2135.

Université de Montréal, Faculty of Graduate Studies, Faculty of Arts and Sciences, School of Library and Information Sciences, Montréal, QC H3C 3J7, Canada. Offers archival (Certificate); information sciences (MBSI, PhD), including information systems and resources (PhD), information transfer (PhD); management of numerical information (Certificate). *Accreditation:* ALA (one or more programs are accredited). *Faculty:* 14 full-time (5 women), 2 part-time/adjunct (1 woman). *Students:* 159 full-time (123 women), 25 part-time (20 women). 196 applicants, 48% accepted, 87 enrolled. In 2006, 81 degrees awarded. *Degree requirements:* For master's, thesis optional. *Entrance requirements:* For master's, interview, master's degree in library and information science or equivalent. *Application deadline:* For fall admission, 2/1 priority date for domestic students; for winter admission, 11/1 priority date for domestic students; for spring admission, 2/1 priority date for domestic students. Application fee: $30. Electronic applications accepted. *Financial support:* Fellowships available. *Unit head:* Jean-Michel Salaün, Director, 514-343-7400, Fax: 514-343-5753. *Application contact:* Diane Mayer, Information Contact, 514-343-6044, Fax: 514-343-5753, E-mail: mayerdi@ere.umontreal.ca.

University at Buffalo, the State University of New York, Graduate School, Graduate School of Education, Department of Library and Information Studies, Buffalo, NY 14260. Offers MLS, Certificate. *Accreditation:* ALA (one or more programs are accredited). Part-time and evening/weekend programs available. *Faculty:* 14 full-time (8 women), 7 part-time/adjunct (5 women). *Students:* 156 full-time (119 women), 150 part-time (115 women); includes 14 minority (6 African Americans, 2 Asian Americans or Pacific Islanders, 6 Hispanic Americans), 8 international. Average age 34. 211 applicants, 50% accepted, 90 enrolled. In 2006, 132 degrees awarded. *Degree requirements:* For master's, thesis optional; for Certificate, thesis. *Entrance requirements:* For master's, minimum GPA of 3.0. Additional exam requirements/recommendations for international students: Required—TOEFL (minimum score 550 paper-based; 213 computer-based), GRE. *Application deadline:* For fall admission, 4/1 priority date for domestic students; for spring admission, 10/15 priority date for domestic students. Applications are processed on a rolling basis. Application fee: $35. Electronic applications accepted. *Financial support:* In 2006–07, 5 fellowships (averaging $10,000 per year), 2 research assistantships with full tuition reimbursements (averaging $5,000 per year) were awarded; teaching assistantships, career-related internships or fieldwork, Federal Work-Study, institutionally sponsored loans, tuition waivers (full and partial), and unspecified assistantships also available. Support available to part-time students. Financial award application deadline: 3/1; financial award applicants required to submit FAFSA. *Faculty research:* Information user behavior, storage and information retrieval, digital libraries, information management services to information users. Total annual research expenditures: $296,881. *Unit head:* Dr. Judith Robinson, Chair, 716-645-2412, Fax: 716-645-3775, E-mail: ub-lis@buffalo.edu. *Application contact:* Dr. Radhika Suresh, Director of Graduate Admissions and Student Services, 716-645-2110 Ext. 1209, Fax: 716-645-7937, E-mail: gse-info@buffalo.edu.

The University of Alabama, Graduate School, College of Communication and Information Sciences, School of Library and Information Studies, Tuscaloosa, AL 35487. Offers book arts (MFA); library and information studies (MLIS, PhD). *Accreditation:* ALA (one or more programs are accredited). Part-time programs available. Postbaccalaureate distance learning degree programs offered (minimal on-campus study). *Faculty:* 11 full-time (6 women). *Students:* 75 full-time (51 women), 170 part-time (132 women); includes 15 minority (11 African Americans, 1 American Indian/Alaska Native, 1 Asian American or Pacific Islander, 2 Hispanic Americans), 1 international. Average age 33. 191 applicants, 86% accepted, 43 enrolled. In 2006, 119 degrees awarded. *Median time to degree:* Master's–1.4 years full-time, 2.3 years part-time. *Entrance requirements:* For master's, GRE General Test or MAT, minimum GPA of 3.0. Additional exam requirements/recommendations for international students: Required—TOEFL. *Application deadline:* For fall admission, 7/1 priority date for domestic and international students; for spring admission, 11/1 priority date for domestic and international students. Applications are processed on a rolling basis. Application fee: $25. Electronic applications accepted. *Financial support:* In 2006–07, 64 students received support, including 4 fellowships with tuition reimbursements available (averaging $14,778 per year), 13 research assistantships with full and partial tuition reimbursements available (averaging $4,912 per year), 18 teaching assistantships with full and partial tuition reimbursements available (averaging $4,912 per year); career-related internships or fieldwork, Federal Work-Study, scholarships/grants, and unspecified assistantships also available. Financial award application deadline: 3/20. *Faculty research:* Instructional design, information equity, youth services, rural information services, book history. *Unit head:* Dr. Elizabeth Aversa, Director and Professor, 205-348-4610, Fax: 205-348-3746, E-mail: eaversa@slis.ua.edu. *Application contact:* Dr. Elizabeth Aversa, Director and Professor, 205-348-4610, Fax: 205-348-3746, E-mail: eaversa@slis.ua.edu.

University of Alberta, Faculty of Graduate Studies and Research, School of Library and Information Studies, Edmonton, AB T6G 2E1, Canada. Offers MLIS. *Accreditation:* ALA. *Faculty:* 6 full-time (5 women), 12 part-time/adjunct (7 women). *Students:* 76 full-time (65 women), 22 part-time (20 women). Average age 32. 142 applicants, 32% accepted, 42 enrolled. In 2006, 24 degrees awarded. *Entrance requirements:* Additional exam requirements/recommendations for international students: Required—TOEFL, Canadian Academic English Language Assessment. *Application deadline:* For fall admission, 7/1 for domestic students, 5/1 for international students. Applications are processed on a rolling basis. Electronic applications accepted. *Financial support:* In 2006–07, 68 students received support, including 12 research assistantships with partial tuition reimbursements available (averaging $3,536 per year); fellowships, career-related internships or fieldwork and scholarships/grants also available. Support available to part-time students. Financial award application deadline: 7/1. *Faculty research:* Intellectual freedom, materials for children and young adults, library classification, multi-media literacy. Total annual research expenditures: $63,000. *Unit head:* Anna Altmann, Acting Director, 780-492-4140, Fax: 403-492-2430, E-mail: anna.altmann@ualberta.ca. *Application contact:* Joanne Hilger, Student Services Administrator, 780-492-4578, Fax: 780-492-2430, E-mail: slis@ualberta.ca.

The University of Arizona, Graduate College, College of Social and Behavioral Sciences, School of Information Resources and Library Science, Tucson, AZ 85721. Offers MA, PhD. *Accreditation:* ALA (one or more programs are accredited). Part-time programs available. *Degree requirements:* For master's, proficiency in disk operating system (DOS); for doctorate, thesis/dissertation. *Entrance requirements:* For master's, GRE, minimum GPA of 3.0; for doctorate, GRE General Test. Additional exam requirements/recommendations for international students: Required—TOEFL. *Faculty research:* Microcomputer applications; quantitative methods systems; information transfer, planning, evaluation, and technology.

The University of British Columbia, Faculty of Arts, School of Library, Archival and Information Studies, Program in Archival Studies/Library and Information Studies, Vancouver, BC V6T 1Z1, Canada. Offers MLIS/MAS. *Faculty:* 10 full-time (7 women), 34 part-time/adjunct (28 women). *Students:* 33 full-time (26 women), 1 (woman) part-time. 25 applicants, 64% accepted, 12 enrolled. *Entrance requirements:* Additional exam requirements/recommendations for international students: Required—TOEFL (minimum score 600 paper-based; 250 computer-based; 100 iBT). *Application deadline:* For fall admission, 2/1 for domestic and international students; for winter admission, 5/1 for domestic and international students. Applications are processed on a rolling basis. Application fee: $90 Canadian dollars ($150 Canadian dollars for international students). Electronic applications accepted. *Financial support:* In 2006–07, fellowships (averaging $16,000 per year), 15 research assistantships were awarded; Federal Work-Study, institutionally sponsored loans, scholarships/grants, tuition waivers (partial), and unspecified assistantships also available. *Application contact:* Graduate Admissions Secretary, 604-822-2404, Fax: 604-822-6006, E-mail: slais.admissions@ubc.ca.

The University of British Columbia, Faculty of Arts, School of Library, Archival and Information Studies, Program in Library and Information Studies, Vancouver, BC V6T 1Z1, Canada. Offers MLIS. Part-time programs available. *Faculty:* 9 full-time (7 women), 26 part-time/adjunct (20 women). *Students:* 136 full-time (106 women), 9 part-time (6 women). Average age 34. 220 applicants, 37% accepted, 55 enrolled. In 2006, 83 degrees awarded. *Degree requirements:* For master's, thesis optional. *Entrance requirements:* For master's, minimum GPA of 3.3 in undergraduate upper-division courses. Additional exam requirements/recommendations for international students: Required—TOEFL (minimum score 600 paper-based; 250 computer-based; 100 iBT). *Application deadline:* For fall admission, 2/1 for domestic and international students; for winter admission, 5/1 for domestic and international students. Application fee: $90 ($150 for international students). Electronic applications accepted. *Financial support:* In 2006–07, 31 students received support, including fellowships (averaging $16,000 per year), 2 research assistantships; teaching assistantships, Federal Work-Study, institutionally sponsored loans, scholarships/grants, and unspecified assistantships also available. *Faculty research:* Computer systems/database design; digital libraries; metadata/classification; censorship and intellectual freedom; children's literature and services. *Application contact:* Graduate Admissions Secretary, 604-822-2404, Fax: 604-822-6006, E-mail: slais.admissions@ubc.ca.

University of California, Berkeley, Graduate Division, School of Information Management and Systems, Berkeley, CA 94720-1500. Offers MIMS, PhD. *Degree requirements:* For doctorate, thesis/dissertation, qualifying exam. *Entrance requirements:* For master's, GRE General Test, minimum GPA of 3.0, previous course work in java or C programming; for doctorate, GRE General Test, minimum GPA of 3.0. Additional exam requirements/recommendations for international students: Required—TOEFL. Application fee: $60 ($80 for international students). *Financial support:* Fellowships, research assistantships, teaching assistantships, unspecified assistantships available. *Faculty research:* Information retrieval research, design and evaluation of information systems, work practice-based design of information systems, economics of information, intellectual property law. *Unit head:* AnnaLee Saxenian, Dean, School of Information Management and Systems, 510-642-9980, E-mail: anna@sims.berkeley.edu. *Application contact:* Leticia Sanchez, Student Affairs Officer, 510-642-1464, Fax: 510-642-5814, E-mail: admissions@sims.berkeley.edu.

University of California, Los Angeles, Graduate Division, Graduate School of Education and Information Studies, Department of Information Studies, Los Angeles, CA 90095. Offers archival studies (MLIS); informatics (MLIS); information studies (PhD); library and information science (Certificate); library studies (MLIS); MBA/MLIS; MLIS/MA. *Accreditation:* ALA (one or more programs are accredited). *Faculty:* 13 full-time (7 women), 5 part-time/adjunct (4 women). *Students:* 186 full-time (145 women), 33 part-time (23 women); includes 83 minority (7 African Americans, 2 American Indian/Alaska Native, 46 Asian Americans or Pacific Islanders, 28 Hispanic Americans), 6 international. Average age 28. 192 applicants, 71% accepted, 105 enrolled. In 2006, 77 master's, 4 doctorates awarded. Terminal master's awarded for partial completion of doctoral program. *Degree requirements:* For master's, thesis or alternative, professional portfolio; for doctorate, thesis/dissertation, oral and written qualifying exams, professional portfolio. *Entrance requirements:* For master's, GRE General Test, previous course work in computer programming and statistics; for doctorate, GRE General Test, previous course work in statistics, 2 samples of research writing in English. Additional exam requirements/recommendations for international students: Required—TOEFL (paper-based 613, computer-based 220) or IELTS or TWE (5). *Application deadline:* For fall admission, 12/15 for domestic and international students. Applications are processed on a rolling basis. Application fee: $60. Electronic applications accepted. *Financial support:* In 2006–07, 41 fellowships (averaging $12,013 per year) were awarded; research assistantships with partial tuition reimbursements, teaching assistantships with partial tuition reimbursements, career-related internships or fieldwork, Federal Work-Study, institutionally sponsored loans, scholarships/grants, and tuition waivers (full and partial) also available. Support available to part-time students. Financial award application deadline: 3/1; financial award applicants required to submit FAFSA. *Faculty research:* Multimedia, digital libraries, archives and electronic records, interface design, information technology and policy, preservation, access. *Unit head:* Anne J. Gilliland, Professor and Chair, 310-825-8799, E-mail: agilliland@ucla.edu. *Application contact:* Susan S. Abler, Student Affairs Officer, 310-825-5269, Fax: 310-206-4460, E-mail: abler@gseis.ucla.edu.

University of Central Missouri, The Graduate School, College of Education, Department of Educational Leadership and Human Development, Program in Library Science and Information Services, Warrensburg, MO 64093. Offers human services/learning resources (Ed S); library science and information services (MS). Part-time programs available. *Faculty:* 4 full-time (3 women). *Students:* 3 full-time (2 women), 57 part-time (54 women); includes 4 minority (2 African Americans, 2 Hispanic Americans), 1 international. Average age 39. 17 applicants, 82% accepted, 14 enrolled. In 2006, 21 master's, 2 other advanced degrees awarded. *Degree requirements:* For master's and Ed S, thesis or alternative. *Entrance requirements:* For master's, minimum GPA of 2.75, interview, 2 years of teaching experience; for Ed S, minimum GPA of 3.25, master's degree, teaching certificate. Additional exam requirements/recommendations for international students: Required—TOEFL (minimum score 500 paper-based; 173 computer-based). *Application deadline:* For fall admission, 6/1 priority date for domestic students, 5/1 priority date for international students; for spring admission, 10/1 priority date for domestic students, 10/1 for international students. Applications are processed on a rolling basis. Application fee: $30 ($50 for international students). *Expenses:* Tuition, state resident: full-time $5,448; part-time $227 per credit hour. Tuition, nonresident: full-time $10,896; part-time $454 per credit hour. Required fees: $336; $14 per credit hour. *Financial support:* In 2006–07, 6 students received support. Federal Work-Study, scholarships/grants, unspecified assistantships, and administrative assistantships available. Support available to part-time students. Financial award application deadline: 3/1; financial award applicants required to submit FAFSA. *Faculty research:* Promoting information literacy; collaboration between teachers and librarians; student retention; K-12 virtual schools; leadership in school libraries.

University of Denver, University College, Denver, CO 80208. Offers applied communication (MAS, MPS); computer information systems (MAS); environmental policy and management (MAS); geographic information systems (MAS); human resource administration (MPS); knowledge and information technologies (MAS); liberal studies (MLS); modern languages (MLS); organizational leadership (MPS); technology management (MAS); telecommunications (MAS). Part-time and evening/weekend programs available. Postbaccalaureate distance learning degree programs offered (no on-campus study). *Students:* 57 full-time (28 women), 453 part-time (253 women); includes 84 minority (37 African Americans, 1 American Indian/Alaska Native, 21 Asian Americans or Pacific Islanders, 25 Hispanic Americans), 39 international. Average age 26. 159 applicants, 84% accepted. In 2006, 171 master's awarded. *Entrance requirements:* Additional exam requirements/recommendations for international students: Required—TOEFL (minimum score 550 paper-based; 213 computer-based). *Application deadline:* Applications are processed on a rolling basis. Application fee: $75. Electronic applications accepted. *Expenses: Contact institution. Financial support:* Applicants required to submit FAFSA. *Unit head:* Dr. James Davis, Dean, 303-871-2291, Fax: 303-871-4047, E-mail: jdavis@du.edu. *Application contact:* Information Contact, 303-871-3069.

University of Hawaii at Manoa, Graduate Division, Colleges of Arts and Sciences, College of Natural Sciences, Department of Information and Computer Sciences, Library and Information Science Program, Honolulu, HI 96822. Offers advanced library and information science (Graduate Certificate); communication and information science (PhD); library and information science (MLI Sc). *Accreditation:* ALA (one or more programs are accredited). Part-time programs available. *Faculty:* 6 full-time (4 women), 6 part-time/adjunct (5 women). *Students:* 48 full-time (36 women), 78 part-time (63 women); includes 74 minority (1 African American, 71 Asian Americans or Pacific Islanders, 2 Hispanic Americans), 7 international. Average age 34. 78 applicants, 71% accepted, 35 enrolled. In 2006, 52 degrees awarded. *Degree requirements:* For master's, thesis optional. *Entrance requirements:* For master's, GRE General Test. Additional exam requirements/recommendations for international students: Required—TOEFL (minimum score 600 paper-based; 250 computer-based). *Application deadline:* For fall admission, 4/1 for domestic students; for spring admission, 11/1 for domestic students. Applications are processed on a rolling basis. Application fee: $50. Electronic applications accepted. *Financial support:* In 2006–07, 25 students received support; research assistantships with full tuition reimbursements available, career-related internships or fieldwork, Federal Work-Study, institutionally sponsored loans, scholarships/grants, and tuition waivers (full and partial) available. *Faculty research:* Information behavior, evaluation of electronic information sources, online learning, history of libraries, information literacy. *Application contact:* Gail Morimoto, Administrative Assistant, E-mail: morimoto@hawaii.edu.

University of Illinois at Urbana–Champaign, Graduate College, Graduate School of Library and Information Science, Champaign, IL 61820. Offers MS, PhD, CAS. *Accreditation:* ALA (one or more programs are accredited). *Faculty:* 21 full-time (9 women), 4 part-time/adjunct (3 women). *Students:* 249 full-time (189 women), 292 part-time (222 women); includes 51 minority (23 African Americans, 24 Asian Americans or Pacific Islanders, 4 Hispanic Americans), 38 international. Average age 31. 571 applicants, 53% accepted, 99 enrolled. In 2006, 197 master's, 4 doctorates, 2 other advanced degrees awarded. *Degree requirements:* For doctorate, thesis/dissertation; for CAS, project. *Entrance requirements:* For master's, GRE General Test, minimum GPA of 3.0; for doctorate, interview; for CAS, master's degree in library and information science or related field, minimum GPA of 3.0. *Application deadline:* For fall admission, 1/16 priority date for domestic students; for spring admission, 10/16 for domestic students. Applications are processed on a rolling basis. Application fee: $50 ($60 for international students). Electronic applications accepted. *Financial support:* In 2006–07, 33 fellowships, 39 research assistantships, 22 teaching assistantships were awarded; tuition waivers (full and partial) also available. Financial award application deadline: 2/1. *Unit head:* John Unsworth, Dean, 217-333-3281, Fax: 217-244-3302, E-mail: unsworth@uiuc.edu. *Application contact:* Valerie Youngen, Admissions, 217-333-0734, Fax: 217-244-3302, E-mail: vyoungen@uiuc.edu.

See Close-Up on page 2137.

The University of Iowa, Graduate College, School of Library and Information Science, Iowa City, IA 52242-1316. Offers MA, MA/Certificate, MBA/MA. *Accreditation:* ALA (one or more programs are accredited). *Faculty:* 4 full-time, 9 part-time/adjunct. *Students:* 43 full-time (38 women), 23 part-time (19 women); includes 2 minority (1 African American, 1 Hispanic American), 3 international. 88 applicants, 56% accepted, 27 enrolled. In 2006, 28 degrees awarded. *Degree requirements:* For master's, exam, portfolio, thesis optional. *Entrance requirements:* For master's, GRE General Test, minimum GPA of 3.0. Additional exam requirements/recommendations for international students: Required—TOEFL (minimum score 550 paper-based; 213 computer-based; 81 iBT). *Application deadline:* For fall admission, 2/1 for domestic and international students. Application fee: $60 ($85 for international students). Electronic applications accepted. *Financial support:* In 2006–07, 1 fellowship, 11 research assistantships with partial tuition reimbursements, 6 teaching assistantships with partial tuition reimbursements were awarded. Financial award applicants required to submit FAFSA. *Unit head:* James Elmborg, Director, 319-335-5707.

University of Maryland, College Park, Graduate Studies, College of Information Studies, College Park, MD 20742. Offers MIM, MLS, PhD, MA/MLS. *Accreditation:* ALA (one or more programs are accredited). Part-time and evening/weekend programs available. *Faculty:* 18 full-time (9 women), 24 part-time/adjunct (13 women). *Students:* 205 full-time (151 women), 222 part-time (171 women); includes 52 minority (29 African Americans, 1 American Indian/Alaska Native, 13 Asian Americans or Pacific Islanders, 9 Hispanic Americans), 37 international. 417 applicants, 62% accepted, 128 enrolled. In 2006, 147 degrees awarded. Terminal master's awarded for partial completion of doctoral program. *Degree requirements:* For master's, thesis optional; for doctorate, thesis/dissertation, 1 year residency, comprehensive exam. *Entrance requirements:* For master's and doctorate, GRE General Test, minimum GPA of 3.0, 3 letters of recommendation. Additional exam requirements/recommendations for international students: Required—TOEFL. *Application deadline:* For fall admission, 2/1 for domestic and international students; for spring admission, 10/1 for domestic students, 6/1 for international students. Applications are processed on a rolling basis. Application fee: $60. Electronic applications accepted. *Financial support:* In 2006–07, 1 fellowship with full tuition reimbursement (averaging $14,140 per year), 6 research assistantships (averaging $17,780 per year), 60 teaching assistantships with tuition reimbursements (averaging $13,992 per year) were awarded; career-related internships or fieldwork, Federal Work-Study, scholarships/grants, and tuition waivers (full and partial) also available. Support available to part-time students. Financial award application deadline: 2/1; financial award applicants required to submit FAFSA. Total annual research expenditures: $291,944. *Unit head:* Dr. Jennifer Preece, Dean, 301-405-2036, Fax: 301-314-9145, E-mail: preece@umd.edu. *Application contact:* Dean of Graduate School, 301-405-0358, Fax: 301-314-9305.

See Close-Up on page 2139.

University of Michigan, Horace H. Rackham School of Graduate Studies, School of Information, Ann Arbor, MI 48109-1107. Offers archives and records management (MS); human-computer interaction (MS); information (MS, PhD); information economics, management and policy (MS); library and information services (MS). *Accreditation:* ALA (one or more programs are accredited). Part-time programs available. *Degree requirements:* For master's, variable foreign language requirement, thesis optional; for doctorate, one foreign language, thesis/dissertation, oral defense of dissertation, preliminary exam. *Entrance requirements:* For master's and doctorate, GRE General Test. Additional exam requirements/recommendations for international students: Required—TOEFL (minimum score 600 paper-based; 250 computer-based). Electronic applications accepted.

See Close-Up on page 2141.

University of Missouri–Columbia, Graduate School, College of Education, School of Information Science and Learning Technologies, Columbia, MO 65211. Offers educational technology (M Ed, Ed S); information science and learning technology (PhD); library science (MA). *Accreditation:* ALA (one or more programs are accredited). Part-time and evening/weekend programs available. *Faculty:* 15 full-time (7 women). *Students:* 140 full-time (105 women), 260 part-time (200 women); includes 15 minority (5 African Americans, 4 American Indian/Alaska Native, 3 Asian Americans or Pacific Islanders, 3 Hispanic Americans), 37 international. In 2006, 175 master's, 7 doctorates, 3 other advanced degrees awarded. *Entrance requirements:* For master's, GRE General Test or MAT, minimum GPA of 3.0. *Application deadline:* For fall admission, 3/1 priority date for domestic students; for winter admission, 10/1 priority date for domestic students; for spring admission, 3/1 priority date for domestic students. Applications are processed on a rolling basis. Application fee: $45 ($60 for international students). *Financial support:* Fellowships, teaching assistantships available. *Unit head:* Dr. John Wedman, Director of Graduate Studies, 573-882-9424, E-mail: wedmanj@missouri.edu.

The University of North Carolina at Chapel Hill, Graduate School, School of Information and Library Science, Chapel Hill, NC 27599. Offers MSIS, MSLS, PhD, CAS. *Accreditation:* ALA (one or more programs are accredited). Part-time programs available. *Faculty:* 22 full-time (13 women), 46 part-time/adjunct (23 women). *Students:* 289 full-time (186 women), 34 part-time (20 women); includes 30 minority (19 African Americans, 3 American Indian/Alaska Native, 5 Asian Americans or Pacific Islanders, 3 Hispanic Americans), 19 international. Average age 28. 326 applicants, 62% accepted, 120 enrolled. In 2006, 105 master's, 4 doctorates awarded. Terminal master's awarded for partial completion of doctoral program. *Median time to degree:* Of those who began their doctoral program in fall 1998, 75% received their degree in 8 years or less. *Degree requirements:* For master's, paper or project; for doctorate, thesis/dissertation. *Entrance requirements:* For master's and doctorate, GRE General Test. Additional exam requirements/recommendations for international students: Required—TOEFL (minimum score 625 paper-based; 263 computer-based). *Application deadline:* For fall admission, 1/1 priority date for domestic and international students; for spring admission, 10/15 for domestic and international students. Applications are processed on a rolling basis. Application fee: $70. Electronic applications accepted. *Financial support:* In 2006–07, 71 fellowships with full tuition reimbursements (averaging $2,445 per year), 138 research assistantships with full tuition reimbursements (averaging $11,836 per year), 4 teaching assistantships with full tuition reimbursements (averaging $11,000 per year) were awarded; career-related internships or fieldwork, Federal Work-Study, institutionally sponsored loans, health care benefits, and unspecified assistantships also available. Financial award application deadline: 1/1. *Faculty research:* Information retrieval, digital libraries, management of information resources, archives and cultural heritage, information management. *Unit head:* Dr. Jose-Marie Griffiths, Dean, 919-962-8366, Fax: 919-962-8071, E-mail: info@ils.unc.edu. *Application contact:* Lara Bailey, Student Services Manager, 919-962-8366, Fax: 919-962-8071, E-mail: info@ils.unc.edu.

The University of North Carolina at Greensboro, Graduate School, School of Education, Department of Library and Information Studies, Greensboro, NC 27412-5001. Offers MLIS. *Accreditation:* ALA. Part-time and evening/weekend programs available. Postbaccalaureate distance learning degree programs offered (no on-campus study). *Faculty:* 8 full-time (6 women), 16 part-time/adjunct (9 women). *Students:* 86 full-time (72 women), 148 part-time (127 women); includes 15 minority (9 African Americans, 4 Asian Americans or Pacific Islanders, 2 Hispanic Americans), 4 international. Average age 35. 146 applicants, 52% accepted, 66 enrolled. In 2006, 104 degrees awarded. *Degree requirements:* For master's, portfolio. *Entrance requirements:* For master's, GRE General Test. Additional exam requirements/recommendations for international students: Required—TOEFL (minimum score 550 paper-based; 213 computer-based), IELTS (minimum score 7). *Application deadline:* For fall admission, 3/31 priority date for domestic students; for spring admission, 10/31 for domestic students. Applications are processed on a rolling basis. Application fee: $45. Electronic applications accepted. *Expenses:* Tuition, state resident: full-time $2,692. Tuition, nonresident: full-time $13,742. *Financial support:* In 2006–07, fellowships (averaging $3,404 per year), 10 research assistantships with full tuition reimbursements (averaging $8,000 per year) were awarded; career-related internships or fieldwork, Federal Work-Study, institutionally sponsored loans, scholarships/grants, and unspecified assistantships also available. Support available to part-time students. Financial award application deadline: 3/1; financial award applicants required to submit FAFSA. *Faculty research:* Library history, gender studies, children's literature, web design, homeless, technical services. *Unit head:* Dr. O Lee Shiflett, Chair, 336-334-3481, E-mail: olshifle@uncg.edu. *Application contact:* Michelle Harkleroad, Director of Graduate Admissions, 336-334-4884, Fax: 336-334-4424, E-mail: mbharkle@uncg.edu.

University of North Texas, Robert B. Toulouse School of Graduate Studies, School of Library and Information Sciences, Denton, TX 76203. Offers information science (MS, PhD); library science (MS). *Accreditation:* ALA (one or more programs are accredited). Part-time and evening/weekend programs available. *Faculty:* 15 full-time (8 women). *Students:* 123 full-time (86 women), 755 part-time (626 women); includes 159 minority (39 African Americans, 6 American Indian/Alaska Native, 21 Asian Americans or Pacific Islanders, 93 Hispanic Americans), 45 international. Average age 36. 355 applicants, 72% accepted, 138 enrolled. In 2006, 362 master's, 11 doctorates awarded. *Degree requirements:* For master's, comprehensive exam; for doctorate, one foreign language, thesis/dissertation, comprehensive exam. *Entrance requirements:* For master's and doctorate, GRE General Test. Additional exam requirements/recommendations for international students: Recommended—TOEFL (minimum score 550 paper-based; 213 computer-based). *Application deadline:* For fall admission, 7/15 for domestic students; for spring admission, 11/30 for domestic students. Applications are processed on a rolling basis. Application fee: $50 ($75 for international students). *Expenses:* Tuition, state resident: full-time $3,573; part-time $198 per credit. Tuition, nonresident: full-time $8,577; part-time $476 per credit. Required fees: $1,258; $126 per credit. One-time fee: $150 full-time. Tuition and fees vary according to course load. *Financial support:* Fellowships, research assistantships, teaching assistantships, career-related internships or fieldwork, Federal Work-Study, institutionally sponsored loans, and library assistantships available. Financial award application deadline: 4/1. *Faculty research:* Information resources and services, information management and retrieval, computer-based information systems. *Unit head:* Dr. Herman Totten, Dean, 940-565-2058, E-mail: totten@lis.admin.unt.edu. *Application contact:* Dr. Brian O'Connor, Graduate Adviser, 940-565-2347, Fax: 940-565-3101, E-mail: boconnor@lis.admin.unt.edu.

University of Oklahoma, Graduate College, College of Arts and Sciences, School of Library and Information Studies, Program in Library and Information Studies, Norman, OK 73019-0390. Offers knowledge management (MS); library and information studies (MLIS); school library media specialist (Certificate); M Ed/MLIS; MBA/MLIS. Part-time and evening/weekend programs available. *Students:* 34 full-time (29 women), 161 part-time (130 women); includes 19 minority (8 African Americans, 8 American Indian/Alaska Native, 1 Asian American or Pacific Islander, 2 Hispanic Americans), 1 international. 52 applicants, 100% accepted, 38 enrolled. In 2006, 56 degrees awarded. *Degree requirements:* For master's, comprehensive exam (MLIS). *Entrance requirements:* For master's, GRE, minimum GPA of 3.2 in last 60 hours or 3.0 overall. Additional exam requirements/recommendations for international students: Required—TOEFL (minimum score 550 paper-based; 213 computer-based). *Application deadline:* For fall admission, 3/1 priority date for domestic students, 4/1 for international students; for spring admission, 10/15 for domestic students, 9/1 for international students. Applications are processed on a rolling basis. Application fee: $40 ($90 for international students). Electronic applications accepted. *Expenses:* Tuition, state resident: full-time $3,180; part-time $133 per credit hour. Tuition, nonresident: full-time $11,347; part-time $473 per credit hour. Required fees: $1,729; $62 per credit hour. $117 per semester. Tuition and fees vary according to course load and program. *Financial support:* Teaching assistantships with partial tuition reimbursements, scholarships/grants and unspecified assistantships available. Financial award applicants required to submit FAFSA. *Faculty research:* Information use in the digital age, equity of access, learning organizations, education of information professionals, information services to special populations. *Application contact:* Maggie Ryan, Coordinator of Admissions, 405-325-3921, Fax: 405-325-7648, E-mail: mryan@ou.edu.

University of Pittsburgh, School of Information Sciences, Department of Library and Information Science, Pittsburgh, PA 15260. Offers MLIS, PhD, Certificate. *Accreditation:* ALA (one or more programs are accredited). Part-time and evening/weekend programs available. Postbaccalaureate distance learning degree programs offered (minimal on-campus study). *Faculty:* 8 full-time (4 women), 11 part-time/adjunct (10 women). *Students:* 148 full-time (113 women),

Information Studies

University of Pittsburgh (continued)
276 part-time (228 women); includes 31 minority (10 African Americans, 11 Asian Americans or Pacific Islanders, 10 Hispanic Americans), 33 international. 298 applicants, 94% accepted, 126 enrolled. In 2006, 196 master's, 6 doctorates, 3 other advanced degrees awarded. *Degree requirements:* For master's, thesis optional; for doctorate, thesis/dissertation, comprehensive exam, registration. *Entrance requirements:* For master's, minimum GPA of 3.0; for doctorate, GRE General Test, minimum GPA of 3.0. Additional exam requirements/recommendations for international students: Required—TOEFL (minimum score 550 paper-based; 213 computer-based; 80 iBT). *Application deadline:* For fall admission, 7/1 priority date for domestic students, 4/1 priority date for international students; for spring admission, 11/1 priority date for domestic students, 10/1 priority date for international students. Applications are processed on a rolling basis. Application fee: $50. Electronic applications accepted. *Expenses: Contact institution. Financial support:* In 2006–07, 186 students received support, including 103 fellowships with full tuition reimbursements available (averaging $3,027 per year), 5 research assistantships with full and partial tuition reimbursements available (averaging $3,887 per year), 78 teaching assistantships with full and partial tuition reimbursements available (averaging $7,554 per year); career-related internships or fieldwork, scholarships/grants, health care benefits, tuition waivers (full and partial), and unspecified assistantships also available. Support available to part-time students. Financial award application deadline: 1/15; financial award applicants required to submit FAFSA. *Faculty research:* Archives, preservation management, children's resources and services, medical informatics, digital libraries, information retrieval. Total annual research expenditures: $93,672. *Unit head:* Dr. Richard Cox, Chair, 412-624-3245, Fax: 412-624-5231, E-mail: rcox@sis.pitt.edu. *Application contact:* Ninette Kay, Admissions Coordinator, 412-624-5146, Fax: 412-624-5231, E-mail: nkay@mail.sis.pitt.edu.

University of Puerto Rico, Río Piedras, Graduate School of Information Sciences and Technologies, San Juan, PR 00931-3300. Offers librarianship (Post-Graduate Certificate); librarianship and information services (MLS). *Accreditation:* ALA. Part-time programs available. *Students:* 38 full-time (27 women), 97 part-time (68 women); includes 134 minority (all Hispanic Americans) In 2006, 18 master's, 28 other advanced degrees awarded. *Degree requirements:* For master's, thesis, portfolio, comprehensive exam. *Entrance requirements:* For master's, PAEG, GRE, interview, minimum GPA of 3.0, 3 letters of recommendation; for Post-Graduate Certificate, PAEG, GRE, minimum GPA of 3.0, IST master's degree. *Application deadline:* For fall admission, 2/1 for domestic and international students. Application fee: $17. *Expenses:* Tuition, state resident: part-time $100 per credit. Tuition, nonresident: part-time $291 per credit. Required fees: $72 per semester. *Financial support:* Fellowships, research assistantships, teaching assistantships, Federal Work-Study, institutionally sponsored loans, and tuition waivers (partial) available. Financial award application deadline: 5/31. *Faculty research:* Evaluation of journals published by the Puerto Rican system. *Unit head:* Dr. Nitza M. Hernández, Director, 787-764-0000 Ext. 5207, Fax: 787-764-2311. *Application contact:* Information Contact, 787-764-0000 Ext. 5827, Fax: 787-764-2311.

University of Rhode Island, Graduate School, College of Arts and Sciences, Graduate School of Library and Information Studies, Kingston, RI 02881. Offers MLIS. *Accreditation:* ALA. In 2006, 64 degrees awarded. *Application deadline:* For fall admission, 4/15 priority date for domestic students. Applications are processed on a rolling basis. Application fee: $35. *Expenses:* Tuition, state resident: full-time $6,032; part-time $335 per credit. Tuition, nonresident: full-time $17,288; part-time $960 per credit. Required fees: $65 per credit. $30 per semester. One-time fee: $80 part-time. *Unit head:* Dr. W. Gale Eaton, Director, 401-874-4651.

University of South Carolina, The Graduate School, College of Mass Communications and Information Studies, School of Library and Information Science, Columbia, SC 29208. Offers MLIS, Certificate, Specialist, MLIS/MA. *Accreditation:* ALA (one or more programs are accredited). Part-time programs available. Postbaccalaureate distance learning degree programs offered (no on-campus study). *Degree requirements:* For master's and other advanced degree, registration. *Entrance requirements:* For master's, GRE General Test, or MAT; for other advanced degree, GRE General Test or MAT. Additional exam requirements/recommendations for international students: Required—TOEFL. Electronic applications accepted. *Faculty research:* Information technology management, distance education, library services for children and young adults, special libraries.

University of South Florida, Graduate School, College of Arts and Sciences, School of Library and Information Science, Tampa, FL 33620-9951. Offers library and information sciences (MA). *Accreditation:* ALA. Part-time and evening/weekend programs available. Postbaccalaureate distance learning degree programs offered (minimal on-campus study). *Faculty:* 20 full-time (15 women), 20 part-time/adjunct (9 women). *Students:* 111 full-time (73 women), 437 part-time (363 women); includes 123 minority (41 African Americans, 14 Asian Americans or Pacific Islanders, 68 Hispanic Americans), 15 international. 237 applicants, 82% accepted, 117 enrolled. In 2006, 177 degrees awarded. *Median time to degree:* Master's–1.5 years full-time, 2.5 years part-time. *Entrance requirements:* For master's, GRE General Test or minimum GPA of 2.5 upper division course work, minimum GPA of 2.5 in last 60 hours of course work. *Application deadline:* For fall admission, 6/1 for domestic students; for spring admission, 10/15 for domestic students. Applications are processed on a rolling basis. Application fee: $30. Electronic applications accepted. *Financial support:* In 2006–07, 11 fellowships with full tuition reimbursements, 13 teaching assistantships with full tuition reimbursements (averaging $11,750 per year) were awarded; career-related internships or fieldwork, scholarships/grants, and unspecified assistantships also available. Support available to part-time students. Financial award application deadline: 6/30; financial award applicants required to submit FAFSA. *Faculty research:* Youth services in libraries, community engagement and libraries, information architecture, biomedical informatics. Total annual research expenditures: $226,470. *Unit head:* Vicki L. Gregory, Chairperson and Program Director, 813-974-3520, Fax: 813-974-6840, E-mail: gregory@luna.cas.usf.edu. *Application contact:* Mel Pace, Information Contact, 813-974-6837, Fax: 813-974-6840, E-mail: lis@luna.cas.usf.edu.

The University of Texas at Austin, Graduate School, Graduate School of Library and Information Science, Austin, TX 78712-1111. Offers MLIS, PhD. *Accreditation:* ALA (one or more programs are accredited). Part-time programs available. *Degree requirements:* For doctorate, 2 foreign languages, thesis/dissertation. *Entrance requirements:* For master's and doctorate, GRE General Test. Electronic applications accepted. *Faculty research:* Information retrieval and artificial intelligence, library history and administration, classification and cataloguing.

University of Toronto, School of Graduate Studies, Social Sciences Division, Faculty of Information Studies, Toronto, ON M5S 1A1, Canada. Offers MI St, PhD, Diploma, JD/M I St. *Accreditation:* ALA (one or more programs are accredited). Part-time programs available. *Degree requirements:* For master's, thesis optional; for doctorate, thesis/dissertation, oral exam/thesis defense. *Entrance requirements:* For master's, minimum B average overall, mid-B in final year; 2 letters of reference; for doctorate, 3 letters of reference, minimum B+ average; for Diploma, MI St, MLS, or MIS degree or equivalent; minimum B+ average overall. Additional exam requirements/recommendations for international students: Required—TOEFL (minimum score 600 paper-based; 250 computer-based), TWE (minimum score 6), MELAB (95) or IELTS (8). Expenses: Contact institution.

The University of Western Ontario, Faculty of Graduate Studies, Faculty of Information and Media Studies, Programs in Library and Information Science, London, ON N6A 5B8, Canada. Offers MLIS, PhD. Program conducted on a trimester basis. *Accreditation:* ALA (one or more programs are accredited). Part-time and evening/weekend programs available. *Faculty:* 20 full-time (12 women), 15 part-time/adjunct (8 women). *Students:* 172 full-time (130 women), 68 part-time (47 women). 262 applicants, 81% accepted, 162 enrolled. In 2006, 160 master's, 1 doctorate awarded. *Median time to degree:* Of those who began their doctoral program in fall 1998, 100% received their degree in 8 years or less. *Degree requirements:* For master's, registration; for doctorate, thesis/dissertation, comprehensive exam, registration. *Entrance requirements:* For master's, honors degree, minimum B average during previous 2 years of course work; for doctorate, MLIS or equivalent. Additional exam requirements/recommendations for international students: Required—TOEFL (minimum score 625 paper-based; 263 computer-based), TWE (minimum score 5). *Application deadline:* For fall admission, 6/29 for domestic students; for winter admission, 11/3 for domestic students; for spring admission, 3/16 for domestic students. Applications are processed on a rolling basis. Application fee: $50 Canadian dollars. Electronic applications accepted. *Financial support:* In 2006–07, 89 students received support, including 17 teaching assistantships with partial tuition reimbursements available (averaging $9,699 Canadian dollars per year); research assistantships, career-related internships or fieldwork, institutionally sponsored loans, scholarships/grants, health care benefits, and unspecified assistantships also available. *Faculty research:* Information, individuals, and society; information systems, policy, power, and institutions. *Application contact:* Shelley Long, Student Services Graduate Secretary, 519-661-4017, Fax: 519-661-3506, E-mail: mlis@uwo.ca.

University of Wisconsin–Madison, Graduate School, College of Letters and Science, School of Library and Information Studies, Madison, WI 53706-1380. Offers MA, PhD, Certificate. *Accreditation:* ALA (one or more programs are accredited). Part-time programs available. *Degree requirements:* For doctorate, thesis/dissertation, comprehensive exam. Electronic applications accepted. *Faculty research:* Intellectual freedom, children's literature, print culture history, information systems design and evaluation, school library media centers.

University of Wisconsin–Milwaukee, Graduate School, School of Information Studies, Milwaukee, WI 53201-0413. Offers MLIS, CAS, MLIS/MA, MLIS/MM, MLIS/MS. *Accreditation:* ALA (one or more programs are accredited). Part-time programs available. *Faculty:* 14 full-time (5 women). *Students:* 99 full-time (75 women), 391 part-time (312 women); includes 32 minority (11 African Americans, 12 Asian Americans or Pacific Islanders, 9 Hispanic Americans), 20 international. Average age 36. 239 applicants, 82% accepted, 121 enrolled. In 2006, 120 degrees awarded. *Entrance requirements:* For master's, GRE General Test or MAT. *Application deadline:* For fall admission, 1/1 priority date for domestic students; for spring admission, 9/1 for domestic students. Applications are processed on a rolling basis. Application fee: $45 ($75 for international students). *Expenses:* Tuition, state resident: part-time $510 per credit. Tuition, nonresident: part-time $1,408 per credit. Tuition and fees vary according to program. *Financial support:* In 2006–07, 3 fellowships were awarded; research assistantships, teaching assistantships, career-related internships or fieldwork, Federal Work-Study, and unspecified assistantships also available. Support available to part-time students. Financial award application deadline: 4/15. *Unit head:* Johannes Britz, Dean, 414-229-4709, Fax: 414-229-4848.

Valdosta State University, Graduate School, Program in Library and Information Science, Valdosta, GA 31698. Offers MLIS. *Accreditation:* ALA. *Degree requirements:* For master's, comprehensive exam. *Entrance requirements:* For master's, GRE. Additional exam requirements/recommendations for international students: Required—TOEFL (minimum score 523 paper-based; 193 computer-based).

Wayne State University, Graduate School, Library and Information Science Program, Detroit, MI 48202. Offers archival administration (Certificate); library and information science (MLIS, Spec); library science (MS, Spec). *Accreditation:* ALA (one or more programs are accredited). Part-time and evening/weekend programs available. *Faculty:* 20 full-time (13 women), 4 part-time/adjunct (all women). *Students:* 115 full-time (92 women), 458 part-time (389 women); includes 75 minority (54 African Americans, 3 American Indian/Alaska Native, 11 Asian Americans or Pacific Islanders, 7 Hispanic Americans), 9 international. Average age 35. 162 applicants, 88% accepted, 98 enrolled. In 2006, 234 degrees awarded. *Entrance requirements:* Additional exam requirements/recommendations for international students: Required—TOEFL (minimum score 550 paper-based; 213 computer-based); Recommended—TWE (minimum score 6). *Application deadline:* For fall admission, 7/1 for domestic students, 6/1 for international students; for winter admission, 10/1 for international students; for spring admission, 2/1 for international students. Applications are processed on a rolling basis. Application fee: $30 ($50 for international students). Electronic applications accepted. *Financial support:* Research assistantships, career-related internships or fieldwork, Federal Work-Study, institutionally sponsored loans, and scholarships/grants available. Support available to part-time students. Financial award application deadline: 5/15. *Faculty research:* Convergence of academic libraries and other academic services, competitive intelligence and data mining, impact of digitization on libraries, international librarianship, consumer health information. Total annual research expenditures: $6,040. *Unit head:* Joseph J. Mika, Director, 313-577-1825, Fax: 313-577-7563, E-mail: aa2500@wayne.edu. *Application contact:* Jennifer Bondy, Education Director, 313-577-2523, E-mail: j.l.bondy@wayne.edu.

Library Science

Appalachian State University, Cratis D. Williams Graduate School, College of Education, Department of Leadership and Educational Studies, Program in Library Science, Boone, NC 28608. Offers MLS. *Students:* 24 full-time (18 women), 59 part-time (51 women); includes 1 minority (African American), 1 international. 25 applicants, 100% accepted, 23 enrolled. In 2006, 37 degrees awarded. *Degree requirements:* For master's, thesis or alternative, comprehensive exam. *Entrance requirements:* For master's, GRE General Test or MAT. *Application deadline:* For fall admission, 7/1 for domestic students. Application fee: $50. *Expenses:* Tuition, state resident: full-time $2,600; part-time $127 per hour. Tuition, nonresident: full-time $13,200; part-time $597 per hour. Required fees: $2,000; $546 per term. *Financial support:* Fellowships, research assistantships, teaching assistantships, career-related internships or fieldwork, Federal Work-Study, scholarships/grants, and unspecified assistantships available. Support available to part-time students. Financial award application deadline: 7/1. *Faculty research:* Multicultural issues in library science curriculum. *Unit head:* Dr. Robert Sanders, Director, 828-262-3115.

Azusa Pacific University, School of Education, Department of Advanced Studies, Program in School Librarianship, Azusa, CA 91702-7000. Offers MA. In 2006, 2 degrees awarded. Application fee: $45 ($65 for international students). *Expenses:* Tuition: Part-time $475 per credit. *Unit head:* Dr. Maria Pacino, Chair, Department of Advanced Studies, 626-815-5416, E-mail: mpacino@apu.edu.

The Catholic University of America, School of Library and Information Science, Washington, DC 20064. Offers MSLS, JD/MSLS, MSLS/MA, MSLS/MS. *Accreditation:* ALA (one or more programs are accredited). Part-time and evening/weekend programs available. Postbaccalaureate distance learning degree programs offered (minimal on-campus study). *Faculty:* 7 full-time (5 women), 19 part-time/adjunct (9 women). *Students:* 36 full-time (33 women), 207 part-time (166 women); includes 26 minority (17 African Americans, 2 Asian Americans or Pacific Islanders, 7 Hispanic Americans), 3 international. Average age 35. 155 applicants, 86% accepted, 64 enrolled. In 2006, 80 degrees awarded. *Degree requirements:* For master's, comprehensive exam. *Entrance requirements:* For master's, GRE General Test, 3 letters of recommendation. Additional exam requirements/recommendations for international students: Required—TOEFL (minimum score 550 paper-based; 213 computer-based). *Application deadline:* For fall admission, 2/1 priority date for domestic students; for spring admission, 11/15 priority date for domestic students. Applications are processed on a rolling basis. Application fee: $55. Electronic applications accepted. *Expenses: Contact institution.* Part-time tuition and fees vary according to campus/location and program. *Financial support:* Fellowships, research assistantships, career-related internships or fieldwork, Federal Work-Study, scholarships/grants, tuition waivers (full and partial), and unspecified assistantships available. Support available to part-time students. Financial award application deadline: 2/1; financial award applicants required to submit FAFSA. *Faculty research:* Information transfer, archives and manuscripts, legal libraries, information seeking, information storage and retrieval, special collections, information systems. *Unit head:* Dr. Martha L. Hale, Dean, 202-319-5085, Fax: 202-319-5574, E-mail: halem@cua.edu.

Chicago State University, School of Graduate and Professional Studies, College of Education, Department of Reading, Elementary Education, Library Information and Media Studies, Program in Library Information and Media Studies, Chicago, IL 60628. Offers MS Ed. *Entrance requirements:* For master's, minimum GPA of 2.75.

Clarion University of Pennsylvania, Office of Research and Graduate Studies, College of Education and Human Services, Department of Library Science, Clarion, PA 16214. Offers MSLS, CAS. *Accreditation:* ALA (one or more programs are accredited). Part-time programs available. *Faculty:* 8 full-time (4 women). *Students:* 45 full-time (31 women), 227 part-time (186 women); includes 16 minority (8 African Americans, 1 American Indian/Alaska Native, 1 Asian American or Pacific Islander, 6 Hispanic Americans). 79 applicants, 77% accepted. In 2006, 114 degrees awarded. *Degree requirements:* For master's, thesis or alternative. *Entrance requirements:* For master's, minimum QPA of 3.0. Additional exam requirements/recommendations for international students: Required—TOEFL (minimum score 550 paper-based; 213 computer-based; 80 iBT). *Application deadline:* For fall admission, 8/1 priority date for domestic students, 4/15 priority date for international students; for spring admission, 12/1 priority date for domestic students, 9/15 priority date for international students. Applications are processed on a rolling basis. Application fee: $30. Electronic applications accepted. *Expenses:* Tuition, state resident: part-time $336 per credit. Tuition, nonresident: part-time $538 per credit. *Financial support:* In 2006–07, 14 research assistantships with partial tuition reimbursements (averaging $2,001 per year) were awarded. Financial award application deadline: 3/1. *Unit head:* Dr. Bernard VRavrek, Chair, 814-393-2271, Fax: 814-393-2150, E-mail: bvavrek@clarion.edu.

College of St. Catherine, Graduate Programs, Program in Library and Information Science, St. Paul, MN 55105-1789. Offers MA. Part-time and evening/weekend programs available. *Degree requirements:* For master's, microcomputer competency. *Entrance requirements:* For master's, minimum GPA of 3.2 or GRE. Additional exam requirements/recommendations for international students: Required—Michigan English Language Assessment Battery or TOEFL.

Columbia University, School of Continuing Education, Program in Information and Archive Management, New York, NY 10027. Offers MS. *Entrance requirements:* Additional exam requirements/recommendations for international students: Required—American Language Program (ALP) placement test. *Application deadline:* For fall admission, 7/15 for domestic students; for spring admission, 11/11 for domestic students. Application fee: $50. *Faculty research:* Library science technology, information systems. *Unit head:* Paul McNeil, Head, 212-854-9699, E-mail: ce-info@columbia.edu. *Application contact:* 212-854-9666, E-mail: ce-advis@columbia.edu.

Dalhousie University, Faculty of Graduate Studies, Faculty of Management, School of Library and Information Studies, Halifax, NS B3H 4R2, Canada. Offers MLIS, LL B/MLIS. *Accreditation:* ALA (one or more programs are accredited). Part-time programs available. *Degree requirements:* For master's, one foreign language, thesis optional. *Entrance requirements:* Additional exam requirements/recommendations for international students: Required—TOEFL. *Faculty research:* Information-seeking behavior, electronic text design, browsing in digital environments, information diffusion among scientists.

Dominican University, Graduate School of Library and Information Science, River Forest, IL 60305-1099. Offers MLIS, CSS, MBA/MLIS, MLIS/M Div, MLIS/MA, MLIS/MM. *Accreditation:* ALA (one or more programs are accredited). Part-time and evening/weekend programs available. Postbaccalaureate distance learning degree programs offered (minimal on-campus study). *Faculty:* 15 full-time (10 women), 28 part-time/adjunct (19 women). *Students:* 137 full-time (101 women), 588 part-time (484 women); includes 43 minority (11 African Americans, 1 American Indian/Alaska Native, 12 Asian Americans or Pacific Islanders, 19 Hispanic Americans), 5 international. Average age 36. 179 applicants, 99% accepted, 127 enrolled. In 2006, 269 degrees awarded. *Entrance requirements:* For master's, minimum GPA of 3.0 or GRE General Test or MAT. Additional exam requirements/recommendations for international students: Required—TOEFL. *Application deadline:* For fall admission, 6/1 priority date for domestic students; for winter admission, 3/1 priority date for domestic students; for spring admission, 10/1 priority date for domestic students. Applications are processed on a rolling basis. Application fee: $25. *Expenses: Contact institution.* Tuition and fees vary according to campus/location and program. *Financial support:* Fellowships, research assistantships, career-related internships or fieldwork, Federal Work-Study, scholarships/grants, and tuition waivers (partial) available. Support available to part-time students. Financial award application deadline: 4/15; financial award applicants required to submit FAFSA. *Faculty research:* Productivity and the information environment, bibliometrics, library history, subject access, library materials and services for children. *Unit head:* Susan Roman, Dean, 708-524-6986, Fax: 708-524-6657, E-mail: sroman@dom.edu. *Application contact:* Tracie Hall, Assistant Dean, 708-524-6848, Fax: 708-524-6657, E-mail: thall@dom.edu.

Drexel University, College of Information Science and Technology, Philadelphia, PA 19104-2875. Offers information science and technology (PhD); information studies (PhD, CAS); information systems (MSIS); library and information science (MS). *Accreditation:* ALA (one or more programs are accredited). Part-time and evening/weekend programs available. Postbaccalaureate distance learning degree programs offered (no on-campus study). *Degree requirements:* For doctorate, thesis/dissertation. *Entrance requirements:* For master's and doctorate, GRE General Test. Additional exam requirements/recommendations for international students: Required—TOEFL. Electronic applications accepted. Expenses: Contact institution. *Faculty research:* Human-computer interaction, computer-supported cooperative work, digital libraries, software engineering, information retrieval/information visualization/bibliometrics.

See Close-Up on page 2129.

East Carolina University, Graduate School, College of Education, Department of Library Science and Instructional Technology, Greenville, NC 27858-4353. Offers instruction technology specialist (MA Ed); library science (MLS, CAS). *Accreditation:* NCATE. Part-time and evening/weekend programs available. Postbaccalaureate distance learning degree programs offered (no on-campus study). *Students:* 26 full-time (21 women), 314 part-time (284 women); includes 33 minority (24 African Americans, 1 American Indian/Alaska Native, 5 Asian Americans or Pacific Islanders, 3 Hispanic Americans), 1 international. Average age 37. 56 applicants, 20% accepted, 10 enrolled. In 2006, 104 master's, 2 other advanced degrees awarded. *Degree requirements:* For master's, thesis optional. *Entrance requirements:* For master's, GRE General Test or MAT, interview, minimum GPA of 2.5, bachelor's degree in related field, teaching license (MA Ed). Additional exam requirements/recommendations for international students: Required—TOEFL. *Application deadline:* For fall admission, 6/1 priority date for domestic students. Applications are processed on a rolling basis. Application fee: $50. *Financial support:* Research assistantships, teaching assistantships, Federal Work-Study available. Support available to part-time students. Financial award application deadline: 6/1. *Unit head:* Dr. Wiliam Suger, Interim Chair, 252-328-4373, Fax: 252-328-4368, E-mail: sugerw@ecu.edu. *Application contact:* Dean of Graduate School, 252-328-6012, Fax: 252-328-6071, E-mail: gradschool@ecu.edu.

Emporia State University, School of Graduate Studies, School of Library and Information Management, Program in Legal Information Management, Emporia, KS 66801-5087. Offers MLM, Certificate. Part-time and evening/weekend programs available. Postbaccalaureate distance learning degree programs offered (minimal on-campus study). *Entrance requirements:* For master's, GRE. Additional exam requirements/recommendations for international students: Required—TOEFL (minimum score 450 paper-based; 133 computer-based). *Application deadline:* For fall admission, 8/15 priority date for domestic students. Applications are processed on a rolling basis. Application fee: $30 ($75 for international students). Electronic applications accepted. *Expenses:* Tuition, state resident: full-time $3,438; part-time $143 per credit hour. Tuition, nonresident: full-time $10,398; part-time $433 per credit hour. Required fees: $724; $44 per credit hour. *Financial support:* Application deadline: 3/15;

Emporia State University, School of Graduate Studies, School of Library and Information Management, Program in Library and Information Management, Emporia, KS 66801-5087. Offers MLS, PhD, Certificate. Part-time and evening/weekend programs available. Postbaccalaureate distance learning degree programs offered (minimal on-campus study). *Faculty:* 10 full-time (8 women). *Students:* 9 full-time (4 women), 302 part-time (244 women); includes 11 minority (3 African Americans, 3 Asian Americans or Pacific Islanders, 5 Hispanic Americans), 5 international. 46 applicants, 74% accepted, 26 enrolled. In 2006, 123 master's, 1 doctorate, 4 other advanced degrees awarded. *Entrance requirements:* For master's, GRE. Additional exam requirements/recommendations for international students: Required—TOEFL. *Application deadline:* For fall admission, 8/15 priority date for domestic students. Applications are processed on a rolling basis. Application fee: $30 ($75 for international students). Electronic applications accepted. *Expenses:* Tuition, state resident: full-time $3,438; part-time $143 per credit hour. Tuition, nonresident: full-time $10,398; part-time $433 per credit hour. Required fees: $724; $44 per credit hour. *Financial support:* In 2006–07, 2 research assistantships (averaging $6,752 per year), 10 teaching assistantships (averaging $6,752 per year) were awarded; Federal Work-Study, institutionally sponsored loans, and unspecified assistantships also available. Financial award application deadline: 3/15; financial award applicants required to submit FAFSA. *Application contact:* Daniel Roland, Assistant to the Dean, 620-341-5064, Fax: 620-341-5233, E-mail: droland@emporia.edu.

Florida State University, Graduate Studies, College of Information, Tallahassee, FL 32306. Offers library and information studies (MS, PhD, Specialist). *Accreditation:* ALA (one or more programs are accredited). Part-time and evening/weekend programs available. Postbaccalaureate distance learning degree programs offered (no on-campus study). *Faculty:* 29 full-time (14 women), 8 part-time/adjunct (4 women). *Students:* 47 full-time (31 women), 746 part-time (541 women); includes 151 minority (76 African Americans, 4 American Indian/Alaska Native, 23 Asian Americans or Pacific Islanders, 48 Hispanic Americans), 47 international. Average age 35. 502 applicants, 75% accepted, 263 enrolled. In 2006, 202 master's, 5 doctorates, 4 other advanced degrees awarded. *Median time to degree:* Master's–2.6 years full-time; doctorate–6.6 years full-time; Specialist–2.8 years full-time. *Degree requirements:* For master's, thesis optional; for doctorate, thesis/dissertation, comprehensive exam, registration; for Specialist, thesis or alternative, registration. *Entrance requirements:* For master's, GRE or minimum GPA of 3.0 on last 2 years of baccalaureate degree; for doctorate, GRE, minimum GPA of 3.0 on last degree program; research paper; resumé; 3 letters of recommendation; for Specialist, GRE, minimum graduate GPA of 3.2, resumé, 3 letters of recommendation. Additional exam requirements/recommendations for international students: Required—TOEFL (minimum score 550 paper-based; 80 iBT). *Application deadline:* For fall admission, 6/1 priority date for domestic students, 6/1 for international students. Applications are processed on a rolling basis. Application fee: $30. Electronic applications accepted. *Expenses:* Tuition, state resident: full-time $5,822; part-time $243 per credit hour. Tuition, nonresident: full-time $20,976; part-time $874 per credit hour. Tuition and fees vary according to program. *Financial support:* In 2006–07, 209 students received support, including 13 fellowships with full tuition reimbursements available, 102 research assistantships with full tuition reimbursements available, 94 teaching assistantships with full tuition reimbursements available; career-related internships or fieldwork, Federal Work-Study, scholarships/grants, and unspecified assistantships also available. Financial award application deadline: 3/1; financial award applicants required to submit FAFSA. *Faculty research:* Needs assessment, information policy, usability analysis, human information behavior, youth services. Total annual research expenditures: $654,946. *Unit head:* Dr. Lawrence Dennis, Dean, 850-644-2216, Fax: 850-644-9763, E-mail: ldennis@ci.fsu.edu. *Application contact:* Delores Bryant, Graduate Program Assistant, 850-644-5775, Fax: 850-644-9763, E-mail: grad@ci.fsu.edu.

Gratz College, Graduate Programs, Program in Judaica Librarianship, Melrose Park, PA 19027. Offers Certificate, MIS/Certificate. Part-time programs available. *Degree requirements:* For Certificate, one foreign language.

Indiana University Bloomington, School of Library and Information Science, Bloomington, IN 47405-7000. Offers MIS, MLS, PhD, Sp LIS, JD/MLS, MIS/MA, MLS/MA, MPA/MIS, MPA/MLS. PhD offered through the University Graduate School. *Accreditation:* ALA (one or more programs are accredited). Part-time programs available. *Faculty:* 12 full-time (7 women). *Students:* 211 full-time (152 women), 120 part-time (81 women); includes 28 minority (9 African Americans, 1 American Indian/Alaska Native, 7 Asian Americans or Pacific Islanders, 11 Hispanic Americans), 31 international. Average age 30. In 2006, 165 master's, 1 doctorate awarded. *Degree requirements:* For doctorate, thesis/dissertation. *Entrance requirements:* For master's and doctorate, GRE General Test, 3 letters of reference. Additional exam requirements/recommendations for international students: Required—TOEFL (minimum score 600 paper-based; 250 computer-based). *Application deadline:* For fall admission, 5/15 priority date for domestic students, 12/1 priority date for international students; for spring admission, 3/15 priority date for domestic students, 9/1 priority date for international students. Applications are processed on a rolling basis. Application fee: $50 ($60 for international students). Electronic applications accepted. *Expenses: Contact institution. Financial support:* Fellowships with full and partial tuition reimbursements, Federal Work-Study, institutionally sponsored loans, and scholarships/grants available. Support available to part-time students. *Faculty research:* Scholarly communication, interface design, public library policy, computer-mediated communication, information retrieval. Total annual research expenditures: $179,634. *Unit head:* Debora Shaw, Dean, 812-855-2018, Fax: 812-855-6166. *Application contact:* Rhonda Spencer, Information Contact, 812-855-2018, Fax: 812-855-6166.

See Close-Up on page 2131.

Indiana University–Purdue University Indianapolis, School of Library and Information Science, Indianapolis, IN 46202-2896. Offers MLS. Part-time and evening/weekend programs available. *Faculty:* 3 full-time (2 women). *Students:* 52 full-time (42 women), 237 part-time (198 women); includes 20 minority (14 African Americans, 3 Asian Americans or Pacific Islanders, 3 Hispanic Americans), 1 international. Average age 36. In 2006, 97 degrees awarded. *Entrance requirements:* For master's, GRE General Test. Additional exam requirements/recommendations for international students: Required—TOEFL (minimum score 600 paper-based). *Application deadline:* For fall admission, 7/15 priority date for domestic students; for spring admission, 11/15 priority date for domestic students. Applications are processed on a rolling basis. Application fee: $50 ($60 for international students). *Expenses:* Tuition, state resident: full-time $5,437; part-time $227 per credit hour. Tuition, nonresident: full-time $15,694; part-time $654 per credit hour. Required fees: $620. Tuition and fees vary according to course load, campus/location and program. *Financial support:* Career-related internships or fieldwork, Federal Work-Study, institutionally sponsored loans, and scholarships/grants available. Support avail-

Library Science

Indiana University–Purdue University Indianapolis (continued)
able to part-time students. *Unit head:* Dr. Daniel Collison, Executive Associate Dean, 317-278-2375, Fax: 317-278-1807, E-mail: slisindy@iupui.edu.

Instituto Tecnológico y de Estudios Superiores de Monterrey, Campus Irapuato, Graduate Programs, Irapuato, Mexico. Offers administration (MBA); administration of information technology (MAIT); administration of telecommunications (MAT); architecture (M Arch); computer science (MCS); education (M Ed); educational administration (MEA); educational innovation and technology (DEIT); educational technology (MET); electronic commerce (MBA); environmental administration and planning (MEAP); environmental systems (MES); finances (MBA); humanistic studies (MHS); international management for Latin American executives (MIMLAE); library and information science (MLIS); manufacturing quality management (MMQM); marketing research (MBA).

Inter American University of Puerto Rico, San Germán Campus, Graduate Studies Center, Graduate Program in Library and Information Sciences, San Germán, PR 00683-5008. Offers MLS. Part-time and evening/weekend programs available. *Faculty:* 2 full-time (0 women). *Students:* 35. In 2006, 7 degrees awarded. *Degree requirements:* For master's, comprehensive exam. *Entrance requirements:* For master's, GRE General Test or EXADEP, minimum GPA of 3.0. *Application deadline:* For fall admission, 4/30 priority date for domestic students; for spring admission, 11/15 for domestic students. Applications are processed on a rolling basis. Application fee: $31. *Expenses:* Tuition: Part-time $175 per credit. Required fees: $238 per semester. Tuition and fees vary according to degree level. *Financial support:* Teaching assistantships, Federal Work-Study and unspecified assistantships available. *Application contact:* Dr. Aurora Graniela, Graduate Coordinator, 787-264-1912 Ext. 7355, Fax: 787-892-7510, E-mail: aurora@sg.inter.edu.

Kent State University, College of Communication and Information, School of Library and Information Science, Kent, OH 44242-0001. Offers MLS, MS. *Accreditation:* ALA (one or more programs are accredited). *Degree requirements:* For master's, thesis optional. *Entrance requirements:* For master's, GRE General Test, minimum GPA of 2.75.

Kent State University, Graduate School of Education, Health, and Human Services, Department of Educational Foundations and Special Services, Program in Instructional Technology, Kent, OH 44242-0001. Offers computer technology (M Ed, MA); instructional technology general (M Ed, MA); library media (M Ed, MA). *Accreditation:* NCATE. *Faculty:* 9 full-time (5 women), 1 (woman) part-time/adjunct. *Students:* 8 full-time (7 women), 45 part-time (26 women); includes 3 minority (2 African Americans, 1 American Indian/Alaska Native), 1 international. 12 applicants, 58% accepted. In 2006, 18 degrees awarded. *Degree requirements:* For master's, thesis (for some programs), registration. *Entrance requirements:* For master's, GRE General Test. Additional exam requirements/recommendations for international students: Required—TOEFL. *Application deadline:* Applications are processed on a rolling basis. Application fee: $30. *Financial support:* In 2006–07, fellowships with full tuition reimbursements (averaging $7,210 per year); research assistantships with full tuition reimbursements, teaching assistantships with full tuition reimbursements, career-related internships or fieldwork, Federal Work-Study, institutionally sponsored loans, scholarships/grants, health care benefits, and unspecified assistantships also available. Support available to part-time students. Financial award application deadline: 4/1; financial award applicants required to submit FAFSA. *Faculty research:* Cooperative learning, aesthetics, computers in schools. *Unit head:* Dr. Albert Ingram, Coordinator, 330-672-2294, E-mail: aingram@kent.edu. *Application contact:* Nancy Miller, Academic Program Coordinator, Office of Graduate Student Services, 330-672-2576, Fax: 330-672-9162, E-mail: ogs@kent.edu.

Kutztown University of Pennsylvania, College of Graduate Studies and Extended Learning, College of Education, Program in Library Science, Kutztown, PA 19530-0730. Offers MLS, Certificate. Part-time and evening/weekend programs available. *Faculty:* 3 full-time (2 women), 1 (woman) part-time/adjunct. *Students:* 8 full-time (7 women), 36 part-time (31 women); includes 2 minority (1 African American, 1 Asian American or Pacific Islander). Average age 36. 45 applicants, 73% accepted, 13 enrolled. In 2006, 11 degrees awarded. *Degree requirements:* For master's, comprehensive exam. *Entrance requirements:* For master's, GRE General Test. Additional exam requirements/recommendations for international students: Required—TOEFL. *Application deadline:* Applications are processed on a rolling basis. Application fee: $35. Electronic applications accepted. *Expenses:* Tuition, state resident: full-time $6,048; part-time $336 per credit. Tuition, nonresident: full-time $9,678; part-time $538 per credit. *Financial support:* In 2006–07, research assistantships with full tuition reimbursements (averaging $5,000 per year); career-related internships or fieldwork, Federal Work-Study, and unspecified assistantships also available. Financial award application deadline: 3/15; financial award applicants required to submit FAFSA. *Unit head:* Dr. M. Kathryn Holland, Chairperson, 610-683-4300, Fax: 610-683-4636, E-mail: holland@kutztown.edu.

Long Island University, C.W. Post Campus, College of Information and Computer Science, Palmer School of Library and Information Science, Brookville, NY 11548-1300. Offers archives and records management (Certificate); information studies (PhD); library and information science (MS); library media specialist (MS); public library management (Certificate). *Accreditation:* ALA (one or more programs are accredited). Part-time and evening/weekend programs available. Postbaccalaureate distance learning degree programs offered (minimal on-campus study). *Degree requirements:* For master's, internship, thesis optional; for doctorate, thesis/dissertation, qualifying exam. *Entrance requirements:* For master's, GRE or MAT, minimum undergraduate GPA of 3.0, resumé. Electronic applications accepted. *Faculty research:* Information retrieval, digital libraries, scientometric and infometric studies, preservation/archiving and electronic records.

Announcement: Students will learn to manage the world of information at the College of Information and Computer Science at Long Island University—the school with vision and a focus on information, technology, and people. The College is comprised of the Palmer School of Library and Information Science and the Department of Computer Science and Management Engineering. The Palmer School offers an MS in library and information science and a PhD in information studies. Selected master's courses are offered at the Manhattan location in the Bobst Library at NYU, at SUNY Purchase in Westchester County, and at LIU's Brentwood Campus in Suffolk County. In addition, The Palmer School offers a dual-degree program with NYU. Advanced certificate programs are offered in archives and records management and public library administration. Concentrations are available in library media specialist, rare books and special collections, and public library management. The College offers master's degrees in information systems, management engineering, and information technology education. For information, contact the College of Information and Computer Science, Long Island University, 720 Northern Boulevard, Brookville, NY 11548. Telephone: 516-299-2866 or 212-998-2680, fax: 516-299-4168, email:cics@liu.edu, www.liu.edu/cics, or the Palmer School: e-mail: palmer@liu.edu, Web site: http://palmer.liu.edu/.

Long Island University, Westchester Graduate Campus, Program in Library and Information Science, Purchase, NY 10577. Offers MS. Part-time and evening/weekend programs available. *Faculty:* 1 (woman) full-time, 19 part-time/adjunct (11 women). *Students:* 110 (88 women). 22 applicants, 91% accepted, 18 enrolled. In 2006, 35 degrees awarded. *Application deadline:* Applications are processed on a rolling basis. Application fee: $30. *Expenses:* Tuition: Part-time $790 per credit. *Financial support:* In 2006–07, 24 students received support. Scholarships/grants, tuition waivers, and unspecified assistantships available. *Unit head:* Trudy Katz, Coordinator, 914-831-2712, E-mail: trudy.katz@liu.edu. *Application contact:* Ellen Brief, Coordinator of Admissions, Marketing, Student Services and Public Relations, 914-831-2701, Fax: 914-251-5959, E-mail: ellen.brief@liu.edu.

Louisiana State University and Agricultural and Mechanical College, Graduate School, School of Library and Information Science, Baton Rouge, LA 70803. Offers MLIS, CAS. *Accreditation:* ALA (one or more programs are accredited). Evening/weekend programs available. *Faculty:* 11 full-time (9 women). *Students:* 63 full-time (47 women), 101 part-time (90 women); includes 19 minority (13 African Americans, 5 American Indian/Alaska Native, 1 Asian American or Pacific Islander), 6 international. Average age 36. 48 applicants, 73% accepted, 17 enrolled. In 2006, 63 master's awarded. *Degree requirements:* For master's, thesis optional. *Entrance requirements:* For master's, GRE General Test, minimum GPA of 3.0. Additional exam requirements/recommendations for international students: Required—TOEFL (minimum score 550 paper-based; 213 computer-based; 79 iBT). *Application deadline:* For fall admission, 1/25 priority date for domestic students, 5/15 for international students; for spring admission, 10/15 for international students. Applications are processed on a rolling basis. Application fee: $25. Electronic applications accepted. *Financial support:* In 2006–07, 33 students received support, including 10 research assistantships with partial tuition reimbursements available (averaging $8,878 per year), 14 teaching assistantships with partial tuition reimbursements available (averaging $10,730 per year); fellowships, career-related internships or fieldwork, Federal Work-Study, institutionally sponsored loans, scholarships/grants, and unspecified assistantships also available. Support available to part-time students. Financial award applicants required to submit FAFSA. *Faculty research:* Information retrieval, management, collection development, public libraries. Total annual research expenditures: $16,801. *Unit head:* Dr. Beth M. Paskoff, Dean, 225-578-3158, Fax: 225-578-4581, E-mail: lspask@lsu.edu.

Mansfield University of Pennsylvania, Graduate Studies, Program in School Library and Information Technologies, Mansfield, PA 16933. Offers library science (M Ed). Part-time and evening/weekend programs available. Postbaccalaureate distance learning degree programs offered. *Faculty:* 1 (woman) full-time, 13 part-time/adjunct (all women). *Students:* 7 full-time (all women), 202 part-time (182 women); includes 26 minority (18 African Americans, 3 American Indian/Alaska Native, 2 Asian Americans or Pacific Islanders, 3 Hispanic Americans). Average age 39. 374 applicants, 48% accepted, 68 enrolled. In 2006, 34 degrees awarded. *Degree requirements:* For master's, thesis optional. *Entrance requirements:* For master's, minimum GPA of 3.0. Additional exam requirements/recommendations for international students: Required—TOEFL (minimum score 550 paper-based; 220 computer-based). *Application deadline:* Applications are processed on a rolling basis. Application fee: $25. Electronic applications accepted. *Expenses: Contact institution.* Tuition and fees vary according to course load and reciprocity agreements. *Financial support:* In 2006–07, 41 students received support. Unspecified assistantships available. Financial award application deadline: 5/1; financial award applicants required to submit FAFSA. *Unit head:* Cindy Keller, Chair, E-mail: ckeller@mansfield.edu. *Application contact:* Judi Brayer, Assistant Director of Enrollment Management/Graduate Admissions, 570-662-4818, Fax: 570-662-4121, E-mail: jbrayer@mansfield.edu.

Marywood University, Academic Affairs, Insalaco College of Creative Arts and Management, Department of Communication Arts, Program in Communication Arts, Scranton, PA 18509-1598. Offers corporate communication (Certificate); e-business (Certificate); health communication (Certificate); instructional technology (Certificate); interdisciplinary (MA); library science/information specialist (Certificate); media management (MA); production (MA). *Students:* 13 full-time (7 women), 14 part-time (6 women); includes 3 minority (1 African American, 2 Hispanic Americans), 1 international. Average age 28. In 2006, 3 degrees awarded. Application fee: $30. *Expenses:* Tuition: Part-time $672 per credit. Tuition and fees vary according to degree level, campus/location and program. *Application contact:* Dr. Deborah M. Flynn, Coordinator of Graduate Advising (Enrollment Management), 570-348-6211, E-mail: flynn@ac.marywood.edu.

Marywood University, Academic Affairs, Insalaco College of Creative Arts and Management, Department of Communication Arts, Program in Information Sciences, Scranton, PA 18509-1598. Offers corporate communication (MS); e-business (MS); health communication (MS); instructional technology (MS); library science/information science (MS). *Students:* 4 full-time (2 women), 18 part-time (16 women); includes 1 minority (African American) Average age 40.Application fee: $30. *Expenses:* Tuition: Part-time $672 per credit. Tuition and fees vary according to degree level, campus/location and program. *Application contact:* Dr. Deborah M. Flynn, Coordinator of Graduate Advising (Enrollment Management), 570-348-6211, E-mail: flynn@ac.marywood.edu.

McDaniel College, Graduate and Professional Studies, Program in Media/Library Science, Westminster, MD 21157-4390. Offers MS. Part-time and evening/weekend programs available. *Degree requirements:* For master's, thesis optional. *Entrance requirements:* For master's, GRE General Test, MAT, or NTE/PRAXIS I, letters of reference (3). Additional exam requirements/recommendations for international students: Required—TOEFL (minimum score 213 computer-based).

McGill University, Faculty of Graduate and Postdoctoral Studies, Faculty of Education, Graduate School of Library and Information Studies, Montréal, QC H3A 2T5, Canada. Offers MLIS, PhD, Certificate, Diploma. *Accreditation:* ALA (one or more programs are accredited). Part-time programs available. *Degree requirements:* For master's, registration; for doctorate, thesis/dissertation, registration. *Entrance requirements:* For master's, minimum GPA of 3.0; for doctorate, MLIS or equivalent. Additional exam requirements/recommendations for international students: Required—TOEFL (minimum score 600 paper-based; 250 computer-based), IELTS (minimum score 8). Electronic applications accepted. *Faculty research:* Information seeking behavior, information resources in context, knowledge management and representation, human computer interaction.

North Carolina Central University, Division of Academic Affairs, School of Library and Information Sciences, Durham, NC 27707-3129. Offers MIS, MLS. *Accreditation:* ALA (one or more programs are accredited). Part-time and evening/weekend programs available. *Degree requirements:* For master's, one foreign language. *Entrance requirements:* For master's, GRE, 90 hours in liberal arts, minimum B average. Additional exam requirements/recommendations for international students: Required—TOEFL. *Faculty research:* African-American resources, planning and evaluation, analysis of economic and physical resources, geography of information, artificial intelligence.

Old Dominion University, Darden College of Education, Program in Elementary/Middle Education, Norfolk, VA 23529. Offers educational media (MS Ed); elementary education (MS Ed); instructional technology (MS Ed); library science (MS Ed); middle school education (MS Ed). *Accreditation:* NCATE. Part-time and evening/weekend programs available. Postbaccalaureate distance learning degree programs offered (no on-campus study). *Faculty:* 20 full-time (9 women). *Students:* 116 full-time (103 women), 217 part-time (178 women); includes 32 minority (22 African Americans, 2 American Indian/Alaska Native, 3 Asian Americans or Pacific Islanders, 5 Hispanic Americans). Average age 35. 127 applicants, 56% accepted, 61 enrolled. In 2006, 167 degrees awarded. *Degree requirements:* For master's, comprehensive exam. *Entrance requirements:* For master's, GRE General Test or MAT and PRAXIS I or SAT or ACT, minimum GPA of 2.8. *Application deadline:* For fall admission, 6/1 priority date for domestic students; for winter admission, 11/1 priority date for domestic students; for spring admission, 3/1 priority date for domestic students. Applications are processed on a rolling basis. Application fee: $40. Electronic applications accepted. *Expenses:* Tuition, area resident: Part-time $285 per credit hour. Tuition, nonresident: part-time $715 per credit hour. Required fees: $94 per semester. *Financial support:* In 2006–07, 180 students received support, including 4 research assistantships with tuition reimbursements available (averaging $9,000 per year), teaching assistantships (averaging $8,000 per year); fellowships, career-related internships or fieldwork, Federal Work-Study, institutionally sponsored loans, scholarships/grants, and tuition waivers (partial) also available. Support available to part-time students. Financial award application deadline: 2/15; financial award applicants required to submit FAFSA. *Faculty research:* Education pre-K to 6, school librarianship. *Unit head:* Dr. Gail S. Taylor, Graduate Program Director, 757-683-4180, E-mail: eciegpd@odu.edu.

Old Dominion University, Darden College of Education, Programs in Secondary Education, Norfolk, VA 23529. Offers biology (MS Ed); chemistry (MS Ed); English (MS Ed); instructional technology (MS Ed); library science (MS Ed); secondary education (MS Ed). *Accreditation:* NCATE. Part-time and evening/weekend programs available. Postbaccalaureate distance learning degree programs offered (minimal on-campus study). *Faculty:* 28 full-time (11 women). *Students:* 61 full-time (45 women), 119 part-time (72 women); includes 21 minority (13 African Americans, 4 Asian Americans or Pacific Islanders, 4 Hispanic Americans), 1 international. Average age 35. 47 applicants, 87% accepted. In 2006, 119 degrees awarded. *Degree requirements:* For master's, thesis optional. *Entrance requirements:* For master's, GRE General Test, or MAT, PRAXIS I for master's with licensure, minimum GPA of 2.8, teaching certificate. Additional exam requirements/recommendations for international students: Required—TOEFL. *Application deadline:* Applications are processed on a rolling basis. Application fee: $40. Electronic applications accepted. *Expenses:* Tuition, area resident: Part-time $285 per credit hour. Tuition, nonresident: part-time $715 per credit hour. Required fees: $94 per semester. *Financial support:* In 2006–07, 58 students received support, including 2 research assistantships with tuition reimbursements available (averaging $6,777 per year), 3 teaching assistantships with tuition reimbursements available (averaging $5,333 per year); fellowships, career-related internships or fieldwork, Federal Work-Study, institutionally sponsored loans, scholarships/grants, and tuition waivers (partial) also available. Support available to part-time students. Financial award application deadline: 2/15; financial award applicants required to submit FAFSA. *Faculty research:* Mathematics retraining, writing project for teachers, geography teaching, reading. *Unit head:* Dr. Robert Lucking, Graduate Program Director, 757-683-5545, Fax: 757-683-5862, E-mail: rlucking@odu.edu.

Pratt Institute, School of Information and Library Science, Brooklyn, NY 11205-3899. Offers MS, Adv C, JD/MS, MS/MS. *Accreditation:* ALA. Part-time and evening/weekend programs available. *Faculty:* 9 full-time (6 women), 27 part-time/adjunct (15 women). *Students:* 121 full-time (93 women), 224 part-time (165 women); includes 78 minority (33 African Americans, 1 American Indian/Alaska Native, 21 Asian Americans or Pacific Islanders, 23 Hispanic Americans), 9 international. Average age 33. 254 applicants, 81% accepted, 110 enrolled. In 2006, 100 degrees awarded. *Degree requirements:* For master's, thesis. *Entrance requirements:* Additional exam requirements/recommendations for international students: Required—TOEFL (minimum score 550 paper-based; 213 computer-based). *Application deadline:* For fall admission, 2/1 for domestic students; for spring admission, 10/1 for domestic students. Application fee: $40 ($90 for international students). Electronic applications accepted. *Expenses: Contact institution.* Tuition and fees vary according to course load and program. *Financial support:* In 2006–07, 10 fellowships (averaging $2,000 per year), 10 research assistantships (averaging $2,500 per year) were awarded; career-related internships or fieldwork, Federal Work-Study, institutionally sponsored loans, scholarships/grants, and unspecified assistantships also available. Support available to part-time students. Financial award application deadline: 2/1; financial award applicants required to submit FAFSA. *Faculty research:* Development of urban libraries and information centers, medical and law librarianship, information management. *Unit head:* Tula Gianinni, Dean, 212-647-7682. *Application contact:* Young Hah, Director of Graduate Admissions, 718-636-3683, Fax: 718-399-4242, E-mail: yhah@pratt.edu.

See Close-Up on page 2133.

Queens College of the City University of New York, Division of Graduate Studies, Social Science Division, Graduate School of Library and Information Studies, Flushing, NY 11367-1597. Offers MLS, AC. *Accreditation:* ALA (one or more programs are accredited). Part-time and evening/weekend programs available. *Faculty:* 17 full-time (11 women). *Students:* 29 full-time (25 women), 348 part-time (249 women). 259 applicants, 92% accepted, 184 enrolled. In 2006, 188 degrees awarded. *Degree requirements:* For master's, thesis; for AC, thesis optional. *Entrance requirements:* For master's, minimum GPA of 3.0; for AC, master's degree or equivalent. Additional exam requirements/recommendations for international students: Required—TOEFL. *Application deadline:* For fall admission, 4/1 for domestic students; for spring admission, 11/1 for domestic students. Applications are processed on a rolling basis. Application fee: $125. *Financial support:* Career-related internships or fieldwork, Federal Work-Study, institutionally sponsored loans, and tuition waivers (partial) available. Support available to part-time students. Financial award application deadline: 4/1; financial award applicants required to submit FAFSA. *Faculty research:* Multimedia and video studies, ethnicity and librarianship, information science and computer applications. *Unit head:* Dr. Virgil Blake, Director/Chair, 718-997-3790. *Application contact:* Dr. Karen Smith, Graduate Adviser, 718-997-3790, E-mail: karen_smith@qc.edu.

Rowan University, Graduate School, College of Education, Department of Foundations of Education, Program in School and Public Librarianship, Glassboro, NJ 08028-1701. Offers MA. *Accreditation:* NCATE. Part-time and evening/weekend programs available. *Students:* 6 full-time (all women), 34 part-time (31 women); includes 5 minority (4 African Americans, 1 Hispanic American). Average age 38. 7 applicants, 71% accepted, 5 enrolled. In 2006, 16 degrees awarded. *Degree requirements:* For master's, thesis, comprehensive exam. *Entrance requirements:* For master's, GRE General Test, minimum GPA of 2.8. Additional exam requirements/recommendations for international students: Required—TOEFL. *Application deadline:* Applications are processed on a rolling basis. Application fee: $50. Electronic applications accepted. *Expenses:* Tuition, state resident: full-time $9,882; part-time $549 per credit. Tuition, nonresident: full-time $9,882; part-time $549 per credit. Tuition and fees vary according to degree level. *Financial support:* Career-related internships or fieldwork, Federal Work-Study, and unspecified assistantships available. Support available to part-time students. *Unit head:* Dr. Holly Willett, Program Adviser, 856-256-4751.

Rutgers, The State University of New Jersey, New Brunswick, School of Communication, Information and Library Studies, Department of Library and Information Science, New Brunswick, NJ 08901-1281. Offers MLS. *Accreditation:* ALA. Part-time programs available. Postbaccalaureate distance learning degree programs offered (no on-campus study). *Faculty:* 18 full-time (8 women), 14 part-time/adjunct (7 women). *Students:* 166 full-time (138 women), 179 part-time (136 women); includes 40 minority (12 African Americans, 1 American Indian/Alaska Native, 16 Asian Americans or Pacific Islanders, 11 Hispanic Americans), 14 international. Average age 34. 232 applicants, 65% accepted, 57 enrolled. In 2006, 155 degrees awarded. *Entrance requirements:* For master's, GRE General Test. Additional exam requirements/recommendations for international students: Required—TOEFL. *Application deadline:* For fall admission, 3/1 priority date for domestic students, 2/1 for international students; for spring admission, 10/1 priority date for domestic and international students. Applications are processed on a rolling basis. Application fee: $50. Electronic applications accepted. *Financial support:* Career-related internships or fieldwork, Federal Work-Study, institutionally sponsored loans, and scholarships/grants available. Support available to part-time students. Financial award application deadline: 2/1; financial award applicants required to submit FAFSA. *Faculty research:* Information science, library services, management of information services. *Unit head:* Dr. Ross Todd, Director, 732-932-7500 Ext. 8223, Fax: 732-932-4912, E-mail: rtodd@scils.rutgers.edu.

St. John's University, St. John's College of Liberal Arts and Sciences, Division of Library and Information Science, Queens, NY 11439. Offers MLS, Adv C, MA/MLS, MS/MLS. *Accreditation:* ALA (one or more programs are accredited). Part-time and evening/weekend programs available. *Faculty:* 5 full-time (3 women), 3 part-time/adjunct (1 woman). *Students:* 7 full-time (all women), 85 part-time (69 women); includes 14 minority (4 African Americans, 4 Asian Americans or Pacific Islanders, 6 Hispanic Americans), 3 international. Average age 34. 45 applicants, 84% accepted, 18 enrolled. In 2006, 35 degrees awarded. *Degree requirements:* For master's, residence. *Entrance requirements:* For master's, interview, minimum GPA of 3.0. Additional exam requirements/recommendations for international students: Required—TOEFL (minimum score 500 paper-based; 173 computer-based). *Application deadline:* For fall admission, 5/1 priority date for domestic and international students; for spring admission, 11/1 priority date for domestic and international students. Applications are processed on a rolling basis. Application fee: $40. Electronic applications accepted. *Expenses: Contact institution.* Tuition and fees vary according to program. *Financial support:* Research assistantships, career-related internships or fieldwork and scholarships/grants available. Support available to part-time students. Financial award application deadline: 3/1; financial award applicants required to submit FAFSA. *Faculty research:* On-line database management, public library patronage, medieval monastic libraries and archives, children's literature, indexing. *Unit head:* Dr. Jeffrey Olson, Director, 718-990-5705, E-mail: olsonj@stjohns.edu. *Application contact:* Matthew Whelan, Director, Office of Admissions, 718-990-2000, Fax: 718-990-2096, E-mail: admissions@stjohns.edu.

Sam Houston State University, College of Education and Applied Science, Department of Library Science, Huntsville, TX 77341. Offers MLS. Part-time and evening/weekend programs available. *Faculty:* 4 full-time (3 women). *Students:* 11 full-time (10 women), 160 part-time (158 women); includes 3 African Americans, 74 Hispanic Americans. Average age 36. In 2006, 74 degrees awarded. *Entrance requirements:* For master's, GRE General Test, minimum GPA of 2.8. *Application deadline:* For fall admission, 8/1 for domestic students; for spring admission, 12/1 for domestic students. Applications are processed on a rolling basis. Application fee: $20. *Expenses:* Tuition, state resident: full-time $5,904; part-time $164 per semester hour. Tuition, nonresident: full-time $15,804; part-time $439 per semester hour. Required fees: $1,374; $462 per semester. *Financial support:* Teaching assistantships, career-related internships or fieldwork and Federal Work-Study available. Support available to part-time students. Financial award application deadline: 5/31; financial award applicants required to submit FAFSA. *Unit head:* Dr. Mary Berry, Chair, 936-294-1150, Fax: 936-294-1153, E-mail: lis_mab@shsu.edu.

San Jose State University, Graduate Studies and Research, College of Applied Sciences and Arts, School of Library and Information Science, San Jose, CA 95192-0001. Offers MLIS. *Accreditation:* ALA. Part-time and evening/weekend programs available. *Students:* 238 full-time (177 women), 577 part-time (458 women); includes 169 minority (19 African Americans, 8 American Indian/Alaska Native, 84 Asian Americans or Pacific Islanders, 58 Hispanic Americans), 1 international. Average age 37. 672 applicants, 80% accepted, 211 enrolled. In 2006, 338 degrees awarded. *Degree requirements:* For master's, comprehensive exam. *Entrance requirements:* Additional exam requirements/recommendations for international students: Required—TOEFL (minimum score 600 paper-based). *Application deadline:* For fall admission, 6/29 for domestic students; for spring admission, 11/30 for domestic students. Applications are processed on a rolling basis. Application fee: $59. Electronic applications accepted. *Financial support:* Career-related internships or fieldwork, Federal Work-Study, and institutionally sponsored loans available. Support available to part-time students. Financial award application deadline: 8/20; financial award applicants required to submit FAFSA. *Faculty research:* Evaluation of information services online, search strategy, organizational behavior. *Unit head:* Ken Haycock, Director, 408-924-2490, Fax: 408-924-2476.

Simmons College, Graduate School of Library and Information Science, Boston, MA 02115. Offers library and information science (PhD); school library teacher (MS, Certificate); MS/MA. MS/DA and MS/MA offered jointly with Department of History. *Accreditation:* ALA (one or more programs are accredited). Part-time and evening/weekend programs available. *Faculty:* 17 full-time (11 women), 30 part-time/adjunct (21 women). *Students:* 26 full-time (20 women), 528 part-time (412 women); includes 41 minority (13 African Americans, 2 American Indian/Alaska Native, 16 Asian Americans or Pacific Islanders, 10 Hispanic Americans), 7 international. Average age 35. 342 applicants, 86% accepted, 159 enrolled. In 2006, 314 master's, 1 doctorate awarded. *Degree requirements:* For master's, technology competency. *Entrance requirements:* For master's, GRE General Test or minimum GPA of 3.0; interview; for doctorate, GRE General Test or MAT, interview. Additional exam requirements/recommendations for international students: Required—TOEFL (minimum score 550 paper-based; 213 computer-based; 79 iBT). *Application deadline:* For fall admission, 3/1 priority date for domestic students, 3/1 for international students; for spring admission, 7/1 priority date for domestic students. Applications are processed on a rolling basis. Application fee: $35. Electronic applications accepted. *Expenses: Contact institution. Financial support:* In 2006–07, 4 research assistantships with full tuition reimbursements were awarded; career-related internships or fieldwork, Federal Work-Study, institutionally sponsored loans, scholarships/grants, and tuition waivers (full and partial) also available. Support available to part-time students. Financial award application deadline: 3/1; financial award applicants required to submit FAFSA. *Faculty research:* Visual communications, database management, information policy, digitization of libraries, international librarianship. Total annual research expenditures: $475,862. *Unit head:* Dr. Michele V. Cloonan, Dean, 617-521-2806, Fax: 617-521-3192, E-mail: cloonan@simmons.edu. *Application contact:* Denise Davis, Assistant Dean for Admission and Recruitment, 617-521-2801, Fax: 617-521-3192, E-mail: denise.davis@simmons.edu.

Southern Arkansas University–Magnolia, Graduate Programs, Magnolia, AR 71753. Offers computer and information sciences (MS); counseling (MS); education (M Ed), including counseling and development, educational administration and supervision, elementary education, secondary education; kinesiology (MS); library media and information specialist (M Ed); school counseling (M Ed); teaching (MAT). *Accreditation:* NCATE. Part-time and evening/weekend programs available. *Degree requirements:* For master's, thesis optional. *Entrance requirements:* For master's, GRE or MAT, minimum GPA of 2.75. *Faculty research:* Alternative certification for teachers, supervision of instruction, instructional leadership, counseling.

Southern Connecticut State University, School of Graduate Studies, School of Communication, Information and Library Science, Department of Library Science and Instructional Technology, New Haven, CT 06515-1355. Offers instructional technology (MS); library science (MLS); library/information studies (Diploma); JD/MLS; MLS/MA; MLS/MS. Part-time and evening/weekend programs available. Postbaccalaureate distance learning degree programs offered (no on-campus study). *Faculty:* 12 full-time, 5 part-time/adjunct. *Students:* 50 full-time (38 women), 255 part-time (223 women); includes 18 minority (5 African Americans, 10 Asian Americans or Pacific Islanders, 3 Hispanic Americans). 139 applicants, 86% accepted, 104 enrolled. In 2006, 127 master's, 12 other advanced degrees awarded. *Degree requirements:* For master's and Diploma, thesis or alternative. *Entrance requirements:* For master's, GRE General Test, interview, minimum QPA of 2.7, introductory computer science course; for Diploma, master's degree in library science or information science. *Application deadline:* For fall admission, 7/15 priority date for domestic students. Applications are processed on a rolling basis. Application fee: $50. Electronic applications accepted. *Financial support:* Research assistantships available. Financial award application deadline: 4/15; financial award applicants required to submit FAFSA. *Unit head:* Dr. Josephine Sche, Chairperson, 203-392-5710, Fax: 203-392-5780, E-mail: schej1@southernct.edu.

Syracuse University, Graduate School, School of Information Studies, Library and Information Science Program, Syracuse, NY 13244. Offers library and information science (MS); school media (MS). *Accreditation:* ALA. Part-time and evening/weekend programs available. Postbaccalaureate distance learning degree programs offered (minimal on-campus study). *Students:* 64 full-time (49 women), 232 part-time (204 women); includes 24 African Americans, 5 Asian Americans or Pacific Islanders, 10 Hispanic Americans, 10 international. 112 applicants, 85% accepted, 33 enrolled. *Degree requirements:* For master's, fieldwork or research paper. *Entrance requirements:* For master's, GRE General Test. Additional exam requirements/recommendations for international students: Required—TOEFL. *Application deadline:* For fall admission, 2/14 priority date for domestic students; for spring admission, 11/1 priority date for domestic students. Application fee: $65. Electronic applications accepted. *Expenses:* Tuition: Full-time $16,920; part-time $940 per credit hour. Required fees: $930; $930 per year. *Unit head:* Dr. Gisela von Dran, Head, 315-443-2086, Fax: 315-443-6886, E-mail: gmvondra@syr.edu. *Application contact:* Susan Corieri, Director of Enrollment Management, 315-443-6885, E-mail: ist@syr.edu.

See Close-Up on page 2135.

Syracuse University, Graduate School, School of Information Studies, Program in Digital Libraries, Syracuse, NY 13244. Offers CAS. Part-time and evening/weekend programs available. Postbaccalaureate distance learning degree programs offered. *Students:* 14 applicants, 100% accepted, 11 enrolled. *Application deadline:* For fall admission, 2/14 for domestic students. Application fee: $65. Electronic applications accepted. *Expenses:* Tuition: Full-time $16,920; part-time $940 per credit hour. Required fees: $930; $930 per year. *Unit head:* Dr.

Library Science

Syracuse University (continued)
Jian Qin, Head, 315-443-5642, Fax: 315-443-6886, E-mail: jqin@syr.edu. *Application contact:* Susan Corieri, Director of Enrollment Management, 315-443-6885, E-mail: ist@syr.edu.

Tennessee Technological University, Graduate School, College of Education, Department of Curriculum and Instruction, Program in Library Science, Cookeville, TN 38505. Offers MA, Ed S. *Students:* 4 full-time (all women), 5 part-time (all women). 10 applicants, 100% accepted, 4 enrolled. In 2006, 12 degrees awarded. *Entrance requirements:* For master's and Ed S, MAT or GRE. *Application deadline:* For fall admission, 3/1 priority date for domestic students; for spring admission, 8/1 for domestic students. Application fee: $25 ($30 for international students). *Expenses:* Tuition, state resident: full-time $8,748; part-time $319 per hour. Tuition, nonresident: full-time $23,524; part-time $740 per hour. *Financial support:* In 2006–07, research assistantships (averaging $4,000 per year), 2 teaching assistantships (averaging $4,000 per year) were awarded. Financial award application deadline: 4/1. *Application contact:* Dr. Francis O. Otuonye, Associate Vice President for Research and Graduate Studies, 931-372-3233, Fax: 931-372-3497, E-mail: fotuonye@tntech.edu.

Texas Woman's University, Graduate School, College of Professional Education, School of Library and Information Studies, Denton, TX 76201. Offers library science (MA, MLS, PhD). *Accreditation:* ALA (one or more programs are accredited). Part-time and evening/weekend programs available. Postbaccalaureate distance learning degree programs offered (minimal on-campus study). *Students:* 100 full-time (95 women), 492 part-time (467 women); includes 116 minority (37 African Americans, 2 American Indian/Alaska Native, 14 Asian Americans or Pacific Islanders, 63 Hispanic Americans), 12 international. Average age 38. In 2006, 173 master's, 1 doctorate awarded. *Degree requirements:* For doctorate, thesis/dissertation, comprehensive exam. *Entrance requirements:* For master's, GRE, GMAT, MCAT, 3 letters of recommendation, resumé (optional); for doctorate, interview, master's degree in library science, minimum GPA of 3.0. Additional exam requirements/recommendations for international students: Required—TOEFL (minimum score 550 paper-based; 213 computer-based; 79 iBT). *Application deadline:* For fall admission, 4/1 for international students; for spring admission, 8/1 for international students. Applications are processed on a rolling basis. Application fee: $30 ($50 for international students). Electronic applications accepted. *Expenses:* Tuition, area resident: Part-time $168 per unit. Tuition, state resident: full-time $4,369. Tuition, nonresident: full-time $9,373; part-time $443 per unit. Required fees: $20 per unit. $177 per term. *Financial support:* In 2006–07, 19 research assistantships (averaging $11,592 per year), 2 teaching assistantships (averaging $11,592 per year) were awarded; career-related internships or fieldwork, Federal Work-Study, institutionally sponsored loans, scholarships/grants, traineeships, health care benefits, and unspecified assistantships also available. Support available to part-time students. Financial award application deadline: 3/1; financial award applicants required to submit FAFSA. *Faculty research:* Children's literature, health information, information needs analysis, information policy, library management. *Unit head:* Dr. Ling Hwey Jeng, Director, 940-898-2602, Fax: 940-898-2611, E-mail: ljeng@mail.twu.edu. *Application contact:* Samuel Wheeler, Coordinator of Graduate Admissions, 940-898-3188, Fax: 940-898-3081, E-mail: wheelersr@twu.edu.

Trevecca Nazarene University, Graduate Division, School of Education, Major in Library and Information Science, Nashville, TN 37210-2877. Offers MLI Sc. Evening/weekend programs available. *Students:* 14 full-time (13 women); includes 1 minority (African American) Average age 34. In 2006, 17 degrees awarded. *Degree requirements:* For master's, exit assessment. *Entrance requirements:* For master's, GRE General Test, MAT, technology pre-assessment, minimum GPA of 2.7, 2 reference forms. Additional exam requirements/recommendations for international students: Required—TOEFL. *Application deadline:* Applications are processed on a rolling basis. Application fee: $25. *Expenses: Contact institution.* Tuition and fees vary according to degree level and program. *Financial support:* Applicants required to submit FAFSA. *Application contact:* Admissions Office, 615-248-1201, Fax: 615-248-1597, E-mail: admissions_ged@trevecca.edu.

Université de Montréal, Faculty of Graduate Studies, Faculty of Arts and Sciences, School of Library and Information Sciences, Montréal, QC H3C 3J7, Canada. Offers archival (Certificate); information sciences (MBSI, PhD), including information systems and resources (PhD), information transfer (PhD); management of numerical information (Certificate). *Accreditation:* ALA (one or more programs are accredited). *Faculty:* 14 full-time (5 women), 2 part-time/adjunct (1 woman). *Students:* 159 full-time (123 women), 25 part-time (20 women). 196 applicants, 48% accepted, 87 enrolled. In 2006, 81 degrees awarded. *Degree requirements:* For master's, thesis optional. *Entrance requirements:* For master's, interview, master's degree in library and information science or equivalent. *Application deadline:* For fall admission, 2/1 priority date for domestic students; for winter admission, 11/1 priority date for domestic students; for spring admission, 2/1 priority date for domestic students. Application fee: $30. Electronic applications accepted. *Financial support:* Fellowships available. *Unit head:* Jean-Michel Salaün, Director, 514-343-7400, Fax: 514-343-5753. *Application contact:* Diane Mayer, Information Contact, 514-343-6044, Fax: 514-343-5753, E-mail: mayerdi@ere.umontreal.ca.

University at Albany, State University of New York, College of Computing and Information, Albany, NY 12222-0001. Offers computer science (MS, PhD); information science (MS, PhD); information science and policy (CAS); library science (MLS); MLS/MA. *Accreditation:* ALA (one or more programs are accredited). Part-time and evening/weekend programs available. *Students:* 192 full-time (109 women), 134 part-time (84 women); includes 9 African Americans, 9 Asian Americans or Pacific Islanders, 11 Hispanic Americans, 60 international. Average age 33. In 2006, 129 master's, 5 doctorates awarded. *Degree requirements:* For doctorate, thesis/dissertation. *Entrance requirements:* For doctorate, GRE General Test. Additional exam requirements/recommendations for international students: Required—TOEFL (minimum score 550 paper-based; 213 computer-based). *Application deadline:* For fall admission, 3/1 for domestic students. Applications are processed on a rolling basis. Application fee: $75. Electronic applications accepted. *Expenses:* Tuition, state resident: full-time $6,900; part-time $288 per credit. Tuition, nonresident: full-time $10,920; part-time $455 per credit. Required fees: $1,139. *Financial support:* Fellowships, Federal Work-Study available. Financial award application deadline: 4/1. *Faculty research:* Human-computer interaction, government information management, library information science, web development, social implications of technology. *Unit head:* Peter Bloniarz, Dean, 518-442-5115. *Application contact:* Brian Goodale, Senior Counselor for Graduate and International Admissions, 518-442-3980.

University at Buffalo, the State University of New York, Graduate School, Graduate School of Education, Department of Library and Information Studies, Buffalo, NY 14260. Offers MLS, Certificate. *Accreditation:* ALA (one or more programs are accredited). Part-time and evening/weekend programs available. *Faculty:* 14 full-time (8 women), 7 part-time/adjunct (5 women). *Students:* 156 full-time (119 women), 150 part-time (115 women); includes 14 minority (6 African Americans, 2 Asian Americans or Pacific Islanders, 6 Hispanic Americans), 8 international. Average age 34. 211 applicants, 50% accepted, 90 enrolled. In 2006, 132 degrees awarded. *Degree requirements:* For master's, thesis optional; for Certificate, thesis. *Entrance requirements:* For master's, minimum GPA of 3.0. Additional exam requirements/recommendations for international students: Required—TOEFL (minimum score 550 paper-based; 213 computer-based), GRE. *Application deadline:* For fall admission, 4/1 priority date for domestic students; for spring admission, 10/15 priority date for domestic students. Applications are processed on a rolling basis. Application fee: $35. Electronic applications accepted. *Financial support:* In 2006–07, 5 fellowships (averaging $10,000 per year), 2 research assistantships with full tuition reimbursements (averaging $5,000 per year) were awarded; teaching assistantships, career-related internships or fieldwork, Federal Work-Study, institutionally sponsored loans, tuition waivers (full and partial), and unspecified assistantships also available. Support available to part-time students. Financial award application deadline: 3/1; financial award applicants required to submit FAFSA. *Faculty research:* Information user behavior, storage and information retrieval, digital libraries, information management services to information users. Total annual research expenditures: $296,881. *Unit head:* Dr. Judith Robinson, Chair, 716-645-2412, Fax: 716-645-3775, E-mail: ub-lis@buffalo.edu. *Application contact:* Dr. Radhika Suresh, Director of Graduate Admissions and Student Services, 716-645-2110 Ext. 1209, Fax: 716-645-7937, E-mail: gse-info@buffalo.edu.

The University of Alabama, Graduate School, College of Communication and Information Sciences, School of Library and Information Studies, Tuscaloosa, AL 35487. Offers book arts (MFA); library and information studies (MLIS, PhD). *Accreditation:* ALA (one or more programs are accredited). Part-time programs available. Postbaccalaureate distance learning degree programs offered (minimal on-campus study). *Faculty:* 11 full-time (6 women). *Students:* 75 full-time (51 women), 170 part-time (132 women); includes 15 minority (11 African Americans, 1 American Indian/Alaska Native, 1 Asian American or Pacific Islander, 2 Hispanic Americans), 1 international. Average age 33. 191 applicants, 86% accepted, 43 enrolled. In 2006, 119 degrees awarded. *Median time to degree:* Master's–1.4 years full-time, 2.3 years part-time. *Entrance requirements:* For master's, GRE General Test or MAT, minimum GPA of 3.0. Additional exam requirements/recommendations for international students: Required—TOEFL. *Application deadline:* For fall admission, 7/1 priority date for domestic and international students; for spring admission, 11/1 priority date for domestic and international students. Applications are processed on a rolling basis. Application fee: $25. Electronic applications accepted. *Financial support:* In 2006–07, 64 students received support, including 4 fellowships with tuition reimbursements available (averaging $14,778 per year), 13 research assistantships with full and partial tuition reimbursements available (averaging $4,912 per year), 18 teaching assistantships with full and partial tuition reimbursements available (averaging $4,912 per year); career-related internships or fieldwork, Federal Work-Study, scholarships/grants, and unspecified assistantships also available. Financial award application deadline: 3/20. *Faculty research:* Instructional design, information equity, youth services, rural information services, book history. *Unit head:* Dr. Elizabeth Aversa, Director and Professor, 205-348-4610, Fax: 205-348-3746, E-mail: eaversa@slis.ua.edu. *Application contact:* Dr. Elizabeth Aversa, Director and Professor, 205-348-4610, Fax: 205-348-3746, E-mail: eaversa@slis.ua.edu.

University of Alberta, Faculty of Graduate Studies and Research, School of Library and Information Studies, Edmonton, AB T6G 2E1, Canada. Offers MLIS. *Accreditation:* ALA. *Faculty:* 6 full-time (5 women), 12 part-time/adjunct (7 women). *Students:* 76 full-time (65 women), 22 part-time (20 women). Average age 32. 142 applicants, 32% accepted, 42 enrolled. In 2006, 24 degrees awarded. *Entrance requirements:* Additional exam requirements/recommendations for international students: Required—TOEFL, Canadian Academic English Language Assessment. *Application deadline:* For fall admission, 7/1 for domestic students, 5/1 for international students. Applications are processed on a rolling basis. Electronic applications accepted. *Financial support:* In 2006–07, 68 students received support, including 12 research assistantships with partial tuition reimbursements available (averaging $3,536 per year); fellowships, career-related internships or fieldwork and scholarships/grants also available. Support available to part-time students. Financial award application deadline: 7/1. *Faculty research:* Intellectual freedom, materials for children and young adults, library classification, multi-media literacy. Total annual research expenditures: $63,000. *Unit head:* Anna Altmann, Acting Director, 780-492-4140, Fax: 403-492-2430, E-mail: anna.altmann@ualberta.ca. *Application contact:* Joanne Hilger, Student Services Administrator, 780-492-4578, Fax: 780-492-2430, E-mail: slis@ualberta.ca.

The University of Arizona, Graduate College, College of Social and Behavioral Sciences, School of Information Resources and Library Science, Tucson, AZ 85721. Offers MA, PhD. *Accreditation:* ALA (one or more programs are accredited). Part-time programs available. *Degree requirements:* For master's, proficiency in disk operating system (DOS); for doctorate, thesis/dissertation. *Entrance requirements:* For master's, GRE, minimum GPA of 3.0; for doctorate, GRE General Test. Additional exam requirements/recommendations for international students: Required—TOEFL. *Faculty research:* Microcomputer applications; quantitative methods systems; information transfer, planning, evaluation, and technology.

The University of British Columbia, Faculty of Arts, School of Library, Archival and Information Studies, Program in Archival Studies/Library and Information Studies, Vancouver, BC V6T 1Z1, Canada. Offers MLIS/MAS. *Faculty:* 10 full-time (7 women), 34 part-time/adjunct (28 women). *Students:* 33 full-time (26 women), 1 (woman) part-time. 25 applicants, 64% accepted, 12 enrolled. *Entrance requirements:* Additional exam requirements/recommendations for international students: Required—TOEFL (minimum score 600 paper-based; 250 computer-based; 100 iBT). *Application deadline:* For fall admission, 2/1 for domestic and international students; for winter admission, 5/1 for domestic and international students. Applications are processed on a rolling basis. Application fee: $90 Canadian dollars ($150 Canadian dollars for international students). Electronic applications accepted. *Financial support:* In 2006–07, fellowships (averaging $16,000 per year), 15 research assistantships were awarded; Federal Work-Study, institutionally sponsored loans, scholarships/grants, tuition waivers (partial), and unspecified assistantships also available. *Application contact:* Graduate Admissions Secretary, 604-822-2404, Fax: 604-822-6006, E-mail: slais.admissions@ubc.ca.

The University of British Columbia, Faculty of Arts, School of Library, Archival and Information Studies, Program in Library and Information Studies, Vancouver, BC V6T 1Z1, Canada. Offers MLIS. Part-time programs available. *Faculty:* 9 full-time (7 women), 26 part-time/adjunct (20 women). *Students:* 136 full-time (106 women), 9 part-time (6 women). Average age 34. 220 applicants, 37% accepted, 55 enrolled. In 2006, 83 degrees awarded. *Degree requirements:* For master's, thesis optional. *Entrance requirements:* For master's, minimum GPA of 3.3 in undergraduate upper-division courses. Additional exam requirements/recommendations for international students: Required—TOEFL (minimum score 600 paper-based; 250 computer-based; 100 iBT). *Application deadline:* For fall admission, 2/1 for domestic and international students; for winter admission, 5/1 for domestic and international students. Application fee: $90 ($150 for international students). Electronic applications accepted. *Financial support:* In 2006–07, 31 students received support, including fellowships (averaging $16,000 per year), 2 research assistantships; teaching assistantships, Federal Work-Study, institutionally sponsored loans, scholarships/grants, and unspecified assistantships also available. *Faculty research:* Computer systems/database design; digital libraries; metadata/classification; censorship and intellectual freedom; children's literature and services. *Application contact:* Graduate Admissions Secretary, 604-822-2404, Fax: 604-822-6006, E-mail: slais.admissions@ubc.ca.

University of California, Los Angeles, Graduate Division, Graduate School of Education and Information Studies, Department of Information Studies, Los Angeles, CA 90095. Offers archival studies (MLIS); informatics (MLIS); information studies (PhD); library and information science (Certificate); library studies (MLIS); MBA/MLIS; MLIS/MA. *Accreditation:* ALA (one or more programs are accredited). *Faculty:* 13 full-time (7 women), 5 part-time/adjunct (4 women). *Students:* 186 full-time (145 women), 33 part-time (23 women); includes 83 minority (7 African Americans, 2 American Indian/Alaska Native, 46 Asian Americans or Pacific Islanders, 28 Hispanic Americans), 6 international. Average age 28. 192 applicants, 71% accepted, 105 enrolled. In 2006, 77 master's, 4 doctorates awarded. Terminal master's awarded for partial completion of doctoral program. *Degree requirements:* For master's, thesis or alternative, professional portfolio; for doctorate, thesis/dissertation, oral and written qualifying exams, professional portfolio. *Entrance requirements:* For master's, GRE General Test, previous course work in computer programming and statistics; for doctorate, GRE General Test, previous course work in statistics, 2 samples of research writing in English. Additional exam requirements/recommendations for international students: Required—TOEFL (paper-based 613, computer-based 220) or IELTS or TWE (5). *Application deadline:* For fall admission, 12/15 for domestic and international students. Applications are processed on a rolling basis. Application fee: $60. Electronic applications accepted. *Financial support:* In 2006–07, 41 fellowships (averaging $12,013 per year) were awarded; research assistantships with partial tuition reimbursements, teaching assistantships with partial tuition reimbursements, career-related internships or fieldwork, Federal Work-Study, institutionally sponsored loans, scholarships/grants, and tuition waivers (full and partial) also available. Support available to part-time students. Financial award application deadline: 3/1; financial award applicants required to submit FAFSA. *Faculty research:* Multimedia, digital libraries, archives and electronic records, interface design, information technology and policy, preservation, access. *Unit head:* Anne J. Gilliland, Professor and Chair, 310-825-8799, E-mail: agilliland@ucla.edu. *Application contact:* Susan S. Abler, Student Affairs Officer, 310-825-5269, Fax: 310-206-4460, E-mail: abler@gseis.ucla.edu.

University of California, Los Angeles, Graduate Division, Graduate School of Education and Information Studies, Program in Library and Information Science, Los Angeles, CA 90095. Offers Ed D. *Entrance requirements:* For doctorate, GRE General Test, minimum undergraduate GPA of 3.0, resumé. Electronic applications accepted.

University of Central Arkansas, Graduate School, College of Education, Department of Middle/Secondary Education and Instructional Technologies, Program in Education Media and Library Science, Conway, AR 72035-0001. Offers MS. Part-time programs available. *Students:* 9 full-time (all women), 96 part-time (93 women); includes 15 minority (6 African Americans, 9 Asian Americans or Pacific Islanders). In 2006, 22 degrees awarded. *Degree requirements:* For master's, comprehensive exam. *Entrance requirements:* For master's, GRE General Test, minimum GPA of 2.7. Additional exam requirements/recommendations for international students: Required—TOEFL (minimum score 550 paper-based; 213 computer-based). *Application deadline:* For fall admission, 3/1 priority date for domestic and international students; for spring admission, 10/1 priority date for domestic and international students. Applications are processed on a rolling basis. *Application fee:* $25 ($40 for international students). *Expenses:* Tuition, state resident: full-time $4,194; part-time $233 per semester. Tuition, nonresident: full-time $5,963; part-time $429 per semester. International tuition: $6,162 full-time. Required fees: $65; $23 per semester. One-time fee: $65 part-time. *Financial support:* Federal Work-Study, scholarships/grants, and tuition waivers (partial) available. Financial award application deadline: 2/15; financial award applicants required to submit FAFSA. *Unit head:* Stephanie Huffman, Head, 501-450-5430, Fax: 501-450-5680, E-mail: stephanieh@uca.edu. *Application contact:* Brenda Herring, Admissions Assistant, 501-450-5065, Fax: 501-450-5678, E-mail: bherring@uca.edu.

University of Central Missouri, The Graduate School, College of Education, Department of Educational Leadership and Human Development, Program in Library Science and Information Services, Warrensburg, MO 64093. Offers human services/learning resources (Ed S); library science and information services (MS). Part-time programs available. *Faculty:* 4 full-time (3 women). *Students:* 3 full-time (2 women), 57 part-time (54 women); includes 4 minority (2 African Americans, 2 Hispanic Americans), 1 international. Average age 39. 17 applicants, 82% accepted, 14 enrolled. In 2006, 21 master's, 2 other advanced degrees awarded. *Degree requirements:* For master's and Ed S, thesis or alternative. *Entrance requirements:* For master's, minimum GPA of 2.75, interview, 2 years of teaching experience; for Ed S, minimum GPA of 3.25, master's degree, teaching certificate. Additional exam requirements/recommendations for international students: Required—TOEFL (minimum score 500 paper-based; 173 computer-based). *Application deadline:* For fall admission, 6/1 priority date for domestic students, 5/1 priority date for international students; for spring admission, 10/1 priority date for domestic students, 10/1 for international students. Applications are processed on a rolling basis. *Application fee:* $30 ($50 for international students). *Expenses:* Tuition, state resident: full-time $5,448; part-time $227 per credit hour. Tuition, nonresident: full-time $10,896; part-time $454 per credit hour. Required fees: $336; $14 per credit hour. *Financial support:* In 2006–07, 6 students received support. Federal Work-Study, scholarships/grants, unspecified assistantships, and administrative assistantships available. Support available to part-time students. Financial award application deadline: 3/1; financial award applicants required to submit FAFSA. *Faculty research:* Promoting information literacy; collaboration between teachers and librarians; student retention; K-12 virtual schools; leadership in school libraries.

University of Denver, College of Education, Denver, CO 80208. Offers counseling psychology (MA, PhD); curriculum and instruction (MA, PhD, Certificate), including curriculum leadership (MA, PhD); educational administration and policy studies (Certificate); educational psychology (MA, PhD, Ed S), including child and family studies (MA, PhD), quantitative research methods (MA, PhD); school psychology (PhD, Ed S); higher education and adult studies (MA, PhD); library and information science (MLIS); library and information sciences (Certificate); school administration (PhD). *Accreditation:* ALA; APA (one or more programs are accredited). Part-time and evening/weekend programs available. Postbaccalaureate distance learning degree programs offered (no on-campus study). *Faculty:* 28 full-time (18 women). *Students:* 293 full-time (240 women), 439 part-time (357 women); includes 102 minority (28 African Americans, 7 American Indian/Alaska Native, 14 Asian Americans or Pacific Islanders, 53 Hispanic Americans), 11 international. Average age 34. 574 applicants, 72% accepted. In 2006, 168 master's, 28 doctorates, 67 other advanced degrees awarded. Terminal master's awarded for partial completion of doctoral program. *Degree requirements:* For master's, comprehensive exam; for doctorate, 2 foreign languages, thesis/dissertation, comprehensive exam. *Entrance requirements:* For master's, GRE General Test or MAT (for most programs); for doctorate, GRE General Test or MAT. *Application deadline:* Applications are processed on a rolling basis. *Application fee:* $50. Electronic applications accepted. *Expenses:* Tuition: Full-time $29,628; part-time $823 per credit. *Financial support:* In 2006–07, 51 teaching assistantships with full and partial tuition reimbursements (averaging $6,700 per year) were awarded; career-related internships or fieldwork, Federal Work-Study, institutionally sponsored loans, and scholarships/grants also available. Support available to part-time students. Financial award application deadline: 3/1; financial award applicants required to submit FAFSA. *Faculty research:* Parkinson's disease, personnel training, development and assessments, gifted education, service learning, transportation, public schools. Total annual research expenditures: $172,000. *Unit head:* Dr. Virginia Maloney, Dean, 303-871-2509. *Application contact:* Linda McCarthy, Contact, 303-871-2509, E-mail: edinfo@du.edu.

University of Hawaii at Manoa, Graduate Division, Colleges of Arts and Sciences, College of Natural Sciences, Department of Information and Computer Sciences, Library and Information Science Program, Honolulu, HI 96822. Offers advanced library and information science (Graduate Certificate); communication and information science (PhD); library and information science (MLI Sc). *Accreditation:* ALA (one or more programs are accredited). Part-time programs available. *Faculty:* 6 full-time (4 women), 6 part-time/adjunct (5 women). *Students:* 48 full-time (36 women), 78 part-time (63 women); includes 74 minority (1 African American, 71 Asian Americans or Pacific Islanders, 2 Hispanic Americans), 7 international. Average age 34. 78 applicants, 71% accepted, 35 enrolled. In 2006, 52 degrees awarded. *Degree requirements:* For master's, thesis optional. *Entrance requirements:* For master's, GRE General Test. Additional exam requirements/recommendations for international students: Required—TOEFL (minimum score 600 paper-based; 250 computer-based). *Application deadline:* For fall admission, 4/1 for domestic students; for spring admission, 11/1 for domestic students. Applications are processed on a rolling basis. *Application fee:* $50. Electronic applications accepted. *Financial support:* In 2006–07, 25 students received support; research assistantships with full tuition reimbursements available, career-related internships or fieldwork, Federal Work-Study, institutionally sponsored loans, scholarships/grants, and tuition waivers (full and partial) available. *Faculty research:* Information behavior, evaluation of electronic information sources, online learning, history of libraries, information literacy. *Application contact:* Gail Morimoto, Administrative Assistant, E-mail: morimoto@hawaii.edu.

Announcement: Founded in 1965, the ALA-accredited Library and Information Science Program prepares information professionals for work in all types of libraries and organizations through its Master of Library and Information Science (MLISc) degree and the Certificate in Advanced Library and Information Science (CALIS) programs. The program is one of 4 sponsors of the interdisciplinary PhD program in communication and information sciences. Dual master's degrees are offered in Pacific Islands studies (MA/MLISc), American studies (MA/MLISc), Asian studies (MA/MLISc), computer science (MS/MLISc), history (MA/MLISc), and law (JD/MLISc). Internships and a limited number of tuition waivers are available. Contact Program Chair, Library and Information Science Program, University of Hawaii at Manoa, 2550 The Mall, Honolulu, HI 96822-2233; 808-956-7321; fax: 808-956-5835; e-mail: slis@hawaii.edu.

University of Houston–Clear Lake, School of Education, Program in Curriculum and Instruction, Houston, TX 77058-1098. Offers curriculum and instruction (MS); early childhood education (MS); reading (MS); school library and information science (MS). Part-time and evening/weekend programs available. *Faculty:* 17 full-time (15 women), 9 part-time/adjunct (7 women). *Students:* 40 full-time (39 women), 185 part-time (176 women); includes 66 minority (32 African Americans, 7 Asian Americans or Pacific Islanders, 27 Hispanic Americans), 6 international. Average age 34. In 2006, 80 degrees awarded. *Degree requirements:* For master's, thesis (for some programs). *Entrance requirements:* For master's, GRE or minimum GPA of 3.0 in last 60 hours. Additional exam requirements/recommendations for international students: Required—TOEFL (minimum score 550 paper-based; 213 computer-based). *Application deadline:* For fall admission, 7/1 for domestic students, 6/1 for international students; for spring admission, 10/1 for domestic and international students. Applications are processed on a rolling basis. *Application fee:* $35 ($75 for international students). Electronic applications accepted. *Financial support:* Career-related internships or fieldwork, Federal Work-Study, institutionally sponsored loans, and scholarships/grants available. Support available to part-time students. Financial award application deadline: 5/1; financial award applicants required to submit FAFSA. *Unit head:* Dr. Suzanne Brown, Chair, 281-283-3540, E-mail: brownsue@uhcl.edu. *Application contact:* Janis S. Bigelow, Assistant Director of Admissions, Recruitment and Communications, 281-283-2540, Fax: 281-283-2530, E-mail: bigelow@uhcl.edu.

University of Illinois at Urbana–Champaign, Graduate College, Graduate School of Library and Information Science, Champaign, IL 61820. Offers MS, PhD, CAS. *Accreditation:* ALA (one or more programs are accredited). *Faculty:* 21 full-time (9 women), 4 part-time/adjunct (3 women). *Students:* 249 full-time (189 women), 292 part-time (222 women); includes 51 minority (23 African Americans, 24 Asian Americans or Pacific Islanders, 4 Hispanic Americans), 38 international. Average age 31. 571 applicants, 53% accepted, 99 enrolled. In 2006, 197 master's, 4 doctorates, 2 other advanced degrees awarded. *Degree requirements:* For doctorate, thesis/dissertation; for CAS, project. *Entrance requirements:* For master's, GRE General Test, minimum GPA of 3.0; for doctorate, interview; for CAS, master's degree in library and information science or related field, minimum GPA of 3.0. *Application deadline:* For fall admission, 1/16 priority date for domestic students; for spring admission, 10/16 for domestic students. Applications are processed on a rolling basis. *Application fee:* $50 ($60 for international students). Electronic applications accepted. *Financial support:* In 2006–07, 33 fellowships, 39 research assistantships, 22 teaching assistantships were awarded; tuition waivers (full and partial) also available. Financial award application deadline: 2/1. *Unit head:* John Unsworth, Dean, 217-333-3281, Fax: 217-244-3302, E-mail: unsworth@uiuc.edu. *Application contact:* Valerie Youngen, Admissions, 217-333-0734, Fax: 217-244-3302, E-mail: vyoungen@uiuc.edu.

See Close-Up on page 2137.

The University of Iowa, Graduate College, School of Library and Information Science, Iowa City, IA 52242-1316. Offers MA, MA/Certificate, MBA/MA. *Accreditation:* ALA (one or more programs are accredited). *Faculty:* 4 full-time, 9 part-time/adjunct. *Students:* 43 full-time (38 women), 23 part-time (19 women); includes 2 minority (1 African American, 1 Hispanic American), 3 international. 88 applicants, 56% accepted, 27 enrolled. In 2006, 28 degrees awarded. *Degree requirements:* For master's, exam, portfolio, thesis optional. *Entrance requirements:* For master's, GRE General Test, minimum GPA of 3.0. Additional exam requirements/recommendations for international students: Required—TOEFL (minimum score 550 paper-based; 213 computer-based; 81 iBT). *Application deadline:* For fall admission, 2/1 for domestic and international students. *Application fee:* $60 ($85 for international students). Electronic applications accepted. *Financial support:* In 2006–07, 1 fellowship, 11 research assistantships with partial tuition reimbursements, 6 teaching assistantships with partial tuition reimbursements were awarded. Financial award applicants required to submit FAFSA. *Unit head:* James Elmborg, Director, 319-335-5707.

University of Kentucky, Graduate School, College of Communications and Information Studies, Program in Library and Information Science, Lexington, KY 40506-0032. Offers library science (MA, MSLS). *Accreditation:* ALA (one or more programs are accredited). Part-time programs available. *Faculty:* 6 full-time (3 women). *Students:* 82 full-time (64 women), 147 part-time (128 women); includes 5 minority (3 African Americans, 2 Hispanic Americans), 2 international. Average age 33. 171 applicants, 55% accepted, 61 enrolled. In 2006, 109 degrees awarded. *Degree requirements:* For master's, variable foreign language requirement, comprehensive exam. *Entrance requirements:* For master's, GRE General Test, minimum undergraduate GPA of 2.75. Additional exam requirements/recommendations for international students: Required—TOEFL (minimum score 550 paper-based; 213 computer-based). *Application deadline:* For fall admission, 7/17 priority date for domestic students, 2/1 priority date for international students; for spring admission, 12/13 priority date for domestic students, 6/15 priority date for international students. Applications are processed on a rolling basis. *Application fee:* $40 ($55 for international students). *Expenses:* Tuition, state resident: full-time $7,670; part-time $401 per credit hour. Tuition, nonresident: full-time $16,158; part-time $873 per credit hour. *Financial support:* In 2006–07, 3 fellowships with full tuition reimbursements (averaging $1,470 per year), 3 research assistantships with full tuition reimbursements (averaging $6,200 per year) were awarded; teaching assistantships, career-related internships or fieldwork, Federal Work-Study, scholarships/grants, traineeships, health care benefits, tuition waivers (partial), and unspecified assistantships also available. Support available to part-time students. Financial award application deadline: 3/15. *Faculty research:* Information retrieval systems, information-seeking behavior, organizational behavior, computer cataloging, library resource sharing. Total annual research expenditures: $24,000. *Unit head:* Dr. Timothy Sineath, Director of Graduate Studies, 859-257-8100, Fax: 859-257-4205, E-mail: tsineath@uky.edu. *Application contact:* Dr. Brian Jackson, Senior Associate Dean, 859-257-4667, Fax: 859-257-4676, E-mail: brian.jackson@uky.edu.

University of Maryland, College Park, Graduate Studies, Interdepartmental Programs, Program in Geography, Library, and Information Services, College Park, MD 20742. Offers MA/MLS. *Application deadline:* For fall admission, 1/15 for domestic and international students. Applications are processed on a rolling basis. *Application fee:* $60. Electronic applications accepted. *Financial support:* Fellowships, research assistantships, teaching assistantships available. Financial award application deadline: 2/1; financial award applicants required to submit FAFSA. *Unit head:* Dr. Diane Barlow, Associate Dean, 301-405-2042, Fax: 301-314-9145, E-mail: dbarlow@umd.edu. *Application contact:* Dean of Graduate School, 301-405-0358, Fax: 301-314-9305.

See Close-Up on page 2139.

University of Maryland, College Park, Graduate Studies, Interdepartmental Programs, Program in History, Library, and Information Services, College Park, MD 20742. Offers MA/MLS. *Students:* 16 full-time (10 women), 5 part-time (all women), 1 international. 29 applicants, 48% accepted, 7 enrolled. *Entrance requirements:* Additional exam requirements/recommendations for international students: Required—TOEFL. *Application deadline:* For fall admission, 12/15 for domestic students, 2/1 for international students. Applications are processed on a rolling basis. *Application fee:* $60. Electronic applications accepted. *Financial support:* In 2006–07, 1 fellowship (averaging $11,000 per year) was awarded; research assistantships, teaching assistantships. Financial award applicants required to submit FAFSA. *Unit head:* Dr. Diane Barlow, Associate Dean, 301-405-2042, Fax: 301-314-9145, E-mail: dbarlow@umd.edu. *Application contact:* Dean of Graduate School, 301-405-0358, Fax: 301-314-9305.

See Close-Up on page 2139.

University of Michigan, Horace H. Rackham School of Graduate Studies, School of Information, Ann Arbor, MI 48109-1107. Offers archives and records management (MS); human-computer interaction (MS); information (MS, PhD); information economics, management and policy (MS); library and information services (MS). *Accreditation:* ALA (one or more programs are accredited). Part-time programs available. *Degree requirements:* For master's, variable foreign language requirement, thesis optional; for doctorate, one foreign language, thesis/dissertation, oral defense of dissertation, preliminary exam. *Entrance requirements:* For master's and doctorate, GRE General Test. Additional exam requirements/recommendations for inter-

Library Science

University of Michigan *(continued)*
national students: Required—TOEFL (minimum score 600 paper-based; 250 computer-based). Electronic applications accepted.

See Close-Up on page 2141.

University of Missouri–Columbia, Graduate School, College of Education, School of Information Science and Learning Technologies, Columbia, MO 65211. Offers educational technology (M Ed, Ed S); information science and learning technology (PhD); library science (MA). *Accreditation:* ALA (one or more programs are accredited). Part-time and evening/weekend programs available. *Faculty:* 15 full-time (7 women). *Students:* 140 full-time (105 women), 260 part-time (200 women); includes 15 minority (5 African Americans, 4 American Indian/Alaska Native, 3 Asian Americans or Pacific Islanders, 3 Hispanic Americans), 37 international. In 2006, 175 master's, 7 doctorates, 3 other advanced degrees awarded. *Entrance requirements:* For master's, GRE General Test or MAT, minimum GPA of 3.0. *Application deadline:* For fall admission, 3/1 priority date for domestic students; for winter admission, 10/1 priority date for domestic students; for spring admission, 3/1 priority date for domestic students. Applications are processed on a rolling basis. Application fee: $45 ($60 for international students). *Financial support:* Fellowships, teaching assistantships available. *Unit head:* Dr. John Wedman, Director of Graduate Studies, 573-882-9424, E-mail: wedmanj@missouri.edu.

University of Nevada, Las Vegas, Graduate College, College of Education, Department of Curriculum and Instruction, Las Vegas, NV 89154-9900. Offers curriculum and instruction (Ed D, PhD, Ed S); elementary education (M Ed, MS); English education (M Ed, MS); library science (M Ed, MS); literacy education (M Ed, MS); mathematics education (M Ed, MS); multicultural education (M Ed, MS); reading specialist (M Ed, MS); secondary education (M Ed, MS); teacher leadership (M Ed, MS); teaching English as a second language (M Ed, MS); technology integration and leadership (M Ed, MS). *Accreditation:* NCATE. Part-time and evening/weekend programs available. *Faculty:* 40 full-time (19 women), 21 part-time/adjunct (14 women). *Students:* 257 full-time (189 women), 387 part-time (296 women); includes 114 minority (28 African Americans, 5 American Indian/Alaska Native, 34 Asian Americans or Pacific Islanders, 47 Hispanic Americans), 7 international. 261 applicants, 70% accepted, 168 enrolled. In 2006, 231 master's, 5 doctorates awarded. *Degree requirements:* For master's, thesis (for some programs), comprehensive exam (for some programs); for doctorate, thesis/dissertation, oral exam. *Entrance requirements:* For master's, minimum GPA of 3.0; for doctorate, GRE General Test, minimum graduate GPA of 3.0. Additional exam requirements/recommendations for international students: Required—TOEFL (minimum score 550 paper-based; 213 computer-based; 80 iBT). *Application deadline:* For fall admission, 2/15 for domestic and international students; for spring admission, 9/30 for domestic and international students. Application fee: $60 ($75 for international students). Electronic applications accepted. *Financial support:* In 2006–07, 30 research assistantships with partial tuition reimbursements (averaging $10,000 per year), 7 teaching assistantships with partial tuition reimbursements (averaging $12,000 per year) were awarded; career-related internships or fieldwork, Federal Work-Study, institutionally sponsored loans, scholarships/grants, health care benefits, and unspecified assistantships also available. Support available to part-time students. Financial award application deadline: 3/1. *Unit head:* Dr. Greg Levitt, Chair, 702-895-3241. *Application contact:* Graduate College Admissions Evaluator, 702-895-3320, E-mail: gradcollege@unlv.edu.

The University of North Carolina at Chapel Hill, Graduate School, School of Information and Library Science, Chapel Hill, NC 27599. Offers MSIS, MSLS, PhD, CAS. *Accreditation:* ALA (one or more programs are accredited). Part-time programs available. *Faculty:* 22 full-time (13 women), 46 part-time/adjunct (23 women). *Students:* 289 full-time (186 women), 34 part-time (20 women); includes 30 minority (19 African Americans, 3 American Indian/Alaska Native, 5 Asian Americans or Pacific Islanders, 3 Hispanic Americans), 19 international. Average age 28. 326 applicants, 62% accepted, 120 enrolled. In 2006, 105 master's, 4 doctorates awarded. Terminal master's awarded for partial completion of doctoral program. *Median time to degree:* Of those who began their doctoral program in fall 1998, 75% received their degree in 8 years or less. *Degree requirements:* For master's, paper or project; for doctorate, thesis/dissertation. *Entrance requirements:* For master's and doctorate, GRE General Test. Additional exam requirements/recommendations for international students: Required—TOEFL (minimum score 625 paper-based; 263 computer-based). *Application deadline:* For fall admission, 1/1 priority date for domestic and international students; for spring admission, 10/15 for domestic and international students. Applications are processed on a rolling basis. Application fee: $70. Electronic applications accepted. *Financial support:* In 2006–07, 71 fellowships with full tuition reimbursements (averaging $2,445 per year), 138 research assistantships with full tuition reimbursements (averaging $11,836 per year), 4 teaching assistantships with full tuition reimbursements (averaging $11,000 per year) were awarded; career-related internships or fieldwork, Federal Work-Study, institutionally sponsored loans, health care benefits, and unspecified assistantships also available. Financial award application deadline: 1/1. *Faculty research:* Information retrieval, digital libraries, management of information resources, archives and cultural heritage, information management. *Unit head:* Dr. Jose-Marie Griffiths, Dean, 919-962-8366, Fax: 919-962-8071, E-mail: info@ils.unc.edu. *Application contact:* Lara Bailey, Student Services Manager, 919-962-8366, Fax: 919-962-8071, E-mail: info@ils.unc.edu.

The University of North Carolina at Greensboro, Graduate School, School of Education, Department of Library and Information Studies, Greensboro, NC 27412-5001. Offers MLIS. *Accreditation:* ALA. Part-time and evening/weekend programs available. Postbaccalaureate distance learning degree programs offered (no on-campus study). *Faculty:* 8 full-time (6 women), 16 part-time/adjunct (9 women). *Students:* 86 full-time (72 women), 148 part-time (127 women); includes 15 minority (9 African Americans, 4 Asian Americans or Pacific Islanders, 2 Hispanic Americans), 4 international. Average age 35. 146 applicants, 52% accepted, 66 enrolled. In 2006, 104 degrees awarded. *Degree requirements:* For master's, portfolio. *Entrance requirements:* For master's, GRE General Test. Additional exam requirements/recommendations for international students: Required—TOEFL (minimum score 550 paper-based; 213 computer-based), IELTS (minimum score 7). *Application deadline:* For fall admission, 3/31 priority date for domestic students; for spring admission, 10/31 for domestic students. Applications are processed on a rolling basis. Application fee: $45. Electronic applications accepted. *Expenses:* Tuition, state resident: full-time $2,692. Tuition, nonresident: full-time $13,742. *Financial support:* In 2006–07, fellowships (averaging $3,404 per year), 10 research assistantships with full tuition reimbursements (averaging $8,000 per year) were awarded; career-related internships or fieldwork, Federal Work-Study, institutionally sponsored loans, scholarships/grants, and unspecified assistantships also available. Support available to part-time students. Financial award application deadline: 3/1; financial award applicants required to submit FAFSA. *Faculty research:* Library history, gender studies, children's literature, web design, homeless, technical services. *Unit head:* Dr. O Lee Shiflett, Chair, 336-334-3481, E-mail: olshifle@uncg.edu. *Application contact:* Michelle Harkleroad, Director of Graduate Admissions, 336-334-4884, Fax: 336-334-4424, E-mail: mbharkle@uncg.edu.

University of North Texas, Robert B. Toulouse School of Graduate Studies, School of Library and Information Sciences, Denton, TX 76203. Offers information science (MS, PhD); library science (MS). *Accreditation:* ALA (one or more programs are accredited). Part-time and evening/weekend programs available. *Faculty:* 15 full-time (8 women). *Students:* 123 full-time (86 women), 755 part-time (626 women); includes 159 minority (39 African Americans, 6 American Indian/Alaska Native, 21 Asian Americans or Pacific Islanders, 93 Hispanic Americans), 45 international. Average age 36. 355 applicants, 72% accepted, 138 enrolled. In 2006, 362 master's, 11 doctorates awarded. *Degree requirements:* For master's, comprehensive exam; for doctorate, one foreign language, thesis/dissertation, comprehensive exam. *Entrance requirements:* For master's and doctorate, GRE General Test. Additional exam requirements/recommendations for international students: Recommended—TOEFL (minimum score 550 paper-based; 213 computer-based). *Application deadline:* For fall admission, 7/15 for domestic students; for spring admission, 11/30 for domestic students. Applications are processed on a rolling basis. Application fee: $50 ($75 for international students). *Expenses:* Tuition, state

resident: full-time $3,573; part-time $198 per credit. Tuition, nonresident: full-time $8,577; part-time $476 per credit. Required fees: $1,258; $126 per credit. One-time fee: $150 full-time. Tuition and fees vary according to course load. *Financial support:* Fellowships, research assistantships, teaching assistantships, career-related internships or fieldwork, Federal Work-Study, institutionally sponsored loans, and library assistantships available. Financial award application deadline: 4/1. *Faculty research:* Information resources and services, information management and retrieval, computer-based information systems. *Unit head:* Dr. Herman Totten, Dean, 940-565-2058, E-mail: totten@lis.admin.unt.edu. *Application contact:* Dr. Brian O'Connor, Graduate Adviser, 940-565-2347, Fax: 940-565-3101, E-mail: boconnor@lis.admin.unt.edu.

University of Oklahoma, Graduate College, College of Arts and Sciences, School of Library and Information Studies, Program in Library and Information Studies, Norman, OK 73019-0390. Offers knowledge management (MS); library and information studies (MLIS); school library media specialist (Certificate); M Ed/MLIS; MBA/MLIS. Part-time and evening/weekend programs available. *Students:* 34 full-time (29 women), 161 part-time (130 women); includes 19 minority (8 African Americans, 8 American Indian/Alaska Native, 1 Asian American or Pacific Islander, 2 Hispanic Americans), 1 international. 52 applicants, 100% accepted, 38 enrolled. In 2006, 56 degrees awarded. *Degree requirements:* For master's, comprehensive exam (MLIS). *Entrance requirements:* For master's, GRE, minimum GPA of 3.2 in last 60 hours or 3.0 overall. Additional exam requirements/recommendations for international students: Required—TOEFL (minimum score 550 paper-based; 213 computer-based). *Application deadline:* For fall admission, 3/1 priority date for domestic students, 4/1 for international students; for spring admission, 10/15 for domestic students, 9/1 for international students. Applications are processed on a rolling basis. Application fee: $40 ($90 for international students). Electronic applications accepted. *Expenses:* Tuition, state resident: full-time $3,180; part-time $133 per credit hour. Tuition, nonresident: full-time $11,347; part-time $473 per credit hour. Required fees: $1,729; $62 per credit hour. $117 per semester. Tuition and fees vary according to course load and program. *Financial support:* Teaching assistantships with partial tuition reimbursements, scholarships/grants and unspecified assistantships available. Financial award applicants required to submit FAFSA. *Faculty research:* Information use in the digital age, equity of access, learning organizations, education of information professionals, information services to special populations. *Application contact:* Maggie Ryan, Coordinator of Admissions, 405-325-3921, Fax: 405-325-7648, E-mail: mryan@ou.edu.

University of Pittsburgh, School of Information Sciences, Department of Library and Information Science, Pittsburgh, PA 15260. Offers MLIS, PhD, Certificate. *Accreditation:* ALA (one or more programs are accredited). Part-time and evening/weekend programs available. Post-baccalaureate distance learning degree programs offered (minimal on-campus study). *Faculty:* 8 full-time (4 women), 11 part-time/adjunct (10 women). *Students:* 148 full-time (113 women), 276 part-time (228 women); includes 31 minority (10 African Americans, 11 Asian Americans or Pacific Islanders, 10 Hispanic Americans), 33 international. 298 applicants, 94% accepted, 126 enrolled. In 2006, 196 master's, 6 doctorates, 3 other advanced degrees awarded. *Degree requirements:* For master's, thesis optional; for doctorate, thesis/dissertation, comprehensive exam, registration. *Entrance requirements:* For master's, minimum GPA of 3.0; for doctorate, GRE General Test, minimum GPA of 3.0. Additional exam requirements/recommendations for international students: Required—TOEFL (minimum score 550 paper-based; 213 computer-based; 80 iBT). *Application deadline:* For fall admission, 7/1 priority date for domestic students, 4/1 priority date for international students; for spring admission, 11/1 priority date for domestic students, 10/1 priority date for international students. Applications are processed on a rolling basis. Application fee: $50. Electronic applications accepted. *Expenses:* Contact institution. *Financial support:* In 2006–07, 186 students received support, including 103 fellowships with full tuition reimbursements available (averaging $3,027 per year), 5 research assistantships with full and partial tuition reimbursements available (averaging $3,887 per year), 78 teaching assistantships with full and partial tuition reimbursements available (averaging $7,554 per year); career-related internships or fieldwork, scholarships/grants, health care benefits, tuition waivers (full and partial), and unspecified assistantships also available. Support available to part-time students. Financial award application deadline: 1/15; financial award applicants required to submit FAFSA. *Faculty research:* Archives, preservation management, children's resources and services, medical informatics, digital libraries, information retrieval. Total annual research expenditures: $93,672. *Unit head:* Dr. Richard Cox, Chair, 412-624-3245, Fax: 412-624-5231, E-mail: rcox@sis.pitt.edu. *Application contact:* Ninette Kay, Admissions Coordinator, 412-624-5146, Fax: 412-624-5231, E-mail: nkay@mail.sis.pitt.edu.

University of Puerto Rico, Río Piedras, Graduate School of Information Sciences and Technologies, San Juan, PR 00931-3300. Offers librarianship (Post-Graduate Certificate); librarianship and information services (MLS). *Accreditation:* ALA. Part-time programs available. *Students:* 38 full-time (27 women), 97 part-time (68 women); includes 134 minority (all Hispanic Americans) In 2006, 18 master's, 28 other advanced degrees awarded. *Degree requirements:* For master's, thesis, portfolio, comprehensive exam. *Entrance requirements:* For master's, PAEG, GRE, interview, minimum GPA of 3.0, 3 letters of recommendation; for Post-Graduate Certificate, PAEG, GRE, minimum GPA of 3.0, IST master's degree. *Application deadline:* For fall admission, 2/1 for domestic and international students. Application fee: $17. *Expenses:* Tuition, state resident: part-time $100 per credit. Tuition, nonresident: part-time $291 per credit. Required fees: $72 per semester. *Financial support:* Fellowships, research assistantships, teaching assistantships, Federal Work-Study, institutionally sponsored loans, and tuition waivers (partial) available. Financial award application deadline: 5/31. *Faculty research:* Evaluation of journals published by the Puerto Rican system. *Unit head:* Dr. Nitza M. Hernández, Director, 787-764-0000 Ext. 5207, Fax: 787-764-2311. *Application contact:* Information Contact, 787-764-0000 Ext. 5827, Fax: 787-764-2311.

University of Rhode Island, Graduate School, College of Arts and Sciences, Graduate School of Library and Information Studies, Kingston, RI 02881. Offers MLIS. *Accreditation:* ALA. In 2006, 64 degrees awarded. *Application deadline:* For fall admission, 4/15 priority date for domestic students. Applications are processed on a rolling basis. Application fee: $35. *Expenses:* Tuition, state resident: full-time $6,032; part-time $335 per credit. Tuition, nonresident: full-time $17,288; part-time $960 per credit. Required fees: $65 per credit. $30 per semester. One-time fee: $80 part-time. *Unit head:* Dr. W. Gale Eaton, Director, 401-874-4651.

University of South Carolina, The Graduate School, College of Mass Communications and Information Studies, School of Library and Information Science, Columbia, SC 29208. Offers MLIS, Certificate, Specialist, MLIS/MA. *Accreditation:* ALA (one or more programs are accredited). Part-time programs available. Postbaccalaureate distance learning degree programs offered (no on-campus study). *Degree requirements:* For master's and other advanced degree, registration. *Entrance requirements:* For master's, GRE General Test, or MAT; for other advanced degree, GRE General Test or MAT. Additional exam requirements/recommendations for international students: Required—TOEFL. Electronic applications accepted. *Faculty research:* Information technology management, distance education, library services for children and young adults, special libraries.

University of Southern Mississippi, Graduate School, College of Education and Psychology, School of Library and Information Science, Hattiesburg, MS 39406-0001. Offers MLIS, SLS. *Accreditation:* ALA (one or more programs are accredited). Part-time and evening/weekend programs available. Postbaccalaureate distance learning degree programs offered (minimal on-campus study). *Faculty:* 7 full-time (6 women). *Students:* 20 full-time (19 women), 151 part-time (126 women); includes 32 minority (28 African Americans, 1 American Indian/Alaska Native, 1 Asian American or Pacific Islander, 2 Hispanic Americans). Average age 38. 78 applicants, 56% accepted, 34 enrolled. In 2006, 54 degrees awarded. *Degree requirements:* For master's, research project, thesis optional; for SLS, field project, thesis optional. *Entrance requirements:* For master's, GRE General Test, minimum GPA of 3.0; for SLS, GRE General Test, MLIS, minimum graduate GPA of 3.25. Additional exam requirements/recommendations for international students: Required—TOEFL. *Application deadline:* For fall admission, 3/15 priority date for domestic students, 3/15 for international students. Applications are processed on a rolling basis. Application fee: $25 ($30 for international students). Electronic applications accepted. *Financial support:* In 2006–07, 8 students received support, including 7 research assistantships with full tuition reimbursements available (averaging $6,150 per year), 2 teaching assistantships (averaging $6,150 per year); fellowships with tuition reimbursements available, career-related internships or fieldwork, Federal Work-Study, institutionally sponsored loans, scholarships/grants, tuition waivers (full and partial), and unspecified assistantships also available. Financial award application deadline: 3/15. *Faculty research:* Printing, library history, children's literature, telecommunications, management. Total annual research expenditures: $14,185. *Unit head:* Dr. Melanie J. Norton, Director, 601-266-4228, Fax: 601-266-5774.

University of South Florida, Graduate School, College of Arts and Sciences, School of Library and Information Science, Tampa, FL 33620-9951. Offers library and information sciences (MA). *Accreditation:* ALA. Part-time and evening/weekend programs available. Postbaccalaureate distance learning degree programs offered (minimal on-campus study). *Faculty:* 20 full-time (15 women), 20 part-time/adjunct (9 women). *Students:* 111 full-time (73 women), 437 part-time (363 women); includes 123 minority (41 African Americans, 14 Asian Americans or Pacific Islanders, 68 Hispanic Americans), 15 international. 237 applicants, 82% accepted, 117 enrolled. In 2006, 177 degrees awarded. *Median time to degree:* Master's–1.5 years full-time, 2.5 years part-time. *Entrance requirements:* For master's, GRE General Test or minimum GPA of 2.5 upper division course work, minimum GPA of 2.5 in last 60 hours of course work. *Application deadline:* For fall admission, 6/1 for domestic students; for spring admission, 10/15 for domestic students. Applications are processed on a rolling basis. Application fee: $30. Electronic applications accepted. *Financial support:* In 2006–07, 11 fellowships with full tuition reimbursements, 13 teaching assistantships with full tuition reimbursements (averaging $11,750 per year) were awarded; career-related internships or fieldwork, scholarships/grants, and unspecified assistantships also available. Support available to part-time students. Financial award application deadline: 6/30; financial award applicants required to submit FAFSA. *Faculty research:* Youth services in libraries, community engagement and libraries, information architecture, biomedical informatics. Total annual research expenditures: $226,470. *Unit head:* Vicki L. Gregory, Chairperson and Program Director, 813-974-3520, Fax: 813-974-6840, E-mail: gregory@luna.cas.usf.edu. *Application contact:* Mel Pace, Information Contact, 813-974-6837, Fax: 813-974-6840, E-mail: lis@luna.cas.usf.edu.

The University of Texas at Austin, Graduate School, Graduate School of Library and Information Science, Austin, TX 78712-1111. Offers MLIS, PhD. *Accreditation:* ALA (one or more programs are accredited). Part-time programs available. *Degree requirements:* For doctorate, 2 foreign languages, thesis/dissertation. *Entrance requirements:* For master's and doctorate, GRE General Test. Electronic applications accepted. *Faculty research:* Information retrieval and artificial intelligence, library history and administration, classification and cataloguing.

University of Toronto, School of Graduate Studies, Social Sciences Division, Faculty of Information Studies, Toronto, ON M5S 1A1, Canada. Offers MI St, PhD, Diploma, JD/M I St. *Accreditation:* ALA (one or more programs are accredited). Part-time programs available. *Degree requirements:* For master's, thesis optional; for doctorate, thesis/dissertation, oral exam/thesis defense. *Entrance requirements:* For master's, minimum B average overall, mid-B in final year; 2 letters of reference; for doctorate, 3 letters of reference, minimum B+ average; for Diploma, MI St, MLS, or MIS degree or equivalent; minimum B+ average overall. Additional exam requirements/recommendations for international students: Required—TOEFL (minimum score 600 paper-based; 250 computer-based), TWE (minimum score 6), MELAB (95) or IELTS (8). Expenses: Contact institution.

University of Washington, Graduate School, The Information School, Seattle, WA 98195. Offers information management (MSIM); information science (PhD); library and information science (MLIS). *Accreditation:* ALA (one or more programs are accredited). Part-time and evening/weekend programs available. Postbaccalaureate distance learning degree programs offered (minimal on-campus study). *Faculty:* 32 full-time (13 women), 15 part-time/adjunct (8 women). *Students:* 201 full-time (138 women), 291 part-time (218 women); includes 67 minority (9 African Americans, 6 American Indian/Alaska Native, 36 Asian Americans or Pacific Islanders, 16 Hispanic Americans), 33 international. Average age 33. 585 applicants, 52% accepted, 193 enrolled. In 2006, 138 master's, 2 doctorates awarded. *Degree requirements:* For master's, thesis optional; for doctorate, thesis/dissertation. *Entrance requirements:* For master's, GRE General Test, GMAT, minimum GPA of 3.0; for doctorate, GRE General Test, minimum GPA of 3.0. Additional exam requirements/recommendations for international students: Required—TOEFL (minimum score 550 paper-based; 173 computer-based; 45 iBT). *Application deadline:* For fall admission, 1/15 for domestic students, 11/1 for international students. Application fee: $45. Electronic applications accepted. *Financial support:* In 2006–07, 38 fellowships with tuition reimbursements (averaging $3,000 per year), 51 research assistantships with tuition reimbursements (averaging $12,308 per year) were awarded; teaching assistantships with tuition reimbursements, career-related internships or fieldwork, Federal Work-Study, institutionally sponsored loans, scholarships/grants, health care benefits, tuition waivers (full and partial), and unspecified assistantships also available. Support available to part-time students. Financial award application deadline: 2/28; financial award applicants required to submit FAFSA. *Faculty research:* Metadata, impact of networked information, human factors in information and communication technology, human-information behavior. Total annual research expenditures: $2 million. *Unit head:* Harry Bruce, Professor and Dean, 206-685-9937, Fax: 206-616-3152, E-mail: harryb@u.washington.edu. *Application contact:* Office and Student and Academic Services (OSAS), 206-543-1794, Fax: 206-616-3152, E-mail: info@ischool.washington.edu.

The University of Western Ontario, Faculty of Graduate Studies, Faculty of Information and Media Studies, Programs in Library and Information Science, London, ON N6A 5B8, Canada. Offers MLIS, PhD. Program conducted on a trimester basis. *Accreditation:* ALA (one or more programs are accredited). Part-time and evening/weekend programs available. *Faculty:* 20 full-time (12 women), 15 part-time/adjunct (8 women). *Students:* 172 full-time (130 women), 68 part-time (47 women). 262 applicants, 81% accepted, 162 enrolled. In 2006, 160 master's, 1 doctorate awarded. *Median time to degree:* Of those who began their doctoral program in fall 1998, 100% received their degree in 8 years or less. *Degree requirements:* For master's, registration; for doctorate, thesis/dissertation, comprehensive exam, registration. *Entrance requirements:* For master's, honors degree, minimum B average during previous 2 years of course work; for doctorate, MLIS or equivalent. Additional exam requirements/recommendations for international students: Required—TOEFL (minimum score 625 paper-based; 263 computer-based), TWE (minimum score 5). *Application deadline:* For fall admission, 6/29 for domestic students; for winter admission, 11/3 for domestic students; for spring admission, 3/16 for domestic students. Applications are processed on a rolling basis. Application fee: $50 Canadian dollars. Electronic applications accepted. *Financial support:* In 2006–07, 89 students received support, including 17 teaching assistantships with partial tuition reimbursements available (averaging $9,699 Canadian dollars per year); research assistantships, career-related internships or fieldwork, institutionally sponsored loans, scholarships/grants, health care benefits, and unspecified assistantships also available. *Faculty research:* Information, individuals, and society; information systems, policy, power, and institutions. *Application contact:* Shelley Long, Student Services Graduate Secretary, 519-661-4017, Fax: 519-661-3506, E-mail: mlis@uwo.ca.

University of Wisconsin–Madison, Graduate School, College of Letters and Science, School of Library and Information Studies, Madison, WI 53706-1380. Offers MA, PhD, Certificate. *Accreditation:* ALA (one or more programs are accredited). Part-time programs available. *Degree requirements:* For doctorate, thesis/dissertation, comprehensive exam. Electronic applications accepted. *Faculty research:* Intellectual freedom, children's literature, print culture history, information systems design and evaluation, school library media centers.

University of Wisconsin–Milwaukee, Graduate School, School of Information Studies, Milwaukee, WI 53201-0413. Offers MLIS, CAS, MLIS/MA, MLIS/MM, MLIS/MS. *Accreditation:* ALA (one or more programs are accredited). Part-time programs available. *Faculty:* 14 full-time (5 women). *Students:* 99 full-time (75 women), 391 part-time (312 women); includes 32 minority (11 African Americans, 12 Asian Americans or Pacific Islanders, 9 Hispanic Americans), 20 international. Average age 36. 239 applicants, 82% accepted, 121 enrolled. In 2006, 120 degrees awarded. *Entrance requirements:* For master's, GRE General Test or MAT. *Application deadline:* For fall admission, 1/1 priority date for domestic students; for spring admission, 9/1 for domestic students. Applications are processed on a rolling basis. Application fee: $45 ($75 for international students). *Expenses:* Tuition, state resident: part-time $510 per credit. Tuition, nonresident: part-time $1,408 per credit. Tuition and fees vary according to program. *Financial support:* In 2006–07, 3 fellowships were awarded; research assistantships, teaching assistantships, career-related internships or fieldwork, Federal Work-Study, and unspecified assistantships also available. Support available to part-time students. Financial award application deadline: 4/15. *Unit head:* Johannes Britz, Dean, 414-229-4709, Fax: 414-229-4848.

Valdosta State University, Graduate School, Program in Library and Information Science, Valdosta, GA 31698. Offers MLIS. *Accreditation:* ALA. *Degree requirements:* For master's, comprehensive exam. *Entrance requirements:* For master's, GRE. Additional exam requirements/recommendations for international students: Required—TOEFL (minimum score 523 paper-based; 193 computer-based).

Wayne State University, Graduate School, Library and Information Science Program, Detroit, MI 48202. Offers archival administration (Certificate); library and information science (MLIS, Spec); library science (MS, Spec). *Accreditation:* ALA (one or more programs are accredited). Part-time and evening/weekend programs available. *Faculty:* 20 full-time (13 women), 4 part-time/adjunct (all women). *Students:* 115 full-time (92 women), 458 part-time (389 women); includes 75 minority (54 African Americans, 3 American Indian/Alaska Native, 11 Asian Americans or Pacific Islanders, 7 Hispanic Americans), 9 international. Average age 35. 162 applicants, 88% accepted, 98 enrolled. In 2006, 234 degrees awarded. *Entrance requirements:* Additional exam requirements/recommendations for international students: Required—TOEFL (minimum score 550 paper-based; 213 computer-based); Recommended—TWE (minimum score 6). *Application deadline:* For fall admission, 7/1 for domestic students, 6/1 for international students; for winter admission, 10/1 for international students; for spring admission, 2/1 for international students. Applications are processed on a rolling basis. Application fee: $30 ($50 for international students). Electronic applications accepted. *Financial support:* Research assistantships, career-related internships or fieldwork, Federal Work-Study, institutionally sponsored loans, and scholarships/grants available. Support available to part-time students. Financial award application deadline: 5/15. *Faculty research:* Convergence of academic libraries and other academic services, competitive intelligence and data mining, impact of digitization on libraries, international librarianship, consumer health information. Total annual research expenditures: $6,040. *Unit head:* Joseph J. Mika, Director, 313-577-1825, Fax: 313-577-7563, E-mail: aa2500@wayne.edu. *Application contact:* Jennifer Bondy, Education Director, 313-577-2523, E-mail: j.l.bondy@wayne.edu.

Wright State University, School of Graduate Studies, College of Education and Human Services, Department of Teacher Education, Programs in Workforce Education, Dayton, OH 45435. Offers career, technology and vocational education (M Ed, MA); computer/technology education (M Ed, MA); library/media (M Ed, MA); vocational education (M Ed, MA). *Accreditation:* NCATE. *Students:* 5 full-time (3 women), 30 part-time (27 women), 1 international. 17 applicants, 94% accepted. In 2006, 14 degrees awarded. *Degree requirements:* For master's, thesis (for some programs). *Entrance requirements:* For master's, GRE General Test, MAT. Additional exam requirements/recommendations for international students: Required—TOEFL. Application fee: $25. *Financial support:* Available to part-time students. Applicants required to submit FAFSA. *Unit head:* Dr. Stephanie Davis, Associate Dean and Program Advisor, 937-775-2880, Fax: 937-775-3308, E-mail: stephanie.davis@wright.edu. *Application contact:* John Kimble, Associate Director of Graduate Admissions and Records, 937-775-2957, Fax: 937-775-2453, E-mail: john.kimble@wright.edu.

DREXEL UNIVERSITY

College of Information Science and Technology

Programs of Study
Drexel University's College of Information Science and Technology (the *iSchool* at Drexel) prepares practitioners and researchers for the information professions. Five graduate degrees are awarded: Master of Science (M.S.) in library and information science, which is offered on campus and online, with recommended course sequences in management of digital information and information/library services; Master of Science in Information Systems (M.S.I.S.), offered both online and on campus; Master of Science in Software Engineering (M.S.S.E.), offered online and on campus; an Executive Master of Science in Information Technology Leadership (Executive M.S.I.T.L.); and a Ph.D. The Post-Master's Certificate of Advanced Study (C.A.S.) program requires eight courses and enrolls professionals who already hold a master's in library science, information systems, or software engineering. Drexel's M.S. program is ranked eleventh in the country, according to *U.S. News & World Report*'s America's Best Graduate Schools 2008.

The M.S. requires fifteen courses and may be completed on a full- or part-time basis. The University calendar includes four terms per calendar year. Students complete required courses (six courses) and pursue an individual program of study. The curriculum is accredited by the American Library Association. A student's individual program may include preparation for a professional specialization. For example, the College offers a Pennsylvania Department of Education–approved curriculum leading to school library media certification. Course work is offered that relates to library and information work in legal, medical, scientific, and business settings, as well as studies in medical informatics, computerized library information systems, Web-mastery, and print-oriented information services. The Ph.D. program comprises advanced course work, research apprenticeships, a portfolio, journal club, and a dissertation. A minimum of three consecutive terms of full-time residency are required; otherwise, doctoral students may pursue studies on either a full- or part-time basis.

The College of Information Science and Technology is also known as "the *iSchool* at Drexel." This identity highlights the College's participation in the iSchools Caucus and its status as a founding member of the organization. The iSchools Caucus is a national alliance of colleges that offer degrees in information science and technology–related fields. Its purpose is to raise awareness and understanding of the information sciences as a cutting-edge and progressive field of study.

Research Facilities
The College's Computing Resource Center (CRC) provides faculty members and administrative personnel with hardware and software support, technical support for its seven presentation classrooms, two student computer laboratories, a video conference room, and a usability lab. The CRC, student labs, and classrooms have access to networked databases, print and file resources within the College, and the Internet via the University's network.

The University's three libraries share an extensive collection of materials for all major areas of library and information science, computer science, systems engineering, information systems, and technology. Electronic resources compose the majority of the collection, delivered to the desktop on or off campus, with several hundred databases holding more than 19,000 full-text electronic journal titles and more than 60,000 electronic books. Students also have easy access to the many libraries and information centers in the Philadelphia area. Librarian assistance is available every day and night, 114 hours per week.

Financial Aid
The College of Information Science and Technology awards scholarships once a year in the fall term and only accepts online scholarship applications from the Web site. The College offers many different types of assistance, including research assistantships for new, full-time Ph.D. students (there are no assistantships for master's-level students); endowed scholarships; Dean's Fellowships; and IST Alumni loan funds. All eligible, degree-seeking, continuing students and newly accepted, degree-seeking applicants are encouraged to apply. The *iSchool* scholarship committee generally awards the scholarships evenly between new and continuing students. There is no distinction made between online and on-campus students; all who are eligible are encouraged to apply. Prospective students should visit the Web site at http://www.ischool.drexel.edu for complete information, deadlines, and additional criteria.

Cost of Study
In 2007–08, tuition is $835 per credit. Each term, on-campus students are also charged a general University fee based on full-time ($220) or part-time ($110) status.

Living and Housing Costs
Ample housing is available in the neighborhood bordering the campus.

Student Group
The College's graduate students represent diverse academic and professional backgrounds and have varied career expectations. Many of the 780 master's students come from the mid-Atlantic region; other regions and countries are also represented. The age range is wide because many students have professional work experience or have pursued graduate studies in other disciplines. The College also enrolls undergraduates pursuing B.S. degrees in information systems, software engineering, and information technology.

The College of Information Science and Technology maintains its own Career Services Office. The office helps students find preprofessional positions and internships and assists graduates in locating professional employment. Many graduates find jobs in libraries and information centers. A number of graduates work in nontraditional positions.

Location
Drexel's 60-acre University City main campus is located in the University City district of Philadelphia, Pennsylvania, about a 10-minute walk from Center City, Philadelphia's downtown neighborhood. As one of the nation's oldest and largest cities, Philadelphia is rich in cultural, historical, and academic institutions and is a leading center for business, industry, and government. These resources provide ample opportunities for information science and technology students to pursue preprofessional employment, internships, and permanent employment.

The University
Drexel is a private institution with an enrollment of 6,976 graduate and professional students and 12,906 undergraduate students. In addition to the information science and technology curricula, degree programs are offered in arts and sciences, biomedical engineering, business, education, engineering, law, media and design arts, medicine, nursing and health sciences, professional studies, and public health.

With College approval, graduate students may include courses from other Drexel units in their program of study. Related curricula include computer science, management, neuropsychology, and technical and science communication.

Applying
Graduate students may apply for admission in the fall, winter, or spring terms; doctoral students are admitted in the fall term. An application and fee, transcripts, a resume, letters of recommendation, and a personal statement are required. Scores for the GRE General Test are required for all master's and Ph.D. applicants. Master's applicants may receive a GRE waiver at the College's discretion based on GPA. Official Test of English as a Foreign Language (TOEFL) scores are required for applicants whose bachelor's degree is from a non-U.S. institution. Students must obtain a minimum score of 600 on the written exam, 250 on the computer-based test, or 100 on the Internet-based exam. Students should visit the College's Web site at http://www.ischool.drexel.edu for additional requirements.

Correspondence and Information
Master's Program Director
College of Information Science and Technology
Drexel University
Philadelphia, Pennsylvania 19104
Phone: 215-895-2474
Web site: http://www.ischool.drexel.edu

Drexel University

THE FACULTY AND THEIR RESEARCH

Eileen G. Abels, Associate Professor and Master's Program Director; Ph.D., UCLA. Digital reference, information-seeking behaviors, information access, business information needs.

Denise E. Agosto, Associate Professor; Ph.D., Rutgers. Information seeking, decision making, World Wide Web, Web site evaluation, gender, children, young adults, multicultural materials.

Robert B. Allen, Associate Professor; Ph.D., California, San Diego. Digital libraries, information organization, knowledge management, scholarly publishing, information retrieval, decision processes.

Michael E. Atwood, Professor and Associate Dean for Academic Affairs and Research; Ph.D., Colorado. Human-computer interaction, computer-supported cooperative work, organizational memory.

Laurie J. Bonnici, Assistant Professor; Ph.D., Florida State. Change management, information technology, memetics, decision sciences, leadership, socialization processes, information science education.

Glenn Booker, Auxiliary Associate Professor; M.S., Berkeley. Software engineering, systems analysis and design, software and process measurement, process improvement, object-oriented analysis and design, bioinformatics, modeling of biological systems.

Chaomei Chen, Associate Professor; Ph.D., Liverpool. Information visualization, visual analytics, knowledge domain visualization, information diffusion, structural and temporal analysis of networks, multiuser virtual environments, hypertext, human-computer interaction, digital libraries.

Thomas A. Childers, Professor Emeritus; Ph.D., Rutgers. Measurement, evaluation, and planning of information and library services; effectiveness of information organizations.

Belinha De Abreu, Auxiliary Assistant Professor; M.L.S., Southern Connecticut State. Media literacy, media effects, information literacy, critical thinking, teacher training, young adults, children services, middle school, school libraries.

M. Carl Drott, Associate Professor; Ph.D., Michigan. Systems analysis techniques, Web usage, competitive intelligence.

David E. Fenske, Isaac L. Auerbach Professor of Information Science and Dean of the College; Ph.D., Wisconsin–Madison. Digital libraries, informatics, knowledge management and information technologies.

Susan Gasson, Associate Professor; Ph.D., Warwick. Codesign of business and IT systems, early requirements analysis for boundary-spanning information systems, human-centered collaborative systems design, social informatics, distributed cognition and knowledge management, wicked problems.

Peter Grillo, Auxiliary Assistant Professor and Executive M.S.I.T.L. Principal; Ph.D., Temple. Strategic applications of technology within organizations.

John B. Hall, Professor Emeritus; Ph.D., Florida State. Academic library service, library administration, organization of materials.

Hyoil Han, Assistant Professor; Ph.D., Texas at Arlington. Text/data mining and understanding, data management/integration, semantic knowledge discovery (e.g., ontology learning), natural language processing, Semantic Web, stream data mining/management, information extraction/retrieval (IE/IR), digital library and life sciences (medical informatics and bioinformatics).

Lewis Hassell, Auxiliary Associate Professor; Ph.D., Drexel. Computer-mediated communication (CMC), neurobiology of information processing and trust, psychological and sociotechnical aspects of information assurance, philosophy of IS, Web design, database design.

Gregory W. Hislop, Associate Professor; Ph.D., Drexel. Information technology for teaching and learning, online education, structure and organization of the information disciplines, computing education research, software evaluation and characterization.

Xiaohua Tony Hu, Assistant Professor; Ph.D., Regina (Canada). Data mining and databases, including data-mining algorithms and methods; Web mining; bioinformatics; data-mining applications in biomedical systems; real-time data warehousing and OLAP.

Randy M. Kaplan, Auxiliary Associate Professor; Ph.D., Temple. Natural language processing, artificial intelligence, information systems management, computer languages, object-oriented technologies, database architecture, knowledge management.

Lee Leitner, Auxiliary Associate Professor; Ph.D., Nova Southeastern. Information security and assurance, software engineering, networking and distributed computing, systems analysis and programming languages.

Xia Lin, Associate Professor; Ph.D., Maryland. Information retrieval and information visualization, visual interface design and visual data analysis, knowledge organization, human-computer interactions, object-oriented programming, Java

and XML, digital libraries and information architecture, information-seeking behaviors in digital environments.

Jacqueline C. Mancall, Professor; Ph.D., Drexel. Information resources and services for children and young adults, collection development, school media centers, instructional role of the information specialist.

Linda S. Marion, Auxiliary Associate Professor; Ph.D., Drexel. Formal and informal communication, bibliometric studies of scholarly communication, diffusion of information, information use in the social sciences, academic and public libraries, information science education.

Katherine W. McCain, Professor; Ph.D., Drexel. Scholarly communication, information production and use in the research process, development and structure of scientific specialties, diffusion of innovation, bibliometrics, evaluation of information retrieval systems.

Carol Hansen Montgomery, Research Professor and Dean of Libraries Emeritus; Ph.D., Drexel. Selection and use of electronic collections, evaluation of library and information systems, digital libraries, economics of libraries and digital collections.

Edward J. O'Connor, Auxiliary Assistant Professor; M.C.S., M.S.M., Polytechnic of New York. Database management systems, programming languages, system analysis and design.

Jung-ran Park, Assistant Professor; Ph.D., Hawaii. Knowledge organization in general (cataloging and classification, metadata schemes, thesauri, lexicons, ontologies, Semantic Web), human language technology, multilingual and multimodal information systems, cross-cultural communication, computer-mediated discourse analysis, applied linguistics, academic libraries/librarianship.

Scott Paul Robertson, Associate Professor; Ph.D., Yale. Digital government and electronic voting, digital libraries, collaborative systems, cognitive science, educational applications of information technologies, knowledge management, knowledge sharing.

Henrry Rodriguez, Visiting Assistant Professor; Ph.D., Royal Institute of Technology (Stockholm). Visualization of persistent conversation, design methods, computer-supported collaborative writing, computer-supported collaborative learning, technology and society.

Scot M. Silverstein, Assistant Professor of Healthcare Informatics and Information Technology and Director of the Institute for Healthcare Informatics (joint appointment with the College of Nursing and Health Professions and the School of Public Health); M.D., Boston University. Medical informatics, electronic medical records, clinical decision support, biomedical information seeking, human-computer interaction, sociotechnical issues in clinical IT, clinical IT project leadership.

Thomas J. Smith, Auxiliary Assistant Professor; M.S., Iowa; M.B.A., Pennsylvania. Internet technologies, programming languages, software design and development processes, software engineering, information science education.

Il-Yeol Song, Professor; Ph.D., LSU. Database modeling and design; design and performance optimization of data warehouses and OLAP; database support for Web-based systems; object-oriented analysis and design with UML; modeling, integration, and analysis of medical and bioinformatics data and digital forensics.

Gerry Stahl, Associate Professor; Ph.D., Colorado; Ph.D., Northwestern. Human-computer interaction, computer-supported cooperative work, computer-supported collaborative learning, theory of collaboration.

Rosina Weber, Assistant Professor and Undergraduate Program Director; Ph.D., Federal University of Santa Catarina (Brazil). Knowledge-based systems; case-based reasoning; textual case-based reasoning; computational intelligence; knowledge discovery; uncertainty, mainly targeting knowledge management goals in different domains, e.g., software engineering, military, finance, law, bioinformatics, and health sciences.

Howard D. White, Professor Emeritus and Visiting Research Professor; Ph.D., Berkeley. Literature information systems, bibliometrics, research methods, collection development, online searching.

Susan Wiedenbeck, Professor and Ph.D. Program Director; Ph.D., Pittsburgh. Human-computer interaction, end-user programming/end-user development, empirical studies of programmers, interface design and evaluation.

Valerie Ann Yonker, Auxiliary Associate Professor; Ph.D., Drexel. Human service information systems, telemedicine, measurement in software evaluation, knowledge engineering, research methods.

Lisl Zach, Assistant Professor; Ph.D., Maryland. Knowledge management/competitive intelligence, disaster-related information services, information-seeking behavior of decision makers, measuring and communicating the value of information, organizational use of information.

A view of the campus at Drexel University.

The Alumni Garden.

INDIANA UNIVERSITY BLOOMINGTON

School of Library and Information Science

Programs of Study	Indiana University's School of Library and Information Science (SLIS) on the Bloomington campus (IUB) offers students a wide choice from among several degree options, where they select a master's or Ph.D. program that best meets their individual needs and career objectives. Master's degrees in library science are also offered at the Indiana University-Purdue University (IUPUI) campus in Indianapolis.
	The Master of Information Science (M.I.S.), a 42-graduate-credit-hour program, places emphasis on the social and behavioral dimensions of information technology. Specialization tracks are human-computer interaction and communication, information architecture, information retrieval systems design, and strategic information management and leadership. This program prepares students for careers in areas such as information management, usability analysis, information architecture, online searching and information brokerage, competitive intelligence and research analysis, Webmaster and Web site design, digital libraries, and database development.
	The Master of Library Science (M.L.S.), a 36-graduate-credit-hour program, explores the role of both print-based and electronic libraries in society. Policy issues and technological trends, how these influence libraries and information centers, how to manage and evaluate collections, responding to patrons' information needs, and using technology to improve access to strategic information resources are all emphasized. Specializations are available in African studies, chemical information, library technology management, music librarianship, and in special collections in two distinct areas: rare books and manuscripts or archives administration. This program prepares students for careers such as library administration, technical services, reference librarianship, and collection development at public, school, academic, corporate, and special libraries.
	The Ph.D. in information science prepares students for advanced research and teaching positions. Students develop a broad understanding of the content, methods, research, and theories of information science and of their relation to other fields of knowledge.
	The Specialist in Library and Information Science degree program (post-master's) offers a means of updating knowledge in a given area or of repositioning oneself to take advantage of changing career options and allows the student in-depth focus on a subject of particular interest.
	SLIS offers a wide range of dual master's degrees: the M.A./M.I.S. in folklore and ethnomusicology and in Russian and East European studies; the M.A./M.L.S. in African American and African diaspora studies, art history, comparative literature, English, folklore and ethnomusicology, history, history and philosophy of science, journalism, Latin American and Caribbean studies, musicology, music theory, and Russian and East European studies; the M.I.S./M.L.S. in information science and library science; the M.I.S./M.P.A. or M.L.S./M.P.A. in public affairs; and the M.L.S./J.D. in law.
	Indiana University School of Library and Information Science M.I.S. and M.L.S. degrees are each accredited by the American Library Association.
Research Facilities	The School's numerous computer laboratories provide students access to a variety of platforms and an array of applications software, including database systems and Web development tools. Labs are designed to encourage experimentation, collaborative project work, and prototype development. One 28-workstation Mac lab offers the latest graphics and Web design tools and allows students to work with UNIX. SLIS is also home to the Laboratory for Applied Informatics Research (LAIR), an Information Processing Laboratory, and an Information Visualization Laboratory (InfoVis).
	Campus resources include the IU libraries, ranked fourteenth in North America in terms of holdings; University Information Technology Services (UITS), which operates one of the world's largest distributed computer networks; and the Lilly Library, one of the preeminent rare-book collections in the nation.
	SLIS is home to the Center for Social Informatics (CSI), where work focuses on social aspects of computerization, including the roles of information technology in social and organizational change and the ways that information technologies are influenced by social forces and practices.
Financial Aid	Scholarships, assistantships, fellowships, guaranteed hourly positions, professional organization awards, and internships are available. The number of applications far exceeds the number of available awards, however. To be eligible for financial aid, a student must be admitted to a degree program. Information is available on the SLIS Web site.
Cost of Study	Tuition rates for 2006–07 were $277.60 per credit hour for Indiana residents and $808.65 per credit hour for nonresidents. Student activity, technology, health, and related fees of approximately $500 per semester also apply.
Living and Housing Costs	IU Bloomington offers graduate housing for both single and married students. University apartments cost approximately $600 per month; dormitory rooms with variable meal plans are also offered. Off-campus housing options, at monthly rents of approximately $500, are also available.
Student Group	SLIS has an enrollment of approximately 300 students on the Bloomington campus and an additional 300 students on the IUPUI campus. Students come from all over the U.S. and from countries around the world. Their major areas of undergraduate study vary widely. All majors are welcome and many students have undergraduate degrees in liberal arts, humanities, social sciences, business, sciences, education, computer science, and information technology.
Student Outcomes	Career prospects for SLIS graduates in library and information science, usability, collection management, information architecture, human-computer interaction, digital library development, and other information professions are generally good because those graduates have learned skills that do not become obsolete as technology and job markets change.
Location	IU Bloomington, with more than 36,000 students, is the primary residential campus of Indiana University. Known for its physical beauty, the 1,931-acre campus is set in the rolling hills of southern Indiana and centered in a beautiful, small, college town. Cultural and social activities flourish; there are hundreds of student organizations and nearly 1,000 musical and theatrical events each year. Students can enjoy Big Ten sports events and participate in an outstanding recreational sports program. The IUPUI campus is located in the downtown area of Indianapolis with access to all the amenities of a major urban city.
The School	SLIS has long been considered one of the top programs of its kind in the nation. The School has the expertise and resources to ensure a first-rate education and solid career preparation. The faculty members, among the most productive in the nation, have backgrounds which include information science, librarianship, law, psychology, political science, sociology, engineering, linguistics, and educational technology.
Applying	Admission depends on scholastic achievement, reference letters, and a professional goals statement. Applicants must hold a bachelor's (all majors are welcome) and an undergraduate minimum GPA of 3.0 on a 4.0 scale. Admission decisions are made as application files are completed.

Correspondence and Information	Director of Admissions
	School of Library and Information Science
	Indiana University Bloomington
	1320 East Tenth Street, LI 011
	Bloomington, Indiana 47405-3907
	Phone: 812-855-2018
	    888-335-SLIS (7547) (toll-free)
	Fax: 812-855-6166
	E-mail: slis@indiana.edu
	Web site: http://www.slis.indiana.edu
	    http://www.slis.iupui.edu

Indiana University Bloomington

THE FACULTY AND THEIR RESEARCH

Rachel Applegate, Assistant Professor; Ph.D., Wisconsin–Madison, 1995. Academic librarianship, evaluation of library resources and services, and literature of the humanities.

Mary Alice Ball, Assistant Professor, IUPUI; Ph.D., Arizona, 2000. Online information retrieval, library automation, digital libraries, and systems analysis.

Katy Börner, Associate Professor, IUB; Ph.D., Kaiserslautern (Germany), 1997. Information visualization, 3-D collaborative virtual environments, virtual reality interfaces, human-computer interaction, user modeling.

Daniel J. Callison, Professor, IUPUI; Director, School Media Education; and Executive Associate Dean, SLIS; Ed.D., Indiana, 1982. Information literacy and inquiry, collection development, management of school media programs.

Kenneth Crews, Professor, IUPUI and Associate Dean, Faculties for Copyright Management, IUPUI; Ph.D., UCLA, 1990; J.D., Washington University, 1980. Copyright and higher education, intellectual property, information access.

Blaise Cronin, Rudy Professor and Dean; Ph.D., 1983, D.S.Sc., 1998, Queen's (Belfast). Scholarly communication, social networks, evaluative bibliometrics, information marketing, strategic intelligence management, information warfare, education for information professionals.

Ronald E. Day, Associate Professor, IUB; Ph.D., SUNY at Binghamton, 1990. History, culture, and political economy of information, documentation, communication, knowledge, and digital media, particularly in the twentieth century and into the twenty-first century.

Noriko Hara, Assistant Professor, IUB; Ph.D., Indiana, 2000. Organizational learning, knowledge management, social and organizational informatics, ecological research methods, online learning.

Susan Herring, Professor, IUB; Ph.D., Berkeley, 1991. Discourse analysis, computer-mediated communication, gender and technology, functional grammar, historical linguistics.

Marilyn M. Irwin, Associate Professor, IUPUI; Ph.D., Indiana, 1991. The evolving role of the public library in the digital era, including information literacy, information services, the tensions of resource allocation, the library as a cultural and community center, and literature for children and youth as a reflection of social change.

Elin K. Jacob, Associate Professor, IUB; Ph.D., North Carolina at Chapel Hill, 1994. Categorization and the cognitive organization of information, theoretical approaches to representation and classification, development, and evaluation of indexing systems.

Lokman I. Meho, Assistant Professor, IUB; Ph.D., North Carolina at Chapel Hill, 2001. Bibliometrics, information retrieval and organization, information-seeking behavior, and scholarly communication.

Javed Mostafa, Victor H. Yngve Associate Professor, IUB; Ph.D., Texas at Austin, 1994. Intelligent interfaces for information retrieval and filtering, automated document representation techniques, knowledge discovery, user modeling, personalized delivery of information.

Thomas E. Nisonger, Associate Professor, IUB; Ph.D., Columbia, 1976. Collection management and evaluation, bibliometrics, serials.

John Paolillo, Associate Professor, IUB; Ph.D., Stanford, 1992. Sociolinguistics and language acquisition, computational linguistics, information retrieval, computer-mediated communication, statistical models and quantitative research methods, second language acquisition.

Jean L. Preer, Associate Professor, IUPUI; J.D., 1975, Ph.D., 1980, George Washington. Library history and management.

Alice R. Robbin, Associate Professor, IUB; Ph.D., Wisconsin–Madison, 1984. Information policy, resource management, and technology; social and organizational informatics, including communication and information behavior in complex organizations; qualitative and quantitative research methods.

Howard Rosenbaum, Associate Professor, IUB; Ph.D., Syracuse, 1996. Electronic commerce, computer-mediated communication, managers and information in organizations, information policy and electronic networking, the intersection of sociological and library and information science theories.

Katherine Schilling, Assistant Professor, IUPUI; Ed.D., Boston, 2002. Health and medical librarianship, reference sources and services, information user education, management of libraries and special information systems.

Pnina Shachaf, Assistant Professor, IUB; Ph.D., North Carolina at Chapel Hill, 2003. Library administration and cooperation, reference services, comparative librarianship, global virtual teams, distributed work, computer-mediated intercultural communication.

Debora Shaw, Professor, IUB and Associate Dean; Ph.D., Indiana, 1983. Information seeking and use, design and impact of electronic information sources.

Joyce Taylor, Senior Lecturer, (part-time) IUPUI; Ph.D., Indiana, 1993. History of black visual artists and library collections of these artists in academic, public, art school, and museum libraries.

Carol Tilley, Lecturer, IUPUI; M.L.S., Indiana, 1993. School library media services, social psychological aspects of reference services provision, e-mail based and other online reference services, education for library and information professionals, young adult literature, instruction for information literacy.

Kiduk Yang, Assistant Professor, IUB; Ph.D., North Carolina at Chapel Hill, 2002. Technology applications for information processing, management, and transfer; dynamic information retrieval; information discovery.

Emeritus Faculty
Marian L. Armstrong, Assistant Professor; A.M., Indiana, 1958.
Stephen P. Harter, Professor; Ph.D., Chicago, 1974.
David Kaser, Distinguished Professor; Ph.D., Michigan, 1956.
Verna Pungitore, Associate Professor; Ph.D., Pittsburgh, 1983.
Judith Serebnick, Associate Professor; Ph.D., Rutgers, 1978.
Herbert S. White, Distinguished Professor; M.S.L.S., Syracuse, 1950.

Senior Fellow
Charles H. Davis, Ph.D., Indiana, 1969.

Visiting Professors
Barbara Albee, Visiting Lecturer, IUPUI; M.L.S., Pittsburgh, 1994. Academic libraries, e-resources, collection development and serials.
Annette Lamb, Visiting Professor, IUPUI; Ph.D., Iowa State, 1987. Effective integration of technology into the classroom. Dr. Lamb hosts the Eduscapes.com Web site, which includes a wide range of award-winning free resources for educators.

Visiting Scholar
Elisabeth R. Davenport, Ph.D., Strathclyde (Glasgow), 1994.
Yvonne Rogers, Professor; Ph.D., Wales, 1988.

PRATT INSTITUTE

School of Information and Library Science

Programs of Study

Distinguished as the only ALA-accredited graduate school of information and library science based in Manhattan and the oldest library and information science (LIS) school in North America, Pratt's School of Information and Library Science (SILS) was established in 1890 and has been continuously accredited since 1923, when accreditation was first introduced to the field. Building upon Pratt's national reputation as a leading school in art and design, Pratt brings creativity and innovation to library science education to offer students exciting and cutting-edge programs and courses from archives and digital libraries, to special libraries and school library media. In addition to the 36-credit Master of Science in Library and Information Science (M.S.L.I.S.) degree, Pratt offers two dual-degree programs, one with Pratt's History of Art Department (M.S.L.I.S./M.S. in art history, 60 credits) and one with the Brooklyn Law School (M.S.L.I.S./J.D., 86 credits); a 12-credit Archives Certificate Program within the M.S.L.I.S.; and a 12-credit Museum Libraries Certificate.

The School of Information and Library Science prepares students for leadership positions in the information professions, including special opportunities in arts and humanities librarianship for students pursuing careers in academic and research libraries, art and museum libraries, and archives and special collections. The program combines a core curriculum (information professions, information services and sources, information technologies, and knowledge organization) with elective courses, such as advanced Web design, digital libraries, human information behavior, information architecture, information policy, and projects in digital archives. Some courses are taught on location in museums and libraries, such as the New York Public Library, the Watson Library, and the Metropolitan Museum of Art. Other courses are held on the Brooklyn Campus in the Pratt Library, and students in the library and media specialist (LMS) studies program take courses in the Art and Design Education Department. SILS maintains a dean's office in North Hall. Students carry out practicum internships at many of New York's leading cultural institutions. Students may choose from a number of program concentrations, depending on their interests and career goals, including business, cultural informatics, digital technology and knowledge organization, legal and health information, library media specialist studies, management and leadership, public urban libraries, and reference and information literacy.

The master's program may be completed in as little as two semesters and one summer and must be completed within four years of enrollment. Courses are offered in the evening, during the day, and on Saturday and Sunday to accommodate students who work.

Research Facilities

The program's teaching and research facilities occupy the entire sixth floor of a seven-story facility in its home at 144 West 14th Street, Manhattan, in a beautifully restored landmark building, designated the Pratt Manhattan Center (PMC). Here, students find faculty and staff offices, smart classrooms, large computer labs, an elegant conference room, and the student cyber place. The fifth-floor computer lab adds to SILS resources, and a separate scanning lab supports digital library projects. The fourth floor is home to the PMC library, containing extensive LIS collections of books, journals, and full-text online databases. Special SILS events and lectures are held in a 150-person lecture hall adjoining the second-floor gallery space. This rich complex of facilities, all with wireless access and convenient to students and faculty members, adds greatly to effective operations and enhances the learning environment.

Financial Aid

Financial aid is available through a variety of programs funded by institutions, New York State, and the federal government. These include the Federal Perkins Loan and the Federal Work-Study Program, the Tuition Assistance Program of New York State, and Pratt scholarships, loans, and student aid. Continuing students in all departments may apply for fellowships and assistantships on a competitive basis. Special alumni-sponsored fellowships are also available.

Cost of Study

In 2007–08, tuition is $850 per credit for the M.S.L.I.S. degree, and student fees are approximately $1105 per year. The cost of books and supplies varies widely among the different programs.

Living and Housing Costs

Housing is available for single students. The cost averages $10,722 per year. The Office of Residential Life maintains listings of off-campus housing to help students find suitable accommodations.

Student Group

Graduate students at Pratt are drawn from all parts of the United States (forty-seven states) and forty other countries. The SILS graduate program average age is 33, with most students working full-time while taking M.S.L.I.S. courses. The employment outlook for Pratt graduates is bright. At present, more than 95 percent of the graduates obtain positions in a broad range of work environments from academic libraries and museums, to special libraries, including those in the corporate, business, and medical fields. The growth potential of the job market is seemingly unlimited. Job opportunities have been increasing for graduates of the information and library science program.

Location

Pratt-SILS is headquartered in the heart of Manhattan. Here, most SILS courses are offered at times convenient to those students who wish to work and pursue their M.S.L.I.S. The main campus of Pratt Institute is located in the Clinton Hill section of Brooklyn. Some courses are offered there to support programs such as the joint degree with Brooklyn Law School and program courses in urban librarianship at Brooklyn Public Library. In Manhattan, courses are taught at Cornell Medical Center for health sciences specialization and the New York Public Library/Research Libraries for special collections. SILS students enjoy the advantages of New York's position as a world center for the information professions. Students also benefit from the wealth of professional experience and expertise that complement their formal study. A vast variety of cultural and recreational activities are available in the neighborhood, in Brooklyn, in the city, and in the region. Pratt has a parklike campus in a quiet neighborhood of Victorian buildings set in the midst of one of the most vibrant cities in the world.

The Institute

A private, nonsectarian institute of higher education, Pratt was founded in 1887 by industrialist and philanthropist Charles Pratt. Changing with the requirements of the professions for which it educates, Pratt today prepares a student body of approximately 4,700 undergraduate and graduate students for a wide range of careers in architecture and planning, design and fine arts, and information science.

Applying

Applications should be submitted by January 1 for anticipated entrance in the fall semester and by October 1 for anticipated entrance in the spring semester. Applications received after these deadlines are considered if there is available space. Information and application forms may be obtained from the Graduate Admissions Office or the Web site. Applications may also be submitted online at http://www.pratt.edu/admiss/apply.

Correspondence and Information

Graduate Admissions Office
DeKalb Hall, Lower Level
Pratt Institute
200 Willoughby Avenue
Brooklyn, New York 11205
Phone: 718-636-3514
 800-331-0834 (toll-free)
Fax: 718-399-4242
Web site: http://www.pratt.edu/admiss

School of Information and Library Science
Pratt Institute
144 West 14th Street, 6th Floor
New York, New York 10011
Phone: 212-647-7682
E-mail: infosils@pratt.edu
Web site: http://www.pratt.edu/sils

Pratt Institute

THE FACULTY AND THEIR RESEARCH

Tula Giannini, Associate Professor and Dean; M.L.S., Rutgers; Ph.D., Bryn Mawr.

Jane Bambrick, Visiting Assistant Professor; M.L.S., Rutgers. Reference/Online Searching, William Paterson University Library.

Glen Bencivengo, Associate Professor; M.L.S., J.D., Rutgers. Information professions, legal research and law literature, online databases: law.

John Berry III, Visiting Associate Professor; M.S.L.S., Simmons. Information professions, professional writing. Editor-in-Chief, *Library Journal.*

Rick Block, Visiting Associate Professor; M.A. (political science), M.A. (library science), Wisconsin–Madison. Knowledge organization, advanced cataloging and classification. Head, Original and Special Materials Cataloging, Columbia University Libraries.

Helen-Ann Brown, Visiting Assistant Professor; M.L.S., Maryland. Reference/Online Searching, Samuel J. Wood Library, Cornell University Medical Center.

Kay Ann Cassell, Visiting Instructor; M.L.S., Rutgers. Associate Director for Programs and Services, New York Public Library.

Linda Cooper, Associate Professor and Coordinator, Library Media Specialist; M.L.S., CUNY, Queens; Ph.D., Rutgers. Human information behavior, library media centers, student teaching.

Anthony M. Cucchiara, Visiting Assistant Professor; M.S. (library and information science), Pratt; M.B.A. (finance), LIU. Management of archives and social collections. Librarian, Special Collections.

Paula DeStefano, Visiting Assistant Professor; M.L.S., Columbia. Conservation and preservation. Barbara Goldsmith Curator for Preservation and Head, Preservation Department, Bobst Library, New York University.

Ernest DiMattia, Visiting Associate Professor; M.B.A., Connecticut; M.S.L.S., Simmons. Management of libraries and information centers, marketing libraries, organizational behavior. President, Ferguson Library, Stamford, Connecticut.

Susan S. DiMattia, Visiting Associate Professor; M.L.S., Simmons; M.B.A. (marketing), Connecticut. Information professions, special libraries. Business Information Consultant.

Deirdre Donahue, Visiting Assistant Professor; M.S.L.I.S., Pratt. Thesaurus design and construction. Librarian, International Center of Photography.

Erminio D'Onofrio, Visiting Assistant Professor; M.S. (library and information science), Pratt. Government information sources. Coordinator, Government Information and Patents, Science, Industry and Business Library, New York Public Library.

Richard Eiger, Visiting Professor; M.B.A. (marketing and economics), NYU. The book publishing business: history and development. Pratt Institute Trustee, former President of Macmillan Education Corp.

Donna Fleming, Visiting Assistant Professor; Postgraduate Diploma (library and information science), West Indies. Urban public library service. Regional Librarian, Brooklyn Public Library.

Bruce Ford, Visiting Assistant Professor; M.L.S., Rutgers. Knowledge organization. Assistant Director for Access Services, Newark Public Library.

Judy Freeman, Visiting Professor; M.L.S., Rutgers. Storytelling. Well-known consultant and writer on children's literature.

Sharareh S. Goldsmith, Visiting Assistant Professor; M.S. (library and information science) and Certificate of Advanced Study (library and information science), Pratt. Director, Corporate Records Management, KeySpan Energy.

Anne Kelly, Associate Professor; M.L.S., Columbia.

Alice Knapp, Visiting Assistant Professor; M.A. (history), M.L.S., SUNY at Albany. Collection development. Director of Public Services, the Ferguson Library, Stamford, Connecticut.

Ellen Loughran, Visiting Associate Professor; M.L.S., Pratt. Library services for children and young adults, materials for children, materials for young adults. Reference Librarian (Adjunct), Hunter College Libraries.

David Marcinkowski, Visiting Assistant Professor; M.A. (media studies and philosophy), New School. Web design. Associate Director, Academic Computing Services, Pratt Manhattan Center.

Michael Miller, Visiting Assistant Professor; M.L.S., Rutgers; M.S. (educational technology), Lehigh. Digital libraries. Coordinator of Access Services, Rosenthal Library, Queens College.

John Parsons, Visiting Assistant Professor; M.S. (library and information science), Pratt. Projects in digital archives. Technical Project Manager, Digital Library Program, New York Public Library; Technical Project Manager, The African-American Migration Experience.

Marilyn Pettit, Visiting Associate Professor; Ph.D. (history), NYU. Management of archives and special collections. Vice-President of Collections, Brooklyn Historical Society.

AnnaMaria Poma-Swank, Visiting Associate Professor; M.L.S., Kent State; D.Lett., Florence (Italy). Cataloging, advanced cataloging, Summer Program in Florence. Librarian, Italian Academy, Columbia University.

Debbie Rabina, Assistant Professor; M.L.S., Hebrew (Jerusalem); Ph.D., Rutgers. Information services and sources, information policy.

Lee Robinson, Visiting Associate Professor; M.S. (library service), Columbia; M.A. (art history), CUNY, Hunter. Art collections. Supervising Librarian, Art and Architecture Department, Humanities and Social Sciences Library, New York Public Library.

Pamela Rollo, Visiting Professor; M.S. (library service), Columbia. Sources and services: business. Consultant; President-Elect, Special Libraries Association.

Charles P. Rubenstein, Professor and Academic Coordinator; M.S. (library and information science), Pratt; Ph.D., Polytechnic of New York.

Nasser Sharify, Visiting Professor; D.L.S., Columbia. Collection management.

Kenneth Soehner, Visiting Associate Professor; M.S. (library service), M.A. (art history), Columbia. Art librarianship. Arthur K. Watson Chief Librarian, Thomas J. Watson Library, Metropolitan Museum of Art.

David Walczyk, Assistant Professor; Ed.D., Columbia Teachers College. Information technologies, instructional technology, information architecture.

James Walther, Visiting Associate Professor; M.L.S., Wisconsin; Ph.D., George Washington. Management of libraries and information centers, communication skills for library managers.

Gary Wasdin, Visiting Associate Professor; M.S. (instructional technology), M.L.S., Southern Connecticut State. Advanced reference, library use instruction. Director, Fogelman Library, New School University.

Tony White, Visiting Assistant Professor; M.F.A., Art Institute of Chicago; M.L.S., Indiana. Art librarianship.

Kevin Winkler, Visiting Assistant Professor; M.A., CUNY, Hunter; M.L.S., Columbia. Performing arts librarianship.

SYRACUSE UNIVERSITY

School of Information Studies
Master of Science in Information Management
Master of Science in Library and Information Science
Master of Science in Telecommunications and Network Management

Programs of Study

The School of Information Studies, the Original School for the Information Age®, offers M.S. degree programs in three areas to prepare students for a growing number of dynamic careers that involve the management and use of information, twenty-first-century librarianship, computers and databases, networks, and telecommunications technologies. Students can earn any of these degrees through on-campus education or through distance learning formats, with some requiring brief residencies in Syracuse.

Ranked number one in the country by *U.S. News & World Report*, the M.S. in information management requires the completion of 42 credit hours. Each student completes courses in management approaches and strategies, user information needs, technological infrastructures, and electives. There is also an exit requirement. The program provides an integrated approach to the effective management and use of information and communication technologies within organizations. Prior work experience and a familiarity with computers are desirable but not required.

Accredited by the American Library Association (ALA), the M.S. in library and information science requires the completion of 36 credit hours. Students work with interdisciplinary faculty advisers to set up their programs of study, which may include course work in other academic areas. The program offers a concentration in school media and two certificates of advanced study in digital libraries and school media, both of which earned the School top positions in the 2006 *U.S. News & World Report* rankings.

The M.S. in telecommunications and network management requires the completion of 36 credit hours. It provides an integrated approach to the effective management, operation, and implementation of telecommunication systems, including voice and data networks, within organizations. Faculty members engage students in research and classroom lessons in a wide variety of areas, including data administration and information engineering, expert systems, group-based decision support systems, information policy, management information systems, online retrieval systems, project management, strategic planning, and telecommunications management.

All three degree programs focus on employing technology and digital tools to find, evaluate, organize, and use information for the betterment of people. Graduates of the programs work in a broad range of managerial and technical positions in business, government, education, health care, and other fields.

The School also offers a Ph.D. in information science and technology. In addition, the School offers certificates of advanced study in information security management, information systems and telecommunications management, digital libraries, and school media.

Research Facilities

Ranked as one of the most connected campuses by Princeton Review/forbes.com, Syracuse University offers wireless capabilities from most buildings and public spaces on campus and provides students with hundreds of computer workstations in public clusters. The School of Information Studies has moved most of its resources into its newly renovated building, which features the latest technologies and innovative teaching and meeting spaces to encourage collaborative and interactive learning. The School's seven research-and-development centers, which have achieved national and international distinction, allow students to apply classroom lessons to authentic problems—sometimes using technologies that have not yet made it to market.

The University's library system includes collections of 3.1 million volumes, 21,000 serials and periodicals, and 34,000 online and electronic resources, which can be accessed from academic and residence hall computer clusters. Among its special collections is the Belfer Audio Laboratory and Archive, which contains more than 300,000 historical sound recordings in all formats.

Financial Aid

Fellowships, scholarships, and assistantships are available to full-time students. The most prestigious and competitive are Syracuse University graduate fellowships, which include a scholarship and a stipend for the academic year. University scholarships provide 24 credit hours of tuition, and graduate assistantships provide tuition and a stipend for the academic year. The University also participates in the federal Scholarship for Service program, which awards full scholarships plus a stipend and paid internship opportunities to U.S. citizens who are interested in earning graduate degrees in fields related to information assurance and security. Syracuse also offers fellowships through the National Science Foundation's Alliance for Graduate Education in the Professoriate program and the Institute of Museum and Library Science's Future Professoriate for Librarianship Project. Tuition scholarships and other small scholarships are available to part-time students.

Loans are available through the University Financial Aid Office. For Federal Work-Study Program contracts, students work through the University Student Employment Office. Financial aid is awarded according to federal financial need guidelines.

Cost of Study

Tuition for 2006–07 was $940 per graduate credit hour. Fees were approximately $900 for one year of full-time study.

Living and Housing Costs

Academic-year living expenses are about $11,000 for single students. The University has residence hall rooms and on-campus apartments for single and married graduate students. Many also live off campus.

Student Group

Syracuse University has about 18,000 students, including about 6,000 graduate students. Approximately 550 graduate students are enrolled in the School of Information Studies. Thirty percent are international students, with the remainder coming from all parts of the United States. Students have diverse backgrounds, with undergraduate majors in the liberal arts, fine arts, business administration, computer science, and engineering. They participate in more than 300 student groups and extracurricular activities, including Women in Information Technology, Information Studies Graduate Organization, Black and Latino Information Studies Support, and chapters of national information and library associations.

Student Outcomes

Career opportunities for graduates of the programs are excellent. Approximately 95 percent of the information management graduates find lucrative professional positions within six months of graduation in a wide variety of organizations, with responsibilities ranging from information systems analysis and database design to software evaluation and systems management. Approximately 70 percent of the library and information science graduates work in library settings, while the remainder hold professional positions in corporations, museums, government agencies, and universities. Telecommunications and network management graduates find success in three main sectors of industry: information systems positions within organizations requiring data and voice network management; telecommunications organizations involved in voice, data, or video transmissions; and such communications businesses as phone companies and voice, data, and video system vendors.

Location

The Syracuse metropolitan area is home to more than a half million people and is the commercial, industrial, medical, and cultural center of central New York State. The 200-acre Main Campus is spacious and attractive, and new University facilities extend the campus into the heart of downtown Syracuse, which is only a 20-minute walk from the University. Winters are snowy and summers are pleasant. Lake Ontario, the Finger Lakes, and the Adirondack and Catskill Mountains are nearby. Boston, Toronto, New York, and Philadelphia are within a day's drive.

The School

The School of Information Studies is a leading center for innovative graduate programs in information fields. It stands out from other institutions that offer computer science, management, and related programs because it focuses on information users and understanding their information needs. The interdisciplinary faculty combines expertise in information science, telecommunications, public administration, business management and management information systems, linguistics, computer science, library science, and communications. The School also offers a unique undergraduate degree program in information management and technology.

Applying

Students are encouraged to apply for the fall semester. Students applying for a master's degree program must have a bachelor's degree from an accredited undergraduate institution and an academic record that is satisfactory for admission to the graduate school. They must also supply three letters of recommendation and an essay on their academic plans and professional goals. All applicants for the master's degree and Ph.D. programs are required to submit scores from the Graduate Record Examinations (GRE). Whenever possible, an interview is recommended. International students should plan to take the Test of English as a Foreign Language (TOEFL); a score of at least 580 on the paper-based test is expected. Students interested in University fellowships must apply by January 8. Other financial aid applicants must submit all materials by February 12.

Correspondence and Information

School of Information Studies
343 Hinds Hall
Syracuse University
Syracuse, New York 13244-4100
Phone: 315-443-2911
E-mail: ist@syr.edu
Web site: http://ist.syr.edu

Syracuse University

THE FACULTY AND THEIR RESEARCH

Marilyn Arnone, Research Associate Professor; Ph.D. (instructional design, development, and evaluation), Syracuse. Information literacy education, children's learning and curiosity in interactive multimedia environments.

Robert Benjamin, Professor; B.S. (economics), Pennsylvania (Wharton). Strategic applications of information technology, managing information technology–enabled change.

Scott Bernard, Assistant Professor; Ph.D. (public administration and policy), Virginia Tech. Enterprise architecture and capital planning, public- and private-sector chief information officers, federal policy on information technology.

Susan Bonzi, Associate Professor; Ph.D. (library and information science), Illinois. Image retrieval systems. Received the first Information Science Doctoral Dissertation Award from the American Society for Information Science (ASIS), 1982.

Derrick Cogburn, Assistant Professor; Ph.D. (political science), Howard. Global information and communication technology (ICT) policy, global governance, use of ICTs for socioeconomic development.

Kevin Crowston, Professor; Ph.D. (information technologies), MIT. Organizational implications of technology, coordination-intensive processes in human organizations.

Michael D'Eredita, Assistant Professor; Ph.D. (experimental/cognitive psychology), Syracuse. Organizational behavior, knowledge management, group and team dynamics.

Anne Diekema, Assistant Research Professor; Ph.D. (information transfer), Syracuse. Classification, cross-language information retrieval, digital libraries, natural-language processing, question answering, metadata.

David Dischiave, Senior Instructor; M.S. (computer information technology), Regis. Systems analysis and design, database management and design, project management, computer hardware and operating system architecture.

Susan Dischiave, Senior Instructor; M.B.A. (business administration), Le Moyne. Systems analysis and design, database management and design, project management, secure enterprises.

Paul Gandel, Professor and Chief Information Officer; Ph.D. (information studies), Syracuse. Software engineering, information networks, cooperative computing environments, knowledge management.

Jon Gant, Assistant Professor; Ph.D. (information technology and organizations), Carnegie Mellon. E-government, IT and service management, social network analysis.

Martha A. Garcia-Murillo, Associate Professor; Ph.D. (international political economy and telecommunications), USC. Electronic commerce, business policy and strategy, international management, technology and innovation management.

William Gibbons, Senior Instructor; M.S. (industrial administration), Union (New York). Collaboration in the online learning environment, wireless network security.

Robert Heckman, Associate Professor; Ph.D. (information systems), Pittsburgh. Vendor-provided information systems, user satisfaction, end-user computing.

Michelle Lynn Kaarst-Brown, Associate Professor; Ph.D. (organizational theory and management information systems), York. Strategic alignment of information technology with business strategy, Internet-based business.

Bruce Kingma, Professor and Associate Dean; Ph.D. (economics), Rochester. Economics of digital libraries, library and nonprofit management.

Barbara Kwasnik, Professor; Ph.D. (library and information studies), Rutgers. Classification research, knowledge representation and organization, research methods.

R. David Lankes, Associate Professor; Ph.D. (information transfer), Syracuse. Building and managing Internet services, designing multimedia with the Internet.

Kenneth Lavender, Assistant Professor; Ph.D. (English), California, Santa Barbara. Digital reference, rare books, archives, preservation.

Elizabeth Liddy, Professor; Ph.D. (information transfer), Syracuse. Indexing, data mining, natural-language processing, information retrieval.

Ian MacInnes, Associate Professor; Ph.D. (political economy and public policy), USC. Electronic commerce, information technology and globalization, public policy, standardization and network economics.

Thomas H. Martin, Associate Professor; Ph.D. (communications), Stanford. Information policy, system design, human interaction with computers, human information processing, organizational communication, the foundations of information science.

Nancy McCracken, Research Professor; Ph.D. (computer and information science), Syracuse. Natural-language processing, question answering, knowledge representation.

Lee McKnight, Associate Professor; Ph.D. (political science, communication, and international relations), MIT. Wireless grids, nomadicity, Internet economics and policy, national and international technology policy.

David Molta, Assistant Dean, Technology Integration; M.P.A., North Texas. Computer and operating systems, high-speed networks, client/server computing.

Milton L. Mueller, Professor; Ph.D. (telecommunication), Pennsylvania. Telecommunication policy and deregulation, universal service.

Scott Nicholson, Assistant Professor; Ph.D. (information studies), North Texas. Internet resources and information services.

Michael Nilan, Associate Professor; Ph.D. (communication research), Washington (Seattle). Employing user behaviors for the design of collaborative work environments in a global electronic network environment, user-based system design.

Megan Oakleaf, Assistant Professor; Ph.D. (information and library science), North Carolina at Chapel Hill. Evolution and assessment of information services; theories, methods, and assessment of user education; information literacy frameworks and instruction; information services in academic libraries.

Carsten Osterlund, Assistant Professor; Ph.D. (organization studies and behavioral policy science), MIT. Distributed work, organizational learning and knowledge.

Joon Park, Assistant Professor; Ph.D. (information technology and information security), George Mason. Information and systems security; security policies, models, mechanisms, evaluation, survivability, and applications.

Jian Qin, Associate Professor; Ph.D. (library and information science), Illinois at Urbana-Champaign. Web-based information architecture, bibliographic databases, communication in science and bibliometrics.

Jeffrey Rubin, Senior Instructor; M.S. (telecommunications and network management), Syracuse. Managing Web sites, designing Internet services, information networking.

Joanne Silverstein, Director of Research and Development; Ph.D. (information transfer), Syracuse. Ontology, metadata, digital reference, human intermediation.

Ruth V. Small, Professor; Ph.D. (instructional design, development, and evaluation), Syracuse. Motivational aspects of information literacy, design and use of information and information technologies in education.

Jeffrey Stanton, Associate Professor; Ph.D. (information studies), Connecticut. Organizational psychology and data collection.

Zixiang (Alex) Tan, Associate Professor; Ph.D. (telecommunications management and policy), Rutgers. Telecommunications policy and regulations, economic and social impacts of new technology, standardization policy, telecommunications in Asia.

Murali Venkatesh, Associate Professor; Ph.D. (management), Indiana. Group-based decision support systems, human-computer interaction, telecommunications.

Gisela von Dran, Assistant Professor; Ph.D. (public administration), Arizona State. Management of information-based organizations, information interfaces, Web design.

Raymond F. von Dran, Professor and Dean; Ph.D. (library and information science), Wisconsin. Leadership and change in the management of communication and information technology; competencies, curriculum, and organization structures in information education; modes of delivery in information education.

Alex Wilkinson, Professor of Practice; Ph.D. (psychology), Michigan. Human-computer interaction, systems engineering, integration testing, network operations, product management.

Ping Zhang, Associate Professor; Ph.D. (information systems), Texas at Austin. Computer technology, information visualization for decision making, human-computer interaction.

UNIVERSITY OF ILLINOIS AT URBANA–CHAMPAIGN

Graduate School of Library and Information Science

Programs of Study

The University of Illinois at Urbana-Champaign Graduate School of Library and Information Science (GSLIS) is recognized as a premier institution. It is frequently ranked among the top three LIS schools in the country. For more than 100 years, GSLIS has prepared students for careers as leaders in information professions and research and has helped establish and develop the methods used in the field of library and information science today. Graduates are adept at using the latest technology and methods for reference, research, information organization, and other professional tasks. The field is necessarily interdisciplinary, and the School recruits faculty members with strong theoretical and methodological foundations who understand libraries and the broader context of information systems and services. Students work with professors on projects that range from community use of information systems to the impact of story on children's development to the design and evaluation of information retrieval systems.

Students may pursue M.S. and Ph.D. degrees and a Certificate of Advanced Study (CAS); a CAS concentration in digital libraries launched in 2004. There is also a K–12 Library Information Specialist Certification Program. Many master's students and recent graduates cite the opportunity to design their own programs of study as a major advantage at Illinois; examples of specializations include history, economics, and policy; information organization; information systems; management; social informatics; user services; and youth services.

A master's degree candidate with a full-time load can complete the 40-hour program in two semesters and one summer, although many students choose to continue in the program for an additional semester or two. Students have flexible scheduling options for M.S. degree and CAS course work; students may pursue their degrees either full-time or part-time and can take courses on campus, through the LEEP online education option, or a combination of both. The LEEP online education option brings students to campus only for brief periods of study; remaining course work is completed remotely, using varied formats that include Internet-based courses with real-time audio and visuals. A few site-based courses in Chicago, offered as part of the Community Informatics Corps, are also available.

Research Facilities

Research is supported by several School resources: the Library Research Center, which conducts research on all types of libraries and information centers; the Information Science Research Laboratory, which supports research into and about design, impacts, analysis, and evaluation of information technologies; the Center for Children's Books, home of a 16,000-book examination collection; the Publications Office, publisher of *Library Trends* and *The Bulletin of the Center for Children's Books;* and the Community Informatics Initiative, a major component of which is Prairienet, the East-Central Illinois community information network. Illinois has the third-largest academic research library in the U.S., which includes a separate Library and Information Science Library. The University hosts the National Center for Supercomputing Applications. These resources provide research opportunities as well as student employment.

Financial Aid

Generous financial assistance is available in the form of fellowships, graduate assistantships, and student loans. All fellowships and assistantships include both a stipend and a tuition and service fee waiver of at least the base in-state rate. Graduate assistantships are the primary source of financial aid and are awarded by the School, the University Library, and a variety of other campus units. Approximately 70 percent of all GSLIS on-campus students received support in 2005–06.

Cost of Study

In 2006–07, the tuition per semester for full-time, on-campus students is $4432 for Illinois residents and $9630 for nonresidents. Additional fees (including University and general services, health insurance, health service, and transportation) total $1772. Complete information about tuition and fee assessments, exemptions, and refunds is available by contacting the Office of Admissions and Records, 901 West Illinois Street, Urbana, Illinois 61801; telephone: 217-333-0302; Web site: http://www.oar.uiuc.edu/.

Living and Housing Costs

On-campus housing for graduate students is available through the University; costs range from $4311 to $5298 for single-occupancy rooms for the academic year; double-occupancy rooms and meal contracts are also available. Most students live in off-campus locations, including private apartments and University-operated family housing.

Student Group

Total enrollment in degree programs in fall 2006 is 377 (95 men, 282 women), of whom 252 are from the state of Illinois, 125 are from out-of-state, including 31 from outside the U.S. There are several active student organizations that sponsor social and educational events throughout the year, including such job search assistance workshops as resume preparation, interviewing, and salary negotiation.

Student Outcomes

Recent master's graduates have accepted posts in all types of libraries and in a variety of other organizations, including consulting firms, library vendors, and technology companies. Employers include Yale University Library; the Chicago Public Library; Microsoft; Amazon.com; Google; Abbott Laboratories; National Library of Medicine; North Carolina State University Libraries; NASA; Coca-Cola; the Memphis-Shelby County (Tennessee) Public Library; the Ohio Legislative Services Commission; the Illinois Supreme Court Library; Illinois State Library; and the Library of Congress. Almost all Ph.D. graduates assume academic faculty, research, and administrative positions. Illinois has an active placement office that maintains an online list of positions and helps students and alumni locate position listings.

Location

Urbana-Champaign has a population of about 100,000 and is situated about 140 miles south of Chicago, 120 miles west of Indianapolis, and 170 miles northeast of St. Louis.

The University and The School

The University was founded in 1867. With 40,670 students, of whom 10,217 are graduate students, it is consistently ranked as one of the top universities in the country. The Graduate School of Library and Information Science, founded in 1893 at the Armour Institute in Chicago, maintains a reputation of excellence and quality. In 1993 and 1996, library educators ranked Illinois first overall in providing the highest quality education for librarianship at both the master's level (accredited by the American Library Association) and the doctoral level; and faculty members who contribute most significantly to the advancement of the profession through research, publication, and leadership among schools of library and information science. In 1999 and 2006, *U.S. News & World Report* ranked Illinois as the top library science school in the country.

Applying

Applicants for graduate programs must hold a bachelor's degree, have a minimum grade point average of 3.0 (on a 4.0 scale) for the last two years of undergraduate work, and submit an essay, a personal statement, a resume, official transcripts from all schools attended, and three letters of recommendation. The GRE General Test is required of applicants with a GPA below 3.0. Prospective doctoral students must also complete an interview with the School's Doctoral Studies Committee after the initial application has been received and reviewed. Applicants for the Certificate of Advanced Study program must hold a master's degree in library and information science; have a minimum grade point average of 3.0 (on a 4.0 scale) in the library and information science course work, plus a minimum grade point average of 3.0 (on a 4.0 scale) in the last two years of undergraduate course work, submit three letters of recommendation, and one essay. Most on-campus students begin study in the fall. Occasionally students can begin in spring or summer semesters; LEEP M.S. degree students must begin study in the summer semester.

Correspondence and Information

Dr. John M. Unsworth, Dean
Graduate School of Library and Information Science
University of Illinois at Urbana-Champaign
501 East Daniel Street
Champaign, Illinois 61820-6211
Phone: 217-333-7197 (Admissions)
      800-982-0914 (toll-free)
Fax: 217-244-3302
E-mail: lis-apply@uiuc.edu
Web site: http://www.lis.uiuc.edu

University of Illinois at Urbana–Champaign

THE FACULTY AND THEIR RESEARCH

Ann P. Bishop, Associate Professor; Ph.D., Syracuse. Use and impact of computer-based information systems, social equity in access to information, human-centered approaches to designing and evaluating information systems.

Bertram (Chip) Bruce, Professor; Ph.D., Texas at Austin. Building environments to support inquiry-based learning, studying collaboration in knowledge making, analyzing new literacy practices.

Susan Davis, Professor; Ph.D., Pennsylvania. Politics of contemporary public and commercial space, nature and its relation to mass commercial culture, history and memory on the landscape, the contemporary history of tourism, southern California and San Diego history and culture.

J. Stephen Downie, Associate Professor; Ph.D., Western Ontario. Design and evaluation of IR systems, including multimedia music information retrieval; the political economy of internetworked communication systems; database design; Web-based technologies.

Fernando Elichirigoity, Assistant Professor; Ph.D., Illinois. Globalization and information infrastructures, industrial classification and transnational spaces of production and consumption, knowledge management and new forms of corporate structures, the use of the Web for personal investing and business information, Spanish-language Internet portals and the virtual construction of Latin America, history of coordination and collaborative technologies, selection and exhibition of foreign language materials in public libraries.

Leigh S. Estabrook, Professor; Ph.D., Boston University. Municipal official and librarian assessments of the public library in the political process, the way in which small businesses use information to solve problems, marketing information services.

Les Gasser, Associate Professor; Ph.D., California, Irvine. Coordination of information, coordination theory/tools, multiagent systems, manufacturing research, intensive industry liaison, R&D project management.

Caroline Haythornthwaite, Associate Professor; Ph.D., Toronto. Organizations and information technology, adoption and diffusion of innovations, computer-mediated communication supporting informal information exchange, organization theory, social network analysis.

Elizabeth (Betsy) G. Hearne, Professor; Ph.D., Chicago. Literary and artistic analysis of children's books, elements of folklore and mythology that survive in children's literature, publishing history of juvenile literature in the nineteenth and twentieth centuries, cultural and social trends reflected in children's books, developmental role of literature and storytelling from birth to adolescence, impact of story on children's psychological adjustment and reading motivation.

P. Bryan Heidorn, Associate Professor; Ph.D., Pittsburgh. Image database design; shape and spatial semantics; natural language processing, particularly as related to images; bioinformatics.

Christine A. Jenkins, Associate Professor; Ph.D., Wisconsin–Madison. History of youth services librarianship as women's history, censorship and intellectual freedom issues, representations of minority-status groups in children's and young adult literature, reading engagement, reader-response research and the reader-text interaction.

Lori Kendall, Associate Professor; Ph.D., California, Davis. Online community and identity, the social aspects of computing, gender and technology.

Kathryn A. La Barre, Assistant Professor; Ph.D., Indiana. Information organization and access systems and structures; historical and theoretical foundations of the field of library and information science, especially as relating to information organization and access and information architecture; cognitive processing of information; category and concept formation.

Jerome McDonough, Assistant Professor; Ph.D., Berkeley. Digital libraries, digital preservation, metadata design, human-computer interaction and user interface design, sociotechnical and participatory design approaches to information systems development.

Kate McDowell, Assistant Professor; Ph.D., Illinois. Library services for youth, literature for children and young adults, history of gender in children's librarianship, gender in children's literature, technology in youth services librarianship, distance education pedagogy.

Carole L. Palmer, Associate Professor; Ph.D., Illinois. Information use in the research process, development of cross-disciplinary information services, boundary-crossing practices of interdisciplinary researchers, scholarly and professional communication, synthesis of research results and integration of knowledge, social and cultural contexts of information in research organization, problem-centered information tools.

W. Boyd Rayward, Professor; Ph.D., Chicago. Historical studies related to the evolution of aspects of information infrastructure, especially libraries and museums; utopian schemes for managing knowledge; the emergence of information science; systems for the international organization and dissemination of information; museum informatics.

Allen Renear, Associate Professor; Ph.D., Brown. How digital documents function as knowledge representation systems: developing models of how documents organize and structure knowledge and then exploring how these models can improve document-intensive applications, such as digital libraries, scientific collaboration systems, publishing systems, educational technology, and humanities textbases.

Dan Schiller, Professor; Ph.D., Pennsylvania. Telecommunications history, role of cultural production in the socioeconomic development of the market system.

Linda C. Smith, Professor and Associate Dean; Ph.D., Syracuse. Information system design, education for library and information science, impact of new technologies on reference and information services.

Michael Twidale, Associate Professor; Ph.D., Lancaster (England). Computer-supported cooperative working and learning, collaborative technologies in digital libraries and museums, user interface design and evaluation, user error analysis, visualization of information and algorithms, the development of interfaces to support the articulation of plans, goals, and beliefs.

John M. Unsworth, Professor and Dean; Ph.D., Virginia. Humanities computing, digital libraries, electronic publishing.

Terry L. Weech, Associate Professor; Ph.D., Illinois. Collection management, evaluation of library services, library education, library cooperation and networking.

Emeritus Faculty

Pauline Atherton Cochrane, Professor Emerita; M.A., Rosary College.
Charles H. Davis, Professor Emeritus; Ph.D., Indiana.
James L. Divilbiss, Associate Professor Emeritus; Ph.D., Illinois.
Herbert Goldhor, Professor Emeritus; Ph.D., Chicago.
Kathryn Luther Henderson, Professor Emerita; M.S., Illinois.
William T. Henderson, Associate Professor Emeritus, M.S., Chicago
Donald W. Krummel, Professor Emeritus; Ph.D., Michigan.
F. W. Lancaster, Professor Emeritus; Fellow, Library Association of Great Britain.
Selma K. Richardson, Professor Emerita; Ph.D., Michigan.
Tim L. Wentling, Professor Emeritus; Ph.D., Illinois.
Martha E. Williams, Research Professor Emerita; M.A., Loyola Chicago.

UNIVERSITY OF MARYLAND, COLLEGE PARK

College of Information Studies

Programs of Study

The academic programs available within the College of Information Studies connect students with career opportunities in the region, the nation, and the world. Degrees include the Master of Information Management (M.I.M.), the Master of Library Science (M.L.S.), the dual Master of Library Science and Master of Arts in history, and Doctor of Philosophy (Ph.D.) in information studies.

The Master of Information Management program is an innovative program that addresses the growing need of organizations for skilled information professionals who can strategically manage information and technology. Every cutting-edge organization needs people with the skills the M.I.M. degree offers. The program meets the need for information professionals who understand the issues of information management, business management, computer science, and information systems. The M.I.M. program fills an empty space among those disciplines. It is in that space where the M.I.M. program excels at teaching future information professionals to understand and mange issues related to users of information, organization, content, technology, and the global environment. Those five points differentiate the M.I.M. degree from others. The program uses a cross-disciplinary approach that combines cutting-edge theory and problem-based learning. The program requires successful completion of 36 credit hours, including the team experience and independent case work.

The courses are integrated into four main blocks: core courses, specialized courses, applied courses, and elective courses. The M.I.M. program offers an Individual Program Plan and two concentrations: the Strategic Management of Information concentration and the Socio-Tech Information Systems concentration.

The Master of Library Science (M.L.S.) program focuses on areas central to research and practice in information science. The M.L.S. program and the dual-degree program with history are accredited by the American Library Association. The M.L.S. degree requires successful completion of 36 hours of course work (a thesis option is available). The dual-degree program requires 54 hours of course work to earn both the M.L.S. and the M.A.

Students may choose to specialize in one of two areas: Archives, Records, and Information Management or School Library Media. Students may also choose from two concentrations: e-Government concentration or Lifelong Access concentration.

The interdisciplinary doctoral program prepares students for careers in teaching, research, system design and development, and administration. Students are introduced to a breadth of research and scholarship in information studies through doctoral seminars. Students also complete course work in research methods and design and specialized areas. Admission to the program is limited so that each student may receive the mentoring that a theory-based program requires.

Research Facilities

Information Studies uses McKeldin as its primary library, but students have access to other libraries in the University of Maryland System, including specialized branches, such as art and computer science. Microcomputer facilities are maintained by Information Studies and by the University of Maryland. All students have access to campus mainframe computer resources, such as e-mail and library catalogs, and to the resources available on the Internet.

Information Studies students enrich their programs through use of other resources close at hand. The University is home to Archives II, an expansion facility of the National Archives. Three national libraries (Library of Congress, National Agricultural Library, and National Library of Medicine) and hundreds of special libraries extend study opportunities for Information Studies students.

Financial Aid

Opportunities include fellowships, assistantships, and scholarships. Awards range from stipends of approximately $12,500 and tuition remission for nine months to one-time awards of $1000. Financial assistance is rarely available to international students. Many employment opportunities in libraries on campus and in the Washington, D.C.–Baltimore area, such as the National Agricultural Library and National Archives, are available.

Cost of Study

In 2005–06, graduate tuition for the academic year (fall and spring semesters) was $393 per credit for Maryland residents and $820 for nonresidents. Mandatory fees for each semester were $279.50 for students taking 1 to 8 credit hours and $458.50 for students taking 9 or more credit hours. The University of Maryland reserves the right to make changes in tuition, fees, and other charges at any time such changes are deemed necessary by the University and the University System of Maryland Board of Regents.

Living and Housing Costs

On-campus living costs for the nine-month 2005–06 academic year were about $5000 for housing with telephone (traditional housing) and approximately $3500 for dining (Department of Resident Life, 301-314-2100). Off-campus living in group rentals cost approximately $550 for rent and utilities and $260 for food per month. The Off-Campus Housing Program maintains a housing location office (301-314-3645).

Student Group

Enrollment in the program was 463 students in fall 2006; 74 percent of the students were women; 62 percent were part-time; 69 percent were from Maryland, the District of Columbia, and Virginia; 57 percent were between the ages of 25 and 39; and 7 percent were international. The Student Services Office and active student chapters of professional organizations (ASIST, SLA, SAA) provide social and educational programs. Graduates find professional positions in academic, special, public, and government libraries and in nontraditional settings as information specialists.

Location

College Park is located in the center of the Washington, D.C.–Baltimore metropolitan area, a cosmopolitan center of cultural and intellectual activity and political power. Information Studies students have opportunities for experience with agencies such as NASA, the Smithsonian Institution, the National Archives and Maryland State Archives, the Library of Congress, the National Library of Medicine, and the National Agricultural Library. The Maryland countryside offers settings for a variety of leisure activities, from the mountains in the west to the Atlantic beaches on the Eastern Shore.

The University and The College

The College Park campus is the flagship campus of the University of Maryland System, with more than 9,000 graduate students. The University is committed to fostering academic excellence through diversity in its faculty, staff, and students. The College has been a leader in preparing information professionals since its inception in 1965. Today, Information Studies is forging new connections with other academic disciplines to facilitate the exploration of vital questions about information policy and services in the twenty-first century. Students interested in joining faculty members and other students in this challenge are invited to seek further information.

Applying

Applicants to the master's programs are evaluated on these criteria: a baccalaureate degree from a regionally accredited college or university with at least a 3.0 GPA on a 4.0 scale on all academic work attempted, strength of three recommendations, strength of the applicant's essay, and scores on the General Test of the Graduate Record Examinations. All applicants are encouraged to submit scores on the General Test. However, applicants with an undergraduate GPA of 3.25 or above, and applicants with an undergraduate GPA of 3.0 or above who have earned other graduate degrees are not required to submit GRE scores. All applicants who do not fall in one of these categories must submit GRE scores.

All international applicants are required to submit GRE scores. Applicants who took the GRE prior to October 2002 must obtain a combined score of at least 1000 in any two of the sections of the General Test (verbal, quantitative, and analytical). Applicants who took the GRE after September 2002 must obtain a score of at least 1000 in the verbal and quantitative sections combined and at least a 4.5 on the analytical writing section. GRE scores must be no more than five years old at the time of application.

Applicants to the doctoral program are evaluated on the basis on their scholarly potential and the appropriateness of their intellectual interests to the Information Studies research environment. Applicants must have earned a baccalaureate degree from a regionally accredited college or university with at least a 3.0 GPA on a 4.0 scale on all academic work attempted for consideration. All applicants are required to submit scores on the General Test of the Graduate Record Examinations, an essay describing their research interests, and three letters of recommendation. An interview may be required.

Application deadlines vary by program and semester. Students should visit the Information Studies Web site for specific program deadlines.

Correspondence and Information

Student Services Office
College of Information Studies
Room 4110 Hornbake South Wing
University of Maryland, College Park
College Park, Maryland 20742-4345

Phone: 301-405-2038
TTD: 301-405-4345
E-mail: lbscgrad@deans.umd.edu
Web site: http://www.informationstudies.umd.edu

University of Maryland, College Park

THE FACULTY AND THEIR RESEARCH

Bruce I. Ambacher, Visiting Professor; Ph.D., Temple. Archives administration, electronic records, digital preservation, national and international digital standards.

Diane L. Barlow, Associate Dean and Lecturer; Ph.D., Maryland. Communication and information transfer.

Susan E. Davis, Assistant Professor; Ph.D., Wisconsin. Archives.

Vedat G. Diker, Assistant Professor; Ph.D., SUNY at Albany. Modeling and simulation of socioeconomic systems, social and human impacts of information and communication technologies.

Allison Druin, Associate Professor; Ph.D., New Mexico. Children's information access and use, digital libraries for children, user interface design, children's storytelling processes and tools.

Kenneth Fleischmann, Assistant Professor; Ph.D., Rensselaer. Human-computer interaction, social informatics, information ethics, computational models and digital libraries.

Trudi B. Hahn, Professor of the Practice; Ph.D., Drexel. Research methods, information environments.

Paul T. Jaeger, Assistant Professor and Director, CIPEG; Ph.D., J.D., Florida State. Information law and policy, information access, e-Government, accessibility and information needs of persons with disabilities, social theory and information, diversity and LIS education, evaluation of networked information services and resources.

Judith L. Klavens, Research Professor; Ph.D., London. Linguistics.

Jimmy Lin, Assistant Professor; Ph.D., MIT. Computational linguistics, information retrieval, question answering, search interfaces, theoretical linguistics.

Charles B. Lowry, Professor and Dean of Libraries; Ph.D., Florida. Information technology, management, academic libraries.

M. Delia Neuman, Associate Professor; Ph.D., Ohio State. Computer-based education, instructional systems design, special education, qualitative research, writing and editing.

Douglas W. Oard, Associate Professor; Ph.D., Maryland. Information technology, computer applications, text filtering, information retrieval.

Jennifer J. Preece, Dean; Ph.D., Open University. Computer-mediated communication, human-computer interaction, management of online communities of practice, health, education, and knowledge

Yan Qu, Assistant Professor; Ph.D., Michigan. Information seeking and organization, sensemaking and learning, information system design, human-computer interaction.

Dagobert Soergel, Professor; D.Phil., Freiburg (Germany). Information storage and retrieval, development of indexing languages, computer applications.

Claude E. Walston, Professor; Ph.D., Ohio State. Computer applications, systems analysis, software management.

Ping Wang, Assistant Professor; Ph.D., UCLA. Management of information technology innovations in organizations, technology entrepreneurship, institutional analysis of technological and organizational change.

Ann Weeks, Professor of the Practice; Ph.D., Pittsburgh. School library media, digital libraries.

Bo Xie, Assistant Professor; Ph.D. Rensselaer. Older adults' learning and use of computers and the Internet, computer literacy, lifelong learning, civic engagement, volunteering, social relationships, social support, online communities, health and well-being.

Emeritus Faculty

Frank G. Burke, Professor Emeritus; Ph.D., Chicago. Archives, records management, manuscript and collection administration, archival automation, documentary editing.

Jerry S. Kidd, Professor Emeritus; Ph.D., Northwestern. Systems analysis, research methods, science communication including popularization, user needs.

James W. Liesener, Professor Emeritus; Ph.D., Michigan. School library media services, young adult services, management.

Anne S. MacLeod, Professor Emerita; Ph.D., Maryland. Children's literature in its historical context.

Ann E. Prentice, Professor Emerita; D.L.S., Columbia. Management of information environments, governance, planning, financial administration, political considerations, community analysis, research methodology, education for the information professions, outcome assessment.

Paul Wasserman, Professor Emeritus; Ph.D., Michigan. Administration, bibliography, publishing, comparative librarianship.

Marilyn Domas White, Professor Emerita; Ph.D., Illinois. Information access, information seeking behavior, questioning behavior, search strategy, user-centered design of retrieval systems, scholarly communication, computer-mediated communication.

Adjunct Faculty

Jason R. Baron, J.D., Boston. Archives.

Lewis Bellardo, Ph.D., Kentucky. Archives.

Diane L. Boehr, M.L.S., Maryland. advanced cataloging.

Allen Brewer, Ph.D., Maryland. Information science.

Lauren Brown, M.L.S., Berkeley. Archives.

Anne S. Caputo, M.A.L.S., San Jose State. Electronic reference services and sources.

Susan R. Clabaugh, M.S., Oklahoma. Instructional materials design, computer science.

Keith Cogdill, Ph.D., North Carolina. Outreach librarianship.

Thomas J. Connors, Adjunct Professor, M.I.A.I., Brown. Archives.

Lisa Covi, Ph.D., California, Irvine. Users and use context.

Walter Cybulski, M.L.S., SUNY at Albany. Preservation.

Bruce W. Dearstyne, Ph.D., Syracuse. Archives, records management.

Aimee Felker, M.A., Boston. Federal records.

John Fleckner, M.A., Wisconsin. Archives.

Geraldine Foudy, M.S.L.I.S., Long Island. Government and politics, public policy, law librarianship.

Maralita Freeny, M.L.S., Catholic University. Children's materials, children's services in public libraries.

Marjorie B. Geldon, M.S., Maryland. School library media.

Robert S. Gresehover, M.L.S., Maryland. Information services

Ronald Grim, Ph.D., Maryland. Map librarianship.

Stephen Hannestad, M.I.M., Maryland. Director of Research, Center for Information Policy.

Carla Hayden, Ph.D., Chicago. Library administration, public library.

Ellen Jay, Adjunct Professor, Ph.D., Kent State. Consultant.

Neal K. Kaske, Ph.D., Oklahoma. Networks, effectiveness of information services.

Deborah Klein, M.L.S., Maryland. Consultant.

William Kules, M.S., Maryland. Consultant.

Michael J. Kurtz, Ph.D., Georgetown. Archives, records management.

Eric Lindquist, Ph.D., Harvard. Humanities reference.

Johnnie Love, M.L.S., Denver. Coordinator.

Michael L. Miller, Ph.D., Ohio State. Archives, electronic records.

Deborah Ozga, M.L.S., Maryland. Information access.

Sabrina I. Pacifici, M.S.L.I.S., Catholic. Founder, solo editor, publisher, and Web manager of LLRX.com.

Thomas C. Phelps, M.L.S., Oregon. Library administration.

Marietta A. Plank, A.M.L.S., Michigan. McKeldin Library.

Mary Ramos, M.L.S., Maryland. Faculty Research Assistant.

Vera T. Rhoads, M.S., Syracuse. Senior manager, intranet, Fannie Mae.

Nancy K. Roderer, M.L.S., Maryland. Director, Welch Medical Library.

Marianne Ryan, Ph.D., Iowa. Government documents and maps.

Maria Salvadore, Adjunct Professor, M.L.S., Maryland. Consultant.

Susan Schreibman, Ph.D., University College (Dublin). Assistant Dean and Head of Digital Collections and Research.

Anne L. Sheldon, M.L.S., Maryland. Storytelling, children's literature.

Wendy Simmons, Ph.D., Maryland. Foreign service library specialist, U.S. Department of State.

Simmona Simmons-Hodo, M.L.S., Maryland. Field study.

Lee Strickland, J.D., Florida. Information policy, legal issues.

Kanti Srikantaiah, Ph.D., Southern California. Knowledge management.

Joan Stahl, M.A., Maryland. Branch manager, Art and Architecture Libraries.

Deborah Taylor, M.L.S., Maryland. Coordinator, School and Student Services.

J. Maurice Travillian, Adjunct Professor, M.A.L.S., Vanderbilt. Consultant.

William G. Wilson, A.M.L.S., Michigan. Reference, public library, academic library.

Arthuree Wright, Ph.D., Maryland. Reference.

UNIVERSITY OF MICHIGAN

School of Information

SCHOOL OF INFORMATION
UNIVERSITY OF MICHIGAN

Programs of Study

The University of Michigan (U-M) School of Information (SI) is a graduate-level teaching and research environment connecting people, information, and technology in more valuable ways. Students from all academic backgrounds are encouraged to challenge the status quo of the information professions and meet the needs of today's employers.

The School of Information offers a 48-credit-hour Master of Science in Information (M.S.I.). Students may elect to take the M.S.I. with one or more of the following specializations: archives and records management, community informatics, human-computer interaction (HCI), incentive-centered design, information analysis and retrieval, information policy, library and information services, preservation of information, and social computing. Students may also elect to self-tailor the M.S.I. to meet their individual career goals. A full-time student can complete the M.S.I. in four semesters. All master's students take three core curriculum foundations courses and must demonstrate competency in research methods and management. Students choose advanced courses related to their specialization(s), electives, and cognates that are available elsewhere at the University of Michigan. Each specialization has its own additional requirements. Students also participate in a Practical Engagement Program that provides invaluable experience in applying knowledge before graduation.

The School's innovative doctoral program prepares students for a research career in this growing field. Researchers investigate the role of information technology in a variety of human activities. Projects include work on collaboratories, community systems, cultural preservation, electronic archives, digital libraries, global teams, information economics, and visualization.

Upon graduation, alumni become Webmasters, chief information officers, information economists, information architects, librarians, digital preservationists, entrepreneurs, consultants, software engineers, records managers, usability specialists, and more.

Research Facilities

The University of Michigan provides access to technologically advanced, thriving research and computing environments. School of Information students have access to a robust networking environment, including computers, telecommunications, and video; to the Duderstadt Center, a 24-hour facility that houses multidisciplinary projects that explore uses of leading-edge information technology; and to libraries that contain more than 7 million volumes and 70,000 serial titles, accessible through online catalogs and digital libraries. The School of Information maintains an advanced computing infrastructure with equipment, software, and services related to media integration (digitization, multimedia authoring, and video editing) and advanced graphics work. The School's Digital Information Access and Dissemination classroom/laboratory provides a general computing and teaching facility with both PC and Macintosh workstations.

Financial Aid

The School of Information offers a limited number of merit-based full- and partial-tuition scholarships to incoming students. The U-M also offers several competitive scholarship and grant opportunities for all students. Numerous opportunities for on-campus and off-campus employment exist.

Cost of Study

In 2007–08, tuition per semester (four months) for a full-time Michigan resident School of Information student is $7779 ($15,734 for a full-time nonresident).

Living and Housing Costs

Off-campus living costs for a single student may average $1300 per month. The U-M also offers several on-campus housing options for both single and married students. The University Housing Office can assist students in locating both on- and off-campus housing.

Student Group

The approximately 300 students in the master's program represent more than seventy different undergraduate majors. The current class of admitted master's students had an average undergraduate GPA of 3.5 and an average GRE combined score of 1250 on the quantitative and verbal sections. Approximately 56 percent of the students are women. About 15 percent attend the program on a part-time basis.

Student Outcomes

Upon graduation, approximately 95 percent of graduates accept professional employment within three to six months. Graduates find challenging work throughout the world in libraries (the M.S.I. program is ALA accredited), corporations, consulting firms, Internet commerce companies, K–12 schools, nonprofit agencies, colleges, universities, and government agencies. Recent graduates are employed as project managers, librarians, usability engineers, digital curators, online community managers, IT consultants, information architects, electronic records archivists, information economists, and more.

Location

Ann Arbor is approximately 40 miles west of Detroit, with easy access to airports, railroads, and all major east-west and north-south highways. The city of approximately 114,000 residents is convenient to major automotive manufacturers, research firms, banking centers, and Internet ventures. Ann Arbor is a cultural center showcasing musical concerts, theatrical performances, film series, and much more.

The University and The School

The University of Michigan is known internationally for its fine higher education and its base of nearly 400,000 living alumni. The U-M is committed to diversity among students, faculty members, and staff members. Approximately 34,000 students attend the Ann Arbor campus, of whom 13,000 are graduate students. Independent rankings place U-M schools and colleges at the top among their peers. The School of Information consistently ranks among the top-rated master's programs in the information fields.

Applying

Applicants for the master's degree program must hold a bachelor's degree and must submit the General Test scores from the GRE, taken within the past five years. The School prefers an overall undergraduate grade point average of at least 3.0 on a 4.0 scale. Three letters of recommendation, an essay, and a resume must be submitted. Deadlines for regular admission with financial assistance are February 1 for fall term or October 1 for winter term. Deadlines for regular admission without financial assistance are May 1 for fall term or November 1 for winter term (October 1 for winter-term international applicants).

It is recommended, but not required, that applicants for the doctoral program hold a master's degree (ideally in an information-related field relevant to the student's proposed area of research). Students without a master's degree may need to adjust their required course work. Other Ph.D. program requirements include a superior academic record, scores from the GRE taken within the past five years, and TOEFL or IELTS scores from within the past three years (international applicants only).

Correspondence and Information

School of Information
304 West Hall
University of Michigan
1085 South University Avenue
Ann Arbor, Michigan 48109-1107

Phone: 734-763-2285
Fax: 734-615-3587
E-mail: si.admissions@umich.edu
Web site: http://si.umich.edu

University of Michigan

THE FACULTY AND THEIR RESEARCH

Steven P. Abney, Associate Professor; Ph.D., MIT. Computational linguistics, learning, syntax.

Mark S. Ackerman, Associate Professor; Ph.D., MIT. Computer-supported cooperative work, sociology of information, organizational memory, multimedia information systems.

Lada A. Adamic, Assistant Professor; Ph.D., Stanford. Information dynamics in networks, navigating social networks.

Charles Antonelli, Assistant Research Scientist; Ph.D., Michigan. Distributed file systems, operating systems, network security.

Daniel E. Atkins, Professor (on leave); Director, Office of Cyberinfrastructure, NSF; Ph.D., Illinois at Urbana-Champaign. Advanced information and collaborative systems and services, digital library architecture, community technology.

Francis X. Blouin, Professor and Director of the Bentley Historical Library; Ph.D., Minnesota. Archival administration, international archival affairs.

Yan Chen, Associate Professor; Ph.D., Caltech. Experimental economics, mechanism design, theory of committees and voting.

Gavin Clarkson, Assistant Professor; J.D., D.B.A., Harvard. Intellectual property management and tribal economic development, including tribal access to capital markets and the determinants of success for tribal entrepreneurship.

Michael D. Cohen, Professor; Ph.D., California, Irvine. Organizational decision making, processes of learning and adaptation within organizations, organizational effects of information technology, complex systems.

Paul Conway, Associate Professor; Ph.D., Michigan. Challenges of representing and interpreting visual and textual resources in digital form, extracting knowledge from large-scale image databases, modeling incentive systems for digital preservation.

Paul N. Courant, Professor; Ph.D., Princeton. Economics of universities, economics of libraries and archives, IT-driven changes in the system of scholarly communication.

Edmund Durfee, Professor; Ph.D., Massachusetts Amherst. Distributed artificial intelligence, planning, cooperative robotics, real-time problem solving.

Joan C. Durrance, Professor; Ph.D., Michigan. Public libraries, community information systems and services, information behavior, community roles of public libraries, professional practice and the reference interview.

Paul N. Edwards, Associate Professor; Ph.D., California, Santa Cruz. History, culture, and politics of computers; networks; artificial intelligence; global environmental change; computer models of climate and other Earth systems.

Ixchel M. Faniel, Assistant Professor; Ph.D., USC. Knowledge sharing and reuse across organizational boundaries, creativity and innovation, socially shared and distributed cognition environments, knowledge-intensive organizations.

J. Bruce Fields, Assistant Research Scientist; Ph.D., Michigan. Networking, cryptography.

Thomas Finholt, Research Professor and Associate Dean for Research and Innovation; Ph.D., Carnegie Mellon. Impact of collaboratories, impact of computer communication technology on information processing in organizations.

Barry Fishman, Associate Professor; Ph.D., Northwestern. Teacher learning, learning technologies, human-computer interaction, learner-centered design, school reform, leadership.

C. Olivia Frost, Professor; Ph.D., Chicago. Intellectual access to information, information searching behavior in a networked environment, organization and retrieval of networked and digital information.

Robert L. Frost, Associate Professor; Ph.D., Wisconsin–Madison. Industrial rationalization, domestic consumerism, industrial informatics, gender and IT, digital divide, history of IT.

George Furnas, Professor and Associate Dean for Academic Strategy; Ph.D., Stanford. Information access and visualization, multivariate statistics, statistical semantics, filtering, multitrees, space-scale diagrams.

Joseph Hardin, Clinical Assistant Professor; B.A., Illinois at Urbana-Champaign. Online collaboration and learning environments, Semantic Web.

Margaret Hedstrom, Associate Professor; Ph.D., Wisconsin–Madison. Management and preservation of electronic records, digital preservation strategies, impact of electronic communications on organizational memory and documentation, remote access to archival materials, cultural preservation and outreach in developing countries.

Maurita P. Holland, Associate Professor and Assistant to the Dean for Academic and Strategic Initiatives; A.M.L.S., Michigan. Special libraries and information centers, knowledge management, distance-independent learning, technology-assisted community networks and programs.

Peter Honeyman, Research Professor; Ph.D., Princeton. Middleware for file systems, security, and mobile computing.

Steven J. Jackson, Assistant Professor; Ph.D., California, San Diego. Information and communication policy; IT and democratic governance; simulation, expertise, and public policy; sociohistorical studies of information infrastructure.

John L. King, Professor and Vice Provost for Academic Information, U-M; Ph.D., California, Irvine. Design and development of sociotechnical information infrastructures in complex organizational settings, technical and institutional coevolution of standards and technical infrastructure in telephony, technical and institutional foundations of global electronic commerce.

Jessica D. Litman, Professor; J.D., Columbia. Digital copyright, cyberspace law, trademark, intellectual property law.

Jeffrey K. MacKie-Mason, Professor; Ph.D., MIT. Economics of information technology and content, telecommunications, industrial organization, public finance, finance.

Karen M. Markey, Professor; Ph.D., Syracuse. Subject searching in online catalogs, subject access to visual resources collections, subject authority control, enhancing bibliographic databases using a library classification.

Shawn P. McKee, Assistant Research Scientist; Ph.D., Michigan. Collaborative tools, grids, and networks.

Michael J. McQuaid, Assistant Professor; Ph.D., Arizona. Systems analysis, information management, visualization tools, information navigation.

Barbara Mirel, Visiting Associate Professor; D.A., Michigan. Interactive design, usability, user-interface design.

Mark Newman, Assistant Professor; Ph.D., Berkeley. End-user programming; design, prototyping, and evaluation of interactive systems.

Gary M. Olson, Professor; Ph.D., Stanford. Human-computer interaction, applied cognitive science, computer-supported cooperative work, design and evaluation of collaboratories.

Judy S. Olson, Professor and Associate Dean for Academic Affairs; Ph.D., Michigan. Human-computer interaction, design and evaluation of software for human problem solving in business, computer-supported cooperative work.

Martha E. Pollack, Professor and Dean; Ph.D., Pennsylvania. Using information and computing to improve quality of life, developing applied technologies for people with cognitive impairment.

Dragomir Radev, Associate Professor; Ph.D., Columbia. Natural-language processing, digital libraries, computational linguistics, information retrieval, artificial intelligence.

Paul Resnick, Professor; Ph.D., MIT. Reputation systems, sociotechnical capital.

Soo Young Rieh, Assistant Professor; Ph.D., Rutgers. Web search behavior, information quality and cognitive authority, human-computer interaction in information systems, evaluation of interactive information retrieval systems, role of intermediaries in digital library environments.

Victor Rosenberg, Associate Professor; Ph.D., Chicago. Information retrieval, information policy, technology in the humanities, software development, entrepreneurship.

Rahul Sami, Assistant Professor; Ph.D., Yale. Incentives in computation, algorithmic mechanism design, distributed mechanisms, incentives in Internet protocols and applications, information markets.

Elliot Soloway, Professor; Ph.D., Massachusetts Amherst. Use of technology in education, developing software that takes into consideration the unique needs of learners.

Stephanie Teasley, Research Associate Professor; Ph.D., Pittsburgh. Social and cognitive processes in collaboration, user needs.

Douglas E. Van Houweling, Professor (on leave); President and CEO, Internet2; Ph.D., Indiana. Information systems planning and management, strategic planning, simulation models of political and public policy processes, economic models of politics, technology assessment.

David A. Wallace, Lecturer; Ph.D., Pittsburgh. Computerization of government records, strategies for preserving electronic records of collaborative processes, U.S. government information secrecy and classification/declassification policies.

Terry Weymouth, Associate Research Scientist; Ph.D., Massachusetts Amherst. Development of collaboration technology for the support of medical diagnosis, technology development, large-scale collaboration test beds for remote distributed science.

Elizabeth Yakel, Associate Professor; Ph.D., Michigan. Recordkeeping practices, representation and categorization of archival records, access to archival information on the World Wide Web, use and user needs.

Kai Zheng, Assistant Professor; Ph.D., Carnegie Mellon. Health informatics, information systems in health care.

Part-Time and Adjunct Faculty

Nancy Bartlett, Adjunct Lecturer; M.A., Michigan.
Gail Beaver, Adjunct Lecturer; A.M.L.S., Michigan.
Jack Bernard, Adjunct Lecturer; J.D., Michigan.
Mark Burde, Adjunct Lecturer; Ph.D., Washington (St. Louis).
Clare Canham-Eaton, Adjunct Lecturer; A.M.L.S., Michigan.
Bonnie A. Dede, Adjunct Lecturer; A.M.L.S., Michigan.
Paul A. Green, Adjunct Associate Professor; Ph.D., Michigan.
Andreas Hug, Adjunct Lecturer; M.Des., IIT.
Brian Kahin, Adjunct Professor and Research Investigator; J.D., Harvard.
Marilyn Kiefer, Adjunct Lecturer; A.M.L.S., Michigan.
Daniel Klyn, Adjunct Lecturer; M.L.I.S., Wayne State.
Hans Masing, Adjunct Lecturer; M.S.I., Michigan.
S. Alan McCord, Adjunct Lecturer; Ph.D., Wayne State.
Catherine Morse, Adjunct Lecturer; M.L.I.S., Dominican.
Peter Morville, Adjunct Lecturer; M.I.L.S., Michigan.
Darlene Nichols, Adjunct Lecturer; A.M.L.S., Michigan.
Thomas E. Powers, Adjunct Professor; A.M.L.S., Michigan.
Virginia Rezmierski, Adjunct Associate Professor; Ph.D., Michigan.
Colleen Seifert, Adjunct Professor; Ph.D., Yale.
Margaret T. Taylor, Adjunct Lecturer; Ph.D., Michigan.
Marshall Van Alstyne, Adjunct Assistant Professor; Ph.D., MIT.
Shannon Zachary, Adjunct Lecturer; M.I.L.S., Michigan.

ACADEMIC AND PROFESSIONAL PROGRAMS IN THE MEDICAL PROFESSIONS AND SCIENCES

Section 34
Acupuncture and Oriental Medicine

This section contains a directory of institutions offering graduate work in acupuncture and oriental medicine, followed by in-depth entries submitted by institutions that chose to prepare detailed program descriptions. Additional information about programs listed in the directory but not augmented by an in-depth entry may be obtained by writing directly to the dean of a graduate school or chair of a department at the address given in the directory.

CONTENTS

Acupuncture and Oriental Medicine

Academy of Chinese Culture and Health Sciences, Program in Traditional Chinese Medicine, Oakland, CA 94612. Offers MS. *Accreditation:* ACAOM. Part-time and evening/weekend programs available. *Degree requirements:* For master's, thesis, comprehensive exam. *Entrance requirements:* Additional exam requirements/recommendations for international students: Required—TOEFL (minimum score 500 paper-based; 173 computer-based). *Faculty research:* Herbs, acupuncture.

Academy of Oriental Medicine at Austin, Program in Acupuncture and Oriental Medicine, Austin, TX 78757. Offers MAOM. *Accreditation:* ACAOM. *Entrance requirements:* For master's, minimum GPA of 2.5.

Acupuncture & Integrative Medicine College, Berkeley, Program in Oriental Medicine, Berkeley, CA 94704. Offers MS. *Accreditation:* ACAOM. Part-time programs available. *Faculty:* 1 full-time (0 women), 20 part-time/adjunct (10 women). *Students:* 90 full-time (74 women), 32 part-time (26 women); includes 36 minority (8 African Americans, 17 Asian Americans or Pacific Islanders, 11 Hispanic Americans). Average age 41. 36 applicants, 86% accepted, 26 enrolled. *Degree requirements:* For master's, comprehensive exam. *Entrance requirements:* For master's, interview, minimum GPA of 2.5, 60 semester units of course work at the baccalaureate level. Additional exam requirements/recommendations for international students: Required—TOEFL (minimum score 500 paper-based; 173 computer-based). *Application deadline:* For fall admission, 8/1 priority date for domestic students; for winter admission, 12/1 priority date for domestic students; for spring admission, 3/1 priority date for domestic students. Applications are processed on a rolling basis. Application fee: $100 ($200 for international students). *Expenses:* Tuition: Full-time $13,500; part-time $224 per term. *Financial support:* In 2006–07, 98 students received support. Application deadline: 7/31; *Faculty research:* Stimulus therapy, oxygen hemoglobin, acupuncture needling, classical Chinese medicine. *Unit head:* Skye Sturgeon, President, 510-666-8248 Ext. 132, Fax: 510-666-0111, E-mail: ssturgeon@aimc.edu. *Application contact:* Nellie E. Wilson, Admissions and Programs Director, 510-666-8248 Ext. 106, Fax: 510-666-0111, E-mail: nwilson@aimc.edu.

Acupuncture and Massage College, Program in Oriental Medicine, Miami, FL 33176. Offers MOM. *Accreditation:* ACAOM.

American College of Acupuncture and Oriental Medicine, Graduate Studies, Houston, TX 77063. Offers MAOM. *Accreditation:* ACAOM. Part-time programs available. *Entrance requirements:* For master's, 60 undergraduate credit hours. Additional exam requirements/recommendations for international students: Required—TOEFL.

American College of Traditional Chinese Medicine, Graduate Program, San Francisco, CA 94107. Offers acupuncture and Oriental medicine (DAOM); shiatsu massage (Certificate); traditional Chinese medicine (MSTCM); tui na massage (Certificate). *Accreditation:* ACAOM. Part-time programs available. *Faculty:* 36 full-time (17 women), 27 part-time/adjunct (17 women). *Students:* 176 full-time (131 women), 96 part-time (70 women); includes 99 minority (6 African Americans, 77 Asian Americans or Pacific Islanders, 16 Hispanic Americans), 9 international. Average age 33. 62 applicants, 82% accepted, 35 enrolled. In 2006, 90 master's awarded. *Median time to degree:* Of those who began their doctoral program in fall 1998, 0% received their degree in 8 years or less. *Degree requirements:* For master's, one foreign language, comprehensive exam, registration. *Entrance requirements:* For master's, 90 semester or 135 quarter units from an accredited institution, minimum GPA of 3.0, interview, starting the application process 3—6 months prior to start date is recommended. Additional exam requirements/recommendations for international students: Required—TOEFL (minimum score 550 paper-based; 213 computer-based). *Application deadline:* For fall admission, 9/1 for domestic and international students; for winter admission, 12/1 for domestic and international students; for spring admission, 3/1 for domestic and international students. Applications are processed on a rolling basis. Application fee: $100 ($150 for international students). *Expenses:* Tuition: Part-time $185 per credit. *Financial support:* In 2006–07, 190 students received support, including 14 teaching assistantships (averaging $3,200 per year); career-related internships or fieldwork, Federal Work-Study, institutionally sponsored loans, and scholarships/grants also available. Support available to part-time students. Financial award application deadline: 3/2; financial award applicants required to submit FAFSA. *Faculty research:* Herbs, acupuncture, qi gong/tai chi. Total annual research expenditures: $114,000. *Unit head:* Lixin Huang, President, 415-282-7600 Ext. 12, Fax: 415-282-0856, E-mail: lixinhuang@actcm.edu. *Application contact:* Matt Munday, Admissions Officer, 415-282-7600 Ext. 14, Fax: 415-282-0856, E-mail: admissions@actcm.edu.

Atlantic Institute of Oriental Medicine, Graduate Program, Fort Lauderdale, FL 33301. Offers MS. *Accreditation:* ACAOM. Evening/weekend programs available. *Faculty:* 7 full-time (2 women), 14 part-time/adjunct (2 women). *Students:* 94 full-time (69 women); includes 33 minority (3 African Americans, 18 Asian Americans or Pacific Islanders, 12 Hispanic Americans), 3 international. 62 applicants, 52% accepted, 32 enrolled. In 2006, 28 degrees awarded. *Entrance requirements:* Additional exam requirements/recommendations for international students: Required—TOEFL (minimum score 500 paper-based). *Application deadline:* For fall admission, 7/1 for domestic students, 5/1 for international students; for spring admission, 11/30 for domestic students, 2/28 for international students. Applications are processed on a rolling basis. Application fee: $20 ($100 for international students). *Expenses:* Tuition: Full-time $12,000. Required fees: $1,200. *Unit head:* Dr. Johanna C. Yen, President, 954-763-9840 Ext. 202, Fax: 954-763-9844, E-mail: president@atom.edu. *Application contact:* Milafros Ferreira, Registrar, 954-763-9840 Ext. 207, Fax: 954-763-9844, E-mail: registrar@atom.edu.

Bastyr University, Graduate and Professional Programs, School of Acupuncture and Oriental Medicine, Kenmore, WA 98028-4966. Offers acupuncture (MS); acupuncture and Oriental medicine (MS, DAOM); Chinese herbal medicine (Certificate). *Accreditation:* ACAOM. *Students:* 94 full-time (63 women), 33 part time (25 women); includes 20 minority (2 American Indian/Alaska Native, 14 Asian Americans or Pacific Islanders, 4 Hispanic Americans), 13 international. Average age 36. 75 applicants, 73% accepted, 32 enrolled. In 2006, 41 master's, 5 doctorates, 3 other advanced degrees awarded. *Entrance requirements:* For master's, BS or BA with course work in biology, chemistry, college algebra and psychology; for doctorate, MS in acupuncture or certificate and 10 years clinical experience. Additional exam requirements/recommendations for international students: Required—TOEFL (minimum score 550 paper-based; 213 computer-based). *Application deadline:* For fall admission, 3/15 priority date for domestic and international students. Applications are processed on a rolling basis. Application fee: $75. *Expenses:* Tuition: Full-time $18,845; part-time $325 per credit hour. Required fees: $1,365. Tuition and fees vary according to course load and degree level. *Financial support:* Career-related internships or fieldwork, Federal Work-Study, and scholarships/grants available. Support available to part-time students. Financial award application deadline: 4/15; financial award applicants required to submit FAFSA. *Unit head:* Terry Courtney, Chair, 425-823-1300, Fax: 425-823-6222. *Application contact:* Admissions Office, 425-602-3330, Fax: 425-602-3090, E-mail: admiss@bastyr.edu.

See Close-Up on page 2149.

Colorado School of Traditional Chinese Medicine, Graduate Programs, Denver, CO 80206-2127. Offers traditional Chinese medicine (MS). *Accreditation:* ACAOM. Part-time and evening/weekend programs available. *Faculty:* 36 part-time/adjunct (11 women). *Students:* 80 full-time (56 women), 36 part-time (29 women); includes 20 minority (1 African American, 9 Asian Americans or Pacific Islanders, 10 Hispanic Americans), 4 international. 28 applicants, 100% accepted. In 2006, 22 degrees awarded. *Entrance requirements:* For master's, 60 semester credits from an accredited college. Additional exam requirements/recommendations for international students: Required—TOEFL (minimum score 500 paper-based; 173 computer-based; 61 iBT). *Application deadline:* Applications are processed on a rolling basis. Application fee: $50 ($100 for international students). *Expenses:* Tuition: Full-time $13,275. Required fees: $495. Tuition and fees vary according to course load. *Financial support:* In 2006–07, 86 students received support. Applicants required to submit FAFSA. *Unit head:* Vladimir Dibrigida, Administrative Director, 303-996-6663, Fax: 303-388-8165, E-mail: director@cstcm.edu. *Application contact:* Kari L. Abarca, Registrar, 303-329-6355 Ext. 12, Fax: 303-388-8165, E-mail: registrar@cstcm.edu.

Dongguk Royal University, Program in Oriental Medicine, Los Angeles, CA 90020. Offers MS. *Accreditation:* ACAOM. Part-time and evening/weekend programs available.

East West College of Natural Medicine, Graduate Programs, Sarasota, FL 34234. Offers MSOM. *Accreditation:* ACAOM.

Emperor's College of Traditional Oriental Medicine, Graduate Programs, Santa Monica, CA 90403. Offers MTOM, DAOM. *Accreditation:* ACAOM. Part-time and evening/weekend programs available. *Entrance requirements:* For master's, minimum 2 years of undergraduate course work, interview; for doctorate, CA acupuncture licensure. *Faculty research:* Menopause, dysmenorrhea.

Five Branches Institute: College of Traditional Chinese Medicine, Program in Traditional Chinese Medicine, Santa Cruz, CA 95062. Offers MTCM. *Accreditation:* ACAOM. *Degree requirements:* For master's, comprehensive exam. *Entrance requirements:* For master's, 6 units in anatomy and physiology, 9 units in basic sciences, minimum GPA of 2.5. Electronic applications accepted.

Florida College of Integrative Medicine, Graduate Program, Orlando, FL 32809. Offers MSOM. *Accreditation:* ACAOM. Evening/weekend programs available. *Faculty:* 3 full-time (2 women), 7 part-time/adjunct (4 women). *Students:* 110 full-time (80 women); includes 29 minority (3 African Americans, 16 Asian Americans or Pacific Islanders, 10 Hispanic Americans), 3 international. Average age 32. 35 applicants, 77% accepted. In 2006, 16 degrees awarded. *Entrance requirements:* For master's, minimum 60 semester hours of undergraduate course-work. *Application deadline:* For fall admission, 6/15 priority date for domestic students; for spring admission, 12/15 priority date for domestic students. Applications are processed on a rolling basis. Application fee: $50. Electronic applications accepted. *Expenses:* Tuition: Full-time $11,500. Required fees: $500. *Financial support:* Application deadline: 6/15; *Unit head:* Dr. Lin Chai, Academic Dean, 407-888-8689, Fax: 407-888-8211, E-mail: lchai@fcim.edu. *Application contact:* Jon Diament, Admissions Officer, 407-888-8689 Ext. 15, Fax: 407-888-8211, E-mail: jdiament@fcim.edu.

Institute of Clinical Acupuncture and Oriental Medicine, Program in Oriental Medicine, Honolulu, HI 96813. Offers MSOM. *Accreditation:* ACAOM.

Midwest College of Oriental Medicine, Graduate Programs, Racine, WI 53403-9747. Offers acupuncture (Certificate); oriental medicine (MSOM). *Accreditation:* ACAOM. Part-time and evening/weekend programs available. *Degree requirements:* For master's and Certificate, thesis, comprehensive exam. *Entrance requirements:* For master's and Certificate, 60 semester credit hours from accredited school, 2 letters of recommendation, interview. Additional exam requirements/recommendations for international students: Required—TOEFL. *Faculty research:* Pharmacology.

Midwest College of Oriental Medicine, Graduate Programs-Chicago, Chicago, IL 60613. Offers acupuncture (Certificate); oriental medicine (MSOM). Part-time and evening/weekend programs available. *Degree requirements:* For master's and Certificate, thesis, comprehensive exam. *Entrance requirements:* For master's and Certificate, 60 semester credit hours from accredited school, 2 letters of recommendation, interview. Additional exam requirements/recommendations for international students: Required—TOEFL.

National College of Natural Medicine, Program in Classical Chinese Medicine, Portland, OR 97201. Offers MSOM. *Accreditation:* ACAOM. *Faculty:* 10 full-time (4 women), 21 part-time/adjunct (7 women). *Students:* 116 full-time (84 women), 2 part-time (both women); includes 14 minority (1 African American, 8 Asian Americans or Pacific Islanders, 5 Hispanic Americans). Average age 29. 61 applicants, 89% accepted, 35 enrolled. In 2006, 33 master's awarded. *Median time to degree:* Of those who began their doctoral program in fall 1998, 99% received their degree in 8 years or less. *Degree requirements:* For master's, thesis. *Entrance requirements:* Additional exam requirements/recommendations for international students: Required—TOEFL (minimum score 550 paper-based; 213 computer-based). *Application deadline:* For fall admission, 11/1 priority date for domestic and international students; for winter admission, 2/1 priority date for domestic and international students. Applications are processed on a rolling basis. Application fee: $75. *Expenses: Contact institution. Financial support:* In 2006–07, 77 students received support. Federal Work-Study and scholarships/grants available. Financial award application deadline: 4/30; financial award applicants required to submit FAFSA. *Faculty research:* Cases on herbs and acupuncture for asthma, diabetes, depression associated with menopause, Qi Gong to maintain weight loss. *Unit head:* Dr. Laurie Regan, Dean, 503-552-1775, Fax: 503-499-0027, E-mail: admissions@ncnm.edu. *Application contact:* Kendra Lapp, Admissions Coordinator, 503-552-1660, Fax: 503-499-0027, E-mail: admissions@ncnm.edu.

National University of Health Sciences, College of Professional Studies, Lombard, IL 60148-4583. Offers acupuncture (MSAC); chiropractic medicine (DC); naturopathic medicine (ND); Oriental medicine (MSOM). *Accreditation:* CCE. *Faculty:* 49 full-time (10 women), 40 part-time/adjunct (15 women). *Students:* 394 full-time (186 women); includes 80 minority (19 African Americans, 47 Asian Americans or Pacific Islanders, 14 Hispanic Americans), 12 international. Average age 27. In 2006, 86 DCs, 2 master's awarded. *Degree requirements:* For first-professional, internship, community service. *Entrance requirements:* Bachelor's degree with strong background in sciences. Additional exam requirements/recommendations for international students: Required—TOEFL (minimum score 500 paper-based; 172 computer-based). *Application deadline:* For fall admission, 8/22 for domestic and international students; for winter admission, 11/22 for domestic and international students; for spring admission, 4/18 for domestic and international students. Applications are processed on a rolling basis. Application fee: $55. Electronic applications accepted. *Expenses:* Tuition: Full-time $16,187. Full-time tuition and fees vary according to course load. *Financial support:* Fellowships, research assistantships, teaching assistantships, Federal Work-Study, scholarships/grants, and tuition waivers (partial) available. Support available to part-time students. Financial award applicants required to submit FAFSA. *Faculty research:* Chiropractic procedures, spinal stenosis, evidence-based practices, secondary effects of manual procedures, autonomic effects of manual procedures. Total annual research expenditures: $502,000. *Unit head:* Dr. James F. Winterstein, President, 630-889-6604, Fax: 630-889-6600, E-mail: jwinterstein@nuhs.edu. *Application contact:* Victoria Sweeney, Director of Admissions, 800-826-6285 Ext. 6572, Fax: 630-889-6554, E-mail: v.sweeney@nuhs.edu.

See Close-Up on page 2161.

New England School of Acupuncture, Program in Acupuncture and Oriental Medicine, Watertown, MA 02472. Offers acupuncture (M Ac); acupuncture and Oriental medicine (MAOM). *Accreditation:* ACAOM (one or more programs are accredited). Part-time programs available. *Degree requirements:* For master's, comprehensive exam. *Entrance requirements:* For master's, previous course work in anatomy, biology, physiology, and psychology. Additional exam requirements/recommendations for international students: Required—TOEFL (minimum score 550 paper-based; 213 computer-based). *Faculty research:* Acupuncture and women's health, acupuncture and stroke rehabilitation, tai chi and cardiovascular health, tai chi and balance, cancer.

See Close-Up on page 2151.

New York Chiropractic College, Program in Acupuncture and Oriental Medicine, Seneca Falls, NY 13148-0800. Offers acupuncture (MS); acupuncture and Oriental medicine (MS). *Faculty:* 9 full-time (6 women), 6 part-time/adjunct (3 women). *Students:* 59 full-time (47 women), 39 part-time (19 women); includes 10 minority (2 American Indian/Alaska Native, 7 Asian Americans or Pacific Islanders, 1 Hispanic American), 2 international. Average age 34. 39 applicants, 90% accepted, 30 enrolled. In 2006, 28 master's awarded. *Degree requirements:* For master's, clinical internship. *Entrance requirements:* For master's, 9 hours of course work in bioscience, minimum GPA of 2.5. Additional exam requirements/recommendations for international students: Recommended—TOEFL (minimum score 550 paper-based; 213 computer-based). *Application deadline:* Applications are processed on a rolling basis. Application fee: $60. Electronic applications accepted. *Expenses:* Tuition: Full-time $14,960. Required fees: $680. *Financial support:* In 2006–07, 88 students received support, including 1 fellowship with tuition reimbursement available (averaging $30,000 per year); Federal Work-Study and scholarships/grants also available. Financial award applicants required to submit FAFSA. *Unit head:* Marilee Murphy, Dean of School of Acupuncture and Oriental Medicine, 315-568-3268, E-mail: mmurphy@nycc.edu. *Application contact:* Michael Lynch, Director of Admissions, 315-568-3052, Fax: 315-568-3087, E-mail: mlynch@nycc.edu.

New York College of Health Professions, Graduate School of Oriental Medicine, Syosset, NY 11791-4413. Offers acupuncture (MS); Oriental medicine (MS). *Accreditation:* ACAOM. Part-time programs available. *Degree requirements:* For master's, thesis. *Entrance requirements:* For master's, minimum GPA of 2.5, 60 semester credits in undergraduate course work. Additional exam requirements/recommendations for international students: Required—TOEFL. *Faculty research:* Breast cancer, diabetic neuropathy hemolysis.

New York College of Traditional Chinese Medicine, Graduate Programs, Mineola, NY 11501. Offers oriental medicine (MAOM). *Accreditation:* ACAOM.

Northwestern Health Sciences University, Minnesota College of Acupuncture and Oriental Medicine, Bloomington, MN 55431-1599. Offers acupuncture (M Ac); oriental medicine (MOM). *Accreditation:* ACAOM. *Entrance requirements:* Additional exam requirements/recommendations for international students: Required—TOEFL (minimum score 540 paper-based; 207 computer-based). Electronic applications accepted.

Oregon College of Oriental Medicine, Graduate Program in Acupuncture and Oriental Medicine, Portland, OR 97216. Offers M Ac OM, MAcOM, DAOM. *Accreditation:* ACAOM. Part-time programs available. *Faculty:* 12 full-time (5 women), 47 part-time/adjunct (26 women). *Students:* 243 full-time (184 women), 23 part-time (20 women); includes 38 minority (5 African Americans, 1 American Indian/Alaska Native, 30 Asian Americans or Pacific Islanders, 2 Hispanic Americans), 2 international. Average age 35. 142 applicants, 70% accepted, 74 enrolled. In 2006, 63 master's, 15 doctorates awarded. *Entrance requirements:* For master's, minimum 3 years of college; course work in chemistry, biology, and psychology; for doctorate, documentation of clinical practice, 3 years of clinical experience. Additional exam requirements/recommendations for international students: Required—TOEFL (minimum score 550 paper-based). *Application deadline:* Applications are processed on a rolling basis. Application fee: $50. *Financial support:* In 2006–07, 208 students received support, including 5 fellowships (averaging $14,000 per year), 1 research assistantship (averaging $14,175 per year); Federal Work-Study also available. Support available to part-time students. Financial award applicants required to submit FAFSA. *Unit head:* Dr. Michael Gaeta, President, 503-253-3443 Ext. 107, Fax: 503-253-2701. *Application contact:* Nicola Moll, Admissions Coordinator, 503-253-3443 Ext. 113, Fax: 503-253-2701, E-mail: nmoll@ocom.edu.

See Close-Up on page 2153.

Pacific College of Oriental Medicine, Graduate Program, San Diego, CA 92108. Offers MSTOM, DAOM. *Accreditation:* ACAOM. Part-time and evening/weekend programs available. *Entrance requirements:* For master's, 2 letters of reference, interviews, minimum GPA of 3.0. *Faculty research:* PMS, acupuncture, herbs, Tai Ji Quan, sports medicine.

Pacific College of Oriental Medicine-Chicago, Graduate Program, Chicago, IL 60613. Offers MTOM. *Accreditation:* ACAOM. Part-time and evening/weekend programs available. *Entrance requirements:* For master's, 2 letters of reference, interview, minimum GPA of 3.0. *Faculty research:* AIDS, cancer, mental health, clinical counseling.

Pacific College of Oriental Medicine-New York, Graduate Program, New York, NY 10010. Offers MSTOM. *Accreditation:* ACAOM. Part-time and evening/weekend programs available. *Entrance requirements:* For master's, 2 letters of reference, interview, minimum GPA of 3.0. *Faculty research:* Energy medicine, acupuncture in the treatment of neurological disorders.

Samra University of Oriental Medicine, Program in Oriental Medicine, Los Angeles, CA 90034. Offers MS, DAOM. *Accreditation:* ACAOM. Part-time and evening/weekend programs available. *Faculty:* 10 full-time (5 women), 60 part-time/adjunct (30 women). *Students:* 322 full-time, 138 part-time. *Degree requirements:* For master's, comprehensive exam. *Entrance requirements:* For master's, 60 semester (90 quarter) units with a 'C' average in general education from an accredited college. *Application deadline:* Applications are processed on a rolling basis. Application fee: $100. *Financial support:* Available to part-time students. *Faculty research:* Herbal therapy; alleviation of AIDS symptoms, cancer, colds, flu. *Unit head:* Dr. Katsuyuki P. Sakamoto, Provost, 310-202-6444 Ext. 113, Fax: 310-202-6004, E-mail: ksakamoto@samra.edu. *Application contact:* Taula Jackson, Admissions Director, 310-202-6444 Ext. 104, Fax: 310-202-6007, E-mail: tjackson@samra.edu.

Seattle Institute of Oriental Medicine, Graduate Program, Seattle, WA 98115. Offers M Ac OM. *Accreditation:* ACAOM. *Faculty:* 2 full-time (0 women), 9 part-time/adjunct (3 women). *Students:* 31 full-time (23 women). Average age 37. 38 applicants, 55% accepted, 14 enrolled. In 2006, 12 degrees awarded. *Median time to degree:* Master's–3 years full-time. *Degree requirements:* For master's, one foreign language, comprehensive exam. *Entrance requirements:* For master's, course work in biology, psychology, chemistry, anatomy, physiology; CPR/first aid certification; 3 years (90 semester credits) post secondary coursework. Additional exam requirements/recommendations for international students: Recommended—TOEFL (minimum score 500 paper-based). *Application deadline:* Applications are processed on a rolling basis. Application fee: $50. *Expenses:* Tuition: Part-time $5,100 per trimester. *Unit head:* Paul D. Karsten, President, 206-517-4541, Fax: 206-526-1932, E-mail: pkarsten@siom.edu. *Application contact:* Anna Couch, Registrar, 206-517-4541 Ext. 1, Fax: 206-526-1932, E-mail: acouch@siom.edu.

South Baylo University, Program in Oriental Medicine and Acupuncture, Anaheim, CA 92801-1701. Offers MS. *Accreditation:* ACAOM. Evening/weekend programs available. *Degree requirements:* For master's, 3 foreign languages, comprehensive exam, registration. *Entrance requirements:* Additional exam requirements/recommendations for international students: Required—TOEFL (minimum score 500 paper-based; 173 computer-based). Electronic applications accepted. *Faculty research:* Effectiveness of acupuncture therapy.

Southern California University of Health Sciences, College of Acupuncture and Oriental Medicine, Whittier, CA 90609-1166. Offers MAOM. *Accreditation:* ACAOM. Part-time and evening/weekend programs available. *Faculty:* 10 full-time (3 women), 15 part-time/adjunct (8 women). *Students:* 66 full-time (40 women), 92 part-time (41 women); includes 104 minority (5 African Americans, 2 American Indian/Alaska Native, 84 Asian Americans or Pacific Islanders, 13 Hispanic Americans). Average age 28. 97 applicants, 51% accepted, 39 enrolled. In 2006, 33 degrees awarded. *Entrance requirements:* For master's, 60 semester hours or 90 quarter credits of undergraduate course work, interview. Additional exam requirements/recommendations for international students: Required—TOEFL (minimum score 500 paper-based; 173 computer-based). *Application deadline:* Applications are processed on a rolling basis. Application fee: $50. Electronic applications accepted. *Financial support:* In 2006–07, 104 students received support. Federal Work-Study available. Financial award applicants required to submit FAFSA. *Unit head:* Dr. Wen–Shuo Wu, Dean, 562-947-8755 Ext. 7028, E-mail: wen-shuowu@scuhs.edu. *Application contact:* Len Rosenthal, Executive Director of Marketing and Enrollment, 562-947-8755 Ext. 305, Fax: 562-947-5724, E-mail: lenrosenthal@scuhs.edu.

Southwest Acupuncture College, Program in Oriental Medicine, Albuquerque Campus, Albuquerque, NM 87109. Offers MS. *Accreditation:* ACAOM. Part-time programs available. *Faculty:* 4 full-time (2 women), 14 part-time/adjunct (7 women). *Students:* 96 full-time (72 women), 2 part-time (both women); includes 11 minority (2 American Indian/Alaska Native, 4 Asian Americans or Pacific Islanders, 5 Hispanic Americans), 1 international. Average age 36. 38 applicants, 92% accepted, 32 enrolled. In 2006, 29 degrees awarded. *Entrance requirements:* For master's, minimum 2 years of college general education. Additional exam requirements/recommendations for international students: Required—TOEFL (minimum score 500 paper-based). *Application deadline:* For fall admission, 5/15 priority date for domestic students; for winter admission, 12/15 priority date for domestic students. Applications are processed on a rolling basis. Application fee: $50. Electronic applications accepted. *Expenses:* Tuition: Full-time $10,657. Required fees: $130. *Financial support:* In 2006–07, 39 students received support. Scholarships/grants available. Financial award application deadline: 5/31; financial award applicants required to submit FAFSA. *Unit head:* Dr. Li Xu, Campus Director, 505-888-8898, Fax: 505-888-1380, E-mail: drlixu@acupuncturecollege.edu. *Application contact:* Dr. Bing zeng Zou, Academic Dean, 505-888-8898, E-mail: admin@acupuncturecollege.edu.

Southwest Acupuncture College, Program in Oriental Medicine, Boulder Campus, Boulder, CO 80301. Offers MS. *Accreditation:* ACAOM. Part-time programs available. *Faculty:* 6 full-time (2 women), 23 part-time/adjunct (17 women). *Students:* 128 full-time (82 women), 3 part-time (2 women); includes 9 minority (1 African American, 7 Asian Americans or Pacific Islanders, 1 Hispanic American), 1 international. Average age 30. 60 applicants, 90% accepted, 45 enrolled. In 2006, 34 degrees awarded. *Entrance requirements:* For master's, minimum 2 years of college general education. *Application deadline:* For fall admission, 5/15 priority date for domestic students; for winter admission, 12/15 priority date for domestic students. Applications are processed on a rolling basis. Application fee: $50. *Expenses:* Tuition: Full-time $10,657. Required fees: $130. *Financial support:* Scholarships/grants available. Financial award application deadline: 5/31; financial award applicants required to submit FAFSA. *Unit head:* Valerie L. Hobbs, Campus Director, 303-581-9955, Fax: 303-581-9944, E-mail: boulder@acupuncturecollege.edu. *Application contact:* Melanie Crane, Academic Dean, 303-581-9955, Fax: 303-581-9944, E-mail: boulder@acupuncturecollege.edu.

Southwest Acupuncture College, Program in Oriental Medicine, Santa Fe Campus, Santa Fe, NM 87505. Offers MS. *Accreditation:* ACAOM. Part-time programs available. *Faculty:* 9 full-time (3 women), 14 part-time/adjunct (6 women). *Students:* 80 full-time (54 women), 4 part-time (2 women); includes 4 minority (1 African American, 1 American Indian/Alaska Native, 2 Asian Americans or Pacific Islanders), 3 international. Average age 33. 31 applicants, 100% accepted, 28 enrolled. In 2006, 20 degrees awarded. *Entrance requirements:* For master's, minimum 2 years of college general education. *Application deadline:* For fall admission, 5/15 priority date for domestic students; for winter admission, 12/15 priority date for domestic students. Applications are processed on a rolling basis. Application fee: $50. *Expenses:* Tuition: Full-time $10,657. Required fees: $130. *Financial support:* In 2006–07, 12 students received support. Scholarships/grants available. Financial award application deadline: 5/31; financial award applicants required to submit FAFSA. *Unit head:* Terry Lopez, Campus Director, 505-438-8884, Fax: 505-438-8883, E-mail: admin@acupuncturecollege.edu. *Application contact:* Dr. Dawei Shao, Academic Dean, 505-438-8884, Fax: 505-438-8883, E-mail: admin@acupuncturecollege.edu.

Swedish Institute, College of Health Sciences, Graduate Program, New York, NY 10001-6700. Offers acupuncture (MS). *Accreditation:* ACAOM. Part-time and evening/weekend programs available. *Faculty:* 6 full-time (4 women), 32 part-time/adjunct (16 women). *Students:* 71 full-time (48 women), 40 part-time (29 women); includes 30 minority (3 African Americans, 19 Asian Americans or Pacific Islanders, 8 Hispanic Americans). Average age 36. 36 applicants, 67% accepted, 20 enrolled. In 2006, 19 degrees awarded. *Median time to degree:* Master's–3 years full-time, 5 years part-time. *Entrance requirements:* Additional exam requirements/recommendations for international students: Required—TOEFL (minimum score 72 iBT). *Application deadline:* For fall admission, 11/9 priority date for domestic and international students; for winter admission, 7/13 priority date for domestic and international students. Application fee: $50. *Expenses:* Tuition: Full-time $8,700. Required fees: $180. One-time fee: $50 full-time. Tuition and fees vary according to class time, course load and student level. *Financial support:* In 2006–07, 3 teaching assistantships with full and partial tuition reimbursements were awarded.

Tai Sophia Institute for the Healing Arts, Program in Acupuncture, Laurel, MD 20723. Offers MA. *Accreditation:* ACAOM. *Faculty research:* Philosophical roots of oriental medicine, meridian pathways, points, pulses.

Tai Sophia Institute for the Healing Arts, Program in Applied Healing Arts, Laurel, MD 20723. Offers MA. *Faculty research:* Healing habits of mind and heart, an expanded vision, bringing of one's vision and practices to a special arena.

Tai Sophia Institute for the Healing Arts, Program in Botanical Healing, Laurel, MD 20723. Offers MA. *Faculty research:* Philosophical roots of holistic healing, botany, herbal pharmacology; materia medica, holistic healing.

Texas College of Traditional Chinese Medicine, Program in Acupuncture and Oriental Medicine, Austin, TX 78704. Offers MAOM. *Accreditation:* ACAOM. Part-time and evening/weekend programs available. *Entrance requirements:* For master's, minimum GPA of 2.0. Additional exam requirements/recommendations for international students: Required—TOEFL (minimum score 500 paper-based; 173 computer-based), TWE. Electronic applications accepted.

Traditional Chinese Medical College of Hawaii, Graduate Programs, Kamuela, HI 96743-2288. Offers MSOM. *Accreditation:* ACAOM.

Tri State College of Acupuncture, Program in Acupuncture, New York, NY 10011. Offers acupuncture (MS); oriental medicine (MS); traditional Chinese herbology (Certificate). *Accreditation:* ACAOM. Evening/weekend programs available.

University of Bridgeport, Acupuncture Institute, Bridgeport, CT 06604. Offers MS. *Faculty:* 2 full-time (1 woman), 5 part-time/adjunct (1 woman). *Students:* 15 full-time (12 women), 8 part-time (5 women); includes 6 minority (2 African Americans, 4 Asian Americans or Pacific Islanders), 2 international. Average age 39. 24 applicants, 38% accepted, 8 enrolled. In 2006, 9 degrees awarded. *Application deadline:* For fall admission, 3/1 priority date for domestic students; for spring admission, 12/1 priority date for domestic students. Applications are processed on a rolling basis. Application fee: $75. Electronic applications accepted. *Expenses:* Contact institution. *Unit head:* Dr. Jennifer Brett, Director, 203-576-4122, Fax: 203-576-4107, E-mail: acup@bridgeport.edu.

World Medicine Institute: College of Acupuncture and Herbal Medicine, Program in Acupuncture and Oriental Medicine, Honolulu, HI 96828. Offers M Ac OM. *Accreditation:* ACAOM. Part-time and evening/weekend programs available. *Entrance requirements:* For master's, minimum 60 college credits.

Yo San University of Traditional Chinese Medicine, Program in Acupuncture and Traditional Chinese Medicine, Los Angeles, CA 90066. Offers MATCM. *Accreditation:* ACAOM. Part-time programs available. Postbaccalaureate distance learning degree programs offered (no on-campus study). *Degree requirements:* For master's, observation and practice internships, exam. *Entrance requirements:* For master's, minimum 2 years of college, interview, minimum GPA of 2.5.

BASTYR UNIVERSITY

School of Acupuncture and Oriental Medicine

Programs of Study

Bastyr University, a small private university featuring a strong sense of community that fosters both academic and personal growth, offers two Master of Science degree programs in the field of acupuncture and Oriental medicine and a Doctorate of Acupuncture and Oriental Medicine (D.A.O.M.). The master's-level curriculum is based on traditional Chinese medicine (TCM). The 3½-year Master of Science in Acupuncture and Oriental Medicine (M.S.A.O.M.) is the model comprehensive program and encompasses Chinese herbal medicine and Chinese medical language in addition to the core theory, TCM diagnosis, TCM pathology, TCM techniques, acupuncture therapeutics, and clinical training required for licensure. The shorter three-year M.S.A. is a viable choice for medical professionals who desire advanced comprehensive training in acupuncture. Clinical training takes place at Bastyr Center for Natural Health, an integrated, multidisciplinary clinic that provides training for students in all of the University's graduate programs. The clinic includes a fully stocked Chinese herbal dispensary. Students also have the opportunity to train at external clinic sites with diverse populations from the community. Students in good academic standing may apply to complete clinical internship credits at the Chengdu University of Traditional Chinese Medicine and/or Shanghai University of Traditional Chinese Medicine.

The Bastyr Doctorate of Acupuncture and Oriental Medicine trains qualified practitioners in an integrated clinical approach to oncology and pain management. Students have the option of full-time study in seven quarters or part-time study in nine quarters. The curriculum includes advanced concepts in TCM and in biomedical theory as well as experience in collaborative clinical settings. Graduates of the M.S. programs are eligible to apply for licensure in the state of Washington as well as in most other states that offer similar licensure. Currently, acupuncture is legal to practice in forty-three states and the District of Columbia. All of the acupuncture and Oriental medicine degree programs at Bastyr University are accredited by the Accreditation Commission for Acupuncture and Oriental Medicine (ACAOM). The M.S.A.O.M. program and the M.S.A. combined with the Chinese herbal medicine certificate (M.S.A./CCHM) are approved by the California Acupuncture Committee.

Research Facilities

The University's mission includes the pursuit of scientific research on nonallopathic therapies in the management and treatment of health-care problems and in the prevention of chronic disease. The University maintains a medical library with current journals; special collections in the areas of Oriental medicine, nutrition, and naturopathic medicine; and audiovisual equipment and materials. Students also have access to the University of Washington Health Sciences Libraries.

Financial Aid

Students are eligible to participate in the University Scholarship Program, as well as the Federal Stafford Student Loan program, the Federal Perkins Loan program, and the Federal Work-Study Program. Washington State residents are also eligible to participate in the Washington State Work-Study Program. In addition, there are private donor scholarships earmarked for students entering the M.S.A.O.M. program. D.A.O.M. students are also eligible for financial aid. Applicants seeking financial aid should complete the application process by May 15. Complete financial aid information is available on the Bastyr University Web site, listed in this description. Students may request a financial aid packet by contacting the Office of Financial Aid at 425-602-3407.

Cost of Study

Tuition for 2007–08 is charged per credit according to the credit load. The cost of 1 to 12 credits is $370 per credit (for all credits from 1 to 11.5); 12 to 16 credits cost $340 per credit (for all credits from 1 to 16). Credits above 16 are charged at $220 per credit. Total tuition and fees for a full-time M.S. student in the first year are $20,210 for the academic year, and books and supplies are approximately $1770 per year. For D.A.O.M. students, tuition and fees are $15,015, and books and supplies cost approximately $990 per year.

Living and Housing Costs

The University provides limited housing. Many students live in shared housing off campus; the average cost per person ranges from $500 to $900 per month. The Student Services Office can direct students to listings of available housing. The Washington Association of Student Financial Aid Administrators estimates that living expenses, including transportation and personal expenses, average $1360 per month.

Student Group

The University's total enrollment in 2006–07 was 1,138. Of the 885 graduate and professional students who attended the University, 213 were graduate students in the School of Acupuncture and Oriental Medicine. Sixty percent of the students are women. The average age is 31. Twenty-five percent are Washington residents; thirty-six other states are represented. Five percent of the students are from other countries.

Location

The academic and administrative campus is on a 50-acre site adjoining Saint Edward State Park in Kenmore, Washington, about 15 miles northeast of Seattle. Several hiking trails to Lake Washington begin at the edge of the campus; abundant opportunities for outdoor activities exist nearby in the Puget Sound area. The teaching clinic is located in a Seattle neighborhood. The city offers a full range of activities and facilities, including museums, theaters, ethnic restaurants, a major opera and symphony orchestra, major-league sports, and outdoor activities. The Puget Sound area has a large number of academic institutions, including seven universities and many colleges, community colleges, and professional schools.

The University

Bastyr University was founded as a naturopathic medical college in 1978. The University's mission includes serving as an effective leader in the improvement of the health and well-being of the human community. Since 1984, as a part of its mission to provide comprehensive education in natural medicine, the University has added graduate and undergraduate programs in nutrition, health psychology, herbal sciences, and exercise science and wellness as well as an M.A. program in applied behavioral science through the Leadership Institute of Seattle (LIOS). Bastyr University is accredited by the Northwest Commission on Colleges and Universities. A comprehensive administrative fee enables all students to receive health care at Bastyr Center for Natural Health, the University's teaching clinic (a minimal co-pay is due at each visit). Counseling services, acupuncture, physical medicine, and the herbal dispensary are all accessible to students.

Applying

Admission is based on academic achievement, personal and social development, relevant experience, and demonstrated humanistic qualities. Credentials to be submitted are all official transcripts, two letters of recommendation, a completed application form, and a $75 application fee. Minimum prerequisites are a baccalaureate degree with a C or better in one course of college-level algebra or precalculus, one course of general psychology, one course of general biology with lab, and two courses of general chemistry with lab. Specific information is available from the Admissions Office or by viewing the catalog on the University's Web site. An interview is required for admission to the program. Applications should be received by the University by March 15 for admission the following fall, although late applications are considered if space is available.

Correspondence and Information

Office of Admissions
Bastyr University
14500 Juanita Drive, NE
Kenmore, Washington 98028
Phone: 425-602-3330
Fax: 425-602-3090
E-mail: admissions@bastyr.edu
Web site: http://www.bastyr.edu/sub/adtrack.asp?adid=pe03

Bastyr University

THE FACULTY

Daniel Altschuler, Ph.D., Guangzhou Chinese Medical, 2005; LAc.
Benjamin Apichai, M.D., Jinan (China); LAc.
Sara Bayer, M.A., Michigan, 1982; LAc.
Qiang Cao, O.M.D., Shanghai University of Traditional Chinese Medicine, 1977; N.D., Bastyr, 1989.
Terry Courtney, Dean, School of Acupuncture and Oriental Medicine; M.P.H., Boston University, 1996.
Wei Yi Ding, O.M.D., Shanghai University of Traditional Chinese Medicine, 1985.
James Dowling, M.Ac., Northwest Institute of Acupuncture and Oriental Medicine; RN, LAc.
Matt Ferguson, M.S.A., Bastyr; LAc.
Steve Given, M.T.C.M., Emperor's College of Traditional Oriental Medicine, 1992.
Jianxin Huang, M.D., Nonjing University of Traditional Chinese Medicine, 1979.
Angela Hughes, M.Ac., Northwest Institute of Acupuncture and Oriental Medicine; LAc.
Randi Jensen, M.A., Antioch, 2004.
Susan Kaetz, M.P.H., Yale, 1975; M.Ac., Northwest Institute of Acupuncture and Oriental Medicine, 1997; LAc.
Mark Kestin, Ph.D., Flinders (Australia), 1989; M.P.H., Harvard, 1990.
Kayo King, M.Ac., Northwest Institute of Acupuncture and Oriental Medicine; LAc.
Elizabeth Kirk, Ph.D., Washington (Seattle), 1994.
Samer Koutoubi, M.D., University of Medicine and Pharmacy (Cluj-Napoca, Romania), 1988; Ph.D., Florida International, 2001.
Chongyun Liu, M.D., Luzhou Medical College (China), 1982.
Tong Lu, M.D., Harbin University of Traditional Chinese Medicine (China); LAc.
Yuanming Lu, M.D., Qinghai Medical School (China); LAc.
Rosie Xin Dong Ma, M.D., Heilongjiang University of Traditional Chinese Medicine (China); LAc.
Andrew McIntyre, M.S.A., Bastyr, 1994.
Kyo Mitchell, M.P.H., Northern Illinois, 1994; M.S.A., Bastyr, 1999; LAc.
Jeffrey Novack, Ph.D., Washington (Seattle), 1991.
Rebecca Love Steward, D.V.M., Washington State, 1987.
Masahiro Takakura, N.D., 2002, M.S.A.O.M., 2003, Bastyr; D.C., National University of Health Sciences, 2005.
Angela Tseng, M.S.A., Bastyr; LAc.
Jianli Wang, N.D., Bastyr; LAc.
Ying Wang, O.M.D., Harbin University of Traditional Chinese Medicine (China), 1988.
Sue Yang, M.S.A., Bastyr, 2000.

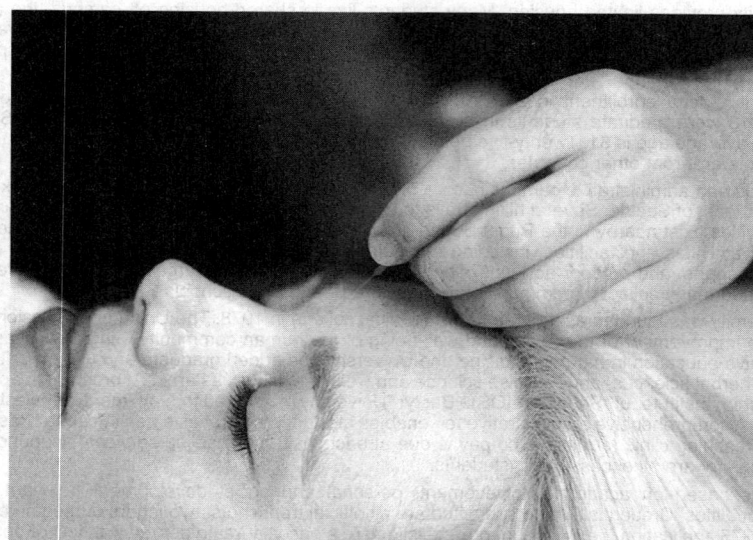

Woman receives an acupuncture treatment from a Bastyr clinician-in-training.

NEW ENGLAND SCHOOL OF ACUPUNCTURE

Graduate Programs in Acupuncture and Oriental Medicine

Program of Study	The New England School of Acupuncture (NESA) is the oldest college of Oriental medicine in the United States. The two master's degree options—the Master of Acupuncture and the Master of Acupuncture and Oriental Medicine—offer students the choice to pursue specific areas of interest. All students complete a comprehensive core curriculum providing theoretical and practical training in Traditional Chinese Medicine (TCM) and Chinese acupuncture. In addition, all students complete a concentration either in Japanese acupuncture styles, Chinese herbal medicine, or both. NESA also offers a varied selection of elective courses to match a student's professional interests.

From the outset, NESA's programs emphasize extensive, hands-on clinical training in small groups. NESA's philosophy is that theoretical material is best learned when taught in careful coordination with corresponding clinical practice sessions. Students also receive training in Western sciences and biomedicine, nutrition, Oriental body work, and research. The program culminates in supervised clinical internships that offer a wide range of clinical experiences in hospitals and community health settings throughout Boston. |
| **Research Facilities** | NESA's research program is a leading contributor in the field of Oriental medicine research. Supported by grants from the National Institutes of Health (NIH), the research department works collaboratively with leading Western medical research institutes and hospitals in the Boston area. Through courses, internships, and research assistantships, students learn about contemporary research in Oriental medicine.

NESA's library maintains a very extensive collection of journals and books on Oriental medicine. The library has a rich collection of electronic resources relevant to Oriental medicine and offers open access to its state-of-the-art online catalog of the library's holdings through the Internet. |
Financial Aid	NESA participates in the Federal Family Education Loan (FFEL) program, which includes subsidized and unsubsidized Federal Stafford Student Loans and various supplemental loan programs.
Cost of Study	For the 2006–07 academic year, full-time tuition (three terms) for the first year of study was approximately $14,240 for the Japanese Acupuncture Track, $15,040 for the Chinese Herbal Medicine Track, and $15,680 for the Dual Track, which includes Chinese Herbal Medicine and Japanese Acupuncture; the tuition rate varies depending on the actual number of credits taken. The cost of books and supplies is estimated to be between $2300 and $2500 for the entire program.
Living and Housing Costs	NESA students find available housing in many communities in and around the Watertown and Boston areas. NESA does not provide housing for students. The College Board estimates that the cost of housing, transportation, and other living expenses for the Boston metropolitan area is approximately $20,000 per academic year.
Student Group	NESA attracts a well-educated and highly motivated group of students that ranges in age from the early 20s to the mid-50s. NESA students reflect many different educational and cultural backgrounds, careers, and life experiences, yet they share a deep commitment to the study and practice of acupuncture and Oriental medicine. Many NESA students have advanced degrees in other fields and are making midcareer changes. Approximately 230 students attend NESA.
Student Outcomes	More than 1,200 practitioners have graduated from NESA, many of whom have made significant contributions to the field. NESA alumni have founded colleges of Oriental medicine; authored well-known texts; established acupuncture clinics in hospitals, community health centers, and extended-care facilities; established acupuncture clinics for the treatment of HIV/AIDS and substance abuse; and initiated groundbreaking research.
Location	NESA's campus consists of two buildings located in Watertown and Newton, Massachusetts. These two facilities provide more than 34,000 square feet of space for the study and practice of Oriental medicine. NESA is located a few miles away from downtown Boston and Cambridge's Harvard Square. The campus is easily accessible via public transportation and major highways. The metropolitan area is rich in history, culture, and entertainment. The Atlantic Ocean and the natural beauty of New England are just a short distance away.
The School	The New England School of Acupuncture was founded in 1975 by master acupuncturist James Tin Yau So. NESA's mission is to be a leader in the development of traditional and modern Oriental medicine as a medical art and science by offering outstanding professional programs. NESA is a not-for-profit institution that is authorized by the Massachusetts Board of Higher Education to grant a master's degree in either acupuncture or acupuncture and Oriental medicine.
Applying	Prospective students are strongly encouraged to visit the School and observe classes before applying. Applicants to the program must have a bachelor's degree. In addition, all applicants must have an admission interview. NESA admits students on a rolling basis. Prospective students who have completed the application process, including the admission interview, before December 1 receive early acceptance decisions by the end of January. Applicants are strongly urged to submit applications by the May 1 deadline. Applications received after May 1 are considered on a space-available basis. Students accepted into the program matriculate at the beginning of the fall semester only. NESA accepts a limited number of part-time and transfer students.
Correspondence and Information	Office of Admissions New England School of Acupuncture 150 California Street Newton, Massachusetts 02458 Phone: 617-558-1788 Fax: 617-558-1789 E-mail: admissions@nesa.edu Web site: http://www.nesa.edu

New England School of Acupuncture

THE FACULTY

Collins J Allen, Lic.Ac.
Jonathan Ammen, Chair, Chinese Acupuncture Department; M.Ac., M.Ed.
Robert Ayers, M.S.
Sarah Barlotta, Lic.Ac.
Linda Barnes, Ph.D., M.T.S.
James Belanger, N.D.; MT (ASCP).
J. Christopher Belskis, LMT, ABT.
Katherine Billings, M.Ac.; Lic.Ac.
Karen Braga, N.D.
Loocie Brown, M.Ac.; Lic.Ac.
Stephen Cina, Lic.Ac.; LATC.
Lisa Conboy, Ph.D.
John Coville, Lic.Ac.
Patrick Cunningham, Chair, Manual Therapy and Internal Arts Department; M.Ac.; Lic.Ac., ABT, RCST.
Linda Davis.
Anne Drogin, M.Ac.; Lic.Ac.
Martin Feldman, M.Ac.; Lic.Ac.
Cheryl Fraser-Bacon, M.Ac.; Lic.Ac.
Anne Geraghty, M.Ac.; Lic.Ac.
Sabrina Hawthorne.
DeGuang He, Lic.Ac.
Emma Heart, Ph.D.
Julia Herskowitz, M.Ac.; Lic.Ac.
Ellen Highfield, Lic.Ac.
Stephen Howard, M.Ac.; Dipl.C.H., Lic.Ac.
Amy Hull, Academic Dean; M.A.O.M., M.Ed.; Lic.Ac.
Diane Iuliano, Co-Chair, Japanese Acupuncture Styles Department; Lic.Ac.
Yan Ping Jin, Lic.Ac.
Ted Kaptchuk, Lic.Ac.
Joseph Kay, Co-Chair, Japanese Acupuncture Styles Department; Lic.Ac.
Joseph Kelliher, Lic.Ac.
Cathy Kerr, Ph.D.
Mary Kinneavy, M.Ac.; Lic.Ac.
Kellie Kirkpatrick.
Takayuki Koei Kuwahara, Lic.Ac.
Yelena Lebedinsky, M.Ac., Ph.D.; Lic.Ac.
Sanford Lee, M.F.A.; Lic.Ac.

Mitchell Levine, M.D.
Sharon Levy, Lic.Ac.
A. Lisa Lipson, M.P.H., M.Ac.; Lic.Ac.
Weidong Lu, Lic.Ac.
Richard Mandell, Lic.Ac.
Barbara Marcel, Research Advisor; Ph.D.
Steve Markus, M.D.
Jeff Matrician, Lic.Ac.
Anne McCaffrey, M.D.
Qin Meng, Lic.Ac.
Lorie Miller, M.B.A.
Susan Miller, Lic.Ac.
Bridie Minehan, Ph.D.
William Mueller, Lic.Ac.
Janis Oliker, Lic.Ac., RN.
Henry Oliveras.
Zachary Parsons, M.Ac.; Lic.Ac.
Sabrina Popp, M.D.
Kristen Porter, M.Ac.; Lic.Ac.
Dana Quinn, Lic.Ac.
Shaune Ralph, M.Ac.; Lic.Ac.
Karla Renaud, M.Ac.; Lic.Ac.
Suzahne Riendeau, M.Ac.; Lic.Ac.
James Roth, Ph.D.
Sharon Rubrake, M.D.; Lic.Ac.
Marcus Schulkind, Lic.Ac.
Kathy Seltzer, Lic.Ac.
Valerie Smith, Lic.Ac.
Meredith St. John, M.Ac.; Lic.Ac.
Peter Valaskatgis, M.Ac.; Lic.Ac.
Elaine Walsh, Lic.Ac.
Bing Yang, Chair, Chinese Herbal Medicine Department, Lic.Ac.
Dongyan Yu.
Vivien Zhang, Chinese Herbal Pharmacy Manager; Lic.Ac.
Yue (Joy) Zhang, Lic.Ac.
Zhen-Zhen Zhang, Lic.Ac.
Li Zheng, Lic.Ac.
Quan Zhou, Lic.Ac.

OREGON COLLEGE of ORIENTAL MEDICINE

OREGON COLLEGE OF ORIENTAL MEDICINE

Program in Acupuncture and Oriental Medicine

Program of Study
Candidates who complete this three-calendar-year (four-academic-year) graduate program at the Oregon College of Oriental Medicine (OCOM) are awarded the Master of Acupuncture and Oriental Medicine (M.Ac.O.M.) degree, are qualified to sit for the national certification exams, and are prepared to enter into independent health-care practice as regulated by each individual state. The academic program presents course work and training in all aspects of traditional Oriental medicine, including the theory and practice of acupuncture, herbal medicine, traditional Chinese physiotherapy, exercise, and qi cultivation; adjunctive courses in Western biomedicine, including anatomy, physiology, pathology, pharmacology, and clinical diagnosis; and relevant course work in public and community health, clinical research, practice management, and practitioner/patient dynamics.

At the heart of the academic program is the Acupuncture and Herbal Clinic, whose mission is to provide high-quality, affordable health care to the public and to support the development of Oriental medicine as a vital healing methodology complementary to Western medicine. Acupuncture and Oriental medical services are provided in the clinic by student interns who practice under the direct supervision of experienced acupuncturists, many from China, who are licensed in the state of Oregon. Students complete 960 hours of supervised clinical training and as third-year interns treat more than 425 patients in supervised clinical settings. All students complete an internship rotation in a community health clinic, underscoring the College's commitment to practitioner training in public health. A specialized certificate program in teacher training is also available to advanced students of qigong.

Research Facilities
The College has incorporated clinical research into the core curriculum by providing the didactic course Topics in Clinical Research as well as the project-oriented research practicum experience. The College clinic supports student research projects through the organization and accessibility of patient demographics and outcomes data. Students, faculty members, and alumni involved in research have full access to the College's outstanding library and computerized online search services as well as Internet access. By virtue of their enrollment, students have library privileges at the Oregon Health & Science University, National College of Natural Medicine, and Western States Chiropractic College. In addition, OCOM is a full participant in four National Institutes of Health–funded research projects, in conjunction with Oregon Health & Science University and Kaiser Permanente's Center for Health Research.

Financial Aid
Federal financial aid is available through the Federal Stafford Student Loan program, veteran's benefits, and the Federal Work-Study Program. A college payment plan is also available.

Cost of Study
Projected tuition costs for full-time students in the thirty-six-month program in 2006–07 totaled $51,864. Books and medical supplies cost an additional $800 per academic year (approximately).

Living and Housing Costs
The College is located in a residential area, with rentals available at reasonable rates. Many students share housing with monthly costs as low as $300–$400. Students can often find housing by utilizing the bulletin board maintained for this purpose in the student lounge. For financial aid purposes, living expenses for nine months are estimated at $9736.

Student Group
A diverse student body of 41 D.A.O.M. students and 230 M.Ac.O.M. students from across the United States, Canada, Mexico, Asia, and Europe bring impressive knowledge and experience to the study of Oriental medicine. Many students are engaged in a major career change from such fields as law, computer science, research, and teaching as well as from the medical fields of nursing, physical therapy, and therapeutic massage. Increasingly, younger students pursue this educational path as their first professional degree program. The academic environment encourages cooperative study among students, who form supportive practice and study groups in support of their learning process.

Student Outcomes
The majority of the College's 790 graduates enter into private practice or group practice with complementary health-care providers. Several pursue careers in public health settings and have accepted positions with public agencies that provide services to clients with HIV/AIDS, chemical dependency, and mental illness. These treatment settings include homeless shelters, residential treatment facilities, jails and prisons, and outpatient drop-in clinics.

Location
The College is situated on a 1-acre campus 10 miles east of downtown Portland, Oregon. A city of 540,000, Portland is heralded by many observers as one of America's most livable cities. Surrounded by the exhilarating beauty of the Pacific Northwest, Portland is blessed with lively commerce, a burgeoning performing arts scene, a symphony orchestra, an NBA franchise, and a beautiful urban parks system. Mount Hood and the Columbia Gorge offer some of the best hiking, skiing, fishing, boating, and windsurfing in the country. Eighty miles to the west is the rugged Oregon coastline, a favorite weekend retreat for city dwellers.

The College
The Oregon College of Oriental Medicine was established as a nonprofit educational institution in 1983 in response to the growing need for comprehensive professional training in traditional Oriental medicine. OCOM has grown significantly in recent years and now includes 320 individuals—students, faculty and staff members, and members of the board of trustees—who learn, practice, and support traditional medicine within the school's own campus and facilities. Through the efforts of this community, the College has emerged as an important contributor to national and regional health care and education. In addition to academic excellence, the OCOM's mission includes a commitment to public health as evidenced by its relationships with numerous clinics offering affordable community health care. The learning environment is supportive and conducive to the development of academic and clinical competencies requisite for success in independent health-care practice. The four-academic-year professional master's degree program in acupuncture and Oriental medicine is accredited by the Accreditation Commission for Acupuncture and Oriental Medicine (ACAOM), a specialized accrediting agency recognized by the U.S. Department of Education. Approval to grant the degree of Master of Acupuncture and Oriental Medicine has been conferred by the state of Oregon Office of Educational Policy and Planning.

Applying
Candidates for admission must demonstrate the potential to become caring, dedicated, and skilled practitioners of traditional Oriental medicine and evidence the maturity and preparation necessary to undertake the challenging academic program. Minimum requirements for admission include the successful completion of at least three years of college at a federally accredited institution, although it is recommended that incoming students have completed a four-year college degree. As part of the required undergraduate education, or in addition to it, applicants must also have completed college-level courses in general biology, general chemistry, and psychology. The application process includes a completed application form and $50 fee as well as complete and official academic transcripts, two admission essays, and two formal letters of recommendation. An on-campus interview is required of all qualified applicants. Applicants are accepted beginning in September for enrollment in the following year's entering class.

Correspondence and Information
Office of Admissions
Oregon College of Oriental Medicine
10525 Southeast Cherry Blossom Drive
Portland, Oregon 97216
Phone: 503-253-3443 Ext. 113
Fax: 503-253-2701
E-mail: admissions@ocom.edu
Web site: http://www.ocom.edu

Oregon College of Oriental Medicine

CLASSROOM AND CLINICAL FACULTY

OCOM faculty members are designated as core, adjunct, or visiting. Core faculty members are ongoing faculty members; adjunct faculty members teach periodically at OCOM; and visiting faculty members teach weekend, day, or weeklong seminars. Faculty members are also designated as full-time or part-time.

Nigel David Adler, D.C., L.Ac.
Harry Affley, B.S.
Satya Ambrose, N.D., L.Ac.
Cynthia J. Anderson, M.Ac.O.M., L.Ac.
David Berkshire, M.Ac.O.M., L.Ac.
Elizabeth B. Burch, N.D.
Edward Chiu, M.Ac., L.Ac.
Joseph J. Coletto, N.D., L.Ac.
Forrest Cooper, M.Ac.O.M., L.Ac.
Steven Dardis, D.A.O.M., L.Ac.
Regina Dehen, N.D., M.Ac.O.M., L.Ac.
David C. Eisen, M.S.W., L.Ac.
Linda Faust, M.Ac.O.M., L.Ac.
Muir Ferdun, M.Ac.O.M., L.Ac.
Mark Goldby, M.Ac.O.M., L.Ac.
Richard Hammerschlag, Ph.D.
Taiping Jia, B.Med. (PR China), L.Ac.
Hong Jin, B.Med. (PR China), L.Ac.
Robert Kaneko, B.A., L.Ac.
Patricia Kuchar, M.Ac.O.M., L.Ac.
Tsuey-Hwa Lai, M.Ac.O.M., L.Ac.
Lily Li, L.Ac.
Zhenbo Li, Ph.D. (PR China), L.Ac.
Guohui Liu, M.Med. (PR China), L.Ac.
He Liu.
Lei Liu, B.Med. (PR China), L.Ac.
Roger Lore, D.A.O.M., L.Ac.
Gwen Lovetere, M.Ac.O.M., L.Ac.

Yan Lu, B.Med. (PR China), L.Ac.
Zhaoxue Lu, Ph.D. (PR China), L.Ac.
Yunpeng Luo, M.Med. (PR China), L.Ac.
Cole Magbanua, M.Ac.O.M., L.Ac.
Elizabeth March, M.Ac.O.M., L.Ac.
Michael McCarron, M.Ac.O.M., L.Ac.
Carmel McMinn, M.Ac.O.M., L.Ac.
Sharon McNichols, M.Ac.O.M., L.Ac.
Nikki Medgalchy, M.Ac.O.M., L.Ac.
Debra Mulrooney, L.Ac.
Frank Mussell, J.D.
Xavier Preciado, LMT.
Anne Prescott, D.C., LMT.
Bob Quinn, M.Ac.O.M., L.Ac., LMT.
Stephen Saeks, Ph.D., M.Ac.O.M., L.Ac.
Catherine Salveson, Ph.D., RN.
Laura Santi, L.Ac.
Joyce Sherpa, Ph.D., M.Ac.O.M., L.Ac.
Mitchell Bebel Stargrove, N.D., L.Ac.
Eric F. Stephens, D.A.O.M., L.Ac.
Sandra Szabat, N.D.
Carol Taub, M.A.T., L.Ac.
Catherine Travis, M.Ac., L.Ac.
Shelly Wagar, LMT.
Yufang Xue, Ph.D. (PR China), L.Ac.
Fang Zhang, M.Med. (PR China), L.Ac.
Lili Zheng, D.A.O.M., L.Ac.

Section 35
Chiropractic

This section contains a directory of institutions offering graduate work in chiropractic, followed by in-depth entries submitted by institutions that chose to prepare detailed program descriptions. Additional information about programs listed in the directory but not augmented by an in-depth entry may be obtained by writing directly to the dean of a graduate school or chair of a department at the address given in the directory.

CONTENTS

Chiropractic

Canadian Memorial Chiropractic College, Certificate Programs, Toronto, ON M2H 3J1, Canada. Offers chiropractic clinical sciences (Certificate); chiropractic radiology (Certificate); chiropractic sports sciences (Certificate). *Degree requirements:* For Certificate, thesis. *Entrance requirements:* For degree, DC, board certification. *Faculty research:* Theories and concepts of chiropractic, sciences related to chiropractic, assessments of the efficacy and efficiency of chiropractic.

Canadian Memorial Chiropractic College, Professional Program, Toronto, ON M2H 3J1, Canada. Offers DC. *Entrance requirements:* 3 full years of university (15 full courses or 90 hours). *Faculty research:* Theories and concepts of chiropractic, sciences related to chiropractic, assessment of the efficacy and efficiency of chiropractic.

Cleveland Chiropractic College-Kansas City Campus, Professional Program, Kansas City, MO 64131-1181. Offers DC. *Accreditation:* CCE. Part-time programs available. *Faculty:* 37 full-time (6 women), 13 part-time/adjunct (3 women). *Students:* 386 full-time (127 women), 7 part-time (2 women); includes 39 minority (10 African Americans, 5 American Indian/Alaska Native, 13 Asian Americans or Pacific Islanders, 11 Hispanic Americans), 6 international. Average age 33. 271 applicants, 51% accepted, 71 enrolled. In 2006, 114 degrees awarded. *Degree requirements:* For first-professional, comprehensive exam. *Entrance requirements:* 90 semester hours of pre-professional study. Additional exam requirements/recommendations for international students: Required—TOEFL (minimum score 550 paper-based; 213 computer-based; 79 iBT). *Application deadline:* For fall admission, 7/1 priority date for domestic and international students; for winter admission, 11/1 priority date for domestic and international students; for spring admission, 3/1 priority date for domestic and international students. Applications are processed on a rolling basis. Application fee: $50. Electronic applications accepted. *Financial support:* Federal Work-Study, institutionally sponsored loans, and scholarships/grants available. Financial award application deadline: 3/1; financial award applicants required to submit FAFSA. *Faculty research:* Effectiveness and efficacy of chiropractic care. *Unit head:* Dr. Paul Barlett, Academic Dean, 816-501-0254. *Application contact:* Melissa Denton, Director of Admissions, 816-501-0161, Fax: 816-501-0205, E-mail: melissa.denton@cleveland.edu.

See Close-Up on page 2159.

Cleveland Chiropractic College-Los Angeles Campus, Professional Program, Los Angeles, CA 90004-2196. Offers DC. *Accreditation:* CCE. *Faculty:* 26 full-time (9 women), 9 part-time/adjunct (2 women). *Students:* 261 full-time (100 women), 15 part-time (5 women); includes 92 minority (9 African Americans, 1 American Indian/Alaska Native, 59 Asian Americans or Pacific Islanders, 23 Hispanic Americans), 15 international. Average age 29. 306 applicants, 15% accepted, 33 enrolled. In 2006, 75 degrees awarded. *Degree requirements:* For first-professional, internship. *Entrance requirements:* 90 semester units of course work in liberal arts; 2 semesters of biology, general chemistry, organic chemistry, and general physics. Additional exam requirements/recommendations for international students: Required—TOEFL. *Application deadline:* For fall admission, 8/1 for domestic and international students; for spring admission, 12/1 for domestic and international students. Applications are processed on a rolling basis. Application fee: $50. Electronic applications accepted. *Expenses:* Tuition: Part-time $274 per contact hour. Required fees: $145 per term. *Financial support:* Fellowships, research assistantships with partial tuition reimbursements, teaching assistantships with partial tuition reimbursements, Federal Work-Study, scholarships/grants, and tuition waivers (partial) available. Financial award application deadline: 5/1; financial award applicants required to submit FAFSA. *Faculty research:* Biomechanics, basic science, neurobiology, neurophysiology, neuroendocrine. Total annual research expenditures: $88,275. *Unit head:* Dr. Ruth Sandefur, Vice President for Academic Affairs, 816-501-0100, Fax: 323-660-5387. *Application contact:* Theresa Moore, Director of Admission, 800-466-CCLA, Fax: 323-906-2094, E-mail: theresa.moore@cleveland.edu.

See Close-Up on page 2159.

D'Youville College, Department of Holistic Health Studies, Buffalo, NY 14201-1084. Offers chiropractic (DC). *Accreditation:* CCE. *Faculty:* 2 full-time (0 women), 6 part-time/adjunct (4 women). *Students:* 31 full-time (16 women), 6 international. Average age 25. 47 applicants, 55% accepted, 14 enrolled.Application fee: $25. *Unit head:* Dr. Paul Hageman, Chair of Holistic Health Studies, 716-829-7606 Ext. 7793, Fax: 716-829-7893, E-mail: hagemanp@dyc.edu. *Application contact:* Linda Fisher, Graduate Admissions Director, 716-829-8400, Fax: 716-829-7900, E-mail: graduateadmissions@dyc.edu.

Institut Franco-Européen de Chiropratique, Professional Program, 94200 Ivry-sur-Seine, France. Offers DC.

Life Chiropractic College West, Professional Program, Hayward, CA 94545. Offers DC. *Accreditation:* CCE. *Entrance requirements:* Minimum GPA of 2.5. Additional exam requirements/recommendations for international students: Required—TOEFL (minimum score 550 paper-based). *Faculty research:* Chiropractic adjustment, neurology.

Announcement: Located in Hayward, California, near San Francisco, Life West offers a 12-quarter program with a 14-quarter option. Students appreciate the distinguished faculty and 12 techniques, taught through core and elective programs. Outstanding classroom and clinic experiences prepare students for a rewarding career in chiropractic health care.

Life University, College of Chiropractic, Marietta, GA 30060-2903. Offers DC. *Accreditation:* CCE. Part-time programs available. *Degree requirements:* For first-professional, thesis or alternative, comprehensive exam, registration. *Entrance requirements:* Minimum 3 years of college; course work in biology, chemistry, physics, humanities, psychology, and English; minimum GPA of 2.5. Additional exam requirements/recommendations for international students: Required—TOEFL (minimum score 500 paper-based; 173 computer-based). Electronic applications accepted. *Faculty research:* Chiropractic clinical trial, spinal modeling, biomechanics, clinical evaluation studies, chiropractic technique development, sports performance.

Logan University-College of Chiropractic, Chiropractic Program, Chesterfield, MO 63006-1065. Offers DC. *Accreditation:* CCE. *Faculty:* 53 full-time (16 women), 52 part-time/adjunct (26 women). *Students:* 921 full-time (294 women), 52 part-time (21 women); includes 76 minority (30 African Americans, 4 American Indian/Alaska Native, 19 Asian Americans or Pacific Islanders, 23 Hispanic Americans), 40 international. Average age 27. 240 applicants, 96% accepted, 147 enrolled. In 2006, 229 degrees awarded. *Degree requirements:* For first-professional, comprehensive exam. *Entrance requirements:* 90 hours of pre-chiropractic including biology, chemistry, physics, and social sciences; minimum GPA of 2.5. Additional exam requirements/recommendations for international students: Required—TOEFL (minimum score 500 paper-based; 172 computer-based). *Application deadline:* For fall admission, 7/15 priority date for domestic and international students; for winter admission, 11/15 priority date for domestic and international students; for spring admission, 3/15 priority date for domestic students, 3/15 for international students. Applications are processed on a rolling basis. Application fee: $50. Electronic applications accepted. *Expenses:* Tuition: Full-time $12,800; part-time $400 per credit hour. Required fees: $270. *Financial support:* In 2006–07, 100 students received support. Federal Work-Study and scholarships/grants available. Support available to part-time students. Financial award applicants required to submit FAFSA. *Faculty research:* Chiropractic manipulative therapy; low-back and pelvic pain in pregnancy; balance and somatosensory integration; radiology: FMRI and digital motion x-ray; electrophysiology: N&S EMG, heart rate variability, F-waves and H-reflex. Total annual research expenditures: $16,534. *Unit head:* Dr. Carl Saubert, Associate Vice President, Academic Affairs, 636-227-2100, Fax: 636-207-2431, E-mail: carl.saubert@logan.edu. *Application contact:* Cindy Sutton, Associate Director, Admissions, 636-227-2100 Ext. 1756, Fax: 636-207-2425, E-mail: loganadm@logan.edu.

Logan University-College of Chiropractic, University Programs, Chesterfield, MO 63006-1065. Offers MS. *Faculty:* 3 full-time (0 women). *Students:* Average age 26. *Degree requirements:* For master's, comprehensive exam. *Entrance requirements:* For master's, GRE or NBCE, minimum GPA of 2.5. Additional exam requirements/recommendations for international students: Required—TOEFL (minimum score 500 paper-based; 172 computer-based). *Application deadline:* For fall admission, 7/15 priority date for domestic and international students; for winter admission, 11/15 priority date for domestic and international students; for spring admission, 3/15 priority date for domestic students, 3/15 for international students. Application fee: $50. *Expenses:* Tuition: Full-time $12,800; part-time $400 per credit hour. Required fees: $270. *Financial support:* Federal Work-Study available. Support available to part-time students. Financial award applicants required to submit FAFSA. *Faculty research:* Chiropractic manipulative therapy; low-back and pelvic pain in pregnancy; balance and somatosensory integration; radiology: FMRI and digital motion x-ray; electrophysiology: N&S EMG, heart rate variability, F-wavs and H-reflex. *Unit head:* Dr. Allen Schwab, Academic Dean, 636-230-1864, E-mail: allen.schwab@logan.edu. *Application contact:* Cindy Sutton, Associate Director, Admissions, 636-227-2100 Ext. 1756, Fax: 636-207-2425, E-mail: loganadm@logan.edu.

National University of Health Sciences, College of Professional Studies, Lombard, IL 60148-4583. Offers acupuncture (MSAC); chiropractic medicine (DC); naturopathic medicine (ND); Oriental medicine (MSOM). *Accreditation:* CCE. *Faculty:* 49 full-time (10 women), 40 part-time/adjunct (15 women). *Students:* 394 full-time (186 women); includes 80 minority (19 African Americans, 47 Asian Americans or Pacific Islanders, 14 Hispanic Americans), 12 international. Average age 27. In 2006, 86 DCs, 2 master's awarded. *Degree requirements:* For first-professional, internship, community service. *Entrance requirements:* Bachelor's degree with strong background in sciences. Additional exam requirements/recommendations for international students: Required—TOEFL (minimum score 500 paper-based; 172 computer-based). *Application deadline:* For fall admission, 8/22 for domestic and international students; for winter admission, 11/22 for domestic and international students; for spring admission, 4/18 for domestic and international students. Applications are processed on a rolling basis. Application fee: $55. Electronic applications accepted. *Expenses:* Tuition: Full-time $16,187. Full-time tuition and fees vary according to course load. *Financial support:* Fellowships, research assistantships, teaching assistantships, Federal Work-Study, scholarships/grants, and tuition waivers (partial) available. Support available to part-time students. Financial award applicants required to submit FAFSA. *Faculty research:* Chiropractic procedures, spinal stenosis, evidence-based practices, secondary effects of manual procedures, autonomic effects of manual procedures. Total annual research expenditures: $502,000. *Unit head:* Dr. James F. Winterstein, President, 630-889-6604, Fax: 630-889-6600, E-mail: jwinterstein@nuhs.edu. *Application contact:* Victoria Sweeney, Director of Admissions, 800-826-6285 Ext. 6572, Fax: 630-889-6554, E-mail: v.sweeney@nuhs.edu.

See Close-Up on page 2161.

New York Chiropractic College, Professional Program, Seneca Falls, NY 13148-0800. Offers DC. *Accreditation:* CCE. *Faculty:* 48 full-time (19 women), 24 part-time/adjunct (8 women). *Students:* 645 full-time (272 women), 2 part-time (1 woman); includes 76 minority (17 African Americans, 28 Asian Americans or Pacific Islanders, 31 Hispanic Americans), 85 international. Average age 25. 368 applicants, 65% accepted, 191 enrolled. In 2006, 189 degrees awarded. *Degree requirements:* For first-professional, internship in health center (clinic). *Entrance requirements:* 24 credit hours of course work in science (90 credit hours with minimum GPA of 2.5). Additional exam requirements/recommendations for international students: Recommended—TOEFL (minimum score 550 paper-based; 213 computer-based). *Application deadline:* Applications are processed on a rolling basis. Application fee: $60. Electronic applications accepted. *Expenses:* Tuition: Full-time $14,960. Required fees: $680. *Financial support:* In 2006–07, 583 students received support, including 5 fellowships with full tuition reimbursements available (averaging $30,000 per year); Federal Work-Study and scholarships/grants also available. Financial award applicants required to submit FAFSA. *Faculty research:* Anatomy, pathophysiology, neurophysiology biomechanics, musculoskeletal pain syndrome. Total annual research expenditures: $289,850. *Unit head:* Dr. Mike Mestan, Interim Executive Vice President of Academic Affairs, 315-568-3864, Fax: 315-568-3087, E-mail: mlynch@nycc.edu. *Application contact:* Michael Lynch, Director of Admissions, 315-568-3052, Fax: 315-568-3087, E-mail: mlynch@nycc.edu.

See Close-Up on page 2163.

Northwestern Health Sciences University, Northwestern College of Chiropractic, Bloomington, MN 55431-1599. Offers DC. *Accreditation:* CCE. *Entrance requirements:* 90 semester hours of course work in health or science, minimum GPA of 2.5. Additional exam requirements/recommendations for international students: Required—TOEFL (minimum score 540 paper-based; 207 computer-based). Electronic applications accepted. *Faculty research:* Headache, low back pain, neck pain, sciatica, rehabilitative exercise.

Palmer College of Chiropractic, Professional Program, Davenport, IA 52803-5287. Offers DC. *Accreditation:* CCE. Part-time programs available. *Faculty:* 133 full-time (40 women). *Students:* 1,395 full-time (493 women), 15 part-time (4 women). Average age 25. In 2006, 480 degrees awarded. *Entrance requirements:* Previous course work in science, minimum GPA of 2.5. *Application deadline:* For fall admission, 10/1 priority date for domestic students; for spring admission, 2/1 priority date for domestic students. Applications are processed on a rolling basis. Application fee: $50. *Expenses:* Tuition: Full-time $21,690; part-time $282 per credit hour. Required fees: $60. *Financial support:* Federal Work-Study, institutionally sponsored loans, scholarships/grants, and tuition waivers available. Support available to part-time students. Financial award applicants required to submit FAFSA. *Faculty research:* Studies to advance the understanding of chiropractic. *Unit head:* Dr. Dennis Marchiori, Vice President for Academic Affairs, 563-884-5466, Fax: 563-884-5624, E-mail: marchiori_d@palmer.edu. *Application contact:* Karen Eden, Director of Admissions, 563-884-5656, Fax: 563-884-5414, E-mail: pcadmit@palmer.edu.

See Close-Up on page 2165.

Palmer College of Chiropractic, Professional Program–West Campus, San Jose, CA 95134-1617. Offers DC. *Accreditation:* CCE. *Faculty:* 26 full-time (5 women), 14 part-time/adjunct (4 women). *Students:* 249 full-time (94 women), 18 part-time (9 women); includes 81 minority (1 African American, 2 American Indian/Alaska Native, 62 Asian Americans or Pacific Islanders, 16 Hispanic Americans). Average age 28. 73 applicants, 60% accepted, 35 enrolled. In 2006, 117 degrees awarded. *Degree requirements:* For first-professional, clinical internship. *Entrance requirements:* Minimum GPA of 2.5. Additional exam requirements/recommendations for international students: Required—TOEFL. *Application deadline:* Applications are processed on a rolling basis. Application fee: $50. Electronic applications accepted. *Expenses:* Tuition: Full-time $21,690; part-time $282 per credit hour. Required fees: $60. *Financial support:* Career-related internships or fieldwork and Federal Work-Study available. Support available to part-time students. Financial award applicants required to submit FAFSA. *Faculty research:* Low back pain complaints, spinal manipulation therapy, cervical biomechanics, clinical trials, practice guidelines. *Application contact:* Armando Andrews, Senior Admissions Representative, 408-944-6031, Fax: 408-944-6032, E-mail: armando.andrews@palmer.edu.

Parker College of Chiropractic, First Professional Degree Program, Dallas, TX 75229-5668. Offers DC. *Accreditation:* CCE. Part-time programs available. *Faculty:* 100 full-time. *Students:* 950 full-time. Average age 26. 300 applicants, 47% accepted. In 2006, 360 degrees awarded. *Entrance requirements:* Minimum GPA of 2.65. Additional exam requirements/recommendations for international students: Required—TOEFL (minimum score 550 paper-based; 213 computer-based). *Application deadline:* For fall admission, 6/1 priority date for domestic students; for spring admission, 10/1 priority date for domestic students. Applications are processed on a rolling basis. Application fee: $50. Electronic applications accepted. *Financial support:* Federal Work-Study and institutionally sponsored loans available. Support available to part-time students. *Faculty research:* Arterial tonometry, bioenergetics, outcome assessment for clinical care. *Unit head:* Dr. Fabrizio Mancini, President, 972-438-6932. *Application contact:* Selena Reagan, Assistant Director of Recruitment, 972-438-6932 Ext. 7007, E-mail: sreagan@parkercc.edu.

Sherman College of Straight Chiropractic, Professional Program, Spartanburg, SC 29304-1452. Offers DC. *Accreditation:* CCE. *Faculty:* 33 full-time (12 women), 10 part-time/adjunct (8 women). *Students:* 311 full-time (141 women). Average age 28. 101 applicants, 60% accepted, 37 enrolled. In 2006, 102 degrees awarded. *Application deadline:* Applications are processed on a rolling basis. Application fee: $35. Electronic applications accepted. *Financial support:* Career-related internships or fieldwork, Federal Work-Study, institutionally sponsored loans, and scholarships/grants available. Support available to part-time students. Financial award applicants required to submit FAFSA. *Faculty research:* Chiropractic effect of immune response, biomechanics, videofluoroscopy, dynamic motion. Total annual research expenditures: $124,000. *Application contact:* Susan Newlin, Vice President for Enrollment Management, 864-578-8770 Ext. 223, Fax: 864-599-4860, E-mail: admissions@sherman.edu.

Announcement: Sherman College offers an exceptional program in the philosophy, science, and art of chiropractic, leading to a Doctor of Chiropractic degree. Specialized approach, limited enrollment, spacious campus, modern facilities, low student-faculty ratio. Accredited by the Commission on Accreditation of the Council on Chiropractic Education and the Commission on Colleges of the Southern Association of Colleges and Schools.

Southern California University of Health Sciences, Los Angeles College of Chiropractic, Whittier, CA 90609-1166. Offers DC. *Accreditation:* CCE. *Faculty:* 35 full-time (9 women), 59 part-time/adjunct (32 women). *Students:* 456 full-time (163 women), 15 part-time (5 women); includes 200 minority (9 African Americans, 4 American Indian/Alaska Native, 129 Asian Americans or Pacific Islanders, 58 Hispanic Americans). Average age 28. 244 applicants, 61% accepted, 89 enrolled. In 2006, 131 degrees awarded. *Degree requirements:* For first-professional, clinical internship. *Entrance requirements:* Minimum GPA of 2.5, 90 incoming units in required pre-requisite coursework. Additional exam requirements/recommendations for international students: Required—TOEFL (minimum score 500 paper-based; 173 computer-based). *Application deadline:* Applications are processed on a rolling basis. Application fee: $50. Electronic applications accepted. *Financial support:* In 2006–07, 469 students received support. Career-related internships or fieldwork, Federal Work-Study, and scholarships/grants available. Financial award applicants required to submit FAFSA. *Faculty research:* X-rays, motion palpation. *Unit head:* Dr. Todd Knudsen, Dean, 562-947-8755 Ext. 522, Fax: 562-947-5724, E-mail: toddknudsen@scuhs.edu. *Application contact:* Len Rosenthal, Executive Director of Marketing and Enrollment, 562-947-8755 Ext. 305, Fax: 562-947-5724, E-mail: lenrosenthal@scuhs.edu.

Texas Chiropractic College, Professional Program, Pasadena, TX 77505-1699. Offers DC. *Accreditation:* CCE. Part-time programs available. *Degree requirements:* For first-professional, clinical internship. *Entrance requirements:* 2 years of college (90 hours with 30 upper-level hours), minimum 2.5 GPA in last 3 years (90 hours). Additional exam requirements/recommendations for international students: Required—TOEFL. *Faculty research:* Range of motion comparison male vs. female student stress levels.

University of Bridgeport, College of Chiropractic, Bridgeport, CT 06604. Offers DC. *Accreditation:* CCE. *Faculty:* 18 full-time (3 women), 16 part-time/adjunct (4 women). *Students:* 193 full-time (74 women), 3 part-time (1 woman); includes 46 minority (17 African Americans, 1 American Indian/Alaska Native, 20 Asian Americans or Pacific Islanders, 8 Hispanic Americans), 9 international. Average age 29. 153 applicants, 46% accepted, 39 enrolled. In 2006, 36 degrees awarded. *Degree requirements:* For first-professional, thesis. *Application deadline:* For fall admission, 3/1 priority date for domestic students; for spring admission, 7/1 for domestic students. Applications are processed on a rolling basis. Application fee: $75. Electronic applications accepted. *Expenses: Contact institution. Financial support:* In 2006–07, 190 students received support. Federal Work-Study and institutionally sponsored loans available. Support available to part-time students. Financial award application deadline: 6/1; financial award applicants required to submit FAFSA. *Unit head:* Dr. Francis A. Zolli, Dean, 203-576-4279, E-mail: zolli@bridgeport.edu. *Application contact:* Michael Grandison, Director of Chiropractic Admissions, 203-576-4348, Fax: 203-576-4941, E-mail: chiro@bridgeport.edu.

Western States Chiropractic College, Professional Program, Portland, OR 97230-3099. Offers DC. *Accreditation:* CCE. *Degree requirements:* For first-professional, internship. *Entrance requirements:* 3 years of pre-chiropractic study in biological sciences, minimum GPA of 2.5. *Faculty research:* Low back pain.

Cleveland
Chiropractic
College
Kansas City | Los Angeles

CLEVELAND CHIROPRACTIC COLLEGE

Graduate Studies

Programs of Study

Cleveland Chiropractic College maintains campuses in Kansas City, Missouri, and Los Angeles, California. Both offer a Doctor of Chiropractic (D.C.) degree program and a Bachelor of Science (B.S.) degree program in human biology, which includes accelerated prerequisite courses for the D.C. degree program, and an Associate of Arts degree in biological sciences. A student may pursue the B.S. and D.C. degree programs concurrently.

The D.C. degree program allows students to select a twelve-trimester (forty-eight month) or an accelerated ten-trimester (forty-month) course of study. Course work is offered in the basic sciences (anatomy, chemistry, microbiology, pathology, physiology, public health), clinical sciences (diagnosis, radiology), chiropractic sciences (chiropractic principles, practice management, techniques), and practicums (clinical experience). The final trimesters of the program are devoted primarily to clinical practice under the supervision of licensed Doctors of Chiropractic. Both campuses maintain public clinics for this practical experience.

Research Facilities

Both campuses are involved in clinical science research. Students often assist in research in cooperation with faculty members and, in certain instances, may receive financial assistance for research.

Financial Aid

Qualified students at each of the campuses are eligible for federally guaranteed loans. Both campuses of Cleveland Chiropractic College participate in the following federal student financial aid programs: Federal Pell Grant, Federal Work-Study, Federal Perkins Loan (LA), Federal Supplemental Educational Opportunity Grant, Federal Stafford Student Loan, and PLUS Loans. In addition, there are other private loan programs available, including Smart Funds Educational Cash Loans, Sallie Mae Signature Loans, Wells Fargo Education Connection Loans, and Richland Loans. Students may also be eligible for private grants and scholarships.

Cost of Study

For 2006–07, the tuition at Cleveland-KC was $251 per credit for the D.C. degree program and $185 per credit for the B.S. degree program. The tuition at Cleveland-LA was $274 per credit for the D.C. degree program and $230 per credit for the B.S. degree program. Special arrangements may be made for a student who enrolls for less than a full trimester load. The campuses do not charge additional out-of-state fees.

Living and Housing Costs

Monthly rents in the greater Kansas City area start at approximately $400 for a small or shared apartment, and housing is readily available close to campus. In Los Angeles, many apartments are located in the immediate neighborhood of the College. Monthly rent ranges from $600 to $900 for studios and singles.

Student Group

Cleveland-KC and Cleveland-LA currently enroll a combined 847 students, 35 percent of whom are women. Both campuses include students from most states and from many other countries, and each campus subscribes to a nondiscriminatory equal opportunity policy for admission of qualified students.

Location

Noted for its fountains and parks, greater Kansas City has many opportunities for cultural events, education, recreation, and spectator sports. Highlights include the Kansas City Chiefs and Royals, Worlds of Fun, the Nelson Art Gallery, the Kansas City Museum, and the world-famous Country Club Plaza shopping district.

Greater Los Angeles abounds in cultural opportunities and landmarks, such as Disneyland, Universal Studios, Beverly Hills, Hollywood, Mann's Chinese Theater, the Getty Museum, and Will Rogers State Park. One of the entertainment capitals of the world, Los Angeles offers numerous sports activities for the spectator (Angels, Clippers, Dodgers, Kings, Lakers) or the participant (from surfing in the Pacific to snow skiing at nearby areas such as Big Bear).

The College

Cleveland Chiropractic College is a multicampus system with campuses in Kansas City, Missouri, and Los Angeles, California. The College is a private, coeducational, not-for-profit institution of higher education. The primary focus is the preparation of students for the D.C. degree.

The mission of the College lies in the areas of education, scholarship, and service. The educational mission consists of the preparation of competent, entry-level Doctors of Chiropractic who offer the focused, nonduplicated specialty in the detection of the vertebral subluxation complex and its management, primarily through the use of chiropractic spinal adjustments; the preparation of Doctors of Chiropractic as portal-of-entry, primary health-care providers within the health-care delivery system, who are well educated to diagnose, care for the human body, understand and relate fundamental scientific information, and consult with and/or refer to other health-care providers when it is in the best interest of the patient; the continuing education of Doctors of Chiropractic; and the presentation of undergraduate education that leads to a baccalaureate degree or an Associate of Arts degree. The scholarship mission consists of conducting research and scholarly activities that will further chiropractic education and health-care and scholarly collaboration with other institutions of higher education or health-care providers. The service mission consists of clinical service to the community, services to alumni and other professionals, involvement with community health and professional issues, and patient education.

The College is regionally accredited, and its D.C. program is professionally accredited. The College attracts students from all parts of the world and has graduates practicing in all fifty states and internationally.

Applying

Applications may be obtained online or by writing or calling either campus (information given below). Applicants must submit the completed application form, official copies of all transcripts, completed recommendations, and a statement of motivation. Preprofessional requirements include 6 semester hours of biology, 6 semester hours of physics and related studies, 12 semester hours of general and organic chemistry, 6 semester hours of English composition, 3 semester hours of psychology, and 15 semester hours of humanities and/or social sciences. The minimum GPA is 2.5, with no science grade below C. The international equivalency for courses may be accepted. Applicants must have a minimum of 90 preprofessional credit hours to be admitted. Classes matriculate in September, January, and May.

Correspondence and Information

Director of Admissions
Cleveland Chiropractic College–Kansas City Campus
6401 Rockhill Road
Kansas City, Missouri 64131-1181
Phone: 816-501-0100
    800-467-CCKC (toll-free)
Fax: 816-501-0205
E-mail: kc.admissions@cleveland.edu
Web site: http://www.cleveland.edu

Director of Admissions
Cleveland Chiropractic College–Los Angeles Campus
590 North Vermont Avenue
Los Angeles, California 90004-2196
Phone: 323-906-2095
    800-466-CCLA (toll-free)
Fax: 323-906-2024
E-mail: la.admissions@cleveland.edu
Web site: http://www.cleveland.edu

Cleveland Chiropractic College

THE FACULTY AND THEIR RESEARCH

Kansas City Campus

Steve Agocs, Clinician, D.C., Palmer Chiropractic, 2000. Paul B. Barlett, Professor, Ph.D., Ohio State, 1984. D. Clark Beckley, Professor, D.C., Cleveland Chiropractic (Kansas City), 1975. Lawrence D. Beem, Associate Professor, D.C., Cleveland Chiropractic (Kansas City), 1970. Bryan M. Bond, Assistant Professor, D.C., National University of Health Sciences, 1997. Geracimo Bracho, Associate Professor, Ph.D., California, Davis, 1987. Ashley Cleveland, Associate Professor, D.C., Cleveland Chiropractic (Kansas City), 1995. Carl S. Cleveland III, President, D.C., Cleveland Chiropractic (Kansas City), 1975. Jill M. Davis, Associate Professor, D.C., Cleveland Chiropractic (Kansas City), 2007. David L. Deupree, Associate Professor, Ph.D., Arizona, 1986. Charles F. Dorlac, Assistant Professor, Ph.D., Missouri–Kansas City, 1981. Kenneth Elkins, Professor, M.S., Oklahoma, 1968. David Fray, Instructor, D.C., Cleveland Chiropractic (Kansas City), 1975. Mark H. Gilgus, Instructor, J.D., Missouri–Kansas City, 1978. Clinton Gowan III, Assistant Professor, D.C., Cleveland Chiropractic (Kansas City), 1995. Sheldon D. Guenther, Adjunct Faculty, D.C., Cleveland Chiropractic (Kansas City), 2001. Kim R. Hamilton, Associate Professor, D.C., Cleveland Chiropractic (Kansas City), 1992. Ned U. Heese, Assistant Professor, D.C., Logan Chiropractic, 1974. Lawrence J. Hurd, Assistant Professor, D.C., Palmer Chiropractic, 1978. Sabina Jawaid, Instructor, Ph.D., Aberdeen (Scotland), 2000. Tobi Jeurink, Instructor, D.C., Cleveland Chiropractic (Kansas City), 2001. Michelle Kalatsky, Instructor, D.C., Cleveland Chiropractic (Kansas City), 2003. Reid Ketteler, Instructor, D.C., Cleveland Chiropractic (Kansas City), 1998. Matthew B. Kounkel, Instructor, D.C., Cleveland Chiropractic (Kansas City), 2002. Curt A. Krause, Instructor, D.C., Palmer Chiropractic, 1999. Stephen P. Larsen, Professor; Ph.D., North Texas State, 1972. Catherine Leduc, Assistant Professor, D.C., Cleveland Chiropractic (Kansas City), 1993. J. Alan Lovejoy, Associate Professor, D.C., Palmer Chiropractic, 1978. Alexander Makarov, Associate Professor, M.D., Odessa Medical, 1994. John D. McGlaughlin, Instructor, M.A., Missouri–Kansas City, 2001. Michael D. Moore, Associate Professor, D.C., Palmer Chiropractic, 1982. Robert Moore, Associate Professor, D.C., Cleveland Chiropractic (Kansas City), 1995. Thomas K. Nichols, Professor, D.C., Palmer Chiropractic, 1977. Mark Pfefer, Assistant Professor, D.C., Cleveland Chiropractic (Kansas City), 1988. Michael Ramcharan, Instructor, D.C., Life University, 2003. Daniel Redwood, Associate Professor, D.C., Palmer Chiropractic, 1979. Debra K. Robertson-Moore, Assistant Professor, D.C., Cleveland Chiropractic (Kansas City), 1996. J. Kevin Robinson, Instructor, M.B.A., Phoenix–San Francisco, 1999. Ruth Sandefur, Professor, D.C., Cleveland Chiropractic (Kansas City), 1967. Timothy Schoof, Associate Professor, Ed.D., Missouri–Kansas City, 2003. Max Joseph Skidmore, Instructor, M.F.A., Missouri–Kansas City, 2004. Thomas G. Smallridge, Instructor, M.A., Central Missouri State, 1970. Richard Strunk, Clinician, D.C., Palmer Chiropractic, 2003. Stephanie N. Teasley, Instructor, M.A., Colorado, 1997. Marcia Thomas, Professor, M.A., Missouri, 1975. Rickard Thomas, Professor, D.C., Cleveland Chiropractic (Kansas City), 1977. William E. Tuttle, Associate Professor, D.C., Cleveland Chiropractic (Kansas City), 1980. Nathan L. Uhl, Instructor, D.C., Cleveland Chiropractic (Kansas City), 2004. Adi S. Virgi, Assistant Professor, Ph.D., London, 1967. G. Michael Whitehead, Professor, D.C., Logan Chiropractic, 1979.

Los Angeles Campus

Assibi Z. Abudu, Associate Professor, M.D., USC, 1975. William W. Adler, Assistant Professor, D.C., Los Angeles College of Chiropractic, 1992. Cecilia L. Anderson, Professor, D.C., Cleveland Chiropractic (Los Angeles), 1979. Alexander Annala, Associate Professor, Ph.D., USC, 1995. Lydia Baghdaseriani, Assistant Professor, D.C., Cleveland Chiropractic (Los Angeles), 1995, FICPA. James Brantingham, Associate Professor, D.C., Los Angeles Chiropractic, 1983. FCC. Gary Bustin, Assistant Professor, D.C., 1981, D.A.C.B.R., 1987, Los Angeles Chiropractic. Lily Cabellon, Associate Professor, M.D., Manila Central, 1952. Lucila T. Calimag, Associate Professor, M.D., Far Eastern (Philippines), 1966. Daryl Capen, Instructor, D.C., Cleveland Chiropractic (Los Angeles), 2003. Richard Carr, Assistant Professor, Psy.D., American Behavioral Studies Institute, 2000. Mitchell Carter, Assistant Professor, D.C., Cleveland Chiropractic (Los Angeles), 1995. Carol A. Claus, Professor, D.C., Cleveland Chiropractic (Los Angeles), 1988, FICPA. Carl S. Cleveland III, Professor, D.C., Cleveland Chiropractic (Kansas City), 1975. Susan Deno, Assistant Professor, M.A., Boston University, 1994. Clarence E. Franklin, Associate Professor and Counselor, M.Ed., Albertson College of Idaho, 1968, D.C., Los Angeles Chiropractic, 1983. David F. Gendreau, Assistant Professor, D.C., 1989, D.A.C.B.R., Los Angeles Chiropractic, 1993. Gary Globe, Associate Professor, D.C., Cleveland Chiropractic (Los Angeles), 1981, M.B.A., Redlands, 1994. Antonio J. Gonsalves Jr., Assistant Professor, D.C., Cleveland Chiropractic (Los Angeles), 1991. Keith Henry, Assistant Professor, D.C., Cleveland Chiropractic (Los Angeles), 1996. Marian A. Hicks, Assistant Professor, M.S.L.S., North Carolina at Chapel Hill, 1979. Leila L. Iler, Professor, Ed.D., Pepperdine, 1994. Muffit Jensen, Professor, D.C., Cleveland Chiropractic (Los Angeles), 1990. Glenn Johnson, Professor, D.C., Cleveland Chiropractic (Los Angeles), 1985, FICPA. Ray Kato, Assistant Professor, Pharm.D., USC, 1962. Milad Keshavarz, Instructor, D.C., Cleveland Chiropractic (Los Angeles), 2004. Gyaneshwar Khare, Professor, D.V.M., Agra (India), 1961, Ph.D., Kansas State, 1966. Bryant Koh, Instructor, D.C., Cleveland Chiropractic (Los Angeles), 1998, FICPA. Felix Lee, Assistant Professor, D.C., Los Angeles College of Chiropractic, 2000. Howard Maize, Instructor, D.C., Cleveland Chiropractic (Los Angeles), 1994. Stephan M. Mayer, Associate Professor, D.C., Cleveland Chiropractic (Los Angeles), 1986. Anita Mork, Associate Professor, M.S., UCLA, 1980. Craig Morris, Professor, D.C., Cleveland Chiropractic (Los Angeles), 1981. Andrew Park, Assistant Professor, D.C., Los Angeles College of Chiropractic, 1998. Shawn Steel, Assistant Professor, J.D., Northrop, 1978. William Strickland, Assistant Professor, D.C., Cleveland Chiropractic (Los Angeles), 1994. Randy P. Talai, Instructor, D.C., Cleveland Chiropractic (Los Angeles), 1999. Victor Tong, Radiologist, Professor, D.C., Logan Chiropractic, 1979, D.A.C.B.R., Los Angeles Chiropractic, 1983. Michael Valentine, Assistant Professor, Ph.D., City of Hope/Beckman, 2000.

NATIONAL UNIVERSITY OF HEALTH SCIENCES

Doctor of Chiropractic Medicine
Doctor of Naturopathic Medicine
Master of Science in Acupuncture
Master of Science in Oriental Medicine

Programs of Study

National University of Health Sciences (NUHS), formerly The National College of Chiropractic, was founded in 1906 and proudly claims a 100-year history as the standard bearer in educating chiropractic physicians. With an emphasis on rigorous science education, broad-scope clinical training, and evidence-based treatment modalities, National trains its students to enter the health-care arena as primary-care chiropractic physicians.

As the institution moves into its second century, National is transforming its campus into a hub of complementary health-care education. National's goal is to develop, encourage, and promote collegiality among members of the chiropractic profession, the complementary and alternative professions, and allopathic medicine.

In addition to its ten-trimester Doctor of Chiropractic degree, National University is accredited by the Higher Learning Commission of the North Central Association of Colleges and Schools to offer a ten-trimester Doctor of Naturopathic Medicine degree, a seven-trimester Master of Science in Acupuncture, a nine-trimester Master of Science in Oriental Medicine, a Bachelor of Biomedical Science completion degree, an Associate of Applied Science in Massage Therapy, a Massage Therapy Certificate, and a Chiropractic Assistant Certificate. National's massage program is accredited by the Commission on Massage Therapy Accreditation (COMTA).

As one of only two institutions in the U.S. to combine chiropractic, oriental, and naturopathic medicine on one campus, National students have the unique opportunity to participate in integrated learning situations. While these professions often compete with each other, NUHS students are able to dialogue together, share collaborative research and clinical-care opportunities, and take a leading role in mainstream health care.

In addition to the above programs, NUHS also offers its Doctor of Chiropractic graduates the opportunity to enter residency programs in family practice and research, as well as residencies in diagnostic imaging and clinical practice, which can lead to a Master of Science in Diagnostic Imaging and a Master of Science in Advanced Clinical Practice.

Research Facilities

National University has one of the most prestigious research facilities among chiropractic colleges, with laboratories dedicated to spinal biomechanics, interdisciplinary research, and biological resources. The NUHS Department of Research promotes the advancement of knowledge pertaining to the practice of chiropractic and other aspects of complementary and alternative medicine by performing and encouraging high-quality, efficiently conducted ethical research. In the last seven years alone, NUHS researchers and faculty have received more than thirty-eight grants for research and have written over eighty-five journal articles and sixty-seven abstract and submission presentations.

National is the only chiropractic college to publish three scientific journals: the *Journal of Chiropractic Humanities*, the *Journal of Chiropractic Medicine*, and the *Journal of Manipulative and Physiological Therapeutics (JMPT)*, the official research journal of the American Chiropractic Association.

The first chiropractic college to own its own Magnetic Resonance Imaging (MRI), the University's MRI Center is utilized for student, patient, and research situations.

Financial Aid

The University's Office of Financial Aid helps students finance their chiropractic education through grants, loans, scholarships, and employment on campus. Federal funds for higher education become available when there is a gap between educational costs and the ability of the student to pay. The principal responsibility for educational costs rests with the student. Most of the University's students take advantage of financial aid in one form or another and augment their income with employment. A comprehensive packet of information on all financial aid programs is available from the Office of Financial Aid. The University's institutional loan default rate is 1.3 percent.

Cost of Study

For the 2006–07 academic year, tuition in the doctoral and master's programs was $329 per credit hour, averaging $8934 per trimester. Tuition for the certificate programs was $13.18 per clock hour. Additional costs that students incur during their study are for books, diagnostic instruments, and supplies.

Living and Housing Costs

The University offers on-campus dormitory and apartment-style housing. Costs range from $1487 per trimester for a dorm room for a single student to $3261 per trimester for a two-bedroom apartment. The University is currently undergoing a multimillion-dollar renovation of its four residence halls. Private apartments and rental homes are also available in nearby suburbs.

Student Group

The total student enrollment for all programs stands at approximately 550 students with 53 percent women and 47 percent men. The average age of an NUHS student is about 22. The majority of the professional degree students are recent college graduates or career changers, with men making up approximately 65 percent of this group. The majority of the certificate program students are women.

Location

The University is just 20 miles from Chicago, a cultural and industrial hub and home to some of the nation's finest museums, entertainment and sports centers, zoos, restaurants, stores, beaches, and other recreation areas. National's location in west suburban Lombard places it in a community of 42,000 that is characterized by a broad-based economy and a moderate cost-of-living level, excellent public and private schools, diverse employment opportunities, and an abundance of shopping, restaurants, and sports and entertainment venues.

The University

The 32-acre campus has a student center, lecture halls, a fitness center, teaching and research laboratories, and housing facilities. A Training and Assessment Center (TAC) allows for remote observation and recording of student-patient interactions with standardized patients and assessment of their clinical competency. The Learning Resource Center offers bibliographic collections and services carefully tailored to meet the needs of health-care students, faculty members, and professionals.

National's teaching clinics include a campus health-care center and student clinic, the Chicago General Health Service, a suburban Aurora clinic, and two nonprofit clinics serving the uninsured and underprivileged in downtown Chicago.

Approximately thirty clubs are active under the auspices of the Student Council, ranging from sports clubs to religious organizations and professional fraternities. Also available to students are an academic advising program, a tutorial service, and many health services at no charge.

Applying

NUHS admits new classes in January, May, and September. Students are encouraged to apply one year in advance. All doctoral and master's degree students must have earned a bachelor's degree in the arts or sciences from an accredited college or university, with a minimum cumulative grade point average of 2.5 on a 4.0 scale.

In order for chiropractic students to be successful at National, the University maintains specific course requirements, including 6 semester hours of English language skills, 3 of psychology, 15 of social sciences or humanities, 6 of biological sciences, 12 of chemistry, and 6 of physics and related studies. For details on the required science courses, prospective students should consult the University Bulletin. A Prerequisite Program is available for applicants who do not meet specific science requirements.

Correspondence and Information

Office of Admissions
National University of Health Sciences
200 East Roosevelt Road
Lombard, Illinois 60148-4583

Phone: 630-629-2000
       800-826-6285 (toll-free)
E-mail: admissions@nuhs.edu
Web site: http://www.nuhs.edu

National University of Health Sciences

THE FACULTY

Faculty of the University
Corrine Acosta, B.A.A., CMT.
Joe Adkins, CMT.
Shawn Allen, D.C., DABCO.
Brian Anderson, D.C., CCN.
Robert F. Appleyard, Ph.D.
Cindy Belles, Ph.D.
Antonio Bifero, D.C.
Jeffrey K. Bergin, D.C., DABCI., FAACP.
Edward J. Bifulco, D.C.
William Bogar, D.C., DACBR.
Marcia Brandes, CMT.
Samson Cahill, D.C., DACBR.
Jerrilyn A. Cambron, D.C., M.P.H., Ph.D.
James A. Christiansen, Ph.D.
Karin Chrysty, CMT.
Patricia Coe, D.C.
Ezra Cohen, D.C., CMT.
Kristina Conner, N.D., M.Ac.
Ann Marie Craig, CMT.
Gregory D. Cramer, D.C., Ph.D.
Susan A. Darby, Ph.D.
Vincent F. DeBono, D.C., CSCS.
Veronica DeLaCruz, Ph.D.
Daniel R. Driscoll, D.C.
Manuel A. Duarte, D.C., DABCO, DACBSP, CCSP, CSCS.
Terry M. Elder, D.C.
Robert Frysztak, Ph.D.
Brian Fuller, D.C.
David A. Gidcumb, D.C., DABCO.
Behty Harrison, D.O.M., L.Ac.
Larry L. Hill, D.C., CCSP.
Amanda Hobbs, CMT.
Bruce Hodges, D.C.
Ann Hoeffel, B.S., CMT.
William J. Hogan, D.C., D.N., DABCI.
C. Robert Humphreys, D.C., DACNB.
Grant C. Iannelli, D.C., DABCI.
Russell A. Iwami, M.A.L.S.
James Jedlicka, D.C.
Claire Johnson, D.C.
Theodore L. Johnson Jr., D.C., DABCI.
Simone J. Joseph, D.C.
Anna Jurik, D.C.; RD., LDN.
Muhammad A. Khan, M.D., DTCD, MCPS.
Charles J. Kuehner, D.C.
Yihyun Kwon, D.C.
Stephen C. Lee, M.S.
Thomas Lotus, D.C.
David Luyando, D.C.
Christine Lynch, Reflexology Certificate.
Barbara Malik, CMT.
Marc McRae, D.C., DACBN, CNS.
Robert F. Metcalf, D.C.

Bridget Murphy, CMT.
Christena V. Nicholson, D.C., DACBI.
Nicholas Nowicki, D.C.
David Parish, D.C., DACBSP, CSCS., CCSP.
Sandy Pearce, CMT.
Josephine Polich, D.C., DCAH.
Jaya Prakash, M.D.
Tari S. Reinke, D.C.
Daniel L. Richardson, Ph.D., D.N., DAANC.
Bonnie Ricicia, CMT.
Matthew Schipma, Ph.D.
Scott Selby, D.C.
Robert C. Shiel, Ph.D.
Monica Silva, D.C.
Fraser Smith, N.D.
Keith Smith, Ed.D., M.B.A.
Jonathan Soltys, D.C., DABFP.
Joseph Stiefel, D.C.
Nancy Steinke, M.Sc.
Michelle Steinys, D.C.
Virgil J. Stoia, D.C.
Frank Strehl, D.C., DABCI.
Howard Streit, D.C., RPh.
Barbara Sullivan, Ph.D.
Randy L. Swenson, D.C., M.H.P.E.
Charles C. Tasharski, D.C.
Derek Talbot, D.C., CNC.
Vrajlal H. Vyas, M.D.
Lurlean Washington, CMT.
Joyce E. Whitehead, M.A.L.S.
Debbie Wilkonski, D.C., CMT.
James F. Winterstein, D.C., DACBR.
Heather Wisniewski, D.C.
Sarah Zender, CMT.

Postprofessional Faculty
Shawn Allen, D.C., DABCO.
Barclay W. Bakkum, D.C., Ph.D.
Jeffrey K. Bergin, D.C., DABCI., FAACP.
Edward J. Bifulco, D.C.
John L. Black, D.C., Ph.D., DABCO., CCSP.
Michael T. Buehler, D.C., DACBR.
Sam Cahill, D.C., DACBR.
Corey Campbell, D.C.
Joseph R. Carter, D.C.
Scott A. Chapman, D.C., DABCO.
James M. Cox, D.C., DACBR.
Leanne N. Cupon, D.C., DABFP, DACRB.
Gregory D. Cramer, D.C., Ph.D.
Susan A. Darby, Ph.D.
Vincent DeBono, D.C., CSCS.
Gary Ditson, D.C.
Manuel A. Duarte, D.C., DABCO., DACBSP, CCSP, CSCS.
Terry M. Elder, D.C.
Patricia Flynn, D.C., DABCO.

Scott D. Fonda, D.C., DABCO.
Nicholas Gatto, D.C., NCCAOM.
Robert Gordon, D.C.
Douglas Gregerson, D.C., DACBR.
Zhengang Guo, D.O.M.
Leena Guptha, N.D., D.O., L.Ac., Ph.D.
Warren I. Hammer, D.C., DABCO.
Larry L. Hill, D.C., CCSP.
Ann Hoeffel, B.S., CMT.
Robert Humphreys, D.C., DACBN.
Grant C. Iannelli, D.C., DACBI.
Warren T. Jahn, D.C., DABCC, DABCO, DABFP, DABIME, DACBSP.
Gayle M. Jasinski, D.C., DACBO.
Mary Jennings, D.C., DNCCAOM.
Kathy Joy, M.B.A.
Clifford L. Kearns, D.C., DNBHE.
Leo M. Kenney, D.C., CCSP.
Jack Kessinger, D.C., DABCI.
David D. Kessler, D.C., DABCO, CCSP.
Natasha Kim, D.C., DABCO, NCCAOM.
Alan B. Korbett, D.C., D.O., DABCO, DABCN, CCSP.
Matthew Kowalski, D.C., DABCO.
Robert Leach, D.C.
Richard A. Leverone, D.C.
Kat Linaker, D.C., DACBR.
Thomas Lotus, D.C.
Timothy McCullough, D.C.
James Michael Menke, D.C.
Pamela A. Olson, DNCCAOM.
John C. Pammer, D.C., DACBR.
David B. Parish, D.C., DACBSP. CCSP, CSCS.
Stephen M. Perle, D.C., CCSP.
Tricia A. Pike, D.C., DABCO.
Julie A. Plezbert, D.C., DNBHE.
David Radford, D.C., DAAPM.
Daniel L. Richardson, Ph.D.
David Seaman, D.C., DABCN, DACBN.
William Shelton, D.C., DABCI.
Robert C. Shiel, Ph.D.
Jerrold J. Simon, D.C., DACBN, DACRB, DABDA., FACCN, CCN.
Dennis R. Skogsbergh, D.C., DABCO, DACBR.
Jonathan Soltys, D.C., DABFP.
Louis Sportelli, D.C.
Frank Strehl, D.C., DABCI.
Jon A. Sunderlage, D.C., DNCCAOM.
Joy A. Sunderlage, D.C., DNCCAOM, DICACCP.
Rand S. Swenson, Ph.D., D.C., M.D.
Randy L. Swenson, D.C., M.H.P.E.
Charles C. Tasharski, D.C.
Scott Varley, D.C.
James F. Winterstein, D.C., DACBR.
Steven Yeomans, D.C., DABCO.

National University of Health Sciences.

NEW YORK CHIROPRACTIC COLLEGE

Program of Study

New York Chiropractic College offers a rigorous but highly rewarding program leading to the degree of Doctor of Chiropractic (D.C.) and prepares students for a professional career in chiropractic health care as well as in related research and teaching. The program is ten trimesters in length and takes five academic years to complete. New York Chiropractic College offers classes year round, and students generally complete the program in forty months of continuous study. The program is open only to full-time students. It includes three trimesters of internship at one of the College's three health centers.

Several 3+1 joint-degree B.S./D.C. programs, which enable the student to save a year in the completion of the two degrees, are offered. NYCC's Postgraduate Division offers continuing education for chiropractors to further their professional development and to satisfy the license renewal requirements of various states.

Research Facilities

NYCC research department activity encompasses a wide variety of research interests. The research programs incorporate sports medicine and chiropractic geriatric studies, biomechanics, nutrition, and pathophysiology. The College supports three primary research laboratories: a biochemistry laboratory; a biodynamics laboratory, where sports chiropractic and related ergonomic and neurophysiology research is conducted; and a biomechanical/gait research laboratory. All laboratories are equipped with state-of-the-art technology capable of supporting extensive research activity in those respective areas. The laboratories are housed in an 8,000-square-foot research facility that contains administrative offices as well as a bone histology and microscopy laboratory and several computer graphics and data analysis workstations.

Financial Aid

Financial aid is generally available on the basis of need, as evidenced by information supplied on the FAFSA as well as an institutional application. Federal sources of aid include Federal Perkins Loans, Federal Work-Study, and veterans' benefits to eligible students. Limited grants are available under New York State's Tuition Assistance Program (TAP). Students may obtain Federal Stafford Student Loans and may compete for scholarships offered by chiropractic associations, private foundations, and NYCC.

Cost of Study

Only full-time students are admitted into the doctoral program. For 2007–08, tuition is $8000 per trimester; tuition and fees for the calendar year (three trimesters) from September 2007 through summer 2008 are estimated at $24,000. The estimated cost of textbooks, equipment, and supplies is an additional $800 per trimester.

Living and Housing Costs

NYCC offers excellent on-campus housing in eight residence halls. The cost of a single room is $1970; a double room is $1015; suites for married students are $2460 to $2805 (these are trimester rates). Meal plans are additional and range from $325 to $950 per trimester. Off-campus housing is available and comparatively priced. The cost of living in the area is substantially lower than that of urban areas.

Student Group

New York Chiropractic College's 700 students (including senior interns) come from more than twenty states and several other countries. The majority are residents of the Northeast. Students range in age from 21 to over 55, with the largest age group consisting of those in their mid-20s. Thirty percent of the students are women, and 80 percent of all students hold a baccalaureate or higher degree. Many students participate in intramural sports and student government as well as in the more than thirty student organizations that pursue such special interests as nutrition, sports injuries, publications, and research. Numerous technique clubs (e.g., Applied Kinesiology, Gonstead) are active on campus.

Location

New York Chiropractic College is located in Seneca Falls, New York, in the scenic wine-growing region of the Finger Lakes, a popular vacation spot less than a 45-minute drive from Syracuse, Rochester, and Ithaca. Outpatient clinics are located in Buffalo, Seneca Falls, and Levittown (Long Island). The 286-acre campus has 250 feet of frontage property on Cayuga Lake, the largest of the Finger Lakes. The College borders a state park and has a nine-hole, par 3 golf course on the campus.

The College

Established in 1919 in New York City as Columbia Institute of Chiropractic, the College is the oldest chiropractic institution in the Northeast. In 1976, it moved to Nassau County on suburban Long Island and moved again to a larger campus in upstate New York in 1991. The College is accredited by the Middle States Association of Colleges and Schools and by the Council on Chiropractic Education. It holds an Absolute Charter from the Board of Regents of the University of the State of New York.

Applying

Information and application forms may be obtained by visiting NYCC's Web site or by calling 800-234-6922 (toll-free). Admission is a continuous process; there are entering classes in September, January, and May of each year. Approximately 300 students are admitted for each year, and applicants are encouraged to apply ten to twelve months in advance of their desired entrance date. Reference forms are supplied upon receipt of an application.

Correspondence and Information

Admissions Office
New York Chiropractic College
2360 Route 89
Seneca Falls, New York 13148-0800
Phone: 315-568-3040
        800-234-6922 (toll-free)
E-mail: enrolnow@nycc.edu
Web site: http://www.nycc.edu

New York Chiropractic College

THE FACULTY

Anatomy

M. Elizabeth Bedford, Ph.D., Kent State, 1994.
Andrew S. Choi, D.C., New York Chiropractic, 2000.
Michael L. Lentini, D.C., National Chiropractic, 1991.
Raj J. Philomin, Ph.D., Madras Medical College (India), 1986.
Maria Thomadaki, D.C., New York Chiropractic, 1994.
Robert A. Walker, Ph.D., Kent State, 1989.
Michael P. Zumpano, Ph.D., SUNY at Buffalo, 1997.

Physiopathology

David S. Aberant, M.S., LIU, C.W. Post, 1970.
Mary E. Balliett, D.C., New York Chiropractic, 1988.
Deborah A. Barr, Sc.D., Boston University, 1988.
Scott Coon, D.C., New York Chiropractic, 1994.
Chithambaram S. Philomin, M.B.B.S., Stanley Medical College, 1989.
Carolyn M. Pover, Ph.D., Bristol, 1986.
Veronica M. Sciotti, Ph.D., SUNY at Buffalo, 1988.
Lee C. VanDusen, D.C., National Chiropractic, 1985.

Diagnosis and Clinical Practice

Lisa K. Bloom, D.C., New York Chiropractic, 1990.
Susan E. Conley, D.C., New York Chiropractic, 1995.
Christine M. Cunningham, M.S., SUNY at Stony Brook, 1988.
Paul E. Dougherty, D.C., Logan Chiropractic, 1990.
Margaret M. Finn, D.C., New York Chiropractic, 1992.
Fiona Jarrett-Thelwell, D.C., New York Chiropractic, 1994.
Stephen J. Mesiti, D.C., New York Chiropractic, 1997.
Joseph A. Miller, D.C., National Chiropractic, 1991.
Michael J. O'Connor, D.C., New York Chiropractic, 1982.
Julie A. Plezbert, D.C., National Chiropractic, 1986.
Robert Ruddy, D.C., New York Chiropractic, 1996.
Fred L. SanFilipo, D.C., New York Chiropractic, 1982.
Judy M. Silvestrone, D.C., Palmer Chiropractic, 1984.
John A. M. Taylor, D.C., Canadian Memorial Chiropractic, 1979.
Meghan B. VanLoon, D.C., Northwestern Chiropractic, 1991.
Jeneen L. Wallace, D.C., New York Chiropractic, 1997.

Technique and Principles

Karen A. Bobak, D.C., National Chiropractic, 1986.
Brian M. Cunningham, D.C., New York Chiropractic, 1986.
John L. DeCicco, D.C., New York Chiropractic, 1982.
James R. Ebbets, D.C., New York Chiropractic, 1992.
Lillian M. Ford, D.C., New York Chiropractic, 1985.

Christopher J. Good, D.C., Palmer Chiropractic, 1982.
Sandra Hartwell-Ford, D.C., New York Chiropractic, 1996.
Lloyd E. Henby, D.C., National Chiropractic, 1952.
Michael E. Howard, D.C., Life Chiropractic, 1981.
Thomas McCloughan, D.C., New York Chiropractic, 1993.
Hunter A. Mollin, D.C., New York Chiropractic, 1980.
David F. Petters, D.C., New York Chiropractic, 1986.
Christopher P. Ryan, D.C., New York Chiropractic, 1987.
Paul W. Ryan, D.C., New York Chiropractic, 1989.
Eileen C. Santipadri, D.C., Palmer Chiropractic, 1981.
David A. Shinherr, D.C., New York Chiropractic, 1995.
Edward J. Sullivan, D.C., Northwestern Chiropractic, 1991.
Michael S. Young, D.C., New York Chiropractic, 1996.

Research

JeanMarie Burke, Ph.D., Indiana, 1991.

Depew Health Center

Margaret M. Anticola, D.C., Life Chiropractic, 1986.
Charles D. Coyle, D.C., National Chiropractic, 1988.
Mark A. Dux, D.C., Western States Chiropractic, 1980.
Daniel R. Johnson, D.C., Logan Chiropractic, 1981.
Sherri L. LaShomb, D.C., Palmer Chiropractic, 1988.
David L. Ribakove, D.C., New York Chiropractic, 1992.
Mark D. Sokolowski, D.C., Palmer Chiropractic, 1985.
Mercedes M. Trzcinski, D.C., Palmer Chiropractic, 1981.

Levittown Health Center

Patricia M. Flynn, D.C., National Chiropractic, 1996.
Charles A. Hemsey, D.C., Life Chiropractic, 1981.
Lloyd H. Kupferman, D.C., New York Chiropractic, 1981.
Frank S. Lizzio, D.C., New York Chiropractic, 1980.
Mariangela Penna, D.C., New York Chiropractic, 1986.
Michael G. Perillo, D.C., National Chiropractic, 1978.
Joseph E. Pfeifer, D.C., New York Chiropractic, 1984.
Lana K. Slinkard, D.C., National Chiropractic, 1985.
Veronica A. Wicks, D.C., New York Chiropractic, 1988.

Seneca Falls Health Center

Steven Feldman, D.C., New York Chiropractic, 1981.
Dennis M. Homack, D.C., New York Chiropractic, 1997.
Wendy L. Maneri, D.C., New York Chiropractic, 1999.
William H. Sherwood, D.C., National Chiropractic, 1990.

NYCC's newest academic building.

A radiology faculty member reviews X-rays with students.

PALMER COLLEGE OF CHIROPRACTIC

Division of Graduate Studies

Programs of Study

Palmer College of Chiropractic was founded to train students to become chiropractors. The orientation toward and focus on health, rather than on symptoms and disease, is central to the College's philosophy. Students are trained for a practice in which they serve as primary-care providers who apply their skills toward wellness promotion and health assessment. The College is accredited by The Higher Learning Commission and is a member of the North Central Association of Colleges and Schools. The Doctor of Chiropractic (D.C.) degree program is accredited by the Commission on Accreditation of the Council on Chiropractic Education.

Offered on all three campuses, the D.C. program offers more hours in anatomy, physiology, diagnosis, and neurology than typical medical school programs. During the first year, students learn all about the basic sciences that are the foundation of chiropractic, such as anatomy, physiology, chemistry, diagnosis, and neurology, along with pathology and bacteriology. During the second year, courses in chiropractic technique, X ray, and practice management are added. The third year is devoted to caring for patients in an outpatient clinic setting, as well as business preparation.

The Davenport campus also offers master's degrees. The Master of Science in anatomy prepares students for doctoral programs and continuing careers in higher education. Students may opt for a research emphasis in anatomy, biomechanics, or neuroscience. The Master of Science in clinical research, offered in partnership with the University of Iowa College of Public Health, trains doctors of chiropractic for careers as clinical scientists. The curriculum consists of 36 credit hours, including required courses, independent study, research ethics, biostatistics, presentation skills, original research, and elective courses.

Research Facilities

The David D. Palmer Health Sciences Library on the Davenport campus is the most comprehensive library of any chiropractic school. Serving as an important health science resource for the entire state of Iowa, it houses almost 50,000 volumes of scientific and biomedical journals and texts. The library also houses the most extensive chiropractic archives in the world.

The Palmer Center for Chiropractic Research, also on the Davenport campus, is one of only thirteen NIH-funded complementary and alternative medicine (CAM) research centers in the nation. Shared facilities include a computer lab, research library, and protected data storage. The biomechanics laboratories contain the equipment to support biomechanics and interdisciplinary research, and the investigators assist in developing equipment used in the neuroscience laboratories. The microscopy laboratories support all forms of imaging of specimens, including preparatory equipment, light microscopy, and electron microscopy. The animal care laboratories include an animal behavioral laboratory and veterinary surgical suites. Animal use complies with U.S. regulatory agencies and the Animals Welfare Act.

The San Jose campus library houses 9,650 books and more than 12,000 periodicals, and its assets include nearly 1,000 videotapes and audiotapes on chiropractic history, practice management, and patient-care procedures, as well as a journal center that subscribes to more than 300 magazines, trade publications, and chiropractic association newsletters from around the world.

Financial Aid

Teaching and research assistantships may be granted to qualified students for a maximum of two years, depending upon availability of funds and the recommendation of their department. Under the Stafford Student Loan Program, graduate students may borrow up to $8500 per year in subsidized loans and $22,500 in unsubsidized loans. Federal Work-Study is available for students who are enrolled at least half-time and are in good academic standing. Veterans and their dependents may be eligible for aid under the Veterans Educational Assistance Program. To be eligible for most types of financial aid, students must submit the Free Application for Federal Student Aid (FAFSA).

Cost of Study

In 2006–07, students paid $295 per academic credit, plus an activity fee of $20 per trimester and a one-time Intent To Graduate Fee of $80. During each academic term, students must purchase textbooks that will be used throughout the program. The cost of books and equipment is estimated to be less than $600 each trimester.

Living and Housing Costs

The school owns eight apartment buildings within three blocks of the campus. Students typically pay $225–$400 per month for a one-bedroom apartment or $350–$500 per month for a two-bedroom apartment. Other apartments and houses are available within a few blocks of the school. Rent varies depending on the accommodation's size and location.

Student Group

The average student is 27 years old, but the students range from 19 to 56. Thirty percent of the students are married, and approximately 35 percent are women. Most students come from throughout the United States, but other countries, including Canada and Korea, are well represented.

Student Outcomes

Graduates of the College are able to secure employment in a number of organizations and perform a variety of functions. Alumni are currently working as sole practitioners, group practitioners, sports team chiropractors, hospital staff members, researchers, educators, speakers, and administrators.

Location

Nestled along the banks of the Mississippi River, Davenport is a great place to live and to visit. It offers the Figge Art Museum, art galleries, a symphony, a theater, and a botanical center, as well as fifteen public golf courses, eighty local parks, and 60 miles of bike trails. The PGA's John Deere Classic attracts 80,000 spectators each year, and the Bix Biederbeck Jazz Festival draws another 20,000. A second campus is in San Jose, California. Founded in 1980 and a part of California's Bay Area, the campus is close to the sights, sounds, entertainment, and culture of San Francisco. The College's third campus is located in Port Orange, Florida, a thriving resort community of 50,000 near Daytona Beach.

The College

Palmer College of Chiropractic was founded by D. D. Palmer, the founder of chiropractic, in 1897. The College currently operates three campuses, each with a mission to educate and prepare students to become Doctors of Chiropractic qualified to serve as primary health care providers who are competent in wellness promotion, health assessment, diagnosis, and the chiropractic management of the patient's health-care needs. Palmer alumni make up one third of the chiropractors currently in practice worldwide, with many holding leadership positions in chiropractic organizations and establishing successful careers in education and research.

Applying

Prospective students are required to submit an application form, online or by mail, at least one year prior to their desired term of entry; a copy of their high school diploma or transcripts; transcripts of previous college or university work, with a minimum 2.5 GPA; a two-page typewritten essay covering the development of their interest in chiropractic, their career goals, and their reason for choosing one of the Palmer campuses; and a $50 nonrefundable application fee. Two letters of recommendation (one from a doctor of chiropractic and one from a college faculty member) are suggested but not required. An interview may be required for some candidates. The deadline to apply is August 1. Admission is granted to the fall-winter trimester. International students must also submit proof of English proficiency. TOEFL scores of at least 500 on the paper-based test (173 computer-based test) are a suitable means of establishing such proficiency. June 1 is the application deadline for international students.

Correspondence and Information

Division of Graduate Studies
Palmer College of Chiropractic
1000 Brady Street
Davenport, Iowa 52803
Phone: 563-884-5307
        800-682-1625 (toll-free)
Fax: 563-884-5227
E-mail: graduate.studies@palmer.edu
Web site: http://www.palmer.edu/gs/

Palmer College of Chiropractic

THE FACULTY AND THEIR RESEARCH

Jean Murray, Dean of Graduate Studies; Ph.D., Walden, 2000.

James DeVocht, Assistant Professor of Biomechanics; Ph.D., Iowa, 1996. Finite element modeling, biomechanical evaluation of a small animal model, quantification of the biomechanical effects of orthopedic devices.

Stephen M. Duray, Professor of Anatomy; Ph.D., Kent State, 1992. Anthropology and human skeletal morphometry.

Ram Gudavalli, Associate Professor of Biomechanics; Ph.D., Cincinnati, 1989. Clinically oriented biomechanics.

Charles Henderson, Associate Professor of Neuroscience; Ph.D., South Florida, 1992. Nature and consequences of spinal subluxation and adjustment in animal model.

Maria Hondras, Associate Professor of Clinical Research; M.P.H., Illinois at Chicago, 1993. Efficacy and effectiveness of chiropractic care, health outcomes assessment, medical informatics.

Se-Pyo Hong, Associate Professor of Anatomy; Ph.D., Southern Illinois, 1981. Ultrastructural changes in articular surfaces.

Dana Lawrence, Associate Professor of Clinical Research; D.C., National Chiropractic, 1979. Development of chiropractic best practices, validity and reliability of chiropractic technique procedures, journalology.

Cynthia R. Long, Associate Professor of Research; Ph.D., Iowa, 1995. Efficacy and effectiveness studies of chiropractic, evaluation and improvement of research reports.

Katherine Manley-Buser, Assistant Professor of Anatomy; Ph.D., California, Davis, 1991. Anthropology, human skeletal morphometry.

Dennis M. Marchiori, Associate Professor of Radiology and Academic Dean; M.S., Palmer Chiropractic, 1992. Behavior of chiropractors and patient trust, empowerment of chiropractic faculty, radiographic and MRI findings in chiropractic patient populations.

Brian A. McMaster, Associate Professor of Anatomy and Neuroscience; Ph.D., Illinois State, 1983. Receptors of trigeminal, muscle spindle distribution in paraspinal muscles.

William C. Meeker, Vice President for Research; M.P.H., San Jose State, 1988. Clinical trials comparing chiropractic to other forms of care, investigating relationships of patient characteristics to optimum chiropractic care, development of chiropractic best practices, validity and reliability of chiropractic technique.

Edward F. Owens Jr., Associate Professor; D.C., Life Chiropractic, 1986.

Joel G. Pickar, Professor of Neuroscience; Ph.D., California, Davis, 1990. Neurophysiological consequences of spinal subluxation, electrophysiological response from mechanoreceptors, autonomic response to spinal subluxation.

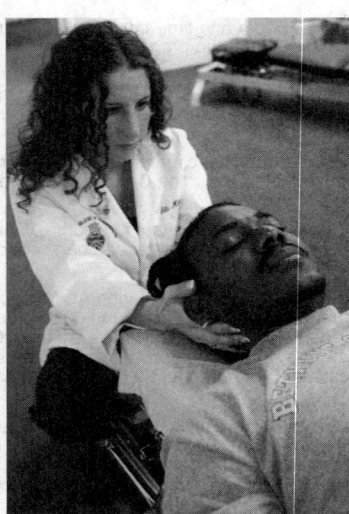
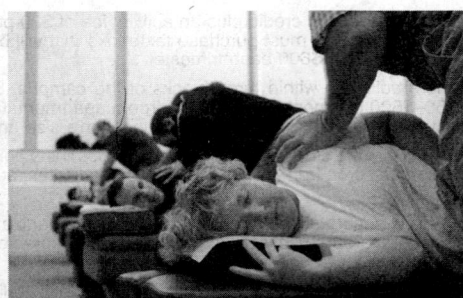
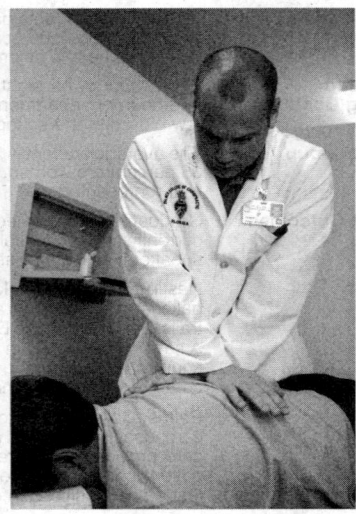

Palmer students learn chiropractic techniques.

Section 36
Dentistry and Dental Sciences

This section contains a directory of institutions offering graduate work in dentistry and dental sciences, followed by in-depth entries submitted by institutions that chose to prepare detailed program descriptions. Additional information about programs listed in the directory but not augmented by an in-depth entry may be obtained by writing directly to the dean of a graduate school or chair of a department at the address given in the directory.

For programs offering related work, see also in this book Allied Health; and in Book 3, Anatomy; Biological and Biomedical Sciences; Cell, Molecular, and Structural Biology; Microbiological Sciences; and Pathology and Pathobiology.

CONTENTS

Program Directories

Announcement

Close-Ups

Dentistry

Boston University, Goldman School of Dental Medicine, Graduate Programs in Dentistry, Boston, MA 02215. Offers advanced general dentistry (CAGS); dental public health (MS, MSD, D Sc D, CAGS); dentistry (DMD); endodontics (MSD, D Sc D, CAGS); implantology (CAGS); operative dentistry (MSD, D Sc D, CAGS); oral and maxillofacial surgery (MSD, D Sc D, CAGS); oral biology (MSD, D Sc, D Sc D, PhD); orthodontics (MSD, D Sc D, CAGS); pediatric dentistry (MSD, D Sc D, CAGS); periodontology (MSD, D Sc D, CAGS); prosthodontics (MSD, D Sc D, CAGS). *Students:* 152 full-time (62 women); includes 13 minority (1 African American, 11 Asian Americans or Pacific Islanders, 1 Hispanic American), 75 international. Average age 29. In 2006, 224 first professional degrees, 22 master's, 10 doctorates, 63 other advanced degrees awarded. *Degree requirements:* For master's and doctorate, thesis/dissertation; for CAGS, thesis (for some programs). *Entrance requirements:* For DMD, DAT, minimum GPA of 3.0; for CAGS, dental degree. *Application deadline:* For fall admission, 5/1 for domestic students. Applications are processed on a rolling basis. Application fee: $60. *Expenses: Contact institution. Financial support:* Career-related internships or fieldwork and institutionally sponsored loans available. Financial award application deadline: 4/15; financial award applicants required to submit CSS PROFILE or FAFSA. *Faculty research:* Defensive mechanisms, bone-cell regulation, protein biochemistry, molecular biology, biomaterials. *Application contact:* 617-638-4787, Fax: 617-638-4798.

See Close-Up on page 2179.

Case Western Reserve University, School of Dental Medicine, Professional Program in Dentistry, Cleveland, OH 44106. Offers DMD. *Accreditation:* ADA. *Faculty:* 44 full-time (13 women), 140 part-time/adjunct (20 women). *Students:* 288 full-time (84 women); includes 55 minority (5 African Americans, 1 American Indian/Alaska Native, 46 Asian Americans or Pacific Islanders, 3 Hispanic Americans). Average age 25. 2,940 applicants, 9% accepted, 70 enrolled. In 2006, 71 degrees awarded. *Degree requirements:* For first-professional, thesis. *Entrance requirements:* DAT. Additional exam requirements/recommendations for international students: Required—TOEFL (minimum score 550 paper-based; 213 computer-based). *Application deadline:* For fall admission, 1/1 for domestic and international students. Applications are processed on a rolling basis. Application fee: $45. *Expenses: Contact institution. Financial support:* In 2006–07, 257 students received support. Federal Work-Study, institutionally sponsored loans, and scholarships/grants available. Financial award application deadline: 4/20; financial award applicants required to submit FAFSA. *Faculty research:* Periodontal disease; overall health; natural antibodies; obesity and periodontal disease; 3D cone beam computerized tomography. *Unit head:* Dr. Marsha A. Pyle, Associate Dean for Education, 216-368-6731, Fax: 216-368-3204, E-mail: marsha.pyle@case.edu. *Application contact:* David A. Dalsky, Director of Admissions, 216-368-2460, Fax: 216-368-3204, E-mail: david.dalsky@case.edu.

Columbia University, School of Dental and Oral Surgery, Professional Program in Dental and Oral Surgery, New York, NY 10032. Offers DDS, DDS/MBA, DDS/MPH, DDS/MS. *Accreditation:* ADA. *Entrance requirements:* DAT, previous course work in biology, organic chemistry, inorganic chemistry, physics, and English.

Creighton University, School of Dentistry, Omaha, NE 68178-0001. Offers DDS. *Accreditation:* ADA. *Entrance requirements:* DAT. Expenses: Contact institution. *Faculty research:* Dental implants, bone calcification, dental materials, laser usage in dentistry.

Dalhousie University, Faculty of Dentistry, Professional Program in Dentistry, Halifax, NS B3H 4R2, Canada. Offers DDS. *Accreditation:* ADA. *Entrance requirements:* DAT, minimum 2 years of university; course work in biochemistry, biology, chemistry, physics, physiology, and microbiology. Additional exam requirements/recommendations for international students: Required—TWE (minimum score 5), TOEFL (580 paper-based; 237 computer-based) or IELTS (7 paper-based). Expenses: Contact institution.

Harvard University, School of Dental Medicine, Advanced Graduate Programs in Dentistry, Cambridge, MA 02138. Offers advanced general dentistry (Certificate); dental public health (Certificate); endodontics (Certificate); general practice residency (Certificate); oral biology (M Med Sc, D Med Sc); oral pathology (Certificate); oral surgery (Certificate); orthodontics (Certificate); pediatric dentistry (Certificate); periodontics (Certificate); prosthodontics (Certificate). *Expenses:* Tuition: Full-time $30,275. Full-time tuition and fees vary according to program and student level.

Harvard University, School of Dental Medicine, Professional Program in Dental Medicine, Cambridge, MA 02138. Offers DMD. *Accreditation:* ADA. *Entrance requirements:* Dental Admissions Test, 1 year each: biology, general chemistry, organic chemistry, physics, calculus, English. *Expenses:* Tuition: Full-time $30,275. Full-time tuition and fees vary according to program and student level.

Howard University, College of Dentistry, Washington, DC 20059-0002. Offers advanced education program general dentistry (Certificate); dentistry (DDS); general dentistry (Certificate); oral and maxillofacial surgery (Certificate); orthodontics (Certificate); pediatric dentistry (Certificate). *Accreditation:* ADA (one or more programs are accredited). *Degree requirements:* For first-professional, didactic and clinical exams. *Entrance requirements:* DAT, 8 semester hours of course work in each biology, inorganic chemistry, organic chemistry. Expenses: Contact institution. *Faculty research:* Epidemiological, biomaterial, molecular genetic, behavioral modification, and clinical trial studies.

Idaho State University, Office of Graduate Studies, Kasiska College of Health Professions, Department of Dental Sciences, Pocatello, ID 83209. Offers advanced general dentistry (Post-Doctoral Certificate); dental hygiene (MS). Postbaccalaureate distance learning degree programs offered (minimal on-campus study). *Faculty:* 6 full-time (all women). *Students:* 18 full-time (5 women), 21 part-time (all women); includes 3 minority (1 Asian American or Pacific Islander, 2 Hispanic Americans), 1 international. Average age 27. In 2006, 4 degrees awarded. *Degree requirements:* For master's, thesis, one year sequences, practicum, comprehensive exam, registration; for Post-Doctoral Certificate, 1 year residency, thesis optional. *Entrance requirements:* For master's, GRE and/or MAT, minimum GPA of 3.0 in upper division undergraduate courses, current dental hygiene license, 2 letters of recommendation; for Post-Doctoral Certificate, DAT. Additional exam requirements/recommendations for international students: Required—TOEFL (minimum score 600 paper-based; 213 computer-based). *Application deadline:* For fall admission, 7/1 for domestic students, 6/1 for international students; for spring admission, 12/1 for domestic students, 11/1 for international students. Applications are processed on a rolling basis. Application fee: $55. *Expenses: Contact institution. Financial support:* In 2006–07, 1 teaching assistantship with full and partial tuition reimbursement (averaging $8,694 per year) was awarded. Financial award application deadline: 1/1. *Unit head:* Dr. Brian Crawford, Chair, 208-282-5275, Fax: 208-282-5834, E-mail: crawbri3@isu.edu. *Application contact:* Ellen Combs, Graduate School Technical Records Specialist, 208-282-2150, Fax: 208-282-4847.

Indiana University–Purdue University Indianapolis, School of Dentistry, Indianapolis, IN 46202-2896. Offers DDS, MS, MSD, PhD, Certificate. *Accreditation:* ADA (one or more programs are accredited). *Faculty:* 16 full-time (2 women). *Students:* 452 full-time (176 women), 60 part-time (27 women); includes 69 minority (10 African Americans, 3 American Indian/Alaska Native, 42 Asian Americans or Pacific Islanders, 14 Hispanic Americans), 45 international. Average age 27. In 2006, 98 DDSs, 30 master's, 2 doctorates awarded. *Degree requirements:* For master's and doctorate, thesis/dissertation, qualifying exam. *Entrance requirements:* For DDS, DAT; for master's, DDS or DMD; for doctorate, GRE, DDS or DMD. Additional exam requirements/recommendations for international students: Required—TOEFL (minimum score 550 paper-based; 213 computer-based). *Application deadline:* For fall admission, 10/1 for domestic students, 10/1 priority date for international students; for spring admission, 2/1 for domestic and international students. Application fee: $50 ($60 for international students). *Expenses: Contact institution.* Tuition and fees vary according to course load, campus/location and program. *Financial support:* In 2006–07, 43 students received support; fellowships, research assistantships, teaching assistantships, Federal Work-Study, institutionally sponsored loans, and scholarships/grants available. Financial award application deadline: 3/1; financial award applicants required to submit FAFSA. *Faculty research:* Preventive dentistry, dental materials, bone metabolism, enzyme metabolism. Total annual research expenditures: $3 million. *Unit head:* Lawrence I. Goldblatt, Dean, 317-274-7461. *Application contact:* Robert Kasberg, Associate Dean for Student Affairs and Director of Admissions, 317-274-8173, Fax: 317-274-2419, E-mail: blerner@iupui.edu.

Loma Linda University, School of Dentistry, Loma Linda, CA 92350. Offers DDS, MS, Certificate, DDS/MS, DDS/PhD, MS/Certificate. *Accreditation:* ADA. *Entrance requirements:* DAT. Expenses: Contact institution.

Louisiana State University Health Sciences Center, School of Dentistry, New Orleans, LA 70112-2223. Offers DDS. *Accreditation:* ADA. *Entrance requirements:* DAT, interview. Expenses: Contact institution. *Faculty research:* HIV/AIDS, implants, metallurgy, lipids, DNA.

Marquette University, School of Dentistry, Professional Program in Dentistry, Milwaukee, WI 53201-1881. Offers DDS. *Accreditation:* ADA. *Entrance requirements:* DAT, 1 year course work in each biology, inorganic chemistry, organic chemistry, physics, and English. Additional exam requirements/recommendations for international students: Required—TOEFL. *Faculty research:* Biomaterials, wound healing, diabetes, biocompatibility, cancer, aging, lasers.

McGill University, Faculty of Graduate and Postdoctoral Studies, Faculty of Dentistry, Montréal, QC H3A 2T5, Canada. Offers forensic dentistry (Certificate); oral and maxillofacial surgery (M Sc, PhD). *Degree requirements:* For master's and doctorate, thesis/dissertation, registration. *Entrance requirements:* For master's, GRE General Test, DDS/DMD or B Sc with a minimum GPA of 3.0 in any of the disciplines in the health sciences or related disciplines. Additional exam requirements/recommendations for international students: Required—TOEFL (minimum score 550 paper-based; 213 computer-based). Electronic applications accepted. *Faculty research:* Extracellular matrix, implant dentistry, longitudinal evaluation of oral health complications of patients with AIDS.

McGill University, Professional Program in Dentistry, Montréal, QC H3A 2T5, Canada. Offers DMD. *Accreditation:* ADA. *Faculty:* 18 full-time (3 women), 135 part-time/adjunct (24 women). *Students:* Average age 25. In 2006, 34 degrees awarded. *Entrance requirements:* DAT, B Sc; course work in biology, general chemistry, organic chemistry, physics, and biochemistry. Additional exam requirements/recommendations for international students: Required—TOEFL. *Application deadline:* For fall admission, 11/15 for domestic students; for winter admission, 1/15 for domestic students. Applications are processed on a rolling basis. Application fee: $80 Canadian dollars. Electronic applications accepted. *Faculty research:* Extracellular matrix, implant dentistry, longitudinal evaluation of oral health, complications of patients with AIDS. *Unit head:* Dr. James P. Lund, Dean, 514-398-7219, Fax: 514-398-8900, E-mail: james.lund@mcgill.ca. *Application contact:* Patricia Bassett, Graduate Secretary, 514-398-7203 Ext. 00091, Fax: 514-398-2028, E-mail: patricia.bassett@mcgill.ca.

Medical College of Georgia, School of Dentistry, Augusta, GA 30912. Offers DMD, DMD/MS, DMD/PhD. *Accreditation:* ADA. *Faculty:* 68 full-time (12 women), 31 part-time/adjunct (3 women). *Students:* 63 full-time (21 women); includes 19 minority (4 African Americans, 1 American Indian/Alaska Native, 10 Asian Americans or Pacific Islanders, 4 Hispanic Americans). Average age 25. 267 applicants, 29% accepted, 63 enrolled. In 2006, 56 degrees awarded. *Entrance requirements:* DAT, previous course work in biology, English, organic chemistry, and general chemistry; 1 semester of course work in physics. *Application deadline:* For fall admission, 10/15 for domestic students. Application fee: $30. Electronic applications accepted. *Expenses: Contact institution. Financial support:* Federal Work-Study and scholarships/grants available. Financial award application deadline: 5/1; financial award applicants required to submit FAFSA. *Faculty research:* Biocompatibility, dentin bonding, oral cancer, ceramic strengthening, resin polymerization. Total annual research expenditures: $1.5 million. *Unit head:* Connie Drisko, Dean, 706-721-2117, Fax: 706-721-6276, E-mail: cdrisko@mcg.edu. *Application contact:* Dr. Carole M. Hanes, Associate Dean for Student and Alumni Affairs, 706-721-3587, Fax: 706-721-6276, E-mail: chanes@mcg.edu.

Medical University of South Carolina, College of Dental Medicine, Charleston, SC 29425-0002. Offers DMD, DMD/PhD. *Accreditation:* ADA. *Faculty:* 47 full-time (8 women), 25 part-time/adjunct (5 women). *Students:* 220 full-time (93 women); includes 32 minority (12 African Americans, 1 American Indian/Alaska Native, 13 Asian Americans or Pacific Islanders, 6 Hispanic Americans). Average age 26. 467 applicants, 13% accepted, 54 enrolled. In 2006, 49 degrees awarded. *Degree requirements:* For first-professional, National Board of Dental Examinations Part I and Part II. *Entrance requirements:* DAT, interview, 52 hours of specific pre-dental course work. Additional exam requirements/recommendations for international students: Required—TOEFL (minimum score 600 paper-based; 250 computer-based). *Application deadline:* For fall admission, 2/1 for domestic and international students. Application fee: $75. Electronic applications accepted. *Expenses: Contact institution. Financial support:* In 2006–07, 197 students received support. Federal Work-Study, scholarships/grants, and tuition waivers (partial) available. Support available to part-time students. Financial award application deadline: 3/15; financial award applicants required to submit FAFSA. *Faculty research:* Scoral health, genetics, health disparities, chlamydia, oral cancer. Total annual research expenditures: $2.9 million. *Unit head:* Dr. John J. Sanders, Dean, 843-792-3811, Fax: 843-792-1376, E-mail: sandersjj@musc.edu. *Application contact:* Jill R. Stevens, Graduate Studies Admissions, 843-792-4892, Fax: 843-792-6615, E-mail: stevensj@musc.edu.

Meharry Medical College, School of Dentistry, Nashville, TN 37208-9989. Offers DDS. *Accreditation:* ADA. *Entrance requirements:* DAT.

New York University, College of Dentistry, Professional Program in Dentistry, New York, NY 10012-1019. Offers DDS. *Accreditation:* ADA. *Faculty:* 227 full-time, 663 part-time/adjunct. *Students:* 1,216 full-time (658 women); includes 769 minority (38 African Americans, 2 American Indian/Alaska Native, 679 Asian Americans or Pacific Islanders, 50 Hispanic Americans). Average age 25. 4,792 applicants, 13% accepted, 350 enrolled. In 2006, 308 degrees awarded. *Entrance requirements:* DAT. Additional exam requirements/recommendations for international students: Required—TOEFL (minimum score 230 computer-based). *Application deadline:* For fall admission, 4/1 priority date for domestic students. Applications are processed on a rolling basis. Application fee: $75. *Expenses:* Tuition: Part-time $1,080 per unit. Required fees: $56 per unit. $329 per term. Tuition and fees vary according to program. *Financial support:* In 2006–07, 1,139 students received support, including fellowships with tuition reimbursements available (averaging $25,000 per year); Federal Work-Study, institutionally sponsored loans, and scholarships/grants also available. Support available to part-time students. Financial award application deadline: 3/1; financial award applicants required to submit FAFSA. *Application contact:* Amy Knowles, Assistant Dean for Student Affairs and Admissions, 212-998-5333, Fax: 212-995-4302, E-mail: ak96@nyu.edu.

Nova Southeastern University, Health Professions Division, College of Dental Medicine, Fort Lauderdale, FL 33314-7796. Offers dental medicine (DMD); dentistry (MS). *Accreditation:* ADA. *Faculty:* 76 full-time (20 women), 175 part-time/adjunct (36 women). *Students:* 437 full-time (189 women), 9 part-time (4 women); includes 129 minority (9 African Americans, 4 American Indian/Alaska Native, 55 Asian Americans or Pacific Islanders, 61 Hispanic Americans), 57 international. Average age 24. 2,285 applicants, 8% accepted, 105 enrolled. In 2006, 100 degrees awarded. *Degree requirements:* For master's, thesis. *Entrance requirements:* DAT, minimum GPA of 2.75. Additional exam requirements/recommendations for international students:

Required—TOEFL (minimum score 550 paper-based; 225 computer-based). *Application deadline:* For fall admission, 2/1 for domestic students, 2/15 for international students. Applications are processed on a rolling basis. Application fee: $50. *Expenses:* Contact institution. *Financial support:* In 2006–07, 372 students received support, including 8 teaching assistantships with full tuition reimbursements available; fellowships with full tuition reimbursements available also available. Financial award application deadline: 4/3; financial award applicants required to submit FAFSA. *Unit head:* Dr. Robert A. Uchin, Dean, 954-262-7312, Fax: 954-262-1782, E-mail: ruchin@nova.edu. *Application contact:* Su-Ann Zarrett, Dental Admissions Counselor, 954-262-1108, Fax: 954-262-2282, E-mail: zarrett@nsu.nova.edu.

The Ohio State University, College of Dentistry, Programs in Dentistry, Columbus, OH 43210. Offers DDS, MS, DDS/PhD. *Accreditation:* ADA. *Faculty:* 97 full-time (29 women), 155 part-time/adjunct (30 women). *Students:* 494 full-time (174 women), 3 part-time; includes 68 minority (14 African Americans, 2 American Indian/Alaska Native, 47 Asian Americans or Pacific Islanders, 5 Hispanic Americans), 9 international. Average age 26. In 2006, 99 DDSs, 24 master's awarded. *Entrance requirements:* DAT. *Application deadline:* For fall admission, 11/15 for domestic students. Applications are processed on a rolling basis. Application fee: $60 ($70 for international students). Electronic applications accepted. *Expenses:* Tuition, state resident: full-time $9,438. Tuition, nonresident: full-time $22,791. Tuition and fees vary according to course load, campus/location and program. *Financial support:* Fellowships, teaching assistantships, Federal Work-Study and institutionally sponsored loans available. Financial award application deadline: 3/1; financial award applicants required to submit FAFSA. Total annual research expenditures: $3.4 million. *Unit head:* Ann L. Griffen, Graduate Studies Committee Chair, 614-292-1150, Fax: 614-292-7619, E-mail: griffen.l@osu.edu. *Application contact:* Graduate Admissions, 614-292-9444, Fax: 614-292-3985, E-mail: domestic.grad@osu.edu.

Oregon Health & Science University, School of Dentistry, Professional Program in Dentistry, Portland, OR 97239-3098. Offers DMD, MD/DMD. *Accreditation:* ADA. *Entrance requirements:* DAT. Electronic applications accepted. *Faculty research:* Dentin permeability, tooth sensations, fluoride metabolism, immunology of periodontal disease, craniofacial growth.

Southern Illinois University Edwardsville, School of Dental Medicine, Edwardsville, IL 62026-0001. Offers DMD. *Accreditation:* ADA. *Faculty:* 19 full-time (1 woman). *Students:* 205 full-time (93 women); includes 31 minority (12 African Americans, 1 American Indian/Alaska Native, 13 Asian Americans or Pacific Islanders, 5 Hispanic Americans). Average age 25. In 2006, 49 degrees awarded. *Entrance requirements:* DAT. *Application deadline:* For fall admission, 2/1 priority date for domestic students. Application fee: $20. *Expenses:* Contact institution. *Unit head:* Dr. Ann Boyle, Dean, 618-474-7120, E-mail: aboyle@siue.edu.

Stony Brook University, State University of New York, Stony Brook University Medical Center, Health Sciences Center, School of Dental Medicine, Professional Program in Dental Medicine, Stony Brook, NY 11794. Offers dental medicine (DDS); endodontics (Certificate); orthodontics (Certificate); periodontics (Certificate). *Accreditation:* ADA (one or more programs are accredited). *Faculty:* 29 full-time (11 women), 61 part-time/adjunct (16 women). *Students:* 157 full-time (76 women), 21 part-time (7 women); includes 48 minority (1 African American, 42 Asian Americans or Pacific Islanders, 5 Hispanic Americans). Average age 25. 729 applicants, 6% accepted. In 2006, 40 DDSs, 9 other advanced degrees awarded. *Entrance requirements:* DAT. *Application deadline:* For fall admission, 1/15 for domestic students. Application fee: $75. *Expenses:* Tuition, state resident: full-time $6,900; part-time $288 per credit. Tuition, nonresident: full-time $10,920; part-time $455 per credit. *Financial support:* Fellowships, Federal Work-Study available. Support available to part-time students. Total annual research expenditures: $386,069. *Application contact:* Kim M. Lambiase Hammer, Director of Admissions, 631-632-8980.

Temple University, Health Sciences Center, School of Dentistry, Professional Program in Dentistry, Philadelphia, PA 19122-6096. Offers DMD, DMD/MBA. *Accreditation:* ADA. *Faculty:* 55 full-time (16 women), 86 part-time/adjunct (19 women). *Students:* 488 full-time (163 women); includes 135 minority (13 African Americans, 1 American Indian/Alaska Native, 94 Asian Americans or Pacific Islanders, 27 Hispanic Americans), 21 international. Average age 24. 3,566 applicants, 9% accepted, 125 enrolled. In 2006, 113 degrees awarded. *Entrance requirements:* DAT, 6 credits of course work in each biology, chemistry, organic chemistry, physics, and English. *Application deadline:* For fall admission, 2/1 for domestic and international students. Applications are processed on a rolling basis. Application fee: $30. *Expenses:* Contact institution. Tuition and fees vary according to program. *Financial support:* In 2006–07, 440 students received support. Institutionally sponsored loans and scholarships/grants available. Financial award application deadline: 3/1; financial award applicants required to submit FAFSA. *Unit head:* Dr. Lisa P. Deem, Associate Dean for Admissions and Student Affairs, 215-707-2801, Fax: 215-707-5461, E-mail: lisa.deem@temple.edu.

Texas A&M Health Science Center, Baylor College of Dentistry, Professional Program in Dentistry, College Station, TX 77840. Offers DDS. *Entrance requirements:* DAT. Expenses: Contact institution. *Faculty research:* Bleaching, implants, craniofacial growth, oral oncology, pulp biology.

Tufts University, School of Dental Medicine, International Student Program in Dental Medicine, Medford, MA 02155. Offers DMD. *Accreditation:* ADA. *Entrance requirements:* National Dental Hygiene Board Exam Part I, BDS, DDS, or equivalent. Additional exam requirements/recommendations for international students: Required—TOEFL. *Expenses:* Tuition: Full-time $33,672. Tuition and fees vary according to degree level and program.

Tufts University, School of Dental Medicine, Professional Program in Dental Medicine, Medford, MA 02155. Offers DMD, DMD/PhD. *Accreditation:* ADA. *Entrance requirements:* DAT. *Expenses:* Tuition: Full-time $33,672. Tuition and fees vary according to degree level and program.

Universidad Iberoamericana, Graduate School, Santo Domingo D.N., Dominican Republic. Offers dentistry (DMD); education (M Ed); international business (IMBA).

Universidad Nacional Pedro Henriquez Urena, School of Dentistry, Santo Domingo, Dominican Republic. Offers DDS.

Université de Montréal, Faculty of Graduate Studies, Faculty of Dental Medicine and Faculty of Graduate Studies, Graduate Programs in Dentistry, Montréal, QC H3C 3J7, Canada. Offers multidisciplinary residency (Certificate); oral and dental sciences (M Sc); orthodontics (M Sc); pediatric dentistry (M Sc); prosthodontics rehabilitation (M Sc); stomatology residency (Certificate). *Application deadline:* For fall admission, 10/1 for domestic students. Application fee: $30. Electronic applications accepted. *Unit head:* Arlette Kolta, Associate Dean for Research, 514-343-7112, Fax: 514-343-2233.

Université Laval, Faculty of Dentistry, Professional Programs in Dentistry, Québec, QC G1K 7P4, Canada. Offers DMD. *Accreditation:* ADA. *Entrance requirements:* Visual perception exam, manual dexterity exam, interview, knowledge of French. Electronic applications accepted.

University at Buffalo, the State University of New York, Graduate School, School of Dental Medicine, Graduate Programs in Dental Medicine, Buffalo, NY 14214. Offers advanced education in general dentistry (Certificate); combined prosthodontics (Certificate); endodontics (Certificate); general practice residency (Certificate); oral and maxillofacial pathology (Certificate); oral and maxillofacial surgery (Certificate); oral biology (PhD); oral diagnostic sciences (MS), including biomaterials; oral sciences (MS); orthodontics (MS, Certificate); pediatric dentistry (Certificate); periodontics (Certificate); temporomandibular disorders and oralfacial pain (Certificate). *Faculty:* 69 full-time (25 women), 109 part-time/adjunct (26 women). *Students:* 72 full-time (29 women), 7 part-time (2 women); includes 8 minority (all Asian Americans or Pacific Islanders), 44 international. Average age 28. 289 applicants, 11% accepted, 25 enrolled. In 2006, 14 master's, 1 doctorate awarded. *Degree requirements:* For master's and doctorate,

thesis/dissertation. *Entrance requirements:* For doctorate, GRE General Test, GRE Subject Test in biology or DDS; for Certificate, DDS, DMD or equivalent. Additional exam requirements/recommendations for international students: Required—TOEFL. *Application deadline:* For fall admission, 10/1 for domestic and international students. Application fee: $35. Electronic applications accepted. *Expenses:* Contact institution. *Financial support:* Fellowships with full and partial tuition reimbursements, research assistantships with full and partial tuition reimbursements, Federal Work-Study, institutionally sponsored loans, scholarships/grants, traineeships, and unspecified assistantships available. Financial award applicants required to submit FAFSA. *Faculty research:* Immunology and microbiology of dental disease, surface science, saliva biochemistry, bone biology. Total annual research expenditures: $5.8 million. *Unit head:* Dr. Russell J. Nisengard, Associate Dean, 716-829-2839, Fax: 716-833-3517, E-mail: nisengar@buffalo.edu. *Application contact:* Kristin Yager, Admissions Secretary, 716-829-2839, Fax: 716-833-3517, E-mail: kmyager2@buffalo.edu.

University at Buffalo, the State University of New York, Graduate School, School of Dental Medicine, Professional Program in Dental Medicine, Buffalo, NY 14260. Offers DDS. *Accreditation:* ADA. *Faculty:* 69 full-time (25 women), 109 part-time/adjunct (26 women). *Students:* 345 full-time (133 women); includes 64 minority (1 African American, 55 Asian Americans or Pacific Islanders, 8 Hispanic Americans), 14 international. 1,368 applicants, 12% accepted, 88 enrolled. In 2006, 77 degrees awarded. *Degree requirements:* For first-professional, National Dental Board Exams. *Entrance requirements:* DAT. *Application deadline:* For fall admission, 2/1 for domestic and international students. Applications are processed on a rolling basis. Application fee: $50. *Financial support:* Federal Work-Study, institutionally sponsored loans, and scholarships/grants available. Financial award application deadline: 2/28; financial award applicants required to submit FAFSA. *Application contact:* Dr. Robert Joynt, Director of Admissions, 716-829-2839, Fax: 716-833-3517, E-mail: joynt@buffalo.edu.

The University of Alabama at Birmingham, School of Dentistry, Professional Program in Dentistry, Birmingham, AL 35294. Offers DMD. *Accreditation:* ADA. *Students:* 223 full-time (96 women); includes 33 minority (17 African Americans, 3 American Indian/Alaska Native, 9 Asian Americans or Pacific Islanders, 4 Hispanic Americans), 1 international. Average age 26. 714 applicants, 8% accepted. In 2006, 56 degrees awarded. *Entrance requirements:* DAT. *Application deadline:* For fall admission, 4/1 for domestic students. Electronic applications accepted. *Expenses:* Tuition, state resident: part-time $170 per credit hour. Tuition, nonresident: part-time $425 per credit hour. Required fees: $15 per credit hour. $122 per term. Tuition and fees vary according to program. *Financial support:* Fellowships, Federal Work-Study available. *Faculty research:* Etiology and pathogenesis of dental diseases, dental biomaterials, therapy of dental diseases. *Application contact:* Dr. Steven J. Filler, Director of Dentistry Admissions, 205-934-5424, Fax: 205-975-6519, E-mail: sfiller@uab.edu.

University of Alberta, Faculty of Medicine and Dentistry, Department of Dentistry, Professional Program in Dentistry, Edmonton, AB T6G 2E1, Canada. Offers DDS. *Accreditation:* ADA. *Faculty:* 29 full-time (6 women), 113 part-time/adjunct (28 women). *Students:* 138 full-time (63 women). 322 applicants, 12% accepted, 34 enrolled. In 2006, 35 degrees awarded. *Entrance requirements:* DAT (Canadian version), interview. Additional exam requirements/recommendations for international students: Required—TOEFL. *Application deadline:* For fall admission, 11/1 for domestic and international students. Application fee: $75. Electronic applications accepted. *Faculty research:* Oral biology, biochemistry of connective tissues, preventive dentistry, applied clinical orthodontics, biomaterials. *Application contact:* Melanie Grams, Administrative Assistant, 780-492-1319, Fax: 780-492-7536, E-mail: melanie.grams@ualberta.ca.

The University of British Columbia, Faculty of Dentistry, Professional Program in Dentistry, Vancouver, BC V6T 1Z1, Canada. Offers DMD. *Accreditation:* ADA. *Faculty:* 34 full-time, 150 part-time/adjunct. *Students:* 176 full-time (94 women). Average age 27. 352 applicants, 11% accepted. In 2006, 48 degrees awarded. *Entrance requirements:* DAT, ACFD, interview, psychomotor assessment. Additional exam requirements/recommendations for international students: Required—IELTS. *Application deadline:* For fall admission, 11/2 for domestic students; for spring admission, 6/8 for international students. Application fee: $200 ($400 for international students). Electronic applications accepted. *Expenses:* Contact institution. *Financial support:* In 2006–07, 75 students received support. Institutionally sponsored loans and scholarships/grants available. Financial award application deadline: 9/15. *Unit head:* Dr. Alan A. Lowe, Chair, 604-822-3414, Fax: 604-822-3562, E-mail: alowe@interchange.ubc.ca. *Application contact:* Connie A. Reynolds, Manager, Admissions and Academic Progress, 604-822-1847, Fax: 604-822-8279, E-mail: connier@interchange.ubc.ca.

University of California, Los Angeles, School of Dentistry, Professional Program in Dentistry, Los Angeles, CA 90095. Offers DDS, Certificate, DDS/MS, DDS/PhD, MS/Certificate, PhD/Certificate. *Accreditation:* ADA (one or more programs are accredited). *Entrance requirements:* DAT.

University of California, San Francisco, School of Dentistry, San Francisco, CA 94143-0150. Offers DDS. *Accreditation:* ADA. *Entrance requirements:* DAT. *Expenses:* Contact institution.

University of Colorado at Denver and Health Sciences Center, School of Dentistry, Denver, CO 80217-3364. Offers DDS. *Accreditation:* ADA. *Faculty:* 54 full-time (11 women), 4 part-time/adjunct (0 women). *Students:* 192 full-time (80 women); includes 26 minority (2 African Americans, 15 Asian Americans or Pacific Islanders, 9 Hispanic Americans), 1 international. Average age 27. 1,322 applicants, 5% accepted, 50 enrolled. In 2006, 46 degrees awarded. *Entrance requirements:* DAT, 1 semester of course work in English composition; 2 semesters of course work in each chemistry/lab, organic chemistry/lab, general biology/lab, general physics/lab, and humanities; 3 letters of recommendation. Additional exam requirements/recommendations for international students: Required—TOEFL (minimum score 580 paper-based; 237 computer-based). *Application deadline:* For fall admission, 1/1 for domestic students, 3/31 for international students. Application fee: $50 ($125 for international students). *Expenses:* Contact institution. *Financial support:* Federal Work-Study and institutionally sponsored loans available. Financial award application deadline: 3/15; financial award applicants required to submit FAFSA. *Faculty research:* Pain control, materials research, geriatric dentistry, restorative dentistry, periodontics. *Unit head:* Dr. Denise K. Kassebaum, Interim ean, 303-724-7100. *Application contact:* Dr. Randy L. Kluender, Assistant Dean for Admissions and Student Affairs, 303-724-7120.

University of Connecticut Health Center, School of Dental Medicine, Professional Program in Dental Medicine, Farmington, CT 06030. Offers DMD, Certificate, DMD/MPH, DMD/PhD, PhD/Certificate. *Accreditation:* ADA. *Entrance requirements:* DAT. *Faculty research:* Neurobiology, cell and molecular biology.

University of Detroit Mercy, School of Dentistry, Professional Program in Dentistry, Detroit, MI 48221. Offers DDS. *Accreditation:* ADA. *Entrance requirements:* DAT. *Expenses:* Tuition: Full-time $15,750; part-time $875 per credit hour. Required fees: $570. *Faculty research:* Peer evaluation in teaching, evaluation of restorative materials, HIV and periodontal disease.

University of Florida, College of Dentistry, Professional Programs in Dentistry, Gainesville, FL 32611. Offers dentistry (DMD); foreign trained dentistry (Certificate). *Accreditation:* ADA. *Faculty:* 101 full-time (10 women), 36 part-time/adjunct (10 women). *Students:* Average age 29. 1,039 applicants, 11% accepted, 93 enrolled. In 2006, 76 DMDs, 11 other advanced degrees awarded. *Degree requirements:* For DMD, registration; for Certificate, National Dental Boards Parts I and II. *Entrance requirements:* For DMD, DAT, interview; for Certificate, interview. Additional exam requirements/recommendations for international students: Required—TOEFL (minimum score 550 paper-based; 213 computer-based). *Application deadline:* For fall admission, 1/1 for domestic students, 11/1 for international students. Application fee: $30. *Expenses:* Tuition, state resident: full-time $6,827. Tuition, nonresident: full-time $21,951. Required fees: $999. *Financial support:* In 2006–07, 296 students received support. Federal Work-Study and

Dentistry

University of Florida (continued)

institutionally sponsored loans available. Financial award applicants required to submit FAFSA. *Faculty research:* Actinobacillus, critical thinking, DNA adenine, methylase, LJP. *Unit head:* Dr. Robert Eliot Primosch, Associate Dean for Education, 352-392-2949, Fax: 352-846-3818, E-mail: rprimosch@dental.ufl.edu. *Application contact:* Dr. Venita Sposetti, Assistant Dean for Admissions and Financial Aid, 352-392-4866, Fax: 352-846-0311, E-mail: sposetti@dental.ufl.edu.

University of Illinois at Chicago, College of Dentistry, Professional Program in Dentistry, Chicago, IL 60607-7128. Offers DDS, DDS/MPH, DDS/PhD. *Accreditation:* ADA. *Entrance requirements:* DAT. Additional exam requirements/recommendations for international students: Required—TOEFL. Electronic applications accepted.

The University of Iowa, College of Dentistry and Graduate College, Graduate Programs in Dentistry, Iowa City, IA 52242-1316. Offers endodontics (MS, Certificate); operative dentistry (MS, Certificate); oral and maxillofacial surgery (MS, Certificate); oral pathology, radiology and medicine (MS, Certificate), including oral and maxillofacial pathology (Certificate), oral and maxillofacial radiology (Certificate), stomatology (MS); oral science (MS, PhD); orthodontics (MS, Certificate); pediatric dentistry (Certificate); periodontics (MS, Certificate); preventive and community dentistry (MS), including dental public health; prosthodontics (MS, Certificate). *Accreditation:* ADA. *Degree requirements:* For master's and doctorate, thesis/dissertation. *Entrance requirements:* For master's, GRE, DDS; for Certificate, DDS. Additional exam requirements/recommendations for international students: Required—TOEFL. Expenses: Contact institution.

The University of Iowa, College of Dentistry, Professional Program in Dentistry, Iowa City, IA 52242-1316. Offers DDS. *Accreditation:* ADA. *Entrance requirements:* DAT, minimum 90 semester hours with minimum GPA of 2.5.

University of Kentucky, College of Dentistry, Lexington, KY 40506-0032. Offers DMD, MS. *Accreditation:* ADA (one or more programs are accredited). *Degree requirements:* For master's, thesis, comprehensive exam. *Entrance requirements:* For DMD, DAT, minimum undergraduate GPA of 3.0; for master's, GRE General Test, minimum undergraduate GPA of 3.0. *Expenses:* Tuition, state resident: full-time $7,670; part-time $401 per credit hour. Tuition, nonresident: full-time $16,158; part-time $873 per credit hour. *Faculty research:* Dental amalgams and mercury, Alzheimer's and aging in oral health.

University of Louisville, School of Dentistry, Professional Programs in Dentistry, Louisville, KY 40292-0001. Offers DMD. *Accreditation:* ADA. *Students:* 316 full-time (132 women), 2 part-time (1 woman); includes 45 minority (22 African Americans, 2 American Indian/Alaska Native, 16 Asian Americans or Pacific Islanders, 5 Hispanic Americans), 2 international. Average age 28. In 2006, 77 degrees awarded. *Degree requirements:* For first-professional, National Board exams. *Entrance requirements:* DAT, 32 hours of course work in science. *Application deadline:* For fall admission, 2/1 for domestic students. Application fee: $25. *Financial support:* Scholarships/grants available. Financial award application deadline: 3/15. *Unit head:* Dr. Gary A. Crim, Head, 502-852-1303, Fax: 502-852-3364, E-mail: gary.crim@louisville.edu. *Application contact:* Dr. Gary A. Crim, Head, 502-852-1303, Fax: 502-852-3364, E-mail: gary.crim@louisville.edu.

University of Manitoba, Faculty of Dentistry, Professional Program in Dentistry, Winnipeg, MB R3T 2N2, Canada. Offers DMD. *Accreditation:* ADA. *Faculty:* 46 full-time (6 women), 84 part-time/adjunct (5 women). *Students:* 135 full-time (65 women). Average age 23. 270 applicants, 9% accepted. In 2006, 26 degrees awarded. *Entrance requirements:* DAT, interview. *Application deadline:* For fall admission, 2/25 for domestic students. Application fee: $50 Canadian dollars. *Financial support:* Career-related internships or fieldwork and institutionally sponsored loans available. Financial award application deadline: 6/30. *Faculty research:* Oral physiology, microbiology, and biochemistry of the oral cavity in health and disease; application of clinical research. Total annual research expenditures: $972,000. *Application contact:* Dr. J. Elliott Scott, Associate Dean (Research), 204-789-3535, Fax: 204-789-3913, E-mail: jscott@cc.umanitoba.ca.

University of Maryland, Baltimore, Professional and Advanced Education Programs in Dentistry, Baltimore, MD 21201-1627. Offers advanced general dentistry (Certificate); dentistry (DDS); endodontics (Certificate); oral and experimental pathology (Certificate); oral biology (MS); oral-maxillofacial surgery (Certificate); orthodontics (Certificate); pediatric dentistry (Certificate); periodontics (Certificate); prosthodontics (Certificate); DDS/PhD. *Accreditation:* ADA. *Faculty:* 123 full-time (48 women), 95 part-time/adjunct (22 women). *Students:* 551 full-time (280 women); includes 161 minority (32 African Americans, 1 American Indian/Alaska Native, 111 Asian Americans or Pacific Islanders, 17 Hispanic Americans), 35 international. Average age 25. 2,375 applicants, 130 enrolled. In 2006, 103 DDSs, 11 other advanced degrees awarded. *Degree requirements:* For DDS and master's, registration. *Entrance requirements:* DAT. Additional exam requirements/recommendations for international students: Required—TOEFL. *Application deadline:* For fall admission, 1/15 for domestic students. Application fee: $65. *Expenses: Contact institution. Financial support:* In 2006–07, research assistantships (averaging $23,000 per year); career-related internships or fieldwork, Federal Work-Study, institutionally sponsored loans, scholarships/grants, and unspecified assistantships also available. Financial award application deadline: 3/1; financial award applicants required to submit FAFSA. *Faculty research:* Neuroscience, cell and molecular biology, infectious diseases and immune function. Total annual research expenditures: $12 million. *Unit head:* Dr. Christian S. Stohler, Dean, 410-706-7461, Fax: 410-706-0406, E-mail: cstohler@dental.umaryland.edu. *Application contact:* Dr. Patricia Meehan, Assistant Dean for Admissions and Recruitment, 410-706-7472, Fax: 410-706-0945, E-mail: pmeehan@umaryland.edu.

University of Medicine and Dentistry of New Jersey, New Jersey Dental School, Newark, NJ 07103-2400. Offers advanced education in general dentistry (Certificate); dental science (MDS); dentistry (DMD, MS); endodontics (Certificate); oral biology (PhD); oral medicine (Certificate); orthodontics (Certificate); pediatric dentistry (Certificate); periodontics (Certificate); prosthodontics (Certificate); DMD/MPH; DMD/MS; DMD/PhD. *Accreditation:* ADA (one or more programs are accredited). *Faculty:* 90 full-time (26 women), 118 part-time/adjunct (20 women). *Students:* 404 full-time (224 women), 1 part-time; includes 141 minority (16 African Americans, 1 American Indian/Alaska Native, 106 Asian Americans or Pacific Islanders, 18 Hispanic Americans), 14 international. Average age 26. 1,391 applicants, 14% accepted, 96 enrolled. In 2006, 80 DMDs, 4 master's, 17 other advanced degrees awarded. *Entrance requirements:* DAT. *Application deadline:* Applications are processed on a rolling basis. Application fee: $75. Electronic applications accepted. *Expenses: Contact institution. Financial support:* Fellowships, research assistantships, teaching assistantships, Federal Work-Study and institutionally sponsored loans available. Financial award application deadline: 5/1. *Unit head:* Dr. Cecile A. Feldman, Dean, 973-972-4633, Fax: 973-972-3689, E-mail: feldman@umdnj.edu. *Application contact:* Dr. Jeffrey Linfante, Director of Admissions and Student Recruitment, 973-972-5362, Fax: 973-972-0309, E-mail: linfante@umdnj.edu.

University of Michigan, School of Dentistry, Professional Program in Dentistry, Ann Arbor, MI 48109. Offers DDS. *Accreditation:* ADA. *Degree requirements:* For first-professional, Parts I and II of National Board Exams. *Entrance requirements:* DAT, 6 credits of course work in English; 8 credits of course work in each chemistry, organic chemistry, biology, and physics. Electronic applications accepted. Expenses: Contact institution.

University of Minnesota, Twin Cities Campus, School of Dentistry, Professional Program in Dentistry, Minneapolis, MN 55455-0213. Offers DDS. *Accreditation:* ADA. *Entrance requirements:* DAT. Additional exam requirements/recommendations for international students: Required—TOEFL. *Expenses:* Tuition, state resident: full-time $9,302; part-time $775 per credit. Tuition, nonresident: full-time $16,400; part-time $1,367 per credit. Full-time tuition and fees vary according to class time, course load, program, reciprocity agreements and student level.

University of Mississippi Medical Center, School of Dentistry, Jackson, MS 39216-4505. Offers DMD, MS, PhD. *Accreditation:* ADA. *Faculty:* 28 full-time (6 women), 36 part-time/adjunct (7 women). *Students:* 124 full-time (55 women); includes 25 minority (18 African Americans, 4 Asian Americans or Pacific Islanders, 3 Hispanic Americans). Average age 25. 97 applicants, 32% accepted, 30 enrolled. In 2006, 28 degrees awarded. *Entrance requirements:* DAT. *Application deadline:* For fall admission, 12/1 for domestic students. Applications are processed on a rolling basis. Application fee: $10. *Expenses: Contact institution. Financial support:* Institutionally sponsored loans and scholarships/grants available. Financial award application deadline: 4/1; financial award applicants required to submit FAFSA. *Faculty research:* Bone growth factors, salivary markers of disease, biomaterial synthesis and evaluation, metabolic bone disease, periodontal disease. Total annual research expenditures: $4 million. *Unit head:* Dr. James Hupp, Dean, 601-984-6000, Fax: 601-984-6014, E-mail: dentistry@sod.umsmed.edu. *Application contact:* Barbara Westerfield, Director, Student Records and Registrar, 601-984-1080, Fax: 601-984-1079, E-mail: bwesterfield@registrar.umsmed.edu.

University of Missouri–Kansas City, School of Dentistry, Kansas City, MO 64110-2499. Offers advanced education in dentistry (Graduate Dental Certificate); dental hygiene education (MS); dental specialties (Graduate Dental Certificate); dentistry (DDS); diagnostic sciences (Graduate Dental Certificate); oral and maxillofacial surgery (Graduate Dental Certificate); oral biology (MS, PhD); orthodontics and dentofacial orthopedics (Graduate Dental Certificate); pediatric dentistry (Graduate Dental Certificate); periodontics (Graduate Dental Certificate); prosthodontics (Graduate Dental Certificate). *Accreditation:* ADA (one or more programs are accredited). *Faculty:* 102 full-time (36 women), 77 part-time/adjunct (22 women). *Students:* 424 full-time (155 women), 34 part-time (27 women); includes 60 minority (10 African Americans, 2 American Indian/Alaska Native, 38 Asian Americans or Pacific Islanders, 10 Hispanic Americans), 12 international. Average age 27. 687 applicants, 17% accepted, 110 enrolled. In 2006, 92 DDSs, 25 other advanced degrees awarded. *Degree requirements:* For master's and doctorate, thesis/dissertation. *Entrance requirements:* For DDS, DAT; for master's, DAT, letters of evaluation, personal interview; for Graduate Dental Certificate, DDS. Additional exam requirements/recommendations for international students: Required—TOEFL. Application fee: $35 ($50 for international students). *Expenses: Contact institution. Financial support:* In 2006–07, 8 fellowships (averaging $42,540 per year), 28 research assistantships (averaging $21,670 per year) were awarded; career-related internships or fieldwork, Federal Work-Study, institutionally sponsored loans, and tuition waivers (full and partial) also available. Support available to part-time students. Financial award applicants required to submit FAFSA. *Faculty research:* Biomaterials, dental use of lasers, effectiveness of periodontal treatments, temporomandibular joint dysfunction. Total annual research expenditures: $3 million. *Unit head:* Dr. Michael Reed, Dean, 816-235-2010, E-mail: reedm@umkc.edu. *Application contact:* 816-235-2080.

University of Nebraska Medical Center, College of Dentistry, Professional Program in Dentistry, Omaha, NE 68198. Offers DDS. *Accreditation:* ADA. *Faculty:* 57 full-time (9 women), 30 part-time/adjunct (6 women). *Students:* 181 full-time (82 women), 1 part-time; includes 16 minority (3 African Americans, 1 American Indian/Alaska Native, 6 Asian Americans or Pacific Islanders, 6 Hispanic Americans), 1 international. Average age 26. 881 applicants, 6% accepted, 45 enrolled. In 2006, 43 degrees awarded. *Entrance requirements:* DAT. *Application deadline:* For fall admission, 12/1 priority date for domestic students; for spring admission, 2/1 for domestic students. Application fee: $50. *Expenses: Contact institution. Financial support:* Federal Work-Study and scholarships/grants available. Support available to part-time students. Financial award applicants required to submit FAFSA. *Application contact:* Glenda Canfield, Admissions Secretary, 402-472-1363, Fax: 402-472-5290, E-mail: gmcanfie@unmc.edu.

University of Nebraska Medical Center, College of Dentistry, Program in Dentistry, Omaha, NE 68198. Offers Certificate. *Faculty:* 12 full-time (2 women). *Students:* 31 full-time (12 women); includes 3 minority (2 Asian Americans or Pacific Islanders, 1 Hispanic American). Average age 31. 224 applicants, 7% accepted. *Degree requirements:* For Certificate, thesis or alternative. *Entrance requirements:* For degree, GRE or National Board Dental Exam, DDS or DMD. *Application deadline:* For fall admission, 9/1 for domestic students. Application fee: $50. *Financial support:* In 2006–07, 5 students received support. Scholarships/grants, health care benefits, and stipends available. Support available to part-time students. Financial award application deadline: 3/1; financial award applicants required to submit FAFSA. *Unit head:* Dr. David G. Brown, Executive Associate Dean, 402-472-1341, E-mail: dgbrown@unmc.edu. *Application contact:* Diane M. Thompson, Staff Assistant, 402-472-6261, Fax: 402-472-6668, E-mail: dmthompson@unmc.edu.

The University of North Carolina at Chapel Hill, School of Dentistry, Professional Program in Dentistry, Chapel Hill, NC 27599. Offers DDS, DDS/PhD. *Accreditation:* ADA. *Faculty:* 124 full-time, 428 part-time/adjunct. *Students:* 319 full-time (142 women); includes 100 minority (50 African Americans, 6 American Indian/Alaska Native, 34 Asian Americans or Pacific Islanders, 10 Hispanic Americans). 1,498 applicants, 6% accepted, 81 enrolled. In 2006, 78 degrees awarded. *Entrance requirements:* DAT, interview. Additional exam requirements/recommendations for international students: Required—TOEFL (minimum score 550 paper-based; 213 computer-based). *Application deadline:* For fall admission, 11/1 for domestic and international students. Application fee: $74. Electronic applications accepted. *Expenses: Contact institution. Financial support:* In 2006–07, 15 fellowships (averaging $9,000 per year), 2 research assistantships (averaging $1,000 per year) were awarded; Federal Work-Study, institutionally sponsored loans, and scholarships/grants also available. Financial award application deadline: 3/1; financial award applicants required to submit FAFSA. *Unit head:* Dr. Janet Guthmiller, Associate Dean for Academic Affairs, 919-966-4451, Fax: 919-966-5795, E-mail: janet.guthmiller@dentistry.unc.edu. *Application contact:* Dr. Albert David Guckes, Assistant Dean for Predoctoral Education, 919-966-4451, Fax: 919-966-5795, E-mail: ad_guckes@dentistry.unc.edu.

University of Oklahoma Health Sciences Center, College of Dentistry, Professional Program in Dentistry, Oklahoma City, OK 73190. Offers DDS. *Accreditation:* ADA. *Faculty:* 38 full-time (9 women), 64 part-time/adjunct (14 women). *Students:* 236 full-time (73 women); includes 46 minority (2 African Americans, 24 American Indian/Alaska Native, 16 Asian Americans or Pacific Islanders, 4 Hispanic Americans), 8 international. Average age 26. 651 applicants, 9% accepted, 58 enrolled. In 2006, 60 degrees awarded. *Degree requirements:* For first-professional, National Board Dental Exam Part 1. *Entrance requirements:* DAT, minimum GPA of 2.5; course work in English, general psychology, biology, general chemistry, organic chemistry, physics, and biochemistry. Additional exam requirements/recommendations for international students: Required—TOEFL (minimum score 570 paper-based; 230 computer-based). *Application deadline:* For fall admission, 9/1 for domestic and international students; for winter admission, 12/1 for domestic students. Applications are processed on a rolling basis. Application fee: $65 ($90 for international students). Electronic applications accepted. *Financial support:* In 2006–07, 214 students received support. Institutionally sponsored loans available. Financial award application deadline: 5/1; financial award applicants required to submit FAFSA. *Faculty research:* Dental caries, microwave sterilization, dental care delivery systems, dental materials, oral health of Native Americans. *Unit head:* Dr. Randy P. Jones, Director of Admissions and Student Affairs, 405-271-3530, Fax: 405-271-3423, E-mail: randolph-jones@ouhsc.edu. *Application contact:* Judy E. Peterson, Admissions Coordinator, 405-271-3530, Fax: 405-271-3423, E-mail: judy.peterson@ouhsc.edu.

University of Pennsylvania, School of Dental Medicine, Philadelphia, PA 19104. Offers DMD, DMD/MS Ed. *Accreditation:* ADA. *Faculty:* 68 full-time (21 women), 376 part-time/adjunct (70 women). *Students:* 516 full-time (294 women); includes 248 minority (33 African Americans, 1 American Indian/Alaska Native, 194 Asian Americans or Pacific Islanders, 20 Hispanic Americans). Average age 24. 2,205 applicants, 13% accepted, 117 enrolled. In 2006, 128 DMDs awarded. *Median time to degree:* 4 years full-time. Of those who began their doctoral program in fall 1998, 100% received their degree in 8 years or less. *Entrance requirements:* DAT. *Application deadline:* For fall admission, 1/1 for domestic students. Applications are processed on a rolling basis. Application fee: $50. *Expenses: Contact institution. Financial support:* In 2006–07, 223 students received support. Federal Work-Study and scholarships/grants available. Financial award application deadline: 6/30; financial award applicants required to submit FAFSA. *Faculty research:* Bone, teeth and extracellular matrix; craniofacial genetic anomalies; infection and host response; periodonatal diseases; stem cells. *Unit head:* Dr. Marjorie Jeffcoat, Dean, 215-898-8941, Fax: 215-573-4075. *Application contact:* Corky Cacas, Director of Admissions, 215-898-8943, Fax: 215-898-5243, E-mail: dental-admissions@pobox.upenn.edu.

University of Pittsburgh, School of Dental Medicine, Professional Program in Dental Medicine, Pittsburgh, PA 15260. Offers DMD. *Accreditation:* ADA. *Faculty:* 86 full-time (31 women), 81 part-time/adjunct (17 women). *Students:* 322 full-time (125 women); includes 91 minority (5 African Americans, 3 American Indian/Alaska Native, 59 Asian Americans or Pacific Islanders, 24 Hispanic Americans), 11 international. Average age 26. 1,880 applicants, 14% accepted, 78 enrolled. In 2006, 65 degrees awarded. *Entrance requirements:* DAT, minimum GPA of 3.2 (science and non-science). Additional exam requirements/recommendations for international students: Required—TOEFL (minimum score 600 paper-based; 250 computer-based; 100 iBT). *Application deadline:* For fall admission, 12/1 for domestic and international students. Applications are processed on a rolling basis. Application fee: $35 ($50 for international students). *Expenses:* Contact institution. *Financial support:* In 2006–07, 300 students received support, including 1 fellowship (averaging $50,436 per year), 1 teaching assistantship with full tuition reimbursement available (averaging $13,555 per year); scholarships/grants also available. Financial award application deadline: 4/30; financial award applicants required to submit FAFSA. *Faculty research:* Human genetics, tissue engineering, public health, periodontal disease, cavities. Total annual research expenditures: $3.7 million. *Unit head:* Dr. Kenneth Etzel, Associate Dean of Education, Director for Student Services, 412-648-8422, Fax: 412-648-9751, E-mail: kre@pitt.edu. *Application contact:* Rosemary Mangold, Recruitment/Financial Aid Officer, 412-648-8437, Fax: 412-648-9571, E-mail: mangold@pitt.edu.

University of Pittsburgh, School of Dental Medicine, Residency Programs in Dental Medicine, Department of Pediatric Dentistry, Pittsburgh, PA 15260. Offers MDS, Certificate. *Accreditation:* ADA. *Faculty:* 3 full-time (2 women), 1 part-time/adjunct (0 women). *Students:* 1 (woman) full-time. Average age 27. 42 applicants, 5% accepted. In 2006, 1 degree awarded. *Degree requirements:* For Certificate, clinical research. *Entrance requirements:* For degree, National Dental Board Exam: Parts 1 and 2, US or Canadian dental degree. *Application deadline:* For fall admission, 10/15 for domestic students. Application fee: $50. Electronic applications accepted. *Financial support:* In 2006–07, 1 student received support, including 1 fellowship (averaging $25,000 per year). *Faculty research:* Sports dentistry, behavior management, women's oral health, adolescent oral health. *Unit head:* Dr. Deborah A. Studen-Pavlovich, Chair and Professor, 412-648-8183, Fax: 412-648-8435, E-mail: das12@pitt.edu. *Application contact:* Sharon Hohman, Departmental Secretary, 412-648-8416, Fax: 412-648-8435, E-mail: sah10@pitt.edu.

University of Pittsburgh, School of Dental Medicine, Residency Programs in Dental Medicine, Program in Advanced Education in General Dentistry, Pittsburgh, PA 15260. Offers Certificate. *Accreditation:* ADA. *Faculty:* 3 part-time/adjunct (1 woman). *Students:* 3 full-time (1 woman); includes 1 minority (Asian American or Pacific Islander) Average age 28. 35 applicants, 9% accepted, 3 enrolled. In 2006, 3 degrees awarded. *Degree requirements:* For degree, registration. *Entrance requirements:* For degree, American or Canadian DDS or DMD degree. *Application deadline:* For fall admission, 12/15 for domestic and international students. Applications are processed on a rolling basis. *Financial support:* In 2006–07, 3 fellowships (averaging $23,000 per year) were awarded. *Unit head:* Dr. Maribeth Krzesinski, Director AEGD, 412-648-8093, Fax: 412-383-7796, E-mail: mbk3@pitt.edu.

University of Puerto Rico, Medical Sciences Campus, School of Dentistry, Professional Program in Dentistry, San Juan, PR 00936-5067. Offers DMD. *Accreditation:* ADA. *Faculty:* 91 full-time (36 women), 53 part-time/adjunct (18 women). *Students:* 208 full-time (121 women); includes 204 minority (all Hispanic Americans) Average age 25. 302 applicants, 13% accepted, 40 enrolled. In 2006, 40 degrees awarded. *Degree requirements:* For first-professional, registration. *Entrance requirements:* DAT, interview. *Application deadline:* For fall admission, 12/1 for domestic and international students. Application fee: $20. *Expenses:* Contact institution. *Financial support:* In 2006–07, 110 students received support, including 9 research assistantships (averaging $3,600 per year), 24 teaching assistantships (averaging $3,600 per year); Federal Work-Study, institutionally sponsored loans, scholarships/grants, and tuition waivers (partial) also available. Financial award application deadline: 5/12; financial award applicants required to submit FAFSA. *Faculty research:* Analgesic drugs, anti-inflammatory drugs, saliva cytoanalysis, dental material and cariology, oral health condition of school-age population. Total annual research expenditures: $1.7 million. *Unit head:* Dr. Aileen Marie Torres, Assistant Dean of Student Affairs, 787-758-2525 Ext. 1113, Fax: 787-751-0990, E-mail: citorres@rcm.upr.edu.

University of Saskatchewan, College of Dentistry, Saskatoon, SK S7N 5A2, Canada. Offers DMD. *Accreditation:* ADA. *Faculty:* 23 full-time (5 women), 61 part-time/adjunct (14 women). *Students:* 111 full-time (40 women). Average age 25. 347 applicants, 8% accepted, 28 enrolled. In 2006, 28 degrees awarded. *Entrance requirements:* DAT. Additional exam requirements/recommendations for international students: Required—TOEFL (minimum score 550 paper-based; 213 computer-based; 80 iBT), IELTS (minimum score 7), Michigan English Language Assessment Battery (85); CanTEST (4.0); CAEL (60); CPE (C). *Application deadline:* For fall admission, 1/15 for domestic and international students. Application fee: $125 Canadian dollars. Electronic applications accepted. *Expenses:* Contact institution. *Financial support:* In 2006–07, 15 students received support. Career-related internships or fieldwork and scholarships/grants available. *Faculty research:* Protein structure, oral cavity, immunology, bone densitometry, biological sciences. Total annual research expenditures: $32,113. *Unit head:* Dr. Gerry Stephen Uswak, Acting Dean, 306-966-5122, Fax: 306-966-5126, E-mail: gerry.uswak@usask.ca. *Application contact:* Jacquie Fraser, Director of Academic and Student Affairs, 306-966-5119, Fax: 306-966-5126, E-mail: jacquie.fraser@usask.ca.

University of Southern California, Graduate School, School of Dentistry, Professional Program in Dentistry, Los Angeles, CA 90089. Offers DDS, Certificate, DDS/MBA, DDS/MS. *Accreditation:* ADA (one or more programs are accredited). *Students:* 744 full-time (307 women); includes 301 minority (11 African Americans, 2 American Indian/Alaska Native, 256 Asian Americans or Pacific Islanders, 32 Hispanic Americans), 52 international. In 2006, 142 degrees awarded. *Entrance requirements:* DAT. Application fee: $85. *Expenses:* Tuition: Full-time $33,314; part-time $1,121 per credit. Required fees: $522. Full-time tuition and fees vary according to program. *Financial support:* Fellowships, research assistantships, teaching assistantships, Federal Work-Study, institutionally sponsored loans, and scholarships/grants available. Support available to part-time students. Financial award application deadline: 2/15; financial award applicants required to submit FAFSA. *Unit head:* Dr. Ilan Rotstein, Chair, 213-740-2841, E-mail: scdental@hsc.usc.edu.

The University of Tennessee Health Science Center, College of Dentistry, Memphis, TN 38163-0002. Offers dentistry (DDS); oral and maxillofacial surgery (Certificate); orthodontics (MS); pediatric dentistry (MS, Certificate); periodontics (MS); prosthodontics (Certificate). *Accreditation:* ADA (one or more programs are accredited). *Faculty:* 57 full-time (8 women), 66 part-time/adjunct (6 women). *Students:* 357 full-time (149 women); includes 80 minority (42 African Americans, 32 Asian Americans or Pacific Islanders, 6 Hispanic Americans). Average age 23. 255 applicants, 37% accepted, 95 enrolled. In 2006, 72 DDSs, 6 master's awarded. *Degree requirements:* For master's, thesis. *Entrance requirements:* For DDS, DAT, interview, pre-professional evaluation; for master's, GRE, interviews. Additional exam requirements/recommendations for international students: Required—TOEFL (minimum score 275 computer-based). *Application deadline:* For fall admission, 12/31 for domestic and international students. Applications are processed on a rolling basis. Application fee: $50. Electronic applications accepted. *Expenses:* Contact institution. One-time fee: $55 full-time. *Financial support:* In 2006–07, 278 students received support. Federal Work-Study and minority scholarships available. Support available to part-time students. Financial award application deadline: 2/15; financial award applicants required to submit FAFSA. *Faculty research:* Oral cancer, proteomics,

inflammation mechanisms, defensins, periopathogens, dental material. Total annual research expenditures: $275,000. *Unit head:* Dr. Russell O. Gilpatrick, Dean, 901-448-6202, Fax: 901-448-1625, E-mail: rgilpatrick@utmem.edu. *Application contact:* Dr. Wisdom F. Coleman, Admissions, Associate Dean, 901-448-4200, Fax: 901-448-1625, E-mail: wcoleman@utmem.edu.

The University of Texas Health Science Center at Houston, The University of Texas Dental Branch at Houston, Houston, TX 77225-0036. Offers DDS, MS. *Accreditation:* ADA. *Faculty:* 88 full-time (29 women), 72 part-time/adjunct (21 women). *Students:* 282 full-time (136 women); includes 120 minority (12 African Americans, 1 American Indian/Alaska Native, 107 Hispanic Americans). Average age 26. 1,193 applicants, 14% accepted, 84 enrolled. In 2006, 62 degrees awarded. *Entrance requirements:* DAT, 90 semester hours of prerequisite courses. *Application deadline:* For fall admission, 10/15 for domestic students. Applications are processed on a rolling basis. Application fee: $80. Electronic applications accepted. *Financial support:* In 2006–07, 23 students received support. Institutionally sponsored loans and scholarships/grants available. Financial award applicants required to submit FAFSA. *Unit head:* Dr. Catherine M. Flaitz, Dean, 713-500-4021, Fax: 713-500-4089. *Application contact:* Dr. H. Philip Pierpont, Associate Dean for Student and Alumni Affairs, 713-500-4151, Fax: 713-500-4425, E-mail: dbstudentaffairs@uthouston.edu.

The University of Texas Health Science Center at San Antonio, Dental School, San Antonio, TX 78229-3900. Offers DDS, MS, Certificate, DDS/PhD. *Accreditation:* ADA (one or more programs are accredited). *Faculty:* 110 full-time (28 women), 85 part-time/adjunct (18 women). *Students:* 353 full-time (159 women); includes 112 minority (8 African Americans, 1 American Indian/Alaska Native, 40 Asian Americans or Pacific Islanders, 63 Hispanic Americans). Average age 26. 1,025 applicants, 9% accepted, 94 enrolled. In 2006, 81 first professional degrees, 10 master's awarded. *Degree requirements:* For DDS, comprehensive exam, registration; for master's, thesis. *Entrance requirements:* For DDS, DAT; for master's, GRE General Test, DDS; for Certificate, DDS. *Application deadline:* For fall admission, 10/1 for domestic students. Application fee: $75. Electronic applications accepted. *Expenses:* Tuition, state resident: part-time $50 per credit hour. Tuition, nonresident: part-time $325 per credit hour. Required fees: $7.5 per credit hour. $155 per term. *Financial support:* In 2006–07, 311 students received support; teaching assistantships, institutionally sponsored loans and scholarships/grants available. Financial award application deadline: 3/1; financial award applicants required to submit FAFSA. *Faculty research:* Nutrition and oral health, periodontal disease, biomaterials, bone mineralization, caries prevention. *Unit head:* Dr. D. Denee Thomas, Associate Dean for Student Affairs, 210-567-3752, Fax: 210-567-4776, E-mail: thomasd@uthscsa.edu. *Application contact:* Sofia Almeda, Office of Admissions and Student Services, 210-567-2659, Fax: 210-567-2685, E-mail: almedas@uthscsa.edu.

University of the Pacific, Arthur A. Dugoni School of Dentistry, Professional Program in Dentistry, Stockton, CA 95211-0197. Offers DDS. *Accreditation:* ADA. In 2006, 137 degrees awarded. *Entrance requirements:* DAT. *Application deadline:* For fall admission, 2/1 priority date for domestic students; for winter admission, 2/1 for domestic students. Applications are processed on a rolling basis. Electronic applications accepted. *Expenses:* Tuition: Full-time $26,920. Required fees: $430. Tuition and fees vary according to course load. *Financial support:* In 2006–07, 374 students received support. Institutionally sponsored loans, scholarships/grants, and stipends available. Support available to part-time students. Financial award application deadline: 3/2; financial award applicants required to submit FAFSA. *Faculty research:* Cell kinetics, cell membrane transport, virus/cell fusion, implants, bioenergy transduction. *Unit head:* Dr. Craig S. Yarborough, Associate Dean for Institutional Advancement and Student Services, 415-929-6491. *Application contact:* Kathy Candito, Director, 415-929-6495, Fax: 415-929-6654.

University of the Pacific, Arthur A. Dugoni School of Dentistry, Program in Advanced Education in General Dentistry, Stockton, CA 95211-0197. Offers Certificate. *Accreditation:* ADA. In 2006, 14 degrees awarded. *Entrance requirements:* For degree, DDS/DMD. *Application deadline:* For fall admission, 10/1 priority date for domestic students. *Expenses:* Contact institution. Tuition and fees vary according to course load. *Financial support:* Stipend available. *Unit head:* Dr. Paul Glassman, Director, 415-929-6490, Fax: 415-749-3334, E-mail: pglassman@pacific.edu. *Application contact:* Gloria Sue, Coordinator, 415-749-6677, Fax: 415-749-3334, E-mail: gsue@pacific.edu.

University of the Pacific, Arthur A. Dugoni School of Dentistry, Program in International Dental Studies, San Francisco, CA 94115. Offers DDS. *Accreditation:* ADA. *Entrance requirements:* National Board Dental Exam I, foreign dental degree. Additional exam requirements/recommendations for international students: Required—TOEFL (minimum score 580 paper-based; 237 computer-based). *Application deadline:* For fall admission, 10/15 for domestic students, 9/15 priority date for international students. Applications are processed on a rolling basis. *Expenses:* Contact institution. Tuition and fees vary according to course load. *Financial support:* Institutionally sponsored loans available. Financial award application deadline: 3/2; financial award applicants required to submit FAFSA. *Faculty research:* Temporomandibular joint, facial pain, cell kinetics, cell membrane transport, virus/cell fusion. *Unit head:* Dr. David B. Nielsen, Associate Dean, Postgraduate and Community Programs, 415-929-6486. *Application contact:* Patricia King, Director, 415-929-6688.

University of the Pacific, Arthur A. Dugoni School of Dentistry, Program in Orthodontics, Stockton, CA 95211-0197. Offers dentistry (MSD). *Degree requirements:* For master's, thesis, comprehensive exam. *Entrance requirements:* For master's, GRE General Test, DDS/DMD. Additional exam requirements/recommendations for international students: Required—TOEFL. *Application deadline:* For fall admission, 10/1 for domestic and international students. *Expenses:* Contact institution. Tuition and fees vary according to course load. *Financial support:* Institutionally sponsored loans and stipends available. Financial award application deadline: 2/1. *Faculty research:* Osteoblast cell studies, digitized orthodontic records, periodontal orthodontic relationships, orthotreatment outcomes. *Unit head:* Dr. Robert Boyd, Chairperson, 415-929-6555. *Application contact:* Loretta Giglione, Information Contact, 415-929-6556, Fax: 415-749-3390.

University of Toronto, Faculty of Dentistry, Professional Program in Dentistry, Toronto, ON M5S 1A1, Canada. Offers DDS. *Accreditation:* ADA. *Entrance requirements:* Canadian Dental Aptitude Test (or equivalent), minimum GPA of 2.7; completion of at least 2 courses in life sciences and 1 course in humanities or social sciences. Additional exam requirements/recommendations for international students: Required—Michigan English Language Assessment Battery, TOEFL, IELTS or COPE. Expenses: Contact institution.

University of Washington, School of Dentistry, Professional Program in Dentistry, Seattle, WA 98195. Offers DDS, DDS/MS. *Accreditation:* ADA. *Entrance requirements:* DAT.

The University of Western Ontario, Schulich School of Medicine and Dentistry, School of Dentistry, Professional Program in Dentistry, London, ON N6A 5B8, Canada. Offers DDS. *Accreditation:* ADA. *Entrance requirements:* DAT (Canadian version), minimum B average. *Application deadline:* For fall admission, 12/1 for domestic students. Application fee: $0 Canadian dollars. *Financial support:* Federal Work-Study and institutionally sponsored loans available. *Unit head:* Dr. Stanley Kogon, Director, 519-661-2111 Ext. 83330. *Application contact:* Dr. H. S. Sandhu, Director, 519-661-2111 Ext. 86141, Fax: 519-661-3875, E-mail: harinder.sandhu@schulich.uwo.ca.

Virginia Commonwealth University, Medical College of Virginia-Professional Programs, School of Dentistry, Richmond, VA 23284-9005. Offers DDS, DDS/MS, DDS/PhD. *Accreditation:* ADA. *Faculty:* 46 full-time (7 women). *Students:* 397 full-time (134 women); includes 78 minority (14 African Americans, 1 American Indian/Alaska Native, 55 Asian Americans or Pacific Islanders, 8 Hispanic Americans), 19 international. 122 applicants, 98% accepted, 109 enrolled. In 2006, 85 DDSs awarded. *Entrance requirements:* DAT. *Application deadline:* For fall admission, 1/1 for domestic students. Electronic applications accepted. *Expenses:* Contact institution. *Financial support:* Fellowships available. *Unit head:* Dr. Ronald J. Hunt, Dean,

Dentistry

Virginia Commonwealth University (continued)
804-828-9184, Fax: 804-828-6072, E-mail: rjhunt@vcu.edu. *Application contact:* Dr. Carolyn L. Booker, Assistant Dean of Student Affairs and Admissions, 804-828-9953, Fax: 804-828-5288, E-mail: clbooker@vcu.edu.

See Close-Up on page 2185.

West Virginia University, School of Dentistry, Professional Program in Dentistry, Morgantown, WV 26506. Offers DDS. *Accreditation:* ADA. *Students:* 193 full-time (88 women); includes 15 minority (2 African Americans, 7 Asian Americans or Pacific Islanders, 6 Hispanic Americans), 5 international. Average age 25. In 2006, 43 degrees awarded. *Degree requirements:* For first-professional, comprehensive exam, registration. *Entrance requirements:* DAT, Letters of recommendation, interview, and pre-requisite courses. *Application deadline:* For fall admission, 11/30 for domestic and international students. Applications are processed on a rolling basis. Application fee: $50. *Expenses:* Tuition, state resident: full-time $4,926; part-time $276 per credit hour. Tuition, nonresident: full-time $14,278; part-time $796 per credit hour. Tuition and fees vary according to program. *Financial support:* In 2006–07, 161 students received support. Federal Work-Study, institutionally sponsored loans, scholarships/grants, and tuition waivers (partial) available. Financial award application deadline: 3/1; financial award applicants required to submit FAFSA. *Faculty research:* Bimaterials, topical drug placement and immunmodualtion, pharmacological evaluation of analgesics, local anesthetics, oral health disparities. *Unit head:* Dr. Sheila Price, Associate Dean for Admissions, Recruitment, and Access, 304-293-1980, E-mail: sprice@hsc.wvu.edu.

Oral and Dental Sciences

A.T. Still University of Health Sciences, Arizona School of Dentistry and Oral Health, Mesa, AZ 85206. Offers dental medicine (DMD). *Accreditation:* ADA. *Faculty:* 26 full-time (12 women), 226 part-time/adjunct (71 women). *Students:* 216 full-time (100 women); includes 56 minority (2 African Americans, 12 American Indian/Alaska Native, 28 Asian Americans or Pacific Islanders, 14 Hispanic Americans). Average age 25. 2,915 applicants, 54 enrolled. *Degree requirements:* For first-professional, National Board Exams I and II. *Entrance requirements:* DAT, minimum GPA of 2.5 overall and in science. *Application deadline:* For fall admission, 12/1 for domestic students. Applications are processed on a rolling basis. Application fee: $60. Electronic applications accepted. *Expenses: Contact institution. Financial support:* In 2006–07, 214 students received support. Federal Work-Study and scholarships/grants available. Financial award application deadline: 5/1; financial award applicants required to submit FAFSA. *Unit head:* Dr. Jack Dillenberg, Dean, 480-219-6000, Fax: 480-219-6110, E-mail: jdillenberg@atsu.edu. *Application contact:* Donna Sparks, Associate Director for Admissions, 660-626-2237, Fax: 660-626-2969, E-mail: admissions@atsu.edu.

Boston University, Goldman School of Dental Medicine, Graduate Programs in Dentistry, Boston, MA 02215. Offers advanced general dentistry (CAGS); dental public health (MS, MSD, D Sc D, CAGS); dentistry (DMD); endodontics (MSD, D Sc D, CAGS); implantology (CAGS); operative dentistry (MSD, D Sc D, CAGS); oral and maxillofacial surgery (MSD, D Sc D, CAGS); oral biology (MSD, D Sc, D Sc D, PhD); orthodontics (MSD, D Sc D, CAGS); pediatric dentistry (MSD, D Sc D, CAGS); periodontology (MSD, D Sc D, CAGS); prosthodontics (MSD, D Sc D, CAGS). *Students:* 152 full-time (62 women); includes 13 minority (1 African American, 11 Asian Americans or Pacific Islanders, 1 Hispanic American), 75 international. Average age 29. In 2006, 224 first professional degrees, 22 master's, 10 doctorates, 63 other advanced degrees awarded. *Degree requirements:* For master's and doctorate, thesis/dissertation; for CAGS, thesis (for some programs). *Entrance requirements:* For DMD, DAT, minimum GPA of 3.0; for CAGS, dental degree. *Application deadline:* For fall admission, 5/1 for domestic students. Applications are processed on a rolling basis. Application fee: $60. *Expenses: Contact institution. Financial support:* Career-related internships or fieldwork and institutionally sponsored loans available. Financial award application deadline: 4/15; financial award applicants required to submit CSS PROFILE or FAFSA. *Faculty research:* Defensive mechanisms, bone-cell regulation, protein biochemistry, molecular biology, biomaterials. *Application contact:* 617-638-4787, Fax: 617-638-4798.

See Close-Up on page 2179.

Case Western Reserve University, School of Dental Medicine and School of Graduate Studies, Advanced Specialty Education Programs in Dentistry, Cleveland, OH 44106. Offers advanced general dentistry (Certificate); endodontics (MSD, Certificate); oral surgery (Certificate); orthodontics (MSD, Certificate); pedodontics (MSD, Certificate); periodontics (MSD, Certificate). *Faculty:* 28 full-time (5 women), 90 part-time/adjunct (30 women). *Students:* 53 full-time (20 women), 2 part-time (both women); includes 13 minority (5 African Americans, 6 Asian Americans or Pacific Islanders, 2 Hispanic Americans), 15 international. Average age 31. 483 applicants, 5% accepted, 22 enrolled. In 2006, 14 master's awarded. *Median time to degree:* Of those who began their doctoral program in fall 1998, 100% received their degree in 8 years or less. *Degree requirements:* For master's, thesis, registration. *Entrance requirements:* For master's, National Dental Board Exam, DDS, minimum GPA of 3.0; for Certificate, DDS. Additional exam requirements/recommendations for international students: Required—TOEFL (minimum score 550 paper-based; 213 computer-based; 79 iBT). *Application deadline:* For fall admission, 9/1 for domestic and international students. Applications are processed on a rolling basis. Application fee: $50. *Expenses: Contact institution. Financial support:* In 2006–07, 19 students received support. Federal Work-Study, institutionally sponsored loans, and health care benefits available. Financial award application deadline: 4/20; financial award applicants required to submit FAFSA. *Faculty research:* Natural antibiotics, obesity and periodontal disease, perioninfection and CV disease, periodontal disease and overall health, 3D cone beam computerized tomography. *Unit head:* Dr. Stanley A. Hirsch, Associate Dean for Graduate Studies, 216-368-4262, Fax: 216-368-3204, E-mail: sah4@cwru.edu. *Application contact:* Loretta Dahlstrom, Department Assistant for Graduate Studies, 216-368-6731, Fax: 216-368-3204, E-mail: lxd29@cwru.edu.

Columbia University, School of Dental and Oral Surgery and Graduate School of Arts and Sciences, Graduate Program in Dental and Oral Surgery, New York, NY 10027. Offers clinical specialty (MA). *Degree requirements:* For master's, thesis, presentation of seminar. *Entrance requirements:* For master's, GRE General Test, DDS or equivalent. Expenses: Contact institution. *Faculty research:* Analysis of growth/form, pulpal microcirculation, implants, microbiology of oral environment, calcified tissues.

Dalhousie University, Faculty of Dentistry, Halifax, NS B3H 4R2, Canada. Offers dental hygiene (Diploma); dentistry (DDS); prosthodontics (MS); MD/M Sc. *Entrance requirements:* For DDS, DAT, 2 years undergraduate university study; for master's and Diploma, DDS. Additional exam requirements/recommendations for international students: Required—TWE (minimum score 5), TOEFL (580 paper-based; 237 computer-based) or IELTS (7 paper-based). Expenses: Contact institution.

Dalhousie University, Faculty of Graduate Studies and Faculty of Dentistry, Graduate Programs in Dentistry, Department of Oral and Maxillofacial Sciences, Halifax, NS B3H 4R2, Canada. Offers MD/M Sc. Expenses: Contact institution. *Faculty research:* Cleft lip/palate, jaw biomechanics.

The George Washington University, School of Medicine and Health Sciences, Health Sciences Programs, Program in Oral Biology, Washington, DC 20052. Offers MSHS. Offered jointly with the National Naval Dental Center and open only to selected active duty military personnel. *Entrance requirements:* For master's, active duty military, 4 years of service as dental officer.

Harvard University, Graduate School of Arts and Sciences, Program in Biological Sciences in Dental Medicine, Cambridge, MA 02138. Offers PhD. *Expenses:* Tuition: Full-time $30,275. Full-time tuition and fees vary according to program and student level. *Unit head:* Gamalia Pharms, Administrator, 617-432-2875.

Harvard University, School of Dental Medicine, Advanced Graduate Programs in Dentistry, Cambridge, MA 02138. Offers advanced general dentistry (Certificate); dental public health (Certificate); endodontics (Certificate); general practice residency (Certificate); oral biology (M Med Sc, D Med Sc); oral pathology (Certificate); oral surgery (Certificate); orthodontics (Certificate); pediatric dentistry (Certificate); periodontics (Certificate); prosthodontics (Certificate). *Expenses:* Tuition: Full-time $30,275. Full-time tuition and fees vary according to program and student level.

Howard University, College of Dentistry, Washington, DC 20059-0002. Offers advanced education program general dentistry (Certificate); dentistry (DDS); general dentistry (Certificate); oral and maxillofacial surgery (Certificate); orthodontics (Certificate); pediatric dentistry (Certificate). *Accreditation:* ADA (one or more programs are accredited). *Degree requirements:* For first-professional, didactic and clinical exams. *Entrance requirements:* DAT, 8 semester hours of course work in each biology, inorganic chemistry, organic chemistry. Expenses: Contact institution. *Faculty research:* Epidemiological, biomaterial, molecular genetic, behavioral modification, and clinical trial studies.

Idaho State University, Office of Graduate Studies, Kasiska College of Health Professions, Department of Dental Sciences, Pocatello, ID 83209. Offers advanced general dentistry (Post-Doctoral Certificate); dental hygiene (MS). Postbaccalaureate distance learning degree programs offered (minimal on-campus study). *Faculty:* 6 full-time (all women). *Students:* 18 full-time (5 women), 21 part-time (all women); includes 3 minority (1 Asian American or Pacific Islander, 2 Hispanic Americans), 1 international. Average age 27. In 2006, 4 degrees awarded. *Degree requirements:* For master's, thesis, one year sequences, practicum, comprehensive exam, registration; for Post-Doctoral Certificate, 1 year residency, thesis optional. *Entrance requirements:* For master's, GRE and/or MAT, minimum GPA of 3.0 in upper division undergraduate courses, current dental hygiene license, 2 letters of recommendation; for Post-Doctoral Certificate, DAT. Additional exam requirements/recommendations for international students: Required—TOEFL (minimum score 600 paper-based; 213 computer-based). *Application deadline:* For fall admission, 7/1 for domestic students, 6/1 for international students; for spring admission, 12/1 for domestic students, 11/1 for international students. Applications are processed on a rolling basis. Application fee: $55. *Expenses: Contact institution. Financial support:* In 2006–07, 1 teaching assistantship with full and partial tuition reimbursement (averaging $8,694 per year) was awarded. Financial award application deadline: 1/1. *Unit head:* Dr. Brian Crawford, Chair, 208-282-5275, Fax: 208-282-5834, E-mail: crawbri3@isu.edu. *Application contact:* Ellen Combs, Graduate School Technical Records Specialist, 208-282-2150, Fax: 208-282-4847.

Jacksonville University, College of Arts and Sciences, School of Orthodontics, Jacksonville, FL 32211-3394. Offers Certificate. *Accreditation:* ADA. *Entrance requirements:* Additional exam requirements/recommendations for international students: Required—TOEFL. Expenses: Contact institution.

Loma Linda University, School of Dentistry, Graduate Programs in Dentistry, Program in Endodontics, Loma Linda, CA 92350. Offers MS, Certificate, MS/Certificate. *Degree requirements:* For master's, thesis. *Entrance requirements:* For master's, GRE General Test, DDS or DMD, minimum GPA of 3.0.

Loma Linda University, School of Dentistry, Graduate Programs in Dentistry, Program in Implant Dentistry, Loma Linda, CA 92350. Offers MS, Certificate, MS/Certificate. *Degree requirements:* For master's, thesis. *Entrance requirements:* For master's, GRE General Test, DDS or DMD, minimum GPA of 3.0.

Loma Linda University, School of Dentistry, Graduate Programs in Dentistry, Program in Oral and Maxillofacial Surgery, Loma Linda, CA 92350. Offers MS, Certificate, MS/Certificate. *Degree requirements:* For master's, thesis. *Entrance requirements:* For master's, GRE General Test, DDS or DMD, minimum GPA of 3.0.

Loma Linda University, School of Dentistry, Graduate Programs in Dentistry, Program in Orthodontics, Loma Linda, CA 92350. Offers MS, Certificate, MS/Certificate. *Degree requirements:* For master's, thesis. *Entrance requirements:* For master's, GRE General Test, DDS or DMD, minimum GPA of 3.0.

Loma Linda University, School of Dentistry, Graduate Programs in Dentistry, Program in Periodontics, Loma Linda, CA 92350. Offers MS. *Degree requirements:* For master's, thesis. *Entrance requirements:* For master's, GRE General Test, DDS or DMD, minimum GPA of 3.0.

Marquette University, School of Dentistry and Graduate School, Graduate Programs in Dentistry, Program in Advanced Training in General Dentistry, Milwaukee, WI 53201-1881. Offers MS. *Entrance requirements:* Additional exam requirements/recommendations for international students: Required—TOEFL. *Faculty research:* Biochemistry.

Marquette University, School of Dentistry and Graduate School, Graduate Programs in Dentistry, Program in Dental Biomaterials, Milwaukee, WI 53201-1881. Offers MS. Part-time programs available. *Degree requirements:* For master's, thesis. *Entrance requirements:* For master's, GRE General Test. Additional exam requirements/recommendations for international students: Required—TOEFL. *Faculty research:* Composite resins, dentin bonding agents.

Marquette University, School of Dentistry and Graduate School, Graduate Programs in Dentistry, Program in Endodontics, Milwaukee, WI 53201-1881. Offers MS. *Degree requirements:* For master's, thesis or alternative. *Entrance requirements:* For master's, DDS or equivalent. Additional exam requirements/recommendations for international students: Required—TOEFL. *Faculty research:* Mechanical properties of endodontic files, use of lasers in endodontics.

Marquette University, School of Dentistry and Graduate School, Graduate Programs in Dentistry, Program in Orthodontics, Milwaukee, WI 53201-1881. Offers MS. *Degree requirements:* For master's, thesis or alternative. *Entrance requirements:* For master's, DDS or equivalent. Additional exam requirements/recommendations for international students: Required—TOEFL. *Faculty research:* Biomaterials, adhesion.

Marquette University, School of Dentistry and Graduate School, Graduate Programs in Dentistry, Program in Prosthodontics, Milwaukee, WI 53201-1881. Offers MS. *Degree requirements:* For master's, thesis or alternative. *Entrance requirements:* For master's, DDS or equivalent. Additional exam requirements/recommendations for international students: Required—TOEFL. *Faculty research:* Biomaterials, implants.

McGill University, Faculty of Graduate and Postdoctoral Studies, Faculty of Dentistry, Graduate Program in Oral and Maxillofacial Surgery, Montréal, QC H3A 2T5, Canada. Offers M Sc, PhD. *Degree requirements:* For master's and doctorate, thesis/dissertation, registration. *Entrance requirements:* For master's, GRE General Test, minimum GPA of 3.0, DMD or equivalent. Additional exam requirements/recommendations for international students: Required—TOEFL (minimum score 550 paper-based; 213 computer-based), IELTS (minimum score 7). Electronic applications accepted.

Medical College of Georgia, School of Graduate Studies, Department of Oral Biology and Maxillofacial Pathology, Augusta, GA 30912. Offers MS, PhD. Part-time programs available. *Faculty:* 25 full-time (5 women). *Students:* 3 full-time (1 woman), 12 part-time (1 woman); includes 6 minority (1 African American, 3 Asian Americans or Pacific Islanders, 2 Hispanic Americans), 3 international. Average age 32. 19 applicants, 63% accepted, 3 enrolled. In 2006, 2 degrees awarded. *Degree requirements:* For master's and doctorate, thesis/dissertation. *Entrance requirements:* For master's, DAT or GRE General Test, DDS, DMD, or equivalent degree or dental student; for doctorate, DAT or GRE General Test. Additional exam requirements/recommendations for international students: Required—TOEFL (minimum score 550 paper-based; 213 computer-based). *Application deadline:* For fall admission, 1/15 for domestic students. Applications are processed on a rolling basis. Application fee: $30. Electronic applications accepted. *Expenses:* Tuition, state resident: full-time $2,293; part-time $192 per credit hour. Tuition, nonresident: full-time $9,169; part-time $765 per credit hour. Required fees: $293 per semester. *Financial support:* In 2006–07, 2 students received support; research assistantships with partial tuition reimbursements available, Federal Work-Study, institutionally sponsored loans, scholarships/grants, and tuition waivers available. Support available to part-time students. Financial award application deadline: 5/31; financial award applicants required to submit FAFSA. *Faculty research:* Oral cancer and chemoprevention, properties of biomaterials including biocompatibility and shear stress responses, taurine and blood pressure in diabetes, dentin biology, induction of periodontal regeneration. *Unit head:* Dr. George S. Schuster, Chair, 706-721-2991, Fax: 706-721-3392, E-mail: gschuste@mail.mcg.edu. *Application contact:* Dr. Jill Lewis, Director, 706-721-2991, Fax: 706-721-3392, E-mail: jillewis@mail.mcg.edu.

New York University, College of Dentistry, Postgraduate Programs in Dentistry, New York, NY 10012-1019. Offers endodontics (Advanced Certificate); oral and maxillofacial surgery (Advanced Certificate); orthodontics (Advanced Certificate); pediatric dentistry (Advanced Certificate); periodontics (Advanced Certificate); prosthodontics (Advanced Certificate); prosthodontics (implantology) (Advanced Certificate). Part-time programs available. *Faculty:* 227 full-time, 663 part-time/adjunct. *Students:* 47 full-time (23 women), 9 part-time (5 women); includes 21 minority (3 African Americans, 16 Asian Americans or Pacific Islanders, 2 Hispanic Americans). Average age 33. 571 applicants, 10% accepted, 56 enrolled. In 2006, 43 degrees awarded. *Entrance requirements:* For degree, DDS. Additional exam requirements/recommendations for international students: Required—TOEFL (minimum score 230 computer-based). *Application deadline:* For fall admission, 12/1 for domestic students. Application fee: $75. Electronic applications accepted. *Expenses:* Tuition: Part-time $1,080 per unit. Required fees: $56 per unit. $329 per term. Tuition and fees vary according to program. *Financial support:* Scholarships/grants and unspecified assistantships available. Financial award application deadline: 3/1; financial award applicants required to submit FAFSA. *Application contact:* Dr. Anthony M. Palatta, Assistant Dean for Student Affairs and Admissions, 212-998-9918, Fax: 212-995-4240, E-mail: ap16@nyu.edu.

New York University, Graduate School of Arts and Science, Department of Biology, New York, NY 10012-1019. Offers biology (PhD); biomedical journalism (MS); cancer and molecular biology (PhD); computational biology (PhD); computers in biological research (MS); developmental genetics (PhD); general biology (MS); immunology and microbiology (PhD); molecular genetics (PhD); neurobiology (PhD); oral biology (MS); plant biology (PhD); recombinant DNA technology (MS); MS/MBA. Part-time programs available. *Faculty:* 24 full-time (5 women), 8 part-time/adjunct. *Students:* 90 full-time (51 women), 41 part-time (24 women); includes 24 minority (1 African American, 17 Asian Americans or Pacific Islanders, 6 Hispanic Americans), 47 international. Average age 28. 255 applicants, 64% accepted, 42 enrolled. In 2006, 42 master's, 6 doctorates awarded. Terminal master's awarded for partial completion of doctoral program. *Degree requirements:* For master's, thesis or alternative, qualifying paper; for doctorate, thesis/dissertation, comprehensive exam. *Entrance requirements:* For master's, GRE General Test; for doctorate, GRE General Test, GRE Subject Test. Additional exam requirements/recommendations for international students: Required—TOEFL. *Application deadline:* For fall admission, 1/4 priority date for domestic students. Application fee: $80. *Expenses:* Tuition: Part-time $1,080 per unit. Required fees: $56 per unit. $329 per term. Tuition and fees vary according to program. *Financial support:* Fellowships with tuition reimbursements, research assistantships with tuition reimbursements, teaching assistantships with tuition reimbursements, career-related internships or fieldwork, Federal Work-Study, institutionally sponsored loans, scholarships/grants, health care benefits, and unspecified assistantships available. Financial award application deadline: 1/4; financial award applicants required to submit FAFSA. *Faculty research:* Genomics, molecular and cell biology, development and molecular genetics, molecular evolution of plants and animals. *Unit head:* Gloria Coruzzi, Chair, 212-998-8200, Fax: 212-995-4015, E-mail: biology@nyu.edu. *Application contact:* Stephen Small, Director of Graduate Studies, 212-998-8200, Fax: 212-995-4015, E-mail: biology@nyu.edu.

New York University, Graduate School of Arts and Science and College of Dentistry, Department of Biomaterials and Biomimetics, New York, NY 10012-1019. Offers biomaterials science (MS). *Faculty:* 5 full-time (2 women). *Students:* 5 full-time (2 women), 10 part-time (6 women); includes 4 minority (3 Asian Americans or Pacific Islanders, 1 Hispanic American), 7 international. Average age 31. 16 applicants, 100% accepted, 7 enrolled. In 2006, 4 degrees awarded. *Degree requirements:* For master's, thesis. *Entrance requirements:* For master's, DDS or DMD. Additional exam requirements/recommendations for international students: Required—TOEFL. *Application deadline:* For fall admission, 4/15 for domestic students. Application fee: $80. *Expenses:* Tuition: Part-time $1,080 per unit. Required fees: $56 per unit. $329 per term. Tuition and fees vary according to program. *Financial support:* Application deadline: 5/15; *Faculty research:* Calcium phosphate, composite restoratives, surfactants, dental metallurgy, impression materials. *Unit head:* Dr. Van Thompson, Director of Graduate Studies, 212-998-9703, Fax: 212-995-4244, E-mail: gsas.graduate.biomaterials@nyu.edu. *Application contact:* Carmen Chilsom, Information Contact, 212-998-9703, Fax: 212-995-4244, E-mail: graduate.biomaterials@nyu.edu.

The Ohio State University, College of Dentistry, Program in Oral Biology, Columbus, OH 43210. Offers PhD, DDS/PhD. *Faculty:* 29 full-time (6 women). *Students:* 12 full-time (5 women), 11 international. Average age 29. 13 applicants, 31% accepted, 2 enrolled. In 2006, 4 doctorates awarded. *Degree requirements:* For doctorate, thesis/dissertation. *Entrance requirements:* For doctorate, GRE General Test, GRE Subject Test in biology (recommended). Additional exam requirements/recommendations for international students: Required—TOEFL (minimum score 600 paper-based; 250 computer-based). *Application deadline:* For fall admission, 10/1 priority date for domestic and international students. Applications are processed on a rolling basis. Application fee: $40 ($50 for international students). Electronic applications accepted. *Expenses:* Tuition, state resident: full-time $9,438. Tuition, nonresident: full-time $22,791. Tuition and fees vary according to course load, campus/location and program. *Financial support:* In 2006–07, 7 fellowships with tuition reimbursements, 13 research assistantships with tuition reimbursements were awarded; teaching assistantships. Financial award application deadline: 3/1. *Faculty research:* Neurobiology, inflammation and immunity, materials science. Total annual research expenditures: $3.4 million. *Unit head:* Dr. Gene Leys, Head, 614-292-6316. *Application contact:* Graduate Admissions, 614-292-9444, Fax: 614-292-3985, E-mail: domestic.grad@osu.edu.

Oregon Health & Science University, School of Dentistry, Graduate Programs in Dentistry, Portland, OR 97239-3098. Offers dental materials (MS); endodontics (MS, Certificate); oral molecular biology (MS); oral pathology (Certificate); orthodontics (MS, Certificate); periodontology (MS, Certificate). *Degree requirements:* For master's, thesis. *Entrance requirements:* For master's, GRE General Test, DMD/DDS; for Certificate, GRE General Test. Additional exam requirements/recommendations for international students: Required—TOEFL. Expenses: Contact institution.

Saint Louis University, Graduate School, Center for Advanced Dental Education, St. Louis, MO 63103-2097. Offers dentistry (MS). *Faculty:* 7 full-time (1 woman), 34 part-time/adjunct (4 women). *Students:* 59 full-time (20 women), 4 part-time (1 woman); includes 12 minority (1 African American, 2 American Indian/Alaska Native, 7 Asian Americans or Pacific Islanders, 2 Hispanic Americans), 8 international. Average age 29. 256 applicants, 8% accepted, 21 enrolled. In 2006, 19 degrees awarded. *Degree requirements:* For master's, thesis, teaching practicum, comprehensive exam, registration. *Entrance requirements:* For master's, GRE General Test, NBDE (National Dental Exam), DDS or DMD, interview, letters of recommendation. Additional exam requirements/recommendations for international students: Required—TOEFL (minimum score 525 paper-based; 194 computer-based). *Application deadline:* For fall admission, 9/15 for domestic and international students. Application fee: $40. *Expenses:* Tuition: Part-time $800 per credit hour. Required fees: $105 per semester. *Financial support:* In 2006–07, 33 students received support. Application deadline: 6/1; *Faculty research:* Orthodontics, endodontics, periodontics, craniofacial growth. Total annual research expenditures: $5,000. *Unit head:* Dr. Rolf Behrents, Executive Director, 314-977-8600, E-mail: behrents@slu.edu. *Application contact:* Gary Behrman, Associate Dean of the Graduate School, 314-977-3827, E-mail: behrmang@slu.edu.

Stony Brook University, State University of New York, Stony Brook University Medical Center, Health Sciences Center, School of Dental Medicine and Graduate School, Department of Oral Biology and Pathology, Stony Brook, NY 11790. Offers PhD. *Faculty:* 8 full-time (2 women). *Students:* 5 full-time (3 women); includes 1 minority (Hispanic American), 2 international. Average age 34. 4 applicants, 25% accepted. *Entrance requirements:* For doctorate, GRE General Test. Additional exam requirements/recommendations for international students: Required—TOEFL. *Application deadline:* For fall admission, 1/15 for domestic students. Application fee: $60. *Expenses: Contact institution. Financial support:* In 2006–07, 7 research assistantships were awarded; fellowships, teaching assistantships, Federal Work-Study also available. Financial award application deadline: 3/15. *Faculty research:* Collagen metabolism, periodontal disease and diabetes, salivary antimicrobial proteins, dental plaque metabolism and dental caries. Total annual research expenditures: $1.4 million. *Unit head:* Dr. Israel Kleinberg, Chair, 631-632-8920, Fax: 631-632-9704, E-mail: israel.kleinberg@storybrook.edu. *Application contact:* Dr. Bill Kaufman, Director, 631-632-8923, Fax: 631-632-9704.

Announcement: The PhD program in oral biology and pathology can also be combined with the periodontics certificate program. This unique training creates dental scientists who are capable of independent, basic, and applied patient-oriented research and who are clinically competent in periodontics.

See Close-Up on page 2181.

Stony Brook University, State University of New York, Stony Brook University Medical Center, Health Sciences Center, School of Dental Medicine, Professional Program in Dental Medicine, Stony Brook, NY 11794. Offers dental medicine (DDS); endodontics (Certificate); orthodontics (Certificate); periodontics (Certificate). *Accreditation:* ADA (one or more programs are accredited). *Faculty:* 29 full-time (11 women), 61 part-time/adjunct (16 women). *Students:* 157 full-time (76 women), 21 part-time (7 women); includes 48 minority (1 African American, 42 Asian Americans or Pacific Islanders, 5 Hispanic Americans). Average age 25. 729 applicants, 6% accepted. In 2006, 40 DDSs, 9 other advanced degrees awarded. *Entrance requirements:* DAT. *Application deadline:* For fall admission, 1/15 for domestic students. Application fee: $75. *Expenses:* Tuition, state resident: full-time $6,900; part-time $288 per credit. Tuition, nonresident: full-time $10,920; part-time $455 per credit. *Financial support:* Fellowships, Federal Work-Study available. Support available to part-time students. Total annual research expenditures: $386,069. *Application contact:* Kim M. Lambiase Hammer, Director of Admissions, 631-632-8980.

Temple University, Health Sciences Center, School of Dentistry and Graduate School, Graduate Programs in Dentistry, Philadelphia, PA 19122-6096. Offers advanced education in general dentistry (Certificate); endodontology (Certificate); oral biology (MS); orthodontics (Certificate); periodontology (Certificate). *Faculty:* 25 full-time (4 women), 42 part-time/adjunct (2 women). *Students:* 100 full-time; includes 20 minority (all Asian Americans or Pacific Islanders) Average age 30. 1,000 applicants, 3% accepted, 26 enrolled. In 2006, 14 master's, 21 other advanced degrees awarded. *Degree requirements:* For master's, thesis, registration. *Entrance requirements:* For master's, GRE; for Certificate, National Boards Parts I and II, DMD or DDS, 3 letters of recommendation. Additional exam requirements/recommendations for international students: Required—TOEFL. *Application deadline:* For fall admission, 10/1 for domestic and international students. Application fee: $40. *Expenses: Contact institution.* Tuition and fees vary according to program. *Financial support:* In 2006–07, 12 students received support. No tuition plus $31,000 stipend for advanced education in general dentistry available. Financial award application deadline: 12/1; financial award applicants required to submit FAFSA. *Faculty research:* Saliva and salivary glands, implantology, material science, periodontal disease, geriatric dentistry. Total annual research expenditures: $366,430. *Unit head:* Dr. Martin F. Tansy, Dean, 215-707-2799, Fax: 215-707-7669, E-mail: mtansy@temple.edu.

Temple University, Health Sciences Center, School of Dentistry, Program in Oral Biology, Philadelphia, PA 19122-6096. Offers MS. Part-time programs available. *Entrance requirements:* For master's, GRE General Test, minimum GPA of 3.0. Additional exam requirements/recommendations for international students: Required—TOEFL (minimum score 600 paper-based; 250 computer-based). *Application deadline:* For fall admission, 7/1 priority date for domestic students, 12/15 for international students; for spring admission, 11/1 priority date for domestic students, 8/1 for international students. Applications are processed on a rolling basis. Application fee: $50. Electronic applications accepted. *Expenses:* Tuition, state resident: full-time $12,264; part-time $511 per credit. Tuition, nonresident: full-time $17,904; part-time $746 per credit. Required fees: $84 per course. Tuition and fees vary according to program. *Financial support:* Application deadline: 1/15; *Unit head:* Dr. Jon Suzuici, Assistant Dean, 215-707-5461, Fax: 215-707-2536, E-mail: ldeem@temple.edu.

Texas A&M Health Science Center, Baylor College of Dentistry, Graduate Division, Department of Biomaterials Science, Dallas, TX 75266-0677. Offers MS. Part-time programs available. *Degree requirements:* For master's, thesis. *Entrance requirements:* For master's, GRE General Test, DDS or DMD or BS in engineering. Additional exam requirements/recommendations for international students: Required—TOEFL. *Faculty research:* Titanium casting for dental applications, mechanical properties of dental ceramics, metal-ceramic adhesion, fatigue failure of dental implants, orthodontic materials, laser welding.

Texas A&M Health Science Center, Baylor College of Dentistry, Graduate Division, Department of Oral and Maxillofacial Surgery, College Station, TX 77840. Offers MD, Certificate. *Degree requirements:* For Certificate, thesis. *Entrance requirements:* For MD, DAT, MCAT; for Certificate, GRE General Test, National Board Dental Examination, DDS or DMD. Additional exam requirements/recommendations for international students: Required—TOEFL. *Faculty research:* Dental implants, temporomandibular joint, recombinant BMP-2.

Texas A&M Health Science Center, Baylor College of Dentistry, Graduate Division, Department of Orthodontics, College Station, TX 77840. Offers MS, Certificate. *Degree requirements:* For master's and Certificate, thesis. *Entrance requirements:* For master's and Certificate, GRE General Test, National Board Dental Examination, DDS or DMD. Additional exam requirements/recommendations for international students: Required—TOEFL. *Faculty research:* Craniofacial biology, distraction osteogenesis, clinical orthodontics, function and shape memory alloys.

Texas A&M Health Science Center, Baylor College of Dentistry, Graduate Division, Department of Pediatric Dentistry, College Station, TX 77840. Offers MS, Certificate. Part-time

Oral and Dental Sciences

Texas A&M Health Science Center (continued)
programs available. *Degree requirements:* For master's and Certificate, thesis. *Entrance requirements:* For master's and Certificate, GRE General Test, National Board Dental Examination, DDS or DMD. Additional exam requirements/recommendations for international students: Required—TOEFL. *Faculty research:* Pulp biology, pharmacological methods of behavior management.

Texas A&M Health Science Center, Baylor College of Dentistry, Graduate Division, Department of Periodontics, College Station, TX 77840. Offers MS, Certificate. Part-time programs available. *Degree requirements:* For master's and Certificate, thesis. *Entrance requirements:* For master's and Certificate, GRE General Test, National Board Dental Examination, DDS or DMD. Additional exam requirements/recommendations for international students: Required—TOEFL. *Faculty research:* Dental implants, quantification of *candida albicans* in adult periodontitis: a survey, smoking, wound healing, stomatology, gingival overgrowth, diabetes mellitus.

Texas A&M Health Science Center, Baylor College of Dentistry, Graduate Division, Department of Restorative Sciences, Field of Endodontics, College Station, TX 77840. Offers endodontics (Certificate); oral biology (MS, PhD). *Degree requirements:* For master's and doctorate, thesis/dissertation. *Entrance requirements:* For master's and Certificate, GRE General Test, National Board Dental Examination, DDS or DMD; for doctorate, GRE General Test, DDS or DMD. Additional exam requirements/recommendations for international students: Required—TOEFL. *Faculty research:* Periradicular healing in response to a biologically inductive root-end filling material.

Texas A&M Health Science Center, Baylor College of Dentistry, Graduate Division, Department of Restorative Sciences, Field of Prosthodontics, College Station, TX 77840. Offers MS, Certificate. Part-time programs available. *Degree requirements:* For master's, thesis. *Entrance requirements:* For master's and Certificate, GRE General Test, National Board Dental Examination, DDS or DMD. Additional exam requirements/recommendations for international students: Required—TOEFL. *Faculty research:* Biomaterials, implants.

Texas A&M Health Science Center, Baylor College of Dentistry, Graduate Division, Program in Oral and Maxillofacial Pathology, College Station, TX 77840. Offers MS, PhD, Certificate. Part-time programs available. Terminal master's awarded for partial completion of doctoral program. *Degree requirements:* For master's and doctorate, thesis/dissertation. *Entrance requirements:* For master's and doctorate, GRE General Test, DDS or DMD; for Certificate, GRE General Test, National Board Dental Examination, DDS or DMD. Additional exam requirements/recommendations for international students: Required—TOEFL. *Faculty research:* Oral cancer and precancer, odontogenic tumors, stomatology.

Tufts University, School of Dental Medicine, Advanced Education Programs in Dental Medicine, Medford, MA 02155. Offers dentistry (Certificate). *Entrance requirements:* Additional exam requirements/recommendations for international students: Required—TOEFL. Expenses: Contact institution. Tuition and fees vary according to degree level and program.

Tufts University, School of Dental Medicine, Graduate Programs in Dental Medicine, Medford, MA 02155. Offers MS. *Degree requirements:* For master's, thesis. *Entrance requirements:* For master's, DDS, DMD, or equivalent; minimum B average. Additional exam requirements/recommendations for international students: Required—TOEFL. Expenses: Contact institution. Tuition and fees vary according to degree level and program. *Faculty research:* Periodontal research, dental materials, salivary research, epidemiology, bone biology.

Université de Montréal, Faculty of Graduate Studies, Faculty of Dental Medicine and Faculty of Graduate Studies, Graduate Programs in Dentistry, Program in Multidisciplinary Residency, Montréal, QC H3C 3J7, Canada. Offers Certificate. *Application deadline:* For fall admission, 10/1 for domestic students. Application fee: $30. Electronic applications accepted. *Unit head:* Richard Mercier, Co-Chair, 514-343-6111 Ext. 3453. *Application contact:* Arlette Kolta, Associate Dean for Research, 514-343-7112, Fax: 514-343-2233.

Université de Montréal, Faculty of Graduate Studies, Faculty of Dental Medicine and Faculty of Graduate Studies, Graduate Programs in Dentistry, Program in Oral and Dental Sciences, Montréal, QC H3C 3J7, Canada. Offers M Sc. *Application deadline:* For fall admission, 10/1 for domestic students. Application fee: $30. Electronic applications accepted. *Unit head:* Jean Barbeau, Director, 514-343-2366.

Université de Montréal, Faculty of Graduate Studies, Faculty of Dental Medicine and Faculty of Graduate Studies, Graduate Programs in Dentistry, Program in Orthodontics, Montréal, QC H3C 3J7, Canada. Offers M Sc. *Application deadline:* For fall admission, 10/1 for domestic students. Application fee: $30. Electronic applications accepted. *Unit head:* Claude Remise, Director, 514-343-7133. *Application contact:* Arlette Kolta, Associate Dean for Research, 514-343-7112, Fax: 514-343-2233.

Université de Montréal, Faculty of Graduate Studies, Faculty of Dental Medicine and Faculty of Graduate Studies, Graduate Programs in Dentistry, Program in Pediatric Dentistry, Montréal, QC H3C 3J7, Canada. Offers M Sc. *Application deadline:* For fall admission, 10/1 for domestic students. Application fee: $30. Electronic applications accepted. *Unit head:* Hélène Buithieu, Head, 514-343-2262. *Application contact:* Arlette Kolta, Associate Dean for Research, 514-343-7112, Fax: 514-343-2233.

Université de Montréal, Faculty of Graduate Studies, Faculty of Dental Medicine and Faculty of Graduate Studies, Graduate Programs in Dentistry, Program in Prosthodontics Rehabilitation, Montréal, QC H3C 3J7, Canada. Offers M Sc. *Application deadline:* For fall admission, 10/1 for domestic students. Application fee: $30. Electronic applications accepted. *Unit head:* Pierre de Grandmont, Director, 514-343-2268. *Application contact:* Arlette Kolta, Associate Dean for Research, 514-343-7112, Fax: 514-343-2233.

Université Laval, Faculty of Dentistry, Diploma Program in Buccal and Maxillofacial Surgery, Québec, QC G1K 7P4, Canada. Offers DESS. *Degree requirements:* For DESS, comprehensive exam. *Entrance requirements:* For degree, interview, knowledge of French. Electronic applications accepted.

Université Laval, Faculty of Dentistry, Diploma Program in Gerodontology, Québec, QC G1K 7P4, Canada. Offers DESS. Part-time programs available. *Entrance requirements:* For degree, interview, good knowledge of French. Electronic applications accepted.

Université Laval, Faculty of Dentistry, Diploma Program in Multidisciplinary Dentistry, Québec, QC G1K 7P4, Canada. Offers DESS. *Entrance requirements:* For degree, interview, knowledge of French. Electronic applications accepted.

Université Laval, Faculty of Dentistry, Diploma Program in Periodontics, Québec, QC G1K 7P4, Canada. Offers DESS. *Entrance requirements:* For degree, interview, knowledge of French. Electronic applications accepted.

Université Laval, Faculty of Dentistry, Graduate Program in Dentistry, Québec, QC G1K 7P4, Canada. Offers M Sc. *Degree requirements:* For master's, thesis (for some programs). Electronic applications accepted.

University at Buffalo, the State University of New York, Graduate School, School of Dental Medicine, Graduate Programs in Dental Medicine, Department of Oral Biology, Buffalo, NY 14260. Offers PhD. *Faculty:* 10 full-time (3 women). *Students:* 14 full-time (7 women), 3 part-time; includes 2 minority (both Asian Americans or Pacific Islanders), 10 international. Average age 27. 6 applicants, 33% accepted, 2 enrolled. In 2006, 1 degree awarded. *Median time to degree:* Of those who began their doctoral program in fall 1998, 100% received their degree in 8 years or less. *Degree requirements:* For doctorate, thesis/dissertation. *Entrance requirements:* For doctorate, GRE General Test, GRE Subject Test in biology or DDS. Additional exam requirements/recommendations for international students: Required—TOEFL. *Application deadline:* For fall admission, 11/1 priority date for domestic students. Application fee: $35. Electronic applications accepted. *Financial support:* Fellowships with full tuition reimbursements, research assistantships with full and partial tuition reimbursements, Federal Work-Study, institutionally sponsored loans, scholarships/grants, and traineeships available. Financial award applicants required to submit FAFSA. *Faculty research:* Oral immunology and microbiology, bone physiology, biochemistry, molecular genetics, neutrophil biology. Total annual research expenditures: $4.1 million. *Unit head:* Dr. Frank Scannapieco, Chairman, 716-829-2854, Fax: 716-829-3942, E-mail: fas1@buffalo.edu.

University at Buffalo, the State University of New York, Graduate School, School of Dental Medicine, Graduate Programs in Dental Medicine, Department of Oral Diagnostic Sciences, Buffalo, NY 14260. Offers biomaterials (MS). Part-time programs available. *Faculty:* 9 full-time (4 women), 10 part-time/adjunct (2 women). *Students:* 2 full-time (both women), (both international). 22 applicants, 18% accepted, 2 enrolled. In 2006, 2 degrees awarded. *Degree requirements:* For master's, thesis. *Entrance requirements:* Additional exam requirements/recommendations for international students: Required—TOEFL. *Application deadline:* For fall admission, 3/1 priority date for domestic students; for spring admission, 9/1 priority date for domestic students. Applications are processed on a rolling basis. Application fee: $35. Electronic applications accepted. *Financial support:* Research assistantships with full and partial tuition reimbursements, Federal Work-Study, institutionally sponsored loans, scholarships/grants, and unspecified assistantships available. Financial award applicants required to submit FAFSA. *Faculty research:* Bioengineering, surface science, bioadhesion, regulatory sterilization. Total annual research expenditures: $168,000. *Unit head:* Dr. W Scott McCall, Interim Chair. *Application contact:* Dr. Robert E Baier, Program Director, 716-829-3560, Fax: 716-835-4872, E-mail: baier@buffalo.edu.

University at Buffalo, the State University of New York, Graduate School, School of Dental Medicine, Graduate Programs in Dental Medicine, Department of Orthodontics, Buffalo, NY 14260. Offers MS, Certificate. *Faculty:* 2 full-time (1 woman), 4 part-time/adjunct (1 woman). *Students:* 18 full-time (5 women), 1 part-time; includes 2 minority (both Asian Americans or Pacific Islanders), 5 international. Average age 28. 114 applicants, 5% accepted, 6 enrolled. In 2006, 5 degrees awarded. *Degree requirements:* For master's, thesis. *Entrance requirements:* For master's and Certificate, DDS, DMD or equivalent foreign degree. Additional exam requirements/recommendations for international students: Required—TOEFL. *Application deadline:* For fall admission, 10/1 for domestic and international students. Application fee: $35. Electronic applications accepted. *Expenses: Contact institution. Financial support:* Fellowships with full and partial tuition reimbursements, Federal Work-Study and institutionally sponsored loans available. Financial award applicants required to submit FAFSA. *Faculty research:* Psychosocial perception of malocclusion, VLC plastics, positioners. Total annual research expenditures: $80,000. *Unit head:* Dr. C. Brian Preston, Chairman, 716-829-2845, Fax: 716-829-2572. *Application contact:* Kristin Yager, Admissions Secretary, 716-829-2839, Fax: 716-833-3517, E-mail: kmyager2@buffalo.edu.

University at Buffalo, the State University of New York, Graduate School, School of Dental Medicine, Graduate Programs in Dental Medicine, Program in Oral Sciences, Buffalo, NY 14260. Offers MS. *Students:* 24 full-time (9 women), 3 part-time (2 women); includes 3 minority (all Asian Americans or Pacific Islanders), 20 international. Average age 31. 22 applicants, 55% accepted, 9 enrolled. In 2006, 7 degrees awarded. *Degree requirements:* For master's, thesis. *Entrance requirements:* For master's, DDS, DMD or equivalent foreign degree. Additional exam requirements/recommendations for international students: Required—TOEFL. *Application deadline:* For fall admission, 2/1 priority date for domestic and international students. Applications are processed on a rolling basis. Application fee: $35. Electronic applications accepted. *Financial support:* Research assistantships with full and partial tuition reimbursements, scholarships/grants and traineeships available. Financial award applicants required to submit FAFSA. *Faculty research:* Oral biology and pathology, behavioral sciences, neuromuscular physiology, facial pain, oral microbiology. Total annual research expenditures: $5.8 million. *Unit head:* Dr. Ernesto DeNardin, Director, 716-829-3518, Fax: 716-833-3517. *Application contact:* Kristin Yager, Admissions Secretary, 716-829-2839, Fax: 716-833-3517, E-mail: kmyager2@buffalo.edu.

The University of Alabama at Birmingham, School of Dentistry, Graduate Programs in Dentistry and Oral Biology, Birmingham, AL 35294. Offers MS. *Students:* Average age 31. 12 applicants, 75% accepted. In 2006, 12 degrees awarded. *Degree requirements:* For master's, thesis. *Application deadline:* Applications are processed on a rolling basis. Application fee: $35 ($60 for international students). Electronic applications accepted. *Expenses:* Tuition, state resident: part-time $170 per credit hour. Tuition, nonresident: part-time $425 per credit hour. Required fees: $15 per credit hour. $122 per term. Tuition and fees vary according to program.

University of Alberta, Faculty of Medicine and Dentistry, Department of Dentistry, Edmonton, AB T6G 2E1, Canada. Offers dental hygiene (Diploma); dental sciences (M Sc, PhD), including dentistry, orthodontics; dentistry (DDS). *Accreditation:* ADA. In 2006, 35 DDSs, 1 doctorate awarded. *Degree requirements:* For DDS, master's, and doctorate, thesis/dissertation. *Entrance requirements:* DAT (Canadian version), interview. Additional exam requirements/recommendations for international students: Required—TOEFL. *Financial support:* Fellowships, research assistantships, teaching assistantships, institutionally sponsored loans available. *Faculty research:* Oral biology, biochemistry of connective tissues, preventive dentistry, applied clinical orthodontics. *Unit head:* Dr. Douglas N. Dederich, Acting Department Chair, 780-492-3312, Fax: 780-492-7536, E-mail: dederich@ualberta.ca. *Application contact:* Melanie Grams, Admissions Officer, 780-492-1319, Fax: 780-492-7536, E-mail: melanie.grams@ualberta.ca.

University of Alberta, Faculty of Medicine and Dentistry, Department of Dentistry, Graduate Programs in Dental Sciences, Division of Orthodontics, Edmonton, AB T6G 2E1, Canada. Offers M Sc, PhD. *Faculty:* 4 full-time (1 woman), 10 part-time/adjunct (1 woman). *Students:* 15 full-time (4 women). Average age 30. 70 applicants, 6% accepted, 4 enrolled. In 2006, 3 degrees awarded. *Degree requirements:* For master's and doctorate, thesis/dissertation. *Entrance requirements:* Additional exam requirements/recommendations for international students: Required—TOEFL (minimum score 580 paper-based; 237 computer-based). *Application deadline:* For fall admission, 10/1 for domestic and international students. Application fee: $100. Electronic applications accepted. *Financial support:* In 2006–07, 1 student received support, including research assistantships (averaging $3,000 per year); institutionally sponsored loans and scholarships/grants also available. *Unit head:* Dr. Paul Major, Head, 780-492-4469, Fax: 780-492-1624, E-mail: major@ualberta.ca. *Application contact:* Nazleen Madhani, Administrative Assistant, 780-492-4469, Fax: 780-492-7108, E-mail: nazleen@ualberta.ca.

The University of British Columbia, Faculty of Dentistry and Faculty of Graduate Studies, Graduate/Postgraduate and Professional Specialty Programs in Dentistry, Vancouver, BC V6T 1Z1, Canada. Offers dental science (M Sc, PhD); periodontics (Diploma). *Faculty:* 26 full-time (6 women), 8 part-time/adjunct (4 women). *Students:* 37 full-time (24 women), 1 part-time; includes 23 minority (all Asian Americans or Pacific Islanders), 2 international. Average age 25. 50 applicants, 14% accepted, 7 enrolled. In 2006, 1 master's, 2 other advanced degrees awarded. *Degree requirements:* For master's, thesis/dissertation; for doctorate, thesis/dissertation, comprehensive exam. *Entrance requirements:* For degree, dental license, interview. Additional exam requirements/recommendations for international students: Required—TOEFL (minimum score 580 paper-based; 237 computer-based). *Application deadline:* For fall admission, 2/28 for domestic students, 1/31 for international students. Applications are processed on a rolling basis. Application fee: $90 Canadian dollars ($150 Canadian dollars for international students). Electronic applications accepted. *Expenses: Contact institution. Financial support:* In 2006–07, 2 fellowships with partial tuition reimbursements (averaging $15,000 per year), 7 research assistantships with partial tuition reimbursements (averaging $16,000 per year), 5 teaching assistantships with partial tuition reimbursements (averaging $800 per year) were awarded; career-related internships or fieldwork, institutionally sponsored loans, scholarships/grants, tuition waivers (full and partial), and unspecified assistantships also available. Financial award application deadline: 12/5; financial award applicants required to submit FAFSA. *Faculty research:* Cell biology, oral physiology, microbiology, immunology, biomaterials. Total annual research expenditures: $1.8 million. *Unit head:* Dr. Hannu S. Larjava, Associate Dean, Graduate Studies, 604-822-6822, Fax: 604-822-3562, E-mail: larjava@interchange.ubc.ca. *Application contact:* Viki Koulouris, Manager, Graduate Admissions and Student Affairs, 604-822-4486, Fax: 604-822-3562, E-mail: vickybk@interchange.ubc.ca.

University of California, Los Angeles, School of Dentistry and Graduate Division, Graduate Programs in Dentistry, Program in Oral Biology, Los Angeles, CA 90095. Offers MS, PhD, DDS/MS, DDS/PhD, MD/PhD, MS/Certificate, PhD/Certificate. *Degree requirements:* For master's, thesis; for doctorate, thesis/dissertation, oral and written qualifying exams. *Entrance requirements:* For doctorate, GRE General Test. *Faculty research:* Neurophysiology, immunology of periodontal disease.

University of California, San Francisco, Graduate Division, Program in Oral and Craniofacial Sciences, San Francisco, CA 94143. Offers MS, PhD. *Students:* 28 full-time (17 women); includes 12 minority (11 Asian Americans or Pacific Islanders, 1 Hispanic American), 2 international. In 2006, 7 master's, 5 doctorates awarded. Terminal master's awarded for partial completion of doctoral program. *Degree requirements:* For master's and doctorate, thesis/dissertation. *Entrance requirements:* For master's and doctorate, GRE General Test. Application fee: $40. *Financial support:* Application deadline: 1/10. *Unit head:* Peter Sargent, Division Chair, 415-476-6156, E-mail: peter.sargent@ucst.edu. *Application contact:* Dalich Williams, Student Liaison, 415-502-8564, Fax: 415-476-4226, E-mail: williamsd@dentistry.ucst.edu.

University of Connecticut, Graduate School, University of Connecticut Health Center, Field of Dental Science, Storrs, CT 06269. Offers M Dent Sc. *Faculty:* 46 full-time (11 women). *Students:* 1 (woman) full-time, 36 part-time (11 women); includes 7 minority (6 Asian Americans or Pacific Islanders, 1 Hispanic American), 9 international. Average age 29. 22 applicants, 59% accepted, 12 enrolled. In 2006, 11 degrees awarded. *Degree requirements:* For master's, comprehensive exam. *Entrance requirements:* For master's, GRE General Test. Additional exam requirements/recommendations for international students: Required—TOEFL (minimum score 550 paper-based; 213 computer-based). *Application deadline:* For fall admission, 2/1 priority date for domestic and international students; for spring admission, 11/1 for domestic students, 10/1 for international students. Applications are processed on a rolling basis. Application fee: $55. Electronic applications accepted. *Financial support:* In 2006–07, 1 research assistantship with full tuition reimbursement was awarded; Federal Work-Study, scholarships/grants, health care benefits, and unspecified assistantships also available. Financial award application deadline: 2/1; financial award applicants required to submit FAFSA. *Unit head:* Peter Robinson, Dean, 860-679-2808. *Application contact:* Michelle Toucey, Administrative Assistant, 860-679-2175, E-mail: toucey@nso.uchc.edu.

University of Connecticut Health Center, Graduate School, Programs in Biomedical Sciences, Combined Degree Programs in Oral Biology, Farmington, CT 06030. Offers DMD/PhD, PhD/Certificate. *Entrance requirements:* Additional exam requirements/recommendations for international students: Required—TOEFL (minimum score 550 paper-based; 213 computer-based).

University of Connecticut Health Center, Graduate School, Programs in Biomedical Sciences, Program in Skeletal, Craniofacial and Oral Biology, Farmington, CT 06030. Offers PhD, DMD/PhD, MD/PhD. *Degree requirements:* For doctorate, thesis/dissertation, comprehensive exam, registration. *Entrance requirements:* For doctorate, GRE General Test. Additional exam requirements/recommendations for international students: Required—TOEFL (minimum score 600 paper-based; 250 computer-based). Electronic applications accepted. *Faculty research:* Developmental biology, muscle physiology, biology of mineralized tissues.

See Close-Up on page 2183.

University of Connecticut Health Center, Graduate School, Programs in Dental Medicine, Program in Dental Science, Farmington, CT 06030. Offers MDS. *Degree requirements:* For master's, thesis, comprehensive exam. *Entrance requirements:* For master's, National Board Dental Examinations I/II. *Faculty research:* Endodontics, periodontics, orthodontics, pediatric dentistry.

University of Detroit Mercy, School of Dentistry, Department of Endodontics, Detroit, MI 48221. Offers MS, Certificate. *Degree requirements:* For master's, thesis. *Entrance requirements:* For master's, DDS or DMD; for Certificate, DAT, DDS or DMD. *Expenses:* Tuition: Full-time $15,750; part-time $875 per credit hour. Required fees: $570. *Faculty research:* Roof and filling materials, cavity preparations, pulp biology.

University of Detroit Mercy, School of Dentistry, Department of Orthodontics, Detroit, MI 48221. Offers MS, Certificate. *Degree requirements:* For master's, thesis. *Entrance requirements:* For master's, DDS or DMD; for Certificate, DAT, DDS or DMD. *Expenses:* Tuition: Full-time $15,750; part-time $875 per credit hour. Required fees: $570. *Faculty research:* Changes in oral flora due to fixed orthodontic appliances, cranioskeletal osteogenesis.

University of Florida, College of Dentistry and Graduate School, Graduate Programs in Dentistry, Department of Endodontics, Gainesville, FL 32611. Offers MS, Certificate. *Faculty:* 4 full-time (1 woman). *Students:* 8 (1 woman); includes 2 minority (both Hispanic Americans) Average age 30. In 2006, 5 degrees awarded. *Degree requirements:* For master's and Certificate, registration. *Entrance requirements:* For master's, DAT, GRE General Test, National Dental Boards I and II, minimum GPA of 3.0, interview; for Certificate, DAT. Additional exam requirements/recommendations for international students: Required—TOEFL (minimum score 550 paper-based; 213 computer-based). *Application deadline:* For fall admission, 9/1 for domestic and international students. Application fee: $30. *Expenses:* Tuition, state resident: full-time $6,827. Tuition, nonresident: full-time $21,951. Required fees: $999. *Financial support:* In 2006–07, 7 students received support. Scholarships/grants and health care benefits available. Financial award applicants required to submit FAFSA. *Faculty research:* Canal cleanliness, antibiotics, resilon, lasers, microbes. *Unit head:* Dr. Frank J. Vertucci, Chair and Director, 352-392-4301, Fax: 352-392-3651, E-mail: vertucci@dental.ufl.edu. *Application contact:* Dr. Venita Sposetti, Assistant Dean for Admissions and Financial Aid, 352-392-4866, Fax: 352-846-0311, E-mail: sposetti@dental.ufl.edu.

University of Florida, College of Dentistry and Graduate School, Graduate Programs in Dentistry, Department of Oral Biology, Gainesville, FL 32611. Offers PhD. *Faculty:* 22 full-time (6 women), 2 part-time/adjunct (1 woman). *Degree requirements:* For doctorate, thesis/dissertation. *Entrance requirements:* For doctorate, GRE General Test, minimum GPA of 3.0. Additional exam requirements/recommendations for international students: Required—TOEFL. *Application deadline:* For fall admission, 2/15 for domestic students. Applications are processed on a rolling basis. Application fee: $30. Electronic applications accepted. *Expenses:* Tuition, state resident: full-time $6,827. Tuition, nonresident: full-time $21,951. Required fees: $999. *Financial support:* In 2006–07, 3 research assistantships with full tuition reimbursements (averaging $25,500 per year) were awarded; fellowships with full tuition reimbursements, traineeships also available. *Faculty research:* Bacterial genetics, cell adhesion, salivary glands, cell proliferation. *Unit head:* Dr. Robert Burne, Chairman, 352-392-4370, E-mail: rburne@dental.ufl.edu. *Application contact:* Dr. Wayne McCormack, Associate Dean of Graduate Education, 352-392-7413, Fax: 352-846-3466, E-mail: mccormac@pathology.ufl.edu.

University of Florida, College of Dentistry and Graduate School, Graduate Programs in Dentistry, Department of Orthodontics, Gainesville, FL 32611. Offers MS, Certificate. *Faculty:* 10 full-time (2 women). *Students:* 12 (3 women); includes 4 minority (all Asian Americans or Pacific Islanders) Average age 29. In 2006, 3 degrees awarded. *Degree requirements:* For master's, thesis, registration. *Entrance requirements:* For master's, DAT, GRE General Test, National Dental Boards I and II, minimum GPA of 3.0, interview. Additional exam requirements/recommendations for international students: Required—TOEFL (minimum score 550 paper-based; 213 computer-based). *Application deadline:* For fall admission, 10/1 for domestic and

international students. Application fee: $30. *Expenses:* Tuition, state resident: full-time $6,827. Tuition, nonresident: full-time $21,951. Required fees: $999. *Financial support:* In 2006–07, 7 students received support. Scholarships/grants and health care benefits available. Financial award applicants required to submit FAFSA. *Faculty research:* Bone biology, osteoclasts, clinical research, root resorption, pain control. *Unit head:* Dr. Timothy T. Wheeler, Chair and Director, 352-392-4135, Fax: 352-846-3818, E-mail: twheeler@dental.ufl.edu. *Application contact:* Dr. Venita Sposetti, Assistant Dean for Admissions and Financial Aid, 352-392-4866, Fax: 352-846-0311, E-mail: sposetti@dental.ufl.edu.

University of Florida, College of Dentistry and Graduate School, Graduate Programs in Dentistry, Department of Periodontology, Gainesville, FL 32611. Offers MS, Certificate. *Faculty:* 5 full-time (4 women). *Students:* 8 (1 woman); includes 1 minority (Hispanic American) 1 international. Average age 30. 15 applicants, 20% accepted, 3 enrolled. In 2006, 3 degrees awarded. *Degree requirements:* For master's, thesis, registration. *Entrance requirements:* For master's, DAT, GRE General Test, National Dental Boards I and II, minimum GPA of 3.0, interview. Additional exam requirements/recommendations for international students: Required—TOEFL (minimum score 550 paper-based; 213 computer-based). *Application deadline:* For fall admission, 9/1 for domestic and international students. Application fee: $30. *Expenses:* Tuition, state resident: full-time $6,827. Tuition, nonresident: full-time $21,951. Required fees: $999. *Financial support:* In 2006–07, 5 students received support. Scholarships/grants and health care benefits available. Financial award applicants required to submit FAFSA. *Faculty research:* Gingival grafting, periodontal plastic surgery, regenerative periodontal surgery, dental implant complications, osteogenic fibroma. *Unit head:* Dr. Ikramuddin Aukhil, Chairman, 352-392-4305, E-mail: iaukhil@dental.ufl.edu. *Application contact:* Dr. Venita Sposetti, Assistant Dean for Admissions and Financial Aid, 352-392-4866, Fax: 352-846-0311, E-mail: sposetti@dental.ufl.edu.

University of Florida, College of Dentistry and Graduate School, Graduate Programs in Dentistry, Department of Prosthodontics, Gainesville, FL 32611. Offers MS, Certificate. *Faculty:* 8 full-time (2 women). *Students:* 7 (2 women); includes 1 minority (Hispanic American) 4 international. Average age 31. In 2006, 3 degrees awarded. *Degree requirements:* For master's, thesis, registration. *Entrance requirements:* For master's, DAT, GRE General Test, National Dental Boards I and II, minimum GPA of 3.0, interview. Additional exam requirements/recommendations for international students: Required—TOEFL (minimum score 550 paper-based; 213 computer-based). *Application deadline:* For fall admission, 10/15 for domestic and international students. Application fee: $30. *Expenses:* Tuition, state resident: full-time $6,827. Tuition, nonresident: full-time $21,951. Required fees: $999. *Financial support:* In 2006–07, 5 students received support. Federal Work-Study, scholarships/grants, and health care benefits available. Financial award applicants required to submit FAFSA. *Faculty research:* Computer panograph, dental implants, resin provisional materials wear rate, implant surface variation, Sjorgen's Syndrome. *Unit head:* Dr. Glenn Earl Turner, Director, 352-392-4231, Fax: 352-392-3070, E-mail: gturner@dental.ufl.edu. *Application contact:* Dr. Venita Sposetti, Assistant Dean for Admissions and Financial Aid, 352-392-4866, Fax: 352-846-0311, E-mail: sposetti@dental.ufl.edu.

University of Illinois at Chicago, College of Dentistry and Graduate College, Graduate Programs in Oral Sciences, Chicago, IL 60607-7128. Offers MS. *Degree requirements:* For master's, thesis. *Entrance requirements:* For master's, GRE General Test, DDS, DVM, or MD. Additional exam requirements/recommendations for international students: Required—TOEFL. Electronic applications accepted. Expenses: Contact institution.

The University of Iowa, College of Dentistry and Graduate College, Graduate Programs in Dentistry, Department of Endodontics, Iowa City, IA 52242-1316. Offers MS, Certificate. *Degree requirements:* For master's, thesis. *Entrance requirements:* For master's, GRE, DDS; for Certificate, DDS. Additional exam requirements/recommendations for international students: Required—TOEFL.

The University of Iowa, College of Dentistry and Graduate College, Graduate Programs in Dentistry, Department of Operative Dentistry, Iowa City, IA 52242-1316. Offers MS, Certificate. *Degree requirements:* For master's, thesis. *Entrance requirements:* For master's, GRE, DDS; for Certificate, DDS. Additional exam requirements/recommendations for international students: Required—TOEFL.

The University of Iowa, College of Dentistry and Graduate College, Graduate Programs in Dentistry, Department of Oral and Maxillofacial Surgery, Iowa City, IA 52242-1316. Offers MS, Certificate. *Degree requirements:* For master's, thesis. *Entrance requirements:* For master's, GRE, DDS; for Certificate, DDS.

The University of Iowa, College of Dentistry and Graduate College, Graduate Programs in Dentistry, Department of Oral Pathology, Radiology and Medicine, Iowa City, IA 52242-1316. Offers oral and maxillofacial pathology (Certificate); oral and maxillofacial radiology (Certificate); stomatology (MS). *Degree requirements:* For master's, thesis. *Entrance requirements:* For master's, GRE, DDS, minimum GPA of 2.7. Additional exam requirements/recommendations for international students: Required—TOEFL.

The University of Iowa, College of Dentistry and Graduate College, Graduate Programs in Dentistry, Department of Orthodontics, Iowa City, IA 52242-1316. Offers MS, Certificate. *Degree requirements:* For master's, thesis. *Entrance requirements:* For master's, GRE, DDS; for Certificate, DDS. Additional exam requirements/recommendations for international students: Required—TOEFL.

The University of Iowa, College of Dentistry and Graduate College, Graduate Programs in Dentistry, Department of Pediatric Dentistry, Iowa City, IA 52242-1316. Offers Certificate. *Entrance requirements:* For degree, DDS. Additional exam requirements/recommendations for international students: Required—TOEFL.

The University of Iowa, College of Dentistry and Graduate College, Graduate Programs in Dentistry, Department of Periodontics, Iowa City, IA 52242-1316. Offers MS, Certificate. *Degree requirements:* For master's, thesis. *Entrance requirements:* For master's, GRE, DDS; for Certificate, DDS. Additional exam requirements/recommendations for international students: Required—TOEFL.

The University of Iowa, College of Dentistry and Graduate College, Graduate Programs in Dentistry, Department of Preventive and Community Dentistry, Iowa City, IA 52242-1316. Offers dental public health (MS). *Degree requirements:* For master's, thesis. *Entrance requirements:* For master's, GRE, DDS. Additional exam requirements/recommendations for international students: Required—TOEFL.

The University of Iowa, College of Dentistry and Graduate College, Graduate Programs in Dentistry, Department of Prosthodontics, Iowa City, IA 52242-1316. Offers MS, Certificate. *Degree requirements:* For master's, thesis. *Entrance requirements:* For master's, GRE, DDS; for Certificate, DDS. Additional exam requirements/recommendations for international students: Required—TOEFL.

The University of Iowa, College of Dentistry and Graduate College, Graduate Programs in Dentistry, Oral Science Graduate Program, Iowa City, IA 52242-1316. Offers MS, PhD. *Degree requirements:* For master's and doctorate, thesis/dissertation. *Entrance requirements:* For master's, GRE, DDS. Additional exam requirements/recommendations for international students: Required—TOEFL.

University of Kentucky, College of Dentistry, Graduate Program in Dentistry, Lexington, KY 40506-0032. Offers MS. *Degree requirements:* For master's, thesis, comprehensive exam. *Entrance requirements:* For master's, GRE General Test, minimum undergraduate GPA of 2.5. Additional exam requirements/recommendations for international students: Required—TOEFL (minimum score 550 paper-based; 213 computer-based). Electronic applications accepted.

Oral and Dental Sciences

University of Kentucky (continued)
Expenses: Tuition, state resident: full-time $7,670; part-time $401 per credit hour. Tuition, nonresident: full-time $16,158; part-time $873 per credit hour.

University of Louisville, School of Dentistry, Graduate Programs in Dentistry, Program of Oral Biology, Louisville, KY 40292-0001. Offers MS. *Students:* 21 full-time (4 women), 11 part-time; includes 3 minority (1 African American, 1 Asian American or Pacific Islander, 1 Hispanic American), 2 international. Average age 31. In 2006, 7 degrees awarded. *Degree requirements:* For master's, thesis. *Entrance requirements:* For master's, DAT or GRE General Test, minimum GPA of 2.75. *Application deadline:* Applications are processed on a rolling basis. Application fee: $50. *Unit head:* Dr. David A Scott, Director, 502-852-2288, Fax: 502-852-7240, E-mail: david.scott@louisville.edu.

University of Manitoba, Faculty of Dentistry and Faculty of Graduate Studies, Graduate Programs in Dentistry, Department of Dental Diagnostic and Surgical Sciences, Winnipeg, MB R3T 2N2, Canada. Offers oral and maxillofacial surgery (M Dent); periodontology (M Dent). *Faculty:* 7 full-time (1 woman). *Students:* 10 full-time (3 women). In 2006, 3 degrees awarded. *Entrance requirements:* For master's, dental degree. Application fee: $50 Canadian dollars. *Financial support:* Career-related internships or fieldwork available. Financial award application deadline: 6/30. *Faculty research:* Implantology, clinical trials, tobacco use, periodontal disease. *Unit head:* Dr. J. Curran, Head, 204-789-3367, Fax: 204-789-3913, E-mail: curranjb@cc.umanitoba.ca.

University of Manitoba, Faculty of Dentistry and Faculty of Graduate Studies, Graduate Programs in Dentistry, Department of Oral Biology, Winnipeg, MB R3T 2N2, Canada. Offers M Sc, PhD. *Faculty:* 9 full-time (1 woman). *Students:* 8 full-time (5 women). Average age 80. 10 applicants, 40% accepted, 4 enrolled. In 2006, 2 degrees awarded. *Degree requirements:* For master's, thesis/dissertation; for doctorate, thesis/dissertation, comprehensive exam. *Entrance requirements:* For master's, B Sc or pre-M Sc; for doctorate, master's degree. Additional exam requirements/recommendations for international students: Required—TOEFL (minimum score 250 computer-based). *Application deadline:* Applications are processed on a rolling basis. Application fee: $50 Canadian dollars ($90 Canadian dollars for international students). *Financial support:* In 2006–07, 3 fellowships (averaging $16,000 per year) were awarded. Financial award application deadline: 6/30. *Faculty research:* Oral bacterial ecology and metabolism, biofilms, saliva and oral health, secretory mechanisms. Total annual research expenditures: $400,000. *Unit head:* Dr. R. P. Bhullar, Head, 204-789-3590, Fax: 204-888-4113, E-mail: bhullar@ms.umanitoba.ca. *Application contact:* Dr. A. C. Karim, Information Officer, 204-789-3780, Fax: 204-789-3913, E-mail: karim@ms.umanitoba.ca.

University of Manitoba, Faculty of Dentistry and Faculty of Graduate Studies, Graduate Programs in Dentistry, Department of Preventive Dental Science, Winnipeg, MB R3T 2N2, Canada. Offers orthodontics (M Sc). *Faculty:* 3 full-time (0 women), 5 part-time/adjunct (0 women). *Students:* 9 full-time (5 women), 1 international. Average age 30. 60 applicants, 5% accepted, 3 enrolled. In 2006, 3 degrees awarded. *Degree requirements:* For master's, thesis. *Entrance requirements:* For master's, dental degree. *Application deadline:* For fall admission, 9/1 for domestic students. Application fee: $100 Canadian dollars. Electronic applications accepted. *Financial support:* In 2006–07, 6 teaching assistantships (averaging $6,000 per year) were awarded. Financial award application deadline: 6/30. Total annual research expenditures: $40,000. *Unit head:* Dr. W. A. Wiltshire, Head, 204-789-3856, Fax: 204-789-3913, E-mail: wa_wiltshire@umanitoba.ca.

University of Manitoba, Faculty of Dentistry and Faculty of Graduate Studies, Graduate Programs in Dentistry, Department of Restorative Dentistry, Winnipeg, MB R3T 2N2, Canada. Offers dental materials (M Sc); oral surgery (M Dent); periodontics (M Dent). Program will be offered pending future operational funding. *Faculty:* 3 full-time (0 women). *Students:* 4 full-time (2 women). Average age 30. *Degree requirements:* For master's, thesis. *Entrance requirements:* For master's, DDS, DMD, or equivalent. Application fee: $50 Canadian dollars. *Financial support:* Fellowships available. Financial award application deadline: 6/30. *Faculty research:* Bonding to teeth and other materials, laser degradation of materials, polishing and finishing of dental composites. Total annual research expenditures: $70,000. *Unit head:* Dr. I. Pesun, Head, 204-789-3594, Fax: 204-789-3916, E-mail: pesun@cc.umanitoba.ca.

University of Maryland, Baltimore, Graduate School, Graduate Programs in Dentistry, Department of Oral Pathology, Baltimore, MD 21201. Offers MS, PhD. *Degree requirements:* For master's, thesis or alternative; for doctorate, thesis/dissertation. *Entrance requirements:* For master's and doctorate, GRE General Test, DDS, DMD. Additional exam requirements/recommendations for international students: Required—TOEFL, TOEFL or IELTS; Recommended—IELTS. Electronic applications accepted. *Faculty research:* Histopathology, epidemiology of oral lesions, embryology.

University of Maryland, Baltimore, Graduate School, Graduate Programs in Dentistry, Graduate Program in Biomedical Sciences—Dental School, Baltimore, MD 21201. Offers MS, PhD, DDS/PhD. *Faculty:* 30 full-time (7 women), 1 part-time/adjunct (0 women). *Students:* Average age 25. *Degree requirements:* For doctorate, thesis/dissertation. *Entrance requirements:* For master's and doctorate, GRE General Test. Additional exam requirements/recommendations for international students: Required—TOEFL (minimum score 550 paper-based; 213 computer-based), TOEFL or IELTS; Recommended—IELTS (minimum score 7). *Application deadline:* For fall admission, 7/1 for domestic students, 1/15 for international students. Application fee: $50. Electronic applications accepted. *Financial support:* In 2006–07, research assistantships with full tuition reimbursements (averaging $23,000 per year). *Faculty research:* Neuroscience, molecular and cell biology, infectious diseases. *Unit head:* Dr. Ronald Dubner, Professor and Chair, 410-706-0860, Fax: 410-706-0865, E-mail: rdubner@dental.umaryland.edu. *Application contact:* Dr. Norman Capra, Graduate Program Director, 410-706-4219, Fax: 410-706-0865, E-mail: ncapra@umaryland.edu.

University of Maryland, Baltimore, Professional and Advanced Education Programs in Dentistry, Baltimore, MD 21201-1627. Offers advanced general dentistry (Certificate); dentistry (DDS); endodontics (Certificate); oral and experimental pathology (Certificate); oral biology (MS); oral-maxillofacial surgery (Certificate); orthodontics (Certificate); pediatric dentistry (Certificate); periodontics (Certificate); prosthodontics (Certificate); DDS/PhD. *Accreditation:* ADA. *Faculty:* 123 full-time (48 women), 95 part-time/adjunct (22 women). *Students:* 551 full-time (280 women); includes 161 minority (32 African Americans, 1 American Indian/Alaska Native, 111 Asian Americans or Pacific Islanders, 17 Hispanic Americans), 35 international. Average age 25. 2,375 applicants, 130 enrolled. In 2006, 103 DDSs, 11 other advanced degrees awarded. *Degree requirements:* For DDS and master's, registration. *Entrance requirements:* DAT. Additional exam requirements/recommendations for international students: Required—TOEFL. *Application deadline:* For fall admission, 1/15 for domestic students. Application fee: $65. *Expenses:* Contact institution. *Financial support:* In 2006–07, research assistantships (averaging $23,000 per year); career-related internships or fieldwork, Federal Work-Study, institutionally sponsored loans, scholarships/grants, and unspecified assistantships also available. Financial award application deadline: 3/1; financial award applicants required to submit FAFSA. *Faculty research:* Neuroscience, cell and molecular biology, infectious diseases and immune function. Total annual research expenditures: $12 million. *Unit head:* Dr. Christian S. Stohler, Dean, 410-706-7461, Fax: 410-706-0406, E-mail: cstohler@dental.umaryland.edu. *Application contact:* Dr. Patricia Meehan, Assistant Dean for Admissions and Recruitment, 410-706-7472, Fax: 410-706-0945, E-mail: pmeehan@umaryland.edu.

University of Medicine and Dentistry of New Jersey, New Jersey Dental School, Newark, NJ 07103-2400. Offers advanced education in general dentistry (Certificate); dental science (MDS); dentistry (DMD, MS); endodontics (Certificate); oral biology (PhD); oral medicine (Certificate); orthodontics (Certificate); pediatric dentistry (Certificate); periodontics (Certificate); prosthodontics (Certificate); DMD/MPH; DMD/MS; DMD/PhD. *Accreditation:* ADA (one or more programs are accredited). *Faculty:* 90 full-time (26 women), 118 part-time/adjunct (20 women). *Students:* 404 full-time (224 women), 1 part-time; includes 141 minority (16 African Americans, 1 American Indian/Alaska Native, 106 Asian Americans or Pacific Islanders, 18 Hispanic Americans), 14 international. Average age 26. 1,391 applicants, 14% accepted, 96 enrolled. In 2006, 80 DMDs, 4 master's, 17 other advanced degrees awarded. *Entrance requirements:* DAT. *Application deadline:* Applications are processed on a rolling basis. Application fee: $75. Electronic applications accepted. *Expenses:* Contact institution. *Financial support:* Fellowships, research assistantships, teaching assistantships, Federal Work-Study and institutionally sponsored loans available. Financial award application deadline: 5/1. *Unit head:* Dr. Cecile A. Feldman, Dean, 973-972-4633, Fax: 973-972-3689, E-mail: feldman@umdnj.edu. *Application contact:* Dr. Jeffrey Linfante, Director of Admissions and Student Recruitment, 973-972-5362, Fax: 973-972-0309, E-mail: linfante@umdnj.edu.

University of Michigan, School of Dentistry and Horace H. Rackham School of Graduate Studies, Graduate Programs in Dentistry, Ann Arbor, MI 48109. Offers MS, PhD, Certificate. *Degree requirements:* For master's, thesis; for doctorate, oral defense of dissertation, preliminary exam. *Entrance requirements:* For master's, GRE (orthodontics), national boards (pediatric and orthodontics); for doctorate, GRE. Additional exam requirements/recommendations for international students: Required—TOEFL (minimum score 220 computer-based). Electronic applications accepted. *Expenses:* Contact institution.

University of Minnesota, Twin Cities Campus, School of Dentistry and Graduate School, Graduate Programs in Dentistry, Advanced Education Program in Periodontology, Minneapolis, MN 55455-0213. Offers MS. *Degree requirements:* For master's, thesis, comprehensive exam, registration. *Entrance requirements:* For master's, DDS/DMD, letter from Dental Dean, specific GGP/class rank, two letters of recommendation. Additional exam requirements/recommendations for international students: Required—TOEFL (minimum score 590 paper-based; 243 computer-based). *Expenses:* Tuition, state resident: full-time $9,302; part-time $775 per credit. Tuition, nonresident: full-time $16,400; part-time $1,367 per credit. Full-time tuition and fees vary according to class time, course load, program, reciprocity agreements and student level. *Faculty research:* Periodontitis, risk factors, regenerating, diabetes immunology.

University of Minnesota, Twin Cities Campus, School of Dentistry and Graduate School, Graduate Programs in Dentistry, Division of Endodontics, Minneapolis, MN 55455-0213. Offers MS, Certificate. *Degree requirements:* For master's, thesis. *Entrance requirements:* Additional exam requirements/recommendations for international students: Required—TOEFL. *Expenses:* Tuition, state resident: full-time $9,302; part-time $775 per credit. Tuition, nonresident: full-time $16,400; part-time $1,367 per credit. Full-time tuition and fees vary according to class time, course load, program, reciprocity agreements and student level. *Faculty research:* Pain, inflammation, neuropharmacology, neuropeptides, cytokines.

University of Minnesota, Twin Cities Campus, School of Dentistry and Graduate School, Graduate Programs in Dentistry, Division of Orthodontics, Minneapolis, MN 55455-0213. Offers MS. *Degree requirements:* For master's, thesis. *Entrance requirements:* Additional exam requirements/recommendations for international students: Required—TOEFL (minimum score 587 paper-based; 240 computer-based). *Expenses:* Tuition, state resident: full-time $9,302; part-time $775 per credit. Tuition, nonresident: full-time $16,400; part-time $1,367 per credit. Full-time tuition and fees vary according to class time, course load, program, reciprocity agreements and student level. *Faculty research:* Bone biology, 3-D imaging.

University of Minnesota, Twin Cities Campus, School of Dentistry and Graduate School, Graduate Programs in Dentistry, Division of Pediatric Dentistry, Minneapolis, MN 55455-0213. Offers MS. *Degree requirements:* For master's, thesis. *Entrance requirements:* Additional exam requirements/recommendations for international students: Required—TOEFL. *Expenses:* Tuition, state resident: full-time $9,302; part-time $775 per credit. Tuition, nonresident: full-time $16,400; part-time $1,367 per credit. Full-time tuition and fees vary according to class time, course load, program, reciprocity agreements and student level. *Faculty research:* Molecular genetics of facial growth, dental material/adhesion, expanded functions dental auxiliary utilization.

University of Minnesota, Twin Cities Campus, School of Dentistry and Graduate School, Graduate Programs in Dentistry, Division of Prosthodontics, Minneapolis, MN 55455-0213. Offers MS. *Degree requirements:* For master's, thesis, clinical. *Entrance requirements:* Additional exam requirements/recommendations for international students: Required—TOEFL. *Expenses:* Tuition, state resident: full-time $9,302; part-time $775 per credit. Tuition, nonresident: full-time $16,400; part-time $1,367 per credit. Full-time tuition and fees vary according to class time, course load, program, reciprocity agreements and student level.

University of Minnesota, Twin Cities Campus, School of Dentistry and Graduate School, Graduate Programs in Dentistry, Program in Oral Biology, Minneapolis, MN 55455-0213. Offers MS, PhD. *Degree requirements:* For master's, thesis. *Expenses:* Tuition, state resident: full-time $9,302; part-time $775 per credit. Tuition, nonresident: full-time $16,400; part-time $1,367 per credit. Full-time tuition and fees vary according to class time, course load, program, reciprocity agreements and student level. *Faculty research:* Microbiology, neuroscience, biomaterials, biochemistry, cancer biology.

University of Minnesota, Twin Cities Campus, School of Dentistry and Graduate School, Graduate Programs in Dentistry, Program in Oral Health Services for Older Adults (Geriatrics), Minneapolis, MN 55455-0213. Offers MS, Certificate. *Degree requirements:* For master's, thesis (for some programs), registration. *Entrance requirements:* For master's, DDS degree or equivalent. Additional exam requirements/recommendations for international students: Required—TOEFL (minimum score 560 paper-based; 233 computer-based). Electronic applications accepted. *Expenses:* Tuition, state resident: full-time $9,302; part-time $775 per credit. Tuition, nonresident: full-time $16,400; part-time $1,367 per credit. Full-time tuition and fees vary according to class time, course load, program, reciprocity agreements and student level. *Faculty research:* Geriatrics dental care, long-term care dental services, oral-systemic health relationships, utilization of care by older adults.

University of Minnesota, Twin Cities Campus, School of Dentistry and Graduate School, Graduate Programs in Dentistry, Program in Temporomandibular Joint Disorders, Minneapolis, MN 55455-0213. Offers MS. *Degree requirements:* For master's, thesis, comprehensive exam, registration (for some programs). *Entrance requirements:* Additional exam requirements/recommendations for international students: Required—TOEFL. Electronic applications accepted. *Expenses:* Tuition, state resident: full-time $9,302; part-time $775 per credit. Tuition, nonresident: full-time $16,400; part-time $1,367 per credit. Full-time tuition and fees vary according to class time, course load, program, reciprocity agreements and student level. *Faculty research:* Clinical trials, TMJ mechanicals, diagnostic criteria, biomarkers, genetics.

University of Mississippi Medical Center, School of Dentistry, Department of Craniofacial and Dental Research, Jackson, MS 39216-4505. Offers MS, PhD. *Students:* 2 full-time (1 woman); includes 1 minority (African American). *Expenses:* Tuition, state resident: full-time $4,523. Tuition, nonresident: full-time $10,566. *Unit head:* Dr. Charles E. Streckfus, Director, 601-984-6171, Fax: 601-984-6087.

University of Missouri–Kansas City, School of Dentistry, Kansas City, MO 64110-2499. Offers advanced education in dentistry (Graduate Dental Certificate); dental hygiene education (MS); dental specialties (Graduate Dental Certificate); dentistry (DDS); diagnostic sciences (Graduate Dental Certificate); oral and maxillofacial surgery (Graduate Dental Certificate); oral biology (MS, PhD); orthodontics and dentofacial orthopedics (Graduate Dental Certificate); pediatric dentistry (Graduate Dental Certificate); periodontics (Graduate Dental Certificate); prosthodontics (Graduate Dental Certificate). *Accreditation:* ADA (one or more programs are accredited). *Faculty:* 102 full-time (36 women), 77 part-time/adjunct (22 women). *Students:* 424 full-time (155 women), 34 part-time (27 women); includes 60 minority (10 African Americans, 2 American Indian/Alaska Native, 38 Asian Americans or Pacific Islanders, 10 Hispanic Americans), 12 international. Average age 27. 687 applicants, 17% accepted, 110 enrolled. In

2006, 92 DDSs, 25 other advanced degrees awarded. *Degree requirements:* For master's and doctorate, thesis/dissertation. *Entrance requirements:* For DDS, DAT; for master's, DAT, letters of evaluation, personal interview; for Graduate Dental Certificate, DDS. Additional exam requirements/recommendations for international students: Required—TOEFL. Application fee: $35 ($50 for international students). *Expenses: Contact institution. Financial support:* In 2006–07, 8 fellowships (averaging $42,540 per year), 28 research assistantships (averaging $21,670 per year) were awarded; career-related internships or fieldwork, Federal Work-Study, institutionally sponsored loans, and tuition waivers (full and partial) also available. Support available to part-time students. Financial award applicants required to submit FAFSA. *Faculty research:* Biomaterials, dental use of lasers, effectiveness of periodontal treatments, temporomandibular joint dysfunction. Total annual research expenditures: $3 million. *Unit head:* Dr. Michael Reed, Dean, 816-235-2010, E-mail: reedm@umkc.edu. *Application contact:* 816-235-2080.

The University of North Carolina at Chapel Hill, School of Dentistry and Graduate School, Graduate Programs in Dentistry, Chapel Hill, NC 27599. Offers dentistry (MS); oral biology (PhD). *Faculty:* 82 full-time (28 women). *Students:* 90 full-time (46 women); includes 20 minority (7 African Americans, 10 Asian Americans or Pacific Islanders, 3 Hispanic Americans), 30 international. Average age 28. 475 applicants, 7% accepted, 31 enrolled. In 2006, 20 master's, 2 doctorates awarded. *Degree requirements:* For master's and doctorate, thesis/dissertation. *Entrance requirements:* For master's, dental degree; for doctorate, GRE General Test. Additional exam requirements/recommendations for international students: Required—TOEFL (minimum score 550 paper-based; 213 computer-based). *Application deadline:* For fall admission, 10/1 for domestic students. Application fee: $70. Electronic applications accepted. *Expenses: Contact institution. Financial support:* In 2006–07, research assistantships with full tuition reimbursements (averaging $22,000 per year), teaching assistantships with full tuition reimbursements (averaging $9,500 per year) were awarded; fellowships also available. Financial award application deadline: 3/1; financial award applicants required to submit FAFSA. *Faculty research:* Inflammation, cell biology, immunology, microbiology, neuroscience, molecular biology. Total annual research expenditures: $6 million. *Unit head:* Dr. Carroll-Ann Trotman, Assistant Dean for Graduate Education and Faculty Development, 919-966-4451, Fax: 919-966-5795, E-mail: carroll-ann_trotman@dentistry.unc.edu. *Application contact:* Tami Rice, Graduate Registrar, 919-966-4451, Fax: 919-966-5795, E-mail: tami_rice@dentistry.unc.edu.

University of Oklahoma Health Sciences Center, College of Dentistry and Graduate College, Graduate Programs in Dentistry, Department of Orthodontics, Oklahoma City, OK 73190. Offers MS. *Faculty:* 2 full-time (0 women), 14 part-time/adjunct (0 women). *Students:* 9 full-time (1 woman); includes 1 minority (Asian American or Pacific Islander), 1 international. Average age 29. 148 applicants, 3% accepted, 4 enrolled. In 2006, 4 degrees awarded. *Degree requirements:* For master's, thesis. *Entrance requirements:* For master's, minimum GPA of 3.0, DDS/DMD. Additional exam requirements/recommendations for international students: Required—TOEFL. *Application deadline:* For fall admission, 10/1 priority date for domestic and international students. Applications are processed on a rolling basis. Application fee: $65 ($90 for international students). Electronic applications accepted. *Financial support:* In 2006–07, 8 teaching assistantships (averaging $6,000 per year) were awarded; institutionally sponsored loans also available. Financial award application deadline: 3/1; financial award applicants required to submit FAFSA. *Faculty research:* Craniofacial growth and development, biomechanical principles in orthodontics. Total annual research expenditures: $10,000. *Unit head:* Dr. G. Frans Currier, Director, 405-271-6087, Fax: 405-271-1178, E-mail: frans-currier@ouhsc.edu. *Application contact:* Angel Miller, Administrative Secretary, 405-271-4271, Fax: 405-271-1178, E-mail: angel-miller@ouhsc.edu.

University of Oklahoma Health Sciences Center, College of Dentistry and Graduate College, Graduate Programs in Dentistry, Department of Periodontics, Oklahoma City, OK 73190. Offers MS. *Faculty:* 3 full-time (0 women), 8 part-time/adjunct (1 woman). *Students:* 6 full-time (0 women). Average age 30. 15 applicants, 13% accepted, 2 enrolled. In 2006, 2 degrees awarded. *Degree requirements:* For master's, thesis. *Entrance requirements:* For master's, DDS/DMD, minimum GPA of 3.0. Additional exam requirements/recommendations for international students: Required—TOEFL (minimum score 550 paper-based; 213 computer-based). *Application deadline:* For fall admission, 9/15 for domestic and international students. Applications are processed on a rolling basis. Application fee: $65 ($90 for international students). Electronic applications accepted. *Financial support:* In 2006–07, 6 students received support, including 6 teaching assistantships (averaging $6,000 per year); institutionally sponsored loans and tuition waivers (partial) also available. Financial award application deadline: 3/1; financial award applicants required to submit FAFSA. *Faculty research:* Lasers, antimicrobial mouth rinses, GBR, GTR dental implants, systemic effects of periodontitis. Total annual research expenditures: $10,000. *Unit head:* Dr. Robert E. Carson, Director, 405-271-6531, Fax: 405-271-3794, E-mail: robert-carson@ouhsc.edu. *Application contact:* Anne Sullivan, Office Manager, 405-271-6531, Fax: 405-271-3794, E-mail: anne-sullivan@ouhsc.edu.

University of Pittsburgh, School of Dental Medicine, Residency Programs in Dental Medicine, Department of Endodontics, Pittsburgh, PA 15260. Offers MDS, Certificate. *Faculty:* 1 full-time (0 women), 3 part-time/adjunct (0 women). *Students:* 7 full-time (3 women). Average age 27. 116 applicants, 3% accepted. In 2006, 3 degrees awarded. *Median time to degree:* 3 years full-time. *Degree requirements:* For master's, thesis. *Application deadline:* For fall admission, 11/1 for domestic students. Application fee: $50. *Financial support:* Federal Work-Study and institutionally sponsored loans available. Financial award application deadline: 4/15. *Faculty research:* Pulpal neurobiology, root canal therapy, root fracture/resorption repair, osseous grafts related to endodontics, endodontic surgery. Total annual research expenditures: $10,000. *Unit head:* Dr. James A. Wallace, Director, 412-648-8647, Fax: 412-383-7796, E-mail: skipp@pitt.edu. *Application contact:* Pamela A. Edwards, Administrator, Office of Resident Education, 412-648-8406, Fax: 412-648-8219, E-mail: pae3@pitt.edu.

University of Pittsburgh, School of Dental Medicine, Residency Programs in Dental Medicine, Department of Oral and Maxillofacial Surgery, Pittsburgh, PA 15260. Offers craniofacial and maxillofacial surgery (Certificate); oral and maxillofacial surgery (Certificate). *Faculty:* 11 full-time (1 woman). *Students:* 12 full-time (2 women); includes 1 minority (Asian American or Pacific Islander) Average age 25. 137 applicants, 3% accepted, 4 enrolled. In 2006, 4 degrees awarded. *Degree requirements:* For Certificate, comprehensive exam, registration. *Entrance requirements:* For degree, US or Canadian dental degree (DDS or DMD). *Application deadline:* For fall admission, 10/15 for domestic students. Applications are processed on a rolling basis. Electronic applications accepted. *Expenses: Contact institution. Financial support:* In 2006–07, 8 students received support, including 4 fellowships (averaging $36,000 per year); scholarships/grants, health care benefits, and tuition waivers also available. *Faculty research:* Clefts, craniofacial anomalies, facial trauma, head and neck cancer, pain management. Total annual research expenditures: $26,000. *Unit head:* Dr. Bernard J. Costello, Program Director, 412-648-6801, Fax: 412-648-6835. *Application contact:* Andrea Ford, Residency and Fellowship Coordinator, 412-648-6801, Fax: 412-648-6835, E-mail: fordam@upmc.edu.

University of Pittsburgh, School of Dental Medicine, Residency Programs in Dental Medicine, Department of Orthodontics, Pittsburgh, PA 15260. Offers MDS, Certificate. *Faculty:* 3 full-time (1 woman), 10 part-time/adjunct (2 women). *Students:* 9 full-time (5 women). Average age 27. 184 applicants, 2% accepted. In 2006, 5 degrees awarded. *Degree requirements:* For master's, thesis, comprehensive exam, registration. *Entrance requirements:* For master's and Certificate, National Boards Parts I and II. *Application deadline:* For fall admission, 10/1 for domestic students. Application fee: $135. *Faculty research:* Muscle physiology, orthodontic outcomes. *Unit head:* Dr. Joseph F. A. Petrone, Director of Residency Education, 412-648-8406, E-mail: jfap@pitt.edu. *Application contact:* Brian Geibel, Department Administrator, 412-648-8419, Fax: 412-648-8817, E-mail: bjg24@pitt.edu.

University of Pittsburgh, School of Dental Medicine, Residency Programs in Dental Medicine, Department of Periodontics, Pittsburgh, PA 15260. Offers MDS, Certificate. *Faculty:* 4 full-time (1 woman), 6 part-time/adjunct (1 woman). *Students:* 6 full-time (3 women); includes 2 minority (both Asian Americans or Pacific Islanders), 1 international. Average age 28. 36 applicants, 6% accepted, 2 enrolled. In 2006, 2 degrees awarded. *Entrance requirements:* For degree, DMD, DDS. *Application deadline:* For fall admission, 9/30 priority date for domestic students. Applications are processed on a rolling basis. *Financial support:* In 2006–07, 2 fellowships (averaging $23,000 per year) were awarded. *Faculty research:* Bone tissue engineering, transcriptional regulation, periodontics, implantology, gene delivery. Total annual research expenditures: $50,000. *Unit head:* Dr. Pouran Famili, Department of Periodontics, Director, Periodontics Residency; Interim Chair, 412-648-8598, Fax: 412-648-8594, E-mail: paf@pitt.edu.

University of Pittsburgh, School of Dental Medicine, Residency Programs in Dental Medicine, Prosthodontic Residency Program, Pittsburgh, PA 15260. Offers MDS, Certificate. *Faculty:* 5 full-time (0 women), 5 part-time/adjunct (0 women). *Students:* 6 full-time (3 women). Average age 28. 10 applicants, 20% accepted, 2 enrolled. *Application deadline:* For fall admission, 11/15 for domestic students. Application fee: $50. Electronic applications accepted. *Financial support:* In 2006–07, 6 fellowships (averaging $25,000 per year) were awarded; career-related internships or fieldwork and institutionally sponsored loans also available. Financial award application deadline: 4/15; financial award applicants required to submit FAFSA. *Faculty research:* Implant dentistry, occlusion, biomechanics, microbiology. *Unit head:* Dr. Mohsen Azarbal, Director, Prosthodontic Residency Program, 412-624-8840, Fax: 412-624-8850, E-mail: moa5@pitt.edu. *Application contact:* Pamela A. Edwards, Administrator, Office of Resident Education, 412-648-8406, Fax: 412-648-8219, E-mail: pae3@pitt.edu.

University of Puerto Rico, Medical Sciences Campus, School of Dentistry, Graduate Programs in Dentistry, San Juan, PR 00936-5067. Offers dentistry (Certificate); general dentistry (Certificate); oral and maxillofacial surgery (MSD, Certificate); orthodontics (MSD, Certificate); pediatric dentistry (MSD, Certificate); prosthodontics (MSD, Certificate). *Faculty:* 20 full-time (5 women), 11 part-time/adjunct (4 women). *Students:* 40 full-time (25 women); all minorities (all Hispanic Americans) Average age 27. 176 applicants, 9% accepted, 15 enrolled. In 2006, 2 master's, 19 other advanced degrees awarded. *Degree requirements:* For master's, thesis, registration. *Entrance requirements:* For master's, DDS or DMD, postdoctoral certificate; for Certificate, National Board Dental Exam I, National Board Dental Exam II, DDS or DMD, interview. *Application deadline:* For fall admission, 10/15 for domestic students. Application fee: $0. Electronic applications accepted. *Expenses: Contact institution. Financial support:* In 2006–07, 40 students received support, including 12 research assistantships (averaging $5,000 per year), 12 teaching assistantships (averaging $5,000 per year); Federal Work-Study, institutionally sponsored loans, scholarships/grants, traineeships, and stipends also available. Financial award application deadline: 3/30. *Faculty research:* Analgesic drugs, anti-inflammatory drugs, saliva cytoanalysis, dental materials, oral epidemiology and dental caries. Total annual research expenditures: $1.7 million. *Unit head:* Dr. Ramon F. Gonzalez, Assistant Dean, 787-758-2525 Ext. 2509, Fax: 787-751-5279, E-mail: rfgonzalez@ram.upr.edu.

University of Rochester, School of Medicine and Dentistry, Graduate Programs in Medicine and Dentistry, Center for Oral Biology, Rochester, NY 14627-0250. Offers MS. *Degree requirements:* For master's, thesis. *Entrance requirements:* For master's, GRE General Test, DDS or equivalent.

University of Southern California, Graduate School, School of Dentistry and Graduate School, Program in Craniofacial Biology, Los Angeles, CA 90089. Offers MS, PhD. *Students:* 35 full-time (19 women), 1 (woman) part-time; includes 10 minority (8 Asian Americans or Pacific Islanders, 2 Hispanic Americans), 13 international. In 2006, 7 master's, 4 doctorates awarded. *Degree requirements:* For master's and doctorate, thesis/dissertation. *Entrance requirements:* For master's and doctorate, GRE General Test. *Application deadline:* For fall admission, 6/1 priority date for domestic students; for spring admission, 10/15 for domestic students. Application fee: $85. *Expenses:* Tuition: Full-time $33,314; part-time $1,121 per credit. Required fees: $522. Full-time tuition and fees vary according to program. *Financial support:* In 2006–07, 2 research assistantships (averaging $18,500 per year), teaching assistantships (averaging $18,500 per year) were awarded; fellowships, Federal Work-Study, institutionally sponsored loans, and scholarships/grants also available. Support available to part-time students. Financial award application deadline: 2/15; financial award applicants required to submit FAFSA. *Unit head:* Dr. Charles Schuler, Director, 213-740-1001, E-mail: shuler@zygote.hsc.usc.edu.

The University of Tennessee Health Science Center, College of Dentistry, Memphis, TN 38163-0002. Offers dentistry (DDS); oral and maxillofacial surgery (Certificate); orthodontics (MS); pediatric dentistry (MS, Certificate); periodontics (MS); prosthodontics (Certificate). *Accreditation:* ADA (one or more programs are accredited). *Faculty:* 57 full-time (8 women), 66 part-time/adjunct (6 women). *Students:* 357 full-time (149 women); includes 80 minority (42 African Americans, 32 Asian Americans or Pacific Islanders, 6 Hispanic Americans). Average age 23. 255 applicants, 37% accepted, 95 enrolled. In 2006, 72 DDSs, 6 master's awarded. *Degree requirements:* For master's, thesis. *Entrance requirements:* For DDS, DAT, interview, pre-professional evaluation; for master's, GRE, interviews. Additional exam requirements/recommendations for international students: Required—TOEFL (minimum score 275 computer-based). *Application deadline:* For fall admission, 12/31 for domestic and international students. Applications are processed on a rolling basis. Application fee: $50. Electronic applications accepted. *Expenses: Contact institution.* One-time fee: $55 full-time. *Financial support:* In 2006–07, 278 students received support. Federal Work-Study and minority scholarships available. Support available to part-time students. Financial award application deadline: 2/15; financial award applicants required to submit FAFSA. *Faculty research:* Oral cancer, proteomics, inflammation mechanisms, defensins, periopathogens, dental material. Total annual research expenditures: $275,000. *Unit head:* Dr. Russell O. Gilpatrick, Dean, 901-448-6202, Fax: 901-448-1625, E-mail: rgilpatrick@utmem.edu. *Application contact:* Dr. Wisdom F. Coleman, Admissions, Associate Dean, 901-448-4200, Fax: 901-448-1625, E-mail: wcoleman@utmem.edu.

The University of Texas Health Science Center at San Antonio, Dental School and Graduate School of Biomedical Sciences, Graduate Program in Dentistry, San Antonio, TX 78229-3900. Offers MS, Certificate. *Faculty:* 110 full-time (28 women), 85 part-time/adjunct (19 women). *Students:* 100 full-time (26 women). In 2006, 10 master's, 17 other advanced degrees awarded. *Degree requirements:* For master's, thesis, registration (for some programs). *Entrance requirements:* For master's, GRE General Test, DDS; for Certificate, DDS. *Application deadline:* For fall admission, 10/15 for domestic students. Application fee: $0. *Expenses:* Tuition, state resident: part-time $50 per credit hour. Tuition, nonresident: part-time $325 per credit hour. Required fees: $7.5 per credit hour. $155 per term. *Financial support:* In 2006–07, 10 students received support; teaching assistantships, institutionally sponsored loans and unspecified assistantships available. Financial award application deadline: 3/1; financial award applicants required to submit FAFSA. *Application contact:* Sofia Almeda, Office of Admissions and Student Services, 210-567-2659, Fax: 210-567-2685, E-mail: almedas@uthscsa.edu.

University of the Pacific, Arthur A. Dugoni School of Dentistry, Program in Oral and Maxillofacial Surgery, Stockton, CA 95211-0197. Offers Certificate. Program offered with Highland General Hospital. *Students:* 120 applicants, 2% accepted, 2 enrolled. In 2006, 2 degrees awarded. *Entrance requirements:* For degree, DDS/DMD. *Application deadline:* For fall admission, 9/1 for domestic students. *Expenses: Contact institution.* Tuition and fees vary according to course load. *Financial support:* In 2006–07, 2 students received support, including 2 fellowships (averaging $40,000 per year); health care benefits also available. *Faculty research:* Trauma surgery, implants, esthetic surgery. Total annual research expenditures: $50,000. *Unit head:* Dr. A. Thomas Indresano, Chair. *Application contact:* Angela Holland, Assistant, 510-437-4548, Fax: 510-437-5728, E-mail: aholland@acmedctr.org.

University of the Pacific, Arthur A. Dugoni School of Dentistry, Program in Orthodontics, Stockton, CA 95211-0197. Offers dentistry (MSD). *Degree requirements:* For master's, thesis, comprehensive exam. *Entrance requirements:* For master's, GRE General Test, DDS/DMD. Additional exam requirements/recommendations for international students: Required—TOEFL. *Application deadline:* For fall admission, 10/1 for domestic and international students. *Expenses:*

Oral and Dental Sciences

University of the Pacific (continued)
Contact institution. Tuition and fees vary according to course load. *Financial support:* Institutionally sponsored loans and stipends available. Financial award application deadline: 2/1. *Faculty research:* Osteoblast cell studies, digitized orthodontic records, periodontal orthodontic relationships, orthotreatment outcomes. *Unit head:* Dr. Robert Boyd, Chairperson, 415-929-6555. *Application contact:* Loretta Giglione, Information Contact, 415-929-6556, Fax: 415-749-3390.

The University of Toledo, College of Graduate Studies, College of Medicine, Department of Oral Biology, Toledo, OH 43606-3390. Offers MS. Part-time programs available. *Faculty:* 4 full-time (1 woman), 1 part-time/adjunct (0 women). *Students:* 1 full-time (0 women), 1 part-time, 1 international. Average age 37. In 2006, 1 degree awarded. *Degree requirements:* For master's, thesis, qualifying exam. *Entrance requirements:* For master's, GRE General Test, minimum undergraduate GPA of 3.0. Application fee: $45. *Financial support:* Federal Work-Study and institutionally sponsored loans available. Financial award applicants required to submit FAFSA. *Faculty research:* Oral biology-tissue cultures. *Unit head:* Dr. William Davis, Program Director, 419-383-4117, Fax: 419-383-6140, E-mail: mcogradschool@mco.edu. *Application contact:* Joann Braatz, Secretary, 419-383-4117, Fax: 419-383-6140, E-mail: mcogradschool@mco.edu.

University of Toronto, Faculty of Dentistry, Graduate Programs in Dentistry, Toronto, ON M5S 1A1, Canada. Offers M Sc, PhD. Part-time programs available. Terminal master's awarded for partial completion of doctoral program. *Degree requirements:* For master's and doctorate, thesis/dissertation. *Entrance requirements:* For master's, honors B Sc., minimum B average, 2 letters of reference; for doctorate, M Sc., minimum B+ average. Additional exam requirements/recommendations for international students: Required—Michigan English Language Assessment Battery, IELTS, TOEFL or COPE. Electronic applications accepted. Expenses: Contact institution. *Faculty research:* Plaque, periodontal biology, biomaterials/dental implants, community dentistry, growth and development.

University of Toronto, Faculty of Dentistry, Specialty Master's Programs, Toronto, ON M5S 1A1, Canada. Offers dental anesthesia (M Sc); dental public health (M Sc); endodontics (M Sc); oral and maxillofacial surgery and anesthesia (M Sc); oral pathology (M Sc); oral radiology (M Sc); orthodontics (M Sc); pediatric dentistry (M Sc); periodontology (M Sc); prosthodontics (M Sc). *Degree requirements:* For master's, thesis, clinical requirements by specialty per CDA, research. *Entrance requirements:* For master's, completion of professional degree of DDS/BDS, DMD, minimum B average, 2 letters of reference. Additional exam requirements/recommendations for international students: Required—TOEFL, Michigan English Language Assessment Battery, IELTS or COPE. Expenses: Contact institution. *Faculty research:* Plaque and periodontal biology, biomaterials/dental implants, community dentistry, growth development, neurophysiology.

University of Washington, School of Dentistry and Graduate School, Graduate Programs in Dentistry, Seattle, WA 98195. Offers MS, MSD, PhD, MSD/PhD. *Degree requirements:* For master's, thesis optional. Expenses: Contact institution.

The University of Western Ontario, Schulich School of Medicine and Dentistry, School of Dentistry, Division of Graduate Orthodontics, London, ON N6A 5B8, Canada. Offers M Cl D. *Faculty:* 2 full-time (0 women), 11 part-time/adjunct (1 woman). *Degree requirements:* For master's, thesis. *Entrance requirements:* For master's, GRE General Test, minimum B average, 1 year of general practice preferred. Additional exam requirements/recommendations for international students: Required—TOEFL (minimum score 600 paper-based; 250 computer-based). *Application deadline:* For fall admission, 10/1 for domestic students. Application fee: $100 Canadian dollars. *Financial support:* Career-related internships or fieldwork available. *Unit head:* Dr. Sahza Hatibovic-Kofman, Chair, 519-661-2111 Ext. 86131, Fax: 519-661-2075, E-mail: sahza.kofman@fmd.uwo.ca.

West Virginia University, School of Dentistry, Division of Dental Hygiene, Morgantown, WV 26506. Offers MS. Part-time programs available. *Degree requirements:* For master's, thesis. *Entrance requirements:* For master's, GRE, MAT, BS in dental hygiene or equivalent, minimum GPA of 2.75. Additional exam requirements/recommendations for international students: Required—TOEFL. *Application deadline:* For fall admission, 7/1 for domestic students; for spring admission, 11/15 priority date for domestic students. Applications are processed on a rolling basis. Application fee: $50. *Expenses:* Tuition, state resident: full-time $4,926; part-time $276 per credit hour. Tuition, nonresident: full-time $14,278; part-time $796 per credit hour. Tuition and fees vary according to program. *Financial support:* In 2006–07, 1 research assistantship with partial tuition reimbursement was awarded; Federal Work-Study and institutionally sponsored loans also available. Financial award application deadline: 3/1; financial award applicants required to submit FAFSA. *Faculty research:* Curriculum and instruction, infection control, special patient care, diversity and cultural sensitivity, oral health disparities. *Unit head:* Amy D. Funk, Interim Director of Dental Hygiene, 304-293-3418, E-mail: afunk@hsc.wvu.edu. *Application contact:* Loreen Hurley, Administrative Associate, 304-293-3417, E-mail: lhurley@hsc.wvu.edu.

West Virginia University, School of Dentistry, Graduate Programs in Dentistry, Morgantown, WV 26506. Offers endodontics (MS); orthodontics (MS); prosthodontics (MS). *Students:* 17 full-time (6 women); includes 1 minority (Asian American or Pacific Islander), 1 international. Average age 30. In 2006, 6 degrees awarded. *Degree requirements:* For master's, thesis, registration. *Entrance requirements:* For master's, National Dental Hygiene Board Exam, DDS/DMD from accredited U.S. or Canadian Dental School. Additional exam requirements/recommendations for international students: Required—TOEFL. *Application deadline:* For fall admission, 9/15 for domestic and international students. Application fee: $50. *Expenses:* Contact institution. Tuition and fees vary according to program. *Financial support:* In 2006–07, 16 students received support, including 9 teaching assistantships with partial tuition reimbursements available (averaging $8,264 per year); research assistantships. Financial award application deadline: 3/1; financial award applicants required to submit FAFSA. *Faculty research:* Growth and development, cephalographics, endodontic interpretation and therapy. *Unit head:* Dr. Christina H. DeBiase, Associate Dean for Academic Affairs, 304-293-3922, E-mail: cdebiase@hsc.wvu.edu. *Application contact:* Karen B. Davis, Administrative Associate, 304-293-3549, Fax: 304-293-4915, E-mail: kdavis@hsc.wvu.edu.

BOSTON UNIVERSITY

Goldman School of Dental Medicine
Ph.D. Program in Oral Biology

Program of Study	The Division of Oral Biology, Boston University Goldman School of Dental Medicine, now offers a Ph.D. in oral biology. The Ph.D. Program in Oral Biology recruits students with backgrounds in the life and basic sciences who are interested in additional advanced training in dental and medical sciences. The aim of the program is to educate students in modern scientific approaches to oral biology and oral disease. The program is designed for the student whose primary goal is to pursue a career in oral biology research, either in an academic or industrial setting. The oral cavity is unique in regard to its microbiology, connective tissue structures, and host responses. Moreover, oral diseases present unsolved scientific challenges and novel biological phenomena, including interactions with systemic diseases.
	Postbaccalaureate Ph.D. degree candidates complete at least 40 credits of didactic course work and 24 credits in dissertation-directed laboratory research. Most candidates require four to five years to fulfill these requirements. Didactic courses are taken principally during the first 1½ to 2 years of the program. Ph.D. qualifying examinations are administered at the end of the first year (written) and second year (oral), respectively. Students perform research rotations during the first year, and a research mentor from the Division of Oral Biology is selected by the end of the first year. Each student meets with a pre-thesis committee at least once annually beginning in the second year to monitor research progress. Successful completion of a dissertation and final thesis defense is required for the Ph.D. Active areas of research include studies of the structure and function of salivary proteins, oral microbiology, host-defense mechanisms, extracellular matrix biosynthesis structure and function, and molecular and cellular interactions that occur in systemic and oral diseases.
Research Facilities	Research laboratories of the Division of Oral Biology are located principally on the second floor of the Center for Advanced Biomedical Research. This facility is a state-of-the-art building that was completed in 1994, and it also houses sophisticated core facilities available to the Medical Center as a whole. The Laboratory Animal Sciences Facility is also located in this building, thus allowing easy access to animal colonies for research. Additional research laboratories are located in the Goldman School of Dental Medicine building and at Boston University School of Medicine. The faculty has research collaborations both at the Goldman School of Dental Medicine and at the School of Medicine.
Financial Aid	Accepted Ph.D. candidates are supported by fellowships awarded by the Boston University Goldman School of Dental Medicine, NIH training grants for U.S. residents and citizens, NIH and other research grants, and other scholarship funds that may be available from the Division of Graduate Medical Sciences, Boston University School of Medicine. These awards generally cover tuition and stipend costs. Stipend awards are approximately $26,000 per year.
Cost of Study	The above awards generally cover tuition and stipend costs.
Living and Housing Costs	Limited University housing on the Medical Center campus is available, with a variety of one- and two-bedroom apartments. Laundry facilities, an exercise room, and other amenities are provided. Rents range from $1200 to $2300 per month. Other housing resources are available in and around Boston, and advice is available regarding these opportunities by calling Housing Resources at Boston University Goldman School of Dental Medicine at 617-638-4787.
Student Group	The Ph.D. Program in Oral Biology was initiated in 1998. Up to 3 new students are accepted each year. Successful candidates must have a strong scientific background, usually with a bachelor's degree in a basic science discipline or with a doctoral degree in medicine or dentistry. A strong interest in pursuing a career in oral biology research is essential.
Location	Boston University Goldman School of Dental Medicine is an integral part of Boston University Medical Center. Located in Boston, Massachusetts, there is an extensive and unique availability of scientific, academic, and cultural resources at both Boston University and at neighboring institutions. The home of numerous biotechnology firms and universities, Boston is a prime location for graduate studies and allows for exposure to both academic and industrial settings. Near the ocean and near the mountains of New England, Boston offers numerous opportunities for recreation both within and outside the city.
The University	The Ph.D. in oral biology is awarded by the Boston University Goldman School of Dental Medicine and is administered by the Division of Graduate Medical Sciences, Boston University School of Medicine. Thus, there is close collaboration between the medical and dental schools regarding design and teaching of didactic courses and regarding research programs. This results in a rich and active environment for graduate education at a major renowned research university.
Applying	Applications must be received by January 15 for admission the following September. Required exams include the GRE and a GRE Subject Test; international applicants must submit scores on the TOEFL. Personal or telephone interviews are initiated by the admissions committee, which is made up of faculty members of the Division of Oral Biology. Application materials are available from the Division of Graduate Medical Sciences, Room L317, Boston University School of Medicine, 715 Albany Street, Boston, Massachusetts 02118-2394, or from the Division of Oral Biology at the University address.
Correspondence and Information	Dr. Frank G. Oppenheim Dr. Philip C. Trackman Division of Oral Biology Boston University Goldman School of Dental Medicine 700 Albany Street Boston, Massachusetts 02118 Phone: 617-638-4942 Fax: 617-638-4924 E-mail: fropp@bu.edu trackman@bu.edu Web site: http://dentalschool.bu.edu

Boston University

THE FACULTY AND THEIR RESEARCH

Salomon Amar, Professor; D.D.S., 1985; Ph.D., 1989, Louis Pasteur (France). Research activities are focused on the biology and mechanisms of wound healing and inflammation. Dr. Amar's laboratory has identified several candidate genes responsible for periodontal tissue regeneration in animal model systems. In addition, Dr. Amar has identified and sequenced a novel gene that controls the expression of the pro-inflammatory cytokine TNF-α. Current studies are in progress that investigate broader implications of controlling TNF-α in various inflammatory diseases.

Dana T. Graves, Professor; D.D.S., Columbia, 1980; D.M.Sc., Harvard, 1984. Dr. Graves is examining the role of specific cytokines and chemokines in orchestrating the host response to bacterial challenge. These studies involve the use of transgenic mice and function-blocking antibodies to dissect the critical events in disease progression. The goal is to establish which aspects of host-bacteria interactions contribute to destruction of connective tissue and bone, particularly as it relates to increased susceptibility to infection in diabetes.

Frank G. Oppenheim, Professor and Chairman; D.D.S., Zürich, 1963; Ph.D. Boston University, 1973. Dr. Oppenheim's laboratory focuses on the structure and function of salivary proteins, with particular emphasis on mechanisms of host protection of both hard and soft tissues. His research with oral fluid and salivary secretions led to the isolation and characterization of several major proteins, such as the acidic proline-rich proteins, statherin variants, and histatins. These proteins show a high selectivity for hydroxyapatite surfaces and participate in the formation of the acquired enamel pellicle. Micromethods of protein isolation and characterization are being employed in conjunction with proteomic approaches to characterize the structure of the in vivo–formed pellicle. The goal is to gain insights into mechanisms of enamel protection and bacterial colonization. The mechanisms of the antimicrobial activities of histatins are being investigated both in yeasts and oral bacteria, using cellular and molecular tools as well as peptide mimetics.

Philip C. Trackman, Professor; Ph.D., Boston University, 1980. Research is focused on regulation and molecular mechanisms of extracellular matrix accumulation in mineralized and non-mineralized normal tissues and on abnormalities that occur in these pathways in oral and systemic pathologies. The roles of extracellular biosynthetic enzymes, including lysyl oxidase and proteolytic processing enzymes such as procollagen N- and C-proteinases, are of particular interest. Thus, the in vitro and in vivo regulation is being determined of these enzymes, of other extracellular matrix components, and of selected cytokines under normal and pathologic conditions. These studies have relevance to elucidation of molecular events and mechanisms that occur in normal bone formation, altered bone formation in diabetes, drug-induced gingival hyperplasia, and other neoplastic disorders, including cancer.

Thomas Van Dyke, Professor; D.D.S., Case Western Reserve, 1973; Ph.D., SUNY at Buffalo, 1982. Dr. Van Dyke's research has contributed to understanding the pathogenesis and genetic inheritance of localized juvenile periodontitis and other periodontal diseases. This laboratory has shown that interactions between neutrophils and their surrounding environment are critical for the initiation of the inflammatory process. Studies have identified chemotactic receptor changes in subjects with juvenile periodontitis, specific enzyme deficiencies in neutrophils in the same subjects, and a novel functional LPS receptor known as moesin.

STONY BROOK UNIVERSITY, STATE UNIVERSITY OF NEW YORK

Department of Oral Biology and Pathology

Program of Study

The discipline of oral biology deals with the structure, development, and functions of oral tissues and organs and their relation to other organ systems in both health and disease. It integrates the core basic health sciences disciplines so as to understand and develop new knowledge of the biology of the oral cavity. This serves as a foundation for the discovery of new and improved methods for preventing and controlling oral disease. In essence, oral biology is a bridge between the core basic health science disciplines and clinical dentistry.

Graduate education and research programs have been developed that have trained highly competent scientists primarily at the Ph.D. level to engage in oral biological research and education, and who have obtained highly desirable positions in academic and industrial institutions. Since the inception of the graduate program, 40 students have completed their doctoral degrees. A master's degree is also offered and is mainly intended for students who have completed a dental curriculum. In addition to the Department's traditional programs, there is also a combined Ph.D.–Periodontics certificate program.

Didactic and laboratory courses are offered at the graduate level and each student's course of study is flexible depending upon his or her research project. After completion of their course work, students are required to pass an advancement-to-candidacy examination a year prior to submission of their dissertations. The average length of time to complete the Ph.D. is five years.

Research Facilities

A new clinical research facility permits investigation of oral research projects, including clinical trials, on human subjects. The director of this unit is Dr. Lorne Golub.

A two-chair clinical research dental facility for research purposes has been developed in Stony Brook University Hospital in collaboration with the General Clinical Research Center. The director of this unit is Dr. Maria Ryan.

A bacterial anaerobe facility has been established for molecular microbiology research related to dental disease. This facility is supervised by the Department's oral microbiologist, Dr. Steven Walker.

The Living Skin Bank was initiated as part of New York State's mandate to bring state-of-the-art treatment of burn wounds to Suffolk County. Under the guidance of its director, Dr. Marcia Simon, the Living Skin Bank also carries out multidisciplinary research aimed at developing therapeutics to reduce various skin disorders, including cancerous lesions.

Financial Aid

Students customarily receive full stipends through research grants awarded to their faculty advisers. Tuition scholarship monies are currently available through the Graduate School, although they are not guaranteed. Student funding is provided through the National Institutes of Health, foundation, and industrial sources. The Department is a leader in gaining grant funding from a wide variety of commercial companies.

Cost of Study

In 2006–07, full-time tuition at 12 credits for entering in-state residents was $3450 per semester, while out-of-state residents and international students paid $5460. Additional fees for each semester, including (but not limited to) the infirmary, activity, technology, and transportation fee, amount to about $430. International students also pay a service fee of $35 per semester and an orientation fee of $50. Fees for the mandatory Student Health Insurance Plan vary depending on citizenship and employment status.

Living and Housing Costs

For 2006–07, Stony Brook calculated the cost of education excluding tuition, fees, and insurance at $13,520 per year. On-campus apartments range in cost from approximately $316 per month to approximately $1456 per month, depending on the size of the unit and the number of students sharing the space. Off-campus housing options include rooms, houses, and apartments that can be rented from $350 to $2500 per month. Costs including books, food, and transportation may vary depending on academic program and/or personal circumstances.

Student Group

There are currently 5 Ph.D. students and 1 M.Sc. student in the Departmental graduate program. Of these, 3 are dentists from international institutions.

Student Outcomes

Department graduates include 11 D.D.S./Ph.D.'s, 5 M.D./Ph.D.'s, 23 Ph.D.'s, and 1 Ph.D./J.D. All of the Department's Ph.D.'s have found employment in academia, industry, and the private sector. Starting salaries for graduates in oral biology in industry are approximately $60,000 per year. Four of the Department's D.D.S./Ph.D. graduates hold academic positions at the Dental School at Stony Brook in the Departments of Oral Biology and Pathology and General Dentistry.

Location

The campus is located on the north shore of Long Island about 60 miles east of New York City. The area is beautiful and the Stony Brook campus is nestled amid fields and woodlands with the tranquil waters of Long Island Sound just minutes away to the north and the white sandy beaches of the Atlantic Ocean a 45-minute drive to the south.

The University and The Department

Stony Brook is classified by the Carnegie Foundation as Research University (very high research activity), reflecting Stony Brook's high volume of federally sponsored research, high percentage of doctoral students, and emphasis on scholarship. The Department of Oral Biology and Pathology faculty members hold the most patents, FDA approvals, and commercial products on the campus. The Department is uniquely known for its translational research.

Applying

Faculty members seek the most highly qualified and motivated students who wish to become professional research or clinician scientists. The application fee is $60. For application forms and other information, prospective students should visit the University's Web site.

Correspondence and Information

Dr. Marcia Simon
Graduate Program Director
Department of Oral Biology and Pathology
Stony Brook University
Stony Brook, New York 11794-8702
Phone: 631-632-8922
E-mail: marcia.simon@stonybrook.edu
Web site: http://www.grad.sunysb.edu

Stony Brook University, State University of New York

THE FACULTY AND THEIR RESEARCH

Distinguished Professor and Chairman

Israel Kleinberg, D.D.S. (dentistry), Toronto, 1952; Ph.D. (oral biology), Newcastle (England), 1958. Identification of salivary factors involved in the metabolism of mixed bacterial populations, mechanisms of dental plaque formation, pharmaceutical application of salivary components in the control of dental caries and oral malodor, control of microbial populations with growth factors and growth inhibitors, development of new commercial products and oral diagnostics for oral disease.

Professors

Lorne M. Golub, D.M.D. (dentistry), Manitoba, 1963; M.D. (hon.), Helsinki (Finland), 2000. Development of new biologically based oral diagnostic techniques; mechanisms of collagen breakdown during various dental and medical diseases, including the role of matrix metalloproteinases (MMPS); development of tetracycline-based inhibitors (subantimicrobial doxycycline or Periostat and chemically modified tetracyclines) as new therapeutic agents for periodontal disease, osteoporosis, cancer and cardiomyopathies.

Maria E. Ryan, D.D.S. (dentistry), 1989; Ph.D. (oral biology and pathology), 1998, SUNY at Stony Brook. Development of new diagnostic and therapeutic modalities for the management of periodontal disease, diabetes and periodontal disease, oral systemic disease connections.

Marcia Simon, Ph.D. (biochemistry), Brandeis, 1981. Regulation of epithelial mesenchymal retinol metabolism, wound healing and the role of fibroblast phenotype switching, epidermal stem cells and differentiation, development of new therapeutic modalities for the treatment of massive skin loss due to acute and chronic injury.

Associate Professors

Soosan Ghazizadeh, Ph.D. (cellular and developmental biology), SUNY at Stony Brook, 1994. Gene transfer to skin epithelial stem cells for the treatment of inherited disorders, developing strategies for in vivo expansion of gene-modified stem cells and host immune responses to neoantigens expressed in skin. It is expected that the development of new strategies to expand genetically modified stem cells in vivo and to circumvent destructive immune responses will overcome the major obstacles to clinical applications of cutaneous gene therapy.

Steven Walker, Ph.D. (microbiology), British Columbia, 1994. The cell surface of Gram-negative oral bacteria, with emphasis on the lipolysaccharide and outer membrane proteins; attachment of oral bacteria to host cells; microbial assessment of periodontopathic microorganisms in periodontal disease.

Research Assistant Professor

Hsi-ming Lee, Ph.D. (oral biology), SUNY at Stony Brook, 1996. Role of chemically modified nonantimicrobial tetracycline analogues as modulators of cytokines and MMPs in cell culture.

Adjunct Graduate Faculty

Christopher Cutler, Associate Professor of Periodontics; D.D.S. (dentistry), 1986; Ph.D. (experimental pathology), 1990, Emory. Periodontal disease, cytokines, mucosal immune regulation by dendritic cells and Langerhans cells.

Robert A. Greenwald, Professor and Chief of Rheumatology at Long Island Jewish Medical Center, New York; M.D. (medicine) Johns Hopkins. Mechanisms of inflammation and connective tissue degradation, pharmacological inhibition of connective tissue degradation.

Bettie M. Steinberg, Professor and Chief of ENT Research, Long Island Jewish Medical Center, New York; Ph.D. (microbiology), SUNY at Stony Brook, 1976. Interaction between viruses and their host cells, virus induced benign and malignant tumors.

UNIVERSITY OF CONNECTICUT HEALTH CENTER

Graduate Program in Skeletal, Craniofacial, and Oral Biology

Programs of Study

The Graduate Program in Skeletal, Craniofacial, and Oral Biology provides students with interdisciplinary research training in the areas of skeletal, craniofacial, and oral biology, emphasizing contemporary research technologies in cell, molecular, and developmental biology; genetics; and biochemistry. Trainees may enter a Ph.D. program or a combined D.M.D./Ph.D., M.D./Ph.D., or Dental Residency/Ph.D. program. The program prepares trainees for academic or industrial careers in the basic biomedical sciences or for academic careers in medicine or dental medicine.

Areas of research include regulation of the formation, outgrowth, and patterning of the developing limb; control of cartilage differentiation, endochondral ossification, osteogenesis, and joint formation; molecular regulation of gene expression in bone; homeobox gene regulation of osteoblast differentiation; gene therapy of bone diseases; hormonal and cytokine regulation of bone growth, formation, and remodeling; control of craniofacial skeletogenesis and tooth development; biochemistry, function, and regulation of the extracellular matrix; signal transduction and intracellular signaling pathways; cellular and molecular aspects of the pathogenesis of inflammatory disease; microbiology, pathogenesis, and immunology of caries and periodontal disease; neural structure and function in the gustatory system; biomaterial development for tissue engineering; bone cell/implant interactions; and analysis of oral and mucosal function and disease.

Research Facilities

The University complex provides excellent physical facilities for research in both basic and clinical sciences. The Health Center Library is well equipped with extensive journal and book holdings and rapid electronic access to database searching, the World Wide Web, and library holdings. The library also contains the Computer Education Center and the End User Support Center. The Center for Laboratory Animal Care contains a transgenic mouse production facility fully equipped for gene targeting studies and with special facilities for housing immunodeficient animals. Facilities include the Center for Biomaterials, the General Clinical Research Center, the Center for Cell Analysis and Modeling (confocal microscopy, low light level microscopy, two photon microscopy), the Center for Bone Histology and Histomorphometry; the Molecular Imaging Laboratory, the Fluorescence Flow Cytometry Facility, the Electron Microscopy Facility, Gene Targeting and Transgenic Facility, the Microarray Core Facility, the Molecular Core Facility, NMR Structural Biology Facility, National Resource for Cell Analysis and Modeling, and the Center for Molecular Medicine (laser capture microdissection).

Financial Aid

Support for doctoral students engaged in full-time degree programs at the Health Center is provided on a competitive basis. Graduate research assistantships for 2007–08 provide a stipend of $26,000 per year, which includes a waiver of tuition/University fees for the fall and spring semesters and a student health-insurance plan. While financial aid is offered competitively, the Health Center makes every possible effort to address the financial needs of all students during their period of training.

Cost of Study

For 2007–08, tuition is $4221 per semester ($8442 per year) for full-time students (Connecticut residents) and $10,962 per semester ($21,924 per year) for full-time out-of-state residents. General University fees are added to the cost of tuition for students who do not receive a tuition waiver. These costs are usually met by traineeships or research assistantships for doctoral students.

Living and Housing Costs

There is a wide range of affordable housing options in the Greater Hartford area within easy commuting distance of the campus, including an extensive complex that is adjacent to the Health Center. Costs range from $600 to $800 per month for a one-bedroom unit; two or more students sharing an apartment usually pay less. University housing is not available at the Health Center.

Student Group

The Program in Skeletal, Craniofacial, and Oral Biology has approximately 20 trainees. At the Health Center there are about 500 students in the Schools of Medicine and Dental Medicine, 150 Ph.D. students, and about 50 postdoctoral fellows. Graduate students are represented on various administrative committees concerned with curricular affairs. A graduate student organization fosters social contact among graduate students in the Health Center and represents graduate students' needs and concerns to the faculty and administration.

Location

The Health Center is located in the historic town of Farmington, Connecticut. Set in the beautiful New England countryside, on a hill overlooking the Farmington Valley, it is close to ski areas, hiking trails, and facilities for boating, fishing, and swimming. Connecticut's capital city of Hartford, 7 miles east of Farmington, is the center of an urban region of approximately 800,000 people. The beaches of the Long Island Sound are about 50 minutes away to the south, and the beautiful Berkshires are a short drive to the northwest. New York City and Boston can be reached within 2½ hours by car.

Hartford is the home of the acclaimed Hartford Stage Company, TheatreWorks, the Hartford Symphony and Chamber orchestras, two ballet companies, an opera company, the Wadsworth Atheneum (the oldest public art museum in the nation), the Mark Twain house, the Hartford Civic Center, and many other interesting cultural and recreational facilities. The area is also home to several branches of the University of Connecticut, Trinity College, and the University of Hartford, which includes the Hartt School of Music. Bradley International Airport (about 20 minutes from campus) serves the Hartford/Springfield area with frequent airline connections to major cities in this country and abroad. Frequent bus and rail service is also available from Hartford.

The Health Center

The 200-acre Health Center campus at Farmington houses a division of the University of Connecticut Graduate School, as well as the Schools of Medicine and Dental Medicine. The campus also includes the John Dempsey Hospital, associated clinics, and extensive medical research facilities, all in a centralized facility with more than 1 million square feet of floor space. The Health Center's newest research addition, the Academic Research Building, opened in 1999. This impressive eleven-story structure provides 170,000 square feet of state-of-the-art laboratory space. The faculty at the center includes more than 260 full-time members. The institution has a strong commitment to graduate study within an environment that promotes social and intellectual interaction among the various educational programs. Graduate students are represented on various administrative committees concerned with curricular affairs, and the Graduate Student Organization (GSO) represents graduate students' needs and concerns to the faculty and administration, in addition to fostering social contact among graduate students in the Health Center.

Applying

Applications for admission should be submitted on standard forms that can be obtained from the Graduate Admissions Office at the University of Connecticut (UConn) Health Center or from the Web site at http://grad.uchc.edu/oral_bio/oralbio_intro.html. Applications should be filed together with transcripts, three letters of recommendation, a personal statement, and recent results from the General Test of the Graduate Record Examinations. International students must take the Test of English as a Foreign Language (TOEFL) to satisfy Graduate School requirements.

The deadline for completed applications and receipt of all supplemental materials is December 15. Deadlines and application procedures for combined programs vary depending on the program. For further information on combined programs, prospective students should contact Dr. William Upholt in the Center for Regenerative Medicine and Skeletal Development.

In accordance with the laws of the state of Connecticut and of the United States, the University of Connecticut Health Center does not discriminate against any person in its educational and employment activities on the grounds of race, color, creed, national origin, sex, age, or physical disability.

Correspondence and Information

Dr. William B. Upholt
Oral Rehabilitation, Biomaterials, and Skeletal Development
Center for Regenerative Medicine and Skeletal Development
University of Connecticut Health Center
Farmington, Connecticut 06030-3705

Phone: 860-679-3388
E-mail: upholt@nso2.uchc.edu
Web site: http://grad.uchc.edu/oral_bio/oralbio_intro.html

University of Connecticut Health Center

THE FACULTY AND THEIR RESEARCH

Andrew Arnold, Professor of Medicine and Murray-Heilig Chair in Molecular Medicine; M.D., Harvard. The molecular genetic underpinnings of tumors of the endocrine glands, role of the cyclin D1 oncogene, animal modeling of hyperparathyroidism.

Caroline N. Dealy, Associate Professor of Oral Rehabilitation, Biomaterials, and Skeletal Development, Center for Regenerative Medicine and Skeletal Development; Ph.D., Connecticut. Roles of various growth factors and signaling molecules, particularly IGF-I and insulin, in the regulation of chick limb development.

Anne Delaney, Assistant Professor of Medicine; Ph.D., Dartmouth. Study of noncollagenous matrix proteins and metalloproteinases important in bone remodeling, including investigation of function and posttranscriptional regulation of osteonectin or SPARC in bone and function and regulation of the metastasis-associated metalloproteinase, stromelysyin-3, in bone.

Anna Dongari-Bagtzoglou, Assistant Professor, Department of Oral Health and Diagnostic Sciences, Division of Periodontology; D.D.S., Ph.D., Texas Health Science Center at San Antonio. Host-pathogen interactions with emphasis on the pathogenesis of inflammation and the innate immune functions of oral mucosal cells.

Paul M. Epstein, Associate Professor of Cell Biology; Ph.D., Yeshiva (Einstein). Second messengers and signal transduction with particular focus on cyclic nucleotide metabolism and protein phosphorylation, with emphasis on analysis of cyclic nucleotide phosphodiesterase (PDE).

Marion Frank, Professor of Oral Health and Diagnostic Sciences and Director, Center for Neurosciences; Ph.D., Brown. Study of the sense of taste using basic and clinical research; development of a fundamental understanding of gustatory systems in mammals at all levels from receptors to cerebral cortex; application of basic knowledge of gustatory systems to the diagnosis and treatment of taste disorders in humans.

A. Jon Goldberg, Professor of Oral Rehabilitation, Biomaterials, and Skeletal Development, Center for Regenerative Medicine and Skeletal Development; Ph.D., Michigan. Biomaterials, with studies involving structure-property relationships, development of novel systems, clinical evaluations, and surface analysis.

Gloria Gronowicz, Professor of Orthopedic Surgery and Director of Research; Ph.D., Columbia. Effects of hormones and growth factors on the production of extracellular matrix (ECM) proteins, on the regulation of integrins (receptors for ECM proteins), and on apoptosis in bone; response of bone cells to implant biomaterials.

Arthur R. Hand, Professor of Orthodontics and Maxillofacial Surgery, Pediatric Dentistry, and Advanced Education in General Dentistry, Division of Pediatric Dentistry; D.D.S., UCLA. Study of gene expression in rodent salivary glands during normal growth and development and in various experimental conditions employing morphological, immunological, and biochemical methodology.

Marc Hansen, Professor of Medicine; Ph.D., Cincinnati. Molecular genetics of osteosarcoma and related bone diseases.

Marja M. Hurley, Associate Professor of Medicine; M.D., Connecticut. Molecular mechanisms regulating the expression of fibroblast growth factors in bone, mechanisms of signal transduction by growth factors in bone cells, and role of fibroblast growth factors in bone remodeling.

Robert A. Kosher, Professor of Oral Rehabilitation, Biomaterials, and Skeletal Development, Center for Regenerative Medicine and Skeletal Development; Ph.D., Temple. Limb development; roles and relationships among regulatory genes, particularly homeobox-containing genes, secreted signaling molecules, and the extracellular matrix in the regulation of limb formation, outgrowth, patterning, cartilage differentiation, osteogenesis, and joint formation.

Barbara E. Kream, Professor of Medicine; Ph.D., Yale. Hormonal regulation of bone remodeling.

Liisa T. Kuhn, Assistant Professor of Oral Rehabilitation, Biomaterials, and Skeletal Development, Center for Regenerative Medicine and Skeletal Development; Ph.D., California, Santa Barbara. Biomaterials for drug delivery and bone regeneration and repair.

Marc Lalande, Professor and Head of Department of Genetics and Developmental Biology; Ph.D., Ontario Cancer Institute, University of Toronto. Genomic imprinting of human chromosome 15q.

Leo Lefrancois, Professor of Immunology; Ph.D., Wake Forest. T-lymphocyte development, mucosal immunology, intestinal intraepithelial T-lymphocytes, gamma/delta T-cells.

Alexander Lichtler, Associate Professor of Genetics and Developmental Biology; Ph.D., Florida. Hormone regulation of bone collagen synthesis.

Alan G. Lurie, Professor of Oral Health and Diagnostic Sciences and Head, Division of Oral and Maxillofacial Radiology; D.D.S., UCLA; Ph.D., Rochester. Actions and interactions of radiation and chemical carcinogens during epithelial carcinogenesis, DNA mutagenesis and repair by gamma radiation in lymphoblasts from both normal and ataxia telangiectatic humans, clinical research digital imaging.

Sanjay Mallya, Assistant Professor of Oral Health and Diagnostic Sciences, Division of Oral Diagnosis; M.D.S., Bombay; Ph.D., Connecticut. Molecular genetics of oral cancer, effects of parathyroid hormone on bone.

Mina Mina, Professor of Orthodontics, Oral and Maxillofacial Surgery, Pediatric Dentistry, and Advanced Education in General Dentistry and Head, Division of Pediatric Dentistry; D.M.D., National University of Iran; Ph.D., Connecticut Health Center. Development of the mandibular arch, including the elongation and polarized outgrowth of the mandibular primordia and subsequent differentiation of the skeletal tissues in spatially defined patterns; characterization of genetic and epigenetic influences involved in the pattern formation and skeletogenesis of the chick mandible and mouse tooth germ; regulation of patterning in the developing mandible and developing teeth by mandibular epithelium, extracellular matrix molecules, growth factors, and transcription factors.

Carol C. Pilbeam, Professor of Medicine; Ph.D., Yale. Mechanisms of regulation of bone formation and resorption.

Ernst Reichenberger, Assistant Professor of Oral Rehabilitation, Biomaterials, and Skeletal Development, Center for Regenerative Medicine and Skeletal Development; Ph.D., Erlangen (Germany). Study of complex processes required for generating and maintaining the skin and bones through characterization of human genetic disorders in which they are disrupted, including aplasia cutis congenita (ACC), cherubism, and craniometaphyseal dysplasia (CMD).

Blanka Rogina, Assistant Professor of Genetics and Developmental Biology; Ph.D., Zagreb University School of Medicine (Croatia). Molecular and genetic mechanisms underlying aging and cost of reproduction.

David W. Rowe, Professor of Genetics and Developmental Biology; M.D., Vermont. Genetic and hormonal control of type I collagen production, development of strategies for somatic gene therapy for heritable diseases of bone built upon the structural and regulatory principles of collagen production.

Jason M. Tanzer, Professor of Oral Health and Diagnostic Sciences and Head, Division of Microbiology and Oral Medicine; D.M.D., Tufts; Ph.D., Georgetown. Physiological/biochemical/genetic bases of virulence by the mutans streptococci and their expression and modification in both humans and experimental animals; secretion of saliva, its regulation by novel and old cholinomimetic agents, and associated characterization of the pharmacokinetics of these agents and pharmacodynamics of cardiovascular, salivary, and lacrimal responses in experimental animals and humans.

William B. Upholt, Professor of Oral Rehabilitation, Biomaterials, and Skeletal Development, Center for Regenerative Medicine and Skeletal Development and Director, Skeletal, Craniofacial, and Oral Biology Graduate Program; Ph.D., Cal Tech. Molecular mechanisms regulating differentiation and pattern formation during embryonic skeletal development in the limb and mandible, use of transgenic mouse model systems, study of the regulation of the process of chondrogenesis.

VIRGINIA COMMONWEALTH UNIVERSITY

School of Dentistry

Programs of Study

The School of Dentistry at Virginia Commonwealth University (VCU) offers a four-year program in general dentistry leading to the Doctor of Dental Surgery (D.D.S.) degree. Three broad areas are emphasized: the biomedical sciences, clinical sciences, and behavioral sciences. The biomedical sciences include the in-depth study of human anatomy, biochemistry, genetics, material science, microbiology, pathology, pharmacology, and physiology. The clinical sciences prepare the student for the actual practice of dentistry and provide exposure to the various specialties in dentistry. The behavioral sciences cover such topics as dental health needs, the system of health-care delivery, practice management, professional ethics, and behavioral factors. Laboratory and clinical experiences are offered throughout the four years to develop the skills and judgment vital to the practice of general dentistry. The academic year begins in July and extends through June.

Specialized training beyond the D.D.S. degree is available in advanced education in general dentistry, endodontics, oral and maxillofacial surgery, orthodontics, pediatric dentistry, and periodontics. In addition to a certificate, students in the endodontics, orthodontics, pediatric dentistry, and periodontics programs also earn a Master of Science in Dentistry (M.S.D.) upon completion of the requirements for the certificate and successful defense of a thesis. The certificate program and the M.S.D. must be completed concurrently. All programs are accredited by the Commission on Dental Accreditation of the American Dental Association.

In cooperation with the School of Dentistry, students in dentistry with an interest in academic and research careers are afforded the opportunity to undergo advanced-degree training while in dental school or residency. The requirements for a combined M.S./Ph.D. and D.D.S. in basic health sciences are equivalent to those required of students seeking a graduate degree alone and are determined by the individual departments. A time limit of five calendar years for the M.S. and seven calendar years for the Ph.D. degree, beginning at the time of first registration in the graduate school, applies to work to be credited toward degrees for students in combined programs.

Research Facilities

The facilities of the School of Dentistry are housed in the Wood Memorial and Lyons Buildings and contain clinical facilities, research facilities, classrooms, student laboratories, departmental offices, and a computer learning laboratory.

The centerpiece of the growing research efforts of the School is the Philips Institute, where studies related to oral and craniofacial molecular biology are carried out. In addition, investigators in the VCU Clinical Research Center for Periodontal Disease are studying genetic risk, pathogenic mechanisms, and immunologic aspects of periodontal diseases.

VCU libraries provide a combined capacity of more than 1.7 million volumes and 10,200 periodical titles and an online bibliographic search service accessing hundreds of databases. In addition, the Virginia State and Richmond Public Libraries are within walking distance of both VCU campuses. Academic Computing provides a variety of microcomputer, minicomputer, and mainframe computing services to support the research and instructional endeavors of the faculty and students, including consultation, instruction, and computer acquisition.

Financial Aid

Students may apply for need-based assistance with the University's Financial Aid Office. Current information on financial aid programs, policies, and procedures is available at http://www.vcu.edu/enroll/finaid.

Cost of Study

For full-time study (9–15 credits) in 2007–08, Virginia residents pay tuition and fees of $4452 per semester; nonresidents, $8876 per semester. For part-time study, Virginia residents pay tuition and fees of $465 per hour; nonresidents, $954 per hour. Some programs require additional fees. On the Medical College of Virginia (MCV) campus, tuition, fees, and other expenses vary in the medicine, pharmacy, nurse anesthesia, dentistry, and School of Allied Health programs.

Living and Housing Costs

Graduate student housing is available on both the MCV campus and the academic campus of Virginia Commonwealth University. Many graduate students live in off-campus housing, which is reasonably priced and readily available in a variety of styles and settings in nearby residential areas or within easy commuting distance. On- and off-campus housing information is available on the Web at http://www.housing.vcu.edu/.

Student Group

VCU enrolls 30,452 students, 7,611 of whom are graduate students. More than 200 clubs and organizations reflect the diverse social, recreational, educational, political, and religious interests of the student body.

Location

Richmond is Virginia's capital and a major East Coast financial and manufacturing center that offers students a wide range of cultural, educational, and recreational activities. Richmond is located in central Virginia at the intersection of Interstates 95 and 64, 2 hours south of Washington, D.C., and nestled between the Blue Ridge Mountains and the Atlantic coast. The Richmond region is easily accessible by plane, car, and train. With nearly 1 million residents, the historic city of Richmond combines big-city offerings with small-town hospitality. Applicants are encouraged to explore http://www.visit.richmond.com/ for more information on the city.

The University

VCU is a state-supported coeducational university with a graduate school, a major teaching hospital, and twelve academic and professional units that offer fifty-two undergraduate, twenty-two postbaccalaureate certificate, sixty-five master's, six post-master's certificate, and twenty-nine Ph.D. programs. VCU also offers M.D., D.D.S., D.P.T., and Pharm.D. programs as well as cooperative degree programs with other major Virginia colleges and universities. VCU has one of the largest evening colleges in the United States. The academic campus is located in Richmond's historic Fan District. The health sciences campus and hospital are located 2 miles east in the downtown business district. A University bus service provides free intercampus transportation for faculty members and students.

With more than $211 million in annual research funding, Virginia Commonwealth University is classified as one of the nation's top research universities by the Carnegie Foundation for the Advancement of Teaching. More than 29,000 undergraduate, certificate, graduate, post-master's, professional, and doctoral students are enrolled in 162 academic programs, forty of which are unique in the commonwealth of Virginia. The faculty members represent the finest American and international graduate institutions and enhance the University's position among the important institutions of higher learning in the United States and the world via their work in the classroom, laboratory, studio, and clinic and in their scholarly publications.

Applying

Admission procedures and program requirements are detailed in the *Graduate Bulletin*. Application deadlines and materials, including the application and the *Graduate Bulletin*, are available online at the Graduate School Web site at http://www.graduate.vcu.edu. Virginia Commonwealth University is an equal opportunity/affirmative action institution providing access to education and employment without regard to age, race, color, national origin, gender, religion, sexual orientation, veteran's status, political affiliation, or disability.

Correspondence and Information

Joanna Brasington
School of Dentistry
Medical College of Virginia Campus
Virginia Commonwealth University
Box 980566
Richmond, Virginia 23298-0566
Phone: 804-828-3784
E-mail: jbrasington@vcu.edu
Web site: http://www.dentistry.vcu.edu

Virginia Commonwealth University

THE FACULTY

CLINICAL RESEARCH CENTER FOR PERIODONTAL DISEASE
Al Best, Associate Professor; Ph.D., Virginia Commonwealth.
Harvey Schenkein, Assistant Dean for Research and Director of the Clinical Research Center for Periodontal Disease; Ph.D., SUNY at Buffalo.

DENTAL HYGIENE
Coral Diaz, Assistant Professor; M.P.H., Puerto Rico; M.S., Old Dominion.
Kim Isringhausen, Assistant Professor and Director; M.P.H., Virginia Commonwealth.
Joan M. Pellegrini, Assistant Professor; Assistant Professor; M.S., Columbia.
Tammy K. Swecker, Assistant Professor; Ed.M., Virginia Commonwealth.

ENDODONTICS
Chin-Lo Hahn, Associate Professor; Ph.D., Maryland; D.D.S., Missouri.
Frederick Liewehr, Professor; D.D.S., Iowa.
Karan J. Replogle, Assistant Professor and Interim Department Chair; D.D.S., Ohio State.

GENERAL PRACTICE
Robert Barnes, Associate Professor; D.D.S., Virginia Commonwealth.
Carol Brooks, Associate Professor; D.D.S., Virginia Commonwealth.
Gilbert Button, Associate Professor; D.D.S., Virginia Commonwealth.
Alfred Certosimo, Associate Professor; D.M.D., Pennsylvania.
Gloria Fernandez-Ward, Assistant Professor; D.D.S., CES (Colombia).
Riki Gottlieb, Assistant Professor; P.M.D., Chicago.
Debra Haselton, Associate Professor; D.D.S., Virginia Commonwealth.
Larry Hellman, Assistant Professor; D.D.S., Texas.
Michael Huband, Associate Professor; D.D.S., Virginia Commonwealth.
Lawrence Masters, Assistant Professor; D.D.S., Virginia Commonwealth.
Peter Moon, Associate Professor; Ph.D., Virginia.
Elizabeth Nance, Assistant Professor; D.D.S., Virginia Commonwealth.
Tonya Parris-Wilkins, Assistant Professor; D.D.S., Virginia Commonwealth; Ph.D., North Carolina at Chapel Hill.
Francis Robertello, Associate Professor; D.M.D., Pennsylvania.
Vincent Sawicki, Assistant Professor; D.D.S., Virginia Commonwealth; Ph.D., Virginia Commonwealth.
Maria Throckmorton, Assistant Professor.
Paul Wiley, Assistant Professor; D.D.S., Virginia Commonwealth.

ORAL AND MAXILLOFACIAL SURGERY
A. Omar Abubaker, Professor and Chair; Ph.D., Pittsburgh; D.M.D., Pittsburgh.
James A. Giglio, Professor; D.D.S., Maryland.
Daniel M. Laskin, Professor; D.D.S., Indiana.
Gregory M. Ness, Professor; D.D.S., Case Western Reserve.
Robert A. Strauss, Professor; D.D.S., SUNY at Buffalo.

ORAL PATHOLOGY
James C. Burns, Professor and Chair; D.D.S., Virginia Commonwealth; Ph.D., Virginia Commonwealth.
Laurie Carter, Professor; D.D.S., Ph.D., SUNY at Buffalo.
John A. Svirsky, D.D.S., Virginia Commonwealth.

ORTHODONTICS
Steven J. Lindauer, Professor and Chair; D.M.D., Connecticut.
Bhavna Shroff, Professor; D.D.S., Paris.
Eser Tufekci, Assistant Professor; Ph.D., Ohio State.

PEDIATRIC DENTISTRY
Tegwyn H. Brickhouse, Assistant Professor and Director of Research; D.D.S., Nebraska; Ph.D., North Carolina.
Holly C. Lewis, Clinical Instructor; D.M.D., Mississippi.
Diane Howell, Instructor; M.S.N.A., Virginia Commonwealth.
John H. Unkel, Associate Professor and Chair; M.P.A., West Virginia.
Michael D. Webb, Director of Residency; D.D.S., Northwestern.

PERIODONTICS
Thomas E. Koertge, Professor; D.M.D., Southern Illinois; Ph.D., Iowa.
Sharon Lanning, Assistant Professor; D.D.S., SUNY at Buffalo.
Robert Sabatini, Assistant Professor; D.D.S., Virginia Commonwealth.
Thomas C. Waldrop, Professor; D.D.S., Virginia Commonwealth.

PROSTHODONTICS
William C. Betzhold, Assistant Professor; D.D.S., Ohio State.
John J. Boyle Jr., Assistant Professor; D.M.D., Boston University.
Bach D. Bui, Assistant Professor; D.D.S., Virginia Commonwealth.
David R. Burns, Professor; M.D., Oregon Health & Science.
James P. Coffey, Associate Professor; D.D.S., Minnesota.
Hugh B. Douglas, Associate Professor; D.D.S., Virginia Commonwealth.
Charles Janus, Associate Professor; D.D.S., Virginia Commonwealth.
Altug Kazanoglu, Associate Professor; D.M.D., Istanbul; D.M.D., Washington (Seattle).
John W. Unger, Professor and Chair; D.D.S., Illinois.

This section contains a directory of institutions offering graduate work in medicine, followed by in-depth entries submitted by institutions that chose to prepare detailed program descriptions. Additional information about programs listed in the directory but not augmented by an in-depth entry may be obtained by writing directly to the dean of a graduate school or chair of a department at the address given in the directory.

CONTENTS

Allopathic Medicine

Albany Medical College, Professional Program, Albany, NY 12208-3479. Offers MD. *Accreditation:* LCME/AMA. *Faculty:* 97 full-time (31 women), 33 part-time/adjunct (13 women). *Students:* 542 full-time (292 women); includes 193 minority (24 African Americans, 4 American Indian/Alaska Native, 156 Asian Americans or Pacific Islanders, 9 Hispanic Americans), 11 international. Average age 26. 7,189 applicants, 4% accepted. In 2006, 131 degrees awarded. *Degree requirements:* For first-professional, USMLE Step1, Step 2 and Clinical Skills. *Entrance requirements:* MCAT, letters of recommendation, interview. *Application deadline:* For fall admission, 11/15 for domestic students. Applications are processed on a rolling basis. Application fee: $100. Electronic applications accepted. *Expenses: Contact institution. Financial support:* Federal Work-Study, institutionally sponsored loans, and tuition waivers (partial) available. Financial award application deadline: 3/15; financial award applicants required to submit FAFSA. *Unit head:* Dr. Vincent Verdile, Dean, 518-262-6008. *Application contact:* Joanne H. Nanos, Director of Admissions and Student Records, 518-262-5521, Fax: 518-262-5887.

Albert Einstein College of Medicine, Professional Program in Medicine, Bronx, NY 10461. Offers MD, MD/PhD. *Accreditation:* LCME/AMA. *Degree requirements:* For first-professional, independent scholars project. *Entrance requirements:* MCAT, interview. *Faculty research:* Cancer, diabetes mellitus, liver disease, infectious disease, neuroscience.

American University of Beirut, Graduate Programs, Faculty of Medicine, Beirut, Lebanon. Offers biochemistry (MS); human morphology (MS); medicine (MD); microbiology and immunology (MS); neuroscience (MS); pharmacology and therapeutics (MS); physiology (MS). Part-time programs available. *Faculty:* 166 full-time (30 women), 64 part-time/adjunct (12 women). *Students:* 322 full-time (123 women), 34 part-time (22 women). Average age 23. In 2006, 76 first professional degrees, 25 master's awarded. *Degree requirements:* For master's, one foreign language, thesis (for some programs), comprehensive exam, registration. *Entrance requirements:* For master's, letter of recommendation. Additional exam requirements/recommendations for international students: Required—TOEFL (minimum score 600 paper-based; 250 computer-based; 100 iBT), IELTS (minimum score 8). *Application deadline:* For fall admission, 4/30 for domestic and international students; for spring admission, 11/1 for domestic and international students. Application fee: $50. *Financial support:* In 2006–07, 4 students received support. Career-related internships or fieldwork, institutionally sponsored loans, scholarships/grants, health care benefits, and unspecified assistantships available. Financial award application deadline: 2/2. *Faculty research:* Cancer research, stem cell research, genetic research, neuroscience research, bone research. Total annual research expenditures: $685,272. *Unit head:* Nadim Cortas, Dean, 961-1350000 Ext. 4700, Fax: 961-1744464, E-mail: cortasn@aub.edu.lb. *Application contact:* Dr. Salim Kanaan, Director of Admissions Office, 961-1-374374 Ext. 2592, Fax: 961-1-750775, E-mail: admissions@aub.edu.lb.

Baylor College of Medicine, Medical School, Professional Program in Medicine, Houston, TX 77030-3498. Offers MD, MD/PhD. *Accreditation:* LCME/AMA. *Students:* 672 full-time (316 women); includes 378 minority (63 African Americans, 11 American Indian/Alaska Native, 226 Asian Americans or Pacific Islanders, 78 Hispanic Americans). Average age 24. 4,326 applicants, 6% accepted, 168 enrolled. In 2006, 156 MDs awarded. *Entrance requirements:* MCAT, 90 hours of pre-med course work. *Application deadline:* For fall admission, 11/1 for domestic students. Applications are processed on a rolling basis. Application fee: $70. Electronic applications accepted. *Expenses: Contact institution. Financial support:* In 2006–07, 503 students received support. Federal Work-Study, institutionally sponsored loans, and scholarships/grants available. Financial award application deadline: 5/11; financial award applicants required to submit FAFSA. *Unit head:* Dr. Major W. Bradshaw, Dean of Education, 713-798-8878, Fax: 713-798-3096, E-mail: majorb@bcm.edu. *Application contact:* Dr. Lloyd H. Michael, Senior Associate Dean of the Medical School, 713-798-4842, Fax: 713-798-5563, E-mail: lmichael@bcm.edu.

Boston University, School of Medicine, Professional Program in Medicine, Boston, MA 02215. Offers MD, MD/MA, MD/MPH, MD/PhD. *Accreditation:* LCME/AMA. Part-time programs available. *Students:* 622 full-time (339 women), 30 part-time (15 women); includes 206 minority (50 African Americans, 128 Asian Americans or Pacific Islanders, 28 Hispanic Americans), 19 international. Average age 24. In 2006, 153 degrees awarded. *Application deadline:* For fall admission, 11/1 for domestic students. Application fee: $95. *Expenses:* Tuition: Full-time $33,330; part-time $1,042 per credit. Required fees: $462; $40. *Financial support:* Fellowships, Federal Work-Study available. Support available to part-time students. *Application contact:* Dr. Robert Witzburg, Associate Dean for Admissions, 617-638-4630.

Brown University, Program in Medicine, Providence, RI 02912. Offers MD, MD/PhD. *Accreditation:* LCME/AMA. Expenses: Contact institution.

Case Western Reserve University, School of Medicine, Professional Program in Medicine, Cleveland, OH 44106. Offers MD, MD/JD, MD/MA, MD/MBA, MD/MPH, MD/MS, MD/PhD. *Accreditation:* LCME/AMA. *Faculty:* 1,972 full-time (620 women), 1,808 part-time/adjunct (703 women). *Students:* 648 full-time (295 women), 2 part-time; includes 236 minority (66 African Americans, 152 Asian Americans or Pacific Islanders, 18 Hispanic Americans), 25 international. Average age 23. 5,327 applicants, 9% accepted, 170 enrolled. In 2006, 132 degrees awarded. *Entrance requirements:* MCAT, interview. *Application deadline:* For fall admission, 11/1 for domestic students. Applications are processed on a rolling basis. Application fee: $85. Electronic applications accepted. *Financial support:* In 2006–07, 533 students received support. Institutionally sponsored loans, scholarships/grants, and tuition waivers (partial) available. Financial award application deadline: 3/30; financial award applicants required to submit FAFSA. *Unit head:* Dr. Daniel Ornt, Vice Dean for Education and Academic Affairs, 216-368-1948, Fax: 216-368-6159, E-mail: daniel.ornt@case.edu. *Application contact:* Dr. Lina Mehta, Associate Dean for Admissions, 216-368-3450, Fax: 216-368-6011, E-mail: lina.mehta@case.edu.

Charles R. Drew University of Medicine and Science, Professional Program in Medicine, Los Angeles, CA 90059. Offers MD. *Entrance requirements:* MCAT.

Columbia University, College of Physicians and Surgeons, Professional Program in Medicine, New York, NY 10032. Offers MD, MD/DDS, MD/MPH, MD/MS, MD/PhD. *Accreditation:* LCME/AMA. Part-time programs available. *Entrance requirements:* MCAT.

Cornell University, Joan and Sanford I. Weill Medical College and Graduate School of Medical Sciences, Weill Medical College, New York, NY 10021-4896. Offers MD, MS, PhD, MD/PhD. *Accreditation:* LCME/AMA. *Faculty:* 277 full-time (57 women). *Students:* 408 full-time (206 women); includes 177 minority (41 African Americans, 5 American Indian/Alaska Native, 100 Asian Americans or Pacific Islanders, 31 Hispanic Americans), 5 international. Average age 27. 5,235 applicants, 5% accepted, 101 enrolled. In 2006, 101 first professional degrees, 8 master's, 41 doctorates awarded. *Degree requirements:* For first-professional, registration. *Entrance requirements:* MCAT. *Application deadline:* For fall admission, 10/15 for domestic students. Application fee: $75. Electronic applications accepted. *Expenses:* Tuition: Full-time $33,775. Required fees: $1,050. *Financial support:* In 2006–07, 278 students received support. Federal Work-Study, institutionally sponsored loans, and scholarships/grants available. Financial award application deadline: 9/1; financial award applicants required to submit FAFSA. *Unit head:* Dr. Antonio Gotto, Dean, 212-746-6005, Fax: 212-746-8424, E-mail: dean@med.cornell.edu. *Application contact:* Liliana Montano, Assistant Dean of Admissions, 212-746-1067, Fax: 212-746-8052, E-mail: cumc-admissions@med.cornell.edu.

Creighton University, School of Medicine, Professional Program in Medicine, Omaha, NE 68178-0001. Offers MD, MD/PhD. *Accreditation:* LCME/AMA. *Faculty:* 286 full-time (74 women), 19 part-time/adjunct (5 women). *Students:* 498 full-time (234 women); includes 82 minority (13 African Americans, 10 American Indian/Alaska Native, 29 Asian Americans or Pacific Islanders, 30 Hispanic Americans), 2 international. Average age 25. 4,884 applicants, 6% accepted, 126 enrolled. In 2006, 102 degrees awarded. *Entrance requirements:* MCAT. *Application deadline:* For fall admission, 11/1 for domestic and international students. Applications are processed on a rolling basis. Application fee: $75. Electronic applications accepted. *Expenses:* Tuition: Part-time $595 per credit hour. Required fees: $38 per semester. *Financial support:* In 2006–07, 395 students received support. Institutionally sponsored loans and scholarships/grants available. Support available to part-time students. Financial award application deadline: 4/1; financial award applicants required to submit FAFSA. *Faculty research:* Hereditary cancer, osteoporosis, diabetes, immunology, microbiology. Total annual research expenditures: $21.2 million. *Application contact:* Dr. Henry C. Nipper, Assistant Dean for Admissions, 402-280-2799, Fax: 402-280-1241, E-mail: medschadm@creighton.edu.

Dalhousie University, Faculty of Medicine, Professional Program in Medicine, Halifax, NS B3H 4R2, Canada. Offers MD, MD/M Sc, MD/PhD. *Accreditation:* LCME/AMA. *Entrance requirements:* MCAT.

Drexel University, College of Medicine, Professional Program in Medicine, Philadelphia, PA 19104-2875. Offers MD, MD/PhD. *Accreditation:* LCME/AMA. *Degree requirements:* For first-professional, National Board Exam Parts I and II. *Entrance requirements:* MCAT. Electronic applications accepted.

Duke University, School of Medicine, Professional Program in Medicine, Durham, NC 27708-0586. Offers MD, MD/JD, MD/MALS, MD/MBA, MD/MHS, MD/MLS, MD/MPH, MD/MPP, MD/MSIS, MD/PhD. *Accreditation:* LCME/AMA. *Faculty:* 1,840 full-time (637 women). *Students:* 470 full-time (225 women); includes 161 minority (60 African Americans, 9 American Indian/Alaska Native, 82 Asian Americans or Pacific Islanders, 10 Hispanic Americans), 24 international. Average age 25. 5,166 applicants, 4% accepted, 101 enrolled. *Entrance requirements:* MCAT. *Application deadline:* For fall admission, 11/15 for domestic students. Applications are processed on a rolling basis. Application fee: $80. Electronic applications accepted. *Expenses: Contact institution. Financial support:* In 2006–07, 355 students received support. Institutionally sponsored loans and scholarships/grants available. Financial award application deadline: 5/1; financial award applicants required to submit FAFSA. *Application contact:* Dr. Brenda Armstrong, Director of Admissions, 919-684-2985, Fax: 919-684-8893, E-mail: medadm@mc.duke.edu.

East Carolina University, Brody School of Medicine, Department of Medicine, Greenville, NC 27858-4353. Offers MD. *Accreditation:* LCME/AMA. *Faculty:* 375 full-time (110 women), 60 part-time/adjunct (30 women). *Students:* 290 full-time (144 women); includes 90 minority (51 African Americans, 10 American Indian/Alaska Native, 27 Asian Americans or Pacific Islanders, 2 Hispanic Americans). Average age 25. 745 applicants, 10% accepted, 72 enrolled. In 2006, 69 degrees awarded. *Entrance requirements:* MCAT, pre-med courses, interviews, faculty evaluations. *Application deadline:* For fall admission, 11/15 for domestic students. Applications are processed on a rolling basis. Application fee: $60. Electronic applications accepted. *Financial support:* In 2006–07, 261 students received support. Institutionally sponsored loans and scholarships/grants available. *Faculty research:* Diabetes, cardiovascular disease, cancer, neurological disorders. *Unit head:* Dr. Ralph Whatley, Associate Dean for Admissions, 252-744-2202, Fax: 252-744-1926, E-mail: somadimissions@ecu.edu. *Application contact:* Sheila E Lee, Director of Admissions, 252-744-2207, Fax: 252-744-1926, E-mail: somadmissions@ecu.edu.

Eastern Virginia Medical School, Professional Program in Medicine, Norfolk, VA 23501-1980. Offers MD, MD/PhD. *Accreditation:* LCME/AMA. *Students:* 437. In 2006, 94 degrees awarded. *Entrance requirements:* MCAT, bachelor's degree or equivalent, course work in sciences. *Application deadline:* For fall admission, 11/15 priority date for domestic students. Applications are processed on a rolling basis. Application fee: $95. *Financial support:* In 2006–07, 397 students received support. Federal Work-Study and institutionally sponsored loans available. Financial award application deadline: 3/15; financial award applicants required to submit CSS PROFILE or FAFSA. *Unit head:* Dr. Michael J. Solhaug, Associate Dean for Academic Affairs, 757-446-5805, Fax: 757-446-5896, E-mail: solhaumj@evms.edu. *Application contact:* Susan Castora, Director of Admissions, 757-446-5812, Fax: 757-446-5896, E-mail: castorsl@evms.edu.

East Tennessee State University, James H. Quillen College of Medicine, Professional Programs in Medicine, Johnson City, TN 37614. Offers MD. *Accreditation:* LCME/AMA. *Entrance requirements:* MCAT. Additional exam requirements/recommendations for international students: Required—TOEFL (minimum score 550 paper-based; 213 computer-based).

Emory University, School of Medicine, Professional Program in Medicine, Atlanta, GA 30322-4510. Offers MD, MD/MPH, MD/PhD. *Accreditation:* LCME/AMA. *Faculty:* 1,804 full-time (573 women), 1,131 part-time/adjunct (358 women). *Students:* 455 full-time (224 women); includes 132 minority (38 African Americans, 1 American Indian/Alaska Native, 77 Asian Americans or Pacific Islanders, 16 Hispanic Americans), 12 international. Average age 25. 4,055 applicants, 8% accepted, 114 enrolled. In 2006, 110 degrees awarded. *Degree requirements:* For first-professional, USMLE Step 1, Step 2 CK, Step 2 CS. *Entrance requirements:* MCAT. *Application deadline:* For fall admission, 10/15 for domestic and international students. Applications are processed on a rolling basis. Electronic applications accepted. *Expenses: Contact institution. Financial support:* In 2006–07, 366 students received support. Institutionally sponsored loans and scholarships/grants available. Financial award application deadline: 4/1; financial award applicants required to submit CSS PROFILE or FAFSA. *Application contact:* Dr. Ira K. Schwartz, Associate Dean of Student Affairs/Director of Admissions, 404-727-5660, Fax: 404-727-5456, E-mail: medadmissions@emory.edu.

Florida State University, College of Medicine, Tallahassee, FL 32306. Offers biomedical sciences (PhD); medicine (MD). *Accreditation:* LCME/AMA. *Faculty:* 105 full-time (32 women), 568 part-time/adjunct (122 women). *Students:* 284 full-time (165 women); includes 106 minority (36 African Americans, 2 American Indian/Alaska Native, 35 Asian Americans or Pacific Islanders, 33 Hispanic Americans). Average age 25. 1,849 applicants, 10% accepted, 100 enrolled. In 2006, 36 degrees awarded. *Degree requirements:* For first-professional, USMLE steps 1 and 2. *Entrance requirements:* For doctorate, MCAT. *Application deadline:* For fall admission, 12/15 for domestic students. Applications are processed on a rolling basis. Application fee: $30. Electronic applications accepted. *Expenses: Contact institution.* Tuition and fees vary according to program. *Financial support:* In 2006–07, 156 students received support, including 2 fellowships (averaging $5,000 per year); scholarships/grants also available. Financial award application deadline: 7/1; financial award applicants required to submit FAFSA. *Faculty research:* Human genome function, aging and neuroscience, health policy and chronic disease management. Total annual research expenditures: $3.4 million. *Unit head:* Dr. J. Ocie Harris, Dean, 850-644-1855, Fax: 850-645-1420, E-mail: ocie.harris@med.fsu.edu. *Application contact:* Admissions Coordinator, 850-644-7904, Fax: 850-645-2846, E-mail: medadmissions@med.fsu.edu.

Georgetown University, School of Medicine, Washington, DC 20057. Offers MD, MD/MBA, MD/PhD. *Accreditation:* LCME/AMA. *Entrance requirements:* MCAT, minimum 90 credit hours with 1 year of course work in biology, organic chemistry, inorganic chemistry, physics, mathematics, and English. Expenses: Contact institution.

The George Washington University, School of Medicine and Health Sciences, Professional Program in Medicine, Washington, DC 20052. Offers MD, MD/MPH, MD/PhD. *Accreditation:* LCME/AMA. *Entrance requirements:* MCAT, minimum 90 undergraduate semester hours, specific pre-med courses equal to 38 semester hours.

Harvard University, Harvard Medical School and Graduate School of Arts and Sciences, Division of Health Sciences and Technology, Program in Medical Sciences, Cambridge, MA 02138. Offers MD, MD/MM Sc. *Accreditation:* LCME/AMA. *Students:* 199 full-time (65 women);

includes 103 minority (4 African Americans, 88 Asian Americans or Pacific Islanders, 11 Hispanic Americans), 10 international. Average age 26. 592 applicants, 7% accepted, 29 enrolled. In 2006, 26 degrees awarded. *Degree requirements:* For first-professional, thesis. *Entrance requirements:* MCAT. *Application deadline:* For fall admission, 11/15 for domestic students. Application fee: $85. *Expenses: Contact institution.* Full-time tuition and fees vary according to program and student level. *Financial support:* In 2006–07, 60 students received support, including 42 research assistantships with full and partial tuition reimbursements available (averaging $8,582 per year), 12 teaching assistantships with full and partial tuition reimbursements available (averaging $6,617 per year); fellowships with full tuition reimbursements available, institutionally sponsored loans, scholarships/grants, and unspecified assistantships also available. Financial award application deadline: 1/15. *Application contact:* Dr. David Earl Cohen, Director of MD Admissions, HST Division, 617-726-5576.

Harvard University, Harvard Medical School, Professional Program in Medicine, Boston, MA 02115. Offers MD, PhD, MD/MBA, MD/MPH, MD/MPP, MD/PhD. *Accreditation:* LCME/AMA. *Faculty:* 7,393 full-time, 2,816 part-time/adjunct. *Students:* 771 full-time (385 women); includes 363 minority (91 African Americans, 12 American Indian/Alaska Native, 195 Asian Americans or Pacific Islanders, 65 Hispanic Americans), 44 international. Average age 24. 4,598 applicants, 5% accepted, 165 enrolled. In 2006, 147 degrees awarded. *Entrance requirements:* MCAT, previous course work in biology, chemistry, physics, calculus, and expository writing. *Application deadline:* For fall admission, 10/15 for domestic students. Application fee: $85. Electronic applications accepted. *Expenses:* Tuition: Full-time $30,275. Full-time tuition and fees vary according to program and student level. *Financial support:* In 2006–07, 517 students received support; fellowships, research assistantships, teaching assistantships, career-related internships or fieldwork, Federal Work-Study, institutionally sponsored loans, scholarships/grants, and tuition waivers (partial) available. Financial award application deadline: 4/15; financial award applicants required to submit CSS PROFILE or FAFSA. *Unit head:* Dr. Jules Dienstag, Dean for Medical Education, 617-432-6250. *Application contact:* Admissions Office, 617-432-1550, Fax: 617-432-3307, E-mail: admissions_office@hms.harvard.edu.

Howard University, College of Medicine, Professional Program in Medicine, Washington, DC 20059-0002. Offers MD, PhD, MD/PhD. *Accreditation:* LCME/AMA. *Degree requirements:* For first-professional, U.S. Medical Licensing Exam Steps 1 and 2. *Entrance requirements:* MCAT, previous course work in biology, English, general and organic chemistry, mathematics, and physics. *Faculty research:* Infectious diseases, protein modeling, neuropsychopharmacology.

Instituto Tecnologico de Santo Domingo, School of Medicine, Santo Domingo, Dominican Republic. Offers MD, M Bioethics.

The Johns Hopkins University, School of Medicine, Professional Program in Medicine, Baltimore, MD 21218-2699. Offers MD, MD/PhD. *Accreditation:* LCME/AMA. *Faculty:* 2,211 full-time (800 women), 1,216 part-time/adjunct (367 women). *Students:* 482 full-time (230 women); includes 230 minority (46 African Americans, 3 American Indian/Alaska Native, 154 Asian Americans or Pacific Islanders, 27 Hispanic Americans), 13 international. Average age 24. 4,149 applicants, 6% accepted, 120 enrolled. In 2006, 102 degrees awarded. *Median time to degree:* 4 years full-time. *Entrance requirements:* MCAT. *Application deadline:* For fall admission, 10/15 for domestic and international students. Applications are processed on a rolling basis. Application fee: $75. Electronic applications accepted. *Expenses:* Tuition: Full-time $32,976. Tuition and fees vary according to degree level and program. *Financial support:* Fellowships, research assistantships, teaching assistantships available. *Unit head:* Dr. Edward D. Miller, Dean of Medical Faculty and Chief Executive Officer, 410-955-3180. *Application contact:* Dr. James L. Weiss, Associate Dean for Admissions, 410-955-3182, Fax: 410-516-5188.

Loma Linda University, School of Medicine, Loma Linda, CA 92350. Offers MD, MS, PhD. *Accreditation:* LCME/AMA. *Entrance requirements:* MCAT, 1 year course work in biology, chemistry, organic chemistry, and physics. Expenses: Contact institution.

Louisiana State University Health Sciences Center, School of Medicine in New Orleans, New Orleans, LA 70112-2223. Offers MD, MPH, MD/PhD. Open only to Louisiana residents. *Accreditation:* LCME/AMA. *Entrance requirements:* MCAT. Electronic applications accepted. Expenses: Contact institution. *Faculty research:* Medical and basic sciences.

Louisiana State University Health Sciences Center at Shreveport, School of Medicine, Shreveport, LA 71130-3932. Offers MD, MD/PhD. *Accreditation:* LCME/AMA. *Entrance requirements:* MCAT. Expenses: Contact institution. *Faculty research:* Biomedical science, molecular biology, cardiovascular science.

Loyola University Chicago, Stritch School of Medicine, Maywood, IL 60153. Offers MD. *Accreditation:* LCME/AMA. *Faculty:* 641 full-time (220 women), 715 part-time/adjunct (187 women). *Students:* 552 full-time (276 women); includes 114 minority (16 African Americans, 5 American Indian/Alaska Native, 80 Asian Americans or Pacific Islanders, 13 Hispanic Americans). Average age 24. 4,707 applicants, 6% accepted, 140 enrolled. In 2006, 130 MDs awarded. *Median time to degree:* Of those who began their doctoral program in fall 1998, 98% received their degree in 8 years or less. *Degree requirements:* For first-professional, passing scores on U.S. Medical Licensing Exam Step 1, Step 2CS, and Step 2CK. *Entrance requirements:* MCAT, 1 full academic year of general biology or zoology, organic chemistry, physics and inorganic chemistry all with labs. *Application deadline:* For fall admission, 11/15 for domestic students. Applications are processed on a rolling basis. Application fee: $70. *Expenses: Contact institution.* *Financial support:* In 2006–07, 513 students received support. Institutionally sponsored loans and scholarships/grants available. Financial award application deadline: 3/30; financial award applicants required to submit FAFSA. *Faculty research:* Cardiovascular pathophysiology, cancer biology, neuroscience, burn injury, infectious disease. Total annual research expenditures: $38.4 million. *Unit head:* Dr. John M. Lee, Dean, 708-216-3223, Fax: 708-216-4305. *Application contact:* LaDonna E. Norstrom, Assistant Dean for Admissions, 708-216-3229.

Marshall University, Joan C. Edwards School of Medicine, Professional Program in Medicine, Huntington, WV 25755. Offers MD. *Accreditation:* LCME/AMA. *Faculty:* 199 full-time (55 women), 40 part-time/adjunct (15 women). *Students:* 227 full-time (91 women); includes 31 minority (5 African Americans, 1 American Indian/Alaska Native, 23 Asian Americans or Pacific Islanders, 2 Hispanic Americans). Average age 25. 1,573 applicants, 8% accepted, 64 enrolled. In 2006, 42 degrees awarded. *Degree requirements:* For first-professional, U.S. Medical Licensing Exam, Steps 1 and 2. *Entrance requirements:* MCAT, 1 year of course work in biology, physics, chemistry, organic chemistry, English, and social or behavioral sciences. *Application deadline:* For fall admission, 12/1 for domestic students. Applications are processed on a rolling basis. Application fee: $50 ($80 for international students). *Expenses: Contact institution.* *Financial support:* In 2006–07, 220 students received support. Career-related internships or fieldwork, Federal Work-Study, institutionally sponsored loans, and scholarships/grants available. Support available to part-time students. Financial award applicants required to submit FAFSA. *Application contact:* Cynthia A. Warren, Assistant Dean for Admissions and Student Affairs, 304-691-1738, Fax: 304-691-1744, E-mail: warren@marshall.edu.

Mayo Medical School, Professional Program, Rochester, MN 55905. Offers MD, MD/Certificate, MD/PhD. MD offered through the Mayo Foundation's Division of Education. *Accreditation:* LCME/AMA. *Entrance requirements:* MCAT, previous undergraduate course work in biology, chemistry, physics, and biochemistry. Electronic applications accepted.

McGill University, Faculty of Graduate and Postdoctoral Studies, Faculty of Medicine, Department of Surgery, Montréal, QC H3A 2T5, Canada. Offers M Sc, PhD. *Degree requirements:* For master's and doctorate, thesis/dissertation. *Entrance requirements:* For master's and doctorate, minimum GPA of 3.2. *Faculty research:* Cancer (metastasis), immunology (organ transplantation), orthopedic surgery, cardiovascular system, urogenital system.

McGill University, Professional Program in Medicine, Montréal, QC H3A 2T5, Canada. Offers MD/CM, MD/MBA, MD/PhD. *Accreditation:* LCME/AMA. *Faculty:* 824 full-time (334 women), 2,236 part-time/adjunct (906 women). *Students:* 648 full-time (363 women), 65 international. Average age 24. 1,044 applicants, 24% accepted, 172 enrolled. In 2006, 148 degrees awarded. *Degree requirements:* For first-professional, thesis. *Entrance requirements:* MCAT, minimum GPA of 3.5; 2 semesters each of university-level course work in general chemistry, organic chemistry, biology and physics, with labs. *Application deadline:* For fall admission, 1/15 for domestic students, 11/15 for international students. Application fee: $60. Electronic applications accepted. *Financial support:* Fellowships, research assistantships, scholarships/grants and health care benefits available. Financial award application deadline: 1/1. *Faculty research:* Cancer, endocrinology and metabolism, genetics, genomics and proteomics, neurology, neurosurgery and mental health, population health. Total annual research expenditures: $209.7 million. *Unit head:* France Drolet, Director, Admission Office, 514-398-3517, Fax: 514-398-4631, E-mail: admissions.med@mcgill.ca. *Application contact:* Michel Dansereau, Admissions Officer, 514-398-3517, Fax: 514-398-4631, E-mail: michel.dansereau@mcgill.ca.

Medical College of Georgia, School of Medicine, Augusta, GA 30912. Offers MD, MD/PhD. *Accreditation:* LCME/AMA. *Degree requirements:* For first-professional, comprehensive exam. *Entrance requirements:* MCAT, average GPA of 3.6 in sciences, 3.64 overall. Expenses: Contact institution. *Faculty research:* Cancer, cardiovascular diseases, diabetes, neurological diseases, infection and inflammation.

Medical College of Wisconsin, Medical School, Professional Program in Medicine, Milwaukee, WI 53226-0509. Offers MD, MD/MA, MD/MS, MD/PhD. *Accreditation:* LCME/AMA. *Entrance requirements:* MCAT, interview, minimum 4 years of college.

Medical University of South Carolina, College of Medicine, Charleston, SC 29425-0002. Offers MD, MD/MBA, MD/MHA, MD/MPH, MD/PhD. *Accreditation:* LCME/AMA. *Faculty:* 949 full-time (332 women), 136 part-time/adjunct (45 women). *Students:* 600 full-time (284 women); includes 121 minority (56 African Americans, 3 American Indian/Alaska Native, 46 Asian Americans or Pacific Islanders, 16 Hispanic Americans), 7 international. Average age 26. 1,501 applicants, 10% accepted, 135 enrolled. In 2006, 135 degrees awarded. *Degree requirements:* For first-professional, steps 1 and 2 of Clinical Performance Exam and US Medical Licensing Exam. *Entrance requirements:* MCAT, interview. *Application deadline:* For fall admission, 12/1 for domestic and international students. Applications are processed on a rolling basis. Application fee: $75. Electronic applications accepted. *Expenses: Contact institution.* *Financial support:* In 2006–07, 487 students received support. Federal Work-Study and scholarships/grants available. Financial award application deadline: 3/15; financial award applicants required to submit FAFSA. *Faculty research:* Cardiovascular proteomics, translational cancer research, diabetes mellitus, neurodegeneritive diseases, addiction. Total annual research expenditures: $114 million. *Unit head:* Dr. Jerry G. Reves, Dean, 843-792-2842, Fax: 843-792-2967, E-mail: revesj@musc.edu. *Application contact:* Wanda L. Taylor, Director of Admissions, 843-792-2055, Fax: 843-792-0204, E-mail: taylorwl@musc.edu.

Meharry Medical College, School of Medicine, Nashville, TN 37208-9989. Offers MD. *Accreditation:* LCME/AMA. *Entrance requirements:* MCAT. *Faculty research:* Signal transduction, membrane biology, neurophysiology, tropical medicine.

Memorial University of Newfoundland, Faculty of Medicine, Professional Program in Medicine, St. John's, NL A1C 5S7, Canada. Offers MD. *Accreditation:* LCME/AMA. *Degree requirements:* For first-professional, licensing exam. *Entrance requirements:* MCAT, B Sc, previous course work in English.

Mercer University, School of Medicine, Macon, GA 31207-0003. Offers MD, MFT, MPH, MSA. *Accreditation:* AAMFT/COAMFTE; LCME/AMA (one or more programs are accredited). *Students:* 334 full-time (185 women), 18 part-time (all women); includes 88 minority (53 African Americans, 33 Asian Americans or Pacific Islanders, 2 Hispanic Americans). In 2006, 36 master's awarded. *Entrance requirements:* For MD, MCAT; for master's, GRE General Test, MAT, or MCAT. Additional exam requirements/recommendations for international students: Required—TOEFL. *Application deadline:* For fall admission, 11/1 for domestic students, 10/1 for international students. Applications are processed on a rolling basis. Application fee: $50 ($150 for international students). *Financial support:* In 2006–07, 352 students received support. Institutionally sponsored loans available. Financial award application deadline: 4/1; financial award applicants required to submit FAFSA. *Faculty research:* Anatomy, biochemistry/nutrition, genetics, microbiology/immunology, neuroscience. *Unit head:* Dr. Martin Dalton, Dean, 478-301-5570, Fax: 478-301-2547. *Application contact:* Mary C. Putnam, Enrollment Associate, 478-301-2542, Fax: 478-301-2547, E-mail: putnam_mc@mercer.edu.

Michigan State University, College of Human Medicine, Professional Program in Human Medicine, East Lansing, MI 48824. Offers human medicine (MD); human medicine/medical scientist training program (MD). *Accreditation:* LCME/AMA. *Students:* 444 full-time (249 women), 12 part-time (5 women); includes 149 minority (46 African Americans, 2 American Indian/Alaska Native, 62 Asian Americans or Pacific Islanders, 39 Hispanic Americans), 3 international. Average age 26. 192 applicants, 99% accepted. In 2006, 89 degrees awarded. *Entrance requirements:* Additional exam requirements/recommendations for international students: Required—TOEFL, Michigan State University ELT (85), Michigan ELAB (83). *Application deadline:* For fall admission, 11/15 for domestic students. Application fee: $160. Electronic applications accepted. *Expenses:* Tuition, state resident: part-time $346 per credit hour. Tuition, nonresident: part-time $730 per credit hour. Tuition and fees vary according to program. *Financial support:* In 2006–07, 38 fellowships with tuition reimbursements, 7 research assistantships with tuition reimbursements (averaging $12,222 per year) were awarded. *Application contact:* Admissions Officer, 517-353-9620, Fax: 517-432-0021, E-mail: mdadmissions@msu.edu.

Morehouse School of Medicine, Professional Program, Atlanta, GA 30310-1495. Offers MD, MD/MPH. *Accreditation:* LCME/AMA. *Degree requirements:* For first-professional, U.S. Medical Licensing Exam Steps 1 and 2. *Entrance requirements:* MCAT. Electronic applications accepted. Expenses: Contact institution. *Faculty research:* Cardiovascular disease and related sequela, infectious diseases/HIV-AIDS, neurological diseases, cancer.

Mount Sinai School of Medicine of New York University, Medical School, New York, NY 10029-6504. Offers MD, MD/PhD. *Accreditation:* LCME/AMA. *Degree requirements:* For first-professional, United States medical Licensing Examination Steps 1 and 2. *Entrance requirements:* MCAT.

New York Medical College, Professional Program, Vahalla, NY 10595-1691. Offers MD, MD/MPH, MD/PhD. *Accreditation:* LCME/AMA. *Faculty:* 1,346 full-time (462 women), 1,672 part-time/adjunct (438 women). *Students:* 774 full-time (395 women); includes 321 minority (18 African Americans, 1 American Indian/Alaska Native, 293 Asian Americans or Pacific Islanders, 9 Hispanic Americans), 3 international. Average age 25. 9,647 applicants, 8% accepted, 194 enrolled. In 2006, 185 degrees awarded. *Entrance requirements:* MCAT, 2 semesters of course work in general biology, general chemistry, organic chemistry, physics, and English. *Application deadline:* For fall admission, 12/15 for domestic and international students. Applications are processed on a rolling basis. Application fee: $100. Electronic applications accepted. *Expenses: Contact institution.* *Financial support:* In 2006–07, 50 research assistantships with full tuition reimbursements (averaging $22,000 per year) were awarded; Federal Work-Study, institutionally sponsored loans, scholarships/grants, and tuition waivers (full) also available. Support available to part-time students. Financial award application deadline: 4/30; financial award applicants required to submit FAFSA. *Faculty research:* Vascular function, hormonal regulation of blood pressure, physiological and molecular control of heart failure, neuroscience, adult stem cells. Total annual research expenditures: $32.9 million. *Unit head:* Dr. Ralph A. O'Connell, Provost and Dean, School of Medicine, 914-594-4900, Fax: 914-594-4145. *Application contact:* Dr. Fern Juster, Admissions Office, 914-594-4507, Fax: 914-594-4613, E-mail: mdadmit@nymc.edu.

Allopathic Medicine

New York University, School of Medicine, Professional Program in Medicine, New York, NY 10012-1019. Offers MD, MD/MA, MD/MPA, MD/PhD. *Accreditation:* LCME/AMA. *Faculty:* 1,073 full-time (349 women), 318 part-time/adjunct (105 women). *Students:* 663 full-time (337 women); includes 236 minority (36 African Americans, 4 American Indian/Alaska Native, 154 Asian Americans or Pacific Islanders, 42 Hispanic Americans), 6 international. Average age 24. 7,423 applicants, 6% accepted, 160 enrolled. In 2006, 155 degrees awarded. *Entrance requirements:* MCAT. *Application deadline:* For fall admission, 10/15 for domestic students. Applications are processed on a rolling basis. Application fee: $100. Electronic applications accepted. *Expenses: Contact institution. Financial support:* In 2006–07, 486 students received support. Federal Work-Study and scholarships/grants available. Financial award application deadline: 7/15; financial award applicants required to submit FAFSA. *Faculty research:* Vascular biology, cancer genetics, molecular pathogenesis, epithelial pathobiology, microbial pathogenesis/host defense. Total annual research expenditures: $141.6 million. *Unit head:* Dr. Veronica Catanese, Senior Associate Dean for Education and Student Affairs, 212-263-0794, Fax: 212-263-0520, E-mail: veronica.catanese@med.nyu.edu. *Application contact:* Dr. Nancy Genieser, Associate Dean, Admissions, 212-263-5290, Fax: 212-263-0720, E-mail: nancy.genieser@nyumc.org.

Northeastern Ohio Universities College of Medicine, Professional Program, Rootstown, OH 44272-0095. Offers MD, MD/PhD. *Accreditation:* LCME/AMA. *Faculty:* 278 full-time (76 women), 1,631 part-time/adjunct (316 women). *Students:* 459 full-time (240 women); includes 186 minority (16 African Americans, 3 American Indian/Alaska Native, 158 Asian Americans or Pacific Islanders, 9 Hispanic Americans). Average age 24. 2,031 applicants, 11% accepted, 140 enrolled. In 2006, 111 degrees awarded. *Entrance requirements:* MCAT, 1 year of course work in organic chemistry and physics. *Application deadline:* For fall admission, 10/1 for domestic students. Applications are processed on a rolling basis. Application fee: $40. Electronic applications accepted. *Financial support:* In 2006–07, 164 students received support. Institutionally sponsored loans and scholarships/grants available. Financial award application deadline: 4/15; financial award applicants required to submit FAFSA. *Faculty research:* Lipid metabolism/cardiovascular disease, bone diseases/skeletal biology, virology/infectious diseases, clinical outcomes, sensory neurobiology. Total annual research expenditures: $3.5 million. *Unit head:* Dr. Lois Margaret Nora, President and Dean, 330-325-6255. *Application contact:* Jill Byers, Director of Admissions, 330-325-6270, E-mail: admission@neoucom.edu.

Northwestern University, Northwestern University Feinberg School of Medicine, Combined MD/PhD Medical Scientist Training Program, Chicago, IL 60611. Offers MD/PhD. Application must be made to both The Graduate School and the Medical School. *Accreditation:* LCME/AMA. *Students:* 80 full-time (29 women); includes 28 minority (4 African Americans, 2 American Indian/Alaska Native, 20 Asian Americans or Pacific Islanders, 2 Hispanic Americans). Average age 25. 458 applicants, 7% accepted, 12 enrolled. *Application deadline:* For fall admission, 10/15 for domestic and international students. Applications are processed on a rolling basis. Application fee: $70. Electronic applications accepted. *Financial support:* In 2006–07, 35 fellowships with full tuition reimbursements (averaging $24,500 per year) were awarded; tuition waivers (full) also available. Financial award application deadline: 3/1; financial award applicants required to submit FAFSA. *Faculty research:* Cardiovascular epidemiology, cancer epidemiology, nutritional interventions for the prevention of cardiovascular disease and cancer, women's health, outcomes research. *Unit head:* David M. Engman, Director, 312-503-1288, E-mail: d-engman@northwestern.edu. *Application contact:* Dr. Sandra Lee, MSTP Associate Director, 312-503-2900, Fax: 312-908-5253, E-mail: s-lee@northwestern.edu.

The Ohio State University, College of Medicine, School of Biomedical Science, Professional Program in Medicine, Columbus, OH 43210. Offers MD. *Accreditation:* LCME/AMA. *Faculty:* 999 full-time (254 women), 500 part-time/adjunct (132 women). *Students:* 827 full-time (318 women), 4 part-time (2 women); includes 254 minority (56 African Americans, 10 American Indian/Alaska Native, 163 Asian Americans or Pacific Islanders, 25 Hispanic Americans), 6 international. Average age 25. In 2006, 202 degrees awarded. *Entrance requirements:* MCAT. *Application deadline:* For fall admission, 11/1 for domestic students. Applications are processed on a rolling basis. Application fee: $60. Electronic applications accepted. *Expenses:* Tuition, state resident: full-time $9,438. Tuition, nonresident: full-time $22,791. Tuition and fees vary according to course load, campus/location and program. *Financial support:* Fellowships, research assistantships, teaching assistantships, Federal Work-Study, institutionally sponsored loans, and scholarships/grants available. Support available to part-time students. Financial award application deadline: 3/1; financial award applicants required to submit FAFSA. *Faculty research:* Molecular genetics, stress and the immune system, molecular cardiology, transplantation biology. Total annual research expenditures: $39.2 million. *Application contact:* Dr. Mark Notestine, Graduate Admissions, 614-292-9444, Fax: 614-292-6985, E-mail: domestic.grad@osu.edu.

Oregon Health & Science University, School of Medicine, Professional Program in Medicine, Portland, OR 97239-3098. Offers MD, MD/DMD, MD/MPH, MD/PhD. *Accreditation:* LCME/AMA. *Degree requirements:* For first-professional, National Board Exam Parts I and II. *Entrance requirements:* MCAT, 1 year of course work in biology, English, social science and physics, 2 years of course work in chemistry and genetics.

Penn State Hershey Medical Center, College of Medicine, Hershey, PA 17033-2360. Offers MD, MS, PhD, MD/PhD, PhD/MBA. *Accreditation:* LCME/AMA. *Faculty:* 707 full-time (151 women), 65 part-time/adjunct (43 women). *Students:* 541 full-time (297 women); includes 131 minority (39 African Americans, 3 American Indian/Alaska Native, 85 Asian Americans or Pacific Islanders, 4 Hispanic Americans), 19 international. Average age 27. 154 applicants, 49% accepted. In 2006, 116 degrees awarded. *Entrance requirements:* MCAT. Additional exam requirements/recommendations for international students: Required—TOEFL (minimum score 560 paper-based; 220 computer-based). *Application deadline:* For fall admission, 11/15 for domestic students. Application fee: $54. *Expenses: Contact institution. Financial support:* In 2006–07, 10 fellowships, 44 research assistantships, 42 teaching assistantships were awarded; scholarships/grants and health care benefits also available. Financial award application deadline: 2/15; financial award applicants required to submit FAFSA. Total annual research expenditures: $76.2 million. *Unit head:* Dr. Harold L. Paz, Senior Vice President and Dean, 717-531-8521, Fax: 717-531-5351.

Ponce School of Medicine, Professional Program, Ponce, PR 00732-7004. Offers MD. *Accreditation:* LCME/AMA. *Degree requirements:* For first-professional, one foreign language, comprehensive exam, registration. *Entrance requirements:* MCAT, Spanish language requirement, proficiency in Spanish/English, 3 letters of recommendation. Additional exam requirements/recommendations for international students: Required—TOEFL. Electronic applications accepted.

Pontificia Universidad Catolica Madre y Maestra, Department of Medicine, Santiago, Dominican Republic. Offers MD.

Queen's University at Kingston, School of Medicine, Professional Program in Medicine, Kingston, ON K7L 3N6, Canada. Offers MD. *Accreditation:* LCME/AMA. *Entrance requirements:* MCAT.

Rosalind Franklin University of Medicine and Science, The Chicago Medical School, North Chicago, IL 60064-3095. Offers MD, MD/MS, MD/PhD. *Accreditation:* LCME/AMA. *Faculty:* 376 full-time (101 women), 298 part-time/adjunct (81 women). *Students:* 750 full-time (325 women); includes 390 minority (34 African Americans, 1 American Indian/Alaska Native, 346 Asian Americans or Pacific Islanders, 9 Hispanic Americans), 16 international. Average age 26. 7,210 applicants, 6% accepted, 184 enrolled. In 2006, 181 degrees awarded. *Median time to degree:* 4 years full-time. *Degree requirements:* For first-professional, clerkship, step 1 and step 2 exams. *Entrance requirements:* MCAT, 3 years of course work with lab in biology, physics, inorganic chemistry, and organic chemistry. *Application deadline:* For fall admission, 11/1 for domestic and international students. Applications are processed on a rolling basis. Application fee: $95. *Expenses: Contact institution. Financial support:* Federal Work-Study, institutionally sponsored loans, and scholarships/grants available. Financial award application deadline: 5/18; financial award applicants required to submit FAFSA. *Faculty research:* Neurosciences, structural biology, cancer biology, cell biology, developmental biology. *Unit head:* Dr. Arthur J. Ross, Dean, 847-578-3300, E-mail: arthur.ross@rosalindfranklin.edu. *Application contact:* Maryann DeCaire, Executive Director of Admissions, Records, and Financial Aid, 847-578-3204, Fax: 847-578-3284, E-mail: maryann.decaire@rosalindfranklin.edu.

Rush University, Rush Medical College, Chicago, IL 60612. Offers MD, MD/PhD. *Accreditation:* LCME/AMA. *Entrance requirements:* MCAT, interview. Expenses: Contact institution.

Saint Louis University, Graduate School, School of Medicine, Program in Medicine, St. Louis, MO 63103-2097. Offers MD. *Accreditation:* LCME/AMA. *Faculty:* 481 full-time (144 women), 103 part-time/adjunct (38 women). *Students:* 668 full-time (285 women); includes 175 minority (17 African Americans, 1 American Indian/Alaska Native, 144 Asian Americans or Pacific Islanders, 13 Hispanic Americans), 14 international. Average age 25. 5,635 applicants, 11% accepted, 177 enrolled. In 2006, 147 degrees awarded. *Degree requirements:* For first-professional, U.S. Medical Licensing Exam Steps 1 and 2. *Entrance requirements:* MCAT, photograph, letters of recommendation, interview. Additional exam requirements/recommendations for international students: Required—TOEFL (minimum score 550 paper-based; 213 computer-based). *Application deadline:* For fall admission, 2/15 for international students; for winter admission, 2/15 for domestic students. Applications are processed on a rolling basis. Application fee: $100. Electronic applications accepted. *Expenses: Contact institution. Financial support:* Application deadline: 2/15; *Faculty research:* Cardiovascular diseases, neurosciences and aging, liver diseases, cancer and molecular biology, infectious diseases and immunology. Total annual research expenditures: $48.1 million. *Application contact:* Dr. James Willmore, Associate Dean of Admissions, 314-577-8205, Fax: 314-577-8214, E-mail: willmore@slu.edu.

San Juan Bautista School of Medicine, Professional Program, Caguas, PR 00726-4968. Offers MD. *Accreditation:* LCME/AMA. *Faculty:* 30 full-time (12 women), 33 part-time/adjunct (9 women). *Students:* 199 full-time (136 women); all minorities (all Hispanic Americans) 110 applicants, 67% accepted, 48 enrolled. In 2006, 31 degrees awarded. *Entrance requirements:* MCAT, interview. *Application deadline:* For fall admission, 7/20 priority date for domestic students. Applications are processed on a rolling basis. Application fee: $75. *Unit head:* Dr. Myrna Borges, Academic Dean, 787-743-3038 Ext. 254, E-mail: mborges@sanjuanbautists.edu. *Application contact:* Jaymi Sanchez, Admissions/Financial Aid Officer, 787-743-3038 Ext. 236, Fax: 787-746-3093, E-mail: jsanchez@sanjuanbautista.edu.

Stanford University, School of Medicine, Professional Program in Medicine, Stanford, CA 94305-9991. Offers MD. *Accreditation:* LCME/AMA. *Entrance requirements:* MCAT. Electronic applications accepted. Expenses: Contact institution.

State University of New York Downstate Medical Center, College of Medicine, Brooklyn, NY 11203-2098. Offers MD, MPH, MD/MPH, MD/PhD. *Accreditation:* LCME/AMA. *Entrance requirements:* MCAT. Expenses: Contact institution. Tuition and fees vary according to course load. *Faculty research:* AIDS epidemiology, virus/host interaction, molecular genetics, developmental neurobiology, prostate cancer.

State University of New York Downstate Medical Center, School of Graduate Studies, MD/PhD Program, Brooklyn, NY 11203-2098. Offers MD/PhD. *Faculty:* 137. *Students:* 7 full-time (2 women); includes 1 minority (Asian American or Pacific Islander) Average age 29. 47 applicants, 21% accepted, 4 enrolled. *Application deadline:* For fall admission, 12/15 for domestic students. Applications are processed on a rolling basis. Application fee: $35. *Expenses:* Tuition, state resident: full-time $6,900; part-time $288 per credit. Tuition, nonresident: full-time $10,920; part-time $455 per credit. Required fees: $100; $20 per credit. $50 per semester. Tuition and fees vary according to course load. *Financial support:* In 2006–07, teaching assistantships with full tuition reimbursements (averaging $25,000 per year); health care benefits and unspecified assistantships also available. *Unit head:* Dr. Stanley Friedman, Director, 718-270-1335, E-mail: sfriedman@downstate.edu. *Application contact:* Denise Sheares, Admissions Officer, 718-270-2738, Fax: 718-270-3378, E-mail: dsheares@downstate.edu.

State University of New York Upstate Medical University, College of Medicine, Syracuse, NY 13210-2334. Offers MD, MD/PhD. *Accreditation:* LCME/AMA. *Faculty:* 366 full-time (74 women), 182 part-time/adjunct (37 women). *Students:* 611 full-time (312 women); includes 176 minority (47 African Americans, 5 American Indian/Alaska Native, 119 Asian Americans or Pacific Islanders, 5 Hispanic Americans), 30 international. Average age 25. 3,572 applicants, 12% accepted, 151 enrolled. In 2006, 157 degrees awarded. *Median time to degree:* 4 years full-time. *Entrance requirements:* MCAT. Additional exam requirements/recommendations for international students: Required—TOEFL. *Application deadline:* For fall admission, 12/1 for domestic and international students. Applications are processed on a rolling basis. Application fee: $100. Electronic applications accepted. *Expenses: Contact institution. Financial support:* In 2006–07, 545 students received support; research assistantships, teaching assistantships, career-related internships or fieldwork, Federal Work-Study, institutionally sponsored loans, scholarships/grants, and tuition waivers (full and partial) available. Support available to part-time students. Financial award application deadline: 3/1; financial award applicants required to submit FAFSA. *Unit head:* Dr. Steven J. Scheinman, Dean, 315-464-9720, E-mail: scheinms@upstate.edu. *Application contact:* Jennifer Welch, Director of Admissions, 315-464-4570, Fax: 315-464-8867, E-mail: welchj@upstate.edu.

Stony Brook University, State University of New York, Stony Brook University Medical Center, School of Medicine, Medical Scientist Training Program, Stony Brook, NY 11794. Offers MD/PhD. *Application deadline:* For fall admission, 1/15 for domestic students. *Expenses:* Tuition, state resident: full-time $6,900; part-time $288 per credit. Tuition, nonresident: full-time $10,920; part-time $455 per credit. *Financial support:* Tuition waivers (full) available.

Stony Brook University, State University of New York, Stony Brook University Medical Center, School of Medicine, Professional Program in Medicine, Stony Brook, NY 11794. Offers MD, MD/PhD. *Accreditation:* LCME/AMA. *Faculty:* 634. *Students:* 438 full-time (225 women); includes 216 minority (44 African Americans, 2 American Indian/Alaska Native, 149 Asian Americans or Pacific Islanders, 21 Hispanic Americans), 3 international. Average age 26. 3,093 applicants, 10% accepted. In 2006, 118 degrees awarded. *Entrance requirements:* MCAT, interview. *Application deadline:* For fall admission, 1/15 for domestic students. Application fee: $75. *Expenses:* Tuition, state resident: full-time $6,900; part-time $288 per credit. Tuition, nonresident: full-time $10,920; part-time $455 per credit. *Financial support:* Fellowships, teaching assistantships available. Total annual research expenditures: $31.8 million. *Application contact:* Dr. Jack Fuhrer, Associate Dean for Admissions, 631-444-2113, Fax: 631-444-6032, E-mail: admissions@dean.som.sunysb.edu.

Temple University, Health Sciences Center, School of Medicine, Professional Program in Medicine, Philadelphia, PA 19122-6096. Offers MD, MD/MPH, MD/PhD. *Accreditation:* LCME/AMA. *Faculty:* 458 full-time (136 women), 73 part-time/adjunct (19 women). *Students:* 713 full-time (326 women); includes 282 minority (50 African Americans, 2 American Indian/Alaska Native, 182 Asian Americans or Pacific Islanders, 48 Hispanic Americans). Average age 24. 8,410 applicants, 7% accepted, 180 enrolled. In 2006, 208 MDs awarded. *Degree requirements:* For first-professional, USMLE Step 1, USMLE Step 2CK, USMLE Step 2CS. *Entrance requirements:* MCAT. *Application deadline:* For fall admission, 12/15 for domestic students. Applications are processed on a rolling basis. Application fee: $70. Electronic applications accepted. *Expenses: Contact institution.* Tuition and fees vary according to program. *Financial support:* In 2006–07, 13 fellowships with full tuition reimbursements (averaging $14,500 per year), 8 research assistantships with full tuition reimbursements (averaging $19,500 per year) were awarded; Federal Work-Study, institutionally sponsored loans, and scholarships/grants also available. Financial award application deadline: 3/1; financial award applicants required to submit FAFSA. *Faculty research:* Molecular biology and immunology of cancer, cardiovascular pathophysiology and thrombosis, biology of substance abuse, causes and consequences of obesity, molecular mechanisms of neurological dysfunction. Total annual research expenditures: $47.2 million. *Unit head:* Dr. John M. Daly, Dean, 215-707-7000, Fax: 215-707-8431, E-mail: johndaly@temple.edu.

Texas Tech University Health Sciences Center, School of Medicine, Lubbock, TX 79430-0002. Offers MD, MD/MBA, MD/PhD. Open only to residents of Texas, eastern New Mexico, and southwestern Oklahoma. *Accreditation:* LCME/AMA. *Faculty:* 511 full-time (158 women). *Students:* 140 full-time (65 women); includes 46 minority (4 African Americans, 1 American Indian/Alaska Native, 30 Asian Americans or Pacific Islanders, 11 Hispanic Americans). Average age 23. 2,856 applicants, 5% accepted, 140 enrolled. In 2006, 118 MDs awarded. *Median time to degree:* Of those who began their doctoral program in fall 1998, 93% received their degree in 8 years or less. *Entrance requirements:* MCAT. Additional exam requirements/recommendations for international students: Required—TOEFL. *Application deadline:* For winter admission, 10/15 for domestic and international students. Applications are processed on a rolling basis. Application fee: $50. Electronic applications accepted. *Expenses: Contact institution. Financial support:* Career-related internships or fieldwork, institutionally sponsored loans, and scholarships/grants available. Financial award applicants required to submit FAFSA. *Unit head:* Dr. Steven L. Berk, Dean, 806-743-3003, Fax: 806-743-3021, E-mail: steven.berk@ttuhsc.edu. *Application contact:* Linda Prado, Director of Admissions, 806-743-2297, Fax: 806-743-2725, E-mail: linda.prado@ttuhsc.edu.

Thomas Jefferson University, Jefferson College of Graduate Studies, MD/PhD Program, Philadelphia, PA 19107. Offers MD/PhD. *Students:* 10 full-time (5 women); includes 2 minority (both Asian Americans or Pacific Islanders), 1 international. 121 applicants, 40% accepted, 4 enrolled. *Entrance requirements:* Additional exam requirements/recommendations for international students: Required—TOEFL (minimum score 213 computer-based). *Application deadline:* For fall admission, 11/1 for domestic and international students. Applications are processed on a rolling basis. Application fee: $0. Electronic applications accepted. *Expenses:* Tuition: Full-time $15,340; part-time $790 per credit. Required fees: $300. *Financial support:* In 2006–07, 10 fellowships with full tuition reimbursements were awarded; research assistantships, Federal Work-Study and institutionally sponsored loans also available. Financial award application deadline: 5/1; financial award applicants required to submit FAFSA. *Faculty research:* Signal transduction, tumorigenesis, apoptosis, molecular immunology, structural biology. *Unit head:* Dr. Scott A. Waldman, Academic Director, 215-955-6086, Fax: 215-955-5681, E-mail: scott.waldman@jefferson.edu. *Application contact:* Jessie F. Pervall, Director of Admissions, 215-503-0155, Fax: 215-503-9920, E-mail: jcgs-info@jefferson.edu.

Thomas Jefferson University, Jefferson Medical College, Philadelphia, PA 19107. Offers MD, MD/PhD. *Accreditation:* LCME/AMA. *Faculty:* 699 full-time (200 women), 25 part-time/adjunct (13 women). *Students:* 966 full-time (496 women); includes 254 minority (17 African Americans, 4 American Indian/Alaska Native, 199 Asian Americans or Pacific Islanders, 34 Hispanic Americans), 26 international. Average age 26. 7,789 applicants, 6% accepted, 255 enrolled. In 2006, 231 MDs awarded. *Median time to degree:* Of those who began their doctoral program in fall 1998, 96% received their degree in 8 years or less. *Entrance requirements:* MCAT. *Application deadline:* For fall admission, 11/15 for domestic and international students. Applications are processed on a rolling basis. Application fee: $80. Electronic applications accepted. *Expenses: Contact institution. Financial support:* In 2006–07, 806 students received support. Federal Work-Study and institutionally sponsored loans available. Financial award application deadline: 3/1; financial award applicants required to submit FAFSA. *Faculty research:* Translational medicine, Alzheimer's research, pancreatic cancer, oncology and endocrinology. Total annual research expenditures: $77.5 million. *Unit head:* Dr. Thomas J. Nasca, Senior Vice President and Dean for Academic Affairs, 215-955-6980, Fax: 215-923-6939. *Application contact:* Dr. Clara Callahan, Dean for Admissions, 215-955-6983, Fax: 215-923-6939, E-mail: clara.callahan@jefferson.edu.

Tufts University, School of Medicine, Professional Program in Medicine, Medford, MA 02155. Offers MD, MD/MA, MD/MBA, MD/MPH, MD/MSE, MD/PhD. *Accreditation:* LCME/AMA. *Students:* 698 full-time (318 women); includes 258 minority (29 African Americans, 3 American Indian/Alaska Native, 188 Asian Americans or Pacific Islanders, 38 Hispanic Americans), 4 international. 8,573 applicants, 5% accepted, 171 enrolled. In 2006, 174 degrees awarded. *Entrance requirements:* MCAT. *Application deadline:* For fall admission, 2/1 for domestic students. Application fee: $95. *Expenses: Contact institution.* Tuition and fees vary according to degree level and program. *Financial support:* Federal Work-Study, institutionally sponsored loans, and scholarships/grants available. Financial award application deadline: 3/16; financial award applicants required to submit FAFSA. *Application contact:* Thomas Slavin, Director of Admissions, 617-636-6571, E-mail: med-admissions@tufts.edu.

Tulane University, School of Medicine, Professional Programs in Medicine, New Orleans, LA 70118-5669. Offers MD, MD/MBA, MD/MPH, MD/MPHTM, MD/MSPH, MD/PhD. *Accreditation:* LCME/AMA. *Faculty:* 429 full-time, 31 part-time/adjunct. *Students:* 609 full-time (280 women); includes 147 minority (35 African Americans, 11 American Indian/Alaska Native, 78 Asian Americans or Pacific Islanders, 23 Hispanic Americans), 4 international. 6,629 applicants, 6% accepted, 155 enrolled. In 2006, 158 degrees awarded. *Entrance requirements:* MCAT. *Application deadline:* For fall admission, 1/15 for domestic students. Application fee: $95. *Financial support:* Fellowships, research assistantships, career-related internships or fieldwork, Federal Work-Study, institutionally sponsored loans, and scholarships/grants available. Financial award application deadline: 2/1. Total annual research expenditures: $20 million. *Application contact:* Dr. Barbara S. Beckman, Assistant Dean for Admissions, 504-988-3545, Fax: 504-988-6735, E-mail: bbeckman@tulane.edu.

Uniformed Services University of the Health Sciences, School of Medicine, Professional Program in Medicine, Bethesda, MD 20814-4799. Offers MD. *Accreditation:* LCME/AMA. *Entrance requirements:* MCAT, US citizenship, clinical exposure, course work in science.

Universidad Autonoma de Guadalajara, School of Medicine, Guadalajara, Mexico. Offers MD. *Entrance requirements:* MCAT, minimum GPA of 3.0.

Universidad Central del Caribe, School of Medicine, Bayamón, PR 00960-6032. Offers MD, MA, MS. *Accreditation:* LCME/AMA. *Degree requirements:* For first-professional, one foreign language. *Entrance requirements:* MCAT, interview, minimum GPA of 2.5, letter of recommendation. *Faculty research:* Membrane neurotransmitter receptors, brain neurotransmission, cocaine toxicology, membrane transport, antimetabolite pharmacology.

Universidad Central del Este, Medical School, San Pedro de Macoris, Dominican Republic. Offers MD.

Universidad de Ciencias Medicas, Graduate Programs, San Jose, Costa Rica. Offers health of administration (MHA); medical and surgery (MD); pharmacy (Pharm D). Part-time programs available. *Faculty:* 36 full-time (11 women), 250 part-time/adjunct (66 women). *Students:* 1,224 full-time (791 women); includes 1,131 Hispanic Americans. Average age 21. 403 applicants, 100% accepted, 293 enrolled. *Median time to degree:* Of those who began their doctoral program in fall 1998, 40% received their degree in 8 years or less. *Entrance requirements:* For first professional degree, admissions test; for master's, MD or bachelors degree. *Application deadline:* For winter admission, 1/6 priority date for domestic and international students; for spring admission, 7/6 priority date for domestic and international students. *Financial support:* In 2006–07, 150 students received support. Institutionally sponsored loans and scholarships/grants available. Financial award application deadline: 10/1; financial award applicants required to submit FAFSA. *Unit head:* Dr. Misael Chinchilla, President of Academic Affairs, 506-296-3944 Ext. 147, Fax: 506-231-4368, E-mail: chinchillacm@ucimed.com. *Application contact:* Lic. Karol Còrdoba, Assistant of Program of International, 506-296-3944 Ext. 158, Fax: 506-290-6116, E-mail: cordobaak@ucimed.com.

Universidad de Iberoamerica, Graduate School, San Jose, Costa Rica. Offers clinical psychology (M Psych); educational psychology (M Psych); hospital and health services management (MHA); intensive care nursing (MN); medicine (MD). *Entrance requirements:* For master's, 2 letters of recommendation, interview.

Universidad Iberoamericana, School of Medicine, Santo Domingo D.N., Dominican Republic. Offers MD. *Entrance requirements:* 3 letters of recommendation.

Universidad Nacional Pedro Henriquez Urena, School of Medicine, Santo Domingo, Dominican Republic. Offers MD.

Université de Montréal, Faculty of Medicine and Faculty of Graduate Studies, Graduate Programs in Medicine, Program in Specialized Studies, Montréal, QC H3C 3J7, Canada. Offers anesthesia (DESS); diagnostic radiology (DESS); family medicine (DESS); medical biochemistry (DESS); medical genetics (DESS); medicine (DESS); microbiology and infectious diseases (DESS); nuclear medicine (DESS); obstetrics and gynecology (DESS); ophthalmology (DESS); pediatrics (DESS); psychiatry (DESS); radiology-oncology (DESS); surgery (DESS). *Faculty:* 159 full-time (37 women), 345 part-time/adjunct (102 women). *Entrance requirements:* For degree, proficiency in French. *Application deadline:* For fall admission, 2/1 priority date for domestic students; for winter admission, 11/1 priority date for domestic students; for spring admission, 2/1 priority date for domestic students. Application fee: $30. Electronic applications accepted. *Unit head:* Dr. Pierre Boyle, Vice Dean of Studies, 514-343-6300, Fax: 514-343-5751, E-mail: pierre.boyle@umontreal.ca.

Université de Montréal, Faculty of Medicine, Professional Program in Medicine, Montréal, QC H3C 3J7, Canada. Offers MD. Open only to Canadian residents. *Accreditation:* LCME/AMA. *Students:* 459 full-time (281 women), 32 part-time (16 women). 41 applicants, 78% accepted, 21 enrolled. *Entrance requirements:* Proficiency in French. *Application deadline:* For fall admission, 2/1 priority date for domestic students; for winter admission, 11/1 priority date for domestic students; for spring admission, 2/1 priority date for domestic students. Application fee: $30. Electronic applications accepted. *Unit head:* Denis Roy, Director, 514-343-5931.

Université de Sherbrooke, Faculty of Medicine and Health Sciences, Professional Program in Medicine, Sherbrooke, QC J1K 2R1, Canada. Offers MD. *Accreditation:* LCME/AMA. *Students:* 583 full-time (378 women). 1,776 applicants, 23% accepted, 194 enrolled. In 2006, 91 degrees awarded. *Application deadline:* For fall admission, 3/1 for domestic students, 1/15 for international students. Application fee: $30. Electronic applications accepted. *Unit head:* Gaston J. Lacroix, Adjoint Administratif au doyen, 819-564-5200, E-mail: gaston.lacroix@usherbrooke.ca. *Application contact:* Isabelle Berube, Administrative Agent, Admissions Office, 819-564-5208, Fax: 819-820-6809, E-mail: admission_med@usherbrooke.ca.

Université Laval, Faculty of Medicine, Post-Professional Programs in Medical Studies, Québec, QC G1K 7P4, Canada. Offers anatomy–pathology (DESS); anesthesiology (DESS); cardiology (DESS); care of older people (Diploma); clinical research (DESS); community health (DESS); dermatology (DESS); diagnostic radiology (DESS); emergency medicine (Diploma); family medicine (DESS); general surgery (DESS); geriatrics (DESS); hematology (DESS); internal medicine (DESS); maternal and fetal medicine (Diploma); medical biochemistry (DESS); medical microbiology and infectious diseases (DESS); medical oncology (DESS); nephrology (DESS); neurology (DESS); neurosurgery (DESS); obstetrics and gynecology (DESS); ophthalmology (DESS); orthopedic surgery (DESS); oto-rhino-laryngology (DESS); palliative medicine (Diploma); pediatrics (DESS); plastic surgery (DESS); psychiatry (DESS); pulmonary medicine (DESS); radiology–oncology (DESS); thoracic surgery (DESS); urology (DESS). *Degree requirements:* For other advanced degree, comprehensive exam. *Entrance requirements:* For degree, knowledge of French. Electronic applications accepted.

Université Laval, Faculty of Medicine, Professional Program in Medicine, Québec, QC G1K 7P4, Canada. Offers MD. *Accreditation:* LCME/AMA. *Entrance requirements:* Interview, proficiency in French. Electronic applications accepted.

University at Buffalo, the State University of New York, Graduate School, School of Medicine and Biomedical Sciences, Professional Program in Medicine, Buffalo, NY 14260. Offers MD, MD/MBA, MD/MPH, MD/PhD. *Accreditation:* LCME/AMA. *Students:* 555 full-time (294 women); includes 146 minority (17 African Americans, 4 American Indian/Alaska Native, 118 Asian Americans or Pacific Islanders, 7 Hispanic Americans), 3 international. Average age 23. 3,067 applicants, 12% accepted, 140 enrolled. In 2006, 134 degrees awarded. *Entrance requirements:* MCAT, interview. *Application deadline:* For fall admission, 11/15 for domestic students. Applications are processed on a rolling basis. Application fee: $65. Electronic applications accepted. *Financial support:* In 2006–07, 551 students received support. Career-related internships or fieldwork, Federal Work-Study, and institutionally sponsored loans available. Financial award application deadline: 3/1; financial award applicants required to submit FAFSA. *Faculty research:* Microbial pathogenesis, neuronal plasticity, structural biology of ion channels, structural development, cell biology of development. Total annual research expenditures: $117.3 million. *Unit head:* Dr. Charles Severin, Dean for Admissions, 716-829-2803, Fax: 716-829-2798, E-mail: severin@buffalo.edu. *Application contact:* James J. Rosso, Admissions Advisor, 716-829-3466, Fax: 716-829-3849, E-mail: jjrosso@buffalo.edu.

The University of Alabama at Birmingham, School of Medicine, Birmingham, AL 35294. Offers MD, MSBMS, PhD, MD/PhD. *Accreditation:* LCME/AMA (one or more programs are accredited). *Students:* 590 full-time (242 women); includes 126 minority (36 African Americans, 3 American Indian/Alaska Native, 81 Asian Americans or Pacific Islanders, 6 Hispanic Americans). Average age 25. 1,914 applicants, 13% accepted. In 2006, 165 degrees awarded. *Entrance requirements:* For MD and doctorate, MCAT, interview. *Application deadline:* For fall admission, 11/1 for domestic students. Application fee: $65. Electronic applications accepted. *Expenses: Contact institution.* Tuition and fees vary according to program. *Financial support:* Fellowships, career-related internships or fieldwork available. Financial award application deadline: 5/1; financial award applicants required to submit FAFSA. *Unit head:* Dr. Robert R. Rich, Vice President/Dean, School of Medicine, 205-934-1111, Fax: 205-934-0333, E-mail: rrich@uab.edu. *Application contact:* Dr. George S. Hand, Assistant Dean for Admissions, 205-934-2333, Fax: 205-934-8724, E-mail: ghand@uab.edu.

The University of Arizona, College of Medicine, Professional Programs in Medicine, Tucson, AZ 85721. Offers MD, MD/PhD. MD program open only to state residents. *Accreditation:* LCME/AMA. *Entrance requirements:* MCAT, previous course work in general chemistry, organic chemistry, biology/zoology, physics, and English. *Faculty research:* Developmental biology, cellular structure and function, immunology, clinical cancer research, heart and respiratory disease.

The University of British Columbia, Faculty of Medicine, Department of Surgery, Vancouver, BC V6T 1Z1, Canada. Offers M Sc. Part-time programs available. *Faculty:* 25 full-time (3 women). *Students:* 5 applicants, 20% accepted, 1 enrolled. In 2006, 2 degrees awarded. *Degree requirements:* For master's, thesis. *Entrance requirements:* Additional exam requirements/recommendations for international students: Required—TOEFL. *Application deadline:* For fall admission, 4/30 for domestic students, 3/31 for international students; for winter admission, 9/30 for domestic students, 8/31 for international students. Application fee: $90 ($150 for international students). Electronic applications accepted. *Faculty research:* Photodynamic therapy, transplantation immunobiology, isolated cell culture, neurophysiology. *Unit head:* Dr. G. L. Warnock, Head, 604-875-4136, Fax: 604-875-4036, E-mail: gwarnock@interchange.ubc.ca. *Application contact:* Dr. Alice Mui, Graduate Adviser, 604-875-4111 Ext. 62242, E-mail: amui@interchange.ubc.ca.

The University of British Columbia, Faculty of Medicine, Professional Program in Medicine, Vancouver, BC V6T 1Z1, Canada. Offers MD, MD/PhD. *Accreditation:* LCME/AMA. *Students:* Average age 23. *Entrance requirements:* MCAT. *Application deadline:* For fall admission, 12/15 for domestic students. Application fee: $105 ($155 for international students). *Application contact:* Dr. J. Carter, Associate Dean of Admissions, 604-822-4482.

University of Calgary, Faculty of Medicine, Professional Program in Medicine, Calgary, AB T2N 1N4, Canada. Offers MD. *Accreditation:* LCME/AMA. *Students:* 346 full-time (182 women). Average age 23. 1,532 applicants, 8% accepted. In 2006, 110 degrees awarded. *Entrance requirements:* MCAT. *Application deadline:* For fall admission, 10/15 for domestic students.

Allopathic Medicine

University of Calgary (continued)
Application fee: $120. Electronic applications accepted. *Financial support:* Career-related internships or fieldwork available. *Unit head:* Dr. B. Wright, Associate Dean (Medical Education), 403-220-3843, Fax: 403-270-2681, E-mail: umeadm4@ucalgary.ca. *Application contact:* Adele Meyers, Coordinator, Admissions and Student Affairs, 403-220-4357, Fax: 403-210-8148, E-mail: meyers@ucalgary.ca.

University of California, Berkeley, Graduate Division, School of Public Health, Division of Health and Medical Sciences, Berkeley, CA 94720-1500. Offers MD/MS. *Application deadline:* For fall admission, 12/1 for domestic students. Applications are processed on a rolling basis. Application fee: $60 ($80 for international students). *Financial support:* Fellowships, research assistantships, teaching assistantships, Federal Work-Study and unspecified assistantships available. *Unit head:* John Swartzberg, Chair, 510-643-0499, E-mail: jes@berkeley.edu. *Application contact:* Ronnie London, Student Affairs Officer, 510-642-5479, Fax: 510-643-8771, E-mail: jmp@berkeley.edu.

University of California, Davis, School of Medicine, Davis, CA 95616. Offers MD, MD/MBA, MD/MPH, MD/MS, MD/PhD. *Accreditation:* LCME/AMA. *Faculty:* 582 full-time (175 women), 92 part-time/adjunct (40 women). *Students:* 402 full-time (220 women). Average age 28. 4,313 applicants, 5% accepted, 90 enrolled. In 2006, 98 MDs awarded. *Entrance requirements:* MCAT. *Application deadline:* For fall admission, 11/1 for domestic and international students. Applications are processed on a rolling basis. Application fee: $60. Electronic applications accepted. *Expenses: Contact institution. Financial support:* In 2006–07, 371 students received support, including 15 fellowships with full tuition reimbursements available (averaging $22,036 per year), 11 research assistantships with partial tuition reimbursements available (averaging $19,932 per year), 10 teaching assistantships with partial tuition reimbursements available (averaging $3,469 per year); institutionally sponsored loans and scholarships/grants also available. Financial award application deadline: 3/2; financial award applicants required to submit FAFSA. *Faculty research:* Infectious diseases, cancer, neurosciences, vascular disease, health disparities. Total annual research expenditures: $124 million. *Unit head:* Dr. Claire Pomeroy, Dean, School of Medicine; Vice Chancellor, Human Health Services, 916-734-7131, Fax: 916-734-7055, E-mail: claire.pomeroy@ucdmc.ucdavis.edu. *Application contact:* Edward D. Dagang, Director of Admissions and Outreach, 916-734-4800, Fax: 916-734-4050, E-mail: ed.dagang@ucdmc.ucdavis.edu.

University of California, Irvine, College of Medicine, Professional Program in Medicine, Irvine, CA 92697. Offers MD, MD/MBA, MD/MPH, MD/PhD. *Accreditation:* LCME/AMA. *Students:* 396 full-time (194 women); includes 126 minority (3 African Americans, 92 Asian Americans or Pacific Islanders, 31 Hispanic Americans). In 2006, 79 degrees awarded. *Entrance requirements:* MCAT. Additional exam requirements/recommendations for international students: Required—TOEFL (minimum score 550 paper-based; 213 computer-based). *Application deadline:* For fall admission, 11/1 for domestic students. Application fee: $60. Electronic applications accepted. *Financial support:* Fellowships, institutionally sponsored loans, traineeships, health care benefits, and unspecified assistantships available. Financial award application deadline: 3/2; financial award applicants required to submit FAFSA. *Application contact:* Peggy Harvey-Lee, Director of Outreach, 949-824-4618, Fax: 949-824-2485, E-mail: pharveyl@uci.edu.

University of California, Los Angeles, School of Medicine, Professional Program in Medicine, Los Angeles, CA 90095. Offers MD, MD/MBA, MD/PhD. *Accreditation:* LCME/AMA. *Entrance requirements:* MCAT.

University of California, San Diego, School of Medicine, Professional Program in Medicine, La Jolla, CA 92093. Offers MD, MD/PhD. *Accreditation:* LCME/AMA. *Entrance requirements:* MCAT.

University of California, San Francisco, School of Medicine, San Francisco, CA 94143-0408. Offers MD, MD/MPH, MD/MS, MD/PhD. *Accreditation:* LCME/AMA (one or more programs are accredited). *Entrance requirements:* MCAT, interview. Electronic applications accepted. Expenses: Contact institution. *Faculty research:* Neurosciences, human genetics, developmental biology, social/behavioral/policy sciences, immunology.

University of Chicago, Division of the Biological Sciences, Pritzker School of Medicine, Chicago, IL 60637-1513. Offers MD, MD/PhD. *Accreditation:* LCME/AMA. *Faculty:* 867 full-time. *Students:* 443 full-time (223 women); includes 149 minority (34 African Americans, 1 American Indian/Alaska Native, 90 Asian Americans or Pacific Islanders, 24 Hispanic Americans), 17 international. Average age 24. 7,519 applicants, 4% accepted, 106 enrolled. In 2006, 105 degrees awarded. *Entrance requirements:* MCAT, one year of each with lab: chemistry, physics, biology and organic chemistry. *Application deadline:* For fall admission, 10/15 for domestic students. Applications are processed on a rolling basis. Application fee: $75. Electronic applications accepted. *Expenses: Contact institution.* One-time fee: $35 full-time. Full-time tuition and fees vary according to course load, degree level and program. *Financial support:* In 2006–07, 361 students received support, including 10 fellowships with full tuition reimbursements available (averaging $20,500 per year), 75 teaching assistantships; career-related internships or fieldwork, Federal Work-Study, institutionally sponsored loans, and scholarships/grants also available. Financial award application deadline: 4/1; financial award applicants required to submit FAFSA. *Faculty research:* Human genetics, diabetes, developmental biology, structural biology, neurobiology. Total annual research expenditures: $210.3 million. *Unit head:* Dr. James Madara, Dean, 773-702-9000. *Application contact:* Sylvia Robertson, Assistant Dean for Admissions and Financial Aid, 773-702-1937, Fax: 773-834-5412, E-mail: sroberts@bsd.uchicago.edu.

University of Cincinnati, Division of Research and Advanced Studies, College of Allied Health Sciences, Program in Transfusion and Transplantation Sciences, Cincinnati, OH 45221. Offers blood transfusion medicine (MS); cellular therapies (MS). *Faculty:* 6 full-time (2 women), 2 part-time/adjunct (both women). *Students:* 1 (woman) full-time. 2 applicants, 0% accepted. In 2006, 2 degrees awarded. *Degree requirements:* For master's, thesis, comprehensive exam. *Entrance requirements:* For master's, GRE General Test. Additional exam requirements/recommendations for international students: Required—TOEFL (minimum score 570 paper-based). *Application deadline:* For fall admission, 3/1 priority date for domestic and international students. Applications are processed on a rolling basis. Application fee: $40. Electronic applications accepted. *Financial support:* In 2006–07, 2 research assistantships with tuition reimbursements (averaging $15,000 per year) were awarded; scholarships/grants also available. Financial award application deadline: 5/1. *Faculty research:* Preservation of red cells, red cell oxidation and delivery to tissues, cellular therapies, coagulopathies. *Unit head:* Dr. Ronald Sacher, Director, 513-558-1203, Fax: 513-558-1300. *Application contact:* Susan Wilkinson, Director, Graduate Program, 513-558-1271, Fax: 513-558-1279, E-mail: susan.wilkinson@uc.edu.

University of Cincinnati, Division of Research and Advanced Studies, College of Medicine, Physician Scientist Training Program, Cincinnati, OH 45267. Offers MD/PhD. *Faculty:* 110 full-time (28 women). *Students:* 6 full-time; includes 2 minority (1 African American, 1 Asian American or Pacific Islander). Average age 22. 91 applicants, 14% accepted, 6 enrolled. *Median time to degree:* Of those who began their doctoral program in fall 1998, 100% received their degree in 8 years or less. *Entrance requirements:* Additional exam requirements/recommendations for international students: Required—TOEFL. *Application deadline:* For fall admission, 11/15 for domestic students. Applications are processed on a rolling basis. Application fee: $40. Electronic applications accepted. *Financial support:* Fellowships with full tuition reimbursements, research assistantships with full tuition reimbursements, health care benefits and unspecified assistantships available. Financial award application deadline: 5/1. *Unit head:* Dr. Leslie Myatt, Director, 513-558-6587, Fax: 513-558-2850, E-mail: leslie.myatt@uc.edu. *Application contact:* Laurie Mayleben, Program Coordinator, 513-558-2380, Fax: 513-558-2850, E-mail: lauren.mayleben@uc.edu.

University of Cincinnati, Division of Research and Advanced Studies, College of Medicine, Professional Program in Medicine, Cincinnati, OH 45267. Offers MD. *Accreditation:* LCME/AMA. *Entrance requirements:* MCAT. Electronic applications accepted. *Faculty research:* Molecular genetics, environmental health, neuroscience and cell biology, cardiovascular science, developmental biology.

University of Colorado at Denver and Health Sciences Center, School of Medicine, Professional Program in Medicine, Denver, CO 80217-3364. Offers MD, MD/MBA, MD/PhD. *Students:* 574 full-time (277 women), 11 part-time (7 women); includes 115 minority (16 African Americans, 5 American Indian/Alaska Native, 53 Asian Americans or Pacific Islanders, 41 Hispanic Americans), 1 international. 2,779 applicants, 9% accepted, 155 enrolled. In 2006, 125 degrees awarded. *Entrance requirements:* MCAT. Additional exam requirements/recommendations for international students: Required—TOEFL (minimum score 550 paper-based). Application fee: $100. *Application contact:* Dr. Henry Sondheimer, Associate Dean for Admissions, 303-315-7361, E-mail: somadmin@uchsc.edu.

University of Connecticut Health Center, School of Medicine, Farmington, CT 06030. Offers MD, MD/MBA, MD/MPH, MD/PhD. *Accreditation:* LCME/AMA. *Degree requirements:* For first-professional, registration. *Entrance requirements:* MCAT. Electronic applications accepted. Expenses: Contact institution.

University of Florida, College of Medicine, Professional Program in Medicine, Gainesville, FL 32611. Offers MD, MD/PhD. *Accreditation:* LCME/AMA. *Faculty:* 96 full-time (18 women), 4 part-time/adjunct (0 women). *Students:* 717 (397 women); includes 196 minority (35 African Americans, 2 American Indian/Alaska Native, 103 Asian Americans or Pacific Islanders, 56 Hispanic Americans) 24 international. Average age 23. *Entrance requirements:* MCAT, 8 semester hours of course work in biology, general chemistry, and general physics; 4 semester hours of course work in geochemistry and organic chemistry. *Application deadline:* For fall admission, 12/1 for domestic students. Applications are processed on a rolling basis. Application fee: $30. Electronic applications accepted. *Expenses:* Tuition, state resident: full-time $6,827. Tuition, nonresident: full-time $21,951. Required fees: $999. *Financial support:* In 2006–07, 12 research assistantships (averaging $23,141 per year) were awarded; Federal Work-Study, institutionally sponsored loans, and scholarships/grants also available. Financial award application deadline: 4/1. *Faculty research:* Neurobiology, gene therapy and genetic imaging technologies, diabetes and autoimmune diseases, transplantation. *Unit head:* Dr. Lynn J. Romrell, Associate Dean for Medical Education, 352-392-3588, Fax: 352-846-1930, E-mail: lynn@dean.med.ufl.edu. *Application contact:* Robyn Sheppard, Admissions Coordinator, 352-392-4569, Fax: 352-392-1307, E-mail: robyn@dean.med.ufl.edu.

University of Hawaii at Manoa, John A. Burns School of Medicine, Professional Programs in Medicine, Honolulu, HI 96822. Offers MD. *Accreditation:* LCME/AMA. *Entrance requirements:* MCAT. *Application deadline:* For fall admission, 2/1 for domestic students, 12/1 for international students. Application fee: $50. Electronic applications accepted. *Financial support:* Fellowships available. Financial award application deadline: 3/1; financial award applicants required to submit FAFSA. *Application contact:* Marilyn M. Nishiki, Admissions Officer, 808-692-1000, Fax: 808-692-1251, E-mail: mnishiki@hawaii.edu.

University of Illinois at Chicago, College of Medicine, Professional Program in Medicine, Chicago, IL 60607-7128. Offers MD, MD/MS, MD/PhD. Part-time programs available. *Entrance requirements:* MCAT. Electronic applications accepted. *Faculty research:* Biomedical and clinical sciences.

University of Illinois at Urbana–Champaign, Graduate College, Medical Scholars Program, Champaign, IL 61820. Offers MD/JD, MD/MBA, MD/PhD. *Students:* 152 full-time (53 women); includes 55 minority (6 African Americans, 35 Asian Americans or Pacific Islanders, 14 Hispanic Americans). 123 applicants, 31% accepted, 18 enrolled. *Application deadline:* For fall admission, 12/31 for domestic students. Application fee: $0. Electronic applications accepted. *Expenses: Contact institution. Financial support:* Fellowships, research assistantships, teaching assistantships, institutionally sponsored loans available. *Unit head:* Dr. Jennifer Bloom, Associate Dean for Student Affairs and Medical Scholars Program, 217-333-8146, Fax: 217-333-2640, E-mail: jlbloom@uiuc.edu. *Application contact:* Amanda E. Cuevas, Assistant Dean for Student Affairs and Medical Scholars Program, 217-333-8146, Fax: 217-333-2640, E-mail: acuevas@uiuc.edu.

The University of Iowa, Roy J. and Lucille A. Carver College of Medicine and Graduate College, Medical Scientist Training Program, Iowa City, IA 52242-1316. Offers MD/PhD. *Faculty:* 130 full-time (30 women), 5 part-time/adjunct (2 women). *Students:* 62 full-time (21 women); includes 10 minority (1 African American, 1 American Indian/Alaska Native, 6 Asian Americans or Pacific Islanders, 2 Hispanic Americans). Average age 24. 118 applicants, 21% accepted, 8 enrolled. *Application deadline:* For fall admission, 12/15 priority date for domestic students. Applications are processed on a rolling basis. Application fee: $50. Electronic applications accepted. *Financial support:* In 2006–07, 24 fellowships with full tuition reimbursements (averaging $22,500 per year), 34 research assistantships with full tuition reimbursements (averaging $22,500 per year) were awarded; scholarships/grants and traineeships also available. Total annual research expenditures: $750,000. *Unit head:* Dr. C. Michael Knudson, Director, 319-335-8147, E-mail: c-knudson@uiowa.edu. *Application contact:* Leslie Harrington, Program Associate—MSTP, 319-335-8304, Fax: 319-335-7656, E-mail: mstp@uiowa.edu.

The University of Iowa, Roy J. and Lucille A. Carver College of Medicine, Professional Program in Medicine, Iowa City, IA 52242-1316. Offers MD, MD/JD, MD/MBA, MD/MPH, MD/PhD. *Accreditation:* LCME/AMA. *Faculty:* 778 full-time (184 women), 414 part-time/adjunct (72 women). *Students:* 572 full-time (283 women). Average age 24. 2,575 applicants, 11% accepted, 142 enrolled. In 2006, 136 degrees awarded. *Entrance requirements:* MCAT, course work in biology, chemistry, physics, mathematics, English, and social sciences. *Application deadline:* For fall admission, 11/1 for domestic students. Applications are processed on a rolling basis. Application fee: $60. Electronic applications accepted. *Expenses: Contact institution. Financial support:* In 2006–07, 562 students received support, including 62 fellowships with full tuition reimbursements available (averaging $22,500 per year); Federal Work-Study, institutionally sponsored loans, scholarships/grants, and unspecified assistantships also available. Support available to part-time students. Financial award applicants required to submit FAFSA. *Unit head:* Dr. Christopher Cooper, Associate Dean, 319-335-8435, Fax: 319-335-8643. *Application contact:* Catherine M. Solow, Assistant Dean, 319-335-6703, Fax: 319-335-8049, E-mail: medical-admissions@uiowa.edu.

University of Kansas, School of Medicine, Lawrence, KS 66045. Offers MD, MD/MHS, MD/MPH, MD/MS, MD/PhD. *Accreditation:* LCME/AMA. *Faculty:* 157 full-time (48 women), 17 part-time/adjunct (9 women). *Students:* 780 full-time (363 women), 147 part-time (98 women); includes 190 minority (51 African Americans, 12 American Indian/Alaska Native, 99 Asian Americans or Pacific Islanders, 28 Hispanic Americans), 31 international. Average age 27. In 2006, 171 MDs awarded. *Entrance requirements:* Letters of recommendation. Electronic applications accepted. *Expenses:* Tuition, area resident: Part-time $227 per credit. Tuition, state resident: part-time $543 per credit. Tuition and fees vary according to course load, campus/location, program and reciprocity agreements. *Unit head:* Dr. Barbara Atkinson, Executive Dean, 913-588-5287, Fax: 913-588-5259. *Application contact:* Peggy M. Heinen, Admissions Coordinator, 913-588-5283, Fax: 913-588-5259, E-mail: pheinen@kumc.edu.

University of Kentucky, College of Medicine, Professional Program in Medicine, Lexington, KY 40506-0032. Offers MD, MD/PhD. *Accreditation:* LCME/AMA. *Faculty:* 614 full-time (178 women), 283 part-time/adjunct (56 women). *Students:* Average age 23. *Entrance requirements:* MCAT. *Application deadline:* For fall admission, 11/1 for domestic students. Applications are processed on a rolling basis. Application fee: $50. Electronic applications accepted. *Expenses:* Tuition, state resident: full-time $7,670; part-time $401 per credit hour. Tuition, nonresident: full-time $16,158; part-time $873 per credit hour. *Financial support:* Application deadline: 4/1;

Application contact: Kimberly Scott, Assistant Director of Admissions, 859-323-6161, Fax: 859-323-2076, E-mail: kstahlma@email.uky.edu.

University of Louisville, School of Medicine, Professional Programs in Medicine, Louisville, KY 40292-0001. Offers MD, MD/MBA, MD/MS, MD/PhD. *Accreditation:* LCME/AMA. *Students:* 600 full-time (245 women); includes 102 minority (40 African Americans, 1 American Indian/Alaska Native, 57 Asian Americans or Pacific Islanders, 4 Hispanic Americans), 2 international. Average age 27. In 2006, 139 degrees awarded. *Entrance requirements:* MCAT. *Application deadline:* For fall admission, 1/15 for domestic students. Application fee: $100. *Application contact:* Director of Admissions, 502-852-5793, Fax: 502-852-6849.

University of Maryland, Baltimore, School of Medicine, Professional Program in Medicine, Baltimore, MD 21201. Offers MD, MD/PhD. *Accreditation:* LCME/AMA. *Entrance requirements:* MCAT, 1 year lecture and laboratory work in biology, general chemistry, organic chemistry, and physics; 1 year course work in English. Electronic applications accepted. Expenses: Contact institution. *Faculty research:* Vaccine development, genetics, diabetes, schizophrenia, cancer.

University of Massachusetts Worcester, Medical School, Worcester, MA 01655-0115. Offers MD, MD/PhD. *Accreditation:* LCME/AMA. *Faculty:* 939 full-time (300 women), 119 part-time/adjunct (92 women). *Students:* 423 full-time (233 women); includes 87 minority (16 African Americans, 4 American Indian/Alaska Native, 60 Asian Americans or Pacific Islanders, 7 Hispanic Americans). Average age 30. 763 applicants, 21% accepted, 103 enrolled. In 2006, 93 degrees awarded. *Entrance requirements:* MCAT, state residency. *Application deadline:* For fall admission, 12/15 for domestic students. Application fee: $75. *Expenses: Contact institution. Financial support:* In 2006–07, 381 students received support. Federal Work-Study, institutionally sponsored loans, scholarships/grants, and tuition waivers (partial) available. Financial award applicants required to submit CSS PROFILE or FAFSA. Total annual research expenditures: $111.9 million. *Unit head:* Dr. Aaron Lazare, Dean, 508-856-0011. *Application contact:* Dr. Jane Cronin, Director of Admissions, 508-856-2303, Fax: 508-856-3629.

University of Medicine and Dentistry of New Jersey, New Jersey Medical School, Newark, NJ 07103-2714. Offers MD, MD/Certificate, MD/JD, MD/MBA, MD/MPH, MD/PhD. *Accreditation:* LCME/AMA. *Faculty:* 700 full-time (239 women), 89 part-time/adjunct (24 women). *Students:* 708 full-time (341 women); includes 420 minority (90 African Americans, 2 American Indian/Alaska Native, 225 Asian Americans or Pacific Islanders, 103 Hispanic Americans). Average age 25. 4,233 applicants, 10% accepted, 170 enrolled. In 2006, 157 degrees awarded. *Entrance requirements:* MCAT. Additional exam requirements/recommendations for international students: Required—TOEFL. *Application deadline:* For fall admission, 8/1 for domestic students. Applications are processed on a rolling basis. Application fee: $75. Electronic applications accepted. *Expenses: Contact institution. Financial support:* Fellowships, research assistantships, teaching assistantships, Federal Work-Study and institutionally sponsored loans available. Financial award application deadline: 5/1. *Faculty research:* Molecular genetics, neurosciences, membranes, cancer, hypertension. *Unit head:* Dr. Robert L Johnson, Interim Dean, 973-972-4538, Fax: 973-972-7104, E-mail: rjohnson@umdnj.edu. *Application contact:* Dr. George F. Heinrich, Assistant Dean, 973-972-4631, Fax: 973-972-7986, E-mail: heinrich@umdnj.edu.

University of Medicine and Dentistry of New Jersey, Robert Wood Johnson Medical School, Piscataway, NJ 08854-5635. Offers MD, MD/JD, MD/MBA, MD/MPH, MD/MS, MD/MSJ, MD/PhD. *Accreditation:* LCME/AMA (one or more programs are accredited). Part-time and evening/weekend programs available. *Faculty:* 891 full-time (316 women), 144 part-time/adjunct (84 women). *Students:* 659 full-time (349 women); includes 340 minority (75 African Americans, 234 Asian Americans or Pacific Islanders, 31 Hispanic Americans). Average age 25. 2,158 applicants, 16% accepted, 156 enrolled. In 2006, 146 degrees awarded. *Entrance requirements:* MCAT. Additional exam requirements/recommendations for international students: Required—TOEFL. *Application deadline:* For fall admission, 8/1 for domestic students. Applications are processed on a rolling basis. Application fee: $75. Electronic applications accepted. *Expenses: Contact institution. Financial support:* Fellowships, research assistantships, teaching assistantships, career-related internships or fieldwork, Federal Work-Study, institutionally sponsored loans, and tuition waivers (partial) available. Support available to part-time students. Financial award application deadline: 5/1; financial award applicants required to submit FAFSA. *Faculty research:* Protein structure and function, regulation of gene expression, multidrug resistance in cancer, developmental neurobiology and genetics, environmental toxicology. *Unit head:* Dr. Peter Amenta, Interim Dean, 732-235-6300, Fax: 732-235-6315, E-mail: amenta@umdnj.edu. *Application contact:* Dr. David Seiden, Associate Dean for Student Affairs, 732-235-4576, Fax: 732-235-5078, E-mail: seiden@umdnj.edu.

University of Miami, Graduate School, Miller School of Medicine, Professional Program in Medicine, Coral Gables, FL 33124. Offers MD. *Accreditation:* LCME/AMA. *Faculty:* 1,194 full-time (402 women), 18 part-time/adjunct (12 women). *Students:* 651 full-time (310 women); includes 278 minority (38 African Americans, 2 American Indian/Alaska Native, 146 Asian Americans or Pacific Islanders, 92 Hispanic Americans), 2 international. Average age 23. 3,912 applicants, 8% accepted, 176 enrolled. In 2006, 152 degrees awarded. *Degree requirements:* For first-professional, registration. *Entrance requirements:* MCAT, 90 pre-med semester hours. *Application deadline:* For fall admission, 12/1 for domestic students. Applications are processed on a rolling basis. Application fee: $65. Electronic applications accepted. *Financial support:* In 2006–07, 574 students received support. Federal Work-Study, institutionally sponsored loans, and scholarships/grants available. Financial award application deadline: 4/1; financial award applicants required to submit FAFSA. *Faculty research:* AIDS, cancer, diabetes, neuroscience, wound healing. Total annual research expenditures: $187.2 million. *Application contact:* Dr. Robert Hinkley, Associate Dean for Admissions, 305-243-6791, Fax: 305-243-6548, E-mail: med.admissions@miami.edu.

University of Michigan, Medical School and Horace H. Rackham School of Graduate Studies, Medical Scientist Training Program, Ann Arbor, MI 48109. Offers MD/PhD. *Accreditation:* LCME/AMA. Electronic applications accepted.

University of Michigan, Medical School, Professional Program in Medicine, Ann Arbor, MI 48109. Offers MD, MD/MPH, MD/PhD. *Accreditation:* LCME/AMA. *Entrance requirements:* MCAT.

University of Minnesota, Duluth, Medical School, Professional Program in Medicine, Duluth, MN 55812-2496. Offers MD. *Faculty:* 38 full-time (12 women), 282 part-time/adjunct (91 women). *Students:* 110 full-time (54 women); includes 14 minority (11 American Indian/Alaska Native, 3 Asian Americans or Pacific Islanders). Average age 25. 1,281 applicants, 7% accepted, 56 enrolled. *Median time to degree:* Of those who began their doctoral program in fall 1998, 98% received their degree in 8 years or less. *Entrance requirements:* MCAT. *Application deadline:* For fall admission, 11/15 for domestic students. Applications are processed on a rolling basis. Application fee: $75. *Financial support:* In 2006–07, 107 students received support. Institutionally sponsored loans and scholarships/grants available. Financial award applicants required to submit FAFSA. *Application contact:* Dr. Lillian A. Repesh, Associate Dean for Admissions and Student Affairs, 218-726-8511, Fax: 218-726-7057, E-mail: lrepesh@d.umn.edu.

University of Minnesota, Twin Cities Campus, Medical School, Professional Program in Medicine, Minneapolis, MN 55455-0213. Offers MD, JD/MD, MD/MBA, MD/MHI, MD/MPH, MD/MS, MD/PhD. *Accreditation:* LCME/AMA. *Faculty:* 602 full-time, 60 part-time/adjunct. *Students:* 2,528 applicants, 165 enrolled. In 2006, 225 degrees awarded. *Entrance requirements:* MCAT. *Application deadline:* For fall admission, 11/15 for domestic and international students. Applications are processed on a rolling basis. Application fee: $75. Electronic applications accepted. *Expenses: Contact institution.* Full-time tuition and fees vary according to class time, course load, program, reciprocity agreements and student level. *Financial support:* In 2006–07, 858 students received support; research assistantships with partial tuition reimbursements available, teaching assistantships with partial tuition reimbursements available, Federal Work-Study, institutionally sponsored loans, scholarships/grants, and unspecified assistantships available. Support available to part-time students. Financial award applicants required to submit FAFSA. Total annual research expenditures: $107.8 million. *Unit head:* Dr. Kathleen V. Watson, Associate Dean for Students and Student Learning, 612-624-5812, Fax: 612-626-0489. *Application contact:* Paul T. White, Assistant Dean of Admissions, 612-625-7977, Fax: 612-625-8228, E-mail: meded@tc.umn.edu.

University of Mississippi Medical Center, School of Medicine, Jackson, MS 39216-4505. Offers MD, MD/PhD. *Accreditation:* LCME/AMA. *Faculty:* 409 full-time (155 women), 74 part-time/adjunct (35 women). *Students:* 407 full-time (176 women); includes 81 minority (32 African Americans, 1 American Indian/Alaska Native, 41 Asian Americans or Pacific Islanders, 7 Hispanic Americans). Average age 24. In 2006, 103 degrees awarded. *Entrance requirements:* MCAT. *Application deadline:* For fall admission, 9/15 for domestic students; for winter admission, 12/1 for domestic students. Applications are processed on a rolling basis. Application fee: $10. *Expenses:* Tuition, state resident: full-time $4,523. Tuition, nonresident: full-time $10,566. *Financial support:* In 2006–07, 374 students received support. Institutionally sponsored loans and scholarships/grants available. Financial award application deadline: 4/1. *Faculty research:* Cardiovascular physiology (computer simulation), transplant immunology, reproductive endocrinology, protein structure, neurotransmitter vesicle structure. *Unit head:* Dr. Daniel W. Jones, Dean, 601-984-1010. *Application contact:* Dr. Steven T. Case, Associate Dean for Medical School Admissions, 601-984-5010, Fax: 601-984-5008, E-mail: admitmd@som.umsmed.edu.

University of Missouri–Columbia, School of Medicine, Professional Program in Medicine, Columbia, MO 65211. Offers MD, MD/MS, MD/PhD. *Accreditation:* LCME/AMA. *Faculty:* 304 full-time (79 women), 46 part-time/adjunct (17 women). *Students:* 371 full-time (182 women); includes 66 minority (18 African Americans, 2 American Indian/Alaska Native, 44 Asian Americans or Pacific Islanders, 2 Hispanic Americans), 1 international. Average age 26. In 2006, 89 degrees awarded. *Entrance requirements:* MCAT, minimum GPA of 3.49, specified pre-med courses. *Application deadline:* For fall admission, 11/1 for domestic students. Applications are processed on a rolling basis. *Financial support:* In 2006–07, 361 students received support. Career-related internships or fieldwork, institutionally sponsored loans, and scholarships/grants available. Financial award application deadline: 8/15; financial award applicants required to submit FAFSA. *Faculty research:* Basic and clinical biomedical sciences. *Application contact:* Judy A. Nolke, Coordinator, Admissions and Recruitment, 573-882-9219, E-mail: nolkej@missouri.edu.

University of Missouri–Kansas City, School of Medicine, Kansas City, MO 64110-2499. Offers MD, MD/PhD. *Accreditation:* LCME/AMA. *Faculty:* 26 full-time (9 women), 6 part-time/adjunct (2 women). *Students:* 363 full-time (220 women); includes 157 minority (15 African Americans, 3 American Indian/Alaska Native, 130 Asian Americans or Pacific Islanders, 9 Hispanic Americans). Average age 22. 586 applicants, 23% accepted, 102 enrolled. In 2006, 90 degrees awarded. *Degree requirements:* For first-professional, one foreign language, registration. *Entrance requirements:* Interview. *Application deadline:* For fall admission, 12/1 for domestic students. Application fee: $50. *Expenses: Contact institution. Financial support:* In 2006–07, 323 students received support, including 3 fellowships (averaging $31,364 per year), 13 research assistantships (averaging $12,740 per year); career-related internships or fieldwork, Federal Work-Study, institutionally sponsored loans, scholarships/grants, and tuition waivers (partial) also available. Financial award application deadline: 3/15; financial award applicants required to submit FAFSA. *Faculty research:* Cardiovascular disease, women's and children's health, trauma and infectious diseases, neurological, metabolic disease. Total annual research expenditures: $13.8 million. *Unit head:* Dr. Betty Drees, Dean, 816-235-1808, E-mail: dreesb@umkc.edu. *Application contact:* MaryAnne Morgenegg, Selection Administrative Assistant, 816-235-1870, Fax: 816-235-6579, E-mail: morgeneggm@umkc.edu.

University of Nebraska Medical Center, College of Medicine, Omaha, NE 68198. Offers MD, Certificate, MD/MPH, MD/PhD. *Accreditation:* LCME/AMA. *Faculty:* 554 full-time, 107 part-time/adjunct. *Students:* 476 full-time (207 women); includes 35 minority (13 African Americans, 4 American Indian/Alaska Native, 17 Asian Americans or Pacific Islanders, 1 Hispanic American). Average age 22. 1,268 applicants, 13% accepted, 123 enrolled. In 2006, 119 degrees awarded. *Entrance requirements:* MCAT. *Application deadline:* For fall admission, 11/1 for domestic students. Applications are processed on a rolling basis. Application fee: $45. Electronic applications accepted. *Expenses: Contact institution. Financial support:* Career-related internships or fieldwork, Federal Work-Study, institutionally sponsored loans, and tuition waivers (full) available. Support available to part-time students. Financial award application deadline: 2/1; financial award applicants required to submit FAFSA. *Unit head:* Dr. John L. Gollan, Dean, 402-559-4146, Fax: 402-559-4148. *Application contact:* Gigi R. Rogers, Administrative Coordinator, 402-559-2259, Fax: 402-559-6840, E-mail: grrogers@unmc.edu.

University of New Mexico, School of Medicine, Professional Program in Medicine, Albuquerque, NM 87131-2039. Offers MD. *Degree requirements:* For first-professional, research. *Entrance requirements:* MCAT, previous course work in biology, general chemistry, organic chemistry, and physics. Expenses: Contact institution.

The University of North Carolina at Chapel Hill, School of Medicine, Professional Program in Medicine, Chapel Hill, NC 27599. Offers MD, MD/MPH, MD/PhD. *Accreditation:* LCME/AMA. *Entrance requirements:* MCAT.

University of North Dakota, School of Medicine, Professional Program in Medicine, Grand Forks, ND 58202. Offers MD, MD/PhD. *Accreditation:* LCME/AMA. *Faculty:* 99 full-time (42 women). *Students:* 236 full-time (119 women); includes 24 minority (16 American Indian/Alaska Native, 5 Asian Americans or Pacific Islanders, 3 Hispanic Americans), 1 international. Average age 26. 67 applicants, 94% accepted, 61 enrolled. In 2006, 57 degrees awarded. *Entrance requirements:* MCAT, minimum GPA of 3.0. Additional exam requirements/recommendations for international students: Required—TOEFL (minimum score 550 paper-based; 213 computer-based; 79 iBT), IELTS (minimum score 6). *Application deadline:* For fall admission, 11/1 for domestic students. Application fee: $50. Electronic applications accepted. *Expenses:* Tuition, state resident: full-time $5,650; part-time $214 per credit. Tuition, nonresident: full-time $14,248; part-time $572 per credit. Required fees: $1,008; $42 per credit. Tuition and fees vary according to reciprocity agreements. *Financial support:* Institutionally sponsored loans and tuition waivers (full and partial) available. Support available to part-time students. Financial award application deadline: 4/15; financial award applicants required to submit FAFSA. *Unit head:* Judy L. DeMers, Associate Dean, Student Affairs and Admissions, 701-777-4221, Fax: 701-777-4942. *Application contact:* Marilyn M. Martin, Admissions and Records Officer, 701-777-2840, Fax: 701-777-4942.

University of Oklahoma Health Sciences Center, College of Medicine, Professional Program in Medicine, Oklahoma City, OK 73190. Offers MD, MD/PhD. *Accreditation:* LCME/AMA. *Entrance requirements:* MCAT. *Faculty research:* Behavior and drugs, structure and function of endothelium, genetics and behavior, gene structure and function, action of antibiotics.

University of Ottawa, Faculty of Graduate and Postdoctoral Studies, Faculty of Medicine, Ottawa, ON K1N 6N5, Canada. Offers MD, M Sc, PhD. *Accreditation:* LCME/AMA. *Degree requirements:* For master's and doctorate, thesis/dissertation. *Entrance requirements:* For master's, honors degree or equivalent, minimum B average; for doctorate, master's degree, minimum B+ average. Electronic applications accepted.

University of Pennsylvania, School of Medicine, Professional Program in Medicine, Philadelphia, PA 19104. Offers MD, MD/JD, MD/MBA, MD/MS, MD/PhD. *Accreditation:* LCME/AMA. *Faculty:* 2,093 full-time (668 women), 968 part-time/adjunct (357 women). *Students:* 712 full-time (350 women); includes 247 minority (57 African Americans, 7 American Indian/Alaska Native, 131 Asian Americans or Pacific Islanders, 52 Hispanic Americans), 7 international. Average age 25. 5,730 applicants, 4% accepted, 151 enrolled. *Entrance requirements:* MCAT. *Application deadline:* For fall admission, 10/15 for domestic students. Application fee: $85. Electronic applications accepted. *Financial support:* In 2006–07, 621 students received sup-

Allopathic Medicine

University of Pennsylvania (continued)
port; fellowships, research assistantships, teaching assistantships, career-related internships or fieldwork, Federal Work-Study, institutionally sponsored loans, and scholarships/grants available. Financial award application deadline: 5/1; financial award applicants required to submit FAFSA. *Unit head:* Dr. Gail Morrison, Head, 215-898-8034. *Application contact:* Gaye Sheffler, Director, Admissions, 215-898-8001, Fax: 215-898-0833, E-mail: sheffler@mail.med.upenn.edu.

University of Pittsburgh, School of Medicine, Professional Program in Medicine, Pittsburgh, PA 15260. Offers MD. *Accreditation:* LCME/AMA. *Faculty:* 1,896 full-time (594 women). *Students:* 589 full-time (274 women); includes 237 minority (44 African Americans, 178 Asian Americans or Pacific Islanders, 15 Hispanic Americans). Average age 26. 5,297 applicants, 9% accepted, 147 enrolled. In 2006, 130 degrees awarded. *Entrance requirements:* MCAT. *Application deadline:* For fall admission, 11/15 for domestic students. Applications are processed on a rolling basis. Application fee: $75. Electronic applications accepted. *Expenses: Contact institution. Financial support:* In 2006–07, 371 students received support. Institutionally sponsored loans and scholarships/grants available. Financial award application deadline: 4/15; financial award applicants required to submit FAFSA. *Unit head:* Dr. Beth Piraino, Associate Dean, 412-648-9891, Fax: 412-648-8768, E-mail: admissions@medschool.pitt.edu. *Application contact:* Paula K Davis, Assistant Dean, Office of Admissions and Financial Aid, 412-648-9891, Fax: 412-648-8768, E-mail: admissions@medschool.pitt.edu.

University of Puerto Rico, Medical Sciences Campus, School of Medicine, Professional Program in Medicine, San Juan, PR 00936-5067. Offers MD. *Accreditation:* LCME/AMA. *Degree requirements:* For first-professional, one foreign language. *Entrance requirements:* MCAT, interview.

University of Rochester, School of Medicine and Dentistry, Professional Program in Medicine, Rochester, NY 14627-0250. Offers MD, MD/MPH, MD/MS, MD/PhD. *Accreditation:* LCME/AMA. *Entrance requirements:* MCAT.

University of Saskatchewan, College of Medicine, Professional Program in Medicine, Saskatoon, SK S7N 5A2, Canada. Offers MD. *Accreditation:* LCME/AMA. *Students:* 240. In 2006, 55 degrees awarded. *Application deadline:* For fall admission, 7/1 priority date for domestic students. Application fee: $25. *Unit head:* Dr. W. Albritton, Dean, College of Medicine, 306-966-6149, Fax: 306-966-6164, E-mail: william.albritton@usask.ca.

University of South Alabama, College of Medicine, Professional Program in Medicine, Mobile, AL 36688-0002. Offers MD. *Accreditation:* LCME/AMA. *Faculty:* 194 full-time (48 women), 33 part-time/adjunct (12 women). *Students:* 276 full-time (140 women); includes 55 minority (29 African Americans, 1 American Indian/Alaska Native, 24 Asian Americans or Pacific Islanders, 1 Hispanic American), 1 international. In 2006, 60 degrees awarded. *Entrance requirements:* MCAT. Application fee: $25. *Unit head:* Dr. Samuel J Strada, Interim Dean, College of Medicine, 251-460-7189.

University of South Carolina, School of Medicine, Professional Program in Medicine, Columbia, SC 29208. Offers MD, MD/MPH. *Accreditation:* LCME/AMA. *Entrance requirements:* MCAT. Electronic applications accepted. *Faculty research:* Cardiovascular diseases, oncology, reproductive biology, vision, neuroscience.

The University of South Dakota, School of Medicine and Health Sciences, Professional Program in Medicine, Vermillion, SD 57069-2390. Offers MD. *Accreditation:* LCME/AMA. *Faculty:* 265 full-time, 721 part-time/adjunct. *Students:* 207 full-time (96 women); includes 9 minority (5 American Indian/Alaska Native, 4 Asian Americans or Pacific Islanders). Average age 24. 807 applicants, 10% accepted, 51 enrolled. In 2006, 52 degrees awarded. *Median time to degree:* 4 years full-time. *Degree requirements:* For first-professional, USMLE-Step 1 USMLE-Step 2, CK OSCE. *Entrance requirements:* MCAT, previous course work in biology, chemistry, organic chemistry, mathematics and physics. *Application deadline:* For fall admission, 11/15 for domestic and international students. Applications are processed on a rolling basis. Application fee: $35. Electronic applications accepted. *Expenses:* Tuition, state resident: part-time $120 per credit hour. Tuition, nonresident: part-time $355 per credit hour. Required fees: $90 per credit hour. *Financial support:* In 2006–07, 199 students received support. Institutionally sponsored loans and scholarships/grants available. *Application contact:* Dr. Paul C. Bunger, Dean, Medical Student Affairs, 605-677-5233, Fax: 605-677-5109, E-mail: pbunger@usd.edu.

University of Southern California, Keck School of Medicine, Professional Program in Medicine, Los Angeles, CA 90089. Offers MD, MD/MBA, MD/MPH, MD/PhD. *Accreditation:* LCME/AMA. *Faculty:* 959 full-time (296 women), 41 part-time/adjunct (19 women). *Students:* 672 full-time (334 women); includes 283 minority (24 African Americans, 2 American Indian/Alaska Native, 188 Asian Americans or Pacific Islanders, 69 Hispanic Americans), 11 international. Average age 24. 6,308 applicants, 6% accepted, 162 enrolled. In 2006, 160 degrees awarded. *Entrance requirements:* MCAT, 2 semesters or 3 quarters of course work in biology, chemistry, organic chemistry, physics (all with lab); 1 course in molecular biology; 30 units of course work in social sciences, biochemistry. *Application deadline:* For fall admission, 11/1 for domestic students. Applications are processed on a rolling basis. Application fee: $90. Electronic applications accepted. *Expenses: Contact institution.* Full-time tuition and fees vary according to program. *Financial support:* In 2006–07, 550 students received support. Career-related internships or fieldwork available. Financial award application deadline: 2/1; financial award applicants required to submit FAFSA. *Faculty research:* Cancer biology, metabolism and endocrinology, gene regulation and signal transduction, human genetics, virology and immunology. Total annual research expenditures: $115.2 million. *Unit head:* Dr. Erin A. Quinn, Associate Dean for Admissions, 323-442-2552, Fax: 323-442-2433, E-mail: medadmit@usc.edu. *Application contact:* Robert J. McCann, Director of Admissions, 323-442-2553, Fax: 323-442-2433, E-mail: medadmit@usc.edu.

The University of Tennessee Health Science Center, College of Medicine, Memphis, TN 38163-0002. Offers MD, MS, PhD, MD/PhD. *Accreditation:* LCME/AMA. *Faculty:* 1,041 full-time (208 women), 990 part-time/adjunct (198 women). *Students:* 611 full-time (245 women); includes 151 minority (64 African Americans, 4 American Indian/Alaska Native, 76 Asian Americans or Pacific Islanders, 7 Hispanic Americans). Average age 25. 1,355 applicants, 11% accepted. In 2006, 144 degrees awarded. *Entrance requirements:* MCAT, interview, pre-professional evaluation. *Application deadline:* For fall admission, 11/15 for domestic students. Applications are processed on a rolling basis. Application fee: $50. Electronic applications accepted. *Expenses: Contact institution.* One-time fee: $55 full-time. *Financial support:* In 2006–07, 519 students received support. Career-related internships or fieldwork, Federal Work-Study, and institutionally sponsored loans available. Support available to part-time students. Financial award application deadline: 2/28. *Unit head:* Dr. Steve J. Schwab, Dean, 901-448-5529, Fax: 901-448-7683, E-mail: jschwab@utmem.edu. *Application contact:* Eunice Taylor, Interim Director, Enrollment Services, 901-448-5560, Fax: 901-448-7772, E-mail: etaylor@utmem.edu.

The University of Texas Health Science Center at Houston, Medical School, Houston, TX 77225-0036. Offers MD, MD/MPH, MD/PhD. *Accreditation:* LCME/AMA. *Faculty:* 776 full-time (276 women), 94 part-time/adjunct (42 women). *Students:* 868 full-time (398 women); includes 237 minority (26 African Americans, 4 American Indian/Alaska Native, 101 Asian Americans or Pacific Islanders, 106 Hispanic Americans), 1 international. Average age 23. 3,446 applicants, 8% accepted, 226 enrolled. In 2006, 208 degrees awarded. *Entrance requirements:* MCAT. *Application deadline:* For fall admission, 10/1 for domestic and international students. Applications are processed on a rolling basis. Application fee: $55 ($100 for international students). Electronic applications accepted. *Expenses: Contact institution. Financial support:* In 2006–07, 859 students received support. Scholarships/grants and health care benefits available. Financial award application deadline: 3/1; financial award applicants required to submit FAFSA. *Faculty research:* Stroke, infectious diseases, cardiovascular disease, neoplastic disease (cancer), molecular medicine for the prevention of diseases. Total annual research expenditures: $59.2 million. *Unit head:* Dr. Jerry S. Wolinsky, Interim Dean, 713-500-5012, E-mail: jerry.s.wolinsky@uth.tmc.edu. *Application contact:* Dr. Judianne Kellaway, Assistant Dean of Admissions, 713-500-5116, E-mail: judianne.kellaway@uth.tmc.edu.

The University of Texas Health Science Center at San Antonio, Medical School, San Antonio, TX 78229-3900. Offers MD. *Accreditation:* LCME/AMA. *Entrance requirements:* MCAT. Expenses: Contact institution. *Faculty research:* Geriatrics, molecular medicine, diabetes, genetics, anticancer agents, AIDS and children, obesity.

The University of Texas Medical Branch, School of Medicine, Galveston, TX 77555. Offers MD. *Accreditation:* LCME/AMA. *Students:* 861 full-time (429 women); includes 372 minority (79 African Americans, 5 American Indian/Alaska Native, 154 Asian Americans or Pacific Islanders, 134 Hispanic Americans), 4 international. Average age 25. In 2006, 183 degrees awarded. *Entrance requirements:* MCAT. *Application deadline:* For fall admission, 11/1 for domestic students. Application fee: $55 ($100 for international students). *Expenses: Contact institution. Financial support:* Federal Work-Study, institutionally sponsored loans, scholarships/grants, and tuition waivers (full and partial) available. Financial award applicants required to submit FAFSA. *Unit head:* Dr. Garland D. Anderson, Dean, 409-772-4793, Fax: 409-772-9598, E-mail: ganderso@utmb.edu. *Application contact:* Dr. Lauree Thomas, Associate Dean for Admissions and Student Affairs, 409-772-1442, Fax: 409-772-5148, E-mail: lauthoma@utmb.edu.

The University of Texas Southwestern Medical Center at Dallas, Southwestern Medical School, Dallas, TX 75390. Offers MD, MD/PhD. *Accreditation:* LCME/AMA. *Entrance requirements:* MCAT. Electronic applications accepted. Expenses: Contact institution. Tuition and fees vary according to program. *Faculty research:* Endocrinology, molecular biology, immunology, cancer biology, neuroscience.

The University of Toledo, College of Graduate Studies, College of Medicine, Department of Medicine, Toledo, OH 43606-3390. Offers MS. Part-time programs available. *Students:* 1 (woman) full-time. *Degree requirements:* For master's, thesis, qualifying exam. *Entrance requirements:* For master's, GRE. Application fee: $45. *Financial support:* Federal Work-Study and institutionally sponsored loans available. Financial award applicants required to submit FAFSA. *Faculty research:* Hypertension, endocrinology, molecular biology. Total annual research expenditures: $754,479. *Unit head:* Dr. Joseph I. Shapiro, Chairman, 419-383-4117, Fax: 419-383-6140, E-mail: mcogradschool@mco.edu.

University of Toronto, Faculty of Medicine, Toronto, ON M5S 1A1, Canada. Offers MD, M Sc, M Sc BMC, M Sc OT, M Sc PT, MH Sc, PhD, MD/PhD. *Accreditation:* LCME/AMA. *Entrance requirements:* For MD, MCAT, at least 2 courses in life sciences, one course in humanities, social sciences or languages; minimum GPA of 3.6; for doctorate, master's degree in related area, minimum B+ average. Expenses: Contact institution.

University of Utah, School of Medicine, MD/PhD Program in Medicine, Salt Lake City, UT 84112-1107. Offers MD/PhD. Part-time programs available. *Faculty:* 105 full-time. *Students:* 26 full-time (9 women); includes 2 minority (1 Asian American or Pacific Islander, 1 Hispanic American). Average age 28. 33 applicants, 18% accepted, 3 enrolled. *Application deadline:* For fall admission, 4/1 for domestic students; for spring admission, 11/1 for domestic students. Application fee: $100. Electronic applications accepted. *Expenses:* Tuition, state resident: full-time $3,208. Tuition, nonresident: full-time $11,326. Required fees: $608. Tuition and fees vary according to class time and program. *Financial support:* In 2006–07, 26 research assistantships with full tuition reimbursements (averaging $24,000 per year), 4 teaching assistantships were awarded; fellowships with full tuition reimbursements, career-related internships or fieldwork, Federal Work-Study, institutionally sponsored loans, scholarships/grants, traineeships, and tuition waivers (full and partial) also available. Support available to part-time students. *Faculty research:* Molecular biology, biochemistry, cell biology, immunology, bioengineering. *Unit head:* Dr. Jerry Kaplan, Associate Dean of Research, 801-581-7427, Fax: 801-585-6364, E-mail: jerry.kaplan@path.utah.edu. *Application contact:* Janet Bassett, Program Administrator, 801-585-6408, Fax: 801-585-6364, E-mail: janet.bassett@path.utah.edu.

University of Utah, School of Medicine, Professional Program in Medicine, Salt Lake City, UT 84112-1107. Offers MD. *Accreditation:* LCME/AMA. *Faculty:* 118 full-time (26 women). *Students:* 402 full-time (152 women); includes 52 minority (5 African Americans, 2 American Indian/Alaska Native, 29 Asian Americans or Pacific Islanders, 16 Hispanic Americans), 6 international. Average age 26. 1,169 applicants, 11% accepted, 102 enrolled. In 2006, 104 degrees awarded. *Median time to degree:* 4 years full-time. *Entrance requirements:* MCAT, 2 years chemistry with lab, 1 year physics with lab, writing/speech, 2 courses biology, 1 course cell biology or biochemistry, 1 course humanities, 1 course diversity, 1 course social science. *Application deadline:* For fall admission, 11/1 for domestic students. Application fee: $100. Electronic applications accepted. *Expenses: Contact institution.* Tuition and fees vary according to class time and program. *Financial support:* Applicants required to submit FAFSA. *Faculty research:* Molecular biology, genetics, immunology, cardiology, endocrinology. *Unit head:* Dr. David J. Bjorkman, Dean, 801-581-6436, Fax: 801-585-3300, E-mail: david.bjorkman@hsc.utah.edu. *Application contact:* Dr. Wayne M. Samuelson, Associate Dean of Admissions, 801-581-7498, Fax: 801-581-2931, E-mail: wayne.samuelson@hsc.utah.edu.

University of Vermont, College of Medicine, Professional Program in Medicine, Burlington, VT 05405. Offers MD, MD/MS, MD/PhD. *Accreditation:* LCME/AMA. *Students:* 422 (254 women); includes 73 minority (1 African American, 1 American Indian/Alaska Native, 64 Asian Americans or Pacific Islanders, 7 Hispanic Americans) 8 international. Average age 26. 5,440 applicants, 4% accepted, 100 enrolled. In 2006, 97 degrees awarded. *Entrance requirements:* MCAT. Additional exam requirements/recommendations for international students: Required—TOEFL (minimum score 550 paper-based; 213 computer-based). *Application deadline:* For fall admission, 11/1 for domestic and international students. Applications are processed on a rolling basis. Application fee: $85. Electronic applications accepted. *Expenses: Contact institution. Financial support:* In 2006–07, 340 students received support. Institutionally sponsored loans and scholarships/grants available. Support available to part-time students. Financial award application deadline: 2/28; financial award applicants required to submit FAFSA. *Unit head:* Dr. G. Scott Waterman, Associate Dean for Student Affairs, 802-656-2150, Fax: 802-656-9377. *Application contact:* Dr. James P. Rathmell, Interim Associate Dean for Admissions, 802-656-2150.

University of Virginia, School of Medicine, Charlottesville, VA 22903. Offers MD, MPH, MS, PhD, JD/MPH, MD/PhD. *Accreditation:* LCME/AMA. *Faculty:* 896 full-time (255 women), 118 part-time/adjunct (51 women). *Students:* 838 full-time (416 women), 12 part-time (6 women); includes 195 minority (53 African Americans, 1 American Indian/Alaska Native, 124 Asian Americans or Pacific Islanders, 17 Hispanic Americans), 62 international. Average age 26. 78 applicants. In 2006, 136 MDs, 30 master's, 29 doctorates awarded. *Entrance requirements:* MCAT. Additional exam requirements/recommendations for international students: Required—TOEFL. *Financial support:* Institutionally sponsored loans and scholarships/grants available. Financial award applicants required to submit FAFSA. *Unit head:* Arthur Garson, Jr., Vice President and Dean, 434-924-5118. *Application contact:* Beth A. Bailey, Director, Admissions Office, 434-924-5571, Fax: 434-982-2586, E-mail: bab7g@virginia.edu.

University of Washington, School of Medicine, Professional Program in Medicine, Seattle, WA 98195. Offers MD, MD/MPH, MD/PhD. *Accreditation:* LCME/AMA. *Students:* 773 full-time (373 women); includes 183 minority (14 African Americans, 27 American Indian/Alaska Native, 108 Asian Americans or Pacific Islanders, 34 Hispanic Americans). Average age 27. 3,775 applicants, 6% accepted, 182 enrolled. In 2006, 151 degrees awarded. *Entrance requirements:* MCAT or GRE, minimum 3 years of college. *Application deadline:* For fall admission, 11/1 for domestic students. Applications are processed on a rolling basis. Application fee: $35. Electronic applications accepted. *Financial support:* In 2006–07, 607 students received support. Institutionally sponsored loans and tuition waivers (partial) available. Support available to part-time students. Financial award application deadline: 2/28; financial award applicants required to submit FAFSA. *Application contact:* Patricia T. Fero, Admissions Officer, 206-543-7212, E-mail: askuwsom@u.washington.edu.

The University of Western Ontario, Faculty of Graduate Studies, Biosciences Division, Department of Family Medicine, London, ON N6A 5B8, Canada. Offers M Cl Sc. *Accreditation:* LCME/AMA. Part-time programs available. Postbaccalaureate distance learning degree programs offered (minimal on-campus study). *Faculty:* 18 full-time (5 women), 1 (woman) part-time/adjunct. *Students:* 2 full-time (1 woman), 12 part-time (6 women). Average age 45. 5 applicants, 100% accepted. *Degree requirements:* For master's, thesis. *Entrance requirements:* For master's, medical degree, minimum B average. Additional exam requirements/recommendations for international students: Required—TOEFL. *Application deadline:* For fall admission, 7/11 for domestic and international students. Applications are processed on a rolling basis. Application fee: $0. *Financial support:* Application deadline: 4/1. *Faculty research:* Family medicine education, dietary counseling, alcohol problems, palliative care support, multicultural health care. *Unit head:* Dr. Thomas Freeman, Chair, 519-661-2111 Ext. 82037, Fax: 519-661-3878, E-mail: tfreeman@uwo.ca. *Application contact:* Dr. Judith Brown, Graduate Chair, 519-858-5028.

The University of Western Ontario, Schulich School of Medicine and Dentistry, Professional Program in Medicine, London, ON N6A 5B8, Canada. Offers MD. *Accreditation:* LCME/AMA. *Application contact:* Darla McNeil, Officer of Admissions and Student Affairs, 519-661-3744 Ext. 86221, E-mail: darla.mcneil@fmd.uwo.ca.

University of Wisconsin–Madison, School of Medicine and Public Health, Professional Program in Medicine, Madison, WI 53706-1380. Offers MD. *Accreditation:* LCME/AMA. *Unit head:* Dr. Robert N. Golden, Dean, School of Medicine and Public Health, 608-263-4910, Fax: 608-265-3286, E-mail: rngolden@wisc.edu.

Vanderbilt University, School of Medicine, Nashville, TN 37240-1001. Offers MED, MPH, MS, Au D, PhD, MD/PhD. *Accreditation:* LCME/AMA (one or more programs are accredited). *Faculty:* 1,346 full-time, 934 part-time/adjunct. *Students:* 895 full-time. Average age 22. 3,699 applicants, 7% accepted, 104 enrolled. In 2006, 25 master's, 2 doctorates awarded. *Application deadline:* For fall admission, 10/15 for domestic students. Applications are processed on a rolling basis. Application fee: $50. Electronic applications accepted. *Expenses: Contact institution.* One-time fee: $30 full-time. Full-time tuition and fees vary according to course load, degree level and program. *Financial support:* In 2006–07, 333 students received support. Institutionally sponsored loans and scholarships/grants available. Financial award application deadline: 3/1; financial award applicants required to submit FAFSA. Total annual research expenditures: $190 million. *Unit head:* Dr. Steven G. Gabbe, Dean, 615-322-5191, E-mail: steven.gabbe@vanderbilt.edu. *Application contact:* Dr. John A. Zic, Associate Dean for Admissions, 615-322-2145, Fax: 615-343-8397.

Virginia Commonwealth University, Medical College of Virginia-Professional Programs, School of Medicine, Professional Program in Medicine, Richmond, VA 23284-9005. Offers MD, MD/PhD. *Accreditation:* LCME/AMA. *Students:* 4,765 applicants, 8% accepted, 183 enrolled. In 2006, 164 degrees awarded. *Entrance requirements:* MCAT. *Application deadline:* For fall admission, 11/15 for domestic students. Applications are processed on a rolling basis. Electronic applications accepted. *Expenses: Contact institution. Financial support:* Fellowships, research assistantships, teaching assistantships, career-related internships or fieldwork, Federal Work-Study, and tuition waivers (full and partial) available. *Unit head:* Dr. James M. Messmer, Associate Dean, 804-828-8691, E-mail: jmmessme@vcu.edu. *Application contact:* Dr. Cynthia M. Heldberg, Associate Dean, Admissions, 804-828-9629, Fax: 804-828-1246, E-mail: cmheldbe@vcu.edu.

Wake Forest University, School of Medicine, Professional Program in Medicine, Winston-Salem, NC 27109. Offers MD, MD/MA, MD/MBA, MD/MS, MD/PhD. *Accreditation:* LCME/AMA. *Entrance requirements:* MCAT, 32 hours of course work in science. Electronic applications accepted. *Faculty research:* Cancer, stroke, infectious diseases, membrane biology, nutrition.

Washington University in St. Louis, School of Medicine, Professional Program in Medicine, St. Louis, MO 63130-4899. Offers MD, MD/MA, MD/PhD. *Accreditation:* LCME/AMA. *Faculty:* 1,567 full-time (443 women), 1,406 part-time/adjunct (410 women). *Students:* 607 full-time (285 women); includes 216 minority (27 African Americans, 6 American Indian/Alaska Native, 157 Asian Americans or Pacific Islanders, 26 Hispanic Americans), 31 international. Average age 23. 4,064 applicants, 8% accepted, 122 enrolled. In 2006, 118 degrees awarded. *Entrance requirements:* MCAT. *Application deadline:* For fall admission, 12/31 for domestic and international students. Applications are processed on a rolling basis. Application fee: $50. Electronic applications accepted. *Expenses: Contact institution. Financial support:* Career-related internships or fieldwork and institutionally sponsored loans available. *Application contact:* Dr. W. Edwin Dodson, Associate Dean, 314-362-6848, Fax: 314-362-4658, E-mail: wumscoa@msnotes.wustl.edu.

Wayne State University, School of Medicine, Professional Program in Medicine, Detroit, MI 48202. Offers MD, MD/PhD. *Accreditation:* LCME/AMA. Part-time programs available. *Students:* 1,942 full-time (890 women), 78 part-time (49 women); includes 634 minority (210 African Americans, 4 American Indian/Alaska Native, 392 Asian Americans or Pacific Islanders, 28 Hispanic Americans), 295 international. Average age 29. In 2006, 241 degrees awarded. *Entrance requirements:* MCAT. Additional exam requirements/recommendations for international students: Required—TOEFL (minimum score 550 paper-based; 213 computer-based); Recommended—TWE (minimum score 6). *Application deadline:* For fall admission, 12/15 for domestic students, 6/1 for international students; for winter admission, 10/1 for international students; for spring admission, 2/1 for international students. Applications are processed on a rolling basis. Application fee: $20. Electronic applications accepted. *Financial support:* Fellowships available. *Unit head:* Dr. Charles F. Whitten, Associate Dean, 313-577-1546.

West Virginia University, School of Medicine, Professional Program in Medicine, Morgantown, WV 26506. Offers MD, MD/PhD. *Accreditation:* LCME/AMA. *Entrance requirements:* MCAT. *Expenses:* Tuition, state resident: full-time $4,926; part-time $276 per credit hour. Tuition, nonresident: full-time $14,278; part-time $796 per credit hour. Tuition and fees vary according to program.

Wright State University, School of Medicine, Professional Program in Medicine, Dayton, OH 45435. Offers MD. *Accreditation:* LCME/AMA. *Faculty:* 135 full-time (34 women), 17 part-time/adjunct (1 woman). *Students:* 366 full-time (201 women); includes 56 minority (34 African Americans, 18 Asian Americans or Pacific Islanders, 4 Hispanic Americans), 2 international. Average age 24. In 2006, 78 degrees awarded. *Entrance requirements:* MCAT. *Application deadline:* For fall admission, 11/15 for domestic students. Application fee: $50. *Financial support:* Research assistantships, teaching assistantships available. Financial award applicants required to submit FAFSA. *Unit head:* Dr. Paul G. Carlson, Associate Dean for Student Affairs and Admissions, 937-775-2934, Fax: 937-775-3672, E-mail: paul.carlson@wright.edu.

Yale University, School of Medicine, Professional Program in Medicine, New Haven, CT 06510. Offers MD. *Accreditation:* LCME/AMA. *Degree requirements:* For first-professional, thesis. *Entrance requirements:* MCAT. Electronic applications accepted.

Bioethics

Albany Medical College, Alden March Bioethics Institute, Albany, NY 12208-3479. Offers bioethics (MS); clinical ethics (Certificate). Part-time programs available. Postbaccalaureate distance learning degree programs offered (no on-campus study). *Students:* 1 applicant, 100% accepted, 1 enrolled. *Degree requirements:* For master's, thesis. *Application deadline:* For fall admission, 7/1 priority date for domestic students. Applications are processed on a rolling basis. Application fee: $50. Electronic applications accepted. *Faculty research:* Ethics nanotechnology, ethics in genetics, ethics in transplant, philosophy and bioethics, the states and bioethics. *Unit head:* Dr. Glenn E. McGee, Director, Alden March Bioethics Institute, 518-262-6082, Fax: 518-262-6856, E-mail: mcgeeoffice@bioethics.net. *Application contact:* Dr. Summer Johnson, Interim Director of Graduate Studies, 518-262-6082, Fax: 518-262-6856, E-mail: summer.johnson@bioethics.net.

Boston University, School of Public Health, Health Law, Bioethics and Human Rights Department, Boston, MA 02215. Offers MPH. *Students:* 16 full-time (13 women), 18 part-time (13 women); includes 4 minority (3 Asian Americans or Pacific Islanders, 1 Hispanic American), 3 international. Average age 25. *Entrance requirements:* For master's, GRE General Test. Additional exam requirements/recommendations for international students: Required—TOEFL or IELTS. *Application deadline:* For fall admission, 2/1 for domestic students; for spring admission, 10/15 for domestic students. Applications are processed on a rolling basis. Application fee: $95. Electronic applications accepted. *Expenses:* Tuition: Full-time $33,330; part-time $1,042 per credit. Required fees: $462; $40. *Financial support:* Career-related internships or fieldwork, Federal Work-Study, institutionally sponsored loans, scholarships/grants, and tuition waivers (partial) available. Support available to part-time students. *Unit head:* Prof. George Annas, Chair, 617-638-4626. *Application contact:* LePhan Quan, Assistant Director of Admissions, 617-638-4640, Fax: 617-638-5299, E-mail: asksph@bu.edu.

Case Western Reserve University, Frances Payne Bolton School of Nursing, Nursing/Bioethics Program, Cleveland, OH 44106. Offers MSN/MA. *Application deadline:* Applications are processed on a rolling basis. Application fee: $75. *Financial support:* Fellowships, research assistantships, teaching assistantships available. Financial award application deadline: 6/30. *Unit head:* Dr. Barbara Daly, Head, 216-368-5994, E-mail: barbara.daly@case.edu. *Application contact:* Peter Taylor, Recruitment and Retention Specialist, 216-368-0349, Fax: 216-368-0124, E-mail: peter.taylor@case.edu.

Case Western Reserve University, School of Graduate Studies and School of Medicine, Department of Bioethics, Cleveland, OH 44106. Offers MA, PhD, JD/MA, MSN/MA. Part-time programs available. *Faculty:* 10 full-time (4 women). *Students:* 21 full-time (11 women), 3 part-time (2 women); includes 3 minority (2 Asian Americans or Pacific Islanders, 1 Hispanic American), 7 international. Average age 24. 47 applicants, 81% accepted, 24 enrolled. In 2006, 25 degrees awarded. *Degree requirements:* For master's, comprehensive exam. *Entrance requirements:* For master's, GRE General Test. Additional exam requirements/recommendations for international students: Required—TOEFL. *Application deadline:* For fall admission, 3/1 priority date for domestic students. Application fee: $50. *Financial support:* In 2006–07, 7 students received support. Institutionally sponsored loans and tuition waivers (full and partial) available. Support available to part-time students. Financial award application deadline: 3/1. *Faculty research:* Ethical issues in genetics, conflicts of interest, organ donation, end-of-life decision making, clinical ethics consultation. *Unit head:* Stuart Youngner, Director, 216-368-6206, Fax: 216-368-8713, E-mail: stuart.youngner@case.edu. *Application contact:* Marie Norris, Graduate Coordinator, 216-368-8718, Fax: 216-368-8713, E-mail: man12@case.edu.

Cleveland State University, College of Graduate Studies, College of Liberal Arts and Social Sciences, Department of Philosophy, Cleveland, OH 44115. Offers bioethics (MA, Certificate); philosophy (MA). Part-time and evening/weekend programs available. *Faculty:* 9 full-time (4 women). *Students:* 9 full-time (1 woman), 8 part-time (3 women); includes 4 minority (3 African Americans, 1 Asian American or Pacific Islander), 1 international. Average age 33. 9 applicants, 44% accepted, 4 enrolled. In 2006, 3 degrees awarded. *Degree requirements:* For master's, thesis optional. *Entrance requirements:* For master's, minimum GPA of 2.75. Additional exam requirements/recommendations for international students: Required—TOEFL (minimum score 525 paper-based; 197 computer-based). *Application deadline:* For fall admission, 5/1 priority date for domestic and international students. Applications are processed on a rolling basis. Application fee: $30. *Financial support:* In 2006–07, 2 research assistantships with full tuition reimbursements (averaging $2,160 per year), 7 teaching assistantships with full tuition reimbursements (averaging $1,740 per year) were awarded; tuition waivers (full) and unspecified assistantships also available. *Faculty research:* Ethics, history of philosophy. *Unit head:* Dr. Diane Steinberg, Chairperson, 216-687-3900, Fax: 216-523-7482, E-mail: d.steinberg@csuohio.edu.

Drew University, Caspersen School of Graduate Studies, Program in Medical Humanities, Madison, NJ 07940-1493. Offers MMH, DMH, CMH. Part-time and evening/weekend programs available. *Degree requirements:* For master's, thesis. *Faculty research:* Biomedical ethics, medical narrative, history of medicine, medicine and the arts.

Duquesne University, Graduate School of Liberal Arts, Program in Health Care Ethics, Pittsburgh, PA 15282-0001. Offers MA, DHCE, PhD, Certificate. Part-time programs available. Postbaccalaureate distance learning degree programs offered (no on-campus study). *Faculty:* 2 full-time (0 women), 2 part-time/adjunct (both women). *Students:* 23 full-time (15 women), 15 part-time (8 women), 11 international. Average age 42. 16 applicants, 88% accepted, 13 enrolled. In 2006, 2 master's, 3 doctorates awarded. Terminal master's awarded for partial completion of doctoral program. *Degree requirements:* For master's, registration; for doctorate, 2 foreign languages, thesis/dissertation, comprehensive exam, registration. *Entrance requirements:* For master's, GRE General Test; for doctorate, master's degree in health care ethics. Additional exam requirements/recommendations for international students: Required—TOEFL. *Application deadline:* For fall admission, 8/15 for domestic students, 5/1 for international students. Applications are processed on a rolling basis. Application fee: $50. *Expenses:* Tuition: Part-time $723 per credit. Required fees: $71 per credit. Tuition and fees vary according to degree level and program. *Financial support:* Federal Work-Study available. Support available to part-time students. Financial award application deadline: 5/1. *Unit head:* Dr. Aaron Mackler, Director, 412-396-5985.

Indiana University–Purdue University Indianapolis, School of Liberal Arts, Department of Philosophy, Indianapolis, IN 46202-2896. Offers American philosophy (Certificate); bioethics (Certificate); philosophy (MA, PhD). Part-time programs available. *Faculty:* 12 full-time (1 woman), 1 part-time/adjunct (0 women). *Students:* 4 full-time (1 woman), 14 part-time (6 women); includes 2 minority (both African Americans) Average age 32. 12 applicants, 75% accepted, 7 enrolled. *Degree requirements:* For master's, thesis optional. *Entrance requirements:* For master's, GRE. Additional exam requirements/recommendations for international students: Required—TOEFL. *Application deadline:* For fall admission, 3/1 priority date for domestic and international students; for spring admission, 11/15 for domestic and international students. Applications are processed on a rolling basis. Application fee: $50. Electronic applications accepted. *Expenses:* Tuition, state resident: full-time $5,437; part-time $227 per credit hour.

Bioethics

Indiana University–Purdue University Indianapolis (continued)
Tuition, nonresident: full-time $15,694; part-time $654 per credit hour. Required fees: $620. Tuition and fees vary according to course load, campus/location and program. *Financial support:* In 2006–07, 6 students received support, including 3 research assistantships with full tuition reimbursements available (averaging $9,000 per year). Financial award application deadline: 1/15; financial award applicants required to submit FAFSA. *Faculty research:* American philosophy, Peirce bioethics, metaphysics, ethical theory. *Unit head:* Dr. John Tilley, Associate Professor and Chair, 317-274-4690, Fax: 317-278-4579, E-mail: jtilley@iupui.edu. *Application contact:* Dr. Jason Thomas Eberl, Assistant Professor and Graduate Co-Director, 317-278-9239, Fax: 317-278-4579, E-mail: jeberl@iupui.edu.

Kansas City University of Medicine and Biosciences, College of Biosciences, Kansas City, MO 64106-1453. Offers bioethics (MA); biomedical sciences (MS). *Faculty:* 23 full-time, 4 part-time/adjunct. *Students:* 28 full-time (15 women); includes 5 minority (2 African Americans, 3 Asian Americans or Pacific Islanders). Average age 26. 125 applicants, 24% accepted, 25 enrolled.Application fee: $30. *Unit head:* Dr. Douglas Rushing, Dean, College of Biosciences, 816-283-2205. *Application contact:* Phil D. Byrne, Vice President of Admissions, 816-283-2392, Fax: 816-460-0506, E-mail: pbyrne@kcumb.edu.

Loma Linda University, Faculty of Religion, Program in Biomedical and Clinical Ethics, Loma Linda, CA 92350. Offers MA, Certificate. *Entrance requirements:* For master's, GRE General Test.

Loyola Marymount University, Graduate Division, College of Liberal Arts, Program in Bioethics, Los Angeles, CA 90045-2659. Offers MA. *Faculty:* 3 full-time (0 women), 1 part-time/adjunct (0 women). *Students:* 14 full-time (7 women), 15 part-time (10 women); includes 12 minority (2 African Americans, 4 Asian Americans or Pacific Islanders, 6 Hispanic Americans), 3 international. Average age 42. 14 applicants, 29% accepted, 3 enrolled. *Application deadline:* For fall admission, 3/1 for domestic students; for spring admission, 10/1 for domestic students. Application fee: $50. *Financial support:* In 2006–07, research assistantships (averaging $12,370 per year). Financial award application deadline: 6/1; financial award applicants required to submit FAFSA. *Unit head:* Dr. Roberto Dell'Oro, Director, 310-338-2752, E-mail: rdelloro@lmu.edu.

McGill University, Faculty of Graduate and Postdoctoral Studies, Faculty of Arts, Department of Philosophy, Montréal, QC H3A 2T5, Canada. Offers bioethics (MA); philosophy (PhD). Terminal master's awarded for partial completion of doctoral program. *Degree requirements:* For master's, thesis, registration; for doctorate, 2 foreign languages, thesis/dissertation, registration. *Entrance requirements:* For master's, GRE General Test, minimum GPA of 3.0; for doctorate, GRE General Test, writing sample. Additional exam requirements/recommendations for international students: Required—TOEFL (minimum score 550 paper-based; 213 computer-based), IELTS (minimum score 7). *Faculty research:* Ancient philosophy, seventeenth- and eighteenth-century philosophy, philosophy of language and mind, aesthetics, moral and political philosophy.

McGill University, Faculty of Graduate and Postdoctoral Studies, Faculty of Law, Montréal, QC H3A 2T5, Canada. Offers air and space law (LL M, DCL, Certificate); bioethics (LL M); comparative law (LL M, DCL, Certificate); law (LL M, DCL). Applications for LL M with specialization in bioethics are made initially through the Biomedical Ethics Unit in the Faculty of Medicine. *Degree requirements:* For master's, thesis (for some programs), registration; for doctorate, thesis/dissertation, comprehensive exam, registration. *Entrance requirements:* For master's, law degree, minimum GPA of 3.0, knowledge of French preferred or required depending on subject; for doctorate, LL M. Additional exam requirements/recommendations for international students: Required—TOEFL (minimum score 600 paper-based; 250 computer-based), IELTS (minimum score 8), For air and space law degrees: TOEFL 575 paper-based, 233 computer-based; IELTS 7.0. Electronic applications accepted. *Faculty research:* International law, international business law, human rights, legal theory and traditions, regulation and technology.

McGill University, Faculty of Graduate and Postdoctoral Studies, Faculty of Medicine, Department of Medicine, Montréal, QC H3A 2T5, Canada. Offers experimental medicine (M Sc, PhD), including bioethics (M Sc), experimental medicine.

McGill University, Faculty of Graduate and Postdoctoral Studies, Faculty of Medicine, Program in Experimental Medicine, Montréal, QC H3A 2T5, Canada. Offers bioethics (M Sc); experimental medicine (M Sc, PhD). Terminal master's awarded for partial completion of doctoral program. *Degree requirements:* For master's and doctorate, thesis/dissertation. *Entrance requirements:* For doctorate, B Sc or M Sc in medical field or MD, minimum GPA of 3.4. Additional exam requirements/recommendations for international students: Required—TOEFL.

Medical College of Wisconsin, Graduate School of Biomedical Sciences, Program in Bioethics, Milwaukee, WI 53226-0509. Offers MA, MD/MA. Part-time programs available. *Degree requirements:* For master's, thesis. *Entrance requirements:* For master's, GRE General Test. Additional exam requirements/recommendations for international students: Required—TOEFL. *Faculty research:* Ethics committees and consultation, ethics of managed care, discussion of code status by physicians.

Michigan State University, College of Human Medicine and The Graduate School, Graduate Programs in Human Medicine, Program in Bioethics, Humanities, and Society, East Lansing, MI 48824. Offers MA. *Students:* 5 full-time (1 woman), 5 part-time (4 women); includes 2 minority (both African Americans) Average age 30. 10 applicants, 70% accepted. In 2006, 5 degrees awarded. *Degree requirements:* For master's, thesis or alternative, oral defense of thesis. *Entrance requirements:* Additional exam requirements/recommendations for international students: Required—TOEFL (minimum score 550 paper-based; 213 computer-based), Michigan State University ELT (85), Michigan ELAB (83). Electronic applications accepted. *Expenses:* Tuition, state resident: part-time $346 per credit hour. Tuition, nonresident: part-time $730 per credit hour. Tuition and fees vary according to program. *Financial support:* In 2006–07, 2 research assistantships with tuition reimbursements (averaging $12,240 per year) were awarded. *Unit head:* Dr. Harry Perlstadt, Director and Graduate Advisor, 517-432-2691, Fax: 517-353-3289, E-mail: bhs@msu.edu. *Application contact:* Laurie Rashid, Graduate Secretary, 517-432-2691, Fax: 517-353-3289, E-mail: laurie.rashid@ht.msu.edu.

Midwestern University, Glendale Campus, College of Health Sciences, Arizona Campus, Program in Bioethics, Glendale, AZ 85308. Offers MA, Certificate. *Students:* 1 (woman) full-time, 6 part-time (5 women); includes 1 minority (Asian American or Pacific Islander) Average age 45. 12 applicants, 83% accepted, 7 enrolled. In 2006, 6 degrees awarded. Application fee: $50. *Unit head:* Dr. Gregory S. Loeben, Director, 623-572-3622. *Application contact:* James Walters, Director of Admissions, 888-247-9277, Fax: 623-572-3340, E-mail: admissaz@midwestern.edu.

Mount Sinai School of Medicine of New York University, Graduate School of Biological Sciences, The Bioethics Program, New York, NY 10029-6504. Offers MS.

See Close-Up on page 2209.

Rush University, College of Health Sciences, Program in Healthcare Ethics, Chicago, IL 60612-3832. Offers MA, Graduate Certificate. Part-time programs available. *Degree requirements:* For master's, oral presentation of thesis. *Entrance requirements:* For master's, GRE General Test, minimum GPA of 3.0. Electronic applications accepted. *Faculty research:* Daily spirituality in the disease process, training psychiatry residents in spirituality, defining and screening for spiritual struggle.

Saint Louis University, Graduate School, Center for Health Care Ethics, St. Louis, MO 63103-2097. Offers clinical health care ethics (Certificate); health care ethics (PhD). *Faculty:* 4 full-time (1 woman), 1 (woman) part-time/adjunct. *Students:* 14 full-time (7 women), 20 part-time (8 women); includes 3 minority (all Hispanic Americans), 2 international. Average age 37. 37 applicants, 89% accepted, 16 enrolled. In 2006, 1 degree awarded. *Degree requirements:* For doctorate, thesis/dissertation, comprehensive exam. *Entrance requirements:* For doctorate, GRE General Test, master's degree in ethics or a health field, basic competencies in philosophical and applied ethics. Additional exam requirements/recommendations for international students: Required—TOEFL (minimum score 525 paper-based; 194 computer-based). *Application deadline:* For fall admission, 7/1 for domestic and international students. Applications are processed on a rolling basis. Application fee: $40. *Expenses:* Tuition: Part-time $800 per credit hour. Required fees: $105 per semester. *Financial support:* In 2006–07, 11 students received support, including 6 teaching assistantships with full tuition reimbursements available (averaging $11,000 per year); career-related internships or fieldwork, Federal Work-Study, scholarships/grants, traineeships, health care benefits, tuition waivers (full), and unspecified assistantships also available. Support available to part-time students. Financial award application deadline: 6/1; financial award applicants required to submit FAFSA. *Faculty research:* Bioterrorism and ethics, genomics and stem cell research, institutional review boards and ethics committees, medical error and patient safety, pain management and palliative care. *Unit head:* Rev. Gerard Magill, PhD, Executive Director, 314-977-6666, Fax: 314-977-5150, E-mail: magill@slu.edu. *Application contact:* Gary Behrman, Associate Dean of the Graduate School, 314-977-3827, E-mail: behrmang@slu.edu.

Trinity International University, Trinity Graduate School, Deerfield, IL 60015-1284. Offers bioethics (MA); communication and culture (MA); counseling psychology (MA); instructional leadership (M Ed); teaching (MA). Part-time and evening/weekend programs available. Postbaccalaureate distance learning degree programs offered (minimal on-campus study). *Faculty:* 5 full-time (4 women), 39 part-time/adjunct (13 women). *Students:* 109 full-time (85 women), 130 part-time (81 women). In 2006, 29 degrees awarded. *Degree requirements:* For master's, comprehensive exam. *Entrance requirements:* For master's, GRE General Test or MAT, minimum undergraduate GPA of 3.0. Additional exam requirements/recommendations for international students: Required—TOEFL (minimum score 580 paper-based; 237 computer-based), TWE (minimum score 4). *Application deadline:* For fall admission, 7/15 priority date for domestic and international students. Applications are processed on a rolling basis. Application fee: $25. Electronic applications accepted. *Expenses:* Tuition: Full-time $13,200; part-time $630 per hour. Required fees: $43 per semester. *Financial support:* Career-related internships or fieldwork, Federal Work-Study, institutionally sponsored loans, and tuition waivers (partial) available. Support available to part-time students. Financial award application deadline: 4/1; financial award applicants required to submit FAFSA. *Unit head:* Dr. James Stamoolis, Academic Dean, 847-317-7001, Fax: 847-317-4786. *Application contact:* Ken Botton, Director of Enrollment Services for University Records and Graduate Admissions, 800-533-0975, Fax: 847-317-8097, E-mail: kbotton@tiu.edu.

Union Graduate College, Center for Bioethics and Clinical Leadership, Program in Bioethics, Schenectady, NY 12308-3107. Offers MS. Part-time programs available. Postbaccalaureate distance learning degree programs offered (minimal on-campus study). *Students:* Average age 40. 27 applicants, 89% accepted, 20 enrolled. In 2006, 13 master's awarded. *Degree requirements:* For master's, capstone course, project. *Entrance requirements:* For master's, letters of recommendation. Additional exam requirements/recommendations for international students: Required—TOEFL (minimum score 550 paper-based; 213 computer-based). Application fee: $60. *Expenses:* Contact institution. *Financial support:* Federal Work-Study, scholarships/grants, health care benefits, and tuition waivers (partial) available. Support available to part-time students. Financial award applicants required to submit FAFSA. *Application contact:* Rhonda Sheehan, Director of Graduate Admissions Registrar, 518-388-6238, Fax: 518-388-6686, E-mail: sheehanr@union.edu.

See Close-Up on page 2209.

Université de Montréal, Faculty of Graduate Studies, Programs in Bioethics, Montréal, QC H3C 3J7, Canada. Offers MA, DESS. *Students:* 26 full-time (23 women), 18 part-time (15 women). 28 applicants, 50% accepted, 9 enrolled. In 2006, 9 master's, 3 DESSs awarded. *Application deadline:* For fall admission, 2/1 priority date for domestic students; for winter admission, 11/1 priority date for domestic students; for spring admission, 2/1 priority date for domestic students. Application fee: $30. Electronic applications accepted. *Unit head:* Beatrice Godard, Director, 514-343-6832, Fax: 514-343-5738, E-mail: beatrice.godard@umontreal.ca.

University of Pennsylvania, School of Arts and Sciences, Program in Bioethics, Philadelphia, PA 19104. Offers M Bioethics, JD/M Bioethics. Electronic applications accepted.

University of Pittsburgh, School of Arts and Sciences, Center for Bioethics and Health Law, Pittsburgh, PA 15260. Offers bioethics (MA). Part-time programs available. *Faculty:* 4 full-time (1 woman), 3 part-time/adjunct (1 woman). *Students:* 12 full-time (6 women), 6 part-time (2 women). 16 applicants, 56% accepted, 5 enrolled. *Degree requirements:* For master's, thesis. *Entrance requirements:* For master's, GRE General Test, letters of recommendation, writing sample. Additional exam requirements/recommendations for international students: Required—TOEFL. *Application deadline:* For fall admission, 2/1 priority date for domestic students, 6/30 for international students. Applications are processed on a rolling basis. Application fee: $50. Electronic applications accepted. *Financial support:* Tuition waivers (partial) available. *Faculty research:* End of life care, ethics and genetics, health law and policy, organ donation and transplantation, research ethics. *Unit head:* Dr. Lisa S. Parker, Director of Graduate Education, 412-647-5780, Fax: 412-647-5877, E-mail: lisap@pitt.edu. *Application contact:* Karen E. Ferris, Administrative Assistant, 412-647-5785, Fax: 412-647-5877, E-mail: bioethic@pitt.edu.

The University of Tennessee, Graduate School, College of Arts and Sciences, Department of Philosophy, Knoxville, TN 37996. Offers medical ethics (MA, PhD); philosophy (MA, PhD); religious studies (MA). Part-time programs available. *Students:* 39 (9 women); includes 1 African American, 1 Asian American or Pacific Islander, 1 Hispanic American 1 international. In 2006, 10 degrees awarded. *Degree requirements:* For master's, thesis or alternative; for doctorate, one foreign language, thesis/dissertation. *Entrance requirements:* For master's and doctorate, GRE General Test, minimum GPA of 2.7. Additional exam requirements/recommendations for international students: Required—TOEFL. *Application deadline:* For fall admission, 2/1 priority date for domestic students. Applications are processed on a rolling basis. Application fee: $35. Electronic applications accepted. *Expenses:* Tuition, state resident: full-time $5,574. Tuition, nonresident: full-time $16,840. Required fees: $792. *Financial support:* In 2006–07, 23 teaching assistantships were awarded; fellowships, research assistantships, Federal Work-Study, institutionally sponsored loans, and unspecified assistantships also available. Financial award application deadline: 2/1; financial award applicants required to submit FAFSA. *Unit head:* Dr. John Hardnig, Head, 865-974-3255, Fax: 865-974-3509, E-mail: jhardnig@utk.edu. *Application contact:* Dr. John Nolt, Graduate Representative, 865-974-7218, E-mail: nolt@utk.edu.

University of Virginia, College and Graduate School of Arts and Sciences, Center for Biomedical Ethics, Charlottesville, VA 22903. Offers bioethics (MA). *Students:* 1 (woman) full-time. Average age 25. 6 applicants, 0% accepted. In 2006, 2 degrees awarded. *Degree requirements:* For master's, thesis optional. *Entrance requirements:* For master's, GRE General Test. Application fee: $60. Electronic applications accepted. *Financial support:* Applicants required to submit FAFSA. *Unit head:* Jonathan Moreno, Director, Center for Biomedical Ethics, 434-924-5974, E-mail: jdm8n@virginia.edu. *Application contact:* Peter C. Brunjes, Associate Dean for Graduate Programs and Research, 434-924-7184, Fax: 434-924-6737, E-mail: grad-a-s@virginia.edu.

Naturopathic Medicine

Bastyr University, Graduate and Professional Programs, School of Naturopathic Medicine, Kenmore, WA 98028-4966. Offers midwifery (Certificate); naturopathic medicine (ND). *Accreditation:* CNME; MEAC. *Students:* 488 full-time (400 women), 2 part-time (1 woman); includes 64 minority (15 African Americans, 32 Asian Americans or Pacific Islanders, 17 Hispanic Americans), 13 international. Average age 29. 271 applicants, 73% accepted, 120 enrolled. In 2006, 83 doctorates, 1 other advanced degree awarded. *Degree requirements:* For doctorate, comprehensive exam. *Entrance requirements:* For doctorate and Certificate, BS or BA with 1 year of course work in biology, chemistry, organic chemistry and physics. Additional exam requirements/recommendations for international students: Required—TOEFL (minimum score 550 paper-based; 213 computer-based). *Application deadline:* For fall admission, 2/1 priority date for domestic and international students. Applications are processed on a rolling basis. Application fee: $75. *Expenses:* Tuition: Full-time $18,845; part-time $325 per credit hour. Required fees: $1,365. Tuition and fees vary according to course load and degree level. *Financial support:* Career-related internships or fieldwork, Federal Work-Study, and scholarships/grants available. Support available to part-time students. Financial award application deadline: 4/15; financial award applicants required to submit FAFSA. *Unit head:* Dr. Gannady Raskin, Dean, 425-823-1300, Fax: 425-823-6222. *Application contact:* Admissions Office, 425-602-3330, Fax: 425-602-3090, E-mail: admiss@bastyr.edu.

See Close-Up on page 2201.

Canadian College of Naturopathic Medicine, Doctoral Program in Naturopathic Medicine, Toronto, ON M2K 1E2, Canada. Offers ND. *Accreditation:* CNME. *Faculty:* 32 full-time, 85 part-time/adjunct. *Students:* 454 full-time (333 women), 35 part-time (29 women). Average age 27. 163 applicants, 87% accepted, 105 enrolled. In 2006, 130 degrees awarded. *Degree requirements:* For doctorate, 12 month internship. *Entrance requirements:* For doctorate, 1 year of course work in general biology, general chemistry, general psychology; 1 semester of course work in organic chemistry and biochemistry and 1 semester course in the humanities. Additional exam requirements/recommendations for international students: Recommended—TOEFL (minimum score 580 paper-based; 257 computer-based). *Application deadline:* For fall admission, 1/31 priority date for domestic and international students; for winter admission, 5/30 priority date for domestic and international students; for spring admission, 11/30 priority date for domestic and international students. Applications are processed on a rolling basis. Application fee: $150. Tuition and fees charges are reported in Canadian dollars. *Expenses:* Tuition: Full-time $17,239 Canadian dollars; part-time $271 Canadian dollars per credit. Required fees: $430 Canadian dollars. One-time fee: $50 Canadian dollars full-time. Tuition and fees vary according to course load. *Financial support:* In 2006–07, 280 students received support, including 3 research assistantships, 2 teaching assistantships; career-related internships or fieldwork, scholarships/grants, and health care benefits also available. Support available to part-time students. Financial award application deadline: 7/31. *Faculty research:* Botanical medicine, clinical nutrition, North American Naturopathic Research Agenda, reporting guidelines in clinical pharmacology trials, reporting guidelines in blood literature. *Unit head:* Bob Bernhardt, President/CEO, 416-498-1255, Fax: 416-498-3197, E-mail: bbernhardt@ccnm.edu. *Application contact:* Student Services, 416-498-1225 Ext. 245, Fax: 416-498-3197, E-mail: info@ccnm.edu.

See Close-Up on page 2203.

National College of Natural Medicine, Program in Naturopathic Medicine, Portland, OR 97201. Offers naturopathic medicine (ND). *Accreditation:* CNME. *Faculty:* 13 full-time (5 women), 53 part-time/adjunct (31 women). *Students:* 382 full-time (308 women); includes 44 minority (4 African Americans, 2 American Indian/Alaska Native, 11 Asian Americans or Pacific Islanders, 27 Hispanic Americans), 4 international. Average age 29. 199 applicants, 83% accepted, 97 enrolled. In 2006, 65 degrees awarded. *Median time to degree:* Of those who began their doctoral program in fall 1998, 95% received their degree in 8 years or less. *Entrance requirements:* Additional exam requirements/recommendations for international students: Required—TOEFL (minimum score 550 paper-based; 213 computer-based). *Application deadline:* For fall admission, 11/1 priority date for domestic and international students; for winter admission, 2/1 priority date for domestic and international students. Applications are processed on a rolling basis. Application fee: $75. *Expenses:* Tuition: Full-time $19,698; part-time $273 per credit. Required fees: $60. One-time fee: $50 full-time. Tuition and fees vary according to program. *Financial support:* In 2006–07, 308 students received support. Federal Work-Study and scholarships/grants available. Financial award application deadline: 4/30; financial award applicants required to submit FAFSA. *Faculty research:* Diet and diabetes, whole practice research, cruciferous vegetables and cancer, natural medicine and immune function, taraxacum and diuretics. Total annual research expenditures: $350,000. *Unit head:* Dr. Rita Bettenburg, Dean, 503-552-1761, Fax: 503-499-0022, E-mail: rbettenburg@ncnm.edu. *Application contact:* Kendra Lapp, Admissions Coordinator, 503-552-1660, Fax: 503-499-0027, E-mail: admissions@ncnm.edu.

National University of Health Sciences, College of Professional Studies, Lombard, IL 60148-4583. Offers acupuncture (MSAC); chiropractic medicine (DC); naturopathic medicine (ND); Oriental medicine (MSOM). *Accreditation:* CCE. *Faculty:* 49 full-time (10 women), 40 part-time/adjunct (15 women). *Students:* 394 full-time (186 women); includes 80 minority (19 African Americans, 47 Asian Americans or Pacific Islanders, 14 Hispanic Americans), 12 international. Average age 27. In 2006, 86 DCs, 2 master's awarded. *Degree requirements:* For first-professional, internship, community service. *Entrance requirements:* Bachelor's degree with strong background in sciences. Additional exam requirements/recommendations for international students: Required—TOEFL (minimum score 500 paper-based; 172 computer-based). *Application deadline:* For fall admission, 8/22 for domestic and international students; for winter admission, 11/22 for domestic and international students; for spring admission, 4/18 for domestic and international students. Applications are processed on a rolling basis. Application fee: $55. Electronic applications accepted. *Expenses:* Tuition: Full-time $16,187. Full-time tuition and fees vary according to course load. *Financial support:* Fellowships, research assistantships, teaching assistantships, Federal Work-Study, scholarships/grants, and tuition waivers (partial) available. Support available to part-time students. Financial award applicants required to submit FAFSA. *Faculty research:* Chiropractic procedures, spinal stenosis, evidence-based practices, secondary effects of manual procedures, autonomic effects of manual procedures. Total annual research expenditures: $502,000. *Unit head:* Dr. James F. Winterstein, President, 630-889-6604, Fax: 630-889-6600, E-mail: jwinterstein@nuhs.edu. *Application contact:* Victoria Sweeney, Director of Admissions, 800-826-6285 Ext. 6572, Fax: 630-889-6554, E-mail: v.sweeney@nuhs.edu.

See Close-Up on page 2161.

Southwest College of Naturopathic Medicine and Health Sciences, Program in Naturopathic Medicine, Tempe, AZ 85282. Offers ND. *Accreditation:* CNME. *Faculty:* 21 full-time (7 women), 30 part-time/adjunct (20 women). *Students:* 330 full-time (249 women), 5 part-time (4 women); includes 73 minority (36 African Americans, 4 American Indian/Alaska Native, 18 Asian Americans or Pacific Islanders, 15 Hispanic Americans), 13 international. Average age 31. 239 applicants, 54% accepted, 99 enrolled. In 2006, 75 degrees awarded. *Entrance requirements:* For doctorate, minimum GPA of 3.0, letters of recommendation. *Application deadline:* For fall admission, 7/1 priority date for domestic students; for spring admission, 2/1 priority date for domestic students. Applications are processed on a rolling basis. Application fee: $65 ($90 for international students). *Expenses:* Tuition: Full-time $5,456; part-time $4,331 per quarter. *Financial support:* Federal Work-Study and scholarships/grants available. Support available to part-time students. Financial award application deadline: 7/1; financial award applicants required to submit FAFSA. *Faculty research:* Environmental toxicology, microbial infection, diabetes, homeopathy. Total annual research expenditures: $236,458. *Unit head:* Dr. Richard Eberst, Provost, 480-858-9100 Ext. 241, Fax: 480-858-9116, E-mail: r.eberst@scnm.edu.

Announcement: Southwest College offers an accredited, 4-year, professional-level medical program resulting in a Doctor of Naturopathic Medicine Degree (ND). Studies concentrate on basic sciences and natural approaches to therapy; strong emphases on disease prevention and an integrated clinical education. Graduates sit for professional board exams for licensure as naturopathic physicians within licensed states. For more information, visit www.scnm.edu.

See Close-Up on page 2207.

University of Bridgeport, College of Naturopathic Medicine, Bridgeport, CT 06604. Offers ND. *Accreditation:* CNME. *Faculty:* 6 full-time (3 women), 25 part-time/adjunct (7 women). *Students:* 109 full-time (80 women), 2 part-time (1 woman); includes 34 minority (18 African Americans, 1 American Indian/Alaska Native, 10 Asian Americans or Pacific Islanders, 5 Hispanic Americans), 14 international. Average age 34. 91 applicants, 36% accepted, 24 enrolled. In 2006, 18 degrees awarded. *Entrance requirements:* For doctorate, minimum GPA of 2.5. *Application deadline:* For fall admission, 8/1 priority date for domestic students; for spring admission, 12/1 for domestic students. Applications are processed on a rolling basis. Application fee: $75. Electronic applications accepted. *Financial support:* In 2006–07, 80 students received support. Federal Work-Study, institutionally sponsored loans, and scholarships/grants available. Financial award application deadline: 4/1; financial award applicants required to submit FAFSA. *Unit head:* Dr. Guru Sandesh Singh Khalsa, Dean, 203-576-4110. *Application contact:* Michael Grandison, Director of Admissions, 203-576-4108, Fax: 203-576-4107, E-mail: natmed@bridgeport.edu.

Osteopathic Medicine

A.T. Still University of Health Sciences, Kirksville College of Osteopathic Medicine, Kirksville, MO 63501. Offers biomedical sciences (MS); osteopathic medicine (DO). *Accreditation:* AOsA. *Faculty:* 71 full-time (20 women), 17 part-time/adjunct (1 woman). *Students:* 695 full-time (285 women), 20 part-time (11 women); includes 117 minority (7 African Americans, 5 American Indian/Alaska Native, 93 Asian Americans or Pacific Islanders, 12 Hispanic Americans), 12 international. Average age 27. 2,911 applicants, 184 enrolled. In 2006, 156 DOs, 4 master's awarded. *Degree requirements:* For DO, level I and 2 CE comprehensive osteopathic Medical Licensing Exam and COMLEX PE; for master's, thesis. *Entrance requirements:* For DO, MCAT, minimum undergraduate GPA of 2.5 (cumulative and science) or 90 semester hours with minimum GPA of 3.5 (cumulative and science) and minimum MCAT of 28; for master's, GRE, MCAT, or DAT, minimum undergraduate GPA of 2.5 (cumulative and science). *Application deadline:* For fall admission, 2/1 for domestic and international students. Applications are processed on a rolling basis. Application fee: $60. Electronic applications accepted. *Expenses:* Contact institution. *Financial support:* In 2006–07, 624 students received support, including 8 fellowships with full tuition reimbursements available (averaging $12,000 per year); career-related internships or fieldwork, Federal Work-Study, institutionally sponsored loans, and scholarships/grants also available. Financial award application deadline: 5/1; financial award applicants required to submit FAFSA. *Faculty research:* Osteopathic manipulation and pneumonia in the elderly, basis of hypocholestrolemic drug-induced cataracts, membrane structure in cataracts, role of caveolin in the ocular lens, cell membrane. Total annual research expenditures: $869,450. *Unit head:* Dr. Philip C. Slocum, Vice President for Medical Affairs and Dean, 660-626-2354, Fax: 660-626-2080, E-mail: pslocum@atsu.edu. *Application contact:* Donna Sparks, Associate Director for Admissions, 660-626-2237, Fax: 660-626-2969, E-mail: admissions@atsu.edu.

Des Moines University, College of Osteopathic Medicine, Des Moines, IA 50312-4104. Offers DO. *Accreditation:* AOsA. *Faculty:* 40 full-time (16 women), 22 part-time/adjunct (4 women). *Students:* 814 full-time (383 women); includes 72 minority (8 African Americans, 1 American Indian/Alaska Native, 48 Asian Americans or Pacific Islanders, 15 Hispanic Americans), 12 international. Average age 25. 1,637 applicants, 25% accepted, 215 enrolled. In 2006, 198 degrees awarded. *Median time to degree:* 4 years full-time. *Degree requirements:* For first-professional, National Board of Osteopathic Medical Examiners Exam Level 1 and 2. *Entrance requirements:* MCAT, minimum GPA of 3.0; 8 hours of course work in biology, chemistry, organic, physics; 6 hours of course work in English; interview. *Application deadline:* For fall admission, 2/1 for domestic students, 2/1 priority date for international students. Applications are processed on a rolling basis. Application fee: $50. Electronic applications accepted. *Expenses:* Contact institution. *Financial support:* In 2006–07, 102 students received support, including 9 fellowships with tuition reimbursements available (averaging $6,000 per year); institutionally sponsored loans, scholarships/grants, and university employment also available. Support available to part-time students. Financial award application deadline: 7/15; financial award applicants required to submit FAFSA. *Faculty research:* Cardiovascular, infectious disease, cancer immunology, cell signaling nociception. *Unit head:* Dr. Kendall Reed, Dean, 515-271-1515, Fax: 515-271-1532, E-mail: kendall.reed@dmu.edu. *Application contact:* Jamie Rehmann, Director of Admissions, 515-271-1451, Fax: 515-271-7163, E-mail: doadmit@dmu.edu.

Edward Via Virginia College of Osteopathic Medicine, Graduate Program, Blacksburg, VA 24060. Offers DO.

Georgia Campus–Philadelphia College of Osteopathic Medicine, Program in Osteopathic Medicine, Suwanee, GA 30024. Offers DO. *Accreditation:* AOsA.

Kansas City University of Medicine and Biosciences, College of Osteopathic Medicine, Kansas City, MO 64106-1453. Offers DO, DO/MA, DO/MBA. *Accreditation:* AOsA. *Faculty:* 44 full-time (13 women), 13 part-time/adjunct (7 women). *Students:* 960 full-time (480 women). Average age 25. 2,800 applicants, 17% accepted, 268 enrolled. In 2006, 203 DOs awarded. *Degree requirements:* For first-professional, National Board Exam. *Entrance requirements:* MCAT, interview. *Application deadline:* For fall admission, 4/1 for domestic students. Applications are processed on a rolling basis. Application fee: $50. *Financial support:* In 2006–07, 54 students received support, including 2 fellowships with full tuition reimbursements available; career-related internships or fieldwork, institutionally sponsored loans, and scholarships/grants also available. Financial award application deadline: 4/1; financial award applicants required to submit FAFSA. *Faculty research:* 2-Chloroadenine in DNA use in controlling leukemia, dietary isoprenoids role in tumor cell control, preventive medicine and public health research of maternal and child health, nonenzymatic glycosylation in cardiac tissue. Total annual research expenditures: $300,000. *Unit head:* Dr. Sandra K. Willsie, Vice President for Academic Affairs/

Osteopathic Medicine

Kansas City University of Medicine and Biosciences (continued)
Dean, 816-283-2308, Fax: 816-283-2347, E-mail: swillsie@kcumb.edu. *Application contact:* Phil D. Byrne, Vice President of Admissions, 816-283-2392, Fax: 816-460-0506, E-mail: pbyrne@kcumb.edu.

Lake Erie College of Osteopathic Medicine, Professional Programs, Erie, PA 16509-1025. Offers biomedical sciences (Postbaccalaureate Certificate); medical education (MS); osteopathic medicine (DO); pharmacy (Pharm D). *Accreditation:* ACPE; AOsA. *Faculty:* 85 full-time (20 women), 84 part-time/adjunct (19 women). *Students:* 1,355 full-time (700 women); includes 261 minority (57 African Americans, 3 American Indian/Alaska Native, 171 Asian Americans or Pacific Islanders, 30 Hispanic Americans). Average age 25. 4,526 applicants, 15% accepted, 366 enrolled. In 2006, 198 DOs, 88 other advanced degrees awarded. *Median time to degree:* First professional degree–4 years full-time; master's–2 years full-time; Postbaccalaureate Certificate–3 years full-time. *Degree requirements:* For first professional degree, National Osteopathic Medical Licensing Exam, Levels 1 and 2; for Postbaccalaureate Certificate, North American Pharmacist Licensure Examination (NAPLEX). *Entrance requirements:* For first professional degree, MCAT, minimum GPA of 3.2, letters of recommendation; for Postbaccalaureate Certificate, PCAT, letters of recommendation, minimum GPA of 3.5. *Application deadline:* For fall admission, 3/1 for domestic students. Applications are processed on a rolling basis. Application fee: $50. Electronic applications accepted. *Expenses:* Tuition: Full-time $25,000. Required fees: $1,095. *Financial support:* In 2006–07, 1,238 students received support. Institutionally sponsored loans and scholarships/grants available. Financial award application deadline: 6/30; financial award applicants required to submit FAFSA. *Faculty research:* Cardiac smooth and skeletal muscle mechanics, chemotherapeutics and vitamins, osteopathic manipulation. *Unit head:* Dr. Silvia M. Ferretti, Provost Dean Vice President of Academic Affairs, 814-866-6641, Fax: 814-866-8123. *Application contact:* Amy Rowe, Admissions Coordinator, 814-866-6641, Fax: 814-866-8123, E-mail: arowe@lecom.edu.

Michigan State University, College of Osteopathic Medicine, Professional Program in Osteopathic Medicine, East Lansing, MI 48824. Offers DO. *Accreditation:* AOsA. *Students:* 702 full-time (376 women), 7 part-time (4 women); includes 133 minority (23 African Americans, 4 American Indian/Alaska Native, 96 Asian Americans or Pacific Islanders, 10 Hispanic Americans), 2 international. Average age 26. In 2006, 123 degrees awarded. *Application deadline:* Applications are processed on a rolling basis. Application fee: $155. Electronic applications accepted. *Expenses:* Tuition, state resident: part-time $346 per credit hour. Tuition, nonresident: part-time $730 per credit hour. Tuition and fees vary according to program. *Financial support:* In 2006–07, 13 fellowships with tuition reimbursements, 15 research assistantships with tuition reimbursements (averaging $15,630 per year), 1 teaching assistantship with tuition reimbursement (averaging $15,804 per year) were awarded. *Unit head:* Dr. Gail Riegle, Associate Dean, Academic Programs, 517-353-4735, Fax: 517-353-9931, E-mail: riegle@msu.edu. *Application contact:* Kathie Schafer, Director of Admissions, 517-353-7740, Fax: 517-355-3296, E-mail: comadm@com.msu.edu.

Midwestern University, Downers Grove Campus, Chicago College of Osteopathic Medicine, Downers Grove, IL 60515-1235. Offers DO. *Accreditation:* AOsA. *Faculty:* 44 full-time (19 women), 253 part-time/adjunct (54 women). *Students:* 690 full-time (376 women); includes 188 minority (5 African Americans, 175 Asian Americans or Pacific Islanders, 8 Hispanic Americans), 10 international. Average age 26. 3,197 applicants, 12% accepted, 174 enrolled. In 2006, 153 degrees awarded. *Entrance requirements:* MCAT, 1 year course work in each organic chemistry, general chemistry, biology, physics, and English. *Application deadline:* For fall admission, 1/1 for domestic students. Applications are processed on a rolling basis. Application fee: $50. *Expenses:* Contact institution. *Financial support:* In 2006–07, 568 students received support; fellowships with partial tuition reimbursements available, career-related internships or fieldwork, Federal Work-Study, institutionally sponsored loans, and tuition waivers (full and partial) available. Financial award application deadline: 6/1; financial award applicants required to submit FAFSA. *Faculty research:* Cadmium toxicity, amino acid transport, metabolic actions of vanadium, diabetes and obesity. Total annual research expenditures: $1.2 million. *Unit head:* Dr. Karen J. Nichols, Dean, 630-515-6147, E-mail: knicho@midwestern.edu. *Application contact:* Michael Laken, Director of Admissions, 630-515-6148, Fax: 630-971-6086, E-mail: admissil@midwestern.edu.

See Close-Up on page 2205.

Midwestern University, Glendale Campus, Arizona College of Osteopathic Medicine, Phoenix, AZ 85308. Offers DO. *Accreditation:* AOsA. *Faculty:* 28 full-time (8 women), 782 part-time/adjunct (120 women). *Students:* 583 full-time (216 women), 1 (woman) part-time; includes 96 minority (1 African American, 4 American Indian/Alaska Native, 76 Asian Americans or Pacific Islanders, 15 Hispanic Americans), 3 international. Average age 27. 2,358 applicants, 15% accepted, 160 enrolled. In 2006, 130 degrees awarded. *Entrance requirements:* MCAT. *Application deadline:* For fall admission, 11/1 priority date for domestic students; for winter admission, 2/1 for domestic students. Applications are processed on a rolling basis. Application fee: $50. Electronic applications accepted. *Expenses:* Contact institution. *Financial support:* Fellowships with partial tuition reimbursements, career-related internships or fieldwork, Federal Work-Study, institutionally sponsored loans, and tuition waivers (full and partial) available. Financial award application deadline: 6/12; financial award applicants required to submit FAFSA. *Unit head:* Dr. James W. Cole, Dean, 623-572-3202. *Application contact:* James Walters, Director of Admissions, 888-247-9277, Fax: 623-572-3340, E-mail: admissaz@midwestern.edu.

See Close-Up on page 2205.

New York Institute of Technology, New York College of Osteopathic Medicine, Old Westbury, NY 11568-8000. Offers DO, DO/MBA, DO/MS. *Accreditation:* AOsA. *Faculty:* 68 full-time (19 women), 35 part-time/adjunct (10 women). *Students:* 1,206 full-time (663 women); includes 525 minority (101 African Americans, 2 American Indian/Alaska Native, 349 Asian Americans or Pacific Islanders, 73 Hispanic Americans), 1 international. Average age 27. 2,569 applicants, 24% accepted, 304 enrolled. In 2006, 242 degrees awarded. *Degree requirements:* For first-professional, comprehensive exam. *Entrance requirements:* MCAT, 6 hours of course work in biology, English, general chemistry, organic chemistry, and physics; minimum GPA of 2.75. *Application deadline:* For fall admission, 2/1 for domestic students. Application fee: $60. *Expenses:* Contact institution. *Financial support:* In 2006–07, 914 students received support, including fellowships with partial tuition reimbursements available (averaging $17,200 per year); tuition waivers (full and partial) also available. Financial award application deadline: 4/1; financial award applicants required to submit FAFSA. *Faculty research:* Osteopathic manipulation therapy, paleodiet of fossil horses, effect of OMT on range motion of arthritic knee, osteopathic treatment of muscle with compromised innervation, cycling smooth muscle crossbridges as substrates for myosin light chain kinase and phosphatase. *Unit head:* Dr. Barbara Ross-Lee, Dean, 516-686-3722, Fax: 516-686-3830, E-mail: brosslee@nyit.edu. *Application contact:* Michael J. Schaefer, Director of Admissions, 516-686-3747, Fax: 516-686-3831, E-mail: mschaefe@nyit.edu.

Nova Southeastern University, Health Professions Division, College of Osteopathic Medicine, Fort Lauderdale, FL 33314-7796. Offers osteopathic medicine (DO); public health (MPH). *Accreditation:* AOsA. *Faculty:* 90 full-time (28 women), 757 part-time/adjunct (132 women). *Students:* 888 full-time (461 women), 34 part-time (23 women); includes 316 minority (41 African Americans, 5 American Indian/Alaska Native, 152 Asian Americans or Pacific Islanders, 118 Hispanic Americans), 13 international. 2,059 applicants, 16% accepted, 207 enrolled. In 2006, 155 DOs, 21 master's awarded. *Entrance requirements:* MCAT. *Application deadline:* For fall admission, 1/15 for domestic students. Applications are processed on a rolling basis. Application fee: $50. *Expenses:* Contact institution. *Financial support:* In 2006–07, 598 students received support, including 12 fellowships with partial tuition reimbursements available; research assistantships, teaching assistantships, career-related internships or fieldwork, Federal Work-Study, institutionally sponsored loans, and scholarships/grants also available. Financial award application deadline: 6/1; financial award applicants required to submit FAFSA. *Faculty research:* Teaching strategies, simulated patient use, HIV-AIDS education, minority health issues, managed care education. Total annual research expenditures: $2.1 million. *Unit head:* Dr. Anthony J. Silavgni, Dean, 954-262-1407, E-mail: silvagni@hpd.nova.edu. *Application contact:* John Chaffin, Associate Director of Admissions and Student Affairs, 954-262-1113.

Ohio University, College of Osteopathic Medicine, Athens, OH 45701-2979. Offers DO, DO/MA, DO/MBA, DO/MHA, DO/MS, DO/PhD. *Accreditation:* AOsA. *Faculty:* 77 full-time (23 women), 34 part-time/adjunct (10 women). *Students:* 434 full-time (227 women); includes 104 minority (47 African Americans, 4 American Indian/Alaska Native, 34 Asian Americans or Pacific Islanders, 19 Hispanic Americans). Average age 24. 2,736 applicants, 61% accepted, 108 enrolled. In 2006, 102 degrees awarded. *Degree requirements:* For first-professional, thesis (for some programs), National Board Exam Parts I and II, COMLEX-PE, comprehensive exam. *Entrance requirements:* MCAT, interview; course work in English, physics, biology, general chemistry, organic chemistry, and behavioral sciences. *Application deadline:* For fall admission, 2/1 for domestic students. Applications are processed on a rolling basis. Application fee: $30. Electronic applications accepted. *Expenses:* Contact institution. *Financial support:* In 2006–07, 400 students received support, including 10 fellowships with full tuition reimbursements available (averaging $8,600 per year); career-related internships or fieldwork, Federal Work-Study, institutionally sponsored loans, scholarships/grants, and tuition waivers (partial) also available. Financial award application deadline: 4/1; financial award applicants required to submit FAFSA. *Faculty research:* Primary care/rural health, molecular aspects of diabetes and cardiovascular disease, drug development, biomechanics, international medicine. Total annual research expenditures: $2.6 million. *Unit head:* Dr. John A. Brose, Dean, 740-593-2178, Fax: 740-593-0761, E-mail: blue@ohio.edu. *Application contact:* Dr. John D. Schriner, Director of Admissions, 740-593-4313, Fax: 740-593-2256, E-mail: admissions@exchange.oucom.ohiou.edu.

Oklahoma State University Center for Health Sciences, College of Osteopathic Medicine, Tulsa, OK 74107-1898. Offers DO, DO/PhD. *Accreditation:* AOsA. *Students:* 351 full-time (166 women); includes 88 minority (17 African Americans, 38 American Indian/Alaska Native, 26 Asian Americans or Pacific Islanders, 7 Hispanic Americans). Average age 28. 1,454 applicants, 10% accepted, 88 enrolled. In 2006, 92 degrees awarded. *Entrance requirements:* MCAT, interview, minimum 90 hours of college course work, minimum GPA of 3.0. *Application deadline:* For fall admission, 2/1 for domestic students. Applications are processed on a rolling basis. Application fee: $40. *Financial support:* In 2006–07, 337 students received support. Federal Work-Study, institutionally sponsored loans, scholarships/grants, and tuition waivers available. Financial award application deadline: 3/31; financial award applicants required to submit FAFSA. *Faculty research:* Neuroscience, artificial vision, mechanisms of hormone action, vaccines and immunotherapy, pathogenic free-living amoebae. Total annual research expenditures: $900,000. *Unit head:* Dr. John J. Fernandes, President and Dean, Center for Health Sciences, Fax: 918-561-8243. *Application contact:* Leah Haines, Associate Director of Admissions and Registrar, 800-677-1972, Fax: 918-561-8243, E-mail: leah.haines@okstate.edu.

Philadelphia College of Osteopathic Medicine, Graduate and Professional Programs, Program in Osteopathic Medicine, Philadelphia, PA 19131-1694. Offers DO, DO/MBA, DO/MPH, DO/PhD. *Accreditation:* AOsA. *Faculty:* 57 full-time (23 women), 942 part-time/adjunct (73 women). *Students:* 1,047 full-time (582 women); includes 222 minority (63 African Americans, 1 American Indian/Alaska Native, 136 Asian Americans or Pacific Islanders, 22 Hispanic Americans), 6 international. Average age 26. 4,397 applicants, 9% accepted, 268 enrolled. In 2006, 241 degrees awarded. *Degree requirements:* For first-professional, registration. *Entrance requirements:* MCAT, minimum GPA of 3.2; course work in biology, chemistry, English, and physics. *Application deadline:* For fall admission, 2/1 priority date for domestic students. Applications are processed on a rolling basis. Application fee: $50. *Financial support:* In 2006–07, 905 students received support, including 12 fellowships with partial tuition reimbursements available; Federal Work-Study, institutionally sponsored loans, and scholarships/grants also available. Financial award application deadline: 4/15; financial award applicants required to submit FAFSA. *Faculty research:* Alzheimer's disease, non-human stem cells, inflammatory diseases, pain management, physical activity. Total annual research expenditures: $957,475. *Unit head:* Dr. Kenneth J. Veit, Dean, 215-871-6770, Fax: 215-871-6781, E-mail: kenv@pcom.edu. *Application contact:* Carol A. Fox, Associate Vice President for Enrollment Management, 215-871-6700, Fax: 215-871-6719, E-mail: carolf@pcom.edu.

Pikeville College, School of Osteopathic Medicine, Pikeville, KY 41501. Offers DO. *Accreditation:* AOsA. *Entrance requirements:* MCAT. *Faculty research:* Primary care in medically underserved areas.

Touro University College of Osteopathic Medicine, Professional Program, Vallejo, CA 94592. Offers education (MA); osteopathic medicine (DO); pharmacy (Pharm D); physician assistant studies (MS); public health (MPH). *Accreditation:* AOsA; ARC-PA. *Faculty:* 61 full-time (26 women), 30 part-time/adjunct (16 women). *Students:* 950 full-time (579 women); includes 354 minority (39 African Americans, 5 American Indian/Alaska Native, 258 Asian Americans or Pacific Islanders, 52 Hispanic Americans). Average age 26. 2,113 applicants, 13% accepted, 269 enrolled. In 2006, 109 first professional degrees, 43 master's awarded. *Median time to degree:* Of those who began their doctoral program in fall 1998, 98% received their degree in 8 years or less. *Entrance requirements:* For first professional degree and master's, BS/BA. *Application deadline:* For fall admission, 6/1 for domestic students. Applications are processed on a rolling basis. Application fee: $100. Electronic applications accepted. *Financial support:* In 2006–07, 3 fellowships (averaging $3,000 per year) were awarded. *Faculty research:* Diabetes, heart disease. *Application contact:* Steve Davis, Admissions Counselor, 707-638-5527, Fax: 707-638-5270, E-mail: sdavis@touro.edu.

University of Medicine and Dentistry of New Jersey, School of Osteopathic Medicine, Stratford, NJ 08084-1501. Offers DO, DO/MPA, DO/MPH, DO/PhD, JD/DO. *Accreditation:* AOsA. *Faculty:* 164 full-time (62 women), 31 part-time/adjunct (19 women). *Students:* 397 full-time (236 women); includes 205 minority (83 African Americans, 1 American Indian/Alaska Native, 91 Asian Americans or Pacific Islanders, 30 Hispanic Americans), 1 international. Average age 26. 2,779 applicants, 6% accepted, 103 enrolled. In 2006, 88 degrees awarded. *Entrance requirements:* MCAT. *Application deadline:* For fall admission, 2/1 for domestic students. Applications are processed on a rolling basis. Application fee: $75. Electronic applications accepted. *Expenses:* Contact institution. *Financial support:* Fellowships, research assistantships, teaching assistantships, career-related internships or fieldwork, Federal Work-Study, and institutionally sponsored loans available. Financial award application deadline: 5/1. *Unit head:* Dr. Thomas A. Cavalieri, Interim Dean, 856-566-6996, Fax: 856-566-6865, E-mail: cavalita@umdnj.edu.

University of New England, College of Osteopathic Medicine, Program in Osteopathic Medicine, Biddeford, ME 04005-9526. Offers DO. *Faculty:* 58 full-time (29 women), 40 part-time/adjunct (16 women). *Students:* 500 full-time (269 women); includes 41 minority (8 African Americans, 2 American Indian/Alaska Native, 23 Asian Americans or Pacific Islanders, 8 Hispanic Americans), 2 international. Average age 28. 176 applicants, 100% accepted, 127 enrolled. In 2006, 117 degrees awarded. *Entrance requirements:* MCAT, interview. *Application deadline:* For fall admission, 3/1 for domestic students. *Expenses:* Contact institution. *Financial support:* In 2006–07, 8 fellowships (averaging $16,500 per year) were awarded; institutionally sponsored loans and scholarships/grants also available. Financial award application deadline: 5/1; financial award applicants required to submit FAFSA. *Application contact:* Lisa Lane, Assistant Director, Graduate Medical Programs, 207-283-0171 Ext. 2297, Fax: 207-602-5900, E-mail: llacroixlane@une.edu.

University of North Texas Health Science Center at Fort Worth, Texas College of Osteopathic Medicine, Fort Worth, TX 76107-2699. Offers osteopathic medicine (DO); physician assistant studies (MPAS); DO/MPH; DO/MS; DO/PhD; MPAS/MPH. *Accreditation:* AOsA. *Entrance requirements:* MCAT, 1 year course work in each biology, physics and English; 2 years course work in chemistry. Electronic applications accepted. *Faculty research:* Tuberculosis, aging, cardiovascular disease, cancer.

Western University of Health Sciences, College of Osteopathic Medicine of the Pacific, Pomona, CA 91766-1854. Offers DO. *Accreditation:* AOsA. *Faculty:* 36 full-time (5 women), 6 part-time/adjunct (3 women). *Students:* 762 full-time (386 women); includes 344 minority (9 African Americans, 5 American Indian/Alaska Native, 300 Asian Americans or Pacific Islanders, 30 Hispanic Americans), 12 international. Average age 28. 2,631 applicants, 20% accepted, 218 enrolled. In 2006, 150 degrees awarded. *Entrance requirements:* MCAT, minimum GPA of 3.3, interview, letters of recommendation. *Application deadline:* For fall admission, 4/15 for domestic students. Applications are processed on a rolling basis. Application fee: $65. *Financial support:* In 2006–07, 8 research assistantships (averaging $40,000 per year), 81 teaching assistantships (averaging $8,846 per year) were awarded; fellowships, institutionally sponsored loans, scholarships/grants, tuition waivers (full), unspecified assistantships, and Veterans Educational Benefits also available. Financial award application deadline: 3/2; financial award applicants required to submit FAFSA. *Unit head:* Dr. Clinton Adams, Dean, 909-469-5423, Fax: 909-469-5535, E-mail: aclinton@westernu.edu. *Application contact:* Audrey Navarro, Information Contact, 909-469-5335, Fax: 909-469-5570, E-mail: admissions@westernu.edu.

West Virginia School of Osteopathic Medicine, Professional Program, Lewisburg, WV 24901-1196. Offers DO. *Accreditation:* AOsA. *Faculty:* 49 full-time (19 women), 93 part-time/adjunct (48 women). *Students:* 503 full-time (240 women); includes 71 minority (5 African Americans, 1 American Indian/Alaska Native, 57 Asian Americans or Pacific Islanders, 8 Hispanic Americans). Average age 26. 2,321 applicants, 26% accepted, 196 enrolled. In 2006, 85 degrees awarded. *Entrance requirements:* MCAT, 3 hours English, 8 hours biology, 8 hours physics, 8 hours inorganic chemistry, 8 hours organic chemistry. *Application deadline:* For fall admission, 2/15 for domestic students. Applications are processed on a rolling basis. Application fee: $155. Electronic applications accepted. *Expenses:* Tuition, state resident: full-time $18,886. Tuition, nonresident: full-time $46,736. *Financial support:* In 2006–07, 479 students received support, including 9 teaching assistantships with full and partial tuition reimbursements available (averaging $10,560 per year); Federal Work-Study, scholarships/grants, tuition waivers (full), and unspecified assistantships also available. Financial award application deadline: 4/1; financial award applicants required to submit FAFSA. *Faculty research:* Cardiac hypertrophy, diabetic population, myocardial eschemia referfusion, computer animations. *Unit head:* Dr. Olen E. Jones, President, 304-645-6270 Ext. 200, Fax: 304-645-4859. *Application contact:* Donna S. Varney, Director of Admissions, 304-647-6373, Fax: 304-647-6384, E-mail: dvarney@wvsom.edu.

Podiatric Medicine

Barry University, School of Graduate Medical Sciences, Podiatric Medicine and Surgery Program, Miami Shores, FL 33161-6695. Offers DPM, DPM/MBA, DPM/MPH. *Accreditation:* APMA. *Students:* 175 full-time (88 women), 6 part-time (3 women); includes 89 minority (35 African Americans, 1 American Indian/Alaska Native, 9 Asian Americans or Pacific Islanders, 44 Hispanic Americans), 5 international. 294 applicants, 29% accepted, 63 enrolled. In 2006, 45 degrees awarded. *Entrance requirements:* MCAT, GRE General Test, previous course work in science and English. Additional exam requirements/recommendations for international students: Required—TOEFL. *Application deadline:* For fall admission, 6/1 for domestic students. Applications are processed on a rolling basis. Application fee: $50. Electronic applications accepted. *Expenses:* Contact institution. *Financial support:* Fellowships, teaching assistantships with tuition reimbursements available. Financial award applicants required to submit FAFSA. *Unit head:* Dr. Chet Evans, Dean, 305-899-3251, Fax: 305-899-3253, E-mail: cevans@mail.barry.edu. *Application contact:* Marc A. Weiner, Director of Graduate and Medical Sciences Admissions and Marketing, 305-899-3130, Fax: 305-899-3253, E-mail: mweiner@mail.barry.edu.

California School of Podiatric Medicine at Samuel Merritt College, Graduate and Professional Programs, Oakland, CA 94609. Offers DPM. *Accreditation:* APMA. *Faculty:* 12 full-time (2 women), 10 part-time/adjunct (2 women). *Students:* 132 full-time (51 women); includes 42 minority (5 African Americans, 32 Asian Americans or Pacific Islanders, 5 Hispanic Americans), 4 international. Average age 27. 243 applicants, 42% accepted, 40 enrolled. In 2006, 100 degrees awarded. *Entrance requirements:* MCAT, 90 hours of undergraduate course work; 1 year of course work in organic chemistry, inorganic chemistry, and physics; 2 years of course work in biological sciences. *Application deadline:* For fall admission, 4/1 priority date for domestic students. Applications are processed on a rolling basis. Application fee: $50. *Expenses:* Tuition: Full-time $25,599. Required fees: $370. One-time fee: $2,100 full-time. *Financial support:* In 2006–07, 112 fellowships were awarded; Federal Work-Study and institutionally sponsored loans also available. Financial award application deadline: 3/2; financial award applicants required to submit FAFSA. *Faculty research:* Biomechanics, surgery, diabetics, sports medicine. *Unit head:* Irma Walker-Adame, Vice President and Dean of Student Services, 415-292-0481 Ext. 413, E-mail: iadame@ccpm.edu. *Application contact:* Dr. David Tran, Associate Director of Admissions, 800-334-2276 Ext. 483, Fax: 415-292-0439, E-mail: pwhite@ccpm.edu.

Des Moines University, College of Podiatric Medicine and Surgery, Des Moines, IA 50312-4104. Offers DPM. *Accreditation:* APMA. *Faculty:* 5 full-time (1 woman), 1 part-time/adjunct (0 women). *Students:* 181 full-time (51 women); includes 16 minority (4 African Americans, 4 American Indian/Alaska Native, 6 Asian Americans or Pacific Islanders, 2 Hispanic Americans), 4 international. Average age 24. 317 applicants, 28% accepted, 61 enrolled. In 2006, 31 degrees awarded. *Median time to degree:* 4 years full-time. *Entrance requirements:* MCAT, interview; minimum GPA of 2.5; 1 year of organic chemistry, inorganic chemistry, physics, biology, and English. *Application deadline:* For fall admission, 4/15 priority date for domestic and international students. Applications are processed on a rolling basis. Application fee: $0. Electronic applications accepted. *Expenses:* Contact institution. *Financial support:* In 2006–07, 82 students received support. Institutionally sponsored loans, scholarships/grants, and university employment available. Support available to part-time students. Financial award application deadline: 7/15; financial award applicants required to submit FAFSA. *Faculty research:* Physics of Equinus, gait analysis. *Unit head:* Dr. Robert Yoho, Dean, 515-271-1464, Fax: 515-271-1521, E-mail: robert.yoho@dmu.edu. *Application contact:* Meghan Good, Admissions Coordinator, 515-271-7497, E-mail: cpmsadmit@dmu.edu.

Midwestern University, Glendale Campus, College of Health Sciences, Arizona Campus, Program in Podiatric Medicine, Glendale, AZ 85308. Offers DPM. *Faculty:* 7 full-time (1 woman), 47 part-time/adjunct (7 women). *Students:* 79 full-time (42 women); includes 4 minority (2 American Indian/Alaska Native, 2 Hispanic Americans), 2 international. Average age 27. 96 applicants, 44% accepted, 34 enrolled. *Entrance requirements:* MCAT or PCAT, 90 semester hours at an accredited college or university, minimum GPA of 2.75. *Application deadline:* For fall admission, 6/1 for domestic students. Applications are processed on a rolling basis. Application fee: $50. *Expenses:* Contact institution. *Unit head:* Jeffrey C. Page, Director, 623-572-3451. *Application contact:* James Walter, Director of Admissions, 888-247-9277, Fax: 623-572-3229, E-mail: admissaz@midwestern.edu.

New York College of Podiatric Medicine, Professional Program, New York, NY 10035. Offers DPM, DPM/MPH. *Accreditation:* APMA. *Degree requirements:* For first-professional, comprehensive exam. *Entrance requirements:* MCAT or DAT, 1 year course work in biology, physics, English, and general and organic chemistry. Additional exam requirements/recommendations for international students: Required—TOEFL.

Ohio College of Podiatric Medicine, Professional Program, Cleveland, OH 44106-3082. Offers DPM. *Accreditation:* APMA. *Faculty:* 15 full-time (4 women), 12 part-time/adjunct (7 women). *Students:* 309 full-time (156 women), 1 part-time; includes 85 minority (48 African Americans, 2 American Indian/Alaska Native, 27 Asian Americans or Pacific Islanders, 8 Hispanic Americans), 8 international. Average age 26. 365 applicants, 29% accepted, 95 enrolled. In 2006, 45 degrees awarded. *Entrance requirements:* MCAT, GRE, previous course work in biology, chemistry, and physics. *Application deadline:* For fall admission, 6/1 priority date for domestic students. Applications are processed on a rolling basis. Application fee: $50. Electronic applications accepted. *Expenses:* Tuition: Full-time $24,000; part-time $1,200 per credit hour. Required fees: $1,420. *Financial support:* Career-related internships or fieldwork, Federal Work-Study, institutionally sponsored loans, and scholarships/grants available. Financial award application deadline: 5/30; financial award applicants required to submit FAFSA. *Faculty research:* Drug interactions using perfused liver and isolated hepatocytes, effects of diabetes mellitus on bone marrow lymphocytes, microcircuitry of the spinal cord in relation to posture and locomotion. *Unit head:* Dr. Thomas Melillo, President, 216-231-3300. *Application contact:* Lois Lott, Dean of Student Affairs, 216-231-3300 Ext. 8130, Fax: 216-231-1005, E-mail: llott@ocpm.edu.

Rosalind Franklin University of Medicine and Science, The Dr. William M. Scholl College of Podiatric Medicine, North Chicago, IL 60064-3095. Offers DPM. *Accreditation:* APMA. *Entrance requirements:* MCAT (or GRE on approval), 12 semester hours of biology; 8 semester hours of inorganic chemistry, organic chemistry and physics; 6 semester hours of English. Additional exam requirements/recommendations for international students: Required—TOEFL.

Temple University, Health Sciences Center, School of Podiatric Medicine, Philadelphia, PA 19107-2496. Offers DPM, DPM/MBA, DPM/MPA, DPM/PhD. *Accreditation:* APMA. *Degree requirements:* For first-professional, National Board Exam. *Entrance requirements:* MCAT, interview, 8 hours of organic chemistry, inorganic chemistry, physics, biology. *Expenses:* Tuition, state resident: full-time $12,264; part-time $511 per credit. Tuition, nonresident: full-time $17,904; part-time $746 per credit. Required fees: $84 per course. Tuition and fees vary according to program. *Faculty research:* Gait analysis, infectious diseases, diabetic neuropathy, peripheral vascular disease.

BASTYR
UNIVERSITY

BASTYR UNIVERSITY

School of Naturopathic Medicine

Program of Study

Bastyr University offers a four-year program of professional education leading to the Doctor of Naturopathic Medicine (N.D.) degree. The naturopathic medical profession and the University are dedicated to being effective leaders in the promotion of the health and well-being of the human community. Naturopathic physicians are licensed to practice independently as primary health-care providers in fourteen states and several Canadian provinces. The goal of the program is to educate future physicians in the tradition of medical science and the art of natural healing. This is accomplished by providing a comprehensive understanding of the basic medical sciences, accurate diagnostic skills, and the ability to apply the natural and minimally invasive methods of holistic health care. The curriculum is founded on the traditional concepts of naturopathic medicine: prevention of disease, encouragement of the body's inherent healing abilities, treatment of the whole person, responsibility for one's own health, and education of patients in health-promoting lifestyles. During the first two years of the program, students receive a thorough foundation in the basic medical sciences along with instruction in naturopathic medicine, clinical and laboratory diagnosis, nutrition, and counseling. The second two years focus on clinical diagnosis and therapeutics, including clinical studies in nutrition, botanical medicine, homeopathy, obstetrics, pediatrics, geriatrics, and other specialty areas. Students also receive clinical training through supervised practice at Bastyr Center for Natural Health and through externships in the offices of practicing physicians.

The University offers a certificate in midwifery for naturopathic medical students and graduates, which is accredited through the Midwifery Education Accreditation Council and meets the requirements for becoming a licensed midwife in Washington as well as those for certification by the American College of Naturopathic Obstetrics. The naturopathic midwifery program provides academic and clinical training leading to a certificate of naturopathic midwifery. Graduates are uniquely qualified among naturopathic physicians and among midwives. As comprehensive naturopathic family physicians, they enjoy an extended scope of practice in the provision of care to the birthing woman and her family. In their role as naturopathic midwives, they augment the midwifery model of care with the naturopathic principles of practice and exceed the midwifery scope of practice by providing ongoing pediatric, gynecological, and family care. The depth and breadth of naturopathic medicine is wholly embodied in the practitioner of naturopathic midwifery.

Research Facilities

The University's mission includes the pursuit of scientific research on the use of nutrition and natural therapies in the management and treatment of health-care problems and in the prevention of chronic disease. Original research is conducted regularly and a research fellowship has been funded. The University established an AIDS Research Center with funding from the NIH National Center for Complementary and Alternative Medicine. Students are engaged in primary clinical research at Bastyr Center for Natural Health. The University maintains a library with current journals; special collections in alternative medicine, acupuncture, nutrition, midwifery, and naturopathic medicine; and audiovisual aids. Students also have access to the nearby University of Washington Health Sciences Libraries.

Financial Aid

Students are eligible to participate in the University Scholarship Program, as well as the Federal Stafford Student Loan program, the Federal Perkins Loan program, and the Federal Work-Study Program. Washington State residents are also eligible to participate in the Washington State Work-Study Program. Applicants seeking financial aid should complete the application process by May 15. Complete financial aid information is available on the Bastyr University Web site, which is listed in this description. To request a financial aid packet, students should contact the financial aid office at 425-602-3407.

Cost of Study

Tuition for 2007–08 is charged per credit according to the credit load. The cost of 1 to 12 credits is $370 per credit (for all credits from 1 to 11.5); 12 to 16 credits cost $340 per credit (for all credits from 1 to 16). Credits above 16 are charged at $220 per credit. Total tuition and fees for a full-time student in the first year are $23,515 for the academic year. Books and supplies cost approximately $2325 per year.

Living and Housing Costs

The University provides limited housing. Many students live in shared facilities off campus; the average cost per person ranges from $500 to $900 per month. The Student Services Office can direct students to listings of available housing. The Washington Association of Student Financial Aid Administrators estimates that living expenses for nine months, including transportation and personal expenses, average $1360 per month.

Student Group

The University's total enrollment in 2006–07 was 1,138 students, of whom 885 were graduate and professional students. A total of 494 students were enrolled in the naturopathic program. Approximately 80 percent of the students were women. The average age of the 2006 entering class in naturopathic medicine was 31. Bastyr students come from all over the United States and Canada and from a number of other countries; 25 percent are residents of Washington.

Location

The academic and administrative campus is on a 50-acre site adjoining Saint Edward State Park in Kenmore, Washington, about 15 miles northeast of Seattle. Several hiking trails to Lake Washington begin at the edge of the campus; abundant opportunities for outdoor activities exist nearby in the Puget Sound area. The clinical campus is located in a Seattle neighborhood. The city offers a full range of activities and facilities, including museums, theaters, fine restaurants of many cuisines, a major opera and symphony orchestra, and major-league sports.

The University

Bastyr University was founded as a naturopathic medical college in 1978 to meet the growing need for scientifically trained naturopathic physicians, brought about by increased consumer interest in, and demand for, natural health-oriented care and preventive medicine. Since 1984, as a part of its mission to provide comprehensive education in natural medicine, the University has added graduate and undergraduate programs in nutrition, Oriental medicine, acupuncture, health psychology, exercise science and wellness, herbal sciences, and applied behavioral science. Bastyr University is accredited by the Northwest Commission on Colleges and Universities, and the naturopathic medicine program is accredited by the Council on Naturopathic Medical Education.

A comprehensive administration fee enables all students to receive health care at Bastyr Center for Natural Health, the University's teaching clinic (a minimal co-pay is due at each visit). Counseling services, acupuncture, naturopathic health care, physical medicine, and access to the herbal dispensary are all services that are available to the students. The cafeteria serves a buffet of vegetarian food as well as healthy snacks and beverages.

Applying

Admission is based on academic achievement, personal and social development, relevant experience, and demonstrated humanistic qualities. Credentials to be submitted are all official transcripts, two letters of recommendation, a completed application form, and a $75 application fee. While a bachelor's degree is strongly recommended, exceptions are made for outstanding students who have completed at least 135 quarter credits or 90 semester credits (must include at least 45 quarter or 30 semester credits of upper-division course work). In recent years, more than 97 percent of entrants have held a bachelor's degree. Required minimum course work includes one course in college-level algebra or precalculus, four courses in chemistry (including a two-term sequence of organic with lab), three quarters or two semesters of biology with labs (must include work in cell biology and genetics), at least one course in physics (must include mechanics, optics, electricity, and magnetism), and one course in psychology. Additional requirements include two courses in English and two courses in humanities. Courses earning a C- or below are not accepted for prerequisite consideration. Required chemistry and biology courses not taken within seven years of matriculation into the program are subject to review by the Admissions Committee. Additional course work may be required. Applicants who meet the basic admission standards may be invited to campus for an interview. For priority consideration, applications should be received by February 1 for admission the following fall, although late applications are considered on a space-available basis.

Correspondence and Information

Office of Admissions
Bastyr University
14500 Juanita Drive, NE
Kenmore, Washington 98028
Phone: 425-602-3330
Fax: 425-602-3090
E-mail: admissions@bastyr.edu
Web site: http://www.bastyr.edu/sub/adtrack.asp?adid=pe04

Bastyr University

THE FACULTY

Lizbeth Adams, Ph.D., Washington (Seattle), 1989.
Melissa Allbin, LMP, Boulder School of Massage Therapy, 1991.
Paul S. Anderson, N.D., National College of Naturopathic Medicine.
Robert Anderson, M.D., Washington (Seattle), 1954.
Richard Baker, M.D., Case Western Reserve, 1965.
Sheryl Berman, Ph.D., Wayne State, 1992.
Christine Bickson, N.D., Bastyr, 1999.
Catherine Brinton, N.D., Bastyr, 1998.
Pat Buckley, N.D., National College of Naturopathic Medicine, 2002.
Kevin Connor, N.D., Bastyr, 2001.
Walter Crinnion, N.D., Bastyr, 1982.
Laureen Cullen, N.D., Bastyr, 1998; RD.
Robin DiPasquale, Chair of Botanical Medicine; N.D., Bastyr, 1995.
Louise Edwards, N.D., National College of Naturopathic Medicine, 1988.
Petra Eichelsdoerfer, N.D., Bastyr, 2003.
Richard Fredrickson, Ph.D., North Dakota, 1970.
Alicia Gonzales, N.D., Bastyr, 2002.
Jane Guiltinan, N.D., Bastyr, 1985.
Steven M. Hall, M.D., Utah, 1982.
Krista Heron, N.D., National College of Naturopathic Medicine, 1988; DHANP.
John Hibbs, N.D., Bastyr, 1983.
Henry Hochberg, M.D., Yeshiva, 1985.
Eric Jones, N.D., Bastyr, 1983.
Sheila Kingsbury, N.D., Bastyr, 2003; RH (AHG).
Samer Koutoubi, M.D., University of Medicine and Pharmacy (Cluj-Napoca, Romania), 1988; Ph.D., Florida International, 2001.
Mark Lamden, N.D., Bastyr, 1986.
Davis Lamson, Ph.D., Illinois; N.D., Bastyr, 1982.
Debora S. Lantz, N.D., Bastyr.
Christy Lee-Engel, N.D., Bastyr, 1991; LAc.
Douglas Lewis, N.D., Bastyr, 1987.
Brad Lichtenstein, N.D., Bastyr, 1995.
Kent Littleton, N.D., Bastyr, 2003.
Richard Mann, Chair of Homeopathic Medicine; N.D., Bastyr, 1987.

Morgan Martin, Chair of Midwifery; N.D., Bastyr, 1991.
Nancy Mercer, N.D., Bastyr, 1987.
Steve Milkis, N.D., Bastyr, 2000.
John Miller, D.C., Western States Chiropractic, 1982; DACBR.
Harold Modell, Ph.D., Mississippi Medical Center, 1971.
Jana Nalbandian, N.D., Bastyr, 1989.
Dean E. Neary Jr., Chair of Physical Medicine; N.D., Bastyr, 1996.
Jeffrey Novack, Chair of Basic Sciences; Ph.D., Washington (Seattle), 1991.
Andrew Parkinson, N.D., Bastyr, 1994.
Brian Peters, N.D., Bastyr, 1995.
Joseph E. Pizzorno Jr., President Emeritus; N.D., National College of Naturopathic Medicine, 1995.
Steven M. Plaza, N.D., Bastyr, 1999.
Esfandiar Pournadeali, M.D., Ph.D.
Kasra Pournadeali, N.D., Bastyr, 1998.
Dirk Powell, N.D., National College of Naturopathic Medicine, 1976.
Maide Romero, N.D., M.S., Bastyr, 2000; LAc.
Dawn Schmidt, LMP, Seattle Massage School, 1991.
Heather Scott, Ph.D., Missouri–Columbia.
Gowsala Sivam, Ph.D., Maryland.
Pamela Snider, N.D., Bastyr, 1982.
Shailinder Sodhi, N.D., Bastyr, 1993.
Leanna Standish, Ph.D., N.D., Bastyr, 1991; LAc.
Michael Stern, M.D., Guadalajara (Mexico), 1973.
Rebecca Love Steward, D.V.M., Washington State, 1987.
Masa Takakura, N.D., Bastyr, 2001.
Aleyamma Thomas, Ph.D., Manitoba.
Amy Turnbull, N.D., Bastyr, 2000.
Susan Vlasuk, D.C., National Chiropractic, 1970; DACBR.
Jamey Wallace, Clinic Medical Director; N.D., Bastyr, 1996.
Wendy Weber, N.D., Bastyr, 2001.
Nancy Welliver, N.D., Bastyr, 1992.
Eric Yarnell, N.D., Bastyr, 1996; RH.
Phoebe Yin, N.D., Bastyr, 2002.
Joy Yu, N.D., Bastyr, 2002.

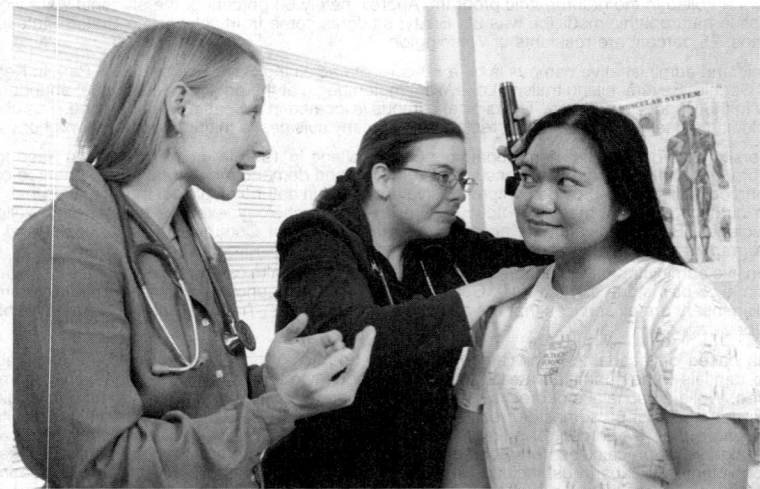

Faculty and student teams deliver health care at Bastyr's teaching clinic, Bastyr Center for Natural Health.

THE CANADIAN COLLEGE OF NATUROPATHIC MEDICINE

Doctor of Naturopathic Medicine Program

Programs of Study

The Canadian College of Naturopathic Medicine (CCNM) is Canada's premier institute for education and research in naturopathic medicine. CCNM brings new thinking, new research, and new approaches to health care, harnessing science to unleash the healing power of nature. Graduates of its intensive four-year postgraduate medical program are recognized for regulation/licensure in all Canadian and most American jurisdictions in which naturopathic medicine is regulated.

CCNM's Doctor of Naturopathic Medicine (N.D.) program comprises more than 4,200 hours of classroom and clinical study. Fourth-year students take the role of senior clinicians in CCNM's Robert Schad Naturopathic Clinic (RSNC), Canada's largest naturopathic teaching clinic. The clinic cares for more than 100 patients a day, of all ages and with a wide range of health concerns. Experience is augmented by participation in pediatrics, sports medicine, and pain management shifts.

The N.D. curriculum involves three major areas of study: basic sciences, clinical sciences, and naturopathic disciplines. Students take courses in the basic sciences of anatomy, histopathology, physiology, biochemistry, microbiology, and immunology. Development of problem-solving skills in applied basic life sciences is achieved through lectures, case discussion, tutorial groups, and clinical simulations. Some of these courses have a laboratory component. Laboratory resources include diagnostic test kits and access to human cadavers for gross anatomy study. A variety of audiovisual resources are also available.

Clinical science disciplines include physical and clinical diagnosis, differential and laboratory diagnosis, advanced imaging, physical assessment, health psychology, primary care, and pathology. The principles and philosophy of naturopathic medicine form the bridgework between the academic and clinical parts of the curriculum.

Six major disciplines define the areas of naturopathic practice: Asian medicine/acupuncture, botanical medicine, clinical nutrition, homeopathic medicine, physical medicine, and health psychology and lifestyle counseling. There are other modalities, as well. Each discipline is a distinct area of practice and includes both diagnostic principles and practices as well as therapeutic skills and techniques. Integration of these disciplines to effectively meet the individual needs of each patient is the objective of the N.D. program. Any of these disciplines may be developed by a naturopathic doctor as a clinical specialty.

In the Asian medicine/acupuncture discipline, the philosophy and principles of Asian medicine are presented. Yin and Yang theory, the meridians and channels system, the five-element theory, and the symptoms and signs involving the twelve master meridians are discussed. Diagnostic and therapeutic methods are introduced with emphasis on the principles of practical acupuncture and the use of therapeutic botanicals.

In botanical medicine, students investigate the medicinal properties of plants and crude plant extracts, including their pharmacognosy, clinical indications, interactions, and toxicology. Examples from traditional herbal lore are examined from a current research perspective. Field trips for identification of local botanicals are part of the course, along with an exploration of herbs in light of their ecological significance and contribution to the history and evolution of medicine.

The clinical nutrition discipline acquaints students with current knowledge and research in clinical nutrition and its application in the prevention and treatment of disease processes. Macro and micro nutrients are studied, and their interacting biochemical roles in human metabolism are investigated. The concept of biochemistry individuality is highlighted. Course content includes etiological considerations and clinical manifestations of nutritional imbalances and food sensitivities. Diagnostic evaluation of nutritional status is presented, and therapeutic strategies such as fasting, detoxification and various diets are studied. Therapeutic approaches based on the biochemical/metabolic focus include supplementation, orthomolecular therapy and the use of food extracts, glandular concentrates, and digestive aids. Inborn errors of metabolism, metabolic disorders, and genetic factors are considered.

In the homeopathic medicine discipline, the history, principles, and philosophy of homeopathy are discussed in-depth. Skills of homeopathic case taking, case analysis, repertorizing, and prescribing (acute and constitutional) are introduced and refined. Practical application of homeopathic therapeutics is emphasized in the latter portion of the course, including case analysis, repertorization, advanced materia medica search, remedy differentiation, and appropriate posology application for each case.

In the physical medicine discipline, lecture practicum courses detail the therapeutic effects of physical modalities. These include electricity, magnetism, sound, light, heat, and cold. The internal and topical therapeutic uses of water are examined, including immersion baths, douching, thermal body wraps and fomentations, colonic irrigation, and constitutional hydrotherapy. Students also learn the significance of integrating structure and function to achieve health. A variety of techniques are taught for manipulating the osseous and soft tissues to correct structural and/or postural imbalance or pathology. Instruction includes active and passive manipulation of spinal, costovertebral, costosternal, and limb articulations. The prescription of restorative and/or preventive exercise for patients requiring these measures is also taught.

Naturopathic medicine is based upon the premise that healing requires a combination of personalized health-care education and counselling to allow patients to achieve optimal levels of control of their health. The cornerstone of this approach rests in lifestyle modification and individualized health-care and counselling programs. These permit patients to begin to change injurious habits and develop a state of high-level wellness. The CCNM health psychology program is oriented toward the acquisition of practical skills, which are augmented by in-depth study of current psychological and educational theory.

CCNM is committed to maintaining its leadership in the exploration of complementary and alternative approaches to medicine. In addition to the six core modalities, in each year of the N.D. program students are provided with instruction in the principles of clinical naturopathic medicine and its application within an N.D.'s practice.

Research Facilities

The Learning Resources Centre houses more than 11,000 resources on naturopathic and complementary health care. CCNM's Department of Research and Clinical Epidemiology is advancing the state of medicine through a better understanding of complementary and alternative medical science. Research department faculty members educate students in their first years in epidemiology, encouraging them to investigate evidence-based medicine throughout their years at the college and to consider a research project of their own. This commitment to evidence-based medicine cultivates research initiatives within the CCNM community, including student and faculty initiatives, through teaching, experiential learning, and mentorship. By fostering this culture of research, CCNM has become a leader in naturopathic and complementary medicine worldwide, investigating topics that not only improve naturopathic treatment practices but also have widespread relevance and international impact.

Results from CCNM research studies help improve treatment options and access to health care and help to influence policy makers on better international health-care policies. This makes CCNM a natural home for the Centre for International Health and Human Rights Studies (http://www.cihhrs.org), the nonprofit research organization dedicated to providing evidence to support equal access to health care for all individuals.

CCNM's research department continues to build a research infrastructure through teaching of students and faculty members and will offer postgraduate programs in advanced research methodologies. To facilitate continued research partnerships, the department is choosing high-profile issues of interest to both the naturopathic and public health communities. The research department receives funding from private and government agency grants and through matched contributions, research partnerships, and a personal and corporate giving program.

CCNM research provides premiere evidence for the use of naturopathic medicine in the workplace. In a study funded by the Canada Post Corporation and Canadian Union of Postal Workers, Orest Szczurko, N.D., and Kieran Cooley, N.D., conducted the first randomized control trial evaluating naturopathic medicine's ability to reduce low back pain. Results showed that naturopathic treatment methods, including acupuncture, mind-body medicine, and nutritional and lifestyle counselling, significantly reduced low back pain and quality of life of participants.

Financial Aid

Qualifying students who enroll with CCNM may take advantage of federal, provincial, and U.S. federal student loan programs. In addition, CCNM offers a number of scholarships, bursaries, loans, and awards through the generosity of its donors. Private and professional school loans may also be available through an individual's financial institution. Government loans may not cover the full cost of tuition. Canadian students enrolled in the naturopathic medicine program may be eligible, if qualified, for assistance under one or more components of Canada Student Loans Program (CSL), Ontario Student Loans Program (OSL), or student loan programs in their province of residence. Private loans are available through participating financial institutions.

Cost of Study

The 2007–08 tuition fee is Can$17,580 for Canadian students. For international students, tuition is Can$21,060. Fees are subject to change.

Living and Housing Costs

Students often live in CCNM's on-site residence. Rooms are single occupancy, and rent is Can$395 per month (subject to change). The residence is equipped with laundry facilities, kitchens, and lounges. CCNM is protected by 24-hour, on-site security. Alternatively, some students occupy off-campus housing. Two-bedroom apartments start at approximately Can$1200 per month and single units start at approximately Can$750 per month.

Student Group

Currently, nearly 500 students are enrolled at CCNM. Students come from every province in Canada, with significant numbers coming from the United States and abroad. The ratio of women to men at CCNM is approximately 4:1. Student ages range from 22 to 40 years and older.

Student Outcomes

Upon graduation, many naturopathic doctors open their own practice. CCNM graduates are building successful practices throughout North America, including remote areas. Some graduates, however, choose to partner with existing naturopathic practices, multidisciplinary clinics, wellness centres, fitness centres, spas, or corporate wellness programs. Many naturopathic doctors conduct special lectures and workshops, represent natural health product companies as spokespeople, develop natural health products, and perform medical and scientific research.

Location

CCNM is located in Toronto, Canada's largest city, with 4.4 million people. Toronto is well maintained, with excellent public transportation and comparatively low living costs. Rated the safest large North American city, Toronto is a welcoming multicultural mosaic. Toronto's distinctive neighbourhoods and vibrant entertainment scenes brim with music, theatre, galleries, sports, shopping, and cuisine. Summer temperatures often climb to more than 30 degrees Celsius.

The College

CCNM's 4.43-acre, 176,000-square-foot campus is conveniently located in Toronto's North York region the Leslie subway station. It is also close to major highways. Campus facilities include a student lounge with satellite TV, games room, meditation room, and piano room; a fitness centre equipped with saunas; a tennis/basketball court; a courtyard and herb garden, which is a relaxing oasis for reflection and meditation, used as a teaching garden for CCNM students and visitors; the Green Life Café, offering healthy foods at reasonable prices in a pleasant atmosphere; and the Body Mind Science Resources bookstore, which sells textbooks, software, and medical equipment and stocks a range of organic foods and healthful snacks.

Applying

To be considered for admission to the N.D. program, applicants must have completed a baccalaureate degree prior to entry. The decision whether or not to admit an applicant is based primarily on the applicant's undergraduate GPA. Additional criteria may include the applicant's academic history, essay, references, autobiographical sketch, and interview. Competitive applications should have a cumulative GPA of at least 3.3 on a four-point scale (equivalent to B+). A lower GPA may be acceptable, depending on the applicant's academic history, interview, essay, references, and autobiographical sketch. Prerequisite courses (general biology, 6 credit hours; biochemistry, 3 credit hours; general chemistry with lab, 6 credit hours; organic chemistry with lab, 3 credit hours; introductory psychology, 6 credit hours; and a humanities elective, 6 credit hours) must be completed with a grade of C– (60 percent) or better for credit to be awarded.

Correspondence and Information

Admissions and Student Services
The Canadian College of Naturopathic Medicine
1255 Sheppard Avenue East
Toronto, Ontario M2K 1E2
Canada

Phone: 416-498-1255 Ext. 245
866-241-2266 Ext. 245 (toll-free)
E-mail: info@ccnm.edu.
Web site: http://www.ccnm.edu

The Canadian College of Naturopathic Medicine

THE FACULTY AND THEIR RESEARCH

Nadia Bakir, N.D., FCAH, DHANP; Associate Professor, Clinic Supervisor, and Coordinator of the Robert Schad Naturopathic Clinic (RSNC) Homeopathy Shifts. Nadia Bakir designed, developed, and implemented the Homeopathy Specialty Clinic at the Robert Schad Naturopathic Clinic, which is now an integral part of the RSNC curriculum. She has committed herself to updating and improving the College's homeopathic curriculum, and coordinates an annual student trip to India to study homeopathy. Bakir believes that maintaining a private practice in addition to her position at CCNM enriches her contribution to students.

Kimberlee Blyden-Taylor, N.D.; Assistant Professor and Associate Dean of Clinical Education. In her position as associate dean of clinical education, Kimberlee Blyden-Taylor oversees the second-, third-, and fourth-year clinical education component of CCNM's academic program. Blyden-Taylor also supervises fourth-year clinic interns, clinical faculty and staff members, and the RSNC's homeopathic medicine specialty groups. In addition to working within the RSNC, Blyden-Taylor teaches and facilitates group studies for a number of CCNM's academic courses. She is also the founder and director of Redhawk Healing Arts in Toronto, where she runs her private practice.

Nick De Groot, N.D.; Dean of Clinical Education. Nick De Groot is responsible for overseeing the day-to-day operations of the clinic. In addition to monitoring and developing the quality of patient care, De Groot supervises the clinical education of students in every stage of the naturopathic program.

Nellie Pachkovskaja, M.D., Ph.D., CMS; Professor, Clinical Sciences, and Associate Dean, Academics. In her role as associate dean of academics, Dr. Nellie Pachkovskaja designs, develops, reviews, and delivers academic curriculum content, course structure, and program-related learning materials. In addition, Dr. Pachkovskaja monitors the program's overall integration and consistency, prepares timetables and exam schedules, and monitors student academic performance. She acts as an academic liaison between students and faculty members.

Cheryl Proctor, N.D., RMT; Associate Professor, Women's Health Studies. Cheryl Proctor lectures on soft tissue manipulation, differential diagnosis, integrated clinical studies, physical and clinical diagnosis, primary care, and women's and men's health. She has made numerous public appearances and presentations on naturopathic approaches to menopause, obstetrics and gynecology, and treating osteoporosis and endometriosis. She has received advanced training in naturopathic approaches to women's health at the Institute of Women's Health and Integrative Medicine in Portland, Oregon. Proctor's primary research interests include osteoporosis, bio-identical hormone replacement therapy, estrogen metabolism, and complementary treatments for menopausal treatments. In addition to her responsibilities at CCNM, Proctor also maintains a private practice in downtown Toronto, specializing in women's health issues.

Jonathan Prousky, N.D., FRSH; Associate Professor of Clinical Nutrition and Chief Naturopathic Medical Officer. In addition to ensuring the delivery of safe and effective naturopathic medical care, Jonathan Prousky develops clinical curriculum for the N.D. program and coordinates educational activities and operations within the Robert Schad Naturopathic Clinic to ensure the competency of all graduates. He coordinates the monthly grand rounds program and supervises the postgraduate residency program in naturopathic medicine. Prousky has also been published in numerous lay publications and peer-reviewed medical journals.

Aubrey Rickford, N.D.; Clinic Faculty. Aubrey Rickford is a professor of Asian medicine and a supervisor in the Robert Schad Naturopathic Clinic, where he has developed North America's only naturopathic sports medicine and pain management group. Attending events across the Greater Toronto area, CCNM's sports medicine group provides athletes with free assessments and onsite naturopathic care for sprains, soreness, and fatigue. In addition, Rickford maintains a practice in Bolton, Ontario, focusing on clinical nutrition, Asian medicine/acupuncture, and sports medicine.

Paul Saunders, N.D., Ph.D., DHANP, CCH; Adjunct Faculty. After earning a Ph.D. in plant ecology from Duke University, Paul Saunders graduated from The Ontario (now The Canadian) College of Naturopathic Medicine and then earned an additional N.D. diploma at National College of Naturopathic Medicine, Portland, Oregon. Dr. Saunders introduced the practice of peer-reviewing during his tenure as editor of the *Canadian Journal of Herbalism* (2000–02). Over the course of his career, he has participated in numerous conferences, delivered lectures for prominent groups, and been honoured with various awards and distinctions. Dr. Saunders currently teaches botanical medicine, parenteral therapy, venipuncture, and art and practice of naturopathic medicine. He currently runs a private practice in Dundas, Ontario.

Dugald Seely, N.D.; Assistant Professor and Research Fellow. As a research fellow in CCNM's Department of Clinical Epidemiology, Dugald Seely is involved in developing clinical trials and research methodology to assess natural health products and therapies used by naturopathic doctors. He also secures funding for conducting and disseminating research projects at CCNM and in collaboration with other institutions. As an assistant professor, Seely teaches the principles of research and clinical epidemiology and assists student research initiatives.

Kavita Sharma, N.D.; Assistant Professor and Associate Dean, Academics. As the associate dean of academics at CCNM, Kavita Sharma is responsible for the curriculum design, delivery, and evaluation of various academic programs at the College. These programs include General Chemistry, the Naturopathic College Preparatory Program (NCPP), the NPLEX Preparatory Program, and both the September and January intakes of the N.D. program. In addition, Sharma is an assistant professor at the College, instructing various academic courses.

Ljubisa Terzic, M.D.; Associate Professor. Ljubisa Terzic practised as a resident neurosurgeon in the University Medical Centre in Sarajevo while completing a postgraduate program in ear, nose, and throat (ENT) and maxillofacial surgery at University of Zagreb and teaching anatomy and general surgery at the local university. Having relocated to Canada, Dr. Terzic teaches anatomy, embriology, and minor surgical procedures at CCNM. A favourite with students, he has been presented with several teaching awards. Dr. Terzic has authored and co-authored a number of published articles and textbooks.

Jonathan Wilde, M.B.A.; Senior Academic Administrator. Jonathan Wilde has dedicated the academic administrative team to restructuring processes including exam marking, grade reporting, and student/faculty evaluation, thereby improving the office's accessibility and responsiveness to students. In addition, Wilde is committed to continuously evaluating and updating the College's academic program.

Ping Wu, M.D.; Research Fellow. Ping Wu joined CCNM in 2003. Her previous experience—practising as an M.D. specializing in neurological diseases—contributes to her present role in CCNM's Department of Clinical Epidemiology. She has performed systematic reviews on topics including herb-drug interactions, acupuncture therapy in cocaine addiction, and the role of complementary and alternative medicine (CAM) on HIV treatment and stroke rehabilitation.

CURRENT RESEARCH PROJECTS

The Department of Research and Clinical Epidemiology is currently involved in three clinical trials.

Clinical trial to assess the effect of melatonin on lung cancer recurrence and mortality. This study funded by the Lotte and John Hecht Memorial Foundation is expected to be completed by 2012.

Clinical trial to compare the effectiveness of two naturopathic-based treatments on shoulder pain in workers at Canada Post. This study funded by Canada Post will be completed by fall 2007.

Clinical trial to test the efficacy of cinnamon as an aid in diabetes to reduce blood sugar levels. This study funded by New Chapter industries is expected to be completed by the end of 2007.

Where time permits and where funding initiatives dictate, the department is also involved in conducting and publishing secondary research in the form of systematic reviews. Current work in this area includes a comparison of trials that have tested Panax ginseng for diabetes from a Western vs. Eastern medicine perspective, a systematic review of all clinical trials that assess for the effect of melatonin on chemotherapy toxicity, and a systematic review of English and Chinese language studies that assess acupuncture as a treatment aid for post stroke rehabilitation.

MIDWESTERN UNIVERSITY

Chicago College of Osteopathic Medicine
Arizona College of Osteopathic Medicine

Program of Study

Midwestern University (MWU) offers a four-year program leading to the Doctor of Osteopathic Medicine (D.O.) degree at two colleges on two campuses: the Chicago College of Osteopathic Medicine (CCOM), located in Downers Grove, Illinois, and the Arizona College of Osteopathic Medicine (AZCOM), located in Glendale, Arizona. As scientists and practitioners of the healing arts, osteopathic physicians subscribe to a philosophy that regards the body as an integrated whole, with structures and functions working interdependently. As an extension of this philosophy, osteopathic physicians treat their patients as unique persons with biological, psychological, and sociological needs—an approach that underscores the osteopathic commitment to patient-oriented versus disease-oriented health care. In recognition of this approach, MWU's colleges of osteopathic medicine have developed and continue to refine curricula that educate students in the biopsychosocial approach to patient care, as well as the basic medical arts and sciences. Within this curricular format, CCOM and AZCOM medical students spend their first two years both completing a rigorous basic science curriculum and preparing for their clinical studies. During their third and fourth years, students rotate through a variety of clinical departments at both ambulatory and hospital sites. Required rotations include family medicine, internal medicine, surgery, pediatrics, psychiatry, community medicine, obstetrics/gynecology, and emergency medicine.

By stimulating intellectual curiosity and teaching problem-solving skills, the CCOM and AZCOM curricula encourage students to regard learning as a lifelong process. Midwestern University is accredited by the Commission on Institutions of Higher Education of the North Central Association (NCA) of Colleges and Schools.

Research Facilities

Midwestern University faculty members are engaged in extramurally funded research programs in the Chicago College of Osteopathic Medicine and the Arizona College of Osteopathic Medicine. The Downers Grove campus has 24,000 square feet of laboratory space, an AAALAC-accredited animal resource facility with 9,000 square feet of space, and a well-equipped library designated as a Resource Library by the National Library of Medicine. The Glendale campus has state-of-the-art laboratories and a modern library with computer resources. Research conducted by the faculty members is supported by the University and through agencies such as the National Institutes of Health, the National Oceanic and Atmospheric Administration, the American Heart Association, the American Diabetes Association, and the Arthritis Foundation. Research expenditures have averaged $2 million in each of the last few years.

Financial Aid

The Office of Financial Aid provides students with information about federal, state, and private sources of financial assistance; helps students coordinate the financial aid application and renewal processes; and assists students in making informed decisions about the financing of their education. All students seeking financial aid must meet general eligibility requirements regarding citizenship, financial need, and satisfactory academic progress. The office helps coordinate three types of financial aid: scholarships and grants, employment programs, and loans. The office automatically mails a financial aid packet to accepted students who return a signed matriculation agreement and submit their initial deposit.

Cost of Study

Tuition for CCOM for the 2006–07 academic year was $36,391 for in-state students and $40,492 for out-of-state students, with a $412 activity fee. Tuition for AZCOM for the 2006–07 academic year was $38,908.

Living and Housing Costs

The University provides on-campus student housing opportunities at both campuses. Off-campus housing is also available in both the Downers Grove and Glendale communities. On-campus housing costs range from $6000 to $8000 annually, with food costs of approximately $2800 per year.

Student Group

The total osteopathic medical student population of Midwestern University for the 2005–06 academic year was approximately 1,200 full-time students, which included a first-year class of 170 for CCOM and 150 for AZCOM. Students come from nearly every state and several other countries. Nearly 50 percent of the students are women. The student body is diverse in terms of age, ethnicity, and background.

Student Outcomes

From 1990 to 2000, approximately 72 percent of CCOM graduates selected an American Osteopathic Association–approved internship for their first year of postdoctoral training. More than 50 percent of CCOM's recent graduates have entered primary-care disciplines of family medicine, pediatrics, and internal medicine. CCOM's alumni have served and continue to serve in hospitals, medical schools, private practices, and government facilities throughout the nation.

Location

Midwestern University operates two campuses. The Downers Grove, Illinois, campus—a 105-acre campus with innovative facilities—is nestled serenely in a wooded setting 25 miles west of downtown Chicago. The Glendale, Arizona, campus—a 137-acre campus that includes state-of-the-art facilities in a peaceful setting—is 15 miles northwest of downtown Phoenix. Both campuses offer suburban environments, with proximity to metropolitan communities and major transportation routes.

The University

Midwestern University is committed to educating the health-care team of the next century. The University's flagship school, the Chicago College of Osteopathic Medicine, was founded in 1900. Midwestern has since encompassed the Chicago College of Pharmacy (1991), the College of Health Sciences (1992), the Arizona College of Osteopathic Medicine (1995), and the College of Pharmacy–Glendale (1998). With two outstanding campuses, hundreds of caring faculty members, and thousands of top-notch graduates, Midwestern University is changing the face of health professions education.

Applying

Interested students should apply directly to the American Association of Colleges of Osteopathic Medicine Application Services (AACOMAS) at 5550 Friendship Boulevard, Suite 310, Chevy Chase, Maryland 20815-7231 (telephone: 301-968-4190). AACOMAS applications are available by May 1. MWU uses a rolling admissions process in which applications are reviewed and interview decisions are made at regular intervals during the admissions cycle. Applicants are notified of their selection status within two to four weeks of their interview date. To be competitive, candidates should apply early. For further information, interested students may visit MWU's Web site.

Correspondence and Information

Office of Admissions
Midwestern University
555 31st Street
Downers Grove, Illinois 60515
Phone: 630-515-7200
    800-458-6253 (toll-free)
E-mail: admissil@midwestern.edu
Web site: http://www.midwestern.edu

Office of Admissions
Midwestern University
19555 North 59th Avenue
Glendale, Arizona 85308
Phone: 623-572-3200
    888-247-9277 (toll-free)
E-mail: admissaz@midwestern.edu
Web site: http://www.midwestern.edu

Midwestern University

THE FACULTY AND THEIR RESEARCH

T. Broderick, Assistant Professor; Ph.D., Alberta. Exercise effects on glucose metabolism in the ischemic diabetic myocardium (funded by the American Heart Association/AZ).

N. Chandar, Associate Professor; Ph.D., Madras (India). Identification of a bone-specific function for p53 (funded by the NIH).

M. Fay, Assistant Professor; Ph.D., Mississippi. Expression and function of CUL-5/VACM-1 in breast cancer (funded by the NIH).

D. Gardner, Assistant Professor; Ph.D., Arizona. Animal model of fetal alcohol syndrome.

T. Kokjohn, Associate Professor; Ph.D., Loyola Chicago. Bacteriophage (or bacterial viruses) dynamics (funded by Phage Therapeutics International, Inc.).

K. LePard, Assistant Professor; Ph.D., Ohio State. Synaptic transmission in diabetic enteric nervous system (funded by the NIH).

A. Mayer, Associate Professor; Ph.D., Buenos Aires. Domoic acid, neonatal microglia neurodegeneration (funded by the NIH); neuroinflammation, microglia, and marine natural products (funded by the California Sea Grant).

K. O'Hagan, Associate Professor; Ph.D., Rutgers. Arterial baroreflex in model of preeclampsia in rabbit (funded by the NIH); regulation of uterine circulation during exercises in pregnancy (funded by the NIH).

J. Peuler, Associate Professor; Ph.D., Penn State. Interaction of oral Ca with K in hypertensive female rats (funded by the NIH).

P. Potter, Assistant Professor; Ph.D., Dalhousie. Muscarinic receptors/G proteins in early Alzheimer's disease (funded by the NIH).

W. Prozialeck, Professor; Ph.D., Thomas Jefferson. Mechanisms of cadmium toxicity in epithelial cells (funded by the NIH).

K. Ramsey, Associate Professor; Ph.D., Arkansas Medical Sciences. Role of nitric oxide in chlamydial infections of mice (funded by the NIH); *Chlamydia pneumoniae* and macrophages in atherosclerosis (funded by the NIH); immunity and latency to chlamydial infections (funded by the NIH).

C. Standley, Assistant Professor; Ph.D., Wayne State. Dicotomous regulation of mitogenic and antimitogenic pathways by vascular smooth muscle (funded by the American Heart Association/AZ).

J. Yodh, Assistant Professor; Ph.D., Johns Hopkins. DNA enzymology in the context of chromatin structure.

SOUTHWEST COLLEGE OF NATUROPATHIC MEDICINE AND HEALTH SCIENCES

Doctor of Naturopathic Medicine Program

Programs of Study

Southwest College of Naturopathic Medicine and Health Sciences (SCNM), founded in 1992, offers a four-year professional degree program leading to the Doctor of Naturopathic Medicine (N.D.). Graduates are educated in the same basic sciences as an M.D., in addition to studying holistic and nontoxic approaches to therapy, with a strong emphasis on disease prevention and optimizing wellness. As part of the N.D. program at Southwest College, students have extensive experience with local hospitals, M.D.'s, and other health-care practitioners. The mission of SCNM is to prepare students to become naturopathic physicians educated and trained in the principles and practice of naturopathic medicine and to serve the public, by providing high-quality education, research, and natural medical care in the science and art of health promotion, disease management, and prevention, based upon these principles.

SCNM is accredited by the Council on Naturopathic Medical Education, the accrediting agency for naturopathic colleges and programs in the United States and Canada. The College is also accredited by the Higher Learning Commission of the North Central Association of Colleges and Schools. In states that license naturopathic physicians, including Arizona, the profession is regulated. In these states, naturopathic physicians must pass either national or state board examinations and must have received an education from an accredited four-year professional-level, naturopathic medical school. Naturopathic physicians are subject to review by a state board of examiners to ensure protection of the patients.

Research Facilities

The Southwest College Research Institute (SCRI), the research division of SCNM, is located on the main campus. SCRI conducts and promotes biomedical research on naturopathic medicine. SCRI provides a full range of research and informational services to support experimental, developmental, and outcomes research and to conduct biomedical research from bench to clinical studies, including patient-care research projects with other academic and medical institutions. Collaboration with other institutions and professionals is fostered through interdisciplinary research models and quality assurance protocols for the naturopathic medicine professional industry. Through clinical trials, the effects and benefits of naturopathic therapies are rigorously studied. Notable collaborations include preclinical and clinical research projects with Arizona State University, the University of Arizona, and the Mayo Clinic in Scottsdale, Arizona.

SCRI performs high-quality research with guidance from the SCNM Institutional Review Board (IRB), the Research Advisory Board, and the Faculty Research Committee. SCRI provides consultation for various fields in medicine and research protocol development and analysis. The Research Institute has resources to provide technical research support for biomedical research. SCNM has developed a network of medical professional groups, academic institutions, and clinical patient-care centers.

The SCNM Medical Center offers multidisciplinary primary medical care for common, serious, and chronic health conditions while providing an engaging clinical experience for students with patients in the community. SCNM requires a great amount of patient contact and numerous clinical training hours. The College's Medical Center and affiliated off-site and extended-site clinics are centers for learning for hundreds of clinical training students pursuing their naturopathic degree, for clinical or research fellows conducting research, and for house staff members facilitating patient care. The Medical Center has numerous off-site facilities and maintains strong business ties in an integrative community.

The SCNM library has more than 11,000 cataloged items, including books, audio and videocassettes, discs, and eighteen user workstations, four of which are at the Medical Center. All workstations are equipped with high-speed Internet access. There are more than 1,500 Internet Explorer Favorites developed and maintained regularly by the library as well as various software programs and about 185 journal titles, including seventy that are currently received. Library hours, schedules, and further information are available at http://199.236.116.16/students/library.php.

Financial Aid

Approximately 90 percent of Southwest College students receive some type of financial aid, including loans and alternative loans. The Financial Aid Office assists students in financing their professional education. Financial resources include the Subsidized Stafford Loan, Unsubsidized Stafford Loan, and alternative loans.

Cost of Study

Tuition for the 2006–07 academic year was $5456 per quarter. Books and fees cost $833 per quarter.

Living and Housing Costs

Arizona has one of the lowest costs of living in the United States. Housing is readily available in the Phoenix area. A two-bedroom, two-bath apartment in Phoenix costs between $800 and $1000 per month.

Student Group

The total enrollment is 340 students. Each year, the fall class has approximately 70 students and the spring class has approximately 30 students. The College's last incoming class hailed from no fewer than fifty-five different colleges, forty different states, and five different countries. The average age of students who are enrolled is 31.

Student Outcomes

Of SCNM graduates, 60 percent practice in Arizona. The N.D. program prepares graduates for a wide range of career opportunities, such as primary-care physicians, respecting the integrated relationship of body and mind while combining the wisdom of traditional healing with the rigor of scientific method; scientific research and professional journal writing; public health education and academia; and advising, sales/marketing, or product development within the medical, environmental, and natural product industry. Practitioners trained in the natural healing arts experience tremendous career opportunities in a climate of support, growth, collaboration, and integration. While some practitioners have a private practice, others work for clinics, wellness centers, and other companies.

Location

SCNM is situated in the tri-city area of Scottsdale, Mesa, and Tempe, Arizona. The environment of the College fosters a positive learning community. The 15-acre campus in Tempe and the medical center in Scottsdale convey the excitement and enthusiasm that the students and faculty and staff members bring to naturopathic medical education. In addition to its beautiful weather, Arizona has much to offer residents. Recreational activities include hiking, mountain biking, walking, water sports, winter sports, golfing, spring training baseball games, and skydiving. Arizona has its share of lakes and rivers as well, including Saguaro Lake, Roosevelt Lake, Lake Powell, Tempe Town Lake, and the Salt River.

The College

SCNM is an accredited, private coeducational naturopathic medical college. The College is one of the best academic and technological leaders of the naturopathic medical schools. The College prepares students to be conscientious and caring naturopathic health-care providers. The SCNM experience is characterized by a high degree of student-faculty interaction, teamwork, practical application, and contact with external organizations. The Naturopathic Residency Program at SCNM is one of the most integrated residency programs available to naturopathic medical school graduates. The program exposes residents to private practice, community clinic, research, and teaching environments. Affiliation agreements with area hospitals and medical clinics allow the College's residents access to hospital facilities, including emergency rooms. The residency program provides broad-based training in diagnostic and treatment strategies, patient management, case presentation, public speaking, teaching, student supervision, and research.

Applying

Applicants are evaluated on their overall academic record, including transcripts, letters of recommendation, personal essay, and work experience. Admission decisions are based on academic performance, occupational history, professional potential, level of maturity, concern for others, and previous experience with natural medicine. Applications are accepted on a year-round basis, and students are admitted for either the fall or spring start. Applications are available at http://www.scnm.edu and http://www.arizonamentor.org.

Correspondence and Information

Admissions Department
Southwest College of Naturopathic Medicine and Health Sciences
2140 East Broadway
Tempe, Arizona 85282
Phone: 888-882-7266
Fax: 480-858-9116
E-mail: admissions@scnm.edu
Web site: http://www.scnm.edu

Southwest College of Naturopathic Medicine and Health Sciences

THE FACULTY AND THEIR RESEARCH

Leslie Axelrod, Professor; N.D., Bastyr, 1987; Southwest Acupuncture, 1999. Dr. Axelrod offers medical services, including acupuncture, homeopathy, craniosacral therapy, nutrition, botanical medicine, family medicine, and women's health. She is also nationally certified in acupuncture.

Matthew Baral, Assistant Professor; N.D., Bastyr, 2000. Dr. Baral is medical director of the Hamilton Elementary School Clinic and teaches pediatrics and nutrition courses at the College. He has a particular interest in childhood diseases and has published papers on ear infection, childhood obesity, and autism. His focus is general pediatric medicine, nutrition, autism, and attention deficit/hyperactivity.

Nick Buratovich, Associate Professor and Chair of Physical Medicine; N.D., National College of Naturopathic Medicine, 1983. Dr. Buratovich specializes in manipulation, acupuncture, and nutrition as well as homeopathy and botanical medicine. In addition to maintaining two busy practices, Dr. Buratovich teaches physical medicine at SCNM and is an active member of the SCNM's Board of Trustees.

Boyd Campbell, Professor of Anatomy and Division Director; M.D., 1963, Ph.D. (anatomy), 1965, Illinois. Dr. Campbell completed a surgical internship at Rush-Presbyterian-St. Luke's Medical Center in Chicago and has done residency training in neurology, neurosurgery, and neuroradiology. He was a faculty member at Indiana University, University of Maryland, University of Puerto Rico, California Institute of Technology, Georgetown University, and the Uniformed Services University of the Health Sciences. He is a retired colonel in the U.S. Army Medical Corps, where he served as a research neurologist at the Walter Reed Army Institute of Research. He teaches gross human anatomy, neuroanatomy, and human histology at SCNM.

Walter J. Crinnion, Professor of Naturopathic Medicine and Director, Environmental Medicine Center of Excellence; N.D., Bastyr,1982. Dr. Crinnion developed a specialty in environmental medicine and opened a comprehensive cleansing center in the Seattle area for twenty years. In addition to directing SCNM's Environmental Medicine Center of Excellence, he is an adjunct faculty member at the National College of Naturopathic Medicine, Bastyr University, and the University of Bridgeport, where he teaches environmental medicine to all four U.S. naturopathic medical schools.

Yong Deng, Professor of Acupuncture and Oriental Medicine; M.D., Chengdu University of Traditional Chinese Medicine (China), 1983; L.Ac. (Arizona), Dipl.Ac., National Certification Commission for Acupuncture and Oriental Medicine. From 1983 through 1996, Dr. Deng taught and practiced acupuncture and Chinese herbal medicine at Chengdu University of Traditional Chinese Medicine and its teaching hospital. He has a practice at Southwest Naturopathic Medical Center. Dr. Deng has more than eighteen years' experience in practicing acupuncture, Chinese herbs, and Tiu Na (Chinese therapeutic massage) for a wide range of diseases and conditions.

John Dye, Professor of Naturopathic Medicine and Department Chair of Mind-Body Medicine; N.D., National College of Naturopathic Medicine, 1979. Dr. Dye teaches endocrinology, mind-body medicine, and geriatrics at SCNM. He is a nationally recognized speaker in the fields of natural hormone replacement, diabetes, and longevity medicine. He is an attending physician and also teaches classes in mind-body healing and stress management and integrates techniques such as imagery, meditation, and stress-release into medical practice.

Richard Eberst, Professor of Medical Education, Provost, and Executive Vice President; Ph.D., Maryland, 1977; CHES, FASHA.

Paul Farnsworth, Professor of Basic Medical Sciences; Ph.D. (developmental biology), London. Dr. Farnsworth has extensive teaching experience at the University of Texas at San Antonio and believes that classes should involve analogies and examples that are relevant to students' current lives and their future careers as healers. He currently teaches microbiology and cell function/organ system at SCNM.

Patricia Gaines, Assistant Professor, Division of Naturopathic Therapeutics; Chair, Department of Botanical Medicine; N.D., Bastyr, 2002.

Christine Girard, Associate Professor of Naturopathic Medicine and Chief Medical Officer/Executive Vice President of Clinical Affairs; N.D., National College of Naturopathic Medicine, 1997.

Richard Laherty, Associate Professor of Anatomy and Chair of Basic Medical Sciences; Ph.D. (human anatomy), Berkeley, 1978. Dr. Laherty's research interest in reproductive endocrinology led him to the Reproductive Endocrinology Center in the Department of Obstetrics and Gynecology at the University of California, San Francisco, School of Medicine. There, he served on the faculties of the School of Dentistry and the School of Medicine and taught histology, gross anatomy, and neuroanatomy. He next served on the faculty of Indiana University School of Medicine where he taught histology and did research in reproductive endocrinology and on the endocrine regulation of the immune system. Dr. Laherty then moved to Kentucky, where he was a faculty member at the University of Kentucky before settling in Arizona. He teaches gross human anatomy, neuroanatomy, and endocrinology.

Arben Lasku, Associate Professor of Pathology and Laboratory Medicine; M.D., 1985, Ph.D. (tumor markers), 1994, Tirana (Albania). Dr. Lasku completed a specialization in nuclear medicine at the University of Genoa Medical Center, Italy. He has trained in clinical chemistry, clinical pathology, and nuclear medicine and has been a faculty member at the University of Tirana. Dr. Lasku teaches human pathology, laboratory diagnosis, and immunology at SCNM.

Pamela Martin, Assistant Professor; M.D., Texas Tech Health Sciences Center. Dr. Martin completed a residency in pediatrics at the Texas Tech Health Sciences Center, Lubbock, Texas. Dr. Martin was in practice for ten years in Amarillo, Texas, and has been an adjunct faculty member at SCNM for several years. Dr. Martin teaches medical ethics, hematology, musculoskeletal and connective tissue disorders, and HEENT.

Stephen Messer, Dolisos Professor of Homeopathy and Director, Division of Naturopathic Therapeutics; N.D., National College of Naturopathic Medicine, 1979. Dr. Messer offers medical services, including nutrition, homeopathy, and family medicine. He has been in practice for twenty-three years and is well known in the world of homeopathy as one the founders of the Homeopathic Academy of Naturopathic Physicians, a board member of the National Center for Homeopathy (NCH), and the dean of the NCH's summer school program.

Paul Mittman, Professor of Naturopathic Medicine, President of SCNM, and Chief Executive Officer; N.D., National College of Naturopathic Medicine, 1985.

Mona Morstein, Associate Professor and Chair of Department of Nutrition; N.D., National College of Naturopathic Medicine, 1988; DHANP. Dr. Morstein did her residency in family practice from 1988 to 1989; and then had a private practice in Great Falls, Montana, from 1989 to 2002 before joining SCNM in 2002. She specializes in the treatment of diabetes, women's medicine, and gastrointestinal disorders, although her private practice encompassed a broad spectrum of family medicine. Dr. Morstein teaches gastroenterology, nutrition, and the grand rounds courses.

Jennifer Nevels, Assistant Professor and Interim Chair of Women's Integrative Medicine; N.D., Southwest College of Naturopathic Medicine and Health Sciences, 2003. Dr. Nevels implements individualized treatments using botanicals, acupuncture, nutrition, and lifestyle counseling. Dr. Nevels enjoys doing research on women's health topics and is involved in coordinating the Annual Women's Integrative Medical Conference held at SCNM.

Thomas Richards, Associate Professor of Anatomy; Ph.D. (anatomy), Michigan, 1971; D.C., Western States Chiropractic College; Diplomate, American Board of Chiropractic Internists. Dr. Richards teaches gross anatomy and neuroanatomy. He did postdoctoral training at the National Institute of Health and Damon Runyon Memorial Fund for Cancer Research. Following a teaching and research career at Oregon Health Sciences University, Dr. Richards obtained the D.C. degree and practiced in Beaverton, Oregon. An outstanding teacher, Dr. Richards received distinguished teaching awards in 1985, 1986, and 1988 at Oregon Health Sciences University.

Timothy Schwaiger, Assistant Professor of Naturopathic Medicine and Director, Division of Clinical Sciences; N.D., Southwest College of Naturopathic Medicine and Health Sciences, 1999. Dr. Schwaiger completed a two-year residency program in naturopathic primary care. He previously served as Medical Director of the Medical Center. His areas of specialty include children's health, adult health, nutrition, food allergies, digestive and liver disorders, pain management, integrative cancer treatment and support, mood disorders, hormonal imbalances, and sleep disorders. He utilizes prolotherapy, which is very helpful in chronic pain involving tendons or ligaments.

Christine Sorensen, Full-time Clinical Faculty and Residency Director; N.D., Southwest College of Naturopathic Medicine and Health Sciences, 2001; RN, Arizona State, 1980.

D. Bryan Stansfield, Library Director; Ph.D., Wisconsin–Madison, 1975. Dr. Stansfield, who began his career as catalog librarian at the main library at Harvard University, has various subsequent professional library work experience, twenty-two years in all, including previous work in academic libraries and extensive work, with a professional publication, in library services for ethnic minority persons. He has served SCNM in his present position with the College since 1999, and for two years was faculty representative to the Board of Trustees.

Eric Udell, Assistant Professor, Division of Naturopathic Therapeutics; N.D., Southwest College of Naturopathic Medicine and Health Sciences, 2002.

Robert Waters, Professor of Biochemistry, Genetics, and Statistics; Ph.D., Montana State, 1975. Dr. Waters earned his doctorate in genetics with graduate minors in biochemistry and statistics. Postdoctoral training and a faculty appointment were added at Kansas State University (KSU) in Manhattan, Kansas. Research duties at KSU included radioactive tracing of DNA involving intergeneric hybridization with publications. During his tenure at KSU, Dr. Waters had the privilege of working with the Nobel Prize Laureate Dr. Norman E. Borlaug in genetics with the International Maize and Wheat Improvement Center near Mexico City (Toluca) and Ciudad Obregón in Sonora, Mexico. Following KSU, Dr. Waters received extensive training in computer science, communications, and programming from IBM, DEC, and many other companies. In computer science, he consulted with the Mexican Ministry of Agriculture in Mexico City and British Petroleum in London. With his varied background he designed, developed, and implemented an extensive emergency medial software system and was a coprinciple investigator for a multimillion dollar federal DOT/NHTSA grant to rewrite the EMT basic curriculum. Following twenty years in private industry, Dr. Waters joined the faculty at the SCNM in 1993 as an Associate Professor of Medical Biochemistry and Medical Genetics. He teaches biochemistry, research methods, and medical genetics.

Debra Wollner, Associate Professor of Physiology and Pharmacology; Ph.D. (pharmacology), Washington (Seattle), 1987. Dr. Wollner teaches physiology, endocrinology, pharmacology, and research. She performed postdoctoral research in the Department of Cell Biology at New York University School of Medicine, the Institute for Cancer Research at the Fox Chase Cancer Center, and the Department of Molecular and Cellular Physiology at Stanford University Medical Center. She has published her research on the development of epithelial polarity, cellular adhesion, and the diversity of the voltage sensitive sodium channel, work that was funded by the NSF, the NIH, and the Cystic Fibrosis Foundation. She currently serves as Chair of the Southwest College Institutional Review Board (IRB).

UNION GRADUATE COLLEGE / MOUNT SINAI SCHOOL OF MEDICINE

The Bioethics Program

Program of Study

The Bioethics Program is a dual-degree program offered by Union Graduate College and the Mount Sinai School of Medicine. The program is designed to provide formal distance and campus-based education in bioethics for doctors, health-care administrators, lawyers, nurses, pharmacists, and students enrolled in professional and graduate programs. Its mission is to provide high-quality master's-level education in bioethics to individuals who, because of the demands of work or obstacles of distance, are unable to participate in campus-based programs.

The Master of Science program is designed to meet the needs of working professionals, comply with the requirements of national accrediting and funding agencies, and impart the clinical skills and knowledge recommended by the American Society of Bioethics and Humanities. Nine of the twelve required courses are taught via distance learning by internationally recognized experts in bioethics. Online courses are complemented by an on-site seminar, practicums, individual master's projects, and capstone assessments. Students are trained in the skills that are essential to competent clinical ethics consultation and mediation or for serving on a research ethics committee (IRB/REC). Students also practice their competencies in clinical ethics and research ethics through interactions with trained actors ("standardized patients") in standardized research and clinical ethics scenarios at Mount Sinai's Morchand Center for Clinical Competence.

Research Facilities

Online connections to 1,750 electronic journals and databases are available through Union Graduate College by means of OVID and other subscription services, including links to the National Reference Center for Bioethics Literature, Medline, PubMed, and dozens of online bioethics and medical humanities journals that are available through JSTORE, MUSE, and other online databases. User support is available online and via phone through the Center for Bioethics and Clinical Leadership at Union Graduate College.

Financial Aid

Course waivers are available based on prior academic work in bioethics and related fields, including bioethics certificates from Montefiore Medical Center, NYU, and other qualified programs. Low-interest, deferred-repayment graduate loans are also available to U.S. citizens with demonstrated need.

Cost of Study

Tuition was $2485 per course in the 2006–07 academic year. The cost of books averaged $100–$200 per course. Students typically take four courses per year, one each term. Students pay a one-time student resource fee of $250. Subscription to a high-speed Internet connection is highly recommended.

Living and Housing Costs

Dormitory rooms and local bed-and-breakfast accommodations are available for summer seminars conducted at Union Graduate College in Schenectady. The on-site practicum is conducted at Mount Sinai School of Medicine in New York City. New York is a major transportation hub that can be reached by plane, train, ship, bus, or automobile. Students have innumerable choices in accommodation, but a list of residential options is provided to assist them in finding lodging.

Student Group

Classes normally consist of up to 18 students, permitting a close working relationship between students and faculty members. The students are diverse, with health-care administrators, physicians and other clinicians, attorneys, political scientists, and others making up a typical class. Relationships begun in the Bioethics Program often continue over a career.

Location

Union Graduate College is located in the Capital District of New York State, the heart of upstate New York. Mount Sinai School of Medicine is located in New York City, which is less than a 3-hour drive from Union.

The College and The School

Union Graduate College and the Mount Sinai School of Medicine in New York City jointly offer degrees and certificates in the Bioethics Program. The program also offers dual-degree programs in law, philosophy, and social work with the Albany Law School and the University at Albany, State University of New York. The Bioethics Program is also a partner in a National Institutes of Health Fogarty International Center Training Grant with Vilnius University.

Applying

Applicants must hold a bachelor's degree and complete an application, including an essay, three letters of recommendation, official transcripts from the institution offering the highest degree attained, a New York State immunization form, and an application fee of $60. Applications are reviewed on a rolling basis. A nonrefundable deposit of $250 is required upon acceptance. Downloadable application forms are available at the Center for Bioethics and Clinical Leadership Web site.

Correspondence and Information

For program information:
Ann Nolte, Assistant Director
The Bioethics Program
Humanities Building, Room 020
Union Graduate College
Schenectady, New York 12308
Phone: 518-388-8045
Fax: 518-388-8046
E-mail: bioethics@union.edu
Web site: http://www.bioethics.union.edu

For admissions information:
Rhonda Sheehan
Director of Admissions and Registrar
Union Graduate College
807 Union Street
Schenectady, New York 12308
Phone: 518-388-6238
Fax: 518-388-6686
E-mail: sheehanr@union.edu
Web site: http://www.bioethics.union.edu

Union Graduate College/Mount Sinai School of Medicine

THE FACULTY

Robert Baker, Ph.D., Professor of Bioethics and Program Director.
Eugenijus Gefanas, M.D., Ph.D., Visiting Associate Professor of Bioethics.
Nada Gligorov, M.A., Assistant Professor of Bioethics.
Jane Greenlaw, J.D., Professor of Bioethics; RN.
Susan Lederer, Ph.D., Visiting Proseminar Health and Human Values Lecturer.
Laurence McCullough, Ph.D., Visiting Proseminar Health and Human Values Lecturer.
Robert D. Orr, M.D., Professor of Bioethics.
Alicia Ouellette, J.D., Professor of Bioethics.
Rosamond Rhodes, Ph.D., Professor of Bioethics and Associate Program Director.
Bonnie Steinbock, Ph.D., Professor of Bioethics.
Martin A. Strosberg, M.P.H., Ph.D., Professor of Bioethics.
Robert Veatch, Ph.D., Visiting Proseminar Health and Human Values Lecturer.

Section 38
Optometry and Vision Sciences

This section contains a directory of institutions offering graduate work in optometry and vision sciences. Additional information about programs listed in the directory but not augmented by an in-depth entry may be obtained by writing directly to the dean of a graduate school or chair of a department at the address given in the directory.

For programs offering related work, see in Book 2 Psychology and Counseling; in Book 3, Biological and Biomedical Sciences, Biophysics, Neuroscience and Neurobiology, and Physiology; in Book 4, Physics; and in Book 5, Biomedical Engineering and Biotechnology.

CONTENTS

Optometry

Ferris State University, Michigan College of Optometry, Big Rapids, MI 49307. Offers OD. *Accreditation:* AOA. *Faculty:* 20 full-time (4 women), 92 part-time/adjunct (33 women). *Students:* 133 full-time (86 women); includes 10 minority (3 African Americans, 7 Asian Americans or Pacific Islanders), 5 international. Average age 27. 255 applicants, 14% accepted. In 2006, 34 degrees awarded. *Entrance requirements:* OAT. Additional exam requirements/recommendations for international students: Required—TOEFL. *Application deadline:* For fall admission, 2/1 for domestic and international students. Applications are processed on a rolling basis. Application fee: $30. Electronic applications accepted. *Expenses:* Tuition, state resident: part-time $355 per credit hour. Tuition, nonresident: part-time $687 per credit hour. *Financial support:* In 2006–07, 122 students received support. Career-related internships or fieldwork, Federal Work-Study, and scholarships/grants available. Financial award application deadline: 3/15; financial award applicants required to submit FAFSA. *Unit head:* Dr. Kevin L. Alexander, Dean, 231-591-3706, Fax: 231-591-2394, E-mail: alexandk@ferris.edu. *Application contact:* Dr. Nancy Peterson-Klein, Associate Dean, 231-591-3703, Fax: 231-591-2394, E-mail: peterson@ferris.edu.

Illinois College of Optometry, Professional Program, Chicago, IL 60616-3878. Offers OD. *Accreditation:* AOA. *Faculty:* 44 full-time (24 women), 37 part-time/adjunct (24 women). *Students:* 604 full-time (399 women); includes 170 minority (12 African Americans, 5 American Indian/Alaska Native, 140 Asian Americans or Pacific Islanders, 13 Hispanic Americans), 94 international. Average age 24. 936 applicants, 31% accepted, 155 enrolled. In 2006, 162 degrees awarded. *Entrance requirements:* OAT. Additional exam requirements/recommendations for international students: Required—OAT. *Application deadline:* For fall admission, 3/15 for domestic and international students. Applications are processed on a rolling basis. Application fee: $75. Electronic applications accepted. *Expenses:* Tuition: Full-time $27,495. *Financial support:* In 2006–07, 525 students received support. Federal Work-Study and scholarships/grants available. Support available to part-time students. Financial award application deadline: 4/15; financial award applicants required to submit FAFSA. *Faculty research:* Eye disease treatment, binocular vision, cataract development, pediatric vision, genetic eye disease. *Unit head:* Dr. Arol Augsburger, President, 312-949-7705, Fax: 312-949-7670, E-mail: aaugsburger@eyecare.ico.edu. *Application contact:* Teisha Johnson, Director of Admissions, 312-949-7400, Fax: 312-949-7680, E-mail: tjohnson@ico.edu.

Indiana University Bloomington, School of Optometry, Bloomington, IN 47405-7000. Offers OD, MS, PhD. PhD offered through the University Graduate School. *Accreditation:* AOA (one or more programs are accredited). *Faculty:* 22 full-time (4 women). *Students:* 323 full-time (195 women), 15 part-time (12 women); includes 37 minority (12 African Americans, 18 Asian Americans or Pacific Islanders, 7 Hispanic Americans), 31 international. Average age 25. 371 applicants, 37% accepted, 75 enrolled. In 2006, 67 ODs, 1 doctorate awarded. Terminal master's awarded for partial completion of doctoral program. *Degree requirements:* For master's, thesis/dissertation, registration; for doctorate, thesis/dissertation, comprehensive exam, registration. *Entrance requirements:* For OD, OAT; for master's and doctorate, GRE, interview, BA in science. Additional exam requirements/recommendations for international students: Required—TOEFL (minimum score 550 paper-based; 213 computer-based; 80 iBT). *Application deadline:* For fall admission, 1/15 for domestic students; for winter admission, 2/1 for domestic and international students; for spring admission, 9/1 for domestic students. Application fee: $50 ($60 for international students). *Expenses: Contact institution. Financial support:* In 2006–07, 15 fellowships with full tuition reimbursements (averaging $20,000 per year), 2 research assistantships with full tuition reimbursements were awarded; Federal Work-Study, institutionally sponsored loans, and scholarships/grants also available. Support available to part-time students. Financial award application deadline: 12/1; financial award applicants required to submit FAFSA. *Faculty research:* Corneal physiology, contact lenses, adaptive optics, dry eye, low vision, refractive anomalies, opthalmic imaging, glaucoma, ocular physiology, infant vision, retinal disease. Total annual research expenditures: $5.6 million. *Unit head:* Dr. Gerald E. Lowther, Dean, 812-855-4440, Fax: 812-855-8664, E-mail: glowther@indiana.edu. *Application contact:* Andrea Waldbieser, Associate Director, Student Administration/Student Services, 812-855-1292, Fax: 812-855-4389.

Inter American University of Puerto Rico School of Optometry, Professional Program, San Juan, PR 00919. Offers OD. *Accreditation:* AOA. *Degree requirements:* For first-professional, thesis, research project. *Entrance requirements:* OAT, interview, minimum GPA of 2.5, 2 letters of recommendation. Electronic applications accepted. Expenses: Contact institution. *Faculty research:* Visual characteristics of special populations, contact lenses, refraction and diabetes.

The New England College of Optometry, Professional Program, Boston, MA 02115-1100. Offers optometry (OD); vision science (MS). *Accreditation:* AOA. *Students:* 436 full-time (309 women), 5 part-time (4 women); includes 129 minority (12 African Americans, 107 Asian Americans or Pacific Islanders, 10 Hispanic Americans), 77 international. Average age 25. 680 applicants, 110 enrolled. In 2006, 116 degrees awarded. *Entrance requirements:* OAT. *Application deadline:* For fall admission, 3/31 for domestic students. Applications are processed on a rolling basis. Application fee: $75. Electronic applications accepted. *Financial support:* In 2006–07, 4 research assistantships (averaging $5,193 per year) were awarded; career-related internships or fieldwork, Federal Work-Study, institutionally sponsored loans, and scholarships/grants also available. Financial award application deadline: 4/1; financial award applicants required to submit FAFSA. *Application contact:* Dr. Taline Farra, Director of Admissions, 617-587-5580, Fax: 617-587-5550, E-mail: farrat@neco.edu.

Announcement: The New England College of Optometry offers 3 programs of study leading to the Doctor of Optometry degree. The standard 4-year program is for applicants who hold a baccalaureate degree or who have completed a minimum of 3 years of specific undergraduate course work. There is an accelerated 27-month program for applicants holding a doctoral degree in science and an advanced-placement International Program for those who have earned a degree in optometry from a recognized international school of optometry. The College also offers postgraduate residency and fellowship programs in specialized areas of optometry. For additional information, visit the Web site at http://www.neco.edu.

Northeastern State University, College of Optometry, Tahlequah, OK 74464-2399. Offers OD. Applicants must be residents of Oklahoma, Arkansas, Kansas, Colorado, New Mexico, Missouri, Texas, or Nebraska. *Accreditation:* AOA. *Faculty:* 24 full-time (10 women), 10 part-time/adjunct (5 women). *Students:* 103 full-time (59 women); includes 17 minority (3 African Americans, 10 American Indian/Alaska Native, 3 Asian Americans or Pacific Islanders, 1 Hispanic American). Average age 26. 108 applicants, 33% accepted, 26 enrolled. In 2006, 25 degrees awarded. *Degree requirements:* For first-professional, research project. *Entrance requirements:* OAT. *Application deadline:* For fall admission, 2/1 for domestic students. Applications are processed on a rolling basis. Application fee: $45. *Expenses: Contact institution. Financial support:* In 2006–07, 42 students received support. Federal Work-Study, institutionally sponsored loans, scholarships/grants, tuition waivers (partial), and residencies available. Financial award application deadline: 5/1; financial award applicants required to submit FAFSA. *Faculty research:* Extended-wear and bifocal contact lenses, methods of vision therapy, glaucoma, low vision, diabetes. Total annual research expenditures: $575,000. *Unit head:* Dr. George E. Foster, Dean, 918-456-5511 Ext. 4000, Fax: 918-458-2104, E-mail: fosterge@nsuok.edu. *Application contact:* Natalie Batt, Student and Alumni Affairs, 918-456-5511 Ext. 4036, Fax: 918-458-2104, E-mail: batt@nsuok.edu.

Nova Southeastern University, Health Professions Division, College of Optometry, Fort Lauderdale, FL 33314-7796. Offers clinical vision research (MS); optometry (OD). *Accreditation:* AOA. Postbaccalaureate distance learning degree programs offered (no on-campus study). *Faculty:* 42 full-time (26 women), 14 part-time/adjunct (7 women). *Students:* 333 full-time (222 women), 106 part-time (73 women); includes 178 minority (24 African Americans, 98 Asian Americans or Pacific Islanders, 56 Hispanic Americans), 9 international. Average age 24. 673 applicants, 77% accepted, 118 enrolled. In 2006, 75 ODs, 3 master's awarded. *Entrance requirements:* OAT, minimum GPA of 3.0. *Application deadline:* For fall admission, 4/1 for domestic and international students. Applications are processed on a rolling basis. Application fee: $50. Electronic applications accepted. *Expenses: Contact institution. Financial support:* Institutionally sponsored loans and scholarships/grants available. Financial award application deadline: 4/1. *Faculty research:* Retinal disease, low vision, binocular vision, contact lenses, accommodation. *Unit head:* Dr. David Loshin, Dean, 954-262-1404, Fax: 954-262-1818. *Application contact:* Fran Franconeri, Admissions Counselor, 954-262-1132, Fax: 954-262-2282.

The Ohio State University, College of Optometry, Professional Program in Optometry, Columbus, OH 43210. Offers OD. *Accreditation:* AOA. *Faculty:* 33 full-time (14 women). *Students:* 252 full-time (153 women), 1 part-time; includes 32 minority (8 African Americans, 17 Asian Americans or Pacific Islanders, 7 Hispanic Americans), 2 international. Average age 25. In 2006, 62 degrees awarded. *Entrance requirements:* OAT. *Application deadline:* For fall admission, 3/1 for domestic and international students. Applications are processed on a rolling basis. Application fee: $40 ($50 for international students). Electronic applications accepted. *Expenses:* Tuition, state resident: full-time $9,438. Tuition, nonresident: full-time $22,791. Tuition and fees vary according to course load, campus/location and program. *Financial support:* In 2006–07, 220 students received support. Federal Work-Study and scholarships/grants available. Financial award application deadline: 3/1; financial award applicants required to submit FAFSA. *Unit head:* Dr. Joseph T. Barr, Head, 614-292-0437. *Application contact:* Graduate Admissions, 614-292-9444, Fax: 614-292-3895, E-mail: domestic.grad@osu.edu.

Pennsylvania College of Optometry, Professional Program, Elkins Park, PA 19027-1598. Offers OD, OD/MS. *Accreditation:* AOA. Postbaccalaureate distance learning degree programs offered. *Degree requirements:* For first-professional, comprehensive exam (for some programs). *Entrance requirements:* OAT, interview. Additional exam requirements/recommendations for international students: Required—TOEFL. Electronic applications accepted. *Faculty research:* Vision research, visual perception, ocular motility, electrodiagnosis, photobiology glaucoma, myopia, keratoconus.

Southern California College of Optometry, Professional Program, Fullerton, CA 92831-1615. Offers OD. *Accreditation:* AOA. *Degree requirements:* For first-professional, thesis. *Entrance requirements:* OAT. Electronic applications accepted. *Faculty research:* Structure and function of the human visual system.

Southern College of Optometry, Professional Program, Memphis, TN 38104-2222. Offers OD. *Accreditation:* AOA. *Degree requirements:* For first-professional, clinical experience. *Entrance requirements:* OAT, 3 years of undergraduate pre-optometry course work.

State University of New York College of Optometry, Professional Program, New York, NY 10036. Offers OD, OD/MPH, OD/MS, OD/PhD. *Accreditation:* AOA. *Faculty:* 45 full-time (10 women), 102 part-time/adjunct (28 women). *Students:* 281 full-time (196 women); includes 130 minority (9 African Americans, 114 Asian Americans or Pacific Islanders, 7 Hispanic Americans), 19 international. Average age 24. 499 applicants, 28% accepted, 74 enrolled. In 2006, 68 degrees awarded. *Entrance requirements:* OAT. Additional exam requirements/recommendations for international students: Required—TOEFL (minimum score 550 paper-based; 220 computer-based). *Application deadline:* For fall admission, 2/15 priority date for domestic and international students. Applications are processed on a rolling basis. Application fee: $75. Electronic applications accepted. *Expenses:* Tuition, state resident: full-time $13,620. Tuition, nonresident: full-time $26,150. Required fees: $370. *Financial support:* In 2006–07, 234 students received support; fellowships, career-related internships or fieldwork, Federal Work-Study, and tuition waivers (full and partial) available. Financial award application deadline: 4/15; financial award applicants required to submit FAFSA. *Faculty research:* Vision research. *Unit head:* Dr. Edward Johnston, Vice President for Student Affairs and Director of Admissions, 212-938-5500, Fax: 212-938-5501, E-mail: johnston@sunyopt.edu.

Université de Montréal, Faculty of Graduate Studies, School of Optometry, Professional Program in Optometry, Montréal, QC H3C 3J7, Canada. Offers OD. Open only to Canadian residents. *Accreditation:* AOA. *Degree requirements:* For first-professional, thesis. *Application deadline:* For fall admission, 2/1 priority date for domestic students; for winter admission, 11/1 priority date for domestic students; for spring admission, 2/1 priority date for domestic students. Application fee: $30. Electronic applications accepted. *Application contact:* Christian Casanova, Chairperson, 514-343-6325, Fax: 514-343-2382.

The University of Alabama at Birmingham, School of Optometry, Professional Program in Optometry, Birmingham, AL 35294. Offers OD. *Students:* 162 full-time (104 women); includes 23 minority (8 African Americans, 3 American Indian/Alaska Native, 12 Asian Americans or Pacific Islanders), 1 international. Average age 25. 212 applicants, 25% accepted. In 2006, 40 degrees awarded. *Entrance requirements:* OAT, interview. *Application deadline:* For fall admission, 3/1 for domestic students. Applications are processed on a rolling basis. Application fee: $40. *Expenses:* Tuition, state resident: part-time $170 per credit hour. Tuition, nonresident: part-time $425 per credit hour. Required fees: $15 per credit hour. $122 per term. Tuition and fees vary according to program. *Financial support:* In 2006–07, 137 students received support. Application deadline: 5/1. *Unit head:* Dr. Jimmy D. Bartlett, Chair, 205-934-6764, E-mail: eyedrug@uab.edu.

University of California, Berkeley, School of Optometry, Berkeley, CA 94720-1500. Offers OD, Certificate. *Accreditation:* AOA. *Students:* 200 applicants, 36% accepted, 61 enrolled. In 2006, 59 degrees awarded. *Degree requirements:* For first-professional, thesis. *Entrance requirements:* OAT. Additional exam requirements/recommendations for international students: Required—TOEFL (minimum score 570 paper-based; 230 computer-based). *Application deadline:* For fall admission, 12/15 for domestic and international students. Application fee: $60. Electronic applications accepted. *Financial support:* Career-related internships or fieldwork, Federal Work-Study, institutionally sponsored loans, scholarships/grants, and unspecified assistantships available. Financial award application deadline: 3/2; financial award applicants required to submit FAFSA. *Faculty research:* Low vision, spatial vision, psychophysics of vision, clinical optics, patient care. *Unit head:* Dr. Dennis M. Levi, Dean, 510-642-3414, Fax: 510-642-7806, E-mail: dlevi@berkeley.edu. *Application contact:* Dr. Richard C. Van Sluyters, Associate Dean for Student Affairs/Head Graduate Adviser, 510-642-9537, Fax: 510-643-5109, E-mail: admissions@optometry.berkeley.edu.

University of Houston, College of Optometry, Professional Program in Optometry, Houston, TX 77204. Offers OD. *Accreditation:* AOA. *Students:* 384 full-time (270 women), 14 part-time (9 women); includes 209 minority (18 African Americans, 2 American Indian/Alaska Native, 155 Asian Americans or Pacific Islanders, 34 Hispanic Americans), 7 international. Average age 25. 96 applicants, 100% accepted, 87 enrolled. In 2006, 89 ODs awarded. *Entrance requirements:* OAT, minimum GPA of 2.7. *Application deadline:* For fall admission, 10/15 priority date for domestic students; for spring admission, 2/1 for domestic students. Applications are processed on a rolling basis. Application fee: $50 ($75 for international students). *Expenses:* Tuition, state resident: full-time $5,429; part-time $226 per credit. Tuition, nonresident: full-time $12,029; part-time $501 per credit. Required fees: $2,454. *Financial support:* Fellowships with full tuition reimbursements, research assistantships with full tuition reimbursements, teaching assistantships with full tuition reimbursements, career-related internships or fieldwork, Federal Work-Study, institutionally sponsored loans, scholarships/grants, health care benefits, and unspecified assistantships available. Support available to part-time students. Financial award application deadline: 3/10. *Faculty research:* Refractive error development, corneal physiology, low vision, binocular vision. *Unit head:* Dr. Roger Boltz, Associate Dean, 713-743-1893, Fax: 713-743-0965, E-mail: boltz@uh.edu. *Application contact:* Paul Pease, Director, Student Affairs and Admission, 713-743-2040, Fax: 713-743-2046, E-mail: ppease@uh.edu.

University of Missouri–St. Louis, College of Optometry, Professional Program in Optometry, St. Louis, MO 63121. Offers OD. *Accreditation:* AOA. *Faculty:* 23 full-time (6 women), 14 part-time/adjunct (4 women). *Students:* 174 full-time (102 women); includes 18 minority (7 African Americans, 2 American Indian/Alaska Native, 6 Asian Americans or Pacific Islanders, 3 Hispanic Americans), 6 international. Average age 23. 360 applicants, 25% accepted, 44 enrolled. In 2006, 34 degrees awarded. *Entrance requirements:* OAT, 90 hours of undergraduate course work. *Application deadline:* For fall admission, 2/15 for domestic and international students. Applications are processed on a rolling basis. Application fee: $50. Electronic applications accepted. *Expenses:* Tuition, state resident: part-time $332 per credit hour. Tuition, nonresident: part-time $770 per credit hour. *Financial support:* In 2006–07, 3 research assistantships (averaging $500 per year), 3 teaching assistantships (averaging $500 per year) were awarded; Federal Work-Study, institutionally sponsored loans, and scholarships/grants also available. Financial award application deadline: 4/1; financial award applicants required to submit FAFSA. *Faculty research:* Visual psychophysics and perception, neurophysiology of visual gulomotor systems, noninvasive assessment of visual processing, aging and Alzheimer's disease, orthokeratology. *Unit head:* Dr. Edward S. Bennett, Director, Student Services, 314-516-6263, Fax: 314-516-6708, E-mail: optstuaff@umsl.edu. *Application contact:* Linda L. Stein, Administrative Assistant, 314-516-5905, Fax: 314-516-6708, E-mail: linda_stein@umsl.edu.

University of Waterloo, Graduate Studies, Faculty of Science, School of Optometry, Waterloo, ON N2L 3G1, Canada. Offers vision science (M Sc, PhD). *Accreditation:* AOA. Part-time programs available. *Faculty:* 32 full-time (14 women), 33 part-time/adjunct (7 women). *Students:* 34 full-time (20 women), 9 part-time (5 women). 18 applicants, 44% accepted, 6 enrolled. In 2006, 10 master's, 3 doctorates awarded. *Degree requirements:* For master's and doctorate, thesis/dissertation. *Entrance requirements:* For master's, honors degree, minimum B average; for doctorate, master's degree, minimum B average. Additional exam requirements/recommendations for international students: Required—TOEFL (minimum score 580 paper-based; 237 computer-based), TWE (minimum score 4). *Application deadline:* For fall admission, 8/1 priority date for domestic students, 3/1 priority date for international students; for winter admission, 12/1 priority date for domestic students, 7/1 priority date for international students; for spring admission, 3/1 priority date for domestic students, 11/1 priority date for international students. Applications are processed on a rolling basis. Application fee: $75 Canadian dollars. Electronic applications accepted. *Financial support:* In 2006–07, 1 fellowship, 9,320 teaching assistantships were awarded; research assistantships, career-related internships or fieldwork, institutionally sponsored loans, scholarships/grants, and health care benefits also available. *Faculty research:* Vision science, fundamental and clinical vision, physiological optics, psychophysics, perception. *Unit head:* Dr. T. Singer, Graduate Officer, 519-888-4567 Ext. 36622, Fax: 519-725-0784, E-mail: tsinger@uwaterloo.ca. *Application contact:* Krista Parsons, Graduate and Research Studies Coordinator, 519-888-4567 Ext. 35039, Fax: 519-725-0784, E-mail: ktparson@uwaterloo.ca.

Vision Sciences

Eastern Virginia Medical School, Ophthalmic Technology Program, Norfolk, VA 23501-1980. Offers Certificate. *Faculty:* 1 full-time. *Students:* 8 full-time (7 women); includes 3 minority (1 African American, 2 Asian Americans or Pacific Islanders). 8 applicants, 50% accepted, 4 enrolled. In 2006, 3 degrees awarded. *Unit head:* Lori J. Williams, Director, 757-388-3747, E-mail: optech@evms.edu.

Emory University, School of Medicine, Programs in Allied Health Professions, The Emory Ophthalmic Technology Program, Atlanta, GA 30322-1100. Offers MM Sc. *Faculty:* 1 full-time (0 women), 4 part-time/adjunct (3 women). *Students:* 3 full-time (1 woman). Average age 31. 2 applicants, 100% accepted, 2 enrolled. *Degree requirements:* For master's, thesis. *Entrance requirements:* For master's, GRE General Test. Additional exam requirements/recommendations for international students: Required—TOEFL. *Application deadline:* For fall admission, 3/31 priority date for domestic and international students. Applications are processed on a rolling basis. Application fee: $50. *Expenses: Contact institution. Financial support:* In 2006–07, 3 students received support. Institutionally sponsored loans and scholarships/grants available. Financial award application deadline: 4/1; financial award applicants required to submit FAFSA. *Faculty research:* Keratocytic density and corneal research involving the confocal corneal microscope. *Unit head:* Paul M. Larson, Director, 404-778-4305, Fax: 404-778-5128, E-mail: plarson@emory.edu.

The New England College of Optometry, Professional Program, Boston, MA 02115-1100. Offers optometry (OD); vision science (MS). *Accreditation:* AOA. *Students:* 436 full-time (309 women), 5 part-time (4 women); includes 129 minority (12 African Americans, 107 Asian Americans or Pacific Islanders, 10 Hispanic Americans), 77 international. Average age 25. 680 applicants, 110 enrolled. In 2006, 116 degrees awarded. *Entrance requirements:* OAT. *Application deadline:* For fall admission, 3/31 for domestic students. Applications are processed on a rolling basis. Application fee: $75. Electronic applications accepted. *Financial support:* In 2006–07, 4 research assistantships (averaging $5,193 per year) were awarded; career-related internships or fieldwork, Federal Work-Study, institutionally sponsored loans, and scholarships/grants also available. Financial award application deadline: 4/1; financial award applicants required to submit FAFSA. *Application contact:* Dr. Taline Farra, Director of Admissions, 617-587-5580, Fax: 617-587-5550, E-mail: farrat@neco.edu.

Nova Southeastern University, Health Professions Division, College of Optometry, Fort Lauderdale, FL 33314-7796. Offers clinical vision research (MS); optometry (OD). *Accreditation:* AOA. Postbaccalaureate distance learning degree programs offered (no on-campus study). *Faculty:* 42 full-time (26 women), 14 part-time/adjunct (7 women). *Students:* 333 full-time (222 women), 106 part-time (73 women); includes 178 minority (24 African Americans, 98 Asian Americans or Pacific Islanders, 56 Hispanic Americans), 9 international. Average age 24. 673 applicants, 77% accepted, 118 enrolled. In 2006, 75 ODs, 3 master's awarded. *Entrance requirements:* OAT, minimum GPA of 3.0. *Application deadline:* For fall admission, 4/1 for domestic and international students. Applications are processed on a rolling basis. Application fee: $50. Electronic applications accepted. *Expenses: Contact institution. Financial support:* Institutionally sponsored loans and scholarships/grants available. Financial award application deadline: 4/1. *Faculty research:* Retinal disease, low vision, binocular vision, contact lenses, accommodation. *Unit head:* Dr. David Loshin, Dean, 954-262-1404, Fax: 954-262-1818. *Application contact:* Fran Franconeri, Admissions Counselor, 954-262-1132, Fax: 954-262-2282.

Pennsylvania College of Optometry, Graduate Studies in Vision Impairment and Audiology, Elkins Park, PA 19027-1598. Offers audiology (Au D); education of children and youth with visual and multiple impairments (M Ed, Certificate); low vision rehabilitation (MS, Certificate); orientation and mobility therapy (MS, Certificate); rehabilitation teaching (MS, Certificate); OD/MS. *Accreditation:* ASHA. Part-time programs available. *Entrance requirements:* For master's, GRE or MAT, letters of reference (3), interviews (2). Additional exam requirements/recommendations for international students: Required—TOEFL, TWE. Expenses: Contact institution. *Faculty research:* Knowledge utilization, technology transfer.

State University of New York College of Optometry, Graduate Programs, New York, NY 10036. Offers MS, PhD, OD/MS, OD/PhD. Part-time programs available. *Faculty:* 28 full-time (3 women), 1 (woman) part-time/adjunct. *Students:* 11 full-time (5 women), 14 part-time (9 women). 11 applicants, 36% accepted, 3 enrolled. In 2006, 4 master's, 1 doctorate awarded. Terminal master's awarded for partial completion of doctoral program. *Degree requirements:* For master's, thesis; for doctorate, thesis/dissertation, specialty exam, comprehensive exam. *Entrance requirements:* For master's and doctorate, GRE General Test. Additional exam requirements/recommendations for international students: Required—TOEFL. *Application deadline:* For fall admission, 3/1 priority date for domestic and international students. Applications are processed on a rolling basis. Application fee: $75. *Expenses: Contact institution. Financial support:* In 2006–07, 9 students received support, including 7 teaching assistantships with full tuition reimbursements available (averaging $18,000 per year); fellowships, research assistantships, Federal Work-Study, tuition waivers (full and partial), and unspecified assistantships also available. Financial award application deadline: 3/1. *Faculty research:* Oculomotor systems, perception, physiological optics, ocular biochemistry, accommodation, color and motion. *Unit head:* Dr. Jerry Feldman, Associate Dean, 212-938-5541, Fax: 212-938-5537, E-mail: jfeldman@sunyopt.edu. *Application contact:* Debra Berger, Assistant to Associate Dean, 212-938-5544, Fax: 212-938-5537, E-mail: berger@sunyopt.edu.

Université de Montréal, Faculty of Graduate Studies, School of Optometry, Graduate Programs in Optometry, Montréal, QC H3C 3J7, Canada. Offers optometry (DESS); vision sciences (M Sc). Part-time programs available. *Degree requirements:* For master's, thesis. *Entrance requirements:* For master's, OD or appropriate bachelor's degree, minimum GPA of 2.7. *Application deadline:* For fall admission, 2/1 priority date for domestic students; for winter admission, 11/1 priority date for domestic students; for spring admission, 2/1 priority date for domestic students. Application fee: $30. Electronic applications accepted. *Financial support:* Research assistantships, teaching assistantships, career-related internships or fieldwork available. Support available to part-time students. *Faculty research:* Binocular vision, visual electrophysiology, eye movements, corneal metabolism, glare sensitivity. *Application contact:* Christian Casanova, Chairperson, 514-343-6325, Fax: 514-343-2382.

Université de Montréal, Faculty of Medicine and Faculty of Graduate Studies, Graduate Programs in Medicine, Program in Specialized Studies, Montréal, QC H3C 3J7, Canada. Offers anesthesia (DESS); diagnostic radiology (DESS); family medicine (DESS); medical biochemistry (DESS); medical genetics (DESS); medicine (DESS); microbiology and infectious diseases (DESS); nuclear medicine (DESS); obstetrics and gynecology (DESS); ophthalmology (DESS); pediatrics (DESS); psychiatry (DESS); radiology-oncology (DESS); surgery (DESS). *Faculty:* 159 full-time (37 women), 345 part-time/adjunct (102 women). *Entrance requirements:* For degree, proficiency in French. *Application deadline:* For fall admission, 2/1 priority date for domestic students; for winter admission, 11/1 priority date for domestic students; for spring admission, 2/1 priority date for domestic students. Application fee: $30. Electronic applications accepted. *Unit head:* Dr. Pierre Boyle, Vice Dean of Studies, 514-343-6300, Fax: 514-343-5751, E-mail: pierre.boyle@umontreal.ca.

The University of Alabama at Birmingham, School of Optometry, Graduate Program in Vision Science, Birmingham, AL 35294. Offers MS, PhD. *Students:* 22 full-time (9 women), 2 part-time (1 woman); includes 3 minority (2 African Americans, 1 Asian American or Pacific Islander), 8 international. Average age 30. 11 applicants, 45% accepted. In 2006, 3 degrees awarded. Terminal master's awarded for partial completion of doctoral program. *Degree requirements:* For master's and doctorate, thesis/dissertation. *Entrance requirements:* For master's and doctorate, GRE General Test, OAT, interview. *Application deadline:* Applications are processed on a rolling basis. Application fee: $35 ($60 for international students). Electronic applications accepted. *Expenses:* Tuition, state resident: part-time $170 per credit hour. Tuition, nonresident: part-time $425 per credit hour. Required fees: $15 per credit hour. $122 per term. Tuition and fees vary according to program. *Unit head:* Dr. Paul Gamlin, Department Chair, 205-934-0322, E-mail: pgamlin@uab.edu.

The University of Alabama in Huntsville, School of Graduate Studies, College of Engineering, Department of Electrical and Computer Engineering, Huntsville, AL 35899. Offers computer engineering (PhD); electrical and computer engineering (MSE); electrical engineering (PhD); optical science and engineering (PhD); software engineering (MSE, MSSE). Part-time programs available. *Faculty:* 23 full-time (3 women), 3 part-time/adjunct (0 women). *Students:* 57 full-time (13 women), 138 part-time (18 women); includes 24 minority (9 African Americans, 2 American Indian/Alaska Native, 11 Asian Americans or Pacific Islanders, 2 Hispanic Americans), 43 international. Average age 30. 215 applicants, 55% accepted, 59 enrolled. In 2006, 52 master's, 6 doctorates awarded. *Degree requirements:* For master's, thesis or alternative, oral and written exams, comprehensive exam, registration; for doctorate, thesis/dissertation, oral and written exams, comprehensive exam, registration. *Entrance requirements:* For master's, GRE General Test, appropriate bachelor's degree, minimum GPA of 3.0; for doctorate, GRE General Test, minimum GPA of 3.0. Additional exam requirements/recommendations for international students: Required—TOEFL (minimum score 500 paper-based; 173 computer-based). *Application deadline:* For fall admission, 5/30 priority date for domestic students, 2/28 priority date for international students; for spring admission, 10/10 priority date for domestic students, 7/10 priority date for international students. Applications are processed on a rolling basis. Application fee: $40. *Expenses:* Tuition, state resident: full-time $6,072; part-time $253 per credit hour. Tuition, nonresident: full-time $12,476; part-time $519 per credit hour. *Financial support:* In 2006–07, 33 students received support, including 10 research assistantships with full and partial tuition reimbursements available (averaging $5,538 per year), 23 teaching assistantships with full and partial tuition reimbursements available (averaging $8,963 per year); fellowships with full and partial tuition reimbursements available, career-related internships or fieldwork, Federal Work-Study, institutionally sponsored loans, scholarships/grants, health care benefits, and unspecified assistantships also available. Support available to part-time students. Financial award application deadline: 4/1; financial award applicants required to submit FAFSA. *Faculty research:* Optical signal processing, electromagnetics, photonics, nonlinear waves, computer architecture. Total annual research expenditures: $717,564. *Unit head:* Dr. Reza Adhami, Chair, 256-824-6316, Fax: 256-824-6803, E-mail: adhami@ece.uah.edu.

University of Alberta, Faculty of Medicine and Dentistry and Faculty of Graduate Studies and Research, Graduate Programs in Medicine, Department of Ophthalmology, Edmonton, AB T6G 2E1, Canada. Offers M Sc, PhD. Part-time programs available. *Faculty:* 1 full-time (0 women), 1 part-time/adjunct (0 women). *Students:* 2 full-time (1 woman). Average age 25. In 2006, 1 degree awarded. Terminal master's awarded for partial completion of doctoral program. *Degree requirements:* For master's, thesis/dissertation; for doctorate, thesis/dissertation, comprehensive exam. *Application deadline:* For fall admission, 4/1 priority date for domestic students. Applications are processed on a rolling basis. Application fee: $60. *Financial support:* In 2006–07, 1 student received support; research assistantships available. *Faculty research:* Ocular genetics. Total annual research expenditures: $240,500. *Unit head:* Dr. G. T. Drummond, Acting Chair, 780-477-4924, Fax: 780-477-4969.

University of California, Berkeley, Graduate Division, Group in Vision Science, Berkeley, CA 94720-1500. Offers MS, PhD. *Degree requirements:* For master's and doctorate, thesis/dissertation. *Entrance requirements:* For master's and doctorate, GRE General Test, GRE Subject Test, minimum GPA of 3.0. *Application deadline:* For fall admission, 1/5 for domestic students. Application fee: $60 ($80 for international students). *Financial support:* Fellowships,

Vision Sciences

University of California, Berkeley (continued)
research assistantships, teaching assistantships, Federal Work-Study, institutionally sponsored loans, scholarships/grants, tuition waivers (partial), and unspecified assistantships available. Financial award applicants required to submit FAFSA. *Faculty research:* Visual neuroscience, bioengineering, computational vision, molecular cell biology, basic and clinical psychophysics. *Unit head:* Stanley Klein, Chair, 510-642-8670, E-mail: klein@spectacle.berkeley.edu. *Application contact:* Fran Stone, Student Affairs Officer, 510-642-9804, Fax: 510-643-5109, E-mail: vision@berkeley.edu.

University of Chicago, Division of the Biological Sciences, Department of Ophthalmology and Visual Science, Chicago, IL 60637-1513. Offers PhD. *Faculty:* 12 full-time (5 women). *Students:* 2 applicants, 0% accepted. *Degree requirements:* For doctorate, thesis/dissertation, registration. *Entrance requirements:* For doctorate, GRE General Test. Additional exam requirements/recommendations for international students: Required—TOEFL. *Application deadline:* For fall admission, 12/28 priority date for domestic and international students. Application fee: $55. *Expenses:* Tuition: Full-time $34,920. Required fees: $612. One-time fee: $35 full-time. Full-time tuition and fees vary according to course load, degree level and program. *Financial support:* In 2006–07, fellowships with tuition reimbursements (averaging $24,758 per year), research assistantships (averaging $24,758 per year) were awarded; institutionally sponsored loans, scholarships/grants, traineeships, and health care benefits also available. Financial award applicants required to submit FAFSA. *Faculty research:* Visual psychophysics, visual molecular biology, immunology, transplantation, infections. Total annual research expenditures: $1.2 million. *Unit head:* Dr. William Mieler, Chairman, 773-702-3838, Fax: 773-702-8094, E-mail: wmieler@bsd.chicago.edu. *Application contact:* Sandra Wallace, Residency Program Coordinator, 773-795-7286, E-mail: swallace@bsd.uchicago.edu.

University of Guelph, Ontario Veterinary College and Graduate Program Services, Graduate Programs in Veterinary Sciences, Department of Clinical Studies, Guelph, ON N1G 2W1, Canada. Offers anesthesiology (M Sc, DV Sc); cardiology (Diploma); clinical studies (Diploma); emergency/critical care (Diploma); medicine (M Sc, DV Sc); neurology (M Sc, DV Sc); ophthalmology (M Sc, DV Sc); surgery (M Sc, DV Sc). *Faculty:* 37. *Students:* 27 (19 women). *Degree requirements:* For master's, thesis/dissertation; for doctorate, thesis/dissertation, comprehensive exam. *Entrance requirements:* Additional exam requirements/recommendations for international students: Required—TOEFL (minimum score 550 paper-based; 213 computer-based), IELTS (minimum score 7). *Application deadline:* For fall admission, 12/6 for domestic students; for winter admission, 10/30 priority date for domestic students; for spring admission, 2/28 priority date for domestic students. Applications are processed on a rolling basis. Application fee: $80. Electronic applications accepted. *Financial support:* Fellowships, research assistantships, teaching assistantships, career-related internships or fieldwork and scholarships/grants available. *Faculty research:* Orthopedics, respirology, oncology, exercise physiology, cardiology. Total annual research expenditures: $1.5 million. *Unit head:* Dr. Dara Allen, Interim Chair, 519-824-4120 Ext. 54001, Fax: 519-767-0311, E-mail: dallen@ouc.uoguelph.ca. *Application contact:* Dr. J. Scott Weese, Graduate Coordinator, 519-824-4120 Ext. 54064, Fax: 519-767-0311, E-mail: jsweese@uoguelph.ca.

University of Houston, College of Optometry, Program in Physiological Optics/Vision Science, Houston, TX 77204. Offers MS Phys Op, PhD. *Students:* 23 full-time (16 women), 7 part-time (4 women); includes 4 minority (3 Asian Americans or Pacific Islanders, 1 Hispanic American), 17 international. Average age 30. 5 applicants, 100% accepted, 5 enrolled. In 2006, 2 master's, 5 doctorates awarded. *Degree requirements:* For master's, thesis; for doctorate, one foreign language, thesis/dissertation, oral or written qualifying exam. *Entrance requirements:* For master's and doctorate, GRE General Test, minimum GPA of 3.0. *Application deadline:* For fall admission, 1/31 for domestic students. Applications are processed on a rolling basis. Application fee: $0 ($25 for international students). *Expenses:* Tuition, state resident: full-time $5,429; part-time $226 per credit. Tuition, nonresident: full-time $12,029; part-time $501 per credit. Required fees: $2,454. *Financial support:* In 2006–07, 13 research assistantships with full tuition reimbursements (averaging $12,950 per year), 14 teaching assistantships with full tuition reimbursements (averaging $12,950 per year) were awarded; fellowships with full tuition reimbursements, career-related internships or fieldwork, Federal Work-Study, institutionally sponsored loans, scholarships/grants, health care benefits, and unspecified assistantships also available. Support available to part-time students. Financial award application deadline: 3/10. *Faculty research:* Space perception, amblyopia, binocular vision, development of visual skills, strabismus, visual cell biology, refractive error. *Unit head:* Laura Frishman, Associate Dean, Graduate Studies/Research, 713-743-1972, Fax: 713-743-1888, E-mail: lfrishman@uh.edu. *Application contact:* Laura Johnson, Graduate Coordinator, 713-743-1885, Fax: 713-743-1888, E-mail: ljohnson@uh.edu.

University of Louisville, School of Medicine, Department of Ophthalmology and Visual Sciences, Louisville, KY 40292-0001. Offers PhD. In 2006, 1 degree awarded. *Application contact:* Director of Admissions, 502-852-5793, Fax: 502-852-6849.

University of Missouri–St. Louis, College of Optometry and Graduate School, Program in Physiological Optics, St. Louis, MO 63121. Offers vision science (MS, PhD). *Faculty:* 11 full-time (1 woman). *Students:* 4 full-time (1 woman), 2 part-time (1 woman); includes 1 minority (Asian American or Pacific Islander), 3 international. Average age 29. 4 applicants, 50% accepted, 1 enrolled. *Degree requirements:* For master's, thesis/dissertation, registration; for doctorate, thesis/dissertation, comprehensive exam, registration. *Entrance requirements:* For master's and doctorate, GRE General Test. Additional exam requirements/recommendations for international students: Required—TOEFL (minimum score 570 paper-based). *Application deadline:* For fall admission, 3/15 for domestic and international students. Applications are processed on a rolling basis. Application fee: $25 ($40 for international students). Electronic applications accepted. *Expenses:* Contact institution. *Financial support:* In 2006–07, 1 research assistantship with full tuition reimbursement, 3 teaching assistantships with full tuition reimbursements (averaging $16,000 per year) were awarded; fellowships with full tuition reimbursements, Federal Work-Study, institutionally sponsored loans, and unspecified assistantships also available. Financial award application deadline: 3/15; financial award applicants required to submit FAFSA. *Faculty research:* Theoretical and applied optics, theoretical and applied psychophysics, eye movements, binocular vision, contact lenses. *Unit head:* Dr. Carl J. Bassi, Director, Research and Graduate Studies, 314-516-6029, Fax: 314-516-5150, E-mail: bassi@umsl.edu.

University of Waterloo, Graduate Studies, Faculty of Science, School of Optometry, Waterloo, ON N2L 3G1, Canada. Offers vision science (M Sc, PhD). *Accreditation:* AOA. Part-time programs available. *Faculty:* 32 full-time (14 women), 33 part-time/adjunct (7 women). *Students:* 34 full-time (20 women), 9 part-time (5 women). 18 applicants, 44% accepted, 6 enrolled. In 2006, 10 master's, 3 doctorates awarded. *Degree requirements:* For master's and doctorate, thesis/dissertation. *Entrance requirements:* For master's, honors degree, minimum B average; for doctorate, master's degree, minimum B average. Additional exam requirements/recommendations for international students: Required—TOEFL (minimum score 580 paper-based; 237 computer-based), TWE (minimum score 4). *Application deadline:* For fall admission, 8/1 priority date for domestic students, 3/1 priority date for international students; for winter admission, 12/1 priority date for domestic students, 7/1 priority date for international students; for spring admission, 3/1 priority date for domestic students, 11/1 priority date for international students. Applications are processed on a rolling basis. Application fee: $75 Canadian dollars. Electronic applications accepted. *Financial support:* In 2006–07, 1 fellowship, 9,320 teaching assistantships were awarded; research assistantships, career-related internships or fieldwork, institutionally sponsored loans, scholarships/grants, and health care benefits also available. *Faculty research:* Vision science, fundamental and clinical vision, physiological optics, psychophysics, perception. *Unit head:* Dr. T. Singer, Graduate Officer, 519-888-4567 Ext. 36622, Fax: 519-725-0784, E-mail: tsinger@uwaterloo.ca. *Application contact:* Krista Parsons, Graduate and Research Studies Coordinator, 519-888-4567 Ext. 35039, Fax: 519-725-0784, E-mail: ktparson@uwaterloo.ca.

Section 39
Pharmacy and Pharmaceutical Sciences

This section contains a directory of institutions offering graduate work in pharmacy and pharmaceutical sciences, followed by in-depth entries submitted by institutions that chose to prepare detailed program descriptions. Additional information about programs listed in the directory but not augmented by an in-depth entry may be obtained by writing directly to the dean of a graduate school or chair of a department at the address given in the directory.

For programs offering related work, see also in this book Allied Health; in Book 3, Biochemistry, Biological and Biomedical Sciences, Nutrition, Pharmacology and Toxicology, and Physiology; in Book 4, Chemistry; and in Book 5, Biomedical Engineering and Biotechnology, and Chemical Engineering.

CONTENTS

Medicinal and Pharmaceutical Chemistry

Duquesne University, School of Pharmacy, Graduate School of Pharmaceutical Sciences, Program in Medicinal Chemistry, Pittsburgh, PA 15282-0001. Offers MS, PhD. *Faculty:* 3 full-time (0 women). *Students:* 16 full-time (5 women), 4 part-time (2 women); includes 1 minority (African American), 19 international. 34 applicants, 12% accepted, 3 enrolled. *Degree requirements:* For master's, thesis/dissertation; for doctorate, thesis/dissertation, comprehensive exam. *Entrance requirements:* For master's and doctorate, GRE General Test. Additional exam requirements/recommendations for international students: Required—TOEFL. *Application deadline:* For fall admission, 2/1 priority date for domestic students. Applications are processed on a rolling basis. Application fee: $50. *Expenses:* Tuition: Part-time $723 per credit. Required fees: $71 per credit. Tuition and fees vary according to degree level and program. *Financial support:* In 2006–07, 16 students received support, including 3 research assistantships with full tuition reimbursements available, 13 teaching assistantships with full tuition reimbursements available; career-related internships or fieldwork, Federal Work-Study, institutionally sponsored loans, scholarships/grants, and unspecified assistantships also available. Support available to part-time students. *Unit head:* Dr. Aleem Gangjee, Head.

See Close-Up on page 2233.

Florida Agricultural and Mechanical University, Division of Graduate Studies, Research, and Continuing Education, College of Pharmacy and Pharmaceutical Sciences, Graduate Programs in Pharmaceutical Sciences, Tallahassee, FL 32307-3200. Offers environmental toxicology (PhD); medicinal chemistry (MS, PhD); pharmaceutics (MS, PhD); pharmacology/toxicology (MS, PhD); pharmacy administration (MS). *Accreditation:* CEPH. *Degree requirements:* For master's and doctorate, thesis/dissertation, publishable paper, comprehensive exam. *Entrance requirements:* For master's and doctorate, GRE General Test, minimum GPA of 3.0 in last 60 hours. Additional exam requirements/recommendations for international students: Required—TOEFL. *Faculty research:* Anticancer agents, anti-inflammatory drugs, chronopharmacology, neuroendocrinology, microbiology.

See Close-Up on page 2235.

Idaho State University, Office of Graduate Studies, College of Pharmacy, Department of Pharmaceutical Sciences, Pocatello, ID 83209. Offers biopharmaceutical analysis (PhD); biopharmaceutics (PhD); pharmaceutical chemistry (MS); pharmaceutical science (PhD); pharmaceutics (MS); pharmacognosy (MS); pharmacokinetics (PhD); pharmacology (MS, PhD). *Faculty:* 11 full-time (2 women). *Students:* 17 full-time (6 women), 4 part-time (2 women); includes 2 minority (both Asian Americans or Pacific Islanders), 14 international. Average age 30. In 2006, 1 master's, 3 doctorates awarded. *Degree requirements:* For master's, one foreign language, thesis, thesis research, comprehensive exam, registration (for some programs); for doctorate, thesis/dissertation, written and oral exams, comprehensive exam, registration. *Entrance requirements:* For master's, GRE General Test, minimum GPA of 3.0, 3 letters of recommendation; for doctorate, GRE General Test, BS degree in pharmacy or related field, minimum GPA of 3.0, 3 letters of recommendation. Additional exam requirements/recommendations for international students: Required—TOEFL (minimum score 550 paper-based; 213 computer-based). *Application deadline:* For fall admission, 7/1 for domestic students, 6/1 priority date for international students; for spring admission, 12/1 for domestic students, 11/1 priority date for international students. Applications are processed on a rolling basis. Application fee: $55. *Expenses:* Tuition, state resident: part-time $251 per credit. Tuition, nonresident: part-time $366 per credit. Tuition and fees vary according to degree level, program and reciprocity agreements. *Financial support:* In 2006–07, 5 teaching assistantships with full and partial tuition reimbursements (averaging $8,694 per year) were awarded; career-related internships or fieldwork, Federal Work-Study, scholarships/grants, traineeships, tuition waivers (full and partial), and unspecified assistantships also available. Support available to part-time students. Financial award application deadline: 1/1. *Faculty research:* Metabolic toxicity of heavy metals, neuroendocrine pharmacology, cardiovascular pharmacology, cancer biology, immunopharmacology. Total annual research expenditures: $1.6 million. *Unit head:* Dr. Fred Risinger, Chair, 208-282-2682, Fax: 208-282-4305, E-mail: risinger@pharmacy.isu.edu. *Application contact:* Ellen Combs, Graduate School Technical Records Specialist, 208-282-2150, Fax: 208-282-4847.

Lehigh University, College of Arts and Sciences, Department of Chemistry, Bethlehem, PA 18015-3094. Offers chemistry (MS, PhD); clinical chemistry (MS); pharmaceutical chemistry (MS, PhD); polymer science and engineering (MS, PhD). Part-time programs available. Post-baccalaureate distance learning degree programs offered (no on-campus study). *Faculty:* 16 full-time (2 women), 1 part-time/adjunct (0 women). *Students:* 34 full-time (16 women), 102 part-time (56 women); includes 21 minority (6 African Americans, 9 Asian Americans or Pacific Islanders, 6 Hispanic Americans), 17 international. 74 applicants, 70% accepted, 42 enrolled. In 2006, 18 master's, 2 doctorates awarded. Terminal master's awarded for partial completion of doctoral program. *Degree requirements:* For master's and doctorate, thesis/dissertation, comprehensive exam, registration. *Entrance requirements:* Additional exam requirements/recommendations for international students: Required—TOEFL (minimum score 230 computer-based). *Application deadline:* For fall admission, 1/15 priority date for domestic and international students. Applications are processed on a rolling basis. Application fee: $65. Electronic applications accepted. *Financial support:* In 2006–07, 3 fellowships with full tuition reimbursements (averaging $20,000 per year), 8 research assistantships with full tuition reimbursements (averaging $20,000 per year), 19 teaching assistantships with full tuition reimbursements (averaging $20,000 per year) were awarded; career-related internships or fieldwork, Federal Work-Study, institutionally sponsored loans, scholarships/grants, tuition waivers (full and partial), and unspecified assistantships also available. Support available to part-time students. Financial award application deadline: 1/15. *Faculty research:* Surfaces and interfaces, polymers, drug conjugates, organometallics. Total annual research expenditures: $1.4 million. *Unit head:* Dr. Robert H. Flowers, Chairman, 610-758-3470, Fax: 610-758-6536, E-mail: rof2@lehigh.edu. *Application contact:* Dr. Rebecca Miller, Graduate Coordinator, 610-758-3471, Fax: 610-758-6536, E-mail: inluchem@lehigh.edu.

Long Island University, C.W. Post Campus, School of Health Professions and Nursing, Department of Biomedical Sciences, Program in Medical Biology, Brookville, NY 11548-1300. Offers hematology (MS); immunology (MS); medical biology (MS); medical chemistry (MS); medical microbiology (MS). Part-time and evening/weekend programs available. *Degree requirements:* For master's, thesis. *Entrance requirements:* For master's, minimum GPA of 2.75 in major. Electronic applications accepted. *Faculty research:* Hematopoiesis, growth factors in cancer, interleukins in allergy, PCR techniques.

The Ohio State University, College of Pharmacy and Graduate School, Graduate Programs in Pharmacy, Division of Medicinal Chemistry and Pharmacognosy, Columbus, OH 43210. Offers MS, PhD. *Faculty:* 9 full-time (0 women). *Students:* 25 full-time (9 women); includes 1 minority (African American), 19 international. Average age 26. 51 applicants, 18% accepted, 4 enrolled. In 2006, 4 master's, 4 doctorates awarded. *Median time to degree:* Master's–2 years full-time. Of those who began their doctoral program in fall 1998, 99% received their degree in 8 years or less. *Degree requirements:* For master's and doctorate, thesis/dissertation. *Entrance requirements:* For master's and doctorate, GRE General Test, minimum GPA of 3.0. Additional exam requirements/recommendations for international students: Required—TOEFL (minimum score 620 paper-based; 250 computer-based; 80 iBT). *Application deadline:* For fall admission, 1/1 priority date for domestic students, 8/31 for international students; for winter admission, 9/1 priority date for domestic students, 11/1 for international students; for spring admission, 11/1 priority date for domestic students, 11/1 for international students. Application fee: $40 ($50 for international students). Electronic applications accepted. *Expenses:* Tuition, state resident: full-time $9,438. Tuition, nonresident: full-time $22,791. Tuition and fees vary according to course load, campus/location and program. *Financial support:* In 2006–07, 25 students received support, including 2 fellowships with full tuition reimbursements available (averaging $23,000 per year), 14 research assistantships with full tuition reimbursements available (averaging $19,600 per year), 9 teaching assistantships with full tuition reimbursements available (averaging $19,100 per year); traineeships also available. Financial award application deadline: 1/1. *Faculty research:* Drug design, natural products, synthesis of enzyme inhibitors, drug metabolism and anticancer agents. *Unit head:* Dr. Pui-Kai Li, Coordinator, 614-688-0253, Fax: 614-292-2435, E-mail: kl.27@osu.edu. *Application contact:* Kathy I. Brooks, Graduate Program Coordinator, 614-292-6822, Fax: 614-292-2588, E-mail: gadmbrks@dendrite.pharmacy.ohio-state.edu.

See Close-Up on page 2239.

Purdue University, College of Pharmacy and Pharmacal Sciences and Graduate School, Graduate Programs in Pharmacy and Pharmacal Sciences, Department of Medicinal Chemistry and Molecular Pharmacology, West Lafayette, IN 47907. Offers analytical medicinal chemistry (PhD); computational and biophysical medicinal chemistry (PhD); medicinal and bioorganic chemistry (PhD); medicinal biochemistry and molecular biology (PhD); molecular pharmacology and toxicology (PhD); natural products and pharmacognosy (PhD); nuclear pharmacy (MS); radiopharmaceutical chemistry and nuclear pharmacy (PhD); MS/PhD. *Faculty:* 23 full-time (2 women), 4 part-time/adjunct (1 woman). *Students:* 66 full-time (41 women), 6 part-time (2 women); includes 6 minority (2 African Americans, 1 Asian American or Pacific Islander, 3 Hispanic Americans), 22 international. Average age 26. 120 applicants, 21% accepted, 12 enrolled. In 2006, 2 master's, 7 doctorates awarded. Terminal master's awarded for partial completion of doctoral program. *Degree requirements:* For master's and doctorate, thesis/dissertation. *Entrance requirements:* For master's, GRE General Test, minimum B average; BS in biology, chemistry, or pharmacy; for doctorate, GRE General Test, minimum B average; BS in biology, chemistry, or pharmacology. Additional exam requirements/recommendations for international students: Required—TOEFL. *Application deadline:* For fall admission, 5/15 for international students; for spring admission, 10/15 for international students. Applications are processed on a rolling basis. Application fee: $55. Electronic applications accepted. *Financial support:* Fellowships, research assistantships, teaching assistantships, traineeships available. Support available to part-time students. Financial award applicants required to submit FAFSA. *Faculty research:* Drug design and development, cancer research, drug synthesis and analysis, chemical pharmacology, environmental toxicology. *Unit head:* Dr. R. F. Borch, Graduate Head, 765-494-1403. *Application contact:* Dr. Eric L. Barker, Chair of the Graduate Committee, 765-494-1454, E-mail: ericb@pharmacy.purdue.edu.

Rutgers, The State University of New Jersey, New Brunswick, Graduate School, Program in Medicinal Chemistry, New Brunswick, NJ 08901-1281. Offers MS, PhD. *Degree requirements:* For master's and doctorate, thesis/dissertation, comprehensive exam. *Entrance requirements:* For master's and doctorate, GRE General Test. Additional exam requirements/recommendations for international students: Required—TOEFL (minimum score 600 paper-based; 250 computer-based). Electronic applications accepted. *Faculty research:* Synthesis and design of anticancer drugs, synthesis of pro-drugs for prostate cancer, natural product synthesis, natural product isolation and structure elucidation, computational chemistry.

Temple University, Health Sciences Center, School of Pharmacy, Department of Pharmaceutical Sciences, Program in Medicinal Chemistry, Philadelphia, PA 19122-6096. Offers MS, PhD. *Students:* 3 full-time (1 woman), 2 part-time (both women), (all international). Average age 28. 25 applicants, 4% accepted. *Degree requirements:* For master's, thesis; for doctorate, 2 foreign languages, thesis/dissertation. *Entrance requirements:* For master's and doctorate, GRE General Test, minimum undergraduate GPA of 3.0. Additional exam requirements/recommendations for international students: Required—TOEFL (minimum score 550 paper-based; 213 computer-based; 79 iBT). *Application deadline:* For fall admission, 1/15 for domestic students, 12/15 for international students. Application fee: $50. Electronic applications accepted. *Expenses:* Tuition, state resident: full-time $12,264; part-time $511 per credit. Tuition, nonresident: full-time $17,904; part-time $746 per credit. Required fees: $84 per course. Tuition and fees vary according to program. *Financial support:* Fellowships with tuition reimbursements, research assistantships with tuition reimbursements, teaching assistantships with tuition reimbursements available. Financial award application deadline: 1/15; financial award applicants required to submit FAFSA. *Unit head:* Dr. Daniel Canney, Director of Graduate Studies, 215-707-4948, E-mail: canney@temple.edu.

University at Buffalo, the State University of New York, Graduate School, College of Arts and Sciences, Department of Chemistry, Buffalo, NY 14260. Offers chemistry (MA, PhD); medicinal chemistry (MS, PhD). Part-time programs available. *Faculty:* 34 full-time (3 women), 5 part-time/adjunct (3 women). *Students:* 127 full-time (46 women), 12 part-time (4 women); includes 11 minority (5 African Americans, 1 American Indian/Alaska Native, 2 Asian Americans or Pacific Islanders, 3 Hispanic Americans), 51 international. Average age 24. 402 applicants, 13% accepted, 32 enrolled. In 2006, 8 master's, 26 doctorates awarded. Terminal master's awarded for partial completion of doctoral program. *Median time to degree:* Of those who began their doctoral program in fall 1998, 100% received their degree in 8 years or less. *Degree requirements:* For master's, thesis or alternative, project; for doctorate, thesis/dissertation, synopsis proposal. *Entrance requirements:* For master's and doctorate, GRE General Test, GRE Subject Test. Additional exam requirements/recommendations for international students: Required—TOEFL. *Application deadline:* For fall admission, 3/1 priority date for domestic students, 3/1 for international students. Applications are processed on a rolling basis. Application fee: $0 ($35 for international students). Electronic applications accepted. *Financial support:* In 2006–07, 10 fellowships with full tuition reimbursements (averaging $21,500 per year), 50 research assistantships with full tuition reimbursements (averaging $21,500 per year), 75 teaching assistantships with full tuition reimbursements (averaging $21,500 per year) were awarded; Federal Work-Study, institutionally sponsored loans, and unspecified assistantships also available. Financial award application deadline: 6/15; financial award applicants required to submit FAFSA. *Faculty research:* Synthesis, measurements, structure theory, translation. Total annual research expenditures: $9.5 million. *Unit head:* Dr. Frank V. Bright, Chairman, 716-645-6800 Ext. 2015, Fax: 716-645-6963, E-mail: chechair@buffalo.edu. *Application contact:* Dr. Huw M. L. Davies, Director of Graduate Studies, 716-645-6800 Ext. 2030, Fax: 716-645-6963, E-mail: hdavies@buffalo.edu.

University of California, San Francisco, School of Pharmacy and Graduate Division, Chemistry and Chemical Biology Graduate Program, San Francisco, CA 94143. Offers PhD. *Faculty:* 43 full-time (8 women). *Students:* 49 full-time (20 women); includes 16 minority (3 African Americans, 8 Asian Americans or Pacific Islanders, 5 Hispanic Americans), 3 international. Average age 27. 128 applicants, 15% accepted, 6 enrolled. In 2006, 5 degrees awarded. *Median time to degree:* Doctorate–6 years full-time. Of those who began their doctoral program in fall 1998, 100% received their degree in 8 years or less. *Degree requirements:* For doctorate, thesis/dissertation. *Entrance requirements:* For doctorate, GRE General Test, GRE Subject Test, minimum GPA of 3.0. Additional exam requirements/recommendations for international students: Required—TOEFL. *Application deadline:* For fall admission, 12/15 for domestic students. Applications are processed on a rolling basis. Application fee: $80. Electronic applications accepted. *Financial support:* In 2006–07, 25 fellowships with partial tuition reimbursements (averaging $17,100 per year), 14 research assistantships with full tuition reimbursements (averaging $26,000 per year), 8 teaching assistantships with partial tuition reimbursements (averaging $7,171 per year) were awarded; institutionally sponsored loans, scholarships/grants, traineeships, and tuition waivers (full) also available. Financial award application deadline: 1/10. *Faculty research:* Biochemistry, macromolecular structure, cellular and molecular pharmacology, physical chemistry and computational biology, synthetic chemistry. *Unit head:* Dr. Charles S. Craik, Director, 415-476-8176, E-mail: craik@cgl.ucsf.edu. *Application contact:* Christine Olson, Senior Administrative Analyst, 415-476-1914, Fax: 415-514-1546, E-mail: olson@cmp.ucsf.edu.

University of Connecticut, Graduate School, School of Pharmacy, Department of Pharmaceutical Sciences, Field of Pharmaceutical Sciences, Program in Medicinal Chemistry, Storrs, CT

06269. Offers MS, PhD. *Faculty:* 8 full-time (2 women). *Students:* 11 full-time (8 women), 1 (woman) part-time, 8 international. Average age 27. 21 applicants, 19% accepted, 3 enrolled. In 2006, 1 master's, 3 doctorates awarded. Terminal master's awarded for partial completion of doctoral program. *Degree requirements:* For master's, thesis/dissertation, comprehensive exam; for doctorate, thesis/dissertation. *Entrance requirements:* Additional exam requirements/recommendations for international students: Required—TOEFL (minimum score 550 paper-based; 213 computer-based). *Application deadline:* For fall admission, 2/1 priority date for domestic and international students; for spring admission, 11/1 for domestic students, 10/1 for international students. Applications are processed on a rolling basis. Application fee: $55. Electronic applications accepted. *Financial support:* In 2006–07, 1 teaching assistantship with full tuition reimbursement was awarded; fellowships, research assistantships with full tuition reimbursements, Federal Work-Study, scholarships/grants, traineeships, health care benefits, and unspecified assistantships also available. Financial award application deadline: 2/1; financial award applicants required to submit FAFSA. *Application contact:* Leslie Lebel, Administrative Assistant, 860-486-4066, Fax: 860-486-4998, E-mail: phrmacy8@uconnvm.uconn.edu.

University of Florida, College of Pharmacy and Graduate School, Graduate Programs in Pharmacy, Department of Medicinal Chemistry, Gainesville, FL 32611. Offers medicinal chemistry (Pharm D); pharmaceutical sciences (MSP, PhD). *Faculty:* 8 full-time (3 women). *Students:* 17 (10 women); includes 2 minority (1 Asian American or Pacific Islander, 1 Hispanic American) 9 international. In 2006, 1 master's, 4 doctorates awarded. *Degree requirements:* For doctorate, thesis/dissertation. *Entrance requirements:* For doctorate, GRE General Test, minimum GPA of 3.0. Additional exam requirements/recommendations for international students: Required—TOEFL. *Application deadline:* For fall admission, 6/1 priority date for domestic students. Applications are processed on a rolling basis. Application fee: $30. *Expenses:* Tuition, state resident: full-time $6,827. Tuition, nonresident: full-time $21,951. Required fees: $999. *Financial support:* In 2006–07, 5 research assistantships (averaging $19,586 per year), 10 teaching assistantships (averaging $19,441 per year) were awarded; fellowships also available. *Faculty research:* Iron chelation, anticancer drug development, drug metabolism and toxicity, dermal delivery of drug and prodrugs. *Unit head:* Dr. Margaret James, Chair, 352-846-1952, Fax: 352-392-9455, E-mail: mojames@ufl.edu. *Application contact:* Dr. Raymond J. Bergeron, Graduate Coordinator, 352-846-1956, Fax: 352-392-9455, E-mail: bergeron@mc.cop.ufl.edu.

University of Georgia, College of Pharmacy, Department of Pharmaceutical and Biomedical Sciences, Athens, GA 30602. Offers medicinal chemistry (MS, PhD); pharmaceutics (MS, PhD); pharmacology (MS, PhD); toxicology (MS, PhD). *Faculty:* 18 full-time (4 women). *Students:* 7 full-time (4 women), 1 part-time; includes 2 minority (both African Americans), 4 international. 138 applicants, 10% accepted, 5 enrolled. In 2006, 1 degree awarded. *Median time to degree:* Of those who began their doctoral program in fall 1998, 100% received their degree in 8 years or less. *Degree requirements:* For master's, thesis; for doctorate, one foreign language, thesis/dissertation. *Entrance requirements:* For master's and doctorate, GRE General Test, minimum GPA of 3.0. Additional exam requirements/recommendations for international students: Required—TOEFL. *Application deadline:* For fall admission, 1/2 priority date for domestic and international students. Application fee: $50. Electronic applications accepted. *Financial support:* In 2006–07, fellowships with full tuition reimbursements (averaging $18,000 per year), 10 research assistantships with full tuition reimbursements (averaging $16,500 per year), 35 teaching assistantships with full tuition reimbursements (averaging $16,500 per year) were awarded; career-related internships or fieldwork, institutionally sponsored loans, tuition waivers (partial), and unspecified assistantships also available. Financial award application deadline: 1/1. *Faculty research:* Cancer and infectious diseases, drug delivery, neuropharmacology, cardiovascular pharmacology, bioanalytical chemistry, structural biology. *Unit head:* Dr. Vasu Nair, Head, 706-542-5610, Fax: 706-542-3398, E-mail: vnair@rx.uga.edu. *Application contact:* Dr. Michael Bartlett, Graduate Coordinator, 706-542-5390, Fax: 706-542-3398, E-mail: bartlett@rx.uga.edu.

University of Kansas, Graduate Studies, School of Pharmacy, Department of Medicinal Chemistry, Lawrence, KS 66045. Offers MS, PhD. *Faculty:* 13. *Students:* 44 full-time (23 women), 3 part-time (1 woman); includes 1 minority (Asian American or Pacific Islander), 21 international. Average age 26. 57 applicants, 25% accepted. In 2006, 3 master's, 5 doctorates awarded. Terminal master's awarded for partial completion of doctoral program. *Degree requirements:* For master's, thesis (for some programs), comprehensive exam, registration; for doctorate, thesis/dissertation, cumulative exams, comprehensive exam, registration. *Entrance requirements:* For master's and doctorate, GRE General Test. Additional exam requirements/recommendations for international students: Required—TOEFL. *Application deadline:* For fall admission, 3/1 priority date for domestic and international students. Applications are processed on a rolling basis. Application fee: $55 ($60 for international students). Electronic applications accepted. *Expenses:* Tuition, area resident: Part-time $227 per credit. Tuition, state resident: part-time $543 per credit. Tuition and fees vary according to course load, campus/location, program and reciprocity agreements. *Financial support:* Fellowships with full tuition reimbursements, research assistantships with full tuition reimbursements, teaching assistantships with full tuition reimbursements, health care benefits and unspecified assistantships available. Financial award application deadline: 3/1. *Faculty research:* Drug design and synthesis, natural products chemistry, drug metabolism and toxicity, enzyme mechanism and inhibition, antiinfective and chemotherapeutic agents. *Unit head:* Prof. Barbara Timmermann, Chair, 785-864-4495. *Application contact:* Prof. Apurba Dutta, Director of Graduate Studies, 785-864-4495, E-mail: medchem@ku.edu.

University of Kansas, Graduate Studies, School of Pharmacy, Department of Pharmaceutical Chemistry, Lawrence, KS 66045. Offers MS, PhD. Postbaccalaureate distance learning degree programs offered. *Faculty:* 16. *Students:* 50 full-time (18 women), 2 part-time; includes 4 minority (1 American Indian/Alaska Native, 1 Asian American or Pacific Islander, 2 Hispanic Americans), 20 international. Average age 28. 32 applicants, 25% accepted. In 2006, 11 master's, 10 doctorates awarded. Terminal master's awarded for partial completion of doctoral program. *Median time to degree:* Of those who began their doctoral program in fall 1998, 100% received their degree in 8 years or less. *Degree requirements:* For master's, thesis/dissertation, qualifying exam; for doctorate, thesis/dissertation, qualifying exam, comprehensive exam, registration. *Entrance requirements:* For master's, GRE General Test, bachelor's degree in biological sciences, chemical engineering, chemistry, or pharmacy; for doctorate, GRE General Test. Additional exam requirements/recommendations for international students: Required—TOEFL. *Application deadline:* For fall admission, 1/20 priority date for domestic and international students. Applications are processed on a rolling basis. Application fee: $55 ($60 for international students). Electronic applications accepted. *Expenses:* Tuition, area resident: Part-time $227 per credit. Tuition, state resident: part-time $543 per credit. Tuition and fees vary according to course load, campus/location, program and reciprocity agreements. *Financial support:* Fellowships with full tuition reimbursements, research assistantships with full and partial tuition reimbursements, teaching assistantships with full and partial tuition reimbursements, career-related internships or fieldwork, scholarships/grants, traineeships, and unspecified assistantships available. Financial award application deadline: 1/20. *Faculty research:* Drug delivery, drug analysis, biotechnology, nanomaterials, protein structure. *Unit head:* Dr. Christian Schöneich, Chair, 785-864-4880, Fax: 785-864-5736, E-mail: schoneic@ku.edu. *Application contact:* Jeffrey Krise, Graduate Director, 785-864-2626, Fax: 785-864-5736, E-mail: krise@ku.edu.

University of Michigan, College of Pharmacy and University of Michigan, Department of Medicinal Chemistry, Ann Arbor, MI 48109. Offers PhD. *Degree requirements:* For doctorate, oral defense of dissertation, preliminary exam. *Entrance requirements:* For doctorate, GRE. Additional exam requirements/recommendations for international students: Required—TOEFL or IELTS. Expenses: Contact institution.

University of Minnesota, Twin Cities Campus, College of Pharmacy and Graduate School, Graduate Programs in Pharmacy, Graduate Program in Medicinal Chemistry, Minneapolis, MN 55455-0213. Offers MS, PhD. Terminal master's awarded for partial completion of doctoral program. *Degree requirements:* For master's and doctorate, thesis/dissertation. *Entrance requirements:* For master's and doctorate, GRE General Test, BS in biology, chemistry, or pharmacy. Additional exam requirements/recommendations for international students: Required—TOEFL. *Expenses:* Tuition, state resident: full-time $9,302; part-time $775 per credit. Tuition, nonresident: full-time $16,400; part-time $1,367 per credit. Full-time tuition and fees vary according to class time, course load, program, reciprocity agreements and student level. *Faculty research:* Drug design and synthesis, molecular modeling, chemical aspects of drug metabolism and toxicity.

University of Mississippi, Graduate School, School of Pharmacy, Graduate Programs in Pharmacy, Oxford, University, MS 38677. Offers medicinal chemistry (MS, PhD); pharmaceutics (MS, PhD); pharmacognosy (MS, PhD); pharmacology (MS, PhD); pharmacy administration (MS, PhD). *Faculty:* 6 full-time (0 women). *Students:* 89 full-time (38 women), 6 part-time (2 women); includes 7 minority (3 African Americans, 3 Asian Americans or Pacific Islanders, 1 Hispanic American), 61 international. 163 applicants. In 2006, 5 master's, 11 doctorates awarded. *Expenses:* Tuition, state resident: full-time $4,602; part-time $256 per credit hour. Tuition, nonresident: full-time $10,566; part-time $587 per credit hour. *Unit head:* Dr. Barbara G. Wells, Dean, School of Pharmacy, 662-915-7265, Fax: 662-915-5704, E-mail: pharmacy@olemiss.edu.

University of Rhode Island, Graduate School, College of Pharmacy, Graduate Programs in Pharmacy, Department of Biomedical and Pharmaceutical Sciences, Kingston, RI 02881. Offers medicinal chemistry and pharmacognosy (MS, PhD); pharmaceutics and pharmacokinetics (MS, PhD); pharmacology and toxicology (MS, PhD). *Expenses:* Tuition, state resident: full-time $6,032; part-time $335 per credit. Tuition, nonresident: full-time $17,288; part-time $960 per credit. Required fees: $65 per credit. $30 per semester. One-time fee: $80 part-time. *Unit head:* Dr. Clinton O. Chichester, Chair, 401-874-5034.

University of the Sciences in Philadelphia, College of Graduate Studies, Program in Chemistry, Biochemistry and Pharmacognosy, Philadelphia, PA 19104-4495. Offers biochemistry (MS, PhD); chemistry (MS, PhD); medicinal chemistry (MS, PhD); pharmacognosy (MS, PhD). Part-time programs available. *Faculty:* 14 full-time (4 women). *Students:* 15 full-time (8 women), 11 part-time (5 women); includes 5 minority (3 African Americans, 2 Asian Americans or Pacific Islanders), 6 international. Average age 28. In 2006, 3 master's, 1 doctorate awarded. *Degree requirements:* For master's, thesis/dissertation, qualifying exams; for doctorate, thesis/dissertation, qualifying exams, comprehensive exam. *Entrance requirements:* For master's and doctorate, GRE General Test, GRE Subject Test. Additional exam requirements/recommendations for international students: Required—TOEFL, TWE. *Application deadline:* For fall admission, 5/1 for international students; for winter admission, 10/1 for international students; for spring admission, 3/1 for international students. Applications are processed on a rolling basis. Application fee: $50. *Expenses:* Tuition: Part-time $1,058 per credit. Tuition and fees vary according to program. *Financial support:* In 2006–07, 19 students received support, including 1 research assistantship with full tuition reimbursement available, 15 teaching assistantships with full tuition reimbursements available (averaging $21,400 per year); fellowships with full tuition reimbursements available, institutionally sponsored loans, scholarships/grants, and tuition waivers (full) also available. Financial award application deadline: 5/1. *Faculty research:* Organic and medicinal synthesis, mass spectroscopy use in protein analysis, study of analogues of taxol, cholesteryl esters. Total annual research expenditures: $341,700. *Unit head:* Dr. James McKee, Director, 215-596-8847, Fax: 215-596-8543, E-mail: jmckee@usip.edu. *Application contact:* Joyce D'Angelo, Administrative Assistant, 215-596-8937, E-mail: j.dangel@usip.edu.

See Close-Up on page 2253.

The University of Toledo, College of Graduate Studies, College of Pharmacy, Department of Medicinal and Biological Chemistry, Program in Medicinal and Biological Chemistry, Toledo, OH 43606-3390. Offers MS, PhD. *Faculty:* 12 full-time (2 women), 6 part-time/adjunct (1 woman). *Students:* 21 full-time (6 women), 13 international. Average age 26. 41 applicants, 22% accepted, 7 enrolled. In 2006, 1 master's, 1 doctorate awarded. Terminal master's awarded for partial completion of doctoral program. *Degree requirements:* For master's and doctorate, thesis/dissertation. *Entrance requirements:* For master's and doctorate, GRE General Test. Additional exam requirements/recommendations for international students: Required—TOEFL (minimum score 550 paper-based; 213 computer-based; 80 iBT). *Application deadline:* For fall admission, 2/1 priority date for domestic students, 1/1 priority date for international students. Application fee: $45. Electronic applications accepted. *Financial support:* In 2006–07, 21 students received support; research assistantships with full tuition reimbursements available, teaching assistantships with full tuition reimbursements available, unspecified assistantships available. *Faculty research:* Neuroscience, molecular modeling, immunotoxicology, organic synthesis, peptide biochemistry. *Unit head:* Dr. Marcia McInerney, Chair, 419-530-1981, Fax: 419-530-7946, E-mail: mmciner@utnet.utoledo.edu. *Application contact:* Linda McPherson, Information Contact, 419-530-2902, Fax: 419-530-7946, E-mail: lmcpher@utnet.utoledo.edu.

University of Utah, College of Pharmacy and The Graduate School, Graduate Programs in Pharmacy, Medicinal Chemistry Program, Salt Lake City, UT 84112-1107. Offers MS, PhD. *Degree requirements:* For doctorate, thesis/dissertation. *Entrance requirements:* For doctorate, minimum GPA of 3.0. *Expenses:* Tuition, state resident: full-time $3,208. Tuition, nonresident: full-time $11,326. Required fees: $608. Tuition and fees vary according to class time and program. *Faculty research:* Cancer chemotherapy, NMR spectroscopy, mass spectrometry, chemotherapeutic agents, antimetabolites.

University of Utah, College of Pharmacy and The Graduate School, Graduate Programs in Pharmacy, Pharmaceutics and Pharmaceutical Chemistry Program, Salt Lake City, UT 84112. Offers MS, PhD. Terminal master's awarded for partial completion of doctoral program. *Degree requirements:* For master's and doctorate, thesis/dissertation. *Entrance requirements:* For master's and doctorate, GRE. Additional exam requirements/recommendations for international students: Required—TOEFL. *Expenses:* Tuition, state resident: full-time $3,208. Tuition, nonresident: full-time $11,326. Required fees: $608. Tuition and fees vary according to class time and program. *Faculty research:* Drug delivery, transdermal delivery, pharmacokinetics, polymer science.

University of Washington, School of Pharmacy and Graduate School, Graduate Programs in Pharmacy, Department of Medicinal Chemistry, Seattle, WA 98195. Offers PhD. *Degree requirements:* For doctorate, thesis/dissertation. *Entrance requirements:* For doctorate, GRE General Test, minimum GPA of 3.0. Additional exam requirements/recommendations for international students: Required—TOEFL. *Faculty research:* Chemical and molecular aspects of drug action, metabolism and drug toxicity, theoretical studies on protein folding, NMR of macromolecules and biomedical mass spectrometry.

Wayne State University, Eugene Applebaum College of Pharmacy and Health Sciences, Department of Pharmacy Practice, Detroit, MI 48202. Offers medicinal chemistry (MS, PhD); pharmaceutical sciences (MS, PhD); pharmaceutics (MS, PhD); pharmacology (MS, PhD); pharmacy (Pharm D). *Faculty:* 33 full-time (23 women), 1 part-time/adjunct (0 women). *Students:* 305 full-time (203 women), 18 part-time (15 women); includes 41 minority (8 African Americans, 1 American Indian/Alaska Native, 30 Asian Americans or Pacific Islanders, 2 Hispanic Americans), 91 international. Average age 25. 103 applicants, 8% accepted, 6 enrolled. In 2006, 46 first professional degrees, 4 doctorates awarded. Terminal master's awarded for partial completion of doctoral program. *Degree requirements:* For master's and doctorate, thesis/dissertation. *Entrance requirements:* For master's, GRE General Test, minimum GPA of 2.6; for doctorate, GRE General Test, minimum GPA of 3.0. Additional exam requirements/recommendations for international students: Required—TOEFL (minimum score 550 paper-based; 213 computer-based); Recommended—TWE (minimum score 6). *Application deadline:* For fall admission, 1/31 priority date for domestic students, 6/1 for international students; for winter admission, 10/1 for international students; for spring admission, 2/1 for international students. Applications are processed on a rolling basis. Application fee: $30 ($50 for international students). Electronic applications accepted. *Financial support:* Fellowships, research assistantships with tuition

Medicinal and Pharmaceutical Chemistry

Wayne State University (continued)
reimbursements, scholarships/grants available. Support available to part-time students. *Faculty research:* Signaling defects as basics of type 1 and type 2 diabetes, dopamine receptor and transporter inhibitors for addition, novel nanoparticles for gene and drug delivery, role of lipocortin 1 in heavy metal mutagenesis, synthesis and anti cancer mechanisms of polyamine and histone deacetylase inhibitors. Total annual research expenditures: $237,898. *Unit head:* Dr. David J. Edwards, Chair, 313-577-0827, Fax: 313-577-5369. *Application contact:* William Lindblad, Associate Professor, 313-577-0513, E-mail: wlindbl@wayne.edu.

West Virginia University, School of Pharmacy, Program in Pharmaceutical and Pharmacological Sciences, Morgantown, WV 26506. Offers administrative pharmacy (PhD); behavioral pharmacy (MS, PhD); biopharmaceutics/pharmacokinetics (MS, PhD); industrial pharmacy (MS); medicinal chemistry (MS, PhD); pharmaceutical chemistry (MS, PhD); pharmaceutics (MS, PhD); pharmacology and toxicology (MS); pharmacy (MS); pharmacy administration (MS). Part-time programs available. *Students:* 29 full-time (12 women), 3 part-time (2 women); includes 1 minority (Asian American or Pacific Islander), 18 international. Average age 30. 47 applicants, 6% accepted, 2 enrolled. In 2006, 3 master's, 9 doctorates awarded. Terminal master's awarded for partial completion of doctoral program. *Median time to degree:* Of those who began their doctoral program in fall 1998, 84% received their degree in 8 years or less. *Degree requirements:* For master's, thesis; for doctorate, one foreign language, thesis/dissertation, comprehensive exam. *Entrance requirements:* For master's and doctorate, GRE General Test, minimum GPA of 2.75. Additional exam requirements/recommendations for international students: Required—TOEFL; Recommended—TWE. *Application deadline:* For fall admission, 3/1 priority date for domestic and international students. Application fee: $50. Electronic applications accepted. *Expenses: Contact institution.* Tuition and fees vary according to program. *Financial support:* In 2006–07, 31 students received support, including 13 research assistantships with full tuition reimbursements available (averaging $23,000 per year), 15 teaching assistantships with full tuition reimbursements available (averaging $23,000 per year); career-related internships or fieldwork, Federal Work-Study, institutionally sponsored loans, health care benefits, tuition waivers (full and partial), and unspecified assistantships also available. Financial award application deadline: 3/1; financial award applicants required to submit FAFSA. *Faculty research:* Pharmaceutics, medicinal chemistry, biopharmaceutics/pharmacokinetics, health outcomes research. Total annual research expenditures: $1.8 million. *Application contact:* Dr. Patrick S. Callery, Assistant Dean for Graduate Programs/Chair, 304-293-1482, Fax: 304-293-2576, E-mail: pcallery@hsc.wvu.edu.

Pharmaceutical Administration

Duquesne University, School of Pharmacy, Graduate School of Pharmaceutical Sciences, Program in Pharmaceutical Administration, Pittsburgh, PA 15282-0001. Offers MS. Part-time programs available. *Faculty:* 4 full-time (0 women). *Students:* 5 full-time (4 women), 3 part-time (1 woman), 5 international. 23 applicants, 9% accepted, 2 enrolled. In 2006, 1 degree awarded. *Degree requirements:* For master's, thesis optional. *Entrance requirements:* For master's, GRE General Test. Additional exam requirements/recommendations for international students: Required—TOEFL. *Application deadline:* For fall admission, 2/1 priority date for domestic students. Applications are processed on a rolling basis. Application fee: $50. *Expenses:* Tuition: Part-time $723 per credit. Required fees: $71 per credit. Tuition and fees vary according to degree level and program. *Financial support:* In 2006–07, 5 students received support, including 5 teaching assistantships with tuition reimbursements available; research assistantships with tuition reimbursements available, career-related internships or fieldwork, Federal Work-Study, institutionally sponsored loans, scholarships/grants, and unspecified assistantships also available. Support available to part-time students. *Unit head:* Dr. Thomas J. Mattei, Head, 412-396-5458.

Fairleigh Dickinson University, Metropolitan Campus, Silberman College of Business, Center for Healthcare Management Studies, Program in Pharmaceutical Studies, Teaneck, NJ 07666-1914. Offers MBA, Certificate. *Students:* 7 full-time (3 women), 17 part-time (9 women), 6 international. Average age 33. 15 applicants, 47% accepted, 1 enrolled. In 2006, 22 degrees awarded. *Application deadline:* Applications are processed on a rolling basis.

Florida Agricultural and Mechanical University, Division of Graduate Studies, Research, and Continuing Education, College of Pharmacy and Pharmaceutical Sciences, Graduate Programs in Pharmaceutical Sciences, Tallahassee, FL 32307-3200. Offers environmental toxicology (PhD); medicinal chemistry (MS, PhD); pharmaceutics (MS, PhD); pharmacology/toxicology (MS, PhD); pharmacy administration (MS). *Accreditation:* CEPH. *Degree requirements:* For master's and doctorate, thesis/dissertation, publishable paper, comprehensive exam. *Entrance requirements:* For master's and doctorate, GRE General Test, minimum GPA of 3.0 in last 60 hours. Additional exam requirements/recommendations for international students: Required—TOEFL. *Faculty research:* Anticancer agents, anti-inflammatory drugs, chronopharmacology, neuroendocrinology, microbiology.

See Close-Up on page 2235.

Idaho State University, Office of Graduate Studies, College of Pharmacy, Department of Pharmacy Practice and Administrative Sciences, Pocatello, ID 83209. Offers pharmacy (Pharm D); pharmacy administration (MS, PhD). *Accreditation:* ACPE (one or more programs are accredited). Postbaccalaureate distance learning degree programs offered (minimal on-campus study). *Faculty:* 4 full-time (1 woman). *Students:* 230 full-time (100 women), 16 part-time (9 women); includes 19 minority (1 American Indian/Alaska Native, 14 Asian Americans or Pacific Islanders, 4 Hispanic Americans), 5 international. Average age 28. In 2006, 63 degrees awarded. *Degree requirements:* For Pharm D, thesis, written and oral exams, comprehensive exam, registration; for master's, one foreign language, thesis (for some programs), thesis research, comprehensive exam, registration (for some programs); for doctorate, thesis/dissertation, oral and written exams, comprehensive exam, registration. *Entrance requirements:* For Pharm D, GRE General Test, minimum GPA of 3.0, 2 years of pre-pharmacy, BS degree in pharmacy or related field, 3 letters of recommendation; for master's, GRE General Test, minimum GPA of 3.0, 3 letters of recommendation; for doctorate, GRE General Test, BS degree in pharmacy or related field, minimum GPA of 3.0, 3 letters of recommendation. Additional exam requirements/recommendations for international students: Required—TOEFL (minimum score 550 paper-based; 213 computer-based; 80 iBT). *Application deadline:* For fall admission, 7/1 for domestic students, 6/1 for international students; for spring admission, 12/1 for domestic students, 11/1 for international students. Applications are processed on a rolling basis. Application fee: $55. *Expenses:* Tuition, state resident: part-time $251 per credit. Tuition, nonresident: part-time $366 per credit. Tuition and fees vary according to degree level, program and reciprocity agreements. *Financial support:* In 2006–07, 8 research assistantships with full and partial tuition reimbursements (averaging $11,303 per year) were awarded; teaching assistantships with full and partial tuition reimbursements, career-related internships or fieldwork, Federal Work-Study, scholarships/grants, and tuition waivers (full and partial) also available. Support available to part-time students. Financial award application deadline: 1/1. *Faculty research:* Pharmaceutical care outcomes, drug use review, pharmacoeconomics. Total annual research expenditures: $131,046. *Unit head:* Dr. Vaughn Culbertson, Chairman, 208-282-4385, Fax: 208-282-4482, E-mail: vculb@pharmacy.isu.edu. *Application contact:* Ellen Combs, Graduate School Technical Records Specialist, 208-282-2150, Fax: 208-282-4847.

Long Island University, Brooklyn Campus, Arnold and Marie Schwartz College of Pharmacy and Health Sciences, Graduate Programs in Pharmacy, Division of Social and Administrative Sciences, Brooklyn, NY 11201-8423. Offers drug regulatory affairs (MS); pharmacy administration (MS). Part-time and evening/weekend programs available. *Faculty:* 6 full-time (1 woman), 21 part-time/adjunct (5 women). *Students:* 49 (20 women); includes 40 minority (14 African Americans, 26 Asian Americans or Pacific Islanders). Average age 28. In 2006, 21 degrees awarded. *Degree requirements:* For master's, thesis optional. *Entrance requirements:* For master's, minimum GPA of 3.0. *Application deadline:* Applications are processed on a rolling basis. Application fee: $30. *Financial support:* In 2006–07, 4 teaching assistantships with full tuition reimbursements (averaging $6,000 per year) were awarded; Federal Work-Study also available. Financial award applicants required to submit FAFSA. *Unit head:* Dr. Donna Dolinsky, Director, 718-488-1105, E-mail: dolinsky@liu.edu. *Application contact:* Edward Dettling, Director of Graduate Admissions, 718-488-1011, Fax: 718-797-2399, E-mail: admissions@brooklyn.liu.edu.

Massachusetts College of Pharmacy and Health Sciences, Graduate Studies, Program in Pharmacy Systems Administration, Boston, MA 02115-5896. Offers MS. Part-time and evening/weekend programs available. *Degree requirements:* For master's, thesis, oral defense of thesis. *Entrance requirements:* For master's, GRE General Test, minimum QPA of 3.0. Additional exam requirements/recommendations for international students: Required—TOEFL.

The Ohio State University, College of Pharmacy and Graduate School, Graduate Programs in Pharmacy, Division of Pharmacy Practice and Administration, Columbus, OH 43210. Offers health-system pharmacy administration (MS); pharmaceutical administration (MS, PhD). Part-time programs available. *Faculty:* 5 full-time (1 woman). *Students:* 27 full-time (16 women), 2 part-time; includes 9 minority (1 African American, 6 Asian Americans or Pacific Islanders, 2 Hispanic Americans), 7 international. Average age 26. 45 applicants, 36% accepted, 12 enrolled. In 2006, 7 master's, 2 doctorates awarded. *Median time to degree:* Of those who began their doctoral program in fall 1998, 100% received their degree in 8 years or less. *Degree requirements:* For doctorate, one foreign language, thesis/dissertation. *Entrance requirements:* For master's and doctorate, GRE General Test, minimum GPA of 3.0. Additional exam requirements/recommendations for international students: Required—TOEFL (minimum score 600 paper-based; 250 computer-based). *Application deadline:* For fall admission, 1/1 priority date for domestic students, 8/31 for international students; for winter admission, 9/1 priority date for domestic students, 9/1 for international students; for spring admission, 11/1 priority date for domestic students, 11/1 for international students. Application fee: $40 ($50 for international students). Electronic applications accepted. *Expenses:* Tuition, state resident: full-time $9,438. Tuition, nonresident: full-time $22,791. Tuition and fees vary according to course load, campus/location and program. *Financial support:* In 2006–07, 25 students received support, including 20 research assistantships with full and partial tuition reimbursements available (averaging $30,000 per year), 5 teaching assistantships with full and partial tuition reimbursements available (averaging $19,000 per year); fellowships with full and partial tuition reimbursements available also available. Financial award application deadline: 1/1. *Faculty research:* Pharmacoeconomic analysis, finance, institutional behavior, drug distribution and public policy. *Unit head:* Dr. Craig Pedersen, Coordinator, 614-292-3011, Fax: 614-292-1335, E-mail: pedersen.18@osu.edu. *Application contact:* Kathy I. Brooks, Graduate Program Coordinator, 614-292-6822, Fax: 614-292-2588, E-mail: gadmbrks@dendrite.pharmacy.ohio-state.edu.

See Close-Up on page 2239.

Purdue University, College of Pharmacy and Pharmacal Sciences and Graduate School, Graduate Programs in Pharmacy and Pharmacal Sciences, Department of Industrial and Physical Pharmacy, West Lafayette, IN 47907. Offers pharmaceutics (PhD); regulatory quality compliance (MS, Certificate). *Faculty:* 9 full-time (3 women), 33 part-time/adjunct (4 women). *Students:* 37 full-time (13 women), 13 part-time (6 women); includes 2 minority (1 Asian American or Pacific Islander, 1 Hispanic American), 20 international. Average age 29. 59 applicants, 32% accepted, 11 enrolled. In 2006, 7 master's, 3 doctorates awarded. *Degree requirements:* For doctorate, thesis/dissertation. *Entrance requirements:* For doctorate, GRE General Test, minimum B average; BS in biology, chemistry, or pharmacy. Additional exam requirements/recommendations for international students: Required—TOEFL. *Application deadline:* For fall admission, 1/1 for domestic and international students. Applications are processed on a rolling basis. Application fee: $55. Electronic applications accepted. *Financial support:* Fellowships, research assistantships, teaching assistantships, traineeships available. Support available to part-time students. Financial award applicants required to submit FAFSA. *Faculty research:* Controlled drug delivery systems, liposomes, antacids, coating technology. *Unit head:* Dr. S. R. Byrn, Graduate Head, 765-494-1460. *Application contact:* Dr. Kenneth R Morris, Graduate Committee Chair, 765-496-3387, E-mail: morris@pharmacy.purdue.edu.

St. John's University, College of Pharmacy and Allied Health Professions, Graduate Programs in Pharmacy, Program in Pharmacy Administration, Queens, NY 11439. Offers MS. Part-time and evening/weekend programs available. *Students:* 3 full-time (1 woman), 19 part-time (9 women), 18 international. Average age 26. 51 applicants, 51% accepted, 9 enrolled. In 2006, 11 degrees awarded. *Degree requirements:* For master's, residency, thesis optional. *Entrance requirements:* For master's, GRE General Test, bachelor's degree in pharmacy, minimum GPA of 3.0. Additional exam requirements/recommendations for international students: Required—TOEFL (minimum score 500 paper-based; 173 computer-based). *Application deadline:* For fall admission, 4/1 for domestic students, 5/1 priority date for international students; for spring admission, 12/1 for domestic students, 11/1 priority date for international students. Applications are processed on a rolling basis. Application fee: $40. Electronic applications accepted. *Expenses: Contact institution.* Tuition and fees vary according to program. *Financial support:* Fellowships, research assistantships, career-related internships or fieldwork available. Support available to part-time students. Financial award application deadline: 3/1; financial award applicants required to submit FAFSA. *Unit head:* Br. Shamus McGrenra, Senior Associate Director, Office of Admission, 718-990-1601, Fax: 718-990-2346, E-mail: gradhelp@stjohns.edu. *Application contact:* Matthew Whelan, Director, Office of Admissions, 718-990-2000, Fax: 718-990-2096, E-mail: admissions@stjohns.edu.

St. Louis College of Pharmacy, Program in Pharmacy Administration, St. Louis, MO 63110-1088. Offers managed care pharmacy (MS, Certificate). Part-time and evening/weekend programs available. Postbaccalaureate distance learning degree programs offered (minimal on-campus study). *Faculty:* 1 full-time (0 women), 3 part-time/adjunct (0 women). *Students:* Average age 35. In 2006, 1 degree awarded. *Degree requirements:* For master's, thesis optional. *Application deadline:* For fall admission, 8/1 priority date for domestic students; for winter admission, 12/20 priority date for domestic students; for spring admission, 3/15 priority date for domestic students. Applications are processed on a rolling basis. Application fee: $50. *Expenses: Contact institution. Faculty research:* Geriatric pharmacy, health economics, pharmacoeconomics, job satisfaction, managed care and insurance.

San Diego State University, Graduate and Research Affairs, College of Sciences, Program in Regulatory Affairs, San Diego, CA 92182. Offers MS. *Students:* 21 applicants, 76% accepted.

In 2006, 6 degrees awarded. *Degree requirements:* For master's, thesis. *Entrance requirements:* For master's, GRE General Test, 3 letters of recommendation, employment/volunteer experience list. Additional exam requirements/recommendations for international students: Required—TOEFL. *Application deadline:* For fall admission, 5/1 for domestic students; for spring admission, 11/1 for domestic students, 10/1 for international students. Applications are processed on a rolling basis. Application fee: $55. Electronic applications accepted. *Unit head:* Larry Gunderson, Director, 619-594-6030, Fax: 619-594-6132, E-mail: cdbd@sciences.sdsu.edu. *Application contact:* Larry Gunderson, Graduate Advisor, 619-594-6030, Fax: 619-594-6132, E-mail: cdbd@sciences.sdsu.edu.

Seton Hall University, Stillman School of Business, Programs in Business Administration, South Orange, NJ 07079-2697. Offers accounting (MBA); finance (MBA); financial markets, institutions and instruments (MBA); healthcare management (MBA); information systems (MBA); international business (MBA); management (MBA); marketing (MBA); pharmaceutical management (MBA); sport management (MBA). Part-time and evening/weekend programs available. *Faculty:* 57 full-time (13 women), 30 part-time/adjunct (3 women). *Students:* 57 full-time (16 women), 180 part-time (57 women); includes 9 African Americans, 10 Asian Americans or Pacific Islanders, 7 Hispanic Americans. Average age 29. 195 applicants, 47% accepted, 48 enrolled. In 2006, 144 degrees awarded. *Median time to degree:* Master's–1.6 years full-time, 2.3 years part-time. *Degree requirements:* For master's, 20 hours of community service (Social Responsibility Project). *Entrance requirements:* For master's, GMAT, minimum GPA of 2.75. Additional exam requirements/recommendations for international students: Required—TOEFL (minimum score 550 paper-based; 213 computer-based). *Application deadline:* For fall admission, 6/1 priority date for domestic students; for spring admission, 11/1 priority date for domestic students. Applications are processed on a rolling basis. Application fee: $75 ($100 for international students). Electronic applications accepted. *Financial support:* In 2006–07, 40 students received support, including research assistantships with full and partial tuition reimbursements available (averaging $5,400 per year); career-related internships or fieldwork, Federal Work-Study, scholarships/grants, and unspecified assistantships also available. Support available to part-time students. Financial award application deadline: 6/1; financial award applicants required to submit FAFSA. *Faculty research:* Financial, hedge funds, international business, legal issues, disclosure and branding. *Unit head:* Dr. Joyce A. Strawser, Associate Dean for Undergraduate and MBA Curricula, 973-761-9225, Fax: 973-761-9217, E-mail: strawsjo@shu.edu. *Application contact:* Catherine Bianchi, Director of Graduate Admissions, 973-761-9220, Fax: 973-761-9208, E-mail: biancha@shu.edu.

University of Arkansas for Medical Sciences, College of Pharmacy, Program in Pharmaceutical Evaluation and Policy, Little Rock, AR 72205-7199. Offers MS. *Students:* 4 full-time. *Entrance requirements:* For master's, GRE, 3 letters of recommendation, resumé. Additional exam requirements/recommendations for international students: Required—TOEFL. *Unit head:* Dr. Bradley C. Martin, Director, E-mail: bmartin@uams.edu.

University of Colorado at Denver and Health Sciences Center, Business School, Executive MBA Program in Health Administration, Denver, CO 80248-0006. Offers health administration (MBA); pharmaceutical management (MBA). *Accreditation:* CAHME. Evening/weekend programs available. Postbaccalaureate distance learning degree programs offered (minimal on-campus study). *Faculty:* 3 full-time (1 woman). *Students:* 30 full-time (14 women), 25 part-time (12 women); includes 5 minority (2 African Americans, 1 Asian American or Pacific Islander, 2 Hispanic Americans), 2 international. 21 applicants, 76% accepted, 13 enrolled. In 2006, 3 degrees awarded. *Entrance requirements:* For master's, 3 years clinical or management experience in health care field. Additional exam requirements/recommendations for international students: Required—TOEFL. *Application deadline:* For fall admission, 4/15 priority date for domestic students. Applications are processed on a rolling basis. Application fee: $50. Electronic applications accepted. *Expenses: Contact institution. Financial support:* Institutionally sponsored loans and scholarships/grants available. Financial award application deadline: 4/1. *Unit head:* W. Scott Guthrie, Director, 303-623-1888, Fax: 800-623-5778, E-mail: scott_guthrie@cudenver.edu. *Application contact:* Peter Taffe, Program Manager, 303-623-1888, Fax: 303-623-6228, E-mail: peter_taffe@cudenver.edu.

University of Florida, College of Pharmacy and Graduate School, Graduate Programs in Pharmacy, Department of Pharmacy Health Care Administration, Gainesville, FL 32611. Offers MSP, PhD. Part-time programs available. *Faculty:* 8 full-time (5 women), 1 part-time/adjunct (0 women). *Students:* 29 (14 women); includes 7 minority (4 African Americans, 3 Hispanic Americans) 12 international. Average age 31. In 2006, 2 master's, 2 doctorates awarded. *Degree requirements:* For doctorate, thesis/dissertation. *Entrance requirements:* For master's, minimum GPA of 3.0; for doctorate, GRE General Test, minimum GPA of 3.0. Additional exam requirements/recommendations for international students: Required—TOEFL. *Application deadline:* For fall admission, 3/1 priority date for domestic students. Applications are processed on a rolling basis. Application fee: $30. Electronic applications accepted. *Expenses:* Tuition, state resident: full-time $6,827. Tuition, nonresident: full-time $21,951. Required fees: $999. *Financial support:* In 2006–07, 14 teaching assistantships (averaging $22,029 per year) were awarded; fellowships, research assistantships, tuition waivers (full) also available. Financial award application deadline: 2/1. *Faculty research:* Pharmaceutical care, drug use systems, drug-related morbidity, pharmacy law. *Unit head:* Dr. Richard Segal, Chair, 352-273-6268, Fax: 352-273-6270, E-mail: segal@cop.health.ufl.edu. *Application contact:* Dr. Carole Kimberlin, Graduate Coordinator, 352-273-6263, Fax: 352-273-6270, E-mail: kimber@cop.ufl.edu.

University of Georgia, College of Pharmacy, Department of Clinical and Administrative Pharmacy, Athens, GA 30602. Offers experimental therapeutics (MS, PhD); pharmacy care administration (MS, PhD). *Faculty:* 10 full-time (4 women). *Students:* Average age 25. 33 applicants, 12% accepted, 2 enrolled.Terminal master's awarded for partial completion of doctoral program. *Degree requirements:* For master's, thesis/dissertation; for doctorate, thesis/dissertation, comprehensive exam. *Entrance requirements:* For master's and doctorate, GRE General Test, minimum GPA of 3.0. Additional exam requirements/recommendations for international students: Required—TOEFL (minimum score 550 paper-based; 213 computer-based). *Application deadline:* For fall admission, 5/15 for domestic students; for spring admission, 10/15 for domestic students. Application fee: $50. Electronic applications accepted. *Financial support:* In 2006–07, 14 teaching assistantships (averaging $11,509 per year) were awarded; tuition waivers (full) and unspecified assistantships also available. Financial award application deadline: 2/15. *Faculty research:* Pharmacy care administration, pharmacoeconomics, cardiovascular therapeutics, central nervous system therapeutics, drug use in populations. *Unit head:* Susan Fagan, Interim Head, 706-721-4915, E-mail: sfagan@mail.mcg.edu. *Application contact:* Dr. Randall L. Tackett, Graduate Coordinator, 706-542-5415, Fax: 706-542-5228.

University of Houston, College of Pharmacy, Houston, TX 77204. Offers hospital pharmacy (MSPHR); medical chemistry and pharmacology (MS); pharmaceutics (MS, PhD); pharmacology (MS, PhD); pharmacy (Pharm D); pharmacy administration (MSPHR). *Accreditation:* ACPE. Part-time programs available. *Faculty:* 15 full-time (4 women), 17 part-time/adjunct (9 women). *Students:* 500 full-time (335 women), 31 part-time (23 women); includes 260 minority (25 African Americans, 192 Asian Americans or Pacific Islanders, 43 Hispanic Americans), 55 international. Average age 25. 573 applicants, 27% accepted, 149 enrolled. In 2006, 106 first professional degrees, 6 master's, 4 doctorates awarded. Terminal master's awarded for partial completion of doctoral program. *Degree requirements:* For master's and doctorate, thesis/dissertation. *Entrance requirements:* For Pharm D, PCAT, interview; for master's and doctorate, GRE General Test. Additional exam requirements/recommendations for international students: Required—TOEFL. *Application deadline:* For spring admission, 3/1 for domestic students. Applications are processed on a rolling basis. Application fee: $25 ($75 for international students). *Expenses:* Tuition, state resident: full-time $5,429; part-time $226 per credit. Tuition, nonresident: full-time $12,029; part-time $501 per credit. Required fees: $2,454. *Financial support:* In 2006–07, 6 research assistantships with full tuition reimbursements (averaging $14,200 per year), 35 teaching assistantships with full tuition reimbursements (averaging $14,200 per year) were awarded; fellowships with full tuition reimbursements, career-related internships or fieldwork, Federal Work-Study, institutionally sponsored loans, scholarships/grants, health care benefits, and unspecified assistantships also available. Support available to part-time students. Financial award application deadline: 3/10. *Faculty research:* Cardiovascular and renal pharmacology, cellular pharmacology, drug delivery systems, geriatrics, pharmacokinetics, pharmacoeconomics, pharmaceutical marketing, pharmaceutical management, behavioral pharmacy, and signal transduction. Total annual research expenditures: $1.3 million. *Unit head:* Dr. Sunny Ohia, Dean, 713-743-1253, Fax: 713-743-1259, E-mail: seohia@uh.edu. *Application contact:* Shara Zatopek, Assistant Dean for Admissions, 713-743-1262, Fax: 713-743-1259, E-mail: szatopek@uh.edu.

University of Illinois at Chicago, College of Pharmacy and Graduate College, Research & Graduate Studies, College of Pharmacy, Chicago, IL 60607-7128. Offers forensic science (MS); medicinal chemistry (MS, PhD); pharmaceutics (MS, PhD); pharmacodynamics (MS, PhD); pharmacognosy (MS, PhD); pharmacy administration (MS, PhD). Terminal master's awarded for partial completion of doctoral program. *Degree requirements:* For master's and doctorate, variable foreign language requirement, thesis/dissertation. *Entrance requirements:* For master's and doctorate, GRE General Test. Additional exam requirements/recommendations for international students: Required—TOEFL. Electronic applications accepted. Expenses: Contact institution.

University of Maryland, Baltimore, Graduate School, Graduate Programs in Pharmacy, Department of Pharmaceutical Health Service Research, Baltimore, MD 21201. Offers epidemiology (MS); pharmacy administration (PhD); Pharm D/PhD. Part-time programs available. *Faculty:* 14 full-time (8 women). *Students:* 21 full-time (10 women), 5 part-time (1 woman); includes 3 minority (2 African Americans, 1 Hispanic American), 20 international. Average age 26. 39 applicants, 15% accepted, 5 enrolled. In 2006, 2 degrees awarded. *Degree requirements:* For doctorate, thesis/dissertation, comprehensive exam. *Entrance requirements:* For doctorate, GRE General Test. Additional exam requirements/recommendations for international students: Required—TOEFL (minimum score 550 paper-based; 215 computer-based), IELTS. *Application deadline:* For fall admission, 7/1 for domestic students, 1/15 for international students; for winter admission, 12/1 for domestic students, 5/1 for international students. Applications are processed on a rolling basis. Application fee: $125. *Financial support:* In 2006–07, 1 fellowship with tuition reimbursement (averaging $20,000 per year), 4 research assistantships with full tuition reimbursements (averaging $21,772 per year), 4 teaching assistantships with full tuition reimbursements (averaging $21,772 per year) were awarded; career-related internships or fieldwork, scholarships/grants, traineeships, and unspecified assistantships also available. Financial award application deadline: 2/15; financial award applicants required to submit FAFSA. *Faculty research:* Pharmacoeconomics, outcomes research, public health policy, drug therapy and aging. Total annual research expenditures: $1.5 million. *Unit head:* Diane Kaufman, Administrative Director, 410-706-3555, E-mail: dkaufman@rx.umaryland.edu. *Application contact:* Tracie Jones, Graduate Coordinator, 410-706-7613, Fax: 410-706-5394, E-mail: tjones@umaryland.edu.

University of Michigan, College of Pharmacy and Horace H. Rackham School of Graduate Studies, Department of Social and Administrative Sciences, Ann Arbor, MI 48109. Offers PhD. Terminal master's awarded for partial completion of doctoral program. *Degree requirements:* For doctorate, oral defense of dissertation, preliminary exam. *Entrance requirements:* For doctorate, GRE General Test. Additional exam requirements/recommendations for international students: Required—TOEFL or IELTS. Electronic applications accepted.

University of Minnesota, Twin Cities Campus, College of Pharmacy and Graduate School, Graduate Programs in Pharmacy, Graduate Program in Social and Administrative Pharmacy, Minneapolis, MN 55455-0213. Offers MS, PhD. *Degree requirements:* For master's, thesis (for some programs); for doctorate, thesis/dissertation. *Entrance requirements:* For master's, GRE General Test, BS in science; for doctorate, GRE General Test. Additional exam requirements/recommendations for international students: Required—TOEFL. *Expenses:* Tuition, state resident: full-time $9,302; part-time $775 per credit. Tuition, nonresident: full-time $16,400; part-time $1,367 per credit. Full-time tuition and fees vary according to class time, course load, program, reciprocity agreements and student level. *Faculty research:* Pharmaceutical economics, pharmaceutical policy, pharmaceutical social/behavioral sciences.

University of Mississippi, Graduate School, School of Pharmacy, Graduate Programs in Pharmacy, Oxford, University, MS 38677. Offers medicinal chemistry (MS, PhD); pharmaceutics (MS, PhD); pharmacognosy (MS, PhD); pharmacology (MS, PhD); pharmacy administration (MS, PhD). *Faculty:* 6 full-time (0 women). *Students:* 89 full-time (38 women), 6 part-time (2 women); includes 7 minority (3 African Americans, 3 Asian Americans or Pacific Islanders, 1 Hispanic American), 61 international. 163 applicants. In 2006, 5 master's, 11 doctorates awarded. *Expenses:* Tuition, state resident: full-time $4,602; part-time $256 per credit hour. Tuition, nonresident: full-time $10,566; part-time $587 per credit hour. *Unit head:* Dr. Barbara G. Wells, Dean, School of Pharmacy, 662-915-7265, Fax: 662-915-5704, E-mail: pharmacy@olemiss.edu.

University of the Sciences in Philadelphia, College of Graduate Studies, Program in Pharmaceutical Business, Philadelphia, PA 19104-4495. Offers MBA. Part-time and evening/weekend programs available. *Faculty:* 5 full-time (0 women), 18 part-time/adjunct (9 women). *Students:* 13 full-time (4 women), 54 part-time (31 women); includes 8 minority (5 African Americans, 3 Asian Americans or Pacific Islanders), 4 international. Average age 33. In 2006, 13 degrees awarded. *Entrance requirements:* Additional exam requirements/recommendations for international students: Required—TOEFL, TWE. *Application deadline:* For fall admission, 5/1 for international students; for winter admission, 10/1 for international students; for spring admission, 3/1 for international students. Applications are processed on a rolling basis. Application fee: $50. *Expenses: Contact institution.* Tuition and fees vary according to program. *Financial support:* In 2006–07, 5 students received support, including 1 fellowship; tuition waivers (partial) also available. *Unit head:* Bruce Rosenthal, Director, 215-596-7439, E-mail: b.rosent@usip.edu. *Application contact:* Joyce D'Angelo, Administrative Assistant, 215-596-8937, E-mail: j.dangel@usip.edu.

University of the Sciences in Philadelphia, College of Graduate Studies, Program in Pharmacy Administration, Philadelphia, PA 19104-4495. Offers MS. Part-time programs available. *Faculty:* 4 full-time (0 women). *Students:* 6 full-time (5 women), 3 part-time (2 women); includes 2 minority (both Asian Americans or Pacific Islanders), 6 international. Average age 25. In 2006, 5 degrees awarded. *Entrance requirements:* Additional exam requirements/recommendations for international students: Required—TOEFL, TWE. *Application deadline:* For fall admission, 5/1 for international students; for winter admission, 10/1 for international students; for spring admission, 3/1 for international students. Applications are processed on a rolling basis. Application fee: $50. *Expenses:* Tuition: Part-time $1,058 per credit. Tuition and fees vary according to program. *Financial support:* In 2006–07, 5 students received support, including teaching assistantships with full tuition reimbursements available (averaging $18,500 per year); fellowships, research assistantships, institutionally sponsored loans, traineeships, tuition waivers (partial), and unspecified assistantships also available. Financial award application deadline: 5/1. *Faculty research:* Cost-effect analysis, pharmaceutical economics, pharmaceutical care, marketing research, health communications. Total annual research expenditures: $20,000. *Unit head:* Dr. William McGhan, Director, 215-596-8852, E-mail: w.mcghan@usip.edu. *Application contact:* Joyce D'Angelo, Administrative Assistant, 215-596-8937, E-mail: j.dangel@usip.edu.

See Close-Up on page 2253.

The University of Toledo, College of Graduate Studies, College of Pharmacy, Department of Pharmacology, Program in Pharmaceutical Science, Toledo, OH 43606-3390. Offers administrative pharmacy (MSPS); industrial pharmacy (MSPS); pharmacology (MSPS). *Faculty:* 15 full-time (4 women), 1 part-time/adjunct (0 women). *Students:* 20 full-time (10 women); includes 2 minority (1 African American, 1 Asian American or Pacific Islander), 5 international. Average age 25. 85 applicants, 14% accepted, 11 enrolled. In 2006, 13 degrees awarded. *Degree*

Pharmaceutical Administration

The University of Toledo (continued)

requirements: For master's, thesis. *Entrance requirements:* For master's, GRE General Test. Additional exam requirements/recommendations for international students: Required—TOEFL (minimum score 550 paper-based; 213 computer-based; 80 iBT). *Application deadline:* For fall admission, 2/1 for domestic students, 1/1 priority date for international students. Application fee: $45. Electronic applications accepted. *Financial support:* In 2006–07, 19 students received support; research assistantships with full tuition reimbursements available, teaching assistantships with full tuition reimbursements available, unspecified assistantships available. *Faculty research:* Drug disposition, neuropharmacology, pharmacokinetics, product stability, pharmacy and health care administration. *Application contact:* Karen F. Papadakis, Graduate Coordinator for Pharmaceutical Sciences, 419-530-1910, Fax: 419-530-1909, E-mail: kpapada@utnet.utoledo.edu.

University of Wisconsin–Madison, School of Pharmacy and Graduate School, Graduate Programs in Pharmacy, Madison, WI 53706-1380. Offers pharmaceutical sciences (MS, PhD); social and administrative sciences in pharmacy (MS, PhD). Terminal master's awarded for partial completion of doctoral program. *Degree requirements:* For master's, thesis (for some programs), registration; for doctorate, thesis/dissertation, comprehensive exam (for some programs), registration. *Entrance requirements:* For master's and doctorate, GRE. Additional exam requirements/recommendations for international students: Required—TOEFL. Electronic applications accepted. Expenses: Contact institution.

Wayne State University, Eugene Applebaum College of Pharmacy and Health Sciences, Department of Pharmaceutical Sciences, Detroit, MI 48202. Offers experimental technology in pharmaceutical sciences (Certificate); health systems pharmacy management (MS); hospital pharmacy (MS); pharmaceutical administration (MS, PhD); pharmacy (Pharm D). *Accreditation:* ACPE (one or more programs are accredited). Part-time programs available. *Faculty:* 39 full-time (0 women). *Students:* 14 full-time (6 women), 3 part-time (2 women); includes 1 minority (African American), 13 international. Average age 31. In 2006, 3 master's, 1 doctorate awarded. *Degree requirements:* For master's, thesis optional. *Entrance requirements:* For Pharm D, bachelor's degree in pharmacy; for master's, GRE General Test, bachelor's degree in pharmacy. Additional exam requirements/recommendations for international students: Required—TOEFL (minimum score 550 paper-based; 213 computer-based); Recommended—TWE (minimum score 6). *Application deadline:* For fall admission, 6/1 for international students; for winter admission, 10/1 for international students; for spring admission, 2/1 for international students. Applications are processed on a rolling basis. Application fee: $30 ($50 for international students). Electronic applications accepted. *Financial support:* In 2006–07, 3 fellowships (averaging $35,000 per year) were awarded; career-related internships or fieldwork and scholarships/grants also available. Support available to part-time students. *Faculty research:* Mechanisms of resistance of bacteria to anti-microbial agents, drug metabolism and disposition in children, treatment strategies for stroke/neurovascular disease, prevalence and treatment of diabetes in Arab-Americans, ethnic variability in development of osteoporosis. Total annual research expenditures: $449,503. *Unit head:* Dr. George B. Corcoran, Chair, 313-577-1737, Fax: 313-577-2033. *Application contact:* Geralynn Smith, Graduate Director, 313-577-5401, E-mail: gbs@wayne.edu.

West Virginia University, School of Pharmacy, Program in Pharmaceutical and Pharmacological Sciences, Morgantown, WV 26506. Offers administrative pharmacy (PhD); behavioral pharmacy (MS, PhD); biopharmaceutics/pharmacokinetics (MS, PhD); industrial pharmacy (MS); medicinal chemistry (MS, PhD); pharmaceutical chemistry (MS, PhD); pharmaceutics (MS, PhD); pharmacology and toxicology (MS); pharmacy (MS); pharmacy administration (MS). Part-time programs available. *Students:* 29 full-time (12 women), 3 part-time (2 women); includes 1 minority (Asian American or Pacific Islander), 18 international. Average age 30. 47 applicants, 6% accepted, 2 enrolled. In 2006, 3 master's, 9 doctorates awarded. Terminal master's awarded for partial completion of doctoral program. *Median time to degree:* Of those who began their doctoral program in fall 1998, 84% received their degree in 8 years or less. *Degree requirements:* For master's, thesis; for doctorate, one foreign language, thesis/dissertation, comprehensive exam. *Entrance requirements:* For master's and doctorate, GRE General Test, minimum GPA of 2.75. Additional exam requirements/recommendations for international students: Required—TOEFL; Recommended—TWE. *Application deadline:* For fall admission, 3/1 priority date for domestic and international students. Application fee: $50. Electronic applications accepted. *Expenses: Contact institution.* Tuition and fees vary according to program. *Financial support:* In 2006–07, 31 students received support, including 13 research assistantships with full tuition reimbursements available (averaging $23,000 per year), 15 teaching assistantships with full tuition reimbursements available (averaging $23,000 per year); career-related internships or fieldwork, Federal Work-Study, institutionally sponsored loans, health care benefits, tuition waivers (full and partial), and unspecified assistantships also available. Financial award application deadline: 3/1; financial award applicants required to submit FAFSA. *Faculty research:* Pharmaceutics, medicinal chemistry, biopharmaceutics/pharmacokinetics, health outcomes research. Total annual research expenditures: $1.8 million. *Application contact:* Dr. Patrick S. Callery, Assistant Dean for Graduate Programs/Chair, 304-293-1482, Fax: 304-293-2576, E-mail: pcallery@hsc.wvu.edu.

Pharmaceutical Sciences

Auburn University, School of Pharmacy and Graduate School, Graduate Program in Pharmacy, Auburn University, AL 36849. Offers pharmacal sciences (MS, PhD); pharmaceutical sciences (PhD); pharmacy care systems (MS, PhD). Part-time programs available. *Faculty:* 19 full-time (5 women). *Students:* 12 full-time (5 women), 10 part-time (5 women); includes 2 minority (both African Americans), 11 international. Average age 32. 47 applicants, 15% accepted, 3 enrolled. In 2006, 4 degrees awarded. *Degree requirements:* For master's and doctorate, thesis/dissertation. *Entrance requirements:* For master's and doctorate, GRE General Test. *Application deadline:* For fall admission, 7/7 for domestic students; for spring admission, 11/24 for domestic students. Applications are processed on a rolling basis. Application fee: $25 ($50 for international students). Electronic applications accepted. *Expenses:* Tuition, state resident: full-time $5,000. Tuition, nonresident: full-time $15,000. Required fees: $416. Tuition and fees vary according to program. *Financial support:* Fellowships, research assistantships, teaching assistantships available. *Faculty research:* Communications, facilities design, substance abuse. Total annual research expenditures: $600,000. *Application contact:* Dr. Joe Pittman, Interim Dean of the Graduate School, 334-844-4700.

Boston University, School of Medicine, Division of Graduate Medical Sciences, Department of Pharmacology and Experimental Therapeutics, Boston, MA 02118. Offers MA, PhD, MD/PhD. *Faculty:* 12 full-time (4 women). Terminal master's awarded for partial completion of doctoral program. *Degree requirements:* For master's and doctorate, thesis/dissertation. *Entrance requirements:* For master's and doctorate, GRE General Test, GRE Subject Test. Additional exam requirements/recommendations for international students: Required—TOEFL. *Application deadline:* For fall admission, 1/15 priority date for domestic students; for spring admission, 10/15 priority date for domestic students. Electronic applications accepted. *Expenses:* Tuition: Full-time $33,330; part-time $1,042 per credit. Required fees: $462; $40. *Financial support:* In 2006–07, fellowships with tuition reimbursements (averaging $19,000 per year), research assistantships with tuition reimbursements (averaging $19,000 per year) were awarded; Federal Work-Study, scholarships/grants, traineeships, tuition waivers, and research stipends also available. *Faculty research:* Molecular pharmacology, neuropharmacology, peptide receptors, psychopharmacology. *Unit head:* Dr. David H. Farb, Chairman, 617-638-4300, Fax: 617-638-4329, E-mail: dfarb@bu.edu. *Application contact:* Dr. Carol T. Walsh, Graduate Director, 617-638-4326, Fax: 617-638-4329, E-mail: ctwalsh@bu.edu.

Butler University, College of Pharmacy, Indianapolis, IN 46208-3485. Offers pharmaceutical science (Pharm D, MS); physician assistance studies (MS). *Accreditation:* ACPE (one or more programs are accredited). Part-time and evening/weekend programs available. *Faculty:* 34 full-time (17 women), 9 part-time/adjunct (7 women). *Students:* 369 full-time (275 women), 9 part-time (7 women); includes 26 minority (7 African Americans, 1 American Indian/Alaska Native, 17 Asian Americans or Pacific Islanders, 1 Hispanic American), 9 international. Average age 24. 135 applicants, 82% accepted, 87 enrolled. In 2006, 84 degrees awarded. *Degree requirements:* For master's, research paper or thesis. *Application deadline:* For fall admission, 8/1 priority date for domestic students; for spring admission, 12/15 for domestic students. Applications are processed on a rolling basis. Application fee: $35. Electronic applications accepted. *Expenses: Contact institution.* Tuition and fees vary according to program. *Financial support:* Applicants required to submit FAFSA. *Faculty research:* Anti-seizure drugs, casein kinase inhibitors, speech recognition interface for prescribing drugs, pharmacoeconomics. Total annual research expenditures: $92,000. *Unit head:* Dr. Mary Andritz, Dean, 317-940-9451, Fax: 317-940-6172, E-mail: mandritz@butler.edu. *Application contact:* Dr. Kent VanTyle, Professor, 317-940-9580, E-mail: kvantyle@butler.edu.

Campbell University, Graduate and Professional Programs, School of Pharmacy, Buies Creek, NC 27506. Offers clinical research (MS); pharmaceutical science (MS); pharmacy (Pharm D). *Accreditation:* ACPE. Part-time and evening/weekend programs available. *Faculty:* 55 full-time (18 women), 119 part-time/adjunct (52 women). *Students:* 435 full-time (296 women), 183 part-time (122 women); includes 50 minority (37 African Americans, 8 American Indian/Alaska Native, 5 Hispanic Americans), 34 international. Average age 23. 1,960 applicants, 7% accepted, 108 enrolled. In 2006, 89 Pharm Ds, 8 master's awarded. *Entrance requirements:* For Pharm D, PCAT; for master's, MCAT, PCAT, GRE, bachelor's degree in health sciences or related field. Additional exam requirements/recommendations for international students: Required—TOEFL (minimum score 550 paper-based; 213 computer-based; 79 iBT). *Application deadline:* For fall admission, 3/1 for domestic and international students. Applications are processed on a rolling basis. Application fee: $25. Electronic applications accepted. *Expenses: Contact institution.* *Financial support:* In 2006–07, 350 students received support, including 4 research assistantships (averaging $3,000 per year), 3 teaching assistantships (averaging $4,000 per year); career-related internships or fieldwork, Federal Work-Study, and scholarships/grants also available. Financial award application deadline: 3/15; financial award applicants required to submit FAFSA. *Faculty research:* Immunology, medicinal chemistry, pharmaceutics, applied pharmacology. Total annual research expenditures: $297,000. *Unit head:* Dr. Ronald W. Maddox, Dean, 910-893-1200 Ext. 1685, Fax: 910-893-1697, E-mail: pharmacy@camel.campbell.edu. *Application contact:* Dr. Mark Moore, Assistant Dean of Admissions and Student Affairs, 910-893-1690, Fax: 910-893-1937, E-mail: pharmacy@campbell.edu.

Creighton University, School of Medicine and Graduate School, Graduate Programs in Medicine and College of Arts and Sciences, Department of Pharmacology, Omaha, NE 68178-0001. Offers pharmaceutical sciences (MS); pharmacology (MS, PhD); Pharm D/MS. *Faculty:* 8 full-time (1 woman), 15 part-time/adjunct (2 women). *Students:* 8 full-time (3 women), 6 international. Average age 25. 35 applicants, 6% accepted, 2 enrolled. In 2006, 1 master's, 1 doctorate awarded. Terminal master's awarded for partial completion of doctoral program. *Median time to degree:* Doctorate–5 years full-time. *Degree requirements:* For master's, thesis, comprehensive exam; for doctorate, thesis/dissertation, oral and written preliminary exams, comprehensive exam. *Entrance requirements:* For master's and doctorate, GRE General Test, minimum GPA of 3.0, undergraduate degree in sciences. Additional exam requirements/recommendations for international students: Required—TOEFL. *Application deadline:* For spring admission, 4/1 priority date for domestic and international students. Applications are processed on a rolling basis. Application fee: $35. Electronic applications accepted. *Expenses:* Tuition: Part-time $595 per credit hour. Required fees: $38 per semester. *Financial support:* In 2006–07, 6 fellowships with full tuition reimbursements (averaging $20,772 per year) were awarded; institutionally sponsored loans and tuition waivers (full and partial) also available. Financial award application deadline: 4/1. *Faculty research:* Pharmacology secretion, cardiovascular-renal pharmacology, adrenergic receptors, signal transduction, genetic regulation of receptors. Total annual research expenditures: $278,221. *Unit head:* Dr. Thomas F. Murray, Chair, 402-280-2983, Fax: 402-280-2142, E-mail: tfmurray@creighton.edu. *Application contact:* Dr. Margaret A. Schofield, Associate Professor, 402-280-2245, Fax: 402-280-2142, E-mail: mscof@creighton.edu.

Creighton University, School of Pharmacy and Health Professions and Department of Pharmacology, Program in Pharmaceutical Sciences, Omaha, NE 68178-0001. Offers MS, Pharm D/MS. *Expenses:* Tuition: Part-time $595 per credit hour. Required fees: $38 per semester.

Dalhousie University, Faculty of Graduate Studies, Faculty of Health Professions, College of Pharmacy, Halifax, NS B3H 4R2, Canada. Offers M Sc, PhD. *Degree requirements:* For master's, thesis; for doctorate, one foreign language, thesis/dissertation. Expenses: Contact institution.

Dartmouth College, Dartmouth Medical School, Program in Experimental and Molecular Medicine, Molecular Pharmacy, Toxicology and Experimental Therapeutics Track, Hanover, NH 03755. Offers PhD. *Expenses:* Tuition: Full-time $33,297.

Duquesne University, School of Pharmacy, Graduate School of Pharmaceutical Sciences, Program in Pharmaceutics, Pittsburgh, PA 15282-0001. Offers MS, PhD, MBA/MS. Part-time programs available. *Faculty:* 5 full-time (1 woman). *Students:* 19 full-time (5 women), 4 part-time (2 women), 15 international. 108 applicants, 5% accepted, 4 enrolled. *Degree requirements:* For master's, thesis/dissertation; for doctorate, thesis/dissertation, comprehensive exam. *Entrance requirements:* For master's and doctorate, GRE General Test. Additional exam requirements/recommendations for international students: Required—TOEFL. *Application deadline:* For fall admission, 2/1 priority date for domestic students. Applications are processed on a rolling basis. Application fee: $50. *Expenses:* Tuition: Part-time $723 per credit. Required fees: $71 per credit. Tuition and fees vary according to degree level and program. *Financial support:* In 2006–07, 19 students received support, including 1 research assistantship, 18 teaching assistantships; career-related internships or fieldwork, Federal Work-Study, institutionally sponsored loans, scholarships/grants, and unspecified assistantships also available. Support available to part-time students. Financial award applicants required to submit FAFSA.

See Close-Up on page 2233.

Florida Agricultural and Mechanical University, Division of Graduate Studies, Research, and Continuing Education, College of Pharmacy and Pharmaceutical Sciences, Graduate Programs in Pharmaceutical Sciences, Tallahassee, FL 32307-3200. Offers environmental toxicology (PhD); medicinal chemistry (MS, PhD); pharmaceutics (MS, PhD); pharmacology/toxicology (MS, PhD); pharmacy administration (MS). *Accreditation:* CEPH. *Degree* *requirements:* For master's and doctorate, thesis/dissertation, publishable paper, comprehensive exam. *Entrance requirements:* For master's and doctorate, GRE General Test, minimum GPA of 3.0 in last 60 hours. Additional exam requirements/recommendations for international students: Required—TOEFL. *Faculty research:* Anticancer agents, anti-inflammatory drugs, chronopharmacology, neuroendocrinology, microbiology.

See Close-Up on page 2235.

Idaho State University, Office of Graduate Studies, College of Pharmacy, Department of Pharmaceutical Sciences, Pocatello, ID 83209. Offers biopharmaceutical analysis (PhD); biopharmaceutics (PhD); pharmaceutical chemistry (MS); pharmaceutical science (PhD); pharmaceutics (MS); pharmacognosy (MS); pharmacokinetics (PhD); pharmacology (MS, PhD). *Faculty:* 11 full-time (2 women). *Students:* 17 full-time (6 women), 4 part-time (2 women); includes 2 minority (both Asian Americans or Pacific Islanders), 14 international. Average age 30. In 2006, 1 master's, 3 doctorates awarded. *Degree requirements:* For master's, one foreign language, thesis, thesis research, comprehensive exam, registration (for some programs); for doctorate, thesis/dissertation, written and oral exams, comprehensive exam, registration. *Entrance requirements:* For master's, GRE General Test, minimum GPA of 3.0, 3 letters of recommendation; for doctorate, GRE General Test, BS degree in pharmacy or related field, minimum GPA of 3.0, 3 letters of recommendation. Additional exam requirements/ recommendations for international students: Required—TOEFL (minimum score 550 paper-based; 213 computer-based). *Application deadline:* For fall admission, 7/1 for domestic students, 6/1 priority date for international students; for spring admission, 12/1 for domestic students, 11/1 priority date for international students. Applications are processed on a rolling basis. Application fee: $55. *Expenses:* Tuition, state resident: part-time $251 per credit. Tuition, nonresident: part-time $366 per credit. Tuition and fees vary according to degree level, program and reciprocity agreements. *Financial support:* In 2006–07, 5 teaching assistantships with full and partial tuition reimbursements (averaging $8,694 per year) were awarded; career-related internships or fieldwork, Federal Work-Study, scholarships/grants, traineeships, tuition waivers (full and partial), and unspecified assistantships also available. Support available to part-time students. Financial award application deadline: 1/1. *Faculty research:* Metabolic toxicity of heavy metals, neuroendocrine pharmacology, cardiovascular pharmacology, cancer biology, immunopharmacology. Total annual research expenditures: $1.6 million. *Unit head:* Dr. Fred Risinger, Chair, 208-282-2682, Fax: 208-282-4305, E-mail: risinger@pharmacy.isu.edu. *Application contact:* Ellen Combs, Graduate School Technical Records Specialist, 208-282-2150, Fax: 208-282-4847.

Long Island University, Brooklyn Campus, Arnold and Marie Schwartz College of Pharmacy and Health Sciences, Graduate Programs in Pharmacy, Division of Pharmaceutical Sciences, Brooklyn, NY 11201-8423. Offers cosmetic science (MS); industrial pharmacy (MS); pharmaceutics (PhD); pharmacology/toxicology (MS). Part-time and evening/weekend programs available. *Faculty:* 18 full-time (2 women), 4 part-time/adjunct (1 woman). *Students:* 277 (105 women); includes 253 minority (21 African Americans, 1 American Indian/Alaska Native, 229 Asian Americans or Pacific Islanders, 2 Hispanic Americans). Average age 30. In 2006, 33 master's, 2 doctorates awarded. Terminal master's awarded for partial completion of doctoral program. *Degree requirements:* For master's, thesis optional; for doctorate, thesis/ dissertation, candidacy exam. *Entrance requirements:* For master's and doctorate, minimum GPA of 3.0. *Application deadline:* Applications are processed on a rolling basis. Application fee: $30. *Financial support:* In 2006–07, 5 fellowships with full tuition reimbursements (averaging $13,500 per year), 18 teaching assistantships with full tuition reimbursements (averaging $6,000 per year) were awarded; Federal Work-Study also available. Financial award applicants required to submit FAFSA. *Unit head:* Dr. Fotios M. Plakogiannis, Director, 718-488-1101, E-mail: fotios.plakogiannis@liu.edu. *Application contact:* Edward Dettling, Director of Graduate Admissions, 718-488-1011, Fax: 718-797-2399, E-mail: admissions@brooklyn.liu.edu.

Long Island University, Rockland Graduate Campus, Graduate School, Program in Pharmaceutics, Orangeburg, NY 10962. Offers cosmetical dermatological sciences (MS); industrial pharmacy (MS).

Massachusetts College of Pharmacy and Health Sciences, Graduate Studies, Program in Drug Discovery and Development, Boston, MA 02115-5896. Offers MS. Part-time and evening/ weekend programs available. *Degree requirements:* For master's, thesis, registration. *Entrance requirements:* For master's, GRE General Test. Additional exam requirements/recommendations for international students: Required—TOEFL. *Faculty research:* Transporters, pharmacokinetics, metabolism, target validation.

Massachusetts College of Pharmacy and Health Sciences, Graduate Studies, Program in Pharmaceutics, Boston, MA 02115-5896. Offers MS, PhD. Terminal master's awarded for partial completion of doctoral program. *Degree requirements:* For master's, thesis, oral defense of thesis; for doctorate, one foreign language, thesis/dissertation, oral defense of dissertation, qualifying exam, comprehensive exam, registration. *Entrance requirements:* For master's and doctorate, GRE General Test, minimum QPA of 3.0. Additional exam requirements/ recommendations for international students: Required—TOEFL (minimum score 600 paper-based; 230 computer-based). *Faculty research:* Pharmacokinetics and drug metabolism, pharmaceutics and physical pharmacy, dosage forms.

See Close-Up on page 2237.

Medical University of South Carolina, College of Pharmacy, Charleston, SC 29425-0002. Offers pharmaceutical sciences (PhD); pharmacy (Pharm D). *Accreditation:* ACPE. *Faculty:* 42 full-time (17 women), 1 part-time/adjunct (0 women). *Students:* 316 full-time (229 women); includes 51 minority (24 African Americans, 2 American Indian/Alaska Native, 19 Asian Americans or Pacific Islanders, 6 Hispanic Americans). Average age 25. 612 applicants, 17% accepted, 81 enrolled. In 2006, 54 degrees awarded. *Entrance requirements:* PCAT, 2 years pre-professional course work, interview, minimum GPA of 2.5. Additional exam requirements/ recommendations for international students: Required—TOEFL (minimum score 600 paper-based; 250 computer-based). *Application deadline:* For fall admission, 1/15 for domestic and international students. Application fee: $75. Electronic applications accepted. *Expenses: Contact institution. Financial support:* In 2006–07, 270 students received support. Career-related internships or fieldwork, Federal Work-Study, institutionally sponsored loans, and scholarships/ grants available. Financial award application deadline: 8/15; financial award applicants required to submit FAFSA. *Faculty research:* Rational and computer aided drug design, drug metabolism and transport, molecular immunology and cellular toxicology, cell injury, death and regeneration. Total annual research expenditures: $1.8 million. *Unit head:* Dr. Arnold W. Karig, Interim Dean, 843-792-8452, Fax: 843-792-9081, E-mail: karigaw@musc.edu.

Memorial University of Newfoundland, School of Graduate Studies, School of Pharmacy, St. John's, NL A1C 5S7, Canada. Offers MSCPharm, PhD. Part-time programs available. *Degree requirements:* For master's, thesis, seminar; for doctorate, thesis/dissertation, oral defense of thesis, comprehensive exam. *Entrance requirements:* For master's, B Sc in pharmacy or related area. Electronic applications accepted. *Faculty research:* Pharmaceutics, medicinal chemistry, physical pharmacy, pharmacology, toxicology.

Mercer University, Graduate Studies, Cecil B. Day Campus, College of Pharmacy and Health Sciences, Macon, GA 31207-0003. Offers medical sciences (MS); pharmacy (Pharm D, Pharm D/MBA, Pharm D/PhD); Pharm D/MBA; Pharm D/PhD. *Accreditation:* ACPE (one or more programs are accredited). *Faculty:* 21 full-time (13 women), 2 part-time/adjunct (1 woman). *Students:* 584 full-time (401 women), 27 part-time (22 women); includes 158 minority (69 African Americans, 3 American Indian/Alaska Native, 71 Asian Americans or Pacific Islanders, 15 Hispanic Americans), 33 international. Average age 26. 2,250 applicants, 12% accepted, 155 enrolled. In 2006, 128 Pharm Ds, 5 doctorates awarded. *Median time to degree:* Of those who began their doctoral program in fall 1998, 95% received their degree in 8 years or less. *Degree requirements:* For doctorate, thesis/dissertation. *Entrance requirements:* For Pharm D, PCAT, minimum GPA of 2.5; for master's, GRE; for doctorate, GRE, Pharm D or BS in pharmacy, minimum GPA of 3.0. *Application deadline:* For fall admission, 1/1 for domestic students. Applications are processed on a rolling basis. Application fee: $25. Electronic applications accepted. *Expenses: Contact institution. Financial support:* In 2006–07, 350 students received support; teaching assistantships with tuition reimbursements available, career-related internships or fieldwork, Federal Work-Study, institutionally sponsored loans, scholarships/grants, and tuition waivers available. Support available to part-time students. Financial award application deadline: 5/1; financial award applicants required to submit FAFSA. *Faculty research:* Stability and compatibility of steroids, synthesis of antihypertensives, disposition of cyclosporine, DUZ-drug research, synthesis of enzyme inhibitors. *Unit head:* Dr. Hewitt W. Matthews, Dean, 678-547-6304, Fax: 678-547-6315, E-mail: matthews_h@mercer.edu. *Application contact:* Dr. James W. Bartling, Associate Dean for Student Affairs and Admissions, 678-547-6232, Fax: 678-547-6063, E-mail: bartling_jw@mercer.edu.

North Dakota State University, The Graduate School, College of Pharmacy, Nursing and Allied Sciences, Department of Pharmaceutical Sciences, Fargo, ND 58105. Offers MS, PhD. *Accreditation:* ACPE. Part-time programs available. *Faculty:* 8 full-time (0 women), 2 part-time/ adjunct (1 woman). *Students:* 23 full-time (13 women); includes 1 minority (Asian American or Pacific Islander), 17 international. Average age 25. 80 applicants, 5% accepted. In 2006, 1 master's, 3 doctorates awarded. Terminal master's awarded for partial completion of doctoral program. *Degree requirements:* For master's and doctorate, thesis/dissertation. *Entrance requirements:* For master's and doctorate, GRE General Test. Additional exam requirements/ recommendations for international students: Required—TOEFL. *Application deadline:* For fall admission, 4/15 for domestic students. Applications are processed on a rolling basis. Application fee: $45 ($60 for international students). *Financial support:* In 2006–07, 19 research assistantships with full tuition reimbursements (averaging $14,000 per year) were awarded; institutionally sponsored loans also available. Financial award application deadline: 4/15. *Faculty research:* Subcellular pharmacokinetics, cancer, cardiovascular drug design, iontophonesis, neuropharmacology. *Unit head:* Dr. Jagdish Singh, Chair, 701-231-7661, E-mail: jagdishsingh@ndsu.edu. *Application contact:* Dr. Jonathan Sheng, Assistant Professor, 701-231-6140, Fax: 701-231-8333, E-mail: jonathan.sheng@ndsu.edu.

Northeastern University, Bouvé College of Health Sciences Graduate School, Program in Pharmacology, Boston, MA 02115-5096. Offers pharmaceutical sciences (PhD); pharmacology (MS). Part-time and evening/weekend programs available. *Faculty:* 39 full-time (13 women). *Students:* 99 full-time (57 women), 22 part-time (13 women). Average age 30. 149 applicants, 46% accepted. In 2006, 15 master's, 6 doctorates awarded. *Degree requirements:* For master's, thesis optional. *Entrance requirements:* For master's, bachelor's degree in science, minimum GPA of 3.0. Additional exam requirements/recommendations for international students: Required—TOEFL. *Application deadline:* Applications are processed on a rolling basis. Application fee: $50. *Financial support:* In 2006–07, 18 research assistantships (averaging $17,238 per year) were awarded; Federal Work-Study and tuition waivers (partial) also available. Support available to part-time students. Financial award application deadline: 3/1; financial award applicants required to submit FAFSA. *Faculty research:* Nicotinic receptor subtypes, G-protein coupled receptors, dopamine receptor pharmacology, path-clamping of ion channel. Total annual research expenditures: $1.6 million. *Unit head:* Dr. Vladimir Torchilin, Director, 617-373-3216, Fax: 617-373-6756. *Application contact:* Margaret Schnabel, Director of Graduate Admissions, 617-373-2708, Fax: 617-373-4704, E-mail: bouvegrad@neu.edu.

Northeastern University, Bouvé College of Health Sciences Graduate School, School of Pharmacy, Boston, MA 02115-5096. Offers Pharm D. Students enter program as undergraduates. *Accreditation:* ACPE. In 2006, 50 degrees awarded. *Entrance requirements:* Prior admission to undergraduate pharmacy program. *Unit head:* Jack Reynolds, Dean, 617-373-8917. *Application contact:* Office of Undergraduate Admissions, 617-373-2200, Fax: 617-373-8780, E-mail: admissions@neu.edu.

The Ohio State University, College of Pharmacy and Graduate School, Graduate Programs in Pharmacy, Division of Medicinal Chemistry and Pharmacognosy, Columbus, OH 43210. Offers MS, PhD. *Faculty:* 9 full-time (0 women). *Students:* 25 full-time (9 women); includes 1 minority (African American), 19 international. Average age 26. 51 applicants, 18% accepted, 4 enrolled. In 2006, 4 master's, 4 doctorates awarded. *Median time to degree:* Master's–2 years full-time. Of those who began their doctoral program in fall 1998, 99% received their degree in 8 years or less. *Degree requirements:* For master's and doctorate, thesis/dissertation. *Entrance requirements:* For master's and doctorate, GRE General Test, minimum GPA of 3.0. Additional exam requirements/recommendations for international students: Required—TOEFL (minimum score 620 paper-based; 250 computer-based; 80 iBT). *Application deadline:* For fall admission, 1/1 priority date for domestic students, 8/31 for international students; for winter admission, 9/1 priority date for domestic students, 11/1 for international students; for spring admission, 11/1 priority date for domestic students, 11/1 for international students. Application fee: $40 ($50 for international students). Electronic applications accepted. *Expenses:* Tuition, state resident: full-time $9,438. Tuition, nonresident: full-time $22,791. Tuition and fees vary according to course load, campus/location and program. *Financial support:* In 2006–07, 25 students received support, including 2 fellowships with full tuition reimbursements available (averaging $23,000 per year), 14 research assistantships with full tuition reimbursements available (averaging $19,600 per year), 9 teaching assistantships with full tuition reimbursements available (averaging $19,100 per year); traineeships also available. Financial award application deadline: 1/1. *Faculty research:* Drug design, natural products, synthesis of enzyme inhibitors, drug metabolism and anticancer agents. *Unit head:* Dr. Pui-Kai Li, Coordinator, 614-688-0253, Fax: 614-292-2435, E-mail: kl.27@osu.edu. *Application contact:* Kathy I. Brooks, Graduate Program Coordinator, 614-292-6822, Fax: 614-292-2588, E-mail: gadmbrks@dendrite.pharmacy.ohio-state.edu.

See Close-Up on page 2239.

The Ohio State University, College of Pharmacy and Graduate School, Graduate Programs in Pharmacy, Division of Pharmaceutics, Columbus, OH 43210. Offers MS, PhD. *Faculty:* 10 full-time (1 woman), 1 part-time/adjunct (0 women). *Students:* 28 full-time (19 women), 3 part-time (1 woman); includes 3 minority (1 African American, 2 Asian Americans or Pacific Islanders), 22 international. Average age 26. 79 applicants, 14% accepted, 7 enrolled. In 2006, 6 degrees awarded. Terminal master's awarded for partial completion of doctoral program. *Median time to degree:* Doctorate–5 years full-time. Of those who began their doctoral program in fall 1998, 100% received their degree in 8 years or less. *Degree requirements:* For doctorate, thesis/dissertation. *Entrance requirements:* For master's and doctorate, GRE General Test, minimum GPA of 3.0. Additional exam requirements/recommendations for international students: Required—TOEFL (minimum score 600 paper-based; 250 computer-based; 80 iBT). *Application deadline:* For fall admission, 1/1 priority date for domestic students, 8/31 for international students; for winter admission, 9/1 priority date for domestic students, 9/1 for international students; for spring admission, 11/1 priority date for domestic students, 11/1 for international students. Application fee: $40 ($50 for international students). Electronic applications accepted. *Expenses:* Tuition, state resident: full-time $9,438. Tuition, nonresident: full-time $22,791. Tuition and fees vary according to course load, campus/location and program. *Financial support:* In 2006–07, 28 students received support, including 4 fellowships with full tuition reimbursements available (averaging $23,000 per year), 15 research assistantships with full tuition reimbursements available (averaging $21,000 per year), 9 teaching assistantships with full tuition reimbursements available (averaging $20,000 per year). Financial award application deadline: 1/1. *Faculty research:* Absorption, metabolism, and elimination of drugs; drug release from emulsions, liposomes, and liquid crystals; clinical and forensic research application. *Unit head:* Dr. Thomas D. Schmittgen, Coordinator, 614-292-3456, Fax: 614-292-7766, E-mail: schmittgen.2@osu.edu. *Application contact:* Kathy I. Brooks, Graduate Program Coordinator, 614-292-6822, Fax: 614-292-2588, E-mail: gadmbrks@dendrite.pharmacy.ohio-state.edu.

See Close-Up on page 2239.

Oregon State University, College of Pharmacy, Corvallis, OR 97331. Offers Pharm D, MAIS, MS, PhD. *Accreditation:* ACPE (one or more programs are accredited). Part-time

Pharmaceutical Sciences

Oregon State University (continued)

programs available. *Faculty:* 35 full-time (16 women). *Students:* 351 full-time (205 women), 8 part-time (5 women); includes 122 minority (4 African Americans, 1 American Indian/Alaska Native, 103 Asian Americans or Pacific Islanders, 14 Hispanic Americans), 15 international. Average age 27. In 2006, 80 first professional degrees, 1 master's, 2 doctorates awarded. Terminal master's awarded for partial completion of doctoral program. *Degree requirements:* For master's and doctorate, thesis/dissertation. *Entrance requirements:* For master's, GRE General Test, minimum GPA of 3.0 in last 90 hours; for doctorate, GRE General Test, minimum GPA of 3.0 in last 90 hours, pre-pharmacy curriculum. Additional exam requirements/recommendations for international students: Required—TOEFL. *Application deadline:* For fall admission, 3/1 for domestic students. Applications are processed on a rolling basis. Application fee: $50. *Financial support:* Fellowships, research assistantships, teaching assistantships, career-related internships or fieldwork, Federal Work-Study, and institutionally sponsored loans available. Support available to part-time students. Financial award application deadline: 2/1. *Faculty research:* Pharmacology/toxicology, pharmacokinetics, biopharmaceutics, neuroscience, natural products. *Unit head:* Dr. Wayne A. Kradjan, Dean, 541-737-3424, Fax: 541-737-3424, E-mail: wayne.kradjan@orst.edu. *Application contact:* 541-737-5784, Fax: 541-737-3999.

Purdue University, College of Pharmacy and Pharmacal Sciences and Graduate School, Graduate Programs in Pharmacy and Pharmacal Sciences, Department of Medicinal Chemistry and Molecular Pharmacology, West Lafayette, IN 47907. Offers analytical medicinal chemistry (PhD); computational and biophysical medicinal chemistry (PhD); medicinal and bioorganic chemistry (PhD); medicinal biochemistry and molecular biology (PhD); molecular pharmacology and toxicology (PhD); natural products and pharmacognosy (PhD); nuclear pharmacy (MS); radiopharmaceutical chemistry and nuclear pharmacy (PhD); MS/PhD. *Faculty:* 23 full-time (2 women), 4 part-time/adjunct (1 woman). *Students:* 66 full-time (41 women), 6 part-time (2 women); includes 6 minority (2 African Americans, 1 Asian American or Pacific Islander, 3 Hispanic Americans), 22 international. Average age 26. 120 applicants, 21% accepted, 12 enrolled. In 2006, 2 master's, 7 doctorates awarded. Terminal master's awarded for partial completion of doctoral program. *Degree requirements:* For master's and doctorate, thesis/dissertation. *Entrance requirements:* For master's, GRE General Test, minimum B average; BS in biology, chemistry, or pharmacy; for doctorate, GRE General Test, minimum B average; BS in biology, chemistry, or pharmacology. Additional exam requirements/recommendations for international students: Required—TOEFL. *Application deadline:* For fall admission, 5/15 for international students; for spring admission, 10/15 for international students. Applications are processed on a rolling basis. Application fee: $55. Electronic applications accepted. *Financial support:* Fellowships, research assistantships, teaching assistantships, traineeships available. Support available to part-time students. Financial award applicants required to submit FAFSA. *Faculty research:* Drug design and development, cancer research, drug synthesis and analysis, chemical pharmacology, environmental toxicology. *Unit head:* Dr. R. F. Borch, Graduate Head, 765-494-1403. *Application contact:* Dr. Eric L. Barker, Chair of the Graduate Committee, 765-494-1454, E-mail: ericb@pharmacy.purdue.edu.

Purdue University, College of Pharmacy and Pharmacal Sciences and Graduate School, Graduate Programs in Pharmacy and Pharmacal Sciences, Department of Pharmacy Practice, West Lafayette, IN 47907. Offers clinical pharmacy (MS, PhD); pharmacy administration (MS, PhD). *Faculty:* 20 full-time (6 women), 5 part-time/adjunct (1 woman). *Students:* 13 full-time (11 women), 1 (woman) part-time; includes 3 minority (2 African Americans, 1 Asian American or Pacific Islander), 9 international. Average age 29. 34 applicants, 32% accepted, 7 enrolled. In 2006, 5 degrees awarded. Terminal master's awarded for partial completion of doctoral program. *Degree requirements:* For master's, thesis optional; for doctorate, thesis/dissertation. *Entrance requirements:* For master's and doctorate, GRE General Test, BS in pharmacy or Pharm D, minimum B average. Additional exam requirements/recommendations for international students: Required—TOEFL. *Application deadline:* For fall admission, 11/1 priority date for domestic students. Applications are processed on a rolling basis. Application fee: $55. Electronic applications accepted. *Financial support:* Fellowships, research assistantships, teaching assistantships, career-related internships or fieldwork and traineeships available. Support available to part-time students. Financial award applicants required to submit FAFSA. *Faculty research:* Clinical drug studies, pharmacy education advancement, administrative studies. *Unit head:* Dr. S. R. Abel, Graduate Head, 765-494-5966. *Application contact:* Dr. Joseph Thomas, Graduate Committee Chair, 765-494-1477, Fax: 765-494-0801, E-mail: jt3@pharmacy.purdue.edu.

Rush University, Graduate College, Division of Pharmacology, Chicago, IL 60612-3832. Offers clinical research (MS); pharmacology (MS, PhD); MD/PhD. Terminal master's awarded for partial completion of doctoral program. *Degree requirements:* For master's and doctorate, thesis/dissertation. *Entrance requirements:* For master's and doctorate, GRE General Test, interview. Additional exam requirements/recommendations for international students: Required—TOEFL (minimum score 550 paper-based; 213 computer-based). *Faculty research:* Dopamine neurobiology and Parkinson's disease; cardiac electrophysiology and clinical pharmacology; neutrophil motility, apoptosis, and adhesion; angiogenesis; pulmonary vascular physiology.

Rutgers, The State University of New Jersey, New Brunswick, Graduate School, Program in Pharmaceutical Science, New Brunswick, NJ 08901-1281. Offers MS, PhD. Part-time programs available. Terminal master's awarded for partial completion of doctoral program. *Degree requirements:* For master's and doctorate, thesis/dissertation. *Entrance requirements:* For master's and doctorate, GRE General Test. Additional exam requirements/recommendations for international students: Required—TOEFL (minimum score 550 paper-based; 213 computer-based; 83 iBT). *Faculty research:* Drug transport, drug delivery, pharmacokinetics, cancer chemoprevention, pharmacogenomics.

St. John's University, College of Pharmacy and Allied Health Professions, Graduate Programs in Pharmacy, Program in Pharmaceutical Sciences, Queens, NY 11439. Offers MS, PhD. Part-time and evening/weekend programs available. *Students:* 17 full-time (13 women), 134 part-time (61 women); includes 14 minority (1 African American, 12 Asian Americans or Pacific Islanders, 1 Hispanic American), 118 international. Average age 27. 315 applicants, 39% accepted, 44 enrolled. In 2006, 16 master's, 3 doctorates awarded. Terminal master's awarded for partial completion of doctoral program. *Median time to degree:* Of those who began their doctoral program in fall 1998, 71% received their degree in 8 years or less. *Degree requirements:* For master's, residency, thesis optional; for doctorate, thesis/dissertation, qualifying exams, residency, comprehensive exam. *Entrance requirements:* For master's, GRE General Test, minimum GPA of 3.0; for doctorate, GRE General Test, minimum GPA of 3.5 (undergraduate), 3.0 (graduate). Additional exam requirements/recommendations for international students: Required—TOEFL (minimum score 500 paper-based; 173 computer-based). *Application deadline:* For fall admission, 4/1 for domestic students, 5/1 priority date for international students; for spring admission, 12/1 for domestic students, 11/1 priority date for international students. Applications are processed on a rolling basis. Application fee: $40. Electronic applications accepted. *Expenses:* Contact institution. Tuition and fees vary according to program. *Financial support:* Fellowships, research assistantships, career-related internships or fieldwork and scholarships/grants available. Support available to part-time students. Financial award application deadline: 3/1; financial award applicants required to submit FAFSA. *Faculty research:* Neurotoxicology, biochemical toxicology, molecular pharmacology, neuropharmacology, intermediary metabolism. *Unit head:* Dr. Louis Trombetta, Chair, 718-990-6025, E-mail: trombetl@stjohns.edu. *Application contact:* Br. Shamus McGrenra, Senior Associate Director, Office of Admission, 718-990-1601, Fax: 718-990-2346, E-mail: gradhelp@stjohns.edu.

South Dakota State University, Graduate School, College of Pharmacy, Department of Pharmaceutical Sciences, Brookings, SD 57007. Offers biological science (MS, PhD). *Faculty:* 8 full-time (0 women). *Students:* 11 full-time (3 women); includes 10 Asian Americans or Pacific Islanders. *Degree requirements:* For master's, thesis/dissertation, oral exam; for doctorate, thesis/dissertation, oral exam, comprehensive exam. *Entrance requirements:* For master's and doctorate, GRE General Test. Additional exam requirements/recommendations for international students: Required—TOEFL (minimum score 550 paper-based; 213 computer-based). *Application deadline:* For fall admission, 3/1 for domestic and international students. Applications are processed on a rolling basis. Application fee: $35. *Financial support:* In 2006–07, 1 fellowship, 3 research assistantships with partial tuition reimbursements, 7 teaching assistantships with partial tuition reimbursements were awarded; Federal Work-Study, scholarships/grants, and unspecified assistantships also available. Financial award application deadline: 3/1; financial award applicants required to submit FAFSA. *Faculty research:* Drugs of abuse, anti-cancer drugs, sustained drug delivery, drug metabolism. *Unit head:* Dr. Chandradhar Dwivedi, Head, 605-688-5598, Fax: 605-688-5993, E-mail: chandradhar.dwivedi@sdstate.edu. *Application contact:* Dr. Xiangming Guan, Graduate Coordinator, 605-688-5598, Fax: 605-688-5993, E-mail: xiangming.guan@sdstate.edu.

Stevens Institute of Technology, Graduate School, Charles V. Schaefer Jr. School of Engineering, Department of Mechanical Engineering, Program in Pharmaceutical Manufacturing, Hoboken, NJ 07030. Offers M Eng, MS, Certificate.

Stevens Institute of Technology, Graduate School, Wesley J. Howe School of Technology Management, Program in Business Administration, Hoboken, NJ 07030. Offers engineering management (MBA); financial management (MBA); global technology management (MBA); information management (MBA); information technology in financial services (MBA); information technology in the pharmaceutical industry (MBA); information technology outsourcing (MBA); pharmaceutical technology management (MBA); project management (MBA); telecommunications management (MBA).

Temple University, Health Sciences Center, School of Pharmacy, Department of Pharmaceutical Sciences, Program in Pharmaceutics, Philadelphia, PA 19122-6096. Offers MS, PhD. *Faculty:* 7 full-time (1 woman). *Students:* 10 full-time (4 women), 13 part-time (6 women). Average age 29. 125 applicants, 2% accepted. In 2006, 3 degrees awarded. *Degree requirements:* For master's, thesis; for doctorate, 2 foreign languages, thesis/dissertation. *Entrance requirements:* For master's, GRE General Test, minimum undergraduate GPA of 3.0; for doctorate, GRE General Test, minimum GPA of 3.0. Additional exam requirements/recommendations for international students: Required—TOEFL (minimum score 550 paper-based; 213 computer-based; 79 iBT). Application fee: $50. Electronic applications accepted. *Expenses:* Tuition, state resident: full-time $12,264; part-time $511 per credit. Tuition, nonresident: full-time $17,904; part-time $746 per credit. Required fees: $84 per course. Tuition and fees vary according to program. *Financial support:* Fellowships with tuition reimbursements, research assistantships with tuition reimbursements, teaching assistantships with tuition reimbursements available. Financial award application deadline: 1/15; financial award applicants required to submit FAFSA. *Unit head:* Dr. Daniel Canney, Director of Graduate Studies, 215-707-4948, E-mail: canney@temple.edu.

See Close-Up on page 2243.

Temple University, Health Sciences Center, School of Pharmacy, Department of Pharmaceutical Sciences, Program in Quality Assurance/Regulatory Affairs, Philadelphia, PA 19122-6096. Offers MS. Part-time and evening/weekend programs available. Postbaccalaureate distance learning degree programs offered (minimal on-campus study). *Faculty:* 20 part-time/adjunct (3 women). *Students:* 7 full-time (6 women), 250 part-time (177 women); includes 44 minority (19 African Americans, 1 American Indian/Alaska Native, 13 Asian Americans or Pacific Islanders, 11 Hispanic Americans). 87 applicants, 61% accepted, 51 enrolled. In 2006, 82 degrees awarded. *Degree requirements:* For master's, thesis. *Entrance requirements:* For master's, GRE or GMAT, minimum undergraduate GPA of 3.0. Additional exam requirements/recommendations for international students: Required—TOEFL (minimum score 550 paper-based; 213 computer-based; 79 iBT). *Application deadline:* For fall admission, 8/1 for domestic students, 12/15 for international students; for spring admission, 12/15 for domestic students, 8/1 for international students. Applications are processed on a rolling basis. Application fee: $50. Electronic applications accepted. *Expenses:* Tuition, state resident: full-time $12,264; part-time $511 per credit. Tuition, nonresident: full-time $17,904; part-time $746 per credit. Required fees: $84 per course. Tuition and fees vary according to program. *Financial support:* Application deadline: 1/15; *Unit head:* Dr. Daniel Canney, Director of Graduate Studies, 215-707-4948, E-mail: canney@temple.edu.

Texas Tech University Health Sciences Center, Graduate School of Biomedical Sciences, Department of Pharmaceutical Sciences, Lubbock, TX 79430. Offers MS, PhD, MS/PhD. *Accreditation:* ACPE. *Faculty:* 18 full-time (2 women), 4 part-time/adjunct (0 women). *Students:* 34 full-time (15 women); includes 27 minority (26 Asian Americans or Pacific Islanders, 1 Hispanic American). Average age 28. 36 applicants, 81% accepted, 16 enrolled. In 2006, 1 master's, 7 doctorates awarded. Terminal master's awarded for partial completion of doctoral program. *Median time to degree:* Of those who began their doctoral program in fall 1998, 3% received their degree in 8 years or less. *Degree requirements:* For master's and doctorate, thesis/dissertation. *Entrance requirements:* For master's and doctorate, GRE General Test, minimum GPA of 3.0. Additional exam requirements/recommendations for international students: Required—TOEFL (minimum score 213 computer-based). *Application deadline:* For fall admission, 4/15 priority date for domestic and international students; for spring admission, 10/15 for domestic and international students. Application fee: $45. Electronic applications accepted. *Financial support:* In 2006–07, 32 students received support, including research assistantships (averaging $20,500 per year); scholarships/grants also available. Financial award application deadline: 4/15. *Faculty research:* Drug design and delivery, pharmacology, pharmacokinetics, drug receptor modeling, molecular and reproductive biology. Total annual research expenditures: $2.2 million. *Unit head:* Dr. Quentin R. Smith, Chair, 806-356-4016, Fax: 806-356-4034, E-mail: quentin@ama.ttuhsc.edu. *Application contact:* Dr. Thomas Abbruscato, Director of Graduate Program, 806-356-4015, Fax: 806-356-4034, E-mail: pharmsci.gradadv@ttuhsc.edu.

Université de Montréal, Faculty of Graduate Studies, Faculty of Pharmacy, Montréal, QC H3C 3J7, Canada. Offers development of medicine (DESS); master pharmacist (DESS); pharmaceutical cares (DESS); pharmaceutical practice (M Sc); pharmaceutical sciences (M Sc, PhD). Part-time programs available. *Faculty:* 24 full-time (13 women), 29 part-time/adjunct (16 women). *Students:* 224 full-time (153 women), 91 part-time (71 women). 236 applicants, 49% accepted, 101 enrolled. In 2006, 83 master's, 7 doctorates, 50 other advanced degrees awarded. Terminal master's awarded for partial completion of doctoral program. *Degree requirements:* For master's and doctorate, thesis/dissertation. *Entrance requirements:* For master's and doctorate, proficiency in French. *Application deadline:* For fall admission, 2/1 priority date for domestic students; for winter admission, 11/1 priority date for domestic students; for spring admission, 2/1 priority date for domestic students. Application fee: $30. Electronic applications accepted. *Financial support:* Fellowships, teaching assistantships, career-related internships or fieldwork, Federal Work-Study, and institutionally sponsored loans available. *Faculty research:* Novel drug delivery systems, immunoassay development, medicinal chemistry of CNS compounds, pharmacokinetics and biopharmaceutical compounds. *Unit head:* Pierre Moreau, Dean, 514-343-6440, Fax: 514-343-2102. *Application contact:* Daniel Lamontagne, Vice Dean, 514-343-6467, Fax: 514-343-2102.

Université Laval, Faculty of Pharmacy, Program in Hospital Pharmacy, Québec, QC G1K 7P4, Canada. Offers M Sc. *Entrance requirements:* For master's, knowledge of French, interview. Electronic applications accepted.

Université Laval, Faculty of Pharmacy, Programs in Community Pharmacy, Québec, QC G1K 7P4, Canada. Offers Diploma. Part-time programs available. *Entrance requirements:* For degree, knowledge of French. Electronic applications accepted.

Université Laval, Faculty of Pharmacy, Programs in Pharmacy, Québec, QC G1K 7P4, Canada. Offers M Sc, PhD. Part-time programs available. Terminal master's awarded for partial completion of doctoral program. *Degree requirements:* For master's, thesis/dissertation; for doctorate, thesis/dissertation, comprehensive exam. *Entrance requirements:* For master's and doctorate, knowledge of French. Electronic applications accepted.

University at Buffalo, the State University of New York, Graduate School, School of Pharmacy and Pharmaceutical Sciences, Department of Pharmaceutical Sciences, Buffalo, NY 14260. Offers MS, PhD. Postbaccalaureate distance learning degree programs offered (minimal on-campus study). *Faculty:* 15 full-time (2 women), 1 part-time/adjunct (0 women). *Students:* 44 full-time (24 women), 4 part-time (1 woman); includes 6 minority (5 Asian Americans or Pacific Islanders, 1 Hispanic American), 39 international. Average age 25. 134 applicants, 19% accepted, 15 enrolled. In 2006, 1 master's, 5 doctorates awarded. Terminal master's awarded for partial completion of doctoral program. *Median time to degree:* Of those who began their doctoral program in fall 1998, 100% received their degree in 8 years or less. *Degree requirements:* For master's, project, thesis optional; for doctorate, thesis/dissertation, comprehensive exam, registration. *Entrance requirements:* For master's, GRE, BS, B Eng, or Pharm D; for doctorate, GRE, BS, MS, B Eng, M Eng, or Pharm D. Additional exam requirements/recommendations for international students: Required—TOEFL (minimum score 550 paper-based; 213 computer-based). *Application deadline:* For fall admission, 2/15 for domestic and international students. Applications are processed on a rolling basis. Application fee: $50. Electronic applications accepted. *Financial support:* In 2006–07, 26 students received support, including 8 fellowships with full tuition reimbursements available (averaging $22,565 per year), 18 research assistantships with full tuition reimbursements available (averaging $22,565 per year); teaching assistantships, institutionally sponsored loans, health care benefits, and unspecified assistantships also available. Financial award application deadline: 2/28; financial award applicants required to submit FAFSA. *Faculty research:* Pharmacokinetics, biopharmaceutics, drug delivery systems, pharmacodynamics, drug metabolism and analysis. Total annual research expenditures: $2.6 million. *Unit head:* Dr. William J. Jusko, Chair, 716-645-2855 Ext. 225, Fax: 716-645-3693, E-mail: wjjusko@acsu.buffalo.edu. *Application contact:* Dr. Joseph P. Balthasar, Director of Graduate Studies, 716-645-2842 Ext. 270, Fax: 716-645-3693, E-mail: jb@buffalo.edu.

See Close-Up on page 2247.

University of Alberta, Faculty of Graduate Studies and Research, Faculty of Pharmacy and Pharmaceutical Sciences, Edmonton, AB T6G 2E1, Canada. Offers M Sc, PhD. *Faculty:* 35. *Students:* 47. Average age 30. 562 applicants, 2% accepted, 11 enrolled. In 2006, 3 master's, 5 doctorates awarded. Terminal master's awarded for partial completion of doctoral program. *Degree requirements:* For master's and doctorate, thesis/dissertation. *Entrance requirements:* Additional exam requirements/recommendations for international students: Required—Michigan English Language Assessment Battery or IELTS. *Application deadline:* For fall admission, 6/1 for international students; for winter admission, 9/15 for international students. Applications are processed on a rolling basis. Electronic applications accepted. *Financial support:* In 2006–07, 13 students received support, including 6 teaching assistantships; research assistantships, tuition waivers (partial) also available. *Faculty research:* Radiopharmacy, pharmacokinetics, bionucleonics, medicinal chemistry, microbiology. Total annual research expenditures: $2 million. *Unit head:* Dr. Franco M. Pasutto, Dean, 780-492-0204, E-mail: fpasutto@pharmacy.ualberta.ca. *Application contact:* Dr. Edward E. Knaus, Director of Graduate Affairs, 780-492-5993, Fax: 780-492-1217.

The University of Arizona, Graduate College, College of Pharmacy, Program in Pharmaceutical Sciences, Tucson, AZ 85721. Offers medicinal and natural products chemistry (MS, PhD); pharmaceutical economics (MS, PhD); pharmaceutics and pharmacokinetics (MS, PhD). *Faculty:* 14 full-time (4 women). *Students:* 39 full-time (18 women), 11 part-time (6 women); includes 5 minority (3 Asian Americans or Pacific Islanders, 2 Hispanic Americans), 18 international. Average age 30. 58 applicants, 22% accepted, 11 enrolled. In 2006, 1 master's, 7 doctorates awarded. *Degree requirements:* For master's, thesis; for doctorate, one foreign language, thesis/dissertation. *Entrance requirements:* For master's and doctorate, GRE General Test, minimum GPA of 3.0. Additional exam requirements/recommendations for international students: Required—TOEFL. *Application deadline:* For fall admission, 1/1 for domestic students, 12/1 for international students. Applications are processed on a rolling basis. Application fee: $50. *Financial support:* In 2006–07, 25 research assistantships (averaging $20,000 per year), 3 teaching assistantships (averaging $20,000 per year) were awarded; fellowships, scholarships/grants, health care benefits, tuition waivers (full), and unspecified assistantships also available. Financial award application deadline: 3/1. *Faculty research:* Drug design, natural products isolation, biological applications of NMR and mass spectrometry, drug formulation and delivery, pharmacokinetics. *Unit head:* Dr. A. Jay Gandolfi, Head, 520-626-6696, Fax: 520-626-2466, E-mail: gandolfi@pharmacy.arizona.edu. *Application contact:* Nancy Faye Colbert, Information Contact, 520-626-7265, Fax: 520-626-2466, E-mail: colbert@pharmacy.arizona.edu.

University of Arkansas for Medical Sciences, College of Pharmacy, Program in Pharmaceutical Evaluation and Policy, Little Rock, AR 72205-7199. Offers MS. *Students:* 4 full-time. *Entrance requirements:* For master's, GRE, 3 letters of recommendation, resumé. Additional exam requirements/recommendations for international students: Required—TOEFL. *Unit head:* Dr. Bradley C. Martin, Director, E-mail: bmartin@uams.edu.

The University of British Columbia, Faculty of Graduate Studies, Faculty of Pharmaceutical Sciences, Vancouver, BC V6T 1Z1, Canada. Offers Pharm D, M Sc, PhD. *Faculty:* 30 full-time (9 women), 26 part-time/adjunct (11 women). *Students:* 40 full-time (10 women). Average age 28. 61 applicants, 36% accepted, 19 enrolled. In 2006, 8 first professional degrees, 4 master's, 4 doctorates awarded. *Median time to degree:* Of those who began their doctoral program in fall 1998, 100% received their degree in 8 years or less. *Degree requirements:* For master's, thesis/dissertation, seminar; for doctorate, thesis/dissertation, seminar, comprehensive exam. *Entrance requirements:* B Sc in pharmacy, Canadian pharmacy license, interview. Additional exam requirements/recommendations for international students: Required—TOEFL (minimum score 600 paper-based; 250 computer-based; 100 iBT). *Application deadline:* For fall admission, 3/15 for domestic students, 2/15 for international students; for spring admission, 4/1 for domestic students. Applications are processed on a rolling basis. Application fee: $90 Canadian dollars ($150 Canadian dollars for international students). Electronic applications accepted. *Financial support:* In 2006–07, fellowships (averaging $16,000 per year), 24 research assistantships (averaging $17,000 per year), 17 teaching assistantships (averaging $10,100 per year) were awarded; career-related internships or fieldwork, institutionally sponsored loans, scholarships/grants, traineeships, health care benefits, tuition waivers (full and partial), and unspecified assistantships also available. *Faculty research:* Biopharmaceutics, pharmaceutical chemistry, pharmacology, toxicology, formulation. Total annual research expenditures: $4.4 million Canadian dollars. *Unit head:* Dr. Robert D. Sindelar, Dean, 604-822-2343, Fax: 604-822-3035, E-mail: sindelar@interchange.ubc.ca. *Application contact:* Dr. Barb Conway, Research Grants Facilitator and Graduate Program Coordinator, 604-822-2390, Fax: 604-822-3035, E-mail: baconway@interchange.ubc.ca.

University of California, San Francisco, School of Pharmacy and Graduate Division, Pharmaceutical Sciences and Pharmacogenomics Graduate Group, San Francisco, CA 94143. Offers PhD. *Students:* 48 full-time (24 women); includes 15 minority (3 African Americans, 10 Asian Americans or Pacific Islanders, 2 Hispanic Americans). Average age 28. 100 applicants, 14% accepted. In 2006, 7 doctorates awarded. *Median time to degree:* Doctorate–5.6 years full-time. *Degree requirements:* For doctorate, thesis/dissertation, comprehensive exam. *Entrance requirements:* For doctorate, GRE General Test, minimum GPA of 3.0. Additional exam requirements/recommendations for international students: Required—TOEFL. *Application deadline:* For fall admission, 12/15 for domestic students. Application fee: $60 ($80 for international students). *Financial support:* In 2006–07, 7 fellowships with full tuition reimbursements (averaging $26,000 per year), 27 research assistantships with full tuition reimbursements (averaging $26,000 per year), 11 teaching assistantships with full tuition reimbursements (averaging $9,000 per year) were awarded; career-related internships or fieldwork, institutionally sponsored loans, scholarships/grants, traineeships, tuition waivers (full), and unspecified assistantships also available. Financial award application deadline: 4/6. *Faculty research:* Drug development, drug delivery, molecular pharmacology. *Unit head:* Francis C. Szoka, Program Director, 415-476-3895, Fax: 415-476-0688, E-mail: szoka@cgl.ucsf.edu. *Application contact:* Debbie Acoba-Idlebi, Program Coordinator, 415-476-1947, Fax: 415-476-4929, E-mail: acobad@pharmacy.ucsf.edu.

University of Cincinnati, Division of Research and Advanced Studies, College of Pharmacy, Division of Pharmaceutical Sciences, Cincinnati, OH 45221. Offers MS, PhD. *Degree requirements:* For master's and doctorate, thesis/dissertation. *Entrance requirements:* For master's and doctorate, GRE General Test, minimum GPA of 3.0. Additional exam requirements/recommendations for international students: Required—TOEFL.

University of Colorado at Denver and Health Sciences Center, School of Pharmacy, Programs in Pharmacy, Denver, CO 80217-3364. Offers pharmaceutical sciences (PhD); toxicology (PhD). *Students:* 41 full-time (18 women); includes 4 minority (3 Asian Americans or Pacific Islanders, 1 Hispanic American), 13 international. 41 applicants, 80% accepted, 8 enrolled. In 2006, 11 degrees awarded. *Degree requirements:* For doctorate, thesis/dissertation, comprehensive exam. *Entrance requirements:* For doctorate, GRE General Test, minimum GPA of 3.0. Additional exam requirements/recommendations for international students: Required—TOEFL (minimum score 550 paper-based; 213 computer-based). Application fee: $50. Electronic applications accepted. *Financial support:* Career-related internships or fieldwork, Federal Work-Study, and institutionally sponsored loans available. Support available to part-time students. Financial award application deadline: 3/15; financial award applicants required to submit FAFSA. *Faculty research:* Mechanistic studies of viral assembly, synthetic gene delivery systems for use in gene therapy, mechanisms of toxicity, pulmonary drug delivery. *Application contact:* Jackie Milowski, Information Contact, 303-315-0565.

See Close-Up on page 2249.

University of Connecticut, Graduate School, School of Pharmacy, Department of Pharmaceutical Sciences, Field of Pharmaceutical Sciences, Program in Pharmaceutics, Storrs, CT 06269. Offers MS, PhD. *Faculty:* 9 full-time (2 women). *Students:* 20 full-time (7 women), 4 part-time (1 woman); includes 4 minority (1 African American, 3 Asian Americans or Pacific Islanders), 16 international. Average age 30. 58 applicants, 9% accepted, 4 enrolled. In 2006, 2 master's, 4 doctorates awarded. Terminal master's awarded for partial completion of doctoral program. *Degree requirements:* For master's, thesis/dissertation, comprehensive exam; for doctorate, thesis/dissertation. *Entrance requirements:* For master's and doctorate, GRE General Test. Additional exam requirements/recommendations for international students: Required—TOEFL (minimum score 550 paper-based; 213 computer-based). *Application deadline:* For fall admission, 2/1 priority date for domestic and international students; for spring admission, 11/1 for domestic students, 10/1 for international students. Applications are processed on a rolling basis. Application fee: $55. Electronic applications accepted. *Financial support:* In 2006–07, 8 research assistantships with full tuition reimbursements, 5 teaching assistantships with full tuition reimbursements were awarded; fellowships, Federal Work-Study, scholarships/grants, health care benefits, and unspecified assistantships also available. Financial award application deadline: 2/1; financial award applicants required to submit FAFSA. *Application contact:* Leslie Lebel, Administrative Assistant, 860-486-4066, Fax: 860-486-4998, E-mail: phrmacy8@uconnvm.uconn.edu.

University of Florida, College of Pharmacy and Graduate School, Graduate Programs in Pharmacy, Department of Pharmaceutics, Gainesville, FL 32611. Offers pharmaceutical sciences (PhD). *Faculty:* 6 full-time (1 woman). *Students:* 136 (101 women); includes 17 minority (5 African Americans, 5 Asian Americans or Pacific Islanders, 7 Hispanic Americans) 6 international. *Degree requirements:* For doctorate, thesis/dissertation. *Entrance requirements:* For doctorate, GRE General Test, minimum GPA of 3.0. Additional exam requirements/recommendations for international students: Required—TOEFL. *Application deadline:* For fall admission, 6/1 priority date for domestic students. Applications are processed on a rolling basis. Application fee: $30. Electronic applications accepted. *Expenses:* Tuition, state resident: full-time $6,827. Tuition, nonresident: full-time $21,951. Required fees: $999. *Financial support:* In 2006–07, 4 research assistantships (averaging $16,901 per year), 20 teaching assistantships (averaging $19,245 per year) were awarded; fellowships, tuition waivers (full) and unspecified assistantships also available. *Unit head:* Dr. Hartmut Derendorf, Chair, 352-846-2726, Fax: 352-392-4447, E-mail: hartmut@cop.ufl.edu. *Application contact:* Dr. Jeff Hughes, Graduate Coordinator, 352-846-2725, Fax: 352-392-4447, E-mail: hughes@cop.ufl.edu.

University of Florida, College of Pharmacy and Graduate School, Graduate Programs in Pharmacy, Department of Pharmacy Practice, Gainesville, FL 32611. Offers clinical pharmaceutical sciences (PhD). *Faculty:* 10 full-time (3 women). *Students:* 41 (21 women); includes 8 minority (2 African Americans, 5 Asian Americans or Pacific Islanders, 1 Hispanic American) 25 international. In 2006, 2 doctorates awarded. *Expenses:* Tuition, state resident: full-time $6,827. Tuition, nonresident: full-time $21,951. Required fees: $999. *Financial support:* In 2006–07, 2 research assistantships (averaging $35,777 per year), 7 teaching assistantships (averaging $16,412 per year) were awarded. *Unit head:* Julie Johnson, Chair, 352-273-6007, E-mail: johnson@cop.ufl.edu.

University of Georgia, College of Pharmacy, Department of Clinical and Administrative Pharmacy, Athens, GA 30602. Offers experimental therapeutics (MS, PhD); pharmacy care administration (MS, PhD). *Faculty:* 10 full-time (4 women). *Students:* Average age 25. 33 applicants, 12% accepted, 2 enrolled.Terminal master's awarded for partial completion of doctoral program. *Degree requirements:* For master's, thesis/dissertation; for doctorate, thesis/dissertation, comprehensive exam. *Entrance requirements:* For master's and doctorate, GRE General Test, minimum GPA of 3.0. Additional exam requirements/recommendations for international students: Required—TOEFL (minimum score 550 paper-based; 213 computer-based). *Application deadline:* For fall admission, 5/15 for domestic students; for spring admission, 10/15 for domestic students. Application fee: $50. Electronic applications accepted. *Financial support:* In 2006–07, 14 teaching assistantships (averaging $11,509 per year) were awarded; tuition waivers (full) and unspecified assistantships also available. Financial award application deadline: 2/15. *Faculty research:* Pharmacy care administration, pharmacoeconomics, cardiovascular therapeutics, central nervous system therapeutics, drug use in populations. *Unit head:* Susan Fagan, Interim Head, 706-721-4915, E-mail: sfagan@mail.mcg.edu. *Application contact:* Dr. Randall L. Tackett, Graduate Coordinator, 706-542-5415, Fax: 706-542-5228.

University of Georgia, College of Pharmacy, Department of Pharmaceutical and Biomedical Sciences, Athens, GA 30602. Offers medicinal chemistry (MS, PhD); pharmaceutics (MS, PhD); pharmacology (MS, PhD); toxicology (MS, PhD). *Faculty:* 18 full-time (4 women). *Students:* 7 full-time (4 women), 1 part-time; includes 2 minority (both African Americans), 4 international. 138 applicants, 10% accepted, 5 enrolled. In 2006, 1 degree awarded. *Median time to degree:* Of those who began their doctoral program in fall 1998, 100% received their degree in 8 years or less. *Degree requirements:* For master's, thesis; for doctorate, one foreign language, thesis/dissertation. *Entrance requirements:* For master's and doctorate, GRE General Test, minimum GPA of 3.0. Additional exam requirements/recommendations for international students: Required—TOEFL. *Application deadline:* For fall admission, 1/2 priority date for domestic and international students. Application fee: $50. Electronic applications accepted. *Financial support:* In 2006–07, fellowships with full tuition reimbursements (averaging $18,000 per year), 10 research assistantships with full tuition reimbursements (averaging $16,500 per year), 35 teaching assistantships with full tuition reimbursements (averaging $16,500 per year) were awarded; career-related internships or fieldwork, institutionally sponsored loans, tuition waivers (partial), and unspecified assistantships also available. Financial award application deadline: 1/1. *Faculty research:* Cancer and infectious diseases, drug delivery, neuropharmacology, cardiovascular pharmacology, bioanalytical chemistry, structural biology. *Unit head:* Dr. Vasu Nair, Head, 706-542-5610, Fax: 706-542-3398, E-mail: vnair@rx.uga.edu. *Application contact:* Dr. Michael Bartlett, Graduate Coordinator, 706-542-5390, Fax: 706-542-3398, E-mail: bartlett@rx.uga.edu.

Pharmaceutical Sciences

University of Houston, College of Pharmacy, Houston, TX 77204. Offers hospital pharmacy (MSPHR); medical chemistry and pharmacology (MS); pharmaceutics (MS, PhD); pharmacology (MS, PhD); pharmacy (Pharm D); pharmacy administration (MSPHR). *Accreditation:* ACPE. Part-time programs available. *Faculty:* 15 full-time (4 women), 17 part-time/adjunct (9 women). *Students:* 500 full-time (335 women), 31 part-time (23 women); includes 260 minority (25 African Americans, 192 Asian Americans or Pacific Islanders, 43 Hispanic Americans), 55 international. Average age 25. 573 applicants, 27% accepted, 149 enrolled. In 2006, 106 first professional degrees, 6 master's, 4 doctorates awarded. Terminal master's awarded for partial completion of doctoral program. *Degree requirements:* For master's and doctorate, thesis/dissertation. *Entrance requirements:* For Pharm D, PCAT, interview; for master's and doctorate, GRE General Test. Additional exam requirements/recommendations for international students: Required—TOEFL. *Application deadline:* For spring admission, 3/1 for domestic students. Applications are processed on a rolling basis. Application fee: $25 ($75 for international students). *Expenses:* Tuition, state resident: full-time $5,429; part-time $226 per credit. Tuition, nonresident: full-time $12,029; part-time $501 per credit. Required fees: $2,454. *Financial support:* In 2006–07, 6 research assistantships with full tuition reimbursements (averaging $14,200 per year), 35 teaching assistantships with full tuition reimbursements (averaging $14,200 per year) were awarded; fellowships with full tuition reimbursements, career-related internships or fieldwork, Federal Work-Study, institutionally sponsored loans, scholarships/grants, health care benefits, and unspecified assistantships also available. Support available to part-time students. Financial award application deadline: 3/10. *Faculty research:* Cardiovascular and renal pharmacology, cellular pharmacology, drug delivery systems, geriatrics, pharmacokinetics, pharmacoeconomics, pharmaceutical marketing, pharmaceutical management, behavioral pharmacy, and signal transduction. Total annual research expenditures: $1.3 million. *Unit head:* Dr. Sunny Ohia, Dean, 713-743-1253, Fax: 713-743-1259, E-mail: seohia@uh.edu. *Application contact:* Shara Zatopek, Assistant Dean for Admissions, 713-743-1262, Fax: 713-743-1259, E-mail: szatopek@uh.edu.

University of Illinois at Chicago, College of Pharmacy and Graduate College, Research & Graduate Studies, College of Pharmacy, Chicago, IL 60607-7128. Offers forensic science (MS); medicinal chemistry (MS, PhD); pharmaceutics (MS, PhD); pharmacodynamics (MS, PhD); pharmacognosy (MS, PhD); pharmacy administration (MS, PhD). Terminal master's awarded for partial completion of doctoral program. *Degree requirements:* For master's and doctorate, variable foreign language requirement, thesis/dissertation. *Entrance requirements:* For master's and doctorate, GRE General Test. Additional exam requirements/recommendations for international students: Required—TOEFL. Electronic applications accepted. Expenses: Contact institution.

University of Kansas, Graduate Studies, School of Pharmacy, Department of Pharmacy Practice, Lawrence, KS 66045. Offers hospital pharmacy (MS). *Faculty:* 10. *Students:* 1 (woman) full-time, 2 part-time. Average age 27. 2 applicants, 50% accepted. In 2006, 3 degrees awarded. *Degree requirements:* For master's, thesis. *Entrance requirements:* For master's, GRE General Test, Pharm D, Kansas pharmacy license, ASHP Resident Matching Program. *Application deadline:* For fall admission, 2/1 priority date for domestic students. Application fee: $55 ($60 for international students). Electronic applications accepted. *Expenses:* Tuition, area resident: Part-time $227 per credit. Tuition, state resident: part-time $543 per credit. Tuition and fees vary according to course load, campus/location, program and reciprocity agreements. *Financial support:* Fellowships with partial tuition reimbursements, research assistantships, health care benefits and residencies available. Financial award application deadline: 2/15. *Faculty research:* Drug trials, drug stability, pharmacoeconomics, education, outcomes. *Unit head:* Dennis W. Grauer, Chair, 785-864-4881, Fax: 785-864-2399, E-mail: dgrauer@kumc.edu.

University of Kentucky, College of Pharmacy and Graduate School, Graduate Programs in Pharmaceutical Sciences, Lexington, KY 40536-0082. Offers MS, PhD. *Faculty:* 47 full-time (9 women), 11 part-time/adjunct (1 woman). *Students:* 64 full-time (32 women); includes 7 minority (2 African Americans, 4 Asian Americans or Pacific Islanders, 1 Hispanic American), 31 international. Average age 28. 178 applicants, 10% accepted, 16 enrolled. In 2006, 1 master's, 12 doctorates awarded. Terminal master's awarded for partial completion of doctoral program. *Median time to degree:* Master's–1 year full-time; doctorate–5 years full-time. Of those who began their doctoral program in fall 1998, 83% received their degree in 8 years or less. *Degree requirements:* For master's, thesis optional; for doctorate, thesis/dissertation, comprehensive exam. *Entrance requirements:* For master's, GRE General Test, minimum undergraduate GPA of 3.2; for doctorate, GRE General Test, minimum graduate GPA of 3.2. Additional exam requirements/recommendations for international students: Required—TOEFL (minimum score 550 paper-based; 213 computer-based; 79 iBT). *Application deadline:* For fall admission, 7/15 for domestic students, 2/1 for international students. Applications are processed on a rolling basis. Application fee: $40 ($55 for international students). Electronic applications accepted. *Expenses:* Tuition, state resident: full-time $7,670; part-time $401 per credit hour. Tuition, nonresident: full-time $16,158; part-time $873 per credit hour. *Financial support:* In 2006–07, 64 students received support, including 12 fellowships with full tuition reimbursements available (averaging $20,000 per year), 35 research assistantships with full tuition reimbursements available (averaging $20,000 per year), 13 teaching assistantships with full tuition reimbursements available (averaging $20,000 per year); career-related internships or fieldwork, institutionally sponsored loans, scholarships/grants, traineeships, health care benefits, and unspecified assistantships also available. Financial award application deadline: 4/15; financial award applicants required to submit FAFSA. *Faculty research:* Drug development, biotechnology, cardiology, pharmacokinetics, CNS pharmacology, clinical pharmacology. Total annual research expenditures: $18,703. *Unit head:* Dr. Janice Buss, Director of Graduate Studies, 859-257-1998, Fax: 859-257-7564, E-mail: jbuss2@email.uky.edu. *Application contact:* Catina Rossoll, Graduate Program Student Affairs Coordinator, 859-257-1998, Fax: 859-257-7564, E-mail: cross2@email.uky.edu.

University of Louisiana at Monroe, Graduate Studies and Research, College of Pharmacy, Program in Pharmaceutical Sciences, Monroe, LA 71209-0001. Offers MS. *Students:* 10 full-time (4 women), 6 international. Average age 27. In 2006, 2 degrees awarded. *Entrance requirements:* For master's, GRE General Test or GMAT, minimum GPA of 2.5. *Application deadline:* For fall admission, 5/1 priority date for domestic students; for spring admission, 11/1 for domestic students. Applications are processed on a rolling basis. Application fee: $20 ($30 for international students). *Expenses:* Tuition, state resident: part-time $124 per credit hour. Tuition, nonresident: part-time $124 per credit hour. *Financial support:* Research assistantships, teaching assistantships, Federal Work-Study and unspecified assistantships available. Financial award application deadline: 5/1. *Unit head:* Dr. Karen Briski, Interim Head, 318-342-3283.

University of Manitoba, Faculty of Graduate Studies, Faculty of Pharmacy, Winnipeg, MB R3T 2N2, Canada. Offers M Sc, PhD. *Degree requirements:* For master's, one foreign language, thesis.

University of Maryland, Baltimore, Graduate School, Graduate Programs in Pharmacy, Department of Pharmaceutical Sciences, Baltimore, MD 21201. Offers PhD. Part-time programs available. *Faculty:* 25 full-time (5 women). *Students:* 72 full-time (33 women); includes 25 minority (10 African Americans, 13 Asian Americans or Pacific Islanders, 2 Hispanic Americans), 4 international. Average age 24. 129 applicants, 13% accepted, 14 enrolled. In 2006, 12 degrees awarded. *Degree requirements:* For doctorate, thesis/dissertation, comprehensive exam, registration. *Entrance requirements:* For doctorate, GRE General Test. Additional exam requirements/recommendations for international students: Required—TOEFL (minimum score 600 paper-based; 260 computer-based), IELTS. *Application deadline:* For fall admission, 2/1 for domestic and international students. Application fee: $125. *Financial support:* In 2006–07, fellowships with full tuition reimbursements (averaging $6,000 per year), research assistantships with full tuition reimbursements (averaging $21,772 per year), teaching assistantships with full tuition reimbursements (averaging $21,772 per year) were awarded; career-related internships or fieldwork, scholarships/grants, traineeships, and unspecified assistantships also available. Financial award application deadline: 2/15; financial award applicants required to submit FAFSA. *Faculty research:* Drug delivery, cellular and biological chemistry, clinical pharmaceutical sciences, biopharmaceutics, neuroscience. *Unit head:* Dr. Paul Shapiro, Graduate Program Director, 410-706-8522, E-mail: pshapiro@rx.umaryland.edu. *Application contact:* Colleen Day, Graduate Coordinator, 410-706-0760, Fax: 410-706-0528, E-mail: cday@rx.umaryland.edu.

University of Michigan, College of Pharmacy and Horace H. Rackham School of Graduate Studies, Department of Pharmaceutical Sciences, Ann Arbor, MI 48109. Offers PhD. Terminal master's awarded for partial completion of doctoral program. *Degree requirements:* For doctorate, oral defense of dissertation, preliminary exam. *Entrance requirements:* For doctorate, GRE General Test. Additional exam requirements/recommendations for international students: Required—TOEFL or IELTS. Electronic applications accepted. *Faculty research:* New drug design, new drug delivery systems, new biotechnology, pharmacy and the public sector.

University of Minnesota, Twin Cities Campus, College of Pharmacy and Graduate School, Graduate Programs in Pharmacy, Graduate Program in Pharmaceutics, Minneapolis, MN 55455-0213. Offers MS, PhD. Terminal master's awarded for partial completion of doctoral program. *Degree requirements:* For master's and doctorate, thesis/dissertation. *Entrance requirements:* For master's, GRE General Test, BS in science; for doctorate, GRE General Test, BS in biology, biomedical engineering, chemical engineering, chemistry, pharmacy, or other science. Additional exam requirements/recommendations for international students: Required—TOEFL. *Expenses:* Tuition, state resident: full-time $9,302; part-time $775 per credit. Tuition, nonresident: full-time $16,400; part-time $1,367 per credit. Full-time tuition and fees vary according to class time, course load, program, reciprocity agreements and student level. *Faculty research:* Molecular biopharmaceutics, pharmacokinetics, drug delivery, drug metabolism, pharmacodynamics, crystal engineering, biophysical chemistry.

University of Minnesota, Twin Cities Campus, College of Pharmacy and Graduate School, Graduate Programs in Pharmacy, Graduate Program in Social and Administrative Pharmacy, Minneapolis, MN 55455-0213. Offers MS, PhD. *Degree requirements:* For master's, thesis (for some programs); for doctorate, thesis/dissertation. *Entrance requirements:* For master's, GRE General Test, BS in science; for doctorate, GRE General Test. Additional exam requirements/recommendations for international students: Required—TOEFL. *Expenses:* Tuition, state resident: full-time $9,302; part-time $775 per credit. Tuition, nonresident: full-time $16,400; part-time $1,367 per credit. Full-time tuition and fees vary according to class time, course load, program, reciprocity agreements and student level. *Faculty research:* Pharmaceutical economics, pharmaceutical policy, pharmaceutical social/behavioral sciences.

University of Mississippi, Graduate School, School of Pharmacy, Graduate Programs in Pharmacy, Oxford, University, MS 38677. Offers medicinal chemistry (MS, PhD); pharmaceutics (MS, PhD); pharmacognosy (MS, PhD); pharmacology (MS, PhD); pharmacy administration (MS, PhD). *Faculty:* 6 full-time (0 women). *Students:* 89 full-time (38 women), 6 part-time (2 women); includes 7 minority (3 African Americans, 3 Asian Americans or Pacific Islanders, 1 Hispanic American), 61 international. 163 applicants. In 2006, 5 master's, 11 doctorates awarded. *Expenses:* Tuition, state resident: full-time $4,602; part-time $256 per credit hour. Tuition, nonresident: full-time $10,566; part-time $587 per credit hour. *Unit head:* Dr. Barbara G. Wells, Dean, School of Pharmacy, 662-915-7265, Fax: 662-915-5704, E-mail: pharmacy@olemiss.edu.

University of Missouri–Kansas City, School of Pharmacy, Kansas City, MO 64110-2499. Offers pharmaceutical sciences (MS, PhD); pharmacy (Pharm D). *Accreditation:* ACPE (one or more programs are accredited). Postbaccalaureate distance learning degree programs offered (minimal on-campus study). *Faculty:* 34 full-time (17 women), 11 part-time/adjunct (4 women). *Students:* 238 full-time (159 women), 5 part-time (2 women); includes 30 minority (10 African Americans, 1 American Indian/Alaska Native, 17 Asian Americans or Pacific Islanders, 2 Hispanic Americans), 7 international. Average age 26. 567 applicants, 39% accepted, 213 enrolled. In 2006, 77 first professional degrees, 3 master's awarded. *Degree requirements:* For Pharm D, registration; for master's, thesis, comprehensive exam (for some programs), registration. *Entrance requirements:* For Pharm D, PCAT, interview, minimum GPA of 2.5, specified pre-pharmacy course work; for master's, GRE General Test, minimum undergraduate GPA of 3.0, graduate 3.5, 3 letters of reference. Additional exam requirements/recommendations for international students: Required—TOEFL (minimum score 580 paper-based). *Application deadline:* For fall admission, 3/1 for domestic students; for spring admission, 10/1 for domestic students. Applications are processed on a rolling basis. Application fee: $35 ($50 for international students). Electronic applications accepted. *Expenses:* Contact institution. *Financial support:* In 2006–07, 2 fellowships (averaging $28,200 per year), 17 research assistantships with full and partial tuition reimbursements (averaging $13,800 per year), 10 teaching assistantships with full tuition reimbursements (averaging $12,819 per year) were awarded; career-related internships or fieldwork, Federal Work-Study, institutionally sponsored loans, tuition waivers (full and partial), and unspecified assistantships also available. Financial award application deadline: 3/1; financial award applicants required to submit FAFSA. *Faculty research:* Bio-organic and medicinal chemistry, drug delivery, pharmaceutics, molecular neurobiology, neurology. Total annual research expenditures: $3.1 million. *Unit head:* Dr. Robert W. Piepho, Dean, 816-235-1609, Fax: 816-235-5190, E-mail: piephor@umkc.edu. *Application contact:* Shelly M. Janasz, Director, Student Services, 816-235-2400, Fax: 816-235-5190, E-mail: janaszs@umkc.edu.

The University of Montana, Graduate School, School of Pharmacy and Allied Health Sciences, Department of Biomedical and Pharmaceutical Sciences, Missoula, MT 59812-0002. Offers pharmaceutical sciences (MS); pharmacology (PhD); toxicology (MS, PhD). *Accreditation:* ACPE. *Degree requirements:* For master's, oral defense of thesis; for doctorate, research dissertation defense. *Entrance requirements:* For master's and doctorate, GRE General Test. Additional exam requirements/recommendations for international students: Required—TOEFL (minimum score 540 paper-based; 210 computer-based). Electronic applications accepted. *Faculty research:* Cardiovascular pharmacology, medicinal chemistry, neurosciences, environmental toxicology, pharmacogenetics, cancer.

University of Nebraska Medical Center, Graduate Studies, Department of Pharmaceutical Sciences, Omaha, NE 68198. Offers MS, PhD. *Faculty:* 17 full-time (2 women), 9 part-time/adjunct (2 women). *Students:* 29 full-time (11 women), 2 part-time; includes 1 minority (Hispanic American), 23 international. Average age 27. 48 applicants, 19% accepted, 9 enrolled. In 2006, 1 degree awarded. Terminal master's awarded for partial completion of doctoral program. *Degree requirements:* For master's, thesis/dissertation, registration; for doctorate, thesis/dissertation, comprehensive exam, registration. *Entrance requirements:* For master's, GRE General Test; for doctorate, GRE. Additional exam requirements/recommendations for international students: Required—TOEFL (minimum score 550 paper-based; 213 computer-based). *Application deadline:* For fall admission, 3/1 priority date for domestic and international students; for spring admission, 10/1 for domestic students, 8/1 for international students. Applications are processed on a rolling basis. Application fee: $45. Electronic applications accepted. *Financial support:* In 2006–07, fellowships with full tuition reimbursements (averaging $20,000 per year), 4 research assistantships with full tuition reimbursements (averaging $20,000 per year), 5 teaching assistantships with full tuition reimbursements (averaging $20,000 per year) were awarded; institutionally sponsored loans also available. Support available to part-time students. Financial award application deadline: 3/1. *Faculty research:* Pharmaceutics, medicinal chemistry, toxicology, chemical carcinogenesis, pharmacokinetics. *Unit head:* Dr. Uday B. Kompella, Chair, Graduate Committee, 402-559-2974, Fax: 402-559-9543, E-mail: psgp@unmc.edu. *Application contact:* April Greene, Office Associate, 402-559-6422, E-mail: acgreene@unmc.edu.

University of New Mexico, Graduate School, College of Pharmacy, Graduate Programs in Pharmaceutical Sciences, Albuquerque, NM 87131-2039. Offers MS, PhD. Part-time programs available. *Students:* 1 full-time (0 women), 8 part-time (6 women); includes 2 minority (both Hispanic Americans), 1 international. Average age 34. 22 applicants, 0% accepted.

In 2006, 3 master's, 1 doctorate awarded. *Degree requirements:* For master's and doctorate, thesis/dissertation, comprehensive exam. *Entrance requirements:* For master's and doctorate, GRE General Test, letters of recommendation. Additional exam requirements/recommendations for international students: Required—TOEFL (minimum score 580 paper-based; 237 computer-based). *Application deadline:* For fall admission, 2/1 priority date for domestic students. Application fee: $50. Electronic applications accepted. *Financial support:* In 2006–07, 3 students received support, including research assistantships (averaging $21,500 per year); health care benefits and residencies also available. Financial award application deadline: 3/1; financial award applicants required to submit FAFSA. *Faculty research:* Pharmaceutical research, cancer research, pharmacy administration, radiopharmacy. Total annual research expenditures: $2 million. *Unit head:* Donald Godwin, Assistant Dean, 505-272-0907, Fax: 505-272-5782, E-mail: dgodwin@salud.unm.edu. *Application contact:* Erin Kells, Student Program Advisor, 505-272-0912, Fax: 505-272-5782, E-mail: ekells@salud.unm.edu.

The University of North Carolina at Chapel Hill, School of Pharmacy, Chapel Hill, NC 27599. Offers MS, PhD. *Accreditation:* ACPE (one or more programs are accredited). Part-time programs available. Postbaccalaureate distance learning degree programs offered (minimal on-campus study). *Faculty:* 39 full-time (10 women), 24 part-time/adjunct (5 women). *Students:* 78 full-time (41 women), 2 part-time (1 woman); includes 15 minority (8 African Americans, 6 Asian Americans or Pacific Islanders, 1 Hispanic American), 35 international. Average age 28. 132 applicants, 30% accepted, 25 enrolled. In 2006, 16 degrees awarded. Terminal master's awarded for partial completion of doctoral program. *Median time to degree:* Doctorate–5 years full-time, 7 years part-time. Of those who began their doctoral program in fall 1998, 100% received their degree in 8 years or less. *Degree requirements:* For master's and doctorate, thesis/dissertation, comprehensive exam, registration. *Entrance requirements:* For master's and doctorate, GRE General Test, minimum GPA of 3.0. Additional exam requirements/recommendations for international students: Required—TOEFL (minimum score 550 paper-based; 213 computer-based). *Application deadline:* For fall admission, 4/1 for domestic and international students; for spring admission, 10/15 for domestic and international students. Applications are processed on a rolling basis. Application fee: $65. Electronic applications accepted. *Financial support:* In 2006–07, 15 fellowships with full tuition reimbursements (averaging $21,000 per year), 25 research assistantships with full tuition reimbursements (averaging $21,000 per year), 35 teaching assistantships with full tuition reimbursements (averaging $21,000 per year) were awarded; career-related internships or fieldwork, Federal Work-Study, institutionally sponsored loans, scholarships/grants, traineeships, health care benefits, and unspecified assistantships also available. Financial award application deadline: 4/1. *Faculty research:* Health services research, pharmacokinetics, molecular modeling, infectious disease, genomics/proteomics, translational research. Total annual research expenditures: $5.8 million. *Unit head:* Dr. Robert A. Blouin, Dean, 919-966-1122, Fax: 919-966-6919, E-mail: bob_blouin@unc.edu. *Application contact:* Amber M. Allen, Graduate Services Manager, 919-843-9759, Fax: 919-966-3525, E-mail: amber_allen@unc.edu.

University of Oklahoma Health Sciences Center, College of Pharmacy and Graduate College, Graduate Programs in Pharmacy, Oklahoma City, OK 73190. Offers MS, PhD, MS/MBA. Terminal master's awarded for partial completion of doctoral program. *Degree requirements:* For master's and doctorate, thesis/dissertation, comprehensive exam. *Entrance requirements:* For master's and doctorate, GRE General Test. Additional exam requirements/recommendations for international students: Required—TOEFL. *Faculty research:* Medicinal chemistry, pharmacokinetics/biopharmaceutics, nuclear pharmacy, pharmacy administration, pharmacodynamics and toxicology.

University of Puerto Rico, Medical Sciences Campus, School of Pharmacy, San Juan, PR 00936-5067. Offers industrial pharmacy (MS); pharmaceutical sciences (MS); pharmacy (Pharm D). Part-time and evening/weekend programs available. *Faculty:* 31 full-time, 22 part-time/adjunct. *Students:* 234 full-time (178 women), 11 part-time (8 women); all minorities (1 Asian American or Pacific Islander, 244 Hispanic Americans). 130 applicants, 45% accepted, 56 enrolled. In 2006, 35 first professional degrees, 7 master's awarded. *Degree requirements:* For Pharm D, portfolio, research project; for master's, thesis, registration. *Entrance requirements:* For Pharm D, PCAT, interview, letters of reference; for master's, GRE, interview. *Application deadline:* For fall admission, 2/9 for domestic and international students. Application fee: $15. *Expenses:* Contact institution. *Financial support:* In 2006–07, 9 research assistantships with full tuition reimbursements (averaging $6,930 per year) were awarded; fellowships with partial tuition reimbursements, teaching assistantships with full tuition reimbursements, career-related internships or fieldwork, Federal Work-Study, institutionally sponsored loans, scholarships/grants, tuition waivers (full), and unspecified assistantships also available. *Faculty research:* Controlled release, solid dosage form, screening of anti-HIV drugs, pharmacokinetic/pharmacodynamic of drugs. Total annual research expenditures: $175,000. *Unit head:* Dr. Lesbia Hernández, Dean, 787-758-2525 Ext. 5427, Fax: 787-751-5680, E-mail: lhernandez@rcm.upr.edu. *Application contact:* Miriam Vélez, Assistant Dean of Student Affairs, 787-758-2525 Ext. 5407, Fax: 787-751-5680, E-mail: mivelez@rcm.upr.edu.

University of Rhode Island, Graduate School, College of Pharmacy, Graduate Programs in Pharmacy, Department of Biomedical and Pharmaceutical Sciences, Kingston, RI 02881. Offers medicinal chemistry and pharmacognosy (MS, PhD); pharmaceutics and pharmacokinetics (MS, PhD); pharmacology and toxicology (MS, PhD). *Expenses:* Tuition, state resident: full-time $6,032; part-time $335 per credit. Tuition, nonresident: full-time $17,288; part-time $960 per credit. Required fees: $65 per credit. $30 per semester. One-time fee: $80 part-time. *Unit head:* Dr. Clinton O. Chichester, Chair, 401-874-5034.

University of Rhode Island, Graduate School, College of Pharmacy, Graduate Programs in Pharmacy, Department of Pharmacy Practice, Kingston, RI 02881. Offers pharmaceutical sciences (MS, PhD), including pharmacoepidemiology and pharmacoeconomics. *Accreditation:* ACPE. *Application deadline:* For fall admission, 4/15 for domestic students. Application fee: $35. *Expenses:* Tuition, state resident: full-time $6,032; part-time $335 per credit. Tuition, nonresident: full-time $17,288; part-time $960 per credit. Required fees: $65 per credit. $30 per semester. One-time fee: $80 part-time. *Unit head:* Norma Owens, Chair, 401-874-2734.

University of Saskatchewan, College of Graduate Studies and Research, College of Pharmacy and Nutrition, Saskatoon, SK S7N 5A2, Canada. Offers M Sc, PhD. *Degree requirements:* For master's and doctorate, thesis/dissertation, registration. *Entrance requirements:* Additional exam requirements/recommendations for international students: Required—TOEFL.

University of South Carolina, College of Pharmacy and The Graduate School, Department of Basic Pharmaceutical Sciences, Columbia, SC 29208. Offers MS, PhD. Part-time programs available. Terminal master's awarded for partial completion of doctoral program. *Degree requirements:* For master's and doctorate, one foreign language, thesis/dissertation, comprehensive exam. *Entrance requirements:* For master's, GRE General Test, BS in biology, chemistry, pharmacy, or related field; for doctorate, GRE General Test, BS in biology, chemistry, or related field. Additional exam requirements/recommendations for international students: Required—TOEFL. Electronic applications accepted. *Faculty research:* Carcinogenesis synthesis of heterocyclic compounds, pharmacokinetics, neuropharmacology.

University of Southern California, Graduate School, School of Pharmacy, Graduate Programs in Pharmacy, Department of Regulatory Sciences, Los Angeles, CA 90089. Offers MS, Pharm D/MS. *Students:* 8 full-time (6 women), 37 part-time (25 women); includes 14 minority (1 American Indian/Alaska Native, 8 Asian Americans or Pacific Islanders, 5 Hispanic Americans), 6 international. In 2006, 14 degrees awarded. *Degree requirements:* For master's, internship. *Entrance requirements:* For master's, GMAT, GRE or MCAT, minimum GPA of 3.0. *Application deadline:* For fall admission, 12/1 priority date for domestic students. Application fee: $85. *Expenses:* Tuition: Full-time $33,314; part-time $1,121 per credit. Required fees: $522. Full-time tuition and fees vary according to program. *Financial support:* In 2006–07, research assistantships (averaging $18,500 per year), teaching assistantships (averaging $18,500 per year) were awarded; fellowships also available. *Unit head:* Dr. Frances J.R. Richmond, Director, 323-442-3521, Fax: 323-442-2333, E-mail: fjr@hsc.usc.edu.

University of Southern California, Graduate School, School of Pharmacy, Graduate Programs in Pharmacy, Graduate Program in Pharmaceutical Sciences, Los Angeles, CA 90089. Offers MS, PhD, Pharm D/PhD. *Students:* 38 full-time (21 women), 4 part-time (3 women); includes 14 minority (1 African American, 11 Asian Americans or Pacific Islanders, 2 Hispanic Americans), 11 international. In 2006, 3 master's, 3 doctorates awarded. *Degree requirements:* For master's, thesis, research and policy paper; for doctorate, thesis/dissertation. *Entrance requirements:* For master's and doctorate, GRE General Test. *Application deadline:* For fall admission, 12/1 priority date for domestic students. Applications are processed on a rolling basis. Application fee: $85. *Expenses:* Tuition: Full-time $33,314; part-time $1,121 per credit. Required fees: $522. Full-time tuition and fees vary according to program. *Financial support:* In 2006–07, 26 students received support, including research assistantships with full tuition reimbursements available (averaging $18,500 per year), teaching assistantships with full tuition reimbursements available (averaging $18,500 per year); fellowships with full tuition reimbursements available, Federal Work-Study, institutionally sponsored loans, scholarships/grants, and unspecified assistantships also available. Financial award application deadline: 2/15; financial award applicants required to submit FAFSA. *Faculty research:* Molecular mechanisms of drug and hormone action, regulation of microtubule-dependent vesicle transport in intact cells, pharmacokinetics. *Unit head:* Dr. Vincent Lee, Director, 323-442-1368. *Application contact:* Wade Thompson-Harper, Graduate Affairs Office, 323-442-1474, Fax: 323-442-2258, E-mail: wharper@usc.edu.

See Close-Up on page 2251.

University of Southern California, Graduate School, School of Pharmacy, Graduate Programs in Pharmacy, Program in Pharmaceutical Economics and Policy, Los Angeles, CA 90089. Offers MS, PhD. *Faculty:* 5 full-time (1 woman), 1 (woman) part-time/adjunct. *Students:* 22 full-time (13 women), 2 part-time; includes 4 minority (all Asian Americans or Pacific Islanders), 13 international. In 2006, 5 doctorates awarded. Terminal master's awarded for partial completion of doctoral program. *Degree requirements:* For master's, empirical analysis paper; for doctorate, thesis/dissertation. *Entrance requirements:* For master's and doctorate, GRE General Test. Additional exam requirements/recommendations for international students: Required—TOEFL. *Application deadline:* For fall admission, 12/1 priority date for domestic students. Application fee: $85. Electronic applications accepted. *Expenses:* Tuition: Full-time $33,314; part-time $1,121 per credit. Required fees: $522. Full-time tuition and fees vary according to program. *Financial support:* In 2006–07, research assistantships with full tuition reimbursements (averaging $18,500 per year), teaching assistantships with full tuition reimbursements (averaging $18,500 per year) were awarded; fellowships with tuition reimbursements, career-related internships or fieldwork, Federal Work-Study, institutionally sponsored loans, and scholarships/grants also available. Financial award application deadline: 1/1; financial award applicants required to submit FAFSA. *Faculty research:* Pharmacoeconomics, outcomes research, quality of life measurement, cost effective computer models, retrospective data analysis. *Unit head:* Dr. Jeffrey McCombs, Director, 323-442-1460. *Application contact:* Wade Thompson-Harper, Graduate Affairs Office, 323-442-1474, Fax: 323-442-2258, E-mail: wharper@usc.edu.

See Close-Up on page 2251.

The University of Tennessee Health Science Center, College of Graduate Health Sciences and College of Pharmacy, Department of Pharmaceutical Sciences, Memphis, TN 38163-0002. Offers MS, PhD, Pharm D/PhD. *Faculty:* 25 full-time (6 women), 8 part-time/adjunct (2 women). *Students:* 80 full-time (30 women); includes 48 minority (6 African Americans, 40 Asian Americans or Pacific Islanders, 2 Hispanic Americans). Average age 26. 250 applicants, 6% accepted. In 2006, 12 degrees awarded. *Degree requirements:* For master's, thesis, comprehensive exam; for doctorate, thesis/dissertation, oral and written preliminary and comprehensive exams. *Entrance requirements:* For master's and doctorate, GRE General Test, minimum GPA of 3.0. Additional exam requirements/recommendations for international students: Required—TOEFL. *Application deadline:* For fall admission, 5/15 for domestic and international students. Application fee: $0. Electronic applications accepted. *Expenses:* Tuition, state resident: full-time $8,267. Tuition, nonresident: full-time $20,747. Required fees: $60. One-time fee: $55 full-time. *Financial support:* Fellowships, research assistantships, teaching assistantships, tuition waivers (full) available. Financial award application deadline: 2/25. *Unit head:* Dr. Duane D. Miller, Chairman, 901-528-6027, Fax: 901-528-6940, E-mail: dmiller@utmem.edu. *Application contact:* Eunice Taylor, Interim Director, Enrollment Services, 901-448-5560, Fax: 901-448-7772, E-mail: etaylor@utmem.edu.

The University of Texas at Austin, College of Pharmacy, Graduate Programs in Pharmacy, Austin, TX 78712-1111. Offers MS Phr, PhD. *Degree requirements:* For master's and doctorate, thesis/dissertation. *Entrance requirements:* For master's and doctorate, GRE General Test. Electronic applications accepted. *Faculty research:* Synthetic medical chemistry, synthetic molecular biology, bio-organic chemistry, pharmacoeconomics, pharmacy practice.

University of the Pacific, School of Pharmacy and Health Sciences, Pharmaceutical and Chemical Sciences Graduate Program, Stockton, CA 95211-0197. Offers MS, PhD. *Faculty:* 10 full-time (1 woman). *Students:* 7 full-time (2 women), 41 part-time (18 women); includes 9 minority (all Asian Americans or Pacific Islanders), 29 international. Average age 29. 88 applicants, 20% accepted, 9 enrolled. In 2006, 4 master's, 2 doctorates awarded. *Entrance requirements:* Additional exam requirements/recommendations for international students: Required—TOEFL (minimum score 475 paper-based; 150 computer-based). Application fee: $75. *Expenses:* Tuition: Full-time $26,920. Required fees: $430. Tuition and fees vary according to course load. *Financial support:* Application deadline: 3/1; *Unit head:* Dr. Bhaskara Jasti, Head, 209-946-3162, E-mail: bjasti@pacific.edu.

University of the Sciences in Philadelphia, College of Graduate Studies, Program in Pharmaceutics, Philadelphia, PA 19104-4495. Offers MS, PhD. Part-time programs available. *Faculty:* 5 full-time (0 women), 2 part-time/adjunct (both women). *Students:* 12 full-time (9 women), 17 part-time (7 women); includes 7 minority (all Asian Americans or Pacific Islanders), 12 international. Average age 32. In 2006, 3 master's, 2 doctorates awarded. Terminal master's awarded for partial completion of doctoral program. *Degree requirements:* For master's, thesis (for some programs); for doctorate, thesis/dissertation, oral defense, comprehensive exam. *Entrance requirements:* For master's and doctorate, GRE General Test. Additional exam requirements/recommendations for international students: Required—TOEFL, TWE. *Application deadline:* For fall admission, 5/1 for international students; for winter admission, 10/1 for international students; for spring admission, 3/1 for international students. Applications are processed on a rolling basis. Application fee: $50. *Expenses:* Tuition: Part-time $1,058 per credit. Tuition and fees vary according to program. *Financial support:* In 2006–07, 16 students received support, including 5 fellowships with full tuition reimbursements available, 11 teaching assistantships with full tuition reimbursements available (averaging $19,497 per year); research assistantships with full tuition reimbursements available, institutionally sponsored loans and tuition waivers (full and partial) also available. Financial award application deadline: 3/1. *Faculty research:* Pharmacodynamics, disperse systems, peptide-biomembranes interactions, in vitro/in vivo correlations, cellular drug delivery. Total annual research expenditures:$505,690. *Unit head:* Dr. Clyde M. Ofner, Director, 215-596-8881, E-mail: c.ofner@usip.edu. *Application contact:* Joyce D'Angelo, Administrative Assistant, 215-596-8937, E-mail: j.dangel@usip.edu.

See Close-Up on page 2253.

The University of Toledo, College of Graduate Studies, College of Pharmacy, Department of Pharmacology, Program in Pharmaceutical Science, Toledo, OH 43606-3390. Offers administrative pharmacy (MSPS); industrial pharmacy (MSPS); pharmacology (MSPS). *Faculty:* 15 full-time (4 women), 1 part-time/adjunct (0 women). *Students:* 20 full-time (10 women); includes 2 minority (1 African American, 1 Asian American or Pacific Islander), 5 international. Average age 25. 85 applicants, 14% accepted, 11 enrolled. In 2006, 13 degrees awarded. *Degree requirements:* For master's, thesis. *Entrance requirements:* For master's, GRE General Test. Additional exam requirements/recommendations for international students: Required—TOEFL

Pharmaceutical Sciences

The University of Toledo (continued)

(minimum score 550 paper-based; 213 computer-based; 80 iBT). *Application deadline:* For fall admission, 2/1 for domestic students, 1/1 priority date for international students. Application fee: $45. Electronic applications accepted. *Financial support:* In 2006–07, 19 students received support; research assistantships with full tuition reimbursements available, teaching assistantships with full tuition reimbursements available, unspecified assistantships available. *Faculty research:* Drug disposition, neuropharmacology, pharmacokinetics, product stability, pharmacy and health care administration. *Application contact:* Karen F. Papadakis, Graduate Coordinator for Pharmaceutical Sciences, 419-530-1910, Fax: 419-530-1909, E-mail: kpapada@utnet.utoledo.edu.

University of Toronto, School of Graduate Studies, Life Sciences Division, Department of Pharmaceutical Sciences, Toronto, ON M5S 1A1, Canada. Offers M Sc, PhD. Part-time programs available. *Degree requirements:* For master's, thesis, poster presentation, oral thesis defense; for doctorate, thesis/dissertation, oral presentation, qualifying examination. *Entrance requirements:* For master's, GRE General Test (international applicants only), minimum B average in last 2 years of full-time study, 3 letters of reference, resumé; for doctorate, GRE General Test (international applicants only), minimum B+ average, M Sc or equivalent, 3 letters of reference, resumé. Additional exam requirements/recommendations for international students: Required—TOEFL (600 paper-based, 250 computer-based), MELAB (88) or IELTS (7).

University of Washington, School of Pharmacy and Graduate School, Graduate Programs in Pharmacy, Department of Pharmaceutics, Seattle, WA 98195. Offers MS, PhD. Terminal master's awarded for partial completion of doctoral program. *Degree requirements:* For master's, thesis; for doctorate, one foreign language, thesis/dissertation. *Entrance requirements:* For master's and doctorate, GRE General Test. Additional exam requirements/recommendations for international students: Required—TOEFL. Electronic applications accepted. *Faculty research:* Pharmacokinetics, drug-drug interaction.

University of Wisconsin–Madison, School of Pharmacy and Graduate School, Graduate Programs in Pharmacy, Pharmaceutical Sciences Division, Madison, WI 53706-1380. Offers MS, PhD. Terminal master's awarded for partial completion of doctoral program. *Degree requirements:* For master's, thesis optional; for doctorate, thesis/dissertation, comprehensive exam, registration. *Entrance requirements:* For master's and doctorate, GRE. Additional exam requirements/recommendations for international students: Required—TOEFL. Electronic applications accepted. *Faculty research:* Drug action, drug delivery, drug discovery.

University of Wisconsin–Madison, School of Pharmacy and Graduate School, Graduate Programs in Pharmacy, Social and Administrative Sciences in Pharmacy Division, Madison, WI 53706-1380. Offers MS, PhD. Terminal master's awarded for partial completion of doctoral program. *Degree requirements:* For master's, thesis optional; for doctorate, thesis/dissertation, comprehensive exam, registration. *Entrance requirements:* For master's and doctorate, GRE. Additional exam requirements/recommendations for international students: Required—TOEFL. Electronic applications accepted. *Faculty research:* Patient-provider communication, economics, patient care systems.

Virginia Commonwealth University, Medical College of Virginia-Professional Programs, School of Pharmacy, Department of Pharmaceutics, Richmond, VA 23284-9005. Offers Pharm D, MS, PhD. *Faculty:* 9 full-time (3 women). In 2006, 6 degrees awarded. Terminal master's awarded for partial completion of doctoral program. *Degree requirements:* For master's and doctorate, thesis/dissertation. *Entrance requirements:* For master's and doctorate, GRE General Test. Additional exam requirements/recommendations for international students: Required—TOEFL. *Application deadline:* For fall admission, 5/1 for domestic students. Application fee: $30. *Financial support:* Fellowships, research assistantships, teaching assistantships, institutionally sponsored loans available. *Faculty research:* Drug delivery systems, drug development. *Unit head:* Dr. Peter R. Byron, Chair, 804-828-6377, Fax: 804-828-8359. *Application contact:* Dr. Mohamadi A. Sarkar, Director, Graduate Program, 804-828-6321, Fax: 804-828-8359, E-mail: masarkar@vcu.edu.

Announcement: The department offers programs leading to MS and PhD degrees and a combined PharmD/PhD in pharmaceutical sciences. The research interests of the department include drug absorption, macromolecular drug delivery, cell transport mechanisms, pharmacokinetics, pharmacodynamics, drug metabolism, drug delivery and dosage form design, aerosol and inhalation technology, and biopharmaceutical analysis of drugs.

See Close-Up on page 2255.

Wayne State University, Eugene Applebaum College of Pharmacy and Health Sciences, Department of Pharmaceutical Sciences, Detroit, MI 48202. Offers experimental technology in pharmaceutical sciences (Certificate); health systems pharmacy management (MS); hospital pharmacy (MS); pharmaceutical administration (MS, PhD); pharmacy (Pharm D). *Accreditation:* ACPE (one or more programs are accredited). Part-time programs available. *Faculty:* 39 full-time (0 women). *Students:* 14 full-time (6 women), 3 part-time (2 women); includes 1 minority (African American), 13 international. Average age 31. In 2006, 3 master's, 1 doctorate awarded. *Degree requirements:* For master's, thesis optional. *Entrance requirements:* For Pharm D, bachelor's degree in pharmacy; for master's, GRE General Test, bachelor's degree in pharmacy. Additional exam requirements/recommendations for international students: Required—TOEFL (minimum score 550 paper-based; 213 computer-based); Recommended—TWE (minimum score 6). *Application deadline:* For fall admission, 6/1 for international students; for winter admission, 10/1 for international students; for spring admission, 2/1 for international students. Applications are processed on a rolling basis. Application fee: $30 ($50 for international students). Electronic applications accepted. *Financial support:* In 2006–07, 3 fellowships (averaging $35,000 per year) were awarded; career-related internships or fieldwork and scholarships/grants also available. Support available to part-time students. *Faculty research:* Mechanisms of resistance of bacteria to anti-microbial agents, drug metabolism and disposition in children, treatment strategies for stroke/neurovascular disease, prevalence and treatment of diabetes in Arab-Americans, ethnic variability in development of osteoporosis. Total annual research expenditures: $449,503. *Unit head:* Dr. George B. Corcoran, Chair, 313-577-1737, Fax: 313-577-2033. *Application contact:* Geralynn Smith, Graduate Director, 313-577-5401, E-mail: gbs@wayne.edu.

Western University of Health Sciences, College of Pharmacy, Program in Pharmaceutical Sciences, Pomona, CA 91766-1854. Offers MS. *Faculty:* 11 full-time (2 women). *Students:* 8 full-time (3 women); includes 3 minority (all Asian Americans or Pacific Islanders), 5 international. Average age 26. 30 applicants, 20% accepted, 4 enrolled. In 2006, 4 degrees awarded. *Entrance requirements:* Additional exam requirements/recommendations for international students: Required—TOEFL (minimum score 500 paper-based; 213 computer-based; 89 iBT). *Application deadline:* For fall admission, 3/1 for domestic and international students; for spring admission, 11/15 for domestic and international students. Application fee: $65. *Expenses: Contact institution. Financial support:* Institutionally sponsored loans and scholarships/grants available. Financial award application deadline: 3/2; financial award applicants required to submit FAFSA. *Unit head:* Guru Betageri, Chair, 909-469-5682, Fax: 909-469-5539. *Application contact:* Audrey Navarro, Information Contact, 909-469-5335, Fax: 909-469-5570, E-mail: admissions@westernu.edu.

West Virginia University, School of Medicine, Graduate Programs at the Health Sciences Center, Interdisciplinary Graduate Programs in Biomedical Sciences, Program in Pharmaceutical and Pharmacological Sciences, Morgantown, WV 26506. Offers MS, PhD, MD/PhD. *Faculty:* 27 full-time (6 women), 6 part-time/adjunct (0 women). *Students:* 17 full-time (6 women), 4 part-time (3 women), 10 international. Average age 23. In 2006, 2 master's, 4 doctorates awarded. *Median time to degree:* Of those who began their doctoral program in fall 1998, 95% received their degree in 8 years or less. *Degree requirements:* For doctorate, thesis/dissertation, comprehensive exam. *Entrance requirements:* For doctorate, GRE General Test, minimum GPA of 3.0. Additional exam requirements/recommendations for international students: Required—TOEFL. *Application deadline:* For fall admission, 3/1 for domestic students, 1/15 for international students. Applications are processed on a rolling basis. Application fee: $0. Electronic applications accepted. *Expenses:* Tuition, state resident: full-time $4,926; part-time $276 per credit hour. Tuition, nonresident: full-time $14,278; part-time $796 per credit hour. Tuition and fees vary according to program. *Financial support:* In 2006–07, research assistantships with full tuition reimbursements (averaging $23,000 per year); institutionally sponsored loans, traineeships, and health care benefits also available. *Faculty research:* Medicinal chemistry, pharmacokinetics, nano-pharmaceutics, polymer-based drug delivery, molecular therapeutics. Total annual research expenditures: $2 million. *Unit head:* Dr. Peter Gannett, Associate Chair, Graduate Director, 304-293-1480, Fax: 304-293-2576, E-mail: pgannett@hsc.wvu.edu. *Application contact:* Claire Noel, Assistant Director for Health Sciences Graduate Program, 304-293-7116, Fax: 304-293-9257, E-mail: cnoel@hsc.wvu.edu.

See Close-Up on page 2257.

West Virginia University, School of Pharmacy, Program in Pharmaceutical and Pharmacological Sciences, Morgantown, WV 26506. Offers administrative pharmacy (PhD); behavioral pharmacy (MS, PhD); biopharmaceutics/pharmacokinetics (MS, PhD); industrial pharmacy (MS); medicinal chemistry (MS, PhD); pharmaceutical chemistry (MS, PhD); pharmaceutics (MS, PhD); pharmacology and toxicology (MS); pharmacy (MS); pharmacy administration (MS). Part-time programs available. *Students:* 29 full-time (12 women), 3 part-time (2 women); includes 1 minority (Asian American or Pacific Islander), 18 international. Average age 30. 47 applicants, 6% accepted, 2 enrolled. In 2006, 3 master's, 9 doctorates awarded. Terminal master's awarded for partial completion of doctoral program. *Median time to degree:* Of those who began their doctoral program in fall 1998, 84% received their degree in 8 years or less. *Degree requirements:* For master's, thesis; for doctorate, one foreign language, thesis/dissertation, comprehensive exam. *Entrance requirements:* For master's and doctorate, GRE General Test, minimum GPA of 2.75. Additional exam requirements/recommendations for international students: Required—TOEFL; Recommended—TWE. *Application deadline:* For fall admission, 3/1 priority date for domestic and international students. Application fee: $50. Electronic applications accepted. *Expenses: Contact institution.* Tuition and fees vary according to program. *Financial support:* In 2006–07, 31 students received support, including 13 research assistantships with full tuition reimbursements available (averaging $23,000 per year), 15 teaching assistantships with full tuition reimbursements available (averaging $23,000 per year); career-related internships or fieldwork, Federal Work-Study, institutionally sponsored loans, health care benefits, tuition waivers (full and partial), and unspecified assistantships also available. Financial award application deadline: 3/1; financial award applicants required to submit FAFSA. *Faculty research:* Pharmaceutics, medicinal chemistry, biopharmaceutics/pharmacokinetics, health outcomes research. Total annual research expenditures: $1.8 million. *Application contact:* Dr. Patrick S. Callery, Assistant Dean for Graduate Programs/Chair, 304-293-1482, Fax: 304-293-2576, E-mail: pcallery@hsc.wvu.edu.

Pharmacy

Albany College of Pharmacy of Union University, Program in Pharmacy, Albany, NY 12208-3425. Offers Pharm D. *Accreditation:* ACPE. Part-time programs available. *Faculty:* 72 full-time, 12 part-time/adjunct. *Students:* 336 full-time (195 women), 2 part-time; includes 43 minority (7 African Americans, 2 American Indian/Alaska Native, 30 Asian Americans or Pacific Islanders, 4 Hispanic Americans), 20 international. Average age 26. 1,808 applicants, 7% accepted, 73 enrolled. In 2006, 132 Pharm Ds awarded. *Median time to degree:* Of those who began their doctoral program in fall 1998, 71% received their degree in 8 years or less. *Degree requirements:* For first-professional, comprehensive exam. *Entrance requirements:* Minimum GPA of 3.2. Additional exam requirements/recommendations for international students: Required—TOEFL (minimum score 600 paper-based; 250 computer-based). *Application deadline:* For fall admission, 3/1 for domestic and international students. Applications are processed on a rolling basis. Application fee: $100. Electronic applications accepted. *Expenses:* Tuition: Full-time $19,350. Required fees: $635. One-time fee: $145 full-time. *Financial support:* In 2006–07, 145 students received support, including 1 fellowship with tuition reimbursement available (averaging $40,000 per year); Federal Work-Study also available. Support available to part-time students. Financial award application deadline: 3/1; financial award applicants required to submit FAFSA. *Faculty research:* Therapeutic use of drugs, pharmacokinetics, pharmaceutical care. Total annual research expenditures: $1.3 million. *Unit head:* Dr. Mehdi Boroujerdi, Dean, 518-694-7212, Fax: 518-694-7063. *Application contact:* Carly Connors, Director of Admissions, 518-694-7221, Fax: 518-694-7322, E-mail: admissions@acp.edu.

Auburn University, School of Pharmacy, Professional Program in Pharmacy, Auburn University, AL 36849. Offers Pharm D. *Accreditation:* ACPE. Part-time programs available. *Faculty:* 19 full-time (5 women). *Students:* 403 full-time (249 women), 111 part-time (75 women); includes 64 minority (29 African Americans, 2 American Indian/Alaska Native, 30 Asian Americans or Pacific Islanders, 3 Hispanic Americans), 6 international. Average age 25. 880 applicants, 16% accepted, 125 enrolled. In 2006, 106 degrees awarded. *Expenses: Contact institution.* Tuition and fees vary according to program. *Financial support:* Federal Work-Study available. Support available to part-time students.

Butler University, College of Pharmacy, Indianapolis, IN 46208-3485. Offers pharmaceutical science (Pharm D, MS); physician assistance studies (MS). *Accreditation:* ACPE (one or more programs are accredited). Part-time and evening/weekend programs available. *Faculty:* 34 full-time (17 women), 9 part-time/adjunct (7 women). *Students:* 369 full-time (275 women), 9 part-time (7 women); includes 26 minority (7 African Americans, 1 American Indian/Alaska Native, 17 Asian Americans or Pacific Islanders, 1 Hispanic American), 9 international. Average age 24. 135 applicants, 82% accepted, 87 enrolled. In 2006, 84 degrees awarded. *Degree requirements:* For master's, research paper or thesis. *Application deadline:* For fall admission, 8/1 priority date for domestic students; for spring admission, 12/15 for domestic students. Applications are processed on a rolling basis. Application fee: $35. Electronic applications accepted. *Expenses: Contact institution.* Tuition and fees vary according to program. *Financial support:* Applicants required to submit FAFSA. *Faculty research:* Anti-seizure drugs, casein kinase inhibitors, speech recognition interface for prescribing drugs, pharmacoeconomics. Total annual research expenditures: $92,000. *Unit head:* Dr. Mary Andritz, Dean, 317-940-9451, Fax: 317-940-6172, E-mail: mandritz@butler.edu. *Application contact:* Dr. Kent VanTyle, Professor, 317-940-9580, E-mail: kvantyle@butler.edu.

Campbell University, Graduate and Professional Programs, School of Pharmacy, Buies Creek, NC 27506. Offers clinical research (MS); pharmaceutical science (MS); pharmacy (Pharm D).

Accreditation: ACPE. Part-time and evening/weekend programs available. *Faculty:* 55 full-time (18 women), 119 part-time/adjunct (52 women). *Students:* 435 full-time (296 women), 183 part-time (122 women); includes 50 minority (37 African Americans, 8 American Indian/Alaska Native, 5 Hispanic Americans), 34 international. Average age 23. 1,960 applicants, 7% accepted, 108 enrolled. In 2006, 89 Pharm Ds, 8 master's awarded. *Entrance requirements:* For Pharm D, PCAT; for master's, MCAT, PCAT, GRE, bachelor's degree in health sciences or related field. Additional exam requirements/recommendations for international students: Required—TOEFL (minimum score 550 paper-based; 213 computer-based; 79 iBT). *Application deadline:* For fall admission, 3/1 for domestic and international students. Applications are processed on a rolling basis. Application fee: $25. Electronic applications accepted. *Expenses: Contact institution. Financial support:* In 2006–07, 350 students received support, including 4 research assistantships (averaging $3,000 per year), 3 teaching assistantships (averaging $4,000 per year); career-related internships or fieldwork, Federal Work-Study, and scholarships/grants also available. Financial award application deadline: 3/15; financial award applicants required to submit FAFSA. *Faculty research:* Immunology, medicinal chemistry, pharmaceutics, applied pharmacology. Total annual research expenditures: $297,000. *Unit head:* Dr. Ronald W. Maddox, Dean, 910-893-1200 Ext. 1685, Fax: 910-893-1697, E-mail: pharmacy@camel.campbell.edu. *Application contact:* Dr. Mark Moore, Assistant Dean of Admissions and Student Affairs, 910-893-1690, Fax: 910-893-1937, E-mail: pharmacy@campbell.edu.

Creighton University, School of Pharmacy and Health Professions, Professional Program in Pharmacy, Omaha, NE 68178-0001. Offers Pharm D. *Accreditation:* ACPE. Postbaccalaureate distance learning degree programs offered (no on-campus study). Electronic applications accepted. *Expenses:* Tuition: Part-time $595 per credit hour. Required fees: $38 per semester. *Faculty research:* Drug synthesis, Phase II drug studies, molecular mechanism of toxicity, pharmaceutics, pharmacology of the eye.

Drake University, College of Pharmacy and Health Sciences, Program in Pharmacy, Des Moines, IA 50311-4516. Offers Pharm D, Pharm D/JD, Pharm D/MBA, Pharm D/MPA. *Accreditation:* ACPE. *Faculty:* 19 full-time (11 women), 4 part-time/adjunct (3 women). *Students:* 496 full-time (350 women), 2 part-time (both women); includes 79 minority (7 African Americans, 68 Asian Americans or Pacific Islanders, 4 Hispanic Americans), 7 international. Average age 20. 916 applicants, 15% accepted. In 2006, 105 degrees awarded. *Degree requirements:* For first-professional, rotations. *Entrance requirements:* PCAT, interview. *Application deadline:* For fall admission, 3/1 priority date for domestic students. Applications are processed on a rolling basis. Application fee: $135. Electronic applications accepted. *Financial support:* In 2006–07, 10 teaching assistantships (averaging $3,200 per year) were awarded; career-related internships or fieldwork, Federal Work-Study, institutionally sponsored loans, and scholarships/grants also available. Support available to part-time students. Financial award application deadline: 3/1; financial award applicants required to submit FAFSA. *Faculty research:* Cardiomyocytes, health literacy, entrepreneurial leadership, community care. Total annual research expenditures: $171,288. *Application contact:* Dr. Renae J. Chesnut, Associate Dean for Student Affairs, 515-271-3018, Fax: 515-271-4171, E-mail: renae.chesnut@drake.edu.

Duquesne University, School of Pharmacy, Professional Program in Pharmacy, Pittsburgh, PA 15282-0001. Offers Pharm D. Students enter program as first year undergraduates. *Accreditation:* ACPE. *Faculty:* 36 full-time (11 women), 8 part-time/adjunct (0 women). *Students:* 1,068 full-time (696 women), 14 part-time (9 women); includes 38 minority (13 African Americans, 23 Asian Americans or Pacific Islanders, 2 Hispanic Americans), 13 international. 872 applicants, 53% accepted, 221 enrolled. In 2006, 112 Pharm Ds awarded. *Entrance requirements:* PCAT (for transfer students). Additional exam requirements/recommendations for international students: Required—TOEFL. *Application deadline:* For fall admission, 12/1 for domestic and international students. Application fee: $50. Electronic applications accepted. *Expenses:* Tuition: Part-time $723 per credit. Required fees: $71 per credit. Tuition and fees vary according to degree level and program. *Financial support:* Career-related internships or fieldwork, Federal Work-Study, institutionally sponsored loans, and scholarships/grants available. Support available to part-time students. Financial award applicants required to submit FAFSA. *Application contact:* Admissions/Recruitment Coordinator, 412-396-6393, Fax: 412-396-4375, E-mail: dp-adm@duq.edu.

Ferris State University, College of Pharmacy, Big Rapids, MI 49307. Offers Pharm D. *Accreditation:* ACPE. *Faculty:* 38 full-time (22 women), 6 part-time/adjunct (5 women). *Students:* 495 full-time (278 women), 20 part-time (11 women); includes 60 minority (10 African Americans, 3 American Indian/Alaska Native, 44 Asian Americans or Pacific Islanders, 3 Hispanic Americans), 34 international. Average age 28. 734 applicants, 20% accepted. In 2006, 118 degrees awarded. *Entrance requirements:* PCAT, 2 years of pre-pharmacy course work. *Application deadline:* For fall admission, 1/31 for domestic students. Application fee: $0. *Expenses: Contact institution. Financial support:* Institutionally sponsored loans and scholarships/grants available. Financial award applicants required to submit FAFSA. *Faculty research:* Diabetes, rural health education, managed care practice, antimicrobial pharmacotherapy, medicinal flora. Total annual research expenditures: $49,078. *Unit head:* Dr. Ian Mathison, Dean, 231-591-2254, Fax: 231-591-3829, E-mail: mathisol@ferris.edu. *Application contact:* Dr. Rodney A. Larson, Assistant Dean, 231-591-3780, Fax: 231-591-3829, E-mail: larsonr@ferris.edu.

Florida Agricultural and Mechanical University, Division of Graduate Studies, Research, and Continuing Education, College of Pharmacy and Pharmaceutical Sciences, Professional Program in Pharmacy and Pharmaceutical Sciences, Tallahassee, FL 32307-3200. Offers Pharm D, Ex Doc. *Accreditation:* ACPE. *Entrance requirements:* Minimum GPA of 2.5. Additional exam requirements/recommendations for international students: Required—TOEFL.

Harding University, College of Pharmacy, Searcy, AR 72149-0001. Offers Pharm D. *Entrance requirements:* PCAT. Additional exam requirements/recommendations for international students: Required—TOEFL (minimum score 550 paper-based). *Application deadline:* For fall admission, 3/15 priority date for domestic and international students. Applications are processed on a rolling basis. Application fee: $50. Electronic applications accepted. *Expenses: Contact institution. Unit head:* Julie Hixson-Wallace, Dean, 501-279-5205, Fax: 501-279-5525, E-mail: jahixson@harding.edu. *Application contact:* Carol Kell, Director of Admissions, 501-279-5523, Fax: 501-279-5525, E-mail: ckell@harding.edu.

Howard University, College of Pharmacy, Nursing and Allied Health Sciences, School of Pharmacy, Washington, DC 20059-0002. Offers Pharm D, Pharm D/MBA. *Accreditation:* ACPE. Postbaccalaureate distance learning degree programs offered (minimal on-campus study). *Faculty:* 26 full-time (12 women), 390 part-time/adjunct (211 women). *Students:* 368 full-time (228 women); includes 301 minority (213 African Americans, 1 American Indian/Alaska Native, 78 Asian Americans or Pacific Islanders, 9 Hispanic Americans), 32 international. Average age 25. 1,517 applicants, 4% accepted, 49 enrolled. In 2006, 82 Pharm Ds awarded. *Degree requirements:* For first-professional, comprehensive exam. *Entrance requirements:* PCAT, minimum GPA of 2.5. *Application deadline:* For fall admission, 12/1 for domestic and international students. Applications are processed on a rolling basis. Application fee: $45. Electronic applications accepted. *Expenses: Contact institution. Financial support:* In 2006–07, 351 students received support, including 3 fellowships (averaging $52,000 per year), 6 teaching assistantships (averaging $6,000 per year); career-related internships or fieldwork, Federal Work-Study, institutionally sponsored loans, and scholarships/grants also available. Financial award application deadline: 2/15; financial award applicants required to submit FAFSA. *Faculty research:* Kinetics of drug absorption, stealth liposomes, synthesis, opiate analgesics. *Unit head:* Dr. Clarence E. Curry, Associate Dean (Interim), 202-806-6530, Fax: 202-806-4636, E-mail: cecurry@howard.edu. *Application contact:* Dr. Joseph R. Ofosu, Assistant Dean for Student Services, 202-806-6530, Fax: 202-806-4636, E-mail: jofosu@howard.edu.

Idaho State University, Office of Graduate Studies, College of Pharmacy, Department of Pharmacy Practice and Administrative Sciences, Pocatello, ID 83209. Offers pharmacy (Pharm D); pharmacy administration (MS, PhD). *Accreditation:* ACPE (one or more programs are accredited). Postbaccalaureate distance learning degree programs offered (minimal on-campus study). *Faculty:* 4 full-time (1 woman). *Students:* 230 full-time (100 women), 16 part-time (9 women); includes 19 minority (1 American Indian/Alaska Native, 14 Asian Americans or Pacific Islanders, 4 Hispanic Americans), 5 international. Average age 28. In 2006, 63 degrees awarded. *Degree requirements:* For Pharm D, thesis, written and oral exams, comprehensive exam, registration; for master's, one foreign language, thesis (for some programs), thesis research, comprehensive exam, registration (for some programs); for doctorate, thesis/dissertation, oral and written exams, comprehensive exam, registration. *Entrance requirements:* For Pharm D, GRE General Test, minimum GPA of 3.0, 2 years of pre-pharmacy, BS degree in pharmacy or related field, 3 letters of recommendation; for master's, GRE General Test, minimum GPA of 3.0, 3 letters of recommendation; for doctorate, GRE General Test, BS degree in pharmacy or related field, minimum GPA of 3.0, 3 letters of recommendation. Additional exam requirements/recommendations for international students: Required—TOEFL (minimum score 550 paper-based; 213 computer-based; 80 iBT). *Application deadline:* For fall admission, 7/1 for domestic students, 6/1 for international students; for spring admission, 12/1 for domestic students, 11/1 for international students. Applications are processed on a rolling basis. Application fee: $55. *Expenses:* Tuition, state resident: part-time $251 per credit. Tuition, nonresident: part-time $366 per credit. Tuition and fees vary according to degree level, program and reciprocity agreements. *Financial support:* In 2006–07, 8 research assistantships with full and partial tuition reimbursements (averaging $11,303 per year) were awarded; teaching assistantships with full and partial tuition reimbursements, career-related internships or fieldwork, Federal Work-Study, scholarships/grants, and tuition waivers (full and partial) also available. Support available to part-time students. Financial award application deadline: 1/1. *Faculty research:* Pharmaceutical care outcomes, drug use review, pharmacoeconomics. Total annual research expenditures: $131,046. *Unit head:* Dr. Vaughn Culbertson, Chairman, 208-282-4385, Fax: 208-282-4482, E-mail: vculb@pharmacy.isu.edu. *Application contact:* Ellen Combs, Graduate School Technical Records Specialist, 208-282-2150, Fax: 208-282-4847.

Lake Erie College of Osteopathic Medicine, Professional Programs, Erie, PA 16509-1025. Offers biomedical sciences (Postbaccalaureate Certificate); medical education (MS); osteopathic medicine (DO); pharmacy (Pharm D). *Accreditation:* ACPE; AOsA. *Faculty:* 85 full-time (20 women), 84 part-time/adjunct (19 women). *Students:* 1,355 full-time (700 women); includes 261 minority (57 African Americans, 3 American Indian/Alaska Native, 171 Asian Americans or Pacific Islanders, 30 Hispanic Americans). Average age 25. 4,526 applicants, 15% accepted, 366 enrolled. In 2006, 198 DOs, 88 other advanced degrees awarded. *Median time to degree:* First professional degree–4 years full-time; master's–2 years full-time; Postbaccalaureate Certificate–3 years full-time. *Degree requirements:* For first professional degree, National Osteopathic Medical Licensing Exam, Levels 1 and 2; for Postbaccalaureate Certificate, North American Pharmacist Licensure Examination (NAPLEX). *Entrance requirements:* For first professional degree, MCAT, minimum GPA of 3.2, letters of recommendation; for Postbaccalaureate Certificate, PCAT, letters of recommendation, minimum GPA of 3.5. *Application deadline:* For fall admission, 3/1 for domestic students. Applications are processed on a rolling basis. Application fee: $50. Electronic applications accepted. *Expenses:* Tuition: Full-time $25,000. Required fees: $1,095. *Financial support:* In 2006–07, 1,238 students received support. Institutionally sponsored loans and scholarships/grants available. Financial award application deadline: 6/30; financial award applicants required to submit FAFSA. *Faculty research:* Cardiac smooth and skeletal muscle mechanics, chemotherapeutics and vitamins, osteopathic manipulation. *Unit head:* Dr. Silvia M. Ferretti, Provost Dean Vice President of Academic Affairs, 814-866-6641, Fax: 814-866-8123. *Application contact:* Amy Rowe, Admissions Coordinator, 814-866-6641, Fax: 814-866-8123, E-mail: arowe@lecom.edu.

Lebanese American University, School of Pharmacy, Beirut, Lebanon. Offers Pharm D. *Accreditation:* ACPE.

Medical University of South Carolina, College of Pharmacy, Charleston, SC 29425-0002. Offers pharmaceutical sciences (PhD); pharmacy (Pharm D). *Accreditation:* ACPE. *Faculty:* 42 full-time (17 women), 1 part-time/adjunct (0 women). *Students:* 316 full-time (229 women); includes 51 minority (24 African Americans, 2 American Indian/Alaska Native, 19 Asian Americans or Pacific Islanders, 6 Hispanic Americans). Average age 25. 612 applicants, 17% accepted, 81 enrolled. In 2006, 54 degrees awarded. *Entrance requirements:* PCAT, 2 years pre-professional course work, interview, minimum GPA of 2.5. Additional exam requirements/recommendations for international students: Required—TOEFL (minimum score 600 paper-based; 250 computer-based). *Application deadline:* For fall admission, 1/15 for domestic and international students. Application fee: $75. Electronic applications accepted. *Expenses: Contact institution. Financial support:* In 2006–07, 270 students received support. Career-related internships or fieldwork, Federal Work-Study, institutionally sponsored loans, and scholarships/grants also available. Financial award application deadline: 8/15; financial award applicants required to submit FAFSA. *Faculty research:* Rational and computer aided drug design, drug metabolism and transport, molecular immunology and cellular toxicology, cell injury, death and regeneration. Total annual research expenditures: $1.8 million. *Unit head:* Dr. Arnold W. Karig, Interim Dean, 843-792-8452, Fax: 843-792-9081, E-mail: karigaw@musc.edu.

Mercer University, Graduate Studies, Cecil B. Day Campus, College of Pharmacy and Health Sciences, Macon, GA 31207-0003. Offers medical sciences (MS); pharmacy (Pharm D, PhD, Pharm D/MBA, Pharm D/PhD); Pharm D/MBA; Pharm D/PhD. *Accreditation:* ACPE (one or more programs are accredited). *Faculty:* 21 full-time (13 women), 2 part-time/adjunct (1 woman). *Students:* 584 full-time (401 women), 27 part-time (22 women); includes 158 minority (69 African Americans, 3 American Indian/Alaska Native, 71 Asian Americans or Pacific Islanders, 15 Hispanic Americans), 33 international. Average age 26. 2,250 applicants, 12% accepted, 155 enrolled. In 2006, 128 Pharm Ds, 5 doctorates awarded. *Median time to degree:* Of those who began their doctoral program in fall 1998, 95% received their degree in 8 years or less. *Degree requirements:* For doctorate, thesis/dissertation. *Entrance requirements:* For Pharm D, PCAT, minimum GPA of 2.5; for master's, GRE; for doctorate, GRE, Pharm D or BS in pharmacy, minimum GPA of 3.0. *Application deadline:* For fall admission, 1/1 for domestic students. Applications are processed on a rolling basis. Application fee: $25. Electronic applications accepted. *Expenses: Contact institution. Financial support:* In 2006–07, 350 students received support; teaching assistantships with tuition reimbursements available, career-related internships or fieldwork, Federal Work-Study, institutionally sponsored loans, scholarships/grants, and tuition waivers available. Support available to part-time students. Financial award application deadline: 5/1; financial award applicants required to submit FAFSA. *Faculty research:* Stability and compatibility of steroids, synthesis of antihypertensives, disposition of cyclosporine, DUZ-drug research, synthesis of enzyme inhibitors. *Unit head:* Dr. Hewitt W. Matthews, Dean, 678-547-6304, Fax: 678-547-6315, E-mail: matthews_h@mercer.edu. *Application contact:* Dr. James W. Bartling, Associate Dean for Student Affairs and Admissions, 678-547-6232, Fax: 678-547-6063, E-mail: bartling_jw@mercer.edu.

Midwestern University, Downers Grove Campus, Chicago College of Pharmacy, Downers Grove, IL 60515-1235. Offers Pharm D. *Accreditation:* ACPE. Part-time programs available. Postbaccalaureate distance learning degree programs offered (minimal on-campus study). *Faculty:* 45 full-time (33 women), 22 part-time/adjunct (14 women). *Students:* 758 full-time (488 women), 54 part-time (35 women); includes 286 minority (23 African Americans, 2 American Indian/Alaska Native, 244 Asian Americans or Pacific Islanders, 17 Hispanic Americans), 13 international. Average age 25. 1,950 applicants, 20% accepted, 215 enrolled. In 2006, 153 degrees awarded. *Entrance requirements:* PCAT. *Application deadline:* For fall admission, 2/3 for domestic students. Application fee: $50. *Expenses: Contact institution. Financial support:* Federal Work-Study and institutionally sponsored loans available. Support available to part-time students. Financial award applicants required to submit FAFSA. *Unit head:* Dr. Mary W. L. Lee, Dean, 630-515-7311, E-mail: mleexx@midwestern.edu. *Application contact:* Michael Laken, Director of Admissions, 630-515-6148, Fax: 630-971-6086, E-mail: admissil@midwestern.edu.

Announcement: Midwestern University is committed to educating the health-care team of the new century. The University administers the Chicago College of Osteopathic Medicine, the Chicago College of Pharmacy, the College of Health Sciences, the Arizona College of Osteo-

Pharmacy

Midwestern University, Downers Grove Campus (continued)
pathic Medicine, and the College of Pharmacy–Glendale. The Chicago College of Pharmacy in Downers Grove, Illinois, offers the Doctor of Pharmacy (Pharm D) degree. As students complete the curriculum, they work closely with a small group of students and a faculty adviser, completing assignments and focusing on problem-solving skills. This small group approach gives a sense of the team-oriented health-care structure in which students will play an essential role after graduation. The College of Pharmacy in Glendale, Arizona, offers an accelerated three-year program featuring a modern curriculum and early introduction of clinical experiences. Contact the Office of Admissions, Midwestern University, 800-458-6253 (Downers Grove campus); 888-247-9277 (Glendale campus); e-mail: admissil@midwestern.edu (Downers Grove campus), admissaz@midwestern.edu (Glendale campus); WWW: http://www.midwestern.edu.

Midwestern University, Glendale Campus, College of Pharmacy-Glendale, Glendale, AZ 85308. Offers Pharm D. *Accreditation:* ACPE. *Faculty:* 22 full-time (12 women), 10 part-time/adjunct (5 women). *Students:* 392 full-time (208 women), 3 part-time (2 women); includes 92 minority (3 African Americans, 3 American Indian/Alaska Native, 68 Asian Americans or Pacific Islanders, 18 Hispanic Americans), 5 international. Average age 28. 1,505 applicants, 15% accepted, 130 enrolled. In 2006, 125 degrees awarded. *Entrance requirements:* PCAT. *Application deadline:* For fall admission, 2/1 for domestic students. Application fee: $50. *Expenses: Contact institution. Financial support:* Applicants required to submit FAFSA. *Unit head:* Dr. Anne Y. F. Lin, Dean, 623-572-3501. *Application contact:* James Walters, Director of Admissions, 888-247-9277, Fax: 623-572-3340, E-mail: admissaz@midwestern.edu.

Nova Southeastern University, Health Professions Division, College of Pharmacy, Fort Lauderdale, FL 33314-7796. Offers Pharm D. *Accreditation:* ACPE. Postbaccalaureate distance learning degree programs offered (minimal on-campus study). *Faculty:* 52 full-time (32 women), 9 part-time/adjunct (3 women). *Students:* 593 full-time (419 women), 61 part-time (48 women); includes 383 minority (41 African Americans, 1 American Indian/Alaska Native, 78 Asian Americans or Pacific Islanders, 263 Hispanic Americans), 4 international. Average age 25. 1,177 applicants, 22% accepted, 189 enrolled. In 2006, 173 degrees awarded. *Median time to degree:* 4 years full-time, 6 years part-time. *Degree requirements:* For first-professional, thesis (for some programs), comprehensive exam. *Entrance requirements:* PCAT. Additional exam requirements/recommendations for international students: Required—TOEFL (minimum score 550 paper-based; 213 computer-based). *Application deadline:* For fall admission, 3/1 for domestic students, 2/1 for international students. Applications are processed on a rolling basis. Application fee: $50. Electronic applications accepted. *Expenses: Contact institution. Financial support:* Career-related internships or fieldwork, Federal Work-Study, institutionally sponsored loans, and scholarships/grants available. Financial award application deadline: 4/15; financial award applicants required to submit FAFSA. *Faculty research:* Neovascularization, health care delivery, pharmacoeconomics, cardiovascular/metabolic metastasis. Total annual research expenditures: $526,388. *Unit head:* Dr. Andrés Malavé, Dean, 954-262-1300, Fax: 954-262-2278. *Application contact:* Tracy Templin, Admissions Counselor, 954-262-1112, Fax: 954-262-2282, E-mail: dpetracy@nsu.nova.edu.

Ohio Northern University, Raabe College of Pharmacy, Ada, OH 45810-1599. Offers Pharm D. Students enter the program as undergraduates. *Accreditation:* ACPE. Postbaccalaureate distance learning degree programs offered (no on-campus study). *Degree requirements:* For first-professional, 9 clinical rotations, capstone course. *Entrance requirements:* ACT or SAT. Electronic applications accepted. Expenses: Contact institution. *Faculty research:* Alcohol and substance abuse, women in pharmacy, non-traditional educations, continuing pharmaceutical education, medicinal chemistry.

The Ohio State University, College of Pharmacy, Professional Program in Pharmacy, Columbus, OH 43210. Offers Pharm D. *Accreditation:* ACPE. *Faculty:* 13 full-time (3 women), 1 part-time/adjunct (0 women). *Students:* 456 full-time (324 women); includes 58 minority (16 African Americans, 39 Asian Americans or Pacific Islanders, 3 Hispanic Americans), 10 international. Average age 23. 955 applicants, 15% accepted, 118 enrolled. In 2006, 111 degrees awarded. *Entrance requirements:* PCAT. Additional exam requirements/recommendations for international students: Required—TOEFL (minimum score 577 paper-based; 233 computer-based). *Application deadline:* For fall admission, 1/1 for domestic and international students. Applications are processed on a rolling basis. Application fee: $40 ($50 for international students). Electronic applications accepted. *Expenses:* Tuition, state resident: full-time $9,438. Tuition, nonresident: full-time $22,791. Tuition and fees vary according to course load, campus/location and program. *Financial support:* In 2006–07, 90 students received support. Career-related internships or fieldwork, Federal Work-Study, institutionally sponsored loans, and scholarships/grants available. Financial award application deadline: 3/1; financial award applicants required to submit FAFSA. *Faculty research:* Clinical pharmacokinetics, drug metabolism, critical care therapeutics, drug interactions, stereoselective drug dispositions. *Unit head:* Sylvan G. Frank, Associate Dean, 614-292-6343. *Application contact:* Heather Agresta, Director of Admissions, 614-292-5001, Fax: 614-292-6396, E-mail: admissions@dendrite.pharmacy.ohio-state.edu.

See Close-Up on page 2239.

Oregon State University, College of Pharmacy, Corvallis, OR 97331. Offers Pharm D, MAIS, MS, PhD. *Accreditation:* ACPE (one or more programs are accredited). Part-time programs available. *Faculty:* 35 full-time (16 women). *Students:* 351 full-time (205 women), 8 part-time (5 women); includes 122 minority (4 African Americans, 1 American Indian/Alaska Native, 103 Asian Americans or Pacific Islanders, 14 Hispanic Americans), 15 international. Average age 27. In 2006, 80 first professional degrees, 1 master's, 2 doctorates awarded. Terminal master's awarded for partial completion of doctoral program. *Degree requirements:* For master's and doctorate, thesis/dissertation. *Entrance requirements:* For master's, GRE General Test, minimum GPA of 3.0 in last 90 hours; for doctorate, GRE General Test, minimum GPA of 3.0 in last 90 hours, pre-pharmacy curriculum. Additional exam requirements/recommendations for international students: Required—TOEFL. *Application deadline:* For fall admission, 3/1 for domestic students. Applications are processed on a rolling basis. Application fee: $50. *Financial support:* Fellowships, research assistantships, teaching assistantships, career-related internships or fieldwork, Federal Work-Study, and institutionally sponsored loans available. Support available to part-time students. Financial award application deadline: 2/1. *Faculty research:* Pharmacology/toxicology, pharmacokinetics, biopharmaceutics, neuroscience, natural products. *Unit head:* Dr. Wayne A. Kradjan, Dean, 541-737-3424, Fax: 541-737-3424, E-mail: wayne.kradjan@orst.edu. *Application contact:* 541-737-5784, Fax: 541-737-3999.

Pacific University, School of Pharmacy, Forest Grove, OR 97116-1797. Offers Pharm D. *Faculty:* 10 full-time (3 women). *Students:* 68 full-time (32 women); includes 30 minority (4 African Americans, 24 Asian Americans or Pacific Islanders, 2 Hispanic Americans). Average age 27.*Expenses: Contact institution. Financial support:* In 2006–07, 68 students received support; fellowships, research assistantships, teaching assistantships, career-related internships or fieldwork and Federal Work-Study available. *Faculty research:* Informatics, enzyme metabolism, apostosis/cell cycle, neurophysiology of chronic pain, neurophysiology of Alzheimer's. *Unit head:* Dr. Robert Rosenow, Director, 503-352-7271. *Application contact:* Kent Steinmetz, Information Contact, 503-352-7225, Fax: 503-352-7290, E-mail: ksteinmetz@pacificu.edu.

Palm Beach Atlantic University, School of Pharmacy, West Palm Beach, FL 33416-4708. Offers Pharm D. *Accreditation:* ACPE. *Faculty:* 18 full-time (12 women), 4 part-time/adjunct (2 women). *Students:* 300 full-time (192 women), 19 part-time (10 women); includes 123 minority (20 African Americans, 1 American Indian/Alaska Native, 54 Asian Americans or Pacific Islanders, 48 Hispanic Americans), 15 international. Average age 27. 1,201 applicants, 15% accepted, 79 enrolled. In 2006, 45 degrees awarded. *Entrance requirements:* PCAT, minimum GPA of 2.5. Additional exam requirements/recommendations for international students: Required—TOEFL (minimum score 550 paper-based; 213 computer-based). *Application deadline:* For fall admission, 5/31 priority date for domestic and international students. Applications are processed on a rolling basis. Application fee: $50. Electronic applications accepted. *Expenses: Contact institution. Financial support:* Fellowships, unspecified assistantships available. *Unit head:* Dr. Daniel Brown, Dean, 561-803-2702, E-mail: daniel_brown@pba.edu. *Application contact:* Laura A. Leinweber, Director of Graduate and Evening Admissions, 888-468-6722, Fax: 561-803-2115, E-mail: grad@pba.edu.

Purdue University, College of Pharmacy and Pharmacal Sciences, Professional Program in Pharmacy and Pharmacal Sciences, West Lafayette, IN 47907. Offers Pharm D. *Accreditation:* ACPE. *Students:* 636 full-time (406 women), 12 part-time (8 women); includes 94 minority (34 African Americans, 48 Asian Americans or Pacific Islanders, 12 Hispanic Americans), 20 international. Average age 25. 755 applicants, 23% accepted, 2 enrolled. In 2006, 162 degrees awarded. *Entrance requirements:* Minimum 2 years of pre-pharmacy course work, interview. *Application deadline:* For fall admission, 12/1 for domestic and international students. Application fee: $55. *Expenses: Contact institution. Financial support:* Career-related internships or fieldwork, Federal Work-Study, and scholarships/grants available. Financial award application deadline: 3/15; financial award applicants required to submit FAFSA. *Faculty research:* Medicinal chemistry, pharmacology, pharmaceutics, clinical pharmacy, pharmacy administration. *Unit head:* Dr. G. Marc Loudon, Associate Dean, 765-494-1462, Fax: 765-494-7880, E-mail: marc.loudon@purdue.edu. *Application contact:* Brenda Stevens, Contact, 765-494-1357, Fax: 765-494-7880, E-mail: stevenbs@pharmacy.purdue.edu.

Rutgers, The State University of New Jersey, New Brunswick, Ernest Mario School of Pharmacy, New Brunswick, NJ 08901-1281. Offers Pharm D. *Accreditation:* ACPE. *Degree requirements:* For first-professional, one foreign language, registration. *Entrance requirements:* SAT or PCAT, interview, criminal background check. Additional exam requirements/recommendations for international students: Recommended—TOEFL (minimum score 550 paper-based; 213 computer-based). Electronic applications accepted. Expenses: Contact institution. *Faculty research:* Pharmacokinetics, cancer prevention, cardiology, neurology, pharmacodynamics.

St. John Fisher College, Office of the Provost, Wegmans School of Pharmacy, Pharmacy Program, Rochester, NY 14618-3597. Offers Pharm D. *Faculty:* 5 full-time (1 woman). *Students:* 55 full-time (23 women); includes 1 African American, 5 Asian Americans or Pacific Islanders. Average age 24. 216 applicants, 28% accepted, 55 enrolled. *Entrance requirements:* PCAT, 64 credits of specific undergraduate courses. Additional exam requirements/recommendations for international students: Required—TOEFL (minimum score 575 paper-based; 233 computer-based; 80 iBT). *Application deadline:* Applications are processed on a rolling basis. Application fee: $50. *Expenses: Contact institution. Faculty research:* Opioid pharmacology, heavy metal toxicology. *Application contact:* Jose J. Perales, Director of Pharmacy and Transfer Admissions, 585-385-8172, E-mail: jperales@ujfc.edu.

St. John's University, College of Pharmacy and Allied Health Professions, Professional Program in Pharmacy, Queens, NY 11439. Offers Pharm D. *Accreditation:* ACPE. *Students:* 451 full-time (333 women), 45 part-time (35 women); includes 294 minority (24 African Americans, 252 Asian Americans or Pacific Islanders, 18 Hispanic Americans), 16 international. Average age 33. 35 applicants, 20% accepted, 6 enrolled. In 2006, 191 degrees awarded. *Degree requirements:* For first-professional, 2-year residency. *Entrance requirements:* Bachelor's degree from an ACPE-accredited program or BS in pharmacy and license, clinical experience, interview. Additional exam requirements/recommendations for international students: Required—TOEFL (minimum score 500 paper-based; 173 computer-based). *Application deadline:* For fall admission, 4/1 for domestic students, 5/1 priority date for international students; for spring admission, 12/1 for domestic students, 11/1 priority date for international students. Applications are processed on a rolling basis. Application fee: $40. Electronic applications accepted. *Expenses: Contact institution.* Tuition and fees vary according to program. *Financial support:* Research assistantships, career-related internships or fieldwork and unspecified assistantships available. Support available to part-time students. Financial award application deadline: 3/1; financial award applicants required to submit FAFSA. *Faculty research:* Patient outcomes, drug-drug-infections, pharmacokinetics, pharmcodynamics. *Unit head:* Dr. Andrew Skirvin, Chair, 718-990-1417, E-mail: skirvinj@stjohns.edu. *Application contact:* Br. Shamus McGrenra, Senior Associate Director, Office of Admission, 718-990-1601, Fax: 718-990-2346, E-mail: gradhelp@stjohns.edu.

St. Louis College of Pharmacy, Professional Program in Pharmacy, St. Louis, MO 63110-1088. Offers Pharm D. *Accreditation:* ACPE. *Students:* 1,124 full-time (668 women); includes 181 minority (24 African Americans, 1 American Indian/Alaska Native, 147 Asian Americans or Pacific Islanders, 9 Hispanic Americans), 6 international. Average age 22. 538 applicants, 83% accepted, 297 enrolled. In 2006, 67 Pharm Ds awarded. *Median time to degree:* Of those who began their doctoral program in fall 1998, 70% received their degree in 8 years or less. *Entrance requirements:* ACT/PCAT, 2 letters of recommendation. Additional exam requirements/recommendations for international students: Required—TOEFL (minimum score 550 paper-based; 220 computer-based). *Application deadline:* For fall admission, 12/15 for domestic and international students; for spring admission, 2/1 for domestic and international students. Application fee: $50. Electronic applications accepted. *Financial support:* In 2006–07, 583 students received support. Federal Work-Study and scholarships/grants available. Financial award application deadline: 12/15; financial award applicants required to submit FAFSA. *Faculty research:* Geriatrics, cardiology, psychobiology, infectious diseases. *Unit head:* Penny Myers Bryant, Director of Admissions/Registrar, 314-446-8313, Fax: 314-446-8310, E-mail: pbryant@stlcop.edu.

Samford University, McWhorter School of Pharmacy, Birmingham, AL 35229-0002. Offers Pharm D. *Accreditation:* ACPE. Postbaccalaureate distance learning degree programs offered (minimal on-campus study). *Faculty:* 38 full-time (17 women). *Students:* 476 full-time (321 women), 13 part-time (8 women); includes 36 minority (17 African Americans, 2 American Indian/Alaska Native, 15 Asian Americans or Pacific Islanders, 2 Hispanic Americans), 5 international. Average age 24. 1,068 applicants, 12% accepted, 88 enrolled. In 2006, 104 degrees awarded. *Entrance requirements:* Minimum GPA of 2.75. Additional exam requirements/recommendations for international students: Required—TOEFL (minimum score 550 paper-based; 213 computer-based). *Application deadline:* For winter admission, 2/1 for domestic students. Applications are processed on a rolling basis. Application fee: $50. *Expenses: Contact institution.* One-time fee: $25 part-time. Full-time tuition and fees vary according to program and student level. *Financial support:* In 2006–07, 103 students received support. Career-related internships or fieldwork, Federal Work-Study, and institutionally sponsored loans available. Financial award application deadline: 5/2; financial award applicants required to submit FAFSA. *Faculty research:* Biotechnology, transdermal drug delivery, vaccines, human skin models, genetic mapping of disease. *Unit head:* Dr. Bobby G. Bryant, Dean, 205-726-2820, Fax: 205-726-2759, E-mail: bgbryant@samford.edu. *Application contact:* C. Bruce Foster, Assistant Dean for Student/Alumni Affairs, 205-726-2053, Fax: 205-726-2759, E-mail: cbfoster@samford.edu.

Shenandoah University, School of Pharmacy, Winchester, VA 22601-5195. Offers pharmacy and non-traditional pharmacy (Pharm D). *Accreditation:* ACPE. Part-time programs available. Postbaccalaureate distance learning degree programs offered (minimal on-campus study). *Faculty:* 18 full-time (6 women). *Students:* 299 full-time (180 women), 108 part-time (61 women); includes 13 minority (3 African Americans, 8 Asian Americans or Pacific Islanders, 2 Hispanic Americans), 5 international. Average age 30. 1,285 applicants, 14% accepted, 112 enrolled. In 2006, 126 degrees awarded. *Entrance requirements:* PCAT, interview, minimum GPA of 2.5, 3 letters of recommendation. Additional exam requirements/recommendations for international students: Required—TOEFL (minimum score 527 paper-based; 197 computer-based; 71 iBT). *Application deadline:* For fall admission, 2/1 for domestic and international students. Applications are processed on a rolling basis. Application fee: $30. Electronic applications accepted. *Expenses: Contact institution.* Full-time tuition and fees vary according to course load and program. *Financial support:* In 2006–07, 306 students received support.

Institutionally sponsored loans and scholarships/grants available. Support available to part-time students. Financial award application deadline: 3/15; financial award applicants required to submit FAFSA. *Faculty research:* Informatics, medical information systems, biotechnology, clinical practice, managed care, drug metabolism, outcomes research, clinical trials, medications and complaints, promotion of pharmaceutical services. Total annual research expenditures: $15,644. *Unit head:* Dr. Alan McKay, Dean, 540-665-1280, Fax: 540-665-1283, E-mail: amckay@su.edu. *Application contact:* David Anthony, Dean of Admissions, 540-665-4581, Fax: 540-665-4627, E-mail: admit@su.edu.

South Dakota State University, Graduate School, College of Pharmacy, Professional Program in Pharmacy, Brookings, SD 57007. Offers Pharm D. *Accreditation:* ACPE. *Faculty:* 8 full-time (0 women). *Students:* 260 full-time (174 women); includes 2 minority (both American Indian/Alaska Native). 304 applicants, 23% accepted, 70 enrolled. In 2006, 56 degrees awarded. *Entrance requirements:* ACT or PCAT, bachelor's degree in pharmacy. Additional exam requirements/recommendations for international students: Required—TOEFL (minimum score 550 paper-based; 213 computer-based). *Application deadline:* For fall admission, 2/1 for domestic and international students. Applications are processed on a rolling basis. Application fee: $35. *Financial support:* Application deadline: 3/1. *Faculty research:* Geriatric medicine, drugs of abuse, anti-cancer drugs, drug metabolism, sustained drug delivery. *Unit head:* Dr. Brian Kaatz, Dean, 605-688-6197, Fax: 605-688-6232, E-mail: brian.kaatz@sdstate.edu. *Application contact:* Dr. Joel Houglum, Assistant Dean, 605-688-4238, Fax: 605-688-6232, E-mail: joel.houglum@sdstate.edu.

Southern Illinois University Edwardsville, School of Pharmacy, Edwardsville, IL 62026-0001. Offers Pharm D. *Faculty:* 13 full-time (3 women). *Students:* 161 full-time (91 women); includes 24 minority (8 African Americans, 13 Asian Americans or Pacific Islanders, 3 Hispanic Americans). 463 applicants, 19% accepted. *Entrance requirements:* PCAT. *Application deadline:* For fall admission, 12/1 for domestic and international students. Application fee: $40. *Unit head:* Dr. Philip J. Medon, Head.

South University, Graduate Programs, School of Pharmacy, Savannah, GA 31406-4805. Offers Pharm D. *Accreditation:* ACPE.

See Close-Up on page 2241.

Southwestern Oklahoma State University, College of Pharmacy, Weatherford, OK 73096-3098. Offers Pharm D. *Accreditation:* ACPE. *Entrance requirements:* PCAT.

Temple University, Health Sciences Center, School of Pharmacy, Professional Program in Pharmacy, Philadelphia, PA 19122-6096. Offers Pharm D. *Accreditation:* ACPE. *Students:* 540 full-time (322 women); includes 339 minority (126 African Americans, 3 American Indian/Alaska Native, 207 Asian Americans or Pacific Islanders, 3 Hispanic Americans), 13 international. 719 applicants, 27% accepted, 150 enrolled. In 2006, 110 degrees awarded. *Expenses:* Contact institution. Tuition and fees vary according to program. *Unit head:* Dr. Daniel Canney, Director of Graduate Studies, 215-707-4948, E-mail: canney@temple.edu.

Texas Southern University, College of Pharmacy and Health Sciences, Houston, TX 77004-4584. Offers Pharm D, MHCA. *Accreditation:* ACPE. Postbaccalaureate distance learning degree programs offered. *Faculty:* 8 full-time (5 women), 9 part-time/adjunct (4 women). *Students:* 325 full-time (199 women), 224 part-time (138 women); includes 464 minority (288 African Americans, 134 Asian Americans or Pacific Islanders, 42 Hispanic Americans), 54 international. Average age 29. 127 applicants, 100% accepted, 118 enrolled. In 2006, 90 degrees awarded. *Entrance requirements:* For Pharm D, GRE General Test, PCAT; for master's, PCAT. *Application deadline:* For fall admission, 3/15 for domestic students. Application fee: $50 ($75 for international students). *Financial support:* Fellowships, teaching assistantships, career-related internships or fieldwork, scholarships/grants, and tuition waivers (partial) available. Financial award application deadline: 5/1; financial award applicants required to submit FAFSA. *Faculty research:* Basic and clinical pharmacokinetics, metabolism studies, diabetes, hypertension, sickle cell. *Unit head:* Dr. Barbara Hayes, Dean, 713-313-7164, Fax: 713-313-1091. *Application contact:* LaJoy Kay, Head, 713-313-1880.

Thomas Jefferson University, Jefferson College of Health Professions, School of Pharmacy, Philadelphia, PA 19107. Offers Pharm D. *Expenses:* Tuition: Full-time $15,340; part-time $790 per credit. Required fees: $300. *Unit head:* Rebecca S. Finley, Dean, 215-955-6300.

See Close-Up on page 2245.

Touro University College of Osteopathic Medicine, Professional Program, Vallejo, CA 94592. Offers education (MA); osteopathic medicine (DO); pharmacy (Pharm D); physician assistant studies (MS); public health (MPH). *Accreditation:* AOsA; ARC-PA. *Faculty:* 61 full-time (26 women), 30 part-time/adjunct (16 women). *Students:* 950 full-time (579 women); includes 354 minority (39 African Americans, 5 American Indian/Alaska Native, 258 Asian Americans or Pacific Islanders, 52 Hispanic Americans). Average age 26. 2,113 applicants, 13% accepted, 269 enrolled. In 2006, 109 first professional degrees, 43 master's awarded. *Median time to degree:* Of those who began their doctoral program in fall 1998, 98% received their degree in 8 years or less. *Entrance requirements:* For first professional degree and master's, BS/BA. *Application deadline:* For fall admission, 6/1 for domestic students. Applications are processed on a rolling basis. Application fee: $100. Electronic applications accepted. *Financial support:* In 2006–07, 3 fellowships (averaging $3,000 per year) were awarded. *Faculty research:* Diabetes, heart disease. *Application contact:* Steve Davis, Admissions Counselor, 707-638-5527, Fax: 707-638-5270, E-mail: sdavis@touro.edu.

Universidad de Ciencias Medicas, Graduate Programs, San Jose, Costa Rica. Offers health of administration (MHA); medical and surgery (MD); pharmacy (Pharm D). Part-time programs available. *Faculty:* 36 full-time (11 women), 250 part-time/adjunct (66 women). *Students:* 1,224 full-time (791 women); includes 1,131 Hispanic Americans. Average age 21. 403 applicants, 100% accepted, 293 enrolled. *Median time to degree:* Of those who began their doctoral program in fall 1998, 40% received their degree in 8 years or less. *Entrance requirements:* For first professional degree, admissions test; for master's, MD or bachelors degree. *Application deadline:* For winter admission, 1/6 priority date for domestic and international students; for spring admission, 7/6 priority date for domestic and international students. *Financial support:* In 2006–07, 150 students received support. Institutionally sponsored loans and scholarships/grants available. Financial award application deadline: 10/1; financial award applicants required to submit FAFSA. *Unit head:* Dr. Misael Chinchilla, President of Academic Affairs, 506-296-3944 Ext. 147, Fax: 506-231-4368, E-mail: chinchillacm@ucimed.com. *Application contact:* Lic. Karol Còrdoba, Assistant of Program of International, 506-296-3944 Ext. 158, Fax: 506-290-6116, E-mail: cordobaak@ucimed.com.

University at Buffalo, the State University of New York, Graduate School, School of Pharmacy and Pharmaceutical Sciences, Professional Program in Pharmacy, Buffalo, NY 14260. Offers Pharm D, Pharm D/JD, Pharm D/MBA. *Accreditation:* ACPE. *Faculty:* 22 full-time (8 women), 6 part-time/adjunct (3 women). *Students:* 341 full-time (209 women), 3 part-time (all women); includes 68 minority (11 African Americans, 52 Asian Americans or Pacific Islanders, 5 Hispanic Americans), 18 international. Average age 26. 1,375 applicants, 9% accepted, 124 enrolled. In 2006, 112 degrees awarded. *Degree requirements:* For first-professional, project. *Entrance requirements:* PCAT. Additional exam requirements/recommendations for international students: Required—TOEFL (minimum score 550 paper-based; 213 computer-based). *Application deadline:* For fall admission, 2/1 priority date for domestic and international students. Applications are processed on a rolling basis. Application fee: $50. Electronic applications accepted. *Financial support:* Fellowships with full tuition reimbursements, Federal Work-Study, scholarships/grants, and unspecified assistantships available. Financial award application deadline: 2/28; financial award applicants required to submit FAFSA. *Faculty research:* Pharmacokinetics, pharmacoepidemiology, AIDS, renal transplant, Attention Deficit Hyperactivity Disorder (ADHD), HIV/AIDS, oncology, critical care, PKPD, renal transplantation. Total annual research expenditures: $2.2 million. *Unit head:* Dr. Gene Morse, Chairman, 716-645-2828, Fax: 716-645-2886, E-mail: emorse@acsu.buffalo.edu. *Application contact:* Cindy F. Konovitz, Assistant Dean, 716-645-2825, Fax: 716-645-3688, E-mail: pharm-admin@acsu.buffalo.edu.

University of Alberta, Faculty of Graduate Studies and Research, Faculty of Pharmacy and Pharmaceutical Sciences, Edmonton, AB T6G 2E1, Canada. Offers M Sc, PhD. *Faculty:* 35. *Students:* 47. Average age 30. 562 applicants, 2% accepted, 11 enrolled. In 2006, 3 master's, 5 doctorates awarded. Terminal master's awarded for partial completion of doctoral program. *Degree requirements:* For master's and doctorate, thesis/dissertation. *Entrance requirements:* Additional exam requirements/recommendations for international students: Required—Michigan English Language Assessment Battery or IELTS. *Application deadline:* For fall admission, 6/1 for international students; for winter admission, 9/15 for international students. Applications are processed on a rolling basis. Electronic applications accepted. *Financial support:* In 2006–07, 13 students received support, including 6 teaching assistantships; research assistantships, tuition waivers (partial) also available. *Faculty research:* Radiopharmacy, pharmacokinetics, bionucleonics, medicinal chemistry, microbiology. Total annual research expenditures: $2 million. *Unit head:* Dr. Franco M. Pasutto, Dean, 780-492-0204, E-mail: fpasutto@pharmacy.ualberta.ca. *Application contact:* Dr. Edward E. Knaus, Director of Graduate Affairs, 780-492-5993, Fax: 780-492-1217.

The University of Arizona, Graduate College, College of Pharmacy, Program in Pharmacy, Tucson, AZ 85721. Offers Pharm D, MS, PhD. *Accreditation:* ACPE (one or more programs are accredited). Part-time programs available. Terminal master's awarded for partial completion of doctoral program. *Degree requirements:* For master's and doctorate, thesis/dissertation. *Entrance requirements:* For master's and doctorate, GRE General Test, minimum GPA of 3.0. Additional exam requirements/recommendations for international students: Required—TOEFL. *Faculty research:* Health/service administrative pharmacy education, geriatric pharmacy, social and behavioral pharmacy management and economics.

University of Arkansas for Medical Sciences, College of Pharmacy, Little Rock, AR 72205-7199. Offers Pharm D, MS. *Accreditation:* ACPE (one or more programs are accredited). *Students:* 384 full-time, 8 part-time. *Degree requirements:* For master's, thesis. Application fee: $0. *Expenses:* Contact institution. *Financial support:* Research assistantships available. Support available to part-time students. *Unit head:* Dr. Stephanie Gardner, Dean, 501-686-5558. *Application contact:* Dr. Kim Light, Information Contact, 501-686-5557.

The University of British Columbia, Faculty of Graduate Studies, Faculty of Pharmaceutical Sciences, Vancouver, BC V6T 1Z1, Canada. Offers Pharm D, M Sc, PhD. *Faculty:* 30 full-time (9 women), 26 part-time/adjunct (11 women). *Students:* 40 full-time (10 women). Average age 28. 61 applicants, 36% accepted, 19 enrolled. In 2006, 8 first professional degrees, 4 master's, 4 doctorates awarded. *Median time to degree:* Of those who began their doctoral program in fall 1998, 100% received their degree in 8 years or less. *Degree requirements:* For master's, thesis/dissertation, seminar; for doctorate, thesis/dissertation, seminar, comprehensive exam. *Entrance requirements:* B Sc in pharmacy, Canadian pharmacy license, interview. Additional exam requirements/recommendations for international students: Required—TOEFL (minimum score 600 paper-based; 250 computer-based; 100 iBT). *Application deadline:* For fall admission, 3/15 for domestic students, 2/15 for international students; for spring admission, 4/1 for domestic students. Applications are processed on a rolling basis. Application fee: $90 Canadian dollars ($150 Canadian dollars for international students). Electronic applications accepted. *Financial support:* In 2006–07, fellowships (averaging $16,000 per year), 24 research assistantships (averaging $17,000 per year), 17 teaching assistantships (averaging $10,100 per year) were awarded; career-related internships or fieldwork, institutionally sponsored loans, scholarships/grants, traineeships, health care benefits, tuition waivers (full and partial), and unspecified assistantships also available. *Faculty research:* Biopharmaceutics, pharmaceutical chemistry, pharmacology, toxicology, formulation. Total annual research expenditures: $4.4 million Canadian dollars. *Unit head:* Dr. Robert D. Sindelar, Dean, 604-822-2343, Fax: 604-822-3035, E-mail: sindelar@interchange.ubc.ca. *Application contact:* Dr. Barb Conway, Research Grants Facilitator and Graduate Program Coordinator, 604-822-2390, Fax: 604-822-3035, E-mail: baconway@interchange.ubc.ca.

University of California, San Diego, School of Pharmacy and Pharmaceutical Sciences, La Jolla, CA 92093. Offers Pharm D.

University of California, San Francisco, School of Pharmacy, Program in Pharmacy, San Francisco, CA 94143. Offers Pharm D. *Accreditation:* ACPE. *Students:* 488 full-time (365 women); includes 294 minority (10 African Americans, 4 American Indian/Alaska Native, 257 Asian Americans or Pacific Islanders, 23 Hispanic Americans). Average age 25. 1,248 applicants, 10% accepted, 122 enrolled. In 2006, 122 degrees awarded. *Degree requirements:* For first-professional, supervised practice experience. *Entrance requirements:* 2 years of preparatory course work in basic sciences. *Application deadline:* For fall admission, 11/1 for domestic and international students. Application fee: $60 ($80 for international students). Electronic applications accepted. *Financial support:* In 2006–07, 431 students received support; fellowships, research assistantships, teaching assistantships, career-related internships or fieldwork, Federal Work-Study, institutionally sponsored loans, scholarships/grants, and tuition waivers (partial) available. Financial award application deadline: 2/1; financial award applicants required to submit FAFSA. *Faculty research:* Drug delivery, drug metabolism and chemical toxicology, macromolecular structure, molecular parasitology, pharmacokinetics. *Application contact:* Cynthia Watchmaker, Assistant Dean and Director Student Affairs, 415-476-2732, Fax: 415-476-6805, E-mail: osaca@pharmacy.ucsf.edu.

University of Charleston, Robert C. Byrd School of Pharmacy, Charleston, WV 25304-1099. Offers Pharm D. *Faculty:* 16 full-time (9 women). *Students:* 79 full-time (44 women); includes 3 African Americans, 10 Asian Americans or Pacific Islanders. Average age 25. 348 applicants, 40% accepted, 79 enrolled. *Entrance requirements:* PCAT. Application fee: $50. *Financial support:* In 2006–07, 74 students received support. Application deadline: 3/1. *Unit head:* Dr. Richard E. Stull, Dean, School of Pharmacy, 304-357-4858. *Application contact:* Betsy Sager, Administrative Assistant, 304-357-4879, E-mail: richardstull@ucwv.edu.

University of Cincinnati, Division of Research and Advanced Studies, College of Pharmacy, Division of Pharmacy Practice, Cincinnati, OH 45221. Offers Pharm D. *Accreditation:* ACPE. *Entrance requirements:* GRE General Test, BS in pharmacy or equivalent, minimum GPA of 3.0. Additional exam requirements/recommendations for international students: Required—TOEFL.

University of Colorado at Denver and Health Sciences Center, School of Pharmacy, Denver, CO 80217-3364. Offers pharmacy (Pharm D, PhD), including pharmaceutical sciences (PhD), toxicology (PhD). *Accreditation:* ACPE (one or more programs are accredited). *Students:* 505 full-time (354 women), 8 part-time (5 women); includes 158 minority (33 African Americans, 3 American Indian/Alaska Native, 90 Asian Americans or Pacific Islanders, 32 Hispanic Americans), 4 international. Average age 29. 1,630 applicants, 12% accepted, 131 enrolled. In 2006, 143 degrees awarded. *Entrance requirements:* Minimum GPA of 2.75 in pre-pharmacy course work, 3 letters of recommendation. Additional exam requirements/recommendations for international students: Required—TOEFL (minimum score 550 paper-based; 213 computer-based). *Application deadline:* For fall admission, 12/1 for domestic students. Application fee: $50. *Expenses:* Contact institution. *Financial support:* Fellowships, research assistantships, teaching assistantships, career-related internships or fieldwork, Federal Work-Study, and institutionally sponsored loans available. Support available to part-time students. Financial award application deadline: 3/15; financial award applicants required to submit FAFSA. *Faculty research:* Antiviral clinical pharmacology, beriatric pharmacology, pharmacoepidemiology, pharmacogenomics, smoking cessation. *Unit head:* Ralpha Altiere, Dean, 303-315-5055. *Application contact:* Beverly Brunson, Director, 303-315-6100.

University of Connecticut, Graduate School, School of Pharmacy, Professional Program in Pharmacy, Storrs, CT 06269. Offers Pharm D. *Unit head:* Jenna Henderson, Head, 860-486-2216, E-mail: jenna.henderson@uconn.edu.

Pharmacy

University of Florida, College of Pharmacy, Professional Program in Pharmacy, Gainesville, FL 32611. Offers Pharm D, MBA/Pharm D, Pharm D/MPA, Pharm D/MPH, Pharm D/PhD. *Accreditation:* ACPE. Part-time programs available. Postbaccalaureate distance learning degree programs offered (no on-campus study). *Students:* 671 full-time (428 women); includes 164 minority (31 African Americans, 83 Asian Americans or Pacific Islanders, 50 Hispanic Americans), 60 international. 623 applicants, 53% accepted, 274 enrolled. In 2006, 114 degrees awarded. *Entrance requirements:* PCAT, minimum GPA of 2.5. Additional exam requirements/recommendations for international students: Required—TOEFL. *Application deadline:* For fall admission, 3/1 for domestic and international students. Applications are processed on a rolling basis. Application fee: $20. Electronic applications accepted. *Expenses:* Tuition, state resident: full-time $6,827. Tuition, nonresident: full-time $21,951. Required fees: $999. *Financial support:* In 2006–07, 18 fellowships (averaging $19,637 per year), 8 research assistantships (averaging $15,982 per year), 35 teaching assistantships (averaging $13,197 per year) were awarded; Federal Work-Study and institutionally sponsored loans also available. Support available to part-time students. Financial award applicants required to submit FAFSA. *Faculty research:* Drug discovery, drug delivery, pharmacodynamics, socioeconomics of pharmacy, neurobiology of aging. *Unit head:* Dr. Michael W. McKenzie, Associate Dean for Professional Affairs, 352-273-6217, Fax: 352-273-6219, E-mail: mckenzie@cop.ufl.edu.

University of Georgia, College of Pharmacy, Professional Program in Pharmacy, Athens, GA 30602. Offers Pharm D. *Accreditation:* ACPE. *Students:* 510 full-time (323 women), 37 part-time (31 women); includes 96 minority (32 African Americans, 61 Asian Americans or Pacific Islanders, 3 Hispanic Americans), 6 international. In 2006, 113 degrees awarded. *Application contact:* Barbara Smith, Admissions Secretary, 706-542-5278, Fax: 706-542-5269, E-mail: bsmith@mail.rx.uga.edu.

University of Houston, College of Pharmacy, Houston, TX 77204. Offers hospital pharmacy (MSPHR); medical chemistry and pharmacology (MS); pharmaceutics (MS, PhD); pharmacology (MS, PhD); pharmacy (Pharm D); pharmacy administration (MSPHR). *Accreditation:* ACPE. Part-time programs available. *Faculty:* 15 full-time (4 women), 17 part-time/adjunct (9 women). *Students:* 500 full-time (335 women), 31 part-time (23 women); includes 260 minority (25 African Americans, 192 Asian Americans or Pacific Islanders, 43 Hispanic Americans), 55 international. Average age 25. 573 applicants, 27% accepted, 149 enrolled. In 2006, 106 first professional degrees, 6 master's, 4 doctorates awarded. Terminal master's awarded for partial completion of doctoral program. *Degree requirements:* For master's and doctorate, thesis/dissertation. *Entrance requirements:* For Pharm D, PCAT, interview; for master's and doctorate, GRE General Test. Additional exam requirements/recommendations for international students: Required—TOEFL. *Application deadline:* For spring admission, 3/1 for domestic students. Applications are processed on a rolling basis. Application fee: $25 ($75 for international students). *Expenses:* Tuition, state resident: full-time $5,429; part-time $226 per credit. Tuition, nonresident: full-time $12,029; part-time $501 per credit. Required fees: $2,454. *Financial support:* In 2006–07, 6 research assistantships with full tuition reimbursements (averaging $14,200 per year), 35 teaching assistantships with full tuition reimbursements (averaging $14,200 per year) were awarded; fellowships with full tuition reimbursements, career-related internships or fieldwork, Federal Work-Study, institutionally sponsored loans, scholarships/grants, health care benefits, and unspecified assistantships also available. Support available to part-time students. Financial award application deadline: 3/10. *Faculty research:* Cardiovascular and renal pharmacology, cellular pharmacology, drug delivery systems, geriatrics, pharmacokinetics, pharmacoeconomics, pharmaceutical marketing, pharmaceutical management, behavioral pharmacy, and signal transduction. Total annual research expenditures: $1.3 million. *Unit head:* Dr. Sunny Ohia, Dean, 713-743-1253, Fax: 713-743-1259, E-mail: seohia@uh.edu. *Application contact:* Shara Zatopek, Assistant Dean for Admissions, 713-743-1262, Fax: 713-743-1259, E-mail: szatopek@uh.edu.

University of Illinois at Chicago, College of Pharmacy, Academic Programs, College of Pharmacy, Chicago, IL 60607-7128. Offers Pharm D. *Accreditation:* ACPE. *Entrance requirements:* PCAT.

University of Illinois at Chicago, College of Pharmacy, Center for Pharmaceutical Biotechnology, Chicago, IL 60607-7173. Offers MS, PhD.

The University of Iowa, College of Pharmacy, Iowa City, IA 52242-1316. Offers MS, PhD, Pharm D/MPH. *Accreditation:* ACPE (one or more programs are accredited). *Faculty:* 27 full-time, 314 part-time/adjunct. *Students:* 42 full-time (20 women), 36 part-time (9 women); includes 7 minority (2 African Americans, 1 Asian American or Pacific Islander, 4 Hispanic Americans), 46 international. 158 applicants, 18% accepted, 12 enrolled. In 2006, 3 master's, 9 doctorates awarded. *Degree requirements:* For master's, exam, thesis optional; for doctorate, thesis/dissertation, comprehensive exam, registration. *Entrance requirements:* For master's and doctorate, GRE General Test, minimum GPA of 3.0. Additional exam requirements/recommendations for international students: Required—TOEFL (minimum score 550 paper-based; 213 computer-based; 81 iBT). *Application deadline:* For fall admission, 2/1 priority date for domestic and international students; for spring admission, 8/1 for domestic students, 8/1 priority date for international students. Applications are processed on a rolling basis. Application fee: $60 ($85 for international students). Electronic applications accepted. *Financial support:* In 2006–07, 6 fellowships, 50 research assistantships with partial tuition reimbursements, 22 teaching assistantships with partial tuition reimbursements were awarded. Financial award application deadline: 2/1; financial award applicants required to submit FAFSA. *Unit head:* Jordan Cohen, Dean, 319-335-8794, Fax: 319-353-5594.

University of Kentucky, College of Pharmacy, Professional Program in Pharmacy, Lexington, KY 40506-0032. Offers Pharm D. *Accreditation:* ACPE. *Faculty:* 71 full-time (26 women), 23 part-time/adjunct (9 women). *Students:* 457 full-time (289 women); includes 30 minority (14 African Americans, 16 Asian Americans or Pacific Islanders), 5 international. Average age 23. 809 applicants, 16% accepted, 130 enrolled. In 2006, 93 degrees awarded. *Entrance requirements:* PCAT, interview, minimum GPA of 2.5. Additional exam requirements/recommendations for international students: Required—TOEFL (minimum score 550 paper-based; 213 computer-based). *Application deadline:* For fall admission, 1/1 for domestic and international students. Applications are processed on a rolling basis. Application fee: $75. *Expenses: Contact institution. Financial support:* In 2006–07, 366 students received support, including 130 fellowships (averaging $1,300 per year); career-related internships or fieldwork, Federal Work-Study, institutionally sponsored loans, and scholarships/grants also available. Financial award application deadline: 9/15; financial award applicants required to submit FAFSA. *Faculty research:* Cardiology, pharmacokinetics, pediatrics, critical care, nutrition, infectious disease. Total annual research expenditures: $18,703. *Unit head:* Dr. William C. Lubawy, Associate Dean for Academic Affairs, 859-257-5304, Fax: 859-257-7297, E-mail: lubawy@email.uky.edu. *Application contact:* Hope Bertram, Professional Admissions Coordinator, 859-257-5303 Ext. 81313, Fax: 859-323-2979, E-mail: hbert2@uky.edu.

University of Louisiana at Monroe, Graduate Studies and Research, College of Pharmacy, Program in Pharmacy, Monroe, LA 71209-0001. Offers Pharm D, PhD. *Accreditation:* ACPE. *Students:* 458 full-time (291 women), 15 part-time (13 women); includes 81 minority (22 African Americans, 3 American Indian/Alaska Native, 53 Asian Americans or Pacific Islanders, 3 Hispanic Americans), 41 international. Average age 24. In 2006, 79 first professional degrees, 11 doctorates awarded. *Degree requirements:* For doctorate, thesis/dissertation. *Entrance requirements:* For doctorate, GRE General Test or GMAT. *Application deadline:* For fall admission, 5/1 priority date for domestic students. Applications are processed on a rolling basis. Application fee: $20 ($30 for international students). *Expenses:* Tuition, state resident: part-time $124 per credit hour. Tuition, nonresident: part-time $124 per credit hour. *Financial support:* Research assistantships, unspecified assistantships available. Financial award application deadline: 5/1. *Unit head:* Dr. F. Lamar Pritchard, Dean, 318-342-1600, Fax: 318-342-1606, E-mail: Pritchard@ulm.edu.

University of Maryland, Baltimore, Graduate School, Graduate Programs in Pharmacy, Baltimore, MD 21201. Offers pharmaceutical health service research (MS, PhD), including epidemiology (MS), pharmacy administration (PhD); pharmaceutical sciences (PhD); Pharm D/PhD. *Accreditation:* ACPE (one or more programs are accredited). Part-time programs available. *Faculty:* 41 full-time (13 women). *Students:* Average age 28. *Degree requirements:* For doctorate, thesis/dissertation, comprehensive exam (for some programs). *Entrance requirements:* Additional exam requirements/recommendations for international students: Required—TOEFL (minimum score 550 paper-based; 215 computer-based), IELTS. *Application deadline:* Applications are processed on a rolling basis. Electronic applications accepted. *Financial support:* Fellowships with full tuition reimbursements, research assistantships with full tuition reimbursements, teaching assistantships with full tuition reimbursements available. Support available to part-time students. *Faculty research:* Health behavior, clinical and biological chemistry, pharmaceutical policy, pharmaceutical sciences. Total annual research expenditures: $14.1 million. *Unit head:* Dr. Ilene H. Zuckerman, Associate Dean for Research and Graduate Studies, 410-706-3266, Fax: 410-706-1488, E-mail: izuckerm@rx.umaryland.edu. *Application contact:* Dr. Malinda B. Orlin, Dean of the Graduate School, 410-706-1850, Fax: 410-706-0234, E-mail: mborlin@umaryland.edu.

University of Maryland, Baltimore, Professional Program in Pharmacy, Baltimore, MD 21201. Offers Pharm D, JD/Pharm D, Pharm D/MBA, Pharm D/MPH, Pharm D/PhD. *Accreditation:* ACPE. *Faculty:* 66 full-time (15 women), 585 part-time/adjunct (158 women). *Students:* 478 full-time (300 women), 3 part-time (1 woman); includes 209 minority (62 African Americans, 1 American Indian/Alaska Native, 133 Asian Americans or Pacific Islanders, 13 Hispanic Americans), 20 international. Average age 24. 1,400 applicants, 11% accepted, 120 enrolled. In 2006, 122 degrees awarded. *Median time to degree:* 4 years full-time. *Entrance requirements:* PCAT, 63 hours in pre-pharmacy course work, on-site interview. Additional exam requirements/recommendations for international students: Required—TOEFL (minimum score 550 paper-based; 213 computer-based). *Application deadline:* For fall admission, 12/1 for domestic and international students. Application fee: $35. Electronic applications accepted. *Financial support:* In 2006–07, 435 students received support. Career-related internships or fieldwork, Federal Work-Study, institutionally sponsored loans, and scholarships/grants available. Support available to part-time students. Financial award application deadline: 3/1; financial award applicants required to submit FAFSA. *Faculty research:* Pharmaceutics, molecular biology, pharmacology, pharmacoepidemiology, pharmocoeconomics. Total annual research expenditures: $14.1 million. *Unit head:* Dr. Jill Morgan, Associate Dean for Student Affairs, 410-706-4332, Fax: 410-706-2158, E-mail: jmorgan@rx.umaryland.edu. *Application contact:* Admissions Office, 410-706-7653, Fax: 410-706-2158, E-mail: pharmdhelp@umaryland.edu.

University of Michigan, College of Pharmacy, Professional Program in Pharmacy, Ann Arbor, MI 48109. Offers Pharm D, Pharm D/PhD. *Accreditation:* ACPE. *Entrance requirements:* PCAT.

University of Minnesota, Twin Cities Campus, College of Pharmacy, Professional Program in Pharmacy, Minneapolis, MN 55455-0213. Offers Pharm D. *Accreditation:* ACPE. *Degree requirements:* For first-professional, paper and seminar presentation. *Entrance requirements:* 2 years of pharmacy-related course work. *Expenses:* Tuition, state resident: full-time $9,302; part-time $775 per credit. Tuition, nonresident: full-time $16,400; part-time $1,367 per credit. Full-time tuition and fees vary according to class time, course load, program, reciprocity agreements and student level.

University of Mississippi, Graduate School, School of Pharmacy, Professional Program in Pharmacy, Oxford, University, MS 38677. Offers Pharm D. *Accreditation:* ACPE. *Faculty:* 17 full-time (8 women), 5 part-time/adjunct (2 women). *Students:* 156 full-time (107 women), 2 part-time (1 woman); includes 15 minority (4 African Americans, 10 Asian Americans or Pacific Islanders, 1 Hispanic American). 76 applicants, 97% accepted, 72 enrolled. In 2006, 67 degrees awarded. *Application deadline:* For fall admission, 4/1 for domestic students. Applications are processed on a rolling basis. Application fee: $25. *Expenses: Contact institution. Financial support:* Scholarships/grants available. Financial award application deadline: 3/1; financial award applicants required to submit FAFSA. *Unit head:* Dr. Barbara G. Wells, Dean, School of Pharmacy, 662-915-7265, Fax: 662-915-5704, E-mail: pharmacy@olemiss.edu.

University of Missouri–Kansas City, School of Pharmacy, Kansas City, MO 64110-2499. Offers pharmaceutical sciences (MS, PhD); pharmacy (Pharm D). *Accreditation:* ACPE (one or more programs are accredited). Postbaccalaureate distance learning degree programs offered (minimal on-campus study). *Faculty:* 34 full-time (17 women), 11 part-time/adjunct (4 women). *Students:* 238 full-time (159 women), 5 part-time (2 women); includes 30 minority (10 African Americans, 1 American Indian/Alaska Native, 17 Asian Americans or Pacific Islanders, 2 Hispanic Americans), 7 international. Average age 26. 567 applicants, 39% accepted, 213 enrolled. In 2006, 77 first professional degrees, 3 master's awarded. *Degree requirements:* For Pharm D, registration; for master's, thesis, comprehensive exam (for some programs), registration. *Entrance requirements:* For Pharm D, PCAT, interview, minimum GPA of 2.5, specified pre-pharmacy course work; for master's, GRE General Test, minimum undergraduate GPA of 3.0, graduate 3.5, 3 letters of reference. Additional exam requirements/recommendations for international students: Required—TOEFL (minimum score 580 paper-based). *Application deadline:* For fall admission, 3/1 for domestic students; for spring admission, 10/1 for domestic students. Applications are processed on a rolling basis. Application fee: $35 ($50 for international students). Electronic applications accepted. *Expenses: Contact institution. Financial support:* In 2006–07, 2 fellowships (averaging $28,200 per year), 17 research assistantships with full and partial tuition reimbursements (averaging $13,800 per year), 10 teaching assistantships with full tuition reimbursements (averaging $12,819 per year) were awarded; career-related internships or fieldwork, Federal Work-Study, institutionally sponsored loans, tuition waivers (full and partial), and unspecified assistantships also available. Financial award application deadline: 3/1; financial award applicants required to submit FAFSA. *Faculty research:* Bio-organic and medicinal chemistry, drug delivery, pharmaceutics, molecular neurobiology, neurology. Total annual research expenditures: $3.1 million. *Unit head:* Dr. Robert W. Piepho, Dean, 816-235-1609, Fax: 816-235-5190, E-mail: piephor@umkc.edu. *Application contact:* Shelly M. Janasz, Director, Student Services, 816-235-2400, Fax: 816-235-5190, E-mail: janaszs@umkc.edu.

University of Nebraska Medical Center, College of Pharmacy, Omaha, NE 68198. Offers Pharm D. *Accreditation:* ACPE. *Faculty:* 28 full-time (4 women), 4 part-time/adjunct (2 women). *Students:* 256 full-time (191 women), 2 part-time (1 woman); includes 24 minority (6 African Americans, 1 American Indian/Alaska Native, 12 Asian Americans or Pacific Islanders, 5 Hispanic Americans). Average age 23. 256 applicants, 26% accepted, 66 enrolled. In 2006, 65 degrees awarded. *Entrance requirements:* 2 years (60 semester hours) of pre-pharmacy work. *Application deadline:* For fall admission, 1/1 for domestic students. Application fee: $45. Electronic applications accepted. *Expenses: Contact institution. Financial support:* Career-related internships or fieldwork, Federal Work-Study, institutionally sponsored loans, and scholarships/grants available. Support available to part-time students. Financial award application deadline: 4/1; financial award applicants required to submit FAFSA. *Faculty research:* Biopharmaceutics, nanomedicine, drug design, pharmaceutics, pharmacokinetics. *Unit head:* Dr. Clarence T. Ueda, Dean, 402-559-4333, Fax: 402-559-5060, E-mail: cueda@unmc.edu. *Application contact:* Dr. Charles H. Krobot, Associate Dean for Academic Affairs, 402-559-4333, Fax: 402-559-5060, E-mail: ckrobot@unmc.edu.

University of New Mexico, Graduate School, College of Pharmacy, Professional Program in Pharmacy, Albuquerque, NM 87131-2039. Offers Pharm D. Registered pharmacists may pursue the non-traditional Pharm D degree. *Accreditation:* ACPE. *Students:* 338 full-time (221 women), 21 part-time (14 women); includes 175 minority (8 African Americans, 19 American Indian/Alaska Native, 36 Asian Americans or Pacific Islanders, 112 Hispanic Americans), 2 international. Average age 29. *Entrance requirements:* PCAT, recommendations, interview. *Application deadline:* For fall admission, 2/1 for domestic students. Application fee: $20. Electronic applications accepted. *Expenses: Contact institution. Financial support:* In 2006–07, 278 students received support. Institutionally sponsored loans and scholarships/grants available. Financial award application deadline: 3/1; financial award applicants required to submit FAFSA.

Total annual research expenditures: $107,864. *Unit head:* Dr. Donald Godwin, Assistant Dean, 505-272-3241, Fax: 505-272-8324, E-mail: dgodwin@salud.unm.edu. *Application contact:* Krystle McCutchen, Admissions Advisor, 505-272-0912, Fax: 505-272-0583, E-mail: kmccutchen@unm.edu.

University of Oklahoma Health Sciences Center, College of Pharmacy, Professional Program in Pharmacy, Oklahoma City, OK 73190. Offers Pharm D. *Accreditation:* ACPE.

University of Pittsburgh, School of Pharmacy, Professional Program in Pharmacy, Pittsburgh, PA 15260. Offers Pharm D. *Accreditation:* ACPE. *Faculty:* 89 full-time (40 women), 117 part-time/adjunct (57 women). *Students:* 406 full-time (265 women); includes 34 minority (13 African Americans, 19 Asian Americans or Pacific Islanders, 2 Hispanic Americans), 1 international. Average age 24. 951 applicants, 14% accepted, 108 enrolled. In 2006, 93 Pharm Ds awarded. *Median time to degree:* Of those who began their doctoral program in fall 1998, 100% received their degree in 8 years or less. *Degree requirements:* For first-professional, registration. *Entrance requirements:* PCAT. Additional exam requirements/recommendations for international students: Required—PCAT. *Application deadline:* For fall admission, 2/1 for domestic students. Application fee: $65. Electronic applications accepted. *Expenses: Contact institution. Financial support:* In 2006–07, 146 students received support. Career-related internships or fieldwork, Federal Work-Study, and scholarships/grants available. Financial award application deadline: 10/1. *Faculty research:* Drug delivery and targeting, neuroendocrine pharmacology, genomics, proteomics, and drug discovery, clinical pharmaceutical sciences. Total annual research expenditures: $7.2 million. *Unit head:* Dr. Sharon Corey, Assistant Dean of Students, 412-648-8579, Fax: 412-648-1086. *Application contact:* Marcia L. Borrelli, Director of Student Services, 412-383-9000, Fax: 412-383-9995, E-mail: borrelli@pitt.edu.

University of Puerto Rico, Medical Sciences Campus, School of Pharmacy, San Juan, PR 00936-5067. Offers industrial pharmacy (MS); pharmaceutical sciences (MS); pharmacy (Pharm D). Part-time and evening/weekend programs available. *Faculty:* 31 full-time, 22 part-time/adjunct. *Students:* 234 full-time (178 women), 11 part-time (8 women); all minorities (1 Asian American or Pacific Islander, 244 Hispanic Americans). 130 applicants, 45% accepted, 56 enrolled. In 2006, 35 first professional degrees, 7 master's awarded. *Degree requirements:* For Pharm D, portfolio, research project; for master's, thesis, registration. *Entrance requirements:* For Pharm D, PCAT, interview, letters of reference; for master's, GRE, interview. *Application deadline:* For fall admission, 2/9 for domestic and international students. Application fee: $15. *Expenses: Contact institution. Financial support:* In 2006–07, 9 research assistantships with full tuition reimbursements (averaging $6,930 per year) were awarded; fellowships with partial tuition reimbursements, teaching assistantships with full tuition reimbursements, career-related internships or fieldwork, Federal Work-Study, institutionally sponsored loans, scholarships/grants, tuition waivers (full), and unspecified assistantships also available. *Faculty research:* Controlled release, solid dosage form, screening of anti-HIV drugs, pharmacokinetic/pharmacodynamic of drugs. Total annual research expenditures: $175,000. *Unit head:* Dr. Lesbia Hernández, Dean, 787-758-2525 Ext. 5427, Fax: 787-751-5680, E-mail: lhernandez@rcm.upr.edu. *Application contact:* Miriam Vélez, Assistant Dean of Student Affairs, 787-758-2525 Ext. 5407, Fax: 787-751-5680, E-mail: mivelez@rcm.upr.edu.

University of Rhode Island, Graduate School, College of Pharmacy, Graduate Programs in Pharmacy, Department of Pharmacy Practice, Kingston, RI 02881. Offers pharmaceutical sciences (MS, PhD), including pharmacoepidemiology and pharmacoeconomics. *Accreditation:* ACPE. *Application deadline:* For fall admission, 4/15 for domestic students. Application fee: $35. *Expenses:* Tuition, state resident: full-time $6,032; part-time $335 per credit. Tuition, nonresident: full-time $17,288; part-time $960 per credit. Required fees: $65 per credit. $30 per semester. One-time fee: $80 part-time. *Unit head:* Norma Owens, Chair, 401-874-2734.

University of South Alabama, Graduate School, Program in Pharmacy, Mobile, AL 36688-0002. Offers Pharm D. *Unit head:* Dr. B. Keith Harrison, Interim Dean of the Graduate School, Graduate School, 251-460-6310.

University of South Carolina, College of Pharmacy, Professional Program in Pharmacy, Columbia, SC 29208. Offers Pharm D. *Accreditation:* ACPE. *Degree requirements:* For first-professional, one foreign language. *Entrance requirements:* 2 years of preprofessional study. Electronic applications accepted. *Faculty research:* Carcinogenesis, antivirals, pharmaco kinetics, heterocyclic chemistry, neuropharmacology, clinical drug trials.

University of Southern California, Graduate School, School of Pharmacy, Professional Program in Pharmacy, Los Angeles, CA 90089. Offers Pharm D, Pharm D/MBA, Pharm D/MS, Pharm D/PhD. *Accreditation:* ACPE. *Students:* 715 full-time (529 women), 3 part-time (2 women); includes 530 minority (18 African Americans, 482 Asian Americans or Pacific Islanders, 30 Hispanic Americans), 6 international. In 2006, 185 degrees awarded. *Application deadline:* For fall admission, 1/12 priority date for domestic students. Application fee: $85. *Expenses:* Tuition: Full-time $33,314; part-time $1,121 per credit. Required fees: $522. Full-time tuition and fees vary according to program. *Financial support:* In 2006–07, 657 students received support; fellowships with partial tuition reimbursements available, research assistantships, teaching assistantships, Federal Work-Study, institutionally sponsored loans, and scholarships/grants available. Financial award application deadline: 2/15; financial award applicants required to submit FAFSA. *Faculty research:* Infectious diseases, health services research, geriatric pharmacology, clinical psychopharmacology. *Unit head:* Alvin Granderson, Director, 323-442-1369, E-mail: pharmadm@usc.edu. *Application contact:* Jim Granderson, Information Contact, 323-442-1466, E-mail: granders@hsc.usc.edu.

University of Southern Nevada, Program in Pharmacy, Henderson, NV 89014. Offers Pharm D. *Accreditation:* ACPE. *Students:* 460 full-time (273 women); includes 230 minority (19 African Americans, 2 American Indian/Alaska Native, 190 Asian Americans or Pacific Islanders, 19 Hispanic Americans). Average age 26. 1,500 applicants, 194 enrolled. In 2006, 109 degrees awarded. *Median time to degree:* 3 years full-time. *Degree requirements:* For first-professional, comprehensive exam. *Entrance requirements:* Additional exam requirements/recommendations for international students: Required—TOEFL. *Application deadline:* For fall admission, 1/11 for international students; for winter admission, 1/11 for domestic students. Applications are processed on a rolling basis. Application fee: $125. *Expenses:* Tuition: Full-time $34,500. Required fees: $2,700.

The University of Tennessee Health Science Center, College of Pharmacy, Memphis, TN 38163-0002. Offers Pharm D, MS, PhD, Pharm D/PhD. *Accreditation:* ACPE (one or more programs are accredited). *Students:* 699 full-time (449 women); includes 182 minority (101 African Americans, 4 American Indian/Alaska Native, 65 Asian Americans or Pacific Islanders, 12 Hispanic Americans). Average age 24. 850 applicants, 25% accepted, 215 enrolled. In 2006, 121 first professional degrees awarded. Terminal master's awarded for partial completion of doctoral program. *Median time to degree:* Of those who began their doctoral program in fall 1998, 100% received their degree in 8 years or less. *Degree requirements:* For master's and doctorate, thesis/dissertation. *Entrance requirements:* For Pharm D, PCAT; for master's and doctorate, GRE General Test, minimum GPA of 3.0. Additional exam requirements/recommendations for international students: Required—TOEFL. *Application deadline:* For fall admission, 2/1 for domestic students. Applications are processed on a rolling basis. Application fee: $50. Electronic applications accepted. *Expenses: Contact institution.* One-time fee: $55 full-time. *Financial support:* In 2006–07, 215 students received support; fellowships, research assistantships, teaching assistantships, career-related internships or fieldwork, Federal Work-Study, institutionally sponsored loans, and tuition waivers (full) available. Support available to part-time students. Financial award application deadline: 2/15. *Unit head:* Dr. Dick R. Gourley, Dean, 901-528-6036, Fax: 901-528-7053, E-mail: rgourley@utmem.edu. *Application contact:* Paula Webber, Enrollment Services Admissions Coordinator, 901-448-5560, E-mail: pwebber@utmem.edu.

The University of Texas at Austin, College of Pharmacy, Professional Program in Pharmacy, San Antonio, TX 78284. Offers Pharm D. *Accreditation:* ACPE. *Entrance requirements:* GRE General Test.

University of the Incarnate Word, Felk School of Pharmacy, San Antonio, TX 78209-6397. Offers Pharm D. *Faculty:* 10. *Students:* 79 full-time (58 women); includes 44 minority (6 African Americans, 9 Asian Americans or Pacific Islanders, 29 Hispanic Americans), 1 international. *Expenses:* Tuition: Part-time $570 per credit hour. Required fees: $54 per credit hour. One-time fee: $195 part-time. Tuition and fees vary according to degree level. *Unit head:* Dr. Arcelia Johnson-Fannin, Founding Dean, 210-805-3011, Fax: 210-805-3013, E-mail: johnsonf@uiwtx.edu.

University of the Pacific, School of Pharmacy and Health Sciences, Professional Program in Pharmacy, Stockton, CA 95211-0197. Offers Pharm D. *Accreditation:* ACPE. *Faculty:* 43 full-time (16 women), 4 part-time/adjunct (1 woman). *Students:* 620 full-time (383 women), 19 part-time (12 women); includes 413 minority (8 African Americans, 2 American Indian/Alaska Native, 374 Asian Americans or Pacific Islanders, 29 Hispanic Americans), 1 international. Average age 26. 176 applicants, 20% accepted, 18 enrolled. In 2006, 191 Pharm Ds awarded. *Entrance requirements:* Additional exam requirements/recommendations for international students: Required—TOEFL (minimum score 475 paper-based; 150 computer-based). *Application deadline:* For fall admission, 2/1 for domestic students. Application fee: $75. *Expenses:* Tuition: Full-time $26,920. Required fees: $430. Tuition and fees vary according to course load. *Financial support:* Career-related internships or fieldwork, Federal Work-Study, institutionally sponsored loans, and tuition waivers (partial) available. Support available to part-time students. Financial award application deadline: 3/1; financial award applicants required to submit FAFSA.

University of the Sciences in Philadelphia, Philadelphia College of Pharmacy, Professional Program in Pharmacy Practice, Philadelphia, PA 19104-4495. Offers Pharm D. *Accreditation:* ACPE. *Entrance requirements:* BS in pharmacy from an ACPE-accredited program, license to practice pharmacy in the U.S. *Expenses:* Tuition: Part-time $1,058 per credit. Tuition and fees vary according to program. *Faculty research:* Pharmacokinetics, oncology, critical care, pediatrics, cardiology.

University of Utah, College of Pharmacy and The Graduate School, Department of Pharmacy Practice, Salt Lake City, UT 84112-1107. Offers MS. *Degree requirements:* For master's, thesis optional. *Entrance requirements:* For master's, GRE, undergraduate degree in pharmacy. *Expenses:* Tuition, state resident: full-time $3,208. Tuition, nonresident: full-time $11,326. Required fees: $608. Tuition and fees vary according to class time and program.

University of Utah, College of Pharmacy, Professional Program in Pharmacy, Salt Lake City, UT 84112-1107. Offers Pharm D. *Accreditation:* ACPE. *Entrance requirements:* BS in pharmacy. *Expenses:* Tuition, state resident: full-time $3,208. Tuition, nonresident: full-time $11,326. Required fees: $608. Tuition and fees vary according to class time and program. *Faculty research:* Pain management, pharmacokinetic aspects of antiarrhythmics and anticoagulants, patient compliance.

University of Washington, School of Pharmacy, External Pharmacy Program, Seattle, WA 98195. Offers Pharm D. *Accreditation:* ACPE. Part-time and evening/weekend programs available. Postbaccalaureate distance learning degree programs offered (no on-campus study). *Degree requirements:* For first-professional, thesis. *Entrance requirements:* Pharmacy license.

University of Washington, School of Pharmacy, Professional Program in Pharmacy, Seattle, WA 98195. Offers Pharm D. *Accreditation:* ACPE. *Degree requirements:* For first-professional, thesis. *Entrance requirements:* PCAT.

University of Wisconsin–Madison, School of Pharmacy, Professional Program in Pharmacy, Madison, WI 53706-1380. Offers Pharm D. *Accreditation:* ACPE.

University of Wyoming, Graduate School, College of Health Sciences, School of Pharmacy, Laramie, WY 82070. Offers Pharm D. *Accreditation:* ACPE. *Faculty:* 21 full-time (11 women), 2 part-time/adjunct (1 woman). *Students:* 193 full-time (117 women), 8 part-time (5 women); includes 7 minority (2 Asian Americans or Pacific Islanders, 5 Hispanic Americans), 5 international. Average age 25. 319 applicants, 16% accepted. In 2006, 44 degrees awarded. *Entrance requirements:* PCAT. Additional exam requirements/recommendations for international students: Required—TOEFL. *Application deadline:* For fall admission, 1/1 for domestic and international students. Application fee: $130. *Financial support:* Federal Work-Study and scholarships/grants available. *Unit head:* John H. Vandel, Dean, 307-766-6120, Fax: 307-766-2953, E-mail: uwpharmacy@uwyo.edu. *Application contact:* Maria A. Bennett, Information Contact, 307-766-6132, Fax: 307-766-2953, E-mail: uwpharmacy@uwyo.edu.

Virginia Commonwealth University, Medical College of Virginia-Professional Programs, School of Pharmacy, Professional Program in Pharmacy, Richmond, VA 23284-9005. Offers Pharm D, Pharm D/PhD. *Accreditation:* ACPE. Part-time programs available. *Faculty:* 45 full-time (8 women). *Students:* Average age 25. In 2006, 95 degrees awarded. *Degree requirements:* For first-professional, research project. *Entrance requirements:* PCAT. *Application deadline:* Applications are processed on a rolling basis. *Financial support:* Institutionally sponsored loans available. Financial award application deadline: 3/1. *Faculty research:* Oncology, cardiology, infectious diseases, epilepsy, connective tissue. *Unit head:* Dr. James M. Messmer, Associate Dean, 804-828-8691, E-mail: jmmessme@vcu.edu. *Application contact:* Dr. Thomas P. Reinders, Associate Dean, Student Affairs, 804-828-3000, Fax: 804-828-7436, E-mail: tpreinde@vcu.edu.

Washington State University, Graduate School, College of Pharmacy, Department of Pharmaceutical Science, Pullman, WA 99164. Offers Pharm D. *Accreditation:* ACPE. *Faculty:* 15. *Students:* 351 full-time (221 women), 2 part-time; includes 80 minority (8 African Americans, 5 American Indian/Alaska Native, 53 Asian Americans or Pacific Islanders, 14 Hispanic Americans). Average age 26. 226 applicants, 35% accepted, 77 enrolled. In 2006, 73 degrees awarded. *Entrance requirements:* GRE, minimum GPA of 3.0, interview, minimum 60 hours documented pharmacy experience. *Application deadline:* For fall admission, 2/1 for domestic students; for spring admission, 9/1 for domestic students. Applications are processed on a rolling basis. Application fee: $40. *Expenses:* Tuition, state resident: full-time $7,066. Tuition, nonresident: full-time $17,204. *Financial support:* In 2006–07, 329 students received support, including 41 fellowships (averaging $4,355 per year); career-related internships or fieldwork, Federal Work-Study, and scholarships/grants also available. Financial award application deadline: 4/1. *Faculty research:* Enzymes, quality assurance, practices, tumor biology of metastasis, heart disease, anxiety and pain control. Total annual research expenditures: $1.4 million. *Unit head:* Dr. Bryan K. Slinker, Interim Chair, 509-335-6624, Fax: 509-335-4650, E-mail: slinker@vetmed.wsu.edu. *Application contact:* Graduate School Admissions, 800-GRADWSU, Fax: 509-335-1949, E-mail: gradsch@wsu.edu.

Washington State University Spokane, Program in Pharmacy, Spokane, WA 99210-1495. Offers Pharm D. *Faculty:* 29 full-time (11 women), 97 part-time/adjunct (39 women). *Students:* 415 full-time (246 women), 14 part-time (9 women); includes 91 minority (6 African Americans, 6 American Indian/Alaska Native, 66 Asian Americans or Pacific Islanders, 13 Hispanic Americans). Average age 29. 919 applicants, 10% accepted, 94 enrolled. *Degree requirements:* For first-professional, thesis, comprehensive exam. *Entrance requirements:* GRE, 3 letters of recommendation, supplemental pharmacy CAS form, interview. *Application deadline:* For fall admission, 12/15 for domestic students. Applications are processed on a rolling basis. Application fee: $40. *Expenses: Contact institution.* Tuition and fees vary according to program. *Financial support:* In 2006–07, 156 students received support, including 17 fellowships (averaging $3,324 per year); career-related internships or fieldwork, Federal Work-Study, and scholarships/grants also available. Financial award application deadline: 4/1. *Faculty research:* Infectious disease, neuroopsychopharmacology, biotechnology/gene therapy. Total annual research expenditures: $3.8 million. *Unit head:* Dr. Linda Garretts, Interim Chair, 509-335-

Pharmacy

Washington State University Spokane (continued)

8030. *Application contact:* Graduate School Admissions, 800-GRADWSU, Fax: 509-335-1949, E-mail: gradsch@wsu.edu.

Wayne State University, Eugene Applebaum College of Pharmacy and Health Sciences, Department of Pharmaceutical Sciences, Detroit, MI 48202. Offers experimental technology in pharmaceutical sciences (Certificate); health systems pharmacy management (MS); hospital pharmacy (MS); pharmaceutical administration (MS, PhD); pharmacy (Pharm D). *Accreditation:* ACPE (one or more programs are accredited). Part-time programs available. *Faculty:* 39 full-time (0 women). *Students:* 14 full-time (6 women), 3 part-time (2 women); includes 1 minority (African American), 13 international. Average age 31. In 2006, 3 master's, 1 doctorate awarded. *Degree requirements:* For master's, thesis optional. *Entrance requirements:* For Pharm D, bachelor's degree in pharmacy; for master's, GRE General Test, bachelor's degree in pharmacy. Additional exam requirements/recommendations for international students: Required—TOEFL (minimum score 550 paper-based; 213 computer-based); Recommended—TWE (minimum score 6). *Application deadline:* For fall admission, 6/1 for international students; for winter admission, 10/1 for international students; for spring admission, 2/1 for international students. Applications are processed on a rolling basis. Application fee: $30 ($50 for international students). Electronic applications accepted. *Financial support:* In 2006–07, 3 fellowships (averaging $35,000 per year) were awarded; career-related internships or fieldwork and scholarships/grants also available. Support available to part-time students. *Faculty research:* Mechanisms of resistance of bacteria to anti-microbial agents, drug metabolism and disposition in children, treatment strategies for stroke/neurovascular disease, prevalence and treatment of diabetes in Arab-Americans, ethnic variability in development of osteoporosis. Total annual research expenditures: $449,503. *Unit head:* Dr. George B. Corcoran, Chair, 313-577-1737, Fax: 313-577-2033. *Application contact:* Geralynn Smith, Graduate Director, 313-577-5401, E-mail: gbs@wayne.edu.

Wayne State University, Eugene Applebaum College of Pharmacy and Health Sciences, Department of Pharmacy Practice, Detroit, MI 48202. Offers medicinal chemistry (MS, PhD); pharmaceutical sciences (MS, PhD); pharmaceutics (MS, PhD); pharmacology (MS, PhD); pharmacy (Pharm D). *Faculty:* 33 full-time (23 women), 1 part-time/adjunct (0 women). *Students:* 305 full-time (203 women), 18 part-time (15 women); includes 41 minority (8 African Americans, 1 American Indian/Alaska Native, 30 Asian Americans or Pacific Islanders, 2 Hispanic Americans), 91 international. Average age 25. 103 applicants, 8% accepted, 6 enrolled. In 2006, 46 first professional degrees, 4 doctorates awarded. Terminal master's awarded for partial completion of doctoral program. *Degree requirements:* For master's and doctorate, thesis/dissertation. *Entrance requirements:* For master's, GRE General Test, minimum GPA of 2.6; for doctorate, GRE General Test, minimum GPA of 3.0. Additional exam requirements/recommendations for international students: Required—TOEFL (minimum score 550 paper-based; 213 computer-based); Recommended—TWE (minimum score 6). *Application deadline:* For fall admission, 1/31 priority date for domestic students, 6/1 for international students; for winter admission, 10/1 for international students; for spring admission, 2/1 for international students. Applications are processed on a rolling basis. Application fee: $30 ($50 for international students). Electronic applications accepted. *Financial support:* Fellowships, research assistantships with tuition reimbursements, scholarships/grants available. Support available to part-time students. *Faculty research:* Signaling defects as basics of type 1 and type 2 diabetes, dopamine receptor and transporter inhibitors for addition, novel nanoparticles for gene and drug delivery, role of lipocortin 1 in heavy metal mutagenesis, synthesis and anti cancer mechanisms of polyamine and histone deacetylase inhibitors. Total annual research expenditures: $237,898. *Unit head:* Dr. David J. Edwards, Chair, 313-577-0827, Fax: 313-577-5369. *Application contact:* William Lindblad, Associate Professor, 313-577-0513, E-mail: wlindbl@wayne.edu.

Western University of Health Sciences, College of Pharmacy, Program in Pharmacy, Pomona, CA 91766-1854. Offers Pharm D. *Accreditation:* ACPE. *Faculty:* 20 full-time (10 women), 3 part-time/adjunct (2 women). *Students:* 497 full-time (365 women); includes 346 minority (6 African Americans, 1 American Indian/Alaska Native, 327 Asian Americans or Pacific Islanders, 12 Hispanic Americans), 26 international. Average age 29. 1,302 applicants, 18% accepted, 120 enrolled. In 2006, 110 degrees awarded. *Entrance requirements:* Minimum GPA of 2.5, interview, letters of recommendation. Additional exam requirements/recommendations for international students: Required—TOEFL (minimum score 500 paper-based; 213 computer-based). *Application deadline:* For fall admission, 11/1 for domestic and international students. Application fee: $65. *Expenses:* Contact institution. *Financial support:* Institutionally sponsored loans and scholarships/grants available. Financial award application deadline: 3/2; financial award applicants required to submit FAFSA. *Application contact:* Audrey Navarro, Information Contact, 909-469-5335, Fax: 909-469-5570, E-mail: admissions@westernu.edu.

West Virginia University, School of Pharmacy, Professional Program in Pharmacy, Morgantown, WV 26506. Offers clinical pharmacy (Pharm D). Students enter program as undergraduates. *Accreditation:* ACPE. *Students:* 321 full-time (215 women), 1 part-time; includes 14 minority (4 African Americans, 1 American Indian/Alaska Native, 7 Asian Americans or Pacific Islanders, 2 Hispanic Americans), 1 international. Average age 24. 208 applicants, 42% accepted, 82 enrolled. In 2006, 75 degrees awarded. *Entrance requirements:* PCAT, minimum 3.1 GPA. *Application deadline:* For fall admission, 12/1 for domestic and international students. Application fee: $135. Electronic applications accepted. *Expenses:* Tuition, state resident: full-time $4,926; part-time $276 per credit hour. Tuition, nonresident: full-time $14,278; part-time $796 per credit hour. Tuition and fees vary according to program. *Financial support:* In 2006–07, 295 students received support, including 2 teaching assistantships; research assistantships. Financial award application deadline: 3/1; financial award applicants required to submit FAFSA. *Application contact:* Jennifer Clutter, Academic Adviser, 304-293-1552, Fax: 304-293-5483, E-mail: jclutter@hsc.wvu.edu.

West Virginia University, School of Pharmacy, Program in Pharmaceutical and Pharmacological Sciences, Morgantown, WV 26506. Offers administrative pharmacy (PhD); behavioral pharmacy (MS, PhD); biopharmaceutics/pharmacokinetics (MS, PhD); industrial pharmacy (MS); medicinal chemistry (MS, PhD); pharmaceutical chemistry (MS, PhD); pharmaceutics (MS, PhD); pharmacology and toxicology (MS); pharmacy (MS); pharmacy administration (MS). Part-time programs available. *Students:* 29 full-time (12 women), 3 part-time (2 women); includes 1 minority (Asian American or Pacific Islander), 18 international. Average age 30. 47 applicants, 6% accepted, 2 enrolled. In 2006, 3 master's, 9 doctorates awarded. Terminal master's awarded for partial completion of doctoral program. *Median time to degree:* Of those who began their doctoral program in fall 1998, 84% received their degree in 8 years or less. *Degree requirements:* For master's, thesis; for doctorate, one foreign language, thesis/dissertation, comprehensive exam. *Entrance requirements:* For master's and doctorate, GRE General Test, minimum GPA of 2.75. Additional exam requirements/recommendations for international students: Required—TOEFL; Recommended—TWE. *Application deadline:* For fall admission, 3/1 priority date for domestic and international students. Application fee: $50. Electronic applications accepted. *Expenses:* Contact institution. Tuition and fees vary according to program. *Financial support:* In 2006–07, 31 students received support, including 13 research assistantships with full tuition reimbursements available (averaging $23,000 per year), 15 teaching assistantships with full tuition reimbursements available (averaging $23,000 per year); career-related internships or fieldwork, Federal Work-Study, institutionally sponsored loans, health care benefits, tuition waivers (full and partial), and unspecified assistantships also available. Financial award application deadline: 3/1; financial award applicants required to submit FAFSA. *Faculty research:* Pharmaceutics, medicinal chemistry, biopharmaceutics/pharmacokinetics, health outcomes research. Total annual research expenditures: $1.8 million. *Application contact:* Dr. Patrick S. Callery, Assistant Dean for Graduate Programs/Chair, 304-293-1482, Fax: 304-293-2576, E-mail: pcallery@hsc.wvu.edu.

Wilkes University, Graduate Studies and Continued Learning, Nesbitt College of Pharmacy and Nursing, School of Pharmacy, Wilkes-Barre, PA 18766-0002. Offers Pharm D. *Students:* 267 full-time (167 women), 1 (woman) part-time; includes 14 minority (1 American Indian/Alaska Native, 12 Asian Americans or Pacific Islanders, 1 Hispanic American), 1 international. Average age 23. In 2006, 73 degrees awarded. *Entrance requirements:* Additional exam requirements/recommendations for international students: Required—TOEFL (minimum score 500 paper-based; 173 computer-based).

Wingate University, School of Pharmacy, Wingate, NC 28174-0159. Offers Pharm D. *Faculty:* 23 full-time (13 women). *Students:* 242 full-time (143 women), 2 part-time; includes 27 minority (8 African Americans, 3 American Indian/Alaska Native, 14 Asian Americans or Pacific Islanders, 2 Hispanic Americans), 4 international. Average age 25. 771 applicants, 9% accepted, 60 enrolled. *Degree requirements:* For first-professional, comprehensive exam. *Entrance requirements:* PCAT. *Application deadline:* For fall admission, 2/1 for domestic and international students. Applications are processed on a rolling basis. Application fee: $0. Electronic applications accepted. *Expenses:* Contact institution. *Financial support:* In 2006–07, 182 students received support; fellowships, research assistantships, teaching assistantships, career-related internships or fieldwork and scholarships/grants available. Financial award application deadline: 5/30. *Faculty research:* Stress response in aging, arthritis therapy educational processes, professional development, sarcopenia in aging, geriatric–psych drug therapy. *Unit head:* Dr. Robert Supernaw, Dean, 704-233-8015, Fax: 704-233-8332, E-mail: supernaw@wingate.edu. *Application contact:* Erinn Nichols, Assistant to the Dean of Pharmacy, 704-233-8331, Fax: 704-233-8332, E-mail: enichols@wingate.edu.

Xavier University of Louisiana, College of Pharmacy, New Orleans, LA 70125-1098. Offers Pharm D. *Accreditation:* ACPE. *Faculty:* 34 full-time (11 women), 4 part-time/adjunct (0 women). *Students:* 637 full-time (464 women); includes 499 minority (328 African Americans, 1 American Indian/Alaska Native, 161 Asian Americans or Pacific Islanders, 9 Hispanic Americans), 7 international. Average age 23. 704 applicants, 28% accepted, 163 enrolled. In 2006, 113 degrees awarded. *Entrance requirements:* Additional exam requirements/recommendations for international students: Required—TOEFL. *Application deadline:* For fall admission, 12/15 for domestic students. Application fee: $25. Electronic applications accepted. *Expenses:* Contact institution. *Financial support:* Career-related internships or fieldwork, Federal Work-Study, institutionally sponsored loans, and scholarships/grants available. Support available to part-time students. Financial award application deadline: 4/1; financial award applicants required to submit FAFSA. *Unit head:* Dr. Wayne T. Harris, Dean, 504-520-7421, Fax: 504-520-7930, E-mail: wharris@xula.edu. *Application contact:* Gwendolyn Hudson, Admissions Liaison, 504-520-7369, Fax: 504-520-7977, E-mail: ghudson@xula.edu.

DUQUESNE UNIVERSITY

Graduate School of Pharmaceutical Sciences

Programs of Study

The Graduate School of Pharmaceutical Sciences offers the M.S. and Ph.D. degrees in pharmaceutics, medicinal chemistry, and pharmacology and the M.S. in pharmacy administration. M.S. programs require a minimum of 30 postbaccalaureate semester hours; 24 credits are for course work, including 2 credits of seminar, and an additional 6 credits are for thesis research. Ph.D. programs require a minimum of 60 postbaccalaureate semester hours; 48 credits are for course work, including 4 credits of seminar, and an additional 12 credits are for dissertation research. The M.S. in pharmacy administration thesis option requires 27 credits of course work, including 2 credits of seminar and 9 credits of thesis research; the nonthesis option requires 33 credits of course work, including 2 credits of seminar. In conjunction with the Graduate School of Business Administration, the department offers an M.B.A./M.S. in industrial pharmacy, an 85-credit, nonthesis program that requires concurrent graduate-level enrollment in both business administration and the pharmaceutical sciences. Fifty-seven credits in core business administration course work and 28 credits of course work in the pharmaceutical sciences are required.

Research Facilities

The Graduate School of Pharmaceutical Sciences is centered in the Richard King Mellon Hall of Science. Laboratory instrumentation includes scanning and transmission electron microscopes, NIR imager, nuclear magnetic resonance spectrometers, infrared spectrometers, near-infrared spectrometers, near-infrared microscope, confocal microscopes, ultraviolet-visible spectrophotometers, atomic absorption spectrophotometers, gas chromatographs, high-pressure liquid chromatographs, rheometers, dissolution and disintegration testing equipment, a benchtop quadruple GC-mass spectrometer with electron impact and positive ion and negative ion chemical ionizations, a liquid chromatograph with a UV diode array detector, a gel permeation chromatograph with laser light scattering, differential pressure viscometry, refractive index detectors, capillary electrophoresis with UV diode array detector, PCR thermocyclers, a cell/tissue culture facility, DNA synthesizer, automatic film developer, gamma counter, and image analyzer. Mellon Hall facilities include the Duquesne University Center for Pharmaceutical Technology and a fully equipped manufacturing laboratory/pilot plant with slant cone and high shear mixers, a microfluidizer, fluid bed and spray dryers, coaters, a capsule-filling machine, and a fully computer controlled/monitored 38-station Hata tablet press. Modern animal facilities in adjacent Bayer Hall provide the opportunity for physiological, pharmacological, and toxicological evaluations of drugs and chemicals. The Academic Research Center for Pharmacy Care in Bayer Learning Center holds cardiovascular, endocrine, and skeletal systems diagnostic and therapeutic treatment equipment. The Gumberg Library at Duquesne houses a state-of-the-art integrated, online library system complete with a computerized card catalog, advanced computer disk (CD-ROM) system, online networked databases, and an array of technical support functions. The system enables students to access extensive local, national, and international databases and library catalogs around the world. Students have direct access to other university and research libraries in the Pittsburgh area.

Financial Aid

Teaching and research assistantships, which may include full remission of tuition and fees, are available.

Cost of Study

In 2007–08, tuition is $914 per credit plus a University fee of $74 per credit.

Living and Housing Costs

For 2007–08, room and board in University dormitories cost $8546 per student per academic year for double occupancy. Food and clothing costs are similar to those in other cities of comparable size. The University offers a Student Health Care package, required for all graduate students.

Student Group

The University enrolls almost 10,000 students; typically, 70 students, representing a mix of U.S. (30 percent) and international (70 percent), are enrolled in graduate programs in the Graduate School of Pharmaceutical Sciences.

Student Outcomes

Most recent M.S. graduates have continued studies at the doctoral level or are employed in a variety of research laboratory settings. Graduates of Ph.D. programs are employed in research and administrative positions in industry and in research and teaching in academia.

Location

Allegheny County has a population of about 1 million; one third live in the city of Pittsburgh. Downtown is headquarters for several major corporations and the hub of cultural and recreational activities. Pittsburgh fields professional teams in football, baseball, and hockey. Perhaps the most engaging quality is the "hometown" flavor of the many neighborhoods that make up Pittsburgh.

The University

Duquesne is a private, Catholic, coeducational university. The 48-acre self-enclosed campus overlooks the Monongahela River. Students and 429 full-time faculty members are organized into the College and Graduate School of Liberal Arts and the Schools of Pharmacy, Nursing, Law, Business Administration, Education, Music, Health Sciences, Natural and Environmental Sciences, and Leadership and Professional Advancement. All campus facilities have been refurbished, with recent additions of current computer labs, a multipurpose athletic complex, and student living-learning centers. The University supports many intercollegiate and intramural athletics programs. The Tamburitzans and the Red Masquers are well-established ethnic dance and theatrical groups.

Applying

Students are admitted for the fall or spring semester. Assistantships are normally awarded in spring for the following academic year. Applicants should have earned a baccalaureate degree in chemistry, biology, pharmacy, allied health sciences, or social/behavioral or business sciences, depending on the proposed field of study. Any deficiencies in undergraduate course work must be resolved. Challenge examinations are not accepted for graduate credit. The completed application and supporting documents (official transcripts of all undergraduate and graduate course work, a brief statement of purpose and intent with regard to the specific area of graduate study chosen, three letters of recommendation from persons acquainted with the academic abilities of the applicant, and results of the GRE General Test) must be sent to the Director of Graduate Studies. Applicants whose native language or principal language of instruction is not English are required to submit TOEFL scores to the Graduate School and to sit for on-campus English language competency testing. International students who are applying for a teaching assistantship are required to submit TSE scores.

Correspondence and Information

Director of Graduate Studies
Graduate School of Pharmaceutical Sciences
School of Pharmacy
409 Mellon Hall
Duquesne University
Pittsburgh, Pennsylvania 15282
Phone: 412-396-1172
E-mail: gsps-adm@duq.edu
Web site: http://www.pharmacy.duq.edu

Duquesne University

THE FACULTY AND THEIR RESEARCH

Medicinal Chemistry

Patrick Flaherty, Assistant Professor of Medicinal Chemistry; Ph.D., Iowa. Synthetic medicinal chemistry and rational drug design, with emphasis on emerging biochemical targets relevant to human disease states, modern synthetic methodology, and iterative rounds of computation, synthesis, then biochemical analysis; general therapeutic areas of CNS agents and anticancer agents; current biological targets of CDK5, microtubules, DXR, alpha-synuclein.

Aleem Gangjee, Professor of Medicinal Chemistry and Mylan School of Pharmacy Distinguished Professor; Ph.D., Iowa. Synthetic medicinal chemistry, computer-assisted drug design, inhibitors of folate-metabolizing enzymes, receptor tyrosine kinase inhibitors, antimitotic agents, antitumor agents, design of combination chemotherapeutic potential in signal agents, antiopportunistic infection agents, heterocyclic chemistry, stereochemistry.

Marc W. Harrold, Professor of Medicinal Chemistry; Ph.D., Ohio State. Development of computer-based educational tools, instructional strategies in medicinal chemistry, drug design.

David J. Lapinsky, Assistant Professor of Medicinal Chemistry; Ph.D., Ohio State. Synthetic organic medicinal chemistry, rational drug design, computer-assisted drug design, emphasis on nicotinic acetylcholine receptor ligands and central nervous system biochemical targets relevant to human disease.

Pharmaceutical Administration

Vincent J. Giannetti, Professor of Pharmaceutical Administration; Ph.D., Pittsburgh. Prescription drug adherence, mental health, substance abuse, pharmacist counseling behaviors, health-care policy and ethics, coping with medication errors.

Khalid M. Kamal, Assistant Professor of Pharmaceutical Administration; Ph.D, West Virginia. Application of decision and cost-effectiveness analysis in health policy and medicine; health outcomes assessment in chronic conditions such as rheumatoid arthritis, ankylosing spondylitis, and chronic obstructive pulmonary disease.

David J. Tipton, Associate Professor of Pharmaceutical Administration and Division Head, Clinical, Social, and Administrative Sciences; Ph.D., St. Louis. Medication errors, services marketing.

Pharmaceutics

Moji Christianah Adeyeye, Professor of Pharmaceutics; Ph.D., Georgia. Preformulation, development, stability, quality assurance, and bioavailability evaluation of immediate and sustained released liquid, semisolid, and solid dosage forms; excipient characterization; biopharmaceutical product technology; unit process optimization.

Carl A. Anderson, Assistant Professor of Pharmaceutical Sciences; Ph.D., Texas at Austin. Sensor technology for the study and control of pharmaceutical manufacturing, employing technologies such as acoustic and near-infrared spectroscopy processed by chemometric methods.

Lawrence H. Block, Professor of Pharmaceutics; Ph.D., Maryland. Theoretical aspects of pharmacokinetics and pharmacodynamics; controlled and modified release drug and cosmetic delivery system development; pharmaceutic aspects of chitin, chitosan, and chitinosans; pharmaceutical engineering, especially scale-up of processing of nonparenteral liquids and semisolids; hydrophilic gels as drug delivery systems.

James K. Drennen III, Associate Professor of Pharmaceutics and Associate Dean of Graduate Programs and Research; Ph.D., Kentucky. Pharmaceutical and medical applications of near-infrared spectroscopy, process control, chemometrics, process analytical technology.

Wilson S. Meng, Associate Professor of Pharmaceutical Sciences; Ph.D., USC. Structure-based design of tumor-reactive T-cell epitopes and development of particle-based DNA delivery systems.

Peter L. D. Wildfong, Assistant Professor of Pharmaceutics; Ph.D., Purdue. Pharmaceutical materials science, with current research projects exploring how specific physicochemical and structural properties of small molecule organic solid materials impact large-scale manufacturing and final-dosage-form performance; emphasis on mechanically activated solid-state phase transformations of APIs and excipients; potential for high-shear induction of polymorphism and amorphization.

Pharmacology

J. Douglas Bricker, Professor of Pharmacology and Dean of the Mylan School of Pharmacy; Ph.D., Duquesne. Effects of drugs, chemicals, and disease states on the regulation of calcium uptake mechanisms, development, and screening of antidotal agents for clinical use and in vitro toxicity testing methods.

Jane E. Cavanaugh, Assistant Professor of Pharmacology; Ph.D., Penn State Hershey Medical Center. Mechanisms of cell death and survival in the diseased (Parkinson's disease, Alzheimer's disease) and nondiseased (normal aging) brain.

Vicki L. Davis, Assistant Professor of Pharmacology; Ph.D., North Carolina. Effects of pharmaceutical, environmental, plant, and natural estrogen exposure on the development of breast cancer and cataracts in women, with emphasis on using various techniques to determine potential methods of decreasing the risk factors.

David A. Johnson, Associate Professor of Pharmacology and Director of Graduate Studies; Ph.D., Massachusetts College of Pharmacy. Drugs that enhance the function of neuronal pathways involved with learning and memory, neuropathology and treatment of eating disorders.

Christopher K. Surratt, Associate Professor of Pharmacology and Division Head of Pharmaceutical Sciences; Ph.D., Virginia. Molecular mechanisms of brain receptors that recognize antidepressants, anxiolytics, and psychostimulant drugs of abuse.

Paula A. Witt-Enderby, Associate Professor of Pharmacology; Ph.D., Arizona. Molecular pharmacology of melatonin receptors, and its associated signaling cascades, with emphasis on the role of melatonin in stem cell differentiation.

FLORIDA AGRICULTURAL AND MECHANICAL UNIVERSITY

College of Pharmacy and Pharmaceutical Sciences
Graduate Programs in Pharmaceutical Sciences and Public Health

Program of Study	The College of Pharmacy and Pharmaceutical Sciences offers a comprehensive program of course work and research leading to the Doctor of Philosophy (Ph.D.) and Master of Science (M.S.) degrees in pharmaceutical sciences with concentrations in environmental toxicology (Ph.D. only), medicinal chemistry, pharmaceutics, pharmacology/toxicology, and pharmacy administration (M.S. only); the Doctor of Public Health (Dr.P.H) with concentrations in behavioral science and health education and epidemiology; and the Master of Public Health (M.P.H.). The courses of study are designed to give students a strong background in modern principles of their chosen area of specialization and in a variety of research subspecialties. Theoretical principles are presented, and application of these principles in research is emphasized. Students may pursue research in any of the areas of specialization of the faculty members listed in this In-Depth Description. The student selects a research adviser and, in conjunction with that adviser, proposes a program of study, presents a tentative thesis/dissertation subject and outline, and selects a committee that oversees their progress in research. At least 3 faculty members sit on an M.S. advisory committee and at least 5 on a Ph.D. committee. After completion of course work, the student takes a comprehensive written exam; doctoral students must also take a comprehensive oral exam. During the course of their research, students are required to make presentations at national meetings. Students seeking the M.S. are required to complete at least one paper for publication in a refereed scientific journal; students seeking the Ph.D. are required to complete at least two. Final degree requirements include completion of a thesis (M.S. candidates) or dissertation (Ph.D. candidates) on research conducted by the student and a public oral defense of the work. Students seeking the Dr.P.H. and M.P.H. degree must do so through the Institute of Public Health. They must select an adviser and complete a special project in public health.
	The College provides research internships at pharmaceutical research laboratories, as well as federal research laboratories. Graduate students are encouraged to gain research experience in these laboratories.
Research Facilities	The College is housed in the New Pharmacy Building, and most of the research laboratories are housed in the new state-of-the-art Science Research Facility and the New Pharmacy Building Research Wing. The Science Research Facility also houses an animal facility, a biomedical research library, and all the infrastructure needed for research. Major laboratory equipment includes a mass spectrometer, a scintillation counter, an ultracentrifuge (L8-80M), environmental chambers, gas and liquid chromatographs, a spectrofluorometer, and a variety of physiographs. Recent additions include a computer-assisted Perkin-Elmer 1480 spectrophotometer, a Perkin-Elmer 3030 atomic absorption spectrometer, and a Beckman DU-65 UV-VIS spectrophotometer. The College also maintains two off-campus facilities in Miami and Tampa, Florida. Clinical research and student training are conducted at these campuses.
Financial Aid	Stipends paying from $12,000 to $16,200 per year are available in the form of research assistantships, work-study funds, and fellowships for qualified students. Tuition waivers may also be available. Students in need of financial assistance should indicate this in a letter accompanying their application for admission.
Cost of Study	In 2006–07, graduate tuition was not less than $213 per semester credit hour for in-state students and $834 per semester credit hour for out-of-state students. These fees are subject to change.
Living and Housing Costs	Dormitory rooms rent for $1333 to $2210 per semester. Apartments are available in University-owned married student housing. Off-campus housing is available at a wide range of prices in locations throughout the city.
Student Group	Total enrollment in the College of Pharmacy and Pharmaceutical Sciences is approximately 800 graduate and Pharm.D. students. While the academic backgrounds of the graduate students are varied, they include undergraduate degrees in scientific fields such as biology, chemistry, microbiology, and pharmacy.
Location	Tallahassee has a population of approximately 268,000. It is the capital of Florida and the home of two state universities and a community college. These institutions support a wide variety of cultural, social, and recreational activities. In addition, the Civic Center makes the city a regional entertainment center. The beaches of the north Florida coast are easily reached from Tallahassee.
The University and The College	Florida A&M University was founded in 1887 and currently comprises eleven schools and colleges and a School of Graduate Studies, Research, and Continuing Education. The University was named College of the Year in 1997 by *Time Magazine Princeton Review*. The College of Pharmacy and Pharmaceutical Sciences has achieved national and international prominence in various areas of research, and each year sponsors a highly successful clinical pharmacy symposium that addresses clinical research aspects in areas of current interest in medicine, pharmacy, and the pharmaceutical sciences. The College is one of the top schools of pharmacy in the nation in attracting National Institutes of Health research funds.
Applying	Applications are accepted for the fall semester only. Applications should be received on or before the end of March. All applicants must have a bachelor's degree from an accredited college or university. A minimum cumulative grade point average of 3.0 in the last 60 semester hours while working for a baccalaureate degree or a minimum combined score of 1000 on the quantitative and verbal sections of the General Test of the Graduate Record Examinations is required for admission to the M.S. and M.P.H. programs. Applicants to the Ph.D. program must have both a GPA of at least 3.0 and a combined GRE General Test score of 1000 or must have an M.S. degree from an accredited institution. Regardless of their GPA, all students must take the GRE and have their scores on record as part of the admission process. While the GPA and the GRE scores are important, the Graduate Committee considers other factors such as the availability of space and letters of recommendation.
Correspondence and Information	Dean, College of Pharmacy and Pharmaceutical Sciences Florida Agricultural and Mechanical University Tallahassee, Florida 32307-3800 Phone: 850-599-3301 Web site: http://pharmacy.famu.edu/

Florida Agricultural and Mechanical University

THE FACULTY AND THEIR RESEARCH

Medicinal Chemistry
Seth Y. Ablordeppey, Professor and Director, Basic Sciences; Ph.D., Mississippi, 1990. Molecular modeling, drug design and synthesis.
R. Renee Reams Brown, Associate Professor; Ph.D., Brigham Young, 1984. Protein chemistry and biological calorimetry.
John Cooperwood, Assistant Professor; Ph.D., Georgia, 1999. Synthesis of antiviral and anticancer agents.
Nazarius Lamango, Assistant Professor; Ph.D., Leeds, 1994. Isoprenylation biochemistry in disease.
Henry Lee, Professor; Ph.D., Oklahoma State, 1971. Biochemistry, synthesis of medicinal compounds and anti-inflammatory steroids.
K. Ken Redda, Professor; Ph.D., Alberta, 1978. Synthesis of anticancer compounds, anti-inflammatory agents.

Pharmaceutics
Kayarna Kandimilla, Assistant Professor; Ph.D., Iowa, 2003. Biopharmaceutics and pharmacokinetics.
Mandip S. Sachdeva, Professor; Ph.D., Dalhousie, 1989. Formulation and in vivo evaluation of targeted drug-delivery systems.
Saber Samaan, Professor; Ph.D., London, 1981. Drug pharmacokinetics and chronopharmacology.
Shawn Spencer, Assistant Professor; Ph.D., Temple, 2004. Solid state binding processes, nucleotide inhibitors.

Pharmacology/Toxicology/Environmental Toxicology
Carl B. Goodman, Associate Professor; Ph.D., Florida A&M, 1992. Drugs of abuse, neurotoxicology/neuropharmacology.
Ann S. Heiman, Professor; Ph.D., Florida, 1984. Immunopharmacology, pharmacologic modulation of activation-coupling events.
Maurice S. Holder, Professor; Ph.D., Howard, 1978. Cardiovascular physiology, angiotensin, antihypertensive drugs, calcium channel blockers.
Malak G. Kolta, Professor; Ph.D., Auburn, 1982. Neuropharmacology/neurotoxicology, drugs of abuse, diabetes.
Ebenezer T. Oriaku, Associate Professor; Ph.D., Florida A&M, 1991. Neuropharmacology/gastrointestinal pharmacology, biochemical pharmacology.
Donald Palm, Associate Professor; Ph.D., Penn State, 1991. Neuropharmacology, stroke and cardiovascular research, neurodegenerative diseases.
Karam F. Soliman, Distinguished Professor and Assistant Dean, Research; Ph.D., Georgia, 1972. Neuroendocrine pharmacology, adrenal pharmacology, neuropharmacology of drug abuse.
Magdi R. I. Soliman, Professor; Ph.D., Georgia, 1972. Heavy-metal toxicology, chronopharmacology and chronobiotic research.
Ronald Thomas, Associate Professor; Ph.D., Alabama, 1995. Environmental/estrogen-induced carcinogenesis.

Pharmacy Administration
Janet Barber, Assistant Professor; Ph.D., Kansas, 1983. Gerontology, demography, health policies.
Ellen Campbell, Assistant Professor; Ph.D., Florida State, 1989. Empirical research on health-care utilization.
Folakemi Odedina, Associate Professor and Director; Ph.D., Florida, 1994. Sociopsychological and economic aspects of health care.
Hong Xiao, Associate Professor; Ph.D., Iowa, 1997. Health services research, resource allocation.

Public Health
Alicestine Ashford, Assistant Professor; Ph.D., California, San Francisco, 1996. Health policy and management access to care, geriatrics.
C. Perry Brown, Professor; Dr.Ph.H., UCLA, 1982. Chronic disease prevention, HIV epidemiology and prevention.
Fran Gordon-Close, Associate Professor; Ph.D., Florida A&M, 1995. Reproductive toxicology and women's health issues.
Cynthia M. Harris, Associate Professor and Director; Ph.D., Meharry Medical College, 1985; DABT. Nutritional biochemistry, environmental toxicology, risk assessment, risk communication.
Gebre E. Kiros, Assistant Professor; Ph.D., Brown, 2000. Adolescence health, statistical research, demographics.
Ivette A. Lopez, Assistant Professor; Dr.P.H., South Florida, 2004. Community and family health.
Saleh M. Rahman, Assistant Professor; Ph.D., Alabama at Birmingham, 2001. Health behavior, international health.
Levi Ross, Assistant Professor; Ph.D., Alabama at Birmingham, 2004. Health education, health promotion.
Sandra G. Suther, Assistant Professor; Ph.D., Texas A&M, 2003. Health education, health promotion, medical anthropology.

MASSACHUSETTS COLLEGE OF PHARMACY AND HEALTH SCIENCES

Graduate Studies

Programs of Study

The size of the Massachusetts College of Pharmacy and Health Sciences (MCPHS) encourages close relationships between students and faculty members. Through an integrated curriculum, programs of graduate study in the pharmaceutical sciences are designed on an individual basis, depending on the academic background and research interests of the student. The College offers graduate programs leading to M.S. and Ph.D. degrees in medicinal chemistry, pharmaceutics, and pharmacology, as well as master's degrees in applied natural products, drug regulatory affairs and health policy, and drug discovery and development.

Medicinal chemistry specifically focuses on providing a student with a greater education of the behavior of chemical substances at the molecular level. Students in the program examine the composition of molecules and their interactions in both a chemic and physical sense with the aim of predicting behavior and properties of new substances. One key aspect of medicinal chemistry is fully understanding the pharmacological actions of substances that lead to improved drug design. Research programs include the synthesis and evaluation of antiviral and anticancer drugs or characterization of natural products from plants.

Pharmaceutics is the area of pharmacy that takes chemicals and creates medication that is safe for consumption. In the MCPHS program, students are exposed to theory and concepts used to promote the materials and technologies associated with pharmaceutical product development, manufacture, and evaluation. A student at MCPHS comes to fully understand dosage forms, drug dissolution and absorption, and pharmacokinetics. Pharmacokinetics analyzes the release of drugs from its dosage form, its distribution and elimination. Research in pharmaceutics has included the development of new drug products, dosage forms, release of drugs from those forms, and new drug entities.

The pharmacology program at MCPHS studies how substances interact with the human body or other living organisms to create a change. This is also true of the reaction of drugs and environmental chemicals. Graduates of the pharmacology program are fully prepared to begin careers in a position of leadership in academia, industry, or government.

An increased demand for dietary and herbal supplements has emerged. With this growing interest also comes a demand for career advancement in the area of natural products. The master's program in applied natural products gives graduates academic training to develop expertise in this field. In addition, the graduates can find jobs in pharmaceutical industries, federal regulatory agencies, or drug information centers. Students also gain experience in natural product dosage, DSHEA regulations, and regulations outside the United States.

The M.S. program in drug discovery and development is designed for students who currently hold a bachelor's degree and who have a strong interest in pharmaceutics and the drug discovery process. Students enroll in 30 credits of course work and gain extensive knowledge of the discovery process and learn to communicate effectively with senior scientists and internal management employed in the field. The graduates typically find employment in the pharmaceutical industry.

Students who are enrolled in the M.S. program in drug regulatory affairs and health policy receive extensive academic training in the regulation of drugs, devices and biologics, law, marketing, and health policy. The graduates pursue careers in regulatory affairs, product management, quality assurance, quality control, manufacturing, marketing, research, and agency work. Students also graduate with a firm understanding of economics, business, policy development, and law.

The M.S. degree programs require a minimum of 30 semester hours of credit, a thesis based on original research, and a final oral examination. The Ph.D. degree requires 50 semester hours of course and research credit, major and minor qualifying examinations, a dissertation based on original research, and a final oral examination.

Research Facilities

The research facilities are well equipped for each of the areas of specialization. In addition, there are such specialized facilities as a suite for radioisotope research and a product development laboratory equipped for tableting, coating, encapsulation, and the manufacture of liquids, ointments, and sterile products. Instruments available include infrared, ultraviolet, and nuclear magnetic resonance spectrometers; gas chromatographs; and high-pressure liquid chromatographs. Computer and animal facilities are also available. In addition, research instrument facilities are available at other institutions in the greater Boston/Cambridge area. The Sheppard Library contains approximately 27,000 volumes and receives more than 700 periodicals. MCPHS is also part of the Fenway library system, as well as the Boston Public Library Consortium. Graduate students and faculty members may also use the facilities of other nearby university libraries. In addition, MCPHS has two other locations, in Worcester, Massachusetts, and in Manchester, New Hampshire. The Worcester and Manchester campuses house programs in Pharm.D., master of physician assistant studies, and nursing.

Financial Aid

Full-time graduate students receive financial assistance from the College in the form of a limited number of graduate assistantships or faculty research grants and contracts. Personal sources or other non-College sources may also be available. Summer assistantships are also available. Tuition remission is available for teaching assistants.

Cost of Study

Students should visit the College's Web site (http://www.mcphs.edu) for up-to-date cost information.

Living and Housing Costs

College housing is not available, but apartments and rooms are available in the metropolitan Boston area and in the immediate Longwood Medical and Academic Area. The large number of students in the area makes sharing apartments feasible, at costs that are affordable for graduate students. The estimated cost of food, housing, books and supplies, personal expenses, and transportation for a single student is more than $20,000 for twelve months.

Student Group

MCPHS has an enrollment of approximately 2,800 students. The Ph.D. programs include students enrolled in pharmacology, pharmaceutics, and medicinal chemistry.

Student Outcomes

Over the past four years, 80 percent of the graduates of the program have entered the pharmaceutical industry as research scientists in their respective disciplines. The remaining 20 percent of students have gone on to medical school, postdoctoral study, government research laboratories, or academia.

Location

Boston, a center of internationally renowned teaching hospitals, research centers, and universities and colleges, is an invigorating and stimulating environment in which to live and learn. Boston is a home of the arts and provides numerous cultural and social opportunities, including classical and jazz concerts, opera, ballet, museums, theaters, and professional sports; outdoor activities are abundant.

The College

The Massachusetts College of Pharmacy and Health Sciences was founded in 1823. It is the oldest private, coeducational college located in Boston. The Longwood Medical and Academic Area offers an educational, professional, and cultural environment and a unique opportunity for graduate study. The George Robert White Building was constructed on the present site during 1917–18 and serves both undergraduate and graduate students. In 2005, the Ronald A. Matricaria Academic and Student Center was opened. The center features state-of-the-art laboratories, classrooms, a library, and residential space for 230 students.

Applying

The priority filing deadline for pharmaceutics, pharmacology, and medicinal chemistry is February 1 for September admission. Application forms are available on request. Candidates for applied natural products, drug discovery and development, and drug regulatory affairs and health policy should apply by July 1. Candidates for graduate degrees must hold a bachelor's degree in a field that is acceptable to the Graduate Council. Applicants must complete and submit the graduate application, paying particular attention to the second page where specific directions are listed. Students from countries in which English has not been the primary educational language must submit TOEFL scores and a CED evaluation. In addition to the general degree requirements described in the College catalog, individual programs may establish additional requirements. Detailed information can be obtained by contacting the Coordinator of Graduate Admission.

Correspondence and Information

Tara M. Hennessy
Coordinator of Graduate Admission
Massachusetts College of Pharmacy and Health Sciences
179 Longwood Avenue
Boston, Massachusetts 02115
Phone: 617-732-2850
Fax: 617-732-2118
E-mail: admissions@mcphs.edu
Web site: http://www.mcphs.edu

Massachusetts College of Pharmacy and Health Sciences

THE FACULTY AND THEIR RESEARCH

Drug Regulatory Affairs and Health Policy Research Faculty

J. Babiarz, Esq., Assistant Professor of Pharmacy Administration; J.D., Suffolk. Law and health policy of drugs and devices.

D. J. Pisano, Professor of Pharmacy Administration, Associate Provost for Pharmacy Education, and Dean, School of Pharmacy; Ph.D., Northeastern. Pharmacy practice and regulatory affairs law and regulation, professional practice dilemmas and professional liability.

Medicinal Chemistry Research Faculty

C. J. Friel, Associate Professor of Medicinal Chemistry; Ph.D., Northeastern. Synthetic organic chemistry, novel compounds for breast cancer.

M. Froimowitz, Research Professor of Chemistry; Ph.D., NYU.

A. R. Garafolo, Professor of Chemistry; Ph.D., Northeastern. Teaching methodology; integrating physics, chemistry, and biology instruction.

L. M. Gracz, Assistant Professor of Biochemistry; Ph.D., California, Santa Barbara. Neurochemistry, membrane biophysics, molecular mechanisms of drug addition, membrane biochemistry.

C. J. Kelley, Associate Professor of Chemistry; Ph.D., Indiana. Structural characterization of natural products, organic synthesis of nuorescent dyes, indicators and laser dyes, design and organic synthesis of novel chemical agents for prevention of HIV transmission.

S. G. Kerr, Assistant Professor of Medicinal Chemistry; Ph.D., SUNY at Buffalo. HIV and herpes simplex enzymology and drug design, designing prodrugs of existing antiviral and anticancer agents, cyclooxygenase enzymes (COX 1 and 2) in neuroblastoma cells for possible roles in dementia-related diseases.

A. S. Mehanna, Professor of Chemistry; Ph.D., Pittsburgh. Development of cardiovascular drugs and anti-AIDS drugs.

D. A. Williams, Professor Emeritus; Ph.D., Minnesota. Analytical methods development, drug stability, free-radical oxidation mechanisms, P450 oxidative metabolism, glucuronidation, sulfation metabolism.

Pharmaceutics Research Faculty

L. Pereira, Assistant Professor of Pharmaceutical Sciences; Ph.D., Iowa. Biopharmaceutics, pharmacokinetics, and pharmacodynamics.

Pharmacology Research Faculty

S. D. Cohen, Professor of Pharmacology and Toxicology and Chair, Department of Pharmaceutical Sciences–Worcester; D.Sc., Harvard. RC1 toxicology, liver-kidney injury.

A. Gardner, Associate Professor of Pharmacology and Toxicology–Worcester; Ph.D., Saint Louis. Signal transduction pathways, NPY-mediated inhibition of neurotransmitter release.

M. Kalis, Professor of Pharmacology and Acting Vice President for Academic Affairs/Provost; Ph.D., Emory. Cardiovascular pharmacology, pharmacy education.

D. Kiel, Assistant Professor of Pharmacology; Ph.D., Columbia. Regulation and function of G protein–coupled receptors, novel therapies for diabetes and obesity.

B. LeDuc, Associate Professor of Pharmacology; Ph.D., Tufts. Drug metabolism, clinical pharmacokinetics, pharmacogenetics.

T. J. Maher, Professor of Pharmacology and Sawyer Professor of Pharmaceutical Sciences; Ph.D., Massachusetts College of Pharmacy and Health Sciences. Neuropharmacology; effects of nutrients or components of nutrients (especially amino acids) on neuronal systems using biochemical, physiological, and behavioral approaches.

R. Sarangarajan, Associate Professor of Pharmacology and Toxicology; Ph.D., Cincinnati. Genetic regulation of pigmentation and pigment, cell biology and protein sorting, kidney function and ion transport and toxicity.

THE OHIO STATE UNIVERSITY

College of Pharmacy

Programs of Study

The College of Pharmacy offers programs leading to the degrees of Master of Science (M.S.), Doctor of Philosophy (Ph.D.), and Doctor of Pharmacy (Pharm.D.). M.S. and Ph.D. degree programs are offered in four areas of specialization. The pharmaceutical administration discipline focuses on issues related to the pharmaceutical care delivery system, pharmacoeconomics, drug distribution and public policy, strategic planning for pharmaceutical organizations, and drug-use behavior and evaluation. The medicinal chemistry and pharmacognosy discipline focuses on the interdisciplinary application of chemical, biochemical, and molecular principles to the identification and development of therapeutic agents. The pharmaceutics area focuses on pharmacodynamics and pharmacokinetics, with a special emphasis on drug-delivery and targeting systems. The pharmacology area focuses on determination of biochemical and physiological mechanisms by which drugs exert their effects. Graduates of these programs are prepared for careers that exploit research skills and independent thinking in pharmaceutical sciences. The M.S. in health-system pharmacy administration educates students to conceptualize, plan, coordinate, and evaluate pharmaceutical care in organized health-care settings. The Doctor of Pharmacy program is a four-year postbaccalaureate professional doctoral degree program that leads to licensure to practice as a pharmacist.

Research Facilities

Ample laboratory space to provide an excellent research environment for all students working on laboratory-based projects is found in modern laboratories in the Riffe Building and in laboratories in Parks Hall. An outstanding Pharmacy and Bioscience Library subscribes to approximately 1,500 journals and contains more than 150,000 books. Modern equipment that is necessary for sophisticated research in chemistry, biochemistry, molecular biology, and biotechnology is available in the College. This includes such items as NMR and ESR spectrometers, radioisotope equipment, gas chromatographs, liquid chromatographs, and physiological recording systems. Cell-culture facilities and an animal vivarium provide additional capabilities.

Financial Aid

Financial support is granted on a competitive basis. Graduate associates are normally appointed on a twelve-month basis. In 2005–06, stipends for graduate associateships ranged from $18,000 to $25,000 per year. In addition, tuition and fees are waived for all graduate associates. A limited number of government and industrial fellowships, University fellowships, and research associateships are also available.

Cost of Study

In 2006–07, tuition and fees for graduate students enrolled in any quarter for 10 or more credit hours were $3121 for Ohio residents and $7572 for nonresidents. Health insurance is required for all students; however, domestic students can choose alternate plans. International students are required to purchase the University's student health insurance plan or graduate associate health insurance. After the University's contribution of 80 percent for the student health insurance comprehensive plan, the single rate for 2006–07 was $91 per quarter.

Living and Housing Costs

University housing is available for single students, married students, or single parents with dependent children. The University provides information on available apartments and rooming houses in the community as well as counseling for students who have questions concerning rental procedures.

Student Group

The Ohio State University includes 10,418 graduate students in its total annual enrollment of about 55,000 students. The graduate programs in the College of Pharmacy enroll approximately 100 U.S. and international students, who come from a wide geographic distribution and represent a variety of undergraduate academic disciplines and institutions.

Student Outcomes

Nearly half of the graduates find positions in the pharmaceutical industry, nearly half enter academia, and a small number switch to a career outside of the pharmaceutical sciences. Those entering academic careers are nearly evenly distributed between institutions in which teaching is the major expected job function and those in which a high level of research is expected along with teaching.

Location

The state's capital and largest city, Columbus is the only city in the northeast quadrant of the country that grew in population during the last census period. Currently, the city has a metropolitan population of approximately 1 million. Columbus is primarily a service-industry community, although there is some light manufacturing. The city has all the amenities of a major metropolitan area—a thriving downtown complete with excellent restaurants, a symphony, a ballet company, theaters, museums, sporting events, and art galleries. Whether they are weekend athletes, amateur musicians, or fine arts buffs, students find a wealth of recreational and cultural pursuits to complement their life in the laboratory, library, or classroom at The Ohio State University and in Columbus.

The University and The College

The Ohio State University, established in 1870, is the premier graduate degree–granting university in Ohio and is among the most prominent institutions of higher education in the world. The University offers 170 fields of specialization for the baccalaureate degree; 120 graduate programs offer a total of 209 degrees, with eighty-eight leading to the Ph.D.

Although pharmacy was first studied at The Ohio State University in the Department of Chemistry, a School of Pharmacy was founded in 1885 and the College of Pharmacy was established in 1895. Today, the College is internationally recognized as a major teaching and research institute in the field of pharmacy.

Applying

Applicants should have a bachelor's degree in pharmacy or in another appropriate field, depending on the area of study selected. Applications are accepted throughout the year, but students seeking financial assistance should apply before February 1. International students whose native language is not English must submit proof of proficiency in English to be considered for admission. A minimum TOEFL score of 250 (computer-based) or 80 (Internet-based) is required. Students who are awarded graduate associateships are required to take a spoken English examination upon arrival at the University. If the score is below the requirement, students must complete the spoken English series within the first three quarters of admission. GRE General Test scores must be submitted by all applicants.

Correspondence and Information

For further information, students should contact:
Office of Graduate Studies and Research
College of Pharmacy
The Ohio State University
500 West 12th Avenue
Columbus, Ohio 43210-1291
Phone: 614-292-6822
Fax: 614-292-2588
E-mail: gadmbrks@dendrite.pharmacy.ohio-state.edu
Web site: http://www.pharmacy.ohio-state.edu

The Ohio State University

THE FACULTY AND THEIR RESEARCH

Division of Medicinal Chemistry and Pharmacognosy

Robert W. Brueggemeier, Ph.D., Professor and Dean. Aromatase inhibitors, steroid biochemistry, hormones and cancer, radiochemicals.

Ching-Shih Chen, Ph.D., Professor. Mechanism-based design of novel therapeutic agents that selectively target apoptosis machinery in cancer cells at cellular or epigenetic levels.

Robert W. Curley, Ph.D., Professor. Vitamin A and its retinoid analogues, stereoselective syntheses of stable isotope-labeled amino acids, NMR studies of drug-receptor interactions.

A. Douglas Kinghorn, Ph.D., Professor. Discovery of therapeutic agents from plant sources, isolating potential agents for cancer chemotherapy and chemoprevention.

Chenglong Li, Ph.D., Assistant Professor. Computer-aided drug design and molecular modeling.

Pui-Kai Li, Ph.D., Associate Professor. Sulfatase inhibitors, neurosteroids, synthesis of melatonin ligands, thalidomide analogues, KGFR antagonists.

Werner Tjarks, Ph.D., Assistant Professor. Synthesis and biological evaluation of boronated nucleosides, folates, texaphyrins for neutron capture therapy.

Karl Werbovetz, Ph.D., Assistant Professor. Discovery and development of drugs to treat disease caused by parasitic organisms.

Division of Pharmaceutics

Jessie L.-S. Au, Pharm.D., Ph.D., Dorothy M. Davis Professor. Pharmacodynamics of anticancer drugs in cultured cells, tissues, animals, and patients; treatment of bladder, head and neck, prostate, breast, and ovarian cancers.

Kenneth K. Chan, Ph.D., Professor. Pharmacokinetics, metabolism, and mechanism of action; preclinical and clinical cancer drug development; antisense oligomers and histone protein deacetylase inhibitors; liquid chromatography mass spectrometry; analytical method development.

James T. Dalton, Ph.D., Professor. Preclinical pharmacology, pharmacokinetics, and metabolism of selective androgen receptor modulators and novel anticancer agents.

Sylvan G. Frank, Ph.D., Professor. Design and evaluation of drug-delivery systems.

Ram Ganapathi, Ph.D., Associate Professor. Molecular pharmacology of antitumor drug resistance.

Williams L. Hayton, Ph.D., Professor. Pharmacokinetics and metabolism in aquatic species, scaling for body size and environmental factors, aquaculture drug development.

Mamuka Kvaratskhelia, Ph.D., Assistant Professor. Study of the drug-protein-DNA/RNA interactions in HIV and cancer using novel powerful proteomic approaches.

Robert J. Lee, Ph.D., Associate Professor. Receptor-mediated targeted drug-delivery systems.

Wolfgang Sadee, Ph.D., Professor. Pharmacogenomic factors that determine treatment of complex diseases, including coronary artery disease, cancer, and CNS disorders.

Thomas G. Schmittgen, Ph.D., Associate Professor. Development of nucleic acid, aptamers as diagnostic and therapeutic targeting agents for prostate and breast cancer.

Duxin Sun, Ph.D., Assistant Professor. Transporters in drug absorption, prodrug design, and targeted drug delivery of small molecules for cancer therapy.

M. Guillaume Wientjes, Ph.D., Professor. Pharmacokinetics and pharmacodynamics of drugs for bladder and prostate cancer in patients, animals, and cell culture; use of regional and targeted drug delivery.

Division of Pharmacology

Terry S. Elton, Ph.D., Professor. Angiotensin II receptors: gene regulation, alternative splice variants, and signaling pathways.

Dale G. Hoyt, Ph.D., Associate Professor. Endothelial-cell DNA damage, DNA repair, and signal transduction.

Kari R. Hoyt, Ph.D., Assistant Professor. Transgenic models of neurodegeneration, oxidative, and mitochondrial mechanisms in neuronal death; primary neuronal culture and fluorescence imaging.

Keli Hu, Ph.D., Assistant Professor. Roles, regulation, and physiological significance of ion-channel function and trafficking.

Lakhu Keshvara, Ph.D., Assistant Professor. Signaling pathways that govern neurodevelopment as well as neuroinflammation, with a focus on protein and lipid phosphorylation as regulatory mechanisms.

Dennis B. McKay, Ph.D., Professor. Cellular and molecular neuropharmacology, neuronal nicotinic receptors, drug discovery and development, neurosecretory mechanisms, autonomic regulation in heart failure.

Lane J. Wallace, Ph.D., Professor. Mechanisms of drug addiction and neurodegeneration caused by addicting drugs, computational neuroscience.

Anthony P. Young, Ph.D., Professor. Molecular and cellular pharmacology, regulation of glutamine synthetase gene expression during retinal development, and glucocorticoid-mediated muscle atrophy; nitric oxide synthase gene expression.

Division of Pharmacy Practice and Administration

Rajesh Balkrishnan, Ph.D., Merrell Dow Professor. Pharmaceutical outcomes research, quantitative research methodology, economic evaluation, health-care effectiveness issues, medication-use behaviors, access and equity to pharmaceuticals.

Robert A. Buerki, Ph.D., Professor. Professional ethics, history of pharmacy, pharmacy education.

Esperanza J. Carache de Blanco, Ph.D., Assistant Professor. Natural products drug discovery, development of dietary supplements.

Cynthia Carnes, Pharm.D., Ph.D., Associate Professor. Cardiovascular pharmacotherapy, emphasizing electrophysiology and electropharmacology.

James D. Coyle, Pharm.D., Assistant Professor. Prevention and treatment of cardiovascular and kidney disease in at-risk patients, particularly patients with chronic kidney disease; clinical pharmacokinetics and dynamics.

Joseph F. Dasta, M.S., Professor. Critical care, health economics.

George Hinkle, M.S., Associate Professor. Nuclear pharmacy, medical use of radionuclides, radiolabeled antibodies, peptides and receptor-binding compounds.

Daren L. Knoell, Pharm.D., Associate Professor. Investigation of mechanisms responsible for lung pathogenesis, development of innovative strategies to treat or prevent lung disease.

James W. McAuley, Ph.D., Professor. Neurology clinical and translational research.

Milap C. Nahata, Pharm.D., Professor. Clinical pharmacokinetics; efficacy, safety, and health outcomes associated with pharmacotherapy.

Craig A. Pedersen, Ph.D., Associate Professor. Medication-use system epidemiology, patient safety technologies, pharmacy workforce/labor economics, leadership.

Philip J. Schneider, M.S., Clinical Professor. Medication-use safety, the impact of technology on medication use, gaps between standards and actual practice, job satisfaction in the workforce.

Enrique Seoane-Vazquez, Ph.D., Assistant Professor. Access to pharmaceutical drug prices and generic prices and competition in the market, pharmacoeconomics.

Sheryl L. Szeinbach, Ph.D., Professor. Distribution of pharmaceutical products and services; service delivery decision-making processes that involve utility analysis (pharmacoeconomics) and risk assessment; organizational structure, automation, and information technology.

SouthUniversity℠

SOUTH UNIVERSITY

Savannah Campus
School of Pharmacy
Doctor of Pharmacy

Program of Study

The South University School of Pharmacy, accredited by the Accreditation Council for Pharmacy Education (ACPE), is one of only three schools of pharmacy in the state of Georgia and one of only six in the U.S. to offer an accelerated three-year curriculum. The mission of the South University School of Pharmacy is to serve the public's health-care needs by preparing pharmacists to provide pharmaceutical care that improves health outcomes for patients.

The School of Pharmacy strives for excellence in teaching, scholarship, professional service, and community service. Faculty members provide students with the knowledge, skills, abilities, and values necessary to become a successful practitioner. While at South University, students are encouraged to foster a desire for lifelong learning, engage in scholarship, learn about the process of research, and develop an understanding of the value of interdisciplinary care. At South University, students are encouraged to become involved in their community and develop an understanding of the importance of volunteerism and its impact on the community.

Following acceptance into the program, Pharm.D. students begin an accelerated, full-time, twelve-quarter schedule designed to provide four academic years of study within three calendar years. This accelerated pace is only available at a handful of institutions across the country. South University's program was designed to meet the increasing demand of well-trained pharmacists. The program is tailored to accentuate the future of the pharmacy profession while also developing pharmacists who are familiar with contemporary practice. The curriculum is structured to educate and prepare competent pharmaceutical practitioners who can provide care in a variety of institutional, community, and other settings. Students learn the skills to assess, monitor, initiate, or adjust drug therapy programs. In those roles, they are prepared to educate patients on the proper use of pharmaceuticals, develop drug therapy plans through data evaluation, and partner with other health-care providers to contribute to a patient's well-being.

Research Facilities

South University's Savannah campus is home to the School of Business, the School of Health Professions, and the School of Pharmacy. The campus houses classroom and laboratory facilities for the health sciences and pharmacy programs. In addition, the University opened an $8-million School of Pharmacy building in December 2004. This facility provides wireless instructional, laboratory, and office facilities for pharmacy students, faculty members, and administrators. In addition to eight small classrooms, two large tiered lecture halls, and two 50-seat classrooms, the building houses two general-purpose laboratories that accommodate 34 students each, a sterile dilutions facility, six patient examination rooms equipped with audio/video monitoring, a drug information center, and a suite of eight laboratories to accommodate basic faculty research. Practice sites to provide both intermediate and advanced practice experiences include community pharmacies, hospitals, long-term-care facilities, pharmaceutical companies, and other venues that have been recruited to support the experiential component of the curriculum. South University's facilities are designed to offer personalized and technically sophisticated instructional delivery.

The campus library provides comfortable study space for students, wireless Internet capabilities for laptop network connectivity, a separate computer lab, and reference and interlibrary loan services.

Financial Aid

A wide range of financial aid options is available to students who qualify. The Savannah campus of South University offers access to federal and state aid, including grants, loans, and work-study programs. Eligible students may apply for veterans' educational benefits and are encouraged to investigate the availability of grants and scholarships through community resources. As a first step, students should complete the Free Application for Federal Student Aid (FAFSA). Students may apply electronically at http://www.fafsa.ed.gov or at the campus Student Financial Services department. Applications should be submitted promptly to receive consideration for the maximum amount of aid.

Cost of Study

Tuition information for the Doctor of Pharmacy program may be obtained by contacting the School of Pharmacy via the South University Web site at http://www.southuniversity.edu.

Living and Housing Costs

South University offers school-sponsored student housing at its Savannah campus in conjunction with a local apartment complex. Due to the full-time nature of the program, pharmacy students typically live in rental homes or apartments in the Savannah area. More information is available by contacting the Director of Student Housing at 912-201-8000.

Student Group

The Savannah campus of South University has a diverse student body enrolled in both day and evening classes. Students are primarily commuters who live within 50 miles of the city.

Student Outcomes

The South University Career Services Department has been established to assist currently enrolled students in developing their career plans and reaching their employment goals. Career services include, but are not limited to, one-on-one career counseling, special career-related workshops and programs, coaching for resume and cover letter development, and resume referral to employers.

Location

Located on the south side of the historic city of Savannah, the campus is convenient to the city's bustling midtown section and a full range of educational and cultural activities. The Atlantic Ocean and recreational amenities of Tybee Island, including beaches and numerous outdoor activities, are just a short drive away. In addition, the campus is located just a short drive from Hilton Head Island and Charleston, South Carolina.

The School

The School of Pharmacy is accredited by the American Council on Pharmaceutical Education (ACPE). South University is accredited as a Level V institution by the Commission on Colleges, Southern Association of Colleges and Schools (1866 Southern Lane, Decatur, Georgia 30033-4097; phone: 404-679-4501), to award associate, bachelor's, master's, and doctoral degrees.

Applying

Students are accepted into the Doctor of Pharmacy program once each year in the fall quarter that begins in August. Candidates may choose to qualify for early admission or general admission. Entrance into the program is gained through a formal application review and assessment of the applicant's potential for professional and academic achievement. Prospective students must complete a minimum of two years of prescribed prepharmacy course requirements at a regionally accredited U.S. college or university. A grade of C or better must be earned in each prerequisite course. The cumulative GPA for the current first-year class was 3.41, and their average science GPA was 3.15. Applicants also must submit scores from the Pharmacy College Admissions Test (PCAT), along with three recommendations and a handwritten personal statement.

The South University School of Pharmacy utilizes the Pharmacy College Application Service (PharmCAS), a centralized application service for prospective students applying to colleges and schools of pharmacy.

Correspondence and Information

Applications for admission to the South University Doctor of Pharmacy program are available by contacting:

School of Pharmacy
South University
709 Mall Boulevard
Savannah, Georgia 31406-4805
Phone: 912-201-8120
      866-629-2901 (toll-free)
Fax: 912-201-8070
E-mail: pharmd@southuniversity.edu
Web site: http://www.southuniversity.edu/pharmacy

South University

THE FACULTY

One of the most outstanding aspects of South University's Doctor of Pharmacy program is the dedication of the faculty members and their ability to cultivate a supportive learning environment. Faculty members are committed to their roles as mentors, teachers, and colearners. They are also dedicated to the training of students who can assume positions of leadership within the field of pharmacy. A current list of program faculty members is available at the South University Web site (http://www.southuniversity.edu/pharmacy).

South University's School of Pharmacy is one of only six schools in the country to offer an accelerated three-year Doctor of Pharmacy degree program.

TEMPLE UNIVERSITY
of the Commonwealth System of Higher Education

School of Pharmacy
Programs in the Pharmaceutical Sciences

Programs of Study
The graduate program in the School of Pharmacy offers Doctor of Philosophy (Ph.D.) and thesis-based Master of Science (M.S.) programs in medicinal/pharmaceutical chemistry, pharmaceutics, and pharmacodynamics (Web site: http://www.temple.edu/pharmacy/graduate.htm). Nonthesis Master of Science programs in quality assurance/regulatory affairs (QA/RA) and pharmaceutics are also offered (Web site: http://www.temple.edu/pharmacy_QARA/).

The School of Pharmacy programs are interdepartmental and provide for specialization in the areas described. They are designed to give the superior student an opportunity for the extension of demonstrated talent for the acquisition and application of basic knowledge. The requirements for completing the degrees are those of the Graduate School of Temple University: demonstration of scholarship by performance in appropriate course work, satisfactory performance in comprehensive examinations, selection and prosecution of a significant research problem, and preparation and defense of a scholarly thesis (when appropriate). (More information is available at http://www.temple.edu/grad/policies/gradpolicies.htm.)

Research Facilities
Surrounding the pharmacy building are the Schools of Medicine, Dentistry, and Health Professions, as well as Temple University Hospital, affording ample opportunity for interdisciplinary research. The laboratories located in the pharmacy building at the Health Sciences Center contain a wide array of modern equipment to conduct research. Analytical instrumentation includes capillary electrophoresis; GC/MS systems with chemical ionization and EI capabilities; HPLC systems with UV, fluorescence, refractive index, and electrochemical detectors; and LC/MS and LC/MS/MS systems. A newly constructed state-of-the-art good manufacturing practices (GMP) solid dosage form production facility is now in operation, providing students the ability to engage in hands-on modern pharmaceutical manufacturing techniques. An AAALAC-accredited animal-care facility is located in the pharmacy building, with nearby satellites in the medical school. The pharmacy building is the home of the Fels Cancer Research and Molecular Biology Center, which includes flow cytometry and confocal microscopy centers. An advanced nuclear magnetic resonance spectroscopy center is located a short distance away in the Department of Chemistry at the main campus. A heath sciences and pharmacy/dental library, with a large offering of online databases and bound volumes, is housed in proximity to the School. Temple University has been ranked number four in *The Princeton Review*'s 25 Most Connected Campuses, which examines the technological capabilities of the country's best cutting-edge schools.

Financial Aid
Support, in the form of teaching/research assistantships and fellowships, is available on a competitive basis for the thesis-based degree options only. Doctoral fellowships (stipend and tuition remission) are available from the University to Ph.D. students on a competitive basis. Graduate teaching assistantships (TAs) and research assistantships (RAs) are also available to Ph.D. students on a competitive basis (stipend and tuition remission).

Cost of Study
Temple University is a state-related university. Relevant data about the University and the annual tuition costs for residents and out-of-state students can be found on the Web at http://www.temple.edu/bursar/tuition_rates.htm and at http://www.temple.edu/factbook/.

Living and Housing Costs
Graduate students usually live in apartments or rooms in various sections of the city. Costs vary considerably, but 1 or 2 students often occupy an apartment renting for an average of $800 to $1000 per month.

Student Group
More than 500 graduate students from all over the world are enrolled at the Health Sciences Center as part of a student population of almost 2,700, which includes professional students. The School of Pharmacy has more than 300 graduate students enrolled in its various programs.

Student Outcomes
Graduates from the Doctor of Philosophy and Master of Science degree programs have accepted faculty or postdoctoral positions at universities throughout the country, including Harvard, Washington University, Fox Chase Cancer Center, Florida A&M, and Tufts. The largest concentration of pharmaceutical companies in the nation is located in the tristate area surrounding Philadelphia. Many graduates have accepted employment in the pharmaceutical industry at Wyeth Research, Merck, Bristol-Myers Squibb, AstraZeneca, Norvartis, Roche, Boehringer Ingelgeim, and West Pharmaceuticals, among others. Graduates are currently engaged in research and development, pharmaceutical production, and analytical laboratory work as well as quality assurance/regulatory affairs.

Location
Philadelphia is the second-largest city on the East Coast and plays an important part in the Temple University experience. Every academic program is enhanced by the cultural and intellectual life of the nation's fifth-largest city. The Philadelphia story is expanding beyond the history that is still an important part of the city's image and significance. Philadelphia is at the center of a region that is alive with innovation in commerce and finance, technological and scientific advancement, achievement in medicine and law, and accomplishment in the arts. Philadelphia's Broad Street has been transformed into an axis of theaters, galleries, and performance spaces. The Avenue of the Arts, as it is known, is a ribbon of creativity winding from south Philadelphia, wrapping around city hall, and continuing north through Temple's main campus. In Center City, a few blocks east of the Avenue of the Arts, is a district well known to shoppers, convention visitors, tourists, and historians: Market Street East, with the Reading Terminal Market, the Pennsylvania Convention Center, a smorgasbord of restaurants, and the Liberty Bell. Further east on Market Street is Penn's Landing, a scenic boulevard splashed with clubs and restaurants, at the edge of the Delaware River. Added to these possibilities are Fairmount Park, the nation's largest landscaped city park; the renowned Philadelphia Museum of Art; the nightlife of South Street; the Flyers, Eagles, Phillies, and 76ers; and a mosaic of vibrant neighborhoods. It is easy to see why Temple University is happy to call Philadelphia home.

The University
Temple University, of the Commonwealth System of Higher Education, is a comprehensive public research university with more than 34,000 students. It has a distinguished faculty in seventeen schools and colleges, including the Schools of Law, Medicine, Pharmacy, Podiatry, and Dentistry, and a renowned Health Sciences Center. Temple University is the twenty-eighth-largest university in the United States, and it is the sixth-largest provider of professional education (law, dentistry, medicine, pharmacy, and podiatric medicine) in the country. Based in Philadelphia, Temple has five regional campuses: the flagship main campus, the health sciences campus, and the Center City campus in Philadelphia; a major suburban campus—Temple University at Ambler; and a suburban art campus in Elkins Park—Tyler School of Art. The University has educational centers in Harrisburg and Fort Washington, Pennsylvania, and international campuses in Tokyo and Rome. Temple also offers educational programs in the People's Republic of China, Israel, Greece, Great Britain, France, and other countries throughout the world.

Applying
Applicants should have a bachelor's degree in biology, biochemistry, chemistry, chemical engineering, pharmacy, or a related field, depending on the area of study selected. International students whose native language is not English must submit proof of proficiency in English to be considered for admission. A minimum TOEFL score of 600 (paper-based) or 250 (computer-based) is required.

Students are encouraged to apply as early as possible. Students may apply at any time but are admitted to full-time programs in the fall semester only. Applications, including all transcripts of college work (sent directly from the university, not from the student), three letters of recommendation, a letter of intent written by the student, and GRE General Test scores, should be submitted by December 31. More information regarding minimum GPAs and GRE scores is available on the Web site. Personal interviews may be requested. Notifications of decisions are made as soon as possible.

Correspondence and Information
Daniel J. Canney, Ph.D., Director of Graduate Studies
School of Pharmacy, Suite 528
Temple University
3307 North Broad Street
Philadelphia, Pennsylvania 19140
Phone: 215-707-4972 (Admissions Office)
E-mail: tuspgrad@temple.edu
Web site: http://www.temple.edu/pharmacy/

Temple University

THE FACULTY AND THEIR RESEARCH

Michael R. Borenstein, Ph.D., Associate Professor and Associate Dean of Pharmaceutical Sciences. Synthesis and evaluation of novel pharmacologic agents, especially with regard to the structural prerequisites for anticonvulsant and CNS activity; development of analytical methodologies (GC/MS and HPLC) for therapeutic drug monitoring, pharmacokinetics, drug metabolism, and dosage forms.

Daniel J. Canney, Ph.D., Associate Professor of Medicinal Chemistry and Director of Graduate Studies. Design, synthesis, and biological evaluation (structure-activity relationship (SAR) studies) of novel ligands for cholinergic (muscarinic and nicotinic) and retinoic acid receptor subtypes; design, synthesis, and evaluation of inhibitors of protein-DNA interactions; synthesis of drug conjugates for metabolism studies.

Reza A. Fassihi, Ph.D., Professor of Biopharmaceutics and Industrial Pharmacy. Drug product design, formulation and development of conventional and modified drug dosage forms, intrinsic permeability of the intestinal wall and drug transport, biopharmaceutical aspects of medicine, in vitro and in vivo evaluation of pharmaceuticals.

James M. Gallo, Ph.D., Professor of Pharmacodynamics. Improving anticancer drug therapy through development of novel drug delivery strategies, characterization of pharmacokinetic and pharmacodynamic properties of both single-agent and combination drug regimens.

Marc Ilies, Ph.D., Assistant Professor of Medicinal Chemistry. Design, synthesis, and evaluation of carbonic anhydrase activators and inhibitors; bioorganic chemistry at membrane interfaces; general aspects of organic and medicinal chemistry.

Evgeny Krynetskiy, Ph.D., Associate Professor of Pharmaceutical Sciences. Characterization of genetic variability in drug-metabolizing enzymes and drug transporter folate carrier (RFC); in particular, development of a genotyping assay of the polymorphic enzyme thiopurine methyltransferase (TPMT) resulted in improved therapy regimens involving thiopurines (U.S. patent issued).

David B. Lebo, Ph.D., Lecturer in Pharmaceutics and Director of cGMP Services. Extensive experience in industrial pharmacy. Past positions include preformulation, formulation development, technical operations, and drug delivery. His research interest is the physical chemical aspects of solubility enhancement.

Swati Nagar, Ph.D., Assistant Professor of Pharmaceutical Sciences. Changes in pharmacokinetics that occur as a result of diseases, including sickle cell anemia and various cancers, and the differences in drug metabolism–attributed pharmacogenetic variability.

Robert B. Raffa, Ph.D., Professor of Pharmacology. In vivo evaluation of opioid and nonopioid peptide and nonpeptide analgesics, mechanisms, tolerance, and dependence; isolated tissue preparations; theoretical pharmacology; synergistic drug interactions; thermodynamics of the drug-receptor interaction.

Scott M. Rawls, Ph.D., Assistant Professor of Pharmacodynamics. Pharmacology of the opioid, cannabinoid, and glutamate systems using microdialysis techniques; studies of nociception and pain.

Ellen A. Walker, Ph.D., Associate Professor of Pharmacodynamics. Behavioral pharmacology of agents acting at opioid and serotonin receptor systems, theoretical aspects of inverse agonists at the 5-HT receptor.

Albert I. Wertheimer, Ph.D., M.B.A., Professor of Pharmacy Practice and Director of Center for Pharmaceutical Services Research. Pharmacoeconomics.

THOMAS JEFFERSON UNIVERSITY

Jefferson School of Pharmacy
Doctor of Pharmacy Program

Program of Study

Thomas Jefferson University's Jefferson School of Pharmacy (JSP) is dedicated to preparing students to play a key role as a member of the health-care team. JSP's presence on an academic health center campus offers students an environment that naturally fosters collaborative relationships with other health-care practitioners and scientists, resulting in the advancement of patient care and safety. Through the provision of a learner-centered, interdisciplinary curriculum, students develop the requisite knowledge, skills, and attitudes that are necessary to provide excellent patient-centered and population-based care.

The School's Doctor of Pharmacy (Pharm.D.) degree reflects this vision. The program's innovative curriculum provides students with the opportunity to develop clinical-practice skills in one of the most prominent health-care systems in the country. For more than forty years, Thomas Jefferson University Hospital has been widely regarded as having one of the most outstanding hospital pharmacies in the country. In addition, the faculty comprises some of the region's top science and health-care researchers.

Students enter the Pharm.D. program with 68 prerequisite credits and complete four years of study and 137 credits at Jefferson. During the first year, students take courses including biochemistry, immunology, pharmacy practice, and pathophysiology. Courses taken during the second year include pharmacology, pharmacy practice, drug delivery systems, and pharmacy management, plus lab courses and electives. During the third year, course work covers clinical diagnosis and pharmacotherapy, pharmacoeconomics and health outcomes, and patient care, plus one professional seminar and 6 credits in elective courses. The final year requires completion of four core experiences, each lasting about six weeks and earning 6 credits, in community pharmacy, hospital and health system pharmacy, ambulatory care, and inpatient and acute care; two elective experiences, each lasting approximately six weeks; a pharmacy law course; and a second professional seminar.

Research Facilities

The Scott Memorial Library includes more than 220,000 bound volumes and over 2,600 journal subscriptions. An additional 2,900 titles are available in full-text electronic format for remote access. In addition, a variety of popular bestseller books and magazines, music CDs, medical education software, and 3-D models complement the library's core book and journal collection. The University Archives houses important university records, manuscripts and personal papers, memorabilia, photographs, rare books, and other historical materials.

Financial Aid

A number of grants and scholarships are available from the University, including the Dean's Scholarship, a merit-based award of $5000 per year, and several other scholarships, which are awarded to students who demonstrate financial need. Other scholarships may be available from private sources.

Under the Federal Stafford Student Loan program, students may receive up to $8500 per year in subsidized loans and $12,000 in unsubsidized loans. Federal Perkins Loans of up to $6000 per year are available to students who demonstrate financial need. Federal Work Study allows students to earn part of their educational expenses by working part-time.

Cost of Study

In 2007–08, tuition is $13,250 per semester for full-time students and $800 per credit for part-time students. Other expenses include a Challenge Examination fee of $50 per credit, lab fees of $50 per course, and activities fees. Students should expect to spend $1495 per year on books and supplies and $855 on miscellaneous costs.

Living and Housing Costs

Students living on campus can expect to spend $805 per month for an efficiency, $935 to $995 for a one-bedroom, $1410 to $1485 for a two-bedroom, or $1665 to $1760 for a three-bedroom apartment. Students living off campus typically spend $850 to $1200 per month for a one-bedroom or $1200 to $2000 for a two-bedroom apartment, depending on size and location.

Student Group

Students in the program come from a wide range of backgrounds, but all have a sufficient background in pharmacy studies and related fields.

Location

Thomas Jefferson University is located in historic Center City Philadelphia, the fourth-largest city in the United States. It is within walking distance of theaters, museums, art galleries, and many places of historical interest. Convenient bus, rail, and subway lines offer transportation to Jefferson as well as to a variety of interesting tourist attractions. Philadelphia combines the historic and the modern. Each distinct neighborhood offers a variety of shops and restaurants, while other sites, such as South Street and Independence Mall, have historic sites standing side-by-side with twenty-first-century attractions. Just outside Philadelphia are horse trails and wine trails, while the New Jersey shore and the Pennsylvania mountains offer year-round recreation.

The University

Thomas Jefferson University is a private, nonsectarian academic health center and is one of the first and largest academic health centers in the United States. It was founded as Jefferson Medical College in 1824. In 1969, the College of Graduate Studies and the College of Health Professions joined Jefferson Medical College to form the Thomas Jefferson University. The goals of the University are to educate qualified students as physicians, nurses, biomedical scientists, and health professionals; to expand the understanding of human beings and their environment, especially their health and diseases, through research; and to provide and promote health services as a basis for clinical education. The University fosters a community of biologically, medically, and health-oriented scholars, teachers, and clinicians who are dedicated to these goals.

Applying

All students entering the program must have completed 68 credits of prerequisite course work in several areas, including anatomy and physiology, biology, general chemistry, calculus, organic chemistry, physics, English composition, and social sciences. Prospective students must apply in two steps. First, they must submit a completed application for admission through PharmCAS, which includes official transcripts from all colleges previously attended, official Pharmacy College Admissions Test (PCAT) scores, and two letters of recommendation. Second, they must submit a supplemental Jefferson application online at http://www.jefferson.edu/jchp/admissions, which includes an essay describing extracurricular or community service activities and a $25 fee. Applications are considered on a rolling basis, but the application for admission should be completed by March 3, 2008.

Correspondence and Information

Office of Admissions
Jefferson College of Health Professions
Thomas Jefferson University
130 South 9th Street, Suite 100
Philadelphia, Pennsylvania 19107
Phone: 215-503-8890
        877-JEFF-CHP (533-3247; toll-free)
Web site: http://www.jefferson.edu/jchp/pharmacy/

Thomas Jefferson University

THE DEANS AND FACULTY

Rebecca S. Finley, Founding Dean, Jefferson School of Pharmacy; Pharm.D., Cincinnati, 1979.
Cynthia Sanoski, Chair, Department of Pharmacy Practice; Pharm.D., Illinois at Chicago, 1998.
Elena M. Umland, Associate Dean for Academic Affairs; Pharm.D., Philadelphia College of Pharmacy and Science, 1995.

Accreditation Disclosure Statement

The Accreditation Council for Pharmacy Education (ACPE; http://www.acpe-accredit.org) accredits Doctor of Pharmacy programs offered by Colleges and Schools of Pharmacy in the United States and selected non-U.S. sites. For a Doctor of Pharmacy program offered by a new College or School of Pharmacy, ACPE accreditation involves three steps: Precandidate status, Candidate status, and Full accreditation. Precandidate accreditation status denotes a developmental program, which is expected to mature in accord with stated plans and within a defined time period. Precandidate status is awarded to a new program of a College or School of Pharmacy that has not yet enrolled students in the professional program and authorizes the college or school to admit its first class. Candidate accreditation status is awarded to a Doctor of Pharmacy program that has students enrolled but has not yet had a graduating class. Full accreditation is awarded to a program that has met all ACPE standards for accreditation and has graduated its first class. Graduates of a class designated as having Candidate status have the same rights and privileges of those graduates from a fully accredited program, generally including eligibility for licensure. ACPE conveys its decision to the various boards of pharmacy and makes recommendations in accord with its decisions. It should be noted, however, that decisions concerning eligibility for licensure, by examination or reciprocity, reside with the respective boards of pharmacy in accordance with the statues and administrative rules.

Since students are not enrolling until fall semester 2008, the Thomas Jefferson University, Jefferson School of Pharmacy, has applied for Precandidate accreditation status for its Doctor of Pharmacy program. An on-site evaluation is scheduled to occur during fall 2007. The ACPE Board of Directors will meet in January 2008 to consider the School's application. The School will be notified of the board's decision as soon as feasible following the meeting. Should the board feel that Precandidate status cannot be conferred at that time, the School could respond to the board's concerns and reapply. Should the school enroll and begin instruction of its inaugural class without first achieving Precandidate status or fail to advance to Candidate status before graduation of its first class, the program will be ineligible for accreditation by ACPE until after graduation of its first class. It is unlikely that graduates of an unaccredited Doctor of Pharmacy program will meet licensing requirements in any U.S. jurisdiction.

UNIVERSITY AT BUFFALO, THE STATE UNIVERSITY OF NEW YORK

Graduate Program in Pharmaceutical Sciences

Programs of Study

The M.S. and Ph.D. programs in pharmaceutical sciences at the University at Buffalo (UB) offer didactic instruction and research training in diverse aspects of drug action, ranging from drug discovery to various elements of drug evaluation. These subjects are examined at the molecular, genomic, biochemical, biological, and clinical levels through an interdisciplinary curriculum that is individualized to the needs of each incoming student and his or her particular research interest. The program encompasses laboratory and clinical research in the areas of pharmacokinetics, pharmacodynamics, pharmacometrics, pharmacogenetics, pharmacogenomics, drug delivery, mechanisms of drug action, drug metabolism, drug product formulation, and drug analysis. A special one-year professional M.S. program in pharmacometrics offers intensive training in biometrics with a focus on drug development and evaluation.

The duration of the program is highly dependent on individual progress. M.S. students generally take one to two years, while Ph.D. students take four to five years to complete their training. Students are expected to have prior background in calculus, biochemistry, organic chemistry, physiology, and pharmacology, although deficient areas can be made up during the program. Ph.D. students acquire competence in pharmaceutical mathematics, analytical methods, drug delivery, drug transport, drug metabolism, drug development, pharmacokinetics, and biostatistics. The department also offers training in elective fields such as advanced pharmacokinetics, pharmacodynamics, pharmacogenomics, and various contemporary laboratory techniques such as liquid chromatography/tandem mass spectroscopy (LCMS), pharmaceutical genetics, small animal surgery, and biophysical techniques.

Research Facilities

The department maintains a broad range of contemporary research facilities and equipment for research in pharmaceutical sciences and pharmacology. Among the modern instrumentations are two liquid chromatography/mass spectrometers, suitable for both qualitative and quantitative work. The department also operates a pharmaceutical genetics laboratory for student training and research in molecular biology. For details, students should go to http://pharmsci.buffalo.edu/facilities/.

Financial Aid

Research assistantships are available to all qualified Ph.D. students, for the entire duration of the program, pending satisfactory progress. The stipend rate is the same as that paid to NIH predoctoral trainees (approximately $24,000 for 2007–08). Master's degree students do not receive assistantships but may work as laboratory assistants during semester breaks and summers.

Cost of Study

Full-tuition scholarships (but not fees) are provided to all qualified Ph.D. students. In fall 2006, tuition was $4109.25 per semester for in-state students and $6119.25 per semester for out-of-state students.

Living and Housing Costs

Both on-campus and off-campus housing are available for graduate students. Housing costs are moderate and are readily available around the Amherst suburban campus. For more details, prospective students should visit the Web site at http://www.grad.buffalo.edu/admissions/housing.shtml.

Student Group

The program maintains an ongoing enrollment of about 35 Ph.D. and 10 M.S. students. Ten to 12 new students (M.S. and Ph.D.) are enrolled each year.

Student Outcomes

Both M.S. and Ph.D. graduates are highly recruited by such pharmaceutical industry companies as Pfizer, Lilly, and Merck, with most graduates entertaining multiple offers prior to graduation. A number of graduates have selected postdoctoral training in other institutions in preparation for an academic career. Some graduates are currently employed by regulatory agencies such as the FDA. Past faculty members, graduates, postdoctoral fellows, and visiting scientists of the department form an extensive national and international network for continuing interaction and mutual assistance. For a listing of immediate positions accepted by recent graduates, students should visit http://www.pharmacy.buffalo.edu/psci_adm_grad_caropp.shtml.

Location

Buffalo, nicknamed the "City of Good Neighbors," is the second-largest city in New York State. Buffalo is a big city with a hometown feel. The area is a great place to study, work, and live, with world-class art galleries and museums, a comprehensive city-wide system of parks and green space designed by renowned landscape architect Frederick Law Olmsted, major and minor league sports teams, and a wide array of cultural and recreational elements. Buffalo is only 2–3 hours by car from many interesting areas, ranging from metropolitan Toronto to the scenic Finger Lakes region. Both summer and winter outdoor activities are plentiful.

The School of Pharmacy and Pharmaceutical Sciences is located on UB's North Campus in Amherst, a suburb of Buffalo. Safety in Amherst, New York, is unsurpassed in the country. In the latest edition of *City Crime Rankings*, an annual reference book of crime statistics and rankings by the Morgan Quitno Press research company, which compares crime statistics in 350 cities, Amherst was ranked first as "America's Safest City" for the fourth consecutive year. For more information, students should visit http://www.morganquitno.com/safecity.htm.

The University

The University at Buffalo was founded in 1846 as a private medical college and merged with the State University of New York system in 1962. Today, UB is New York State's premier public center for graduate and professional education as well as the state's largest and most comprehensive public university. A member of the prestigious Association of American Universities, the State University of New York at Buffalo ranks first among the nation's research-intensive public universities.

The School of Pharmacy and Pharmaceutical Sciences has been ranked as one of the top schools in the country, and the department's graduate training program is world-renowned. For more information, prospective students should visit http://www.pharmacy.buffalo.edu/psci_adm_grad_intrep.shtml or http://www.pharmacy.buffalo.edu/psci_adm_grad_alumni.shtml.

Applying

Only online applications are accepted. Application information can be accessed through the Web site at http://www.pharmacy.buffalo.edu/psci_adm_grad_apply.shtml. A fund has been established to pay the application fees of U.S. citizens and permanent residents. To qualify for this waiver, prospective students should contact the Director of Graduate Studies.

Correspondence and Information

Joseph P. Balthasar, Ph.D.
Director of Graduate Studies
Department of Pharmaceutical Sciences
School of Pharmacy and Pharmaceutical Sciences
University at Buffalo, the State University of New York
Buffalo, New York 14260-1200
Phone: 716-645-2842 Ext. 270
Fax: 716-645-3693
E-mail: jb@buffalo.edu
Web site: http://www.pharmacy.buffalo.edu/psci_adm_grad_index.shtml

University at Buffalo, the State University of New York

THE FACULTY AND THEIR RESEARCH

S. Balasubramanian, Ph.D., Assistant Professor. Pharmaceutical biotechnology and biophysics, protein delivery.

Joseph Balthasar, Ph.D., Associate Professor and Director of Graduate Studies. Antibody pharmacokinetics and pharmacodynamics.

Javier Blanco, Ph.D., Assistant Professor. Pharmacogenetics of cancer chemotherapy.

Kathleen M. K. Boje, Ph.D., Associate Professor and Vice Chair. Neuropharmacologic and neuroimmunologic modulation, blood-brain barrier transport.

Daniel Brazeau, Ph.D., Research Assistant Professor. Pharmacogenomics.

Gayle Brazeau, Ph.D., Associate Professor and Associate Dean. Skeletal muscle disease and therapeutics, drug delivery.

Ho-Leung Fung, Ph.D., Professor. Therapeutics of nitric oxide modulation, pharmacologic tolerance.

William J. Jusko, Ph.D., Professor and Chair. Pharmacokinetics and pharmacodynamics of immunosuppressive drugs.

Wojciech Krzyzanski, Ph.D., Assistant Professor. Mathematical modeling in pharmacodynamics.

Donald E. Mager, Pharm.D., Ph.D., Assistant Professor. Integrated and systems pharmacology of antiplatelet and anticancer drugs.

Marilyn E. Morris, Ph.D., Professor. Hepatic, renal, and intestinal drug transport and metabolism.

Murali Ramanathan, Ph.D., Associate Professor. Pharmacogenomics of multiple sclerosis and autoimmune diseases of the central nervous system.

Jerome J. Schentag, Pharm.D., Professor. Clinical pharmacodynamics in the acute-care setting.

Robert M. Straubinger, Ph.D., Associate Professor. Carrier-mediated drug delivery, intracellular processing.

Aiming Yu, Ph.D., Assistant Professor. Pharmacogenetics, drug metabolism and bioanalysis.

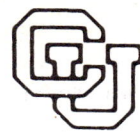

UNIVERSITY OF COLORADO AT DENVER AND HEALTH SCIENCES CENTER
School of Pharmacy

Programs of Study

The School of Pharmacy at the University of Colorado at Denver and Health Sciences Center offers graduate programs leading to the Ph.D. degree in pharmaceutical sciences and in toxicology. Basic and advanced courses are available in the areas of pharmacology, toxicology, medicinal chemistry, pharmacokinetics, and pharmaceutics.

Graduate students currently enrolled have bachelor's degrees in the areas of pharmacy, chemistry, biology, biochemistry, and molecular biology. The diverse backgrounds of the graduate students reflect the broad research interests of the faculty members. These include the mechanisms of toxicity of drugs and environmental chemicals, cancer research, drug addiction research, pharmacokinetics, medicinal chemistry, and the design of novel drug delivery systems.

Research Facilities

The School of Pharmacy has excellent facilities in a building on the University of Colorado at Denver and Health Sciences Center Campus. These include 28,800 square feet of research laboratory space, 6,250 square feet of office space, 4,000 square feet of conference rooms and administrative offices, 7,000 square feet of classroom space, and 3,000 square feet of reading room/lounge/group study rooms. The research space is equipped with modern instrumentation, including liquid chromatograph/mass spectrometer and gas chromatograph/mass spectrometer/computer systems and apparatus for high-performance liquid chromatography, gas chromatography, nuclear magnetic resonance spectroscopy, liquid and gamma scintillation counting, DNA and amino acid sequencing, tissue culture, electrophoresis and differential centrifugation equipment, rodent breeding, and behavior-testing facilities.

Financial Aid

Financial assistance is available in the form of graduate teaching and research assistantships and University doctoral fellowships. In 2006–07, monthly stipends were approximately $1875. For students seeking fellowship support, early application (by mid-January) is recommended.

Cost of Study

Tuition for graduate students in 2006–07 was $123 per quarter hour for residents of Colorado and $575 per quarter hour for nonresidents. Financial assistance in the form of tuition waivers is available for research and teaching assistants. Insurance and activity fees for all graduate students amounted to $3230 annually.

Living and Housing Costs

At present, no University housing is available. Students generally have little difficulty, however, finding suitable inexpensive housing close to campus. The cost of incidentals (rent, food, travel, etc.) is estimated by the Office of Financial Aid at $16,000 a year.

Student Group

Currently, 486 professional students are pursuing Pharm.D. degrees in a four-year program in the School of Pharmacy and 40 graduate students (19 women, 21 men) are seeking Ph.D. degrees. There are also many postdoctoral fellows and professional research assistants in the School of Pharmacy.

Location

The University of Colorado at Denver and Health Sciences Center Campus is located in a quiet residential area of east Denver. A modern city of approximately 2 million, Denver has a wide variety of cultural and recreational facilities. The climate in Denver and its environs is exceptionally pleasant with mild, sunny winters and warm, dry summers, which allows residents to partake of the many recreational opportunities afforded by the Rocky Mountains.

The University

What began in 1883 as a medical school with 2 students has evolved into the largest comprehensive health facility in the region and has gained both national and international recognition for accomplishments in biomedical research and patient care. The Center has undergone considerable expansion in the past decade, and current facilities include the enlarged and modernized Denison Library; the Schools of Medicine, Nursing, Dentistry, and Pharmacy; and a 400-bed teaching hospital. An eight-story biomedical research building was completed in 1991. Expected to take place in 2010 is the move to the new Fitzsimons campus, a 3.4-million-square-foot facility that includes the Anschutz Center for Advanced Medicine.

Applying

Applications for graduate admission can be submitted online at https://app.applyyourself.com/?id=UCHSC-G. The Graduate School Web page (http://www.uchsc.edu/gs/gs) contains specific instructions regarding the completion of forms, the forwarding of academic transcripts, and letters of recommendation. The Graduate Committee should receive all material before mid-February, and admission is normally granted for the fall only.

Correspondence and Information

Graduate Admissions
Department of Pharmaceutical Sciences
School of Pharmacy, Room 456
University of Colorado at Denver and Health Sciences Center
Campus Box C238
4200 East Ninth Avenue
Denver, Colorado 80262
Phone: 303-315-0565
Web site: http://www.uchsc.edu/sop/phd
      http://www.uchsc.edu/sop/phd/2.Ph.D._in_Toxicology

University of Colorado at Denver and Health Sciences Center

THE FACULTY AND THEIR RESEARCH

Rajesh Agarwal, Professor; Ph.D., Lucknow (India), 1981. Cancer pharmacology, phytochemicals and cancer prevention and therapy, signal transduction, cell-cycle regulation, apoptosis.

Ralph J. Altiere, Professor and Dean; Ph.D., New York Medical College, 1979. Pulmonary physiology and pharmacology, neural regulation of airway function, pulmonary vascular pharmacology.

Thomas J. Anchordoquy, Associate Professor; Ph.D., California, Davis, 1989. Gene delivery, physical stabilization and characterization of DNA-based therapeutics, liposome technology.

Peter Anderson, Assistant Professor; Pharm.D., Minnesota, Twin Cities, 1998. Determining the feasibility, safety, and antiviral activity of concentration-controlled antiretroviral therapy contrasted with the conventional approach of standard, fixed-dose therapy in all HIV-infected individuals in the population.

Christina Aquilante, Assistant Professor; Pharm.D., North Carolina at Chapel Hill. The influence of polymorphisms on interindividual variability in the pharmacokinetics, pharmacodynamics, and drug interactions of commonly used drugs in diabetes and cardiovascular disease.

David L. Bain, Assistant Professor; Ph.D., Johns Hopkins, 1994. Human progesterone receptor and its role in transcriptional regulation as it applies to breast cancer, the roles of ligand antagonists and antagonists in regulating assembly and transcriptional activity of the receptor.

John F. Carpenter, Professor; Ph.D., Southwestern Louisiana, 1985. Cellular physiology and pathophysiology, metabolic regulation, protein structure and function, protein preservation and formulation.

Louis Diamond, Professor; Ph.D., Maryland, 1967. Pulmonary physiology, pharmacology, and toxicology.

Dawn Duval, Assistant Professor; Ph.D., Nevada, 1994. The role of Ets transcription factors in development and progression of cancer, mechanisms by which the Ras oncogene activates transcription of the rat prolactin gene through a Pit-1/Etx-1 composite element, identification of the coactivators responsible for mediating Ras signaling to this transcriptional complex.

Christopher C. Franklin, Assistant Professor; Ph.D., Missouri–Columbia, 1989. Elucidation of the signal transduction pathways and molecular mechanisms that regulate apoptotic cell death in response to various extracellular stimuli.

Daniel L. Gustafson, Assistant Professor; Ph.D., Nevada, 1992. Interactions of xenobiotics at both the pharmacokinetic and pharmacodynamic levels.

Numsen Hail Jr., Assistant Professor; Ph.D., Texas–Houston Health Science Center. Investigation of the mechanistic aspects of apoptosis induction by several putative cancer chemopreventive agents in transformed human epithelial cells; exploration of whether changes in cellular bioenergetic and/or redox processes may dictate sensitivity to certain types of chemopreventive agents, e.g., phenolic compounds, selenium compounds, and vitamin E analogues.

Richard D. Irons, Professor; Ph.D., Rochester, 1974. Molecular mechanisms of leukemogenesis.

LaToya S. Jones, Assistant Professor; Ph.D., Colorado Health Sciences Center, 2001. Biophysical characterization of vaccine antigen-adjuvant interactions and polyanion-protein interactions.

Cynthia Ju, Assistant Professor; Ph.D., Toronto. Immune-mediated adverse drug reactions (IADR), T-cell hyporesponsiveness to drug protein adducts, acetaminophen-induced liver injury, immunosuppressive function of hepatic microphages.

Alvin M. Malkinson, Professor; Ph.D., Johns Hopkins, 1968. Genetic, biochemical, and histologic aspects of mouse lung tumor development and inflammation; protein phosphorylation; signal transduction.

N. Karl Maluf, Assistant Professor; Ph.D., Washington (St. Louis), 2003. Mechanism of viral DNA packaging in human adenovirus, role of putative NTPase activity, detailed biochemical and biophysical studies of the IVa2 protein.

Lori Dwyer Nield, Associate Research Professor; Ph.D., Kentucky, 1991. Involvement of protein kinase C signal transduction in lung tumorigenesis.

Manisha Patel, Associate Professor; Ph.D., Purdue, 1992. Neuroscience, oxidative stress, mitochondria, epilepsy, excitotoxicity, neurodegeneration, neurotoxicology.

Dennis R. Petersen, Professor and Vice Chair; Ph.D., Wyoming, 1974. Pharmacogenetics and toxicological aspects of hepatic aldehyde metabolism.

Richard Radcliffe, Assistant Professor; Ph.D., Colorado Health Sciences Center, 1996. Neuroscience, neurotoxicology, alcoholism, alcohol tolerance, mice/zebrafish, drug abuse, genetics, microarrays, QTL mapping, fear conditioning.

David Ross, Professor and Department Chair; Ph.D., Aston (Birmingham), 1982; DABFT. Relationship of metabolism to toxicity, mechanisms of bone marrow toxicity of myelotoxins and leukemogens, mechanisms of selective toxicity of cancer chemotherapeutic agents to human tumor cells.

James A. Ruth, Professor; Ph.D., Northwestern, 1974. Toxic mechanisms in drugs of abuse, mechanisms of drug deposition in hair, forensic toxicology.

Robert I. Scheinman, Assistant Professor; Ph.D., Washington (Seattle), 1990. Regulation of gene expression focusing on NF-κβ and steroid hormone receptors, mechanism of immunosuppression and growth regulation.

John A. Thompson, Professor; Ph.D., UCLA, 1969. Chemical and biochemical aspects of the metabolism and toxicity of drugs and environmental chemicals.

Vasilis K. Vasiliou, Associate Professor; Ph.D., Ioannina School of Medicine (Greece), 1988. Cellular responses to oxidative stress, pharmacogenetics of alcohol drinking preference and toxicity.

CURRENT RESEARCH

Research in the School is supported by a variety of federal and nonfederal agencies. Federal agencies include NCI, NEI, NIGMS, NIAAA, NIAID, NIBIB, NIDDKD, NIEHS, NINDS, and NSF. Current research support exceeds $14 million annually.

Biochemistry and Cellular Biology. Areas of study include mechanistic enzymology and molecular mechanisms of carcinogenesis and tumor promotion. Catalysis at the molecular level is of interest and is investigated in two general research areas: the biochemistry of virus assembly and the molecular mechanisms of genotoxicity. The interactions of compounds that can damage DNA directly or interfere with the proteins that regulate DNA behavior (replication, repair, transcription) are studied. Biochemical, biophysical, and molecular biological methods are extensively utilized to obtain a detailed picture of the processes involved in enzymatic catalysis.

Medicinal Chemistry. The focus of this interdisciplinary program provides students with the foundation necessary for applying chemical theory and techniques to studies of pharmacological and toxicological problems. Course work involves advanced training in organic, biological, and analytical chemistry, together with courses in pharmacology and toxicology. Students participate in an ongoing research program in one of several areas, including neurochemistry, drug metabolism, enzyme mechanisms, and chemical carcinogenesis.

Pharmaceutics. This field is concerned with the stability, the delivery, and the analysis of known drug compounds. Research projects include the design of delivery systems and stable formulations for recombinant protein drugs and genes; mechanistic studies on physical and chemical stabilization of proteins, peptides, and DNA; drug delivery across the blood-brain barrier; lyophilization technology; and advanced spectroscopic structural studies.

Pharmacology. Areas of study include autonomic, cardiovascular, pulmonary, and endocrine pharmacology.

Toxicology and Carcinogenesis. Areas of study are centered on elucidation of mechanisms of toxicity of drugs and environmental pollutants. Major research areas include studies of bone marrow toxicity and leukemogenesis, drug- and toxin-induced hepatic and lung injury, and mechanisms of DNA damage and tumor induction by environmental toxins. The role of metabolic mechanisms in toxicity is a central theme, and the elucidation of pathways of selective toxicity to human tumor cells is an additional focus of research in this area. Genetic analysis and the use of bioinformatics provide exciting tools for further mechanistic dissection.

UNIVERSITY OF SOUTHERN CALIFORNIA

School of Pharmacy

Programs of Study

The School of Pharmacy at the University of Southern California (USC) offers graduate programs in molecular pharmacology and toxicology, pharmaceutical economics and policy, and pharmaceutical sciences. The School also offers an interdisciplinary M.S. in regulatory science.

The programs that lead to the M.S. and Ph.D. degrees in molecular pharmacology and toxicology have an emphasis on molecular pharmacology, gene regulation, neuropharmacology, free-radical biochemistry, toxicology, and neurotoxicology. The molecular pharmacology and toxicology program offers superb interdisciplinary educational opportunities. Faculty members are engaged in research directed toward understanding the mechanisms of drug action, gene regulation, neurobiology of behavior, learning and memory, neurobiology of drug tolerance, and the induction and regulation of signal transduction systems. A major focus of research of the toxicology faculty is the role of free-radical mechanisms in metabolic regulation, carcinogenesis, and membrane-associated disorders. All areas of research emphasize the potential for development of therapeutic agents.

The programs that lead to the Master of Science (M.S.) and Doctor of Philosophy (Ph.D.) degrees in pharmaceutical economics and policy focus on economics and outcomes assessment of pharmaceuticals, pharmacy services, and medical technology. The programs also include research into the finance and delivery of pharmaceuticals and pharmacy services. Graduates have the capability to conduct research and provide training and expertise in assisting health-care organizations to make decisions regarding the costs and benefits of alternative therapeutic strategies.

The programs that lead to the M.S. and Ph.D. degrees in pharmaceutical sciences have an emphasis on cancer pharmacology, cell biology, computational drug design, drug targeting and delivery, medicinal chemistry, membrane biophysics, molecular pharmacology, and pharmacokinetics. The pharmaceutical sciences program provides highly interdisciplinary educational opportunities. Utilizing a broad spectrum of state-of-the-art techniques, faculty members are engaged in research directed toward understanding the mechanisms of drug interactions at transport barriers and target sites and developing new strategies in the design, functional analysis, delivery, and optimization of therapeutic agents.

Regulatory science relates to the regulatory and legal requirements of biomedical product development to the scientific testing and oversight needed to establish product safety and efficacy. The program provides an opportunity for advanced preparation in the fields of regulatory affairs, quality assurance, and clinical research. Offerings include a full- and part-time stand-alone program and a dual Pharm.D./M.S. program.

Research Facilities

The graduate programs of the School of Pharmacy are housed in the seven-story Pharmaceutical Sciences Center and the three-story Center for Health Professionals on the University's Health Science Campus. There are collaborative research programs with the USC Comprehensive Cancer Center, the USC Research Center for Liver Disease, the Doheny Eye Institute and Hospital, and the L.A. County–USC Medical Center, all of which are adjacent to the School of Pharmacy; with the science, public administration, and economics departments on the University Park Campus; and with a number of other prestigious clinical research facilities in the Los Angeles area. The School has the full range of equipment found in any modern research facility. The Norris Medical Library, located on the Health Science Campus, supports computerized searches through Ovid Online. With the University Park Campus libraries, the number of volumes exceeds 1.5 million.

Financial Aid

Fellowships, teaching assistantships, and research assistantships are available. These assistantships also come with an annual stipend award. Assistants also receive full tuition remission (up to 12 units per semester), while quarter-time positions receive up to 8 units of tuition remission per semester and health insurance and mandatory health center fees for the year.

Cost of Study

Tuition fees as of 2007 are $1209 per semester unit.

Living and Housing Costs

A limited number of double rooms are available in Seaver Hall, located next to the School. Rents vary in range (students must contact USC Housing Services for exact costs). Off-campus housing is also available.

Student Group

Of a total University population of 28,000 full-time and part-time students, almost 12,500 are pursuing graduate or professional degrees. Within the School of Pharmacy there are more than 120 graduate students. Approximately 75 percent of the students receive some form of financial assistance. The demand from the pharmaceutical industry, academia, and government for graduates in selected areas is high.

Location

The health sciences campus is 5 miles from downtown Los Angeles and is easily accessible from all parts of greater Los Angeles. The ocean, mountains, and deserts are all close by. Recreational and sporting facilities are excellent. Cultural and entertainment attractions are numerous, including the Los Angeles Philharmonic, the Los Angeles Chamber Orchestra, the Hollywood Bowl, numerous theaters, and the Music Center. Los Angeles supports professional basketball, hockey, soccer, and baseball teams, and numerous college sporting events are held throughout the year. The southern California climate, with mild winters and warm, dry summers, is renowned.

The University

Founded in 1880, the University is the oldest major independent, coeducational, nonsectarian university in the West. The modern health sciences campus, 7 miles from the main campus and adjacent to the L.A. County–USC Medical Center, houses not only the School of Pharmacy but also the School of Medicine, the Doheny Eye Institute and Hospital, and the USC Comprehensive Cancer Center, all of which have active research programs. There are excellent opportunities for collaborative work.

Applying

Applicants must have, or expect to receive, a bachelor's or higher-level degree in an appropriate field prior to beginning graduate studies (students should contact the respective department for details). A GPA of at least 3.0 and qualifying verbal and quantitative GRE test scores are required. International applicants must also submit a TOEFL score. Applicants who meet graduate admission standards are notified of acceptance by the end of May. Fellowships and teaching assistantships are offered to top applicants who have expressed the desire for financial aid. The application deadline for some of the fellowships is February 1.

Correspondence and Information

Graduate Affairs Office
School of Pharmacy
University of Southern California
1985 Zonal Avenue, PSC 713
Los Angeles, California 90089-9121
Phone: 323-442-1474
Fax: 323-442-2258
E-mail: pharmgrd@hsc.usc.edu
Web site: http://www.usc.edu/schools/pharmacy

University of Southern California

THE FACULTY AND THEIR RESEARCH

Pharmaceutical Economics and Policy

Richard L. Ernst, Assistant Research Professor; Ph.D., Berkeley, 1970. Theoretical foundations of cost-effective analysis for the planning of pharmaceutical formularies, provision of health care in general.

Denise R. Globe, Assistant Professor; Ph.D., UCLA, 1998. Health services research, quality of life, utility measurement, health-care finance.

Joel W. Hay, Associate Professor; Ph.D., Yale, 1980. Health economics, pharmaceutical economics, HIV/AIDS medical costs and epidemiology, health insurance reform, economic assessment of medical technology, medical interventions.

Kathleen A. Johnson, Associate Professor (also with Clinical Pharmacy); Ph.D., UCLA, 1991. Health services research, clinical pharmacy, pharmaceutical economics, health economics, OTC nonprescription drugs, women's health issues.

Jeffrey S. McCombs, Associate Professor; Ph.D., California, San Diego, 1982. Health economics, pharmaceutical economics, capitated medical systems, noncompliance with drug therapies and with drug formularies.

Michael B. Nichol, Associate Professor and Chairman; Ph.D., USC, 1987. State health policy, pharmaceutical economics, cost-effectiveness, outcomes research.

Pharmaceutical Sciences

M. B. Bolger, Associate Professor; Ph.D., California, San Francisco, 1978. Molecular mechanisms of drug and hormone action; biophysical, biochemical, and computational study of ligand-receptor interaction.

S. F. Hamm-Alvarez, Associate Professor; Ph.D., Duke, 1990. Role of kinesin and cytoplasmic dynein in vesicle transport along microtubules, regulation of microtubule-dependent vesicle transport in intact cells, regulation of cytoskeletal processes.

I. S. Haworth, Associate Professor; Ph.D., Liverpool, 1989. Computational drug design, NMR spectroscopy, structure and dynamics of DNA and DNA-ligand complexes, molecular modeling, molecular dynamics.

E. J. Lien, Professor; Ph.D., California, San Francisco, 1966. Quantitative structure-activity correlation of chemotherapeutic agents, centrally acting drugs and natural products, design synthesis and testing of new antiviral and antitumor agents, isolation and testing of immunostimulating polysaccharides from plants, especially Chinese medicinal plants.

C. McKenna, Professor of Chemistry and of Pharmaceutical Sciences (secondary appointment); Ph.D., California, San Diego, 1971. Synthetic and biological chemistry of phosphonocarboxylates, phosphinophosphonates, and bisphosphonates.

N. Neamati, Assistant Professor; Ph.D., Texas, 1995. Structure- and mechanism-based drug design, computer modeling, cellular and molecular pharmacology of anti-cancer and anti-viral drugs, pharmacogenomics and target identification.

C. T. Okamoto, Associate Professor; Ph.D., Berkeley, 1989. Protein sorting in epithelial cells.

W. C. Shen, Professor; Ph.D., Boston University, 1972. Endocytosis and transcytosis of proteins in epithelial cells and its applications in oral drug delivery.

W. Wolf, Distinguished Professor; Ph.D., Paris, 1956. Pharmacokinetic imaging, noninvasive studies of drug biodistribution, targeting and metabolism using NMRS and nuclear medicine imaging (including PET) techniques, pharmacokinetics of antitumor agents, synthesis and mechanism of action of radiopharmaceuticals.

A. Yang, Assistant Professor; Ph.D., California, Irvine. Proteomics of the central nervous system.

Molecular Pharmacology and Toxicology

J. D. Adams Jr., Associate Professor; Ph.D., California, San Francisco, 1981. Bioactivation of drugs and toxins in Parkinson's disease and other diseases.

R. L. Alkana, Professor and Assistant Dean, Interdisciplinary Programs; Pharm.D., USC, 1970; Ph.D., California, Irvine, 1975. Mechanisms of psychoactive drug action, neuropharmacology and behavioral pharmacology/toxicology, pharmacogenetics, allosteric signal transduction.

D. K. Ann, Professor; Ph.D., Purdue, 1984. Molecular mechanism(s) governing tissue-specific and inducible gene expression and signal transduction.

R. E. Brinton, Associate Professor (also with Neurosciences); Ph.D., Arizona, 1984. Neurobiology of learning and memory; peptide and steroid induction of morphological, biochemical, and genomic plasticity in cultured nerve cells.

E. Cadenas, Professor and Chairman (also with Biochemistry and Molecular Biology); Ph.D., Buenos Aires, 1977. Free-radical chemistry and biology, cell-cycle regulation by oxidants and antioxidants.

T. M. Chan, Professor and Dean; Ph.D., California, Davis, 1972. Metabolic toxicology, metabolic and hormonal abnormalities in obesity and diabetes, perturbation of cell growth and intermediary metabolism by free radicals and related oxidants.

K. Chen, Research Associate Professor; Ph.D., UCLA, 1976. Mitochondria genesis and protein targeting, serotonin and brain developmental abnormality.

N. S. Cohen, Research Assistant Professor; Ph.D., NYU, 1965. Intracellular organization of the proteins of enzymatic pathways, mRNA transport and localization, protein-protein interactions.

D. L. Davies, Research Assistant Professor and Director of the Alcohol and Brain Research Laboratory; Ph.D., USC, 1996. Neuropharmacology, with an emphasis on alcohol and other psychoactive drugs that act on GABA-A and other ligand-gated ion channels in the central nervous system.

R. F. Duncan, Associate Professor (also with Microbiology); Ph.D., Hawaii, 1978. Function of stress proteins in cell regulation and cell survival during stress, molecular mechanisms that regulate the rate of protein synthesis.

D. Johnson, Professor (also with Biochemistry and Molecular Biology); Ph.D., Georgetown, 1980. Regulation of gene expression by viral proteins and by activation of signal transduction pathways.

F. J. R. Richmond, Research Professor and Director of Regulatory and Clinical Science, Alfred E. Mann Institute of Biomedical Engineering; Ph.D., Queen's University, 1976. Neural control of movement, medical product development and testing, regulatory aspects of product development and commercialization.

A. Sevanian, Professor (also with Pathology); Ph.D., UCLA, 1977. Mechanisms of lipid peroxidation in biological membranes and lipoproteins, lipoprotein oxidation and atherosclerosis, effect of lipid oxidation products on vascular cell signaling.

J. C. Shih, Professor; Ph.D., California, Riverside, 1968. Biochemistry and molecular biology of serotonin receptors and enzymes related to catecholamine metabolism, molecular basis of mental disorders, neurodegeneration and aggressive behavior.

R. S. Sohal, Professor; Ph.D., Tulane, 1965. Role of oxidative stress in the aging process.

UNIVERSITY OF THE SCIENCES IN PHILADELPHIA
College of Graduate Studies

Programs of Study
University of the Sciences in Philadelphia (USP) offers Doctor of Philosophy degrees with research specializations in biochemistry, chemistry, health policy, pharmaceutics, pharmacognosy, and pharmacology and toxicology. Master of Science degrees with research specializations are offered in biochemistry, bioinformatics, cell biology and biotechnology, chemistry, health psychology, pharmaceutics, pharmacognosy, and pharmacology and toxicology. M.S. (nonthesis) degrees are offered in biochemistry, biomedical writing, cell biology and biotechnology, chemistry, health policy, health psychology, pharmaceutics, and pharmacy administration. An M.B.A. degree is offered in pharmaceutical business, and an M.P.H. degree with a health policy concentration is also offered. Each is administered by the appropriate department, with general supervision by the Graduate Subcouncil and the College of Graduate Studies. A minimum of 20 semester hours of didactic credits has been established for either the M.S. or the Ph.D. degree and 30 semester hours for the M.S. (nonthesis) degree. A student must satisfactorily complete a minimum of 10 research credits at USP to receive the M.S. thesis degree and a minimum of 20 research credits to receive the Ph.D. degree. Courses can be taken either on a full-time (9 or more credits per semester) or part-time (less than 9 credits per semester) basis.

Research Facilities
The new 77,000-square-foot Science and Technology Center supports learning and research with state-of-the-art classrooms and laboratories for biology, bioinformatics, and physics. The McNeil Research Center includes well-equipped laboratories and an experimental greenhouse for graduate study and research in pharmaceutics, chemistry, biochemistry, and pharmacognosy. The pharmaceutical development and manufacturing laboratory in Griffith Hall is among the most complete of any college of pharmaceutical sciences. The Pharmacology/Toxicology Center provides modern laboratories and AAALAC-accredited animal-care facilities for instruction and research in pharmacology and toxicology. Throughout the campus there are special laboratories equipped with instrumentation for cell biology, fluorescence DNA sequencing, receptor binding, high-pressure liquid chromatography, mass spectrometry, calorimetry, capillary electrophoresis, kinetics, rheology, radioisotope methodology, and nuclear magnetic resonance spectroscopy studies (proton, carbon, fluorine, phosphorus, and other commonly used techniques). The West Center for Computer-Aided Drug Discovery provides an environment for research in bioinformatics, computer-aided drug design, and computational chemistry. The Center for Advanced Pharmacy Studies (CAPS) provides a unique learning environment for students in a variety of majors, such as health policy students conducting health services research.
USP's library provides access to the world's research literature through its 8,000 print and electronic journals and its specialized collection of 85,000 print volumes. Major scientific databases are available both on and off campus. Graduate students also receive free and unlimited interlibrary loans from libraries around the world.

Financial Aid
Graduate students may be supported by fellowships funded directly through the American Foundation for Pharmaceutical Education, other national associations (such as the Society of Toxicology), the federal government (such as NIH), and the pharmaceutical industry. Information on these fellowships is available from the program directors. In addition, the University awards tuition scholarships, competitive stipends, and tuition waivers.

Cost of Study
Tuition and fees are $1123 per credit for all programs except the Online and Executive M.B.A. programs, which are $1727 per credit, and the Science Teacher Certification program, which is $562 per credit. All tuition and fee information is subject to change.

Living and Housing Costs
Costs in Philadelphia are comparable to those in other urban areas of the eastern United States. Apartments and furnished rooms are available nearby. For a single student, the cost of living, excluding tuition and fees, is approximately $17,000 per year.

Student Group
Of a total student body of 2,808, 369 are graduate students. Approximately 100 graduate students study full-time. In the graduate population, several international areas (Asia, Europe, Middle East, South America) are always represented. The average age of the graduate students is 32.

Student Outcomes
Graduates have accepted doctoral and postdoctoral positions at Harvard, the University of North Carolina, Duke University, the University of Florida, and the University of Pennsylvania and have accepted employment in the pharmaceutical industry at Merck, West Pharmaceuticals, Astra Zeneca, FMC Corporation, Cephalon, Warner-Lambert, Robert Wood Johnson Pharmaceutical Research Institute, Bayer Corporation, and Wyeth-Ayerst Research. Additional employers include the University of Virginia, Vanderbilt University, and the Fox Chase Cancer Center.

Location
Metropolitan Philadelphia is the home of eighty-nine universities, colleges, and seminaries; a world-renowned orchestra; famous museums; and numerous historic landmarks. Growth and community development have greatly improved the city; its suburban environs are unexcelled. As a founder-member of the West Philadelphia Corporation, the University City Science Center, and Campus Philadelphia, USP participates actively in community development and improvement. Within a 12-minute streetcar ride to the center of the city are fine shops, restaurants, theaters, and places of cultural and historical interest. Frequent train service reaches New York City in less than 1½ hours and Washington, D.C., in less than 2 hours.

The University
Founded in 1821 as America's first college of pharmacy, USP programs prepare students, at the undergraduate level, for professional careers in biochemistry, bioinformatics, biology, chemistry, computer science, environmental science, health psychology, medical technology, microbiology, occupational therapy, pharmaceutical chemistry, pharmaceutical marketing and management, pharmaceutical technology, pharmacology and toxicology, pharmacy, physical therapy, physician assistant studies, premed, and science teacher certification.
USP has sixteen buildings on a 25-acre site in the University City section of Philadelphia. Students get hands-on experience in eighty state-of-the-art laboratories. USP is an active and lively campus, offering eleven varsity and eighteen intramural sports and a wide variety of professional clubs, honor societies, religious organizations, service and social fraternities, a student government organization, and a campus newspaper.

Applying
Application forms are available from the USP Graduate Office or the USP Web site. An online application is also available on the USP Web site. Early submission is encouraged since appointments are limited. Specific requirements for each program are outlined on the checklist enclosed with the form. Applications requesting financial aid and applications from international students for fall admission must be complete by May 1; for spring admission, October 1; for summer, March 1. Applications from domestic students who are not applying for financial aid must be complete by the Wednesday prior to the start of courses each semester (fall, spring, and summer), except for the Ph.D. program in health policy; pharmacology/toxicology M.S. and Ph.D. programs; pharmaceutics M.S.; and Ph.D. and health psychology programs, which only accept applications for fall admission.
Requirements for international applicants include a Certification of Finances form and bank statement, guaranteeing sufficient funds for at least one year; official TOEFL and TWE scores for applicants whose native language is not English; and official TSE for those requesting financial aid. Applicants who are not U.S. citizens or permanent residents may obtain a student visa request form from USP after they have been accepted for admission and have paid their deposit.

Correspondence and Information
Rodney J. Wigent, Ph.D., Dean
College of Graduate Studies
Box 15
University of the Sciences in Philadelphia
600 South 43rd Street
Philadelphia, Pennsylvania 19104
Phone: 866-GRAD-USP
Fax: 215-895-1185
E-mail: graduate@usip.edu
Web site: http://gradschool.usip.edu

University of the Sciences in Philadelphia

THE FACULTY

Up-to-date information about the faculty members can be found at http://gradfaculty.usip.edu/directory/results?title=Alphabetical+Listing+of+All+Faculty&alpha=1.

CURRENT RESEARCH

Cell Biology and Biotechnology. This master's degree program is designed to give a theoretical and practical background in biotechnological techniques and applications, functions of cells at the molecular and cellular levels, methods for studying cell systems, and study of the genetics of cell systems. The major research emphasis includes studies of cell adhesion, RNA-protein interactions, plant-microbe interactions, cell-signal transduction, oncogene function, molecular studies of viruses, prokaryotes and eukaryotes, bacterial metabolism, bioluminescence, and novel approaches to medicinal natural products.

Chemistry, Biochemistry, and Pharmacognosy. The Department of Chemistry and Biochemistry offers graduate programs in chemistry (specialties in analytical, medicinal, organic, or physical chemistry), biochemistry, and pharmacognosy (specialties in analytical pharmacognosy, biotechnology and cell culture, and natural product synthesis). Research areas related to drug discovery are emphasized, including computer modeling, synthesis, and analytical characterization of potential drug candidates.

Health Policy. The Health Policy Program offers Ph.D. and M.S. degrees that train students in the range of skills needed to perform health policy analysis and research in professional settings, including health economics, law, epidemiology, information technology, ethics, and statistics. Areas of research interest include health services evaluation, outcomes analysis, regulatory policy, mental health policy, and health care finance.

Health Psychology. Health Psychology faculty members are currently conducting funded research on developing a prevention program for children at risk for the development of anxiety disorders; developing models of adaptation and survival following the diagnosis of colorectal cancer, neuropsychological dysfunction in head trauma patients, the suicide-activation process in persons suffering from both psychiatric and health disorders, classical conditioning of the immune system, the development of a walking index for spinal cord injury, and the development of psychometric measures of specific health functioning.

Pharmaceutics. Pharmaceutics applies the theories and techniques of the mathematical, chemical, biological, and pharmaceutical sciences to develop and evaluate drug delivery systems and to test their in vivo performance. Major areas of research are the specialized systemic delivery of drugs, receptor binding of drugs, applications of spheronized granules, rheological properties of pharmaceutical systems, physics of tablet compression, suspension and emulsion technology, controlled release of drugs, pharmacokinetics, pharmacodynamics, cross linking in proteins, membrane characterization, and utilization of physical models.

Pharmacology and Toxicology. The faculty members and their students work in several fields of interdisciplinary research: autonomic, cardiovascular, and systems integrative pharmacology; neuropsychopharmacology; cancer biology; drug metabolism; therapeutic targeting of tumors and imaging, and renal and hepatic toxicology.

Pharmacy Administration. Major areas of study and research in the Pharmacy Administration Program include pharmaceutical economics, cost effectiveness analysis, pharmaceutical care, marketing research, health communications, and management sciences. Additional areas of research include technology assessment and decision analysis as well as patient education and compliance. The University is strategically located near several major health science centers, business schools, and international pharmaceutical firms and has collaborative arrangements for learning and research.

Public Health. The USP Master of Public Health (M.P.H.) degree program provides students with the knowledge, practical training, and analytical skills they need to realize their full potential in improving public health. Through the M.P.H. program, students can focus their studies on areas such as assuring public health through access to high-quality prevention and health promotion; tracking epidemics to their source, such as bird flu-like illnesses; creating educational campaigns to combat childhood obesity by encouraging healthy lifestyles; and advocating for improved health policies through both regulatory and legislative channels.

VIRGINIA COMMONWEALTH UNIVERSITY

Department of Pharmaceutics

Programs of Study

The Department of Pharmaceutics offers graduate programs leading to the M.S. or the Ph.D. in pharmaceutical sciences as well as a Pharm.D./Ph.D dual-degree program. These programs provide the preparation and research experience for academic, federal, and industrial careers. Students are required to participate in a common core of entry-level graduate courses, including statistics, biopharmaceutics, drug metabolism, pharmacokinetics, physical pharmacy, and pharmaceutical analysis and seminars in drug development. Building upon this core, graduate students then choose, through advanced course work and research, a concentration such as biopharmaceutical analysis, biopharmaceutics/physical pharmacy, medicinal chemistry, pharmacokinetics/pharmacodynamics, pharmacotherapy, pharmacy administration, or pharmacology and toxicology. For the M.S., a minimum of 24 credit hours, exclusive of research credits, is generally required. In practice, a minimum of two years of study, including research, is necessary to complete all requirements. Ph.D. candidates must complete a minimum of 30 credit hours, exclusive of research credits. Four years of study, including research, is necessary to complete all requirements. In addition to the core curriculum, Ph.D. students are required to take elective courses, selected based upon the mutual consent of the student and major adviser. The Pharm.D./Ph.D. is a full-time program of professional education with advanced study in pharmaceutical sciences. The program addresses the need for pharmacy practitioners by preparing students with excellent research skills in clinical, academic, industrial, and regulatory environments. Most students complete both degrees within six years.

Research Facilities

The school is well-equipped for graduate research and provides leadership to the VCU Institute for Structural Biology and Drug Discovery at the Virginia BioTechnology Research Park. The institute makes use of synthetic medicinal chemistry, X-ray crystallography, NMR, protein and nucleic acid chemistry, bacterial enzymology, and molecular pharmacology to promote drug development. Several businesses have been spawned through the institute, and two new drugs have entered clinical trials. The Department of Pharmacy supports the Center for Drug Studies (CDS), a fully staffed facility for conducting Phase I–III research in humans. The center is supported by an FDA-compliant biopharmaceutical analysis laboratory, conducting drug and metabolite analyses to support the Department's reputation for innovative studies in drug absorption, distribution, metabolism, and excretion.

Financial Aid

There are a limited number of graduate teaching and research assistantships in the School of Pharmacy awarded each year only to the most outstanding Ph.D. applicants. M.S. students are not eligible for assistantships. These assistantships may include waiver of tuition and fees and also provide a stipend for twelve months' service. Outstanding applicants may be eligible for a range of University fellowships. Students may apply for need-based assistance with the University's Financial Aid Office. Current information on financial aid programs, policies, and procedures is available at http://www.vcu.edu/enroll/finaid.

Cost of Study

For full-time study (9–15 credits) in 2007–08, Virginia residents pay tuition and fees of $4452 per semester; nonresidents, $8876 per semester. For part-time study, Virginia residents pay tuition and fees of $465 per hour; nonresidents, $954 per hour. Some programs require additional fees. On the Medical College of Virginia (MCV) campus, tuition, fees, and other expenses vary in the medicine, pharmacy, nurse anesthesia, dentistry, and School of Allied Health programs.

Living and Housing Costs

Graduate student housing is available on both the MCV campus and the academic campus of Virginia Commonwealth University. Many graduate students live in off-campus housing, which is reasonably priced and readily available in a variety of styles and settings in nearby residential areas or within easy commuting distance. On- and off-campus housing information is available on the Web at http://www.housing.vcu.edu/.

Student Group

VCU enrolls 30,452 students, 7,611 of whom are graduate students. More than 200 clubs and organizations reflect the diverse social, recreational, educational, political, and religious interests of the student body.

Location

Richmond is Virginia's capital and a major East Coast financial and manufacturing center that offers students a wide range of cultural, educational, and recreational activities. Richmond is located in central Virginia at the intersection of Interstates 95 and 64, 2 hours south of Washington, D.C., and nestled between the Blue Ridge Mountains and the Atlantic coast. The Richmond region is easily accessible by plane, car, and train. With nearly 1 million residents, the historic city of Richmond combines big-city offerings with small-town hospitality. Applicants are encouraged to explore http://www.visit.richmond.com/ for more information on the city.

The University

VCU is a state-supported coeducational university with a graduate school, a major teaching hospital, and twelve academic and professional units that offer fifty-two undergraduate, twenty-two postbaccalaureate certificate, sixty-five master's, six post-master's certificate, and twenty-nine Ph.D. programs. VCU also offers M.D., D.D.S., D.P.T., and Pharm.D. programs as well as cooperative degree programs with other major Virginia colleges and universities. VCU has one of the largest evening colleges in the United States. The academic campus is located in Richmond's historic Fan District. The health sciences campus and hospital are located 2 miles east in the downtown business district. A University bus service provides free intercampus transportation for faculty members and students.

With more than $211 million in annual research funding, Virginia Commonwealth University is classified as one of the nation's top research universities by the Carnegie Foundation for the Advancement of Teaching. More than 29,000 undergraduate, certificate, graduate, post-master's, professional, and doctoral students are enrolled in 162 academic programs, forty of which are unique in the commonwealth of Virginia. The faculty members represent the finest American and international graduate institutions and enhance the University's position among the important institutions of higher learning in the United States and the world via their work in the classroom, laboratory, studio, and clinic and in their scholarly publications.

Applying

Admission procedures and program requirements are detailed in the *Graduate Bulletin*. Application deadlines and materials, including the application and the *Graduate Bulletin*, are available online at the Graduate School Web site at http://www.graduate.vcu.edu. Virginia Commonwealth University is an equal opportunity/affirmative action institution providing access to education and employment without regard to age, race, color, national origin, gender, religion, sexual orientation, veteran's status, political affiliation, or disability.

Correspondence and Information

Susanna Wu-Pong, Director
Dean's Office
School of Pharmacy
Virginia Commonwealth University
410 North 12th Street
P.O. Box 980581
Richmond, Virginia 23298-0581

Phone: 804-828-4328
Fax: 804-828-7536
E-mail: swupong@vcu.edu
Web site: http://dev.pharmacy.vcu.edu/pharmaceutics/index.html

Virginia Commonwealth University

THE FACULTY AND THEIR RESEARCH

F. Douglas Boudinot, Professor and Dean of Graduate Studies; Ph.D., SUNY at Buffalo. Pharmacokinetics, biopharmaceutics, drug metabolism and pharmacodynamics in drug discovery and development.

The use of Monte Carlo simulations to study the effect of poor compliance on the steady state concentrations of valproic acid following administration of enteric-coated and extended release divalproex dodium formulations. *Biopharma. Drug Disposition* 26:417–25, 2005. With Ahmad, Barr, Reed, and Garnett.

Peter R. Byron, Professor and Chairman; Ph.D., Manchester. Optimal design and evaluation of aerosol drug delivery systems, including physical, chemical, and formulation factors, and the impact of the aerosol generation device.

Mitigating producer risk in a highly regulated environment. *Resp. Drug Delivery* 59–168, 2006. With Christopher, Falco, and Vanneste.

Helen L. Fillmore, Assistant Professor; Ph.D., Tennessee. Stem cell therapeutics, gene delivery for cancer.

Ectopic telomerase expression inhibits neuronal differentiation of NT2 neural progenitor cells. *Neurosci. Lett.* 421(2):168–72, 2007. With Richardson, Nguyen, Holt, and Broaddus.

Phillip M. Gerk, Assistant Professor; Pharm.D., Illinois; Ph.D., Kentucky. ABC transporters on maternal-fetal drug transport pharmacokinetics, maternal and fetal health during pregnancy and after birth, optimizing maternal and fetal exposure through appropriate drug therapy.

Lack of interaction between tauroursodeoxycholate (TUDC) on transport mediated by the ATP-Binding Cassette transporter isoform G2 (ABCG2). *Mol. Pharma.* 3(3):303–6, 2006. With Vaidya.

Michael Hindle, Research Associate Professor; Ph.D., Bradford. Novel aerosol drug delivery devices, including in vitro particle size analysis, aerosol characterization, and inhaler design.

Novel chemo-enzymatic oligomers of cinnamic acids as direct and indirect inhibitors of coagulation proteinases. *Bioorganic Med. Chem.* 14:7988–98, 2006. With Monien et al.

John (Randy) James, Research Assistant Professor; Ph.D., Virginia Commonwealth. Nicotine's mechanism of action in the central nervous system.

Nicotinic receptor inactivation after acute and repeated in-vivo nicotine exposures in rats. *Brain Res.* 1086(1):98–103, 2006. With Vann, Rosecrans, and Robinson.

H. Thomas Karnes, Professor and Graduate Program Director; Ph.D., Florida. Bioanalysis using novel luminescence, mass spectroscopy, immunoreactor, and laser spectroscopy systems; drug metabolism, drug release, and biological drug distribution.

Profiling in vitro drug release from subcutaneous implants: A review of current status and potential implications on drug product development. *Biopharma. Drug Disposition* 27(4):157–70, 2006. With Iyer and Barr.

P. Worth Longest Jr., Assistant Professor, Ph.D., North Carolina State. Multiphase biofluid transport with applications to respiratory and cardiovascular therapies.

Transport and deposition of micro-aerosols in realistic and simplified models of the oral airway. *Ann. Biomed. Eng.* 35(4):560–81, 2007. With Xi.

Gary R. Matzke, Professor and Associate Dean for Clinical Research and Public Policy; Pharm.D., Minnesota; FCCP, FCP. Renal pharmacotherapy, hemodialysis, public policy.

Effect of conjugated equine estrogens on oxidative metabolism in middle-aged and elderly postmenopausal women. *J. Clin. Pharmacol.* 46(11):1299–307, 2006. With O'Connell et al.

Joanne Peart, Associate Professor; Ph.D., Bath. Aerosol electrostatics, aerosolization; formulation, regional lung deposition, and in vitro testing aspects of powder aerosols and metered dose inhalers (MDIs); role of packaging components on aerosol electrostatics.

Using and interpreting aerosol electrostatic data using the electrical low pressure impactor (ELPI). *Respiratory Drug Delivery* 267–78, 2006. With Keil and Kotian.

Wesley Poynor, Associate Professor; Ph.D., Texas at Austin. Hepatic pharmacokinetics, pharmacokinetics of lead and discontinuous processes (e.g., peritoneal dialysis), information technology for pharmacokinetic data analysis and instruction.

Masahiro Sakagami, Assistant Professor; Ph.D., Virginia Commonwealth. Solute and fluid disposition (absorption, metabolism, and clearance) in the lung, alveolar transporters and metabolic enzymes for macromolecular proteins and peptides along with epithelial tight junctions and mucociliary clearance.

Expression and transport functionality of FcRn within rat alveolar epithelium: A study in primary cell culture and in the isolated perfused lung. *Pharm. Res.* 23: 270–9, 2006. With Omidi et al.

Patricia W. Slattum, Associate Professor; Pharm.D./Ph.D., Virginia Commonwealth, 1992. Medication-related problems in older adults, drug-induced cognitive impairment.

An exploratory study of drug abuse and dependence information in package inserts. *J. Addict. Dis.* 26(2):25–34, 2007. With Phipps, Balster, and Kirkwood.

Jurgen Venitz, Associate Professor and Vice Chairman; M.D., Ph.D., Saarbrucken. Design, implementation, and analysis of safety and toleration; PK and PD studies in the early clinical drug development; dose-response and pharmacological effect-plasma concentration relationships.

Characterization of in vitro and in vivo metabolic pathways of the investigational anticancer agent, 2-methoxyestradiol. *J. Pharm. Sci.* 96(7):1821–31, 2007. With Lakhani et al.

Victor A. Yanchick, Professor and Dean; Ph.D., Purdue. Curricular development, geriatrics, interprofessional education and practice.

WEST VIRGINIA UNIVERSITY

Graduate Program in Pharmaceutical and Pharmacological Sciences

Programs of Study

The Graduate Program in Pharmaceutical and Pharmacological Sciences is one of seven graduate programs in West Virginia University (WVU) Schools of Medicine and Pharmacy offering interdisciplinary biomedical research training leading to the Ph.D. or M.D./Ph.D. degree. Research interests are complementary to a focus on drug discovery and development. Key areas of research and expertise are in the fundamentals of drug design and synthesis, drug metabolism and drug discovery, drug delivery, cardiovascular, pulmonary and neuropharmacology, and translational research collaborations for preclinical and clinical testing. The Computational Chemistry Molecular Modeling (CCMM) Laboratory is a focal point for drug discovery at WVU.

Students benefit from individual attention by faculty members within a research environment that is dynamic, collaborative, and interdisciplinary. In addition to course work and laboratory research, students participate in seminars, journal clubs, and research conferences. Graduate trainees also attend national scientific meetings and obtain valuable speaking and teaching experience. The Ph.D. typically takes five years to complete. During year 1, students matriculate into a common integrated core curriculum. This integrated first year allows students to build competence in key areas of contemporary science, gain exposure to the various training program options, meet potential dissertation advisers, and network scientifically and socially. In the second semester, students customize their course work by selecting from an array of program-specific electives. At the end of year 1, students select a research adviser and can select Pharmaceutical and Pharmacological Sciences as their training program. Year 2 consists of advanced course work, research, teaching, and the candidacy examination. Years 3 to 5 are devoted to dissertation research. The Graduate Program in Pharmaceutical and Pharmacological Sciences also participates in the combined M.D./Ph.D. Scholars Program. M.D./Ph.D. Scholars take the first two years of the medical curriculum, followed typically by three years of research as required for the Ph.D. degree before returning to the M.D. program.

Research Facilities

Institutional facilities include a computer-based learning center, a centralized animal facility with a transgenic barrier, and a library housing more than 205,000 volumes and 2,400 journals. Core facilities are available for examining gene expression or genetic variation (Affymetrix platform), image analysis, confocal and electron microscopy and laser capture microdissection, live-cell imaging, mass spectrometry, flow cytometry with high-speed cell sorting, proteomics, recombinant DNA technology, transgenic rodent biology, and functional neuroimaging (fMRI, PET/CT). Affiliated research centers include the National Institute for Occupational Safety and Health (NIOSH), Center for Advanced Imaging, Blanchette Rockefeller Neurosciences Institute, Sensory Neuroscience Research Center, and Mary Babb Randolph Cancer Center.

Financial Aid

Ph.D. and M.D./Ph.D. students in the biomedical sciences receive financial support during their training, provided they remain in good academic standing and excel in research. Such support includes full tuition, health insurance, and an annual stipend of $23,000. Combined M.D./Ph.D. students also receive medical tuition waivers.

Cost of Study

Students' tuition costs are covered.

Living and Housing Costs

The cost of an efficiency apartment in University-owned housing is approximately $400 per month. A limited number of University apartments are available for married students. Privately owned apartments in Morgantown cost $400 to $600 per month. In general, the cost of living is lower than other, larger cities.

Student Group

The University's total enrollment is approximately 26,000 students, which includes 6,500 graduate and professional students. Graduate students come from all parts of the United States and many other countries.

Location

Morgantown is a vibrant university community of 80,000 residents in northern West Virginia. Located near the Pennsylvania border at the western edge of the Appalachian Mountains, abundant opportunities exist for activities such as world-class white-water rafting and kayaking, hiking and camping, mountain biking, fishing, and skiing. Morgantown has a cosmopolitan atmosphere with a range of activities usually found in much larger cities. It also enjoys proximity to major metropolitan centers: Pittsburgh is a 90-minute drive to the north, and Washington, D.C., is a 3-hour drive to the east.

The University

West Virginia University is a comprehensive, land-grant, Carnegie-designated Doctoral/Research University–Extensive public institution. The University's academic Health Sciences Center includes the Schools of Medicine, Dentistry. Nursing, and Pharmacy, all of which offer graduate degree programs. There are seven Ph.D. biomedical research training programs in the Schools of Medicine and Pharmacy that benefit from the Schools' common, undifferentiated first year: Biochemistry and Molecular Biology, Cancer Cell Biology, Cellular and Integrative Physiology, Exercise Physiology, Immunology and Microbial Pathogenesis, Neuroscience, and Pharmaceutical and Pharmacological Sciences. Graduate faculty members in these programs are from various basic science and clinical departments throughout WVU and are members of interdisciplinary research centers in six health-related areas: cancer cell biology, cardiovascular sciences, diabetes and obesity, immunopathology and microbial pathogenesis, neuroscience, and respiratory biology and lung diseases.

WVU participates in NCAA Division I sports as a member of the Big East conference and also offers a wide variety of creative arts, theater, and entertainment opportunities.

Applying

Applicants must have a bachelor's degree and an excellent GPA and GRE scores. Three letters of recommendation and a personal statement are required. Students are invited in groups of 10 for a paid two-day visit/interview in January through March. Prospective students can find more information and an online application at http://www.hsc.wvu.edu/som/resoff/gradprograms/PhD.asp.

Correspondence and Information

Peter Gannett, Ph.D., Graduate Director
Graduate Program in Pharmaceutical and Pharmacological
   Sciences
West Virginia University
P.O. Box 9530
Morgantown, West Virginia 26506
Phone: 304-293-1480
E-mail: pgannett@hsc.wvu.edu
Web site: http://www.hsc.wvu.edu/som/resoff/gradprograms/
   PhD.asp

Office of Research and Graduate Education
Health Sciences Center
West Virginia University
P.O. Box 9104
Morgantown, West Virginia 26506
Phone: 304-293-7116
E-mail: cnoel@hsc.wvu.edu

West Virginia University

THE FACULTY AND THEIR RESEARCH

Marie Abate, Professor; Pharm.D., Michigan. Drug information and clinical pharmacy.

Patrick Callery, Professor; Ph.D., California, San Francisco. Drug design, drug metabolism, mass spectrometry.

Vincent Castranova, Adjunct Professor (NIOSH); Ph.D., West Virginia. Free-radical biology, pulmonary toxicology, silica-induced carcinogenesis.

Eugene Demchuk, Adjunct Associate Professor (NIOSH); Ph.D., Moscow. Computational chemistry and molecular modeling.

Jeffrey Fedan, Adjunct Professor (NIOSH); Ph.D., Alabama. Inhalation studies, respiratory diseases, pharmacology.

Peter Gannett, Professor; Ph.D., Wisconsin. Carcinogenesis, drug-protein interactions, DNA structure and conformation, EPR and NMR, molecular modeling.

Jason Huber, Assistant Professor; Ph.D., Florida A&M. Pharmacology, blood-brain barrier, diabetes.

Joseph Ma, Professor; Ph.D., Duquesne. Lung toxicology of diesel particulates, pharmaceutics, drug delivery.

Jamal Mustafa, Professor; Ph.D., Lucknow (India). Cardiovascular pharmacology and physiology, blood flow regulation to the heart.

James O'Donnell, Professor; Ph.D., Chicago. Pharmacology, phosphodiesterases and depression.

William Petros, Associate Professor; Pharm.D., Philadelphia College of Pharmacy and Science. Pharmacokinetics, pharmacodynamics, pharmacogenomics, oncology.

Yongyut Rojanasakul, Professor; Ph.D., Wisconsin. Apoptosis, drug delivery, pharmaceutics.

Xianglin Shi, Adjunct Assistant Professor (NIOSH); Ph.D., West Virginia. Free-radical biology, chromium toxicology, carcinogenesis.

Paul Siegel, Adjunct Associate Professor (NIOSH); Ph.D., Tulane. Asthmatogen biomarkers, pharmacology.

Paula Stout, Associate Professor; Ph.D., West Virginia. Biodegradable polymers, drug delivery, nutraceuticals, solid-state and surface chemistry.

Grazyna Szklarz, Associate Professor; Ph.D., Clarkson. Structure and function of cytochrome P-450, P-450-mediated drug metabolism, carcinogenesis, molecular modeling.

Val Vallyathan, Adjunct Professor (NIOSH); Ph.D., Baroda. Inflammation, oxidant injury, pathogenesis.

Section 40
Veterinary Medicine and Sciences

This section contains a directory of institutions offering graduate work in veterinary medicine and sciences. Additional information about programs listed in the directory but not augmented by an in-depth entry may be obtained by writing directly to the dean of a graduate school or chair of a department at the address given in the directory.

For programs offering related work, see in Book 2 Economics (Agricultural Economics and Agribusiness); in Book 3, Biological and Biomedical Sciences and Zoology; in Book 4, Agricultural and Food Sciences, Marine Sciences and Oceanography, and Natural Resources; and in Book 5, Agricultural Engineering and Bioengineering and Biomedical Engineering and Biotechnology.

CONTENTS

Program Directories

Veterinary Medicine

Auburn University, College of Veterinary Medicine, Professional Program in Veterinary Medicine, Auburn University, AL 36849. Offers DVM, DVM/MS. *Accreditation:* AVMA. *Faculty:* 84 full-time (29 women), 1 part-time/adjunct (0 women). *Students:* 371 full-time (256 women); includes 14 minority (7 African Americans, 4 Asian Americans or Pacific Islanders, 3 Hispanic Americans). Average age 26. 868 applicants, 11% accepted, 93 enrolled. In 2006, 91 degrees awarded. *Degree requirements:* For first-professional, preceptorship. *Application deadline:* For fall admission, 7/7 for domestic students; for spring admission, 11/24 for domestic students. Applications are processed on a rolling basis. Application fee: $25. *Expenses: Contact institution.* Tuition and fees vary according to program. *Financial support:* Fellowships available. Financial award application deadline: 3/15. *Application contact:* Dr. Joe Pittman, Interim Dean of the Graduate School, 334-844-4700.

Colorado State University, College of Veterinary Medicine and Biomedical Sciences, Professional Program in Veterinary Medicine, Fort Collins, CO 80523-0015. Offers DVM, DVM/PhD, MBA/DVM. *Accreditation:* AVMA. *Students:* 534 full-time (424 women); includes 61 minority (3 African Americans, 4 American Indian/Alaska Native, 26 Asian Americans or Pacific Islanders, 28 Hispanic Americans), 3 international. Average age 27. 1,393 applicants, 10% accepted, 137 enrolled. In 2006, 135 degrees awarded. *Entrance requirements:* GRE General Test, Colorado Supplemental Application. Additional exam requirements/recommendations for international students: Required—TOEFL. *Application deadline:* For fall admission, 10/1 for domestic students. Application fee: $60. Electronic applications accepted. *Expenses:* Tuition, state resident: full-time $4,248; part-time $236 per credit. Tuition, nonresident: full-time $15,642; part-time $869 per credit. Required fees: $66 per credit. Tuition and fees vary according to program. *Financial support:* Fellowships, research assistantships, teaching assistantships available. Financial award application deadline: 3/1; financial award applicants required to submit FAFSA. *Faculty research:* Animal reproduction, infectious diseases, cancer biology, musculoskeletal research, neurobiology. Total annual research expenditures: $653,187. *Application contact:* Dr. Sherry Stewart, Assistant Dean of Admissions and Student Affairs, 970-491-7052, Fax: 970-491-2250, E-mail: sherry.stewart@colostate.edu.

Cornell University, College of Veterinary Medicine, Ithaca, NY 14853-0001. Offers comparative biomedical science (PhD); immunology (PhD); pharmacology (PhD); physiology (PhD); veterinary medicine (DVM); zoology (PhD). *Accreditation:* AVMA. *Faculty:* 156 full-time (48 women). *Students:* 479 full-time (355 women); includes 94 minority (24 African Americans, 1 American Indian/Alaska Native, 31 Asian Americans or Pacific Islanders, 38 Hispanic Americans), 67 international. Average age 26. 853 applicants, 12% accepted, 84 enrolled. In 2006, 85 DVMs, 15 doctorates awarded. *Median time to degree:* Of those who began their doctoral program in fall 1998, 100% received their degree in 8 years or less. *Degree requirements:* For DVM, thesis or alternative, on-site clinical training; for doctorate, thesis/dissertation, admission to candidacy exam, comprehensive exam, registration. *Entrance requirements:* For DVM, GRE General Test or MCAT, undergraduate pre-medical science program, animal or veterinary experience, letter of recommendation; for doctorate, GRE General Test, letters of recommendation. Additional exam requirements/recommendations for international students: Required—TOEFL. *Application deadline:* For fall admission, 10/1 for domestic and international students. Application fee: $40. Electronic applications accepted. *Expenses: Contact institution.* Full-time tuition and fees vary according to program. *Financial support:* In 2006–07, 452 students received support, including 30 fellowships (averaging $27,162 per year), 119 research assistantships with tuition reimbursements available (averaging $27,162 per year); Federal Work-Study, institutionally sponsored loans, scholarships/grants, and unspecified assistantships also available. Financial award application deadline: 2/1; financial award applicants required to submit CSS PROFILE or FAFSA. *Faculty research:* Extensive biomedical research, comparative cancer, food safety. Total annual research expenditures: $49.3 million. *Unit head:* Dr. Donald F. Smith, Dean, 607-253-3771. *Application contact:* Jennifer A. Mailey, Director of Admissions, 607-253-3700, Fax: 607-253-3709, E-mail: jam333@cornell.edu.

Iowa State University of Science and Technology, College of Veterinary Medicine and Graduate College, Graduate Programs in Veterinary Medicine, Department of Veterinary Diagnostic and Production Animal Medicine, Ames, IA 50011. Offers veterinary diagnostic and production animal medicine (MS); veterinary preventative medicine (MS). *Faculty:* 25 full-time, 1 part-time/adjunct. *Students:* 4 full-time (0 women), 1 part-time; includes 1 minority (Asian American or Pacific Islander), 1 international. 4 applicants, 25% accepted, 1 enrolled. In 2006, 1 degree awarded. *Degree requirements:* For master's, thesis or alternative. *Entrance requirements:* For master's, GRE General Test. Additional exam requirements/recommendations for international students: Required—TOEFL (paper-based 550; computer-based 213; iBT 79) or IELTS (6.0). *Application deadline:* Applications are processed on a rolling basis. Application fee: $30 ($70 for international students). Electronic applications accepted. *Expenses:* Tuition, state resident: full-time $5,936; part-time $330 per credit. Tuition, nonresident: full-time $16,350; part-time $330 per credit. *Financial support:* In 2006–07, 2 research assistantships with partial tuition reimbursements (averaging $19,500 per year), 2 teaching assistantships with partial tuition reimbursements (averaging $19,500 per year) were awarded; institutionally sponsored loans, scholarships/grants, health care benefits, and unspecified assistantships also available. *Unit head:* Dr. Patrick Halbur, Chair, 515-294-3837. *Application contact:* Dr. Richard Evans, Director of Graduate Education, 515-294-3836, E-mail: revans@iastate.edu.

Iowa State University of Science and Technology, College of Veterinary Medicine, Professional Program in Veterinary Medicine, Ames, IA 50011. Offers DVM. *Students:* 436 full-time (325 women), 3 part-time (all women); includes 7 minority (2 African Americans, 3 Asian Americans or Pacific Islanders, 2 Hispanic Americans), 1 international. In 2006, 104 degrees awarded. *Expenses:* Tuition, state resident: full-time $5,936; part-time $330 per credit. Tuition, nonresident: full-time $16,350; part-time $330 per credit. *Financial support:* Federal Work-Study available. *Unit head:* Dr. John Thomson, Dean, College of Veterinary Medicine, 515-294-1250.

Kansas State University, College of Veterinary Medicine, Professional Program in Veterinary Medicine, Manhattan, KS 66506. Offers DVM. *Accreditation:* AVMA. *Students:* 428 full-time (297 women); includes 16 minority (1 African American, 1 American Indian/Alaska Native, 5 Asian Americans or Pacific Islanders, 9 Hispanic Americans), 2 international. Average age 24. In 2006, 106 degrees awarded. *Entrance requirements:* GRE General Test, 70 hours of pre-professional requirements. *Application deadline:* For fall admission, 2/1 for domestic students. Applications are processed on a rolling basis. Application fee: $50. *Expenses: Contact institution.* *Financial support:* Research assistantships, teaching assistantships, Federal Work-Study, institutionally sponsored loans, and scholarships/grants available. Financial award application deadline: 3/15. *Faculty research:* Surgery and medicine, epithelial function, infectious disease of animals, neuroscience, analytical pharmacology. Total annual research expenditures:$184,041. *Application contact:* Ralph Richardson, Dean, 785-532-4005, Fax: 785-532-5884, E-mail: dean@vet.ksu.edu.

Louisiana State University and Agricultural and Mechanical College, School of Veterinary Medicine, Professional Program in Veterinary Medicine, Baton Rouge, LA 70803. Offers DVM. Available to state and contract students and a limited number of highly qualified out-of-state applicants. *Students:* 323 full-time (247 women); includes 23 minority (7 African Americans, 1 American Indian/Alaska Native, 3 Asian Americans or Pacific Islanders, 12 Hispanic Americans). Average age 26. 92 applicants, 100% accepted. In 2006, 83 degrees awarded. *Entrance requirements:* GRE General Test or MCAT. Additional exam requirements/recommendations for international students: Required—TOEFL. *Application deadline:* For fall admission, 3/1 priority date for domestic students. Applications are processed on a rolling basis. Application fee: $25. *Expenses: Contact institution.* *Financial support:* In 2006–07, 6 fellowships with full and partial tuition reimbursements (averaging $13,646 per year) were awarded; research assistantships with full and partial tuition reimbursements, teaching assistantships with full and partial tuition reimbursements, tuition waivers (full and partial) also available. Financial award applicants required to submit FAFSA. *Faculty research:* Veterinary microbiology, pathology, immunology, anatomy, epidemiology. *Application contact:* Dr. Thomas R. Klei, Associate Dean for Research and Advanced Studies, 225-578-9727, Fax: 225-578-9916, E-mail: klei@vetmed.lsu.edu.

Michigan State University, College of Veterinary Medicine, Professional Program in Veterinary Medicine, East Lansing, MI 48824. Offers veterinary medicine (DVM); veterinary medicine/medical scientist training program (DVM). *Accreditation:* AVMA. *Students:* 427 full-time (346 women), 10 part-time (8 women); includes 49 minority (5 African Americans, 5 American Indian/Alaska Native, 19 Asian Americans or Pacific Islanders, 20 Hispanic Americans), 2 international. Average age 26. 118 applicants, 97% accepted. In 2006, 102 degrees awarded. *Entrance requirements:* Additional exam requirements/recommendations for international students: Required—TOEFL. Application fee: $137. Electronic applications accepted. *Expenses: Contact institution.* Tuition and fees vary according to program. *Financial support:* In 2006–07, 15 fellowships with tuition reimbursements (averaging $8,028 per year), 2 research assistantships with tuition reimbursements (averaging $14,664 per year) were awarded. *Unit head:* Dr. David Sprecher, Acting Associate Dean for Academic Programs, 517-355-7624, Fax: 517-432-1037, E-mail: sprecher@cvm.msu.edu. *Application contact:* 517-353-9793, Fax: 517-353-3041, E-mail: admiss@cvm.msu.edu.

Mississippi State University, College of Veterinary Medicine, Professional Program in Veterinary Medicine, Mississippi State, MS 39762. Offers DVM. *Accreditation:* AVMA. *Entrance requirements:* VCAT, GRE, minimum GPA of 3.0 in math and science coursework, 2.8 overall. Expenses: Contact institution. Tuition and fees vary according to course load.

North Carolina State University, College of Veterinary Medicine, Professional Program in Veterinary Medicine, Raleigh, NC 27695. Offers DVM, DVM/PhD. *Accreditation:* AVMA. *Faculty:* 137 full-time, 146 part-time/adjunct. *Students:* 306 full-time (262 women); includes 21 minority (9 African Americans, 1 American Indian/Alaska Native, 5 Asian Americans or Pacific Islanders, 6 Hispanic Americans). 564 applicants, 16% accepted, 78 enrolled. *Entrance requirements:* GRE. *Application deadline:* For fall admission, 10/1 for domestic students. Application fee: $130. *Expenses: Contact institution.* *Financial support:* Fellowships, research assistantships, teaching assistantships, Federal Work-Study available. Financial award applicants required to submit FAFSA. *Unit head:* Dr. David Bristol, Associate Dean, 919-513-6212, Fax: 919-513-4452, E-mail: david_bristol@ncsu.edu. *Application contact:* Association of American Veterinary Medical Colleges, 202-371-9195, Fax: 202-842-0073, E-mail: vmcas@nmaa.org.

North Carolina State University, College of Veterinary Medicine, Program in Specialized Veterinary Medicine, Raleigh, NC 27695. Offers MSpVM. *Accreditation:* AVMA. *Degree requirements:* For master's, thesis optional. *Entrance requirements:* For master's, GRE General Test. Additional exam requirements/recommendations for international students: Required—TOEFL (minimum score 550 paper-based; 213 computer-based). Electronic applications accepted. *Faculty research:* Cell biology, infectious diseases, pharmacology and toxicology, genomics, pathology and population medicine.

North Carolina State University, College of Veterinary Medicine, Program in Veterinary Public Health, Raleigh, NC 27695. Offers MVPH. *Degree requirements:* For master's, thesis optional. Electronic applications accepted.

The Ohio State University, College of Veterinary Medicine, Professional Program in Veterinary Medicine, Columbus, OH 43210. Offers DVM, DVM/MS, DVM/PhD. *Accreditation:* AVMA. *Students:* 555 full-time (440 women), 5 part-time (all women); includes 27 minority (4 African Americans, 1 American Indian/Alaska Native, 15 Asian Americans or Pacific Islanders, 7 Hispanic Americans), 1 international. Average age 25. In 2006, 133 degrees awarded. *Entrance requirements:* GRE General Test, MCAT, or VCAT, 96 hours of pre-veterinary course work. *Application deadline:* For fall admission, 11/1 for domestic students. Applications are processed on a rolling basis. Application fee: $60 ($70 for international students). Electronic applications accepted. *Expenses:* Tuition, state resident: full-time $9,438. Tuition, nonresident: full-time $22,791. Tuition and fees vary according to course load, campus/location and program. *Financial support:* Fellowships, Federal Work-Study and institutionally sponsored loans available. Support available to part-time students. *Application contact:* Graduate Admissions, 614-292-9444, Fax: 614-292-3895.

Oklahoma State University, Center for Veterinary Health Sciences, Professional Program in Veterinary Medicine, Stillwater, OK 74078. Offers DVM. *Accreditation:* AVMA. *Students:* 308 full-time (217 women); includes 34 minority (2 African Americans, 24 American Indian/Alaska Native, 3 Asian Americans or Pacific Islanders, 5 Hispanic Americans). Average age 24. 481 applicants, 17% accepted, 80 enrolled. In 2006, 74 degrees awarded. *Entrance requirements:* GRE General Test, GRE Subject Test (biology). *Application deadline:* For fall admission, 10/1 for domestic students. Application fee: $50. Electronic applications accepted. *Expenses:* Tuition, state resident: part-time $146 per credit hour. Tuition, nonresident: part-time $516 per credit hour. Required fees: $44 per credit hour. Tuition and fees vary according to program. *Financial support:* In 2006–07, 21 research assistantships (averaging $22,032 per year), 8 teaching assistantships (averaging $22,032 per year) were awarded; career-related internships or fieldwork, Federal Work-Study, and tuition waivers (partial) also available. Support available to part-time students. Financial award application deadline: 3/1. *Faculty research:* Infectious diseases, physiology, toxicology, biomedical lasers, clinical studies. *Application contact:* Robin K. Wilson, Manager of Admissions, 405-744-6653, Fax: 405-744-0356, E-mail: robin.wilson@okstate.edu.

Oregon State University, College of Veterinary Medicine, Professional Program in Veterinary Medicine, Corvallis, OR 97331. Offers DVM. DVM admissions open only to residents of Oregon and other states participating in the Western Interstate Commission for Higher Education (WICHE). *Accreditation:* AVMA. *Students:* 195 full-time (162 women), 1 part-time; includes 10 minority (1 African American, 2 American Indian/Alaska Native, 5 Asian Americans or Pacific Islanders, 2 Hispanic Americans). Average age 26. In 2006, 38 degrees awarded. *Entrance requirements:* VCAT and/or GRE, minimum GPA of 3.3 during previous 2 years, 3.2 overall. *Application deadline:* For fall admission, 11/1 for domestic students. Application fee: $50. *Financial support:* Federal Work-Study, institutionally sponsored loans, and scholarships/grants available. Support available to part-time students. Financial award application deadline: 2/1. *Unit head:* Dr. Susan J. Tornquist, Associate Dean, 541-737-2098, Fax: 541-737-4245. *Application contact:* Associate Dean, 541-737-2098, Fax: 541-737-4245.

Purdue University, School of Veterinary Medicine, Professional Program in Veterinary Medicine, West Lafayette, IN 47907. Offers DVM, DVM/MS, DVM/PhD. *Accreditation:* AVMA. *Faculty:* 100 full-time (31 women), 8 part-time/adjunct (4 women). *Students:* 269 full-time (215 women), 1 (woman) part-time; includes 16 minority (2 African Americans, 4 Asian Americans or Pacific Islanders, 10 Hispanic Americans), 2 international. Average age 23. 604 applicants, 16% accepted. In 2006, 58 degrees awarded. *Entrance requirements:* GRE General Test. Additional exam requirements/recommendations for international students: Required—TOEFL. *Application deadline:* For fall admission, 10/1 for domestic and international students. Application fee: $0. *Financial support:* Federal Work-Study, institutionally sponsored loans, and scholarships/grants available. Support available to part-time students. Financial award application deadline: 3/1; financial award applicants required to submit FAFSA. *Unit head:* J. F. Van Vleet, Associate Dean, 765-494-9185. *Application contact:* Denise A. Ottinger, Director, Student Services and Admissions, 765-494-7893, Fax: 765-496-2891, E-mail: vetadmissions@purdue.edu.

Texas A&M University, College of Veterinary Medicine, Graduate Programs in Veterinary Medicine, Department of Veterinary Large Animal Clinical Sciences, College Station, TX 77843. Offers veterinary medicine and surgery (MS). *Faculty:* 20 full-time (2 women). *Students:* 2 full-time (both women), 2 part-time (1 woman); includes 1 minority (Hispanic American)

Average age 30. 1 applicant, 100% accepted, 0 enrolled. In 2006, 1 degree awarded. *Degree requirements:* For master's, thesis (for some programs). *Entrance requirements:* For master's, GRE General Test. Additional exam requirements/recommendations for international students: Required—TOEFL. Application fee: $50 ($75 for international students). *Expenses:* Tuition, state resident: full-time $4,697. Tuition, nonresident: full-time $11,297. Required fees: $2,272. *Financial support:* In 2006–07, fellowships with tuition reimbursements (averaging $37,500 per year), research assistantships (averaging $30,700 per year), teaching assistantships (averaging $37,500 per year) were awarded. Financial award application deadline: 4/1; financial award applicants required to submit FAFSA. *Faculty research:* Epidemiology including environmental and food safety; veterinary clinical studies. *Unit head:* Dr. William Moyer, Head, 979-845-9127, Fax: 979-847-8863, E-mail: wmoyer@cvm.tamu.edu. *Application contact:* Dr. James A. Thompson, Graduate Advisor, 979-845-9158, Fax: 979-847-8863, E-mail: jthompson@cvm.tamu.edu.

Texas A&M University, College of Veterinary Medicine, Professional Programs in Veterinary Medicine, College Station, TX 77843. Offers DVM, DVM/PhD. *Accreditation:* AVMA. *Faculty:* 1 (woman) part-time/adjunct. *Students:* 509 full-time (377 women); includes 55 minority (3 African Americans, 1 American Indian/Alaska Native, 17 Asian Americans or Pacific Islanders, 34 Hispanic Americans). Average age 24. 131 applicants, 100% accepted, 131 enrolled. In 2006, 125 degrees awarded. *Entrance requirements:* GRE. *Application deadline:* For fall admission, 9/1 for domestic students. Application fee: $100. *Expenses:* Contact institution. *Financial support:* Application deadline: 4/1; *Faculty research:* Reproductive biology, theriogenology, genetics, endocrinology, animal behavior. *Unit head:* Dr. E. Dean Gage, Associate Dean Professional Programs, 979-845-3878, Fax: 979-845-5088, E-mail: dgage@cvm.tamu.edu. *Application contact:* Yolanda Brinkman, Coordinator of Admissions, 979-845-5038, Fax: 979-845-5088, E-mail: ymbrinkman@cvm.tamu.edu.

Tufts University, Cummings School of Veterinary Medicine, Professional Program in Veterinary Medicine, Medford, MA 02155. Offers DVM, DVM/MPH, DVM/MS. *Accreditation:* AVMA. *Faculty:* 85 full-time (35 women), 147 part-time/adjunct (59 women). *Students:* 319 full-time (274 women); includes 22 minority (1 African American, 19 Asian Americans or Pacific Islanders, 2 Hispanic Americans). Average age 27. 696 applicants, 23% accepted, 80 enrolled. In 2006, 77 degrees awarded. *Degree requirements:* For first-professional, thesis optional. *Entrance requirements:* GRE General Test. Additional exam requirements/recommendations for international students: Required—TOEFL. *Application deadline:* For fall admission, 11/1 for domestic and international students. Application fee: $60. Electronic applications accepted. *Expenses:* Contact institution. Tuition and fees vary according to degree level and program. *Financial support:* In 2006–07, 53 students received support. Career-related internships or fieldwork, Federal Work-Study, institutionally sponsored loans, and institutional aid awards available. Financial award application deadline: 3/10. *Faculty research:* Infectious disease, reproductive biology, respiratory physiology. *Application contact:* Rebecca Russo, Director of Admissions, 508-839-7920, Fax: 508-839-2953, E-mail: rebecca.russo@tufts.edu.

Tuskegee University, Graduate Programs, College of Veterinary Medicine, Nursing and Allied Health, Department of Veterinary Medicine, Tuskegee, AL 36088. Offers DVM. *Accreditation:* AVMA. *Faculty:* 62 full-time (6 women). *Students:* 233 full-time (183 women), 3 part-time (2 women); includes 122 minority (117 African Americans, 1 American Indian or Pacific Islander, 4 Hispanic Americans), 10 international. Average age 26. 264 applicants, 23% accepted. In 2006, 50 degrees awarded. *Entrance requirements:* VCAT. Additional exam requirements/recommendations for international students: Required—TOEFL (minimum score 500 paper-based; 173 computer-based). *Application deadline:* For fall admission, 7/15 for domestic students. Applications are processed on a rolling basis. Application fee: $25 ($35 for international students). *Expenses:* Tuition: Full-time $13,520; part-time $390 per semester. Required fees: $480; $405 per semester. *Financial support:* Application deadline: 4/15. *Unit head:* Dr. Tsegaye Habtemariam, Dean, College of Veterinary Medicine, Nursing and Allied Health, 334-727-8174, Fax: 334-727-8177.

Universidad Nacional Pedro Henriquez Urena, Graduate School, Santo Domingo, Dominican Republic. Offers accounting and auditing (M Acct); animal production (M Agr); business administration (MBA, PhD); Caribbean tropical architecture (M Arch); conservation of monuments and cultural goods (M Arch); economics (M Econ); education (PhD); environmental engineering (MEE); horticulture (M Agr); hospital administration (PhD); humanities (PhD); international relations (MPS); management of natural resources (MNRM); project management (M Man, MPM); public administration (MPS); sanitary engineering (ME); social science (PhD); veterinary medicine (DVM).

Université de Montréal, Faculty of Graduate Studies, Faculty of Veterinary Medicine, Professional Program in Veterinary Medicine, Montréal, QC H3C 3J7, Canada. Offers DVM. Open only to Canadian residents. Part-time programs available. *Faculty:* 106. *Application deadline:* For fall admission, 2/1 priority date for domestic students; for winter admission, 11/1 priority date for domestic students; for spring admission, 2/1 priority date for domestic students. Application fee: $30. Electronic applications accepted. *Financial support:* Teaching assistantships, career-related internships or fieldwork available. *Faculty research:* Animal reproduction, infectious diseases of swine, physiology of exercise in horses, viral diseases of cattle, health management and epidemiology. *Unit head:* Andre Urins, Unit Head, 514-343-6111 Ext. 8289. *Application contact:* Ginette Richer, Assistant, Professional Program, 450-773-8521 Ext. 8271, Fax: 450-778-8132, E-mail: saefmv@medvet.umontreal.ca.

University of California, Davis, School of Veterinary Medicine, Program in Veterinary Medicine, Davis, CA 95616. Offers DVM, DVM/MPVM. *Accreditation:* AVMA. *Entrance requirements:* GRE General Test. Additional exam requirements/recommendations for international students: Required—TOEFL. Electronic applications accepted.

University of Florida, College of Veterinary Medicine, Professional Program in Veterinary Medicine, Gainesville, FL 32611. Offers DVM. *Accreditation:* AVMA. *Faculty:* 1 (woman) full-time. *Students:* 763 applicants, 10% accepted. *Entrance requirements:* GRE General Test. *Application deadline:* For fall admission, 10/1 for domestic students. Application fee: $155. *Expenses:* Tuition, state resident: full-time $6,827. Tuition, nonresident: full-time $21,951. Required fees: $999. *Financial support:* Career-related internships or fieldwork, Federal Work-Study, institutionally sponsored loans, and scholarships/grants available. Financial award application deadline: 7/1; financial award applicants required to submit FAFSA. *Unit head:* Dr. James P. Thompson, Interim Dean, 352-392-4700 Ext. 5000, Fax: 352-392-8351, E-mail: thompsonji@ @mail.vetmed.ufl.edu.

University of Georgia, College of Veterinary Medicine, Professional Program in Veterinary Medicine, Athens, GA 30602. Offers DVM. *Accreditation:* AVMA. *Faculty:* 131 full-time (47 women), 8 part-time/adjunct (0 women). *Students:* 365 full-time (278 women); includes 15 minority (8 African Americans, 7 Asian Americans or Pacific Islanders). Average age 26. 524 applicants, 20% accepted, 96 enrolled. In 2006, 88 DVMs awarded. *Entrance requirements:* GRE General Test, GRE Subject Test (biology). *Application deadline:* For fall admission, 10/1 for domestic students. Application fee: $155. Electronic applications accepted. *Financial support:* In 2006–07, 298 students received support. Career-related internships or fieldwork and scholarships/grants available. Financial award application deadline: 8/1; financial award applicants required to submit FAFSA. *Faculty research:* Vascular biomedicine, environmental toxicology, food safety, vaccines and emerging diseases. Total annual research expenditures: $7.1 million. *Unit head:* Scott A. Brown, Acting Associate Dean for Academic Affairs, 706-542-5728, Fax: 706-542-1004, E-mail: sbrown@vet.uga.edu. *Application contact:* Teresa A. McClure, Admissions Counselor, 706-542-5727, Fax: 706-542-1004, E-mail: tmcclure@vet.uga.edu.

University of Guelph, Ontario Veterinary College and Graduate Program Services, Graduate Programs in Veterinary Sciences, Department of Clinical Studies, Guelph, ON N1G 2W1, Canada. Offers anesthesiology (M Sc, DV Sc); cardiology (Diploma); clinical studies (Diploma); emergency/critical care (Diploma); medicine (M Sc, DV Sc); neurology (M Sc, DV Sc); ophthalmology (M Sc, DV Sc); surgery (M Sc, DV Sc). *Faculty:* 37. *Students:* 27 (19 women). *Degree requirements:* For master's, thesis/dissertation; for doctorate, thesis/dissertation, comprehensive exam. *Entrance requirements:* Additional exam requirements/recommendations for international students: Required—TOEFL (minimum score 550 paper-based; 213 computer-based), IELTS (minimum score 7). *Application deadline:* For fall admission, 12/6 for domestic students; for winter admission, 10/30 priority date for domestic students; for spring admission, 2/28 priority date for domestic students. Applications are processed on a rolling basis. Application fee: $80. Electronic applications accepted. *Financial support:* Fellowships, research assistantships, teaching assistantships, career-related internships or fieldwork and scholarships/grants available. *Faculty research:* Orthopedics, respirology, oncology, exercise physiology, cardiology. Total annual research expenditures: $1.5 million. *Unit head:* Dr. Dara Allen, Interim Chair, 519-824-4120 Ext. 54001, Fax: 519-767-0311, E-mail: dallen@ouc.uoguelph.ca. *Application contact:* Dr. J. Scott Weese, Graduate Coordinator, 519-824-4120 Ext. 54064, Fax: 519-767-0311, E-mail: jsweese@uoguelph.ca.

University of Illinois at Urbana–Champaign, College of Veterinary Medicine, Professional Program in Veterinary Medicine, Champaign, IL 61820. Offers DVM. *Accreditation:* AVMA. *Faculty:* 62 full-time (22 women), 9 part-time/adjunct (6 women). *Students:* 413 full-time (324 women); includes 27 minority (2 African Americans, 2 American Indian/Alaska Native, 18 Asian Americans or Pacific Islanders, 5 Hispanic Americans), 2 international. 266 applicants, 73% accepted, 112 enrolled. In 2006, 96 degrees awarded. *Entrance requirements:* VCAT, GRE. Application fee: $50 ($60 for international students). Electronic applications accepted. *Expenses:* Contact institution. *Financial support:* In 2006–07, 2 fellowships, 1 research assistantship were awarded; teaching assistantships, career-related internships or fieldwork, Federal Work-Study, and tuition waivers (full) also available. Financial award application deadline: 3/15. Total annual research expenditures: $4.1 million. *Application contact:* Mary Anna Kelm, Assistant Dean for Academic and Student Affairs, 217-333-1192, Fax: 217-333-4628, E-mail: marykelm@uiuc.edu.

University of Maryland, College Park, Graduate Studies, College of Agriculture and Natural Resources, Maryland Campus of VA/MD Regional College of Veterinary Medicine, Professional Program in Veterinary Medicine, College Park, MD 20742. Offers DVM. *Students:* 129 full-time (102 women); includes 5 minority (1 African American, 4 Asian Americans or Pacific Islanders), 11 international. 30 applicants, 100% accepted, 30 enrolled. In 2006, 29 degrees awarded. *Degree requirements:* For first-professional, thesis, oral exam, public seminar. *Application deadline:* For fall admission, 5/1 for domestic students, 2/1 for international students; for spring admission, 10/1 for domestic students, 6/1 for international students. Application fee: $60. *Financial support:* In 2006–07, 2 fellowships (averaging $1,000 per year) were awarded. *Unit head:* Dr. Siba K. Samal, Chair/Associate Dean, Maryland Campus of VA/MD Regional College of Veterinary Medicine, 301-314-6830, Fax: 301-314-6855, E-mail: ssamal@umd.edu.

University of Minnesota, Twin Cities Campus, College of Veterinary Medicine, Professional Program in Veterinary Medicine, Minneapolis, MN 55455-0213. Offers DVM, DVM/PhD. *Accreditation:* AVMA. *Faculty:* 137 full-time (54 women). *Students:* 361 full-time (305 women); includes 18 minority (2 American Indian/Alaska Native, 13 Asian Americans or Pacific Islanders, 3 Hispanic Americans), 1 international. Average age 24. 916 applicants, 14% accepted, 90 enrolled. In 2006, 82 degrees awarded. *Entrance requirements:* GRE General Test. *Application deadline:* For fall admission, 10/1 for domestic students. Application fee: $50. Electronic applications accepted. *Expenses:* Contact institution. Full-time tuition and fees vary according to class time, course load, program, reciprocity agreements and student level. *Financial support:* In 2006–07, 308 students received support. Career-related internships or fieldwork, Federal Work-Study, and scholarships/grants available. Financial award application deadline: 4/1; financial award applicants required to submit FAFSA. *Faculty research:* Infectious toxic diseases of animals, zoonotic animal models of human disease, epidemiologic and preventive medicine. Total annual research expenditures: $18 million. *Unit head:* Dr. Laura Molgaard, Associate Dean, 612-624-4747, Fax: 612-624-1276. *Application contact:* Larry D. Bjorklund, Director, Student Affairs and Admissions, 612-624-4747, Fax: 612-624-1276, E-mail: dvminfo@umn.edu.

University of Missouri–Columbia, College of Veterinary Medicine, Professional Program in Veterinary Medicine, Columbia, MO 65211. Offers veterinary medicine (DVM). *Accreditation:* AVMA. *Faculty:* 109 full-time (32 women), 3 part-time/adjunct (2 women). *Students:* 266 full-time (190 women); includes 11 minority (3 African Americans, 2 Asian Americans or Pacific Islanders, 6 Hispanic Americans). Average age 23. In 2006, 64 degrees awarded. *Entrance requirements:* VCAT, minimum GPA of 2.5 for state residents, 3.0 for nonresidents. *Application deadline:* For fall admission, 11/1 for domestic students. Electronic applications accepted. *Financial support:* In 2006–07, 58 students received support; fellowships, research assistantships, career-related internships or fieldwork, institutionally sponsored loans, tuition waivers (full), and research associateships available. *Faculty research:* Cardiovascular physiology, food safety, infectious diseases, laboratory animal medicine, ophthalmology. Total annual research expenditures: $4 million. *Unit head:* Dr. James L. Cook, Assistant Professor, 573-882-1371, E-mail: cookjl@missouri.edu. *Application contact:* Dr. John R. Dodam, Associate Dean of Academic Affairs, 573-884-6774, E-mail: dodamj@missouri.edu.

University of Pennsylvania, School of Veterinary Medicine, Philadelphia, PA 19104. Offers VMD, VMD/MBA, VMD/PhD. *Accreditation:* AVMA. *Faculty:* 185 full-time (80 women). *Students:* 438 full-time (346 women); includes 38 minority (8 African Americans, 2 American Indian/Alaska Native, 22 Asian Americans or Pacific Islanders, 6 Hispanic Americans). Average age 24. 1,478 applicants, 11% accepted, 112 enrolled. *Entrance requirements:* GRE. Additional exam requirements/recommendations for international students: Required—TOEFL. *Application deadline:* For fall admission, 10/1 for domestic students. Application fee: $0. *Expenses:* Contact institution. *Financial support:* Career-related internships or fieldwork, Federal Work-Study, and institutionally sponsored loans available. Total annual research expenditures: $25 million. *Unit head:* Dr. Joan C. Hendricks, Dean, 215-898-8841, Fax: 215-573-8837, E-mail: vetdean@vet.upenn.edu. *Application contact:* Malcolm Keiter, Assistant Dean for Admissions, 215-898-5434, Fax: 215-573-8819, E-mail: admissions@vet.upenn.edu.

University of Prince Edward Island, Atlantic Veterinary College, Professional Program in Veterinary Medicine, Charlottetown, PE C1A 4P3, Canada. Offers DVM. *Accreditation:* AVMA. *Faculty:* 71 full-time (20 women), 61 part-time/adjunct (13 women). *Students:* 237 full-time (197 women). 190 applicants, 33% accepted, 61 enrolled. In 2006, 59 degrees awarded. *Entrance requirements:* GRE. Additional exam requirements/recommendations for international students: Required—TOEFL (minimum score 550 paper-based; 213 computer-based; 80 iBT), Canadian Academic English Language Assessment, Michigan English Language Assessment Battery, Canadian Test of English for Scholars and Trainees. *Application deadline:* For fall admission, 11/1 for domestic students, 10/1 for international students. Application fee: $50. *Financial support:* Research assistantships available. *Faculty research:* Shellfish toxicology, animal nutrition, fish health, toxicology, animal health management. *Unit head:* Dr. Lisa Miller, Associate Dean of Academic Affairs, 902-566-0858, Fax: 902-566-0958. *Application contact:* Jack MacDougall, Registrar's Office, 902-566-0781, Fax: 902-566-0795, E-mail: registrar@upei.ca.

University of Saskatchewan, Western College of Veterinary Medicine and College of Graduate Studies and Research, Graduate Programs in Veterinary Medicine, Department of Large Animal Clinical Sciences, Saskatoon, SK S7N 5A2, Canada. Offers herd medicine and theriogenology (M Sc, M Vet Sc, PhD). *Faculty:* 11 full-time (3 women). *Students:* 16 full-time (10 women); includes 1 minority (African American) In 2006, 7 master's, 1 doctorate awarded. *Degree requirements:* For master's, thesis (for some programs); for doctorate, thesis/dissertation. *Faculty research:* Reproduction, infectious diseases, epidemiology, food safety. *Unit head:* Dr. David Wilson, Head, 306-966-7087, Fax: 306-966-7159, E-mail: david.wilson@usask.ca.

University of Saskatchewan, Western College of Veterinary Medicine and College of Graduate Studies and Research, Graduate Programs in Veterinary Medicine, Department of Small Animal Clinical Sciences, Saskatoon, SK S7N 5A2, Canada. Offers small animal clinical

Veterinary Medicine

University of Saskatchewan (continued)
sciences (M Sc, PhD); veterinary anesthesiology, radiology and surgery (M Vet Sc); veterinary internal medicine (M Vet Sc). *Faculty:* 8 full-time (7 women). *Students:* 9 full-time (5 women). In 2006, 1 degree awarded. *Degree requirements:* For master's, thesis (for some programs); for doctorate, thesis/dissertation. *Faculty research:* Orthopedics, wildlife, cardiovascular exercise/myelopathy, ophthalmology. *Unit head:* Dr. Klaas Post, Head, 306-966-7084, Fax: 306-966-7174, E-mail: klaas.post@usask.ca.

University of Saskatchewan, Western College of Veterinary Medicine, Professional Program in Veterinary Medicine, Saskatoon, SK S7N 5A2, Canada. Offers DVM. *Accreditation:* AVMA. In 2006, 70 degrees awarded. *Degree requirements:* For first-professional, thesis. *Application deadline:* For fall admission, 7/1 priority date for domestic students. Application fee: $50. *Financial support:* Fellowships, teaching assistantships available. Financial award application deadline: 1/31. *Unit head:* Dr. J. Bailey, Associate Dean, 306-966-7409.

The University of Tennessee, Graduate School, College of Veterinary Medicine, Knoxville, TN 37996. Offers DVM. *Accreditation:* AVMA. *Faculty:* 92 full-time (35 women). *Students:* 274 full-time (215 women), 2 part-time (both women); includes 11 minority (4 African Americans, 3 Asian Americans or Pacific Islanders, 4 Hispanic Americans). In 2006, 65 degrees awarded. *Entrance requirements:* VCAT, interview, minimum GPA of 2.7. Additional exam requirements/recommendations for international students: Required—TOEFL. *Application deadline:* For fall admission, 11/1 for domestic students. Application fee: $25. *Expenses: Contact institution. Financial support:* In 2006–07, 1 fellowship, 10 research assistantships, 5 teaching assistantships were awarded; career-related internships or fieldwork, institutionally sponsored loans, and unspecified assistantships also available. Financial award application deadline: 2/1; financial award applicants required to submit FAFSA. *Unit head:* Dr. Michael J. Blackwell, Dean, 865-974-7263, Fax: 865-974-4773. *Application contact:* Dr. James Brace, Associate Dean, 865-974-7263, E-mail: jbrace@utk.edu.

University of Wisconsin–Madison, School of Veterinary Medicine, Professional Program in Veterinary Medicine, Madison, WI 53706-1380. Offers DVM. *Accreditation:* AVMA. *Entrance requirements:* GRE General Test.

Virginia Polytechnic Institute and State University, Virginia-Maryland Regional College of Veterinary Medicine, Professional Program in Veterinary Medicine, Blacksburg, VA 24061. Offers DVM. *Accreditation:* AVMA. *Faculty:* 87 full-time (23 women). *Students:* 356 full-time (294 women); includes 24 minority (4 African Americans, 1 American Indian/Alaska Native, 11 Asian Americans or Pacific Islanders, 8 Hispanic Americans). Average age 27. 874 applicants, 10% accepted, 90 enrolled. In 2006, 90 degrees awarded. *Degree requirements:* For first-professional, registration. *Application deadline:* For fall admission, 10/1 for domestic and international students. Application fee: $137. *Expenses: Contact institution. Financial support:* Career-related internships or fieldwork, Federal Work-Study, scholarships/grants, and unspecified assistantships available. Financial award application deadline: 3/1. *Unit head:* Dr. Grant H. Turnwald, Academic Affairs, 540-231-4090, E-mail: acadaff@vt.edu. *Application contact:* Joyce B. Massie, Admissions Coordinator, 540-231-4699, Fax: 540-231-9290, E-mail: dvmadmit@vt.edu.

Washington State University, College of Veterinary Medicine, Professional Program in Veterinary Medicine, Pullman, WA 99164. Offers DVM, DVM/MS, DVM/PhD. *Accreditation:* AVMA. *Students:* 383 full-time (296 women); includes 22 minority (3 African Americans, 3 American Indian/Alaska Native, 9 Asian Americans or Pacific Islanders, 7 Hispanic Americans). Average age 26. 784 applicants, 12% accepted, 96 enrolled. In 2006, 69 degrees awarded. *Entrance requirements:* GRE. *Application deadline:* For fall admission, 10/2 for domestic and international students. Applications are processed on a rolling basis. Application fee: $40. Electronic applications accepted. *Expenses:* Tuition, state resident: full-time $7,066. Tuition, nonresident: full-time $17,204. *Financial support:* Research assistantships, teaching assistantships, scholarships/grants available. Financial award application deadline: 3/1; financial award applicants required to submit FAFSA. *Faculty research:* Biotechnology, immunology, pathology, neurosciences, clinical sciences. *Unit head:* Dr. Gilbert A. Burns, Associate Dean, 509-355-1531, Fax: 509-335-5063. *Application contact:* Barbara Hodson, Program Coordinator, 509-335-1532, Fax: 509-335-6133, E-mail: bhodson@vetmed.wsu.edu.

Western University of Health Sciences, College of Veterinary Medicine, Pomona, CA 91766-1854. Offers DVM. *Faculty:* 42 full-time (21 women), 3 part-time/adjunct (1 woman). *Students:* 359 full-time (285 women); includes 79 minority (1 African American, 4 American Indian/Alaska Native, 47 Asian Americans or Pacific Islanders, 27 Hispanic Americans), 5 international. Average age 29. 441 applicants, 42% accepted, 103 enrolled. *Entrance requirements:* MCAT or GRE General Test, minimum GPA of 2.5, letters of recommendation, interview. Additional exam requirements/recommendations for international students: Required—TOEFL (minimum score 550 paper-based; 213 computer-based). *Application deadline:* For fall admission, 10/1 for domestic students. Application fee: $75. *Expenses: Contact institution. Financial support:* Institutionally sponsored loans, scholarships/grants, and Veterans Educational Benefits available. Financial award application deadline: 3/2; financial award applicants required to submit FAFSA. *Unit head:* Dr. Phil Nelson, Interim Dean, 909-469-5637, Fax: 909-469-5635. *Application contact:* Audrey Navarro, Information Contact, 909-469-5335, Fax: 909-469-5570, E-mail: admissions@westernu.edu.

Veterinary Sciences

Auburn University, College of Veterinary Medicine and Graduate School, Graduate Programs in Veterinary Medicine, Auburn University, AL 36849. Offers biomedical sciences (MS, PhD), including anatomy, physiology and pharmacology (MS), biomedical sciences (PhD), clinical sciences (MS), large animal surgery and medicine (MS), pathobiology (MS), radiology (MS), small animal surgery and medicine (MS); DVM/MS. Part-time programs available. *Faculty:* 84 full-time (29 women), 1 part-time/adjunct (0 women). *Students:* 19 full-time (10 women), 34 part-time (24 women); includes 2 minority (both Hispanic Americans), 18 international. Average age 32. 49 applicants, 39% accepted, 9 enrolled. In 2006, 8 master's, 4 doctorates awarded. *Degree requirements:* For doctorate, thesis/dissertation. *Entrance requirements:* For master's, GRE General Test; for doctorate, GRE General Test, GRE Subject Test. *Application deadline:* For fall admission, 7/7 for domestic students; for spring admission, 11/24 for domestic students. Applications are processed on a rolling basis. Application fee: $25 ($50 for international students). Electronic applications accepted. *Expenses:* Tuition, state resident: full-time $5,000. Tuition, nonresident: full-time $15,000. Required fees: $416. Tuition and fees vary according to program. *Financial support:* Research assistantships, teaching assistantships, Federal Work-Study available. Support available to part-time students. Financial award application deadline: 3/15. *Application contact:* Dr. Joe Pittman, Interim Dean of the Graduate School, 334-844-4700.

Clemson University, Graduate School, College of Agriculture, Forestry and Life Sciences, Department of Animal and Veterinary Sciences, Program in Animal and Veterinary Sciences, Clemson, SC 29634. Offers MS, PhD. Offered in cooperation with the Department of Poultry Science. *Students:* 8 full-time (6 women), 5 part-time (4 women), 1 international. Average age 26. 8 applicants, 25% accepted, 2 enrolled. In 2006, 3 degrees awarded. *Degree requirements:* For master's and doctorate, thesis/dissertation. *Entrance requirements:* For master's and doctorate, GRE General Test. Additional exam requirements/recommendations for international students: Required—TOEFL. *Application deadline:* For fall admission, 6/1 priority date for domestic students, 4/15 for international students; for spring admission, 11/1 priority date for domestic students, 9/15 for international students. Applications are processed on a rolling basis. Application fee: $50. Electronic applications accepted. *Expenses:* Tuition, state resident: full-time $8,812; part-time $450 per hour. Tuition, nonresident: full-time $18,036; part-time $760 per hour. Required fees: $474; $5 per term. *Financial support:* Fellowships, research assistantships, teaching assistantships, career-related internships or fieldwork available. Financial award application deadline: 6/1; financial award applicants required to submit FAFSA. *Faculty research:* Reproductive physiology, endocrinology, stress physiology, immunology. *Unit head:* Dr. Tom Scott, Coordinator, 864-656-4027, Fax: 864-656-3131, E-mail: trscott@clemson.edu.

Colorado State University, College of Veterinary Medicine and Biomedical Sciences, Department of Clinical Sciences, Fort Collins, CO 80523-0015. Offers MS, PhD. Part-time programs available. *Faculty:* 49 full-time (16 women), 1 part-time/adjunct (0 women). *Students:* 10 full-time (6 women), 58 part-time (34 women); includes 6 minority (5 Asian Americans or Pacific Islanders, 1 Hispanic American), 15 international. Average age 32. 13 applicants, 100% accepted, 12 enrolled. In 2006, 10 degrees awarded. Terminal master's awarded for partial completion of doctoral program. *Degree requirements:* For master's, thesis (for some programs), exam; for doctorate, thesis/dissertation, exam. *Entrance requirements:* For master's, GRE General Test, minimum GPA of 3.0, DVM (for some) or other equivalent medical degree; for doctorate, GRE General Test, DVM (for some) or other equivalent medical degree. Additional exam requirements/recommendations for international students: Required—TOEFL (minimum score 550 paper-based). *Application deadline:* For fall admission, 2/1 priority date for domestic students. Applications are processed on a rolling basis. Application fee: $50. Electronic applications accepted. *Expenses:* Tuition, state resident: full-time $4,248; part-time $236 per credit. Tuition, nonresident: full-time $15,642; part-time $869 per credit. Required fees: $66 per credit. Tuition and fees vary according to program. *Financial support:* In 2006–07, 40 research assistantships with full and partial tuition reimbursements (averaging $29,020 per year) were awarded; fellowships, teaching assistantships, Federal Work-Study, institutionally sponsored loans, and traineeships also available. Financial award application deadline: 2/15; financial award applicants required to submit FAFSA. *Faculty research:* Bone densitometry, orthopedics, oncology, epidemiology, infectious diseases. Total annual research expenditures: $7 million. *Unit head:* D. Paul Lunn, Head, 970-297-1274, Fax: 970-297-1275, E-mail: david.lunn@colostate.edu. *Application contact:* Morna J. Mynard, Information Contact, 970-297-4030, Fax: 970-297-1275, E-mail: mmynard@colostate.edu.

Drexel University, College of Medicine, Biomedical Graduate Programs, Program in Laboratory Animal Science, Philadelphia, PA 19104-2875. Offers MLAS. Part-time programs available. *Degree requirements:* For master's, comprehensive exam. *Entrance requirements:* For master's, GRE General Test, minimum GPA of 3.0. Additional exam requirements/recommendations for international students: Required—TOEFL. Electronic applications accepted. *Faculty research:* Laboratory animal medicine, experimental surgery, development of animal models for human diseases.

Iowa State University of Science and Technology, College of Veterinary Medicine and Graduate College, Graduate Programs in Veterinary Medicine, Department of Veterinary Clinical Sciences, Ames, IA 50011. Offers MS. Part-time programs available. *Faculty:* 26 full-time. *Students:* 1 (woman) full-time, 2 part-time (both women). 1 applicant, 100% accepted, 1 enrolled. In 2006, 2 degrees awarded. *Degree requirements:* For master's, thesis or alternative. *Entrance requirements:* For master's, DVM. Additional exam requirements/recommendations for international students: Required—TOEFL (paper-based 550; computer-based 213; iBT 79) or IELTS (6.5). *Application deadline:* Applications are processed on a rolling basis. Application fee: $30 ($70 for international students). Electronic applications accepted. *Expenses:* Tuition, state resident: full-time $5,936; part-time $330 per credit. Tuition, nonresident: full-time $16,350; part-time $330 per credit. *Financial support:* Fellowships, research assistantships with partial tuition reimbursements, teaching assistantships with partial tuition reimbursements, career-related internships or fieldwork, scholarships/grants, health care benefits, and unspecified assistantships available. *Faculty research:* Theriogenology, veterinary medicine, veterinary surgery, extracorporeal shock waves, therapy, orthopedic research in animals. *Unit head:* Dr. James Toombs, Chair, 515-294-2199, E-mail: jptoombs@iastate.edu. *Application contact:* Dr. Albert Jergens, Director of Graduate Education, 515-294-6411.

Iowa State University of Science and Technology, College of Veterinary Medicine and Graduate College, Graduate Programs in Veterinary Medicine, Department of Veterinary Microbiology and Preventive Medicine, Ames, IA 50011. Offers veterinary microbiology (MS, PhD). *Faculty:* 23 full-time, 10 part-time/adjunct. *Students:* 29 full-time (15 women), 12 part-time (9 women); includes 2 minority (both Hispanic Americans), 12 international. 16 applicants, 25% accepted, 4 enrolled. In 2006, 3 master's, 4 doctorates awarded. *Degree requirements:* For master's, thesis or alternative; for doctorate, thesis/dissertation. *Entrance requirements:* For master's and doctorate, GRE General Test. Additional exam requirements/recommendations for international students: Required—TOEFL (paper-based 550; computer-based 213; iBT 79) or IELTS (6.5). *Application deadline:* For fall admission, 2/1 priority date for domestic and international students. Applications are processed on a rolling basis. Application fee: $30 ($70 for international students). Electronic applications accepted. *Expenses:* Tuition, state resident: full-time $5,936; part-time $330 per credit. Tuition, nonresident: full-time $16,350; part-time $330 per credit. *Financial support:* In 2006–07, 20 research assistantships with full tuition reimbursements (averaging $18,775 per year), 1 teaching assistantship with full tuition reimbursement (averaging $18,696 per year) were awarded; fellowships, scholarships/grants, health care benefits, and unspecified assistantships also available. *Faculty research:* Bacteriology, immunology, virology, public health and food safety. *Unit head:* Dr. Lisa Nolan, Chair, 515-294-5776, E-mail: vetmicro@iastate.edu. *Application contact:* Dr. Eileen Thacker, Director of Graduate Education, 515-294-5097, E-mail: vetmicro@instate.edu.

Kansas State University, College of Veterinary Medicine and Graduate School, Graduate Programs in Veterinary Medicine, Department of Clinical Sciences, Manhattan, KS 66506. Offers biomedical science (MS). *Faculty:* 19 full-time (6 women), 11 part-time/adjunct (3 women). *Students:* 8 full-time (3 women), 7 part-time (4 women); includes 1 minority (American Indian/Alaska Native), 2 international. Average age 27. 14 applicants, 100% accepted, 14 enrolled. In 2006, 1 degree awarded. *Degree requirements:* For master's, thesis. *Entrance requirements:* For master's, GRE, DVM. Additional exam requirements/recommendations for international students: Required—TOEFL (minimum score 550 paper-based; 213 computer-based). *Application deadline:* For fall admission, 2/1 priority date for domestic students; for spring admission, 10/1 for domestic students. Applications are processed on a rolling basis. Application fee: $30 ($55 for international students). Electronic applications accepted. *Expenses:* Tuition, state resident: full-time $6,352; part-time $240 per credit hour. Tuition, nonresident: full-time $14,296; part-time $571 per credit hour. Required fees: $585. *Financial support:* In 2006–07, 13 research assistantships (averaging $16,687 per year) were awarded; teaching assistantships, institutionally sponsored loans and scholarships/grants also available. Financial award application deadline: 3/1; financial award applicants required to submit FAFSA. *Faculty research:* Clinical trials, equine gastrointestinal ulceration, leptospirosis, food animal pharmacology, equine immunology, diabetes. Total annual research expenditures: $976,864. *Unit* *head:* Bonnie Rush, Interim Department Head, 785-532-4249, E-mail: brush@vet.ksu.edu. *Application contact:* David Anderson, Director, 785-532-4259, E-mail: danderso@vet.ksu.edu.

Louisiana State University and Agricultural and Mechanical College, School of Veterinary Medicine and Graduate School, Department of Comparative Biomedical Sciences, Baton Rouge, LA 70803. Offers MS, PhD. *Faculty:* 17 full-time (0 women). *Students:* 13 full-time (5 women), 2 part-time (1 woman); includes 1 American Indian/Alaska Native, 7 international. Average age 30. 3 applicants, 67% accepted, 1 enrolled. In 2006, 1 degree awarded. *Degree requirements:* For master's, thesis; for doctorate, thesis/dissertation, final exam. *Entrance requirements:* For master's and doctorate, GRE, minimum GPA of 3.0. Additional exam requirements/recommendations for international students: Required—TOEFL (minimum score 550 paper-based; 213 computer-based; 79 iBT). *Application deadline:* For fall admission, 5/15 for international students; for spring admission, 10/15 for international students. Electronic applications accepted. *Financial support:* In 2006–07, 3 fellowships with full and partial tuition reimbursements (averaging $23,813 per year), 10 research assistantships with full and partial tuition reimbursements (averaging $20,300 per year) were awarded; teaching assistantships, Federal Work-Study, institutionally sponsored loans, scholarships/grants, and unspecified assistantships also available. Support available to part-time students. Financial award applicants required to submit FAFSA. *Faculty research:* Gene therapy, metastasis, DNA repair, cytokines in cardiovascular function, aguatic toxicology. Total annual research expenditures: $1.9 million. *Unit head:* Dr. Gary E. Wise, Head, 225-578-9889, Fax: 225-578-9895, E-mail: gwise@mail.vetmed.lsu.edu. *Application contact:* Dr. George M. Strain, Graduate Adviser, 225-578-9758, Fax: 225-578-9895, E-mail: strain@lsu.edu.

Louisiana State University and Agricultural and Mechanical College, School of Veterinary Medicine and Graduate School, Department of Pathobiological Sciences, Baton Rouge, LA 70803. Offers MS, PhD. *Faculty:* 30 full-time (6 women), 1 part-time/adjunct (0 women). *Students:* 25 full-time (14 women), 8 part-time (4 women); includes 1 African American, 9 international. Average age 32. 18 applicants, 39% accepted, 5 enrolled. In 2006, 2 master's, 4 doctorates awarded. *Entrance requirements:* Additional exam requirements/recommendations for international students: Required—TOEFL (minimum score 550 paper-based; 213 computer-based; 79 iBT). *Application deadline:* For fall admission, 5/15 for international students; for spring admission, 10/15 for international students. Electronic applications accepted. *Financial support:* In 2006–07, 26 students received support, including fellowships with full tuition reimbursements available (averaging $23,279 per year), 23 research assistantships with full and partial tuition reimbursements available (averaging $24,308 per year); teaching assistantships with full and partial tuition reimbursements available, Federal Work-Study, scholarships/grants, and unspecified assistantships also available. Support available to part-time students. Financial award applicants required to submit FAFSA. *Faculty research:* Infectious disease, host-pathogen interaction, vaccinology. Total annual research expenditures: $3.6 million. *Unit head:* Dr. Ronald Thune, Head, 225-578-9680, Fax: 225-578-9701, E-mail: thune@mail.vetmed.lsu.edu. *Application contact:* Dr. James E. Miller, Graduate Adviser, 225-578-9652, Fax: 225-578-9701, E-mail: jmille1@lsu.edu.

Louisiana State University and Agricultural and Mechanical College, School of Veterinary Medicine and Graduate School, Department of Veterinary Clinical Sciences, Baton Rouge, LA 70803. Offers MS, PhD. *Faculty:* 27 full-time (14 women), 1 part-time/adjunct (0 women). *Students:* 5 full-time (3 women), 7 part-time (4 women), 6 international. Average age 34. 6 applicants, 67% accepted, 1 enrolled. In 2006, 1 degree awarded. *Entrance requirements:* For master's and doctorate, GRE, DVM or equivalent degree. Additional exam requirements/recommendations for international students: Required—TOEFL (minimum score 550 paper-based; 213 computer-based; 79 iBT). *Application deadline:* For fall admission, 5/15 for domestic and international students; for spring admission, 10/15 for international students. Application fee: $25. Electronic applications accepted. *Financial support:* In 2006–07, 9 students received support, including 5 research assistantships with full and partial tuition reimbursements available (averaging $19,480 per year); fellowships, teaching assistantships, Federal Work-Study, institutionally sponsored loans, scholarships/grants, and unspecified assistantships also available. Support available to part-time students. Financial award applicants required to submit FAFSA. *Faculty research:* Urology/nephrology, equine arthroscopy orthopedics and laser surgery, physical rehabilitation on companion animals, cardiology, gastroenterology, infectious diseases, medical oncology, mare infertility. Total annual research expenditures: $302,736. *Unit head:* Dr. David Senior, Head, 225-578-9551, Fax: 225-578-9559, E-mail: dsenior@vetmed.lsu.edu. *Application contact:* Dr. Giselle Hosgood, Graduate Adviser, 225-578-9551, Fax: 225-578-9559, E-mail: ghosgood@mail.vetmed.lsu.edu.

Michigan State University, College of Veterinary Medicine and The Graduate School, Graduate Programs in Veterinary Medicine, East Lansing, MI 48824. Offers comparative medicine and integrative biology (MS, PhD); food safety and toxicology (MS), including food safety; integrative toxicology (PhD), including animal science–environmental toxicology, biochemistry and molecular biology–environmental toxicology, chemistry–environmental toxicology, crop and soil sciences–environmental toxicology, environmental engineering–environmental toxicology, environmental geosciences–environmental toxicology, fisheries and wildlife–environmental toxicology, food science–environmental toxicology, forestry–environmental toxicology, microbiology–environmental toxicology, pathology–environmental toxicology, pharmacology and toxicology–environmental toxicology, zoology–environmental toxicology; large animal clinical sciences (MS, PhD); microbiology and molecular genetics (MS, PhD), including industrial microbiology (MS), microbiology, microbiology and molecular genetics, microbiology–environmental toxicology (PhD); pathobiology and diagnostic investigation (MS, PhD), including pathology, pathology–environmental toxicology (PhD); small animal clinical sciences (MS). *Students:* 55 full-time (27 women), 56 part-time (38 women); includes 20 minority (11 African Americans, 2 American Indian/Alaska Native, 5 Asian Americans or Pacific Islanders, 2 Hispanic Americans), 30 international. Average age 34. *Application deadline:* For fall admission, 12/27 for domestic students. Applications are processed on a rolling basis. Application fee: $50. Electronic applications accepted. *Expenses:* Tuition, state resident: part-time $346 per credit hour. Tuition, nonresident: part-time $730 per credit hour. Tuition and fees vary according to program. *Faculty research:* Molecular genetics, food safety/toxicology, comparative orthopedics, airway disease, population medicine. *Unit head:* Dr. John C. Baker, Associate Dean for Research and Graduate Studies, 517-432-2388, Fax: 517-432-1037, E-mail: baker@cvm.msu.edu. *Application contact:* Dr. Victoria Hoelzer-Maddox, Administrative Assistant, 517-353-3118, Fax: 517-432-1037, E-mail: hoelzer-maddox@cvm.msu.edu.

Mississippi State University, College of Veterinary Medicine, Graduate Programs in Veterinary Medical Science, Mississippi State, MS 39762. Offers environmental toxicology (PhD); veterinary medical science (MS, PhD). Part-time programs available. Terminal master's awarded for partial completion of doctoral program. *Degree requirements:* For master's, thesis (for some programs); for doctorate, thesis/dissertation. *Entrance requirements:* For master's and doctorate, minimum GPA of 3.0. Additional exam requirements/recommendations for international students: Required—TOEFL. Electronic applications accepted. Expenses: Contact institution. Tuition and fees vary according to course load. *Faculty research:* Food animal health (poultry and warm-water aquaculture) using immunology, microbiology, molecular biology, parasitology, pathology, pharmacology, and environmental toxicology.

Montana State University, College of Graduate Studies, College of Agriculture, Department of Veterinary Molecular Biology, Bozeman, MT 59717. Offers MS, PhD. Part-time programs available. *Faculty:* 4 full-time (0 women), 1 (woman) part-time/adjunct. *Students:* 3 full-time (1 woman), 10 part-time (5 women); includes 1 minority (Hispanic American), 3 international. Average age 28. 8 applicants, 50% accepted, 4 enrolled. In 2006, 2 master's, 3 doctorates awarded. *Degree requirements:* For master's, comprehensive exam, registration; for doctorate, thesis/dissertation, comprehensive exam, registration. *Entrance requirements:* For master's and doctorate, GRE General Test. Additional exam requirements/recommendations for international students: Required—TOEFL (minimum score 550 paper-based; 213 computer-based). *Application deadline:* For fall admission, 7/15 priority date for domestic students, 5/15 for international students; for spring admission, 12/1 priority date for domestic students, 10/1 priority date for international students. Applications are processed on a rolling basis. Application fee: $30. Electronic applications accepted. *Expenses:* Tuition, state resident: full-time $5,113. Tuition, nonresident: full-time $12,501. *Financial support:* In 2006–07, 13 students received support, including 11 research assistantships with full tuition reimbursements available (averaging $18,000 per year), 2 teaching assistantships with full tuition reimbursements available (averaging $18,000 per year); health care benefits and unspecified assistantships also available. Financial award application deadline: 3/1; financial award applicants required to submit FAFSA. *Faculty research:* Infectious diseases, immunology, functional genomics, vaccine delivery systems, embryonic development. Total annual research expenditures: $11.2 million. *Unit head:* Dr. Mark G. Quinn, Head, 406-994-5721, Fax: 406-994-4303, E-mail: mquinn@montana.edu.

North Carolina State University, College of Veterinary Medicine, Program in Comparative Biomedical Sciences, Raleigh, NC 27695. Offers cell biology and morphology (MS, PhD); epidemiology and population medicine (MS, PhD); immunology (MS, PhD); microbiology and immunology (MS, PhD); pathology (MS, PhD); pharmacology (MS, PhD); specialized veterinary medicine (MS). Part-time programs available. *Degree requirements:* For master's and doctorate, thesis/dissertation. *Entrance requirements:* For master's and doctorate, GRE General Test. Additional exam requirements/recommendations for international students: Required—TOEFL (minimum score 550 paper-based; 213 computer-based). Electronic applications accepted. Expenses: Contact institution. *Faculty research:* Infectious diseases, cell biology, pharmacology and toxicology, genomics, pathology and population medicine.

North Dakota State University, The Graduate School, College of Agriculture, Food Systems, and Natural Resources, Department of Veterinary and Microbiological Sciences, Fargo, ND 58105. Offers microbiology (MS); molecular pathogenesis (PhD); natural resource management (MS). Part-time programs available. *Degree requirements:* For master's, thesis; for doctorate, thesis/dissertation, oral and written preliminary exams. *Entrance requirements:* For master's and doctorate, GRE. Additional exam requirements/recommendations for international students: Required—TOEFL. *Application deadline:* For fall admission, 3/15 priority date for domestic students. Applications are processed on a rolling basis. Application fee: $25. *Financial support:* Fellowships with full tuition reimbursements, research assistantships with full tuition reimbursements, teaching assistantships with full tuition reimbursements, Federal Work-Study and institutionally sponsored loans available. Financial award application deadline: 4/15. *Faculty research:* Bacterial gene regulation, antibiotic resistance, molecular virology, mechanisms of bacterial pathogenesis, immunology of animals. *Unit head:* Dr. Doug Freeman, Chair, 701-231-7511. *Application contact:* Dr. Eugene S. Berry, Associate Professor, 701-231-7520, Fax: 701-231-7514, E-mail: eugene.berry@ndsu.edu.

The Ohio State University, College of Veterinary Medicine, Department of Veterinary Biosciences, Columbus, OH 43210. Offers anatomy and cellular biology (MS, PhD); pathobiology (MS, PhD); pharmacology (MS, PhD); toxicology (MS, PhD); veterinary physiology (MS, PhD). *Faculty:* 45. *Students:* 35 full-time (24 women), 16 part-time (6 women); includes 5 minority (2 African Americans, 3 Asian Americans or Pacific Islanders), 24 international. Average age 30. 2 applicants, 100% accepted. In 2006, 5 master's, 5 doctorates awarded. *Entrance requirements:* For master's and doctorate, GRE. *Application deadline:* Applications are processed on a rolling basis. Application fee: $40 ($50 for international students). Electronic applications accepted. *Expenses:* Tuition, state resident: full-time $9,438. Tuition, nonresident: full-time $22,791. Tuition and fees vary according to course load, campus/location and program. *Faculty research:* Microvasculature, muscle biology, neonatal lung and bone development. *Unit head:* Dr. Michael J. Oglesbee, Graduate Studies Committee Chair, 614-292-5661, Fax: 614-292-6473, E-mail: oglesbee.1@osu.edu. *Application contact:* Graduate Admissions, 614-292-9444, Fax: 614-292-3895, E-mail: domestic.grad@osu.edu.

The Ohio State University, College of Veterinary Medicine, Department of Veterinary Clinical Sciences, Columbus, OH 43210. Offers MS, PhD. *Faculty:* 54. *Students:* 40 full-time (24 women), 3 part-time (2 women); includes 1 minority (Asian American or Pacific Islander), 11 international. Average age 30. 13 applicants, 100% accepted, 11 enrolled. In 2006, 11 master's, 3 doctorates awarded. *Entrance requirements:* For master's and doctorate, GRE for graduates of institutions not accredited by the AVMA. *Application deadline:* For fall admission, 1/2 for domestic students. Applications are processed on a rolling basis. Application fee: $40 ($50 for international students). Electronic applications accepted. *Expenses:* Tuition, state resident: full-time $9,438. Tuition, nonresident: full-time $22,791. Tuition and fees vary according to course load, campus/location and program. *Faculty research:* Equine exercise physiology, orthopedic surgery, oncology. *Unit head:* Kenneth W. Hinchcliff, Graduate Studies Committee Chair, 614-292-7105, Fax: 614-292-0895, E-mail: hinchcliff.2@osu.edu. *Application contact:* Graduate Admissions, 614-292-9444, Fax: 614-292-3895, E-mail: domestic.grad@osu.edu.

The Ohio State University, College of Veterinary Medicine, Department of Veterinary Preventive Medicine, Columbus, OH 43210. Offers MS, PhD. *Faculty:* 34. *Students:* 21 full-time (15 women), 2 part-time; includes 2 minority (1 African American, 1 American Indian/Alaska Native), 11 international. Average age 31. 6 applicants, 100% accepted, 5 enrolled. In 2006, 7 master's, 5 doctorates awarded. *Entrance requirements:* For master's and doctorate, GRE for graduates of institutions not accredited by the AVMA. *Application deadline:* Applications are processed on a rolling basis. Application fee: $40 ($50 for international students). Electronic applications accepted. *Expenses:* Tuition, state resident: full-time $9,438. Tuition, nonresident: full-time $22,791. Tuition and fees vary according to course load, campus/location and program. *Faculty research:* Epidemiology; herd health; environmental health; animal health research pertaining to diagnosis, prevention, and control. *Unit head:* Dr. Paivi Rajala-Schultz, Graduate Studies Committee Chair, 614-292-1206, Fax: 614-292-4142, E-mail: rajala-schultz@osu.edu. *Application contact:* Graduate Admissions, 614-292-94444, Fax: 614-292-3895, E-mail: domestic.grad@osu.edu.

Oklahoma State University, Center for Veterinary Health Sciences and Graduate College, Graduate Program in Veterinary Biomedical Sciences, Stillwater, OK 74078. Offers MS, PhD. Postbaccalaureate distance learning degree programs offered (minimal on-campus study). *Faculty:* 85 full-time (14 women). *Students:* 51 full-time (23 women); includes 20 minority (1 African American, 17 Asian Americans or Pacific Islanders, 2 Hispanic Americans). Average age 30. In 2006, 2 master's, 2 doctorates awarded. Terminal master's awarded for partial completion of doctoral program. *Degree requirements:* For master's and doctorate, thesis/dissertation. *Entrance requirements:* For master's and doctorate, GRE General Test, GRE Subject Test. Additional exam requirements/recommendations for international students: Required—TOEFL. *Application deadline:* For fall admission, 7/1 priority date for domestic students; for spring admission, 10/1 priority date for domestic students. Applications are processed on a rolling basis. Application fee: $50 ($75 for international students). Electronic applications accepted. *Expenses:* *Contact institution.* Tuition and fees vary according to program. *Financial support:* In 2006–07, 38 students received support, including 5 fellowships with tuition reimbursements available (averaging $18,000 per year), 24 research assistantships with partial tuition reimbursements available (averaging $21,396 per year), 9 teaching assistantships with partial tuition reimbursements available (averaging $21,396 per year); career-related internships or fieldwork, Federal Work-Study, institutionally sponsored loans, scholarships/grants, and tuition waivers (full) also available. Support available to part-time students. Financial award application deadline: 3/1; financial award applicants required to submit FAFSA. *Faculty research:* Infectious diseases, physiology, toxicology, biomedical lasers, clinical studies. *Unit head:* Dr. Jerry Malayer, Associate Dean, Graduate Studies, 405-744-6750, Fax: 405-744-5275, E-mail: jerry.malayer@okstate.edu. *Application contact:* Diana Moffeit, Assistant, 405-744-6750, Fax: 405-744-5275, E-mail: diana.moffeit@okstate.edu.

Oregon State University, College of Veterinary Medicine, Program in Comparative Veterinary Medicine, Corvallis, OR 97331. Offers PhD. *Degree requirements:* For doctorate, one foreign language, thesis/dissertation. *Entrance requirements:* For doctorate, minimum GPA of 3.0 in last 90 hours of course work. Additional exam requirements/recommendations for international students: Required—TOEFL. *Application deadline:* For fall admission, 11/1 for domestic students.

Veterinary Sciences

Oregon State University (continued)

Application fee: $50. *Financial support:* Fellowships, research assistantships, Federal Work-Study and institutionally sponsored loans available. Support available to part-time students. Financial award application deadline: 2/1. *Faculty research:* Microbiology, virology, toxicology. *Unit head:* Dr. Susan J. Tornquist, Associate Dean, 541-737-2098, Fax: 541-737-4245.

Oregon State University, College of Veterinary Medicine, Program in Veterinary Science, Corvallis, OR 97331. Offers microbiology (MS); pathology (MS); toxicology (MS). Part-time programs available. *Students:* 3 full-time (1 woman), 1 international. Average age 27. *Degree requirements:* For master's, thesis. *Entrance requirements:* For master's, minimum GPA of 3.0 in last 90 hours. Additional exam requirements/recommendations for international students: Required—TOEFL. *Application deadline:* For fall admission, 11/1 for domestic students. Application fee: $50. *Expenses: Contact institution. Financial support:* Research assistantships, Federal Work-Study, institutionally sponsored loans, and scholarships/grants available. Support available to part-time students. Financial award application deadline: 2/1. *Faculty research:* Calf diseases, bovine foot rot, caliciviruses, effects of toxic agents on immune systems. *Unit head:* Dr. Susan J. Tornquist, Associate Dean, 541-737-2098, Fax: 541-737-4245.

Penn State Hershey Medical Center, College of Medicine, Graduate School Programs in the Biomedical Sciences, Graduate Program in Laboratory Animal Medicine, Hershey, PA 17033-2360. Offers MS. *Students:* Average age 27. *Median time to degree:* Of those who began their doctoral program in fall 1998, 100% received their degree in 8 years or less. *Degree requirements:* For master's, thesis or alternative, registration. *Entrance requirements:* For master's, GRE, DVM or DMV. Additional exam requirements/recommendations for international students: Required—TOEFL (minimum score 550 paper-based; 213 computer-based). *Application deadline:* For fall admission, 2/1 priority date for domestic and international students. Applications are processed on a rolling basis. Application fee: $45. Electronic applications accepted. *Financial support:* In 2006–07, 2 students received support; fellowships with tuition reimbursements available, research assistantships with tuition reimbursements available, scholarships/grants, traineeships, health care benefits, and unspecified assistantships available. Financial award applicants required to submit FAFSA. *Faculty research:* Veterinary pathology; pain, analgesia and anesthesia of lab animals; genetically modified animal models of cancer; transgenic animals. *Unit head:* Dr. Ronald P. Wilson, Chair, 717-531-8460, Fax: 717-531-5001, E-mail: grad-hmc@psu.edu.

Penn State University Park, Graduate School, College of Agricultural Sciences, Department of Veterinary and Biomedical Sciences, State College, University Park, PA 16802-1503. Offers pathobiology (PhD). *Unit head:* Dr. C. Channa Reddy, Head, 814-865-7696, Fax: 814-863-6140, E-mail: crrl@psu.edu. *Application contact:* Information Contact, E-mail: vjk1@psu.edu.

Purdue University, School of Veterinary Medicine and Graduate School, Graduate Programs in Veterinary Medicine, Department of Basic Medical Sciences, West Lafayette, IN 47907. Offers anatomy (MS, PhD); pharmacology (MS, PhD); physiology (MS, PhD). Part-time programs available. *Faculty:* 18 full-time (5 women), 2 part-time/adjunct (1 woman). *Students:* 21 full-time (12 women), 3 part-time (all women); includes 2 minority (1 African American, 1 Hispanic American), 15 international. Average age 27. 23 applicants, 17% accepted, 4 enrolled. In 2006, 1 master's, 3 doctorates awarded. Terminal master's awarded for partial completion of doctoral program. *Median time to degree:* Of those who began their doctoral program in fall 1998, 33% received their degree in 8 years or less. *Degree requirements:* For master's and doctorate, thesis/dissertation. *Entrance requirements:* For master's and doctorate, GRE General Test. Additional exam requirements/recommendations for international students: Required—TOEFL. *Application deadline:* For fall admission, 12/31 priority date for domestic students, 12/31 for international students. Application fee: $55. Electronic applications accepted. *Financial support:* In 2006–07, 4 fellowships with partial tuition reimbursements (averaging $13,251 per year), 12 research assistantships with partial tuition reimbursements (averaging $15,012 per year), 2 teaching assistantships with partial tuition reimbursements (averaging $17,800 per year) were awarded. Financial award application deadline: 3/1; financial award applicants required to submit FAFSA. *Faculty research:* Development and regeneration, tissue injury and shock, biomedical engineering, ovarian function, bone and cartilage biology, cell and molecular biology. *Unit head:* Dr. Gordon L. Coppoc, Head, 765-494-8592, Fax: 765-494-0781, E-mail: coppoc@purdue.edu. *Application contact:* Dr. Kevin M. Hannon, Chairman, Graduate Committee, 765-494-5949, Fax: 765-494-0781, E-mail: bmsgrad@purdue.edu.

Purdue University, School of Veterinary Medicine and Graduate School, Graduate Programs in Veterinary Medicine, Department of Comparative Pathobiology, West Lafayette, IN 47907. Offers biochemistry and molecular biology (MS, PhD); comparative epidemiology (MS, PhD); epidemiology (MS, PhD); immunology (MS, PhD); infectious diseases (MS, PhD); interdisciplinary genetics (PhD); laboratory animal medicine (MS, PhD); microbiology (MS, PhD); molecular virology (MS, PhD); parasitology (MS, PhD); pathobiology (MS, PhD); public health epidemiology (MS, PhD); toxicology (MS, PhD); veterinary anatomic pathology (MS, PhD); veterinary clinical pathology (MS, PhD); virology (MS, PhD). *Faculty:* 34 full-time (8 women). *Students:* 45 full-time (19 women), 3 part-time (1 woman); includes 1 minority (African American), 29 international. Average age 35. In 2006, 3 master's, 2 doctorates awarded. Terminal master's awarded for partial completion of doctoral program. *Degree requirements:* For master's, thesis (for some programs); for doctorate, thesis/dissertation. *Entrance requirements:* For master's and doctorate, GRE General Test. Additional exam requirements/recommendations for international students: Required—TOEFL (minimum score 575 paper-based; 232 computer-based), IELTS (minimum score 7), TWE (minimum score 4). *Application deadline:* For fall admission, 8/12 for domestic students, 6/15 for international students; for spring admission, 1/12 for domestic students, 10/15 for international students. Application fee: $55. Electronic applications accepted. *Financial support:* Fellowships, research assistantships, teaching assistantships available. Financial award application deadline: 3/1; financial award applicants required to submit FAFSA. *Unit head:* Dr. H. Hogen Esch, Head, 765-494-7543.

Purdue University, School of Veterinary Medicine and Graduate School, Graduate Programs in Veterinary Medicine, Department of Veterinary Clinical Sciences, West Lafayette, IN 47907. Offers MS, PhD. Degrees offered are post-DVM. *Faculty:* 48 full-time (18 women), 6 part-time/adjunct (3 women). *Students:* 4 full-time (2 women), 20 part-time (13 women); includes 1 minority (African American), 4 international. In 2006, 8 degrees awarded. Terminal master's awarded for partial completion of doctoral program. *Degree requirements:* For master's, thesis (for some programs); for doctorate, thesis/dissertation. *Entrance requirements:* For master's and doctorate, DVM. *Application deadline:* For fall admission, 7/1 for domestic students, 5/1 for international students; for winter admission, 12/1 for domestic students, 10/1 for international students; for spring admission, 6/15 for domestic students, 3/15 for international students. Application fee: $55. *Financial support:* In 2006–07, 2 fellowships with full tuition reimbursements, 4 research assistantships were awarded; teaching assistantships, institutionally sponsored loans and tuition waivers (full) also available. Financial award application deadline: 3/1; financial award applicants required to submit FAFSA. *Faculty research:* Flow cytometry, chemotherapy, biologic response modifiers, broncho-alveolar lavage, lithotripsy. *Unit head:* Peter Constable, Head, 765-494-9900, Fax: 765-496-1108.

South Dakota State University, Graduate School, College of Agriculture and Biological Sciences, Department of Veterinary Science, Brookings, SD 57007. Offers biological sciences (MS, PhD). Part-time and evening/weekend programs available. *Faculty:* 10 full-time (3 women), 10 part-time/adjunct (2 women). *Students:* 20 full-time (14 women). In 2006, 1 degree awarded. *Degree requirements:* For master's, thesis (for some programs), oral exam; for doctorate, thesis/dissertation, preliminary oral and written exams, comprehensive exam. *Entrance requirements:* Additional exam requirements/recommendations for international students: Required—TOEFL (minimum score 525 paper-based; 197 computer-based; 71 iBT). *Application deadline:* For fall admission, 4/15 for international students; for spring admission, 8/15 for international students. Applications are processed on a rolling basis. Application fee: $35. *Financial support:* In 2006–07, 4 fellowships, 9 research assistantships with partial tuition reimbursements, 7 teaching assistantships with partial tuition reimbursements were awarded; career-related internships or fieldwork, Federal Work-Study, and unspecified assistantships also available. *Faculty research:* Infectious disease, food animal, virology, immunology. *Unit head:* Dr. David H. Zeman, Head, 605-688-5171, Fax: 605-688-6003, E-mail: david.zeman@sdstate.edu. *Application contact:* Dr. Christopher C.L. Chase, Graduate Coordinator, 605-688-5171, Fax: 605-688-6003, E-mail: christopher.chase@sdstate.edu.

Texas A&M University, College of Veterinary Medicine, Graduate Programs in Veterinary Medicine, Department of Veterinary Small Animal Medicine and Surgery, College Station, TX 77843. Offers veterinary medicine and surgery (MS). *Faculty:* 23 full-time (13 women). *Students:* 3 full-time (all women), 1 international. Average age 25. 2 applicants, 100% accepted, 2 enrolled. In 2006, 1 degree awarded. *Degree requirements:* For master's, thesis. *Entrance requirements:* For master's, GRE General Test. Additional exam requirements/recommendations for international students: Required—TOEFL. Application fee: $50 ($75 for international students). *Expenses:* Tuition, state resident: full-time $4,697. Tuition, nonresident: full-time $11,297. Required fees: $2,272. *Financial support:* In 2006–07, research assistantships with full tuition reimbursements (averaging $13,800 per year); fellowships, teaching assistantships also available. Financial award application deadline: 3/1; financial award applicants required to submit FAFSA. *Faculty research:* Gastroenterology, anesthesiology, nephrology and urology, cardiology, nutrition. *Unit head:* Dr. Sandee Hartsfield, Head, 979-845-2351, Fax: 979-845-6978, E-mail: shartsfield@cvm.tamu.edu.

Tufts University, Cummings School of Veterinary Medicine, Program in Animals and Public Policy, Medford, MA 02155. Offers MS. *Faculty:* 2 full-time (0 women), 25 part-time/adjunct. *Students:* 13 full-time (11 women); includes 1 African American. 35 applicants, 43% accepted, 13 enrolled. In 2006, 7 degrees awarded. *Degree requirements:* For master's, thesis or alternative. *Entrance requirements:* For master's, GRE General Test. Additional exam requirements/recommendations for international students: Required—TOEFL. *Application deadline:* For fall admission, 4/1 for domestic and international students. Application fee: $60. Electronic applications accepted. *Expenses: Contact institution.* Tuition and fees vary according to degree level and program. *Faculty research:* Veterinary ethics, veterinary jurisprudence, companion animal demographics and control, human/animal relationships, wildlife policy issues, animal research ethics. *Unit head:* Dr. Paul Waldau, Director, Center for Animals and Public Policy, 508-839-4671, E-mail: paul.waldau@tufts.edu. *Application contact:* Rebecca Russo, Director of Admissions, 508-839-7920, Fax: 508-839-2953, E-mail: rebecca.russo@tufts.edu.

Tufts University, Cummings School of Veterinary Medicine, Program in Comparative Biomedical Sciences, Medford, MA 02155. Offers PhD, DVM/MS. *Faculty:* 13 full-time. *Students:* 6 full-time (all women); includes 5 minority (all Asian Americans or Pacific Islanders) Average age 27. 2 applicants, 100% accepted, 1 enrolled. *Degree requirements:* For doctorate, thesis/dissertation. *Entrance requirements:* For doctorate, GRE General Test. Additional exam requirements/recommendations for international students: Required—TOEFL. *Application deadline:* For fall admission, 2/1 for domestic and international students. Application fee: $75. Electronic applications accepted. *Expenses:* Tuition: Full-time $33,672. Tuition and fees vary according to degree level and program. *Financial support:* In 2006–07, 6 research assistantships with full tuition reimbursements (averaging $20,774 per year), 2 teaching assistantships with full tuition reimbursements (averaging $5,000 per year) were awarded. Financial award application deadline: 3/10. *Faculty research:* Infectious disease, reproductive biology. *Unit head:* Dr. Charles Shoemaker, Head, 508-887-4324, E-mail: charles.shoemaker@tufts.edu. *Application contact:* Rebecca Russo, Director of Admissions, 508-839-7920, Fax: 508-839-2953, E-mail: rebecca.russo@tufts.edu.

Tufts University, Cummings School of Veterinary Medicine, Program in Laboratory Animal Medicine, Medford, MA 02155. Offers DVM/MS. *Faculty:* 6 full-time (4 women), 2 part-time/adjunct (0 women). *Students:* 7 full-time (6 women); includes 1 minority (Asian American or Pacific Islander) Average age 25. 3 applicants, 100% accepted, 3 enrolled. *Application deadline:* For fall admission, 5/15 for domestic and international students. Application fee: $100. *Expenses:* Tuition: Full-time $33,672. Tuition and fees vary according to degree level and program. *Financial support:* In 2006–07, 7 students received support, including 4 fellowships with tuition reimbursements available. Financial award application deadline: 5/10. *Faculty research:* Animal research alternatives, pain management. *Unit head:* Dr. Angeline Warner, Associate Dean for Academic Affairs, 508-887-4200, E-mail: angie.warner@tufts.edu.

Tuskegee University, Graduate Programs, College of Veterinary Medicine, Nursing and Allied Health, Department of Veterinary Medicine, Tuskegee, AL 36088. Offers MS. *Faculty:* 62 full-time (6 women). *Students:* 25 full-time (17 women), 4 part-time (2 women); includes 13 minority (12 African Americans, 1 Asian American or Pacific Islander), 8 international. Average age 35. 17 applicants, 76% accepted. In 2006, 5 degrees awarded. *Degree requirements:* For master's, thesis. *Entrance requirements:* For master's, GRE General Test. *Application deadline:* For fall admission, 7/15 for domestic students. Applications are processed on a rolling basis. Application fee: $25 ($35 for international students). *Expenses:* Tuition: Full-time $13,520; part-time $390 per semester. Required fees: $480; $405 per semester. *Financial support:* Application deadline: 4/15. *Unit head:* Dr. Tsegaye Habtemariam, Dean, College of Veterinary Medicine, Nursing and Allied Health, 334-727-8174, Fax: 334-727-8177.

Université de Montréal, Faculty of Graduate Studies, Faculty of Veterinary Medicine and Faculty of Graduate Studies, Graduate Programs in Veterinary Sciences, Montréal, QC H3C 3J7, Canada. Offers M Sc, DES, PhD, Certificate, DESS. *Faculty:* 106. *Students:* Average age 29. *Degree requirements:* For master's, one foreign language, thesis optional. *Application deadline:* For fall admission, 2/1 priority date for domestic students; for winter admission, 11/1 priority date for domestic students; for spring admission, 2/1 priority date for domestic students. Application fee: $30. Electronic applications accepted. *Financial support:* Research assistantships, teaching assistantships, career-related internships or fieldwork and scholarships/grants available. *Faculty research:* Animal reproduction, infectious diseases of swine, physiology of exercise in horses, viral diseases of cattle, health management and epidemiology. *Unit head:* Mario Jacques, Unit Head, 514-343-6111 Ext. 8348. *Application contact:* Micheline St-Germain, Assistant, Graduate Studies, 450-773-8521 Ext. 8520, Fax: 450-778-8132, E-mail: saefmv@medvet.umontreal.ca.

University of California, Davis, School of Veterinary Medicine and Graduate Studies, Program in Preventive Veterinary Medicine, Davis, CA 95616. Offers MPVM, DVM/MPVM. Part-time programs available. *Degree requirements:* For master's, thesis. *Entrance requirements:* For master's, DVM or equivalent. Additional exam requirements/recommendations for international students: Required—TOEFL (minimum score 550 paper-based; 213 computer-based). *Faculty research:* Epidemiology, zoonoses, veterinary public health, wildlife and ecosystem health.

University of California, Davis, School of Veterinary Medicine, Residency Training Program, Davis, CA 95616. Offers Certificate. *Entrance requirements:* For degree, DVM or equivalent, 1 year of related experience. *Faculty research:* Small animal and large animal medicine, surgery, infectious diseases, pathology.

University of Florida, College of Veterinary Medicine, Graduate Program in Veterinary Medical Sciences, Gainesville, FL 32611. Offers forensic toxicology (Certificate); veterinary medical sciences (MS, PhD), including forensic toxicology (MS). Postbaccalaureate distance learning degree programs offered (no on-campus study). *Faculty:* 114. In 2006, 29 master's, 9 doctorates awarded. Terminal master's awarded for partial completion of doctoral program. *Degree requirements:* For master's and doctorate, thesis/dissertation. *Entrance requirements:* For master's and doctorate, GRE General Test, minimum GPA of 3.0. Additional exam requirements/recommendations for international students: Required—TOEFL (minimum score 550 paper-based; 213 computer-based). *Application deadline:* For fall admission, 6/1 priority date for domestic students. Applications are processed on a rolling basis. Application fee: $30. Electronic applications accepted. *Expenses: Contact institution. Financial support:* In 2006–07, 1 fellowship with partial tuition reimbursement (averaging $14,000 per year), 32 research assistantships with partial tuition reimbursements (averaging $15,623 per year), 14 teaching assistantships with partial tuition reimbursements (averaging $15,921 per year) were awarded;

institutionally sponsored loans also available. *Unit head:* Dr. Charles H. Courtney, Associate Dean for Research and Graduate Studies, 352-392-4700 Ext. 5100, Fax: 352-392-8351, E-mail: courtneyc@mail.vetmed.ufl.edu. *Application contact:* Dr. Louis Archbald, Coordinator, 352-392-4700 Ext. 5641, Fax: 352-392-8351, E-mail: archbaldl@mail.vetmed.ufl.edu.

University of Georgia, College of Veterinary Medicine and Graduate School, Graduate Programs in Veterinary Medicine, Athens, GA 30602. Offers infectious diseases (MS, PhD), including infectious diseases; pathology (MS, PhD); physiology and pharmacology (MS, PhD), including pharmacology, physiology; population health (MAM, MFAM), including food animal medicine (MFAM), population health (MAM); toxicology (MS, PhD); veterinary anatomy and radiology (MS), including veterinary anatomy. *Faculty:* 71 full-time (25 women). *Students:* 105 full-time (61 women), 11 part-time (8 women); includes 8 minority (4 African Americans, 2 Asian Americans or Pacific Islanders, 2 Hispanic Americans), 39 international. Average age 27. 88 applicants, 39% accepted, 24 enrolled. In 2006, 6 master's, 4 doctorates awarded. *Degree requirements:* For master's and doctorate, thesis/dissertation, comprehensive exam, registration. *Entrance requirements:* For master's and doctorate, GRE General Test, 3 letters of recommendation. Additional exam requirements/recommendations for international students: Required—TOEFL (minimum score 550 paper-based; 213 computer-based). *Application deadline:* For fall admission, 7/1 for domestic students, 4/15 for international students; for spring admission, 11/15 for domestic students, 10/15 for international students. Applications are processed on a rolling basis. Application fee: $50. *Expenses:* Contact institution. *Financial support:* In 2006–07, 102 research assistantships with full tuition reimbursements (averaging $23,000 per year) were awarded; unspecified assistantships also available. Financial award application deadline: 3/1; financial award applicants required to submit FAFSA. *Faculty research:* Vascular biomedicine, environmental toxicology, food safety, vaccines and emergency diseases. Total annual research expenditures: $11.3 million. *Unit head:* Dr. Harry W. Dickerson, Associate Dean for Research and Graduate Affairs, 706-542-5734, Fax: 706-542-8254, E-mail: hwd@vet.uga.edu.

University of Guelph, Ontario Veterinary College and Graduate Program Services, Graduate Programs in Veterinary Sciences, Guelph, ON N1G 2W1, Canada. Offers M Sc, DV Sc, PhD, Diploma. *Accreditation:* AVMA (one or more programs are accredited). *Faculty:* 115. *Students:* 206 (120 women). *Degree requirements:* For master's, thesis/dissertation; for doctorate, thesis/dissertation, comprehensive exam. *Entrance requirements:* Additional exam requirements/recommendations for international students: Required—TOEFL. *Application deadline:* Applications are processed on a rolling basis. Application fee: $75. *Financial support:* In 2006–07, 1 fellowship (averaging $28,000 per year) was awarded; research assistantships, teaching assistantships, career-related internships or fieldwork and scholarships/grants also available. *Faculty research:* Veterinary and comparative medicine, biomedical sciences, population medicine, pathology, microbiology. Total annual research expenditures: $10 million. *Unit head:* Dr. Robert Jacobs, Associate Dean, 519-524-4120 Ext. 54796, Fax: 519-837-3230, E-mail: rjacobs@uoguelph.ca. *Application contact:* Barb Gaudette, Graduate Coordinator, Dean's Office, 519-824-4120 Ext. 54406, Fax: 519-837-3230, E-mail: bgaudett@ovc.uogelph.ca.

University of Idaho, College of Graduate Studies, College of Agricultural and Life Sciences, Department of Animal and Veterinary Science, Moscow, ID 83844-2282. Offers animal physiology (PhD); animal science (MS); veterinary science (MS). *Students:* 23 (11 women). Average age 36. In 2006, 5 master's, 2 doctorates awarded. *Degree requirements:* For doctorate, thesis/dissertation. *Entrance requirements:* For master's, GRE General Test, minimum GPA of 2.8; for doctorate, minimum undergraduate GPA of 2.8, graduate GPA of 3.0. *Application deadline:* For fall admission, 8/1 for domestic students; for spring admission, 12/15 for domestic students. Application fee: $55 ($60 for international students). *Expenses:* Tuition, nonresident: full-time $9,600; part-time $140 per credit. Required fees: $4,740; $227 per credit. *Financial support:* Research assistantships, teaching assistantships available. Financial award application deadline: 2/15. *Faculty research:* Agribusiness, range-livestock management. *Unit head:* Dr. Richard A. Battaglia, Head, 208-885-6345.

University of Illinois at Urbana–Champaign, College of Veterinary Medicine and Graduate College, Graduate Programs in Veterinary Medicine, Department of Pathobiology, Champaign, IL 61820. Offers MS, PhD. Part-time programs available. Postbaccalaureate distance learning degree programs offered (minimal on-campus study). *Faculty:* 24 full-time (7 women). *Students:* 17 full-time (10 women), 1 (woman) part-time; includes 3 minority (1 African American, 1 Asian American or Pacific Islander, 1 Hispanic American), 7 international. Average age 26. 26 applicants, 23% accepted, 1 enrolled. In 2006, 4 master's, 6 doctorates awarded. Terminal master's awarded for partial completion of doctoral program. *Degree requirements:* For master's and doctorate, thesis/dissertation. *Entrance requirements:* For master's and doctorate, GRE, minimum GPA of 3.0. *Application deadline:* Applications are processed on a rolling basis. Application fee: $50 ($60 for international students). Electronic applications accepted. *Financial support:* In 2006–07, 6 fellowships, 7 research assistantships, 4 teaching assistantships were awarded; tuition waivers (full and partial) also available. *Faculty research:* Epidemiology, immunology, microbiology, parasitology, clinical pathology. *Unit head:* Daniel L. Rock, Head, 217-333-2449, Fax: 217-244-7421, E-mail: dlrock@uiuc.edu. *Application contact:* Tish Lehigh, Graduate Program Coordinator, 217-244-8924, Fax: 217-244-7421, E-mail: lehigh@uiuc.edu.

University of Illinois at Urbana–Champaign, College of Veterinary Medicine and Graduate College, Graduate Programs in Veterinary Medicine, Department of Veterinary Biosciences, Champaign, IL 61820. Offers MS, PhD. *Faculty:* 15 full-time (6 women), 2 part-time/adjunct (both women). *Students:* 17 full-time (10 women), 9 international. 15 applicants, 40% accepted, 4 enrolled. In 2006, 2 master's, 1 doctorate awarded. *Degree requirements:* For master's and doctorate, thesis/dissertation. *Entrance requirements:* For master's and doctorate, minimum GPA of 3.0. *Application deadline:* Applications are processed on a rolling basis. Application fee: $50 ($60 for international students). Electronic applications accepted. *Financial support:* In 2006–07, 2 fellowships, 12 research assistantships, 1 teaching assistantship were awarded; tuition waivers (full and partial) also available. *Unit head:* Dr. Val Beasley, Head, 217-333-2506, Fax: 217-244-1652. *Application contact:* Linda Swett, Graduate Records Secretary, 217-333-2506, Fax: 217-244-1652, E-mail: lswett@uiuc.edu.

University of Illinois at Urbana–Champaign, College of Veterinary Medicine and Graduate College, Graduate Programs in Veterinary Medicine, Department of Veterinary Clinical Medicine, Champaign, IL 61820. Offers MS, PhD. *Faculty:* 21 full-time (9 women), 4 part-time/adjunct (2 women). *Students:* 22 full-time (14 women), 5 part-time (all women); includes 2 minority (1 African American, 1 Asian American or Pacific Islander), 13 international. 9 applicants, 89% accepted, 7 enrolled. In 2006, 7 master's, 2 doctorates awarded. *Degree requirements:* For master's, thesis; for doctorate, one foreign language, thesis/dissertation. *Entrance requirements:* For master's and doctorate, minimum GPA of 3.0. *Application deadline:* Applications are processed on a rolling basis. Application fee: $50 ($60 for international students). Electronic applications accepted. *Financial support:* In 2006–07, 6 research assistantships were awarded; fellowships, teaching assistantships, career-related internships or fieldwork and tuition waivers (full and partial) also available. *Unit head:* David A. Williams, Head, 217-333-5310, Fax: 217-244-1475, E-mail: daw@uiuc.edu. *Application contact:* Barbara Huffman, Staff Secretary, 217-333-5343, Fax: 217-244-1475, E-mail: bhuffman@uiuc.edu.

University of Kentucky, Graduate School, College of Agriculture, Program in Veterinary Science, Lexington, KY 40506-0032. Offers MS, PhD. *Faculty:* 30 full-time (5 women), 1 part-time/adjunct (0 women). *Students:* 21 full-time (15 women), 1 (woman) part-time, 9 international. Average age 31. 34 applicants, 44% accepted, 13 enrolled. In 2006, 2 master's, 4 doctorates awarded. *Median time to degree:* Of those who began their doctoral program in fall 1998, 78% received their degree in 8 years or less. *Degree requirements:* For master's and doctorate, thesis/dissertation, comprehensive exam. *Entrance requirements:* For master's, GRE General Test, minimum undergraduate GPA of 2.75; for doctorate, GRE General Test, minimum graduate GPA of 3.0. Additional exam requirements/recommendations for international students: Required—TOEFL (minimum score 550 paper-based; 213 computer-based). *Application deadline:* For fall admission, 7/17 priority date for domestic students, 2/1 priority date for international students; for spring admission, 12/13 priority date for domestic students, 6/15 priority date for international students. Application fee: $40 ($55 for international students). Electronic applications accepted. *Expenses:* Tuition, state resident: full-time $7,670; part-time $401 per credit hour. Tuition, nonresident: full-time $16,158; part-time $873 per credit hour. *Financial support:* In 2006–07, 2 fellowships with full tuition reimbursements (averaging $10,666 per year), 20 research assistantships with full tuition reimbursements (averaging $17,500 per year) were awarded; teaching assistantships with full tuition reimbursements, Federal Work-Study, institutionally sponsored loans, scholarships/grants, traineeships, health care benefits, tuition waivers (partial), and unspecified assistantships also available. Support available to part-time students. Financial award application deadline: 3/15. *Faculty research:* Microbiology, reproductive physiology, genetics, pharmacology/toxicology, parasitology. *Unit head:* Dr. Barry Fitzgerald, Director of Graduate Studies, 859-257-4557, Fax: 859-257-8542, E-mail: bfitz@pop.uky.edu. *Application contact:* Dr. Brian Jackson, Senior Associate Dean, 859-257-4667, Fax: 859-257-4676, E-mail: brian.jackson@uky.edu.

University of Maryland, College Park, Graduate Studies, College of Agriculture and Natural Resources, Maryland Campus of VA/MD Regional College of Veterinary Medicine, Veterinary Medical Sciences Program, College Park, MD 20742. Offers MS, PhD. *Students:* 14 full-time (4 women), 11 international. 10 applicants, 40% accepted, 4 enrolled. In 2006, 1 master's, 1 doctorate awarded. *Degree requirements:* For master's, thesis, oral exam; for doctorate, thesis/dissertation, oral exam, public seminar. *Entrance requirements:* For doctorate, GRE General Test. *Application deadline:* For fall admission, 5/1 for domestic students, 2/1 for international students; for spring admission, 10/1 for domestic students, 6/1 for international students. Applications are processed on a rolling basis. Application fee: $60. Electronic applications accepted. *Financial support:* In 2006–07, 2 fellowships (averaging $550 per year) were awarded; research assistantships, teaching assistantships. *Unit head:* Dr. Siba K. Samal, Chair/Associate Dean, Maryland Campus of VA/MD Regional College of Veterinary Medicine, 301-314-6830, Fax: 301-314-6855, E-mail: ssamal@umd.edu.

University of Minnesota, Twin Cities Campus, College of Veterinary Medicine and Graduate School, Graduate Programs in Veterinary Medicine, Program in Comparative and Molecular Bioscience, Minneapolis, MN 55455-0213. Offers MS, PhD, DVM/PhD. Part-time programs available. *Faculty:* 45 full-time (10 women). *Students:* 33 full-time (20 women); includes 1 minority (African American), 16 international. 32 applicants, 16% accepted, 4 enrolled. In 2006, 1 master's, 4 doctorates awarded. Terminal master's awarded for partial completion of doctoral program. *Median time to degree:* Master's–3 years full-time; doctorate–5 years full-time. Of those who began their doctoral program in fall 1998, 100% received their degree in 8 years or less. *Degree requirements:* For master's and doctorate, thesis/dissertation, comprehensive exam. *Entrance requirements:* For master's and doctorate, GRE. Additional exam requirements/recommendations for international students: Required—TOEFL (minimum score 550 paper-based; 213 computer-based; 79 iBT). *Application deadline:* For fall admission, 1/15 for domestic and international students. Application fee: $55 ($75 for international students). Electronic applications accepted. *Expenses:* Tuition, state resident: full-time $9,302; part-time $775 per credit. Tuition, nonresident: full-time $16,400; part-time $1,367 per credit. Full-time tuition and fees vary according to class time, course load, program, reciprocity agreements and student level. *Financial support:* In 2006–07, 2 fellowships (averaging $21,000 per year), 24 research assistantships with full tuition reimbursements (averaging $20,772 per year), 1 teaching assistantship with full tuition reimbursement (averaging $26,500 per year) were awarded; traineeships, health care benefits, and unspecified assistantships also available. *Faculty research:* Molecular regulation of immunity; mechanisms of bacterial, viral, and parasite pathogenesis; structural and functional comparative physiology and pathology. *Unit head:* Dr. Bruce Walcheck, Director of Graduate Studies, 612-624-2282, E-mail: walch003@umn.edu. *Application contact:* Erin Mann, Graduate Program Administrative Specialist, 612-624-2744, Fax: 612-625-4734, E-mail: mann0162@umn.edu.

University of Minnesota, Twin Cities Campus, College of Veterinary Medicine and Graduate School, Graduate Programs in Veterinary Medicine, Program in Veterinary Medicine, Minneapolis, MN 55455-0213. Offers MS, PhD. Part-time programs available. *Faculty:* 85 full-time (25 women). *Students:* 61 full-time (33 women); includes 5 minority (2 Asian Americans or Pacific Islanders, 3 Hispanic Americans), 30 international. 25 applicants, 44% accepted, 11 enrolled. In 2006, 7 master's, 6 doctorates awarded. Terminal master's awarded for partial completion of doctoral program. *Median time to degree:* Master's–3.3 years full-time; doctorate–6.5 years full-time. Of those who began their doctoral program in fall 1998, 70% received their degree in 8 years or less. *Degree requirements:* For master's and doctorate, thesis/dissertation, comprehensive exam. *Entrance requirements:* For master's and doctorate, GRE (recommended). Additional exam requirements/recommendations for international students: Required—TOEFL (minimum score 550 paper-based; 213 computer-based; 79 iBT). *Application deadline:* For fall admission, 3/1 for domestic and international students; for spring admission, 10/1 for domestic and international students. Application fee: $55 ($75 for international students). Electronic applications accepted. *Expenses:* Tuition, state resident: full-time $9,302; part-time $775 per credit. Tuition, nonresident: full-time $16,400; part-time $1,367 per credit. Full-time tuition and fees vary according to class time, course load, program, reciprocity agreements and student level. *Financial support:* In 2006–07, 24 research assistantships with full tuition reimbursements (averaging $20,772 per year), 14 teaching assistantships with full tuition reimbursements (averaging $26,500 per year) were awarded; traineeships, health care benefits, and unspecified assistantships also available. *Faculty research:* Infectious diseases, internal medicine, population medicine, surgery/radiology/anesthesiology, theriogenology. *Unit head:* Dr. Sagar Goyal, Director of Graduate Studies, 612-625-2714, E-mail: goyal001@umn.edu. *Application contact:* Erin Mann, Graduate Program Administrative Specialist, 612-624-2744, Fax: 612-625-4734, E-mail: mann0162@umn.edu.

University of Missouri–Columbia, College of Veterinary Medicine and Graduate School, Graduate Programs in Veterinary Medicine, Columbia, MO 65211. Offers veterinary biomedical sciences (MS); veterinary medicine and surgery (MS), including veterinary clinical sciences; veterinary pathobiology (MS, PhD), including laboratory animal medicine (MS), pathobiology. *Faculty:* 109 full-time (32 women), 3 part-time/adjunct (2 women). *Students:* 55 full-time (27 women), 38 part-time (21 women); includes 13 minority (5 African Americans, 1 American Indian/Alaska Native, 4 Asian Americans or Pacific Islanders, 3 Hispanic Americans), 24 international. In 2006, 9 master's, 9 doctorates awarded. *Degree requirements:* For master's, thesis; for doctorate, 2 foreign languages, thesis/dissertation. *Entrance requirements:* For master's and doctorate, GRE General Test, minimum GPA of 3.0. Additional exam requirements/recommendations for international students: Required—TOEFL (minimum score 600 paper-based; 250 computer-based). Application fee: $45 ($60 for international students). *Expenses:* Contact institution. *Financial support:* Fellowships with full tuition reimbursements, research assistantships with full tuition reimbursements, teaching assistantships with full tuition reimbursements, institutionally sponsored loans also available. *Unit head:* Dr. Ronald Terjung, Associate Dean for Research and Postdoctoral Studies, 573-882-2635, E-mail: terjungr@missouri.edu.

University of Nebraska–Lincoln, Graduate College, College of Agricultural Sciences and Natural Resources, Department of Veterinary and Biomedical Sciences, Lincoln, NE 68588. Offers MS, PhD. Postbaccalaureate distance learning degree programs offered (minimal on-campus study). *Degree requirements:* For master's, thesis optional; for doctorate, thesis/dissertation, comprehensive exam. *Entrance requirements:* For master's, GRE General Test; for doctorate, GRE General Test, MCAT, or VCAT. Additional exam requirements/recommendations for international students: Required—TOEFL (minimum score 550 paper-based; 213 computer-based). Electronic applications accepted. *Faculty research:* Virology, immunobiology, molecular biology, mycotoxins, ocular degeneration.

University of Prince Edward Island, Atlantic Veterinary College, Graduate Program in Veterinary Medicine, Charlottetown, PE C1A 4P3, Canada. Offers anatomy (M Sc, PhD); bacteriology (M Sc, PhD); clinical pharmacology (M Sc, PhD); clinical sciences (M Sc, PhD); epidemiology (M Sc, PhD), including reproduction; fish health (M Sc, PhD); food animal nutrition (M Sc, PhD); immunology (M Sc, PhD); microanatomy (M Sc, PhD); parasitology

Veterinary Sciences

University of Prince Edward Island (continued)
(M Sc, PhD); pathology (M Sc, PhD); pharmacology (M Sc, PhD); physiology (M Sc, PhD); toxicology (M Sc, PhD); veterinary science (M Vet Sc); virology (M Sc, PhD). Part-time programs available. *Faculty:* 76 full-time (25 women), 49 part-time/adjunct (8 women). *Students:* 55 full-time (28 women), 5 part-time (all women). Average age 30. 37 applicants, 51% accepted, 18 enrolled. In 2006, 5 master's, 7 doctorates awarded. *Degree requirements:* For master's and doctorate, thesis/dissertation. *Entrance requirements:* For master's, DVM, B Sc honors degree, or equivalent; for doctorate, M Sc. Additional exam requirements/recommendations for international students: Required—TOEFL (minimum score 550 paper-based; 213 computer-based; 80 iBT). *Application deadline:* Applications are processed on a rolling basis. Application fee: $75 ($100 for international students). *Expenses: Contact institution. Financial support:* In 2006–07, 4 fellowships (averaging $25,000 Canadian dollars per year), 4 research assistantships (averaging $16,500 Canadian dollars per year) were awarded; career-related internships or fieldwork also available. *Faculty research:* Animal health management, infectious diseases, fin fish and shellfish health, basic biomedical sciences, ecosystem health. Total annual research expenditures: $1.2 million Canadian dollars. *Unit head:* Dr. James Bellamy, Associate Dean of Graduate Studies and Research, 902-566-0856, E-mail: bellamy@upei.ca. *Application contact:* Jack MacDougall, Registrar's Office, 902-566-0781, Fax: 902-566-0795, E-mail: registrar@upei.ca.

University of Saskatchewan, Western College of Veterinary Medicine and College of Graduate Studies and Research, Graduate Programs in Veterinary Medicine, Saskatoon, SK S7N 5A2, Canada. Offers large animal clinical sciences (M Sc, M Vet Sc, PhD), including herd medicine and theriogenology; small animal clinical sciences (M Sc, M Vet Sc, PhD), including small animal clinical sciences (M Sc, PhD), veterinary anesthesiology, radiology and surgery (M Vet Sc), veterinary internal medicine (M Vet Sc); veterinary biomedical sciences (M Sc, M Vet Sc, PhD), including veterinary anatomy (M Sc), veterinary biomedical sciences (M Vet Sc), veterinary physiological sciences (M Sc, PhD); veterinary medicine (M Sc, PhD); veterinary microbiology (M Sc, M Vet Sc, PhD); veterinary pathology (M Sc, M Vet Sc, PhD). *Faculty:* 84 full-time, 34 part-time/adjunct. *Degree requirements:* For master's, thesis (for some programs), comprehensive exam; for doctorate, thesis/dissertation, comprehensive exam. *Entrance requirements:* Additional exam requirements/recommendations for international students: Required—IELTS or TOEFL. *Application deadline:* For fall admission, 7/1 priority date for domestic students. Application fee: $50. *Expenses: Contact institution. Financial support:* Fellowships, teaching assistantships available. Financial award application deadline: 1/31. *Faculty research:* Reproduction, toxicology, wildlife diseases, food animal medicine, equine health. *Application contact:* Dr. Norman C. Rawlings, Associate Dean, Research, 306-966-7068, Fax: 306-966-8747, E-mail: norman.rawlings@usask.ca.

University of Washington, School of Medicine and Graduate School, Graduate Programs in Medicine, Department of Comparative Medicine, Seattle, WA 98195. Offers veterinary science (MS).

University of Wisconsin–Madison, School of Veterinary Medicine, Graduate Program in Veterinary Medicine, Madison, WI 53706-1380. Offers MS, PhD. Postbaccalaureate distance learning degree programs offered (minimal on-campus study). Terminal master's awarded for partial completion of doctoral program. *Degree requirements:* For master's and doctorate, thesis/dissertation. *Entrance requirements:* For master's and doctorate, GRE, minimum GPA of 3.0. Additional exam requirements/recommendations for international students: Required—TOEFL.

Utah State University, School of Graduate Studies, College of Agriculture, Department of Animal, Dairy and Veterinary Sciences, Logan, UT 84322. Offers animal science (MS, PhD); bioveterinary science (MS, PhD); dairy science (MS). Part-time programs available. *Faculty:* 18 full-time (2 women), 2 part-time/adjunct (0 women). *Students:* 15 full-time (4 women), 1 part-time; includes 1 minority (Hispanic American), 1 international. Average age 25. 9 applicants, 56% accepted, 4 enrolled. In 2006, 4 master's, 1 doctorate awarded. *Degree requirements:* For master's, thesis (for some programs), registration; for doctorate, thesis/dissertation, comprehensive exam, registration. *Entrance requirements:* For master's and doctorate, GRE General Test, minimum GPA of 3.0. Additional exam requirements/recommendations for international students: Required—TOEFL. *Application deadline:* For fall admission, 5/15 priority date for domestic students; for spring admission, 10/15 for domestic students. Applications are processed on a rolling basis. Application fee: $50 ($60 for international students). Electronic applications accepted. *Financial support:* In 2006–07, 10 fellowships with full and partial tuition reimbursements (averaging $12,000 per year), 4 research assistantships with full and partial tuition reimbursements (averaging $13,300 per year), 3 teaching assistantships with full and partial tuition reimbursements (averaging $13,300 per year) were awarded; career-related internships or fieldwork, Federal Work-Study, institutionally sponsored loans, scholarships/grants, and tuition waivers (partial) also available. Financial award application deadline: 3/15. *Faculty research:* Monoclonal antibodies, antiviral chemotherapy, management systems, biotechnology, rumen fermentation manipulation. *Unit head:* Dr. Mark C. Healey, Head, 435-797-2162, Fax: 435-797-2118, E-mail: mchealey@cc.usu.edu. *Application contact:* Dr. Jeffrey L. Walters, Graduate Program Coordinator, 435-797-2161, Fax: 435-797-2118, E-mail: jwalters@cc.usu.edu.

Virginia Polytechnic Institute and State University, Virginia-Maryland Regional College of Veterinary Medicine and Graduate School, Graduate Programs in Biomedical and Veterinary Sciences, Blacksburg, VA 24061. Offers MS, PhD. Part-time programs available. *Faculty:* 32 full-time (5 women). *Students:* 76 full-time (41 women), 6 part-time (3 women); includes 8 minority (3 African Americans, 2 Asian Americans or Pacific Islanders, 3 Hispanic Americans), 34 international. Average age 29. 53 applicants, 40% accepted, 21 enrolled. In 2006, 13 master's, 7 doctorates awarded. *Degree requirements:* For master's and doctorate, thesis/dissertation. *Entrance requirements:* For master's and doctorate, GRE General Test, 3 letters of recommendation. Additional exam requirements/recommendations for international students: Required—TOEFL (minimum score 510 paper-based; 230 computer-based; 90 iBT). *Application deadline:* For fall admission, 5/15 for international students; for spring admission, 10/15 for international students. Applications are processed on a rolling basis. Application fee: $45. Electronic applications accepted. *Expenses: Contact institution. Financial support:* In 2006–07, research assistantships with tuition reimbursements (averaging $18,561 per year), teaching assistantships with tuition reimbursements (averaging $18,561 per year) were awarded; fellowships, career-related internships or fieldwork, Federal Work-Study, scholarships/grants, health care benefits, and unspecified assistantships also available. *Faculty research:* Infectious diseases, nanotechnology and neuroscience, immunology, nutrition, toxicology and pharmacology. *Unit head:* Dr. Roger Avery, Associate Dean of Research and Graduate Studies, 540-231-5649, Fax: 540-231-2574, E-mail: vmsgrad@vt.edu. *Application contact:* Tara V Craig, Office of Research and Graduate Studies, 540-231-4992, Fax: 540-231-2574, E-mail: vmsgrad@vt.edu.

Washington State University, College of Veterinary Medicine and Graduate School, Graduate Programs in Veterinary Science, Department of Veterinary and Comparative Anatomy, Pharmacology, and Physiology, Pullman, WA 99164. Offers neuroscience (MS, PhD); veterinary science (MS, PhD). Part-time programs available. *Faculty:* 25 full-time (7 women), 3 part-time/adjunct (1 woman). *Students:* 1 full-time (0 women), 1 international. Average age 32. 4 applicants, 0% accepted. Terminal master's awarded for partial completion of doctoral program. *Degree requirements:* For master's, thesis, written exam; for doctorate, thesis/dissertation, written exam, oral exam. *Entrance requirements:* For master's and doctorate, GRE General Test, minimum GPA of 3.0. Additional exam requirements/recommendations for international students: Required—TOEFL. *Application deadline:* For fall admission, 12/31 priority date for domestic students. Applications are processed on a rolling basis. Application fee: $50. Electronic applications accepted. *Expenses:* Tuition, state resident: full-time $7,066. Tuition, nonresident: full-time $17,204. *Financial support:* In 2006–07, research assistantships with partial tuition reimbursements (averaging $20,088 per year), teaching assistantships with partial tuition reimbursements (averaging $20,088 per year) were awarded; career-related internships or fieldwork, Federal Work-Study, and institutionally sponsored loans also available. Financial award application deadline: 12/31. *Faculty research:* Cardiovascular, neuroscience, muscle, behavior, feeding. Total annual research expenditures: $4.8 million. *Unit head:* Dr. Bryan K. Slinker, Chairman, 509-335-6624, Fax: 509-335-4650, E-mail: slinker@vetmed.wsu.edu. *Application contact:* Pam Colbert, Coordinator, 509-335-0986, Fax: 509-335-4650, E-mail: colbertp@vetmed.wsu.edu.

Washington State University, College of Veterinary Medicine and Graduate School, Graduate Programs in Veterinary Science, Department of Veterinary Clinical Sciences, Pullman, WA 99164. Offers MS. Part-time programs available. *Faculty:* 25 full-time (3 women). *Students:* 21 full-time (12 women); includes 1 minority (African American), 9 international. Average age 30. 8 applicants, 100% accepted, 8 enrolled. In 2006, 2 degrees awarded. *Degree requirements:* For master's, thesis/dissertation, oral exam. *Entrance requirements:* For master's, GRE General Test, minimum GPA of 3.0, DVM or equivalent. *Application deadline:* For fall admission, 12/31 priority date for domestic students. Application fee: $50. Electronic applications accepted. *Expenses:* Tuition, state resident: full-time $7,066. Tuition, nonresident: full-time $17,204. *Financial support:* In 2006–07, research assistantships with full tuition reimbursements (averaging $20,800 per year). Financial award application deadline: 3/1. *Faculty research:* Oncology, mastitis, nuclear medicine, neuroanesthesia, exercise physiology. Total annual research expenditures: $500,000. *Unit head:* Dr. Stephen A. Greene, Interim Chair, 509-335-8707, Fax: 509-335-0880. *Application contact:* Connie M. Sakamoto, Administrative Manager, 509-335-0779, Fax: 509-335-0880, E-mail: cmf@vetmed.wsu.edu.

Washington State University, College of Veterinary Medicine and Graduate School, Graduate Programs in Veterinary Science, Department of Veterinary Microbiology and Pathology, Pullman, WA 99164. Offers veterinary science (MS, PhD). *Faculty:* 24 full-time (5 women), 1 (woman) part-time/adjunct. *Students:* 39 full-time (19 women); includes 2 minority (1 Asian American or Pacific Islander, 1 Hispanic American), 15 international. Average age 32. 26 applicants, 35% accepted, 7 enrolled. In 2006, 3 degrees awarded. Terminal master's awarded for partial completion of doctoral program. *Median time to degree:* Of those who began their doctoral program in fall 1998, 100% received their degree in 8 years or less. *Degree requirements:* For master's and doctorate, thesis/dissertation, oral exam. *Entrance requirements:* For master's and doctorate, minimum GPA of 3.0. Additional exam requirements/recommendations for international students: Required—TOEFL (minimum score 550 paper-based; 213 computer-based). *Application deadline:* Applications are processed on a rolling basis. Application fee: $50. Electronic applications accepted. *Expenses:* Tuition, state resident: full-time $7,066. Tuition, nonresident: full-time $17,204. *Financial support:* In 2006–07, fellowships (averaging $2,400 per year), 28 research assistantships (averaging $33,018 per year) were awarded; scholarships/grants, traineeships, health care benefits, and unspecified assistantships also available. Financial award application deadline: 3/1. *Faculty research:* Microbial pathogenesis, veterinary and wildlife parasitology, laboratory animal pathology, immune responses to infectious diseases. *Unit head:* Dr. David J. Prieur, Chair, 509-335-6030, Fax: 509-335-8529, E-mail: dprieur@vetmed.wsu.edu. *Application contact:* Dr. Guy Palmer, Professor, 509-335-6033, Fax: 509-335-8529, E-mail: gpalmer@vetmed.wsu.edu.

ACADEMIC AND PROFESSIONAL PROGRAMS IN PHYSICAL EDUCATION, SPORTS, AND RECREATION

Section 41
Leisure Studies and Recreation

This section contains a directory of institutions offering graduate work in leisure studies and recreation, followed by in-depth entries submitted by institutions that chose to prepare detailed program descriptions. Additional information about programs listed in the directory but not augmented by an in-depth entry may be obtained by writing directly to the dean of a graduate school or chair of a department at the address given in the directory.

For programs offering related work, in Book 2, see Performing Arts and in Book 4, see Natural Resources.

CONTENTS

Program Directories

Close-Ups

Leisure Studies

Aurora University, George Williams College of Aurora University, School of Experiential Leadership, Aurora, IL 60506-4892. Offers administration of leisure services (MS); outdoor pursuits recreation administration (MS). Part-time and evening/weekend programs available. *Faculty:* 2 full-time (1 woman), 2 part-time/adjunct (1 woman). *Students:* 21 full-time (13 women), 15 part-time (10 women); includes 3 minority (2 African Americans, 1 Asian American or Pacific Islander). Average age 31. 30 applicants, 100% accepted, 22 enrolled. In 2006, 30 degrees awarded. *Degree requirements:* For master's, thesis optional. *Entrance requirements:* For master's, minimum GPA of 2.75. Additional exam requirements/recommendations for international students: Required—TOEFL (minimum score 550 paper-based; 213 computer-based). *Application deadline:* For fall admission, 8/25 priority date for domestic students. Applications are processed on a rolling basis. Application fee: $25. Electronic applications accepted. *Expenses: Contact institution.* Tuition and fees vary according to campus/location and program. *Financial support:* In 2006–07, 27 students received support, including 6 fellowships (averaging $5,609 per year); research assistantships, teaching assistantships, Federal Work-Study, scholarships/grants, and unspecified assistantships also available. Support available to part-time students. Financial award application deadline: 4/15. *Application contact:* Dr. Rita Yerkes, Dean, 262-245-8572, E-mail: ryerkes@aurora.edu.

Bowling Green State University, Graduate College, College of Education and Human Development, School of Human Movement, Sport, and Leisure Studies, Bowling Green, OH 43403. Offers developmental kinesiology (M Ed); recreation and leisure (M Ed); sport administration (M Ed). Part-time programs available. *Faculty:* 26 full-time (13 women), 4 part-time/adjunct (2 women). *Students:* 36 full-time (22 women), 14 part-time (6 women); includes 6 minority (all African Americans), 5 international. Average age 27. 54 applicants, 50% accepted, 20 enrolled. In 2006, 33 degrees awarded. *Degree requirements:* For master's, thesis or alternative. *Entrance requirements:* For master's, GRE General Test, minimum GPA of 2.7. Additional exam requirements/recommendations for international students: Required—TOEFL. *Application deadline:* For fall admission, 1/15 priority date for domestic students. Applications are processed on a rolling basis. Application fee: $30. Electronic applications accepted. *Expenses:* Tuition, state resident: part-time $535 per hour. Tuition, nonresident: part-time $884 per hour. *Financial support:* In 2006–07, 13 research assistantships with full tuition reimbursements (averaging $7,926 per year), 18 teaching assistantships with full tuition reimbursements (averaging $6,263 per year) were awarded; career-related internships or fieldwork, Federal Work-Study, and unspecified assistantships also available. Financial award applicants required to submit FAFSA. *Faculty research:* Teacher-learning process, travel and tourism, sport marketing and management, exercise physiology and sport psychology, life-span motor development. *Unit head:* Dr. Lynn Darby, Acting Director, 419-372-2334. *Application contact:* Dr. Geoff Meek, Graduate Coordinator, 419-372-0501.

California State University, Long Beach, Graduate Studies, College of Health and Human Services, Department of Recreation and Leisure Studies, Long Beach, CA 90840. Offers recreation administration (MS). Part-time programs available. *Faculty:* 8 full-time (4 women), 5 part-time/adjunct (4 women). *Students:* 17 full-time (14 women), 17 part-time (11 women); includes 4 minority (2 African Americans, 1 American Indian/Alaska Native, 1 Hispanic American), 6 international. Average age 32. 27 applicants, 74% accepted, 13 enrolled. In 2006, 2 degrees awarded. *Degree requirements:* For master's, comprehensive exam or thesis. *Entrance requirements:* For master's, GRE General Test. *Application deadline:* For fall admission, 7/1 for domestic students; for spring admission, 12/1 for domestic students. Applications are processed on a rolling basis. Application fee: $55. Electronic applications accepted. *Financial support:* Federal Work-Study, institutionally sponsored loans, and scholarships/grants available. Financial award application deadline: 3/2. *Unit head:* Dr. Maridith Janssen, Chair, 562-985-4071, Fax: 562-985-8154, E-mail: mjanssen@csulb.edu. *Application contact:* Dr. Katherine James, Information Contact, 562-985-4071, Fax: 562-985-8154, E-mail: kjames@csulb.edu.

Central Michigan University, College of Graduate Studies, College of Education and Human Services, Department of Recreation, Parks, and Leisure Studies Administration, Mount Pleasant, MI 48859. Offers recreation and park administration (MA); therapeutic recreation (MA). *Degree requirements:* For master's, thesis or alternative, registration. *Entrance requirements:* For master's, minimum GPA of 2.75 in last 60 hours of course work. *Faculty research:* Study of ethics in parks and recreation professionals in Michigan, computer touch-tone information services at visitor centers, creative play spaces for children.

Dalhousie University, Faculty of Graduate Studies, Faculty of Health Professions, School of Health and Human Performance, Division of Leisure Studies, Halifax, NS B3H 4R2, Canada. Offers MA. Part-time programs available. *Degree requirements:* For master's, thesis. *Entrance requirements:* Additional exam requirements/recommendations for international students: Required—TOEFL. *Faculty research:* Leisure and lifestyles of social groups, historical analysis of leisure, sport and leisure administration.

East Carolina University, Graduate School, College of Health and Human Performance, Department of Recreation and Leisure Studies, Greenville, NC 27858-4353. Offers recreation and leisure services administration (MS); therapeutic recreation administration (MS). Part-time and evening/weekend programs available. Postbaccalaureate distance learning degree programs offered (minimal on-campus study). *Students:* 22 full-time (14 women), 6 part-time (1 woman); includes 1 minority (Asian American or Pacific Islander) Average age 26. 7 applicants, 14% accepted, 1 enrolled. In 2006, 10 degrees awarded. *Degree requirements:* For master's, thesis optional. *Entrance requirements:* For master's, GRE General Test or MAT. Additional exam requirements/recommendations for international students: Required—TOEFL. *Application deadline:* For fall admission, 6/1 priority date for domestic students. Applications are processed on a rolling basis. Application fee: $50. *Financial support:* In 2006–07, 8 students received support, including 1 research assistantship, 4 teaching assistantships with partial tuition reimbursements available (averaging $7,500 per year). Financial award application deadline: 6/1. *Faculty research:* Therapeutic recreation, stress and coping behavior, medicine carrying capacity, choice behavior, tourism preferences. Total annual research expenditures: $124,923. *Unit head:* Dr. Joseph Fridgen, Chair, 252-328-4640, Fax: 252-328-4642, E-mail: fridgenj@ecu.edu.

Florida International University, College of Education, Department of Health, Physical Education, and Recreation, Program in Parks and Recreation Management, Miami, FL 33199. Offers leisure services (MS); therapeutic recreation (MS). Part-time and evening/weekend programs available. *Faculty:* 3 full-time (2 women). *Students:* 2 full-time (1 woman), 6 part-time (5 women); includes 3 minority (1 African American, 1 Asian American or Pacific Islander, 1 Hispanic American). Average age 30. 4 applicants, 50% accepted, 2 enrolled. In 2006, 1 degree awarded. *Entrance requirements:* For master's, GRE General Test or minimum GPA of 3.0. Additional exam requirements/recommendations for international students: Required—TOEFL (minimum score 550 paper-based; 213 computer-based; 80 iBT), IELTS (minimum score 6). *Application deadline:* For fall admission, 6/1 priority date for domestic students, 4/1 for international students; for winter admission, 10/1 priority date for domestic students, 9/1 for international students; for spring admission, 3/1 priority date for domestic students, 2/1 for international students. Applications are processed on a rolling basis. Application fee: $30. Electronic applications accepted. *Expenses:* Tuition, state resident: part-time $249 per credit hour. Tuition, nonresident: part-time $753 per credit hour. Tuition and fees vary according to program. *Financial support:* Fellowships, research assistantships, teaching assistantships, Federal Work-Study and tuition waivers (full and partial) available. Support available to part-time students. *Faculty research:* Effects of prosocial behavior interventions on children and adolescents with behavior disorders or who are considered to be at risk. *Application contact:* Marisa Salazar, Student Recruiter, 305-348-3002, Fax: 305-348-3227, E-mail: marisa.salazar@fiu.edu.

Gallaudet University, The Graduate School, School of Education and Human Services, Department of Physical Education and Recreation, Washington, DC 20002-3625. Offers leisure services administration (MS). *Entrance requirements:* For master's, GRE General Test or MAT.

Howard University, Graduate School, Department of Health, Human Performance and Leisure Studies, Washington, DC 20059-0002. Offers exercise physiology (MS); health education (MS); sport studies (MS), including sociology of sport, sport management; urban recreation (MS), including leisure studies. Part-time and evening/weekend programs available. *Degree requirements:* For master's, thesis, comprehensive exam, registration. *Entrance requirements:* For master's, BS in human performance or related field. Electronic applications accepted. *Faculty research:* Health promotion, cardiovascular hypertension, physical activity, sport and human rights issues.

Howard University, Graduate School, Department of Physical Education, Recreation, and Health Education, Washington, DC 20059-0002. Offers exercise physiology (MS); recreation and leisure studies (MS); school and community health education (MS). Part-time programs available. *Degree requirements:* For master's, thesis or alternative, comprehensive exam. *Entrance requirements:* For master's, GRE General Test, minimum GPA of 3.0. *Faculty research:* Women's health, work and health, AIDS, men's health, hypertension, sports nutrition, social science, urban recreation, therapeutic recreation, commercial recreation.

Indiana University Bloomington, School of Health, Physical Education and Recreation, Department of Recreation and Park Administration, Bloomington, IN 47405-7000. Offers leisure behavior (PhD); outdoor recreation management (MS); park and recreation administration (MS); recreation (Re Dir); recreational sports administration (MS); therapeutic recreation (MS). PhD offered through the University Graduate School. *Faculty:* 11 full-time (4 women). *Students:* 18 full-time (7 women), 11 part-time (6 women); includes 2 minority (both African Americans), 3 international. Average age 28. In 2006, 9 degrees awarded. Terminal master's awarded for partial completion of doctoral program. *Degree requirements:* For doctorate, thesis/dissertation; for Re Dir, thesis optional. *Entrance requirements:* For master's, GRE General Test, minimum GPA of 2.8; for doctorate and Re Dir, GRE. *Application deadline:* For fall admission, 1/1 for international students; for spring admission, 9/1 for international students. Applications are processed on a rolling basis. Application fee: $50 ($60 for international students). *Expenses:* Tuition, state resident: full-time $5,791; part-time $241 per credit hour. Tuition, nonresident: full-time $16,866; part-time $703 per credit hour. *Financial support:* Fellowships, research assistantships, teaching assistantships with partial tuition reimbursements, career-related internships or fieldwork, Federal Work-Study, institutionally sponsored loans, scholarships/grants, tuition waivers (partial), unspecified assistantships, and fee remissions available. Financial award application deadline: 3/1. *Faculty research:* Leisure counseling, gerontology, special populations, planning and development. *Unit head:* Dr. Lynne Jamieson, Chairperson, 812-855-4711. *Application contact:* Program Office, 812-855-4711, Fax: 812-855-3998, E-mail: recpark@indiana.edu.

Murray State University, College of Health Sciences and Human Services, Department of Wellness and Therapeutic Sciences, Program in Exercise and Leisure Studies, Murray, KY 42071. Offers MS. Part-time programs available. *Faculty:* 3 full-time (1 woman), 2 part-time/adjunct (1 woman). *Students:* 6 full-time (3 women), 9 part-time (3 women); includes 2 minority (both African Americans) Average age 24. 5 applicants, 100% accepted. In 2006, 4 degrees awarded. *Degree requirements:* For master's, thesis optional. *Entrance requirements:* For master's, GRE General Test or MAT. Additional exam requirements/recommendations for international students: Required—TOEFL. *Application deadline:* Applications are processed on a rolling basis. Application fee: $25. *Financial support:* In 2006–07, research assistantships (averaging $5,000 per year), teaching assistantships (averaging $5,000 per year) were awarded; Federal Work-Study also available. Financial award application deadline: 5/1. *Faculty research:* Exercise and cancer recovery. *Unit head:* Dr. Matt Wiggins, Graduate Coordinator, 270-809-6285, Fax: 270-809-6803, E-mail: matt.wiggins@murraystate.edu.

Oklahoma State University, College of Education, School of Applied Health and Educational Psychology, Stillwater, OK 74078. Offers applied behavioral studies (MS, Ed D, PhD); counseling and student personnel (MS, PhD); educational psychology (PhD); health (MS, Ed D); leisure sciences (MS, Ed D); physical education (MS, Ed D); physical education and leisure sciences (Ed D); school psychology (Ed S). *Accreditation:* APA (one or more programs are accredited). Part-time programs available. *Faculty:* 37 full-time (17 women), 12 part-time/adjunct (8 women). *Students:* 189 full-time (137 women), 180 part-time (113 women); includes 75 minority (25 African Americans, 34 American Indian/Alaska Native, 5 Asian Americans or Pacific Islanders, 11 Hispanic Americans), 27 international. Average age 33. 275 applicants, 28% accepted, 64 enrolled. In 2006, 45 master's, 21 doctorates awarded. *Degree requirements:* For master's, thesis or alternative; for doctorate, thesis/dissertation. *Entrance requirements:* For master's, GRE or MAT; for doctorate, GRE (PhD). Additional exam requirements/recommendations for international students: Required—TOEFL. *Application deadline:* For fall admission, 7/1 priority date for domestic students, 3/1 priority date for international students; for spring admission, 8/1 priority date for international students. Applications are processed on a rolling basis. Application fee: $40 ($75 for international students). Electronic applications accepted. *Expenses:* Tuition, state resident: part-time $146 per credit hour. Tuition, nonresident: part-time $516 per credit hour. Required fees: $44 per credit hour. Tuition and fees vary according to program. *Financial support:* In 2006–07, 29 research assistantships (averaging $6,452 per year), 64 teaching assistantships (averaging $8,263 per year) were awarded; career-related internships or fieldwork, Federal Work-Study, scholarships/grants, health care benefits, tuition waivers (partial), and unspecified assistantships also available. Support available to part-time students. Financial award application deadline: 3/1. *Unit head:* Dr. John Romans, Head, 405-744-6040.

Penn State University Park, Graduate School, College of Health and Human Development, Department of Recreation, Park and Tourism Management, Program in Leisure Studies, State College, University Park, PA 16802-1503. Offers MS, PhD. *Students:* 31 full-time (17 women), 2 part-time (both women); includes 1 minority (African American), 18 international. 47 applicants, 19% accepted, 8 enrolled. In 2006, 4 master's, 2 doctorates awarded. *Unit head:* Dr. Harry Zinn, Head, 814-863-7849, E-mail: hzimm@psu.edu.

See Close-Up on page 1813.

Prescott College, Graduate Programs, Program in Adventure Education/Wilderness Leadership, Prescott, AZ 86301. Offers MA. Part-time programs available. Postbaccalaureate distance learning degree programs offered (minimal on-campus study). *Faculty:* 1 full-time (0 women), 20 part-time/adjunct (11 women). *Students:* 18 full-time (9 women), 14 part-time (5 women). Average age 32. In 2006, 9 degrees awarded. *Degree requirements:* For master's, thesis, fieldwork or internship, practicum. *Entrance requirements:* For master's, 2 letters of recommendation, resumé. *Application deadline:* For fall admission, 5/1 priority date for domestic students; for spring admission, 11/1 priority date for domestic students. Applications are processed on a rolling basis. Application fee: $40. Electronic applications accepted. *Expenses:* Tuition: Full-time $12,408; part-time $517 per credit. One-time fee: $130. *Financial support:* Career-related internships or fieldwork and Federal Work-Study available. Financial award applicants required to submit FAFSA. *Unit head:* Dr. Rick Medrick, Head, 303-320-0372. *Application contact:* Kerstin Alicki, Admissions Counselor, 877-350-2100 Ext. 2102, Fax: 928-776-5242, E-mail: admissions@prescott.edu.

San Francisco State University, Division of Graduate Studies, College of Health and Human Services, Department of Recreation and Leisure Studies, San Francisco, CA 94132-1722. Offers recreation (MS). Part-time programs available. *Faculty:* 3 full-time (1 woman). *Entrance requirements:* For master's, minimum GPA of 2.5 in last 60 units. *Application deadline:* For fall admission, 11/30 priority date for domestic students. Applications are processed on a rolling basis. Application fee: $55. *Financial support:* Career-related internships or fieldwork available. Financial award application deadline: 3/1. *Faculty research:* Leisure systems, leisure education, play theory and leadership, ethnic and cultural diversity, commercial recreation and tour-

Section 41
Leisure Studies and Recreation

This section contains a directory of institutions offering graduate work in leisure studies and recreation, followed by in-depth entries submitted by institutions that chose to prepare detailed program descriptions. Additional information about programs listed in the directory but not augmented by an in-depth entry may be obtained by writing directly to the dean of a graduate school or chair of a department at the address given in the directory.

For programs offering related work, in Book 2, see Performing Arts and in Book 4, see Natural Resources.

CONTENTS

Program Directories

Close-Ups

Leisure Studies

Aurora University, George Williams College of Aurora University, School of Experiential Leadership, Aurora, IL 60506-4892. Offers administration of leisure services (MS); outdoor pursuits recreation administration (MS). Part-time and evening/weekend programs available. *Faculty:* 2 full-time (1 woman), 2 part-time/adjunct (1 woman). *Students:* 21 full-time (13 women), 15 part-time (10 women); includes 3 minority (2 African Americans, 1 Asian American or Pacific Islander). Average age 31. 30 applicants, 100% accepted, 22 enrolled. In 2006, 30 degrees awarded. *Degree requirements:* For master's, thesis optional. *Entrance requirements:* For master's, minimum GPA of 2.75. Additional exam requirements/recommendations for international students: Required—TOEFL (minimum score 550 paper-based; 213 computer-based). *Application deadline:* For fall admission, 8/25 priority date for domestic students. Applications are processed on a rolling basis. Application fee: $25. Electronic applications accepted. *Expenses: Contact institution.* Tuition and fees vary according to campus/location and program. *Financial support:* In 2006–07, 27 students received support, including 6 fellowships (averaging $5,609 per year); research assistantships, teaching assistantships, Federal Work-Study, scholarships/grants, and unspecified assistantships also available. Support available to part-time students. Financial award application deadline: 4/15. *Application contact:* Dr. Rita Yerkes, Dean, 262-245-8572, E-mail: ryerkes@aurora.edu.

Bowling Green State University, Graduate College, College of Education and Human Development, School of Human Movement, Sport, and Leisure Studies, Bowling Green, OH 43403. Offers developmental kinesiology (M Ed); recreation and leisure (M Ed); sport administration (M Ed). Part-time programs available. *Faculty:* 26 full-time (13 women), 4 part-time/adjunct (2 women). *Students:* 36 full-time (22 women), 14 part-time (6 women); includes 6 minority (all African Americans), 5 international. Average age 27. 54 applicants, 50% accepted, 20 enrolled. In 2006, 33 degrees awarded. *Degree requirements:* For master's, thesis or alternative. *Entrance requirements:* For master's, GRE General Test, minimum GPA of 2.7. Additional exam requirements/recommendations for international students: Required—TOEFL. *Application deadline:* For fall admission, 1/15 priority date for domestic students. Applications are processed on a rolling basis. Application fee: $30. Electronic applications accepted. *Expenses:* Tuition, state resident: part-time $535 per hour. Tuition, nonresident: part-time $884 per hour. *Financial support:* In 2006–07, 13 research assistantships with full tuition reimbursements (averaging $7,926 per year), 18 teaching assistantships with full tuition reimbursements (averaging $6,263 per year) were awarded; career-related internships or fieldwork, Federal Work-Study, and unspecified assistantships also available. Financial award applicants required to submit FAFSA. *Faculty research:* Teacher-learning process, travel and tourism, sport marketing and management, exercise physiology and sport psychology, life-span motor development. *Unit head:* Dr. Lynn Darby, Acting Director, 419-372-2334. *Application contact:* Dr. Geoff Meek, Graduate Coordinator, 419-372-0501.

California State University, Long Beach, Graduate Studies, College of Health and Human Services, Department of Recreation and Leisure Studies, Long Beach, CA 90840. Offers recreation administration (MS). Part-time programs available. *Faculty:* 8 full-time (4 women), 5 part-time/adjunct (4 women). *Students:* 17 full-time (14 women), 17 part-time (11 women); includes 4 minority (2 African Americans, 1 American Indian/Alaska Native, 1 Hispanic American), 6 international. Average age 32. 27 applicants, 74% accepted, 13 enrolled. In 2006, 2 degrees awarded. *Degree requirements:* For master's, comprehensive exam or thesis. *Entrance requirements:* For master's, GRE General Test. *Application deadline:* For fall admission, 7/1 for domestic students; for spring admission, 12/1 for domestic students. Applications are processed on a rolling basis. Application fee: $55. Electronic applications accepted. *Financial support:* Federal Work-Study, institutionally sponsored loans, and scholarships/grants available. Financial award application deadline: 3/2. *Unit head:* Dr. Maridith Janssen, Chair, 562-985-4071, Fax: 562-985-8154, E-mail: mjanssen@csulb.edu. *Application contact:* Dr. Katherine James, Information Contact, 562-985-4071, Fax: 562-985-8154, E-mail: kjames@csulb.edu.

Central Michigan University, College of Graduate Studies, College of Education and Human Services, Department of Recreation, Parks, and Leisure Studies Administration, Mount Pleasant, MI 48859. Offers recreation and park administration (MA); therapeutic recreation (MA). *Degree requirements:* For master's, thesis or alternative, registration. *Entrance requirements:* For master's, minimum GPA of 2.75 in last 60 hours of course work. *Faculty research:* Study of ethics in parks and recreation professionals in Michigan, computer touch-tone information services at visitor centers, creative play spaces for children.

Dalhousie University, Faculty of Graduate Studies, Faculty of Health Professions, School of Health and Human Performance, Division of Leisure Studies, Halifax, NS B3H 4R2, Canada. Offers MA. Part-time programs available. *Degree requirements:* For master's, thesis. *Entrance requirements:* Additional exam requirements/recommendations for international students: Required—TOEFL. *Faculty research:* Leisure and lifestyles of social groups, historical analysis of leisure, sport and leisure administration.

East Carolina University, Graduate School, College of Health and Human Performance, Department of Recreation and Leisure Studies, Greenville, NC 27858-4353. Offers recreation and leisure services administration (MS); therapeutic recreation administration (MS). Part-time and evening/weekend programs available. Postbaccalaureate distance learning degree programs offered (minimal on-campus study). *Students:* 22 full-time (14 women), 6 part-time (1 woman); includes 1 minority (Asian American or Pacific Islander) Average age 26. 7 applicants, 14% accepted, 1 enrolled. In 2006, 10 degrees awarded. *Degree requirements:* For master's, thesis optional. *Entrance requirements:* For master's, GRE General Test or MAT. Additional exam requirements/recommendations for international students: Required—TOEFL. *Application deadline:* For fall admission, 6/1 priority date for domestic students. Applications are processed on a rolling basis. Application fee: $50. *Financial support:* In 2006–07, 8 students received support, including 1 research assistantship, 4 teaching assistantships with partial tuition reimbursements available (averaging $7,500 per year). Financial award application deadline: 6/1. *Faculty research:* Therapeutic recreation, stress and coping behavior, medicine carrying capacity, choice behavior, tourism preferences. Total annual research expenditures: $124,923. *Unit head:* Dr. Joseph Fridgen, Chair, 252-328-4640, Fax: 252-328-4642, E-mail: fridgenj@ecu.edu.

Florida International University, College of Education, Department of Health, Physical Education, and Recreation, Program in Parks and Recreation Management, Miami, FL 33199. Offers leisure services (MS); therapeutic recreation (MS). Part-time and evening/weekend programs available. *Faculty:* 3 full-time (2 women). *Students:* 2 full-time (1 woman), 6 part-time (5 women); includes 3 minority (1 African American, 1 Asian American or Pacific Islander, 1 Hispanic American). Average age 30. 4 applicants, 50% accepted, 2 enrolled. In 2006, 1 degree awarded. *Entrance requirements:* For master's, GRE General Test or minimum GPA of 3.0. Additional exam requirements/recommendations for international students: Required—TOEFL (minimum score 550 paper-based; 213 computer-based; 80 iBT), IELTS (minimum score 6). *Application deadline:* For fall admission, 6/1 priority date for domestic students, 4/1 for international students; for winter admission, 10/1 priority date for domestic students, 9/1 for international students; for spring admission, 3/1 priority date for domestic students, 2/1 for international students. Applications are processed on a rolling basis. Application fee: $30. Electronic applications accepted. *Expenses:* Tuition, state resident: part-time $249 per credit hour. Tuition, nonresident: part-time $753 per credit hour. Tuition and fees vary according to program. *Financial support:* Fellowships, research assistantships, teaching assistantships, Federal Work-Study and tuition waivers (full and partial) available. Support available to part-time students. *Faculty research:* Effects of prosocial behavior interventions on children and adolescents with behavior disorders or who are considered to be at risk. *Application contact:* Marisa Salazar, Student Recruiter, 305-348-3002, Fax: 305-348-3227, E-mail: marisa.salazar@fiu.edu.

Gallaudet University, The Graduate School, School of Education and Human Services, Department of Physical Education and Recreation, Washington, DC 20002-3625. Offers leisure services administration (MS). *Entrance requirements:* For master's, GRE General Test or MAT.

Howard University, Graduate School, Department of Health, Human Performance and Leisure Studies, Washington, DC 20059-0002. Offers exercise physiology (MS); health education (MS); sport studies (MS), including sociology of sport, sport management; urban recreation (MS), including leisure studies. Part-time and evening/weekend programs available. *Degree requirements:* For master's, thesis, comprehensive exam, registration. *Entrance requirements:* For master's, BS in human performance or related field. Electronic applications accepted. *Faculty research:* Health promotion, cardiovascular hypertension, physical activity, sport and human rights issues.

Howard University, Graduate School, Department of Physical Education, Recreation, and Health Education, Washington, DC 20059-0002. Offers exercise physiology (MS); recreation and leisure studies (MS); school and community health education (MS). Part-time programs available. *Degree requirements:* For master's, thesis or alternative, comprehensive exam. *Entrance requirements:* For master's, GRE General Test, minimum GPA of 3.0. *Faculty research:* Women's health, work and health, AIDS, men's health, hypertension, sports nutrition, social science, urban recreation, therapeutic recreation, commercial recreation.

Indiana University Bloomington, School of Health, Physical Education and Recreation, Department of Recreation and Park Administration, Bloomington, IN 47405-7000. Offers leisure behavior (PhD); outdoor recreation management (MS); park and recreation administration (MS); recreation (Re Dir); recreational sports administration (MS); therapeutic recreation (MS). PhD offered through the University Graduate School. *Faculty:* 11 full-time (4 women). *Students:* 18 full-time (7 women), 11 part-time (6 women); includes 2 minority (both African Americans), 3 international. Average age 28. In 2006, 9 degrees awarded. Terminal master's awarded for partial completion of doctoral program. *Degree requirements:* For doctorate, thesis/dissertation; for Re Dir, thesis optional. *Entrance requirements:* For master's, GRE General Test, minimum GPA of 2.8; for doctorate and Re Dir, GRE. *Application deadline:* For fall admission, 1/1 for international students; for spring admission, 9/1 for international students. Applications are processed on a rolling basis. Application fee: $50 ($60 for international students). *Expenses:* Tuition, state resident: full-time $5,791; part-time $241 per credit hour. Tuition, nonresident: full-time $16,866; part-time $703 per credit hour. *Financial support:* Fellowships, research assistantships, teaching assistantships with partial tuition reimbursements, career-related internships or fieldwork, Federal Work-Study, institutionally sponsored loans, scholarships/grants, tuition waivers (partial), unspecified assistantships, and fee remissions available. Financial award application deadline: 3/1. *Faculty research:* Leisure counseling, gerontology, special populations, planning and development. *Unit head:* Dr. Lynne Jamieson, Chairperson, 812-855-4711. *Application contact:* Program Office, 812-855-4711, Fax: 812-855-3998, E-mail: recpark@indiana.edu.

Murray State University, College of Health Sciences and Human Services, Department of Wellness and Therapeutic Sciences, Program in Exercise and Leisure Studies, Murray, KY 42071. Offers MS. Part-time programs available. *Faculty:* 3 full-time (1 woman), 2 part-time/adjunct (1 woman). *Students:* 6 full-time (3 women), 9 part-time (3 women); includes 2 minority (both African Americans) Average age 24. 5 applicants, 100% accepted. In 2006, 4 degrees awarded. *Degree requirements:* For master's, thesis optional. *Entrance requirements:* For master's, GRE General Test or MAT. Additional exam requirements/recommendations for international students: Required—TOEFL. *Application deadline:* Applications are processed on a rolling basis. Application fee: $25. *Financial support:* In 2006–07, research assistantships (averaging $5,000 per year), teaching assistantships (averaging $5,000 per year) were awarded; Federal Work-Study also available. Financial award application deadline: 5/1. *Faculty research:* Exercise and cancer recovery. *Unit head:* Dr. Matt Wiggins, Graduate Coordinator, 270-809-6285, Fax: 270-809-6803, E-mail: matt.wiggins@murraystate.edu.

Oklahoma State University, College of Education, School of Applied Health and Educational Psychology, Stillwater, OK 74078. Offers applied behavioral studies (MS, Ed D, PhD); counseling and student personnel (MS, PhD); educational psychology (PhD); health (MS, Ed D); leisure sciences (MS, Ed D); physical education (MS, Ed D); physical education and leisure sciences (Ed D); school psychology (Ed S). *Accreditation:* APA (one or more programs are accredited). Part-time programs available. *Faculty:* 37 full-time (17 women), 12 part-time/adjunct (8 women). *Students:* 189 full-time (137 women), 180 part-time (113 women); includes 75 minority (25 African Americans, 34 American Indian/Alaska Native, 5 Asian Americans or Pacific Islanders, 11 Hispanic Americans), 27 international. Average age 33. 275 applicants, 28% accepted, 64 enrolled. In 2006, 45 master's, 21 doctorates awarded. *Degree requirements:* For master's, thesis or alternative; for doctorate, thesis/dissertation. *Entrance requirements:* For master's, GRE or MAT; for doctorate, GRE (PhD). Additional exam requirements/recommendations for international students: Required—TOEFL. *Application deadline:* For fall admission, 7/1 priority date for domestic students, 3/1 priority date for international students; for spring admission, 8/1 priority date for international students. Applications are processed on a rolling basis. Application fee: $40 ($75 for international students). Electronic applications accepted. *Expenses:* Tuition, state resident: part-time $146 per credit hour. Tuition, nonresident: part-time $516 per credit hour. Required fees: $44 per credit hour. Tuition and fees vary according to program. *Financial support:* In 2006–07, 29 research assistantships (averaging $6,452 per year), 64 teaching assistantships (averaging $8,263 per year) were awarded; career-related internships or fieldwork, Federal Work-Study, scholarships/grants, health care benefits, tuition waivers (partial), and unspecified assistantships also available. Support available to part-time students. Financial award application deadline: 3/1. *Unit head:* Dr. John Romans, Head, 405-744-6040.

Penn State University Park, Graduate School, College of Health and Human Development, Department of Recreation, Park and Tourism Management, Program in Leisure Studies, State College, University Park, PA 16802-1503. Offers MS, PhD. *Students:* 31 full-time (17 women), 2 part-time (both women); includes 1 minority (African American), 18 international. 47 applicants, 19% accepted, 8 enrolled. In 2006, 4 master's, 2 doctorates awarded. *Unit head:* Dr. Harry Zinn, Head, 814-863-7849, E-mail: hzimm@psu.edu.

See Close-Up on page 1813.

Prescott College, Graduate Programs, Program in Adventure Education/Wilderness Leadership, Prescott, AZ 86301. Offers MA. Part-time programs available. Postbaccalaureate distance learning degree programs offered (minimal on-campus study). *Faculty:* 1 full-time (0 women), 20 part-time/adjunct (11 women). *Students:* 18 full-time (9 women), 14 part-time (5 women). Average age 32. In 2006, 9 degrees awarded. *Degree requirements:* For master's, thesis, fieldwork or internship, practicum. *Entrance requirements:* For master's, 2 letters of recommendation, resumé. *Application deadline:* For fall admission, 5/1 priority date for domestic students; for spring admission, 11/1 priority date for domestic students. Applications are processed on a rolling basis. Application fee: $40. Electronic applications accepted. *Expenses:* Tuition: Full-time $12,408; part-time $517 per credit. One-time fee: $130. *Financial support:* Career-related internships or fieldwork and Federal Work-Study available. Financial award applicants required to submit FAFSA. *Unit head:* Dr. Rick Medrick, Head, 303-320-0372. *Application contact:* Kerstin Alicki, Admissions Counselor, 877-350-2100 Ext. 2102, Fax: 928-776-5242, E-mail: admissions@prescott.edu.

San Francisco State University, Division of Graduate Studies, College of Health and Human Services, Department of Recreation and Leisure Studies, San Francisco, CA 94132-1722. Offers recreation (MS). Part-time programs available. *Faculty:* 3 full-time (1 woman). *Entrance requirements:* For master's, minimum GPA of 2.5 in last 60 units. *Application deadline:* For fall admission, 11/30 priority date for domestic students. Applications are processed on a rolling basis. Application fee: $55. *Financial support:* Career-related internships or fieldwork available. Financial award application deadline: 3/1. *Faculty research:* Leisure systems, leisure education, play theory and leadership, ethnic and cultural diversity, commercial recreation and tourism. *Unit head:* Dr. James Murphy, Chair, 415-338-2030. *Application contact:* Dr. Rene Dahl, Graduate Coordinator, 415-338-7575, E-mail: rdahl@sfsu.edu.

Southeast Missouri State University, School of Graduate Studies, Department of Health, Human Performance and Recreation, Cape Girardeau, MO 63701-4799. Offers community wellness and leisure services (MPA); nutrition and exercise science (MS). Part-time and evening/weekend programs available. *Faculty:* 7 full-time (2 women). *Students:* 7 full-time (5 women), 8 part-time (4 women); includes 2 minority (both African Americans) Average age 25. 8 applicants, 100% accepted. In 2006, 8 degrees awarded. *Degree requirements:* For master's, thesis or alternative. *Entrance requirements:* For master's, GRE General Test (MS), minimum GPA of 3.0 (MS), minimum GPA of 2.7 (MPA). Additional exam requirements/recommendations for international students: Required—TOEFL (minimum score 550 paper-based; 213 computer-based). *Application deadline:* For fall admission, 8/1 for domestic students, 4/1 for international students; for spring admission, 11/21 for domestic students, 10/1 for international students. Applications are processed on a rolling basis. Application fee: $20 ($100 for international students). Electronic applications accepted. *Financial support:* In 2006–07, 12 students received support, including 6 research assistantships with full tuition reimbursements available (averaging $7,100 per year), 3 teaching assistantships with full tuition reimbursements available (averaging $7,100 per year); unspecified assistantships also available. Financial award applicants required to submit FAFSA. *Faculty research:* Health issues of athletes, body composition assessment, exercise training. *Unit head:* Dr. Joe Pujol, Chairperson, 573-651-2664, Fax: 573-651-5150, E-mail: jpujol@semo.edu. *Application contact:* Marsha L. Arant, Senior Administrative Assistant, Office of Graduate Studies, 573-651-2192, Fax: 573-651-2001, E-mail: marant@semo.edu.

Southern Connecticut State University, School of Graduate Studies, School of Health and Human Services, Department of Recreation and Leisure Studies, New Haven, CT 06515-1355. Offers MS. Part-time and evening/weekend programs available. *Faculty:* 2 full-time, 1 part-time/adjunct. *Students:* 11 full-time (8 women), 22 part-time (12 women); includes 2 minority (1 Asian American or Pacific Islander, 1 Hispanic American). 13 applicants, 77% accepted, 9 enrolled. In 2006, 10 degrees awarded. *Degree requirements:* For master's, thesis or alternative. *Entrance requirements:* For master's, interview, minimum undergraduate QPA of 3.0 in graduate major field or 2.5 overall. *Application deadline:* For fall admission, 7/15 priority date for domestic students. Applications are processed on a rolling basis. Application fee: $50. Electronic applications accepted. *Financial support:* In 2006–07, 1 teaching assistantship was awarded; career-related internships or fieldwork also available. Financial award application deadline: 4/15; financial award applicants required to submit FAFSA. *Unit head:* Dr. Robert Cipriano, Chairperson, 203-392-6387, Fax: 203-392-6965, E-mail: cipriano@southernct.edu. *Application contact:* Dr. James MacGregor, Graduate Coordinator, 203-392-6385, Fax: 203-392-6147, E-mail: macgregorj1@southernct.edu.

State University of New York College at Brockport, School of Professions, Department of Recreation and Leisure Studies, Brockport, NY 14420-2997. Offers MS. Part-time programs available. *Students:* 9 full-time (4 women), 8 part-time (all women); includes 4 minority (3 African Americans, 1 Hispanic American), 1 international. 8 applicants, 88% accepted, 7 enrolled. In 2006, 11 degrees awarded. *Degree requirements:* For master's, thesis or alternative. *Entrance requirements:* For master's, minimum GPA of 3.0, letters of recommendation, written critical analysis. Additional exam requirements/recommendations for international students: Required—TOEFL (minimum score 550 paper-based; 213 computer-based; 80 iBT). *Application deadline:* For fall admission, 7/15 for domestic and international students; for spring admission, 11/15 for domestic and international students. Application fee: $50. *Expenses:* Tuition, state resident: full-time $6,900; part-time $288 per credit. Tuition, nonresident: full-time $10,920; part-time $455 per credit. *Financial support:* In 2006–07, 1 fellowship with tuition reimbursement (averaging $7,500 per year) was awarded; career-related internships or fieldwork, Federal Work-Study, scholarships/grants, and unspecified assistantships also available. Support available to part-time students. Financial award application deadline: 3/15; financial award applicants required to submit FAFSA. *Faculty research:* Leisure service delivery systems; therapeutic recreation; international issues in recreation and leisure; tourism; customer service, customer behavior and perceived value/satisfaction; leisure motivation among Baby Boomers. *Unit head:* Dr. Joel Frater, Chair, 585-395-2994, E-mail: jfrater@brockport.edu.

Temple University, Graduate School, School of Tourism and Hospitality Management, Program in Sport and Recreation Administration, Philadelphia, PA 19122-6096. Offers Ed M. Part-time and evening/weekend programs available. *Faculty:* 5 full-time (2 women). *Students:* 44 full-time (27 women), 34 part-time (13 women); includes 17 minority (all African Americans), 3 international. 98 applicants, 48% accepted, 27 enrolled. In 2006, 36 degrees awarded. *Entrance requirements:* For master's, GRE General Test or MAT, minimum undergraduate GPA of 3.0. Additional exam requirements/recommendations for international students: Required—TOEFL (minimum score 550 paper-based; 213 computer-based; 79 iBT). *Application deadline:* For fall admission, 4/15 priority date for domestic students, 12/15 for international students; for spring admission, 9/30 priority date for domestic students, 8/1 for international students. Application fee: $50. Electronic applications accepted. *Expenses:* Tuition, state resident: full-time $12,264; part-time $511 per credit. Tuition, nonresident: full-time $17,904; part-time $746 per credit. Required fees: $84 per course. Tuition and fees vary according to program. *Financial support:* Teaching assistantships available. Financial award application deadline: 1/15; financial award applicants required to submit FAFSA. *Unit head:* Dr. Michael W. Jackson, Director, 215-204-6298, Fax: 215-204-8705, E-mail: pierre@temple.edu.

See Close-Up on page 507.

Texas State University-San Marcos, Graduate School, College of Education, Department of Health, Physical Education, and Recreation, Program in Recreation and Leisure Services, San Marcos, TX 78666. Offers MSRLS. *Faculty:* 2 full-time (1 woman). *Students:* 13 full-time (10 women), 12 part-time (6 women); includes 4 minority (1 African American, 3 Hispanic Americans). Average age 28. 8 applicants, 100% accepted, 6 enrolled. In 2006, 6 degrees awarded. *Degree requirements:* For master's, thesis optional. *Entrance requirements:* For master's, GRE General Test, minimum GPA of 2.75 in last 60 hours of course work. Additional exam requirements/recommendations for international students: Required—TOEFL. *Application deadline:* For fall admission, 6/15 priority date for domestic students; for spring admission, 10/15 priority date for domestic students. Applications are processed on a rolling basis. Application fee: $40 ($90 for international students). *Financial support:* In 2006–07, 16 students received support, including 6 research assistantships (averaging $8,331 per year), 2 teaching assistantships (averaging $11,502 per year). Financial award application deadline: 4/1; financial award applicants required to submit FAFSA. *Unit head:* Dr. Tom Gustafson, Graduate Advisor, 512-245-2972, Fax: 512-245-8678, E-mail: tg08@txstate.edu.

Universidad Metropolitana, Graduate Programs in Education, Program in Managing Leisure Services, San Juan, PR 00928-1150. Offers MA. Part-time programs available. *Degree requirements:* For master's, thesis or alternative. *Entrance requirements:* For master's, EXADEP, interview. Electronic applications accepted.

Université du Québec à Trois-Rivières, Graduate Programs, Program in Leisure, Culture and Tourism Sciences, Trois-Rivières, QC G9A 5H7, Canada. Offers MA, DESS. Part-time programs available. *Degree requirements:* For master's, thesis optional. *Entrance requirements:* For master's, appropriate bachelor's degree, proficiency in French.

University of Connecticut, Graduate School, Neag School of Education, Department of Kinesiology, Storrs, CT 06269. Offers kinesiology (MA, PhD), including exercise science, sport management and sociology. *Faculty:* 16 full-time (5 women). *Students:* 78 full-time (42 women), 15 part-time (4 women); includes 14 minority (6 African Americans, 6 Asian Americans or Pacific Islanders, 2 Hispanic Americans), 8 international. Average age 26. 110 applicants, 43% accepted, 47 enrolled. In 2006, 29 master's, 7 doctorates awarded. Terminal master's awarded for partial completion of doctoral program. *Degree requirements:* For master's, thesis or alternative, comprehensive exam; for doctorate, thesis/dissertation. *Entrance requirements:* For doctorate, GRE General Test. Additional exam requirements/recommendations for international students: Required—TOEFL (minimum score 550 paper-based; 213 computer-based). *Application deadline:* For fall admission, 2/1 priority date for domestic students, 2/1 for international students; for spring admission, 11/1 for domestic students, 10/1 for international students. Application fee: $55. *Financial support:* In 2006–07, 49 research assistantships with full tuition reimbursements were awarded; fellowships, teaching assistantships with full tuition reimbursements, Federal Work-Study, scholarships/grants, health care benefits, and unspecified assistantships also available. Financial award application deadline: 2/1; financial award applicants required to submit FAFSA. *Unit head:* Carl Maresh, Head, 860-486-3623, Fax: 860-486-1123. *Application contact:* Lisa Rasicot, Graduate Coordinator, 860-486-3065, Fax: 860-486-0210, E-mail: soeadm02@uconnvm.uconn.edu.

University of Connecticut, Graduate School, Neag School of Education, Department of Kinesiology, Field of Kinesiology, Program in Sport Management and Sociology, Storrs, CT 06269. Offers MA, PhD. *Faculty:* 6 full-time (4 women). *Students:* 34 full-time (19 women), 9 part-time (4 women); includes 7 minority (4 African Americans, 2 Asian Americans or Pacific Islanders, 1 Hispanic American), 3 international. Average age 24. 48 applicants, 52% accepted, 25 enrolled. In 2006, 15 degrees awarded. Terminal master's awarded for partial completion of doctoral program. *Degree requirements:* For master's, thesis or alternative, comprehensive exam; for doctorate, thesis/dissertation. *Entrance requirements:* For doctorate, GRE General Test. Additional exam requirements/recommendations for international students: Required—TOEFL (minimum score 550 paper-based; 213 computer-based). *Application deadline:* For fall admission, 2/1 priority date for domestic and international students; for spring admission, 11/1 for domestic students, 10/1 for international students. Applications are processed on a rolling basis. Application fee: $55. Electronic applications accepted. *Financial support:* In 2006–07, 18 research assistantships with full tuition reimbursements were awarded; fellowships, teaching assistantships with full tuition reimbursements, Federal Work-Study, scholarships/grants, health care benefits, and unspecified assistantships also available. Financial award application deadline: 2/1; financial award applicants required to submit FAFSA. *Application contact:* Lisa Rasicot, Graduate Coordinator, 860-486-3065, Fax: 860-486-0210, E-mail: soeadm02@uconnvm.uconn.edu.

University of Illinois at Urbana–Champaign, Graduate College, College of Applied Health Studies, Department of Recreation, Sport and Tourism, Champaign, IL 61820. Offers MS, PhD. *Faculty:* 13 full-time (7 women). *Students:* 50 full-time (24 women), 17 part-time (9 women); includes 9 minority (5 African Americans, 2 Asian Americans or Pacific Islanders, 2 Hispanic Americans), 19 international. 62 applicants, 52% accepted, 20 enrolled. In 2006, 18 master's, 2 doctorates awarded. *Degree requirements:* For doctorate, 2 foreign languages, thesis/dissertation. *Entrance requirements:* For master's, GRE General Test, minimum GPA of 3.0. *Application deadline:* For fall admission, 4/15 for domestic students. Applications are processed on a rolling basis. Application fee: $50 ($60 for international students). Electronic applications accepted. *Financial support:* In 2006–07, 1 fellowship, 21 research assistantships, 14 teaching assistantships were awarded; tuition waivers (full and partial) also available. Financial award application deadline: 2/15. *Unit head:* Cary McDonald, Head, 217-333-4410, Fax: 217-244-1935, E-mail: carym@uiuc.edu. *Application contact:* Angela Ronk, Secretary, 217-333-4410, Fax: 217-244-1935, E-mail: aronk@uiuc.edu.

The University of Iowa, Graduate College, College of Liberal Arts and Sciences, Program in Leisure Studies, Iowa City, IA 52242-1316. Offers leisure and recreational sport management (MA); therapeutic recreation (MA). *Faculty:* 4 full-time, 1 part-time/adjunct. *Students:* 16 full-time (11 women), 5 part-time (1 woman); includes 2 minority (both African Americans), 1 international. 21 applicants, 86% accepted, 16 enrolled. In 2006, 6 degrees awarded. *Degree requirements:* For master's, exam, thesis optional. *Entrance requirements:* For master's, GRE General Test, minimum GPA of 3.0. Additional exam requirements/recommendations for international students: Required—TOEFL (minimum score 550 paper-based; 213 computer-based; 81 iBT). *Application deadline:* For spring admission, 11/15 priority date for domestic students. Applications are processed on a rolling basis. Application fee: $60 ($85 for international students). Electronic applications accepted. *Financial support:* In 2006–07, 16 teaching assistantships with partial tuition reimbursements were awarded; fellowships, research assistantships with partial tuition reimbursements also available. Financial award applicants required to submit FAFSA. *Unit head:* Kenneth Mobily, Academic Coordinator, 319-335-0172, Fax: 319-335-3884.

University of Memphis, Graduate School, College of Education, Department of Health and Sport Sciences, Memphis, TN 38152. Offers clinical nutrition (MS); exercise and sport science (MS); health promotion (MS); physical education teacher education (MS), including teacher education; sport and leisure commerce (MS). Part-time and evening/weekend programs available. *Faculty:* 26 full-time (10 women), 8 part-time/adjunct (5 women). *Students:* Average age 28. 50 applicants, 62% accepted. In 2006, 14 degrees awarded. *Degree requirements:* For master's, thesis, comprehensive exam. *Entrance requirements:* For master's, GRE General Test or GMAT (sport and leisure commerce). *Application deadline:* For fall admission, 5/1 priority date for domestic students; for spring admission, 11/1 for domestic students. Applications are processed on a rolling basis. Application fee: $25 ($50 for international students). *Financial support:* In 2006–07, 13 research assistantships with full tuition reimbursements (averaging $6,000 per year), 4 teaching assistantships with full tuition reimbursements (averaging $6,000 per year) were awarded; career-related internships or fieldwork, tuition waivers (partial), and community assistantships also available. *Faculty research:* Sport marketing and consumer analysis, health psychology, smoking cessation, psychosocial aspects of cardiovascular disease, global health promotion. Total annual research expenditures: $1.3 million. *Unit head:* Dr. Michael H. Hamrick, Chairman, 901-678-4165, Fax: 901-678-3591, E-mail: mhamrick@memphis.edu. *Application contact:* Christina Little, Academic Services Coordinator, 901-678-4316, Fax: 901-678-3591, E-mail: aclittle@memphis.edu.

University of Minnesota, Twin Cities Campus, Graduate School, College of Education and Human Development, School of Kinesiology, Division of Recreation, Park, and Leisure Studies, Minneapolis, MN 55455-0213. Offers M Ed, MA, PhD. Part-time programs available. *Students:* 29 full-time (17 women), 8 part-time (4 women); includes 1 minority (American Indian/Alaska Native), 8 international. Average age 32. 34 applicants, 50% accepted, 12 enrolled. In 2006, 28 master's, 12 doctorates awarded. Terminal master's awarded for partial completion of doctoral program. *Degree requirements:* For master's, thesis (for some programs), final oral exam; for doctorate, thesis/dissertation, preliminary written/oral exam, final oral exam. *Entrance requirements:* For master's, GRE or MAT, minimum GPA of 3.0; for doctorate, GRE or MAT, minimum GPA of 3.0, writing sample. *Application deadline:* For fall admission, 7/15 for domestic students; for spring admission, 12/15 for domestic students. Applications are processed on a rolling basis. *Expenses:* Tuition, state resident: full-time $9,302; part-time $775 per credit. Tuition, nonresident: full-time $16,400; part-time $1,367 per credit. Full-time tuition and fees vary according to class time, course load, program, reciprocity agreements and student level. *Financial support:* Fellowships, research assistantships, teaching assistantships, career-related internships or fieldwork, Federal Work-Study, institutionally sponsored loans, and tuition waivers (full and partial) available. Support available to part-time students. *Application contact:* Dr. Mary Bents, Associate Dean, 612-625-6501, Fax: 612-626-1580, E-mail: mbents@tc.umn.edu.

University of Mississippi, Graduate School, School of Applied Sciences, Department of Health, Exercise Science, and Recreation Management, Oxford, University, MS 38677. Offers exercise science (MA, MS); exercise science and leisure management (PhD); leisure management (MA); park and recreation management (MA); wellness (MS). *Faculty:* 13 full-time (2 women), 4 part-time/adjunct (3 women). *Students:* 24 full-time (12 women), 7 part-time (4 women); includes 7 minority (5 African Americans, 2 Hispanic Americans), 2 international. In 2006, 9 master's, 4 doctorates awarded. *Degree requirements:* For master's, thesis (for some programs); for doctorate, thesis/dissertation. *Entrance requirements:* For master's, GRE General Test, minimum GPA of 3.0; for doctorate, GRE General Test. Additional exam requirements/recommendations for international students: Required—TOEFL. *Application deadline:* For fall

Leisure Studies

University of Mississippi (continued)
admission, 4/1 for domestic students; for spring admission, 10/1 for domestic students. Applications are processed on a rolling basis. Application fee: $25. *Expenses:* Tuition, state resident: full-time $4,602; part-time $256 per credit hour. Tuition, nonresident: full-time $10,566; part-time $587 per credit hour. *Financial support:* Scholarships/grants available. Financial award application deadline: 3/1; financial award applicants required to submit FAFSA. *Unit head:* Dr. James Gilbert, Interim Chair, 662-915-5521, Fax: 662-915-5525, E-mail: dgilbert@olemiss.edu.

University of Nevada, Las Vegas, Graduate College, William F. Harrah College of Hotel Administration, Department of Leisure Studies, Las Vegas, NV 89154-9900. Offers MS. Part-time programs available. *Faculty:* 5 full-time (2 women). *Students:* 10 full-time (5 women), 15 part-time (8 women); includes 2 minority (1 African American, 1 Hispanic American). 25 applicants, 48% accepted, 11 enrolled. In 2006, 5 degrees awarded. *Degree requirements:* For master's, thesis (for some programs), professional paper. *Entrance requirements:* For master's, GRE General Test, minimum GPA of 3.0 during previous 2 years, 2.75 overall. Additional exam requirements/recommendations for international students: Required—TOEFL (minimum score 550 paper-based; 213 computer-based; 80 iBT). *Application deadline:* For fall admission, 6/15 for domestic students, 5/1 for international students; for spring admission, 11/15 for domestic students, 10/1 for international students. Application fee: $60 ($75 for international students). Electronic applications accepted. *Financial support:* In 2006–07, 5 research assistantships with partial tuition reimbursements (averaging $10,000 per year) were awarded; teaching assistantships with partial tuition reimbursements, career-related internships or fieldwork, Federal Work-Study, institutionally sponsored loans, scholarships/grants, health care benefits, and unspecified assistantships also available. Support available to part-time students. Financial award application deadline: 3/1. *Unit head:* Dr. Patti J. Shock, Chair, 702-895-3930. *Application contact:* Graduate College Admissions Evaluator, 702-895-3320, Fax: 702-895-4180, E-mail: gradcollege@unlv.edu.

The University of North Carolina at Chapel Hill, Graduate School, College of Arts and Sciences, Department of Recreation and Leisure Studies, Chapel Hill, NC 27599. Offers MSRA. Part-time programs available. *Degree requirements:* For master's, thesis or alternative, comprehensive exam. *Entrance requirements:* For master's, GRE General Test, minimum GPA of 3.0. Additional exam requirements/recommendations for international students: Required—TOEFL. Electronic applications accepted. *Faculty research:* Leisure research related to gender, youth, inclusion, and family; social psychology of leisure; leisure democracy.

University of Northern Iowa, Graduate College, College of Education, School of Health, Physical Education, and Leisure Services, Program in Leisure Services, Cedar Falls, IA 50614. Offers leisure services (Ed D); program administration (MA); youth/human services administration (MA). *Students:* 36 full-time (22 women), 14 part-time (7 women); includes 16 minority (14 African Americans, 2 Hispanic Americans), 15 international. 26 applicants, 69% accepted, 18 enrolled. In 2006, 13 degrees awarded. *Degree requirements:* For master's, thesis or alternative, comprehensive exam; for doctorate, thesis/dissertation. *Entrance requirements:* For master's, 3 years of educational experience, minimum GPA of 3.5; for doctorate, GRE. Additional exam requirements/recommendations for international students: Required—TOEFL (minimum score 500 paper-based; 180 computer-based; 61 iBT). *Application deadline:* Applications are processed on a rolling basis. Application fee: $30 ($50 for international students). Electronic applications accepted. *Expenses:* Tuition, state resident: full-time $5,936. Tuition, nonresident: full-time $14,074. *Financial support:* Career-related internships or fieldwork, Federal Work-Study, institutionally sponsored loans, tuition waivers (full), and unspecified assistantships available. Financial award application deadline: 2/1. *Unit head:* Dr. Samuel Lankford, Interim Director, 319-273-6840, Fax: 319-273-5958, E-mail: sam.lankford@uni.edu.

University of North Texas, Robert B. Toulouse School of Graduate Studies, College of Education, Department of Kinesiology, Health Promotion, and Recreation, Program in Recreation and Leisure Studies, Denton, TX 76203. Offers MS, Certificate. Part-time programs available. *Students:* 21 full-time (15 women), 11 part-time (8 women); includes 7 minority (2 African Americans, 5 Hispanic Americans), 1 international. Average age 25. 18 applicants, 83% accepted, 11 enrolled. In 2006, 7 degrees awarded. *Entrance requirements:* For master's, GRE General Test. Additional exam requirements/recommendations for international students: Recommended—TOEFL (minimum score 550 paper-based; 213 computer-based). *Application deadline:* For fall admission, 7/15 for domestic students. Application fee: $50 ($75 for international students). *Expenses:* Tuition, state resident: full-time $3,573; part-time $198 per credit. Tuition, nonresident: full-time $8,577; part-time $476 per credit. Required fees: $1,258; $126 per credit. One-time fee: $150 full-time. Tuition and fees vary according to course load. *Financial support:* Teaching assistantships, career-related internships or fieldwork, Federal Work-Study, and institutionally sponsored loans available. Financial award application deadline: 4/1. *Application contact:* Dr. John Collins, Adviser, 940-565-3422, Fax: 940-565-4904, E-mail: collins@unt.edu.

University of South Alabama, Graduate School, College of Education, Department of Health, Physical Education and Leisure Services, Mobile, AL 36688-0002. Offers exercise science (MS); health education (M Ed); physical education (M Ed); therapeutic recreation (MS). *Accreditation:* NCATE (one or more programs are accredited). Part-time programs available. *Faculty:* 9 full-time (1 woman). *Students:* 26 full-time (18 women), 11 part-time (8 women); includes 11 minority (9 African Americans, 1 Asian American or Pacific Islander, 1 Hispanic American), 2 international. 12 applicants, 83% accepted, 5 enrolled. In 2006, 17 degrees awarded. *Degree requirements:* For master's, comprehensive exam. *Entrance requirements:* For master's, GRE General Test or MAT. *Application deadline:* For fall admission, 9/1 priority date for domestic students. Applications are processed on a rolling basis. Application fee: $25. *Financial support:* In 2006–07, 10 teaching assistantships were awarded; career-related internships or fieldwork also available. Support available to part-time students. Financial award application deadline: 4/1. *Unit head:* Dr. Frederick M. Scaffidi, Chair, 251-460-7131.

University of Southern Mississippi, Graduate School, College of Health, School of Human Performance and Recreation, Hattiesburg, MS 39406-0001. Offers human performance (MS, Ed D, PhD); interscholastic athletic administration (MS); recreation and leisure management (MS); sport administration (MS); sport and coaching education (MS); sport management (MS); sports and high performance materials (MS). Part-time and evening/weekend programs available. *Faculty:* 15 full-time (3 women). *Students:* 63 full-time (21 women), 36 part-time (11 women); includes 16 minority (13 African Americans, 1 Asian American or Pacific Islander, 2 Hispanic Americans), 6 international. Average age 27. 75 applicants, 64% accepted, 38 enrolled. In 2006, 37 master's, 5 doctorates awarded. *Degree requirements:* For master's, thesis optional; for doctorate, thesis/dissertation, comprehensive exam, registration. *Entrance requirements:* For master's, GRE General Test, minimum GPA of 2.75 in last 60 hours; for doctorate, GRE General Test, minimum GPA of 3.5. Additional exam requirements/recommendations for international students: Required—TOEFL. *Application deadline:* For fall admission, 3/1 priority date for domestic students, 3/1 for international students. Applications are processed on a rolling basis. Application fee: $25 ($30 for international students). Electronic applications accepted. *Financial support:* In 2006–07, 5 research assistantships with full tuition

reimbursements (averaging $10,426 per year), 10 teaching assistantships with full tuition reimbursements (averaging $10,426 per year) were awarded; fellowships, career-related internships or fieldwork, Federal Work-Study, institutionally sponsored loans, and tuition waivers (partial) also available. Financial award application deadline: 3/15. *Faculty research:* Exercise physiology, health behaviors, resource management, activity interaction, site development. *Unit head:* Dr. Louis Marciani, Director, 601-266-5379, Fax: 601-266-4445. *Application contact:* Dr. Dennis Phillips, Graduate Coordinator, 601-266-5379, Fax: 601-266-4445.

The University of Tennessee, Graduate School, College of Education, Health and Human Sciences, Department of Exercise, Sport, and Leisure Studies, Knoxville, TN 37996. Offers exercise science (MS, PhD), including biomechanics/sports medicine, exercise physiology; recreation and leisure studies (MS); sport management (MS); sport studies (MS, PhD); therapeutic recreation (MS). Part-time and evening/weekend programs available. *Students:* 28 (21 women); includes 1 minority (African American) 4 international. In 2006, 5 degrees awarded. *Degree requirements:* For master's, thesis optional. *Entrance requirements:* For master's, minimum GPA of 2.7. Additional exam requirements/recommendations for international students: Required—TOEFL. *Application deadline:* For fall admission, 2/1 priority date for domestic students. Applications are processed on a rolling basis. Application fee: $35. Electronic applications accepted. *Expenses:* Tuition, state resident: full-time $5,574. Tuition, nonresident: full-time $16,840. Required fees: $792. *Financial support:* In 2006–07, 2 fellowships, 1 research assistantship, 24 teaching assistantships were awarded; career-related internships or fieldwork, Federal Work-Study, institutionally sponsored loans, and unspecified assistantships also available. Financial award application deadline: 2/1; financial award applicants required to submit FAFSA. *Unit head:* Dr. Edward Howley, Head, 865-974-8555, Fax: 865-974-5781, E-mail: ehowley@utk.edu.

The University of Toledo, College of Graduate Studies, College of Health Science and Human Service, Division of Human Services, Department of Recreation and Leisure, Toledo, OH 43606-3390. Offers MA. *Students:* 11 full-time (6 women), 5 part-time (1 woman); includes 5 minority (all African Americans) Average age 25. 12 applicants, 75% accepted, 7 enrolled. In 2006, 10 degrees awarded.

University of Utah, The Graduate School, College of Health, Department of Parks, Recreation, and Tourism, Salt Lake City, UT 84112-1107. Offers M Phil, MS, Ed D, PhD. *Faculty:* 10 full-time (3 women). *Students:* 32 full-time (14 women), 32 part-time (18 women); includes 1 minority (Asian American or Pacific Islander), 6 international. Average age 33. 49 applicants, 39% accepted, 14 enrolled. In 2006, 13 master's, 4 doctorates awarded. Terminal master's awarded for partial completion of doctoral program. *Median time to degree:* Of those who began their doctoral program in fall 1998, 100% received their degree in 8 years or less. *Degree requirements:* For master's, thesis or alternative, comprehensive exam; for doctorate, thesis/dissertation. *Entrance requirements:* For master's, minimum GPA of 3.0; for doctorate, GRE General Test or MAT, minimum GPA of 3.2. Additional exam requirements/recommendations for international students: Required—TOEFL (minimum score 500 paper-based; 173 computer-based). *Application deadline:* For fall admission, 4/1 for domestic students, 2/15 for international students; for spring admission, 11/1 for domestic students. Application fee: $45 ($65 for international students). Electronic applications accepted. *Expenses:* Tuition, state resident: full-time $3,208. Tuition, nonresident: full-time $11,326. Required fees: $608. Tuition and fees vary according to class time and program. *Financial support:* Teaching assistantships with full tuition reimbursements, career-related internships or fieldwork available. Financial award application deadline: 2/15; financial award applicants required to submit FAFSA. *Faculty research:* Commercial, therapeutic, community, and outdoor recreation; tourism. Total annual research expenditures: $40,922. *Unit head:* Dr. Dan Dustin, Chair, 801-581-7560, E-mail: daniel.dustin@health.utah.edu. *Application contact:* Dr. Edward J. Ruddell, Director of Graduate Studies, 801-585-8085, Fax: 801-581-4930, E-mail: edward.ruddell@health.utah.edu.

University of Victoria, Faculty of Graduate Studies, Faculty of Education, School of Physical Education, Victoria, BC V8W 2Y2, Canada. Offers coaching studies (co-operative education) (M Ed); kinesiology (M Sc, MA); leisure service administration (MA); physical education (MA). Part-time programs available. *Degree requirements:* For master's, thesis (for some programs), comprehensive exam (for some programs), registration. *Entrance requirements:* For master's, minimum B average. Additional exam requirements/recommendations for international students: Required—TOEFL (minimum score 575 paper-based; 233 computer-based), IELTS (minimum score 7). Electronic applications accepted. *Faculty research:* Children and exercise, mental skills in sports, teaching effectiveness, neural control of human movement, physical performance and health.

University of Waterloo, Graduate Studies, Faculty of Applied Health Sciences, Department of Recreation and Leisure Studies, Waterloo, ON N2L 3G1, Canada. Offers MA, PhD. Part-time programs available. *Faculty:* 14 full-time (6 women), 8 part-time/adjunct (3 women). *Students:* 32 full-time (28 women), 7 part-time (3 women). 33 applicants, 42% accepted, 14 enrolled. In 2006, 4 master's, 2 doctorates awarded. *Degree requirements:* For master's, thesis/dissertation, registration; for doctorate, thesis/dissertation, comprehensive exam, registration. *Entrance requirements:* For master's, honors degree, minimum B average, writing sample, resumé; for doctorate, GRE (recommended), master's degree, minimum B average, writing sample, resumé. Additional exam requirements/recommendations for international students: Required—TOEFL, TWE. *Application deadline:* For fall admission, 2/1 for domestic and international students. Application fee: $75 Canadian dollars. Electronic applications accepted. *Financial support:* Research assistantships, teaching assistantships, career-related internships or fieldwork, Federal Work-Study, institutionally sponsored loans, and scholarships/grants available. *Faculty research:* Tourism, leisure behavior, special populations, leisure service management, outdoor resources, aging, health and well-being, work and health. *Application contact:* Tracy Taves, Graduate Studies Coordinator, 519-888-4567 Ext. 36149, Fax: 519-746-6776, E-mail: tltaves@uwaterloo.ca.

University of West Florida, College of Professional Studies, Division of Health, Leisure, and Exercise Science, Program in Health, Leisure, and Exercise Science, Pensacola, FL 32514-5750. Offers exercise science (MS); physical education (MS). *Students:* 25 full-time (16 women), 21 part-time (16 women); includes 5 minority (4 African Americans, 1 Hispanic American), 1 international. Average age 31. 24 applicants, 83% accepted, 15 enrolled. In 2006, 6 degrees awarded. *Degree requirements:* For master's, thesis or alternative. *Entrance requirements:* For master's, GRE General Test, minimum GPA of 3.0. Additional exam requirements/recommendations for international students: Required—TOEFL (minimum score 550 paper-based; 213 computer-based). *Application deadline:* For fall admission, 6/1 for domestic students, 5/15 for international students; for spring admission, 11/1 for domestic students, 10/1 for international students. Applications are processed on a rolling basis. Application fee: $30. *Expenses:* Tuition, state resident: full-time $5,871; part-time $245 per credit hour. Tuition, nonresident: full-time $21,241; part-time $885 per credit hour. *Financial support:* Fellowships, research assistantships with partial tuition reimbursements, teaching assistantships, Federal Work-Study, scholarships/grants, tuition waivers (full and partial), and unspecified assistantships available. Financial award application deadline: 4/15; financial award applicants required to submit FAFSA. *Unit head:* Dr. Stuart W. Ryan, Chairperson, Division of Health, Leisure, and Exercise Science, 850-474-2592.

Recreation and Park Management

Acadia University, Faculty of Professional Studies, School of Recreation Management and Kinesiology, Wolfville, NS B4P 2R6, Canada. Offers MR. In 2006, 2 degrees awarded. *Entrance requirements:* Additional exam requirements/recommendations for international students: Required—TOEFL (minimum score 580 paper-based; 237 computer-based). Application fee: $50. *Unit head:* Dr. Gary Ness, Director, 902-585-1566, Fax: 902-585-1702, E-mail: gary.ness@acadiau.ca. *Application contact:* Krista Robertson, Secretary, 902-585-1457, Fax: 902-585-1702, E-mail: krista.robertson@acadiau.ca.

Arizona State University, Division of Graduate Studies, College of Public Programs, School of Community Resources and Development, Tempe, AZ 85287. Offers recreation (MS). *Degree requirements:* For master's, thesis or alternative.

Baker College Center for Graduate Studies, Programs in Business, Flint, MI 48507-9843. Offers accounting (MBA); computer information systems (MBA); finance (MBA); general business (MBA); health and recreation services management (MBA); health care management (MBA); human resource management (MBA); industrial management (MBA); international business (MBA); leadership (MBA); marketing (MBA). MBA in health and recreation services management enrollment limited to international students. Part-time and evening/weekend programs available. *Faculty:* 15 full-time (6 women), 425 part-time/adjunct (200 women). *Students:* 370 full-time (190 women), 1,060 part-time (560 women); includes 372 minority (205 African Americans, 27 American Indian/Alaska Native, 66 Asian Americans or Pacific Islanders, 74 Hispanic Americans), 30 international. Average age 38. 780 applicants, 85% accepted, 567 enrolled. In 2006, 202 degrees awarded. *Degree requirements:* For master's, portfolio. *Entrance requirements:* For master's, 3 years of work experience, minimum undergraduate GPA of 2.5, writing sample, letters of recommendation. Additional exam requirements/recommendations for international students: Required—TOEFL (minimum score 550 paper-based; 213 computer-based). *Application deadline:* For fall admission, 8/6 priority date for domestic students; for winter admission, 12/15 priority date for domestic students; for spring admission, 2/15 priority date for domestic students. Applications are processed on a rolling basis. Application fee: $25. Electronic applications accepted. *Expenses:* Tuition: Full-time $7,200; part-time $300 per credit hour. *Financial support:* In 2006–07, 410 students received support. Scholarships/grants available. Support available to part-time students. Financial award applicants required to submit FAFSA. *Unit head:* Dr. Michael Heberling, President, 800-469-3165, Fax: 810-766-4399, E-mail: heberling@baker.edu. *Application contact:* Chuck J. Gurden, Vice President for Graduate and Online Admissions, 800-469-3165, Fax: 810-766-2051, E-mail: chuck@baker.edu.

Bowling Green State University, Graduate College, College of Education and Human Development, School of Human Movement, Sport, and Leisure Studies, Bowling Green, OH 43403. Offers developmental kinesiology (M Ed); recreation and leisure (M Ed); sport administration (M Ed). Part-time programs available. *Faculty:* 26 full-time (13 women), 4 part-time/adjunct (2 women). *Students:* 36 full-time (22 women), 14 part-time (6 women); includes 6 minority (all African Americans), 5 international. Average age 27. 54 applicants, 50% accepted, 20 enrolled. In 2006, 33 degrees awarded. *Degree requirements:* For master's, thesis or alternative. *Entrance requirements:* For master's, GRE General Test, minimum GPA of 2.7. Additional exam requirements/recommendations for international students: Required—TOEFL. *Application deadline:* For fall admission, 1/15 priority date for domestic students. Applications are processed on a rolling basis. Application fee: $30. Electronic applications accepted. *Expenses:* Tuition, state resident: part-time $535 per hour. Tuition, nonresident: part-time $884 per hour. *Financial support:* In 2006–07, 13 research assistantships with full tuition reimbursements (averaging $7,926 per year), 18 teaching assistantships with full tuition reimbursements (averaging $6,263 per year) were awarded; career-related internships or fieldwork, Federal Work-Study, and unspecified assistantships also available. Financial award applicants required to submit FAFSA. *Faculty research:* Teacher-learning process, travel and tourism, sport marketing and management, exercise physiology and sport psychology, life-span motor development. *Unit head:* Dr. Lynn Darby, Acting Director, 419-372-2334. *Application contact:* Dr. Geoff Meek, Graduate Coordinator, 419-372-0501.

Brigham Young University, Graduate Studies, College of Health and Human Performance, Department of Recreation Management and Youth Leadership, Provo, UT 84602-1001. Offers youth and family recreation (MS). *Faculty:* 7 full-time (1 woman). *Students:* 7 full-time (4 women), 7 part-time (3 women); includes 1 Asian American or Pacific Islander. Average age 30. 8 applicants, 63% accepted, 5 enrolled. In 2006, 3 degrees awarded. *Degree requirements:* For master's, thesis, oral defense. *Entrance requirements:* For master's, GRE General Test, minimum GPA of 3.0 in last 60 hours. Additional exam requirements/recommendations for international students: Required—TOEFL (minimum score 580 paper-based; 237 computer-based; 85 iBT), IELTS (minimum score 7). *Application deadline:* For fall admission, 2/1 priority date for domestic students. Application fee: $50. Electronic applications accepted. *Expenses:* Contact institution. *Financial support:* In 2006–07, 8 students received support, including 8 research assistantships with full tuition reimbursements available (averaging $2,200 per year); fellowships, teaching assistantships with tuition reimbursements available, career-related internships or fieldwork, institutionally sponsored loans, scholarships/grants, tuition waivers (full and partial), unspecified assistantships, and administrative aides also available. Support available to part-time students. Financial award application deadline: 3/1. *Faculty research:* Family recreation, adolescent development, leisure behavior, families with child with disability inclusive and adaptive recreation. *Unit head:* Dr. Patti Ann Freeman, Chair, 801-422-1286, Fax: 801-422-0609, E-mail: patti.freeman@byu.edu. *Application contact:* Dr. Ramon Zabriskie, Graduate Coordinator, 801-422-1667, Fax: 801-422-0609, E-mail: zabriskie@byu.edu.

California State University, Chico, Graduate School, College of Communication and Education, Department of Recreation and Parks Management, Chico, CA 95929-0560. Offers recreation administration (MA). *Students:* Average age 35. *Degree requirements:* For master's, thesis or alternative, oral exam. *Entrance requirements:* For master's, GRE General Test, 3 letters of recommendation, resumé. Additional exam requirements/recommendations for international students: Required—TOEFL (minimum score 550 paper-based; 213 computer-based). *Application deadline:* For fall admission, 3/1 for domestic and international students. Applications are processed on a rolling basis. Application fee: $55. Electronic applications accepted. *Financial support:* Fellowships, career-related internships or fieldwork and stipends available. *Unit head:* Dr. James Fletcher, Graduate Coordinator, 530-898-4365.

California State University, Long Beach, Graduate Studies, College of Health and Human Services, Department of Recreation and Leisure Studies, Long Beach, CA 90840. Offers recreation administration (MS). Part-time programs available. *Faculty:* 8 full-time (4 women), 5 part-time/adjunct (4 women). *Students:* 17 full-time (14 women), 17 part-time (11 women); includes 4 minority (2 African Americans, 1 American Indian/Alaska Native, 1 Hispanic American), 6 international. Average age 32. 27 applicants, 74% accepted, 13 enrolled. In 2006, 2 degrees awarded. *Degree requirements:* For master's, comprehensive exam or thesis. *Entrance requirements:* For master's, GRE General Test. *Application deadline:* For fall admission, 7/1 for domestic students; for spring admission, 12/1 for domestic students. Applications are processed on a rolling basis. Application fee: $55. Electronic applications accepted. *Financial support:* Federal Work-Study, institutionally sponsored loans, and scholarships/grants available. Financial award application deadline: 3/2. *Unit head:* Dr. Maridith Janssen, Chair, 562-985-4071, Fax: 562-985-8154, E-mail: mjanssen@csulb.edu. *Application contact:* Dr. Katherine James, Information Contact, 562-985-4071, Fax: 562-985-8154, E-mail: kjames@csulb.edu.

California State University, Northridge, Graduate Studies, College of Health and Human Development, Department of Recreation and Tourism Management, Northridge, CA 91330. Offers recreation administration (MS). *Faculty:* 8 full-time (4 women), 5 part-time/adjunct (4 women). *Students:* Average age 33. 2 applicants, 0% accepted. In 2006, 3 degrees awarded. *Degree requirements:* For master's, thesis (for some programs). *Entrance requirements:* For master's, GRE. Additional exam requirements/recommendations for international students: Required—TOEFL. *Application deadline:* For fall admission, 11/30 for domestic students. Application fee: $55. *Expenses:* Tuition, nonresident: full-time $8,136; part-time $4,068 per year. Required fees: $3,624; $1,161 per term. *Financial support:* Application deadline: 3/1. *Unit head:* Dr. Craig Finney, Chair, 818-677-3202. *Application contact:* Information Contact, 818-677-3202.

California State University, Sacramento, Graduate Studies, College of Health and Human Services, Department of Recreation and Leisure Studies, Sacramento, CA 95819-6048. Offers recreation administration (MS). Part-time programs available. *Students:* 10 full-time (8 women), 17 part-time (8 women); includes 8 minority (1 African American, 1 American Indian/Alaska Native, 2 Asian Americans or Pacific Islanders, 4 Hispanic Americans). Average age 30. 18 applicants, 61% accepted, 8 enrolled. *Degree requirements:* For master's, thesis or alternative, writing proficiency exam. *Entrance requirements:* Additional exam requirements/recommendations for international students: Required—TOEFL. *Application deadline:* Applications are processed on a rolling basis. Application fee: $55. Electronic applications accepted. *Financial support:* Research assistantships, teaching assistantships, career-related internships or fieldwork and Federal Work-Study available. Support available to part-time students. Financial award application deadline: 3/1. *Unit head:* Beth Kivel, Chair, 916-278-6752, Fax: 916-278-5053.

Central Michigan University, College of Graduate Studies, College of Education and Human Services, Department of Recreation, Parks, and Leisure Studies Administration, Mount Pleasant, MI 48859. Offers recreation and park administration (MA); therapeutic recreation (MA). *Degree requirements:* For master's, thesis or alternative, registration. *Entrance requirements:* For master's, minimum GPA of 2.75 in last 60 hours of course work. *Faculty research:* Study of ethics in parks and recreation professionals in Michigan, computer touch-tone information services at visitor centers, creative play spaces for children.

Central Michigan University, College of Graduate Studies, Program in Administration, Mount Pleasant, MI 48859. Offers general administration (MSA); health services administration (MSA); hospitality and tourism administration (MSA); human resource administration (MSA); information resource administration (MSA); international administration (MSA); leadership (MSA); organizational communications (MSA); public administration (MSA); recreation and park administration (MSA); software engineering (MSA); sports administration (MSA). *Accreditation:* AACSB. *Degree requirements:* For master's, thesis or alternative. *Entrance requirements:* For master's, minimum undergraduate GPA of 2.5.

See Close-Up on page 253.

Clemson University, Graduate School, College of Health, Education, and Human Development, Department of Parks, Recreation, and Tourism Management, Clemson, SC 29634. Offers MPRTM, MS, PhD. Part-time programs available. *Faculty:* 20 full-time (7 women). *Students:* 44 full-time (26 women), 16 part-time (10 women); includes 1 minority (Hispanic American), 13 international. Average age 25. 60 applicants, 62% accepted, 20 enrolled. In 2006, 5 master's, 6 doctorates awarded. *Degree requirements:* For master's, thesis (for some programs); for doctorate, thesis/dissertation. *Entrance requirements:* For master's, GRE General Test, minimum undergraduate GPA of 3.0; for doctorate, GRE General Test, minimum graduate GPA of 3.0. Additional exam requirements/recommendations for international students: Required—TOEFL. *Application deadline:* For fall admission, 5/1 priority date for domestic students; for spring admission, 10/1 for domestic students. Application fee: $50. *Expenses:* Tuition, state resident: full-time $8,812; part-time $450 per hour. Tuition, nonresident: full-time $18,036; part-time $760 per hour. Required fees: $474; $5 per term. *Financial support:* Fellowships, research assistantships, teaching assistantships, career-related internships or fieldwork, tuition waivers (partial), and unspecified assistantships available. Financial award application deadline: 4/15; financial award applicants required to submit FAFSA. *Faculty research:* Recreation resource management, leisure behavior, therapeutic recreation, community leisure services. *Unit head:* Dr. Brett A Wright, Chair, 864-656-3036, Fax: 864-656-2226, E-mail: wright@clemson.edu. *Application contact:* Dr. Fran McGuire, Graduate Coordinator, 864-656-2183, Fax: 864-656-2226, E-mail: lefty@clemson.edu.

See Close-Ups on pages 2279 and 2281.

Colorado State University, Graduate School, Warner College of Natural Resources, Department of Human Dimensions of Natural Resources, Fort Collins, CO 80523-0015. Offers MS, PhD. Part-time programs available. *Faculty:* 9 full-time (2 women). *Students.* 24 full-time (12 women), 15 part-time (10 women); includes 2 minority (both Hispanic Americans), 7 international. Average age 30. 56 applicants, 32% accepted, 13 enrolled. In 2006, 3 master's, 4 doctorates awarded. Terminal master's awarded for partial completion of doctoral program. *Degree requirements:* For master's, thesis or alternative, comprehensive exam, registration; for doctorate, thesis/dissertation, comprehensive exam, registration. *Entrance requirements:* For master's, GRE General Test with a score of 1000 or more on the quantitative and verbal sections, minimum GPA of 3.0, 3 letters of recommendation, transcripts, personal statement; for doctorate, GRE General Test with a score of 1000 or more, minimum GPA of 3.0, 3 letters of recommendation, transcripts, personal statement, copy of master's thesis or professional paper, interview. Additional exam requirements/recommendations for international students: Required—TOEFL. *Application deadline:* For fall admission, 3/1 priority date for domestic students. Applications are processed on a rolling basis. Application fee: $50. Electronic applications accepted. *Expenses:* Tuition, state resident: full-time $4,248; part-time $236 per credit. Tuition, nonresident: full-time $15,642; part-time $869 per credit. Required fees: $66 per credit. Tuition and fees vary according to program. *Financial support:* In 2006–07, 6 research assistantships with tuition reimbursements (averaging $14,000 per year), 8 teaching assistantships with tuition reimbursements (averaging $14,000 per year) were awarded; fellowships, career-related internships or fieldwork, Federal Work-Study, scholarships/grants, and traineeships also available. Support available to part-time students. Financial award application deadline: 2/1; financial award applicants required to submit FAFSA. *Faculty research:* International tourism, wilderness preservation, resource interpretation, human dimensions in natural resources, protected areas management. Total annual research expenditures: $669,843. *Unit head:* Dr. Michael J. Manfredo, Chair, 970-491-6591, Fax: 970-491-2255, E-mail: manfredo@cnr.colostate.edu. *Application contact:* Linda Adams, Coordinator of Administration, 970-491-6591, Fax: 970-491-2255, E-mail: linda.adams@colostate.edu.

Delta State University, Graduate Programs, College of Education, Division of Health, Physical Education and Recreation, Cleveland, MS 38733-0001. Offers physical education and recreation (M Ed). Part-time and evening/weekend programs available. *Degree requirements:* For master's, thesis optional. *Entrance requirements:* For master's, GRE General Test or MAT, Class A teaching certificate. *Application deadline:* For fall admission, 8/1 priority date for domestic students; for spring admission, 12/1 priority date for domestic students. Applications are processed on a rolling basis. Application fee: $0. *Financial support:* In 2006–07, research assistantships (averaging $4,000 per year); career-related internships or fieldwork, Federal Work-Study, and institutionally sponsored loans also available. Support available to part-time students. Financial award application deadline: 6/1. *Faculty research:* Blood pressure, body fat, power and reaction time, learning disorders for athletes, effects of walking. *Unit head:* Dr. Duke Barnes, Chair, 662-846-4555, Fax: 662-846-4571, E-mail: dbarnes@deltastate.edu.

East Carolina University, Graduate School, College of Health and Human Performance, Department of Recreation and Leisure Studies, Greenville, NC 27858-4353. Offers recreation and leisure services administration (MS); therapeutic recreation administration (MS). Part-time and evening/weekend programs available. Postbaccalaureate distance learning degree programs offered (minimal on-campus study). *Students:* 22 full-time (14 women), 6 part-time (1 woman); includes 1 minority (Asian American or Pacific Islander) Average age 26. 7 applicants, 14%

Recreation and Park Management

East Carolina University (continued)
accepted, 1 enrolled. In 2006, 10 degrees awarded. *Degree requirements:* For master's, thesis optional. *Entrance requirements:* For master's, GRE General Test or MAT. Additional exam requirements/recommendations for international students: Required—TOEFL. *Application deadline:* For fall admission, 6/1 priority date for domestic students. Applications are processed on a rolling basis. Application fee: $50. *Financial support:* In 2006–07, 8 students received support, including 1 research assistantship, 4 teaching assistantships with partial tuition reimbursements available (averaging $7,500 per year). Financial award application deadline: 6/1. *Faculty research:* Therapeutic recreation, stress and coping behavior, medicine carrying capacity, choice behavior, tourism preferences. Total annual research expenditures: $124,923. *Unit head:* Dr. Joseph Fridgen, Chair, 252-328-4640, Fax: 252-328-4642, E-mail: fridgenj@ecu.edu.

Eastern Kentucky University, The Graduate School, College of Health Sciences, Department of Recreation and Park Administration, Richmond, KY 40475-3102. Offers MS. Part-time programs available. *Faculty:* 3 full-time (0 women). *Students:* 6 full-time (3 women), 6 part-time (2 women), 1 international. Average age 29. 8 applicants, 63% accepted, 3 enrolled. In 2006, 5 degrees awarded. *Entrance requirements:* For master's, GRE General Test, minimum GPA of 2.5. Application fee: $35. *Expenses:* Tuition, state resident: full-time $5,610. Tuition, nonresident: full-time $15,910. *Financial support:* Research assistantships, teaching assistantships, Federal Work-Study available. Support available to part-time students. *Unit head:* Dr. Charles Everett, Acting Chair, 859-622-1833, Fax: 859-622-2971.

Florida Agricultural and Mechanical University, Division of Graduate Studies, Research, and Continuing Education, College of Education, Department of Health, Physical Education, and Recreation, Tallahassee, FL 32307-3200. Offers M Ed, MS Ed. *Accreditation:* NCATE. Part-time and evening/weekend programs available. *Degree requirements:* For master's, thesis optional. *Entrance requirements:* For master's, GRE General Test, minimum GPA of 3.0. Additional exam requirements/recommendations for international students: Required—TOEFL. *Faculty research:* Administration/curriculum, work behavior, psychology.

Florida Gulf Coast University, College of Health Professions, Geriatric Recreational Therapy Program, Fort Myers, FL 33965-6565. Offers MS. *Faculty:* 42 full-time (35 women), 21 part-time/adjunct (14 women). *Students:* 2 full-time (both women). Average age 41. *Expenses:* Tuition, state resident: full-time $4,326. Tuition, nonresident: full-time $18,523. Required fees: $1,211. One-time fee: $5 full-time. *Unit head:* Dr. Joan Glacken, Chair, 239-590-7498, Fax: 239-590-7474, E-mail: jglacken@fgcu.edu.

Florida International University, College of Education, Department of Health, Physical Education, and Recreation, Program in Parks and Recreation Management, Miami, FL 33199. Offers leisure services (MS); therapeutic recreation (MS). Part-time and evening/weekend programs available. *Faculty:* 3 full-time (2 women). *Students:* 2 full-time (1 woman), 6 part-time (5 women); includes 3 minority (1 African American, 1 Asian American or Pacific Islander, 1 Hispanic American). Average age 30. 4 applicants, 50% accepted, 2 enrolled. In 2006, 1 degree awarded. *Entrance requirements:* For master's, GRE General Test or minimum GPA of 3.0. Additional exam requirements/recommendations for international students: Required—TOEFL (minimum score 550 paper-based; 213 computer-based; 80 iBT), IELTS (minimum score 6). *Application deadline:* For fall admission, 6/1 priority date for domestic students, 4/1 for international students; for winter admission, 10/1 priority date for domestic students, 9/1 for international students; for spring admission, 3/1 priority date for domestic students, 2/1 for international students. Applications are processed on a rolling basis. Application fee: $30. Electronic applications accepted. *Expenses:* Tuition, state resident: part-time $249 per credit hour. Tuition, nonresident: part-time $753 per credit hour. Tuition and fees vary according to program. *Financial support:* Fellowships, research assistantships, teaching assistantships, Federal Work-Study and tuition waivers (full and partial) available. Support available to part-time students. *Faculty research:* Effects of prosocial behavior interventions on children and adolescents with behavior disorders or who are considered to be at risk. *Application contact:* Marisa Salazar, Student Recruiter, 305-348-3002, Fax: 305-348-3227, E-mail: marisa.salazar@fiu.edu.

Florida State University, Graduate Studies, College of Education, Department of Sport Management, Recreation Management, and Physical Education, Tallahassee, FL 32306. Offers physical education (MS, Ed D, PhD, Ed S); recreation management (MS); sport management (MS, Ed D, PhD, Ed S). *Faculty:* 18 full-time (9 women), 5 part-time/adjunct (3 women). *Students:* 93 full-time (35 women), 87 part-time (39 women); includes 65 minority (21 African Americans, 34 Asian Americans or Pacific Islanders, 10 Hispanic Americans). 226 applicants, 56% accepted, 75 enrolled. In 2006, 57 master's, 13 doctorates, 1 other advanced degree awarded. *Degree requirements:* For master's and Ed S, thesis optional; for doctorate, thesis/dissertation, comprehensive exam. *Entrance requirements:* For master's, doctorate, and Ed S, GRE General Test, minimum GPA of 3.0. Additional exam requirements/recommendations for international students: Required—TOEFL (minimum score 550 paper-based; 213 computer-based). *Application deadline:* For fall admission, 7/1 priority date for domestic students, 5/1 for international students; for spring admission, 11/1 for domestic students, 9/1 for international students. Applications are processed on a rolling basis. Application fee: $30. Electronic applications accepted. *Expenses:* Tuition, state resident: full-time $5,822; part-time $243 per credit hour. Tuition, nonresident: full-time $20,976; part-time $874 per credit hour. Tuition and fees vary according to program. *Financial support:* In 2006–07, 1 fellowship, 35 research assistantships, 38 teaching assistantships were awarded; career-related internships or fieldwork also available. Financial award applicants required to submit FAFSA. *Faculty research:* Sport marketing, teacher career cycle, gender issues. *Unit head:* Dr. Cheryl Beeler, Chair, 850-644-4813, Fax: 850-644-0975, E-mail: beeler@coe.fsu.edu. *Application contact:* Cynthia Bailey, Program Assistant, 850-644-4813, Fax: 850-644-0975, E-mail: bailey@coe.fsu.edu.

Frostburg State University, Graduate School, College of Education, Program in Parks and Recreational Management, Frostburg, MD 21532-1099. Offers MS. Part-time and evening/weekend programs available. *Degree requirements:* For master's, thesis. *Entrance requirements:* For master's, resumé. Electronic applications accepted.

Georgia Southern University, Jack N. Averitt College of Graduate Studies, College of Health and Human Sciences, Department of Hospitality, Tourism, and Family and Consumer Sciences, Program in Recreation Administration, Statesboro, GA 30460. Offers MS. Part-time and evening/weekend programs available. *Students:* 11 full-time (4 women), 2 part-time (1 woman); includes 3 minority (2 African Americans, 1 Hispanic American). Average age 26. 8 applicants, 100% accepted, 6 enrolled. In 2006, 1 degree awarded. *Degree requirements:* For master's, exam, thesis optional. *Entrance requirements:* For master's, GMAT, GRE General Test, or MAT, minimum GPA of 2.75, undergraduate major in recreation or related field, faculty interview. Additional exam requirements/recommendations for international students: Required—TOEFL (minimum score 550 paper-based; 213 computer-based; 80 iBT). *Application deadline:* For fall admission, 3/1 priority date for domestic students, 3/1 for international students; for spring admission, 10/1 priority date for domestic students, 10/1 for international students. Applications are processed on a rolling basis. Application fee: $50. Electronic applications accepted. *Financial support:* In 2006–07, 12 students received support, including research assistantships with partial tuition reimbursements available (averaging $5,500 per year), teaching assistantships with partial tuition reimbursements available (averaging $5,500 per year); Federal Work-Study, scholarships/grants, tuition waivers (partial), and unspecified assistantships also available. Support available to part-time students. Financial award application deadline: 4/15; financial award applicants required to submit FAFSA. *Faculty research:* Tourism management, economic development, urban planning and design, commercial recreation, clinical therapeutic recreation. Total annual research expenditures: $1,583. *Unit head:* Dr. John Naught, Director, 912-468-7427, Fax: 912-681-0386, E-mail: jnaurigh@georgiasouthern.edu. *Application contact:* 912-681-5384, Fax: 912-681-0740, E-mail: gradadmissions@georgiasouthern.edu.

Hardin-Simmons University, Graduate School, Irvin School of Education, Department of Fitness and Sport Sciences, Program in Sports and Recreation Management, Abilene, TX 79698-0001. Offers M Ed. Part-time programs available. *Faculty:* 4 full-time (1 woman), 1 part-time/adjunct (0 women). *Students:* 7 full-time (1 woman), 18 part-time (8 women); includes 7 minority (3 African Americans, 4 Hispanic Americans). Average age 26. 11 applicants, 100% accepted, 8 enrolled. In 2006, 10 degrees awarded. *Degree requirements:* For master's, internship, project, thesis optional. *Entrance requirements:* For master's, minimum undergraduate GPA of 3.0 in major, 2.7 overall; interview; writing sample; letters of recommendation; resumé. Additional exam requirements/recommendations for international students: Required—TOEFL (minimum score 550 paper-based; 213 computer-based). *Application deadline:* For fall admission, 8/15 priority date for domestic students; for spring admission, 1/5 priority date for domestic students. Applications are processed on a rolling basis. Application fee: $50 ($100 for international students). *Expenses:* Tuition: Full-time $9,090; part-time $505 per hour. Required fees: $490; $66 per semester. One-time fee: $50. Tuition and fees vary according to course load and degree level. *Financial support:* In 2006–07, 25 students received support, including 20 fellowships (averaging $1,000 per year); career-related internships or fieldwork, scholarships/grants, and recreation assistantships also available. Support available to part-time students. Financial award application deadline: 6/30; financial award applicants required to submit FAFSA. *Unit head:* Dr. Ray Galloway, Director, 325-670-1470, Fax: 325-670-1572, E-mail: rgallow@hsutx.edu. *Application contact:* Dr. Gary Stanlake, Dean of Graduate Studies, 325-670-1298, Fax: 325-670-1564, E-mail: gradoff@hsutx.edu.

Howard University, Graduate School, Department of Physical Education, Recreation, and Health Education, Washington, DC 20059-0002. Offers exercise physiology (MS); recreation and leisure studies (MS); school and community health education (MS). Part-time programs available. *Degree requirements:* For master's, thesis or alternative, comprehensive exam. *Entrance requirements:* For master's, GRE General Test, minimum GPA of 3.0. *Faculty research:* Women's health, work and health, AIDS, men's health, hypertension, sports nutrition, social science, urban recreation, therapeutic recreation, commercial recreation.

Indiana University Bloomington, School of Health, Physical Education and Recreation, Department of Recreation and Park Administration, Bloomington, IN 47405-7000. Offers leisure behavior (PhD); outdoor recreation management (MS); park and recreation administration (MS); recreation (Re Dir); recreational sports administration (MS); therapeutic recreation (MS). PhD offered through the University Graduate School. *Faculty:* 11 full-time (4 women). *Students:* 18 full-time (7 women), 11 part-time (6 women); includes 2 minority (both African Americans), 3 international. Average age 28. In 2006, 9 degrees awarded. Terminal master's awarded for partial completion of doctoral program. *Degree requirements:* For doctorate, thesis/dissertation; for Re Dir, thesis optional. *Entrance requirements:* For master's, GRE General Test, minimum GPA of 2.8; for doctorate and Re Dir, GRE. *Application deadline:* For fall admission, 1/1 for international students; for spring admission, 9/1 for international students. Applications are processed on a rolling basis. Application fee: $50 ($60 for international students). *Expenses:* Tuition, state resident: full-time $5,791; part-time $241 per credit hour. Tuition, nonresident: full-time $16,866; part-time $703 per credit hour. *Financial support:* Fellowships, research assistantships, teaching assistantships with partial tuition reimbursements, career-related internships or fieldwork, Federal Work-Study, institutionally sponsored loans, scholarships/grants, tuition waivers (partial), unspecified assistantships, and fee remissions available. Financial award application deadline: 3/1. *Faculty research:* Leisure counseling, gerontology, special populations, planning and development. *Unit head:* Dr. Lynne Jamieson, Chairperson, 812-855-4711. *Application contact:* Program Office, 812-855-4711, Fax: 812-855-3998, E-mail: recpark@indiana.edu.

Kent State University, Graduate School of Education, Health, and Human Services, Program in Exercise, Leisure, and Sport, Kent, OH 44242-0001. Offers athletic training (MA); exercise physiology (MA); physical teacher education (MA); sport and recreation management (MA); sports studies (MA). *Faculty:* 15 full-time (7 women). *Students:* 47 full-time (25 women), 34 part-time (13 women); includes 11 minority (10 African Americans, 1 Hispanic American), 4 international. 46 applicants, 74% accepted. In 2006, 9 degrees awarded. Application fee: $30. *Unit head:* Dr. Steve Mitchell, Coordinator, 330-672-0206, E-mail: smitchel@kent.edu. *Application contact:* Nancy Miller, Academic Program Coordinator, Office of Graduate Student Services, 330-672-2576, Fax: 330-672-9162, E-mail: ogs@kent.edu.

Lehman College of the City University of New York, Division of Natural and Social Sciences, Department of Health Sciences, Program in Recreation, Bronx, NY 10468-1589. Offers recreation education (MA, MS Ed). Part-time and evening/weekend programs available. *Degree requirements:* For master's, thesis or alternative, comprehensive exam. *Entrance requirements:* For master's, minimum GPA of 2.7. *Faculty research:* Therapeutic recreation philosophy, curriculum, current approaches to treatment, impact of societal trends, ethical issues.

Michigan State University, The Graduate School, College of Agriculture and Natural Resources, Department of Community, Agriculture, Recreation, and Resource Studies, East Lansing, MI 48824. Offers MS, PhD. *Faculty:* 24 full-time (5 women). *Students:* 57 full-time (35 women), 21 part-time (15 women); includes 11 minority (3 African Americans, 2 American Indian/Alaska Native, 4 Asian Americans or Pacific Islanders, 2 Hispanic Americans), 35 international. Average age 34. 57 applicants, 42% accepted. In 2006, 4 master's, 1 doctorate awarded. *Entrance requirements:* Additional exam requirements/recommendations for international students: Required—TOEFL. Electronic applications accepted. *Expenses:* Tuition, state resident: part-time $346 per credit hour. Tuition, nonresident: part-time $730 per credit hour. Tuition and fees vary according to program. *Financial support:* In 2006–07, 14 fellowships with tuition reimbursements, 29 research assistantships with tuition reimbursements (averaging $13,671 per year), 6 teaching assistantships with tuition reimbursements (averaging $12,456 per year) were awarded. Total annual research expenditures: $2 million. *Unit head:* Dr. Scott G. Witter, Chairperson, 517-432-0263, Fax: 517-432-3597, E-mail: witter@msu.edu. *Application contact:* Diane Davis, Graduate Secretary, 517-432-0275, Fax: 517-432-3597, E-mail: davisdia@msu.edu.

Middle Tennessee State University, College of Graduate Studies, College of Education and Behavioral Science, Department of Health, Physical Education, Recreation and Safety, Murfreesboro, TN 37132. Offers exercise science and health promotion (MS); health, physical education, recreation and safety (MS); human performance (PhD); physical education (PhD). *Accreditation:* NCATE (one or more programs are accredited). Part-time and evening/weekend programs available. Postbaccalaureate distance learning degree programs offered. *Faculty:* 26 full-time (12 women). *Students:* 10 full-time (6 women), 130 part-time (64 women); includes 27 minority (21 African Americans, 1 American Indian/Alaska Native, 5 Asian Americans or Pacific Islanders). Average age 28. 64 applicants, 94% accepted. In 2006, 39 master's, 7 doctorates awarded. *Entrance requirements:* For master's and doctorate, GRE or MAT. Additional exam requirements/recommendations for international students: Required—TOEFL (minimum score 525 paper-based; 195 computer-based). *Application deadline:* For fall admission, 8/1 priority date for domestic students. Applications are processed on a rolling basis. Application fee: $25. Electronic applications accepted. *Financial support:* In 2006–07, 31 students received support. Application deadline: 5/1; *Faculty research:* Cardiovascular disease and psychosocial stress, pediatric health and fitness, obesity, fitness testing, anaerobic power and lactate kinetics. *Unit head:* Dr. Dianne Bartley, Chair, 615-898-2811, Fax: 615-898-5020, E-mail: dbartley@mtsu.edu.

Naropa University, Graduate Programs, Program in Transpersonal Counseling Psychology, Concentration in Wilderness Therapy, Boulder, CO 80302-6697. Offers MA. *Faculty:* 1 (woman) full-time, 9 part-time/adjunct (7 women). *Students:* 28 full-time (17 women), 12 part-time (6 women); includes 1 minority (Hispanic American), 6 international. Average age 30. 20 applicants, 75% accepted, 12 enrolled. In 2006, 9 degrees awarded. *Median time to degree:* Master's–3 years full-time. *Degree requirements:* For master's, internship. *Entrance requirements:* For master's, in-person interview, outdoor experience, course work in psychology. Additional exam requirements/recommendations for international students: Required—TOEFL (minimum score

600 paper-based; 250 computer-based). *Application deadline:* For fall admission, 1/15 priority date for domestic and international students; for spring admission, 10/15 for domestic students. Applications are processed on a rolling basis. Application fee: $60. Electronic applications accepted. *Expenses:* Tuition: Full-time $15,070; part-time $646 per credit. Tuition and fees vary according to course load. *Financial support:* In 2006–07, 7 students received support, including research assistantships with partial tuition reimbursements available (averaging $3,000 per year); career-related internships or fieldwork, Federal Work-Study, scholarships/grants, tuition waivers (partial), and unspecified assistantships also available. Support available to part-time students. Financial award application deadline: 3/1; financial award applicants required to submit FAFSA. *Unit head:* Dr. Deb Piranian, Coordinator, 303-245-4838. *Application contact:* Alice Di Tullio, Admissions Counselor, 303-546-3598, Fax: 303-546-3583, E-mail: aliced@naropa.edu.

North Carolina Central University, Division of Academic Affairs, College of Arts and Sciences, Department of Physical Education and Recreation, Durham, NC 27707-3129. Offers general physical education (MS); recreation administration (MS); special physical education (MS); therapeutic recreation (MS). Part-time and evening/weekend programs available. *Degree requirements:* For master's, one foreign language, thesis, comprehensive exam. *Entrance requirements:* For master's, GRE, minimum GPA of 3.0 in major, 2.5 overall. Additional exam requirements/recommendations for international students: Required—TOEFL. *Faculty research:* Physical activity patterns of children with disabilities, physical fitness test of North Carolina school children, exercise physiology, motor learning/development.

North Carolina State University, Graduate School, College of Natural Resources, Department of Parks, Recreation and Tourism Management, Raleigh, NC 27695. Offers geographic information systems (MS); maintenance management (MRRA, MS); parks, recreation and tourism management (PhD); recreation planning (MRRA, MS); recreation resources administration/public administration (MRRA); recreation/park management (MRRA, MS); sports management (MRRA, MS); travel and tourism management (MS). *Degree requirements:* For master's, thesis (for some programs); for doctorate, thesis/dissertation. *Entrance requirements:* For master's and doctorate, GRE General Test. Additional exam requirements/recommendations for international students: Required—TOEFL. Electronic applications accepted. *Faculty research:* Tourism policy and development, spatial information systems, natural resource management, recreational sports management, park and recreation management.

Northwest Missouri State University, Graduate School, College of Education and Human Services, Department of Health, Physical Education, Recreation and Dance, Maryville, MO 64468-6001. Offers health and physical education (MS Ed); recreation (MS). *Accreditation:* NCATE. Part-time programs available. *Faculty:* 10 full-time (4 women). *Students:* 36 full-time (16 women), 6 part-time (1 woman); includes 2 minority (1 African American, 1 Asian American or Pacific Islander). 36 applicants, 69% accepted, 16 enrolled. In 2006, 12 degrees awarded. *Degree requirements:* For master's, comprehensive exam. *Entrance requirements:* For master's, GRE General Test, minimum undergraduate GPA of 2.75, teaching certificate, writing sample. Additional exam requirements/recommendations for international students: Required—TOEFL (minimum score 550 paper-based; 213 computer-based). *Application deadline:* For fall admission, 7/1 for domestic and international students; for spring admission, 11/15 for domestic and international students. Applications are processed on a rolling basis. Application fee: $0 ($50 for international students). *Financial support:* In 2006–07, 23 teaching assistantships with full tuition reimbursements (averaging $6,000 per year) were awarded; research assistantships, unspecified assistantships also available. Financial award application deadline: 3/1; financial award applicants required to submit FAFSA. *Unit head:* Dr. Loren Butler, Program Director, 660-562-1066. *Application contact:* Dr. Frances Shipley, Dean of Graduate School, 660-562-1145, Fax: 660-562-1096, E-mail: gradsch@nwmissouri.edu.

Ohio University, Graduate Studies, College of Health and Human Services, School of Recreation and Sport Sciences, Program in Recreation Studies, Athens, OH 45701-2979. Offers MS. *Faculty:* 4 full-time (3 women), 5 part-time/adjunct (1 woman). *Students:* 14 full-time (6 women), 2 international. Average age 20. 13 applicants, 77% accepted, 9 enrolled. In 2006, 10 degrees awarded. *Degree requirements:* For master's, thesis or alternative. *Entrance requirements:* For master's, GRE. Additional exam requirements/recommendations for international students: Required—TOEFL (minimum score 575 paper-based; 233 computer-based). *Application deadline:* For fall admission, 3/1 priority date for domestic and international students; for winter admission, 11/1 priority date for domestic and international students; for spring admission, 1/1 priority date for domestic and international students. Application fee: $45. *Financial support:* In 2006–07, 4 fellowships with full tuition reimbursements, 4 teaching assistantships with full tuition reimbursements (averaging $7,900 per year) were awarded; scholarships/grants, tuition waivers (full), and unspecified assistantships also available. *Faculty research:* Recreation, leisure studies, physical education, national parks. Total annual research expenditures: $7,500. *Unit head:* Dr. Jennifer Hinton, Coordinator, 740-597-1757, Fax: 740-593-0284, E-mail: hinton@ohio.edu. *Application contact:* Molly de Laval, Graduate Records, 740-593-9787, Fax: 740-593-0284, E-mail: delaval@ohio.edu.

Old Dominion University, Darden College of Education, Program in Physical Education, Recreation and Tourism Studies Emphasis, Norfolk, VA 23529. Offers MS Ed. Part-time and evening/weekend programs available. *Faculty:* 2 full-time (0 women). *Students:* 2 full-time (0 women), 4 part-time (all women); includes 1 minority (African American) Average age 28. 10 applicants, 60% accepted, 5 enrolled. In 2006, 1 degree awarded. *Degree requirements:* For master's, thesis or alternative, internship, research project, comprehensive exam. *Entrance requirements:* For master's, GRE, minimum GPA of 2.8 overall, 3.0 in major. Additional exam requirements/recommendations for international students: Required—TOEFL (minimum score 500 paper-based; 200 computer-based). *Application deadline:* For fall admission, 7/1 for domestic students; for spring admission, 11/1 for domestic students. Applications are processed on a rolling basis. Application fee: $40. *Expenses:* Tuition, area resident: Part-time $285 per credit hour. Tuition, nonresident: part-time $715 per credit hour. Required fees: $94 per semester. *Financial support:* In 2006–07, 1 student received support, including 1 research assistantship with partial tuition reimbursement available (averaging $9,000 per year); career-related internships or fieldwork and scholarships/grants also available. Financial award application deadline: 4/15; financial award applicants required to submit FAFSA. *Faculty research:* Ethnicity and recreation, recreation programming, recreation and resiliency, tourism development, dog parks, recreation and diabetes. Total annual research expenditures: $12,000. *Unit head:* Dr. Edward Lee Hill, Graduate Program Director, 757-683-4881, Fax: 757-683-4270, E-mail: ehill@odu.edu. *Application contact:* Dr. Edward Lee Hill, Graduate Program Director, 757-683-4881, Fax: 757-683-4270, E-mail: ehill@odu.edu.

Penn State University Park, Graduate School, College of Health and Human Development, Department of Recreation, Park and Tourism Management, State College, University Park, PA 16802-1503. Offers leisure studies (MS, PhD); recreation, park and tourism management (M Ed). *Unit head:* Dr. John P. Dattilo, Head, 814-863-0720, E-mail: jxd8@psu.edu.

San Francisco State University, Division of Graduate Studies, College of Health and Human Services, Department of Recreation and Leisure Studies, San Francisco, CA 94132-1722. Offers recreation (MS). Part-time programs available. *Faculty:* 3 full-time (1 woman). *Entrance requirements:* For master's, minimum GPA of 2.5 in last 60 units. *Application deadline:* For fall admission, 11/30 priority date for domestic students. Applications are processed on a rolling basis. Application fee: $55. *Financial support:* Career-related internships or fieldwork available. Financial award application deadline: 3/1. *Faculty research:* Leisure systems, leisure education, play theory and leadership, ethnic and cultural diversity, commercial recreation and tourism. *Unit head:* Dr. James Murphy, Chair, 415-338-2030. *Application contact:* Dr. Rene Dahl, Graduate Coordinator, 415-338-7575, E-mail: rdahl@sfsu.edu.

San Jose State University, Graduate Studies and Research, College of Applied Sciences and Arts, Department of Hospitality, Recreation and Tourism Management, San Jose, CA 95192-0001. Offers recreation (MS). *Students:* 13 full-time (9 women), 10 part-time (7 women); includes 5 minority (1 African American, 1 Asian American or Pacific Islander, 3 Hispanic Americans), 6 international. Average age 31. 18 applicants, 61% accepted, 8 enrolled. In 2006, 4 degrees awarded. *Application deadline:* For fall admission, 6/27 for domestic students; for spring admission, 11/30 for domestic students. Applications are processed on a rolling basis. Application fee: $59. Electronic applications accepted. *Financial support:* Applicants required to submit FAFSA. *Unit head:* Jill Cody, Chair, 408-924-3000, Fax: 408-924-3061.

South Dakota State University, Graduate School, College of Arts and Science, Department of Health, Physical Education and Recreation, Brookings, SD 57007. Offers MS. Part-time programs available. *Faculty:* 4 full-time (1 woman), 1 part-time/adjunct (0 women). *Students:* 13 full-time (5 women), 12 part-time (2 women); includes 1 minority (African American) In 2006, 12 degrees awarded. *Degree requirements:* For master's, thesis, oral and written exams. *Entrance requirements:* For master's, GRE. Additional exam requirements/recommendations for international students: Required—TOEFL (minimum score 550 paper-based; 213 computer-based). *Application deadline:* For fall admission, 10/15 priority date for domestic students, 4/15 for international students; for spring admission, 3/15 for domestic students, 8/15 for international students. Applications are processed on a rolling basis. Application fee: $35. *Financial support:* In 2006–07, 1 research assistantship with partial tuition reimbursement (averaging $15,750 per year), 9 teaching assistantships with partial tuition reimbursements (averaging $15,750 per year) were awarded; career-related internships or fieldwork, Federal Work-Study, scholarships/grants, and unspecified assistantships also available. *Faculty research:* Effective teaching behaviors in physical education, sports nutrition, muscle/bone interaction, hormonal response to exercise. *Unit head:* Fred Oien, Head, 605-688-4668, Fax: 605-688-6446, E-mail: fred.oien@sdstate.edu. *Application contact:* Dr. Mathew Vukovich, Graduate Coordinator, 605-688-4668, Fax: 605-688-6446, E-mail: matt.vukovich@sdstate.edu.

Southern Connecticut State University, School of Graduate Studies, School of Health and Human Services, Department of Recreation and Leisure Studies, New Haven, CT 06515-1355. Offers MS. Part-time and evening/weekend programs available. *Faculty:* 2 full-time, 1 part-time/adjunct. *Students:* 11 full-time (8 women), 22 part-time (12 women); includes 2 minority (1 Asian American or Pacific Islander, 1 Hispanic American). 13 applicants, 77% accepted, 9 enrolled. In 2006, 10 degrees awarded. *Degree requirements:* For master's, thesis or alternative. *Entrance requirements:* For master's, interview, minimum undergraduate QPA of 3.0 in graduate major field or 2.5 overall. *Application deadline:* For fall admission, 7/15 priority date for domestic students. Applications are processed on a rolling basis. Application fee: $50. Electronic applications accepted. *Financial support:* In 2006–07, 1 teaching assistantship was awarded; career-related internships or fieldwork also available. Financial award application deadline: 4/15; financial award applicants required to submit FAFSA. *Unit head:* Dr. Robert Cipriano, Chairperson, 203-392-6387, Fax: 203-392-6965, E-mail: cipriano@southernct.edu. *Application contact:* Dr. James MacGregor, Graduate Coordinator, 203-392-6385, Fax: 203-392-6147, E-mail: macgregorj1@southernct.edu.

Southern Illinois University Carbondale, Graduate School, College of Education, Department of Health Education and Recreation, Program in Recreation, Carbondale, IL 62901-4701. Offers MS Ed. Part-time programs available. *Faculty:* 5 full-time (2 women). *Students:* 7 full-time (1 woman), 8 part-time (1 woman); includes 2 minority (1 African American, 1 American Indian/Alaska Native), 2 international. Average age 26. 16 applicants, 38% accepted, 2 enrolled. In 2006, 9 degrees awarded. *Degree requirements:* For master's, thesis. *Entrance requirements:* For master's, minimum GPA of 2.7. Additional exam requirements/recommendations for international students: Required—TOEFL. *Application deadline:* Applications are processed on a rolling basis. Application fee: $20. *Financial support:* In 2006–07, 15 students received support, including 4 research assistantships with full tuition reimbursements available, 4 teaching assistantships with full tuition reimbursements available; fellowships with full tuition reimbursements available, career-related internships or fieldwork, Federal Work-Study, institutionally sponsored loans, and tuition waivers (full) also available. Support available to part-time students. Financial award application deadline: 2/1. *Faculty research:* Leisure across the life span, outdoor recreation, recreation therapy, leisure service administration. *Application contact:* Carol Reynolds, Administrative Assistant, 618-453-2415, Fax: 618-453-1829, E-mail: creynolds@siu.edu.

Southern University and Agricultural and Mechanical College, Graduate School, College of Education, Program in Leisure and Recreation Studies, Baton Rouge, LA 70813. Offers therapeutic recreation (MS). *Degree requirements:* For master's, thesis optional. *Entrance requirements:* For master's, GMAT or GRE General Test. Additional exam requirements/recommendations for international students: Required—TOEFL (minimum score 525 paper-based; 193 computer-based).

Southwestern Oklahoma State University, College of Professional and Graduate Studies, School of Behavioral Sciences and Education, Specialization in Parks and Recreation Management, Weatherford, OK 73096-3098. Offers M Ed.

Springfield College, Graduate Programs, Programs in Sport Management and Recreation, Springfield, MA 01109-3797. Offers outdoor recreational management (M Ed, MS); recreational management (M Ed, MS); sport management (M Ed, MS); therapeutic recreational management (M Ed, MS). Part-time and evening/weekend programs available. *Faculty:* 5 full-time (1 woman), 6 part-time/adjunct (4 women). *Students:* 43. Average age 26. 31 applicants, 84% accepted, 20 enrolled. In 2006, 22 degrees awarded. *Degree requirements:* For master's, research project or thesis. *Entrance requirements:* Additional exam requirements/recommendations for international students: Required—TOEFL (minimum score 550 paper-based; 213 computer-based). *Application deadline:* For fall admission, 1/15 for domestic students; for winter admission, 11/1 for domestic students; for spring admission, 12/1 for domestic students. Applications are processed on a rolling basis. Application fee: $50. Electronic applications accepted. *Expenses:* Tuition: Full-time $12,222; part-time $679 per credit. Required fees: $25; $25 per year. One-time fee: $25 full-time. *Financial support:* In 2006–07, 2 teaching assistantships with partial tuition reimbursements were awarded; fellowships with partial tuition reimbursements, career-related internships or fieldwork, Federal Work-Study, institutionally sponsored loans, and tuition waivers (full and partial) also available. Financial award application deadline: 3/1. *Faculty research:* Leisure behavior, public relations, therapeutic recreation in the community, outdoor recreation, leadership. *Unit head:* Dr. Donald R. Snyder, Director, 413-748-3272, Fax: 413-748-3685, E-mail: donald_snyder@spfldcol.edu. *Application contact:* Donald James Shaw, Director of Graduate Admissions, 413-748-3060, Fax: 413-748-3069, E-mail: donald_shaw_jr@spfldcol.edu.

State University of New York College at Brockport, School of Professions, Department of Recreation and Leisure Studies, Brockport, NY 14420-2997. Offers MS. Part-time programs available. *Students:* 9 full-time (4 women), 8 part-time (all women); includes 4 minority (3 African Americans, 1 Hispanic American), 1 international. 8 applicants, 88% accepted, 7 enrolled. In 2006, 11 degrees awarded. *Degree requirements:* For master's, thesis or alternative. *Entrance requirements:* For master's, minimum GPA of 3.0, letters of recommendation, written critical analysis. Additional exam requirements/recommendations for international students: Required—TOEFL (minimum score 550 paper-based; 213 computer-based; 80 iBT). *Application deadline:* For fall admission, 7/15 for domestic and international students; for spring admission, 11/15 for domestic and international students. Application fee: $50. *Expenses:* Tuition, state resident: full-time $6,900; part-time $288 per credit. Tuition, nonresident: full-time $10,920; part-time $455 per credit. *Financial support:* In 2006–07, 1 fellowship with tuition reimbursement (averaging $7,500 per year) was awarded; career-related internships or fieldwork, Federal Work-Study, scholarships/grants, and unspecified assistantships also available. Support available to part-time students. Financial award application deadline: 3/15; financial award applicants required to submit FAFSA. *Faculty research:* Leisure service delivery systems; therapeutic recreation; international issues in recreation and leisure; tourism; customer service, customer behavior and perceived value/satisfaction; leisure motivation among Baby Boomers. *Unit head:* Dr. Joel Frater, Chair, 585-395-2994, E-mail: jfrater@brockport.edu.

Recreation and Park Management

State University of New York College at Cortland, Graduate Studies, School of Professional Studies, Department of Recreation and Leisure Studies, Cortland, NY 13045. Offers MS, MS Ed. Part-time and evening/weekend programs available. *Degree requirements:* For master's, thesis (for some programs), comprehensive exam. *Entrance requirements:* Additional exam requirements/recommendations for international students: Required—TOEFL.

State University of New York College of Environmental Science and Forestry, Faculty of Forest and Natural Resources Management, Syracuse, NY 13210-2779. Offers environmental and natural resource policy (MS, PhD); environmental and natural resources policy (MPS); forest management and operations (MF); forestry ecosystems science and applications (MPS, MS, PhD); natural resources management (MPS, MS, PhD); quantitative methods and management in forest science (MPS, MS, PhD); recreation and resource management (MPS, MS, PhD); watershed management and forest hydrology (MPS, MS, PhD). *Faculty:* 25 full-time (6 women), 1 part-time/adjunct (0 women). *Students:* 42 full-time (18 women), 26 part-time (12 women); includes 4 minority (1 American Indian/Alaska Native, 2 Asian Americans or Pacific Islanders, 1 Hispanic American), 19 international. Average age 30. 62 applicants, 68% accepted, 20 enrolled. In 2006, 20 master's, 6 doctorates awarded. *Median time to degree:* Of those who began their doctoral program in fall 1998, 50% received their degree in 8 years or less. *Degree requirements:* For master's, thesis (for some programs), registration; for doctorate, thesis/dissertation, comprehensive exam, registration. *Entrance requirements:* For master's and doctorate, GRE General Test, minimum GPA of 3.0. Additional exam requirements/recommendations for international students: Required—TOEFL (minimum score 550 paper-based; 213 computer-based; 80 iBT), IELTS (minimum score 6). *Application deadline:* For fall admission, 2/1 priority date for domestic and international students; for spring admission, 11/1 priority date for domestic and international students. Applications are processed on a rolling basis. Application fee: $60. *Financial support:* In 2006–07, 43 students received support, including 5 fellowships with full and partial tuition reimbursements available (averaging $10,500 per year), 13 research assistantships with full and partial tuition reimbursements available (averaging $12,500 per year), 25 teaching assistantships with full and partial tuition reimbursements available (averaging $12,500 per year); career-related internships or fieldwork, Federal Work-Study, institutionally sponsored loans, scholarships/grants, health care benefits, and unspecified assistantships also available. Financial award application deadline: 6/30; financial award applicants required to submit FAFSA. *Faculty research:* Silviculture recreation management, tree improvement, operations management, economics. Total annual research expenditures: $2.1 million. *Unit head:* Dr. David Newman, Chair, 315-470-6536, Fax: 315-470-6535. *Application contact:* Dr. Dudley J. Raynal, Dean, Instruction and Graduate Studies, 315-470-6599, Fax: 315-470-6978, E-mail: esfgrad@esf.edu.

Temple University, Graduate School, School of Tourism and Hospitality Management, Program in Sport and Recreation Administration, Philadelphia, PA 19122-6096. Offers Ed M. Part-time and evening/weekend programs available. *Faculty:* 5 full-time (2 women). *Students:* 44 full-time (27 women), 34 part-time (13 women); includes 17 minority (all African Americans), 3 international. 98 applicants, 48% accepted, 27 enrolled. In 2006, 36 degrees awarded. *Entrance requirements:* For master's, GRE General Test or MAT, minimum undergraduate GPA of 3.0. Additional exam requirements/recommendations for international students: Required—TOEFL (minimum score 550 paper-based; 213 computer-based; 79 iBT). *Application deadline:* For fall admission, 4/15 priority date for domestic students, 12/15 for international students; for spring admission, 9/30 priority date for domestic students, 8/1 for international students. Application fee: $50. Electronic applications accepted. *Expenses:* Tuition, state resident: full-time $12,264; part-time $511 per credit. Tuition, nonresident: full-time $17,904; part-time $746 per credit. Required fees: $84 per course. Tuition and fees vary according to program. *Financial support:* Teaching assistantships available. Financial award application deadline: 1/15; financial award applicants required to submit FAFSA. *Unit head:* Dr. Michael W. Jackson, Director, 215-204-6298, Fax: 215-204-8705, E-mail: pierre@temple.edu.

See Close-Up on page 507.

Temple University, Health Sciences Center and Graduate School, College of Health Professions, Department of Therapeutic Recreation, Philadelphia, PA 19122-6096. Offers Ed M. Part-time and evening/weekend programs available. *Faculty:* 12 full-time (8 women). *Students:* 2 full-time (both women), 5 part-time (all women). 4 applicants, 75% accepted, 1 enrolled. In 2006, 3 degrees awarded. *Degree requirements:* For master's, thesis optional. *Entrance requirements:* For master's, GRE or MAT. Additional exam requirements/recommendations for international students: Required—TOEFL (minimum score 550 paper-based; 213 computer-based; 79 iBT). *Application deadline:* For fall admission, 6/1 for domestic students, 12/15 for international students; for spring admission, 10/15 for domestic students, 8/1 for international students. Applications are processed on a rolling basis. Application fee: $50. Electronic applications accepted. *Expenses:* Tuition, state resident: full-time $12,264; part-time $511 per credit. Tuition, nonresident: full-time $17,904; part-time $746 per credit. Required fees: $84 per course. Tuition and fees vary according to program. *Financial support:* Research assistantships with tuition reimbursements, teaching assistantships with tuition reimbursements, unspecified assistantships available. Financial award application deadline: 1/15; financial award applicants required to submit FAFSA. *Faculty research:* Quality of life, curriculum issues, disability issues, adaptive equipment/technology. *Unit head:* Dr. John Shank, Chair, 215-204-6278, Fax: 215-204-1386, E-mail: jshank@temple.edu.

Texas A&M University, College of Agriculture and Life Sciences, Department of Recreation, Park and Tourism Sciences, College Station, TX 77843. Offers natural resources development (M Agr); recreation resources development (M Agr); recreation, park, and tourism sciences (MS, PhD). *Faculty:* 12 full-time (3 women), 4 part-time/adjunct (1 woman). *Students:* 63 full-time (41 women), 18 part-time (10 women); includes 12 minority (5 African Americans, 1 American Indian/Alaska Native, 1 Asian American or Pacific Islander, 5 Hispanic Americans), 33 international. Average age 28. 51 applicants, 59% accepted, 20 enrolled. In 2006, 5 master's, 4 doctorates awarded. *Degree requirements:* For master's, thesis (for some programs), internship and professional paper (M Agr); for doctorate, thesis/dissertation. *Entrance requirements:* For master's and doctorate, GRE General Test. Additional exam requirements/recommendations for international students: Required—TOEFL. *Application deadline:* For fall admission, 4/15 priority date for domestic students; for spring admission, 10/15 priority date for domestic students. Applications are processed on a rolling basis. Application fee: $50 ($75 for international students). Electronic applications accepted. *Expenses:* Tuition, state resident: full-time $4,697; part-time $196 per semester hour. Tuition, nonresident: full-time $11,297; part-time $471 per semester hour. Required fees: $2,272; $2,272 per year. *Financial support:* Fellowships, research assistantships, teaching assistantships, career-related internships or fieldwork, institutionally sponsored loans, and scholarships/grants available. Financial award application deadline: 4/15; financial award applicants required to submit FAFSA. *Faculty research:* Administration and tourism, outdoor recreation, commercial recreation, environmental law, system planning. *Unit head:* Dr. Joseph T. O'Leary, Head, 979-845-5412, Fax: 979-845-0446, E-mail: joleary@rpts.tamu.edu. *Application contact:* Marguerite M. Van Dyke, Graduate Recruitment Coordinator, 979-845-5412, Fax: 979-845-0446, E-mail: mvandyke@rpts.tamu.edu.

Texas State University-San Marcos, Graduate School, College of Education, Department of Health, Physical Education, and Recreation, Program in Recreation and Leisure Services, San Marcos, TX 78666. Offers MSRLS. *Faculty:* 2 full-time (1 woman). *Students:* 13 full-time (10 women), 12 part-time (6 women); includes 4 minority (1 African American, 3 Hispanic Americans). Average age 28. 8 applicants, 100% accepted, 6 enrolled. In 2006, 6 degrees awarded. *Degree requirements:* For master's, thesis optional. *Entrance requirements:* For master's, GRE General Test, minimum GPA of 2.75 in last 60 hours of course work. Additional exam requirements/recommendations for international students: Required—TOEFL. *Application deadline:* For fall admission, 6/15 priority date for domestic students; for spring admission, 10/15 priority date for domestic students. Applications are processed on a rolling basis. Application fee: $40 ($90 for international students). *Financial support:* In 2006–07, 16 students received support, including 6 research assistantships (averaging $8,331 per year), 2 teaching assistantships (averaging $11,502 per year). Financial award application deadline: 4/1; financial award applicants required to submit FAFSA. *Unit head:* Dr. Tom Gustafson, Graduate Advisor, 512-245-2972, Fax: 512-245-8678, E-mail: tg08@txstate.edu.

Texas State University-San Marcos, Graduate School, Interdisciplinary Studies Program in Health, Physical Education, and Recreation, San Marcos, TX 78666. Offers MAIS. Part-time and evening/weekend programs available. *Degree requirements:* For master's, thesis or alternative, comprehensive exam. *Entrance requirements:* For master's, GRE General Test, minimum GPA of 2.75 in last 60 hours of course work. Additional exam requirements/recommendations for international students: Required—TOEFL. *Application deadline:* For fall admission, 6/15 priority date for domestic students; for spring admission, 10/15 priority date for domestic students. Applications are processed on a rolling basis. Application fee: $40 ($90 for international students). *Financial support:* Career-related internships or fieldwork, Federal Work-Study, and institutionally sponsored loans available. Support available to part-time students. Financial award application deadline: 4/1; financial award applicants required to submit FAFSA. *Unit head:* Dr. John Walker, Head, 512-245-8106, Fax: 512-245-8678, E-mail: jw18@txstate.edu. *Application contact:* Dr. J. Michael Willoughby, Dean of Graduate School, 512-245-2581, Fax: 512-245-8365, E-mail: gradcollege@txstate.edu.

Universidad Metropolitana, Graduate Programs in Education, Program in Managing Leisure Services, San Juan, PR 00928-1150. Offers MA. Part-time programs available. *Degree requirements:* For master's, thesis or alternative. *Entrance requirements:* For master's, EXADEP, interview. Electronic applications accepted.

University of Alberta, Faculty of Graduate Studies and Research, Faculty of Physical Education and Recreation, Edmonton, AB T6G 2E1, Canada. Offers physical education (M Sc); recreation and physical education (MA, PhD). Part-time programs available. *Faculty:* 30 full-time (10 women). *Students:* 60 full-time (34 women), 55 part-time (28 women), 10 international. 69 applicants, 36% accepted. In 2006, 13 master's, 7 doctorates awarded. Terminal master's awarded for partial completion of doctoral program. *Degree requirements:* For master's, thesis (for some programs); for doctorate, thesis/dissertation. *Entrance requirements:* For master's, bachelor's degree in related field; for doctorate, master's degree in related field with thesis. Additional exam requirements/recommendations for international students: Required—TOEFL. *Application deadline:* For fall admission, 1/1 priority date for domestic students. Applications are processed on a rolling basis. *Financial support:* In 2006–07, 63 students received support, including 28 research assistantships, 35 teaching assistantships; career-related internships or fieldwork and scholarships/grants also available. Support available to part-time students. *Faculty research:* Motivation and adherence to physical ability, performance enhancement, adapted physical activity, exercise physiology, sport administration, tourism. *Unit head:* Dr. D. Marshall, Assistant Dean, 780-492-3198, Fax: 403-492-2364. *Application contact:* Anne Jordan, Department Office, 403-492-3198, Fax: 403-492-2364, E-mail: pergrad@ualberta.ca.

University of Arkansas, Graduate School, College of Education and Health Professions, Department of Health Science, Kinesiology, Recreation and Dance, Program in Recreation, Fayetteville, AR 72701-1201. Offers M Ed, Ed D. *Students:* 20 full-time (9 women), 19 part-time (10 women); includes 6 minority (5 African Americans, 1 Hispanic American). 22 applicants, 55% accepted. In 2006, 17 degrees awarded. *Degree requirements:* For master's, thesis optional; for doctorate, thesis/dissertation. *Entrance requirements:* For doctorate, GRE General Test. Application fee: $40 ($50 for international students). *Financial support:* In 2006–07, 3 fellowships with tuition reimbursements, 1 teaching assistantship were awarded; research assistantships, career-related internships or fieldwork and Federal Work-Study also available. Support available to part-time students. Financial award application deadline: 4/1; financial award applicants required to submit FAFSA. *Application contact:* Dr. Dean Gorman, Coordinator of Graduate Studies, 479-575-6625, E-mail: dgorman@comp.uark.edu.

University of Florida, Graduate School, College of Health and Human Performance, Department of Tourism, Recreation and Sport Management, Gainesville, FL 32611. Offers health and human performance (PhD), including natural resource recreation (MS, PhD), sport management (MS, PhD), therapeutic recreation (MS, PhD), tourism; recreational studies (MS), including campus recreation programming and administration, natural resource recreation (MS, PhD), recreation administration and supervision, sport management (MS, PhD), therapeutic recreation (MS, PhD), tourism and commercial recreation. *Faculty:* 17 full-time (5 women). *Students:* 71 (23 women); includes 11 minority (6 African Americans, 1 American Indian/Alaska Native, 4 Hispanic Americans) 5 international. Average age 33. In 2006, 35 degrees awarded. *Degree requirements:* For master's, thesis optional. *Entrance requirements:* For master's, GRE General Test, minimum GPA of 3.0. Additional exam requirements/recommendations for international students: Required—TOEFL (minimum score 550 paper-based; 213 computer-based). *Application deadline:* For fall admission, 6/1 priority date for domestic students. Applications are processed on a rolling basis. Application fee: $30. Electronic applications accepted. *Expenses:* Tuition, state resident: full-time $6,827. Tuition, nonresident: full-time $21,951. Required fees: $999. *Financial support:* In 2006–07, 19 research assistantships (averaging $8,932 per year), 9 teaching assistantships (averaging $9,441 per year) were awarded; fellowships, career-related internships or fieldwork, Federal Work-Study, and unspecified assistantships also available. *Faculty research:* Recreation resource planning, commercial recreation, campus recreation. *Unit head:* Dr. Stephen M. Holland, Chair, 352-392-4042 Ext. 1313, Fax: 352-392-7588, E-mail: sholland@hhp.ufl.edu. *Application contact:* Dr. Myron F. Floyd, Coordinator, 352-392-4042 Ext. 1242, Fax: 352-392-7588, E-mail: mfloyd@hhp.ufl.edu.

University of Idaho, College of Graduate Studies, College of Education, Department of Health, Physical Education, Recreation, and Dance, Program in Recreation, Moscow, ID 83844-2282. Offers MS. *Students:* 21 (6 women). Average age 26. In 2006, 10 degrees awarded. *Entrance requirements:* For master's, minimum GPA of 2.8. *Application deadline:* For fall admission, 8/1 for domestic students; for spring admission, 12/15 for domestic students. Application fee: $55 ($60 for international students). *Expenses:* Tuition, nonresident: full-time $9,600; part-time $140 per credit. Required fees: $4,740; $227 per credit. *Financial support:* Research assistantships available. Financial award application deadline: 2/15. *Unit head:* Dr. Kathy Browder, Chair, Department of Health, Physical Education, Recreation, and Dance, 208-885-2192.

The University of Iowa, Graduate College, College of Liberal Arts and Sciences, Program in Leisure Studies, Iowa City, IA 52242-1316. Offers leisure and recreational sport management (MA); therapeutic recreation (MA). *Faculty:* 4 full-time, 1 part-time/adjunct. *Students:* 16 full-time (11 women), 5 part-time (1 woman); includes 2 minority (both African Americans), 1 international. 21 applicants, 86% accepted, 16 enrolled. In 2006, 6 degrees awarded. *Degree requirements:* For master's, exam, thesis optional. *Entrance requirements:* For master's, GRE General Test, minimum GPA of 3.0. Additional exam requirements/recommendations for international students: Required—TOEFL (minimum score 550 paper-based; 213 computer-based; 81 iBT). *Application deadline:* For spring admission, 11/15 priority date for domestic students. Applications are processed on a rolling basis. Application fee: $60 ($85 for international students). Electronic applications accepted. *Financial support:* In 2006–07, 16 teaching assistantships with partial tuition reimbursements were awarded; fellowships, research assistantships with partial tuition reimbursements also available. Financial award applicants required to submit FAFSA. *Unit head:* Kenneth Mobily, Academic Coordinator, 319-335-0172, Fax: 319-335-3884.

University of Manitoba, Faculty of Graduate Studies, Faculty of Physical Education and Recreation Studies, Winnipeg, MB R3T 2N2, Canada. Offers M Sc.

University of Minnesota, Twin Cities Campus, Graduate School, College of Education and Human Development, School of Kinesiology, Division of Recreation, Park, and Leisure Studies, Minneapolis, MN 55455-0213. Offers M Ed, MA, PhD. Part-time programs available. *Students:* 29 full-time (17 women), 8 part-time (4 women); includes 1 minority (American Indian/Alaska Native), 8 international. Average age 32. 34 applicants, 50% accepted, 12 enrolled. In 2006, 28 master's, 12 doctorates awarded. Terminal master's awarded for partial completion of doctoral program. *Degree requirements:* For master's, thesis (for some programs), final oral exam; for doctorate, thesis/dissertation, preliminary written/oral exam, final oral exam. *Entrance requirements:* For master's, GRE or MAT, minimum GPA of 3.0; for doctorate, GRE or MAT, minimum GPA of 3.0, writing sample. *Application deadline:* For fall admission, 7/15 for domestic students; for spring admission, 12/15 for domestic students. Applications are processed on a rolling basis. *Expenses:* Tuition, state resident: full-time $9,302; part-time $775 per credit. Tuition, nonresident: full-time $16,400; part-time $1,367 per credit. Full-time tuition and fees vary according to class time, course load, program, reciprocity agreements and student level. *Financial support:* Fellowships, research assistantships, teaching assistantships, career-related internships or fieldwork, Federal Work-Study, institutionally sponsored loans, and tuition waivers (full and partial) available. Support available to part-time students. *Application contact:* Dr. Mary Bents, Associate Dean, 612-625-6501, Fax: 612-626-1580, E-mail: mbents@tc.umn.edu.

University of Mississippi, Graduate School, School of Applied Sciences, Department of Health, Exercise Science, and Recreation Management, Oxford, University, MS 38677. Offers exercise science (MA, MS); exercise science and leisure management (PhD); leisure management (MA); park and recreation management (MA); wellness (MS). *Faculty:* 13 full-time (2 women), 4 part-time/adjunct (3 women). *Students:* 24 full-time (12 women), 7 part-time (4 women); includes 7 minority (5 African Americans, 2 Hispanic Americans), 2 international. In 2006, 9 master's, 4 doctorates awarded. *Degree requirements:* For master's, thesis (for some programs); for doctorate, thesis/dissertation. *Entrance requirements:* For master's, GRE General Test, minimum GPA of 3.0; for doctorate, GRE General Test. Additional exam requirements/recommendations for international students: Required—TOEFL. *Application deadline:* For fall admission, 4/1 for domestic students; for spring admission, 10/1 for domestic students. Applications are processed on a rolling basis. Application fee: $25. *Expenses:* Tuition, state resident: full-time $4,602; part-time $256 per credit hour. Tuition, nonresident: full-time $10,566; part-time $587 per credit hour. *Financial support:* Scholarships/grants available. Financial award application deadline: 3/1; financial award applicants required to submit FAFSA. *Unit head:* Dr. James Gilbert, Interim Chair, 662-915-5521, Fax: 662-915-5525, E-mail: dgilbert@olemiss.edu.

University of Missouri–Columbia, Graduate School, School of Natural Resources, Department of Parks, Recreation and Tourism, Columbia, MO 65211. Offers MS. *Faculty:* 3 full-time (0 women). *Students:* 8 full-time (3 women), 3 part-time (1 woman), 1 international. In 2006, 7 degrees awarded. *Entrance requirements:* For master's, GRE General Test, minimum GPA of 3.0. Additional exam requirements/recommendations for international students: Required—TOEFL (minimum score 500 paper-based; 173 computer-based). *Application deadline:* Applications are processed on a rolling basis. Application fee: $45 ($60 for international students). *Financial support:* Research assistantships, teaching assistantships, institutionally sponsored loans and scholarships/grants available. *Unit head:* Dr. Randy Vessell, Director of Graduate Studies, 573-882-9515, E-mail: vessellc@missouri.edu.

The University of Montana, Graduate School, College of Forestry and Conservation, Missoula, MT 59812-0002. Offers ecosystem management (MEM, MS); fish and wildlife biology (PhD); forestry (MS, PhD); recreation management (MS); resource conservation (MS); wildlife biology (MS). *Degree requirements:* For doctorate, thesis/dissertation. *Entrance requirements:* For master's and doctorate, GRE General Test. Additional exam requirements/recommendations for international students: Required—TOEFL (minimum score 575 paper-based; 213 computer-based).

University of Nebraska at Omaha, Graduate Studies and Research, College of Education, School of Health, Physical Education, and Recreation, Omaha, NE 68182. Offers MA, MS. Part-time and evening/weekend programs available. *Faculty:* 12 full-time (2 women). *Students:* 49 full-time (28 women), 52 part-time (37 women); includes 7 minority (3 Asian Americans or Pacific Islanders, 4 Hispanic Americans), 7 international. Average age 28. 66 applicants, 55% accepted, 21 enrolled. In 2006, 31 degrees awarded. *Degree requirements:* For master's, thesis (for some programs), comprehensive exam. *Entrance requirements:* For master's, minimum GPA of 3.0, vary by concentration. Additional exam requirements/recommendations for international students: Required—TOEFL (minimum score 550 paper-based; 213 computer-based; 80 iBT). *Application deadline:* For fall admission, 7/1 priority date for domestic students; for spring admission, 12/1 priority date for domestic students. Applications are processed on a rolling basis. Application fee: $45. Electronic applications accepted. *Financial support:* In 2006–07, 71 students received support, including 8 research assistantships with tuition reimbursements available; fellowships, Federal Work-Study, institutionally sponsored loans, scholarships/grants, tuition waivers (full), and unspecified assistantships also available. Support available to part-time students. Financial award application deadline: 3/1; financial award applicants required to submit FAFSA. *Unit head:* Dr. Dan Blanke, Director, 402-554-2670.

University of Nebraska–Lincoln, Graduate College, College of Education and Human Services, Department of Health and Human Performance, Lincoln, NE 68588. Offers health, physical education, and recreation (M Ed, MPE). *Accreditation:* NCATE. *Degree requirements:* For master's, thesis (for some programs). *Entrance requirements:* For master's, curriculum vitae. Additional exam requirements/recommendations for international students: Required—TOEFL (minimum score 500 paper-based; 173 computer-based). Electronic applications accepted. *Faculty research:* Exercise science, health behaviors, fitness, teacher effectiveness.

University of New Brunswick Fredericton, School of Graduate Studies, Faculty of Kinesiology, Fredericton, NB E3B 5A3, Canada. Offers exercise and sport science (M Sc); sport and recreation administration (MA, MBA/MA); MBA/MA. Part-time programs available. *Faculty:* 16 full-time (6 women). *Students:* 45 full-time (20 women), 8 part-time (6 women). In 2006, 8 degrees awarded. *Degree requirements:* For master's, thesis (for some programs). *Entrance requirements:* For master's, minimum GPA of 3.0, written statement of research goals and interests. Additional exam requirements/recommendations for international students: Required—TOEFL (minimum score 600 paper-based; 250 computer-based), TWE (minimum score 5). *Application deadline:* For fall admission, 3/1 priority date for domestic students. Applications are processed on a rolling basis. Application fee: $50 Canadian dollars. Electronic applications accepted. *Financial support:* In 2006–07, 24 research assistantships, 23 teaching assistantships were awarded; fellowships with tuition reimbursements, career-related internships or fieldwork and scholarships/grants also available. *Unit head:* Dr. Chris Stevenson, Acting Director of Graduate Studies, 506-453-5063, Fax: 506-453-3511, E-mail: cls@unb.ca. *Application contact:* Linda O'Brien, Graduate Secretary, 506-453-4576, Fax: 506-453-3511, E-mail: lobrien@unb.ca.

University of New Hampshire, Graduate School, School of Health and Human Services, Department of Recreation Management and Policy, Durham, NH 03824. Offers recreation administration (MS); therapeutic recreation (MS). Part-time programs available. *Faculty:* 6 full-time. *Students:* 7 full-time (3 women), 8 part-time (6 women). Average age 27. 9 applicants, 89% accepted, 3 enrolled. In 2006, 9 degrees awarded. *Degree requirements:* For master's, thesis optional. *Entrance requirements:* For master's, GRE. Additional exam requirements/recommendations for international students: Required—TOEFL (minimum score 550 paper-based; 213 computer-based); Recommended—TWE. *Application deadline:* For fall admission, 4/1 priority date for domestic and international students. Application fee: $60. Electronic applications accepted. *Expenses:* Tuition, state resident: full-time $8,540; part-time $474 per credit hour. Tuition, nonresident: full-time $20,990; part-time $862 per credit hour. Required fees: $1,343; $356 per term. Tuition and fees vary according to course load, program and reciprocity agreements. *Financial support:* In 2006–07, 4 teaching assistantships were awarded; fellowships, research assistantships also available. *Unit head:* Dr. Janet Sable, Chairperson, 603-862-3401. *Application contact:* Louise Craig, Administrative Assistant, 603-862-2391, E-mail: rmp.graduate@unh.edu.

The University of North Carolina at Chapel Hill, Graduate School, College of Arts and Sciences, Department of Recreation and Leisure Studies, Chapel Hill, NC 27599. Offers MSRA. Part-time programs available. *Degree requirements:* For master's, thesis or alternative, comprehensive exam. *Entrance requirements:* For master's, GRE General Test, minimum GPA of 3.0. Additional exam requirements/recommendations for international students: Required—TOEFL. Electronic applications accepted. *Faculty research:* Leisure research related to gender, youth, inclusion, and family; social psychology of leisure; leisure democracy.

The University of North Carolina at Greensboro, Graduate School, School of Health and Human Performance, Department of Recreation, Tourism, and Hospitality Management, Greensboro, NC 27412-5001. Offers parks and recreation management (MS). *Faculty:* 10 full-time (5 women), 6 part-time/adjunct (all women). *Students:* 16 full-time (9 women), 5 part-time (2 women); includes 3 minority (1 African American, 2 Asian Americans or Pacific Islanders). 17 applicants, 53% accepted. *Degree requirements:* For master's, thesis. *Entrance requirements:* For master's, GRE General Test. Additional exam requirements/recommendations for international students: Required—TOEFL. *Application deadline:* For fall admission, 7/1 priority date for domestic students; for spring admission, 11/1 for domestic students. Applications are processed on a rolling basis. Application fee: $45. Electronic applications accepted. *Expenses:* Tuition, state resident: full-time $2,692. Tuition, nonresident: full-time $13,742. *Financial support:* Fellowships with full tuition reimbursements, research assistantships with full tuition reimbursements, teaching assistantships with full tuition reimbursements, career-related internships or fieldwork, Federal Work-Study, scholarships/grants, and traineeships available. Support available to part-time students. *Unit head:* Dr. Stuart J. Schelein, Head, 336-334-5327, Fax: 336-334-3238, E-mail: sjs@uncg.edu. *Application contact:* Michelle Harkleroad, Director of Graduate Admissions, 336-334-4884, Fax: 336-334-4424, E-mail: mbharkle@uncg.edu.

University of North Texas, Robert B. Toulouse School of Graduate Studies, College of Education, Department of Kinesiology, Health Promotion, and Recreation, Program in Recreation and Leisure Studies, Denton, TX 76203. Offers MS, Certificate. Part-time programs available. *Students:* 21 full-time (15 women), 11 part-time (8 women); includes 7 minority (2 African Americans, 5 Hispanic Americans), 1 international. Average age 25. 18 applicants, 83% accepted, 11 enrolled. In 2006, 7 degrees awarded. *Entrance requirements:* For master's, GRE General Test. Additional exam requirements/recommendations for international students: Recommended—TOEFL (minimum score 550 paper-based; 213 computer-based). *Application deadline:* For fall admission, 7/15 for domestic students. Application fee: $50 ($75 for international students). *Expenses:* Tuition, state resident: full-time $3,573; part-time $198 per credit. Tuition, nonresident: full-time $8,577; part-time $476 per credit. Required fees: $1,258; $126 per credit. One-time fee: $150 full-time. Tuition and fees vary according to course load. *Financial support:* Teaching assistantships, career-related internships or fieldwork, Federal Work-Study, and institutionally sponsored loans available. Financial award application deadline: 4/1. *Application contact:* Dr. John Collins, Adviser, 940-565-3422, Fax: 940-565-4904, E-mail: collins@unt.edu.

University of Rhode Island, Graduate School, College of Human Science and Services, Department of Kinesiology, Kingston, RI 02881. Offers exercise science (MS); physical education (MS); physical therapy (DPT); psychosocial aspects of physical activity and sport (MS); teaching and administration (MS). *Accreditation:* NCATE (one or more programs are accredited). In 2006, 14 degrees awarded. *Entrance requirements:* For master's, MAT or GRE. *Application deadline:* For fall admission, 4/15 priority date for domestic students; for spring admission, 11/15 for domestic students. Applications are processed on a rolling basis. Application fee: $35. *Expenses:* Tuition, state resident: full-time $6,032; part-time $335 per credit. Tuition, nonresident: full-time $17,288; part-time $960 per credit. Required fees: $65 per credit. $30 per semester. One-time fee: $80 part-time. *Financial support:* Career-related internships or fieldwork available. *Unit head:* Dr. Deborah Riebe, Chair, 401-874-5444.

University of South Alabama, Graduate School, College of Education, Department of Health, Physical Education and Leisure Services, Mobile, AL 36688-0002. Offers exercise science (MS); health education (M Ed); physical education (M Ed); therapeutic recreation (MS). *Accreditation:* NCATE (one or more programs are accredited). Part-time programs available. *Faculty:* 9 full-time (1 woman). *Students:* 26 full-time (18 women), 11 part-time (8 women); includes 11 minority (9 African Americans, 1 Asian American or Pacific Islander, 1 Hispanic American), 2 international. 12 applicants, 83% accepted, 5 enrolled. In 2006, 17 degrees awarded. *Degree requirements:* For master's, comprehensive exam. *Entrance requirements:* For master's, GRE General Test or MAT. *Application deadline:* For fall admission, 9/1 priority date for domestic students. Applications are processed on a rolling basis. Application fee: $25. *Financial support:* In 2006–07, 10 teaching assistantships were awarded; career-related internships or fieldwork also available. Support available to part-time students. Financial award application deadline: 4/1. *Unit head:* Dr. Frederick M. Scaffidi, Chair, 251-460-7131.

University of Southern Mississippi, Graduate School, College of Health, School of Human Performance and Recreation, Hattiesburg, MS 39406-0001. Offers human performance (MS, Ed D, PhD); interscholastic athletic administration (MS); recreation and leisure management (MS); sport administration (MS); sport and coaching education (MS); sport management (MS); sports and high performance materials (MS). Part-time and evening/weekend programs available. *Faculty:* 15 full-time (3 women). *Students:* 63 full-time (21 women), 36 part-time (11 women); includes 16 minority (13 African Americans, 1 Asian American or Pacific Islander, 2 Hispanic Americans), 6 international. Average age 27. 75 applicants, 64% accepted, 38 enrolled. In 2006, 37 master's, 5 doctorates awarded. *Degree requirements:* For master's, thesis optional; for doctorate, thesis/dissertation, comprehensive exam, registration. *Entrance requirements:* For master's, GRE General Test, minimum GPA of 2.75 in last 60 hours; for doctorate, GRE General Test, minimum GPA of 3.5. Additional exam requirements/recommendations for international students: Required—TOEFL. *Application deadline:* For fall admission, 3/1 priority date for domestic students, 3/1 for international students. Applications are processed on a rolling basis. Application fee: $25 ($30 for international students). Electronic applications accepted. *Financial support:* In 2006–07, 5 research assistantships with full tuition reimbursements (averaging $10,426 per year), 10 teaching assistantships with full tuition reimbursements (averaging $10,426 per year) were awarded; fellowships, career-related internships or fieldwork, Federal Work-Study, institutionally sponsored loans, and tuition waivers (partial) also available. Financial award application deadline: 3/15. *Faculty research:* Exercise physiology, health behaviors, resource management, activity interaction, site development. *Unit head:* Dr. Louis Marciani, Director, 601-266-5379, Fax: 601-266-4445. *Application contact:* Dr. Dennis Phillips, Graduate Coordinator, 601-266-5379, Fax: 601-266-4445.

The University of Tennessee, Graduate School, College of Education, Health and Human Sciences, Department of Exercise, Sport, and Leisure Studies, Knoxville, TN 37996. Offers exercise science (MS, PhD), including biomechanics/sports medicine, exercise physiology; recreation and leisure studies (MS); sport management (MS); sport studies (MS, PhD); therapeutic recreation (MS). Part-time and evening/weekend programs available. *Students:* 28 (21 women); includes 1 minority (African American) 4 international. In 2006, 5 degrees awarded. *Degree requirements:* For master's, thesis optional. *Entrance requirements:* For master's, minimum GPA of 2.7. Additional exam requirements/recommendations for international students: Required—TOEFL. *Application deadline:* For fall admission, 2/1 priority date for domestic students. Applications are processed on a rolling basis. Application fee: $35. Electronic applications accepted. *Expenses:* Tuition, state resident: full-time $5,574. Tuition, nonresident: full-time $16,840. Required fees: $792. *Financial support:* In 2006–07, 2 fellowships, 1 research assistantship, 24 teaching assistantships were awarded; career-related internships or fieldwork, Federal Work-Study, institutionally sponsored loans, and unspecified assistantships also available. Financial award application deadline: 2/1; financial award applicants required to submit FAFSA. *Unit head:* Dr. Edward Howley, Head, 865-974-8555, Fax: 865-974-5781, E-mail: ehowley@utk.edu.

University of Utah, The Graduate School, College of Health, Department of Parks, Recreation, and Tourism, Salt Lake City, UT 84112-1107. Offers M Phil, MS, Ed D, PhD. *Faculty:* 10 full-time (3 women). *Students:* 32 full-time (14 women), 32 part-time (18 women); includes 1 minority (Asian American or Pacific Islander), 6 international. Average age 33. 49 applicants,

Recreation and Park Management

University of Utah (continued)
39% accepted, 14 enrolled. In 2006, 13 master's, 4 doctorates awarded. Terminal master's awarded for partial completion of doctoral program. *Median time to degree:* Of those who began their doctoral program in fall 1998, 100% received their degree in 8 years or less. *Degree requirements:* For master's, thesis or alternative, comprehensive exam; for doctorate, thesis/dissertation. *Entrance requirements:* For master's, minimum GPA of 3.0; for doctorate, GRE General Test or MAT, minimum GPA of 3.2. Additional exam requirements/recommendations for international students: Required—TOEFL (minimum score 500 paper-based; 173 computer-based). *Application deadline:* For fall admission, 4/1 for domestic students, 2/15 for international students; for spring admission, 11/1 for domestic students. Application fee: $45 ($65 for international students). Electronic applications accepted. *Expenses:* Tuition, state resident: full-time $3,208. Tuition, nonresident: full-time $11,326. Required fees: $608. Tuition and fees vary according to class time and program. *Financial support:* Teaching assistantships with full tuition reimbursements, career-related internships or fieldwork available. Financial award application deadline: 2/15; financial award applicants required to submit FAFSA. *Faculty research:* Commercial, therapeutic, community, and outdoor recreation; tourism. Total annual research expenditures: $40,922. *Unit head:* Dr. Dan Dustin, Chair, 801-581-7560, E-mail: daniel.dustin@health.utah.edu. *Application contact:* Dr. Edward J. Ruddell, Director of Graduate Studies, 801-585-8085, Fax: 801-581-4930, E-mail: edward.ruddell@health.utah.edu.

University of Waterloo, Graduate Studies, Faculty of Applied Health Sciences, Department of Recreation and Leisure Studies, Waterloo, ON N2L 3G1, Canada. Offers MA, PhD. Part-time programs available. *Faculty:* 14 full-time (6 women), 8 part-time/adjunct (3 women). *Students:* 32 full-time (28 women), 7 part-time (3 women). 33 applicants, 42% accepted, 14 enrolled. In 2006, 4 master's, 2 doctorates awarded. *Degree requirements:* For master's, thesis/dissertation, registration; for doctorate, thesis/dissertation, comprehensive exam, registration. *Entrance requirements:* For master's, honors degree, minimum B average, writing sample, resumé; for doctorate, GRE (recommended), master's degree, minimum B average, writing sample, resumé. Additional exam requirements/recommendations for international students: Required—TOEFL, TWE. *Application deadline:* For fall admission, 2/1 for domestic and international students. Application fee: $75 Canadian dollars. Electronic applications accepted. *Financial support:* Research assistantships, teaching assistantships, career-related internships or fieldwork, Federal Work-Study, institutionally sponsored loans, and scholarships/grants available. *Faculty research:* Tourism, leisure behavior, special populations, leisure service management, outdoor resources, aging, health and well-being, work and health. *Application contact:* Tracy Taves, Graduate Studies Coordinator, 519-888-4567 Ext. 36149, Fax: 519-746-6776, E-mail: tltaves@uwaterloo.ca.

University of Wisconsin–La Crosse, Office of University Graduate Studies, College of Science and Health, Department of Recreation Management and Therapeutic Recreation, La Crosse, WI 54601-3742. Offers recreation (MS), including recreation administration, therapeutic recreation. Part-time programs available. *Faculty:* 7 full-time (4 women). *Students:* 23 full-time (15 women), 10 part-time (5 women); includes 1 minority (American Indian/Alaska Native), 4 international. Average age 28. 24 applicants, 92% accepted, 14 enrolled. In 2006, 6 degrees awarded. *Degree requirements:* For master's, thesis or alternative, graduate project or internship. *Entrance requirements:* Additional exam requirements/recommendations for international students: Required—TOEFL (minimum score 550 paper-based; 213 computer-based). *Application deadline:* For fall admission, 3/15 priority date for domestic students. Applications are processed on a rolling basis. Application fee: $45. Electronic applications accepted. *Financial support:* In 2006–07, 5 research assistantships with full tuition reimbursements (averaging $6,654 per year) were awarded; career-related internships or fieldwork, Federal Work-Study, health care benefits, unspecified assistantships, and grant-funded positions also available. Support available to part-time students. Financial award application deadline: 3/15; financial award applicants required to submit FAFSA. *Unit head:* Dr. Steve Simpson, Program Director, 608-785-8216, Fax: 608-785-8206, E-mail: simpson.stev@uwlax.edu. *Application contact:* Kathryn Kiefer, Associate Director of Admissions, 608-785-8939, E-mail: admissions@uwlax.edu.

University of Wisconsin–Madison, Graduate School, College of Agricultural and Life Sciences, School of Natural Resources, Recreation Resources Management Program, Madison, WI 53706-1380. Offers MS.

Utah State University, School of Graduate Studies, College of Natural Resources, Department of Environment and Society, Logan, UT 84322. Offers bioregional planning (MS); geography (MA, MS); human dimensions of ecosystem science and management (MS, PhD); recreation resource management (MS, PhD). *Faculty:* 13 full-time (3 women). *Students:* 8 full-time (2 women), 11 part-time (5 women), 2 international. Average age 32. 18 applicants, 67% accepted, 10 enrolled. In 2006, 19 master's, 1 doctorate awarded. *Degree requirements:* For master's, thesis (for some programs), comprehensive exam. *Entrance requirements:* For master's and doctorate, GRE General Test, minimum GPA of 3.0. Additional exam requirements/recommendations for international students: Required—TOEFL. *Application deadline:* For fall admission, 6/15 for domestic students; for spring admission, 10/15 priority date for domestic students. Applications are processed on a rolling basis. Application fee: $50 ($60 for international students). Electronic applications accepted. *Financial support:* In 2006–07, 21 research assistantships with partial tuition reimbursements (averaging $11,000 per year), 5 teaching assistantships with partial tuition reimbursements (averaging $10,000 per year) were awarded; fellowships with partial tuition reimbursements, career-related internships or fieldwork, Federal Work-Study, tuition waivers (full and partial), and unspecified assistantships also available. Financial award applicants required to submit FAFSA. *Faculty research:* Geographic information systems/geographic and environmental education, bioregional planning, natural resource and environmental policy, outdoor recreation and tourism, natural resource and environmental management. Total annual research expenditures: $1.4 million. *Unit head:* Dr. Terry L. Sharik, Head and Professor, 435-797-3270, Fax: 435-797-4048, E-mail: tlsharik@cc.usu.edu. *Application contact:* Becky D. Hirst, Staff Assistant, 435-797-3781, Fax: 435-797-4048, E-mail: becky.hirst@usu.edu.

Virginia Commonwealth University, Graduate School, School of Education, Program in Recreation, Parks and Sports Leadership, Richmond, VA 23284-9005. Offers MS. *Faculty:* 2 full-time (0 women). *Students:* 66 applicants, 80% accepted, 43 enrolled. In 2006, 56 degrees awarded. *Entrance requirements:* For master's, GRE General Test or MAT. *Application deadline:* For fall admission, 5/15 for domestic students; for spring admission, 11/15 for domestic students. Applications are processed on a rolling basis. Application fee: $50. *Financial support:* Tuition waivers (full and partial) available. Financial award application deadline: 3/1. *Unit head:* Dr. Jack Schiltz, Chair, 804-828-1130. *Application contact:* Dr. Michael D. Davis, Director, Graduate Studies, 804-828-6530, Fax: 804-827-0676, E-mail: mddavis@vcu.edu.

See Close-Up on page 2283.

Virginia Polytechnic Institute and State University, Graduate School, College of Natural Resources, Department of Forestry, Blacksburg, VA 24061. Offers forest biology (MF, MS, PhD); forest biometry (MF, MS, PhD); forest management/economics (MF, MS, PhD); industrial forestry operations (MF, MS, PhD); outdoor recreation (MF, MS, PhD). *Entrance requirements:* For master's and doctorate, GRE General Test. Additional exam requirements/recommendations for international students: Required—TOEFL (minimum score 550 paper-based; 213 computer-based). *Application deadline:* For fall admission, 5/15 for international students; for spring admission, 10/15 for international students. Applications are processed on a rolling basis. Application fee: $45. Electronic applications accepted. *Financial support:* Research assistantships with full tuition reimbursements, teaching assistantships with full tuition reimbursements, career-related internships or fieldwork, Federal Work-Study, scholarships/grants, and unspecified assistantships available. Financial award application deadline: 4/1. *Unit head:* Dr. Harold E. Burkhart, Head, 540-231-6952, Fax: 540-231-3698, E-mail: burkhart@vt.edu. *Application contact:* Sue Snow, Information Contact, 540-231-5483, Fax: 540-231-3698, E-mail: suesnow@vt.edu.

Wayne State University, College of Education, Division of Kinesiology, Health and Sports Studies, Detroit, MI 48202. Offers health education (M Ed); kinesiology (M Ed); physical education (M Ed); recreation and park services (MA); sports administration (MA). *Faculty:* 9 full-time (2 women). *Students:* 40 full-time (16 women), 73 part-time (24 women); includes 25 minority (22 African Americans, 1 Asian American or Pacific Islander, 2 Hispanic Americans), 6 international. Average age 31. 39 applicants, 95% accepted, 26 enrolled. In 2006, 39 degrees awarded. *Degree requirements:* For master's, thesis (for some programs). *Entrance requirements:* For master's, GRE General Test. Additional exam requirements/recommendations for international students: Required—TOEFL; Recommended—TWE (minimum score 6). *Application deadline:* For fall admission, 7/1 for domestic students, 6/1 for international students; for winter admission, 10/1 for international students; for spring admission, 2/1 for international students. Application fee: $30 ($50 for international students). Electronic applications accepted. *Financial support:* In 2006–07, 3 research assistantships with tuition reimbursements (averaging $13,222 per year), 2 teaching assistantships with tuition reimbursements (averaging $13,222 per year) were awarded; career-related internships or fieldwork also available. *Faculty research:* Fitness in urban children, motor development of crack babies, effects of caffeine on metabolism/exercise, body composition of elite youth sports participants, systematic observation of teaching. Total annual research expenditures: $437,871. *Unit head:* Dr. Sally Erbaugh, Assistant Dean, 313-577-6210, Fax: 313-577-5999, E-mail: serbaugh@coe.wayne.edu. *Application contact:* John Wirth, Assistant Professor, 313-993-7972, Fax: 313-577-5999, E-mail: johnwirth@wayne.edu.

Western Illinois University, School of Graduate Studies, College of Education and Human Services, Department of Recreation, Park, and Tourism Administration, Macomb, IL 61455-1390. Offers MS. Part-time programs available. *Students:* 30 full-time (9 women), 4 part-time (3 women); includes 3 minority (1 African American, 2 Asian Americans or Pacific Islanders), 2 international. Average age 28. 30 applicants, 57% accepted. In 2006, 19 degrees awarded. *Degree requirements:* For master's, thesis or alternative. *Entrance requirements:* Additional exam requirements/recommendations for international students: Required—TOEFL (minimum score 550 paper-based; 213 computer-based; 80 iBT). *Application deadline:* Applications are processed on a rolling basis. Application fee: $30. Electronic applications accepted. *Expenses:* Tuition, state resident: part-time $200 per credit hour. Tuition, nonresident: part-time $400 per credit hour. *Financial support:* In 2006–07, 27 students received support, including 27 research assistantships with full tuition reimbursements available (averaging $6,568 per year). Financial award applicants required to submit FAFSA. *Unit head:* Dr. K. Dale Adkins, Chairperson, 309-298-1967. *Application contact:* Dr. Barbara Baily, Director of Graduate Studies/Associate Provost, 309-298-1806, Fax: 309-298-2345, E-mail: grad-office@wiu.edu.

Western Kentucky University, Graduate Studies, College of Health and Human Services, Department of Physical Education and Recreation, Bowling Green, KY 42101. Offers physical education (MS); recreation (MS). Part-time and evening/weekend programs available. *Faculty:* 9 full-time (0 women), 1 part-time/adjunct (0 women). *Students:* 19 full-time (6 women), 46 part-time (11 women); includes 4 minority (all African Americans), 4 international. Average age 27. 26 applicants, 77% accepted, 15 enrolled. In 2006, 17 degrees awarded. *Degree requirements:* For master's, thesis optional. *Entrance requirements:* For master's, GRE General Test, minimum GPA of 2.75. Additional exam requirements/recommendations for international students: Required—TOEFL (minimum score 555 paper-based; 213 computer-based; 79 iBT). *Application deadline:* For fall admission, 7/1 priority date for domestic students, 4/1 for international students; for spring admission, 11/1 for domestic students, 9/1 for international students. Applications are processed on a rolling basis. Application fee: $35. *Expenses:* Tuition, state resident: full-time $6,520; part-time $226 per hour. Tuition, nonresident: full-time $7,140; part-time $357 per hour. International tuition: $15,820 full-time. *Financial support:* In 2006–07, 2 teaching assistantships with partial tuition reimbursements (averaging $9,000 per year) were awarded; career-related internships or fieldwork, Federal Work-Study, institutionally sponsored loans, and service awards also available. Support available to part-time students. Financial award application deadline: 4/1; financial award applicants required to submit FAFSA. *Faculty research:* Orthopedic rehabilitation, fitness center coordination, heat acclimation, biomechanical and physiological parameters. *Unit head:* Dr. Thaddeus Crews, Department Head, 270-745-3347, Fax: 270-745-6043, E-mail: thad.crews@wku.edu.

West Virginia University, Davis College of Agriculture, Forestry and Consumer Sciences, Division of Forestry, Program in Recreation, Parks and Tourism Resources, Morgantown, WV 26506. Offers MS. Part-time programs available. *Students:* 10 full-time (6 women). Average age 27. 10 applicants, 30% accepted, 3 enrolled. In 2006, 7 degrees awarded. *Degree requirements:* For master's, thesis (for some programs), registration. *Entrance requirements:* For master's, GRE, minimum GPA of 3.0. Additional exam requirements/recommendations for international students: Required—TOEFL. *Application deadline:* Applications are processed on a rolling basis. Application fee: $50. *Expenses:* Tuition, state resident: full-time $4,926; part-time $276 per credit hour. Tuition, nonresident: full-time $14,278; part-time $796 per credit hour. Tuition and fees vary according to program. *Financial support:* In 2006–07, 9 students received support, including 6 research assistantships (averaging $12,000 per year), 2 teaching assistantships (averaging $8,164 per year); Federal Work-Study, institutionally sponsored loans, tuition waivers (full and partial), and graduate administrative assistantships also available. Financial award application deadline: 2/1; financial award applicants required to submit FAFSA. *Faculty research:* Attitudes, use patterns and impacts of outdoor recreation in West Virginia. *Unit head:* Dr. Steve W. Selin, Program Coordinator, 304-293-2941 Ext. 2441, Fax: 304-293-3441, E-mail: steve.selin@mail.wvu.edu.

Wright State University, School of Graduate Studies, College of Education and Human Services, Department of Health, Physical Education, and Recreation, Dayton, OH 45435. Offers M Ed, MA. *Accreditation:* NCATE. *Students:* 1 (woman) full-time, 2 part-time (1 woman). Average age 30. 3 applicants, 67% accepted. In 2006, 3 degrees awarded. *Degree requirements:* For master's, thesis (for some programs), comprehensive exam. *Entrance requirements:* For master's, GRE General Test, MAT. Additional exam requirements/recommendations for international students: Required—TOEFL. Application fee: $25. *Financial support:* Available to part-time students. Applicants required to submit FAFSA. *Faculty research:* Motor learning, motor development, exercise physiology, adapted physical education. *Unit head:* Dr. D. Drew Pringle, Chair, 937-775-3223, Fax: 937-775-4252, E-mail: d.pringle@wright.edu. *Application contact:* John Kimble, Associate Director of Graduate Admissions and Records, 937-775-2957, Fax: 937-775-2453, E-mail: john.kimble@wright.edu.

CLEMSON UNIVERSITY

Department of Parks, Recreation and Tourism Management
Master's Degree Programs

Programs of Study	The Department of Parks, Recreation and Tourism Management (PRTM) offers the Master of Parks, Recreation and Tourism Management (M.P.R.T.M.) and the Master of Science (M.S.) degree programs.
	The M.P.R.T.M. is a professional degree program in which the students increase their depth and breadth of knowledge while developing practical administrative and management skills. This program should be selected by those who intend to enter or reenter the workplace upon the completion of degree requirements. All candidates must complete an independent project and a minimum of 36 credit hours of course work.
	The M.S. program places greater emphasis on research design and methodology and requires a thesis that represents an original contribution to scholarship that is acceptable to the faculty and the Graduate School. This program is designed for those planning to undertake doctoral study or seek employment in research-related positions. Candidates must complete a minimum of 30 credit hours of course work and 6 credit hours of research culminating in a thesis.
	The flexibility of Clemson's programs allows students to develop their skills in such professional interest areas as therapeutic recreation, travel and tourism management, recreation resource management and interpretation, and administration of recreation, park, or tourism systems. All students have the opportunity to tailor their programs to suit their personal and professional goals. The course of study is uniquely developed for each student in consultation with a graduate advisory committee. Factors determining the course of study include the student's interests and goals, the undergraduate course of study, the student's employment history, and the degree program.
Research Facilities	Students have access to the modern, well-equipped laboratories within both the Department and the College. These facilities include a PC laboratory equipped with microcomputer hardware and software, several remote computer terminals for communicating with the Clemson University Computer Center, and the Geographic Information System (GIS) Laboratory. In addition, there are two federal cooperative research units—the U.S. Forest Service Cooperative Study Unit and the U.S. Fish and Wildlife Cooperative Study Unit—housed in Lehotsky Hall. Adjacent to the campus are the 17,000-acre Clemson Experimental Forest and the approximately 200-acre Outdoor Laboratory. Students also have access to research and scholarly pursuits within the Strom Thurmond Institute of Government and Public Affairs, the Osher Lifelong Learning Institute, and the Recreation, Travel, and Tourism Institute.
Financial Aid	A limited number of assistantships and University fellowships are available. The Conover Graduate Fellowship is sponsored by Richard and Sandra Conover to further graduate study in recreation resource management. The award consists of a 20-hour-per-week, twelve-month-per-year graduate assistantship, plus a fellowship, totaling up to $15,000 for M.S. (thesis) students. Fellowships are awarded for one year only; however, the same student may receive the fellowship in succeeding years based on annual recommendations by the Department of Parks, Recreation and Tourism Management.
Cost of Study	Tuition for 2007–08 is $3641 per semester for in-state students and $7285 per semester for nonresidents. Part-time rates are $330 per hour for in-state students and $660 per hour for nonresidents. Graduate assistants pay a flat fee of $950 per semester. Graduate fellows pay South Carolina resident fees.
Living and Housing Costs	On-campus housing is available. For information, students should visit http://www.housing.clemson.edu. The cost of living in Clemson is quite low compared to the national average. Students who choose to live off campus typically spend $300–$400 per month for rent, depending on location, amenities, roommates, and other factors.
Student Group	Of the 51 graduate students currently enrolled, 41 are full-time, and 25 are women. Ten percent of the students in the program are international students.
Location	Clemson is a small, beautiful college town near the Blue Ridge Mountains and Lake Hartwell in Upstate South Carolina. The Upstate is one of the country's fastest-growing areas and is an important part of the I-85 corridor, a multistate area along Interstate 85 that runs from metro Atlanta to Richmond, Virginia, and encompasses Charlotte, North Carolina, and North Carolina's Research Triangle. Atlanta and Charlotte are each a 2-hour drive away. Many financial institutions and other industries have a national headquarters or a major presence in the Upstate, including Wachovia, Bank of America, BMW, Bon Secours St. Francis Health System, Bosch North America, Bowater, Charter Communications, Ernst & Young, Fluor Corporation, IBM, Microsoft, Michelin of North America, and many others.
The University and The Department	Clemson is classified by the Carnegie Foundation as an RU/H: Research University (high research activity), a category comprising just 10 percent of all graduate degree–granting universities in America. The University's mission is to fulfill the covenant between its founder and the people of South Carolina to establish a "high seminary of learning" through its responsibilities of teaching, research, and extended public service. The University has identified eight areas of academic emphasis that create collaborations that, in turn, help fulfill the University's mission.
	The Department of Parks, Recreation and Tourism Management is one of the largest programs of its type in the country, consisting of more than 500 undergraduate and 51 graduate students. In total, the Department has 22 faculty members, of whom 11 have qualifications for teaching and conducting research in the recreation resource management area.
Applying	Applicants may apply on the Web at http://www.grad.clemson.edu/p_apply.html. Successful candidates most often hold a bachelor's degree and have a minimum GPA of 3.0. Applicants must submit the completed application form, the $50 application fee, undergraduate transcripts, letters of recommendation, Graduate Record Examinations (GRE) scores, and a statement of purpose (goals). Applications are accepted and encouraged from those whose undergraduate education did not include the formal study of recreation and parks. Applicants are encouraged to apply by February 15 for the fall semester and October 15 for the spring.
Correspondence and Information	Fran McGuire, Coordinator of Graduate Studies Department of Parks, Recreation and Tourism Management 263 Lehotsky Hall Clemson University Clemson, South Carolina 29634-0735 Phone: 864-656-3400 Fax: 864-656-2226 E-mail: lefty@clemson.edu Web site: http://www.clemson.edu/PRTM/indexflash.html

Clemson University

THE FACULTY AND THEIR RESEARCH

Lawrence R. Allen, Professor, Academy of Leisure Sciences Fellow, and Dean of the College of Health, Education, and Human Development; Ph.D. Community and tourism development, benefits-based programming, youth development, impact of recreation and tourism.

Denise M. Anderson, Assistant Professor; Ph.D. Girls' and women's participation in leisure, professional development of recreation professionals, youth programming, health and wellness.

Skye Arthur-Banning, Assistant Professor; Ph.D. Youth sports, sportsmanship and referee behaviors.

Kenneth F. Backman, Associate Professor; Ph.D. Tourism marketing, recreational fishing, ecotourism planning, community tourism development.

Sheila J. Backman, Professor and Coordinator of Graduate Studies; Ph.D. Incentive travel, consumer behavior and judgments, recreation service loyalty.

Elizabeth Baldwin, Assistant Professor; Ph.D. Large-scale conservation policy and planning, environmental conflict and collaboration, outdoor literature, qualitative inquiry.

Robert H. Becker, Professor, Director of Strom Thurmond Institute of Government and Public Affairs, Co-Founder and Executive Faculty Member for the Doctoral Program in Policy Studies, and Academy of Leisure Sciences Fellow; Ph.D. Regional and community development, natural resource policy.

Robert Bixler, Associate Professor; Ph.D. Environmental socialization, formative and summative evaluation of nonformal educational programs, environmental education and interpretation, human dimensions of natural resources.

Bob Brookover, Lecturer, Executive Director of the South Carolina Recreation Development Project, and Leisure Skills Curriculum Coordinator; Ph.D. Community development, pricing models for recreation/leisure services, facility design and operation, organizational commitment among recreational professionals, admission standards for college athletes.

G. W. Burnett, Professor and Fellow of the Royal Geographical Society; Ph.D. Planning and park management, biological conservation, Third World parks.

Lynne Cory, Assistant Professor; Ph.D. Quality of life across the lifespan for individuals with and without disabilities, community-based inclusive recreation, community integration and reintegration for individuals with developmental or acquired disabilities.

Keith G. Diem, Professor, Director of South Carolina 4-H Development Program, Clemson University Cooperative Extension Service Project Director for the Science Discovery Series and Exploring the Treasures of 4-H Curricula, and Design Team Member for the Heads on, Hands on, the Power of Experiential Learning Curriculum; Ph.D. Youth development and nonformal education (K–12); program development, management, and evaluation; science education for youth and adults working with elementary school youth; experiential learning processes applied to youth development programs and curricula; marketing communications for nonprofit/educational institutions and programs.

Caroline Goasguen, Lecturer; B.A., PGA. Golfer development and recruitment.

William E. Hammitt, Professor and Academy of Leisure Sciences Fellow; Ph.D. Recreation and parkland management, visitor preference and management strategies, recreation behavior, visual resources assessment.

Laura W. Jodice, Research Associate in the Recreation, Travel and Tourism Institute; M.S. Marine and coastal tourism management, recreational fisheries management, natural resource management training, environmental education and outreach.

Rick Lucas, Lecturer and Director of the Professional Golf Management Program; M.B.A. Golf facility management, accessible golf.

Fran Mainella, Visiting Scholar; M.S., Honorary Doctorate. Natural and cultural resources, partnerships and volunteerism, meaning and importance of parks and recreation in today's society, ecotourism.

Norman McGee Jr., Senior Lecturer and Director of the Clemson University Outdoor Lab; J.D. Camp administration, experiential education, legal issues.

Francis A. McGuire, Alumni Distinguished Professor, Academy of Leisure Sciences Fellow, and Fellow in the Strom Thurmond Institute of Government and Public Affairs; Ph.D. Therapeutic recreation, leisure behavior, aging.

William C. Norman, Associate Professor and Director of the Recreation, Travel and Tourism Institute; Ph.D. Travel behavior and decision making, tourism marketing, sport tourism, community tourism development.

Chiok Oh, Assistant Professor; Ph.D. Human dimensions of recreation resources, recreation specialization in recreationists' populations, economic valuation of natural resources, recreationists' attitudes toward resource conservation.

Nancy M. Porter, Professor, Co-Chair of the National Cooperative Extension, Adviser to the South Carolina Association of Family and Community Leaders, and Extension Family Resource Management Specialist; Ph.D., CFCS. Family financial management and consumer education.

Robert B. Powell, Assistant Professor; Ph.D. Protected-area management, human dimensions of resource management, human-environment interactions, ecotourism and nature-based tourism, environmental interpretation, biodiversity conservation.

Adam R. Savedra, Lecturer; M.B.A., PGA. Internship coordinator, membership development.

Dorothy L. Schmalz, Assistant Professor; Ph.D. Stereotypes in leisure and sport; adolescents' leisure participation, weight concerns, and physical activity.

Bonnie W. Stevens, Assistant Professor, Director of the HEHD Development Office of Training and Education for Practicing Professionals, and Director of the Clemson University American Humanics Program; Ed.D. Mental health, leadership, and nonprofit management; service provision in community settings; outcome-based assessment.

J. Herbert Stevens Jr., Lecturer and Academic Advisor; M.R.P.A.

Deborah J. Thomason, Professor, State Program Leader for Extension Family and Consumer Sciences, and Family and Youth Development Specialist; Ed.D. Life skills development in rural and nonrural 4-H youth, building family strengths, family and youth development, human growth and development.

Judith E. Voelkl, Professor and Coordinator of Therapeutic Recreation; Ph.D., CTRS. Therapeutic recreation, aging, families and leisure, long-term care, daily experiences.

Willard H. Warmath Jr., Lecturer, Team Ventures Facilitator, and Trainer for the Clemson University Outdoor Laboratory; M.B.A. Adventure and experiential education, youth and adult development, leadership development, group dynamics and interpersonal communications.

David E. Weatherford, Professor and 4-H and Youth Development Specialist; Ed.D. Responsible for the development and coordination of 4-H volunteer systems within the state, 4-H science and technology curriculum areas, and staff development.

Mary Sara Wells, Assistant Professor and Extension Specialist for Community Youth Development at the Sandhill Research and Education Center and PRTM; Ph.D. Youth development.

Brett Wright, Professor and Department Chair; Ph.D. Human dimensions of natural resources management, park management, recreation resources policy, private lands, ecotourism.

Andrew Yiannakis, Professor and Director of the Clemson Institute for Tourism, Research and Development; Ph.D. Sociology of sport and leisure, sociology/social psychology, research methods with computer applications, social science aspects of tourism, leisure and sport, participation in recreational sports.

Adjunct Faculty
Doug Kleiber, Ph.D.
Aloyce Nzuki, Ph.D.

CLEMSON UNIVERSITY

Department of Parks, Recreation and Tourism Management
Ph.D. Program

Program of Study

The Department of Parks, Recreation and Tourism Management (PRTM) offers the Doctor of Philosophy (Ph.D.) degree program. This program is based on students' understanding of recreation subject matter, competency to plan and conduct research, and ability to effectively and professionally use written and oral communication. The course of study is uniquely developed for each student in consultation with a graduate advisory committee. Factors determining the course of study include the student's interests and goals, the undergraduate course of study, the student's employment history, and the degree program.

Comprehensive and final examinations and 18 hours of dissertation research are required of all doctoral students. Course work is determined by students' doctoral committees. Candidates must pass the comprehensive examination, gain the Graduate School's approval of the dissertation, and defend the dissertation within the five-year period prior to graduation. As many as 48 semester hours of work may be transferred. Students must complete at least 15 semester hours of graduate credit, including research credit, on the Clemson University campus in a continuous twelve-month period.

Research Facilities

Students have access to the modern, well-equipped laboratories within both the Department and the College. These facilities include a PC laboratory equipped with microcomputer hardware and software, several remote computer terminals for communicating with the Clemson University Computer Center, and the Geographic Information System (GIS) Laboratory. In addition, there are two federal cooperative research units—the U.S. Forest Service Cooperative Study Unit and the U.S. Fish and Wildlife Cooperative Study Unit housed in Lehotsky Hall. Adjacent to the campus are the 17,000-acre Clemson Experimental Forest and the approximately 200-acre Outdoor Laboratory. Students also have access to research and scholarly pursuits within the Strom Thurmond Institute of Government and Public Affairs, the Osher Lifelong Learning Institute, and the Recreation, Travel and Tourism Institute.

Financial Aid

A limited number of assistantships and University fellowships are available. The Conover Graduate Fellowship is sponsored by Richard and Sandra Conover to further graduate study in recreation resource management. The award consists of a 20-hour-per-week, twelve-month-per-year graduate assistantship, plus a fellowship, totaling up to $20,000 per year (including tuition waiver) for Ph.D. students. Fellowships are awarded for one year only; however, the same student may receive the fellowship in succeeding years based on annual recommendations by the Department of Parks, Recreation and Tourism Management.

Cost of Study

Tuition for 2007–08 is $3641 per semester for in-state students and $7285 per semester for nonresidents. Part-time rates are $330 per hour for in-state students and $660 per hour for nonresidents. Graduate assistants pay a flat fee of $950 per semester. Graduate fellows pay South Carolina resident fees.

Living and Housing Costs

On-campus housing is available. For information, students should visit http://www.housing.clemson.edu. The cost of living in Clemson is quite low compared to the national average. Students who choose to live off campus typically spend $300–$400 per month for rent, depending on location, amenities, roommates, and other factors.

Student Group

Of the 51 graduate students currently enrolled, 41 are full-time, and 25 are women. Ten percent of the students in the program are international students.

Location

Clemson is a small, beautiful college town near the Blue Ridge Mountains and Lake Hartwell in Upstate South Carolina. The Upstate is one of the country's fastest-growing areas and is an important part of the I-85 corridor, a multistate area along Interstate 85 that runs from metro Atlanta to Richmond, Virginia, and encompasses Charlotte, North Carolina, and North Carolina's Research Triangle. Atlanta and Charlotte are each a 2-hour drive away. Many financial institutions and other industries have a national headquarters or a major presence in the Upstate, including Wachovia, Bank of America, BMW, Bon Secours St. Francis Health System, Bosch North America, Bowater, Charter Communications, Ernst & Young, Fluor Corporation, IBM, Microsoft, Michelin of North America, and many others.

The University and The Department

Clemson is classified by the Carnegie Foundation as an RU/H: Research University (high research activity), a category comprising just 10 percent of all graduate degree–granting universities in America. The University's mission is to fulfill the covenant between its founder and the people of South Carolina to establish a "high seminary of learning" through its responsibilities of teaching, research, and extended public service. The University has identified eight areas of academic emphasis that create collaborations that, in turn, help fulfill the University's mission.

The Department of Parks, Recreation and Tourism Management is one of the largest programs of its type in the country, consisting of more than 500 undergraduate and 51 graduate students. In total, the Department has 22 faculty members, of whom 11 have qualifications for teaching and conducting research in the recreation resource management area.

Applying

Applicants may apply on the Web at http://www.grad.clemson.edu/p_apply.html. Successful candidates typically have a minimum GPA of 3.0 for all graduate work and at least 1500 on the verbal, quantitative, and analytical sections of the Graduate Record Examinations (GRE). Applicants must submit the completed application form, the $50 application fee, undergraduate transcripts, letters of recommendation, GRE scores, and a statement of purpose (goals). Applicants are encouraged to apply by February 15 for the fall semester and October 15 for the spring.

Correspondence and Information

Fran McGuire, Coordinator of Graduate Studies
Department of Parks, Recreation and Tourism Management
263 Lehotsky Hall
Clemson University
Clemson, South Carolina 29634-0735
Phone: 864-656-3400
Fax: 864-656-2226
E-mail: lefty@clemson.edu
Web site: http://www.clemson.edu/PRTM/indexflash.html

Clemson University

THE FACULTY AND THEIR RESEARCH

Lawrence R. Allen, Professor, Academy of Leisure Sciences Fellow, and Dean of the College of Health, Education, and Human Development; Ph.D. Community and tourism development, benefits-based programming, youth development, impact of recreation and tourism.

Denise M. Anderson, Assistant Professor; Ph.D. Girls' and women's participation in leisure, professional development of recreation professionals, youth programming, health and wellness.

Skye Arthur-Banning, Assistant Professor; Ph.D. Youth sports, sportsmanship, and referee behaviors.

Kenneth F. Backman, Associate Professor; Ph.D. Tourism marketing, recreational fishing, ecotourism planning, community tourism development.

Sheila J. Backman, Professor and Coordinator of Graduate Studies; Ph.D. Incentive travel, consumer behavior and judgments, recreation service loyalty.

Elizabeth Baldwin, Assistant Professor; Ph.D. Large-scale conservation policy and planning, environmental conflict and collaboration, outdoor literature, qualitative inquiry.

Robert H. Becker, Professor, Director of Strom Thurmond Institute of Government and Public Affairs, Co-Founder and Executive Faculty Member for the Doctoral Program in Policy Studies, and Academy of Leisure Sciences Fellow; Ph.D. Regional and community development and natural resource policy.

Robert Bixler, Associate Professor; Ph.D. Environmental socialization, formative and summative evaluation of nonformal educational programs, environmental education and interpretation, human dimensions of natural resources.

Bob Brookover, Lecturer, Executive Director of the South Carolina Recreation Development Project, and Leisure Skills Curriculum Coordinator; Ph.D. Community development, pricing models for recreation/leisure services, facility design and operation, organizational commitment among recreational professionals, admission standards for college athletes.

G. W. Burnett, Professor and Fellow of the Royal Geographical Society; Ph.D. Planning and park management, biological conservation, Third World parks.

Lynne Cory, Assistant Professor; Ph.D. Quality of life across the lifespan for individuals with and without disabilities, community-based inclusive recreation, community integration and reintegration for individuals with developmental or acquired disabilities.

Keith G. Diem, Professor, Director of South Carolina 4-H Development Program, Clemson University Cooperative Extension Service Project Director for the Science Discovery Series and Exploring the Treasures of 4-H Curricula, and Design Team Member for the Heads on, Hands on, the Power of Experiential Learning Curriculum; Ph.D. Youth development and nonformal education (K–12); program development, management, and evaluation; science education for youth and adults working with elementary school youth; experiential learning processes applied to youth development programs and curricula; marketing communications for nonprofit/educational institutions and programs.

Caroline Goasguen, Lecturer; B.A., PGA. Golfer development and recruitment.

William E. Hammitt, Professor and Academy of Leisure Sciences Fellow; Ph.D. Recreation and parkland management, visitor preference and management strategies, recreation behavior, visual resources assessment.

Laura W. Jodice, Research Associate in the Recreation, Travel and Tourism Institute; M.S. Marine and coastal tourism management, recreational fisheries management, natural resource management training, environmental education and outreach.

Rick Lucas, Lecturer and Director of the Professional Golf Management Program; M.B.A. Golf facility management, accessible golf.

Fran Mainella, Visiting Scholar; M.S., Honorary Doctorate. Natural and cultural resources, partnerships and volunteerism, meaning and importance of parks and recreation in today's society, ecotourism.

Norman McGee Jr., Senior Lecturer and Director of the Clemson University Outdoor Lab; J.D. Camp administration, experiential education, legal issues.

Francis A. McGuire, Alumni Distinguished Professor, Academy of Leisure Sciences Fellow, and Fellow in the Strom Thurmond Institute of Government and Public Affairs; Ph.D. Therapeutic recreation, leisure behavior, aging.

William C. Norman, Associate Professor and Director of the Recreation, Travel and Tourism Institute; Ph.D. Travel behavior and decision making, tourism marketing, sport tourism, community tourism development.

Chiok Oh, Assistant Professor; Ph.D. Human dimensions of recreation resources, recreation specialization in recreationists' populations, economic valuation of natural resources, recreationists' attitudes toward resource conservation.

Nancy M. Porter, Professor, Co-Chair of the National Cooperative Extension, Advisor to the South Carolina Association of Family and Community Leaders, and Extension Family Resource Management Specialist; Ph.D., CFCS. Family financial management and consumer education.

Robert B. Powell, Assistant Professor; Ph.D. Protected-area management, human dimensions of resource management, human-environment interactions, ecotourism and nature-based tourism, environmental interpretation, biodiversity conservation.

Adam R. Savedra, Lecturer; M.B.A., PGA. Internship coordinator, membership development.

Dorothy L. Schmalz, Assistant Professor; Ph.D. Stereotypes in leisure and sport; adolescents' leisure participation, weight concerns, and physical activity.

Bonnie W. Stevens, Assistant Professor, Director of the HEHD Development Office of Training and Education for Practicing Professionals, and Director of the Clemson University American Humanics Program; Ed.D. Mental health, leadership, and nonprofit management; service provision in community settings; outcome-based assessment.

J. Herbert Stevens Jr., Lecturer and Academic Adviser; M.R.P.A.

Deborah J. Thomason, Professor, State Program Leader for Extension Family and Consumer Sciences, and Family and Youth Development Specialist; Ed.D. Life skills development in rural and nonrural 4-H youth, building family strengths, family and youth development, human growth and development.

Judith E. Voelkl, Professor and Coordinator of Therapeutic Recreation; Ph.D., CTRS. Therapeutic recreation, aging, families and leisure, long-term care, daily experiences.

Willard H. Warmath Jr., Lecturer, Team Ventures Facilitator, and Trainer for the Clemson University Outdoor Laboratory; M.B.A. Adventure and experiential education, youth and adult development, leadership development, group dynamics and interpersonal communications.

David E. Weatherford, Professor and 4-H and Youth Development Specialist; Ed.D. Responsible for the development and coordination of 4-H volunteer systems within the state, 4-H science and technology curriculum areas, and staff development.

Mary Sara Wells, Assistant Professor and Extension Specialist for Community Youth Development at the Sandhill Research and Education Center and PRTM.; Ph.D. Youth development.

Brett Wright, Professor and Department Chair; Ph.D. Human dimensions of natural resources management, park management, recreation resources policy, private lands, ecotourism.

Andrew Yiannakis, Professor and Director of the Clemson Institute for Tourism, Research and Development; Ph.D. Sociology of sport and leisure, sociology/social psychology, research methods with computer applications, social science aspects of tourism, leisure and sport, participation in recreational sports.

Adjunct Faculty
Doug Kleiber, Ph.D.
Aloyce Nzuki, Ph.D.

VIRGINIA COMMONWEALTH UNIVERSITY

Program in Sports Leadership

Program of Study

Virginia Commonwealth University (VCU), through its SportsCenter, offers structured graduate programs combining classroom theory with exposure to relevant field experiences. In the sports leadership program, students are prepared to assume the responsibilities for developing professional and amateur athletes and for managing sports programs in a variety of academic, public, and private sectors. The interdisciplinary faculty and curriculum give students the opportunity to concentrate on areas most important to them and most relevant to the sports business. Courses are also available online. Currently, three classes are available each semester.

Students must complete 36 credits to obtain the Master of Science in sport leadership. Required courses—including Research Methods, Action Learning, Sport and Society, Sports Business, Coaching & Administration, Sport Leadership, and the internship/final project—make up 24 credits. The rest of the curriculum comprises electives, such as Practical Experience, Contemporary Issues in Sports, Sports Psychology, Sports Marketing, Advanced Coaching, NCAA and College Athletics, Ethical Issues in Sports, Sports Law and Facilities Management, Perspectives on Professional Sports, Global Perspectives on Sports, Media and Event Management, American Sports Model, and European Sports Model.

Research Facilities

VCU libraries provide a combined capacity of more than 1.7 million volumes and 10,200 periodical titles and an online bibliographic search service accessing hundreds of databases. In addition, the Virginia State and Richmond Public libraries are within walking distance of both VCU campuses. Academic Computing provides a variety of microcomputer, minicomputer, and mainframe computing services to support the research and instructional endeavors of its faculty and students, including consultation, instruction, and computer acquisition.

The Alltel Pavilion at the Stuart C. Siegel Center is a high-quality multipurpose indoor facility that can accommodate Division I–level NCAA intercollegiate athletics, serve as a general-purpose assembly space for special events, and provide expanded recreational sports activity space. The latest addition to VCU facilities is the Sports Medicine Building, which opened in July 2001. This 30,000-square-foot, two-story building houses a student health clinic and has offices for many VCU coaches, in addition to housing the athletic department's academic advising, compliance, sports information, and athletic-training staffs. There is ample meeting space for special events, and the building also serves as the headquarters for the VCU SportsCenter. Sports Backers Stadium serves as the home facility for the University's men's and women's soccer team and track-and-field teams. The stadium's international-caliber track provides an ideal setting for regional, national, and even international track-and-field meets. The eight 48-inch lanes with the Martin surface and the full complement of throwing facilities within the main stadium make this an ideal event facility. The Diamond, the home of the Richmond Braves, is recognized as one of the finest facilities in all of minor league baseball. Men's and women's tennis teams practice and compete at the Thalhimer Tennis Center. The facility, which includes six courts and seating for 250 people, served as the site for the 1998 NCAA Men's Region II Championship. An air-supported structure known as "the bubble" allows for play during the winter. Former home to the VCU men's and women's basketball teams, Franklin Street is a two-gymnasium facility that provides an indoor practice facility for all the University's varsity teams at VCU. In addition, Franklin Street is used for athletic camps and physical education and recreation classes. Cary Street Field is the home for Virginia Commonwealth field hockey. The 1,200-seat venue features an artificial turf playing surface.

Financial Aid

Students may apply for need-based assistance through the University's Financial Aid Office. Current information on financial aid programs, policies, and procedures is available at http://www.vcu.edu/enroll/finaid.

Cost of Study

For full-time study (9–15 credits) in 2007–08, Virginia residents pay tuition and fees of $4452 per semester; nonresidents, $8876 per semester. For part-time study, Virginia residents pay tuition and fees of $465 per hour; nonresidents, $954 per hour. Some programs require additional fees. On the Medical College of Virginia (MCV) campus, tuition, fees, and other expenses vary in the medicine, pharmacy, nurse anesthesia, dentistry, and School of Allied Health programs.

Living and Housing Costs

Graduate student housing is available on both the MCV campus and the academic campus of Virginia Commonwealth University. Many graduate students live in off-campus housing, which is reasonably priced and readily available in a variety of styles and settings in nearby residential areas or within easy commuting distance. On- and off-campus housing information is available on the Web at http://www.housing.vcu.edu/.

Student Group

VCU enrolls 30,452 students, 7,611 of whom are graduate students. More than 200 clubs and organizations reflect the diverse social, recreational, educational, political, and religious interests of the student body.

Location

Richmond is Virginia's capital and a major East Coast financial and manufacturing center that offers students a wide range of cultural, educational, and recreational activities. Richmond is located in central Virginia at the intersection of Interstates 95 and 64, 2 hours south of Washington, D.C., and nestled between the Blue Ridge Mountains and the Atlantic coast. The Richmond region is easily accessible by plane, car, and train. With nearly 1 million residents, the historic city of Richmond combines big-city offerings with small-town hospitality. Applicants are encouraged to explore http://www.visit.richmond.com/ for more information on the city.

The University

VCU is a state-supported coeducational university with a graduate school, a major teaching hospital, and twelve academic and professional units that offer fifty-two undergraduate, twenty-two postbaccalaureate certificate, sixty-five master's, six post-master's certificate, and twenty-nine Ph.D. programs. VCU also offers M.D., D.D.S., D.P.T., and Pharm.D. programs as well as cooperative degree programs with other major Virginia colleges and universities. VCU has one of the largest evening colleges in the United States. The academic campus is located in Richmond's historic Fan District. The health sciences campus and hospital are located 2 miles east in the downtown business district. A University bus service provides free intercampus transportation for faculty members and students.

With more than $211 million in annual research funding, Virginia Commonwealth University is classified as one of the nation's top research universities by the Carnegie Foundation for the Advancement of Teaching. More than 29,000 undergraduate, certificate, graduate, post-master's, professional, and doctoral students are enrolled in 162 academic programs, forty of which are unique in the commonwealth of Virginia. The faculty members represent the finest American and international graduate institutions and enhance the University's position among the important institutions of higher learning in the United States and the world via their work in the classroom, laboratory, studio, and clinic and in their scholarly publications.

Applying

Admission procedures and program requirements are detailed in the *Graduate Bulletin*. Application deadlines and materials, including the application and the *Graduate Bulletin*, are available online at the Graduate School Web site at http://www.graduate.vcu.edu. Virginia Commonwealth University is an equal opportunity/affirmative action institution providing access to education and employment without regard to age, race, color, national origin, gender, religion, sexual orientation, veteran's status, political affiliation, or disability.

Correspondence and Information

Leslie R. Winston, Assistant Director
VCU SportsCenter
1300 West Broad Street
Virginia Commonwealth University
P.O. Box 842003
Richmond, Virginia 23284-2020
Phone: 804-828-8498
Fax: 804-828-4938
E-mail: lrsander @vcu.edu
Web site: http://www.vcu.edu/sportscenter/

Virginia Commonwealth University

THE FACULTY AND THEIR RESEARCH

Michael Burch, Adjunct Professor and Director of Business Development, Speedway Motorsports Inc. (SMI); M.S., Georgia Southern.
Joe Cantafio, Adjunct Professor; M.S., Virginia Commonwealth.
Steven Danish, Counseling Director at the Life Skills Center; Ph.D., Michigan State.
Tanya Taylor Forneris, Adjunct Professor; M.S., New Brunswick.
Tim Lampe, Adjunct Professor and Director of Facilities and the Siegel Center; M.S., New Mexico.
Gijs Langevoort, Adjunct Professor; M.D., Free University of Amsterdam.
Tracey Leverty, Adjunct Professor and Founder and President, Echelon Event Management; M.S., Richmond.
Joseph Marolla, Director of the Center for Teaching Excellence; Ph.D., Denver.
Gary Ness, Adjunct Professor of Sport Management; Ph.D., Stanford.
Richard L. Sander, Executive Director; Ed.D., Cincinnati.
Tom Shupe, Adjunct Professor and Associate Athletic Director for External Affairs; B.S., Slippery Rock State.
Domenic Sica, Professor of Medicine and Pharmacology; M.D., Virginia Commonwealth.
Pat Stauffer, Adjunct Professor and Assistant Athletic Director for Olympic Sports; M.S., Richmond; M.S., Arizona.
Beverly Warren, Dean of the School of Education; Ph.D., Auburn; Ed.D., Alabama.

Section 42
Physical Education and Kinesiology

This section contains a directory of institutions offering graduate work in physical education and kinesiology, followed by in-depth entries submitted by institutions that chose to prepare detailed program descriptions. Additional information about programs listed in the directory but not augmented by an in-depth entry may be obtained by writing directly to the dean of a graduate school or chair of a department at the address given in the directory.

For programs offering related work, see also in this book Business Administration and Management, Education, and Sports Management; and in Book 2, Performing Arts.

CONTENTS

Program Directories

Close-Ups

Athletic Training and Sports Medicine

Armstrong Atlantic State University, School of Graduate Studies, Program in Sports Medicine, Savannah, GA 31419-1997. Offers sports health sciences (MSSM). Part-time programs available. *Faculty:* 4 full-time (0 women). *Students:* 18 full-time (14 women), 12 part-time (6 women); includes 3 minority (2 African Americans, 1 Hispanic American), 2 international. Average age 27. In 2006, 11 degrees awarded. *Degree requirements:* For master's, project, thesis optional. *Entrance requirements:* For master's, GRE General Test, MAT, GMAT, minimum GPA of 2.5. Additional exam requirements/recommendations for international students: Required—TOEFL (minimum score 523 paper-based; 193 computer-based). *Application deadline:* For fall admission, 7/1 priority date for domestic and international students; for spring admission, 11/15 priority date for domestic and international students. Application fee: $25. *Expenses:* Tuition, state resident: full-time $2,286; part-time $127 per credit. Tuition, nonresident: full-time $9,144; part-time $508 per credit. One-time fee: $257. *Financial support:* In 2006–07, research assistantships with partial tuition reimbursements (averaging $2,500 per year); scholarships/grants, tuition waivers (full), and unspecified assistantships also available. Financial award applicants required to submit FAFSA. *Unit head:* Dr. James Streater, Department Head, 912-921-7346, Fax: 912-921-7350, E-mail: mssm@mail.armstrong.edu. *Application contact:* Dr. Robert Lefavi, Graduate Coordinator, 912-921-5482, E-mail: lefaviro@mail.armstrong.edu.

Barry University, School of Human Performance and Leisure Sciences, Program in Movement Science, Specialization in Athletic Training, Miami Shores, FL 33161-6695. Offers MS. Part-time and evening/weekend programs available. *Students:* 11 applicants, 55% accepted, 5 enrolled. In 2006, 2 degrees awarded. *Degree requirements:* For master's, project or thesis. *Entrance requirements:* For master's, GRE General Test, minimum GPA of 3.0. *Application deadline:* Applications are processed on a rolling basis. Application fee: $30. Electronic applications accepted. *Financial support:* In 2006–07, 2 teaching assistantships with full tuition reimbursements were awarded. *Faculty research:* Pain management, prevention and injury analysis, low energy static magnetic field therapy, upper extremity biomechanics. *Application contact:* Dave Fletcher, Director of Graduate Admissions, 305-899-3113, Fax: 305-899-2971, E-mail: dfletcher@mail.barry.edu.

Boston University, College of Health and Rehabilitation Sciences—Sargent College, Department of Physical Therapy and Athletic Training, Boston, MA 02215. Offers physical therapy (DPT); rehabilitation sciences (D Sc). *Accreditation:* APTA (one or more programs are accredited). Postbaccalaureate distance learning degree programs offered (minimal on-campus study). *Faculty:* 15 full-time (11 women), 22 part-time/adjunct (15 women). *Students:* 117 full-time (96 women), 185 part-time (128 women); includes 32 minority (3 African Americans, 18 Asian Americans or Pacific Islanders, 11 Hispanic Americans), 5 international. Average age 32. 185 applicants, 56% accepted, 33 enrolled. In 2006, 212 doctorates awarded. *Degree requirements:* For doctorate, thesis/dissertation (for some programs). *Entrance requirements:* For doctorate, GRE General Test, master's degree. Additional exam requirements/recommendations for international students: Required—TOEFL (minimum score 550 paper-based). *Application deadline:* For fall admission, 1/5 for domestic students. Applications are processed on a rolling basis. Application fee: $70. Electronic applications accepted. *Expenses:* Tuition: Full-time $33,330; part-time $1,042 per credit. Required fees: $462; $40. *Financial support:* In 2006–07, 3 research assistantships with full tuition reimbursements, 10 teaching assistantships with full tuition reimbursements were awarded; career-related internships or fieldwork, Federal Work-Study, institutionally sponsored loans, scholarships/grants, and tuition waivers (partial) also available. Financial award application deadline: 4/15. *Faculty research:* EMG, gait, infant assessment, motor control, orthopedics. *Unit head:* Dr. Julie Keysor, Chairman, 617-353-2735, E-mail: jkeysor@bu.edu. *Application contact:* Sharon Sankey, Director, Student Services, 617-353-2713, Fax: 617-353-7500, E-mail: ssankey@bu.edu.

Brigham Young University, Graduate Studies, College of Health and Human Performance, Department of Exercise Sciences, Provo, UT 84602-1001. Offers athletic training (MS); exercise physiology (MS, PhD); health promotion (MS, PhD); physical medicine and rehabilitation (PhD); sports pedagogy (MS). *Faculty:* 19 full-time (3 women), 1 (woman) part-time/adjunct. *Students:* 23 full-time (10 women), 48 part-time (21 women); includes 7 minority (3 American Indian/Alaska Native, 1 Asian American or Pacific Islander, 3 Hispanic Americans). Average age 28. 30 applicants, 70% accepted, 14 enrolled. In 2006, 9 master's, 4 doctorates awarded. *Median time to degree:* Of those who began their doctoral program in fall 1998, 100% received their degree in 8 years or less. *Degree requirements:* For master's, thesis, oral defense; for doctorate, thesis/dissertation, oral defense, oral and written exams, comprehensive exam. *Entrance requirements:* For master's, GRE General Test, minimum GPA of 3.0 in last 60 hours of course work; for doctorate, GRE General Test, minimum GPA of 3.5 in last 60 hours of course work. Additional exam requirements/recommendations for international students: Required—TOEFL (minimum score 580 paper-based; 237 computer-based; 85 iBT), IELTS (minimum score 7). *Application deadline:* For fall admission, 2/1 for domestic and international students. Application fee: $50. Electronic applications accepted. *Financial support:* In 2006–07, 18 research assistantships with full and partial tuition reimbursements (averaging $3,324 per year), 45 teaching assistantships with full and partial tuition reimbursements (averaging $11,080 per year) were awarded; fellowships, career-related internships or fieldwork, institutionally sponsored loans, tuition waivers (full and partial), and unspecified assistantships also available. Financial award application deadline: 3/1. *Faculty research:* Injury prevention and rehabilitation, human skeletal muscle adaptation, cardiovascular health and fitness, lifestyle modification and health promotion. Total annual research expenditures: $250,125. *Unit head:* Dr. Larry Hall, Chair, 801-422-7303, Fax: 801-422-0543, E-mail: larry_hall@byu.edu. *Application contact:* Dr. J. William Myrer, Graduate Coordinator, 801-422-2690, Fax: 801-422-0557, E-mail: bill_myrer@byu.edu.

California University of Pennsylvania, School of Graduate Studies and Research, School of Education, Department of Athletic Training, California, PA 15419-1394. Offers athletic training (MS); exercise science and health promotion (MS), including fitness and wellness, performance enhancement and injury prevention, rehabilitation sciences, sport management, sport psychology. Summer admission only. *Faculty:* 34 full-time (15 women), 7 part-time/adjunct (0 women). *Students:* 18 full-time (11 women); includes 4 minority (1 African American, 3 Asian Americans or Pacific Islanders). Average age 23. 4 applicants, 50% accepted, 1 enrolled. In 2006, 18 degrees awarded. *Median time to degree:* Master's–1.5 years full-time, 1.8 years part-time. *Degree requirements:* For master's, thesis, comprehensive exam. *Entrance requirements:* For master's, minimum GPA of 3.0. Additional exam requirements/recommendations for international students: Required—TOEFL (minimum score 550 paper-based; 213 computer-based; 80 iBT). *Application deadline:* For fall admission, 4/1 priority date for domestic students, 4/1 for international students. Applications are processed on a rolling basis. Application fee: $25. *Expenses:* Tuition, state resident: full-time $6,048; part-time $336 per credit. Tuition, nonresident: full-time $9,678; part-time $538 per credit. Required fees: $1,854; $263 per credit. Full-time tuition and fees vary according to course load, campus/location and program. *Financial support:* Traineeships and unspecified assistantships available. Financial award applicants required to submit FAFSA. *Faculty research:* Exercise physiology, pedagogy, athletic training, biomechanical engineering, case studies in injury and athletic medicine. Total annual research expenditures: $88,000. *Unit head:* Dr. William Biddington, Chairperson, 724-938-4562, Fax: 724-938-4342, E-mail: biddington@cup.edu.

Eastern Michigan University, Graduate School, College of Health and Human Services, School of Health Promotion and Human Performance, Program in Orthotics and Prosthetics, Ypsilanti, MI 48197. Offers MS. Part-time and evening/weekend programs available. Postbaccalaureate distance learning degree programs offered (minimal on-campus study). *Students:* 4 full-time (3 women), 2 part-time (both women); includes 1 minority (Hispanic American) Average age 26. *Entrance requirements:* Additional exam requirements/recommendations for international students: Required—TOEFL. *Application deadline:* For fall admission, 5/15 priority date for domestic students, 5/1 priority date for international students; for winter admission, 10/15 priority date for domestic students, 10/1 priority date for international students; for spring

admission, 3/15 priority date for domestic students, 3/1 priority date for international students. Applications are processed on a rolling basis. Application fee: $35. *Expenses:* Tuition, state resident: part-time $341 per credit hour. Tuition, nonresident: full-time $16,104; part-time $671 per credit hour. Required fees: $816; $34 per credit hour. $40 per term. One-time fee: $82 full-time. Tuition and fees vary according to course level, course load, degree level and reciprocity agreements. *Financial support:* Fellowships, research assistantships with full tuition reimbursements, teaching assistantships with full tuition reimbursements, career-related internships or fieldwork, Federal Work-Study, institutionally sponsored loans, scholarships/grants, tuition waivers (partial), and unspecified assistantships available. Support available to part-time students. Financial award applicants required to submit FAFSA.

Eastern Michigan University, Graduate School, College of Health and Human Services, School of Health Promotion and Human Performance, Program in Sports Medicine, Ypsilanti, MI 48197. Offers MS. Part-time and evening/weekend programs available. Postbaccalaureate distance learning degree programs offered (minimal on-campus study). *Students:* 3 full-time (all women), 6 part-time (4 women). Average age 28. In 2006, 6 degrees awarded. *Entrance requirements:* Additional exam requirements/recommendations for international students: Required—TOEFL. *Application deadline:* For fall admission, 5/15 priority date for domestic students, 5/1 priority date for international students; for winter admission, 10/15 priority date for domestic students, 10/1 priority date for international students; for spring admission, 3/15 priority date for domestic students, 3/1 priority date for international students. Applications are processed on a rolling basis. Application fee: $35. *Expenses:* Tuition, state resident: part-time $341 per credit hour. Tuition, nonresident: full-time $16,104; part-time $671 per credit hour. Required fees: $816; $34 per credit hour. $40 per term. One-time fee: $82 full-time. Tuition and fees vary according to course level, course load, degree level and reciprocity agreements. *Financial support:* Fellowships, research assistantships, teaching assistantships, career-related internships or fieldwork, Federal Work-Study, institutionally sponsored loans, scholarships/grants, tuition waivers (partial), and unspecified assistantships available. Support available to part-time students. Financial award applicants required to submit FAFSA.

Florida International University, College of Education, Department of Health, Physical Education, and Recreation, Program in Exercise and Sports Science, Miami, FL 33199. Offers advanced athletic injury training/sports medicine (MS); strength and conditioning (MS). *Accreditation:* NCATE. Part-time and evening/weekend programs available. *Faculty:* 4 full-time (2 women), 8 part-time/adjunct (all women). *Students:* 21 full-time (14 women), 12 part-time (6 women); includes 16 minority (4 African Americans, 1 Asian American or Pacific Islander, 11 Hispanic Americans). Average age 27. 34 applicants, 85% accepted, 29 enrolled. In 2006, 2 master's awarded. *Entrance requirements:* Additional exam requirements/recommendations for international students: Required—TOEFL (minimum score 550 paper-based; 213 computer-based; 80 iBT), IELTS (minimum score 6). *Application deadline:* For fall admission, 6/1 priority date for domestic students, 4/1 for international students; for winter admission, 10/1 priority date for domestic students, 9/1 for international students; for spring admission, 3/1 priority date for domestic students, 2/1 for international students. Applications are processed on a rolling basis. Application fee: $30. Electronic applications accepted. *Expenses:* Tuition, state resident: part-time $249 per credit hour. Tuition, nonresident: part-time $753 per credit hour. Tuition and fees vary according to program. *Financial support:* Fellowships, research assistantships, teaching assistantships, Federal Work-Study and tuition waivers (full and partial) available. Support available to part-time students. *Faculty research:* Strength and conditioning, women in athletic training, celiac disease. *Application contact:* Marisa Salazar, Student Recruiter, 305-348-3002, Fax: 305-348-3227, E-mail: marisa.salazar@fiu.edu.

Georgia State University, College of Education, Department of Kinesiology and Health, Program in Sports Medicine, Atlanta, GA 30303-3083. Offers MS. *Students:* 14 full-time (9 women); includes 3 minority (all African Americans), 1 international. Average age 24. 13 applicants, 92% accepted. *Degree requirements:* For master's, comprehensive exam. *Entrance requirements:* For master's, GRE General Test, minimum GPA of 2.5. *Application deadline:* For fall admission, 5/1 for domestic students; for spring admission, 10/1 for domestic students. Application fee: $25. *Financial support:* Research assistantships available. *Faculty research:* Athletic training. *Unit head:* Dr. J. Andrew Doyle, Chair, Department of Kinesiology and Health, 404-651-4258, E-mail: adoyle@gsu.edu.

Humboldt State University, Graduate Studies, College of Professional Studies, Department of Kinesiology, Arcata, CA 95521-8299. Offers athletic training education (MS); exercise science/wellness management (MS); pre-physical therapy (MS); teaching/coaching (MS). *Students:* 10 full-time (5 women), 5 part-time (1 woman); includes 4 minority (1 African American, 3 Asian Americans or Pacific Islanders). Average age 31. 15 applicants, 73% accepted, 6 enrolled. In 2006, 3 degrees awarded. *Degree requirements:* For master's, thesis or alternative. *Entrance requirements:* For master's, GMAT, minimum GPA of 2.5. Additional exam requirements/recommendations for international students: Required—TOEFL. *Application deadline:* Applications are processed on a rolling basis. Application fee: $55. *Financial support:* Teaching assistantships, career-related internships or fieldwork, Federal Work-Study, and institutionally sponsored loans available. Financial award application deadline: 3/1; financial award applicants required to submit FAFSA. *Faculty research:* Human performance, adapted physical education, physical therapy. *Unit head:* Dr. Sue MacConnie, Chair, 707-826-4536, Fax: 707-826-5451, E-mail: sem1@humboldt.edu. *Application contact:* Dr. Kathy Munoz, Coordinator, 707-826-3840, Fax: 707-826-5451, E-mail: kdm1@humboldt.edu.

Indiana State University, School of Graduate Studies, College of Arts and Sciences, Department of Life Sciences, Terre Haute, IN 47809-1401. Offers ecology (PhD); life sciences (MS); microbiology (PhD); physiology (PhD); science education (MS); sports medicine (PhD). *Faculty:* 22 full-time (6 women), 4 part-time/adjunct (1 woman). *Students:* 49 full-time (21 women), 15 part-time (7 women); includes 2 minority (both Asian Americans or Pacific Islanders), 14 international. Average age 28. 42 applicants, 64% accepted, 21 enrolled. In 2006, 14 master's, 2 doctorates awarded. *Degree requirements:* For master's, thesis (for some programs); for doctorate, thesis/dissertation, comprehensive exam. *Entrance requirements:* For master's and doctorate, GRE General Test. *Application deadline:* For fall admission, 7/1 priority date for domestic students; for spring admission, 11/1 priority date for domestic students. Applications are processed on a rolling basis. Application fee: $35. Electronic applications accepted. *Expenses:* Tuition, state resident: part-time $278 per credit. Tuition, nonresident: part-time $552 per credit. *Financial support:* In 2006–07, 23 teaching assistantships with partial tuition reimbursements (averaging $8,478 per year) were awarded; research assistantships with partial tuition reimbursements, Federal Work-Study, institutionally sponsored loans, and tuition waivers (partial) also available. Financial award application deadline: 3/1; financial award applicants required to submit FAFSA. *Unit head:* Dr. Swapan Ghosh, Interim Chairperson, 812-237-2400.

Indiana State University, School of Graduate Studies, College of Health and Human Performance, Department of Athletic Training, Terre Haute, IN 47809-1401. Offers MS. *Faculty:* 3 full-time (2 women), 1 part-time/adjunct (0 women). *Students:* 12 full-time (8 women), 1 (woman) part-time; includes 1 minority (American Indian/Alaska Native), 4 international. Average age 24. 3 applicants, 67% accepted, 2 enrolled. In 2006, 12 degrees awarded. *Degree requirements:* For master's, thesis or alternative. *Entrance requirements:* For master's, GRE General Test. *Application deadline:* For fall admission, 7/1 priority date for domestic students; for spring admission, 11/1 priority date for domestic students. Applications are processed on a rolling basis. Application fee: $35. Electronic applications accepted. *Expenses:* Tuition, state resident: part-time $278 per credit. Tuition, nonresident: part-time $552 per credit. *Financial support:* In 2006–07, 12 research assistantships with partial tuition reimbursements (averaging $6,300 per year) were awarded; teaching assistantships with partial tuition reimbursements, tuition waivers (partial) also available. Financial award application deadline: 3/1; financial award applicants required to submit FAFSA. *Unit head:* Dr. Jeffrey Edwards, Chairperson, 812-237-8232.

Indiana University Bloomington, School of Health, Physical Education and Recreation, Department of Kinesiology, Bloomington, IN 47405-7000. Offers adapted physical education (MS); applied sport science (MS); athletic training (MS); biomechanics (MS); clinical exercise physiology (MS); ergonomics (MS); exercise physiology (MS); human performance (MS, PhD, PE Dir); motor control (MS); sport management (MS). PhD offered through the University Graduate School. Part-time programs available. *Faculty:* 10 full-time (1 woman). *Students:* 106 full-time (47 women), 41 part-time (15 women); includes 16 minority (15 African Americans, 1 American Indian/Alaska Native), 26 international. Average age 26.Terminal master's awarded for partial completion of doctoral program. *Degree requirements:* For master's and PE Dir, thesis optional; for doctorate, variable foreign language requirement, thesis/dissertation. *Entrance requirements:* For master's, GRE General Test, minimum GPA of 2.8; for doctorate, GRE General Test, minimum graduate GPA of 3.5, minimum undergraduate GPA of 3.0; for PE Dir, GRE. *Application deadline:* For fall admission, 1/1 for international students; for spring admission, 9/1 for international students. Applications are processed on a rolling basis. Application fee: $50 ($60 for international students). *Expenses:* Tuition, state resident: full-time $5,791; part-time $241 per credit hour. Tuition, nonresident: full-time $16,866; part-time $703 per credit hour. *Financial support:* Fellowships, research assistantships with full tuition reimbursements, teaching assistantships with full tuition reimbursements, career-related internships or fieldwork, Federal Work-Study, institutionally sponsored loans, scholarships/grants, tuition waivers (partial), and fee remissions available. Financial award application deadline: 3/1. *Faculty research:* Exercise physiology and biochemistry, sports biomechanics, human motor control, adaptation of fitness and exercise to special populations. *Unit head:* John Shea, Chairperson, 812-855-3114. *Application contact:* Program Office, 812-855-5523, Fax: 812-855-9417, E-mail: kines@indiana.edu.

Kent State University, Graduate School of Education, Health, and Human Services, Program in Exercise, Leisure, and Sport, Kent, OH 44242-0001. Offers athletic training (MA); exercise physiology (MA); physical teacher education (MA); sport and recreation management (MA); sports studies (MA). *Faculty:* 15 full-time (7 women). *Students:* 47 full-time (25 women), 34 part-time (13 women); includes 11 minority (10 African Americans, 1 Hispanic American), 4 international. 46 applicants, 74% accepted. In 2006, 9 degrees awarded. Application fee: $30. *Unit head:* Dr. Steve Mitchell, Coordinator, 330-672-0206, E-mail: smitchel@kent.edu. *Application contact:* Nancy Miller, Academic Program Coordinator, Office of Graduate Student Services, 330-672-2576, Fax: 330-672-9162, E-mail: ogs@kent.edu.

Long Island University, Brooklyn Campus, School of Health Professions, Division of Sports Sciences, Brooklyn, NY 11201-8423. Offers adapted physical education (MS); athletic training and sports sciences (MS); exercise physiology (MS); health sciences (MS). Part-time and evening/weekend programs available. *Entrance requirements:* For master's, 2 letters of recommendation. Additional exam requirements/recommendations for international students: Required—TOEFL (minimum score 500 paper-based; 173 computer-based). Electronic applications accepted.

Montana State University–Billings, College of Allied Health Professions, Department of Health and Human Performance, Billings, MT 59101-0298. Offers athletic training (MS); sport management (MS). *Faculty:* 6 full-time (3 women). *Students:* 25. 7 applicants, 100% accepted, 7 enrolled. *Degree requirements:* For master's, thesis optional. *Entrance requirements:* For master's, GRE General Test, minimum undergraduate GPA of 3.0. Application fee: $40. *Expenses:* Tuition, state resident: full-time $4,599. Tuition, nonresident: full-time $10,786. *Financial support:* Teaching assistantships, career-related internships or fieldwork, Federal Work-Study, institutionally sponsored loans, scholarships/grants, tuition waivers (partial), and unspecified assistantships available. Support available to part-time students. Financial award application deadline: 5/1; financial award applicants required to submit FAFSA. *Unit head:* Dr. Ernie Randolfi, Chair, 406-657-2370, Fax: 406-657-2399, E-mail: randolfi@msubillings.edu. *Application contact:* David M. Sullivan, Graduate Studies Counselor, 406-657-2053, Fax: 406-657-2299, E-mail: dsullivan@msubillings.edu.

Ohio University, Graduate Studies, College of Health and Human Services, School of Recreation and Sport Sciences, Program in Athletic Training Education, Athens, OH 45701-2979. Offers MS RSS. *Faculty:* 4 full-time (1 woman), 2 part-time/adjunct (1 woman). *Students:* 16 full-time (9 women). 35 applicants, 49% accepted, 16 enrolled. In 2006, 17 degrees awarded. *Entrance requirements:* For master's, GRE, NATA certification. Additional exam requirements/recommendations for international students: Required—TOEFL. Application fee: $45. *Financial support:* In 2006–07, 3 teaching assistantships with full tuition reimbursements (averaging $9,000 per year) were awarded; unspecified assistantships also available. *Faculty research:* Athletic training, heart, injuries, health, muscles, exercise, sport. *Unit head:* Dr. Jeff Seegmiller, Coordinator, 740-593-9497, Fax: 740-593-0284, E-mail: seegmill@ohio.edu.

Old Dominion University, Darden College of Education, Program in Physical Education, Athletic Training Emphasis, Norfolk, VA 23529. Offers MS Ed. Part-time programs available. *Faculty:* 2 full-time (1 woman). *Students:* 10 full-time (9 women), 1 (woman) part-time; includes 3 minority (all African Americans) Average age 23. 40 applicants, 58% accepted, 11 enrolled. In 2006, 10 degrees awarded. *Degree requirements:* For master's, thesis or research project, thesis optional. *Entrance requirements:* For master's, GRE, minimum GPA of 3.0. Additional exam requirements/recommendations for international students: Required—TOEFL (minimum score 500 paper-based; 200 computer-based). *Application deadline:* For spring admission, 2/1 priority date for domestic and international students. Applications are processed on a rolling basis. Application fee: $40. Electronic applications accepted. *Expenses:* Tuition, area resident: Part-time $285 per credit hour. Tuition, nonresident: part-time $715 per credit hour. Required fees: $94 per semester. *Financial support:* In 2006–07, 23 research assistantships with partial tuition reimbursements (averaging $11,000 per year), 1 teaching assistantship with partial tuition reimbursement (averaging $9,000 per year) were awarded; fellowships, career-related internships or fieldwork, scholarships/grants, and unspecified assistantships also available. Financial award application deadline: 4/15; financial award applicants required to submit FAFSA. *Faculty research:* ACL injury prevention, lower extremity biomechanical program satisfaction, muscle energy techniques, tissue temperature. *Unit head:* Dr. Bonnie L. Van Lunen, Graduate Program Director, 757-683-3516, Fax: 757-683-4270, E-mail: bvanlune@odu.edu. *Application contact:* Dr. Bonnie L. Van Lunen, Graduate Program Director, 757-683-3516, Fax: 757-683-4270, E-mail: bvanlune@odu.edu.

Plymouth State University, College of Graduate Studies, Graduate Studies in Education, Program in Athletic Training, Plymouth, NH 03264-1595. Offers M Ed, MS. Part-time and evening/weekend programs available. *Students:* 2 full-time (0 women), 14 part-time (8 women); includes 2 minority (1 African American, 1 Asian American or Pacific Islander). Average age 27. 4 applicants, 100% accepted. In 2006, 3 degrees awarded. *Entrance requirements:* For master's, MAT, GRE General Test. *Application deadline:* For fall admission, 4/1 for domestic students. Applications are processed on a rolling basis. Application fee: $75. *Expenses:* Tuition, state resident: part-time $369 per credit. Tuition, nonresident: part-time $407 per credit. Tuition and fees vary according to course level. *Financial support:* Career-related internships or fieldwork, scholarships/grants, and unspecified assistantships available. Support available to part-time students. Financial award application deadline: 4/15; financial award applicants required to submit FAFSA. *Unit head:* Dr. Marjorie A. King, Program Coordinator, 603-535-3108, E-mail: making1@plymouth.edu.

Seton Hall University, School of Graduate Medical Education, Program in Athletic Training, South Orange, NJ 07079-2697. Offers MS. *Faculty:* 4 full-time (3 women), 8 part-time/adjunct (3 women). *Students:* 21 full-time (13 women); includes 8 minority (3 African Americans, 1 Asian American or Pacific Islander, 4 Hispanic Americans). 33 applicants, 70% accepted, 14 enrolled. In 2006, 10 degrees awarded. *Degree requirements:* For master's, research project. *Entrance requirements:* Additional exam requirements/recommendations for international students: Required—TOEFL. *Application deadline:* For fall admission, 11/15 for domestic and international students; for spring admission, 2/15 for domestic and international students. Applications are processed on a rolling basis. Application fee: $75. Electronic applications accepted. *Financial support:* Unspecified assistantships available. *Faculty research:* Electrotherapy. *Unit head:* Prof. Carolyn Goeckel, Chair, 973-275-2826, Fax: 973-275-2370. *Application contact:* Deborah Ann Verderosa, Director of Admissions, 973-275-2062, Fax: 973-275-2370, E-mail: verderde@shu.edu.

See Close-Up on page 2327.

Shenandoah University, School of Health Professions, Division of Athletic Training, Winchester, VA 22601-5195. Offers MS. *Faculty:* 3 full-time (1 woman), 1 part-time/adjunct (0 women). *Students:* 22 full-time (12 women), 1 part-time, 1 international. Average age 25. In 2006, 6 degrees awarded. *Entrance requirements:* For master's, SAT, GRE General Test, minimum GPA of 2.8, interview, athletic experience, 3 letters of recommendation. Additional exam requirements/recommendations for international students: Required—TOEFL (minimum score 527 paper-based; 197 computer-based; 71 iBT). *Application deadline:* Applications are processed on a rolling basis. Application fee: $30. Electronic applications accepted. *Expenses: Contact institution.* Full-time tuition and fees vary according to course load and program. *Financial support:* In 2006–07, 12 students received support. Institutionally sponsored loans available. Support available to part-time students. Financial award application deadline: 3/15; financial award applicants required to submit FAFSA. *Faculty research:* Cervical radiculopathy, validation of clinical field experience performance instrument, survey research on pre-participation physical examination in NCAA sports program. *Unit head:* Dr. Rose A. Schmieg, Director, 540-665-5534, Fax: 540-545-7387, E-mail: rschmieg@su.edu. *Application contact:* David Anthony, Dean of Admissions, 540-665-4581, Fax: 540-665-4627, E-mail: admit@su.edu.

Stephen F. Austin State University, Graduate School, College of Education, Department of Kinesiology and Health Science, Nacogdoches, TX 75962. Offers athletic training (MS); kinesiology (M Ed). *Degree requirements:* For master's, comprehensive exam. *Entrance requirements:* For master's, GRE General Test. Additional exam requirements/recommendations for international students: Required—TOEFL.

Texas Tech University Health Sciences Center, School of Allied Health Sciences, Program in Athletic Training, Lubbock, TX 79430. Offers MAT. *Faculty:* 4 full-time (2 women). *Students:* 43 full-time (26 women); includes 12 minority (5 African Americans, 1 American Indian/Alaska Native, 1 Asian American or Pacific Islander, 5 Hispanic Americans). Average age 25. 49 applicants, 49% accepted, 24 enrolled. In 2006, 17 degrees awarded. *Entrance requirements:* Additional exam requirements/recommendations for international students: Required—TOEFL. *Application deadline:* For fall admission, 10/15 priority date for domestic students; for spring admission, 2/1 priority date for domestic students. Application fee: $35. Electronic applications accepted. *Financial support:* Career-related internships or fieldwork, institutionally sponsored loans, and scholarships/grants available. Financial award applicants required to submit FAFSA. *Unit head:* Dr. Steve Sawyer, Chair, 806-743-3226, Fax: 806-743-3249, E-mail: steve.sawyer@ttuhsc.edu. *Application contact:* Jeri Moravcik, Assistant Director of Admissions and Student Affairs, 806-743-3220, Fax: 806-743-2994, E-mail: jeri.moravcik@ttuhsc.edu.

United States Sports Academy, Graduate Programs, Department of Sports Medicine, Daphne, AL 36526-7055. Offers MSS. Part-time programs available. Postbaccalaureate distance learning degree programs offered (minimal on-campus study). *Faculty:* 1 full-time (0 women), 5 part-time/adjunct (0 women). *Students:* 3 full-time (1 woman), 13 part-time (6 women); includes 2 minority (both Hispanic Americans) *Degree requirements:* For master's, thesis optional. *Entrance requirements:* For master's, GRE General Test, GMAT, or MAT, minimum GPA of 2.5, 3 letters of recommendation, resumé. Additional exam requirements/recommendations for international students: Required—TOEFL (minimum score 500 paper-based; 213 computer-based). *Application deadline:* Applications are processed on a rolling basis. Application fee: $50 ($125 for international students). Electronic applications accepted. *Financial support:* Career-related internships or fieldwork, Federal Work-Study, scholarships/grants, and service assistantships available. Support available to part-time students. Financial award application deadline: 8/15; financial award applicants required to submit FAFSA. *Faculty research:* Psychiatric aspects of injury rehabilitation, geriatric exercises and mobility. *Unit head:* Dr. Enrico Esposito, Chair, 251-626-3303 Ext. 155, Fax: 251-626-1149, E-mail: esposito@ussa.edu. *Application contact:* Dr. Albert G. Applin, Dean of Student Services, 251-626-3303 Ext. 147, Fax: 251-626-1035, E-mail: applin@ussa.edu.

See Close-Up on page 2353.

The University of Findlay, Graduate and Professional Studies, College of Health Professions, Program in Athletic Training, Findlay, OH 45840-3653. Offers MAT. *Students:* 15 full-time (9 women), 2 part-time (1 woman). 4 applicants, 25% accepted, 1 enrolled. In 2006, 5 degrees awarded. *Entrance requirements:* For master's, minimum GPA of 3.0, 75 hours of supervised clinical experience, 3 letters of recommendation. Additional exam requirements/recommendations for international students: Required—TOEFL (minimum score 550 paper-based). *Application deadline:* For fall admission, 2/1 for domestic and international students. Applications are processed on a rolling basis. Application fee: $25. Electronic applications accepted. *Unit head:* Dr. Donald Fuller, Director, Master of Athletic Training, 419-434-6739, Fax: 419-434-4822, E-mail: dfuller@findlay.edu. *Application contact:* Heather Riffle, Director, Graduate and Special Programs, 419-434-4640, Fax: 419-434-5517, E-mail: rifle@findlay.edu.

University of Florida, Graduate School, College of Health and Human Performance, Department of Applied Physiology and Kinesiology, Gainesville, FL 32611. Offers athletic training/sport medicine (MS, PhD); biomechanics (MS, PhD); clinical exercise physiology (MS); exercise physiology (MS, PhD); health and human performance (PhD); human performance (MS); motor learning/control (MS, PhD); sport and exercise psychology (MS). *Faculty:* 14 full-time (2 women), 1 part-time/adjunct (0 women). *Degree requirements:* For doctorate, thesis/dissertation. *Entrance requirements:* For doctorate, GRE General Test. *Application deadline:* For fall admission, 6/1 priority date for domestic students. Applications are processed on a rolling basis. Application fee: $20. Electronic applications accepted. *Expenses:* Tuition, state resident: full-time $6,827. Tuition, nonresident: full-time $21,951. Required fees: $999. *Financial support:* In 2006–07, 16 research assistantships (averaging $13,060 per year), 28 teaching assistantships (averaging $12,925 per year) were awarded; fellowships, unspecified assistantships also available. *Unit head:* Dr. Steven Dodd, Chair, 352-392-0584 Ext. 1342, E-mail: sdodd@hhp.ufl.edu. *Application contact:* Dr. Paul A. Borsa, Coordinator, 352-392-0584 Ext. 1261, Fax: 352-392-5262, E-mail: pborsa@hhp.ufl.edu.

University of Miami, Graduate School, School of Education, Department of Exercise and Sport Sciences, Program in Sports Medicine, Coral Gables, FL 33124. Offers MS Ed. *Students:* 2 full-time (both women), 1 (woman) part-time; includes 2 minority (both Hispanic Americans) Average age 25. 6 applicants, 100% accepted, 2 enrolled. In 2006, 3 degrees awarded. *Degree requirements:* For master's, special project, thesis optional. *Entrance requirements:* For master's, GRE General Test, GRE Subject Test. Additional exam requirements/recommendations for international students: Required—TOEFL. *Application deadline:* Applications are processed on a rolling basis. Application fee: $50. Electronic applications accepted. *Financial support:* In 2006–07, 3 students received support; research assistantships, teaching assistantships, career-related internships or fieldwork, Federal Work-Study, institutionally sponsored loans, tuition waivers (full and partial), and unspecified assistantships available. Financial award application deadline: 3/1; financial award applicants required to submit FAFSA. *Faculty research:* Care, prevention, and treatment of athletic injuries. *Unit head:* Dr. Gianluca Del Rossi, Coordinator, 305-284-3011, Fax: 305-284-3001, E-mail: delrossi@miami.edu. *Application contact:* Marissa Stevenson, Graduate Admissions Coordinator, 305-284-2167, Fax: 305-284-3003, E-mail: mstevenson@miami.edu.

The University of North Carolina at Chapel Hill, Graduate School, College of Arts and Sciences, Department of Exercise and Sport Science, Chapel Hill, NC 27599. Offers athletic training (MA); exercise physiology (MA); sport administration (MA). *Degree requirements:* For

Athletic Training and Sports Medicine

The University of North Carolina at Chapel Hill (continued)
master's, thesis, comprehensive exam. *Entrance requirements:* For master's, GRE General Test, minimum GPA of 3.0. Additional exam requirements/recommendations for international students: Required—TOEFL (minimum score 550 paper-based). Electronic applications accepted. *Faculty research:* Mild head injury in sport, endocrine system's response to exercise, obesity and children, effect of aerobic exercise on cerebral bloodflow in elderly population.

University of Pittsburgh, School of Health and Rehabilitation Sciences, Program in Health and Rehabilitation Sciences, Pittsburgh, PA 15260. Offers dietetics (MS); health and rehabilitation sciences (MS), including clinical dietetics, coordinated with dietetics, health care supervision and management, health information systems, occupational therapy, physical therapy, rehabilitation counseling, rehabilitation science and technology, sports medicine; wellness and human performance (MS). *Accreditation:* APTA. Part-time and evening/weekend programs available. *Faculty:* 40 full-time (23 women), 3 part-time/adjunct (2 women). *Students:* 93 full-time (67 women), 54 part-time (35 women); includes 31 minority (12 African Americans, 18 Asian Americans or Pacific Islanders, 1 Hispanic American), 15 international. Average age 30. 122 applicants, 82% accepted, 64 enrolled. In 2006, 28 degrees awarded. *Entrance requirements:* For master's, minimum GPA of 3.0. Additional exam requirements/recommendations for international students: Required—TOEFL, IELTS. *Application deadline:* Applications are processed on a rolling basis. Application fee: $50. Electronic applications accepted. *Financial support:* In 2006–07, 11 research assistantships with full tuition reimbursements (averaging $16,918 per year) were awarded; teaching assistantships, Federal Work-Study, institutionally sponsored loans, traineeships, and unspecified assistantships also available. Support available to part-time students. Financial award applicants required to submit FAFSA. *Faculty research:* Assistive technology, seating and wheeled mobility, cellular neurophysiology, low back syndrome, augmentative communication. Total annual research expenditures: $953,246. *Application contact:* Shameem Gangjee, Director of Admissions, 412-383-6558, Fax: 412-383-6535, E-mail: admissions@shrs.pitt.edu.

The University of Tennessee, Graduate School, College of Education, Health and Human Sciences, Department of Exercise, Sport, and Leisure Studies, Program in Exercise Science, Knoxville, TN 37996. Offers biomechanics/sports medicine (MS, PhD); exercise physiology (MS, PhD). *Accreditation:* CEPH (one or more programs are accredited). Part-time programs available. *Faculty:* 13 full-time (4 women). *Students:* 28 (21 women); includes 1 African American 4 international. In 2006, 5 degrees awarded. *Degree requirements:* For master's, thesis optional. *Entrance requirements:* For master's, minimum GPA of 2.7. Additional exam requirements/recommendations for international students: Required—TOEFL. *Application deadline:* For fall admission, 2/1 priority date for domestic students. Application fee: $35. Electronic applications accepted. *Expenses:* Tuition, state resident: full-time $5,574. Tuition, nonresident: full-time $16,840. Required fees: $792. *Financial support:* In 2006–07, 1 fellowship, 10 teaching assistantships were awarded; research assistantships, career-related internships or fieldwork, Federal Work-Study, institutionally sponsored loans, and unspecified assistantships also available. Financial award application deadline: 2/1; financial award applicants required to submit FAFSA. *Unit head:* Dr. Delores Smith, Interim Head, 865-974-5041, Fax: 865-974-6439, E-mail: delsmith@utk.edu.

The University of West Alabama, School of Graduate Studies, College of Education, Department of Physical Education and Athletic Training, Livingston, AL 35470. Offers physical education (M Ed, MAT). Part-time programs available. *Faculty:* 3 full-time (0 women). *Students:* 21 full-time (3 women), 24 part-time (8 women); includes 18 minority (all African Americans) In 2006, 9 degrees awarded. *Entrance requirements:* For master's, GRE General Test, MAT, minimum GPA of 2.75. *Application deadline:* For fall admission, 9/10 priority date for domestic students; for spring admission, 3/24 for domestic students. Applications are processed on a rolling basis. Application fee: $20 ($50 for international students). *Financial support:* Career-related internships or fieldwork, Federal Work-Study, scholarships/grants, and unspecified assistantships available. Support available to part-time students. Financial award applicants required to submit FAFSA. *Unit head:* Dr. R. T. Floyd, Chairperson, 205-652-3714, Fax: 205-652-3706, E-mail: rtf@uwa.edu.

University of Wisconsin–La Crosse, Office of University Graduate Studies, College of Science and Health, Department of Exercise and Sport Science, Program in Human Performance, La Crosse, WI 54601-3742. Offers athletic training (MS); human performance (MS). Part-time and evening/weekend programs available. *Students:* 25 full-time (10 women), 7 part-time (3 women); includes 2 minority (1 African American, 1 American Indian/Alaska Native), 2 international. Average age 25. 30 applicants, 73% accepted, 15 enrolled. In 2006, 14 degrees awarded. *Degree requirements:* For master's, thesis optional. *Entrance requirements:* For master's, GRE, course work in anatomy, physiology, biomechanics, and exercise physiology. Additional exam requirements/recommendations for international students: Required—TOEFL (minimum score 550 paper-based; 213 computer-based). *Application deadline:* For fall admission, 2/1 priority date for domestic students; for spring admission, 10/1 for domestic students. Applications are processed on a rolling basis. Application fee: $45. Electronic applications accepted. *Financial support:* In 2006–07, 11 research assistantships (averaging $7,020 per year) were awarded; career-related internships or fieldwork, Federal Work-Study, institutionally sponsored loans, scholarships/grants, health care benefits, tuition waivers (full and partial), unspecified assistantships, and grant-funded positions also available. Support available to part-time students. Financial award application deadline: 3/15; financial award applicants required to submit FAFSA. *Faculty research:* Athletic performance, strength and conditioning, anaerobic metabolism, body composition. *Unit head:* Dr. Glenn Wright, Director, 608-785-8689, Fax: 608-785-6520, E-mail: wright.glen@uwlax.edu. *Application contact:* Kathryn Kiefer, Associate Director of Admissions, 608-785-8939, E-mail: admissions@uwlax.edu.

Virginia Commonwealth University, Graduate School, School of Education, Department of Health and Human Performance, Richmond, VA 23284-9005. Offers athletic training (MS); exercise science (MS); rehabilitation and movement science (PhD); teacher education (MS). *Faculty:* 7 full-time (2 women). *Students:* 13 full-time (8 women), 28 part-time (17 women); includes 3 minority (2 African Americans, 1 American Indian/Alaska Native), 1 international. 8 applicants, 100% accepted, 8 enrolled. *Entrance requirements:* For master's, GRE General Test or MAT. *Application deadline:* For fall admission, 5/15 for domestic students; for spring admission, 11/15 for domestic students. Applications are processed on a rolling basis. Application fee: $50. *Financial support:* Career-related internships or fieldwork, Federal Work-Study, and institutionally sponsored loans available. Support available to part-time students. Financial award application deadline: 3/1. *Unit head:* Dr. Edmund Acevedo, Chair, 804-828-1948, Fax: 804-828-1946, E-mail: eoacevedo@vcu.edu. *Application contact:* Dr. Michael D. Davis, Director, Graduate Studies, 804-828-6530, Fax: 804-827-0676, E-mail: mddavis@vcu.edu.

See Close-Ups on pages 2331, 2333, and 1751.

West Chester University of Pennsylvania, Graduate Studies, School of Business and Public Affairs, Program in Administration, West Chester, PA 19383. Offers health services (MSA); human research management (MSA); individualized (MSA); leadership for women (MSA); long-term care (MSA); public administration (MSA); regional planning (MSA); sport and athletic training (MSA); training and development (MSA). Part-time and evening/weekend programs available. *Students:* 3 full-time (all women), 4 part-time (1 woman); includes 1 minority (African American) Average age 31. 20 applicants, 90% accepted. In 2006, 31 degrees awarded. *Degree requirements:* For master's, comprehensive exam. *Entrance requirements:* For master's, GMAT, GRE General Test, or MAT, interview, minimum GPA of 3.0. *Application deadline:* For fall admission, 4/15 priority date for domestic students; for spring admission, 10/15 for domestic students. Applications are processed on a rolling basis. Application fee: $35. *Financial support:* In 2006–07, research assistantships with full tuition reimbursements (averaging $5,000 per year); career-related internships or fieldwork and unspecified assistantships also available. Support available to part-time students. Financial award application deadline: 2/15; financial award applicants required to submit FAFSA. *Unit head:* Dr. Duane Milne, Director, 610-436-2448, E-mail: dmilne@wcupa.edu.

Western Michigan University, Graduate College, College of Education, Department of Health, Physical Education and Recreation, Kalamazoo, MI 49008-5202. Offers administration (MA); athletic training (MA); coaching and sports studies (MA); exercise science (MA); motor development (MA); physical education (MA); special education for handicapped children (MA).

West Virginia University, School of Physical Education, Morgantown, WV 26506. Offers athletic coaching (MS); athletic training (MS); exercise physiology (Ed D); physical education/teacher education (MS, Ed D), including administration of physical education (Ed D), curriculum and instruction (Ed D), motor development (Ed D), special physical education (Ed D); sport management (MS); sport psychology (MS, Ed D). *Degree requirements:* For doctorate, thesis/dissertation, oral exam, comprehensive exam. *Entrance requirements:* For master's, GRE or MAT, minimum GPA of 3.0; for doctorate, GRE General Test or MAT, minimum GPA of 3.5. Additional exam requirements/recommendations for international students: Required—TOEFL (minimum score 550 paper-based; 213 computer-based). Electronic applications accepted. *Expenses:* Tuition, state resident: full-time $4,926; part-time $276 per credit hour. Tuition, nonresident: full-time $14,278; part-time $796 per credit hour. Tuition and fees vary according to program. *Faculty research:* Sport psychosociology, teacher education, exercise psychology, counseling.

Exercise and Sports Science

American University, College of Arts and Sciences, School of Education, Teaching, and Health, Program in Health Promotion Management, Washington, DC 20016-8001. Offers MS. *Expenses:* Tuition: Full-time $18,864; part-time $1,048 per credit. Required fees: $380. Tuition and fees vary according to program. *Unit head:* Dr. Robert Karch, Director, 202-885-6285, Fax: 202-885-6288.

Appalachian State University, Cratis D. Williams Graduate School, College of Fine and Applied Arts, Department of Health, Leisure, and Exercise Science, Boone, NC 28608. Offers exercise science (MS). *Faculty:* 21 full-time (5 women). *Students:* 26 full-time (11 women), 4 part-time; includes 1 minority (Asian American or Pacific Islander) 28 applicants, 89% accepted, 20 enrolled. In 2006, 10 degrees awarded. *Degree requirements:* For master's, comprehensive exam. *Entrance requirements:* For master's, GRE General Test. Additional exam requirements/recommendations for international students: Required—TOEFL (minimum score 570 paper-based; 230 computer-based). *Application deadline:* For fall admission, 7/1 for domestic students, 1/1 for international students; for spring admission, 11/1 for domestic students, 6/1 for international students. Application fee: $50. *Expenses:* Tuition, state resident: full-time $2,600; part-time $127 per hour. Tuition, nonresident: full-time $13,200; part-time $597 per hour. Required fees: $2,000; $546 per term. *Financial support:* In 2006–07, 10 research assistantships (averaging $9,000 per year) were awarded; fellowships, teaching assistantships, career-related internships or fieldwork, Federal Work-Study, scholarships/grants, and unspecified assistantships also available. Support available to part-time students. Financial award application deadline: 7/1. *Faculty research:* Exercise immunology, biomechanics, exercise and chronic disease, muscle damage, strength and conditioning. Total annual research expenditures: $29,832. *Unit head:* Dr. Paul Gaskill, Head, 828-262-6336. *Application contact:* Dr. Charles Dumke, Director, 828-262-8652, E-mail: dumkecl@appstate.edu.

Arizona State University, Division of Graduate Studies, College of Liberal Arts and Sciences, Division of Natural Sciences and Mathematics, Interdisciplinary Program in Exercise Science, Tempe, AZ 85287. Offers PhD. *Degree requirements:* For doctorate, thesis/dissertation. *Entrance requirements:* For doctorate, GRE. *Faculty research:* Biomechanics, physiology of exercise, motor behavior/sport psychology.

Arizona State University at the Polytechnic Campus, East College, Department of Exercise and Wellness, Mesa, AZ 85212. Offers exercise and wellness (MS); physical activity, nutrition and wellness (PhD). *Faculty:* 6 full-time (3 women). *Students:* 32 full-time (22 women), 6 part-time (3 women); includes 1 minority (Hispanic American), 2 international. Average age 31. 33 applicants, 70% accepted, 20 enrolled. In 2006, 10 degrees awarded. *Degree requirements:* For master's, thesis, oral defense. *Entrance requirements:* For master's, GRE, letters of recommendation. Additional exam requirements/recommendations for international students: Required—TOEFL (minimum score 550 paper-based; 213 computer-based; 83 iBT); Recommended—TWE. *Application deadline:* For fall admission, 1/15 for domestic and international students. Applications are processed on a rolling basis. Application fee: $50. Electronic applications accepted. *Expenses:* Tuition, state resident: part-time $310 per credit hour. Tuition, nonresident: part-time $688 per credit hour. *Financial support:* In 2006–07, 1 research assistantship with partial tuition reimbursement (averaging $7,750 per year), 13 teaching assistantships (averaging $9,256 per year) were awarded; career-related internships or fieldwork, scholarships/grants, traineeships, health care benefits, and unspecified assistantships also available. Support available to part-time students. Financial award application deadline: 3/1; financial award applicants required to submit FAFSA. *Faculty research:* Fitness, health and wellness benefits of healthy lifestyles; disease prevention and fitness; physical activity and fitness program effectiveness; women's health issues; motivation, assessment, environmental health and fitness. Total annual research expenditures: $67,874. *Unit head:* Dr. William Stone, Chair, 480-727-1933, E-mail: william.stone@asu.edu. *Application contact:* Barbara Mattingly, Administrative Associate, 480-727-1959, Fax: 480-727-1051.

Arkansas State University, Graduate School, College of Education, Department of Health, Physical Education, and Sport Sciences, Jonesboro, State University, AR 72467. Offers exercise science (MS); physical education (MS, MSE, SCCT). Part-time programs available. *Faculty:* 4 full-time (1 woman), 1 part-time/adjunct (0 women). *Students:* 5 full-time (3 women), 9 part-time (2 women); includes 3 minority (all African Americans), 1 international. Average age 24. 12 applicants, 50% accepted, 6 enrolled. In 2006, 10 degrees awarded. *Degree requirements:* For master's, thesis or alternative, comprehensive exam. *Entrance requirements:* For master's, GRE General Test or MAT, appropriate bachelor's degree, official transcript; for SCCT, GRE General Test or MAT, interview, master's degree, official transcript. Additional exam requirements/recommendations for international students: Required—TOEFL (minimum score 213 computer-based). *Application deadline:* Applications are processed on a rolling basis. Application fee: $30 ($40 for international students). Electronic applications accepted. *Expenses:* Tuition, state resident: full-time $3,393; part-time $189 per hour. Tuition, nonresident: full-time $8,577; part-time $477 per hour. Required fees: $752; $39 per hour. $25 per semester. *Financial support:* Teaching assistantships, career-related internships or fieldwork, scholarships/grants, and unspecified assistantships available. Financial award application deadline: 7/1; financial award applicants required to submit FAFSA. *Unit head:* Dr. Jim Stillwell, Chair, 870-972-3066, Fax: 870-972-3096, E-mail: jstillwel@astate.edu.

Armstrong Atlantic State University, School of Graduate Studies, Program in Sports Medicine, Savannah, GA 31419-1997. Offers sports health sciences (MSSM). Part-time programs available. *Faculty:* 4 full-time (0 women). *Students:* 18 full-time (14 women), 12 part-time (6 women); includes 3 minority (2 African Americans, 1 Hispanic American), 2 international. Average age 27. In 2006, 11 degrees awarded. *Degree requirements:* For master's, project, thesis optional. *Entrance requirements:* For master's, GRE General Test, MAT, GMAT, minimum GPA of 2.5. Additional exam requirements/recommendations for international students: Required—TOEFL (minimum score 523 paper-based; 193 computer-based). *Application deadline:* For fall admission, 7/1 priority date for domestic and international students; for spring admission, 11/15 priority date for domestic and international students. Application fee: $25. *Expenses:* Tuition, state resident: full-time $2,286; part-time $127 per credit. Tuition, nonresident: full-time $9,144; part-time $508 per credit. One-time fee: $257. *Financial support:* In 2006–07, research assistantships with partial tuition reimbursements (averaging $2,500 per year); scholarships/grants, tuition waivers (full), and unspecified assistantships also available. Financial award applicants required to submit FAFSA. *Unit head:* Dr. James Streater, Department Head, 912-921-7346, Fax: 912-921-7350, E-mail: mssm@mail.armstrong.edu. *Application contact:* Dr. Robert Lefavi, Graduate Coordinator, 912-921-5482, E-mail: lefaviro@mail.armstrong.edu.

Ashland University, College of Education, Graduate Studies in Education, Department of Sport Sciences, Ashland, OH 44805-3702. Offers adapted physical education (M Ed); applied exercise science (M Ed); sport education (M Ed); sport management (M Ed). Part-time programs available. *Faculty:* 6 full-time (1 woman), 1 (woman) part-time/adjunct. *Students:* 26 full-time (12 women), 28 part-time (11 women); includes 4 minority (all African Americans) Average age 31. In 2006, 29 degrees awarded. *Degree requirements:* For master's, thesis or alternative, practicum, seminar. *Entrance requirements:* For master's, GRE General Test or MAT, minimum GPA of 2.75. Additional exam requirements/recommendations for international students: Required—TOEFL. *Application deadline:* For fall admission, 8/27 for domestic students; for spring admission, 1/14 for domestic students. Applications are processed on a rolling basis. Application fee: $30. *Expenses:* Tuition: Part-time $403 per credit. Tuition and fees vary according to degree level and program. *Financial support:* In 2006–07, 16 students received support, including teaching assistantships with full tuition reimbursements available (averaging $6,000 per year); institutionally sponsored loans and scholarships/grants also available. Financial award application deadline: 4/15. *Faculty research:* Coaching, legal issues, strength and conditioning, sport management rating of perceived exertion. *Unit head:* Dr. Glen Fincher, Chair, 419-289-5450, E-mail: gfincher@ashland.edu.

A.T. Still University of Health Sciences, Arizona School of Health Sciences, Mesa, AZ 85206. Offers advanced occupational therapy (MS); advanced physician assistant (MS); audiology (Au D); human movement (MS); medical informatics (MS); occupational therapy (MS); physical therapy (MS, DPT); physician assistant (MS); sports health care (MS); transitional physical therapy (DPT). *Accreditation:* AOTA (one or more programs are accredited); APTA. Postbaccalaureate distance learning degree programs offered (no on-campus study). *Faculty:* 47 full-time (27 women), 101 part-time/adjunct (60 women). *Students:* 442 full-time (277 women), 732 part-time (579 women); includes 143 minority (38 African Americans, 11 American Indian/Alaska Native, 55 Asian Americans or Pacific Islanders, 39 Hispanic Americans), 4 international. Average age 33. 1,471 applicants, 547 enrolled. In 2006, 104 master's, 432 doctorates awarded. *Degree requirements:* For master's and doctorate, thesis/dissertation (for some programs). *Entrance requirements:* For master's, GRE General Test, minimum GPA of 2.5; for doctorate, GRE, Evaluation of Practicing Audiologists Capabilities (Au D), Physical Therapy Evaluation Tool (DPT), current state licensure, master's degree or equivalent (Au D), minimum GPA of 2.7. *Application deadline:* For fall admission, 2/1 priority date for domestic and international students. Applications are processed on a rolling basis. Application fee: $60. *Expenses:* Contact institution. *Financial support:* In 2006–07, 382 students received support. Federal Work-Study and scholarships/grants available. Financial award application deadline: 5/1. *Faculty research:* Constraint-induced therapy, scapular motion analysis, shoulder mobility, biomechanics, quadriceps. *Unit head:* Dr. Randy Danielsen, Dean, 480-219-6000, Fax: 480-219-6110, E-mail: rdanielsen@atsu.edu. *Application contact:* Donna Sparks, Associate Director for Admissions, 660-626-2237, Fax: 660-626-2969, E-mail: admissions@atsu.edu.

Auburn University, Graduate School, College of Education, Department of Health and Human Performance, Auburn University, AL 36849. Offers exercise science (M Ed, MS, PhD); health promotion (M Ed, MS); physical education/teacher education (M Ed, MS, Ed D, Ed S). *Accreditation:* NCATE. Part-time programs available. *Faculty:* 13 full-time (5 women). *Students:* 40 full-time (18 women), 27 part-time (6 women); includes 7 minority (5 African Americans, 2 Hispanic Americans), 6 international. Average age 28. 67 applicants, 79% accepted, 24 enrolled. In 2006, 17 master's, 2 doctorates awarded. *Degree requirements:* For master's, thesis (for some programs); for doctorate, thesis/dissertation; for Ed S, exam, field project. *Entrance requirements:* For master's, GRE General Test; for doctorate and Ed S, GRE General Test, interview, master's degree. *Application deadline:* For fall admission, 7/7 for domestic students; for spring admission, 11/24 for domestic students. Applications are processed on a rolling basis. Application fee: $25 ($50 for international students). Electronic applications accepted. *Expenses:* Tuition, state resident: full-time $5,000. Tuition, nonresident: full-time $15,000. Required fees: $416. Tuition and fees vary according to program. *Financial support:* Research assistantships, teaching assistantships, Federal Work-Study available. Support available to part-time students. Financial award application deadline: 3/15. *Faculty research:* Biomechanics, exercise physiology, motor skill learning, school health, curriculum development. *Unit head:* Dr. Mary E Rudisill, Acting Head, 334-844-4483. *Application contact:* Dr. Joe Pittman, Interim Dean of the Graduate School, 334-844-4700.

Austin Peay State University, College of Graduate Studies, College of Professional Programs and Social Sciences, Department of Health and Human Performance, Clarksville, TN 37044. Offers health and physical education (MS). Part-time and evening/weekend programs available. Postbaccalaureate distance learning degree programs offered. *Faculty:* 6 full-time (4 women), 1 (woman) part-time/adjunct. *Students:* 31 full-time (16 women), 35 part-time (25 women); includes 30 minority (26 African Americans, 4 Hispanic Americans). Average age 30. In 2006, 29 degrees awarded. *Degree requirements:* For master's, thesis optional. *Entrance requirements:* For master's, GRE General Test, minimum GPA of 2.5, 2 letters of recommendation. Additional exam requirements/recommendations for international students: Required—TOEFL (minimum score 500 paper-based; 173 computer-based). *Application deadline:* For fall admission, 7/31 priority date for domestic students; for spring admission, 12/17 priority date for domestic students. Applications are processed on a rolling basis. Application fee: $25. Electronic applications accepted. *Expenses:* Tuition, state resident: full-time $5,138; part-time $272 per credit hour. Tuition, nonresident: full-time $14,832; part-time $693 per credit hour. Required fees: $1,009. *Financial support:* In 2006–07, fellowships (averaging $9,000 per year), research assistantships (averaging $10,270 per year) were awarded; career-related internships or fieldwork, Federal Work-Study, institutionally sponsored loans, scholarships/grants, and unspecified assistantships also available. Support available to part-time students. Financial award application deadline: 3/1; financial award applicants required to submit FAFSA. *Faculty research:* Aging and physical activity. *Unit head:* Dr. Dixie Dennis, Professor and Chair, 931-221-6111, Fax: 931-221-7040, E-mail: dennisdi@apsu.edu.

Ball State University, Graduate School, College of Applied Science and Technology, Interdepartmental Program in Human Bioenergetics, Muncie, IN 47306-1099. Offers PhD. *Students:* 4 full-time (2 women), 2 part-time. 3 applicants, 67% accepted, 2 enrolled. In 2006, 2 degrees awarded. *Degree requirements:* For doctorate, thesis/dissertation. *Entrance requirements:* For doctorate, GRE General Test, interview, minimum graduate GPA of 3.2, resumé. Application fee: $25 ($35 for international students). *Financial support:* In 2006–07, 3 research assistantships with full tuition reimbursements (averaging $10,815 per year), 5 teaching assistantships (averaging $15,661 per year) were awarded. Financial award application deadline: 3/1. *Unit head:* Dr. Bruce Craig, Director, 765-285-1156, Fax: 765-285-8596.

Barry University, School of Human Performance and Leisure Sciences, Program in Movement Science, Specialization in Exercise Science, Miami Shores, FL 33161-6695. Offers MS. *Students:* 4 full-time (3 women), 2 part-time, 1 international. 10 applicants, 50% accepted, 1 enrolled. In 2006, 4 degrees awarded. *Degree requirements:* For master's, thesis, comprehensive exam. *Entrance requirements:* For master's, GRE, minimum GPA of 3.0. *Application deadline:* Applications are processed on a rolling basis. Application fee: $30. Electronic applications accepted. *Faculty research:* Physiological adaptations to exercise. *Unit head:* Dr. Constance Mier, Coordinator, 305-899-3573, Fax: 305-899-3556, E-mail: cmier@mail.barry.edu. *Application contact:* Dave Fletcher, Director of Graduate Admissions, 305-899-3113, Fax: 305-899-2971, E-mail: dfletcher@mail.barry.edu.

Baylor University, Graduate School, School of Education, Department of Health, Human Performance and Recreation, Waco, TX 76798. Offers exercise, nutrition and preventive health (PhD); health, human performance and recreation (MS Ed). *Accreditation:* NCATE. Part-time programs available. *Faculty:* 13 full-time (5 women), 3 part-time/adjunct (1 woman). *Students:* 58 full-time (33 women), 31 part-time (16 women); includes 14 minority (7 African Americans, 4 American Indian/Alaska Native, 1 Asian American or Pacific Islander, 2 Hispanic Americans), 5 international. 30 applicants, 87% accepted. In 2006, 41 master's, 5 doctorates awarded. *Degree requirements:* For master's, thesis optional. *Entrance requirements:* For master's, GRE General Test. *Application deadline:* For fall admission, 4/1 priority date for domestic students; for spring admission, 10/1 for domestic students. Applications are processed on a rolling basis. Application fee: $25. Electronic applications accepted. *Financial support:* In 2006–07, 35 students received support, including 22 teaching assistantships; career-related internships or fieldwork, Federal Work-Study, institutionally sponsored loans, tuition waivers (partial), and recreation supplements also available. *Faculty research:* Behavior change theory, pedagogy, nutrition and enzyme therapy, exercise testing, health planning. *Unit head:* Dr. Mike Greenwood, Graduate Program Director, 254-710-3505, Fax: 254-710-3527, E-mail: mike_greenwood@baylor.edu. *Application contact:* Suzanne Keener, Administrative Assistant, 254-710-3588, Fax: 254-710-3870.

Bemidji State University, School of Graduate Studies, College of Professional Studies, Field of Sport Studies, Bemidji, MN 56601-2699. Offers MS. Part-time programs available. *Faculty:* 11 full-time (4 women). *Students:* 3 full-time (2 women), 16 part-time (4 women); includes 1 minority (American Indian/Alaska Native). Average age 34. 11 applicants, 100% accepted. In 2006, 5 degrees awarded. *Degree requirements:* For master's, thesis, departmental qualifying exam. *Entrance requirements:* Additional exam requirements/recommendations for international students: Required—TOEFL. *Application deadline:* For fall admission, 5/1 for domestic students. Applications are processed on a rolling basis. Application fee: $20. Electronic applications accepted. *Expenses:* Tuition, nonresident: part-time $284 per credit. Required fees: $86 per credit. *Financial support:* In 2006–07, 15 research assistantships with partial tuition reimbursements (averaging $8,250 per year), 12 teaching assistantships with partial tuition reimbursements (averaging $8,250 per year) were awarded; career-related internships or fieldwork, Federal Work-Study, scholarships/grants, health care benefits, and unspecified assistantships also available. Support available to part-time students. Financial award application deadline: 5/1. *Unit head:* Dr. Muriel Gilman, Chair, 218-755-2740, Fax: 218-755-3898, E-mail: mgilman@bemidjistate.edu.

Benedictine University, Graduate Programs, Program in Clinical Exercise Physiology, Lisle, IL 60532-0900. Offers MS. Part-time programs available. *Faculty:* 1 full-time (0 women), 3 part-time/adjunct (1 woman). *Students:* 20 (16 women); includes 3 minority (all Asian Americans or Pacific Islanders) 1 international. Average age 28. 15 applicants, 87% accepted, 9 enrolled. In 2006, 8 degrees awarded. *Entrance requirements:* Additional exam requirements/recommendations for international students: Required—TOEFL (minimum score 550 paper-based; 213 computer-based). *Application deadline:* For fall admission, 9/1 for domestic students; for winter admission, 12/1 for domestic students; for spring admission, 2/15 for domestic students. Applications are processed on a rolling basis. Application fee: $40. Electronic applications accepted. *Expenses:* Tuition: Full-time $12,150; part-time $450 per credit hour. *Financial support:* Career-related internships or fieldwork and health care benefits available. Support available to part-time students. *Faculty research:* Protein synthesis cell signaling control, aging. *Unit head:* Dr. Craig Broeder, Director, 630-829-6227, Fax: 630-960-1126, E-mail: cbroeder@ben.edu. *Application contact:* Kari Gibbons, Director, Admissions, 630-829-6200, Fax: 630-829-6584, E-mail: kgibbons@ben.edu.

Bloomsburg University of Pennsylvania, School of Graduate Studies, College of Liberal Arts, Department of Exercise Science and Athletics, Bloomsburg, PA 17815-1301. Offers exercise science (MS). *Faculty:* 8 full-time (2 women). *Students:* 16 full-time (10 women), 6 part-time (4 women). Average age 25. 17 applicants, 100% accepted, 11 enrolled. In 2006, 11 degrees awarded. *Degree requirements:* For master's, thesis, practical clinical experience. *Entrance requirements:* For master's, GRE General Test or MAT, minimum QPA of 3.0. Additional exam requirements/recommendations for international students: Required—TOEFL (minimum score 550 paper-based; 213 computer-based; 79 iBT). *Application deadline:* Applications are processed on a rolling basis. Application fee: $30. Electronic applications accepted. *Expenses:* Tuition, state resident: full-time $6,048; part-time $336 per credit. Tuition, nonresident: full-time $9,678; part-time $538 per credit. Required fees: $1,415. *Financial support:* Unspecified assistantships available. *Unit head:* Dr. Swapan Mookerjee, Chair, 570-389-4743, Fax: 570-389-5047, E-mail: smookerj@bloomu.edu. *Application contact:* Dr. Timothy McConnell, Coordinator, 570-389-4376, Fax: 570-389-5047, E-mail: tmmcconne@bloomu.edu.

Boise State University, Graduate College, College of Education, Department of Kinesiology, Program in Exercise and Sports Studies, Boise, ID 83725-0399. Offers MS. Part-time programs available. *Faculty:* 14 full-time (5 women), 6 part-time/adjunct (0 women). *Students:* 7 full-time (2 women), 29 part-time (18 women), 2 international. Average age 31. 25 applicants, 100% accepted, 9 enrolled. In 2006, 9 degrees awarded. *Degree requirements:* For master's, thesis. *Entrance requirements:* For master's, minimum GPA of 3.0. *Application deadline:* For fall admission, 3/1 priority date for domestic students; for spring admission, 10/1 priority date for domestic students. Applications are processed on a rolling basis. Application fee: $0. Electronic applications accepted. *Financial support:* In 2006–07, 8 students received support. Career-related internships or fieldwork, Federal Work-Study, institutionally sponsored loans, and unspecified assistantships available. Support available to part-time students. Financial award application deadline: 3/1. *Unit head:* Dr. Chad Harris, Coordinator, 208-426-3973, Fax: 208-426-1894, E-mail: charris@boisestate.edu.

Brigham Young University, Graduate Studies, College of Health and Human Performance, Department of Exercise Sciences, Provo, UT 84602-1001. Offers athletic training (MS); exercise physiology (MS, PhD); health promotion (MS, PhD); physical medicine and rehabilitation (PhD); sports pedagogy (MS). *Faculty:* 19 full-time (3 women), 1 (woman) part-time/adjunct. *Students:* 23 full-time (10 women), 48 part-time (21 women); includes 7 minority (3 American Indian/Alaska Native, 1 Asian American or Pacific Islander, 3 Hispanic Americans). Average age 28. 30 applicants, 70% accepted, 14 enrolled. In 2006, 9 master's, 4 doctorates awarded. *Median time to degree:* Of those who began their doctoral program in fall 1998, 100% received their degree in 8 years or less. *Degree requirements:* For master's, thesis, oral defense; for doctorate, thesis/dissertation, oral defense, oral and written exams, comprehensive exam. *Entrance requirements:* For master's, GRE General Test, minimum GPA of 3.0 in last 60 hours of course work; for doctorate, GRE General Test, minimum GPA of 3.5 in last 60 hours of course work. Additional exam requirements/recommendations for international students: Required—TOEFL (minimum score 580 paper-based; 237 computer-based; 85 iBT), IELTS (minimum score 7). *Application deadline:* For fall admission, 2/1 for domestic and international students. Application fee: $50. Electronic applications accepted. *Financial support:* In 2006–07, 18 research assistantships with full and partial tuition reimbursements (averaging $3,324 per year), 45 teaching assistantships with full and partial tuition reimbursements (averaging

Exercise and Sports Science

Brigham Young University (continued)
$11,080 per year) were awarded; fellowships, career-related internships or fieldwork, institutionally sponsored loans, tuition waivers (full and partial), and unspecified assistantships also available. Financial award application deadline: 3/1. *Faculty research:* Injury prevention and rehabilitation, human skeletal muscle adaptation, cardiovascular health and fitness, lifestyle modification and health promotion. Total annual research expenditures: $250,125. *Unit head:* Dr. Larry Hall, Chair, 801-422-7303, Fax: 801-422-0543, E-mail: larry_hall@byu.edu. *Application contact:* Dr. J. William Myrer, Graduate Coordinator, 801-422-2690, Fax: 801-422-0557, E-mail: bill_myrer@byu.edu.

Brooklyn College of the City University of New York, Division of Graduate Studies, Department of Physical Education and Exercise Science, Brooklyn, NY 11210-2889. Offers exercise science and rehabilitation (MS), including psychosocial aspects of physical activity, sports management; physical education (MS, MS Ed). Part-time programs available. *Students:* 1 (woman) full-time, 52 part-time (16 women); includes 15 minority (10 African Americans, 5 Hispanic Americans), 16 international. 37 applicants, 84% accepted, 13 enrolled. In 2006, 21 degrees awarded. *Degree requirements:* For master's, comprehensive exam or thesis. *Entrance requirements:* For master's, previous course work in physical education and education, minimum GPA of 3.0, 2 letters of recommendation, essay. Additional exam requirements/recommendations for international students: Required—TOEFL. *Application deadline:* For fall admission, 3/1 priority date for domestic students, 2/1 priority date for international students; for spring admission, 11/1 priority date for domestic students, 10/1 priority date for international students. Applications are processed on a rolling basis. Application fee: $125. Electronic applications accepted. *Expenses:* Tuition, state resident: full-time $6,400; part-time $270 per credit. Tuition, nonresident: full-time $12,000; part-time $500 per credit. Required fees: $118 per semester. *Financial support:* Career-related internships or fieldwork, Federal Work-Study, institutionally sponsored loans, and scholarships/grants available. Support available to part-time students. Financial award application deadline: 5/1; financial award applicants required to submit FAFSA. *Faculty research:* Exercise physiology, motor learning, sports psychology, women in athletics. Total annual research expenditures: $9,231. *Unit head:* Dr. Charles Tobey, Chairperson, 718-951-5514, E-mail: ctobey@brooklyn.cuny.edu. *Application contact:* Karen Alleyne-Pierre, Director of Admissions Services and Enrollment Communications, 718-951-5902, Fax: 718-951-4506, E-mail: grads@brooklyn.cuny.edu.

California State University, Fresno, Division of Graduate Studies, College of Health and Human Services, Department of Kinesiology, Fresno, CA 93740-8027. Offers exercise science (MA); sport psychology (MA). Part-time and evening/weekend programs available. *Degree requirements:* For master's, thesis or alternative. *Entrance requirements:* For master's, GRE General Test, minimum GPA of 2.7. Additional exam requirements/recommendations for international students: Required—TOEFL. Electronic applications accepted. *Faculty research:* Refugee education, homeless, geriatrics, fitness.

California University of Pennsylvania, School of Graduate Studies and Research, School of Education, Department of Athletic Training, Program in Exercise Science and Health Promotion, California, PA 15419-1394. Offers fitness and wellness (MS); performance enhancement and injury prevention (MS); rehabilitation sciences (MS); sport management (MS); sport psychology (MS). Part-time and evening/weekend programs available. Postbaccalaureate distance learning degree programs offered (no on-campus study). *Faculty:* 34 full-time (15 women), 7 part-time/adjunct (0 women). *Students:* 382 full-time (167 women), 44 part-time (15 women); includes 68 minority (35 African Americans, 2 American Indian/Alaska Native, 17 Asian Americans or Pacific Islanders, 14 Hispanic Americans). Average age 31. In 2006, 176 degrees awarded. *Median time to degree:* Master's–1.5 years full-time, 2.25 years part-time. *Degree requirements:* For master's, thesis optional. *Entrance requirements:* For master's, minimum QPA of 3.0. Additional exam requirements/recommendations for international students: Required—TOEFL (minimum score 550 paper-based; 213 computer-based; 80 iBT). *Application deadline:* For fall admission, 8/1 priority date for domestic and international students; for winter admission, 12/1 priority date for domestic and international students; for spring admission, 5/1 priority date for domestic and international students. Applications are processed on a rolling basis. Application fee: $25. Electronic applications accepted. *Expenses:* Contact institution. *Financial support:* Career-related internships or fieldwork, scholarships/grants, and unspecified assistantships available. Financial award applicants required to submit FAFSA. *Faculty research:* Reducing obesity in children, sport performance, creating unique biomechanical assessment techniques, Web-based training for fitness professionals, Webcams. Total annual research expenditures: $25,000. *Unit head:* Prof. Barry McGlumphy, Graduate Coordinator, 724-938-1694, Fax: 724-938-4342, E-mail: mcglumphy@cup.edu.

Central Connecticut State University, School of Graduate Studies, School of Education and Professional Studies, Department of Physical Education and Health Fitness Studies, New Britain, CT 06050-4010. Offers physical education (MS, Certificate). Part-time and evening/weekend programs available. *Faculty:* 16 full-time (8 women), 21 part-time/adjunct (16 women). *Students:* 20 full-time (6 women), 35 part-time (12 women); includes 3 minority (2 African Americans, 1 Hispanic American), 1 international. Average age 29. 38 applicants, 79% accepted, 17 enrolled. In 2006, 19 master's, 1 other advanced degree awarded. *Degree requirements:* For master's, thesis or alternative, comprehensive exam. *Entrance requirements:* For master's, minimum GPA of 2.7, bachelor's degree in physical education (preferred). Additional exam requirements/recommendations for international students: Required—TOEFL. *Application deadline:* For fall admission, 7/1 priority date for domestic students; for spring admission, 12/1 for domestic students. Applications are processed on a rolling basis. Application fee: $50. Electronic applications accepted. *Expenses:* Tuition, area resident: Full-time $3,970; part-time $380 per credit. Tuition, state resident: full-time $5,955; part-time $380 per credit. Tuition, nonresident: full-time $11,061; part-time $380 per credit. Required fees: $3,189. One-time fee: $62 part-time. Tuition and fees vary according to degree level and program. *Financial support:* In 2006–07, 5 students received support, including 5 research assistantships; career-related internships or fieldwork, Federal Work-Study, scholarships/grants, and unspecified assistantships also available. Support available to part-time students. Financial award application deadline: 3/1; financial award applicants required to submit FAFSA. *Faculty research:* Exercise science, athletic training, preparation of physical education for schools. *Unit head:* Dr. David Harackiewicz, Chair, 860-832-2155.

Central Michigan University, College of Graduate Studies, The Herbert H. and Grace A. Dow College of Health Professions, Department of Physical Education and Sport, Mount Pleasant, MI 48859. Offers athletic administration (MA); coaching (MA); exercise science (MA); sport administration (MA); teaching (MA). *Degree requirements:* For master's, thesis or alternative, registration. *Faculty research:* Biomechanical analysis of sports skills, sociological studies, psychological studies.

Cleveland State University, College of Graduate Studies, College of Education and Human Services, Department of Health, Physical Education, Recreation and Dance, Cleveland, OH 44115. Offers community health education (M Ed); exercise science (M Ed); human performance (M Ed); physical education pedagogy (M Ed); school health education (M Ed); sport and exercise psychology (M Ed); sports management (M Ed). Part-time programs available. *Faculty:* 9 full-time (5 women), 3 part-time/adjunct (0 women). *Students:* 12 full-time (7 women), 62 part-time (32 women); includes 16 minority (15 African Americans, 1 Asian American or Pacific Islander), 4 international. Average age 30. 52 applicants, 52% accepted, 19 enrolled. In 2006, 36 degrees awarded. *Degree requirements:* For master's, thesis optional. *Entrance requirements:* For master's, GRE General Test or MAT (if undergraduate GPA is below 2.75), minimum undergraduate GPA of 2.75. Additional exam requirements/recommendations for international students: Required—TOEFL (minimum score 525 paper-based; 197 computer-based), IELTS (minimum score 6). *Application deadline:* For fall admission, 7/15 priority date for domestic students; for spring admission, 12/15 priority date for domestic students. Applications are processed on a rolling basis. Application fee: $30. Electronic applications accepted. *Financial support:* In 2006–07, 6 research assistantships with full and partial tuition reimbursements (averaging $3,480 per year), 1 teaching assistantship with full and partial tuition reimbursement (averaging $3,480 per year) were awarded; career-related internships or fieldwork, tuition waivers (full), and unspecified assistantships also available. Financial award application deadline: 3/15. *Faculty research:* Childhood obesity, bone density, marketing fitness centers, motor development of disabled, mental skills training. Total annual research expenditures: $102,615. *Unit head:* Dr. Sheila M. Patterson, Chairperson, 216-687-4870, Fax: 216-687-5410, E-mail: s.m.patterson@csuohio.edu.

The College of St. Scholastica, Graduate Studies, Department of Exercise Physiology, Duluth, MN 55811-4199. Offers MA. Part-time programs available. *Faculty:* 4 full-time (0 women). *Students:* 12 full-time (6 women), 1 (woman) part-time. Average age 30. 15 applicants, 73% accepted, 10 enrolled. In 2006, 15 degrees awarded. *Degree requirements:* For master's, thesis (for some programs). *Entrance requirements:* For master's, minimum GPA of 2.7. Additional exam requirements/recommendations for international students: Required—TOEFL (minimum score 550 paper-based; 213 computer-based; 79 iBT). *Application deadline:* For fall admission, 8/1 priority date for domestic students, 8/1 for international students; for spring admission, 11/15 priority date for domestic students, 11/15 for international students. Applications are processed on a rolling basis. Application fee: $50. Electronic applications accepted. *Financial support:* In 2006–07, 13 students received support, including 8 teaching assistantships (averaging $1,895 per year); Federal Work-Study and scholarships/grants also available. Support available to part-time students. Financial award applicants required to submit FAFSA. *Faculty research:* Cardiovascular and metabolic responses, cardiorespiratory effects, orthostatic intolerance, lower extremity asymmetry. *Unit head:* Dr. Larry Birnbaum, Director, 218-723-6297, Fax: 218-723-5991. *Application contact:* Tonya J. Roth, Graduate Recruitment Counselor, 218-723-6285, Fax: 218-733-2275, E-mail: gradstudies@css.edu.

Colorado State University, Graduate School, College of Applied Human Sciences, Department of Health and Exercise Science, Fort Collins, CO 80523-0015. Offers health and exercise science (MS); human bioenergetics (PhD). Part-time programs available. *Faculty:* 11 full-time (3 women). *Students:* 22 full-time (13 women), 14 part-time (7 women), 1 international. Average age 27. 58 applicants, 43% accepted, 14 enrolled. In 2006, 12 degrees awarded. *Degree requirements:* For master's, thesis optional. *Entrance requirements:* For master's, GRE General Test, minimum GPA of 3.0. Additional exam requirements/recommendations for international students: Required—TOEFL. *Application deadline:* For fall admission, 1/31 for domestic and international students; for spring admission, 9/30 for domestic and international students. Application fee: $50. Electronic applications accepted. *Expenses:* Tuition, state resident: full-time $4,248; part-time $236 per credit. Tuition, nonresident: full-time $15,642; part-time $869 per credit. Required fees: $66 per credit. Tuition and fees vary according to program. *Financial support:* In 2006–07, 9 fellowships (averaging $1,555 per year), 2 research assistantships with full tuition reimbursements (averaging $12,500 per year), 19 teaching assistantships with full tuition reimbursements (averaging $12,000 per year) were awarded; Federal Work-Study, institutionally sponsored loans, and traineeships also available. Support available to part-time students. *Faculty research:* Metabolism and metabolic disease, obesity, diabetes, hypertension, physical activity and health across the lifespan, bioenergetics. Total annual research expenditures: $608,063. *Unit head:* Richard Gay Israel, Head, 970-491-3785, Fax: 970-491-0216, E-mail: israel@cahs.colostate.edu. *Application contact:* Noehl Robin, Department Operations, 970-491-7161, Fax: 970-491-0445, E-mail: noehl@cahs.colostate.edu.

Concordia University, College of Arts and Sciences, Program in Human Services, River Forest, IL 60305-1499. Offers human services (MA), including administration, exercise science. Part-time and evening/weekend programs available. *Degree requirements:* For master's, thesis, comprehensive exam. *Entrance requirements:* For master's, minimum GPA of 2.9. Additional exam requirements/recommendations for international students: Required—TOEFL (minimum score 550 paper-based; 195 computer-based). Electronic applications accepted.

Concordia University, School of Graduate Studies, Faculty of Arts and Science, Department of Exercise Science, Montréal, QC H3G 1M8, Canada. Offers M Sc. *Students:* 9 full-time (8 women). 28 applicants, 46% accepted, 7 enrolled.Application fee: $50. *Unit head:* Dr. Robert Kilgour, Chair, 514-842-2424 Ext. 3322. *Application contact:* Dr. Richard Courtmanche, Assistant Professor.

East Carolina University, Graduate School, College of Health and Human Performance, Department of Exercise and Sports Science, Greenville, NC 27858-4353. Offers bioenergetics (PhD); exercise and sport science (MA, MA Ed). *Students:* 66 full-time (25 women), 26 part-time (10 women); includes 8 minority (all African Americans), 2 international. Average age 25. 12 applicants, 17% accepted, 0 enrolled. In 2006, 40 master's, 1 doctorate awarded. *Degree requirements:* For master's, thesis optional; for doctorate, thesis/dissertation, comprehensive exam, registration. *Entrance requirements:* For master's, GRE General Test or MAT; for doctorate, GRE. Additional exam requirements/recommendations for international students: Required—TOEFL. *Application deadline:* For fall admission, 2/1 priority date for domestic students, 2/1 for international students. Applications are processed on a rolling basis. Application fee: $50. *Financial support:* In 2006–07, 40 students received support, including 12 research assistantships with tuition reimbursements available (averaging $17,500 per year), 28 teaching assistantships (averaging $5,800 per year). Support available to part-time students. Financial award application deadline: 2/1. *Faculty research:* Diabetes metabolism, pediatric obesity, biomechanics of arthritis, physical activity measurement. *Unit head:* Dr. Peter Farrell, Chair, 252-328-4635, Fax: 252-328-4634, E-mail: farrellp@ecu.edu.

Eastern Michigan University, Graduate School, College of Health and Human Services, School of Health Promotion and Human Performance, Ypsilanti, MI 48197. Offers health and physical education (MS); orthotics and prosthetics (MS); sports management (MS); sports medicine (MS). Part-time and evening/weekend programs available. Postbaccalaureate distance learning degree programs offered (minimal on-campus study). *Faculty:* 19 full-time (10 women). *Students:* 9 full-time (6 women), 67 part-time (31 women); includes 10 minority (9 African Americans, 1 Hispanic American), 4 international. Average age 29. In 2006, 22 degrees awarded. *Entrance requirements:* Additional exam requirements/recommendations for international students: Required—TOEFL. *Application deadline:* For fall admission, 5/15 priority date for domestic students, 5/1 priority date for international students; for winter admission, 10/15 priority date for domestic students, 10/1 priority date for international students; for spring admission, 3/15 priority date for domestic students, 3/1 priority date for international students. Applications are processed on a rolling basis. Application fee: $35. *Expenses:* Tuition, state resident: part-time $341 per credit hour. Tuition, nonresident: full-time $16,104; part-time $671 per credit hour. Required fees: $816; $34 per credit hour. $40 per term. One-time fee: $82 full-time. Tuition and fees vary according to course level, course load, degree level and reciprocity agreements. *Financial support:* Fellowships, research assistantships with full tuition reimbursements, teaching assistantships with full tuition reimbursements, career-related internships or fieldwork, Federal Work-Study, institutionally sponsored loans, scholarships/grants, tuition waivers (partial), and unspecified assistantships available. Support available to part-time students. Financial award applicants required to submit FAFSA. *Unit head:* Dr. Murali Nair, Director, 734-487-0090, Fax: 734-487-2024, E-mail: murali.nair@emich.edu.

East Stroudsburg University of Pennsylvania, Graduate School, School of Health Sciences and Human Performance, Department of Exercise Science, East Stroudsburg, PA 18301-2999. Offers cardiac rehabilitation and exercise science (MS). Part-time and evening/weekend programs available. *Faculty:* 4 full-time (1 woman), 1 part-time/adjunct (0 women). *Students:* 25 full-time (16 women), 6 part-time (2 women); includes 1 minority (African American), 4 international. Average age 28. In 2006, 32 degrees awarded. *Degree requirements:* For master's, comprehensive exam. *Entrance requirements:* Additional exam requirements/recommendations for international students: Required—TOEFL (minimum score 560 paper-based; 220 computer-based; 83 iBT). *Application deadline:* For fall admission, 7/31 priority date for domestic students, 5/1 priority date for international students; for spring admission, 11/30 for domestic students, 10/1 for international students. Applications are processed on a rolling basis. Application fee: $50. *Expenses:* Tuition, state resident: full-time $6,048; part-time

$336 per credit. Tuition, nonresident: full-time $9,678; part-time $538 per credit. Required fees: $1,353; $67 per credit. One-time fee: $37 part-time. *Financial support:* In 2006–07, 19 research assistantships with full and partial tuition reimbursements were awarded; Federal Work-Study and institutionally sponsored loans also available. Financial award application deadline: 3/1. *Unit head:* Dr. Shala Davis, Graduate Coordinator, 570-422-3302, Fax: 570-422-3616, E-mail: sdavis@po-box.esu.edu.

East Stroudsburg University of Pennsylvania, Graduate School, School of Health Sciences and Human Performance, Department of Sports Studies, East Stroudsburg, PA 18301-2999. Offers management and leadership (MS); sports management (MS). *Faculty:* 4 full-time (1 woman). *Students:* 23 full-time (12 women), 20 part-time (4 women); includes 5 minority (4 African Americans, 1 Hispanic American). Average age 27. *Entrance requirements:* Additional exam requirements/recommendations for international students: Required—TOEFL (minimum score 560 paper-based; 220 computer-based; 83 iBT). *Application deadline:* For fall admission, 7/31 priority date for domestic students, 5/1 priority date for international students; for spring admission, 11/30 for domestic students, 10/1 for international students. Application fee: $50. *Expenses:* Tuition, state resident: full-time $6,048; part-time $336 per credit. Tuition, nonresident: full-time $9,678; part-time $538 per credit. Required fees: $1,353; $67 per credit. One-time fee: $37 part-time. *Financial support:* In 2006–07, 15 research assistantships were awarded; Federal Work-Study and unspecified assistantships also available. Financial award application deadline: 3/1; financial award applicants required to submit FAFSA. *Unit head:* Dr. Robert Fleischman, Graduate Coordinator, 570-422-3316.

East Tennessee State University, School of Graduate Studies, College of Education, Department of Physical Education, Exercise and Sport Sciences, Johnson City, TN 37614. Offers exercise physiology (MA); fitness leadership (MA); physical education (M Ed, MA); sports management (MA); sports sciences (MA). Part-time and evening/weekend programs available. *Degree requirements:* For master's, comprehensive exam (M Ed), oral and written comprehensive exams, thesis (MA). *Entrance requirements:* For master's, GRE General Test, major or minor in physical education or equivalent, interview, minimum GPA of 2.7. Additional exam requirements/recommendations for international students: Required—TOEFL (minimum score 550 paper-based; 213 computer-based). *Faculty research:* Resistance training for various populations, self actualization using challenging courses, park and recreation industry needs relative to recent university graduates, funding sport operations.

Florida Atlantic University, College of Education, Department of Exercise Science and Health Promotion, Boca Raton, FL 33431-0991. Offers M Ed, MS. Part-time and evening/weekend programs available. *Faculty:* 8 full-time (2 women), 4 part-time/adjunct (2 women). *Students:* 19 full-time (11 women), 7 part-time (6 women); includes 7 minority (1 African American, 2 Asian Americans or Pacific Islanders, 4 Hispanic Americans), 3 international. Average age 28. 22 applicants, 64% accepted, 7 enrolled. In 2006, 10 degrees awarded. *Degree requirements:* For master's, thesis optional. *Entrance requirements:* For master's, GRE General Test, minimum GPA of 3.0 during last 60 hours of course work. Additional exam requirements/recommendations for international students: Required—TOEFL (minimum score 500 paper-based). *Application deadline:* For fall admission, 7/1 priority date for domestic students; for spring admission, 4/1 priority date for domestic students. Applications are processed on a rolling basis. Application fee: $30. *Expenses:* Tuition, area resident: Full-time $4,394. Tuition, nonresident: full-time $16,441. *Financial support:* In 2006–07, 4 research assistantships with partial tuition reimbursements (averaging $12,000 per year), 11 teaching assistantships with partial tuition reimbursements (averaging $12,000 per year) were awarded; career-related internships or fieldwork also available. *Faculty research:* Pulmonary limitations during exercise, metabolism regulation, determinants of performance, age related change in functional mobility and geriatric exercise, behavioral change aimed at promoting active lifestyles. Total annual research expenditures: $280,000. *Unit head:* Dr. Sue Graves, Chair, 954-236-1261, Fax: 954-236-1259. *Application contact:* Dr. Joseph A. O'Kroy, Graduate Coordinator, 954-236-1266, Fax: 954-236-1259, E-mail: okroy@fau.edu.

Florida International University, College of Education, Department of Health, Physical Education, and Recreation, Program in Exercise and Sports Science, Miami, FL 33199. Offers advanced athletic injury training/sports medicine (MS); strength and conditioning (MS). *Accreditation:* NCATE. Part-time and evening/weekend programs available. *Faculty:* 4 full-time (2 women), 8 part-time/adjunct (all women). *Students:* 21 full-time (14 women), 12 part-time (6 women); includes 16 minority (4 African Americans, 1 Asian American or Pacific Islander, 11 Hispanic Americans). Average age 27. 34 applicants, 85% accepted, 29 enrolled. In 2006, 2 master's awarded. *Entrance requirements:* Additional exam requirements/recommendations for international students: Required—TOEFL (minimum score 550 paper-based; 213 computer-based; 80 iBT), IELTS (minimum score 6). *Application deadline:* For fall admission, 6/1 priority date for domestic students, 4/1 for international students; for winter admission, 10/1 priority date for domestic students, 9/1 for international students; for spring admission, 3/1 priority date for domestic students, 2/1 for international students. Applications are processed on a rolling basis. Application fee: $30. Electronic applications accepted. *Expenses:* Tuition, state resident: part-time $249 per credit hour. Tuition, nonresident: part-time $753 per credit hour. Tuition and fees vary according to program. *Financial support:* Fellowships, research assistantships, teaching assistantships, Federal Work-Study and tuition waivers (full and partial) available. Support available to part-time students. *Faculty research:* Strength and conditioning, women in athletic training, celiac disease. *Application contact:* Marisa Salazar, Student Recruiter, 305-348-3002, Fax: 305-348-3227, E-mail: marisa.salazar@fiu.edu.

Florida State University, Graduate Studies, College of Human Sciences, Department of Nutrition, Food, and Exercise Sciences, Tallahassee, FL 32306. Offers exercise science (PhD), including exercise physiology, motor learning and control; nutrition and food science (PhD); nutrition and food sciences (MS), including clinical nutrition, food science, nutrition and sport, nutrition science, nutrition, education and health promotion. *Faculty:* 15 full-time (9 women). *Students:* 44 full-time (35 women), 28 part-time (16 women); includes 16 minority (9 African Americans, 2 Asian Americans or Pacific Islanders, 5 Hispanic Americans), 12 international. 76 applicants, 72% accepted, 28 enrolled. In 2006, 17 master's, 4 doctorates awarded. *Degree requirements:* For master's, thesis optional; for doctorate, thesis/dissertation, registration. *Entrance requirements:* For master's and doctorate, GRE General Test, minimum GPA of 3.0. Additional exam requirements/recommendations for international students: Required—TOEFL (minimum score 80 iBT). *Application deadline:* For fall admission, 7/1 for domestic students, 5/1 for international students; for spring admission, 11/1 for domestic students, 12/1 for international students. Application fee: $30. Electronic applications accepted. *Expenses:* Tuition, state resident: full-time $5,822; part-time $243 per credit hour. Tuition, nonresident: full-time $20,976; part-time $874 per credit hour. Tuition and fees vary according to program. *Financial support:* In 2006–07, 43 students received support, including 3 fellowships with partial tuition reimbursements available (averaging $10,000 per year), 9 research assistantships with partial tuition reimbursements available (averaging $8,000 per year), 22 teaching assistantships with partial tuition reimbursements available (averaging $8,000 per year); career-related internships or fieldwork, Federal Work-Study, institutionally sponsored loans, scholarships/grants, and unspecified assistantships also available. Financial award application deadline: 1/15; financial award applicants required to submit FAFSA. *Faculty research:* Nutrition and exercise, vitamin A deficiency, protein biochemistry, cardiovascular responses to exercises, physiological effects of cigarette smoking related to health and wellness. *Unit head:* Dr. Bahram Arjmandi, Chair, 850-644-1828, Fax: 850-645-5000. *Application contact:* Olga Garmash, Program Assistant, 850-644-4800, Fax: 850-645-5000, E-mail: ogarmash@fsu.edu.

Gardner-Webb University, Graduate School, Department of Physical Education, Wellness, and Sports Studies, Boiling Springs, NC 28017. Offers sport science and pedagogy (MA). Part-time and evening/weekend programs available. *Faculty:* 1 (woman) full-time. *Students:* 1 full-time (0 women), 14 part-time (9 women); includes 3 minority (2 African Americans, 1 Asian American or Pacific Islander). Average age 25. 4 applicants, 100% accepted, 4 enrolled. In 2006, 6 degrees awarded. *Degree requirements:* For master's, comprehensive exam. *Entrance requirements:* For master's, GRE General Test or NTE, PRAXIS, minimum GPA of 2.5. *Application deadline:* For fall admission, 8/1 priority date for domestic students. Applications are processed on a rolling basis. Application fee: $25. Electronic applications accepted. *Expenses:* Tuition: Full-time $3,144; part-time $262 per hour. *Financial support:* Unspecified assistantships available. *Unit head:* Dr. Ken Baker, Chair, 704-406-4481, Fax: 704-406-4739.

George Mason University, Graduate School of Education, Program in Health Science, Fairfax, VA 22030. Offers exercise, fitness and health promotion (MS). *Faculty:* 21 full-time (8 women), 39 part-time/adjunct (24 women). *Students:* 8 full-time (all women), 25 part-time (18 women); includes 18 minority (8 African Americans, 7 Asian Americans or Pacific Islanders, 3 Hispanic Americans), 2 international. Average age 33. 15 applicants, 80% accepted, 8 enrolled. In 2006, 11 degrees awarded. *Degree requirements:* For master's, thesis optional. *Entrance requirements:* For master's, minimum GPA of 3.0 in last 60 hours of course work. *Application deadline:* For fall admission, 5/1 for domestic students; for spring admission, 11/1 for domestic students. Application fee: $60 ($75 for international students). Electronic applications accepted. *Expenses:* Tuition, state resident: full-time $5,724; part-time $238 per credit. Tuition, nonresident: full-time $16,896; part-time $704 per credit. Required fees: $1,656; $69 per credit. *Financial support:* Available to part-time students. Application deadline: 3/1; *Unit head:* Dr. David Wiggins, Chair, 703-993-2057, E-mail: dwiggin1@gmu.edu.

The George Washington University, School of Public Health and Health Services, Department of Exercise Science, Washington, AA 20052. Offers MS. *Degree requirements:* For master's, thesis, comprehensive exam. *Entrance requirements:* For master's, GRE General Test or MAT. Additional exam requirements/recommendations for international students: Required—TOEFL. *Faculty research:* Fitness and cardiac rehabilitation, exercise testing, women in exercise.

Georgia State University, College of Education, Department of Kinesiology and Health, Program in Exercise Science, Atlanta, GA 30303-3083. Offers MS. *Students:* 17 full-time (15 women), 13 part-time (6 women); includes 8 minority (5 African Americans, 2 Asian Americans or Pacific Islanders, 1 Hispanic American). Average age 28. 20 applicants, 80% accepted. In 2006, 13 degrees awarded. *Degree requirements:* For master's, comprehensive exam. *Entrance requirements:* For master's, GRE General Test, minimum GPA of 2.5. *Application deadline:* For fall admission, 5/1 for domestic students; for spring admission, 10/1 for domestic students. Application fee: $25. *Financial support:* Research assistantships available. *Faculty research:* Aging, exercise metabolism, biomechanics and ergonomics, blood pressure regulation, exercise performance. *Unit head:* Dr. J. Andrew Doyle, Chair, Department of Kinesiology and Health, 404-651-4258, E-mail: adoyle@gsu.edu.

Georgia State University, College of Education, Department of Kinesiology and Health, Program in Sport Science, Atlanta, GA 30303-3083. Offers PhD. *Students:* 4 full-time (0 women), 4 part-time; includes 1 minority (Asian American or Pacific Islander), 3 international. Average age 33. 5 applicants, 20% accepted. In 2006, 2 degrees awarded. *Degree requirements:* For doctorate, thesis/dissertation, comprehensive exam. *Entrance requirements:* For doctorate, GRE General Test or MAT, minimum GPA of 3.3. *Application deadline:* For fall admission, 3/1 for domestic students; for spring admission, 10/1 for domestic students. Application fee: $25. *Financial support:* Research assistantships, teaching assistantships available. *Faculty research:* Aging, exercise metabolism, biomechanics and ergonomics, blood pressure regulation, exercise performance. *Unit head:* Dr. J. Andrew Doyle, Chair, Department of Kinesiology and Health, 404-651-4258, E-mail: adoyle@gsu.edu.

High Point University, Norcross Graduate School, High Point, NC 27262-3598. Offers business administration (MBA); educational leadership (M Ed); elementary education (M Ed); history (MA); nonprofit organizations (MPA); special education (M Ed); sport studies (MS). *Accreditation:* ACBSP; NCATE. Part-time and evening/weekend programs available. *Faculty:* 31 full-time (11 women), 1 part-time/adjunct (0 women). *Students:* 49 full-time (29 women), 202 part-time (130 women); includes 72 minority (66 African Americans, 1 American Indian/Alaska Native, 2 Asian Americans or Pacific Islanders, 3 Hispanic Americans), 11 international. Average age 33. 171 applicants, 71% accepted, 94 enrolled. In 2006, 95 degrees awarded. *Degree requirements:* For master's, thesis (for some programs), comprehensive exam (for some programs), registration. *Entrance requirements:* For master's, GMAT (MBA), GRE, MAT, minimum GPA of 3.0. Additional exam requirements/recommendations for international students: Required—TOEFL (minimum score 550 paper-based). *Application deadline:* For fall admission, 4/15 priority date for domestic and international students; for spring admission, 10/15 priority date for domestic and international students. Applications are processed on a rolling basis. Application fee: $50. Electronic applications accepted. *Expenses:* Tuition: Full-time $9,270; part-time $1,545 per course. *Financial support:* In 2006–07, 190 students received support. Federal Work-Study, scholarships/grants, and unspecified assistantships available. Support available to part-time students. Financial award application deadline: 3/1; financial award applicants required to submit FAFSA. *Application contact:* Dr. Alberta Haynes Herron, Dean of Norcross Graduate School, 336-841-9198, Fax: 336-888-6378, E-mail: aherron@highpoint.edu.

Howard University, Graduate School, Department of Health, Human Performance and Leisure Studies, Washington, DC 20059-0002. Offers exercise physiology (MS); health education (MS); sport studies (MS), including sociology of sport, sport management; urban recreation (MS), including leisure studies. Part-time and evening/weekend programs available. *Degree requirements:* For master's, thesis, comprehensive exam, registration. *Entrance requirements:* For master's, BS in human performance or related field. Electronic applications accepted. *Faculty research:* Health promotion, cardiovascular hypertension, physical activity, sport and human rights issues.

Howard University, Graduate School, Department of Physical Education, Recreation, and Health Education, Washington, DC 20059-0002. Offers exercise physiology (MS); recreation and leisure studies (MS); school and community health education (MS). Part-time programs available. *Degree requirements:* For master's, thesis or alternative, comprehensive exam. *Entrance requirements:* For master's, GRE General Test, minimum GPA of 3.0. *Faculty research:* Women's health, work and health, AIDS, men's health, hypertension, sports nutrition, social science, urban recreation, therapeutic recreation, commercial recreation.

Humboldt State University, Graduate Studies, College of Professional Studies, Department of Kinesiology, Arcata, CA 95521-8299. Offers athletic training education (MS); exercise science/wellness management (MS); pre-physical therapy (MS); teaching/coaching (MS). *Students:* 10 full-time (5 women), 5 part-time (1 woman); includes 4 minority (1 African American, 3 Asian Americans or Pacific Islanders). Average age 31. 15 applicants, 73% accepted, 6 enrolled. In 2006, 3 degrees awarded. *Degree requirements:* For master's, thesis or alternative. *Entrance requirements:* For master's, GMAT, minimum GPA of 2.5. Additional exam requirements/recommendations for international students: Required—TOEFL. *Application deadline:* Applications are processed on a rolling basis. Application fee: $55. *Financial support:* Teaching assistantships, career-related internships or fieldwork, Federal Work-Study, and institutionally sponsored loans available. Financial award application deadline: 3/1; financial award applicants required to submit FAFSA. *Faculty research:* Human performance, adapted physical education, physical therapy. *Unit head:* Dr. Sue MacConnie, Chair, 707-826-4536, Fax: 707-826-5451, E-mail: sem1@humboldt.edu. *Application contact:* Dr. Kathy Munoz, Coordinator, 707-826-3840, Fax: 707-826-5451, E-mail: kdm1@humboldt.edu.

Indiana State University, School of Graduate Studies, College of Health and Human Performance, Department of Physical Education, Terre Haute, IN 47809-1401. Offers adult fitness (MA, MS); coaching (MA, MS); exercise science (MA, MS); master teacher (MA, MS). *Faculty:* 7 full-time (3 women), 2 part-time/adjunct (0 women). *Students:* 19 full-time (5 women), 13 part-time (4 women); includes 1 minority (African American), 5 international. Average age 27. 19 applicants, 89% accepted, 8 enrolled. In 2006, 18 degrees awarded. *Degree requirements:* For master's, thesis (for some programs). *Entrance requirements:* For master's, minor in physical education. *Application deadline:* For fall admission, 7/1 priority date

Exercise and Sports Science

Indiana State University (continued)
for domestic students; for spring admission, 11/1 priority date for domestic students. Applications are processed on a rolling basis. Application fee: $35. Electronic applications accepted. *Expenses:* Tuition, state resident: part-time $278 per credit. Tuition, nonresident: part-time $552 per credit. *Financial support:* In 2006–07, 10 research assistantships with partial tuition reimbursements (averaging $6,300 per year) were awarded; teaching assistantships with partial tuition reimbursements, tuition waivers (partial) also available. Financial award application deadline: 3/1; financial award applicants required to submit FAFSA. *Faculty research:* Exercise science. *Unit head:* Dr. Jeffrey Edwards, Chairperson, 812-237-4048.

Indiana University Bloomington, School of Health, Physical Education and Recreation, Department of Kinesiology, Bloomington, IN 47405-7000. Offers adapted physical education (MS); applied sport science (MS); athletic training (MS); biomechanics (MS); clinical exercise physiology (MS); ergonomics (MS); exercise physiology (MS); human performance (MS, PhD, PE Dir); motor control (MS); sport management (MS). PhD offered through the University Graduate School. Part-time programs available. *Faculty:* 10 full-time (1 woman). *Students:* 106 full-time (47 women), 41 part-time (15 women); includes 16 minority (15 African Americans, 1 American Indian/Alaska Native), 26 international. Average age 26.Terminal master's awarded for partial completion of doctoral program. *Degree requirements:* For master's and PE Dir, thesis optional; for doctorate, variable foreign language requirement, thesis/dissertation. *Entrance requirements:* For master's, GRE General Test, minimum GPA of 2.8; for doctorate, GRE General Test, minimum graduate GPA of 3.5, minimum undergraduate GPA of 3.0; for PE Dir, GRE. *Application deadline:* For fall admission, 1/1 for international students; for spring admission, 9/1 for international students. Applications are processed on a rolling basis. Application fee: $50 ($60 for international students). *Expenses:* Tuition, state resident: full-time $5,791; part-time $241 per credit hour. Tuition, nonresident: full-time $16,866; part-time $703 per credit hour. *Financial support:* Fellowships, research assistantships with full tuition reimbursements, teaching assistantships with full tuition reimbursements, career-related internships or fieldwork, Federal Work-Study, institutionally sponsored loans, scholarships/grants, tuition waivers (partial), and fee remissions available. Financial award application deadline: 3/1. *Faculty research:* Exercise physiology and biochemistry, sports biomechanics, human motor control, adaptation of fitness and exercise to special populations. *Unit head:* John Shea, Chairperson, 812-855-3114. *Application contact:* Program Office, 812-855-5523, Fax: 812-855-9417, E-mail: kines@indiana.edu.

Indiana University of Pennsylvania, School of Graduate Studies and Research, College of Health and Human Services, Department of Health and Physical Education, Program in Sport Science, Indiana, PA 15705-1087. Offers MS. Part-time programs available. *Students:* 24 full-time (11 women), 25 part-time (14 women); includes 2 minority (both African Americans), 12 international. Average age 26. 52 applicants, 71% accepted. In 2006, 18 degrees awarded. *Degree requirements:* For master's, thesis optional. *Entrance requirements:* For master's, 2 letters of recommendation. Additional exam requirements/recommendations for international students: Required—TOEFL. *Application deadline:* For fall admission, 7/1 priority date for domestic students; for spring admission, 11/1 for domestic students. Applications are processed on a rolling basis. Application fee: $30. *Expenses:* Tuition, state resident: full-time $6,048; part-time $336 per credit. Tuition, nonresident: full-time $9,678; part-time $538 per credit. Required fees: $1,069; $148 per year. *Financial support:* In 2006–07, 5 research assistantships (averaging $4,990 per year) were awarded. Financial award application deadline: 3/15; financial award applicants required to submit FAFSA.

Iowa State University of Science and Technology, Graduate College, College of Human Sciences, Department of Health and Human Performance, Ames, IA 50011. Offers education (M Ed); exercise and sport science (MS); health and human performance (PhD). *Faculty:* 15 full-time. *Students:* 31 full-time (14 women), 5 part-time (4 women); includes 2 minority (both African Americans), 5 international. 40 applicants, 28% accepted, 8 enrolled. In 2006, 8 master's, 1 doctorate awarded. *Degree requirements:* For master's, thesis or alternative; for doctorate, thesis/dissertation. *Entrance requirements:* For master's and doctorate, GRE General Test. Additional exam requirements/recommendations for international students: Required—TOEFL (paper-based 560; computer-based 220; iBT 79) or IELTS (6.5). *Application deadline:* For fall admission, 2/1 priority date for domestic and international students; for spring admission, 11/1 priority date for domestic and international students. Application fee: $30 ($70 for international students). Electronic applications accepted. *Expenses:* Tuition, state resident: full-time $5,936; part-time $330 per credit. Tuition, nonresident: full-time $16,350; part-time $330 per credit. *Financial support:* In 2006–07, 17 research assistantships with full and partial tuition reimbursements (averaging $17,180 per year), 13 teaching assistantships with full and partial tuition reimbursements (averaging $16,096 per year) were awarded; fellowships, career-related internships or fieldwork, scholarships/grants, health care benefits, and unspecified assistantships also available. *Unit head:* Dr. Jerry Thomas, Chair, 515-294-8009, Fax: 515-294-8740, E-mail: hhpgrad@iastate.edu. *Application contact:* Dr. Warren Franke, Chair, 515-294-8257, Fax: 515-294-8740, E-mail: wfranke@iastate.edu.

Ithaca College, Graduate Studies, School of Health Sciences and Human Performance, Program in Exercise and Sport Sciences, Ithaca, NY 14850-7020. Offers MS. Part-time programs available. *Faculty:* 11 full-time (3 women). *Students:* 20 full-time (13 women), 7 part-time (4 women), 3 international. Average age 25. 44 applicants, 45% accepted, 16 enrolled. In 2006, 19 master's awarded. *Degree requirements:* For master's, thesis optional. *Entrance requirements:* For master's, GRE General Test, minimum GPA of 3.0. Additional exam requirements/recommendations for international students: Required—TOEFL (minimum score 550 paper-based; 213 computer-based). *Application deadline:* Applications are processed on a rolling basis. Application fee: $40. *Financial support:* In 2006–07, 23 students received support, including 18 teaching assistantships (averaging $8,694 per year); career-related internships or fieldwork, Federal Work-Study, institutionally sponsored loans, scholarships/grants, and unspecified assistantships also available. Support available to part-time students. Financial award application deadline: 3/1; financial award applicants required to submit FAFSA. *Faculty research:* Analysis of teaching and coaching behavior, exercise physiology across the age spectrum, optimizing exercise performance, physiological and psychological factors that affect human performance, sport and exercise psychology. *Unit head:* Dr. John Sigg, Chairperson, 607-274-7055.

Kean University, College of Education, Program in Exercise Science, Union, NJ 07083. Offers MS. *Faculty:* 17 full-time (9 women). *Students:* 6 full-time (3 women), 17 part-time (9 women); includes 2 minority (1 African American, 1 Asian American or Pacific Islander). Average age 30. 6 applicants, 83% accepted, 3 enrolled. In 2006, 3 degrees awarded. *Degree requirements:* For master's, thesis, comprehensive exam. *Entrance requirements:* For master's, GRE General Test, minimum GPA of 3.0, interview, 2 letters of recommendation, minimum B average in undergraduate prerequisites. *Application deadline:* For fall admission, 5/1 for domestic students; for spring admission, 11/1 for domestic students. Application fee: $60 ($150 for international students). Electronic applications accepted. *Expenses:* Tuition, state resident: full-time $8,856; part-time $369 per credit. Tuition, nonresident: full-time $11,256; part-time $469 per credit. *Financial support:* In 2006–07, 4 research assistantships with full tuition reimbursements (averaging $3,217 per year) were awarded. *Unit head:* Dr. Walter D. Andzel, Program Coordinator, 908-737-5436, E-mail: wandzel@kean.edu. *Application contact:* Joanne Morris, Director of Graduate Admissions, 908-737-3355, Fax: 908-737-3354, E-mail: grad-adm@kean.edu.

Kent State University, Graduate School of Education, Health, and Human Services, Program in Exercise and Sport, Kent, OH 44242-0001. Offers exercise physiology (PhD). *Faculty:* 11 full-time (6 women). *Students:* 5 full-time (2 women), 3 part-time (2 women); includes 1 minority (African American) 6 applicants, 33% accepted.Application fee: $30. *Unit head:* Dr. Steve Mitchell, Coordinator, 330-672-0206, E-mail: smitchel@kent.edu. *Application contact:* Nancy Miller, Academic Program Coordinator, Office of Graduate Student Services, 330-672-2576, Fax: 330-672-9162, E-mail: ogs@kent.edu.

Kent State University, Graduate School of Education, Health, and Human Services, Program in Exercise, Leisure, and Sport, Kent, OH 44242-0001. Offers athletic training (MA); exercise physiology (MA); physical teacher education (MA); sport and recreation management (MA); sports studies (MA). *Faculty:* 15 full-time (7 women). *Students:* 47 full-time (25 women), 34 part-time (13 women); includes 11 minority (10 African Americans, 1 Hispanic American), 4 international. 46 applicants, 74% accepted. In 2006, 9 degrees awarded. Application fee: $30. *Unit head:* Dr. Steve Mitchell, Coordinator, 330-672-0206, E-mail: smitchel@kent.edu. *Application contact:* Nancy Miller, Academic Program Coordinator, Office of Graduate Student Services, 330-672-2576, Fax: 330-672-9162, E-mail: ogs@kent.edu.

Kent State University, Graduate School of Education, Health, and Human Services, School of Exercise, Leisure and Sport, Kent, OH 44242-0001. Offers MA, PhD. *Faculty:* 26 full-time (13 women). *Students:* 52 full-time (27 women), 37 part-time (15 women); includes 12 minority (11 African Americans, 1 Hispanic American), 4 international. 52 applicants, 69% accepted. In 2006, 9 degrees awarded. *Degree requirements:* For master's, thesis optional; for doctorate, thesis/dissertation. *Entrance requirements:* For master's, minimum GPA of 2.75; for doctorate, minimum GPA of 3.0. *Application deadline:* For fall admission, 7/18 for domestic students; for spring admission, 11/29 for domestic students. Applications are processed on a rolling basis. Application fee: $30. Electronic applications accepted. *Financial support:* Fellowships with full tuition reimbursements, research assistantships with full tuition reimbursements, teaching assistantships with full tuition reimbursements, career-related internships or fieldwork, Federal Work-Study, institutionally sponsored loans, and tuition waivers (full) available. Financial award application deadline: 3/15. *Unit head:* Wayne Munson, Interim Director, 330-672-2012, Fax: 330-672-4106, E-mail: wmunson@kent.edu. *Application contact:* Aaron L. Mulroony, Graduate Coordinator, 330-672-2857, Fax: 330-672-4106, E-mail: amulroon@kent.edu.

Lakehead University, Graduate Studies, School of Kinesiology, Thunder Bay, ON P7B 5E1, Canada. Offers applied sport science and coaching (M Sc, MA). Part-time programs available. *Degree requirements:* For master's, thesis. *Entrance requirements:* For master's, minimum B average. Additional exam requirements/recommendations for international students: Required—TOEFL. *Faculty research:* Social psychology and physical education, sport history, sports medicine, exercise physiology, gerontology.

Life University, College of Arts and Sciences, Program in Sport Health Science, Marietta, GA 30060-2903. Offers chiropractic sport science (MS); exercise and sport science (MS); sport coaching (MS); sport injury management (MS). Part-time programs available. *Faculty:* 4 full-time (1 woman), 3 part-time/adjunct (1 woman). *Students:* 5 full-time (2 women), 22 part-time (8 women); includes 7 minority (5 African Americans, 2 Asian Americans or Pacific Islanders). 23 applicants, 78% accepted, 10 enrolled. In 2006, 9 degrees awarded. *Degree requirements:* For master's, thesis optional. *Entrance requirements:* For master's, GRE General Test or MAT, minimum GPA of 3.0, 3 letters of recommendation. Additional exam requirements/recommendations for international students: Required—TOEFL (minimum score 500 paper-based; 173 computer-based). *Application deadline:* For fall admission, 4/1 priority date for domestic and international students; for winter admission, 12/1 priority date for domestic and international students; for spring admission, 3/1 priority date for domestic and international students. Applications are processed on a rolling basis. Application fee: $50. Electronic applications accepted. *Financial support:* Career-related internships or fieldwork, Federal Work-Study, and tuition waivers (full and partial) available. Support available to part-time students. Financial award application deadline: 9/1; financial award applicants required to submit FAFSA. *Unit head:* Dr. Deloss Brubaker, Department Head, 770-426-2771, Fax: 770-426-2861, E-mail: brubaker@life.edu. *Application contact:* Dr. Deborah Heairlston, Director of New Student Development, 770-426-2703, Fax: 770-426-2895, E-mail: drdeb@life.edu.

Long Island University, Brooklyn Campus, School of Health Professions, Division of Sports Sciences, Brooklyn, NY 11201-8423. Offers adapted physical education (MS); athletic training and sports sciences (MS); exercise physiology (MS); health sciences (MS). Part-time and evening/weekend programs available. *Entrance requirements:* For master's, 2 letters of recommendation. Additional exam requirements/recommendations for international students: Required—TOEFL (minimum score 500 paper-based; 173 computer-based). Electronic applications accepted.

Louisiana Tech University, Graduate School, College of Education, Department of Health Exercise Science, Ruston, LA 71272. Offers MS. *Accreditation:* NCATE. Part-time programs available. *Degree requirements:* For master's, thesis or alternative. *Entrance requirements:* For master's, GRE General Test.

Manhattanville College, Graduate Programs, School of Education, Program in Physical Education and Sport Pedagogy, Purchase, NY 10577-2132. Offers MAT. *Students:* 62 full-time (17 women), 75 part-time (20 women); includes 4 African Americans, 1 Asian American or Pacific Islander, 4 Hispanic Americans, 1 international. Application fee: $55. *Application contact:* Alyce Ware Poli, Director of Admissions, 914-373-3718, Fax: 914-694-1732, E-mail: edschool@mville.edu.

Marshall University, Academic Affairs Division, College of Education and Human Services, Division of Exercise Science, Sports and Recreation, Program in Exercise Science, Huntington, WV 25755. Offers MS. *Faculty:* 11 full-time (4 women). *Students:* 37 full-time (16 women), 4 part-time; includes 6 minority (4 African Americans, 2 Asian Americans or Pacific Islanders), 1 international. Average age 25. In 2006, 18 degrees awarded. *Degree requirements:* For master's, comprehensive assessment, thesis optional. *Entrance requirements:* For master's, GRE General Test. Application fee: $40. *Unit head:* Dr. William Marley, Director Human Performance Laboratory Programs, 304-696-2936, E-mail: marley@marshall.edu. *Application contact:* Information Contact, 304-746-1900, Fax: 304-746-1902, E-mail: services@marshall.edu.

Marywood University, Academic Affairs, College of Health and Human Services, Department of Nutrition and Dietetics, Program in Sports Nutrition and Exercise Science, Scranton, PA 18509-1598. Offers MS. *Students:* 17 full-time (11 women), 8 part-time (6 women), 3 international. Average age 27. *Expenses:* Tuition: Part-time $672 per credit. Tuition and fees vary according to degree level, campus/location and program. *Application contact:* Dr. Deborah M. Flynn, Coordinator of Graduate Advising (Enrollment Management), 570-348-6211, E-mail: flynn@ac.marywood.edu.

McNeese State University, Graduate School, College of Education, Department of Health and Human Performance, Lake Charles, LA 70609. Offers exercise physiology (MS); health promotion (MS). *Accreditation:* NCATE. Evening/weekend programs available. *Faculty:* 5 full-time (2 women). *Students:* 18 full-time (11 women), 8 part-time (5 women); includes 4 minority (3 African Americans, 1 Asian American or Pacific Islander), 3 international. In 2006, 13 degrees awarded. *Entrance requirements:* For master's, GRE, UG major or minor in health and human performance or related field of study. *Application deadline:* For fall admission, 5/15 priority date for domestic students. Applications are processed on a rolling basis. Application fee: $20 ($30 for international students). *Expenses:* Tuition, area resident: Full-time $2,226; part-time $193 per hour. Required fees: $919; $106 per hour. *Financial support:* Application deadline: 5/1. *Unit head:* Dr. Michael Soileau, Head, 337-475-5374, Fax: 337-475-5947, E-mail: msoileau@mcneese.edu.

Memorial University of Newfoundland, School of Graduate Studies, School of Human Kinetics and Recreation, St. John's, NL A1C 5S7, Canada. Offers administration, curriculum and supervision (MPE); biomechanics/ergonomics (MS Kin); exercise and work physiology (MS Kin); sport psychology (MS Kin). Part-time programs available. *Degree requirements:* For master's, seminars, thesis presentations, thesis optional. *Entrance requirements:* For master's, bachelor's degree in a related field, minimum B average. Electronic applications accepted. *Faculty research:* Administration, sociology of sports, kinesiology, physiology/recreation.

Miami University, Graduate School, School of Education and Allied Professions, Department of Physical Education, Health, and Sports Studies, Oxford, OH 45056. Offers exercise and health studies (MS); sport studies (MS). Part-time programs available. *Entrance requirements:* For master's, minimum undergraduate GPA of 3.0 during previous 2 years or 2.75 overall. Additional exam requirements/recommendations for international students: Required—TOEFL (minimum score 550 paper-based; 213 computer-based), TWE (minimum score 4).

Middle Tennessee State University, College of Graduate Studies, College of Education and Behavioral Science, Department of Health, Physical Education, Recreation and Safety, Murfreesboro, TN 37132. Offers exercise science and health promotion (MS); health, physical education, recreation and safety (MS); human performance (PhD); physical education (PhD). *Accreditation:* NCATE (one or more programs are accredited). Part-time and evening/weekend programs available. Postbaccalaureate distance learning degree programs offered. *Faculty:* 26 full-time (12 women). *Students:* 10 full-time (6 women), 130 part-time (64 women); includes 27 minority (21 African Americans, 1 American Indian/Alaska Native, 5 Asian Americans or Pacific Islanders). Average age 28. 64 applicants, 94% accepted. In 2006, 39 master's, 7 doctorates awarded. *Entrance requirements:* For master's and doctorate, GRE or MAT. Additional exam requirements/recommendations for international students: Required—TOEFL (minimum score 525 paper-based; 195 computer-based). *Application deadline:* For fall admission, 8/1 priority date for domestic students. Applications are processed on a rolling basis. Application fee: $25. Electronic applications accepted. *Financial support:* In 2006–07, 31 students received support. Application deadline: 5/1; *Faculty research:* Cardiovascular disease and psychosocial stress, pediatric health and fitness, obesity, fitness testing, anaerobic power and lactate kinetics. *Unit head:* Dr. Dianne Bartley, Chair, 615-898-2811, Fax: 615-898-5020, E-mail: dbartley@mtsu.edu.

Mississippi State University, College of Education, Department of Kinesiology, Mississippi State, MS 39762. Offers exercise science (MS); health education/health promotion (MS); sports administration (MS); teaching/coaching (MS). Part-time programs available. Postbaccalaureate distance learning degree programs offered (minimal on-campus study). *Faculty:* 15 full-time (4 women), 6 part-time/adjunct (4 women). *Students:* 34 full-time (13 women), 13 part-time (6 women); includes 6 minority (all African Americans), 1 international. Average age 25. 49 applicants, 69% accepted, 26 enrolled. In 2006, 25 degrees awarded. *Degree requirements:* For master's, comprehensive oral or written exam, thesis optional. *Entrance requirements:* For master's, GRE General Test, minimum GPA of 3.0. Additional exam requirements/recommendations for international students: Required—TOEFL. *Application deadline:* For fall admission, 7/1 for domestic students; for spring admission, 11/1 for domestic students. Applications are processed on a rolling basis. Application fee: $30. Electronic applications accepted. *Expenses:* Tuition, state resident: full-time $4,550; part-time $253 per hour. Tuition, nonresident: full-time $10,552; part-time $584 per hour. International tuition: $10,882 full-time. Tuition and fees vary according to course load. *Financial support:* In 2006–07, 13 students received support, including 7 teaching assistantships with full tuition reimbursements available (averaging $7,772 per year); research assistantships with full tuition reimbursements available, career-related internships or fieldwork, Federal Work-Study, institutionally sponsored loans, and unspecified assistantships also available. Financial award applicants required to submit FAFSA. *Faculty research:* Static balance and stepping performance of older adults, organizational justice, public health, strength training and recovery drinks, high risk drinking perceptions and behaviors. *Unit head:* Dr. Joseph Chromiak, Interim Head, 662-325-2963, Fax: 662-325-4525, E-mail: jchrom@colled.msstate.edu. *Application contact:* Dr. Phil Bonfanti, Director of Admissions, 662-325-4104, Fax: 662-325-8872, E-mail: admit@msstate.edu.

Montclair State University, The Graduate School, College of Education and Human Services, Department of Exercise Science and Physical Education, Montclair, NJ 07043-1624. Offers health and physical education (Certificate); nutrition and exercise science (Certificate); physical education (MA, Certificate), including coaching and sports administration (MA), exercise science (MA), physical education (MA), teaching and supervision of physical education (MA). Part-time and evening/weekend programs available. *Faculty:* 14 full-time (8 women), 12 part-time/adjunct (7 women). *Students:* 23 full-time (10 women), 54 part-time (33 women); includes 10 minority (5 African Americans, 1 Asian American or Pacific Islander, 4 Hispanic Americans). 36 applicants, 47% accepted, 12 enrolled. In 2006, 11 master's, 13 other advanced degrees awarded. *Degree requirements:* For master's, comprehensive exam. *Entrance requirements:* For master's, GRE General Test, 2 letters of recommendation; for Certificate, 2 letters of recommendation (nutrition and exercise science concentration). Additional exam requirements/recommendations for international students: Required—TOEFL (minimum score 83 computer-based). *Application deadline:* For fall admission, 6/1 for international students; for spring admission, 10/1 for international students. Applications are processed on a rolling basis. Application fee: $60. Electronic applications accepted. *Expenses:* Tuition, state resident: part-time $450 per credit. Tuition, nonresident: part-time $682 per credit. Tuition and fees vary according to degree level and program. *Financial support:* In 2006–07, 4 research assistantships with full tuition reimbursements (averaging $5,000 per year) were awarded; Federal Work-Study, scholarships/grants, and unspecified assistantships also available. Support available to part-time students. Financial award application deadline: 3/1; financial award applicants required to submit FAFSA. *Unit head:* Dr. Joseph Donnelly, Chairperson, 973-655-4154.

Morehead State University, Graduate Programs, College of Education, Department of Health, Physical Education and Sport Sciences, Morehead, KY 40351. Offers exercise physiology (MA); health and physical education (MA); sports management (MA). *Accreditation:* NCATE. Part-time and evening/weekend programs available. *Faculty:* 12 full-time (8 women), 5 part-time/adjunct (2 women). *Students:* 16 full-time (10 women), 12 part-time (7 women), 2 international. Average age 32. In 2006, 11 degrees awarded. *Degree requirements:* For master's, oral exam, written core exam, thesis optional. *Entrance requirements:* For master's, GRE General Test or MAT, minimum GPA of 2.5; undergraduate major/minor in health, physical education, or recreation. Additional exam requirements/recommendations for international students: Required—TOEFL (minimum score 500 paper-based; 173 computer-based). *Application deadline:* For fall admission, 8/1 priority date for domestic and international students; for spring admission, 12/1 priority date for domestic and international students. Applications are processed on a rolling basis. Application fee: $0 ($55 for international students). Electronic applications accepted. *Financial support:* In 2006–07, 4 teaching assistantships (averaging $6,000 per year) were awarded; career-related internships or fieldwork, Federal Work-Study, and unspecified assistantships also available. Financial award application deadline: 4/1; financial award applicants required to submit FAFSA. *Faculty research:* Child growth and performance, instructional strategies, outdoor leadership qualities, exercise science, athletic training. *Unit head:* Dr. Lynne Fitzgerald, Chair, 606-783-2180, Fax: 606-783-5058. *Application contact:* Michelle Barber, Graduate Admissions Counselor, 606-783-2039, Fax: 606-783-5061, E-mail: m.barber@moreheadstate.edu.

Murray State University, College of Health Sciences and Human Services, Department of Wellness and Therapeutic Sciences, Program in Exercise and Leisure Studies, Murray, KY 42071. Offers MS. Part-time programs available. *Faculty:* 3 full-time (1 woman), 2 part-time/adjunct (1 woman). *Students:* 6 full-time (3 women), 9 part-time (3 women); includes 2 minority (both African Americans) Average age 24. 5 applicants, 100% accepted. In 2006, 4 degrees awarded. *Degree requirements:* For master's, thesis optional. *Entrance requirements:* For master's, GRE General Test or MAT. Additional exam requirements/recommendations for international students: Required—TOEFL. *Application deadline:* Applications are processed on a rolling basis. Application fee: $25. *Financial support:* In 2006–07, research assistantships (averaging $5,000 per year), teaching assistantships (averaging $5,000 per year) were awarded; Federal Work-Study also available. Financial award application deadline: 5/1. *Faculty research:* Exercise and cancer recovery. *Unit head:* Dr. Matt Wiggins, Graduate Coordinator, 270-809-6285, Fax: 270-809-6803, E-mail: matt.wiggins@murraystate.edu.

New Mexico Highlands University, Graduate Studies, School of Education, Department of Exercise and Sport Sciences, Las Vegas, NM 87701. Offers human performance and sport (MA); sports administration (MA); teacher education (MA). Part-time programs available. *Faculty:* 2 full-time (1 woman). *Students:* 16 full-time (5 women), 44 part-time (13 women); includes 29 minority (7 African Americans, 1 Asian American or Pacific Islander, 21 Hispanic Americans), 1 international. Average age 31. 23 applicants, 78% accepted, 8 enrolled. In 2006, 10 degrees awarded. *Degree requirements:* For master's, thesis or alternative, comprehensive exam, registration. *Entrance requirements:* For master's, minimum undergraduate GPA of 3.0. Additional exam requirements/recommendations for international students: Required—TOEFL (minimum score 540 paper-based; 190 computer-based). *Application deadline:* For fall admission, 8/1 priority date for domestic students. Applications are processed on a rolling basis. Application fee: $15. *Expenses:* Tuition, state resident: part-time $101 per credit hour. Tuition, nonresident: part-time $101 per credit hour. *Financial support:* In 2006–07, 22 students received support, including 8 teaching assistantships with full and partial tuition reimbursements available (averaging $6,500 per year); career-related internships or fieldwork, Federal Work-Study, institutionally sponsored loans, scholarships/grants, tuition waivers (partial), and unspecified assistantships also available. Support available to part-time students. Financial award application deadline: 3/1; financial award applicants required to submit FAFSA. *Unit head:* Dr. Kathy Jenkins, Chair, 505-454-3287, Fax: 505-454-3001, E-mail: kjenkins@nmhu.edu. *Application contact:* Diane Trujillo, Administrative Assistant Graduate Studies, 505-454-3266, Fax: 505-454-3558, E-mail: dtrujillo@nmhu.edu.

North Dakota State University, The Graduate School, College of Human Development and Education, Department of Health, Nutrition, and Exercise Sciences, Fargo, ND 58105. Offers dietetics (MS); entry level athletic training (MS); exercise science (MS); nutrition science (MS); public health (MS); sport pedagogy (MS); sports recreation management (MS). Part-time and evening/weekend programs available. Postbaccalaureate distance learning degree programs offered (no on-campus study). *Faculty:* 12 full-time (6 women). *Students:* 30 full-time, 50 part-time; includes 6 minority (2 African Americans, 1 American Indian/Alaska Native, 2 Asian Americans or Pacific Islanders, 1 Hispanic American), 3 international. 19 applicants, 100% accepted, 15 enrolled. In 2006, 4 degrees awarded. *Degree requirements:* For master's, thesis (for some programs), registration. *Entrance requirements:* For master's, minimum GPA of 3.0. *Application deadline:* For fall admission, 3/1 priority date for domestic and international students. Application fee: $45 ($60 for international students). Electronic applications accepted. *Financial support:* In 2006–07, 28 students received support, including 18 teaching assistantships with full tuition reimbursements available (averaging $6,500 per year). Financial award application deadline: 3/31. *Faculty research:* Biomechanics, sport specialization, recreation, nutrition, athletic training. Total annual research expenditures: $10,000. *Unit head:* Brad Strand, Head, 701-231-9718, Fax: 701-231-8872, E-mail: bradford.strand@ndsu.edu.

Northeastern University, Bouvé College of Health Sciences Graduate School, Department of Cardiopulmonary and Exercise Sciences, Program in Clinical Exercise Physiology, Boston, MA 02115-5096. Offers MS. Part-time and evening/weekend programs available. *Faculty:* 6 full-time (3 women), 3 part-time/adjunct. *Students:* 32 full-time (29 women), 1 (woman) part-time. Average age 29. 44 applicants, 61% accepted. In 2006, 10 degrees awarded. *Degree requirements:* For master's, thesis optional. *Entrance requirements:* For master's, GRE General Test or MAT. *Application deadline:* Applications are processed on a rolling basis. Application fee: $50. *Financial support:* In 2006–07, 2 teaching assistantships (averaging $13,832 per year) were awarded; research assistantships, career-related internships or fieldwork, Federal Work-Study, tuition waivers (partial), and unspecified assistantships also available. Support available to part-time students. Financial award application deadline: 3/1; financial award applicants required to submit FAFSA. *Faculty research:* Exercise in cardiovascular pulmonary and metabolic diseases, mechanisms related to lactate and ventilation threshold, body composition assessment techniques. *Application contact:* Margaret Schnabel, Director of Graduate Admissions, 617-373-2708, Fax: 617-373-4704, E-mail: bouvegrad@neu.edu.

Northern Arizona University, Consortium of Professional Schools and Colleges, College of Health Professions, Department of Exercise Science and Athletic Training, Flagstaff, AZ 86011. Offers exercise science (MS); physical education (MS). Part-time programs available. *Degree requirements:* For master's, thesis optional. *Entrance requirements:* For master's, GRE General Test, minimum GPA of 3.0. *Faculty research:* Muscle fiber type conversions, small animal locomotive study, electromyographic patterns.

Northern Michigan University, College of Graduate Studies, College of Professional Studies, Department of Health, Physical Education and Recreation, Marquette, MI 49855-5301. Offers exercise science (MS). Part-time programs available. *Degree requirements:* For master's, thesis or alternative. *Entrance requirements:* For master's, GRE General Test, minimum GPA of 3.0 in major, 2.75 overall; 9 hours of course work in human anatomy, physiology, kinesiology.

Oakland University, Graduate Study and Lifelong Learning, School of Health Sciences, Program in Exercise Science, Rochester, MI 48309-4401. Offers MS, Certificate. *Faculty:* 3 full-time (0 women), 1 part-time/adjunct (0 women). *Students:* 20 full-time (12 women), 15 part-time (11 women), 6 international. Average age 29. 20 applicants, 100% accepted, 16 enrolled. In 2006, 4 master's, 2 other advanced degrees awarded. *Degree requirements:* For master's, thesis (for some programs). *Entrance requirements:* For master's, minimum GPA of 3.0 for unconditional admission. Additional exam requirements/recommendations for international students: Required—TOEFL (minimum score 550 paper-based; 213 computer-based). *Application deadline:* For fall admission, 7/15 priority date for domestic students, 5/1 priority date for international students; for winter admission, 12/1 priority date for domestic students, 9/1 priority date for international students; for spring admission, 3/15 priority date for domestic students. Applications are processed on a rolling basis. Application fee: $35. Electronic applications accepted. *Expenses: Contact institution. Financial support:* Federal Work-Study, institutionally sponsored loans, and tuition waivers (full) available. Financial award application deadline: 3/1; financial award applicants required to submit FAFSA. *Unit head:* Dr. Brian Goslin, Director, 248-370-4038, Fax: 248-370-4227, E-mail: goslin@oakland.edu.

Ohio University, Graduate Studies, College of Arts and Sciences, Department of Biological Sciences, Athens, OH 45701-2979. Offers biological sciences (MS, PhD); cell biology and physiology (MS, PhD); ecology and evolutionary biology (MS, PhD); exercise physiology and muscle biology (MS, PhD); microbiology (MS, PhD); neuroscience (MS, PhD). *Faculty:* 51 full-time (17 women), 6 part-time/adjunct (1 woman). *Students:* 63 full-time (33 women), 1 part-time; includes 2 minority (1 African American, 1 Hispanic American), 29 international. Average age 24. 52 applicants, 25% accepted, 10 enrolled. In 2006, 5 master's, 5 doctorates awarded. *Median time to degree:* Of those who began their doctoral program in fall 1998, 90% received their degree in 8 years or less. *Degree requirements:* For master's, thesis, 1 quarter of teaching experience; for doctorate, thesis/dissertation, 2 quarters of teaching experience, comprehensive exam. *Entrance requirements:* For master's and doctorate, GRE General Test. Additional exam requirements/recommendations for international students: Required—TOEFL (minimum score 620 paper-based; 260 computer-based; 105 iBT). *Application deadline:* For fall admission, 1/15 for domestic and international students. Application fee: $45. Electronic applications accepted. *Financial support:* In 2006–07, 64 students received support, including 2 fellowships with full tuition reimbursements available (averaging $16,360 per year), 10 research assistantships with full tuition reimbursements available (averaging $16,360 per year), 52 teaching assistantships with full tuition reimbursements available (averaging $16,360 per year); Federal Work-Study, institutionally sponsored loans, and tuition waivers (full) also available. Financial award application deadline: 1/15. *Faculty research:* Ecology and evolutionary biology, exercise physiology and muscle biology, neurobiology, cell biology, physiology. Total annual research expenditures: $2.8 million. *Unit head:* Dr. Ralph DiCaprio, Chair, 740-593-2290, Fax: 740-593-0300, E-mail: dicaprir@ohio.edu. *Application contact:* Dr. Donald Holzschu, Graduate Chair, 740-593-0425, E-mail: holzschu@ohio.edu.

Ohio University, Graduate Studies, College of Health and Human Services, School of Recreation and Sport Sciences, Program in Physiology of Exercise, Athens, OH 45701-2979. Offers MSP Ex. *Faculty:* 5 full-time (2 women), 2 part-time/adjunct (0 women). *Students:* 9 full-time (6 women). Average age 20. 20 applicants, 65% accepted, 9 enrolled. In 2006, 5 degrees awarded. *Degree requirements:* For master's, thesis or alternative. *Entrance requirements:* For master's, GRE General Test or MAT, minimum GPA of 3.0. Additional exam requirements/recommendations for international students: Required—TOEFL (minimum score

Exercise and Sports Science

Ohio University *(continued)*

575 paper-based; 233 computer-based). *Application deadline:* For fall admission, 3/1 priority date for domestic and international students. Application fee: $45. *Financial support:* In 2006–07, 4 research assistantships with tuition reimbursements (averaging $8,577 per year), 4 teaching assistantships with full tuition reimbursements (averaging $8,577 per year) were awarded; Federal Work-Study, institutionally sponsored loans, scholarships/grants, tuition waivers (full), and stipends also available. Financial award application deadline: 3/15. *Faculty research:* Blood pressure, heart rate, health skeleton, muscles, training. *Unit head:* Dr. Roger Gilders, Coordinator, 740-593-0101, Fax: 740-593-0285, E-mail: gilders@ohio.edu. *Application contact:* Molly de Laval, Graduate Records, 740-593-9787, Fax: 740-593-0284, E-mail: delaval@ohio.edu.

Old Dominion University, Darden College of Education, Program in Physical Education, Exercise and Wellness Emphasis, Norfolk, VA 23529. Offers MS Ed. Part-time and evening/weekend programs available. *Faculty:* 7 full-time (4 women). *Students:* 20 full-time (13 women), 2 part-time (1 woman); includes 3 minority (all African Americans), 4 international. Average age 26. 12 applicants, 92% accepted, 8 enrolled. In 2006, 3 degrees awarded. *Degree requirements:* For master's, thesis or alternative, internship, research project, comprehensive exam. *Entrance requirements:* For master's, GRE, minimum GPA of 2.8 overall, minimum of 3.0 in major. Additional exam requirements/recommendations for international students: Required—TOEFL (minimum score 500 paper-based; 200 computer-based). *Application deadline:* For fall admission, 7/1 for domestic students; for spring admission, 11/1 for domestic students. Applications are processed on a rolling basis. Application fee: $40. *Expenses:* Tuition, area resident: Part-time $285 per credit hour. Tuition, nonresident: part-time $715 per credit hour. Required fees: $94 per semester. *Financial support:* In 2006–07, fellowships (averaging $1,500 per year), 2 research assistantships with partial tuition reimbursements (averaging $9,000 per year), 1 teaching assistantship with partial tuition reimbursement (averaging $9,000 per year) were awarded; career-related internships or fieldwork and scholarships/grants also available. Financial award application deadline: 4/15. *Faculty research:* Diabetes, exercise, prescription, gait and balance. Total annual research expenditures: $105,000. *Unit head:* Liz Dowling, Graduate Program Director, 757-683-4514, E-mail: ldowling@odu.edu. *Application contact:* Robert Spina, Graduate Program Director, 757-683-6029, E-mail: rspina@odu.edu.

Oregon State University, Graduate School, College of Health and Human Sciences, Department of Nutrition and Exercise Sciences, Program in Human Performance, Corvallis, OR 97331. Offers MAIS, MS, PhD. *Students:* Average age 29. In 2006, 1 degree awarded. Terminal master's awarded for partial completion of doctoral program. *Degree requirements:* For master's, thesis; for doctorate, thesis/dissertation, 2 languages (may include foreign, statistical, computer, Braille, or sign). *Entrance requirements:* For master's and doctorate, minimum GPA of 3.0 in last 90 hours of course work. Additional exam requirements/recommendations for international students: Required—TOEFL. *Application deadline:* For fall admission, 2/1 priority date for domestic students. Application fee: $50. *Financial support:* Research assistantships, teaching assistantships, career-related internships or fieldwork, Federal Work-Study, and institutionally sponsored loans available. Support available to part-time students. Financial award application deadline: 2/1. *Faculty research:* Exercise metabolism, biomechanics of sports, bone metabolism, sport psychology, teacher behavior. *Application contact:* Linda Johnson, Head Adviser, 541-737-3718, Fax: 541-737-4230, E-mail: linda.johnson@orst.edu.

Purdue University, Graduate School, College of Liberal Arts, Department of Health and Kinesiology, West Lafayette, IN 47907. Offers exercise, human physiology of movement and sport (PhD); health and fitness (MS); health promotion (MS); health promotion and disease prevention (PhD); movement and sport science (MS); pedagogy and administration (MS); pedagogy of physical activity and health (PhD); psychology of sport and exercise, and motor behavior (PhD). Part-time programs available. *Faculty:* 16 full-time (5 women), 6 part-time/adjunct (0 women). *Students:* 60 full-time (37 women), 25 part-time (12 women); includes 8 minority (3 African Americans, 1 American Indian/Alaska Native, 1 Asian American or Pacific Islander, 3 Hispanic Americans), 15 international. Average age 28. 92 applicants, 63% accepted, 33 enrolled. In 2006, 13 master's, 3 doctorates awarded. *Degree requirements:* For master's, thesis (for some programs); for doctorate, thesis/dissertation. *Entrance requirements:* For master's and doctorate, GRE General Test. Additional exam requirements/recommendations for international students: Required—TOEFL. *Application deadline:* For fall admission, 2/1 for domestic and international students. Applications are processed on a rolling basis. Application fee: $55. Electronic applications accepted. *Financial support:* In 2006–07, 4 fellowships with partial tuition reimbursements (averaging $12,000 per year), 2 research assistantships with partial tuition reimbursements (averaging $10,000 per year), 22 teaching assistantships with partial tuition reimbursements (averaging $10,000 per year) were awarded; Federal Work-Study also available. Support available to part-time students. Financial award applicants required to submit FAFSA. *Faculty research:* Wellness, motivation, teaching effectiveness, learning and development. *Unit head:* Dr. William Harper, Head, 765-494-3178, Fax: 765-494-496-1239. *Application contact:* Graduate Studies Office, 765-494-3162, Fax: 765-496-1239, E-mail: hkgrad@purdue.edu.

Queens College of the City University of New York, Division of Graduate Studies, Mathematics and Natural Sciences Division, Department of Family, Nutrition and Exercise Sciences, Flushing, NY 11367-1597. Offers home economics (MS Ed); physical education and exercise sciences (MS Ed). Part-time and evening/weekend programs available. *Faculty:* 12 full-time (7 women). *Students:* 2 full-time (0 women), 57 part-time (46 women). 53 applicants, 100% accepted, 32 enrolled. In 2006, 2 degrees awarded. *Degree requirements:* For master's, research project. *Entrance requirements:* For master's, minimum GPA of 3.0. Additional exam requirements/recommendations for international students: Required—TOEFL. *Application deadline:* For fall admission, 4/1 for domestic students; for spring admission, 11/1 for domestic students. Applications are processed on a rolling basis. Application fee: $125. *Financial support:* Career-related internships or fieldwork, Federal Work-Study, institutionally sponsored loans, tuition waivers (partial), and adjunct lectureships available. Support available to part-time students. Financial award application deadline: 4/1; financial award applicants required to submit FAFSA. *Faculty research:* Exercise and environmental physiology, interdisciplinary approaches to school curricula using outdoor education, program development in cardiac rehabilitation and adult fitness, nutrition education. *Unit head:* Dr. Elizabeth Lowe, Chairperson, 718-997-4168. *Application contact:* Mario Caruso, Director of Graduate Admissions, 718-997-5200, Fax: 718-997-5193, E-mail: graduate_admissions@qc.edu.

Queen's University at Kingston, School of Graduate Studies and Research, School of Physical and Health Education, Kingston, ON K7L 3N6, Canada. Offers applied exercise science (PhD); biomechanics/ergonomics (M Sc); exercise physiology rehabilitation (M Sc); social psychology of sport and exercise rehabilitation (MA); sociology of sport (MA). Part-time programs available. *Degree requirements:* For master's, thesis (for some programs); for doctorate, thesis/dissertation, comprehensive exam. *Entrance requirements:* For master's and doctorate, minimum B+ average. Additional exam requirements/recommendations for international students: Required—TOEFL. Electronic applications accepted. *Faculty research:* Expert performance ergonomics, obesity research, pregnancy and exercise, gender and sport participation.

St. Cloud State University, School of Graduate Studies, College of Education, Department of Health, Physical Education, Recreation, and Sport Science, St. Cloud, MN 56301-4498. Offers exercise science (MS); physical education (MS); sports management (MS). *Faculty:* 16 full-time (8 women), 1 (woman) part-time/adjunct. *Students:* 12 full-time (6 women), 3 part-time (1 woman), 2 international. 82 applicants, 43% accepted. In 2006, 18 degrees awarded. *Degree requirements:* For master's, thesis or alternative. *Entrance requirements:* For master's, GRE General Test, minimum GPA of 2.75. Additional exam requirements/recommendations for international students: Required—MELAB; Recommended—TOEFL (minimum score 550 paper-based; 213 computer-based), IELTS (minimum score 7). *Application deadline:* For fall admis-

sion, 6/1 priority date for domestic students, 4/1 for international students; for spring admission, 10/1 priority date for domestic students, 8/1 for international students. Applications are processed on a rolling basis. Application fee: $35. Electronic applications accepted. *Financial support:* Federal Work-Study, scholarships/grants, and unspecified assistantships available. Financial award application deadline: 3/1. *Unit head:* Dr. Caryl Martin, Chairperson, 320-308-4251, E-mail: clmartin@stcloudstate.edu. *Application contact:* Linda Lou Krueger, School of Graduate Studies, 320-308-2113, Fax: 320-308-5371, E-mail: lekrueger@stcloudstate.edu.

San Diego State University, Graduate and Research Affairs, College of Professional Studies and Fine Arts, Department of Exercise and Nutritional Sciences, Program in Exercise Physiology, San Diego, CA 92182. Offers MA. *Students:* 8 full-time (7 women), 3 part-time (all women). 29 applicants, 45% accepted, 3 enrolled. In 2006, 7 degrees awarded. *Degree requirements:* For master's, thesis. *Entrance requirements:* For master's, GRE General Test, 2 letters of reference. Additional exam requirements/recommendations for international students: Required—TOEFL. *Application deadline:* For fall admission, 2/1 for domestic and international students. Applications are processed on a rolling basis. Application fee: $55. Electronic applications accepted. *Financial support:* Teaching assistantships, unspecified assistantships available. *Unit head:* Larry Verity, Graduate Advisor, 619-594-5541, Fax: 619-594-6553, E-mail: ensgrad@mail.sdsu.edu. *Application contact:* Larry Verity, Graduate Advisor, 619-594-6489, Fax: 619-594-6553, E-mail: ensgrad@mail.sdsu.edu.

Smith College, Graduate Programs, Department of Exercise and Sport Studies, Northampton, MA 01063. Offers MS. Part-time programs available. *Faculty:* 4 full-time (2 women), 1 part-time/adjunct (0 women). *Students:* 16 full-time (14 women), 1 (woman) part-time, 2 international. Average age 25. 23 applicants, 48% accepted, 8 enrolled. In 2006, 7 degrees awarded. *Degree requirements:* For master's, thesis or special studies. *Entrance requirements:* For master's, GRE General Test. Additional exam requirements/recommendations for international students: Required—TOEFL. *Application deadline:* For fall admission, 4/1 for domestic students, 1/15 for international students; for spring admission, 12/1 for domestic students. Application fee: $60. *Expenses:* Tuition: Full-time $32,320; part-time $1,010 per credit. Tuition and fees vary according to course load. *Financial support:* In 2006–07, 17 students received support, including fellowships with full tuition reimbursements available (averaging $11,150 per year), 10 teaching assistantships with full tuition reimbursements available (averaging $11,150 per year); career-related internships or fieldwork, institutionally sponsored loans, scholarships/grants, and tuition waivers (partial) also available. Support available to part-time students. Financial award application deadline: 1/15; financial award applicants required to submit CSS PROFILE or FAFSA. *Faculty research:* Women in sport, perceived exertion, motor programming, race in sport, stress management. *Unit head:* James Johnson, Graduate Student Adviser, 413-585-3975, E-mail: jjohnson@smith.edu. *Application contact:* Jane Stangl, Graduate Student Adviser, 413-585-3972, E-mail: jstangl@smith.edu.

Southeast Missouri State University, School of Graduate Studies, Department of Health, Human Performance and Recreation, Cape Girardeau, MO 63701-4799. Offers community wellness and leisure services (MPA); nutrition and exercise science (MS). Part-time and evening/weekend programs available. *Faculty:* 7 full-time (2 women). *Students:* 7 full-time (5 women), 8 part-time (4 women); includes 2 minority (both African Americans) Average age 25. 8 applicants, 100% accepted. In 2006, 8 degrees awarded. *Degree requirements:* For master's, thesis or alternative. *Entrance requirements:* For master's, GRE General Test (MS), minimum GPA of 3.0 (MS), minimum GPA of 2.7 (MPA). Additional exam requirements/recommendations for international students: Required—TOEFL (minimum score 550 paper-based; 213 computer-based). *Application deadline:* For fall admission, 8/1 for domestic students, 4/1 for international students; for spring admission, 11/21 for domestic students, 10/1 for international students. Applications are processed on a rolling basis. Application fee: $20 ($100 for international students). Electronic applications accepted. *Financial support:* In 2006–07, 12 students received support, including 6 research assistantships with full tuition reimbursements available (averaging $7,100 per year), 3 teaching assistantships with full tuition reimbursements available (averaging $7,100 per year); unspecified assistantships also available. Financial award applicants required to submit FAFSA. *Faculty research:* Health issues of athletes, body composition assessment, exercise training. *Unit head:* Dr. Joe Pujol, Chairperson, 573-651-2664, Fax: 573-651-5150, E-mail: jpujol@semo.edu. *Application contact:* Marsha L. Arant, Senior Administrative Assistant, Office of Graduate Studies, 573-651-2192, Fax: 573-651-2001, E-mail: marant@semo.edu.

Southern Connecticut State University, School of Graduate Studies, School of Education, Department of Exercise Science, New Haven, CT 06515-1355. Offers human performance (MS); physical education (MS); sport psychology (MS). Part-time and evening/weekend programs available. *Faculty:* 8 full-time. *Students:* 28 full-time (13 women), 54 part-time (28 women); includes 6 minority (2 African Americans, 4 Hispanic Americans), 1 international. 43 applicants, 44% accepted, 13 enrolled. In 2006, 18 degrees awarded. *Degree requirements:* For master's, thesis or alternative. *Entrance requirements:* For master's, interview. *Application deadline:* For fall admission, 7/15 priority date for domestic students. Applications are processed on a rolling basis. Application fee: $50. Electronic applications accepted. *Financial support:* In 2006–07, 8 teaching assistantships were awarded. Financial award application deadline: 4/15; financial award applicants required to submit FAFSA. *Unit head:* Dr. David Martens, Chairperson, 203-392-6094, Fax: 203-392-6911. *Application contact:* Dr. Robert Axtell, Coordinator, 203-392-6037, Fax: 203-392-6093, E-mail: axtell@southernct.edu.

Springfield College, Graduate Programs, Programs in Exercise Science and Sport Studies, Springfield, MA 01109-3797. Offers biomechanics (MS); exercise physiology (MS, DPE), including clinical exercise physiology (MS); science and research (MS); interdisciplinary movement sciences (MS); sport psychology (MS, DPE). Part-time programs available. *Faculty:* 3 full-time (0 women), 4 part-time/adjunct (1 woman). *Students:* 43. Average age 26. 57 applicants, 77% accepted, 20 enrolled. In 2006, 31 master's awarded. *Degree requirements:* For master's, thesis. *Entrance requirements:* For master's, GRE General Test. Additional exam requirements/recommendations for international students: Required—TOEFL (minimum score 550 paper-based; 213 computer-based). *Application deadline:* For fall admission, 1/15 for domestic students; for winter admission, 11/1 for domestic students; for spring admission, 12/1 for domestic students. Applications are processed on a rolling basis. Application fee: $50. Electronic applications accepted. *Expenses:* Tuition: Full-time $12,222; part-time $679 per credit. Required fees: $25; $25 per year. One-time fee: $25 full-time. *Financial support:* In 2006–07, 6 teaching assistantships with partial tuition reimbursements were awarded; fellowships with partial tuition reimbursements, career-related internships or fieldwork, Federal Work-Study, institutionally sponsored loans, and tuition waivers (full and partial) also available. Financial award application deadline: 3/1. *Faculty research:* Fitness in renal disease, environmental exercise physiology. *Unit head:* Charles J. Redmond, Director, 413-748-3231, Fax: 413-748-3371, E-mail: credmond@spfldcol.edu. *Application contact:* Donald James Shaw, Director of Graduate Admissions, 413-748-3060, Fax: 413-748-3069, E-mail: donald_shaw_jr@spfldcol.edu.

Springfield College, Graduate Programs, Programs in Physical Education, Springfield, MA 01109-3797. Offers adapted physical education (M Ed, MPE, MS); advanced level coaching (M Ed, MPE, MS); athletic administration (M Ed, MPE, MS); general physical education (DPE, CAS); health education licensure (MPE, MS); health education licensure program (M Ed); physical education licensure (MPE, MS); physical education licensure program (M Ed); sport performance (M Ed, MPE, MS); teaching and administration (MS). Part-time and evening/weekend programs available. *Faculty:* 25 full-time (13 women), 2 part-time/adjunct (0 women). *Students:* 97. Average age 27. 78 applicants, 86% accepted, 45 enrolled. In 2006, 22 master's, 4 doctorates awarded. Terminal master's awarded for partial completion of doctoral program. *Degree requirements:* For master's, research project; for doctorate, thesis/dissertation. *Entrance requirements:* For master's, GRE General Test; for doctorate, GRE General Test, interview. Additional exam requirements/recommendations for international students: Required—TOEFL (minimum score 550 paper-based; 213 computer-based). *Application deadline:* For fall admission, 1/15 priority date for domestic students; for winter admission,

11/1 for domestic students; for spring admission, 12/1 for domestic students. Applications are processed on a rolling basis. Application fee: $50. Electronic applications accepted. *Expenses:* Tuition: Full-time $12,222; part-time $679 per credit. Required fees: $25; $25 per year. One-time fee: $25 full-time. *Financial support:* Fellowships with partial tuition reimbursements, teaching assistantships with partial tuition reimbursements, career-related internships or fieldwork, Federal Work-Study, institutionally sponsored loans, and tuition waivers (full and partial) available. Financial award application deadline: 3/1. *Faculty research:* Pedagogy, motor learning, history of physical education. *Unit head:* Dr. Stephen C. Coulon, Director, 413-748-3029, Fax: 413-748-3537, E-mail: stephen_coulon@spfldcol.edu. *Application contact:* Donald James Shaw, Director of Graduate Admissions, 413-748-3060, Fax: 413-748-3069, E-mail: donald_shaw_jr@spfldcol.edu.

State University of New York College at Cortland, Graduate Studies, School of Professional Studies, Department of Exercise Science and Sport Studies, Cortland, NY 13045. Offers MS.

See Close-Up on page 2329.

Syracuse University, Graduate School, School of Education, Program in Exercise Science, Syracuse, NY 13244. Offers MS. Part-time and evening/weekend programs available. *Students:* 24 full-time (13 women), 4 part-time (2 women); includes 4 minority (3 Asian Americans or Pacific Islanders, 1 Hispanic American), 1 international. 22 applicants, 73% accepted, 8 enrolled. *Degree requirements:* For master's, thesis or alternative. *Entrance requirements:* For master's, GRE, resumé. Additional exam requirements/recommendations for international students: Required—TOEFL. *Application deadline:* For fall admission, 2/1 priority date for domestic students. Applications are processed on a rolling basis. Application fee: $65. Electronic applications accepted. *Expenses:* Tuition: Full-time $16,920; part-time $940 per credit hour. Required fees: $930; $930 per year. *Financial support:* Fellowships, research assistantships with full and partial tuition reimbursements, teaching assistantships with full and partial tuition reimbursements available. *Faculty research:* Bone density, obesity in females, cardiovascular functioning, attitudes toward physical education, sports management and psychology. *Unit head:* Dr. Lori Ploutz-Snyder, Interim Chair, 315-443-2114, E-mail: llploutz@syr.edu. *Application contact:* Liza Rochelson, Graduate Admission Recruiter, 315-443-2505, Fax: 315-443-2258, E-mail: gradcrt@gwmail.syr.edu.

Tennessee State University, The School of Graduate Studies and Research, College of Education, Department of Human Performance and Sports Science, Nashville, TN 37209-1561. Offers MA Ed. *Faculty:* 7 full-time (2 women). *Students:* 17 full-time (9 women), 12 part-time (4 women); includes 25 minority (all African Americans), 1 international. Average age 29. 31 applicants, 35% accepted, 9 enrolled. In 2006, 13 degrees awarded. *Degree requirements:* For master's, thesis optional. *Entrance requirements:* For master's, GRE General Test or MAT. Application fee: $25. *Unit head:* Dr. Catona R. Starks, Head, 615-963-5581, Fax: 615-963-5594, E-mail: cstarks@tnstate.edu.

Texas Tech University, Graduate School, College of Arts and Sciences, Department of Health, Exercise and Sport Sciences, Lubbock, TX 79409. Offers exercise and sport sciences (MS); sports health (MS). Part-time programs available. *Faculty:* 13 full-time (8 women). *Students:* 50 full-time (16 women), 12 part-time (4 women); includes 10 minority (3 African Americans, 7 Hispanic Americans), 2 international. Average age 25. 78 applicants, 45% accepted, 16 enrolled. In 2006, 27 degrees awarded. *Degree requirements:* For master's, thesis or alternative. *Entrance requirements:* For master's, GRE General Test. Additional exam requirements/recommendations for international students: Required—TOEFL (minimum score 550 paper-based; 213 computer-based). *Application deadline:* For fall admission, 3/1 priority date for international students; for spring admission, 11/1 priority date for international students. Applications are processed on a rolling basis. Application fee: $50 ($60 for international students). Electronic applications accepted. *Expenses:* Tuition, state resident: full-time $4,440. Tuition, nonresident: full-time $11,040. Required fees: $2,136. *Financial support:* In 2006–07, 34 students received support, including 21 teaching assistantships with partial tuition reimbursements available (averaging $8,814 per year); research assistantships with partial tuition reimbursements available, Federal Work-Study and institutionally sponsored loans also available. Support available to part-time students. Financial award application deadline: 4/15; financial award applicants required to submit FAFSA. *Faculty research:* Cardiopulmonary physiology: chronic lung disease, upper airway control and rehabilitation; muscle physiology, balance and biomechanics. Total annual research expenditures: $49,917. *Unit head:* Dr. Rick Carter, Chair, 806-742-3371, Fax: 806-742-1688, E-mail: rick.carter@ttu.edu. *Application contact:* Graduate Adviser, 806-742-3371, Fax: 806-742-1688.

Texas Woman's University, Graduate School, College of Health Sciences, Department of Nutrition and Food Sciences, Program in Exercise and Sports Nutrition, Denton, TX 76201. Offers MS. Part-time programs available. *Students:* 14 full-time (10 women), 11 part-time (all women); includes 6 minority (3 African Americans, 3 Hispanic Americans), 2 international. Average age 28. In 2006, 2 degrees awarded. *Degree requirements:* For master's, thesis, comprehensive exam. *Entrance requirements:* For master's, GRE General Test, bachelor's degree in kinesiology or nutrition, minimum GPA of 3.0 in the last 60 hours, 9 hours of course work in chemistry, 3 hours of course work in each physiology and nutrition, 6 hours of upper-level course work in nutrition. Additional exam requirements/recommendations for international students: Required—TOEFL (minimum score 550 paper-based; 213 computer-based; 79 iBT). *Application deadline:* For fall admission, 4/1 for international students; for spring admission, 8/1 for international students. Applications are processed on a rolling basis. Application fee: $30 ($50 for international students). Electronic applications accepted. *Expenses:* Tuition, area resident: Part-time $168 per unit. Tuition, state resident: full-time $4,369. Tuition, nonresident: full-time $9,373; part-time $443 per unit. Required fees: $20 per unit. $177 per term. *Financial support:* In 2006–07, research assistantships (averaging $9,468 per year), teaching assistantships (averaging $9,468 per year) were awarded. Financial award application deadline: 3/1; financial award applicants required to submit FAFSA. *Unit head:* Dr. Kyle Biggerstaff, Program Director, 940-898-2575, Fax: 940-898-2793. *Application contact:* Samuel Wheeler, Coordinator of Graduate Admissions, 940-898-3188, Fax: 940-898-3081, E-mail: wheelersr@twu.edu.

United States Sports Academy, Graduate Programs, Department of Health and Fitness Management, Daphne, AL 36526-7055. Offers MSS. Part-time programs available. Postbaccalaureate distance learning degree programs offered (minimal on-campus study). *Faculty:* 1 full-time (0 women), 1 part-time/adjunct (0 women). *Students:* 2 full-time (0 women), 3 part-time (1 woman). *Degree requirements:* For master's, thesis optional. *Entrance requirements:* For master's, GRE General Test, GMAT, or MAT, minimum GPA of 2.5, 3 letters of recommendation, resumé. Additional exam requirements/recommendations for international students: Required—TOEFL (minimum score 500 paper-based; 213 computer-based). *Application deadline:* Applications are processed on a rolling basis. Application fee: $50 ($125 for international students). Electronic applications accepted. *Financial support:* Application deadline: 8/15; *Faculty research:* Exercise physiology, conditioning. *Unit head:* Dr. Brian Wallace, Chair, 251-626-3303 Ext. 137, Fax: 251-625-1035, E-mail: bwallace@ussd.edu. *Application contact:* Dr. Albert G. Applin, Dean of Student Services, 251-626-3303 Ext. 147, Fax: 251-626-1035, E-mail: applin@ussa.edu.

United States Sports Academy, Graduate Programs, Department of Sport Studies, Daphne, AL 36526-7055. Offers MSS. Part-time programs available. Postbaccalaureate distance learning degree programs offered (minimal on-campus study). *Faculty:* 1 full-time (0 women). *Students:* 6 full-time (1 woman), 21 part-time (5 women); includes 3 minority (2 African Americans, 1 Hispanic American). Average age 28. *Degree requirements:* For master's, thesis optional. *Entrance requirements:* For master's, GRE General Test, GMAT, or MAT, minimum GPA of 2.5, 3 letters of recommendation, resumé. Additional exam requirements/recommendations for international students: Required—TOEFL (minimum score 500 paper-based; 213 computer-based). *Application deadline:* Applications are processed on a rolling basis. Application fee: $50 ($125 for international students). Electronic applications accepted. *Unit head:* Fred Cromartie, Department Chair, 251-626-3303 Ext. 151, Fax: 251-625-1035, E-mail: cromarti@ussa.edu. *Application contact:* Dr. Albert G. Applin, Dean of Student Services, 251-626-3303 Ext. 147, Fax: 251-626-1035, E-mail: applin@ussa.edu.

University at Buffalo, the State University of New York, Graduate School, School of Public Health and Health Professions, Department of Exercise and Nutrition Sciences, Buffalo, NY 14260. Offers exercise science (MS, PhD); nutrition (MS). Part-time programs available. *Faculty:* 16 full-time (4 women), 14 part-time/adjunct (12 women). *Students:* 57 full-time (34 women), 31 part-time (26 women); includes 9 minority (4 African Americans, 3 Asian Americans or Pacific Islanders, 2 Hispanic Americans), 11 international. Average age 23. 109 applicants, 50% accepted, 39 enrolled. In 2006, 26 master's, 2 doctorates awarded. *Median time to degree:* Of those who began their doctoral program in fall 1998, 100% received their degree in 8 years or less. *Degree requirements:* For master's, comprehensive exam or thesis; for doctorate, thesis/dissertation, comprehensive exam. *Entrance requirements:* For master's, GRE General Test (nutrition), minimum GPA of 3.0; for doctorate, GRE General Test, minimum GPA of 3.0 (PhD). Additional exam requirements/recommendations for international students: Required—TOEFL (minimum score 550 paper-based; 213 computer-based; 79 iBT), IELTS (minimum score 7). *Application deadline:* Applications are processed on a rolling basis. Application fee: $50. Electronic applications accepted. *Financial support:* In 2006–07, 12 students received support, including 1 research assistantship with tuition reimbursement available (averaging $18,000 per year), 11 teaching assistantships with full and partial tuition reimbursements available (averaging $11,000 per year); career-related internships or fieldwork, Federal Work-Study, institutionally sponsored loans, scholarships/grants, health care benefits, tuition waivers (full and partial), unspecified assistantships, and stipends also available. Financial award application deadline: 3/15; financial award applicants required to submit FAFSA. *Faculty research:* Cardiovascular disease-diet and exercise, respiratory control and muscle function, plasticity of connective and neural tissue, exercise nutrition, diet and cancer. Total annual research expenditures: $413,549. *Unit head:* Dr. John X. Wilson, Chair, 716-829-2941 Ext. 208, Fax: 716-829-2428, E-mail: jxwilson@buffalo.edu. *Application contact:* Dr. Gaspar Farkas, Director of Graduate Studies, 76-829-2941 Ext. 311, Fax: 716-829-2428, E-mail: farkas@buffalo.edu.

The University of Akron, Graduate School, College of Education, Department of Sport Science and Wellness Education, Program in Exercise Physiology/Adult Fitness, Akron, OH 44325. Offers MA, MS. *Students:* 16 full-time (8 women), 11 part-time (6 women); includes 2 minority (both African Americans) Average age 29. 14 applicants, 86% accepted, 12 enrolled. In 2006, 9 degrees awarded. *Degree requirements:* For master's, thesis optional. *Entrance requirements:* For master's, minimum GPA of 2.75. Additional exam requirements/recommendations for international students: Required—TOEFL (minimum score 550 paper-based; 213 computer-based; 79 iBT). *Application deadline:* For fall admission, 8/15 for domestic students. Applications are processed on a rolling basis. Application fee: $30 ($40 for international students). Electronic applications accepted. *Expenses:* Tuition, state resident: full-time $6,164; part-time $342 per credit. Tuition, nonresident: full-time $10,575; part-time $588 per credit. Required fees: $806; $43 per credit. $12 per term. Tuition and fees vary according to course load, degree level and program. *Unit head:* Dr. Ron Otterstetter, Coordinator, 330-972-7738, E-mail: ro5@uakron.edu.

The University of Akron, Graduate School, College of Education, Department of Sport Science and Wellness Education, Program in Sports Science/Coaching, Akron, OH 44325. Offers MA, MS. *Students:* 24 full-time (8 women), 10 part-time (5 women); includes 1 minority (African American), 3 international. Average age 26. 17 applicants, 82% accepted, 9 enrolled. In 2006, 17 degrees awarded. *Degree requirements:* For master's, thesis optional. *Entrance requirements:* For master's, minimum GPA of 2.75. Additional exam requirements/recommendations for international students: Required—TOEFL (minimum score 550 paper-based; 213 computer-based; 79 iBT). *Application deadline:* For fall admission, 8/15 for domestic students. Applications are processed on a rolling basis. Application fee: $30 ($40 for international students). Electronic applications accepted. *Expenses:* Tuition, state resident: full-time $6,164; part-time $342 per credit. Tuition, nonresident: full-time $10,575; part-time $588 per credit. Required fees: $806; $43 per credit. $12 per term. Tuition and fees vary according to course load, degree level and program. *Unit head:* Dr. Alan Kornspan, 330-972-8145, E-mail: alan3@uakron.edu.

The University of Alabama, Graduate School, College of Education, Department of Kinesiology, Tuscaloosa, AL 35487. Offers alternative sport pedagogy (MA); exercise science (MA, PhD); human performance (MA); sport management (MA); sport pedagogy (MA, PhD). Part-time programs available. *Faculty:* 9 full-time (1 woman). *Students:* 39 full-time (18 women), 20 part-time (11 women); includes 2 minority (both African Americans), 11 international. Average age 30. 35 applicants, 63% accepted, 7 enrolled. In 2006, 3 master's, 13 doctorates awarded. *Median time to degree:* Of those who began their doctoral program in fall 1998, 100% received their degree in 8 years or less. *Degree requirements:* For master's, thesis optional; for doctorate, thesis/dissertation, comprehensive exam. *Entrance requirements:* For master's and doctorate, GRE, MAT, minimum GPA of 3.0. Additional exam requirements/recommendations for international students: Required—TOEFL. *Financial support:* In 2006–07, 14 students received support, including 13 teaching assistantships with full tuition reimbursements available (averaging $8,678 per year). *Faculty research:* Race gender and sexuality in sports, physical education curriculum reform, disability sports, physical activity and health, environmental physiology. Total annual research expenditures: $9,290. *Unit head:* Dr. Matt Curtner-Smith, Department Head and Professor, 205-348-9209, Fax: 205-348-0867, E-mail: msmith@bamed.ua.edu.

University of Alberta, Faculty of Graduate Studies and Research, Faculty of Physical Education and Recreation, Edmonton, AB T6G 2E1, Canada. Offers physical education (M Sc); recreation and physical education (MA, PhD). Part-time programs available. *Faculty:* 30 full-time (10 women). *Students:* 60 full-time (34 women), 55 part-time (28 women), 10 international. 69 applicants, 36% accepted. In 2006, 13 master's, 7 doctorates awarded. Terminal master's awarded for partial completion of doctoral program. *Degree requirements:* For master's, thesis (for some programs); for doctorate, thesis/dissertation. *Entrance requirements:* For master's, bachelor's degree in related field; for doctorate, master's degree in related field with thesis. Additional exam requirements/recommendations for international students: Required—TOEFL. *Application deadline:* For fall admission, 1/1 priority date for domestic students. Applications are processed on a rolling basis. *Financial support:* In 2006–07, 63 students received support, including 28 research assistantships, 35 teaching assistantships; career-related internships or fieldwork and scholarships/grants also available. Support available to part-time students. *Faculty research:* Motivation and adherence to physical ability, performance enhancement, adapted physical activity, exercise physiology, sport administration, tourism. *Unit head:* Dr. D. Marshall, Assistant Dean, 780-492-3198, Fax: 403-492-2364. *Application contact:* Anne Jordan, Department Office, 403-492-3198, Fax: 403-492-2364, E-mail: pergrad@ualberta.ca.

University of Calgary, Faculty of Graduate Studies, Faculty of Kinesiology, Calgary, AB T2N 1N4, Canada. Offers biomedical engineering (M Sc, PhD); kinesiology (M Kin, M Sc, PhD), including biomechanics (PhD), health and exercise physiology (PhD). *Faculty:* 59 full-time (13 women), 18 part-time/adjunct (8 women). *Students:* 75 full-time (38 women), 3 part-time (1 woman). Average age 26. 52 applicants, 62% accepted, 25 enrolled. In 2006, 6 master's, 4 doctorates awarded. *Degree requirements:* For master's, thesis (M Sc); for doctorate, thesis/dissertation. *Entrance requirements:* Additional exam requirements/recommendations for international students: Required—TOEFL. *Application deadline:* For fall admission, 3/31 for domestic students. Applications are processed on a rolling basis. Application fee: $100 ($130 for international students). Electronic applications accepted. *Financial support:* In 2006–07, 21 students received support, including 3 research assistantships, 18 teaching assistantships; career-related internships or fieldwork and unspecified assistantships also available. Financial award application deadline: 3/31. *Faculty research:* Load acting on the human body, muscle mechanics and physiology, optimizing high performance athlete performance, eye movement in sports, analysis of body composition. Total annual research expenditures: $1.5 million. *Unit head:* Brian R. MacIntosh, Associate Dean, 403-220-3421, Fax: 403-220-0105, E-mail: brian@

Exercise and Sports Science

University of Calgary (continued)
kin.ucalgary.ca. *Application contact:* Rosalie Kolstad, Graduate Program Administrator, 403-220-5183, Fax: 403-220-0105, E-mail: knesgrad@ucalgary.ca.

University of California, Davis, Graduate Studies, Graduate Group in Exercise Science, Davis, CA 95616. Offers MS. *Degree requirements:* For master's, thesis. *Entrance requirements:* For master's, GRE, minimum GPA of 3.25. Additional exam requirements/recommendations for international students: Required—TOEFL (minimum score 550 paper-based; 213 computer-based). Electronic applications accepted.

University of Central Florida, College of Education, Department of Child, Family and Community Sciences, Program in Physical Education-Exercise Physiology, Orlando, FL 32816. Offers M Ed, MA. Part-time and evening/weekend programs available. *Students:* 19 full-time (9 women), 20 part-time (11 women); includes 4 minority (all African Americans) In 2006, 16 master's awarded. *Entrance requirements:* For master's, GRE General Test. Additional exam requirements/recommendations for international students: Required—TOEFL. *Application deadline:* For fall admission, 7/15 for domestic students; for spring admission, 12/1 for domestic students. Application fee: $30. Electronic applications accepted. *Expenses:* Tuition, state resident: full-time $6,167; part-time $257 per credit hour. Tuition, nonresident: full-time $22,790; part-time $950 per credit hour. *Financial support:* In 2006–07, 2 research assistantships with partial tuition reimbursements (averaging $6,400 per year) were awarded; fellowships with partial tuition reimbursements, teaching assistantships with partial tuition reimbursements, career-related internships or fieldwork, Federal Work-Study, institutionally sponsored loans, tuition waivers (partial), and unspecified assistantships also available. Financial award application deadline: 3/1; financial award applicants required to submit FAFSA. *Unit head:* Dr. Patricia Higginbotham, Coordinator, 407-823-2050, E-mail: higginbp@mail.ucf.edu.

University of Central Missouri, The Graduate School, College of Health and Human Services, Department of Health and Human Performance, Warrensburg, MO 64093. Offers physical education/exercise and sports science (MS). Part-time programs available. *Faculty:* 16 full-time (7 women). *Students:* 3 full-time (0 women), 44 part-time (18 women); includes 10 minority (4 African Americans, 1 American Indian/Alaska Native, 1 Asian American or Pacific Islander, 4 Hispanic Americans). Average age 29. 20 applicants, 90% accepted, 11 enrolled. In 2006, 13 degrees awarded. *Degree requirements:* For master's, research project, thesis or internship. *Entrance requirements:* For master's, minimum GPA of 2.5, bachelor's degree in physical education. Additional exam requirements/recommendations for international students: Required—TOEFL (minimum score 500 paper-based; 173 computer-based). *Application deadline:* For fall admission, 6/1 priority date for domestic students, 5/1 priority date for international students; for spring admission, 10/1 priority date for domestic students, 10/1 for international students. Applications are processed on a rolling basis. Application fee: $30 ($50 for international students). *Expenses:* Tuition, state resident: full-time $5,448; part-time $227 per credit hour. Tuition, nonresident: full-time $10,896; part-time $454 per credit hour. Required fees: $336; $14 per credit hour. *Financial support:* In 2006–07, 4 students received support. Federal Work-Study, scholarships/grants, unspecified assistantships, and administrative and laboratory assistantships available. Support available to part-time students. Financial award application deadline: 3/1; financial award applicants required to submit FAFSA. *Faculty research:* Walking gait kinetics with external loads, maximum oxygen uptake, resting energy expenditure. Total annual research expenditures: $19,000. *Unit head:* Dr. Dirk Nelson, Chair, 660-543-4256, Fax: 660-543-4168, E-mail: nelson@ucmo.edu.

University of Connecticut, Graduate School, Neag School of Education, Department of Kinesiology, Storrs, CT 06269. Offers kinesiology (MA, PhD), including exercise science, sport management and sociology. *Faculty:* 16 full-time (5 women). *Students:* 78 full-time (42 women), 15 part-time (4 women); includes 14 minority (6 African Americans, 6 Asian Americans or Pacific Islanders, 2 Hispanic Americans), 8 international. Average age 26. 110 applicants, 43% accepted, 47 enrolled. In 2006, 29 master's, 7 doctorates awarded. Terminal master's awarded for partial completion of doctoral program. *Degree requirements:* For master's, thesis or alternative, comprehensive exam; for doctorate, thesis/dissertation. *Entrance requirements:* For doctorate, GRE General Test. Additional exam requirements/recommendations for international students: Required—TOEFL (minimum score 550 paper-based; 213 computer-based). *Application deadline:* For fall admission, 2/1 priority date for domestic students, 2/1 for international students; for spring admission, 11/1 for domestic students, 10/1 for international students. Application fee: $55. *Financial support:* In 2006–07, 49 research assistantships with full tuition reimbursements were awarded; fellowships, teaching assistantships with full tuition reimbursements, Federal Work-Study, scholarships/grants, health care benefits, and unspecified assistantships also available. Financial award application deadline: 2/1; financial award applicants required to submit FAFSA. *Unit head:* Carl Maresh, Head, 860-486-3623, Fax: 860-486-1123. *Application contact:* Lisa Rasicot, Graduate Coordinator, 860-486-3065, Fax: 860-486-0210, E-mail: soeadm02@uconnvm.uconn.edu.

University of Connecticut, Graduate School, Neag School of Education, Department of Kinesiology, Field of Kinesiology, Program in Exercise Science, Storrs, CT 06269. Offers MA, PhD. *Faculty:* 11 full-time (2 women). *Students:* 39 full-time (22 women); includes 7 minority (2 African Americans, 4 Asian Americans or Pacific Islanders, 1 Hispanic American), 3 international. Average age 25. 60 applicants, 45% accepted, 21 enrolled. In 2006, 10 degrees awarded. Terminal master's awarded for partial completion of doctoral program. *Degree requirements:* For master's, thesis or alternative, comprehensive exam; for doctorate, thesis/dissertation. *Entrance requirements:* For doctorate, GRE General Test. Additional exam requirements/recommendations for international students: Required—TOEFL (minimum score 550 paper-based; 213 computer-based). *Application deadline:* For fall admission, 2/1 priority date for domestic and international students; for spring admission, 11/1 for domestic students, 10/1 for international students. Applications are processed on a rolling basis. Application fee: $55. Electronic applications accepted. *Financial support:* In 2006–07, 22 research assistantships with full tuition reimbursements were awarded; teaching assistantships with full tuition reimbursements, Federal Work-Study, scholarships/grants, health care benefits, and unspecified assistantships also available. Financial award application deadline: 2/1; financial award applicants required to submit FAFSA. *Application contact:* Lisa Rasicot, Graduate Coordinator, 860-486-3065, Fax: 860-486-0210, E-mail: soeadm02@uconnvm.uconn.edu.

University of Dayton, Graduate School, School of Education and Allied Professions, Department of Health and Sport Science, Dayton, OH 45469-1300. Offers exercise sports science (MS Ed); physical education (MS Ed). Part-time and evening/weekend programs available. *Faculty:* 15 full-time (5 women). *Students:* 30 full-time (21 women), 7 part-time (5 women); includes 3 African Americans, 1 American Indian/Alaska Native, 2 international. Average age 32. 72 applicants, 63% accepted, 31 enrolled. In 2006, 1 degree awarded. *Median time to degree:* Master's–2 years full-time. *Degree requirements:* For master's and doctorate, thesis/dissertation. *Entrance requirements:* For master's, GRE General Test, MAT, minimum GPA of 2.75; for doctorate, GRE General Test, minimum GPA of 3.0, 80 observation hours. Additional exam requirements/recommendations for international students: Required—TOEFL (minimum score 550 paper-based; 213 computer-based). *Application deadline:* For fall admission, 3/15 priority date for domestic students, 3/1 priority date for international students. Applications are processed on a rolling basis. Application fee: $0. Electronic applications accepted. *Expenses:* Tuition: Part-time $601 per semester hour. Tuition and fees vary according to degree level and program. *Financial support:* In 2006–07, 4 students received support, including 4 teaching assistantships with tuition reimbursements available (averaging $8,000 per year); research assistantships, career-related internships or fieldwork, institutionally sponsored loans, health care benefits, and unspecified assistantships also available. Financial award applicants required to submit FAFSA. *Faculty research:* Energy expenditure, strength, training, teaching nutrition and calcium intake of children and families in Head-Start. *Unit head:* Dr. Paul Vanderburgh, Chair, 937-229-4240, Fax: 937-229-4244. *Application contact:* Erika Eavers, Graduate Admission Processor, 937-229-3065, Fax: 937-229-4729, E-mail: erika.eavers@notes.udayton.edu.

University of Delaware, College of Health Sciences, Department of Health, Nutrition, and Exercise Sciences, Newark, DE 19716. Offers exercise science (MS), including biomechanics, exercise physiology, motor control; health promotion (MS); human nutrition (MS). Part-time programs available. *Degree requirements:* For master's, thesis, registration. *Entrance requirements:* For master's, GRE General Test, interview, minimum GPA of 3.0. Additional exam requirements/recommendations for international students: Required—TOEFL (minimum score 550 paper-based; 213 computer-based). Electronic applications accepted. *Faculty research:* Sport biomechanics, rehabilitation biomechanics, vascular dynamics.

University of Florida, Graduate School, College of Health and Human Performance, Department of Applied Physiology and Kinesiology, Gainesville, FL 32611. Offers athletic training/sport medicine (MS, PhD); biomechanics (MS, PhD); clinical exercise physiology (MS); exercise physiology (MS, PhD); health and human performance (PhD); human performance (MS); motor learning/control (MS, PhD); sport and exercise psychology (MS). *Faculty:* 14 full-time (2 women), 1 part-time/adjunct (0 women). *Degree requirements:* For doctorate, thesis/dissertation. *Entrance requirements:* For doctorate, GRE General Test. *Application deadline:* For fall admission, 6/1 priority date for domestic students. Applications are processed on a rolling basis. Application fee: $20. Electronic applications accepted. *Expenses:* Tuition, state resident: full-time $6,827. Tuition, nonresident: full-time $21,951. Required fees: $999. *Financial support:* In 2006–07, 16 research assistantships (averaging $13,060 per year), 28 teaching assistantships (averaging $12,925 per year) were awarded; fellowships, unspecified assistantships also available. *Unit head:* Dr. Steven Dodd, Chair, 352-392-0584 Ext. 1342, E-mail: sdodd@hhp.ufl.edu. *Application contact:* Dr. Paul A. Borsa, Coordinator, 352-392-0584 Ext. 1261, Fax: 352-392-5262, E-mail: pborsa@hhp.ufl.edu.

University of Houston, College of Education, Department of Health and Human Performance, Houston, TX 77204. Offers allied health (M Ed, Ed D); exercise science (MS); health education (M Ed); kinesiology (PhD); physical education (M Ed, Ed D). *Accreditation:* NCATE (one or more programs are accredited). Part-time and evening/weekend programs available. *Faculty:* 11 full-time (5 women), 6 part-time/adjunct (3 women). *Students:* 35 full-time (19 women), 33 part-time (17 women); includes 22 minority (12 African Americans, 1 Asian American or Pacific Islander, 9 Hispanic Americans), 1 international. Average age 29. 35 applicants, 54% accepted, 11 enrolled. In 2006, 24 master's, 4 doctorates awarded. *Degree requirements:* For master's, comprehensive exam or thesis; for doctorate, thesis/dissertation, comprehensive exam. *Entrance requirements:* For master's, GRE General Test or MAT; for doctorate, GRE General Test, interview. *Application deadline:* For fall admission, 7/3 for domestic students. Application fee: $35 ($75 for international students). *Expenses:* Tuition, state resident: full-time $5,429; part-time $226 per credit. Tuition, nonresident: full-time $12,029; part-time $501 per credit. Required fees: $2,454. *Financial support:* In 2006–07, 5 fellowships with full tuition reimbursements (averaging $9,500 per year), 4 research assistantships with full tuition reimbursements (averaging $9,850 per year), 9 teaching assistantships with full tuition reimbursements (averaging $9,850 per year) were awarded; career-related internships or fieldwork, Federal Work-Study, institutionally sponsored loans, scholarships/grants, health care benefits, and unspecified assistantships also available. Support available to part-time students. Financial award application deadline: 3/10. *Faculty research:* Motor development, physical fitness, comprehensive school health, leadership, sports law. *Unit head:* Dr. Chuck Layne, Chairperson, 713-743-9868, Fax: 713-743-9860, E-mail: clayne2@uh.edu.

University of Houston–Clear Lake, School of Human Sciences and Humanities, Programs in Human Sciences, Houston, TX 77058-1098. Offers behavioral sciences (MA), including behavioral sciences-general, behavioral sciences-psychology, behavioral sciences-sociology; clinical psychology (MA); criminology (MA); cross-cultural studies (MA); family therapy (MA); fitness and human performance (MA); school psychology (MA). *Accreditation:* AAMFT/COAMFTE. Part-time and evening/weekend programs available. Postbaccalaureate distance learning degree programs offered (minimal on-campus study). *Faculty:* 37 full-time (19 women), 35 part-time/adjunct (22 women). *Students:* 299 full-time (221 women), 411 part-time (282 women); includes 262 minority (133 African Americans, 2 American Indian/Alaska Native, 31 Asian Americans or Pacific Islanders, 96 Hispanic Americans), 28 international. Average age 34. In 2006, 163 degrees awarded. *Degree requirements:* For master's, thesis or alternative. *Entrance requirements:* For master's, GRE General Test. Additional exam requirements/recommendations for international students: Required—TOEFL (minimum score 550 paper-based; 213 computer-based). *Application deadline:* For fall admission, 8/1 for domestic students, 6/1 for international students; for spring admission, 12/1 for domestic students, 10/1 for international students. Applications are processed on a rolling basis. Application fee: $35 ($75 for international students). Electronic applications accepted. *Financial support:* Fellowships, research assistantships, teaching assistantships, career-related internships or fieldwork, Federal Work-Study, institutionally sponsored loans, and scholarships/grants available. Support available to part-time students. Financial award application deadline: 5/1; financial award applicants required to submit FAFSA. *Faculty research:* Smoking cessation, adolescent sexuality, white collar crime, serial murder, human factors/human computer interaction. *Unit head:* Dr. Hilary Karp, Division Chair, 281-283-3383, E-mail: karp@cl.uh.edu. *Application contact:* Janis S. Bigelow, Assistant Director of Admissions, Recruitment and Communications, 281-283-2540, Fax: 281-283-2530, E-mail: bigelow@uhcl.edu.

The University of Iowa, Graduate College, College of Liberal Arts and Sciences, Department of Health and Sport Studies, Iowa City, IA 52242-1316. Offers psychology of sport and physical activity (MA, PhD); sports studies (MA, PhD). *Faculty:* 8 full-time, 7 part-time/adjunct. *Students:* 22 full-time (16 women), 11 part-time (7 women); includes 5 minority (all African Americans) 55 applicants, 36% accepted, 12 enrolled. In 2006, 15 master's, 2 doctorates awarded. *Degree requirements:* For master's, exam, thesis optional; for doctorate, thesis/dissertation, comprehensive exam, registration. *Entrance requirements:* For master's and doctorate, GRE General Test, minimum GPA of 3.0. Additional exam requirements/recommendations for international students: Required—TOEFL (minimum score 550 paper-based; 230 computer-based; 81 iBT). *Application deadline:* For fall admission, 3/1 for domestic and international students. Application fee: $60 ($85 for international students). Electronic applications accepted. *Financial support:* In 2006–07, 3 research assistantships with partial tuition reimbursements, 28 teaching assistantships with partial tuition reimbursements were awarded; fellowships also available. Financial award applicants required to submit FAFSA. *Unit head:* Susan Birrell, Chair, 319-335-9337, Fax: 319-335-6669.

The University of Iowa, Graduate College, College of Liberal Arts and Sciences, Department of Integrative Physiology, Iowa City, IA 52242-1316. Offers exercise science (MS); integrative physiology (PhD). *Faculty:* 9 full-time, 3 part-time/adjunct. *Students:* 8 full-time (4 women), 5 part-time (1 woman), 1 international. 30 applicants, 23% accepted, 6 enrolled. In 2006, 3 degrees awarded. *Degree requirements:* For master's, exam, thesis optional; for doctorate, thesis/dissertation, comprehensive exam, registration. *Entrance requirements:* For master's and doctorate, GRE General Test, minimum GPA of 3.0. Additional exam requirements/recommendations for international students: Required—TOEFL (minimum score 550 paper-based; 213 computer-based; 81 iBT). *Application deadline:* Applications are processed on a rolling basis. Application fee: $60 ($85 for international students). Electronic applications accepted. *Financial support:* In 2006–07, 6 research assistantships with partial tuition reimbursements, 14 teaching assistantships with partial tuition reimbursements were awarded; fellowships also available. Financial award applicants required to submit FAFSA. *Unit head:* Jerry Maynard, Chair, 319-335-9495, Fax: 319-335-6966.

University of Kentucky, Graduate School, College of Education, Program in Kinesiology and Health Promotion, Lexington, KY 40506-0032. Offers exercise science (PhD); kinesiology (MS, Ed D). *Faculty:* 13 full-time (4 women). *Students:* 82 full-time (46 women), 31 part-time (12 women); includes 15 minority (10 African Americans, 3 Asian Americans or Pacific Islanders, 2 Hispanic Americans), 2 international. Average age 29. 127 applicants, 55% accepted, 46 enrolled. In 2006, 37 master's, 3 doctorates awarded. Terminal master's awarded for partial completion of doctoral program. *Median time to degree:* Of those who began their doctoral program in fall 1998, 75% received their degree in 8 years or less. *Degree requirements:* For master's, thesis optional; for doctorate, thesis/dissertation, comprehensive exam. *Entrance requirements:* For master's, GRE General Test, minimum undergraduate GPA of 2.75; for doctorate, GRE General Test, minimum graduate GPA of 3.0. Additional exam requirements/recommendations for international students: Required—TOEFL (minimum score 550 paper-based; 213 computer-based). *Application deadline:* For fall admission, 7/17 priority date for domestic students, 2/1 priority date for international students; for spring admission, 12/13 priority date for domestic students, 6/15 priority date for international students. Application fee: $40 ($55 for international students). Electronic applications accepted. *Expenses:* Tuition, state resident: full-time $7,670; part-time $401 per credit hour. Tuition, nonresident: full-time $16,158; part-time $873 per credit hour. *Financial support:* In 2006–07, 2 fellowships with full tuition reimbursements (averaging $4,500 per year), 17 research assistantships with full tuition reimbursements (averaging $9,500 per year), 19 teaching assistantships with full tuition reimbursements (averaging $7,446 per year) were awarded; career-related internships or fieldwork, Federal Work-Study, institutionally sponsored loans, scholarships/grants, traineeships, health care benefits, tuition waivers (partial), and unspecified assistantships also available. Support available to part-time students. Financial award application deadline: 3/15. *Unit head:* Dr. Richard Riggs, Director of Graduate Studies, 859-257-3645, Fax: 859-323-1090. *Application contact:* Dr. Brian Jackson, Senior Associate Dean, 859-257-4667, Fax: 859-257-4676, E-mail: brian.jackson@uky.edu.

University of Lethbridge, School of Graduate Studies, Lethbridge, AB T1K 3M4, Canada. Offers accounting (MScM); addictions counseling (M Sc); agricultural biotechnology (M Sc); agricultural studies (M Sc, MA); anthropology (MA); archaeology (MA); art (MA); biochemistry (M Sc); biological sciences (M Sc); biomolecular science (PhD); biosystems and biodiversity (PhD); Canadian studies (MA); chemistry (M Sc); computer science (M Sc); computer science and geographical information science (M Sc); counseling psychology (M Ed); dramatic arts (MA); earth, space, and physical science (PhD); economics (MA); educational leadership (M Ed); English (MA); environmental science (M Sc); evolution and behavior (PhD); exercise science (M Sc); finance (MScM); French (MA); French/German (MA); French/Spanish (MA); general education (M Ed); general management (MScM); geography (M Sc, MA); German (MA); health sciences (M Sc, MA); history (MA); human resource management and labour relations (MScM); individualized multidisciplinary (M Sc, MA); information systems (MScM); international management (MScM); kinesiology (M Sc, MA); management (M Sc, MA); marketing (MScM); mathematics (M Sc); music (MA); Native American studies (MA); neuroscience (M Sc, PhD); new media (MA); nursing (M Sc); philosophy (MA); physics (M Sc); policy and strategy (MScM); political science (MA); psychology (M Sc, MA); religious studies (MA); sociology (MA); theoretical and computational science (PhD); urban and regional studies (MA). Part-time and evening/weekend programs available. *Students:* 200 full-time, 90 part-time. In 2006, 105 master's, 3 doctorates awarded. *Degree requirements:* For doctorate, thesis/dissertation, comprehensive exam. *Entrance requirements:* For master's, GMAT (M Sc management), bachelor's degree in related field, minimum GPA of 3.0 during previous 20 graded semester courses, 2 years teaching or related experience (M Ed); for doctorate, master's degree, minimum graduate GPA of 3.5. Additional exam requirements/recommendations for international students: Required—TOEFL. Application fee: $60 Canadian dollars. *Financial support:* Fellowships, research assistantships, teaching assistantships, scholarships/grants, health care benefits, and unspecified assistantships available. *Faculty research:* Movement and brain plasticity, gibberellin physiology, photosynthesis, carbon cycling, molecular properties of main-group ring components. *Unit head:* Dr. Jo-Anne Fiske, Interim Dean, 403-329-2121, Fax: 403-329-2097. *Application contact:* Kathy Schrage, Administrative Assistant, Office of the Academic Vice President, 403-329-2121, Fax: 403-329-2097, E-mail: inquiries@uleth.ca.

University of Louisiana at Monroe, Graduate Studies and Research, College of Education and Human Development, Department of Kinesiology, Monroe, LA 71209-0001. Offers exercise science (MS). Part-time and evening/weekend programs available. *Faculty:* 6 full-time (3 women). *Students:* 11 full-time (7 women), 4 part-time (2 women); includes 1 minority (African American), 1 international. Average age 26. In 2006, 8 degrees awarded. *Degree requirements:* For master's, thesis optional. *Entrance requirements:* For master's, GRE General Test. *Application deadline:* For fall admission, 6/1 priority date for domestic students; for spring admission, 11/1 for domestic students. Applications are processed on a rolling basis. Application fee: $20 ($30 for international students). *Expenses:* Tuition, state resident: part-time $124 per credit hour. Tuition, nonresident: part-time $124 per credit hour. *Financial support:* Research assistantships, teaching assistantships, career-related internships or fieldwork and unspecified assistantships available. Financial award application deadline: 7/1. *Faculty research:* Cardiovascular disease risk factors; exercise and immunological system; attitude, exercise, and the aged. *Unit head:* Dr. Wilson Campbell, Head, 318-342-1305, Fax: 318-342-1308, E-mail: wcampbell@ulm.edu.

University of Louisville, Graduate School, College of Education and Human Development, Department of Health and Sports Sciences, Program in Exercise Physiology, Louisville, KY 40292-0001. Offers MS. *Students:* 17 full-time (6 women), 7 part-time (4 women); includes 2 minority (1 African American, 1 Asian American or Pacific Islander). Average age 29. In 2006, 7 degrees awarded. *Degree requirements:* For master's, thesis optional. *Entrance requirements:* For master's, GRE General Test. *Application deadline:* Applications are processed on a rolling basis. Application fee: $50. Electronic applications accepted. *Financial support:* Fellowships, research assistantships, teaching assistantships, Federal Work-Study and scholarships/grants available. *Unit head:* Dr. Ann Swank, Program Head, 502-852-8351, Fax: 502-852-4534, E-mail: ann.swank@louisville.edu.

University of Mary Hardin-Baylor, College of Education, Belton, TX 76513. Offers educational administration (M Ed, Ed D); educational psychology (M Ed); exercise and sport science (M Ed); general studies (M Ed); reading education (M Ed). Part-time and evening/weekend programs available. *Faculty:* 10 full-time (5 women), 1 part-time/adjunct (0 women). *Students:* 8 full-time (3 women), 36 part-time (26 women); includes 8 minority (3 African Americans, 5 Hispanic Americans). Average age 24. In 2006, 18 degrees awarded. *Degree requirements:* For master's, comprehensive exam, registration. *Entrance requirements:* For master's, GRE General Test, minimum GPA of 2.75, Texas teaching certificate. *Application deadline:* For fall admission, 6/1 priority date for domestic students; for spring admission, 11/1 for domestic students. Applications are processed on a rolling basis. Application fee: $35 ($135 for international students). Electronic applications accepted. *Expenses:* Tuition: Full-time $8,910; part-time $495 per hour. Required fees: $906; $47 per hour. $30 per term. Tuition and fees vary according to course load. *Financial support:* Federal Work-Study, scholarships/grants, and scholarships (for some active duty military personnel only) available. Support available to part-time students. Financial award application deadline: 6/1; financial award applicants required to submit FAFSA. *Unit head:* Dr. Marlene Zipperlen, Dean, 254-295-4572, Fax: 254-295-4480, E-mail: mzipperlen@umhb.edu. *Application contact:* Dr. Shirley Dahl, Director, Graduate Programs in Education, 254-295-4185, Fax: 254-295-4480, E-mail: sdahl@umhb.edu.

University of Memphis, Graduate School, College of Education, Department of Health and Sport Sciences, Memphis, TN 38152. Offers clinical nutrition (MS); exercise and sport science (MS); health promotion (MS); physical education teacher education (MS), including teacher education; sport and leisure commerce (MS). Part-time and evening/weekend programs available. *Faculty:* 26 full-time (10 women), 8 part-time/adjunct (5 women). *Students:* Average age 28. 50 applicants, 62% accepted. In 2006, 14 degrees awarded. *Degree requirements:* For master's, thesis, comprehensive exam. *Entrance requirements:* For master's, GRE General Test or GMAT (sport and leisure commerce). *Application deadline:* For fall admission, 5/1 priority date for domestic students; for spring admission, 11/1 for domestic students. Applications are processed on a rolling basis. Application fee: $25 ($50 for international students). *Financial support:* In 2006–07, 13 research assistantships with full tuition reimbursements (averaging $6,000 per year), 4 teaching assistantships with full tuition reimbursements (averaging $6,000 per year) were awarded; career-related internships or fieldwork, tuition waivers (partial), and community assistantships also available. *Faculty research:* Sport marketing and consumer analysis, health psychology, smoking cessation, psychosocial aspects of cardiovascular disease, global health promotion. Total annual research expenditures: $1.3 million. *Unit head:* Dr. Michael H. Hamrick, Chairman, 901-678-4165, Fax: 901-678-3591, E-mail: mhamrick@memphis.edu. *Application contact:* Christina Little, Academic Services Coordinator, 901-678-4316, Fax: 901-678-3591, E-mail: aclittle@memphis.edu.

University of Miami, Graduate School, School of Education, Department of Exercise and Sport Sciences, Program in Exercise Physiology, Coral Gables, FL 33124. Offers MS Ed, PhD. Part-time programs available. *Students:* 20 full-time (9 women), 1 (woman) part-time; includes 3 minority (1 African American, 2 Hispanic Americans), 6 international. Average age 24. 10 applicants, 80% accepted, 1 enrolled. In 2006, 2 master's, 2 doctorates awarded. *Degree requirements:* For master's, special project, thesis optional; for doctorate, thesis/dissertation. *Entrance requirements:* For master's and doctorate, GRE General Test, GRE Subject Test. Additional exam requirements/recommendations for international students: Required—TOEFL (minimum score 550 paper-based; 212 computer-based). *Application deadline:* Applications are processed on a rolling basis. Application fee: $50. Electronic applications accepted. *Financial support:* In 2006–07, 6 students received support, including 6 research assistantships (averaging $18,000 per year); teaching assistantships with full tuition reimbursements available, career-related internships or fieldwork and unspecified assistantships also available. Financial award application deadline: 3/1; financial award applicants required to submit FAFSA. *Faculty research:* Women's health, cardiovascular health, aging, metabolism, obesity. *Application contact:* Marissa Stevenson, Graduate Admissions Coordinator, 305-284-2167, Fax: 305-284-3003, E-mail: mstevenson@miami.edu.

University of Minnesota, Twin Cities Campus, Graduate School, College of Education and Human Development, School of Kinesiology, Minneapolis, MN 55455-0213. Offers adapted physical education (MA, PhD); biomechanics (MA); biomechanics and neural control (PhD); coaching (Certificate); developmental adapted physical education (M Ed); exercise physiology (MA, PhD); human factors/ergonomics (MA, PhD); international/comparative sport (MA, PhD); kinesiology (M Ed, MA, PhD); leisure services/management (MA, PhD); motor development (MA, PhD); motor learning/control (MA, PhD); outdoor education/recreation (MA, PhD); physical education (M Ed); recreation, park, and leisure studies (M Ed, MA, PhD); sport and exercise science (M Ed); sport management (M Ed, MA, PhD); sport psychology (MA, PhD); sport sociology (MA, PhD); therapeutic recreation (MA, PhD). Part-time programs available. *Faculty:* 14 full-time (6 women). *Students:* 142 full-time (70 women), 68 part-time (28 women); includes 9 minority (3 African Americans, 1 American Indian/Alaska Native, 2 Asian Americans or Pacific Islanders, 3 Hispanic Americans), 21 international. Average age 30. 186 applicants, 60% accepted, 88 enrolled. In 2006, 141 master's, 57 doctorates, 12 other advanced degrees awarded. Terminal master's awarded for partial completion of doctoral program. *Degree requirements:* For master's, final oral exam; for doctorate, thesis/dissertation, preliminary written/oral exam, final oral exam. *Entrance requirements:* For master's, GRE or MAT, minimum GPA of 3.0; for doctorate, GRE or MAT, minimum GPA of 3.0, writing sample. *Expenses:* Tuition, state resident: full-time $9,302; part-time $775 per credit. Tuition, nonresident: full-time $16,400; part-time $1,367 per credit. Full-time tuition and fees vary according to class time, course load, program, reciprocity agreements and student level. *Financial support:* In 2006–07, 1 fellowship (averaging $24,775 per year), 13 research assistantships with full tuition reimbursements (averaging $24,775 per year), 34 teaching assistantships with full tuition reimbursements (averaging $24,775 per year) were awarded; career-related internships or fieldwork, Federal Work-Study, institutionally sponsored loans, and tuition waivers (full and partial) also available. Support available to part-time students. *Faculty research:* Exercise for health promotion and disease prevention and management; female athletes and bone health; affordance perception-action; gender and youth sport and psychosocial outcomes; outdoor behavioral healthcare. Total annual research expenditures: $708,598. *Unit head:* Dr. Mary Jo Kane, Director, 612-625-3870, Fax: 612-626-7700, E-mail: maryjo@umn.edu. *Application contact:* Dr. Mary Bents, Associate Dean, 612-625-6501, Fax: 612-626-1580, E-mail: mbents@tc.umn.edu.

University of Mississippi, Graduate School, School of Applied Sciences, Department of Health, Exercise Science, and Recreation Management, Oxford, University, MS 38677. Offers exercise science (MA, MS); exercise science and leisure management (PhD); leisure management (MA); park and recreation management (MA); wellness (MS). *Faculty:* 13 full-time (2 women), 4 part-time/adjunct (3 women). *Students:* 24 full-time (12 women), 7 part-time (4 women); includes 7 minority (5 African Americans, 2 Hispanic Americans), 2 international. In 2006, 9 master's, 4 doctorates awarded. *Degree requirements:* For master's, thesis (for some programs); for doctorate, thesis/dissertation. *Entrance requirements:* For master's, GRE General Test, minimum GPA of 3.0; for doctorate, GRE General Test. Additional exam requirements/recommendations for international students: Required—TOEFL. *Application deadline:* For fall admission, 4/1 for domestic students; for spring admission, 10/1 for domestic students. Applications are processed on a rolling basis. Application fee: $25. *Expenses:* Tuition, state resident: full-time $4,602; part-time $256 per credit hour. Tuition, nonresident: full-time $10,566; part-time $587 per credit hour. *Financial support:* Scholarships/grants available. Financial award application deadline: 3/1; financial award applicants required to submit FAFSA. *Unit head:* Dr. James Gilbert, Interim Chair, 662-915-5521, Fax: 662-915-5525, E-mail: dgilbert@olemiss.edu.

University of Missouri–Columbia, Graduate School, College of Human Environmental Science, Department of Nutritional Sciences, Columbia, MO 65211. Offers exercise physiology (MA, PhD); nutritional sciences (MS, PhD). *Faculty:* 6 full-time (4 women). *Students:* 14 full-time (7 women), 5 part-time (3 women); includes 2 minority (1 African American, 1 Asian American or Pacific Islander), 3 international. In 2006, 3 degrees awarded. *Degree requirements:* For doctorate, thesis/dissertation. *Entrance requirements:* For master's and doctorate, GRE General Test, minimum GPA of 3.0. Additional exam requirements/recommendations for international students: Required—TOEFL (minimum score 500 paper-based; 173 computer-based). *Application deadline:* Applications are processed on a rolling basis. Application fee: $45 ($60 for international students). *Financial support:* Fellowships, research assistantships, teaching assistantships, institutionally sponsored loans available. *Unit head:* Dr. Kevin Fritsche, Director of Graduate Studies, 573-882-4288.

The University of Montana, Graduate School, School of Education, Department of Health and Human Performance, Missoula, MT 59812-0002. Offers exercise science (MS); health and human performance (MS); health promotion (MS). *Accreditation:* NCATE. Part-time programs available. *Entrance requirements:* For master's, GRE General Test. Additional exam requirements/recommendations for international students: Required—TOEFL. *Faculty research:* Exercise physiology, performance psychology, nutrition, pre-employment physical screening, program evaluation.

University of Nebraska at Kearney, College of Graduate Study, College of Education, Department of Health, Physical Education, Recreation, and Leisure Studies, Kearney, NE 68849-0001. Offers adapted physical education (MA Ed); exercise science (MA Ed); master teacher (MA Ed). Part-time and evening/weekend programs available. *Faculty:* 6 full-time (3 women). *Students:* 11 full-time (4 women), 18 part-time (6 women); includes 1 minority (African American), 3 international. 14 applicants, 79% accepted. In 2006, 9 degrees awarded. *Degree requirements:* For master's, thesis optional. *Entrance requirements:* For master's, GRE General Test. Additional exam requirements/recommendations for international students: Required—TOEFL (minimum score 550 paper-based; 213 computer-based). *Application deadline:* For fall admission, 5/1 for domestic and international students; for spring admission, 8/15 for domestic students, 8/1 for international students. Applications are processed on a rolling basis. Application fee: $45. Electronic applications accepted. *Expenses:* Tuition, state resident: part-time $161 per hour. Tuition, nonresident: part-time $332 per hour. Required fees: $57 per hour. *Financial support:* In 2006–07, 2 research assistantships with full tuition reimbursements (averaging $8,200 per year), 8 teaching assistantships with full tuition reimbursements (averaging $8,200 per year) were awarded; career-related internships or fieldwork, scholarships/grants, and unspecified assistantships also available. Support available to part-time students. Financial award application deadline: 3/1; financial award applicants required to submit FAFSA.

Exercise and Sports Science

University of Nebraska at Kearney (continued)
Faculty research: Ergonomic aids, nutrition, motor development, sports pedagogy, applied behavior analysis. *Unit head:* Dr. Nita Unruh, Chair, 308-865-8331, E-mail: unruhnc@unk.edu.

University of Nevada, Las Vegas, Graduate College, Division of Health Sciences, Department of Kinesiology, Las Vegas, NV 89154-9900. Offers exercise physiology (MS); kinesiology (MS). Part-time programs available. *Faculty:* 11 full-time (2 women), 2 part-time/adjunct (both women). *Students:* 19 full-time (8 women), 22 part-time (12 women); includes 6 minority (2 African Americans, 3 Asian Americans or Pacific Islanders, 1 Hispanic American), 1 international. 47 applicants, 57% accepted, 13 enrolled. In 2006, 11 degrees awarded. *Degree requirements:* For master's, thesis (for some programs), comprehensive exam (for some programs). *Entrance requirements:* For master's, GRE General Test, minimum GPA of 3.0 during previous 2 years, 2.75 overall. Additional exam requirements/recommendations for international students: Required—TOEFL (minimum score 550 paper-based; 213 computer-based; 80 iBT). *Application deadline:* For fall admission, 6/15 for domestic students, 5/1 for international students; for spring admission, 11/15 for domestic students, 10/1 for international students. Application fee: $60 ($75 for international students). Electronic applications accepted. *Financial support:* In 2006–07, 10 research assistantships with partial tuition reimbursements (averaging $10,000 per year), 3 teaching assistantships with partial tuition reimbursements (averaging $10,000 per year) were awarded; career-related internships or fieldwork, Federal Work-Study, institutionally sponsored loans, scholarships/grants, health care benefits, and unspecified assistantships also available. Support available to part-time students. Financial award application deadline: 3/1. *Unit head:* Dr. John Mercer, Chair, 702-895-3766. *Application contact:* Graduate College Admissions Evaluator, 702-895-3320, Fax: 702-895-4180, E-mail: gradcollege@unlv.edu.

University of New Brunswick Fredericton, School of Graduate Studies, Faculty of Kinesiology, Fredericton, NB E3B 5A3, Canada. Offers exercise and sport science (M Sc); sport and recreation administration (MA, MBA/MA); MBA/MA. Part-time programs available. *Faculty:* 16 full-time (6 women). *Students:* 45 full-time (20 women), 8 part-time (6 women). In 2006, 8 degrees awarded. *Degree requirements:* For master's, thesis (for some programs). *Entrance requirements:* For master's, minimum GPA of 3.0, written statement of research goals and interests. Additional exam requirements/recommendations for international students: Required—TOEFL (minimum score 600 paper-based; 250 computer-based), TWE (minimum score 5). *Application deadline:* For fall admission, 3/1 priority date for domestic students. Applications are processed on a rolling basis. Application fee: $50 Canadian dollars. Electronic applications accepted. *Financial support:* In 2006–07, 24 research assistantships, 23 teaching assistantships were awarded; fellowships with tuition reimbursements, career-related internships or fieldwork and scholarships/grants also available. *Unit head:* Dr. Chris Stevenson, Acting Director of Graduate Studies, 506-453-5063, Fax: 506-453-3511, E-mail: cls@unb.ca. *Application contact:* Linda O'Brien, Graduate Secretary, 506-453-4576, Fax: 506-453-3511, E-mail: lobrien@unb.ca.

The University of North Carolina at Chapel Hill, Graduate School, College of Arts and Sciences, Department of Exercise and Sport Science, Chapel Hill, NC 27599. Offers athletic training (MA); exercise physiology (MA); sport administration (MA). *Degree requirements:* For master's, thesis, comprehensive exam. *Entrance requirements:* For master's, GRE General Test, minimum GPA of 3.0. Additional exam requirements/recommendations for international students: Required—TOEFL (minimum score 550 paper-based). Electronic applications accepted. *Faculty research:* Mild head injury in sport, endocrine system's response to exercise, obesity and children, effect of aerobic exercise on cerebral bloodflow in elderly population.

The University of North Carolina at Charlotte, Graduate School, College of Health and Human Services, Department of Kinesiology, Charlotte, NC 28223-0001. Offers clinical exercise physiology (MS). *Faculty:* 4 full-time (2 women). *Students:* 11 full-time (8 women), 8 part-time (all women); includes 2 minority (1 African American, 1 Asian American or Pacific Islander). Average age 26. 12 applicants, 83% accepted, 6 enrolled. In 2006, 2 degrees awarded. *Entrance requirements:* For master's, GRE or MAT. Additional exam requirements/recommendations for international students: Required—TOEFL (minimum score 557 paper-based; 220 computer-based). *Application deadline:* For fall admission, 7/1 for domestic students, 5/1 for international students; for spring admission, 11/1 for domestic students, 10/1 for international students. Applications are processed on a rolling basis. Application fee: $55. Electronic applications accepted. *Expenses:* Tuition, state resident: full-time $2,719; part-time $170 per credit. Tuition, nonresident: full-time $12,926; part-time $808 per credit. Required fees: $1,555. *Financial support:* In 2006–07, 7 research assistantships (averaging $11,607 per year), 4 teaching assistantships (averaging $12,000 per year) were awarded; fellowships, career-related internships or fieldwork, Federal Work-Study, institutionally sponsored loans, scholarships/grants, traineeships, and unspecified assistantships also available. Support available to part-time students. Financial award application deadline: 4/1; financial award applicants required to submit FAFSA. *Faculty research:* Genetic determinants of physical activity, cardiac muscle apoptosis with aging, sensorimotor deficits in knee osteoarthritis, mechanical laxity in functionally ankle instability. *Unit head:* Dr. Mitchell L. Cordova, Chair, 704-687-4695, Fax: 704-687-3180, E-mail: mcordova@email.uncc.edu. *Application contact:* Kathy B. Giddings, Director of Graduate Admissions, 704-687-3366, Fax: 704-687-3279, E-mail: gradadm@email.uncc.edu.

The University of North Carolina at Greensboro, Graduate School, School of Health and Human Performance, Department of Exercise and Sports Science, Greensboro, NC 27412-5001. Offers M Ed, MS, Ed D, PhD. *Faculty:* 19 full-time (9 women), 6 part-time/adjunct (4 women). *Students:* 56 full-time (17 women), 64 part-time (49 women); includes 24 minority (10 African Americans, 10 Asian Americans or Pacific Islanders, 4 Hispanic Americans). 127 applicants, 33% accepted. *Degree requirements:* For master's, thesis (for some programs); for doctorate, thesis/dissertation. *Entrance requirements:* For master's and doctorate, GRE General Test. Additional exam requirements/recommendations for international students: Required—TOEFL. *Application deadline:* For fall admission, 2/15 priority date for domestic students; for spring admission, 11/1 for domestic students. Applications are processed on a rolling basis. Application fee: $45. Electronic applications accepted. *Expenses:* Tuition, state resident: full-time $2,692. Tuition, nonresident: full-time $13,742. *Financial support:* Fellowships with full tuition reimbursements, research assistantships with full tuition reimbursements, teaching assistantships with full tuition reimbursements, career-related internships or fieldwork, Federal Work-Study, scholarships/grants, traineeships, and unspecified assistantships available. Support available to part-time students. *Unit head:* Dr. Kathleen Williams, Head, 336-334-5573, Fax: 336-334-3238, E-mail: k_willia@uncg.edu. *Application contact:* Michelle Harkleroad, Director of Graduate Admissions, 336-334-4884, Fax: 336-334-4424, E-mail: mbharkle@uncg.edu.

University of Northern Colorado, Graduate School, College of Natural and Health Sciences, School of Sport and Exercise Science, Greeley, CO 80639. Offers exercise science (MS, PhD); sport administration (MS, PhD); sport pedagogy (MS, PhD). Part-time and evening/weekend programs available. *Faculty:* 12 full-time (6 women). *Students:* 69 full-time (18 women), 20 part-time (9 women); includes 7 minority (2 American Indian/Alaska Native, 3 Asian Americans or Pacific Islanders, 2 Hispanic Americans), 16 international. Average age 30. 140 applicants, 69% accepted, 31 enrolled. In 2006, 64 master's, 8 doctorates awarded. *Degree requirements:* For master's, comprehensive exam; for doctorate, thesis/dissertation, comprehensive exam. *Entrance requirements:* For master's, 2 letters of recommendation, resumé; for doctorate, GRE General Test, 3 letters of recommendation, resumé. *Application deadline:* Applications are processed on a rolling basis. Application fee: $50 ($60 for international students). Electronic applications accepted. *Expenses:* Tuition, state resident: full-time $5,118; part-time $213 per credit hour. Tuition, nonresident: full-time $14,832; part-time $618 per credit hour. Required fees: $674; $34 per credit hour. *Financial support:* In 2006–07, 71 students received support, including 6 fellowships (averaging $2,417 per year), 18 research assistantships (averaging $6,834 per year), 14 teaching assistantships (averaging $8,725 per year); unspecified assistantships also available. Financial award application deadline: 3/1; financial award applicants required to submit FAFSA. *Unit head:* Dr. Dianna Gray, Director, 970-351-2535, Fax: 970-351-1762.

University of Oklahoma, Graduate College, College of Arts and Sciences, Department of Health and Exercise Science, Norman, OK 73019-0390. Offers MS, PhD. Part-time programs available. *Faculty:* 11 full-time (4 women). *Students:* 20 full-time (9 women), 8 part-time (3 women); includes 1 minority (Hispanic American), 5 international. 21 applicants, 76% accepted, 10 enrolled. In 2006, 5 degrees awarded. *Degree requirements:* For master's, thesis, comprehensive exam (for some programs). *Entrance requirements:* For master's, GRE General Test, minimum GPA of 3.0 in last 60 hours of undergraduate course work, interview, 3 letters of recommendation; for doctorate, GRE General Test, 3 letters of recommendation, curriculum vitae. Additional exam requirements/recommendations for international students: Required—TOEFL (minimum score 550 paper-based; 213 computer-based). *Application deadline:* For fall admission, 3/15 priority date for domestic students, 4/1 for international students; for spring admission, 9/1 for international students. Applications are processed on a rolling basis. Application fee: $40 ($90 for international students). *Expenses:* Tuition, state resident: full-time $3,180; part-time $133 per credit hour. Tuition, nonresident: full-time $11,347; part-time $473 per credit hour. Required fees: $1,729; $62 per credit hour. $117 per semester. Tuition and fees vary according to course load and program. *Financial support:* In 2006–07, 23 students received support, including 23 teaching assistantships with partial tuition reimbursements available (averaging $11,900 per year); research assistantships with partial tuition reimbursements available, scholarships/grants, health care benefits, tuition waivers (partial), and unspecified assistantships also available. Financial award applicants required to submit FAFSA. *Faculty research:* Neuromuscular function, aging body composition, endocrine, sports nutrition, bone, balance, physical activity. Total annual research expenditures: $2,140. *Unit head:* Dr. E. Laurette Taylor, Chairperson, 405-325-5211, Fax: 405-325-0594, E-mail: eltaylor@ou.edu. *Application contact:* Debra Bemben, Graduate Liaison, 405-325-2709, Fax: 405-325-0594, E-mail: dbemben@ou.edu.

University of Pittsburgh, School of Education, Department of Health and Physical Activity, Program in Developmental Movement, Pittsburgh, PA 15260. Offers MS. *Students:* 7 full-time (2 women), 4 part-time (1 woman); includes 3 minority (1 African American, 2 Asian Americans or Pacific Islanders), 4 international. 2 applicants, 100% accepted, 2 enrolled. In 2006, 3 degrees awarded. *Degree requirements:* For master's, thesis. *Entrance requirements:* Additional exam requirements/recommendations for international students: Required—TOEFL. *Application deadline:* For fall admission, 2/1 for domestic students. Application fee: $50. Electronic applications accepted. *Financial support:* Traineeships and unspecified assistantships available. Financial award application deadline: 3/1; financial award applicants required to submit FAFSA. *Application contact:* Joan M. Cutone, Director, School of Education Student Service Center, 412-648-2230, Fax: 412-648-1899, E-mail: soeinfo@pitt.edu.

University of Pittsburgh, School of Education, Department of Health and Physical Activity, Program in Exercise Physiology, Pittsburgh, PA 15260. Offers MS, PhD. *Students:* 65 full-time (41 women), 25 part-time (16 women); includes 6 minority (3 African Americans, 1 American Indian/Alaska Native, 1 Asian American or Pacific Islander, 1 Hispanic American), 6 international. 56 applicants, 80% accepted, 31 enrolled. In 2006, 26 master's, 6 doctorates awarded. Application fee: $50. *Application contact:* Joan M. Cutone, Director, School of Education Student Service Center, 412-648-2230, Fax: 412-648-1899, E-mail: soeinfo@pitt.edu.

University of Pittsburgh, School of Health and Rehabilitation Sciences, Program in Health and Rehabilitation Sciences, Pittsburgh, PA 15260. Offers dietetics (MS); health and rehabilitation sciences (MS), including clinical dietetics, coordinated with dietetics, health care supervision and management, health information systems, occupational therapy, physical therapy, rehabilitation counseling, rehabilitation science and technology, sports medicine; wellness and human performance (MS). *Accreditation:* APTA. Part-time and evening/weekend programs available. *Faculty:* 40 full-time (23 women), 3 part-time/adjunct (2 women). *Students:* 93 full-time (67 women), 54 part-time (35 women); includes 31 minority (12 African Americans, 18 Asian Americans or Pacific Islanders, 1 Hispanic American), 15 international. Average age 30. 122 applicants, 82% accepted, 64 enrolled. In 2006, 28 degrees awarded. *Entrance requirements:* For master's, minimum GPA of 3.0. Additional exam requirements/recommendations for international students: Required—TOEFL, IELTS. *Application deadline:* Applications are processed on a rolling basis. Application fee: $50. Electronic applications accepted. *Financial support:* In 2006–07, 11 research assistantships with full tuition reimbursements (averaging $16,918 per year) were awarded; teaching assistantships, Federal Work-Study, institutionally sponsored loans, traineeships, and unspecified assistantships also available. Support available to part-time students. Financial award applicants required to submit FAFSA. *Faculty research:* Assistive technology, seating and wheeled mobility, cellular neurophysiology, low back syndrome, augmentative communication. Total annual research expenditures: $953,246. *Application contact:* Shameem Gangjee, Director of Admissions, 412-383-6558, Fax: 412-383-6535, E-mail: admissions@shrs.pitt.edu.

University of Puerto Rico, Río Piedras, College of Education, Program in Exercise Sciences, San Juan, PR 00931-3300. Offers MS. *Students:* 4 full-time (2 women), 10 part-time (5 women); all Hispanic Americans *Entrance requirements:* For master's, PAEG or GRE, minimum GPA of 3.0. Application fee: $17. *Expenses:* Tuition, state resident: part-time $100 per credit. Tuition, nonresident: part-time $291 per credit. Required fees: $72 per semester. *Unit head:* Dr. Loyda Martinez, Coordinator, 787-764-0000 Ext. 4361, Fax: 787-763-4130.

University of Rhode Island, Graduate School, College of Human Science and Services, Department of Kinesiology, Kingston, RI 02881. Offers exercise science (MS); physical education (MS); physical therapy (DPT); psychosocial aspects of physical activity and sport (MS); teaching and administration (MS). *Accreditation:* NCATE (one or more programs are accredited). In 2006, 14 degrees awarded. *Entrance requirements:* For master's, MAT or GRE. *Application deadline:* For fall admission, 4/15 priority date for domestic students; for spring admission, 11/15 for domestic students. Applications are processed on a rolling basis. Application fee: $35. *Expenses:* Tuition, state resident: full-time $6,032; part-time $335 per credit. Tuition, nonresident: full-time $17,288; part-time $960 per credit. Required fees: $65 per credit. $30 per semester. One-time fee: $80 part-time. *Financial support:* Career-related internships or fieldwork available. *Unit head:* Dr. Deborah Riebe, Chair, 401-874-5444.

University of South Alabama, Graduate School, College of Education, Department of Health, Physical Education and Leisure Services, Mobile, AL 36688-0002. Offers exercise science (MS); health education (M Ed); physical education (M Ed); therapeutic recreation (MS). *Accreditation:* NCATE (one or more programs are accredited). Part-time programs available. *Faculty:* 9 full-time (1 woman). *Students:* 26 full-time (18 women), 11 part-time (8 women); includes 11 minority (9 African Americans, 1 Asian American or Pacific Islander, 1 Hispanic American), 2 international. 12 applicants, 83% accepted, 5 enrolled. In 2006, 17 degrees awarded. *Degree requirements:* For master's, comprehensive exam. *Entrance requirements:* For master's, GRE General Test or MAT. *Application deadline:* For fall admission, 9/1 priority date for domestic students. Applications are processed on a rolling basis. Application fee: $25. *Financial support:* In 2006–07, 10 teaching assistantships were awarded; career-related internships or fieldwork also available. Support available to part-time students. Financial award application deadline: 4/1. *Unit head:* Dr. Frederick M. Scaffidi, Chair, 251-460-7131.

University of South Carolina, The Graduate School, Arnold School of Public Health, Department of Exercise Science, Columbia, SC 29208. Offers MS, DPT, PhD. Part-time programs available. *Degree requirements:* For master's, thesis (for some programs), project, comprehensive exam; for doctorate, thesis/dissertation, comprehensive exam. *Entrance requirements:* For master's and doctorate, GRE General Test. Additional exam requirements/recommendations for international students: Required—TOEFL (minimum score 570 paper-based; 230 computer-based). Electronic applications accepted. *Faculty research:* Effects of acute and chronic exercise on human function and health, motor control.

University of Southern Mississippi, Graduate School, College of Health, School of Human Performance and Recreation, Hattiesburg, MS 39406-0001. Offers human performance (MS, Ed D, PhD); interscholastic athletic administration (MS); recreation and leisure management (MS); sport administration (MS); sport and coaching education (MS); sport management (MS); sports and high performance materials (MS). Part-time and evening/weekend programs available. *Faculty:* 15 full-time (3 women). *Students:* 63 full-time (21 women), 36 part-time (11 women); includes 16 minority (13 African Americans, 1 Asian American or Pacific Islander, 2 Hispanic Americans), 6 international. Average age 27. 75 applicants, 64% accepted, 38 enrolled. In 2006, 37 master's, 5 doctorates awarded. *Degree requirements:* For master's, thesis optional; for doctorate, thesis/dissertation, comprehensive exam, registration. *Entrance requirements:* For master's, GRE General Test, minimum GPA of 2.75 in last 60 hours; for doctorate, GRE General Test, minimum GPA of 3.5. Additional exam requirements/ recommendations for international students: Required—TOEFL. *Application deadline:* For fall admission, 3/1 priority date for domestic students, 3/1 for international students. Applications are processed on a rolling basis. Application fee: $25 ($30 for international students). Electronic applications accepted. *Financial support:* In 2006–07, 5 research assistantships with full tuition reimbursements (averaging $10,426 per year), 10 teaching assistantships with full tuition reimbursements (averaging $10,426 per year) were awarded; fellowships, career-related internships or fieldwork, Federal Work-Study, institutionally sponsored loans, and tuition waivers (partial) also available. Financial award application deadline: 3/15. *Faculty research:* Exercise physiology, health behaviors, resource management, activity interaction, site development. *Unit head:* Dr. Louis Marciani, Director, 601-266-5379, Fax: 601-266-4445. *Application contact:* Dr. Dennis Phillips, Graduate Coordinator, 601-266-5379, Fax: 601-266-4445.

The University of Tennessee, Graduate School, College of Education, Health and Human Sciences, Department of Exercise, Sport, and Leisure Studies, Program in Exercise Science, Knoxville, TN 37996. Offers biomechanics/sports medicine (MS, PhD); exercise physiology (MS, PhD). *Accreditation:* CEPH (one or more programs are accredited). Part-time programs available. *Faculty:* 13 full-time (4 women). *Students:* 28 (21 women); includes 1 African American 4 international. In 2006, 5 degrees awarded. *Degree requirements:* For master's, thesis optional. *Entrance requirements:* For master's, minimum GPA of 2.7. Additional exam requirements/recommendations for international students: Required—TOEFL. *Application deadline:* For fall admission, 2/1 priority date for domestic students. Application fee: $35. Electronic applications accepted. *Expenses:* Tuition, state resident: full-time $5,574. Tuition, nonresident: full-time $16,840. Required fees: $792. *Financial support:* In 2006–07, 1 fellowship, 10 teaching assistantships were awarded; research assistantships, career-related internships or fieldwork, Federal Work-Study, institutionally sponsored loans, and unspecified assistantships also available. Financial award application deadline: 2/1; financial award applicants required to submit FAFSA. *Unit head:* Dr. Delores Smith, Interim Head, 865-974-5041, Fax: 865-974-6439, E-mail: delsmith@utk.edu.

The University of Tennessee, Graduate School, College of Education, Health and Human Sciences, Program in Education, Knoxville, TN 37996. Offers art education (MS); counseling education (PhD); cultural studies in education (PhD); curriculum (MS, Ed S); curriculum, educational research and evaluation (Ed D, PhD); early childhood education (PhD); early childhood special education (MS); education of deaf and hard of hearing (MS); educational administration and policy studies (Ed D, PhD); educational administration and supervision (Ed S); educational psychology (Ed D, PhD); elementary education (MS, Ed S); elementary teaching (MS); English education (MS, Ed S); exercise science (PhD); foreign language/ESL education (MS, Ed S); instructional technology (MS, Ed D, PhD, Ed S); literacy, language and ESL education (PhD); literacy, language education, and ESL education (Ed D); mathematics education (MS, Ed S); modified and comprehensive special education (MS); reading education (MS, Ed S); school counseling (Ed S); school psychology (PhD, Ed S); science education (MS, Ed S); secondary teaching (MS); social foundations (MS); social science education (MS, Ed S); socio-cultural foundations of sports and education (PhD); special education (Ed S); teacher education (Ed D, PhD). *Accreditation:* NCATE. Part-time and evening/weekend programs available. *Students:* 529 (401 women); includes 39 minority (23 African Americans, 2 American Indian/Alaska Native, 9 Asian Americans or Pacific Islanders, 5 Hispanic Americans) 34 international. 420 applicants, 50% accepted. In 2006, 258 master's, 28 doctorates awarded. *Degree requirements:* For master's and Ed S, thesis optional; for doctorate, variable foreign language requirement, thesis/dissertation. *Entrance requirements:* For master's, minimum GPA of 2.7; for doctorate and Ed S, GRE General Test, minimum GPA of 2.7. Additional exam requirements/recommendations for international students: Required—TOEFL. *Application deadline:* For fall admission, 2/1 priority date for domestic students. Applications are processed on a rolling basis. Application fee: $35. Electronic applications accepted. *Expenses:* Tuition, state resident: full-time $5,574. Tuition, nonresident: full-time $16,840. Required fees: $792. *Financial support:* In 2006–07, 4 fellowships, 9 teaching assistantships were awarded; career-related internships or fieldwork, Federal Work-Study, institutionally sponsored loans, and unspecified assistantships also available. Financial award application deadline: 2/1; financial award applicants required to submit FAFSA. *Unit head:* Dr. Lester Knight, Head, 865-974-0907, Fax: 865-974-8718, E-mail: lknight@utk.edu.

The University of Texas at Arlington, Graduate School, College of Education, Arlington, TX 76019. Offers curriculum and instruction (M Ed); educational leadership and policy studies (M Ed); physiology of exercise (MS); teaching (M Ed T). *Accreditation:* NCATE. Part-time and evening/weekend programs available. Postbaccalaureate distance learning degree programs offered (minimal on-campus study). *Faculty:* 19 full-time (11 women), 3 part-time/adjunct (2 women). *Students:* 171 full-time (107 women), 579 part-time (474 women); includes 278 minority (130 African Americans, 6 American Indian/Alaska Native, 20 Asian Americans or Pacific Islanders, 122 Hispanic Americans), 40 international. Average age 36. 579 applicants, 88% accepted, 368 enrolled. In 2006, 101 degrees awarded. *Degree requirements:* For master's, thesis (for some programs), comprehensive activity, research project, comprehensive exam (for some programs), registration. *Entrance requirements:* For master's, GRE General Test, minimum undergraduate GPA of 3.0 in last 60 hours of course work, writing sample, 3 letters of recommendation. Additional exam requirements/recommendations for international students: Required—TOEFL (minimum score 550 paper-based; 213 computer-based). *Application deadline:* For fall admission, 6/16 priority date for domestic students, 4/9 priority date for international students; for winter admission, 10/22 priority date for domestic students, 9/10 priority date for international students; for spring admission, 3/25 priority date for domestic and international students. Applications are processed on a rolling basis. Application fee: $35 ($50 for international students). Electronic applications accepted. *Expenses:* Tuition, state resident: full-time $5,528. Tuition, nonresident: full-time $10,478. International tuition: $10,608 full-time. *Financial support:* In 2006–07, 11 fellowships (averaging $1,000 per year), teaching assistantships with tuition reimbursements (averaging $9,000 per year) were awarded; career-related internships or fieldwork, Federal Work-Study, scholarships/grants, and unspecified assistantships also available. Financial award application deadline: 6/1; financial award applicants required to submit FAFSA. *Unit head:* Dr. Jeanne M. Gerlach, Dean, 817-272-2591, Fax: 817-272-2530, E-mail: soeadvising@uta.edu. *Application contact:* Brendan Hardy, Graduate Advisor, 817-272-2956, Fax: 817-272-7624, E-mail: coedadvising@uta.edu.

The University of Texas at El Paso, Graduate School, College of Health Sciences, School of Allied Health, Program in Kinesiology and Sports Studies, El Paso, TX 79968-0001. Offers MS. Part-time and evening/weekend programs available. *Degree requirements:* For master's, thesis optional. *Entrance requirements:* For master's, GRE General Test. Additional exam requirements/recommendations for international students: Required—TOEFL. Electronic applications accepted.

The University of Texas at Tyler, College of Nursing and Health Sciences, Department of Health and Kinesiology, Tyler, TX 75799-0001. Offers clinical exercise physiology (MS); health and kinesiology (M Ed); kinesiology (MS). Part-time programs available. Postbaccalaureate distance learning degree programs offered. *Faculty:* 8 full-time (2 women), 8 part-time/adjunct (5 women). *Students:* 16 full-time (10 women), 29 part-time (15 women); includes 7 minority (5 African Americans, 1 Asian American or Pacific Islander, 1 Hispanic American).

Average age 27. 27 applicants, 21 enrolled. In 2006, 20 degrees awarded. *Degree requirements:* For master's, thesis (for some programs), comprehensive exam (for some programs). *Application deadline:* Applications are processed on a rolling basis. Application fee: $0 ($50 for international students). Electronic applications accepted. *Expenses:* Tuition, state resident: part-time $50 per credit hour. Tuition, nonresident: part-time $328 per credit hour. Required fees: $107 per credit hour. $426 per term. *Financial support:* In 2006–07, 2 teaching assistantships (averaging $6,000 per year) were awarded; research assistantships, Federal Work-Study and scholarships/grants also available. Financial award application deadline: 7/1. *Faculty research:* Osteoporosis, muscle soreness, economy of locomotion, adoption of rehabilitation programs, effect of inactivity and aging on muscle blood vessels, territoriality. *Unit head:* Dr. James Schwane, Chairperson, 903-566-7306, Fax: 903-566-7065, E-mail: jschwane@mail. uttyl.edu. *Application contact:* Bonnie Purser, Office of Graduate Studies, 903-566-7142, Fax: 903-566-7068, E-mail: bpurser@uttyler.edu.

University of the Pacific, College of the Pacific, Department of Sport Sciences, Stockton, CA 95211-0197. Offers MA. *Faculty:* 9 full-time (5 women). *Students:* Average age 26. 12 applicants, 25% accepted, 0 enrolled. In 2006, 8 degrees awarded. *Degree requirements:* For master's, thesis (for some programs), comprehensive exam (for some programs). *Entrance requirements:* For master's, GRE General Test. Additional exam requirements/recommendations for international students: Required—TOEFL (minimum score 475 paper-based; 150 computer-based). *Application deadline:* For fall admission, 3/1 priority date for domestic students; for spring admission, 10/1 for domestic students. Applications are processed on a rolling basis. Application fee: $75. *Expenses:* Tuition: Full-time $26,920. Required fees: $430. Tuition and fees vary according to course load. *Financial support:* In 2006–07, 7 teaching assistantships were awarded; institutionally sponsored loans also available. Support available to part-time students. Financial award application deadline: 3/1; financial award applicants required to submit FAFSA. *Unit head:* Dr. Christopher Snell, Chairperson, 209-946-2703, E-mail: csnell@pacific.edu.

The University of Toledo, College of Graduate Studies, College of Health Science and Human Service, Division of Human Services, Department of Kinesiology, Toledo, OH 43606-3390. Offers exercise science (MSX, PhD). *Faculty:* 8 full-time (0 women), 5 part-time/ adjunct (4 women). *Students:* 32 full-time (17 women), 6 part-time (3 women); includes 1 minority (Hispanic American), 6 international. Average age 28. 30 applicants, 53% accepted, 15 enrolled. In 2006, 10 degrees awarded. *Application deadline:* For fall admission, 3/1 priority date for domestic students. Application fee: $45. *Financial support:* In 2006–07, 1 research assistantship with tuition reimbursement (averaging $15,000 per year), 15 teaching assistantships with tuition reimbursements (averaging $12,000 per year) were awarded. *Unit head:* Dr. Charles Armstrong, Chair, 419-530-5369.

University of Utah, The Graduate School, College of Health, Department of Exercise and Sport Science, Salt Lake City, UT 84112-1107. Offers MS, PhD. *Faculty:* 15 full-time (6 women), 1 part-time/adjunct (0 women). *Students:* 41 full-time (18 women), 24 part-time (9 women); includes 1 minority (Asian American or Pacific Islander), 6 international. Average age 31. 63 applicants, 60% accepted, 17 enrolled. In 2006, 19 master's, 2 doctorates awarded. Terminal master's awarded for partial completion of doctoral program. *Median time to degree:* Of those who began their doctoral program in fall 1998, 80% received their degree in 8 years or less. *Degree requirements:* For master's, thesis (for some programs), comprehensive exam (for some programs); for doctorate, thesis/dissertation, comprehensive exam. *Entrance requirements:* For master's, GRE General Test, minimum undergraduate GPA of 3.0; for doctorate, GRE General Test, minimum undergraduate GPA of 3.0, acceptance by mentor. Additional exam requirements/recommendations for international students: Required—TOEFL (minimum score 500 paper-based; 173 computer-based). *Application deadline:* For fall admission, 1/15 for domestic and international students. Application fee: $45 ($65 for international students). Electronic applications accepted. *Expenses:* Tuition, state resident: full-time $3,208. Tuition, nonresident: full-time $11,326. Required fees: $608. Tuition and fees vary according to class time and program. *Financial support:* In 2006–07, research assistantships with full tuition reimbursements (averaging $11,000 per year), 35 teaching assistantships with full and partial tuition reimbursements (averaging $11,000 per year) were awarded; career-related internships or fieldwork, institutionally sponsored loans, scholarships/grants, and health care benefits also available. Financial award application deadline: 2/15; financial award applicants required to submit FAFSA. *Faculty research:* Exercise physiology, psychosocial aspects of sports and physical education, special physical education, elementary/secondary physical education. Total annual research expenditures: $49,104. *Unit head:* Barry Shultz, Chair, 801-585-3125. *Application contact:* Janet Shaw, Director of Graduate Studies, 801-581-5107, Fax: 801-585-3992, E-mail: janet.shaw@health.utah.edu.

University of West Florida, College of Professional Studies, Division of Health, Leisure, and Exercise Science, Program in Health, Leisure, and Exercise Science, Pensacola, FL 32514-5750. Offers exercise science (MS); physical education (MS). *Students:* 25 full-time (16 women), 21 part-time (16 women); includes 5 minority (4 African Americans, 1 Hispanic American), 1 international. Average age 31. 24 applicants, 83% accepted, 15 enrolled. In 2006, 6 degrees awarded. *Degree requirements:* For master's, thesis or alternative. *Entrance requirements:* For master's, GRE General Test, minimum GPA of 3.0. Additional exam requirements/recommendations for international students: Required—TOEFL (minimum score 550 paper-based; 213 computer-based). *Application deadline:* For fall admission, 6/1 for domestic students, 5/15 for international students; for spring admission, 11/1 for domestic students, 10/1 for international students. Applications are processed on a rolling basis. Application fee: $30. *Expenses:* Tuition, state resident: full-time $5,871; part-time $245 per credit hour. Tuition, nonresident: full-time $21,241; part-time $885 per credit hour. *Financial support:* Fellowships, research assistantships with partial tuition reimbursements, teaching assistantships, Federal Work-Study, scholarships/grants, tuition waivers (full and partial), and unspecified assistantships available. Financial award application deadline: 4/15; financial award applicants required to submit FAFSA. *Unit head:* Dr. Stuart W. Ryan, Chairperson, Division of Health, Leisure, and Exercise Science, 850-474-2592.

University of Wisconsin–La Crosse, Office of University Graduate Studies, College of Science and Health, Department of Exercise and Sport Science, Program in Clinical Exercise Physiology, La Crosse, WI 54601-3742. Offers MS. *Students:* 16 full-time (12 women), 3 part-time (1 woman); includes 1 minority (Hispanic American), 2 international. Average age 26. 31 applicants, 52% accepted, 15 enrolled. In 2006, 13 degrees awarded. *Degree requirements:* For master's, thesis optional. *Entrance requirements:* Additional exam requirements/ recommendations for international students: Required—TOEFL (minimum score 550 paper-based; 213 computer-based). *Application deadline:* For fall admission, 2/1 for domestic and international students; for spring admission, 10/1 for domestic and international students. Application fee: $45. *Financial support:* In 2006–07, 6 research assistantships (averaging $5,601 per year) were awarded; career-related internships or fieldwork, Federal Work-Study, institutionally sponsored loans, health care benefits, tuition waivers (full and partial), and unspecified assistantships also available. Financial award application deadline: 2/1; financial award applicants required to submit FAFSA. *Faculty research:* Cardiovascular physiology, wellness, risk factors for heart disease, obesity, exercise adherence. *Unit head:* Dr. John Porcari, Director, 608-785-8684, Fax: 608-785-8686, E-mail: porcari.john@uwlax.edu. *Application contact:* Kathryn Kiefer, Associate Director of Admissions, 608-785-8939, E-mail: admissions@uwlax.edu.

University of Wisconsin–La Crosse, Office of University Graduate Studies, College of Science and Health, Department of Exercise and Sport Science, Program in Human Performance, La Crosse, WI 54601-3742. Offers athletic training (MS); human performance (MS). Part-time and evening/weekend programs available. *Students:* 25 full-time (10 women), 7 part-time (3 women); includes 2 minority (1 African American, 1 American Indian/Alaska Native), 2 international. Average age 25. 30 applicants, 73% accepted, 15 enrolled. In 2006, 14 degrees awarded. *Degree requirements:* For master's, thesis optional. *Entrance requirements:* For master's, GRE, course work in anatomy, physiology, biomechanics, and exercise physiology.

Exercise and Sports Science

University of Wisconsin–La Crosse (continued)

Additional exam requirements/recommendations for international students: Required—TOEFL (minimum score 550 paper-based; 213 computer-based). *Application deadline:* For fall admission, 2/1 priority date for domestic students; for spring admission, 10/1 for domestic students. Applications are processed on a rolling basis. Application fee: $45. Electronic applications accepted. *Financial support:* In 2006–07, 11 research assistantships (averaging $7,020 per year) were awarded; career-related internships or fieldwork, Federal Work-Study, institutionally sponsored loans, scholarships/grants, health care benefits, tuition waivers (full and partial), unspecified assistantships, and grant-funded positions also available. Support available to part-time students. Financial award application deadline: 3/15; financial award applicants required to submit FAFSA. *Faculty research:* Athletic performance, strength and conditioning, anaerobic metabolism, body composition. *Unit head:* Dr. Glenn Wright, Director, 608-785-8689, Fax: 608-785-6520, E-mail: wright.glen@uwlax.edu. *Application contact:* Kathryn Kiefer, Associate Director of Admissions, 608-785-8939, E-mail: admissions@uwlax.edu.

Virginia Commonwealth University, Graduate School, School of Education, Department of Health and Human Performance, Richmond, VA 23284-9005. Offers athletic training (MS); exercise science (MS); rehabilitation and movement science (PhD); teacher education (MS). *Faculty:* 7 full-time (2 women). *Students:* 13 full-time (8 women), 28 part-time (17 women); includes 3 minority (2 African Americans, 1 American Indian/Alaska Native), 1 international. 8 applicants, 100% accepted, 8 enrolled. *Entrance requirements:* For master's, GRE General Test or MAT. *Application deadline:* For fall admission, 5/15 for domestic students; for spring admission, 11/15 for domestic students. Applications are processed on a rolling basis. Application fee: $50. *Financial support:* Career-related internships or fieldwork, Federal Work-Study, and institutionally sponsored loans available. Support available to part-time students. Financial award application deadline: 3/1. *Unit head:* Dr. Edmund Acevedo, Chair, 804-828-1948, Fax: 804-828-1946, E-mail: eoacevedo@vcu.edu. *Application contact:* Dr. Michael D. Davis, Director, Graduate Studies, 804-828-6530, Fax: 804-827-0676, E-mail: mddavis@vcu.edu.

See Close-Ups on pages 2331, 2333, and 1751.

Wake Forest University, Graduate School, Department of Health and Exercise Science, Winston-Salem, NC 27109. Offers MS. *Faculty:* 9 full-time (2 women). *Students:* 14 full-time (12 women); includes 1 minority (Asian American or Pacific Islander), 1 international. Average age 24. 16 applicants, 44% accepted, 7 enrolled. In 2006, 7 degrees awarded. *Degree requirements:* For master's, one foreign language, thesis, registration. *Entrance requirements:* For master's, GRE General Test, resumé. Additional exam requirements/recommendations for international students: Required—TOEFL (minimum score 213 computer-based). *Application deadline:* For fall admission, 1/15 for domestic and international students. Application fee: $45 ($55 for international students). Electronic applications accepted. *Financial support:* In 2006–07, 14 students received support, including 14 teaching assistantships with full tuition reimbursements available (averaging $8,500 per year); fellowships with full tuition reimbursements available, scholarships/grants and tuition waivers (full) also available. Financial award application deadline: 1/15; financial award applicants required to submit FAFSA. *Faculty research:* Cardiac rehabilitation, biomechanics, health psychology, exercise physiology. *Unit head:* Dr. Anthony Marsh, Director, 336-758-4643, Fax: 336-758-4680, E-mail: marshap@wfu.edu.

Washington State University, Graduate School, College of Education, Department of Teaching and Learning, Pullman, WA 99164. Offers curriculum and instruction (Ed D, PhD); diverse languages (M Ed, MA); elementary education (M Ed, MA, MIT); exercise science (MS); literacy education (M Ed, MA, PhD); math education (PhD); secondary education (M Ed, MA). *Accreditation:* NCATE. *Faculty:* 27. *Students:* 54 full-time (43 women), 20 part-time (14 women); includes 13 minority (4 African Americans, 2 American Indian/Alaska Native, 2 Asian Americans or Pacific Islanders, 5 Hispanic Americans), 5 international. Average age 34. 244 applicants, 16% accepted, 11 enrolled. In 2006, 20 master's, 3 doctorates awarded. *Degree requirements:* For master's, thesis (for some programs), oral or written exam, comprehensive exam (for some programs); for doctorate, thesis/dissertation, oral, written exam, comprehensive exam. *Entrance requirements:* For master's and doctorate, GRE General Test, minimum GPA of 3.0, 3 letters of recommendation. Additional exam requirements/recommendations for international students: Required—TOEFL. *Application deadline:* For fall admission, 2/1 for domestic students, 3/1 for international students; for spring admission, 9/1 for domestic students, 7/1 for international students. Applications are processed on a rolling basis. Application fee: $50. *Expenses:* Tuition, state resident: full-time $7,066. Tuition, nonresident: full-time $17,204. *Financial support:* In 2006–07, 13 research assistantships with partial tuition reimbursements (averaging $13,917 per year), 22 teaching assistantships with partial tuition reimbursements (averaging $13,056 per year) were awarded; career-related internships or fieldwork, Federal Work-Study, institutionally sponsored loans, tuition waivers (partial), unspecified assistantships, and staff assistantships, teaching associateships also available. Financial award application deadline: 4/1. *Faculty research:* Evolution of middle school education issues in special education, computer-assisted language learning. Total annual research expenditures: $1.1 million. *Unit head:* Dr. Corinne Mantle-Bromley, Chair, 509-335-5027. *Application contact:* Graduate School Admissions, 800-GRADWSU, Fax: 509-335-1949, E-mail: gradsch@wsu.edu.

Washington State University Spokane, Graduate Programs, Program in Exercise Science, Spokane, WA 99210-1495. Offers cellular physiology (MS); clinical exercise physiology (MS); clinical physiology (MS). *Faculty:* 4. *Students:* 5 full-time (3 women); includes 1 minority (Hispanic American) Average age 27. 10 applicants, 40% accepted, 2 enrolled. *Degree requirements:* For master's, thesis optional. *Entrance requirements:* For master's, GRE, minimum GPA of 3.0. Additional exam requirements/recommendations for international students: Required—TOEFL (minimum score 550 paper-based; 213 computer-based). *Application deadline:* For fall admission, 7/15 priority date for domestic students, 3/1 for international students; for spring admission, 10/15 priority date for domestic students, 7/1 for international students. Application fee: $50. *Expenses:* Tuition, state resident: full-time $7,066. Tuition, nonresident: full-time $17,204. Tuition and fees vary according to program. *Financial support:* In 2006–07, 4 students received support, including 3 research assistantships with full and partial tuition reimbursements available (averaging $13,917 per year), teaching assistantships with full and partial tuition reimbursements available (averaging $13,056 per year); career-related internships or fieldwork, Federal Work-Study, scholarships/grants, health care benefits, and unspecified assistantships also available. *Faculty research:* Experimental exercise physiology, cellular and molecular mechanisms. *Unit head:* Dr. Sally Blank, Associate Professor/Director, 509-358-7633, E-mail: seblank@wsu.edu. *Application contact:* Graduate School Admissions, 800-GRADWSU, Fax: 509-335-1949, E-mail: gradsch@wsu.edu.

Wayne State College, School of Natural and Social Sciences, Department of Health, Human Performance and Sport, Wayne, NE 68787. Offers exercise science (MSE); organization management (MSE), including sport and recreation management. Part-time and evening/weekend programs available. *Faculty:* 6 part-time/adjunct (2 women). *Students:* 15 full-time (3 women), 6 part-time (1 woman); includes 3 minority (all African Americans), 2 international. Average age 27. In 2006, 11 degrees awarded. *Degree requirements:* For master's, thesis optional. *Entrance requirements:* For master's, GRE General Test, minimum GPA of 3.0. Additional exam requirements/recommendations for international students: Required—TOEFL (minimum score 550 paper-based; 213 computer-based). *Application deadline:* Applications are processed on a rolling basis. Application fee: $30. Electronic applications accepted. *Expenses:* Tuition, state resident: full-time $3,114; part-time $130 per credit hour. Tuition, nonresident: full-time $6,228; part-time $260 per credit hour. Required fees: $894; $37 per credit hour. Tuition and fees vary according to course load. *Financial support:* In 2006–07, 3 teaching assistantships with full tuition reimbursements (averaging $4,000 per year) were awarded; career-related internships or fieldwork also available. Financial award applicants required to submit FAFSA. *Unit head:* Dr. Kevin Hill, Dean, 402-375-7030.

West Chester University of Pennsylvania, Graduate Studies, School of Health Sciences, Department of Kinesiology, West Chester, PA 19383. Offers driver education (Certificate); exercise and sport physiology (MS); physical education (MS); sport and athletic administration (MSA). Part-time and evening/weekend programs available. *Students:* 9 full-time (6 women), 30 part-time (8 women); includes 2 African Americans, 1 Hispanic American, 1 international. Average age 29. 35 applicants, 94% accepted, 12 enrolled. In 2006, 21 degrees awarded. *Degree requirements:* For master's, thesis optional. *Entrance requirements:* For master's, GRE or MAT, interview. *Application deadline:* For fall admission, 4/15 priority date for domestic students; for spring admission, 10/15 for domestic students. Applications are processed on a rolling basis. Application fee: $35. *Financial support:* In 2006–07, 7 research assistantships with full tuition reimbursements were awarded; unspecified assistantships also available. Support available to part-time students. Financial award application deadline: 2/15; financial award applicants required to submit FAFSA. *Faculty research:* Weight lifting and type 1 diabetes mellitus, martial arts, sexual harassment in sports. *Unit head:* Dr. Raymond Zetts, Chair, 610-436-2610, E-mail: czetts@wcupa.edu. *Application contact:* Dr. Sheri Melton, Graduate Coordinator, 610-436-2610, E-mail: smelton@wcupa.edu.

Western Michigan University, Graduate College, College of Education, Department of Health, Physical Education and Recreation, Kalamazoo, MI 49008-5202. Offers administration (MA); athletic training (MA); coaching and sports studies (MA); exercise science (MA); motor development (MA); physical education (MA); special education for handicapped children (MA).

Western Washington University, Graduate School, College of Humanities and Social Sciences, Department of Physical Education, Health, and Recreation, Bellingham, WA 98225-5996. Offers exercise science (MS); sport psychology (MS). Part-time programs available. *Faculty:* 12. *Students:* 12 full-time (6 women), 1 part-time; includes 2 minority (1 African American, 1 American Indian/Alaska Native), 1 international. 16 applicants, 81% accepted, 7 enrolled. In 2006, 3 degrees awarded. *Degree requirements:* For master's, thesis. *Entrance requirements:* For master's, GRE General Test, minimum GPA of 3.0 in last 60 semester hours or last 90 quarter hours. Additional exam requirements/recommendations for international students: Required—TOEFL (minimum score 567 paper-based; 227 computer-based). *Application deadline:* For fall admission, 4/15 priority date for domestic students; for winter admission, 10/1 for domestic students; for spring admission, 2/1 for domestic students. Applications are processed on a rolling basis. Application fee: $50. *Expenses:* Tuition, state resident: full-time $6,609; part-time $199 per credit. Tuition, nonresident: full-time $16,845; part-time $540 per credit. *Financial support:* In 2006–07, 3 teaching assistantships with partial tuition reimbursements (averaging $9,339 per year) were awarded; Federal Work-Study, institutionally sponsored loans, scholarships/grants, tuition waivers (partial), and unspecified assistantships also available. Support available to part-time students. Financial award application deadline: 2/15; financial award applicants required to submit FAFSA. *Unit head:* Dr. LeaAnn Martin, Chair, 360-650-3054. *Application contact:* Dr. Dennis Caine, Graduate Adviser, 360-650-3056.

West Texas A&M University, College of Education and Social Sciences, Department of Sports and Exercise Science, Canyon, TX 79016-0001. Offers MS. Part-time and evening/weekend programs available. *Degree requirements:* For master's, thesis or alternative, comprehensive exam, registration. *Entrance requirements:* For master's, GRE General Test, minimum GPA of 3.0. Additional exam requirements/recommendations for international students: Required—TOEFL (minimum score 550 paper-based). Electronic applications accepted. *Faculty research:* Coronary heart disease, athletic performance, pain coping, cardiovascular fitness, nutritional status of NCAA athletes.

West Virginia University, School of Medicine, Graduate Programs at the Health Sciences Center, Interdisciplinary Graduate Programs in Biomedical Sciences, Exercise Physiology Program, Morgantown, WV 26506. Offers MS, PhD, MD/PhD. *Faculty:* 17 full-time (4 women). *Students:* 37 full-time (23 women); includes 2 minority (1 Asian American or Pacific Islander, 1 Hispanic American), 1 international. Average age 24. In 2006, 11 master's, 1 doctorate awarded. *Median time to degree:* Of those who began their doctoral program in fall 1998, 96% received their degree in 8 years or less. *Degree requirements:* For doctorate, thesis/dissertation, comprehensive exam. *Entrance requirements:* For doctorate, GRE General Test, minimum GPA of 3.0. Additional exam requirements/recommendations for international students: Required—TOEFL. *Application deadline:* For fall admission, 3/1 priority date for domestic students, 1/15 for international students. Applications are processed on a rolling basis. Application fee: $0. Electronic applications accepted. *Expenses:* Tuition, state resident: full-time $4,926; part-time $276 per credit hour. Tuition, nonresident: full-time $14,278; part-time $796 per credit hour. Tuition and fees vary according to program. *Financial support:* In 2006–07, research assistantships with full tuition reimbursements (averaging $23,000 per year); institutionally sponsored loans, traineeships, and health care benefits also available. *Faculty research:* Cardiovascular function in health and disease, circulatory adaptations to exercise training, aging, microgravity, muscle adaptation and injury. Total annual research expenditures:$250,000. *Unit head:* Dr. Michael Delp, Professor, Graduate Director, 304-293-7767, Fax: 304-293-7105, E-mail: mdelp@hsc.wvu.edu. *Application contact:* Claire Noel, Assistant Director, Health Sciences Graduate Programs, 304-293-7116, Fax: 304-293-9257, E-mail: cnoel@hsc.wvu.edu.

See Close-Up on page 2335.

West Virginia University, School of Physical Education, Morgantown, WV 26506. Offers athletic coaching (MS); athletic training (MS); exercise physiology (Ed D); physical education/teacher education (MS, Ed D), including administration of physical education (Ed D), curriculum and instruction (Ed D), motor development (Ed D), special physical education (Ed D); sport management (MS); sport psychology (MS, Ed D). *Degree requirements:* For doctorate, thesis/dissertation, oral exam, comprehensive exam. *Entrance requirements:* For master's, GRE or MAT, minimum GPA of 3.0; for doctorate, GRE General Test or MAT, minimum GPA of 3.5. Additional exam requirements/recommendations for international students: Required—TOEFL (minimum score 550 paper-based; 213 computer-based). Electronic applications accepted. *Expenses:* Tuition, state resident: full-time $4,926; part-time $276 per credit hour. Tuition, nonresident: full-time $14,278; part-time $796 per credit hour. Tuition and fees vary according to program. *Faculty research:* Sport psychosociology, teacher education, exercise psychology, counseling.

Wichita State University, Graduate School, College of Education, Department of Kinesiology and Sport Studies, Wichita, KS 67260. Offers physical education (M Ed), including exercise science and wellness; sports administration (M Ed), including exercise science and wellness. Part-time programs available. *Degree requirements:* For master's, thesis optional. *Entrance requirements:* For master's, minimum GPA of 2.75. Additional exam requirements/recommendations for international students: Required—TOEFL. Electronic applications accepted.

Kinesiology and Movement Studies

Acadia University, Faculty of Professional Studies, School of Recreation Management and Kinesiology, Wolfville, NS B4P 2R6, Canada. Offers MR. In 2006, 2 degrees awarded. *Entrance requirements:* Additional exam requirements/recommendations for international students: Required—TOEFL (minimum score 580 paper-based; 237 computer-based). Application fee: $50. *Unit head:* Dr. Gary Ness, Director, 902-585-1566, Fax: 902-585-1702, E-mail: gary.ness@acadiau.ca. *Application contact:* Krista Robertson, Secretary, 902-585-1457, Fax: 902-585-1702, E-mail: krista.robertson@acadiau.ca.

Angelo State University, College of Graduate Studies, College of Education, Department of Kinesiology, San Angelo, TX 76909. Offers MS. Part-time and evening/weekend programs available. *Faculty:* 6 full-time (3 women). *Students:* 9 full-time (4 women), 10 part-time (3 women); includes 5 minority (2 African Americans, 3 Hispanic Americans). Average age 24. 11 applicants, 82% accepted, 5 enrolled. In 2006, 9 degrees awarded. *Degree requirements:* For master's, comprehensive exam. *Entrance requirements:* For master's, GRE General Test. Additional exam requirements/recommendations for international students: Required—TOEFL or IELTS. *Application deadline:* For fall admission, 7/15 priority date for domestic students, 6/10 for international students; for spring admission, 12/8 for domestic students, 11/1 for international students. Applications are processed on a rolling basis. Application fee: $40 ($50 for international students). Electronic applications accepted. *Expenses:* Tuition, state resident: full-time $2,340; part-time $130 per hour. Tuition, nonresident: full-time $7,290; part-time $405 per hour. Required fees: $906; $56 per hour. *Financial support:* In 2006–07, 16 students received support, including 2 teaching assistantships (averaging $10,251 per year); career-related internships or fieldwork, Federal Work-Study, scholarships/grants, and unspecified assistantships also available. Support available to part-time students. Financial award application deadline: 3/1; financial award applicants required to submit FAFSA. *Unit head:* Dr. Doyle Carter, Department Head, 325-942-2365 Ext. 225, E-mail: doyle.carter@angelo.edu. *Application contact:* Dr. Steven Snowden, Graduate Advisor, 325-942-2173 Ext. 224, E-mail: steven.snowden@angelo.edu.

Arizona State University, Division of Graduate Studies, College of Liberal Arts and Sciences, Division of Natural Sciences and Mathematics, Department of Kinesiology, Tempe, AZ 85287. Offers MS, PhD. *Degree requirements:* For master's and doctorate, thesis/dissertation. *Entrance requirements:* For master's, GRE.

See Close-Up on page 2325.

A.T. Still University of Health Sciences, Arizona School of Health Sciences, Mesa, AZ 85206. Offers advanced occupational therapy (MS); advanced physician assistant (MS); audiology (Au D); human movement (MS); medical informatics (MS); occupational therapy (MS); physical therapy (MS, DPT); physician assistant (MS); sports health care (MS); transitional physical therapy (DPT). *Accreditation:* AOTA (one or more programs are accredited); APTA. Postbaccalaureate distance learning degree programs offered (no on-campus study). *Faculty:* 47 full-time (27 women), 101 part-time/adjunct (60 women). *Students:* 442 full-time (277 women), 732 part-time (579 women); includes 143 minority (38 African Americans, 11 American Indian/Alaska Native, 55 Asian Americans or Pacific Islanders, 39 Hispanic Americans), 4 international. Average age 33. 1,471 applicants, 547 enrolled. In 2006, 104 master's, 432 doctorates awarded. *Degree requirements:* For master's and doctorate, thesis/dissertation (for some programs). *Entrance requirements:* For master's, GRE General Test, minimum GPA of 2.5; for doctorate, GRE, Evaluation of Practicing Audiologists Capabilities (Au D), Physical Therapy Evaluation Tool (DPT), current state licensure, master's degree or equivalent (Au D), minimum GPA of 2.7. *Application deadline:* For fall admission, 2/1 priority date for domestic and international students. Applications are processed on a rolling basis. Application fee: $60. *Expenses: Contact institution. Financial support:* In 2006–07, 382 students received support. Federal Work-Study and scholarships/grants available. Financial award application deadline: 5/1. *Faculty research:* Constraint-induced therapy, scapular motion analysis, shoulder mobility, biomechanics, quadriceps. *Unit head:* Dr. Randy Danielsen, Dean, 480-219-6000, Fax: 480-219-6110, E-mail: rdanielsen@atsu.edu. *Application contact:* Donna Sparks, Associate Director for Admissions, 660-626-2237, Fax: 660-626-2969, E-mail: admissions@atsu.edu.

Barry University, School of Human Performance and Leisure Sciences, Program in Movement Science, General Movement Science Program, Miami Shores, FL 33161-6695. Offers MS. *Students:* 2 full-time (both women), 4 part-time (all women), 2 international. In 2006, 3 degrees awarded. *Application contact:* Dave Fletcher, Director of Graduate Admissions, 305-899-3113, Fax: 305-899-2971, E-mail: dfletcher@mail.barry.edu.

Barry University, School of Human Performance and Leisure Sciences, Program in Movement Science, Specialization in Biomechanics, Miami Shores, FL 33161-6695. Offers MS. *Students:* 7 full-time (4 women), 4 part-time (3 women); includes 1 minority (Hispanic American), 2 international. 15 applicants, 33% accepted, 5 enrolled. In 2006, 1 degree awarded. *Entrance requirements:* For master's, GRE General Test, minimum GPA of 3.0. *Application deadline:* Applications are processed on a rolling basis. Application fee: $30. Electronic applications accepted. *Faculty research:* Upper extremity biomechanics, orthopedic biomechanics. *Unit head:* Dr. G. Monique Mokha, Coordinator, 305-899-3064, Fax: 305-899-3556, E-mail: mbutcher@mail.barry.edu. *Application contact:* Dave Fletcher, Director of Graduate Admissions, 305-899-3113, Fax: 305-899-2971, E-mail: dfletcher@mail.barry.edu.

Bowling Green State University, Graduate College, College of Education and Human Development, School of Human Movement, Sport, and Leisure Studies, Bowling Green, OH 43403. Offers developmental kinesiology (M Ed); recreation and leisure (M Ed); sport administration (M Ed). Part-time programs available. *Faculty:* 26 full-time (13 women), 4 part-time/adjunct (2 women). *Students:* 36 full-time (22 women), 14 part-time (6 women); includes 6 minority (all African Americans), 5 international. Average age 27. 54 applicants, 50% accepted, 20 enrolled. In 2006, 33 degrees awarded. *Degree requirements:* For master's, thesis or alternative. *Entrance requirements:* For master's, GRE General Test, minimum GPA of 2.7. Additional exam requirements/recommendations for international students: Required—TOEFL. *Application deadline:* For fall admission, 1/15 priority date for domestic students. Applications are processed on a rolling basis. Application fee: $30. Electronic applications accepted. *Expenses:* Tuition, state resident: part-time $535 per hour. Tuition, nonresident: part-time $884 per hour. *Financial support:* In 2006–07, 13 research assistantships with full tuition reimbursements (averaging $7,926 per year), 18 teaching assistantships with full tuition reimbursements (averaging $6,263 per year) were awarded; career-related internships or fieldwork, Federal Work-Study, and unspecified assistantships also available. Financial award applicants required to submit FAFSA. *Faculty research:* Teacher-learning process, travel and tourism, sport marketing and management, exercise physiology and sport psychology, life-span motor development. *Unit head:* Dr. Lynn Darby, Acting Director, 419-372-2334. *Application contact:* Dr. Geoff Meek, Graduate Coordinator, 419-372-0501.

California Baptist University, Program in Kinesiology, Riverside, CA 92504-3206. Offers MS. Part-time programs available. *Faculty:* 2 full-time (1 woman), 1 (woman) part-time/adjunct. *Students:* 23 full-time (7 women), 14 part-time (5 women); includes 14 minority (3 African Americans, 1 American Indian/Alaska Native, 3 Asian Americans or Pacific Islanders, 7 Hispanic Americans), 1 international. 30 applicants, 70% accepted, 14 enrolled. In 2006, 22 degrees awarded. *Degree requirements:* For master's, thesis or alternative, field experience. *Entrance requirements:* For master's, 12 semester units of course work in kinesiology, including basic movement anatomy or a related course, minimum undergraduate GPA of 2.75. Additional exam requirements/recommendations for international students: Required—TOEFL (minimum score 575 paper-based; 230 computer-based), IELTS (minimum score 7). *Application deadline:* For fall admission, 9/1 for domestic students, 7/15 priority date for international students; for spring admission, 1/3 for domestic students, 11/1 priority date for international students. Applications are processed on a rolling basis. Application fee: $45. Electronic applications accepted. *Expenses:* Tuition: Full-time $7,812; part-time $434 per unit. Required fees: $120 per semester. Tuition and fees vary according to program. *Financial support:* Federal Work-Study available. Support available to part-time students. Financial award applicants required to submit FAFSA. *Unit head:* Dr. Sean Sullivan, Chair, Department of Kinesiology, 951-343-4528, E-mail: ssullivan@calbaptist.edu. *Application contact:* Gail Ronveaux, Dean of Graduate Enrollment, 951-343-5045, Fax: 951-343-5095, E-mail: graduateadmissions@calbaptist.edu.

California Polytechnic State University, San Luis Obispo, College of Science and Mathematics, Department of Kinesiology, San Luis Obispo, CA 93407. Offers MS. Part-time programs available. *Faculty:* 4 full-time (3 women), 2 part-time/adjunct (both women). *Students:* 14 full-time (9 women), 5 part-time (4 women); includes 5 minority (1 African American, 2 Asian Americans or Pacific Islanders, 2 Hispanic Americans). 18 applicants, 72% accepted, 7 enrolled. In 2006, 11 degrees awarded. *Degree requirements:* For master's, thesis (for some programs), comprehensive exam (for some programs). *Entrance requirements:* For master's, minimum GPA of 2.75 in last 90 quarter units of course work. Additional exam requirements/recommendations for international students: Required—TOEFL (minimum score 550 paper-based; 213 computer-based), TWE (minimum score 4.5). *Application deadline:* For fall admission, 7/1 for domestic students, 11/30 for international students; for winter admission, 11/1 for domestic students, 6/30 for international students; for spring admission, 2/1 for domestic students. Application fee: $55. *Financial support:* Teaching assistantships, career-related internships or fieldwork, Federal Work-Study, and scholarships/grants available. Support available to part-time students. Financial award application deadline: 3/2; financial award applicants required to submit FAFSA. *Unit head:* Dr. Kris Jankovitz, Graduate Coordinator, 805-756-2534, Fax: 805-756-7273, E-mail: kjankovi@calpoly.edu.

California State Polytechnic University, Pomona, Academic Affairs, College of Letters, Arts, and Social Sciences, Program in Kinesiology, Pomona, CA 91768-2557. Offers MS. Part-time programs available. *Students:* 1 (woman) full-time, 10 part-time (7 women); includes 1 Asian American or Pacific Islander, 1 Hispanic American. Average age 32. 13 applicants, 38% accepted, 2 enrolled. In 2006, 6 degrees awarded. *Degree requirements:* For master's, thesis or alternative. *Application deadline:* For fall admission, 5/1 priority date for domestic students; for winter admission, 10/15 priority date for domestic students; for spring admission, 1/20 priority date for domestic students. Applications are processed on a rolling basis. Application fee: $55. Electronic applications accepted. *Expenses:* Tuition, state resident: part-time $226 per unit. Tuition, nonresident: part-time $226 per unit. Required fees: $2,486 per year. *Financial support:* Federal Work-Study and institutionally sponsored loans available. Support available to part-time students. Financial award application deadline: 3/2; financial award applicants required to submit FAFSA. *Unit head:* Dr. Thomas Spalding, Graduate Coordinator, 909-869-2772.

California State University, Chico, Graduate School, College of Communication and Education, Department of Kinesiology, Chico, CA 95929-0330. Offers MA. *Students:* 25 full-time (12 women), 17 part-time (10 women); includes 7 minority (1 African American, 3 American Indian/Alaska Native, 1 Asian American or Pacific Islander, 2 Hispanic Americans). Average age 29. 20 applicants, 100% accepted, 15 enrolled. In 2006, 19 degrees awarded. *Degree requirements:* For master's, thesis or alternative, oral exam. *Entrance requirements:* For master's, GRE General Test, 2 letters of recommendation. Additional exam requirements/recommendations for international students: Required—TOEFL (minimum score 550 paper-based; 213 computer-based). *Application deadline:* For fall admission, 3/1 for domestic and international students; for spring admission, 9/15 for domestic and international students. Applications are processed on a rolling basis. Application fee: $55. Electronic applications accepted. *Financial support:* Fellowships, teaching assistantships available. *Unit head:* David Swanson, Graduate Coordinator, 530-898-4841.

California State University, Fresno, Division of Graduate Studies, College of Health and Human Services, Department of Kinesiology, Fresno, CA 93740-8027. Offers exercise science (MA); sport psychology (MA). Part-time and evening/weekend programs available. *Degree requirements:* For master's, thesis or alternative. *Entrance requirements:* For master's, GRE General Test, minimum GPA of 2.7. Additional exam requirements/recommendations for international students: Required—TOEFL. Electronic applications accepted. *Faculty research:* Refugee education, homeless, geriatrics, fitness.

California State University, Long Beach, Graduate Studies, College of Health and Human Services, Department of Kinesiology and Physical Education, Long Beach, CA 90840. Offers kinesiology (MA, MS). Part-time programs available. *Faculty:* 28 full-time (12 women), 33 part-time/adjunct (19 women). *Students:* 53 full-time (29 women), 96 part-time (52 women); includes 15 minority (5 African Americans, 2 Asian Americans or Pacific Islanders, 8 Hispanic Americans), 4 international. Average age 29. 126 applicants, 53% accepted, 44 enrolled. In 2006, 42 degrees awarded. *Degree requirements:* For master's, oral and written comprehensive exams or thesis. *Entrance requirements:* For master's, GRE General Test, minimum GPA of 2.75 during previous 2 years of course work. *Application deadline:* For fall admission, 7/1 for domestic students; for spring admission, 12/1 for domestic students. Applications are processed on a rolling basis. Application fee: $55. Electronic applications accepted. *Financial support:* Federal Work-Study, institutionally sponsored loans, and scholarships/grants available. Financial award application deadline: 3/2. *Faculty research:* Pulmonary functioning, feedback and practice structure, strength training, history and politics of sports, special population research issues. *Unit head:* Dr. Keith W Freeseman, Chair, 562-985-4051, Fax: 562-985-8067, E-mail: kfreesmn@csulb.edu. *Application contact:* Dr. Sharon Guthrie, Graduate Coordinator, 562-985-7487, Fax: 562-985-8067.

California State University, Los Angeles, Graduate Studies, College of Health and Human Services, Department of Kinesiology and Nutritional Sciences, Major in Physical Education and Kinesiology, Los Angeles, CA 90032-8530. Offers kinesiology (MA); physical education (MA). *Students:* 9 full-time (5 women), 30 part-time (18 women); includes 25 minority (3 African Americans, 10 Asian Americans or Pacific Islanders, 12 Hispanic Americans), 3 international. In 2006, 11 degrees awarded. *Expenses:* Tuition, nonresident: part-time $226 per unit. *Unit head:* Dr. Steve Hawkins, Coordinator, 323-343-4650.

California State University, Northridge, Graduate Studies, College of Health and Human Development, Department of Kinesiology, Northridge, CA 91330. Offers MS. Part-time and evening/weekend programs available. *Faculty:* 24 full-time (12 women), 28 part-time/adjunct (14 women). *Students:* 12 full-time (4 women), 30 part-time (11 women); includes 9 minority (1 African American, 3 Asian Americans or Pacific Islanders, 5 Hispanic Americans), 9 international. Average age 31. 35 applicants, 49% accepted, 9 enrolled. In 2006, 19 degrees awarded. *Degree requirements:* For master's, thesis or alternative. *Entrance requirements:* For master's, GRE General Test or minimum GPA of 3.0. Additional exam requirements/recommendations for international students: Required—TOEFL. *Application deadline:* For fall admission, 11/30 for domestic students. Application fee: $55. *Expenses:* Tuition, nonresident: full-time $8,136; part-time $4,068 per year. Required fees: $3,624; $1,161 per term. *Financial support:* Teaching assistantships available. Financial award application deadline: 3/1. *Unit head:* Dr. Carole Oglesby, Chair, 818-677-3205. *Application contact:* Dr. William Whiting, Graduate Coordinator, 818-677-4917.

California State University, San Bernardino, Graduate Studies, College of Natural Sciences, Department of Kinesiology, San Bernardino, CA 92407-2397. Offers MA Ed. Part-time and evening/weekend programs available. *Faculty:* 11 full-time, 23 part-time/adjunct. *Students:* 3 full-time (2 women), 12 part-time (7 women); includes 7 minority (1 African American, 6 Hispanic Americans). Average age 31. 8 applicants, 75% accepted, 3 enrolled. *Application deadline:* Applications are processed on a rolling basis. Application fee: $55. *Financial support:* Career-related internships or fieldwork, Federal Work-Study, and institutionally sponsored

Kinesiology and Movement Studies

California State University, San Bernardino (continued)
loans available. Support available to part-time students. *Unit head:* Dr. Terry Rizzo, Chair, 909-537-5355, Fax: 909-537-2397, E-mail: trizzo@csusb.edu.

Columbia University, College of Physicians and Surgeons, Programs in Occupational Therapy, New York, NY 10032. Offers movement science (Ed D), including occupational therapy; occupational therapy (professional) (MS); occupational therapy administration or education (post-professional) (MS); MPH/MS. *Accreditation:* AOTA. *Faculty:* 9 full-time (8 women), 6 part-time/adjunct (4 women). *Students:* 114 full-time (106 women), 6 part-time (all women); includes 28 minority (5 African Americans, 17 Asian Americans or Pacific Islanders, 6 Hispanic Americans), 5 international. Average age 26. In 2006, 47 degrees awarded. *Degree requirements:* For master's, project, 6 months of fieldwork, thesis for post-professional students; for doctorate, thesis/dissertation, comprehensive exam. *Entrance requirements:* For master's, undergraduate course work in anatomy, physiology, statistics, psychology, social sciences, humanities, English composition; NBCOT eligibility; for doctorate, NBCOT certified. Additional exam requirements/recommendations for international students: Required—TOEFL (minimum score 250 computer-based), TWE (minimum score 4). *Application deadline:* For fall admission, 12/31 for domestic and international students. Application fee: $75. Electronic applications accepted. *Expenses: Contact institution. Financial support:* In 2006–07, 80 students received support. Career-related internships or fieldwork, Federal Work-Study, institutionally sponsored loans, and scholarships/grants available. Financial award application deadline: 4/15; financial award applicants required to submit FAFSA. *Faculty research:* Community mental health, developmental tasks of late life, infant play, cognition, obesity, motor learning. Total annual research expenditures: $30,000. *Unit head:* Dr. Janet Falk-Kessler, Director, 212-305-5267, Fax: 212-305-4569, E-mail: jf6@columbia.edu. *Application contact:* Marilyn Harper, Administrative Assistant, 212-305-5267, Fax: 212-305-4569, E-mail: mh15@columbia.edu.

Dalhousie University, Faculty of Graduate Studies, Faculty of Health Professions, School of Health and Human Performance, Division of Kinesiology, Halifax, NS B3H 4R2, Canada. Offers M Sc. Part-time programs available. *Degree requirements:* For master's, thesis. *Entrance requirements:* Additional exam requirements/recommendations for international students: Required—TOEFL. *Faculty research:* Sport science, fitness, neuromuscular physiology, biomechanics, ergonomics, sport psychology.

Florida State University, Graduate Studies, College of Human Sciences, Department of Nutrition, Food, and Exercise Sciences, Tallahassee, FL 32306. Offers exercise science (PhD), including exercise physiology, motor learning and control; nutrition and food science (PhD); nutrition and food sciences (MS), including clinical nutrition, food science, nutrition and sport, nutrition science, nutrition, education and health promotion. *Faculty:* 15 full-time (9 women). *Students:* 44 full-time (35 women), 28 part-time (16 women); includes 16 minority (9 African Americans, 2 Asian Americans or Pacific Islanders, 5 Hispanic Americans), 12 international. 76 applicants, 72% accepted, 28 enrolled. In 2006, 17 master's, 4 doctorates awarded. *Degree requirements:* For master's, thesis optional; for doctorate, thesis/dissertation, registration. *Entrance requirements:* For master's and doctorate, GRE General Test, minimum GPA of 3.0. Additional exam requirements/recommendations for international students: Required—TOEFL (minimum score 80 iBT). *Application deadline:* For fall admission, 7/1 for domestic students, 5/1 for international students; for spring admission, 11/1 for domestic students, 12/1 for international students. Application fee: $30. Electronic applications accepted. *Expenses:* Tuition, state resident: full-time $5,822; part-time $243 per credit hour. Tuition, nonresident: full-time $20,976; part-time $874 per credit hour. Tuition and fees vary according to program. *Financial support:* In 2006–07, 43 students received support, including 3 fellowships with partial tuition reimbursements available (averaging $10,000 per year), 9 research assistantships with partial tuition reimbursements available (averaging $8,000 per year), 22 teaching assistantships with partial tuition reimbursements available (averaging $8,000 per year); career-related internships or fieldwork, Federal Work-Study, institutionally sponsored loans, scholarships/grants, and unspecified assistantships also available. Financial award application deadline: 1/15; financial award applicants required to submit FAFSA. *Faculty research:* Nutrition and exercise, vitamin A deficiency, protein biochemistry, cardiovascular responses to exercises, physiological effects of cigarette smoking related to health and wellness. *Unit head:* Dr. Bahram Arjmandi, Chair, 850-644-1828, Fax: 850-645-5000. *Application contact:* Olga Garmash, Program Assistant, 850-644-4800, Fax: 850-645-5000, E-mail: ogarmash@fsu.edu.

Fresno Pacific University, Graduate Programs, Program in Kinesiology, Fresno, CA 93702-4709. Offers MA. *Students:* 1 (woman) full-time. Average age 28. *Application deadline:* For fall admission, 7/15 for domestic and international students; for spring admission, 11/15 for domestic and international students. *Expenses:* Tuition: Full-time $7,470; part-time $415 per credit. *Unit head:* Jim Ave, Program Director, 559-453-7186, Fax: 559-453-7182, E-mail: jimave@fresno.edu.

Georgia Southern University, Jack N. Averitt College of Graduate Studies, College of Health and Human Sciences, Department of Health and Kinesiology, Statesboro, GA 30460. Offers MS. *Students:* 34 full-time (18 women), 4 part-time (3 women); includes 7 minority (5 African Americans, 2 Asian Americans or Pacific Islanders), 3 international. Average age 24. 34 applicants, 74% accepted, 16 enrolled. In 2006, 14 degrees awarded. *Degree requirements:* For master's, thesis optional. *Entrance requirements:* For master's, GRE, minimum GPA of 2.75, resumé, reference list. *Financial support:* In 2006–07, 35 students received support, including research assistantships with partial tuition reimbursements available (averaging $5,500 per year), teaching assistantships with partial tuition reimbursements available (averaging $5,500 per year); tuition waivers (partial) also available. *Unit head:* Dr. Barry A. Joyner, Chair, 912-681-0200, E-mail: joyner@georgiasouthen.edu. *Application contact:* 912-681-5384, Fax: 912-681-0740, E-mail: gradadmissions@georgiasouthern.edu.

Humboldt State University, Graduate Studies, College of Professional Studies, Department of Kinesiology, Arcata, CA 95521-8299. Offers athletic training education (MS); exercise science/wellness management (MS); pre-physical therapy (MS); teaching/coaching (MS). *Students:* 10 full-time (5 women), 5 part-time (1 woman); includes 4 minority (1 African American, 3 Asian Americans or Pacific Islanders). Average age 31. 15 applicants, 73% accepted, 6 enrolled. In 2006, 3 degrees awarded. *Degree requirements:* For master's, thesis or alternative. *Entrance requirements:* For master's, GMAT, minimum GPA of 2.5. Additional exam requirements/recommendations for international students: Required—TOEFL. *Application deadline:* Applications are processed on a rolling basis. Application fee: $55. *Financial support:* Teaching assistantships, career-related internships or fieldwork, Federal Work-Study, and institutionally sponsored loans available. Financial award application deadline: 3/1; financial award applicants required to submit FAFSA. *Faculty research:* Human performance, adapted physical education, physical therapy. *Unit head:* Dr. Sue MacConnie, Chair, 707-826-4536, Fax: 707-826-5451, E-mail: sem1@humboldt.edu. *Application contact:* Dr. Kathy Munoz, Coordinator, 707-826-3840, Fax: 707-826-5451, E-mail: kdm1@humboldt.edu.

Indiana University Bloomington, School of Health, Physical Education and Recreation, Department of Kinesiology, Bloomington, IN 47405-7000. Offers adapted physical education (MS); applied sport science (MS); athletic training (MS); biomechanics (MS); clinical exercise physiology (MS); ergonomics (MS); exercise physiology (MS); human performance (MS, PhD, PE Dir); motor control (MS); sport management (MS). PhD offered through the University Graduate School. Part-time programs available. *Faculty:* 10 full-time (1 woman). *Students:* 106 full-time (47 women), 41 part-time (15 women); includes 16 minority (15 African Americans, 1 American Indian/Alaska Native), 26 international. Average age 26.Terminal master's awarded for partial completion of doctoral program. *Degree requirements:* For master's and PE Dir, thesis optional; for doctorate, variable foreign language requirement, thesis/dissertation. *Entrance requirements:* For master's, GRE General Test, minimum GPA of 2.8; for doctorate, GRE General Test, minimum graduate GPA of 3.5, minimum undergraduate GPA of 3.0; for PE Dir, GRE. *Application deadline:* For fall admission, 1/1 for international students; for spring admission, 9/1 for international students. Applications are processed on a rolling basis. Application fee: $50 ($60 for international students). *Expenses:* Tuition, state resident: full-time $5,791; part-time $241 per credit hour. Tuition, nonresident: full-time $16,866; part-time $703 per credit hour. *Financial support:* Fellowships, research assistantships with full tuition reimbursements, teaching assistantships with full tuition reimbursements, career-related internships or fieldwork, Federal Work-Study, institutionally sponsored loans, scholarships/grants, tuition waivers (partial), and fee remissions available. Financial award application deadline: 3/1. *Faculty research:* Exercise physiology and biochemistry, sports biomechanics, human motor control, adaptation of fitness and exercise to special populations. *Unit head:* John Shea, Chairperson, 812-855-3114. *Application contact:* Program Office, 812-855-5523, Fax: 812-855-9417, E-mail: kines@indiana.edu.

Inter American University of Puerto Rico, San Germán Campus, Graduate Studies Center, Graduate Program in Physical Education and Scientific Analysis of Human Body Movement, San Germán, PR 00683-5008. Offers MA. Part-time and evening/weekend programs available. *Faculty:* 8 full-time, 11 part-time/adjunct. *Students:* 17. In 2006, 2 degrees awarded. *Degree requirements:* For master's, comprehensive exam. *Entrance requirements:* For master's, GRE General Test or EXADEP, minimum GPA of 3.0. *Application deadline:* For fall admission, 4/30 priority date for domestic students; for spring admission, 11/15 for domestic students. Applications are processed on a rolling basis. Application fee: $31. *Expenses:* Tuition: Part-time $175 per credit. Required fees: $238 per semester. Tuition and fees vary according to degree level. *Financial support:* Teaching assistantships available. *Application contact:* Dr. Aurora Graniela, Graduate Coordinator, 787-264-1912 Ext. 7355, Fax: 787-892-7510, E-mail: aurora@sg.inter.edu.

James Madison University, College of Graduate and Outreach Programs, College of Integrated Science and Technology, Department of Kinesiology, Harrisonburg, VA 22807. Offers MS. Part-time and evening/weekend programs available. *Faculty:* 10 full-time (4 women). *Students:* 51 full-time (29 women), 19 part-time (8 women); includes 6 minority (4 African Americans, 1 Asian American or Pacific Islander, 1 Hispanic American). Average age 27. In 2006, 45 degrees awarded. *Degree requirements:* For master's, thesis or alternative. *Entrance requirements:* For master's, GRE General Test. Additional exam requirements/recommendations for international students: Required—TOEFL. *Application deadline:* For fall admission, 5/1 priority date for domestic students; for spring admission, 9/1 priority date for domestic students. Applications are processed on a rolling basis. Application fee: $55. Electronic applications accepted. *Expenses:* Tuition, state resident: full-time $6,336; part-time $264 per credit hour. Tuition, nonresident: full-time $17,832; part-time $743 per credit hour. *Financial support:* In 2006–07, 27 students received support, including 11 teaching assistantships with full tuition reimbursements available (averaging $8,167 per year); Federal Work-Study and unspecified assistantships also available. Financial award application deadline: 3/1; financial award applicants required to submit FAFSA. *Unit head:* Dr. Michael S. Goldberger, Academic Unit Head, 540-568-6145.

Kansas State University, Graduate School, College of Arts and Sciences, Department of Kinesiology, Manhattan, KS 66506. Offers MS. Part-time programs available. *Faculty:* 5 full-time (2 women). *Students:* 25 full-time (16 women), 6 part-time (4 women); includes 4 minority (2 African Americans, 1 Asian American or Pacific Islander, 1 Hispanic American), 3 international. Average age 24. 17 applicants, 100% accepted, 9 enrolled. In 2006, 9 degrees awarded. *Degree requirements:* For master's, thesis optional. *Entrance requirements:* For master's, GRE General Test, bachelor's degree in kinesiology or exercise science, minimum GPA of 3.0. Additional exam requirements/recommendations for international students: Required—TOEFL. *Application deadline:* For fall admission, 2/1 priority date for domestic and international students; for spring admission, 10/1 for domestic students, 8/1 priority date for international students. Applications are processed on a rolling basis. Application fee: $30 ($55 for international students). *Expenses:* Tuition, state resident: full-time $6,352; part-time $240 per credit hour. Tuition, nonresident: full-time $14,296; part-time $571 per credit hour. Required fees: $585. *Financial support:* In 2006–07, 2 teaching assistantships (averaging $8,327 per year) were awarded; fellowships, research assistantships, career-related internships or fieldwork, Federal Work-Study, institutionally sponsored loans, scholarships/grants, and tuition waivers (full) also available. Support available to part-time students. Financial award application deadline: 3/1; financial award applicants required to submit FAFSA. *Faculty research:* Exercise physiology, vascular function, cardiorespiratory disease, exercise adherence and compliance, public health/physical activity. Total annual research expenditures: $1,428. *Unit head:* Tom Barstow, Head, 785-532-0712, Fax: 785-532-6486, E-mail: tbarsto@ksu.edu.

Lamar University, College of Graduate Studies, College of Education and Human Development, Department of Health and Kinesiology, Beaumont, TX 77710. Offers kinesiology (MS). *Faculty:* 9 full-time (6 women), 8 part-time/adjunct (6 women). *Students:* 7 full-time (4 women), 1 (woman) part-time; includes 2 minority (1 African American, 1 Asian American or Pacific Islander), 2 international. Average age 28. 16 applicants, 25% accepted, 3 enrolled. In 2006, 3 degrees awarded. *Degree requirements:* For master's, thesis optional. *Entrance requirements:* For master's, GRE General Test, minimum GPA of 2.5. Additional exam requirements/recommendations for international students: Required—TOEFL. *Application deadline:* For fall admission, 8/1 for domestic students; for spring admission, 12/1 for domestic students. Applications are processed on a rolling basis. Application fee: $25. *Expenses:* Tuition, nonresident: part-time $33 per hour. Required fees: $43 per hour. $110 per semester. *Financial support:* In 2006–07, 4 teaching assistantships (averaging $7,500 per year) were awarded. Financial award application deadline: 4/1. *Faculty research:* Motor learning, exercise physiology, pedagogy. *Unit head:* Dr. Charles L. Nix, Chair, 409-880-2226, Fax: 409-880-1761, E-mail: nixcl@hal.lamar.edu. *Application contact:* Dr. Daniel R. Chilek, Graduate Coordinator, 409-880-8090, Fax: 409-880-1761, E-mail: chilekdr@hal.lamar.edu.

Louisiana State University and Agricultural and Mechanical College, Graduate School, College of Education, Department of Kinesiology, Baton Rouge, LA 70803. Offers MS, PhD. *Faculty:* 14 full-time (5 women). *Students:* 47 full-time (20 women), 27 part-time (12 women); includes 12 minority (8 African Americans, 3 Asian Americans or Pacific Islanders, 1 Hispanic American), 7 international. Average age 29. 49 applicants, 47% accepted, 3 enrolled. In 2006, 27 master's, 7 doctorates awarded. Terminal master's awarded for partial completion of doctoral program. *Degree requirements:* For master's, thesis (for some programs); for doctorate, one foreign language, thesis/dissertation, residency. *Entrance requirements:* For master's and doctorate, GRE General Test, minimum GPA of 3.0. Additional exam requirements/recommendations for international students: Required—TOEFL (minimum score 550 paper-based; 213 computer-based; 79 iBT). *Application deadline:* For fall admission, 1/25 priority date for domestic students, 5/15 for international students; for spring admission, 10/15 for international students. Applications are processed on a rolling basis. Application fee: $25. Electronic applications accepted. *Financial support:* In 2006–07, 35 students received support, including fellowships with full and partial tuition reimbursements available (averaging $19,711 per year), 2 research assistantships with full and partial tuition reimbursements available (averaging $11,000 per year), 22 teaching assistantships with full and partial tuition reimbursements available (averaging $13,682 per year); career-related internships or fieldwork, Federal Work-Study, tuition waivers (full and partial), and unspecified assistantships also available. Financial award applicants required to submit FAFSA. *Faculty research:* Physical activity promotion in schools, wellness centers, hospitals and sports settings, healthy aging, rehabilitation studies. Total annual research expenditures: $178,359. *Unit head:* Dr. Amelia M. Lee, Chair, 225-578-2036, Fax: 225-578-3680, E-mail: amlee@lsu.edu. *Application contact:* Dr. Richard Magill, Coordinator of Graduate Studies, 225-578-3548, Fax: 225-578-3680, E-mail: rmagill@lsu.edu.

McGill University, Faculty of Graduate and Postdoctoral Studies, Faculty of Education, Department of Kinesiology and Physical Education, Montréal, QC H3A 2T5, Canada. Offers M Sc, MA, PhD, Certificate, Diploma. Part-time programs available. *Degree requirements:* For master's and doctorate, thesis/dissertation, registration. *Entrance requirements:* For master's, minimum GPA of 3.0, bachelor's degree in kinesiology, physical education or a related biological or behavioral science. Additional exam requirements/recommendations for international students: Required—TOEFL (minimum score 550 paper-based; 213 computer-based), IELTS (minimum score 7). Electronic applications accepted. *Faculty research:* Biomechanics, exercise physiology, adapted physical education, psychology of motor behavior, pedagogy.

McMaster University, School of Graduate Studies, Faculty of Social Sciences, Department of Kinesiology, Hamilton, ON L8S 4M2, Canada. Offers human biodynamics (M Sc, PhD). *Faculty:* 16 full-time, 4 part-time/adjunct. *Students:* 46 full-time, 3 part-time. 43 applicants, 21% accepted. *Degree requirements:* For master's, thesis. *Entrance requirements:* For master's, minimum B+ average in undergraduate course work. Additional exam requirements/ recommendations for international students: Required—TOEFL (minimum score 580 paper-based; 237 computer-based). *Application deadline:* For fall admission, 3/1 priority date for domestic students. Applications are processed on a rolling basis. Application fee: $90. *Financial support:* In 2006–07, teaching assistantships (averaging $8,440 per year); research assistantships, scholarships/grants also available. *Faculty research:* Motor learning and control, neuromuscular physiology, exercise rehabilitation, cellular responses to exercise, management. Total annual research expenditures: $176,479. *Unit head:* Dr. Neil McCartney, Chair, 905-525-9140 Ext. 24469, Fax: 905-525-7629, E-mail: mccartne@mcmaster.ca. *Application contact:* Dr. Cameron Blimkie, Director, Graduate Program, 905-525-9140 Ext. 24702, Fax: 905-523-6011, E-mail: blimkie@mcmaster.ca.

Memorial University of Newfoundland, School of Graduate Studies, School of Human Kinetics and Recreation, St. John's, NL A1C 5S7, Canada. Offers administration, curriculum and supervision (MPE); biomechanics/ergonomics (MS Kin); exercise and work physiology (MS Kin); sport psychology (MS Kin). Part-time programs available. *Degree requirements:* For master's, seminars, thesis presentations, thesis optional. *Entrance requirements:* For master's, bachelor's degree in a related field, minimum B average. Electronic applications accepted. *Faculty research:* Administration, sociology of sports, kinesiology, physiology/recreation.

Michigan State University, The Graduate School, College of Education, Department of Kinesiology, East Lansing, MI 48824. Offers MS, PhD. *Faculty:* 11 full-time (7 women). *Students:* 73 full-time (34 women), 14 part-time (7 women); includes 11 minority (7 African Americans, 2 Asian Americans or Pacific Islanders, 2 Hispanic Americans), 5 international. Average age 27. 112 applicants, 45% accepted. In 2006, 30 master's, 12 doctorates awarded. *Entrance requirements:* Additional exam requirements/recommendations for international students: Required—TOEFL. Electronic applications accepted. *Expenses:* Tuition, state resident: part-time $346 per credit hour. Tuition, nonresident: part-time $730 per credit hour. Tuition and fees vary according to program. *Financial support:* In 2006–07, 12 fellowships with tuition reimbursements, 30 research assistantships with tuition reimbursements (averaging $13,948 per year), 33 teaching assistantships with tuition reimbursements (averaging $13,838 per year) were awarded. Total annual research expenditures: $36,376. *Unit head:* Dr. Deborah L. Feltz, Chairperson, 517-355-4732, Fax: 517-353-2944, E-mail: dfeltz@msu.edu. *Application contact:* JoAnne Janes, Graduate Studies Secretary, 517-355-4736, Fax: 517-355-2944, E-mail: janes@msu.edu.

Midwestern State University, Graduate Studies, College of Health Sciences and Human Services, Program in Kinesiology, Wichita Falls, TX 76308. Offers MSK. Part-time and evening/ weekend programs available. *Faculty:* 4 full-time (2 women). *Students:* 8 full-time (4 women), 15 part-time (4 women); includes 4 minority (1 African American, 1 Asian American or Pacific Islander, 2 Hispanic Americans), 6 international. Average age 28. 9 applicants, 67% accepted, 4 enrolled. In 2006, 6 degrees awarded. *Degree requirements:* For master's, thesis optional. *Entrance requirements:* For master's, GRE General Test or MAT. Additional exam requirements/ recommendations for international students: Required—TOEFL (minimum score 550 paper-based; 213 computer-based). *Application deadline:* For fall admission, 7/1 for domestic students, 4/1 for international students; for spring admission, 11/1 for domestic students, 8/1 for international students. Applications are processed on a rolling basis. Application fee: $35 ($50 for international students). Electronic applications accepted. *Financial support:* In 2006–07, 16 students received support, including 13 teaching assistantships with partial tuition reimbursements available (averaging $7,617 per year); career-related internships or fieldwork, Federal Work-Study, institutionally sponsored loans, scholarships/grants, tuition waivers (partial), and unspecified assistantships also available. Support available to part-time students. Financial award application deadline: 5/1; financial award applicants required to submit FAFSA. *Unit head:* Dr. Frank Wyatt, Chair, 940-397-4829, Fax: 940-397-4901, E-mail: frank.wyatt@mwsu.edu. *Application contact:* 800-842-1922, Fax: 940-397-4672, E-mail: admissions@mwsu.edu.

Mississippi State University, College of Education, Department of Kinesiology, Mississippi State, MS 39762. Offers exercise science (MS); health education/health promotion (MS); sports administration (MS); teaching/coaching (MS). Part-time programs available. Postbaccalaureate distance learning degree programs offered (minimal on-campus study). *Faculty:* 15 full-time (4 women), 6 part-time/adjunct (4 women). *Students:* 34 full-time (13 women), 13 part-time (6 women); includes 6 minority (all African Americans), 1 international. Average age 25. 49 applicants, 69% accepted, 26 enrolled. In 2006, 25 degrees awarded. *Degree requirements:* For master's, comprehensive oral or written exam, thesis optional. *Entrance requirements:* For master's, GRE General Test, minimum GPA of 3.0. Additional exam requirements/recommendations for international students: Required—TOEFL. *Application deadline:* For fall admission, 7/1 for domestic students; for spring admission, 11/1 for domestic students. Applications are processed on a rolling basis. Application fee: $30. Electronic applications accepted. *Expenses:* Tuition, state resident: full-time $4,550; part-time $253 per hour. Tuition, nonresident: full-time $10,552; part-time $584 per hour. International tuition: $10,882 full-time. Tuition and fees vary according to course load. *Financial support:* In 2006–07, 13 students received support, including 7 teaching assistantships with full tuition reimbursements available (averaging $7,772 per year); research assistantships with full tuition reimbursements available, career-related internships or fieldwork, Federal Work-Study, institutionally sponsored loans, and unspecified assistantships also available. Financial award applicants required to submit FAFSA. *Faculty research:* Static balance and stepping performance of older adults, organizational justice, public health, strength training and recovery drinks, high risk drinking perceptions and behaviors. *Unit head:* Dr. Joseph Chromiak, Interim Head, 662-325-2963, Fax: 662-325-4525, E-mail: jchrom@colled.msstate.edu. *Application contact:* Dr. Phil Bonfanti, Director of Admissions, 662-325-4104, Fax: 662-325-8872, E-mail: admit@msstate.edu.

New York University, Steinhardt School of Culture, Education and Human Development, Department of Physical Therapy, New York, NY 10012-1019. Offers physical therapists pathokinesiology (MA); physical therapy (DPT); practicing physical therapist (DPT); research in physical therapy (PhD). *Accreditation:* APTA (one or more programs are accredited). Part-time and evening/weekend programs available. *Faculty:* 10 full-time (5 women), 6 part-time/ adjunct (1 woman). *Students:* 89 full-time (70 women), 9 part-time (5 women); includes 24 minority (6 African Americans, 1 American Indian/Alaska Native, 12 Asian Americans or Pacific Islanders, 5 Hispanic Americans), 12 international. 135 applicants, 68% accepted, 37 enrolled. In 2006, 11 master's, 22 doctorates awarded. Terminal master's awarded for partial completion of doctoral program. *Degree requirements:* For master's, thesis (for some programs); for doctorate, thesis/dissertation. *Entrance requirements:* For master's, physical therapy certificate; for doctorate, GRE General Test, interview, physical therapy certificate. Additional exam requirements/recommendations for international students: Required—TOEFL. *Application deadline:* For fall admission, 12/15 priority date for domestic and international students; for spring admission, 11/1 for domestic and international students. Applications are processed on a rolling basis. Application fee: $50. *Expenses:* Tuition: Part-time $1,080 per unit. Required fees: $56 per unit. $329 per term. Tuition and fees vary according to program. *Financial support:* Fellowships with full and partial tuition reimbursements, research assistantships with full and partial tuition reimbursements, career-related internships or fieldwork, Federal Work-Study, scholarships/grants, tuition waivers (partial), and unspecified assistantships available. Support available to part-time students. Financial award application deadline: 2/1; financial award applicants required to submit FAFSA. *Faculty research:* Motor learning and control, neuromuscular disorders, biomechanics and ergonomics, movement analysis, exercise physiology. *Unit head:* Dr. Wen K. Ling, Chairperson, 212-998-9400, Fax: 212-995-4190. *Application contact:* 212-998-5030, Fax: 212-995-4328, E-mail: steinhardt.gradadmissions@nyu.edu.

Old Dominion University, Darden College of Education, Doctoral Program in Human Movement Science, Norfolk, VA 23529. Offers PhD. *Faculty:* 3 full-time (2 women). *Students:* Average age 34. 9 applicants, 89% accepted, 6 enrolled. *Degree requirements:* For doctorate, thesis/dissertation, comprehensive exam. *Entrance requirements:* For doctorate, GRE, minimum GPA of 3.0. Additional exam requirements/recommendations for international students: Required—TOEFL. *Application deadline:* For spring admission, 2/1 priority date for domestic and international students. Applications are processed on a rolling basis. Application fee: $40. Electronic applications accepted. *Expenses:* Tuition, area resident: Part-time $285 per credit hour. Tuition, nonresident: part-time $715 per credit hour. Required fees: $94 per semester. *Financial support:* In 2006–07, 6 students received support, including 1 fellowship with full tuition reimbursement available (averaging $15,000 per year), 5 teaching assistantships with full tuition reimbursements available (averaging $15,000 per year); career-related internships or fieldwork, scholarships/grants, and unspecified assistantships also available. *Faculty research:* Prevention of ACL injury, lower extremity mechanics muscle energy techniques, athletic training, program satisfaction, evidence based practice outcomes. Total annual research expenditures: $10,000. *Unit head:* Dr. Bonnie L. Van Lunen, Graduate Program Director, 757-683-3516, Fax: 757-683-4270, E-mail: bvanlune@odu.edu.

Oregon State University, Graduate School, College of Health and Human Sciences, Department of Nutrition and Exercise Sciences, Program in Movement Studies in Disabilities, Corvallis, OR 97331. Offers MAIS, MS. *Students:* 2 full-time (0 women); includes 1 minority (Asian American or Pacific Islander), 1 international. Average age 26. In 2006, 2 degrees awarded. *Degree requirements:* For master's, thesis. *Entrance requirements:* For master's, minimum GPA of 3.0 in last 90 hours. Additional exam requirements/recommendations for international students: Required—TOEFL. *Application deadline:* For fall admission, 3/1 for domestic students. Applications are processed on a rolling basis. Application fee: $50. *Financial support:* Research assistantships, teaching assistantships, career-related internships or fieldwork, Federal Work-Study, and institutionally sponsored loans available. Support available to part-time students. Financial award application deadline: 2/1. *Faculty research:* Fitness testing of disabled, biomechanics of disabled, assessment of disabled athletes, biomechanics of wheeling, energy cost of wheeling. *Unit head:* Dr. Jeffrey A. McCubbin, Director, 541-737-2176.

Penn State University Park, Graduate School, College of Health and Human Development, Department of Kinesiology, State College, University Park, PA 16802-1503. Offers MS, PhD. *Unit head:* Dr. Philip E. Martin, Head, 814-863-0847, E-mail: pem11@psu.edu. *Application contact:* Jacque McKinney, Graduate Program Staff Assistant, E-mail: kinesgrad@psu.edu.

See Close-Up on page 1813.

Saint Mary's College of California, School of Liberal Arts, Department of Kinesiology, Moraga, CA 94575. Offers MA. Part-time programs available. *Faculty:* 4 full-time (1 woman), 3 part-time/adjunct (1 woman). *Students:* 49 full-time (14 women); includes 15 minority (4 African Americans, 3 Asian Americans or Pacific Islanders, 8 Hispanic Americans). Average age 28. 17 applicants, 82% accepted, 14 enrolled. In 2006, 19 degrees awarded. *Degree requirements:* For master's, thesis or special project. *Entrance requirements:* For master's, minimum GPA of 2.75, BA in physical education or related field, or professional experience. *Application deadline:* For fall admission, 4/30 priority date for domestic and international students. Applications are processed on a rolling basis. Application fee: $25. *Expenses: Contact institution. Financial support:* In 2006–07, fellowships (averaging $3,000 per year), research assistantships (averaging $3,000 per year) were awarded; teaching assistantships, career-related internships or fieldwork, institutionally sponsored loans, scholarships/grants, tuition waivers (partial), and unspecified assistantships also available. Support available to part-time students. Financial award applicants required to submit FAFSA. *Faculty research:* Moral development in sport, applied motor learning, achievement motivation, sport history. Total annual research expenditures: $1,500. *Unit head:* Deane Lamont, Chair, 925-631-4024, Fax: 925-631-4965. *Application contact:* Jeanne Abate, Administrative Assistant, 925-631-4377, Fax: 925-631-4965, E-mail: jabate@stmarys-ca.edu.

Sam Houston State University, College of Education and Applied Science, Department of Health and Kinesiology, Huntsville, TX 77341. Offers M Ed, MA. Part-time and evening/ weekend programs available. *Faculty:* 4 full-time (1 woman). *Students:* 10 full-time (5 women), 15 part-time (6 women); includes 3 minority (2 African Americans, 1 Hispanic American). Average age 26. In 2006, 12 degrees awarded. *Entrance requirements:* For master's, GRE, MAT. *Application deadline:* For fall admission, 8/1 for domestic students; for spring admission, 12/1 for domestic students. Application fee: $20. *Expenses:* Tuition, state resident: full-time $5,904; part-time $164 per semester hour. Tuition, nonresident: full-time $15,804; part-time $439 per semester hour. Required fees: $1,374; $462 per semester. *Financial support:* Research assistantships, teaching assistantships, career-related internships or fieldwork, Federal Work-Study, and institutionally sponsored loans available. Financial award application deadline: 5/31; financial award applicants required to submit FAFSA. *Unit head:* Dr. Alice Fisher, Chair, 936-294-1165, Fax: 936-294-3891.

San Francisco State University, Division of Graduate Studies, College of Health and Human Services, Department of Kinesiology, San Francisco, CA 94132-1722. Offers MS. *Faculty:* 6 full-time (4 women), 2 part-time/adjunct (1 woman). *Students:* Average age 28. In 2006, 7 degrees awarded. *Degree requirements:* For master's, thesis, exam, project. *Entrance requirements:* For master's, minimum GPA of 2.75. *Application deadline:* For fall admission, 11/30 priority date for domestic students. Applications are processed on a rolling basis. Application fee: $55. *Financial support:* In 2006–07, 2 teaching assistantships were awarded. Financial award application deadline: 3/1. *Faculty research:* Metabolism, movement analysis, nutrition, ventilation, skill development. Total annual research expenditures: $20,000. *Unit head:* Dr. David Anderson, Chair, 415-338-1258. *Application contact:* Dr. Allen Abraham, Director of Advising, 415-338-2705, E-mail: aabraham@sfsu.edu.

San Jose State University, Graduate Studies and Research, College of Applied Sciences and Arts, Department of Kinesiology, San Jose, CA 95192-0001. Offers MA. *Students:* 49 full-time (26 women), 38 part-time (23 women); includes 19 minority (6 African Americans, 5 Asian Americans or Pacific Islanders, 8 Hispanic Americans), 8 international. Average age 29. 92 applicants, 72% accepted, 37 enrolled. In 2006, 35 degrees awarded. *Degree requirements:* For master's, comprehensive exam. *Entrance requirements:* For master's, bachelor's degree in physical education. *Application deadline:* For fall admission, 6/27 for domestic students; for spring admission, 11/30 for domestic students. Applications are processed on a rolling basis. Application fee: $59. Electronic applications accepted. *Financial support:* Applicants required to submit FAFSA. *Unit head:* Dr. Shirley Reekie, Chair, 408-924-3010, Fax: 408-924-3053, E-mail: sreekie@kin.sjsu.edu. *Application contact:* Dr. Ted Butryn, Graduate Coordinator, 408-924-3068, E-mail: tbutryn1@kin.sjsu.edu.

Simon Fraser University, Graduate Studies, Faculty of Applied Science, School of Kinesiology, Burnaby, BC V5A 1S6, Canada. Offers M Sc, PhD. *Degree requirements:* For master's and doctorate, thesis/dissertation. *Entrance requirements:* For master's, minimum GPA of 3.0; for doctorate, minimum GPA of 3.5. Additional exam requirements/recommendations for international students: Required—TOEFL or IELTS. *Faculty research:* Biomechanics, human factors/ ergonomics, behavioral neuroscience/motor control, cardiovascular/respiratory physiology, endocrine and immune systems.

Sonoma State University, School of Science and Technology, Department of Kinesiology, Rohnert Park, CA 94928-3609. Offers MA. Part-time programs available. *Faculty:* 5 full-time (3 women). *Students:* Average age 33. 14 applicants, 86% accepted, 8 enrolled. *Degree requirements:* For master's, thesis, oral exam. *Entrance requirements:* For master's, minimum GPA of 2.8. *Application deadline:* For fall admission, 11/30 for domestic students; for spring admission, 9/1 for domestic students. Applications are processed on a rolling basis. Applica-

Kinesiology and Movement Studies

Sonoma State University (continued)

tion fee: $55. *Expenses:* Tuition, nonresident: part-time $339 per unit. Required fees: $1,464 per term. *Financial support:* Career-related internships or fieldwork available. Financial award application deadline: 3/2. *Faculty research:* Exercise physiology, adult fitness, prosocial behavior, moral development, sport psychology. *Unit head:* Dr. Thomas Ormond, Chair, 707-664-2357, E-mail: thomas.ormond@sonoma.edu. *Application contact:* Dr. Lea Ann Schell, Graduate Coordinator, 707-664-2678.

Southeastern Louisiana University, College of Nursing and Health Sciences, Department of Kinesiology and Health Studies, Hammond, LA 70402. Offers health and kinesiology (MA). *Accreditation:* NCATE. Part-time programs available. *Faculty:* 10 full-time (4 women). *Students:* 21 full-time (15 women), 22 part-time (19 women); includes 11 minority (all African Americans), 3 international. Average age 29. 20 applicants, 95% accepted, 13 enrolled. In 2006, 15 degrees awarded. *Degree requirements:* For master's, thesis optional. *Entrance requirements:* For master's, GRE General Test, 30 hours of physical education, minimum GPA of 2.5. Additional exam requirements/recommendations for international students: Required—TOEFL (minimum score 500 paper-based; 173 computer-based). *Application deadline:* For fall admission, 7/15 priority date for domestic students, 6/1 priority date for international students; for spring admission, 12/1 priority date for domestic students, 10/1 priority date for international students. Applications are processed on a rolling basis. Application fee: $20 ($30 for international students). Electronic applications accepted. *Expenses:* Tuition, state resident: full-time $2,216; part-time $123 per credit. Tuition, nonresident: full-time $6,212; part-time $345 per credit. Required fees: $986; $55 per credit. Part-time tuition and fees vary according to course load. *Financial support:* In 2006–07, 8 research assistantships with full tuition reimbursements (averaging $5,500 per year), 3 teaching assistantships with full tuition reimbursements (averaging $5,500 per year) were awarded; Federal Work-Study, institutionally sponsored loans, unspecified assistantships, and administrative assistantships also available. Support available to part-time students. Financial award application deadline: 5/1; financial award applicants required to submit FAFSA. *Faculty research:* Relationship of exercise on body hormones; sexuality knowledge, attitudes and behaviors; drug and tobacco use and abuse; relationship of health and spirituality; exercise adherence and motivation. *Unit head:* Dr. Edward Hebert, Department Head, 985-549-2130, Fax: 985-549-5119, E-mail: ehebert@selu.edu. *Application contact:* Sandra Meyers, Graduate Admissions Analyst, 985-549-2066, Fax: 985-549-5632, E-mail: admissions@selu.edu.

Southern Arkansas University–Magnolia, Graduate Programs, Magnolia, AR 71753. Offers computer and information sciences (MS); counseling (MS); education (M Ed), including counseling and development, educational administration and supervision, elementary education, secondary education; kinesiology (MS); library media and information specialist (M Ed); school counseling (M Ed); teaching (MAT). *Accreditation:* NCATE. Part-time and evening/weekend programs available. *Degree requirements:* For master's, thesis optional. *Entrance requirements:* For master's, GRE or MAT, minimum GPA of 2.75. *Faculty research:* Alternative certification for teachers, supervision of instruction, instructional leadership, counseling.

Southern Illinois University Edwardsville, Graduate Studies and Research, School of Education, Department of Kinesiology and Health Education, Edwardsville, IL 62026-0001. Offers exercise physiology (Postbaccalaureate Certificate); kinesiology (MS Ed); pedagogy administration (Postbaccalaureate Certificate); sport and exercise behavior (Postbaccalaureate Certificate). *Accreditation:* NCATE. Part-time and evening/weekend programs available. *Faculty:* 12 full-time (5 women). *Students:* 20 full-time (10 women), 55 part-time (26 women); includes 8 minority (7 African Americans, 1 Hispanic American), 4 international. Average age 33. 53 applicants, 70% accepted. In 2006, 23 degrees awarded. *Degree requirements:* For master's, thesis or alternative, final exam. *Entrance requirements:* Additional exam requirements/recommendations for international students: Required—TOEFL. *Application deadline:* For fall admission, 7/20 for domestic students, 6/1 for international students; for spring admission, 12/14 for domestic students, 10/1 for international students. Application fee: $30. Electronic applications accepted. *Financial support:* In 2006–07, 5 teaching assistantships with full tuition reimbursements were awarded; fellowships, research assistantships with full tuition reimbursements, Federal Work-Study, institutionally sponsored loans, and unspecified assistantships also available. Support available to part-time students. Financial award application deadline: 3/1; financial award applicants required to submit FAFSA. *Unit head:* Dr. E. William Vogler, Chair, 618-650-3252, E-mail: wvogler@siue.edu.

Southwestern Oklahoma State University, College of Professional and Graduate Studies, School of Behavioral Sciences and Education, Specialization in Kinesiology, Weatherford, OK 73096-3098. Offers M Ed. Part-time programs available. *Degree requirements:* For master's, exam. *Entrance requirements:* For master's, GRE General Test or minimum undergraduate GPA of 3.0. Additional exam requirements/recommendations for international students: Required—TOEFL.

Springfield College, Graduate Programs, Programs in Exercise Science and Sport Studies, Springfield, MA 01109-3797. Offers biomechanics (MS); exercise physiology (MS, DPE), including clinical exercise physiology (MS), science and research (MS); interdisciplinary movement sciences (MS); sport psychology (MS, DPE). Part-time programs available. *Faculty:* 3 full-time (0 women), 4 part-time/adjunct (1 woman). *Students:* 43. Average age 26. 57 applicants, 77% accepted, 20 enrolled. In 2006, 31 master's awarded. *Degree requirements:* For master's, thesis. *Entrance requirements:* For master's, GRE General Test. Additional exam requirements/recommendations for international students: Required—TOEFL (minimum score 550 paper-based; 213 computer-based). *Application deadline:* For fall admission, 1/15 for domestic students; for winter admission, 11/1 for domestic students; for spring admission, 12/1 for domestic students. Applications are processed on a rolling basis. Application fee: $50. Electronic applications accepted. *Expenses:* Tuition: Full-time $12,222; part-time $679 per credit. Required fees: $25; $25 per year. One-time fee: $25 full-time. *Financial support:* In 2006–07, 6 teaching assistantships with partial tuition reimbursements were awarded; fellowships with partial tuition reimbursements, career-related internships or fieldwork, Federal Work-Study, institutionally sponsored loans, and tuition waivers (full and partial) also available. Financial award application deadline: 3/1. *Faculty research:* Fitness in renal disease, environmental exercise physiology. *Unit head:* Charles J. Redmond, Director, 413-748-3231, Fax: 413-748-3371, E-mail: credmond@spfldcol.edu. *Application contact:* Donald James Shaw, Director of Graduate Admissions, 413-748-3060, Fax: 413-748-3069, E-mail: donald_shaw_jr@spfldcol.edu.

Stephen F. Austin State University, Graduate School, College of Education, Department of Kinesiology and Health Science, Nacogdoches, TX 75962. Offers athletic training (MS); kinesiology (M Ed). *Degree requirements:* For master's, comprehensive exam. *Entrance requirements:* For master's, GRE General Test. Additional exam requirements/recommendations for international students: Required—TOEFL.

Teachers College Columbia University, Graduate Faculty of Education, Department of Biobehavioral Studies, Program in Motor Learning/Movement Science, New York, NY 10027-6696. Offers Ed M, MA, Ed D. Part-time and evening/weekend programs available. *Faculty:* 4 full-time (1 woman). *Students:* 1 (woman) full-time, 17 part-time (11 women). Average age 35. 18 applicants, 78% accepted, 9 enrolled. In 2006, 4 master's, 1 doctorate awarded. Terminal master's awarded for partial completion of doctoral program. *Degree requirements:* For master's, integrative paper; for doctorate, thesis/dissertation. *Entrance requirements:* For doctorate, GRE General Test. *Application deadline:* For fall admission, 5/15 for domestic students; for spring admission, 12/1 for domestic students. Application fee: $65. *Expenses:* Tuition: Full-time $23,400; part-time $975 per credit. Required fees: $320 per term. *Financial support:* Teaching assistantships, career-related internships or fieldwork, Federal Work-Study, institutionally sponsored loans, traineeships, and tuition waivers (full and partial) available. Support available to part-time students. Financial award application deadline: 2/1. *Faculty research:* Motor control, analysis of tasks, biomechanical aspect of learning, skill acquisition, recovery of motor behavior. *Application contact:* Debbie Lesperance, Assistant Director of Admission, 212-678-3710, Fax: 212-678-4171.

See Close-Up on page 1739.

Temple University, Health Sciences Center and Graduate School, College of Health Professions, Department of Kinesiology, Philadelphia, PA 19122-6096. Offers kinesiology (Ed M, PhD), including behavioral sciences, somatic sciences. Part-time programs available. *Faculty:* 11 full-time (5 women). *Students:* 45 full-time (26 women), 57 part-time (31 women); includes 12 minority (6 African Americans, 2 Asian Americans or Pacific Islanders, 4 Hispanic Americans), 6 international. 95 applicants, 42% accepted, 30 enrolled. In 2006, 21 master's, 8 doctorates awarded. Terminal master's awarded for partial completion of doctoral program. *Degree requirements:* For master's and doctorate, thesis/dissertation. *Entrance requirements:* For master's, GRE General Test or MAT, minimum undergraduate GPA of 3.0; for doctorate, GRE General Test, minimum undergraduate GPA of 3.0. Additional exam requirements/recommendations for international students: Required—TOEFL (minimum score 550 paper-based; 213 computer-based; 79 iBT). *Application deadline:* For fall admission, 1/15 for domestic students, 12/15 for international students; for spring admission, 10/1 for domestic students, 8/1 for international students. Application fee: $50. *Expenses:* Tuition, state resident: full-time $12,264; part-time $511 per credit. Tuition, nonresident: full-time $17,904; part-time $746 per credit. Required fees: $84 per course. Tuition and fees vary according to program. *Financial support:* Fellowships, research assistantships with full tuition reimbursements, teaching assistantships with full tuition reimbursements, career-related internships or fieldwork and Federal Work-Study available. Financial award application deadline: 1/15; financial award applicants required to submit FAFSA. *Unit head:* Dr. Michael R. Sitler, Chair, 215-204-1950, Fax: 215-204-8705, E-mail: sitler@temple.edu.

Tennessee Technological University, Graduate School, College of Education, Department of Exercise Science, Physical Education and Wellness, Cookeville, TN 38505. Offers MA. *Accreditation:* NCATE. Part-time programs available. *Faculty:* 7 full-time (0 women). *Students:* 12 full-time (7 women), 32 part-time (14 women); includes 5 minority (all African Americans) Average age 27. 24 applicants, 88% accepted, 17 enrolled. In 2006, 9 degrees awarded. *Entrance requirements:* For master's, MAT. Additional exam requirements/recommendations for international students: Required—TOEFL. *Application deadline:* For fall admission, 3/1 priority date for domestic students; for spring admission, 8/1 for domestic students. Application fee: $25 ($30 for international students). *Expenses:* Tuition, state resident: full-time $8,748; part-time $319 per hour. Tuition, nonresident: full-time $23,524; part-time $740 per hour. *Financial support:* In 2006–07, fellowships (averaging $8,000 per year), 3 research assistantships (averaging $4,000 per year), 4 teaching assistantships (averaging $4,000 per year) were awarded; career-related internships or fieldwork also available. Financial award application deadline: 4/1. *Unit head:* Dr. Patricia Jordan, Interim Chairperson, 931-372-3467, Fax: 931-372-6319. *Application contact:* Dr. Francis O. Otuonye, Associate Vice President for Research and Graduate Studies, 931-372-3233, Fax: 931-372-3497, E-mail: fotuonye@tntech.edu.

Texas A&M University, College of Education and Human Development, Department of Health and Kinesiology, College Station, TX 77843. Offers health education (M Ed, MS, Ed D, PhD); kinesiology (M Ed, MS, Ed D, PhD), including kinesiology (MS, PhD), physical education (M Ed, Ed D). Part-time programs available. *Faculty:* 25 full-time (7 women). *Students:* 121 full-time (50 women), 19 part-time (7 women); includes 23 minority (10 African Americans, 2 Asian Americans or Pacific Islanders, 11 Hispanic Americans), 24 international. Average age 23. 110 applicants, 65% accepted, 48 enrolled. In 2006, 30 master's, 13 doctorates awarded. *Degree requirements:* For master's, thesis (for some programs), registration; for doctorate, thesis/dissertation, comprehensive exam, registration. *Entrance requirements:* For master's and doctorate, GRE General Test. Additional exam requirements/recommendations for international students: Required—TOEFL. *Application deadline:* Applications are processed on a rolling basis. Application fee: $50 ($75 for international students). Electronic applications accepted. *Expenses:* Tuition, state resident: full-time $4,697. Tuition, nonresident: full-time $11,297. Required fees: $2,272. *Financial support:* Fellowships with partial tuition reimbursements, research assistantships, teaching assistantships, career-related internships or fieldwork and institutionally sponsored loans available. Financial award application deadline: 2/15; financial award applicants required to submit FAFSA. *Unit head:* Dr. Steve Dorman, Head, 979-845-3109, Fax: 979-847-8987. *Application contact:* Eva Parkerson, Information Contact, 979-458-2673, Fax: 979-847-8987, E-mail: eva@hlkn.tamu.edu.

Texas A&M University–Commerce, Graduate School, College of Education and Human Services, Department of Health, Kinesiology and Sports Studies, Commerce, TX 75429-3011. Offers M Ed, MS, Ed D. Part-time programs available. *Degree requirements:* For master's, thesis (for some programs), comprehensive exam. *Entrance requirements:* For master's, GRE General Test. Electronic applications accepted. *Faculty research:* Teaching, physical fitness.

Texas A&M University–Corpus Christi, Graduate Studies and Research, College of Education, Corpus Christi, TX 78412-5503. Offers counseling (MS, PhD), including counseling (MS), counselor education (PhD); curriculum and instruction (MS, Ed D); early childhood education (MS); educational administration (MS); educational leadership (Ed D); educational technology (MS); elementary education (MS); kinesiology (MS); occupational training and development (MS); reading (MS); secondary education (MS); special education (MS). Part-time and evening/weekend programs available. *Degree requirements:* For master's, thesis (for some programs), comprehensive exam, registration; for doctorate, thesis/dissertation, comprehensive exam, registration. *Entrance requirements:* For master's, GRE General Test. Additional exam requirements/recommendations for international students: Required—TOEFL. Electronic applications accepted.

Texas A&M University–Kingsville, College of Graduate Studies, College of Education, Department of Health and Kinesiology, Kingsville, TX 78363. Offers MA, MS. Part-time programs available. *Degree requirements:* For master's, thesis or alternative, comprehensive exam. *Entrance requirements:* For master's, GRE General Test, minimum GPA of 3.0. *Faculty research:* Body composition, electromyography.

Texas Christian University, Harris College of Nursing and Health Sciences, Department of Kinesiology, Fort Worth, TX 76129-0002. Offers MS. Part-time and evening/weekend programs available. *Degree requirements:* For master's, thesis optional. *Entrance requirements:* For master's, GRE General Test, course work in physical education. Additional exam requirements/recommendations for international students: Required—TOEFL. *Application deadline:* For fall admission, 3/1 for domestic students; for spring admission, 12/1 for domestic students. Applications are processed on a rolling basis. Application fee: $0. *Expenses:* Tuition: Part-time $800 per credit hour. *Financial support:* Unspecified assistantships available. Financial award application deadline: 3/1. *Unit head:* Dr. Joel Mitchell, Chairperson, 817-257-7665, E-mail: j.mitchell@tcu.edu.

Texas Woman's University, Graduate School, College of Health Sciences, Department of Kinesiology, Denton, TX 76201. Offers MS, PhD. Part-time and evening/weekend programs available. *Students:* 51 full-time (27 women), 71 part-time (49 women); includes 16 minority (4 African Americans, 1 Asian American or Pacific Islander, 11 Hispanic Americans), 27 international. Average age 33. In 2006, 44 master's, 5 doctorates awarded. Terminal master's awarded for partial completion of doctoral program. *Degree requirements:* For master's, thesis or alternative; for doctorate, thesis/dissertation, qualifying exam, comprehensive exam. *Entrance requirements:* For master's, 2 letters of reference; for doctorate, interview, 3 letters of reference, curriculum vitae. Additional exam requirements/recommendations for international students: Required—TOEFL (minimum score 550 paper-based; 213 computer-based; 79 iBT). *Application deadline:* For fall admission, 4/1 for international students; for spring admission, 8/1 for international students. Applications are processed on a rolling basis. Application fee: $30 ($50 for international students). Electronic applications accepted. *Expenses:* Tuition, area resident: Part-time $168 per unit. Tuition, state resident: full-time $4,369. Tuition, nonresident: full-time $9,373; part-time $443 per unit. Required fees: $20 per unit. $177 per term. *Financial support:*

In 2006–07, 13 research assistantships (averaging $10,494 per year), 12 teaching assistantships (averaging $10,494 per year) were awarded; career-related internships or fieldwork, Federal Work-Study, institutionally sponsored loans, scholarships/grants, traineeships, health care benefits, and unspecified assistantships also available. Support available to part-time students. Financial award application deadline: 3/1; financial award applicants required to submit FAFSA. *Faculty research:* Kinematics and kinetics of sport activities, autism students, lipoprotein-cholesterol metabolism, obesity in children, bone mineral density in children. *Unit head:* Dr. Charlotte Sanborn, Chair, 940-898-2575, Fax: 940-898-2581. *Application contact:* Samuel Wheeler, Coordinator of Graduate Admissions, 940-898-3188, Fax: 940-898-3081, E-mail: wheelersr@twu.edu.

Université de Montréal, Faculty of Graduate Studies, Department of Kinesiology, Montréal, QC H3C 3J7, Canada. Offers kinesiology (M Sc, DESS); physical activity (M Sc, PhD); physical activity and health promotion (DESS). *Faculty:* 14 full-time (5 women), 8 part-time/adjunct (2 women). *Students:* 50 full-time (14 women), 14 part-time (10 women). Average age 26. 49 applicants, 45% accepted, 19 enrolled. In 2006, 11 master's, 7 doctorates awarded. *Degree requirements:* For master's, one foreign language, thesis (for some programs); for doctorate, one foreign language, thesis/dissertation, general exam. *Application deadline:* For fall admission, 2/1 priority date for domestic students; for winter admission, 11/1 priority date for domestic students; for spring admission, 2/1 priority date for domestic students. Application fee: $30. Electronic applications accepted. *Financial support:* In 2006–07, 3 fellowships (averaging $20,000 per year), 10 research assistantships (averaging $5,000 per year), 6 teaching assistantships (averaging $7,000 per year) were awarded. Financial award application deadline: 2/1. *Faculty research:* Physiology of exercise, psychology of sports, biomechanics, dance, sociology of sports. Total annual research expenditures: $600,000. *Unit head:* Director, 514-343-6166, Fax: 514-343-2181. *Application contact:* Francine Normandeau, Information Contact, 514-343-6152, E-mail: francine.normandeau@umontreal.ca.

Université de Sherbrooke, Faculty of Physical Education, Program in Physical Education, Sherbrooke, QC J1K 2R1, Canada. Offers kinanthropology (M Sc); physical activity (Diploma). *Degree requirements:* For master's, thesis. *Entrance requirements:* For master's, minimum GPA of 2.7; for Diploma, bachelor's degree in physical education. *Faculty research:* Physical fitness, nutrition, human factors, sociology, teaching.

Université du Québec à Montréal, Graduate Programs, Program in Human Movement Studies, Montréal, QC H3C 3P8, Canada. Offers M Sc. Part-time programs available. *Degree requirements:* For master's, thesis optional. *Entrance requirements:* For master's, appropriate bachelor's degree or equivalent and proficiency in French.

Université Laval, Faculty of Medicine, Graduate Programs in Medicine, Programs in Kinesiology, Québec, QC G1K 7P4, Canada. Offers M Sc, PhD. Terminal master's awarded for partial completion of doctoral program. *Degree requirements:* For master's, thesis/dissertation; for doctorate, thesis/dissertation, comprehensive exam. *Entrance requirements:* For master's and doctorate, French exam, knowledge of French, comprehension of written English. Electronic applications accepted.

The University of Alabama, Graduate School, College of Education, Department of Kinesiology, Tuscaloosa, AL 35487. Offers alternative sport pedagogy (MA); exercise science (MA, PhD); human performance (MA); sport management (MA); sport pedagogy (MA, PhD). Part-time programs available. *Faculty:* 9 full-time (1 woman). *Students:* 39 full-time (18 women), 20 part-time (11 women); includes 2 minority (both African Americans), 11 international. Average age 30. 35 applicants, 63% accepted, 7 enrolled. In 2006, 3 master's, 13 doctorates awarded. *Median time to degree:* Of those who began their doctoral program in fall 1998, 100% received their degree in 8 years or less. *Degree requirements:* For master's, thesis optional; for doctorate, thesis/dissertation, comprehensive exam. *Entrance requirements:* For master's and doctorate, GRE, MAT, minimum GPA of 3.0. Additional exam requirements/recommendations for international students: Required—TOEFL. *Financial support:* In 2006–07, 14 students received support, including 13 teaching assistantships with full tuition reimbursements available (averaging $8,678 per year). *Faculty research:* Race gender and sexuality in sports, physical education curriculum reform, disability sports, physical activity and health, environmental physiology. Total annual research expenditures: $9,290. *Unit head:* Dr. Matt Curtner-Smith, Department Head and Professor, 205-348-9209, Fax: 205-348-0867, E-mail: msmith@bamed.ua.edu.

University of Arkansas, Graduate School, College of Education and Health Professions, Department of Health Science, Kinesiology, Recreation and Dance, Program in Kinesiology, Fayetteville, AR 72701-1201. Offers MS, PhD. *Students:* 45 full-time (26 women), 24 part-time (14 women); includes 11 minority (8 African Americans, 1 Asian American or Pacific Islander, 2 Hispanic Americans), 11 international. 58 applicants, 28% accepted. In 2006, 13 master's, 5 doctorates awarded. *Degree requirements:* For doctorate, thesis/dissertation. *Entrance requirements:* For doctorate, GRE General Test. Application fee: $40 ($50 for international students). *Financial support:* In 2006–07, 8 fellowships with tuition reimbursements, 7 research assistantships, 5 teaching assistantships were awarded; career-related internships or fieldwork and Federal Work-Study also available. Support available to part-time students. Financial award application deadline: 4/1; financial award applicants required to submit FAFSA. *Unit head:* Dr. Dean Gorman, Coordinator of Graduate Studies, 479-575-6625, E-mail: dgorman@comp.uark.edu.

The University of British Columbia, Faculty of Graduate Studies, Faculty of Education, School of Human Kinetics, Vancouver, BC V6T 1Z1, Canada. Offers M Sc, MA, MHK, PhD. Part-time programs available. *Faculty:* 22 full-time (6 women), 4 part-time/adjunct (1 woman). *Students:* 93 full-time (56 women), 1 part-time; includes 1 African American, 14 Asian Americans or Pacific Islanders. Average age 25. 51 applicants, 61% accepted, 25 enrolled. In 2006, 10 master's, 6 doctorates awarded. *Median time to degree:* Of those who began their doctoral program in fall 1998, 100% received their degree in 8 years or less. *Degree requirements:* For master's, thesis (for some programs), registration; for doctorate, thesis/dissertation, comprehensive exam, registration. *Entrance requirements:* For doctorate, thesis-based master's degree. Additional exam requirements/recommendations for international students: Required—TOEFL (minimum score 550 paper-based; 213 computer-based), IELTS. *Application deadline:* For fall admission, 3/1 for domestic students, 2/1 for international students; for winter admission, 8/1 for domestic students, 7/1 for international students. Applications are processed on a rolling basis. Application fee: $90 Canadian dollars ($150 Canadian dollars for international students). Electronic applications accepted. *Financial support:* In 2006–07, 5 fellowships, 5 research assistantships, 55 teaching assistantships (averaging $5,000 per year) were awarded; career-related internships or fieldwork, Federal Work-Study, institutionally sponsored loans, scholarships/grants, and tuition waivers (full and partial) also available. Financial award application deadline: 3/15. *Faculty research:* Exercise physiology, biomechanics, motor learning, natural sciences, socio-managerial. *Unit head:* Dr. Robert E. Sparks, Director, 604-822-2767, Fax: 604-822-6842, E-mail: robert.sparks@ubc.ca. *Application contact:* Rochelle de la Giroday, Graduate Secretary, 604-822-2767, Fax: 604-822-6842, E-mail: hkin-gradsec@interchange.ubc.ca.

University of Calgary, Faculty of Graduate Studies, Faculty of Kinesiology, Calgary, AB T2N 1N4, Canada. Offers biomedical engineering (M Sc, PhD); kinesiology (M Kin, M Sc, PhD), including biomechanics (PhD), health and exercise physiology (PhD). *Faculty:* 59 full-time (13 women), 18 part-time/adjunct (8 women). *Students:* 75 full-time (38 women), 3 part-time (1 woman). Average age 26. 52 applicants, 62% accepted, 25 enrolled. In 2006, 6 master's, 4 doctorates awarded. *Degree requirements:* For master's, thesis (M Sc); for doctorate, thesis/dissertation. *Entrance requirements:* Additional exam requirements/recommendations for international students: Required—TOEFL. *Application deadline:* For fall admission, 3/31 for domestic students. Applications are processed on a rolling basis. Application fee: $100 ($130 for international students). Electronic applications accepted. *Financial support:* In 2006–07, 21 students received support, including 3 research assistantships, 18 teaching assistantships; career-related internships or fieldwork and unspecified assistantships also available. Financial award application deadline: 3/31. *Faculty research:* Load acting on the human body, muscle mechanics and physiology, optimizing high performance athlete performance, eye movement in sports, analysis of body composition. Total annual research expenditures: $1.5 million. *Unit head:* Brian R. MacIntosh, Associate Dean, 403-220-3421, Fax: 403-220-0105, E-mail: brian@kin.ucalgary.ca. *Application contact:* Rosalie Kolstad, Graduate Program Administrator, 403-220-5183, Fax: 403-220-0105, E-mail: knesgrad@ucalgary.ca.

University of Central Arkansas, Graduate School, College of Health and Behavioral Sciences, Department of Kinesiology, Conway, AR 72035-0001. Offers MS. *Faculty:* 5 full-time (1 woman), 1 (woman) part-time/adjunct. *Students:* 8 full-time (3 women), 9 part-time (3 women), 3 international. 5 applicants, 100% accepted, 5 enrolled. In 2006, 1 degree awarded. *Degree requirements:* For master's, thesis optional. *Entrance requirements:* For master's, GRE General Test, minimum GPA of 2.7. Additional exam requirements/recommendations for international students: Required—TOEFL (minimum score 550 paper-based; 213 computer-based). *Application deadline:* For fall admission, 3/1 priority date for domestic students; for spring admission, 10/1 for domestic students. Applications are processed on a rolling basis. Application fee: $25 ($40 for international students). *Expenses:* Tuition, state resident: full-time $4,194; part-time $233 per semester. Tuition, nonresident: full-time $5,963; part-time $429 per semester. International tuition: $6,162 full-time. Required fees: $65; $23 per semester. One-time fee: $65 part-time. *Financial support:* Federal Work-Study, scholarships/grants, tuition waivers (partial), and unspecified assistantships available. Financial award application deadline: 2/15; financial award applicants required to submit FAFSA. *Unit head:* Dr. Deborah Howell-Creswell, Chairperson, 501-450-3148, Fax: 501-450-5503, E-mail: debbieh@uca.edu. *Application contact:* Nanette Fitzhugh, Administrative Assistant, 501-450-5063, Fax: 501-450-5678, E-mail: fitzhugh@uca.edu.

University of Colorado at Boulder, Graduate School, College of Arts and Sciences, Department of Integrative Physiology, Boulder, CO 80309. Offers MS, PhD. *Faculty:* 20 full-time (6 women). *Students:* 45 full-time (25 women), 9 part-time (4 women); includes 9 minority (1 African American, 4 Asian Americans or Pacific Islanders, 4 Hispanic Americans), 3 international. Average age 28. 30 applicants, 83% accepted. In 2006, 15 master's, 6 doctorates awarded. *Degree requirements:* For master's, thesis or alternative, comprehensive exam; for doctorate, thesis/dissertation. *Entrance requirements:* For master's, GRE General Test, minimum undergraduate GPA of 2.75. *Application deadline:* For fall admission, 1/15 priority date for domestic students, 12/15 for international students. Applications are processed on a rolling basis. Application fee: $50 ($60 for international students). *Financial support:* In 2006–07, 23 fellowships (averaging $3,872 per year), 14 research assistantships (averaging $14,237 per year), 33 teaching assistantships (averaging $11,787 per year) were awarded. Financial award application deadline: 2/1. *Faculty research:* Integrative or cellular kinesiology. Total annual research expenditures: $7.3 million. *Unit head:* Roger Enoka, Chair, 303-492-7232, Fax: 303-492-4009, E-mail: roger.enoka@spot.colorado.edu. *Application contact:* Marsha Cook, Graduate Program Administrator, 303-492-5362, Fax: 303-492-4009, E-mail: iphygrad@colorado.edu.

University of Connecticut, Graduate School, Neag School of Education, Department of Kinesiology, Field of Kinesiology, Storrs, CT 06269. Offers exercise science (MA, PhD); sport management and sociology (MA, PhD). *Faculty:* 13 full-time (4 women). *Students:* 78 full-time (42 women), 15 part-time (4 women); includes 14 minority (6 African Americans, 6 Asian Americans or Pacific Islanders, 2 Hispanic Americans), 8 international. Average age 26. 110 applicants, 43% accepted, 47 enrolled. In 2006, 29 master's, 7 doctorates awarded. Terminal master's awarded for partial completion of doctoral program. *Degree requirements:* For master's, thesis or alternative, comprehensive exam; for doctorate, thesis/dissertation. *Entrance requirements:* For doctorate, GRE General Test. Additional exam requirements/recommendations for international students: Required—TOEFL (minimum score 550 paper-based; 213 computer-based). *Application deadline:* For fall admission, 2/1 priority date for domestic and international students; for spring admission, 11/1 for domestic students, 10/1 for international students. Applications are processed on a rolling basis. Application fee: $55. Electronic applications accepted. *Financial support:* In 2006–07, 49 research assistantships with full tuition reimbursements were awarded; teaching assistantships with full tuition reimbursements, Federal Work-Study, health care benefits, and unspecified assistantships also available. Financial award application deadline: 2/1; financial award applicants required to submit FAFSA. *Application contact:* Lisa Rasicot, Graduate Coordinator, 860-486-3065, Fax: 860-486-0210, E-mail: soeadm02@uconnvm.uconn.edu.

University of Delaware, College of Arts and Sciences, Interdisciplinary Program in Biomechanics and Movement Science, Newark, DE 19716. Offers MS, PhD. Part-time programs available. Terminal master's awarded for partial completion of doctoral program. *Degree requirements:* For master's and doctorate, thesis/dissertation. *Entrance requirements:* For master's and doctorate, GRE General Test, minimum undergraduate GPA of 3.0. Additional exam requirements/recommendations for international students: Required—TOEFL (minimum score 550 paper-based; 213 computer-based). Electronic applications accepted. *Faculty research:* Muscle modeling, gait, motor control, human movement.

University of Delaware, College of Health Sciences, Department of Health, Nutrition, and Exercise Sciences, Newark, DE 19716. Offers exercise science (MS), including biomechanics, exercise physiology, motor control; health promotion (MS); human nutrition (MS). Part-time programs available. *Degree requirements:* For master's, thesis, registration. *Entrance requirements:* For master's, GRE General Test, interview, minimum GPA of 3.0. Additional exam requirements/recommendations for international students: Required—TOEFL (minimum score 550 paper-based; 213 computer-based). Electronic applications accepted. *Faculty research:* Sport biomechanics, rehabilitation biomechanics, vascular dynamics.

University of Florida, Graduate School, College of Health and Human Performance, Department of Applied Physiology and Kinesiology, Gainesville, FL 32611. Offers athletic training/sport medicine (MS, PhD); biomechanics (MS, PhD); clinical exercise physiology (MS); exercise physiology (MS, PhD); health and human performance (PhD); human performance (MS); motor learning/control (MS, PhD); sport and exercise psychology (MS). *Faculty:* 14 full-time (2 women), 1 part-time/adjunct (0 women). *Degree requirements:* For doctorate, thesis/dissertation. *Entrance requirements:* For doctorate, GRE General Test. *Application deadline:* For fall admission, 6/1 priority date for domestic students. Applications are processed on a rolling basis. Application fee: $20. Electronic applications accepted. *Expenses:* Tuition, state resident: full-time $6,827. Tuition, nonresident: full-time $21,951. Required fees: $999. *Financial support:* In 2006–07, 16 research assistantships (averaging $13,060 per year), 28 teaching assistantships (averaging $12,925 per year) were awarded; fellowships, unspecified assistantships also available. *Unit head:* Dr. Steven Dodd, Chair, 352-392-0584 Ext. 1342, E-mail: sdodd@hhp.ufl.edu. *Application contact:* Dr. Paul A. Borsa, Coordinator, 352-392-0584 Ext. 1261, Fax: 352-392-5262, E-mail: pborsa@hhp.ufl.edu.

University of Georgia, Graduate School, College of Education, Department of Kinesiology, Athens, GA 30602. Offers M Ed, MA, Ed D, PhD, Ed S. *Faculty:* 16 full-time (4 women). *Students:* 102 full-time (49 women), 23 part-time (9 women); includes 14 minority (11 African Americans, 3 Hispanic Americans), 14 international. Average age 27. 180 applicants, 43% accepted, 48 enrolled. In 2006, 44 master's, 8 doctorates awarded. *Entrance requirements:* For master's and Ed S, GRE General Test or MAT; for doctorate, GRE General Test. Additional exam requirements/recommendations for international students: Required—TOEFL. *Application deadline:* For fall admission, 7/1 priority date for domestic students; for spring admission, 11/15 for domestic students. Application fee: $50. Electronic applications accepted. *Unit head:* Dr. Kirk J. Cureton, Head, 706-542-4378, Fax: 706-542-3148, E-mail: kcureton@uga.edu. *Application contact:* Dr. Ted A. Baumgartner, Graduate Coordinator, 706-542-4424, Fax: 706-542-3148, E-mail: tbaumgar@uga.edu.

University of Hawaii at Manoa, Graduate Division, College of Education, Department of Kinesiology and Leisure Science, Honolulu, HI 96822. Offers kinesiology (MS). *Faculty:* 9 full-time (4 women). *Students:* 30 full-time (22 women), 12 part-time (4 women); includes 11 minority (2 African Americans, 1 American Indian/Alaska Native, 7 Asian Americans or Pacific

Kinesiology and Movement Studies

University of Hawaii at Manoa (continued)
Islanders, 1 Hispanic American), 1 international. Average age 32. 41 applicants, 41% accepted, 13 enrolled. In 2006, 9 degrees awarded. *Degree requirements:* For master's, thesis optional. *Entrance requirements:* For master's, GRE General Test. Additional exam requirements/recommendations for international students: Required—TOEFL (minimum score 540 paper-based; 207 computer-based; 76 iBT). *Application deadline:* For fall admission, 4/1 for domestic and international students; for spring admission, 11/1 for domestic and international students. Application fee: $50. *Financial support:* In 2006–07, 2 research assistantships (averaging $16,176 per year), 12 teaching assistantships (averaging $13,296 per year) were awarded. *Application contact:* Dr. Nathan Murata, Chairperson, 808-956-7606, Fax: 808-956-7976.

University of Houston, College of Education, Department of Health and Human Performance, Houston, TX 77204. Offers allied health (M Ed, Ed D); exercise science (MS); health education (M Ed); kinesiology (PhD); physical education (M Ed, Ed D). *Accreditation:* NCATE (one or more programs are accredited). Part-time and evening/weekend programs available. *Faculty:* 11 full-time (5 women), 6 part-time/adjunct (3 women). *Students:* 35 full-time (19 women), 33 part-time (17 women); includes 22 minority (12 African Americans, 1 Asian American or Pacific Islander, 9 Hispanic Americans), 1 international. Average age 29. 35 applicants, 54% accepted, 11 enrolled. In 2006, 24 master's, 4 doctorates awarded. *Degree requirements:* For master's, comprehensive exam or thesis; for doctorate, thesis/dissertation, comprehensive exam. *Entrance requirements:* For master's, GRE General Test or MAT; for doctorate, GRE General Test, interview. *Application deadline:* For fall admission, 7/3 for domestic students. Application fee: $35 ($75 for international students). *Expenses:* Tuition, state resident: full-time $5,429; part-time $226 per credit. Tuition, nonresident: full-time $12,029; part-time $501 per credit. Required fees: $2,454. *Financial support:* In 2006–07, 5 fellowships with full tuition reimbursements (averaging $9,500 per year), 4 research assistantships with full tuition reimbursements (averaging $9,850 per year), 9 teaching assistantships with full tuition reimbursements (averaging $9,850 per year) were awarded; career-related internships or fieldwork, Federal Work-Study, institutionally sponsored loans, scholarships/grants, health care benefits, and unspecified assistantships also available. Support available to part-time students. Financial award application deadline: 3/10. *Faculty research:* Motor development, physical fitness, comprehensive school health, leadership, sports law. *Unit head:* Dr. Chuck Layne, Chairperson, 713-743-9868, Fax: 713-743-9860, E-mail: clayne2@uh.edu.

University of Illinois at Chicago, Graduate College, College of Applied Health Sciences, School of Movement Sciences, Chicago, IL 60607-7128. Offers MS. Part-time programs available. *Degree requirements:* For master's, thesis. *Entrance requirements:* For master's, GRE General Test, minimum GPA of 2.75. Additional exam requirements/recommendations for international students: Required—TOEFL. Electronic applications accepted. *Faculty research:* Mitochondrial biogenesis, glucocorticoid lipid metabolism, at-risk youth, motor control.

University of Illinois at Urbana–Champaign, Graduate College, College of Applied Health Studies, Department of Kinesiology and Community Health, Champaign, IL 61820. Offers community health (MS, MSPH, PhD); kinesiology (MS, PhD). *Faculty:* 26 full-time (12 women), 1 part-time/adjunct (0 women). *Students:* 87 full-time (55 women), 4 part-time (2 women); includes 17 minority (11 African Americans, 5 Asian Americans or Pacific Islanders, 1 Hispanic American), 13 international. 95 applicants, 52% accepted, 29 enrolled. In 2006, 15 master's, 6 doctorates awarded. *Degree requirements:* For doctorate, thesis/dissertation. *Entrance requirements:* For master's, GRE General Test, minimum GPA of 3.0; for doctorate, GRE, minimum graduate GPA of 3.5. Additional exam requirements/recommendations for international students: Required—TOEFL. *Application deadline:* For fall admission, 1/15 priority date for domestic students. Applications are processed on a rolling basis. Application fee: $50 ($60 for international students). Electronic applications accepted. *Financial support:* In 2006–07, 13 fellowships, 43 research assistantships, 76 teaching assistantships were awarded; tuition waivers (full and partial) also available. Financial award application deadline: 2/15. *Unit head:* Wojtek Chodzko-Zajko, Head, 217-244-0823, Fax: 217-244-7322, E-mail: wojtek@uiuc.edu. *Application contact:* Deb Shilts, Administrative Aide, 217-333-1083, Fax: 217-244-7322, E-mail: dshilts@uiuc.edu.

University of Kentucky, Graduate School, College of Education, Program in Kinesiology and Health Promotion, Lexington, KY 40506-0032. Offers exercise science (PhD); kinesiology (MS, Ed D). *Faculty:* 13 full-time (4 women). *Students:* 82 full-time (46 women), 31 part-time (12 women); includes 15 minority (10 African Americans, 3 Asian Americans or Pacific Islanders, 2 Hispanic Americans), 2 international. Average age 29. 127 applicants, 55% accepted, 46 enrolled. In 2006, 37 master's, 3 doctorates awarded. Terminal master's awarded for partial completion of doctoral program. *Median time to degree:* Of those who began their doctoral program in fall 1998, 75% received their degree in 8 years or less. *Degree requirements:* For master's, thesis optional; for doctorate, thesis/dissertation, comprehensive exam. *Entrance requirements:* For master's, GRE General Test, minimum undergraduate GPA of 2.75; for doctorate, GRE General Test, minimum graduate GPA of 3.0. Additional exam requirements/recommendations for international students: Required—TOEFL (minimum score 550 paper-based; 213 computer-based). *Application deadline:* For fall admission, 7/17 priority date for domestic students, 2/1 priority date for international students; for spring admission, 12/13 priority date for domestic students, 6/15 priority date for international students. Application fee: $40 ($55 for international students). Electronic applications accepted. *Expenses:* Tuition, state resident: full-time $7,670; part-time $401 per credit hour. Tuition, nonresident: full-time $16,158; part-time $873 per credit hour. *Financial support:* In 2006–07, 2 fellowships with full tuition reimbursements (averaging $4,500 per year), 17 research assistantships with full tuition reimbursements (averaging $9,500 per year), 19 teaching assistantships with full tuition reimbursements (averaging $7,446 per year) were awarded; career-related internships or fieldwork, Federal Work-Study, institutionally sponsored loans, scholarships/grants, traineeships, health care benefits, tuition waivers (partial), and unspecified assistantships also available. Support available to part-time students. Financial award application deadline: 3/15. *Unit head:* Dr. Richard Riggs, Director of Graduate Studies, 859-257-3645, Fax: 859-323-1090. *Application contact:* Dr. Brian Jackson, Senior Associate Dean, 859-257-4667, Fax: 859-257-4676, E-mail: brian.jackson@uky.edu.

University of Lethbridge, School of Graduate Studies, Lethbridge, AB T1K 3M4, Canada. Offers accounting (MScM); addictions counseling (M Sc); agricultural biotechnology (M Sc); agricultural studies (M Sc, MA); anthropology (MA); archaeology (MA); art (MA); biochemistry (M Sc); biological sciences (M Sc); biomolecular science (PhD); biosystems and biodiversity (PhD); Canadian studies (MA); chemistry (M Sc); computer science (M Sc); computer science and geographical information science (M Sc); counseling psychology (M Ed); dramatic arts (MA); earth, space, and physical science (PhD); economics (MA); educational leadership (M Ed); English (MA); environmental science (M Sc); evolution and behavior (PhD); exercise science (M Sc); finance (MScM); French (MA); French/German (MA); French/Spanish (MA); general education (M Ed); general management (MScM); geography (M Sc, MA); German (MA); health sciences (M Sc, MA); history (MA); human resource management and labour relations (MScM); individualized multidisciplinary (M Sc, MA); information systems (MScM); international management (MScM); kinesiology (M Sc, MA); management (M Sc, MA); marketing (MScM); mathematics (M Sc); music (MA); Native American studies (MA); neuroscience (M Sc, PhD); new media (MA); nursing (M Sc); philosophy (MA); physics (M Sc); policy and strategy (MScM); political science (MA); psychology (M Sc, MA); religious studies (MA); sociology (MA); theoretical and computational science (PhD); urban and regional studies (MA). Part-time and evening/weekend programs available. *Students:* 200 full-time, 90 part-time. In 2006, 105 master's, 3 doctorates awarded. *Degree requirements:* For doctorate, thesis/dissertation, comprehensive exam. *Entrance requirements:* For master's, GMAT (M Sc management), bachelor's degree in related field, minimum GPA of 3.0 during previous 20 graded semester courses, 2 years teaching or related experience (M Ed); for doctorate, master's degree, minimum graduate GPA of 3.5. Additional exam requirements/recommendations for international students: Required—TOEFL. Application fee: $60 Canadian dollars. *Financial support:* Fellowships, research assistantships, teaching assistantships, scholarships/grants, health care benefits, and unspecified assistantships available. *Faculty research:* Movement and brain plasticity, gibberellin physiology, photosynthesis, carbon cycling, molecular properties of main-group ring components. *Unit head:* Dr. Jo-Anne Fiske, Interim Dean, 403-329-2121, Fax: 403-329-2097. *Application contact:* Kathy Schrage, Administrative Assistant, Office of the Academic Vice President, 403-329-2121, Fax: 403-329-2097, E-mail: inquiries@uleth.ca.

University of Maine, Graduate School, College of Education and Human Development, Program in Kinesiology and Physical Education, Orono, ME 04469. Offers M Ed, MS. Part-time and evening/weekend programs available. *Students:* 13 full-time (5 women), 17 part-time (9 women); includes 1 minority (Hispanic American), 1 international. Average age 30. 8 applicants, 88% accepted, 7 enrolled. In 2006, 8 degrees awarded. *Degree requirements:* For master's, thesis or alternative. *Entrance requirements:* For master's, MAT. Additional exam requirements/recommendations for international students: Required—TOEFL. *Application deadline:* For fall admission, 2/1 priority date for domestic students. Applications are processed on a rolling basis. Application fee: $50. Electronic applications accepted. *Financial support:* In 2006–07, teaching assistantships with tuition reimbursements (averaging $9,010 per year); research assistantships with tuition reimbursements, career-related internships or fieldwork, Federal Work-Study, institutionally sponsored loans, tuition waivers (full and partial), and unspecified assistantships also available. Support available to part-time students. Financial award application deadline: 3/1. *Unit head:* Dr. Dorothy Breen, Coordinator, 207-581-2444, Fax: 207-581-2423. *Application contact:* Scott G. Delcourt, Associate Dean of the Graduate School, 207-581-3219, Fax: 207-581-3232, E-mail: graduate@maine.edu.

University of Maryland, College Park, Graduate Studies, College of Health and Human Performance, Department of Kinesiology, College Park, MD 20742. Offers MA, PhD. Part-time and evening/weekend programs available. *Faculty:* 31 full-time (7 women), 5 part-time/adjunct (4 women). *Students:* 68 full-time (33 women), 8 part-time (3 women); includes 9 minority (4 African Americans, 5 Asian Americans or Pacific Islanders), 26 international. 73 applicants, 19% accepted, 12 enrolled. In 2006, 5 master's, 5 doctorates awarded. *Median time to degree:* Of those who began their doctoral program in fall 1998, 42% received their degree in 8 years or less. *Degree requirements:* For master's, thesis optional; for doctorate, thesis/dissertation. *Entrance requirements:* For master's, GRE General Test, minimum GPA of 3.0, 3 letters of recommendation; for doctorate, GRE General Test, minimum GPA of 3.5, 3 letters of recommendation. *Application deadline:* For fall admission, 12/1 for domestic students, 2/1 for international students; for spring admission, 6/1 for domestic and international students. Applications are processed on a rolling basis. Application fee: $60. Electronic applications accepted. *Financial support:* In 2006–07, 10 fellowships with full tuition reimbursements (averaging $15,517 per year), 11 research assistantships with tuition reimbursements (averaging $14,699 per year), 28 teaching assistantships with tuition reimbursements (averaging $14,229 per year) were awarded; career-related internships or fieldwork, Federal Work-Study, and scholarships/grants also available. Support available to part-time students. Financial award applicants required to submit FAFSA. *Faculty research:* Sports, biophysical and professional studies, cognitive motor behavior, exercise physiology. Total annual research expenditures: $2.9 million. *Unit head:* Dr. Jane E. Clark, Chairman, 301-405-2450, Fax: 301-405-5578, E-mail: jeclark@umd.edu. *Application contact:* Dean of Graduate School, 301-405-4190, Fax: 301-314-9305.

University of Massachusetts Amherst, Graduate School, School of Public Health and Health Sciences, Department of Kinesiology, Amherst, MA 01003. Offers MS, PhD. Part-time programs available. *Faculty:* 11 full-time (3 women). *Students:* 24 full-time (12 women), 22 part-time (12 women); includes 5 minority (1 African American, 4 Hispanic Americans), 10 international. Average age 28. 64 applicants, 33% accepted, 16 enrolled. In 2006, 12 master's, 3 doctorates awarded. Terminal master's awarded for partial completion of doctoral program. *Degree requirements:* For master's, thesis optional; for doctorate, thesis/dissertation. *Entrance requirements:* For master's and doctorate, GRE General Test. Additional exam requirements/recommendations for international students: Required—TOEFL (minimum score 530 paper-based; 197 computer-based). *Application deadline:* For fall admission, 2/1 priority date for domestic and international students. Applications are processed on a rolling basis. Application fee: $40 ($65 for international students). Electronic applications accepted. *Expenses:* Tuition, state resident: full-time $2,640; part-time $110 per credit. Tuition, nonresident: full-time $9,936; part-time $414 per credit. Required fees: $8,969; $3,129 per term. One-time fee: $257 full-time. Tuition and fees vary according to class time, course load, campus/location and reciprocity agreements. *Financial support:* In 2006–07, 3 fellowships with full tuition reimbursements (averaging $17,402 per year), 29 research assistantships with full tuition reimbursements (averaging $7,417 per year), 27 teaching assistantships with full tuition reimbursements (averaging $6,471 per year) were awarded; career-related internships or fieldwork, Federal Work-Study, scholarships/grants, traineeships, and unspecified assistantships also available. Support available to part-time students. Financial award application deadline: 2/1. *Unit head:* Dr. Patty Freedson, Head, 413-545-070, Fax: 413-545-2906, E-mail: psf@kin.umass.edu.

University of Medicine and Dentistry of New Jersey, School of Health Related Professions, Department of Interdisciplinary Studies, Program in Health Sciences, Newark, NJ 07107-1709. Offers cardiopulmonary sciences (PhD); clinical laboratory sciences (PhD); health sciences (MS); interdisciplinary studies (PhD); nutrition (PhD); physical therapy/movement science (PhD). *Degree requirements:* For doctorate, thesis/dissertation. *Entrance requirements:* For doctorate, interview, writing sample. Additional exam requirements/recommendations for international students: Required—TOEFL. *Application deadline:* For fall admission, 3/1 for domestic students. Applications are processed on a rolling basis. Application fee: $50. Electronic applications accepted. *Unit head:* Dr. Margaret Kildoff, Director, 973-972-4989, Fax: 973-972-7854, E-mail: ms-phd-hs@umdnj.edu.

University of Michigan, Horace H. Rackham School of Graduate Studies, Division of Kinesiology, Ann Arbor, MI 48109. Offers kinesiology (MS, PhD); sport management (AM). Terminal master's awarded for partial completion of doctoral program. *Degree requirements:* For master's, thesis (for some programs); for doctorate, thesis/dissertation, oral defense of dissertation, comprehensive exam. *Entrance requirements:* For master's and doctorate, GRE General Test. Additional exam requirements/recommendations for international students: Required—TOEFL. Electronic applications accepted. Expenses: Contact institution. *Faculty research:* Motor development, exercise endocrinology, biomechanics, body composition and weight control, sport management.

University of Minnesota, Twin Cities Campus, Graduate School, College of Education and Human Development, School of Kinesiology, Division of Kinesiology, Minneapolis, MN 55455-0213. Offers M Ed, MA, PhD. Part-time programs available. *Students:* 113 full-time (53 women), 60 part-time (24 women); includes 8 minority (3 African Americans, 2 Asian Americans or Pacific Islanders, 3 Hispanic Americans), 13 international. Average age 29. 152 applicants, 30% accepted, 36 enrolled. In 2006, 113 master's, 45 doctorates awarded. Terminal master's awarded for partial completion of doctoral program. *Degree requirements:* For master's, thesis (for some programs), final oral exam; for doctorate, thesis/dissertation, preliminary written/oral exam, final oral exam. *Entrance requirements:* For master's, GRE or MAT, minimum GPA of 3.0; for doctorate, GRE or MAT, minimum GPA of 3.0, writing sample. *Application deadline:* Applications are processed on a rolling basis. *Expenses:* Tuition, state resident: full-time $9,302; part-time $775 per credit. Tuition, nonresident: full-time $16,400; part-time $1,367 per credit. Full-time tuition and fees vary according to class time, course load, program, reciprocity agreements and student level. *Financial support:* Fellowships, research assistantships, teaching assistantships, career-related internships or fieldwork, Federal Work-Study, institutionally sponsored loans, and tuition waivers (full and partial) available. Support available to part-time students. *Application contact:* Dr. Mary Bents, Associate Dean, 612-625-6501, Fax: 612-626-1580, E-mail: mbents@tc.umn.edu.

University of Nevada, Las Vegas, Graduate College, Division of Health Sciences, Department of Kinesiology, Las Vegas, NV 89154-9900. Offers exercise physiology (MS); kinesiology (MS).

Part-time programs available. *Faculty:* 11 full-time (2 women), 2 part-time/adjunct (both women). *Students:* 19 full-time (8 women), 22 part-time (12 women); includes 6 minority (2 African Americans, 3 Asian Americans or Pacific Islanders, 1 Hispanic American), 1 international. 47 applicants, 57% accepted, 13 enrolled. In 2006, 11 degrees awarded. *Degree requirements:* For master's, thesis (for some programs), comprehensive exam (for some programs). *Entrance requirements:* For master's, GRE General Test, minimum GPA of 3.0 during previous 2 years, 2.75 overall. Additional exam requirements/recommendations for international students: Required—TOEFL (minimum score 550 paper-based; 213 computer-based; 80 iBT). *Application deadline:* For fall admission, 6/15 for domestic students, 5/1 for international students; for spring admission, 11/15 for domestic students, 10/1 for international students. Application fee: $60 ($75 for international students). Electronic applications accepted. *Financial support:* In 2006–07, 10 research assistantships with partial tuition reimbursements (averaging $10,000 per year), 3 teaching assistantships with partial tuition reimbursements (averaging $10,000 per year) were awarded; career-related internships or fieldwork, Federal Work-Study, institutionally sponsored loans, scholarships/grants, health care benefits, and unspecified assistantships also available. Support available to part-time students. Financial award application deadline: 3/1. *Unit head:* Dr. John Mercer, Chair, 702-895-3766. *Application contact:* Graduate College Admissions Evaluator, 702-895-3320, Fax: 702-895-4180, E-mail: gradcollege@unlv.edu.

University of New Hampshire, Graduate School, School of Health and Human Services, Department of Kinesiology, Durham, NH 03824. Offers MS. Part-time programs available. *Faculty:* 11 full-time. *Students:* 8 full-time (4 women), 12 part-time (6 women), 1 international. Average age 27. 19 applicants, 58% accepted, 7 enrolled. In 2006, 10 degrees awarded. *Degree requirements:* For master's, thesis or alternative. *Entrance requirements:* For master's, GRE General Test. Additional exam requirements/recommendations for international students: Required—TOEFL (minimum score 550 paper-based; 213 computer-based). *Application deadline:* For fall admission, 4/1 priority date for domestic students, 4/1 for international students; for winter admission, 12/1 for domestic students; for spring admission, 2/1 for domestic students. Applications are processed on a rolling basis. Application fee: $60. *Expenses:* Tuition, state resident: full-time $8,540; part-time $474 per credit hour. Tuition, nonresident: full-time $20,990; part-time $862 per credit hour. Required fees: $1,343; $356 per term. Tuition and fees vary according to course load, program and reciprocity agreements. *Financial support:* In 2006–07, 1 fellowship, 7 teaching assistantships were awarded; research assistantships, career-related internships or fieldwork, Federal Work-Study, scholarships/grants, and tuition waivers (full and partial) also available. Support available to part-time students. Financial award application deadline: 2/15. *Faculty research:* Exercise specialist, sports studies, special physical education, pediatric exercises and motor behavior. *Unit head:* Dr. Heather Barber, Chairperson, 603-862-2058. *Application contact:* Kate Mallen, Administrative Assistant, 603-862-2071, E-mail: kinesiology.dept@unh.edu.

The University of North Carolina at Chapel Hill, School of Medicine and Graduate School, Graduate Programs in Medicine, Chapel Hill, NC 27599. Offers allied health sciences (MPT, MS, Au D, DPT, PhD), including human movement science (MS, PhD), occupational science (MS, PhD), physical therapy (MPT, MS, DPT), rehabilitation counseling and psychology (MS), speech and hearing sciences (MS, Au D, PhD); biochemistry and biophysics (MS, PhD); biomedical engineering (MS, PhD); cell and developmental biology (PhD); cell and molecular physiology (PhD); genetics and molecular biology (PhD); microbiology and immunology (MS, PhD), including immunology, microbiology; neurobiology (PhD); pathology and laboratory medicine (PhD), including experimental pathology; pharmacology (PhD); MD/PhD. Post-baccalaureate distance learning degree programs offered. *Faculty:* 470 full-time (156 women), 101 part-time/adjunct (17 women). *Students:* 730 full-time (447 women), 36 part-time (27 women); includes 110 minority (43 African Americans, 6 American Indian/Alaska Native, 48 Asian Americans or Pacific Islanders, 13 Hispanic Americans), 79 international. In 2006, 73 master's, 62 doctorates awarded. Terminal master's awarded for partial completion of doctoral program. *Degree requirements:* For master's, comprehensive exam; for doctorate, thesis/dissertation. *Application deadline:* Applications are processed on a rolling basis. Application fee: $65. Electronic applications accepted. *Expenses:* Contact institution. *Financial support:* In 2006–07, 77 fellowships with full and partial tuition reimbursements, 309 research assistantships with full tuition reimbursements, 23 teaching assistantships with full tuition reimbursements were awarded; career-related internships or fieldwork, Federal Work-Study, institutionally sponsored loans, traineeships, tuition waivers (full and partial), and unspecified assistantships also available. Support available to part-time students. Financial award applicants required to submit FAFSA. *Unit head:* Dr. William L. Roper, Dean, 919-966-4161, Fax: 919-966-6354.

The University of North Carolina at Chapel Hill, School of Medicine and Graduate School, Graduate Programs in Medicine, Department of Allied Health Sciences, Curriculum in Human Movement Science, Chapel Hill, NC 27599. Offers PhD. *Faculty:* 14 full-time (10 women), 3 part-time/adjunct (2 women). *Students:* 18 full-time (13 women), 2 part-time (both women); includes 5 minority (4 Asian Americans or Pacific Islanders, 1 Hispanic American). Average age 29. 38 applicants, 16% accepted, 4 enrolled. In 2006, 1 degree awarded. *Degree requirements:* For doctorate, thesis/dissertation or alternative, comprehensive exam. *Entrance requirements:* For doctorate, GRE General Test, curriculum vitae, minimum GPA of 3.0. Additional exam requirements/recommendations for international students: Required—TOEFL (minimum score 550 paper-based; 79 computer-based). *Application deadline:* For fall admission, 12/1 priority date for domestic students, 12/1 for international students. Applications are processed on a rolling basis. Application fee: $70. Electronic applications accepted. *Financial support:* In 2006–07, 3 fellowships with tuition reimbursements (averaging $15,000 per year), 5 research assistantships with tuition reimbursements (averaging $5,833 per year), 4 teaching assistantships (averaging $12,000 per year) were awarded; career-related internships or fieldwork also available. Financial award application deadline: 12/1. *Faculty research:* Orthopaedics, neuromuscular, biomedical endocrinology, postural cortol developmental disabilities. Total annual research expenditures: $217,647. *Unit head:* Carol A. Giuliani, Director, 919-843-8792, Fax: 919-966-3678, E-mail: carol-giuliani@med.unc.edu. *Application contact:* William C. Smithson, Registrar, 919-966-4708, Fax: 919-966-3678, E-mail: willsmit@med.unc.edu.

The University of North Carolina at Chapel Hill, School of Medicine and Graduate School, Graduate Programs in Medicine, Department of Allied Health Sciences, Program in Human Movement Science, Chapel Hill, NC 27599. Offers MS. *Faculty:* 14 full-time (10 women), 3 part-time/adjunct (2 women). *Students:* 1 full-time (0 women). Average age 33. 3 applicants, 33% accepted, 1 enrolled. *Degree requirements:* For master's, thesis or alternative, comprehensive exam. *Entrance requirements:* For master's, GRE General Test, course work, 1 year of experience, curriculum vitae, minimum GPA of 3.0. Additional exam requirements/recommendations for international students: Required—TOEFL (minimum score 550 paper-based; 79 computer-based). *Application deadline:* For fall admission, 12/1 priority date for domestic students, 12/1 for international students. Applications are processed on a rolling basis. Application fee: $55. Electronic applications accepted. *Financial support:* In 2006–07, 2 research assistantships with tuition reimbursements (averaging $5,000 per year), 1 teaching assistantship (averaging $6,000 per year) were awarded; fellowships with tuition reimbursements, career-related internships or fieldwork also available. Financial award application deadline: 12/1; financial award applicants required to submit FAFSA. Total annual research expenditures: $217,647. *Unit head:* Darlene K. Sekerak, Associate Professor, Director, 919-843-8660, Fax: 919-966-3678, E-mail: darlene_sekerak@med.unc.edu. *Application contact:* William C. Smithson, Registrar, 919-966-4708, Fax: 919-966-3678, E-mail: willsmit@med.unc.edu.

The University of North Carolina at Chapel Hill, School of Medicine and Graduate School, Graduate Programs in Medicine, Department of Allied Health Sciences, Program in Physical Therapy, Chapel Hill, NC 27599. Offers human movement science (MS); physical therapy (MPT, DPT). *Accreditation:* APTA. Part-time and evening/weekend programs available. Post-baccalaureate distance learning degree programs offered (no on-campus study). *Faculty:* 14 full-time (10 women), 3 part-time/adjunct (2 women). *Students:* 57 full-time (47 women), 32 part-time (24 women); includes 10 minority (6 African Americans, 1 American Indian/Alaska Native, 3 Asian Americans or Pacific Islanders). Average age 43. 189 applicants, 39% accepted, 54 enrolled. In 2006, 16 master's, 15 doctorates awarded. *Degree requirements:* For master's, thesis/dissertation or alternative, comprehensive exam; for doctorate, thesis/dissertation or alternative. *Entrance requirements:* For master's, GRE General Test, minimum GPA of 3.0, prerequisite coursework, experience with physical therapy; for doctorate, physical therapy license. Additional exam requirements/recommendations for international students: Required—TOEFL (minimum score 550 paper-based; 79 computer-based). *Application deadline:* For fall admission, 11/1 for domestic and international students. Application fee: $70. Electronic applications accepted. *Financial support:* In 2006–07, 49 students received support, including 2 fellowships with tuition reimbursements available (averaging $9,000 per year); research assistantships with tuition reimbursements available, career-related internships or fieldwork and institutionally sponsored loans also available. Financial award application deadline: 11/1; financial award applicants required to submit FAFSA. *Faculty research:* Traumatic brain injury, quality of life after heart and/or lung transplant, cultural diversity, life care planning, rehabilitation education and supervision. Total annual research expenditures: $253,511. *Unit head:* Dr. Darlene K. Sekerak, Associate Professor and Director, 919-843-8660, Fax: 919-966-3678, E-mail: darlene_sekerak@med.unc.edu. *Application contact:* William C. Smithson, Registrar, 919-966-4708, Fax: 919-966-3678, E-mail: willsmit@med.unc.edu.

The University of North Carolina at Charlotte, Graduate School, College of Health and Human Services, Department of Kinesiology, Charlotte, NC 28223-0001. Offers clinical exercise physiology (MS). *Faculty:* 4 full-time (2 women). *Students:* 11 full-time (8 women), 8 part-time (all women); includes 2 minority (1 African American, 1 Asian American or Pacific Islander). Average age 26. 12 applicants, 83% accepted, 6 enrolled. In 2006, 2 degrees awarded. *Entrance requirements:* For master's, GRE or MAT. Additional exam requirements/recommendations for international students: Required—TOEFL (minimum score 557 paper-based; 220 computer-based). *Application deadline:* For fall admission, 7/1 for domestic students, 5/1 for international students; for spring admission, 11/1 for domestic students, 10/1 for international students. Applications are processed on a rolling basis. Application fee: $55. Electronic applications accepted. *Expenses:* Tuition, state resident: full-time $2,719; part-time $170 per credit. Tuition, nonresident: full-time $12,926; part-time $808 per credit. Required fees: $1,555. *Financial support:* In 2006–07, 7 research assistantships (averaging $11,607 per year), 4 teaching assistantships (averaging $12,000 per year) were awarded; fellowships, career-related internships or fieldwork, Federal Work-Study, institutionally sponsored loans, scholarships/grants, traineeships, and unspecified assistantships also available. Support available to part-time students. Financial award application deadline: 4/1; financial award applicants required to submit FAFSA. *Faculty research:* Genetic determinants of physical activity, cardiac muscle apoptosis with aging, sensorimotor deficits in knee osteoarthritis, mechanical laxity in functionally ankle instability. *Unit head:* Dr. Mitchell L. Cordova, Chair, 704-687-4695, Fax: 704-687-3180, E-mail: mcordova@email.uncc.edu. *Application contact:* Kathy B. Giddings, Director of Graduate Admissions, 704-687-3366, Fax: 704-687-3279, E-mail: gradadm@email.uncc.edu.

University of North Dakota, Graduate School, College of Education and Human Development, Department of Kinesiology, Grand Forks, ND 58202. Offers MS. Part-time programs available. *Faculty:* 5 full-time (1 woman), 1 part-time/adjunct (0 women). *Students:* 15 full-time (6 women); includes 1 minority (American Indian/Alaska Native), 3 international. 21 applicants, 48% accepted, 10 enrolled. In 2006, 11 degrees awarded. *Degree requirements:* For master's, thesis or alternative, final exam or comprehensive examination. *Entrance requirements:* For master's, GRE General Test, minimum GPA of 3.0. Additional exam requirements/recommendations for international students: Required—TOEFL (minimum score 550 paper-based; 213 computer-based; 79 iBT), IELTS (minimum score 6). *Application deadline:* For fall admission, 2/15 priority date for domestic and international students; for spring admission, 10/15 priority date for domestic and international students. Applications are processed on a rolling basis. Application fee: $35. Electronic applications accepted. *Expenses:* Tuition, state resident: full-time $5,650; part-time $214 per credit. Tuition, nonresident: full-time $14,248; part-time $572 per credit. Required fees: $1,008; $42 per credit. Tuition and fees vary according to reciprocity agreements. *Financial support:* In 2006–07, 1 research assistantship (averaging $5,206 per year), 5 teaching assistantships with full tuition reimbursements (averaging $6,074 per year) were awarded; fellowships, Federal Work-Study, institutionally sponsored loans, scholarships/grants, tuition waivers (full and partial), and unspecified assistantships also available. Support available to part-time students. Financial award application deadline: 3/15; financial award applicants required to submit FAFSA. *Faculty research:* Exercise physiology, exercise biomechanics, anatomy and physiology, exercise psychology. *Unit head:* Dr. Sandra E. Short, Graduate Director, 701-777-4325, Fax: 701-777-3619, E-mail: sandra_short@und.nodak.edu. *Application contact:* Brenda Halle, Admissions Specialist, 701-777-2947, Fax: 701-777-3619, E-mail: brendahalle@mail.und.edu.

University of North Texas, Robert B. Toulouse School of Graduate Studies, College of Education, Department of Kinesiology, Health Promotion, and Recreation, Program in Kinesiology, Denton, TX 76203. Offers MS. Part-time programs available. *Students:* 21 full-time (13 women), 24 part-time (13 women); includes 17 minority (9 African Americans, 2 Asian Americans or Pacific Islanders, 6 Hispanic Americans). Average age 28. 50 applicants, 60% accepted, 20 enrolled. In 2006, 30 degrees awarded. *Entrance requirements:* For master's, GRE General Test. Additional exam requirements/recommendations for international students: Recommended—TOEFL (minimum score 550 paper-based; 213 computer-based). *Application deadline:* For fall admission, 7/15 for domestic students. Application fee: $50 ($75 for international students). *Expenses:* Tuition, state resident: full-time $3,573; part-time $198 per credit. Tuition, nonresident: full-time $8,577; part-time $476 per credit. Required fees: $1,258; $126 per credit. One-time fee: $150 full-time. Tuition and fees vary according to course load. *Financial support:* Teaching assistantships, career-related internships or fieldwork, Federal Work-Study, and institutionally sponsored loans available. Financial award application deadline: 4/1. *Application contact:* Dr. Noreen Goggin, Graduate Adviser, 940-565-2212, Fax: 940-565-4904, E-mail: goggin@unt.edu.

University of Ottawa, Faculty of Graduate and Postdoctoral Studies, Faculty of Health Sciences, School of Human Kinetics, Ottawa, ON K1N 6N5, Canada. Offers MA. *Degree requirements:* For master's, thesis or alternative. *Entrance requirements:* For master's, honors degree or equivalent, minimum B average. Electronic applications accepted. *Faculty research:* Psychosocial sciences, physical and health administration of sport and physical activity, intervention and consultation in sport, physical activity and health.

University of Regina, Faculty of Graduate Studies and Research, Faculty of Kinesiology and Health Studies, Regina, SK S4S 0A2, Canada. Offers kinesiology and health studies (PhD); physical activity studies (M Sc). *Faculty:* 14 full-time (3 women), 3 part-time/adjunct (0 women). *Students:* 19 full-time (11 women), 11 part-time (6 women). 10 applicants, 100% accepted. In 2006, 3 degrees awarded. *Degree requirements:* For master's and doctorate, thesis/dissertation, registration. *Entrance requirements:* Additional exam requirements/recommendations for international students: Required—TOEFL (minimum score 580 paper-based; 237 computer-based; 88 iBT). *Application deadline:* Applications are processed on a rolling basis. Application fee: $60 ($100 for international students). *Financial support:* In 2006–07, 3 fellowships (averaging $14,886 per year), 1 research assistantship (averaging $12,750 per year), 3 teaching assistantships (averaging $13,501 per year) were awarded; scholarships/grants also available. *Unit head:* Dr. Craig Chamberlin, Dean, 306-585-4876, Fax: 306-585-4854, E-mail: craig.chamberlin@uregina.ca. *Application contact:* Dr. Kim Dorsch, Program Coordinator, 306-585-4742, E-mail: kim.dorsch@uregina.ca.

University of Saskatchewan, College of Graduate Studies and Research, College of Kinesiology, Saskatoon, SK S7N 5A2, Canada. Offers M Sc, PhD, Diploma. *Degree requirements:* For master's and doctorate, thesis/dissertation, registration. *Entrance requirements:* Additional exam requirements/recommendations for international students: Required—TOEFL.

University of Southern California, Graduate School, Independent Health Professions, Department of Biokinesiology and Physical Therapy, Program in Biokinesiology, Los Angeles, CA

Kinesiology and Movement Studies

University of Southern California (continued)
90089. Offers MS, PhD. *Students:* 29 full-time (20 women), 4 part-time (1 woman); includes 4 minority (2 Asian Americans or Pacific Islanders, 2 Hispanic Americans), 17 international. In 2006, 1 degree awarded. *Degree requirements:* For doctorate, thesis/dissertation. *Entrance requirements:* For master's and doctorate, GRE General Test. *Application deadline:* For fall admission, 12/1 priority date for domestic students. Application fee: $85. *Expenses:* Tuition: Full-time $33,314; part-time $1,121 per credit. Required fees: $522. Full-time tuition and fees vary according to program. *Financial support:* In 2006–07, research assistantships with full tuition reimbursements (averaging $18,500 per year), teaching assistantships with full tuition reimbursements (averaging $18,500 per year) were awarded; fellowships, Federal Work-Study and institutionally sponsored loans also available. Support available to part-time students. Financial award application deadline: 2/15; financial award applicants required to submit FAFSA.

The University of Tennessee, Graduate School, College of Education, Health and Human Sciences, Department of Exercise, Sport, and Leisure Studies, Program in Exercise Science, Knoxville, TN 37996. Offers biomechanics/sports medicine (MS, PhD); exercise physiology (MS, PhD). *Accreditation:* CEPH (one or more programs are accredited). Part-time programs available. *Faculty:* 13 full-time (4 women). *Students:* 28 (21 women); includes 1 African American 4 international. In 2006, 5 degrees awarded. *Degree requirements:* For master's, thesis optional. *Entrance requirements:* For master's, minimum GPA of 2.7. Additional exam requirements/recommendations for international students: Required—TOEFL. *Application deadline:* For fall admission, 2/1 priority date for domestic students. Application fee: $35. Electronic applications accepted. *Expenses:* Tuition, state resident: full-time $5,574. Tuition, nonresident: full-time $16,840. Required fees: $792. *Financial support:* In 2006–07, 1 fellowship, 10 teaching assistantships were awarded; research assistantships, career-related internships or fieldwork, Federal Work-Study, institutionally sponsored loans, and unspecified assistantships also available. Financial award application deadline: 2/1; financial award applicants required to submit FAFSA. *Unit head:* Dr. Delores Smith, Interim Head, 865-974-5041, Fax: 865-974-6439, E-mail: delsmith@utk.edu.

The University of Texas at Austin, Graduate School, College of Education, Department of Kinesiology and Health Education, Austin, TX 78712-1111. Offers health education (M Ed, MA, Ed D, PhD); kinesiology (M Ed, MA, Ed D, PhD). Part-time programs available. Terminal master's awarded for partial completion of doctoral program. *Degree requirements:* For master's, thesis (for some programs); for doctorate, thesis/dissertation. *Entrance requirements:* For master's and doctorate, GRE General Test. Additional exam requirements/recommendations for international students: Required—TOEFL. Electronic applications accepted. *Faculty research:* Health promotion, human performance and exercise biochemistry, motor behavior and biomechanics, sport management, aging and pediatric development.

The University of Texas at El Paso, Graduate School, College of Health Sciences, School of Allied Health, Program in Kinesiology and Sports Studies, El Paso, TX 79968-0001. Offers MS. Part-time and evening/weekend programs available. *Degree requirements:* For master's, thesis optional. *Entrance requirements:* For master's, GRE General Test. Additional exam requirements/recommendations for international students: Required—TOEFL. Electronic applications accepted.

The University of Texas at Tyler, College of Nursing and Health Sciences, Department of Health and Kinesiology, Tyler, TX 75799-0001. Offers clinical exercise physiology (MS); health and kinesiology (M Ed); kinesiology (MS). Part-time programs available. Postbaccalaureate distance learning degree programs offered. *Faculty:* 8 full-time (2 women), 8 part-time/adjunct (5 women). *Students:* 16 full-time (10 women), 29 part-time (15 women); includes 7 minority (5 African Americans, 1 Asian American or Pacific Islander, 1 Hispanic American). Average age 27. 27 applicants, 21 enrolled. In 2006, 20 degrees awarded. *Degree requirements:* For master's, thesis (for some programs), comprehensive exam (for some programs). *Application deadline:* Applications are processed on a rolling basis. Application fee: $0 ($50 for international students). Electronic applications accepted. *Expenses:* Tuition, state resident: part-time $50 per credit hour. Tuition, nonresident: part-time $328 per credit hour. Required fees: $107 per credit hour. $426 per term. *Financial support:* In 2006–07, 2 teaching assistantships (averaging $6,000 per year) were awarded; research assistantships, Federal Work-Study and scholarships/grants also available. Financial award application deadline: 7/1. *Faculty research:* Osteoporosis, muscle soreness, economy of locomotion, adoption of rehabilitation programs, effect of inactivity and aging on muscle blood vessels, territoriality. *Unit head:* Dr. James Schwane, Chairperson, 903-566-7306, Fax: 903-566-7065, E-mail: jschwane@mail.uttyl.edu. *Application contact:* Bonnie Purser, Office of Graduate Studies, 903-566-7142, Fax: 903-566-7068, E-mail: bpurser@uttyler.edu.

The University of Texas of the Permian Basin, Office of Graduate Studies, College of Arts and Sciences, Department of Behavioral Science, Program in Kinesiology, Odessa, TX 79762-0001. Offers MS. Part-time and evening/weekend programs available. Postbaccalaureate distance learning degree programs offered (no on-campus study). *Degree requirements:* For master's, thesis (for some programs), comprehensive exam (for some programs), registration. *Entrance requirements:* For master's, GRE General Test, minimum GPA of 2.5. Additional exam requirements/recommendations for international students: Required—TOEFL (minimum score 550 paper-based; 213 computer-based).

The University of Texas–Pan American, College of Education, Department of Health and Kinesiology, Edinburg, TX 78541-2999. Offers kinesiology (MS). Part-time and evening/weekend programs available. Postbaccalaureate distance learning degree programs offered (no on-campus study). *Degree requirements:* For master's, oral exam, thesis optional. *Entrance requirements:* For master's, minimum GPA of 3.0 in last 60 hours. *Expenses:* Tuition, state resident: full-time $2,577; part-time $143 per credit hour. Tuition, nonresident: full-time $7,527; part-time $418 per credit hour. Required fees: $561. *Faculty research:* History, physiology of exercise, fitness levels, Mexican-American children, winter tourist profiles, sports psychology.

University of the Incarnate Word, School of Graduate Studies and Research, Dreeben School of Education, Programs in Education, San Antonio, TX 78209-6397. Offers adult education (M Ed, MA); diversity education (M Ed, MA); early childhood education (M Ed, MA); instructional technology (M Ed, MA); international education and entrepreneurship (PhD); kinesiology (M Ed, MA); mathematics education (PhD); organizational leadership (PhD); organizational learning (M Ed, MA); reading (M Ed, MA); special education (M Ed, MA). *Students:* 15 full-time (8 women), 179 part-time (117 women); includes 70 minority (20 African Americans, 1 American Indian/Alaska Native, 1 Asian American or Pacific Islander, 48 Hispanic Americans), 54 international. Average age 39. In 2006, 15 degrees awarded. Application fee: $20. *Expenses:* Tuition: Part-time $570 per credit hour. Required fees: $54 per credit hour. One-time fee: $195 part-time. Tuition and fees vary according to degree level. *Financial support:* Federal Work-Study and scholarships/grants available. *Unit head:* Dr. Richard Gray, Director, 210-829-3138, Fax: 210-829-3134, E-mail: gray@uiwtx.edu. *Application contact:* Andrea Cyterski-Acosta, Dean of Enrollment, 210-829-6005, Fax: 210-829-3921, E-mail: cyterski@uiwtx.edu.

University of the Incarnate Word, School of Graduate Studies and Research, School of Nursing and Health Professions, Program in Human Performance, San Antonio, TX 78209-6397. Offers kinesiology (MS); sports management (MS). *Students:* Average age 27. In 2006, 3 degrees awarded. *Entrance requirements:* Additional exam requirements/recommendations for international students: Required—TOEFL. *Application deadline:* For fall admission, 8/15 priority date for domestic students; for spring admission, 12/31 for domestic students. Applications are processed on a rolling basis. Application fee: $20. *Expenses:* Tuition: Part-time $570 per credit hour. Required fees: $54 per credit hour. One-time fee: $195 part-time. Tuition and fees vary according to degree level. *Financial support:* Federal Work-Study and scholarships/grants available. *Unit head:* Dr. William Carleton, Coordinator, 210-829-3966, Fax: 210-829-3174, E-mail: carleton@uiwtx.edu. *Application contact:* Andrea Cyterski-Acosta, Dean of Enrollment, 210-829-6005, Fax: 210-829-3921, E-mail: cyterski@uiwtx.edu.

University of Victoria, Faculty of Graduate Studies, Faculty of Education, School of Physical Education, Victoria, BC V8W 2Y2, Canada. Offers coaching studies (co-operative education) (M Ed); kinesiology (M Sc, MA); leisure service administration (MA); physical education (MA). Part-time programs available. *Degree requirements:* For master's, thesis (for some programs), comprehensive exam (for some programs), registration. *Entrance requirements:* For master's, minimum B average. Additional exam requirements/recommendations for international students: Required—TOEFL (minimum score 575 paper-based; 233 computer-based), IELTS (minimum score 7). Electronic applications accepted. *Faculty research:* Children and exercise, mental skills in sports, teaching effectiveness, neural control of human movement, physical performance and health.

University of Virginia, Curry School of Education, Department of Human Services, Program in Health and Physical Education, Charlottesville, VA 22903. Offers kinesiology (M Ed, Ed D). *Students:* 37 full-time (19 women), 2 part-time; includes 2 minority (1 African American, 1 Asian American or Pacific Islander). Average age 25. 28 applicants, 68% accepted, 8 enrolled. In 2006, 33 degrees awarded. *Degree requirements:* For master's, thesis (for some programs), comprehensive exam (for some programs); for doctorate, thesis/dissertation, comprehensive exam. *Entrance requirements:* For master's and doctorate, GRE General Test. *Application deadline:* Applications are processed on a rolling basis. Application fee: $60. Electronic applications accepted. *Financial support:* Applicants required to submit FAFSA. *Unit head:* Glenn A. Gaesser, Chair, 434-924-3543. *Application contact:* Roberta Camb, Information Contact, 434-924-6207, E-mail: rcl8b@virginia.edu.

University of Waterloo, Graduate Studies, Faculty of Applied Health Sciences, Department of Kinesiology, Waterloo, ON N2L 3G1, Canada. Offers M Sc, PhD. Part-time programs available. *Faculty:* 22 full-time (5 women), 29 part-time/adjunct (6 women). *Students:* 53 full-time (26 women), 10 part-time (7 women). 41 applicants, 46% accepted, 19 enrolled. In 2006, 15 master's, 3 doctorates awarded. *Degree requirements:* For master's, thesis/dissertation, registration; for doctorate, thesis/dissertation, comprehensive exam, registration. *Entrance requirements:* For master's, honors degree, minimum B average, writing sample; for doctorate, GRE (recommended), master's degree, minimum B average, writing sample. Additional exam requirements/recommendations for international students: Required—TOEFL, TWE. *Application deadline:* For fall admission, 2/1 for domestic students. Application fee: $75 Canadian dollars. Electronic applications accepted. *Financial support:* In 2006–07, 17 research assistantships, 45 teaching assistantships (averaging $6,021 per year) were awarded; institutionally sponsored loans, scholarships/grants, and university sponsored bursaries also available. *Faculty research:* Work physiology, biomechanics and neural control of human movement, psychomotor learning and performance, aging, health and well-being, work and health. *Unit head:* Dr. Nancy Theberge, Associate Chair, Graduate Studies, 519-888-4567 Ext. 33534, Fax: 519-746-6776, E-mail: theberge@healthy.uwaterloo.ca. *Application contact:* Ruth Gooding, Graduate Studies Coordinator, 519-888-4567 Ext. 32476, Fax: 519-746-6776, E-mail: gooding@uwaterloo.ca.

The University of Western Ontario, Faculty of Graduate Studies, Biosciences Division, School of Kinesiology, London, ON N6A 5B8, Canada. Offers M Sc, MA, PhD. *Faculty:* 30. *Students:* 67 full-time (30 women), 2 part-time. Average age 25. 69 applicants, 51% accepted. In 2006, 11 master's, 4 doctorates awarded. *Degree requirements:* For master's, thesis optional; for doctorate, thesis/dissertation, comprehensive exam. *Entrance requirements:* For doctorate, MA in physical education or kinesiology. Additional exam requirements/recommendations for international students: Required—Michigan English Language Assessment Battery, TOEFL or IELTS. *Application deadline:* Applications are processed on a rolling basis. Application fee: $50 Canadian dollars. *Financial support:* In 2006–07, 3 research assistantships, 45 teaching assistantships (averaging $9,000 Canadian dollars per year) were awarded; scholarships/grants and unspecified assistantships also available. Financial award application deadline: 4/1. *Faculty research:* Exercise physiology/biochemistry, sports injuries, sport psychology, sport history, sport philosophy. *Unit head:* Dr. Earl Noble, Director, 519-661-2111 Ext. 83541, Fax: 519-661-2008, E-mail: enoble@uwo.ca. *Application contact:* Dr. Albert Carron, Director, 519-661-2111 Ext. 85475, Fax: 519-661-2008, E-mail: bcarron@uwo.ca.

University of Windsor, Faculty of Graduate Studies and Research, Faculty of Human Kinetics, Windsor, ON N9B 3P4, Canada. Offers MHK. Part-time programs available. *Degree requirements:* For master's, thesis optional. *Entrance requirements:* For master's, minimum B average. Additional exam requirements/recommendations for international students: Required—TOEFL (minimum score 600 paper-based; 250 computer-based). Electronic applications accepted. *Faculty research:* Movement sciences, sport and lifestyle management, historical and sociological studies of sport.

University of Wisconsin–Madison, Graduate School, School of Education, Department of Kinesiology, Madison, WI 53706-1380. Offers kinesiology (MS, PhD); occupational therapy (MS, PhD); therapeutic science (MS). *Accreditation:* AOTA. *Degree requirements:* For doctorate, thesis/dissertation. *Entrance requirements:* For master's and doctorate, GRE General Test. Application fee: $45. Electronic applications accepted. *Financial support:* Fellowships with full tuition reimbursements, research assistantships with full tuition reimbursements, teaching assistantships with full tuition reimbursements, project assistantships available. *Unit head:* Dr. Li Li Ji, Chair, 608-262-0048.

University of Wisconsin–Milwaukee, Graduate School, College of Health Sciences, Program in Kinesiology, Milwaukee, WI 53201-0413. Offers MS. Part-time programs available. *Faculty:* 10 full-time (8 women). *Students:* 9 full-time (4 women), 13 part-time (7 women). 17 applicants, 47% accepted, 1 enrolled. In 2006, 6 degrees awarded. *Entrance requirements:* For master's, GRE General Test. *Application deadline:* For fall admission, 1/1 priority date for domestic students; for spring admission, 9/1 for domestic students. Applications are processed on a rolling basis. Application fee: $45 ($75 for international students). *Expenses:* Tuition, state resident: part-time $510 per credit. Tuition, nonresident: part-time $1,408 per credit. Tuition and fees vary according to program. *Financial support:* In 2006–07, 1 fellowship, 10 teaching assistantships were awarded; research assistantships, career-related internships or fieldwork and unspecified assistantships also available. Support available to part-time students. Financial award application deadline: 4/15. *Unit head:* Barbara Hart, Representative, 414-229-6080, Fax: 414-906-3935, E-mail: hart@uwm.edu.

Washington University in St. Louis, Graduate School of Arts and Sciences, Interdisciplinary Program in Movement Science, St. Louis, MO 63130-4899. Offers PhD. *Degree requirements:* For doctorate, thesis/dissertation. *Entrance requirements:* For doctorate, GRE General Test. Electronic applications accepted.

Wayne State University, College of Education, Division of Kinesiology, Health and Sports Studies, Detroit, MI 48202. Offers health education (M Ed); kinesiology (M Ed); physical education (M Ed); recreation and park services (MA); sports administration (MA). *Faculty:* 9 full-time (2 women). *Students:* 40 full-time (16 women), 73 part-time (24 women); includes 25 minority (22 African Americans, 1 Asian American or Pacific Islander, 2 Hispanic Americans), 6 international. Average age 31. 39 applicants, 95% accepted, 26 enrolled. In 2006, 39 degrees awarded. *Degree requirements:* For master's, thesis (for some programs). *Entrance requirements:* For master's, GRE General Test. Additional exam requirements/recommendations for international students: Required—TOEFL; Recommended—TWE (minimum score 6). *Application deadline:* For fall admission, 7/1 for domestic students, 6/1 for international students; for winter admission, 10/1 for international students; for spring admission, 2/1 for international students. Application fee: $30 ($50 for international students). Electronic applications accepted. *Financial support:* In 2006–07, 3 research assistantships with tuition reimbursements (averaging $13,222 per year), 2 teaching assistantships with tuition reimbursements (averaging $13,222 per year) were awarded; career-related internships or fieldwork also available. *Faculty research:* Fitness in urban children, motor development of crack babies, effects of caffeine on metabolism/exercise, body composition of elite youth sports participants, systematic observation of teaching. Total annual research expenditures: $437,871. *Unit head:* Dr. Sally Erbaugh, Assistant Dean, 313-577-6210, Fax: 313-577-5999, E-mail: serbaugh@coe.wayne.edu. *Applica-*

tion contact: John Wirth, Assistant Professor, 313-993-7972, Fax: 313-577-5999, E-mail: johnwirth@wayne.edu.

West Chester University of Pennsylvania, Graduate Studies, School of Health Sciences, Department of Kinesiology, West Chester, PA 19383. Offers driver education (Certificate); exercise and sport physiology (MS); physical education (MS); sport and athletic administration (MSA). Part-time and evening/weekend programs available. *Students:* 9 full-time (6 women), 30 part-time (8 women); includes 2 African Americans, 1 Hispanic American, 1 international. Average age 29. 35 applicants, 94% accepted, 12 enrolled. In 2006, 21 degrees awarded. *Degree requirements:* For master's, thesis optional. *Entrance requirements:* For master's, GRE or MAT, interview. *Application deadline:* For fall admission, 4/15 priority date for domestic students; for spring admission, 10/15 for domestic students. Applications are processed on a rolling basis. Application fee: $35. *Financial support:* In 2006–07, 7 research assistantships with full tuition reimbursements were awarded; unspecified assistantships also available. Support available to part-time students. Financial award application deadline: 2/15; financial award applicants required to submit FAFSA. *Faculty research:* Weight lifting and type 1 diabetes mellitus, martial arts, sexual harassment in sports. *Unit head:* Dr. Raymond Zetts, Chair, 610-436-2610, E-mail: czetts@wcupa.edu. *Application contact:* Dr. Sheri Melton, Graduate Coordinator, 610-436-2610, E-mail: smelton@wcupa.edu.

Western Illinois University, School of Graduate Studies, College of Education and Human Services, Department of Kinesiology, Program in Kinesiology, Macomb, IL 61455-1390. Offers MS. Part-time programs available. *Students:* 20 full-time (11 women), 11 part-time (6 women); includes 2 minority (1 American Indian/Alaska Native, 1 Hispanic American), 1 international. Average age 30. 22 applicants, 64% accepted. In 2006, 12 degrees awarded. *Entrance requirements:* For master's, minimum GPA of 3.0. Additional exam requirements/recommendations for international students: Required—TOEFL (minimum score 550 paper-based; 213 computer-based; 80 iBT). *Application deadline:* Applications are processed on a rolling basis. Application fee: $30. Electronic applications accepted. *Expenses:* Tuition, state resident: part-time $200 per credit hour. Tuition, nonresident: part-time $400 per credit hour. *Financial support:* In 2006–07, 16 students received support, including 8 research assistantships with full tuition reimbursements available (averaging $6,568 per year), 8 teaching assistantships with full tuition reimbursements available (averaging $7,576 per year). *Unit head:* Dr. Chris Kovacs, Graduate Committee Chairperson, 309-298-1981.

Wilfrid Laurier University, Faculty of Graduate Studies, Faculty of Science, Department of Kinesiology and Physical Education, Waterloo, ON N2L 3C5, Canada. Offers M Sc. *Faculty:* 13 full-time. *Students:* 6 full-time. 12 applicants, 50% accepted, 6 enrolled. *Degree requirements:* For master's, thesis. *Entrance requirements:* For master's, honours degree in kinesiology, health, physical education with a minimum B+ in kinesiology and health-related courses. Additional exam requirements/recommendations for international students: Required—TOEFL (minimum score 230 computer-based; 89 iBT). *Application deadline:* For fall admission, 2/1 priority date for domestic students. Application fee: $75. Electronic applications accepted. *Financial support:* Fellowships, research assistantships, teaching assistantships available. *Faculty research:* Biomechanics, health, exercise physiology, motor control, sport psychology. *Unit head:* Dr. Peter Tiidus, Chairperson, 519-884-0710 Ext. 4157. *Application contact:* Dianne Duffy, Student Contact, 519-884-0710 Ext. 3127, Fax: 519-884-1020, E-mail: gradstudies@wlu.ca.

York University, Faculty of Graduate Studies, Faculty of Health, Program in Kinesiology and Health Science, Toronto, ON M3J 1P3, Canada. Offers M Sc, MA, PhD. Part-time programs available. *Faculty:* 26 full-time (10 women), 4 part-time/adjunct (1 woman). *Students:* 74 full-time (43 women), 4 part-time (3 women). 66 applicants, 29% accepted, 12 enrolled. In 2006, 12 degrees awarded. *Degree requirements:* For master's, thesis or alternative, registration; for doctorate, thesis/dissertation, comprehensive exam, registration. *Application deadline:* For fall admission, 2/15 priority date for domestic students. Application fee: $80. Electronic applications accepted. *Financial support:* In 2006–07, fellowships (averaging $11,986 per year), research assistantships (averaging $11,278 per year), teaching assistantships (averaging $8,628 per year) were awarded; tuition waivers (partial) and fee bursaries also available. *Unit head:* Barry Fowler, Director, 416-736-5728.

Physical Education

Adams State College, The Graduate School, Department of Health and Physical Education, Alamosa, CO 81102. Offers MA. *Accreditation:* Teacher Education Accreditation Council. Part-time programs available. *Degree requirements:* For master's, comprehensive exam. *Entrance requirements:* For master's, GRE General Test or MAT, minimum undergraduate GPA of 2.75.

Adelphi University, School of Education, Program in Physical Education and Human Performance Science, Garden City, NY 11530-0701. Offers aging (Certificate); physical/educational human performance science (MA). Part-time and evening/weekend programs available. *Students:* 47 full-time (22 women), 97 part-time (47 women); includes 12 minority (5 African Americans, 1 Asian American or Pacific Islander, 6 Hispanic Americans), 2 international. Average age 28. In 2006, 80 degrees awarded. *Degree requirements:* For master's, internship. *Entrance requirements:* For master's, 3 letters of recommendation, resumé. Additional exam requirements/recommendations for international students: Required—TOEFL (minimum score 550 paper-based; 213 computer-based). *Application deadline:* Applications are processed on a rolling basis. Application fee: $50. Electronic applications accepted. *Financial support:* In 2006–07, 4 research assistantships with full and partial tuition reimbursements (averaging $1,500 per year) were awarded; fellowships, teaching assistantships, career-related internships or fieldwork, Federal Work-Study, institutionally sponsored loans, and tuition waivers (full) also available. Support available to part-time students. Financial award application deadline: 2/15; financial award applicants required to submit FAFSA. *Faculty research:* Physical education for the handicapped, sport sociology, sport pedagogy. *Unit head:* Dr. Stephen J. Virgilio, Chair, 516-877-4262, E-mail: virgilio@adelphi.edu. *Application contact:* Christine Murphy, Director of Admissions, 516-877-3050, Fax: 516-877-3039, E-mail: graduateadmissions@adelphi.edu.

Alabama Agricultural and Mechanical University, School of Graduate Studies, School of Education, Department of Curriculum and Instruction, Area in Health and Physical Education, Huntsville, AL 35811. Offers physical education (M Ed, MS). Part-time and evening/weekend programs available. *Faculty:* 3 full-time (2 women). *Students:* 5 full-time (4 women), 12 part-time (3 women); includes 14 minority (all African Americans), 2 international. In 2006, 1 degree awarded. *Degree requirements:* For master's, comprehensive exam. *Entrance requirements:* For master's, GRE General Test. *Application deadline:* For fall admission, 5/1 for domestic students. Applications are processed on a rolling basis. Application fee: $25. Electronic applications accepted. *Financial support:* Career-related internships or fieldwork available. Financial award application deadline: 4/1. *Faculty research:* Cardiorespiratory assessment. *Unit head:* Dr. Rodney Whittle, Chairperson, 256-372-8260.

Alabama State University, School of Graduate Studies, College of Education, Department of Health, Physical Education, and Recreation, Montgomery, AL 36101-0271. Offers health education (M Ed); physical education (M Ed). Part-time programs available. *Faculty:* 4 full-time (all women), 1 part-time/adjunct (0 women). *Students:* 7 full-time (2 women), 15 part-time (8 women); includes 18 minority (all African Americans) In 2006, 8 degrees awarded. *Degree requirements:* For master's, comprehensive exam. *Entrance requirements:* For master's, GRE General Test, MAT, graduate writing competency test. Additional exam requirements/recommendations for international students: Required—TOEFL (minimum score 500 paper-based; 173 computer-based). *Application deadline:* For fall admission, 7/15 for domestic students; for spring admission, 12/15 for domestic students. Applications are processed on a rolling basis. Application fee: $10. *Expenses:* Tuition, state resident: full-time $1,728; part-time $192 per hour. Tuition, nonresident: full-time $3,456; part-time $334 per hour. *Financial support:* In 2006–07, research assistantships (averaging $9,450 per year). *Faculty research:* Risk factors for heart disease in the college-age population, cardiovascular reactivity for the Cold Pressor Test. *Unit head:* Dr. Doris Screws, Chair, 334-229-4504, Fax: 334-229-4928.

Albany State University, College of Education, Program in Health and Physical Education, Albany, GA 31705-2717. Offers M Ed. *Accreditation:* NCATE. Part-time programs available. *Degree requirements:* For master's, thesis optional. *Entrance requirements:* For master's, GRE General Test, MAT or NTE. Electronic applications accepted.

Alcorn State University, School of Graduate Studies, School of Psychology and Education, Alcorn State, MS 39096-7500. Offers agricultural education (MS Ed); elementary education (MS Ed, Ed S); guidance and counseling (MS Ed); industrial education (MS Ed); secondary education (MS Ed), including health and physical education; special education (MS Ed). *Accreditation:* NCATE. *Faculty:* 14 full-time (9 women), 21 part-time/adjunct (13 women). *Students:* 76 full-time (44 women), 271 part-time (226 women); includes 333 minority (all African Americans) In 2006, 119 degrees awarded. *Degree requirements:* For master's, thesis optional. *Application deadline:* For fall admission, 7/15 priority date for domestic students; for spring admission, 11/25 for domestic students. Applications are processed on a rolling basis. Application fee: $0 ($10 for international students). *Financial support:* Career-related internships or fieldwork available. Support available to part-time students. *Unit head:* Dr. Josephine M. Posey, Dean, 601-877-6141, Fax: 601-877-3867.

American University of Puerto Rico, Program in Education, Bayamón, PR 00960-2037. Offers art history (M Ed); elementary education (4-6) (M Ed); elementary education (k-3) (M Ed); general science education (M Ed); physical education (k-12) (M Ed); special education at secondary level (transition) (M Ed). *Entrance requirements:* For master's, EXADEP or GRE or MAT, 2 letters of recommendation, minimum GPA of 2.5.

Arizona State University at the Polytechnic Campus, The School of Educational Innovation and Teacher Preparation, Mesa, AZ 85212. Offers administration/supervision (M Ed); curriculum and instruction (M Ed); physical education (MPE, PhD). *Faculty:* 9 full-time (6 women), 1 part-time/adjunct (0 women). *Students:* 86 full-time (74 women), 119 part-time (92 women); includes 18 minority (1 African American, 1 American Indian/Alaska Native, 5 Asian Americans or Pacific Islanders, 11 Hispanic Americans), 1 international. Average age 33. 94 applicants, 84% accepted, 65 enrolled. In 2006, 19 degrees awarded. *Degree requirements:* For master's, written comprehensive exam or applied project; for doctorate, thesis/dissertation. *Entrance requirements:* For master's, 3 letters of recommendation, minimum GPA of 3.0. *Application deadline:* For fall admission, 4/15 priority date for domestic and international students; for spring admission, 10/15 priority date for domestic and international students. Applications are processed on a rolling basis. Application fee: $50. Electronic applications accepted. *Expenses:* Tuition, state resident: part-time $310 per credit hour. Tuition, nonresident: part-time $688 per credit hour. *Financial support:* In 2006–07, 4 teaching assistantships with full tuition reimbursements (averaging $12,978 per year) were awarded; fellowships, research assistantships with full tuition reimbursements also available. Financial award applicants required to submit FAFSA.

Arkansas State University, Graduate School, College of Education, Department of Health, Physical Education, and Sport Sciences, Jonesboro, State University, AR 72467. Offers exercise science (MS); physical education (MS, MSE, SCCT). Part-time programs available. *Faculty:* 4 full-time (1 woman), 1 part-time/adjunct (0 women). *Students:* 5 full-time (3 women), 9 part-time (2 women); includes 3 minority (all African Americans), 1 international. Average age 24. 12 applicants, 50% accepted, 6 enrolled. In 2006, 10 degrees awarded. *Degree requirements:* For master's, thesis or alternative, comprehensive exam. *Entrance requirements:* For master's, GRE General Test or MAT, appropriate bachelor's degree, official transcript; for SCCT, GRE General Test or MAT, interview, master's degree, official transcript. Additional exam requirements/recommendations for international students: Required—TOEFL (minimum score 213 computer-based). *Application deadline:* Applications are processed on a rolling basis. Application fee: $30 ($40 for international students). Electronic applications accepted. *Expenses:* Tuition, state resident: full-time $3,393; part-time $189 per hour. Tuition, nonresident: full-time $8,577; part-time $477 per hour. Required fees: $752; $39 per hour. $25 per semester. *Financial support:* Teaching assistantships, career-related internships or fieldwork, scholarships/grants, and unspecified assistantships available. Financial award application deadline: 7/1; financial award applicants required to submit FAFSA. *Unit head:* Dr. Jim Stillwell, Chair, 870-972-3066, Fax: 870-972-3096, E-mail: jstillwel@astate.edu.

Ashland University, College of Education, Graduate Studies in Education, Department of Sport Sciences, Ashland, OH 44805-3702. Offers adapted physical education (M Ed); applied exercise science (M Ed); sport education (M Ed); sport management (M Ed). Part-time programs available. *Faculty:* 6 full-time (1 woman), 1 (woman) part-time/adjunct. *Students:* 26 full-time (12 women), 28 part-time (11 women); includes 4 minority (all African Americans) Average age 31. In 2006, 29 degrees awarded. *Degree requirements:* For master's, thesis or alternative, practicum, seminar. *Entrance requirements:* For master's, GRE General Test or MAT, minimum GPA of 2.75. Additional exam requirements/recommendations for international students: Required—TOEFL. *Application deadline:* For fall admission, 8/27 for domestic students; for spring admission, 1/14 for domestic students. Applications are processed on a rolling basis. Application fee: $30. *Expenses:* Tuition: Part-time $403 per credit. Tuition and fees vary according to degree level and program. *Financial support:* In 2006–07, 16 students received support, including teaching assistantships with full tuition reimbursements available (averaging $6,000 per year); institutionally sponsored loans and scholarships/grants also available. Financial award application deadline: 4/15. *Faculty research:* Coaching, legal issues, strength and conditioning, sport management rating of perceived exertion. *Unit head:* Dr. Glen Fincher, Chair, 419-289-5450, E-mail: gfincher@ashland.edu.

Auburn University, Graduate School, College of Education, Department of Health and Human Performance, Auburn University, AL 36849. Offers exercise science (M Ed, MS, PhD); health promotion (M Ed, MS); physical education/teacher education (M Ed, MS, Ed D, Ed S). *Accreditation:* NCATE. Part-time programs available. *Faculty:* 13 full-time (5 women). *Students:* 40 full-time (18 women), 27 part-time (6 women); includes 7 minority (5 African Americans, 2 Hispanic Americans), 6 international. Average age 28. 67 applicants, 79% accepted, 24 enrolled. In 2006, 17 master's, 2 doctorates awarded. *Degree requirements:* For master's, thesis (for some programs); for doctorate, thesis/dissertation; for Ed S, exam, field project. *Entrance requirements:* For master's, GRE General Test; for doctorate and Ed S, GRE General Test, interview, master's degree. *Application deadline:* For fall admission, 7/7 for domestic students; for spring admission, 11/24 for domestic students. Applications are processed on a rolling basis. Application fee: $25 ($50 for international students). Electronic applica-

Physical Education

Auburn University (continued)

tions accepted. *Expenses:* Tuition, state resident: full-time $5,000. Tuition, nonresident: full-time $15,000. Required fees: $416. Tuition and fees vary according to program. *Financial support:* Research assistantships, teaching assistantships, Federal Work-Study available. Support available to part-time students. Financial award application deadline: 3/15. *Faculty research:* Biomechanics, exercise physiology, motor skill learning, school health, curriculum development. *Unit head:* Dr. Mary E Rudisill, Acting Head, 334-844-4483. *Application contact:* Dr. Joe Pittman, Interim Dean of the Graduate School, 334-844-4700.

Auburn University Montgomery, School of Education, Department of Foundations, Secondary, and Physical Education, Montgomery, AL 36124-4023. Offers physical education (M Ed); secondary education (M Ed, Ed S). *Accreditation:* NCATE. Part-time and evening/weekend programs available. *Faculty:* 9 full-time (5 women), 1 (woman) part-time/adjunct. *Students:* 22 full-time (13 women), 59 part-time (50 women); includes 29 minority (27 African Americans, 2 Hispanic Americans). Average age 33. In 2006, 27 master's, 4 other advanced degrees awarded. *Degree requirements:* For master's and Ed S, thesis optional. *Entrance requirements:* For master's, GRE General Test or MAT, certification, BS in teaching; for Ed S, GRE General Test or MAT, certification. *Application deadline:* Applications are processed on a rolling basis. Application fee: $25. Electronic applications accepted. *Financial support:* In 2006–07, 3 teaching assistantships were awarded; career-related internships or fieldwork and scholarships/grants also available. Support available to part-time students. Financial award application deadline: 3/1; financial award applicants required to submit FAFSA. *Unit head:* Dr. Henry N. Williford, Head, 334-244-3548, Fax: 334-244-3547, E-mail: hwilliford@mail.aum.edu.

Augusta State University, Graduate Studies, College of Education, Program in Health and Physical Education, Augusta, GA 30904-2200. Offers M Ed. *Faculty:* 3 full-time (2 women). *Students:* 4 full-time (2 women), 4 part-time (all women); includes 1 minority (Asian American or Pacific Islander) Average age 31. 3 applicants, 100% accepted, 3 enrolled. In 2006, 3 degrees awarded. *Entrance requirements:* For master's, GRE, MAT, minimum GPA of 2.5. Application fee: $20. *Expenses:* Tuition, state resident: full-time $3,044; part-time $127 per credit hour. Tuition, nonresident: full-time $12,172; part-time $508 per credit hour. *Financial support:* Career-related internships or fieldwork, Federal Work-Study, institutionally sponsored loans, and unspecified assistantships available. Support available to part-time students. *Unit head:* Dr. Paula J Dohoney, Chair, 706-731-7922, Fax: 706-667-4140, E-mail: pdohoney@aug.edu. *Application contact:* Andrea M Scott, Secretary to the Dean, 706-737-1499, Fax: 706-667-4706, E-mail: ascott@aug.edu.

Austin College, Program in Education, Sherman, TX 75090-4400. Offers art education (MA); elementary education (MA); middle school education (MA); music education (MA); physical education and coaching (MA); secondary education (MA). Applicants must meet Austin College's undergraduate curriculum requirements. Part-time programs available. *Faculty:* 5 full-time (3 women), 1 (woman) part-time/adjunct. *Students:* 33 full-time (26 women); includes 3 minority (2 Asian Americans or Pacific Islanders, 1 Hispanic American). Average age 25. In 2006, 24 degrees awarded. *Degree requirements:* For master's, one foreign language, thesis or alternative. *Entrance requirements:* For master's, Texas Academic Skills Program Test. *Application deadline:* For fall admission, 5/1 priority date for domestic students; for spring admission, 1/15 priority date for domestic students. Applications are processed on a rolling basis. Application fee: $35. Electronic applications accepted. *Expenses:* Tuition: Full-time $27,385. Required fees: $160. *Financial support:* In 2006–07, 27 students received support. Career-related internships or fieldwork, Federal Work-Study, scholarships/grants, and unspecified assistantships available. Support available to part-time students. Financial award application deadline: 4/1; financial award applicants required to submit FAFSA. *Unit head:* Dr. Barbara Sylvester, Director of Teaching Program, 903-813-2498, Fax: 903-813-2326, E-mail: bsylvester@austincollege.edu.

Austin Peay State University, College of Graduate Studies, College of Professional Programs and Social Sciences, Department of Health and Human Performance, Clarksville, TN 37044. Offers health and physical education (MS). Part-time and evening/weekend programs available. Postbaccalaureate distance learning degree programs offered. *Faculty:* 6 full-time (4 women), 1 (woman) part-time/adjunct. *Students:* 31 full-time (16 women), 35 part-time (25 women); includes 30 minority (26 African Americans, 4 Hispanic Americans). Average age 30. In 2006, 29 degrees awarded. *Degree requirements:* For master's, thesis optional. *Entrance requirements:* For master's, GRE General Test, minimum GPA of 2.5, 2 letters of recommendation. Additional exam requirements/recommendations for international students: Required—TOEFL (minimum score 500 paper-based; 173 computer-based). *Application deadline:* For fall admission, 7/31 priority date for domestic students; for spring admission, 12/17 priority date for domestic students. Applications are processed on a rolling basis. Application fee: $25. Electronic applications accepted. *Expenses:* Tuition, state resident: full-time $5,138; part-time $272 per credit hour. Tuition, nonresident: full-time $14,832; part-time $693 per credit hour. Required fees: $1,009. *Financial support:* In 2006–07, fellowships (averaging $9,000 per year), research assistantships (averaging $10,270 per year) were awarded; career-related internships or fieldwork, Federal Work-Study, institutionally sponsored loans, scholarships/grants, and unspecified assistantships also available. Support available to part-time students. Financial award application deadline: 3/1; financial award applicants required to submit FAFSA. *Faculty research:* Aging and physical activity. *Unit head:* Dr. Dixie Dennis, Professor and Chair, 931-221-6111, Fax: 931-221-7040, E-mail: dennisdi@apsu.edu.

Averett University, Graduate Studies in Education, Danville, VA 24541-3692. Offers art education (M Ed); biology (M Ed); chemistry (M Ed); curriculum and instruction (M Ed); elementary education (M Ed); English (M Ed); health and physical education (M Ed); history and social studies (M Ed); mathematics education (M Ed); physical science (M Ed); reading (M Ed); special education (learning disabilities specialization PK-12) (M Ed). Part-time and evening/weekend programs available. *Faculty:* 10 full-time (4 women), 7 part-time/adjunct (6 women). *Students:* 14 full-time (10 women), 85 part-time (67 women); includes 20 minority (18 African Americans, 2 Asian Americans or Pacific Islanders). Average age 33. 52 applicants, 100% accepted, 40 enrolled. In 2006, 48 degrees awarded. *Degree requirements:* For master's, thesis optional. *Entrance requirements:* For master's, PRAXIS, GRE General Test, MAT or NTE, writing proficiency exam, 3 letters of recommendation, current teacher's licensure or eligibility for licensure, minimum undergraduate GPA of 3.0 in previous 2 years. Additional exam requirements/recommendations for international students: Required—TOEFL (minimum score 600 paper-based; 200 computer-based). *Application deadline:* Applications are processed on a rolling basis. Application fee: $20. *Expenses:* Contact institution. *Financial support:* In 2006–07, 23 students received support. Federal Work-Study and scholarships/grants available. Financial award application deadline: 4/1; financial award applicants required to submit FAFSA. *Faculty research:* Literary assessment-PreK-6, handwriting instruction and assessment-PreK-6, written language instruction and assessment-PreK-6 and special needs students learning styles, curriculum and instruction processes. *Unit head:* Dr. Lynn H. Wolf, Chair, 434-793-3995, Fax: 434-791-4392, E-mail: lynn.wolf@averett.edu.

Azusa Pacific University, School of Education, Department of Advanced Studies, Program in Physical Education, Azusa, CA 91702-7000. Offers M Ed. Evening/weekend programs available. *Students:* 2 full-time (1 woman), 127 part-time (46 women); includes 31 minority (5 African Americans, 1 American Indian/Alaska Native, 6 Asian Americans or Pacific Islanders, 19 Hispanic Americans), 1 international. In 2006, 81 degrees awarded. *Degree requirements:* For master's, core exams, oral exam, oral presentation. *Entrance requirements:* For master's, BA in physical education or 12 units of course work in education, minimum GPA of 3.0. Application fee: $45 ($65 for international students). *Expenses:* Tuition: Part-time $475 per credit. *Unit head:* Dr. Teri Marcos, Director, 626-969-5457, E-mail: tmarcos@apu.edu.

Ball State University, Graduate School, College of Applied Science and Technology, School of Physical Education, Muncie, IN 47306-1099. Offers MA, MAE, MS, PhD. *Faculty:* 32. *Students:* 49 full-time (26 women), 104 part-time (39 women); includes 5 minority (4 African Americans, 1 Asian American or Pacific Islander), 9 international. Average age 24. 139 applicants, 51% accepted, 45 enrolled. In 2006, 76 master's, 2 doctorates awarded. *Degree requirements:* For doctorate, thesis/dissertation. *Entrance requirements:* For master's, resumé; for doctorate, GRE General Test, minimum graduate GPA of 3.2. Application fee: $25 ($35 for international students). *Financial support:* In 2006–07, 1 research assistantship (averaging $11,947 per year), 40 teaching assistantships with full tuition reimbursements (averaging $10,326 per year) were awarded. Financial award application deadline: 3/1. *Unit head:* Dr. Mitchell Whaley, Director, 765-285-1748, Fax: 765-285-8254.

Bayamón Central University, Graduate Programs, Program in Education, Bayamón, PR 00960-1725. Offers administration and supervision (MA Ed); commercial education (MA Ed); education of the autistic (MA Ed); elementary education (K–3) (MA Ed); elementary education (K–6) (MA Ed); elementary physical education (MA Ed); guidance and counseling (MA Ed); pre-elementary teacher (MA Ed); special education (MA Ed), including attention deficit disorder, learning disabilities. Part-time and evening/weekend programs available. *Degree requirements:* For master's, comprehensive exam. *Entrance requirements:* For master's, EXADEP, bachelor's degree in education or related field.

Baylor University, Graduate School, School of Education, Department of Health, Human Performance and Recreation, Waco, TX 76798. Offers exercise, nutrition and preventive health (PhD); health, human performance and recreation (MS Ed). *Accreditation:* NCATE. Part-time programs available. *Faculty:* 13 full-time (5 women), 3 part-time/adjunct (1 woman). *Students:* 58 full-time (33 women), 31 part-time (16 women); includes 14 minority (7 African Americans, 4 American Indian/Alaska Native, 1 Asian American or Pacific Islander, 2 Hispanic Americans), 5 international. 30 applicants, 87% accepted. In 2006, 41 master's, 5 doctorates awarded. *Degree requirements:* For master's, thesis optional. *Entrance requirements:* For master's, GRE General Test. *Application deadline:* For fall admission, 4/1 priority date for domestic students; for spring admission, 10/1 for domestic students. Applications are processed on a rolling basis. Application fee: $25. Electronic applications accepted. *Financial support:* In 2006–07, 35 students received support, including 22 teaching assistantships; career-related internships or fieldwork, Federal Work-Study, institutionally sponsored loans, tuition waivers (partial), and recreation supplements also available. *Faculty research:* Behavior change theory, pedagogy, nutrition and enzyme therapy, exercise testing, health planning. *Unit head:* Dr. Mike Greenwood, Graduate Program Director, 254-710-3505, Fax: 254-710-3527, E-mail: mike_greenwood@baylor.edu. *Application contact:* Suzanne Keener, Administrative Assistant, 254-710-3588, Fax: 254-710-3870.

Bethel College, Program in Education, McKenzie, TN 38201. Offers administration and supervision (MA Ed); biology education K8-12 (MAT); elementary education (MAT); English education K8-12 (MAT); history education K8-12 (MAT); physical education K8-12 (MAT); special education K8-12 (MAT). Part-time and evening/weekend programs available. *Degree requirements:* For master's, thesis (for some programs). *Entrance requirements:* For master's, GRE General Test or MAT, minimum undergraduate GPA of 2.5.

Boston University, School of Education, Department of Curriculum and Teaching, Program in Physical Education and Coaching, Boston, MA 02215. Offers Ed M, Ed D, CAGS. *Students:* 9 full-time (3 women), 9 part-time (4 women), 1 international. Average age 28. 28 applicants, 86% accepted. In 2006, 12 master's, 1 doctorate awarded. *Degree requirements:* For master's, thesis optional; for doctorate, thesis/dissertation, comprehensive exam. *Entrance requirements:* For master's, doctorate, and CAGS, GRE General Test or MAT. Additional exam requirements/recommendations for international students: Required—TOEFL. *Application deadline:* For fall admission, 2/15 priority date for domestic students; for winter admission, 10/1 priority date for domestic students. Applications are processed on a rolling basis. Application fee: $70. Electronic applications accepted. *Expenses:* Tuition: Full-time $33,330; part-time $1,042 per credit. Required fees: $462; $40. *Financial support:* Application deadline: 2/15. *Faculty research:* Sports theory, biofeedback, exercise. *Unit head:* Dr. Eileen C. Sullivan, Coordinator, 617-353-3300, E-mail: eileensu@bu.edu. *Application contact:* 617-353-4231, Fax: 617-353-8937, E-mail: sedgrad@bu.edu.

Bridgewater State College, School of Graduate Studies, School of Education and Allied Science, Department of Movement Arts, Health Promotion, and Leisure Studies, Program in Physical Education, Bridgewater, MA 02325-0001. Offers MS. Part-time and evening/weekend programs available. *Degree requirements:* For master's, thesis or alternative. *Entrance requirements:* For master's, GRE General Test. *Application deadline:* For fall admission, 3/1 priority date for domestic students; for spring admission, 10/1 priority date for domestic students. Application fee: $50. *Financial support:* Career-related internships or fieldwork, health care benefits, and unspecified assistantships available. Support available to part-time students.

Brigham Young University, Graduate Studies, College of Health and Human Performance, Department of Exercise Sciences, Provo, UT 84602-1001. Offers athletic training (MS); exercise physiology (MS, PhD); health promotion (MS, PhD); physical medicine and rehabilitation (PhD); sports pedagogy (MS). *Faculty:* 19 full-time (3 women), 1 (woman) part-time/adjunct. *Students:* 23 full-time (10 women), 48 part-time (21 women); includes 7 minority (3 American Indian/Alaska Native, 1 Asian American or Pacific Islander, 3 Hispanic Americans). Average age 28. 30 applicants, 70% accepted, 14 enrolled. In 2006, 9 master's, 4 doctorates awarded. *Median time to degree:* Of those who began their doctoral program in fall 1998, 100% received their degree in 8 years or less. *Degree requirements:* For master's, thesis, oral defense; for doctorate, thesis/dissertation, oral defense, oral and written exams, comprehensive exam. *Entrance requirements:* For master's, GRE General Test, minimum GPA of 3.0 in last 60 hours of course work; for doctorate, GRE General Test, minimum GPA of 3.5 in last 60 hours of course work. Additional exam requirements/recommendations for international students: Required—TOEFL (minimum score 580 paper-based; 237 computer-based; 85 iBT), IELTS (minimum score 7). *Application deadline:* For fall admission, 2/1 for domestic and international students. Application fee: $50. Electronic applications accepted. *Financial support:* In 2006–07, 18 research assistantships with full and partial tuition reimbursements (averaging $3,324 per year), 45 teaching assistantships with full and partial tuition reimbursements (averaging $11,080 per year) were awarded; fellowships, career-related internships or fieldwork, institutionally sponsored loans, tuition waivers (full and partial), and unspecified assistantships also available. Financial award application deadline: 3/1. *Faculty research:* Injury prevention and rehabilitation, human skeletal muscle adaptation, cardiovascular health and fitness, lifestyle modification and health promotion. Total annual research expenditures: $250,125. *Unit head:* Dr. Larry Hall, Chair, 801-422-7303, Fax: 801-422-0543, E-mail: larry_hall@byu.edu. *Application contact:* Dr. J. William Myrer, Graduate Coordinator, 801-422-2690, Fax: 801-422-0557, E-mail: bill_myrer@byu.edu.

Brooklyn College of the City University of New York, Division of Graduate Studies, Department of Physical Education and Exercise Science, Brooklyn, NY 11210-2889. Offers exercise science and rehabilitation (MS), including psychosocial aspects of physical activity, sports management; physical education (MS, MS Ed). Part-time programs available. *Students:* 1 (woman) full-time, 52 part-time (16 women); includes 15 minority (10 African Americans, 5 Hispanic Americans), 16 international. 37 applicants, 84% accepted, 13 enrolled. In 2006, 21 degrees awarded. *Degree requirements:* For master's, comprehensive exam or thesis. *Entrance requirements:* For master's, previous course work in physical education and education, minimum GPA of 3.0, 2 letters of recommendation, essay. Additional exam requirements/recommendations for international students: Required—TOEFL. *Application deadline:* For fall admission, 3/1 priority date for domestic students, 2/1 priority date for international students; for spring admission, 11/1 priority date for domestic students, 10/1 priority date for international students. Applications are processed on a rolling basis. Application fee: $125. Electronic applications accepted. *Expenses:* Tuition, state resident: full-time $6,400; part-time $270 per credit. Tuition, nonresident: full-time $12,000; part-time $500 per credit. Required fees: $118 per semester. *Financial support:* Career-related internships or fieldwork, Federal Work-Study, institutionally sponsored loans, and scholarships/grants available. Support available to part-time students. Financial award application deadline: 5/1; financial award applicants required to submit FAFSA. *Faculty research:* Exercise physiology, motor learning, sports psychology, women in athletics. Total annual research expenditures: $9,231. *Unit head:* Dr. Charles Tobey, Chairperson, 718-951-5514, E-mail: ctobey@brooklyn.cuny.edu. *Application contact:* Karen Alleyne-Pierre, Director of Admissions Services and Enrollment Communications, 718-951-5902, Fax: 718-951-4506, E-mail: grads@brooklyn.cuny.edu.

Brooklyn College of the City University of New York, Division of Graduate Studies, School of Education, Program in Adolescence Education and Special Subjects, Brooklyn, NY 11210-2889. Offers art teacher (MA); biology teacher (MA); chemistry teacher (MA); English teacher (MA); French teacher (MA); health and nutrition sciences: health teacher (MS Ed); mathematics teacher (MA); music education (CAS); music teacher (MA); physical education teacher (MS Ed); physics teacher (MA); social studies teacher (MA); Spanish teacher (MA). Part-time and evening/weekend programs available. *Students:* 30 full-time (22 women), 450 part-time (257 women); includes 167 minority (101 African Americans, 21 Asian Americans or Pacific Islanders, 45 Hispanic Americans), 21 international. 277 applicants, 84% accepted, 113 enrolled. In 2006, 172 master's, 6 other advanced degrees awarded. *Degree requirements:* For master's, comprehensive exam (for some programs). *Entrance requirements:* For master's, LAST, previous course work in education, resumé, 2 letters of recommendation, essay. Additional exam requirements/recommendations for international students: Required—TOEFL. *Application deadline:* For fall admission, 3/1 priority date for domestic students, 2/1 priority date for international students; for spring admission, 11/1 priority date for domestic students, 10/1 priority date for international students. Applications are processed on a rolling basis. Application fee: $125. Electronic applications accepted. *Expenses:* Tuition, state resident: full-time $6,400; part-time $270 per credit. Tuition, nonresident: full-time $12,000; part-time $500 per credit. Required fees: $118 per semester. *Financial support:* Career-related internships or fieldwork, Federal Work-Study, institutionally sponsored loans, and scholarships/grants available. Support available to part-time students. Financial award application deadline: 5/1; financial award applicants required to submit FAFSA. *Faculty research:* Interdisciplinary education, semiotics, discourse analysis, autobiography, teacher identity. *Unit head:* Prof. Stephen Phillips, Program Facilitator, 718-951-5214, E-mail: phillips@brooklyn.cuny.edu. *Application contact:* Karen Alleyne-Pierre, Director of Admissions Services and Enrollment Communications, 718-951-5902, Fax: 718-951-4506, E-mail: grads@brooklyn.cuny.edu.

California State University, Dominguez Hills, College of Health and Human Services, Program in Physical Education Administration, Carson, CA 90747-0001. Offers MA. Part-time programs available. *Faculty:* 2 full-time (1 woman). *Students:* 2 full-time (1 woman), 19 part-time (7 women); includes 13 minority (6 African Americans, 2 Asian Americans or Pacific Islanders, 5 Hispanic Americans). Average age 33. 11 applicants, 91% accepted, 2 enrolled. In 2006, 7 degrees awarded. *Degree requirements:* For master's, comprehensive exam. *Entrance requirements:* For master's, minimum GPA of 2.75. *Application deadline:* For fall admission, 6/1 for domestic students. Applications are processed on a rolling basis. Application fee: $55. *Expenses:* Tuition, nonresident: part-time $339 per unit. Required fees: $1,148 per term. Tuition and fees vary according to program. *Faculty research:* Teaching pedagogy, physical activity. *Unit head:* Dr. Michael Ernst, Head, 310-243-3761. *Application contact:* 310-243-3600.

California State University, East Bay, Academic Programs and Graduate Studies, College of Education and Allied Studies, Department of Kinesiology and Physical Education, Hayward, CA 94542-3000. Offers physical education (MS), including exercise physiology, professional perspectives, skill acquisition and sport psychology, sports humanities. *Faculty:* 4 full-time (1 woman). *Students:* 15 full-time (9 women), 23 part-time (12 women); includes 12 minority (3 African Americans, 1 American Indian/Alaska Native, 3 Asian Americans or Pacific Islanders, 5 Hispanic Americans), 3 international. Average age 30. 22 applicants, 55% accepted, 9 enrolled. In 2006, 13 degrees awarded. *Degree requirements:* For master's, project or thesis. *Entrance requirements:* For master's, GRE or MAT, minimum GPA of 3.0. Additional exam requirements/recommendations for international students: Required—TOEFL (minimum score 550 paper-based; 213 computer-based). *Application deadline:* For fall admission, 5/31 for domestic students, 4/30 for international students; for winter admission, 9/30 for domestic and international students; for spring admission, 12/31 for domestic students, 11/30 for international students. Applications are processed on a rolling basis. Application fee: $55. Electronic applications accepted. *Financial support:* Federal Work-Study, institutionally sponsored loans, and scholarships/grants available. Support available to part-time students. Financial award application deadline: 3/2. *Unit head:* Dr. Rita Liberti, Chair, 510-885-3061, Fax: 510-885-2282, E-mail: rita.liberti@csueastbay.edu. *Application contact:* My Huynh, Graduate Prospect Specialist, 510-885-2989, Fax: 510-885-4059, E-mail: my.huynh@csueastbay.edu.

California State University, Fullerton, Graduate Studies, College of Health and Human Development, Department of Kinesiology, Fullerton, CA 92834-9480. Offers physical education (MS). Part-time programs available. *Students:* 36 full-time (18 women), 56 part-time (35 women); includes 30 minority (5 African Americans, 9 Asian Americans or Pacific Islanders, 16 Hispanic Americans), 3 international. Average age 27. 78 applicants, 69% accepted, 40 enrolled. In 2006, 30 degrees awarded. *Degree requirements:* For master's, project or thesis. *Entrance requirements:* For master's, minimum GPA of 3.0 in field, 2.5 overall. Application fee: $55. *Expenses:* Tuition, nonresident: part-time $339 per unit. Required fees: $1,155 per semester. *Financial support:* Teaching assistantships, career-related internships or fieldwork, Federal Work-Study, institutionally sponsored loans, and scholarships/grants available. Support available to part-time students. Financial award application deadline: 3/1. *Unit head:* Dr. Kathy Koser, Head, 714-278-3320. *Application contact:* Dr. William Beam, Adviser, 714-278-3316.

California State University, Long Beach, Graduate Studies, College of Health and Human Services, Department of Kinesiology and Physical Education, Long Beach, CA 90840. Offers kinesiology (MA, MS). Part-time programs available. *Faculty:* 28 full-time (12 women), 33 part-time/adjunct (19 women). *Students:* 53 full-time (29 women), 96 part-time (52 women); includes 15 minority (5 African Americans, 2 Asian Americans or Pacific Islanders, 8 Hispanic Americans), 4 international. Average age 29. 126 applicants, 53% accepted, 44 enrolled. In 2006, 42 degrees awarded. *Degree requirements:* For master's, oral and written comprehensive exams or thesis. *Entrance requirements:* For master's, GRE General Test, minimum GPA of 2.75 during previous 2 years of course work. *Application deadline:* For fall admission, 7/1 for domestic students; for spring admission, 12/1 for domestic students. Applications are processed on a rolling basis. Application fee: $55. Electronic applications accepted. *Financial support:* Federal Work-Study, institutionally sponsored loans, and scholarships/grants available. Financial award application deadline: 3/2. *Faculty research:* Pulmonary functioning, feedback and practice structure, strength training, history and politics of sports, special population research issues. *Unit head:* Dr. Keith W Freeseman, Chair, 562-985-4051, Fax: 562-985-8067, E-mail: kfreesmn@csulb.edu. *Application contact:* Dr. Sharon Guthrie, Graduate Coordinator, 562-985-7487, Fax: 562-985-8067.

California State University, Los Angeles, Graduate Studies, College of Health and Human Services, Department of Kinesiology and Nutritional Sciences, Major in Physical Education and Kinesiology, Los Angeles, CA 90032-8530. Offers kinesiology (MA); physical education (MA). *Students:* 9 full-time (5 women), 30 part-time (18 women); includes 25 minority (3 African Americans, 10 Asian Americans or Pacific Islanders, 12 Hispanic Americans), 3 international. In 2006, 11 degrees awarded. *Expenses:* Tuition, nonresident: part-time $226 per unit. *Unit head:* Dr. Steve Hawkins, Coordinator, 323-343-4650.

California State University, Sacramento, Graduate Studies, College of Health and Human Services, Department of Kinesiology and Health Science, Sacramento, CA 95819-6048. Offers physical education (MS). *Accreditation:* APTA. Part-time programs available. *Students:* 13 full-time (6 women), 46 part-time (12 women); includes 16 minority (4 African Americans, 5 Asian Americans or Pacific Islanders, 7 Hispanic Americans). Average age 29. 54 applicants, 56% accepted, 19 enrolled. *Degree requirements:* For master's, thesis or alternative, writing proficiency exam. *Entrance requirements:* Additional exam requirements/recommendations for international students: Required—TOEFL. *Application deadline:* Applications are processed on a rolling basis. Application fee: $55. Electronic applications accepted. *Financial support:* Research assistantships, teaching assistantships, career-related internships or fieldwork and Federal Work-Study available. Support available to part-time students. Financial award application deadline: 3/1. *Unit head:* Dr. Fred Baldini, Chair, 916-278-6441, Fax: 916-278-7664.

Campbell University, Graduate and Professional Programs, School of Education, Buies Creek, NC 27506. Offers administration (MSA); community counseling (MA); elementary education (M Ed); English education (M Ed); interdisciplinary studies (M Ed); mathematics education (M Ed); middle grades education (M Ed); physical education (M Ed); school counseling (M Ed); secondary education (M Ed); social science education (M Ed). *Accreditation:* NCATE. Part-time and evening/weekend programs available. *Faculty:* 14 full-time (9 women), 12 part-time/adjunct (7 women). *Students:* 27 full-time (25 women), 183 part-time (146 women); includes 30 minority (24 African Americans, 3 American Indian/Alaska Native, 3 Hispanic Americans), 1 international. Average age 31. 112 applicants, 74% accepted, 74 enrolled. In 2006, 65 degrees awarded. *Degree requirements:* For master's, comprehensive exam. *Entrance requirements:* For master's, GRE General Test, minimum GPA of 2.7. *Application deadline:* For fall admission, 8/1 priority date for domestic students; for spring admission, 1/2 priority date for domestic students. Applications are processed on a rolling basis. Application fee: $65. *Expenses:* Tuition: Part-time $380 per semester hour. *Financial support:* In 2006–07, 67 students received support. Career-related internships or fieldwork and Federal Work-Study available. Financial award application deadline: 4/15; financial award applicants required to submit FAFSA. *Faculty research:* Spiritual values and wellness issues in counseling, stress and professional burnout among counselors, thinking strategies, leadership, adaptive technology. *Unit head:* Dr. Karen P. Nery, Dean, 910-893-1630, Fax: 910-893-1999, E-mail: nery@campbell.edu. *Application contact:* James S. Farthing, Director of Graduate Admissions for Business and Education, 910-893-1200 Ext. 1318, Fax: 910-814-4718, E-mail: farthing@campbell.edu.

Canisius College, Graduate Division, School of Education and Human Services, Department of Physical Education, Buffalo, NY 14208-1098. Offers physical education (MS); physical education—birth to 12 (MS). Part-time and evening/weekend programs available. Post-baccalaureate distance learning degree programs offered (minimal on-campus study). *Faculty:* 8 full-time (1 woman), 18 part-time/adjunct (7 women). *Students:* 79 full-time (31 women), 63 part-time (25 women); includes 5 minority (3 African Americans, 2 Hispanic Americans), 22 international. Average age 26. In 2006, 46 degrees awarded. *Degree requirements:* For master's, research project or thesis. *Entrance requirements:* For master's, GRE General Test, minimum GPA of 2.5. *Application deadline:* Applications are processed on a rolling basis. Application fee: $25. *Expenses:* Tuition: Part-time $645 per credit hour. Required fees: $19 per credit hour. Tuition and fees vary according to program. *Financial support:* Teaching assistantships with full tuition reimbursements, career-related internships or fieldwork, institutionally sponsored loans, scholarships/grants, health care benefits, tuition waivers (full and partial), and unspecified assistantships available. Financial award application deadline: 7/1; financial award applicants required to submit FAFSA. *Faculty research:* Sport psychology, adapted physical education, current health issues, teaching methods. *Unit head:* Dr. Gregory K. Reeds, Chair, 716-888-2952, Fax: 716-888-3219, E-mail: reedsg@canisius.edu. *Application contact:* James D. Bagwell, Director of Graduate Recruitment and Admissions, 716-888-2544, Fax: 716-888-3290, E-mail: bagwellj@canisius.edu.

Caribbean University, Graduate School, Bayamón, PR 00960-0493. Offers accounting (MBA); administration and supervision (MA Ed); criminal justice (MA); curriculum and instruction (MA Ed); education (PhD); gerontology (MSN); human resources (MBA); museology, archiving and art history (MA Ed); neonatal pediatrics (MSN); physical education (MA Ed); special education (MA Ed). *Entrance requirements:* For master's, interview, minimum GPA of 2.5.

Central Connecticut State University, School of Graduate Studies, School of Education and Professional Studies, Department of Physical Education and Health Fitness Studies, New Britain, CT 06050-4010. Offers physical education (MS, Certificate). Part-time and evening/weekend programs available. *Faculty:* 16 full-time (8 women), 21 part-time/adjunct (16 women). *Students:* 20 full-time (6 women), 35 part-time (12 women); includes 3 minority (2 African Americans, 1 Hispanic American), 1 international. Average age 29. 38 applicants, 79% accepted, 17 enrolled. In 2006, 19 master's, 1 other advanced degree awarded. *Degree requirements:* For master's, thesis or alternative, comprehensive exam. *Entrance requirements:* For master's, minimum GPA of 2.7, bachelor's degree in physical education (preferred). Additional exam requirements/recommendations for international students: Required—TOEFL. *Application deadline:* For fall admission, 7/1 priority date for domestic students; for spring admission, 12/1 for domestic students. Applications are processed on a rolling basis. Application fee: $50. Electronic applications accepted. *Expenses:* Tuition, area resident: Full-time $3,970; part-time $380 per credit. Tuition, state resident: full-time $5,955; part-time $380 per credit. Tuition, nonresident: full-time $11,061; part-time $380 per credit. Required fees: $3,189. One-time fee: $62 part-time. Tuition and fees vary according to degree level and program. *Financial support:* In 2006–07, 5 students received support, including 5 research assistantships; career-related internships or fieldwork, Federal Work-Study, scholarships/grants, and unspecified assistantships also available. Support available to part-time students. Financial award application deadline: 3/1; financial award applicants required to submit FAFSA. *Faculty research:* Exercise science, athletic training, preparation of physical education for schools. *Unit head:* Dr. David Harackiewicz, Chair, 860-832-2155.

Central Michigan University, College of Graduate Studies, The Herbert H. and Grace A. Dow College of Health Professions, Department of Physical Education and Sport, Mount Pleasant, MI 48859. Offers athletic administration (MA); coaching (MA); exercise science (MA); sport administration (MA); teaching (MA). *Degree requirements:* For master's, thesis or alternative, registration. *Faculty research:* Biomechanical analysis of sports skills, sociological studies, psychological studies.

Central Washington University, Graduate Studies, Research and Continuing Education, College of Education and Professional Studies, Department of Health, Human Performance and Nutrition, Ellensburg, WA 98926. Offers health, physical education and nutrition (MS). *Accreditation:* NCATE. Part-time programs available. *Faculty:* 19 full-time (5 women). *Students:* 6 full-time (3 women), 15 part-time (9 women); includes 3 minority (2 African Americans, 1 Asian American or Pacific Islander). 22 applicants, 77% accepted, 15 enrolled. In 2006, 11 degrees awarded. *Degree requirements:* For master's, thesis or alternative. *Entrance requirements:* For master's, minimum GPA of 3.0. Additional exam requirements/recommendations for international students: Required—TOEFL (minimum score 550 paper-based; 213 computer-based; 79 iBT). *Application deadline:* For fall admission, 4/1 priority date for domestic students; for winter admission, 10/1 for domestic students; for spring admission, 1/1 for domestic students. Applications are processed on a rolling basis. Application fee: $50. Electronic applications accepted. *Expenses:* Tuition, state resident: full-time $6,312. Tuition, nonresident: full-time $14,112. Tuition and fees vary according to course load and degree level. *Financial support:* In 2006–07, 18 teaching assistantships with partial tuition reimbursements (averaging $8,100 per year) were awarded; research assistantships, Federal Work-Study and health care benefits also available. Financial award application deadline: 3/1; financial award applicants required to submit FAFSA. *Unit head:* Dr. Robert McGowan, Chair, 509-963-1911. *Application contact:* Justine Eason, Admissions Program Coordinator, 509-963-3103, Fax: 509-963-1799, E-mail: masters@cwu.edu.

Chicago State University, School of Graduate and Professional Studies, College of Education, Department of Health, Physical Education and Recreation, Chicago, IL 60628. Offers physical education (MS Ed). Part-time and evening/weekend programs available. Post-baccalaureate distance learning degree programs offered. *Degree requirements:* For master's, thesis optional. *Entrance requirements:* For master's, minimum GPA of 2.75. *Faculty research:* Sports psychology, recreation and leisure studies administration.

The Citadel, The Military College of South Carolina, College of Graduate and Professional Studies, Department of Health, Exercise, and Sport Science, Charleston, SC 29409. Offers

Physical Education

The Citadel, The Military College of South Carolina (continued)
health, exercise, and sports science (MS); physical education (MAT). *Accreditation:* NCATE. Part-time and evening/weekend programs available. *Students:* 3 full-time (all women), 29 part-time (13 women); includes 2 minority (both African Americans) Average age 26. In 2006, 13 degrees awarded. *Entrance requirements:* For master's, GRE General Test, MAT, or 12 hours of graduate course work with a minimum GPA of 3.0. Additional exam requirements/ recommendations for international students: Required—TOEFL (minimum score 550 paper-based; 213 computer-based). *Application deadline:* Applications are processed on a rolling basis. Application fee: $30. *Expenses:* Tuition, state resident: part-time $259 per credit hour. Tuition, nonresident: part-time $482 per credit hour. *Financial support:* Application deadline: 7/1; *Unit head:* Dr. John Carter, Interim Head, 843-953-5060, Fax: 843-953-6798, E-mail: john.carter@citadel.edu. *Application contact:* Dr. Raymond S. Jones, Associate Dean, College of Graduate and Professional Studies, 843-953-5089, Fax: 843-953-7630, E-mail: ray.jones@citadel.edu.

Cleveland State University, College of Graduate Studies, College of Education and Human Services, Department of Health, Physical Education, Recreation and Dance, Cleveland, OH 44115. Offers community health education (M Ed); exercise science (M Ed); human performance (M Ed); physical education pedagogy (M Ed); school health education (M Ed); sport and exercise psychology (M Ed); sports management (M Ed). Part-time programs available. *Faculty:* 9 full-time (5 women), 3 part-time/adjunct (0 women). *Students:* 12 full-time (7 women), 62 part-time (32 women); includes 16 minority (15 African Americans, 1 Asian American or Pacific Islander), 4 international. Average age 30. 52 applicants, 52% accepted, 19 enrolled. In 2006, 36 degrees awarded. *Degree requirements:* For master's, thesis optional. *Entrance requirements:* For master's, GRE General Test or MAT (if undergraduate GPA is below 2.75), minimum undergraduate GPA of 2.75. Additional exam requirements/recommendations for international students: Required—TOEFL (minimum score 525 paper-based; 197 computer-based), IELTS (minimum score 6). *Application deadline:* For fall admission, 7/15 priority date for domestic students; for spring admission, 12/15 priority date for domestic students. Applications are processed on a rolling basis. Application fee: $30. Electronic applications accepted. *Financial support:* In 2006–07, 6 research assistantships with full and partial tuition reimbursements (averaging $3,480 per year), 1 teaching assistantship with full and partial tuition reimbursement (averaging $3,480 per year) were awarded; career-related internships or fieldwork, tuition waivers (full), and unspecified assistantships also available. Financial award application deadline: 3/15. *Faculty research:* Childhood obesity, bone density, marketing fitness centers, motor development of disabled, mental skills training. Total annual research expenditures: $102,615. *Unit head:* Dr. Sheila M. Patterson, Chairperson, 216-687-4870, Fax: 216-687-5410, E-mail: s.m.patterson@csuohio.edu.

The College of New Jersey, Graduate Division, School of Nursing, Health and Exercise Science, Department of Health and Exercise Science, Program in Health Education, Ewing, NJ 08628. Offers health (MAT); physical education (M Ed). *Accreditation:* NCATE. *Students:* 3 applicants, 100% accepted. *Degree requirements:* For master's, comprehensive exam. *Entrance requirements:* For master's, MAT or GRE, minimum GPA of 3.0 in field or 2.75 overall. Additional exam requirements/recommendations for international students: Required—TOEFL. *Application deadline:* For fall admission, 4/15 for domestic students; for spring admission, 10/15 for domestic students. Application fee: $60. Electronic applications accepted. *Financial support:* Unspecified assistantships available. Financial award application deadline: 5/1; financial award applicants required to submit FAFSA. *Unit head:* Dr. Aristomen Chilakos, Coordinator, 609-771-3160, Fax: 609-637-5153, E-mail: chilako@tcnj.edu. *Application contact:* Susan L. Hydro, Office of Graduate Studies, Assistant Dean, 609-771-2300, Fax: 609-637-5105, E-mail: graduate@tcnj.edu.

The College of New Jersey, Graduate Division, School of Nursing, Health and Exercise Science, Department of Health and Exercise Science, Program in Physical Education, Ewing, NJ 08628. Offers M Ed, MAT. Part-time and evening/weekend programs available. *Students:* 4 full-time (0 women), 13 part-time (9 women); includes 2 minority (both Hispanic Americans) 11 applicants, 100% accepted. In 2006, 11 degrees awarded. *Degree requirements:* For master's, comprehensive exam. *Entrance requirements:* For master's, MAT or GRE, minimum GPA of 2.75 overall or 3.0 in field. Additional exam requirements/recommendations for international students: Required—TOEFL. *Application deadline:* For fall admission, 4/15 for domestic students; for spring admission, 10/15 for domestic students. Application fee: $60. Electronic applications accepted. *Financial support:* Unspecified assistantships available. Financial award application deadline: 5/1; financial award applicants required to submit FAFSA. *Unit head:* Dr. Aristomen Chilakos, Coordinator, 609-771-3160, Fax: 609-637-5153, E-mail: chilako@tcnj.edu. *Application contact:* Susan L. Hydro, Office of Graduate Studies, Assistant Dean, 609-771-2300, Fax: 609-637-5105, E-mail: graduate@tcnj.edu.

Columbus State University, Graduate Studies, College of Education, Department of Teacher Education, Columbus, GA 31907-5645. Offers early childhood education (M Ed, Ed S); instructional technology (MS); middle grades education (M Ed, Ed S); physical education (M Ed); secondary education (M Ed, Ed S), including English/language arts, general science (M Ed), mathematics, science (Ed S), social science; special education (Ed S), including behavior disorders, learning disabilities, mental retardation. *Accreditation:* NCATE. Part-time and evening/weekend programs available. Postbaccalaureate distance learning degree programs offered (minimal on-campus study). *Faculty:* 16 full-time (8 women), 2 part-time/adjunct (1 woman). *Students:* 61 full-time (45 women), 128 part-time (89 women); includes 44 minority (36 African Americans, 3 Asian Americans or Pacific Islanders, 5 Hispanic Americans), 1 international. Average age 36. 77 applicants, 49% accepted, 26 enrolled. In 2006, 66 master's, 13 other advanced degrees awarded. *Degree requirements:* For master's, thesis, exit exam; for Ed S, thesis or alternative. *Entrance requirements:* For master's, GRE General Test, minimum GPA of 2.75; for Ed S, GRE General Test. Additional exam requirements/ recommendations for international students: Required—TOEFL (minimum score 550 paper-based; 213 computer-based). *Application deadline:* For fall admission, 5/1 priority date for domestic students, 5/1 for international students; for spring admission, 11/1 for domestic and international students. Applications are processed on a rolling basis. Application fee: $25. Electronic applications accepted. *Expenses:* Tuition, state resident: part-time $127 per semester hour. Tuition, nonresident: part-time $508 per semester hour. Required fees: $264 per semester. Tuition and fees vary according to course load. *Financial support:* In 2006–07, 118 students received support, including 21 research assistantships with partial tuition reimbursements available (averaging $3,000 per year); career-related internships or fieldwork, Federal Work-Study, institutionally sponsored loans, scholarships/grants, tuition waivers (partial), and unspecified assistantships also available. Support available to part-time students. Financial award application deadline: 5/1; financial award applicants required to submit FAFSA. *Unit head:* Dr. Deborah Gober, Acting Chair, 706-568-2255, Fax: 706-568-3134, E-mail: gober_deborah@colstate.edu. *Application contact:* Katie Thornton, Graduate Admissions Specialist, 706-568-2035, Fax: 706-568-2462, E-mail: thornton_katie@colstate.edu.

Concordia University, School of Arts and Sciences, Irvine, CA 92612-3299. Offers coaching and athletic administration (MA). *Faculty:* 3 full-time, 4 part-time/adjunct. *Students:* 51 full-time (13 women); includes 7 minority (1 African American, 1 Asian American or Pacific Islander, 5 Hispanic Americans), 1 international. *Degree requirements:* For master's, exam or thesis. *Entrance requirements:* Additional exam requirements/recommendations for international students: Required—TOEFL. *Application deadline:* Applications are processed on a rolling basis. Application fee: $50 ($300 for international students). *Unit head:* Dr. Kenneth Mangels, Dean, 949-854-8002 Ext. 1350, Fax: 949-854-6854, E-mail: kenneth.mangels@cui.edu. *Application contact:* Roberto Marquez, Coordinator of Graduate Enrollment, 949-854-8002 Ext. 1133, Fax: 949-854-6854, E-mail: roberto.marquez@cui.edu.

Delta State University, Graduate Programs, College of Education, Division of Health, Physical Education and Recreation, Cleveland, MS 38733-0001. Offers physical education and recreation (M Ed). Part-time and evening/weekend programs available. *Degree requirements:* For master's, thesis optional. *Entrance requirements:* For master's, GRE General Test or MAT, Class A teaching certificate. *Application deadline:* For fall admission, 8/1 priority date for domestic students; for spring admission, 12/1 priority date for domestic students. Applications are processed on a rolling basis. Application fee: $0. *Financial support:* In 2006–07, research assistantships (averaging $4,000 per year); career-related internships or fieldwork, Federal Work-Study, and institutionally sponsored loans also available. Support available to part-time students. Financial award application deadline: 6/1. *Faculty research:* Blood pressure, body fat, power and reaction time, learning disorders for athletes, effects of walking. *Unit head:* Dr. Duke Barnes, Chair, 662-846-4555, Fax: 662-846-4571, E-mail: dbarnes@deltastate.edu.

DePaul University, School of Education, Chicago, IL 60604-2287. Offers bilingual and bicultural education (M Ed, MA); curriculum studies (M Ed, MA); education (Ed D), including curriculum studies, educational leadership; educational leadership (M Ed, MA), including administration and supervision, Catholic school leadership, physical education; human development and learning (MA); human services and counseling (M Ed, MA), including agencies, family concerns, and higher education, elementary schools, human services management, secondary schools; reading and learning disabilities (M Ed, MA); social culture studies in education and development (M Ed, MA), including curriculum studies/development; teaching and learning (early childhood, elementary and secondary) (M Ed), including elementary education (M Ed, MA), secondary education (M Ed, MA); teaching and learning (early childhood, elementary, and secondary) (MA), including elementary education (M Ed, MA), secondary education (M Ed, MA). *Accreditation:* NCATE. Part-time and evening/weekend programs available. *Faculty:* 61 full-time (40 women), 76 part-time/adjunct (46 women). *Students:* 1,371 full-time (1,103 women), 474 part-time (362 women); includes 435 minority (144 African Americans, 7 American Indian/ Alaska Native, 89 Asian Americans or Pacific Islanders, 195 Hispanic Americans), 11 international. Average age 30. 993 applicants, 80% accepted, 617 enrolled. In 2006, 324 master's, 7 doctorates awarded. *Degree requirements:* For doctorate, thesis/dissertation. *Entrance requirements:* For master's, interview, minimum GPA of 2.75, 2 letters of recommendation; for doctorate, interview, master's degree, 2 years of work experience (recommended), writing sample, 3 letters of recommendation. Application fee: $25. Electronic applications accepted. *Financial support:* In 2006–07, 16 research assistantships with tuition reimbursements (averaging $4,370 per year), 1 teaching assistantship (averaging $6,000 per year) were awarded; career-related internships or fieldwork also available. *Faculty research:* Reflective teaching, children at risk, loss, ethnicity, urban education. Total annual research expenditures: $556,194. *Unit head:* Dr. Clara Jennings, Dean, 773-325-7581, Fax: 773-325-7728, E-mail: cjennings@depaul.edu. *Application contact:* Dr. John Bollwark, Data Project Manager, 773-325-7582, Fax: 773-325-7713, E-mail: jbollwar@depaul.edu.

Drury University, Graduate Programs in Education, Program in Physical Education, Springfield, MO 65802. Offers M Ed. Part-time and evening/weekend programs available. *Degree requirements:* For master's, thesis. *Entrance requirements:* For master's, GRE or MAT, minimum GPA of 2.75. *Faculty research:* Technology and physical education.

Eastern Illinois University, Graduate School, College of Education and Professional Studies, Department of Physical Education, Charleston, IL 61920-3099. Offers MS. Part-time programs available. *Faculty:* 15 full-time (3 women). In 2006, 33 degrees awarded. *Application deadline:* For fall admission, 7/31 priority date for domestic students. Applications are processed on a rolling basis. Application fee: $30. *Expenses:* Tuition, state resident: part-time $169 per semester hour. Tuition, nonresident: part-time $508 per semester hour. Required fees: $60 per semester hour. *Financial support:* In 2006–07, 9 teaching assistantships with tuition reimbursements (averaging $7,200 per year) were awarded; Federal Work-Study also available. Support available to part-time students. *Unit head:* Dr. Jill Owen, Chairperson, 217-581-2215, E-mail: jdowen@eiu.edu. *Application contact:* Dr. Scott Crawford, Coordinator, 217-581-6363, E-mail: agcrawford@eiu.edu.

Eastern Kentucky University, The Graduate School, College of Education, Department of Curriculum and Instruction, Program in Secondary and Higher Education, Richmond, KY 40475-3102. Offers agricultural education (MA Ed); allied health sciences education (MA Ed); art education (MA Ed); biological sciences education (MA Ed); business education (MA Ed); chemistry education (MA Ed); earth science education (MA Ed); English education (MA Ed); general science education (MA Ed); geography education (MA Ed); history education (MA Ed); home economics education (MA Ed); industrial education (MA Ed); mathematical sciences education (MA Ed); physical education (MA Ed); physics education (MA Ed); political science education (MA Ed); psychology education (MA Ed); reading (MA Ed); school health education (MA Ed); sociology education (MA Ed). *Accreditation:* NCATE. Part-time programs available. *Students:* 16 full-time (8 women), 63 part-time (43 women); includes 5 minority (2 African Americans, 2 American Indian/Alaska Native, 1 Asian American or Pacific Islander). Average age 32. *Entrance requirements:* For master's, GRE General Test, minimum GPA of 2.5. Application fee: $30. *Expenses:* Tuition, state resident: full-time $5,610. Tuition, nonresident: full-time $15,910. *Financial support:* Research assistantships, teaching assistantships, Federal Work-Study available. Support available to part-time students. *Unit head:* Dr. Michael Martin, Chair, Department of Curriculum and Instruction, 859-622-2154, Fax: 859-622-2004.

Eastern Kentucky University, The Graduate School, College of Health Sciences, Department of Exercise and Sport Science, Richmond, KY 40475-3102. Offers physical education (MS); sports administration (MS). Part-time programs available. *Faculty:* 3 full-time (1 woman), 1 part-time/adjunct (0 women). *Students:* 27 full-time (11 women), 25 part-time (11 women); includes 9 minority (all African Americans), 1 international. Average age 27. 38 applicants, 76% accepted, 18 enrolled. In 2006, 18 degrees awarded. *Entrance requirements:* For master's, GRE General Test, minimum GPA of 2.5. *Application deadline:* For fall admission, 8/15 for domestic students. Application fee: $30. *Expenses:* Tuition, state resident: full-time $5,610. Tuition, nonresident: full-time $15,910. *Financial support:* Research assistantships, teaching assistantships, Federal Work-Study available. Support available to part-time students. *Faculty research:* Nutrition and exercise. *Unit head:* Dr. Lonnie Davis, Chair, 859-622-1887, Fax: 859-622-1254, E-mail: lonnie.davis@eku.edu.

Eastern Michigan University, Graduate School, College of Health and Human Services, School of Health Promotion and Human Performance, Programs in Health and Physical Education, Ypsilanti, MI 48197. Offers MS. Part-time and evening/weekend programs available. Postbaccalaureate distance learning degree programs offered (minimal on-campus study). *Students:* 2 full-time (0 women), 31 part-time (18 women); includes 3 minority (all African Americans), 4 international. Average age 32. In 2006, 10 degrees awarded. *Entrance requirements:* Additional exam requirements/recommendations for international students: Required—TOEFL. *Application deadline:* For fall admission, 5/15 priority date for domestic students, 5/1 priority date for international students; for winter admission, 10/15 priority date for domestic students, 10/1 priority date for international students; for spring admission, 3/15 priority date for domestic students, 3/1 priority date for international students. Applications are processed on a rolling basis. Application fee: $35. *Expenses:* Tuition, state resident: part-time $341 per credit hour. Tuition, nonresident: full-time $16,104; part-time $671 per credit hour. Required fees: $816; $34 per credit hour. $40 per term. One-time fee: $82 full-time. Tuition and fees vary according to course level, course load, degree level and reciprocity agreements. *Financial support:* Fellowships, research assistantships with full tuition reimbursements, teaching assistantships with full tuition reimbursements, career-related internships or fieldwork, Federal Work-Study, institutionally sponsored loans, scholarships/grants, tuition waivers (partial), and unspecified assistantships available. Support available to part-time students. Financial award applicants required to submit FAFSA.

Eastern New Mexico University, Graduate School, College of Education and Technology, Department of Health and Physical Education, Portales, NM 88130. Offers physical education (MS). Part-time programs available. *Faculty:* 3 full-time (2 women). *Students:* 1 full-time (0 women), 27 part-time (12 women); includes 10 minority (3 African Americans, 7 Hispanic Americans). Average age 28. 27 applicants, 81% accepted. In 2006, 10 degrees awarded. *Degree requirements:* For master's, thesis optional. *Entrance requirements:* For master's, minimum

GPA of 2.5. *Application deadline:* For fall admission, 8/20 priority date for domestic students. Applications are processed on a rolling basis. Application fee: $0. Electronic applications accepted. *Expenses:* Tuition, state resident: full-time $2,478; part-time $103 per credit hour. Tuition, nonresident: full-time $8,034; part-time $335 per credit hour. Required fees: $35 per credit hour. *Financial support:* In 2006–07, fellowships (averaging $1,025 per year), 4 research assistantships (averaging $8,200 per year), 15 teaching assistantships (averaging $8,200 per year) were awarded; Federal Work-Study also available. Support available to part-time students. Financial award application deadline: 3/1. *Unit head:* Dr. Sarah Wall, Graduate Coordinator, 505-562-2915, E-mail: sarah.wall@enmu.edu.

Eastern Washington University, Graduate Studies, College of Education and Human Development, Department of Physical Education, Health and Recreation, Cheney, WA 99004-2431. Offers college instruction in physical education (MS); physical education (MS). *Degree requirements:* For master's, thesis or alternative, comprehensive exam. *Entrance requirements:* For master's, minimum GPA of 3.0.

East Stroudsburg University of Pennsylvania, Graduate School, School of Health Sciences and Human Performance, Department of Exercise Science, East Stroudsburg, PA 18301-2999. Offers cardiac rehabilitation and exercise science (MS). Part-time and evening/weekend programs available. *Faculty:* 4 full-time (1 woman), 1 part-time/adjunct (0 women). *Students:* 25 full-time (16 women), 6 part-time (2 women); includes 1 minority (African American), 4 international. Average age 28. In 2006, 32 degrees awarded. *Degree requirements:* For master's, comprehensive exam. *Entrance requirements:* Additional exam requirements/recommendations for international students: Required—TOEFL (minimum score 560 paper-based; 220 computer-based; 83 iBT). *Application deadline:* For fall admission, 7/31 priority date for domestic students, 5/1 priority date for international students; for spring admission, 11/30 for domestic students, 10/1 for international students. Applications are processed on a rolling basis. Application fee: $50. *Expenses:* Tuition, state resident: full-time $6,048; part-time $336 per credit. Tuition, nonresident: full-time $9,678; part-time $538 per credit. Required fees: $1,353; $67 per credit. One-time fee: $37 part-time. *Financial support:* In 2006–07, 19 research assistantships with full and partial tuition reimbursements were awarded; Federal Work-Study and institutionally sponsored loans also available. Financial award application deadline: 3/1. *Unit head:* Dr. Shala Davis, Graduate Coordinator, 570-422-3302, Fax: 570-422-3616, E-mail: sdavis@po-box.esu.edu.

East Stroudsburg University of Pennsylvania, Graduate School, School of Health Sciences and Human Performance, Department of Physical Education, East Stroudsburg, PA 18301-2999. Offers health and physical education (M Ed). *Faculty:* 2 full-time (both women). *Students:* 17 full-time (9 women), 9 part-time (1 woman); includes 3 minority (2 African Americans, 1 Hispanic American). Average age 30. In 2006, 20 degrees awarded. *Entrance requirements:* Additional exam requirements/recommendations for international students: Required—TOEFL (minimum score 560 paper-based; 220 computer-based; 83 iBT). *Application deadline:* For fall admission, 7/31 for domestic students, 5/1 for international students; for spring admission, 11/30 for domestic students, 10/1 for international students. Applications are processed on a rolling basis. Application fee: $50. *Expenses:* Tuition, state resident: full-time $6,048; part-time $336 per credit. Tuition, nonresident: full-time $9,678; part-time $538 per credit. Required fees: $1,353; $67 per credit. One-time fee: $37 part-time. *Financial support:* In 2006–07, 5 research assistantships were awarded; Federal Work-Study and unspecified assistantships also available. Financial award application deadline: 3/1; financial award applicants required to submit FAFSA. *Unit head:* Dr. Suzanne Mueller, Graduate Coordinator, 570-422-3104, E-mail: smueller@po-box.esu.edu.

East Tennessee State University, School of Graduate Studies, College of Education, Department of Physical Education, Exercise and Sport Sciences, Johnson City, TN 37614. Offers exercise physiology (MA); fitness leadership (MA); physical education (M Ed, MA); sports management (MA); sports sciences (MA). Part-time and evening/weekend programs available. *Degree requirements:* For master's, comprehensive exam (M Ed), oral and written comprehensive exams, thesis (MA). *Entrance requirements:* For master's, GRE General Test, major or minor in physical education or equivalent, interview, minimum GPA of 2.7. Additional exam requirements/recommendations for international students: Required—TOEFL (minimum score 550 paper-based; 213 computer-based). *Faculty research:* Resistance training for various populations, self actualization using challenging courses, park and recreation industry needs relative to recent university graduates, funding sport operations.

Emporia State University, School of Graduate Studies, The Teachers College, Department of Health, Physical Education and Recreation, Emporia, KS 66801-5087. Offers physical education (MS). Part-time programs available. Postbaccalaureate distance learning degree programs offered (no on-campus study). *Faculty:* 14 full-time (8 women), 1 (woman) part-time/adjunct. *Students:* 14 full-time (10 women), 152 part-time (62 women); includes 14 minority (8 African Americans, 1 Asian American or Pacific Islander, 5 Hispanic Americans). 28 applicants, 75% accepted, 7 enrolled. In 2006, 70 degrees awarded. *Degree requirements:* For master's, comprehensive exam or thesis. *Entrance requirements:* For master's, bachelor's degree in physical education, health, and recreation; letters of recommendation. Additional exam requirements/recommendations for international students: Required—TOEFL. *Application deadline:* For fall admission, 8/15 priority date for domestic students. Applications are processed on a rolling basis. Application fee: $30 ($75 for international students). Electronic applications accepted. *Expenses:* Tuition, state resident: full-time $3,438; part-time $143 per credit hour. Tuition, nonresident: full-time $10,398; part-time $433 per credit hour. Required fees: $724; $44 per credit hour. *Financial support:* In 2006–07, 5 teaching assistantships with full tuition reimbursements (averaging $6,752 per year) were awarded; career-related internships or fieldwork, Federal Work-Study, institutionally sponsored loans, health care benefits, and unspecified assistantships also available. Financial award application deadline: 3/15; financial award applicants required to submit FAFSA. *Unit head:* Dr. Kathy Ermler, Chair, 620-341-5926, E-mail: kermler@emporia.edu.

Florida Agricultural and Mechanical University, Division of Graduate Studies, Research, and Continuing Education, College of Education, Department of Health, Physical Education, and Recreation, Tallahassee, FL 32307-3200. Offers M Ed, MS Ed. *Accreditation:* NCATE. Part-time and evening/weekend programs available. *Degree requirements:* For master's, thesis optional. *Entrance requirements:* For master's, GRE General Test, minimum GPA of 3.0. Additional exam requirements/recommendations for international students: Required—TOEFL. *Faculty research:* Administration/curriculum, work behavior, psychology.

Florida International University, College of Education, Department of Curriculum and Instruction, Miami, FL 33199. Offers art education (MAT, MS, Ed D); curriculum and instruction (Ed S); curriculum development (MS); curriculum studies (PhD); early childhood education (MS, Ed D); elementary education (MS, Ed D); English education (MAT, MS, Ed D); foreign language education—teaching English to speakers of other languages (TESOL) (Certificate), including foreign language education; foreign language education- teaching English to speakers of other languages (TESOL) (MS), including teaching English; French education—initial teacher preparation (MAT); international and intercultural development education (Ed D); international and intercultural developmental education (MS); language, literacy and culture (PhD); learning technologies (MS, Ed D, PhD); mathematics education (MAT, MS, Ed D, PhD); modern language education/bilingual education (MS, Ed D); physical education (MS); reading education (MS, Ed D); science education (MAT, MS, Ed D, PhD); social studies education (MAT, MS, Ed D); Spanish education—initial teacher preparation (MAT); special education (MS). Part-time and evening/weekend programs available. *Faculty:* 19 full-time (11 women). *Students:* 89 full-time (66 women), 258 part-time (221 women); includes 99 minority (72 African Americans, 10 Asian Americans or Pacific Islanders, 17 Hispanic Americans). Average age 35. 167 applicants, 50% accepted, 81 enrolled. In 2006, 141 master's, 8 doctorates, 1 other advanced degree awarded. *Degree requirements:* For doctorate, thesis/dissertation, comprehensive exam, registration. *Entrance requirements:* For master's, GRE General Test, Florida General Knowledge Test or Florida College Level Academic Skills Test; for doctorate

and other advanced degree, GRE General Test. Additional exam requirements/recommendations for international students: Required—TOEFL (minimum score 550 paper-based; 213 computer-based; 80 iBT), IELTS (minimum score 6). *Application deadline:* For fall admission, 6/1 priority date for domestic students, 4/1 for international students; for winter admission, 10/1 priority date for domestic students, 9/1 for international students; for spring admission, 3/1 priority date for domestic students, 2/1 for international students. Applications are processed on a rolling basis. Application fee: $30. Electronic applications accepted. *Expenses:* Tuition, state resident: part-time $249 per credit hour. Tuition, nonresident: part-time $753 per credit hour. Tuition and fees vary according to program. *Financial support:* Research assistantships with full and partial tuition reimbursements, teaching assistantships with full and partial tuition reimbursements available. *Unit head:* Dr. Lisbeth Dixon-Krauss, Interim Chairperson, 305-348-3609, Fax: 305-348-2086, E-mail: kraussl@fiu.edu. *Application contact:* Marisa Salazar, Student Recruiter, 305-348-3002, Fax: 305-348-3227, E-mail: marisa.salazar@fiu.edu.

Florida International University, College of Education, Department of Health, Physical Education, and Recreation, Program in Physical Education, Miami, FL 33199. Offers advanced teacher preparation (MS); sports management (MS). Part-time and evening/weekend programs available. *Faculty:* 3 full-time (2 women). *Students:* 7 full-time (2 women), 16 part-time (9 women); includes 17 minority (7 African Americans, 1 Asian American or Pacific Islander, 9 Hispanic Americans). Average age 31. 8 applicants, 38% accepted, 3 enrolled. In 2006, 7 degrees awarded. *Entrance requirements:* For master's, GRE General Test or minimum GPA of 3.0, teaching certificate in physical education. Additional exam requirements/recommendations for international students: Required—TOEFL (minimum score 550 paper-based; 213 computer-based; 80 iBT), IELTS (minimum score 6). *Application deadline:* For fall admission, 6/1 priority date for domestic students, 4/1 for international students; for winter admission, 10/1 priority date for domestic students, 9/1 for international students; for spring admission, 3/1 priority date for domestic students, 2/1 for international students. Applications are processed on a rolling basis. Application fee: $30. Electronic applications accepted. *Expenses:* Tuition, state resident: part-time $249 per credit hour. Tuition, nonresident: part-time $753 per credit hour. Tuition and fees vary according to program. *Financial support:* Fellowships, research assistantships, teaching assistantships, Federal Work-Study available. Support available to part-time students. *Application contact:* Marisa Salazar, Student Recruiter, 305-348-3002, Fax: 305-348-3227, E-mail: marisa.salazar@fiu.edu.

Florida State University, Graduate Studies, College of Education, Department of Sport Management, Recreation Management, and Physical Education, Tallahassee, FL 32306. Offers physical education (MS, Ed D, PhD, Ed S); recreation management (MS); sport management (MS, Ed D, PhD, Ed S). *Faculty:* 18 full-time (9 women), 5 part-time/adjunct (3 women). *Students:* 93 full-time (35 women), 87 part-time (39 women); includes 65 minority (21 African Americans, 34 Asian Americans or Pacific Islanders, 10 Hispanic Americans). 226 applicants, 56% accepted, 75 enrolled. In 2006, 57 master's, 13 doctorates, 1 other advanced degree awarded. *Degree requirements:* For master's and Ed S, thesis optional; for doctorate, thesis/dissertation, comprehensive exam. *Entrance requirements:* For master's, doctorate, and Ed S, GRE General Test, minimum GPA of 3.0. Additional exam requirements/recommendations for international students: Required—TOEFL (minimum score 550 paper-based; 213 computer-based). *Application deadline:* For fall admission, 7/1 priority date for domestic students, 5/1 for international students; for spring admission, 11/1 for domestic students, 9/1 for international students. Applications are processed on a rolling basis. Application fee: $30. Electronic applications accepted. *Expenses:* Tuition, state resident: full-time $5,822; part-time $243 per credit hour. Tuition, nonresident: full-time $20,976; part-time $874 per credit hour. Tuition and fees vary according to program. *Financial support:* In 2006–07, 1 fellowship, 35 research assistantships, 38 teaching assistantships were awarded; career-related internships or fieldwork also available. Financial award applicants required to submit FAFSA. *Faculty research:* Sport marketing, teacher career cycle, gender issues. *Unit head:* Dr. Cheryl Beeler, Chair, 850-644-4813, Fax: 850-644-0975, E-mail: beeler@coe.fsu.edu. *Application contact:* Cynthia Bailey, Program Assistant, 850-644-4813, Fax: 850-644-0975, E-mail: bailey@coe.fsu.edu.

Fort Hays State University, Graduate School, College of Health and Life Sciences, Department of Health and Human Performance, Hays, KS 67601-4099. Offers MS. Part-time programs available. *Faculty:* 7 full-time (1 woman). *Students:* 16 full-time (6 women), 22 part-time (7 women); includes 3 minority (2 African Americans, 1 Hispanic American). Average age 29. 21 applicants, 100% accepted. In 2006, 15 degrees awarded. *Degree requirements:* For master's, thesis optional. *Entrance requirements:* For master's, GRE General Test or MAT. Additional exam requirements/recommendations for international students: Required—TOEFL (minimum score 550 paper-based; 213 computer-based). *Application deadline:* For fall admission, 7/1 priority date for domestic students. Applications are processed on a rolling basis. Application fee: $35. Electronic applications accepted. *Financial support:* In 2006–07, 8 teaching assistantships (averaging $5,000 per year) were awarded; research assistantships. *Faculty research:* Isoproterenol hydrochloride and exercise, dehydrogenase and high-density lipoprotein levels in athletics, venous blood parameters to adipose fat. *Unit head:* Glen McNeil, Chair, 785-628-4352, E-mail: gmcneil@fhsu.edu.

Frostburg State University, Graduate School, College of Education, Program in Human Performance, Frostburg, MD 21532-1099. Offers MS. Part-time and evening/weekend programs available. *Degree requirements:* For master's, thesis. *Entrance requirements:* For master's, interview. Electronic applications accepted.

Gardner-Webb University, Graduate School, Department of Physical Education, Wellness, and Sports Studies, Boiling Springs, NC 28017. Offers sport science and pedagogy (MA). Part-time and evening/weekend programs available. *Faculty:* 1 (woman) full-time. *Students:* 1 full-time (0 women), 14 part-time (9 women); includes 3 minority (2 African Americans, 1 Asian American or Pacific Islander). Average age 25. 4 applicants, 100% accepted, 4 enrolled. In 2006, 6 degrees awarded. *Degree requirements:* For master's, comprehensive exam. *Entrance requirements:* For master's, GRE General Test or NTE, PRAXIS, minimum GPA of 2.5. *Application deadline:* For fall admission, 8/1 priority date for domestic students. Applications are processed on a rolling basis. Application fee: $25. Electronic applications accepted. *Expenses:* Tuition: Full-time $3,144; part-time $262 per hour. *Financial support:* Unspecified assistantships available. *Unit head:* Dr. Ken Baker, Chair, 704-406-4481, Fax: 704-406-4739.

Georgia College & State University, Graduate School, School of Health Sciences, Department of Kinesiology, Milledgeville, GA 31061. Offers health and physical education (M Ed, Ed S). *Accreditation:* NCATE (one or more programs are accredited). *Students:* 16 full-time (8 women), 5 part-time (4 women), 2 international. Average age 26. 19 applicants, 74% accepted, 10 enrolled. In 2006, 8 master's awarded. *Degree requirements:* For master's, comprehensive exam; for Ed S, research project. *Entrance requirements:* For master's, GRE General Test or MAT, minimum GPA of 2.75 in upper-level undergraduate courses; for Ed S, GRE General Test or MAT, master's degree, minimum graduate GPA of 3.25, 2 years teaching experience. Additional exam requirements/recommendations for international students: Required—TOEFL (minimum score 500 paper-based; 173 computer-based). *Application deadline:* For fall admission, 7/15 priority date for domestic students. Applications are processed on a rolling basis. Application fee: $25. Electronic applications accepted. *Expenses:* Tuition, state resident: full-time $3,222; part-time $179 per credit hour. Tuition, nonresident: full-time $12,870; part-time $715 per credit hour. Required fees: $391 per semester. Tuition and fees vary according to course load. *Financial support:* In 2006–07, 13 research assistantships were awarded; career-related internships or fieldwork, Federal Work-Study, and unspecified assistantships also available. Support available to part-time students. Financial award application deadline: 3/1; financial award applicants required to submit FAFSA. *Unit head:* Dr. James Lidstone, Chair, 478-445-4072, E-mail: jim.lidstone@gcsu.edu.

Georgia Southern University, Jack N. Averitt College of Graduate Studies, College of Education, Department of Teaching and Learning, Program in Health and Physical Education, Statesboro, GA 30460. Offers M Ed. *Accreditation:* NCATE. Part-time and evening/weekend

Physical Education

Georgia Southern University (continued)
programs available. *Students:* 2 full-time (1 woman). Average age 24. *Degree requirements:* For master's, comprehensive exam. *Entrance requirements:* For master's, GRE General Test or MAT, minimum GPA of 2.5. Additional exam requirements/recommendations for international students: Required—TOEFL (minimum score 550 paper-based; 213 computer-based; 80 iBT). *Application deadline:* For fall admission, 3/1 priority date for domestic students, 3/1 for international students; for spring admission, 10/1 priority date for domestic students, 10/1 for international students. Applications are processed on a rolling basis. Application fee: $50. Electronic applications accepted. *Financial support:* In 2006–07, 2 students received support, including research assistantships with partial tuition reimbursements available (averaging $5,500 per year), teaching assistantships with partial tuition reimbursements available (averaging $5,500 per year); career-related internships or fieldwork, Federal Work-Study, and tuition waivers (partial) also available. Support available to part-time students. Financial award application deadline: 4/15; financial award applicants required to submit FAFSA. *Unit head:* Dr. Tony Pritchard, Coordinator, 912-871-1323, Fax: 912-681-0026, E-mail: tpritchard@georgiasouthen.edu. *Application contact:* 912-681-5384, Fax: 912-681-0740, E-mail: gradadmissions@georgiasouthern.edu.

Georgia Southwestern State University, Graduate Studies, School of Education, Americus, GA 31709-4693. Offers early childhood education (M Ed, Ed S); health and physical education (M Ed); middle grades education (M Ed, Ed S); reading (M Ed); secondary education (M Ed); special education (M Ed). *Accreditation:* NCATE. *Degree requirements:* For master's, comprehensive exam. *Entrance requirements:* For master's, GRE General Test or MAT, minimum GPA of 2.5; for Ed S, GRE General Test or MAT, minimum graduate GPA of 3.25, M Ed from accredited college or university, 3 years teaching experience. Electronic applications accepted.

Georgia State University, College of Education, Department of Kinesiology and Health, Program in Health and Physical Education, Atlanta, GA 30303-3083. Offers M Ed. Part-time and evening/weekend programs available. *Students:* Average age 34. 1 applicant, 100% accepted. In 2006, 1 degree awarded. *Degree requirements:* For master's, comprehensive exam. *Entrance requirements:* For master's, GRE General Test, minimum GPA of 2.5. *Application deadline:* For fall admission, 5/1 for domestic students; for spring admission, 10/1 for domestic students. Application fee: $25. *Financial support:* Teaching assistantships, career-related internships or fieldwork available. *Faculty research:* Exercise science, teacher behavior. *Unit head:* Dr. J. Andrew Doyle, Chair, Department of Kinesiology and Health, 404-651-4258, E-mail: adoyle@gsu.edu.

Hardin-Simmons University, Graduate School, Irvin School of Education, Department of Fitness and Sport Sciences, Program in Advanced Physical Education, Abilene, TX 79698-0001. Offers M Ed. Part-time programs available. In 2006, 1 degree awarded. *Degree requirements:* For master's, professional project. *Entrance requirements:* For master's, GRE, minimum undergraduate GPA of 3.0 in major, 2.7 overall; writing sample; letters of recommendation; resumé. Additional exam requirements/recommendations for international students: Required—TOEFL (minimum score 550 paper-based; 213 computer-based). *Application deadline:* For fall admission, 8/15 priority date for domestic students; for spring admission, 1/5 priority date for domestic students. Applications are processed on a rolling basis. Application fee: $50 ($100 for international students). *Expenses:* Tuition: Full-time $9,090; part-time $505 per hour. Required fees: $490; $66 per semester. One-time fee: $50. Tuition and fees vary according to course load and degree level. *Financial support:* Fellowships, career-related internships or fieldwork, scholarships/grants, and unspecified assistantships available. Support available to part-time students. Financial award application deadline: 6/30; financial award applicants required to submit FAFSA. *Unit head:* Dr. Ray Galloway, Director, 325-670-1470, Fax: 325-670-1572, E-mail: rgallow@hsutx.edu. *Application contact:* Dr. Gary Stanlake, Dean of Graduate Studies, 325-670-1298, Fax: 325-670-1564, E-mail: gradoff@hsutx.edu.

Henderson State University, Graduate Studies, School of Education, Department of Health, Physical Education and Recreation, Arkadelphia, AR 71999-0001. Offers recreation (MS); sports administration (MS). *Faculty:* 6 full-time (1 woman). *Students:* 24 full-time (7 women), 29 part-time (11 women); includes 9 minority (8 African Americans, 1 Hispanic American), 18 international. Average age 27. In 2006, 8 degrees awarded. *Entrance requirements:* For master's, GRE General Test or MAT, minimum GPA of 2.7. *Application deadline:* For fall admission, 5/1 for international students; for winter admission, 10/1 for international students; for spring admission, 4/1 for international students. Application fee: $0 ($30 for international students). *Expenses:* Tuition, state resident: full-time $3,294; part-time $183 per credit hour. Tuition, nonresident: full-time $6,588; part-time $366 per credit hour. Required fees: $176 per term. *Unit head:* Dr. Hal McAfee, Chair of HPER, 870-230-5189, E-mail: mcafeeh@hsu.edu. *Application contact:* Dr. Marck L. Beggs, Graduate Dean, 870-230-5126, Fax: 870-230-5479, E-mail: beggsm@hsu.edu.

Hofstra University, School of Education and Allied Human Services, Department of Physical Education and Sports Sciences, Hempstead, NY 11549. Offers physical education (MS). Part-time programs available. *Faculty:* 6 full-time (2 women), 11 part-time/adjunct (5 women). *Students:* 49 full-time (20 women), 35 part-time (11 women); includes 9 minority (1 African American, 3 Asian Americans or Pacific Islanders, 5 Hispanic Americans). Average age 26. 50 applicants, 86% accepted, 29 enrolled. In 2006, 45 degrees awarded. *Degree requirements:* For master's, registration. *Entrance requirements:* For master's, 2 letters of recommendation, interview, essay. Additional exam requirements/recommendations for international students: Required—TOEFL (minimum score 550 paper-based; 213 computer-based). *Application deadline:* Applications are processed on a rolling basis. Application fee: $60. Electronic applications accepted. *Expenses:* Tuition: Full-time $13,320; part-time $740 per credit. Required fees: $930; $155 per term. *Financial support:* In 2006–07, 22 students received support, including 1 fellowship with tuition reimbursement available (averaging $3,000 per year), 3 research assistantships with full and partial tuition reimbursements available (averaging $6,834 per year); scholarships/grants and tuition waivers (full and partial) also available. Financial award applicants required to submit FAFSA. *Faculty research:* Adventure education, youth development: after school programs and fitness, childhood obesity, motor skills acquisition. *Unit head:* Dr. Nancy E. Halliday, Chairperson, 516-463-5811, E-mail: hprneh@hofstra.edu. *Application contact:* Carol Drummer, Dean of Graduate Admissions, 516-463-4876, Fax: 516-463-4664, E-mail: gradstudent@hofstra.edu.

Howard University, Graduate School, Department of Health, Human Performance and Leisure Studies, Washington, DC 20059-0002. Offers exercise physiology (MS); health education (MS); sport studies (MS), including sociology of sport, sport management; urban recreation (MS), including leisure studies. Part-time and evening/weekend programs available. *Degree requirements:* For master's, thesis, comprehensive exam, registration. *Entrance requirements:* For master's, BS in human performance or related field. Electronic applications accepted. *Faculty research:* Health promotion, cardiovascular hypertension, physical activity, sport and human rights issues.

Humboldt State University, Graduate Studies, College of Professional Studies, Department of Kinesiology, Arcata, CA 95521-8299. Offers athletic training education (MS); exercise science/wellness management (MS); pre-physical therapy (MS); teaching/coaching (MS). *Students:* 10 full-time (5 women), 5 part-time (1 woman); includes 4 minority (1 African American, 3 Asian Americans or Pacific Islanders). Average age 31. 15 applicants, 73% accepted, 6 enrolled. In 2006, 3 degrees awarded. *Degree requirements:* For master's, thesis or alternative. *Entrance requirements:* For master's, GMAT, minimum GPA of 2.5. Additional exam requirements/recommendations for international students: Required—TOEFL. *Application deadline:* Applications are processed on a rolling basis. Application fee: $55. *Financial support:* Teaching assistantships, career-related internships or fieldwork, Federal Work-Study, and institutionally sponsored loans available. Financial award application deadline: 3/1; financial award applicants required to submit FAFSA. *Faculty research:* Human performance, adapted physical education, physical therapy. *Unit head:* Dr. Sue MacConnie, Chair, 707-826-4536, Fax: 707-826-5451, E-mail: sem1@humboldt.edu. *Application contact:* Dr. Kathy Munoz, Coordinator, 707-826-3840, Fax: 707-826-5451, E-mail: kdm1@humboldt.edu.

Idaho State University, Office of Graduate Studies, College of Education, Department of Sports Science and Physical Education, Pocatello, ID 83209. Offers physical education (MPE). Part-time programs available. *Faculty:* 4 full-time (1 woman). *Students:* 20 full-time (2 women), 36 part-time (13 women); includes 6 minority (1 African American, 1 American Indian/Alaska Native, 4 Asian Americans or Pacific Islanders), 2 international. Average age 30. In 2006, 29 degrees awarded. *Degree requirements:* For master's, internship, oral defense of dissertation, or written exams, thesis optional. *Entrance requirements:* For master's, MAT or GRE General Test, minimum GPA of 3.0 in upper division classes. Additional exam requirements/recommendations for international students: Required—TOEFL (minimum score 550 paper-based; 213 computer-based; 80 iBT). *Application deadline:* For fall admission, 7/1 for domestic students, 6/1 for international students; for spring admission, 12/1 for domestic students, 11/1 for international students. Applications are processed on a rolling basis. Application fee: $55. *Expenses:* Tuition, state resident: part-time $251 per credit. Tuition, nonresident: part-time $366 per credit. Tuition and fees vary according to degree level, program and reciprocity agreements. *Financial support:* In 2006–07, 1 teaching assistantship with full and partial tuition reimbursement (averaging $8,694 per year) was awarded; career-related internships or fieldwork, Federal Work-Study, institutionally sponsored loans, scholarships/grants, tuition waivers, and unspecified assistantships also available. Support available to part-time students. Financial award application deadline: 1/1. *Faculty research:* Youth fitness, school-based physical education, athletic administration, leadership. *Unit head:* Dr. Michael Lester, Chair, 208-282-4563, Fax: 208-282-4697. *Application contact:* Dr. Peter Denner, Assistant Dean, 208-282-3807, Fax: 208-282-4697, E-mail: dennpete@isu.edu.

Illinois State University, Graduate School, College of Applied Science and Technology, School of Kinesiology and Recreation, Normal, IL 61790-2200. Offers health education (MS); physical education (MS). *Faculty:* 20 full-time (10 women). *Students:* 77 full-time (40 women), 17 part-time (10 women); includes 9 minority (3 African Americans, 1 Asian American or Pacific Islander, 5 Hispanic Americans), 7 international. 86 applicants, 80% accepted. In 2006, 44 degrees awarded. *Degree requirements:* For master's, thesis or alternative. *Entrance requirements:* For master's, GRE General Test, minimum GPA of 2.6 in last 60 hours of course work. *Application deadline:* Applications are processed on a rolling basis. Application fee: $40. *Expenses:* Tuition, state resident: full-time $3,330; part-time $185 per credit hour. Tuition, nonresident: full-time $6,948; part-time $438 per credit hour. Required fees: $1,259; $52 per credit hour. *Financial support:* In 2006–07, 38 teaching assistantships (averaging $6,694 per year) were awarded; career-related internships or fieldwork, Federal Work-Study, tuition waivers (full and partial), and unspecified assistantships also available. Financial award application deadline: 4/1. *Faculty research:* Physical education obesity prevention and lifestyle enhancement program, development of a physical activity and nutrition resource web page. *Unit head:* David Thomas, Acting Chairperson, 309-438-8661.

Indiana State University, School of Graduate Studies, College of Health and Human Performance, Department of Physical Education, Terre Haute, IN 47809-1401. Offers adult fitness (MA, MS); coaching (MA, MS); exercise science (MA, MS); master teacher (MA, MS). *Faculty:* 7 full-time (3 women), 2 part-time/adjunct (0 women). *Students:* 19 full-time (5 women), 13 part-time (4 women); includes 1 minority (African American), 5 international. Average age 27. 19 applicants, 89% accepted, 8 enrolled. In 2006, 18 degrees awarded. *Degree requirements:* For master's, thesis (for some programs). *Entrance requirements:* For master's, minor in physical education. *Application deadline:* For fall admission, 7/1 priority date for domestic students; for spring admission, 11/1 priority date for domestic students. Applications are processed on a rolling basis. Application fee: $35. Electronic applications accepted. *Expenses:* Tuition, state resident: part-time $278 per credit. Tuition, nonresident: part-time $552 per credit. *Financial support:* In 2006–07, 10 research assistantships with partial tuition reimbursements (averaging $6,300 per year) were awarded; teaching assistantships with partial tuition reimbursements, tuition waivers (partial) also available. Financial award application deadline: 3/1; financial award applicants required to submit FAFSA. *Faculty research:* Exercise science. *Unit head:* Dr. Jeffrey Edwards, Chairperson, 812-237-4048.

Indiana University Bloomington, School of Health, Physical Education and Recreation, Department of Kinesiology, Bloomington, IN 47405-7000. Offers adapted physical education (MS); applied sport science (MS); athletic training (MS); biomechanics (MS); clinical exercise physiology (MS); ergonomics (MS); exercise physiology (MS); human performance (MS, PhD, PE Dir); motor control (MS); sport management (MS). PhD offered through the University Graduate School. Part-time programs available. *Faculty:* 10 full-time (1 woman). *Students:* 106 full-time (47 women), 41 part-time (15 women); includes 16 minority (15 African Americans, 1 American Indian/Alaska Native), 26 international. Average age 26. Terminal master's awarded for partial completion of doctoral program. *Degree requirements:* For master's and PE Dir, thesis optional; for doctorate, variable foreign language requirement, thesis/dissertation. *Entrance requirements:* For master's, GRE General Test, minimum GPA of 2.8; for doctorate, GRE General Test, minimum graduate GPA of 3.5, minimum undergraduate GPA of 3.0; for PE Dir, GRE. *Application deadline:* For fall admission, 1/1 for international students; for spring admission, 9/1 for international students. Applications are processed on a rolling basis. Application fee: $50 ($60 for international students). *Expenses:* Tuition, state resident: full-time $5,791; part-time $241 per credit hour. Tuition, nonresident: full-time $16,866; part-time $703 per credit hour. *Financial support:* Fellowships, research assistantships with full tuition reimbursements, teaching assistantships with full tuition reimbursements, career-related internships or fieldwork, Federal Work-Study, institutionally sponsored loans, scholarships/grants, tuition waivers (partial), and fee remissions available. Financial award application deadline: 3/1. *Faculty research:* Exercise physiology and biochemistry, sports biomechanics, human motor control, adaptation of fitness and exercise to special populations. *Unit head:* John Shea, Chairperson, 812-855-3114. *Application contact:* Program Office, 812-855-5523, Fax: 812-855-9417, E-mail: kines@indiana.edu.

Indiana University of Pennsylvania, School of Graduate Studies and Research, College of Health and Human Services, Department of Health and Physical Education, Indiana, PA 15705-1087. Offers aquatics administration and facilities management (MS); exercise science (MS); sport management (MS); sport science (MS). Part-time programs available. *Faculty:* 8 full-time (4 women). *Students:* 33 full-time (17 women), 39 part-time (21 women); includes 3 minority (2 African Americans, 1 Asian American or Pacific Islander), 12 international. Average age 27. 75 applicants, 75% accepted. In 2006, 18 degrees awarded. *Degree requirements:* For master's, thesis optional. *Entrance requirements:* For master's, 2 letters of recommendation. Additional exam requirements/recommendations for international students: Required—TOEFL. *Application deadline:* For fall admission, 7/1 priority date for domestic students; for spring admission, 11/1 for domestic students. Applications are processed on a rolling basis. Application fee: $30. *Expenses:* Tuition, state resident: full-time $6,048; part-time $336 per credit. Tuition, nonresident: full-time $9,678; part-time $538 per credit. Required fees: $1,069; $148 per year. *Financial support:* In 2006–07, 6 research assistantships with full and partial tuition reimbursements (averaging $4,990 per year) were awarded. Financial award application deadline: 3/15; financial award applicants required to submit FAFSA. *Unit head:* Dr. Elaine Blair, Chairperson, 724-357-2770, E-mail: eblair@iup.edu.

Indiana University–Purdue University Indianapolis, School of Physical Education and Tourism Management, Indianapolis, IN 46202-2896. Offers MS. *Faculty:* 4 full-time (2 women). *Students:* 8 full-time (6 women), 8 part-time (3 women); includes 3 minority (1 African American, 2 Asian Americans or Pacific Islanders), 1 international. Average age 30. In 2006, 5 degrees awarded. *Expenses:* Tuition, state resident: full-time $5,437; part-time $227 per credit hour. Tuition, nonresident: full-time $15,694; part-time $654 per credit hour. Required fees: $620. Tuition and fees vary according to course load, campus/location and program. *Financial support:* Career-related internships or fieldwork, Federal Work-Study, institutionally sponsored loans, and scholarships/grants available. Support available to part-time students. *Unit head:* P. Nicholas Kellum, Dean, 317-274-0606, Fax: 317-278-2041, E-mail: pkellum@iupui.edu.

Inter American University of Puerto Rico, Metropolitan Campus, Faculty of Education, Program in Health and Physical Education, San Juan, PR 00919-1293. Offers MA. *Degree requirements:* For master's, comprehensive exam. *Entrance requirements:* For master's, GRE or EXADEP, interview. Electronic applications accepted.

Inter American University of Puerto Rico, San Germán Campus, Graduate Studies Center, Graduate Program in Physical Education and Scientific Analysis of Human Body Movement, San Germán, PR 00683-5008. Offers MA. Part-time and evening/weekend programs available. *Faculty:* 8 full-time, 11 part-time/adjunct. *Students:* 17. In 2006, 2 degrees awarded. *Degree requirements:* For master's, comprehensive exam. *Entrance requirements:* For master's, GRE General Test or EXADEP, minimum GPA of 3.0. *Application deadline:* For fall admission, 4/30 priority date for domestic students; for spring admission, 11/15 for domestic students. Applications are processed on a rolling basis. Application fee: $31. *Expenses:* Tuition: Part-time $175 per credit. Required fees: $238 per semester. Tuition and fees vary according to degree level. *Financial support:* Teaching assistantships available. *Application contact:* Dr. Aurora Graniela, Graduate Coordinator, 787-264-1912 Ext. 7355, Fax: 787-892-7510, E-mail: aurora@sg.inter.edu.

Iowa State University of Science and Technology, Graduate College, College of Human Sciences, Department of Health and Human Performance, Ames, IA 50011. Offers education (M Ed); exercise and sport science (MS); health and human performance (PhD). *Faculty:* 15 full-time. *Students:* 31 full-time (14 women), 5 part-time (4 women); includes 2 minority (both African Americans), 5 international. 40 applicants, 28% accepted, 8 enrolled. In 2006, 8 master's, 1 doctorate awarded. *Degree requirements:* For master's, thesis or alternative; for doctorate, thesis/dissertation. *Entrance requirements:* For master's and doctorate, GRE General Test. Additional exam requirements/recommendations for international students: Required—TOEFL (paper-based 560; computer-based 220; iBT 79) or IELTS (6.5). *Application deadline:* For fall admission, 2/1 priority date for domestic and international students; for spring admission, 11/1 priority date for domestic and international students. Application fee: $30 ($70 for international students). Electronic applications accepted. *Expenses:* Tuition, state resident: full-time $5,936; part-time $330 per credit. Tuition, nonresident: full-time $16,350; part-time $330 per credit. *Financial support:* In 2006–07, 17 research assistantships with full and partial tuition reimbursements (averaging $17,180 per year), 13 teaching assistantships with full and partial tuition reimbursements (averaging $16,096 per year) were awarded; fellowships, career-related internships or fieldwork, scholarships/grants, health care benefits, and unspecified assistantships also available. *Unit head:* Dr. Jerry Thomas, Chair, 515-294-8009, Fax: 515-294-8740, E-mail: hhpgrad@iastate.edu. *Application contact:* Dr. Warren Franke, Chair, 515-294-8257, Fax: 515-294-8740, E-mail: wfranke@iastate.edu.

Ithaca College, Graduate Studies, School of Health Sciences and Human Performance, Program in Physical Education, Ithaca, NY 14850-7020. Offers MS. Part-time programs available. *Faculty:* 7 full-time (5 women). *Students:* 5 full-time (3 women), 1 international. Average age 24. 9 applicants, 67% accepted, 5 enrolled. *Degree requirements:* For master's, thesis optional. *Entrance requirements:* For master's, GRE General Test, minimum GPA of 3.0. Additional exam requirements/recommendations for international students: Required—TOEFL (minimum score 550 paper-based; 213 computer-based). *Application deadline:* For fall admission, 3/1 for domestic students; for spring admission, 12/1 for domestic students. Application fee: $40. *Expenses:* Contact institution. *Financial support:* In 2006–07, 5 students received support, including 5 teaching assistantships (averaging $4,656 per year); career-related internships or fieldwork, Federal Work-Study, institutionally sponsored loans, scholarships/grants, and unspecified assistantships also available. Support available to part-time students. Financial award application deadline: 3/1; financial award applicants required to submit FAFSA. *Unit head:* Mary Bentley, Chairperson, 607-274-3105, Fax: 607-274-1263, E-mail: gradstudies@ithaca.edu.

Jackson State University, Graduate School, School of Education, Department of Health, Physical Education and Recreation, Jackson, MS 39217. Offers MS Ed. *Accreditation:* NCATE. Part-time and evening/weekend programs available. *Faculty:* 5 full-time (0 women). *Students:* 6 full-time (5 women), 8 part-time (1 woman); includes 13 minority (all African Americans) In 2006, 5 degrees awarded. *Degree requirements:* For master's, thesis or alternative, comprehensive exam. *Entrance requirements:* For master's, GRE General Test. Additional exam requirements/recommendations for international students: Required—TOEFL. *Application deadline:* For fall admission, 3/1 priority date for domestic students; for spring admission, 10/1 for domestic students. Applications are processed on a rolling basis. Application fee: $20. *Financial support:* In 2006–07, 8 students received support. Career-related internships or fieldwork, Federal Work-Study, scholarships/grants, and unspecified assistantships available. Support available to part-time students. Financial award application deadline: 3/1; financial award applicants required to submit FAFSA. *Unit head:* Dr. Hill Williams, Chair, 601-979-2373, Fax: 601-979-2374, E-mail: hill.williams@jsums.edu. *Application contact:* Curtis Gore, Director of Graduate Admissions, 601-979-2455, Fax: 601-974-4325, E-mail: cgore@ccaix.jsums.edu.

Jacksonville State University, College of Graduate Studies and Continuing Education, College of Education and Professional Studies, Program in Health and Physical Education, Jacksonville, AL 36265-1602. Offers MS Ed. *Accreditation:* NCATE. Part-time and evening/weekend programs available. *Faculty:* 4 full-time (0 women). *Students:* 7 full-time (2 women), 48 part-time (19 women); includes 7 minority (6 African Americans, 1 American Indian/Alaska Native). In 2006, 14 degrees awarded. *Entrance requirements:* For master's, GRE General Test or MAT. *Application deadline:* Applications are processed on a rolling basis. Application fee: $20. *Expenses:* Tuition, state resident: full-time $5,400; part-time $225 per credit hour. Tuition, nonresident: full-time $10,800; part-time $450 per credit hour. One-time fee: $20 full-time. *Financial support:* Available to part-time students. Application deadline: 4/1. *Unit head:* Dr. Jeff Chandler, Head, 256-782-5973. *Application contact:* 256-782-5329.

Kent State University, Graduate School of Education, Health, and Human Services, Program in Exercise, Leisure, and Sport, Kent, OH 44242-0001. Offers athletic training (MA); exercise physiology (MA); physical teacher education (MA); sport and recreation management (MA); sports studies (MA). *Faculty:* 15 full-time (7 women). *Students:* 47 full-time (25 women), 34 part-time (13 women); includes 11 minority (10 African Americans, 1 Hispanic American), 4 international. 46 applicants, 74% accepted. In 2006, 9 degrees awarded. Application fee: $30. *Unit head:* Dr. Steve Mitchell, Coordinator, 330-672-0206, E-mail: smitchel@kent.edu. *Application contact:* Nancy Miller, Academic Program Coordinator, Office of Graduate Student Services, 330-672-2576, Fax: 330-672-9162, E-mail: ogs@kent.edu.

Kent State University, Graduate School of Education, Health, and Human Services, School of Exercise, Leisure and Sport, Kent, OH 44242-0001. Offers MA, PhD. *Faculty:* 26 full-time (13 women). *Students:* 52 full-time (27 women), 37 part-time (15 women); includes 12 minority (11 African Americans, 1 Hispanic American), 4 international. 52 applicants, 69% accepted. In 2006, 9 degrees awarded. *Degree requirements:* For master's, thesis optional; for doctorate, thesis/dissertation. *Entrance requirements:* For master's, minimum GPA of 2.75; for doctorate, minimum GPA of 3.0. *Application deadline:* For fall admission, 7/18 for domestic students; for spring admission, 11/29 for domestic students. Applications are processed on a rolling basis. Application fee: $30. Electronic applications accepted. *Financial support:* Fellowships with full tuition reimbursements, research assistantships with full tuition reimbursements, teaching assistantships with full tuition reimbursements, career-related internships or fieldwork, Federal Work-Study, institutionally sponsored loans, and tuition waivers (full) available. Financial award application deadline: 3/15. *Unit head:* Wayne Munson, Interim Director, 330-672-2012, Fax: 330-672-4106, E-mail: wmunson@kent.edu. *Application contact:* Aaron L. Mulroony, Graduate Coordinator, 330-672-2857, Fax: 330-672-4106, E-mail: amulroon@kent.edu.

Lakehead University, Graduate Studies, School of Kinesiology, Thunder Bay, ON P7B 5E1, Canada. Offers applied sport science and coaching (M Sc, MA). Part-time programs available. *Degree requirements:* For master's, thesis. *Entrance requirements:* For master's, minimum B average. Additional exam requirements/recommendations for international students: Required—TOEFL. *Faculty research:* Social psychology and physical education, sport history, sports medicine, exercise physiology, gerontology.

Long Island University, Brooklyn Campus, School of Health Professions, Division of Sports Sciences, Brooklyn, NY 11201-8423. Offers adapted physical education (MS); athletic training and sports sciences (MS); exercise physiology (MS); health sciences (MS). Part-time and evening/weekend programs available. *Entrance requirements:* For master's, 2 letters of recommendation. Additional exam requirements/recommendations for international students: Required—TOEFL (minimum score 500 paper-based; 173 computer-based). Electronic applications accepted.

Louisiana Tech University, Graduate School, College of Education, Department of Curriculum, Instruction and Leadership, Ruston, LA 71272. Offers curriculum and instruction (MS, Ed D); educational leadership (Ed D); secondary education (M Ed), including business education, English education, foreign language education, health and physical education, mathematics education, science education, social studies education, speech education. *Accreditation:* NCATE. Part-time programs available. *Degree requirements:* For doctorate, thesis/dissertation. *Entrance requirements:* For master's and doctorate, GRE General Test.

McDaniel College, Graduate and Professional Studies, Program in Physical Education, Westminster, MD 21157-4390. Offers MS. Part-time and evening/weekend programs available. *Degree requirements:* For master's, thesis optional. *Entrance requirements:* For master's, letters of reference (3). Additional exam requirements/recommendations for international students: Required—TOEFL (minimum score 213 computer-based).

McGill University, Faculty of Graduate and Postdoctoral Studies, Faculty of Education, Department of Kinesiology and Physical Education, Montréal, QC H3A 2T5, Canada. Offers M Sc, MA, PhD, Certificate, Diploma. Part-time programs available. *Degree requirements:* For master's and doctorate, thesis/dissertation, registration. *Entrance requirements:* For master's, minimum GPA of 3.0, bachelor's degree in kinesiology, physical education or a related biological or behavioral science. Additional exam requirements/recommendations for international students: Required—TOEFL (minimum score 550 paper-based; 213 computer-based), IELTS (minimum score 7). Electronic applications accepted. *Faculty research:* Biomechanics, exercise physiology, adapted physical education, psychology of motor behavior, pedagogy.

Memorial University of Newfoundland, School of Graduate Studies, School of Human Kinetics and Recreation, St. John's, NL A1C 5S7, Canada. Offers administration, curriculum and supervision (MPE); biomechanics/ergonomics (MS Kin); exercise and work physiology (MS Kin); sport psychology (MS Kin). Part-time programs available. *Degree requirements:* For master's, seminars, thesis presentations, thesis optional. *Entrance requirements:* For master's, bachelor's degree in a related field, minimum B average. Electronic applications accepted. *Faculty research:* Administration, sociology of sports, kinesiology, physiology/recreation.

Middle Tennessee State University, College of Graduate Studies, College of Education and Behavioral Science, Department of Health, Physical Education, Recreation and Safety, Murfreesboro, TN 37132. Offers exercise science and health promotion (MS); health, physical education, recreation and safety (MS); human performance (PhD); physical education (PhD). *Accreditation:* NCATE (one or more programs are accredited). Part-time and evening/weekend programs available. Postbaccalaureate distance learning degree programs offered. *Faculty:* 26 full-time (12 women). *Students:* 10 full-time (6 women), 130 part-time (64 women); includes 27 minority (21 African Americans, 1 American Indian/Alaska Native, 5 Asian Americans or Pacific Islanders). Average age 28. 64 applicants, 94% accepted. In 2006, 39 master's, 7 doctorates awarded. *Entrance requirements:* For master's and doctorate, GRE or MAT. Additional exam requirements/recommendations for international students: Required—TOEFL (minimum score 525 paper-based; 195 computer-based). *Application deadline:* For fall admission, 8/1 priority date for domestic students. Applications are processed on a rolling basis. Application fee: $25. Electronic applications accepted. *Financial support:* In 2006–07, 31 students received support. Application deadline: 5/1; *Faculty research:* Cardiovascular disease and psychosocial stress, pediatric health and fitness, obesity, fitness testing, anaerobic power and lactate kinetics. *Unit head:* Dr. Dianne Bartley, Chair, 615-898-2811, Fax: 615-898-5020, E-mail: dbartley@mtsu.edu.

Minnesota State University Mankato, College of Graduate Studies, College of Allied Health and Nursing, Department of Human Performance, Mankato, MN 56001. Offers MA, MS, MT, SP. Part-time programs available. *Students:* 37 full-time (18 women), 47 part-time (16 women). Average age 28. In 2006, 24 degrees awarded. *Degree requirements:* For master's, thesis, comprehensive exam; for SP, thesis. *Entrance requirements:* For master's, minimum GPA of 3.0 during previous 2 years; for SP, minimum GPA of 3.0. Additional exam requirements/recommendations for international students: Required—TOEFL. *Application deadline:* For fall admission, 7/1 for domestic students, 5/1 for international students; for spring admission, 11/1 for domestic students, 10/1 for international students. Applications are processed on a rolling basis. Application fee: $40. *Financial support:* Research assistantships with full tuition reimbursements, teaching assistantships with full tuition reimbursements, career-related internships or fieldwork, Federal Work-Study, institutionally sponsored loans, and unspecified assistantships available. Support available to part-time students. Financial award application deadline: 3/15; financial award applicants required to submit FAFSA. *Faculty research:* Exercise physiology. *Unit head:* Dr. Gary Rushing, Graduate Coordinator, 507-389-2212. *Application contact:* 507-389-2321, E-mail: grad@mnsu.edu.

Mississippi State University, College of Education, Department of Kinesiology, Mississippi State, MS 39762. Offers exercise science (MS); health education/health promotion (MS); sports administration (MS); teaching/coaching (MS). Part-time programs available. Postbaccalaureate distance learning degree programs offered (minimal on-campus study). *Faculty:* 15 full-time (4 women), 6 part-time/adjunct (4 women). *Students:* 34 full-time (13 women), 13 part-time (6 women); includes 6 minority (all African Americans), 1 international. Average age 25. 49 applicants, 69% accepted, 26 enrolled. In 2006, 25 degrees awarded. *Degree requirements:* For master's, comprehensive oral or written exam, thesis optional. *Entrance requirements:* For master's, GRE General Test, minimum GPA of 3.0. Additional exam requirements/recommendations for international students: Required—TOEFL. *Application deadline:* For fall admission, 7/1 for domestic students; for spring admission, 11/1 for domestic students. Applications are processed on a rolling basis. Application fee: $30. Electronic applications accepted. *Expenses:* Tuition, state resident: full-time $4,550; part-time $253 per hour. Tuition, nonresident: full-time $10,552; part-time $584 per hour. International tuition: $10,882 full-time. Tuition and fees vary according to course load. *Financial support:* In 2006–07, 13 students received support, including 7 teaching assistantships with full tuition reimbursements available (averaging $7,772 per year); research assistantships with full tuition reimbursements available, career-related internships or fieldwork, Federal Work-Study, institutionally sponsored loans, and unspecified assistantships also available. Financial award applicants required to submit FAFSA. *Faculty research:* Static balance and stepping performance of older adults, organizational justice, public health, strength training and recovery drinks, high risk drinking perceptions and behaviors. *Unit head:* Dr. Joseph Chromiak, Interim Head, 662-325-2963, Fax: 662-325-4525, E-mail: jchrom@colled.msstate.edu. *Application contact:* Dr. Phil Bonfanti, Director of Admissions, 662-325-4104, Fax: 662-325-8872, E-mail: admit@msstate.edu.

Missouri State University, Graduate College, College of Health and Human Services, Department of Health, Physical Education, and Recreation, Springfield, MO 65804-0094. Offers health promotion and wellness management (MS); public health (MPH); secondary education (MS Ed), including physical education. Part-time programs available. *Faculty:* 12 full-time (4 women). *Students:* 43 full-time (11 women), 36 part-time (18 women); includes 1 minority (Hispanic American), 45 international. Average age 27. 126 applicants, 73% accepted, 37 enrolled. In 2006, 15 degrees awarded. *Degree requirements:* For master's, thesis or alternative, comprehensive exam. *Entrance requirements:* For master's, GRE (MS, MPH), minimum GPA of 2.8 (MS), minimum GPA of 3.0 (MPH), 9-12 teaching certification (MS Ed). Additional exam requirements/recommendations for international students: Required—TOEFL (minimum

Physical Education

Missouri State University (continued)

score 550 paper-based; 213 computer-based; 79 iBT). *Application deadline:* For fall admission, 7/20 priority date for domestic students; for spring admission, 12/20 priority date for domestic students. Applications are processed on a rolling basis. Application fee: $35. Electronic applications accepted. *Expenses:* Tuition, state resident: full-time $3,582; part-time $199 per credit hour. Tuition, nonresident: full-time $6,984; part-time $199 per credit hour. Required fees: $548. Full-time tuition and fees vary according to course level, course load, program and reciprocity agreements. *Financial support:* In 2006–07, 6 teaching assistantships with full tuition reimbursements (averaging $6,780 per year) were awarded; research assistantships with full tuition reimbursements, Federal Work-Study, scholarships/grants, and unspecified assistantships also available. Financial award application deadline: 3/31; financial award applicants required to submit FAFSA. *Unit head:* Dr. Sarah McCallister, Acting Head, 417-836-6582, Fax: 417-836-5371, E-mail: sarahmccallister@missouristate.edu. *Application contact:* Dr. Sarah McCallister, Acting Head, 417-836-6582, Fax: 417-836-5371, E-mail: sarahmccallister@missouristate.edu.

Montana State University–Billings, College of Allied Health Professions, Department of Health and Human Performance, Billings, MT 59101-0298. Offers athletic training (MS); sport management (MS). *Faculty:* 6 full-time (3 women). *Students:* 25. 7 applicants, 100% accepted, 7 enrolled. *Degree requirements:* For master's, thesis optional. *Entrance requirements:* For master's, GRE General Test, minimum undergraduate GPA of 3.0. Application fee: $40. *Expenses:* Tuition, state resident: full-time $4,599. Tuition, nonresident: full-time $10,786. *Financial support:* Teaching assistantships, career-related internships or fieldwork, Federal Work-Study, institutionally sponsored loans, scholarships/grants, tuition waivers (partial), and unspecified assistantships available. Support available to part-time students. Financial award application deadline: 5/1; financial award applicants required to submit FAFSA. *Unit head:* Dr. Ernie Randolfi, Chair, 406-657-2370, Fax: 406-657-2399, E-mail: randolfi@msubillings.edu. *Application contact:* David M. Sullivan, Graduate Studies Counselor, 406-657-2053, Fax: 406-657-2299, E-mail: dsullivan@msubillings.edu.

Montclair State University, The Graduate School, College of Education and Human Services, Department of Curriculum and Teaching, Montclair, NJ 07043-1624. Offers education (M Ed); educational technology (M Ed); school library media specialist (Certificate); teaching (MAT, Certificate), including art (MAT), biological science (MAT), early childhood education (P-3) (MAT), earth science (MAT), elementary education (K-8) (MAT), English (MAT), French (MAT), health and physical education (MAT), health education (MAT), home economics (MAT), mathematics (MAT), music (MAT), physical education (MAT), physical science (MAT), social studies (MAT), Spanish (MAT), teacher of ESL (MAT), teacher of students with disabilities (MAT). Part-time and evening/weekend programs available. *Faculty:* 16 full-time (12 women), 13 part-time/adjunct (8 women). *Students:* 147 full-time (113 women), 230 part-time (188 women); includes 58 minority (33 African Americans, 1 American Indian/Alaska Native, 12 Asian Americans or Pacific Islanders, 12 Hispanic Americans), 4 international. Average age 33. 118 applicants, 38% accepted, 37 enrolled. In 2006, 166 master's, 11 other advanced degrees awarded. *Degree requirements:* For master's, field experience. *Entrance requirements:* For master's, PRAXIS II, minimum GPA of 2.67, 2 letters of recommendation. Additional exam requirements/recommendations for international students: Required—TOEFL (minimum score 83 computer-based). *Application deadline:* For fall admission, 2/15 for domestic and international students; for spring admission, 9/15 for domestic and international students. Applications are processed on a rolling basis. Application fee: $60. Electronic applications accepted. *Expenses:* Tuition, state resident: part-time $450 per credit. Tuition, nonresident: part-time $682 per credit. Tuition and fees vary according to degree level and program. *Financial support:* In 2006–07, 7 research assistantships with full tuition reimbursements (averaging $7,000 per year) were awarded; Federal Work-Study, scholarships/grants, and unspecified assistantships also available. Support available to part-time students. Financial award application deadline: 3/1; financial award applicants required to submit FAFSA. *Unit head:* Dr. Deborah Eldridge, Chairperson, 973-655-5187.

Montclair State University, The Graduate School, College of Education and Human Services, Department of Exercise Science and Physical Education, Montclair, NJ 07043-1624. Offers health and physical education (Certificate); nutrition and exercise science (Certificate); physical education (MA, Certificate), including coaching and sports administration (MA), exercise science (MA), physical education (MA), teaching and supervision of physical education (MA). Part-time and evening/weekend programs available. *Faculty:* 14 full-time (8 women), 12 part-time/adjunct (7 women). *Students:* 23 full-time (10 women), 54 part-time (33 women); includes 10 minority (5 African Americans, 1 Asian American or Pacific Islander, 4 Hispanic Americans). 36 applicants, 47% accepted, 12 enrolled. In 2006, 11 master's, 13 other advanced degrees awarded. *Degree requirements:* For master's, comprehensive exam. *Entrance requirements:* For master's, GRE General Test, 2 letters of recommendation; for Certificate, 2 letters of recommendation (nutrition and exercise science concentration). Additional exam requirements/recommendations for international students: Required—TOEFL (minimum score 83 computer-based). *Application deadline:* For fall admission, 6/1 for international students; for spring admission, 10/1 for international students. Applications are processed on a rolling basis. Application fee: $60. Electronic applications accepted. *Expenses:* Tuition, state resident: part-time $450 per credit. Tuition, nonresident: part-time $682 per credit. Tuition and fees vary according to degree level and program. *Financial support:* In 2006–07, 4 research assistantships with full tuition reimbursements (averaging $5,000 per year) were awarded; Federal Work-Study, scholarships/grants, and unspecified assistantships also available. Support available to part-time students. Financial award application deadline: 3/1; financial award applicants required to submit FAFSA. *Unit head:* Dr. Joseph Donnelly, Chairperson, 973-655-4154.

Morehead State University, Graduate Programs, College of Education, Department of Health, Physical Education and Sport Sciences, Morehead, KY 40351. Offers exercise physiology (MA); health and physical education (MA); sports management (MA). *Accreditation:* NCATE. Part-time and evening/weekend programs available. *Faculty:* 12 full-time (8 women), 5 part-time/adjunct (2 women). *Students:* 16 full-time (10 women), 12 part-time (7 women), 2 international. Average age 32. In 2006, 11 degrees awarded. *Degree requirements:* For master's, oral exam, written core exam, thesis optional. *Entrance requirements:* For master's, GRE General Test or MAT, minimum GPA of 2.5; undergraduate major/minor in health, physical education, or recreation. Additional exam requirements/recommendations for international students: Required—TOEFL (minimum score 500 paper-based; 173 computer-based). *Application deadline:* For fall admission, 8/1 priority date for domestic and international students; for spring admission, 12/1 priority date for domestic and international students. Applications are processed on a rolling basis. Application fee: $0 ($55 for international students). Electronic applications accepted. *Financial support:* In 2006–07, 4 teaching assistantships (averaging $6,000 per year) were awarded; career-related internships or fieldwork, Federal Work-Study, and unspecified assistantships also available. Financial award application deadline: 4/1; financial award applicants required to submit FAFSA. *Faculty research:* Child growth and performance, instructional strategies, outdoor leadership qualities, exercise science, athletic training. *Unit head:* Dr. Lynne Fitzgerald, Chair, 606-783-2180, Fax: 606-783-5058. *Application contact:* Michelle Barber, Graduate Admissions Counselor, 606-783-2039, Fax: 606-783-5061, E-mail: m.barber@moreheadstate.edu.

Murray State University, College of Education, Department of Adolescent, Career and Special Education, Murray, KY 42071. Offers health, physical education, and recreation (MA), including physical education; industrial and technical education (MS); middle school education (MA Ed, Ed S); secondary education (MA Ed, Ed S); special education (MA Ed), including advanced learning behavior disorders, learning disabilities, moderate/severe disorders. *Accreditation:* NCATE. Part-time programs available. *Students:* 13 full-time (10 women), 218 part-time (164 women); includes 8 minority (7 African Americans, 1 Hispanic American), 2 international. 33 applicants, 100% accepted. *Entrance requirements:* Additional exam requirements/recommendations for international students: Required—TOEFL. *Application deadline:* Applications are processed on a rolling basis. Application fee: $25. *Financial support:*

Research assistantships, teaching assistantships, Federal Work-Study available. Financial award application deadline: 4/1. *Unit head:* Dr. Martin Jacobs, Chairman, 270-809-2593, Fax: 270-809-2540, E-mail: martin.jacobs@coe.murraystate.edu.

North Carolina Agricultural and Technical State University, Graduate School, School of Education, Department of Health and Physical Education, Greensboro, NC 27411. Offers MS. *Accreditation:* NCATE. Part-time and evening/weekend programs available. *Degree requirements:* For master's, thesis or alternative, qualifying exam, comprehensive exam. *Entrance requirements:* For master's, GRE General Test, minimum GPA of 3.0.

North Carolina Central University, Division of Academic Affairs, College of Arts and Sciences, Department of Physical Education and Recreation, Durham, NC 27707-3129. Offers general physical education (MS); recreation administration (MS); special physical education (MS); therapeutic recreation (MS). Part-time and evening/weekend programs available. *Degree requirements:* For master's, one foreign language, thesis, comprehensive exam. *Entrance requirements:* For master's, GRE, minimum GPA of 3.0 in major, 2.5 overall. Additional exam requirements/recommendations for international students: Required—TOEFL. *Faculty research:* Physical activity patterns of children with disabilities, physical fitness test of North Carolina school children, exercise physiology, motor learning/development.

North Dakota State University, The Graduate School, College of Human Development and Education, School of Education, Program in Curriculum and Instruction, Fargo, ND 58105. Offers pedagogy (M Ed, MS); physical education and athletic administration (M Ed, MS). *Faculty:* 10 full-time (3 women). *Students:* 1 (woman) full-time, 11 part-time (10 women). Average age 27. 8 applicants, 75% accepted, 6 enrolled. In 2006, 1 degree awarded. *Degree requirements:* For master's, thesis (for some programs), comprehensive exam. *Entrance requirements:* For master's, Cooperative English Test, GRE General Test, MAT. Additional exam requirements/recommendations for international students: Required—TOEFL. *Application deadline:* For fall admission, 5/1 for domestic students. Applications are processed on a rolling basis. Application fee: $45 ($60 for international students). *Financial support:* Teaching assistantships, career-related internships or fieldwork, Federal Work-Study, institutionally sponsored loans, and tuition waivers (full) available. Financial award application deadline: 4/15. *Application contact:* Dr. Justin Wageman, Associate Professor, 701-231-7108, Fax: 701-231-9685, E-mail: justin.wageman@ndsu.edu.

Northern Arizona University, Consortium of Professional Schools and Colleges, College of Health Professions, Department of Exercise Science and Athletic Training, Flagstaff, AZ 86011. Offers exercise science (MS); physical education (MS). Part-time programs available. *Degree requirements:* For master's, thesis optional. *Entrance requirements:* For master's, GRE General Test, minimum GPA of 3.0. *Faculty research:* Muscle fiber type conversions, small animal locomotive study, electromyographic patterns.

Northern Illinois University, Graduate School, College of Education, Department of Kinesiology and Physical Education, De Kalb, IL 60115-2854. Offers physical education (MS Ed); sport management (MS). Part-time and evening/weekend programs available. *Faculty:* 21 full-time (12 women). *Students:* 75 full-time (30 women), 56 part-time (25 women); includes 11 minority (3 African Americans, 4 Asian Americans or Pacific Islanders, 4 Hispanic Americans), 10 international. Average age 28. 63 applicants, 89% accepted, 38 enrolled. In 2006, 43 degrees awarded. *Degree requirements:* For master's, thesis optional. *Entrance requirements:* For master's, GRE General Test, minimum GPA of 2.75, undergraduate major in related area. Additional exam requirements/recommendations for international students: Required—TOEFL (minimum score 550 paper-based; 213 computer-based). *Application deadline:* For fall admission, 6/1 for domestic students, 5/1 for international students; for spring admission, 11/1 for domestic students, 10/1 for international students. Applications are processed on a rolling basis. Application fee: $30. Electronic applications accepted. *Financial support:* In 2006–07, 31 teaching assistantships with full tuition reimbursements were awarded; fellowships with full tuition reimbursements, research assistantships with full tuition reimbursements, career-related internships or fieldwork, Federal Work-Study, scholarships/grants, tuition waivers (full), and unspecified assistantships also available. Support available to part-time students. Financial award applicants required to submit FAFSA. *Faculty research:* Leadership in athletic training, motor development, dance education, gait analysis, fat phobia. *Unit head:* Dr. Paul Carpenter, Chair, 815-753-1407, Fax: 815-753-1413, E-mail: pcarpenter@niu.edu. *Application contact:* Dr. Laurie Zittel, Director, Graduate Studies, 815-753-3907, E-mail: lzape@niu.edu.

Northern State University, Division of Graduate Studies in Education, Program in Teaching and Learning, Aberdeen, SD 57401-7198. Offers educational studies (MS Ed); elementary classroom teaching (MS Ed); health, physical education, and coaching (MS Ed); language and literacy (MS Ed); secondary classroom teaching (MS Ed); special education (MS Ed). *Accreditation:* NCATE. Part-time and evening/weekend programs available. *Faculty:* 69 full-time (19 women). *Students:* 5 full-time (3 women), 70 part-time (51 women); includes 3 minority (1 African American, 1 American Indian/Alaska Native, 1 Asian American or Pacific Islander). Average age 32. In 2006, 23 degrees awarded. *Degree requirements:* For master's, thesis optional. *Entrance requirements:* For master's, minimum GPA of 2.75. Additional exam requirements/recommendations for international students: Required—TOEFL (minimum score 550 paper-based; 213 computer-based). *Application deadline:* For fall admission, 8/15 priority date for domestic students; for spring admission, 12/15 for domestic students. Applications are processed on a rolling basis. Application fee: $35. Electronic applications accepted. *Expenses:* Tuition, state resident: full-time $3,373; part-time $120 per credit. Tuition, nonresident: full-time $9,943; part-time $355 per credit. International tuition: $13,000 full-time. Required fees: $86 per credit. One-time fee: $35 full-time. Tuition and fees vary according to course load, degree level and reciprocity agreements. *Financial support:* In 2006–07, 17 teaching assistantships with partial tuition reimbursements (averaging $4,812 per year) were awarded; career-related internships or fieldwork, Federal Work-Study, institutionally sponsored loans, scholarships/grants, and unspecified assistantships also available. Support available to part-time students. Financial award application deadline: 3/1; financial award applicants required to submit FAFSA. *Application contact:* Tammy K. Griffith, Senior Secretary, 605-626-2558, Fax: 605-626-2542, E-mail: griffith@northern.edu.

North Georgia College & State University, Graduate Studies, Program in Teacher Education, Dahlonega, GA 30597. Offers early childhood education (M Ed); educational leadership (Ed S); middle grades education (M Ed); secondary education (M Ed), including art education, biology education, chemistry education, English education, history education, mathematics education, physical education, science education, special education (M Ed), including inter-related special education, learning disabilities. *Accreditation:* NCATE. Part-time and evening/weekend programs available. Postbaccalaureate distance learning degree programs offered (minimal on-campus study). *Faculty:* 35 full-time (18 women), 9 part-time/adjunct (6 women). *Students:* 260. Average age 32. 120 applicants, 63% accepted. In 2006, 134 degrees awarded. *Degree requirements:* For master's, thesis optional. *Entrance requirements:* For master's, GRE General Test or MAT, minimum GPA of 2.75; for Ed S, GRE General Test or MAT, 3 years of teaching experience, master's degree, minimum graduate GPA of 3.25. *Application deadline:* For fall admission, 7/1 priority date for domestic students; for spring admission, 12/10 priority date for domestic students. Applications are processed on a rolling basis. Application fee: $25. Electronic applications accepted. *Expenses:* Tuition, state resident: full-time $3,044; part-time $127 per credit hour. Tuition, nonresident: full-time $12,172; part-time $508 per credit hour. Required fees: $892; $458 per semester. *Financial support:* Teaching assistantships, career-related internships or fieldwork and scholarships/grants available. Support available to part-time students. Financial award application deadline: 5/1. *Faculty research:* Computers and teachers' attitudes, rural versus urban teacher attitudes, teacher leadership roles, minority recruitment in teaching force. *Unit head:* Dr. Bob Michael, Dean, School of Education, 706-864-1998, Fax: 706-867-2850, E-mail: bmichael@ngcsu.edu. *Application contact:* Dr. Donna A. Gessell, Director of Graduate Studies and External Programs, 706-864-1528, Fax: 706-867-2795, E-mail: dgessell@ngcsu.edu.

Northwest Missouri State University, Graduate School, College of Education and Human Services, Department of Health, Physical Education, Recreation and Dance, Maryville, MO 64468-6001. Offers health and physical education (MS Ed); recreation (MS). *Accreditation:* NCATE. Part-time programs available. *Faculty:* 10 full-time (4 women). *Students:* 36 full-time (16 women), 6 part-time (1 woman); includes 2 minority (1 African American, 1 Asian American or Pacific Islander). 36 applicants, 69% accepted, 16 enrolled. In 2006, 12 degrees awarded. *Degree requirements:* For master's, comprehensive exam. *Entrance requirements:* For master's, GRE General Test, minimum undergraduate GPA of 2.75, teaching certificate, writing sample. Additional exam requirements/recommendations for international students: Required—TOEFL (minimum score 550 paper-based; 213 computer-based). *Application deadline:* For fall admission, 7/1 for domestic and international students; for spring admission, 11/15 for domestic and international students. Applications are processed on a rolling basis. Application fee: $0 ($50 for international students). *Financial support:* In 2006–07, 23 teaching assistantships with full tuition reimbursements (averaging $6,000 per year) were awarded; research assistantships, unspecified assistantships also available. Financial award application deadline: 3/1; financial award applicants required to submit FAFSA. *Unit head:* Dr. Loren Butler, Program Director, 660-562-1066. *Application contact:* Dr. Frances Shipley, Dean of Graduate School, 660-562-1145, Fax: 660-562-1096, E-mail: gradsch@nwmissouri.edu.

The Ohio State University, Graduate School, College of Education and Human Ecology, School of Physical Activity and Educational Services, Columbus, OH 43210. Offers M Ed, MA, PhD. *Accreditation:* CORE. Part-time programs available. *Faculty:* 57. *Students:* 277 full-time (191 women), 164 part-time (118 women); includes 67 minority (48 African Americans, 1 American Indian/Alaska Native, 6 Asian Americans or Pacific Islanders, 12 Hispanic Americans), 43 international. Average age 31. 225 applicants, 60% accepted, 49 enrolled. In 2006, 135 master's, 44 doctorates awarded. *Degree requirements:* For master's, thesis optional; for doctorate, thesis/dissertation. *Entrance requirements:* For master's and doctorate, GRE General Test or GMAT. Additional exam requirements/recommendations for international students: Required—TOEFL (minimum score 600 paper-based; 250 computer-based). *Application deadline:* For fall admission, 8/15 priority date for domestic students, 7/1 priority date for international students; for winter admission, 12/1 priority date for domestic students, 11/1 priority date for international students; for spring admission, 3/1 priority date for domestic students, 2/1 priority date for international students. Applications are processed on a rolling basis. Application fee: $40 ($50 for international students). Electronic applications accepted. *Expenses:* Tuition, state resident: full-time $9,438. Tuition, nonresident: full-time $22,791. Tuition and fees vary according to course load, campus/location and program. *Financial support:* Fellowships, research assistantships, teaching assistantships, Federal Work-Study and institutionally sponsored loans available. Support available to part-time students. *Unit head:* Philip C. Word, Graduate Studies Commitee Chair, 614-688-4791, Fax: 614-292-2581, E-mail: word.116@osu.edu. *Application contact:* 614-292-9444, Fax: 614-292-3895, E-mail: domestic.grad@osu.edu.

Ohio University, Graduate Studies, College of Health and Human Services, School of Recreation and Sport Sciences, Program in Athletic Training Education, Athens, OH 45701-2979. Offers MS RSS. *Faculty:* 4 full-time (1 woman), 2 part-time/adjunct (1 woman). *Students:* 16 full-time (9 women). 35 applicants, 49% accepted, 16 enrolled. In 2006, 17 degrees awarded. *Entrance requirements:* For master's, GRE, NATA certification. Additional exam requirements/recommendations for international students: Required—TOEFL. Application fee: $45. *Financial support:* In 2006–07, 3 teaching assistantships with full tuition reimbursements (averaging $9,000 per year) were awarded; unspecified assistantships also available. *Faculty research:* Athletic training, heart, injuries, health, muscles, exercise, sport. *Unit head:* Dr. Jeff Seegmiller, Coordinator, 740-593-9497, Fax: 740-593-0284, E-mail: seegmill@ohio.edu.

Ohio University, Graduate Studies, College of Health and Human Services, School of Recreation and Sport Sciences, Program in Coaching Education, Athens, OH 45701-2979. Offers MS. *Faculty:* 5 full-time (2 women). *Students:* 18 full-time (6 women), 1 (woman) part-time; includes 4 minority (all African Americans), 2 international. Average age 23. 28 applicants, 61% accepted, 17 enrolled. In 2006, 12 degrees awarded. *Entrance requirements:* For master's, GRE. Additional exam requirements/recommendations for international students: Required—TOEFL (minimum score 575 paper-based; 233 computer-based). *Application deadline:* For fall admission, 3/1 priority date for domestic and international students. Application fee: $45. *Financial support:* In 2006–07, 4 research assistantships with full tuition reimbursements (averaging $8,577 per year), 17 teaching assistantships with full tuition reimbursements (averaging $8,577 per year) were awarded; scholarships/grants, tuition waivers (full), and stipends also available. *Faculty research:* Sports, physical activity, athletes. *Unit head:* Dr. David Carr, Assistant Professor and Coordinator, 740-593-4651, Fax: 740-593-0284, E-mail: carr@ohio.edu. *Application contact:* Molly de Laval, Graduate Records, 740-593-9787, Fax: 740-593-0284, E-mail: delaval@ohio.edu.

Oklahoma State University, College of Education, School of Applied Health and Educational Psychology, Stillwater, OK 74078. Offers applied behavioral studies (MS, Ed D, PhD); counseling and student personnel (MS, PhD); educational psychology (PhD); health (MS, Ed D); leisure sciences (MS, Ed D); physical education (MS, Ed D); physical education and leisure sciences (Ed D); school psychology (Ed S). *Accreditation:* APA (one or more programs are accredited). Part-time programs available. *Faculty:* 37 full-time (17 women), 12 part-time/adjunct (8 women). *Students:* 189 full-time (137 women), 180 part-time (113 women); includes 75 minority (25 African Americans, 34 American Indian/Alaska Native, 5 Asian Americans or Pacific Islanders, 11 Hispanic Americans), 27 international. Average age 33. 275 applicants, 28% accepted, 64 enrolled. In 2006, 45 master's, 21 doctorates awarded. *Degree requirements:* For master's, thesis or alternative; for doctorate, thesis/dissertation. *Entrance requirements:* For master's, GRE or MAT; for doctorate, GRE (PhD). Additional exam requirements/recommendations for international students: Required—TOEFL. *Application deadline:* For fall admission, 7/1 priority date for domestic students, 3/1 priority date for international students; for spring admission, 8/1 priority date for international students. Applications are processed on a rolling basis. Application fee: $40 ($75 for international students). Electronic applications accepted. *Expenses:* Tuition, state resident: part-time $146 per credit hour. Tuition, nonresident: part-time $516 per credit hour. Required fees: $44 per credit hour. Tuition and fees vary according to program. *Financial support:* In 2006–07, 29 research assistantships (averaging $6,452 per year), 64 teaching assistantships (averaging $8,263 per year) were awarded; career-related internships or fieldwork, Federal Work-Study, scholarships/grants, health care benefits, tuition waivers (partial), and unspecified assistantships also available. Support available to part-time students. Financial award application deadline: 3/1. *Unit head:* Dr. John Romans, Head, 405-744-6040.

Old Dominion University, Darden College of Education, Program in Physical Education, Norfolk, VA 23529. Offers athletic training (MS Ed); curriculum and instruction (MS Ed); exercise and wellness (MS Ed); recreation and tourism studies (MS Ed); sport management (MS Ed). Part-time and evening/weekend programs available. *Faculty:* 12 full-time (6 women), 6 part-time/adjunct (4 women). *Students:* 59 full-time (33 women), 47 part-time (25 women); includes 18 minority (15 African Americans, 2 Asian Americans or Pacific Islanders, 1 Hispanic American), 9 international. Average age 26. 105 applicants, 72% accepted, 55 enrolled. In 2006, 39 degrees awarded. *Degree requirements:* For master's, thesis or alternative, internship, research project, comprehensive exam. *Entrance requirements:* For master's, GRE General Test, minimum GPA of 2.8. Additional exam requirements/recommendations for international students: Required—TOEFL (minimum score 500 paper-based; 200 computer-based). *Application deadline:* For fall admission, 7/1 for domestic students; for spring admission, 11/1 for domestic students. Applications are processed on a rolling basis. Application fee: $40. *Expenses:* Tuition, area resident: Part-time $285 per credit hour. Tuition, nonresident: part-time $715 per credit hour. Required fees: $94 per semester. *Financial support:* In 2006–07, 1 fellowship (averaging $1,500 per year), 2 research assistantships with partial tuition reimbursements (averaging $9,000 per year), 5 teaching assistantships with tuition reimbursements (averaging $9,000 per year) were awarded; career-related internships or fieldwork and scholarships/grants also available. Financial award application deadline: 4/15; financial award applicants required to submit FAFSA. *Faculty research:* Exercise physiology, nutrition and sports, sports psychology, sports management. Total annual research expenditures: $183,251. *Unit head:* Robert Spina, Graduate Program Director, 757-683-6029, E-mail: rspina@odu.edu.

Oregon State University, Graduate School, College of Health and Human Sciences, Program in Physical Education Teacher Education, Corvallis, OR 97331. Offers MAT. *Entrance requirements:* For master's, California Basic Educational Skills Test, GRE General Test, NTE, minimum GPA of 3.0 in last 90 hours. Additional exam requirements/recommendations for international students: Required—TOEFL. *Application deadline:* For fall admission, 1/15 for domestic students. Application fee: $50. *Financial support:* Fellowships, career-related internships or fieldwork, Federal Work-Study, and institutionally sponsored loans available. Support available to part-time students. Financial award application deadline: 2/1. *Unit head:* Dr. Barbara Cusimano, Coordinator, 541-737-5925, E-mail: barbara.cusimano@orst.edu. *Application contact:* Linda Johnson, Head Adviser, 541-737-3718, Fax: 541-737-4230, E-mail: linda.johnson@orst.edu.

Pittsburg State University, Graduate School, College of Education, Department of Health, Physical Education and Recreation, Pittsburg, KS 66762. Offers physical education (MS). *Students:* 15. *Degree requirements:* For master's, thesis or alternative. Application fee: $35 ($60 for international students). *Expenses:* Tuition, state resident: full-time $2,144; part-time $181 per credit hour. Tuition, nonresident: full-time $5,273; part-time $442 per credit hour. Tuition and fees vary according to course load and campus/location. *Financial support:* In 2006–07, teaching assistantships (averaging $5,000 per year); career-related internships or fieldwork, Federal Work-Study, and unspecified assistantships also available. *Faculty research:* Personality of athletes, fitness activities for children, aerobic conditioning, fitness evaluation. *Unit head:* Dr. John Oppliger, Chairperson, 620-235-4668. *Application contact:* Jamie Vanderbeck, Assistant Director, 620-235-4223, Fax: 620-235-4219, E-mail: jvanderb@pittstate.edu.

Prairie View A&M University, Graduate School, College of Education, Department of Health and Human Performance, Prairie View, TX 77446-0519. Offers health education (M Ed, MS); physical education (M Ed, MS). *Accreditation:* NCATE. Part-time and evening/weekend programs available. *Faculty:* 3 part-time/adjunct (2 women). *Students:* 6 full-time (2 women), 30 part-time (11 women); includes 35 minority (33 African Americans, 1 American Indian/Alaska Native, 1 Hispanic American). Average age 27. 36 applicants, 100% accepted, 36 enrolled. In 2006, 9 degrees awarded. *Entrance requirements:* For master's, GRE General Test. *Application deadline:* For fall admission, 10/2 priority date for domestic students; for spring admission, 2/19 for domestic students. Applications are processed on a rolling basis. Application fee: $50. *Financial support:* In 2006–07, 8 fellowships with tuition reimbursements (averaging $1,200 per year), 10 research assistantships with tuition reimbursements (averaging $15,000 per year) were awarded; teaching assistantships with tuition reimbursements, career-related internships or fieldwork, Federal Work-Study, and institutionally sponsored loans also available. Support available to part-time students. Financial award application deadline: 4/1. *Unit head:* Marsha Kay Washington, Head, 936-857-4210, Fax: 936-857-4422. *Application contact:* Dr. William H. Parker, Dean of Graduate School, 936-857-2312, Fax: 936-857-4127, E-mail: william_parker@pvamu.edu.

Purdue University, Graduate School, College of Liberal Arts, Department of Health and Kinesiology, West Lafayette, IN 47907. Offers exercise, human physiology of movement and sport (PhD); health and fitness (MS); health promotion (MS); health promotion and disease prevention (PhD); movement and sport science (MS); pedagogy and administration (MS); pedagogy of physical activity and health (PhD); psychology of sport and exercise, and motor behavior (PhD). Part-time programs available. *Faculty:* 16 full-time (5 women), 6 part-time/adjunct (0 women). *Students:* 60 full-time (37 women), 25 part-time (12 women); includes 8 minority (3 African Americans, 1 American Indian/Alaska Native, 1 Asian American or Pacific Islander, 3 Hispanic Americans), 15 international. Average age 28. 92 applicants, 63% accepted, 33 enrolled. In 2006, 13 master's, 3 doctorates awarded. *Degree requirements:* For master's, thesis (for some programs); for doctorate, thesis/dissertation. *Entrance requirements:* For master's and doctorate, GRE General Test. Additional exam requirements/recommendations for international students: Required—TOEFL. *Application deadline:* For fall admission, 2/1 for domestic and international students. Applications are processed on a rolling basis. Application fee: $55. Electronic applications accepted. *Financial support:* In 2006–07, 4 fellowships with partial tuition reimbursements (averaging $12,000 per year), 2 research assistantships with partial tuition reimbursements (averaging $10,000 per year), 22 teaching assistantships with partial tuition reimbursements (averaging $10,000 per year) were awarded; Federal Work-Study also available. Support available to part-time students. Financial award applicants required to submit FAFSA. *Faculty research:* Wellness, motivation, teaching effectiveness, learning and development. *Unit head:* Dr. William Harper, Head, 765-494-3178, Fax: 765-494-496-1239. *Application contact:* Graduate Studies Office, 765-494-3162, Fax: 765-496-1239, E-mail: hkgrad@purdue.edu.

Saginaw Valley State University, College of Education, Program in Adapted Physical Activity, University Center, MI 48710. Offers MAT. Part-time and evening/weekend programs available. *Students:* Average age 26. In 2006, 1 degree awarded. *Degree requirements:* For master's, capstone course. *Entrance requirements:* For master's, minimum GPA of 3.0. *Application deadline:* Applications are processed on a rolling basis. Application fee: $25. Electronic applications accepted. *Expenses:* Tuition, state resident: full-time $7,225; part-time $301 per credit hour. Tuition, nonresident: full-time $13,888; part-time $579 per credit hour. Required fees: $330; $14 per credit hour. Tuition and fees vary according to course load. *Financial support:* Applicants required to submit FAFSA. *Application contact:* Jeanne Chipman, Certification Officer, 989-964-4053, Fax: 989-964-4385, E-mail: jdc@svsu.edu.

St. Cloud State University, School of Graduate Studies, College of Education, Department of Health, Physical Education, Recreation, and Sport Science, St. Cloud, MN 56301-4498. Offers exercise science (MS); physical education (MS); sports management (MS). *Faculty:* 16 full-time (8 women), 1 (woman) part-time/adjunct. *Students:* 12 full-time (6 women), 3 part-time (1 woman), 2 international. 82 applicants, 43% accepted. In 2006, 18 degrees awarded. *Degree requirements:* For master's, thesis or alternative. *Entrance requirements:* For master's, GRE General Test, minimum GPA of 2.75. Additional exam requirements/recommendations for international students: Required—MELAB; Recommended—TOEFL (minimum score 550 paper-based; 213 computer-based), IELTS (minimum score 7). *Application deadline:* For fall admission, 6/1 priority date for domestic students, 4/1 for international students; for spring admission, 10/1 priority date for domestic students, 8/1 for international students. Applications are processed on a rolling basis. Application fee: $35. Electronic applications accepted. *Financial support:* Federal Work-Study, scholarships/grants, and unspecified assistantships available. Financial award application deadline: 3/1. *Unit head:* Dr. Caryl Martin, Chairperson, 320-308-4251, E-mail: clmartin@stcloudstate.edu. *Application contact:* Linda Lou Krueger, School of Graduate Studies, 320-308-2113, Fax: 320-308-5371, E-mail: lekrueger@stcloudstate.edu.

Salem International University, School of Education, Salem, WV 26426-0500. Offers curriculum and instruction (M Ed), including curriculum and instruction, educational technology leadership, physical education/health, teaching English as a second language; educational administration (M Ed). Part-time and evening/weekend programs available. Postbaccalaureate distance learning degree programs offered. *Faculty:* 5 full-time (4 women), 17 part-time/adjunct (8 women). *Students:* 74 full-time (45 women), 154 part-time (75 women); includes 7 minority (2 African Americans, 5 Asian Americans or Pacific Islanders), 28 international. Average age 41. 200 applicants, 75% accepted, 130 enrolled. In 2006, 18 degrees awarded. *Degree requirements:* For master's, thesis (for some programs), comprehensive exam (for some programs), registration. *Entrance requirements:* For master's, GRE, MAT, NTE, 3 letters of recommendation. Additional exam requirements/recommendations for international students: Required—TOEFL (minimum score 550 paper-based; 213 computer-based). *Application deadline:* Applications are processed on a rolling basis. Application fee: $25. Electronic applications accepted. *Expenses: Contact institution.* One-time fee: $25 part-time. Tuition and

Physical Education

Salem International University (continued)
fees vary according to program. *Financial support:* Application deadline: 4/15; *Faculty research:* Improved classroom effectiveness. *Unit head:* Dean, School of Education, 304-326-1253, Fax: 304-326-1246. *Application contact:* Thomas White, Director of Admissions, 304-326-1549, Fax: 304-326-1246, E-mail: admission@salemiu.edu.

Salem State College, Graduate School, Professional Studies—Physical Education 5-12, Salem, MA 01970-5353. Offers M Ed. Part-time and evening/weekend programs available. *Students:* Average age 32. In 2006, 2 degrees awarded. *Application deadline:* Applications are processed on a rolling basis. Application fee: $35. *Unit head:* MaryLou Breitborde, Associate Dean of Education, 978-542-6262, E-mail: mbreitborde@salemstate.edu.

Salem State College, Graduate School, Professional Studies—Physical Education K-9, Salem, MA 01970-5353. Offers M Ed. Part-time and evening/weekend programs available. *Students:* Average age 32. In 2006, 2 degrees awarded. *Application deadline:* Applications are processed on a rolling basis. Application fee: $35. *Unit head:* MaryLou Breitborde, Associate Dean of Education, 978-542-6262, E-mail: mbreitborde@salemstate.edu.

San Diego State University, Graduate and Research Affairs, College of Professional Studies and Fine Arts, Department of Exercise and Nutritional Sciences, Program in Physical Education, San Diego, CA 92182. Offers MS. *Students:* 25 full-time (14 women), 9 part-time (5 women); includes 3 minority (1 Asian American or Pacific Islander, 2 Hispanic Americans), 1 international. 47 applicants, 57% accepted. In 2006, 16 degrees awarded. *Degree requirements:* For master's, thesis. *Entrance requirements:* For master's, GRE General Test, 2 letters of reference. Additional exam requirements/recommendations for international students: Required—TOEFL. *Application deadline:* For fall admission, 2/1 for domestic and international students. Applications are processed on a rolling basis. Application fee: $55. Electronic applications accepted. *Financial support:* Teaching assistantships, unspecified assistantships available. *Unit head:* Larry Verity, Head, 619-594-5979, Fax: 619-594-6553, E-mail: ensgrad@mail.sdsu.edu. *Application contact:* Larry Verity, Graduate Advisor, 619-594-6489, Fax: 619-594-6553, E-mail: ensgrad@mail.sdsu.edu.

Slippery Rock University of Pennsylvania, Graduate Studies (Recruitment), College of Education, Department of Physical Education, Slippery Rock, PA 16057-1383. Offers M Ed. *Expenses:* Tuition, state resident: part-time $336 per credit. Tuition, nonresident: part-time $538 per credit. Required fees: $84 per credit. $37 per semester. *Unit head:* Dr. Betsy McKinley, Graduate Coordinator, 724-738-2824, Fax: 724-738-2921, E-mail: betsy.mckinley@stu.edu. *Application contact:* April Longwell, Interim Director of Graduate Studies, 724-738-2051 Ext. 2116, Fax: 724-738-2146, E-mail: graduate.studies@sru.edu.

South Dakota State University, Graduate School, College of Arts and Science, Department of Health, Physical Education and Recreation, Brookings, SD 57007. Offers MS. Part-time programs available. *Faculty:* 4 full-time (1 woman), 1 part-time/adjunct (0 women). *Students:* 13 full-time (5 women), 12 part-time (2 women); includes 1 minority (African American) In 2006, 12 degrees awarded. *Degree requirements:* For master's, thesis, oral and written exams. *Entrance requirements:* For master's, GRE. Additional exam requirements/recommendations for international students: Required—TOEFL (minimum score 550 paper-based; 213 computer-based). *Application deadline:* For fall admission, 10/15 priority date for domestic students, 4/15 for international students; for spring admission, 3/15 for domestic students, 8/15 for international students. Applications are processed on a rolling basis. Application fee: $35. *Financial support:* In 2006–07, 1 research assistantship with partial tuition reimbursement (averaging $15,750 per year), 9 teaching assistantships with partial tuition reimbursements (averaging $15,750 per year) were awarded; career-related internships or fieldwork, Federal Work-Study, scholarships/grants, and unspecified assistantships also available. *Faculty research:* Effective teaching behaviors in physical education, sports nutrition, muscle/bone interaction, hormonal response to exercise. *Unit head:* Fred Oien, Head, 605-688-4668, Fax: 605-688-6446, E-mail: fred.oien@sdstate.edu. *Application contact:* Dr. Matthew Vukovich, Graduate Coordinator, 605-688-4668, Fax: 605-688-6446, E-mail: matt.vukovich@sdstate.edu.

Southern Connecticut State University, School of Graduate Studies, School of Education, Department of Exercise Science, New Haven, CT 06515-1355. Offers human performance (MS); physical education (MS); sport psychology (MS). Part-time and evening/weekend programs available. *Faculty:* 8 full-time. *Students:* 28 full-time (13 women), 54 part-time (28 women); includes 6 minority (2 African Americans, 4 Hispanic Americans), 1 international. 43 applicants, 44% accepted, 13 enrolled. In 2006, 18 degrees awarded. *Degree requirements:* For master's, thesis or alternative. *Entrance requirements:* For master's, interview. *Application deadline:* For fall admission, 7/15 priority date for domestic students. Applications are processed on a rolling basis. Application fee: $50. Electronic applications accepted. *Financial support:* In 2006–07, 8 teaching assistantships were awarded. Financial award application deadline: 4/15; financial award applicants required to submit FAFSA. *Unit head:* Dr. David Martens, Chairperson, 203-392-6094, Fax: 203-392-6911. *Application contact:* Dr. Robert Axtell, Coordinator, 203-392-6037, Fax: 203-392-6093, E-mail: axtell@southernct.edu.

Southern Illinois University Carbondale, Graduate School, College of Education, Department of Physical Education, Carbondale, IL 62901-4701. Offers MS Ed. Part-time programs available. *Faculty:* 6 full-time (2 women). *Students:* 23 full-time (7 women), 31 part-time (7 women); includes 4 minority (1 African American, 1 American Indian/Alaska Native, 2 Asian Americans or Pacific Islanders), 8 international. Average age 25. 41 applicants, 54% accepted, 11 enrolled. In 2006, 19 degrees awarded. *Degree requirements:* For master's, thesis. *Entrance requirements:* For master's, GRE, minimum GPA of 2.7. Additional exam requirements/recommendations for international students: Required—TOEFL. *Application deadline:* Applications are processed on a rolling basis. Application fee: $20. *Financial support:* In 2006–07, 17 students received support, including 10 teaching assistantships; fellowships, research assistantships, career-related internships or fieldwork, Federal Work-Study, institutionally sponsored loans, and tuition waivers (full) also available. Support available to part-time students. *Faculty research:* Caffeine and exercise effects, ground reaction forces in walking and running, social psychology of sports. *Unit head:* Dr. Elaine Blinde, Interim Chair, 618-536-2431, E-mail: blinde@siu.edu. *Application contact:* Chasity Jack, Administrative Clerk, 618-453-3134, E-mail: cjack@siu.edu.

Springfield College, Graduate Programs, Programs in Physical Education, Springfield, MA 01109-3797. Offers adapted physical education (M Ed, MPE, MS); advanced level coaching (M Ed, MPE, MS); athletic administration (M Ed, MPE, MS); general physical education (DPE, CAS); health education licensure (MPE, MS); health education licensure program (M Ed); physical education licensure (MPE, MS); physical education licensure program (M Ed); sport performance (M Ed, MPE, MS); teaching and administration (MS). Part-time and evening/weekend programs available. *Faculty:* 25 full-time (13 women), 2 part-time/adjunct (0 women). *Students:* 97. Average age 27. 78 applicants, 86% accepted, 45 enrolled. In 2006, 22 master's, 4 doctorates awarded. Terminal master's awarded for partial completion of doctoral program. *Degree requirements:* For master's, research project; for doctorate, thesis/dissertation. *Entrance requirements:* For master's, GRE General Test; for doctorate, GRE General Test, interview. Additional exam requirements/recommendations for international students: Required—TOEFL (minimum score 550 paper-based; 213 computer-based). *Application deadline:* For fall admission, 1/15 priority date for domestic students; for winter admission, 11/1 for domestic students; for spring admission, 12/1 for domestic students. Applications are processed on a rolling basis. Application fee: $50. Electronic applications accepted. *Expenses:* Tuition: Full-time $12,222; part-time $679 per credit. Required fees: $25; $25 per year. One-time fee: $25 full-time. *Financial support:* Fellowships with partial tuition reimbursements, teaching assistantships with partial tuition reimbursements, career-related internships or fieldwork, Federal Work-Study, institutionally sponsored loans, and tuition waivers (full and partial) available. Financial award application deadline: 3/1. *Faculty research:* Pedagogy, motor learning, history of physical education. *Unit head:* Dr. Stephen C. Coulon, Director,

413-748-3029, Fax: 413-748-3537, E-mail: stephen_coulon@spfldcol.edu. *Application contact:* Donald James Shaw, Director of Graduate Admissions, 413-748-3060, Fax: 413-748-3069, E-mail: donald_shaw_jr@spfldcol.edu.

State University of New York College at Brockport, School of Arts and Performance, Department of Physical Education and Sport, Brockport, NY 14420-2997. Offers MS Ed. Part-time programs available. *Students:* 15 full-time (6 women), 87 part-time (38 women); includes 4 minority (2 African Americans, 2 Hispanic Americans), 1 international. 41 applicants, 85% accepted, 34 enrolled. In 2006, 44 degrees awarded. *Degree requirements:* For master's, thesis or alternative. *Entrance requirements:* For master's, minimum GPA of 3.0. Additional exam requirements/recommendations for international students: Required—TOEFL (minimum score 550 paper-based; 213 computer-based; 80 iBT). *Application deadline:* For fall admission, 3/15 for domestic and international students; for spring admission, 10/15 for domestic and international students. Application fee: $50. *Expenses:* Tuition, state resident: full-time $6,900; part-time $288 per credit. Tuition, nonresident: full-time $10,920; part-time $455 per credit. *Financial support:* In 2006–07, 1 fellowship with tuition reimbursement (averaging $7,500 per year), 1 research assistantship with tuition reimbursement (averaging $6,000 per year), 7 teaching assistantships with tuition reimbursements (averaging $6,000 per year) were awarded; career-related internships or fieldwork, Federal Work-Study, scholarships/grants, and unspecified assistantships also available. Support available to part-time students. Financial award application deadline: 3/15; financial award applicants required to submit FAFSA. *Faculty research:* Athletic administration, adapted physical education, physical education curriculum, physical education teaching/coaching. *Unit head:* Dr. Susan C. Petersen, Chairperson, 585-395-5332, E-mail: speters@brockport.edu. *Application contact:* Dr. William Stier, Graduate Program Director, 585-395-5331, E-mail: bstier@brockport.edu.

State University of New York College at Cortland, Graduate Studies, School of Professional Studies, Department of Physical Education, Cortland, NY 13045. Offers MS Ed. Part-time and evening/weekend programs available. *Entrance requirements:* Additional exam requirements/recommendations for international students: Required—TOEFL.

Stony Brook University, State University of New York, School of Professional Development, Stony Brook, NY 11794. Offers adolescence education: mathematics (Certificate); biology 7-12 (MAT); chemistry-grade 7-12 (MAT); coaching (Certificate); computer integrated engineering (Certificate); cultural studies (Certificate); earth science-grade 7-12 (MAT); educational computing (Advanced Certificate, Certificate); English-grade 7-12 (MAT); environmental and waste management (MS, Advanced Certificate); environmental systems management (Certificate); environmental/occupational health and safety (Certificate); French-grade 7-12 (MAT); German-grade 7-12 (MAT); human resource management (Certificate); industrial management (Certificate); information systems management (Certificate); Italian-grade 7-12 (MAT); liberal studies (MA); liberal studies online (MA); Long Island regional studies (Certificate); operation research (Certificate); physics-grade 7-12 (MAT); Russian-grade 7-12 (MAT); school administration and supervision (Certificate); school district administration (Certificate); social science and the professions (MPS), including human resources management, labor management, public affairs, waste management; social studies 7-12 (MAT); waste management (Certificate); women's studies (Certificate). Part-time and evening/weekend programs available. Postbaccalaureate distance learning degree programs offered. *Faculty:* 1 full-time (0 women), 118 part-time/adjunct (45 women). *Students:* 322 full-time (202 women), 1,188 part-time (728 women); includes 164 minority (69 African Americans, 2 American Indian/Alaska Native, 29 Asian Americans or Pacific Islanders, 64 Hispanic Americans), 11 international. Average age 28. In 2006, 738 master's, 405 other advanced degrees awarded. *Degree requirements:* For master's, one foreign language, thesis or alternative. *Application deadline:* Applications are processed on a rolling basis. Application fee: $62. *Expenses:* Tuition, state resident: full-time $6,900; part-time $288 per credit. Tuition, nonresident: full-time $10,920; part-time $455 per credit. *Financial support:* In 2006–07, 5 teaching assistantships were awarded; fellowships, research assistantships, career-related internships or fieldwork also available. Support available to part-time students. *Unit head:* Dr. Paul J. Edelson, Dean, 631-632-7052, Fax: 631-632-9046, E-mail: paul.edelson@sunysb.edu. *Application contact:* Sandra Romansky, Director of Admissions and Advisement, 631-632-7050, Fax: 631-632-9046, E-mail: sandra.romansky@sunysb.edu.

Sul Ross State University, School of Professional Studies, Department of Physical Education, Alpine, TX 79832. Offers M Ed. Part-time programs available. *Entrance requirements:* For master's, GMAT or GRE General Test, minimum GPA of 2.5 in last 60 hours of undergraduate work.

Tarleton State University, College of Graduate Studies, College of Education, Department of Health and Physical Education, Stephenville, TX 76402. Offers physical education (M Ed). Part-time and evening/weekend programs available. *Faculty:* 1 full-time (0 women), 3 part-time/adjunct (1 woman). *Students:* 10 full-time (6 women), 18 part-time (13 women); includes 6 minority (5 African Americans, 1 Asian American or Pacific Islander). Average age 39. In 2006, 12 degrees awarded. *Degree requirements:* For master's, thesis optional. *Entrance requirements:* For master's, GRE General Test, minimum GPA of 3.0. Additional exam requirements/recommendations for international students: Required—TOEFL (minimum score 550 paper-based; 220 computer-based). *Application deadline:* For fall admission, 8/5 priority date for domestic students; for spring admission, 12/1 for domestic students. Applications are processed on a rolling basis. Application fee: $25 ($75 for international students). *Financial support:* In 2006–07, 9 teaching assistantships with partial tuition reimbursements (averaging $12,000 per year) were awarded; career-related internships or fieldwork, Federal Work-Study, and institutionally sponsored loans also available. Support available to part-time students. Financial award application deadline: 5/1; financial award applicants required to submit FAFSA. *Unit head:* Dr. Steve Crews, Head, 254-968-9377.

Teachers College Columbia University, Graduate Faculty of Education, Department of Biobehavioral Studies, Program in Curriculum and Teaching in Physical Education, New York, NY 10027-6696. Offers Ed M, MA, Ed D. Part-time and evening/weekend programs available. *Faculty:* 1 full-time (0 women). *Students:* 4 full-time (2 women), 41 part-time (23 women); includes 40 minority (10 African Americans, 3 American Indian/Alaska Native, 3 Asian Americans or Pacific Islanders, 24 Hispanic Americans), 5 international. Average age 35. 18 applicants, 78% accepted, 9 enrolled. In 2006, 13 master's, 4 doctorates awarded. Terminal master's awarded for partial completion of doctoral program. *Degree requirements:* For master's, integrative paper; for doctorate, thesis/dissertation. *Entrance requirements:* For doctorate, GRE General Test. *Application deadline:* For fall admission, 5/15 for domestic students; for spring admission, 12/1 for domestic students. Application fee: $65. *Expenses:* Tuition: Full-time $23,400; part-time $975 per credit. Required fees: $320 per term. *Financial support:* Career-related internships or fieldwork, Federal Work-Study, institutionally sponsored loans, and tuition waivers (full and partial) available. Support available to part-time students. Financial award application deadline: 2/1. *Faculty research:* Analysis of teaching, teacher performance, program development, data bank project in physical education. *Unit head:* John H. Saxman, Chair, 212-678-3895, E-mail: jhs37@columbia.edu. *Application contact:* Debbie Lesperance, Assistant Director of Admission, 212-678-3710, Fax: 212-678-4171.

See Close-Up on page 1129.

Temple University, Health Sciences Center and Graduate School, College of Health Professions, Department of Kinesiology, Philadelphia, PA 19122-6096. Offers kinesiology (Ed M, PhD), including behavioral sciences, somatic sciences. Part-time programs available. *Faculty:* 11 full-time (5 women). *Students:* 45 full-time (26 women), 57 part-time (31 women); includes 12 minority (6 African Americans, 2 Asian Americans or Pacific Islanders, 4 Hispanic Americans), 6 international. 95 applicants, 42% accepted, 30 enrolled. In 2006, 21 master's, 8 doctorates awarded. Terminal master's awarded for partial completion of doctoral program. *Degree requirements:* For master's and doctorate, thesis/dissertation. *Entrance requirements:* For master's, GRE General Test or MAT, minimum undergraduate GPA of 3.0; for doctorate, GRE General Test, minimum undergraduate GPA of 3.0. Additional exam requirements/

recommendations for international students: Required—TOEFL (minimum score 550 paper-based; 213 computer-based; 79 iBT). *Application deadline:* For fall admission, 1/15 for domestic students, 12/15 for international students; for spring admission, 10/1 for domestic students, 8/1 for international students. Application fee: $50. *Expenses:* Tuition, state resident: full-time $12,264; part-time $511 per credit. Tuition, nonresident: full-time $17,904; part-time $746 per credit. Required fees: $84 per course. Tuition and fees vary according to program. *Financial support:* Fellowships, research assistantships with full tuition reimbursements, teaching assistantships with full tuition reimbursements, career-related internships or fieldwork and Federal Work-Study available. Financial award application deadline: 1/15; financial award applicants required to submit FAFSA. *Unit head:* Dr. Michael R. Sitler, Chair, 215-204-1950, Fax: 215-204-8705, E-mail: sitler@temple.edu.

Tennessee State University, The School of Graduate Studies and Research, College of Education, Department of Human Performance and Sports Science, Nashville, TN 37209-1561. Offers MA Ed. *Faculty:* 7 full-time (2 women). *Students:* 17 full-time (9 women), 12 part-time (4 women); includes 25 minority (all African Americans), 1 international. Average age 29. 31 applicants, 35% accepted, 9 enrolled. In 2006, 13 degrees awarded. *Degree requirements:* For master's, thesis optional. *Entrance requirements:* For master's, GRE General Test or MAT. Application fee: $25. *Unit head:* Dr. Catona R. Starks, Head, 615-963-5581, Fax: 615-963-5594, E-mail: cstarks@tnstate.edu.

Tennessee Technological University, Graduate School, College of Education, Department of Exercise Science, Physical Education and Wellness, Cookeville, TN 38505. Offers MA. *Accreditation:* NCATE. Part-time programs available. *Faculty:* 7 full-time (0 women). *Students:* 12 full-time (7 women), 32 part-time (14 women); includes 5 minority (all African Americans) Average age 27. 24 applicants, 88% accepted, 17 enrolled. In 2006, 9 degrees awarded. *Entrance requirements:* For master's, MAT. Additional exam requirements/recommendations for international students: Required—TOEFL. *Application deadline:* For fall admission, 3/1 priority date for domestic students; for spring admission, 8/1 for domestic students. Application fee: $25 ($30 for international students). *Expenses:* Tuition, state resident: full-time $8,748; part-time $319 per hour. Tuition, nonresident: full-time $23,524; part-time $740 per hour. *Financial support:* In 2006–07, fellowships (averaging $8,000 per year), 3 research assistantships (averaging $4,000 per year), 4 teaching assistantships (averaging $4,000 per year) were awarded; career-related internships or fieldwork also available. Financial award application deadline: 4/1. *Unit head:* Dr. Patricia Jordan, Interim Chairperson, 931-372-3467, Fax: 931-372-6319. *Application contact:* Dr. Francis O. Otuonye, Associate Vice President for Research and Graduate Studies, 931-372-3233, Fax: 931-372-3497, E-mail: fotuonye@tntech.edu.

Texas A&M University, College of Education and Human Development, Department of Health and Kinesiology, College Station, TX 77843. Offers health education (M Ed, MS, Ed D, PhD); kinesiology (M Ed, MS, Ed D, PhD), including kinesiology (MS, PhD), physical education (M Ed, Ed D). Part-time programs available. *Faculty:* 25 full-time (7 women). *Students:* 121 full-time (50 women), 19 part-time (7 women); includes 23 minority (10 African Americans, 2 Asian Americans or Pacific Islanders, 11 Hispanic Americans), 24 international. Average age 23. 110 applicants, 65% accepted, 48 enrolled. In 2006, 30 master's, 13 doctorates awarded. *Degree requirements:* For master's, thesis (for some programs), registration; for doctorate, thesis/dissertation, comprehensive exam, registration. *Entrance requirements:* For master's and doctorate, GRE General Test. Additional exam requirements/recommendations for international students: Required—TOEFL. *Application deadline:* Applications are processed on a rolling basis. Application fee: $50 ($75 for international students). Electronic applications accepted. *Expenses:* Tuition, state resident: full-time $4,697. Tuition, nonresident: full-time $11,297. Required fees: $2,272. *Financial support:* Fellowships with partial tuition reimbursements, research assistantships, teaching assistantships, career-related internships or fieldwork and institutionally sponsored loans available. Financial award application deadline: 2/15; financial award applicants required to submit FAFSA. *Unit head:* Dr. Steve Dorman, Head, 979-845-3109, Fax: 979-847-8987. *Application contact:* Eva Parkerson, Information Contact, 979-458-2673, Fax: 979-847-8987, E-mail: eva@hlkn.tamu.edu.

Texas A&M University–Commerce, Graduate School, College of Education and Human Services, Department of Health, Kinesiology and Sports Studies, Commerce, TX 75429-3011. Offers M Ed, MS, Ed D. Part-time programs available. *Degree requirements:* For master's, thesis (for some programs), comprehensive exam. *Entrance requirements:* For master's, GRE General Test. Electronic applications accepted. *Faculty research:* Teaching, physical fitness.

Texas Southern University, Graduate School, College of Education, Department of Health, Physical Education and Recreation, Houston, TX 77004-4584. Offers health education (MS); physical education (MS). Part-time and evening/weekend programs available. *Faculty:* 5 full-time (2 women). *Students:* 9 full-time (6 women), 10 part-time (5 women); includes 17 minority (16 African Americans, 1 Hispanic American), 1 international. Average age 32. 7 applicants, 57% accepted, 4 enrolled. In 2006, 10 degrees awarded. *Degree requirements:* For master's, thesis optional. *Entrance requirements:* For master's, GRE General Test, minimum GPA of 2.5. Additional exam requirements/recommendations for international students: Required—TOEFL. *Application deadline:* For fall admission, 7/15 priority date for domestic students. Applications are processed on a rolling basis. Application fee: $50 ($75 for international students). *Financial support:* In 2006–07, 1 fellowship (averaging $1,473 per year) was awarded. Financial award application deadline: 5/1. *Unit head:* Dr. T. Robinson, Head, 713-313-7087.

Texas State University-San Marcos, Graduate School, College of Education, Department of Health, Physical Education, and Recreation, Program in Health and Physical Education, San Marcos, TX 78666. Offers MA. Part-time and evening/weekend programs available. *Degree requirements:* For master's, thesis, comprehensive exam. *Entrance requirements:* For master's, GRE General Test, minimum GPA of 2.75 in last 60 hours of course work. Additional exam requirements/recommendations for international students: Required—TOEFL. *Application deadline:* For fall admission, 6/15 priority date for domestic students; for spring admission, 10/15 priority date for domestic students. Applications are processed on a rolling basis. Application fee: $40 ($90 for international students). *Financial support:* Teaching assistantships, career-related internships or fieldwork, Federal Work-Study, and institutionally sponsored loans available. Financial award application deadline: 4/1; financial award applicants required to submit FAFSA. *Faculty research:* HIV/AIDS, youth fitness, leisure behavior, leisure program services and management evaluation. *Unit head:* Dr. John Walker, Head, 512-245-8106, Fax: 512-245-8678, E-mail: jw18@txstate.edu.

Texas State University-San Marcos, Graduate School, College of Education, Department of Health, Physical Education, and Recreation, Program in Physical Education, San Marcos, TX 78666. Offers M Ed. Part-time and evening/weekend programs available. *Faculty:* 4 full-time (1 woman). *Students:* 48 full-time (20 women), 20 part-time (11 women); includes 21 minority (7 African Americans, 1 Asian American or Pacific Islander, 13 Hispanic Americans), 2 international. Average age 27. 35 applicants, 100% accepted, 27 enrolled. In 2006, 19 degrees awarded. *Degree requirements:* For master's, comprehensive exam. *Entrance requirements:* For master's, GRE General Test, minimum GPA of 2.75 in last 60 hours of course work. Additional exam requirements/recommendations for international students: Required—TOEFL. *Application deadline:* For fall admission, 6/15 priority date for domestic students; for spring admission, 10/15 priority date for domestic students. Applications are processed on a rolling basis. Application fee: $40 ($90 for international students). *Financial support:* In 2006–07, 51 students received support, including 6 research assistantships (averaging $7,325 per year), 17 teaching assistantships (averaging $5,783 per year); career-related internships or fieldwork, Federal Work-Study, and institutionally sponsored loans also available. Support available to part-time students. Financial award application deadline: 4/1; financial award applicants required to submit FAFSA. *Faculty research:* AIDS education, employee wellness, isometric strength evaluation. *Unit head:* Dr. John Walker, Head, 512-245-8106, Fax: 512-245-8678, E-mail: jw18@txstate.edu.

Texas State University-San Marcos, Graduate School, Interdisciplinary Studies Program in Health, Physical Education, and Recreation, San Marcos, TX 78666. Offers MAIS. Part-time and evening/weekend programs available. *Degree requirements:* For master's, thesis or alternative, comprehensive exam. *Entrance requirements:* For master's, GRE General Test, minimum GPA of 2.75 in last 60 hours of course work. Additional exam requirements/recommendations for international students: Required—TOEFL. *Application deadline:* For fall admission, 6/15 priority date for domestic students; for spring admission, 10/15 priority date for domestic students. Applications are processed on a rolling basis. Application fee: $40 ($90 for international students). *Financial support:* Career-related internships or fieldwork, Federal Work-Study, and institutionally sponsored loans available. Support available to part-time students. Financial award application deadline: 4/1; financial award applicants required to submit FAFSA. *Unit head:* Dr. John Walker, Head, 512-245-8106, Fax: 512-245-8678, E-mail: jw18@txstate.edu. *Application contact:* Dr. J. Michael Willoughby, Dean of Graduate School, 512-245-2581, Fax: 512-245-8365, E-mail: gradcollege@txstate.edu.

Union College, Graduate Programs, Department of Education, Barbourville, KY 40906-1499. Offers elementary education (MA); health and physical education (MA); middle grades (MA); music education (MA); principalship (MA); reading specialist (MA); secondary education (MA); special education (MA). *Degree requirements:* For master's, thesis optional. *Entrance requirements:* For master's, GRE General Test, NTE.

United States Sports Academy, Graduate Programs, Department of Sport Coaching, Daphne, AL 36526-7055. Offers MSS. Part-time programs available. Postbaccalaureate distance learning degree programs offered (minimal on-campus study). *Faculty:* 2 full-time (0 women), 11 part-time/adjunct (1 woman). *Students:* 17 full-time (5 women), 58 part-time (10 women); includes 11 minority (8 African Americans, 1 Asian American or Pacific Islander, 2 Hispanic Americans), 2 international. Average age 28. *Degree requirements:* For master's, thesis optional. *Entrance requirements:* For master's, GRE General Test, GMAT, or MAT, minimum GPA of 2.5, 3 letters of recommendation, resumé. Additional exam requirements/recommendations for international students: Required—TOEFL (minimum score 500 paper-based; 213 computer-based). *Application deadline:* Applications are processed on a rolling basis. Application fee: $50 ($125 for international students). Electronic applications accepted. *Financial support:* Career-related internships or fieldwork, Federal Work-Study, scholarships/grants, and service assistantships available. Support available to part-time students. Financial award application deadline: 8/15; financial award applicants required to submit FAFSA. *Faculty research:* Effect of attentional skill on sports performance, survey of coaching qualifications, coaching certification. Total annual research expenditures: $2,500. *Unit head:* Dr. Sally Ford, Chair, 251-626-3303 Ext. 139, Fax: 251-626-1149, E-mail: sford@ussa.edu. *Application contact:* Dr. Albert G. Applin, Dean of Student Services, 251-626-3303 Ext. 147, Fax: 251-626-1035, E-mail: applin@ussa.edu.

See Close-Up on page 2353.

Universidad Metropolitana, Graduate Programs in Education, Program in Teaching of Physical Education, San Juan, PR 00928-1150. Offers MA. *Degree requirements:* For master's, thesis or alternative. *Entrance requirements:* For master's, EXADEP, interview. Electronic applications accepted.

Université de Montréal, Faculty of Graduate Studies, Department of Kinesiology, Montréal, QC H3C 3J7, Canada. Offers kinesiology (M Sc, DESS); physical activity (M Sc, PhD); physical activity and health promotion (DESS). *Faculty:* 14 full-time (5 women), 8 part-time/adjunct (2 women). *Students:* 50 full-time (14 women), 14 part-time (10 women). Average age 26. 49 applicants, 45% accepted, 19 enrolled. In 2006, 11 master's, 7 doctorates awarded. *Degree requirements:* For master's, one foreign language, thesis (for some programs); for doctorate, one foreign language, thesis/dissertation, general exam. *Application deadline:* For fall admission, 2/1 priority date for domestic students; for winter admission, 11/1 priority date for domestic students; for spring admission, 2/1 priority date for domestic students. Application fee: $30. Electronic applications accepted. *Financial support:* In 2006–07, 3 fellowships (averaging $20,000 per year), 10 research assistantships (averaging $5,000 per year), 6 teaching assistantships (averaging $7,000 per year) were awarded. Financial award application deadline: 2/1. *Faculty research:* Physiology of exercise, psychology of sports, biomechanics, dance, sociology of sports. Total annual research expenditures: $600,000. *Unit head:* Director, 514-343-6166, Fax: 514-343-2181. *Application contact:* Francine Normandeau, Information Contact, 514-343-6152, E-mail: francine.normandeau@umontreal.ca.

Université de Sherbrooke, Faculty of Physical Education, Program in Physical Education, Sherbrooke, QC J1K 2R1, Canada. Offers kinanthropology (M Sc); physical activity (Diploma). *Degree requirements:* For master's, thesis. *Entrance requirements:* For master's, minimum GPA of 2.7; for Diploma, bachelor's degree in physical education. *Faculty research:* Physical fitness, nutrition, human factors, sociology, teaching.

Université du Québec à Trois-Rivières, Graduate Programs, Program in Physical Education, Trois-Rivières, QC G9A 5H7, Canada. Offers M Sc. Part-time programs available. *Degree requirements:* For master's, thesis. *Entrance requirements:* For master's, appropriate bachelor's degree, proficiency in French.

The University of Akron, Graduate School, College of Education, Department of Sport Science and Wellness Education, Program in Physical Education K–12, Akron, OH 44325. Offers MA, MS. *Students:* Average age 32. 1 applicant, 100% accepted, 1 enrolled. In 2006, 1 degree awarded. *Degree requirements:* For master's, thesis optional. *Entrance requirements:* For master's, minimum GPA of 2.75. Additional exam requirements/recommendations for international students: Required—TOEFL (minimum score 550 paper-based; 213 computer-based; 79 iBT). *Application deadline:* For fall admission, 8/15 for domestic students. Applications are processed on a rolling basis. Application fee: $30 ($40 for international students). Electronic applications accepted. *Expenses:* Tuition, state resident: full-time $6,164; part-time $342 per credit. Tuition, nonresident: full-time $10,575; part-time $588 per credit. Required fees: $806; $43 per credit. $12 per term. Tuition and fees vary according to course load, degree level and program. *Unit head:* Dr. Sean Cai, Coordinator, 330-972-7986, E-mail: xiang@uakron.edu.

The University of Akron, Graduate School, College of Education, Department of Sport Science and Wellness Education, Program in Sports Science/Coaching, Akron, OH 44325. Offers MA, MS. *Students:* 24 full-time (8 women), 10 part-time (5 women); includes 1 minority (African American), 3 international. Average age 26. 17 applicants, 82% accepted, 9 enrolled. In 2006, 17 degrees awarded. *Degree requirements:* For master's, thesis optional. *Entrance requirements:* For master's, minimum GPA of 2.75. Additional exam requirements/recommendations for international students: Required—TOEFL (minimum score 550 paper-based; 213 computer-based; 79 iBT). *Application deadline:* For fall admission, 8/15 for domestic students. Applications are processed on a rolling basis. Application fee: $30 ($40 for international students). Electronic applications accepted. *Expenses:* Tuition, state resident: full-time $6,164; part-time $342 per credit. Tuition, nonresident: full-time $10,575; part-time $588 per credit. Required fees: $806; $43 per credit. $12 per term. Tuition and fees vary according to course load, degree level and program. *Unit head:* Dr. Alan Kornspan, 330-972-8145, E-mail: alan3@uakron.edu.

The University of Alabama, Graduate School, College of Education, Department of Kinesiology, Tuscaloosa, AL 35487. Offers alternative sport pedagogy (MA); exercise science (MA, PhD); human performance (MA); sport management (MA); sport pedagogy (MA, PhD). Part-time programs available. *Faculty:* 9 full-time (1 woman). *Students:* 39 full-time (18 women), 20 part-time (11 women); includes 2 minority (both African Americans), 11 international. Average age 30. 35 applicants, 63% accepted, 7 enrolled. In 2006, 3 master's, 13 doctorates awarded. *Median time to degree:* Of those who began their doctoral program in fall 1998, 100% received their degree in 8 years or less. *Degree requirements:* For master's, thesis optional; for doctorate, thesis/dissertation, comprehensive exam. *Entrance requirements:* For master's and doctorate, GRE, MAT, minimum GPA of 3.0. Additional exam requirements/recommendations for international students: Required—TOEFL. *Financial support:* In 2006–07, 14 students

Physical Education

The University of Alabama (continued)

received support, including 13 teaching assistantships with full tuition reimbursements available (averaging $8,678 per year). *Faculty research:* Race gender and sexuality in sports, physical education curriculum reform, disability sports, physical activity and health, environmental physiology. Total annual research expenditures: $9,290. *Unit head:* Dr. Matt Curtner-Smith, Department Head and Professor, 205-348-9209, Fax: 205-348-0867, E-mail: msmith@bamed.ua.edu.

The University of Alabama at Birmingham, School of Education, Department of Human Studies, Program in Physical Education, Birmingham, AL 35294. Offers MA Ed. Evening/weekend programs available. *Students:* 11 full-time (8 women), 9 part-time (8 women); includes 1 minority (American Indian/Alaska Native). 13 applicants, 92% accepted. In 2006, 19 degrees awarded. *Degree requirements:* For master's, thesis optional. *Entrance requirements:* For master's, GRE General Test, MAT, or NTE, minimum GPA of 3.0. *Application deadline:* Applications are processed on a rolling basis. Application fee: $35 ($60 for international students). Electronic applications accepted. *Expenses:* Tuition, state resident: part-time $170 per credit hour. Tuition, nonresident: part-time $425 per credit hour. Required fees: $15 per credit hour. $122 per term. Tuition and fees vary according to program. *Unit head:* Dr. David M. Macrina, Chair, Department of Human Studies, 205-934-2446, Fax: 205-975-8040, E-mail: dmacrina@uab.edu.

University of Alberta, Faculty of Graduate Studies and Research, Faculty of Physical Education and Recreation, Edmonton, AB T6G 2E1, Canada. Offers physical education (M Sc); recreation and physical education (MA, PhD). Part-time programs available. *Faculty:* 30 full-time (10 women). *Students:* 60 full-time (34 women), 55 part-time (28 women), 10 international. 69 applicants, 36% accepted. In 2006, 13 master's, 7 doctorates awarded. Terminal master's awarded for partial completion of doctoral program. *Degree requirements:* For master's, thesis (for some programs); for doctorate, thesis/dissertation. *Entrance requirements:* For master's, bachelor's degree in related field; for doctorate, master's degree in related field with thesis. Additional exam requirements/recommendations for international students: Required—TOEFL. *Application deadline:* For fall admission, 1/1 priority date for domestic students. Applications are processed on a rolling basis. *Financial support:* In 2006–07, 63 students received support, including 28 research assistantships, 35 teaching assistantships; career-related internships or fieldwork and scholarships/grants also available. Support available to part-time students. *Faculty research:* Motivation and adherence to physical ability, performance enhancement, adapted physical activity, exercise physiology, sport administration, tourism. *Unit head:* Dr. D. Marshall, Assistant Dean, 780-492-3198, Fax: 403-492-2364. *Application contact:* Anne Jordan, Department Office, 403-492-3198, Fax: 403-492-2364, E-mail: pergrad@ualberta.ca.

University of Arkansas, Graduate School, College of Education and Health Professions, Department of Health Science, Kinesiology, Recreation and Dance, Program in Physical Education, Fayetteville, AR 72701-1201. Offers M Ed, MAT. *Students:* 10 full-time (1 woman); includes 2 minority (1 African American, 1 American Indian/Alaska Native). 4 applicants, 50% accepted. In 2006, 14 degrees awarded. *Degree requirements:* For master's, thesis optional. Application fee: $40 ($50 for international students). *Financial support:* In 2006–07, 1 fellowship with tuition reimbursement was awarded; research assistantships, teaching assistantships, career-related internships or fieldwork and Federal Work-Study also available. Support available to part-time students. Financial award application deadline: 4/1; financial award applicants required to submit FAFSA. *Application contact:* Dr. Dean Gorman, Coordinator of Graduate Studies, 479-575-6625, E-mail: dgorman@comp.uark.edu.

University of Arkansas at Pine Bluff, Program in Education, Pine Bluff, AR 71601-2799. Offers elementary education (M Ed); secondary education (M Ed), including English, general science, mathematics, physical education, social studies. Part-time and evening/weekend programs available. *Degree requirements:* For master's, comprehensive exam. *Entrance requirements:* For master's, GRE, minimum GPA of 2.75, NTE or Standard Arkansas Teaching Certificate. *Faculty research:* Teacher certification, accreditation, assessment, standards, portfolio development, rehabilitation, technology.

The University of British Columbia, Faculty of Graduate Studies, Faculty of Education, Department of Curriculum Studies, Vancouver, BC V6T 1Z1, Canada. Offers art education (M Ed, MA); curriculum studies (M Ed, MA, PhD); home economics education (M Ed, MA); math education (M Ed, MA); music education (M Ed, MA); physical education (M Ed, MA); science education (M Ed, MA); social studies education (M Ed, MA); technical studies education (M Ed, MA). Part-time programs available. *Faculty:* 31 full-time (17 women), 1 (woman) part-time/adjunct. *Students:* 153 full-time (102 women), 101 part-time (67 women), 25 international. Average age 40. 118 applicants, 64% accepted, 62 enrolled. In 2006, 46 master's, 4 doctorates awarded. *Degree requirements:* For master's, thesis (MA); for doctorate, thesis/dissertation, comprehensive exam, registration. *Entrance requirements:* Additional exam requirements/recommendations for international students: Required—TOEFL (minimum score 580 paper-based; 237 computer-based). *Application deadline:* For fall admission, 2/1 for domestic students, 1/1 for international students; for spring admission, 10/1 for domestic students, 9/1 for international students. Application fee: $90 ($150 for international students). Electronic applications accepted. *Expenses:* Contact institution. *Financial support:* In 2006–07, 10 fellowships with partial tuition reimbursements (averaging $16,000 per year), 11 research assistantships with partial tuition reimbursements (averaging $14,000 per year), 27 teaching assistantships with partial tuition reimbursements (averaging $14,000 per year) were awarded; tuition waivers (partial) also available. *Faculty research:* School subjects, teaching and learning. *Unit head:* Dr. Linda Peterat, Interim Head, 604-822-5422, Fax: 604-822-4714. *Application contact:* Basia Zurek, Graduate Secretary, 604-822-5367, Fax: 604-822-4714, E-mail: cust.grad@ubc.ca.

University of California, Berkeley, Graduate Division, School of Education, Division of Language and Literacy, Society and Culture, Berkeley, CA 94720-1500. Offers education and single subject credential: English (MA); language, literacy, and culture (MA, Ed D, PhD), including athletes and academic achievement (MA), language, literacy, and culture (MA); social and cultural studies in education (MA, PhD); PhD/MA. *Degree requirements:* For master's, exam or thesis; for doctorate, thesis/dissertation, oral qualifying exam (PhD). *Entrance requirements:* For master's and doctorate, GRE General Test, minimum GPA of 3.0 during last 2 years of undergraduate course work. *Application deadline:* For fall admission, 12/1 for domestic students. Application fee: $60 ($80 for international students). Electronic applications accepted. *Financial support:* Fellowships, research assistantships, teaching assistantships, unspecified assistantships available. *Faculty research:* Literature, English education, reading education, second language teaching and learning, teacher education. *Application contact:* Admissions Office, 510-642-0841, Fax: 510-642-4808, E-mail: gse_info@uclink.berkeley.edu.

University of Central Florida, College of Education, Department of Child, Family and Community Sciences, Program in Physical Education-Exercise Physiology, Orlando, FL 32816. Offers M Ed, MA. Part-time and evening/weekend programs available. *Students:* 19 full-time (9 women), 20 part-time (11 women); includes 4 minority (all African Americans) In 2006, 16 master's awarded. *Entrance requirements:* For master's, GRE General Test. Additional exam requirements/recommendations for international students: Required—TOEFL. *Application deadline:* For fall admission, 7/15 for domestic students; for spring admission, 12/1 for domestic students. Application fee: $30. Electronic applications accepted. *Expenses:* Tuition, state resident: full-time $6,167; part-time $257 per credit hour. Tuition, nonresident: full-time $22,790; part-time $950 per credit hour. *Financial support:* In 2006–07, 2 research assistantships with partial tuition reimbursements (averaging $6,400 per year) were awarded; fellowships with partial tuition reimbursements, teaching assistantships with partial tuition reimbursements, career-related internships or fieldwork, Federal Work-Study, institutionally sponsored loans, tuition waivers (partial), and unspecified assistantships also available. Financial award application deadline: 3/1; financial award applicants required to submit FAFSA. *Unit head:* Dr. Patricia Higginbotham, Coordinator, 407-823-2050, E-mail: higginbp@mail.ucf.edu.

University of Central Missouri, The Graduate School, College of Health and Human Services, Department of Health and Human Performance, Warrensburg, MO 64093. Offers physical education/exercise and sports science (MS). Part-time programs available. *Faculty:* 16 full-time (7 women). *Students:* 3 full-time (0 women), 44 part-time (18 women); includes 10 minority (4 African Americans, 1 American Indian/Alaska Native, 1 Asian American or Pacific Islander, 4 Hispanic Americans). Average age 29. 20 applicants, 90% accepted, 11 enrolled. In 2006, 13 degrees awarded. *Degree requirements:* For master's, research project, thesis or internship. *Entrance requirements:* For master's, minimum GPA of 2.5, bachelor's degree in physical education. Additional exam requirements/recommendations for international students: Required—TOEFL (minimum score 500 paper-based; 173 computer-based). *Application deadline:* For fall admission, 6/1 priority date for domestic students, 5/1 priority date for international students; for spring admission, 10/1 priority date for domestic students, 10/1 for international students. Applications are processed on a rolling basis. Application fee: $30 ($50 for international students). *Expenses:* Tuition, state resident: full-time $5,448; part-time $227 per credit hour. Tuition, nonresident: full-time $10,896; part-time $454 per credit hour. Required fees: $336; $14 per credit hour. *Financial support:* In 2006–07, 4 students received support. Federal Work-Study, scholarships/grants, unspecified assistantships, and administrative and laboratory assistantships available. Support available to part-time students. Financial award application deadline: 3/1; financial award applicants required to submit FAFSA. *Faculty research:* Walking gait kinetics with external loads, maximum oxygen uptake, resting energy expenditure. Total annual research expenditures: $19,000. *Unit head:* Dr. Dirk Nelson, Chair, 660-543-4256, Fax: 660-543-4168, E-mail: nelson@ucmo.edu.

University of Dayton, Graduate School, School of Education and Allied Professions, Department of Health and Sport Science, Dayton, OH 45469-1300. Offers exercise sports science (MS Ed); physical education (MS Ed). Part-time and evening/weekend programs available. *Faculty:* 15 full-time (5 women). *Students:* 30 full-time (21 women), 7 part-time (5 women); includes 3 African Americans, 1 American Indian/Alaska Native, 2 international. Average age 32. 72 applicants, 63% accepted, 31 enrolled. In 2006, 1 degree awarded. *Median time to degree:* Master's–2 years full-time. *Degree requirements:* For master's and doctorate, thesis/dissertation. *Entrance requirements:* For master's, GRE General Test, MAT, minimum GPA of 2.75; for doctorate, GRE General Test, minimum GPA of 3.0, 80 observation hours. Additional exam requirements/recommendations for international students: Required—TOEFL (minimum score 550 paper-based; 213 computer-based). *Application deadline:* For fall admission, 3/15 priority date for domestic students, 3/1 priority date for international students. Applications are processed on a rolling basis. Application fee: $0. Electronic applications accepted. *Expenses:* Tuition: Part-time $601 per semester hour. Tuition and fees vary according to degree level and program. *Financial support:* In 2006–07, 4 students received support, including 4 teaching assistantships with tuition reimbursements available (averaging $8,000 per year); research assistantships, career-related internships or fieldwork, institutionally sponsored loans, health care benefits, and unspecified assistantships also available. Financial award applicants required to submit FAFSA. *Faculty research:* Energy expenditure, strength, training, teaching nutrition and calcium intake of children and families in Head-Start. *Unit head:* Dr. Paul Vanderburgh, Chair, 937-229-4240, Fax: 937-229-4244. *Application contact:* Erika Eavers, Graduate Admission Processor, 937-229-3065, Fax: 937-229-4729, E-mail: erika.eavers@notes.udayton.edu.

University of Florida, Graduate School, College of Health and Human Performance, Department of Applied Physiology and Kinesiology, Gainesville, FL 32611. Offers athletic training/sport medicine (MS, PhD); biomechanics (MS, PhD); clinical exercise physiology (MS); exercise physiology (MS, PhD); health and human performance (PhD); human performance (MS); motor learning/control (MS, PhD); sport and exercise psychology (MS). *Faculty:* 14 full-time (2 women), 1 part-time/adjunct (0 women). *Degree requirements:* For doctorate, thesis/dissertation. *Entrance requirements:* For doctorate, GRE General Test. *Application deadline:* For fall admission, 6/1 priority date for domestic students. Applications are processed on a rolling basis. Application fee: $20. Electronic applications accepted. *Expenses:* Tuition, state resident: full-time $6,827. Tuition, nonresident: full-time $21,951. Required fees: $999. *Financial support:* In 2006–07, 16 research assistantships (averaging $13,060 per year), 28 teaching assistantships (averaging $12,925 per year) were awarded; fellowships, unspecified assistantships also available. *Unit head:* Dr. Steven Dodd, Chair, 352-392-0584 Ext. 1342, E-mail: sdodd@hhp.ufl.edu. *Application contact:* Dr. Paul A. Borsa, Coordinator, 352-392-0584 Ext. 1261, Fax: 352-392-5262, E-mail: pborsa@hhp.ufl.edu.

University of Houston, College of Education, Department of Health and Human Performance, Houston, TX 77204. Offers allied health (M Ed, Ed D); exercise science (MS); health education (M Ed); kinesiology (PhD); physical education (M Ed, Ed D). *Accreditation:* NCATE (one or more programs are accredited). Part-time and evening/weekend programs available. *Faculty:* 11 full-time (5 women), 6 part-time/adjunct (3 women). *Students:* 35 full-time (19 women), 33 part-time (17 women); includes 22 minority (12 African Americans, 1 Asian American or Pacific Islander, 9 Hispanic Americans), 1 international. Average age 29. 35 applicants, 54% accepted, 11 enrolled. In 2006, 24 master's, 4 doctorates awarded. *Degree requirements:* For master's, comprehensive exam or thesis; for doctorate, thesis/dissertation, comprehensive exam. *Entrance requirements:* For master's, GRE General Test or MAT; for doctorate, GRE General Test, interview. *Application deadline:* For fall admission, 7/3 for domestic students. Application fee: $35 ($75 for international students). *Expenses:* Tuition, state resident: full-time $5,429; part-time $226 per credit. Tuition, nonresident: full-time $12,029; part-time $501 per credit. Required fees: $2,454. *Financial support:* In 2006–07, 5 fellowships with full tuition reimbursements (averaging $9,500 per year), 4 research assistantships with full tuition reimbursements (averaging $9,850 per year), 9 teaching assistantships with full tuition reimbursements (averaging $9,850 per year) were awarded; career-related internships or fieldwork, Federal Work-Study, institutionally sponsored loans, scholarships/grants, health care benefits, and unspecified assistantships also available. Support available to part-time students. Financial award application deadline: 3/10. *Faculty research:* Motor development, physical fitness, comprehensive school health, leadership, sports law. *Unit head:* Dr. Chuck Layne, Chairperson, 713-743-9868, Fax: 713-743-9860, E-mail: clayne2@uh.edu.

University of Idaho, College of Graduate Studies, College of Education, Department of Health, Physical Education, Recreation, and Dance, Program in Physical Education, Moscow, ID 83844-2282. Offers M Ed, MS. *Students:* Average age 26. In 2006, 13 degrees awarded. *Entrance requirements:* For master's, minimum GPA of 2.8. *Application deadline:* For fall admission, 8/1 for domestic students; for spring admission, 12/15 for domestic students. Application fee: $55 ($60 for international students). *Expenses:* Tuition, nonresident: full-time $9,600; part-time $140 per credit. Required fees: $4,740; $227 per credit. *Financial support:* Research assistantships, teaching assistantships available. Financial award application deadline: 2/15. *Unit head:* Dr. Kathy Browder, Chair, Department of Health, Physical Education, Recreation, and Dance, 208-885-2192.

University of Idaho, College of Graduate Studies, College of Education, Doctoral Programs in Education, Moscow, ID 83844-2282. Offers adult and organizational learning (Ed D, PhD); counseliing and human services (PhD); counseling and human services (Ed D); curriculm and intstruction (Ed D); curriculum and instruction (PhD); educational leadership (Ed D, PhD); physical education (PhD); professional-technical and technology education (PhD); professional-technical and tecnology education (Ed D). *Students:* 208 (118 women). In 2006, 50 degrees awarded. *Expenses:* Tuition, nonresident: full-time $9,600; part-time $140 per credit. Required fees: $4,740; $227 per credit. *Application contact:* Shirley Green, Information Contact, 208-885-6773.

University of Indianapolis, Graduate Programs, School of Education, Indianapolis, IN 46227-3697. Offers art education (MAT); biology (MAT); chemistry (MAT); curriculum and instruction (MA); earth sciences (MAT); education (MA, MAT); educational leadership (MA); elementary education (MA); English (MAT); French (MAT); math (MAT); physical education (MAT); physics (MAT); secondary education (MA), including art education, education, English education, social studies education; social studies (MAT); Spanish (MAT). *Accreditation:* NCATE. Part-time and evening/weekend programs available. *Faculty:* 4 full-time (2 women), 6 part-time/

adjunct (2 women). *Students:* 32 full-time (16 women), 70 part-time (42 women); includes 2 minority (1 African American, 1 Hispanic American). Average age 31. In 2006, 51 degrees awarded. *Entrance requirements:* For master's, GRE Subject Test, minimum GPA of 2.5, 3 letters of recommendation, interview, Praxis I, writing exercise, be within 9 hours of completing content requirements. Additional exam requirements/recommendations for international students: Required—TOEFL (minimum score 550 paper-based; 213 computer-based). *Application deadline:* Applications are processed on a rolling basis. Application fee: $50. *Financial support:* Federal Work-Study available. Financial award application deadline: 5/1; financial award applicants required to submit FAFSA. *Faculty research:* Assessment of teacher education, perceptions of prospective teachers by parents. *Unit head:* Dr. E. Lynne Weisenbach, Dean, 317-788-3446, Fax: 317-788-3300, E-mail: weisenbach@uindy.edu.

The University of Iowa, Graduate College, College of Liberal Arts and Sciences, Department of Health and Sport Studies, Iowa City, IA 52242-1316. Offers psychology of sport and physical activity (MA, PhD); sports studies (MA, PhD). *Faculty:* 8 full-time, 7 part-time/adjunct. *Students:* 22 full-time (16 women), 11 part-time (7 women); includes 5 minority (all African Americans) 55 applicants, 36% accepted, 12 enrolled. In 2006, 15 master's, 2 doctorates awarded. *Degree requirements:* For master's, exam, thesis optional; for doctorate, thesis/dissertation, comprehensive exam, registration. *Entrance requirements:* For master's and doctorate, GRE General Test, minimum GPA of 3.0. Additional exam requirements/recommendations for international students: Required—TOEFL (minimum score 550 paper-based; 230 computer-based; 81 iBT). *Application deadline:* For fall admission, 3/1 for domestic and international students. Application fee: $60 ($85 for international students). Electronic applications accepted. *Financial support:* In 2006–07, 3 research assistantships with partial tuition reimbursements, 28 teaching assistantships with partial tuition reimbursements were awarded; fellowships also available. Financial award applicants required to submit FAFSA. *Unit head:* Susan Birrell, Chair, 319-335-9337, Fax: 319-335-6669.

University of Kansas, Graduate Studies, School of Education, Department of Health, Sport, and Exercise Sciences, Lawrence, KS 66045. Offers health, sports, and exercise sciences (Ed D); physical education (MS Ed, PhD). *Accreditation:* NCATE. Part-time and evening/weekend programs available. *Faculty:* 12. *Students:* 49 full-time (25 women), 45 part-time (22 women); includes 9 minority (6 African Americans, 1 American Indian/Alaska Native, 2 Hispanic Americans), 3 international. Average age 28. 54 applicants, 46% accepted. In 2006, 66 master's, 5 doctorates awarded. *Degree requirements:* For master's, thesis (for some programs), comprehensive exam; for doctorate, variable foreign language requirement, thesis/dissertation, comprehensive exam. *Entrance requirements:* For master's, GRE General Test, minimum GPA of 3.0; for doctorate, GRE General Test, minimum master's GPA of 3.5, minimum bachelor's GPA of 3.0. Additional exam requirements/recommendations for international students: Required—TOEFL. *Application deadline:* For fall admission, 3/15 priority date for domestic students; for spring admission, 10/15 priority date for domestic students. Applications are processed on a rolling basis. Application fee: $55 ($60 for international students). Electronic applications accepted. *Expenses:* Tuition, area resident: Part-time $227 per credit. Tuition, state resident: part-time $543 per credit. Tuition and fees vary according to course load, campus/location, program and reciprocity agreements. *Financial support:* Research assistantships with full and partial tuition reimbursements, teaching assistantships with full and partial tuition reimbursements available. Financial award application deadline: 4/1. *Faculty research:* Character education, health education, ACE genotype, obesity prevention, force and torque production. *Unit head:* Bob Frederick, Chair, 785-864-0784, Fax: 785-864-3343, E-mail: bfrederick@ku.edu. *Application contact:* Dr. James D. LaPoint, Graduate Coordinator, 785-864-0785, Fax: 785-864-3343, E-mail: jdl@ku.edu.

University of Louisville, Graduate School, College of Education and Human Development, Department of Health and Sports Sciences, Program in Physical Education (Teacher Preparation), Louisville, KY 40292-0001. Offers M Ed, MAT. *Students:* 10 full-time (4 women), 3 part-time (2 women); includes 1 minority (African American), 2 international. Average age 30. In 2006, 10 degrees awarded. *Entrance requirements:* For master's, GRE General Test. *Application deadline:* Applications are processed on a rolling basis. Application fee: $50. Electronic applications accepted. *Financial support:* Fellowships, research assistantships, teaching assistantships, Federal Work-Study and scholarships/grants available.

University of Maine, Graduate School, College of Education and Human Development, Program in Kinesiology and Physical Education, Orono, ME 04469. Offers M Ed, MS. Part-time and evening/weekend programs available. *Students:* 13 full-time (5 women), 17 part-time (9 women); includes 1 minority (Hispanic American), 1 international. Average age 30. 8 applicants, 88% accepted, 7 enrolled. In 2006, 8 degrees awarded. *Degree requirements:* For master's, thesis or alternative. *Entrance requirements:* For master's, MAT. Additional exam requirements/recommendations for international students: Required—TOEFL. *Application deadline:* For fall admission, 2/1 priority date for domestic students. Applications are processed on a rolling basis. Application fee: $50. Electronic applications accepted. *Financial support:* In 2006–07, teaching assistantships with tuition reimbursements (averaging $9,010 per year); research assistantships with tuition reimbursements, career-related internships or fieldwork, Federal Work-Study, institutionally sponsored loans, tuition waivers (full and partial), and unspecified assistantships also available. Support available to part-time students. Financial award application deadline: 3/1. *Unit head:* Dr. Dorothy Breen, Coordinator, 207-581-2444, Fax: 207-581-2423. *Application contact:* Scott G. Delcourt, Associate Dean of the Graduate School, 207-581-3219, Fax: 207-581-3232, E-mail: graduate@maine.edu.

University of Manitoba, Faculty of Graduate Studies, Faculty of Physical Education and Recreation Studies, Winnipeg, MB R3T 2N2, Canada. Offers M Sc.

University of Massachusetts Amherst, Graduate School, School of Education, Program in Education, Amherst, MA 01003. Offers cultural diversity and curriculum reform (M Ed, Ed D, CAGS); early childhood education and development (M Ed, Ed D, CAGS); educational administration (M Ed, Ed D, CAGS); elementary teacher education (M Ed, Ed D, CAGS); higher education (M Ed, Ed D, CAGS); international education (M Ed, Ed D, CAGS); mathematics, science, and instructional technology (M Ed, Ed D, CAGS); physical education teacher education (M Ed, Ed D, CAGS); reading and writing (M Ed, Ed D, CAGS); research and evaluation methods (M Ed, Ed D, CAGS); school psychology and school counseling (M Ed, Ed D, CAGS); secondary teacher education (M Ed, Ed D, CAGS); social justice education (M Ed, Ed D, CAGS); special education (M Ed, Ed D, CAGS). *Accreditation:* NCATE. *Students:* 418 full-time (286 women), 447 part-time (319 women); includes 147 minority (70 African Americans, 4 American Indian/Alaska Native, 28 Asian Americans or Pacific Islanders, 45 Hispanic Americans), 81 international. Average age 36. In 2006, 260 master's, 30 doctorates awarded. *Degree requirements:* For doctorate, thesis/dissertation. *Entrance requirements:* For master's and doctorate, GRE General Test. Additional exam requirements/recommendations for international students: Required—TOEFL (minimum score 530 paper-based; 197 computer-based). *Application deadline:* For fall admission, 1/15 for domestic and international students; for spring admission, 10/1 for domestic and international students. Applications are processed on a rolling basis. Application fee: $40 ($65 for international students). Electronic applications accepted. *Expenses:* Tuition, state resident: full-time $2,640; part-time $110 per credit. Tuition, nonresident: full-time $9,936; part-time $414 per credit. Required fees: $8,969; $3,129 per term. One-time fee: $257 full-time. Tuition and fees vary according to class time, course load, campus/location and reciprocity agreements. *Financial support:* Fellowships with full tuition reimbursements, research assistantships with full tuition reimbursements, teaching assistantships with full tuition reimbursements, career-related internships or fieldwork, Federal Work-Study, scholarships/grants, traineeships, and unspecified assistantships available. Support available to part-time students. Financial award application deadline: 1/15. *Unit head:* Linda L. Griffin, Professor, 413-545-6984.

University of Memphis, Graduate School, College of Education, Department of Health and Sport Sciences, Memphis, TN 38152. Offers clinical nutrition (MS); exercise and sport science (MS); health promotion (MS); physical education teacher education (MS), including teacher education; sport and leisure commerce (MS). Part-time and evening/weekend programs available. *Faculty:* 26 full-time (10 women), 8 part-time/adjunct (5 women). *Students:* Average age 28. 50 applicants, 62% accepted. In 2006, 14 degrees awarded. *Degree requirements:* For master's, thesis, comprehensive exam. *Entrance requirements:* For master's, GRE General Test or GMAT (sport and leisure commerce). *Application deadline:* For fall admission, 5/1 priority date for domestic students; for spring admission, 11/1 for domestic students. Applications are processed on a rolling basis. Application fee: $25 ($50 for international students). *Financial support:* In 2006–07, 13 research assistantships with full tuition reimbursements (averaging $6,000 per year), 4 teaching assistantships with full tuition reimbursements (averaging $6,000 per year) were awarded; career-related internships or fieldwork, tuition waivers (partial), and community assistantships also available. *Faculty research:* Sport marketing and consumer analysis, health psychology, smoking cessation, psychosocial aspects of cardiovascular disease, global health promotion. Total annual research expenditures: $1.3 million. *Unit head:* Dr. Michael H. Hamrick, Chairman, 901-678-4165, Fax: 901-678-3591, E-mail: mhamrick@memphis.edu. *Application contact:* Christina Little, Academic Services Coordinator, 901-678-4316, Fax: 901-678-3591, E-mail: aclittle@memphis.edu.

University of Minnesota, Twin Cities Campus, Graduate School, College of Education and Human Development, School of Kinesiology, Minneapolis, MN 55455-0213. Offers adapted physical education (MA, PhD); biomechanics (MA); biomechanics and neural control (PhD); coaching (Certificate); developmental adapted physical education (M Ed); exercise physiology (MA, PhD); human factors/ergonomics (MA, PhD); international/comparative sport (MA, PhD); kinesiology (M Ed, MA, PhD); leisure services/management (MA, PhD); motor development (MA, PhD); motor learning/control (MA, PhD); outdoor education/recreation (MA, PhD); physical education (M Ed); recreation, park, and leisure studies (M Ed, MA, PhD); sport and exercise science (M Ed); sport management (M Ed, MA, PhD); sport psychology (MA, PhD); sport sociology (MA, PhD); therapeutic recreation (MA, PhD). Part-time programs available. *Faculty:* 14 full-time (6 women). *Students:* 142 full-time (70 women), 68 part-time (28 women); includes 9 minority (3 African Americans, 1 American Indian/Alaska Native, 2 Asian Americans or Pacific Islanders, 3 Hispanic Americans), 21 international. Average age 30. 186 applicants, 60% accepted, 88 enrolled. In 2006, 141 master's, 57 doctorates, 12 other advanced degrees awarded. Terminal master's awarded for partial completion of doctoral program. *Degree requirements:* For master's, final oral exam; for doctorate, thesis/dissertation, preliminary written/oral exam, final oral exam. *Entrance requirements:* For master's, GRE or MAT, minimum GPA of 3.0; for doctorate, GRE or MAT, minimum GPA of 3.0, writing sample. *Expenses:* Tuition, state resident: full-time $9,302; part-time $775 per credit. Tuition, nonresident: full-time $16,400; part-time $1,367 per credit. Full-time tuition and fees vary according to class time, course load, program, reciprocity agreements and student level. *Financial support:* In 2006–07, 1 fellowship (averaging $24,775 per year), 13 research assistantships with full tuition reimbursements (averaging $24,775 per year), 34 teaching assistantships with full tuition reimbursements (averaging $24,775 per year) were awarded; career-related internships or fieldwork, Federal Work-Study, institutionally sponsored loans, and tuition waivers (full and partial) also available. Support available to part-time students. *Faculty research:* Exercise for health promotion and disease prevention and management; female athletes and bone health; affordance perception-action; gender and youth sport and psychosocial outcomes; outdoor behavioral healthcare. Total annual research expenditures: $708,598. *Unit head:* Dr. Mary Jo Kane, Director, 612-625-3870, Fax: 612-626-7700, E-mail: maryjo@umn.edu. *Application contact:* Dr. Mary Bents, Associate Dean, 612-625-6501, Fax: 612-626-1580, E-mail: mbents@tc.umn.edu.

The University of Montana, Graduate School, School of Education, Department of Health and Human Performance, Missoula, MT 59812-0002. Offers exercise science (MS); health and human performance (MS); health promotion (MS). *Accreditation:* NCATE. Part-time programs available. *Entrance requirements:* For master's, GRE General Test. Additional exam requirements/recommendations for international students: Required—TOEFL. *Faculty research:* Exercise physiology, performance psychology, nutrition, pre-employment physical screening, program evaluation.

University of Nebraska at Kearney, College of Graduate Study, College of Education, Department of Health, Physical Education, Recreation, and Leisure Studies, Kearney, NE 68849-0001. Offers adapted physical education (MA Ed); exercise science (MA Ed); master teacher (MA Ed). Part-time and evening/weekend programs available. *Faculty:* 6 full-time (3 women). *Students:* 11 full-time (4 women), 18 part-time (6 women); includes 1 minority (African American), 3 international. 14 applicants, 79% accepted. In 2006, 9 degrees awarded. *Degree requirements:* For master's, thesis optional. *Entrance requirements:* For master's, GRE General Test. Additional exam requirements/recommendations for international students: Required—TOEFL (minimum score 550 paper-based; 213 computer-based). *Application deadline:* For fall admission, 5/1 for domestic and international students; for spring admission, 8/15 for domestic students, 8/1 for international students. Applications are processed on a rolling basis. Application fee: $45. Electronic applications accepted. *Expenses:* Tuition, state resident: part-time $161 per hour. Tuition, nonresident: part-time $332 per hour. Required fees: $57 per hour. *Financial support:* In 2006–07, 2 research assistantships with full tuition reimbursements (averaging $8,200 per year), 8 teaching assistantships with full tuition reimbursements (averaging $8,200 per year) were awarded; career-related internships or fieldwork, scholarships/grants, and unspecified assistantships also available. Support available to part-time students. Financial award application deadline: 3/1; financial award applicants required to submit FAFSA. *Faculty research:* Ergonomic aids, nutrition, motor development, sports pedagogy, applied behavior analysis. *Unit head:* Dr. Nita Unruh, Chair, 308-865-8331, E-mail: unruhnc@unk.edu.

University of Nebraska at Omaha, Graduate Studies and Research, College of Education, School of Health, Physical Education, and Recreation, Omaha, NE 68182. Offers MA, MS. Part-time and evening/weekend programs available. *Faculty:* 12 full-time (2 women). *Students:* 49 full-time (28 women), 52 part-time (37 women); includes 7 minority (3 Asian Americans or Pacific Islanders, 4 Hispanic Americans), 7 international. Average age 28. 66 applicants, 55% accepted, 21 enrolled. In 2006, 31 degrees awarded. *Degree requirements:* For master's, thesis (for some programs), comprehensive exam. *Entrance requirements:* For master's, minimum GPA of 3.0, vary by concentration. Additional exam requirements/recommendations for international students: Required—TOEFL (minimum score 550 paper-based; 213 computer-based; 80 iBT). *Application deadline:* For fall admission, 7/1 priority date for domestic students; for spring admission, 12/1 priority date for domestic students. Applications are processed on a rolling basis. Application fee: $45. Electronic applications accepted. *Financial support:* In 2006–07, 71 students received support, including 8 research assistantships with tuition reimbursements available; fellowships, Federal Work-Study, institutionally sponsored loans, scholarships/grants, tuition waivers (full), and unspecified assistantships also available. Support available to part-time students. Financial award application deadline: 3/1; financial award applicants required to submit FAFSA. *Unit head:* Dr. Dan Blanke, Director, 402-554-2670.

University of Nebraska–Lincoln, Graduate College, College of Education and Human Services, Department of Health and Human Performance, Lincoln, NE 68588. Offers health, physical education, and recreation (M Ed, MPE). *Accreditation:* NCATE. *Degree requirements:* For master's, thesis (for some programs). *Entrance requirements:* For master's, curriculum vitae. Additional exam requirements/recommendations for international students: Required—TOEFL (minimum score 500 paper-based; 173 computer-based). Electronic applications accepted. *Faculty research:* Exercise science, health behaviors, fitness, teacher effectiveness.

University of Nevada, Las Vegas, Graduate College, College of Education, Department of Sports Education Leadership, Las Vegas, NV 89154-9900. Offers M Ed, MS, PhD. *Faculty:* 6 full-time (3 women), 5 part-time/adjunct (1 woman). *Students:* 13 full-time (4 women), 26 part-time (4 women); includes 7 minority (5 African Americans, 1 American Indian/Alaska Native, 1 Asian American or Pacific Islander), 1 international. 21 applicants, 62% accepted, 9 enrolled. In 2006, 3 master's, 2 doctorates awarded. *Entrance requirements:* Additional exam requirements/recommendations for international students: Required—TOEFL (minimum score 550 paper-based; 213 computer-based; 80 iBT). *Application deadline:* For fall admission, 5/1

Physical Education

University of Nevada, Las Vegas (continued)
for domestic and international students; for spring admission, 10/1 for domestic and international students. Application fee: $60 ($75 for international students). Electronic applications accepted. *Financial support:* In 2006–07, 4 research assistantships (averaging $10,500 per year), 5 teaching assistantships (averaging $11,000 per year) were awarded; career-related internships or fieldwork, Federal Work-Study, institutionally sponsored loans, scholarships/grants, health care benefits, and unspecified assistantships also available. Support available to part-time students. *Unit head:* Dr. Monica Lounsbery, Chair, 702-895-5057. *Application contact:* Graduate College Admissions Evaluator, 702-895-3320, Fax: 702-895-4180, E-mail: gradcollege@unlv.edu.

University of New Brunswick Fredericton, School of Graduate Studies, Faculty of Kinesiology, Fredericton, NB E3B 5A3, Canada. Offers exercise and sport science (M Sc); sport and recreation administration (MA, MBA/MA); MBA/MA. Part-time programs available. *Faculty:* 16 full-time (6 women). *Students:* 45 full-time (20 women), 8 part-time (6 women). In 2006, 8 degrees awarded. *Degree requirements:* For master's, thesis (for some programs). *Entrance requirements:* For master's, minimum GPA of 3.0, written statement of research goals and interests. Additional exam requirements/recommendations for international students: Required—TOEFL (minimum score 600 paper-based; 250 computer-based), TWE (minimum score 5). *Application deadline:* For fall admission, 3/1 priority date for domestic students. Applications are processed on a rolling basis. Application fee: $50 Canadian dollars. Electronic applications accepted. *Financial support:* In 2006–07, 24 research assistantships, 23 teaching assistantships were awarded; fellowships with tuition reimbursements, career-related internships or fieldwork and scholarships/grants also available. *Unit head:* Dr. Chris Stevenson, Acting Director of Graduate Studies, 506-453-5063, Fax: 506-453-3511, E-mail: cls@unb.ca. *Application contact:* Linda O'Brien, Graduate Secretary, 506-453-4576, Fax: 506-453-3511, E-mail: lobrien@unb.ca.

University of New Mexico, Graduate School, College of Education, Department of Physical Performance and Development, Program in Physical Education, Albuquerque, NM 87131-2039. Offers MS, Ed D, PhD, EDSPC. Part-time programs available. *Students:* 58 full-time (22 women), 47 part-time (18 women); includes 30 minority (10 African Americans, 1 American Indian/Alaska Native, 3 Asian Americans or Pacific Islanders, 16 Hispanic Americans), 14 international. Average age 37. 82 applicants, 50% accepted, 25 enrolled. In 2006, 11 master's, 7 doctorates awarded. *Degree requirements:* For master's, thesis optional; for doctorate, thesis/dissertation, comprehensive exam. *Entrance requirements:* For master's and doctorate, GRE, 3 letters of reference, minimum cumulative GPA of 3.0 in last 2 years of bachelor's degree. Additional exam requirements/recommendations for international students: Required—TOEFL (minimum score 550 paper-based; 213 computer-based). *Application deadline:* For fall admission, 6/15 priority date for domestic students; for spring admission, 11/1 priority date for domestic students. Application fee: $50. Electronic applications accepted. *Financial support:* In 2006–07, 29 students received support, including 17 teaching assistantships with full tuition reimbursements available (averaging $9,517 per year); career-related internships or fieldwork, institutionally sponsored loans, scholarships/grants, health care benefits, and unspecified assistantships also available. Financial award application deadline: 3/1; financial award applicants required to submit FAFSA. *Faculty research:* Physical education pedagogy, sports psychology, sports administration, cardiac rehabilitation, sports physiology, physical fitness assessment, exercise prescription. *Unit head:* Dr. David Scott, Chair, 505-277-8173, Fax: 505-277-6227, E-mail: dscott@unm.edu. *Application contact:* Carol Catania, Department Office, 505-277-8173, Fax: 505-277-6227, E-mail: catania@unm.edu.

The University of North Carolina at Chapel Hill, Graduate School, College of Arts and Sciences, Department of Exercise and Sport Science, Chapel Hill, NC 27599. Offers athletic training (MA); exercise physiology (MA); sport administration (MA). *Degree requirements:* For master's, thesis, comprehensive exam. *Entrance requirements:* For master's, GRE General Test, minimum GPA of 3.0. Additional exam requirements/recommendations for international students: Required—TOEFL (minimum score 550 paper-based). Electronic applications accepted. *Faculty research:* Mild head injury in sport, endocrine system's response to exercise, obesity and children, effect of aerobic exercise on cerebral bloodflow in elderly population.

The University of North Carolina at Pembroke, Graduate Studies, Department of Health, Physical Education, and Recreation, Pembroke, NC 28372-1510. Offers physical education (MA, MAT). Part-time and evening/weekend programs available. *Faculty:* 3 full-time (0 women), 1 part-time/adjunct (0 women). *Students:* 15 full-time (8 women), 20 part-time (6 women); includes 5 minority (3 African Americans, 1 American Indian/Alaska Native, 1 Hispanic American). Average age 34. 35 applicants, 100% accepted, 35 enrolled. In 2006, 13 degrees awarded. *Degree requirements:* For master's, thesis optional. *Entrance requirements:* For master's, MAT or GRE, minimum GPA of 3.0 in major, 2.5 overall. Additional exam requirements/recommendations for international students: Required—TOEFL. *Application deadline:* For fall admission, 7/15 priority date for domestic and international students; for spring admission, 12/1 priority date for domestic and international students. Applications are processed on a rolling basis. Application fee: $40. *Expenses:* Tuition, state resident: full-time $3,516; part-time $1,091 per semester. Tuition, nonresident: full-time $12,924; part-time $4,619 per semester. Tuition and fees vary according to class time, course load, degree level and campus/location. *Financial support:* In 2006–07, 18 research assistantships with full tuition reimbursements (averaging $6,000 per year) were awarded; unspecified assistantships also available. Support available to part-time students. Financial award application deadline: 4/15; financial award applicants required to submit FAFSA. *Unit head:* Dr. Tommy Thompson, Chair, 910-521-6220, Fax: 910-521-6554, E-mail: tommy.thompson@uncp.edu. *Application contact:* Dr. Kathleen C. Hilton, Dean of Graduate Studies, 910-521-6271, Fax: 910-521-6751, E-mail: grad@uncp.edu.

University of Northern Colorado, Graduate School, College of Natural and Health Sciences, School of Sport and Exercise Science, Greeley, CO 80639. Offers exercise science (MS, PhD); sport administration (MS, PhD); sport pedagogy (MS, PhD). Part-time and evening/weekend programs available. *Faculty:* 12 full-time (6 women). *Students:* 69 full-time (18 women), 20 part-time (9 women); includes 7 minority (2 American Indian/Alaska Native, 3 Asian Americans or Pacific Islanders, 2 Hispanic Americans), 16 international. Average age 30. 140 applicants, 69% accepted, 31 enrolled. In 2006, 64 master's, 8 doctorates awarded. *Degree requirements:* For master's, comprehensive exam; for doctorate, thesis/dissertation, comprehensive exam. *Entrance requirements:* For master's, 2 letters of recommendation, resumé; for doctorate, GRE General Test, 3 letters of recommendation, resumé. *Application deadline:* Applications are processed on a rolling basis. Application fee: $50 ($60 for international students). Electronic applications accepted. *Expenses:* Tuition, state resident: full-time $5,118; part-time $213 per credit hour. Tuition, nonresident: full-time $14,832; part-time $618 per credit hour. Required fees: $674; $34 per credit hour. *Financial support:* In 2006–07, 71 students received support, including 6 fellowships (averaging $2,417 per year), 18 research assistantships (averaging $6,834 per year), 14 teaching assistantships (averaging $8,725 per year); unspecified assistantships also available. Financial award application deadline: 3/1; financial award applicants required to submit FAFSA. *Unit head:* Dr. Dianna Gray, Director, 970-351-2535, Fax: 970-351-1762.

University of Northern Iowa, Graduate College, College of Education, School of Health, Physical Education, and Leisure Services, Program in Physical Education, Cedar Falls, IA 50614. Offers physical education (MA); scientific basis of physical education (MA); teaching/coaching (MA). Part-time and evening/weekend programs available. *Students:* 53 full-time (19 women), 7 part-time (3 women); includes 2 minority (both African Americans), 5 international. 58 applicants, 78% accepted, 37 enrolled. In 2006, 14 degrees awarded. *Degree requirements:* For master's, thesis or alternative, comprehensive exam. *Entrance requirements:* For master's, minimum GPA of 3.5, 3 years of educational experience. Additional exam requirements/recommendations for international students: Required—TOEFL (minimum score 500 paper-based; 180 computer-based; 61 iBT). *Application deadline:* For fall admission, 8/1 priority date for domestic students. Applications are processed on a rolling basis. Application fee: $30 ($50 for international students). Electronic applications accepted. *Expenses:* Tuition, state resident: full-time $5,936. Tuition, nonresident: full-time $14,074. *Financial support:* Career-related internships or fieldwork, Federal Work-Study, and tuition waivers (full and partial) available. Support available to part-time students. Financial award application deadline: 2/1.

University of Rhode Island, Graduate School, College of Human Science and Services, Department of Kinesiology, Kingston, RI 02881. Offers exercise science (MS); physical education (MS); physical therapy (DPT); psychosocial aspects of physical activity and sport (MS); teaching and administration (MS). *Accreditation:* NCATE (one or more programs are accredited). In 2006, 14 degrees awarded. *Entrance requirements:* For master's, MAT or GRE. *Application deadline:* For fall admission, 4/15 priority date for domestic students; for spring admission, 11/15 for domestic students. Applications are processed on a rolling basis. Application fee: $35. *Expenses:* Tuition, state resident: full-time $6,032; part-time $335 per credit. Tuition, nonresident: full-time $17,288; part-time $960 per credit. Required fees: $65 per credit. $30 per semester. One-time fee: $80 part-time. *Financial support:* Career-related internships or fieldwork available. *Unit head:* Dr. Deborah Riebe, Chair, 401-874-5444.

University of South Alabama, Graduate School, College of Education, Department of Health, Physical Education and Leisure Services, Mobile, AL 36688-0002. Offers exercise science (MS); health education (M Ed); physical education (M Ed); therapeutic recreation (MS). *Accreditation:* NCATE (one or more programs are accredited). Part-time programs available. *Faculty:* 9 full-time (1 woman). *Students:* 26 full-time (18 women), 11 part-time (8 women); includes 11 minority (9 African Americans, 1 Asian American or Pacific Islander, 1 Hispanic American), 2 international. 12 applicants, 83% accepted, 5 enrolled. In 2006, 17 degrees awarded. *Degree requirements:* For master's, comprehensive exam. *Entrance requirements:* For master's, GRE General Test or MAT. *Application deadline:* For fall admission, 9/1 priority date for domestic students. Applications are processed on a rolling basis. Application fee: $25. *Financial support:* In 2006–07, 10 teaching assistantships were awarded; career-related internships or fieldwork also available. Support available to part-time students. Financial award application deadline: 4/1. *Unit head:* Dr. Frederick M. Scaffidi, Chair, 251-460-7131.

University of South Carolina, The Graduate School, College of Education, Department of Physical Education, Columbia, SC 29208. Offers IMA, MAT, MS, PhD. Part-time programs available. *Degree requirements:* For master's, thesis (for some programs), comprehensive exam; for doctorate, thesis/dissertation, comprehensive exam. *Entrance requirements:* For master's and doctorate, GRE General Test, writing sample. *Faculty research:* Teaching/learning processes, anthropometric measurement, growth and development, motor development.

The University of South Dakota, Graduate School, School of Education, Division of Health, Physical Education and Recreation, Vermillion, SD 57069-2390. Offers MA. *Accreditation:* NCATE. Part-time programs available. *Faculty:* 5 full-time (2 women), 1 (woman) part-time/adjunct. *Students:* 26 (8 women). In 2006, 22 degrees awarded. *Degree requirements:* For master's, thesis or alternative, comprehensive exam. *Entrance requirements:* For master's, GRE General Test, MAT, minimum GPA of 2.7. Additional exam requirements/recommendations for international students: Required—TOEFL (minimum score 550 paper-based; 213 computer-based; 79 iBT). *Application deadline:* Applications are processed on a rolling basis. Application fee: $35. Electronic applications accepted. *Expenses:* Tuition, state resident: part-time $120 per credit hour. Tuition, nonresident: part-time $355 per credit hour. Required fees: $90 per credit hour. *Financial support:* In 2006–07, research assistantships with partial tuition reimbursements (averaging $4,626 per year), teaching assistantships with partial tuition reimbursements (averaging $4,626 per year) were awarded; Federal Work-Study and unspecified assistantships also available. Financial award applicants required to submit FAFSA. *Unit head:* Dr. Garreth Zalud, Acting Chair/Graduate Director, 605-677-5310, Fax: 605-677-5338, E-mail: rkoch@usd.edu.

University of Southern Mississippi, Graduate School, College of Health, School of Human Performance and Recreation, Hattiesburg, MS 39406-0001. Offers human performance (MS, Ed D, PhD); interscholastic athletic administration (MS); recreation and leisure management (MS); sport administration (MS); sport and coaching education (MS); sport management (MS); sports and high performance materials (MS). Part-time and evening/weekend programs available. *Faculty:* 15 full-time (3 women). *Students:* 63 full-time (21 women), 36 part-time (11 women); includes 16 minority (13 African Americans, 1 Asian American or Pacific Islander, 2 Hispanic Americans), 6 international. Average age 27. 75 applicants, 64% accepted, 38 enrolled. In 2006, 37 master's, 5 doctorates awarded. *Degree requirements:* For master's, thesis optional; for doctorate, thesis/dissertation, comprehensive exam, registration. *Entrance requirements:* For master's, GRE General Test, minimum GPA of 2.75 in last 60 hours; for doctorate, GRE General Test, minimum GPA of 3.5. Additional exam requirements/recommendations for international students: Required—TOEFL. *Application deadline:* For fall admission, 3/1 priority date for domestic students, 3/1 for international students. Applications are processed on a rolling basis. Application fee: $25 ($30 for international students). Electronic applications accepted. *Financial support:* In 2006–07, 5 research assistantships with full tuition reimbursements (averaging $10,426 per year), 10 teaching assistantships with full tuition reimbursements (averaging $10,426 per year) were awarded; fellowships, career-related internships or fieldwork, Federal Work-Study, institutionally sponsored loans, and tuition waivers (partial) also available. Financial award application deadline: 3/15. *Faculty research:* Exercise physiology, health behaviors, resource management, activity interaction, site development. *Unit head:* Dr. Louis Marciani, Director, 601-266-5379, Fax: 601-266-4445. *Application contact:* Dr. Dennis Phillips, Graduate Coordinator, 601-266-5379, Fax: 601-266-4445.

University of South Florida, Graduate School, College of Education, School of Physical Education, Wellness, and Sport Studies, Tampa, FL 33620-9951. Offers physical education (MA). Part-time and evening/weekend programs available. *Faculty:* 6 full-time (4 women), 3 part-time/adjunct (0 women). *Students:* 14 full-time (7 women), 25 part-time (12 women); includes 4 minority (2 African Americans, 1 Asian American or Pacific Islander, 1 Hispanic American). 39 applicants, 77% accepted, 19 enrolled. In 2006, 4 degrees awarded. *Entrance requirements:* For master's, GRE General Test, minimum GPA of 3.5 in last 60 hours of coursework. Additional exam requirements/recommendations for international students: Required—TOEFL (minimum score 550 paper-based; 213 computer-based). *Application deadline:* For fall admission, 6/1 for domestic students; for spring admission, 10/15 for domestic students. Application fee: $30. Electronic applications accepted. *Financial support:* Unspecified assistantships available. Financial award application deadline: 7/3. Total annual research expenditures:$52,251. *Unit head:* Dr. Michael Stewart, Director, 813-974-3443, Fax: 813-974-4979, E-mail: mstewart@tempest.coedu.usf.edu.

The University of Tennessee at Chattanooga, Graduate School, College of Health, Education and Professional Studies, Department of Health and Human Performance, Program in Health and Human Performance, Chattanooga, TN 37403-2598. Offers MS. *Faculty:* 4 full-time (1 woman), 1 (woman) part-time/adjunct. *Students:* 32 full-time (26 women), 4 part-time (1 woman); includes 6 minority (5 African Americans, 1 Hispanic American), 1 international. Average age 26. In 2006, 21 degrees awarded. *Entrance requirements:* For master's, GRE General Test or MAT. *Application deadline:* For fall admission, 8/1 priority date for domestic students; for spring admission, 12/1 priority date for domestic students. Applications are processed on a rolling basis. Application fee: $30. *Expenses:* Tuition, state resident: full-time $5,434; part-time $339 per hour. Tuition, nonresident: full-time $14,830; part-time $861 per hour. Required fees: $940; $178 per hour. *Financial support:* Application deadline: 4/1. *Faculty research:* Therapeutic exercise, lumbar spine biomechanics, functional rehabilitation outcomes, metabolic health. Total annual research expenditures: $536,199. *Unit head:* Dr. Gary Wilkerson, Coordinator, 423-425-5394, E-mail: gary-wilkerson@utc.edu.

The University of Texas at Arlington, Graduate School, College of Education, Arlington, TX 76019. Offers curriculum and instruction (M Ed); educational leadership and policy studies (M Ed); physiology of exercise (MS); teaching (M Ed T). *Accreditation:* NCATE. Part-time and evening/weekend programs available. Postbaccalaureate distance learning degree programs offered (minimal on-campus study). *Faculty:* 19 full-time (11 women), 3 part-time/adjunct (2 women). *Students:* 171 full-time (107 women), 579 part-time (474 women); includes 278 minority (130 African Americans, 6 American Indian/Alaska Native, 20 Asian Americans or Pacific Islanders, 122 Hispanic Americans), 40 international. Average age 36. 579 applicants, 88% accepted, 368 enrolled. In 2006, 101 degrees awarded. *Degree requirements:* For master's, thesis (for some programs), comprehensive activity, research project, comprehensive exam (for some programs), registration. *Entrance requirements:* For master's, GRE General Test, minimum undergraduate GPA of 3.0 in last 60 hours of course work, writing sample, 3 letters of recommendation. Additional exam requirements/recommendations for international students: Required—TOEFL (minimum score 550 paper-based; 213 computer-based). *Application deadline:* For fall admission, 6/16 priority date for domestic students, 4/9 priority date for international students; for winter admission, 10/22 priority date for domestic students, 9/10 priority date for international students; for spring admission, 3/25 priority date for domestic and international students. Applications are processed on a rolling basis. Application fee: $35 ($50 for international students). Electronic applications accepted. *Expenses:* Tuition, state resident: full-time $5,528. Tuition, nonresident: full-time $10,478. International tuition: $10,608 full-time. *Financial support:* In 2006–07, 11 fellowships (averaging $1,000 per year), teaching assistantships with tuition reimbursements (averaging $9,000 per year) were awarded; career-related internships or fieldwork, Federal Work-Study, scholarships/grants, and unspecified assistantships also available. Financial award application deadline: 6/1; financial award applicants required to submit FAFSA. *Unit head:* Dr. Jeanne M. Gerlach, Dean, 817-272-2591, Fax: 817-272-2530, E-mail: soeadvising@uta.edu. *Application contact:* Brendan Hardy, Graduate Advisor, 817-272-2956, Fax: 817-272-7624, E-mail: coedadvising@uta.edu.

The University of Texas at El Paso, Graduate School, College of Health Sciences, School of Allied Health, Department of Health and Physical Education, El Paso, TX 79968-0001. Offers MS. Part-time and evening/weekend programs available. *Degree requirements:* For master's, thesis optional. *Entrance requirements:* For master's, GRE General Test. Additional exam requirements/recommendations for international students: Required—TOEFL. Electronic applications accepted.

University of the Incarnate Word, School of Graduate Studies and Research, School of Nursing and Health Professions, Program in Human Performance, San Antonio, TX 78209-6397. Offers kinesiology (MS); sports management (MS). *Students:* Average age 27. In 2006, 3 degrees awarded. *Entrance requirements:* Additional exam requirements/recommendations for international students: Required—TOEFL. *Application deadline:* For fall admission, 8/15 priority date for domestic students; for spring admission, 12/31 for domestic students. Applications are processed on a rolling basis. Application fee: $20. *Expenses:* Tuition: Part-time $570 per credit hour. Required fees: $54 per credit hour. One-time fee: $195 part-time. Tuition and fees vary according to degree level. *Financial support:* Federal Work-Study and scholarships/grants available. *Unit head:* Dr. William Carleton, Coordinator, 210-829-3966, Fax: 210-829-3174, E-mail: carleton@uiwtx.edu. *Application contact:* Andrea Cyterski-Acosta, Dean of Enrollment, 210-829-6005, Fax: 210-829-3921, E-mail: cyterski@uiwtx.edu.

The University of Toledo, College of Graduate Studies, College of Education, Department of Early Childhood, Physical and Special Education, Program in Physical Education, Toledo, OH 43606-3390. Offers ME. *Students:* 4 full-time (1 woman), 2 part-time (both women). Average age 26. 2 applicants, 100% accepted, 1 enrolled. *Unit head:* Dr. Laurie Dinnebeil, Chair, Department of Early Childhood, Physical and Special Education, 419-530-4330.

University of Toronto, School of Graduate Studies, Life Sciences Division, Faculty of Physical Education and Health, Toronto, ON M5S 1A1, Canada. Offers M Sc, PhD. *Degree requirements:* For master's, thesis, oral defense of thesis; for doctorate, defense of thesis. *Entrance requirements:* For master's, background in physical education and health, minimum B+ average in final year of undergraduate study, 2 letters of reference, resumé, 2 writing samples; for doctorate, master's degree with successful defense of thesis, background in exercise sciences, minimum A– average, 2 letters of reference.

University of Victoria, Faculty of Graduate Studies, Faculty of Education, School of Physical Education, Victoria, BC V8W 2Y2, Canada. Offers coaching studies (co-operative education) (M Ed); kinesiology (M Sc, MA); leisure service administration (MA); physical education (MA). Part-time programs available. *Degree requirements:* For master's, thesis (for some programs), comprehensive exam (for some programs), registration. *Entrance requirements:* For master's, minimum B average. Additional exam requirements/recommendations for international students: Required—TOEFL (minimum score 575 paper-based; 233 computer-based), IELTS (minimum score 7). Electronic applications accepted. *Faculty research:* Children and exercise, mental skills in sports, teaching effectiveness, neural control of human movement, physical performance and health.

University of Virginia, Curry School of Education, Department of Human Services, Program in Health and Physical Education, Charlottesville, VA 22903. Offers kinesiology (M Ed, Ed D). *Students:* 37 full-time (19 women), 2 part-time; includes 2 minority (1 African American, 1 Asian American or Pacific Islander). Average age 25. 28 applicants, 68% accepted, 8 enrolled. In 2006, 33 degrees awarded. *Degree requirements:* For master's, thesis (for some programs), comprehensive exam (for some programs); for doctorate, thesis/dissertation, comprehensive exam. *Entrance requirements:* For master's and doctorate, GRE General Test. *Application deadline:* Applications are processed on a rolling basis. Application fee: $60. Electronic applications accepted. *Financial support:* Applicants required to submit FAFSA. *Unit head:* Glenn A. Gaesser, Chair, 434-924-3543. *Application contact:* Roberta Camb, Information Contact, 434-924-6207, E-mail: rcl8b@virginia.edu.

The University of West Alabama, School of Graduate Studies, College of Education, Department of Physical Education and Athletic Training, Livingston, AL 35470. Offers physical education (M Ed, MAT). Part-time programs available. *Faculty:* 3 full-time (0 women). *Students:* 21 full-time (3 women), 24 part-time (8 women); includes 18 minority (all African Americans) In 2006, 9 degrees awarded. *Entrance requirements:* For master's, GRE General Test, MAT, minimum GPA of 2.75. *Application deadline:* For fall admission, 9/10 priority date for domestic students; for spring admission, 3/24 for domestic students. Applications are processed on a rolling basis. Application fee: $20 ($50 for international students). *Financial support:* Career-related internships or fieldwork, Federal Work-Study, scholarships/grants, and unspecified assistantships available. Support available to part-time students. Financial award applicants required to submit FAFSA. *Unit head:* Dr. R. T. Floyd, Chairperson, 205-652-3714, Fax: 205-652-3706, E-mail: rtf@uwa.edu.

University of West Florida, College of Professional Studies, Division of Health, Leisure, and Exercise Science, Program in Health, Leisure, and Exercise Science, Pensacola, FL 32514-5750. Offers exercise science (MS); physical education (MS). *Students:* 25 full-time (16 women), 21 part-time (16 women); includes 5 minority (4 African Americans, 1 Hispanic American), 1 international. Average age 31. 24 applicants, 83% accepted, 15 enrolled. In 2006, 6 degrees awarded. *Degree requirements:* For master's, thesis or alternative. *Entrance requirements:* For master's, GRE General Test, minimum GPA of 3.0. Additional exam requirements/recommendations for international students: Required—TOEFL (minimum score 550 paper-based; 213 computer-based). *Application deadline:* For fall admission, 6/1 for domestic students, 5/15 for international students; for spring admission, 11/1 for domestic students, 10/1 for international students. Applications are processed on a rolling basis. Application fee: $30. *Expenses:* Tuition, state resident: full-time $5,871; part-time $245 per credit hour. Tuition, nonresident: full-time $21,241; part-time $885 per credit hour. *Financial support:* Fellowships, research assistantships with partial tuition reimbursements, teaching assistantships, Federal Work-Study, scholarships/grants, tuition waivers (full and partial), and unspecified assistantships available. Financial award application deadline: 4/15; financial award applicants required to submit FAFSA. *Unit head:* Dr. Stuart W. Ryan, Chairperson, Division of Health, Leisure, and Exercise Science, 850-474-2592.

University of West Georgia, Graduate School, College of Education, Department of Physical Education and Recreation, Carrollton, GA 30118. Offers physical education (M Ed, Ed S). Part-time and evening/weekend programs available. *Faculty:* 9 full-time (6 women). *Students:* 5 full-time (3 women), 5 part-time (2 women); includes 1 minority (African American) Average age 20. In 2006, 1 degree awarded. *Degree requirements:* For master's, comprehensive exam; for Ed S, research project. *Entrance requirements:* For master's, GRE General Test, minimum GPA of 2.5; for Ed S, GRE General Test, master's degree, minimum graduate GPA of 3.0. *Application deadline:* For fall admission, 8/1 for domestic students. Applications are processed on a rolling basis. Application fee: $20. *Expenses:* Tuition, state resident: full-time $2,286; part-time $127 per credit. Tuition, nonresident: full-time $9,144; part-time $508 per credit. Required fees: $494; $27 per credit. $121 per semester. *Financial support:* In 2006–07, 4 research assistantships with full tuition reimbursements (averaging $3,000 per year) were awarded; career-related internships or fieldwork, scholarships/grants, and unspecified assistantships also available. Support available to part-time students. Financial award applicants required to submit FAFSA. *Faculty research:* Biomechanics, physical education pedagogy, sport management, sport marketing. Total annual research expenditures: $3,000. *Unit head:* Dr. Deborah Bainer Jenkins, Interim Chair, 678-839-6181, Fax: 678-839-6195, E-mail: bsnow@westga.edu. *Application contact:* Dr. Charles W. Clark, Chair, 678-839-6508, E-mail: cclark@westga.edu.

University of Wisconsin–La Crosse, Office of University Graduate Studies, College of Science and Health, Department of Exercise and Sport Science, Program in Physical Education Teaching, La Crosse, WI 54601-3742. Offers MS. Part-time and evening/weekend programs available. *Students:* 12 full-time (3 women), 18 part-time (9 women), 1 international. Average age 29. 17 applicants, 94% accepted, 10 enrolled. In 2006, 27 degrees awarded. *Degree requirements:* For master's, thesis optional. *Entrance requirements:* For master's, minimum GPA of 3.0 during previous 2 years, 2.85 overall; BA in physical education. Additional exam requirements/recommendations for international students: Required—TOEFL (minimum score 550 paper-based; 213 computer-based). *Application deadline:* For fall admission, 3/1 priority date for domestic students. Applications are processed on a rolling basis. Application fee: $45. Electronic applications accepted. *Financial support:* In 2006–07, 8 research assistantships (averaging $6,459 per year) were awarded; career-related internships or fieldwork, Federal Work-Study, institutionally sponsored loans, health care benefits, tuition waivers (full and partial), and grant-funded assistantships, external contracts also available. Financial award application deadline: 3/15; financial award applicants required to submit FAFSA. *Unit head:* Dr. Jeff Steffen, Director, 608-785-6535, E-mail: steffen.jeff@uwlax.edu. *Application contact:* Kathryn Kiefer, Associate Director of Admissions, 608-785-8939, E-mail: admissions@uwlax.edu.

University of Wyoming, Graduate School, College of Health Sciences, Division of Kinesiology and Health, Laramie, WY 82070. Offers MS. *Accreditation:* NCATE. Part-time programs available. Postbaccalaureate distance learning degree programs offered (no on-campus study). *Faculty:* 11 full-time (2 women). *Students:* 13 full-time (8 women), 24 part-time (13 women); includes 2 minority (both Hispanic Americans), 3 international. Average age 29. 25 applicants, 36% accepted. In 2006, 7 degrees awarded. *Degree requirements:* For master's, thesis (for some programs), comprehensive exam (for some programs), registration. *Entrance requirements:* For master's, GRE General Test, minimum GPA of 3.0. Additional exam requirements/recommendations for international students: Required—TOEFL. *Application deadline:* For fall admission, 6/1 priority date for domestic students; for spring admission, 11/1 for domestic students. Applications are processed on a rolling basis. Application fee: $50. Electronic applications accepted. *Financial support:* In 2006–07, 7 teaching assistantships with tuition reimbursements (averaging $10,062 per year) were awarded; career-related internships or fieldwork and unspecified assistantships also available. Financial award application deadline: 3/1. *Faculty research:* Teacher effectiveness, effects of exercising on heart function, physiological responses of overtraining, psychological benefits of physical activity, health behavior. Total annual research expenditures: $25,000. *Unit head:* Dr. Mark Byra, Director, 307-766-5285, Fax: 307-766-4098, E-mail: byra@uwyo.edu. *Application contact:* Dr. Mark Byra, Graduate Coordinator, 307-766-5227, Fax: 307-766-4098, E-mail: byra@uwyo.edu.

Utah State University, School of Graduate Studies, College of Education and Human Services, Department of Health, Physical Education and Recreation, Logan, UT 84322. Offers M Ed, MS. *Accreditation:* NCATE. Part-time and evening/weekend programs available. Postbaccalaureate distance learning degree programs offered (minimal on-campus study). *Faculty:* 6 full-time (1 woman). *Students:* 43 full-time (16 women), 9 part-time (6 women); includes 3 minority (2 African Americans, 1 Hispanic American), 5 international. Average age 34. 45 applicants, 80% accepted, 32 enrolled. In 2006, 15 degrees awarded. *Degree requirements:* For master's, thesis (for some programs). *Entrance requirements:* For master's, GRE General Test or MAT, minimum GPA of 3.0. Additional exam requirements/recommendations for international students: Required—TOEFL. *Application deadline:* For fall admission, 3/15 priority date for domestic students, 3/15 for international students; for spring admission, 6/15 priority date for domestic students, 6/15 for international students. Applications are processed on a rolling basis. Application fee: $50 ($60 for international students). *Financial support:* In 2006–07, 5 research assistantships with partial tuition reimbursements (averaging $6,488 per year), 15 teaching assistantships with partial tuition reimbursements (averaging $6,488 per year) were awarded; career-related internships or fieldwork, Federal Work-Study, institutionally sponsored loans, and tuition waivers (full) also available. Financial award application deadline: 2/10. *Faculty research:* Sport psychology intervention, motor learning biomechanics, pedagogy, physiology. Total annual research expenditures: $21,000. *Unit head:* Dr. Dennis A. Nelson, Interim Head, 435-797-1509, Fax: 435-797-3759, E-mail: dane@cc.usu.edu. *Application contact:* Dr. Richard D. Gordin, Graduate Chair, 435-797-1506, Fax: 435-797-3759, E-mail: gordin@cc.usu.edu.

Valdosta State University, Graduate School, College of Education, Department of Kinesiology and Physical Education, Valdosta, GA 31698. Offers health and physical education (M Ed). *Accreditation:* NCATE. Part-time and evening/weekend programs available. *Degree requirements:* For master's, comprehensive written and/or oral exams. *Entrance requirements:* For master's, GRE General Test or MAT. Additional exam requirements/recommendations for international students: Required—TOEFL (minimum score 523 paper-based; 193 computer-based). Electronic applications accepted.

Virginia Commonwealth University, Graduate School, School of Education, Department of Health and Human Performance, Richmond, VA 23284-9005. Offers athletic training (MS); exercise science (MS); rehabilitation and movement science (PhD); teacher education (MS). *Faculty:* 7 full-time (2 women). *Students:* 13 full-time (8 women), 28 part-time (17 women); includes 3 minority (2 African Americans, 1 American Indian/Alaska Native), 1 international. 8 applicants, 100% accepted, 8 enrolled. *Entrance requirements:* For master's, GRE General Test or MAT. *Application deadline:* For fall admission, 5/15 for domestic students; for spring admission, 11/15 for domestic students. Applications are processed on a rolling basis. Application fee: $50. *Financial support:* Career-related internships or fieldwork, Federal Work-Study, and institutionally sponsored loans available. Support available to part-time students. Financial award application deadline: 3/1. *Unit head:* Dr. Edmund Acevedo, Chair, 804-828-1948, Fax: 804-828-1946, E-mail: eoacevedo@vcu.edu. *Application contact:* Dr. Michael D. Davis, Director, Graduate Studies, 804-828-6530, Fax: 804-827-0676, E-mail: mddavis@vcu.edu.

See Close-Ups on pages 2331, 2333, and 1751.

Virginia Polytechnic Institute and State University, Graduate School, College of Liberal Arts and Human Sciences, School of Education, Department of Teaching and Learning, Blacksburg, VA 24061. Offers curriculum and instruction (MA Ed, Ed D, PhD, Ed S); health and physical education (MS Ed); instructional technology (ITMA). *Accreditation:* NCATE. Postbaccalaureate distance learning degree programs offered (no on-campus study). *Students:* 274 full-time (184 women), 400 part-time (271 women); includes 83 minority (55 African Americans, 2 American Indian/Alaska Native, 18 Asian Americans or Pacific Islanders, 8

Physical Education

Virginia Polytechnic Institute and State University (continued)
Hispanic Americans), 36 international. Average age 34. 374 applicants, 71% accepted, 237 enrolled. In 2006, 245 master's, 21 doctorates, 4 other advanced degrees awarded. *Entrance requirements:* Additional exam requirements/recommendations for international students: Required—TOEFL (minimum score 550 paper-based; 213 computer-based). *Application deadline:* For fall admission, 5/15 for international students; for spring admission, 10/15 for international students. Applications are processed on a rolling basis. Application fee: $45. Electronic applications accepted. *Expenses:* Tuition, state resident: full-time $7,017; part-time $390 per credit hour. Tuition, nonresident: full-time $12,414; part-time $690 per credit hour. International tuition: $11,296 full-time. Required fees: $1,523; $256 per term. *Financial support:* Career-related internships or fieldwork, Federal Work-Study, scholarships/grants, and unspecified assistantships available. Financial award application deadline: 4/1. *Faculty research:* Instructional technology, teacher evaluation, school change, literacy, teaching strategies. *Unit head:* Dr. Daisy L. Stewart, Head, 540-231-8327, Fax: 540-231-3717. *Application contact:* Nancy Nolen, Information Contact, 540-231-5348, Fax: 540-231-3717, E-mail: nanolen@vt.edu.

Wayne State College, School of Natural and Social Sciences, Department of Health, Human Performance and Sport, Wayne, NE 68787. Offers exercise science (MSE); organization management (MSE), including sport and recreation management. Part-time and evening/weekend programs available. *Faculty:* 6 part-time/adjunct (2 women). *Students:* 15 full-time (3 women), 6 part-time (1 woman); includes 3 minority (all African Americans), 2 international. Average age 27. In 2006, 11 degrees awarded. *Degree requirements:* For master's, thesis optional. *Entrance requirements:* For master's, GRE General Test, minimum GPA of 3.0. Additional exam requirements/recommendations for international students: Required—TOEFL (minimum score 550 paper-based; 213 computer-based). *Application deadline:* Applications are processed on a rolling basis. Application fee: $30. Electronic applications accepted. *Expenses:* Tuition, state resident: full-time $3,114; part-time $130 per credit hour. Tuition, nonresident: full-time $6,228; part-time $260 per credit hour. Required fees: $894; $37 per credit hour. Tuition and fees vary according to course load. *Financial support:* In 2006–07, 3 teaching assistantships with full tuition reimbursements (averaging $4,000 per year) were awarded; career-related internships or fieldwork also available. Financial award applicants required to submit FAFSA. *Unit head:* Dr. Kevin Hill, Dean, 402-375-7030.

Wayne State University, College of Education, Division of Kinesiology, Health and Sports Studies, Detroit, MI 48202. Offers health education (M Ed); kinesiology (M Ed); physical education (M Ed); recreation and park services (MA); sports administration (MA). *Faculty:* 9 full-time (2 women). *Students:* 40 full-time (16 women), 73 part-time (24 women); includes 25 minority (22 African Americans, 1 Asian American or Pacific Islander, 2 Hispanic Americans), 6 international. Average age 31. 39 applicants, 95% accepted, 26 enrolled. In 2006, 39 degrees awarded. *Degree requirements:* For master's, thesis (for some programs). *Entrance requirements:* For master's, GRE General Test. Additional exam requirements/recommendations for international students: Required—TOEFL; Recommended—TWE (minimum score 6). *Application deadline:* For fall admission, 7/1 for domestic students, 6/1 for international students; for winter admission, 10/1 for international students; for spring admission, 2/1 for international students. Application fee: $30 ($50 for international students). Electronic applications accepted. *Financial support:* In 2006–07, 3 research assistantships with tuition reimbursements (averaging $13,222 per year), 2 teaching assistantships with tuition reimbursements (averaging $13,222 per year) were awarded; career-related internships or fieldwork also available. *Faculty research:* Fitness in urban children, motor development of crack babies, effects of caffeine on metabolism/exercise, body composition of elite youth sports participants, systematic observation of teaching. Total annual research expenditures: $437,871. *Unit head:* Dr. Sally Erbaugh, Assistant Dean, 313-577-6210, Fax: 313-577-5999, E-mail: serbaugh@coe.wayne.edu. *Application contact:* John Wirth, Assistant Professor, 313-993-7972, Fax: 313-577-5999, E-mail: johnwirth@wayne.edu.

West Chester University of Pennsylvania, Graduate Studies, School of Health Sciences, Department of Kinesiology, West Chester, PA 19383. Offers driver education (Certificate); exercise and sport physiology (MS); physical education (MS); sport and athletic administration (MSA). Part-time and evening/weekend programs available. *Students:* 9 full-time (6 women), 30 part-time (8 women); includes 2 African Americans, 1 Hispanic American, 1 international. Average age 29. 35 applicants, 94% accepted, 12 enrolled. In 2006, 21 degrees awarded. *Degree requirements:* For master's, thesis optional. *Entrance requirements:* For master's, GRE or MAT, interview. *Application deadline:* For fall admission, 4/15 priority date for domestic students; for spring admission, 10/15 for domestic students. Applications are processed on a rolling basis. Application fee: $35. *Financial support:* In 2006–07, 7 research assistantships with full tuition reimbursements were awarded; unspecified assistantships also available. Support available to part-time students. Financial award application deadline: 2/15; financial award applicants required to submit FAFSA. *Faculty research:* Weight lifting and type 1 diabetes mellitus, martial arts, sexual harassment in sports. *Unit head:* Dr. Raymond Zetts, Chair, 610-436-2610, E-mail: czetts@wcupa.edu. *Application contact:* Dr. Sheri Melton, Graduate Coordinator, 610-436-2610, E-mail: smelton@wcupa.edu.

Western Carolina University, Graduate School, College of Education and Allied Professions, Department of Educational Leadership and Foundations, Programs in Secondary Education, Cullowhee, NC 28723. Offers art education (MAT); biology (MAT); chemistry (MAT); comprehensive education (MA Ed), including art, biology, English, mathematics, music, physical education, reading, social sciences; English (MAT); family and consumer sciences (MAT); mathematics (MAT); physical education (MAT); reading (MAT); social sciences (MAT). *Accreditation:* NCATE (one or more programs are accredited). Part-time and evening/weekend programs available. *Degree requirements:* For master's, comprehensive exam. *Entrance requirements:* For master's, GRE General Test, portfolio. Additional exam requirements/recommendations for international students: Required—TOEFL (minimum score 550 paper-based; 213 computer-based).

Western Carolina University, Graduate School, College of Education and Allied Professions, Department of Health and Human Performance, Cullowhee, NC 28723. Offers comprehensive education (MA Ed), including physical education; physical education (MA Ed, MAT). Part-time and evening/weekend programs available. *Degree requirements:* For master's, thesis optional. *Entrance requirements:* For master's, GRE General Test. Additional exam requirements/recommendations for international students: Required—TOEFL (minimum score 550 paper-based; 213 computer-based).

Western Kentucky University, Graduate Studies, College of Health and Human Services, Department of Physical Education and Recreation, Bowling Green, KY 42101. Offers physical education (MS); recreation (MS). Part-time and evening/weekend programs available. *Faculty:* 9 full-time (0 women), 1 part-time/adjunct (0 women). *Students:* 19 full-time (6 women), 46 part-time (11 women); includes 4 minority (all African Americans), 4 international. Average age 27. 26 applicants, 77% accepted, 15 enrolled. In 2006, 17 degrees awarded. *Degree requirements:* For master's, thesis optional. *Entrance requirements:* For master's, GRE General Test, minimum GPA of 2.75. Additional exam requirements/recommendations for international students: Required—TOEFL (minimum score 555 paper-based; 213 computer-based; 79 iBT). *Application deadline:* For fall admission, 7/1 priority date for domestic students, 4/1 for international students; for spring admission, 11/1 for domestic students, 9/1 for international students. Applications are processed on a rolling basis. Application fee: $35. *Expenses:* Tuition, state resident: full-time $6,520; part-time $226 per hour. Tuition, nonresident: full-time $7,140; part-time $357 per hour. International tuition: $15,820 full-time. *Financial support:* In 2006–07, 2 teaching assistantships with partial tuition reimbursements (averaging $9,000 per year) were awarded; career-related internships or fieldwork, Federal Work-Study, institutionally sponsored loans, and service awards also available. Support available to part-time students. Financial award application deadline: 4/1; financial award applicants required to submit FAFSA. *Faculty research:* Orthopedic rehabilitation, fitness center coordination, heat acclimation,

biomechanical and physiological parameters. *Unit head:* Dr. Thaddeus Crews, Department Head, 270-745-3347, Fax: 270-745-6043, E-mail: thad.crews@wku.edu.

Western Michigan University, Graduate College, College of Education, Department of Health, Physical Education and Recreation, Kalamazoo, MI 49008-5202. Offers administration (MA); athletic training (MA); coaching and sports studies (MA); exercise science (MA); motor development (MA); physical education (MA); special education for handicapped children (MA).

Western Washington University, Graduate School, College of Humanities and Social Sciences, Department of Physical Education, Health, and Recreation, Bellingham, WA 98225-5996. Offers exercise science (MS); sport psychology (MS). Part-time programs available. *Faculty:* 12. *Students:* 12 full-time (6 women), 1 part-time; includes 2 minority (1 African American, 1 American Indian/Alaska Native), 1 international. 16 applicants, 81% accepted, 7 enrolled. In 2006, 3 degrees awarded. *Degree requirements:* For master's, thesis. *Entrance requirements:* For master's, GRE General Test, minimum GPA of 3.0 in last 60 semester hours or last 90 quarter hours. Additional exam requirements/recommendations for international students: Required—TOEFL (minimum score 567 paper-based; 227 computer-based). *Application deadline:* For fall admission, 4/15 priority date for domestic students; for winter admission, 10/1 for domestic students; for spring admission, 2/1 for domestic students. Applications are processed on a rolling basis. Application fee: $50. *Expenses:* Tuition, state resident: full-time $6,609; part-time $199 per credit. Tuition, nonresident: full-time $16,845; part-time $540 per credit. *Financial support:* In 2006–07, 3 teaching assistantships with partial tuition reimbursements (averaging $9,339 per year) were awarded; Federal Work-Study, institutionally sponsored loans, scholarships/grants, tuition waivers (partial), and unspecified assistantships also available. Support available to part-time students. Financial award application deadline: 2/15; financial award applicants required to submit FAFSA. *Unit head:* Dr. LeaAnn Martin, Chair, 360-650-3054. *Application contact:* Dr. Dennis Caine, Graduate Adviser, 360-650-3056.

Westfield State College, Division of Graduate and Continuing Education, Department of Movement Science, Sport, and Leisure, Westfield, MA 01086. Offers physical education (M Ed). Part-time and evening/weekend programs available. *Degree requirements:* For master's, comprehensive exam. *Entrance requirements:* For master's, GRE General Test or MAT, minimum GPA of 2.7.

West Virginia University, School of Physical Education, Morgantown, WV 26506. Offers athletic coaching (MS); athletic training (MS); exercise physiology (Ed D); physical education/teacher education (MS, Ed D), including administration of physical education (Ed D), curriculum and instruction (Ed D), motor development (Ed D), special physical education (Ed D); sport management (MS); sport psychology (MS, Ed D). *Degree requirements:* For doctorate, thesis/dissertation, oral exam, comprehensive exam. *Entrance requirements:* For master's, GRE or MAT, minimum GPA of 3.0; for doctorate, GRE General Test or MAT, minimum GPA of 3.5. Additional exam requirements/recommendations for international students: Required—TOEFL (minimum score 550 paper-based; 213 computer-based). Electronic applications accepted. *Expenses:* Tuition, state resident: full-time $4,926; part-time $276 per credit hour. Tuition, nonresident: full-time $14,278; part-time $796 per credit hour. Tuition and fees vary according to program. *Faculty research:* Sport psychosociology, teacher education, exercise psychology, counseling.

Wichita State University, Graduate School, College of Education, Department of Kinesiology and Sport Studies, Wichita, KS 67260. Offers physical education (M Ed), including exercise science and wellness; sports administration (M Ed), including exercise science and wellness. Part-time programs available. *Degree requirements:* For master's, thesis optional. *Entrance requirements:* For master's, minimum GPA of 2.75. Additional exam requirements/recommendations for international students: Required—TOEFL. Electronic applications accepted.

Wilfrid Laurier University, Faculty of Graduate Studies, Faculty of Science, Department of Kinesiology and Physical Education, Waterloo, ON N2L 3C5, Canada. Offers M Sc. *Faculty:* 13 full-time. *Students:* 6 full-time. 12 applicants, 50% accepted, 6 enrolled. *Degree requirements:* For master's, thesis. *Entrance requirements:* For master's, honours degree in kinesiology, health, physical education with a minimum B+ in kinesiology and health-related courses. Additional exam requirements/recommendations for international students: Required—TOEFL (minimum score 230 computer-based; 89 iBT). *Application deadline:* For fall admission, 2/1 priority date for domestic students. Application fee: $75. Electronic applications accepted. *Financial support:* Fellowships, research assistantships, teaching assistantships available. *Faculty research:* Biomechanics, health, exercise physiology, motor control, sport psychology. *Unit head:* Dr. Peter Tiidus, Chairperson, 519-884-0710 Ext. 4157. *Application contact:* Dianne Duffy, Student Contact, 519-884-0710 Ext. 3127, Fax: 519-884-1020, E-mail: gradstudies@wlu.ca.

Wingate University, Program in Education, Wingate, NC 28174-0159. Offers educational leadership (MA Ed); elementary education (MA Ed, MAT); physical education (MA Ed); sport administration (MA Ed). *Accreditation:* NCATE. Part-time and evening/weekend programs available. *Faculty:* 4 full-time (3 women), 4 part-time/adjunct (1 woman). *Students:* 1 (woman) full-time, 127 part-time (96 women); includes 2 minority (both African Americans) Average age 35. 19 applicants, 58% accepted, 11 enrolled. In 2006, 12 degrees awarded. *Degree requirements:* For master's, portfolio. *Entrance requirements:* For master's, GRE General Test or MAT, teaching certificate (MA Ed). *Application deadline:* For fall admission, 8/15 priority date for domestic students; for spring admission, 12/15 for domestic students. Applications are processed on a rolling basis. Application fee: $0. *Expenses:* Tuition: Full-time $3,330; part-time $185 per credit hour. *Financial support:* In 2006–07, 20 students received support. Scholarships/grants available. Support available to part-time students. Financial award applicants required to submit FAFSA. *Faculty research:* Teaching/learning styles, principles of teaching, homework, stress management, student's rights. *Unit head:* Dr. Robert Shaw, Dean, Thayer School of Education, 704-233-8128, Fax: 704-233-8273, E-mail: rshaw@wingate.edu. *Application contact:* Marsha Luke, Secretary, Thayer School of Education, 704-233-8127, Fax: 704-233-8273, E-mail: mluke@wingate.edu.

Winthrop University, College of Education, Program in Physical Education, Rock Hill, SC 29733. Offers MS. Part-time programs available. *Students:* 11 full-time (5 women), 6 part-time (5 women); includes 3 minority (all African Americans), 1 international. Average age 24. In 2006, 2 degrees awarded. *Degree requirements:* For master's, thesis optional. *Entrance requirements:* For master's, GRE General Test or PRAXIS, minimum GPA of 3.0. *Application deadline:* For fall admission, 7/15 priority date for domestic students; for spring admission, 12/1 for domestic students. Applications are processed on a rolling basis. Application fee: $35 ($50 for international students). Electronic applications accepted. *Expenses:* Tuition, state resident: full-time $9,148; part-time $383 per hour. Tuition, nonresident: full-time $16,864; part-time $704 per hour. *Financial support:* Career-related internships or fieldwork, Federal Work-Study, scholarships/grants, and unspecified assistantships available. Support available to part-time students. Financial award application deadline: 2/1; financial award applicants required to submit FAFSA. *Unit head:* Dr. Steveda Chepko, Chair, 803-323-3693. *Application contact:* 800-411-7041, Fax: 803-323-2292, E-mail: graduatestu@winthrop.edu.

Wright State University, School of Graduate Studies, College of Education and Human Services, Department of Health, Physical Education, and Recreation, Dayton, OH 45435. Offers M Ed, MA. *Accreditation:* NCATE. *Students:* 1 (woman) full-time, 2 part-time (1 woman). Average age 30. 3 applicants, 67% accepted. In 2006, 3 degrees awarded. *Degree requirements:* For master's, thesis (for some programs), comprehensive exam. *Entrance requirements:* For master's, GRE General Test, MAT. Additional exam requirements/recommendations for international students: Required—TOEFL. Application fee: $25. *Financial support:* Available to part-time students. Applicants required to submit FAFSA. *Faculty research:* Motor learning, motor development, exercise physiology, adapted physical education. *Unit head:* Dr. D. Drew Pringle, Chair, 937-775-3223, Fax: 937-775-4252, E-mail: d.pringle@wright.edu. *Application contact:* John Kimble, Associate Director of Graduate Admissions and Records, 937-775-2957, Fax: 937-775-2453, E-mail: john.kimble@wright.edu.

ARIZONA STATE UNIVERSITY

Department of Kinesiology

Program of Study

Kinesiology is the study of the body's organ systems' responses to movement, muscle contraction, and exercise training. The mission of the Department of Kinesiology at Arizona State University (ASU) is to promote the creation of new knowledge in the field of kinesiology, to use this knowledge to create an invigorating learning environment, and to better the health of society through education and research. Students have numerous opportunities to learn in the laboratory, and cutting-edge knowledge produced by the faculty is translated directly into an enhanced learning environment.

The Master of Science in kinesiology program requires a minimum of 30 graduate credits, at least 21 of which must be courses from the Department. Required courses for all students include Research Methods and Research Statistics. A thesis is also required. Remaining course work is selected by the student in consultation with an adviser and the supervisory committee. Applicants may choose from five areas of specialization: biomechanics, exercise and sport psychology, exercise physiology, motor control, and motor development and learning.

The Ph.D. in the kinesiology program prepares scholars for careers in kinesiology research. Emphases are available in biomechanics, exercise physiology, human physiology, motor behavior, and sport/exercise psychology. Entering students are required to take a graduate student seminar and a graduate survey of kinesiology, plus three laboratory rotations. Subsequent semesters are devoted to completing didactic course work and developing a dissertation research plan. During the fifth semester, the student takes a comprehensive examination consisting of written and oral portions. The program culminates in a written dissertation followed by a public presentation and dissertation defense. A master's degree is not required for admission to the Ph.D. program.

Research Facilities

Research in the Laboratory for Integrative Motor Behavior seeks to discover fundamental principles of biomechanics and motor control, interpret these principles in the context of the physical and occupational environment, and apply basic research discoveries to problems in biomedicine and public health. The Motor Control Laboratory is dedicated to research investigating how movement is regulated and controlled, with special emphasis on examining motor deficits attributed to aging and basal ganglia dysfunction. Work at the Neural Control of Movement Laboratory focuses on understanding the control of complex movements. Approaches range from measuring the electrical activity of muscles to quantifying motion and forces during the execution of single-joint and multijoint movements. Research in the Center for Metabolic Biology revolves around answering central questions regarding the pathogenesis of insulin resistance in muscle. Its Proteomics Laboratory provides state-of-the-art mass spectrometry instruments, and the Department of Kinesiology Clinical Research Unit provides a venue for human physiology experiments.

Collectively, the ASU University Libraries are among the premier research libraries in the country. Its collections comprise nearly 4 million volumes, more than 34,000 periodical and serial subscriptions, thousands of sound recordings and videos, and hundreds of thousands of government documents and maps.

Financial Aid

Graduate assistantships involve 20 hours each week of research and teaching responsibilities at an annual stipend of $12,450 for master's students and $13,540 for Ph.D. students, plus health insurance. Twelve-month graduate assistantships involve 20 hours each week of research and teaching responsibilities at an annual stipend of $20,750 for Ph.D. students, plus health insurance. The annual stipend for 13 hours per week is $8575. The Achievement Rewards for College Scientists Foundation provides fellowships to outstanding students who are in need of financial assistance. Dissertation Fellowships are designed to support doctoral students who are in the final stages of postcandidacy doctoral work. Doctoral Enrichment Fellowships are designed to enhance recruitment of doctoral students who will contribute to the achievements of diversity in the student population.

Cost of Study

In 2007–08, tuition is $310 per academic credit for residents or $688 per credit for out-of-state students, plus $150 in fees. Students can also expect to spend approximately $2180 for books and supplies, $3090 for transportation, and $2950 in miscellaneous personal costs. Health insurance costs an additional $1264 per year.

Living and Housing Costs

Students living on campus pay $5319 for double occupancy and $6033 for single occupancy. Meal plans range from $1900 to $3500. Other fees include an annual $30 data connectivity fee and an annual $40 RHA fee. Students living off campus typically pay between $680 and $900 per month in rent, depending on the size and location of the apartment.

Student Group

The number of students accepted into the different areas of specialization varies depending upon the number of faculty members available to advise students. However, acceptance into the program remains highly competitive. There are currently 20–25 students enrolled in the program during any semester.

Student Outcomes

The M.S. program provides adequate preparation for admission to a Ph.D. program in the biosciences, and the Ph.D. program readies the student for an academic or industry career as an independent scientist.

Location

Tempe, the seventh-largest city in Arizona, has been voted one of the top ten college towns by the *New York Times.* The city is packed with history, culture, shopping, dining, nightlife, and sports, while Tempe Town Lake provides a haven for kayaking, sailing, rowing, jogging, skating, and picnicking. The Tempe campus is just minutes from downtown Phoenix, Scottsdale, and Phoenix Sky Harbor International Airport.

The University

Since its establishment in 1886, Arizona State University has emerged as a leading national and international research institution. Its mission is to provide outstanding programs in instruction, research, and creative activity; to promote and support economic development; and to provide service that is appropriate for the nation and the region. The University offers undergraduate and graduate programs for more than 58,000 students through five campuses throughout Arizona and other instructional, research, and public service sites throughout Maricopa County.

Applying

Each applicant is required to provide a completed online application, official transcripts of previous college work, a letter of intent designating a potential area of interest, a professional resume, three letters of recommendation, official GRE scores, and a $50 nonrefundable application fee. The deadline to apply is January 1 for fall admission and August 15 for spring admission.

Correspondence and Information

Lawrence Mandarino, Department Chair
Arizona State University
P.O. Box 870701
Tempe, Arizona 85287-0701
Phone: 480-965-3591
E-mail: lawrence.mandarino@asu.edu
Web site: http://www.asu.edu/clas/kines/index.html

Arizona State University

THE FACULTY AND THEIR RESEARCH

Donna Cataldo, Lecturer; Ph.D., New Mexico, 2001.

Natalia Dounskaia, Assistant Professor; Ph.D., Institute of Control Sciences (Russia). How movement control strategies used by the central nervous system are adjusted to the biomechanical properties of human limbs.

Jennifer Fay, Lecturer; M.S., Arizona State, 2005. Exercise, strength training, adolescents and research methods.

Kristinn I. Heinrichs, Lecturer; Ph.D., Virginia. Evidence-based medicine, curriculum development, scholarship of teaching.

Richard Herman, Visiting Professor; M.D., Queen's (Belfast). Device-oriented research to investigate mechanisms of function and dysfunction and test conventional therapies, new therapeutic tools.

Richard N. Hinrichs, Associate Professor; Ph.D., Penn State, 1982. Sport biomechanics, aquatics and locomotion.

Devin L. Jindrich, Assistant Professor; Ph.D., Berkeley, 2001. Fundamental principles of biomechanics and motor control.

Christos S. Katsanos, Assistant Professor; Ph.D., Florida State. Nutrient metabolism in humans.

Pamela Hodges Kulinna, Associate Professor; Ph.D., Illinois at Urbana-Champaign. Study of physical activity patterns in and outside of school settings, measuring student learning and teaching behaviors.

Daniel Landers, Regents' Professor. Effects of exercise on selected mental health variables.

Donna Landers, Senior Lecturer; M.S., Washington (Seattle).

Lawrence Mandarino, Professor and Department Chair; Ph.D., Arizona State. Molecular mechanisms responsible for insulin resistance in human skeletal muscle.

Miya Kato Rand, Associate Professor, Research; Ph.D., Copenhagen, 1993. Understanding of movement control, locomotion in humans, motor skill acquisition in primates, kinematic analysis and coordination among different body segments.

Shannon Ringenbach, Associate Professor; Ph.D., Purdue, 1998. Learning and development of bimanual coordination.

Marco Santello, Associate Professor; Ph.D., Birmingham, 1995. Neural mechanisms underlying control of the hand.

George Stelmach, Professor; Ed.D., Berkeley, 1967. Multijoint coordination mechanisms, visuomotor adaptation, sensorimotor integration, handwriting control, reaching and grasping, force control.

Arend W. A. Van Gemmert, Associate Professor, Research; Ph.D., Nijmegen (Netherlands), 1997. Understanding of movement control in fine motor tasks, mechanisms behind changes in movement control.

Wayne Willis, Associate Professor; Ph.D., Berkeley, 1986. Control of respiration in skeletal muscle.

SETON HALL UNIVERSITY

School of Graduate Medical Education
Athletic Training Program

Program of Study	As integral members of the sports medicine team, athletic trainers (AT) provide health care to individuals in the areas of injury prevention, evaluation, management, and rehabilitation. The athletic trainer functions as an essential member of the health team in a variety of settings, including secondary schools, colleges and universities, sports medicine clinics, industrial settings, and professional sport programs. Accredited by the Commission on Accreditation of Athletic Training Education since October 2003, the program is the only entry-level Master of Science in Athletic Training (M.S.A.T.) in New Jersey and one of fewer than twenty such programs in the country.
	Throughout the two-year, 64-credit program, students focus on quality of care and the uniqueness of each patient needing treatment. Distinctive courses, such as Clinical Imaging and Evaluation of the Spine, are taught by University faculty and physicians who have practical experience in the field. Foundational courses are "cross-program," meaning students gain an appreciation from their peers in other health professions, including occupational therapy and physical therapy, and learn from a distinguished faculty. Clinical rotations begin in the first semester, allowing students early on to integrate their classroom knowledge with clinical learning in varied working environments. The program boasts a competitive admissions process. Students accepted into the program include undergraduates enrolled in the University's 3-2 dual-degree program. For more information on this program, students should visit the Web site at http://www.shu.edu/academics/gradmeded/bs-ms-athletic-training.cfm.
Research Facilities	Dynamic clinical research is a major focus of the M.S.A.T. program. Student topics include hamstring flexibility as it relates to the injury, Mulligan taping techniques in ankle sprains, and the public's perception of athletic trainers. Students present their research at professional conferences and at an annual on-campus colloquium. Graduates of the program possess an understanding of the research process and recognize the importance of applying evidence-based research to clinical practice.
Financial Aid	Nearly 90 percent of the students who entered Seton Hall University (SHU) last year received some form of financial aid. Graduate assistantships are available for tuition remission and a small stipend, as are teaching, research, and administrative positions throughout the University. Loans are available to students enrolled in at least 6 credits per semester, though some require full-time study.
Cost of Study	Tuition for the 2007–08 academic year is $826 per credit. University fees are $105 per semester for full-time students. Additional fees are required for technology, parking, and use of the recreation center.
Living and Housing Costs	Limited housing space is available for graduate students at Ora Manor Apartments, approximately 1 mile from campus. Seton Hall provides a shuttle service to campus during the academic year; public transportation is also available. In addition, South Orange residents rent space to students. Off-campus listings are available through the Department of Housing and Residence Life.
Student Group	The SHU Athletic Training Student Association is a student-run organization that provides opportunities and activities to promote the advancement of future AT professionals and the profession of athletic training.
Student Outcomes	M.S.A.T. students are well-prepared for the Board of Certification examination. The curriculum also prepares students for the National Strength and Conditioning Specialist examination. This program prepares graduates to critically analyze and convey information to patients, colleagues, and other health professionals. These practitioners provide a broad range of patient-care services and perform research and administrative responsibilities. Students develop the skills they need to perform as entry-level practitioners and to grow and adapt to the rapid changes in the profession. Graduates of this program seek leadership positions in a variety of settings, including secondary schools, colleges, universities, sports medicine clinics, and professional sports programs as well as influence the development of policy and standard setting in athletic training practice.
Location	Seton Hall is located 14 miles southwest of New York City on 58 green acres in South Orange, New Jersey, at the foot of South Mountain. South Orange is a suburban neighborhood with tree-lined streets and large, gracious homes. The town center is just a 10-minute walk from campus and has a variety of quaint shops and conveniences, including a train station that is about a 25-minute ride from New York City.
The School	The School of Graduate Medical Education, established in 1987, is a graduate professional school within the University structure utilizing a multi-institutional/integrated approach to graduate education. In recent years, the School expanded its mission and direction to include the graduate education of health-care providers other than physicians and dentists. In response to the changing health-care needs of society, the School of Graduate Medical Education seeks to utilize community and University resources to establish a nationally recognized educational center for health professionals. The School's innovative approach provides students with effective tools for becoming leaders in today's health-care arena.
Applying	Students accepted into the program include students with a non-AT bachelor's degree who want to become a certified AT. Admission to the program requires a bachelor's degree from an accredited institution, official transcripts, an overall cumulative GPA of 3.0 or better, completion of certain prerequisite courses with a minimum GPA of 3.0, 50 hours of clinical observation with a certified athletic trainer, one letter of recommendation from an observational experience, two additional letters of recommendation, and completion of the applicant essay question. The preferred deadline for application is February 15.
Correspondence and Information	Master of Science in Athletic Training Program School of Graduate Medical Education McQuaid Hall Seton Hall University 400 South Orange Avenue South Orange, New Jersey 07079 Phone: 973-275-2826 Fax: 973-275-2171 E-mail: gradmeded@shu.edu Web site: http://www.shu.edu/academics/gradmeded/ms-athletic-training/

Seton Hall University

THE FACULTY

Core Faculty
Carolyn Goeckel, Program Chair; M.A., ATC.
Mary Murray, Director of Clinical Education; M.A., ATC.
Vicci Hill-Lombardi, Ed.D., ATC.

Support Faculty
Ben Brennan, Ph.D.
Deborah Deluca, J.D., CH-E.
Diana Glendinning, Ph.D.
John Mitchell, Ph.D.
H. James Phillips, Ph.D., PT, OCS, ATC, FAAOMPT.
Tom Sowa, Ph.D.
Doreen Stiskal, Chair, DPT Program; Ph.D., PT.

STATE UNIVERSITY OF NEW YORK COLLEGE AT CORTLAND

Program in Exercise Science and Sport Studies

Program of Study

The State University of New York (SUNY) College at Cortland's Department of Exercise Science and Sport Studies was formed when Cortland's physical education department was split into two departments in the late 1990s. The department currently assembles a diverse collection of disciplines that examine a wide range of topics involving exercise science, sport studies, athletic training, and fitness development. The M.S. in exercise science degree program provides students with an in-depth study of the scientific aspects of exercise and sport. This program prepares individuals for careers in exercise and sport research and in the fitness, wellness, and associated industries, as well as for further graduate study in the subdisciplines of exercise science and in the allied health professions.

The program requires completion of 30 credit hours. The 15 required credit hours of core courses include one course each in biomechanics, exercise physiology, and motor control; one course in research methods; and one course in statistics. Another 9 credit hours come from electives chosen from an approved list of courses, including behavior in sport, perceptual motor development, and nutritional aspects of athletic performance. The program culminates in a 6-credit-hour thesis as the final integrative experience for the degree. Students may enter the program at the beginning of any semester, and the program is expected to take two years to complete.

Research Facilities

The Sport Media & Technology Learning Center (SMTLC) provides sports-specific information technology training to students who are enrolled in sport management courses. The center includes three state-of-the-art student computer labs/classrooms, with a total of ninety-six seats, loaded with the latest hardware and software used in the sport industry, as well as a mobile lab and a video editing suite. The center includes training on XOS software, the world's largest provider of digital solutions for the sport industry. Dartfish, the world's leading producer of performance-enhancing sport video training applications, houses its Northeast Training Center in the SMTLC. Memorial Library houses a collection of more than 400,000 volumes, 1,200 journal subscriptions, an extensive microtext collection, and a strong collection of electronic resources, including videotapes, compact discs, and digital video recordings. The library has two networked computer labs, one for Macintosh and one for PC users, and there are Macintoshes and PCs in the Late Night Reading Room. In addition, there are sixteen public computing labs, including a lab that is open 24 hours a day, seven days a week.

Financial Aid

Diversity Fellowships of up to $10,000 are awarded to students who contribute to the diversity of the College. Graduate assistantships are presented to students for teaching labs or performing various other functions in academic or administrative departments. The award includes a partial tuition waiver of 6 credits per semester and a stipend. An Arethusa Scholarship of up to $1000 each year is awarded to a graduate student with demonstrated financial need and leadership and community involvement. Non-Traditional Student Scholarships are awarded to students who do not fit the traditional college student profile. Students may fund their education through loans, scholarships, and grants from private sources or through employment and tuition reimbursement through an employer.

Cost of Study

In 2006–07, tuition was $288 per academic credit hour for New York residents and $455 per credit for nonresidents. Other fees included a college fee of $0.85 per credit and a program services fee of $42.30 per credit.

Living and Housing Costs

Housing is not available on campus for graduate students. However, housing is available at rents ranging from $1900 to $2500 per month, depending on size and location. Some units have parking fees ranging from $50 to $75 per month.

Student Group

Students enrolling in the program are already working in the fields of exercise science and sports management or have undergraduate course experience in these and related fields and wish to continue their education.

Student Outcomes

Graduates of the program are prepared for careers in exercise and sport research and in the fitness, wellness, and associated industries or for further graduate study in the subdisciplines of biomechanics, exercise physiology, and motor control and in medicine, nursing, and physical therapy.

Location

The campus is located in Cortland, just blocks from the downtown area, with numerous opportunities for shopping, dining, entertainment, and socializing. Cortland County lies in the northern part of the Allegheny Plateau and is the eastern gateway to the Finger Lakes Region. Cortland is located about 40 minutes from Syracuse, and New York City is a 4- to 5-hour drive to the south.

The University

Since its beginnings in 1868, the State University of New York College at Cortland has been committed to excellence in teaching, scholarship, research, and service to the community. The College is committed to a comprehensive curriculum, building on traditional strengths in education and enhancing high-quality programs in the arts, humanities, and sciences. As one of thirteen colleges in the SUNY system, SUNY at Cortland has approximately 7,300 students enrolled in more than 100 degree programs. The College campus covers 191 acres and is located within walking distance of Cortland's business district.

Applying

Prospective students are required to submit an application for admission, official college transcripts showing an undergraduate GPA of 3.0 or higher, official combined GRE scores of 1000 or higher, two letters of recommendation, a personal statement of approximately 250 words describing the applicant's professional and education goals, and a $65 application fee. The deadline to apply is July 1 for fall admission and December 1 for spring admission.

Correspondence and Information

Dr. Peter McGinnis
Department of Exercise Science and Sport Studies
138 Studio West
State University of New York College at Cortland
P.O. Box 2000
Cortland, New York 13045
Phone: 607-753-4300
E-mail: pmcginnis@cortland.edu
Web site: http://www.cortland.edu/esss/

State University of New York College at Cortland

THE FACULTY

Jeff Bauer, Associate Professor.
Tim Bryant, Lecturer.
Phil Buckenmeyer, Assistant Professor.
Sonya Comins, Clinical Instructor and Athletic Trainer.
John Cottone, Associate Professor and Department Chair.
Alyson Dearie, Clinical Instructor and Athletic Trainer.
Patrick Donnelly, Clinical Instructor and Athletic Trainer.
Joy L. Hendrick, Professor; Ph.D., Indiana, 1988. Authentic assessment in physical education, interactive knowledge of results, statistics, information processing in older adults, cell phone use and its effect on reaction time, psychological refractory period, reaction time.
Jim Hokanson, Assistant Professor.
Wendy Hurley, Assistant Professor.
Yomee Lee, Assistant Professor.
Kristin Luther, Clinical Instructor and Athletic Trainer.
Peter McGinnis, Professor.
Steve Meyer, Clinical Instructor and Athletic Trainer.
Katherine Polasek, Assistant Professor.
Susan Rayl, Assistant Professor.
Brian Richardson, Lecturer.
Gerri Smith, Keyboard Specialist.

VIRGINIA COMMONWEALTH UNIVERSITY

Program in Athletic Training

Program of Study

Virginia Commonwealth University (VCU) offers the M.S. in athletic training (MSAT), an entry-level program for students interested in becoming certified as athletic trainers. Athletic training is recognized by the American Medical Association as an allied health profession. Certified athletic trainers (ATCs) are unique health-care providers who specialize in the prevention, assessment, treatment, and rehabilitation of injuries and illnesses that occur to athletes and the physically active. The course of study is a twenty-four-month program beginning during the summer semester, in July, in the first year. Students who successfully complete the program are required to pass an entry-level examination administered by the National Athletic Trainers' Association Board of Certification to be awarded the MSAT. Virginia requires state licensure by the Virginia Board of Medicine to practice as an athletic trainer.

The MSAT program applied for accreditation by the Commission on Accreditation of Athletic Training Education (CAATE) in September 2007 with an expected program evaluation in the spring semester of 2008. Application for CAATE accreditation does not guarantee accreditation, and if accreditation is not awarded to the MSAT program following their anticipated site visit, students enrolled in the program will not be eligible to register with the Board of Certification and take the certifying examination. Students will receive a M.S. in health and movement sciences if accreditation is not awarded.

Research Facilities

VCU libraries provide a combined capacity of more than 1.7 million volumes and 10,200 periodical titles and an online bibliographic search service accessing hundreds of databases. In addition, the Virginia State and Richmond Public libraries are within walking distance of both VCU campuses. Academic Computing provides a variety of microcomputer, minicomputer, and mainframe computing services to support the research and instructional endeavors of its faculty and students, including consultation, instruction, and computer acquisition.

The Sports Medicine Research Laboratory is a 1,500-square-foot facility dedicated to the training of researchers and faculty member research. The general focus of the laboratory is lower-extremity injury, with emphases on anatomical, biomechanical, and proprioceptive factors contributing to injury. Tools used in the laboratory include Motion Monitor motion-analysis systems, a Myopack sixteen-channel EMG system, three AMTI force plates, two nonconductive Bertec force plates, a Biodex isokinetic dynamometer, a Primus isotonic dynamometer, a TELOS stress device, a Fluoroscan Encore Premiere mini C-arm fluoroscope, two Sensotec load cells, a PCB Piezotronics triaxial accelerometer, a Grass telefactor stimulator with constant current and stimulus isolation units, a Tektronix oscilloscope (4ch, 100 MHz, 1 GS/s), NI Developer Suite, and Datapack data collection software.

Financial Aid

Students may apply for need-based assistance through the University's Financial Aid Office. Current information on financial aid programs, policies, and procedures is available at http://www.vcu.edu/enroll/finaid.

Cost of Study

For full-time study (9–15 credits) in 2007–08, Virginia residents pay tuition and fees of $4452 per semester; nonresidents, $8876 per semester. For part-time study, Virginia residents pay tuition and fees of $465 per hour; nonresidents, $954 per hour. Some programs require additional fees. On the Medical College of Virginia (MCV) campus, tuition, fees, and other expenses vary in the medicine, pharmacy, nurse anesthesia, dentistry, and School of Allied Health programs.

Living and Housing Costs

Graduate student housing is available on both the MCV campus and the academic campus of Virginia Commonwealth University. Many graduate students live in off-campus housing, which is reasonably priced and readily available in a variety of styles and settings in nearby residential areas or within easy commuting distance. On- and off-campus housing information is available on the Web at http://www.housing.vcu.edu/.

Student Group

VCU enrolls 30,452 students, 7,611 of whom are graduate students. More than 200 clubs and organizations reflect the diverse social, recreational, educational, political, and religious interests of the student body.

Location

Richmond is Virginia's capital and a major East Coast financial and manufacturing center that offers students a wide range of cultural, educational, and recreational activities. Richmond is located in central Virginia at the intersection of Interstates 95 and 64, 2 hours south of Washington, D.C., and nestled between the Blue Ridge Mountains and the Atlantic coast. The Richmond region is easily accessible by plane, car, and train. With nearly 1 million residents, the historic city of Richmond combines big-city offerings with small-town hospitality. Applicants are encouraged to explore http://www.visit.richmond.com/ for more information on the city.

The University

VCU is a state-supported coeducational university with a graduate school, a major teaching hospital, and twelve academic and professional units that offer fifty-two undergraduate, twenty-two postbaccalaureate certificate, sixty-five master's, six post-master's certificate, and twenty-nine Ph.D. programs. VCU also offers M.D., D.D.S., D.P.T., and Pharm.D. programs as well as cooperative degree programs with other major Virginia colleges and universities. VCU has one of the largest evening colleges in the United States. The academic campus is located in Richmond's historic Fan District. The health sciences campus and hospital are located 2 miles east in the downtown business district. A University bus service provides free intercampus transportation for faculty members and students. With more than $211 million in annual research funding, Virginia Commonwealth University is classified as one of the nation's top research universities by the Carnegie Foundation for the Advancement of Teaching. More than 29,000 undergraduate, certificate, graduate, post-master's, professional, and doctoral students are enrolled in 162 academic programs, forty of which are unique in the commonwealth of Virginia. The faculty members represent the finest American and international graduate institutions and enhance the University's position among the important institutions of higher learning in the United States and the world via their work in the classroom, laboratory, studio, and clinic and in their scholarly publications.

Applying

Admission procedures and program requirements are detailed in the *Graduate Bulletin*. Application deadlines and materials, including the application and the *Graduate Bulletin*, are available online at the Graduate School Web site at http://www.graduate.vcu.edu.

Application to the athletic training program is a two step process. First, students must apply directly to the graduate school and complete all application materials requested by the graduate school. Then, supplemental application materials must be completed. Supplemental application forms for the athletic training program are available at: http://www.soe.vcu.edu/pdf/hhp/ATSupplementary%20Application.pdf. Applications should be sent to Athletic Training Program Director, P.O. Box 842020, Richmond, Virginia 23284-2020.

Items to be included in the supplemental application are proof of physical exam, proof of hepatitis B vaccination, and a content verification form and syllabus for each prerequisite course (valid syllabi must include daily or weekly schedules of course content). In addition, an interview with the athletic training major admissions committee may be required. If an interview is required, interviews will be scheduled through the Department of Health and Human Performance administrative office (804-828-1948). The selection of students for the athletic training major is competitive. The application deadline for admission is March 15, but priority is given to applications received by February 1. Review of applications begins February 1 and continues until the class is full.

Virginia Commonwealth University is an equal opportunity/affirmative action institution providing access to education and employment without regard to age, race, color, national origin, gender, religion, sexual orientation, veteran's status, political affiliation, or disability.

Correspondence and Information

Brent L. Arnold, Ph.D., ATC
Director, Graduate Studies
Department of Health and Human Performance
School of Education
1015 West Main Street
Virginia Commonwealth University
Richmond, Virginia 23284-2020
Phone: 804-828-1948
Fax: 804-828-1323
E-mail: barnold @vcu.edu
Web site: http://www.soe.vcu.edu/departments/hhp/MS_hlthMovSc_athletic.htm

Virginia Commonwealth University

THE FACULTY AND THEIR RESEARCH

Brent L. Arnold, Associate Professor; Ph.D., Virginia, 1994. Proprioceptive loss in functional ankle instability, ability to perceive force and its relationship to joint stability, impairments in balance and movement following lower extremity injury.

Alan D. Freedman, Instructor; M.Ed., Virginia, 1991. Educational standards in athletic training; clinical education in athletic training; hip-joint pathology, proprioception, and kinesthesia.

Scott E. Ross, Assistant Professor; Ph.D., North Carolina at Chapel Hill, 2003. Effects of functional ankle instability on postural stability, effects of functional ankle instability on time to stabilization measures following single-leg jump landings, improving postural stability with balance training exercises and stochastic resonance stimulation.

VIRGINIA COMMONWEALTH UNIVERSITY

Program in Health and Movement Sciences

Programs of Study	The Master of Science Program in Health and Movement Sciences (HEMS) at Virginia Commonwealth University (VCU) provides advanced course work for students interested in the application of health and movement science principles to exercise science, teaching, and sports medicine. This degree program has a central focus on the sciences and is flexible enough so that students, with the assistance of an adviser, can design a program that truly meets their professional goals. The HEMS program is also an excellent progression of study for those students who teach in the health and physical education field. This program does not provide opportunities for initial licensure in health and physical education. The program of study offers thesis and nonthesis options. Both require a minimum of 36 total graduate credit hours for completion of the degree program. After completing at least 12 but not more than 18 graduate credits with a minimum GPA of 3.0, all students must apply for advancement to candidacy. In the thesis option, students must complete 30 hours of prescribed course work and HEMS 798 Thesis for 6 credit hours. Students enrolling in this option are not required to complete a comprehensive examination. In the nonthesis option, students must complete 36 hours of prescribed course work and must pass a comprehensive examination, which is taken after completing 30 hours of course work.
Research Facilities	The 1,000-square-foot Health and Human Performance Laboratory houses the exercise physiology research and instructional laboratory capacities, with equipment related to both applied physiology and biochemistry applications. Equipment includes a Sensormedics VMax Spectra 29S metabolic cart with integrated Cardiosoft Electrocardiography module; ergometers, such as a Trackmaster JAS Fitness treadmill, Monark cycle ergometers, Monark anaerobic (Peak) cycle ergometers, Medgraphics V2.23 cycle ergometer, and a Monark arm ergometer; a Biopac Systems MP150 data acquisition system with noninvasive cardiac output and heart-rate modules; an Arcon-VerNova Functional testing system; a dual energy x-ray absorptiometry (DEXA) system; an EX Comp 500 bioelectric impedance analyzer; a Genesys 2 Spectrophotometer; a YSI 2300 STAT Plus glucose and lactate analyzer; a lactate scout; an IEC Centra CL3R Thermo Centrifuge; a Biorad gel electrophoresis system; and a Millipore Elix 3 water-purification system.
	The Sports Medicine Research Laboratory is a 1,500-square-foot facility dedicated to the training of researchers and faculty member research. The general focus of the laboratory is lower-extremity injury, with emphases on anatomical, biomechanical, and proprioceptive factors contributing to injury. Tools used in the laboratory include Motion Monitor motion-analysis systems, a Myopack sixteen-channel EMG system, three AMTI force plates, two nonconductive Bertec force plates, a Biodex Isokinetic dynamometer, a Primus Isotonic dynamometer, a TELOS stress device, a Fluoroscan Encore Premiere mini C-arm fluoroscope, two Sensotec load cells, a PCB Piezotronics triaxial accelerometer, a Grass Telefactor Stimulator with Constant Current and Stimulus Isolation Units, a Tektronix Oscilloscope (4ch, 100 MHz, 1 GS/s), NI Developer Suite, and Datapack data collection software.
	VCU libraries provide a combined capacity of more than 1.7 million volumes and 10,200 periodical titles and an online bibliographic search service accessing hundreds of databases. In addition, the Virginia State and Richmond Public Libraries are within walking distance of both VCU campuses. Academic Computing provides a variety of microcomputer, minicomputer, and mainframe computing services to support the research and instructional endeavors of the faculty and students, including consultation, instruction, and computer acquisition.
Financial Aid	Students may apply for need-based assistance with the University's Financial Aid Office. Current information on financial aid programs, policies, and procedures is available at http://www.vcu.edu/enroll/finaid.
Cost of Study	For full-time study (9–15 credits) in 2007–08, Virginia residents pay tuition and fees of $4452 per semester; nonresidents, $8876 per semester. For part-time study, Virginia residents pay tuition and fees of $465 per hour; nonresidents, $954 per hour. Some programs require additional fees. On the Medical College of Virginia (MCV) campus, tuition, fees, and other expenses vary in the medicine, pharmacy, nurse anesthesia, dentistry, and School of Allied Health programs.
Living and Housing Costs	Graduate student housing is available on both the MCV campus and the academic campus of Virginia Commonwealth University. Many graduate students live in off-campus housing, which is reasonably priced and readily available in a variety of styles and settings in nearby residential areas or within easy commuting distance. On- and off-campus housing information is available on the Web at http://www.housing.vcu.edu/.
Student Group	VCU enrolls 30,452 students, 7,611 of whom are graduate students. More than 200 clubs and organizations reflect the diverse social, recreational, educational, political, and religious interests of the student body.
Location	Richmond is Virginia's capital and a major East Coast financial and manufacturing center that offers students a wide range of cultural, educational, and recreational activities. Richmond is located in central Virginia at the intersection of Interstates 95 and 64, 2 hours south of Washington, D.C., and nestled between the Blue Ridge Mountains and the Atlantic coast. The Richmond region is easily accessible by plane, car, and train. With nearly 1 million residents, the historic city of Richmond combines big-city offerings with small-town hospitality. Applicants are encouraged to explore http://www.visit.richmond.com/ for more information on the city.
The University	VCU is a state-supported coeducational university with a graduate school, a major teaching hospital, and twelve academic and professional units that offer fifty-two undergraduate, twenty-two postbaccalaureate certificate, sixty-five master's, six post-master's certificate, and twenty-nine Ph.D. programs. VCU also offers M.D., D.D.S., D.P.T., and Pharm.D. programs as well as cooperative degree programs with other major Virginia colleges and universities. VCU has one of the largest evening colleges in the United States. The academic campus is located in Richmond's historic Fan District. The health sciences campus and hospital are located 2 miles east in the downtown business district. A University bus service provides free intercampus transportation for faculty members and students.
	With more than $211 million in annual research funding, Virginia Commonwealth University is classified as one of the nation's top research universities by the Carnegie Foundation for the Advancement of Teaching. More than 29,000 undergraduate, certificate, graduate, post-master's, professional, and doctoral students are enrolled in 162 academic programs, forty of which are unique in the commonwealth of Virginia. The faculty members represent the finest American and international graduate institutions and enhance the University's position among the important institutions of higher learning in the United States and the world via their work in the classroom, laboratory, studio, and clinic and in their scholarly publications.
Applying	Admission procedures and program requirements are detailed in the *Graduate Bulletin*. Application deadlines and materials, including the application and the *Graduate Bulletin*, are available online at the Graduate School Web site at http://www.graduate.vcu.edu. Virginia Commonwealth University is an equal opportunity/affirmative action institution providing access to education and employment without regard to age, race, color, national origin, gender, religion, sexual orientation, veteran's status, political affiliation, or disability.
Correspondence and Information	Edmund O. Acevedo, Chair Department of Health and Human Performance School of Education Virginia Commonwealth University 1015 West Main Street Richmond, Virginia 23284-2020 Phone: 804-828-1948 Fax: 804-828-1323 E-mail: eoacevedo@vcu.edu Web site: http://www.soe.vcu.edu/departments/hhp

Virginia Commonwealth University

THE FACULTY AND THEIR RESEARCH

Edmund Acevedo, Professor and Chair; Ph.D., North Carolina at Greensboro. Impact of stress and fitness level on an individual's health.

Brent Arnold, Associate Professor; Ph.D., Virginia. Proprioceptive loss in functional ankle instability, ability to perceive force and its relationship to joint stability, impairments in balance and movement following lower-extremity injury.

Ted Conway, Professor and Associate Dean, Research Services; Ph.D. Optimization of an accurate elastic and time-dependent load-deformation relationship for biological tissues to develop a more robust human joint mechanics model; inclusion of underrepresented groups in science, technology, engineering, and math education.

Robert Davis, Professor; Ph.D., Maryland. Children's fitness.

Ronald Evans, Assistant Professor; Ph.D., Auburn. Skeletal and myocardial alterations associated with myocardial volume overload and chronic heart failure, lactate transport and metabolism, physical activity and obesity in children and adolescents, role of physical activity in successful weight loss following gastric bypass surgery.

Alan Freedman, Instructor; M.Ed., Virginia. Educational standards in athletic training; clinical education in athletic training; hip-joint pathology, proprioception, and kinesthesia.

Richard Gayle, Associate Professor; Ed.D., Tennessee. Measurement of habitual physical activity, relationship of habitual physical activity to risks for chronic degenerative diseases.

Deborah Getty, Assistant Professor; Ph.D., Berkeley. Gender issues in sport and physical activity, character development and healthy competition in sport, team-building and positive coaching in physical activity.

Joann Richardson, Associate Professor; Ph.D., Virginia Commonwealth. Women's health, minority health (i.e., African American), rural health, international health, secondary prevention of chronic disease (i.e., breast and prostate cancer, cardiovascular disease), accessibility for underserved populations.

Scott Ross, Assistant Professor; Ph.D., North Carolina at Chapel Hill. Effects of functional ankle instability on postural stability, effects of functional ankle instability on time to stabilization measures following single-leg jump landings, improving postural stability with balance training exercises and stochastic resonance.

Beverly Warren, Dean and Professor; Ed.D., Alabama; Ph.D., Auburn; FACSM. Impact of physical activity on weight loss and weight maintenance in weight-challenged populations, environmental influences on obesity treatment and prevention strategies for decreasing childhood obesity.

WEST VIRGINIA UNIVERSITY

Graduate Program in Exercise Physiology

Programs of Study

The Graduate Program in Exercise Physiology is one of seven graduate programs in West Virginia University (WVU) Schools of Medicine and Pharmacy offering interdisciplinary biomedical research training leading to the Ph.D., M.D./Ph.D., or M.S. degree. Exercise physiology provides a well-rounded and rigorous academic environment with a high degree of collaboration between clinical and basic researchers. Research areas include cardiovascular function in health and disease, circulatory adaptation to exercise training, microgravity, aging and diabetes, muscle adaptation and injury, genetic basis for and effect of strength training on muscle strength, and aging and vascular and bone adaptations to microgravity—experimentations with NASA and the space shuttle. The Division of Exercise Physiology is also actively engaged in patient care, including rehabilitation, disease prevention, and risk-factor management, with an emphasis on cardiovascular disease, obesity, and diabetes.

Students benefit from individual attention by faculty members within a research environment that is dynamic, collaborative, and interdisciplinary. In addition to course work and laboratory research, students participate in seminars, journal clubs, and research conferences. Graduate trainees also attend national scientific meetings and obtain valuable speaking and teaching experience. The Ph.D. typically takes five years to complete. During Year 1, students matriculate in a common integrated core curriculum. This integrated first year allows students to build competence in key areas of contemporary science, gain exposure to the various training program options, meet potential dissertation advisers, and network scientifically and socially. In the second semester, students customize their course work by selecting from an array of program-specific electives. At the end of Year 1, students select a research adviser and can select exercise physiology as their training program. Year 2 consists of advanced course work, research, teaching, and the candidacy examination. Years 3 to 5 are devoted to dissertation research. The M.S. degree is a one-year clinically based program. An alternate M.S. degree program with a thesis option, requiring one additional year of research training and participation in the integrated core curriculum, is available for students considering subsequent Ph.D. training. The Graduate Program in Exercise Physiology also participates in the combined M.D./Ph.D. Scholars Program. M.D./Ph.D. Scholars take the first two years of the medical curriculum, followed typically by three years of research as required for the Ph.D. degree before returning to the M.D. program.

Research Facilities

Institutional facilities include a computer-based learning center, a centralized animal facility with a transgenic barrier, and a library housing more than 205,000 volumes and 2,400 journals. Core facilities are available for examining gene expression or genetic variation (Affymetrix platform), image analysis, confocal and electron microscopy and laser capture microdissection, live-cell imaging, mass spectrometry, flow cytometry with high-speed cell sorting, proteomics, recombinant DNA technology, transgenic rodent biology, and functional neuroimaging (fMRI, PET/CT). Affiliated research centers include the National Institute for Occupational Safety and Health (NIOSH), Center for Advanced Imaging, Blanchette Rockefeller Neurosciences Institute, Sensory Neuroscience Research Center, and Mary Babb Randolph Cancer Center.

Financial Aid

All Ph.D. and M.D./Ph.D. students in the biomedical sciences receive financial support during their training, provided they remain in good academic standing and excel in research. Such support includes full tuition, health insurance, and an annual stipend of $23,000. Combined M.D./Ph.D. students also receive medical tuition waivers. M.S. students are not eligible for institutional tuition waivers or stipends, but may be supported on a grant if funds are available.

Cost of Study

Students' tuition costs are covered.

Living and Housing Costs

The cost of an efficiency apartment in University-owned housing is approximately $400 per month. A limited number of University apartments are available for married students. Privately owned apartments in Morgantown cost $400 to $600 per month. In general, the cost of living is lower than other, larger cities.

Student Group

Total University enrollment is approximately 26,000 students, which includes 6,500 graduate and professional students. Graduate students come from all parts of the United States and many other countries.

Location

Morgantown is a vibrant university community of 80,000 residents in northern West Virginia. Located near the Pennsylvania border at the western edge of the Appalachian Mountains, abundant opportunities exist for activities such as world-class white-water rafting and kayaking, hiking and camping, mountain biking, fishing, and skiing. Morgantown has a cosmopolitan atmosphere with a range of activities usually found in much larger cities. It also enjoys proximity to major metropolitan centers: Pittsburgh is a 90-minute drive north, and Washington, D.C., is a 3-hour drive east.

The University

West Virginia University is a comprehensive, land-grant, Carnegie-designated Doctoral/Research University–Extensive public institution. The University's academic Health Sciences Center includes the Schools of Medicine, Dentistry, Nursing, and Pharmacy, all of which offer graduate degree programs. There are seven Ph.D. biomedical research training programs in the Schools of Medicine and Pharmacy that benefit from the Schools' common, undifferentiated first year: Biochemistry and Molecular Biology; Cancer Cell Biology, Cellular and Integrative Physiology; Exercise Physiology; Immunology and Microbial Pathogenesis; Neuroscience; and Pharmaceutical and Pharmacological Sciences. Graduate faculty members in these programs come from various basic science and clinical departments throughout WVU and are members of interdisciplinary research centers in six health-related areas: cancer cell biology, cardiovascular sciences, diabetes and obesity, immunopathology, neuroscience, and respiratory biology and lung diseases.

WVU participates in NCAA Division I sports as a member of the Big East Conference and also offers a wide variety of creative arts, theater, and entertainment opportunities.

Applying

Applicants must have a bachelor's degree and an excellent GPA and GRE scores. Three letters of recommendation and a personal statement are required. Prospective students are invited in groups of 10 for a paid two-day visit/interview in January through March. Students can find more information and an online application at http://www.hsc.wvu.edu/som/resoff/gradprograms/PhD.asp.

Correspondence and Information

Michael Delp, Ph.D., Graduate Director
Graduate Program in Exercise Physiology
West Virginia University
P.O. Box 9277
Morgantown, West Virginia 26506
Phone: 304-293-7767
E-mail: mdelp@hsc.wvu.edu
Web site: http://www.hsc.wvu.edu/som/resoff/gradprograms/
PhD.asp

Office of Research and Graduate Education
Health Sciences Center
West Virginia University
P.O. Box 9104
Morgantown, West Virginia 26506
Phone: 304-293-7116
E-mail: cnoel@hsc.wvu.edu

West Virginia University

THE FACULTY AND THEIR RESEARCH

Stephen Alway, Associate Professor; Ph.D., McMaster. Aging and sarcopenia in skeletal muscle, cellular and molecular adaptations of skeletal muscle to overload and disuse.

Matthew Boegehold, Professor; Ph.D., Arizona. Physiology and pathophysiology of the microcirculation, local and neural mechanisms of blood flow control, endothelium-dependent regulation of microvascular tone, microvascular alterations in hypertension.

Randall Bryner, Associate Professor; Ed.D., West Virginia. Role of uncoupling protein-3 in aging and exercise, effects of exercise on prostate cancer development, metabolic changes with weight loss, ergogenic aids and exercise.

Robert G. Cutlip, Adjunct Associate Professor (NIOSH); Ph.D., West Virginia. Biomechanical, biochemical, and molecular investigation of acute and chronic skeletal muscle injury.

Michael Delp, Professor; Ph.D., Georgia. Circulatory remodeling with microgravity, exercise training on endothelial function, arterial remodeling with microgravity, vascular biology and aging.

Jeffrey Frisbee, Assistant Professor; Ph.D., Guelph. Microvascular reactivity, microvessel density, microvascular dysfunction with the metabolic syndrome, regulation of tissue and organ perfusion.

Paul Gordon, Associate Professor; Ph.D., M.P.H., Pittsburgh. Physical activity and public health, physical activity epidemiology, genetic influences on individual responses to exercise.

Laurie Gutmann, Associate Professor; M.D., West Virginia. Neuromuscular physiology and pathophysiology of skeletal muscle, neuromuscular diseases, myopathic investigations and treatment of amyotrophic lateral sclerosis (ALS) and muscular dystrophy.

John Hollander, Assistant Professor; Ph.D., Wisconsin. Heat-shock proteins, transgenic models, ischemia reperfusion injury in the heart.

Judy Muller-Delp, Associate Professor; Ph.D., Missouri. Effects of aging on vascular reactivity of resistance arterioles in cardiac and skeletal muscles, gender specificity, role of sex hormones and exercise in cardiovascular aging.

Ming Pei, Assistant Professor; Ph.D., Peking (China). Musculoskeletal tissue engineering, cartilage, nanobiomaterials, cell-biomaterial interface, mechanical stimulation and tissue regeneration, drug delivery and gene therapy.

Section 43
Sports Management

This section contains a directory of institutions offering graduate work in sports management, followed by in-depth entries submitted by institutions that chose to prepare detailed program descriptions. Additional information about programs listed in the directory but not augmented by an in-depth entry may be obtained by writing directly to the dean of a graduate school or chair of a department at the address given in the directory.

For programs offering related work, see also in this book Business Administration and Management, Education, and Physical Education and Kinesiology.

CONTENTS

Program Directory

Sports Management

American Public University System, AMU/APU Graduate Programs, Charles Town, WV 25414. Offers business administration (MBA); criminal justice (MA); emergency and disaster management (MA); environmental policy and management (MS); history (MA); homeland security (MA); humanities (MA); intelligence (MA Strategic Intelligence); international relations and conflict resolution (MA); management (MA); military history (MA); national security studies (MA); political science (MA); public administration (MA); public health (MA); security management (MA); space studies (MS); sports management (MA); transportation and logistics management (MA). Programs offered via distance learning only. Part-time and evening/weekend programs available. Postbaccalaureate distance learning degree programs offered (no on-campus study). *Faculty:* 10 full-time (3 women), 188 part-time/adjunct (57 women). *Students:* 498 full-time (104 women), 5,272 part-time (1,209 women). Average age 34. 6,574 applicants, 100% accepted, 3508 enrolled. In 2006, 358 degrees awarded. *Degree requirements:* For master's, comprehensive exam, registration. *Entrance requirements:* For master's, bachelor's degree or equivalent, minimum GPA of 2.7 in last 60 hours of course work. *Application deadline:* For fall admission, 9/1 priority date for domestic students; for winter admission, 1/1 priority date for domestic students; for spring admission, 5/1 priority date for domestic students. Applications are processed on a rolling basis. Application fee: $0. Electronic applications accepted. *Expenses:* Tuition: Full-time $4,950; part-time $275 per credit. One-time fee: $200 full-time. *Financial support:* Applicants required to submit FAFSA. *Faculty research:* Military history, criminal justice, management performance, national security. *Unit head:* Dr. Frank McCluskey, Provost, 877-468-6268, Fax: 304-724-3780. *Application contact:* Terry Grant, Director of Enrollment Management, 877-468-6268, Fax: 304-724-3780, E-mail: info@apus.edu.

Ashland University, College of Education, Graduate Studies in Education, Department of Sport Sciences, Ashland, OH 44805-3702. Offers adapted physical education (M Ed); applied exercise science (M Ed); sport education (M Ed); sport management (M Ed). Part-time programs available. *Faculty:* 6 full-time (1 woman), 1 (woman) part-time/adjunct. *Students:* 26 full-time (12 women), 28 part-time (11 women); includes 4 minority (all African Americans) Average age 31. In 2006, 29 degrees awarded. *Degree requirements:* For master's, thesis or alternative, practicum, seminar. *Entrance requirements:* For master's, GRE General Test or MAT, minimum GPA of 2.75. Additional exam requirements/recommendations for international students: Required—TOEFL. *Application deadline:* For fall admission, 8/27 for domestic students; for spring admission, 1/14 for domestic students. Applications are processed on a rolling basis. Application fee: $30. *Expenses:* Tuition: Part-time $403 per credit. Tuition and fees vary according to degree level and program. *Financial support:* In 2006–07, 16 students received support, including teaching assistantships with full tuition reimbursements available (averaging $6,000 per year); institutionally sponsored loans and scholarships/grants also available. Financial award application deadline: 4/15. *Faculty research:* Coaching, legal issues, strength and conditioning, sport management rating of perceived exertion. *Unit head:* Dr. Glen Fincher, Chair, 419-289-5450, E-mail: gfincher@ashland.edu.

Barry University, School of Human Performance and Leisure Sciences, Program in Sport Management, Miami Shores, FL 33161-6695. Offers MS. Part-time and evening/weekend programs available. *Students:* 25 full-time (11 women), 17 part-time (7 women); includes 13 minority (7 African Americans, 6 Hispanic Americans), 10 international. 45 applicants, 53% accepted, 17 enrolled. In 2006, 18 degrees awarded. *Degree requirements:* For master's, project or thesis. *Entrance requirements:* For master's, GMAT or GRE General Test, minimum GPA of 3.0. *Application deadline:* Applications are processed on a rolling basis. Application fee: $30. Electronic applications accepted. *Financial support:* In 2006–07, 10 teaching assistantships with full and partial tuition reimbursements were awarded. *Faculty research:* Economic impact of professional sports, sport marketing. *Unit head:* Dr. Annie Clement, Coordinator, 305-899-3493, Fax: 305-899-3556, E-mail: aclement@mail.barry.edu. *Application contact:* Dave Fletcher, Director of Graduate Admissions, 305-899-3113, Fax: 305-899-2971, E-mail: dfletcher@mail.barry.edu.

See Close-Up on page 2349.

Barry University, School of Human Performance and Leisure Sciences and Andreas School of Business, Program in Sport Management and Business Administration, Miami Shores, FL 33161-6695. Offers MS/MBA. Part-time and evening/weekend programs available. *Students:* 10 full-time (4 women), 1 part-time; includes 2 minority (1 African American, 1 Hispanic American), 1 international. 19 applicants, 58% accepted, 6 enrolled. *Application deadline:* Applications are processed on a rolling basis. Application fee: $30. Electronic applications accepted. *Financial support:* Teaching assistantships with full tuition reimbursements, career-related internships or fieldwork available. Support available to part-time students. Financial award application deadline: 5/1; financial award applicants required to submit FAFSA. *Faculty research:* Economic impact of professional sports, sport marketing. *Unit head:* Dr. Annie Clement, Coordinator, 305-899-3493, Fax: 305-899-3556, E-mail: aclement@mail.barry.edu. *Application contact:* Dave Fletcher, Director of Graduate Admissions, 305-899-3113, Fax: 305-899-2971, E-mail: dfletcher@mail.barry.edu.

See Close-Up on page 2349.

Belmont University, College of Arts and Sciences, School of Education, Nashville, TN 37212-3757. Offers education (MAT); elementary education (M Ed), including early childhood education, elementary education, gifted education, language arts education; English (M Ed); history (M Ed); mathematics (M Ed); middle grade education (M Ed); science (M Ed); secondary education (M Ed), including gifted education; sports administration (MSA); technology (M Ed). *Accreditation:* NCATE. Part-time and evening/weekend programs available. *Faculty:* 9 full-time (7 women), 20 part-time/adjunct (15 women). *Students:* 50 full-time (36 women), 116 part-time (76 women); includes 23 minority (20 African Americans, 1 Asian American or Pacific Islander, 2 Hispanic Americans), 1 international. Average age 30. 55 applicants, 60% accepted, 30 enrolled. In 2006, 82 degrees awarded. *Degree requirements:* For master's, thesis, comprehensive exam. *Entrance requirements:* For master's, MAT or GRE, minimum GPA of 2.75. Additional exam requirements/recommendations for international students: Required—TOEFL. *Application deadline:* For fall admission, 8/1 priority date for domestic students, 5/1 for international students; for spring admission, 12/1 priority date for domestic students, 9/1 for international students. Applications are processed on a rolling basis. Application fee: $50. *Expenses: Contact institution. Financial support:* In 2006–07, 25 students received support; fellowships with partial tuition reimbursements available, institutionally sponsored loans and tuition waivers (partial) available. Financial award application deadline: 4/15; financial award applicants required to submit FAFSA. *Faculty research:* Technology grant, professional development schools. Total annual research expenditures: $6,500. *Unit head:* Dr. Trevor F. Hutchins, Associate Dean, 615-460-6232, Fax: 615-460-6414, E-mail: hutchinst@mail.belmont.edu. *Application contact:* Julie Hullett, Admission/Licensure Officer, 615-460-6879, Fax: 615-460-5556, E-mail: hullettj@email.belmont.edu.

Boise State University, Graduate College, College of Education, Department of Kinesiology, Program in Physical Education, Boise, ID 83725-0399. Offers athletic administration (MPE). Part-time programs available. *Students:* 4 full-time (1 woman), 10 part-time (2 women); includes 1 minority (Hispanic American), 1 international. Average age 32. 8 applicants, 100% accepted, 4 enrolled. *Degree requirements:* For master's, thesis. *Entrance requirements:* For master's, minimum GPA of 3.0. *Application deadline:* For fall admission, 3/1 priority date for domestic students; for spring admission, 10/1 priority date for domestic students. Applications are processed on a rolling basis. Application fee: $0. Electronic applications accepted. *Financial support:* Career-related internships or fieldwork, Federal Work-Study, institutionally sponsored loans, and unspecified assistantships available. Support available to part-time students. Financial award application deadline: 3/1. *Unit head:* Dr. Linda Petlichkoff, Director, 208-426-1231, Fax: 208-426-1894.

Bowling Green State University, Graduate College, College of Education and Human Development, School of Human Movement, Sport, and Leisure Studies, Bowling Green, OH 43403. Offers developmental kinesiology (M Ed); recreation and leisure (M Ed); sport administration (M Ed). Part-time programs available. *Faculty:* 26 full-time (13 women), 4 part-time/adjunct (2 women). *Students:* 36 full-time (22 women), 14 part-time (6 women); includes 6 minority (all African Americans), 5 international. Average age 27. 54 applicants, 50% accepted, 20 enrolled. In 2006, 33 degrees awarded. *Degree requirements:* For master's, thesis or alternative. *Entrance requirements:* For master's, GRE General Test, minimum GPA of 2.7. Additional exam requirements/recommendations for international students: Required—TOEFL. *Application deadline:* For fall admission, 1/15 priority date for domestic students. Applications are processed on a rolling basis. Application fee: $30. Electronic applications accepted. *Expenses:* Tuition, state resident: part-time $535 per hour. Tuition, nonresident: part-time $884 per hour. *Financial support:* In 2006–07, 13 research assistantships with full tuition reimbursements (averaging $7,926 per year), 18 teaching assistantships with full tuition reimbursements (averaging $6,263 per year) were awarded; career-related internships or fieldwork, Federal Work-Study, and unspecified assistantships also available. Financial award applicants required to submit FAFSA. *Faculty research:* Teacher-learning process, travel and tourism, sport marketing and management, exercise physiology and sport psychology, life-span motor development. *Unit head:* Dr. Lynn Darby, Acting Director, 419-372-2334. *Application contact:* Dr. Geoff Meek, Graduate Coordinator, 419-372-0501.

Brooklyn College of the City University of New York, Division of Graduate Studies, Department of Physical Education and Exercise Science, Brooklyn, NY 11210-2889. Offers exercise science and rehabilitation (MS), including psychosocial aspects of physical activity, sports management; physical education (MS, MS Ed). Part-time programs available. *Students:* 1 (woman) full-time, 52 part-time (16 women); includes 15 minority (10 African Americans, 5 Hispanic Americans), 16 international. 37 applicants, 84% accepted, 13 enrolled. In 2006, 21 degrees awarded. *Degree requirements:* For master's, comprehensive exam or thesis. *Entrance requirements:* For master's, previous course work in physical education and education, minimum GPA of 3.0, 2 letters of recommendation, essay. Additional exam requirements/recommendations for international students: Required—TOEFL. *Application deadline:* For fall admission, 3/1 priority date for domestic students, 2/1 priority date for international students; for spring admission, 11/1 priority date for domestic students, 10/1 priority date for international students. Applications are processed on a rolling basis. Application fee: $125. Electronic applications accepted. *Expenses:* Tuition, state resident: full-time $6,400; part-time $270 per credit. Tuition, nonresident: full-time $12,000; part-time $500 per credit. Required fees: $118 per semester. *Financial support:* Career-related internships or fieldwork, Federal Work-Study, institutionally sponsored loans, and scholarships/grants available. Support available to part-time students. Financial award application deadline: 5/1; financial award applicants required to submit FAFSA. *Faculty research:* Exercise physiology, motor learning, sports psychology, women in athletics. Total annual research expenditures: $9,231. *Unit head:* Dr. Charles Tobey, Chairperson, 718-951-5514, E-mail: ctobey@brooklyn.cuny.edu. *Application contact:* Karen Alleyne-Pierre, Director of Admissions Services and Enrollment Communications, 718-951-5902, Fax: 718-951-4506, E-mail: grads@brooklyn.cuny.edu.

California University of Pennsylvania, School of Graduate Studies and Research, School of Education, Department of Athletic Training, Program in Exercise Science and Health Promotion, California, PA 15419-1394. Offers fitness and wellness (MS); performance enhancement and injury prevention (MS); rehabilitation sciences (MS); sport management (MS); sport psychology (MS). Part-time and evening/weekend programs available. Postbaccalaureate distance learning degree programs offered (no on-campus study). *Faculty:* 34 full-time (15 women), 7 part-time/adjunct (0 women). *Students:* 382 full-time (167 women), 44 part-time (15 women); includes 68 minority (35 African Americans, 2 American Indian/Alaska Native, 17 Asian Americans or Pacific Islanders, 14 Hispanic Americans). Average age 31. In 2006, 176 degrees awarded. *Median time to degree:* Master's–1.5 years full-time, 2.25 years part-time. *Degree requirements:* For master's, thesis optional. *Entrance requirements:* For master's, minimum QPA of 3.0. Additional exam requirements/recommendations for international students: Required—TOEFL (minimum score 550 paper-based; 213 computer-based; 80 iBT). *Application deadline:* For fall admission, 8/1 priority date for domestic and international students; for winter admission, 12/1 priority date for domestic and international students; for spring admission, 5/1 priority date for domestic and international students. Applications are processed on a rolling basis. Application fee: $25. Electronic applications accepted. *Expenses: Contact institution. Financial support:* Career-related internships or fieldwork, scholarships/grants, and unspecified assistantships available. Financial award applicants required to submit FAFSA. *Faculty research:* Reducing obesity in children, sport performance, creating unique biomechanical assessment techniques, Web-based training for fitness professionals, Webcams. Total annual research expenditures: $25,000. *Unit head:* Prof. Barry McGlumphy, Graduate Coordinator, 724-938-1694, Fax: 724-938-4342, E-mail: mcglumphy@cup.edu.

Canisius College, Graduate Division, School of Education and Human Services, Department of Sport Administration, Buffalo, NY 14208-1098. Offers MS. *Faculty:* 3 part-time/adjunct (1 woman). *Students:* 43 full-time (17 women), 23 part-time (6 women); includes 8 minority (6 African Americans, 1 Asian American or Pacific Islander, 1 Hispanic American), 6 international. Average age 26. In 2006, 40 degrees awarded. *Degree requirements:* For master's, research project. *Entrance requirements:* For master's, GRE General Test. *Application deadline:* Applications are processed on a rolling basis. Application fee: $25. *Expenses:* Tuition: Part-time $645 per credit hour. Required fees: $19 per credit hour. Tuition and fees vary according to program. *Financial support:* Research assistantships with full tuition reimbursements, career-related internships or fieldwork, institutionally sponsored loans, scholarships/grants, health care benefits, tuition waivers (full and partial), and unspecified assistantships available. *Faculty research:* Organizational effectiveness, economic impact, sponsorship and marketing, ethics, leadership. *Unit head:* Staci C. Carney Studesville, Director, 716-888-3165, Fax: 716-888-3174, E-mail: studesvs@canisius.edu. *Application contact:* James D. Bagwell, Director of Graduate Recruitment and Admissions, 716-888-2544, Fax: 716-888-3290, E-mail: bagwellj@canisius.edu.

Central Michigan University, Central Michigan University Off-Campus Programs, Program in Sport Administration, Mount Pleasant, MI 48859. Offers MA. *Unit head:* Dr. Scott J. Smith, Head, 989-774-2859, E-mail: scott.j.smith@cmich.edu. *Application contact:* 877-268-4636, E-mail: cmuoffcampus@cmich.edu.

Central Michigan University, College of Graduate Studies, The Herbert H. and Grace A. Dow College of Health Professions, Department of Physical Education and Sport, Mount Pleasant, MI 48859. Offers athletic administration (MA); coaching (MA); exercise science (MA); sport administration (MA); teaching (MA). *Degree requirements:* For master's, thesis or alternative, registration. *Faculty research:* Biomechanical analysis of sports skills, sociological studies, psychological studies.

Central Michigan University, College of Graduate Studies, Program in Administration, Mount Pleasant, MI 48859. Offers general administration (MSA); health services administration (MSA); hospitality and tourism administration (MSA); human resource administration (MSA); information resource administration (MSA); international administration (MSA); leadership (MSA); organizational communications (MSA); public administration (MSA); recreation and park administration (MSA); software engineering (MSA); sports administration (MSA). *Accreditation:* AACSB. *Degree requirements:* For master's, thesis or alternative. *Entrance requirements:* For master's, minimum undergraduate GPA of 2.5.

See Close-Up on page 253.

Cleveland State University, College of Graduate Studies, College of Education and Human Services, Department of Health, Physical Education, Recreation and Dance, Cleveland, OH

44115. Offers community health education (M Ed); exercise science (M Ed); human performance (M Ed); physical education pedagogy (M Ed); school health education (M Ed); sport and exercise psychology (M Ed); sports management (M Ed). Part-time programs available. *Faculty:* 9 full-time (5 women), 3 part-time/adjunct (0 women). *Students:* 12 full-time (7 women), 62 part-time (32 women); includes 16 minority (15 African Americans, 1 Asian American or Pacific Islander), 4 international. Average age 30. 52 applicants, 52% accepted, 19 enrolled. In 2006, 36 degrees awarded. *Degree requirements:* For master's, thesis optional. *Entrance requirements:* For master's, GRE General Test or MAT (if undergraduate GPA is below 2.75), minimum undergraduate GPA of 2.75. Additional exam requirements/recommendations for international students: Required—TOEFL (minimum score 525 paper-based; 197 computer-based), IELTS (minimum score 6). *Application deadline:* For fall admission, 7/15 priority date for domestic students; for spring admission, 12/15 priority date for domestic students. Applications are processed on a rolling basis. Application fee: $30. Electronic applications accepted. *Financial support:* In 2006–07, 6 research assistantships with full and partial tuition reimbursements (averaging $3,480 per year), 1 teaching assistantship with full and partial tuition reimbursement (averaging $3,480 per year) were awarded; career-related internships or fieldwork, tuition waivers (full), and unspecified assistantships also available. Financial award application deadline: 3/15. *Faculty research:* Childhood obesity, bone density, marketing fitness centers, motor development of disabled, mental skills training. Total annual research expenditures: $102,615. *Unit head:* Dr. Sheila M. Patterson, Chairperson, 216-687-4870, Fax: 216-687-5410, E-mail: s.m.patterson@csuohio.edu.

Concordia University, School of Arts and Sciences, Irvine, CA 92612-3299. Offers coaching and athletic administration (MA). *Faculty:* 3 full-time, 4 part-time/adjunct. *Students:* 51 full-time (13 women); includes 7 minority (1 African American, 1 Asian American or Pacific Islander, 5 Hispanic Americans), 1 international. *Degree requirements:* For master's, exam or thesis. *Entrance requirements:* Additional exam requirements/recommendations for international students: Required—TOEFL. *Application deadline:* Applications are processed on a rolling basis. Application fee: $50 ($300 for international students). *Unit head:* Dr. Kenneth Mangels, Dean, 949-854-8002 Ext. 1350, Fax: 949-854-6854, E-mail: kenneth.mangels@cui.edu. *Application contact:* Roberto Marquez, Coordinator of Graduate Enrollment, 949-854-8002 Ext. 1133, Fax: 949-854-6854, E-mail: roberto.marquez@cui.edu.

Concordia University, School of Graduate Studies, John Molson School of Business, Montréal, QC H3G 1M8, Canada. Offers administration (M Sc, Diploma); aviation management (Certificate, Diploma); business administration (MBA, UA Undergraduate Associate, PhD), including international aviation (UA Undergraduate Associate); chartered accountancy (Diploma); community organizational development (Certificate); event management and fundraising (Certificate); executive business administration (EMBA); investment management (Diploma); investment management option (MBA); management accounting (Certificate); management of healthcare organizations (Certificate); sport administration (Diploma). *Accreditation:* AACSB. Part-time and evening/weekend programs available. *Students:* 447 full-time (174 women), 448 part-time (206 women). 925 applicants, 59% accepted, 319 enrolled. In 2006, 183 master's, 6 doctorates, 62 other advanced degrees awarded. *Degree requirements:* For master's, one foreign language, thesis (for some programs), research project; for doctorate, one foreign language, thesis/dissertation; for other advanced degree, one foreign language. *Entrance requirements:* For master's and doctorate, GMAT. Additional exam requirements/recommendations for international students: Required—TOEFL. Application fee: $50. *Expenses: Contact institution.* *Financial support:* Fellowships, career-related internships or fieldwork available. *Faculty research:* General business, capital markets, international business. *Unit head:* Dr. Jerry Tomberlin, Dean, 514-848-2424 Ext. 2700, Fax: 514-848-4502. *Application contact:* Dr. Michel Magnan, Associate Dean, Graduate Programs, 514-848-2424 Ext. 4145, Fax: 514-848-4208.

Eastern Kentucky University, The Graduate School, College of Health Sciences, Department of Exercise and Sport Science, Richmond, KY 40475-3102. Offers physical education (MS); sports administration (MS). Part-time programs available. *Faculty:* 3 full-time (1 woman), 1 part-time/adjunct (0 women). *Students:* 27 full-time (11 women), 25 part-time (11 women); includes 9 minority (all African Americans), 1 international. Average age 27. 38 applicants, 76% accepted, 18 enrolled. In 2006, 18 degrees awarded. *Entrance requirements:* For master's, GRE General Test, minimum GPA of 2.5. *Application deadline:* For fall admission, 8/15 for domestic students. Application fee: $30. *Expenses:* Tuition, state resident: full-time $5,610. Tuition, nonresident: full-time $15,910. *Financial support:* Research assistantships, teaching assistantships, Federal Work-Study available. Support available to part-time students. *Faculty research:* Nutrition and exercise. *Unit head:* Dr. Lonnie Davis, Chair, 859-622-1887, Fax: 859-622-1254, E-mail: lonnie.davis@eku.edu.

Eastern Michigan University, Graduate School, College of Health and Human Services, School of Health Promotion and Human Performance, Program in Sports Management, Ypsilanti, MI 48197. Offers MS. Part-time and evening/weekend programs available. Postbaccalaureate distance learning degree programs offered (minimal on-campus study). *Students:* Average age 28. In 2006, 6 degrees awarded. *Entrance requirements:* Additional exam requirements/recommendations for international students: Required—TOEFL. *Application deadline:* For fall admission, 5/15 priority date for domestic students, 5/1 priority date for international students; for winter admission, 10/15 priority date for domestic students, 10/1 priority date for international students; for spring admission, 3/15 priority date for domestic students, 3/1 priority date for international students. Applications are processed on a rolling basis. Application fee: $35. *Expenses:* Tuition, state resident: part-time $341 per credit hour. Tuition, nonresident: full-time $16,104; part-time $671 per credit hour. Required fees: $816; $34 per credit hour. $40 per term. One-time fee: $82 full-time. Tuition and fees vary according to course level, course load, degree level and reciprocity agreements. *Financial support:* Fellowships, research assistantships with full tuition reimbursements, teaching assistantships with full tuition reimbursements, career-related internships or fieldwork, Federal Work-Study, institutionally sponsored loans, scholarships/grants, tuition waivers (partial), and unspecified assistantships available. Support available to part-time students. Financial award applicants required to submit FAFSA.

East Stroudsburg University of Pennsylvania, Graduate School, School of Health Sciences and Human Performance, Department of Sports Studies, East Stroudsburg, PA 18301-2999. Offers management and leadership (MS); sports management (MS). *Faculty:* 4 full-time (1 woman). *Students:* 23 full-time (12 women), 20 part-time (4 women); includes 5 minority (4 African Americans, 1 Hispanic American). Average age 27. *Entrance requirements:* Additional exam requirements/recommendations for international students: Required—TOEFL (minimum score 560 paper-based; 220 computer-based; 83 iBT). *Application deadline:* For fall admission, 7/31 priority date for domestic students, 5/1 priority date for international students; for spring admission, 11/30 for domestic students, 10/1 for international students. Application fee: $50. *Expenses:* Tuition, state resident: full-time $6,048; part-time $336 per credit. Tuition, nonresident: full-time $9,678; part-time $538 per credit. Required fees: $1,353; $67 per credit. One-time fee: $37 part-time. *Financial support:* In 2006–07, 15 research assistantships were awarded; Federal Work-Study and unspecified assistantships also available. Financial award application deadline: 3/1; financial award applicants required to submit FAFSA. *Unit head:* Dr. Robert Fleischman, Graduate Coordinator, 570-422-3316.

East Tennessee State University, School of Graduate Studies, College of Education, Department of Physical Education, Exercise and Sport Sciences, Johnson City, TN 37614. Offers exercise physiology (MA); fitness leadership (MA); physical education (M Ed, MA); sports management (MA); sports sciences (MA). Part-time and evening/weekend programs available. *Degree requirements:* For master's, comprehensive exam (M Ed), oral and written comprehensive exams, thesis (MA). *Entrance requirements:* For master's, GRE General Test, major or minor in physical education or equivalent, interview, minimum GPA of 2.7. Additional exam requirements/recommendations for international students: Required—TOEFL (minimum score 550 paper-based; 213 computer-based). *Faculty research:* Resistance training for various populations, self actualization using challenging courses, park and recreation industry needs relative to recent university graduates, funding sport operations.

Endicott College, Van Loan School of Graduate and Professional Studies, Program in Sport Management, Beverly, MA 01915-2096. Offers M Ed. Part-time and evening/weekend programs available. *Faculty:* 8 part-time/adjunct (5 women). *Students:* Average age 30. *Degree requirements:* For master's, thesis, practicum. *Entrance requirements:* For master's, GRE or MAT, letters of recommendation. *Expenses:* Tuition: Part-time $279 per credit. Tuition and fees vary according to program. *Unit head:* Dr. Jayanti Bandyopadhyay, Associate Dean of Graduate School, 978-232-2744, Fax: 978-232-3000, E-mail: jbandyop@endicott.edu. *Application contact:* Dr. Jayanti Bandyopadhyay, Associate Dean of Graduate School, 978-232-2744, Fax: 978-232-3000, E-mail: jbandyop@endicott.edu.

Florida Atlantic University, College of Business, Department of Management, International Business and Entrepreneurship, Boca Raton, FL 33431-0991. Offers business administration (Exec MBA, MBA), including accounting (MBA), electronic commerce (MBA), finance (MBA), financial planning (MBA), global entrepreneurship (MBA), health administration (MBA), international business (MBA), marketing (MBA), operations management (MBA), real estate (MBA), sport management (MBA). *Faculty:* 64 full-time (17 women), 15 part-time/adjunct (3 women). *Students:* 215 full-time (89 women), 365 part-time (189 women); includes 150 minority (49 African Americans, 2 American Indian/Alaska Native, 36 Asian Americans or Pacific Islanders, 63 Hispanic Americans), 54 international. Average age 32. 414 applicants, 55% accepted, 167 enrolled. In 2006, 196 master's awarded. *Degree requirements:* For master's, thesis optional. *Entrance requirements:* For master's, GMAT, minimum GPA of 3.0. Additional exam requirements/recommendations for international students: Required—TOEFL (minimum score 600 paper-based; 250 computer-based). *Application deadline:* For fall admission, 7/1 priority date for domestic students, 2/15 priority date for international students; for winter admission, 11/1 priority date for domestic students, 8/15 priority date for international students; for spring admission, 4/1 priority date for domestic students, 1/15 priority date for international students. Applications are processed on a rolling basis. Application fee: $30. Electronic applications accepted. *Expenses:* Tuition, area resident: Full-time $4,394. Tuition, nonresident: full-time $16,441. *Financial support:* Research assistantships, teaching assistantships, career-related internships or fieldwork, Federal Work-Study, institutionally sponsored loans, tuition waivers (partial), and unspecified assistantships available. Support available to part-time students. Financial award application deadline: 3/1; financial award applicants required to submit FAFSA. *Unit head:* Dr. Brenda Richey, Head, 561-297-3194, E-mail: brichey@fau.edu. *Application contact:* Fredrick G. Taylor, Graduate Adviser, 561-297-2768, Fax: 561-297-1315, E-mail: mba@fau.edu.

Florida International University, College of Education, Department of Health, Physical Education, and Recreation, Program in Physical Education, Miami, FL 33199. Offers advanced teacher preparation (MS); sports management (MS). Part-time and evening/weekend programs available. *Faculty:* 3 full-time (2 women). *Students:* 7 full-time (2 women), 16 part-time (9 women); includes 17 minority (7 African Americans, 1 Asian American or Pacific Islander, 9 Hispanic Americans). Average age 31. 8 applicants, 38% accepted, 3 enrolled. In 2006, 7 degrees awarded. *Entrance requirements:* For master's, GRE General Test or minimum GPA of 3.0, teaching certificate in physical education. Additional exam requirements/recommendations for international students: Required—TOEFL (minimum score 550 paper-based; 213 computer-based; 80 iBT), IELTS (minimum score 6). *Application deadline:* For fall admission, 6/1 priority date for domestic students, 4/1 for international students; for winter admission, 10/1 priority date for domestic students, 9/1 for international students; for spring admission, 3/1 priority date for domestic students, 2/1 for international students. Applications are processed on a rolling basis. Application fee: $30. Electronic applications accepted. *Expenses:* Tuition, state resident: part-time $249 per credit hour. Tuition, nonresident: part-time $753 per credit hour. Tuition and fees vary according to program. *Financial support:* Fellowships, research assistantships, teaching assistantships, Federal Work-Study available. Support available to part-time students. *Application contact:* Marisa Salazar, Student Recruiter, 305-348-3002, Fax: 305-348-3227, E-mail: marisa.salazar@fiu.edu.

Florida State University, Graduate Studies, College of Education, Department of Sport Management, Recreation Management, and Physical Education, Tallahassee, FL 32306. Offers physical education (MS, Ed D, PhD, Ed S); recreation management (MS); sport management (MS, Ed D, PhD, Ed S). *Faculty:* 18 full-time (9 women), 5 part-time/adjunct (3 women). *Students:* 93 full-time (35 women), 87 part-time (39 women); includes 65 minority (21 African Americans, 34 Asian Americans or Pacific Islanders, 10 Hispanic Americans). 226 applicants, 56% accepted, 75 enrolled. In 2006, 57 master's, 13 doctorates, 1 other advanced degree awarded. *Degree requirements:* For master's and Ed S, thesis optional; for doctorate, thesis/dissertation, comprehensive exam. *Entrance requirements:* For master's, doctorate, and Ed S, GRE General Test, minimum GPA of 3.0. Additional exam requirements/recommendations for international students: Required—TOEFL (minimum score 550 paper-based; 213 computer-based). *Application deadline:* For fall admission, 7/1 priority date for domestic students, 5/1 for international students; for spring admission, 11/1 for domestic students, 9/1 for international students. Applications are processed on a rolling basis. Application fee: $30. Electronic applications accepted. *Expenses:* Tuition, state resident: full-time $5,822; part-time $243 per credit hour. Tuition, nonresident: full-time $20,976; part-time $874 per credit hour. Tuition and fees vary according to program. *Financial support:* In 2006–07, 1 fellowship, 35 research assistantships, 38 teaching assistantships were awarded; career-related internships or fieldwork also available. Financial award applicants required to submit FAFSA. *Faculty research:* Sport marketing, teacher career cycle, gender issues. *Unit head:* Dr. Cheryl Beeler, Chair, 850-644-4813, Fax: 850-644-0975, E-mail: beeler@coe.fsu.edu. *Application contact:* Cynthia Bailey, Program Assistant, 850-644-4813, Fax: 850-644-0975, E-mail: bailey@coe.fsu.edu.

The George Washington University, School of Business, Department of Tourism and Hospitality Management, Washington, DC 20052. Offers event management (MTA, Professional Certificate); sport management (MTA); tourism administration (MTA); tourism and hospitality management (MBA); tourism destination management (Professional Certificate). Part-time programs available. *Degree requirements:* For master's, thesis, comprehensive exam. *Entrance requirements:* For master's, GRE General Test. Additional exam requirements/recommendations for international students: Required—TOEFL. *Faculty research:* Tourism policy, tourism impact forecasting, geotourism.

Georgia Southern University, Jack N. Averitt College of Graduate Studies, College of Health and Human Sciences, Department of Hospitality, Tourism, and Family and Consumer Sciences, Program in Sport Management, Statesboro, GA 30460. Offers MS. Part-time programs available. *Students:* 19 full-time (8 women), 5 part-time (1 woman); includes 1 minority (African American), 2 international. Average age 25. 20 applicants, 70% accepted, 9 enrolled. In 2006, 17 degrees awarded. *Degree requirements:* For master's, internship, terminal exam, thesis optional. *Entrance requirements:* For master's, GMAT, GRE General Test, MAT, minimum GPA of 2.75, interview. Additional exam requirements/recommendations for international students: Required—TOEFL (minimum score 550 paper-based; 213 computer-based; 80 iBT). *Application deadline:* For fall admission, 3/1 priority date for domestic students, 3/1 for international students; for spring admission, 10/1 priority date for domestic students, 10/1 for international students. Applications are processed on a rolling basis. Application fee: $50. Electronic applications accepted. *Financial support:* In 2006–07, 18 students received support, including research assistantships with partial tuition reimbursements available (averaging $5,500 per year), teaching assistantships with partial tuition reimbursements available (averaging $5,500 per year); career-related internships or fieldwork, Federal Work-Study, scholarships/grants, tuition waivers (partial), and unspecified assistantships also available. Support available to part-time students. Financial award application deadline: 4/15; financial award applicants required to submit FAFSA. *Faculty research:* Sport marketing, sport sociology, sport law, sports finance and economics. *Unit head:* Dr. John Nauright, Director, 912-468-7427, Fax: 912-681-0386, E-mail: jnaurigh@georgiasouthern.edu. *Application contact:* 912-681-5384, Fax: 912-681-0740, E-mail: gradadmissions@georgiasouthern.edu.

Georgia State University, College of Education, Department of Kinesiology and Health, Program in Sports Administration, Atlanta, GA 30303-3083. Offers MS. *Students:* 32 full-time

Sports Management

Georgia State University (continued)
(15 women), 27 part-time (14 women); includes 21 minority (18 African Americans, 1 American Indian/Alaska Native, 2 Hispanic Americans), 3 international. Average age 27. 39 applicants, 74% accepted. In 2006, 22 degrees awarded. *Degree requirements:* For master's, comprehensive exam. *Entrance requirements:* For master's, GRE General Test, minimum GPA of 2.5. *Application deadline:* For fall admission, 5/1 for domestic students; for spring admission, 10/1 for domestic students. Application fee: $25. *Financial support:* Research assistantships available. *Faculty research:* Sports marketing. *Unit head:* Dr. J. Andrew Doyle, Chair, Department of Kinesiology and Health, 404-651-4258, E-mail: adoyle@gsu.edu.

Gonzaga University, School of Education, Program in Sports and Athletic Administration, Spokane, WA 99258. Offers MASPAA. *Students:* 8 full-time (2 women), 21 part-time (8 women); includes 3 minority (1 African American, 1 Asian American or Pacific Islander, 1 Hispanic American), 1 international. Average age 25. In 2006, 7 degrees awarded. *Degree requirements:* For master's, comprehensive exam. *Entrance requirements:* Additional exam requirements/recommendations for international students: Required—TOEFL. Application fee: $40. *Expenses:* Tuition: Full-time $10,620; part-time $590 per credit. *Unit head:* Dr. John Sunderland, Chairperson, 509-328-4220 Ext. 3503.

Grambling State University, School of Graduate Studies and Research, College of Education, Department of Kinesiology, Sports and Leisure Studies, Grambling, LA 71245. Offers sports administration (MS). Part-time programs available. *Faculty:* 4 full-time (2 women). *Students:* 41 full-time (13 women), 6 part-time (4 women); includes 46 minority (45 African Americans, 1 Asian American or Pacific Islander). Average age 28. In 2006, 20 degrees awarded. *Degree requirements:* For master's, comprehensive exam. *Entrance requirements:* For master's, GRE General Test, minimum GPA of 2.5 in last degree. Additional exam requirements/recommendations for international students: Required—TOEFL. *Application deadline:* For fall admission, 7/1 for domestic students; for spring admission, 12/1 for domestic students. Application fee: $20 ($30 for international students). *Expenses:* Tuition, state resident: full-time $2,232; part-time $124 per credit hour. Tuition, nonresident: full-time $7,582; part-time $124 per credit hour. Required fees: $1,127. *Financial support:* In 2006–07, 35 students received support, including 5 research assistantships (averaging $4,700 per year); teaching assistantships, institutionally sponsored loans and unspecified assistantships also available. Financial award application deadline: 5/31. *Faculty research:* Sports psychology, sport history. *Unit head:* Dr. Willie Daniel, Head, 318-274-2294, Fax: 318-274-6053. *Application contact:* Shelia Griffin, Secretary, 318-274-2499, Fax: 318-274-6053, E-mail: griffins@alpha0.gram.edu.

Hardin-Simmons University, Graduate School, Irvin School of Education, Department of Fitness and Sport Sciences, Program in Sports and Recreation Management, Abilene, TX 79698-0001. Offers M Ed. Part-time programs available. *Faculty:* 4 full-time (1 woman), 1 part-time/adjunct (0 women). *Students:* 7 full-time (1 woman), 18 part-time (8 women); includes 7 minority (3 African Americans, 4 Hispanic Americans). Average age 26. 11 applicants, 100% accepted, 8 enrolled. In 2006, 10 degrees awarded. *Degree requirements:* For master's, internship, project, thesis optional. *Entrance requirements:* For master's, minimum undergraduate GPA of 3.0 in major, 2.7 overall; interview; writing sample; letters of recommendation; resumé. Additional exam requirements/recommendations for international students: Required—TOEFL (minimum score 550 paper-based; 213 computer-based). *Application deadline:* For fall admission, 8/15 priority date for domestic students; for spring admission, 1/5 priority date for domestic students. Applications are processed on a rolling basis. Application fee: $50 ($100 for international students). *Expenses:* Tuition: Full-time $9,090; part-time $505 per hour. Required fees: $490; $66 per semester. One-time fee: $50. Tuition and fees vary according to course load and degree level. *Financial support:* In 2006–07, 25 students received support, including 20 fellowships (averaging $1,000 per year); career-related internships or fieldwork, scholarships/grants, and recreation assistantships also available. Support available to part-time students. Financial award application deadline: 6/30; financial award applicants required to submit FAFSA. *Unit head:* Dr. Ray Galloway, Director, 325-670-1470, Fax: 325-670-1572, E-mail: rgallow@hsutx.edu. *Application contact:* Dr. Gary Stanlake, Dean of Graduate Studies, 325-670-1298, Fax: 325-670-1564, E-mail: gradoff@hsutx.edu.

Henderson State University, Graduate Studies, School of Education, Department of Health, Physical Education and Recreation, Arkadelphia, AR 71999-0001. Offers recreation (MS); sports administration (MS). *Faculty:* 6 full-time (1 woman). *Students:* 24 full-time (7 women), 29 part-time (11 women); includes 9 minority (8 African Americans, 1 Hispanic American), 18 international. Average age 27. In 2006, 8 degrees awarded. *Entrance requirements:* For master's, GRE General Test or MAT, minimum GPA of 2.7. *Application deadline:* For fall admission, 5/1 for international students; for winter admission, 10/1 for international students; for spring admission, 4/1 for international students. Application fee: $0 ($30 for international students). *Expenses:* Tuition, state resident: full-time $3,294; part-time $183 per credit hour. Tuition, nonresident: full-time $6,588; part-time $366 per credit hour. Required fees: $176 per term. *Unit head:* Dr. Hal McAfee, Chair of HPER, 870-230-5189, E-mail: mcafeeh@hsu.edu. *Application contact:* Dr. Marck L. Beggs, Graduate Dean, 870-230-5126, Fax: 870-230-5479, E-mail: beggsm@hsu.edu.

Howard University, Graduate School, Department of Health, Human Performance and Leisure Studies, Washington, DC 20059-0002. Offers exercise physiology (MS); health education (MS); sport studies (MS), including sociology of sport, sport management; urban recreation (MS), including leisure studies. Part-time and evening/weekend programs available. *Degree requirements:* For master's, thesis, comprehensive exam, registration. *Entrance requirements:* For master's, BS in human performance or related field. Electronic applications accepted. *Faculty research:* Health promotion, cardiovascular hypertension, physical activity, sport and human rights issues.

Indiana State University, School of Graduate Studies, College of Health and Human Performance, Department of Physical Education, Terre Haute, IN 47809-1401. Offers adult fitness (MA, MS); coaching (MA, MS); exercise science (MA, MS); master teacher (MA, MS). *Faculty:* 7 full-time (3 women), 2 part-time/adjunct (0 women). *Students:* 19 full-time (5 women), 13 part-time (4 women); includes 1 minority (African American), 5 international. Average age 27. 19 applicants, 89% accepted, 8 enrolled. In 2006, 18 degrees awarded. *Degree requirements:* For master's, thesis (for some programs). *Entrance requirements:* For master's, minor in physical education. *Application deadline:* For fall admission, 7/1 priority date for domestic students; for spring admission, 11/1 priority date for domestic students. Applications are processed on a rolling basis. Application fee: $35. Electronic applications accepted. *Expenses:* Tuition, state resident: part-time $278 per credit. Tuition, nonresident: part-time $552 per credit. *Financial support:* In 2006–07, 10 research assistantships with partial tuition reimbursements (averaging $6,300 per year) were awarded; teaching assistantships with partial tuition reimbursements, tuition waivers (partial) also available. Financial award application deadline: 3/1; financial award applicants required to submit FAFSA. *Faculty research:* Exercise science. *Unit head:* Dr. Jeffrey Edwards, Chairperson, 812-237-4048.

Indiana State University, School of Graduate Studies, College of Health and Human Performance, Department of Recreation and Sport Management, Terre Haute, IN 47809-1401. Offers MA, MS. *Faculty:* 4 full-time (1 woman), 2 part-time/adjunct (1 woman). *Students:* 27 full-time (8 women), 28 part-time (7 women); includes 6 minority (5 African Americans, 1 Hispanic American), 25 international. Average age 27. 41 applicants, 95% accepted, 20 enrolled. In 2006, 13 degrees awarded. *Degree requirements:* For master's, thesis (for some programs), comprehensive exam (for some programs). *Entrance requirements:* For master's, GRE General Test, undergraduate major in related field. *Application deadline:* For fall admission, 7/1 priority date for domestic students; for spring admission, 11/1 priority date for domestic students. Applications are processed on a rolling basis. Application fee: $35. Electronic applications accepted. *Expenses:* Tuition, state resident: part-time $278 per credit. Tuition, nonresident: part-time $552 per credit. *Financial support:* In 2006–07, research assistantships with partial tuition reimbursements (averaging $6,300 per year). Financial award application deadline: 3/1; financial award applicants required to submit FAFSA. *Unit head:* Dr. Daniel McLean, Chairperson, 812-237-2183, Fax: 812-237-4338.

Indiana University Bloomington, School of Health, Physical Education and Recreation, Department of Kinesiology, Bloomington, IN 47405-7000. Offers adapted physical education (MS); applied sport science (MS); athletic training (MS); biomechanics (MS); clinical exercise physiology (MS); ergonomics (MS); exercise physiology (MS); human performance (MS, PhD, PE Dir); motor control (MS); sport management (MS). PhD offered through the University Graduate School. Part-time programs available. *Faculty:* 10 full-time (1 woman). *Students:* 106 full-time (47 women), 41 part-time (15 women); includes 16 minority (15 African Americans, 1 American Indian/Alaska Native), 26 international. Average age 26.Terminal master's awarded for partial completion of doctoral program. *Degree requirements:* For master's and PE Dir, thesis optional; for doctorate, variable foreign language requirement, thesis/dissertation. *Entrance requirements:* For master's, GRE General Test, minimum GPA of 2.8; for doctorate, GRE General Test, minimum graduate GPA of 3.5, minimum undergraduate GPA of 3.0; for PE Dir, GRE. *Application deadline:* For fall admission, 1/1 for international students; for spring admission, 9/1 for international students. Applications are processed on a rolling basis. Application fee: $50 ($60 for international students). *Expenses:* Tuition, state resident: full-time $5,791; part-time $241 per credit hour. Tuition, nonresident: full-time $16,866; part-time $703 per credit hour. *Financial support:* Fellowships, research assistantships with full tuition reimbursements, teaching assistantships with full tuition reimbursements, career-related internships or fieldwork, Federal Work-Study, institutionally sponsored loans, scholarships/grants, tuition waivers (partial), and fee remissions available. Financial award application deadline: 3/1. *Faculty research:* Exercise physiology and biochemistry, sports biomechanics, human motor control, adaptation of fitness and exercise to special populations. *Unit head:* John Shea, Chairperson, 812-855-3114. *Application contact:* Program Office, 812-855-5523, Fax: 812-855-9417, E-mail: kines@indiana.edu.

Indiana University Bloomington, School of Health, Physical Education and Recreation, Department of Recreation and Park Administration, Bloomington, IN 47405-7000. Offers leisure behavior (PhD); outdoor recreation management (MS); park and recreation administration (MS); recreation (Re Dir); recreational sports administration (MS); therapeutic recreation (MS). PhD offered through the University Graduate School. *Faculty:* 11 full-time (4 women). *Students:* 18 full-time (7 women), 11 part-time (6 women); includes 2 minority (both African Americans), 3 international. Average age 28. In 2006, 9 degrees awarded. Terminal master's awarded for partial completion of doctoral program. *Degree requirements:* For doctorate, thesis/dissertation; for Re Dir, thesis optional. *Entrance requirements:* For master's, GRE General Test, minimum GPA of 2.8; for doctorate and Re Dir, GRE. *Application deadline:* For fall admission, 1/1 for international students; for spring admission, 9/1 for international students. Applications are processed on a rolling basis. Application fee: $50 ($60 for international students). *Expenses:* Tuition, state resident: full-time $5,791; part-time $241 per credit hour. Tuition, nonresident: full-time $16,866; part-time $703 per credit hour. *Financial support:* Fellowships, research assistantships, teaching assistantships with partial tuition reimbursements, career-related internships or fieldwork, Federal Work-Study, institutionally sponsored loans, scholarships/grants, tuition waivers (partial), unspecified assistantships, and fee remissions available. Financial award application deadline: 3/1. *Faculty research:* Leisure counseling, gerontology, special populations, planning and development. *Unit head:* Dr. Lynne Jamieson, Chairperson, 812-855-4711. *Application contact:* Program Office, 812-855-4711, Fax: 812-855-3998, E-mail: recpark@indiana.edu.

Indiana University of Pennsylvania, School of Graduate Studies and Research, College of Health and Human Services, Department of Health and Physical Education, Indiana, PA 15705-1087. Offers aquatics administration and facilities management (MS); exercise science (MS); sport management (MS); sport science (MS). Part-time programs available. *Faculty:* 8 full-time (4 women). *Students:* 33 full-time (17 women), 39 part-time (21 women); includes 3 minority (2 African Americans, 1 Asian American or Pacific Islander), 12 international. Average age 27. 75 applicants, 75% accepted. In 2006, 18 degrees awarded. *Degree requirements:* For master's, thesis optional. *Entrance requirements:* For master's, 2 letters of recommendation. Additional exam requirements/recommendations for international students: Required—TOEFL. *Application deadline:* For fall admission, 7/1 priority date for domestic students; for spring admission, 11/1 for domestic students. Applications are processed on a rolling basis. Application fee: $30. *Expenses:* Tuition, state resident: full-time $6,048; part-time $336 per credit. Tuition, nonresident: full-time $9,678; part-time $538 per credit. Required fees: $1,069; $148 per year. *Financial support:* In 2006–07, 6 research assistantships with full and partial tuition reimbursements (averaging $4,990 per year) were awarded. Financial award application deadline: 3/15; financial award applicants required to submit FAFSA. *Unit head:* Dr. Elaine Blair, Chairperson, 724-357-2770, E-mail: eblair@iup.edu.

Ithaca College, Graduate Studies, School of Health Sciences and Human Performance, Program in Sport Management, Ithaca, NY 14850-7020. Offers MS. Part-time programs available. *Faculty:* 7 full-time (3 women). *Students:* 14 full-time (6 women), 1 part-time. Average age 26. 27 applicants, 59% accepted, 14 enrolled. *Degree requirements:* For master's, thesis optional. *Entrance requirements:* For master's, GRE General Test, minimum GPA of 3.0. Additional exam requirements/recommendations for international students: Required—TOEFL (minimum score 550 paper-based; 213 computer-based). *Application deadline:* For fall admission, 4/1 priority date for domestic students; for spring admission, 12/1 for domestic students. Application fee: $40. *Financial support:* In 2006–07, 10 teaching assistantships (averaging $8,325 per year) were awarded; career-related internships or fieldwork, Federal Work-Study, institutionally sponsored loans, and scholarships/grants also available. Support available to part-time students. Financial award application deadline: 4/1; financial award applicants required to submit FAFSA. *Unit head:* Wayne Blann, Chairperson, 607-274-3155, E-mail: wblann@ithaca.edu.

Kent State University, Graduate School of Education, Health, and Human Services, Program in Exercise, Leisure, and Sport, Kent, OH 44242-0001. Offers athletic training (MA); exercise physiology (MA); physical teacher education (MA); sport and recreation management (MA); sports studies (MA). *Faculty:* 15 full-time (7 women). *Students:* 47 full-time (25 women), 34 part-time (13 women); includes 11 minority (10 African Americans, 1 Hispanic American), 4 international. 46 applicants, 74% accepted. In 2006, 9 degrees awarded. Application fee: $30. *Unit head:* Dr. Steve Mitchell, Coordinator, 330-672-0206, E-mail: smitchel@kent.edu. *Application contact:* Nancy Miller, Academic Program Coordinator, Office of Graduate Student Services, 330-672-2576, Fax: 330-672-9162, E-mail: ogs@kent.edu.

Lindenwood University, Graduate Programs, Division of Management, St. Charles, MO 63301-1695. Offers accounting (MBA, MS); business administration (MBA); entrepreneurial studies (MBA); finance (MBA, MS); human resource management (MBA); human resources (MS); international business (MBA, MS); management (MBA, MS); management information systems (MBA, MS); managing business to business (MA); managing human resources (MA); managing international business (MA); managing investment management (MA); managing leadership (MA); managing marketing (MA); managing organizational behavior (MA); managing sales (MA); managing, training and development (MA); marketing (MBA, MS); nonprofit administration (MA); public management (MBA, MS); sport management (MA). Part-time and evening/weekend programs available. *Faculty:* 38 full-time (15 women), 20 part-time/adjunct (5 women). *Students:* 177 full-time (78 women), 138 part-time (67 women); includes 43 minority (27 African Americans, 4 American Indian/Alaska Native, 6 Asian Americans or Pacific Islanders, 6 Hispanic Americans), 73 international. Average age 30. In 2006, 159 degrees awarded. *Degree requirements:* For master's, thesis (for some programs). *Entrance requirements:* For master's, interview, minimum GPA of 3.0. Additional exam requirements/recommendations for international students: Required—TOEFL (minimum score 550 paper-based; 173 computer-based). *Application deadline:* For fall admission, 7/30 priority date for domestic students, 9/30 priority date for international students; for winter admission, 12/30 priority date for domestic and international students; for spring admission, 3/30 priority date for domestic and international students. Applications are processed on a rolling basis. Application fee: $30 ($100 for international students). Electronic applications accepted. *Expenses:* Tuition: Part-time $340 per credit hour. Tuition and fees vary according to course level, course load, degree level and program. *Financial support:* Career-related internships or fieldwork, Federal Work-Study, institutionally sponsored loans, and tuition waivers (partial) available. Financial award application deadline: 6/30; financial award applicants required to submit FAFSA. *Unit head:* Ed Morris, Dean, 636-949-4832, Fax: 636-949-4910, E-mail: emorris@lindenwood.edu. *Application contact:* Brett Barger, Dean Adult, Corporate and Graduate Admissions, 636-949-4366, Fax: 636-949-4109, E-mail: bbarger@lindenwood.edu.

Lynn University, College of Business and Management, Boca Raton, FL 33431-5598. Offers aviation management (MBA); financial valuation and investment management (MBA); global leadership (PhD); hospitality management (MBA); international business (MBA); marketing (MBA); mass communication and media management (MBA); sports and athletics administration (MBA). Part-time and evening/weekend programs available. Postbaccalaureate distance learning degree programs offered. *Faculty:* 13 full-time (5 women), 7 part-time/adjunct (3 women). *Students:* 71 full-time (37 women), 113 part-time (47 women); includes 35 minority (13 African Americans, 6 Asian Americans or Pacific Islanders, 16 Hispanic Americans), 55 international. Average age 32. 114 applicants, 88% accepted, 71 enrolled. In 2006, 83 master's, 9 doctorates awarded. *Degree requirements:* For master's, project; for doctorate, thesis/dissertation, qualifying paper. *Entrance requirements:* For master's, GMAT or GRE, minimum undergraduate GPA of 3.0, resumé, 2 letters of recommendation; for doctorate, GRE or GMAT, minimum graduate GPA of 3.25, resumé, 2 letters of recommendation. Additional exam requirements/recommendations for international students: Required—TOEFL (minimum score 550 paper-based; 213 computer-based). *Application deadline:* Applications are processed on a rolling basis. Application fee: $50. Electronic applications accepted. *Expenses:* Tuition: Full-time $26,200. Required fees: $1,500. Tuition and fees vary according to class time, course load and degree level. *Financial support:* In 2006–07, 160 students received support. Career-related internships or fieldwork, Federal Work-Study, institutionally sponsored loans, scholarships/grants, tuition waivers (full and partial), and unspecified assistantships available. Support available to part-time students. Financial award application deadline: 8/1; financial award applicants required to submit FAFSA. *Faculty research:* Labor relations, dynamic balance in leisure-time skills, ethics in athletics, hotel development. *Unit head:* Dr. Russell Boisjoly, Dean, 561-237-7458, Fax: 561-237-7014, E-mail: rboisjoly@lynn.edu. *Application contact:* Dr. Larissa Baia, Assistant Director of Graduate Admissions, 561-237-7916, Fax: 561-237-7100, E-mail: admissionpm@lynn.edu.

Manhattanville College, Graduate Programs, Humanities and Social Sciences Programs, Program in Sports Business Management, Purchase, NY 10577-2132. Offers MS. *Students:* 14 full-time (5 women), 13 part-time (6 women), 3 international. Application fee: $55. *Application contact:* Natalia Fernandez, Director of Admissions, 914-323-5418, E-mail: gps@mylllle.edu.

Marshall University, Academic Affairs Division, College of Education and Human Services, Division of Exercise Science, Sports and Recreation, Program in Sport Administration, Huntington, WV 25755. Offers MS. *Faculty:* 6 full-time (3 women). *Students:* Average age 28. In 2006, 28 degrees awarded. *Degree requirements:* For master's, comprehensive assessment, thesis optional. *Entrance requirements:* For master's, GRE General Test. Application fee: $40. *Unit head:* Dr. Robert Barnett, Graduate Program Director, Sport Administration, 304-696-6491, E-mail: barnett@marshall.edu. *Application contact:* Information Contact, 304-746-1900, Fax: 304-746-1902, E-mail: services@marshall.edu.

Millersville University of Pennsylvania, Graduate School, School of Education, Department of Wellness and Sports Science, Program in Sport Management, Millersville, PA 17551-0302. Offers athletic coaching (M Ed); athletic management (M Ed). Part-time and evening/weekend programs available. *Faculty:* 12 full-time (5 women), 1 part-time/adjunct (0 women). *Students:* 15 full-time (9 women), 31 part-time (9 women). Average age 27. 16 applicants, 94% accepted, 7 enrolled. In 2006, 23 degrees awarded. *Degree requirements:* For master's, internships. *Entrance requirements:* For master's, GRE or MAT, minimum undergraduate GPA of 2.75. Additional exam requirements/recommendations for international students: Required—TOEFL (minimum score 500 paper-based; 183 computer-based). *Application deadline:* For fall admission, 3/1 priority date for domestic students; for winter admission, 10/1 priority date for domestic students; for spring admission, 10/1 priority date for domestic students. Applications are processed on a rolling basis. Application fee: $35. *Expenses:* Tuition, state resident: full-time $6,048; part-time $336 per credit. Tuition, nonresident: full-time $9,678; part-time $538 per credit. Required fees: $1,244. Tuition and fees vary according to course load. *Financial support:* In 2006–07, 6 students received support, including 6 research assistantships with full tuition reimbursements available (averaging $4,250 per year); career-related internships or fieldwork, Federal Work-Study, institutionally sponsored loans, and unspecified assistantships also available. Support available to part-time students. Financial award application deadline: 3/15; financial award applicants required to submit FAFSA. *Unit head:* Dr. Rebecca J. Mowrey, Coordinator, 717-872-3794, Fax: 717-871-2393, E-mail: rebecca.mowrey@millersville.edu. *Application contact:* Dr. Victor S. DeSantis, Dean of Graduate Studies, 717-872-3099, Fax: 717-871-2022, E-mail: victor.desantis@millersville.edu.

Mississippi State University, College of Education, Department of Kinesiology, Mississippi State, MS 39762. Offers exercise science (MS); health education/health promotion (MS); sports administration (MS); teaching/coaching (MS). Part-time programs available. Postbaccalaureate distance learning degree programs offered (minimal on-campus study). *Faculty:* 15 full-time (4 women), 6 part-time/adjunct (4 women). *Students:* 34 full-time (13 women), 13 part-time (6 women); includes 6 minority (all African Americans), 1 international. Average age 25. 49 applicants, 69% accepted, 26 enrolled. In 2006, 25 degrees awarded. *Degree requirements:* For master's, comprehensive oral or written exam, thesis optional. *Entrance requirements:* For master's, GRE General Test, minimum GPA of 3.0. Additional exam requirements/recommendations for international students: Required—TOEFL. *Application deadline:* For fall admission, 7/1 for domestic students; for spring admission, 11/1 for domestic students. Applications are processed on a rolling basis. Application fee: $30. Electronic applications accepted. *Expenses:* Tuition, state resident: full-time $4,550; part-time $253 per hour. Tuition, nonresident: full-time $10,552; part-time $584 per hour. International tuition: $10,882 full-time. Tuition and fees vary according to course load. *Financial support:* In 2006–07, 13 students received support, including 7 teaching assistantships with full tuition reimbursements available (averaging $7,772 per year); research assistantships with full tuition reimbursements available, career-related internships or fieldwork, Federal Work-Study, institutionally sponsored loans, and unspecified assistantships also available. Financial award applicants required to submit FAFSA. *Faculty research:* Static balance and stepping performance of older adults, organizational justice, public health, strength training and recovery drinks, high risk drinking perceptions and behaviors. *Unit head:* Dr. Joseph Chromiak, Interim Head, 662-325-2963, Fax: 662-325-4525, E-mail: jchrom@colled.msstate.edu. *Application contact:* Dr. Phil Bonfanti, Director of Admissions, 662-325-4104, Fax: 662-325-8872, E-mail: admit@msstate.edu.

Missouri State University, Graduate College, Interdisciplinary Program in Administrative Studies, Springfield, MO 65804-0094. Offers applied communication (MSAS); criminal justice (MSAS); environmental management (MSAS); project management (MSAS); sports management (MSAS). Part-time programs available. Postbaccalaureate distance learning degree programs offered (no on-campus study). *Students:* 9 full-time (4 women), 68 part-time (44 women); includes 2 minority (both African Americans), 3 international. Average age 35. 22 applicants, 86% accepted, 15 enrolled. In 2006, 29 degrees awarded. *Degree requirements:* For master's, thesis or alternative, comprehensive exam. *Entrance requirements:* For master's, GRE, GMAT, 3 years of work experience. Additional exam requirements/recommendations for international students: Required—TOEFL (minimum score 550 paper-based; 213 computer-based; 79 iBT). *Application deadline:* For fall admission, 7/20 priority date for domestic students; for spring admission, 12/20 priority date for domestic students. Applications are processed on a rolling basis. Application fee: $35. Electronic applications accepted. *Expenses:* Tuition, state resident: full-time $3,582; part-time $199 per credit hour. Tuition, nonresident: full-time $6,984; part-time $199 per credit hour. Required fees: $548. Full-time tuition and fees vary according to course level, course load, program and reciprocity agreements. *Financial support:* In 2006–07, 1 research assistantship (averaging $6,780 per year) was awarded; teaching assistantships, career-related internships or fieldwork, Federal Work-Study, institutionally sponsored loans, scholarships/grants, and unspecified assistantships also available. Support available to part-time students. Financial award application deadline: 3/31; financial award applicants required to submit FAFSA. *Unit head:* John Bourhis, Director, 417-836-6390, E-mail: johnbourhis@missouristate.edu.

Montana State University–Billings, College of Allied Health Professions, Department of Health and Human Performance, Billings, MT 59101-0298. Offers athletic training (MS); sport management (MS). *Faculty:* 6 full-time (3 women). *Students:* 25. 7 applicants, 100% accepted, 7 enrolled. *Degree requirements:* For master's, thesis optional. *Entrance requirements:* For master's, GRE General Test, minimum undergraduate GPA of 3.0. Application fee: $40. *Expenses:* Tuition, state resident: full-time $4,599. Tuition, nonresident: full-time $10,786. *Financial support:* Teaching assistantships, career-related internships or fieldwork, Federal Work-Study, institutionally sponsored loans, scholarships/grants, tuition waivers (partial), and unspecified assistantships available. Support available to part-time students. Financial award application deadline: 5/1; financial award applicants required to submit FAFSA. *Unit head:* Dr. Ernie Randolfi, Chair, 406-657-2370, Fax: 406-657-2399, E-mail: randolfi@msubillings.edu. *Application contact:* David M. Sullivan, Graduate Studies Counselor, 406-657-2053, Fax: 406-657-2299, E-mail: dsullivan@msubillings.edu.

Montclair State University, The Graduate School, College of Education and Human Services, Department of Exercise Science and Physical Education, Montclair, NJ 07043-1624. Offers health and physical education (Certificate); nutrition and exercise science (Certificate); physical education (MA, Certificate), including coaching and sports administration (MA), exercise science (MA), physical education (MA), teaching and supervision of physical education (MA). Part-time and evening/weekend programs available. *Faculty:* 14 full-time (8 women), 12 part-time/adjunct (7 women). *Students:* 23 full-time (10 women), 54 part-time (33 women); includes 10 minority (5 African Americans, 1 Asian American or Pacific Islander, 4 Hispanic Americans). 36 applicants, 47% accepted, 12 enrolled. In 2006, 11 master's, 13 other advanced degrees awarded. *Degree requirements:* For master's, comprehensive exam. *Entrance requirements:* For master's, GRE General Test, 2 letters of recommendation; for Certificate, 2 letters of recommendation (nutrition and exercise science concentration). Additional exam requirements/recommendations for international students: Required—TOEFL (minimum score 83 computer-based). *Application deadline:* For fall admission, 6/1 for international students; for spring admission, 10/1 for international students. Applications are processed on a rolling basis. Application fee: $60. Electronic applications accepted. *Expenses:* Tuition, state resident: part-time $450 per credit. Tuition, nonresident: part-time $682 per credit. Tuition and fees vary according to degree level and program. *Financial support:* In 2006–07, 4 research assistantships with full tuition reimbursements (averaging $5,000 per year) were awarded; Federal Work-Study, scholarships/grants, and unspecified assistantships also available. Support available to part-time students. Financial award application deadline: 3/1; financial award applicants required to submit FAFSA. *Unit head:* Dr. Joseph Donnelly, Chairperson, 973-655-4154.

Morehead State University, Graduate Programs, College of Education, Department of Health, Physical Education and Sport Sciences, Morehead, KY 40351. Offers exercise physiology (MA); health and physical education (MA); sports management (MA). *Accreditation:* NCATE. Part-time and evening/weekend programs available. *Faculty:* 12 full-time (8 women), 5 part-time/adjunct (2 women). *Students:* 16 full-time (10 women), 12 part-time (7 women), 2 international. Average age 32. In 2006, 11 degrees awarded. *Degree requirements:* For master's, oral exam, written core exam, thesis optional. *Entrance requirements:* For master's, GRE General Test or MAT, minimum GPA of 2.5; undergraduate major/minor in health, physical education, or recreation. Additional exam requirements/recommendations for international students: Required—TOEFL (minimum score 500 paper-based; 173 computer-based). *Application deadline:* For fall admission, 8/1 priority date for domestic and international students; for spring admission, 12/1 priority date for domestic and international students. Applications are processed on a rolling basis. Application fee: $0 ($55 for international students). Electronic applications accepted. *Financial support:* In 2006–07, 4 teaching assistantships (averaging $6,000 per year) were awarded; career-related internships or fieldwork, Federal Work-Study, and unspecified assistantships also available. Financial award application deadline: 4/1; financial award applicants required to submit FAFSA. *Faculty research:* Child growth and performance, instructional strategies, outdoor leadership qualities, exercise science, athletic training. *Unit head:* Dr. Lynne Fitzgerald, Chair, 606-783-2180, Fax: 606-783-5058. *Application contact:* Michelle Barber, Graduate Admissions Counselor, 606-783-2039, Fax: 606-783-5061, E-mail: m.barber@moreheadstate.edu.

Neumann College, Program in Sports Management, Aston, PA 19014-1298. Offers MS. Part-time programs available. *Faculty:* 5 full-time (2 women). *Students:* 5 full-time (4 women), 21 part-time (8 women); includes 6 minority (all African Americans) Average age 29. 10 applicants, 100% accepted, 8 enrolled. In 2006, 9 degrees awarded. *Degree requirements:* For master's, thesis or alternative, experiential component. *Application deadline:* Applications are processed on a rolling basis. Application fee: $50. *Financial support:* Available to part-time students. Application deadline: 3/15; *Unit head:* Dr. Sandra L. Slabik, Coordinator, 610-361-5291, Fax: 610-558-5574, E-mail: slabiks@neumann.edu. *Application contact:* Louise Bank, Assistant Director of Admissions, Graduate and Evening Programs, 610-558-5604, Fax: 610-459-1370, E-mail: bankl@neumann.edu.

New Mexico Highlands University, Graduate Studies, School of Education, Department of Exercise and Sport Sciences, Las Vegas, NM 87701. Offers human performance and sport (MA); sports administration (MA); teacher education (MA). Part-time programs available. *Faculty:* 2 full-time (1 woman). *Students:* 16 full-time (5 women), 44 part-time (13 women); includes 29 minority (7 African Americans, 1 Asian American or Pacific Islander, 21 Hispanic Americans), 1 international. Average age 31. 23 applicants, 78% accepted, 8 enrolled. In 2006, 10 degrees awarded. *Degree requirements:* For master's, thesis or alternative, comprehensive exam, registration. *Entrance requirements:* For master's, minimum undergraduate GPA of 3.0. Additional exam requirements/recommendations for international students: Required—TOEFL (minimum score 540 paper-based; 190 computer-based). *Application deadline:* For fall admission, 8/1 priority date for domestic students. Applications are processed on a rolling basis. Application fee: $15. *Expenses:* Tuition, state resident: part-time $101 per credit hour. Tuition, nonresident: part-time $101 per credit hour. *Financial support:* In 2006–07, 22 students received support, including 8 teaching assistantships with full and partial tuition reimbursements available (averaging $6,500 per year); career-related internships or fieldwork, Federal Work-Study, institutionally sponsored loans, scholarships/grants, tuition waivers (partial), and unspecified assistantships also available. Support available to part-time students. Financial award application deadline: 3/1; financial award applicants required to submit FAFSA. *Unit head:* Dr. Kathy Jenkins, Chair, 505-454-3287, Fax: 505-454-3001, E-mail: kjenkins@nmhu.edu. *Application contact:* Diane Trujillo, Administrative Assistant Graduate Studies, 505-454-3266, Fax: 505-454-3558, E-mail: dtrujillo@nmhu.edu.

New York University, School of Continuing and Professional Studies, Tisch Center for Hospitality, Tourism and Sports Management, Program in Sports Business, New York, NY 10012-1019. Offers MS, Advanced Certificate. *Faculty:* 6 full-time (1 woman), 26 part-time/adjunct (4 women). *Students:* 63 full-time (21 women), 77 part-time (28 women); includes 28 minority (8 African Americans, 13 Asian Americans or Pacific Islanders, 7 Hispanic Americans), 8 international. Average age 27. 113 applicants, 66% accepted, 42 enrolled. In 2006, 22 master's, 3 other advanced degrees awarded. *Degree requirements:* For master's, thesis, comprehensive exam (for some programs). *Entrance requirements:* For master's, GMAT or GRE General Test, 1 year of work experience. Additional exam requirements/recommendations for international students: Required—TOEFL (minimum score 600 paper-based; 250 computer-based; 100 iBT), TWE. *Application deadline:* For fall admission, 3/15 priority date for domestic and international students; for spring admission, 10/15 priority date for domestic students, 8/15 priority date for

Sports Management

New York University (continued)

international students. Application fee: $75. *Expenses:* Tuition: Part-time $1,080 per unit. Required fees: $56 per unit. $329 per term. Tuition and fees vary according to program. *Financial support:* In 2006–07, fellowships (averaging $1,358 per year). Financial award application deadline: 3/1; financial award applicants required to submit FAFSA. *Faculty research:* Implications of college football's bowl coalition series from a legal, economic, and academic perspective; social history of sports. *Unit head:* Dr. Mark M. Warner, Director, Graduate Programs, 212-998-9107, Fax: 212-995-4676, E-mail: mmw4@nyu.edu.

See Close-Up on page 505.

North Carolina State University, Graduate School, College of Natural Resources, Department of Parks, Recreation and Tourism Management, Raleigh, NC 27695. Offers geographic information systems (MS); maintenance management (MRRA, MS); parks, recreation and tourism management (PhD); recreation planning (MRRA, MS); recreation resources administration/public administration (MRRA); recreation/park management (MRRA, MS); sports management (MRRA, MS); travel and tourism management (MS). *Degree requirements:* For master's, thesis (for some programs); for doctorate, thesis/dissertation. *Entrance requirements:* For master's and doctorate, GRE General Test. Additional exam requirements/recommendations for international students: Required—TOEFL. Electronic applications accepted. *Faculty research:* Tourism policy and development, spatial information systems, natural resource management, recreational sports management, park and recreation management.

North Dakota State University, The Graduate School, College of Human Development and Education, Department of Health, Nutrition, and Exercise Sciences, Fargo, ND 58105. Offers dietetics (MS); entry level athletic training (MS); exercise science (MS); nutrition science (MS); public health (MS); sport pedagogy (MS); sports recreation management (MS). Part-time and evening/weekend programs available. Postbaccalaureate distance learning degree programs offered (no on-campus study). *Faculty:* 12 full-time (6 women). *Students:* 30 full-time, 50 part-time; includes 6 minority (2 African Americans, 1 American Indian/Alaska Native, 2 Asian Americans or Pacific Islanders, 1 Hispanic American), 3 international. 19 applicants, 100% accepted, 15 enrolled. In 2006, 4 degrees awarded. *Degree requirements:* For master's, thesis (for some programs), registration. *Entrance requirements:* For master's, minimum GPA of 3.0. *Application deadline:* For fall admission, 3/1 priority date for domestic and international students. Application fee: $45 ($60 for international students). Electronic applications accepted. *Financial support:* In 2006–07, 28 students received support, including 18 teaching assistantships with full tuition reimbursements available (averaging $6,500 per year). Financial award application deadline: 3/31. *Faculty research:* Biomechanics, sport specialization, recreation, nutrition, athletic training. Total annual research expenditures: $10,000. *Unit head:* Brad Strand, Head, 701-231-9718, Fax: 701-231-8872, E-mail: bradford.strand@ndsu.edu.

North Dakota State University, The Graduate School, College of Human Development and Education, School of Education, Program in Curriculum and Instruction, Fargo, ND 58105. Offers pedagogy (M Ed, MS); physical education and athletic administration (M Ed, MS). *Faculty:* 10 full-time (3 women). *Students:* 1 (woman) full-time, 11 part-time (10 women). Average age 27. 8 applicants, 75% accepted, 6 enrolled. In 2006, 1 degree awarded. *Degree requirements:* For master's, thesis (for some programs), comprehensive exam. *Entrance requirements:* For master's, Cooperative English Test, GRE General Test, MAT. Additional exam requirements/recommendations for international students: Required—TOEFL. *Application deadline:* For fall admission, 5/1 for domestic students. Applications are processed on a rolling basis. Application fee: $45 ($60 for international students). *Financial support:* Teaching assistantships, career-related internships or fieldwork, Federal Work-Study, institutionally sponsored loans, and tuition waivers (full) available. Financial award application deadline: 4/15. *Application contact:* Dr. Justin Wageman, Associate Professor, 701-231-7108, Fax: 701-231-9685, E-mail: justin.wageman@ndsu.edu.

Northern Illinois University, Graduate School, College of Education, Department of Kinesiology and Physical Education, De Kalb, IL 60115-2854. Offers physical education (MS Ed); sport management (MS). Part-time and evening/weekend programs available. *Faculty:* 21 full-time (12 women). *Students:* 75 full-time (30 women), 56 part-time (25 women); includes 11 minority (3 African Americans, 4 Asian Americans or Pacific Islanders, 4 Hispanic Americans), 10 international. Average age 28. 63 applicants, 89% accepted, 38 enrolled. In 2006, 43 degrees awarded. *Degree requirements:* For master's, thesis optional. *Entrance requirements:* For master's, GRE General Test, minimum GPA of 2.75, undergraduate major in related area. Additional exam requirements/recommendations for international students: Required—TOEFL (minimum score 550 paper-based; 213 computer-based). *Application deadline:* For fall admission, 6/1 for domestic students, 5/1 for international students; for spring admission, 11/1 for domestic students, 10/1 for international students. Applications are processed on a rolling basis. Application fee: $30. Electronic applications accepted. *Financial support:* In 2006–07, 31 teaching assistantships with full tuition reimbursements were awarded; fellowships with full tuition reimbursements, research assistantships with full tuition reimbursements, career-related internships or fieldwork, Federal Work-Study, scholarships/grants, tuition waivers (full), and unspecified assistantships also available. Support available to part-time students. Financial award applicants required to submit FAFSA. *Faculty research:* Leadership in athletic training, motor development, dance education, gait analysis, fat phobia. *Unit head:* Dr. Paul Carpenter, Chair, 815-753-1407, Fax: 815-753-1413, E-mail: pcarpenter@niu.edu. *Application contact:* Dr. Laurie Zittel, Director, Graduate Studies, 815-753-3907, E-mail: lzape@niu.edu.

Nova Southeastern University, Fischler School of Education and Human Services, Graduate Teacher Education Program, Fort Lauderdale, FL 33314-7796. Offers athletic administration (MS); cognitive and behavioral disabilities (MS); computer science education (Ed S); computer science education (K-12) (MS); curriculum and teaching (Ed S); curriculum, instruction and technology (MS); curriculum, instruction, management and administration (Ed S); early childhood special education (MS); early literacy and reading (Ed S); early literacy education (MS); education technology (MS); educational leadership (administration K–12) (MS, Ed S); educational media (Ed S); educational media (K-12) (MS); elementary education (MS, Ed S), including ESOL endorsement (MS); English (MS, Ed S); exceptional student education (MS), including ESOL endorsement; gifted education (MS, Ed S); interdisciplinary arts education (MS); management and administration of educational programs (MS); mathematics (MS, Ed S); multicultural early intervention (MS); pre-kindergarten/primary (MS); preschool education (MS); reading (MS, Ed S); science (MS, Ed S); secondary education (MS); social studies (MS, Ed S); Spanish language (MS); teaching and learning (MA, MS), including curriculum and instruction (MA), elementary mathematics (MA), elementary reading (MA), K-12 technology integration (MA); teaching English to speakers of other languages (MS, Ed S); technology management and administration (Ed S); urban studies education (MS); varying exceptionalities (Ed S). Part-time and evening/weekend programs available. Postbaccalaureate distance learning degree programs offered. *Faculty:* 131 full-time (78 women), 548 part-time/adjunct (342 women). *Students:* 1,418 full-time (1,139 women), 3,464 part-time (2,877 women); includes 2,462 minority (1,732 African Americans, 13 American Indian/Alaska Native, 44 Asian Americans or Pacific Islanders, 673 Hispanic Americans), 77 international. Average age 38. 1,771 applicants, 80% accepted, 1419 enrolled. In 2006, 2,078 master's, 425 other advanced degrees awarded. *Degree requirements:* For master's and Ed S, thesis, practicum, internship. *Entrance requirements:* For master's, MAT, GRE, CLAST, CBEST, PRAXIS I, GKT, minimum GPA of 2.5; for Ed S, MAT or GRE, master's degree, teaching certificate, minimum GPA of 3.0. Additional exam requirements/recommendations for international students: Recommended—TOEFL (minimum score 550 paper-based; 213 computer-based), IELTS (minimum score 6). *Application deadline:* For fall admission, 8/11 priority date for domestic and international students; for winter admission, 12/28 priority date for domestic and international students; for spring admission, 4/22 priority date for domestic and international students. Applications are processed on a rolling basis. Application fee: $50. Electronic applications accepted. *Financial support:* Federal Work-Study available. Support available to part-time students. Financial award application deadline: 1/7. *Faculty research:* School effectiveness, critical thinking, leadership skills acquisition, child education, multicultural education. *Unit head:* Dr. Meline Kevorkian, Associate Dean of Master's and Educational Programs, 954-262-8500, Fax: 954-262-3606, E-mail: melinek@nova.edu. *Application contact:* Jennifer Quiñones Nottingham, Dean of Student Affairs, 800-986-3223 Ext. 8624, Fax: 954-262-3911, E-mail: jlquinon@nova.edu.

Ohio University, Graduate Studies, College of Health and Human Services, School of Recreation and Sport Sciences, Program in Coaching Education, Athens, OH 45701-2979. Offers MS. *Faculty:* 5 full-time (2 women). *Students:* 18 full-time (6 women), 1 (woman) part-time; includes 4 minority (all African Americans), 2 international. Average age 23. 28 applicants, 61% accepted, 17 enrolled. In 2006, 12 degrees awarded. *Entrance requirements:* For master's, GRE. Additional exam requirements/recommendations for international students: Required—TOEFL (minimum score 575 paper-based; 233 computer-based). *Application deadline:* For fall admission, 3/1 priority date for domestic and international students. Application fee: $45. *Financial support:* In 2006–07, 4 research assistantships with full tuition reimbursements (averaging $8,577 per year), 17 teaching assistantships with full tuition reimbursements (averaging $8,577 per year) were awarded; scholarships/grants, tuition waivers (full), and stipends also available. *Faculty research:* Sports, physical activity, athletes. *Unit head:* Dr. David Carr, Assistant Professor and Coordinator, 740-593-4651, Fax: 740-593-0284, E-mail: carr@ohio.edu. *Application contact:* Molly de Laval, Graduate Records, 740-593-9787, Fax: 740-593-0284, E-mail: delaval@ohio.edu.

Ohio University, Graduate Studies, College of Health and Human Services, School of Recreation and Sport Sciences, Program in Sports Administration and Facility Management, Athens, OH 45701-2979. Offers MSA. Postbaccalaureate distance learning degree programs offered (minimal on-campus study). *Faculty:* 6 full-time (2 women), 3 part-time/adjunct (0 women). *Students:* 27 full-time (6 women); includes 1 minority (African American), 1 international. Average age 26. 135 applicants, 23% accepted, 20 enrolled. In 2006, 26 degrees awarded. *Median time to degree:* Master's–2 years full-time. *Degree requirements:* For master's, 11 week internship. *Entrance requirements:* For master's, GMAT or LSAT, interview. Additional exam requirements/recommendations for international students: Required—TOEFL (minimum score 250 computer-based). *Application deadline:* For fall admission, 2/1 for domestic and international students. Application fee: $45. *Financial support:* In 2006–07, 25 students received support, including 6 fellowships with full tuition reimbursements available, 15 research assistantships with full and partial tuition reimbursements available (averaging $8,577 per year); Federal Work-Study, institutionally sponsored loans, scholarships/grants, tuition waivers (partial), and stipends also available. Financial award application deadline: 3/15. *Faculty research:* Sport management, sport marketing, sports and technology, career development. *Unit head:* James Kahler, Executive Director, 740-593-4666, Fax: 740-593-0539, E-mail: kahler@ohio.edu. *Application contact:* Teresa Tedrow, Administrative Associate, 740-593-4666, Fax: 740-593-0539, E-mail: tedrow@ohio.edu.

Old Dominion University, Darden College of Education, Program in Physical Education, Sport Management Emphasis, Norfolk, VA 23529. Offers MS Ed. Part-time and evening/weekend programs available. *Faculty:* 3 full-time (1 woman), 2 part-time/adjunct (both women). *Students:* 30 full-time (15 women), 18 part-time (8 women); includes 17 minority (8 African Americans, 6 Asian Americans or Pacific Islanders, 3 Hispanic Americans), 3 international. Average age 25. 42 applicants, 71% accepted, 28 enrolled. In 2006, 23 degrees awarded. *Degree requirements:* For master's, thesis or alternative, internship, research project, comprehensive exam. *Entrance requirements:* For master's, GRE, minimum GPA of 2.8 overall, 3.0 in major. Additional exam requirements/recommendations for international students: Required—TOEFL (minimum score 500 paper-based; 200 computer-based). *Application deadline:* For fall admission, 7/1 for domestic students; for spring admission, 11/1 for domestic students. Applications are processed on a rolling basis. Application fee: $40. *Expenses:* Tuition, area resident: Part-time $285 per credit hour. Tuition, nonresident: part-time $715 per credit hour. Required fees: $94 per semester. *Financial support:* In 2006–07, fellowships (averaging $1,500 per year), 1 research assistantship with partial tuition reimbursement (averaging $9,000 per year), teaching assistantships with partial tuition reimbursements (averaging $9,000 per year) were awarded; career-related internships or fieldwork and scholarships/grants also available. Financial award application deadline: 4/15; financial award applicants required to submit FAFSA. *Faculty research:* Leadership, fan motives, sport communications, curriculum development in sport management, violence in sport. Total annual research expenditures: $185,000. *Unit head:* Dr. Robert Spina, Chair, 757-683-4995, Fax: 757-683-4995, E-mail: rspina@odu.edu. *Application contact:* Dr. Robert Case, Graduate Program Director, 757-683-5962, Fax: 757-683-5962, E-mail: rcase@odu.edu.

Robert Morris University, Graduate Studies, School of Business, Moon Township, PA 15108-1189. Offers accounting (MS); business administration and management (MBA); finance (MS); human resource management (MS); nonprofit management (MS); sport management (MS); taxation (MS). Part-time and evening/weekend programs available. *Faculty:* 27 full-time (12 women), 6 part-time/adjunct (1 woman). *Students:* Average age 31. 253 applicants, 59% accepted, 103 enrolled. In 2006, 139 degrees awarded. *Entrance requirements:* For master's, GMAT, letters of recommendation. Additional exam requirements/recommendations for international students: Required—TOEFL (minimum score 550 paper-based; 213 computer-based). *Application deadline:* For fall admission, 7/1 priority date for domestic and international students; for spring admission, 11/1 priority date for domestic and international students. Applications are processed on a rolling basis. Application fee: $35. Electronic applications accepted. *Expenses:* Tuition: Part-time $580 per credit. Part-time tuition and fees vary according to degree level and program. *Financial support:* Research assistantships with partial tuition reimbursements, Federal Work-Study, institutionally sponsored loans, and unspecified assistantships available. Support available to part-time students. Financial award application deadline: 5/1; financial award applicants required to submit FAFSA. *Unit head:* Dr. Derya A. Jacobs, Dean, 412-262-8451, Fax: 412-262-8494, E-mail: jacobs@rmu.edu. *Application contact:* Kellie L. Laurenzi, Dean of Enrollment, 412-262-8235, Fax: 412-299-2425, E-mail: laurenzi@rmu.edu.

St. Cloud State University, School of Graduate Studies, College of Education, Department of Health, Physical Education, Recreation, and Sport Science, St. Cloud, MN 56301-4498. Offers exercise science (MS); physical education (MS); sports management (MS). *Faculty:* 16 full-time (8 women), 1 (woman) part-time/adjunct. *Students:* 12 full-time (6 women), 3 part-time (1 woman), 2 international. 82 applicants, 43% accepted. In 2006, 18 degrees awarded. *Degree requirements:* For master's, thesis or alternative. *Entrance requirements:* For master's, GRE General Test, minimum GPA of 2.75. Additional exam requirements/recommendations for international students: Required—MELAB; Recommended—TOEFL (minimum score 550 paper-based; 213 computer-based), IELTS (minimum score 7). *Application deadline:* For fall admission, 6/1 priority date for domestic students, 4/1 for international students; for spring admission, 10/1 priority date for domestic students, 8/1 for international students. Applications are processed on a rolling basis. Application fee: $35. Electronic applications accepted. *Financial support:* Federal Work-Study, scholarships/grants, and unspecified assistantships available. Financial award application deadline: 3/1. *Unit head:* Dr. Caryl Martin, Chairperson, 320-308-4251, E-mail: clmartin@stcloudstate.edu. *Application contact:* Linda Lou Krueger, School of Graduate Studies, 320-308-2113, Fax: 320-308-5371, E-mail: lekrueger@stcloudstate.edu.

St. Edward's University, School of Management and Business, Program in Human Services, Austin, TX 78704. Offers conflict resolution (Certificate); human services (MA), including administration, conflict resolution, human resource management, sports management; sports management (Certificate). Part-time and evening/weekend programs available. *Students:* 9 full-time (8 women), 46 part-time (34 women); includes 19 minority (4 African Americans, 2 Asian Americans or Pacific Islanders, 13 Hispanic Americans), 2 international. Average age 34. 43 applicants, 84% accepted, 28 enrolled. In 2006, 28 degrees awarded. *Degree requirements:* For master's, minimum 24 resident hours. *Entrance requirements:* For master's, GRE General Test, GMAT, minimum GPA of 2.75 in last 60 hours of course work. Additional exam requirements/recommendations for international students: Required—TOEFL (minimum score 550 paper-based; 213 computer-based; 79 iBT). *Application deadline:* For fall admission, 8/1 for domestic students, 7/1 for international students; for spring admission, 12/1 for domestic students, 11/1 for international students. Applications are processed on a rolling basis. Application fee: $45 ($50 for international students). Electronic applications accepted. *Expenses:* Tuition: Full-time $11,682; part-time $649 per credit hour. Full-time tuition and fees vary according to course load and program. *Financial support:* In 2006–07, 4 students received support. Scholarships/grants available. Financial award applicants required to submit FAFSA. *Faculty research:* Leadership development, organizational management, public policy, emotional intelligence. *Unit head:* Dr. Constance D Porter, Director, 512-416-5827, Fax: 512-448-8492, E-mail: constanp@stedwards.edu. *Application contact:* Kay L. Arnold, Graduate Admissions Coordinator, 512-233-1636, Fax: 512-428-1032, E-mail: kayla@stedwards.edu.

Saint Leo University, Graduate Business Studies, Saint Leo, FL 33574-6665. Offers accounting (MBA); business (MBA); criminal justice (MBA); human resource administration (MBA); information security management (MBA); sport business (MBA). Part-time and evening/weekend programs available. Postbaccalaureate distance learning degree programs offered (no on-campus study). *Faculty:* 17 full-time (5 women), 24 part-time/adjunct (6 women). *Students:* 298 full-time (187 women), 368 part-time (215 women); includes 195 minority (132 African Americans, 3 American Indian/Alaska Native, 23 Asian Americans or Pacific Islanders, 37 Hispanic Americans), 6 international. Average age 36. 863 applicants, 59% accepted, 282 enrolled. In 2006, 156 degrees awarded. *Degree requirements:* For master's, thesis. *Entrance requirements:* For master's, GMAT, 5 years of professional work experience, resumé, 2 letters of recommendation. Additional exam requirements/recommendations for international students: Required—TOEFL (minimum score 550 paper-based; 213 computer-based). *Application deadline:* For fall admission, 7/1 priority date for domestic students; for spring admission, 11/12 priority date for domestic students. Applications are processed on a rolling basis. Application fee: $45. Electronic applications accepted. *Expenses: Contact institution. Financial support:* In 2006–07, 39 students received support. Career-related internships or fieldwork, Federal Work-Study, and scholarships/grants available. Support available to part-time students. Financial award application deadline: 3/1; financial award applicants required to submit FAFSA. *Unit head:* Dr. Robert Robertson, Director, 352-588-8758, Fax: 352-588-8912, E-mail: mba@saintleo.edu. *Application contact:* Scott Cathcart, Vice President of Enrollment, 800-707-8846, Fax: 352-588-7873, E-mail: grad.admission@saintleo.edu.

Seattle University, College of Arts and Sciences, Center for the Study of Sport and Exercise, Seattle, WA 98122-1090. Offers MSAL. *Faculty:* 2 full-time (0 women). *Students:* 4 full-time (0 women), 41 part-time (18 women); includes 9 minority (4 African Americans, 1 American Indian/Alaska Native, 4 Asian Americans or Pacific Islanders), 2 international. Average age 27. *Unit head:* Dr. Daniel Tripps, Director, 206-296-5440, E-mail: trippsd@seattleu.edu.

Seton Hall University, Stillman School of Business, Programs in Business Administration, South Orange, NJ 07079-2697. Offers accounting (MBA); finance (MBA); financial markets, institutions and instruments (MBA); healthcare management (MBA); information systems (MBA); international business (MBA); management (MBA); marketing (MBA); pharmaceutical management (MBA); sport management (MBA). Part-time and evening/weekend programs available. *Faculty:* 57 full-time (13 women), 30 part-time/adjunct (3 women). *Students:* 57 full-time (16 women), 180 part-time (57 women); includes 9 African Americans, 10 Asian Americans or Pacific Islanders, 7 Hispanic Americans. Average age 29. 195 applicants, 47% accepted, 48 enrolled. In 2006, 144 degrees awarded. *Median time to degree:* Master's–1.6 years full-time, 2.3 years part-time. *Degree requirements:* For master's, 20 hours of community service (Social Responsibility Project). *Entrance requirements:* For master's, GMAT, minimum GPA of 2.75. Additional exam requirements/recommendations for international students: Required—TOEFL (minimum score 550 paper-based; 213 computer-based). *Application deadline:* For fall admission, 6/1 priority date for domestic students; for spring admission, 11/1 priority date for domestic students. Applications are processed on a rolling basis. Application fee: $75 ($100 for international students). Electronic applications accepted. *Financial support:* In 2006–07, 40 students received support, including research assistantships with full and partial tuition reimbursements available (averaging $5,400 per year); career-related internships or fieldwork, Federal Work-Study, scholarships/grants, and unspecified assistantships also available. Support available to part-time students. Financial award application deadline: 6/1; financial award applicants required to submit FAFSA. *Faculty research:* Financial, hedge funds, international business, legal issues, disclosure and branding. *Unit head:* Dr. Joyce A. Strawser, Associate Dean for Undergraduate and MBA Curricula, 973-761-9225, Fax: 973-761-9217, E-mail: strawsjo@shu.edu. *Application contact:* Catherine Bianchi, Director of Graduate Admissions, 973-761-9220, Fax: 973-761-9208, E-mail: biancha@shu.edu.

Slippery Rock University of Pennsylvania, Graduate Studies (Recruitment), College of Education, Department of Sport Management, Slippery Rock, PA 16057-1383. Offers MS. Part-time and evening/weekend programs available. *Degree requirements:* For master's, thesis (for some programs), comprehensive exam (for some programs). *Entrance requirements:* For master's, GRE General Test, MAT, minimum GPA of 2.75. Additional exam requirements/recommendations for international students: Required—TOEFL (minimum score 550 paper-based; 213 computer-based). *Application deadline:* For fall admission, 7/1 priority date for domestic and international students; for spring admission, 11/1 priority date for domestic and international students. Applications are processed on a rolling basis. Application fee: $25. Electronic applications accepted. *Expenses:* Tuition, state resident: part-time $336 per credit. Tuition, nonresident: part-time $538 per credit. Required fees: $84 per credit. $37 per semester. *Financial support:* Career-related internships or fieldwork, Federal Work-Study, scholarships/grants, and unspecified assistantships available. Support available to part-time students. Financial award application deadline: 5/1. *Unit head:* Dr. Brian Crow, Graduate Coordinator, 724-738-2392, Fax: 724-738-2921, E-mail: brain.crow@sru.edu. *Application contact:* Director of Graduate Studies, 724-738-2051, Fax: 724-738-2146, E-mail: graduate.studies@sru.edu.

Southern New Hampshire University, School of Business, Manchester, NH 03106-1045. Offers accounting (MS); business administration (MBA, Certificate), including accounting (Certificate), business administration (MBA), finance (Certificate), forensic accounting (Certificate), human resources management (Certificate), international business (Certificate), international sport management (Certificate), leadership of not for profit organizations (Certificate), marketing (Certificate), operations management (Certificate), sport management (Certificate), taxation (Certificate); finance (MS); hospitality and tourism leadership (Certificate); information technology (MS, Certificate); information technology/international business (Certificate); integrated marketing communications (Certificate); international business (MS, DBA); marketing (MS); operations and project management (MS); organizational leadership (MS); project management (Certificate); sport management (MS); MBA/Certificate. *Accreditation:* ACBSP. Part-time and evening/weekend programs available. Postbaccalaureate distance learning degree programs offered (no on-campus study). *Faculty:* 45 full-time, 75 part-time/adjunct. *Students:* 427 full-time (184 women), 774 part-time (428 women). Average age 32. In 2006, 682 master's, 1 doctorate awarded. Terminal master's awarded for partial completion of doctoral program. *Degree requirements:* For master's, one foreign language, thesis or alternative, comprehensive exam (for some programs); for doctorate, one foreign language, thesis/dissertation, comprehensive exam. *Entrance requirements:* For master's, minimum GPA of 2.5; for doctorate, GMAT. Additional exam requirements/recommendations for international students: Required—TOEFL (minimum score 500 paper-based). *Application deadline:* Applications are processed on a rolling basis. Application fee: $25. Electronic applications accepted. *Financial support:* Career-related internships or fieldwork, Federal Work-Study, institutionally sponsored loans, tuition waivers (partial), and unspecified assistantships available. Support available to part-time students. Financial award applicants required to submit FAFSA. *Unit head:* Dr. Martin Bradley, Dean, 603-644-3102, Fax: 603-644-3144, E-mail: m.bradley@snhu.edu. *Application contact:* Scott Durand, Director of Graduate Enrollment Services, 603-644-3102 Ext. 3338, Fax: 603-644-3144, E-mail: s.durand@snhu.edu.

See Close-Up on page 325.

Springfield College, Graduate Programs, Programs in Physical Education, Springfield, MA 01109-3797. Offers adapted physical education (M Ed, MPE, MS); advanced level coaching (M Ed, MPE, MS); athletic administration (M Ed, MPE, MS); general physical education (DPE, CAS); health education licensure (MPE, MS); health education licensure program (M Ed); physical education licensure (MPE, MS); physical education licensure program (M Ed); sport performance (M Ed, MPE, MS); teaching and administration (MS). Part-time and evening/weekend programs available. *Faculty:* 25 full-time (13 women), 2 part-time/adjunct (0 women). *Students:* 97. Average age 27. 78 applicants, 86% accepted, 45 enrolled. In 2006, 22 master's, 4 doctorates awarded. Terminal master's awarded for partial completion of doctoral program. *Degree requirements:* For master's, research project; for doctorate, thesis/dissertation. *Entrance requirements:* For master's, GRE General Test; for doctorate, GRE General Test, interview. Additional exam requirements/recommendations for international students: Required—TOEFL (minimum score 550 paper-based; 213 computer-based). *Application deadline:* For fall admission, 1/15 priority date for domestic students; for winter admission, 11/1 for domestic students; for spring admission, 12/1 for domestic students. Applications are processed on a rolling basis. Application fee: $50. Electronic applications accepted. *Expenses:* Tuition: Full-time $12,222; part-time $679 per credit. Required fees: $25; $25 per year. One-time fee: $25 full-time. *Financial support:* Fellowships with partial tuition reimbursements, teaching assistantships with partial tuition reimbursements, career-related internships or fieldwork, Federal Work-Study, institutionally sponsored loans, and tuition waivers (full and partial) available. Financial award application deadline: 3/1. *Faculty research:* Pedagogy, motor learning, history of physical education. *Unit head:* Dr. Stephen C. Coulon, Director, 413-748-3029, Fax: 413-748-3537, E-mail: stephen_coulon@spfldcol.edu. *Application contact:* Donald James Shaw, Director of Graduate Admissions, 413-748-3060, Fax: 413-748-3069, E-mail: donald_shaw_jr@spfldcol.edu.

Springfield College, Graduate Programs, Programs in Sport Management and Recreation, Springfield, MA 01109-3797. Offers outdoor recreational management (M Ed, MS); recreational management (M Ed, MS); sport management (M Ed, MS); therapeutic recreational management (M Ed, MS). Part-time and evening/weekend programs available. *Faculty:* 5 full-time (1 woman), 6 part-time/adjunct (4 women). *Students:* 43. Average age 26. 31 applicants, 84% accepted, 20 enrolled. In 2006, 22 degrees awarded. *Degree requirements:* For master's, research project or thesis. *Entrance requirements:* Additional exam requirements/recommendations for international students: Required—TOEFL (minimum score 550 paper-based; 213 computer-based). *Application deadline:* For fall admission, 1/15 for domestic students; for winter admission, 11/1 for domestic students; for spring admission, 12/1 for domestic students. Applications are processed on a rolling basis. Application fee: $50. Electronic applications accepted. *Expenses:* Tuition: Full-time $12,222; part-time $679 per credit. Required fees: $25; $25 per year. One-time fee: $25 full-time. *Financial support:* In 2006–07, 2 teaching assistantships with partial tuition reimbursements were awarded; fellowships with partial tuition reimbursements, career-related internships or fieldwork, Federal Work-Study, institutionally sponsored loans, and tuition waivers (full and partial) also available. Financial award application deadline: 3/1. *Faculty research:* Leisure behavior, public relations, therapeutic recreation in the community, outdoor recreation, leadership. *Unit head:* Dr. Donald R. Snyder, Director, 413-748-3272, Fax: 413-748-3685, E-mail: donald_snyder@spfldcol.edu. *Application contact:* Donald James Shaw, Director of Graduate Admissions, 413-748-3060, Fax: 413-748-3069, E-mail: donald_shaw_jr@spfldcol.edu.

State University of New York College at Cortland, Graduate Studies, School of Professional Studies, Department of Sport Management, Cortland, NY 13045. Offers international sport management (MS); sport management (MS). *Entrance requirements:* For master's, GMAT or GRE, 2 letters of recommendation.

See Close-Up on page 2351.

Temple University, Graduate School, School of Tourism and Hospitality Management, Program in Sport and Recreation Administration, Philadelphia, PA 19122-6096. Offers Ed M. Part-time and evening/weekend programs available. *Faculty:* 5 full-time (2 women). *Students:* 44 full-time (27 women), 34 part-time (13 women); includes 17 minority (all African Americans), 3 international. 98 applicants, 48% accepted, 27 enrolled. In 2006, 36 degrees awarded. *Entrance requirements:* For master's, GRE General Test or MAT, minimum undergraduate GPA of 3.0. Additional exam requirements/recommendations for international students: Required—TOEFL (minimum score 550 paper-based; 213 computer-based; 79 iBT). *Application deadline:* For fall admission, 4/15 priority date for domestic students, 12/15 for international students; for spring admission, 9/30 priority date for domestic students, 8/1 for international students. Application fee: $50. Electronic applications accepted. *Expenses:* Tuition, state resident: full-time $12,264; part-time $511 per credit. Tuition, nonresident: full-time $17,904; part-time $746 per credit. Required fees: $84 per course. Tuition and fees vary according to program. *Financial support:* Teaching assistantships available. Financial award application deadline: 1/15; financial award applicants required to submit FAFSA. *Unit head:* Dr. Michael W. Jackson, Director, 215-204-6298, Fax: 215-204-8705, E-mail: pierre@temple.edu.

See Close-Up on page 507.

Tiffin University, Program in Business Administration, Tiffin, OH 44883-2161. Offers general management (MBA); leadership (MBA); safety and security (MBA); sports management (MBA). *Accreditation:* ACBSP. Part-time and evening/weekend programs available. Postbaccalaureate distance learning degree programs offered (no on-campus study). *Faculty:* 29 full-time (8 women), 28 part-time/adjunct (9 women). *Students:* 89 full-time (54 women), 159 part-time (87 women); includes 31 minority (28 African Americans, 3 Hispanic Americans), 8 international. Average age 31. 182 applicants, 68% accepted, 88 enrolled. In 2006, 145 degrees awarded. *Entrance requirements:* For master's, minimum undergraduate GPA of 2.5, work experience. Additional exam requirements/recommendations for international students: Required—TOEFL (minimum score 550 paper-based; 213 computer-based). *Application deadline:* For fall admission, 9/3 for domestic students, 8/1 for international students; for spring admission, 1/9 for domestic students, 12/1 for international students. Applications are processed on a rolling basis. Application fee: $50. Electronic applications accepted. *Expenses:* Tuition: Part-time $700 per credit hour. *Financial support:* In 2006–07, 94 students received support. Available to part-time students. Application deadline: 7/31; *Faculty research:* Small business, executive development operations, research and statistical analysis, market research, management information systems. *Unit head:* Dr. Shawn P. Daly, Dean of the School of Business, 419-448-3404, Fax: 419-443-5002, E-mail: sdaly@tiffin.edu. *Application contact:* Kristi Krintzline, Director of Graduate Admissions, 800-968-6446 Ext. 3445, Fax: 419-443-5002, E-mail: krintzlineka@tiffin.edu.

Troy University, Graduate School, College of Health and Human Services, Program in Sport and Fitness Management, Troy, AL 36082. Offers MS. Part-time and evening/weekend programs available. *Students:* 20 full-time (11 women), 31 part-time (10 women); includes 12 minority (all African Americans) Average age 27. In 2006, 16 degrees awarded. *Degree requirements:* For master's, thesis optional. *Entrance requirements:* For master's, GRE or MAT. Application fee: $40. *Expenses:* Tuition, state resident: full-time $4,368; part-time $182 per hour. Tuition, nonresident: full-time $8,736; part-time $364 per hour. Required fees: $50 per term. *Financial support:* Career-related internships or fieldwork and unspecified assistantships available. *Faculty research:* Sport marketing, fitness, sport law. *Unit head:* Dr. Fred Green, Interim Chairman, 334-670-3764, Fax: 334-670-3936, E-mail: fegreen@troy.edu. *Application contact:* Brenda K. Campbell, Director of Graduate Admissions, 334-670-3178, Fax: 334-670-3733, E-mail: bcamp@troy.edu.

United States Sports Academy, Graduate Programs, Department of Health and Fitness Management, Daphne, AL 36526-7055. Offers MSS. Part-time programs available. Postbaccalaureate distance learning degree programs offered (minimal on-campus study). *Faculty:* 1 full-time (0 women), 1 part-time/adjunct (0 women). *Students:* 2 full-time (0 women), 3 part-time (1 woman). *Degree requirements:* For master's, thesis optional. *Entrance requirements:* For master's, GRE General Test, GMAT, or MAT, minimum GPA of 2.5, 3 letters of recommendation, resumé. Additional exam requirements/recommendations for international students: Required—TOEFL (minimum score 500 paper-based; 213 computer-based). *Application*

Sports Management

United States Sports Academy (continued)

deadline: Applications are processed on a rolling basis. Application fee: $50 ($125 for international students). Electronic applications accepted. *Financial support:* Application deadline: 8/15; *Faculty research:* Exercise physiology, conditioning. *Unit head:* Dr. Brian Wallace, Chair, 251-626-3303 Ext. 137, Fax: 251-625-1035, E-mail: bwallace@ussd.edu. *Application contact:* Dr. Albert G. Applin, Dean of Student Services, 251-626-3303 Ext. 147, Fax: 251-626-1035, E-mail: applin@ussa.edu.

United States Sports Academy, Graduate Programs, Department of Sport Management, Daphne, AL 36526-7055. Offers MSS, DSM, Ed D. Part-time programs available. Postbaccalaureate distance learning degree programs offered (minimal on-campus study). *Faculty:* 5 full-time (1 woman), 12 part-time/adjunct (0 women). *Students:* 84 full-time (14 women), 259 part-time (76 women); includes 73 minority (42 African Americans, 26 Asian Americans or Pacific Islanders, 5 Hispanic Americans), 10 international. Average age 36. *Degree requirements:* For master's, thesis optional; for doctorate, thesis/dissertation, comprehensive exam. *Entrance requirements:* For master's, GRE General Test, GMAT, or MAT, minimum GPA of 2.5, 3 letters of recommendation, resumé; for doctorate, GRE General Test, GMAT, or MAT, master's degree, 3 letters of recommendation, resumé. Additional exam requirements/recommendations for international students: Required—TOEFL (minimum score 500 paper-based; 213 computer-based). *Application deadline:* Applications are processed on a rolling basis. Application fee: $50 ($125 for international students). Electronic applications accepted. *Financial support:* In 2006–07, 95 students received support, including 2 research assistantships with full tuition reimbursements available (averaging $10,000 per year); career-related internships or fieldwork, Federal Work-Study, scholarships/grants, and service assistantships also available. Support available to part-time students. Financial award application deadline: 8/15; financial award applicants required to submit FAFSA. *Faculty research:* Sport law, leadership behavior, personnel evaluation. Total annual research expenditures: $2,500. *Unit head:* Dr. Albert G. Applin, Dean of Student Services, 251-626-3303 Ext. 147, Fax: 251-626-1035, E-mail: applin@ussa.edu.

See Close-Up on page 2353.

The University of Alabama, Graduate School, College of Education, Department of Kinesiology, Tuscaloosa, AL 35487. Offers alternative sport pedagogy (MA); exercise science (MA, PhD); human performance (MA); sport management (MA); sport pedagogy (MA, PhD). Part-time programs available. *Faculty:* 9 full-time (1 woman). *Students:* 39 full-time (18 women), 20 part-time (11 women); includes 2 minority (both African Americans), 11 international. Average age 30. 35 applicants, 63% accepted, 7 enrolled. In 2006, 3 master's, 13 doctorates awarded. *Median time to degree:* Of those who began their doctoral program in fall 1998, 100% received their degree in 8 years or less. *Degree requirements:* For master's, thesis optional; for doctorate, thesis/dissertation, comprehensive exam. *Entrance requirements:* For master's and doctorate, GRE, MAT, minimum GPA of 3.0. Additional exam requirements/recommendations for international students: Required—TOEFL. *Financial support:* In 2006–07, 14 students received support, including 13 teaching assistantships with full tuition reimbursements available (averaging $8,678 per year). *Faculty research:* Race gender and sexuality in sports, physical education curriculum reform, disability sports, physical activity and health, environmental physiology. Total annual research expenditures: $9,290. *Unit head:* Dr. Matt Curtner-Smith, Department Head and Professor, 205-348-9209, Fax: 205-348-0867, E-mail: msmith@bamed.ua.edu.

University of Alberta, Faculty of Graduate Studies and Research, Program in Business Administration, Edmonton, AB T6G 2E1, Canada. Offers international business (MBA); leisure and sport management (MBA); natural resources and energy (MBA); technology commercialization (MBA); MBA/LL B; MBA/M Ag; MBA/M Eng; MBA/MF; MBA/PhD. *Accreditation:* AACSB. Part-time and evening/weekend programs available. *Faculty:* 77 full-time, 20 part-time/adjunct. *Students:* 131 full-time (56 women), 109 part-time (51 women). Average age 29. 525 applicants, 30% accepted, 90 enrolled. In 2006, 114 degrees awarded. *Degree requirements:* For master's, thesis or alternative. *Entrance requirements:* For master's, GMAT. Additional exam requirements/recommendations for international students: Required—TOEFL (minimum score 600 paper-based; 250 computer-based). *Application deadline:* For fall admission, 4/30 priority date for domestic students, 4/30 for international students. Applications are processed on a rolling basis. Application fee: $0. Electronic applications accepted. *Financial support:* Fellowships, research assistantships, teaching assistantships, career-related internships or fieldwork, scholarships/grants, health care benefits, and unspecified assistantships available. *Faculty research:* Natural resources and energy/management and policy/family enterprise/international business/healthcare research management. Total annual research expenditures: $1 million. *Unit head:* Dr. Douglas Olsen, Associate Dean, 780-492-5412, Fax: 780-492-7825. *Application contact:* Joan A. White, Secretary, 780-492-3679, Fax: 780-492-2024, E-mail: mba@ualberta.ca.

University of Central Florida, College of Business Administration, Department of Sport Business Management, Orlando, FL 32816. Offers MSBM. *Faculty:* 3 full-time (0 women), 1 part-time/adjunct (0 women). *Students:* 59 full-time (29 women); includes 15 minority (11 African Americans, 1 Asian American or Pacific Islander, 3 Hispanic Americans), 8 international. In 2006, 24 master's awarded. *Degree requirements:* For master's, thesis or alternative, internship. *Entrance requirements:* For master's, GMAT, minimum GPA of 3.0, letters of recommendation. Additional exam requirements/recommendations for international students: Required—TOEFL. *Application deadline:* For fall admission, 2/15 priority date for domestic students. Application fee: $30. Electronic applications accepted. *Expenses:* Tuition, state resident: full-time $6,167; part-time $257 per credit hour. Tuition, nonresident: full-time $22,790; part-time $950 per credit hour. *Financial support:* In 2006–07, 24 fellowships with partial tuition reimbursements (averaging $2,000 per year), 36 research assistantships with partial tuition reimbursements (averaging $6,000 per year) were awarded; teaching assistantships. *Unit head:* Dr. Richard Lapchick, Head.

University of Central Florida, College of Education, Department of Teaching and Learning Principles, Orlando, FL 32816. Offers art education (M Ed, MA); coaching (Certificate); educational media (M Ed); elementary education (M Ed, MA); English language arts education (M Ed, MA); foreign language education (Certificate); health and wellness (Certificate); K-8 mathematics and science education (M Ed, Certificate); mathematics education (M Ed, MA); music education (M Ed, MA); online educational media (Certificate); reading education (M Ed, MA, Certificate); science education (M Ed, MA); social science education (M Ed, MA); sports leadership (Certificate); vocational education (M Ed, MA); world studies education (Certificate); writing education (Certificate). Part-time and evening/weekend programs available. *Faculty:* 57 full-time (44 women), 62 part-time/adjunct (42 women). *Students:* 101 full-time (77 women), 323 part-time (269 women); includes 60 minority (24 African Americans, 13 Asian Americans or Pacific Islanders, 23 Hispanic Americans), 5 international. 221 applicants, 76% accepted, 115 enrolled. In 2006, 158 master's, 40 other advanced degrees awarded. *Degree requirements:* For Certificate, thesis or alternative. *Entrance requirements:* For degree, GRE General Test, minimum GPA of 3.0. Additional exam requirements/recommendations for international students: Required—TOEFL. *Application deadline:* For fall admission, 7/15 for domestic students; for spring admission, 12/15 for domestic students. Application fee: $30. Electronic applications accepted. *Expenses:* Tuition, state resident: full-time $6,167; part-time $257 per credit hour. Tuition, nonresident: full-time $22,790; part-time $950 per credit hour. *Financial support:* Fellowships with partial tuition reimbursements, research assistantships with partial tuition reimbursements, teaching assistantships with partial tuition reimbursements, career-related internships or fieldwork, Federal Work-Study, institutionally sponsored loans, tuition waivers (partial), and unspecified assistantships available. Financial award application deadline: 3/1; financial award applicants required to submit FAFSA. *Unit head:* Dr. Robert Williams, Chair, 407-823-1768, E-mail: rdwilliams@mail.ucf.edu. *Application contact:* Information Contact, 407-823-2053.

University of Dallas, Graduate School of Management, Irving, TX 75062-4736. Offers accounting (MBA, MS); business management (MBA); corporate finance (MBA, MM); engineering management (MBA, MM); entrepreneurship (MBA, MM); financial services (MBA, MM); global business (MBA, MM); health services management (MBA, MM); human resource management (MBA, MM, MS); information assurance (MBA, MM, MS); information technology (MBA, MM, MS); information technology service management (MBA); IT service management (MS); marketing (MM); marketing management (MBA); not-for-profit management (MBA); organization development (MBA); project management (MBA, MM); sports and entertainment management (MBA, MM); strategic leadership (MBA); supply chain management (MBA); supply chain management and market logistics (MM); telecommunications management (MBA, MM). *Accreditation:* ACBSP. Part-time and evening/weekend programs available. Postbaccalaureate distance learning degree programs offered (no on-campus study). *Faculty:* 26 full-time (5 women), 85 part-time/adjunct (18 women). *Students:* 227 full-time (98 women), 1,160 part-time (446 women); includes 473 minority (209 African Americans, 3 American Indian/Alaska Native, 143 Asian Americans or Pacific Islanders, 118 Hispanic Americans), 224 international. Average age 34. 556 applicants, 86% accepted, 291 enrolled. In 2006, 476 degrees awarded. *Entrance requirements:* Additional exam requirements/recommendations for international students: Required—TOEFL. *Application deadline:* Applications are processed on a rolling basis. Application fee: $50. Electronic applications accepted. *Expenses:* Contact institution. *Financial support:* In 2006–07, 468 students received support. Scholarships/grants and unspecified assistantships available. Financial award application deadline: 2/15; financial award applicants required to submit FAFSA. *Unit head:* Dr. J. Lee Whittington, Dean, 972-721-5230. *Application contact:* Sarah Stivison, Director of Graduate Admissions, 972-721-5198, Fax: 972-721-4009, E-mail: admiss@gsm.udallas.edu.

University of Florida, Graduate School, Warrington College of Business Administration, Programs in Business Administration, Gainesville, FL 32611. Offers accounting (MBA); arts administration (MBA); business strategy and public policy (MBA); competitive strategy (MBA); decision and information sciences (MBA); electronic commerce (MBA); finance (MBA); general business (MBA); global management (MBA); Graham-Buffett security analysis (MBA); health administration (MBA); human resources management (MBA); international studies (MBA); Latin American business (MBA); management (MBA); marketing (MBA); sports administration (MBA); JD/MBA; MBA/MS; MBA/PhD; MBA/Pharm D; MD/MBA. *Accreditation:* AACSB. Part-time and evening/weekend programs available. Postbaccalaureate distance learning degree programs offered. *Faculty:* 14. *Students:* 950 (282 women); includes 189 minority (31 African Americans, 2 American Indian/Alaska Native, 66 Asian Americans or Pacific Islanders, 90 Hispanic Americans) 56 international. In 2006, 481 degrees awarded. *Entrance requirements:* For master's, GMAT, minimum GPA of 3.0, interview. Additional exam requirements/recommendations for international students: Required—TOEFL (minimum score 550 paper-based; 213 computer-based). *Application deadline:* For fall admission, 4/15 for domestic students; for winter admission, 10/15 priority date for domestic students; for spring admission, 2/15 for domestic students. Applications are processed on a rolling basis. Application fee: $30. Electronic applications accepted. *Expenses:* Tuition, state resident: full-time $6,827. Tuition, nonresident: full-time $21,951. Required fees: $999. *Financial support:* Fellowships, research assistantships, teaching assistantships, career-related internships or fieldwork, scholarships/grants, and unspecified assistantships available. Support available to part-time students. Financial award application deadline: 2/15; financial award applicants required to submit FAFSA. *Faculty research:* Accounting, finance, insurance, management, real estate and urban analysis marketing. *Unit head:* Alex Sevilla, Director, 352-392-7992 Ext. 1206. *Application contact:* Patrick Foran, Associate Director of Admissions, 352-392-7992 Ext. 282, Fax: 352-392-8791, E-mail: patrick.foran@cba.ufl.edu.

The University of Iowa, Graduate College, College of Liberal Arts and Sciences, Program in Leisure Studies, Iowa City, IA 52242-1316. Offers leisure and recreational sport management (MA); therapeutic recreation (MA). *Faculty:* 4 full-time, 1 part-time/adjunct. *Students:* 16 full-time (11 women), 5 part-time (1 woman); includes 2 minority (both African Americans), 1 international. 21 applicants, 86% accepted, 16 enrolled. In 2006, 6 degrees awarded. *Degree requirements:* For master's, exam, thesis optional. *Entrance requirements:* For master's, GRE General Test, minimum GPA of 3.0. Additional exam requirements/recommendations for international students: Required—TOEFL (minimum score 550 paper-based; 213 computer-based; 81 iBT). *Application deadline:* For spring admission, 11/15 priority date for domestic students. Applications are processed on a rolling basis. Application fee: $60 ($85 for international students). Electronic applications accepted. *Financial support:* In 2006–07, 16 teaching assistantships with partial tuition reimbursements were awarded; fellowships, research assistantships with partial tuition reimbursements also available. Financial award applicants required to submit FAFSA. *Unit head:* Kenneth Mobily, Academic Coordinator, 319-335-0172, Fax: 319-335-3884.

University of Louisville, Graduate School, College of Education and Human Development, Department of Health and Sports Sciences, Program in Sport Administration, Louisville, KY 40292-0001. Offers MS. *Students:* 41 full-time (21 women), 22 part-time (7 women); includes 7 minority (all African Americans), 10 international. Average age 27. In 2006, 31 degrees awarded. Application fee: $50. *Unit head:* Dr. Anita Moorman, Program Head, 502-852-0553, Fax: 502-852-6683, E-mail: anita.moorman@louisville.edu.

University of Mary Hardin-Baylor, College of Business, Graduate Studies in Business Administration, Belton, TX 76513. Offers accounting (MBA); management (MBA); sport management (MBA). Part-time and evening/weekend programs available. *Faculty:* 10 full-time (3 women), 3 part-time/adjunct (1 woman). *Students:* 4 full-time (2 women), 19 part-time (10 women); includes 3 minority (all Hispanic Americans) Average age 24. In 2006, 9 degrees awarded. *Degree requirements:* For master's, practicum. *Entrance requirements:* For master's, GMAT, minimum GPA of 3.0, work experience, interview. *Application deadline:* For fall admission, 6/1 priority date for domestic students; for spring admission, 11/1 for domestic students. Applications are processed on a rolling basis. Application fee: $35 ($135 for international students). Electronic applications accepted. *Expenses:* Tuition: Full-time $8,910; part-time $495 per hour. Required fees: $906; $47 per hour. $30 per term. Tuition and fees vary according to course load. *Financial support:* Federal Work-Study and scholarships (for some active duty military personnel only) available. Financial award applicants required to submit FAFSA. *Unit head:* Dr. Chrisann Merriman, Director, 254-295-4647, E-mail: chrisann.merriman@umhb.edu.

University of Massachusetts Amherst, Graduate School, Isenberg School of Management, Department of Sport Management, Amherst, MA 01003. Offers MS, PhD, MBA/MS. Part-time programs available. *Faculty:* 12 full-time (3 women). *Students:* 17 full-time (7 women), 6 part-time (2 women); includes 2 minority (1 Asian American or Pacific Islander, 1 Hispanic American), 7 international. Average age 28. 69 applicants, 67% accepted, 12 enrolled. In 2006, 27 master's, 1 doctorate awarded. *Degree requirements:* For master's, thesis or alternative; for doctorate, thesis/dissertation. *Entrance requirements:* For master's, GMAT; for doctorate, GMAT or GRE. Additional exam requirements/recommendations for international students: Required—TOEFL (minimum score 530 paper-based; 197 computer-based). *Application deadline:* For fall admission, 2/1 priority date for domestic and international students. Applications are processed on a rolling basis. Application fee: $40 ($65 for international students). Electronic applications accepted. *Expenses:* Tuition, state resident: full-time $2,640; part-time $110 per credit. Tuition, nonresident: full-time $9,936; part-time $414 per credit. Required fees: $8,969; $3,129 per term. One-time fee: $257 full-time. Tuition and fees vary according to class time, course load, campus/location and reciprocity agreements. *Financial support:* In 2006–07, 14 research assistantships with full tuition reimbursements (averaging $6,058 per year), 17 teaching assistantships with full tuition reimbursements (averaging $7,208 per year) were awarded; fellowships with full tuition reimbursements, career-related internships or fieldwork, Federal Work-Study, scholarships/grants, traineeships, and unspecified assistantships also available. Support available to part-time students. Financial award application deadline: 2/1. *Unit head:* Dr. Lisa P. Masteralexis, Head, 413-545-5061, Fax: 413-577-0642, E-mail: lpmaster@sportstudy.umass.edu.

University of Miami, Graduate School, School of Education, Department of Exercise and Sport Sciences, Program in Sport Administration, Coral Gables, FL 33124. Offers MS Ed.

Part-time programs available. *Students:* 16 full-time (6 women), 16 part-time (8 women); includes 4 minority (2 African Americans, 2 Hispanic Americans), 4 international. Average age 24. 46 applicants, 76% accepted, 10 enrolled. In 2006, 14 degrees awarded. *Degree requirements:* For master's, special project, thesis optional. *Entrance requirements:* For master's, GRE General Test, GRE Subject Test. Additional exam requirements/recommendations for international students: Required—TOEFL (minimum score 550 paper-based; 212 computer-based). *Application deadline:* Applications are processed on a rolling basis. Application fee: $50. Electronic applications accepted. *Financial support:* In 2006–07, 27 students received support; fellowships, research assistantships, teaching assistantships, career-related internships or fieldwork, Federal Work-Study, institutionally sponsored loans, tuition waivers (full and partial), and unspecified assistantships available. Financial award application deadline: 3/1; financial award applicants required to submit FAFSA. *Faculty research:* Constitutional procedural due process, legal liability, tort law, moral development in sports administration, ethics intervention. *Unit head:* Dr. Jeremy S. Jordan, Coordinator, 305-284-8345, Fax: 305-284-3001, E-mail: ssjordan@miami.edu. *Application contact:* Marissa Stevenson, Graduate Admissions Coordinator, 305-284-2167, Fax: 305-284-3003, E-mail: mstevenson@miami.edu.

University of Michigan, Horace H. Rackham School of Graduate Studies, Division of Kinesiology, Ann Arbor, MI 48109. Offers kinesiology (MS, PhD); sport management (AM). Terminal master's awarded for partial completion of doctoral program. *Degree requirements:* For master's, thesis (for some programs); for doctorate, thesis/dissertation, oral defense of dissertation, comprehensive exam. *Entrance requirements:* For master's and doctorate, GRE General Test. Additional exam requirements/recommendations for international students: Required—TOEFL. Electronic applications accepted. Expenses: Contact institution. *Faculty research:* Motor development, exercise endocrinology, biomechanics, body composition and weight control, sport management.

University of Minnesota, Twin Cities Campus, Graduate School, College of Education and Human Development, School of Kinesiology, Minneapolis, MN 55455-0213. Offers adapted physical education (MA, PhD); biomechanics (MA); biomechanics and neural control (PhD); coaching (Certificate); developmental adapted physical education (M Ed); exercise physiology (MA, PhD); human factors/ergonomics (MA, PhD); international/comparative sport (MA, PhD); kinesiology (M Ed, MA, PhD); leisure services/management (MA, PhD); motor development (MA, PhD); motor learning/control (MA, PhD); outdoor education/recreation (MA, PhD); physical education (M Ed); recreation, park, and leisure studies (M Ed, MA, PhD); sport and exercise science (M Ed); sport management (M Ed, MA, PhD); sport psychology (MA, PhD); sport sociology (MA, PhD); therapeutic recreation (MA, PhD). Part-time programs available. *Faculty:* 14 full-time (6 women). *Students:* 142 full-time (70 women), 68 part-time (28 women); includes 9 minority (3 African Americans, 1 American Indian/Alaska Native, 2 Asian Americans or Pacific Islanders, 3 Hispanic Americans), 21 international. Average age 30. 186 applicants, 60% accepted, 88 enrolled. In 2006, 141 master's, 57 doctorates, 12 other advanced degrees awarded. Terminal master's awarded for partial completion of doctoral program. *Degree requirements:* For master's, final oral exam; for doctorate, thesis/dissertation, preliminary written/oral exam, final oral exam. *Entrance requirements:* For master's, GRE or MAT, minimum GPA of 3.0; for doctorate, GRE or MAT, minimum GPA of 3.0, writing sample. *Expenses:* Tuition, state resident: full-time $9,302; part-time $775 per credit. Tuition, nonresident: full-time $16,400; part-time $1,367 per credit. Full-time tuition and fees vary according to class time, course load, program, reciprocity agreements and student level. *Financial support:* In 2006–07, 1 fellowship (averaging $24,775 per year), 13 research assistantships with full tuition reimbursements (averaging $24,775 per year), 34 teaching assistantships with full tuition reimbursements (averaging $24,775 per year) were awarded; career-related internships or fieldwork, Federal Work-Study, institutionally sponsored loans, and tuition waivers (full and partial) also available. Support available to part-time students. *Faculty research:* Exercise for health promotion and disease prevention and management; female athletes and bone health; affordance perception-action; gender and youth sport and psychosocial outcomes; outdoor behavioral healthcare. Total annual research expenditures: $708,598. *Unit head:* Dr. Mary Jo Kane, Director, 612-625-3870, Fax: 612-626-7700, E-mail: maryjo@umn.edu. *Application contact:* Dr. Mary Bents, Associate Dean, 612-625-6501, Fax: 612-626-1580, E-mail: mbents@tc.umn.edu.

University of Nevada, Las Vegas, Graduate College, College of Education, Department of Sports Education Leadership, Las Vegas, NV 89154-9900. Offers M Ed, MS, PhD. *Faculty:* 6 full-time (3 women), 5 part-time/adjunct (1 woman). *Students:* 13 full-time (4 women), 26 part-time (4 women); includes 7 minority (5 African Americans, 1 American Indian/Alaska Native, 1 Asian American or Pacific Islander), 1 international. 21 applicants, 62% accepted, 9 enrolled. In 2006, 3 master's, 2 doctorates awarded. *Entrance requirements:* Additional exam requirements/recommendations for international students: Required—TOEFL (minimum score 550 paper-based; 213 computer-based; 80 iBT). *Application deadline:* For fall admission, 5/1 for domestic and international students; for spring admission, 10/1 for domestic and international students. Application fee: $60 ($75 for international students). Electronic applications accepted. *Financial support:* In 2006–07, 4 research assistantships (averaging $10,500 per year), 5 teaching assistantships (averaging $11,000 per year) were awarded; career-related internships or fieldwork, Federal Work-Study, institutionally sponsored loans, scholarships/grants, health care benefits, and unspecified assistantships also available. Support available to part-time students. *Unit head:* Dr. Monica Lounsbery, Chair, 702-895-5057. *Application contact:* Graduate College Admissions Evaluator, 702-895-3320, Fax: 702-895-4180, E-mail: gradcollege@unlv.edu.

University of New Brunswick Fredericton, School of Graduate Studies, Faculty of Kinesiology, Fredericton, NB E3B 5A3, Canada. Offers exercise and sport science (M Sc); sport and recreation administration (MA, MBA/MA); MBA/MA. Part-time programs available. *Faculty:* 16 full-time (6 women). *Students:* 45 full-time (20 women), 8 part-time (6 women). In 2006, 8 degrees awarded. *Degree requirements:* For master's, thesis (for some programs). *Entrance requirements:* For master's, minimum GPA of 3.0, written statement of research goals and interests. Additional exam requirements/recommendations for international students: Required—TOEFL (minimum score 600 paper-based; 250 computer-based), TWE (minimum score 5). *Application deadline:* For fall admission, 3/1 priority date for domestic students. Applications are processed on a rolling basis. Application fee: $50 Canadian dollars. Electronic applications accepted. *Financial support:* In 2006–07, 24 research assistantships, 23 teaching assistantships were awarded; fellowships with tuition reimbursements, career-related internships or fieldwork and scholarships/grants also available. *Unit head:* Dr. Chris Stevenson, Acting Director of Graduate Studies, 506-453-5063, Fax: 506-453-3511, E-mail: cls@unb.ca. *Application contact:* Linda O'Brien, Graduate Secretary, 506-453-4576, Fax: 506-453-3511, E-mail: lobrien@unb.ca.

University of New Haven, Graduate School, School of Business, Program in Business Administration, West Haven, CT 06516-1916. Offers accounting (MBA); business policy and strategy (MBA); finance (MBA); health care management (MBA); human resources management (MBA); international business (MBA); marketing (MBA); public relations (MBA); sports management (MBA); technology management (MBA); MBA/MPA; MBA/MSIE. Part-time and evening/weekend programs available. *Degree requirements:* For master's, thesis or alternative. *Entrance requirements:* For master's, GMAT.

University of New Haven, Graduate School, School of Business, Program in Sports Management, West Haven, CT 06516-1916. Offers MS.

The University of North Carolina at Chapel Hill, Graduate School, College of Arts and Sciences, Department of Exercise and Sport Science, Chapel Hill, NC 27599. Offers athletic training (MA); exercise physiology (MA); sport administration (MA). *Degree requirements:* For master's, thesis, comprehensive exam. *Entrance requirements:* For master's, GRE General Test, minimum GPA of 3.0. Additional exam requirements/recommendations for international students: Required—TOEFL (minimum score 550 paper-based). Electronic applications accepted. *Faculty research:* Mild head injury in sport, endocrine system's response to exercise, obesity and children, effect of aerobic exercise on cerebral bloodflow in elderly population.

The University of North Carolina at Charlotte, Graduate School, Belk College of Business Administration, Program in Sports Marketing Management, Charlotte, NC 28223-0001. Offers MS. *Expenses:* Tuition, state resident: full-time $2,719; part-time $170 per credit. Tuition, nonresident: full-time $12,926; part-time $808 per credit. Required fees: $1,555. *Application contact:* Kathy B. Giddings, Director of Graduate Admissions, 704-687-3366, Fax: 704-687-3279, E-mail: gradadm@email.uncc.edu.

University of Northern Colorado, Graduate School, College of Natural and Health Sciences, School of Sport and Exercise Science, Greeley, CO 80639. Offers exercise science (MS, PhD); sport administration (MS, PhD); sport pedagogy (MS, PhD). Part-time and evening/weekend programs available. *Faculty:* 12 full-time (6 women). *Students:* 69 full-time (18 women), 20 part-time (9 women); includes 7 minority (2 American Indian/Alaska Native, 3 Asian Americans or Pacific Islanders, 2 Hispanic Americans), 16 international. Average age 30. 140 applicants, 69% accepted, 31 enrolled. In 2006, 64 master's, 8 doctorates awarded. *Degree requirements:* For master's, comprehensive exam; for doctorate, thesis/dissertation, comprehensive exam. *Entrance requirements:* For master's, 2 letters of recommendation, resumé; for doctorate, GRE General Test, 3 letters of recommendation, resumé. *Application deadline:* Applications are processed on a rolling basis. Application fee: $50 ($60 for international students). Electronic applications accepted. *Expenses:* Tuition, state resident: full-time $5,118; part-time $213 per credit hour. Tuition, nonresident: full-time $14,832; part-time $618 per credit hour. Required fees: $674; $34 per credit hour. *Financial support:* In 2006–07, 71 students received support, including 6 fellowships (averaging $2,417 per year), 18 research assistantships (averaging $6,834 per year), 14 teaching assistantships (averaging $8,725 per year); unspecified assistantships also available. Financial award application deadline: 3/1; financial award applicants required to submit FAFSA. *Unit head:* Dr. Dianna Gray, Director, 970-351-2535, Fax: 970-351-1762.

University of Northern Iowa, Graduate College, College of Education, School of Health, Physical Education, and Leisure Services, Program in Leisure Services, Cedar Falls, IA 50614. Offers leisure services (Ed D); program administration (MA); youth/human services administration (MA). *Students:* 36 full-time (22 women), 14 part-time (7 women); includes 16 minority (14 African Americans, 2 Hispanic Americans), 15 international. 26 applicants, 69% accepted, 18 enrolled. In 2006, 13 degrees awarded. *Degree requirements:* For master's, thesis or alternative, comprehensive exam; for doctorate, thesis/dissertation. *Entrance requirements:* For master's, 3 years of educational experience, minimum GPA of 3.5; for doctorate, GRE. Additional exam requirements/recommendations for international students: Required—TOEFL (minimum score 500 paper-based; 180 computer-based; 61 iBT). *Application deadline:* Applications are processed on a rolling basis. Application fee: $30 ($50 for international students). Electronic applications accepted. *Expenses:* Tuition, state resident: full-time $5,936. Tuition, nonresident: full-time $14,074. *Financial support:* Career-related internships or fieldwork, Federal Work-Study, institutionally sponsored loans, tuition waivers (full), and unspecified assistantships available. Financial award application deadline: 2/1. *Unit head:* Dr. Samuel Lankford, Interim Director, 319-273-6840, Fax: 319-273-5958, E-mail: sam.lankford@uni.edu.

University of Rhode Island, Graduate School, College of Business Administration, Kingston, RI 02881. Offers accounting (MS); business administration (PhD), including finance, management, management science and information systems, marketing; finance (MBA); international business (MBA); international sports management (MBA); management (MBA); management science (MBA), including management information systems, manufacturing; marketing (MBA). *Accreditation:* AACSB. In 2006, 86 master's, 1 doctorate awarded. *Entrance requirements:* For master's and doctorate, GMAT. Additional exam requirements/recommendations for international students: Required—TOEFL. *Application deadline:* For fall admission, 4/15 priority date for domestic students. Applications are processed on a rolling basis. Application fee: $35. *Expenses:* Tuition, state resident: full-time $6,032; part-time $335 per credit. Tuition, nonresident: full-time $17,288; part-time $960 per credit. Required fees: $65 per credit. $30 per semester. One-time fee: $80 part-time. *Financial support:* Unspecified assistantships available. *Unit head:* Mark Higgins, Dean, 401-874-2337. *Application contact:* Dr. Laura Beauvais, Director of Graduate Programs, 401-874-4341.

University of San Francisco, College of Arts and Sciences, Program in Sport Management, San Francisco, CA 94117-1080. Offers MA. Evening/weekend programs available. *Faculty:* 4 full-time (0 women), 21 part-time/adjunct (8 women). *Students:* 183 full-time (78 women), 6 part-time (1 woman); includes 48 minority (13 African Americans, 19 Asian Americans or Pacific Islanders, 16 Hispanic Americans), 18 international. Average age 27. 214 applicants, 69% accepted, 68 enrolled. In 2006, 87 degrees awarded. *Degree requirements:* For master's, thesis or alternative. *Entrance requirements:* For master's, interview, minimum GPA of 2.75. *Application deadline:* For fall admission, 3/31 priority date for domestic students. Applications are processed on a rolling basis. Application fee: $55 ($65 for international students). *Expenses:* Tuition: Full-time $17,370; part-time $965 per unit. Tuition and fees vary according to degree level, campus/location and program. *Financial support:* In 2006–07, 120 students received support. Career-related internships or fieldwork, Federal Work-Study, and institutionally sponsored loans available. Financial award application deadline: 3/2; financial award applicants required to submit FAFSA. *Faculty research:* Media and sports, sports marketing, sports law, management and organization. *Unit head:* Daniel Rascher, Graduate Director, 415-422-2678, Fax: 415-422-6267, E-mail: sport.management@usfca.edu.

University of South Carolina, The Graduate School, College of Hospitality, Retail, and Sport Management, Department of Sport and Entertainment Management, Columbia, SC 29208. Offers live sport and entertainment events (MS); public assembly facilities management (MS). Part-time and evening/weekend programs available. Postbaccalaureate distance learning degree programs offered (minimal on-campus study). *Degree requirements:* For master's, thesis optional. *Entrance requirements:* For master's, GRE General Test or GMAT (preferred), minimum GPA of 3.0, 1 year of management experience. Electronic applications accepted. Expenses: Contact institution. *Faculty research:* Public assembly marketing, operations, box office, booking and scheduling, law/economic impacts.

University of Southern Maine, College of Education and Human Development, Educational Leadership Program, Portland, ME 04104-9300. Offers assistant principal (Certificate); athletic administration (Certificate); educational leadership (MS Ed, CAS); middle-level education (Certificate). *Accreditation:* NCATE. Part-time and evening/weekend programs available. Postbaccalaureate distance learning degree programs offered (minimal on-campus study). *Faculty:* 7 full-time (1 woman), 5 part-time/adjunct (2 women). *Students:* 4 full-time (3 women), 111 part-time (63 women), 1 international. 20 applicants, 65% accepted, 8 enrolled. In 2006, 36 master's, 23 CASs awarded. *Degree requirements:* For master's, thesis or alternative, practicum; for other advanced degree, thesis or alternative. *Entrance requirements:* For master's, GRE General Test or MAT; for other advanced degree, master's degree. Additional exam requirements/recommendations for international students: Required—TOEFL. *Application deadline:* For fall admission, 2/1 for domestic students; for spring admission, 9/15 for domestic students. Application fee: $50. Electronic applications accepted. *Expenses:* Tuition, state resident: full-time $4,860; part-time $270 per credit hour. Tuition, nonresident: full-time $13,572; part-time $754 per credit hour. Required fees: $222 per semester. Tuition and fees vary according to course load. *Financial support:* In 2006–07, 3 students received support, including 2 research assistantships with tuition reimbursements available (averaging $4,500 per year); career-related internships or fieldwork, Federal Work-Study, institutionally sponsored loans, scholarships/grants, and unspecified assistantships also available. Financial award application deadline: 3/1; financial award applicants required to submit FAFSA. *Unit head:* Dr. James Curry, Chair, Professional Education Department, 270-780-5400, Fax: 270-780-5674,

Sports Management

University of Southern Maine (continued)

E-mail: jcurry@usm.maine.edu. *Application contact:* Robin Audesse, Associate Director of Graduate Admissions, 207-780-5306, Fax: 207-780-5193, E-mail: raudesse@usm.maine.edu.

University of Southern Mississippi, Graduate School, College of Health, School of Human Performance and Recreation, Hattiesburg, MS 39406-0001. Offers human performance (MS, Ed D, PhD); interscholastic athletic administration (MS); recreation and leisure management (MS); sport administration (MS); sport and coaching education (MS); sport management (MS); sports and high performance materials (MS). Part-time and evening/weekend programs available. *Faculty:* 15 full-time (3 women). *Students:* 63 full-time (21 women), 36 part-time (11 women); includes 16 minority (13 African Americans, 1 Asian American or Pacific Islander, 2 Hispanic Americans), 6 international. Average age 27. 75 applicants, 64% accepted, 38 enrolled. In 2006, 37 master's, 5 doctorates awarded. *Degree requirements:* For master's, thesis optional; for doctorate, thesis/dissertation, comprehensive exam, registration. *Entrance requirements:* For master's, GRE General Test, minimum GPA of 2.75 in last 60 hours; for doctorate, GRE General Test, minimum GPA of 3.5. Additional exam requirements/recommendations for international students: Required—TOEFL. *Application deadline:* For fall admission, 3/1 priority date for domestic students, 3/1 for international students. Applications are processed on a rolling basis. Application fee: $25 ($30 for international students). Electronic applications accepted. *Financial support:* In 2006–07, 5 research assistantships with full tuition reimbursements (averaging $10,426 per year), 10 teaching assistantships with full tuition reimbursements (averaging $10,426 per year) were awarded; fellowships, career-related internships or fieldwork, Federal Work-Study, institutionally sponsored loans, and tuition waivers (partial) also available. Financial award application deadline: 3/15. *Faculty research:* Exercise physiology, health behaviors, resource management, activity interaction, site development. *Unit head:* Dr. Louis Marciani, Director, 601-266-5379, Fax: 601-266-4445. *Application contact:* Dr. Dennis Phillips, Graduate Coordinator, 601-266-5379, Fax: 601-266-4445.

The University of Tennessee, Graduate School, College of Education, Health and Human Sciences, Department of Exercise, Sport, and Leisure Studies, Knoxville, TN 37996. Offers exercise science (MS, PhD), including biomechanics/sports medicine, exercise physiology; recreation and leisure studies (MS); sport management (MS); sport studies (MS, PhD); therapeutic recreation (MS). Part-time and evening/weekend programs available. *Students:* 28 (21 women); includes 1 minority (African American) 4 international. In 2006, 5 degrees awarded. *Degree requirements:* For master's, thesis optional. *Entrance requirements:* For master's, minimum GPA of 2.7. Additional exam requirements/recommendations for international students: Required—TOEFL. *Application deadline:* For fall admission, 2/1 priority date for domestic students. Applications are processed on a rolling basis. Application fee: $35. Electronic applications accepted. *Expenses:* Tuition, state resident: full-time $5,574. Tuition, nonresident: full-time $16,840. Required fees: $792. *Financial support:* In 2006–07, 2 fellowships, 1 research assistantship, 24 teaching assistantships were awarded; career-related internships or fieldwork, Federal Work-Study, institutionally sponsored loans, and unspecified assistantships also available. Financial award application deadline: 2/1; financial award applicants required to submit FAFSA. *Unit head:* Dr. Edward Howley, Head, 865-974-8555, Fax: 865-974-5781, E-mail: ehowley@utk.edu.

University of the Incarnate Word, School of Graduate Studies and Research, H-E-B School of Business and Administration, Programs in Administration, San Antonio, TX 78209-6397. Offers adult education (MAA); applied administration (MAA); communication arts (MAA); English (MAA); instructional technology (MAA); international business (Certificate); multidisciplinary sciences (MAA); nutrition (MAA); organizational development (MAA, Certificate); project management (Certificate); sports management (MAA); urban administration (MAA). *Students:* 1 (woman) full-time, 161 part-time (102 women); includes 17 African Americans, 1 American Indian/Alaska Native, 82 Hispanic Americans, 18 international. Average age 34. In 2006, 78 degrees awarded. *Entrance requirements:* For master's, GMAT, GRE, MAT. Additional exam requirements/recommendations for international students: Required—TOEFL. *Application deadline:* For fall admission, 8/15 priority date for domestic students; for spring admission, 12/31 for domestic students. Applications are processed on a rolling basis. Application fee: $20. *Expenses:* Tuition: Part-time $570 per credit hour. Required fees: $54 per credit hour. One-time fee: $195 part-time. Tuition and fees vary according to degree level. *Financial support:* Federal Work-Study and scholarships/grants available. *Unit head:* Dr. Dan Dominguez, MAA Director, 210-829-3180, Fax: 210-805-3564, E-mail: domingue@uiwtx.edu. *Application contact:* Andrea Cyterski-Acosta, Dean of Enrollment, 210-829-6005, Fax: 210-829-3921, E-mail: cyterski@uiwtx.edu.

University of the Incarnate Word, School of Graduate Studies and Research, H-E-B School of Business and Administration, Programs in Business Administration, San Antonio, TX 78209-6397. Offers international business (MBA); sports management (MBA); MBA/MSN. *Accreditation:* ACBSP. Part-time and evening/weekend programs available. *Students:* 19 full-time (13 women), 219 part-time (120 women); includes 123 minority (13 African Americans, 3 American Indian/Alaska Native, 4 Asian Americans or Pacific Islanders, 103 Hispanic Americans), 35 international. Average age 31. In 2006, 99 degrees awarded. *Entrance requirements:* For master's, GMAT. Additional exam requirements/recommendations for international students: Required—TOEFL. *Application deadline:* For fall admission, 8/15 priority date for domestic students; for spring admission, 12/31 for domestic students. Applications are processed on a rolling basis. Application fee: $20. *Expenses:* Tuition: Part-time $570 per credit hour. Required fees: $54 per credit hour. One-time fee: $195 part-time. Tuition and fees vary according to degree level. *Financial support:* Federal Work-Study, scholarships/grants, and tuition waivers (partial) available. Financial award application deadline: 5/31. *Faculty research:* Small business, Mexico/U.S. business, organizational development. *Unit head:* Dr. Connie Green, MBA Director, 210-829-3182, Fax: 210-805-3564, E-mail: greenc@uiwtx.edu. *Application contact:* Andrea Cyterski-Acosta, Dean of Enrollment, 210-829-6005, Fax: 210-829-3921, E-mail: cyterski@uiwtx.edu.

University of the Incarnate Word, School of Graduate Studies and Research, School of Nursing and Health Professions, Program in Human Performance, San Antonio, TX 78209-6397. Offers kinesiology (MS); sports management (MS). *Students:* Average age 27. In 2006, 3 degrees awarded. *Entrance requirements:* Additional exam requirements/recommendations for international students: Required—TOEFL. *Application deadline:* For fall admission, 8/15 priority date for domestic students; for spring admission, 12/31 for domestic students. Applications are processed on a rolling basis. Application fee: $20. *Expenses:* Tuition: Part-time $570 per credit hour. Required fees: $54 per credit hour. One-time fee: $195 part-time. Tuition and fees vary according to degree level. *Financial support:* Federal Work-Study and scholarships/grants available. *Unit head:* Dr. William Carleton, Coordinator, 210-829-3966, Fax: 210-829-3174, E-mail: carleton@uiwtx.edu. *Application contact:* Andrea Cyterski-Acosta, Dean of Enrollment, 210-829-6005, Fax: 210-829-3921, E-mail: cyterski@uiwtx.edu.

University of Wisconsin–La Crosse, Office of University Graduate Studies, College of Science and Health, Department of Exercise and Sport Science, Program in Sport Administration, La Crosse, WI 54601-3742. Offers MS. Part-time programs available. *Students:* 29 full-time (13 women), 29 part-time (5 women); includes 3 minority (2 African Americans, 1 American Indian/Alaska Native). Average age 28. 48 applicants, 69% accepted, 7 enrolled. In 2006, 39 degrees awarded. *Degree requirements:* For master's, internship, thesis optional. *Entrance requirements:* For master's, minimum GPA of 2.85, course work in anatomy and physiology. Additional exam requirements/recommendations for international students: Required—TOEFL (minimum score 550 paper-based; 213 computer-based). *Application deadline:* For fall admission, 3/1 priority date for domestic students. Applications are processed on a rolling basis. Application fee: $45. *Financial support:* In 2006–07, 13 research assistantships (averaging $6,480 per year) were awarded; career-related internships or fieldwork, Federal Work-Study, institutionally sponsored loans, health care benefits, and unspecified assistantships also available. Financial award application deadline: 3/15; financial award applicants required to submit FAFSA. *Faculty research:* Sport economics, sport sponsorship, leadership behaviors in sport, management/leadership competencies, team culture in sports. *Unit head:* Dr. David Waters, Director, 608-785-8167, Fax: 608-785-8674, E-mail: waters.davi@uwlax.edu. *Application contact:* Kathryn Kiefer, Associate Director of Admissions, 608-785-8939, E-mail: admissions@uwlax.edu.

Valparaiso University, Graduate Division, Program in Sports Administration, Valparaiso, IN 46383. Offers MS, JD/MS. Part-time and evening/weekend programs available. *Students:* 34 full-time (12 women), 17 part-time (7 women); includes 5 minority (all African Americans) Average age 26. In 2006, 18 degrees awarded. *Entrance requirements:* For master's, minimum GPA of 3.0. Additional exam requirements/recommendations for international students: Required—TOEFL (minimum score 550 paper-based; 213 computer-based). *Application deadline:* Applications are processed on a rolling basis. Application fee: $30 ($50 for international students). Electronic applications accepted. *Expenses:* Tuition: Part-time $390 per credit hour. Required fees: $60 per term. Tuition and fees vary according to program. *Financial support:* Available to part-time students. Applicants required to submit FAFSA. *Application contact:* Jamie Haney, Coordinator of Recruitment Activities, 219-464-5313, Fax: 219-464-5381, E-mail: jamie.haney@valpo.edu.

Washington State University, Graduate School, College of Education, Department of Educational Leadership and Counseling Psychology, Pullman, WA 99164. Offers counseling psychology (Ed M, MA, PhD); educational leadership (M Ed, MA, Ed D, PhD); educational psychology (Ed M, MA, PhD); higher education (Ed M, MA, Ed D, PhD), including higher education administration (PhD), sport management (PhD), student affairs (PhD); higher education with sport management (Ed M). *Accreditation:* NCATE. *Faculty:* 25. *Students:* 109 full-time (63 women), 54 part-time (34 women); includes 42 minority (11 African Americans, 2 American Indian/Alaska Native, 12 Asian Americans or Pacific Islanders, 17 Hispanic Americans). Average age 34. 107 applicants, 67% accepted, 30 enrolled. In 2006, 33 master's, 20 doctorates awarded. Terminal master's awarded for partial completion of doctoral program. *Degree requirements:* For master's, thesis (for some programs), oral exam or written exam, comprehensive exam (for some programs); for doctorate, thesis/dissertation, oral and written exams, comprehensive exam. *Entrance requirements:* For master's and doctorate, GRE General Test, minimum GPA of 3.0, 3 letters of recommendation. Additional exam requirements/recommendations for international students: Required—TOEFL (minimum score 550 paper-based; 213 computer-based). *Application deadline:* For fall admission, 3/1 for domestic and international students; for spring admission, 10/1 for domestic students, 7/1 for international students. Application fee: $50. *Expenses:* Tuition, state resident: full-time $7,066. Tuition, nonresident: full-time $17,204. *Financial support:* In 2006–07, research assistantships (averaging $13,917 per year), teaching assistantships (averaging $13,056 per year) were awarded; career-related internships or fieldwork, Federal Work-Study, institutionally sponsored loans, scholarships/grants, tuition waivers (partial), and unspecified assistantships also available. Financial award application deadline: 4/1; financial award applicants required to submit FAFSA. *Faculty research:* Attentional processes, cross cultural psychology, faculty development in higher education. Total annual research expenditures: $854,827. *Unit head:* Dr. Phyllis Erdman, Chair, 509-335-9117. *Application contact:* Graduate School Admissions, 800-GRADWSU, Fax: 509-335-1949, E-mail: gradsch@wsu.edu.

Wayne State University, College of Education, Division of Kinesiology, Health and Sports Studies, Detroit, MI 48202. Offers health education (M Ed); kinesiology (M Ed); physical education (M Ed); recreation and park services (MA); sports administration (MA). *Faculty:* 9 full-time (2 women). *Students:* 40 full-time (16 women), 73 part-time (24 women); includes 25 minority (22 African Americans, 1 Asian American or Pacific Islander, 2 Hispanic Americans), 6 international. Average age 31. 39 applicants, 95% accepted, 26 enrolled. In 2006, 39 degrees awarded. *Degree requirements:* For master's, thesis (for some programs). *Entrance requirements:* For master's, GRE General Test. Additional exam requirements/recommendations for international students: Required—TOEFL; Recommended—TWE (minimum score 6). *Application deadline:* For fall admission, 7/1 for domestic students, 6/1 for international students; for winter admission, 10/1 for international students; for spring admission, 2/1 for international students. Application fee: $30 ($50 for international students). Electronic applications accepted. *Financial support:* In 2006–07, 3 research assistantships with tuition reimbursements (averaging $13,222 per year), 2 teaching assistantships with tuition reimbursements (averaging $13,222 per year) were awarded; career-related internships or fieldwork also available. *Faculty research:* Fitness in urban children, motor development of crack babies, effects of caffeine on metabolism/exercise, body composition of elite youth sports participants, systematic observation of teaching. Total annual research expenditures: $437,871. *Unit head:* Dr. Sally Erbaugh, Assistant Dean, 313-577-6210, Fax: 313-577-5999, E-mail: serbaugh@coe.wayne.edu. *Application contact:* John Wirth, Assistant Professor, 313-993-7972, Fax: 313-577-5999, E-mail: johnwirth@wayne.edu.

Webber International University, Graduate School of Business, Babson Park, FL 33827-0096. Offers accounting (MBA); management (MBA); sports management (MBA). Part-time and evening/weekend programs available. *Degree requirements:* For master's, thesis or alternative. *Entrance requirements:* For master's, previous course work in financial and managerial accounting. Additional exam requirements/recommendations for international students: Required—TOEFL. *Faculty research:* Finance strategy, market research, investments, intranet.

See Close-Up on page 375.

West Chester University of Pennsylvania, Graduate Studies, School of Health Sciences, Department of Kinesiology, West Chester, PA 19383. Offers driver education (Certificate); exercise and sport physiology (MS); physical education (MS); sport and athletic administration (MSA). Part-time and evening/weekend programs available. *Students:* 9 full-time (6 women), 30 part-time (8 women); includes 2 African Americans, 1 Hispanic American, 1 international. Average age 29. 35 applicants, 94% accepted, 12 enrolled. In 2006, 21 degrees awarded. *Degree requirements:* For master's, thesis optional. *Entrance requirements:* For master's, GRE or MAT, interview. *Application deadline:* For fall admission, 4/15 priority date for domestic students; for spring admission, 10/15 for domestic students. Applications are processed on a rolling basis. Application fee: $35. *Financial support:* In 2006–07, 7 research assistantships with full tuition reimbursements were awarded; unspecified assistantships also available. Support available to part-time students. Financial award application deadline: 2/15; financial award applicants required to submit FAFSA. *Faculty research:* Weight lifting and type 1 diabetes mellitus, martial arts, sexual harassment in sports. *Unit head:* Dr. Raymond Zetts, Chair, 610-436-2610, E-mail: czetts@wcupa.edu. *Application contact:* Dr. Sheri Melton, Graduate Coordinator, 610-436-2610, E-mail: smelton@wcupa.edu.

Western Illinois University, School of Graduate Studies, College of Education and Human Services, Department of Kinesiology, Program in Sport Management, Macomb, IL 61455-1390. Offers MS. Part-time programs available. *Students:* 37 full-time (15 women), 13 part-time (2 women); includes 4 minority (2 African Americans, 2 Hispanic Americans), 1 international. Average age 25. 48 applicants, 75% accepted. In 2006, 23 degrees awarded. *Entrance requirements:* For master's, minimum GPA of 3.0. Additional exam requirements/recommendations for international students: Required—TOEFL (minimum score 550 paper-based; 213 computer-based; 80 iBT). *Application deadline:* Applications are processed on a rolling basis. Application fee: $30. Electronic applications accepted. *Expenses:* Tuition, state resident: part-time $200 per credit hour. Tuition, nonresident: part-time $400 per credit hour. *Financial support:* In 2006–07, 22 students received support, including 20 research assistantships (averaging $6,568 per year), 2 teaching assistantships (averaging $7,576 per year). *Unit head:* Dr. Darlene Young, Graduate Committee Chairperson, 309-298-1981.

Western Michigan University, Graduate College, College of Education, Department of Health, Physical Education and Recreation, Kalamazoo, MI 49008-5202. Offers administration (MA); athletic training (MA); coaching and sports studies (MA); exercise science (MA); motor development (MA); physical education (MA); special education for handicapped children (MA).

West Virginia University, School of Physical Education, Morgantown, WV 26506. Offers athletic coaching (MS); athletic training (MS); exercise physiology (Ed D); physical education/

teacher education (MS, Ed D), including administration of physical education (Ed D), curriculum and instruction (Ed D), motor development (Ed D), special physical education (Ed D); sport management (MS); sport psychology (MS, Ed D). *Degree requirements:* For doctorate, thesis/dissertation, oral exam, comprehensive exam. *Entrance requirements:* For master's, GRE or MAT, minimum GPA of 3.0; for doctorate, GRE General Test or MAT, minimum GPA of 3.5. Additional exam requirements/recommendations for international students: Required—TOEFL (minimum score 550 paper-based; 213 computer-based). Electronic applications accepted. *Expenses:* Tuition, state resident: full-time $4,926; part-time $276 per credit hour. Tuition, nonresident: full-time $14,278; part-time $796 per credit hour. Tuition and fees vary according to program. *Faculty research:* Sport psychosociology, teacher education, exercise psychology, counseling.

Wichita State University, Graduate School, College of Education, Department of Kinesiology and Sport Studies, Wichita, KS 67260. Offers physical education (M Ed), including exercise science and wellness; sports administration (M Ed), including exercise science and wellness. Part-time programs available. *Degree requirements:* For master's, thesis optional. *Entrance requirements:* For master's, minimum GPA of 2.75. Additional exam requirements/recommendations for international students: Required—TOEFL. Electronic applications accepted.

Wingate University, Program in Education, Wingate, NC 28174-0159. Offers educational leadership (MA Ed); elementary education (MA Ed, MAT); physical education (MA Ed); sport administration (MA Ed). *Accreditation:* NCATE. Part-time and evening/weekend programs available. *Faculty:* 4 full-time (3 women), 4 part-time/adjunct (1 woman). *Students:* 1 (woman) full-time, 127 part-time (96 women); includes 2 minority (both African Americans) Average age 35. 19 applicants, 58% accepted, 11 enrolled. In 2006, 12 degrees awarded. *Degree requirements:* For master's, portfolio. *Entrance requirements:* For master's, GRE General Test or MAT, teaching certificate (MA Ed). *Application deadline:* For fall admission, 8/15 priority date for domestic students; for spring admission, 12/15 for domestic students. Applications are processed on a rolling basis. Application fee: $0. *Expenses:* Tuition: Full-time $3,330; part-time $185 per credit hour. *Financial support:* In 2006–07, 20 students received support. Scholarships/grants available. Support available to part-time students. Financial award applicants required to submit FAFSA. *Faculty research:* Teaching/learning styles, principles of teaching, homework, stress management, student's rights. *Unit head:* Dr. Robert Shaw, Dean, Thayer School of Education, 704-233-8128, Fax: 704-233-8273, E-mail: rshaw@wingate.edu. *Application contact:* Marsha Luke, Secretary, Thayer School of Education, 704-233-8127, Fax: 704-233-8273, E-mail: mluke@wingate.edu.

Xavier University, College of Social Sciences, Health and Education, Department of Sports Studies, Cincinnati, OH 45207. Offers sport administration (M Ed). Part-time and evening/weekend programs available. *Faculty:* 3 full-time (1 woman), 8 part-time/adjunct (3 women). *Students:* 25 full-time (17 women), 53 part-time (33 women); includes 11 minority (10 African Americans, 1 Hispanic American). Average age 28. 52 applicants, 75% accepted, 28 enrolled. In 2006, 49 degrees awarded. *Degree requirements:* For master's, internship, research proposal. *Entrance requirements:* For master's, GRE or MAT, minimum GPA of 2.8. Additional exam requirements/recommendations for international students: Required—TOEFL (minimum score 550 paper-based; 213 computer-based). *Application deadline:* For fall admission, 8/15 priority date for domestic students. Applications are processed on a rolling basis. Application fee: $35. Electronic applications accepted. *Expenses:* Tuition: Part-time $462 per credit hour. Part-time tuition and fees vary according to degree level, campus/location and program. *Financial support:* Career-related internships or fieldwork, scholarships/grants, and unspecified assistantships available. Support available to part-time students. Financial award applicants required to submit FAFSA. *Faculty research:* Sport management, youth sport, coaching education, sport medicine, sport economics. *Unit head:* Dr. Douglas Olberding, Chair, 513-745-3653, Fax: 513-745-4291, E-mail: olberding@xavier.edu. *Application contact:* Roger Bosse, Interim Director of Graduate Studies, 513-745-3357, Fax: 513-745-1048, E-mail: bosse@xavier.edu.

BARRY UNIVERSITY

School of Human Performance and Leisure Sciences

Program of Study

Through Barry University's School of Human Performance and Leisure Studies (HPLS), students can earn the Master of Science in movement science, with specializations in athletic training, biomechanics, exercise science, and sport and exercise psychology; the Master of Science in sport management; or the Master of Science in sport management/Master of Business Administration (M.S./M.B.A.).

In the 36-credit M.S. in movement science program, the athletic training specialization combines both the theory and practice that prepare students for a leadership position as an allied health practitioner in athletic training, such as in college/university athletic training administration, clinical administration, athletic training curriculum clinical education, and clinical research in any athletic training setting. Students can prepare for predoctoral research by choosing the thesis option. With the biomechanics specialization, students are well prepared for a career as a movement analyst in orthopedics, coaching, teaching, sports medicine, and research. Graduates can also continue their research and study at the doctoral level. Exercise science students receive training for career opportunities in fitness and wellness, with emphasis on developing professional practices in clinical settings and on exercise physiology research. The 36-credit curriculum offers advanced course work as well as extensive opportunities for research and clinical practice in the state-of-the-art Human Performance Laboratory. Sport and exercise psychology provides the basis for understanding the thought processes and attitudes of athletes and individuals involved in sport or exercise activities. Since sport psychology and exercise psychology are two separate subdisciplines, they are two distinct concentrations within the graduate degree program. The sport psychology curriculum includes courses in performance enhancement, motor learning and development, and psychophysiology of human performance. The exercise psychology track emphasizes courses in exercise psychology and health psychology. Students in the movement science program who do not choose a specialization can customize a program of advanced study, which requires a total of 36 credits of course work.

The 36-credit M.S. in sport management combines both academic excellence and practical experience to prepare students for opportunities in management in a variety of sport, recreation, and health promotion areas, including arena and dome management, amateur and professional sports, high school and college athletics, resort and tourism industries, parks and recreational centers, and fitness and wellness centers. This program is designed for working professionals, with evening and weekend classes available.

The 57-credit M.S./M.B.A. program provides students with both sport industry–specific skills and in-depth business knowledge. A combination of courses in the Department of Sport and Exercise Science and the Andreas School of Business gives students the opportunity to develop top management, marketing, and financial skills and allows students to develop a comprehensive knowledge of the sport enterprise.

Research Facilities

Barry's Health and Sports Center's state-of-the-art athletic training facility serves as a working medical area for Barry's top-ranked Division II athletics program. The facility is equipped with the most modern treatment modalities available in the field. Barry's 780-square-foot Biomechanics Lab contains the latest equipment and computer software programs used for analyzing human movement. The hands-on experience laboratory enables students to gain the skills necessary to correctly apply selected quantitative movement analysis techniques to activities of daily living, sports, and the workplace. The equipment includes high-speed cameras (used for 3-D high-speed videography); force-measurement devices, such as Biodex; electromyography; and computer software, such as Labview. The 2,100-square-foot Human Performance Laboratory is equipped for cycle ergometer and treadmill exercise testing, oxygen uptake measures, body composition assessment, blood analyses, pulmonary function analyses, and twelve-lead EKG assessment. The Performance Behavior Lab is equipped with the latest hardware and software, as well as equipment that allows for research opportunities with a variety of psychophysiological recordings, including electroencephalography (EEG), evoked related potentials (ERP), electromyography (EMG), heart rate (HR), galvanic skin response (GSR), respiration breathing (RB), and skin temperature (ST). A new clinical space enables students to learn and practice sport psychology intervention and counseling skills under the guidance of the faculty. The facility includes two observation rooms with one-way mirrors, in which students practice and observe real-time interventions with athletes. Digital video analysis equipment allows for structured performance recall as an effective tool in enhancing athletic performance and polishing students' counseling/psychological intervention skills. The proximity of the classrooms and computer lab makes the clinic a convenient learning environment.

Financial Aid

Financial aid is available for qualified students. Some programs offer assistantships and/or scholarships; students should contact the School for more details. Barry University also participates in the Federal Family Loan Program and applicable state of Florida financial aid programs. Additional information is available from the Associate Director of Financial Aid (phone: 305-899-3673; e-mail: finaid@mail.barry.edu).

Cost of Study

Tuition for 2006–07 was $725 per credit hour; fees were additional.

Living and Housing Costs

Campus housing is available for full-time graduate students, space permitting. Costs range from $3500 to $4900 per semester. Barry University provides assistance in locating off-campus housing.

Student Group

The majority of graduate students are studying part-time in evening and weekend classes.

Location

The University's 122-acre campus is located in Miami Shores, which is between the cities of Miami and Fort Lauderdale. This ideal location provides students with access to one of the nation's most dynamic multicultural environments and all of its business, cultural, and recreational opportunities.

The University and The School

Barry University is an independent, coeducational university, with a history of distinguished graduate programs. Founded in 1940, the University has grown steadily in size and diversity, while maintaining a low student-faculty ratio, thus providing for the individual needs of its academic community. Three departments make up the School of Human Performance and Leisure Sciences: the Department of Sport and Exercise Sciences, the Department of Intercollegiate Athletics, and the Department of Campus Recreation and Wellness.

Applying

All applicants should have a bachelor's degree from a regionally accredited or internationally listed institution, but specific course work prerequisites vary by program. In general, students should submit the completed application, the application fee, two copies of official transcripts, GRE or GMAT scores (depending on the program), two letters of recommendation, and a short essay. Applications are processed on a rolling basis. An interview may be required. Students should check online for specific requirements.

Correspondence and Information

Department of Sport and Exercise Sciences
School of Human Performance and Leisure Sciences
Barry University
11300 Northeast Second Avenue
Miami Shores, Florida 33161-6695
Phone: 305-899-3490 or 3550
        800-756-6000 Ext. 3490 (toll-free)
E-mail: sportsciences@mail.barry.edu
Web site: http://www.barry.edu/hpls

Barry University

THE FACULTY AND THEIR RESEARCH

G. Jean Cerra, Professor and Dean; Ph.D., Missouri–Columbia.

Paul Choi, Assistant Professor and Coordinator of Sport Management–Golf Industry; Ph.D., Oklahoma State. Developing a golf management competencies model, investigating economic impacts and consumer behavior in golf.

Carl Cramer, Professor and Director of Athletic Training Programs; Ed.D., Kansas State. Athletic training academic program structure and content.

Gualberto Cremades, Associate Professor and Coordinator of Sport and Exercise Psychology; Ed.D., Ph.D., Houston. Psychophysiological aspects of human performance, using techniques such as electroencephalography (EEG) recordings to measure brain wave activity and electromyography (EMG) to measure muscle activation.

Ann Gibson, Associate Professor of Exercise Science; Ph.D., New Mexico. Body composition, gender differences in performance and responses to exercise, physical activity and aging, physiological responses to altitude.

Leta Hicks, Associate Professor and Director of Graduate Programs; Ed.D., Oklahoma State. Wellness education in middle schools, physical activity for the older adult population.

Sharon Kegeles, Assistant Professor and Facilitator of Sport Management–Diving Industry; M.S., Barry.

Doris Lu, Assistant Professor of Sport Management; Ph.D., Florida State. Sport marketing, consumer behavior, sponsorship.

Kathryn Ludwig, Associate Professor and Coordinator of Physical Education; Ph.D., Texas Woman's. Biomechanics of soccer, particularly the skill of heading.

Constance Mier, Associate Professor and Coordinator of Exercise Science; Ph.D., Texas at Austin. Investigating the role of physical activity in the fitness and health of prepubescent children.

Monique Mokha, Associate Professor and Coordinator of Biomechanics; Ph.D., Texas Woman's. Applied sport and sport-injury mechanics, including disability.

Cesar Odio, Instructor and Men's Head Basketball Coach; M.S., Nova Southeastern.

Artur Poczwardowski, Associate Professor; Ph.D., Utah. Applied sport psychology.

Daniel Rosenberg, Associate Professor and Interim Coordinator of Sport Management; Ed.D., Massachusetts Amherst. Sport management and athletic administration.

George Samuel, Assistant Professor and Men's and Women's Head Tennis Coach; Ph.D., Southern Illinois Carbondale. Sport and exercise science.

Sue B. Shapiro, Associate Professor of Athletic Training; Ed.D., Virginia. Sports medicine and curriculum design.

Gayle Workman, Associate Professor, Associate Dean, and Department Chair; Ph.D., Ohio State. The meaning of leisure throughout the life span, particularly in the lives of older adults; dynamics of groups and roles of leadership in wilderness settings; integration of experiential, outdoor, and physical education within school settings; the interwoven phenomena and experience of ecotourism and the meaning of adventure travel.

STATE UNIVERSITY OF NEW YORK COLLEGE AT CORTLAND

Department of Sport Management

Programs of Study

Sport has become a dynamic growth industry, generating more than $400 billion in the United States and more than $600 billion worldwide. Over the years, the scope of the industry has greatly diversified and is expanding to incorporate new growth areas such as e-commerce and new technologies. The Department of Sport Management at the State University of New York (SUNY) College at Cortland provides the formal educational foundation and the practical experiences necessary to gain access to a career in this extremely competitive industry.

The Department offers two distinctive tracks to earn a Master of Science (M.S.) degree in sport management. Both tracks require the completion of 30 credit hours of course work. The Full-Time Residential Track is designed for students who are interested in the traditional on-campus, full-time degree program. This program may be completed in approximately one calendar year. The Part-Time Professional Track was created for sport professionals who are currently employed in the industry. This track may be completed in approximately two calendar years and consists of a mix of online and blended (on-campus and online) courses completed part-time. This track requires three 5-day residencies on campus during each of the summers while enrolled in the program. Students in both tracks are required to complete 18 hours of required courses, 6 hours of electives, and a culminating 6-hour master's or thesis project. Core courses focus on business, marketing, sport law, information technology, the globalization of sport, strategic planning and management, and finance. The final project is concentrated on a topic of the student's choice.

Research Facilities

The Sport Media & Technology Learning Center (SMTLC) provides sports-specific information technology training to students who are enrolled in sport management courses. The center includes three state-of-the-art student computer labs/classrooms, with a total of ninety-six seats, loaded with the latest hardware and software used in the sport industry, as well as a mobile lab and a video editing suite. The center includes training on XOS software, the world's largest provider of digital solutions for the sport industry. Dartfish, the world's leading producer of performance-enhancing sport video training applications, houses its Northeast Training Center in the SMTLC. Memorial Library houses a collection of more than 400,000 volumes, 1,200 journal subscriptions, an extensive microtext collection, and a strong collection of electronic resources, including videotapes, compact discs, and digital video recordings. The library has two networked computer labs, one for Macintosh and one for PC users, and there are Macintoshes and PCs in the Late Night Reading Room. In addition, there are sixteen public computing labs, including a 24-hour-a-day, seven-day-a-week lab.

Financial Aid

Diversity Fellowships of up to $10,000 are awarded to students who contribute to the diversity of the College. Graduate assistantships are presented to students for teaching labs or performing various other functions in academic or administrative departments. The award includes a partial tuition waiver of 6 credits per semester and a stipend. An Arethusa Scholarship of up to $1000 each year is awarded to a graduate student with demonstrated financial need and leadership and community involvement. Non-Traditional Student Scholarships are awarded to students who do not fit the traditional college student profile. Students may fund their education through loans, scholarships, and grants from private sources or through employment and tuition reimbursement through an employer.

Cost of Study

In 2006–07, tuition was $288 per academic credit hour for New York residents and $455 per hour for nonresidents. Other costs included a College fee of $0.85 per hour and a program services fee of $42.30 per hour.

Living and Housing Costs

Housing is not available on campus for graduate students. However, housing is available at rents ranging from $1900 to $2500 per month, depending on size and location. Some units have parking fees ranging from $50 to $75 per month.

Student Group

Students in the program are either currently working in the field of sport management or hoping to establish a career in the field.

Student Outcomes

Graduates of the program are well prepared to enter the sport business industry in areas such as marketing, public relations, sales, facility management, information technology, law, media, event management, finance, economics, and athletic management.

Location

The campus is located in Cortland, just blocks from the downtown area, with numerous opportunities for shopping, dining, entertainment, and socializing. Cortland County lies in the northern part of the Allegheny Plateau and is the eastern gateway to the Finger Lakes region. Cortland is located about 40 minutes from Syracuse, and New York City is a 4- to 5-hour drive to the south.

The University

Since its beginnings in 1868, the State University of New York College at Cortland has been committed to excellence in teaching, scholarship, research, and service to the community. The College is committed to a comprehensive curriculum, building on traditional strengths in education and enhancing high-quality programs in the arts, humanities, and sciences. As one of thirteen colleges in the SUNY system, SUNY at Cortland has approximately 7,300 students enrolled in more than 100 degree programs. The College campus covers 191 acres and is located within walking distance of Cortland's business district.

Applying

Prospective students are required to submit an application for admission, official college transcripts showing an undergraduate GPA of at least 2.8, official GRE or GMAT scores, a personal statement of approximately 250 words describing the applicant's academic and professional goals, two letters of recommendation, and a $65 application fee. The deadline to apply is July 1 for fall admission and December 1 for spring admission.

Correspondence and Information

James T. Reese Jr., Ed.D.
Associate Professor and Graduate Program Coordinator
Department of Sport Management
Studio West 156-G
State University of New York College at Cortland
Cortland, New York 13045
Phone: 607-753-4118
Fax: 607-753-5795
E-mail: reesej@cortland.edu
Web site: http://www.cortland.edu/spmg/home.htm

State University of New York College at Cortland

THE FACULTY AND THEIR RESEARCH

Graduate Faculty

Ted Fay, Associate Professor and Chair; Ph.D., Massachusetts Amherst. International sport, strategic management, disability in sport, race and gender in sport, the Olympic Games, the Paralympic Games.

James Reese, Associate Professor and Graduate Program Coordinator; Ed.D., Northern Colorado. Ticket operations and sales, ethics in sport, event management, sport marketing and sponsorship, college athletic reform, internships.

David Snyder, Associate Professor; J.D., Tennessee; Ph.D. candidate, German Sport University. Sport law, sport marketing, Japanese baseball, naming rights, sport sponsorship, Asian sports, contract negotiation.

Departmental and Support Faculty

Daniel DePerno, Assistant Professor and Director, Sport Media & Technology Learning Center; M.S., Canisius. Information technology in sport, sport public relations, sport journalism, digital video analysis in sport, Web design, graphic design, NASCAR, fantasy sports, sport video games, sport sponsorship value.

Lisa Scherer, Assistant Professor and Internship Coordinator; M.A., Ohio State. Sport event management, sport marketing, sponsorship sales, internships.

Matthew Seyfried, Lecturer; Ph.D. candidate, German Sport University. Sport media management, sport broadcasting, sport media relations, television production, videography.

Tara Derbick, Lecturer and Assistant Athletics Director, SUNY at Cortland; M.A., Minnesota State. Sport event management, sport event practicum.

Peter Han, Visiting Assistant Professor of Sport Studies; Ph.D. candidate, German Sport University. Information technology in sport, international sport management, Web design, graphic design.

Aaron Zipp, Visiting Lecturer; M.S., Virginia Commonwealth. International sport, strategic management of sport organizations, individual/alternative sport, ethical leadership and management.

Sarah Zipp, Visiting Lecturer; M.S., Virginia Commonwealth. International sport, college athletics, sport marketing, internships and practicum, research.

Joseph Manhertz, Adjunct Professor and Associate Director of Leadership Gifts, Hamilton College. Applied sport sales and marketing.

UNITED STATES SPORTS ACADEMY

Graduate School

Programs of Study

The United States Sports Academy, "America's Sports University," is a sport-specific institution that offers a Master of Sports Science (M.S.S.) degree in sports coaching, sports fitness, sports management, sports medicine, and sports studies. The Doctor of Education (Ed.D.) degree in sports management is also offered, as well as the Doctor of Education in sports management with an emphasis in sports medicine. The Academy offers a flexible program consisting of both online and resident study. The practical experience, or mentorship program, enables the student to gain hands-on experience in the areas of coaching, corporate wellness, fitness-center management, athletics administration, clinical and institutional sports medicine, and research.

Research Facilities

The Fitness Performance Lab has the capability of assessing the metabolic parameters of human performance, including oxygen intake, carbon dioxide production, pulmonary function testing, and body composition.

The Fitness Performance Center is equipped with a range of rehabilitative equipment, including ultrasound, electrical modalities, isokinetic rehabilitation equipment, and hydrotherapy modalities. Students learn to use evaluation devices such as the BodPod and Ariel CES systems.

The Academy maintains a library learning center and computer laboratory for student research. The library collection includes reference materials, books, periodicals, journals, films, and audiocassettes and videocassettes on sport-related subjects. The library also participates in online computerized data search programs, allowing students access to citations and full-text articles in sport and sport-related areas. The Academy is a member of the Network of Alabama Academic Libraries and the area's arm of OCLC, SOLINET.

Financial Aid

A variety of financial aid programs are available to qualified students. Federal programs include Federal Stafford Student Loans, Federal Work-Study, and military and veterans' benefits. Campus programs include doctoral assistantships that pay stipends and offer tuition waivers. Recipients are determined by consideration of academic performance, prior work experience, and their ability to benefit from graduate study. Interested students should contact the Office of Financial Aid at 800-223-2668 Ext. 7143 for assistance.

Cost of Study

The tuition for the Master of Sports Science degree program is $435 per credit hour. Tuition for the Doctor of Education degree program is $540 per credit hour.

Living and Housing Costs

The Academy is surrounded by a range of high-quality, low-cost apartments with long-term or short-term leases that meet the needs of students. The estimated cost of room, board, transportation, and miscellaneous living expenses is $18,000 per year. Students should contact Student Services (800-223-2668) at least four months in advance if they are planning on relocating to the Daphne area.

Student Group

The Academy enrolls students from all over the United States and from several countries. The diversity of ethnic and economic backgrounds enables students to increase their knowledge and awareness of global trends and concepts in sports.

Location

The Academy is located in Daphne, Alabama, on the beautiful eastern shore of historic Mobile Bay, just off Interstate 10. The Gulf Coast is famous for its boating, fishing, and white sand beaches. The area enjoys semitropical weather most of the year. Several large urban communities, such as New Orleans, Atlanta, and Pensacola, are within driving distance.

The Academy

The United States Sports Academy is an independent nonprofit, accredited, special mission sports university created to serve the nation and the world with programs in instruction, research, and service. The role of the Academy is to prepare men and women for careers in the profession of sports. The Academy is accredited by the Commission on Colleges of the Southern Association of Colleges and Schools (1866 Southern Lane, Decatur, Georgia 30033-4097; telephone: 404-679-4501) to award the Bachelor of Sports Science degree (level II), the Master of Sports Science degree (level III), and the Doctor of Sports Management degree (level V). The Academy accepts graduate students regardless of race, religion, gender, age, disability, or national origin.

The degrees are on the approved list of the Sport Management Program Review Council, a joint program of the National Association for Sport and Physical Education (NASPE) and the North American Society of Sport Management (NASSM).

Applying

For full-standing admission to the master's degree program, an applicant must be a graduate of a four-year, regionally accredited undergraduate institution and must have maintained a cumulative grade point average of 2.5 or better (on a 4.0 scale) in all undergraduate work. Continuing full-standing status in all master's programs may be achieved if students score at least 800 on the GRE, 27 on the MAT, or 400 on the GMAT. In the case in which a student's reported standardized test score is below the stipulated score, the student may attain full standing by achieving a minimum 3.0 grade point average in the first 9 credits of course work.

A student applying for admission to the master's degree program is required to submit the following to the Office of Student Services: a completed application form accompanied by a $50 application fee (the fee is nonrefundable and constitutes part of the admission credentials); an official copy of all college transcripts; three letters of recommendation; an official score report of GRE, MAT, or GMAT results taken within the last five years; a written personal statement detailing personal reasons for desiring a master's degree; and a resume or vita.

A student applying for admission to the doctoral degree program is required to submit a completed application form accompanied by a $100 application fee; an official copy of all college transcripts; three letters of recommendation; an official GRE, MAT, or GMAT score report from within the last five years with a minimum score of 950 (GRE), 40 (MAT), or 500 (GMAT); a qualifying essay (in narrative form, not to exceed 3,000 words); and a resume or vita.

The Academy catalogs can be viewed at the Academy Web site.

Correspondence and Information

Office of Student Services
United States Sports Academy
One Academy Drive
Daphne, Alabama 36526
Phone: 251-626-3303
    800-223-2668 (toll-free)
Fax: 251-625-1035
E-mail: admissions@ussa.edu
Web site: http://www.ussa.edu

United States Sports Academy

DIVISION OF ACADEMIC AFFAIRS

MASTER OF SPORTS SCIENCE DEGREE PROGRAM

The Master of Sports Science degree program consists of 33-semester-hour majors. Students may take a dual major by combining any two majors; between 42 and 48 semester hours are required depending on the combination chosen. Students in the sports fitness and sports medicine programs must complete a mentorship in their field of study. Students in the sports coaching, sports management, and sports studies programs must select one of three options: a mentorship (minimum of 9 semester hours/450 contact hours in the field), thesis (a minimum of 6 semester hours and SAR 575 Professional Writing and Applied Research), or the elective track (a minimum of 9 semester hours of course electives).

Department of Sports Fitness

Those interested in pursuing a degree in sports fitness may be accepted from a variety of backgrounds. Generally, undergraduate majors with a strong background in exercise physiology, physical education, biology, health sciences, and business are more suitable, although successful experience in the field may substitute if a person did not pursue a suitable undergraduate major. The fitness major is versatile in that it offers opportunities to pursue careers in corporate, private, public, and not-for-profit organizations. The program also examines issues in health and physical fitness, such as obesity.

Department of Sports Coaching

Those interested in sports coaching should have a background in sports as a player or coach. Generally, undergraduate majors in health, physical education, recreation, or sports training are most suitable. The graduate program in sports coaching is designed to prepare a student for leadership in the dynamic career of sports coaching. Program objectives are established to prepare each student for the multiplicity of demands involved in the control and operation of individual and team sports.

Department of Sports Management

Those interested in sports management generally have undergraduate majors associated with business administration, management, finance, marketing, human relations, physical education, communications, or sports. The graduate curriculum in sports management is designed to prepare each student for the increasing number of career leadership opportunities in the field of sport and recreational management. Program objectives prepare the student for a multiplicity of demands involved in the operation of sports programs at various levels. Sports management students are prepared for careers as sports facility managers, sports information directors, sports front office administrators, or community relations directors.

Department of Sports Medicine

Those interested in pursuing a degree in sports medicine may be accepted from a variety of backgrounds. Undergraduate majors with backgrounds in an allied health field, sports medicine, and the medical sciences are most suitable, especially in biology, physical education, nursing, physical therapy, or athletic training. Those with strong backgrounds in the natural sciences are encouraged to apply. Program objectives prepare the student for the prevention, management, rehabilitation of athletic injuries, and the multiplicity of demands involved with the successful operation of sports medicine programs at various levels.

Department of Sports Studies

Those interested in sports studies may enter the program from a variety of backgrounds. Undergraduate degrees in physical education, sport health, human relations, and business are appropriate. Students must have a high level of interest in the field of sports. The graduate curriculum is designed to prepare students for further study in sports at a higher level or to allow students to develop and build individual concentrations. The courses are selected in accordance with each student's interest.

DOCTOR OF EDUCATION PROGRAM

The Doctor of Education degree program, like the master's degree program, is designed for the working professional. The 60 semester hours required to complete the degree may be earned through a combination of on-campus study and distance learning online, mentorship, and directed individualized study. The doctoral program is designed to prepare students to perform with a high degree of efficiency and proficiency in the sports industry, including sports education. There are three specialization areas: leadership, marketing, and human resource management. There is also an emphasis in sports medicine for those already licensed or certified in the area. The curriculum is designed to enable students who are recent master's degree graduates, working professionals, sports enthusiasts, athletic administrators, and sports education instructors to achieve personal, educational, and professional objectives in a sport-specific environment. The degree normally requires three to five years to complete.

DELIVERY OPTIONS

Students may take course work through a variety of delivery options to best meet their needs. These options may be combined in some cases to provide flexibility. The master's and bachelor's degree programs may be completed entirely online.

While the doctoral program course work can be completed entirely online, the comprehensive exam, dissertation proposal, and dissertation final defense must be completed in residence.

Distance Learning

Distance learning offers students the opportunity to earn degrees through a combination of independent and practical activities. Master's students are able to complete degrees at their homes or places of work without having to travel to the campus. In addition, doctoral students may complete all of their course work through the distance learning option, but must complete their comprehensive exam, dissertation proposal, and final defense on campus. Distance learning at the Academy is computer mediated and asynchronous, meaning the professor and student do not have to be in simultaneous contact with each other for learning to take place or assignments to be completed. The Master of Sports Science degree program can be taken entirely online.

Summer Residential Master's Degree Program

Under the guidance of on-campus faculty members, students study in a traditional classroom setting. The two-summer plus residential master's degree program is a specially designed program of two summers plus a mentorship that can be completed in one year. Resident study allows a student to combine classroom instruction with practical work or applied research, providing flexibility designed to meet the specific needs of the individual.

Three Summer Residential Doctoral Degree Program

The Doctor of Education degree program can be completed in three summer schools with a combination of mentorship and online study. The residential summer semester is normally seven weeks during the months of June and July. The program can also be completed through full-time residential study under the guidance of on-campus faculty members. Financial aid is available.

Mentorship Option

Mentorship study provides many opportunities for valuable practical learning experiences because students can select, within established guidelines, both the site and the type of experience desired. The flexibility of the mentorship study is particularly important for the teaching or working professional who seeks career advancement but prefers to remain employed while pursuing a degree. To insure high-quality experiences, established guidelines require that the duties and responsibilities for the mentorship be completed apart and different from the student's regular workplace. Master's degree students have the option of completing a thesis or electives instead of participating in the mentorship.

DIVISION OF CONTINUING EDUCATION AND PROFESSIONAL STUDIES

The Academy offers open enrollment and flexible online delivery of all sports management, sports coaching, human performance, and sports medicine continuing education courses and certification programs for working sports professionals who want to enhance their professional positions. Academy courses provide an efficient and flexible curriculum for those who seek to earn CEUs for professional development, for those who want to maintain certification/licensure, and for those who want to obtain concise, cutting-edge topical information.

ACADEMIC AND PROFESSIONAL PROGRAMS IN SOCIAL WORK

This section contains a directory of institutions offering graduate work in social work, followed by in-depth entries submitted by institutions that chose to prepare detailed program descriptions. Additional information about programs listed in the directory but not augmented by an in-depth entry may be obtained by writing directly to the dean of a graduate school or chair of a department at the address given in the directory.

For programs offering related work, see also in this book Allied Health and Education. In Book 2, see Criminology and Forensics, Family and Consumer Sciences, Psychology and Counseling, and Sociology, Anthropology, and Archaeology.

CONTENTS

Human Services

Abilene Christian University, Graduate School, College of Arts and Sciences, Department of Sociology and Family Studies, Abilene, TX 79699-9100. Offers family studies (MS, Certificate); gerontology (MS, Certificate). Part-time programs available. *Faculty:* 4 part-time/adjunct (0 women). *Students:* 1 (woman) full-time, 5 part-time (3 women); includes 2 minority (1 African American, 1 Asian American or Pacific Islander). 2 applicants, 50% accepted, 1 enrolled. In 2006, 1 degree awarded. *Degree requirements:* For master's, comprehensive exam. *Entrance requirements:* For master's, GRE General Test or MAT. *Application deadline:* For fall admission, 4/1 priority date for domestic students; for spring admission, 11/1 for domestic students. Applications are processed on a rolling basis. Application fee: $40 ($45 for international students). Electronic applications accepted. *Expenses:* Tuition: Full-time $12,504; part-time $521 per hour. Required fees: $700; $34 per hour. *Financial support:* Career-related internships or fieldwork and Federal Work-Study available. Support available to part-time students. Financial award application deadline: 4/1. *Unit head:* Dr. David Gother, Department Chair, 325-674-2349, Fax: 325-674-6524, E-mail: gotherd@acu.edu. *Application contact:* William Horn, Graduate Admissions Counselor, 325-674-2656, Fax: 325-674-6717, E-mail: gradinfo@acu.edu.

Abilene Christian University, Graduate School, College of Education and Human Services, Abilene, TX 79699-9100. Offers M Ed, MS, MSSW, Certificate. *Faculty:* 15 part-time/adjunct (11 women). *Students:* 38 full-time (32 women), 74 part-time (48 women); includes 10 minority (4 African Americans, 6 Hispanic Americans), 1 international. 128 applicants, 66% accepted, 76 enrolled. In 2006, 24 degrees awarded. *Degree requirements:* For master's, comprehensive exam. *Expenses:* Tuition: Full-time $12,504; part-time $521 per hour. Required fees: $700; $34 per hour. *Unit head:* Dr. Malesa Breeding, Dean, 325-674-2700, Fax: 325-674-2552, E-mail: breedingm@acu.edu. *Application contact:* William Horn, Graduate Admissions Counselor, 325-674-2656, Fax: 325-674-6717, E-mail: gradinfo@acu.edu.

Andrews University, School of Graduate Studies, College of Arts and Sciences, Department of Behavioral Science, Berrien Springs, MI 49104. Offers community services management (MSA); international development (MSA).

Anna Maria College, Graduate Division, Program in Human Services Administration, Paxton, MA 01612. Offers MS. Part-time and evening/weekend programs available. *Faculty:* 1 (woman) part-time/adjunct. *Degree requirements:* For master's, capstone project. *Application deadline:* For fall admission, 3/1 priority date for domestic and international students; for spring admission, 11/1 priority date for domestic and international students. Applications are processed on a rolling basis. Application fee: $40. Electronic applications accepted. *Unit head:* Dr. Michael Boover, Director, 508-849-2931, Fax: 508-849-3343, E-mail: mboover@annamaria.edu. *Application contact:* Janet LaPointe, Admissions Coordinator, Graduate and Continuing Education, 508-849-3234, Fax: 508-819-3362, E-mail: jlapointe@annamaria.edu.

Bellevue University, Graduate School, Bellevue, NE 68005-3098. Offers business (MBA); communications studies (MA, MS); computer information systems (MS); health care administration (MS); human services (MS); leadership (MA); management (MA); security management (MS). MA is delivered in an accelerated executive format. Part-time and evening/weekend programs available. Postbaccalaureate distance learning degree programs offered (no on-campus study). *Degree requirements:* For master's, thesis or project. *Entrance requirements:* For master's, minimum GPA of 2.5 in last 60 hours. Additional exam requirements/recommendations for international students: Required—TOEFL (minimum score 538 paper-based; 200 computer-based).

Boricua College, Program in Human Services, New York, NY 10032-1560. Offers MS. Evening/weekend programs available. *Faculty:* 3 full-time (2 women). *Students:* 37 full-time (32 women); includes 32 minority (all Hispanic Americans), 5 international. 31 applicants, 65% accepted, 20 enrolled. In 2006, 41 degrees awarded. *Median time to degree:* Master's–1 year full-time. *Degree requirements:* For master's, thesis. *Entrance requirements:* For master's, interview. *Application deadline:* Applications are processed on a rolling basis. Application fee: $100. *Expenses:* Tuition: Full-time $9,000. Required fees: $50. One-time fee: $100 full-time. Full-time tuition and fees vary according to degree level and program. *Financial support:* Career-related internships or fieldwork and Federal Work-Study available. Financial award applicants required to submit FAFSA. *Unit head:* Dr. Basilisa Colón, Chair, 212-694-7000 Ext. 655, E-mail: bcolon@boricuacollege.edu. *Application contact:* Miriam Pfeiffer, Director of Student Services, 718-782-2200 Ext. 211, E-mail: mpfeiffer@boricuacollege.edu.

Brandeis University, The Heller School for Social Policy and Management, Program in Human Services, Waltham, MA 02454-9110. Offers child, youth, and family services (MBA); health care administration (MBA); human services (MBA); MBA/MA. Part-time and evening/weekend programs available. *Degree requirements:* For master's, team consulting project. *Entrance requirements:* For master's, GMAT. Additional exam requirements/recommendations for international students: Required—TOEFL (minimum score 600 paper-based). Electronic applications accepted. Expenses: Contact institution. *Faculty research:* Health care, child and family, elder and disabled services, general human services.

See Close-Up on page 247.

California State University, Sacramento, Graduate Studies, College of Health and Human Services, Division of Social Work, Sacramento, CA 95819-6048. Offers family and children's services (MSW); health care (MSW); mental health (MSW); social justice and corrections (MSW). *Accreditation:* CSWE. *Students:* 284 full-time (233 women), 38 part-time (31 women); includes 158 minority (43 African Americans, 3 American Indian/Alaska Native, 63 Asian Americans or Pacific Islanders, 49 Hispanic Americans), 3 international. Average age 33. 369 applicants, 53% accepted, 137 enrolled. *Degree requirements:* For master's, thesis or alternative, writing proficiency exam. *Entrance requirements:* For master's, minimum GPA of 2.5 during previous 2 years of course work. Additional exam requirements/recommendations for international students: Required—TOEFL. *Application deadline:* Applications are processed on a rolling basis. Application fee: $55. Electronic applications accepted. *Financial support:* Career-related internships or fieldwork and Federal Work-Study available. Support available to part-time students. Financial award application deadline: 3/1. *Unit head:* Dr. Robin Carter, Chair, 916-278-6943, Fax: 916-278-7167.

Canisius College, Graduate Division, School of Education and Human Services, Department of Counseling and Human Services, Buffalo, NY 14208-1098. Offers community mental health counseling (MS); counseling and human services (MS); school and agency counseling (MS). Part-time and evening/weekend programs available. *Faculty:* 5 full-time (3 women), 9 part-time/adjunct (3 women). *Students:* 70 full-time (58 women), 56 part-time (44 women); includes 17 minority (14 African Americans, 1 Asian American or Pacific Islander, 2 Hispanic Americans), 2 international. Average age 28. 82 applicants, 87% accepted, 34 enrolled. In 2006, 75 degrees awarded. *Degree requirements:* For master's, thesis, research project. *Entrance requirements:* For master's, interview, minimum GPA of 2.5. *Application deadline:* Applications are processed on a rolling basis. Application fee: $25. Electronic applications accepted. *Expenses:* Tuition: Part-time $645 per credit hour. Required fees: $19 per credit hour. Tuition and fees vary according to program. *Financial support:* In 2006–07, 2 research assistantships with partial tuition reimbursements (averaging $8,708 per year) were awarded; career-related internships or fieldwork, Federal Work-Study, institutionally sponsored loans, health care benefits, and unspecified assistantships also available. Support available to part-time students. Financial award applicants required to submit FAFSA. *Faculty research:* Positive psychology, wellness, school violence prevention, lifespan development. *Unit head:* Dr. David L. Farrugia, Chairman, 716-888-2393, Fax: 716-888-3290, E-mail: farrugia@canisius.edu. *Application contact:* James D. Bagwell, Director of Graduate Recruitment and Admissions, 716-888-2544, Fax: 716-888-3290, E-mail: bagwellj@canisius.edu.

Capella University, School of Human Services, Minneapolis, MN 55402. Offers addictions counseling (Certificate); counseling studies (MS, PhD); criminal justice (MS, PhD, Certificate); diversity studies (Certificate); general human services (MS, PhD); health care administration (MS, PhD, Certificate); management of nonprofit agencies (MS, PhD, Certificate); marital, couple and family counseling/therapy (MS); marriage and family services (Certificate); mental health counseling (MS); professional counseling (Certificate); social and community services (MS, PhD, Certificate). Part-time and evening/weekend programs available. Postbaccalaureate distance learning degree programs offered (minimal on-campus study). Terminal master's awarded for partial completion of doctoral program. *Degree requirements:* For master's, integrative project, thesis optional; for doctorate, thesis/dissertation, comprehensive exam, registration. *Entrance requirements:* Additional exam requirements/recommendations for international students: Required—TOEFL (minimum score 550 paper-based; 213 computer-based), TWE (minimum score 4). Electronic applications accepted. *Faculty research:* Compulsive and addictive behaviors, substance abuse, assessment of psychopathology and neuropsychology.

Chestnut Hill College, School of Graduate Studies, Division of Psychology, Program in Counseling Psychology and Human Services, Philadelphia, PA 19118-2693. Offers MA, MS, CAS. Part-time and evening/weekend programs available. *Faculty:* 8 full-time (3 women), 28 part-time/adjunct (11 women). *Students:* 73 full-time (63 women), 152 part-time (128 women); includes 43 minority (36 African Americans, 3 Asian Americans or Pacific Islanders, 4 Hispanic Americans). Average age 34. In 2006, 75 degrees awarded. *Degree requirements:* For master's, practica, thesis optional. *Entrance requirements:* For master's, GRE or MAT, writing sample; for CAS, Master's degree in counseling or a related discipline. Additional exam requirements/recommendations for international students: Required—TOEFL (minimum score 550 paper-based). *Application deadline:* For fall admission, 7/15 priority date for domestic students, 7/15 for international students; for spring admission, 12/15 priority date for domestic students, 12/15 for international students. Applications are processed on a rolling basis. Application fee: $50. *Expenses:* Tuition: Part-time $470 per credit hour. Required fees: $30 per semester. Tuition and fees vary according to degree level. *Financial support:* Institutionally sponsored loans available. Financial award application deadline: 7/15; financial award applicants required to submit FAFSA. *Faculty research:* Child and adolescent therapy and clinical issues; supervision and training of clinicians; acute and chronic trauma disorders; ethical and legal issues in clinical practice; family therapy with adolescents. *Application contact:* Jayne Mashett, Director of Graduate Admissions, 215-248-7020, Fax: 215-248-7161, E-mail: mashettj@chc.edu.

Chestnut Hill College, School of Graduate Studies, Program in Administration of Human Services, Philadelphia, PA 19118-2693. Offers administration of human services (MS); adult and aging services (CAS); leadership development (CAS). Part-time and evening/weekend programs available. *Students:* 21 full-time (17 women), 24 part-time (17 women); includes 26 minority (23 African Americans, 3 Hispanic Americans). Average age 36. *Entrance requirements:* For master's, GRE General Test or MAT, 100 hours volunteer or 1 year work related human services experience, writing sample. Additional exam requirements/recommendations for international students: Required—TOEFL (minimum score 500 paper-based). *Application deadline:* For fall admission, 7/15 priority date for domestic students, 7/15 for international students; for spring admission, 12/15 priority date for domestic students, 12/15 for international students. Applications are processed on a rolling basis. Application fee: $50. *Expenses:* Tuition: Part-time $470 per credit hour. Required fees: $30 per semester. Tuition and fees vary according to degree level. *Financial support:* Institutionally sponsored loans available. Financial award application deadline: 7/15; financial award applicants required to submit FAFSA. *Faculty research:* Volunteer services management, diversity issues, life satisfaction and quality of life, adult and aging services, health psychology. *Unit head:* Dr. Elaine Green, Coordinator, 215-248-7071, Fax: 215-248-7155, E-mail: green@chc.edu. *Application contact:* Jayne Mashett, Director of Graduate Admissions, 215-248-7020, Fax: 215-248-7161, E-mail: mashettj@chc.edu.

Concordia University, College of Arts and Sciences, Program in Human Services, River Forest, IL 60305-1499. Offers human services (MA), including administration, exercise science. Part-time and evening/weekend programs available. *Degree requirements:* For master's, thesis, comprehensive exam. *Entrance requirements:* For master's, minimum GPA of 2.9. Additional exam requirements/recommendations for international students: Required—TOEFL (minimum score 550 paper-based; 195 computer-based). Electronic applications accepted.

Concordia University Wisconsin, Graduate Programs, School of Health and Human Services, Mequon, WI 53097-2402. Offers MOT, MSN, MSPT, MSRS, DPT. *Application contact:* Mary Eberhardt, Graduate Admissions, 262-243-4551, Fax: 262-243-4428, E-mail: mary.eberhardt@cuw.edu.

Coppin State University, Division of Graduate Studies, Division of Arts and Sciences, Department of Social Sciences, Baltimore, MD 21216-3698. Offers human services administration (MS). Part-time and evening/weekend programs available. *Faculty:* 2 part-time/adjunct (both women). *Students:* 28 full-time (23 women), 25 part-time (20 women); includes 51 minority (all African Americans), 2 international. Average age 37. 20 applicants, 90% accepted, 14 enrolled. In 2006, 14 degrees awarded. *Entrance requirements:* For master's, resumé, references, interview. *Application deadline:* For fall admission, 8/15 priority date for domestic students; for spring admission, 12/15 priority date for domestic students. Applications are processed on a rolling basis. Application fee: $45. *Financial support:* Application deadline: 6/30; *Unit head:* Dr. John Hudgins, Interim Chair, 410-951-3528, Fax: 410-951-3045, E-mail: jhudgins@coppin.edu.

DePaul University, School of Education, Chicago, IL 60604-2287. Offers bilingual and bicultural education (M Ed, MA); curriculum studies (M Ed, MA); education (Ed D), including curriculum studies, educational leadership; educational leadership (M Ed, MA), including administration and supervision, Catholic school leadership, physical education; human development and learning (MA); human services and counseling (M Ed, MA), including agencies, family concerns, and higher education, elementary schools, human services management, secondary schools; reading and learning disabilities (M Ed, MA); social culture studies in education and development (M Ed, MA), including curriculum studies/development; teaching and learning (early childhood, elementary and secondary) (M Ed), including elementary education (M Ed, MA), secondary education (M Ed, MA); teaching and learning (early childhood, elementary, and secondary) (MA), including elementary education (M Ed, MA), secondary education (M Ed, MA). *Accreditation:* NCATE. Part-time and evening/weekend programs available. *Faculty:* 61 full-time (40 women), 76 part-time/adjunct (46 women). *Students:* 1,371 full-time (1,103 women), 474 part-time (362 women); includes 435 minority (144 African Americans, 7 American Indian/Alaska Native, 89 Asian Americans or Pacific Islanders, 195 Hispanic Americans), 11 international. Average age 30. 993 applicants, 80% accepted, 617 enrolled. In 2006, 324 master's, 7 doctorates awarded. *Degree requirements:* For doctorate, thesis/dissertation. *Entrance requirements:* For master's, interview, minimum GPA of 2.75, 2 letters of recommendation; for doctorate, interview, master's degree, 2 years of work experience (recommended), writing sample, 3 letters of recommendation. Application fee: $25. Electronic applications accepted. *Financial support:* In 2006–07, 16 research assistantships with tuition reimbursements (averaging $4,370 per year), 1 teaching assistantship (averaging $6,000 per year) were awarded; career-related internships or fieldwork also available. *Faculty research:* Reflective teaching, children at risk, loss, ethnicity, urban education. Total annual research expenditures: $556,194. *Unit head:* Dr. Clara Jennings, Dean, 773-325-7581, Fax: 773-325-7728, E-mail: cjennings@depaul.edu. *Application contact:* Dr. John Bollwark, Data Project Manager, 773-325-7582, Fax: 773-325-7713, E-mail: jbollwar@depaul.edu.

Drury University, Graduate Programs in Education, Program in Human Services, Springfield, MO 65802. Offers M Ed. Part-time and evening/weekend programs available. *Degree requirements:*

For master's, thesis. *Entrance requirements:* For master's, GRE or MAT, minimum GPA of 2.75. *Faculty research:* Grant writing, multicultural education.

Eastern New Mexico University, Graduate School, College of Liberal Arts and Sciences, Department of Health and Human Services, Portales, NM 88130. Offers speech pathology and audiology (MS). *Accreditation:* ASHA. Part-time programs available. Postbaccalaureate distance learning degree programs offered (minimal on-campus study). *Faculty:* 4 full-time (3 women). *Students:* 9 full-time (7 women), 34 part-time (32 women); includes 18 minority (1 African American, 1 American Indian/Alaska Native, 2 Asian Americans or Pacific Islanders, 14 Hispanic Americans). Average age 43. 29 applicants, 93% accepted. In 2006, 7 degrees awarded. *Degree requirements:* For master's, thesis optional. *Entrance requirements:* For master's, minimum GPA of 2.5. *Application deadline:* For fall admission, 8/20 priority date for domestic students. Applications are processed on a rolling basis. Application fee: $0. Electronic applications accepted. *Expenses:* Tuition, state resident: full-time $2,478; part-time $103 per credit hour. Tuition, nonresident: full-time $8,034; part-time $335 per credit hour. Required fees: $35 per credit hour. *Financial support:* In 2006–07, 12 research assistantships (averaging $8,200 per year) were awarded; fellowships, teaching assistantships, Federal Work-Study also available. Support available to part-time students. Financial award application deadline: 3/1. *Unit head:* Dr. Linda Weems, Graduate Coordinator, 505-562-2700, E-mail: linda.weems@enmu.edu.

Ferris State University, College of Education and Human Services, Big Rapids, MI 49307. Offers M Ed, MS, MSCTE. Part-time and evening/weekend programs available. Postbaccalaureate distance learning degree programs offered. *Faculty:* 19 full-time (11 women), 27 part-time/adjunct (19 women). *Students:* 49 full-time (33 women), 301 part-time (193 women); includes 48 minority (37 African Americans, 2 American Indian/Alaska Native, 2 Asian Americans or Pacific Islanders, 7 Hispanic Americans), 1 international. Average age 36. In 2006, 113 degrees awarded. *Entrance requirements:* For master's, minimum GPA of 3.0. *Application deadline:* For fall admission, 8/31 for domestic students; for winter admission, 12/10 for domestic students. Applications are processed on a rolling basis. Application fee: $30. *Expenses:* Tuition, state resident: part-time $355 per credit hour. Tuition, nonresident: part-time $687 per credit hour. *Financial support:* In 2006–07, 8 students received support, including research assistantships with full tuition reimbursements available (averaging $3,960 per year), 1 teaching assistantship with partial tuition reimbursement available (averaging $3,800 per year); career-related internships or fieldwork and tuition waivers (full and partial) also available. Support available to part-time students. *Faculty research:* Competency testing, teaching methodologies, assessment of teaching effectiveness, suicide prevention, women in education, special needs. *Unit head:* Michelle Johnston, Dean, 231-591-3646, Fax: 231-592-3792, E-mail: michelle_johnston@ferris.edu.

Georgia State University, College of Health and Human Sciences, School of Social Work, Atlanta, GA 30303-3083. Offers community partnerships (MSW). *Accreditation:* CSWE. Part-time programs available. *Faculty:* 16 full-time (11 women), 2 part-time/adjunct (1 woman). *Students:* 50 full-time (46 women), 5 part-time (4 women); includes 19 minority (16 African Americans, 3 Asian Americans or Pacific Islanders), 2 international. Average age 32. 83 applicants, 55% accepted, 21 enrolled. In 2006, 32 degrees awarded. *Degree requirements:* For master's, community project. *Entrance requirements:* For master's, GRE General Test. Additional exam requirements/recommendations for international students: Required—TOEFL (minimum score 550 paper-based; 213 computer-based). *Application deadline:* For fall admission, 2/1 priority date for domestic students. Applications are processed on a rolling basis. Application fee: $50. Electronic applications accepted. *Financial support:* In 2006–07, research assistantships with full and partial tuition reimbursements (averaging $3,108 per year); Federal Work-Study, scholarships/grants, tuition waivers (partial), and unspecified assistantships also available. Support available to part-time students. Financial award application deadline: 4/1; financial award applicants required to submit FAFSA. *Faculty research:* Social work education, child welfare, labor unions and child care workers, secondary victimization in death penalty cases. Total annual research expenditures: $431,852. *Unit head:* Dr. Nancy Kropf, Director, 404-651-3526. *Application contact:* Renanda Dear, Director, Student and Community Services, 404-651-3526, Fax: 404-651-1863, E-mail: rwood@gsu.edu.

Indiana University Northwest, School of Public and Environmental Affairs, Gary, IN 46408-1197. Offers criminal justice (MPA); environmental affairs (Certificate); health services administration (MPA); human services administration (MPA); nonprofit management (Certificate); public administration (MPA); public management (MPA, Certificate). *Accreditation:* NASPAA (one or more programs are accredited). Part-time programs available. *Faculty:* 5 full-time (3 women). *Students:* 16 full-time (12 women), 118 part-time (92 women); includes 89 minority (76 African Americans, 1 Asian American or Pacific Islander, 12 Hispanic Americans). Average age 39. In 2006, 30 master's, 31 other advanced degrees awarded. *Degree requirements:* For master's, registration. *Entrance requirements:* For master's, GRE General Test or GMAT, letters of recommendation. *Application deadline:* For fall admission, 8/15 priority date for domestic students. Applications are processed on a rolling basis. Application fee: $25. *Expenses:* Tuition, state resident: full-time $4,332; part-time $181 per credit hour. Tuition, nonresident: full-time $10,081; part-time $420 per credit hour. Tuition and fees vary according to course load, campus/location and program. *Financial support:* Career-related internships or fieldwork, Federal Work-Study, and tuition waivers (partial) available. Support available to part-time students. Financial award application deadline: 3/1. *Faculty research:* Employment in income security policies, evidence in criminal justice, equal employment law, social welfare policy and welfare reform, public finance in developing countries. *Unit head:* Karen Evans, Interim Assistant Dean/Division Director, 219-980-6695, Fax: 219-980-6737. *Application contact:* Sandra Hall Smith, Secretary, 219-980-6695, Fax: 219-980-6737, E-mail: shsmith@iun.edu.

Kansas State University, Graduate School, College of Human Ecology, School of Family Studies and Human Services, Manhattan, KS 66506. Offers family studies and human services (MS). *Accreditation:* AAMFT/COAMFTE; ASHA. Part-time programs available. *Faculty:* 19 full-time (13 women), 6 part-time/adjunct (3 women). *Students:* 170 full-time (116 women), 56 part-time (42 women); includes 27 minority (21 African Americans, 2 American Indian/Alaska Native, 2 Asian Americans or Pacific Islanders, 2 Hispanic Americans), 6 international. 153 applicants, 61% accepted, 34 enrolled. In 2006, 45 degrees awarded. *Degree requirements:* For master's, thesis or alternative, oral exam, residency. *Entrance requirements:* For master's, GRE, minimum GPA of 3.0 in last 2 years of undergraduate study. Additional exam requirements/recommendations for international students: Required—TOEFL (minimum score 600 paper-based; 250 computer-based). *Application deadline:* For fall admission, 2/1 priority date for domestic students, 1/15 priority date for international students; for spring admission, 10/1 priority date for domestic students, 8/1 for international students. Applications are processed on a rolling basis. Application fee: $30 ($55 for international students). *Expenses:* Tuition, state resident: full-time $6,352; part-time $240 per credit hour. Tuition, nonresident: full-time $14,296; part-time $571 per credit hour. Required fees: $585. *Financial support:* In 2006–07, 4 research assistantships (averaging $11,050 per year), 6 teaching assistantships with full and partial tuition reimbursements (averaging $10,167 per year) were awarded; Federal Work-Study, institutionally sponsored loans, scholarships/grants, and unspecified assistantships also available. Support available to part-time students. Financial award application deadline: 3/1; financial award applicants required to submit FAFSA. *Faculty research:* Health and security of military families, personal and family risk assessment and evaluation, disorders of communication and swallowing, families and health. Total annual research expenditures: $1.9 million. *Unit head:* Dr. William Meredith, Head, 785-532-1472, Fax: 785-532-5505, E-mail: meredith@ksu.edu. *Application contact:* Esther Maddux, Director, 785-532-1940, Fax: 785-532-5505, E-mail: emaddux@ksu.edu.

Kent State University, Graduate School of Education, Health, and Human Services, Kent, OH 44242-0001. Offers M Ed, MA, MAT, MPH, MS, Au D, PhD, Ed S. *Accreditation:* NCATE. Part-time and evening/weekend programs available. Postbaccalaureate distance learning degree programs offered (no on-campus study). *Faculty:* 115 full-time (67 women), 87 part-time/adjunct (71 women). *Students:* 769 full-time (616 women), 964 part-time (757 women); includes 158 minority (125 African Americans, 5 American Indian/Alaska Native, 11 Asian Americans or Pacific Islanders, 17 Hispanic Americans), 76 international. 670 applicants, 63% accepted. In 2006, 422 master's, 31 doctorates, 25 other advanced degrees awarded. *Degree requirements:* For master's, thesis (for some programs), registration; for doctorate, thesis/dissertation, comprehensive exam, registration. *Entrance requirements:* For doctorate and Ed S, GRE General Test. Additional exam requirements/recommendations for international students: Required—TOEFL (minimum score 525 paper-based; 197 computer-based). *Application deadline:* Applications are processed on a rolling basis. Application fee: $30. Electronic applications accepted. *Financial support:* In 2006–07, 21 fellowships with full tuition reimbursements (averaging $8,497 per year), 124 research assistantships with full tuition reimbursements were awarded; teaching assistantships with full tuition reimbursements, career-related internships or fieldwork, Federal Work-Study, institutionally sponsored loans, scholarships/grants, health care benefits, and unspecified assistantships also available. Support available to part-time students. Financial award application deadline: 4/1; financial award applicants required to submit FAFSA. *Unit head:* Dr. David A. England, Dean, 330-672-2808, Fax: 330-672-3407, E-mail: denglan1@kent.edu. *Application contact:* Nancy Miller, Office of Student Services, Academic Program Coordinator, 330-672-2576, Fax: 330-672-9162, E-mail: nmiller1@kent.edu.

Lehigh University, College of Education, Department of Education and Human Services, Program in Counseling Psychology, Bethlehem, PA 18015-3094. Offers counseling and human services (M Ed); counseling psychology (PhD); international counseling (M Ed, Certificate); school counseling (M Ed). *Accreditation:* APA (one or more programs are accredited). Part-time and evening/weekend programs available. *Faculty:* 29 full-time (16 women), 17 part-time/adjunct (9 women). *Students:* 56 full-time (44 women), 47 part-time (43 women); includes 13 minority (5 African Americans, 1 American Indian/Alaska Native, 4 Asian Americans or Pacific Islanders, 3 Hispanic Americans), 9 international. 140 applicants, 39% accepted, 19 enrolled. In 2006, 37 master's, 2 doctorates awarded. *Degree requirements:* For doctorate, thesis/dissertation. *Entrance requirements:* For master's, GRE General Test or MAT, minimum GPA of 3.0; for doctorate, GRE General Test or MAT. Additional exam requirements/recommendations for international students: Required—TOEFL (minimum score 500 paper-based; 250 computer-based). Application fee: $60. Electronic applications accepted. *Financial support:* Fellowships with full and partial tuition reimbursements, research assistantships with full and partial tuition reimbursements, career-related internships or fieldwork, Federal Work-Study, institutionally sponsored loans, scholarships/grants, and tuition waivers (full and partial) available. Financial award application deadline: 1/31. *Faculty research:* Multicultural counseling, career development, family systems. *Unit head:* Dr. Tina Richardson, Coordinator, 610-758-3250, Fax: 610-758-3227, E-mail: tgr0@lehigh.edu.

Lincoln University, Graduate Program in Human Services, Lincoln University, PA 19352. Offers M Hum Svcs. Evening/weekend programs available. *Degree requirements:* For master's, thesis. *Entrance requirements:* For master's, 5 years of work experience in human services. *Faculty research:* Gerontology/minority aging, computers in composition instruction.

Louisiana State University in Shreveport, College of Liberal Arts, Program in Human Services Administration, Shreveport, LA 71115-2399. Offers MS. Part-time and evening/weekend programs available. Postbaccalaureate distance learning degree programs offered. *Faculty:* 4 full-time (0 women), 4 part-time/adjunct (2 women). *Students:* Average age 37. 48 applicants, 100% accepted. In 2006, 16 degrees awarded. *Degree requirements:* For master's, comprehensive exam. *Entrance requirements:* For master's, GRE, interview, minimum GPA of 3.0. *Application deadline:* For fall admission, 8/5 priority date for domestic students; for spring admission, 12/15 priority date for domestic students. Applications are processed on a rolling basis. Application fee: $10 ($20 for international students). *Financial support:* In 2006–07, 5 research assistantships (averaging $6,000 per year) were awarded; Federal Work-Study and scholarships/grants also available. Support available to part-time students. *Faculty research:* Collaboration, small nonprofits, volunteerism, financial management. Total annual research expenditures: $32,506. *Unit head:* Dr. Norman A. Dolch, Director, 318-797-5235, Fax: 318-797-5358, E-mail: ndolch@pilot.lsus.edu.

McDaniel College, Graduate and Professional Studies, Program in Human Service Management in Special Education, Westminster, MD 21157-4390. Offers MS. *Accreditation:* NCATE. Evening/weekend programs available. *Degree requirements:* For master's, internship. *Entrance requirements:* For master's, letters of reference (3). Additional exam requirements/recommendations for international students: Required—TOEFL (minimum score 213 computer-based).

Minnesota State University Mankato, College of Graduate Studies, College of Social and Behavioral Sciences, Department of Sociology and Corrections, Mankato, MN 56001. Offers human services planning and administration (MS); sociology (MA); sociology: corrections (MS). Part-time programs available. *Students:* 16 full-time (11 women), 29 part-time (21 women). Average age 32. In 2006, 17 degrees awarded. *Degree requirements:* For master's, thesis or alternative, comprehensive exam. *Entrance requirements:* For master's, minimum GPA of 3.0 during previous 2 years, 3 letters of reference, resumé. Additional exam requirements/recommendations for international students: Required—TOEFL. *Application deadline:* For fall admission, 7/1 priority date for domestic students; for spring admission, 11/1 for domestic students. Applications are processed on a rolling basis. Application fee: $40. Electronic applications accepted. *Financial support:* Research assistantships with full tuition reimbursements, teaching assistantships with full tuition reimbursements, career-related internships or fieldwork, Federal Work-Study, institutionally sponsored loans, and unspecified assistantships available. Support available to part-time students. Financial award application deadline: 3/15; financial award applicants required to submit FAFSA. *Faculty research:* Women's suffrage movements. *Unit head:* Dr. Kimberly Greer, Chairperson, 507-389-1561. *Application contact:* 507-389-2321, E-mail: grad@mnsu.edu.

Minnesota State University Moorhead, Graduate Studies, College of Education and Human Services, Moorhead, MN 56563-0002. Offers counseling and student affairs (MS); curriculum and instruction (MS); educational leadership (MS, Ed S); nursing (MS); reading (MS); special education (MS); speech-language pathology (MS). *Accreditation:* NCATE. Part-time and evening/weekend programs available. *Faculty:* 18 full-time (11 women), 25 part-time/adjunct (13 women). *Students:* 45 full-time (42 women), 167 part-time (130 women); includes 4 minority (2 American Indian/Alaska Native, 2 Hispanic Americans), 4 international. 154 applicants, 56% accepted. In 2006, 60 degrees awarded. *Degree requirements:* For master's, final oral exam, project or thesis. *Entrance requirements:* Additional exam requirements/recommendations for international students: Required—TOEFL. *Application deadline:* For fall admission, 4/15 priority date for domestic students; for spring admission, 11/1 priority date for domestic students. Applications are processed on a rolling basis. Application fee: $20. Electronic applications accepted. *Financial support:* Career-related internships or fieldwork, Federal Work-Study, and unspecified assistantships available. Financial award application deadline: 7/15; financial award applicants required to submit FAFSA. *Unit head:* Dr. Michael Parsons, Dean of Education and Human Services, 218-477-2096. *Application contact:* Karla Wenger, Graduate Studies Office, 218-477-2344, Fax: 218-477-2482, E-mail: wengerk@mnstate.edu.

Minnesota State University Moorhead, Graduate Studies, College of Social and Natural Sciences, Program in Public, Human Services, and Health Administration, Moorhead, MN 56563-0002. Offers MS. Part-time and evening/weekend programs available. *Faculty:* 5 full-time (2 women), 2 part-time/adjunct (1 woman). *Students:* 6 full-time (2 women), 15 part-time (8 women); includes 1 African American, 1 Hispanic American, 2 international. 4 applicants, 100% accepted. In 2006, 12 degrees awarded. *Degree requirements:* For master's, final oral exam, final project paper or thesis. *Entrance requirements:* For master's, GRE General Test, minimum GPA of 2.75. Additional exam requirements/recommendations for international students: Required—TOEFL (minimum score 550 paper-based; 213 computer-based). *Application deadline:* For fall admission, 4/15 priority date for domestic students, 3/15 for international students; for spring admission, 11/1 priority date for domestic students. Applications are

Human Services

Minnesota State University Moorhead (continued)
processed on a rolling basis. Application fee: $20. Electronic applications accepted. *Financial support:* In 2006–07, 1 research assistantship (averaging $3,000 per year) was awarded; career-related internships or fieldwork, Federal Work-Study, and unspecified assistantships also available. Financial award application deadline: 7/15; financial award applicants required to submit FAFSA. *Unit head:* Dr. Steven Bolduc, Coordinator, 218-477-4683, E-mail: bolduc@mnstate.edu.

Montana State University–Billings, College of Allied Health Professions, Program in Rehabilitation and Human Services, Billings, MT 59101-0298. Offers MSRC. *Accreditation:* CORE. Part-time programs available. *Students:* 55. 9 applicants, 100% accepted, 9 enrolled. In 2006, 10 degrees awarded. *Degree requirements:* For master's, thesis or professional paper and/or field experience, thesis optional. *Entrance requirements:* For master's, GRE General Test or MAT, minimum GPA of 3.0. *Application deadline:* Applications are processed on a rolling basis. Application fee: $40. *Expenses:* Tuition, state resident: full-time $4,599. Tuition, nonresident: full-time $10,786. *Financial support:* Teaching assistantships, career-related internships or fieldwork, Federal Work-Study, institutionally sponsored loans, scholarships/grants, tuition waivers (partial), and unspecified assistantships available. Support available to part-time students. Financial award application deadline: 5/1; financial award applicants required to submit FAFSA. *Unit head:* Dr. Kyle Colling, Acting Chairperson, 406-657-5830, E-mail: kcolling@msubillings.edu. *Application contact:* David M. Sullivan, Graduate Studies Counselor, 406-657-2053, Fax: 406-657-2299, E-mail: dsullivan@msubillings.edu.

Murray State University, College of Education, Department of Educational Studies, Leadership and Counseling, Program in Human Development and Leadership, Murray, KY 42071. Offers MS. Part-time programs available. *Students:* 76. 28 applicants, 100% accepted. *Degree requirements:* For master's, thesis optional. *Entrance requirements:* Additional exam requirements/recommendations for international students: Required—TOEFL. *Application deadline:* Applications are processed on a rolling basis. Application fee: $25. *Financial support:* Research assistantships, teaching assistantships, Federal Work-Study available. Financial award application deadline: 4/1. *Unit head:* Dr. Thomas Holcomb, Chairman, 270-809-2795, Fax: 270-809-3799, E-mail: tom.holcomb@coe.murraystate.edu.

National-Louis University, College of Arts and Sciences, Department of Counseling and Human Services, Chicago, IL 60603. Offers addictions counseling (Certificate); addictions treatment (Certificate); career counseling and development studies (Certificate); community counseling (MS); community wellness and prevention (Certificate); counseling (Certificate); eating disorders counseling (Certificate); employee assistance programs (MS, Certificate); gerontology administration (Certificate); gerontology counseling (MS, Certificate); human services administration (MS, Certificate); long-term care administration (Certificate); school counseling (MS). Part-time programs available. *Students:* 15 full-time (11 women), 229 part-time (187 women); includes 69 minority (56 African Americans, 1 American Indian/Alaska Native, 2 Asian Americans or Pacific Islanders, 10 Hispanic Americans). Average age 38. 71 applicants, 96% accepted. In 2006, 53 master's, 6 other advanced degrees awarded. *Degree requirements:* For master's and Certificate, internship. *Entrance requirements:* For master's and Certificate, GRE, MAT, or Watson-Glaser Critical Thinking Appraisal, interview, minimum GPA of 3.0. *Application deadline:* Applications are processed on a rolling basis. Application fee: $25. *Expenses:* Tuition: Full-time $17,685. One-time fee: $40 full-time. *Financial support:* Federal Work-Study, institutionally sponsored loans, scholarships/grants, and tuition waivers available. Support available to part-time students. Financial award applicants required to submit FAFSA. *Faculty research:* Religion and aging, drug abuse prevention, hunger, homelessness, multicultural diversity. *Unit head:* Dr. Susan Thorne-Devin, Assistant Dean, 847-475-1100 Ext.4511. *Application contact:* David McCulloch, Vice President for University Services, 800-443-5522 Ext. 5127, Fax: 847-465-0593, E-mail: dmcc@wheeling1.nl.edu.

National University, Academic Affairs, School of Health and Human Services, La Jolla, CA 92037-1011. Offers MHCA, MS. Part-time and evening/weekend programs available. Postbaccalaureate distance learning degree programs offered (no on-campus study). *Faculty:* 2 full-time (0 women), 1 (woman) part-time/adjunct. *Students:* 6 full-time (5 women), 8 part-time (3 women); includes 6 minority (2 African Americans, 4 Hispanic Americans). Average age 33. 16 applicants, 12 enrolled. *Degree requirements:* For master's, thesis. *Entrance requirements:* For master's, interview, minimum GPA of 2.5. Additional exam requirements/recommendations for international students: Required—TOEFL (minimum score 550 paper-based; 213 computer-based; 80 iBT), IELTS (minimum score 6). *Application deadline:* Applications are processed on a rolling basis. Application fee: $60 ($65 for international students). Electronic applications accepted. *Expenses:* Tuition: Full-time $7,722; part-time $286 per unit. One-time fee: $60. *Financial support:* Career-related internships or fieldwork, institutionally sponsored loans, and scholarships/grants available. Support available to part-time students. Financial award application deadline: 6/30; financial award applicants required to submit FAFSA. *Unit head:* Dr. Thomas M. Green, Interim Dean, 858-642-8107 Fax: 858-642-8716, E-mail: tgreen@nu.edu. *Application contact:* Dominick Giovanniello, Associate Regional Dean—San Diego, 800-NAT-UNIV, Fax: 858-642-8709, E-mail: dgiovann@nu.edu.

New England College, Program in Community Mental Health Counseling, Henniker, NH 03242-3293. Offers human services (MS); mental health counseling (MS). Part-time and evening/weekend programs available. *Degree requirements:* For master's, internship.

Nova Southeastern University, Fischler School of Education and Human Services, Program in Education, Fort Lauderdale, FL 33314-7796. Offers educational leadership (Ed D); health care education (Ed D); higher education (Ed D); human serviced administration (Ed D); instructional leadership (Ed D); instructional technology distance education (Ed D); organizational leadership (Ed D); special education (Ed D); speech language pathology (Ed D). *Students:* 619 full-time (452 women), 615 part-time (473 women); includes 737 minority (616 African Americans, 2 American Indian/Alaska Native, 14 Asian Americans or Pacific Islanders, 105 Hispanic Americans), 8 international. Average age 38. 480 applicants, 83% accepted, 398 enrolled. *Degree requirements:* For doctorate, thesis/dissertation. *Entrance requirements:* For doctorate, MAT or GRE, master's degree, 2 letters of recommendation, work experience. Additional exam requirements/recommendations for international students: Required—TSE (recommended) with a minimum score of 50; Recommended—TOEFL (minimum score 550 paper-based; 213 computer-based), IELTS (minimum score 6). *Application deadline:* For fall admission, 8/11 priority date for domestic and international students; for winter admission, 12/28 priority date for domestic and international students; for spring admission, 4/22 priority date for domestic and international students. Applications are processed on a rolling basis. Application fee: $50. Electronic applications accepted. *Financial support:* In 2006–07, 2 fellowships (averaging $9,375 per year) were awarded; scholarships/grants and tuition waivers (full) also available. Support available to part-time students. Financial award application deadline: 1/7; financial award applicants required to submit FAFSA. *Unit head:* Dr. Karen D. Bowser, Associate Dean of Doctoral Programs, 954-262-8500, Fax: 954-262-3912, E-mail: bowserk@nova.edu. *Application contact:* Jennifer Quiñones Nottingham, Dean of Student Affairs, 800-986-3223 Ext. 8624, Fax: 954-262-3911, E-mail: jlquinon@nova.edu.

Pontifical Catholic University of Puerto Rico, Institute of Graduate Studies in Behavioral Science and Community Affairs, Ponce, PR 00717-0777. Offers clinical psychology (MA, MS); clinical social work (MSW); criminology (MA); industrial psychology (MS); psychology (PhD); public administration (MA). Part-time and evening/weekend programs available. *Entrance requirements:* For master's, EXADEP, GRE, 3 letters of recommendation, interview, minimum GPA of 2.75.

Roberts Wesleyan College, Division of Social Work, Rochester NY 14624-1997. Offers child and family practice (MSW); congregational and community practice (MSW); mental health practice (MSW). *Accreditation:* CSWE. *Faculty:* 11. *Students:* 75 full-time (66 women), 23 part-time (16 women). Average age 35. 75 applicants, 75% accepted. In 2006, 49 degrees awarded. *Entrance requirements:* For master's, minimum GPA of 2.75. *Application deadline:* For fall admission, 4/1 priority date for domestic students. Applications are processed on a rolling basis. Application fee: $35. *Financial support:* In 2006–07, 84 students received support, including 35 fellowships (averaging $1,863 per year); career-related internships or fieldwork, scholarships/grants, and tuition waivers (partial) also available. Financial award applicants required to submit FAFSA. *Faculty research:* Religion and social work, family studies, values and ethics. *Unit head:* Dr. Harmon Meldrim, Chair, 585-594-6487, E-mail: meldrimh@roberts.edu. *Application contact:* Beverly Keim, Graduate Admissions Coordinator, 585-594-6232, E-mail: keimb@roberts.edu.

Rosemont College, Graduate School, Program in Counseling Psychology, Rosemont, PA 19010-1699. Offers human services (MA); school counseling (MA). Part-time and evening/weekend programs available. *Degree requirements:* For master's, thesis or alternative. *Entrance requirements:* For master's, GRE or MAT. Additional exam requirements/recommendations for international students: Required—TOEFL. Electronic applications accepted. Expenses: Contact institution.

Sage Graduate School, Graduate School, Division of Management, Communications and Legal Studies, Program in Public Administration, Troy, NY 12180-4115. Offers human services administration (MS); public management (MS). Part-time and evening/weekend programs available. *Faculty:* 3 full-time (1 woman), 4 part-time/adjunct (2 women). *Students:* 3 full-time (all women), 16 part-time (15 women); includes 6 minority (5 African Americans, 1 Hispanic American). Average age 32. 11 applicants, 91% accepted, 7 enrolled. In 2006, 3 degrees awarded. *Entrance requirements:* For master's, minimum GPA of 2.75. Additional exam requirements/recommendations for international students: Required—TOEFL (minimum score 550 paper-based; 213 computer-based). *Application deadline:* Applications are processed on a rolling basis. Application fee: $40. *Expenses:* Tuition: Full-time $9,270; part-time $515 per credit hour. *Financial support:* Career-related internships or fieldwork, scholarships/grants, and unspecified assistantships available. Support available to part-time students. Financial award application deadline: 3/1; financial award applicants required to submit FAFSA. *Application contact:* Shannon K. Easton, Director of Graduate and Adult Admission, 518-244-2443, Fax: 518-244-6880, E-mail: sgsadm@sage.edu.

St. Edward's University, School of Management and Business, Program in Human Services, Austin, TX 78704. Offers conflict resolution (Certificate); human services (MA), including administration, conflict resolution, human resource management, sports management; sports management (Certificate). Part-time and evening/weekend programs available. *Students:* 9 full-time (8 women), 46 part-time (34 women); includes 19 minority (4 African Americans, 2 Asian Americans or Pacific Islanders, 13 Hispanic Americans), 2 international. Average age 34. 43 applicants, 84% accepted, 28 enrolled. In 2006, 28 degrees awarded. *Degree requirements:* For master's, minimum 24 resident hours. *Entrance requirements:* For master's, GRE General Test, GMAT, minimum GPA of 2.75 in last 60 hours of course work. Additional exam requirements/recommendations for international students: Required—TOEFL (minimum score 550 paper-based; 213 computer-based; 79 iBT). *Application deadline:* For fall admission, 8/1 for domestic students, 7/1 for international students; for spring admission, 12/1 for domestic students, 11/1 for international students. Applications are processed on a rolling basis. Application fee: $45 ($50 for international students). Electronic applications accepted. *Expenses:* Tuition: Full-time $11,682; part-time $649 per credit hour. Full-time tuition and fees vary according to course load and program. *Financial support:* In 2006–07, 4 students received support. Scholarships/grants available. Financial award applicants required to submit FAFSA. *Faculty research:* Leadership development, organizational management, public policy, emotional intelligence. *Unit head:* Dr. Constance D Porter, Director, 512-416-5827, Fax: 512-448-8492, E-mail: constanp@stedwards.edu. *Application contact:* Kay L. Arnold, Graduate Admissions Coordinator, 512-233-1636, Fax: 512-428-1032, E-mail: kayla@stedwards.edu.

St. John Fisher College, Office of the Provost, School of Arts and Sciences, Human Service Administration Program, Rochester, NY 14618-3597. Offers MS. Part-time and evening/weekend programs available. *Faculty:* 1 full-time (0 women), 1 (woman) part-time/adjunct. *Students:* 1 full-time (0 women), 8 part-time (6 women); includes 4 minority (all African Americans) Average age 38. In 2006, 3 degrees awarded. *Degree requirements:* For master's, project. *Entrance requirements:* For master's, minimum GPA of 3.0. Additional exam requirements/recommendations for international students: Required—TOEFL (minimum score 575 paper-based; 233 computer-based; 80 iBT). *Application deadline:* For fall admission, 7/1 for domestic students; for spring admission, 10/30 for domestic students. Applications are processed on a rolling basis. Application fee: $30. *Expenses:* Tuition: Part-time $615 per credit. Tuition and fees vary according to program. *Financial support:* In 2006–07, 3 students received support. Federal Work-Study and scholarships/grants available. Financial award application deadline: 2/15; financial award applicants required to submit FAFSA. *Faculty research:* Group dynamics, self and social relationships. *Unit head:* Dr. John Seem, Graduate Director, 585-385-2142, E-mail: jseem@sjfc.edu. *Application contact:* Shannon Cleverley, Director of Graduate Admissions, 585-385-8161, Fax: 585-385-8344, E-mail: scleverley@sjfc.edu.

Saint Joseph's University, College of Arts and Sciences, Program in Gerontological Services, Philadelphia, PA 19131-1395. Offers gerontological counseling (MS); gerontological services (Post-Master's Certificate); human services administration (MS). Evening/weekend programs available. *Students:* 2 full-time (1 woman), 9 part-time (8 women); includes 4 minority (3 African Americans, 1 Hispanic American), 1 international. Average age 31. In 2006, 7 degrees awarded. *Entrance requirements:* For master's, 2 letters of recommendation. Additional exam requirements/recommendations for international students: Required—TOEFL. *Application deadline:* For fall admission, 7/15 for domestic students; for spring admission, 11/15 for domestic students. Application fee: $35. *Financial support:* Fellowships available. *Unit head:* Dr. Catherine Murray, Director, 610-660-1805.

St. Mary's University of San Antonio, Graduate School, Department of Counseling and Human Services, San Antonio, TX 78228-8507. Offers community counseling (MA); counseling (Sp C); counseling education and supervision (PhD); marriage and family relations (Certificate); marriage and family therapy (MA, PhD); mental health (MA); mental health and substance abuse counseling (Certificate); substance abuse (MA). *Accreditation:* AAMFT/COAMFTE (one or more programs are accredited); ACA (one or more programs are accredited). Postbaccalaureate distance learning degree programs offered (minimal on-campus study). *Faculty:* 5 full-time (1 woman), 10 part-time/adjunct (3 women). *Students:* 121; includes 43 minority (5 African Americans, 3 Asian Americans or Pacific Islanders, 35 Hispanic Americans), 2 international. Average age 34. In 2006, 25 master's, 7 doctorates awarded. *Degree requirements:* For master's, internship, thesis optional; for doctorate, thesis/dissertation, internship, comprehensive exam, registration. *Entrance requirements:* For master's, GRE General Test, MAT; for doctorate, GRE General Test, recommendation from employers, admissions committee and department faculty. Additional exam requirements/recommendations for international students: Required—TOEFL (minimum score 550 paper-based; 213 computer-based). *Application deadline:* Applications are processed on a rolling basis. Application fee: $30. Electronic applications accepted. *Expenses:* Contact institution. Tuition and fees vary according to degree level. *Financial support:* Career-related internships or fieldwork, Federal Work-Study, institutionally sponsored loans, scholarships/grants, and health care benefits available. Financial award application deadline: 3/31; financial award applicants required to submit FAFSA.

Sojourner-Douglass College, Graduate Program, Baltimore, MD 21205-1814. Offers human services (MASS); public administration (MASS); urban education (reading) (MASS).

South Carolina State University, School of Graduate Studies, Department of Human Services, Orangeburg, SC 29117-0001. Offers elementary counselor education (M Ed); rehabilitation counseling (MA); secondary counselor education (M Ed). *Accreditation:* CORE. Part-time and evening/weekend programs available. *Faculty:* 9 full-time (6 women), 3 part-time/adjunct (2 women). *Students:* 106 full-time (79 women), 37 part-time (25 women); includes 137 minority (136 African Americans, 1 Asian American or Pacific Islander), 1 international. Average age 31. 76 applicants, 71% accepted, 43 enrolled. In 2006, 45 degrees awarded. *Degree requirements:*

For master's, departmental qualifying exam, internship, thesis optional. *Entrance requirements:* For master's, GRE, MAT, minimum GPA of 2.7. *Application deadline:* For fall admission, 6/15 priority date for domestic students, 6/15 for international students; for spring admission, 11/1 for domestic and international students. Applications are processed on a rolling basis. Application fee: $25. Electronic applications accepted. *Expenses:* Tuition, state resident: full-time $7,278. Tuition, nonresident: full-time $14,322. *Financial support:* In 2006–07, 35 students received support; fellowships, research assistantships, career-related internships or fieldwork, institutionally sponsored loans, and unspecified assistantships available. Financial award application deadline: 6/1. *Faculty research:* Handicap, disability, rehabilitation evaluation, vocation. *Unit head:* Dr. Christine Boone, Interim Chair, 803-533-3968, Fax: 803-533-3666, E-mail: boonec@scsu.edu. *Application contact:* Annette Hazzard-Jones, Program Coordinator II, 803-536-8809, Fax: 803-536-8812, E-mail: zs_ahazzard@scsu.edu.

Southern Oregon University, Graduate Studies, School of Social Sciences, Department of Psychology, Ashland, OR 97520. Offers applied psychology (MAP); human service-organizational training and development (MA, MS); social science (MA, MS), including professional counseling, psychology. Part-time programs available. *Degree requirements:* For master's, thesis, portfolio and oral defense. *Entrance requirements:* For master's, GRE General Test, minimum GPA of 3.0. Electronic applications accepted.

Springfield College, Graduate Programs, Program in Human Services, Springfield, MA 01109-3797. Offers MS. Part-time and evening/weekend programs available. *Faculty:* 28 full-time (19 women), 74 part-time/adjunct (41 women). *Students:* 536. Average age 39. 335 applicants, 53% accepted, 160 enrolled. In 2006, 245 degrees awarded. *Degree requirements:* For master's, project. *Entrance requirements:* Additional exam requirements/recommendations for international students: Required—TOEFL (minimum score 550 paper-based; 213 computer-based). *Application deadline:* For fall admission, 7/15 priority date for domestic students; for spring admission, 11/15 priority date for domestic students. Applications are processed on a rolling basis. Application fee: $50. Electronic applications accepted. *Expenses: Contact institution.* One-time fee: $25 full-time. *Financial support:* Federal Work-Study and scholarships/grants available. Support available to part-time students. Financial award application deadline: 7/15. *Faculty research:* Social justice, organizational management and leadership, counseling, education and criminal justice. *Unit head:* Dr. Robert J. Willey, Dean, 413-748-3985, Fax: 413-748-3557, E-mail: rwilley@spfldcol.edu. *Application contact:* Donald James Shaw, Director of Graduate Admissions, 413-748-3060, Fax: 413-748-3069, E-mail: donald_shaw_jr@spfldcol.edu.

State University of New York at Oswego, Graduate Studies, School of Education, Department of Counseling and Psychological Services, Program in Human Services/Community Counseling, Oswego, NY 13126. Offers MS. Part-time programs available. *Faculty:* 7 full-time, 10 part-time/adjunct. *Students:* 22 full-time (18 women), 11 part-time (7 women); includes 2 minority (1 African American, 1 Hispanic American), 1 international. Average age 31. 20 applicants, 80% accepted. In 2006, 21 degrees awarded. *Degree requirements:* For master's, comprehensive exam. *Entrance requirements:* For master's, GRE General Test, interview, minimum GPA of 3.0. Additional exam requirements/recommendations for international students: Required—TOEFL (minimum score 560 paper-based; 220 computer-based). *Application deadline:* For fall admission, 2/1 for domestic students. Application fee: $50. *Expenses:* Tuition, state resident: part-time $288 per credit. Tuition, nonresident: part-time $455 per credit. Tuition and fees vary according to program. *Financial support:* Career-related internships or fieldwork, Federal Work-Study, institutionally sponsored loans, and scholarships/grants available. Support available to part-time students. Financial award application deadline: 4/1; financial award applicants required to submit FAFSA. *Unit head:* Jodi Mullen, Coordinator, 315-312-3234.

Texas Southern University, Graduate School, College of Liberal Arts and Behavioral Sciences, Department of Human Services and Consumer Sciences, Houston, TX 77004-4584. Offers human services and consumer sciences (MS), including child development, comprehensive human services and consumer sciences, foods and nutrition. Part-time and evening/weekend programs available. *Faculty:* 2 full-time (both women), 2 part-time/adjunct (1 woman). *Students:* 8 full-time (all women), 15 part-time (14 women); includes 22 minority (20 African Americans, 1 American Indian/Alaska Native, 1 Hispanic American). Average age 38. 9 applicants, 100% accepted, 7 enrolled. *Degree requirements:* For master's, thesis (for some programs), comprehensive exam. *Entrance requirements:* For master's, GRE General Test, minimum GPA of 2.5. Additional exam requirements/recommendations for international students: Required—TOEFL. *Application deadline:* For fall admission, 7/15 priority date for domestic students. Applications are processed on a rolling basis. Application fee: $50 ($75 for international students). *Financial support:* Research assistantships, teaching assistantships, career-related internships or fieldwork and institutionally sponsored loans available. Financial award application deadline: 5/1. *Faculty research:* Food radiation/food for space travel, adolescent parenting, gerontology/grandparenting. *Unit head:* Dr. Shirley R. Nealy, Chair, 713-313-7638, Fax: 713-313-7228, E-mail: nealy_sr@tsu.edu.

Thomas University, Department of Human Services, Thomasville, GA 31792-7499. Offers community counseling (MSCC); rehabilitation counseling (MRC). *Accreditation:* CORE. Part-time programs available. *Faculty:* 3 full-time (2 women). *Students:* 24 full-time (17 women), 30 part-time (23 women); includes 23 minority (all African Americans), 2 international. Average age 33. *Entrance requirements:* For master's, resumé, 3 academic/professional references. Additional exam requirements/recommendations for international students: Required—TOEFL (minimum score 600 paper-based; 250 computer-based). *Application deadline:* For fall admission, 8/1 priority date for domestic students, 6/1 for international students; for spring admission, 2/1 priority date for domestic students, 10/1 for international students. Applications are processed on a rolling basis. Application fee: $50 ($125 for international students). Electronic applications accepted. *Expenses:* Tuition: Part-time $376 per credit. Required fees: $130 per semester. *Financial support:* Applicants required to submit FAFSA. *Unit head:* Dr. Theresa Reese, Assistant Professor, Chair of Human Services, 229-226-1621, Fax: 229-226-1653, E-mail: treese@thomasu.edu. *Application contact:* Adrienne Diggs, Assistant Director of Admissions, 229-226-1621 Ext. 127, Fax: 229-227-6919, E-mail: adiggs@thomasu.edu.

Universidad del Turabo, Graduate Programs, Programs in Public Affairs, Program in Human Services Administration, Gurabo, PR 00778-3030. Offers MPA. *Entrance requirements:* For master's, GRE, EXADEP, interview.

Université de Montréal, Faculty of Graduate Studies, Programs in Applied Human Sciences, Montréal, QC H3C 3J7, Canada. Offers PhD. *Students:* 47 full-time (29 women), 5 part-time (4 women). 25 applicants, 52% accepted, 13 enrolled. In 2006, 5 degrees awarded. *Degree requirements:* For doctorate, thesis/dissertation, general exam. *Application deadline:* For fall admission, 2/1 priority date for domestic students; for winter admission, 11/1 priority date for domestic students; for spring admission, 2/1 priority date for domestic students. Application fee: $30. Electronic applications accepted. *Unit head:* Claude Lessard, Director, 514-343-7165, Fax: 514-343-2393, E-mail: claude.lessard@umontreal.ca.

University of Baltimore, Graduate School, The Yale Gordon College of Liberal Arts, Division of Applied Behavioral Sciences, Program in Human Services Administration, Baltimore, MD 21201-5779. Offers MS. Part-time and evening/weekend programs available. *Faculty:* 5 full-time (1 woman), 7 part-time/adjunct (1 woman). *Students:* 12 full-time (all women), 32 part-time (30 women); includes 37 minority (all African Americans) Average age 33. 15 applicants, 80% accepted, 12 enrolled. In 2006, 22 degrees awarded. *Entrance requirements:* For master's, interview. Additional exam requirements/recommendations for international students: Required—TOEFL (minimum score 550 paper-based; 213 computer-based). *Application deadline:* For fall admission, 7/15 priority date for domestic students; for spring admission, 12/15 priority date for domestic students. Applications are processed on a rolling basis. Application fee: $45. Electronic applications accepted. *Expenses:* Tuition, state resident: full-time $5,322; part-time $591 per credit. Tuition, nonresident: full-time $7,527; part-time $830 per credit. *Financial support:* Career-related internships or fieldwork and Federal Work-Study available. Support available to part-time students. Financial award application deadline: 4/1; financial award applicants required to submit FAFSA. *Unit head:* Dr. Bridal Pearson, Director, 410-837-5251, E-mail: bpearson@ubalt.edu. *Application contact:* Dean Dreibelbis, Assistant Director, Office of Graduate Admissions, 410-837-6565, Fax: 410-837-4793, E-mail: gradadmissions@ubalt.edu.

University of Bridgeport, School of Education and Human Resources, Division of Human Resources, Bridgeport, CT 06604. Offers college student personnel (MS); community counseling (MS); human resource development (MS). Part-time and evening/weekend programs available. *Faculty:* 6 full-time (3 women), 14 part-time/adjunct (9 women). *Students:* 27 full-time (21 women), 76 part-time (59 women); includes 42 minority (30 African Americans, 1 American Indian/Alaska Native, 1 Asian American or Pacific Islander, 10 Hispanic Americans), 23 international. Average age 34. 84 applicants, 70% accepted, 37 enrolled. In 2006, 25 degrees awarded. *Degree requirements:* For master's, thesis optional. *Application deadline:* For fall admission, 8/1 priority date for domestic students; for spring admission, 12/1 priority date for domestic students. Applications are processed on a rolling basis. Application fee: $25 ($35 for international students). Electronic applications accepted. *Financial support:* In 2006–07, 27 students received support; fellowships, research assistantships, teaching assistantships, career-related internships or fieldwork, Federal Work-Study, and institutionally sponsored loans available. Support available to part-time students. Financial award application deadline: 6/1; financial award applicants required to submit FAFSA. *Faculty research:* Corporate elder care programs. *Unit head:* Dr. Joseph T. Cullen, Head, 203-576-4175.

University of Central Missouri, The Graduate School, College of Education, Department of Educational Leadership and Human Development, Program in Counselor Education, Warrensburg, MO 64093. Offers counseling (MS); human service/guidance counseling (Ed S). *Students:* 6 full-time (5 women), 95 part-time (85 women); includes 6 minority (4 African Americans, 2 Hispanic Americans), 1 international. Average age 36. 20 applicants. In 2006, 17 degrees awarded. *Entrance requirements:* Additional exam requirements/recommendations for international students: Required—TOEFL (minimum score 500 paper-based; 173 computer-based). *Application deadline:* For fall admission, 6/1 priority date for domestic students, 5/1 priority date for international students; for spring admission, 10/1 priority date for domestic students, 10/1 for international students. *Expenses:* Tuition, state resident: full-time $5,448; part-time $227 per credit hour. Tuition, nonresident: full-time $10,896; part-time $454 per credit hour. Required fees: $336; $14 per credit hour. *Faculty research:* School counselor certification issues, counselor licensing issues, counselor personnel and professional development. *Unit head:* Dr. Janelle Cowles, Coordinator, 660-543-8204, E-mail: cowles@ucmo.edu.

University of Central Missouri, The Graduate School, College of Health and Human Services, Department of Safety Sciences, Warrensburg, MO 64093. Offers fire science (MS); human services/public services (Ed S); industrial hygiene (MS); industrial safety management (MS); loss control (MS); occupational safety management (MS); public safety (MS); security (MS); transportation safety (MS). *Accreditation:* ABET (one or more programs are accredited). Part-time programs available. *Faculty:* 18 full-time (3 women). *Students:* 14 full-time (4 women), 18 part-time (6 women); includes 6 minority (2 African Americans, 1 American Indian/Alaska Native, 3 Hispanic Americans), 1 international. Average age 36. 9 applicants, 78% accepted, 6 enrolled. In 2006, 6 degrees awarded. *Degree requirements:* For master's, comprehensive exam. *Entrance requirements:* For master's, GRE General Test, minimum GPA of 2.5, 15 hours of course work in related area; for Ed S, master's degree in related field. Additional exam requirements/recommendations for international students: Required—TOEFL (minimum score 500 paper-based; 173 computer-based). *Application deadline:* For fall admission, 6/1 priority date for domestic students, 5/1 priority date for international students; for spring admission, 10/1 priority date for domestic students, 10/1 for international students. Applications are processed on a rolling basis. Application fee: $30 ($50 for international students). *Expenses:* Tuition, state resident: full-time $5,448; part-time $227 per credit hour. Tuition, nonresident: full-time $10,896; part-time $454 per credit hour. Required fees: $336; $14 per credit hour. *Financial support:* In 2006–07, 5 students received support. Federal Work-Study, scholarships/grants, unspecified assistantships, and administrative and laboratory assistantships available. Support available to part-time students. Financial award application deadline: 3/1; financial award applicants required to submit FAFSA. *Faculty research:* Workplace and school safety, industrial hygiene assessment methods, lead and take-home toxins, rural emergency management, cultural aspects of safety, health, and the environment. Total annual research expenditures: $60,999. *Unit head:* Dr. Dennis Laster, Interim Chair, 660-543-4017, E-mail: laster@cmsu1.cmsu.edu.

University of Colorado at Colorado Springs, Graduate School, College of Education, Colorado Springs, CO 80933-7150. Offers counseling and human services (MA); curriculum and instruction (MA); educational administration (MA); educational leadership (MA, PhD); special education (MA). *Accreditation:* ACA; NCATE. Part-time and evening/weekend programs available. *Faculty:* 22 full-time (15 women), 29 part-time/adjunct (17 women). *Students:* 331 full-time (246 women), 173 part-time (135 women); includes 85 minority (26 African Americans, 4 American Indian/Alaska Native, 13 Asian Americans or Pacific Islanders, 42 Hispanic Americans). Average age 35. 107 applicants, 93% accepted, 49 enrolled. In 2006, 234 degrees awarded. *Degree requirements:* For master's, thesis or alternative, microcomputer proficiency, comprehensive exam; for doctorate, doctoral research lab requirement. *Entrance requirements:* For master's, GRE General Test, MAT. *Application deadline:* For fall admission, 6/15 for domestic students; for spring admission, 10/15 for domestic students. Applications are processed on a rolling basis. Application fee: $60 ($75 for international students). *Expenses:* Tuition, state resident: part-time $303 per credit hour. Tuition, nonresident: part-time $840 per credit hour. Tuition and fees vary according to course load, campus/location and program. *Financial support:* Fellowships, career-related internships or fieldwork and Federal Work-Study available. *Faculty research:* Job training for special populations, materials development for classroom. Total annual research expenditures: $961,803. *Unit head:* Dr. LaVonne Neal, Dean, 719-262-4111, Fax: 719-262-4110, E-mail: lneal@uccs.edu. *Application contact:* Connie Wroten, Professional Assistant, 719-262-4102, Fax: 719-262-4110, E-mail: cwroten@uccs.edu.

University of Great Falls, Graduate Studies, Program in Human Services Administration, Great Falls, MT 59405. Offers organizational management (MS). Part-time and evening/weekend programs available. Postbaccalaureate distance learning degree programs offered (minimal on-campus study). *Faculty:* 2 full-time (both women), 4 part-time/adjunct (1 woman). *Students:* 2 full-time (1 woman), 2 part-time (both women); includes 2 minority (both American Indian/Alaska Native). Average age 37. 8 applicants, 88% accepted. In 2006, 4 degrees awarded. *Degree requirements:* For master's, thesis optional. *Entrance requirements:* For master's, GRE General Test or MAT, 3 letters of recommendation. Additional exam requirements/recommendations for international students: Required—TOEFL (minimum score 500 paper-based; 205 computer-based). *Application deadline:* For fall admission, 8/15 priority date for domestic students, 6/15 priority date for international students; for spring admission, 12/15 priority date for domestic students, 10/15 priority date for international students. Applications are processed on a rolling basis. Application fee: $50. Electronic applications accepted. *Financial support:* In 2006–07, 3 students received support. Career-related internships or fieldwork, Federal Work-Study, and institutionally sponsored loans available. Support available to part-time students. Financial award application deadline: 6/1; financial award applicants required to submit FAFSA. *Unit head:* Dr. Craig A. Ganster, Director, 406-791-5363, E-mail: cganster01@ugf.edu.

University of Illinois at Springfield, Graduate Programs, College of Education and Human Services, Program in Human Services, Springfield, IL 62703-5407. Offers alcoholism and substance abuse (MA); child and family services (MA); gerontology (MA); social services administration (MA). Part-time and evening/weekend programs available. Postbaccalaureate distance learning degree programs offered. *Faculty:* 5 full-time (4 women), 1 (woman) part-time/adjunct. *Students:* 24 full-time (22 women), 72 part-time (57 women); includes 22 minority

Human Services

University of Illinois at Springfield (continued)
(18 African Americans, 2 Asian Americans or Pacific Islanders, 2 Hispanic Americans), 2 international. Average age 36. 44 applicants, 59% accepted, 23 enrolled. In 2006, 24 degrees awarded. *Degree requirements:* For master's, internship, thesis optional. *Entrance requirements:* For master's, interview, 2 letters of reference, minimum undergraduate GPA of 3.0, prerequisite courses in lifespan development and research methods. Additional exam requirements/recommendations for international students: Required—TOEFL (minimum score 550 paper-based; 213 computer-based). *Application deadline:* For fall admission, 2/15 priority date for domestic and international students; for spring admission, 9/15 priority date for domestic and international students. Application fee: $50 ($60 for international students). *Expenses:* Tuition, state resident: full-time $4,722; part-time $197 per credit hour. Tuition, nonresident: full-time $12,558; part-time $523 per credit hour. Required fees: $1,614; $8 per credit hour. $597 per term. *Financial support:* In 2006–07, research assistantships with full tuition reimbursements (averaging $7,425 per year), teaching assistantships with full tuition reimbursements (averaging $7,425 per year) were awarded; career-related internships or fieldwork, scholarships/grants, health care benefits, and unspecified assistantships also available. Support available to part-time students. Financial award application deadline: 11/15. *Faculty research:* Delinquency prevention, organizational development. *Unit head:* Dr. Carolyn Peck, Program Administrator, 217-206-7577, Fax: 217-206-6775, E-mail: peck.carolyn@uis.edu.

University of Maryland, Baltimore County, Graduate School, College of Arts, Humanities and Social Sciences, Department of Psychology, Program in Human Services Psychology, Baltimore, MD 21250. Offers applied behavioral analysis (MA); human services psychology/clinical (PhD). *Faculty:* 28 full-time (11 women), 11 part-time/adjunct (6 women). *Students:* 69 full-time (58 women), 23 part-time (16 women); includes 21 minority (10 African Americans, 6 Asian Americans or Pacific Islanders, 5 Hispanic Americans). Average age 29. 164 applicants, 18% accepted, 18 enrolled. In 2006, 26 master's, 13 doctorates awarded. *Median time to degree:* Of those who began their doctoral program in fall 1998, 73% received their degree in 8 years or less. *Degree requirements:* For doctorate, thesis/dissertation, comprehensive exam. *Entrance requirements:* For master's, GRE General Test, minimum GPA of 3.0; for doctorate, GRE General Test, GRE Subject Test, minimum GPA of 3.0. Additional exam requirements/recommendations for international students: Required—TOEFL. *Application deadline:* For fall admission, 12/1 for domestic students. Application fee: $50. Electronic applications accepted. *Expenses:* Tuition, state resident: part-time $412 per credit hour. Tuition, nonresident: part-time $681 per credit hour. Required fees: $91 per credit hour. One-time fee: $75 part-time. *Financial support:* In 2006–07, 3 fellowships with full tuition reimbursements (averaging $22,000 per year), 31 research assistantships with full tuition reimbursements (averaging $14,280 per year), 17 teaching assistantships with full tuition reimbursements (averaging $14,280 per year) were awarded; career-related internships or fieldwork, Federal Work-Study, scholarships/grants, and tuition waivers (full and partial) also available. Financial award application deadline: 3/1; financial award applicants required to submit FAFSA. *Faculty research:* Addictive behaviors, cardiovascular and cerebrovascular disease, family violence, pediatric psychology, community prevention. Total annual research expenditures: $1.4 million. *Unit head:* Dr. Steven C. Pitts, Director, 410-455-2567, Fax: 410-455-1055, E-mail: spitts@umbc.edu. *Application contact:* Tamara D. Brown, Program Management Specialist, 410-455-2567, Fax: 410-455-1055, E-mail: psycdept@umbc.edu.

University of Massachusetts Boston, Office of Graduate Studies, College of Public and Community Service, Program in Human Services, Boston, MA 02125-3393. Offers MS. Part-time and evening/weekend programs available. *Students:* 20 full-time (15 women), 13 part-time (10 women). Average age 41. 24 applicants, 83% accepted, 13 enrolled. In 2006, 8 degrees awarded. *Median time to degree:* Master's–4 years full-time. *Degree requirements:* For master's, practicum, final project. *Entrance requirements:* For master's, MAT, GRE, minimum GPA of 2.75. *Application deadline:* For fall admission, 3/1 priority date for domestic students; for spring admission, 11/1 for domestic students. Application fee: $25 ($40 for international students). *Expenses:* Tuition, state resident: full-time $2,590; part-time $301 per credit. Tuition, nonresident: full-time $9,758; part-time $427 per credit. One-time fee: $495 full-time. *Financial support:* In 2006–07, 1 research assistantship with full tuition reimbursement (averaging $13,000 per year), teaching assistantships with full tuition reimbursements (averaging $13,000 per year) were awarded; career-related internships or fieldwork, Federal Work-Study, and unspecified assistantships also available. Support available to part-time students. Financial award application deadline: 3/1; financial award applicants required to submit FAFSA. *Faculty research:* Institutional and policy context of human services, ethics and social policy, public law and human services, social welfare, politics and human services. *Unit head:* Dr. Sylvia Mignon, Director, 617-287-7384. *Application contact:* Peggy Roldan, Graduate Admissions Coordinator, 617-287-6400, Fax: 617-287-6236, E-mail: bos.gadm@dpc.umassp.edu.

University of Oklahoma, Graduate College, College of Arts and Sciences, Department of Human Relations, Norman, OK 73019-0390. Offers MHR. Part-time and evening/weekend programs available. Postbaccalaureate distance learning degree programs offered (minimal on-campus study). *Faculty:* 45 full-time (23 women), 42 part-time/adjunct (25 women). *Students:* 385 full-time (245 women), 788 part-time (493 women); includes 400 minority (240 African Americans, 35 American Indian/Alaska Native, 64 Asian Americans or Pacific Islanders, 61 Hispanic Americans), 26 international. 288 applicants, 99% accepted, 213 enrolled. In 2006, 447 degrees awarded. *Degree requirements:* For master's, thesis optional. *Entrance requirements:* For master's, minimum GPA of 3.0 in last 60 hours of undergraduate course work, resumé, 3 letters of reference. Additional exam requirements/recommendations for international students: Required—TOEFL (minimum score 550 paper-based; 213 computer-based). *Application deadline:* For fall admission, 6/1 priority date for domestic students, 4/1 for international students; for spring admission, 11/1 for domestic students, 9/1 for international students. Applications are processed on a rolling basis. Application fee: $40 ($90 for international students). *Expenses:* Tuition, state resident: full-time $3,180; part-time $133 per credit hour. Tuition, nonresident: full-time $11,347; part-time $473 per credit hour. Required fees: $1,729; $62 per credit hour. $117 per semester. Tuition and fees vary according to course load and program. *Financial support:* In 2006–07, 321 students received support, including 29 research assistantships with partial tuition reimbursements available (averaging $9,686 per year), 3 teaching assistantships (averaging $12,368 per year); career-related internships or fieldwork, Federal Work-Study, institutionally sponsored loans, scholarships/grants, health care benefits, tuition waivers (partial), and unspecified assistantships also available. Financial award applicants required to submit FAFSA. *Faculty research:* Counseling and adolescent issues, child welfare women's criminality, substance abuse, diversity, leadership and organization. Total annual research expenditures: $4,782. *Unit head:* Dr. Susan Marcus-Mendoza, Chair, 405-325-1756, Fax: 405-325-4402, E-mail: smmendoza@ou.edu. *Application contact:* Jacob Smith, Admissions Coordinator, 405-325-1756, Fax: 405-325-1756, E-mail: jacosmith@ou.edu.

University of Phoenix–Maryland Campus, The Artemis School, College of Health and Human Services, Columbia, MD 21045-5424. Offers administration of justice and security (MS); nursing (MSN); nursing education (MSN); psychology (MS); MSN/MBA; MSN/MHA. Evening/weekend programs available. *Faculty:* 8 part-time/adjunct (7 women). *Students:* 1 (woman) full-time; minority (African American) Average age 27. *Degree requirements:* For master's, thesis (for some programs), registration. *Entrance requirements:* For master's, minimum undergraduate GPA of 2.5, 3 years work experience. Additional exam requirements/recommendations for international students: Required—TOEFL (minimum score 550 paper-based; 213 computer-based; 79 iBT). *Application deadline:* Applications are processed on a rolling basis. Application fee: $45. Electronic applications accepted. *Expenses:* Tuition: Full-time $13,200. Required fees: $760. *Financial support:* Institutionally sponsored loans and scholarships/grants available. Financial award applicants required to submit FAFSA. *Unit head:* Dr. Gil Linne, Dean/Executive Director, 480-557-1751, E-mail: gil.line@phoenix.com. *Application contact:* Campus Chair, 410-872-9001.

University of Phoenix–Richmond Campus, The Artemis School, College of Health and Human Services, Richmond, VA 23230. Offers administration of justice and security (MS); health administration (MHA); health care management (MBA); nursing (MSN); psychology (MS). Evening/weekend programs available. *Faculty:* 4 part-time/adjunct (1 woman). *Students:* 2 full-time (1 woman); includes 1 minority (African American) Average age 38. *Degree requirements:* For master's, thesis (for some programs), registration. *Entrance requirements:* For master's, minimum undergraduate GPA of 2.5, 3 years work experience, current RN license for nursing programs. Additional exam requirements/recommendations for international students: Required—TOEFL (minimum score 500 paper-based; 213 computer-based; 79 iBT). *Application deadline:* Applications are processed on a rolling basis. Application fee: $45. Electronic applications accepted. *Financial support:* Institutionally sponsored loans and scholarships/grants available. Financial award applicants required to submit FAFSA. *Unit head:* Dr. Gil Linne, Dean/Executive Director, 480-557-1751, E-mail: gil.linne@phoenix.edu. *Application contact:* Chair, 804-288-3390.

Upper Iowa University, Online Master's Programs, Fayette, IA 52142-1857. Offers accounting (MBA); corporate financial management (MBA); global business (MBA); health and human services (MPA); homeland security (MPA); human resources management (MBA); justice administration (MPA); organizational development (MBA); public personnel management (MPA); quality management (MBA). MBA also available at Madison, Wisconsin campus. Part-time and evening/weekend programs available. Postbaccalaureate distance learning degree programs offered (no on-campus study). *Degree requirements:* For master's, research project. *Entrance requirements:* For master's, GMAT, GRE, or minimum GPA of 2.7 during last 60 hours. Additional exam requirements/recommendations for international students: Required—TOEFL (minimum score 570 paper-based; 230 computer-based). Electronic applications accepted. *Faculty research:* Total quality management, CQI, teams, organization culture and climate, management.

Walden University, Graduate Programs, School of Health and Human Services, Minneapolis, MN 55401. Offers health services (PhD); human services (PhD); nursing (MS); public health (MPH, PhD). Part-time and evening/weekend programs available. Postbaccalaureate distance learning degree programs offered (minimal on-campus study). *Faculty:* 100. *Students:* 2,383 full-time (2,074 women), 1,082 part-time (876 women); includes 840 minority (662 African Americans, 18 American Indian/Alaska Native, 83 Asian Americans or Pacific Islanders, 77 Hispanic Americans), 24 international. Average age 42. 1,164 applicants, 85% accepted, 813 enrolled. In 2006, 212 master's, 30 doctorates awarded. *Degree requirements:* For master's, thesis (for some programs); for doctorate, thesis/dissertation. *Entrance requirements:* For master's, minimum GPA of 3.0; for doctorate, 3 years of professional experience, master's degree. Additional exam requirements/recommendations for international students: Required—TOEFL (minimum score 550 paper-based; 213 computer-based), IELTS (minimum score 7). *Application deadline:* For fall admission, 8/15 priority date for domestic and international students; for winter admission, 11/15 priority date for domestic and international students; for spring admission, 12/15 priority date for domestic and international students. Applications are processed on a rolling basis. Application fee: $50. Electronic applications accepted. *Financial support:* Fellowships with partial tuition reimbursements, tuition waivers (partial) available. Support available to part-time students. Financial award applicants required to submit FAFSA. *Unit head:* Dr. Gary J. Burkholder, Dean, 800-925-3368, Fax: 612-338-5092. *Application contact:* 866-4-WALDEN, Fax: 410-843-8780, E-mail: request@waldenu.edu.

Wayne State University, Graduate School, Interdisciplinary Program in Developmental Disabilities, Detroit, MI 48202. Offers Certificate. *Entrance requirements:* For degree, master's degree. Additional exam requirements/recommendations for international students: Required—TOEFL (minimum score 550 paper-based; 213 computer-based); Recommended—TWE (minimum score 6). *Application deadline:* For fall admission, 6/1 for international students; for winter admission, 10/1 for international students; for spring admission, 2/1 for international students. Applications are processed on a rolling basis. Application fee: $30 ($50 for international students). Electronic applications accepted. *Unit head:* Dr. Barbara Leroy, Director, 313-577-0334, Fax: 313-577-3770.

West Virginia University, Eberly College of Arts and Sciences, School of Applied Social Science, Division of Social Work, Morgantown, WV 26506. Offers aging and health care (MSW); children and families (MSW); community mental health (MSW). *Accreditation:* CSWE. Part-time programs available. *Faculty:* 13 full-time (10 women), 9 part-time/adjunct (8 women). *Students:* 97 full-time (79 women), 167 part-time (145 women); includes 25 minority (22 African Americans, 1 American Indian/Alaska Native, 2 Hispanic Americans), 1 international. Average age 33. 190 applicants, 73% accepted, 104 enrolled. In 2006, 46 degrees awarded. *Degree requirements:* For master's, fieldwork. *Entrance requirements:* For master's, GRE, minimum GPA of 2.75, 2 letters of reference. Additional exam requirements/recommendations for international students: Required—TOEFL. *Application deadline:* For fall admission, 3/1 for domestic students. Application fee: $45. *Expenses:* Tuition, state resident: full-time $4,926; part-time $276 per credit hour. Tuition, nonresident: full-time $14,278; part-time $796 per credit hour. Tuition and fees vary according to program. *Financial support:* In 2006–07, 179 students received support, including 7 research assistantships with full tuition reimbursements available (averaging $9,000 per year), 11 teaching assistantships with full tuition reimbursements available (averaging $9,000 per year); career-related internships or fieldwork, Federal Work-Study, institutionally sponsored loans, scholarships/grants, tuition waivers (full and partial), and stipends also available. Financial award application deadline: 3/1; financial award applicants required to submit FAFSA. *Faculty research:* Rural and small town social work practice, gerontology, health and mental health, welfare reform, child welfare. Total annual research expenditures: $208,000. *Unit head:* Dr. Virginia Majewski, Chairperson, 304-293-3501 Ext. 3129, Fax: 304-293-5936, E-mail: ginny.majewski@mail.wvu.edu. *Application contact:* Brenda Morgan-Patrick, Academic Advisor, 304-293-3501 Ext. 3128, Fax: 304-293-5936, E-mail: brenda.morgan-patrick@mail.wvu.edu.

Wichita State University, Graduate School, Fairmount College of Liberal Arts and Sciences, School of Community Affairs, Wichita, KS 67260. Offers criminal justice (MA); gerontology (MA). Part-time programs available. Electronic applications accepted.

Wilmington College, Division of Behavioral Science, New Castle, DE 19720-6491. Offers administration of human services (MS); administration of justice (MS); community counseling (MS). *Accreditation:* ACA. Part-time and evening/weekend programs available. *Faculty:* 3 full-time (1 woman). *Students:* 63 full-time (50 women), 170 part-time (125 women); includes 40 minority (34 African Americans, 1 Asian American or Pacific Islander, 5 Hispanic Americans). Average age 36. 78 applicants, 100% accepted, 39 enrolled. In 2006, 69 degrees awarded. *Entrance requirements:* Additional exam requirements/recommendations for international students: Required—TOEFL (minimum score 500 paper-based; 173 computer-based). *Application deadline:* Applications are processed on a rolling basis. Application fee: $25. *Financial support:* Applicants required to submit FAFSA. *Unit head:* Dr. Thomas Cupples, Chair, 302-328-9401 Ext. 162, Fax: 302-328-5164, E-mail: thomas.b.cupples@wilmcoll.edu. *Application contact:* Chris Ferguson, Director of Admissions and Financial Aid, 302-328-9407 Ext. 256, Fax: 302-328-5164, E-mail: inquire@wilmcoll.edu.

Youngstown State University, Graduate School, College of Health and Human Services, Department of Health Professions, Youngstown, OH 44555-0001. Offers health and human services (MHHS); public health (MPH). *Accreditation:* NAACLS. Part-time and evening/weekend programs available. *Degree requirements:* For master's, thesis optional. *Entrance requirements:* For master's, GRE General Test, minimum GPA of 3.0. Additional exam requirements/recommendations for international students: Required—TOEFL. *Faculty research:* Drug prevention, multiskilling in health care, organizational behavior, health care management, health behaviors, research management.

Social Work

Abilene Christian University, Graduate School, College of Education and Human Services, School of Social Work, Abilene, TX 79699-9100. Offers MSSW. *Expenses:* Tuition: Full-time $12,504; part-time $521 per hour. Required fees: $700; $34 per hour. *Unit head:* Dr. Paul Ammons, Unit Head, 325-674-2072.

Adelphi University, School of Social Work, Garden City, NY 11530-0701. Offers social welfare (DSW); social work (MSW). *Accreditation:* CSWE (one or more programs are accredited). Part-time and evening/weekend programs available. *Faculty:* 22 full-time (14 women). *Students:* 212 full-time (193 women), 688 part-time (597 women); includes 270 minority (187 African Americans, 1 American Indian/Alaska Native, 15 Asian Americans or Pacific Islanders, 67 Hispanic Americans), 7 international. Average age 36. 624 applicants, 71% accepted, 297 enrolled. In 2006, 280 master's, 4 doctorates awarded. *Degree requirements:* For master's, field internships; for doctorate, thesis/dissertation. *Entrance requirements:* For master's, minimum undergraduate GPA of 3.0, paid or volunteer work experience, 3 letters of recommendation, interview; for doctorate, GRE, MSW with GPA of at least 3.3, 3 years post-MSW work experience, 3 letters of reference; 3 examples of professional writing. Additional exam requirements/recommendations for international students: Required—TOEFL (minimum score 587 paper-based; 240 computer-based). *Application deadline:* For fall admission, 5/1 for international students; for spring admission, 12/1 for domestic and international students. Application fee: $50. Electronic applications accepted. *Financial support:* In 2006–07, 72 research assistantships with full and partial tuition reimbursements (averaging $2,317 per year) were awarded; career-related internships or fieldwork, Federal Work-Study, institutionally sponsored loans, scholarships/grants, traineeships, tuition waivers (full and partial), and unspecified assistantships also available. Financial award application deadline: 2/15; financial award applicants required to submit FAFSA. *Faculty research:* Services for rape victims, immigrants research methods, remarriage and step families, social health indicators. *Unit head:* Dr. Andrew Safyer, Dean, 516-877-4300, E-mail: asafyer@adelphi.edu. *Application contact:* Christine Murphy, Director of Admissions, 516-877-3050, Fax: 516-877-3039, E-mail: graduateadmissions@adelphi.edu.

See Close-Up on page 2381.

Alabama Agricultural and Mechanical University, School of Graduate Studies, School of Arts and Sciences, Department of Social Work, Huntsville, AL 35811. Offers MSW. *Accreditation:* CSWE. *Faculty:* 2 full-time (both women), 4 part-time/adjunct (2 women). *Students:* 80 full-time (72 women), 18 part-time (17 women); includes 81 minority (80 African Americans, 1 Hispanic American). In 2006, 37 degrees awarded. *Degree requirements:* For master's, thesis. *Entrance requirements:* For master's, GRE General Test, portfolio. *Application deadline:* For fall admission, 5/1 priority date for domestic students. Applications are processed on a rolling basis. Application fee: $25. Electronic applications accepted. *Financial support:* Application deadline: 4/1. *Unit head:* Dr. Shelley Wyckoff, Chair, 256-372-5478, Fax: 256-372-5970.

American Jewish University, Graduate School, David Lieber School of Graduate Studies, Program in Jewish Communal Studies, Bel Air, CA 90077-1599. Offers MAJCS. *Degree requirements:* For master's, thesis. *Entrance requirements:* For master's, GMAT or GRE General Test, interview.

Andrews University, School of Graduate Studies, College of Arts and Sciences, Department of Social Work, Berrien Springs, MI 49104. Offers MSW. *Accreditation:* CSWE.

Appalachian State University, Cratis D. Williams Graduate School, College of Arts and Sciences, Department of Sociology, Program in Social Work, Boone, NC 28608. Offers MSW. *Expenses:* Tuition, state resident: full-time $2,600; part-time $127 per hour. Tuition, nonresident: full-time $13,200; part-time $597 per hour. Required fees: $2,000; $546 per term. *Application contact:* Dr. Leon Ginsberg, Program Director, E-mail: ginsberglh@appstate.edu.

Arizona State University, Division of Graduate Studies, College of Public Programs, School of Social Work, Tempe, AZ 85287. Offers MSW, PhD. *Accreditation:* CSWE (one or more programs are accredited). *Degree requirements:* For doctorate, thesis/dissertation. *Entrance requirements:* For master's, GRE or MAT.

Arizona State University at the West campus, College of Human Services, Program in Social Work, Phoenix, AZ 85069-7100. Offers MSW. *Accreditation:* CSWE. Part-time and evening/weekend programs available. *Faculty:* 10 full-time (6 women), 9 part-time/adjunct (6 women). *Students:* 114 full-time (100 women), 16 part-time (12 women); includes 32 minority (9 African Americans, 4 American Indian/Alaska Native, 2 Asian Americans or Pacific Islanders, 17 Hispanic Americans). Average age 34. 82 applicants, 65% accepted, 36 enrolled. In 2006, 69 degrees awarded. *Median time to degree:* Master's–1 year full-time, 3 years part-time. *Degree requirements:* For master's, applied project. *Entrance requirements:* For master's, GRE or MAT, 3 letters of recommendation. Additional exam requirements/recommendations for international students: Required—TOEFL (minimum score 550 paper-based; 213 computer-based; 83 iBT). *Application deadline:* For fall admission, 2/1 priority date for domestic students. Applications are processed on a rolling basis. Application fee: $50. Electronic applications accepted. *Expenses:* Tuition, state resident: full-time $5,930. Tuition, nonresident: full-time $16,516. Tuition and fees vary according to course load. *Financial support:* Career-related internships or fieldwork, Federal Work-Study, scholarships/grants, traineeships, and tuition waivers (full and partial) available. Support available to part-time students. Financial award applicants required to submit FAFSA. *Faculty research:* Behavioral healthcare, differential assessment, child sexual abuse, poverty and gender, ethical dilemmas in practice. *Unit head:* Dr. Wendy Hultzman, Interim Chair, 602-543-6620, Fax: 602-543-6612, E-mail: wendy.hultzman@asu.edu. *Application contact:* Margaret Carbonel, Administrative Assistant, 602-543-4679, Fax: 602-543-6612, E-mail: margaret.carbonel@asu.edu.

Arkansas State University, Graduate School, College of Nursing and Health Professions, Department of Social Work, Jonesboro, State University, AR 72467. Offers MSW. Part-time programs available. *Degree requirements:* For master's, thesis (for some programs), comprehensive exam. *Entrance requirements:* For master's, GRE, appropriate bachelor's degree, letters of reference, official transcript. Additional exam requirements/recommendations for international students: Required—TOEFL (minimum score 213 computer-based). Application fee: $30 ($40 for international students). *Expenses:* Tuition, state resident: full-time $3,393; part-time $189 per hour. Tuition, nonresident: full-time $8,577; part-time $477 per hour. Required fees: $752; $39 per hour. $25 per semester. *Financial support:* Scholarships/grants and unspecified assistantships available. Financial award application deadline: 7/1; financial award applicants required to submit FAFSA.

Augsburg College, Program in Social Work, Minneapolis, MN 55454-1351. Offers MSW. *Accreditation:* CSWE. Part-time and evening/weekend programs available. *Faculty:* 8 full-time (5 women), 5 part-time/adjunct (2 women). *Students:* 74 full-time (61 women), 16 part-time (13 women); includes 15 minority (8 African Americans, 1 American Indian/Alaska Native, 2 Asian Americans or Pacific Islanders, 4 Hispanic Americans). Average age 31. 359 applicants, 20% accepted, 36 enrolled. In 2006, 32 degrees awarded. *Degree requirements:* For master's, thesis optional. *Entrance requirements:* For master's, previous course work in human biology and statistics. *Application deadline:* For fall admission, 1/15 for domestic students; for spring admission, 10/1 for domestic students. Application fee: $35. *Expenses:* Tuition: Full-time $10,584; part-time $1,764 per course. Required fees: $300; $35 per course. Tuition and fees vary according to program. *Financial support:* In 2006–07, 38 students received support. Career-related internships or fieldwork, institutionally sponsored loans, and tuition waivers (partial) available. Support available to part-time students. Financial award application deadline: 4/15. *Unit head:* Dr. Tony Bibus, Director, 612-330-1746, Fax: 612-330-1493, E-mail: bibus@augsburg.edu. *Application contact:* Holley Locher, Program Coordinator, 612-330-1763, Fax: 612-330-1493, E-mail: locherh@augsburg.edu.

Aurora University, College of Professional Studies, School of Social Work, Aurora, IL 60506-4892. Offers MSW. *Accreditation:* CSWE. Part-time and evening/weekend programs available. *Faculty:* 10 full-time (8 women), 12 part-time/adjunct (11 women). *Students:* 186 full-time (167 women), 107 part-time (89 women); includes 50 minority (24 African Americans, 5 Asian Americans or Pacific Islanders, 21 Hispanic Americans). Average age 33. 228 applicants, 97% accepted, 133 enrolled. In 2006, 122 degrees awarded. *Degree requirements:* For master's, thesis optional. *Entrance requirements:* For master's, minimum GPA of 3.0. Additional exam requirements/recommendations for international students: Required—TOEFL (minimum score 550 paper-based; 213 computer-based). *Application deadline:* For fall admission, 8/25 priority date for domestic students. Applications are processed on a rolling basis. Application fee: $25. Electronic applications accepted. *Expenses:* Contact institution. Tuition and fees vary according to campus/location and program. *Financial support:* In 2006–07, 224 students received support; fellowships, research assistantships, teaching assistantships, Federal Work-Study and scholarships/grants available. Support available to part-time students. Financial award application deadline: 4/15; financial award applicants required to submit FAFSA. *Unit head:* Dr. Fred Mckenzie, Dean, 630-844-5420, E-mail: mckenzie@aurora.edu. *Application contact:* Melissa Yovich-Whattam, Graduate Recruiter for MSW Program, 630-844-5292, E-mail: auadmission@aurora.edu.

Barry University, School of Social Work, Doctoral Program in Social Work, Miami Shores, FL 33161-6695. Offers PhD. Part-time and evening/weekend programs available. *Students:* 4 applicants, 0% accepted. In 2006, 8 degrees awarded. *Degree requirements:* For doctorate, thesis/dissertation. *Entrance requirements:* For doctorate, GRE, MSW from an accredited school of social work, 2 years of professional experience. *Application deadline:* For fall admission, 7/1 for domestic and international students; for spring admission, 12/1 for domestic and international students. Application fee: $30. Electronic applications accepted. *Financial support:* Tuition waivers (full) available. *Faculty research:* Family and children services, homelessness, gerontology, school social work. *Unit head:* Dr. Elane Nuehring, Director, 305-899-3922, Fax: 305-899-3934, E-mail: nuehring@aquinas.barry.edu. *Application contact:* Phillip Mack, Director of Admissions, 305-899-3919, Fax: 305-899-3934, E-mail: pmack@mail.barry.edu.

Barry University, School of Social Work, Master's Program in Social Work, Miami Shores, FL 33161-6695. Offers MSW. *Accreditation:* CSWE. Part-time and evening/weekend programs available. *Students:* 143 full-time (122 women), 142 part-time (123 women); includes 173 minority (124 African Americans, 1 American Indian/Alaska Native, 5 Asian Americans or Pacific Islanders, 43 Hispanic Americans), 12 international. 276 applicants, 61% accepted, 127 enrolled. In 2006, 152 degrees awarded. *Degree requirements:* For master's, fieldwork. *Entrance requirements:* For master's, minimum GPA of 3.0, minimum of 30 liberal arts credits. Additional exam requirements/recommendations for international students: Required—TOEFL (minimum score 550 paper-based; 173 computer-based). *Application deadline:* For fall admission, 7/1 for domestic and international students; for spring admission, 12/1 for domestic and international students. Application fee: $30. Electronic applications accepted. *Financial support:* In 2006–07, 75 fellowships with partial tuition reimbursements (averaging $6,000 per year), 5 research assistantships (averaging $8,000 per year) were awarded; career-related internships or fieldwork, scholarships/grants, and tuition waivers (partial) also available. Support available to part-time students. Financial award application deadline: 6/2; financial award applicants required to submit FAFSA. *Faculty research:* Family and children services, homelessness, gerontology, school social work. *Unit head:* Dr. Phyllis Scott, Director, 305-899-3914, Fax: 305-899-3934. *Application contact:* Phillip Mack, Director of Admissions, 305-899-3919, Fax: 305-899-3934, E-mail: pmack@mail.barry.edu.

See Close-Up on page 2383.

Baylor University, Graduate School, College of Arts and Sciences, School of Social Work, Waco, TX 76798. Offers MSW, M Div/MSW. *Accreditation:* CSWE. *Students:* 50 full-time (44 women), 7 part-time (5 women); includes 10 minority (6 African Americans, 1 Asian American or Pacific Islander, 3 Hispanic Americans). In 2006, 39 degrees awarded. Application fee: $25. *Unit head:* Dr. Dennis Myers, Graduate Program Director, 254-710-6404, E-mail: dennis_myers@baylor.edu. *Application contact:* Suzanne Keener, Administrative Assistant, 254-710-3588, Fax: 254-710-3870.

Boise State University, Graduate College, College of Social Sciences and Public Affairs, School of Social Work, Boise, ID 83725-0399. Offers MSW. *Accreditation:* CSWE. Part-time programs available. *Faculty:* 9 full-time (5 women), 1 part-time/adjunct (0 women). *Students:* 41 full-time (28 women), 1 (woman) part-time; includes 5 minority (1 African American, 1 American Indian/Alaska Native, 1 Asian American or Pacific Islander, 2 Hispanic Americans), 1 international. Average age 33. 35 applicants, 43% accepted, 8 enrolled. In 2006, 29 degrees awarded. *Entrance requirements:* For master's, GRE General Test, minimum GPA of 3.0. *Application deadline:* For fall admission, 1/1 priority date for domestic students; for spring admission, 8/1 priority date for domestic students. Applications are processed on a rolling basis. Application fee: $0. Electronic applications accepted. *Financial support:* In 2006–07, 8 students received support. Career-related internships or fieldwork, Federal Work-Study, institutionally sponsored loans, and unspecified assistantships available. Support available to part-time students. Financial award application deadline: 3/1. *Unit head:* Dr. William H. Whitaker, Coordinator, 208-426-2579, Fax: 208-426-4291, E-mail: wwhitak@boisestate.edu.

Boston College, Graduate School of Social Work, Chestnut Hill, MA 02467-3800. Offers MSW, PhD, JD/MSW, MSW/MA, MSW/MBA. *Accreditation:* CSWE (one or more programs are accredited). Part-time programs available. *Faculty:* 21 full-time (12 women), 35 part-time/adjunct (21 women). *Students:* 391 full-time (351 women), 125 part-time (112 women); includes 86 minority (32 African Americans, 2 American Indian/Alaska Native, 27 Asian Americans or Pacific Islanders, 25 Hispanic Americans), 11 international. 733 applicants, 67% accepted, 208 enrolled. In 2006, 179 master's, 4 doctorates awarded. *Degree requirements:* For master's, 2 internships; for doctorate, thesis/dissertation. *Entrance requirements:* For doctorate, GRE. Additional exam requirements/recommendations for international students: Required—TOEFL (minimum score 550 paper-based; 213 computer-based). *Application deadline:* For fall admission, 3/1 for domestic students. Applications are processed on a rolling basis. Application fee: $40. *Expenses:* Contact institution. *Financial support:* In 2006–07, 354 students received support, including 15 fellowships with full tuition reimbursements available (averaging $18,000 per year), 2 research assistantships with full tuition reimbursements available (averaging $6,000 per year); teaching assistantships, career-related internships or fieldwork, Federal Work-Study, institutionally sponsored loans, scholarships/grants, traineeships, tuition waivers (partial), and unspecified assistantships also available. Support available to part-time students. Financial award applicants required to submit FAFSA. *Faculty research:* Healthy aging communities, balancing work and family, service options for persons with disabilities, abuse and trauma of children and adolescents/family interventions, older workers. Total annual research expenditures: $2.6 million. *Unit head:* Dr. Alberto Godenzi, Dean, 617-552-0866, Fax: 617-552-2374, E-mail: godenzi@bc.edu. *Application contact:* Dr. William Howard, Director of Admission, 617-552-4024, Fax: 617-552-1690, E-mail: william.howard@bc.edu.

See Close-Up on page 2385.

Boston University, Graduate School of Arts and Sciences, Interdisciplinary Program in Sociology and Social Work, Boston, MA 02215. Offers PhD. *Students:* 23 full-time (18 women), 2 part-time (both women); includes 7 minority (3 African Americans, 1 Asian American or Pacific Islander, 3 Hispanic Americans), 5 international. Average age 37. 20 applicants, 75% accepted, 4 enrolled. *Degree requirements:* For doctorate, one foreign language, thesis/dissertation, critical essay, comprehensive exam, registration. *Entrance requirements:* For doctorate, GRE General Test or MAT, sample of written work. Additional exam requirements/recommendations for international students: Required—TOEFL. *Application deadline:* For fall

Social Work

Boston University (continued)

admission, 1/15 for domestic and international students. Application fee: $70. Electronic applications accepted. *Expenses:* Tuition: Full-time $33,330; part-time $1,042 per credit. Required fees: $462; $40. *Financial support:* In 2006–07, 12 students received support, including 5 research assistantships with full tuition reimbursements available (averaging $15,500 per year); fellowships, career-related internships or fieldwork, Federal Work-Study, and scholarships/grants also available. Support available to part-time students. Financial award application deadline: 1/15; financial award applicants required to submit FAFSA. *Faculty research:* Mental health, child welfare, aging, substance abuse. *Unit head:* Mary E. Collins, Director, 617-353-3748, Fax: 617-353-5612, E-mail: mcollins@bu.edu. *Application contact:* Rilda Letouneau, Staff Coordinator, 617-353-3765, Fax: 617-353-5612, E-mail: sswphd@bu.edu.

Boston University, School of Social Work, Boston, MA 02215. Offers clinical practice with groups (MSW); clinical practice with individuals and families (MSW); macro social work practice (MSW); social work and sociology (PhD); D Min/MSW; M Div/MSW; MSW/Ed D; MSW/Ed M; MSW/MPH; MSW/MTS. *Accreditation:* CSWE (one or more programs are accredited). Part-time programs available. *Faculty:* 22 full-time (16 women), 29 part-time/adjunct (23 women). *Students:* 165 full-time (144 women), 194 part-time (169 women); includes 41 minority (16 African Americans, 1 American Indian/Alaska Native, 5 Asian Americans or Pacific Islanders, 19 Hispanic Americans), 4 international. Average age 30. 507 applicants, 87% accepted, 192 enrolled. In 2006, 161 degrees awarded. *Degree requirements:* For doctorate, one foreign language, thesis/dissertation, critical essay. *Entrance requirements:* For master's, minimum GPA of 3.0 or GRE General Test or MAT; for doctorate, GRE General Test or MAT, writing sample. Additional exam requirements/recommendations for international students: Required—TOEFL (minimum score 550 paper-based; 213 computer-based). *Application deadline:* For fall admission, 3/1 for domestic and international students. Applications are processed on a rolling basis. Application fee: $70. Electronic applications accepted. *Expenses:* Contact institution. *Financial support:* In 2006–07, 95 students received support, including 1 research assistantship with full tuition reimbursement available (averaging $8,000 per year); career-related internships or fieldwork, Federal Work-Study, institutionally sponsored loans, and scholarships/grants also available. Support available to part-time students. Financial award application deadline: 3/1; financial award applicants required to submit FAFSA. *Faculty research:* Health and aging, child and adolescent substance abuse, mental health. Total annual research expenditures: $1.3 million. *Unit head:* Wilma Peebles-Wilkins, Dean, 617-353-3760, Fax: 617-353-5612. *Application contact:* Edward M. Greene, Director of Admissions, 617-353-3765, Fax: 617-353-5612, E-mail: busswad@bu.edu.

Bridgewater State College, School of Graduate Studies, School of Arts and Sciences, Department of Social Work, Bridgewater, MA 02325-0001. Offers MSW. *Accreditation:* CSWE. *Application deadline:* For fall admission, 2/1 for domestic students. Application fee: $50. *Financial support:* Career-related internships or fieldwork, health care benefits, and unspecified assistantships available. Support available to part-time students. *Application contact:* Dr. Raymond Charles Guillette, Assistant Dean School of Graduate Studies, 508-531-2919, Fax: 508-531-6162, E-mail: rguillette@bridgew.edu.

Brigham Young University, Graduate Studies, College of Family, Home, and Social Sciences, School of Social Work, Provo, UT 84602-1001. Offers MSW. *Accreditation:* CSWE. *Faculty:* 11 full-time (5 women). *Students:* 81 full-time (52 women); includes 12 minority (2 African Americans, 3 American Indian/Alaska Native, 5 Asian Americans or Pacific Islanders, 2 Hispanic Americans), 7 international. Average age 28. 154 applicants, 31% accepted, 41 enrolled. In 2006, 39 degrees awarded. *Median time to degree:* Master's–1.66 years full-time. *Degree requirements:* For master's, thesis optional. *Entrance requirements:* Additional exam requirements/recommendations for international students: Required—TOEFL (minimum score 580 paper-based; 237 computer-based), IELTS (minimum score 7). *Application deadline:* For fall admission, 1/15 for domestic and international students. Application fee: $50. Electronic applications accepted. *Financial support:* In 2006–07, 23 students received support, including 5 fellowships with tuition reimbursements available (averaging $4,000 per year), 14 research assistantships (averaging $1,820 per year), 4 teaching assistantships (averaging $3,640 per year); career-related internships or fieldwork, tuition waivers (partial), and administrative aides, paid field practicum also available. Financial award application deadline: 6/1. *Faculty research:* Adoptions, depression, spirituality, child welfare, marriage and family. Total annual research expenditures: $62,011. *Unit head:* Dr. Kevin M. Marett, Director, 801-422-3282, Fax: 801-422-0624, E-mail: socialwork@byu.edu. *Application contact:* Lisa Willey, Graduate Secretary, 801-422-5681, Fax: 801-422-0624, E-mail: lisa_willey@byu.edu.

Bryn Mawr College, Graduate School of Social Work and Social Research, Bryn Mawr, PA 19010-2899. Offers MLSP, MSS, PhD. *Accreditation:* CSWE (one or more programs are accredited). Part-time programs available. *Faculty:* 14 full-time (8 women), 39 part-time/adjunct (33 women). *Students:* 163 full-time (142 women), 89 part-time (79 women); includes 63 minority (52 African Americans, 7 Asian Americans or Pacific Islanders, 4 Hispanic Americans), 7 international. Average age 34. 208 applicants, 74% accepted, 90 enrolled. In 2006, 108 master's, 4 doctorates awarded. *Median time to degree:* Of those who began their doctoral program in fall 1998, 75% received their degree in 8 years or less. *Degree requirements:* For master's, fieldwork; for doctorate, thesis/dissertation, comprehensive exam. *Entrance requirements:* For master's, interview, 3 letters of reference; for doctorate, GRE General Test, interview, 3 letters of reference, master's degree. Additional exam requirements/recommendations for international students: Required—TOEFL (minimum score 620 paper-based). *Application deadline:* For fall admission, 3/31 priority date for domestic and international students. Applications are processed on a rolling basis. Application fee: $50. *Expenses:* Contact institution. *Financial support:* In 2006–07, 190 students received support, including 17 fellowships with full and partial tuition reimbursements available (averaging $3,271 per year), 12 teaching assistantships with full and partial tuition reimbursements available (averaging $9,722 per year); research assistantships with full and partial tuition reimbursements available, career-related internships or fieldwork, Federal Work-Study, institutionally sponsored loans, scholarships/grants, tuition waivers (full and partial), and PhD dissertation award also available. Support available to part-time students. Financial award application deadline: 3/1; financial award applicants required to submit FAFSA. *Faculty research:* Ethical issues, children and adolescents, poverty, mental health, child and family welfare. Total annual research expenditures: $3 million. *Unit head:* Dr. Marcia L. Martin, Co-Dean, 610-520-2603, Fax: 610-520-2613, E-mail: mmartin@brynmawr.edu. *Application contact:* Nancy J. Kirby, Assistant Dean and Director of Admissions, 610-520-2601, Fax: 610-520-2655, E-mail: swadmiss@brynmawr.edu.

California State University, Bakersfield, Division of Graduate Studies and Research, School of Humanities and Social Sciences, Program in Social Work, Bakersfield, CA 93311-1022. Offers MSW. *Accreditation:* CSWE. *Students:* 81 full-time (67 women), 15 part-time (11 women); includes 45 minority (13 African Americans, 6 Asian Americans or Pacific Islanders, 26 Hispanic Americans), 1 international. Average age 35. In 2006, 35 degrees awarded. *Application deadline:* Applications are processed on a rolling basis. Application fee: $55. *Unit head:* Dr. Debra Morrison-Octon, Graduate Coordinator, 661-664-3208, Fax: 661-665-6928.

California State University, Chico, Graduate School, College of Behavioral and Social Sciences, School of Social Work, Chico, CA 95929-0550. Offers MSW. *Accreditation:* CSWE. *Students:* 57 full-time (45 women), 38 part-time (28 women); includes 28 minority (4 African Americans, 2 American Indian/Alaska Native, 9 Asian Americans or Pacific Islanders, 13 Hispanic Americans). Average age 35. 85 applicants, 100% accepted, 66 enrolled. In 2006, 28 degrees awarded. *Degree requirements:* For master's, thesis or alternative, oral exam. *Entrance requirements:* For master's, 3 letters of recommendation on departmental form. Additional exam requirements/recommendations for international students: Required—TOEFL (minimum score 550 paper-based; 213 computer-based). *Application deadline:* For fall admission, 3/1 for domestic and international students. Applications are processed on a rolling basis. Electronic applications accepted. *Unit head:* Jean Schuldberg, Graduate Coordinator, 530-898-4187.

California State University, Dominguez Hills, College of Health and Human Services, Program in Social Work, Carson, CA 90747-0001. Offers MSW. Part-time and evening/weekend programs available. *Faculty:* 4 full-time (2 women). *Students:* 15 full-time (12 women); includes 12 minority (7 African Americans, 1 Asian American or Pacific Islander, 4 Hispanic Americans), 1 international. Average age 30. 17 applicants, 94% accepted, 15 enrolled. *Degree requirements:* For master's, thesis. *Entrance requirements:* For master's, minimum GPA of 2.75 in last 60 units; 3 courses in behavioral science, 2 in humanities, 1 in English composition, 1 in elementary statistics, and 1 in human biology. *Application deadline:* For fall admission, 4/30 for domestic students. Applications are processed on a rolling basis. *Expenses:* Tuition, nonresident: part-time $339 per unit. Required fees: $1,148 per term. Tuition and fees vary according to program. *Faculty research:* HIV/AIDS, community capacity, program evaluation. *Unit head:* Dr. Larry Ortiz, Professor and Director, 310-243-5464, E-mail: lortiz@csudh.edu. *Application contact:* Susan Nakaoka, Director of Admissions, 310-243-2181, Fax: 310-217-6800, E-mail: snakaoka@csudh.edu.

California State University, East Bay, Academic Programs and Graduate Studies, College of Letters, Arts, and Social Sciences, Department of Social Work, Hayward, CA 94542-3000. Offers MSW. *Accreditation:* CSWE. *Faculty:* 10 full-time (7 women), 9 part-time/adjunct (6 women). *Students:* 124 full-time (97 women), 45 part-time (36 women); includes 103 minority (47 African Americans, 28 Asian Americans or Pacific Islanders, 28 Hispanic Americans), 4 international. Average age 35. 183 applicants, 55% accepted, 75 enrolled. In 2006, 69 degrees awarded. *Entrance requirements:* For master's, resumé, 3 letters of recommendation, minimum GPA of 2.6 in last 60 hours of course work. Additional exam requirements/recommendations for international students: Required—TOEFL (minimum score 550 paper-based; 213 computer-based). *Application deadline:* For fall admission, 5/31 for domestic students, 4/30 for international students; for winter admission, 9/30 for domestic and international students; for spring admission, 12/31 for domestic students, 11/30 for international students. Applications are processed on a rolling basis. Application fee: $55. Electronic applications accepted. *Unit head:* Terry Jones, Chair, 510-885-4916, Fax: 510-885-7580, E-mail: terry.jones@csueastbay.edu. *Application contact:* My Huynh, Graduate Prospect Specialist, 510-885-2989, Fax: 510-885-4059, E-mail: my.huynh@csueastbay.edu.

California State University, Fresno, Division of Graduate Studies, College of Health and Human Services, Department of Social Work Education, Fresno, CA 93740-8027. Offers MSW. *Accreditation:* CSWE. Part-time and evening/weekend programs available. *Degree requirements:* For master's, thesis or alternative. *Entrance requirements:* For master's, GRE General Test, minimum GPA of 2.5. Additional exam requirements/recommendations for international students: Required—TOEFL. Electronic applications accepted. *Faculty research:* Children at risk, international cooperation, child welfare training, nutrition.

California State University, Long Beach, Graduate Studies, College of Health and Human Services, Department of Social Work, Long Beach, CA 90840. Offers MSW. *Accreditation:* CSWE. Part-time and evening/weekend programs available. Postbaccalaureate distance learning degree programs offered (no on-campus study). *Faculty:* 26 full-time (17 women), 33 part-time/adjunct (26 women). *Students:* 394 full-time (343 women), 154 part-time (139 women); includes 325 minority (61 African Americans, 4 American Indian/Alaska Native, 71 Asian Americans or Pacific Islanders, 189 Hispanic Americans), 2 international. Average age 33. 608 applicants, 52% accepted, 226 enrolled. In 2006, 176 degrees awarded. *Degree requirements:* For master's, thesis. *Application deadline:* For fall admission, 7/1 for domestic students; for spring admission, 12/1 for domestic students. Applications are processed on a rolling basis. Application fee: $55. Electronic applications accepted. *Financial support:* Federal Work-Study, institutionally sponsored loans, and scholarships/grants available. Financial award application deadline: 3/2. *Unit head:* Dr. John Oliver, Director, 562-985-5655, Fax: 562-985-5514, E-mail: joliver@csulb.edu. *Application contact:* Dr. Christine Kleinpeter, Graduate Coordinator, 562-985-5655, Fax: 562-985-5514, E-mail: ckleinpe@csulb.edu.

California State University, Los Angeles, Graduate Studies, College of Health and Human Services, School of Social Work, Los Angeles, CA 90032-8530. Offers MSW. *Accreditation:* CSWE. *Faculty:* 17 full-time (13 women), 12 part-time/adjunct (4 women). *Students:* 116 full-time (97 women), 165 part-time (134 women); includes 203 minority (27 African Americans, 1 American Indian/Alaska Native, 32 Asian Americans or Pacific Islanders, 143 Hispanic Americans), 8 international. In 2006, 109 degrees awarded. *Entrance requirements:* Additional exam requirements/recommendations for international students: Required—TOEFL. *Application deadline:* For fall admission, 6/30 for domestic students; for spring admission, 2/1 for domestic students. Applications are processed on a rolling basis. Application fee: $55. *Expenses:* Tuition, nonresident: part-time $226 per unit. *Financial support:* Application deadline: 3/1. *Unit head:* Dr. Karin Elliott-Brown, Chair, 323-343-4680, Fax: 323-343-5009.

California State University, Northridge, Graduate Studies, College of Social and Behavioral Sciences, Department of Sociology, Northridge, CA 91330. Offers social work (MSW), including advanced practice with urban families; sociology (MA). Part-time and evening/weekend programs available. *Faculty:* 27 full-time (13 women), 32 part-time/adjunct (20 women). *Students:* 76 full-time (12 women), 14 part-time (5 women); includes 45 minority (5 African Americans, 1 American Indian/Alaska Native, 7 Asian Americans or Pacific Islanders, 32 Hispanic Americans), 2 international. Average age 30. 119 applicants, 54% accepted, 37 enrolled. In 2006, 3 degrees awarded. *Degree requirements:* For master's, thesis or alternative. *Entrance requirements:* For master's, GRE General Test or minimum GPA of 3.0. Additional exam requirements/recommendations for international students: Required—TOEFL. *Application deadline:* For fall admission, 11/30 for domestic students. Application fee: $55. *Expenses:* Tuition, nonresident: full-time $8,136; part-time $4,068 per year. Required fees: $3,624; $1,161 per term. *Financial support:* Career-related internships or fieldwork, Federal Work-Study, and institutionally sponsored loans available. Support available to part-time students. Financial award application deadline: 3/1. *Faculty research:* Crime and corrections, relationships between adult children and parents. *Unit head:* Dr. Nathan Weinberg, Chair, 818-677-3591. *Application contact:* Dr. David Boyns, Graduate Advisor, 818-677-6803.

California State University, Sacramento, Graduate Studies, College of Health and Human Services, Division of Social Work, Sacramento, CA 95819-6048. Offers family and children's services (MSW); health care (MSW); mental health (MSW); social justice and corrections (MSW). *Accreditation:* CSWE. *Students:* 284 full-time (233 women), 38 part-time (31 women); includes 158 minority (43 African Americans, 3 American Indian/Alaska Native, 63 Asian Americans or Pacific Islanders, 49 Hispanic Americans), 3 international. Average age 33. 369 applicants, 53% accepted, 137 enrolled. *Degree requirements:* For master's, thesis or alternative, writing proficiency exam. *Entrance requirements:* For master's, minimum GPA of 2.5 during previous 2 years of course work. Additional exam requirements/recommendations for international students: Required—TOEFL. *Application deadline:* Applications are processed on a rolling basis. Application fee: $55. Electronic applications accepted. *Financial support:* Career-related internships or fieldwork and Federal Work-Study available. Support available to part-time students. Financial award application deadline: 3/1. *Unit head:* Dr. Robin Carter, Chair, 916-278-6943, Fax: 916-278-7167.

California State University, San Bernardino, Graduate Studies, College of Social and Behavioral Sciences, Department of Social Work, San Bernardino, CA 92407-2397. Offers MSW. *Accreditation:* CSWE. Part-time and evening/weekend programs available. *Faculty:* 9 full-time, 10 part-time/adjunct. *Students:* 162 full-time (134 women), 2 part-time (both women); includes 97 minority (31 African Americans, 3 American Indian/Alaska Native, 8 Asian Americans or Pacific Islanders, 55 Hispanic Americans). Average age 31. 156 applicants, 58% accepted, 70 enrolled. In 2006, 56 degrees awarded. *Degree requirements:* For master's, field practicum, research project. *Entrance requirements:* For master's, minimum GPA of 2.75 in last 2 years of course work, liberal arts background. *Application deadline:* For fall admission, 8/31 priority date for domestic students. Application fee: $55. *Financial support:* Fellowships, research assistantships, career-related internships or fieldwork, Federal Work-Study, institutionally sponsored loans, and stipends for practicum available. Support available to part-time students.

Financial award application deadline: 5/1. *Faculty research:* Addiction, computers in social work practice, minority issues, gerontology. *Unit head:* Dr. Teresa Morris, Chair, 909-537-5501, Fax: 909-537-7029, E-mail: tmorris@csusb.edu.

California State University, Stanislaus, Graduate School, College of Arts, Letters, and Sciences, Department of Social Work, Turlock, CA 95382. Offers MSW. *Accreditation:* CSWE. *Degree requirements:* For master's, thesis. *Entrance requirements:* For master's, minimum GPA of 2.5 required, 3.0 preferred; letters of reference. Electronic applications accepted.

California University of Pennsylvania, School of Graduate Studies and Research, School of Education, Department of Social Work and Gerontology, California, PA 15419-1394. Offers social work (MSW). *Accreditation:* CSWE. Part-time programs available. *Faculty:* 14 full-time (13 women). *Students:* 32 full-time (27 women), 18 part-time (13 women); includes 4 minority (all African Americans) Average age 34. 26 applicants, 85% accepted, 19 enrolled. In 2006, 14 degrees awarded. *Median time to degree:* Master's–1.5 years full-time, 3 years part-time. *Degree requirements:* For master's, comprehensive exam. *Entrance requirements:* For master's, GRE, letters of reference. Additional exam requirements/recommendations for international students: Required—TOEFL. *Application deadline:* For fall admission, 8/1 priority date for domestic and international students; for winter admission, 12/1 priority date for domestic and international students; for spring admission, 5/1 priority date for domestic and international students. Applications are processed on a rolling basis. Application fee: $25. Electronic applications accepted. *Expenses:* Tuition, state resident: full-time $6,048; part-time $336 per credit. Tuition, nonresident: full-time $9,678; part-time $538 per credit. Required fees: $1,854; $263 per credit. Full-time tuition and fees vary according to course load, campus/location and program. *Financial support:* Career-related internships or fieldwork, scholarships/grants, traineeships, and unspecified assistantships available. Financial award applicants required to submit FAFSA. *Faculty research:* Social welfare and policy, housing and community development, health and mental health, Black Appalachian, aging. Total annual research expenditures: $30,000. *Unit head:* Dr. Pamela Twiss, Coordinator, 724-938-4053, Fax: 724-938-5977, E-mail: twiss@cup.edu. *Application contact:* Coordinator, 724-938-4053.

Campbellsville University, Carver School of Social Work, Campbellsville, KY 42718-2799. Offers M Ed/MLIS. Evening/weekend programs available. *Faculty:* 6 full-time (3 women), 2 part-time/adjunct (0 women). *Students:* 15 full-time (12 women); includes 2 minority (both African Americans) 15 applicants, 67% accepted, 10 enrolled.Application fee: $25. Electronic applications accepted. *Expenses:* Tuition: Full-time $6,570; part-time $365 per hour. Tuition and fees vary according to program. *Financial support:* Applicants required to submit FAFSA. *Unit head:* Dr. Darlene F. Eastridge, Program Director, 270-789-5178, Fax: 270-789-5542, E-mail: dfeastridge@campbellsville.edu.

Carleton University, Faculty of Graduate Studies, Faculty of Public Affairs and Management, School of Social Work, Ottawa, ON K1S 5B6, Canada. Offers MSW. Part-time programs available. *Degree requirements:* For master's, thesis optional. *Entrance requirements:* For master's, basic research methods course. Additional exam requirements/recommendations for international students: Required—TOEFL. *Application deadline:* Applications are processed on a rolling basis. Application fee: $75 Canadian dollars. *Financial support:* Fellowships, research assistantships, teaching assistantships, institutionally sponsored loans, scholarships/grants, and unspecified assistantships available. *Faculty research:* Social administration, program evaluation, history of Canadian social welfare, women's issues, education in social work. *Unit head:* Roy Hanes, Director, 613-520-2600 Ext. 5601, Fax: 613-520-7496, E-mail: chair_social_work@carleton.ca. *Application contact:* Sue Brady, Graduate Secretary, 613-520-2600 Ext. 5601, Fax: 613-520-7496, E-mail: chair_social_work@carleton.ca.

Case Western Reserve University, Mandel School of Applied Social Sciences, Cleveland, OH 44106. Offers nonprofit organizations (MNO, CNM); social administration (MSSA); social welfare (PhD); JD/MSSA; MSSA/MBA; MSSA/MNO. *Accreditation:* CSWE (one or more programs are accredited). Evening/weekend programs available. *Degree requirements:* For master's, fieldwork; for doctorate, thesis/dissertation. *Entrance requirements:* For master's, GRE General Test, MAT, or minimum GPA of 2.7; for doctorate, GRE General Test or MAT, minimum GPA of 2.7. Additional exam requirements/recommendations for international students: Required—TOEFL. Expenses: Contact institution. *Faculty research:* Models of social work practice, improved delivery in health and social services, evaluating community-based initiatives, center for community development, center on urban poverty and social change.

See Close-Up on page 2387.

The Catholic University of America, National Catholic School of Social Service, Washington, DC 20064. Offers MSW, PhD, JD/MSW. *Accreditation:* CSWE (one or more programs are accredited). Part-time programs available. *Faculty:* 17 full-time (15 women), 22 part-time/adjunct (19 women). *Students:* 101 full-time (87 women), 136 part-time (112 women); includes 36 minority (26 African Americans, 4 Asian Americans or Pacific Islanders, 6 Hispanic Americans), 6 international. Average age 34. 178 applicants, 80% accepted, 94 enrolled. In 2006, 71 master's, 4 doctorates awarded. *Degree requirements:* For master's, thesis or alternative, comprehensive exam; for doctorate, one foreign language, thesis/dissertation, comprehensive exam. *Entrance requirements:* For master's, GRE or MAT, 3 letters of recommendation, resumé; for doctorate, GRE or MAT, MSW, 3 letters of recommendation, resumé. Additional exam requirements/recommendations for international students: Required—TOEFL (minimum score 600 paper-based; 250 computer-based). *Application deadline:* For fall admission, 2/1 priority date for domestic students; for spring admission, 11/15 priority date for domestic students. Applications are processed on a rolling basis. Application fee: $55. Electronic applications accepted. *Expenses: Contact institution.* Part-time tuition and fees vary according to campus/location and program. *Financial support:* Fellowships, career-related internships or fieldwork, Federal Work-Study, scholarships/grants, and unspecified assistantships available. Support available to part-time students. Financial award application deadline: 2/1; financial award applicants required to submit FAFSA. *Faculty research:* Family and child services, social policy, health and mental health, ethics, spirituality and social work practice. *Unit head:* Dr. James R. Zabora, Dean, 202-319-5454, Fax: 202-319-5093, E-mail: zabora@cua.edu. *Application contact:* Christine Mica, Director, University Admissions, 202-319-5305, Fax: 202-319-6533, E-mail: cua-admissions@cua.edu.

See Close-Up on page 2389.

Chicago State University, School of Graduate and Professional Studies, College of Arts and Sciences, Program in Social Work, Chicago, IL 60628. Offers MSW. *Accreditation:* CSWE. Electronic applications accepted.

Clark Atlanta University, School of Social Work, Atlanta, GA 30314. Offers MSW, PhD. *Accreditation:* CSWE (one or more programs are accredited). Part-time programs available. Terminal master's awarded for partial completion of doctoral program. *Degree requirements:* For master's, thesis; for doctorate, one foreign language, thesis/dissertation.

Cleveland State University, College of Graduate Studies, College of Liberal Arts and Social Sciences, School of Social Work, Cleveland, OH 44115. Offers MSW. *Accreditation:* CSWE. Part-time and evening/weekend programs available. Postbaccalaureate distance learning degree programs offered (no on-campus study). *Faculty:* 11 full-time (4 women), 5 part-time/adjunct (2 women). *Students:* 129 full-time (111 women), 54 part-time (46 women); includes 71 minority (66 African Americans, 1 American Indian/Alaska Native, 4 Hispanic Americans), 3 international. Average age 35. 150 applicants, 61% accepted, 76 enrolled. In 2006, 59 degrees awarded. *Entrance requirements:* For master's, 3 letters of reference. Additional exam requirements/recommendations for international students: Required—TOEFL (minimum score 525 paper-based; 197 computer-based); Recommended—IELTS (minimum score 6). *Application deadline:* For fall admission, 2/28 for domestic students. Application fee: $30. *Financial support:* In 2006–07, 15 students received support, including 2 research assistantships with full and partial tuition reimbursements available (averaging $3,480 per year); tuition waivers (full) also available. *Faculty research:* Mental health, aging. Total annual research expenditures: $1.2 million. *Unit head:* Dr. Maggie Jackson, Director, 216-687-4599, Fax: 216-687-5590, E-mail: m.jackson@csuohio.edu.

College of St. Catherine, Graduate Programs, Program in Social Work, St. Paul, MN 55105-1789. Offers MSW. *Accreditation:* CSWE. Part-time and evening/weekend programs available. *Degree requirements:* For master's, clinical research paper. *Entrance requirements:* For master's, minimum GPA of 3.0. Additional exam requirements/recommendations for international students: Required—Michigan English Language Assessment Battery or TOEFL. Expenses: Contact institution.

Colorado State University, Graduate School, College of Applied Human Sciences, School of Social Work, Fort Collins, CO 80523-0015. Offers MSW. *Accreditation:* CSWE. Postbaccalaureate distance learning degree programs offered (minimal on-campus study). *Faculty:* 11 full-time (6 women). *Students:* 77 full-time (63 women), 32 part-time (30 women); includes 11 minority (4 African Americans, 2 Asian Americans or Pacific Islanders, 5 Hispanic Americans). Average age 33. 130 applicants, 38% accepted, 32 enrolled. In 2006, 82 degrees awarded. *Degree requirements:* For master's, thesis or alternative, research paper. *Entrance requirements:* For master's, minimum GPA of 3.0; 18 credits of course work in social or behavioral science, human biology, statistics, and human development; 450 hours of verifiable human service work and/or volunteer experience. Additional exam requirements/recommendations for international students: Required—TOEFL. *Application deadline:* For fall admission, 1/31 for domestic and international students. Application fee: $50. Electronic applications accepted. *Expenses:* Tuition, state resident: full-time $4,248; part-time $236 per credit. Tuition, nonresident: full-time $15,642; part-time $869 per credit. Required fees: $66 per credit. Tuition and fees vary according to program. *Financial support:* In 2006–07, 7 fellowships (averaging $1,514 per year), 3 research assistantships with partial tuition reimbursements (averaging $9,325 per year), 3 teaching assistantships with partial tuition reimbursements (averaging $9,333 per year) were awarded; career-related internships or fieldwork, Federal Work-Study, and institutionally sponsored loans also available. Financial award application deadline: 12/30. *Faculty research:* Environmental health, child welfare, mental health, international social work, disabilities, social advocacy. Total annual research expenditures: $542,005. *Unit head:* Dr. Deborah P. Valentine, Director, 970-491-2536, Fax: 970-491-7280. *Application contact:* Dawn Carlson, MSW Program Coordinator, 970-491-2536, Fax: 970-491-7280, E-mail: dcarlson@cahs.colostate.edu.

Columbia University, School of Social Work, New York, NY 10027. Offers MSSW, PhD, JD/MS, MBA/MS, MPA/MS, MPH/MS, MS/M Div, MS/MA, MS/MS, MS/MS Ed. PhD offered through the Graduate School of Arts and Sciences. *Accreditation:* CSWE (one or more programs are accredited). *Faculty:* 50 full-time. *Students:* 850. Average age 26. 1,104 applicants, 425 enrolled. In 2006, 437 master's, 17 doctorates awarded. *Degree requirements:* For doctorate, thesis/dissertation. *Entrance requirements:* For master's, 3 letters of reference; for doctorate, GRE General Test, 3 letters of recommendation. Additional exam requirements/recommendations for international students: Required—TOEFL, TWE. *Application deadline:* For fall admission, 3/1 priority date for domestic students; for winter admission, 11/15 priority date for domestic students. Applications are processed on a rolling basis. Application fee: $65. Electronic applications accepted. *Expenses: Contact institution. Financial support:* Fellowships, research assistantships, teaching assistantships with partial tuition reimbursements, career-related internships or fieldwork, Federal Work-Study, institutionally sponsored loans, scholarships/grants, health care benefits, and unspecified assistantships available. Support available to part-time students. Financial award application deadline: 2/15; financial award applicants required to submit CSS PROFILE or FAFSA. *Unit head:* Dr. Jeanette Takamura, Dean. *Application contact:* Debbie Lesperance, Director of Admissions, 212-851-2211, Fax: 212-851-2305, E-mail: dl635@columbia.edu.

See Close-Up on page 2391.

Cornell University, Graduate School, Graduate Fields of Human Ecology, Field of Policy Analysis and Management, Ithaca, NY 14853-0001. Offers consumer policy (PhD); evaluation (PhD); family and social welfare policy (PhD); health administration (MHA); health management and policy (PhD). *Faculty:* 33 full-time (14 women). *Students:* 54 full-time (30 women); includes 12 minority (3 African Americans, 6 Asian Americans or Pacific Islanders, 3 Hispanic Americans), 15 international. Average age 28. 69 applicants, 35% accepted, 16 enrolled. In 2006, 17 master's, 3 doctorates awarded. *Degree requirements:* For master's and doctorate, thesis/dissertation, registration. *Entrance requirements:* For master's, GRE General Test or GMAT, 2 letters of recommendation; for doctorate, GRE General Test, 2 letters of recommendation. Additional exam requirements/recommendations for international students: Required—TOEFL (minimum score 550 paper-based; 213 computer-based). *Application deadline:* For fall admission, 1/15 for domestic students. Application fee: $60. Electronic applications accepted. *Expenses:* Tuition: Full-time $32,800. Full-time tuition and fees vary according to program. *Financial support:* In 2006–07, 33 students received support, including 6 fellowships with full and partial tuition reimbursements available, 12 research assistantships with full and partial tuition reimbursements available, 15 teaching assistantships with full and partial tuition reimbursements available; institutionally sponsored loans, scholarships/grants, health care benefits, tuition waivers (full and partial), and unspecified assistantships also available. Financial award applicants required to submit FAFSA. *Faculty research:* Health policy, family policy, social welfare policy, program evaluation, consumer policy. *Unit head:* Director of Graduate Studies, 607-255-7772. *Application contact:* Graduate Field Assistant, 607-255-7772, Fax: 607-255-4071, E-mail: pam_phd@cornell.edu.

Dalhousie University, Faculty of Graduate Studies, Faculty of Health Professions, The Maritime School of Social Work, Halifax, NS B3H 4R2, Canada. Offers MSW. Part-time programs available. Postbaccalaureate distance learning degree programs offered (no on-campus study). *Degree requirements:* For master's, field placement, thesis optional. *Entrance requirements:* For master's, bachelor's degree in social work, 2 years work experience in social work, minimum GPA of 3.0. Additional exam requirements/recommendations for international students: Required—TOEFL. Expenses: Contact institution. *Faculty research:* Family and child welfare, public policy, physical and mental health, elder abuse, violence against women.

Delaware State University, Graduate Programs, Department of Social Work, Program in Social Work, Dover, DE 19901-2277. Offers MSW. *Accreditation:* CSWE. Evening/weekend programs available. *Entrance requirements:* For master's, GRE, minimum GPA of 3.0 in major, 2.75 overall. Electronic applications accepted. *Faculty research:* Gerontology, human behavior, corrections, child welfare, adolescent behavior policy.

Dominican University, Graduate School of Social Work, River Forest, IL 60305-1099. Offers MSW. *Accreditation:* CSWE. *Faculty:* 5 full-time (2 women), 14 part-time/adjunct (8 women). *Students:* 75 full-time (68 women), 69 part-time (58 women); includes 20 minority (10 African Americans, 2 Asian Americans or Pacific Islanders, 8 Hispanic Americans), 3 international. Average age 31. 118 applicants, 98% accepted, 57 enrolled. In 2006, 53 degrees awarded. *Entrance requirements:* For master's, minimum GPA of 2.75 for regular standing, 3.0 for advanced standing. Additional exam requirements/recommendations for international students: Required—TOEFL (minimum score 550 paper-based; 213 computer-based). *Application deadline:* Applications are processed on a rolling basis. Application fee: $25. *Expenses:* Tuition: Full-time $12,420; part-time $690 per credit hour. Required fees: $10 per course. Tuition and fees vary according to campus/location and program. *Financial support:* Career-related internships or fieldwork and scholarships/grants available. *Faculty research:* Human trafficking, domestic violence, gerontology, school social work, child welfare. *Unit head:* Dr. Mark Rodgers, Dean, 708-366-3316, E-mail: mrodgers@dom.edu. *Application contact:* Felicia Towsend, Director of Admissions, 708-771-5298, Fax: 708-366-3446, E-mail: ftownsend@dom.edu.

East Carolina University, Graduate School, College of Human Ecology, School of Social Work, Greenville, NC 27858-4353. Offers MSW. *Accreditation:* CSWE. Postbaccalaureate distance learning degree programs offered (no on-campus study). *Students:* 108 full-time (100

Social Work

East Carolina University (continued)

women), 49 part-time (41 women); includes 64 minority (58 African Americans, 1 American Indian/Alaska Native, 2 Asian Americans or Pacific Islanders, 3 Hispanic Americans). Average age 32. 34 applicants, 24% accepted, 8 enrolled. In 2006, 102 degrees awarded. *Degree requirements:* For master's, comprehensive exam. *Entrance requirements:* For master's, GRE or MAT. *Additional exam requirements/recommendations for international students:* Required—TOEFL. *Application deadline:* For fall admission, 2/1 priority date for domestic and international students. Application fee: $50. *Financial support:* In 2006–07, 16 students received support, including 1 fellowship (averaging $350 per year), 16 research assistantships (averaging $1,875 per year). Financial award application deadline: 6/1. *Faculty research:* Social research, gerontology, women's issues, social services in schools, human behavior. Total annual research expenditures: $691,409. *Unit head:* Dr. Glen Stone, Director, 252-328-2281, Fax: 252-328-6071, E-mail: stoneg@ecu.edu.

Eastern Michigan University, Graduate School, College of Health and Human Services, School of Social Work, Ypsilanti, MI 48197. Offers Alzheimer's education (Graduate Certificate); gerontology (Graduate Certificate); social work (MSW). *Accreditation:* CSWE. Part-time and evening/weekend programs available. Postbaccalaureate distance learning degree programs offered (minimal on-campus study). *Faculty:* 16 full-time (14 women). *Students:* 43 full-time (36 women), 145 part-time (118 women); includes 70 minority (61 African Americans, 2 American Indian/Alaska Native, 2 Asian Americans or Pacific Islanders, 5 Hispanic Americans), 1 international. Average age 34. In 2006, 93 degrees awarded. *Entrance requirements:* Additional exam requirements/recommendations for international students: Required—TOEFL. *Application deadline:* For fall admission, 5/15 priority date for domestic students, 5/1 priority date for international students; for winter admission, 10/15 priority date for domestic students, 10/1 priority date for international students; for spring admission, 3/15 priority date for domestic students, 3/1 priority date for international students. Applications are processed on a rolling basis. Application fee: $35. *Expenses:* Tuition, state resident: part-time $341 per credit hour. Tuition, nonresident: full-time $16,104; part-time $671 per credit hour. Required fees: $816; $34 per credit hour. $40 per term. One-time fee: $82 full-time. Tuition and fees vary according to course level, course load, degree level and reciprocity agreements. *Financial support:* Fellowships, research assistantships with full tuition reimbursements, teaching assistantships with full tuition reimbursements, career-related internships or fieldwork, Federal Work-Study, institutionally sponsored loans, scholarships/grants, tuition waivers (partial), and unspecified assistantships available. Support available to part-time students. Financial award applicants required to submit FAFSA. *Unit head:* Prof. Marjorie Ziefert, Director, 734-487-0393, Fax: 734-487-6832, E-mail: marjorie.ziefert@emich.edu.

Eastern Washington University, Graduate Studies, School of Social Work and Human Services, Cheney, WA 99004-2431. Offers MSW, MPA/MSW. *Accreditation:* CSWE. Part-time programs available. *Degree requirements:* For master's, comprehensive exam. *Entrance requirements:* For master's, minimum GPA of 3.0.

East Tennessee State University, School of Graduate Studies, College of Arts and Sciences, Department of Social Work, Johnson City, TN 37614. Offers MSW. *Accreditation:* CSWE. *Entrance requirements:* For master's, GRE. Additional exam requirements/recommendations for international students: Required—TOEFL (minimum score 550 paper-based; 213 computer-based).

Edinboro University of Pennsylvania, Graduate Studies and Research, School of Liberal Arts, Department of Social Work, Edinboro, PA 16444. Offers MSW. *Accreditation:* CSWE. Evening/weekend programs available. *Faculty:* 6 full-time (3 women). *Students:* 30 full-time (27 women), 23 part-time (19 women); includes 6 minority (3 African Americans, 3 Hispanic Americans), 1 international. Average age 33. In 2006, 19 degrees awarded. *Degree requirements:* For master's, competency exam. *Application deadline:* Applications are processed on a rolling basis. Application fee: $30. Electronic applications accepted. *Expenses:* Tuition, state resident: full-time $6,048; part-time $336 per credit. Tuition, nonresident: full-time $9,678; part-time $538 per credit. Required fees: $1,849; $42 per credit. *Financial support:* In 2006–07, 2 research assistantships with full and partial tuition reimbursements (averaging $3,850 per year) were awarded; career-related internships or fieldwork, Federal Work-Study, scholarships/grants, and unspecified assistantships also available. Support available to part-time students. Financial award application deadline: 2/15; financial award applicants required to submit FAFSA. *Unit head:* Dr. Donna Hixon, Chairperson, 814-732-1588, E-mail: dhixon@edinboro.edu. *Application contact:* Dr. R. Scott Baldwin, Dean, 814-732-2752, Fax: 814-732-2268, E-mail: sbaldwin@edinboro.edu.

Fayetteville State University, Graduate School, Program in Social Work, Fayetteville, NC 28301-4298. Offers MSW. *Accreditation:* CSWE. *Faculty:* 28 full-time (21 women), 2 part-time/adjunct (0 women). *Students:* 58 full-time (52 women), 4 part-time (3 women); includes 48 minority (44 African Americans, 1 American Indian/Alaska Native, 3 Hispanic Americans). Average age 36. 26 applicants, 100% accepted, 21 enrolled. In 2006, 22 degrees awarded. *Application deadline:* For fall admission, 7/1 for domestic students; for spring admission, 12/1 for domestic students. Application fee: $25. *Expenses:* Tuition, state resident: full-time $2,118. Tuition, nonresident: full-time $11,708. Required fees: $1,099. Tuition and fees vary according to course load. *Faculty research:* Cultural diversity, child welfare, student mentoring within undergraduate and graduate social work programs, g programs and assessment in family social work practice, foster care and African American families. Total annual research expenditures: $1,000. *Unit head:* Dr. Terri Moore-Brown, Department Chair, 910-672-1853, E-mail: tmbrown@uncfsu.edu.

Florida Agricultural and Mechanical University, Division of Graduate Studies, Research, and Continuing Education, College of Arts and Sciences, Division of History and Political Sciences, Program in Applied Social Science, Tallahassee, FL 32307-3200. Offers African American history (MASS); criminal justice (MASS); economics (MASS); history (MASS); political science (MASS); public administration (MASS); public management (MASS); social work (MASS); sociology (MASS). Part-time programs available. *Degree requirements:* For master's, thesis optional. *Entrance requirements:* For master's, GRE General Test, minimum GPA of 3.0. *Faculty research:* Southern history, black history, election trends, presidential history.

Florida Agricultural and Mechanical University, Division of Graduate Studies, Research, and Continuing Education, College of Arts and Sciences, Division of History and Political Sciences, Program in Social Work, Tallahassee, FL 32307-3200. Offers MSW. *Accreditation:* CSWE. *Entrance requirements:* For master's, GRE General Test, minimum GPA of 3.0, 3 letters of recommendation. Additional exam requirements/recommendations for international students: Required—TOEFL.

Florida Atlantic University, College of Architecture, Urban and Public Affairs, School of Social Work, Boca Raton, FL 33431-0991. Offers MSW. *Accreditation:* CSWE. Part-time and evening/weekend programs available. *Faculty:* 15 full-time (8 women), 10 part-time/adjunct (7 women). *Students:* 55 full-time (51 women), 72 part-time (63 women); includes 38 minority (15 African Americans, 1 Asian American or Pacific Islander, 22 Hispanic Americans), 1 international. Average age 34. 128 applicants, 52% accepted, 43 enrolled. In 2006, 50 degrees awarded. *Application deadline:* For fall admission, 6/1 priority date for domestic students; for spring admission, 10/20 priority date for domestic students. Applications are processed on a rolling basis. Application fee: $30. *Expenses:* Tuition, area resident: Full-time $4,394. Tuition, nonresident: full-time $16,441. *Financial support:* In 2006–07, 2 research assistantships with tuition reimbursements (averaging $7,000 per year) were awarded; fellowships with tuition reimbursements, career-related internships or fieldwork, Federal Work-Study, institutionally sponsored loans, and tuition waivers (partial) also available. Financial award application deadline: 4/1. *Faculty research:* Child welfare, special work education. *Unit head:* Dr. Michele Hawkins, Director, 561-297-3234, Fax: 561-297-2866, E-mail: mhawkins@fau.edu. *Application contact:* Dr. Elwood Hamlin, Professor, 501-297-3234, E-mail: ehamlin@fau.edu.

Florida Atlantic University, Jupiter Campus, College of Architecture, Urban and Public Affairs, Jupiter, FL 33458. Offers MPA, MSW.

Florida Gulf Coast University, College of Public and Social Services, Program in Social Work, Fort Myers, FL 33965-6565. Offers MSW. *Accreditation:* CSWE. Part-time and evening/weekend programs available. *Faculty:* 29 full-time (14 women), 15 part-time/adjunct (5 women). *Students:* 19 full-time (18 women), 25 part-time (22 women); includes 10 minority (4 African Americans, 1 Asian American or Pacific Islander, 5 Hispanic Americans). Average age 33. 37 applicants, 92% accepted, 27 enrolled. In 2006, 24 degrees awarded. *Entrance requirements:* For master's, GRE General Test, MAT, minimum GPA of 3.0. Additional exam requirements/recommendations for international students: Required—TOEFL (minimum score 550 paper-based; 213 computer-based). *Application deadline:* For fall admission, 2/15 priority date for domestic students. Applications are processed on a rolling basis. Application fee: $30. Electronic applications accepted. *Expenses:* Tuition, state resident: full-time $4,326. Tuition, nonresident: full-time $18,523. Required fees: $1,211. One-time fee: $5 full-time. *Financial support:* In 2006–07, 6 research assistantships were awarded; career-related internships or fieldwork and tuition waivers (partial) also available. Support available to part-time students. *Faculty research:* Gerontology, clinical case management, domestic violence, homelessness, migrant workers. *Unit head:* Dr. Sakinah Salahu-Din, Director, 239-590-7867, Fax: 239-590-7842, E-mail: ssalahud@fgcu.edu.

Florida International University, College of Social Work, Justice and Public Affairs, School of Social Work, Miami, FL 33199. Offers MSW, PhD. *Accreditation:* CSWE (one or more programs are accredited). Part-time and evening/weekend programs available. *Faculty:* 12 full-time (5 women), 1 (woman) part-time/adjunct. *Students:* 125 full-time (107 women), 98 part-time (79 women); includes 178 minority (64 African Americans, 5 Asian Americans or Pacific Islanders, 109 Hispanic Americans), 2 international. Average age 38. 131 applicants, 66% accepted, 58 enrolled. In 2006, 88 master's, 3 doctorates awarded. *Degree requirements:* For doctorate, thesis/dissertation, comprehensive exam. *Entrance requirements:* For master's, GRE General Test, minimum GPA of 3.0; for doctorate, GRE General Test, minimum graduate GPA of 3.5. Additional exam requirements/recommendations for international students: Required—TOEFL. *Application deadline:* For fall admission, 4/1 priority date for domestic students; for spring admission, 10/1 for domestic students. Applications are processed on a rolling basis. Application fee: $25. *Expenses:* Tuition, state resident: part-time $249 per credit hour. Tuition, nonresident: part-time $753 per credit hour. Tuition and fees vary according to program. *Unit head:* Dr. Gary Lowe, Acting Dean, 305-348-7196, Fax: 305-348-5848, E-mail: gary.lowe@fiu.edu.

See Close-Up on page 2393.

Florida State University, Graduate Studies, College of Social Work, Tallahassee, FL 32306. Offers clinical social work (MSW); social policy and administration (MSW); social work (PhD); JD/MSW; MPA/MSW; MS/MSW. *Accreditation:* CSWE (one or more programs are accredited). Part-time and evening/weekend programs available. Postbaccalaureate distance learning degree programs offered (no on-campus study). *Faculty:* 33 full-time (19 women), 28 part-time/adjunct (24 women). *Students:* 241 full-time (208 women), 138 part-time (114 women); includes 86 minority (55 African Americans, 3 American Indian/Alaska Native, 6 Asian Americans or Pacific Islanders, 22 Hispanic Americans). Average age 30. 343 applicants, 62% accepted, 138 enrolled. In 2006, 151 master's, 7 doctorates awarded. *Degree requirements:* For doctorate, thesis/dissertation, comprehensive exam. *Entrance requirements:* For master's and doctorate, GRE General Test, minimum GPA of 3.0. Additional exam requirements/recommendations for international students: Required—TOEFL. *Application deadline:* For fall admission, 6/1 priority date for domestic students; for winter admission, 3/1 priority date for domestic students; for spring admission, 11/1 priority date for domestic students. Applications are processed on a rolling basis. Electronic applications accepted. *Expenses:* Tuition, state resident: full-time $5,822; part-time $243 per credit hour. Tuition, nonresident: full-time $20,976; part-time $874 per credit hour. Tuition and fees vary according to program. *Financial support:* In 2006–07, 79 students received support, including 9 fellowships with full tuition reimbursements available, 35 research assistantships with partial tuition reimbursements available (averaging $3,500 per year), 21 teaching assistantships with full tuition reimbursements available (averaging $15,000 per year); career-related internships or fieldwork, Federal Work-Study, institutionally sponsored loans, scholarships/grants, traineeships, health care benefits, and unspecified assistantships also available. Support available to part-time students. Financial award application deadline: 3/1; financial award applicants required to submit FAFSA. *Faculty research:* Family violence, AIDS, aging, family therapy, substance abuse. Total annual research expenditures: $2.6 million. *Unit head:* Dr. C. Aaron McNeece, Dean, 850-644-4752, Fax: 850-644-9750. *Application contact:* Vicky Verano, Director of Recruitment and Admissions, 800-378-9550, Fax: 850-644-9750, E-mail: vveranoc@mailer.fsu.edu.

Fordham University, Graduate School of Social Service, New York, NY 10023. Offers social work (MSW, PhD); JD/MSW. *Accreditation:* CSWE (one or more programs are accredited). Part-time and evening/weekend programs available. *Faculty:* 50 full-time (38 women), 85 part-time/adjunct (61 women). *Students:* 972 full-time (866 women), 373 part-time (326 women); includes 506 minority (280 African Americans, 28 Asian Americans or Pacific Islanders, 198 Hispanic Americans). Average age 32. 1,701 applicants, 61% accepted, 694 enrolled. In 2006, 539 degrees awarded. *Median time to degree:* Master's–2 years full-time, 3 years part-time. *Degree requirements:* For master's, 1200 hours field placement. *Entrance requirements:* For master's, BA degree in liberal arts; for doctorate, GRE. Additional exam requirements/recommendations for international students: Required—TOEFL (minimum score 575 paper-based; 231 computer-based). *Application deadline:* For fall admission, 6/1 priority date for domestic students; for spring admission, 12/1 priority date for domestic students. Applications are processed on a rolling basis. Application fee: $50. *Expenses:* Contact institution. *Financial support:* In 2006–07, 838 students received support, including 39 research assistantships with partial tuition reimbursements available (averaging $1,980 per year); fellowships with partial tuition reimbursements available, career-related internships or fieldwork, scholarships/grants, tuition waivers (partial), and unspecified assistantships also available. Support available to part-time students. Financial award application deadline: 9/1; financial award applicants required to submit FAFSA. *Faculty research:* Aging, children and family, healthcare, domestic violence, substance abuse. *Unit head:* Dr. Peter B. Vaughan, Dean, 212-636-6616. *Application contact:* Elaine Gerald, Assistant Dean, 212-636-6600, Fax: 212-636-6613, E-mail: gssadmission@fordham.edu.

See Close-Up on page 2395.

Gallaudet University, The Graduate School, College of Arts and Sciences, Department of Social Work, Washington, DC 20002-3625. Offers MSW. *Accreditation:* CSWE. *Degree requirements:* For master's, thesis optional. *Entrance requirements:* For master's, GRE General Test or MAT.

George Mason University, College of Health and Human Services, Fairfax, VA 22030. Offers advanced clinical nursing (MSN); nurse practitioner (MSN); nursing (MSN, PhD); nursing administration (MSN); nursing education (Certificate); nursing educator (MSN); social work (MSW). *Accreditation:* AACN. *Faculty:* 69 full-time (55 women), 75 part-time/adjunct (66 women). *Students:* 98 full-time (81 women), 301 part-time (260 women); includes 121 minority (60 African Americans, 45 Asian Americans or Pacific Islanders, 16 Hispanic Americans), 27 international. Average age 39. 326 applicants, 61% accepted, 121 enrolled. In 2006, 89 master's, 7 doctorates, 11 other advanced degrees awarded. *Degree requirements:* For doctorate, thesis/dissertation, oral/written exams. *Entrance requirements:* For master's, RN license, minimum GPA of 3.0 in last 60 hours of course work; for doctorate, MAT, 3 years of nursing experience, master's degree, minimum GPA of 3.25, professional liability insurance. *Application deadline:* For fall admission, 5/1 for domestic students; for spring admission, 11/1 for domestic students. Application fee: $60 ($75 for international students). Electronic applications accepted. *Expenses:* Tuition, state resident: full-time $5,724; part-time $238 per credit. Tuition, nonresident: full-time $16,896; part-time $704 per credit. Required fees: $1,656;

$69 per credit. *Financial support:* Fellowships, research assistantships, teaching assistantships, tuition waivers (partial) available. Support available to part-time students. Financial award application deadline: 3/1; financial award applicants required to submit FAFSA. *Unit head:* Dr. Shirley S. Travis, Dean, 703-993-1918. *Application contact:* Dr. James D. Vail, Associate Dean, Graduate Programs and Research, 703-993-1947, Fax: 703-993-1942, E-mail: nursinfo@gmu.edu.

George Mason University, College of Humanities and Social Sciences, Program in Social Work, Fairfax, VA 22030. Offers MSW. *Accreditation:* CSWE. *Faculty:* 10 full-time (7 women), 15 part-time/adjunct (13 women). *Students:* 38 full-time (35 women), 18 part-time (15 women); includes 16 minority (7 African Americans, 3 Asian Americans or Pacific Islanders, 6 Hispanic Americans), 1 international. Average age 32. 106 applicants, 53% accepted, 23 enrolled. In 2006, 26 degrees awarded. Application fee: $60 ($75 for international students). *Expenses:* Tuition, state resident: full-time $5,724; part-time $238 per credit. Tuition, nonresident: full-time $16,896; part-time $704 per credit. Required fees: $1,656; $69 per credit. *Unit head:* Dr. Sunny Harris Rome, Chair, 703-993-2072, Fax: 703-993-4249, E-mail: srome@gmu.edu.

Georgia State University, College of Health and Human Sciences, School of Social Work, Atlanta, GA 30303-3083. Offers community partnerships (MSW). *Accreditation:* CSWE. Part-time programs available. *Faculty:* 16 full-time (11 women), 2 part-time/adjunct (1 woman). *Students:* 50 full-time (46 women), 5 part-time (4 women); includes 19 minority (16 African Americans, 3 Asian Americans or Pacific Islanders), 2 international. Average age 32. 83 applicants, 55% accepted, 21 enrolled. In 2006, 32 degrees awarded. *Degree requirements:* For master's, community project. *Entrance requirements:* For master's, GRE General Test. Additional exam requirements/recommendations for international students: Required—TOEFL (minimum score 550 paper-based; 213 computer-based). *Application deadline:* For fall admission, 2/1 priority date for domestic students. Applications are processed on a rolling basis. Application fee: $50. Electronic applications accepted. *Financial support:* In 2006–07, research assistantships with full and partial tuition reimbursements (averaging $3,108 per year); Federal Work-Study, scholarships/grants, tuition waivers (partial), and unspecified assistantships also available. Support available to part-time students. Financial award application deadline: 4/1; financial award applicants required to submit FAFSA. *Faculty research:* Social work education, child welfare, labor unions and child care workers, secondary victimization in death penalty cases. Total annual research expenditures: $431,852. *Unit head:* Dr. Nancy Kropf, Director, 404-651-3526. *Application contact:* Renanda Dear, Director, Student and Community Services, 404-651-3526, Fax: 404-651-1863, E-mail: rwood@gsu.edu.

Governors State University, College of Health Professions, Program in Social Work, University Park, IL 60466-0975. Offers MSW. *Accreditation:* CSWE. *Students:* 16 full-time, 89 part-time. Average age 34. *Application deadline:* For fall admission, 2/15 for domestic students. Application fee: $25. *Expenses:* Tuition, state resident: full-time $4,104; part-time $171 per hour. Tuition, nonresident: part-time $513 per hour. *Financial support:* Application deadline: 5/1. *Unit head:* Geraldine Outlaw, Coordinator, 708-235-2178.

Graduate School and University Center of the City University of New York, Graduate Studies, Program in Social Welfare, New York, NY 10016-4039. Offers DSW, PhD. *Faculty:* 17 full-time (7 women). *Students:* 85 full-time (60 women), 3 part-time (all women); includes 33 minority (16 African Americans, 3 Asian Americans or Pacific Islanders, 14 Hispanic Americans), 4 international. Average age 45. 36 applicants, 39% accepted, 11 enrolled. In 2006, 6 degrees awarded. *Degree requirements:* For doctorate, thesis/dissertation, project, qualifying exam. *Entrance requirements:* For doctorate, MSW or equivalent, 3 years of post-master's work experience. Additional exam requirements/recommendations for international students: Required—TOEFL. *Application deadline:* For fall admission, 3/1 for domestic students. Application fee: $125. Electronic applications accepted. *Financial support:* In 2006–07, 59 fellowships, 1 teaching assistantship were awarded; research assistantships, career-related internships or fieldwork, Federal Work-Study, institutionally sponsored loans, and tuition waivers (full and partial) also available. Financial award application deadline: 2/1; financial award applicants required to submit FAFSA. *Unit head:* Dr. Michael Fabricant, Executive Officer, 212-452-7023, Fax: 212-452-7440, E-mail: mfabrica@hunter.cuny.edu.

Grambling State University, School of Graduate Studies and Research, College of Professional Studies, School of Social Work, Grambling, LA 71245. Offers MSW. *Accreditation:* CSWE. Part-time programs available. *Faculty:* 1 full-time (0 women), 1 part-time/adjunct (0 women). *Students:* 72 full-time (64 women), 1 (woman) part-time; includes 55 minority (all African Americans), 1 international. Average age 32. In 2006, 35 degrees awarded. *Degree requirements:* For master's, thesis (for some programs), comprehensive exam (for some programs). *Entrance requirements:* For master's, GRE, minimum GPA of 3.0 on last degree, 36 hours in liberal arts, autobiography, interview. Additional exam requirements/recommendations for international students: Required—TOEFL. *Application deadline:* For fall admission, 2/1 priority date for domestic students. Application fee: $20 ($30 for international students). *Expenses:* Tuition, state resident: full-time $2,232; part-time $124 per credit hour. Tuition, nonresident: full-time $7,582; part-time $124 per credit hour. Required fees: $1,127. *Financial support:* In 2006–07, 54 students received support, including 3 research assistantships (averaging $3,000 per year); career-related internships or fieldwork, Federal Work-Study, institutionally sponsored loans, and unspecified assistantships also available. Financial award application deadline: 5/31; financial award applicants required to submit FAFSA. *Faculty research:* Welfare history, social services in Louisiana, stress and child abuse, the black family, rurality. *Unit head:* Dr. Marvin Arnold, Director, 318-274-3305, E-mail: arnoldm@gram.edu. *Application contact:* LaVerne Junior, Secretary, 318-274-3146, Fax: 318-274-3254, E-mail: juniorls@gram.edu.

Grand Valley State University, College of Community and Public Service, School of Social Work, Allendale, MI 49401-9403. Offers MSW. *Accreditation:* CSWE. Part-time programs available. *Faculty:* 20 full-time (13 women), 13 part-time/adjunct (9 women). *Students:* 124 full-time (109 women), 251 part-time (221 women); includes 60 minority (36 African Americans, 9 American Indian/Alaska Native, 2 Asian Americans or Pacific Islanders, 13 Hispanic Americans). Average age 33. 131 applicants, 74% accepted, 70 enrolled. In 2006, 110 degrees awarded. *Entrance requirements:* Additional exam requirements/recommendations for international students: Required—TOEFL. *Application deadline:* For fall admission, 5/1 priority date for domestic students; for winter admission, 10/1 priority date for domestic students; for spring admission, 3/15 priority date for domestic students. Applications are processed on a rolling basis. Application fee: $30. Electronic applications accepted. *Expenses:* Tuition, state resident: full-time $5,850; part-time $325 per credit. Tuition, nonresident: full-time $10,800; part-time $600 per credit. Tuition and fees vary according to course load. *Financial support:* In 2006–07, 22 students received support, including 22 research assistantships with full and partial tuition reimbursements available (averaging $6,000 per year); career-related internships or fieldwork, Federal Work-Study, institutionally sponsored loans, and unspecified assistantships also available. *Faculty research:* Drug addiction, aging, management, effectiveness of therapy. *Unit head:* Dr. Elaine Schott, Director, 616-331-6550, Fax: 616-771-6570, E-mail: schottl@gvsu.edu. *Application contact:* Prof. Lois Smith Owens, Chair, Admissions, 616-331-6577, E-mail: owensl@gvsu.edu.

Gratz College, Graduate Programs, Program in Jewish Communal Studies, Melrose Park, PA 19027. Offers MA, Certificate, MA/Certificate, MBA/Certificate, MSW/Certificate. Part-time and evening/weekend programs available. *Degree requirements:* For master's, one foreign language.

Hawai'i Pacific University, College of Liberal Arts, Honolulu, HI 96813. Offers diplomacy and military studies (MA); social work (MA). Part-time and evening/weekend programs available. *Faculty:* 3 full-time (0 women), 5 part-time/adjunct (1 woman). *Students:* 86 full-time (45 women), 49 part-time (18 women); includes 47 minority (7 African Americans, 5 American Indian/Alaska Native, 31 Asian Americans or Pacific Islanders, 4 Hispanic Americans), 11 international. Average age 35. 134 applicants, 69% accepted, 46 enrolled. In 2006, 3 degrees awarded. *Degree requirements:* For master's, thesis. *Entrance requirements:* Additional exam requirements/recommendations for international students: Recommended—TOEFL (minimum score 550 paper-based; 213 computer-based), TWE (minimum score 5). *Application deadline:* For fall admission, 2/15 priority date for domestic students; for spring admission, 10/15 priority date for domestic students. Applications are processed on a rolling basis. Application fee: $50. Electronic applications accepted. *Expenses:* Tuition: Full-time $10,080; part-time $560 per credit. *Financial support:* In 2006–07, 60 students received support. Career-related internships or fieldwork, Federal Work-Study, scholarships/grants, and unspecified assistantships available. Support available to part-time students. Financial award application deadline: 3/1; financial award applicants required to submit FAFSA. *Unit head:* Dr. Leslie Correa, Associate Vice President and Dean, 808-544-0228, Fax: 808-544-1424, E-mail: lcorrea@hpu.edu. *Application contact:* Danny Lam, Assistant Director of Graduate Admissions, 808-544-1135, Fax: 808-544-0280, E-mail: graduate@hpu.edu.

Hebrew Union College–Jewish Institute of Religion, School of Jewish Communal Service, Los Angeles, CA 90007-3796. Offers MAJCS, Certificate, MAJCS/MA, MAJCS/MAJE, MAJCS/MAJS, MAJCS/MBA, MAJCS/MPA, MAJCS/MSW, MCM/MAJCS. *Faculty:* 3 full-time (2 women), 9 part-time/adjunct (3 women). *Students:* 25 full-time (19 women), 1 (woman) part-time, 2 international. Average age 25. 11 applicants, 100% accepted, 7 enrolled. In 2006, 9 master's, 9 other advanced degrees awarded. *Median time to degree:* Master's–2 years full-time, 3 years part-time. *Degree requirements:* For master's, one foreign language. *Entrance requirements:* For master's, GRE General Test, interview, minimum undergraduate GPA of 3.0. Additional exam requirements/recommendations for international students: Required—TOEFL (minimum score 550 paper-based). *Application deadline:* For fall admission, 2/1 for domestic and international students. Application fee: $50. *Expenses:* Tuition: Full-time $16,000; part-time $680 per unit. One-time fee: $100 full-time. *Financial support:* Career-related internships or fieldwork and scholarships/grants available. Financial award application deadline: 3/2; financial award applicants required to submit FAFSA. *Unit head:* Macla Abraham, Interim Director, 213-749-3424 Ext. 4218, Fax: 213-747-6128, E-mail: mabraham@huc.edu. *Application contact:* Director of Admissions and Recruitment, 213-749-3424 Ext. 4221, Fax: 213-747-6128.

Howard University, School of Social Work, Washington, DC 20059. Offers MSW, PhD. *Accreditation:* CSWE (one or more programs are accredited). Part-time programs available. *Degree requirements:* For doctorate, thesis/dissertation, qualifying exam, comprehensive exam. *Entrance requirements:* For master's, minimum GPA of 2.5; for doctorate, GRE General Test, minimum GPA of 3.3, MSW or master's in related field. Additional exam requirements/recommendations for international students: Required—TOEFL. *Faculty research:* Infant mortality, child and family services, displaced populations, social work practice, domestic violence, black males, mental health.

Humboldt State University, Graduate Studies, College of Professional Studies, Social Work Program, Arcata, CA 95521-8299. Offers MSW. *Accreditation:* CSWE. *Students:* 47 full-time (35 women), 12 part-time (all women); includes 16 minority (3 African Americans, 6 American Indian/Alaska Native, 2 Asian Americans or Pacific Islanders, 5 Hispanic Americans). Average age 37. 55 applicants, 49% accepted, 19 enrolled. In 2006, 29 degrees awarded. *Entrance requirements:* Additional exam requirements/recommendations for international students: Required—TOEFL (minimum score 500 paper-based; 173 computer-based). *Application deadline:* For fall admission, 2/1 for domestic and international students. Application fee: $55. *Financial support:* Application deadline: 3/1; *Unit head:* Ken Nakamura, Director of MSW Program, 707-826-4448, Fax: 707-826-4418, E-mail: kkn1@humboldt.edu. *Application contact:* Ken Nakamura, Director of MSW Program, 707-826-4448, Fax: 707-826-4418, E-mail: kkn1@humboldt.edu.

Hunter College of the City University of New York, Graduate School, School of Social Work, New York, NY 10021-5085. Offers MSW, DSW. *Accreditation:* CSWE (one or more programs are accredited). *Faculty:* 32 full-time (21 women), 37 part-time/adjunct (23 women). *Students:* 460 full-time (384 women), 374 part-time (286 women); includes 187 minority (88 African Americans, 18 Asian Americans or Pacific Islanders, 81 Hispanic Americans). Average age 35. 1,115 applicants, 37% accepted, 372 enrolled. In 2006, 275 degrees awarded. *Degree requirements:* For master's, major paper. *Entrance requirements:* Additional exam requirements/recommendations for international students: Required—TOEFL. *Application deadline:* For fall admission, 1/15 for domestic and international students. Applications are processed on a rolling basis. Application fee: $125. *Expenses:* Tuition, state resident: part-time $270 per credit. Tuition, nonresident: part-time $500 per credit. Required fees: $45 per semester. *Financial support:* In 2006–07, 120 fellowships (averaging $1,000 per year) were awarded; career-related internships or fieldwork, Federal Work-Study, and tuition waivers (partial) also available. Support available to part-time students. *Faculty research:* Child welfare, AIDS, homeless, aging, mental health. *Unit head:* Dr. Jacqueline B. Mondros, Dean, 212-452-7085. *Application contact:* Raymond Montero, Coordinator of Admissions, 212-452-7005, E-mail: grad.socworkadvisor@hunter.cuny.edu.

Illinois State University, Graduate School, College of Arts and Sciences, School of Social Work, Normal, IL 61790-2200. Offers MSW. *Accreditation:* CSWE. *Faculty:* 11 full-time (9 women). *Students:* 41 full-time (37 women), 18 part-time (all women); includes 11 minority (8 African Americans, 3 Hispanic Americans), 1 international. 57 applicants, 91% accepted. In 2006, 23 degrees awarded. Application fee: $40. *Expenses:* Tuition, state resident: full-time $3,330; part-time $185 per credit hour. Tuition, nonresident: full-time $6,948; part-time $438 per credit hour. Required fees: $1,259; $52 per credit hour. *Financial support:* In 2006–07, 13 research assistantships (averaging $6,562 per year) were awarded. Financial award application deadline: 4/1. *Faculty research:* Adoption studies, risk for HIV among middle-aged African American women, developing professional careers in child welfare, Evan B. Donaldson Adoption Institute. Total annual research expenditures: $233,960. *Unit head:* Dr. Wanda Bracy, Director, 309-438-3631.

Indiana University Northwest, Division of Social Work, Gary, IN 46408-1197. Offers MSW. *Accreditation:* CSWE. Part-time and evening/weekend programs available. *Faculty:* 1 full-time (0 women). *Students:* 29 full-time (27 women), 88 part-time (73 women); includes 54 minority (46 African Americans, 1 American Indian/Alaska Native, 2 Asian Americans or Pacific Islanders, 5 Hispanic Americans), 1 international. Average age 34. *Degree requirements:* For master's, registration. *Entrance requirements:* For master's, minimum GPA of 3.0. *Application deadline:* For fall admission, 2/1 for domestic students. Application fee: $25. *Expenses:* Contact institution. Tuition and fees vary according to course load, campus/location and program. *Financial support:* In 2006–07, 43 students received support. Career-related internships or fieldwork, Federal Work-Study, tuition waivers (partial), and tuition remissions available. Support available to part-time students. Financial award application deadline: 6/1; financial award applicants required to submit FAFSA. *Faculty research:* Educational outcomes, generalist practice, homelessness. Total annual research expenditures: $1,000. *Unit head:* Dr. Denise Travis, Director, 219-980-7111, Fax: 219-981-4264, E-mail: dtravis@iun.edu. *Application contact:* Kellie Branch, Assistant to the Director, 219-980-7111.

Indiana University–Purdue University Indianapolis, School of Social Work, Indianapolis, IN 46202-2896. Offers MSW, PhD, Certificate. *Accreditation:* CSWE (one or more programs are accredited). Part-time and evening/weekend programs available. *Faculty:* 16 full-time (7 women). *Students:* 291 full-time (250 women), 294 part-time (251 women); includes 85 minority (66 African Americans, 2 American Indian/Alaska Native, 6 Asian Americans or Pacific Islanders, 11 Hispanic Americans), 5 international. Average age 32. In 2006, 250 master's, 2 doctorates awarded. Terminal master's awarded for partial completion of doctoral program. *Degree requirements:* For master's, field practicum; for doctorate, thesis/dissertation, residential internship. *Entrance requirements:* For master's, minimum GPA of 2.5; course work in social behavior, statistics, research methodology, and human biology; for doctorate, GRE General Test. Additional exam requirements/recommendations for international students: Required—TOEFL. Application fee: $50 ($60 for international students). *Expenses:* Contact institution. Tuition and fees vary according to course load, campus/location and program. *Financial support:* In 2006–07, 27 students received support; fellowships with full tuition reimbursements available, research assistantships with partial tuition reimbursements avail-

Social Work

Indiana University–Purdue University Indianapolis (continued)
able, teaching assistantships, Federal Work-Study, institutionally sponsored loans, scholarships/grants, and tuition waivers (partial) available. Support available to part-time students. Financial award applicants required to submit FAFSA. *Faculty research:* Social justice, institutional child welfare, mental health, aging, AIDS/HIV disease. Total annual research expenditures: $145,580. *Unit head:* Michael Patchner, Dean, 317-274-8362, Fax: 317-274-8630, E-mail: patchner@iupui.edu. *Application contact:* Sherry Gass, Student Services Secretary, 317-274-6727, Fax: 317-274-8630, E-mail: stgass@iupui.edu.

Indiana University South Bend, School of Social Work, South Bend, IN 46634-7111. Offers MSW. *Accreditation:* CSWE. Part-time and evening/weekend programs available. *Faculty:* 4 full-time (2 women). *Students:* 35 full-time (33 women), 69 part-time (60 women); includes 14 minority (8 African Americans, 1 American Indian/Alaska Native, 1 Asian American or Pacific Islander, 4 Hispanic Americans), 1 international. Average age 35. *Application deadline:* For fall admission, 2/1 priority date for domestic students. Application fee: $40. *Expenses:* Contact institution. Tuition and fees vary according to course load, campus/location and program. *Financial support:* Career-related internships or fieldwork and Federal Work-Study available. Support available to part-time students. Financial award application deadline: 3/1; financial award applicants required to submit FAFSA. *Unit head:* Dr. Paul R. Newcomb, Program Director, 574-520-4880, Fax: 574-520-4876, E-mail: msn@iusb.edu.

Institute for Clinical Social Work, Graduate Programs, Chicago, IL 60601. Offers PhD. Part-time programs available. *Degree requirements:* For doctorate, thesis/dissertation, supervised practicum. *Entrance requirements:* For doctorate, 2 years of experience, master's degree. *Faculty research:* Impact of AIDS on partners, effects of learning disabilities on children and families, clinical social work issues.

Inter American University of Puerto Rico, Metropolitan Campus, School of Social Work, San Juan, PR 00919-1293. Offers clinical services (MSW); social administration (MSW). *Accreditation:* CSWE. Evening/weekend programs available. *Degree requirements:* For master's, comprehensive exam. *Entrance requirements:* For master's, GRE or EXADEP, interview. Electronic applications accepted.

Jackson State University, Graduate School, School of Social Work, Jackson, MS 39217. Offers MSW, PhD. *Accreditation:* CSWE (one or more programs are accredited). Evening/weekend programs available. *Faculty:* 5 full-time (4 women). *Students:* 86 full-time (72 women), 25 part-time (21 women); includes 83 minority (82 African Americans, 1 American Indian/Alaska Native), 1 international. In 2006, 12 degrees awarded. *Degree requirements:* For master's, comprehensive exam; for doctorate, thesis/dissertation, comprehensive exam. *Entrance requirements:* For master's, GRE General Test; for doctorate, MAT. Additional exam requirements/recommendations for international students: Required—TOEFL. *Application deadline:* For fall admission, 2/1 for domestic students. Application fee: $20. *Financial support:* In 2006–07, 20 students received support. Career-related internships or fieldwork, Federal Work-Study, scholarships/grants, tuition waivers, and unspecified assistantships available. Support available to part-time students. Financial award application deadline: 3/1; financial award applicants required to submit FAFSA. *Unit head:* Dr. Gwednolyn Prater, Dean, 601-979-8836, Fax: 601-979-8837, E-mail: deanofcps@jsums.edu. *Application contact:* Curtis Gore, Director of Graduate Admissions, 601-979-2455, Fax: 601-974-4325, E-mail: cgore@ccaix.jsums.edu.

Kean University, College of Humanities and Social Sciences, Program in Social Work, Union, NJ 07083. Offers advanced standing (MSW); social work (MSW). *Accreditation:* CSWE. Part-time and evening/weekend programs available. *Faculty:* 11 full-time (9 women). *Students:* 88 full-time (70 women); includes 43 minority (32 African Americans, 2 Asian Americans or Pacific Islanders, 9 Hispanic Americans). Average age 32. 159 applicants, 78% accepted, 47 enrolled. In 2006, 51 degrees awarded. *Degree requirements:* For master's, field work, thesis optional. *Entrance requirements:* For master's, minimum undergraduate GPA of 2.8, undergraduate course work in social sciences, 3 letters of recommendation, minimum 3.5 GPA (for advanced standing). *Application deadline:* For fall admission, 3/15 for domestic students. Application fee: $60 ($150 for international students). Electronic applications accepted. *Expenses:* Tuition, state resident: full-time $8,856; part-time $369 per credit. Tuition, nonresident: full-time $11,256; part-time $469 per credit. *Financial support:* In 2006–07, 2 research assistantships with full tuition reimbursements (averaging $3,217 per year) were awarded. *Unit head:* Dr. Alan Lightfoot, Program Coordinator, 908-737-4037, E-mail: alightfo@kean.edu. *Application contact:* Dr. Dorothy Rowe, Director of MSW Admissions and Agency Recruitment, 908-737-4047, E-mail: drowe@kean.edu.

Kennesaw State University, College of Health and Human Services, Program in Social Work, Kennesaw, GA 30144-5591. Offers MSW. *Students:* 33 full-time (32 women); includes 10 minority (8 African Americans, 2 Asian Americans or Pacific Islanders). Average age 34. 55 applicants, 69% accepted, 33 enrolled. *Entrance requirements:* For master's, GRE, criminal history check, minimum GPA of 2.75, 3 letters of recommendation, resumé. Additional exam requirements/recommendations for international students: Required—TOEFL (minimum score 550 paper-based; 213 computer-based; 80 iBT), IELTS (minimum score 6). *Application deadline:* For fall admission, 3/15 for domestic students. Application fee: $50. Electronic applications accepted. *Expenses:* Tuition, state resident: full-time $3,044; part-time $127 per semester hour. Tuition, nonresident: full-time $12,172; part-time $508 per semester hour. Required fees: $353 per semester. Full-time tuition and fees vary according to campus/location and program. *Financial support:* Unspecified assistantships available. *Unit head:* Dr. Alan Kirk, Department Chair, 770-423-6630, E-mail: akirk@kennesaw.edu. *Application contact:* Vilma Marquez, Admissions Counselor, 770-420-4377, Fax: 770-423-6885, E-mail: vmarquez@kennesaw.edu.

Kutztown University of Pennsylvania, College of Graduate Studies and Extended Learning, College of Liberal Arts and Sciences, Program in Social Work, Kutztown, PA 19530-0730. Offers MSW. *Accreditation:* CSWE. *Faculty:* 5 full-time (2 women). *Students:* 30 full-time (26 women), 9 part-time (7 women); includes 10 minority (4 African Americans, 2 American Indian/Alaska Native, 4 Hispanic Americans), 3 international. Average age 31. 44 applicants, 55% accepted, 17 enrolled. In 2006, 11 degrees awarded. *Degree requirements:* For master's, comprehensive exam. Application fee: $35. *Expenses:* Tuition, state resident: full-time $6,048; part-time $336 per credit. Tuition, nonresident: full-time $9,678; part-time $538 per credit. *Financial support:* In 2006–07, research assistantships with full tuition reimbursements (averaging $5,000 per year). *Unit head:* Dr. John Vafeas, Head, 610-683-4329, E-mail: vafeas@kutztown.edu.

Lakehead University, Graduate Studies, Gerontology Collaborative Program-Northern Educational Center for Aging and Health, Thunder Bay, ON P7B 5E1, Canada. Offers specialization gerontology (M Ed, M Sc, MA, MSW). Part-time programs available. *Degree requirements:* For master's, thesis (for some programs). *Entrance requirements:* Additional exam requirements/recommendations for international students: Required—TOEFL. *Faculty research:* Integrated health information systems.

Lakehead University, Graduate Studies, School of Social Work, Thunder Bay, ON P7B 5E1, Canada. Offers MSW. Part-time programs available. *Degree requirements:* For master's, thesis or project. *Entrance requirements:* For master's, minimum B average. Additional exam requirements/recommendations for international students: Required—TOEFL. *Faculty research:* Clinical psychology, social work and practice theory, long-term care, health care for frail elderly, women's studies.

Laurentian University, School of Graduate Studies and Research, School of Social Work, Sudbury, ON P3E 2C6, Canada. Offers MSS. Open only to French-speaking students. Part-time programs available. *Degree requirements:* For master's, thesis. *Faculty research:* Income security, poverty, violence against women, child poverty, effects of economic crisis on families.

Loma Linda University, School of Science and Technology, Department of Social Work and Social Ecology, Loma Linda, CA 92350. Offers social policy and research (PhD); social work (MSW). *Accreditation:* CSWE. *Entrance requirements:* For master's, GRE General Test.

Louisiana State University and Agricultural and Mechanical College, Graduate School, School of Social Work, Baton Rouge, LA 70803. Offers MSW, PhD. *Accreditation:* CSWE (one or more programs are accredited). Part-time programs available. *Faculty:* 12 full-time (8 women). *Students:* 174 full-time (162 women), 48 part-time (37 women); includes 57 minority (51 African Americans, 3 American Indian/Alaska Native, 1 Asian American or Pacific Islander, 2 Hispanic Americans), 3 international. Average age 31. 116 applicants, 73% accepted, 34 enrolled. In 2006, 75 master's, 2 doctorates awarded. *Degree requirements:* For master's, field instruction. *Entrance requirements:* For master's and doctorate, GRE General Test, minimum GPA of 3.0. Additional exam requirements/recommendations for international students: Required—TOEFL (minimum score 550 paper-based; 213 computer-based; 79 iBT). *Application deadline:* For fall admission, 3/1 for domestic students, 5/15 for international students; for spring admission, 10/15 for international students. Application fee: $25. Electronic applications accepted. *Financial support:* In 2006–07, 26 students received support, including 4 research assistantships with partial tuition reimbursements available (averaging $10,750 per year), 13 teaching assistantships with partial tuition reimbursements available (averaging $9,717 per year); fellowships, career-related internships or fieldwork, Federal Work-Study, scholarships/grants, and unspecified assistantships also available. Support available to part-time students. Financial award applicants required to submit FAFSA. *Faculty research:* Child welfare, gerontology addictions, mental health. Total annual research expenditures: $64,434. *Unit head:* Dr. Pamela Ann Monroe, Dean, 225-578-5875, E-mail: pmonroe@lsu.edu. *Application contact:* Denise Chiasson Breaux, Director of Student Services, 225-578-1234, Fax: 225-578-1357, E-mail: dchiass@lsu.edu.

Loyola University Chicago, School of Social Work, Programs in Social Work, Chicago, IL 60611-2196. Offers MSW, PhD, JD/MSW, M Div/MSW, MJ/MSW, MSW/M Ed, MSW/MA. Part-time programs available. *Degree requirements:* For master's, 2 clinical practica; for doctorate, clinical practicum. *Entrance requirements:* Additional exam requirements/recommendations for international students: Required—TOEFL (minimum score 550 paper-based; 213 computer-based), IELTS (minimum score 7). Electronic applications accepted. *Faculty research:* Clinical social work, ethics, health care, school social work.

Marywood University, Academic Affairs, College of Education and Human Development, Department of Human Development, Emphasis in Social Work, Scranton, PA 18509-1598. Offers PhD. *Students:* Average age 49. *Expenses:* Tuition: Part-time $672 per credit. Tuition and fees vary according to degree level, campus/location and program. *Unit head:* Dr. Marie Loftus, Director, Department of Human Development, 570-348-6292, E-mail: loftus@es.marywood.edu.

Marywood University, Academic Affairs, College of Health and Human Services, School of Social Work, Scranton, PA 18509-1598. Offers MSW, MPA/MSW. *Accreditation:* CSWE. Part-time and evening/weekend programs available. *Faculty:* 18 full-time (12 women). *Students:* 179 full-time (151 women), 125 part-time (109 women); includes 29 minority (14 African Americans, 1 American Indian/Alaska Native, 3 Asian Americans or Pacific Islanders, 11 Hispanic Americans). Average age 33. *Entrance requirements:* For master's, minimum undergraduate GPA of 3.0. *Application deadline:* For fall admission, 5/15 for domestic students; for spring admission, 10/15 for domestic students. Application fee: $30. *Expenses:* Contact institution. Tuition and fees vary according to degree level, campus/location and program. *Financial support:* Research assistantships, career-related internships or fieldwork, scholarships/grants, and tuition waivers (partial) available. Support available to part-time students. Financial award application deadline: 5/1; financial award applicants required to submit FAFSA. *Faculty research:* Impaired professionals, ethics, child welfare, communities, professional gatekeeping. *Unit head:* Dr. Joyce White, Director, 570-348-6211 Ext. 2396, E-mail: jzwhite@marywood.edu. *Application contact:* Virginia Haskett, Director of Admissions, 717-348-6282, Fax: 717-961-4742.

See Close-Up on page 2397.

McGill University, Faculty of Graduate and Postdoctoral Studies, Faculty of Arts, School of Social Work, Montréal, QC H3A 2T5, Canada. Offers MSW, PhD, Diploma, MSW/LL B. Part-time programs available. *Degree requirements:* For master's, thesis or alternative, registration; for doctorate, one foreign language, thesis/dissertation, registration. *Entrance requirements:* For master's, BSW, minimum GPA of 3.0, introductory course in statistics; for doctorate, BSW, MSW, bilingual (English and French), work experience. Additional exam requirements/recommendations for international students: Required—TOEFL (minimum score 577 paper-based; 233 computer-based). Electronic applications accepted. *Faculty research:* Child and family welfare, health and well being through the life cycle, community development.

McMaster University, School of Graduate Studies, Faculty of Social Sciences, School of Social Work, Hamilton, ON L8S 4M2, Canada. Offers analysis of social welfare policy (MSW); analysis of social work practice (MSW). Part-time programs available. *Faculty:* 10 full-time. *Students:* 11 full-time, 28 part-time. 57 applicants, 39% accepted. *Entrance requirements:* For master's, minimum B+ average in final year, BSW from accredited program, half course each in introductory statistics and introductory social research methods. Additional exam requirements/recommendations for international students: Required—TOEFL (minimum score 580 paper-based; 237 computer-based). *Application deadline:* For fall admission, 2/15 priority date for domestic students. Applications are processed on a rolling basis. Application fee: $90. *Financial support:* In 2006–07, 6 teaching assistantships (averaging $8,440 per year) were awarded; scholarships/grants also available. *Faculty research:* Health policy, income maintenance, child welfare, native issues, immigration policies, racism. Total annual research expenditures:$875,550. *Unit head:* Dr. Jane Aronson, Director, 905-525-9140 Ext. 24596, Fax: 905-577-4667, E-mail: aronsonj@mcmaster.ca. *Application contact:* Darlene Savoy, Graduate Secretary, 905-525-9140 Ext. 24596, Fax: 905-577-4667, E-mail: dsavoy@mcmaster.ca.

Memorial University of Newfoundland, School of Graduate Studies, School of Social Work, St. John's, NL A1C 5S7, Canada. Offers MSW. Part-time and evening/weekend programs available. *Degree requirements:* For master's, internship, thesis optional. *Entrance requirements:* For master's, BSW with a minimum of 2nd-class standing or equivalent. Electronic applications accepted. *Faculty research:* Violence, child abuse, sexual abuse, social policy, gerontology.

Miami University, Graduate School, School of Education and Allied Professions, Department of Family Studies and Social Work, Oxford, OH 45056. Offers child and family studies (MS). Part-time programs available. *Degree requirements:* For master's, thesis or alternative, final exam. *Entrance requirements:* For master's, MAT, minimum undergraduate GPA of 3.0 during previous 2 years or 2.75 overall.

Michigan State University, The Graduate School, College of Social Science, School of Social Work, East Lansing, MI 48824. Offers clinical social work (MSW); organizational and community practice (MSW); social work (PhD). *Accreditation:* CSWE. Part-time programs available. Postbaccalaureate distance learning degree programs offered (minimal on-campus study). *Faculty:* 20 full-time (12 women). *Students:* 162 full-time (138 women), 199 part-time (178 women); includes 77 minority (46 African Americans, 5 American Indian/Alaska Native, 8 Asian Americans or Pacific Islanders, 18 Hispanic Americans), 7 international. Average age 32. 280 applicants, 65% accepted. In 2006, 96 master's, 5 doctorates awarded. *Entrance requirements:* Additional exam requirements/recommendations for international students: Required—TOEFL. Electronic applications accepted. *Expenses:* Tuition, state resident: part-time $346 per credit hour. Tuition, nonresident: part-time $730 per credit hour. Tuition and fees vary according to program. *Financial support:* In 2006–07, 66 fellowships with tuition reimbursements, 12 research assistantships with tuition reimbursements (averaging $12,340 per year), 3 teaching assistantships with tuition reimbursements (averaging $12,222 per year) were awarded. Total annual research expenditures: $107,502. *Unit head:* Dr. Gary R. Anderson, Director, 517-355-7515, Fax: 517-

353-3038, E-mail: gary.anderson@ssc.msu.edu. *Application contact:* Nancy Gray, Graduate Office Assistant, 517-353-8632, Fax: 517-353-3038, E-mail: nancy.gray@ssc.msu.edu.

Millersville University of Pennsylvania, Graduate School, School of Humanities and Social Sciences, Department of Social Work, Millersville, PA 17551-0302. Offers MSW. *Faculty:* 7 full-time (5 women), 3 part-time/adjunct (all women). *Students:* 10 full-time (9 women), 9 part-time (all women). Average age 31. 25 applicants, 72% accepted, 14 enrolled. *Entrance requirements:* For master's, MAT or GRE, minimum GPA of 2.8, 3 professional references, resumé. Additional exam requirements/recommendations for international students: Required—TOEFL (minimum score 500 paper-based; 183 computer-based). *Application deadline:* For fall admission, 3/1 priority date for domestic and international students; for winter admission, 10/1 priority date for domestic students; for spring admission, 10/1 priority date for domestic students. Application fee: $35. *Expenses:* Tuition, state resident: full-time $6,048; part-time $336 per credit. Tuition, nonresident: full-time $9,678; part-time $538 per credit. Required fees: $1,244. Tuition and fees vary according to course load. *Financial support:* In 2006–07, 3 students received support, including 3 research assistantships with full tuition reimbursements available (averaging $4,250 per year). Financial award application deadline: 3/15. *Unit head:* Dr. Kathryn A. Gregoire, 717-871-2475, Fax: 717-871-2022, E-mail: kathryn.gregoire@millersville.edu. *Application contact:* Dr. Victor S. DeSantis, Dean of Graduate Studies and Research, 717-872-3099, Fax: 717-871-2022, E-mail: victor.desantis@millersville.edu.

Missouri State University, Graduate College, College of Health and Human Services, School of Social Work, Springfield, MO 65804-0094. Offers MSW. *Accreditation:* CSWE. Part-time programs available. *Faculty:* 10 full-time (7 women), 3 part-time/adjunct (2 women). *Students:* 78 full-time (66 women), 34 part-time (31 women); includes 12 minority (7 African Americans, 2 American Indian/Alaska Native, 3 Hispanic Americans), 1 international. Average age 33. 52 applicants, 71% accepted, 33 enrolled. In 2006, 44 degrees awarded. *Degree requirements:* For master's, thesis or alternative, comprehensive exam. *Entrance requirements:* For master's, GRE, minimum GPA of 3.0. Additional exam requirements/recommendations for international students: Required—TOEFL (minimum score 550 paper-based; 213 computer-based; 79 iBT). *Application deadline:* For fall admission, 1/5 priority date for domestic students. Application fee: $35. Electronic applications accepted. *Expenses:* Tuition, state resident: full-time $3,582; part-time $199 per credit hour. Tuition, nonresident: full-time $6,984; part-time $199 per credit hour. Required fees: $548. Full-time tuition and fees vary according to course level, course load, program and reciprocity agreements. *Financial support:* In 2006–07, 4 research assistantships with full tuition reimbursements (averaging $6,780 per year) were awarded; teaching assistantships with full tuition reimbursements, Federal Work-Study, scholarships/grants, and unspecified assistantships also available. Financial award application deadline: 3/31; financial award applicants required to submit FAFSA. *Unit head:* Dr. Etta Madden, Acting Director, 417-836-6967, Fax: 417-836-7688, E-mail: socialwork@missouristate.edu.

Monmouth University, Graduate School, Department of Social Work, West Long Branch, NJ 07764-1898. Offers community and international development (MSW); practice with families and children (MSW). *Accreditation:* CSWE. Part-time and evening/weekend programs available. *Faculty:* 13 full-time (10 women), 11 part-time/adjunct (10 women). *Students:* 110 full-time (96 women), 87 part-time (76 women); includes 32 minority (21 African Americans, 1 Asian American or Pacific Islander, 10 Hispanic Americans), 2 international. Average age 32. 214 applicants, 90% accepted, 93 enrolled. In 2006, 77 degrees awarded. *Degree requirements:* For master's, thesis, internship. *Entrance requirements:* For master's, minimum GPA of 3.0 in major, 2.75 overall. Additional exam requirements/recommendations for international students: Required—TOEFL (minimum score 550 paper-based; 213 computer-based; 79 iBT), IELTS (minimum score 5), MELAB 77, Cambridge A, B, C. *Application deadline:* For fall admission, 3/15 priority date for domestic students. Applications are processed on a rolling basis. Application fee: $50. Electronic applications accepted. *Expenses:* Tuition: Full-time $12,780; part-time $710 per credit. Required fees: $628; $314 per term. *Financial support:* In 2006–07, 122 fellowships (averaging $3,508 per year), 5 research assistantships (averaging $8,790 per year) were awarded; scholarships/grants and unspecified assistantships also available. Support available to part-time students. Financial award application deadline: 3/1; financial award applicants required to submit FAFSA. *Faculty research:* Child welfare citizen participation, cultural diversity, diversity issues, employee help. *Unit head:* Dr. Robin Mama, Chair, 732-571-3543, Fax: 732-263-5217, E-mail: swdept@monmouth.edu. *Application contact:* Kevin Roane, Director, Office of Graduate Admission, 732-571-3452, Fax: 732-263-5123, E-mail: gradadm@monmouth.edu.

Morgan State University, School of Graduate Studies, School of Education and Urban Studies, Department of Social Work, Baltimore, MD 21251. Offers MSW, PhD. *Accreditation:* CSWE. *Faculty:* 8. *Students:* 77. *Entrance requirements:* For doctorate, GRE. *Application deadline:* Applications are processed on a rolling basis. Application fee: $0. *Expenses:* Tuition, state resident: part-time $272 per credit. Tuition, nonresident: part-time $478 per credit. Required fees: $38 per credit. *Financial support:* Fellowships, research assistantships, teaching assistantships available. *Unit head:* Dr. Anna McPhatter, Chairperson, 443-885-3537, E-mail: amcphatter@moac.morgan.edu. *Application contact:* Dr. Maurice C. Taylor, Dean, 443-885-3185, Fax: 443-885-8226, E-mail: mctaylor@moac.morgan.edu.

Nazareth College of Rochester, Graduate Studies, Department of Social Work, Rochester, NY 14618-3790. Offers MSW. *Students:* 56 full-time (53 women), 75 part-time (66 women); includes 28 minority (23 African Americans, 1 Asian American or Pacific Islander, 4 Hispanic Americans). Average age 27. 136 applicants, 80% accepted, 37 enrolled. In 2006, 39 degrees awarded. *Entrance requirements:* For master's, minimum GPA of 3.0. *Application deadline:* For fall admission, 3/15 for domestic students. *Financial support:* Research assistantships with partial tuition reimbursements available. Financial award application deadline: 3/1; financial award applicants required to submit FAFSA. *Unit head:* Dr. Carol Brownstein-Evans, Director, 585-395-8459, E-mail: cbrown3@naz.edu. *Application contact:* Judith G. Baker, Director, Graduate Admissions, 585-389-2050, Fax: 585-389-2817, E-mail: gradstudies@naz.edu.

Newman University, School of Social Work, Wichita, KS 67213-2097. Offers MSW. *Accreditation:* CSWE. Postbaccalaureate distance learning degree programs offered (no on-campus study). *Faculty:* 7 full-time (2 women), 6 part-time/adjunct (2 women). *Students:* 54 full-time (49 women), 81 part-time (70 women); includes 31 minority (18 African Americans, 1 American Indian/Alaska Native, 3 Asian Americans or Pacific Islanders, 9 Hispanic Americans), 2 international. Average age 36. 88 applicants, 78% accepted, 55 enrolled. In 2006, 41 degrees awarded. *Degree requirements:* For master's, fieldwork, thesis optional. *Entrance requirements:* For master's, interview, minimum GPA of 3.0, 3 letters of reference. Additional exam requirements/recommendations for international students: Required—TOEFL (minimum score 600 paper-based; 250 computer-based). *Application deadline:* For fall admission, 8/15 for domestic students. Applications are processed on a rolling basis. Application fee: $25 ($40 for international students). *Financial support:* In 2006–07, 7 students received support. Federal Work-Study, scholarships/grants, and tuition waivers (full) available. Financial award application deadline: 8/15; financial award applicants required to submit FAFSA. *Unit head:* Dr. Kevin Brown, Dean, 316-942-4291 Ext. 2458, Fax: 316-942-4483. *Application contact:* Linda Kay Sabala, Director of Graduate Admissions, 316-942-4291 Ext. 2230, Fax: 316-942-4483, E-mail: sabalal@newmanu.edu.

New Mexico Highlands University, Graduate Studies, School of Social Work, Las Vegas, NM 87701. Offers bilingual/bicultural social work practice (MSW); clinical practice (MSW); community organization (MSW). *Accreditation:* CSWE. Part-time programs available. *Faculty:* 11 full-time (4 women), 12 part-time/adjunct (6 women). *Students:* 225 full-time (181 women), 65 part-time (51 women); includes 140 minority (9 African Americans, 31 American Indian/Alaska Native, 2 Asian Americans or Pacific Islanders, 98 Hispanic Americans), 2 international. Average age 37. 136 applicants, 94% accepted, 102 enrolled. In 2006, 135 degrees awarded. *Degree requirements:* For master's, thesis or alternative, comprehensive exam, registration. *Entrance requirements:* For master's, minimum undergraduate GPA of 3.0. *Application deadline:* For fall admission, 8/1 priority date for domestic students. Applications are processed on a rolling basis. Application fee: $15. *Expenses:* Tuition, state resident: part-time $101 per credit hour. Tuition, nonresident: part-time $101 per credit hour. *Financial support:* In 2006–07, 201 students received support. Career-related internships or fieldwork, Federal Work-Study, institutionally sponsored loans, scholarships/grants, tuition waivers (partial), and unspecified assistantships available. Support available to part-time students. Financial award application deadline: 3/1; financial award applicants required to submit FAFSA. *Unit head:* Dr. Alfredo Garcia, Dean, 505-891-9053, Fax: 505-454-3290, E-mail: a_garcia@nmhu.edu. *Application contact:* Diane Trujillo, Administrative Assistant Graduate Studies, 505-454-3266, Fax: 505-454-3558, E-mail: dtrujillo@nmhu.edu.

New Mexico State University, Graduate School, College of Health and Social Services, School of Social Work, Las Cruces, NM 88003-8001. Offers MSW. *Accreditation:* CSWE. Part-time and evening/weekend programs available. *Faculty:* 15 full-time (6 women), 3 part-time/adjunct (2 women). *Students:* 104 full-time (90 women), 89 part-time (77 women); includes 88 minority (4 African Americans, 10 American Indian/Alaska Native, 1 Asian American or Pacific Islander, 73 Hispanic Americans). Average age 35. 124 applicants, 73% accepted. In 2006, 66 degrees awarded. *Degree requirements:* For master's, research project, oral exam, thesis optional. *Entrance requirements:* For master's, minimum GPA of 3.0. Additional exam requirements/recommendations for international students: Required—TOEFL (minimum score 637 paper-based; 270 computer-based). *Application deadline:* For fall admission, 1/15 priority date for domestic and international students. Applications are processed on a rolling basis. Application fee: $30 ($50 for international students). Electronic applications accepted. *Financial support:* In 2006–07, 2 research assistantships, 10 teaching assistantships with tuition reimbursements were awarded; fellowships, career-related internships or fieldwork, traineeships, health care benefits, and unspecified assistantships also available. Financial award application deadline: 3/1. *Faculty research:* Attachment issues, border issues, substance abuse, sexual orientation, family diversity. *Unit head:* Dr. Stephen Anderson, Interim Head, 505-646-4300, Fax: 505-646-4343, E-mail: stephean@nmsu.edu. *Application contact:* Dr. Alice Chornesky, Graduate Program Coordinator, 505-646-2143, Fax: 505-646-4116, E-mail: achornes@nmsu.edu.

New York University, School of Social Work, New York, NY 10012-1019. Offers MSW, PhD, MSW/JD, MSW/MA, MSW/MS. *Accreditation:* CSWE (one or more programs are accredited). Part-time and evening/weekend programs available. *Faculty:* 39 full-time (32 women), 129 part-time/adjunct (94 women). *Students:* 631 full-time (558 women), 369 part-time (310 women); includes 291 minority (108 African Americans, 3 American Indian/Alaska Native, 62 Asian Americans or Pacific Islanders, 118 Hispanic Americans), 25 international. Average age 27. 1,341 applicants, 81% accepted, 397 enrolled. In 2006, 465 master's, 12 doctorates awarded. *Degree requirements:* For doctorate, thesis/dissertation. *Entrance requirements:* For doctorate, GRE or MAT, MSW. Additional exam requirements/recommendations for international students: Required—TOEFL, TWE. *Application deadline:* For fall admission, 3/1 for domestic students, 3/15 for international students; for spring admission, 11/3 for domestic students, 11/2 for international students. Application fee: $50. *Expenses: Contact institution.* Tuition and fees vary according to program. *Financial support:* In 2006–07, 650 students received support, including 5 research assistantships with full and partial tuition reimbursements available (averaging $5,000 per year); career-related internships or fieldwork, Federal Work-Study, scholarships/grants, tuition waivers (partial), and unspecified assistantships also available. Support available to part-time students. Financial award application deadline: 3/1; financial award applicants required to submit FAFSA. *Faculty research:* Social welfare policies, foster care, aging. *Unit head:* Dr. Suzanne England, Dean, 212-998-5959, Fax: 212-995-4172. *Application contact:* Robert W. Sommo, Assistant Dean for Enrollment Services, 212-998-5910, Fax: 212-995-4171, E-mail: ssw.admissions@nyu.edu.

See Close-Up on page 2399.

Norfolk State University, School of Graduate Studies, School of Social Work, Norfolk, VA 23504. Offers MSW, PhD. *Accreditation:* CSWE (one or more programs are accredited). Part-time programs available. *Degree requirements:* For doctorate, thesis/dissertation. *Entrance requirements:* For master's, minimum GPA of 2.7. Additional exam requirements/recommendations for international students: Required—TOEFL.

North Carolina Agricultural and Technical State University, Graduate School, College of Arts and Sciences, Department of Sociology and Social Work, Greensboro, NC 27411. Offers MSW. *Accreditation:* CSWE. Part-time and evening/weekend programs available. *Degree requirements:* For master's, qualifying exam. *Entrance requirements:* For master's, GRE General Test.

Northwest Nazarene University, Graduate Studies, Program in Social Work, Nampa, ID 83686-5897. Offers MSW. *Accreditation:* CSWE. *Faculty:* 8 full-time (5 women), 2 part-time/adjunct (1 woman). *Students:* 77 full-time (48 women), 10 part-time (5 women); includes 8 minority (2 African Americans, 2 Asian Americans or Pacific Islanders, 4 Hispanic Americans), 2 international. Average age 34. In 2006, 27 degrees awarded. *Degree requirements:* For master's, comprehensive exam. *Application deadline:* Applications are processed on a rolling basis. Application fee: $25. Electronic applications accepted. *Unit head:* Mary Curran, Director, 208-467-8679, E-mail: msw@nnu.edu.

The Ohio State University, Graduate School, College of Social Work, Columbus, OH 43210. Offers MSW, PhD. *Accreditation:* CSWE (one or more programs are accredited). Part-time programs available. *Faculty:* 31. *Students:* 262 full-time (229 women), 188 part-time (158 women); includes 75 minority (59 African Americans, 3 American Indian/Alaska Native, 8 Asian Americans or Pacific Islanders, 5 Hispanic Americans), 9 international. Average age 31. 271 applicants, 86% accepted, 79 enrolled. In 2006, 170 master's, 2 doctorates awarded. *Degree requirements:* For master's, thesis optional; for doctorate, thesis/dissertation. *Entrance requirements:* For master's and doctorate, GRE General Test or minimum GPA of 3.0. Additional exam requirements/recommendations for international students: Required—TOEFL (paper-based 550; computer-based 213) or IELTS (7) or Michigan English Language Assessment Battery (82). *Application deadline:* For fall admission, 8/15 priority date for domestic students, 7/1 priority date for international students; for winter admission, 12/1 priority date for domestic students, 11/1 priority date for international students; for spring admission, 3/1 priority date for domestic students, 2/1 priority date for international students. Applications are processed on a rolling basis. Application fee: $40 ($50 for international students). Electronic applications accepted. *Expenses:* Tuition, state resident: full-time $9,438. Tuition, nonresident: full-time $22,791. Tuition and fees vary according to course load, campus/location and program. *Financial support:* Fellowships, research assistantships, teaching assistantships, Federal Work-Study, institutionally sponsored loans, and unspecified assistantships available. Support available to part-time students. *Unit head:* William Meezan, Dean, 614-292-5300, Fax: 614-292-6940, E-mail: meezan.1@osu.edu. *Application contact:* 614-292-9444, Fax: 614-292-3895, E-mail: domestic.grad@osu.edu.

The Ohio State University at Lima, Graduate Programs, Lima, OH 45804. Offers early childhood education (M Ed); education (MA); middle childhood education (M Ed); social work (MSW). *Students:* 46 full-time (37 women), 32 part-time (27 women), 1 international. Average age 30. *Degree requirements:* For master's, thesis (for some programs), comprehensive exam (for some programs). *Entrance requirements:* For master's, GRE, minimum GPA of 3.0. Additional exam requirements/recommendations for international students: Required—TOEFL, IELTS or Michigan English Language Assessment Battery. *Application deadline:* For fall admission, 8/15 priority date for domestic students, 7/1 priority date for international students; for winter admission, 12/1 priority date for domestic students, 11/1 priority date for international students; for spring admission, 3/1 priority date for domestic students, 2/1 priority date for international students. Applications are processed on a rolling basis. Application fee: $40 ($50 for international students). Electronic applications accepted. *Expenses:* Tuition, state resident: full-time $8,919. Tuition, nonresident: full-time $22,272. Tuition and fees vary according to course load, campus/location and program. *Unit head:* Dr. John Snyder, Dean/Director, 419-995-8481, E-mail: snyder.4@osu.edu. *Application contact:* Graduate Admissions, 614-292-9444, Fax: 614-292-3895, E-mail: domestic.grad@osu.edu.

Social Work

The Ohio State University at Marion, Graduate Programs, Marion, OH 43302-5695. Offers early childhood education (pre-K to grade 3) (M Ed); integrated teaching and learning (MA); middle childhood education (grades 4-9) (M Ed); nursing (MS, PhD); social work (MSW); MS/PhD. *Students:* 63 full-time (56 women), 43 part-time (41 women); includes 2 minority (both African Americans), 1 international. Average age 32. *Degree requirements:* For master's, thesis (for some programs), comprehensive exam (for some programs). *Entrance requirements:* For master's and doctorate, GRE, minimum undergraduate GPA of 3.0. Additional exam requirements/recommendations for international students: Required—TOEFL, IELTS or Michigan English Language Assessment Battery. *Application deadline:* For fall admission, 8/15 priority date for domestic students, 7/1 priority date for international students; for winter admission, 12/1 priority date for domestic students, 11/1 priority date for international students; for spring admission, 3/1 priority date for domestic students, 2/1 priority date for international students. Applications are processed on a rolling basis. Application fee: $40 ($50 for international students). Electronic applications accepted. *Expenses:* Tuition, state resident: full-time $8,919. Tuition, nonresident: full-time $22,272. Tuition and fees vary according to course load, campus/location and program. *Unit head:* Gregory S. Rose, Dean/Director, 740-389-6786 Ext. 6218, E-mail: rose.9@osu.edu. *Application contact:* Graduate Admissions, 614-292-9444, Fax: 614-292-3895, E-mail: domestic.grad@osu.edu.

The Ohio State University–Mansfield Campus, Graduate Programs, Mansfield, OH 44906-1599. Offers early and middle childhood education (MA); early childhood education (M Ed); middle childhood education (M Ed); social work (MSW). *Faculty:* 8 full-time (4 women). *Students:* 35 full-time (32 women), 46 part-time (42 women); includes 4 minority (all African Americans), 1 international. Average age 32. *Degree requirements:* For master's, thesis (for some programs), comprehensive exam (for some programs). *Entrance requirements:* For master's, GRE, minimum GPA of 3.0. Additional exam requirements/recommendations for international students: Required—TOEFL (minimum score 550 paper-based; 213 computer-based). *Application deadline:* For fall admission, 8/15 priority date for domestic students, 7/1 priority date for international students; for winter admission, 12/1 priority date for domestic students, 11/1 priority date for international students; for spring admission, 3/1 priority date for domestic students, 2/1 priority date for international students. Applications are processed on a rolling basis. Application fee: $40 ($50 for international students). Electronic applications accepted. *Expenses:* Tuition, state resident: full-time $8,919. Tuition, nonresident: full-time $22,272. Tuition and fees vary according to course load, campus/location and program. *Financial support:* In 2006–07, 14 students received support, including 3 teaching assistantships with full tuition reimbursements available (averaging $9,000 per year); Federal Work-Study and scholarships/grants also available. Support available to part-time students. Financial award application deadline: 7/1. *Application contact:* Graduate Admissions, 614-292-9444, Fax: 614-292-3895, E-mail: domestic.grad@osu.edu.

The Ohio State University–Newark Campus, Graduate Programs, Newark, OH 43055-1797. Offers early/middle childhood education (M Ed); integrated teaching and learning (MA); social work (MSW). *Students:* 31 full-time (25 women), 39 part-time (34 women); includes 3 minority (1 African American, 1 Asian American or Pacific Islander, 1 Hispanic American), 1 international. Average age 33. *Degree requirements:* For master's, thesis (for some programs), comprehensive exam (for some programs). *Entrance requirements:* For master's, GRE, minimum GPA of 3.0. Additional exam requirements/recommendations for international students: Required—TOEFL, IELTS or Michigan English Language Assessment Battery. *Application deadline:* For fall admission, 8/15 priority date for domestic students, 7/1 priority date for international students; for winter admission, 12/1 priority date for domestic students, 11/1 priority date for international students; for spring admission, 3/1 priority date for domestic students, 2/1 priority date for international students. Applications are processed on a rolling basis. Application fee: $40 ($50 for international students). Electronic applications accepted. *Expenses:* Tuition, state resident: full-time $8,919. Tuition, nonresident: full-time $22,272. Tuition and fees vary according to course level, campus/location and program. *Unit head:* Dr. William L. MacDonald, Dean/Director, 740-366-9333 Ext. 330, E-mail: macdonald.24@osu.edu. *Application contact:* Graduate Admissions, 614-292-9444, Fax: 614-292-3985, E-mail: domestic.grad@osu.edu.

Ohio University, Graduate Studies, College of Arts and Sciences, Department of Social Work, Athens, OH 45701-2979. Offers MSW. *Accreditation:* CSWE. *Faculty:* 8 full-time (6 women), 6 part-time/adjunct (4 women). *Students:* 18 full-time (17 women), 32 part-time (30 women). Average age 29. 160 applicants, 25% accepted, 25 enrolled. In 2006, 14 degrees awarded. *Median time to degree:* Master's–2 years full-time, 3 years part-time. *Degree requirements:* For master's, fieldwork. *Entrance requirements:* For master's, GRE General Test or minimum GPA of 3.0, liberal arts background. Additional exam requirements/recommendations for international students: Required—TOEFL (minimum score 600 paper-based), IELTS. *Application deadline:* For fall admission, 9/1 priority date for international students; for spring admission, 2/1 priority date for domestic students. Applications are processed on a rolling basis. Application fee: $45. Electronic applications accepted. *Financial support:* In 2006–07, 9 research assistantships with full tuition reimbursements (averaging $9,000 per year), 2 teaching assistantships with full tuition reimbursements (averaging $9,000 per year) were awarded; career-related internships or fieldwork and tuition waivers (partial) also available. Financial award application deadline: 2/1; financial award applicants required to submit FAFSA. *Faculty research:* Violence, suicide, ethics, technology, field education, families. Total annual research expenditures: $65,000. *Unit head:* Dr. Susan Kiss Sarnoff, Graduate Chair, 740-593-1301, Fax: 740-593-0427, E-mail: sarnoff@ohio.edu.

Our Lady of the Lake University of San Antonio, Worden School of Social Service, San Antonio, TX 78207-4689. Offers MSW. *Accreditation:* CSWE. Part-time programs available. *Degree requirements:* For master's, practicum, thesis optional. *Entrance requirements:* For master's, GRE General Test or MAT. Additional exam requirements/recommendations for international students: Required—TOEFL. Electronic applications accepted. *Faculty research:* Cross-cultural social work practice, mental health, adult literacy, spirituality, maternal health care, experiential learning.

Phillips Theological Seminary, Programs in Theology, Tulsa, OK 74116. Offers administration of church agencies (M Div); campus ministry (M Div); church-related social work (M Div); college and seminary teaching (M Div); global mission work (M Div); institutional chaplaincy (M Div); ministerial vocations in Christian education (M Div); ministry (D Min), including parish ministry, pastoral counseling, practices of ministry; ministry and culture (MAMC), including Christian education, congregational leadership, history and practice of Christian spirituality, theology, ethics, and culture; ministry of music (M Div); pastoral care and counseling (M Div); pastoral ministry (M Div); theological studies (MTS). *Accreditation:* ATS. Part-time programs available. Postbaccalaureate distance learning degree programs offered (minimal on-campus study). *Degree requirements:* For master's, thesis (for some programs); for doctorate, thesis/dissertation. *Entrance requirements:* For master's, minimum GPA of 2.5; for doctorate, M Div, minimum GPA of 3.0. *Faculty research:* Biblical studies, historical studies, theology and culture, practical theology, theology and film.

Pontifical Catholic University of Puerto Rico, Institute of Graduate Studies in Behavioral Science and Community Affairs, Ponce, PR 00717-0777. Offers clinical psychology (MA, MS); clinical social work (MSW); criminology (MA); industrial psychology (MS); psychology (PhD); public administration (MA). Part-time and evening/weekend programs available. *Entrance requirements:* For master's, EXADEP, GRE, 3 letters of recommendation, interview, minimum GPA of 2.75.

Portland State University, Graduate Studies, Graduate School of Social Work, Portland, OR 97207-0751. Offers social work (MSW); social work and social research (PhD). *Accreditation:* CSWE (one or more programs are accredited). Part-time programs available. *Faculty:* 35 full-time (24 women), 14 part-time/adjunct (6 women). *Students:* 314 full-time (248 women), 154 part-time (127 women); includes 69 minority (15 African Americans, 9 American Indian/Alaska Native, 15 Asian Americans or Pacific Islanders, 30 Hispanic Americans), 4 international. Average age 35. 474 applicants, 69% accepted, 221 enrolled. In 2006, 141 master's, 2 doctorates awarded. *Degree requirements:* For doctorate, thesis/dissertation. *Entrance requirements:* For master's, minimum GPA of 3.0 in upper-division course work or 2.75 overall. Additional exam requirements/recommendations for international students: Required—TOEFL (minimum score 550 paper-based; 213 computer-based). *Application deadline:* For fall admission, 2/1 for domestic and international students. Application fee: $50. *Expenses:* Tuition, state resident: full-time $6,426; part-time $238 per credit. Tuition, nonresident: full-time $11,016; part-time $408 per credit. Tuition and fees vary according to course load. *Financial support:* In 2006–07, 8 research assistantships with full tuition reimbursements (averaging $10,022 per year), 2 teaching assistantships with full tuition reimbursements (averaging $13,161 per year) were awarded; career-related internships or fieldwork, Federal Work-Study, scholarships/grants, tuition waivers (partial), and unspecified assistantships also available. Support available to part-time students. Financial award application deadline: 3/1; financial award applicants required to submit FAFSA. *Faculty research:* Child welfare; child mental health; social welfare policies and services; work, family, and dependent care; adult mental health. Total annual research expenditures: $8.4 million. *Unit head:* Dr. Kristine E. Nelson, Dean, 503-725-4712, Fax: 503-725-5545, E-mail: nelsonk@pdx.edu. *Application contact:* Janet Putnam, Director of Student Affairs, 503-725-4712, Fax: 503-725-5545, E-mail: putnamj@pdx.edu.

Radford University, Graduate College, Waldron College of Health and Human Services, School of Social Work, Radford, VA 24142. Offers MSW. *Accreditation:* CSWE. Part-time programs available. Postbaccalaureate distance learning degree programs offered (minimal on-campus study). *Faculty:* 6 full-time (5 women), 10 part-time/adjunct (8 women). *Students:* 61 full-time (60 women), 43 part-time (37 women); includes 13 minority (12 African Americans, 1 Hispanic American). Average age 33. 39 applicants, 92% accepted, 28 enrolled. In 2006, 27 degrees awarded. *Degree requirements:* For master's, comprehensive exam. *Entrance requirements:* Additional exam requirements/recommendations for international students: Required—TOEFL. *Application deadline:* For fall admission, 2/15 priority date for domestic students, 4/1 for international students; for spring admission, 10/1 for domestic students, 8/1 for international students. Applications are processed on a rolling basis. Application fee: $40. Electronic applications accepted. *Expenses:* Tuition, state resident: full-time $4,680; part-time $260 per credit hour. Tuition, nonresident: full-time $8,604; part-time $478 per credit hour. *Financial support:* In 2006–07, 35 students received support, including 21 research assistantships with partial tuition reimbursements available (averaging $8,000 per year), teaching assistantships with partial tuition reimbursements available (averaging $8,700 per year); career-related internships or fieldwork, Federal Work-Study, institutionally sponsored loans, and scholarships/grants also available. Financial award application deadline: 3/1; financial award applicants required to submit FAFSA. *Unit head:* Dr. Cathryne L. Schmitz, Director, 540-831-7689, Fax: 540-831-6053, E-mail: cschmitz2@radford.edu.

Rhode Island College, School of Graduate Studies, School of Social Work, Providence, RI 02908-1991. Offers MSW. *Accreditation:* CSWE. Part-time programs available. *Faculty:* 10 full-time (8 women), 6 part-time/adjunct (5 women). *Students:* 101 full-time (87 women), 22 part-time (19 women); includes 13 minority (3 African Americans, 3 Asian Americans or Pacific Islanders, 7 Hispanic Americans). Average age 34. In 2006, 61 degrees awarded. *Entrance requirements:* For master's, 3 letters of recommendation. *Application deadline:* For fall admission, 2/15 for domestic students. Applications are processed on a rolling basis. Application fee: $50. *Expenses:* Contact institution. Tuition and fees vary according to degree level, program and reciprocity agreements. *Financial support:* Career-related internships or fieldwork, Federal Work-Study, scholarships/grants, health care benefits, and unspecified assistantships available. Support available to part-time students. Financial award application deadline: 5/15; financial award applicants required to submit FAFSA. *Unit head:* Dr. Carol Bennett-Speight, Dean, 401-456-8043.

Roberts Wesleyan College, Division of Social Work, Rochester, NY 14624-1997. Offers child and family practice (MSW); congregational and community practice (MSW); mental health practice (MSW). *Accreditation:* CSWE. *Faculty:* 11. *Students:* 75 full-time (66 women), 23 part-time (16 women). Average age 35. 75 applicants, 75% accepted. In 2006, 49 degrees awarded. *Entrance requirements:* For master's, minimum GPA of 2.75. *Application deadline:* For fall admission, 4/1 priority date for domestic students. Applications are processed on a rolling basis. Application fee: $35. *Financial support:* In 2006–07, 84 students received support, including 35 fellowships (averaging $1,863 per year); career-related internships or fieldwork, scholarships/grants, and tuition waivers (partial) also available. Financial award applicants required to submit FAFSA. *Faculty research:* Religion and social work, family studies, values and ethics. *Unit head:* Dr. Harmon Meldrim, Chair, 585-594-6487, E-mail: meldrimh@roberts.edu. *Application contact:* Beverly Keim, Graduate Admissions Coordinator, 585-594-6232, E-mail: keimb@roberts.edu.

Rutgers, The State University of New Jersey, New Brunswick, Graduate School, Doctoral Program in Social Work, New Brunswick, NJ 08901-1281. Offers direct intervention in interpersonal situations (PhD); social policy analysis and administration (PhD); social work (PhD). Part-time programs available. *Degree requirements:* For doctorate, thesis/dissertation. *Entrance requirements:* For doctorate, GRE General Test, MSW or related master's degree. *Faculty research:* Women, substance abuse, aging, organizational behavior, social service needs assessment.

Rutgers, The State University of New Jersey, New Brunswick, School of Social Work, Program in Social Work, New Brunswick, NJ 08901-1281. Offers MSW, PhD, JD/MSW, M Div/MSW. Part-time programs available. *Entrance requirements:* For master's, GRE General Test, social work experience. Additional exam requirements/recommendations for international students: Required—TOEFL. Electronic applications accepted.

St. Ambrose University, College of Arts and Sciences, Program in Social Work, Davenport, IA 52803-2898. Offers MSW. *Accreditation:* CSWE. Part-time and evening/weekend programs available. *Faculty:* 7 full-time (3 women), 3 part-time/adjunct (all women). *Students:* 49 full-time (45 women), 17 part-time (14 women); includes 8 minority (5 African Americans, 3 Hispanic Americans), 2 international. Average age 31. 53 applicants, 72% accepted, 27 enrolled. In 2006, 26 degrees awarded. *Degree requirements:* For master's, thesis or alternative, integration projects, comprehensive exam (for some programs), registration. *Entrance requirements:* For master's, minimum GPA of 3.0, course work in statistics, bachelor's degree in liberal arts. Additional exam requirements/recommendations for international students: Required—TOEFL. *Application deadline:* For fall admission, 8/1 priority date for domestic students; for winter admission, 12/15 priority date for domestic students; for spring admission, 1/1 priority date for domestic students. Applications are processed on a rolling basis. Application fee: $25. Electronic applications accepted. *Financial support:* In 2006–07, 61 students received support, including 6 research assistantships with partial tuition reimbursements available (averaging $3,600 per year); career-related internships or fieldwork, scholarships/grants, and tuition waivers (partial) also available. Support available to part-time students. Financial award application deadline: 8/15; financial award applicants required to submit FAFSA. *Faculty research:* Social work practice, cults/sects, family therapy, developmental disabilities. *Unit head:* Dr. Brenda DuBois, Associate Director, 563-333-6379, Fax: 563-333-6243, E-mail: bdubois@sau.edu. *Application contact:* Elizabeth Berridge, Director of Graduate Student Recruitment, 563-333-6271, Fax: 563-333-6268, E-mail: berridgeelizabethb@sau.edu.

Saint Louis University, Graduate School, College of Public Service, School of Social Work, St. Louis, MO 63103-2097. Offers MSW. *Accreditation:* CSWE. Part-time programs available. *Faculty:* 14 full-time (7 women), 12 part-time/adjunct (9 women). *Students:* 90 full-time (81 women), 85 part-time (77 women); includes 38 minority (34 African Americans, 1 Asian American or Pacific Islander, 3 Hispanic Americans), 3 international. Average age 31. 125 applicants, 83% accepted, 51 enrolled. In 2006, 64 degrees awarded. *Entrance requirements:* For master's, minimum GPA of 3.0, letters of recommendation. Additional exam requirements/recommendations for international students: Required—TOEFL (minimum score 550 paper-based; 215 computer-based). *Application deadline:* For fall admission, 4/1 priority date for domestic students, 9/1 for international students; for spring admission, 11/1 priority date for domestic students, 11/1 for international students. Applications are processed on a rolling basis. Application fee: $40. *Expenses: Contact institution. Financial support:* In 2006–07, 114 students received support, including 5 research assistantships with tuition reimbursements available (averaging $3,600 per year); career-related internships or fieldwork, Federal Work-Study, institutionally sponsored loans, scholarships/grants, traineeships, health care benefits, tuition waivers (partial), and unspecified assistantships also available. Support available to part-time students. Financial award application deadline: 4/1; financial award applicants required to submit FAFSA. *Faculty research:* Gerontology, mental health issues, child welfare (especially abuse and neglect), social justice, and peace making, homelessness. Total annual research expenditures: $125,000. *Unit head:* Dr. Susan C. Tebb, PhD, Director, 314-977-2730, Fax: 314-977-2731, E-mail: tebbsc@slu.edu. *Application contact:* Jane Sprankel, Director of Admission, 314-977-2722, Fax: 314-977-2731.

Salem State College, Graduate School, Program in Social Work, Salem, MA 01970-5353. Offers MSW. *Accreditation:* CSWE. Part-time and evening/weekend programs available. *Faculty:* 8 full-time (5 women), 6 part-time/adjunct (2 women). *Students:* 84 full-time (77 women), 145 part-time (123 women); includes 23 minority (13 African Americans, 1 American Indian/Alaska Native, 2 Asian Americans or Pacific Islanders, 7 Hispanic Americans), 2 international. Average age 35. In 2006, 74 degrees awarded. *Entrance requirements:* For master's, GRE General Test or MAT. *Application deadline:* Applications are processed on a rolling basis. Application fee: $35. *Unit head:* Cheryl Springer, Coordinator, 978-542-6317, E-mail: cspringer@salemsatate.edu.

Salisbury University, Graduate Division, Program in Social Work, Salisbury, MD 21801-6837. Offers MSW. *Accreditation:* CSWE. Part-time and evening/weekend programs available. *Faculty:* 10 full-time (8 women), 1 part-time/adjunct (0 women). *Students:* 61 full-time (56 women), 30 part-time (24 women); includes 26 minority (23 African Americans, 1 Asian American or Pacific Islander, 2 Hispanic Americans), 1 international. Average age 32. 90 applicants, 61% accepted, 51 enrolled. In 2006, 45 degrees awarded. *Entrance requirements:* Additional exam requirements/recommendations for international students: Required—TOEFL (minimum score 550 paper-based; 213 computer-based). *Application deadline:* Applications are processed on a rolling basis. Application fee: $45. Electronic applications accepted. *Expenses:* Tuition, state resident: part-time $260 per credit hour. Tuition, nonresident: part-time $546 per credit hour. Required fees: $52 per credit hour. *Financial support:* Applicants required to submit FAFSA. *Unit head:* Dr. Marvin Tossey, Director, 410-543-6305.

San Diego State University, Graduate and Research Affairs, College of Health and Human Services, School of Social Work, San Diego, CA 92182. Offers MSW, JD/MSW, MSW/MPH. *Accreditation:* CSWE. Part-time programs available. *Students:* 192 full-time (171 women), 62 part-time (57 women); includes 85 minority (11 African Americans, 1 American Indian/Alaska Native, 25 Asian Americans or Pacific Islanders, 48 Hispanic Americans), 4 international. Average age 31. 276 applicants, 53% accepted, 80 enrolled. In 2006, 108 degrees awarded. *Degree requirements:* For master's, thesis optional. *Entrance requirements:* For master's, GRE General Test. Additional exam requirements/recommendations for international students: Required—TOEFL. *Application deadline:* For fall admission, 5/1 for domestic and international students. Application fee: $55. Electronic applications accepted. *Financial support:* In 2006–07, 10 research assistantships were awarded; fellowships, career-related internships or fieldwork and unspecified assistantships also available. Financial award applicants required to submit FAFSA. *Faculty research:* Child maltreatment, substance abuse, neighborhood studies, child welfare. Total annual research expenditures: $11.8 million. *Unit head:* Anita S. Harbert, Director, 619-594-6310, Fax: 619-594-5991, E-mail: aharbert@mail.sdsu.edu. *Application contact:* Lucinda Rasmussen, Graduate Coordinator, 619-594-6459, Fax: 619-594-5991, E-mail: rasmuss2@mail.sdsu.edu.

San Francisco State University, Division of Graduate Studies, College of Health and Human Services, School of Social Work, San Francisco, CA 94132-1722. Offers MSW. *Accreditation:* CSWE. Part-time programs available. *Faculty:* 22 full-time (11 women), 7 part-time/adjunct (3 women). *Students:* Average age 33. In 2006, 75 degrees awarded. *Degree requirements:* For master's, thesis optional. *Entrance requirements:* For master's, minimum GPA of 2.5 in last 60 units. *Application deadline:* For fall admission, 1/31 priority date for domestic students. Applications are processed on a rolling basis. Application fee: $55. *Financial support:* In 2006–07, 102 students received support, including 40 fellowships, 2 teaching assistantships; career-related internships or fieldwork, Federal Work-Study, and fieldwork stipends also available. Financial award application deadline: 3/1. *Faculty research:* U.S. social policy alternatives, aging and health care, mental health in communities of color, community organizing in minority communities, racism and oppression. *Unit head:* Dr. Eileen Levy, Director, 415-338-1005. *Application contact:* Dr. Felix Rivera, Graduate Coordinator, 415-338-1005, E-mail: felixr@dnai.com.

San Jose State University, Graduate Studies and Research, College of Applied Sciences and Arts, School of Social Work, San Jose, CA 95192-0001. Offers MSW, Certificate. *Accreditation:* CSWE. *Students:* 261 full-time (224 women), 68 part-time (60 women); includes 158 minority (19 African Americans, 1 American Indian/Alaska Native, 47 Asian Americans or Pacific Islanders, 91 Hispanic Americans), 1 international. Average age 33. 317 applicants, 66% accepted, 149 enrolled. In 2006, 157 degrees awarded. *Application deadline:* For fall admission, 6/29 for domestic students; for spring admission, 11/30 for domestic students. Applications are processed on a rolling basis. Application fee: $59. Electronic applications accepted. *Financial support:* Application deadline: 5/31; *Unit head:* Alice Hines, Director, 408-924-5800.

Savannah State University, Program in Social Work, Savannah, GA 31404. Offers MSW. *Accreditation:* CSWE. *Entrance requirements:* For master's, GRE General Test, minimum GPA of 2.6. *Faculty research:* Clinical and administrative social work.

Shippensburg University of Pennsylvania, School of Graduate Studies, College of Education and Human Services, Department of Social Work and Gerontology, Shippensburg, PA 17257-2299. Offers social work (MSW). Part-time and evening/weekend programs available. Post-baccalaureate distance learning degree programs offered. *Faculty:* 4 full-time (3 women). *Students:* 7 full-time (6 women), 11 part-time (10 women); includes 2 minority (both African Americans) Average age 36. 27 applicants, 56% accepted, 13 enrolled. In 2006, 4 degrees awarded. *Degree requirements:* For master's, internship or practicum. *Entrance requirements:* For master's, GRE or MAT, 3 letters of reference, resumé, interview. Additional exam requirements/recommendations for international students: Required—TOEFL (minimum score 560 paper-based; 220 computer-based). *Application deadline:* For fall admission, 3/1 for domestic and international students. Applications are processed on a rolling basis. Application fee: $30. Electronic applications accepted. *Expenses:* Tuition, state resident: part-time $336 per credit. Tuition, nonresident: part-time $538 per credit. *Financial support:* In 2006–07, 1 research assistantship with full tuition reimbursement (averaging $3,125 per year) was awarded; career-related internships or fieldwork, scholarships/grants, and unspecified assistantships also available. Support available to part-time students. Financial award application deadline: 3/1; financial award applicants required to submit FAFSA. *Application contact:* Renee Payne, Associate Dean of Graduate Admissions, 717-477-1231, Fax: 717-477-4016, E-mail: rmpayn@ship.edu.

Simmons College, School of Social Work, Boston, MA 02115. Offers clinical social work (MSW, PhD); MSW/Certificate. *Accreditation:* CSWE (one or more programs are accredited). Part-time programs available. *Faculty:* 21 full-time (17 women), 68 part-time/adjunct (46 women). *Students:* 234 full-time (201 women), 136 part-time (122 women); includes 60 minority (32 African Americans, 12 Asian Americans or Pacific Islanders, 16 Hispanic Americans), 7 international. Average age 27. 540 applicants, 85% accepted, 160 enrolled. In 2006, 141 master's, 4 doctorates awarded. *Degree requirements:* For master's, thesis or alternative; for doctorate, thesis/dissertation. *Entrance requirements:* For master's, minimum GPA of 3.0 in last 2 years of undergraduate course work; for doctorate, MAT, interview, minimum GPA of 3.0 in last 2 years of undergraduate course work. Additional exam requirements/recommendations for international students: Required—TOEFL (minimum score 600 paper-based; 250 computer-based). *Application deadline:* For fall admission, 12/15 priority date for domestic students; for winter admission, 2/15 for domestic students. Application fee: $45. *Expenses: Contact institution. Financial support:* Fellowships with full tuition reimbursements, career-related internships or fieldwork, Federal Work-Study, institutionally sponsored loans, and tuition waivers (full) available. Support available to part-time students. Financial award application deadline: 3/1; financial award applicants required to submit FAFSA. *Faculty research:* Adolescence and depression, multicultural social work, competence, domestic violence, narrative theory. *Unit head:* Dr. Stefan Krug, Dean, 617-521-3929, Fax: 617-521-3980, E-mail: stefan.krug@simmons.edu.

Smith College, School for Social Work, Northampton, MA 01063. Offers MSW, PhD. *Accreditation:* CSWE (one or more programs are accredited). *Faculty:* 10 full-time (7 women), 98 part-time/adjunct (75 women). *Students:* 373 full-time (332 women); includes 74 minority (33 African Americans, 4 American Indian/Alaska Native, 11 Asian Americans or Pacific Islanders, 26 Hispanic Americans), 6 international. Average age 32. 346 applicants, 70% accepted, 124 enrolled. In 2006, 114 master's, 6 doctorates awarded. *Median time to degree:* Of those who began their doctoral program in fall 1998, 63% received their degree in 8 years or less. *Degree requirements:* For master's and doctorate, thesis/dissertation. *Entrance requirements:* For doctorate, MAT. Additional exam requirements/recommendations for international students: Required—TOEFL. *Application deadline:* For fall admission, 2/21 for domestic students. Applications are processed on a rolling basis. Application fee: $60. *Expenses: Contact institution.* Tuition and fees vary according to course load. *Financial support:* In 2006–07, 218 students received support. Career-related internships or fieldwork, institutionally sponsored loans, and scholarships/grants available. Financial award application deadline: 4/1; financial award applicants required to submit FAFSA. *Faculty research:* Social work practice, human behavior in the social environment, social welfare policy, social work research. *Unit head:* Dr. Carolyn Jacobs, Dean, 413-585-7977, E-mail: cjacobs@smith.edu. *Application contact:* Irene Rodriguez Martin, Director of Enrollment Management and Continuing Education, 413-585-7960, Fax: 413-585-7994, E-mail: imartin@smith.edu.

See Close-Up on page 2401.

Southern Connecticut State University, School of Graduate Studies, School of Health and Human Services, Department of Social Work, New Haven, CT 06515-1355. Offers MSW, MSW/MS. *Accreditation:* CSWE. Part-time and evening/weekend programs available. *Faculty:* 16 full-time, 7 part-time/adjunct. *Students:* 87 full-time (73 women), 57 part-time (47 women); includes 24 minority (11 African Americans, 2 Asian Americans or Pacific Islanders, 11 Hispanic Americans), 1 international. 358 applicants, 22% accepted, 66 enrolled. In 2006, 49 degrees awarded. *Degree requirements:* For master's, thesis. *Entrance requirements:* For master's, minimum undergraduate QPA of 3.0 in graduate major field or 2.5 overall, interview. *Application deadline:* For fall admission, 3/1 for domestic students; for spring admission, 12/1 for domestic students. Application fee: $50. Electronic applications accepted. *Financial support:* Application deadline: 4/15; *Faculty research:* Social work practice; social service development; services for women, the aging, children, and families in educational and health care systems. *Unit head:* Dr. Anthony Maltese, Chairperson, 203-392-6554, Fax: 203-392-6580, E-mail: maltesea1@southernct.edu. *Application contact:* Dr. Barbara Worden, Graduate Coordinator, 203-392-6563, Fax: 203-392-6580, E-mail: wordenb1@southernct.edu.

Southern Illinois University Carbondale, Graduate School, College of Education, School of Social Work, Carbondale, IL 62901-4701. Offers MSW, JD/MSW. *Accreditation:* CSWE. *Faculty:* 10 full-time (6 women). *Students:* 69 full-time (62 women), 17 part-time (9 women); includes 11 minority (10 African Americans, 1 Asian American or Pacific Islander), 10 international. Average age 30. 57 applicants, 35% accepted, 4 enrolled. In 2006, 48 degrees awarded. *Entrance requirements:* For master's, GRE General Test, minimum GPA of 2.7. Additional exam requirements/recommendations for international students: Required—TOEFL. *Application deadline:* For fall admission, 3/1 for domestic students. Applications are processed on a rolling basis. Application fee: $20. *Financial support:* In 2006–07, 19 students received support, including 6 research assistantships with full tuition reimbursements available; fellowships with full tuition reimbursements available, teaching assistantships with full tuition reimbursements available, career-related internships or fieldwork and tuition waivers (full) also available. Financial award application deadline: 5/1. *Faculty research:* Service delivery systems, comparative race relations, advocacy research, gerontology, child welfare and health. *Unit head:* Dr. Mizanur Miah, Director, 618-453-2243. *Application contact:* Judy Wright, Assistant to Graduate Director, 618-453-1202, Fax: 618-453-1219, E-mail: mmmjw@siu.edu.

Southern Illinois University Edwardsville, Graduate Studies and Research, College of Arts and Sciences, Department of Social Work, Edwardsville, IL 62026-0001. Offers MSW. *Accreditation:* CSWE. Part-time and evening/weekend programs available. *Faculty:* 7 full-time (3 women). *Students:* 32 full-time (28 women), 7 part-time (all women); includes 5 minority (all African Americans) Average age 33. 69 applicants, 55% accepted. In 2006, 29 degrees awarded. *Degree requirements:* For master's, thesis or alternative, final exam. *Entrance requirements:* For master's, GRE General Test or MAT. Additional exam requirements/recommendations for international students: Required—TOEFL. *Application deadline:* For fall admission, 2/15 for domestic and international students. Application fee: $30. Electronic applications accepted. *Financial support:* Fellowships with full tuition reimbursements, research assistantships with full tuition reimbursements, teaching assistantships with full tuition reimbursements, unspecified assistantships available. Financial award application deadline: 3/1. *Unit head:* Dr. Venessa Brown, Director, 618-650-2450, E-mail: vbrown@siue.edu. *Application contact:* Dr. Venessa Brown, Director, 618-650-2450, E-mail: vbrown@siue.edu.

Southern University at New Orleans, School of Social Work, New Orleans, LA 70126-1009. Offers MSW. *Accreditation:* CSWE. Part-time and evening/weekend programs available. *Degree requirements:* For master's, thesis. *Faculty research:* Service needs of people with AIDS, suicidal rate of people with AIDS.

Spalding University, Graduate Studies, College of Social Sciences and Humanities, School of Social Work, Louisville, KY 40203-2188. Offers MSW. *Accreditation:* CSWE. Evening/weekend programs available. *Degree requirements:* For master's, thesis or alternative, project presentation. *Entrance requirements:* For master's, 18 hours of course work in social sciences including statistics, human biology; GRE General Test (if undergraduate GPA is less than 2.8). Additional exam requirements/recommendations for international students: Required—TOEFL. Electronic applications accepted. *Faculty research:* Addictions, spirituality, feminist studies, mental retardation, action research.

Springfield College, School of Social Work, Springfield, MA 01109-3797. Offers advanced generalist (MSW); advanced standing (MSW); practice with children and adolescents (PMC); JD/MSW. *Accreditation:* CSWE. Part-time and evening/weekend programs available. *Faculty:* 11 full-time (5 women), 29 part-time/adjunct (20 women). *Students:* 249. Average age 34. 244 applicants, 72% accepted, 110 enrolled. In 2006, 97 degrees awarded. *Degree requirements:* For master's, fieldwork. *Entrance requirements:* For master's, minimum GPA of 3.0 during previous 2 years. Additional exam requirements/recommendations for international students: Required—TOEFL (minimum score 550 paper-based; 213 computer-based). *Application deadline:* For fall admission, 3/1 priority date for domestic students. Applications are processed on a rolling basis. Application fee: $50. Electronic applications accepted. *Expenses:* Tuition: Full-time $12,222; part-time $679 per credit. Required fees: $25; $25 per year. One-time fee: $25 full-time. *Financial support:* Fellowships with partial tuition reimbursements, teaching assistantships with partial tuition reimbursements, career-related internships or fieldwork, Federal Work-Study, institutionally sponsored loans, scholarships/grants, and unspecified assistantships available. Financial award application deadline: 3/1. *Faculty research:* Child and adolescent practice, health and aging, human rights, mental health. *Unit head:* Dr. Francine Vecchiolla, Dean, 413-748-3060, Fax: 413-748-3069, E-mail: francine_vecchiolla@spfldcol.edu. *Application contact:* Donald James Shaw, Director of Graduate Admissions, 413-748-3060, Fax: 413-748-3069, E-mail: donald_shaw_jr@spfldcol.edu.

See Close-Up on page 2403.

Social Work

State University of New York College at Brockport, School of Professions, Greater Rochester Collaborative Master of Social Work Program, Brockport, NY 14420-2997. Offers MSW. Part-time programs available. *Students:* 56 full-time (53 women), 75 part-time (66 women); includes 27 minority (20 African Americans, 1 Asian American or Pacific Islander, 6 Hispanic Americans). 74 applicants, 100% accepted, 74 enrolled. In 2006, 30 degrees awarded. *Degree requirements:* For master's, thesis or alternative. *Entrance requirements:* For master's, minimum GPA of 3.0, letters of recommendation. Additional exam requirements/recommendations for international students: Required—TOEFL (minimum score 550 paper-based; 213 computer-based; 80 iBT). *Application deadline:* For fall admission, 3/15 for domestic students, 3/15 priority date for international students. Application fee: $50. *Expenses:* Contact institution. *Financial support:* Career-related internships or fieldwork, Federal Work-Study, scholarships/grants, and unspecified assistantships available. Support available to part-time students. Financial award application deadline: 3/15; financial award applicants required to submit FAFSA. *Faculty research:* Care giving, child welfare, substance abuse, gerontological social work, home-school-community partnerships. *Unit head:* Dr. Carol Brownstein-Evans, Director, 585-395-8450, E-mail: cbrownst@brockport.edu. *Application contact:* Linda Fleming, Admissions Coordinator, 585-395-8450, E-mail: rcmsw@brockport.edu.

Stephen F. Austin State University, Graduate School, College of Applied Arts and Science, School of Social Work, Nacogdoches, TX 75962. Offers MSW. *Accreditation:* CSWE. *Degree requirements:* For master's, thesis optional. *Entrance requirements:* For master's, GRE General Test, interview. Additional exam requirements/recommendations for international students: Required—TOEFL (minimum score 550 paper-based).

Stony Brook University, State University of New York, Stony Brook University Medical Center, Health Sciences Center, School of Social Welfare, Doctoral Program in Social Welfare, Stony Brook, NY 11794. Offers PhD. *Faculty:* 23 full-time (14 women), 17 part-time/adjunct (8 women). *Students:* 29 full-time (20 women), 5 part-time (all women); includes 10 minority (6 African Americans, 2 Asian Americans or Pacific Islanders, 2 Hispanic Americans), 2 international. 18 applicants, 28% accepted. In 2006, 3 degrees awarded. *Degree requirements:* For doctorate, thesis/dissertation. *Entrance requirements:* For doctorate, GRE General Test. *Application deadline:* For fall admission, 2/1 for domestic students. Application fee: $60. *Expenses:* Tuition, state resident: full-time $6,900; part-time $288 per credit. Tuition, nonresident: full-time $10,920; part-time $455 per credit. *Financial support:* In 2006–07, 7 fellowships, 10 teaching assistantships were awarded. Financial award application deadline: 2/1. *Application contact:* Dr. Joel Blau, Director, 631-444-3149, Fax: 631-444-7565, E-mail: jblau@notes.cc.sunysb.edu.

Announcement: The PhD program is one of the few social welfare doctoral programs focusing exclusively on policy-related research. Emphasizing health, mental health, and social welfare issues, such as aging, poverty, and homelessness, this interdisciplinary program prepares students for teaching and research positions in government, the university, and throughout the nonprofit sector.

See Close-Up on page 2405.

Stony Brook University, State University of New York, Stony Brook University Medical Center, Health Sciences Center, School of Social Welfare, Master's Program in Social Work, Stony Brook, NY 11794. Offers MSW. *Accreditation:* CSWE. *Students:* 363 full-time (298 women), 10 part-time (6 women); includes 115 minority (71 African Americans, 3 American Indian/Alaska Native, 3 Asian Americans or Pacific Islanders, 38 Hispanic Americans), 6 international. Average age 35. 401 applicants, 66% accepted. In 2006, 173 degrees awarded. *Degree requirements:* For master's, project or thesis. *Entrance requirements:* For master's, interview. *Application deadline:* For fall admission, 3/1 for domestic students. Application fee: $60. *Expenses:* Tuition, state resident: full-time $6,900; part-time $288 per credit. Tuition, nonresident: full-time $10,920; part-time $455 per credit. *Financial support:* Application deadline: 3/1. *Application contact:* Dr. Michael Lewis, Director, 631-444-3166, Fax: 631-444-7565, E-mail: michaell@ssw.hsc.sunysb.edu.

Syracuse University, Graduate School, College of Human Services and Health Professions, School of Social Work, Syracuse, NY 13244. Offers MSW. *Accreditation:* CSWE. Part-time and evening/weekend programs available. *Students:* 136 full-time (120 women), 59 part-time (49 women); includes 21 minority (14 African Americans, 2 American Indian/Alaska Native, 2 Asian Americans or Pacific Islanders, 3 Hispanic Americans). 175 applicants, 86% accepted, 82 enrolled. *Entrance requirements:* For master's, 3 letters of recommendation. Additional exam requirements/recommendations for international students: Required—TOEFL. *Application deadline:* For fall admission, 4/15 for domestic students; for spring admission, 11/1 for domestic students. Applications are processed on a rolling basis. Application fee: $65. Electronic applications accepted. *Expenses:* Tuition: Full-time $16,920; part-time $940 per credit hour. Required fees: $930; $930 per year. *Financial support:* Fellowships with tuition reimbursements, research assistantships with partial tuition reimbursements, teaching assistantships with tuition reimbursements, tuition waivers (partial) available. Financial award applicants required to submit FAFSA. *Faculty research:* Aging policy, healthcare, criminal justice, disability, rights of passage. *Unit head:* Dr. Alejandro Garcia, Director, 315-443-5562, Fax: 315-443-2562. *Application contact:* Amy Pangborn, Information Contact, 315-443-5555, E-mail: inquire@hshp.syr.edu.

Temple University, Graduate School, School of Social Administration, Program in Social Work, Philadelphia, PA 19122-6096. Offers MSW. *Accreditation:* CSWE. Part-time and evening/weekend programs available. *Faculty:* 18 full-time (11 women). *Students:* 209 full-time (178 women), 290 part-time (224 women); includes 147 minority (123 African Americans, 6 Asian Americans or Pacific Islanders, 18 Hispanic Americans), 5 international. 400 applicants, 71% accepted, 183 enrolled. In 2006, 160 degrees awarded. *Entrance requirements:* For master's, minimum GPA of 3.0. Additional exam requirements/recommendations for international students: Required—TOEFL (minimum score 550 paper-based; 213 computer-based; 79 iBT). *Application deadline:* For fall admission, 2/15 priority date for domestic students, 12/15 for international students; for spring admission, 11/1 priority date for domestic students, 8/1 for international students. Applications are processed on a rolling basis. Application fee: $50. Electronic applications accepted. *Expenses:* Tuition, state resident: full-time $12,264; part-time $511 per credit. Tuition, nonresident: full-time $17,904; part-time $746 per credit. Required fees: $84 per course. Tuition and fees vary according to program. *Financial support:* Fellowships, research assistantships, teaching assistantships with tuition reimbursements, career-related internships or fieldwork, Federal Work-Study, institutionally sponsored loans, traineeships, tuition waivers (partial), and field assistantships available. Financial award application deadline: 1/15; financial award applicants required to submit FAFSA. *Unit head:* Dr. Bernie Sue Newman, Director of MSW Program, 215-204-1205, Fax: 215-204-9606, E-mail: bnewman@temple.edu.

Texas A&M University–Commerce, Graduate School, College of Arts and Sciences, Department of Social Work, Commerce, TX 75429-3011. Offers MSW. *Accreditation:* CSWE. *Entrance requirements:* For master's, GRE General Test.

Texas State University-San Marcos, Graduate School, College of Health Professions, School of Social Work, San Marcos, TX 78666. Offers MSW. *Accreditation:* CSWE. *Faculty:* 11 full-time (8 women), 1 (woman) part-time/adjunct. *Students:* 56 full-time (54 women), 72 part-time (62 women); includes 50 minority (18 African Americans, 1 American Indian/Alaska Native, 1 Asian American or Pacific Islander, 30 Hispanic Americans). Average age 32. 63 applicants, 94% accepted, 38 enrolled. In 2006, 44 degrees awarded. *Degree requirements:* For master's, comprehensive exam. *Entrance requirements:* For master's, GRE General Test, minimum GPA of 2.75 in last 60 hours of course work. Additional exam requirements/recommendations for international students: Required—TOEFL. *Application deadline:* For fall admission, 2/1 priority date for domestic students, 2/1 for international students. Applications are processed on a rolling basis. Application fee: $40 ($90 for international students). *Financial support:* In 2006–07, 114 students received support, including 1 research assistantship (averaging $13,880 per year), 3 teaching assistantships (averaging $5,027 per year); career-related internships or fieldwork, Federal Work-Study, institutionally sponsored loans, and unspecified assistantships also available. Support available to part-time students. Financial award application deadline: 4/1; financial award applicants required to submit FAFSA. *Faculty research:* Domestic or workplace violence, parental participation and school social work, addictions and co-dependency. *Unit head:* Dr. Dorinda Noble, Director, 512-245-2592, Fax: 512-245-8097, E-mail: dn12@txstate.edu.

Tulane University, School of Social Work, New Orleans, LA 70118-5669. Offers MSW, JD/MSW, MSW/MPH. *Accreditation:* CSWE (one or more programs are accredited). Part-time programs available. *Faculty:* 18 full-time (13 women), 37 part-time/adjunct (22 women). *Students:* 29 full-time (22 women), 5 part-time (3 women); includes 12 minority (9 African Americans, 3 Hispanic Americans). Average age 28. 5 applicants, 100% accepted, 4 enrolled. *Degree requirements:* For master's, thesis. *Entrance requirements:* Additional exam requirements/recommendations for international students: Required—TOEFL. *Application deadline:* For fall admission, 3/31 priority date for domestic students. Applications are processed on a rolling basis. Application fee: $25. Electronic applications accepted. *Financial support:* Fellowships, Federal Work-Study available. Financial award applicants required to submit FAFSA. *Unit head:* Dr. Ronald Marks, Dean, 504-865-5314, Fax: 504-862-8727, E-mail: rmarks@tulane.edu. *Application contact:* Dr. Michael J Zakour, Director, 504-865-5314, Fax: 504-862-8727.

Universidad del Este, Graduate School, Carolina, PR 00983. Offers accounting (MBA); administration (M Ed); criminal justice and criminology (MA); education (M Ed); elementary education (M Ed); human resources (MBA); management (MBA); social work (MA); teaching English (M Ed); teaching Spanish (M Ed).

Université de Moncton, Faculty of Social Sciences, School of Social Work, Moncton, NB E1A 3E9, Canada. Offers MSS. *Degree requirements:* For master's, one foreign language. *Entrance requirements:* For master's, minimum GPA of 3.0. *Faculty research:* Burnout and education, mental health (institutionalization), unemployment's effect on youth, women and health services.

Université de Montréal, Faculty of Graduate Studies, Faculty of Arts and Sciences, School of Social Service, Program in Social Administration, Montréal, QC H3C 3J7, Canada. Offers DESS. *Application deadline:* For fall admission, 2/1 priority date for domestic students; for winter admission, 11/1 priority date for domestic students; for spring admission, 2/1 priority date for domestic students. Application fee: $30. Electronic applications accepted. *Unit head:* Claude Larivière, Director, 514-343-7224, Fax: 514-343-2493, E-mail: claude.lariviere@umontreal.ca.

Université de Sherbrooke, Faculty of Letters and Human Sciences, Department of Social Service, Sherbrooke, QC J1K 2R1, Canada. Offers MSS.

Université du Québec à Montréal, Graduate Programs, Program in Social Intervention, Montréal, QC H3C 3P8, Canada. Offers MA. Part-time programs available. *Degree requirements:* For master's, thesis. *Entrance requirements:* For master's, appropriate bachelor's degree or equivalent, proficiency in French.

Université du Québec en Outaouais, Graduate Programs, Program in Social Work, Gatineau, QC J8X 3X7, Canada. Offers MA. *Students:* 10 full-time, 28 part-time, 1 international. *Application deadline:* For fall admission, 6/1 priority date for domestic students, 3/1 for international students; for winter admission, 11/1 priority date for domestic students, 10/1 for international students. Application fee: $30 Canadian dollars. *Financial support:* Research assistantships available. *Unit head:* Yao Assogba, Director, 819-595-3900 Ext. 2201, Fax: 819-595-2384, E-mail: yao.assogba@uqo.ca. *Application contact:* Registrar's Office, 819-773-1850, Fax: 819-773-1835, E-mail: registraire@uqo.ca.

Université Laval, Faculty of Social Sciences, School of Social Work, Programs in Social Work, Québec, QC G1K 7P4, Canada. Offers M Serv Soc, PhD. Terminal master's awarded for partial completion of doctoral program. *Degree requirements:* For master's, thesis (for some programs); for doctorate, thesis/dissertation, comprehensive exam. *Entrance requirements:* For master's and doctorate, knowledge of French, comprehension of written English. Electronic applications accepted.

University at Albany, State University of New York, School of Social Welfare, Albany, NY 12222-0001. Offers MSW, PhD, MSW/MA. *Accreditation:* CSWE (one or more programs are accredited). Part-time and evening/weekend programs available. *Students:* 253 full-time (220 women), 150 part-time (126 women); includes 77 minority (40 African Americans, 2 American Indian/Alaska Native, 7 Asian Americans or Pacific Islanders, 28 Hispanic Americans), 15 international. Average age 34. In 2006, 133 master's, 8 doctorates awarded. *Degree requirements:* For doctorate, thesis/dissertation. *Entrance requirements:* For doctorate, GRE General Test. Additional exam requirements/recommendations for international students: Required—TOEFL (minimum score 550 paper-based; 213 computer-based). *Application deadline:* For fall admission, 2/15 for domestic and international students. Application fee: $75. Electronic applications accepted. *Expenses:* Tuition, state resident: full-time $6,900; part-time $288 per credit. Tuition, nonresident: full-time $10,920; part-time $455 per credit. Required fees: $1,139. *Financial support:* Fellowships, career-related internships or fieldwork and Federal Work-Study available. Financial award application deadline: 2/15. *Faculty research:* Welfare reform, homelessness, children and families, mental health, substance abuse. *Unit head:* Katharine Briar-Lawson, Dean, 518-442-5324. *Application contact:* Brian Goodale, Senior Counselor for Graduate and International Admissions, 518-442-3980.

University at Buffalo, the State University of New York, Graduate School, School of Social Work, Buffalo, NY 14260. Offers MSW, PhD, JD/MSW, MBA/MSW. MSW available in Buffalo, Rochester, Jamestown, and Corning, New York. *Accreditation:* CSWE (one or more programs are accredited). Part-time programs available. *Faculty:* 21 full-time (12 women), 40 part-time/adjunct (28 women). *Students:* 278 full-time (251 women), 206 part-time (175 women); includes 81 minority (53 African Americans, 2 American Indian/Alaska Native, 4 Asian Americans or Pacific Islanders, 22 Hispanic Americans), 10 international. Average age 32. 425 applicants, 72% accepted, 212 enrolled. In 2006, 160 master's, 1 doctorate awarded. *Median time to degree:* Of those who began their doctoral program in fall 1998, 75% received their degree in 8 years or less. *Degree requirements:* For master's, 900 hours of field work; for doctorate, thesis/dissertation, comprehensive exam. *Entrance requirements:* For master's, minimum GPA of 3.0 for advanced standing, 24 credits of course work in liberal arts; for doctorate, GRE General Test, MSW or equivalent. Additional exam requirements/recommendations for international students: Required—TOEFL (minimum score 600 paper-based; 250 computer-based; 100 iBT). *Application deadline:* For fall admission, 3/1 priority date for domestic and international students. Applications are processed on a rolling basis. Application fee: $50. Electronic applications accepted. *Financial support:* In 2006–07, 67 students received support, including 4 fellowships with full tuition reimbursements available (averaging $7,500 per year), 3 research assistantships with full tuition reimbursements available (averaging $15,000 per year), 6 teaching assistantships with full tuition reimbursements available (averaging $15,000 per year); Federal Work-Study, scholarships/grants, health care benefits, tuition waivers (partial), unspecified assistantships, and instructorships and research grants for PhD students also available. Financial award application deadline: 2/1; financial award applicants required to submit FAFSA. *Faculty research:* Trauma, substance abuse, child welfare, aging, developmental disabilities. Total annual research expenditures: $1.3 million. *Unit head:* Dr. Nancy J. Smyth, Dean, 716-645-3381 Ext. 221, Fax: 716-645-3883, E-mail: njsmyth@buffalo.edu. *Application contact:* Maria Soos, Admissions Processor, 716-645-3381, Fax: 716-645-3456, E-mail: sw-info@buffalo.edu.

The University of Akron, Graduate School, College of Fine and Applied Arts, School of Social Work, Akron, OH 44325. Offers MS. *Accreditation:* CSWE. *Faculty:* 6 full-time (4 women), 30 part-time/adjunct (21 women). *Students:* 62 full-time (51 women), 21 part-time (15 women); includes 22 minority (15 African Americans, 3 American Indian/Alaska Native, 1 Asian American or Pacific Islander, 3 Hispanic Americans). Average age 35. 54 applicants, 74% accepted, 33 enrolled. In 2006, 35 degrees awarded. *Entrance requirements:* For master's, undergraduate major in social work or related field, minimum GPA of 2.75, resumé, letters of recommendation.

Additional exam requirements/recommendations for international students: Required—TOEFL (minimum score 550 paper-based; 213 computer-based; 79 iBT). *Application deadline:* For fall admission, 2/15 for domestic students. Applications are processed on a rolling basis. Application fee: $30 ($40 for international students). Electronic applications accepted. *Expenses:* Tuition, state resident: full-time $6,164; part-time $342 per credit. Tuition, nonresident: full-time $10,575; part-time $588 per credit. Required fees: $806; $43 per credit. $12 per term. Tuition and fees vary according to course load, degree level and program. *Financial support:* In 2006–07, 8 research assistantships with full tuition reimbursements, 1 teaching assistantship were awarded; Federal Work-Study also available. *Unit head:* Dr. Virginia Fitch, Director, 330-972-5975, E-mail: vfitch@uakron.edu.

The University of Alabama, Graduate School, School of Social Work, Tuscaloosa, AL 35487. Offers MSW, PhD. *Accreditation:* CSWE (one or more programs are accredited). Postbaccalaureate distance learning degree programs offered (no on-campus study). *Faculty:* 25 full-time (17 women), 13 part-time/adjunct (9 women). *Students:* 248 full-time (214 women), 50 part-time (39 women); includes 112 minority (103 African Americans, 3 Asian Americans or Pacific Islanders, 6 Hispanic Americans), 11 international. Average age 29. 245 applicants, 54% accepted, 121 enrolled. In 2006, 119 master's, 3 doctorates awarded. *Median time to degree:* Master's–1.4 years full-time, 2 years part-time; doctorate–6.3 years full-time, 6.6 years part-time. Of those who began their doctoral program in fall 1998, 50% received their degree in 8 years or less. *Degree requirements:* For doctorate, thesis/dissertation. *Entrance requirements:* For master's, GRE or MAT (if GPA less than 3.0), minimum GPA of 2.5; for doctorate, GRE, minimum GPA of 3.0. Additional exam requirements/recommendations for international students: Required—TOEFL. *Application deadline:* For fall admission, 2/1 priority date for domestic students. Applications are processed on a rolling basis. Application fee: $30. Electronic applications accepted. *Financial support:* In 2006–07, 113 students received support, including 4 fellowships (averaging $3,750 per year), 9 research assistantships with full tuition reimbursements available (averaging $9,394 per year), 3 teaching assistantships with full tuition reimbursements available (averaging $9,396 per year); career-related internships or fieldwork, scholarships/grants, health care benefits, tuition waivers (partial), and unspecified assistantships also available. Financial award application deadline: 2/1. *Faculty research:* Mental health, family and child welfare, aging, social policy, healthcare. Total annual research expenditures: $134,129. *Unit head:* Dr. James P. Adams, Dean, 205-348-3924, Fax: 205-348-9419, E-mail: jadams@sw.ua.edu. *Application contact:* Dr. Ginny Raymond, Associate Dean, 205-348-3943, Fax: 205-348-9419, E-mail: graymond@sw.ua.edu.

University of Alaska Anchorage, College of Health and Social Welfare, School of Social Work, Anchorage, AK 99508-8060. Offers clinical social work practice (Certificate); social work (MSW); social work management (Certificate). *Accreditation:* CSWE. Part-time and evening/weekend programs available. Postbaccalaureate distance learning degree programs offered (no on-campus study). *Students:* 38 full-time (30 women), 33 part-time (27 women); includes 12 minority (2 African Americans, 5 American Indian/Alaska Native, 3 Asian Americans or Pacific Islanders, 2 Hispanic Americans). 43 applicants, 58% accepted. In 2006, 23 degrees awarded. *Degree requirements:* For master's, thesis or alternative, research project, comprehensive exam (for some programs), registration. *Entrance requirements:* For master's, GRE General Test, writing sample. Additional exam requirements/recommendations for international students: Required—TOEFL (minimum score 550 paper-based; 213 computer-based). *Application deadline:* For fall admission, 1/15 for domestic and international students. Application fee: $45. Electronic applications accepted. *Expenses:* Contact institution. *Financial support:* Application deadline: 4/1; *Unit head:* Dr. Elizabeth Sirles, Director, 907-786-6160, Fax: 907-786-1008. *Application contact:* Dr. Randy Magen, MSW Coordinator, 907-786-6901, Fax: 907-786-6912, E-mail: afrhm1@uaa.alaska.edu.

University of Arkansas, Graduate School, J. William Fulbright College of Arts and Sciences, School of Social Work, Fayetteville, AR 72701-1201. Offers MSW. *Accreditation:* CSWE. *Students:* 23 full-time (19 women); includes 2 minority (1 American Indian/Alaska Native, 1 Asian American or Pacific Islander). 37 applicants, 49% accepted. In 2006, 24 degrees awarded. *Entrance requirements:* For master's, GRE General Test. Application fee: $40 ($50 for international students). *Financial support:* In 2006–07, 3 fellowships with tuition reimbursements, 2 research assistantships, 5 teaching assistantships were awarded. *Unit head:* Dr. Joe Schriver, Departmental Chairperson, 479-575-5039, Fax: 479-575-4145, E-mail: jschrive@uark.edu. *Application contact:* Melody Greer, Graduate Coordinator, 479-575-7190, E-mail: melodyg@uark.edu.

University of Arkansas at Little Rock, Graduate School, College of Professional Studies, School of Social Work, Program in Social Work, Little Rock, AR 72204-1099. Offers clinical social work (MSW); social program administration (MSW). *Accreditation:* CSWE. *Entrance requirements:* For master's, GRE General Test or MAT.

The University of British Columbia, Faculty of Arts and Faculty of Graduate Studies, School of Social Work and Family Studies, Vancouver, BC V6T 1Z1, Canada. Offers family studies (MA); social work (MSW); social work and family studies (PhD). Part-time programs available. *Faculty:* 23 full-time (10 women). *Students:* 49 full-time (45 women), 27 part-time (22 women). Average age 36. 100 applicants, 57% accepted, 57 enrolled. In 2006, 48 degrees awarded. *Degree requirements:* For master's, thesis (for some programs), thesis or essay; for doctorate, thesis/dissertation, comprehensive exam. *Entrance requirements:* For master's, BSW (MSW); for doctorate, MSW or MA. Additional exam requirements/recommendations for international students: Required—TOEFL (minimum score 580 paper-based; 237 computer-based). *Application deadline:* For fall admission, 1/31 for domestic and international students. Application fee: $90 Canadian dollars ($150 Canadian dollars for international students). Electronic applications accepted. *Financial support:* In 2006–07, 3 fellowships (averaging $2,521 Canadian dollars per year), 26 research assistantships (averaging $5,400 Canadian dollars per year), 15 teaching assistantships (averaging $6,600 Canadian dollars per year) were awarded; career-related internships or fieldwork, Federal Work-Study, institutionally sponsored loans, scholarships/grants, and unspecified assistantships also available. Financial award application deadline:4/1. *Faculty research:* Families and work, gerontology, family resources, diversity, social inequality. Total annual research expenditures: $838,644. *Unit head:* Prof. Graham Riches, Director, 604-822-0782, Fax: 604-822-8656, E-mail: griches@interchange.ubc.ca. *Application contact:* Christine Graham, Program Advisor, 604-822-4119, Fax: 604-822-8656, E-mail: swfs.advisor@ubc.ca.

University of Calgary, Faculty of Graduate Studies, Faculty of Social Work, Calgary, AB T2N 1N4, Canada. Offers MSW, PhD, Postgraduate Diploma. *Degree requirements:* For master's, thesis (for some programs), registration; for doctorate, thesis/dissertation, candidacy exam. *Entrance requirements:* For master's, BSW, minimum undergraduate GPA of 3.4 (1 year program), minimum GPA of 3.5 (2 year program); for doctorate, minimum graduate GPA of 3.5, MSW (preferred); for Postgraduate Diploma, MSW, minimum graduate GPA of 3.5. Additional exam requirements/recommendations for international students: Required—TOEFL (paper-based 550; computer-based 213) or IELTS (paper-based 7). Electronic applications accepted. *Faculty research:* Family violence, direct practice, gerontology, child welfare, community development.

University of California, Berkeley, Graduate Division, School of Social Welfare, Berkeley, CA 94720-1500. Offers MSW, PhD, MSW/PhD. *Accreditation:* CSWE (one or more programs are accredited). Terminal master's awarded for partial completion of doctoral program. *Degree requirements:* For master's, thesis optional; for doctorate, thesis/dissertation, qualifying exam. *Entrance requirements:* For master's and doctorate, GRE General Test, minimum GPA of 3.0. Additional exam requirements/recommendations for international students: Required—TOEFL, TWE. *Application deadline:* Applications are processed on a rolling basis. Application fee: $60 ($80 for international students). *Financial support:* Fellowships, research assistantships with partial tuition reimbursements, teaching assistantships with partial tuition reimbursements, career-related internships or fieldwork, Federal Work-Study, scholarships/grants, traineeships, health care benefits, and unspecified assistantships available. Financial award applicants required to submit FAFSA. *Faculty research:* Child welfare, law and social welfare, minority mental health, social welfare policy analysis, health services. *Unit head:* Lorraine Midanik, Dean, School of Social Welfare, 510-642-5039, E-mail: swdean@berkeley.edu. *Application contact:* Rafael Herrera, Director of Admissions, 510-642-9042, Fax: 510-643-6126, E-mail: socwelf@berkeley.edu.

University of California, Los Angeles, Graduate Division, School of Public Policy and Social Research, Program in Social Welfare, Los Angeles, CA 90095. Offers MSW, PhD, JD/MSW. *Accreditation:* CSWE (one or more programs are accredited). *Degree requirements:* For master's, research project; for doctorate, thesis/dissertation, oral and written qualifying exams. *Entrance requirements:* For master's, GRE General Test, minimum GPA of 3.0; for doctorate, GRE General Test, minimum undergraduate GPA of 3.0. Additional exam requirements/recommendations for international students: Required—TOEFL. Electronic applications accepted.

University of Central Florida, College of Health and Public Affairs, School of Social Work, Orlando, FL 32816. Offers addictions (Certificate); aging studies (Certificate); children's services (Certificate); school social work (Certificate); social work (MSW); social work administration (Certificate). *Accreditation:* CSWE. Part-time and evening/weekend programs available. *Faculty:* 17 full-time (11 women), 20 part-time/adjunct (18 women). *Students:* 122 full-time (111 women), 100 part-time (85 women); includes 66 minority (33 African Americans, 2 Asian Americans or Pacific Islanders, 31 Hispanic Americans), 1 international. In 2006, 103 master's, 18 other advanced degrees awarded. *Degree requirements:* For master's, thesis or alternative, field education. *Entrance requirements:* For master's, resumé. Additional exam requirements/recommendations for international students: Required—TOEFL. *Application deadline:* For fall admission, 3/1 for domestic students. Application fee: $30. Electronic applications accepted. *Expenses:* Tuition, state resident: full-time $6,167; part-time $257 per credit hour. Tuition, nonresident: full-time $22,790; part-time $950 per credit hour. *Financial support:* In 2006–07, 1 fellowship with partial tuition reimbursement (averaging $5,000 per year), 14 research assistantships with partial tuition reimbursements (averaging $5,400 per year) were awarded; teaching assistantships with partial tuition reimbursements, career-related internships or fieldwork, Federal Work-Study, institutionally sponsored loans, and unspecified assistantships also available. Financial award application deadline: 3/1; financial award applicants required to submit FAFSA. *Unit head:* Dr. John Ronnau, Director, 407-823-2208, Fax: 407-823-5697, E-mail: jronnau@mail.ucf.edu.

University of Chicago, School of Social Service Administration, Chicago, IL 60637. Offers social service administration (PhD); social work (AM); AM/M Div; MBA/AM; MPP/AM. *Accreditation:* CSWE (one or more programs are accredited). Part-time and evening/weekend programs available. *Faculty:* 33 full-time (21 women), 48 part-time/adjunct (32 women). *Students:* 421 full-time (365 women), 62 part-time (47 women); includes 130 minority (65 African Americans, 2 American Indian/Alaska Native, 28 Asian Americans or Pacific Islanders, 35 Hispanic Americans), 12 international. Average age 28. 594 applicants, 64% accepted, 187 enrolled. In 2006, 188 master's, 3 doctorates awarded. *Degree requirements:* For master's, 2 field placements; for doctorate, thesis/dissertation, comprehensive exam, registration. *Entrance requirements:* For master's, 4 letters of recommendation; for doctorate, writing sample, 4 letters of recommendation. Additional exam requirements/recommendations for international students: Required—TOEFL (minimum score 600 paper-based; 250 computer-based). *Application deadline:* For fall admission, 4/1 priority date for domestic and international students. Applications are processed on a rolling basis. Application fee: $60 ($70 for international students). Electronic applications accepted. *Expenses:* Contact institution. One-time fee: $35 full-time. Full-time tuition and fees vary according to course load, degree level and program. *Financial support:* In 2006–07, 415 students received support, including 20 research assistantships with full tuition reimbursements available (averaging $15,000 per year), 20 teaching assistantships with full tuition reimbursements available (averaging $12,000 per year); fellowships, career-related internships or fieldwork, Federal Work-Study, institutionally sponsored loans, scholarships/grants, health care benefits, and unspecified assistantships also available. Support available to part-time students. Financial award application deadline: 4/15; financial award applicants required to submit FAFSA. *Faculty research:* Family treatment, mental health, the aged, child welfare, health administration. *Unit head:* Dr. Jeanne Marsh, Dean, 773-702-1144, Fax: 773-834-1582, E-mail: j-marsh@uchicago.edu. *Application contact:* Quenette Walton, Assistant Director of Admissions, 773-834-8104, Fax: 773-834-4751, E-mail: qlwalton@uchicago.edu.

See Close-Up on page 2407.

University of Cincinnati, Division of Research and Advanced Studies, School of Social Work, Cincinnati, OH 45221. Offers MSW. *Accreditation:* CSWE. Part-time programs available. *Entrance requirements:* Additional exam requirements/recommendations for international students: Required—TOEFL. Electronic applications accepted. *Faculty research:* Fatherhood, mediation, mental illness, child welfare, elderly.

University of Connecticut, Graduate School, School of Social Work, Field of Social Work, Storrs, CT 06269. Offers MSW, PhD, JD/MSW, MBA/MSW, MPA/MSW. *Faculty:* 32 full-time (23 women). *Students:* 316 full-time (261 women), 88 part-time (73 women); includes 129 minority (75 African Americans, 3 American Indian/Alaska Native, 8 Asian Americans or Pacific Islanders, 43 Hispanic Americans), 4 international. Average age 32. 487 applicants, 55% accepted, 236 enrolled. In 2006, 158 degrees awarded. *Degree requirements:* For master's, comprehensive exam; for doctorate, thesis/dissertation. *Entrance requirements:* Additional exam requirements/recommendations for international students: Required—TOEFL (minimum score 550 paper-based; 213 computer-based). *Application deadline:* For fall admission, 2/1 priority date for domestic and international students; for spring admission, 11/1 for domestic students, 10/1 for international students. Applications are processed on a rolling basis. Application fee: $55. Electronic applications accepted. *Financial support:* In 2006–07, 9 research assistantships with full tuition reimbursements were awarded; teaching assistantships with full tuition reimbursements, Federal Work-Study, health care benefits, and unspecified assistantships also available. Financial award application deadline: 2/1; financial award applicants required to submit FAFSA. *Unit head:* Michie Hesselbrock, Chairperson, 860-570-9146, E-mail: michie.hesselbrock@uconnvm.uconn.edu. *Application contact:* Tilitha Conyers, Director of Admissions, 860-570-9118, Fax: 860-570-9139, E-mail: sswadmit1@uconnvm.uconn.edu.

University of Denver, Graduate School of Social Work, Denver, CO 80208. Offers MSW, PhD, Certificate. *Accreditation:* CSWE (one or more programs are accredited). Part-time and evening/weekend programs available. *Faculty:* 24 full-time (18 women). *Students:* 350 full-time (320 women), 30 part-time (24 women); includes 52 minority (11 African Americans, 3 American Indian/Alaska Native, 12 Asian Americans or Pacific Islanders, 26 Hispanic Americans), 6 international. Average age 29. 474 applicants, 89% accepted. In 2006, 187 master's, 6 doctorates, 16 other advanced degrees awarded. *Degree requirements:* For doctorate, thesis/dissertation. *Entrance requirements:* For doctorate, GRE General Test, MSW. *Application deadline:* Applications are processed on a rolling basis. Application fee: $60. Electronic applications accepted. *Expenses:* Tuition: Full-time $29,628; part-time $823 per credit. *Financial support:* In 2006–07, 12 teaching assistantships with full and partial tuition reimbursements (averaging $9,625 per year) were awarded; Federal Work-Study, institutionally sponsored loans, scholarships/grants, and tuition waivers (partial) also available. Support available to part-time students. Financial award application deadline: 2/1; financial award applicants required to submit FAFSA. *Faculty research:* Children, youth, and families; mental health; drug dependency; gerontology; child welfare. Total annual research expenditures: $271,000. *Unit head:* Dr. Christian Molidor, Interim Dean, 303-871-2841. *Application contact:* Colin Schneider, Director of Admission and Financial Aid, 303-871-2841, Fax: 303-871-2845, E-mail: gssw-admission@du.edu.

See Close-Up on page 2409.

University of Georgia, Graduate School, School of Social Work, Athens, GA 30602. Offers MA, MSW, PhD, Certificate. *Accreditation:* CSWE (one or more programs are accredited). Part-time and evening/weekend programs available. *Faculty:* 20 full-time (11 women). *Students:*

Social Work

University of Georgia (continued)

290 full-time (251 women), 63 part-time (52 women); includes 104 minority (94 African Americans, 1 American Indian/Alaska Native, 3 Asian Americans or Pacific Islanders, 6 Hispanic Americans), 9 international. Average age 34. 338 applicants, 65% accepted, 138 enrolled. In 2006, 149 master's, 9 doctorates awarded. *Median time to degree:* Of those who began their doctoral program in fall 1998, 80% received their degree in 8 years or less. *Degree requirements:* For master's, thesis or alternative; for doctorate, one foreign language, thesis/dissertation. *Entrance requirements:* For master's and doctorate, GRE General Test. *Application deadline:* For fall admission, 7/1 priority date for domestic students, 7/1 for international students; for spring admission, 11/15 for domestic and international students. Applications are processed on a rolling basis. Application fee: $50. Electronic applications accepted. *Financial support:* In 2006–07, 39 students received support, including 4 fellowships (averaging $25,000 per year), 35 research assistantships with tuition reimbursements available (averaging $7,500 per year); teaching assistantships with tuition reimbursements available, career-related internships or fieldwork, Federal Work-Study, scholarships/grants, tuition waivers (full and partial), and unspecified assistantships also available. Support available to part-time students. Financial award application deadline: 2/10; financial award applicants required to submit FAFSA. *Faculty research:* Juvenile justice, substance abuse, civil rights and social justice, gerontology, social policy. Total annual research expenditures: $2.6 million. *Unit head:* Dr. Maurice Daniels, Dean, 706-542-5424, Fax: 706-542-3845.

University of Hawaii at Manoa, Graduate Division, College of Health Sciences and Social Welfare, School of Social Work, Honolulu, HI 96822. Offers social welfare (PhD); social work (MSW). *Accreditation:* CSWE (one or more programs are accredited). Part-time programs available. *Faculty:* 26 full-time (15 women). *Students:* 151 full-time (124 women), 41 part-time (33 women); includes 29 minority (3 African Americans, 19 Asian Americans or Pacific Islanders, 7 Hispanic Americans), 2 international. 212 applicants, 75% accepted, 111 enrolled. In 2006, 73 master's, 1 doctorate awarded. *Median time to degree:* Of those who began their doctoral program in fall 1998, 20% received their degree in 8 years or less. *Degree requirements:* For doctorate, thesis/dissertation, comprehensive exam. *Entrance requirements:* For doctorate, master's degree (MSW preferred), minimum GPA of 3.0. Additional exam requirements/recommendations for international students: Required—TOEFL (minimum score 560 paper-based; 220 computer-based; 83 iBT). *Application deadline:* For fall admission, 1/15 for domestic and international students. Applications are processed on a rolling basis. Application fee: $50. *Financial support:* In 2006–07, 7 research assistantships with full and partial tuition reimbursements (averaging $16,939 per year) were awarded; fellowships with full and partial tuition reimbursements, career-related internships or fieldwork, Federal Work-Study, institutionally sponsored loans, and tuition waivers (full) also available. Support available to part-time students. Financial award application deadline: 2/1; financial award applicants required to submit FAFSA. *Faculty research:* Health, mental health, AIDS, substance abuse, rural health, community-based research, social policy. Total annual research expenditures: $2 million. *Application contact:* Ann Alverez, Information Contact, 808-956-3833, Fax: 808-956-5964.

University of Houston, Graduate School of Social Work, Houston, TX 77204. Offers MSW, PhD. *Accreditation:* CSWE (one or more programs are accredited). Part-time programs available. *Faculty:* 16 full-time (9 women), 15 part-time/adjunct (10 women). *Students:* 204 full-time (173 women), 160 part-time (142 women); includes 172 minority (90 African Americans, 1 American Indian/Alaska Native, 15 Asian Americans or Pacific Islanders, 66 Hispanic Americans), 9 international. Average age 33. 251 applicants, 53% accepted, 119 enrolled. In 2006, 114 master's, 6 doctorates awarded. *Degree requirements:* For master's, field internship, thesis optional; for doctorate, thesis/dissertation, comprehensive exam. *Entrance requirements:* For master's, GRE, minimum GPA of 3.0. Additional exam requirements/recommendations for international students: Required—TOEFL. *Application deadline:* For fall admission, 3/1 priority date for domestic students. Applications are processed on a rolling basis. Application fee: $50 ($125 for international students). *Expenses:* Tuition, state resident: full-time $5,429; part-time $226 per credit. Tuition, nonresident: full-time $12,029; part-time $501 per credit. Required fees: $2,454. *Financial support:* In 2006–07, 13 fellowships with full tuition reimbursements (averaging $12,850 per year), 8 research assistantships with full tuition reimbursements (averaging $8,800 per year), 4 teaching assistantships with full tuition reimbursements (averaging $8,800 per year) were awarded; career-related internships or fieldwork, Federal Work-Study, institutionally sponsored loans, scholarships/grants, health care benefits, and unspecified assistantships also available. Support available to part-time students. Financial award application deadline: 3/10; financial award applicants required to submit FAFSA. *Faculty research:* Health care, gerontology, political social work, mental health, children and families. Total annual research expenditures: $3.7 million. *Unit head:* Dr. Ira C. Colby, Dean, 713-743-8085, Fax: 713-743-3267, E-mail: icolby@uh.edu. *Application contact:* Colen Skinner, Admissions Office, 713-743-8078, Fax: 713-743-8149, E-mail: cskinner@mail.uh.edu.

University of Illinois at Chicago, Graduate College, Jane Addams College of Social Work, Chicago, IL 60607-7128. Offers MSW, PhD. *Accreditation:* CSWE (one or more programs are accredited). Part-time programs available. Terminal master's awarded for partial completion of doctoral program. *Degree requirements:* For doctorate, thesis/dissertation. *Entrance requirements:* For master's, GMAT, minimum GPA of 2.75; for doctorate, GRE General Test or MAT, minimum GPA of 2.75. Additional exam requirements/recommendations for international students: Required—TOEFL. Electronic applications accepted.

University of Illinois at Urbana–Champaign, Graduate College, School of Social Work, Champaign, IL 61820. Offers MSW, PhD, MS/MSW. *Accreditation:* CSWE (one or more programs are accredited). *Faculty:* 17 full-time (12 women), 3 part-time/adjunct (2 women). *Students:* 213 full-time (196 women), 61 part-time (58 women); includes 49 minority (27 African Americans, 8 Asian Americans or Pacific Islanders, 14 Hispanic Americans), 12 international. 270 applicants, 56% accepted, 41 enrolled. In 2006, 143 master's, 2 doctorates awarded. *Degree requirements:* For doctorate, thesis/dissertation. *Entrance requirements:* For master's and doctorate, GRE, minimum GPA of 3.0. *Application deadline:* For fall admission, 3/1 for domestic students; for spring admission, 3/1 for domestic students. Applications are processed on a rolling basis. Application fee: $50 ($60 for international students). *Financial support:* In 2006–07, 11 fellowships, 16 research assistantships, 3 teaching assistantships were awarded; career-related internships or fieldwork and tuition waivers (full and partial) also available. Financial award application deadline: 2/15. *Unit head:* Wynne S. Korr, Dean, 217-333-2260, Fax: 217-244-5220, E-mail: wkorr@uiuc.edu. *Application contact:* Michele Winfrey, Officer II, 217-333-2261, Fax: 217-244-5220, E-mail: mwinfrey@uiuc.edu.

The University of Iowa, Graduate College, College of Liberal Arts and Sciences, School of Social Work, Iowa City, IA 52242-1316. Offers MSW, PhD, MSW/MA, MSW/MS. *Accreditation:* CSWE. *Faculty:* 11 full-time, 68 part-time/adjunct. *Students:* 109 full-time (93 women), 115 part-time (101 women); includes 17 minority (11 African Americans, 1 American Indian/Alaska Native, 5 Hispanic Americans), 3 international. 120 applicants, 73% accepted, 58 enrolled. In 2006, 57 master's, 3 doctorates awarded. *Degree requirements:* For master's, thesis optional; for doctorate, thesis/dissertation, comprehensive exam, registration. *Entrance requirements:* For master's, minimum GPA of 3.0; for doctorate, GRE General Test, minimum GPA of 3.0. Additional exam requirements/recommendations for international students: Required—TOEFL (minimum score 600 paper-based; 250 computer-based; 100 iBT). *Application deadline:* For fall admission, 2/1 for domestic and international students. Application fee: $60 ($85 for international students). Electronic applications accepted. *Financial support:* In 2006–07, 14 fellowships, 21 research assistantships with partial tuition reimbursements, 17 teaching assistantships with partial tuition reimbursements were awarded. Financial award applicants required to submit FAFSA. *Unit head:* Edward Saunders, Director, 319-335-3316, Fax: 319-335-1711.

University of Kentucky, Graduate School, College of Social Work, Program in Social Work, Lexington, KY 40506-0032. Offers MSW, PhD. *Accreditation:* CSWE (one or more programs are accredited). *Faculty:* 20 full-time (13 women). *Students:* 124 full-time (114 women), 171 part-time (148 women); includes 21 minority (16 African Americans, 2 Asian Americans or Pacific Islanders, 3 Hispanic Americans), 3 international. Average age 33. 229 applicants, 72% accepted, 131 enrolled. In 2006, 97 master's, 4 doctorates awarded. *Median time to degree:* Of those who began their doctoral program in fall 1998, 67% received their degree in 8 years or less. *Degree requirements:* For master's, comprehensive exam; for doctorate, thesis/dissertation, comprehensive exam. *Entrance requirements:* For master's, GRE General Test, minimum undergraduate GPA of 2.75; for doctorate, GRE General Test, minimum undergraduate GPA of 3.0. Additional exam requirements/recommendations for international students: Required—TOEFL (minimum score 550 paper-based; 213 computer-based). *Application deadline:* For fall admission, 7/17 priority date for domestic students, 2/1 priority date for international students; for spring admission, 12/13 priority date for domestic students, 6/15 priority date for international students. Application fee: $40 ($55 for international students). Electronic applications accepted. *Expenses:* Tuition, state resident: full-time $7,670; part-time $401 per credit hour. Tuition, nonresident: full-time $16,158; part-time $873 per credit hour. *Financial support:* In 2006–07, 17 students received support, including 7 research assistantships with full tuition reimbursements available (averaging $1,500 per year), 10 teaching assistantships with full tuition reimbursements available (averaging $3,000 per year); fellowships with full tuition reimbursements available, career-related internships or fieldwork, Federal Work-Study, institutionally sponsored loans, scholarships/grants, traineeships, health care benefits, tuition waivers (partial), and unspecified assistantships also available. Support available to part-time students. Financial award application deadline: 3/15. *Faculty research:* Aging, family and children, domestic violence, delinquency, health and mental health. Total annual research expenditures: $93,993. *Unit head:* Dr. Janet Ford, Director of Graduate Studies, 859-257-6660, Fax: 859-323-1030, E-mail: janet.ford@uky.edu. *Application contact:* Dr. Brian Jackson, Senior Associate Dean, 859-257-4667, Fax: 859-257-4676, E-mail: brian.jackson@uky.edu.

University of Louisville, Graduate School, Raymond A. Kent School of Social Work, Louisville, KY 40292-0001. Offers marriage and family therapy (PMC); social work (MSSW, PhD). *Accreditation:* AAMFT/COAMFTE; CSWE (one or more programs are accredited). *Faculty:* 25 full-time (16 women), 40 part-time/adjunct (24 women). *Students:* 302 full-time (251 women), 96 part-time (83 women); includes 78 minority (71 African Americans, 1 American Indian/Alaska Native, 4 Asian Americans or Pacific Islanders, 2 Hispanic Americans), 10 international. Average age 33. In 2006, 141 master's, 7 doctorates awarded. *Degree requirements:* For doctorate, thesis/dissertation. *Entrance requirements:* For master's, GRE or minimum GPA of 2.75; for doctorate, GRE General Test, interview, writing sample. *Application deadline:* Applications are processed on a rolling basis. Application fee: $50. *Financial support:* In 2006–07, 3 fellowships with full tuition reimbursements (averaging $18,000 per year), 11 research assistantships with full tuition reimbursements (averaging $18,000 per year) were awarded; tuition waivers (full) also available. Financial award application deadline: 4/1. *Faculty research:* Child welfare, substance abuse, gerontology, family functioning, health behavior. *Unit head:* Dr. Terry Singer, Dean, 502-852-6402, Fax: 502-852-0422, E-mail: terry.singer@louisville.edu.

University of Maine, Graduate School, College of Business, Public Policy and Health, School of Social Work, Orono, ME 04469. Offers MSW. *Accreditation:* CSWE. *Faculty:* 8 full-time. *Students:* 117 full-time (98 women), 9 part-time (7 women); includes 6 minority (1 African American, 5 American Indian/Alaska Native), 1 international. Average age 37. 44 applicants, 84% accepted, 26 enrolled. In 2006, 35 degrees awarded. *Entrance requirements:* For master's, GRE General Test. Additional exam requirements/recommendations for international students: Required—TOEFL. *Application deadline:* For fall admission, 2/1 priority date for domestic students. Applications are processed on a rolling basis. Application fee: $50. Electronic applications accepted. *Financial support:* In 2006–07, 3 research assistantships with tuition reimbursements (averaging $9,010 per year) were awarded. Financial award application deadline: 3/1. *Unit head:* Dr. Sandra Butler, Director, 207-581-2382, Fax: 207-581-2396. *Application contact:* Scott G. Delcourt, Associate Dean of the Graduate School, 207-581-3219, Fax: 207-581-3232, E-mail: graduate@maine.edu.

University of Manitoba, Faculty of Graduate Studies, Faculty of Social Work, Winnipeg, MB R3T 2N2, Canada. Offers MSW. *Degree requirements:* For master's, thesis or alternative.

University of Maryland, Baltimore, Graduate School, Graduate Programs in Social Work, Doctoral Program in Social Work, Baltimore, MD 21201. Offers PhD. Part-time programs available. *Degree requirements:* For doctorate, thesis/dissertation. *Entrance requirements:* For doctorate, GRE General Test, minimum GPA of 3.5, MSW. *Faculty research:* Breast cancer, child abuse, parental abduction, homelessness, elderly.

University of Maryland, Baltimore, Graduate School, Graduate Programs in Social Work, Master's Program in Social Work, Baltimore, MD 21201. Offers MSW, MBA/MSW, MSW/MA, MSW/MPH. *Accreditation:* CSWE. *Entrance requirements:* For master's, minimum GPA of 3.0. Electronic applications accepted. *Faculty research:* Child welfare, occupational social work, homelessness, community organization, multiculturalism.

University of Maryland, College Park, Graduate Studies, Robert H. Smith School of Business, Combined MSW/MBA Program, College Park, MD 20742. Offers MSW/MBA. *Accreditation:* AACSB. *Students:* 2 applicants, 0% accepted. *Entrance requirements:* Additional exam requirements/recommendations for international students: Required—TOEFL. *Application deadline:* For fall admission, 2/1 for domestic and international students. Application fee: $60. *Financial support:* In 2006–07, 1 fellowship (averaging $25,961 per year) was awarded. *Application contact:* Dean of Graduate School, 301-405-0358, Fax: 301-314-9305.

University of Michigan, School of Social Work, Ann Arbor, MI 48109. Offers MSW, PhD, MSW/JD, MSW/MBA, MSW/MPH, MSW/MPP, MSW/MSI, MSW/MUP. PhD offered through the Horace H. Rackham School of Graduate Studies. *Accreditation:* CSWE (one or more programs are accredited). *Degree requirements:* For doctorate, oral defense of dissertation, preliminary exam. *Entrance requirements:* For doctorate, GRE General Test. Additional exam requirements/recommendations for international students: Required—TOEFL (minimum score 600 paper-based; 250 computer-based), TWE. Electronic applications accepted. Expenses: Contact institution. *Faculty research:* Children and adults, aging, community organization, health and mental health, policy and evaluation.

See Close-Up on page 2411.

University of Minnesota, Duluth, Graduate School, College of Education and Human Service Professions, Department of Social Work, Duluth, MN 55812-2496. Offers MSW. *Accreditation:* CSWE. Part-time and evening/weekend programs available. Postbaccalaureate distance learning degree programs offered (minimal on-campus study). *Faculty:* 8 full-time (5 women), 7 part-time/adjunct (4 women). *Students:* 88 full-time (71 women), 3 part-time (all women); includes 17 minority (1 African American, 13 American Indian/Alaska Native, 2 Asian Americans or Pacific Islanders, 1 Hispanic American). Average age 30. 94 applicants, 73% accepted, 48 enrolled. In 2006, 35 degrees awarded. *Entrance requirements:* For master's, minimum GPA of 3.0. Additional exam requirements/recommendations for international students: Required—TOEFL (minimum score 550 paper-based; 213 computer-based). *Application deadline:* For fall admission, 1/12 priority date for domestic students, 1/12 for international students. Application fee: $55 ($75 for international students). *Financial support:* In 2006–07, 9 fellowships with partial tuition reimbursements (averaging $4,111 per year), 5 teaching assistantships with partial tuition reimbursements (averaging $11,583 per year) were awarded; career-related internships or fieldwork, Federal Work-Study, institutionally sponsored loans, scholarships/grants, and traineeships also available. Support available to part-time students. Financial award application deadline: 1/13. *Faculty research:* Domestic abuse, substance abuse, minority health, child welfare, gerontology. Total annual research expenditures: $110,000. *Unit head:* Dr. Lynn Bye, Director of Graduate Studies, 218-726-8492, Fax: 218-726-7185, E-mail: 1bye@d.umn.edu. *Application contact:* Sandy Maturi, Student Support Assistant, 218-726-8497, Fax: 218-726-7185, E-mail: smaturi@d.umn.edu.

University of Minnesota, Twin Cities Campus, Graduate School, College of Education and Human Development, School of Social Work, Minneapolis, MN 55455-0213. Offers MSW, PhD. *Accreditation:* CSWE (one or more programs are accredited). Part-time and evening/weekend programs available. Postbaccalaureate distance learning degree programs offered. *Faculty:* 21 full-time (8 women). *Students:* 204 full-time (177 women), 90 part-time (71 women); includes 55 minority (21 African Americans, 5 American Indian/Alaska Native, 19 Asian Americans or Pacific Islanders, 10 Hispanic Americans), 9 international. Average age 33. 262 applicants, 65% accepted, 105 enrolled. In 2006, 122 master's, 5 doctorates awarded. *Degree requirements:* For doctorate, thesis/dissertation. *Entrance requirements:* For master's, minimum GPA of 3.0, 1 year of work experience; for doctorate, GRE, minimum GPA of 3.0, MSW. *Application deadline:* For fall admission, 1/15 for domestic students. Application fee: $40 ($50 for international students). *Expenses:* Tuition, state resident: full-time $9,302; part-time $775 per credit. Tuition, nonresident: full-time $16,400; part-time $1,367 per credit. Full-time tuition and fees vary according to class time, course load, program, reciprocity agreements and student level. *Financial support:* In 2006–07, 142 students received support, including 5 fellowships (averaging $24,775 per year), 26 research assistantships (averaging $24,775 per year), 6 teaching assistantships (averaging $24,775 per year); career-related internships or fieldwork, Federal Work-Study, institutionally sponsored loans, and tuition waivers (full and partial) also available. Support available to part-time students. Financial award applicants required to submit FAFSA. *Faculty research:* Child welfare, family and community violence prevention, aging, mental health, disability policy. Total annual research expenditures: $4.4 million. *Unit head:* James Reinardy, Director, 612-624-3673, Fax: 612-624-3746, E-mail: jreinard@umn.edu. *Application contact:* Rachel Grewell, Information Contact, 612-625-0477.

University of Missouri–Columbia, Graduate School, School of Social Work, Columbia, MO 65211. Offers MSW. *Accreditation:* CSWE. Part-time programs available. *Faculty:* 17 full-time (12 women). *Students:* 153 full-time (138 women), 33 part-time (28 women); includes 16 minority (12 African Americans, 2 Asian Americans or Pacific Islanders, 2 Hispanic Americans), 8 international. In 2006, 108 degrees awarded. *Entrance requirements:* For master's, GRE General Test, minimum GPA of 3.0. *Application deadline:* For fall admission, 1/15 priority date for domestic students. Applications are processed on a rolling basis. Application fee: $45 ($60 for international students). *Financial support:* Fellowships, research assistantships, teaching assistantships, institutionally sponsored loans available. *Unit head:* Dr. Colleen Galambos, Director of Graduate Studies, 573-882-3701, E-mail: galambos@missouri.edu.

University of Missouri–Kansas City, College of Arts and Sciences, School of Social Work, Kansas City, MO 64110-2499. Offers MSW. *Accreditation:* CSWE. Part-time and evening/weekend programs available. *Faculty:* 7 full-time (all women), 16 part-time/adjunct (12 women). *Students:* 118 full-time (103 women), 41 part-time (33 women); includes 46 minority (36 African Americans, 1 American Indian/Alaska Native, 3 Asian Americans or Pacific Islanders, 6 Hispanic Americans), 3 international. Average age 34. 118 applicants, 87% accepted, 83 enrolled. In 2006, 66 degrees awarded. *Entrance requirements:* For master's, minimum GPA of 3.0, 3 letters of reference. *Application deadline:* For fall admission, 4/1 priority date for domestic students, 7/31 priority date for international students; for winter admission, 12/15 priority date for international students; for spring admission, 9/1 priority date for domestic students. Applications are processed on a rolling basis. Application fee: $35 ($50 for international students). *Expenses:* Tuition, state resident: full-time $4,975; part-time $276 per credit. Tuition, nonresident: full-time $12,847; part-time $713 per credit. Required fees: $595; $595 per year. *Financial support:* In 2006–07, 37 students received support, including 4 research assistantships with partial tuition reimbursements available (averaging $11,280 per year); career-related internships or fieldwork and institutionally sponsored loans also available. *Faculty research:* Social justice, LGBT issues, deinstitutionalization, community collaboration and partnerships, evaluation of strengths model with addiction model. *Unit head:* Dr. Walter Boulden, Chair, 816-235-6308, E-mail: bouldenw@umkc.edu.

University of Missouri–St. Louis, College of Arts and Sciences, School of Social Work, St. Louis, MO 63121. Offers MSW. *Accreditation:* CSWE. *Faculty:* 9 full-time (8 women). *Students:* 53 full-time (50 women), 38 part-time (36 women); includes 13 minority (11 African Americans, 1 Asian American or Pacific Islander, 1 Hispanic American), 1 international. Average age 31. In 2006, 34 degrees awarded. *Entrance requirements:* For master's, 3 letters of recommendation, supplemental application. Additional exam requirements/recommendations for international students: Required—TOEFL (minimum score 550 paper-based; 213 computer-based). *Application deadline:* For fall admission, 2/15 for domestic students. Application fee: $35 ($40 for international students). *Expenses:* Tuition, state resident: part-time $332 per credit hour. Tuition, nonresident: part-time $770 per credit hour. *Financial support:* In 2006–07, 10 teaching assistantships with full tuition reimbursements (averaging $10,125 per year) were awarded; research assistantships. *Faculty research:* Family violence, child abuse/neglect, immigration, community economic development. *Unit head:* Dr. Lois Pierce, Director, 314-516-6364, Fax: 314-516-5816, E-mail: socialwork@umsl.edu. *Application contact:* 314-516-5458, Fax: 314-516-6996, E-mail: gradadm@umsl.edu.

University of Nebraska at Omaha, Graduate Studies and Research, College of Public Affairs and Community Service, School of Social Work, Omaha, NE 68182. Offers MSW. *Accreditation:* CSWE. *Faculty:* 12 full-time (10 women). *Students:* 89 full-time (80 women), 66 part-time (62 women); includes 12 minority (3 African Americans, 3 Asian Americans or Pacific Islanders, 6 Hispanic Americans), 2 international. Average age 29. 99 applicants, 74% accepted, 42 enrolled. In 2006, 63 degrees awarded. *Degree requirements:* For master's, thesis (for some programs), comprehensive exam. *Entrance requirements:* For master's, minimum GPA of 3.0, letters of recommendation, essay, resumé. Additional exam requirements/recommendations for international students: Required—TOEFL (minimum score 500 paper-based; 173 computer-based; 61 iBT). *Application deadline:* For fall admission, 3/1 for domestic students. Applications are processed on a rolling basis. Application fee: $45. Electronic applications accepted. *Financial support:* In 2006–07, 115 students received support; fellowships, research assistantships with tuition reimbursements available, career-related internships or fieldwork, Federal Work-Study, institutionally sponsored loans, scholarships/grants, tuition waivers (full), and unspecified assistantships available. Support available to part-time students. Financial award application deadline: 3/1; financial award applicants required to submit FAFSA. *Unit head:* Dr. Theresa Barron-McKeagney, Director, 402-554-2791.

University of Nevada, Las Vegas, Graduate College, Greenspun College of Urban Affairs, School of Social Work, Las Vegas, NV 89154-9900. Offers MSW. *Accreditation:* CSWE. *Faculty:* 14 full-time (11 women), 3 part-time/adjunct (all women). *Students:* 122 full-time (99 women), 35 part-time (31 women); includes 39 minority (18 African Americans, 8 Asian Americans or Pacific Islanders, 13 Hispanic Americans), 2 international. 159 applicants, 60% accepted, 60 enrolled. In 2006, 55 degrees awarded. *Degree requirements:* For master's, thesis optional. *Entrance requirements:* For master's, minimum GPA of 3.0 during previous 2 years, 2.75 overall; bachelor's degree in social work. Additional exam requirements/recommendations for international students: Required—TOEFL (minimum score 550 paper-based; 231 computer-based; 80 iBT). *Application deadline:* For fall admission, 3/1 for domestic and international students. Application fee: $60 ($75 for international students). Electronic applications accepted. *Financial support:* In 2006–07, 4 research assistantships (averaging $10,000 per year) were awarded; career-related internships or fieldwork, Federal Work-Study, institutionally sponsored loans, scholarships/grants, health care benefits, and unspecified assistantships also available. Support available to part-time students. Financial award application deadline: 3/1. *Unit head:* Dr. Joanne Thompson, Director, 702-895-3311. *Application contact:* Graduate College Admissions Evaluator, 702-895-3320, Fax: 702-895-4180, E-mail: gradcollege@unlv.edu.

University of Nevada, Reno, Graduate School, College of Health and Human Sciences, School of Social Work, Reno, NV 89557. Offers MSW. *Accreditation:* CSWE. Part-time and evening/weekend programs available. *Faculty:* 12. *Students:* 34 full-time (24 women), 11 part-time (all women); includes 2 minority (both Asian Americans or Pacific Islanders) Average age 34. 46 applicants, 59% accepted, 19 enrolled. In 2006, 28 degrees awarded. *Degree requirements:* For master's, thesis optional. *Entrance requirements:* For master's, GRE General Test, minimum GPA of 2.75, statistics course. Additional exam requirements/recommendations for international students: Required—TOEFL. *Application deadline:* For fall admission, 2/1 priority date for domestic students. Applications are processed on a rolling basis. Application fee: $60 ($95 for international students). *Financial support:* In 2006–07, 7 research assistantships were awarded; teaching assistantships, institutionally sponsored loans and tuition waivers (full) also available. Financial award application deadline: 3/1. *Faculty research:* Policy practice, poverty, women's issues, race and diversity, vulnerable family. *Unit head:* Dr. Jill Jones, Graduate Program Director, 775-682-8704, E-mail: jbjones@unr.edu.

University of New England, College of Health Professions, School of Social Work, Biddeford, ME 04005-9526. Offers addictions counseling (Certificate); gerontology (Certificate); social work (MSW). *Accreditation:* CSWE. Part-time programs available. *Faculty:* 14 full-time (8 women), 5 part-time/adjunct (4 women). *Students:* 116 full-time (103 women), 41 part-time (34 women); includes 4 minority (1 African American, 2 American Indian/Alaska Native, 1 Asian American or Pacific Islander), 4 international. Average age 32. 110 applicants, 86% accepted, 55 enrolled. In 2006, 55 master's, 1 other advanced degree awarded. *Degree requirements:* For master's, field internships. *Entrance requirements:* Additional exam requirements/recommendations for international students: Required—TOEFL (minimum score 550 paper-based; 213 computer-based). *Application deadline:* For fall admission, 1/15 priority date for domestic students; for spring admission, 3/31 priority date for domestic students, 3/31 for international students. Applications are processed on a rolling basis. Application fee: $40. Electronic applications accepted. *Financial support:* In 2006–07, 40 students received support. Scholarships/grants and tuition waivers (partial) available. Financial award application deadline: 5/1; financial award applicants required to submit FAFSA. *Faculty research:* Domestic violence, solution focused practice, empowerment models, adverse childhood experiences. *Unit head:* Martha Wilson, Director, 207-283-0171 Ext. 4513, E-mail: mwilson@une.edu. *Application contact:* Peggy Warden, Assistant Dean of Graduate Admissions, 207-221-4225, Fax: 207-221-4898, E-mail: admissions@une.edu.

University of New Hampshire, Graduate School, School of Health and Human Services, Department of Social Work, Durham, NH 03824. Offers MSW. *Accreditation:* CSWE. Part-time programs available. *Faculty:* 9 full-time. *Students:* 92 full-time (81 women), 49 part-time (44 women); includes 4 minority (3 African Americans, 1 Hispanic American). Average age 37. 119 applicants, 86% accepted, 52 enrolled. In 2006, 58 degrees awarded. *Entrance requirements:* Additional exam requirements/recommendations for international students: Required—TOEFL (minimum score 550 paper-based; 213 computer-based). *Application deadline:* For fall admission, 2/1 for domestic and international students. Applications are processed on a rolling basis. Application fee: $60. Electronic applications accepted. *Expenses:* Tuition, state resident: full-time $8,540; part-time $474 per credit hour. Tuition, nonresident: full-time $20,990; part-time $862 per credit hour. Required fees: $1,343; $356 per term. Tuition and fees vary according to course load, program and reciprocity agreements. *Financial support:* In 2006–07, 1 fellowship, 6 teaching assistantships were awarded; research assistantships, career-related internships or fieldwork, Federal Work-Study, and scholarships/grants also available. Support available to part-time students. Financial award application deadline: 2/15. *Unit head:* Dr. Jerry Marx, Chairperson, 603-862-0274. *Application contact:* Karen Franrie, Contact, 603-862-0215, E-mail: kfrarie@cisunix.unh.edu.

University of New Hampshire at Manchester, Center for Graduate and Professional Studies, Manchester, NH 03101-1113. Offers business administration (MBA); counseling (M Ed); education (M Ed, MAT); educational administration and supervision (M Ed, CAGS); industrial statistics (Certificate); public administration (MPA); public health (MPH, Certificate); social work (MSW).

The University of North Carolina at Chapel Hill, Graduate School, School of Social Work, Chapel Hill, NC 27599. Offers MSW, PhD, JD/MSW, MPA/MSW, MSPH/MSW. *Accreditation:* CSWE (one or more programs are accredited). Part-time programs available. Terminal master's awarded for partial completion of doctoral program. *Degree requirements:* For doctorate, thesis/dissertation, qualifying exam. *Entrance requirements:* For master's and doctorate, GRE General Test, minimum GPA of 3.0. Electronic applications accepted. *Faculty research:* School success, risk and resiliency, welfare reform, aging, substance abuse.

The University of North Carolina at Charlotte, Graduate School, College of Health and Human Services, Department of Social Work, Charlotte, NC 28223-0001. Offers MSW. *Accreditation:* CSWE. Part-time programs available. *Faculty:* 7 full-time (4 women), 7 part-time/adjunct (5 women). *Students:* 76 full-time (67 women), 28 part-time (24 women); includes 20 minority (16 African Americans, 3 Asian Americans or Pacific Islanders, 1 Hispanic American). Average age 29. 131 applicants, 76% accepted, 62 enrolled. In 2006, 24 degrees awarded. *Entrance requirements:* For master's, GRE, minimum GPA of 2.7 overall, 3.0 in last 30 hours of course work. Additional exam requirements/recommendations for international students: Required—TOEFL (minimum score 557 paper-based; 220 computer-based). *Application deadline:* For fall admission, 7/1 for domestic students, 5/1 for international students; for spring admission, 11/1 for domestic students, 10/1 for international students. Applications are processed on a rolling basis. Application fee: $55. Electronic applications accepted. *Expenses:* Tuition, state resident: full-time $2,719; part-time $170 per credit. Tuition, nonresident: full-time $12,926; part-time $808 per credit. Required fees: $1,555. *Financial support:* In 2006–07, 6 research assistantships (averaging $3,283 per year), 1 teaching assistantship (averaging $4,000 per year) were awarded; fellowships, career-related internships or fieldwork, Federal Work-Study, institutionally sponsored loans, scholarships/grants, and unspecified assistantships also available. Support available to part-time students. Financial award application deadline: 4/1; financial award applicants required to submit FAFSA. *Faculty research:* Social work practice with lesbian and gay youth, aging, welfare reform; non-custodial fathers, grandparents as caregivers of grandchildren. *Unit head:* Dr. Dennis Long, Interim Chair, 704-687-7935, Fax: 704-687-2343. *Application contact:* Kathy B. Giddings, Director of Graduate Admissions, 704-687-3366, Fax: 704-687-3279, E-mail: gradadm@email.uncc.edu.

The University of North Carolina at Greensboro, Graduate School, School of Human Environmental Sciences, Department of Social Work, Greensboro, NC 27412-5001. Offers MSW. *Accreditation:* CSWE. *Faculty:* 9 full-time (7 women), 1 (woman) part-time/adjunct. *Students:* 98 full-time (89 women); includes 48 minority (45 African Americans, 3 Hispanic Americans). *Entrance requirements:* For master's, GRE General Test. Additional exam requirements/recommendations for international students: Required—TOEFL. *Application deadline:* For fall admission, 3/22 for domestic students. Application fee: $45. Electronic applications accepted. *Expenses:* Tuition, state resident: full-time $2,692. Tuition, nonresident: full-time $13,742. *Financial support:* Fellowships with full tuition reimbursements, research assistantships with full tuition reimbursements, teaching assistantships with full tuition reimbursements, career-related internships or fieldwork, Federal Work-Study, scholarships/grants, and traineeships available. Support available to part-time students. *Unit head:* Dr. Elizabeth Lindsey, Interim Chair, 336-334-5147, Fax: 336-334-5210. *Application contact:* Michelle Harkleroad, Director of Graduate Admissions, 336-334-4884, Fax: 336-334-4424, E-mail: mbharkle@uncg.edu.

The University of North Carolina Wilmington, College of Arts and Sciences, Department of Social Work, Wilmington, NC 28403-3297. Offers MSW. *Students:* 44 full-time (36 women), 3 part-time (all women); includes 3 African Americans, 1 American Indian/Alaska Native, 3 Hispanic Americans. Average age 34. 63 applicants, 59% accepted, 25 enrolled. *Entrance requirements:* For master's, GMAT, GRE General Test. *Application deadline:* For fall admission, 6/1 for domestic students, 3/15 for international students; for spring admission, 11/1 for domestic students, 10/1 for international students. Application fee: $45. *Unit head:* Dr. Reginald O. York, Chair, 910-962-7801.

University of North Dakota, Graduate School, College of Education and Human Development, School of Social Work, Grand Forks, ND 58202. Offers MSW. *Accreditation:* CSWE. *Faculty:* 8 full-time (3 women). *Students:* 45 applicants, 53% accepted, 24 enrolled. In 2006, 16 degrees awarded. *Degree requirements:* For master's, thesis or alternative,

Social Work

University of North Dakota (continued)

comprehensive exam. *Entrance requirements:* For master's, minimum GPA of 3.0. Additional exam requirements/recommendations for international students: Required—TOEFL (minimum score 550 paper-based; 213 computer-based; 79 iBT), IELTS (minimum score 6). *Application deadline:* For fall admission, 1/15 for domestic and international students. Application fee: $35. Electronic applications accepted. *Expenses:* Tuition, state resident: full-time $5,650; part-time $214 per credit. Tuition, nonresident: full-time $14,248; part-time $572 per credit. Required fees: $1,008; $42 per credit. Tuition and fees vary according to reciprocity agreements. *Financial support:* In 2006–07, 5 research assistantships with full tuition reimbursements (averaging $6,074 per year), 1 teaching assistantship with full tuition reimbursement (averaging $5,206 per year) were awarded; fellowships, Federal Work-Study, institutionally sponsored loans, scholarships/grants, tuition waivers (full and partial), and unspecified assistantships also available. Support available to part-time students. Financial award application deadline: 3/15; financial award applicants required to submit FAFSA. *Faculty research:* Mental health, gerontology, chemical abuse, children and families. *Unit head:* Dr. Carenlee Barkdull, Graduate Director, 701-777-2947, Fax: 701-777-3619. *Application contact:* Brenda Halle, Admissions Specialist, 701-777-2947, Fax: 701-777-3619, E-mail: brendahalle@mail.und.edu.

University of Northern British Columbia, Office of Graduate Studies, Prince George, BC V2N 4Z9, Canada. Offers business administration (Diploma); community health science (M Sc); disability management (MA); education (M Ed); first nations studies (MA); gender studies (MA); history (MA); interdisciplinary studies (MA); international studies (MA); mathematical, computer and physical sciences (M Sc); natural resources and environmental studies (M Sc, MA, MNRES, PhD); political science (MA); psychology (M Sc, PhD); social work (MSW). Part-time and evening/weekend programs available. Postbaccalaureate distance learning degree programs offered (no on-campus study). *Degree requirements:* For master's and doctorate, thesis/dissertation. *Entrance requirements:* For master's, GRE, minimum B average in undergraduate course work; for doctorate, candidacy exam, minimum A average in graduate course work.

University of Northern Iowa, Graduate College, College of Social and Behavioral Sciences, Department of Social Work, Cedar Falls, IA 50614. Offers MSW. *Accreditation:* CSWE. *Faculty:* 8 full-time (5 women), 1 (woman) part-time/adjunct. *Students:* 40 full-time (32 women), 3 part-time (2 women); includes 5 minority (2 American Indian/Alaska Native, 1 Asian American or Pacific Islander, 2 Hispanic Americans), 1 international. 57 applicants, 42% accepted, 12 enrolled. In 2006, 27 degrees awarded. *Entrance requirements:* Additional exam requirements/recommendations for international students: Required—TOEFL (minimum score 500 paper-based; 180 computer-based; 61 iBT). *Application deadline:* For fall admission, 8/1 priority date for domestic students. Applications are processed on a rolling basis. Application fee: $30 ($50 for international students). Electronic applications accepted. *Expenses:* Tuition, state resident: full-time $5,936. Tuition, nonresident: full-time $14,074. *Financial support:* Application deadline: 2/1. *Unit head:* Dr. Thomas W. Keefe, III, Head, 319-273-6249, Fax: 319-273-2738, E-mail: thomas.keefe@uni.edu.

University of Oklahoma, Graduate College, College of Arts and Sciences, School of Social Work, Norman, OK 73019-0390. Offers MSW. *Accreditation:* CSWE. Part-time programs available. *Faculty:* 21 full-time (11 women), 22 part-time/adjunct (18 women). *Students:* 141 full-time (130 women), 90 part-time (78 women); includes 65 minority (17 African Americans, 30 American Indian/Alaska Native, 5 Asian Americans or Pacific Islanders, 13 Hispanic Americans). 155 applicants, 72% accepted, 101 enrolled. In 2006, 95 degrees awarded. *Entrance requirements:* For master's, GRE, minimum GPA of 3.0, 3 letters of reference. Additional exam requirements/recommendations for international students: Required—TOEFL (minimum score 550 paper-based; 213 computer-based). *Application deadline:* For fall admission, 3/1 priority date for domestic students, 4/1 for international students; for spring admission, 11/1 for domestic students, 9/1 for international students. Application fee: $40 ($90 for international students). *Expenses:* Tuition, state resident: full-time $3,180; part-time $133 per credit hour. Tuition, nonresident: full-time $11,347; part-time $473 per credit hour. Required fees: $1,729; $62 per credit hour. $117 per semester. Tuition and fees vary according to course load and program. *Financial support:* In 2006–07, 141 students received support, including 6 research assistantships with partial tuition reimbursements available (averaging $9,124 per year), 2 teaching assistantships with partial tuition reimbursements available (averaging $9,124 per year); career-related internships or fieldwork, Federal Work-Study, institutionally sponsored loans, scholarships/grants, traineeships, health care benefits, and unspecified assistantships also available. Support available to part-time students. Financial award application deadline: 3/1; financial award applicants required to submit FAFSA. *Faculty research:* Community-based participatory research: homelessness; co-occuring disorder (substance abuse and mental illness); child welfare, working retention, foster care, poverty, Afro-centric theory. Total annual research expenditures: $208,414. *Unit head:* Dr. Donald R Baker, Interim Director, 405-325-2821, Fax: 405-325-7072, E-mail: drralph@ou.edu. *Application contact:* Dr. Mary L. Samlefer, Staff Assistant III, 405-325-8570, Fax: 405-325-7072, E-mail: maryisand@ou.edu.

University of Ottawa, Faculty of Graduate and Postdoctoral Studies, Faculty of Social Sciences, School of Social Work, Ottawa, ON K1N 6N5, Canada. Offers MSS. Program offered in French. *Degree requirements:* For master's, thesis or alternative. *Entrance requirements:* For master's, honors bachelor's degree or equivalent, minimum B average. Electronic applications accepted. *Faculty research:* Family-children, health.

University of Pennsylvania, School of Social Policy and Practice, Graduate Group on Social Welfare, Philadelphia, PA 19104. Offers PhD. *Faculty:* 29 full-time (12 women). *Students:* 36 full-time (28 women); includes 11 minority (4 African Americans, 7 Asian Americans or Pacific Islanders), 1 international. Average age 30. 46 applicants, 9% accepted, 3 enrolled. In 2006, 3 doctorates awarded. *Degree requirements:* For doctorate, thesis/dissertation. *Entrance requirements:* For doctorate, GRE General Test, MSW or master's degree in related field. Additional exam requirements/recommendations for international students: Required—TOEFL (minimum score 550 paper-based; 213 computer-based). *Application deadline:* For fall admission, 12/15 for domestic and international students. Applications are processed on a rolling basis. Application fee: $70. Electronic applications accepted. *Financial support:* In 2006–07, 3 fellowships with full tuition reimbursements (averaging $17,500 per year), 16 research assistantships with full tuition reimbursements (averaging $17,500 per year) were awarded; teaching assistantships with full tuition reimbursements, career-related internships or fieldwork and institutionally sponsored loans also available. Financial award application deadline: 2/1; financial award applicants required to submit FAFSA. *Faculty research:* Mental health, child welfare, organizational behavior, urban poverty, comparative social welfare. Total annual research expenditures: $3.1 million. *Unit head:* Dr. Ram Cnaan, Director, Doctoral Program, 215-898-5523, Fax: 215-573-2099, E-mail: cnaan@ssw.upenn.edu. *Application contact:* Mary C. Mazzola, Director of Admissions and Recruitment, 215-898-5550, Fax: 215-573-2099, E-mail: mmazzola@sp2.upenn.edu.

See Close-Up on page 2413.

University of Pennsylvania, School of Social Policy and Practice, Program in Social Work, Philadelphia, PA 19104. Offers MSW, JD/MSW, MSW/Certificate, MSW/MBA, MSW/MCP, MSW/MS Ed, MSW/PhD. *Accreditation:* CSWE. *Students:* 213. 301 applicants, 85% accepted, 121 enrolled. In 2006, 129 degrees awarded. *Degree requirements:* For master's, fieldwork. *Entrance requirements:* Additional exam requirements/recommendations for international students: Required—TOEFL. *Application deadline:* For fall admission, 3/15 for domestic students. Application fee: $65. *Financial support:* Fellowships, Federal Work-Study and scholarships/grants available. Support available to part-time students. Financial award application deadline: 3/15. *Application contact:* Mary C. Mazzola, Director of Admissions and Recruitment, 215-898-5550, Fax: 215-573-2099, E-mail: mmazzola@sp2.upenn.edu.

See Close-Up on page 2413.

University of Pittsburgh, School of Social Work, Program in Social Work, Pittsburgh, PA 15260. Offers gerontology (Certificate); social work (MSW, PhD); M Div/MSW; MPA/MSW; MPH/PhD; MPIA/MSW; MSW/MAJCS. *Accreditation:* CSWE (one or more programs are accredited). Part-time programs available. Postbaccalaureate distance learning degree programs offered (no on-campus study). *Faculty:* 22 full-time (10 women), 38 part-time/adjunct (29 women). *Students:* 353 full-time (290 women), 279 part-time (232 women); includes 100 minority (84 African Americans, 1 American Indian/Alaska Native, 10 Asian Americans or Pacific Islanders, 5 Hispanic Americans), 6 international. Average age 31. 431 applicants, 80% accepted, 245 enrolled. In 2006, 206 master's, 6 doctorates awarded. *Degree requirements:* For master's, practicum; for doctorate, thesis/dissertation, comprehensive exam, registration. *Entrance requirements:* For master's, minimum QPA of 3.0, course work in descriptive statistics and human biology; for doctorate, GRE, MSW or related degree, course work in statistics. Additional exam requirements/recommendations for international students: Required—TOEFL (minimum score 600 paper-based; 250 computer-based). *Application deadline:* For fall admission, 3/31 for domestic and international students. Applications are processed on a rolling basis. Application fee: $40. Electronic applications accepted. *Financial support:* In 2006–07, 102 students received support, including 2 research assistantships with full tuition reimbursements available (averaging $12,535 per year), 5 teaching assistantships with full tuition reimbursements available (averaging $13,555 per year); career-related internships or fieldwork, institutionally sponsored loans, scholarships/grants, traineeships, tuition waivers (full), and unspecified assistantships also available. Financial award application deadline: 6/1; financial award applicants required to submit FAFSA. *Faculty research:* Child abuse and neglect, poverty race relations and community empowerment, family preservation, welfare reform, mental health services research. Total annual research expenditures: $20.9 million. *Application contact:* Dr. Chenits Pettigrew, Director of Admissions, 412-624-6346, Fax: 412-624-6323, E-mail: chp14@pitt.edu.

University of Puerto Rico, Río Piedras, College of Social Sciences, Graduate School of Social Work, San Juan, PR 00931-3300. Offers MSW, PhD. *Accreditation:* CSWE. Part-time programs available. *Students:* 138 full-time (118 women), 48 part-time (34 women); includes 185 minority (all Hispanic Americans) Average age 25. In 2006, 50 degrees awarded. *Degree requirements:* For master's and doctorate, thesis/dissertation, comprehensive exam. *Entrance requirements:* For master's, PAEG or GRE, interview, minimum GPA of 3.0, letter of recommendation; for doctorate, PAEG or GRE, interview, minimum GPA of 3.0, 3 letters of recommendation, social work experience. *Application deadline:* For fall admission, 2/1 for domestic and international students. Application fee: $17. *Expenses:* Tuition, state resident: part-time $100 per credit. Tuition, nonresident: part-time $291 per credit. Required fees: $72 per semester. *Financial support:* Fellowships, research assistantships, teaching assistantships, career-related internships or fieldwork, Federal Work-Study, institutionally sponsored loans, and tuition waivers (partial) available. Financial award application deadline: 5/31. *Faculty research:* Social work in Puerto Rico, Cuba, and the Dominican Republic; migration; poverty in Puerto Rico. *Unit head:* Dr. Norma Rodriguez, Director, 787-764-0000 Ext. 4268, Fax: 787-763-3725. *Application contact:* Information Contact, 787-764-0000 Ext. 5831, Fax: 787-763-3725.

University of Regina, Faculty of Graduate Studies and Research, Faculty of Social Work, Regina, SK S4S 0A2, Canada. Offers MASW, MSW, PhD. Part-time programs available. *Faculty:* 16 full-time (8 women), 7 part-time/adjunct (4 women). *Students:* 29 full-time (24 women), 34 part-time (27 women). 32 applicants, 63% accepted. In 2006, 18 degrees awarded. *Degree requirements:* For master's, registration; for doctorate, thesis/dissertation, registration. *Entrance requirements:* For master's, BSW. Additional exam requirements/recommendations for international students: Required—TOEFL (minimum score 580 paper-based; 237 computer-based). *Application deadline:* For fall admission, 2/15 for domestic students. Application fee: $60 ($100 for international students). *Expenses: Contact institution. Financial support:* In 2006–07, 7 fellowships (averaging $14,886 per year), 1 research assistantship (averaging $12,750 per year), 5 teaching assistantships (averaging $13,501 per year) were awarded; career-related internships or fieldwork and scholarships/grants also available. Financial award application deadline: 6/15. *Faculty research:* Social research, social planning, social policy implementation, policy planning, social administration. *Unit head:* Dr. David Schantz, Dean, 306-585-4037, E-mail: david.schantz@uregina.ca. *Application contact:* Dr. David Broad, Graduate Coordinator, 306-585-4588, Fax: 306-585-4872, E-mail: david.broad@uregina.ca.

University of St. Francis, College of Arts and Sciences, Joliet, IL 60435-6169. Offers social work (MSW). Part-time and evening/weekend programs available. *Faculty:* 4 full-time (3 women). *Students:* 12 full-time (9 women), 1 part-time; includes 2 minority (both African Americans) Average age 36. 41 applicants, 49% accepted, 13 enrolled. *Degree requirements:* For master's, registration. *Entrance requirements:* For master's, minimum GPA of 3.0, 2 letters of recommendation. Additional exam requirements/recommendations for international students: Required—TOEFL (minimum score 550 paper-based; 213 computer-based). *Application deadline:* Applications are processed on a rolling basis. Application fee: $30. Electronic applications accepted. *Expenses:* Tuition: Part-time $445 per credit hour. Part-time tuition and fees vary according to campus/location and program. *Financial support:* In 2006–07, 10 students received support. Tuition waivers (partial) available. Support available to part-time students. Financial award applicants required to submit FAFSA. *Unit head:* Dr. Frank Pascoe, Dean, 815-740-3592, Fax: 815-740-6366. *Application contact:* Sandra Sloka, Director of Admissions for Graduate and Degree Completion Programs, 800-735-7500, Fax: 815-740-5032, E-mail: ssloka@stfrancis.edu.

University of St. Thomas, Graduate Studies, School of Social Work, St. Paul, MN 55105-1096. Offers MSW. *Accreditation:* CSWE. Part-time and evening/weekend programs available. Postbaccalaureate distance learning degree programs offered (minimal on-campus study). *Faculty:* 12 full-time (8 women), 17 part-time/adjunct (14 women). *Students:* 174 full-time (161 women), 126 part-time (108 women); includes 34 minority (14 African Americans, 1 American Indian/Alaska Native, 8 Asian Americans or Pacific Islanders, 11 Hispanic Americans), 5 international. Average age 31. 198 applicants, 85% accepted, 111 enrolled. In 2006, 97 degrees awarded. *Degree requirements:* For master's, thesis, fieldwork. *Entrance requirements:* For master's, previous course work in developmental psychology, human biology, and statistics/methods. Additional exam requirements/recommendations for international students: Required—TOEFL (minimum score 600 paper-based; 250 computer-based; 100 iBT). *Application deadline:* For fall admission, 1/10 for domestic students. Application fee: $25. Electronic applications accepted. *Expenses: Contact institution. Financial support:* In 2006–07, 178 students received support, including 19 research assistantships (averaging $1,000 per year); fellowships, career-related internships or fieldwork, institutionally sponsored loans, and scholarships/grants also available. Support available to part-time students. Financial award application deadline: 7/1. *Faculty research:* Clinical supervision, group work, spirituality and social work. *Unit head:* Dr. Barbara W. Shank, Dean and Professor, 651-962-5801, Fax: 651-962-5819, E-mail: bwshank@stthomas.edu. *Application contact:* Lisa Dalsin, Program Manager, 651-962-5810, Fax: 651-962-5819, E-mail: msw@stthomas.edu.

University of South Carolina, The Graduate School, College of Social Work, Columbia, SC 29208. Offers MSW, PhD, JD/MSW, MSW/MPA, MSW/MPH. *Accreditation:* CSWE (one or more programs are accredited). *Degree requirements:* For master's, comprehensive exam; for doctorate, thesis/dissertation. *Entrance requirements:* For master's, minimum undergraduate GPA of 3.0. Additional exam requirements/recommendations for international students: Required—TOEFL (minimum score 570 paper-based; 230 computer-based). Electronic applications accepted. Expenses: Contact institution. *Faculty research:* Victimization, child abuse and neglect, families.

University of Southern California, Graduate School, School of Social Work, Los Angeles, CA 90089. Offers MSW, PhD, JD/MSW, M Pl/MSW, MPA/MSW, MSW/MAJCS, MSW/MS. *Accreditation:* CSWE (one or more programs are accredited). *Students:* 562 full-time (491 women), 111 part-time (101 women); includes 410 minority (91 African Americans, 5 American Indian/Alaska Native, 80 Asian Americans or Pacific Islanders, 234 Hispanic Americans), 28 international. In 2006, 237 master's, 1 doctorate awarded. *Degree requirements:* For doctorate, thesis/dissertation. *Entrance requirements:* For doctorate, GRE General Test. *Application deadline:* For fall admission, 12/1 priority date for domestic students. Application fee: $85. *Expenses:* Tuition: Full-time $33,314; part-time $1,121 per credit. Required fees: $522. Full-time tuition and fees vary according to program. *Financial support:* In 2006–07, research assistantships (averaging $18,500 per year), teaching assistantships (averaging $18,500 per year) were awarded; fellowships, Federal Work-Study, institutionally sponsored loans, and scholarships/grants also available. Support available to part-time students. Financial award application deadline: 2/15; financial award applicants required to submit FAFSA. *Unit head:* Dr. Marilyn L. Flynn, Dean, 213-740-8311, E-mail: sswadm@usc.edu.

University of Southern Indiana, Graduate Studies, College of Education and Human Services, Program in Social Work, Evansville, IN 47712-3590. Offers MSW. *Accreditation:* CSWE. Part-time and evening/weekend programs available. *Faculty:* 11 full-time (7 women), 1 (woman) part-time/adjunct. *Students:* 57 full-time (48 women), 32 part-time (29 women); includes 5 minority (3 African Americans, 1 Asian American or Pacific Islander, 1 Hispanic American), 1 international. Average age 34. 43 applicants, 98% accepted, 32 enrolled. In 2006, 49 degrees awarded. *Entrance requirements:* For master's, minimum GPA of 2.8. Additional exam requirements/recommendations for international students: Required—TOEFL (minimum score 550 paper-based; 213 computer-based). *Application deadline:* For fall admission, 1/12 for domestic and international students. Application fee: $25. *Expenses:* Tuition, state resident: full-time $3,888; part-time $216 per credit hour. Tuition, nonresident: full-time $7,688; part-time $426 per credit hour. Required fees: $220; $23 per term. Tuition and fees vary according to course load and reciprocity agreements. *Financial support:* In 2006–07, 64 students received support. Federal Work-Study, scholarships/grants, tuition waivers (full and partial), and unspecified assistantships available. Financial award application deadline: 3/1; financial award applicants required to submit FAFSA. *Unit head:* Dr. Martha Raske, Director, 812-465-1147, E-mail: mraske@usi.edu.

University of Southern Maine, College of Arts and Sciences, Program in Social Work, Portland, ME 04104-9300. Offers MSW. *Accreditation:* CSWE. *Expenses:* Tuition, state resident: full-time $4,860; part-time $270 per credit hour. Tuition, nonresident: full-time $13,572; part-time $754 per credit hour. Required fees: $222 per semester. Tuition and fees vary according to course load. *Unit head:* David Wagner, Head, 207-780-4764, Fax: 207-780-4902, E-mail: wagner@usm.maine.edu. *Application contact:* Graduate Studies, 207-780-4386, Fax: 207-780-4969, E-mail: gradstudies@usm.maine.edu.

University of Southern Mississippi, Graduate School, College of Health, School of Social Work, Hattiesburg, MS 39406-0001. Offers MSW. *Accreditation:* CSWE. Part-time programs available. *Faculty:* 6 full-time (1 woman). *Students:* 103 full-time (86 women), 42 part-time (41 women); includes 61 minority (60 African Americans, 1 Hispanic American). Average age 32. 80 applicants, 69% accepted, 33 enrolled. In 2006, 34 degrees awarded. *Degree requirements:* For master's, thesis or alternative, practicum, comprehensive exam, registration. *Entrance requirements:* For master's, GRE General Test, minimum GPA of 2.75 in last 60 hours. Additional exam requirements/recommendations for international students: Required—TOEFL. *Application deadline:* For fall admission, 4/1 priority date for domestic students, 4/1 for international students. Applications are processed on a rolling basis. Application fee: $25 ($30 for international students). Electronic applications accepted. *Financial support:* In 2006–07, 15 research assistantships (averaging $6,961 per year), 4 teaching assistantships (averaging $6,961 per year) were awarded; career-related internships or fieldwork, Federal Work-Study, and scholarships/grants also available. Financial award application deadline: 3/15. *Faculty research:* Delinquency prevention, risk and resiliency in youth, successful aging, women in social service management, social work and the law. *Unit head:* Dr. Michael Forster, Director, 601-266-4171, Fax: 601-266-4165, E-mail: michael.forster@usm.edu.

University of South Florida, Graduate School, College of Arts and Sciences, School of Social Work, Tampa, FL 33620-9951. Offers MSW. *Accreditation:* CSWE. Part-time and evening/weekend programs available. *Faculty:* 16 full-time (11 women), 9 part-time/adjunct (all women). *Students:* 111 full-time (102 women), 77 part-time (62 women); includes 47 minority (23 African Americans, 6 Asian Americans or Pacific Islanders, 18 Hispanic Americans), 2 international. 101 applicants, 50% accepted, 30 enrolled. In 2006, 74 degrees awarded. *Degree requirements:* For master's, comprehensive exam. *Entrance requirements:* For master's, GRE General Test, minimum GPA of 3.0 in last 60 hours of course work. *Application deadline:* For fall admission, 2/15 priority date for domestic students. Applications are processed on a rolling basis. Application fee: $30. Electronic applications accepted. *Financial support:* Research assistantships with partial tuition reimbursements, career-related internships or fieldwork, Federal Work-Study, scholarships/grants, and unspecified assistantships available. Support available to part-time students. Financial award application deadline: 6/30; financial award applicants required to submit FAFSA. *Faculty research:* Posttraumatic stress disorder, substance abuse among social work, breast cancer telephone support groups, social service organization change. Total annual research expenditures: $3.4 million. *Unit head:* William Rowe, Chairperson, 813-974-1379, Fax: 813-974-4675. *Application contact:* Aaron A. Smith, Graduate Chair, 813-974-1356, Fax: 813-974-4675, E-mail: asmith@chuma1.cas.usf.edu.

The University of Tennessee, Graduate School, College of Social Work, Knoxville, TN 37996. Offers clinical social work practice (MSSW); social welfare management and community practice (MSSW); social work (PhD). *Accreditation:* CSWE (one or more programs are accredited). Part-time programs available. *Faculty:* 29 full-time (14 women). *Students:* 306 full-time (270 women), 141 part-time (121 women); includes 128 minority (118 African Americans, 4 Asian Americans or Pacific Islanders, 6 Hispanic Americans), 6 international. In 2006, 195 master's, 5 doctorates awarded. *Degree requirements:* For master's, thesis or alternative; for doctorate, thesis/dissertation. *Entrance requirements:* For master's and doctorate, GRE General Test, minimum GPA of 2.7. Additional exam requirements/recommendations for international students: Required—TOEFL. *Application deadline:* For fall admission, 2/1 priority date for domestic students. Applications are processed on a rolling basis. Application fee: $35. Electronic applications accepted. *Expenses:* Tuition, state resident: full-time $5,574. Tuition, nonresident: full-time $16,840. Required fees: $792. *Financial support:* In 2006–07, 8 fellowships, 9 research assistantships were awarded; teaching assistantships, career-related internships or fieldwork, Federal Work-Study, institutionally sponsored loans, and unspecified assistantships also available. Financial award application deadline: 2/1; financial award applicants required to submit FAFSA. *Unit head:* Dr. Karen Sowers, Dean, 865-974-3175, Fax: 865-974-4803, E-mail: kmsowers@utk.edu.

The University of Texas at Arlington, Graduate School, School of Social Work, Arlington, TX 76019. Offers MSSW, PhD. *Accreditation:* CSWE (one or more programs are accredited). Part-time and evening/weekend programs available. Postbaccalaureate distance learning degree programs offered (minimal on-campus study). *Faculty:* 26 full-time (12 women), 10 part-time/adjunct (8 women). *Students:* 341 full-time (301 women), 257 part-time (222 women); includes 212 minority (127 African Americans, 7 American Indian/Alaska Native, 17 Asian Americans or Pacific Islanders, 61 Hispanic Americans), 34 international. Average age 32. 253 applicants, 93% accepted, 185 enrolled. In 2006, 136 master's, 5 doctorates awarded. *Degree requirements:* For master's, thesis optional; for doctorate, thesis/dissertation. *Entrance requirements:* For master's, GRE General Test (if GPA is below 3.0), 3 letters of recommendation; for doctorate, GRE General Test, minimum graduate GPA of 3.4. Additional exam requirements/recommendations for international students: Required—TOEFL (minimum score 550 paper-based; 213 computer-based). *Application deadline:* For fall admission, 3/15 for domestic students. Application fee: $35 ($50 for international students). *Expenses:* Tuition, state resident: full-time $5,528. Tuition, nonresident: full-time $10,478. International tuition: $10,608 full-time. *Financial support:* In 2006–07, 355 students received support, including 14 fellowships (averaging $1,000 per year), 10 teaching assistantships (averaging $8,000 per year); research assistantships, career-related internships or fieldwork, Federal Work-Study, institutionally sponsored loans, scholarships/grants, and unspecified assistantships also available. Financial award application deadline: 6/1; financial award applicants required to submit FAFSA. *Faculty research:* Community practice, administrative practice, mental health and children and families. *Unit head:* Dr. Santos H. Hernandez, Dean, 817-272-3181, Fax: 817-272-5229, E-mail: herns@uta.edu. *Application contact:* Darlene Santee, Director of admissions, 817-272-3613, Fax: 817-272-5229.

The University of Texas at Austin, Graduate School, School of Social Work, Austin, TX 78712-1111. Offers MSSW, PhD. *Accreditation:* CSWE (one or more programs are accredited). Part-time programs available. *Degree requirements:* For doctorate, thesis/dissertation. *Entrance requirements:* For master's and doctorate, GRE General Test. Additional exam requirements/recommendations for international students: Required—TOEFL. *Faculty research:* Substance abuse, child welfare, gerontology, mental health, public policy.

The University of Texas at San Antonio, College of Public Policy, Department of Social Work, San Antonio, TX 78249-0617. Offers MSW. Part-time and evening/weekend programs available. *Faculty:* 9 full-time (6 women). *Students:* 24 full-time (20 women), 49 part-time (37 women); includes 10 African Americans, 1 Asian American or Pacific Islander, 30 Hispanic Americans. Average age 35. 36 applicants, 83% accepted, 22 enrolled. *Entrance requirements:* Additional exam requirements/recommendations for international students: Required—TOEFL (minimum score 500 paper-based; 173 computer-based). *Application deadline:* For fall admission, 7/1 for domestic students, 4/1 for international students; for spring admission, 11/1 for domestic students, 9/1 for international students. Applications are processed on a rolling basis. Application fee: $45 ($80 for international students). Electronic applications accepted. *Expenses:* Tuition, state resident: full-time $1,730; part-time $192 per credit hour. Tuition, nonresident: full-time $6,680; part-time $742 per credit hour. Required fees: $733; $308,359 per credit hour. *Financial support:* In 2006–07, 3 research assistantships (averaging $20,800 per year) were awarded. *Unit head:* Dr. Dennis Haynes, Chair, 210-458-3000, E-mail: dennis.haynes@utsa.edu.

The University of Texas–Pan American, College of Health Sciences and Human Services, Department of Social Work, Edinburg, TX 78541-2999. Offers MSSW. *Accreditation:* CSWE. Part-time programs available. *Faculty:* 11 full-time (6 women), 1 part-time/adjunct (0 women). *Students:* 47 full-time (40 women), 34 part-time (30 women); includes 78 minority (all Hispanic Americans) Average age 33. 43 applicants, 91% accepted, 30 enrolled. In 2006, 27 degrees awarded. *Median time to degree:* Master's–1 year full-time, 2 years part-time. *Entrance requirements:* For master's, minimum GPA of 3.0, basic statistics course completed within 5 years of admission. Additional exam requirements/recommendations for international students: Recommended—TOEFL (minimum score 500 paper-based). *Application deadline:* For fall admission, 3/31 priority date for domestic and international students. Applications are processed on a rolling basis. Application fee: $35. *Expenses:* Tuition, state resident: full-time $2,577; part-time $143 per credit hour. Tuition, nonresident: full-time $7,527; part-time $418 per credit hour. Required fees: $561. *Financial support:* In 2006–07, 4 students received support; fellowships, research assistantships, teaching assistantships, career-related internships or fieldwork, Federal Work-Study, institutionally sponsored loans, scholarships/grants, and traineeships available. Financial award applicants required to submit FAFSA. *Faculty research:* Child welfare, family violence, social justice, Hispanic traditional healing (curanderismo and spirtuality), community development. *Unit head:* Dr. Hector Diaz, Chair, 956-381-3575, E-mail: hdiaz@utpa.edu. *Application contact:* Dr. Alonzo Cavazos, Program director, 956-381-2487, Fax: 956-381-2487, E-mail: alonso@panam.edu.

The University of Toledo, College of Graduate Studies, College of Health Science and Human Service, Division of Human Services, Department of Social Work, Toledo, OH 43606-3390. Offers MS. *Faculty:* 7. *Students:* 29 full-time (26 women), 26 part-time (22 women); includes 13 minority (9 African Americans, 4 Hispanic Americans). Average age 34. 42 applicants, 76% accepted, 25 enrolled.Application fee: $45. *Financial support:* In 2006–07, 1 research assistantship (averaging $9,000 per year) was awarded. *Unit head:* Terry Cluse-Tolar, Chair, E-mail: tcluset@utnet.utoledo.edu.

University of Toronto, School of Graduate Studies, Social Sciences Division, Faculty of Social Work, Toronto, ON M5S 1A1, Canada. Offers MSW, PhD. Part-time programs available. *Degree requirements:* For doctorate, thesis/dissertation, oral exam/thesis defense. *Entrance requirements:* For master's, minimum mid-B average in last 2 years of full-time study, 3 full courses in social sciences, experience in social services recommended, 3 letters of reference, resumé; for doctorate, MSW or equivalent, minimum B+ average, competency in basic statistical methods. Additional exam requirements/recommendations for international students: Required—TOEFL (minimum score 580 paper-based; 237 computer-based), TWE (minimum score 5), IELTS (7) or MELAB (85). Expenses: Contact institution.

University of Utah, The Graduate School, College of Social Work, Salt Lake City, UT 84112-1107. Offers MSW, PhD, MPA/PhD. *Accreditation:* CSWE (one or more programs are accredited). Part-time programs available. *Faculty:* 33 full-time (19 women), 8 part-time/adjunct (3 women). *Students:* 307 full-time (213 women), 36 part-time (25 women); includes 34 minority (4 African Americans, 9 American Indian/Alaska Native, 8 Asian Americans or Pacific Islanders, 13 Hispanic Americans), 14 international. Average age 33. 334 applicants, 50% accepted, 126 enrolled. In 2006, 165 master's, 7 doctorates awarded. *Median time to degree:* Of those who began their doctoral program in fall 1998, 66% received their degree in 8 years or less. *Degree requirements:* For master's, thesis or alternative; for doctorate, thesis/dissertation, comprehensive exam. *Entrance requirements:* For master's, GRE General Test, MAT, minimum GPA of 3.0; for doctorate, GRE General Test. Additional exam requirements/recommendations for international students: Required—TOEFL (minimum score 500 paper-based; 173 computer-based). *Application deadline:* For fall admission, 4/1 for domestic and international students; for spring admission, 11/1 for domestic and international students. Applications are processed on a rolling basis. Application fee: $45 ($65 for international students). *Expenses:* Tuition, state resident: full-time $3,208. Tuition, nonresident: full-time $11,326. Required fees: $608. Tuition and fees vary according to class time and program. *Financial support:* In 2006–07, 66 fellowships with full and partial tuition reimbursements (averaging $3,026 per year), 38 research assistantships with full and partial tuition reimbursements (averaging $6,300 per year), 7 teaching assistantships with full and partial tuition reimbursements (averaging $5,956 per year) were awarded; Federal Work-Study and institutionally sponsored loans also available. Support available to part-time students. Financial award application deadline: 3/15; financial award applicants required to submit FAFSA. *Faculty research:* Clinical/direct practice, health and mental health, gerontology, child welfare, prevention of substance abuse. Total annual research expenditures: $570,255. *Unit head:* Jannah H. Mather, Dean, 801-581-6194, Fax: 801-585-3219, E-mail: jannah.mather@socwk.utah.edu. *Application contact:* Mary Jane Taylor, Associate Dean, 801-581-8828, Fax: 801-585-3219, E-mail: maryjane.taylor@socwk.utah.edu.

University of Vermont, Graduate College, College of Education and Social Services, Department of Social Work, Burlington, VT 05405. Offers MSW. *Accreditation:* CSWE. *Students:* 65 (55 women); includes 2 minority (1 African American, 1 American Indian/Alaska Native) 1 international. 83 applicants, 59% accepted, 29 enrolled. In 2006, 25 degrees awarded. *Entrance requirements:* For master's, GRE General Test, resumé. Additional exam requirements/recommendations for international students: Required—TOEFL (minimum score 550 paper-based; 213 computer-based). *Application deadline:* For fall admission, 2/1 priority date for domestic students. Applications are processed on a rolling basis. Application fee: $40. Electronic applications accepted. *Expenses:* Tuition, state resident: part-time $434 per credit. Tuition, nonresident: part-time $1,096 per credit. *Financial support:* Application deadline: 2/1. *Unit head:* G. Widrick, Acting Chair, 802-656-8800.

University of Victoria, Faculty of Graduate Studies, Faculty of Human and Social Development, School of Social Work, Victoria, BC V8W 2Y2, Canada. Offers MSW. *Entrance requirements:* For master's, BSW. Additional exam requirements/recommendations for international students: Required—TOEFL (minimum score 575 paper-based; 233 computer-based), IELTS (minimum score 7). Electronic applications accepted. *Faculty research:* Women's issues, public policy formation and implementation, child welfare, First Nations, community development.

Social Work

University of Victoria, Faculty of Graduate Studies, Faculty of Human and Social Development, Studies in Policy and Practice in Health and Social Services, Victoria, BC V8W 2Y2, Canada. Offers human and social development (MA). Part-time programs available. *Degree requirements:* For master's, thesis, registration. *Entrance requirements:* For master's, resumé. Additional exam requirements/recommendations for international students: Required—TOEFL (minimum score 575 paper-based; 233 computer-based), IELTS (minimum score 7). Electronic applications accepted. *Faculty research:* Women's issues, public policy formation and implementation, health promotion and education, children, youth and families.

University of Washington, Graduate School, School of Social Work, Seattle, WA 98195. Offers MSW, PhD, MPH/MSW. *Accreditation:* CSWE (one or more programs are accredited). Evening/weekend programs available. Postbaccalaureate distance learning degree programs offered (minimal on-campus study). *Degree requirements:* For master's, thesis optional; for doctorate, thesis/dissertation. *Entrance requirements:* For master's, GRE General Test, minimum GPA of 3.0; for doctorate, master's degree, sample of scholarly work, minimum GPA of 3.0. Additional exam requirements/recommendations for international students: Required—TOEFL. *Faculty research:* Health and mental health; children, youth, and families; multicultural issues; reducing risk and enhancing protective factors in children; etrology of substance use.

University of Washington, Graduate School, School of Social Work, Tacoma Campus, Seattle, WA 98195. Offers MSW. Part-time and evening/weekend programs available. *Degree requirements:* For master's, registration. *Entrance requirements:* For master's, GRE General Test, minimum GPA of 3.0 for last 90 undergraduate credits. Electronic applications accepted. *Faculty research:* Aging, diversity, feminism, spirituality, medical social work.

University of Windsor, Faculty of Graduate Studies and Research, Faculty of Arts and Social Sciences, School of Social Work, Windsor, ON N9B 3P4, Canada. Offers MSW. Part-time programs available. *Degree requirements:* For master's, thesis or alternative. *Entrance requirements:* For master's, minimum B+ average in last year of undergraduate study. Additional exam requirements/recommendations for international students: Required—TOEFL (minimum score 600 paper-based; 250 computer-based). Electronic applications accepted. *Faculty research:* Addiction, social policy analysis, gerontology and health care.

University of Wisconsin–Green Bay, Graduate Studies, Program in Social Work, Green Bay, WI 54311-7001. Offers MSW. *Accreditation:* CSWE. *Faculty:* 5 full-time (3 women), 6 part-time/adjunct (4 women). *Students:* 22 full-time (16 women); includes 4 minority (3 American Indian/Alaska Native, 1 Hispanic American). Average age 29. 21 applicants, 86% accepted, 13 enrolled. In 2006, 10 degrees awarded. *Degree requirements:* For master's, thesis or alternative. *Entrance requirements:* For master's, GRE, minimum GPA of 2.75. *Application deadline:* For fall admission, 8/1 priority date for domestic students; for spring admission, 11/1 priority date for domestic students. Applications are processed on a rolling basis. Application fee: $45. Electronic applications accepted. *Expenses:* Tuition, state resident: full-time $5,910; part-time $246 per credit. Tuition, nonresident: full-time $16,520; part-time $688 per credit. Required fees: $1,148; $48 per credit. *Faculty research:* Child welfare. *Unit head:* Dr. Judith Martin, Coordinator, 920-465-2049, E-mail: martinj@uwgb.edu.

University of Wisconsin–Madison, Graduate School, College of Letters and Science, School of Social Work, Madison, WI 53706-1380. Offers social welfare (PhD); social work (MSSW). *Accreditation:* CSWE (one or more programs are accredited). Terminal master's awarded for partial completion of doctoral program. *Degree requirements:* For doctorate, thesis/dissertation. *Entrance requirements:* For master's, minimum GPA of 3.0 on last 60 credits; for doctorate, GRE General Test, minimum GPA of 3.0 on last 60 credits. Electronic applications accepted. Expenses: Contact institution. *Faculty research:* Poverty, caregiving, child welfare, developmental disabilities, mental health, severe mental illnesses, adolescence, family, social policy, child support.

University of Wisconsin–Milwaukee, Graduate School, School of Social Welfare, Department of Social Work, Milwaukee, WI 53201-0413. Offers MSW, Certificate. *Accreditation:* CSWE. Part-time programs available. *Faculty:* 17 full-time (9 women). *Students:* 186 full-time (174 women), 93 part-time (86 women); includes 42 minority (22 African Americans, 2 American Indian/Alaska Native, 7 Asian Americans or Pacific Islanders, 11 Hispanic Americans), 3 international. 302 applicants, 60% accepted, 113 enrolled. In 2006, 107 degrees awarded. *Degree requirements:* For master's, thesis or alternative. *Application deadline:* For fall admission, 1/1 priority date for domestic students; for spring admission, 9/1 for domestic students. Applications are processed on a rolling basis. Application fee: $45 ($75 for international students). *Expenses:* Tuition, state resident: part-time $510 per credit. Tuition, nonresident: part-time $1,408 per credit. Tuition and fees vary according to program. *Financial support:* In 2006–07, 1 teaching assistantship was awarded; fellowships, research assistantships, career-related internships or fieldwork and unspecified assistantships also available. Support available to part-time students. Financial award application deadline: 4/15. *Unit head:* Deborah Padgett, Representative, 414-229-4852, Fax: 414-229-5311.

University of Wisconsin–Oshkosh, The School of Graduate Studies, Department of Social Work, Oshkosh, WI 54901. Offers MSW. Part-time programs available. *Degree requirements:* For master's, registration. *Entrance requirements:* For master's, GRE, letters of recommendation, previous courses in statistics and human biology, work experience. Additional exam requirements/recommendations for international students: Required—TOEFL (minimum score 550 paper-based; 213 computer-based).

University of Wyoming, Graduate School, College of Health Sciences, Division of Social Work, Laramie, WY 82070. Offers MSW. *Accreditation:* CSWE. *Faculty:* 7 full-time (5 women), 6 part-time/adjunct (3 women). *Students:* 29 full-time (27 women), 37 part-time (34 women); includes 6 minority (1 American Indian/Alaska Native, 1 Asian American or Pacific Islander, 4 Hispanic Americans). Average age 37. 65 applicants, 54% accepted, 30 enrolled. In 2006, 28 degrees awarded. *Degree requirements:* For master's, thesis or alternative, comprehensive exam, registration. *Entrance requirements:* For master's, minimum GPA of 3.0. Additional exam requirements/recommendations for international students: Required—TOEFL. *Application deadline:* For spring admission, 2/15 priority date for domestic students. Application fee: $50. *Expenses:* Contact institution. *Financial support:* In 2006–07, 11 research assistantships with partial tuition reimbursements (averaging $5,031 per year) were awarded; career-related internships or fieldwork, Federal Work-Study, institutionally sponsored loans, scholarships/grants, and unspecified assistantships also available. Support available to part-time students. Financial award application deadline: 3/1. *Faculty research:* Social work education, child welfare, mental health, diversity, school social work. *Unit head:* Gail M. Leedy, Director, 307-766-2562, Fax: 307-766-6839, E-mail: zzleedy@uwyo.edu. *Application contact:* Lori Dockter, Office Associate, Senior, 307-766-5422, Fax: 307-766-6839, E-mail: dockterl@uwyo.edu.

Valdosta State University, Graduate School, Division of Social Work, Valdosta, GA 31698. Offers MSW. *Accreditation:* CSWE. Part-time and evening/weekend programs available. *Degree requirements:* For master's, 5 practica. *Entrance requirements:* For master's, GRE General Test, MAT, minimum GPA of 3.0 in last 2 years of course work. Additional exam requirements/recommendations for international students: Required—TOEFL (minimum score 523 paper-based; 193 computer-based).

Virginia Commonwealth University, Graduate School, School of Social Work, Doctoral Program in Social Work, Richmond, VA 23284-9005. Offers PhD. *Students:* 15 full-time (14 women), 19 part-time (13 women); includes 4 minority (3 African Americans, 1 Asian American or Pacific Islander), 8 international. 21 applicants, 57% accepted, 8 enrolled. In 2006, 6 degrees awarded. *Degree requirements:* For doctorate, thesis/dissertation, comprehensive exam. *Entrance requirements:* For doctorate, GRE General Test, MSW or related degree. *Application deadline:* For fall admission, 3/1 priority date for domestic students. Application fee: $50. *Financial support:* Fellowships, research assistantships, teaching assistantships, career-related internships or fieldwork, Federal Work-Study, institutionally sponsored loans, and tuition waivers (full and partial) available. Support available to part-time students. Financial award application deadline: 5/1. *Unit head:* Dr. Kia J. Bentley, Director, 804-828-0453, E-mail: kbentley@saturn.vcu.edu. *Application contact:* Dr. Ann M. Nichols-Casebolt, Associate Dean, 804-828-0703, Fax: 804-828-0716, E-mail: acasebol@saturn.vcu.edu.

See Close-Up on page 2415.

Virginia Commonwealth University, Graduate School, School of Social Work, Master's Program in Social Work, Richmond, VA 23284-9005. Offers MSW, JD/MSW, MSW/MA. *Accreditation:* CSWE. *Students:* 294 full-time (261 women), 201 part-time (171 women). 469 applicants, 73% accepted, 198 enrolled. In 2006, 171 degrees awarded. *Application deadline:* For fall admission, 2/1 for domestic students. Application fee: $50. *Financial support:* Fellowships, research assistantships, teaching assistantships, career-related internships or fieldwork, Federal Work-Study, institutionally sponsored loans, and tuition waivers (full and partial) available. Support available to part-time students. Financial award application deadline: 3/1. *Unit head:* Dr. Beverly Koerin, Director, 804-828-6692, E-mail: bkoerin@vcu.edu. *Application contact:* Dr. Ann M. Nichols-Casebolt, Associate Dean, 804-828-0703, Fax: 804-828-0716, E-mail: acasebol@saturn.vcu.edu.

Walla Walla College, Graduate School, School of Social Work, College Place, WA 99324-1198. Offers MSW. *Accreditation:* CSWE. Part-time programs available. *Faculty:* 17 full-time (12 women), 15 part-time/adjunct (11 women). *Students:* 183 full-time (145 women), 26 part-time (16 women); includes 46 minority (3 African Americans, 26 American Indian/Alaska Native, 4 Asian Americans or Pacific Islanders, 13 Hispanic Americans), 2 international. Average age 38. 167 applicants, 84% accepted, 105 enrolled. In 2006, 130 master's awarded. *Entrance requirements:* For master's, minimum GPA of 2.75. *Application deadline:* For fall admission, 7/15 priority date for domestic students. Applications are processed on a rolling basis. Application fee: $50. Electronic applications accepted. *Expenses:* Tuition: Full-time $20,124; part-time $516 per quarter hour. *Financial support:* In 2006–07, 184 students received support. Career-related internships or fieldwork, Federal Work-Study, and scholarships/grants available. Support available to part-time students. Financial award application deadline: 4/1; financial award applicants required to submit FAFSA. *Unit head:* Dr. Pamela Cress, Dean, 509-527-2270, Fax: 509-527-2253. *Application contact:* Dr. Joe G. Galusha, Dean of Graduate Studies, 509-527-2421, Fax: 509-527-2237, E-mail: galujo@wwc.edu.

Washburn University, School of Applied Studies, Department of Social Work, Topeka, KS 66621. Offers clinical social work (MSW). *Accreditation:* CSWE. Part-time and evening/weekend programs available. *Faculty:* 9 full-time (4 women), 3 part-time/adjunct (1 woman). *Students:* 82 full-time (70 women), 39 part-time (35 women); includes 20 minority (9 African Americans, 4 American Indian/Alaska Native, 2 Asian Americans or Pacific Islanders, 5 Hispanic Americans). Average age 33. *Entrance requirements:* For master's, course in human biology, course in cultural anthropology. *Application deadline:* For winter admission, 1/15 for domestic and international students. Applications are processed on a rolling basis. Electronic applications accepted. *Expenses:* Tuition, state resident: full-time $4,338; part-time $241 per credit hour. Tuition, nonresident: full-time $8,820; part-time $490 per credit hour. Required fees: $62; $31 per semester. *Financial support:* Career-related internships or fieldwork, Federal Work-Study, institutionally sponsored loans, and scholarships/grants available. Support available to part-time students. Financial award applicants required to submit FAFSA. *Faculty research:* Drug courts; cultural competency; values/ethics; social work practice. *Unit head:* Jay L. Memmott, Chairperson, 785-670-2139, Fax: 785-670-1027, E-mail: jay.memmott@washburn.edu.

Washington University in St. Louis, George Warren Brown School of Social Work, St. Louis, MO 63130-4899. Offers MSW, PhD, JD/MSW, M Arch/MSW, MBA/MSW, MHA/MSW, MSW/M Div, MSW/MAPS. *Accreditation:* CSWE (one or more programs are accredited). Part-time programs available. *Faculty:* 31 full-time (15 women), 49 part-time/adjunct (29 women). *Students:* 369 full-time (322 women), 32 part-time (26 women); includes 84 minority (39 African Americans, 12 American Indian/Alaska Native, 17 Asian Americans or Pacific Islanders, 16 Hispanic Americans), 60 international. Average age 28. 524 applicants, 64% accepted, 166 enrolled. In 2006, 161 master's, 13 doctorates awarded. *Median time to degree:* Master's–7 years part-time. Of those who began their doctoral program in fall 1998, 100% received their degree in 8 years or less. *Degree requirements:* For doctorate, thesis/dissertation, comprehensive exam. *Entrance requirements:* For master's, minimum GPA of 3.0; for doctorate, GRE, MA or MSW. Additional exam requirements/recommendations for international students: Required—TOEFL (minimum score 575 paper-based; 233 computer-based), TWE. *Application deadline:* Applications are processed on a rolling basis. Application fee: $60. Electronic applications accepted. *Financial support:* In 2006–07, 365 students received support, including 273 fellowships with partial tuition reimbursements available (averaging $5,432 per year), 43 research assistantships with full tuition reimbursements available (averaging $3,000 per year), 26 teaching assistantships with full tuition reimbursements available (averaging $1,000 per year); career-related internships or fieldwork, Federal Work-Study, institutionally sponsored loans, scholarships/grants, and tuition waivers (partial) also available. Support available to part-time students. Financial award applicants required to submit FAFSA. *Faculty research:* Mental health services, social development, public child welfare, at-risk teens, social development, dietary risks in African-American women. *Unit head:* Dr. Edward F Lawlor, Dean and William E. Gordon Professor, 314-935-6693, Fax: 314-935-8511, E-mail: elawlor@wush.edu. *Application contact:* Janice Wells-White, Director of Admissions and Recruiting, 314-935-6676, Fax: 314-935-4859, E-mail: msw@gwbmail.wustl.edu.

See Close-Up on page 2417.

Washington University in St. Louis, Graduate School of Arts and Sciences, Program in Social Work, St. Louis, MO 63130-4899. Offers PhD.

Wayne State University, School of Social Work, Detroit, MI 48202. Offers interdisciplinary studies (PhD); social work (MSW); social work practice with families and couples (Certificate). *Accreditation:* CSWE (one or more programs are accredited). Part-time and evening/weekend programs available. *Faculty:* 31 full-time (19 women), 19 part-time/adjunct (11 women). *Students:* 293 full-time (257 women), 183 part-time (157 women); includes 180 minority (151 African Americans, 6 American Indian/Alaska Native, 14 Asian Americans or Pacific Islanders, 9 Hispanic Americans), 12 international. Average age 33. 318 applicants, 61% accepted, 144 enrolled. In 2006, 205 master's, 13 other advanced degrees awarded. *Degree requirements:* For master's, thesis optional. *Entrance requirements:* Additional exam requirements/recommendations for international students: Required—TOEFL (minimum score 550 paper-based; 213 computer-based); Recommended—TWE (minimum score 6). *Application deadline:* For fall admission, 3/31 for domestic students, 6/1 for international students; for winter admission, 10/1 for international students; for spring admission, 2/28 for domestic students, 2/1 for international students. Applications are processed on a rolling basis. Application fee: $20 ($30 for international students). Electronic applications accepted. *Financial support:* In 2006–07, 1 research assistantship with tuition reimbursement (averaging $15,475 per year), 1 teaching assistantship (averaging $13,222 per year) were awarded; career-related internships or fieldwork, institutionally sponsored loans, scholarships/grants, and tuition waivers (partial) also available. Support available to part-time students. Financial award application deadline: 5/1; financial award applicants required to submit FAFSA. *Faculty research:* Clinical treatment of adults, children, adolescents and their families and youth development; capacity-building, asset-building and empowerment of urban and vulnerable people and organizations; international social work; violence and trauma prevention and intervention; reentry and reintegration of ex-offenders. Total annual research expenditures: $44,100. *Unit head:* Phyllis Vroom, Dean, 313-577-4400, Fax: 313-577-8770, E-mail: aa8773@wayne.edu. *Application contact:* Ann Alvarez, Associate Dean, 313-577-4441, E-mail: ann.r.alvarez@wayne.edu.

West Chester University of Pennsylvania, Graduate Studies, School of Business and Public Affairs, Department of Social Work, West Chester, PA 19383. Offers MSW. *Accreditation:* CSWE. Part-time and evening/weekend programs available. *Students:* 54 full-time (41 women), 20 part-time (17 women); includes 12 African Americans, 3 Asian Americans or Pacific Islanders, 1 Hispanic American, 2 international. Average age 31. 96 applicants, 77% accepted, 44 enrolled. In 2006, 37 degrees awarded. *Degree requirements:* For master's, thesis optional. *Entrance requirements:* For master's, GRE, MAT, interview, minimum GPA of 3.0. *Application deadline:* For fall admission, 4/15 priority date for domestic students; for spring admission, 10/15 for domestic students. Applications are processed on a rolling basis. Application fee: $35. *Financial support:* In 2006–07, 4 research assistantships with full tuition reimbursements (averaging $5,000 per year) were awarded; unspecified assistantships also available. Support available to part-time students. Financial award application deadline: 2/15; financial award applicants required to submit FAFSA. *Faculty research:* Teen pregnancy/parenting, adoption, health care advocacy, welfare-to-work, mentoring/alternative education. *Unit head:* Dr. Ann Abbott, Chair and Director, 610-436-2527, E-mail: aabbott@wcupa.edu.

Western Kentucky University, Graduate Studies, College of Health and Human Services, Department of Social Work, Bowling Green, KY 42101. Offers MSW. *Accreditation:* CSWE. *Faculty:* 10 full-time (8 women), 1 (woman) part-time/adjunct. *Students:* 36 full-time (31 women), 19 part-time (15 women); includes 6 minority (all African Americans), 5 international. Average age 32. 21 applicants, 62% accepted, 13 enrolled. In 2006, 19 master's awarded. *Entrance requirements:* Additional exam requirements/recommendations for international students: Required—TOEFL (minimum score 555 paper-based; 213 computer-based; 79 iBT). *Application deadline:* For fall admission, 7/1 priority date for domestic students, 4/1 for international students; for spring admission, 11/1 for domestic students, 9/1 for international students. Applications are processed on a rolling basis. Application fee: $35. *Expenses:* Tuition, state resident: full-time $6,520; part-time $226 per hour. Tuition, nonresident: full-time $7,140; part-time $357 per hour. International tuition: $15,820 full-time. *Financial support:* In 2006–07, 1 research assistantship with partial tuition reimbursement (averaging $9,500 per year) was awarded. Total annual research expenditures: $20,553. *Unit head:* Dr. Dean May, Head, 270-745-5312, E-mail: dean.may@wku.edu.

Western Michigan University, Graduate College, College of Health and Human Services, School of Social Work, Kalamazoo, MI 49008-5202. Offers MSW. *Accreditation:* CSWE. Part-time programs available.

West Virginia University, Eberly College of Arts and Sciences, School of Applied Social Science, Division of Social Work, Morgantown, WV 26506. Offers aging and health care (MSW); children and families (MSW); community mental health (MSW). *Accreditation:* CSWE. Part-time programs available. *Faculty:* 13 full-time (10 women), 9 part-time/adjunct (8 women). *Students:* 97 full-time (79 women), 167 part-time (145 women); includes 25 minority (22 African Americans, 1 American Indian/Alaska Native, 2 Hispanic Americans), 1 international. Average age 33. 190 applicants, 73% accepted, 104 enrolled. In 2006, 46 degrees awarded. *Degree requirements:* For master's, fieldwork. *Entrance requirements:* For master's, GRE, minimum GPA of 2.75, 2 letters of reference. Additional exam requirements/recommendations for international students: Required—TOEFL. *Application deadline:* For fall admission, 3/1 for domestic students. Application fee: $45. *Expenses:* Tuition, state resident: full-time $4,926; part-time $276 per credit hour. Tuition, nonresident: full-time $14,278; part-time $796 per credit hour. Tuition and fees vary according to program. *Financial support:* In 2006–07, 179 students received support, including 7 research assistantships with full tuition reimbursements available (averaging $9,000 per year), 11 teaching assistantships with full tuition reimbursements available (averaging $9,000 per year); career-related internships or fieldwork, Federal Work-Study, institutionally sponsored loans, scholarships/grants, tuition waivers (full and partial), and stipends also available. Financial award application deadline: 3/1; financial award applicants required to submit FAFSA. *Faculty research:* Rural and small town social work practice, gerontology, health and mental health, welfare reform, child welfare. Total annual research expenditures: $208,000. *Unit head:* Dr. Virginia Majewski, Chairperson, 304-293-3501 Ext. 3129, Fax: 304-293-5936, E-mail: ginny.majewski@mail.wvu.edu. *Application contact:* Brenda Morgan-Patrick, Academic Advisor, 304-293-3501 Ext. 3128, Fax: 304-293-5936, E-mail: brenda.morgan-patrick@mail.wvu.edu.

Wheelock College, Graduate Programs, Division of Social Work, Boston, MA 02215-4176. Offers MSW. *Accreditation:* CSWE. *Degree requirements:* For master's, thesis, comprehensive exam. *Entrance requirements:* For master's, minimum GPA of 3.0; undergraduate course work in human biology, statistics. Additional exam requirements/recommendations for international students: Required—TOEFL. Electronic applications accepted.

Wichita State University, Graduate School, Fairmount College of Liberal Arts and Sciences, School of Social Work, Wichita, KS 67260. Offers MSW. *Accreditation:* CSWE.

Widener University, School of Human Service Professions, Center for Social Work Education, Chester, PA 19013-5792. Offers MSW. *Accreditation:* CSWE. Part-time programs available. *Degree requirements:* For master's, field practica. *Entrance requirements:* For master's, minimum GPA of 3.0. Electronic applications accepted. Expenses: Contact institution. *Faculty research:* Clinical practice, clinical supervision, gerontology, child welfare, self-psychology.

Announcement: Widener's MSW program prepares students for agency-based clinical social work practice through small classes, an integrated and individualized field placement, and collaborative relations with faculty and other students. The program has full-time and part-time tracks as well as advanced standing and regular admissions. The Ph.D. program develops academic leaders with skills in scholarly research, teaching, and advanced clinical practice. On a part-time basis, students are engaged in targeted course work and mentoring relationships with faculty such that degree completion can occur within 5 years.

Wilfrid Laurier University, Faculty of Graduate Studies, Faculty of Social Work, Waterloo, ON N2L 3C5, Canada. Offers MSW, PhD. Part-time programs available. *Faculty:* 23 full-time, 30 part-time/adjunct. *Students:* 209 full-time, 93 part-time. 402 applicants, 39% accepted, 120 enrolled. In 2006, 108 master's, 2 doctorates awarded. *Degree requirements:* For master's, thesis optional; for doctorate, thesis/dissertation. *Entrance requirements:* For master's, course work in social science, research methodology, and statistics; honors BA with a minimum B average; for doctorate, master's degree in social work, minimum A- average. Additional exam requirements/recommendations for international students: Required—TOEFL (minimum score 230 computer-based; 89 iBT). *Application deadline:* For fall admission, 1/15 for domestic students. Application fee: $100. Electronic applications accepted. *Expenses: Contact institution.* *Financial support:* Fellowships, research assistantships, teaching assistantships available. *Faculty research:* Individuals, families, and groups/community, policy, planning and organizations/integrated concentration/aboriginal fields of study. *Unit head:* Dr. Lesley Cooper, Dean, 519-884-1970. *Application contact:* Dale Taylor, 519-884-1970, E-mail: socialwork@wlu.ca.

Winthrop University, College of Arts and Sciences, Program in Social Work, Rock Hill, SC 29733. Offers MA. *Faculty:* 4 full-time (3 women), 2 part-time/adjunct (1 woman). *Students:* 18 full-time (17 women), 14 part-time (12 women); includes 14 minority (13 African Americans, 1 Hispanic American), 1 international. Average age 29. *Entrance requirements:* For master's, GRE or MAT, minimum GPA of 3.0. *Application deadline:* For fall admission, 7/15 priority date for domestic students; for spring admission, 12/1 for domestic students. Applications are processed on a rolling basis. Application fee: $35 ($50 for international students). Electronic applications accepted. *Expenses:* Tuition, state resident: full-time $9,148; part-time $383 per hour. Tuition, nonresident: full-time $16,864; part-time $704 per hour. *Unit head:* Dr. Ronald K. Green, Unit Head, 803-323-2646, E-mail: greenr@winthrop.edu. *Application contact:* 800-411-7041, Fax: 803-323-2292, E-mail: graduatestu@winthrop.edu.

Yeshiva University, Wurzweiler School of Social Work, New York, NY 10033-3201. Offers MSW, PhD, MSW/Certificate. *Accreditation:* CSWE (one or more programs are accredited). Part-time and evening/weekend programs available. *Faculty:* 25 full-time (14 women), 38 part-time/adjunct (26 women). *Students:* 273 full-time (182 women), 187 part-time (137 women); includes 217 minority (129 African Americans, 6 Asian Americans or Pacific Islanders, 82 Hispanic Americans). Average age 41. 444 applicants, 73% accepted, 223 enrolled. In 2006, 158 master's, 18 doctorates awarded. *Median time to degree:* Of those who began their doctoral program in fall 1998, 75% received their degree in 8 years or less. *Degree requirements:* For master's, thesis/dissertation; for doctorate, thesis/dissertation, comprehensive exam. *Entrance requirements:* For master's, interview, minimum GPA of 3.0, letters of reference; for doctorate, GRE, interview, letters of reference, writing sample, MSW, minimum 2 years professional social work experience. Additional exam requirements/recommendations for international students: Required—TOEFL (minimum score 550 paper-based; 213 computer-based). *Application deadline:* For fall admission, 5/1 priority date for domestic students; for spring admission, 10/31 for domestic students. Applications are processed on a rolling basis. Application fee: $50. *Expenses: Contact institution.* *Financial support:* In 2006–07, 381 students received support, including 2 teaching assistantships (averaging $5,000 per year); career-related internships or fieldwork, Federal Work-Study, institutionally sponsored loans, and scholarships/grants also available. Financial award application deadline: 4/15; financial award applicants required to submit FAFSA. *Faculty research:* Child abuse, AIDS, day care, nonprofits, gerontology. Total annual research expenditures: $100,000. *Unit head:* Dr. Sheldon R. Gelman, Dean, 212-960-0820, Fax: 212-960-0822, E-mail: srgelman@yu.edu. *Application contact:* Ruth Bigman, Director of Admissions, 212-960-0811, Fax: 212-960-0822, E-mail: rbigman@yu.edu.

York University, Faculty of Graduate Studies, Atkinson Faculty of Liberal and Professional Studies, Program in Social Work, Toronto, ON M3J 1P3, Canada. Offers MSW, PhD. Part-time and evening/weekend programs available. *Faculty:* 33 full-time (24 women). *Students:* 37 full-time (28 women), 69 part-time (58 women). 266 applicants, 33% accepted, 73 enrolled. In 2006, 47 degrees awarded. *Degree requirements:* For master's, thesis or alternative, registration. *Application deadline:* For fall admission, 1/9 for domestic students. Application fee: $80. Electronic applications accepted. *Financial support:* In 2006–07, 1 fellowship (averaging $4,000 per year) was awarded; research assistantships. *Unit head:* Narda Razack, Director, 416-736-5226.

ADELPHI UNIVERSITY

School of Social Work

Programs of Study

The School of Social Work at Adelphi University offers programs leading to the Master of Social Work (M.S.W.) and the Doctor of Philosophy (Ph.D.) in social work and post-master's certificate programs in bilingual school social work and human resources management.

The 64-credit M.S.W. program combines core courses in the foundations of social work with supervised field instruction to give students experience in applying social work theories to professional practice. The program fosters an abiding commitment to professional values and social justice and equips students with knowledge and skills for social work practice with a wide range of clients and diverse communities. All first-year M.S.W. students are required to take ten core courses in a set sequence. The plan of study in the first year includes eight courses plus a minimum of 600 hours of supervised field instruction. In their second year of study, students complete six required courses, two elective courses, plus 600 hours of field instruction in advanced, direct social work practice. In addition, M.S.W. students are eligible to enroll in a joint program with the School of Business leading to a certificate in human resources management that requires only 9 additional credits beyond the M.S.W. degree.

The 51-credit Ph.D. in social work program gives practitioners the skills and knowledge to effect significant change in social welfare policy and practice. The program emphasizes critical thinking and prepares students to develop knowledge for all methods of social work practice. Graduates are able to provide leadership in the profession as scholars, educators, researchers, and administrators in social agencies. Candidates can pursue doctoral study while they continue to work. Classes are offered one day a week in the late afternoon and early evening. Students must pass qualifying examinations that test mastery and integration of the first two years of study, and they must complete and successfully defend a dissertation that evidences original, independent research.

The interdisciplinary 16-credit certificate in bilingual education program is designed for M.S.W. graduates who are bilingual and who work or plan to work in a school setting that requires certification in bilingual education. The program consists of core courses that meet the bilingual certification requirements for pupil personnel service professionals mandated by the New York State Department of Education. Courses are offered jointly by the School of Social Work and the School of Education.

Research Facilities

The University's primary research holdings are at Swirbul Library and include 657,000 volumes (including bound periodicals and government publications), 805,000 microformats, 27,000 audiovisual items, 33,000 electronic journal titles, more than 135 electronic databases, and general and special-accessibility computer facilities.

Financial Aid

The School of Social Work offers various ways to help defray the cost of graduate study. These include scholarships, assistantships, agency tuition remission, and field-placement stipends. More information is available at http://socialwork.adelphi.edu/scholarships/ or from the Office of Student Financial Services at http://ecampus.adelphi.edu/sfs/.

Cost of Study

For the 2006–07 academic year, the tuition rate is $690 per credit. University fees range from $225 to $400 per semester.

Living and Housing Costs

The University assists single and married students in finding suitable accommodations whenever possible. The cost of living depends on the location and number of rooms rented.

Student Group

There are 870 students in the School of Social Work.

Location

Located in historic Garden City, New York, 45 minutes from Manhattan and 20 minutes from Queens, Adelphi's 75-acre suburban campus is known for the beauty of its landscape and architecture. The campus is a short walk from the Long Island Railroad and is convenient to New York's major airports and several major highways. Off-campus centers are located in Manhattan, Hauppauge, and Poughkeepsie.

The University and The School

Founded in 1896, Adelphi is a fully accredited, private university with 8,110 undergraduate, graduate, and returning-adult students in the arts and sciences, business, clinical psychology, education, nursing, and social work. Students come from forty-three states and from thirty-seven countries. *The Princeton Review* named Adelphi University a 2005 Best College in the Northeastern Region, and the *Fiske Guide to Colleges 2007* recognized Adelphi as a "Best Buy" in higher education. The University is the only private institution on Long Island and one of only twenty-six in the nation to earn this recognition.

For more than fifty years, the School of Social Work has trained social work practitioners who are dedicated to improving the lives of individuals, families, groups, and communities. Through its many programs, the School has been a driving force for ethical social work practice and a strong advocate for social justice. The School is committed to the development of new knowledge that can inform the evolution of social policy, the organization and delivery of social services, and the profession's ability to intervene effectively with, and on behalf of, the vulnerable, disenfranchised, and marginalized populations. The scholarship, research, and demonstration projects that the faculty members and graduate students are engaged in respond to the exigencies of contemporary life and contribute to social work's capacity to improve individuals' well-being. The School features small classes in a supportive environment that fosters a close and nurturing relationship between faculty members and students. The faculty members have extensive teaching experience and are recognized as leaders in their respective fields. The broad base of diverse students and professionals seeking advanced degrees enhances the classroom learning and enriches the educational experience for all.

Applying

Master's degree applicants should have a bachelor's degree with a strong science and liberal arts background; doctoral applicants should have an M.S.W. and at least three years' experience in the field. All applicants must submit the completed application form, the $50 application fee, official college transcripts, and three letters of recommendation. Ph.D. applicants must also submit GRE scores. An interview is required. Application deadlines are July 15 for the fall semester and December 1 for the spring semester in the M.S.W. program and May 1 for doctoral applications. For more information, students should contact the School.

Correspondence and Information

Dr. Andrew Safyer, Dean
School of Social Work
Social Work Building, Room 201
Adelphi University
Garden City, New York 11530
Phone: 516-877-4354
Fax: 516-877-4436
E-mail: asafyer@adelphi.edu
Web site: http://socialwork.adelphi.edu/

Adelphi University

THE FACULTY AND THEIR RESEARCH

Julie Cooper Altman, Assistant Professor; Ph.D., Chicago, 1999. Engagement in child welfare services, client use of agency-initiated services, worker use of knowledge, impact of welfare reform, M.S.W. child welfare training outcomes.

Beverly Araujo, Assistant Professor; Ph.D., Michigan, 2004. Impact of psychosocial stressors, such as discrimination and language barriers, on the mental health of Latino immigrants, development of culturally competent interventions for Latino communities.

Richard Belson, Associate Professor; D.S.W., Adelphi, 1977. Marriage and family therapy.

Roni Berger, Professor; Ph.D., Hebrew (Jerusalem), 1993. Immigrants and refugees, qualitative and combined research methods, remarriage and stepfamilies, law guardianship.

Ellen Bogolub, Associate Professor; Ph.D., Rutgers, 1986. Families and divorce, child welfare.

Dianne Cameron-Kelly, Assistant Professor; Ph.D., Fordham, 2002. Early childhood and family systems, civic engagement and civic duty, child and adolescent development.

Peter I. Chernack, Assistant Professor and Associate Dean; D.S.W., Adelphi, 2001. Evaluation of alternative models of field education, education for social work practice in health care, development and measurement of social work practice skills.

Carol S. Cohen, Associate Professor; D.S.W., CUNY, 1993. Social work with groups, agency-based practice, organizational and community practice.

Judy Fenster, Associate Dean; Ph.D., NYU, 2000. Substance abuse, children and families, multiculturalism.

Gertrude Schaffner Goldberg, Professor; D.S.W., Columbia, 1976. Welfare state in cross-national perspective, history of social work and social welfare, public assistance/welfare reform, program development in the social services, organizational change, public assistance, full employment.

Godfrey A. Gregg, Clinical Assistant Professor; M.S.W., Fordham, 1995. Breast cancer, end-of-life issues, sexual orientation, thanatology.

Patricia Joyce, Assistant Professor; D.S.W., CUNY, Hunter, 2001. Trauma, incest, mental illness, nonoffending mothers of sexually abused children, cultural competence and PTSD, secondary trauma and ethnicity, psychoanalytic theory, professionals' constructions of clients, social welfare rhetoric, social process of treatment planning in agency practice.

Roger Levin, Associate Professor; Ph.D., NYU, 1988. Issues In social welfare, history and philosophy of social welfare.

Suzanne Michael, Assistant Professor; Ph.D., CUNY, 1998. Migration and immigration, ethnic communities, social health indicators, health-care access, organizations, program development.

James B. Mullin, Assistant Professor and Director, B.S.W. Program; D.P.A., NYU, 1979. Principles and practice in social work.

Elizabeth Palley, Assistant Professor; Ph.D., Brandeis, 2002. Understanding the impact of federal and state laws on people with disabilities and children.

Geoffrey Ream, Assistant Professor, Ph.D., Cornell, 2005. Contextual mediators between adolescent sexuality and negative outcomes.

Ellen Rosenberg, Associate Professor; D.S.W., Columbia, 1981. Social work assessment and diagnosis.

Philip A. Rozario, Assistant Professor; Ph.D., Washington (St. Louis), 2002. The well-being of caregivers of frail older adults, meaning in later life, successful and productive aging, long-term care issues of frail older adults.

Andrew Safyer, Professor and Dean; Ph.D., Michigan. At-risk youths and their families, ego psychology, defense mechanisms, narcissistic personality disorders.

Zulema Suarez, Associate Professor; Ph.D., Chicago, 1988. Spiritual and religious coping, motherhood as a protective factor, critical consciousness and social work practice, multicultural social work practice and education, positive psychology.

Carol Sussal, Associate Professor; D.S.W., Adelphi, 1978. Social work practice with gay, lesbian, bisexual, and transgendered persons.

Bradley D. Zodikoff, Assistant Professor; Ph.D., Columbia, 2005. Gerontology, geriatric mental health services, family caregiving, social work practice in health care, social work research methods.

School of Social Work Community Partnerships

Adelphi New York Statewide Breast Cancer Hotline and Support Program: The only comprehensive, university-based, breast cancer counseling program in New York State, the program supports, educates, and empowers breast cancer patients, professionals and the community. Director: Hillary Rutter (rutter@adelphi.edu).

Adelphi Practicum Partnership Program (PPP): Funded by the John A. Hartford Foundation through the New York Academy of Medicine, the PPP prepares master's students for practice and leadership roles in gerontology and geriatric mental health. Principal Investigator: Dr. Peter Chernack (chernack@adelphi.edu).

Addictions Advisory Committee: A partnership with executives of substance-abuse treatment agencies and community leaders to enhance the quality of professional-development programming in this arena. Chair: Dr. Peter Chernack (chernack@adelphi.edu).

Building Resilient Immigrant Families: This program was developed to address the impact of immigration stressors on the mental health and the behavioral outcomes of elementary school–age Latino immigrant children through a peer-support-group model. Principal Investigator: Dr. Beverly Araujo (araujo2@adelphi.edu).

Geriatric Mental Health Needs Assessment Project: With funding from the Mental Health Association of Nassau County through a grant from the Long Island Community Foundation, this needs-assessment study helps identify specific barriers to geriatric mental health care on Long Island. Principal Investigator: Dr. Bradley Zodikoff (zodikoff@adelphi.edu); Co-Principal Investigator: Dr. Peter Chernack (chernack@adelphi.edu).

Immigrant Primary Care Project: Funded by the New York Hospital Medical Center of Queens, this project seeks to increase the ability of primary-care medical residents to competently work cross culturally with immigrant Muslim women. Co-Principal Investigator: Dr. Tricia Joyce (joyce2@adelphi.edu); Co-Principal Investigator: Dr. Suzanne Michael (michael@adelphi.edu).

Investigators to Investors: Funded by the Department of Health and Human Services, Children's Bureau, this five-year project trains M.S.W. child-welfare professionals from the New York City Administration for Children's Services (ACS). Principal Investigator: Dr. Julie Cooper Altman (altman@adelphi.edu).

Long Island Center for Excellence in Nonprofit Leadership: This University-based, community-driven leadership-development initiative responds to the immediate and long-term leadership crisis facing Long Island's nonprofit sector. Principal Investigator: Dr. Peter Chernack (chernack@adelphi.edu); Co-Principal Investigator: Dr. Andrew Safyer (asafyer@adelphi.edu).

BARRY UNIVERSITY

School of Social Work

Program of Study	Barry University School of Social Work offers the Master of Social Work (M.S.W.) and prepares students to work as clinical social workers in a variety of public and private social agencies and institutions, in private industry, or in private practice. The School's alumni are employed in a variety of settings and work with individuals, families, groups, or communities; plan, supervise, manage, and evaluate social programs; research social problems; analyze social policy; or organize communities for social change. The School teaches the skills needed to work with a range of individuals, families, groups, and communities with diverse physical, social, and psychological needs. The M.S.W. program consists of 60 credits and can be completed in four consecutive semesters (sixteen months) on a full-time basis or in 2½ years on a part-time basis. Students who possess a B.S.W. degree may be eligible to apply for advanced standing. Students enrolled in advanced standing may complete the M.S.W. program in seven months (May through December), eight months (January through August), or nine months (September through May). All social work students must complete field internships planned and monitored by the School. Full-time and part-time students complete two field internships; each internship extends over two semesters. Advanced standing students complete one field internship over two semesters. The School offers three areas of specialization: clinical practice with children and families, clinical practice in health care, and clinical practice in mental health.
Research Facilities	The Monsignor William Barry Memorial Library provides material and services in support of educational and cultural objectives of the University. Students have access in open stacks to a collection exceeding 600,000 items. This includes more than 2,000 periodical titles. The Barry Library participates in a number of library networks. The Southeast Florida Library Information Network (SEFLIN) provides, by courier service and fax, access to more than 11.4 million items and 30,000 periodical titles held by larger academic and public libraries of Dade, Broward, and Palm Beach Counties. Materials not readily available at this level are obtained through the Florida Library Information Network (FLIN), which provides for the delivery of materials based in the major libraries of the state of Florida, including those in the state university system.
Financial Aid	For the last five years, the School of Social Work has averaged awarding more than $1.5 million in scholarships, grants, and tuition discounts to its students. Students enrolled in the program on a full-time basis are eligible for Barry Scholarships. These scholarships are merit-based awards and range from $7000 to $9000 per academic year. Part-time students who are employed in social service positions receive a 30 percent tuition discount. Ninety-five percent of students in the School receive financial aid, and 90 percent receive scholarships, grants, or tuition discounts other than loans.
Cost of Study	Graduate tuition cost is $685 per credit. Fees are approximately $100 per year.
Living and Housing Costs	There is no graduate housing. Most graduate students live off-campus; many reside with roommates. Studio and one-bedroom apartments range from $500 to $750, while two-bedroom apartments can be found for $800 to $1000 per month. Private transportation is a must.
Student Group	The School of Social Work has more than 300 students enrolled in the master's program. Approximately 80 percent of the students are women, and 50 percent are students of color. The faculty of the School of Social Work looks to admit students who are committed to social work values and practice and who have excellent interpersonal and communication skills.
Location	Located in Miami Shores, Florida, Barry University is situated between the cities of Miami and Fort Lauderdale. This location gives the students the benefits of a small suburb, yet allows easy access to major metropolitan areas. Barry is located near all major Miami highways and is easily accessible by car. Often referred to as the "City of the Future," the Miami–South Florida community is one of the most culturally dynamic, ethnically diverse, and exciting communities in the United States. The School also has a part-time only program, where classes meet on Saturdays in West Palm Beach/Treasure Coast.
The University and The School	The Adrian Dominican Sisters founded Barry University in 1940. From its outset, the University committed itself to a humanitarian value base that emphasized social concern and community service. As such, Barry University is a fitting environment for a school of social work. In response to the need for social workers to assist with the social turbulence of the 1960s in south Florida, Barry established the School of Social Work in 1966. In its relatively brief history, the School has become nationally recognized as a leading educator of social work practitioners. The School was granted full accreditation by the Council on Social Work Education in 1969.
Applying	Individuals seeking admission to the M.S.W. program must have a bachelor's degree from a regionally accredited college or university. Applicants must have a broad liberal arts background that includes study in the social, behavioral, and biological sciences. Applicants must submit a completed application form, official transcripts from all colleges and universities attended, three letters of recommendation, a three-page personal statement, a criminal history disclaimer form, a core performance standard for admission, progression and graduation form, and a $30 application fee. Application deadline dates for each year are as follows: December 15 for spring semester, April 15 for summer semester, and July 15 for fall semester.
Correspondence and Information	Philip S. Mack Director of Admission School of Social Work Barry University 11300 Northeast Second Avenue Miami Shores, Florida 33161-6695 Phone: 305-899-3919 800-756-6000 Ext. 3919 (toll-free) E-mail: pmack@mail.barry.edu Web site: http://www.barry.edu/msw

Barry University

THE FACULTY

Victoria Anyikwa, Assistant Professor, Human Behavior and Practice; Ph.D., Barry.
Preeti Charania, Assistant Director, Field Education; M.S.W., Bombay.
Patricia Cook, Assistant Professor and Director, B.S.W. Program; M.S.W., Columbia.
Linda Cummings, Associate Professor, Social Welfare Policy; Ph.D., Ohio State.
Sally Dodds, Professor, Research and Practice; Ph.D., Barry.
Susan Gray, Professor, Clinical Social Work Practice; Ph.D., Barry.
Montier Haskins, Assistant Director, Field Education; M.S.W., Syracuse.
Mary Kay Houston-Vega, Associate Professor, Clinical Practice; Ph.D., USC.
Sara Lewis, Associate Professor, Research; Ph.D., Florida State.
Philip S. Mack, Associate Professor and Director of Admissions; M.S.W., Columbia.
Debra McPhee, Professor and Associate Dean, Clinical Social Work Practice; Ph.D., Toronto.
Irene Moreda, Associate Professor, Human Behavior; M.S.W., Chicago.
Gala Brown Munnings, Associate Professor and Director, Field Education; M.S.W., Barry.
Elane Nuehring, Professor and Director, Doctoral Program; Ph.D., Florida State.
Walter Pierce, Associate Professor, Social Welfare Policy; Ph.D., Barry.
Phyllis Scott, Associate Professor, Social Welfare Policy, and Director, M.S.W. Program; Ph.D., Barry.
Sharron Singleton-Bowie, Associate Professor and Associate Dean, Human Behavior; D.S.W., Howard.
Mark Smith, Assistant Professor, Practice; Ph.D., Barry.
Gerri Sprague-Damon, Assistant Professor and Director, West Palm Beach Program; M.S.W., Barry.
Maxine Thurston, Associate Professor, Research; Ph.D., Florida State.
Greg Tully, Associate Professor, Group Social Work Practice; Ph.D., NYU.
Joanne Whelley, Associate Professor, Clinical Social Work Practice; Ph.D., Fordham.

Cor Jesu Chapel on the mall.

The School seeks to admit students who are committed to social work values.

The School of Social Work at Barry University.

BOSTON COLLEGE

Graduate School of Social Work

Programs of Study

The Graduate School of Social Work at Boston College offers programs leading to the Master of Social Work (M.S.W.) and Doctor of Philosophy in social work (Ph.D.) degrees. Dual degrees with the Graduate School of Management (M.S.W./M.B.A.), the Law School (M.S.W./J.D.), and the Institute of Religious Education and Pastoral Ministry (M.S.W./M.A.) are also offered. Advanced standing may be applied for by candidates who have graduated from a B.S.W. program accredited by the Council on Social Work Education.

The M.S.W. curriculum consists of foundation requirements common to all students, with method courses and two field internships providing the focus in clinical or macro social work. With an emphasis on skill development, clinical students are prepared to work with individuals, families, and groups, and macro students are prepared to work with organizations and communities. Students also choose a concentration in children, youth, and family; older adults and families; health and mental health; global practice social work; or an individualized concentration.

Students may enroll on a full-time or a part-time basis. The traditional Full-Time Plan consists of concurrent class and field instruction for two academic years. The Part-Time Plan extends class work and fieldwork over three or four years. Foundation courses and practicum placements are also available at part-time sites in Portland, Maine, and Easton and Worcester, Massachusetts. Field placements are arranged in public and private social work agencies.

The Ph.D. program prepares scholars who are committed to pursue knowledge that will advance the field of social welfare and social work practice. Students master a substantive area and gain methodological expertise to excel as teachers and scholars in leading academic and social welfare settings throughout the world. A combined M.S.W. and Ph.D. program is available. All accepted doctoral students receive extensive financial support.

Research Facilities

The twelve libraries and centers that make up the Boston College libraries offer general and specialized collections, services, and other resources to support teaching, learning, and research at Boston College. The Thomas P. O'Neill Jr. Library is the central research library for the university. Collections include approximately 2 million volumes on a broad range of subjects reflecting the university's extensive curriculum. In addition to the print collections, Boston College libraries provide access to more than 350 online research databases, more than 34,000 online full-text journals, and a variety of digital collections.

The Social Work Library, along with the Graduate School of Social Work, is located in McGuinn Hall and houses a distinguished and comprehensive collection of 30,000 monographs, 350 serials, and 300 videos and other multimedia materials that focus on all aspects of professional social work and social work education. Two full-time social work librarians provide training, research, and technical assistance to social work students and faculty members.

Financial Aid

There is a basic two-tier approach to financial aid. All eligible students are expected to pursue university-administered financial aid in the form of Federal Stafford Student Loans, Federal Perkins Loans, and Federal Work-Study Programs. In conjunction with this, all students are eligible to apply for assistantships, scholarships, and agency grants administered by the School. The School-administered funds include VA stipends, graduate assistantships, and scholarships based on diversity and merit.

Cost of Study

Tuition in 2006–07 was $820 per credit hour. Books and fees cost $1000. Stafford Loan fees were $555.

Living and Housing Costs

The cost of living is $16,835, with approximately $1800 added for each dependent. An off-campus housing office assists students in locating individual living accommodations.

Student Group

The total enrollment for the Graduate School of Social Work in the spring of 2006 was 500 students. The student body is diverse, representing many undergraduate colleges and international universities. The School is committed to recruitment of members of ethnic and racial minority groups and other underrepresented groups. The involvement of an active alumni association has contributed significantly to the excellent employment prospects available to graduates.

Location

The College is located on the city line with Newton. There is good access by private and public transportation to the city of Boston, its surrounding suburbs, and the countryside of New England.

The College and The School

Boston College is one of the oldest Jesuit-sponsored universities in the United States. It has professional and graduate schools, doctoral programs, research institutes, community service programs, an excellent faculty, and rich resources of libraries, research equipment, computers, and other facilities.

The Graduate School of Social Work was established in 1936 and is fully accredited by the Council on Social Work Education. The Ph.D. degree program was instituted in 1979.

The educational programs focus upon the development of humanitarian values and social work skills. There is special emphasis on educating value-committed knowledgeable practitioners for work with disadvantaged and high-risk groups that have experienced social, economic, or political discrimination and deprivation.

Applying

Requirements for admission to the M.S.W. program include a baccalaureate degree from an accredited college or university, a minimum of 20 semester hours in social or behavioral sciences, scores on the TOEFL for ESL students, a grade point average indicative of ability to complete graduate study, and the personal qualifications necessary for professional practice. GRE scores are required for doctoral applicants. Early submission of all necessary application materials facilitates decision making on admissions and financial aid.

Correspondence and Information

William C. Howard, Ph.D.
Director of Admissions
Graduate School of Social Work
McGuinn Hall
Boston College
140 Commonwealth Avenue
Chestnut Hill, Massachusetts 02467
Phone: 617-552-4024
Fax: 617-552-1690
E-mail: swadmit@bc.edu
Web site: http://socialwork.bc.edu

Boston College

THE FACULTY AND THEIR RESEARCH

Sandra Bertman, Research Professor; Ph.D., Union (Ohio), 1988. End-of-life, grief, and bereavement issues; arts in health care.

Stephanie Cosner Berzin, Assistant Professor; Ph.D., Berkeley, 2006. Youth in foster care, emerging adulthood, youth and poverty.

Janet Lee Bezanson, Research Professor; M.S., Hartford, 1977. Medicare and long-term care.

Betty Blythe, Professor; Ph.D., Washington (Seattle), 1983. Practice research and children and family services.

Alberto Godenzi, Professor and Dean; Ph.D., Zurich (Switzerland), 1985. Interpersonal violence, peace and conflict, gender and society.

Demetrius S. Iatridis, Professor; Ph.D., Bryn Mawr, 1954. Policy analysis, comparative social services.

Karen K. Kayser, Professor; Ph.D., Michigan, 1988. Health psychology, social work in medical settings, intervention research, couples therapy.

Paul Kline, Adjunct Associate Professor; Ph.D., Boston College, 1990. Homelessness, community violence, and war.

Othelia Lee, Assistant Professor; Ph.D., Columbia, 2000. Spirituality, quality of life, and older adults.

Margaret Lombe, Assistant Professor; Ph.D., Washington (St. Louis), 2004. Social and economic development, asset building and civic service.

James Lubben, Louise McMahon Ahearn Professor; D.S.W., Berkeley, 1984. Social support networks, older adults and families, cross-cultural and cross-national studies of aging.

Kevin J. Mahoney, Professor; Ph.D., Wisconsin–Madison, 1978. Aging, disability, and long-term care policy issues.

Kathleen McInnis-Dittrich, Associate Professor; Ph.D., Wisconsin–Madison, 1987. Aging and psychological well-being, special concerns of older women, nontraditional approaches to mental health.

Kerry Mitchell, Lecturer; Ph.D., Boston College, 1995. Cognitive theory and practice, couples treatment, clinical practice theory integration.

Thomas O'Hare, Associate Professor; Ph.D., Rutgers, 1988. Co-occurring mental health and substance abuse problems and evidence-based social work practice.

Marcie Pitt-Catsouphes, Associate Professor; Ph.D., Boston University, 2000. Work and family issues, corporate culture, and workplace policies and programs.

Richard H. Rowland, Adjunct Associate Professor; Ph.D., Brandeis, 1970. Social welfare policy and services, social administration, gerontology, assisted living and health care.

Ce Shen, Assistant Professor; Ph.D., Boston College, 1996. Social development, children and families, research and statistics.

Susan Lee Tohn, Lecturer; M.S.W., Boston University. Solution-focused treatment, cognitive-behavioral treatment.

Robbie Tourse, Adjunct Associate Professor; Ph.D., Boston College, 1990. Multicultural practice, interprofessional collaboration, and field education policy and practice.

Thanh Van Tran, Professor; Ph.D., Texas at Austin, 1986. Cross-cultural research methodology, evidenced-based research, evaluation, mental health services research.

Nancy W. Veeder, Associate Professor; Ph.D., Brandeis, 1974; M.B.A., Boston College, 1990. Managed care and marketing for social work and human service agencies.

Thomas Walsh, Adjunct Associate Professor and Associate Dean; Ph.D., Boston College, 1995. Substance abuse, violence, treatment of offenders and incarcerated clients.

Robin Warsh, Lecturer; M.S.W., Connecticut, 1983. Family preservation, family reunification, and independent living for adolescents leaving foster care.

Leslie Wind, Assistant Professor; Ph.D., USC, 2003. Child welfare, child and family mental health, organizational processes.

Qingwen Xu, Assistant Professor; Ph.D., Denver, 2002. Comparative social policy, welfare reform, immigrants and refugees, legal issues.

CASE WESTERN RESERVE UNIVERSITY

Mandel School of Applied Social Sciences

Programs of Study	Ranked among the top graduate schools of social work in the country, the Mandel School of Applied Social Sciences at Case Western Reserve University (Case) offers a course of study leading to the Master of Science in Social Administration degree (M.S.S.A.), an advanced program for a Doctor of Philosophy in social welfare (Ph.D.), and several joint degree programs: the Master of Science in Social Administration/Doctor of Jurisprudence (M.S.S.A./J.D.), Master of Science in Social Administration/ Master of Business Administration (M.S.S.A./M.B.A.), Master of Science in Social Administration/Master of Nonprofit Organizations (M.S.S.A./M.N.O.), and Master of Science in Social Administration/Master of Arts in social work/bioethics (M.S.S.A./M.A.).

Master's degree students pursue degrees through a variety of study options, including a traditional two-year course of full-time study, a specialized intensive weekend program for employed professionals, a 3+2 program for undergraduate students of superior ability from approved schools, and twelve-month and eighteen-month advanced standing programs. Ph.D. students pursue their degrees through a full-time or summer-study option program.

Master's degree students pursue their course of study in one of two concentrations, Direct Practice or Community and Social Development. In the Direct Practice concentration, students can choose among the following specializations: children, youth, and families; alcohol and other drug abuse; aging; health; or mental health. The Community and Social Development concentration focuses on the social, economic, political, and physical lives of people in their communities and prepares students to intervene in all of these spheres.

Research Facilities
The Mandel School faculty conducts research in a number of cutting-edge areas as independent researchers and as part of multidisciplinary academic centers. Among issues and populations being investigated at the Mandel School are urban poverty, community development, family care giving, substance abuse, mental illness, mental health services for adolescents, and child welfare. In addition to the numerous research centers, the Mandel School supports its own top-flight on-site library. One of only a few professional social work libraries administered by a school of social work, it is available for use by students, staff and faculty members, alumni, and others in the social work community.

Financial Aid
Case's Mandel School of Applied Social Sciences sets itself apart from most graduate schools of social work in that all full-time master's students receive paid field placements. Additional financial aid is granted on the basis of financial need and promise for the field of social work. Scholarship, grant-in-aid, and college work-study funds are available from the University, the Mandel School Alumni Association, the Louis Stokes Fellowship in Community Development, private groups, individuals, agencies in the community, and federal aid programs. Currently, more than 96 percent of the master's students receive financial assistance. To apply for aid, students must submit the graduate FAFSA and the Case financial aid form.

Cost of Study
For the 2007–08 academic year, full-time tuition is $29,800 for one year for master's students.

Living and Housing Costs
For the 2007–08 academic year, full-time students at the Mandel School of Applied Social Sciences need approximately $46,521 for tuition and living expenses.

Student Group
The University enrolls more than 9,900 students. Approximately 6,200 students are seeking graduate or professional degrees. Although many students are from Ohio, most of the fifty states are represented. Nearly 1,000 international students representing more than ninety-seven different countries provide a contemporary international perspective. On average, 500 students are enrolled at the Mandel School.

Location
Case Western Reserve University is located in University Circle, a 500-acre parklike concentration of educational, scientific, medical, artistic, musical, and cultural institutions on the eastern edge of the city of Cleveland.

The University
Case Western Reserve University is one of the nation's leading independent research universities, with programs that encompass the arts and sciences, engineering, the health sciences, law, management, and social work.

Although its origins date to 1826, the University in its present form is the result of the 1967 merger of Case Institute of Technology and Western Reserve University. The two institutions had shared adjacent campuses since the late nineteenth century and were involved in cooperative efforts for many years. Western Reserve College was founded in 1826 in Hudson, Ohio, a town 26 miles southeast of Cleveland.

Applying
Applications to the master's program must be submitted by June 30, with a $30 nonrefundable application fee. Material considered with application forms includes personal statements submitted by the applicant, reference letters, official transcripts from each college attended, and evidence of superior personal qualifications. A minimum 2.7 GPA is required; a Miller Analogies Test (MAT) score or Graduate Record Exam (GRE) score is required for a grade point average below 2.7.

To be admitted to the Ph.D. program, a candidate should have a master's degree from an accredited school of social work or a master's degree in a related field and should demonstrate a superior record in undergraduate and graduate studies. Application to the Ph.D. program is considered from those with master's degrees in allied fields, with the recognition that their program includes equivalency requirements related to knowledge of social welfare. Scores from the GRE are required for application to the Ph.D. program. Prospective students should see the doctoral program Web site for more details.

Correspondence and Information
Office of Admissions
Mandel School of Applied Social Sciences
Case Western Reserve University
10900 Euclid Avenue
Cleveland, Ohio 44106-7164
Phone: 216-368-2280
     800-863-6772 (toll-free)
Fax: 216-368-5065
E-mail: msassadmit@case.edu
Web site: http://msass.case.edu

Case Western Reserve University

THE FACULTY AND THEIR RESEARCH

Katheryn B. Adams, Ph.D., Maryland. Depression in older adults, theories of aging, persons with early-stage Alzheimer's disease and their caregivers, mental health treatment methods, intervention research.

Sarah Andrews, M.S.S.A., Case Western Reserve. Family development, death, loss and bereavement, women's issues, spirituality and social work practice.

David E. Biegel, Ph.D., Maryland. Mental health, co-occurring substance use and mental disorders, informal support systems, aging, caregiving.

Pranab Chatterjee, Ph.D., Chicago. Organizational behavior/small-group behavior, comparative social welfare systems, technology transfer.

Mark Chupp, Ph.D., Case Western Reserve. Intergroup dialogue and conflict transformation, citizen participation, community building, community organizing and appreciative inquiry.

Claudia J. Coulton, Ph.D., Case Western Reserve. Research and statistics, poverty, neighborhoods, urban affairs.

David Crampton, Ph.D., Michigan. Research/teaching in child welfare.

Kathleen J. Farkas, Ph.D., Case Western Reserve. Alcohol and other drug abuse treatment, co-occurring disorders, criminal justice and reentry, women's issues.

Robert L. Fischer, Ph.D., Vanderbilt. Program evaluation, social/behavioral intervention research, child and family interventions, nonprofit programming, policy studies.

Jerry E. Floersch, Ph.D., Chicago. Adult severe mental illness, recovery, medication management, qualitative research methods, case management.

Grover C. Gilmore, Ph.D., Johns Hopkins. Visual perception and aging, Alzheimer's disease, intelligence.

Wallace J. Gingerich, Ph.D., Washington (St. Louis). Practice evaluation, family therapy, computer applications, assessing educational outcomes.

Victor Groza, Ph.D., Oklahoma. Child welfare, international child welfare, adoptions from the public system and other countries, adoptive family.

Merl C. Hokenstad Jr., Ph.D., Brandeis. International social welfare, social work education, health and social services policy and programs for older people.

Deborah Regenbogen Jacobson, Ph.D., Tulane. Practice evaluation, social work methods, women's health issues, international study-abroad programs.

Mark L. Joseph, Ph.D., Chicago. Community development, urban poverty, mixed-income development, comprehensive community initiatives.

Lenore A. Kola, Ph.D., Boston University. Alcohol and other drug abuse, employee assistance programs.

Jeffrey L. Longhofer, Ph.D., Kansas. Adolescent and adult mental health, culture and emotion, qualitative methods of clinical research.

Gerald Mahoney, Ph.D., Vanderbilt. Early childhood mental health, early intervention, parent education, disabilities.

Oren Meyers, Ph.D., Fordham, Pediatric bipolar disorder, adult attention deficit disorder, pain management, mild cognitive impairment, early dementia.

David Miller, Ph.D., Pittsburgh. African American fatherhood, violence as public health problem, child maltreatment, adolescent resiliency factors, treatment of individuals exposed to violence.

Dorothy Miller, D.S.W., Columbia. Women's economic well-being, equality, public policy.

Sharon E. Milligan, Ph.D., Pittsburgh. Evaluation of community-based initiatives, urban poverty, health and mental health service use among African Americans.

Michelle R. Munson, Ph.D., Washington (St. Louis). Adolescent and emerging-adult mental health services, older foster-care youth, supportive relationships.

G. Regina Nixon, Ph.D., Howard. Poverty/high-risk populations, cultural diversity.

Mark I. Singer, Ph.D., Case Western Reserve. Adolescent mental health, adolescent substance abuse, youth-related violence.

Louis Stokes, J.D., Cleveland State. Public policy, government, social change.

Gerald Strom, M.S.W., Howard. Child abuse, growth and development, sexual abuse investigation and treatment, clinical practice.

Aloen Townsend, Ph.D., Michigan. Adult development and aging, research methods and statistics, mental health, families and formal service systems.

Elizabeth M. Tracy, Ph.D., Washington (Seattle). Co-occurring disorders, school social work, social networks and social support.

Kathleen Wells, Ph.D., Colorado. Research methods, child mental health, child welfare.

Zoe Breen Wood, M.S.W., Virginia Commonwealth. Child welfare policy and practice, social work methods, adoption, social policy and advocacy, field education.

Eric A. Youngstrom, Ph.D., Delaware. Child psychology pathology, bipolar disorders in children and adolescents, evidence-based approaches to assessment, emotions and developmental, psychopathology.

RESEARCH ACTIVITIES

Faculty and staff members conduct cutting-edge research related to social work practice, social problems, and social policy, including interdisciplinary research and collaborative projects with the community. Students are involved in all aspects of the research process, and there is an emphasis on application of research findings to the pressing challenges in the field. Faculty members conduct their research both independently as faculty research projects or through several Mandel School research centers.

Center for Evidence-Based Practices. The Center for Evidence-Based Practices (EBPs) is a technical-assistance organization that promotes knowledge development and the implementation of EBPs for the treatment and recovery of people with severe mental illness and co-occurring severe mental and substance use disorders. The center also implements and studies emerging best practices in an effort to identify innovations that consistently generate improved outcomes and, thus, may become an EBP. The center functions as an umbrella entity for two technical-assistance organizations that disseminate two different, yet related, EBPs—Ohio SAMI CCOE and Ohio SE CCOE.

Ohio SAMI CCOE. The Ohio Substance Abuse and Mental Illness Coordinating Center of Excellence (Ohio SAMI CCOE) disseminates the Integrated Dual Disorder Treatment (IDDT) model, which helps people with co-occurring severe mental illness and substance use disorders reduce and eventually eliminate their substance use and manage symptoms of both disorders simultaneously.

Ohio SE CCOE. The Ohio Supported Employment Coordinating Center of Excellence (SE CCOE) disseminates the evidence-based Supported Employment (SE) model, which helps people with severe mental illness find competitive jobs in their communities with rapid job-search and placement services, as well as time-unlimited individualized follow-along services.

Center on Urban Poverty and Community Development. The focus of the center, which merges two important research centers, is on community-based approaches to addressing the problems of persistent and concentrated urban poverty. Based in Cleveland, the center views the city as both a tool for building communities and producing change locally and as a representative urban center from which nationally relevant research and policy implications can be drawn. The center works closely with policy makers and advocacy organizations to bring its research into the public-policy discussion. The center works with organizations at all levels to raise community capacity, improve service delivery, and analyze community needs and assets. The center maintains a publicly available, Web-based data system (NEO CANDO) to bring neighborhood information, such as census figures, crime statistics, property information, and other demographic details, to the people of Northeast Ohio.

Center on Substance Abuse and Mental Illness. The Center on Substance Abuse and Mental Illness, funded by the National Institute on Drug Abuse, provides education, research, training, and consultation in the fields of substance abuse and mental health, with particular emphasis on the coexistence of substance and mental disorders.

Center on Intervention Children and Families. CICF is a research and training center focused on developing and disseminating evidence-based interdisciplinary treatment models that promote the development and social emotional well-being of young children by enhancing family and social/environmental supports. These include interventions designed to improve parenting/caregiving skills, promote the stability of families, and enhance the social and community supports of families.

Dr. Semi J. and Ruth W. Begun Center for Violence Prevention Research and Education. The Begun Center is a comprehensive multidisciplinary collaboration focused on violence prevention research, development of community-based violence prevention programs, program evaluation, and violence prevention education in the form of conferences, workshops, lectures, and publications. The Begun Center offers services such as training and technical assistance on strategic planning and management indicators that improve community-based violence intervention and prevention initiatives.

Mandel Center for Nonprofit Organizations. This interdisciplinary center was established in 1984 as one of the first university-based programs in the country focused on the education of nonprofit leaders and managers. The center offers a Master of Nonprofit Organization degree (M.N.O.) and a certificate in nonprofit management (CNM) and conducts research on the nonprofit sector.

Grace Brody Institute for Parent-Child Studies. The institute seeks to stimulate, support, and disseminate research that pertains to parent-child relationships in all natural birth, adoptive, and foster care families, including single-parent households, regardless of the age or sexual orientation of the parent(s).

THE CATHOLIC UNIVERSITY OF AMERICA

The National Catholic School of Social Service

Programs of Study

The National Catholic School of Social Service (NCSSS) embraces as its special responsibility the education of social workers who promote the dignity of all people as bio-psycho-social-spiritual beings and who serve the local, national, and international community. As such, graduate study at NCSSS offers several unique features. These include (1) at the M.S.W. level, an enriched curriculum that allows for a clinical, macro, or a combined focus following a broad foundation year; (2) also at the M.S.W. level, a systematic integration of both classroom and field experiences guided by NCSSS faculty; (3) a community of learners in which professors make a strong, personal commitment to each student's professional learning; (4) its location in Washington, D.C., with established alliances for policy, clinical, and research opportunities; (5) an opportunity for interdisciplinary study through the Consortium of Universities in the Washington, D.C., metro area; and (6) a proud heritage of service, diversity, and dynamic academic dialogue guided by the School's social justice commitment; by the values and ethics set forth in the Judeo-Christian tradition; by the NASW professional code of ethics; and by the curriculum standards of the Council for Social Work Education.

NCSSS offers courses of study leading to a Master of Social Work (M.S.W.) degree and a doctoral degree (Ph.D.). The M.S.W. degree is a 60-credit program, fully accredited by CSWE. Three specializations are offered, following a broad foundation year of study: clinical work, macro (policy, planning, and administration), and a combined focus (micro and macro). Both the clinical and combined specializations meet the requirements for clinical licensing exams. NCSSS offers approximately 300 field placement opportunities, providing a very selective level of field instructors, and NCSSS has long-standing relationships with both Washington, D.C., policy and clinical communities. Both full-time and planned part-time courses of study are offered, as is a dual-degree M.S.W./J.D. program with the University's Columbus School of Law. NCSSS has also established the International Center on Global Aging, the National Research Center for Child and Family Services, the Center for International Social Development, the Center for Spirituality and Integral Social Work, the Center for Health and Mental Health, and the Center for Community Development and Social Justice. Electives allow students to individualize their study programs according to professional goals.

The doctoral program, the third-oldest in the country, prepares graduates to be leaders in the field and to work in such settings as universities, federal and local government agencies, associations, think-tanks, nonprofit organizations, health settings, and service agencies. The program's hallmark is the individual attention and professional collegiality offered to each student. The course work is both rigorous and dynamic; it is directed at theory, knowledge building, and research, with focuses on policy, administration, or clinical social work. There is also an option for an individualized educational program.

Research Facilities

The Catholic University libraries contain well over 1 million volumes. Students have access to electronic databases and thousands of electronic journals. In addition, students can travel to many libraries in the Washington, D.C., area, including the Library of Congress and the National Library of Medicine. Students also have access to the libraries in the Consortium of Universities in the Washington metropolitan area. These libraries have a wireless network.

Financial Aid

The University awards a limited number of graduate scholarships to master's and doctoral students on a competitive basis each year; interested applicants must submit their application portfolios and GRE scores by February 1. Departmental scholarships are awarded to qualified doctoral students.

In addition, NCSSS awards several grants to full-time M.S.W. students. Some of these grants require meeting certain requirements set forth by the donors. Financial need is a major consideration in awarding NCSSS grants. All eligible students are expected to pursue University-administered loans. Federal work-study funding may also be awarded for work completed in the field internship.

Cost of Study

Tuition in 2006–07 was $17,800 per academic year for full-time students and $670 per credit hour for part-time students.

Living and Housing Costs

The cost of living is comparable to that of other large East Coast cities. On-campus housing is available for single graduate students. Most students live in adjacent off-campus areas. Additional information about on- and off-campus housing may be obtained from the Office of Resident Life, 106 St. Bonaventure, The Catholic University of America, Washington, D.C. 20064, and the Office of Off-Campus Housing, University Center East, The Catholic University of America, Washington, D.C. 20064.

Student Group

Approximately 6,130 students, 3,077 of whom are graduate students, are enrolled at the University. Of these, about 290 are enrolled at NCSSS. Coming from all over the United States and several other countries, students bring with them diverse work and volunteer experiences as well as varied cultural, religious, ethnic, and age backgrounds.

Location

Catholic University of America's 144-acre, tree-lined campus in the northeast quadrant of Washington, D.C., provides a picturesque setting for study and reflection, just a few miles away from the nation's capital. Campus activities include a wide range of concerts, theater productions, lecture programs, and film series. Cultural, artistic, and scholarly resources of the Washington, D.C., area, within easy subway access of the campus, include the Smithsonian Institution, Capitol Hill, the John F. Kennedy Center for the Performing Arts, the National Institutes of Health, and the Library of Congress.

The University and The School

Established as a graduate institution in 1889, Catholic University has evolved into a modern university committed to graduate, undergraduate, and professional education and to the cultivation of the arts. A community of scholars, the University is dedicated to scholarship and research as well as service to the larger community. CUA is a tier II research university.

Applying

Applications for full-time study are accepted for fall term only. Applications for part-time study are accepted for both the fall and spring terms. The application deadline for spring term is December 1. Early submission of applications is encouraged, especially for those seeking scholarships or grants.

Correspondence and Information

Office of Admissions
National Catholic School of Social Service
Cardinal Station
The Catholic University of America
Washington, D.C. 20064
Phone: 202-319-5496
Fax: 202-319-5093
Web site: http://ncsss.cua.edu

The Catholic University of America

THE FACULTY AND THEIR RESEARCH

Frederick L. Ahearn Jr., Professor and Editor, *Social Thought;* D.S.W., Columbia. Refugees, disasters and disaster victims, planning social services, community organization, international social work.

C. Susanne Bennett, Assistant Professor; Ph.D., Smith. Contemporary psychodynamic theory and attachment research applied to clinical practice, pedagogy, and research on nontraditional and multicultural family structures.

Wendy Whiting Blome, Associate Professor; D.S.W., Catholic University. Child welfare policy and practice in public and private sectors, use of research in organizational and practice decision making, organizational development, administration and management.

Karlynn BrintzenhofeSzoc, Assistant Professor; D.S.W., Catholic University. Oncology social work research, statistics, grief and loss.

Sr. Ann Patrick Conrad, Associate Professor; D.S.W., Catholic University. Social justice, religion and social work, organizational research, object relations theory, social work supervision, social work ethics.

Laura Daughtery, Assistant Professor; Ph.D., Catholic University. Child welfare, foster care, African American dependent children.

Linda Plitt Donaldson, Assistant Professor; Ph.D., Catholic University. Policy advocacy, community organizing, community development, grassroots leadership, homelessness.

Barbara Early, Associate Professor and Co-Chair, Ph.D. Program; D.S.W., Catholic University. Children and families, clinical supervision, family preservation.

Cathleen Gray, Associate Professor; Ph.D., Maryland. Conflict resolution, divorce mediation, meditation and spiritual approaches to social work.

Sr. M. Vincentia Joseph, Professor Emerita; D.S.W., Catholic University. Supervision and consultation, role coping, social work ethics, religion and spirituality in social work practice, organizational burnout, social work education.

David W. M. Kerrigan, Clinical Associate and Assistant Director, Center for Spirituality and Integral Social Work; Ph.D., Catholic University. Spirituality and religion, transpersonal and integral theory, attachment theory, hardiness and resilience, the helping relationship, child and family practice, foster care and adoption, giftedness.

Lynn Milgram Mayer, Assistant Professor and Chair, Baccalaureate Program; Ph.D., Catholic University. Clinical social work with children and families at risk; children with disabilities; infants and toddlers, with an emphasis on research pertaining to early intervention and child development services.

Marie Raber, Assistant Professor, Assistant Dean, and Chair, M.S.W. Program; D.S.W., Fordham. Occupational social work; consultant work in employee assistant programs, career management, and human resources development with organizations; influence of workplace issues on the individual and the family.

Christine Anlauf Sabatino, Associate Professor; D.S.W., Catholic University. Clinical social work practice; public and private school social work practice and research, particularly in areas of early intervention and special education programs; child treatment.

Joseph Shields, Associate Professor; Ph.D., Catholic University. Substance abuse prevention, organizational planning, religion in society.

Elizabeth D. Smith, Associate Professor, Co-Chair of the Ph.D. Program, and Director of the Center for Spirituality and Integral Social Work; D.S.W., Catholic University. Transpersonal and spiritual dimensions of social work with the terminally ill, enhancement of clinical practice through research methods.

Barbara Soniat, Associate Professor; Ph.D., Maryland, Baltimore. Community practice with older adults, minority aging, geriatric mental health, health disparities, interdisciplinary geriatric education.

Elizabeth Timberlake, Professor Emerita; D.S.W., Catholic University. Clinical social work with children, homeless women and children, school social work, children's coping and adaptation with handicapping conditions, mental health, clinical practice research issues.

Mary Jeanne Verdieck, Associate Professor and Associate Dean; Ph.D., Catholic University. Research methodology, child welfare.

James Robert Zabora, Associate Professor, Dean, and Editor, *Journal of Psychosocial Oncology;* Sc.D., Johns Hopkins. Cancer, clinical services in medical settings, palliative and end-of-life care.

Michaela L. Z. Farber, Assistant Professor; D.S.W., Catholic University. Psychosocial issues of early childhood development, partnering, disabilities, and adaptation to trauma.

The International Center on Global Aging

The International Center on Global Aging was established in 1996 to improve the lives of older people throughout the world by advancing the international understanding of the strengths and needs of older people and of policies and programs to serve them. The Center provides opportunities for the direct personal exchange of ideas and information; supports comparative studies of aging policies and programs from social, political, economic, and cultural perspectives among countries; and supports international visitors who come to the United States to study aging, conduct seminars on aging issues, and provide training on aging. The Center currently offers a certificate program.

The National Research Center for Child and Family Services

The mission of the National Research Center for Child and Family Services is to facilitate multidisciplinary exploration of the trends, issues, values, and challenges associated with delivering socially just and culturally competent social work and other services to children and their families. The Center seeks to improve the quality of life, safety, and well-being of children and their families within their own communities through needs assessments and program evaluations.

The Center for International Social Development

The mission of the Center for International Social Development is to promote international development in the interest of peace and justice, with respect for the totality of the human person, through a collaborative, cross-disciplinary program in education, research, and service.

The Center for Spirituality and Integral Social Work

The Center for Spirituality and Integral Social Work (CSISW) is conceived as providing integrated state-of-the-art social work research, training, and service from a bio-psycho-social-spiritual perspective, with a particular emphasis on spirituality, guided by integral theory. As primarily a research center in purpose, the CSISW is committed to performing rigorous research on spiritual practices, needs, assessment, and interventions to serve social work clients and systems. Secondarily, the CSISW provides training and education for social work and other helping professionals at the student and practitioner level, along with spiritually sensitive integral social work services to clients and systems.

The Center for Health and Mental Health

The overall mission of the Center for Health and Mental Health is to develop and conduct research studies that focus on promoting the physical and mental health of individuals, organizations, and society by generating and disseminating knowledge that informs social work practice, enhances the delivery of social services, and influences state and national policy. Currently, the members have focused their research on issues of social oncology, substance abuse, and foster care.

The Center for Community Development and Social Justice

The Center for Community Development and Social Justice is the home within the National Catholic School of Social Service for faculty members throughout The Catholic University of America with shared interests in cooperative, participatory partnerships with communities to build on their strengths and promote individual and community well-being and contribute to social justice. The primary focus of the Center is research, but other activities are supported as well.

COLUMBIA UNIVERSITY

School of Social Work

Programs of Study

Columbia's School of Social Work offers Master of Science and doctoral degrees in social work. Master's students may select from a variety of degree programs, all of which require a combination of classroom instruction and field education. They include the two-year full-time program, advanced standing (for B.S.W. graduates), a reduced residency program (for students who are employed in social service agencies), an extended program (a combination of part- and full-time study over a period of three to four years), and a transfer program (for advanced students transferring from a full-time accredited M.S.W. program). The doctoral program has contributed a disproportionate share of leaders in social work education, with its graduates in an unprecedented thirty-nine deanships in schools of social work all over the world.

Columbia social work students are drawn by the School's diversity and depth—in curriculum, dual-degree opportunities, field education clients and agencies, faculty expertise and practice approach, and student background.

Students in their second year choose to concentrate in one of four social work practice methods—advanced clinical social work practice, advanced generalist practice and programming (AGPP), social enterprise administration, and policy practice—and select among seven fields of practice: aging; contemporary social issues; family, youth, and children's services; health, mental health, and disabilities; international social welfare and services to immigrants and refugees; school-based and school-linked services; and world of work.

Fieldwork is the central component in each student's professional education. An extensive network of more than 400 public and private agencies and organizations includes such training settings as medical and psychiatric hospitals, mental-health clinics, family agencies, facilities for the aging, community programs, courts, unions, employee assistance programs, corporations, schools, and planning and coordinating councils.

A broad selection of dual-degree programs and minors attracts students who seek to combine social work with other professional studies. Dual-degree programs are optional and offered in business, divinity, international affairs, Jewish communal service, law, public health, public policy and administration, special education, and urban planning. Students may minor in business, international social welfare, law, and public policy and administration.

Research Facilities

Columbia's social work faculty has been identified repeatedly as the most influential and productive social work research group in the country; students often assist with their ground-breaking studies. They are supported in their efforts by the School's Whitney M. Young, Jr. Memorial Library. With more than 75,000 bound volumes and an estimated 20,000 pieces of unbound material, it houses one of the most outstanding collections in the field. Students also have access to the many other collections in the field and in the University library system. Cutting-edge technology is available in every classroom—each student has some experience in processing and analyzing data, and computer-based research electives and pilot courses help students understand how computers assist social workers in assessment and treatment processes.

Financial Aid

The School provides a comprehensive program of financial aid—in 2006–07, about 85 percent of social work students receive some form of aid. The School awards general scholarships and work-study. Eligibility for funds is based on an applicant's demonstrated financial need, as determined by the School of Social Work. Financial need is based on the total amount of student tuition and living expenses minus the expected student contribution. Social work students finance their education with funds from various sources, including, but not limited to, federal and state loan programs, Federal Stafford Student Loans, Federal Stafford Unsubsidized Loans, Federal Perkins Loans, Columbia University student loans, school scholarships, Federal Work-Study Program funds, and the New York State Tuition Assistance Program (TAP). Further information regarding financial aid opportunities may be obtained by visiting the Columbia University School of Social Work Web site at http://www.columbia.edu/cu/ssw/finaid.

Cost of Study

For 2007–08, the cost per credit is $970. At 30 credits per year, which is the average for full-time matriculation, tuition is $29,100. Miscellaneous fees are estimated at $2994.

Living and Housing Costs

The cost of living (including housing, books, food, and miscellaneous expenses) for the 2007–08 academic year is estimated at $17,434. Limited University housing is available to full-time social work students.

Student Group

The School is notable for its diversity—90 percent of the students are women. Asian-American, African-American, and Latino students constitute 35 percent of the class; international students make up 10 percent.

Student Outcomes

More than half of Columbia's 16,000 social work graduates are in the greater New York area, giving students access to an extensive local professional network. A recent survey revealed that each grad received an average of two employment offers, and the vast majority had jobs within a few months of graduation; several had received offers prior to graduation. Thirty-five percent of graduates practice in mental health; youth and child welfare services occupy 19 percent, 25 percent choose family services, and 11 percent select medical social work.

Location

New York is arguably the preeminent social work laboratory in the world, where students are involved for 21 hours a week in real-life, on-the-ground social work services. The cultural and social advantages of the city are also hard to beat. The School's Morningside Heights neighborhood offers bookstores, outdoor cafés, ethnic restaurants, music clubs, open-air fruit markets, and other amenities that appeal to a university audience. Tree-filled Morningside Park, Riverside Park, and Central Park are all only a few blocks from the campus.

The University and The School

The Columbia University School of Social Work is the oldest school of social work in the country. It opened in 1898 under the auspices of the Charity Organization Society (now the Community Service Society); tuition was $10. During its first century, the School, its faculty members, and its graduates have played key roles in almost every major development—from establishing the field instruction requirement for social work to helping to write and implement the Social Security Act and from pioneering psychiatric social work to originating the environmental/ecological approach to social work.

As part of New York City's only Ivy League university, the School and its students benefit daily from the resources of Columbia University, with sixteen faculties, sixty-nine departments, 70 Nobel Prize winners, hundreds of academic centers, and more than 20,000 students.

Applying

Applicants for admission into the Columbia M.S. degree program must have a bachelor's degree in arts, letters, philosophy, or science from an accredited college or university. The application consists of a personal statement, all official transcripts, and three letters of reference. GRE scores are not required but are admissible. Applicants for the two-year and advanced-standing programs should submit the necessary materials by January 15, particularly if they seek financial aid or housing assistance. Applicants for the sixteen-month program should submit the necessary materials on or before November 1. In some cases, the Office of Admissions may request an interview.

Dual-degree applicants must apply to each school separately and meet the admission requirements of both schools.

Correspondence and Information

Office of Admissions
School of Social Work
Columbia University
1255 Amsterdam Avenue
New York, New York 10027

Fax: 212-854-2305
E-mail: cussw-admit@columbia.edu
Web site: http://www.socialwork.columbia.edu

Columbia University

FULL-TIME FACULTY

Sheila H. Akabas, Professor of Social Work and Director, Center for Social Policy and Practice in the Workplace; Ph.D., NYU. Labor and social policy, equal employment opportunities, employee assistance programs, substance abuse.

Michelle S. Ballan, Assistant Professor of Social Work; Ph.D., Texas at Austin. Developmental disabilities, sexual counseling for vulnerable populations, sexual offenders, evaluation of clinical interventions.

Barbara Berkman, Professor of Social Work; D.S.W., Columbia. Gerontology, oncology, health, mental health.

Denise Burnette, Professor of Social Work; Ph.D., Berkeley. Social gerontology, grandparents raising grandchildren, aging and quality of life, qualitative and quantitative research methods.

Marcia Carlson, Associate Professor of Social Work and Sociology; Ph.D., Michigan. Family structure and parenting, child and adolescent well being, social policy, poverty and inequality, father involvement.

Fang-Pei Chen, Assistant Professor of Social Work; Ph.D., Wisconsin-Madison. Issues at the interface between the family and the mental health, social work generalist practice in mental health, family caregiving, qualitative research methods.

Grace Christ, Associate Professor of Social Work; D.S.W., Columbia. Psychosocial oncology, hospital social work, AIDS caregivers.

Nabila El-Bassel, Professor of Social Work; D.S.W., Columbia. Alcoholism, substance abuse, AIDS, international social work.

Ronald A. Feldman, Professor of Social Work; Ph.D., Michigan. Adolescent mental health.

Irwin Garfinkel, Professor of Social Work; Ph.D., Michigan. Social policy, child support.

Robin Gearing, Assistant Professor of Social Work; Ph.D., Toronto. Child and adolescent mental health, serious and persistent mental illness, mental health and the family, social work practice with children and families.

Vincent Guilamo-Ramos, Associate Professor of Social Work; Ph.D., SUNY at Albany. Latino families, gay and adolescent youth, psychosocial aspects of HIV/AIDS.

Wen-Jui Han, Associate Professor of Social Work; Ph.D., Columbia. Social welfare policy, with an emphasis on children and families; effects of maternal employment and child care; child-care issues facing immigrant families.

Andre Ivanoff, Associate Professor of Social Work; Ph.D., Washington (Seattle). Suicidal behavior, homeless women.

Sheila B. Kamerman, Professor of Social Work and Co-Director, Cross-National Studies Research Program; D.S.W., Columbia. Income support policies for families with young children, social services, the welfare state.

Neeraj Kaushal, Assistant Professor of Social Work; Ph.D., CUNY Graduate Center. Immigration, welfare reform, social inequality, health insurance, globalization and international social welfare.

Vicki Lens, Assistant Professor of Social Work; J.D., New York Law; Ph.D., Yeshiva. Welfare reform and administrative justice, impact of the judiciary on social policy, advocacy, community organizing and social change.

Dana Lizardi, Assistant Professor of Social Work; Ph.D., Fordham. Suicide attempt, protective factors, Hispanics and mental health, race ethnicity and culture in mental health research, ataques de nervios.

Ellen Lukens, Associate Professor of Social Work; Ph.D., Columbia. Families, mental health, siblings and chronic illness, supervision, clinical services research, qualitative and quantitative methods.

Michael MacKenzie, Assistant Professor of Social Work; Ph.D., Michigan. Dynamic processes in human development over the lifespan; social, familial, and biological transactions in developmental psychopathology; child maltreatment prediction and prevention in early childhood.

James M. Mandiberg, Assistant Professor of Social Work; Ph.D., Michigan. Innovation and its diffusion, including transnationally, social entrepreneurship, and social enterprise; social movements in human services; organizational strategy; organizational theory.

Brenda G. McGowan, Professor of Social Work; D.S.W., Columbia. Child welfare, case advocacy, children's rights.

Ronald B. Mincy, Professor of Social Work; Ph.D., MIT. First occupant of the Maurice V. Russell Professorship in Social Policy and Social Work Practice. Workplace development and welfare, strengthening fragile families.

Ada Chan Yuk-Sim Mui, Associate Professor of Social Work; Ph.D., Washington (St. Louis). Older volunteers, the effectiveness of hospital discharge plans for elderly patients, racial differences in family caregiving.

Edward J. Mullen, Professor of Social Work and Director, Center for the Study of Social Work Practice; D.S.W., Columbia. Expanding research-based knowledge about social work practice.

Rogerio M. Pinto, Assistant Professor of Social Work; Ph.D., Columbia. Clinical practice with immigrants and racial and ethnic minorities, HIV prevention practice and research, research on health-related social interventions.

Mark S. Preston, Assistant Professor of Social Work; Ph.D., SUNY at Albany. Child welfare, human services management and public management, management training, organizational behavior and organizational theory, research methods.

Marion Reidel, Associate Professor of Professional Practice; Ph.D., Columbia. AIDS-affected families, addiction, adolescence.

Victoria M. Rizzo, Assistant Professor of Social Work; Ph.D., SUNY at Albany. Efficacy and cost-effectiveness of social work interventions in health care and aging, impact of parental serious illness on children, palliative care.

Steven Schinke, Professor of Social Work and Director, AIDS Prevention Research Center; Ph.D., Wisconsin. Clinical interventions to prevent social, behavioral, and health problems among early adolescents.

Craig S. Schwalbe, Assistant Professor of Social Work; Ph.D., North Carolina at Chapel Hill. Evidence-based practice, juvenile justice policy and practice, risk assessment and structured decision making, delinquency prevention.

Katherine Shear, Professor of Social Work; Ph.D. Psychotherapy research, anxiety disorder, bereavement and grief, women's mental health.

Barbara Levy Simon, Associate Professor of Social Work; Ph.D., Bryn Mawr. Organizational culture and behavior, social welfare history and policy, feminization of poverty.

Mary E. Sormanti, Associate Professor of Professional Practice; Ph.D., Boston College. Practice, pediatric oncology, health care, families and bereavement.

Fred Ssewamala, Assistant Professor of Professional Practice; Ph.D., Washington (St. Louis). International social and economic development, comparative social welfare policy, antipoverty policies, gender and development, civil society, civic participation, social networks.

Julien O. Teitler, Assistant Professor of Social Work and Director of the Social Indicators Survey Center; Ph.D., Pennsylvania. Social stratification, family, youth sexual behavior, research methods.

Ronald G. Thompson Jr., Assistant Professor of Social Work; Ph.D., Washington (St, Louis). Adolescent mental health, substance use and HIV risk behaviors, HIV/AIDS prevention interventions for adolescents in high risk contexts, child welfare, evidence-based practice, evaluation of programs and services.

Jane Waldfogel, Professor of Social Work; Ph.D., Harvard. Urban studies, econometrics and statistical methods, child protective services.

Suzanne Witte, Associate Professor of Social Work; Ph.D., Columbia. HIV/AIDS interventions with individuals, couples, and families; substance-abuse and violence prevention; female-initiated STD/HIV barrier methods.

Elwin Wu, Assistant Professor of Social Work; Ph.D., Columbia. Offenders and individuals involved with the criminal justice system; comorbidity of substance abuse, violence, and sexual-risk behavior; social networks; services research; intervention research.

Marianne Yoshioka, Assistant Dean of Academic Affairs; Ph.D., Florida State. Marriage and family, cultural competency in practice, intervention design and development, addictions and HIV prevention.

Allen Zweben, Professor of Social Work and Associate Dean for Research; D.S.W., Columbia. Substance abuse interventions, combining medication and behavioral therapy for alcohol problems, motivational enhancement therapy, HIV risk reduction, patient-treatment matching, brief intervention.

FLORIDA INTERNATIONAL UNIVERSITY

College of Social Work, Justice, and Public Affairs
School of Social Work
Master of Social Work (M.S.W.)
Doctor of Philosophy (Ph.D.) in Social Welfare

Programs of Study

The Master of Social Work (M.S.W.) degree program at Florida International University (FIU) prepares qualified individuals for the advanced practice of social work. M.S.W. graduates provide services to individuals, families, and groups. Graduates also organize community groups and administer social agencies. The Ph.D. in social welfare degree program at FIU prepares qualified individuals for careers in research, teaching, and leadership in social work and/or social welfare. Students strengthen their skills in scientific inquiry, in the analysis of social problems and public issues, and in the evaluation of social welfare interventions.

The expertise of the faculty is broad; the School has been nationally recognized as a leader in a number of fields, including substance abuse, Latino youth acculturation, child welfare, immigration and international social work, mental health, and social work and psychopharmacology. Interdisciplinary collaboration is encouraged.

Research Facilities

FIU has state-of-the art library and research facilities. The library houses more than 1.5 million volumes and 24,000 journal subscriptions and hosts a wireless network for computerized searches. The Marc Building opened on campus in 2002 as a facility to house funded research projects. Several doctoral students are involved in large, federally funded investigations conducted by the Community-Based Intervention Research Group, the Institute for Children and Families at Risk, the Latino Drug Abuse Research Center (LDARC), and the Latino HIV Behavioral Science Center (LHIVBSC), all of which are affiliated with the School of Social Work. Other relevant University resources include the Professional Development Center, the Center on Aging, as well as many other research centers and groups throughout the South Florida region.

Financial Aid

The School of Social Work tries to help qualified students secure financial assistance necessary to pursue their educational goals. Scholarships and graduate assistantships, including both research and teaching assistantships, are available to doctoral students. There are also a number of university-wide awards. Information is available from the FIU Financial Aid Office at http://www.fiu.edu/orgs/finaid.

Cost of Study

In 2006–07 tuition was $259.73 per credit hour for Florida residents and $763.80 per credit hour for out-of-state students. Additional per semester fees such as intercollegiate athletics, health services, and transportation access are not included.

Living and Housing Costs

On-campus housing includes apartment-style accommodations ranging from studio apartments to shared units. The supply is limited and should be requested as early as possible. Costs vary within the choice of housing and residential life. Off-campus housing near the University is also available. Information can be obtained from the University Housing Office Web site at http://www.fiu.edu/~housing.

Student Outcomes

The Ph.D. program was established in 1992. Approximately 80 percent of Ph.D. graduates have obtained positions as faculty members in schools of social work. Other graduates occupy administrative and research positions in social welfare agencies.

Location

The University is located in Miami, Florida's largest urban center and a major transportation and business hub for the southeastern United States and the Caribbean. Miami is an exciting, dynamic, global marketplace. Nearby Miami Beach is known for its historic art deco district and the numerous hotels that line its beaches. Miami is a hemispheric crossroads for trade, travel, culture, and communications.

The University

FIU is the public research university of Miami and is ranked among the nation's Research I institutions. For the past five years, FIU was ranked among the top 100 public universities in *U.S. News & World Report's* "America's Best Colleges." FIU has 35,000 students, 1,100 full-time faculty members, and 1,100,000 alumni—making it the largest university in South Florida and among the nation's thirty largest colleges and universities.

Applying

To download an application packet and obtain detailed information on the application process for the M.S.W. and Ph.D. programs, students should visit the Web site at http://swjpa.fiu.edu/SocialWork/admission.htm.

All applicants for admission to the M.S.W. program must have earned a bachelor's degree from an accredited college or university. Several undergraduate courses are required. Applicants with the B.S.W. degree from a program accredited by the Council on Social Work Education (CSWE) are considered for admission to the Advanced Standing Program, which allows students to complete the M.S.W. in one academic year. Applicants for admission to the Ph.D. program must have an M.S.W. degree from a CSWE-accredited school of social work or a master's degree in a related field. (Students who do not have the M.S.W. are expected to complete 6 to 12 credits of M.S.W.-level courses.) M.S.W. applicants should have an undergraduate GPA of 3.0 or higher in upper division work. Applicants for the Ph.D. program should have a minimum undergraduate GPA of 3.0 and a minimum graduate GPA of 3.5, a combined quantitative and verbal Graduate Record Examination score of at least 1120, three letters of reference from academic and/or professional sources, two writing samples (published articles, research reports, or graduate assignments), and a personal statement (three to six double-spaced pages) that indicates the reasons for the pursuit of doctoral studies and outlines specific research interests. Social work experience is highly desired but not required.

Correspondence and Information

Dr. Paul H. Stuart, Director
School of Social Work
University Park Campus, GL-415A
Florida International University
11200 Southwest 8th Street
Miami, Florida 33199
Phone: 305-348-5880
E-mail: paul.stuart@fiu.edu
Web site: http://swjpa.fiu.edu/SocialWork/default.htm

Florida International University

THE FACULTY AND THEIR RESEARCH

Richard Beaulaurier, Associate Professor; Ph.D., USC. Civil and disability rights, mental health and aging, consumer issues, computer technology and social work curricula, community practice, administration and organizational behavior.

David Cohen, Professor and Coordinator of the Ph.D. Program; Ph.D., Berkeley. Psychopharmacology and social work practice, sociocultural aspects of medication usage, critical perspectives in mental health, law and psychiatry.

Mario De La Rosa, Professor and Director, Latino HIV/AIDS Behavioral Science Research Center and Latino Minority Drug Abuse Research Program; Ph.D., Ohio State. Substance abuse and acculturation in Latino populations, drug use and crime problems in Latino populations, social support system and Latino health.

Marian Dumaine, Clinical Associate Professor and Field Practicum Coordinator; Ph.D., Florida International. Mental health systems, dual diagnosis (schizophrenia and substance abuse).

Andres Gil, Professor and Associate Vice President for Research Development; Ph.D., Miami (Florida). Adolescent substance use: epidemiology, risk factors and treatment, and cultural factors in the context of acculturation among immigrant families.

Mary Helen Hayden, Assistant Professor and Associate Director; Ed.D., Florida International. Group work, families, substance abuse, child welfare, service learning.

Rosa Jones, Associate Professor and Vice President, Academic Affairs and Undergraduate Studies; D.S.W., Howard.

Mark Macgowan, Associate Professor; Ph.D., Barry. Assessment and reduction of aggression and violence among children and youth, engagement in group work, family group conferencing.

Miriam Potocky, Associate Professor; Ph.D., Kansas. Refugee resettlement, international and multicultural social work.

Christopher Rice, Assistant Professor; Ph.D., Washington (St. Louis). Health services, substance use, elderly caregiving, technology transfer.

Paul H. Stuart, Professor and Director; Ph.D., Wisconsin-Madison. History of social welfare and social work.

Barbara Thomlison, Professor and Director, Institute for Children and Families at Risk; Ph.D., Toronto. Child welfare, early childhood intervention, evidence-based practice models, children's mental health, social work curriculum.

Ray Thomlison, Professor and Dean; Ph.D., Toronto. Clinical practice, behavior therapy, family therapy, couples therapy, parent training, child welfare, employee assistance, curriculum development, international social work.

Nan Van Den Bergh, Associate Professor; Ph.D., Pittsburgh. Empowerment, feminist practice, addictions, workplace-based practice, employee assistance programs, culturally sensitive interventions, sexual minority issues.

Richard Van Dorn, Assistant Professor; Ph.D., North Carolina at Chapel Hill. Mental health services research, mental health law, juvenile delinquency.

Eric Wagner, Professor and Director, Community-Based Intervention Research Group (C-BIRG); Ph.D., Pittsburgh. Randomized, community-based clinical trials of interventions to reduce substance use problems in youth, evidence-based practice models, development of culturally sensitive approaches to assessment and intervention.

Stephen E. Wong, Associate Professor; Ph.D., Western Michigan. Clinical practice with severe mental disorders, single-case experimental study design, critical perspectives in mental health.

FORDHAM UNIVERSITY

Graduate School of Social Service

Programs of Study

Fordham University's Graduate School of Social Service (GSSS) offers a Master of Social Work (M.S.W.) degree. The School offers a two-year full-time program, a one-year advanced-standing program for B.S.W. graduates, and a program for experienced and employed social service practitioners as well as extended three- to four-year plans of study. Course work leading to the M.S.W. degree may be completed at either of two campuses: Lincoln Center, in midtown New York City, or Marymount College of Fordham University, in Tarrytown, New York. The School offers day, evening, and Saturday classes at both sites. In addition, the School has begun a collaborative program with Molloy College, in Rockville Center, Long Island, in which students from that area may begin their course work at the Molloy campus and eventually finish the program at the Lincoln Center campus. Earning the M.S.W. degree at Fordham is accomplished through a combination of classes focused on social work theory and fieldwork placement. The integration of classroom theory with practical experience is an integral part of the master's program at the Graduate School of Social Service. The complete program comprises 66 credit hours: 48 credit hours in the classroom and 18 credit hours for the fieldwork placement. Students select from three areas of concentration for their advanced course work and fieldwork assignment: clinical, administrative, or research. In addition, Fordham students may elect a specialization in various practice areas: older persons and their families, children and families, substance abuse, social work and law, or global social work. There is also a client-centered management concentration, which combines both clinical practice and administration. Students are placed in more than 700 public or private organizations and agencies for fieldwork instruction throughout the New York tristate area. Students taking their foundation course work complete a placement that engages them in generalist social work practice. The advanced field placement is carefully selected to match the student's desired concentration and specialization. Fieldwork assignments are arranged as closely to the residential area of the student as possible. In addition, the GSSS offers the following interdisciplinary/joint-degree programs: M.S.W./J.D. in conjunction with the Fordham University School of Law, M.S.W./M.Div. in conjunction with the New York Theological Seminary Scholarship, and the M.S.W./Certificate in Psychotherapy or Family Therapy through the Blanton-Peale Institute.

Research Facilities

The Quinn Library at the Lincoln Center campus and the Gloria Gaines Library at the Marymount campus provide reference materials and research facilities for M.S.W. students. Collectively, these facilities hold more that 360,000 bound volumes and 1,400 periodical titles. The social work collection, including social work periodicals and journals, is housed within the Quinn Library. These materials are available to the Tarrytown campus students through interlibrary loan. The School also houses various specialized programs and institutes. These include the Langenfeld Research and Demonstration Center; the Bertram M. Beck Institute on Religion and Poverty; the Children and Families Institute for Research, Support and Training (Children FIRST); the Fordham HIV/AIDS Service Administration (HASA) Training Academy; the Fordham Institute for Innovation in Social Policy; the Interdisciplinary Center for Family and Child Advocacy; the National Center for Schools and Communities; the Ravazzin Center for Social Work Research on Aging; and the newly created Fordham University Center for International Studies.

Financial Aid

Financial aid is available in the form of tuition remission, graduate assistantships, loan programs, scholarships, and fellowships. Tuition remission is awarded to students with demonstrated financial need who are enrolled in fieldwork instruction. Graduate assistantships are awarded to students with demonstrated financial need. The maximum amount of the subsidized and unsubsidized Federal Family Education Loan is $20,500 annually. Scholarships and fellowships awarded in the past include the New York Theological Seminary Scholarship, the Fagan Award, the Edward Kane Trust, the Connolly Scholarship, the Beverly Powers Memorial Scholarship, the Jewish Foundation for Education of Women Scholarship, and the Jesuit High School Scholarship. In addition, the School participates in various outside scholarship programs, including the NYC Board of Education Bilingual Scholarship Program, the James Satterwhite Academy of the New York City Administration for Children's Services, the NYC Mayor's Graduate Scholarship Program, and the New York State Regents Professional Opportunities Scholarship Program.

Cost of Study

For 2007–08, the cost per credit is $680. There are a $113-per-semester general University fee and a $100-per-semester technology fee. In addition, students in fieldwork pay a $30-per-academic-year malpractice insurance fee.

Living and Housing Costs

Off-campus housing options include Fordham-leased apartments, privately leased apartments, and residential hotels. Housing costs in the New York metropolitan area vary considerably according to location and the type of quarters desired.

Student Group

As of January 2004, the school had 1,385 students enrolled in various models of study, from full-time to part-time. The number of students attending the Lincoln Center campus is 976, while 409 are enrolled at the Marymount College site in Tarrytown. The student body of the School ranges from recent B.A. or B.S. graduates to experienced returning students from the social service field as well as various other backgrounds and employment histories. In 2003–04, student ages ranged from early 20s to mid-70s. Roughly 80 percent of students elect a concentration in clinical social work, while 15 percent choose administration and approximately 5 percent choose the research area.

Location

Fordham University's Graduate School of Social Service is located in New York City. The Leon Lowenstein Building is part of the Lincoln Center for the Performing Arts complex. The School also offers the full M.S.W. program in Tarrytown, New York, in Westchester County. The Tarrytown campus is part of Marymount College of Fordham University. The School also offers the option of completing some of the program requirements, including field placement, at the campus of Molloy College in Rockville Centre, Long Island, New York. The School has educated future social workers throughout the New York tristate area since its founding in 1916. Fordham's student body is recruited from all areas of the United States as well as abroad.

The University and The School

Fordham University was founded as a Jesuit institution in 1841. Fordham University is distinguished by a 450-year tradition of Jesuit education. The University is renowned for its esteemed faculty and highly advanced libraries and research facilities as well as the resources of New York City. The Graduate School of Social Service was founded in 1916 and has been located in the Leon Lowenstein Center at the Lincoln Center campus since 1969. The program expanded to the Tarrytown campus in 1975. The goal of the School is to prepare students for the professional practice of social work. Its mission is to prepare advanced social work practitioners who are committed to the goals, values, and ethics of the profession and who will be able to provide high-quality services that promote the well-being of individuals, families, groups, and communities. The School's hope is that its graduates become practitioners and citizens who are committed to working toward a just, equitable, and caring society free from violence, oppression, and discrimination.

Applying

Persons holding a bachelor's degree from an accredited institution are qualified to apply for admission to the program. The School does not require the GRE or any other form of testing. The application deadline for fall admission is June 1 and the deadline for spring admission is December 1. Admissions decisions are made on a rolling basis; priority is given to applications for the upcoming enrollment period. It should be noted that deadlines are not meant to be strictly enforced but rather should be considered as priority guidelines. The Admissions Committee makes every effort to review all completed application materials for any given semester regardless of the time of application.

Correspondence and Information

Office of Admissions
Graduate School of Social Service
Fordham University
113 West 60th Street, Suite 703
New York, New York 10023

Phone: 212-636-6600
Fax: 212-636-6613
E-mail: gssadmission@fordham.edu
Web site: http://www.fordham.edu/gss

Fordham University

THE FACULTY

Gregory Acevedo, Assistant Professor; Ph.D., Bryn Mawr.
Portia Adams, Assistant Professor; Ph.D., Washington (St. Louis).
Lee W. Badger, Professor; Ph.D., Alabama.
Cathy Berkman, Assistant Professor; Ph.D., Yale.
Valerie Borum, Assistant Professor; Ph.D., Howard.
Patricia Brownwell, Assistant Professor; D.S.W., Fordham.
Marjorie H. Cantor, Brookdale Professor; M.A., Columbia.
Robert Chazin, Professor; D.S.W., Case Western Reserve.
Roslyn H. Chernesky, Professor; D.S.W., CUNY, Hunter.
Lisa Colarossi, Assistant Professor; Ph.D., Michigan.
Elaine P. Congress, Professor; D.S.W., CUNY, Hunter.
Marlene Cooper, Associate Professor; Ph.D., NYU.
John Cosgrove, Associate Professor; Ph.D., Fordham.
Carole B. Cox, Associate Professor; D.S.W., Maryland.
Maddy Cunningham, Assistant Professor; D.S.W., Adelphi.
James R. Dumpson, Professor and Dean Emeritus; Ph.D., Dacca (East Pakistan).
Jane H. Edwards, Professor and Assistant Dean; D.S.W., Utah.
Mary Ann Forgey, Professor; Ph.D., Columbia.
Raymond D. Fox, Professor; Ph.D., NYU.
Shirley Gatenio Gabel, Assistant Professor; Ph.D., Columbia.
Ursula M. Gerty, Professor Emerita; D.S.W., Catholic University.
Manny J. Gonzalez, Assistant Professor; D.S.W., Adelphi.
Irene Gutheil, Professor; D.S.W., Columbia.
Meredith Hanson, Associate Professor and Director of Ph.D. Program; D.S.W., Columbia.
Janna C. Heyman, Assistant Professor; Ph.D., Fordham.
W. Dana Holman, Assistant Professor; D.S.W., CUNY, Hunter.
Barbara Kail, Associate Professor; D.S.W., Columbia.
Carol Kaplan, Professor; D.S.W., NYU.
David Koch, Assistant Professor; Ph.D., CUNY Graduate Center.
Winnie Kung, Associate Professor; Ph.D., Chicago.
Ji Seon Lee, Assistant Professor; Ph.D., Fordham.
Laura J. Lee, Associate Professor; D.S.W., Pennsylvania.
Anita Lightburn, Associate Professor; Ed.D., Columbia.
Monica McGoldrick, Distinguished Visiting Lecturer; Ph.D., Smith.
Elaine Norman, Professor; Ph.D., CUNY Graduate Center.
Victoria M. Oids, Professor Emerita; D.S.W., Columbia.
Rosa Perez-Koenig, Associate Professor; D.S.W., NYU.
Tonya Perry, Assistant Professor; Ph.D., Alabama.
Michael H. Phillips, Professor; D.S.W., Columbia.
Chaya S. Piotrkowski, Professor; Ph.D., Michigan.
Cynthia C. Poindexter, Associate Professor; Ph.D., Illinois at Chicago.
Mary Ann Quaranta, Professor and Dean Emerita; D.S.W., Columbia.
Howard Robinson, Assistant Professor; D.S.W., CUNY, Hunter.
Barry Rock, Associate Professor; D.S.W., CUNY, Hunter.
Yvette M. Sealy, Assistant Professor; Ph.D., Fordham.
Lyn Kennedy Slater, Assistant Professor; M.S.W., CUNY, Hunter.
Judith R. Smith, Associate Professor; Ph.D., Columbia.
Virginia Strand, Associate Professor; D.S.W., Columbia.
Sandra G. Turner, Associate Professor; Ph.D., Rutgers.
Ernst O. VanBergeijk, Assistant Professor; Ph.D., Columbia.
Peter B. Vaughan, Professor and Dean; Ph.D., Michigan.
Nancy Boy Webb, Distinguished Professor; D.S.W., Columbia.
Pauline C. Zischka, Professor Emerita; Ph.D., NYU.

MARYWOOD UNIVERSITY

School of Social Work

Program of Study

The M.S.W. program consists of 45 credits of classroom courses and 15 credits of field education. Concentration is in either advanced practice with client systems or administration in social work. The foundation content is designed to develop basic knowledge of social welfare policy; problems and issues of human behavior from the psychosocial and sociocultural perspectives; the ethical foundations of social work practice; attention to qualitative and quantitative research methodologies and their relevance to effective, competent, and ethical social work practice; and theory and methods of intervention. The second year facilitates students' development of advanced social work skills. The first semester incorporates course work in practice with individuals, families, and groups and administration with field experience in the student's chosen practice concentration. Course work and field experience in the specialization continue through the year and, in tandem with electives, support the development of advanced knowledge and skill in the student's chosen area. The full-time program calls for two academic years of study. Summer courses are available for those who prefer a lighter class load in fall or spring. There is a basic part-time plan to complete the program in three years. In Scranton, part-time students do class work on Saturdays; in the Lehigh Valley Program, classes are offered on Monday and Wednesday evenings. A program in Reading has classes available on Tuesday and Thursday evenings. The Central Pennsylvania Program at Bloomsburg University follows the Saturday model. Field agency placements usually can be developed for students in the region in which they live. Field assignments are 16 hours per week and are undertaken in the semesters when the student takes theory and practice classes. Advanced standing is available to those who have earned a B.S.W. degree from a CSWE-accredited program within five years of application to Marywood. An M.P.A. may be earned in combination with the M.S.W. under a dual-degree program. Students with a special interest in work with the aging may earn a Certificate of Specialization in Gerontology by taking 12 credit hours through the Gerontology Institute at Marywood. Students can also take a specialization in behavioral health, and can prepare for certification in practicing social work in schools. A curriculum plan combining the M.S.W. with art therapy is available. Joint M.S.W./Master of Arts in Pastoral Counseling (M.A.P.C.) and M.S.W./M.Div. degree programs are available in cooperation with Moravian Theological Seminary.

Research Facilities

The Learning Resources Center houses the library and media center. The library collection consists of more than 217,290 bound volumes, 881 print journal titles, and more than 44,300 nonprint items. Numerous electronic full-text and indexing/abstracting databases are accessible on campus, through networked workstations, and remotely from a student's home or office computer. Traditional library services are available 91 hours per week during regular semester hours. Most of these services are also available around-the-clock through the library Web page. Research and data analysis may be performed, using SPSS in three major computer labs that are located in the McGowan Center for Graduate and Professional Studies, the Center for Natural and Health Sciences, and the Learning Resources Center. A statistician is available (by appointment) for instruction and consultation. The bookstore offers SPSS software for personal use at a discounted price. The off-site programs have library and computer lab services.

Financial Aid

Partial-tuition scholarships are awarded on the basis of financial need to full- and part-time students. A limited number of assistantships are available. Assistantships are approved for 18 credits and include a stipend for 20 hours of work per week. Applications are available from the School of Social Work. Students enrolled for at least 6 credits per semester can borrow under the Federal Stafford Student Loan. Because tuition for students registered in the Central Pennsylvania Program is reduced, scholarships are not available.

Cost of Study

Tuition for 2007–08 is $695 per credit ($695 at the Scranton, Lehigh Valley, and Reading locations and $560 at the central Pennsylvania location). General fees are $850 per year full-time and $280 per year part-time. Deferred-payment plans are offered.

Living and Housing Costs

Students can pursue off-campus housing. Marywood's Scranton campus is located in a residential area, and rental apartments are available for graduate students.

Student Group

The total enrollment at Marywood University in 2006–07 was 3,180, of whom 1,284 were graduate students. The School of Social Work enrolls about 400 students, (both Ph.D. and B.S.W.). An entering class includes 25 to 35 in each part-time program (Saturday and Lehigh Valley), 20 each at Reading and central Pennsylvania, and about 40 full-time, of whom 15 have advanced standing. About 20 percent receive scholarships. The average age of students is 34 years, and all have related work experience through volunteer activity, internships, or employment. Class size in all programs is typically capped at 20. The group of students who enter as a class can expect to work together throughout their program. Each course is evaluated by students each semester, and faculty members are regularly rated highly for knowledge, quality of teaching, and accessibility. There is an active Student Association in each program.

Student Outcomes

Degree completion rates are 85 percent or better. Graduates move quickly into professional-level employment. More than 80 percent have prepared for work with individuals, families, and small groups and accept positions of direct service in varied fields of practice. Mental health and family/children's service settings employ the largest number of graduates. Health-care and school settings also employ significant numbers. Graduates of the administration concentration are similarly distributed in the full range of social work practice areas.

Location

Marywood University is situated in a suburban section of Scranton, a city of about 75,000. It is located a little more than 100 miles from New York City to the east and from Philadelphia to the south. It is served by the Wilkes-Barre/Scranton International Airport and is easily accessible via a network of interstate highways. The Pocono Mountains, skiing, and several beautiful lakes are nearby. The Lehigh Valley Program is just south of Allentown, Pennsylvania, convenient to the Philadelphia metropolitan area. The program in Reading is equidistant from Philadelphia and Harrisburg. The Central Pennsylvania Program is in Bloomsburg.

The University and The School

Marywood University, which was established in 1915, is an independent, comprehensive Catholic university that is owned and sponsored by the Congregation of Sisters, Servants of the Immaculate Heart of Mary. Graduate studies were inaugurated in 1921. The School of Social Work opened in 1969 and is fully accredited by the Council on Social Work Education. The School prepares students for advanced practice with individuals, families, and groups or in program planning and social service agency administration.

Applying

Application deadlines are for fall semester (full- or part-time), May 15; for summer (full-time advanced standing), February 15; for assistantships, February 15; and for scholarships, April 15. Applications must include two references; official transcripts, showing course work in social and behavior sciences, 6 credits minimum, and humanities; a resume; and a personal statement. Individual interviews are required; telephone interviews can be arranged.

Correspondence and Information

School of Social Work
Marywood University
Scranton, Pennsylvania 18509
Phone: 570-348-6282
      866-279-9663 (toll-free)
Fax: 570-961-4742
E-mail: grad_adm@marywood.edu
Web site: http://www.marywood.edu/ssw/main.stm

Marywood University

THE FACULTY AND THEIR RESEARCH

Packiaraj Arumighan, Assistant Professor; M.S.W., Bishop Heber (India); Ph.D., Bharathidasan (India). Cultural diversity, community development, social work, and religion.

Phyllis Black, Professor; M.S.W., McGill; Ph.D., Catholic University. Gatekeeping in schools of social work, ethical issues in social practice and education, evaluation of student performance in graduate schools of social work.

Stephen Burke, Associate Professor; Ph.D. (social work), Minnesota. Military families in times of deployment, rural service delivery.

Doris Chechotka-McQuade, Assistant Professor; Ph.D. (social work), Fordham. Stress management in hospice settings, grief.

Geraldine Dawson, Associate Professor; M.S.W., Smith; M.D., Yeshiva (Einstein). Psychopharmacology, resiliency in childhood, biopsychosocial models of assessment.

Michelle DiLauro, Assistant Professor; Ph.D. (social work), Fordham. Psychosocial factors associated with child maltreatment, social work in ambulatory care.

George Haskett, Associate Professor; M.P.A., Virginia Commonwealth; D.S.W., Columbia. Social policy and critical thinking, child welfare, privatization.

Joanne M. Hessmiller, Associate Professor; Ph.D. (social work), Maryland, Baltimore. Prevention of intimate violence, social work and law, international social welfare, conflict resolution and dispute mediation.

Diane Keller, Associate Professor; Ph.D. (child and family studies), Syracuse. Intervention for children and families, disabilities and chronic illness, teaching strategies.

Christine Kessen, Assistant Professor; D.S.W., Columbia. Mental health, ethics.

Lloyd L. Lyter, Professor; M.P.A., Temple; Ph.D. (social work), Rutgers. Psychopathology, chemical dependence, HIV disease, ethics.

Jane Strobino, Professor; M.S.W., Washington (St. Louis); Ph.D., Catholic University. Student evaluations of teaching, instructional innovations and teaching strategies.

Cynthia J. Weaver, Assistant Professor; M.S.W., Temple; D.Min., Eastern Baptist Theological Seminary. Practice, family studies, disabilities, death and dying, spirituality.

Joyce Z. White, Professor; M.S.W., Virginia Commonwealth; Ph.D., Case Western Reserve. Disabilities, social work with Native Americans, social work education.

Kenneth White, Assistant Professor; M.Div., Wesley Theological Seminary; Ph.D., Barry. Culturally competent practice, African-centered philosophy, racial identity development, child-rearing socialization practices, substance abuse, mental health.

NEW YORK UNIVERSITY

School of Social Work

Programs of Study

The New York University (NYU) School of Social Work is widely known for professional education in clinical work with individuals, groups, and families. The School offers B.S., M.S.W., and Ph.D. degrees in social work. The School's programs are fully accredited by the Council on Social Work Education. The M.S.W. program is offered in several formats to accommodate the differing circumstances of its highly diverse student body. The Two-Year Program requires four semesters of study. The 16-Month Accelerated Program, an intensive route to a master's degree, provides a concentrated two-year course of study over four continuous semesters, including summer. The Extended M.S.W. Program allows students to complete their M.S.W. over three to four years, with one year of full-time study. The Extended One-Year Residence Program (typically three to four years, with one year of full-time study) is designed for individuals who are employed in social service agencies. Graduates of an accredited undergraduate social work program may apply for advanced-standing admission into the second year of the Two-Year Program. All programs may be completed at the main Washington Square campus and, with the exception of the 16-Month Accelerated Program, at the School's Rockland County campus. Foundation courses may be taken at the School's Staten Island and Westchester sites. The School also offers dual-degree programs with both the School of Law and the Wagner Graduate School of Public Service at NYU and with Sarah Lawrence College. Study for all programs is organized around small classes, articulation of hands-on field placement and academic work, experienced faculty members who practice what they teach, and a uniquely supportive advisement system. The curriculum includes foundation courses that build a knowledge base for work with individuals, families, and groups; an advanced concentration in clinical practice, providing intensive training in human behavior and intervention strategies for direct practice; and a wide selection of electives through which students may pursue individual professional interests. Students in all programs are trained at two or more of the 500 field instruction sites at which the School has arranged experienced on-site supervision. The Ph.D. program in social work at New York University prepares students for leadership in the study, design, and development of clinical social work practice. The program, which is offered on a full- and part-time basis, combines contemporary theory and knowledge related to practice in the urban environment with content related to diversity, the opportunity for interdisciplinary study, and a global perspective on social work. Graduates of the program are faculty members in social work education, scholars of practice, and/or leaders in policy implementation.

Research Facilities

Bobst Library at NYU is one of the largest open-stack research libraries in the nation, with an extraordinary assemblage of accessible print/video/audio resources, ample reading room and individual study spaces, and long, convenient hours of operation. NYU is a wired university, and students and faculty members alike have free, high-powered access for research and study (from campus or home) to computing resources that include e-mail, the Internet, and major databases. The School itself is home to the widely used international Web site for social work research and education (Information for Practice-IP). The University supports leading centers of research on health, social services, and law, including the School's Leslie Glass Center for Mental Health and Practice Research. Students participate with faculty members on research and program development projects with community service agencies.

Financial Aid

The School offers a comprehensive program of both merit-based and need-based financial assistance. Nearly 85 percent of eligible M.S.W. students receive School-based scholarships, and 97 percent of M.S.W. students receive some level of financial assistance. Amounts of financial assistance vary by student and are contingent on the availability of funding each academic year.

Cost of Study

Graduate tuition for 2006–07 was $794 per credit, plus a $56 nonreturnable registration and services fee, per point, for registration after the first point. There are additional health insurance fees for graduate students, which vary based on coverage.

Living and Housing Costs

Graduate student housing at NYU provides the advantages of apartment-style living, with the convenience, security, activities, and supportive environment of residence hall life. Several types of accommodations are offered to suit different preferences and budgets, including shared studios, double rooms in one- and two-bedroom apartments, and a limited number of private rooms in 2- and 3-person suites. Monthly costs for on-campus housing options range from $950 to $1500. Off-campus housing is also available at market rates. Meal plans are available but not required. For further information, students may contact NYU Housing at 212-998-4600 or on the Web at http://www.nyu.edu/housing.

Student Group

The School's commitment to diversity is the governing philosophy that is reflected in every aspect of the student experience. The School's student body, like its faculty, is composed of individuals of varied ages, ethnicities, cultural backgrounds, and interests. Great emphasis is placed on keeping the mix vital.

Student Outcomes

According to the most recent report, more than 92 percent of the School's graduates have jobs in social work within three months of graduation. They work in all areas of social work, with the greatest proportion going into mental health services. Significant numbers find employment in the areas of aging, school social work, hospital social work, child welfare and adoption services, and AIDS/HIV support services.

Location

NYU is an integral part of the metropolitan community of New York City, an international capital of art, culture, business, and finance and home of the United Nations. Located in historic Washington Square in the heart of Greenwich Village, NYU allows students to have the city's extraordinary resources at their doorstep. Museums, art galleries, and theaters enrich both academic programs and life experience and contribute to a dynamic environment for study and learning.

The School

The School is, in many respects, an intimate school within the larger University—in its educational philosophy, program structure, and physical setting. Faculty members and students interact in a teaching culture where faculty members are very accessible. Small classes predominate, typically with 25 or fewer students. Three nineteenth-century town houses facing Washington Square Park are the educational and social center of the School, where students gather for classes, seminars, advisement sessions, and informal meetings.

Established in 1953, the School is one of the few in the country to provide a continuum of social work education from undergraduate through doctoral levels. The School maintains affiliations with more than 500 mental health, social services, and health agencies in the tristate area, which serve as teaching centers for students in field internships.

Applying

Application forms are available from the School's Office of Admissions as well as at the School's Web site and should be returned with a nonrefundable fee of $50. Programs begin in the fall and spring only. The Ph.D. program begins in the fall only. Prospective students should consult the School's Web site for application deadlines. International applications are welcomed. All applications should be sent to Office of Social Work Admissions, Graduate Processing Center, New York University, P.O. Box 919, New York, New York 10003-0919.

Correspondence and Information

For more information and application forms, prospective students should contact:

School of Social Work
New York University
One Washington Square North
New York, New York 10003-6654
Phone: 212-998-5910
E-mail: ssw.admissions@nyu.edu
Web site: http://www.socialwork.nyu.edu

New York University

THE FACULTY AND THEIR RESEARCH

Theresa Aiello, Associate Professor; Ph.D., NYU. Child and adolescent treatment, object relations theory, history of psychoanalysis and social work, HIV/AIDS.

Jeane W. Anastas, Professor; Ph.D., Brandeis. Women's issues, mental health and substance-abuse services research, gay and lesbian issues, research methodology.

Alma J. Carten, Associate Professor; Ph.D., CUNY, Hunter. Child welfare, welfare reform, elderly kinship caretakers, adolescent pregnancy and parenting, public policy development.

Suzanne England, Professor and Dean; Ph.D., Illinois at Chicago. Community and program development, health promotion and disease prevention research, use of new media in professional education, assessment of learning outcomes, creating and managing change in social work education.

Trudy B. Festinger, Professor; D.S.W., Columbia. Foster care and child adoption, research as a basis for public policy.

RoseMarie Perez Foster, Associate Professor; Ph.D., St. John's. Role of language in clinical treatment, long-term impact of trauma, clinical care for immigrants, clinical research.

Martha A. Gabriel, Associate Professor; Ph.D., Smith. Group practice, health care, gay and lesbian issues, HIV/AIDS, secondary trauma.

Daniel S. Gardner, Assistant Professor; Ph.D., Columbia. Aging and social gerontology; end-of-life and palliative care; health-care practice and policy; clinical practice with individuals, couples, and families; program evaluation.

Caroline Rosenthal Gelman, Assistant Professor; Ph.D., Smith. Geriatric social work, culturally sensitive practice, community mental health.

Susan Gerbino, Clinical Assistant Professor; Ph.D., NYU. Bioethics, palliative and end-of-life care, geriatric social work, clinical practice.

Eda G. Goldstein, Professor; D.S.W., Columbia. Clinical practice theory, contemporary psychodynamic developmental theories, borderline and narcissistic disorders, short-term treatment.

Gladys Gonzalez-Ramos, Associate Professor; Ph.D., NYU. Multicultural issues, school-based services, child abuse and neglect, Latino families.

Diane Grodney, Clinical Associate Professor; Ph.D., NYU. HIV/AIDS, substance abuse, bereavement.

Robert Leibson Hawkins, Assistant Professor; Ph.D., Brandeis. Family and children's policy analysis, welfare and poverty, program evaluation, quantitative and qualitative methods, survey design and implementation.

Gary Holden, Professor; D.S.W., Columbia. Applied research for practice, role of new information technologies in social work, psychosocial factors in health, social cognitive theory and self-efficacy, research methodology.

Mary Ann Jones, Associate Professor; D.S.W., Columbia. Child and family welfare, psychotherapy research, gay and lesbian issues, research methodology.

Gerald Landsberg, Professor; D.S.W., CUNY, Hunter. Violence, forensic mental health, mental health and managed care, services in naturally occurring retirement communities.

Shulamith La Straussner, Professor; D.S.W., Columbia. Addictions, EAP/occupational social work, women's issues, research, cross-disciplinary training.

Yuhwa Eva Lu, Associate Professor; Ph.D. (joint degree), Claremont and San Diego State. Cross-cultural psychotherapy, clinical process and outcome research, social work with Asian clients.

James I. Martin, Associate Professor; Ph.D., Illinois at Chicago. HIV prevention, gay and lesbian issues, self-psychology, short-term treatment, clinical practice with gay and lesbian clients.

Linda G. Mills, Professor; Ph.D., Brandeis. Domestic violence, law and social work, women's issues, program and policy research, child welfare training.

Diane Mirabito, Assistant Professor; D.S.W., CUNY, Hunter. Adolescent health/mental health, community mental health, school social work.

Robert E. Moore, Clinical Assistant Professor; Dr.P.H., Columbia. Research methodology; service access by the homeless, children, and adolescents; spirituality approaches in social work.

Peggy Morton, Clinical Assistant Professor; D.S.W., CUNY, Hunter. Reproductive health issues, school-based social services, geriatric social work.

Maryellen Noonan, Associate Professor; Ph.D., NYU. The difficult client, acting-out adolescents, child welfare, homelessness.

Deborah Padgett, Professor; Ph.D., Wisconsin. Mental health services research, ethnicity and aging, women's mental health, quantitative and qualitative research methods.

Marjorie A. Rock, Associate Professor; Dr.P.H., Columbia. Chronic mental illness, public mental health, services for the aging, forensic mental health services.

Dina J. Rosenfeld, Clinical Associate Professor; D.S.W., Yeshiva. Adoption, Holocaust studies, hospice care, field instructor training.

Jeffrey Seinfeld, Professor; Ph.D., NYU. Application of object relations theory to populations with serious emotional/environmental disadvantages.

Judith Siegel, Associate Professor; Ph.D., Virginia Commonwealth. Couples and family therapy.

Carol Tosone, Associate Professor; Ph.D., NYU. Grief and bereavement, women's issues, masochism, short-term treatment, medical social work.

Ellen Tuchman, Assistant Professor; Ph.D., NYU. The intersection of HIV/AIDS, substance abuse, and menopause; evidence-based practice.

Jerome C. Wakefield, Professor; Ph.D., D.S.W., Berkeley. Concept of mental illness, social work practice, philosophy of mind, sexual dysfunction.

Allison V. Werner-Lin, Assistant Professor; Ph.D., Chicago. Psychosocial oncology, genetic testing for hereditary disease, family development, clinical practice with children and families in health-care settings.

Alice K. Wolson, Clinical Assistant Professor; D.S.W., Yeshiva. Supervision, work with the chronically ill, short-term treatment.

SMITH COLLEGE

School for Social Work

Program of Study	The School for Social Work, open to both men and women, offers a concentration in clinical practice leading to the M.S.W. and Ph.D. degrees. Clinical social work practice is concerned with the interdependence between individuals and their environment and the use of relationships to promote healing, growth, and empowerment. The School also recognizes the pernicious consequences of racism and works to identify and overcome the overt and covert aspects of racism. The program is organized on the Block Plan, designed to integrate theory and practice through a carefully devised sequence of summer academic sessions and intervening winter sessions devoted to clinical internships. The summer sessions provide students with the theoretical framework for practice during the winter months. During the winter, students are placed for eight months in 125 affiliated agencies located in twenty-one geographic areas: Alaska, California, Colorado, Connecticut, Georgia, Illinois, Maine, Maryland, Massachusetts, New Hampshire, New Mexico, New York, North Carolina, Ohio, Pennsylvania, Rhode Island, Texas, Vermont, Virginia, Washington, and Washington, D.C. Additional placements are available in Thailand. The School admits a class once a year, in June.
	The M.S.W. program is twenty-seven months in length and comprises three academic ten-week summer sessions and two intervening full-time eight-month field placements in agencies affiliated with the School. The M.S.W. may also be earned through a fifteen-month advanced-standing program (two summers and one winter) that the School offers to graduates of accredited B.S.W. programs who are able to demonstrate second-year-level clinical practice skills and knowledge.
	The Ph.D. program of twenty-seven months is oriented to the preparation of advanced casework practitioner-scholars, supervisors, and educators. Its residency period consists of two 10-week academic sessions, a final five-week summer academic session, two intervening clinical internships of three days a week, and a research internship. This program is open to women and men who have graduated from an accredited school of social work following a period of post-master's practice.
Research Facilities	The School utilizes two of Smith College's four libraries—the William Allen Neilson Library (more than 1.4 million volumes, 96,500 microforms, and 2,300 current periodicals and newspapers) and the Science Library (more than 136,000 volumes, 20,000 microfilms, and 700 periodicals)—in addition to the Five College (Amherst College, Hampshire College, Mount Holyoke College, and the University of Massachusetts) interlibrary loan system. The Reference Department offers students extensive bibliographic and research assistance throughout the summer. Students have access to the Academic Computing Center in Seelye Hall and, through that office, to all computer services of the campus. There are computer databases, including Internet access and access to the Five College computer links. The Clinical Research Institute provides small grants for faculty research and is engaged in ongoing agency-based research.
Financial Aid	Financial assistance is available to students in the M.S.W. program who are U.S. citizens and permanent residents and is based on financial need. Every effort is made to assist students in obtaining loan funds under the federally insured loan program.
Cost of Study	For 2007–08, the total tuition cost of the program is $41,016 for twenty-seven months ($17,202 for each full year and $6612 for the final summer). For the Ph.D. program, the total tuition is $45,596 for twenty-six months. Other fees, books, and supplies average approximately $1000 per year. In addition, students should estimate expenses for typing and copying the research project during the final summer.
Living and Housing Costs	On-campus summer housing is available in coed and single-sex dormitories. The cost of room and board for the 2007 summer session was $3012. Off-campus housing is available, and students make their own arrangements. During the field placement period, students must also make their own living arrangements. Expenses include transportation from the School to the agency assignment, rent, food, utilities, medical insurance, and other normal living costs.
Student Group	In 2007–08, there are 369 students (333 women and 36 men ranging in age from 22 to 62) enrolled full-time: 348 in the master's program and 21 in the doctoral program, coming from twenty-eight states and three countries. Students in the master's program have rich and varied backgrounds of work and volunteer experiences in the helping professions; some have made career changes from such fields as education, law, nursing, and business. Graduates are employed as clinical social workers, consultants, directors of agencies, directors of training, supervisors, and administrators, and some are engaged in private practice in conjunction with teaching or agency work and other similar combinations.
Student Outcomes	Job prospects for Smith graduates have proven quite positive. In a survey of recent graduates, more than 75 percent of respondents were able to secure a job within two months of beginning their search. While graduates were hired into a variety of settings, 34 percent found employment in social service agencies, 24 percent in hospitals, and 22 percent in outpatient mental health clinics. Within these settings, 32 percent described their field of practice as mental health, 19 percent as children and youth, and 13 percent as family services or child welfare.
Location	Smith is located in Northampton, Massachusetts. The Five College area is rich in cultural and recreational opportunities throughout the year.
The School	The School for Social Work, founded in 1918, continues to demonstrate its commitment to excellence in clinical practice. It pursues its mission through the study of individuals, groups, and families; the interrelated social, cultural, ethnic, and organizational factors that shape the environment in which development occurs; and the service processes through which social workers safeguard and facilitate growth. The School implements its educational mission through the degree-conferring master's and doctoral programs, the Program of Continuing Education, the Clinical Research Institute, and the publication of *Smith College Studies in Social Work.*
Applying	The requirements for entry into Plan A of the M.S.W. program include a baccalaureate degree from an accredited college or university and approximately 20 semester hours in the social, biological, and psychological sciences. The advanced-standing program for B.S.W. graduates requires the submission of a case study and second-year-level clinical practice skills and knowledge. The application deadline for the coming June is February 21 and for early decision, January 5. The deadline for receiving all application materials is February 21. Applications received by January 5 are given preference in admission and early review of field placement requests. The deadline for application to the Ph.D. program is February 1; an M.S.W. degree is required. Financial aid applications should be filed as soon after January 1 as possible. The nonrefundable application fee for admission is $60. The School begins accepting applications for the coming June starting September 1.
Correspondence and Information	Office of Admission School for Social Work Smith College Northampton, Massachusetts 01063 Phone: 413-585-7960 E-mail: sswadm@email.smith.edu Web site: http://www.smith.edu/ssw

Smith College

THE FACULTY

Carolyn Jacobs, Dean; Ph.D., Brandeis.
Susan Donner, Associate Dean and Professor; Ph.D., Smith.
Joan Berzoff, Professor and Cochair, Doctoral Program; Ed.D., Boston University.
Joyce Everett, Professor and Cochair, Doctoral Program; Ph.D., Brandeis.
Kathryn Basham, Professor; Ph.D., Smith.
David L. Burton, Assistant Professor; Ph.D., Washington (Seattle).
Joanne Corbin, Associate Professor; Ph.D., Yale.
James Drisko, Professor; Ph.D., Boston College.
Mary F. Hall, Professor; Ph.D., Simmons.
Dennis Miehls, Associate Professor; Ph.D., Smith.
Joshua Miller, Professor; Ph.D., Connecticut.
Catherine Nye, Professor; Ph.D., Chicago.
Yoosun Park, Assistant Professor; Ph.D., Washington (Seattle).
Marsha Kline Pruett, Professor; Ph.D., Berkeley.
Phebe Sessions, Professor; Ph.D., Brandeis.

SPRINGFIELD COLLEGE

School of Social Work

Program of Study

The Springfield College School of Social Work has the mission of teaching social work practice and knowledge to prepare its students to meet universal human needs and to engender mutually beneficial interaction between individuals and societal systems at all levels, based on the principles of economic and social justice, dignity, and human rights.

The School of Social Work offers a 60-credit program leading to the Master of Social Work (M.S.W.) degree through a weekday program (full-time, two years) and a weekend program (part-time, three years). The 60 credits are distributed across four sequences, two field practicums and seminars, and three electives. Guided by the School's mission, the curriculum is designed around a generalist foundation year and an advanced generalist concentration year. Electives enrich the curriculum of the concentration year by providing students the opportunity to explore a specific area of advanced generalist practice in greater depth, depending on individual interests, strengths, and needs.

An advanced-standing Master of Social Work Program (32 credit hours) is available to qualified graduates of Bachelor of Social Work programs that are accredited by the Council of Social Work Education.

Students may also pursue a Master of Social Work/Juris Doctor (M.S.W./J.D.) degree with Western New England College School of Law (full-time, four years), which allows the student to earn both degrees in less time than it would take to pursue each degree separately. Having both a social and legal perspective effectively prepares graduates to meet the social work and legal challenges in many areas of practice, such as child welfare, education, mental health, individual and family practice, family mediation, services to the disabled, legal aid, criminal and juvenile justice, consumer protection, advocacy, employment, housing, community development, human rights, and evaluation of social-service programs. Students must complete the academic requirements of each institution for a total of 124 credits.

Research Facilities

The Babson Library collection mirrors the curriculum and is especially strong in the areas of social services, education, psychology, health, physical education, recreation, and sports. Staffed by professionals who assist in the use of library resources and provide library instruction and interlibrary loan and electronic reserve services, the library is a member of the Cooperating Libraries of Greater Springfield, the Western Massachusetts Regional Library System, NELINET, and the Massachusetts Library and Information Network—all of which provide greater access to resources for students. The library includes spacious reading areas, lounges, and individual and group study areas as well as an open computer lab and several electronic classrooms run by the Information and Technology Services Department. Students can access the catalog and its many databases from the library's home page, and other Web pages provide information about library services and policies and allow students to request help from the reference librarians or to submit interlibrary loan requests.

Financial Aid

Students may apply for a limited number of graduate associateships (which pay a monthly stipend), but financial aid availability varies from year to year. The Springfield College Office of Financial Aid provides associateship applications as well as information about federal loans.

Cost of Study

The 2006–07 cost per credit hour was $679. Tuition charges are based on the number of credits taken.

Living and Housing Costs

There are housing opportunities both on campus and in College-owned apartments off campus. Campus apartments are air conditioned and feature a computer-network connection, cable-television hookup, and local phone service with voice mail. College-owned apartments, located within easy walking distance, offer two to four private bedrooms and are furnished with beds, desks, dressers, chairs, sofas, and appliances. The rent for the academic year, about $6500 for single students, includes heat and utilities. Room and board total about $8100 a year, depending on accommodations and meal plan selected.

Student Group

The School of Social work has 260 graduate students.

Student Outcomes

The School of Social Work administers an alumni survey every two years as a part of the School's effort to maintain an ongoing evaluation of the M.S.W. program. Alumni report employment in social service agencies, hospitals, nursing homes, school systems, the criminal justice system, and private practice. Primary areas of practice include mental health, family and children's services, health, education, aging, and corrections. Most graduates choose to sit for professional social work licensure. Competent, qualified professionals delivering social services are a must in this era of accountability.

Location

The campus is located on Lake Massasoit, about 3 miles from the downtown area of Springfield, Massachusetts, offering the advantages of a small-town setting within a metropolitan area. The campus site covers 156 acres, including the 56-acre campground fronting the lake. The College is within a day's drive of major centers in the northeastern United States. Boston is less than a 2-hour drive away, and New York City is only 3 hours away. The Green Mountains of Vermont and the White Mountains of New Hampshire are easily reached via modern northbound highways. The entire area abounds in lakes, mountains, resorts, historic sites, museums, and other attractions.

The School of Social Work is located at the Brennan Center on Island Pond Road. The Brennan Center, a state-of-the-art facility, is located 1 mile from the main campus and has smart classrooms, an auditorium, a computer lab, a student lounge, and faculty and staff offices.

The College and The School

Since its founding more than 100 years ago, Springfield College continues to be concerned with the preparation of the total person—spirit, mind, and body. Its professional curriculum has been specifically designed to prepare students for careers in what have come to be known as the "human-helping" professions. The College lists more than 30,000 alumni whose professional education at Springfield has enabled them to assume leadership positions in virtually all areas of community service, including recreation, physical education, counseling, psychological services, education, commerce and industry, community leadership and development, rehabilitation services, health promotion, and physical, art, occupational, and recreational therapy.

Through the teaching of social work knowledge and practice, the School of Social Work prepares individuals to promote a commitment to meeting universal human needs that can engender mutually beneficial interaction between individuals and societal systems at all levels, based on principles of economic and social justice, dignity, and human rights.

Applying

M.S.W. applicants must have a bachelor's degree from an accredited institution that reflects a broad background in liberal arts, with at least 20 semester hours in the social, behavioral, and biological sciences, with an emphasis on human biology. Applicants should also have social work experience as an employee or volunteer or in an undergraduate field practicum and a GPA of at least 2.5 for all undergraduate work (3.0 or better in the last two years of academic work). M.S.W. students are admitted for the fall semester. Advanced-standing students are admitted for the summer semester.

Applicants interested in the combined M.S.W./J.D. degree program must successfully meet the separate admission requirements of each institution and be accepted into the combined degree program. Neither the Springfield College School of Social Work nor the Western New England School of Law admits new students for the spring semester.

The completed application, the $50 application fee, official transcripts from all universities attended, three letters of recommendation, and a personal statement that describes a student's relevant education, professional/work experience, personal characteristics, professional goals, and reasons for pursuing a M.S.W. degree must be submitted.

The deadline for applications and all supporting credentials is March 15. Applications that are received after the deadline are considered only if space is available.

Correspondence and Information

Mae E. Chillson, Admissions Coordinator
School of Social Work
Springfield College
263 Alden Street
Springfield, Massachusetts 01109-3797
Phone: 413-748-3060
E-mail: mchillso@spfldcol.edu
Web site: http://www.springfieldcollege.edu/homepage/dept.nsf/ssw

Springfield College

THE FACULTY AND THEIR RESEARCH

The School of Social Work at Springfield College is fortunate to have distinguished and dedicated faculty members who are experienced professionals, accomplished in their fields. Drawing from experience and current practice, they are committed to education and learning that addresses the needs and goals of today's social work students.

Miguel Arce, Assistant Professor; M.S.W., San Jose State, 1976. Program design and technical assistance, community and organizational practice.

James J. Canning, Associate Professor; Ph.D., Smith College, 1997. Clinical research; clinical practice with infants, adolescents, and families; social justice; social work practice.

Ann M. Drennan, Assistant Director of Field Education; M.S.S.W., Boston College, 1951. Social work, child welfare, field education.

William T. Fisher Jr., Associate Professor and Director of Field Education; Ed.D., Columbia Teachers College, 1989. Alcohol and substance abuse counseling, community organizing, community mental-health program evaluation.

Joseph R. Gianesin, Associate Professor; Ph.D., Denver, 1995. School administration, group work, school social work, male adolescent development, therapeutic applications of adventure.

Walter J. Mullin, Assistant Professor; Ph.D., Boston College, 1999. Children and families, adult mental health, couples treatment, ethnicity in clinical practice.

Ann W. Roy, Professor; Ph.D., Case Western Reserve, 1985. Quantitative research, gerontology, policy advocacy, social work.

Linda Anderson Smith, Professor; D.S.W., CUNY, Hunter, 1989. Community mental-health practice, program development and evaluation, clinical practice with overwhelmed families and individuals across the life span, diversity.

Francine J. Vecchiolla, Professor and Dean; Ph.D., Brandeis, 1987. Child welfare, program development, public/private collaboration, administration, management and leadership.

Katherine Walsh, Professor; Ph.D., Boston College, 1990. Oncology social work, therapeutic applications of adventure, family treatment, women's issues, end of life, loss and bereavement.

Joseph Wronka, Professor; Ph.D., Brandeis, 1992. Qualitative research, social-welfare policy, global human rights.

Adjunct Faculty

Al Alissi, Ph.D., D.S.W.
Steven Bogatz, M.S.W.
Mary Brainerd, Ph.D., LICSW.
Jean Carosella, M.S.W.
Kenneth Cunningham, M.S.W., LCSW.
Mary Ann Franco, M.S.W.
Margie Gilberti, M.S.W.
John Habif, M.S.W.
Susan Hauschild, M.S.W., UCSW, ACSW, CADAC.
Terri Haven, M.S.W.
Aura L. Irizarry, M.S.W., LCSW, SAC.
Winston Barrington Johnston, M.S.W., LCSW, ACSW.
Sandra Joyner, M.S.W.
Ellen Lang, M.S.W., LICSW.
Frances Lipsky, M.S.W., LPN.
Luz Marcano, M.S.W.
Jennifer Markens, M.S.W., LICSW.
Blanche Martin, M.S.W.
Anita Minkin, M.S.W.
Aimee Mitchell, M.S.W., LICSW.
Karen Poisson, M.S.W., LICSW.
Edwina Ranganathan, M.S.W.
Karen Reininger, M.S.W., LICSW.
Dora Robinson, M.S.W.
Frank Robinson, M.S.W.
Karen Seltzer, M.S.W., LICSW, LADCI.
Karen Sherping, M.S.W.
Douglas B. Stephens, Ed.D.
Margaret Wynne, M.S.W.
Charlotte Zeller, M.Ed., M.S.W., L.I.C.S.W.

STATE UNIVERSITY OF NEW YORK
STONY BROOK
THE GRADUATE SCHOOL

STONY BROOK UNIVERSITY, STATE UNIVERSITY OF NEW YORK
School of Social Welfare

Programs of Study

The School of Social Welfare is committed to a society organized around the principles of equality, human dignity, and social justice. In fulfillment of this mission, it offers a Master of Social Work (M.S.W.) degree for advanced social work practice and a social work and law dual degree (M.S.W./J.D.) with the Touro Law Center. Also available is a doctoral program leading to a Ph.D. degree, which emphasizes policy and research in the field of health and mental health and prepares students for careers in social welfare research, teaching, and policy analysis.

The M.S.W. program generally requires two years (64 credits) and combines classroom study with field placements in social welfare agencies. The curriculum provides students with the theoretical and practice expertise needed to function with maximum competence at different administrative or policy levels in social welfare and in the provision of direct services to individuals, families, groups, and communities. The first year is a generalist foundation year. In the second year, students concentrate in advanced social work practice. In addition to the regular full-time two-year program, the School has two alternative pathways that extend the time necessary to earn the degree, as well as one specialization in health with subspecializations in alcohol and substance abuse or public health and another specialization in student-community development. Completion of the course work for the Ph.D. program requires three years full-time or four years part-time. A total of 54 course credits are required for the doctorate, including both research and teaching practicums under faculty mentorship before the writing and defense of the dissertation.

Research Facilities

The School of Social Welfare is located within the Health Sciences Center, which includes the University Hospital and the Medical School as well as the Schools of Dental Medicine, Nursing, and Health Technology and Management. These facilities offer a unique opportunity for interdisciplinary practice and research experience at both the master's and doctoral levels. The Health Sciences Center Library contains approximately 275,000 volumes in social welfare and the health sciences. Students may also utilize the 1.7 million volumes of the University's Frank Melville, Jr. Memorial Library for related areas of inquiry. In addition, computer labs are located both in the Health Sciences Center and at other sites on campus.

Financial Aid

A variety of financial aid is available. This aid includes the Graduate Tuition Waiver program for former Educational Opportunity Program students, as well as several fellowships for minority students and tuition waivers for New York State residents in the doctoral program. Doctoral students are also eligible for renewable University-wide fellowships paying more than $15,000 per year, graduate assistantships, tuition waivers, and research stipends.

Cost of Study

In 2006–07, full-time tuition at 12 credits for entering in-state residents was $3450 per semester, while out-of-state residents and international students paid $5460. Additional fees for each semester, including (but not limited to) the infirmary, activity, technology, and transportation fee, amount to about $430. International students also pay a service fee of $35 per semester and an orientation fee of $50. Fees for the mandatory Student Health Insurance Plan vary depending on citizenship and employment status.

Living and Housing Costs

For 2006–07, Stony Brook calculated the cost of education excluding tuition, fees, and insurance at $13,520 per year. On-campus apartments range in cost from approximately $316 per month to approximately $1456 per month, depending on the size of the unit and the number of students sharing the space. Off-campus housing options include rooms, houses, and apartments that can be rented from $350 to $2500 per month. Costs including books, food, and transportation may vary depending on academic program and/or personal circumstances.

Student Group

In the most recent demographic analysis, the M.S.W. program had 355 full-time students and 10 part-time students, including 298 women. One hundred sixty-two students, or 48 percent of the School, were members of minority groups: 70 African Americans, 3 Asian Americans, and 38 Latinos/Hispanics. The average age of students in the M.S.W. program is 30. The doctoral program admits up to 8 full-time and 4 part-time students each year. Its composition is diverse.

Student Outcomes

Graduates of the M.S.W. program hold a wide variety of positions in social welfare. They are employed as social workers in schools, in hospitals, and in facilities dealing with substance abuse. Graduates do counseling in community agencies for different populations, including young people, victims of domestic violence, and the aged. They also advocate and do policy-related work in all these arenas. The Ph.D. program trains students for positions in the field of social welfare as teachers, researchers, and policy analysts.

Location

One of four university centers in the State University of New York system, SUNY at Stony Brook is located 60 miles east of New York City on Long Island's wooded north shore. The campus consists of 1,100 acres, with a total of 105 University buildings. In addition to excellent academic resources, students find diverse cultural and recreational opportunities, including the Staller Center for the Arts, a 26-acre nature preserve, and the nearby beaches of Long Island Sound. The School of Social Welfare is located in the Health Sciences Center on the East Campus.

The University and The Program

The University was founded in 1957 as a small college in Oyster Bay, Long Island, that educated students to become math and science teachers. In 1960, the State Board of Regents mandated the college to become a comprehensive research university. Construction of the new campus at Stony Brook began in 1962. The School of Social Welfare opened in 1971 and has now prepared about 4,000 people for careers in social work.

Applying

The deadline for application and financial aid requests for the M.S.W. programs is March 1. The deadline for the Ph.D. program is February 1. Personal interviews are required for the Ph.D. program but are optional for the M.S.W. program. Applicants to the Ph.D. program are notified by March 15, while M.S.W. applicants are notified by May 1. The Graduate Record Examinations are required only for doctoral applicants.

Correspondence and Information

M.S.W. program inquiries should be directed to:
Dr. Angel Campos
Chairperson, Admissions Committee
School of Social Welfare, Health Sciences Center
Stony Brook University, State University of New York
Stony Brook, New York 11794-8231

Phone: 631-444-3141
E-mail: kalbin@notes.cc.sunysb.edu
Web site: http://www.hsc.stonybrook.edu/ssw

Ph.D. program inquiries should be directed to:
Dr. Joel Blau
Director, Ph.D. Program
School of Social Welfare, Health Sciences Center
Stony Brook University, State University of New York
Stony Brook, New York 11794-8231

Phone: 631-444-3149
E-mail: jblau@notes.cc.sunysb.edu
Web site: http://www.hsc.stonybrook.edu/ssw/phd.cfm

Stony Brook University, State University of New York

THE FACULTY AND THEIR RESEARCH

Gloria Adams, Lecturer and Coordinator, Faith-Based Community Partnerships; D.Min., Hartford Seminary. Spirituality and religion in social work.

Jean Bacon, Clinical Assistant Professor and Assistant Director, Field Instruction; Ph.D., South Carolina. Death and dying, ethnic-sensitive practice, AIDS, child welfare, qualitative methods, mental health, student-community development, women's studies.

Candyce S. Berger, Associate Professor; Ph.D., USC. Health policy, social work practice in health-care settings, structure and financing of health-care delivery, administration and leadership, resizing and restructuring strategies, case management, women's health.

Joel Blau, Professor and Director, Ph.D. Program; D.S.W., Columbia. Social policy, history of social welfare, poverty, homelessness, the political economy of social welfare, comparative social welfare.

Ruth Brandwein, Professor; Ph.D., Brandeis. Family violence, welfare, and poverty; women in administration; organizational and social change; single-parent families; feminist frameworks; history of U.S. social policy; international social welfare.

Frances Brisbane, Professor and Dean; Ph.D., Union (Ohio). Alcoholism and other drug addictions, counseling with people of color, complementary medicine, cultural competence, spirituality, international health and social work, suicide.

Angel P. Campos, Associate Professor and Executive Associate Dean; Ed.D., Columbia. Hispanics/Latinos in the United States, the Hispanic/Latino family, mental health and the Hispanic/Latino, cross-cultural social work practice, cultural competency in social work practice, social gerontology, social work education.

John Colon, Lecturer and Assistant to the Dean; M.A., Inter American of Puerto Rico. Substance abuse, methadone treatment, inner-city community-based organizations.

Harvey A. Farberman, Professor; Ph.D., Minnesota. Philosophy of social work, public mental health services, research.

Jack Farrington, Clinical Associate Professor; Ph.D., Nova Southeastern. Community health orientation, advocacy, human rights for Long Island teenagers, domestic violence.

Jeanne Bertrand Finch, Clinical Associate Professor and Assistant Dean, Field Instruction; D.S.W., Columbia. Child welfare, social work practice, drug-involved women and their children, clinical practice with children in foster care, qualitative research, and quality assurance within nonprofit organizations.

Linda E. Francis, Clinical Assistant Professor and Director, Graduate Program; Ph.D., Indiana. Mental health, health services research, qualitative methods, stress and emotion.

Rose Leung, Assistant Professor; Psy.D., Biola. Community psychology, community mental health, psychosocial models of intervention, Asian American communities' needs and assessments, racial/cultural sensitivity training and education.

Michael A. Lewis, Associate Professor and Assistant Dean, New York City Sites; Ph.D., CUNY Graduate Center. Poverty and social policy, the application of sociology, economics, and moral philosophy to the examination of social policy and social programs.

Abraham Lurie, Professor; Ph.D., NYU. Mental health, case management, the aged.

Kathleen Monahan, Associate Professor; D.S.W., Adelphi. Siblings and sexual abuse, battered women, domestic violence, disability.

Richard Morgan, Clinical Assistant Professor; Ph.D., Fordham. Child welfare policy and programs, child sexual abuse and juvenile sex offenders, research.

Bertha Murphy, Clinical Assistant Professor and Director, Undergraduate Program; M.S.W., SUNY at Stony Brook. Substance abuse and ethnically sensitive practice.

Carolyn Peabody, Clinical Assistant Professor and Assistant Dean, Eastern Long Island Sites; Ph.D., SUNY at Stony Brook. Advocacy/empowerment theory and practice, feminist theory and practice, mental health, lesbian and gay issues, development of political identity among oppressed populations, impact of sexual abuse histories among mental health populations.

Charles Robbins, Associate Professor and Associate Dean, Academic Affairs; D.S.W., Yeshiva. Violence in intimate relationships and as a public health problem, health-care policy, social work and health care, use of complementary medicine, international public health, international social work, gender issues.

Carlos M. Vidal, Associate Professor and Associate Dean, Development and External Affairs; Ph.D., Fordham. Child welfare policy and research methods, Hispanics, empowerment and advocacy, health-care issues among children of color, violence in schools and communities of color.

Betty Jean Wrase, Clinical Assistant Professor and Assistant Director, Field Instruction; M.S.W., SUNY at Stony Brook. Program evaluation, social welfare administration, case management and health.

RESEARCH, SERVICE, AND TRAINING PROJECTS

Center for Health Promotion and Wellness
Centers for Culturally Competent Education and Training
New York State Center for Aging Policy Research
New York State Center for Sudden Infant Death
Project for Aging and Cultural Diversity
Sayville Project
The Child Welfare Training Program
The Family Violence Education and Research Center
The Social Justice Center

UNIVERSITY OF CHICAGO

School of Social Service Administration

Programs of Study	The School of Social Service Administration offers programs of study in social work leading to the Master of Arts and Doctor of Philosophy degrees.
	The Master of Arts program, a two-year curriculum of general study and specialization, prepares students for a wide range of career opportunities in the field of social work. In the first two quarters, students take core courses on the policy and programs of social welfare, the practice of social intervention, research and evaluation, and HBSE (Human Behavior in the Social Environment). These courses stress the common themes and problems that occur in diverse social work efforts. In the remaining four quarters, students select a concentration in advanced clinical social work practice or social administration. Specialization within a concentration is also available. Classroom and field instruction are integrated throughout the course of the program.
	The School also has a part-time evening program that enables students to work full-time and complete the degree requirements in three years. A part-time day program is also available.
	The Doctor of Philosophy program prepares students for careers in research and teaching. Specializations are offered in social development (policy, planning, and management), social treatment, and combined social development and social treatment. Programs are tailored to the student's scholarly and research interests. A dissertation is required.
	The School of Social Service Administration and the Graduate School of Business offer a joint-degree program, which leads to both the A.M. and the M.B.A. degrees in three academic years. A joint-degree program is also offered by the School of Social Service Administration and the Harris School of Public Policy leading to the A.M. and M.P.P. degrees in three years. In addition, the School also offers a joint-degree program with the Divinity School, which leads to both the A.M. and M.Div. degrees in four academic years. The School of Social Service Administration has developed dual-degree arrangements with several schools from the Chicago Cluster of Theological Schools. The concurrent dual-degree program enables students to receive both the A.M. and M.Div. degrees in one less year than it would if both degree programs were taken sequentially. Interested students must apply to both schools in each of the specific programs.
Research Facilities	The Joseph Regenstein Library is a graduate research library in the social sciences and humanities. It is the center of the University library's collections of approximately 3.5 million volumes and is complemented by the library of the School of Social Service Administration.
	Students may participate in the work of various research projects as well as in the Chapin Hall Center for Children, the Committee on Public Policy Studies, the Center for Health Administration Studies, the Center for Urban Research and Policy Studies, and the National Opinion Research Center (NORC).
Financial Aid	More than 90 percent of the students receive scholarship aid from the School and from outside sources. Assistance is available through scholarships and loans drawn from federal funds and School and University sources. A number of research and teaching assistantships are also available.
Cost of Study	Tuition for the full-time program was $30,100 for 2006–07. The cost of the part-time program was $21,522 per year in 2006–07.
Living and Housing Costs	The cost of living for a single student for the 2006–07 academic year, including tuition, academic supplies, room, and board was approximately $49,512; estimated expenses for married students were approximately $53,000. Housing is available in University dormitories and apartments and in private lodgings off campus.
Student Group	Each year, the School admits approximately 175 students to the master's degree program and 8 to the doctoral program. Students come to the School from a wide range of academic disciplines and with a great variety of work experiences in social work and other fields. Students vary widely in age (more than a quarter of the master's degree students are over 30 years old) and by culture, race, and ethnicity. Thirty-two percent of the students in the 2006–07 student body are members of minority groups.
Student Outcomes	Recent SSA graduates are pursuing a variety of careers. They work as clinicians in traditional social work agencies and in such nontraditional settings as corporate headquarters, banks, and industrial plants; as policy analysts with local, state, and federal agencies, as well as with nonprofit advocacy groups; as consultants with management consulting firms; as researchers in academia and agencies; as community planners and organizers working on a wide range of problems; and in a variety of other positions in the private, public, and voluntary sectors.
Location	The University of Chicago is located in Hyde Park, a politically independent and racially integrated neighborhood 15 minutes from the Loop, the heart of downtown Chicago. Students at the School have access to Chicago's outstanding cultural, recreational, and athletic activities. The University is less than a mile from Lake Michigan, which offers picnic areas, beaches, harbors, and miles of walking and bicycle paths. An unusually wide range of cultural and recreational facilities is also available on campus.
The School	The School of Social Service Administration is part of the University of Chicago and shares the University's dedication to excellence in teaching, research, and service. The School was incorporated into the University in 1920, bringing the programs of the Chicago School of Civics and Philanthropy together with programs in other parts of the University. The School has its own building, designed by Ludwig Mies van der Rohe, which opened in 1964. The building is located near the Law School, the National Opinion Research Center, and the University of Chicago Hospitals. The *Social Service Review,* an outstanding scholarly journal in the field, has been published continuously by the School since 1927. The School also works closely with the Woodlawn Social Services Center, which houses a variety of social service agencies and is the site of some training and demonstration programs.
Applying	Students enter the A.M. and Ph.D. programs in the autumn quarter only. The application deadlines for the master's program are December 1, January 15, and April 1; for the Ph.D. program, the deadline is December 15. Interviews are normally not required, but prospective students are encouraged to visit the School. Applicants for financial assistance must file the Free Application for Federal Student Aid, which is available online at http://www.fafsa.gov.
Correspondence and Information	Director of Admissions School of Social Service Administration University of Chicago 969 East 60th Street Chicago, Illinois 60637 Phone: 773-702-1492 Fax: 773-834-4751 E-mail: admissions@ssa.uchicago.edu Web site: http://www.ssa.uchicago.edu/

University of Chicago

THE FACULTY

Beth Angell, Ph.D., Assistant Professor.
Sharon B. Berlin, Ph.D., Helen Ross Professor.
William Borden, Ph.D., Senior Lecturer.
Evelyn Z. Brodkin, Ph.D., Associate Professor.
E. Summerson Carr, Ph.D., Assistant Professor.
Robert Chaskin, Ph.D., Associate Professor and Research Fellow, Chapin Hall Center for Children.
Yoonsun Choi, Ph.D., Assistant Professor and Faculty Associate, Chapin Hall Center for Children.
Mark Courtney, Ph.D., McCormick Tribune Professor and Faculty Associate, Chapin Hall Center for Children.
Malitta Engstrom, Ph.D., Assistant Professor.
Robert P. Fairbanks II, Ph.D., Assistant Professor.
Sarah Gehlert, Ph.D., Professor and Deputy Dean, Research; Director, Center for Health Disparities Research; Faculty, Graduate Program in Health Administration and Policy; Research Associate, Center for Health Administration Studies.
Colleen Grogan, Ph.D., Associate Professor; Director, Center for Health Administration Studies; and Faculty Chair, Graduate Program in Health Administration and Policy.
Neil Guterman, Ph.D., Professor.
Sydney L. Hans, Ph.D., Associate Professor and Chair of the Doctoral Program.
Julia R. Henly, Ph.D., Associate Professor.
Penny Ruff Johnson, Ph.D., Lecturer and Dean of Students.
Waldo E. Johnson Jr., Ph.D., Associate Professor; Faculty Associate, Chapin Hall Center for Children; and Director, Center for the Study of Race, Politics, and Culture.
Susan J. Lambert, Ph.D., Associate Professor.
Judith Levine, Ph.D., Assistant Professor; Research Associate, Population Research Center; Research Associate, Alfred P. Sloan Center on Parents, Children, and Work.
Jeanne C. Marsh, Ph.D., George Herbert Jones Professor and Dean.
Stanley McCracken, Ph.D., Senior Lecturer.
Jennifer Mosley, Ph.D., Assistant Professor.
Dolores G. Norton, Ph.D., Samuel Deutsch Professor.
Virginia Parks, Ph.D., Assistant Professor.
Harold Pollack, Ph.D., Associate Professor and Faculty Chair, Center for Health Administration Studies.
Melissa Roderick, Ph.D., Hermon Dunlap Smith Professor.
Tina L. Rzepnicki, Ph.D., David and Mary Winton-Greene Professor.
Gina Samuels, Ph.D., Assistant Professor and Faculty Associate, Chapin Hall Center for Children.
William Sites, Ph.D., Associate Professor.
Michael Sosin, Ph.D., Emily Klein Gidwitz Professor and Editor, *Social Service Review.*
Karen Teigiser, A.M., Senior Lecturer and Deputy Dean, Master's Program.
Dexter Voisin, Ph.D., Associate Professor Faculty Associate, Chapin Hall Center for Children.
Froma Walsh, Ph.D., Mose and Sylvia Firestone Professor and Co-Director, Center for Family Health.
Henry Webber, M.P.P., Senior Lecturer and Vice President, Community Affairs.

UNIVERSITY OF DENVER

Graduate School of Social Work

Programs of Study	The University of Denver Graduate School of Social Work (GSSW) offers courses of study leading to a doctoral degree (Ph.D.) and a master's degree (M.S.W.) that includes certificates in social work with Latinos/as, trauma response and recovery, and animal-assisted social work. A certificate in couples and family therapy is offered in cooperation with the Denver Family Institute. The University of Denver also offers a dual undergraduate/graduate program through which students may earn a baccalaureate degree and the M.S.W. in a total of five years.
	The two-year M.S.W. program is organized into the foundation year and the concentration year. The foundation year provides knowledge and skills essential to all social work practice. The concentration year prepares students for advanced community practice (administration, community development and organizing, and policy analysis and advocacy) or advanced clinical practice (specializing in child welfare, families, high-risk youth, or adulthood and late-life challenges). Field internships are required both years, and students may choose from among 600 field placement sites. Interdisciplinary dual- and cooperative-degree programs are offered in international studies, law, human communication, and theology. Students may also propose an interdisciplinary dual degree that fits their goals. Part-time, weekend, and evening classes are available to accommodate students who are employed.
	GSSW offers a one-year advanced standing M.S.W. program that is available to students with an undergraduate degree in social work from a college or university whose social work program is accredited by, or in accreditation candidacy with, the Council on Social Work Education at the time the degree is conferred. Advanced-standing students begin in the summer or fall quarter. Full-time advanced-standing students complete their degree requirements in four quarters (one calendar year).
	The program leading to the Ph.D. in social work is both theory- and research-oriented to encourage the development of scholarly and professional competence at an advanced level. It includes three components that are individualized to facilitate achievement of each student's career goals: courses offered by GSSW and other departments within the University, a comprehensive examination, and dissertation research. Students may enroll either full-time or part-time. Course work for full-time students is usually completed during the second year of study. Course work is followed first by the comprehensive examination necessary for advancement to final candidacy and then by dissertation research conducted under the guidance of members of the faculty.
Research Facilities	Craig Hall, a new, state-of-the-art educational facility that was completed in 2005, includes clinical practice suites with audio/videotaping capabilities, a virtual library with access to national research findings, and technology-enhanced classrooms, several of which are equipped to broadcast and simulcast distance education classes. Research at GSSW provides vital information to national and state policy makers and enriches learning among GSSW students. Research and training specialties include child welfare, high-risk youth, mental health, and gerontology. GSSW is home to the Butler Institute for Families, the Institute of Gerontology, and the Institute for Human-Animal Connection.
Financial Aid	Financial aid for M.S.W. students includes federal loans, GSSW scholarships, the Federal Work-Study Program, Colorado Graduate Grants, and child welfare and gerontology stipends. Graduate teaching and research assistantships and Graduate Studies Doctoral Fellowships are forms of financial aid available for doctoral students. Filing the Free Application for Federal Student Aid (FAFSA) is required for any need-based aid.
Cost of Study	In 2006–07, tuition for full-time study (12 to 18 quarter-hour credits) is $29,628 per year, or $9876 per quarter. Part-time students pay $823 per credit hour. Health insurance and other fees are also required.
Living and Housing Costs	The estimated cost of living in 2006–07 for a single student without children is $10,680 per academic year. This estimate is exclusive of tuition costs and fees. Students should contact the Graduate Housing Office for graduate housing information (telephone: 303-282-4311; Web site: http://www.du.edu/housing).
Student Group	The School's total enrollment in the academic year 2005–06 was 392 students, of whom 278 were full-time master's students and 78 were part-time. There were 36 doctoral students. Among the part-time master's students were 25 students enrolled in GSSW's Four Corners Distance Education program based in Durango, Colorado. The School's diverse population includes African-American, Latino/a, Native American, Asian-American, and international students. Approximately 40 percent of the students are from outside of Colorado.
Location	The Denver metropolitan area has an excellent climate because of its location on a mile-high plateau at the foot of the Rockies. Its 2000 population was 2.5 million. As the capital of Colorado, Denver is the center of regional offices of federal services and state social welfare, education, and health programs. It is rich in both public and private agencies, hospitals, schools, and other organizations, offering more than 600 approved field internship sites. Outdoor recreation and outstanding cultural programs in music, art, and drama are readily available. Denver is home to professional sports teams in football, baseball, hockey, basketball, and soccer.
The University	The oldest independent university in the Rocky Mountain region, the University of Denver (DU) was founded in 1864, twelve years before Colorado became a state. A DU education is distinguished by an emphasis on values, racial and cultural awareness, and global perspective. The University offers fifty-six bachelor's degree programs, 103 graduate degree programs, and fourteen certificate programs, representing a full range of disciplines in the arts, humanities, social sciences, natural sciences, business, and other professions. Located in a residential neighborhood in the heart of one of the country's most exciting and livable cities, DU attracts students from all fifty states and around the world.
Applying	Applicants for the master's program must have an undergraduate degree from a regionally accredited college or university and should present a broad background in the liberal arts. It is recommended that incoming students have a basic knowledge of research methods and statistics and be competent in using a personal computer. Admission factors include experience, grade point average, career goals, and references. Applicants are encouraged to submit all application materials by February 1 of the year in which they are seeking admission. Applications are reviewed on a rolling basis.
	Applicants to the doctoral program must have a master's degree conferred by a school of social work accredited by CSWE or a master's degree in another social science with demonstrated evidence of substantial professional experience in social work. They must have a superior academic record, adhere to professional social work values and ethics, and demonstrate evidence of maturity, intellectual ability, and readiness for advance study. At least two years of post-master's practice experience is preferable but not mandatory. Preference is given to prospective doctoral students with an interest in child welfare, high-risk youth, mental health, or gerontology. Applicants must submit a Graduate Record Examinations (GRE) General Test score from within the past five years and have a basic proficiency in descriptive and inferential statistics. Prospective students should apply between September and January prior to the year in which they seek admission. Applications may be accepted until May 1 if space remains available.
Correspondence and Information	Director of Admission Graduate School of Social Work University of Denver 2148 South High Street Denver, Colorado 80208 Phone: 303-871-2841 E-mail: gssw-admission@du.edu Web site: http://www.du.edu/gssw

University of Denver

THE FACULTY AND THEIR RESEARCH INTERESTS

Catherine F. Alter, Professor; Ph.D., Maryland. Networking as a strategy for social change, microenterprise and self-employment programs promoting women's self-sufficiency.

Inna Altschul, Assistant Professor; Ph.D., Michigan. Promoting academic achievement among low-income immigrant and Latino/a youth.

Maria Yellow Horse Brave Heart, Associate Research Professor; Ph.D., Smith. American Indian/Alaska Native mental health and child welfare, genocide, intergenerational trauma and unresolved grief, psychodynamic theory and practice, substance abuse prevention, minority issues and diversity.

Daniel Brisson, Assistant Professor; Ph.D., North Carolina at Chapel Hill. Community practice, community development issues in low-income neighborhoods.

Marian C. Bussey, Associate Professor; Ph.D., Texas at Arlington. Children's mental health, American Indian child welfare, emotionally disturbed children and adults, chronic mental illness, trauma and substance abuse.

William A. Cloud, Professor; Ph.D., Denver. Substance abuse treatment, prevention, and policy.

Susan Stark Connelly, Gerontology Specialist; M.S.S.W., Columbia. Geriatric social work practice.

Enid Opal Cox, Professor; D.S.W., Columbia. Social policy, gerontology, empowerment-oriented practice, elderly care-receivers, housing for the elderly.

Jean Demmler, Research Associate Professor; Ph.D., McMaster. Social policy, evidence-based social system change and service system improvement.

Jean F. East, Associate Professor; Ph.D., Denver. Welfare reform, low-income women, community empowerment, leadership, administration, supervision.

Wanda Ellingson, Clinical Assistant Professor; M.S.W., Minnesota. Distance education, international social work, bilingual/bicultural mental health services, child and family mental health.

Ben Fransua, Clinical Assistant Professor; M.S.W., Denver. M.S.W. field education in southern Colorado.

Stacey Freedenthal, Assistant Professor; Ph.D., Washington (St. Louis). Adult and adolescent mental health, suicide risk and protective factors.

Julie Anne Laser Haddow, Assistant Professor; Ph.D., Michigan State. Adolescent resiliency, including the relevance of specific protective and risk factors by culture and gender.

Michele D. Hanna, Assistant Professor; Ph.D., Texas at Austin. Special-needs adoption, child welfare, foster care, multicultural practice.

Carole Fee Ivanoff, Clinical Associate Professor; Ph.D., Denver. Nature and meaning of mentoring for women in social work academe, direct practice skills, integration of course work and field work.

Jeffrey M. Jenson, Professor; Ph.D., Washington (Seattle). Etiology, prevention, and treatment of juvenile delinquency and adolescent substance abuse; youth violence; juvenile gangs and juvenile justice.

John A. Kayser, Associate Professor; Ph.D., Denver. Child and adult mental health in interprofessional contexts and interdisciplinary practice settings, late life challenges, narrative and oral history research with social work practitioners.

Walter F. LaMendola, Professor; Ph.D., Minnesota. Human service information technology.

Susan S. Manning, Professor; Ph.D., Denver. Empowerment outcomes and interventions for people with serious psychiatric disability, professional ethics as applied to leaders, administrators, and managers.

Christian E. Molidor, Professor and Interim Dean; Ph.D., Illinois at Chicago. Teen dating violence, gang and juvenile violence, female delinquency.

Nicole Nicotera, Assistant Professor; Ph.D., Washington (Seattle). Neighborhood effects on parenting and developmental outcomes; unearned privilege and oppression in social work practice, education, and research.

Kathleen Ohman, Professor and Associate Dean; Ph.D., Illinois at Urbana-Champaign. Child welfare policy and services, legal aspects of social work practice, services for homeless youth, home visitation for infants.

Debora Ortega, Associate Professor; Ph.D., Washington (Seattle). Child welfare, foster care, culturally responsive practice, family therapy, social work with Latinos/as.

Lynn Parker, Associate Professor; Ph.D., Denver. Social justice issues in families, couples, and society; power, privilege, and oppression in therapeutic work.

Ann T. Petrila, Clinical Assistant Professor and Director, Field Education; M.S.W., M.P.A., Denver. M.S.W. field education, children's mental health, child maltreatment, foster care.

Cathryn C. Potter, Associate Professor; Ph.D., Denver. Child welfare, juvenile justice, children's mental health.

Colleen J. Reed, Assistant Professor; Ph.D., Kansas. Gerontology, mental health and aging.

Kathryn Ross, Clinical Assistant Professor; M.S.W., Denver. M.S.W. field education.

Michele Sienkiewicz, Clinical Assistant Professor; M.S.W., Fordham. Student placement and professional development for M.S.W. field education.

Philip Tedeschi, Animal-Assisted Social Work Specialist; M.S.W., Wisconsin–Madison. Animal-assisted social work, forensic social work, experiential therapy.

N. Eugene Walls, Assistant Professor; Ph.D., Notre Dame. Community practice; social stratification; social movements; gender, lesbian, and gay issues; homelessness; stereotypes.

UNIVERSITY OF MICHIGAN

School of Social Work

Programs of Study

The School offers programs leading to the Master of Social Work and a Doctor of Philosophy in Social Work and Social Science. Dual degrees with the School of Public Health (M.S.W./M.P.H.), the Graduate School of Business Administration (M.S.W./M.B.A.), the School of Public Policy Studies (M.S.W./M.P.P.), the College of Architecture and Urban Planning (M.S.W./M.U.P.), the School of Information (M.S.W./M.S.I.), and the Law School (J.D./M.S.W.) are offered; also offered are certificates in aging, Judaic studies and Jewish communal service (child welfare fellowships and geriatric fellowships), and preparation in public school social work.

The M.S.W. is a 60-credit-hour, dual-concentration program that offers opportunities for professional training and field instruction in a choice of practice methods and practice areas. Practice methods include interpersonal practice, community organization, management of human services, and social policy and evaluation. Practice areas include health, mental health, children and youth in families in society, aging in families in society, and community and social systems.

The doctoral program grants a Ph.D. in social work jointly with one of five social sciences disciplines (i.e., anthropology, economics, political science, psychology, or sociology). Students not only gain expertise in knowledge development and research in social work but are also trained as social scientists, thus acquiring broad career options. These include teaching and research positions in schools of social work, social science departments, research institutes, and public and private social planning and social welfare agencies. The specifics of the program vary with each social science department and the student's prior preparation.

Research Facilities

The School has its own library, which has on on-site collection of approximately 45,000 volumes and 180 journal and periodical subscriptions. It is an integral part of the University library system, which has a collection of more than 7 million books, current journals, video and audio tapes, and maps, and access to thousands of online resources. The School also has its own on-site computer laboratory, which provides easy access to numerous microcomputers that are also connected to the Computer Center, whose hardware, statistical packages, and training centers are rated among the best in the world. The School's full-time faculty members are leading scholars in their field. Several hold joint appointments or collaborative relations with other University of Michigan teaching and research units, including the Departments of Anthropology, Education, Psychology, Sociology, Economics, and Psychiatry; School of Public Health; School of Public Policy; Institute for Social Research; Institute of Gerontology; Institute of Labor and Industrial Relations; Population Studies Center; and the Law School's Child Advocacy Clinic.

Financial Aid

In the M.S.W. program, financial aid through the School of Social Work is awarded on the basis of financial need and/or merit. This aid may take the form of grants, scholarships, fellowships, and memorial awards. The University's Office of Financial Aid administers Federal Direct Student Loans, Federal Perkins Loans, and college work-study to eligible students. In the Ph.D. program, all students are guaranteed funding through fellowships or program-related employment. Ph.D. students are also eligible for a wide variety of scholarships, fellowships, and other funding opportunities, which are available in the social science department and through the Rackham School of Graduate Studies.

Cost of Study

M.S.W. student tuition per semester was $8146 for state residents and $13,874 for nonresidents in 2005–06. Tuition charges are subject to approval by the Board of Regents.

Living and Housing Costs

Estimated monthly living expenses are $1600. Rooms, apartments, and houses for single and married students are available for a wide range of rents in Ann Arbor and the surrounding area.

Student Group

In fall 2005, there were 609 students enrolled in the M.S.W. program and 70 active students in the Ph.D. program. The School has a diverse student body with a representation from local, national, and international undergraduate and graduate colleges and universities. In continuing to expand its diversified student body, the School encourages applications from nonresidents, international students, and other underrepresented groups, including the LGBT community and members of minority groups.

Location

Ann Arbor, with a population of 114,000, is located 40 miles southwest of Detroit. It has the charm of a small city and the excitement of a cosmopolitan center. High-technology industry and research activities are centered in Ann Arbor. The landscape is a blend of parks, office buildings, boutiques, malls, bike paths, and tree-lined streets. Cultural, recreational, and social opportunities are plentiful.

The University and The School

The University of Michigan has long been recognized as a leader among institutions of higher education. The University had a fall 2005 student enrollment of approximately 39,990 students, of whom 14,600 were graduate students. The School of Social Work is internationally recognized for its outstanding programs and is ranked first by *U.S. News & World Report.*

Applying

Applicants for the M.S.W. program must have a baccalaureate degree from an accredited college or university with competitive grades; a minimum of 20 semester hours in social sciences; and personal qualifications considered essential for successful professional practice. Admission to the M.S.W. program is limited to the fall term. The priority processing deadline is March 1; the international student application priority processing deadline is February 1.

Applicants for the Ph.D. program must have scholarly potential and promise for advanced interdisciplinary work in social work and their elected social science. Graduate Record Examinations results are required. All materials, including GRE scores, must be received by December 15.

Correspondence and Information

For the M.S.W. program:
Office of Student Services
School of Social Work
University of Michigan
1080 South University, Room 1748
Ann Arbor, Michigan 48109-1106
Phone: 734-764-3309
E-mail: ssw.msw.info@umich.edu
Web site: http://www.ssw.umich.edu

For the Ph.D. program:
Doctoral Program in Social Work and
 Social Science
School of Social Work
University of Michigan
1080 South University, Room 1696
Ann Arbor, Michigan 48109-1106
Phone: 734-763-5768
E-mail: ssw.phd.info@umich.edu
Web site: http://www.ssw.umich.edu

University of Michigan

THE FACULTY AND THEIR RESEARCH

Paula Allen-Meares, Dean and Norma Radin Collegiate Professor; Ph.D., Illinois at Urbana-Champaign. Schools, adolescents, parenting.

Robin S. Axelrod, Clinical Assistant Professor; J.D., Wayne State. Community organizing, planning, organizational development, Jewish communal services and leadership.

Deborah I. Bybee, Assistant Research Scientist and Associate Director, Social Work Research Development Center; Ph.D., Michigan State. Research methodology and applied statistics, longitudinal and contextual modeling, community-based research, violence against women, mental health.

Letha A. Chadiha, Associate Professor; Ph.D., Michigan. Family caregiving involving older African Americans.

Linda M. Chatters, Professor; Ph.D., Michigan. Religious involvement and well-being, social support networks of adult/elderly African Americans, intergenerational family relations, families and health.

Barry N. Checkoway, Professor; Ph.D., Pennsylvania. Community organization, social planning, neighborhood development.

Sandra K. Danziger, Professor; Ph.D., Boston University. Child, adolescent, and family policies and programs; effects of welfare reform.

Jorge Delva, Associate Professor; Ph.D., Hawaii. Prevention and treatment of chemical dependency, drug epidemiology, program evaluation, survey research and cross-cultural and cross-national research, use of multilevel statistics to study individual and contextual-level variables.

Ruth E. Dunkle, Wilbur J. Cohen Collegiate Professor; Ph.D., Syracuse. Clinical gerontology, service delivery to the elderly, the oldest old, coping and service delivery strategies for the elderly, racial and ethnic variations in giving care to the elderly.

Kathleen C. Faller, Professor; Ph.D., Michigan. Child welfare, child abuse/neglect, sexual abuse.

Dale K. Fitch, Assistant Professor; Ph.D., Texas at Arlington. Mental health, child abuse, information technology, systems theory, community practice, administration and policy.

Bridgett C. Ford, Assistant Professor; Ph.D., Pittsburgh. African American families, mental health, violence, DSM-IV.

Larry M. Gant, Associate Professor; Ph.D., Michigan. Program evaluation, African-American populations, HIV/AIDS intervention research.

Elizabeth T. Gershoff, Assistant Professor; Ph.D., Texas at Austin. Child poverty, community violence, youth violence, neighborhoods, school-based violence prevention, and parenting impacts on child behavior.

Andrew C. Grogan-Kaylor, Assistant Professor; Ph.D., Wisconsin–Madison. Poverty, neighborhoods, parenting and child well-being.

Lorraine M. Gutierrez, Professor and Director of Academic Programs; Ph.D., Michigan. Empowerment-oppressed groups, mental health, Latinos.

Joseph A. Himle, Assistant Professor; Ph.D., Michigan. Mental health, anxiety, depression, psychosocial interventions, cognitive-behavioral therapy, interface between neurobiology and psychosocial interventions in mental health.

Leslie D. Hollingsworth, Associate Professor; Ph.D., Purdue. African American families, child welfare, adoption, foster care.

Matthew O. Howard, Professor; Ph.D., Washington (Seattle). Substance use, abuse, and dependence; juvenile delinquency; youth violence; antisocial behavior in youth.

Berit Ingersoll-Dayton, Professor; Ph.D., Michigan. Social support of families in later life, employed caregivers, cross-cultural gerontology.

Srinika D. Jayaratne, Professor and Associate Dean for Faculty and Academic Affairs; Ph.D., Michigan. Work stress, professional practice, client violence toward social workers, human service prevention programs.

Sean Joe, Assistant Professor; Ph.D., Illinois at Urbana-Champaign. Self-destructive behaviors, including suicidal behavior; community organizing; positive youth development.

Edith C. Kieffer, Associate Professor; Ph.D., Hawaii. Ethnic and geographic disparities in health, including maternal and child health, obesity, and diabetes; multilevel community-based intervention research related to supply and demand for healthy food access and use and promotion of regular physical activity.

Sherrie A. Kossoudji, Associate Professor; Ph.D., Michigan. Immigrant work lives, labor market inequalities, migrant worker opportunities, gender economics.

Edith A. Lewis, Associate Professor; Ph.D., Wisconsin–Madison. Culturally competent practice, empowerment, women and families of color, interpersonal practice.

Lydia W. Li, Associate Professor; Ph.D., Wisconsin–Madison. Caregiving, social support, race differences in health and disability, formal and informal care.

Susan C. McDonough, Associate Research Professor; Ph.D., Illinois at Urbana-Champaign. Children's mental health, preventive interventions.

Robert M. Ortega, Associate Professor; Ph.D., Michigan. Child welfare, juvenile justice, serious mental illness.

Daphna R. Oyserman, Professor; Ph.D., Michigan. Culture, race, stigma, prevention, identity, adolescence, cognition, motivation.

Julia F. Paley, Assistant Professor; Ph.D., Harvard. Political anthropology, urban studies, urban neighborhoods, ethnicity, ethnographic methodology.

Janice C. Paul, Assistant Professor; Ph.D., NYU. Prison art, integrated arts curricula in urban schools, university community partnerships in the arts, art programming in community development, perceptual development, children's art.

Thomas J. Powell, Professor; Ph.D., Smith. Mental health policies, self-help and community-based support systems.

Beth G. Reed, Associate Professor; Ph.D., Cincinnati. Gender/ethnicity in social systems, feminist/multicultural practice, alcohol/drugs.

Michael S. Reisch, Professor; Ph.D., SUNY at Binghamton. Social policy, community organization, history/philosophy of social welfare.

Julie W. Ribaudo, Clinical Assistant Professor; M.S.W., Georgia. Infant mental health, post-institutionalized children, attachment patterns and school outcomes.

Lawrence Root, Professor; Ph.D., Chicago. Social welfare/employment, employee assistance plans, workplace education.

Mary C. Ruffolo, Associate Professor and Associate Dean for Educational Programs; Ph.D., Ohio State. Intersection of mental health interventions with children, adolescents, and their families.

Daniel G. Saunders, Professor; Ph.D., Wisconsin–Madison. Domestic and dating violence, direct practice, program evaluation.

Brett A. Seabury, Associate Professor; D.S.W., Columbia. Interpersonal practice, radical critique, indigenous healing systems.

Trina R. Shanks, Assistant Professor; Ph.D., Washington (St. Louis). Poverty, wealth, and child well-being; intergenerational economic inequality; family policies and programs.

Kristine A. Siefert, Professor; Ph.D., Minnesota. Women's health and mental health, maternal and child health, prevention.

Michael Spencer, Associate Professor; Ph.D., Washington (Seattle). Race, poverty, mental health, children and families.

Karen M. Staller, Assistant Professor; Ph.D., Columbia. Runaway and homeless youth, law, social problem construction, history of social welfare, qualitative research methods.

Jose A. Tapia Granados, Adjunct Assistant Professor and Assistant Research Scientist; Ph.D., New School University, New York. Impact of economic fluctuations on morality; intersections between demography, economic history, economic theory, and epidemiology; pathways leading from working and living conditions to changes in mortality.

Robert J. Taylor, Sheila Feld Collegiate Professor and Associate Dean for Research; Ph.D., Michigan. Informal social support networks of adult/elderly African Americans.

Richard M. Tolman, Professor; Ph.D., Wisconsin–Madison. Group work and family violence, interpersonal practice.

John E. Tropman, Professor; Ph.D., Michigan. Decision-making systems, social welfare policy, disadvantaged groups, management of human service organizations, executive burnout and organizational reward systems.

David J. Tucker, Professor; Ph.D., Toronto. Organizational demography, organizational change, dynamic modeling of change processes, knowledge development and production.

Diane K. Vinokur, Associate Professor; Ph.D., Michigan. Nonprofit management, human service workplaces, collaboration between organizations and sectors.

Elizabeth H. Voshel, Director of Field Instruction; M.S.W., Western Michigan. Field education, social work ethics, safety training, school-based violence prevention, clinical supervision, mental health.

Michael Woodford, Assistant Professor; Ph.D., Toronto. Participatory policy analysis, organizational management and change, inclusion of vulnerable communities in HIV/AIDS prevention, community organizing, qualitative methodology.

Michael E. Woolley, Assistant Professor; Ph.D., North Carolina at Chapel Hill. School social work, interpersonal practice with children and families, development of assessment instruments for practice, the cognitive processes of instrument item response.

Mieko Yoshihama, Associate Professor; Ph.D., UCLA. Violence against women/immigrants, race, culture, class, mental health.

UNIVERSITY OF PENNSYLVANIA

School of Social Policy & Practice

Programs of Study

The School of Social Policy & Practice at the University of Pennsylvania offers the degrees of Master of Social Work (M.S.W.), the Master of Science in nonprofit/non-governmental leadership (MNP), the Master of Science in social policy (MSP), the Clinical Doctorate in Social Work (D.S.W.), and Doctor of Philosophy (Ph.D.) in social welfare. In addition, students can combine the M.S.W. with the Master of Bioethics (M.S.W./M.B.E.), the Master of Business Administration (M.S.W./M.B.A.), the Master of City Planning (M.S.W./M.C.P.), the Master of Science in Criminology (M.S.W./M.S.), the Master of Science in Education (M.S.W./M.S.Ed.), the Juris Doctor (M.S.W./J.D.), the Master of Government Administration (M.S.W./M.G.A.), the Master of Nonprofit/Non-Governmental Leadership (M.S.W./M.N.P), the Master of Public Health (M.S.W./M.P.H.), the Master of Science in Social Policy (M.S.W./M.S.P.) and the Doctor of Philosophy (M.S.W./Ph.D.) degree program. In addition, the School offers an M.S.W./Certificate in Jewish Communal Studies, an M.S.W./Certificate in Catholic Social Ministry, and an M.S.W./Certificate in Lutheran Social Ministries.

The School also offers an Advanced Standing (M.S.W.) Program. This program is designed for exceptional B.S.W. students who have graduated from a CSWE-accredited B.S.W. program within the past five years. A limited number of students are accepted into this program. Students begin graduate studies in the summer, followed by two semesters of full-time study. After successful completion of the required two summer courses, plus a no-cost integrated practice seminar and field placement, students enter their advanced year of study. In addition, the program offers a part-time option.

The primary goal of the Master of Social Work (M.S.W.) Program is to prepare social workers for leadership roles in developing and providing services to individuals, families, groups, communities, and organizations. Full-time (two-year) and part-time (three-year) courses of study are available.

The Nonprofit/NGO Leadership (MNP) Program is a full-time, intensive one-year program designed for professionals preparing to assume leadership positions in nonprofit or non-governmental organizations dedicated to enhancing community viability.

The Master of Science in Social Policy (MSP) Program is designed to prepare students for leadership positions in analyzing and shaping social policy at the local, national, and international levels. The MSP is a ten- to eleven-month program spanning three semesters of study, although some students may elect to extend the program over a longer period of time.

The Clinical Doctorate in Social Work (D.S.W.) program is intended for clinicians with at least two years of post-M.S.W. experience. Penn's Clinical D.S.W. program differs from most doctoral programs in that it is a professional-practice degree, designed to prepare students for advanced clinical practice and university-level teaching.

The Ph.D. in Social Welfare program prepares students to address a wide range of social problems related to human welfare. Most graduates of this doctoral program pursue leadership positions in public and private human services organizations or careers in postsecondary teaching and research.

Research Facilities

The School operates six research centers: the Cartographic Modeling Lab; the Center for High Impact Philanthropy; the Field Center for Children's Policy, Practice, and Research; the Center for Research on Youth and Social Policy; the Out-of-School Time Research Center; and the Program for Religion and Social Policy Research.

Financial Aid

Financial aid is based primarily on need. Students applying for aid must file a FAFSA form. More than 80 percent of M.S.W. students receive financial aid. In addition, the School recognizes merit by offering a range of scholarships to those who qualify. Limited financial aid is available for the MNP and MSP programs. The Ph.D. program provides aid in the form of merit fellowships and graduate assistantships, which enable students to gain teaching experience and to collaborate with members of the faculty on research projects. There is no financial aid available for the D.S.W. program.

Cost of Study

For academic year 2007–08, tuition and fees for the full-time M.S.W. program is $33,338 per year, including student fees; for part-time students the cost per course unit, including fees, is $4167. Tuition and fees for the MNP is $37,586. Tuition and fees for the full-time MSP program is $33,338; for part-time students the cost per course unit, including fees, is $4167. Tuition for the Clinical D.S.W. program is calculated on a per-course basis; students must complete 14 courses and the dissertation. Students should expect that the per-course tuition will increase slightly for years two and three, as determined by the University. Tuition and fees per course is $4517. All students accepted into the Ph.D. program and who maintain their academic standing are eligible for financial support, including full-tuition scholarships as well as fellowships or research assistantships for the three years of course work.

Living and Housing Costs

The approximate annual cost of living, including room and board, books, and miscellaneous (e.g., health insurance), for a single student is $20,750 for academic year 2007–08. On-campus living accommodations are available in Sansom Place (graduate student housing).

Student Group

The student body is diverse, representing a wide range of age groups and educational, geographical, and ethnic backgrounds. The School is committed to recruiting a diverse student body. The following are student organizations within the School: Student Council, National Association of Black Social Workers, Women Organized for Social Change, United Community Clinic, Asian Social Work Council, Jewish Social Work Alliance, Latino Social Workers at Penn, Queer Social Workers at Penn, Social Welfare Action Alliance, Students for International Social Work, and Society of Part-Time Students.

Location

The campus of the University of Pennsylvania is located near central Philadelphia, a metropolitan area with a population of more than 5 million. The city of Philadelphia and the University both offer a variety of cultural, recreational, and educational opportunities. Excellent rail and bus services connect Philadelphia to the Washington, D.C. (2½ hours), and New York (2 hours) areas. Philadelphia also operates an international airport that serves all parts of the country and most parts of the world with direct airline service.

The University

The University of Pennsylvania is a private, Ivy League university with a long and distinguished history of education in social work. The University was founded by Benjamin Franklin and is the oldest university in the country. Penn's social work program, one of the oldest in the country, was established in 1908. The University has pioneered in the development of many professional fields of higher education in addition to social work, including city planning, nursing, medicine, law, education, veterinary medicine, dentistry, and business.

Applying

Students are admitted once a year, in the fall, to the School's M.S.W., MNP, MSP, D.S.W., and Ph.D. programs. Students are admitted to the full-time Advanced Standing Program in June.

The application deadline for the M.S.W. Advanced Standing program is March 1; the deadline for the M.S.W. program is March 31. The School must receive applications for the MNP program by April 1. The application deadline for the MSP is April 15.

Applications for the Ph.D. program are accepted between September 15 and December 15. The deadline for D.S.W. applications is March 1. It is important to apply early as enrollment is limited.

Correspondence and Information

Office of Admissions
School of Social Policy & Practice
University of Pennsylvania
3701 Locust Walk
Philadelphia, Pennsylvania 19104-6214

Phone: 215-898-5511
Web site: http://www.sp2.upenn.edu

University of Pennsylvania

THE FACULTY AND THEIR RESEARCH

Joretha Bourjolly, Associate Professor and Associate Dean, Academic Affairs; Ph.D., Bryn Mawr, 1996. Effects of chronic illness on individuals and family members as well as the impact of racial and economic factors on the delivery of health care.

Louis Carter, Associate Professor; M.S.W., Pennsylvania, 1962. Criminal and juvenile justice, family systems, social work practice.

Ram A. Cnaan, Professor and Associate Dean, Research; Ph.D., Pittsburgh, 1981. Social work research methods, social policy, volunteerism and volunteer action, information technology applications.

Dennis Culhane, Associate Professor; Ph.D., Boston College, 1990. Homelessness, housing policy, policy analysis research methods.

Joan K. Davitt, Assistant Professor; Ph.D., Bryn Mawr, 2003. Gerontology, health, and health-care outcomes for older adults and ethical issues in long-term care.

Richard J. Estes, Professor; D.S.W., Berkeley, 1973. International and comparative social welfare, social indicators, mental health, evaluative research, computer technology.

Damon W. Freeman, Assistant Professor; J.D., Ph.D., Indiana, 2004. African American intellectual history, critical race theory, social policy and social movements.

Richard James Gelles, Professor and Dean; Ph.D., New Hampshire, 1973. Child welfare, family violence, child abuse.

Toorjo Ghose, Assistant Professor; Ph.D., UCLA, 2005. Substance abuse, HIV/AIDS in developing countries, mental health service provision, welfare policy.

Roberta Rehner Iversen, Associate Professor; Ph.D., Bryn Mawr, 1991. Practice with children and families, research on women and poverty.

Karin Rhodes, Assistant Professor; M.D., Chicago, 1983. Family violence, quality of emergency services, access to follow-up care, the intersection between acute care and the mental health, social services, and criminal justice systems.

Laura Ann McCloskey, Associate Professor; Ph.D., Michigan, 1986. Family violence and the health impact of domestic violence on women and children.

Roberta G. Sands, Professor; Ph.D., Louisville, 1979. Mental health, women's issues, clinical social work practice, interprofessional communications, ethnographic sociolinguistic research.

Vivian Seltzer, Professor; Ph.D., Bryn Mawr, 1975. Adolescents, psychosocial development, adolescent behavior, adolescent problems, adolescent peer group relations, child development and behavior.

Kenwyn K. Smith, Associate Professor; Ph.D., Yale, 1974. Group and intergroup relations, organizational change, organizational politics, conflict management, impact of organizational dynamics on the health of employees.

Phyllis Solomon, Professor; Ph.D., Case Western Reserve, 1978. Social work research methods, mental health policy and service delivery systems, severely mentally disabled persons and their families.

Susan Sorenson, Professor; Ph.D., Cincinnati, 1985. Public health, epidemiology and prevention of violence, including homicide, suicide, sexual assault, child abuse, battering, and firearms.

Carol Wilson Spigner, Associate Professor; D.S.W., USC, 1980. Children, youth and families, child welfare, program evaluation and administration.

Mark J. Stern, Professor; Ph.D., York (England), 1980. Social welfare policy; social history and social welfare; poverty in the United States, 1900–present.

Yin-Ling Irene Wong, Associate Professor; Ph.D., Wisconsin, 1995. Social policy, homelessness, homelessness prevention and poverty research.

VIRGINIA COMMONWEALTH UNIVERSITY

Doctoral Program in Social Work

Program of Study
Virginia Commonwealth University (VCU) offers the Ph.D. in social work, a research-oriented educational enterprise with a mission to develop scholars and leaders for education and practice in human services. The program is built around excellence in curriculum and a strong sense of community. Graduates become active in teaching, consultation, research, practice and program evaluation, staff and program development, policy analysis, and advocacy. They are employed in universities and colleges and in human service organizations and agencies at the local, state, national, and international levels.

The doctoral program in social work brings together a unique group of diverse faculty members who provide opportunities for professional development and advanced interdisciplinary study to eager-to-learn individuals. The program's signature is its commitment to the mentorship, nurturance, and socialization of doctoral students. Faculty members and students perform research together, write papers together, do presentations together, and participate as colleagues in many activities. Doctoral students are active in the life of the school and in the life of the social work profession. Faculty members report that the doctoral program and its students help stimulate their own scholarship and development as individuals. According to the faculty members, doctoral students not only support their work and serve to affirm their choice to be social workers, but also challenge them to be better and to see the future possibilities of the profession.

A minimum of 38 credit hours of course work beyond the master's degree, plus a minimum of 16 credit hours of dissertation research, is required. The course work includes 26 credit hours of content common for all students and 12 credit hours of concentration content in a substantive area. Full-time students ordinarily complete 18–20 credit hours per academic year.

Research Facilities
VCU libraries provide a combined capacity of more than 1.7 million volumes and 10,200 periodical titles and an online bibliographic search service accessing hundreds of databases. In addition, the Virginia State and Richmond Public Libraries are within walking distance of both VCU campuses. Academic Computing provides a variety of microcomputer, minicomputer, and mainframe computing services to support the research and instructional endeavors of the faculty and students, including consultation, instruction, and computer acquisition.

Financial Aid
Generous financial aid packages in the form of graduate research assistantships, fellowships, and tuition assistance are available to full-time students. Interested students should contact the Program Director for more information. Other information on financial aid programs, policies, and procedures is available at http://www.vcu.edu/enroll/finaid.

Cost of Study
For full-time study (9–15 credits) in 2007–08, Virginia residents pay tuition and fees of $4452 per semester; nonresidents, $8876 per semester. For part-time study, Virginia residents pay tuition and fees of $465 per hour; nonresidents, $954 per hour. Some programs require additional fees. On the Medical College of Virginia (MCV) campus, tuition, fees, and other expenses vary in the medicine, pharmacy, nurse anesthesia, dentistry, and School of Allied Health programs.

Living and Housing Costs
Graduate student housing is available on both the MCV campus and the academic campus of Virginia Commonwealth University. Many graduate students live in off-campus housing, which is reasonably priced and readily available in a variety of styles and settings in nearby residential areas or within easy commuting distance. On- and off-campus housing information is available on the Web at http://www.housing.vcu.edu/.

Student Group
VCU School of Social Work is proud of its active and involved Doctoral Student Association, which participates in program governance and helps create a strong network of support. Currently there are 37 students, with incoming fall cohorts of about 7 to 10 students. The University enrolls 30,452 students, 7,611 of whom are graduate students. More than 200 clubs and organizations reflect the diverse social, recreational, educational, political, and religious interests of the student body.

Location
Richmond is Virginia's capital and a major East Coast financial and manufacturing center that offers students a wide range of cultural, educational, and recreational activities. Richmond is located in central Virginia at the intersection of Interstates 95 and 64, 2 hours south of Washington, D.C., and nestled between the Blue Ridge Mountains and the Atlantic coast. The Richmond region is easily accessible by plane, car, and train. With nearly 1 million residents, the historic city of Richmond combines big-city offerings with small-town hospitality. Applicants are encouraged to explore http://www.visit.richmond.com/ for more information on the city.

The University
VCU is a state-supported coeducational university with a graduate school, a major teaching hospital, and twelve academic and professional units that offer fifty-two undergraduate, twenty-two postbaccalaureate certificate, sixty-five master's, six post-master's certificate, and twenty-nine Ph.D. programs. VCU also offers M.D., D.D.S., D.P.T., and Pharm.D. programs as well as cooperative degree programs with other major Virginia colleges and universities. VCU has one of the largest evening colleges in the United States. The academic campus is located in Richmond's historic Fan District. The health sciences campus and hospital are located 2 miles east in the downtown business district. A University bus service provides free intercampus transportation for faculty members and students.

With more than $211 million in annual research funding, Virginia Commonwealth University is classified as one of the nation's top research universities by the Carnegie Foundation for the Advancement of Teaching. More than 29,000 undergraduate, certificate, graduate, post-master's, professional, and doctoral students are enrolled in 162 academic programs, forty of which are unique in the commonwealth of Virginia. The faculty members represent the finest American and international graduate institutions and enhance the University's position among the important institutions of higher learning in the United States and the world via their work in the classroom, laboratory, studio, and clinic and in their scholarly publications.

Applying
Admission procedures and program requirements are detailed in the *Graduate Bulletin*. Application deadlines and materials, including the application and the *Graduate Bulletin*, are available online at the Graduate School Web site at http://www.graduate. vcu.edu. Virginia Commonwealth University is an equal opportunity/affirmative action institution providing access to education and employment without regard to age, race, color, national origin, gender, religion, sexual orientation, veteran's status, political affiliation, or disability.

Correspondence and Information
Kia J. Bentley, Director
Ph.D. Program in Social Work
School of Social Work
Virginia Commonwealth University
1001 West Franklin Street
P.O. Box 842027
Richmond, Virginia 23284
Phone: 804-828-0453
E-mail: kbentley@vcu.edu
Web site: http://www.vcu.edu/slwweb/academicprograms/programsofstudy/phd.html

Virginia Commonwealth University

THE FACULTY AND THEIR RESEARCH

Melissa L. Abell, Associate Professor; Ph.D., North Carolina. Aggressive behavior in children and youth violence, technology-based group-work practice, and intervention research to develop practice technologies.

Frank R. Baskind, Professor and Dean; Ph.D., Connecticut. Generalist social work practice, leadership in social work education, the ways of scholarship in education for the profession.

Kia J. Bentley, Professor, Director of the Ph.D. Program, and Associate Dean for Strategic Initiatives; Ph.D., Florida State. Mental health and mental illness, psychopharmacology and social work, psychosocial rehabilitation and empowerment practice, practice theories and models, women's issues.

Janice Berry-Edwards, Assistant Professor; D.S.W., Catholic University. Mental health, psychodynamic and relational/cultural theories, social work practice and education, multiple intelligences and social work education.

Shirley Bryant, Associate Professor; D.S.W., Howard. Child welfare, impact of violence on children, African American women.

Randi Buerlein, Assistant Director of Field; M.S.W., Virginia Commonwealth. Student development, student services, career development.

Portia Cole, Assistant Professor; Ph.D., American. Health disparities, health policy, women's health, occupational health, mixed-methods research.

Jacqueline Corcoran, Associate Professor; Ph.D., Texas at Austin. Solution-focused therapy, evidence-based practice, family treatment, treatment of children and adolescents.

Elizabeth Cramer, Associate Professor; Ph.D., South Carolina. Domestic violence, lesbian/gay issues, group methods.

Patrick Dattalo, Associate Professor; Ph.D., Virginia Commonwealth. Anti-poverty policy, social work research methods, organizational behavior.

Timothy L. Davey, Associate Dean for Community Engagement and Director of Field; Ph.D., Florida State. Evaluating intensive case management services to homeless families, multiple-family group work with at-risk families, mental health issues.

Elizabeth Dungee-Anderson, Associate Professor and Director of the M.S.W. Program; D.S.W., Howard. ADHD, cancer in African Americans, multiple personality and borderline personality/trauma/incest.

Humberto Fabelo, Associate Professor and Director of the B.S.W. Program; Ph.D., Florida International. Child welfare, child sexual abuse, refugee and immigration resettlement.

Rosemary Farmer, Associate Professor; Ph.D., Virginia Commonwealth. Schizophrenia, psychopharmacology and social work practice, bringing more of the biological into social work, HBSE models.

David Fauri, Professor; Ph.D., Syracuse. Bereavement service and caregiving, macro-interventions, case-teaching method.

Nicole K. Footen, Director of Student Services; Ph.D., Virginia Commonwealth. International and national human trafficking legislation.

Marcia Harrigan, Associate Professor and Senior Associate Dean for Student and Academic Affairs; Ph.D., Virginia Commonwealth. Family measurement, nontraditional family structures, family caregiving, family intervention.

Elizabeth Hutchison, Associate Professor; Ph.D., SUNY at Albany. Child welfare, substance abuse, practice approaches with involuntary clients, human behavior curriculum.

Jenny Jones, Assistant Professor; Ph.D., Tennessee. Child protective services, supervision and organization change, HIV/AIDS, family copying strategies.

Pamela Kovacs, Associate Professor; Ph.D., Florida International. HIV/AIDS, living with chronic and terminal illness, end-of-life care, health-care social work, caregiving, volunteerism, field instruction.

Anthony Mallon, Assistant Professor; Ph.D., Michigan. Poverty and inequality, policy implementation, welfare reform, workforce development for populations with barriers to employment.

Holly Matto, Associate Professor; Ph.D., Maryland. Substance abuse treatment intervention research, integrative practice model development, clinical interventions with children and families, therapy methods in social work.

Matthias Naleppa, Associate Professor; Ph.D., SUNY at Albany. Practice evaluation, clinical case management, practice with the elderly, task-centered social work, international social work.

F. Ellen Netting, Professor; Ph.D., Chicago. Case management and primary care with frail elderly, long-term-care ombudsman program, continuing-care retirement communities, nonprofit voluntary agencies.

Peter Nguyen, Assistant Professor; Ph.D., Houston. Asian Americans, immigrant populations specializing in acculturation/assimilation, mental health services and access, parent-child relationship issues.

Ann Nichols-Casebolt, Professor and University Vice President, Office of Research; Ph.D., Wisconsin–Madison. Social welfare policy, poverty of single-mother families, women's issues.

Sarah K. Price, Assistant Professor; Ph.D., Washington (St. Louis). Bereavement, maternal depression, pregnancy loss and infant death, women's wellness, mental health services research and community-based participatory program evaluation.

Karen Rotabi, Assistant Professor; Ph.D., North Carolina at Chapel Hill. Child-abuse and child-neglect prevention, child-welfare systems, social support and health outcomes, immigrant integration, families impacted by war.

Mary Katherine (Rodwell) O'Connor, Professor; Ph.D., Kansas. Family and child welfare, field-based education, international social work, organization practice, and qualitative methodology, especially constructivist inquiry.

Robert Schneider, Professor; Ph.D., Tulane. Advocacy, policy practice, state policy, gerontology in social work education.

Jeffrey Schwamm, M.S.W. Associate Director and Coordinator of the Northern Virginia Program; Ph.D., Brandeis. Developmental disability policy and practice, social work field education.

Sanford Schwartz, Associate Professor; Ph.D., Washington (St. Louis). AIDS service organizations, case management, substance abuse.

Mary Secret, Associate Professor; Ph.D., Virginia Commonwealth. Workplace policy and the integration of work and family roles, program evaluation and practice-research collaborations, fatherhood and parenting capacity.

David Stoesz, Professor; D.S.W., Maryland. Social welfare policy.

Joseph Walsh, Professor; Ph.D., Ohio State. Serious mental illness, psychopharmacology, clinical social work, social support, rock 'n' roll music.

WASHINGTON UNIVERSITY IN ST. LOUIS

George Warren Brown School of Social Work

Programs of Study

The George Warren Brown School of Social Work (Brown) offers a curriculum leading to the degree of Master of Social Work and, in collaboration with the Graduate School of Arts and Sciences, the degree of Doctor of Philosophy in social work. The School is characterized by flexibility in the choice of courses, including the practicum, individually planned curricula, interdisciplinary collaboration, and the combination of experimental and traditional courses. Both the M.S.W. and Ph.D. programs require concentrated academic work. Students with superior academic preparation are encouraged to apply.

The master's degree curriculum prepares students for advanced social work practice in the fields of children, youth, and family; gerontology; health; mental health; and social and economic development. Specializations are available in the areas of family therapy, management, and research. The program involves 60 credit hours for graduation and ordinarily requires two academic years of full-time study or four academic years of part-time study for completion. Students with a B.S.W. from a CSWE-accredited school enroll in an advanced-standing program that permits them to complete the requirements in sixteen months.

The Ph.D. program is highly interdisciplinary and is designed to prepare graduates for teaching and research careers. The average time needed to complete all Ph.D. requirements is three years of full-time study for students with the M.S.W. degree and four to five years for those without it.

A special feature of the School is the availability of programs leading to dual degrees in social work and architecture (M.S.W./M.Arch.), business administration (M.S.W./M.B.A.), divinity (M.S.W./M.Div.), Jewish studies (M.S.W./M.A.J.S.), law (M.S.W./J.D.), and pastoral studies (M.S.W./M.A.P.S.). In addition, students often enroll in courses in other graduate schools of the University.

Research Facilities

Brown is housed in two connecting buildings that were built for teaching and research—Goldfarb Hall, opened in 1998, and Brown Hall, the first academic building dedicated to social work in the United States. A wide range of computing equipment and services is available for use by students for classroom instruction and research projects. Library holdings in the social and behavioral sciences and social welfare are strong and up to date. There are ample opportunities for collaborative and interdisciplinary work throughout the University. Most of the faculty members have ongoing research projects in which both M.S.W. and Ph.D. students participate. The School houses the Center for Mental Health Services Research, the Kathryn M. Buder Center for American Indian Studies, the Center for Social Development, Center for Latino Family Research, the Comorbidity and Addictions Center, and the Martha N. Ozawa Center for Social Policy Studies.

Financial Aid

More than 200 scholarships, five loan programs, college work-study arrangements, paid practicums, and part-time employment assistance are among the various types of financial aid administered by the School of Social Work in conjunction with Washington University's Office of Student Financial Services. The School gives full consideration to all applicants for admission and financial aid without regard to age, color, creed, disability, sexual orientation, marital status, national origin, race, or sex. Eighty-eight percent of M.S.W. students receive financial aid.

Cost of Study

The tuition for master's degree students is $913 per credit hour in 2007–08. Tuition for the doctoral program is $34,500 per year. Additional expenses, including the cost of health service, student activity fees, books, and supplies, are about $1900 per year.

Living and Housing Costs

Approximately $1100 per month should be budgeted to provide for living costs. Most students prefer to rent an apartment in the vicinity of the School.

Student Group

In spring 2007, there were 359 full-time and 33 part-time students in the M.S.W. program. Fifty-two students were working toward the Ph.D. degree in social work. Students from forty-seven states and thirty other countries were enrolled in the program.

Location

The St. Louis area offers a variety of musical, cultural, and sports events throughout the academic year. Washington University is contiguous with the city of St. Louis and adjoins its suburbs. There is a delightful potpourri of shops, ethnic restaurants, churches, bookstores, movie theaters, and art museums within a mile of the campus. In addition, St. Louis social agencies offer outstanding practicum opportunities to students.

The University and The School

Brown is ranked among the top schools of social work in the United States. It is one of the eight graduate and professional schools that constitute Washington University in St. Louis—a medium-sized, private, urban institution. Brown profits from all of the University's resources, including an outstanding and internationally recognized faculty, a diverse and talented student body, a superior library, and an overall environment of creative excellence. The School is one of the few social work programs in the country to have its own placement office for graduates. The M.S.W. program is fully accredited by the Council on Social Work Education.

Applying

Applicants must have an undergraduate degree or be in the process of obtaining one. No specific undergraduate major is required; however, a minimum of 30 semester hours in the social sciences and liberal arts is recommended. Undergraduate performance should demonstrate intellectual capacity for graduate study, with a B average as the minimum requirement. Applicants are advised to apply as early as possible.

Correspondence and Information

For the M.S.W. program:
Janice Wells-White
Director of Admissions and Recruitment
George Warren Brown School of Social Work
Box 1196
Washington University in St. Louis
St. Louis, Missouri 63130
Phone: 314-935-6676
   877-321-2426 (toll-free, North America)
Fax: 314-935-4859
E-mail: msw@gwbmail.wustl.edu
Web site: http://gwbweb.wustl.edu

For the Ph.D. program:
Dr. Wendy Auslander
Chairperson, Ph.D. Program
George Warren Brown School of Social Work
Box 1196
Washington University in St. Louis
St. Louis, Missouri 63130
Phone: 314-935-6605
   877-321-2426 (toll-free, North America)
Fax: 314-935-8511
E-mail: phdsw@gwbmail.wustl.edu
Web site: http://gwbweb.wustl.edu

Washington University in St. Louis

THE FACULTY AND THEIR RESEARCH

Professors

Wendy Auslander, Ph.D., Washington (St. Louis). Minority health/health promotion, families and chronic illness, juvenile diabetes, AIDS prevention.

David F. Gillespie, Ph.D., Washington (Seattle). Disaster preparedness, organizational theory, interorganizational relations, measurement.

Shanti K. Khinduka, George Warren Brown Distinguished University Professor; Ph.D., Brandeis. Social work education, international social development.

Eddie F. Lawlor, Ph.D., Brandeis. Health care reform, health care administration, policy for the aged and poor, Medicare policy.

Nancy Morrow-Howell, Ralph and Muriel Pumphrey Professor of Social Work; Ph.D., Berkeley. Gerontology, care for dependent elderly, hospital discharge planning for elderly.

Martha N. Ozawa, Bettie Bofinger Brown Distinguished Professor of Social Policy; Ph.D., Wisconsin–Madison. Policy analysis of social welfare programs, income support programs, social security, unemployment.

Enola K. Proctor, Frank Bruno Professor for Social Work Research; Ph.D., Washington (St. Louis). Mental health and health services; treatment planning in direct practice; evaluation of clinical social work; race, gender, and socioeconomic status.

Mark Rank, Herbert S. Hadley Professor of Social Welfare; Ph.D., Wisconsin–Madison. Poverty, social stratification, family, social policy, social justice.

Michael W. Sherraden, Benjamin E. Youngdahl Professor of Social Development; Ph.D., Michigan. Social policy and administration, youth policy.

Arlene Stiffman, Barbara A. Bailey Professor of Social Work; Ph.D., Washington (St. Louis). Child and adolescent mental health, high-risk behaviors.

Luis H. Zayas, Shanti K. Khinduka Distinguished Professor of Social Work; Ph.D., Columbia. Child socialization and parent interaction, child and adolescent mental health and treatment, ethnoracial minority mental health and intervention research.

Associate Professors

F. Brett Drake, Ph.D., UCLA. Social stress, substance abuse, child abuse and neglect, burnout of child welfare workers.

Tonya Edmond, Ph.D., Texas at Austin. Sexual abuse survivors, women's issues, domestic violence, clinical practice.

Melissa Jonson-Reid, Ph.D., Berkeley. Children and violence, child welfare/juvenile justice services outcomes, interagency school interventions.

Jack A. Kirkland, M.S.W., Syracuse. Community work, group relations, international social development, racism, social planning.

J. Curtis McMillen, Ph.D., Maryland, Baltimore. Child welfare, clinical social work practice, mental health.

Shanta Pandey, Ph.D., Case Western Reserve. Social policy, poverty, program evaluation.

Nancy R. Vosler, Ph.D., Virginia Commonwealth. Families and work, family policy, impact of unemployment on families.

Gautam N. Yadama, Ph.D., Case Western Reserve. International community development, rural farming and forestry.

Assistant Professors

Stephanie C. Boddie, Ph.D., Pennsylvania. Community development organizations, faith-based partnerships, social welfare policy.

Clifton Emery, Ph.D., Chicago. Children, youth and families, domestic abuse.

Peter Hovmand, Ph.D., Michigan State. Domestic violence, women's studies, violence against women, system dynamics.

Patricia Kohl, Ph.D., North Carolina at Chapel Hill. Child welfare, mental health assessments and evaluation.

Carolyn Lesorogol, Ph.D., Washington (St. Louis). International social development, cross-cultural research, land use.

Amanda Moore McBride, Ph.D., Washington (St. Louis). Service/civic engagement, program evaluation, social policy.

Yunju Nam, Ph.D., Michigan. Poverty, policy, social development, socioeconomic equality.

Juan Pena, Ph.D., Columbia. Mental health and Latino populations.

Michelle Putnam, Ph.D., UCLA. Gerontology, disability, public policy.

Paul Shattuck, Ph.D., Wisconsin-Madison. Autism, health, developmental disabilities, health policy.

Renee M. Williams, Ph.D., Washington (St. Louis). Mental health, addictions, gambling.

Visiting Professors

Priscilla Day, Ph.D., Minnesota, Duluth. Indian child welfare.

Daniel Frigo, Ph.D., Washington (St. Louis). Mental health, clinical practice.

John Robertson, Ph.D., Columbia. Poverty, child welfare policy, community development.

Adjunct Professors

Robert Benjamin, J.D., M.S.W., Saint Louis. Family law and social work, mediation.

Cathy Blair, M.S.W., Washington (St. Louis). Health, domestic violence, women's issues.

James Braun, M.S.W., Saint Louis. At-risk children, youth and their families, administration.

Jeffrey Brenneman, M.S.W., Washington (St. Louis). Children's mental health, clinical social work practice, case management.

Web Brown, M.S.W., Washington (St. Louis). HIV/AIDS services, case management, clinical social work practice.

Lorien Carter, M.S.W., Washington (St. Louis). Adolescent development, adolescent mental health, case management.

Linda Griffith, M.S.W., Saint Louis. Mental health, research, clinical practice.

Cheryl Houston, Ph.D., Saint Louis. Public health, nutrition, health promotion, diabetes.

Way Huey, Pharm.D., Nebraska. Pharmacology.

Mark Keeley, M.S.W., Washington (St. Louis). Developmental disability, program development, administration.

Peggy Keilholz, M.S.W., Washington (St. Louis). Family therapy, clinical practice.

Dorothy Kontak, M.S.W., Washington (St. Louis). School social work, conflict resolution, behavioral management, IDEA and related services, gangs.

Suzanne LeLaurin, M.S.W., Washington (St. Louis). Refugees and community-based services, community development.

Barbara Levin, M.S.W., Maryland, Baltimore. Nonprofit boards, volunteers, social entrepreneurship.

Judy Lincoff, M.S.W., Washington (St. Louis). Family therapy, clinical practice.

Larry McEvoy, M.A., SUNY at Binghamton. Statistical analysis, data management.

Bonnie Miller, J.D./M.S.W., Washington (St. Louis). Social work and law, family mediation.

Pamela Mousette, M.S.W., Washington (St. Louis). Family services, child welfare, family preservation.

Diane Beckerle O'Brien, M.S.W., Washington (St. Louis). Gerontology, crisis management, Alzheimer's disease.

Cheryl Oliver, M.A., Utah. Gerontology, with emphasis on healthy aging.

Betul Ozmat, M.S.W., Washington (St. Louis). Marketing, community relations, development.

Nicholas Peppes, M.B.A., Saint Louis. Budgeting and fiscal management.

Barbara Richter, M.S.W., Washington (St. Louis). Management, fiscal management.

Amy Rome, M.S.W., Washington (St. Louis). Program development, management, marketing.

Barry Rosenberg, M.S.W., SUNY at Albany. Working with boards and volunteers, development, nonprofit management.

Meg Schnabel, M.S.W., Washington (St. Louis). Women's issues and domestic violence.

Suzanne Shepard, Ph.D., Washington (St. Louis). Treatment evaluation and research, clinical practice.

Donald Sloane, M.S.W., Washington (St. Louis). Behavioral therapy, clinical practice.

Danny Wedding, Ph.D., Hawaii. Mental health practice and policy, psychotherapies.

Linda Weiner, M.S.W., Missouri–Columbia. Clinical social work, human sexuality.

APPENDIXES

APPENDIXES

Institutional Changes
Since the 2007 Edition

Following is an alphabetical listing of institutions that have recently closed, moved, merged with other institutions, or changed their names or status. In the case of a name change, the former name appears first, followed by the new name.

Alliant International University–San Francisco Bay (San Francisco, CA): name changed to Alliant International University–San Francisco.

American Academy of Nutrition, College of Nutrition (Knoxville, TN): name changed to Huntington College of Health Sciences.

American InterContinental University (Atlanta, GA): name changed to American InterContinental University Buckhead Campus.

American InterContinental University (Atlanta, GA): name changed to American InterContinental University Dunwoody Campus.

Antioch New England Graduate School (Keene, NH): name changed to Antioch University New England.

Argosy University/Atlanta (Atlanta, GA): name changed to Argosy University, Atlanta Campus.

Argosy University/Chicago (Chicago, IL): name changed to Argosy University, Chicago Campus.

Argosy University/Dallas (Dallas, TX): name changed to Argosy University, Dallas Campus.

Argosy University/Denver (Denver, CO): name changed to Argosy University, Denver Campus.

Argosy University/Hawai'i (Honolulu, HI): name changed to Argosy University, Hawai'i Campus.

Argosy University/Nashville (Franklin, TN): name changed to Argosy University, Nashville Campus.

Argosy University/Orange County (Santa Ana, CA): name changed to Argosy University, Orange County Campus.

Argosy University/Phoenix (Phoenix, AZ): name changed to Argosy University, Phoenix Campus.

Argosy University/San Diego (San Diego, CA): name changed to Argosy University, San Diego Campus.

Argosy University/San Francisco Bay Area (Point Richmond, CA): name changed to Argosy University, San Francisco Bay Area Campus.

Argosy University/Santa Monica (Santa Monica, CA): name changed to Argosy University, Santa Monica Campus.

Argosy University/Sarasota (Sarasota, FL): name changed to Argosy University, Sarasota Campus.

Argosy University/Schaumburg (Schaumburg, IL): name changed to Argosy University, Schaumburg Campus.

Argosy University/Seattle (Seattle, WA): name changed to Argosy University, Seattle Campus.

Argosy University/Tampa (Tampa, FL): name changed to Argosy University, Tampa Campus.

Argosy University/Twin Cities (Eagan, MN): name changed to Argosy University, Twin Cities Campus.

Argosy University/Washington D.C. (Arlington, VA): name changed to Argosy University, Washington DC Campus.

Arizona State University West (Phoenix, AZ): name changed to Arizona State University at the West Campus.

Central Missouri State University (Warrensburg, MO): name changed to University of Central Missouri.

Chatham College (Pittsburgh, PA): name changed to Chatham University.

Chicago School of Professional Psychology (Chicago, IL): name changed to The Chicago School of Professional Psychology.

David N. Myers University (Cleveland, OH): name changed to Myers University.

The Dickinson School of Law of The Pennsylvania State University (Carlisle, PA): name changed to Penn State Dickinson School of Law.

Dominican House of Studies (Washington, DC): name changed to Dominican House of Studies, Pontifical Faculty of the Immaculate Conception.

Embry-Riddle Aeronautical University, Extended Campus (Daytona Beach, FL): name changed to Embry-Riddle Aeronautical University Worldwide.

Evangelical School of Theology (Myerstown, PA): name changed to Evangelical Theological Seminary.

The Feinstein Institute for Medical Research (Manhasset, NY): name changed to North Shore–LIJ Graduate School of Molecular Medicine.

Franklin Pierce College (Rindge, NH): name changed to Franklin Pierce University.

International College (Naples, FL): name changed to Hodges University.

Methodist College (Fayetteville, NC): name changed to Methodist University.

Nevada College of Pharmacy (Las Vegas, NV): name changed to University of Southern Nevada.

North American Baptist Seminary (Sioux Falls, SD): name changed to Sioux Falls Seminary.

North Greenville College (Tigerville, SC): name changed to North Greenville University.

The Pennsylvania State University at Erie, The Behrend College (Erie, PA): name changed to Penn State Erie, The Behrend College.

The Pennsylvania State University Great Valley Campus (Malvern, PA): name changed to Penn State Great Valley.

The Pennsylvania State University Harrisburg Campus (Middletown, PA): name changed to Penn State Harrisburg.

The Pennsylvania State University Milton S. Hershey Medical Center (Hershey, PA): name changed to Penn State Hershey Medical Center.

The Pennsylvania State University University Park Campus (University Park, PA): name changed to Penn State University Park.

Piedmont Baptist College (Winston-Salem, NC): name changed to Piedmont Baptist College and Graduate School.

Rutgers, The State University of New Jersey, New Brunswick/Piscataway (New Brunswick, NJ): name changed to Rutgers, The State University of New Jersey, New Brunswick.

Santa Barbara College of Oriental Medicine (Santa Barbara, CA): closing December 2007.

Southwestern University School of Law (Los Angeles, CA): name changed to Southwestern Law School.

State University of New York at Buffalo (Buffalo, NY): name changed to University at Buffalo, the State University of New York.

State University of New York, Fredonia (Fredonia, NY): name changed to State University of New York at Fredonia.

Texas A&M University System Health Science Center (College Station, TX): name changed to Texas A&M Health Science Center.

Thunderbird, The Garvin School of International Management (Glendale, AZ): name changed to Thunderbird School of Global Management.

University of Colorado at Denver and Health Sciences Center–Downtown Denver Campus (Denver, CO): name changed to University of Colorado at Denver and Health Sciences Center.

University of Judaism (Bel Air, CA): name changed to American Jewish University.

University of Maryland (Baltimore, MD): name changed to University of Maryland, Baltimore.

University of Phoenix–Idaho Campus (Boise, ID): name changed to University of Phoenix–Magic View.

University of Phoenix–Nevada Campus (Las Vegas, NV): name changed to University of Phoenix–Las Vegas Campus.

University of Phoenix–South Florida Campus (Fort Lauderdale, FL): name changed to University of Phoenix–Fort Lauderdale Campus.

University of Phoenix–Spokane Campus (Spokane Valley, WA): name changed to University of Phoenix–Eastern Washington Campus.

Whitworth College (Spokane, WA): name changed to Whitworth University.

William Carey College (Hattiesburg, MS): name changed to William Carey University.

Abbreviations Used in the Guides

The following list includes abbreviations of degree names used in the profiles in the 2008 edition of the guides. Because some degrees (e.g., Doctor of Education) can be abbreviated in more than one way (e.g., D.Ed. or Ed.D.), and because the abbreviations used in the guides reflect the preferences of the individual colleges and universities, the list may include two or more abbreviations for a single degree.

Degrees

A Mus D	Doctor of Musical Arts
AC	Advanced Certificate
AD	Artist's Diploma
ADP	Artist's Diploma
Adv C	Advanced Certificate
Adv M	Advanced Master
AGSC	Advanced Graduate Specialist Certificate
ALM	Master of Liberal Arts
AM	Master of Arts
AMRS	Master of Arts in Religious Studies
APC	Advanced Professional Certificate
App Sc	Applied Scientist
App Sc D	Doctor of Applied Science
Au D	Doctor of Audiology
B Th	Bachelor of Theology
CAES	Certificate of Advanced Educational Specialization
CAGS	Certificate of Advanced Graduate Studies
CAL	Certificate in Applied Linguistics
CALS	Certificate of Advanced Liberal Studies
CAMS	Certificate of Advanced Management Studies
CAPS	Certificate of Advanced Professional Studies
CAS	Certificate of Advanced Studies
CASPA	Certificate of Advanced Study in Public Administration
CASR	Certificate in Advanced Social Research
CATS	Certificate of Achievement in Theological Studies
CBHS	Certificate in Basic Health Sciences
CBS	Graduate Certificate in Biblical Studies
CCJA	Certificate in Criminal Justice Administration
CCMBA	Cross-Continent Master of Business Administration
CCSA	Certificate in Catholic School Administration
CE	Civil Engineer
CEM	Certificate of Environmental Management
CET	Certificate in Educational Technologies
CG	Certificate in Gerontology
CGS	Certificate of Graduate Studies
Ch E	Chemical Engineer
CM	Certificate in Management
CMH	Certificate in Medical Humanities
CMM	Master of Church Ministries
CMS	Certificate in Ministerial Studies
CNM	Certificate in Nonprofit Management
CP	Certificate in Performance
CPASF	Certificate Program for Advanced Study in Finance
CPC	Certificate in Professional Counseling Certificate in Publication and Communication
CPH	Certificate in Public Health
CPM	Certificate in Public Management
CPS	Certificate of Professional Studies
CScD	Doctor of Clinical Science
CSD	Certificate in Spiritual Direction
CSS	Certificate of Special Studies
CTS	Certificate of Theological Studies
CURP	Certificate in Urban and Regional Planning
D Arch	Doctor of Architecture
D Ed	Doctor of Education
D Eng	Doctor of Engineering
D Engr	Doctor of Engineering
D Env	Doctor of Environment
D Env M	Doctor of Environmental Management
D Law	Doctor of Law
D Litt	Doctor of Letters
D Med Sc	Doctor of Medical Science
D Min	Doctor of Ministry
D Min PCC	Doctor of Ministry, Pastoral Care, and Counseling
D Miss	Doctor of Missiology
D Mus	Doctor of Music
D Mus A	Doctor of Musical Arts
D Phil	Doctor of Philosophy
D Ps	Doctor of Psychology
D Sc	Doctor of Science
D Sc D	Doctor of Science in Dentistry
D Sc IS	Doctor of Science in Information Systems
D Th	Doctor of Theology
D Th P	Doctor of Practical Theology
DA	Doctor of Arts
DA Ed	Doctor of Arts in Education
DAOM	Doctorate in Acupuncture and Oriental Medicine
DAST	Diploma of Advanced Studies in Teaching
DBA	Doctor of Business Administration
DBS	Doctor of Buddhist Studies
DC	Doctor of Chiropractic
DCC	Doctor of Computer Science
DCD	Doctor of Communications Design
DCL	Doctor of Comparative Law
DCM	Doctor of Church Music
DCN	Doctor of Clinical Nutrition
DCS	Doctor of Computer Science
DDN	Diplôme du Droit Notarial
DDS	Doctor of Dental Surgery
DE	Doctor of Education Doctor of Engineering
DEIT	Doctor of Educational Innovation and Technology
DEM	Doctor of Educational Ministry
DEPD	Diplôme Études Spécialisées
DES	Doctor of Engineering Science
DESS	Diplôme Études Supérieures Spécialisées
DFA	Doctor of Fine Arts
DGP	Diploma in Graduate and Professional Studies
DH Ed	Doctor of Health Education
DH Sc	Doctor of Health Sciences
DHA	Doctor of Health Administration
DHCE	Doctor of Health Care Ethics
DHL	Doctor of Hebrew Letters Doctor of Hebrew Literature

DHS	Doctor of Health Science
	Doctor of Human Services
DHSc	Doctor of Health Science
DIBA	Doctor of International Business Administration
Dip CS	Diploma in Christian Studies
DIT	Doctor of Industrial Technology
DJ Ed	Doctor of Jewish Education
DJS	Doctor of Jewish Studies
DM	Doctor of Management
	Doctor of Music
DMA	Doctor of Musical Arts
DMD	Doctor of Dental Medicine
DME	Doctor of Manufacturing Management
	Doctor of Music Education
DMEd	Doctor of Music Education
DMFT	Doctor of Marital and Family Therapy
DMH	Doctor of Medical Humanities
DML	Doctor of Modern Languages
DMM	Doctor of Music Ministry
DN Sc	Doctor of Nursing Science
DNP	Doctor of Nursing Practice
DNS	Doctor of Nursing Science
DO	Doctor of Osteopathy
DPA	Doctor of Public Administration
DPC	Doctor of Pastoral Counseling
DPDS	Doctor of Planning and Development Studies
DPE	Doctor of Physical Education
DPH	Doctor of Public Health
DPM	Doctor of Plant Medicine
	Doctor of Podiatric Medicine
DPS	Doctor of Professional Studies
DPT	Doctor of Physical Therapy
DPTSc	Doctor of Physical Therapy Science
Dr DES	Doctor of Design
Dr PH	Doctor of Public Health
Dr Sc PT	Doctor of Science in Physical Therapy
DrNP	Doctor of Nursing Practice
DS	Doctor of Science
DS Sc	Doctor of Social Science
DSJS	Doctor of Science in Jewish Studies
DSL	Doctor of Strategic Leadership
DSM	Doctor of Sport Management
DSN	Doctor of Science in Nursing
DSW	Doctor of Social Work
DTL	Doctor of Talmudic Law
DV Sc	Doctor of Veterinary Science
DVM	Doctor of Veterinary Medicine
EAA	Engineer in Aeronautics and Astronautics
ECS	Engineer in Computer Science
Ed D	Doctor of Education
Ed DCT	Doctor of Education in College Teaching
Ed M	Master of Education
Ed S	Specialist in Education
Ed Sp	Specialist in Education
Ed Sp PTE	Specialist in Education in Professional Technical Education
EDBA	Executive Doctor of Business Adminstration
EDM	Executive Doctorate in Management
EDSPC	Education Specialist
EE	Electrical Engineer
EJD	Executive Juris Doctor

EM	Mining Engineer
EMBA	Executive Master of Business Administration
EMCIS	Executive Master of Computer Information Systems
EMHA	Executive Master of Health Administration
EMIB	Executive Master of International Business
EMPA	Executive Master of Public Affairs
EMS	Executive Master of Science
EMTM	Executive Master of Technology Management
Eng	Engineer
Eng Sc D	Doctor of Engineering Science
Engr	Engineer
Ex Doc	Executive Doctor of Pharmacy
Exec Ed D	Executive Doctor of Education
Exec MBA	Executive Master of Business Administration
Exec MPA	Executive Master of Public Administration
Exec MPH	Executive Master of Public Health
Exec MS	Executive Master of Science
GBC	Graduate Business Certificate
GCE	Graduate Certificate in Education
GDM	Graduate Diploma in Management
GDPA	Graduate Diploma in Public Administration
GDRE	Graduate Diploma in Religious Education
GEMBA	Global Executive Master of Business Administration
Geol E	Geological Engineer
GMBA	Global Master of Business Administration
GPD	Graduate Performance Diploma
GSS	Graduate Special Certificate for Students in Special Situations
IMA	Interdisciplinary Master of Arts
IMBA	International Master of Business Administration
ITMA	Master of Instructional Technology
JCD	Doctor of Canon Law
JCL	Licentiate in Canon Law
JD	Juris Doctor
JD/DVM	Juris Doctor/Doctor of Veterinary Medicine
JD/MAP	Juris Doctor/Master of Applied Politics
JD/MCS	Juris Doctor/Master of Computer Science
JD/MHRIR	Juris Doctor/Master of Human Resources and Industrial Relations
JSD	Doctor of Juridical Science
	Doctor of Jurisprudence
	Doctor of the Science of Law
JSM	Master of Science of Law
L Th	Licenciate in Theology
LL B	Bachelor of Laws
LL CM	Master of Laws in Comparative Law
LL D	Doctor of Laws
LL M	Master of Laws
LL M T	Master of Laws in Taxation
M Ac	Master of Accountancy
	Master of Accounting
	Master of Acupuncture
M Ac OM	Master of Acupuncture and Oriental Medicine
M Acc	Master of Accountancy
	Master of Accounting
M Acct	Master of Accountancy
	Master of Accounting
M Accy	Master of Accountancy
M Actg	Master of Accounting
M Acy	Master of Accountancy

M Ad	Master of Administration
M Ad Ed	Master of Adult Education
M Adm	Master of Administration
M Adm Mgt	Master of Administrative Management
M ADU	Master of Architectural Design and Urbanism
M Adv	Master of Advertising
M Aero E	Master of Aerospace Engineering
M AEST	Master of Applied Environmental Science and Technology
M Ag	Master of Agriculture
M Ag Ed	Master of Agricultural Education
M Agr	Master of Agriculture
M Anesth Ed	Master of Anesthesiology Education
M App Comp Sc	Master of Applied Computer Science
M App St	Master of Applied Statistics
M Appl Stat	Master of Applied Statistics
M Aq	Master of Aquaculture
M Ar	Master of Architecture
M Arch	Master of Architecture
M Arch I	Master of Architecture I
M Arch II	Master of Architecture II
M Arch E	Master of Architectural Engineering
M Arch H	Master of Architectural History
M Arch UD	Master of Architecture in Urban Design
M Arch/SMRED	Master of Architecture/Master of Science in Real Estate Development
M Bio E	Master of Bioengineering
M Biomath	Master of Biomathematics
M Ch	Master of Chemistry
M Ch E	Master of Chemical Engineering
M Chem	Master of Chemistry
M Cl D	Master of Clinical Dentistry
M Cl Sc	Master of Clinical Science
M Comp E	Master of Computer Engineering
M Comp Sc	Master of Computer Science
M Coun	Master of Counseling
M Dent	Master of Dentistry
M Dent Sc	Master of Dental Sciences
M Des	Master of Design
M Des S	Master of Design Studies
M Div	Master of Divinity
M E Com	Master of Electronic Commerce
M Ec	Master of Economics
M Econ	Master of Economics
M Ed	Master of Education
M Ed T	Master of Education in Teaching
M En	Master of Engineering
M En S	Master of Environmental Sciences
M Eng	Master of Engineering
M Eng Mgt	Master of Engineering Management
M Eng Tel	Master of Engineering in Telecommunications
M Engr	Master of Engineering
M Env	Master of Environment
M Env Des	Master of Environmental Design
M Env E	Master of Environmental Engineering
M Env Sc	Master of Environmental Science
M Fin	Master of Finance
M Fr	Master of French
M Geo E	Master of Geological Engineering
M Geoenv E	Master of Geoenvironmental Engineering
M Geog	Master of Geography
M Hum	Master of Humanities
M Hum Svcs	Master of Human Services
M Kin	Master of Kinesiology
M Land Arch	Master of Landscape Architecture
M Lit M	Master of Liturgical Music
M Litt	Master of Letters
M Man	Master of Management
M Mat SE	Master of Material Science and Engineering
M Math	Master of Mathematics
M Med Sc	Master of Medical Science
M Mgmt	Master of Management
M Mgt	Master of Management
M Min	Master of Ministries
M Mtl E	Master of Materials Engineering
M Mu	Master of Music
M Mus	Master of Music
M Mus Ed	Master of Music Education
M Nat Sci	Master of Natural Science
M Nurs	Master of Nursing
M Oc E	Master of Oceanographic Engineering
M Pharm	Master of Pharmacy
M Phil	Master of Philosophy
M Phil F	Master of Philosophical Foundations
M Pl	Master of Planning
M Pol	Master of Political Science
M Pr A	Master of Professional Accountancy
M Pr Met	Master of Professional Meteorology
M Prob S	Master of Probability and Statistics
M Prof Past	Master of Professional Pastoral
M Psych	Master of Psychology
M Pub	Master of Publishing
M Rel	Master of Religion
M Sc	Master of Science
M Sc A	Master of Science (Applied)
M Sc AHN	Master of Science in Applied Human Nutrition
M Sc BMC	Master of Science in Biomedical Communications
M Sc CS	Master of Science in Computer Science
M Sc E	Master of Science in Engineering
M Sc Eng	Master of Science in Engineering
M Sc Engr	Master of Science in Engineering
M Sc F	Master of Science in Forestry
M Sc FE	Master of Science in Forest Engineering
M Sc Geogr	Master of Science in Geography
M Sc N	Master of Science in Nursing
M Sc OT	Master of Science in Occupational Therapy
M Sc P	Master of Science in Planning
M Sc Pl	Master of Science in Planning
M Sc PT	Master of Science in Physical Therapy
M Sc T	Master of Science in Teaching
M Soc	Master of Sociology
M Sp Ed	Master of Special Education
M Stat	Master of Statistics
M Sw En	Master of Software Engineering
M Sys Sc	Master of Systems Science
M Tax	Master of Taxation
M Tech	Master of Technology
M Th	Master of Theology
M Th Past	Master of Pastoral Theology
M Tox	Master of Toxicology
M Trans E	Master of Transportation Engineering
M Vet Sc	Master of Veterinary Science

MA	Master of Administration
	Master of Arts
MA Comm	Master of Arts in Communication
MA Ed	Master of Arts in Education
MA Ed Ad	Master of Arts in Educational Administration
MA Ext	Master of Agricultural Extension
MA Islamic	Master of Arts in Islamic Studies
MA Min	Master of Arts in Ministry
MA Missions	Master of Arts in Missions
MA Past St	Master of Arts in Pastoral Studies
MA Ph	Master of Arts in Philosophy
MA Ps	Master of Arts in Psychology
MA Psych	Master of Arts in Psychology
MA Sc	Master of Applied Science
MA Sp	Master of Arts (Spirituality)
MA Th	Master of Arts in Theology
MA-R	Master of Arts (Research)
MAA	Master of Administrative Arts
	Master of Applied Anthropology
	Master of Arts in Administration
MAAA	Master of Arts in Arts Administration
MAAE	Master of Arts in Art Education
MAAT	Master of Arts in Applied Theology
	Master of Arts in Art Therapy
MAB	Master of Agribusiness
MABC	Master of Arts in Biblical Counseling
	Master of Arts in Business Communication
MABE	Master of Arts in Bible Exposition
MABL	Master of Arts in Biblical Languages
MABM	Master of Agribusiness Management
MABS	Master of Arts in Biblical Studies
MABT	Master of Arts in Bible Teaching
MAC	Master of Accounting
	Master of Addictions Counseling
	Master of Arts in Communication
	Master of Arts in Counseling
MACAT	Master of Arts in Counseling Psychology: Art Therapy
MACC	Master of Arts in Christian Counseling
MACCM	Master of Arts in Church and Community Ministry
MACCT	Master of Accounting
MACE	Master of Arts in Christian Education
MACFM	Master of Arts in Children's and Family Ministry
MACH	Master of Arts in Church History
MACJ	Master of Arts in Criminal Justice
MACL	Master of Arts in Classroom Psychology
MACM	Master of Arts in Christian Ministries
	Master of Arts in Church Music
	Master of Arts in Counseling Ministries
MACN	Master of Arts in Counseling
MACO	Master of Arts in Counseling
MAcOM	Master of Acupuncture and Oriental Medicine
MACP	Master of Arts in Counseling Psychology
MACPC	Master of Clinical Pastoral Counseling
MACS	Master of Arts in Catholic Studies
	Master of Arts in Christian Service
MACSE	Master of Arts in Christian School Education
MACT	Master of Arts in Christian Thought
	Master of Arts in Communications and Technology
MACY	Master of Arts in Accountancy
MAD	Master in Educational Institution Administration
	Master of Art and Design

MADR	Master of Arts in Dispute Resolution
MADS	Master of Animal and Dairy Science
	Master of Applied Disability Studies
MAE	Master of Aerospace Engineering
	Master of Agricultural Economics
	Master of Architectural Engineering
	Master of Art Education
	Master of Arts in Economics
	Master of Arts in Education
	Master of Arts in English
	Master of Automotive Engineering
MAEd	Master of Arts Education
MAEE	Master of Arts in Agricultural and Extension Education
MAEL	Master of Arts in Educational Leadership
	Master of Arts in Executive Leadership
MAEM	Master of Arts in Educational Ministries
MAEN	Master of Arts in English
MAEP	Master of Arts in Economic Policy
MAES	Master of Arts in Environmental Sciences
MAESL	Master of Arts in English as a Second Language
MAET	Master of Arts in English Teaching
MAF	Master of Arts in Finance
MAFE	Master of Arts in Financial Economics
MAFLL	Master of Arts in Foreign Language and Literature
MAFM	Master of Accounting and Financial Management
MAFS	Master of Arts in Family Studies
MAG	Master of Applied Geography
MAGC	Master of Arts in Global Communication
MAGP	Master of Arts in Gerontological Psychology
MAGU	Master of Urban Analysis and Management
MAH	Master of Arts in Humanities
MAHA	Master of Arts in Humanitarian Assistance
	Master of Arts in Humanitarian Studies
MAHCM	Master of Arts in Health Care Mission
MAHG	Master of American History and Government
MAHL	Master of Arts in Hebrew Letters
MAHN	Master of Applied Human Nutrition
MAHS	Master of Arts in Human Services
MAHT	Master of Arts in History Teaching
MAIA	Master of Arts in International Administration
MAIB	Master of Arts in International Business
MAICS	Master of Arts in Intercultural Studies
MAIDM	Master of Arts in Interior Design and Merchandising
MAIPCR	Master of Arts in International Peace and Conflict Management
MAIR	Master of Arts in Industrial Relations
MAIS	Master of Accounting and Information Systems
	Master of Arts in Intercultural Studies
	Master of Arts in Interdisciplinary Studies
	Master of Arts in International Studies
MAIT	Master of Administration in Information Technology
	Master of Applied Information Technology
MAJ	Master of Arts in Journalism
MAJ Ed	Master of Arts in Jewish Education
MAJCS	Master of Arts in Jewish Communal Service
MAJE	Master of Arts in Jewish Education
MAJS	Master of Arts in Jewish Studies
MAL	Master in Agricultural Leadership
MALA	Master of Arts in Liberal Arts
MALD	Master of Arts in Law and Diplomacy
MALER	Master of Arts in Labor and Employment Relations

MALM	Master of Arts in Leadership Evangelical Mobilization	**MAS**	Master of Accounting Science
MALP	Master of Arts in Language Pedagogy		Master of Actuarial Science
MALPS	Master of Arts in Liberal and Professional Studies		Master of Administrative Science
MALS	Master of Arts in Liberal Studies		Master of Advanced Study
MALT	Master of Arts in Learning and Teaching		Master of Aeronautical Science
MAM	Master of Acquisition Management		Master of American Studies
	Master of Agriculture and Management		Master of Applied Science
	Master of Applied Mathematics		Master of Applied Statistics
	Master of Applied Mechanics		Master of Archival Studies
	Master of Arts in Management	**MAS/JD**	Master of Accounting Science/Juris Doctor
	Master of Arts in Ministry	**MASA**	Master of Advanced Studies in Architecture
	Master of Arts Management	**MASAC**	Master of Arts in Substance Abuse Counseling
	Master of Avian Medicine	**MASC**	Master of Arts in School Counseling
MAMB	Master of Applied Molecular Biology	**MASD**	Master of Arts in Spiritual Direction
MAMC	Master of Arts in Mass Communication	**MASE**	Master of Arts in Special Education
	Master of Arts in Ministry and Culture	**MASF**	Master of Arts in Spiritual Formation
	Master of Arts in Ministry for a Multicultural Church	**MASJ**	Master of Arts in Systems of Justice
MAME	Master of Arts in Missions/Evangelism	**MASL**	Master of Arts in School Leadership
MAMFC	Master of Arts in Marriage and Family Counseling	**MASLA**	Master of Advanced Studies in Landscape Architecture
MAMFCC	Master of Arts in Marriage, Family, and Child Counseling	**MASM**	Master of Arts in Special Ministries
			Master of Arts in Specialized Ministries
MAMFT	Master of Arts in Marriage and Family Therapy	**MASP**	Master of Applied Social Psychology
MAMM	Master of Arts in Ministry Management		Master of Arts in School Psychology
MAMS	Master of Applied Mathematical Sciences	**MASPAA**	Master of Arts in Sports and Athletic Administration
	Master of Arts in Ministerial Studies	**MASS**	Master of Applied Social Science
	Master of Arts in Ministry and Spirituality		Master of Arts in Social Science
	Master of Associated Medical Sciences	**MAST**	Master of Arts Science Teaching
MAMT	Master of Arts in Mathematics Teaching	**MASW**	Master of Aboriginal Social Work
MAN	Master of Applied Nutrition	**MAT**	Master of Arts in Teaching
MANM	Master of Arts in Nonprofit Management		Master of Arts in Theology
MANT	Master of Arts in New Testament		Master of Athletic Training
MAO	Master of Arts in Organizational Psychology		Master in Administration of Telecommunications
MAOA	Master of Arts in Organizational Administration	**Mat E**	Materials Engineer
MAOL	Master of Arts in Organizational Leadership	**MATCM**	Master of Acupuncture and Traditional Chinese Medicine
MAOM	Master of Acupuncture and Oriental Medicine	**MATDE**	Master of Arts in Theology, Development, and Evangelism
	Master of Arts in Organizational Management	**MATE**	Master of Arts for the Teaching of English
MAOT	Master of Arts in Old Testament	**MATESL**	Master of Arts in Teaching English as a Second Language
MAP	Master of Applied Psychology	**MATESOL**	Master of Arts in Teaching English to Speakers of Other Languages
	Master of Arts in Planning		
	Master of Public Administration	**MATF**	Master of Arts in Teaching English as a Foreign Language/Intercultural Studies
	Masters of Psychology		
MAP Min	Master of Arts in Pastoral Ministry	**MATFL**	Master of Arts in Teaching Foreign Language
MAPA	Master of Arts in Public Administration	**MATH**	Master of Arts in Therapy
MAPC	Master of Arts in Pastoral Counseling	**MATI**	Master of Administration of Information Technology
MAPE	Master of Arts in Political Economy	**MATL**	Master of Arts in Teaching of Languages
MAPM	Master of Arts in Pastoral Ministry		Master of Arts in Transformational Leadership
	Master of Arts in Pastoral Music	**MATM**	Master of Arts in Teaching of Mathematics
	Master of Arts in Practical Ministry	**MATS**	Master of Arts in Theological Studies
MAPP	Master of Arts in Public Policy		Master of Arts in Transforming Spirituality
MAPPS	Master of Arts in Asia Pacific Policy Studies	**MATSL**	Master of Arts in Teaching a Second Language
MAPS	Master of Arts in Pastoral Counseling/Spiritual Formation	**MAUA**	Master of Arts in Urban Affairs
		MAUD	Master of Arts in Urban Design
	Master of Arts in Pastoral Studies	**MAUM**	Master of Arts in Urban Ministry
	Master of Arts in Public Service	**MAURP**	Master of Arts in Urban and Regional Planning
MAPT	Master of Practical Theology	**MAW**	Master of Arts in Writing
MAPW	Master of Arts in Professional Writing	**MAWL**	Master of Arts in Worship Leadership
MAR	Master of Arts in Religion	**MAWS**	Master of Arts in Worship/Spirituality
Mar Eng	Marine Engineer	**MAWSHP**	Master of Arts in Worship
MARC	Master of Arts in Rehabilitation Counseling	**MAYM**	Master of Arts in Youth Ministry
MARE	Master of Arts in Religious Education		
MARL	Master of Arts in Religious Leadership		
MARS	Master of Arts in Religious Studies		

MB	Master of Bioinformatics
MBA	Master of Business Administration
MBA-EP	Master of Business Administration–Experienced Professionals
MBA/M Stat	Master of Business Administration/Master of Statistics
MBA/MEE	Master of Business Administration/Master of Electrical Engineering
MBA/MNO	Master of Business Administration/Master of Nonprofit Organization
MBAA	Master of Business Administration in Aviation
MBAE	Master of Biological and Agricultural Engineering
	Master of Biosystems and Agricultural Engineering
MBAH	Master of Business Administration in Health
MBAi	Master of Business Administration–International
MBAICT	Master of Business Administration in Information and Communication Technology
MBAIM	Master of Business Administration in International Management
MBAPA	Master of Business Administration–Physician Assistant
MBATM	Master of Business Administration in Technology Management
	Master of Business in Telecommunication Management
MBC	Master of Building Construction
MBE	Master of Bilingual Education
	Master of Bioengineering
	Master of Biological Engineering
	Master of Biomedical Engineering
	Master of Business and Engineering
	Master of Business Economics
	Master of Business Education
MBET	Master of Business, Entrepreneurship and Technology
MBI	Master in Business Informatics
MBIOT	Master of Biotechnology
MBIT	Master of Business Information Technology
MBL	Master of Business Law
MBLE	Master in Business Logistics Engineering
MBMSE	Master of Business Management and Software Engineering
MBOL	Master of Business and Organizational Leadership
MBS	Master of Behavioral Science
	Master of Biological Science
	Master of Biomedical Sciences
	Master of Bioscience
	Master of Building Science
MBSI	Master of Business Information Science
MBT	Master of Biblical and Theological Studies
	Master of Biomedical Technology
	Master of Business Taxation
MC	Master of Communication
	Master of Counseling
	Master of Cybersecurity
MC Ed	Master of Continuing Education
MC Sc	Master of Computer Science
MCA	Master of Arts in Applied Criminology
	Master of Commercial Aviation
MCALL	Master of Computer-Assisted Language Learning
MCAM	Master of Computational and Applied Mathematics
MCC	Master of Computer Science
MCCS	Master of Crop and Soil Sciences

MCD	Master of Communications Disorders
	Master of Community Development
MCE	Master in Electronic Commerce
	Master of Christian Education
	Master of Civil Engineering
	Master of Control Engineering
MCEM	Master of Construction Engineering Management
MCH	Master of Community Health
MCHE	Master of Chemical Engineering
MCIS	Master of Communication and Information Studies
	Master of Computer and Information Science
MCIT	Master of Computer and Information Technology
MCJ	Master of Criminal Justice
MCJA	Master of Criminal Justice Administration
MCL	Master in Communication Leadership
	Master of Canon Law
	Master of Civil Law
	Master of Comparative Law
MCM	Master of Christian Ministry
	Master of Church Management
	Master of Church Ministry
	Master of Church Music
	Master of City Management
	Master of Communication Management
	Master of Community Medicine
	Master of Competitive Manufacturing
	Master of Construction Management
	Master of Contract Management
	Master of Corporate Media
MCMS	Master of Clinical Medical Science
MCP	Master in Science
	Master of City Planning
	Master of Community Planning
	Master of Counseling Psychology
	Master of Cytopathology Practice
MCPD	Master of Community Planning and Development
MCRP	Master of City and Regional Planning
MCRS	Master of City and Regional Studies
MCS	Master of Christian Studies
	Master of Clinical Science
	Master of Combined Sciences
	Master of Communication Studies
	Master of Computer Science
MCSE	Master of Computer Science and Engineering
MCSL	Master of Catholic School Leadership
MCSM	Master of Construction Science/Management
MCST	Master of Science in Computer Science and Information Technology
MCTP	Master of Communication Technology and Policy
MCVS	Master of Cardiovascular Science
MD	Doctor of Medicine
MD/CM	Doctor of Medicine and Master of Surgery
MD/MSBS	Doctor of Medicine/Master of Science in Biomedical Science
MDA	Master of Development Administration
	Master of Dietetic Administration
MDE	Master of Developmental Economics
	Master of Distance Education
MDH	Master of Dental Hygiene
MDR	Master of Dispute Resolution
MDS	Master of Defense Studies
	Master of Dental Surgery
ME	Master of Education
	Master of Engineering
	Master of Entrepreneurship
	Master of Evangelism
ME Sc	Master of Engineering Science

MEA	Master of Educational Administration
	Master of Engineering Administration
MEAP	Master of Environmental Administration and Planning
MEBT	Master in Electronic Business Technologies
MEC	Master of Electronic Commerce
MECE	Master of Electrical and Computer Engineering
Mech E	Mechanical Engineer
MED	Master of Education of the Deaf
MEDL	Master of Educational Leadership
MEDS	Master of Environmental Design Studies
MEE	Master in Education
	Master of Electrical Engineering
	Master of Environmental Engineering
MEEM	Master of Environmental Engineering and Management
MEENE	Master of Engineering in Environmental Engineering
MEEP	Master of Environmental and Energy Policy
MEERM	Master of Earth and Environmental Resource Management
MEH	Master in Humanistics Studies
MEHS	Master of Environmental Health and Safety
MEIM	Master of Entertainment Industry Management
MEL	Master of Educational Leadership
	Master of English Literature
MEM	Master of Ecosystem Management
	Master of Electricity Markets
	Master of Engineering Management
	Master of Environmental Management
	Master of Marketing
MEME	Master of Engineering in Manufacturing Engineering
	Master of Engineering in Mechanical Engineering
MEMS	Master of Engineering in Manufacturing Systems
MENG	Master of Arts in English
MENVEGR	Master of Environmental Engineering
MEP	Master of Engineering Physics
	Master of Environmental Planning
MEPC	Master of Environmental Pollution Control
MEPD	Master of Education–Professional Development
MEPM	Master of Environmental Protection Management
MER	Master of Employment Relations
MES	Master of Education and Science
	Master of Engineering Science
	Master of Environmental Science
	Master of Environmental Studies
	Master of Environmental Systems
	Master of Special Education
MESM	Master of Environmental Science and Management
MET	Master of Education in Teaching
	Master of Educational Technology
	Master of Engineering Technology
	Master of Entertainment Technology
	Master of Environmental Toxicology
Met E	Metallurgical Engineer
METM	Master of Engineering and Technology Management
MEVE	Master of Environmental Engineering
MF	Master of Finance
	Master of Forestry
MFA	Master of Financial Administration
	Master of Fine Arts
MFAM	Master in Food Animal Medicine
MFAS	Master of Fisheries and Aquatic Science

MFAW	Master of Fine Arts in Writing
MFC	Master of Forest Conservation
MFCC	Marriage and Family Counseling Certificate
MFCS	Master of Family and Consumer Sciences
MFE	Master of Financial Engineering
	Master of Forest Engineering
MFG	Master of Functional Genomics
MFHD	Master of Family and Human Development
MFM	Master of Financial Mathematics
MFMS	Masters in Food Microbiology and Safety
MFP	Master of Financial Planning
MFPE	Master of Food Process Engineering
MFR	Master of Forest Resources
MFRC	Master of Forest Resources and Conservation
MFS	Master of Financial Services
	Master of Food Science
	Master of Forensic Sciences
	Master of Forest Science
	Master of Forest Studies
	Master of French Studies
MFSA	Master of Forensic Sciences Administration
MFT	Master of Family Therapy
	Master of Food Technology
MFWB	Master of Fishery and Wildlife Biology
MFWS	Master of Fisheries and Wildlife Sciences
MFYCS	Master of Family, Youth and Community Sciences
MG	Master of Genetics
MGA	Master of Government Administration
MGE	Master of Gas Engineering
	Master of Geotechnical Engineering
MGF	Master of Global Finance
MGH	Master of Geriatric Health
MGIS	Master of Geographic Information Science
MGM/MBA	Master in Global Management/Master of Business Administration
MGP	Master of Gestion de Projet
MGS	Master of Gerontological Studies
	Master of Global Studies
MH	Master of Humanities
MH Ed	Master of Health Education
MH Sc	Master of Health Sciences
MHA	Master of Health Administration
	Master of Healthcare Administration
	Master of Hospital Administration
	Master of Hospitality Administration
MHCA	Master of Health Care Administration
MHCI	Master of Human-Computer Interaction
MHCL	Master of Health Care Leadership
MHE	Master of Health Education
MHE Ed	Master of Home Economics Education
MHHS	Master of Health and Human Services
MHI	Master of Health Informatics
MHIIM	Master of Health Informatics and Information Management
MHIS	Master of Health Information Systems
MHK	Master of Human Kinetics
MHL	Master of Hebrew Literature
MHM	Master of Hospitality Management
MHMS	Master of Health Management Systems
MHP	Master of Health Physics
	Master of Heritage Preservation
	Master of Historic Preservation
MHPA	Master of Heath Policy and Administration

MHPE	Master of Health Professions Education
MHR	Master of Human Resources
MHRD	Master in Human Resource Development
MHRDL	Master of Human Resource Development Leadership
MHRIM	Master of Hotel, Restaurant, and Institutional Management
MHRIR	Master of Human Resources and Industrial Relations
MHRIR/JD	Master of Human Resources and Industrial Relations/Juris Doctor
MHRIR/MBA	Master of Human Resources and Industrial Relations/Master of Business Administration
MHRLR	Master of Human Resources and Labor Relations
MHRM	Master of Human Resources Management
MHROD	Master of Human Resources and Organization Development
MHRTM	Master of Hotel, Restaurant, and Tourism Management
MHS	Master of Health Sciences
	Master of Health Studies
	Master of Hispanic Studies
	Master of Humanistic Studies
MHSA	Master of Health Services Administration
MHSM	Master of Health Sector Management
	Master of Health Systems Management
	Master of Human Services Management
MI	Master of Instruction
MI Arch	Master of Interior Architecture
MI St	Master of Information Studies
MIA	Master of Interior Architecture
	Master of International Affairs
MIAA	Master of International Affairs and Administration
MIAM	Master of International Agribusiness Management
MIB	Master of International Business
MIBA	Master of International Business Administration
MICM	Master of International Construction Management
MID	Master of Industrial Design
	Master of Industrial Distribution
	Master of Interior Design
	Master of International Development
MIE	Master of Industrial Engineering
MIEM	Master of Industrial Engineering and Management
MIJ	Master of International Journalism
MILR	Master of Industrial and Labor Relations
MIM	Master of Information Management
	Master of International Management
MIMLAE	Master of International Management for Latin American Executives
MIMS	Master of Information Management and Systems
	Master of Integrated Manufacturing Systems
MIP	Master of Infrastructure Planning
	Master of Intellectual Property
MIPER	Master of International Political Economy of Resources
MIPP	Master of International Policy and Practice
	Master of International Public Policy
MIPS	Master of International Planning Studies
MIR	Master of Industrial Relations
	Master of International Relations

MIS	Master of Industrial Statistics
	Master of Information Science
	Master of Information Systems
	Master of Integrated Science
	Master of Interdisciplinary Studies
	Master of International Service
	Master of International Studies
MISE	Master of Industrial and Systems Engineering
MISKM	Master of Information Sciences and Knowledge Management
MISM	Master of Information Systems Management
MIT	Master in Teaching
	Master of Industrial Technology
	Master of Information Technology
	Master of Initial Teaching
	Master of International Trade
	Master of Internet Technology
MITA	Master of Information Technology Administration
MITE	Master of Information Technology Education
MITM	Master of International Technology Management
MITO	Master of Industrial Technology and Operations
MJ	Master of Journalism
	Master of Jurisprudence
MJ Ed	Master of Jewish Education
MJA	Master of Justice Administration
MJS	Master of Judicial Studies
	Master of Juridical Science
MKM	Master of Knowledge Management
ML	Master of Latin
ML Arch	Master of Landscape Architecture
MLA	Master of Landscape Architecture
	Master of Liberal Arts
MLAS	Master of Laboratory Animal Science
MLAUD	Master of Landscape Architecture in Urban Development
MLBLST	Master of Liberal Studies
MLD	Master of Leadership Development
	Master of Leadership Studies
MLE	Master of Applied Linguistics and Exegesis
MLER	Master of Labor and Employment Relations
MLERE	Master of Land Economics and Real Estate
MLHR	Master of Labor and Human Resources
MLI	Master of Legal Institutions
MLI Sc	Master of Library and Information Science
MLIS	Master of Library and Information Science
	Master of Library and Information Studies
MLM	Master of Library Media
MLOS	Master in Leadership and Organizational Studies
MLRHR	Master of Labor Relations and Human Resources
MLS	Master of Leadership Studies
	Master of Legal Studies
	Master of Liberal Studies
	Master of Library Science
	Master of Life Sciences
MLS/PMC	Master of Library Science/Graduat Certificate in Public Management
MLSP	Master of Law and Social Policy
MLT	Master of Language Technologies
MLW	Master of Studies in Law

MM	Master of Management Master of Mediation Master of Ministry Master of Missiology Master of Music	**MNAS**	Master of Natural and Applied Science
		MNCM	Master of Network and Communications Management
MM Ed	Master of Music Education	**MNE**	Master of Network Engineering Master of Nuclear Engineering
MM Sc	Master of Medical Science	**MNL**	Master in International Business for Latin America
MM St	Master of Museum Studies	**MNM**	Master of Nonprofit Management
MMA	Master of Marine Affairs Master of Media Arts Master of Musical Arts	**MNO**	Master of Nonprofit Organization
		MNO/MSSA	Master of Nonprofit Organization/Master of Arts
MMAE	Master of Mechanical and Aerospace Engineering	**MNPL**	Master of Not-for-Profit Leadership
MMAS	Master of Military Art and Science	**MNPS**	Master of New Professional Studies
MMB	Master of Microbial Biotechnology	**MNR**	Master of Natural Resources
MMBA	Managerial Master of Business Administration	**MNRES**	Master of Natural Resources and Environmental Studies
MMC	Master of Competitive Manufacturing Master of Mass Communications Master of Music Conducting	**MNRM**	Master of Natural Resource Management
		MNRS	Master of Natural Resource Stewardship
MMCM	Master of Music in Church Music	**MNS**	Master of Natural Science
MMCSS	Master of Mathematical Computational and Statistical Sciences	**MO**	Master of Oceanography
		MOA	Maître d'Orthophonie et d'Audiologie
MME	Master of Manufacturing Engineering Master of Mathematics for Educators Master of Mechanical Engineering Master of Medical Engineering Master of Mining Engineering Master of Music Education Mater of Mathematics Education	**MOD**	Master of Organizational Development
		MOGS	Master of Oil and Gas Studies
		MOH	Master of Occupational Health
		MOL	Master of Organizational Leadership
		MOM	Master of Manufacturing Master of Oriental Medicine
MMFT	Master of Marriage and Family Therapy	**MOR**	Master of Operations Research
MMG	Master of Management	**MOT**	Master of Occupational Therapy
MMH	Master of Management in Hospitality Master of Medical History Master of Medical Humanities Master of Military History	**MP**	Master of Physiology Master of Planning
		MP Ac	Master of Professional Accountancy
		MP Acc	Master of Professional Accountancy Master of Professional Accounting Master of Public Accounting
MMIS	Master of Management Information Systems		
MMM	Master of Manufacturing Management Master of Marine Management Master of Medical Management	**MP Aff**	Master of Public Affairs
		MP Th	Master of Pastoral Theology
MMME	Master of Metallurgical and Materials Engineering	**MPA**	Master of Physician Assistant Master of Professional Accountancy Master of Professional Accounting Master of Public Administration Master of Public Affairs
MMMP	Master of Music in Music Performance		
MMP	Master of Marine Policy Master of Music Performance		
MMPA	Master of Management and Professional Accounting	**MPA-URP**	Master of Public Affairs and Urban and Regional Planning
MMQM	Master of Manufacturing Quality Management	**MPAC**	Master in Professional Accounting
MMR	Master of Marketing Research	**MPAID**	Master of Public Administration and International Development
MMRM	Master of Marine Resources Management		
MMS	Master of Management Science Master of Manufacturing Systems Master of Marine Studies Master of Materials Science Master of Medical Science Master of Medieval Studies Master of Modern Studies	**MPAP**	Master of Physician Assistant Practice Master of Public Affairs and Politics
		MPAS	Master of Physician Assistant Science Master of Physician Assistant Studies Master of Public Art Studies
		MPC	Master of Pastoral Counseling Master of Professional Communication Master of Professional Counseling
MMSE	Master of Manufacturing Systems Engineering		
MMSM	Master of Music in Sacred Music		
MMT	Master in Marketing Master of Music Teaching Master of Music Therapy Masters in Marketing Technology	**MPD**	Master of Product Development Master of Public Diplomacy
		MPDS	Master of Planning and Development Studies
MMus	Master of Music	**MPE**	Master of Physical Education
MN	Master of Nursing Master of Nutrition	**MPEM**	Master of Project Engineering and Management
		MPH	Master of Public Health
MN Sc	Master of Nursing Science	**MPHE**	Master of Public Health Education
MNA	Master of Nonprofit Administration Master of Nurse Anesthesia	**MPHTM**	Master of Public Health and Tropical Medicine
		MPIA	Master of Public and International Affairs
MNAL	Master of Nonprofit Administration and Leadership	**MPL**	Master of Pastoral Leadership

MPM	Master of Pastoral Ministry
	Master of Pest Management
	Master of Practical Ministries
	Master of Project Management
	Master of Public Management
MPNA	Master of Public and Nonprofit Administration
MPOD	Master of Positive Organizational Development
MPP	Master of Public Policy
MPPA	Master of Public Policy Administration
	Master of Public Policy and Administration
MPPAL	Master of Public Policy, Administration and Law
MPPM	Master of Public and Private Management
	Master of Public Policy and Management
MPPPM	Master of Plant Protection and Pest Management
MPPUP	Master of Public Policy and Urban Planning
MPRTM	Master of Parks, Recreation, and Tourism Management
MPS	Master of Pastoral Studies
	Master of Perfusion Science
	Master of Political Science
	Master of Preservation Studies
	Master of Professional Studies
	Master of Public Service
MPSA	Master of Public Service Administration
MPSRE	Master of Professional Studies in Real Estate
MPT	Master of Pastoral Theology
	Master of Physical Therapy
MPVM	Master of Preventive Veterinary Medicine
MPW	Master of Professional Writing
	Master of Public Works
MQF	Master of Quantitative Finance
MQM	Master of Quality Management
MQS	Master of Quality Systems
MR	Master of Recreation
MRC	Master of Rehabilitation Counseling
MRCP	Master of Regional and City Planning
	Master of Regional and Community Planning
MRD	Master of Rural Development
MRE	Master of Religious Education
MRED	Master of Real Estate Development
MRLS	Master of Resources Law Studies
MRM	Master of Rehabilitation Medicine
	Master of Resources Management
MRP	Master of Regional Planning
MRP/JD	Master of Regional Planning/Juris Doctor
MRRA	Master of Recreation Resources Administration
MRS	Master of Religious Studies
MRSc	Master of Rehabilitation Science
MS	Master of Science
MS Kin	Master of Science in Kinesiology
MS Acct	Master of Science in Accounting
MS Aero E	Master of Science in Aerospace Engineering
MS Ag	Master of Science in Agriculture
MS Arch	Master of Science in Architecture
MS Arch St	Master of Science in Architectural Studies
MS Bio E	Master of Science in Bioengineering
	Master of Science in Biomedical Engineering
MS Bm E	Master of Science in Biomedical Engineering
MS Ch E	Master of Science in Chemical Engineering
MS Chem	Master of Science in Chemistry
MS Cp E	Master of Science in Computer Engineering
MS Eco	Master of Science in Economics
MS Econ	Master of Science in Economics
MS Ed	Master of Science in Education

MS EI	Master of Science in Educational Leadership and Administration
MS En E	Master of Science in Environmental Engineering
MS Eng	Master of Science in Engineering
MS Engr	Master of Science in Engineering
MS Env E	Master of Science in Environmental Engineering
MS Exp Surg	Master of Science in Experimental Surgery
MS Int A	Master of Science in International Affairs
MS Mat E	Master of Science in Materials Engineering
MS Mat SE	Master of Science in Material Science and Engineering
MS Met E	Master of Science in Metallurgical Engineering
MS Metr	Master of Science in Meteorology
MS Mgt	Master of Science in Management
MS Min	Master of Science in Mining
MS Min E	Master of Science in Mining Engineering
MS Mt E	Master of Science in Materials Engineering
MS Otol	Master of Science in Otolaryngology
MS Pet E	Master of Science in Petroleum Engineering
MS Phr	Master of Science in Pharmacy
MS Phys	Master of Science in Physics
MS Phys Op	Master of Science in Physiological Optics
MS Poly	Master of Science in Polymers
MS Psy	Master of Science in Psychology
MS Pub P	Master of Science in Public Policy
MS RSS	Master of Science in Recreation and Sport Sciences
MS Sc	Master of Science in Social Science
MS SEng	Master of Science in Systems Engineering
MS Sp C	Master of Science in Space Science
MS Sp Ed	Master of Science in Special Education
MS Stat	Master of Science in Statistics
MS Surg	Master of Science in Surgery
MS Tax	Master of Science in Taxation
MS Tc E	Master of Science in Telecommunications Engineering
MS-R	Master of Science (Research)
MSA	Master of School Administration
	Master of Science Administration
	Master of Science in Accountancy
	Master of Science in Accounting
	Master of Science in Administration
	Master of Science in Aeronautics
	Master of Science in Agriculture
	Master of Science in Anesthesia
	Master of Science in Architecture
	Master of Science in Aviation
	Master of Sports Administration
MSA Phy	Master of Science in Applied Physics
MSAA	Master of Science in Astronautics and Aeronautics
MSAAE	Master of Science in Aeronautical and Astronautical Engineering
MSABE	Master of Science in Agricultural and Biological Engineering
MSAC	Master of Science in Acupuncture
MSACC	Master of Science in Accounting
MSaCS	Master of Science in Applied Computer Science
MSAE	Master of Science in Aeronautical Engineering
	Master of Science in Aerospace Engineering
	Master of Science in Agricultural Engineering
	Master of Science in Applied Economics
	Master of Science in Architectural Engineering
	Master of Science in Art Education
MSAH	Master of Science in Allied Health

MSAL	Master of Sport Administration and Leadership
MSAM	Master of Science in Applied Mathematics
MSAOM	Master of Science in Agricultural Operations Management
MSAPM	Master of Security Analysis and Portfolio Management
MSAS	Master of Science in Administrative Studies
	Master of Science in Applied Statistics
	Master of Science in Architectural Studies
MSAT	Master of Science in Advanced Technology
MSB	Master of Science in Bible
	Master of Science in Business
MSBA	Master of Science in Business Administration
MSBAE	Master of Science in Biological and Agricultural Engineering
	Master of Science in Biosystems and Agricultural Engineering
MSBC	Master of Science in Building Construction
MSBE	Master of Science in Biological Engineering
	Master of Science in Biomedical Engineering
	Master of Science in Business Education
MSBENG	Master of Science in Bioengineering
MSBIT	Master of Science in Business Information Technology
MSBM	Master of Sport Business Management
MSBME	Master of Science in Biomedical Engineering
MSBMS	Master of Science in Basic Medical Science
MSBS	Master of Science in Biomedical Sciences
MSC	Master of Science in Commerce
	Master of Science in Communication
	Master of Science in Computers
	Master of Science in Counseling
	Master of Science in Criminology
MSCC	Master of Science in Christian Counseling
	Master of Science in Community Counseling
MSCD	Master of Science in Communication Disorders
	Master of Science in Community Development
MSCE	Master of Science in Civil Engineering
	Master of Science in Clinical Epidemiology
	Master of Science in Computer Engineering
	Master of Science in Continuing Education
MSCEE	Master of Science in Civil and Environmental Engineering
MSCES	Master of Science in Computer and Engineering Sciences
MSCF	Master of Science in Computational Finance
MSCH	Master of Science in Chemical Engineering
MSChE	Master of Science in Chemical Engineering
MSCI	Master of Science in Clinical Investigation
	Master of Science in Curriculum and Instruction
MSCIS	Master of Science in Computer and Information Systems
	Master of Science in Computer Information Science
	Master of Science in Computer Information Systems
MSCIT	Master of Science in Computer Information Technology
MSCJ	Master of Science in Criminal Justice
MSCJA	Master of Science in Criminal Justice Administration
MSCLS	Master of Science in Clinical Laboratory Studies
MSCM	Master of Science in Conflict Management
	Master of Science in Construction Management
MScM	Master of Science in Management
MSCP	Master of Science in Clinical Psychology
	Master of Science in Computer Engineering
	Master of Science in Counseling Psychology
MSCPharm	Master of Science in Pharmacy
MSCRP	Master of Science in City and Regional Planning
	Master of Science in Community and Regional Planning
MSCS	Master of Science in Computer Science
	Master of Science in Construction Science
MSCSD	Master of Science in Communication Sciences and Disorders
MSCSE	Master of Science in Computer Science and Engineering
	Master of Science in Computer Systems Engineering
MSCST	Master of Science in Computer Science Technology
MSCTE	Master of Science in Career and Technical Education
MSD	Master of Science in Dentistry
	Master of Science in Design
MSDD	Master of Software Design and Development
MSDM	Master of Design Methods
MSDR	Master of Dispute Resolution
MSE	Master of Science Education
	Master of Science in Education
	Master of Science in Engineering
	Master of Science in Engineering Managment
	Master of Software Engineering
	Master of Structural Engineering
MSE Mgt	Master of Science in Engineering Management
MSECE	Master of Science in Electrical and Computer Engineering
MSED	Master of Sustainable Economic Development
MSEE	Master of Science in Electrical Engineering
	Master of Science in Environmental Engineering
MSEH	Master of Science in Environmental Health
MSEL	Master of Science in Educational Leadership
	Master of Science in Executive Leadership
	Master of Studies in Environmental Law
MSEM	Master of Science in Engineering Management
	Master of Science in Engineering Mechanics
	Master of Science in Environmental Management
MSENE	Master of Science in Environmental Engineering
MSEO	Master of Science in Electro-Optics
MSEP	Master of Science in Economic Policy
MSES	Master of Science in Embedded Software Engineering
	Master of Science in Engineering Science
	Master of Science in Environmental Science
	Master of Science in Environmental Studies
MSESM	Master of Science in Engineering Science and Mechanics
MSET	Master of Science in Education in Educational Technology
	Master of Science in Engineering Technology
MSETM	Master of Science in Environmental Technology Management
MSEV	Master of Science in Environmental Engineering
MSEVH	Master of Science in Environmental Health and Safety
MSF	Master of Science in Finance
	Master of Science in Forestry
	Master of Social Foundations
MSFA	Master of Science in Financial Analysis
MSFAM	Master of Science in Family Studies

MSFCS	Master of Science in Family and Consumer Science
MSFE	Master of Science in Financial Engineering
MSFOR	Master of Science in Forestry
MSFP	Master of Science in Financial Planning
MSFS	Master of Science in Financial Sciences Master of Science in Forensic Science
MSFT	Master of Science in Family Therapy
MSGC	Master of Science in Genetic Counseling
MSGL	Master of Science in Global Leadership
MSH	Master of Science in Health Master of Science in Hospice
MSHA	Master of Science in Health Administration
MSHCA	Master of Science in Health Care Administration
MSHCI	Master of Science in Human Computer Interaction
MSHCPM	Master of Science in Health Care Policy and Management
MSHCS	Master of Science in Human and Consumer Science
MSHE	Master of Science in Health Education
MSHES	Master of Science in Human Environmental Sciences
MSHFID	Master of Science in Human Factors in Information Design
MSHFS	Master of Science in Human Factors and Systems
MSHP	Master of Science in Health Professions
MSHR	Master of Science in Human Resources
MSHRM	Master of Science in Human Resource Management
MSHROD	Master of Science in Human Resources and Organizational Development
MSHS	Master of Science in Health Science Master of Science in Health Services Master of Science in Health Systems
MSHT	Master of Science in History of Technology
MSI	Master of Science in Instruction
MSIA	Master of Science in Industrial Administration Master of Science in Information Assurance and Computer Security Master of Science in Interior Architecture
MSIB	Master of Science in International Business
MSIDM	Master of Science in Interior Design and Merchandising
MSIDT	Master of Science in Information Design and Technology
MSIE	Master of Science in Industrial Engineering Master of Science in International Economics
MSIEM	Master of Science in Information Engineering and Management
MSIM	Master of Science in Information Management Master of Science in Investment Management
MSIMC	Master of Science in Integrated Marketing Communications
MSIO	Master of Science of Industrial-Organizational Psychology
MSIR	Master of Science in Industrial Relations
MSIS	Master of Science in Information Science Master of Science in Information Systems Master of Science in Interdisciplinary Studies
MSISE	Master of Science in Infrastructure Systems Engineering
MSISM	Master of Science in Information Systems Management

MSISPM	Master of Science in Information Security Policy and Management
MSIST	Master of Science in Information Systems Technology
MSIT	Master of Science in Industrial Technology Master of Science in Information Technology Master of Science in Instructional Technology
MSITM	Master of Science in Information Technology Management
MSJ	Master of Science in Journalism Master of Science in Jurisprudence
MSJE	Master of Science in Jewish Education
MSJFP	Master of Science in Juvenile Forensic Psychology
MSJJ	Master of Science in Juvenile Justice
MSJPS	Master of Science in Justice and Public Safety
MSJS	Master of Science in Jewish Studies
MSK	Master of Science in Kinesiology
MSL	Master of School Leadership Master of Science in Limnology Master of Studies in Law
MSLA	Master of Science in Landscape Architecture Master of Science in Legal Administration
MSLD	Master of Science in Land Development
MSLS	Master of Science in Legal Studies Master of Science in Library Science Master of Science in Logistics Systems
MSLT	Master of Second Language Teaching
MSM	Master of Sacred Ministry Master of Sacred Music Master of School Mathematics Master of Science in Management
MSMA	Master of Science in Marketing Analysis
MSMAE	Master of Science in Materials Engineering
MSMC	Master of Science in Mass Communications
MSME	Master of Science in Mechanical Engineering
MSMFE	Master of Science in Manufacturing Engineering
MSMIS	Master of Science in Management Information Systems
MSMIT	Master of Science in Management and Information Technology
MSMM	Master of Science in Manufacturing Management
MSMO	Master of Science in Manufacturing Operations
MSMOT	Master of Science in Management of Technology
MSMS	Master of Science in Management Science
MSMSE	Master of Science in Manufacturing Systems Engineering Master of Science in Material Science and Engineering Master of Science in Mathematics and Science Education
MSMT	Master of Science in Management and Technology Master of Science in Medical Technology
MSN	Master of Science in Nursing
MSN-R	Master of Science in Nursing (Research)
MSN/Ed D	Master of Science in Nursing/Doctor of Education
MSN/M Div	Master of Science in Nursing/Master of Divinity
MSNA	Master of Science in Nurse Anesthesia
MSNE	Master of Science in Nuclear Engineering
MSNM	Master of Science in Nonprofit Management
MSNS	Master of Science in Natural Science Master's of Science in Nutritional Science
MSOD	Master of Science in Organizational Development

MSOEE	Master of Science in Outdoor and Environmental Education	**MSST**	Master of Science in Systems Technology
MSOES	Master of Science in Occupational Ergonomics and Safety	**MSSW**	Master of Science in Social Work
		MST	Master of Science and Technology
MSOL	Master of Science in Organizational Leadership		Master of Science in Taxation
MSOM	Master of Science in Organization and Management		Master of Science in Teaching
			Master of Science in Technology
	Master of Science in Oriental Medicine		Master of Science in Telecommunications
MSOR	Master of Science in Operations Research		Master of Science Teaching
MSOT	Master of Science in Occupational Technology	**MSTC**	Master of Science in Telecommunications
	Master of Science in Occupational Therapy	**MSTCM**	Master of Science in Traditional Chinese Medicine
MSP	Master of Science in Pharmacy	**MSTE**	Master of Science in Telecommunications Engineering
	Master of Science in Planning		Master of Science in Transportation Engineering
	Master of Speech Pathology	**MSTM**	Master of Science in Technical Management
MSP Ex	Master of Science in Exercise Physiology		Master of Science in Technology Management
MSPA	Master of Science in Physician Assistant	**MSTOM**	Master of Science in Traditional Oriental Medicine
	Master of Science in Professional Accountancy	**MSUD**	Master of Science in Urban Design
MSPAS	Master of Science in Physician Assistant Studies	**MSUESM**	Master of Science in Urban Environmental Systems Management
MSPC	Master of Science in Professional Communications	**MSW**	Master of Social Work
	Master of Science in Professional Counseling	**MSWE**	Master of Software Engineering
MSPE	Master of Science in Petroleum Engineering	**MSWREE**	Master of Science in Water Resources and Environmental Engineering
MSPG	Master of Science in Psychology		
MSPH	Master of Science in Public Health	**MSX**	Master of Science in Exercise Science
MSPHR	Master of Science in Pharmacy	**MT**	Master of Taxation
MSPM	Master of Science in Professional Management		Master of Teaching
MSPNGE	Master of Science in Petroleum and Natural Gas Engineering		Master of Technology
			Master of Textiles
MSPS	Master of Science in Pharmaceutical Science	**MTA**	Master of Arts in Teaching
	Master of Science in Psychological Services		Master of Tax Accounting
MSPT	Master of Science in Physical Therapy		Master of Teaching Arts
MSpVM	Master of Specialized Veterinary Medicine		Master of Tourism Administration
MSQFE	Master of Science in Quantitative Financial Economics	**MTCM**	Master of Traditional Chinese Medicine
		MTD	Master of Training and Development
MSR	Master of Science in Radiology	**MTE**	Master in Educational Technology
	Master of Science in Rehabilitation Sciences		Master of Teacher Education
MSRA	Master of Science in Recreation Administration	**MTEL**	Master of Telecommunications
MSRC	Master of Science in Resource Conservation	**MTESL**	Master in Teaching English as a Second Language
MSRE	Master of Science in Real Estate		
	Master of Science in Religious Education	**MTHM**	Master of Tourism and Hospitality Management
MSRED	Master of Science in Real Estate Development	**MTI**	Master of Information Technology
MSREM	Master of Science in Real Estate Management	**MTIM**	Masters of Trust and Investment Management
MSRLS	Master of Science in Recreation and Leisure Studies	**MTL**	Master of Talmudic Law
		MTLM	Master of Transportation and Logistics Management
MSRMP	Master of Science in Radiological Medical Physics		
		MTM	Master of Technology Management
MSRS	Master of Science in Rehabilitation Science		Master of Telecommunications Management
MSS	Master of Science in Software		Master of the Teaching of Mathematics
	Master of Social Science	**MTMH**	Master of Tropical Medicine and Hygiene
	Master of Social Services	**MTOM**	Master of Traditional Oriental Medicine
	Master of Software Systems	**MTP**	Master of Transpersonal Psychology
	Master of Sports Science	**MTPC**	Master of Technical and Professional Communication
	Master of Strategic Studies		
MSSA	Master of Science in Social Administration	**MTS**	Master of Teaching Science
MSSE	Master of Science in Software Engineering		Master of Theological Studies
MSSEM	Master of Science in Systems and Engineering Management	**MTSC**	Master of Technical and Scientific Communication
		MTSE	Master of Telecommunications and Software Engineering
MSSI	Master of Science in Strategic Intelligence		
MSSL	Master of Science in Strategic Leadership	**MTT**	Master in Technology Management
MSSLP	Master of Science in Speech-Language Pathology	**MTX**	Master of Taxation
MSSM	Master of Science in Sports Medicine	**MUA**	Master of Urban Affairs
MSSPA	Master of Science in Student Personnel Administration	**MUD**	Master of Urban Design
		MUEP	Master of Urban and Environmental Planning
MSSS	Master of Science in Safety Science	**MUP**	Master of Urban Planning
	Master of Science in Systems Science		

MUPDD	Master of Urban Planning, Design, and Development
MUPP	Master of Urban Planning and Policy
MUPRED	Masters of Urban Planning and Real Estate Development
MURP	Master of Urban and Regional Planning
	Master of Urban and Rural Planning
MUS	Master of Urban Studies
Mus Doc	Doctor of Music
Mus M	Master of Music
MVP	Master of Voice Pedagogy
MVPH	Master of Veterinary Public Health
MVTE	Master of Vocational-Technical Education
MWC	Master of Wildlife Conservation
MWE	Master in Welding Engineering
MWPS	Master of Wood and Paper Science
MWR	Master of Water Resources
MWS	Master of Women's Studies
MZS	Master of Zoological Science
Nav Arch	Naval Architecture
Naval E	Naval Engineer
ND	Doctor of Naturopathic Medicine
NE	Nuclear Engineer
Nuc E	Nuclear Engineer
OD	Doctor of Optometry
OTD	Doctor of Occupational Therapy
PBME	Professional Master of Biomedical Engineering
PD	Professional Diploma
PDD	Professional Development Degree
PE Dir	Director of Physical Education
PGC	Post-Graduate Certificate
Ph L	Licentiate of Philosophy
Pharm D	Doctor of Pharmacy
PhD	Doctor of Philosophy
PhD Otol	Doctor of Philosophy in Otolaryngology
Phd Surg	Doctor of Philosophy in Surgery
PhDEE	Doctor of Philosophy in Electrical Engineering
PM Sc	Professional Master of Science
PMBA	Professional Master of Business Administration
PMC	Post Master Certificate
PMD	Post-Master's Diploma
PMS	Professional Master of Science
PPDPT	Postprofessional Doctor of Physical Therapy
PSM	Professional Master of Science
Psy D	Doctor of Psychology
Psy M	Master of Psychology

Psy S	Specialist in Psychology
Psya D	Doctor of Psychoanalysis
Re Dir	Director of Recreation
Rh D	Doctor of Rehabilitation
S Psy S	Specialist in Psychological Services
Sc D	Doctor of Science
Sc M	Master of Science
SCCT	Specialist in Community College Teaching
ScDPT	Doctor of Physical Therapy Science
SD	Doctor of Science
	Specialist Degree
SJD	Doctor of Juridical Science
SLPD	Doctor of Speech-Language Pathology
SLS	Specialist in Library Science
SM	Master of Science
SM Arch S	Master of Science in Architectural Studies
SM Arch S/MCP	Master of Science in Architectural Studies/Master of City Planning
SM Arch S/ SMRED	Master of Science in Architectural Studies/Master of Science in Real Estate Development
SM Vis S	Master of Science in Visual Studies
SMBT	Master of Science in Building Technology
SP	Specialist Degree
Sp C	Specialist in Counseling
Sp Ed	Specialist in Education
Sp LIS	Specialist in Library and Information Science
SPA	Specialist in Arts
SPCM	Special in Church Music
Spec	Specialist's Certificate
Spec M	Specialist in Music
SPEM	Special in Educational Ministries
SPS	School Psychology Specialist
Spt	Specialist Degree
SPTH	Special in Theology
SSP	Specialist in School Psychology
STB	Bachelor of Sacred Theology
STD	Doctor of Sacred Theology
STL	Licentiate of Sacred Theology
STM	Master of Sacred Theology
TDPT	Transitional Doctor of Physical Therapy
Th D	Doctor of Theology
Th M	Master of Theology
VMD	Doctor of Veterinary Medicine
WEMBA	Weekend Executive Master of Business Administration
XMBA	Executive Master of Business Administration

INDEXES

Close-Ups and Announcements

Directories and Subject Areas in Books 2–6

Following is an alphabetical listing of directories and subject areas in Books 2–6. Also listed are cross-references for subject area names not used in the directory structure of the guides, for example, "Arabic (*see* Near and Middle Eastern Languages)."

Accounting—Book 6
Acoustics—Book 4
Actuarial Science—Book 6
Acupuncture and Oriental Medicine—Book 6
Acute Care/Critical Care Nursing—Book 6
Addictions/Substance Abuse Counseling—Book 2
Administration (*see* Arts Administration; Business Administration and Management; Educational Administration; Health Services Management and Hospital Administration; Industrial Administration; Pharmaceutical Administration; Public Administration)
Adult Education—Book 6
Adult Nursing—Book 6
Advanced Practice Nursing (*see* Family Nurse Practitioner Studies)
Advertising and Public Relations—Book 6
Aeronautical Engineering (*see* Aerospace/Aeronautical Engineering)
Aerospace/Aeronautical Engineering—Book 5
Aerospace Studies (*see* Aerospace/Aeronautical Engineering)
African-American Studies—Book 2
African Languages and Literatures (*see* African Studies)
African Studies—Book 2
Agribusiness (*see* Agricultural Economics and Agribusiness)
Agricultural Economics and Agribusiness—Book 2
Agricultural Education—Book 6
Agricultural Engineering—Book 5
Agricultural Sciences—Book 4
Agronomy and Soil Sciences—Book 4
Alcohol Abuse Counseling (*see* Addictions/Substance Abuse Counseling; Counselor Education)
Allied Health—Book 6
Allopathic Medicine—Book 6
American Indian/Native American Studies—Book 2
American Studies—Book 2
Analytical Chemistry—Book 4
Anatomy—Book 3
Anesthesiologist Assistant Studies—Book 6
Animal Behavior—Book 3
Animal Sciences—Book 4
Anthropology—Book 2
Applied Arts and Design—Book 2
Applied Economics—Book 2
Applied History (*see* Public History)
Applied Mathematics—Book 4
Applied Mechanics (*see* Mechanics)
Applied Physics—Book 4
Applied Science and Technology—Book 5
Applied Sciences (*see* Applied Science and Technology; Engineering and Applied Sciences)
Applied Social Research—Book 2
Applied Statistics—Book 4
Aquaculture—Book 4
Arabic (*see* Near and Middle Eastern Languages)
Arab Studies (*see* Near and Middle Eastern Studies)
Archaeology—Book 2
Architectural Engineering—Book 5
Architectural History—Book 2
Architecture—Book 2
Archives Administration (*see* Public History)

Area and Cultural Studies (*see* African-American Studies; African Studies; American Indian/Native American Studies; American Studies; Asian-American Studies; Asian Studies; Canadian Studies; East European and Russian Studies; Ethnic Studies; Gender Studies; Hispanic Studies; Jewish Studies; Latin American Studies; Near and Middle Eastern Studies; Northern Studies; Western European Studies; Women's Studies)
Art Education—Book 6
Art/Fine Arts—Book 2
Art History—Book 2
Arts Administration—Book 2
Art Therapy—Book 2
Artificial Intelligence/Robotics—Book 5
Asian-American Studies—Book 2
Asian Languages—Book 2
Asian Studies—Book 2
Astronautical Engineering (*see* Aerospace/Aeronautical Engineering)
Astronomy—Book 4
Astrophysical Sciences (*see* Astrophysics; Atmospheric Sciences; Meteorology; Planetary Sciences)
Astrophysics—Book 4
Athletics Administration (*see* Exercise and Sports Science; Kinesiology and Movement Studies; Physical Education; Sports Management)
Athletic Training and Sports Medicine—Book 6
Atmospheric Sciences—Book 4
Audiology (*see* Communication Disorders)
Automotive Engineering—Book 5
Aviation—Book 5
Aviation Management—Book 6
Bacteriology—Book 3
Banking (*see* Finance and Banking)
Behavioral Genetics (*see* Biopsychology)
Behavioral Sciences (*see* Biopsychology; Neuroscience; Psychology; Zoology)
Bible Studies (*see* Religion; Theology)
Bilingual and Bicultural Education (*see* Multilingual and Multicultural Education)
Biochemical Engineering—Book 5
Biochemistry—Book 3
Bioengineering—Book 5
Bioethics—Book 6
Bioinformatics—Book 5
Biological and Biomedical Sciences—Book 3
Biological Anthropology—Book 2
Biological Chemistry (*see* Biochemistry)
Biological Engineering (*see* Bioengineering)
Biological Oceanography (*see* Marine Biology; Marine Sciences; Oceanography)
Biomathematics (*see* Biometrics)
Biomedical Engineering—Book 5
Biometrics—Book 4
Biophysics—Book 3
Biopsychology—Book 3
Biostatistics—Book 4
Biosystems Engineering—Book 5
Biotechnology—Book 5
Black Studies (*see* African-American Studies)
Botany—Book 3
Breeding (*see* Animal Sciences; Botany and Plant Biology; Genetics; Horticulture)
Broadcasting (*see* Communication; Media Studies)
Building Science—Book 2

Business Administration and Management—Book 6
Business Education—Book 6
Canadian Studies—Book 2
Cancer Biology/Oncology—Book 3
Cardiovascular Sciences—Book 3
Cell Biology—Book 3
Cellular Physiology (*see* Cell Biology; Physiology)
Celtic Languages—Book 2
Ceramic Engineering (*see* Ceramic Sciences and Engineering)
Ceramic Sciences and Engineering—Book 5
Ceramics (*see* Art/Fine Arts; Ceramic Sciences and Engineering)
Cereal Chemistry (*see* Food Science and Technology)
Chemical Engineering—Book 5
Chemical Physics—Book 4
Chemistry—Book 4
Child and Family Studies—Book 2
Child-Care Nursing (*see* Maternal and Child/Neonatal Nursing)
Child Development—Book 2
Child-Health Nursing (*see* Maternal and Child/Neonatal Nursing)
Chinese—Book 2
Chinese Studies (*see* Asian Languages; Asian Studies)
Chiropractic—Book 6
Christian Studies (*see* Missions and Missiology; Religion; Religious Education; Theology)
Cinema (*see* Film, Television, and Video Production; Media Studies)
City and Regional Planning (*see* Urban and Regional Planning)
Civil Engineering—Book 5
Classical Languages and Literatures (*see* Classics)
Classics—Book 2
Clinical Laboratory Sciences/Medical Technology—Book 6
Clinical Microbiology (*see* Medical Microbiology)
Clinical Psychology—Book 2
Clinical Research—Book 6
Clothing and Textiles—Book 2
Cognitive Sciences—Book 2
Communication—Book 2
Communication Disorders—Book 6
Communication Theory (*see* Communication)
Community Affairs (*see* Urban and Regional Planning; Urban Studies)
Community College Education—Book 6
Community Health—Book 6
Community Health Nursing—Book 6
Community Planning (*see* Architecture; Environmental Design; Urban and Regional Planning; Urban Design; Urban Studies)
Community Psychology (*see* Social Psychology)
Comparative and Interdisciplinary Arts—Book 2
Comparative Literature—Book 2
Composition (*see* Music)
Computational Biology—Book 3
Computational Sciences—Book 4
Computer and Information Systems Security—Book 5
Computer Art and Design—Book 2
Computer Education—Book 6
Computer Engineering—Book 5
Computer Science—Book 5
Computing Technology (*see* Computer Science)
Condensed Matter Physics—Book 4
Conflict Resolution and Mediation/Peace Studies—Book 2
Conservation Biology—Book 3
Construction Engineering—Book 5
Construction Management—Book 5
Consumer Economics—Book 2
Continuing Education (*see* Adult Education)
Corporate and Organizational Communication—Book 2
Corrections (*see* Criminal Justice and Criminology)

Counseling (*see* Addictions/Substance Abuse Counseling; Counseling Psychology; Counselor Education; Genetic Counseling; Pastoral Ministry and Counseling; Rehabilitation Counseling)
Counseling Psychology—Book 2
Counselor Education—Book 6
Crafts (*see* Art/Fine Arts)
Creative Arts Therapies (*see* Art Therapy; Therapies—Dance, Drama, and Music)
Criminal Justice and Criminology—Book 2
Crop Sciences (*see* Agricultural Sciences; Agronomy and Soil Sciences; Botany; Plant Biology; Plant Sciences)
Cultural Studies—Book 2
Curriculum and Instruction—Book 6
Cytology (*see* Cell Biology)
Dairy Science (*see* Animal Sciences)
Dance—Book 2
Dance Therapy (*see* Therapies—Dance, Drama, and Music)
Decorative Arts—Book 2
Demography and Population Studies—Book 2
Dental and Oral Surgery (*see* Oral and Dental Sciences)
Dental Assistant Studies (*see* Dental Hygiene)
Dental Hygiene—Book 6
Dental Services (*see* Dental Hygiene)
Dentistry—Book 6
Design (*see* Applied Arts and Design; Architecture; Art/Fine Arts; Environmental Design; Graphic Design; Industrial Design; Interior Design; Textile Design; Urban Design)
Developmental Biology—Book 3
Developmental Education—Book 6
Developmental Psychology—Book 2
Dietetics (*see* Nutrition)
Diplomacy (*see* International Affairs)
Disability Studies—Book 2
Distance Education Development—Book 6
Drama/Theater Arts (*see* Theater)
Drama Therapy (*see* Therapies—Dance, Drama, and Music)
Dramatic Arts (*see* Theater)
Drawing (*see* Art/Fine Arts)
Drug Abuse Counseling (*see* Addictions/Substance Abuse Counseling; Counselor Education)
Early Childhood Education—Book 6
Earth Sciences (*see* Geosciences)
East Asian Studies (*see* Asian Studies)
East European and Russian Studies—Book 2
Ecology—Book 3
Economics—Book 2
Education—Book 6
Educational Administration—Book 6
Educational Leadership (*see* Educational Administration)
Educational Measurement and Evaluation—Book 6
Educational Media/Instructional Technology—Book 6
Educational Policy—Book 6
Educational Psychology—Book 6
Educational Theater (*see* Therapies—Dance, Drama, and Music; Theater; Education)
Education of the Blind (*see* Special Education)
Education of the Deaf (*see* Special Education)
Education of the Gifted—Book 6
Education of the Hearing Impaired (*see* Special Education)
Education of the Learning Disabled (*see* Special Education)
Education of the Mentally Retarded (*see* Special Education)
Education of the Multiply Handicapped—Book 6
Education of the Physically Handicapped (*see* Special Education)
Education of the Visually Handicapped (*see* Special Education)
Electrical Engineering—Book 5
Electronic Commerce—Book 6
Electronic Materials—Book 5

Electronics Engineering (*see* Electrical Engineering)
Elementary Education—Book 6
Embryology (*see* Developmental Biology)
Emergency Management—Book 2
Emergency Medical Services—Book 6
Endocrinology (*see* Physiology)
Energy and Power Engineering—Book 5
Energy Management and Policy—Book 5
Engineering and Applied Sciences—Book 5
Engineering and Public Affairs (*see* Management of Engineering and Technology; Technology and Public Policy)
Engineering and Public Policy (*see* Management of Engineering and Technology; Technology and Public Policy)
Engineering Design—Book 5
Engineering Management—Book 5
Engineering Mechanics (*see* Mechanics)
Engineering Metallurgy (*see* Metallurgical Engineering and Metallurgy)
Engineering Physics—Book 5
English—Book 2
English as a Second Language—Book 6
English Education—Book 6
Entomology—Book 3
Entrepreneurship—Book 6
Environmental and Occupational Health—Book 6
Environmental Biology—Book 3
Environmental Design—Book 2
Environmental Education—Book 6
Environmental Engineering—Book 5
Environmental Management and Policy—Book 4
Environmental Sciences—Book 4
Environmental Studies (*see* Environmental Management and Policy)
Epidemiology—Book 6
Ergonomics and Human Factors—Book 5
Ethics—Book 2
Ethnic Studies—Book 2
Ethnomusicology (*see* Music)
Evolutionary Biology—Book 3
Exercise and Sports Science—Book 6
Experimental Psychology—Book 2
Experimental Statistics (*see* Statistics)
Facilities Management—Book 6
Family and Consumer Sciences—Book 2
Family Nurse Practitioner Studies—Book 6
Family Studies (*see* Child and Family Studies)
Family Therapy (*see* Marriage and Family Therapy)
Filmmaking (*see* Film, Television, and Video Production)
Film Studies (*see* Film, Television, and Video Production; Media Studies)
Film, Television, and Video Production—Book 2
Film, Television, and Video Theory and Criticism—Book 2
Finance and Banking—Book 6
Financial Engineering—Book 5
Fine Arts (*see* Art/Fine Arts)
Fire Protection Engineering—Book 5
Fish, Game, and Wildlife Management—Book 4
Folklore—Book 2
Food Engineering (*see* Agricultural Engineering)
Foods (*see* Food Science and Technology; Nutrition)
Food Science and Technology—Book 4
Food Services Management (*see* Hospitality Management)
Foreign Languages (*see* specific languages)
Foreign Languages Education—Book 6
Foreign Service (*see* International Affairs)
Forensic Nursing—Book 6
Forensic Psychology—Book 2
Forensics (*see* Speech and Interpersonal Communication)
Forensic Sciences—Book 2

Forestry—Book 4
Foundations and Philosophy of Education—Book 6
French—Book 2
Game and Wildlife Management (*see* Fish, Game, and Wildlife Management)
Gas Engineering (*see* Petroleum Engineering)
Gender Studies—Book 2
General Studies (*see* Liberal Studies)
Genetic Counseling—Book 2
Genetics—Book 3
Genomic Sciences—Book 3
Geochemistry—Book 4
Geodetic Sciences—Book 4
Geographic Information Systems—Book 2
Geography—Book 2
Geological Engineering—Book 5
Geological Sciences (*see* Geology)
Geology—Book 4
Geophysical Fluid Dynamics (*see* Geophysics)
Geophysics—Book 4
Geophysics Engineering (*see* Geological Engineering)
Geosciences—Book 4
Geotechnical Engineering—Book 5
German—Book 2
Gerontological Nursing—Book 6
Gerontology—Book 2
Government (*see* Political Science)
Graphic Design—Book 2
Greek (*see* Classics)
Guidance and Counseling (*see* Counselor Education)
Hazardous Materials Management—Book 5
Health Communication—Book 2
Health Education—Book 6
Health Informatics—Book 5
Health Physics/Radiological Health—Book 6
Health Promotion—Book 6
Health Psychology—Book 2
Health-Related Professions (*see* individual allied health professions)
Health Sciences (*see* Public Health; Community Health)
Health Services Management and Hospital Administration—Book 6
Health Services Research—Book 6
Health Systems (*see* Safety Engineering; Systems Engineering)
Hearing Sciences (*see* Communication Disorders)
Hebrew (*see* Near and Middle Eastern Languages)
Hebrew Studies (*see* Jewish Studies)
Higher Education—Book 6
Highway Engineering (*see* Transportation and Highway Engineering)
Hispanic Studies—Book 2
Histology (*see* Anatomy; Cell Biology)
Historic Preservation—Book 2
History—Book 2
History of Art (*see* Art History)
History of Medicine—Book 2
History of Science and Technology—Book 2
HIV-AIDS Nursing—Book 6
Holocaust Studies—Book 2
Home Economics (*see* Family and Consumer Sciences)
Home Economics Education—Book 6
Homeland Security—Book 2
Horticulture—Book 4
Hospice Nursing—Book 6
Hospital Administration (*see* Health Services Management and Hospital Administration)
Hospitality Administration (*see* Hospitality Management)
Hospitality Management—Book 6
Hotel Management (*see* Travel and Tourism)

Household Economics, Sciences, and Management (*see* Consumer Economics)

Human-Computer Interaction—Book 5

Human Development—Book 2

Human Ecology (*see* Family and Consumer Sciences)

Human Factors (*see* Ergonomics and Human Factors)

Human Genetics—Book 3

Humanistic Psychology (*see* Transpersonal and Humanistic Psychology)

Humanities—Book 2

Human Movement Studies (*see* Dance; Exercise and Sports Sciences; Kinesiology and Movement Studies)

Human Resources Development—Book 6

Human Resources Management—Book 6

Human Services—Book 6

Hydraulics—Book 5

Hydrogeology—Book 4

Hydrology—Book 4

Illustration—Book 2

Immunology—Book 3

Industrial Administration—Book 6

Industrial and Labor Relations—Book 2

Industrial and Manufacturing Management—Book 6

Industrial and Organizational Psychology—Book 2

Industrial Design—Book 2

Industrial Education (*see* Vocational and Technical Education)

Industrial Hygiene—Book 6

Industrial/Management Engineering—Book 5

Infectious Diseases—Book 3

Information Science—Book 5

Information Studies—Book 6

Inorganic Chemistry—Book 4

Instructional Technology (*see* Educational Media/Instructional Technology)

Insurance—Book 6

Interdisciplinary Studies—Book 2

Interior Design—Book 2

International Affairs—Book 2

International and Comparative Education—Book 6

International Business—Book 6

International Commerce (*see* International Business; International Development)

International Development—Book 2

International Economics (*see* Economics; International Affairs; International Business; International Development)

International Health—Book 6

International Service (*see* International Affairs)

International Trade (*see* International Business)

Internet and Interactive Multimedia—Book 2

Interpersonal Communication (*see* Speech and Interpersonal Communication)

Interpretation (*see* Translation and Interpretation)

Investment and Securities (*see* Business Administration and Management; Finance and Banking; Investment Management)

Investment Management—Book 6

Islamic Studies (*see* Near and Middle Eastern Studies; Religion)

Italian—Book 2

Japanese—Book 2

Japanese Studies (*see* Asian Languages; Asian Studies)

Jewelry/Metalsmithing (*see* Art/Fine Arts)

Jewish Studies—Book 2

Journalism—Book 2

Judaic Studies (*see* Jewish Studies; Religion; Religious Education)

Junior College Education (*see* Community College Education)

Kinesiology and Movement Studies—Book 6

Labor Relations (*see* Industrial and Labor Relations)

Laboratory Medicine (*see* Clinical Laboratory Sciences/Medical Technology; Immunology; Microbiology; Pathobiology; Pathology)

Landscape Architecture—Book 2

Latin (*see* Classics)

Latin American Studies—Book 2

Law—Book 6

Law Enforcement (*see* Criminal Justice and Criminology)

Legal and Justice Studies—Book 6

Leisure Studies—Book 6

Liberal Studies—Book 2

Librarianship (*see* Library Science)

Library Science—Book 6

Life Sciences (*see* Biological and Biomedical Sciences)

Limnology—Book 4

Linguistics—Book 2

Literature (*see* Classics; Comparative Literature; specific language)

Logistics—Book 6

Macromolecular Science (*see* Polymer Science and Engineering)

Management (*see* Business Administration and Management)

Management Engineering (*see* Engineering Management; Industrial/Management Engineering)

Management Information Systems—Book 6

Management of Engineering and Technology—Book 5

Management of Technology—Book 5

Management Strategy and Policy—Book 6

Manufacturing Engineering—Book 5

Marine Affairs—Book 4

Marine Biology—Book 3

Marine Engineering (*see* Civil Engineering)

Marine Geology—Book 4

Marine Sciences—Book 4

Marine Studies (*see* Marine Affairs; Marine Geology; Marine Sciences; Oceanography)

Marketing—Book 6

Marketing Research—Book 6

Marriage and Family Therapy—Book 2

Mass Communication—Book 2

Materials Engineering—Book 5

Materials Sciences—Book 5

Maternal and Child Health—Book 6

Maternal and Child/Neonatal Nursing—Book 6

Maternity Nursing (*see* Maternal and Child/Neonatal Nursing)

Mathematical and Computational Finance—Book 4

Mathematical Physics—Book 4

Mathematical Statistics (*see* Statistics)

Mathematics—Book 4

Mathematics Education—Book 6

Mechanical Engineering—Book 5

Mechanics—Book 5

Media Studies—Book 2

Medical Illustration—Book 2

Medical Imaging—Book 6

Medical Informatics—Book 5

Medical Microbiology—Book 3

Medical Nursing (*see* Medical/Surgical Nursing)

Medical Physics—Book 6

Medical Sciences (*see* Biological and Biomedical Sciences)

Medical Science Training Programs (*see* Biological and Biomedical Sciences)

Medical/Surgical Nursing—Book 6

Medical Technology (*see* Clinical Laboratory Sciences/Medical Technology)

Medicinal and Pharmaceutical Chemistry—Book 6

Medicinal Chemistry (*see* Medicinal and Pharmaceutical Chemistry)

Medicine (*see* Allopathic Medicine; Naturopathic Medicine; Osteopathic Medicine; Podiatric Medicine)

Medieval and Renaissance Studies—Book 2

Metallurgical Engineering and Metallurgy—Book 5
Metallurgy (*see* Metallurgical Engineering and Metallurgy)
Metalsmithing (*see* Art/Fine Arts)
Meteorology—Book 4
Microbiology—Book 3
Middle Eastern Studies (*see* Near and Middle Eastern Studies)
Middle School Education—Book 6
Midwifery (*see* Nurse Midwifery)
Military and Defense Studies—Book 2
Mineral Economics—Book 2
Mineral/Mining Engineering—Book 5
Mineralogy—Book 4
Ministry (*see* Pastoral Ministry and Counseling; Theology)
Missions and Missiology—Book 2
Molecular Biology—Book 3
Molecular Biophysics—Book 3
Molecular Genetics—Book 3
Molecular Medicine—Book 3
Molecular Pathogenesis—Book 3
Molecular Pathology—Book 3
Molecular Pharmacology—Book 3
Molecular Physiology—Book 3
Molecular Toxicology—Book 3
Motion Pictures (*see* Film, Television, and Video Production; Media Studies)
Movement Studies (*see* Dance; Exercise and Sports Science; Kinesiology and Movement Studies)
Multilingual and Multicultural Education—Book 6
Museum Education—Book 6
Museum Studies—Book 2
Music—Book 2
Music Education—Book 6
Music History (*see* Music)
Musicology (*see* Music)
Music Theory (*see* Music)
Music Therapy (*see* Therapies—Dance, Drama, and Music)
Nanotechnology—Book 5
National Security—Book 2
Native American Studies (*see* American Indian/Native American Studies)
Natural Resources—Book 4
Natural Resources Management (*see* Environmental Management and Policy; Natural Resources)
Naturopathic Medicine—Book 6
Near and Middle Eastern Languages—Book 2
Near and Middle Eastern Studies—Book 2
Near Environment (*see* Family and Consumer Sciences; Human Development)
Neural Sciences (*see* Biopsychology; Neuroscience)
Neurobiology—Book 3
Neuroendocrinology (*see* Biopsychology; Neuroscience; Physiology)
Neuropharmacology (*see* Biopsychology; Neuroscience; Pharmacology)
Neurophysiology (*see* Biopsychology; Neuroscience; Physiology)
Neuroscience—Book 3
Nonprofit Management—Book 6
North American Studies (*see* Northern Studies)
Northern Studies—Book 2
Nuclear Engineering—Book 5
Nuclear Medical Technology (*see* Clinical Laboratory Sciences/Medical Technology)
Nuclear Physics (*see* Physics)
Nurse Anesthesia—Book 6
Nurse Midwifery—Book 6
Nurse Practitioner Studies (*see* Family Nurse Practitioner Studies)
Nursery School Education (*see* Early Childhood Education)
Nursing—Book 6

Nursing and Healthcare Administration—Book 6
Nursing Education—Book 6
Nursing Informatics—Book 6
Nutrition—Book 3
Occupational Education (*see* Vocational and Technical Education)
Occupational Health (*see* Environmental and Occupational Health; Occupational Health Nursing)
Occupational Health Nursing—Book 6
Occupational Therapy—Book 6
Ocean Engineering—Book 5
Oceanography—Book 4
Oncology—Book 3
Oncology Nursing—Book 6
Operations Research—Book 5
Optical Sciences—Book 4
Optical Technologies (*see* Optical Sciences)
Optics (*see* Applied Physics; Optical Sciences; Physics)
Optometry—Book 6
Oral and Dental Sciences—Book 6
Oral Biology (*see* Oral and Dental Sciences)
Oral Pathology (*see* Oral and Dental Sciences)
Organic Chemistry—Book 4
Organismal Biology (*see* Biological and Biomedical Sciences; Zoology)
Organizational Behavior—Book 6
Organizational Management—Book 6
Organizational Psychology (*see* Industrial and Organizational Psychology)
Oriental Languages (*see* Asian Languages)
Oriental Medicine—Book 6
Oriental Studies (*see* Asian Studies)
Orthodontics (*see* Oral and Dental Sciences)
Osteopathic Medicine—Book 6
Painting/Drawing (*see* Art/Fine Arts)
Paleontology—Book 4
Paper and Pulp Engineering—Book 5
Paper Chemistry (*see* Chemistry)
Parasitology—Book 3
Park Management (*see* Recreation and Park Management)
Pastoral Ministry and Counseling—Book 2
Pathobiology—Book 3
Pathology—Book 3
Peace Studies (*see* Conflict Resolution and Mediation/Peace Studies)
Pediatric Nursing—Book 6
Pedodontics (*see* Oral and Dental Sciences)
Performance (*see* Music)
Performing Arts (*see* Dance; Music; Theater)
Periodontics (*see* Oral and Dental Sciences)
Personnel (*see* Human Resources Development; Human Resources Management; Organizational Behavior; Organizational Management; Student Affairs)
Petroleum Engineering—Book 5
Pharmaceutical Administration—Book 6
Pharmaceutical Chemistry (*see* Medicinal and Pharmaceutical Chemistry)
Pharmaceutical Engineering—Book 5
Pharmaceutical Sciences—Book 6
Pharmacognosy (*see* Pharmaceutical Sciences)
Pharmacology—Book 3
Pharmacy—Book 6
Philanthropic Studies—Book 2
Philosophy—Book 2
Philosophy of Education (*see* Foundations and Philosophy of Education)
Photobiology of Cells and Organelles (*see* Botany and Plant Biology; Cell Biology)
Photography—Book 2
Photonics—Book 4

Physical Chemistry—Book 4
Physical Education—Book 6
Physical Therapy—Book 6
Physician Assistant Studies—Book 6
Physics—Book 4
Physiological Optics (*see* Physiology; Vision Sciences)
Physiology—Book 3
Planetary Sciences—Book 4
Plant Biology—Book 3
Plant Molecular Biology—Book 3
Plant Pathology—Book 3
Plant Physiology—Book 3
Plant Sciences—Book 4
Plasma Physics—Book 4
Plastics Engineering (*see* Polymer Science and Engineering)
Playwriting (*see* Theater; Writing)
Podiatric Medicine—Book 6
Policy Studies (*see* Educational Policy; Energy Management and Policy; Environmental Management and Policy; Public Policy; Strategy and Policy; Technology and Public Policy)
Political Science—Book 2
Polymer Science and Engineering—Book 5
Pomology (*see* Agricultural Sciences; Botany and Plant Biology; Horticulture; Plant Sciences)
Population Studies (*see* Demography and Population Studies)
Portuguese—Book 2
Poultry Science (*see* Animal Sciences)
Power Engineering—Book 5
Preventive Medicine (*see* Public Health; Community Health)
Printmaking (*see* Art/Fine Arts)
Product Design (*see* Environmental Design; Industrial Design)
Project Management—Book 6
Psychiatric Nursing—Book 6
Psychoanalysis and Psychotherapy—Book 2
Psychobiology (*see* Biopsychology)
Psychology—Book 2
Psychopharmacology (*see* Biopsychology; Neuroscience; Pharmacology)
Public Administration—Book 2
Public Affairs—Book 2
Public Health—Book 6
Public Health Nursing (*see* Community Health Nursing)
Public History—Book 2
Public Policy—Book 2
Public Relations (*see* Advertising and Public Relations)
Public Speaking (*see* Mass Communication; Rhetoric; Speech and Interpersonal Communication)
Publishing—Book 2
Quality Management—Book 6
Quantitative Analysis—Book 6
Radiation Biology—Book 3
Radio (*see* Media Studies)
Radiological Health (*see* Health Physics/Radiological Health)
Radiological Physics (*see* Physics)
Range Management (*see* Range Science)
Range Science—Book 4
Reading Education—Book 6
Real Estate—Book 6
Recreation and Park Management—Book 6
Recreation Therapy (*see* Recreation and Park Management)
Regional Planning (*see* Architecture; Environmental Design; Urban and Regional Planning; Urban Design; Urban Studies)
Rehabilitation Counseling—Book 2
Rehabilitation Sciences—Book 6
Rehabilitation Therapy (*see* Physical Therapy)
Reliability Engineering—Book 5
Religion—Book 2

Religious Education—Book 6
Religious Studies (*see* Religion; Theology)
Remedial Education (*see* Special Education)
Renaissance Studies (*see* Medieval and Renaissance Studies)
Reproductive Biology—Book 3
Resource Management (*see* Environmental Management and Policy)
Restaurant Administration (*see* Hospitality Management)
Rhetoric—Book 2
Robotics (*see* Artificial Intelligence/Robotics)
Romance Languages—Book 2
Romance Literatures (*see* Romance Languages)
Rural Planning and Studies—Book 2
Rural Sociology—Book 2
Russian—Book 2
Russian Studies (*see* East European and Russian Studies)
Sacred Music (*see* Music)
Safety Engineering—Book 5
Scandinavian Languages—Book 2
School Nursing—Book 6
School Psychology—Book 2
Science Education—Book 6
Sculpture (*see* Art/Fine Arts)
Secondary Education—Book 6
Security Administration (*see* Criminal Justice and Criminology)
Slavic Languages—Book 2
Slavic Studies (*see* East European and Russian Studies; Slavic Languages)
Social Psychology—Book 2
Social Sciences—Book 2
Social Sciences Education—Book 6
Social Studies Education (*see* Social Sciences Education)
Social Welfare (*see* Social Work)
Social Work—Book 6
Sociobiology (*see* Evolutionary Biology)
Sociology—Book 2
Software Engineering—Book 5
Soil Sciences and Management (*see* Agronomy and Soil Sciences)
Solid-Earth Sciences (*see* Geosciences)
Solid-State Sciences (*see* Materials Sciences)
South and Southeast Asian Studies (*see* Asian Studies)
Space Sciences (*see* Astronomy; Astrophysics; Planetary Sciences)
Spanish—Book 2
Special Education—Book 6
Speech and Interpersonal Communication—Book 2
Speech-Language Pathology (*see* Communication Disorders)
Sport Psychology—Book 2
Sports Management—Book 6
Statistics—Book 4
Strategy and Policy—Book 6
Structural Biology—Book 3
Structural Engineering—Book 5
Student Affairs—Book 6
Studio Art (*see* Art/Fine Arts)
Substance Abuse Counseling (*see* Addictions/Substance Abuse Counseling)
Supply Chain Management—Book 6
Surgical Nursing (*see* Medical/Surgical Nursing)
Surveying Science and Engineering—Book 5
Sustainable Development—Book 2
Systems Analysis (*see* Systems Engineering)
Systems Biology—Book 3
Systems Engineering—Book 5
Systems Management (*see* Management Information Systems)
Systems Science—Book 5
Taxation—Book 6
Teacher Education (*see* Education)

Teaching English as a Second Language (*see* English as a Second Language)

Technical Communication—Book 2

Technical Education (*see* Vocational and Technical Education)

Technical Writing—Book 2

Technology and Public Policy—Book 5

Telecommunications—Book 5

Telecommunications Management—Book 5

Television (*see* Film, Television, and Video Production; Media Studies)

Teratology (*see* Developmental Biology; Environmental and Occupational Health; Pathology)

Textile Design—Book 2

Textile Sciences and Engineering—Book 5

Textiles (*see* Clothing and Textiles; Textile Design; Textile Sciences and Engineering)

Thanatology—Book 2

Theater—Book 2

Theology—Book 2

Theoretical Biology (*see* Biological and Biomedical Sciences)

Theoretical Chemistry—Book 4

Theoretical Physics—Book 4

Theory and Criticism of Film, Television, and Video (*see* Film, Television, and Video Theory and Criticism)

Therapeutic Recreation—Book 6

Therapeutics (*see* Pharmaceutical Sciences; Pharmacology; Pharmacy)

Therapies—Dance, Drama, and Music—Book 2

Toxicology—Book 3

Transcultural Nursing—Book 6

Translational Biology—Book 3

Translation and Interpretation—Book 2

Transpersonal and Humanistic Psychology—Book 2

Transportation and Highway Engineering—Book 5

Transportation Management—Book 6

Travel and Tourism—Book 6

Tropical Medicine (*see* Parasitology)

Urban and Regional Planning—Book 2

Urban Design—Book 2

Urban Education—Book 6

Urban Studies—Book 2

Urban Systems Engineering (*see* Systems Engineering)

Veterinary Medicine—Book 6

Veterinary Sciences—Book 6

Video (*see* Film, Television, and Video Production; Media Studies)

Virology—Book 3

Vision Sciences—Book 6

Visual Arts (*see* Applied Arts and Design; Art/Fine Arts; Film, Television, and Video Production; Graphic Design; Illustration; Media Studies; Photography)

Vocational and Technical Education—Book 6

Vocational Counseling (*see* Counselor Education)

Waste Management (*see* Hazardous Materials Management)

Water Resources—Book 4

Water Resources Engineering—Book 5

Western European Studies—Book 2

Wildlife Biology (*see* Zoology)

Wildlife Management (*see* Fish, Game, and Wildlife Management)

Women's Health Nursing—Book 6

Women's Studies—Book 2

World Wide Web (*see* Internet and Interactive Multimedia)

Writing—Book 2

Zoology—Book 3

Directories and Subject Areas in This Book

NOTES

NOTES

NOTES

NOTES

NOTES

NOTES

NOTES

NOTES

NOTES

NOTES